Presented to

---

By

---

Date

---

Presented to

By

Date

# What Is the Bible?

TThe Bible is made up of a "library" of 73 books, 46 in the Old Testament, 27 in the New. The writings of the **OLD TESTAMENT** first appeared as separate scrolls in Hebrew; we do not know how or when they were first gathered into a single volume. The 46 books of the Old Testament vary in authorship and style and can be divided into four major groupings:

**Law**
Sometimes called the Pentateuch, or "five scrolls."

**History**
Tracing the story of God's people from their entry into the Promised Land to the Exile.

**Poetry and Wisdom**
Full of proverbs, riddles, parables, warnings and wise sayings.

**Prophecy**
God's prophets explained what had happened in the past; spoke out against evil in the present; and told of what God would do in the future.

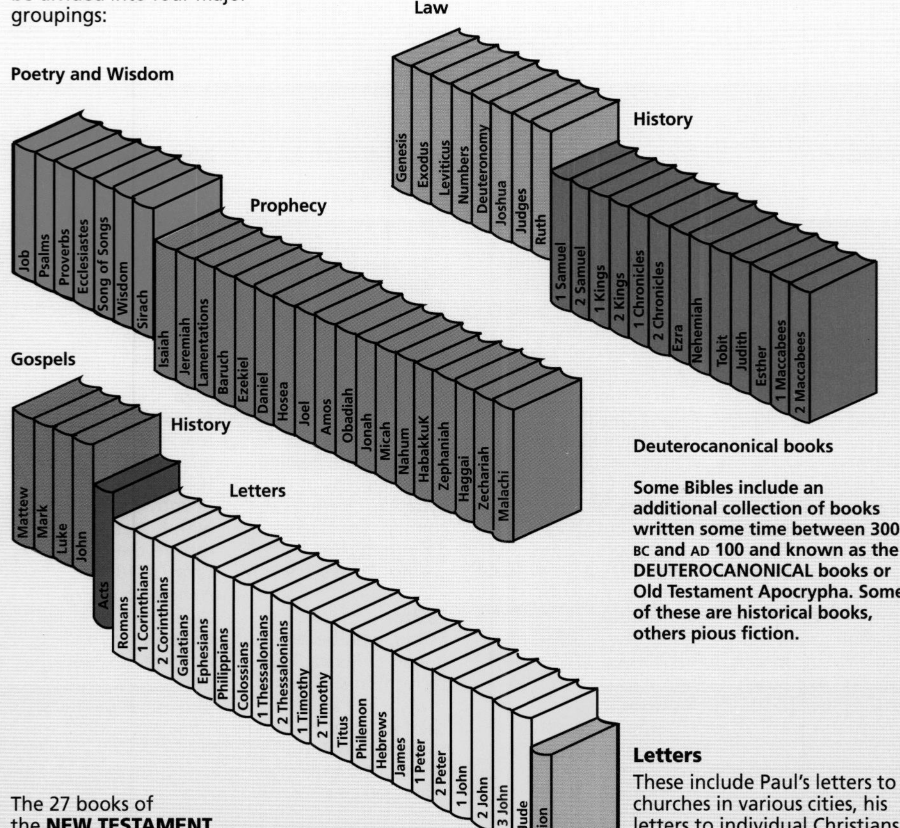


**Deuterocanonical books**

**Some Bibles include an additional collection of books written some time between 300 BC and AD 100 and known as the DEUTEROCANONICAL books or Old Testament Apocrypha. Some of these are historical books, others pious fiction.**

The 27 books of the **NEW TESTAMENT** were written in Greek and can also be divided into different types of writing:

**History**
The book of Acts and the four Gospels. The Gospels, however, are not simply historical records; they were written to persuade readers to believe in Jesus and form portraits of Jesus as the Messiah.

**Letters**
These include Paul's letters to churches in various cities, his letters to individual Christians, and letters written by other Christians.

**Revelation**
This book opens with letters to seven churches in Asia Minor, but continues with disturbing and consoling visions about the Last Days.

# Great Characters of the OLD TESTAMENT



**Aaron**
Aaron, Moses' brother, became the first high priest of Israel. He founded the priesthood of Israel, but gave way to the people's demand in the wilderness for an idol, allowing the making of the golden calf.
*Exodus 4:10-16, 17:10-12, 32:1-35*

**Abram (Abraham)**
The founder of the Jewish nation, Abraham left Ur to travel to the land God had promised to him and his descendants. His barren wife, Sarah, gave birth to a son, Isaac, who enabled God's promise to be fulfilled that Abraham would become father of a great nation.
*Genesis 11:26-25:10*

**Adam**
The first man, Adam, created by God to be like God, was placed in the Garden of Eden. When he disobeyed God's command by eating fruit from the forbidden tree, the whole creation was affected, and death entered the world.
*Genesis 2:4-3:24*

**Daniel**
A high-born Jew, Daniel was taken as a captive to Babylon and trained as an adviser at King Nebuchadnezzar's court. God gave him wisdom, enabling him to interpret the king's dreams. When rivals plotted his downfall, and he was thrown into a lions' den, God saved him.
*Daniel*

**David**
Youngest of Jesse's sons, David was working as a shepherd when Samuel anointed him king to replace Saul. David slew the Philistine champion, Goliath, but aroused Saul's jealousy, as a result of which he had to flee into hiding. After the death of Saul, David was crowned king. He made Jerusalem his capital and brought the Ark of the Covenant there. David was a great king, a poet to whom many of the psalms are attributed.
*1 Samuel 16:1–1 Kings 2:11*

**Deborah**
Deborah, the only woman judge, was one of the most successful judges of Israel. Her commander, Barak, defeated the Philistines, producing 40 years free of foreign domination.
*Judges 4:1-5:31*

**Elijah**
The prophet lived in the time of the wicked King Ahab and was sent to tell Ahab that God was sending a drought. Later, he defeated the prophets of Baal in a contest on Mount Carmel and denounced Ahab for the murder of Naboth. Elijah trained Elisha to take over from him.
*1 Kings 17:1–2 Kings 2:12*

**Elisha**
Elisha took over from Elijah as prophet of Israel. He worked many miracles, including the healing of the leprosy of the Syrian army commander Naaman.
*1 Kings 19:16-21, 2 Kings 2:1-8:15, 9:1-37*

**Esther**
Esther, who became queen of Persia, kept secret that she was Jewish. The king's chief minister planned to wipe out all the Jews, but Esther managed to save her people by pleading with the king. Her victory is remembered every year in the Jewish festival of Purim.
*Esther*

**Eve**
Adam's companion, Eve, was the first woman. When she and Adam ate fruit from the forbidden tree, sin and death entered the world, and Adam and Eve were ejected from Eden.
*Genesis 2:18-3:24*

**Ezekiel**
A Jewish prophet who was taken as a prisoner to Babylon, where he continued prophesying.
*Ezekiel*

**Ezra**
A Jewish priest and teacher of the Law who led some of the Jews back from exile in Babylon. He worked with Nehemiah to restore the Law.
*Ezra 7:1-10:17; Nehemiah 8:1-18*

**Gideon**
A judge of Israel who defeated the Midianites by guile.
*Judges 6:1-8:32*

**Hezekiah**
Judah's twelfth king, Hezekiah restored and re-opened the Temple and introduced religious reforms.
*2 Kings 18:1-20:21; 2 Chronicles 29:1-32:33*

**Isaac**
Isaac was born to Abraham and Sarah when his parents were very old. Later, Abraham was tested by God and told to sacrifice his son, but at the last minute an angel stopped him. Isaac married Rebekah and had twin sons, Esau and Jacob.
*Genesis 21:1-28:5*

**Isaiah**
Isaiah was a great prophet who lived through the reigns of Uzziah, Jotham, Ahaz and Hezekiah. During his time, the nation was threatened by Assyria; Isaiah foretold that, though his people would be taken into exile, they would eventually return. He also prophesied of the coming Messiah.
*2 Kings l9:1-20:19; Isaiah*

**Jacob**
Jacob, Isaac's son, deceived his father into giving him the eldest son's blessing, and also bought his brother Esau's birthright. Jacob married Leah, and, later, her sister Rachel, and had twelve sons. After Jacob wrestled with a stranger, God gave him the name "Israel."
*Genesis 25:21-35:29, 37:1-35, 42:1-49:14*

**Jeremiah**
A prophet who ministered during the reigns of the last five kings of Judah, Jeremiah was unpopular because of his message of doom for the nation.
*Jeremiah; 2 Chronicles 35:25, 36:21-22*

**Jonah**
A Hebrew prophet whom the Bible says God sent to denounce the citizens of Nineveh, Jonah was the first prophet to a heathen nation. He fled to the sea; God saved him from drowning by means of a great fish.
*Jonah*

**Joseph**
Joseph, Jacob's favorite son, was sold into slavery in Egypt as a result of his brothers' jealousy. Thrown into prison on false charges, he later rose to prominence after correctly interpreting Pharaoh's dreams. When famine came, Joseph invited his family to Egypt to escape its effects.
*Genesis 37:2-50:26*

**Joshua**
Moses' successor, Joshua led the Israelites into Canaan, conquered it, and divided it between the twelve tribes.
*Exodus 17:8-14, 24:13 Numbers 14:6-9; Deuteronomy 31:7-8,14,23, 34:9; Joshua*

**Miriam**
As a child, Miriam helped her brother, Moses, escape death. Later she became a prophetess; once she opposed Moses' leadership and was punished with leprosy.
*Exodus 2:4-8, 15:20-21; Numbers 12:1-15, 20:1*

**Moses**
Moses, the leader who freed his people, the Hebrews, from slavery in Egypt, was brought up by the king's daughter. Called by God to set his people free, Moses led his people out of Egypt and across the Red Sea. On Mount Sinai, God gave him the Ten Commandments. Moses died in Moab before the Israelites entered the Promised Land.
*Exodus 2:1–Deuteronomy 34:12*

**Rebekah**
Rebekah married Isaac and suggested to her son Jacob that he trick his father into giving him the blessing.
*Genesis 24:1-28:5*

**Ruth**
Ruth left her home country, Moab, to return to her mother-in-law's home in Bethlehem, where she married Boaz, and became the great-grandmother of David.
*Ruth*

**Samuel**
Samuel, the last of Israel's judges, was also one of the first prophets. At the end of his life he anointed Saul as Israel's first king. When Saul disobeyed God, Samuel anointed David to be king after him.
*1 Samuel 1:1-4:1, 7:2-13:15, 15:1-16:13, 19:18-24, 25:1*

**Sarah**
Abraham's wife, Sarah, became the mother of Isaac in her old age, in fulfilment of God's promise.
*Genesis 11:29-31, 12:5-20, 16:1-9, 18:1-15, 20:1-21:21, 23:1-20*

**Solomon**
Solomon, perhaps Israel's most famous king, was David's son by Bathsheba. Under his rule, the nation prospered, and his wisdom was renowned. He built the first Temple in Jerusalem, but his marriages to foreign wives led to his turning away from God to false gods.
*1 Kings 1-11*

# Old Testament
## TIME CHART

### Abraham

Abraham set out from Mesopotamia on his great journey to the Promised Land. God promised that through him all people would be blessed (Genesis 12:1-25:11). He was given a son, Isaac, in his old age (Genesis 21:1-7, 24:1-28:9).

### Jacob

Isaac's son Jacob was forced by famine to go down to Egypt; his people settled there, and years later, were forced into slavery (Genesis 25:19-35:29, 43:1-50:14).

### Moses

Moses led the Hebrew people, Abraham's descendants, out of Egypt (Exodus 1:1-12:51). In the wilderness they were given the Ten Commandments. Eventually, after the death of Moses, the Israelites entered the Promised Land and occupied it (Joshua 1:1-12:24).

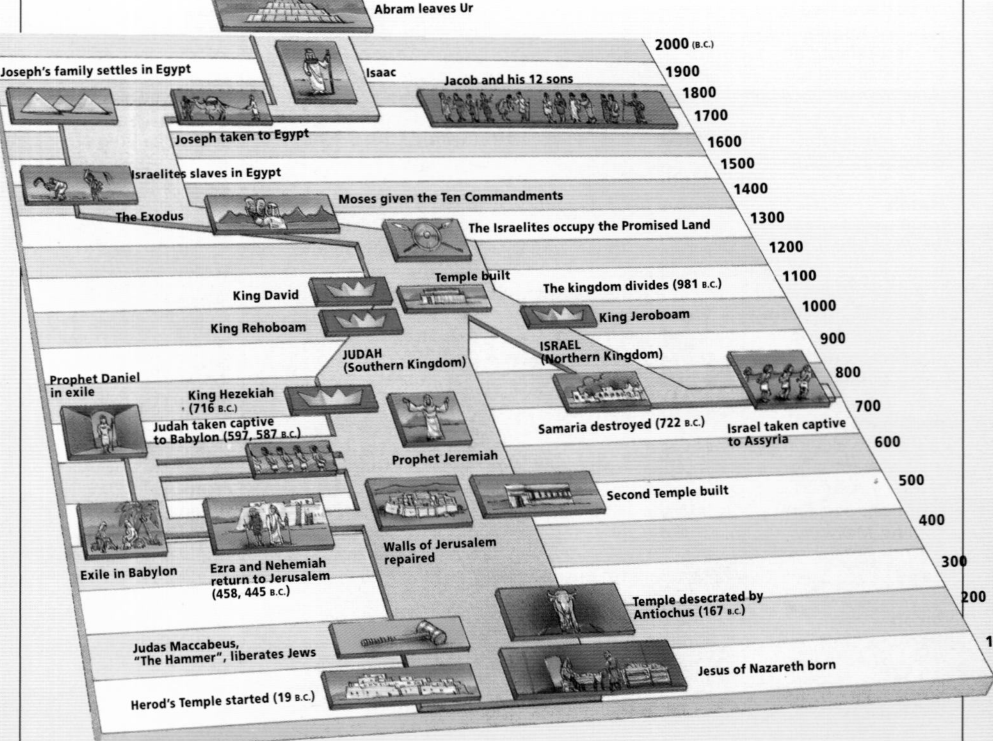


### Judges and Kings

As the nation of Israel developed, they were led first by judges (Judges 2:16-16:31; 1 Samuel 1:1-8:22) and then by a succession of kings (1 Samuel 9:1-31:13; 2 Samuel 1:1-24:23; 1 Kings 1:1-11:43). After the death of Solomon, the kingdom divided into Israel and Judah (1 Kings 12:1-22:53; 2 Kings 1:1-25:30).

### Captivity

When the Assyrian Empire rose to power, Israel was threatened with invasion. Despite God's warnings to his people through the prophets, the northern kingdom (Israel) was taken into captivity by Assyria in 722 B.C., and the southern kingdom (Judah) by Babylon in 587 B.C. (2 Kings 17:1-23, 25:1-30).

### Return

The Jews only returned from exile in Babylon to Palestine by stages, to set about reclaiming their land and rebuilding Jerusalem and the Temple (Ezra 1:1-6:22; Nehemiah 1:1-7:73a). Many of the Jews did not make this journey back to Palestine.

# THE NEW AMERICAN BIBLE

Translated from the Original Languages
with Critical Use of All the Ancient Sources
with

THE REVISED BOOK OF PSALMS
and
THE REVISED NEW TESTAMENT

AUTHORIZED BY THE BOARD OF TRUSTEES
of the
CONFRATERNITY OF CHRISTIAN DOCTRINE
and
APPROVED BY THE ADMINISTRATIVE COMMITTEE/BOARD
of the
NATIONAL CONFERENCE OF CATHOLIC BISHOPS
and the
UNITED STATES CATHOLIC CONFERENCE

**World Catholic Press**
A Division of
Catholic Book Publishing Corp.

THE NEW AMERICAN BIBLE

OLD TESTAMENT

NIHIL OBSTAT: Stephen J. Hartdegen, O.F.M., S.S.L.
Christian P. Ceroke, O. Carm., S.T.D.

IMPRIMATUR: †Patrick Cardinal O'Boyle, D.D.
Archbishop of Washington

JULY 27, 1970

REVISED NEW TESTAMENT

NIHIL OBSTAT: Stephen J. Hartdegen, O.F.M., S.S.L.
Censor Deputatus

IMPRIMATUR: †James A. Hickey, S.T.D., J.C.D.
Archbishop of Washington

August 27, 1986

REVISED PSALMS

IMPRIMATURE: Most Reverend Daniel E. Pilarczyk
President, National Conference of Catholic Biships

September 10, 1991

DICTIONARY/CONCORDANCE
AND NON-BIBLICAL MATERIALS

NIHIL OBSTAT: Reverend Richard L. Schaefer
Censor Deputatus

IMPRIMATUR: Most Reverend Jerome Hanus, O.S.B.
Archbiship of Dubuque

December 29, 1999

REFERENCE/ILLUSTRATION MATERIALS

NIHIT OBSTAT: Reverend Richard L. Schaefer
Censor Deputatus

IMPRIMATUR: Most Reverend Jerome Hanus, O.S.B.
Archbishop of Dubuque

November 7, 2000



Printed in Korea

9 10 11 Q 06 05 04

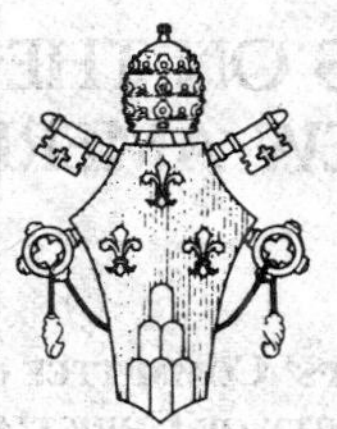

For the faithful in all English-speaking countries the publication of *The New American Bible* represents a notable achievement. Its pages contain a new Catholic version of the Bible in English, along with illustrations and explanations that facilitate the understanding of the text.

For more than a quarter of a century, members of the Catholic Biblical Association of America, sponsored by the Bishops' Committee of the Confraternity of Christian Doctrine, have labored to create this new translation of the Scriptures from the original languages or from the oldest extant form in which the texts exist.

In so doing, the translators have carried out the directive of our predecessor, Pius XII, in his famous Encyclical *Divino Afflante Spiritu,* and the decree of the Second Vatican Council *(Dei Verbum),* which prescribed that "up-to-date and appropriate translations be made in the various languages, by preference from the original texts of the sacred books," and that "with the approval of Church authority, these translations may be produced in cooperation with our separated brethren" so that "all Christians may be able to use them."

The holy task of spreading God's word to the widest possible readership has a special urgency today. Despite all his material achievements, man still struggles with the age-old problems of how to order his life for the glory of God, for the welfare of his fellows and the salvation of his soul. Therefore we are gratified to find in this new translation of the Scriptures a new opportunity for men to give themselves to frequent reading of, and meditation on, the living Word of God. In its pages we recognize His voice, we hear a message of deep significance for every one of us. Through the spiritual dynamism and prophetic force of the Bible, the Holy Spirit spreads his light and his warmth over all men, in whatever historical or sociological situation they find themselves.

On all who have contributed to this translation, and all who seek in its pages the sacred teaching and the promise of salvation of Jesus Christ our Lord, we gladly bestow our paternal Apostolic Blessing.

From the Vatican, September 18, 1970

Paulus PP. VI

# COLLABORATORS ON THE OLD TESTAMENT OF THE NEW AMERICAN BIBLE

## Bishops' Committee of the Confraternity of Christian Doctrine

Most Rev. Charles P. Greco, D.D., *Chairman*
Most Rev. Joseph T. McGucken, S.T.D.
Most Rev. Vincent S. Waters, D.D.
Most Rev. Romeo Blanchette, D.D.
Most Rev. Christopher J. Weldon, D.D.

## EDITORS IN CHIEF

Rev. Louis F. Hartman, C.SS.R., S.S.L., Ling. Or. L., *Chairman*
Rev. Msgr. Patrick W. Skehan, S.T.D., LL.D., *Vice-Chairman*
Rev. Stephen J. Hartdegen, O.F.M., S.S.L., *Secretary*

## ASSOCIATE EDITORS AND TRANSLATORS

Rev. Edward P. Arbez, S.S., S.T.D.
Rev. Msgr. Edward J. Byrne, Ph.D., S.T.D.
Rev. Edward A. Cerny, S.S., S.T.D.
Rev. James E. Coleran, S.J., S.T.L., S.S.L.
Rev. John J. Collins, S.J., M.A., S.S.L.
Sr. M. Emmanuel Collins, O.S.F., Ph.D.
Prof. Frank M. Cross, Jr., Ph.D.
Rev. Patrick Cummins, O.S.B., S.T.D.
Rev. Antonine A. De Guglielmo, O.F.M., S.T.D., S.S.L., S.S. Lect. Gen.
Rev. Alexander A. Di Lella, O.F.M., S.T.L., S.S.L., Ph.D.
Most Rev. John J. Dougherty, S.T.L., S.S.D.
Rev. William A. Dowd, S.J., S.T.D., S.S.L.
Prof. David Noel Freedman, Ph.D.
Rev. Michael J. Gruenthaner, S.J., S.T.D., S.S.D.
Rev. Msgr. Maurice A. Hofer, S.S.L.
Rev. Justin Krellner, O.S.B., S.T.D.
Rev. Joseph L. Lilly, C.M., S.T.D., S.S.L.
Rev. Roderick F. MacKenzie, S.J., M.A., S.S.D.
Rev. Edward A. Mangan, C.SS.R., S.S.L.
Rev. Daniel W. Martin, C.M., S.T.L., S.S.L.
Rev. William H. McClellan, S.J.
Rev. James McGlinchey, C.M., S.T.D.
Rev. Frederick Moriarty, S.J., S.S.L., S.T.D.
Rev. Richard T. Murphy, O.P., S.T.D., S.S.D.
Rev. Roland E. Murphy, O. Carm., M.A., S.T.D., S.S.L.
Rev. Msgr. William R. Newton, M.S., S.S.D.
Rev. Eberhard Olinger, O.S.B.
Rev. Charles H. Pickar, O.S.A., S.T.L., S.S.L.
Rev. Christopher Rehwinkel, O.F.M., S.T.D., S.S. Lect. Gen.
Rev. Msgr. John R. Rowan, S.T.D., S.S.L.
Prof. J. A. Sanders, Ph.D.
Rev. Edward F. Siegman, C.PP.S., S.T.D., S.S.L.
Rev. Msgr. Matthew P. Stapleton, S.T.D., S.S.L.
Rev. Msgr. John E. Steinmueller, S.T.D., S.S.L.
Rev. John Ujlaki, O.S.B., Litt.D.
Rev. Bruce Vawter, C.M., S.T.L., S.S.D.
Rev. John B. Weisengoff, S.T.D., S.S.L.

# Collaborators on the Revised Edition of the New Testament of the New American Bible

## Ad Hoc Bishops' Committee

Most Rev. Theodore E. McCarrick, D.D.
Most Rev. Richard J. Sklba, D.D.
Most Rev. J. Francis Stafford, D.D.
Most Rev. John F. Whealon, D.D., *Chairman*

## BOARD OF EDITORS

Rev. Msgr. Myles M. Bourke
Rev. Francis T. Gignac, S.J., *Chairman*
Rev. Stephen J. Hartdegen, O.F.M., *Secretary*
Rev. Claude J. Peifer, O.S.B.
Rev. John H. Reumann

## REVISERS

Rev. Msgr. Myles M. Bourke
Rev. Frederick W. Danker
Rev. Alexander A. Di Lella, O.F.M.
Rev. Charles H. Giblin, S.J.
Rev. Francis T. Gignac, S.J.
Rev. Stephen J. Hartdegen, O.F.M.
Dr. Maurya P. Horgan
Rev. John R. Keating, S.J.
Rev. John Knox
Dr. Paul J. Kobelski
Dr. J. Rebecca Lyman
Bro. Elliott C. Maloney, O.S.B.
Dr. Janet A. Timbie

## CONSULTANTS

The Rev. Joseph Jensen, O.S.B.
The Rev. Aidan Kavanagh, O.S.B.
Dr. Marianne Sawicki

## BUSINESS MANAGER

Charles A. Buggé

## WORD PROCESSOR

Suzanna Jordan

# Collaborators on the Revised Psalms of the New American Bible

## Bishops' Ad Hoc Committee

Most Rev. Enrique San Pedro, S.J.
Most Rev. Richard Sklba, D.D.
Most Rev. Donald W. Troutman, S.T.D., S.S.L.
Most Rev. Emil A. Wcela
Most Rev. John F. Whealon, S.S.L., *Chairman*

## BOARD OF EDITORS

Rev. Richard Clifford, S.J.
Br. Aloysius Fitzgerald, F.S.C.
Rev. Joseph Jensen, O.S.B.
Rev. Roland E. Murphy, O. Carm.
Sr. Irene Nowell, O.S.B.
Dr. Judith Sanderson

## REVISERS

Prof. Gary Anderson
Rev. Michael L. Barré
Rev. Christopher T. Begg
Dr. Joseph Blenkinsopp
Rev. Anthony R. Ceresko, O.S.F.S.
Rev. Richard J. Clifford, S.J.
Rev. Aelred Cody, O.S.B.
Prof. Michael D. Coogan
Rev. Alexander A. Di Lella, O.F.M.
Dr. Robert A. Di Vito
Br. Aloysius Fitzgerald, F.S.C.
Rev. Michael D. Guinan, O.F.M.
Rev. William L. Holladay
Rev. William Irwin, C.S.B.
Rev. Joseph Jensen, O.S.B.
Rev. John S. Kselman
Dr. Conrad E. L'Heureux
Rev. Leo Laberge, O.M.I.
Dr. Paul G. Mosca
Rev. Roland E. Murphy, O. Carm.
Dr. Michael Patrick O'Connor
Rev. Brian J. Peckham, S.J.
Prof. Jimmy J. Roberts
Sr. Eileen M. Schuller, O.S.U.
Dr. Byron E. Shafer
Prof. Mark S. Smith
Prof. Matitiahu Tsevat
Dr. Eugene C. Ulrich
Prof. James C. VanderKam
Rev. Jerome T. Walsh

## ENGLISH CONSULTANTS

Dr. Catherine Dunn
Br. Daniel Burke, F.S.C.

## BUSINESS MANAGER

Charles A. Buggé

# List of the Popes

1. St. Peter d. 67
2. St. Linus, 67-76
3. St. Anacletus I, 76-88
4. St. Clement I, 88-97
5. St. Evaristus, 97-105
6. St. Alexander I, 105-115
7. St. Sixtus I, 115-125
8. St. Telesphorus, 125-36
9. St. Hyginus, 136-40
10. St. Pius I, 140-55
11. St. Anicetus, 155-66
12. St. Soter, 166-75
13. St. Eleuterius, 175-89
14. St. Victor I, 189-99
15. St. Zephyrinus, 199-217
16. St. Callistus I, 217-22
17. St. Urban I, 222-30
18. St. Pontian, 230-35
19. St. Anterus, 235-36
20. St. Fabian, 236-50
21. St. Cornelius, 251-53
22. St. Lucius I, 253-54
23. St. Stephen I, 254-57
24. St. Sixtus II, 257-58
25. St. Dionysius, 259-68
26. St. Felix I, 269-74
27. St. Eutychian, 275-83
28. St. Caius, 283-96
29. St. Marcellinus, 296-304
30. St. Marcellus I, 304-09
31. St. Eusebius, 309-11
32. St. Melchiades, 311-14
33. St. Sylvester I, 314-35
34. St. Marcus, 336
35. St. Julius I, 337-52
36. Liberius, 352-66
37. St. Damasus I, 366-84
38. St. Siricius, 384-99
39. St. Anastasius I, 399-401
40. St. Innocent I, 401-17
41. St. Zosimus, 417-18
42. St. Boniface I, 418-22
43. St. Celestine I, 422-32
44. St. Sixtus III, 432-40
45. St. Leo I, 440-61
46. St. Hilarius, 461-68
47. St. Simplicius, 468-83
48. St. Felix II, 483-92
49. St. Gelasius I, 492-96
50. Anastasius II, 496-98
51. St. Symmachus, 498-514
52. St. Hormisdas, 514-23
53. St. John I, 523-26
54. St. Felix III, 526-30
55. Boniface II, 530-32
56. John II, 533-35
57. St. Agapitus I, 535-36
58. St. Silverius, 536-37
59. Vigilius, 537-55
60. Pelagius I, 556-61
61. John III, 561-74
62. Benedict I, 575-79
63. Pelagius II, 579-90
64. St. Gregory I, 590-604
65. Sabinianus, 604-06
66. Boniface III, 607
67. St. Boniface IV, 608-15
68. St. Deusdedit, 615-18
69. Boniface V, 619-25
70. Honorius I, 625-38
71. Severinus, 638-40
72. John IV, 640-42
73. Theodore I, 642-49
74. St. Martin I, 649-55
75. St. Eugene I, 655-57
76. St. Vitalian, 657-72
77. Adeodatus, 672-76
78. Donus, 676-78
79. St. Agatho, 678-81
80. St. Leo II, 682-83
81. St. Benedict II, 684-85
82. John V, 685-86
83. Conon, 686-87
84. St. Sergius I, 687-701
85. John VI, 701-05
86. John VII, 705-07

87. Sisinnius, 708
88. Constantine, 708-15
89. St. Gregory II, 715-31
90. St. Gregory III, 731-41
91. St. Zacharias, 741-52
92. Stephen II, 752-57
93. St. Paul I, 757-67
94. Stephen III, 768-72
95. Adrian I, 772-95
96. St. Leo III, 795-816
97. Stephen IV, 816-17
98. St. Paschal I, 817-24
99. Eugene II, 824-27
100. Valentine, 827
101. Gregory IV, 827-44
102. Sergius II, 844-47
103. St. Leo IV, 847-55
104. Benedict III, 855-58
105. St. Nicholas I, 858-67
106. Adrian II, 867-72
107. John VIII, 872-82
108. Marinus I, 882-84
109. St. Adrian III, 884-85
110. Stephen V, 885-91
111. Formosus, 891-96
112. Boniface VI, 896
113. Stephen VI, 896-97
114. Romanus, 897
115. Theodore II, 897
116. John IX, 898-900
117. Benedict IV, 900-03
118. Leo V, 903
119. Sergius III, 904-11
120. Anastasius III, 911-13
121. Lando, 913-14
122. John X, 914-28
123. Leo VI, 928
124. Stephen VII, 928-31
125. John XI, 931-36
126. Leo VII, 936-39
127. Stephen VIII, 939-42
128. Marinus II, 942-46
129. Agaptus II, 946-55
130. John XII, 955-64
131. Leo VIII, 964-65
132. Benedict V, 965
133. John XIII, 965-72
134. Benedict VI, 973-74
135. Benedict VII, 974-83
136. John XIV, 983-84
137. John XV, 985-96
138. Gregory V, 996-99
139. Sylvester II, 999-1003
140. John XVII, 1003
141. John XVIII, 1003-09
142. Sergius IV, 1009-12
143. Benedict VIII, 1012-24
144. John XIX, 1024-32
145. Benedict IX, 1032-45
146. Sylvester III, 1045
147. Benedict IX, 1045 (2nd)
148. Gregory VI, 1045-46
149. Clement II, 1046-47
150. Benedict IX, 1047-48 (3rd)
151. Damasus II, 1048
152. St. Leo IX, 1049-54
153. Victor II, 1055-57
154. Stephen IX, 1057-58
155. Nicholas II, 1059-61
156. Alexander II, 1061-73
157. St. Gregory VII, 1073-85
158. Bl. Victor III, 1087
159. Bl. Urban II, 1088-99
160. Paschal II, 1099-1118
161. Gelasius II, 1118-19
162. Callistus II, 1119-24
163. Honorius II, 1124-30
164. Innocent II, 1130-43
165. Celestine II, 1143-44
166. Lucius, 1144-45
167. Bl. Eugene III, 1145-53
168. Anastasius IV, 1153-54
169. Adrian IV, 1154-59
170. Alexander III, 1159-81
171. Lucius III, 1181-85
172. Urban III, 1185-87
173. Gregory VIII, 1187
174. Clement III, 1187-91
175. Celestine III, 1191-98
176. Innocent III, 1198-1216

177. Honorius III, 1216-27
178. Gregory IX, 1227-41
179. Celestine IV, 1241
180. Innocent IV, 1243-54
181. Alexander IV, 1254-61
182. Urban IV, 1261-64
183. Clement IV, 1265-68
184. Bl. Gregory X, 1271-76
185. Bl. Innocent V, 1276
186. Adrian V, 1276
187. John XXI, 1276-77
188. Nicholas III, 1277-80
189. Martin IV, 1281-85
190. Honorius IV, 1285-87
191. Nicholas IV, 1288-91
192. St. Celestine V, 1294
193. Boniface VIII, 1294-1303
194. Benedict XI, 1303-04
195. Clement V, 1305-14
196. John XXII, 1316-34
197. Benedict XII, 1334-42
198. Clement VI, 1342-52
199. Innocent VI, 1352-62
200. Bl. Urban V, 1362-70
201. Gregory XI, 1370-78
202. Urban VI, 1378-89
203. Boniface IX, 1389-1404
204. Innocent VII, 1404-06
205. Gregory XII, 1406-15 (resigned during Western Schism to permit a proper election of a successor)
206. Martin V, 1417-31
207. Eugene IV, 1431-47
208. Nicholas V, 1447-55
209. Callistus III, 1455-58
210. Pius II, 1458-64
211. Paul II, 1464-71
212. Sixtus IV, 1471-84
213. Innocent VIII, 1484-92
214. Alexander VI, 1492-1503
215. Pius III, 1503
216. Julius II, 1503-13
217. Leo X, 1513-21
218. Adrian VI, 1522-23
219. Clement VII, 1523-34
220. Paul III, 1534-49
221. Julius III, 1550-55
222. Marcellus II, 1555
223. Paul IV, 1555-59
224. Pius IV, 1559-65
225. St. Pius V, 1566-72
226. Gregory XIII, 1572-85
227. Sixtus V, 1585-90
228. Urban VII, 1590
229. Gregory XIV, 1590-91
230. Innocent IX, 1591
231. Clement VIII, 1592-1605
232. Leo XI, 1605
233. Paul V, 1605-21
234. Gregory XV, 1621-23
235. Urban VIII, 1623-44
236. Innocent X, 1644-55
237. Alexander VII, 1655-67
238. Clement IX, 1667-69
239. Clement X, 1670-76
240. Bl. Innocent XI, 1676-89
241. Alexander VIII, 1689-91
242. Innocent XII, 1691-1700
243. Clement XI, 1700-21
244. Innocent XIII, 1721-24
245. Benedict XIII, 1724-30
246. Clement XII, 1730-40
247. Benedict XIV, 1740-58
248. Clement XIII, 1758-69
249. Clement XIV, 1769-74
250. Pius VI, 1775-99
251. Pius VII, 1800-23
252. Leo XII, 1823-29
253. Pius VIII, 1829-30
254. Gregory XVI, 1831-46
255. Pius IX, 1846-78
256. Leo XIII, 1878-1903
257. St. Pius X, 1903-14
258. Benedict XV, 1914-22
259. Pius XI, 1922-1939
260. Pius XII, 1939-1958
261. John XXIII, 1958-1963
262. Paul VI, 1963-1978
263. John Paul I, 1978
264. John Paul II, 1978-2005
265. Benedict XVI, 2005 (now reigning)

# Parables in Chronological Order

| GALILEAN MINISTRY | Mt. | Mk. | Lk. | Jn. |
|---|---|---|---|---|
| **Second Period** | | | | |
| 1. The Two Debtors | | | 7.41-50 | |
| 2. The Sower | 13.1-23 | 4.1-20 | 8.4-15 | |
| 3. The Seed | | 4.26-29 | | |
| 4. The Weeds | 13.24-30, 36-43 | | | |
| 5. The Mustard Seed | 13.31, 32 | 4.30-32 | | |
| 6. The Yeast | 13.33 | | | |
| 7. The Hidden Treasure | 13.44 | | | |
| 8. The Costly Pearl | 13.45, 46 | | | |
| 9. The Drag-net | 13.47-50 | | | |
| **Third Period** | | | | |
| 10. The Unforgiving Servant | 18.21-35 | | | |
| THE PEREAN MINISTRY | | | | |
| 11. The Good Samaritan | | | 10.25-37 | |
| 12. The Rich Fool | | | 12.16-21 | |
| 13. The Barren Fig Tree | | | 13.6-9 | |
| 14. The Wedding Guest | | | 14.7-11 | |
| 15. The Great Feast | | | 14.15-24 | |
| 16. Counting the Cost | | | 14.25-35 | |
| 17. The Lost Sheep | | | 15.1-7 | |
| 18. The Lost Coin | | | 15.8-10 | |
| 19. The Lost Son | | | 15.11-32 | |
| 20. The Dishonest Steward | | | 16.1-13 | |
| 21. The Rich Man and Lazarus | | | 16.19-31 | |
| 22. The Unprofitable Servant | | | 17.1-10 | |
| 23. The Unjust Judge | | | 18.1-8 | |
| 24. The Pharisee and Tax Collector | | | 18.9-14 | |
| 25. The Workers in the Vineyard | 20.1-16 | | | |
| 26. The Ten Gold Coins | | | 19.11-28 | |
| THE PASSION WEEK | | | | |
| **Tuesday** | | | | |
| 27. The Two Sons | 21.28-32 | | | |
| 28. The Tenants | 21.33-46 | 12.1-12 | 20.9-19 | |
| 29. The Wedding Feast | 22.1-14 | | | |
| 30. The Ten Virgins | 25.1-13 | | | |
| 31. The Talents | 25.14-30 | | | |

# Miracles in Chronological Order

| Beginning of His Ministry | Mt. | Mk. | Lk. | Jn. |
|---|---|---|---|---|
| 1. Water Made Wine—at Cana | | | | 2.1-11 |
| **THE GALILEAN MINISTRY** | | | | |
| **First Period** | | | | |
| 2. Healing the Nobleman's Son | | | | 4.46-54 |
| 3. The Catch of Fish | | | 5.1-11 | |
| 4. The Man with an Unclean Demon | | 1.23-26 | 4.33-35 | |
| 5. Cure of Peter's Mother-in-law | 8.14-15 | 1.30, 31 | 4.38-39 | |
| 6. Healing a Leper | 8.2-4 | 1.40-45 | 5.12-14 | |
| 7. Healing the Paralytic | 9.2-8 | 2.1-12 | 5.17-26 | |
| 8. The Ill Man | | | | 5.1-16 |
| 9. The Withered Hand | 12.9-14 | 3.1-6 | 6.6-11 | |
| **Second Period** | | | | |
| 10. The Centurion's Servant | 8.5-13 | | 7.1-10 | |
| 11. The Widow's Son at Nain | | | 7.11-17 | |
| 12. The Man Mute and Blind | 12.22 | | | |
| 13. Calming the Storm | 8.23-27 | 4.35-41 | 8.22-25 | |
| 14. The Gadarene Demoniac | 8.28-34 | 5.1-20 | 8.26-39 | |
| 15. The Daughter of Jairus | 9.18-26 | 5.21-43 | 8.40-56 | |
| 16. The Afflicted Woman | 9.20-22 | 5.25-34 | 8.43-48 | |
| 17. Two Blind Men, Dumb Demoniac | 9.27-34 | | | |
| 18. Feeding the Five Thousand | 14.13-23 | 6.30-46 | 9.10-17 | 6.1-15 |
| 19. Jesus Walking on the Water | 14.24-36 | 6.47-56 | | 6.16-21 |
| **Third Period** | | | | |
| 20. Canaanite Woman's Daughter | 15.21-28 | 7.24-30 | | |
| 21. Deaf and Mute Man | 15.29-31 | 7.31-37 | | |
| 22. Feeding Four Thousand | 15.32-38 | 8.1-9 | | |
| 23. The Blind Man Near Bethsaida | | 8.22-26 | | |
| 24. The Demoniac Boy | 17.14-20 | 9.14-29 | 9.37-43 | |
| 25. The Temple-tax | 17.24-27 | 9.33 | | |
| **THE PEREAN MINISTRY** | | | | |
| 26. The Man Born Blind | | | | 9.1-41 |
| 27. The Mute Demoniac | | | 11.14 | |
| 28. The Crippled Woman | | | 13.10-21 | |
| 29. The Man Having Dropsy | | | 14.1-6 | |
| 30. The Raising of Lazarus | | | | 11.1-46 |
| 31. The Ten Lepers | | | 17.11-19 | |
| 32. The Blind Men Near Jericho | 20.29-34 | 10.46-52 | 18.35-43 | |
| **THE PASSION WEEK** | | | | |
| **Tuesday** | | | | |
| 33. The Withered Fig Tree | 21.20-22 | 11.20-25 | | |
| **Friday** | | | | |
| 34. Healing the Ear of Malchus | 26.50, 51 | 14.47 | 22.49-51 | |
| **AFTER THE RESURRECTION** | | | | |
| 35. The Catch of Fish | | | | 21.6-11 |

# The Books of the Bible

## THE OLD TESTAMENT


| | Abbrev. | Chaps. | Page |
|---|---|---|---|
| **PENTATEUCH** | | | 5 |
| Genesis | Gn | 50 | 7 |
| Exodus | Ex | 40 | 58 |
| Leviticus | Lv | 27 | 95 |
| Numbers | Nm | 36 | 122 |
| Deuteronomy | Dt | 34 | 161 |
| Joshua | Jos | 24 | 195 |
| Judges | Jgs | 21 | 217 |
| Ruth | Ru | 4 | 238 |
| **HISTORICAL BOOKS** | | | 242 |
| 1 Samuel | 1 Sm | 31 | 243 |
| 2 Samuel | 2 Sm | 24 | 272 |
| 1 Kings | 1 Kgs | 22 | 295 |
| 2 Kings | 2 Kgs | 25 | 321 |
| 1 Chronicles | 1 Chr | 29 | 347 |
| 2 Chronicles | 2 Chr | 36 | 374 |
| Ezra | Ezr | 10 | 404 |
| Nehemiah | Neh | 13 | 414 |
| Tobit | Tb | 14 | 428 |
| Judith | Jdt | 16 | 442 |
| Esther | Est | 10 | 456 |
| 1 Maccabees | 1 Mc | 16 | 468 |
| 2 Maccabees | 2 Mc | 15 | 497 |
| **WISDOM BOOKS** | | | 518 |
| Job | Jb | 42 | 519 |
| Psalms | Ps(s) | 150 | 547 |
| Proverbs | Prv | 31 | 634 |
| Ecclesiastes | Eccl | 12 | 664 |
| Song of Songs | Sg | 8 | 673 |
| Wisdom | Wis | 19 | 680 |
| Sirach | Sir | 51 | 699 |
| **PROPHETIC BOOKS** | | | 744 |
| Isaiah | Is | 66 | 746 |
| Jeremiah | Jer | 52 | 803 |
| Lamentations | Lam | 5 | 859 |
| Baruch | Bar | 6 | 866 |
| Ezekiel | Ez | 48 | 874 |
| Daniel | Dn | 14 | 917 |
| Hosea | Hos | 14 | 936 |
| Joel | Jl | 4 | 947 |
| Amos | Am | 9 | 951 |
| Obadiah | Ob | 1 | 959 |
| Jonah | Jon | 4 | 961 |
| Micah | Mi | 7 | 964 |
| Nahum | Na | 3 | 970 |
| Habakkuk | Hb | 3 | 973 |
| Zephaniah | Zep | 3 | 976 |
| Haggai | Hg | 2 | 979 |
| Zechariah | Zec | 14 | 982 |
| Malachi | Mal | 3 | 991 |


## THE NEW TESTAMENT


| | Abbrev. | Chaps. | Page |
|---|---|---|---|
| Matthew | Mt | 28 | 1005 |
| Mark | Mk | 16 | 1063 |
| Luke | Lk | 24 | 1090 |
| John | Jn | 21 | 1135 |
| Acts of the Apostles | Acts | 28 | 1169 |
| Romans | Rom | 16 | 1208 |
| 1 Corinthians | 1 Cor | 16 | 1229 |
| 2 Corinthians | 2 Cor | 13 | 1251 |
| Galatians | Gal | 6 | 1268 |
| Ephesians | Eph | 6 | 1277 |
| Philippians | Phil | 4 | 1285 |
| Colossians | Col | 4 | 1292 |
| 1 Thessalonians | 1 Thes | 5 | 1298 |
| 2 Thessalonians | 2 Thes | 3 | 1302 |
| 1 Timothy | 1 Tm | 6 | 1306 |
| 2 Timothy | 2 Tm | 4 | 1313 |
| Titus | Ti | 3 | 1318 |
| Philemon | Phlm | 1 | 1321 |
| Hebrews | Heb | 13 | 1323 |
| James | Jas | 5 | 1341 |
| 1 Peter | 1 Pt | 5 | 1347 |
| 2 Peter | 2 Pt | 3 | 1354 |
| 1 John | 1 Jn | 5 | 1359 |
| 2 John | 2 Jn | 1 | 1365 |
| 3 John | 3 Jn | 1 | 1367 |
| Jude | Jude | 1 | 1369 |
| Revelation | Rv | 22 | 1372 |

# Alphabetical Index

## OLD TESTAMENT


| | Abbrev. | Page | | Abbrev. | Page |
|---|---|---|---|---|---|
| Amos | Am | 951 | 1 Kings | 1 Kgs | 295 |
| Baruch | Bar | 866 | 2 Kings | 2 Kgs | 321 |
| 1 Chronicles | 1 Chr | 347 | Lamentations | Lam | 859 |
| 2 Chronicles | 2 Chr | 374 | Leviticus | Lv | 95 |
| Daniel | Dn | 917 | 1 Maccabees | 1 Mc | 468 |
| Deuteronomy | Dt | 161 | 2 Maccabees | 2 Mc | 497 |
| Ecclesiastes | Eccl | 664 | Malachi | Mal | 991 |
| Esther | Est | 456 | Micah | Mi | 964 |
| Exodus | Ex | 58 | Nahum | Na | 970 |
| Ezra | Ezr | 404 | Nehemiah | Neh | 414 |
| Ezekiel | Ez | 874 | Numbers | Nm | 122 |
| Genesis | Gn | 7 | Obadiah | Ob | 959 |
| Habakkuk | Hb | 973 | Proverbs | Prv | 634 |
| Haggai | Hg | 979 | Psalms | Ps(s) | 547 |
| Hosea | Hos | 936 | Ruth | Ru | 238 |
| Isaiah | Is | 746 | 1 Samuel | 1 Sm | 243 |
| Jeremiah | Jer | 803 | 2 Samuel | 2 Sm | 272 |
| Job | Jb | 519 | Sirach | Sir | 699 |
| Joel | Jl | 947 | Song of Songs | Sg | 673 |
| Jonah | Jon | 961 | Tobit | Tb | 428 |
| Joshua | Jos | 195 | Wisdom | Wis | 680 |
| Judges | Jgs | 217 | Zechariah | Zec | 982 |
| Judith | Jdt | 442 | Zephaniah | Zep | 976 |


## NEW TESTAMENT


| | Abbrev. | Page | | Abbrev. | Page |
|---|---|---|---|---|---|
| Acts of the Apostles | Acts | 1169 | Mark | Mk | 1063 |
| Colossians | Col | 1292 | Matthew | Mt | 1005 |
| 1 Corinthians | 1 Cor | 1229 | 1 Peter | 1 Pt | 1347 |
| 2 Corinthians | 2 Cor | 1251 | 2 Peter | 2 Pt | 1354 |
| Ephesians | Eph | 1277 | Philemon | Phlm | 1321 |
| Galatians | Gal | 1268 | Philippians | Phil | 1285 |
| Hebrews | Heb | 1323 | Revelation | Rv | 1372 |
| James | Jas | 1341 | Romans | Rom | 1208 |
| John (Gospel) | Jn | 1135 | 1 Thessalonians | 1 Thes | 1298 |
| 1 John | 1 Jn | 1359 | 2 Thessalonians | 2 Thes | 1302 |
| 2 John | 2 Jn | 1365 | 1 Timothy | 1 Tm | 1306 |
| 3 John | 3 Jn | 1367 | 2 Timothy | 2 Tm | 1313 |
| Jude | Jude | 1369 | Titus | Ti | 1318 |
| Luke | Lk | 1090 | | | |

# THE OLD TESTAMENT

# Preface to
# THE NEW AMERICAN BIBLE
## Old Testament

On September 30, 1943, His Holiness Pope Pius XII issued his now famous encyclical on scripture studies, *Divino afflante Spiritu*. He wrote: "We ought to explain the original text which was written by the inspired author himself and has more authority and greater weight than any, even the very best, translation whether ancient or modern. This can be done all the more easily and fruitfully if to the knowledge of languages be joined a real skill in literary criticism of the same text."

Early in 1944, in conformity with the spirit of the encyclical, and with the encouragement of Archbishop Cicognani, Apostolic Delegate to the United States, the Bishops' Committee of the Confraternity of Christian Doctrine requested members of The Catholic Biblical Association of America to translate the sacred scriptures from the original languages or from the oldest extant form of the text, and to present the sense of the biblical text in as correct a form as possible.

The first English Catholic version of the Bible, the Douay-Rheims (1582–1609/10), and its revision by Bishop Challoner (1750) were based on the Latin Vulgate. In view of the relative certainties more recently attained by textual and higher criticism, it has become increasingly desirable that contemporary translations of the sacred books into English be prepared in which due reverence for the text and strict observance of the rules of criticism would be combined.

THE NEW AMERICAN BIBLE has accomplished this in response to the need of the church in America today. It is the achievement of some fifty biblical scholars, the greater number of whom, though not all, are Catholics. In particular, the editors-in-chief have devoted twenty-five years to this work. The collaboration of scholars who are not Catholic fulfills the directive of the Second Vatican Council, not only that "correct translations be made into different languages especially from the original texts of the sacred books," but that, "with the approval of the church authority, these translations be produced in cooperation with separated brothers" so that "all Christians may be able to use them."

The text of the books contained in THE NEW AMERICAN BIBLE is a completely new translation throughout. From the original and the oldest available texts of the sacred books, it aims to convey as directly as possible the thought and individual style of the inspired writers. The better understanding of Hebrew and Greek, and the steady development of the science of textual criticism, the fruit of patient study since the time of St. Jerome, have allowed the translators and editors in their use of all available materials to approach more closely than ever before the sense of what the sacred authors actually wrote.

Where the translation supposes the received text—Hebrew, Aramaic, or Greek, as the case may be—ordinarily contained in the best-known editions, as the original or the oldest extant form, no additional remarks are necessary. But for those who are happily able to study the original text of the scriptures at first-hand, a supplementary series of textual notes pertaining to the Old Testament was added originally in an appendix to the typical edition. (It is now obtainable in a separate booklet from The Catholic Biblical Association of America, The Catholic University of America, Washington, DC 20064.) These notes furnish a guide in those cases in which the editorial board judges that the manuscripts in the original languages, or the evidence of the ancient versions, or some similar source, furnish the correct reading of a passage, or at least a reading more true to the original than that customarily printed in the available editions.

The Massoretic text of 1 and 2 Samuel has in numerous instances been corrected by the more ancient manuscripts Samuel a, b, and c from Cave 4 of Qumran, with the aid of important evidence from the Septuagint in both its oldest form and its Lucianic recension. Fragments of the lost Book of Tobit in Aramaic and in Hebrew, recovered from Cave 4 of Qumran, are in substantial agreement with the Sinaiticus Greek recension used for the translation of this book. The lost original Hebrew text of 1 Maccabees is replaced by its oldest extant form in Greek. Judith, 2 Maccabees, and parts of Esther are also translated from the Greek.

The basic text for the Psalms is not the Massoretic but one which the editors considered closer to the original inspired form, namely the Hebrew text underlying the new Latin Psalter of the Church, the *Liber Psalmorum* (1944[1],

1945[2]). Nevertheless they retained full liberty to establish the reading of the original text on sound critical principles.

The translation of Sirach, based on the original Hebrew as far as it is preserved and corrected from the ancient versions, is often interpreted in the light of the traditional Greek text. In the Book of Baruch the basic text is the Greek of the Septuagint, with some readings derived from an underlying Hebrew form no longer extant. In the deuterocanonical sections of Daniel (3, 24–90; 13, 1–14, 42), the basic text is the Greek text of Theodotion, occasionally revised according to the Greek text of the Septuagint.

In some instances in the Book of Job, in Proverbs, Sirach, Isaiah, Jeremiah, Ezekiel, Hosea, Amos, Micah, Nahum, Habakkuk, and Zechariah there is good reason to believe that the original order of lines was accidentally disturbed in the transmission of the text. The verse numbers given in such cases are always those of the current Hebrew text, though the arrangement differs. In these instances the textual notes advise the reader of the difficulty. Cases of exceptional dislocation are called to the reader's attention by footnotes.

The Books of *Genesis to Ruth* were first published in 1952; the Wisdom Books, *Job to Sirach,* in 1955; the Prophetic Books, *Isaiah to Malachi,* in 1961; and the Books of *Samuel to Maccabees,* in 1969. In the present edition of *Genesis to Ruth* there are certain new features: a general introduction to the Pentateuch, a retranslation of the text of Genesis with an introduction, cross-references, and revised textual notes, besides new and expanded exegetical notes which take into consideration the various sources or literary traditions.

The revision of *Job to Sirach* includes changes in strophe division in Job and Proverbs and in titles of principal parts and sections of Wisdom and Ecclesiastes. Corrections in the text of Sirach are made in 39, 27–44, 17 on the basis of the Masada text, and in 51, 13–30 on the basis of the occurrence of this canticle in the Psalms scroll from Qumran Cave 11. In this typical edition, new corrections are reflected in the textual notes of Job, Proverbs, Wisdom, and Sirach. In the Psalms, the enumeration found in the Hebrew text is followed instead of the double enumeration, according to both the Hebrew and the Latin Vulgate texts, contained in the previous edition of this book.

In the Prophetic Books *Isaiah to Malachi,* only minor revisions have been made in the structure and wording of the texts, and in the textual notes.

The spelling of proper names in THE NEW AMERICAN BIBLE follows the customary forms found in most English Bibles since the Authorized Version.

The work of translating the Bible has been characterized as "the sacred and apostolic work of interpreting the word of God and of presenting it to the laity in translations as clear as the difficulty of the matter and the limitations of human knowledge permit" (A. G. Cicognani, Apostolic Delegate, in *The Catholic Biblical Quarterly,* 6, [1944], 389–90). In the appraisal of the present work, it is hoped that the words of the encyclical *Divino afflante Spiritu* will serve as a guide: "Let all the sons of the church bear in mind that the efforts of these resolute laborers in the vineyard of the Lord should be judged not only with equity and justice but also with the greatest charity; all moreover should abhor that intemperate zeal which imagines that whatever is new should for that very reason be opposed or suspected."

Conscious of their personal limitations for the task thus defined, those who have prepared this text cannot expect that it will be considered perfect; but they can hope that it may deepen in its readers "the right understanding of the divinely given Scriptures," and awaken in them "that piety by which it behooves us to be grateful to the God of all providence, who from the throne of his majesty has sent these books as so many personal letters to his own children" (*Divino afflante Spiritu*).

# THE PENTATEUCH

*The Pentateuch, which consists of the first five books of the Bible (Genesis, Exodus, Leviticus, Numbers, Deuteronomy), enjoys particular prestige among the Jews as the "Law," or "Torah," the concrete expression of God's will in their regard. It is more than a body of legal doctrine, even though such material occupies many chapters, for it contains the story of the formation of the People of God: Abraham and the patriarchs, Moses and the oppressed Hebrews in Egypt, the birth of Israel in the Sinai covenant, the journey to the threshold of the Promised Land, and the "discourses" of Moses.*

*The grandeur of this historic sweep is the result of a careful and complex joining of several historical traditions, or sources. These are primarily four: the so-called Yahwist, Elohist, Priestly and Deuteronomic strands that run through the Pentateuch. (They are conveniently abbreviated as J, E, P and D.) Each brings to the Torah its own characteristics, its own theological viewpoint—a rich variety of interpretation that the sensitive reader will take pains to appreciate. A superficial difference between two of these sources is responsible for their names: the Yahwist prefers the name* Yahweh *(represented in translation as* Lord*) by which God revealed himself to Israel; the Elohist prefers the generic name for God,* Elohim. *The Yahwist is concrete, imaginative, using many anthropomorphisms in its theological approach, as seen, e.g., in the narrative of creation in Gn 2, compared with the Priestly version in Gn 1. The Elohist is more sober, moralistic. The Priestly strand, which emphasizes genealogies, is more severely theological in tone. The Deuteronomic approach is characterized by the intense hortatory style of Dt 5–11, and by certain principles from which it works, such as the centralization of worship in the Jerusalem temple.*

*However, even this analysis of the Pentateuch is an over-simplification, for it is not always possible to distinguish with certainty among the various sources. The fact is that each of these individual traditions incorporates much older material. The Yahwist was himself a collector and adapter. His narrative is made up of many disparate stories that have been reoriented, and given a meaning within the context in which they now stand; e.g., the story of Abraham and Isaac in Gn 22. Within the J and P traditions one has to reckon with many individual units; these had their own history and life-setting before they were brought together into the present more or less connected narrative.*

*This is not to deny the role of Moses in the development of the Pentateuch. It is true we do not conceive of him as the author of the books in the modern sense. But there is no reason to doubt that, in the events described in these traditions, he had a uniquely important role, especially as lawgiver. Even the later laws which have been added in P and D are presented as a Mosaic heritage. Moses is the lawgiver* par excellence, *and all later legislation is conceived in his spirit, and therefore attributed to him. Hence, the reader is not held to undeviating literalness in interpreting the words, "the* LORD *said to Moses." One must keep in mind that the Pentateuch is the crystallization of Israel's age-old relationship with God.*

*In presenting the story of the birth of the People of God, the Pentateuch looks back to the promises made to the patriarchs, and forward to the continuing fulfillment of these promises in later books of the Bible. The promises find their classic expression in Gn 12, 1ff. The "God of the Fathers" challenges Abraham to believe: the patriarch is to receive a people, a land, and through him the nations will somehow be blessed.*

*The mysterious and tortuous way in which this people is brought into being is described: Despite Sarah's sterility, Isaac is finally born—to be offered in sacrifice! The promises are renewed to him eventually, and also to the devious Jacob, as if to show that the divine design will be effected, with or without human cunning. The magnificent story of Joseph is highlighted by the theme of Providence; the promise of a people is taking shape.*

*Israel is not formed in a vacuum, but amid the age-old civilization of Mesopotamia and the Nile. Oppression in Egypt provokes a striking intervention of God.*

*Yahweh reveals himself to Moses as a savior, and the epic story of deliverance is told in Exodus. This book also tells of the Sinai covenant, which is rightfully regarded as the key to the Old Testament. Through the covenant Israel becomes*

*Yahweh's people, and Yahweh becomes Israel's God. This act of grace marks the fulfillment of the first promise; that Abraham will be the father of a great nation, God's special possession. The laws in Exodus and Leviticus (P tradition) are both early and late. They spell out the proper relationship of the federation of the Twelve tribes with the* LORD. *He is a jealous God, demanding exclusive allegiance; he cannot be imaged; he takes vengeance upon the wicked, and shows mercy to the good. Slowly the* LORD *reveals himself to his people; with remarkable honesty, Israel records the unsteady response—the murmurings and rebellions and infidelities through the desert wanderings up to the plain of Moab.*

*This sacred history was formed within the bosom of early Israel, guided by the spirit of God. It was sung beside the desert campfires; it was commemorated in the liturgical feasts, such as Passover; it was transmitted by word of mouth from generation to generation—until all was brought together in writing, about the sixth century* B.C., *when the literary formation of the Pentateuch came to an end.*

*The Book of Deuteronomy has a history quite peculiar to itself. Its old traditions and law code (12–26) are put forth in the form of "discourses" of Moses before his death. The extraordinarily intense and hortatory tone fits the mood of a discourse. The book contains possibly the preaching of the Levites in the northern kingdom of Israel before its fall in 721* B.C. *If this book is situated in its proper historical perspective, its true impact is more vividly appreciated. It is the blueprint of the great "Deuteronomic" reform under King Josiah (640–609* B.C.*). This was an attempt to galvanize the people into a wholehearted commitment to the covenant ideals, into an obedience motivated by the great commandment of love (Dt 6, 4ff). Israel has yet another chance, if it obeys. The people are poised between life and death; and they are exhorted to choose life—today (26, 16–19; 30, 15–20).*

# The Book of

# GENESIS

*Genesis, the first book of the Bible, opens with the Hebrew word* bereshit, *which means "in the beginning." The title "Genesis" was given to the Septuagint (Greek) translation of the book, because of its concern with the origin of the world (Gn 1, 1; 2, 4), of the human race, and, in particular, of the Hebrew people.*

*Eleven structural units* (toledoth), *of unequal length and importance, present the unity and purpose of the books in terms of God's universal sovereignty, his dealings with men, and his choice and formation of a special people to be the instrument of his plan of salvation.*

*The tracing of the direct descendance from Adam to Jacob constitutes the major part of the book, while the genealogical tables of lateral branches are not so developed nor of such interest as those that pertain to the story of the Israelite people. In fact, these lateral branches gradually disappear from the narrative. And with the introduction of Abraham and his covenant with God, the history of humanity as such becomes contracted to the story of the descendants of Abraham through Isaac and Jacob—the chosen people.*

*Despite its unity of plan and purpose, the book is a complex work, not to be attributed to a single original author. Several sources, or literary traditions, that the final redactor used in his composition are discernible. These are the Yahwist (J), Elohist (E) and Priestly (P) sources, which in turn reflect older oral traditions (see Introduction to the Pentateuch).*

*In Genesis, the Yahwist source is the most important by reason of its teaching, its antiquity, and the continuity it gives the book. It constitutes a sacred history, continually drawing attention to the working out of God's design through his interventions in the affairs of men. The Elohist source, less well preserved, is found in fragmentary form only, depicting God's manifestations through visions and dreams rather than theophanies. Angels are God's intermediaries with men. Moreover, there is a solicitude for the divine transcendence and greater sensitivity toward the moral order. The Priestly source contains those elements—chronological data, lists, genealogies—that construct the framework of Genesis and bind its contents together. To the J and E sources it adds such legal institutions as the sabbath rest, circumcision and the alliances between God and Noah and God and Abraham.*

*The interpreter of Genesis will recognize at once the distinct object that sets chapters 1–11 apart: the recounting of the origin of the world and of man (primeval history). To make the truths contained in these chapters intelligible to the Israelite people destined to preserve them, they needed to be expressed through elements prevailing among that people at that time. For this reason, the truths themselves must therefore be clearly distinguished from their literary garb.*

*With the story of the patriarchs Abraham, Isaac and Jacob (Gn 11, 27–50, 26), the character of the narrative changes. While we do not view the account of the patriarchs as history in the strict sense, nevertheless certain of the matters recounted from the time of Abraham onward can be placed in the actual historical and social framework of the Near East in the early part of the second millennium* B.C. *(2000–1500), and documented by non-biblical sources.*

*Genesis contains many religious teachings of basic importance: the preexistence and transcendence of God, his wisdom and goodness, his power through which all things are made and on which they all depend; the special creation of man in God's image and likeness, and of woman from the substance of man; the institution of marriage as the union of one man with one woman; man's original state of innocence; man's sin of pride and disobedience, its consequences for the protoparents and their posterity. Despite the severity of their punishment, hope of reconciliation is offered by God through the first as well as the subsequent promises of salvation and blessing. Abraham is blessed for his faith and obedience, and he is to be a blessing for all nations through his offspring, Isaac, Jacob, and Jacob's sons (Gn 12, 3; 18, 18; 22, 18), of whom the Messiah, mankind's greatest blessing, will eventually be born (Gal 3, 8).*

*Frequent references to Genesis are found in the New Testament. Christ becomes the antithesis of Adam: sin and death comes to mankind through Adam, justification and life through Jesus Christ (Rom 5, 12. 17ff). Noah's ark becomes the symbol of the church, by which men are saved from destruction through the waters of baptism (1 Pt 3, 20ff); Abraham's faith is the model for all believers; the sacrifice of his son Isaac typifies the sacrifice of Christ, Son of the Father. The liturgy, too, relates the persons of Abel, Abraham and Melchizedek to Christ in his act of sacrifice.*

*The Book of Genesis is divided as follows:*
*I. The Primeval History (1, 1–11, 26).*
*II. The Patriarch Abraham (11, 27–25, 18).*
*III. The Patriarchs Isaac and Jacob (25, 19–36, 43).*
*IV. Joseph and His Brothers (37, 1–50, 26).*

## *1: The Primeval History*

### CHAPTER 1

**First Story of Creation.*** **1** In the beginning, when God created the heavens and the
earth,[a] **2** the earth was a formless wasteland,
and darkness covered the abyss,* while a
mighty wind swept over the waters.[b]
**3** Then God said, "Let there be light," and
there was light.[c] **4** God saw how good the light
was. God then separated the light from the darkness. **5** God called the light "day," and the
darkness he called "night." Thus evening
came, and morning followed—the first day.*
**6** Then God said, "Let there be a dome in the
middle of the waters, to separate one body of
water from the other." And so it happened:
**7** God made the dome, and it separated the
water above the dome from the water below it.[d]
**8** God called the dome "the sky." Evening
came, and morning followed—the second day.
**9** Then God said, "Let the water under the
sky be gathered into a single basin, so that the
dry land may appear." And so it happened: the
water under the sky was gathered into its basin,
and the dry land appeared.[e] **10** God called the
dry land "the earth," and the basin of the water
he called "the sea." God saw how good it was.
**11** [f]Then God said, "Let the earth bring forth
vegetation: every kind of plant that bears seed
and every kind of fruit tree on earth that bears
fruit with its seed in it." And so it happened:
**12** the earth brought forth every kind of plant
that bears seed and every kind of fruit tree on
earth that bears fruit with its seed in it. God saw
how good it was. **13** Evening came, and morning followed—the third day.
**14** Then God said: "Let there be lights in the
dome of the sky, to separate day from night. Let
them mark the fixed times, the days and the
years,[g] **15** and serve as luminaries in the dome
of the sky, to shed light upon the earth." And
so it happened: **16** God made the two great
lights, the greater one to govern the day, and the
lesser one to govern the night; and he made the
stars.[h] **17** God set them in the dome of the sky,
to shed light upon the earth, **18** to govern the
day and the night, and to separate the light from
the darkness. God saw how good it was.
**19** Evening came, and morning followed—the
fourth day.
**20** [i]Then God said, "Let the water teem with
an abundance of living creatures, and on the
earth let birds fly beneath the dome of the sky."
And so it happened: **21** God created the great
sea monsters and all kinds of swimming creatures with which the water teems, and all kinds
of winged birds. God saw how good it was,
**22** and God blessed them, saying, "Be fertile,
multiply, and fill the water of the seas; and let

a Gn 2, 1.4: Pss 8, 4; 38—39; 90, 2; Wis 11, 17; Sir 16, 24; Jer 10, 12; 2 Mc 7, 28; Acts 14, 15; Col 1, 16f; Heb 1, 2f; 3, 4; 11, 3; Rv 4, 11.
b Jer 4, 23.
c 2 Cor 4, 6.
d Prv 8, 27f; 2 Pt 3, 5.
e Jb 38, 8; Ps 33, 7; Jer 5, 22.
f Ps 104, 14.
g Jb 26, 10; Ps 19, 1f; Bar 3, 33.
h Dt 4, 19; Ps 136, 7ff; Wis 13, 2ff; Jer 31, 35.
i Jb 12, 7-10.
j Gn 8, 17.

*

1, 1—2, 4a: This section introduces the whole Pentateuch. It shows how God brought an orderly universe out of primordial chaos.

1, 2: The abyss: the primordial ocean according to the ancient Semitic cosmogony. After God's creative activity, part of this vast body forms the salt-water seas (vv 9f); part of it is the fresh water under the earth (Ps 33, 7; Ez 31, 4), which wells forth on the earth as springs and fountains (Gn 7, 11; 8, 2; Prv 3, 20). Part of it, "the upper water" (Ps 148, 4; Dn 3, 60), is held up by the dome of the sky (Gn 1, 6f) from which rain descends on the earth (Gn 7, 11; 2 Kgs 7, 2. 19; Ps 104, 13). A mighty wind: Literally, "a wind of God," or "a spirit of God"; cf Gn 8 1.

1, 5: In ancient Israel a day was considered to begin at sunset. According to the highly artificial literary structure of Gn 1, 1—2, 4a, God's creative activity is divided into six days to teach the sacredness of the sabbath rest on the seventh day in the Israelite religion (Gn 2, 2f).

the birds multiply on the earth."[j] **23** Evening
came, and morning followed—the fifth day.
**24** [k]Then God said, "Let the earth bring
forth all kinds of living creatures: cattle, creeping things, and wild animals of all kinds." And
so it happened: **25** God made all kinds of wild
animals, all kinds of cattle, and all kinds of
creeping things of the earth. God saw how good
it was. **26** [l]Then God said: "Let us make man
in our image, after our likeness. Let them have
dominion over the fish of the sea, the birds of
the air, and the cattle, and over all the wild
animals and all the creatures that crawl on the
ground."*

**27** God created man in his image;
in the divine image he created him;
male and female he created them.

**28** God blessed them, saying: "Be fertile
and multiply; fill the earth and subdue it. Have
dominion over the fish of the sea, the birds of
the air, and all the living things that move on the
earth."[m] **29** [n]God also said: "See, I give you
every seed-bearing plant all over the earth and
every tree that has seed-bearing fruit on it to be
your food; **30** and to all the animals of the land,
all the birds of the air, and all the living creatures that crawl on the ground, I give all the
green plants for food." And so it happened.
**31** God looked at everything he had made, and
he found it very good. Evening came, and
morning followed—the sixth day.[o]

## CHAPTER 2

**1** Thus the heavens and the earth and all their
array were completed.[p] **2** Since on the seventh
day God was finished with the work he had been
doing, he rested on the seventh day from all the
work he had undertaken.[q] **3** So God blessed the
seventh day and made it holy, because on it he
rested from all the work he had done in creation.[r]

**4** Such is the story of the heavens and the
earth at their creation.

**Second Story of Creation.*** At the time
when the LORD God made the earth and the
heavens— **5** while as yet there was no field
shrub on earth and no grass of the field had
sprouted, for the LORD God had sent no rain
upon the earth and there was no man to till the
soil, **6** but a stream was welling up out of the
earth and was watering all the surface of the
ground— **7** the LORD God formed man out of
the clay of the ground* and blew into his nostrils
the breath of life, and so man became a living
being.[s]

**8** Then the LORD God planted a garden in
Eden,* in the east, and he placed there the man
whom he had formed.[t] **9** Out of the ground the
LORD God made various trees grow that were
delightful to look at and good for food, with the
tree of life in the middle of the garden and the
tree of the knowledge of good and bad.[u]

**10** A river rises* in Eden to water the garden;
beyond there it divides and becomes four
branches. **11** The name of the first is the Pishon; it is the one that winds through the whole
land of Havilah, where there is gold. **12** The
gold of that land is excellent; bdellium and lapis
lazuli are also there. **13** The name of the second
river is the Gihon; it is the one that winds all
through the land of Cush.[v] **14** The name of the
third river is the Tigris; it is the one that flows
east of Asshur. The fourth river is the Euphrates.

**15** The LORD God then took the man and
settled him in the garden of Eden, to cultivate
and care for it.[w] **16** The LORD God gave man
this order: "You are free to eat from any of the
trees of the garden[x] **17** except the tree of
knowledge of good and bad. From that tree you
shall not eat; the moment you eat from it you are
surely doomed to die."[y]

**18** The LORD God said: "It is not good for
the man to be alone. I will make a suitable
partner for him."[z] **19** So the LORD God formed
out of the ground various wild animals and various birds of the air, and he brought them to the

k Sir 16, 27f; Bar 3, 32.
l 26f: Gn 5, 1. 3; 9, 6; Ps 8, 5f; Wis 2, 23; 10, 2; Sir 17, 1. 3f; Jas 3, 7; 1 Cor 11, 7; Eph 4, 24; Col 3, 10; Mt 19, 4; Mk 10, 6.
m Gn 8, 17; 9, 1; Pss 8, 6-9; 115, 16; Wis 9, 2.
n 29f: Gn 9, 3; Ps 104, 14f.
o 1 Tm 4, 4.
p Is 45, 12; Jn 1, 3.
q Ex 20, 9ff; 31, 17; Heb 4, 4. 10.
r Ex 20, 11; Dt 5, 14; Neh 9, 14.
s Gn 3, 19; 18, 27; Tb 8, 6; Jb 34, 15; Pss 103, 14; 104, 29; Eccl 3, 20; 12, 7; Wis 7, 1; Sir 33, 10; 1 Cor 15, 45.
t Is 51, 3; Ez 31, 9.
u Gn 3, 22; Prv 3, 18; Rv 2, 7; 22, 2. 14.
v Sir 24, 25.
w Sir 7, 15.
x Ps 104, 14.
y Gn 3, 2f; Rom 6, 23.
z Tb 8, 6; Sir 36, 24; 1 Cor 11, 9; 1 Tm 2, 13.

*

1, 26: Man is here presented as the climax of God's creative activity; he resembles God primarily because of the dominion God gives him over the rest of creation.

2, 4b–25: This section is chiefly concerned with the creation of man. It is much older than the narrative of Gn 1, 1—2, 4a. Here God is depicted as creating man before the rest of his creatures, which are made for man's sake.

2, 7: God is portrayed as a potter molding man's body out of clay. There is a play on words in Hebrew between adam ("man") and adama ("ground"). Being: literally, "soul."

2, 8: Eden: used here as the name of a region in southern Mesopotamia; the term is derived from the Sumerian word eden, "fertile plain." A similar-sounding Hebrew word means "delight"; the garden in Eden could therefore be understood as the "garden of delight," so that, through the Greek version, it is now known also as "paradise," literally, a "pleasure park."

2, 10–14: Rises: in flood to overflow its banks. Beyond there: as one travels upstream. Branches: literally, "heads," i.e., upper courses. Eden is near the head of the Persian Gulf, where the Tigris and the Euphrates join with two other streams to form a single river. The land of Cush here and in Gn 10, 8, is not Ethiopia (Nubia) as elsewhere, but the region of the Kassites east of Mesopotamia.

man to see what he would call them; whatever
the man called each of them would be its name.
**20** The man gave names to all the cattle, all the
birds of the air, and all the wild animals; but
none proved to be the suitable partner for the
man.

**21** So the LORD God cast a deep sleep on the
man, and while he was asleep, he took out one
of his ribs and closed up its place with flesh.[a]
**22** The LORD God then built up into a woman
the rib that he had taken from the man. When
he brought her to the man, **23** the man said:

"This one, at last, is bone of my bones
and flesh of my flesh;
This one shall be called 'woman,'
for out of 'her man' this one has been
taken."*

**24** [b]That is why a man leaves his father and
mother and clings to his wife, and the two of
them become one body.*

**25** The man and his wife were both naked,
yet they felt no shame.

## CHAPTER 3

**The Fall of Man.** 1 Now the serpent was the
most cunning of all the animals that the LORD
God had made. The serpent asked the woman,
"Did God really tell you not to eat from any of
the trees in the garden?" **2** The woman answered the serpent: "We may eat of the fruit of
the trees in the garden; **3** [c]it is only about the
fruit of the tree in the middle of the garden that
God said, 'You shall not eat it or even touch it,
lest you die.' " **4** But the serpent said to the
woman: "You certainly will not die![d] **5** No,
God knows well that the moment you eat of it
your eyes will be opened and you will be like
gods who know* what is good and what is
bad." **6** The woman saw that the tree was good
for food, pleasing to the eyes, and desirable for
gaining wisdom. So she took some of its fruit
and ate it; and she also gave some to her husband, who was with her, and he ate it.[e] **7** Then
the eyes of both of them were opened, and they
realized that they were naked; so they sewed fig
leaves together and made loincloths for themselves.

**8** When they heard the sound of the LORD
God moving about in the garden at the breezy
time of the day,* the man and his wife hid
themselves from the LORD God among the trees
of the garden.[f] **9** The LORD God then called to
the man and asked him, "Where are you?"
**10** He answered, "I heard you in the garden;
but I was afraid, because I was naked, so I hid
myself." **11** Then he asked, "Who told you
that you were naked? You have eaten, then,
from the tree of which I had forbidden you to
eat!" **12** The man replied, "The woman whom
you put here with me—she gave me fruit from
the tree, so I ate it." **13** The LORD God then
asked the woman, "Why did you do such a
thing?" The woman answered, "The serpent
tricked me into it, so I ate it."[g]

**14** Then the LORD God said to the serpent:

"Because you have done this, you shall be
banned
from all the animals
and from all the wild creatures;
On your belly shall you crawl,
and dirt shall you eat
all the days of your life.[h]
**15** I will put enmity between you and the
woman,
and between your offspring and hers;
He will strike at your head,
while you strike at his heel."*[i]
**16** To the woman he said:
"I will intensify the pangs of your
childbearing;
in pain shall you bring forth children.
Yet your urge shall be for your husband,
and he shall be your master."[j]

**17** To the man he said: "Because you listened
to your wife and ate from the tree of which I had
forbidden you to eat,

"Cursed be the ground because of you!
In toil shall you eat its yield
all the days of your life.[k]
**18** Thorns and thistles shall it bring forth to
you,
as you eat of the plants of the field.

---

a Sir 17, 1; 1 Cor 11, 8f; 1 Tm 2, 13.
b Mt 19, 5; Mk 10, 7; 1 Cor 7, 10f; Eph 5, 31.
c Gn 2, 17; Rom 6, 23.
d 4f: Wis 2, 24; Sir 25, 14; Is 14, 14; Jn 8, 44; 2 Cor 11, 3.
e Gn 3, 22; 1 Tm 2, 14.
f Jer 23, 24.
g 2 Cor 11, 3.
h Is 65, 25; Mi 7, 17; Rv 12, 9.
i Is 7, 14; 9, 5; Rom 16, 20; 1 Jn 3, 8; Rv 12, 17.
j 1 Cor 11, 3; Eph 5, 22f; 1 Tm 2, 12.
k Gn 5, 29; Rom 5, 12; 8, 20; Heb 6, 8.

---

2, 23: There is a play on the similar-sounding Hebrew words ishsha ("woman") and ishah ("her man, her husband").

2, 24: One body: literally "one flesh"; classical Hebrew has no specific word for "body." The sacred writer stresses the fact that conjugal union is willed by God.

3, 5: Like gods who know: or "like God who knows."

3, 8: The breezy time of the day: literally "the wind of the day." On most days in Palestine a cooling breeze blows from the sea shortly before sunset.

3, 15: He will strike . . . at his heel: since the antecedent for he and his is the collective noun offspring, i.e., all the descendants of the woman, a more exact rendering of the sacred writer's words would be, "They will strike . . . at their heels." However, later theology saw in this passage more than unending hostility between snakes and men. The serpent was regarded as the devil (Wis 2, 24; Jn 8, 44; Rv 12, 9; 20, 2), whose eventual defeat seems implied in the contrast between head and heel. Because "the Son of God appeared that he might destroy the works of the devil" (1 Jn 3, 8), the passage can be understood as the first promise of a Redeemer for fallen mankind. The woman's offspring then is primarily Jesus Christ.

19 By the sweat of your face
shall you get bread to eat,
Until you return to the ground,
from which you were taken;
For you are dirt,
and to dirt you shall return."[l]

20 The man called his wife Eve, because she
became the mother of all the living.*
21 For the man and his wife the LORD God
made leather garments, with which he clothed
them. 22 Then the LORD God said: "See! The
man has become like one of us, knowing what
is good and what is bad! Therefore, he must not
be allowed to put out his hand to take fruit from
the tree of life also, and thus eat of it and live
forever."[m] 23 The LORD God therefore banished him from the garden of Eden, to till the
ground from which he had been taken.
24 When he expelled the man, he settled him
east of the garden of Eden; and he stationed the
cherubim and the fiery revolving sword, to
guard the way to the tree of life.*

## CHAPTER 4

**Cain and Abel.** 1 The man had relations
with his wife Eve, and she conceived and bore
Cain, saying, "I have produced a man with the
help of the LORD."* 2 Next she bore his brother Abel. Abel became a keeper of flocks, and
Cain a tiller of the soil. 3 In the course of time
Cain brought an offering to the LORD from the
fruit of the soil, 4 while Abel, for his part,
brought one of the best firstlings of his flock.[n]
The LORD looked with favor on Abel and his
offering, 5 but on Cain and his offering he did
not. Cain greatly resented this and was crestfall-
en. 6 So the LORD said to Cain: "Why are you
so resentful and crestfallen? 7 If you do well,
you can hold up your head; but if not, sin is a
demon lurking* at the door: his urge is toward
you, yet you can be his master."[o]
8 Cain said to his brother Abel, "Let us go
out in the field." When they were in the field,
Cain attacked his brother Abel and killed him.[p]
9 Then the LORD asked Cain, "Where is your
brother Abel?" He answered, "I do not know.
Am I my brother's keeper?" 10 The LORD then
said: "What have you done! Listen: Your brother's blood cries out to me from the soil!
11 Therefore you shall be banned from the soil
that opened its mouth to receive your brother's
blood from your hand.[q] 12 If you till the soil,
it shall no longer give you its produce. You shall
become a restless wanderer on the earth."
13 Cain said to the LORD: "My punishment is
too great to bear. 14 Since you have now banished me from the soil, and I must avoid your
presence and become a restless wanderer on the
earth, anyone may kill me at sight." 15 "Not
so!" the LORD said to him. "If anyone kills
Cain, Cain shall be avenged sevenfold." So the
LORD put a mark* on Cain, lest anyone should
kill him at sight. 16 Cain then left the LORD's
presence and settled in the land of Nod,* east of
Eden.

### Descendants of Cain and Seth.

17 *Cain had relations with his wife, and she
conceived and bore Enoch. Cain also became
the founder of a city, which he named after his
son Enoch. 18 To Enoch was born Irad, and
Irad became the father of Mehujael; Mehujael
became the father of Metusael, and Methusael
became the father of Lamech. 19 Lamech took
two wives; the name of the first was Adah, and
the name of the second Zillah. 20 Adah gave
birth to Jabal, the ancestor of all who dwell in
tents and keep cattle. 21 His brother's name
was Jubal; he was the ancestor of all who play
the lyre and the pipe. 22 Zillah, on her part,
gave birth to Tubalcain, the ancestor of all who
forge instruments of bronze and iron. The sister
of Tubalcain was Naamah. 23 Lamech said to
his wives:

"Adah and Zillah, hear my voice;
wives of Lamech, listen to my utterance:
I have killed a man for wounding me,
a boy for bruising me.
24 If Cain is avenged sevenfold,
then Lamech seventy-sevenfold."

25 Adam again had relations with his wife, and

---

l Gn 2, 7; Jb 10, 9; 34, 15; Pss 90, 3; 103, 14; Eccl 3, 20; 12, 7; Wis 15, 8; Sir 10, 9; 17, 2; Rom 5, 12; 1 Cor 15, 21; Heb 9, 27.
m Gn 2, 9; Rv 22, 2. 14.
n Ex 34, 19; Heb 11, 4.
o Sir 7, 1; Jude 11.
p Wis 10, 3; Mt 23, 35; Lk 11, 51; 1 Jn 3, 12; Jude 11.
q Dt 27, 24.

---

3, 20: This verse seems to be out of place; it would fit better after v 24. The Hebrew name hawwa ("Eve") is related to the Hebrew word hay ("living").

3, 24: The above rendering is based on the ancient Greek version; that of the current Hebrew is, When he expelled the man, he settled east of the garden of Eden, the cherubim.

4, 1: The Hebrew name qayin ("Cain") and the term qaniti ("I have produced") present another play on words.

4, 7: Demon lurking: in Hebrew, robes, literally "croucher," is used here, like the similar Akkadian term rabisu, to designate a certain kind of evil spirit.

4, 15: A mark: probably a tattoo. The use of tattooing for tribal marks has always been common among the nomads of the Near Eastern deserts.

4, 16: The land of Nod: not a definite geographic region. The term merely means "the land of nomads."

4, 17–22: In vv 12–16 Cain was presented as the archetype of nomadic peoples. The sacred author in this section follows another ancient tradition that makes Cain the prototype of sedentary peoples with higher material culture.

4, 25f: Has granted: Hebrew shat, a wordplay on the name shet ("Seth"). Enosh: in Hebrew, a synonym of adam ("man"). At the time . . . name: men began to call God by his personal name, Yahweh, rendered as "the Lord" in this version of the Bible. The ancient, so-called Yahwist source used here employs the name Yahweh long before the time of Moses. Another ancient source, the Elohist (from its use of the term Elohim,

she gave birth to a son whom she called Seth. "God has granted* me more offspring in place of Abel," she said, "because Cain slew him." **26** To Seth, in turn, a son was born, and he named him Enosh.

At that time men began to invoke the LORD by name.[r]

## CHAPTER 5

**Generations: Adam to Noah.*** **1** [s]This is the record of the descendants of Adam. When God created man, he made him in the likeness of God; **2** he created them male and female. When they were created, he blessed them and named them "man."

**3** [t]Adam was one hundred and thirty years old when he begot a son in his likeness, after his image; and he named him Seth.[u] **4** Adam lived eight hundred years after the birth of Seth, and he had other sons and daughters. **5** The whole lifetime of Adam was nine hundred and thirty years; then he died.

**6** When Seth was one hundred and five years old, he became the father of Enosh. **7** Seth lived eight hundred and seven years after birth of Enosh, and he had other sons and daughters. **8** The whole lifetime of Seth was nine hundred and twelve years; then he died.

**9** When Enosh was ninety years old, he became the father of Kenan. **10** Enosh lived eight hundred and fifteen years after the birth of Kenan, and he had other sons and daughters. **11** The whole lifetime of Enosh was nine hundred and five years; then he died.

**12** When Kenan was seventy years old, he became the father of Mahalalel. **13** Kenan lived eight hundred and forty years after the birth of Mahalalel, and he had other sons and daughters. **14** The whole lifetime of Kenan was nine hundred and ten years; then he died.

**15** When Mahalalel was sixty-five years old, he became the father of Jared. **16** Mahalalel lived eight hundred and thirty years after the birth of Jared, and he had other sons and daughters. **17** The whole lifetime of Mahalalel was eight hundred and ninety-five years; then he died.

**18** When Jared was one hundred and sixty-two years old, he became the father of Enoch. **19** Jared lived eight hundred years after the birth of Enoch, and he had other sons and daughters. **20** The whole lifetime of Jared was nine hundred and sixty-two years; then he died.

**21** When Enoch was sixty-five years old, he became the father of Methuselah. **22** Enoch lived three hundred years after the birth of Methuselah, and he had other sons and daughters. **23** The whole lifetime of Enoch was three hundred and sixty-five years. **24** Then Enoch walked with God,* and he was no longer here, for God took him.[v]

**25** When Methuselah was one hundred and eighty-seven years old, he became the father of Lamech. **26** Methuselah lived seven hundred and eighty-two years after the birth of Lamech, and he had other sons and daughters. **27** The whole lifetime of Methuselah was nine hundred and sixty-nine years; then he died.

**28** When Lamech was one hundred and eighty-two years old, he begot a son **29** [w]and named him Noah, saying, "Out of the very ground that the LORD has put under a curse, this one shall bring us relief from our work and the toil of our hands."* **30** Lamech lived five hundred and ninety-five years after the birth of Noah, and he had other sons and daughters. **31** The whole lifetime of Lamech was seven hundred and seventy-seven years; then he died.

**32** When Noah was five hundred years old, he became the father of Shem, Ham and Japheth.[x]

## CHAPTER 6

**Origin of the Nephilim.*** **1** When men began to multiply on earth and daughters were

---

r 1 Chr 1, 1; Lk 3, 38.
s Gn 1, 27; Wis 2, 23; Sir 17, 1; 1 Cor 11, 7; Jas 3, 9.
t Gn 4, 25.
u 3-32: 1 Chr 1, 1-4; Lk 3, 36ff.
v Wis 4, 10f; Sir 44, 16; 49, 14; Heb 11, 5.
w Gn 3, 17ff.
x Gn 6, 10; 10, 1.

---

"God," instead of Yahweh, "Lord," for the pre-Mosaic period), makes Moses the first to use Yahweh as the proper name of Israel's God, previously known by other names as well; cf Ex 3, 13ff.

5, 1–32: Although this chapter, with its highly schematic form, belongs to the relatively late "Priestly document," it is based on very ancient traditions. Together with Gn 11, 10–26, its primary purpose is to bridge the genealogical gap between Adam and Abraham. Adam's line is traced through Seth, but several names in the series are the same as, or similar to, certain names in Cain's line (Gn 4, 17ff). The long lifespans attributed to these ten antediluvian patriarchs have a symbolic rather than a historical value. Babylonian tradition also recorded ten kings with fantastically high ages who reigned successively before the flood.

5, 24: In place of the usual formula, Then he died, the change to Enoch walked with God clearly implies that he did not die, but like Elijah (2 Kgs 2, 11f) was taken alive to God's abode.

5, 29: There is a similarity in sound between the Hebrew word noah, "Noah," and the verbal phrase yenahamenu, "he will bring us relief"; this latter refers both to the curse put on the soil because of the fall of man (Gn 3, 17ff) and to Noah's success in agriculture, especially in raising grapes for wine (Gn 9, 20f).

6, 1–4: This is apparently a fragment of an old legend that had borrowed much from ancient mythology. The sacred author incorporates it here, not only in order to account for the prehistoric giants of Palestine, whom the Israelites called the Nephilim, but also to introduce the story of the flood with a moral orientation—the constantly increasing wickedness of mankind.

born to them, 2 the sons of heaven* saw how
beautiful the daughters of man were, and so they
took for their wives as many of them as they
chose.[y] 3 Then the LORD said: "My spirit*
shall not remain in man forever, since he is but
flesh. His days shall comprise one hundred and
twenty years."

4 At that time the Nephilim appeared on
earth (as well as later*), after the sons of heaven
had intercourse with the daughters of man, who
bore them sons. They were the heroes of old, the
men of renown.[z]

**Warning of the Flood.** 5 *When the LORD
saw how great was man's wickedness on earth,
and how no desire that his heart conceived was
ever anything but evil,[a] 6 he regretted that he
had made man on the earth, and his heart was
grieved.

7 So the LORD said: "I will wipe out from the
earth the men whom I have created, and not only
the men, but also the beasts and the creeping
things and the birds of the air, for I am sorry that
I made them." 8 But Noah found favor with the
LORD.

9 These are the descendants of Noah. Noah,
a good man and blameless in that age,[b] 10 for
he walked with God, begot three sons: Shem,
Ham and Japheth.

11 In the eyes of God the earth was corrupt
and full of lawlessness.[c] 12 When God saw
how corrupt the earth had become, since all
mortals led depraved lives on earth,[d] 13 he said
to Noah: "I have decided to put an end to all
mortals on earth; the earth is full of lawlessness
because of them. So I will destroy them and all
life on earth.[e]

**Preparation for the Flood.** 14 "Make
yourself an ark of gopherwood,* put various
compartments in it, and cover it inside and out
with pitch. 15 This is how you shall build it: the
length of the ark shall be three hundred cubits,
its width fifty cubits, and its height thirty cubits.* 16 Make an opening for daylight* in the
ark, and finish the ark a cubit above it. Put an
entrance in the side of the ark, which you shall
make with bottom, second and third decks.
17 I, on my part, am about to bring the flood
[waters] on the earth, to destroy everywhere all
creatures in which there is the breath of life;
everything on earth shall perish.[f] 18 But with
you I will establish my covenant; you and your
sons, your wife and your sons' wives, shall go
into the ark.[g] 19 Of all other living creatures
you shall bring two into the ark, one male and
one female, that you may keep them alive with
you. 20 Of all kinds of birds, of all kinds of
beasts, and of all kinds of creeping things, two
of each shall come into the ark with you, to stay
alive. 21 Moreover, you are to provide yourself
with all the food that is to be eaten, and store
it away, that it may serve as provisions for you
and for them." 22 This Noah did; he carried
out all the commands that God gave him.

## CHAPTER 7

1 Then the LORD said to Noah: "Go into the
ark, you and all your household, for you alone
in this age have I found to be truly just.[h] 2 Of
every clean animal, take with you seven pairs,
a male and its mate; and of the unclean animals,
one pair, a male and its mate; 3 likewise, of
every clean bird of the air, seven pairs, a male
and a female, and of all the unclean birds, one
pair, a male and a female. Thus you will keep
their issue alive over all the earth. 4 Seven days
from now I will bring rain down on the earth for
forty days and forty nights, and so I will wipe

y Mt 24, 38; Lk 17, 26f.
z Wis 14, 6; Bar 3, 26.
a Ps 14, 2f.
b Wis 10, 4; Sir 44, 17.
c Jb 22, 15ff.
d Ps 14, 2.
e Sir 40, 9f; 44, 17; Mt 24, 37ff.
f Gn 7, 4. 21; 2 Pt 2, 5.
g Gn 9, 9; Wis 14, 6; Heb 11, 7; 1 Pt 3, 20.
h Wis 10, 4; Sir 44, 17; 2 Pt 2, 5.
i Gn 6, 17; 2 Pt 2, 5.

*

6, 2: The sons of heaven: literally "the sons of the gods" or "the sons of God," i.e., the celestial beings of mythology.

6, 3: My spirit: the breath of life referred to in Gn 2, 7. His days . . . years: probably the time God would still let men live on earth before destroying them with the flood, rather than the maximum span of life God would allot to individual men in the future.

6, 4: As well as later: According to Nm 13, 33, when the Israelites invaded Palestine and found there the tall aboriginal Anakim, they likened them to the Nephilim; cf Dt 2, 10f. Perhaps the huge megalithic structures in Palestine were thought to have been built by a race of giants, whose superhuman strength was attributed to semi-divine origin. The heroes of old: the legendary worthies of ancient mythology.

6, 5—8, 22: The story of the great flood here recorded is a composite narrative based on two separate sources interwoven into an intricate patchwork. To the Yahwist source, with some later editorial additions, are usually assigned 6, 5–8; 7, 1–5. 7–10. 12. 16b. 17b. 22–23; 8, 2b–3a. 6–12. 13b. 20–22. The other sections come from the "Priestly document." The combination of the two sources produced certain duplications (e.g., 6, 13–22 of the Yahwist source, beside 7, 1–5 of the Priestly source); also certain inconsistencies, such as the number of the various animals taken into the ark (6, 19f; 7, 14f of the Priestly source, beside 7, 2f of the Yahwist source), and the timetable of the flood (8, 3–5. 13f of the Priestly source, beside 7, 4. 10. 12. 17b; 8, 6. 10. 12 of the Yahwist source). Both biblical sources go back ultimately to an ancient Mesopotamian story of a great flood, preserved in the eleventh tablet of the Gilgamesh Epic. The latter account, in some respects remarkably similar to the biblical account, is in others very different from it.

6, 14: Gopherwood: an unidentified wood not mentioned elsewhere; gopher is merely the Hebrew word for it.

6, 15: The dimensions of Noah's ark were approximately 440 × 73 × 44 feet, a foot and a half to the cubit. The ark of the Babylonian flood story was an exact cube, 120 cubits in length, width, and height.

6, 16: Opening for daylight: a conjectural rendering of the Hebrew word sohar, occurring only here. The reference is probably to an open space on all sides near the top of the ark to admit light and air. The ark also had a window or hatch, which could be opened and closed (Gn 8. 6).

out from the surface of the earth every moving
creature that I have made."[i] 5 Noah did just as
the LORD had commanded him.

**The Great Flood.** 6 Noah was six hundred
years old when the flood waters came upon the
earth. 7 Together with his sons, his wife, and
his sons' wives, Noah went into the ark because
of the waters of the flood.[j] 8 Of the clean animals and the unclean, of the birds, and of everything that creeps on the ground, 9 [two by two]
male and female entered the ark with Noah, just
as the LORD had commanded him.[k] 10 As soon
as the seven days were over, the waters of the
flood came upon the earth.

11 In the six hundredth year of Noah's life,
in the second month, on the seventeenth day of
the month: it was on that day that

> All the fountains of the great abyss* burst
> forth,
> and the floodgates of the sky were
> opened.

12 For forty days and forty nights heavy rain
poured down on the earth.

13 On the precise day named, Noah and his
sons Shem, Ham and Japheth, and Noah's wife,
and the three wives of Noah's sons had entered
the ark, 14 together with every kind of wild
beast, every kind of domestic animal, every
kind of creeping thing of the earth, and every
kind of bird. 15 Pairs of all creatures in which
there was the breath of life entered the ark with
Noah. 16 Those that entered were male and
female, and of all species they came, as God had
commanded Noah. Then the LORD shut him in.

17 The flood continued upon the earth for
forty days. As the waters increased, they lifted
the ark, so that it rose above the earth. 18 The
swelling waters increased greatly, but the ark
floated on the surface of the waters. 19 Higher
and higher above the earth rose the waters, until
all the highest mountains everywhere were submerged, 20 the crest rising fifteen cubits higher
than the submerged mountains. 21 All creatures that stirred on earth perished: birds, cattle,
wild animals, and all that swarmed on the earth,
as well as all mankind.[l] 22 Everything on dry
land with the faintest breath of life in its nostrils
died out. 23 The LORD wiped out every living
thing on earth: man and cattle, the creeping
things and the birds of the air; all were wiped out
from the earth. Only Noah and those with him
in the ark were left.

## CHAPTER 8

7, 24 *The waters maintained their crest
over the earth for one hundred and fifty days,
1 and then God remembered Noah and all the
animals, wild and tame, that were with him in
the ark. So God made a wind sweep over the
earth, and the waters began to subside. 2 The
fountains of the abyss and the floodgates of the
sky were closed, and the downpour from the sky
was held back. 3 Gradually the waters receded
from the earth. At the end of one hundred and
fifty days, the waters had so diminished 4 that,
in the seventh month, on the seventeenth day of
the month, the ark came to rest on the mountains
of Ararat.* 5 The waters continued to diminish
until the tenth month, and on the first day of the
tenth month the tops of the mountains appeared.

6 At the end of forty days Noah opened the
hatch he had made in the ark,* 7 and he sent out
a raven, to see if the waters had lessened on the
earth. It flew back and forth until the waters
dried off from the earth. 8 Then he sent out a
dove, to see if the waters had lessened on the
earth. 9 But the dove could find no place to
alight and perch, and it returned to him in the
ark, for there was water all over the earth. Putting out his hand, he caught the dove and drew
it back to him inside the ark. 10 He waited
seven days more and again sent the dove out
from the ark. 11 In the evening the dove came
back to him, and there in its bill was a
plucked-off olive leaf! So Noah knew that the
waters had lessened on the earth. 12 He waited
still another seven days and then released the
dove once more; and this time it did not come
back.

13 In the six hundred and first year of Noah's
life, in the first month, on the first day of the
month, the water began to dry up on the earth.
Noah then removed the covering of the ark and
saw that the surface of the ground was drying
up. 14 In the second month, on the twenty-seventh day of the month, the earth was dry.

15 Then God said to Noah: 16 "Go out of
the ark, together with your wife and your sons
and your sons' wives. 17 Bring out with you
every living thing that is with you—all bodily
creatures, be they birds or animals or creeping
things of the earth—and let them abound on the
earth, breeding and multiplying on it."[m] 18 So
Noah came out, together with his wife and his
sons and his sons' wives; 19 and all the ani-

j Wis 14, 6; 1 Pt 3, 20; 2 Pt 2, 5.
k Gn 6, 19.
l 21ff; Jb 22, 16; Mt 24, 39; Lk 17, 27; 2 Pt 3, 6.
m Gn 1, 22. 28.

*

7, 11: Abyss: the subterranean ocean; see note on Gn 1, 2.

7, 24: This verse belongs to chapter 7 but its contents properly introduce chapter 8.

8, 4: Ararat: ancient Urartu, north of the Mesopotamian plain, part of modern Armenia.

8, 6: In the original Yahwist source, from which this verse is taken, the forty days refer to the full period of the flood itself (cf Gn 7, 4. 17); in the present context, however, they seem to refer to a period following the date just given in v 5 from the Priestly source.

mals, wild and tame, all the birds, and all the
creeping creatures of the earth left the ark, one
kind after another.
**20** Then Noah built an altar to the LORD, and
choosing from every clean animal and every
clean bird, he offered holocausts on the altar.
**21** When the LORD smelled the sweet odor, he
said to himself: "Never again will I doom the
earth because of man, since the desires of man's
heart are evil from the start;* nor will I ever
again strike down all living beings, as I have
done.[n]

**22** As long as the earth lasts,
seedtime and harvest,
cold and heat,
Summer and winter,
and day and night
shall not cease."[o]

## CHAPTER 9

**Covenant with Noah.** **1** God blessed
Noah and his sons and said to them: "Be fertile
and multiply and fill the earth.[p] **2** Dread fear of
you shall come upon all the animals of the earth
and all the birds of the air, upon all the creatures
that move about on the ground and all the fishes
of the sea; into your power they are delivered.
**3** [q]Every creature that is alive shall be yours to
eat; I give them all to you as I did the green
plants.* **4** [r]Only flesh with its lifeblood still in
it you shall not eat.* **5** For your own lifeblood,
too, I will demand an accounting: from every
animal I will demand it, and from man in regard
to his fellow man I will demand an accounting
for human life.[s]

**6** If anyone sheds the blood of man,
by man shall his blood be shed;
For in the image of God
has man been made.[t]

**7** Be fertile, then, and multiply; abound on
earth and subdue it."[u]
**8** God said to Noah and to his sons with him:
**9** "See, I am now establishing my covenant
with you and your descendants after you[v]
**10** and with every living creature that was with
you: all the birds, and the various tame and wild
animals that were with you and came out of the
ark. **11** I will establish my covenant with you,
that never again shall all bodily creatures be
destroyed by the waters of a flood; there shall
not be another flood to devastate the earth."[w]
**12** God added: "This is the sign that I am giving for all ages to come, of the covenant between me and you and every living creature with
you: **13** [x]I set my bow in the clouds to serve as
a sign of the covenant between me and the earth.
**14** When I bring clouds over the earth, and the
bow appears in the clouds, **15** I will recall the
covenant I have made between me and you and
all living beings, so that the waters shall never
again become a flood to destroy all mortal beings.[y] **16** As the bow appears in the clouds, I
will see it and recall the everlasting covenant
that I have established between God and all
living beings—all mortal creatures that are on
earth." **17** God told Noah: "This is the sign of
the covenant I have established between me and
all mortal creatures that are on earth."

**Noah and His Sons.** **18** *The sons of
Noah who came out of the ark were Shem, Ham
and Japheth. (Ham was the father of Canaan.)[z]
**19** These three were the sons of Noah, and from
them the whole earth was peopled.
**20** Now Noah, a man of the soil, was the first
to plant a vineyard. **21** When he drank some of
the wine, he became drunk and lay naked inside
his tent.[a] **22** Ham, the father of Canaan, saw
his father's nakedness, and he told his two
brothers outside about it. **23** Shem and Japheth,
however, took a robe, and holding it on their
backs, they walked backward and covered their
father's nakedness; since their faces were turned
the other way, they did not see their father's
nakedness. **24** When Noah woke up from his
drunkenness and learned what his youngest son
had done to him, **25** he said:

"Cursed be Canaan!
The lowest of slaves
shall he be to his brothers."[b]

---

n Sir 44, 18; Is 54, 9; Rom 7, 18.
o Jer 33, 20. 25.
p Gn 1, 22, 28; 8, 17; Jas 3, 7.
q Gn 1, 29f; Dt 12, 15.
r Lv 7, 26f; 17, 4; Dt 12, 16. 23; 1 Sm 14, 33; Acts 15, 20.
s Gn 4, 10f; Ex 21, 12.
t Gn 1, 26f; Lv 24, 17; Nm 35, 33; Jas 3, 9.
u Gn 1, 28; 8, 17; 9, 2.
v Gn 6, 18.
w Sir 44, 18; Is 54, 9.
x Sir 43, 12.
y Is 54, 9.
z Gn 5, 32; 10, 1.
a Lam 4, 21; Heb 2, 15.
b Dt 27, 16; Wis 12, 11.

---

*

8, 21: From the start: literally "from his youth." It is uncertain whether this means from the beginning of the human race or from the early years of the individual.

9, 3: Antediluvian creatures, including man, are depicted as vegetarians (Gn 1, 29f), becoming carnivorous only after the flood.

9, 4: Because a living being dies when it loses most of its blood, the ancients regarded blood as the seat of life, and therefore as sacred. Although in itself the prohibition against eating meat with blood in it is comparable to the ritual laws of the Mosaic code, the Jews considered it binding on all men, because it was given by God to Noah, the new ancestor of all mankind; therefore the early Christian Church retained it for a time (Acts 15, 20. 29).

9, 18–27: This story seems to be a composite of two earlier accounts; in the one, Ham was guilty, whereas in the other, it was Canaan. One purpose of the story is to justify the Israelites' enslavement of the Canaanites because of certain indecent sexual practices in the Canaanite religion. Obviously the story offers no justification for enslaving African Negroes, even though Canaan is presented as a "son" of Ham because the land of Canaan belonged to Hamitic Egypt at the time of the Israelite invasion.

26 He also said:
"Blessed be the LORD, the God of Shem!*
Let Canaan be his slave.
27 May God expand Japheth,*
so that he dwells among the tents of
Shem;
and let Canaan be his slave."

28 Noah lived three hundred and fifty years
after the flood. 29 The whole lifetime of Noah
was nine hundred and fifty years; then he died.

## CHAPTER 10

**Table of the Nations.*** 1 These are the
descendants of Noah's sons, Shem, Ham and
Japheth, to whom sons were born after the
flood.

2 [c]The descendants of Japheth:
Gomer,* Magog, Madai, Javan, Tubal,
Meschech and Tiras.[d]
3 The descendants of Gomer:
Ashkenaz,* Riphath and Togarmah.
4 The descendants of Javan:
Elishah,* Tarshish, the Kittim and the
Rodanim.

5 These are the descendants of Japheth, and
from them sprang the maritime nations, in their
respective lands—each with its own language
—by their clans within their nations.

6 The descendants of Ham:
Cush,* Mizraim, Put and Canaan.
7 The descendants of Cush:
Seba, Havilah, Sabtah, Raamah and
Sabteca.
The descendants of Raamah: Sheba and
Dedan.

8 Cush* became the father of Nimrod, who
was the first potentate on earth. 9 He was a
mighty hunter by the grace of the LORD; hence
the saying, "Like Nimrod, a mighty hunter by
the grace of the LORD." 10 The chief cities of
his kingdom were Babylon, Erech and Accad,
all of them in the land of Shinar.* 11 From that
land he went forth to Asshur,* where he built
Nineveh, Rehoboth-Ir and Calah, 12 as well as
Resen, between Nineveh and Calah,* the latter
being the principal city.
13 [e]Mizraim became the father of the
Ludim, the Anamim, the Lehabim, the Naphtuhim, 14 the Pathrusim,* the Casluhim, and
the Caphtorim from whom the Philistines
sprang.
15 Canaan became the father of Sidon, his
first-born, and of Heth;* 16 also of the Jebusites, the Amorites, the Girgashites, 17 the Hivites, the Arkites, the Sinites, 18 the Arvadites,
the Zemarites and the Hamathites. Afterward,
the clans of the Canaanites spread out, 19 so
that the Canaanite borders extended from Sidon
all the way to Gerar, near Gaza, and all the way
to Sodom, Gomorrah, Admah and Zeboiim,
near Lasha.*
20 These are the descendants of Ham, according to their clans and languages, by their
lands and nations.
21 To Shem also, Japheth's oldest brother
and the ancestor of all the children of Eber, sons
were born.

22 [f]The descendants of Shem:
Elam, Asshur, Arpachshad, Lud and
Aram.
23 The descendants of Aram:
Uz, Hul, Gether and Mash.

24 Arpachshad became the father of Shelah,

c 2-8: 1 Chr 1, 5-10.
d Ez 38, 2.
e 13-18: 1 Chr 1, 11-16.
f 22-29: 1 Chr 1, 17-23.

*

9, 26: Blessed . . . Shem: perhaps the text read originally, "Blessed of the Lord be Shem," which would be expected in the context.

9, 27: In the Hebrew text there is a play on the words yapt ("expand") and yepet ("Japheth").

10, 1–32: This chapter presents a remarkably good classification of the various peoples known to the ancient Israelites; it is theologically important as stressing the basic family unity of all men on earth. The relationship between the various peoples is based partly on linguistic, partly on geographic, and partly on political grounds according to their . . . languages, . . . lands and nations: (v 31). In general, the descendants of Japheth (vv 2–5) are the peoples of the Indo-European languages to the north and west of Mesopotamia and Syria; the descendants of Ham (vv 6–20) are the Hamitic-speaking peoples of northern Africa; and the descendants of Shem (vv 21–31) are the Semitic-speaking peoples of Mesopotamia, Syria and Arabia. But there are many exceptions to this rule; the Semitic-speaking peoples of Canaan, for instance, are considered descendants of Ham, because at the time they were subject to Hamitic Egypt (vv 6. 15–19). This chapter is a composite from the Yahwist source (vv 8–19. 21. 24–30) of about the ninth century B.C., and the Priestly source (vv 1–7. 20. 22f. 31f) of a few centuries later. That is why certain tribes of Arabia are listed under both Ham (v 7) and Shem (vv 26ff).

10, 2: Gomer: the Cimmerians; Madai: the Medes; Javan: the Greeks.

10, 3: Ashkenaz: the Scythians.

10, 4: Elishah: Cyprus; the Kittim: certain inhabitants of Cyprus; the Rodanim: the inhabitants of Rhodes.

10, 6: Cush: Biblical Ethiopia, modern Nubia. Mizraim: Egypt; Put: either Punt in East Africa or Libya.

10, 8: Cush: here, the Kassites; see note on Gn 2, 10–14. Nimrod: probably Tukulti-Ninurta I (thirteenth century B.C.), the first Assyrian conqueror of Babylonia and a famous city-builder at home.

10, 10: Shinar: ancient Sumer in southern Mesopotamia, mentioned also in Gn 11, 2; 14, 1.

10, 11: Asshur: Assyria. Rehoboth-Ir: literally "wide-streets city," was probably not the name of another city, but an epithet of Nineveh; cf Jon 3, 3.

10, 12: Calah: Assyrian Kalhu, the capital of Assyria in the ninth century B.C.

10, 14: The Pathrusim: the people of upper (southern) Egypt; cf Is 11, 11; Jer 44, 1; Ez 29, 14; 30, 14. Caphtorim: Crete; for Caphtor as the place of origin of the Philistines, cf Dt 2, 23; Am 9, 7; Jer 47, 4.

10, 15: Heth: the biblical Hittites; see note on Gn 23, 3.

10, 19: Lasha: the reading of this name is uncertain; perhaps it should be "Bela"; cf Gn 14, 2.

and Shelah became the father of Eber. **25** To
Eber two sons were born: the name of the first
was Peleg, for in his time the world was divided;* and the name of his brother was Joktan.
**26** Joktan became the father of Almodad,
Sheleph, Hazarmaveth, Jerah, **27** Hadoram,
Uzal, Diklah, **28** Obal, Abimael, Sheba
**29** Ophir, Havilah and Jobab. All these were
descendants of Joktan. **30** Their settlements extended all the way to Sephar, the eastern hill
country.
**31** These are the descendants of Shem, according to their clans and languages, by their
lands and nations.
**32** These are the groupings of Noah's sons,
according to their origins and by their nations.
From these the other nations of the earth
branched out after the flood.

## CHAPTER 11

**The Tower of Babel.*** **1** The whole world
spoke the same language, using the same
words. **2** While men were migrating in the east,
they came upon a valley in the land of Shinar*
and settled there. **3** They said to one another,
"Come, let us mold bricks and harden them
with fire." They used bricks for stone, and
bitumen for mortar. **4** Then they said, "Come,
let us build ourselves a city and a tower with its
top in the sky,* and so make a name for ourselves; otherwise we shall be scattered all over
the earth."
**5** The LORD came down to see the city and
the tower that the men had built. **6** Then the
LORD said: "If now, while they are one people,
all speaking the same language, they have started to do this, nothing will later stop them from
doing whatever they presume to do. **7** Let us
then go down and there confuse their language,
so that one will not understand what another
says." **8** Thus the LORD scattered them from
there all over the earth, and they stopped building the city. **9** That is why it was called Babel,*
because there the LORD confused the speech of
all the world. It was from that place that he
scattered them all over the earth.

**The Line from Shem to Abraham.***
**10** [g]This is the record of the descendants of
Shem. When Shem was one hundred years old,
he became the father of Arpachshad, two years
after the flood. **11** Shem lived five hundred
years after the birth of Arpachshad, and he had
other sons and daughters.
**12** When Arpachshad was thirty-five years
old, he became the father of Shelah.* **13** Arpachshad lived four hundred and three years
after the birth of Shelah, and he had other sons
and daughters.
**14** When Shelah was thirty years old, he became the father of Eber. **15** Shelah lived four
hundred and three years after the birth of Eber,
and he had other sons and daughters.
**16** When Eber* was thirty-four years old, he
became the father of Peleg. **17** Eber lived four
hundred and thirty years after the birth of Peleg,
and he had other sons and daughters.
**18** When Peleg was thirty years old, he became the father of Reu. **19** Peleg lived two
hundred and nine years after the birth of Reu,
and he had other sons and daughters.
**20** When Reu was thirty-two years old, he
became the father of Serug. **21** Reu lived two
hundred and seven years after the birth of Serug,
and he had other sons and daughters.
**22** When Serug was thirty years old, he became the father of Nahor. **23** Serug lived two
hundred years after the birth of Nahor, and he
had other sons and daughters.
**24** When Nahor was twenty-nine years old,
he became the father of Terah. **25** Nahor lived
one hundred and nineteen years after the birth
of Terah, and he had other sons and daughters.
**26** When Terah was seventy years old, he
became the father of Abram, Nahor and Haran. [h]

---

g 10-26: 1 Chr 1, 24-27; Lk 3, 34ff.  h Jos 24, 2; 1 Chr 1, 27.

---

10, 25: In the Hebrew text there is a play on the name Peleg and the word niplega, "was divided."

11, 1-9: This story, based on traditions about the temple towers or ziggurats of Babylonia, is used by the sacred writer primarily to illustrate man's increasing wickedness, shown here in his presumptuous effort to create an urban culture apart from God. The secondary motive in the story is to present an imaginative origin of the diversity of the languages among the various peoples inhabiting the earth, as well as an artificial explanation of the name "Babylon."

11, 2: Shinar: see note on Gn 10, 10.

11, 4: Tower with its top in the sky: a direct reference to the chief ziggurat of Babylon, the E-sag-ila, signifying "the house that raises high its head." Babylonian ziggurats were the earliest skyscrapers.

11, 9: Babel: the Hebrew form of the name "Babylon"; the native name, Bab-ili, means "gate of the gods." The Hebrew word balil, "he confused," has a similar sound. Apparently the name referred originally only to a certain part of the city, the district near the gate that led to the temple area.

11, 10-26: This section is a continuation of the genealogical record given in Gn 5, 1-32; see note there. Although the ages of the patriarchs in this list are much lower than those of the antediluvian patriarchs, they are still artificial and devoid of historical value. The ages given here are from the current Hebrew text; the Samaritan and Greek texts have divergent sets of numbers in most cases.

11, 12: The Greek text has a certain Kenan (cf Gn 5, 9f) between Arpachshad and Shelah. The text is followed in Lk 3, 36.

11, 16: Eber: the eponymous ancestor of the Hebrews, "descendants of Eber" (Gn 10, 21. 24-30); see note on Gn 14, 13.

## II: The Patriarch Abraham

**Terah.** 27 This is the record of the descendants of Terah. Terah became the father of
Abram, Nahor and Haran, and Haran became
the father of Lot. 28 Haran died before his father Terah, in his native land, in Ur of the
Chaldeans.* 29 Abram and Nahor took wives;
the name of Abram's wife was Sarai, and the
name of Nahor's wife was Milcah, daughter of
Haran, the father of Milcah and Iscah.[i] 30 Sarai was barren; she had no child.
31 Terah took his son Abram, his grandson
Lot, son of Haran, and his daughter-in-law Sarai, the wife of his son Abram, and brought
them out of Ur of the Chaldeans, to go to the
land of Canaan.* But when they reached Haran,
they settled there.[j] 32 The lifetime of Terah
was two hundred and five years; then Terah died
in Haran.*

### CHAPTER 12

**Abram's Call and Migration.** 1 The
LORD said to Abram: "Go forth from the land
of your kinsfolk and from your father's house to
a land that I will show you.[k]

2 "I will make of you a great nation,
and I will bless you;
I will make your name great,
so that you will be a blessing.[l]
3 [m]I will bless those who bless you
and curse those who curse you.
All the communities of the earth
shall find blessing in you."*

4 [n]Abram went as the LORD directed him,
and Lot went with him. Abram was seventy-five
years old when he left Haran. 5 Abram took his
wife Sarai, his brother's son Lot, all the possessions that they had accumulated, and the persons* they had acquired in Haran, and they set
out for the land of Canaan. When they came to
the land of Canaan, 6 Abram passed through
the land as far as the sacred place at Shechem,
by the terebinth of Moreh. (The Canaanites
were then in the land.)
7 The LORD appeared to Abram and said,
"To your descendants I will give this land." So
Abram built an altar there to the LORD who had
appeared to him.[o] 8 From there he moved on to
the hill country east of Bethel, pitching his tent
with Bethel to the west and Ai to the east. He
built an altar there to the LORD and invoked the
LORD by name. 9 Then Abram journeyed on by
stages to the Negeb.*

**Abram and Sarai in Egypt.** 10 There was
famine in the land; so Abram went down to
Egypt to sojourn there, since the famine in the
land was severe.[p] 11 When he was about to
enter Egypt, he said to his wife Sarai: "I know
well how beautiful a woman you are. 12 When
the Egyptians see you, they will say, 'She is his
wife'; then they will kill me, but let you live.
13 Please say, therefore, that you are my sister,* so that it may go well with me on your
account and my life may be spared for your
sake."[q] 14 When Abram came to Egypt, the
Egyptians saw how beautiful the woman was;
15 and when Pharaoh's courtiers saw her, they
praised her to Pharaoh. So she was taken into
Pharaoh's palace. 16 On her account it went
very well with Abram, and he received flocks
and herds, male and female slaves, male and
female asses, and camels.*

i Gn 17, 15; 20, 12.
j Jos 24, 3; Neh 9, 7; Jdt 5, 6-9; Acts 7, 4.
k Acts 7, 3; Heb 11, 8.
l Gn 17, 6; Sir 44, 20; Rom 4, 17-22.
m Gn 18, 18; 22, 18; Acts 3, 25; Gal 3, 8.
n 4f: Gn 11, 31; Jos 24, 3; Acts 7, 4.
o Ex 33, 1; Dt 34, 4; Acts 7, 5.
p Gn 26, 1.
q Gn 20, 12f; 26, 7.

*

11, 28: Ur of the Chaldeans: Ur was an extremely ancient city of the Sumerians (later, of the Babylonians) in southern Mesopotamia. The Greek text has "the land of the Chaldeans." In either case, the term Chaldeans is an anachronism, because the Chaldeans were not known to history until approximately a thousand years after Abraham's time.

11, 31: The Samaritan and Greek texts include Nahor and his wife in Terah's migration to Haran. Although this is probably due to scribal harmonization, Nahor's family actually did migrate to Haran; cf Gn 24, 10; 27, 43.

11, 32: Since Terah was seventy years old when his son Abraham was born (v 26), and Abraham was seventy-five when he left Haran (Gn 12, 4), Terah lived in Haran for sixty years after Abraham's departure. According to the tradition in the Samaritan text, Terah died when he was one hundred and forty-five years old, therefore, in the same year in which Abraham left Haran. This is the tradition followed in St. Stephen's speech: Abraham left Haran "after his father's death" (Acts 7, 4).

12, 3: Shall find blessing in you: the sense of the Hebrew expression is probably reflexive, "shall bless themselves through you" (i.e., in giving a blessing they shall say, "May you be as blessed as Abraham"), rather than passive, "shall be blessed in you." Since the term is understood in a passive sense in the New Testament (Acts 3, 25; Gal 3, 8), it is rendered here by a neutral expression that admits of both meanings. So also in the blessings given by God to Isaac (Gn 26, 4) and Jacob (Gn 28, 14).

12, 5: Persons: slaves and retainers that formed the social aggregate under the leadership of Abraham; cf Gn 14, 14.

12, 9: The Negeb: the semidesert land of southern Palestine.

12, 13: You are my sister: although Abraham's deceit may not be fully defensible, his statement was at least a half-truth; Sarah was indeed his relative, called "a sister" in Hebrew; cf Gn 20, 12. Moreover, the ancient traditions on which this story and the parallel ones in Gn 20, 1–18 and 26, 6–11 are based, probably come from the Hurrian custom of wife-sister marriage. Among the Hurrians, with whom Abraham's clan lived in close contact at Haran, a man could adopt his wife as his sister and thus give her higher status.

12, 16: Camels: domesticated camels probably did not come into common use in the ancient Near East until the end of the 2nd millennium B.C. Thus the mention of camels at the time of the patriarchs (Gn 24, 11–64; 30, 43; 31, 17. 34; 32, 8. 16; 37, 25) is seemingly an anachronism.

**17** But the LORD struck Pharaoh and his
household with severe plagues because of
Abram's wife Sarai.[r] **18** Then Pharaoh summoned Abram and said to him: "How could you
do this to me! Why didn't you tell me she was
your wife? **19** Why did you say, 'She is my
sister,' so that I took her for my wife? Here,
then, is your wife. Take her and be gone!"
**20** Then Pharaoh gave men orders concerning him, and they sent him on his way, with his
wife and all that belonged to him.

## CHAPTER 13

**Abram and Lot Part.** **1** From Egypt
Abram went up to the Negeb with his wife and
all that belonged to him, and Lot accompanied
him.[s] **2** Now Abram was very rich in livestock,
silver and gold.[t] **3** From the Negeb he traveled
by stages toward Bethel, to the place between
Bethel and Ai where his tent had formerly
stood, **4** The site where he had first built the
altar; and there he invoked the LORD by name.[u]
**5** Lot, who went with Abram, also had flocks
and herds and tents, **6** so that the land could not
support them if they stayed together; their possessions were so great that they could not dwell
together. **7** There were quarrels between the
herdsmen of Abram's livestock and those of
Lot's. (At this time the Canaanites and the Perizzites were occupying the land.)
**8** So Abram said to Lot: "Let there be no
strife between you and me, or between your
herdsmen and mine, for we are kinsmen. **9** Is
not the whole land at your disposal? Please separate from me. If you prefer the left, I will go
to the right; if you prefer the right, I will go to
the left." **10** Lot looked about and saw how
well watered the whole Jordan Plain was as far
as Zoar, like the LORD's own garden, or like
Egypt. (This was before the LORD had destroyed
Sodom and Gomorrah.) **11** Lot, therefore,
chose for himself the whole Jordan Plain and set
out eastward. Thus they separated from each
other; **12** Abram stayed in the land of Canaan,
while Lot settled among the cities of the Plain,
pitching his tents near Sodom. **13** Now the inhabitants of Sodom were very wicked in the sins
they committed against the LORD.[v]
**14** After Lot had left, the LORD said to
Abram: "Look about you, and from where you
are, gaze to the north and south, east and west;[w]
**15** all the land that you see I will give to you
and your descendants forever.[x] **16** I will make
your descendants like the dust of the earth; if
anyone could count the dust of the earth, your
descendants too might be counted.[y] **17** Set
forth and walk about in the land, through its
length and breadth, for to you I will give it."
**18** Abram moved his tents and went on to settle near the terebinth of Mamre, which is at
Hebron. There he built an altar to the LORD.[z]

## CHAPTER 14

**The Four Kings.** **1** In the days of . . . ,*
Amraphel king of Shinar, Arioch king of Ella-
sar, Chedorlaomer king of Elam, and Tidal king
of Goiim **2** made war on Bera king of Sodom,
Birsha king of Gomorrah, Shinab king of Admah, Shemeber king of Zeboiim, and the king
of Bela (that is, Zoar). **3** All the latter kings
joined forces in the Valley of Siddim (that is, the
Salt Sea*). **4** For twelve years they had been
subject to Chedorlaomer, but in the thirteenth
year they rebelled. **5** *In the fourteenth year
Chedorlaomer and the kings allied with him
came and defeated the Rephaim in Ashteroth-
karnaim, the Zuzim in Ham, the Emim in Sha-
veh-kiriathaim, **6** and the Horites in the hill
country of Seir, as far as Elparan, close by the
wilderness.[a] **7** They then turned back and came
to Enmishpat (that is, Kadesh), and they subdued the whole country both of the Amalekites
and of the Amorites who dwelt in Hazazon-ta-
mar. **8** Thereupon the king of Sodom, the king
of Gomorrah, the king of Admah, the king of
Zeboiim, and the king of Bela (that is, Zoar)
marched out, and in the Valley of Siddim they
went into battle against them: **9** against Chedorlaomer king of Elam, Tidal king of Goiim, Amraphel king of Shinar, and Arioch king of Ella-
sar—four kings against five. **10** Now the
Valley of Siddim was full of bitumen pits; and
as the kings of Sodom and Gomorrah fled, they
fell into these, while the rest fled to the mountains. **11** The victors seized all the possessions
and food supplies of Sodom and Gomorrah and
then went their way, **12** taking with them
Abram's nephew Lot, who had been living in
Sodom, as well as his possessions.[b]
**13** A fugitive came and brought the news to
Abram the Hebrew,* who was camping at the
terebinth of Mamre the Amorite, a kinsman of
Eshcol and Aner; these were in league with
Abram. **14** When Abram heard that his nephew

---

r Ps 105, 14.
s Gn 12, 9.
t Ps 112, 1ff; Prv 10, 22.
u Gn 12, 8.
v Gn 18, 20; Ez 16, 49; 2 Pt 2, 6ff; Jude 1, 7.
w Gn 28, 14.
x Gn 12, 7; Mt 5, 4; Lk 1, 55; Acts 7, 5; Gal 3, 16.
y Gn 22, 17; Nm 23, 10.
z Gn 14, 13.
a Dt 2, 12.
b Gn 13, 10ff.

*

14, 1: In the days of . . . : the personal name by which the event is dated has not been preserved.

14, 3: The Salt Sea: now known as the Dead Sea.

14, 5f: The five kings came from north to south through the land east of the Jordan.

14, 13: Abram the Hebrew: elsewhere in the Old Testament, until the last pre-Christian centuries, the term "Hebrew" is used only by non-Israelites, or by Israelites in speaking to foreigners, since it evidently had a disparaging connotation—something like "immigrant." The account in this chapter may, therefore, have been taken originally from a non-Israelite source, in which Abraham, a warlike sheik of Palestine, appears as a truly historical figure of profane history.

had been captured, he mustered three hundred
and eighteen of his retainers, born in his house,
and went in pursuit as far as Dan. **15** He and his
party deployed against them at night, defeated
them, and pursued them as far as Hobah, which
is north of Damascus. **16** He recovered all the
possessions, besides bringing back his kinsman
Lot and his possessions, along with the women
and the other captives.

**17** When Abram returned from his victory
over Chedorlaomer and the kings who were allied with him, the king of Sodom went out to
greet him in the Valley of Shaveh (that is, the
King's Valley).

**18** Melchizedek, king of Salem,* brought
out bread and wine, and being a priest of God
Most High,* he blessed Abram with these
words:[c]

**19** "Blessed be Abram by God Most High,*
the creator of heaven and earth;
**20** And blessed be God Most High,
who delivered your foes into your hand."

Then Abram gave him* a tenth of everything.

**21** The king of Sodom said to Abram, "Give
me the people; the goods you may keep."
**22** But Abram replied to the king of Sodom: "I
have sworn to the LORD, God Most High,* the
creator of heaven and earth, **23** that I would not
take so much as a thread or a sandal strap from
anything that is yours, lest you should say, 'I
made Abram rich.' **24** Nothing for me except
what my servants have used up and the share
that is due to the men who joined me—Aner,
Eshcol and Mamre; let them take their share."

## CHAPTER 15

**The Covenant with Abram.** **1** Some time
after these events, this word of the LORD came
to Abram in a vision:

"Fear not, Abram!
I am your shield;
I will make your reward very great."

**2** But Abram said, "O Lord GOD, what good
will your gifts be, if I keep on being childless
and have as my heir the steward of my house,
Eliezer?" **3** Abram continued, "See, you have
given me no offspring, and so one of my servants will be my heir." **4** Then the word of the
LORD came to him: "No, that one shall not be
your heir; your own issue shall be your heir."[d]
**5** He took him outside and said, "Look up at
the sky and count the stars, if you can. Just so,"
he added, "shall your descendants be."[e]
**6** [f]Abram put his faith in the LORD, who credited it to him as an act of righteousness.*

**7** He then said to him, "I am the LORD who
brought you from Ur of the Chaldeans to give
you this land as a possession."[g] **8** "O Lord
GOD," he asked, "how am I to know that I shall
possess it?" **9** He answered him, "Bring me a
three-year-old heifer, a three-year-old she-goat,
a three-year-old* ram, a turtle-dove, and a
young pigeon."[h] **10** He brought him all these,
split them in two, and placed each half opposite
the other; but the birds he did not cut up.
**11** Birds of prey swooped down on the carcasses, but Abram stayed with them. **12** As the
sun was about to set, a trance fell upon Abram,
and a deep, terrifying darkness enveloped him.

**13** Then the LORD said to Abram: "Know for
certain that your descendants shall be aliens in
a land not their own, where they shall be enslaved and oppressed for four hundred years.[i]
**14** But I will bring judgment on the nation they
must serve, and in the end they will depart with
great wealth.[j] **15** You, however, shall join your
forefathers in peace; you shall be buried at a
contented old age. **16** In the fourth time-span*
the others shall come back here; the wickedness
of the Amorites will not have reached its full
measure until then."[k]

**17** When the sun had set and it was dark,

c Ps 110, 4; Heb 5, 6. 10; 7, 1.
d Gn 17, 16.
e Gn 22, 17; 28, 14; Ex 32, 13; Dt 1, 10; Sir 44, 21; Rom 4, 18; Heb 11, 12.
f 1 Mc 2, 52; Rom 4, 3. 9. 22; Gal 3, 6f; Jas 2, 23.
g Gn 11, 31; 12, 1; Ex 32, 13; Neh 9, 7f; Acts 7, 2f.
h Lv 1, 14.
i Ex 12, 40; Nm 20, 15; Jdt 5, 9f; Is 52, 4; Acts 13, 20; Gal 3, 17.
j Ex 3, 8. 21f.
k 1 Kgs 21, 26.

*

14, 18: Salem: traditionally identified with Jerusalem (Ps 76, 3), but the Hebrew text is not certain; instead of the present melek shalem ("king of Salem") the original may have been melek shelomo ("a king allied to him"). In Heb 7, 2, "king of Salem" is interpreted as "king of peace" (shalom).

14, 19: God most High: in Hebrew, el-elyon. In Canaanite texts, each element may occur separately as the name of a specific deity, or they may be applied together to a single deity, as is done here by the Canaanite priest Melchizedek. For the Israelites, el became a poetic synonym for elohim ("God"); elyon ("Most High") became one of the titles of their God Yahweh.

14, 20: Abram gave him: literally "he gave him"; but Abram is to be understood as the subject of the sentence, for the tithes were the tenth part assigned to priests; cf Heb 7, 4–10.

14, 22: Abraham uses the name of the Canaanite god el-elyon ("God, the Most High") in apposition to the name of his God, yahweh ("the Lord").

15, 6: Abraham's faith in God's promises was regarded as an act of righteousness, i.e., as expressing the "right" attitude of man toward God. In turn, God credited this to Abraham, i.e., gave him title to the fulfillment of God's promises. St. Paul (Rom 4, 1–25; Gal 3, 6–9) makes Abraham's faith a model for that of Christians.

15, 9: Three-year-old: ritually mature.

15, 16: Time-span: the Hebrew term dor is commonly rendered as "generation," but it may signify a period of varying length. Neither this passage nor the statement about the four hundred years has any value for determining how long the Israelites were in Egypt.

15, 17: Brazier: literally "oven"; a portable one is meant here. The smoke and fire represent God's presence. Although the text does not mention it, Abraham no doubt also walked between the split carcasses. For the meaning of this strange

there appeared a smoking brazier* and a flaming torch, which passed between those pieces.
**18** It was on that occasion that the LORD made
a covenant* with Abram, saying: "To your descendants I give this land, from the Wadi of
Egypt to the Great River [the Euphrates],[l]
**19** [m]the land of the Kenites, the Kenizzites, the
Kadmonites, **20** the Hittites, the Perizzites, the
Rephaim, **21** the Amorites, the Canaanites, the
Girgashites, and the Jebusites."

## CHAPTER 16

**Birth of Ishmael.** **1** *Abram's wife Sarai
had borne him no children. She had, however,
an Egyptian maidservant named Hagar.[n] **2** Sarai said to Abram: "The LORD has kept me from
bearing children. Have intercourse, then, with
my maid; perhaps I shall have sons through
her." Abram heeded Sarai's request.[o] **3** Thus,
after Abram had lived ten years in the land of
Canaan, his wife Sarai took her maid, Hagar the
Egyptian, and gave her to her husband Abram
to be his concubine. **4** He had intercourse with
her, and she became pregnant. When she became aware of her pregnancy, she looked on her
mistress with disdain.[p] **5** [q]So Sarai said to
Abram: "You are responsible for this outrage
against me. I myself gave my maid to your
embrace; but ever since she became aware of
her pregnancy, she has been looking on me with
disdain. May the LORD decide between you and
me!" **6** Abram told Sarai: "Your maid is in
your power. Do to her whatever you please."
Sarai then abused her so much that Hagar ran
away from her.

**7** The LORD's messenger* found her by a
spring in the wilderness, the spring on the road
to Shur,[r] **8** and he asked, "Hagar, maid of
Sarai, where have you come from and where are
you going?" She answered, "I am running
away from my mistress, Sarai." **9** But the
LORD's messenger told her: "Go back to your
mistress and submit to her abusive treatment.
**10** I will make your descendants so numerous," added the LORD's messenger, "that they
will be too many to count.[s] **11** Besides," the
LORD's messenger said to her:

"You are now pregnant and shall bear a
son;
you shall name him Ishmael,*
For the LORD has heard you,
God has answered you.

**12** He shall be a wild ass of a man,
his hand against everyone,
and everyone's hand against him;
In opposition to all his kin
shall he encamp."[t]

**13** To the LORD who spoke to her she gave
a name, saying, "You are the God of Vision";*
she meant, "Have I really seen God and remained alive after my vision?"[u] **14** That is why
the well is called Beer-lahai-roi.* It is between
Kadesh and Bered.

**15** Hagar bore Abram a son, and Abram
named the son whom Hagar bore him Ishmael.[v]
**16** Abram was eighty-six years old when Hagar
bore him Ishmael.

## CHAPTER 17

**Covenant of Circumcision.** **1** When
Abram was ninety-nine years old, the LORD
appeared to him and said: "I am God the Almighty.* Walk in my presence and be blameless.[w] **2** Between you and me I will establish
my covenant, and I will multiply you exceedingly."[x]

**3** When Abram prostrated himself, God continued to speak to him: **4** "My covenant with
you is this: you are to become the father of a host
of nations.[y] **5** No longer shall you be called
Abram; your name shall be Abraham,* for I am
making you the father of a host of nations.[z] **6** I
will render you exceedingly fertile; I will make
nations of you; kings shall stem from you. **7** I
will maintain my covenant with you and your
descendants after you throughout the ages as an
everlasting pact, to be your God and the God of
your descendants after you.[a] **8** I will give to

l Ex 32, 13; Neh 9, 8; Ps 105, 11; Sir 44, 21.
m 19f: Dt 7, 1.
n Gn 11, 30.
o Gn 21, 8f; Gal 4, 22.
p 1 Sm 1, 6; Prv 30, 23.
q 5-16: Gn 21, 10-19.
r Ex 15, 22.
s Gn 17, 20; 21, 13. 18; 25, 12-18.
t Gn 21, 20; 25, 18.
u Gn 24, 62.
v Gn 16, 2; Gal 4, 22.
w Gn 35, 11; Ex 6, 3.
x Gn 12, 2: 13, 16; Ex 32, 13.
y Sir 44, 21; Rom 4, 17.
z Neh 9, 7.
a Ps 105, 42; Lk 1, 72f; Gal 3, 16.
b Ex 32, 13; Dt 1, 8; 14, 2; Lk 1, 55; Acts 7, 5.

*

ceremony, see note on Jer 34, 18ff.

15, 18: Made a covenant: literally "cut a covenant"; the expression derives from the ceremony of cutting the animals in two.

16, 1–6: Sarah's actions are all in keeping with the laws of the time, as known from ancient extra-biblical sources.

16, 7: The Lord's messenger: a manifestation of God in human form; therefore in v 13 the messenger is identified with the Lord himself.

16, 11: Ishmael: in Hebrew the name means "God has heard."

16, 13: The God of Vision: in Hebrew, el-roi; hence the name of the spring. Remained alive: for the ancient notion that a person died on seeing God, cf Gn 32, 31; Ex 20, 19; Dt 4, 33; Jgs 13, 22.

16, 14: Beer-lahai-roi: probably "the well of living sight," i.e., the well where one can see (God) and yet live.

17, 1: The Almighty: traditional but incorrect rendering of the divine title shaddai, of uncertain meaning.

17, 5: Abram and Abraham are merely two forms of the same name, both meaning, "the father is exalted"; another variant form is Abiram (Nm 16, 1; 1 Kgs 16, 34). The additional -ha- in the form Abraham is explained by folk etymology as coming from ab-hamon goyim, "father of a host of nations."

you and to your descendants after you the land
in which you are now staying, the whole land
of Canaan, as a permanent possession; and I will
be their God."[b]

**9** God also said to Abraham: "On your part,
you and your descendants after you must keep
my covenant throughout the ages. **10** This is
my covenant with you and your descendants
after you that you must keep: every male among
you shall be circumcised.[c] **11** Circumcise the
flesh of your foreskin, and that shall be the mark
of the covenant between you and me.[d]
**12** Throughout the ages, every male among
you, when he is eight days old, shall be circumcised, including houseborn slaves and those acquired with money from any foreigner who is
not of your blood.[e] **13** Yes, both the houseborn
slaves and those acquired with money must be
circumcised. Thus my covenant shall be in your
flesh as an everlasting pact. **14** If a male is
uncircumcised, that is, if the flesh of his foreskin has not been cut away, such a one shall be
cut off from his people; he has broken my covenant."

**15** God further said to Abraham: "As for
your wife Sarai, do not call her Sarai; her name
shall be Sarah.* **16** I will bless her, and I will
give you a son by her. Him also will I bless; he
shall give rise to nations, and rulers of peoples
shall issue from him."[f] **17** Abraham prostrated
himself and laughed* as he said to himself,
"Can a child be born to a man who is a hundred
years old? Or can Sarah give birth at ninety?"[g]
**18** Then Abraham said to God, "Let but Ishmael live on by your favor!" **19** God replied:
"Nevertheless, your wife Sarah is to bear you
a son, and you shall call him Isaac. I will maintain my covenant with him as an everlasting
pact, to be his God and the God of his descendants after him.[h] **20** As for Ishmael, I am heeding you: I hereby bless him. I will make him
fertile and will multiply him exceedingly. He
shall become the father of twelve chieftains, and
I will make of him a great nation.[i] **21** But my
covenant I will maintain with Isaac, whom Sarah shall bear to you by this time next year."[j]
**22** When he had finished speaking with him,
God departed from Abraham.

**23** Then Abraham took his son Ishmael and
all his slaves, whether born in his house or
acquired with his money—every male among
the members of Abraham's household—and he
circumcised the flesh of their foreskins on that
same day, as God had told him to do. **24** Abraham was ninety-nine years old when the flesh of
his foreskin was circumcised,[k] **25** and his son
Ishmael was thirteen years old when the flesh of
his foreskin was circumcised. **26** Thus, on that
same day Abraham and his son Ishmael were
circumcised; **27** and all the male members of
his household, including the slaves born in his
house or acquired with his money from foreigners, were circumcised with him.

## CHAPTER 18

**Abraham's Visitors.** **1** The LORD appeared to Abraham by the terebinth of Mamre,
as he sat in the entrance of his tent, while the
day was growing hot. **2** Looking up, he saw
three men standing nearby. When he saw them,
he ran from the entrance of the tent to greet
them; and bowing to the ground,[l] **3** he said:
"Sir,* if I may ask you this favor, please do not
go on past your servant. **4** Let some water be
brought, that you may bathe your feet, and then
rest yourselves under the tree. **5** Now that you
have come this close to your servant, let me
bring you a little food, that you may refresh
yourselves; and afterward you may go on your
way." "Very well," they replied, "do as you
have said."

**6** Abraham hastened into the tent and told
Sarah, "Quick, three seahs* of fine flour!
Knead it and make rolls." **7** He ran to the herd,
picked out a tender, choice steer, and gave it to
a servant, who quickly prepared it. **8** Then he
got some curds* and milk, as well as the steer
that had been prepared, and set these before
them; and he waited on them under the tree
while they ate.

**9** "Where is your wife Sarah?" they asked
him. "There in the tent," he replied. **10** One of
them* said, "I will surely return to you about
this time next year, and Sarah will then have a
son." Sarah was listening at the entrance of the
tent, just behind him.[m] **11** Now Abraham and
Sarah were old, advanced in years, and Sarah
had stopped having her womanly periods.[n]

---

c Jn 7, 22; Acts 7, 8; Rom 4, 11.
d Sir 44, 21.
e Lv 12, 3; Lk 1, 59; 2, 21.
f Gn 18, 10; Gal 4, 23.
g Rom 4, 19; Heb 11, 11f.
h Gn 11, 30; 21, 2; Ex 32, 13; Sir 44, 22.
i Gn 16, 10; 21, 13. 18; 25, 12-16.
j Gn 18, 14; 21, 2; 26, 2-5; Rom 9, 7.
k Gn 17, 10; Rom 4, 11.
l Heb 13, 1f.
m Gn 17, 19; 21, 1; 2 Kgs 4, 16; Rom 9, 9.
n Gn 17, 17; Rom 4, 19; Heb 11, 11f.

---

17, 15: Sarai and Sarah are variant forms of the same name, both meaning "princess."

17, 17: Laughed: yishaq, which is the Hebrew form of the name "Isaac"; other similar explanations of the name are given in Gn 18, 12 and 21, 6.

18, 3: Abraham addresses the leader of the group, whom he does not yet recognize as Yahweh; in the next two verses he speaks to all three men. The other two are later (Gn 19, 1) identified as messengers.

18, 6: Three seahs: one ephah, about half a bushel.

18, 8: Curds: a type of soft cheese or yoghurt.

18, 10: One of them: i.e., the Lord. Abraham now realizes this for the first time when he hears the prediction of a miraculous birth. About this time next year: literally "when the time becomes alive," i.e., at the time when birth is due after the period of gestation; the conception is understood as taking place soon after the prediction.

**12** So Sarah laughed* to herself and said,
"Now that I am so withered and my husband is
so old, am I still to have sexual pleasure?"
**13** But the LORD said to Abraham: "Why did
Sarah laugh and say, 'Shall I really bear a child,
old as I am?' **14** Is anything too marvelous for
the LORD to do? At the appointed time, about
this time next year, I will return to you, and
Sarah will have a son."[o] **15** Because she was
afraid, Sarah dissembled, saying, "I didn't
laugh." But he said, "Yes you did."

**Abraham Intercedes for Sodom** **16** The
men set out from there and looked down toward
Sodom; Abraham was walking with them, to
see them on their way. **17** The LORD reflected:
"Shall I hide from Abraham what I am about to
do, **18** now that he is to become a great and
populous nation, and all the nations of the earth
are to find blessing in him? [p] **19** Indeed, I have
singled him out that he may direct his sons and
his posterity to keep the way of the LORD by
doing what is right and just, so that the LORD
may carry into effect for Abraham the promises
he made about him." **20** [q]Then the LORD said:
"The outcry against Sodom and Gomorrah is so
great, and their sin so grave,* **21** that I must go
down and see whether or not their actions fully
correspond to the cry against them that comes
to me. I mean to find out."

**22** While the two men walked on farther toward Sodom, the LORD remained standing before Abraham. **23** Then Abraham drew nearer
to him and said: "Will you sweep away the
innocent with the guilty? **24** Suppose there
were fifty innocent people in the city; would you
wipe out the place, rather than spare it for the
sake of the fifty innocent people within it?
**25** Far be it from you to do such a thing, to
make the innocent die with the guilty, so that the
innocent and the guilty would be treated alike!
Should not the judge of all the world act with
justice?"[r] **26** The LORD replied, "If I find fifty
innocent people in the city of Sodom, I will
spare the whole place for their sake." **27** Abraham spoke up again: "See how I am presuming
to speak to my Lord, though I am but dust and
ashes![s] **28** What if there are five less than fifty
innocent people? Will you destroy the whole
city because of those five?" "I will not destroy
it," he answered, "if I find forty-five there."
**29** But Abraham persisted, saying, "What if
only forty are found there?" He replied, "I will
forbear doing it for the sake of the forty."
**30** Then he said, "Let not my Lord grow impatient if I go on. What if only thirty are found
there?" He replied, "I will forbear doing it if
I can find but thirty there." **31** Still he went on,
"Since I have thus dared to speak to my Lord,
what if there are no more than twenty?" "I will
not destroy it," he answered, "for the sake of
the twenty." **32** But he still persisted, "Please,
let not my Lord grow angry if I speak up this last
time. What if there are at least ten there?" "For
the sake of those ten," he replied, "I will not
destroy it."[t]

**33** The LORD departed as soon as he had
finished speaking with Abraham, and Abraham
returned home.

## CHAPTER 19

### Destruction of Sodom and Gomorrah.

**1** The two angels reached Sodom in the evening, as Lot was sitting at the gate of Sodom.
When Lot saw them, he got up to greet them;
and bowing down with his face to the ground,
**2** he said, "Please, gentlemen,* come aside
into your servant's house for the night, and
bathe your feet; you can get up early to continue
your journey." But they replied, "No, we shall
pass the night in the town square."[u] **3** He urged
them so strongly, however, that they turned
aside to his place and entered his house. He
prepared a meal for them, baking cakes without
leaven, and they dined.

**4** [v]Before they went to bed, all the townsmen
of Sodom, both young and old—all the people
to the last man—closed in on the house. **5** They
called to Lot and said to him, "Where are the
men who came to your house tonight? Bring
them out to us that we may have intimacies with
them." **6** Lot went out to meet them at the
entrance. When he had shut the door behind
him, **7** he said, "I beg you, my brothers, not to
do this wicked thing. **8** I have two daughters
who have never had intercourse with men. Let
me bring them out to you, and you may do to
them as you please. But don't do anything to
these men, for you know they have come under
the shelter of my roof." **9** They replied, "Stand
back! This fellow," they sneered, "came here
as an immigrant, and now he dares to give orders! We'll treat you worse than them!" With

o Mt 19, 26; Mk 10, 27; Lk 1, 37; 18, 27; Rom 4, 21.
p Lk 1, 55.
q Gn 19, 13; Is 3, 9; Lk 17, 28; Jude 1, 7.
r Dt 32, 4; Jb 8, 3. 20; Wis 12, 15.
s Sir 10, 9; 17, 27.
t Jer 5, 1; Ez 22, 30.
u Wis 10, 6; Sir 16, 8; Ez 16, 50; Heb 13, 1f.
v 4-9; Jgs 19, 22-25; Jude 1, 7.
w Gn 13, 12; 2 Pt 2, 7f.

*

18, 12: Sarah laughed: see note on Gn 17, 17.

18, 20: Israelite tradition was unanimous in ascribing the destruction of Sodom and Gomorrah to the wickedness of these cities, but tradition varied in regard to the nature of this wickedness. According to the present account of the Yahwist, the sin of Sodom was homosexuality (Gn 19, 4f), which is therefore also known as sodomy; but according to Isaiah (1, 9f; 3, 9), it was a lack of social justice; Ezekiel (16, 46–51) described it as a disregard for the poor, whereas Jeremiah (23, 14) saw it as general immorality.

19, 2: Gentlemen: Lot does not yet know that the distinguished-looking men are God's messengers; cf Gn 18, 3.

that, they pressed hard against Lot, moving in
closer to break down the door.[w] **10** But his
guests put out their hands, pulled Lot inside
with them, and closed the door; **11** at the same
time they struck the men at the entrance of the
house, one and all, with such a blinding light*
that they were utterly unable to reach the doorway.

**12** Then the angels said to Lot: "Who else
belongs to you here? Your sons [sons-in-law]*
and your daughters and all who belong to you
in the city—take them away from it![x] **13** We
are about to destroy this place, for the outcry
reaching the LORD against those in the city is so
great that he has sent us to destroy it."[y] **14** So
Lot went out and spoke to his sons-in-law, who
had contracted marriage with his daughters.*
"Get up and leave this place," he told them;
"the LORD is about to destroy the city." But his
sons-in-law thought he was joking.

**15** As dawn was breaking, the angels urged
Lot on, saying, "On your way! Take with you
your wife and your two daughters who are here,
or you will be swept away in the punishment of
the city." **16** When he hesitated, the men, by
the LORD's mercy, seized his hand and the
hands of his wife and his two daughters and led
them to safety outside the city. **17** As soon as
they had been brought outside, he was told:
"Flee for your life! Don't look back or stop
anywhere on the Plain. Get off to the hills at
once, or you will be swept away."[z] **18** "Oh,
no, my lord!" replied Lot. **19** "You have already thought enough of your servant to do me
the great kindness of intervening to save my
life. But I cannot flee to the hills to keep the
disaster from overtaking me, and so I shall die.
**20** Look, this town ahead is near enough to
escape to. It's only a small place.* Let me flee
there—it's a small place, isn't it?—that my life
may be saved." **21** "Well, then," he replied,
"I will also grant you the favor you now ask.
I will not overthrow the town you speak of.
**22** Hurry, escape there! I cannot do anything
until you arrive there." That is why the town is
called Zoar.[a]

**23** The sun was just rising over the earth as
Lot arrived in Zoar;[b] **24** at the same time the
LORD rained down sulphurous fire upon Sodom
and Gomorrah [from the LORD out of heaven].[c]
**25** He overthrew* those cities and the whole
Plain, together with the inhabitants of the cities
and the produce of the soil.[d] **26** But Lot's wife
looked back, and she was turned into a pillar of
salt.[e]

**27** Early the next morning Abraham went to
the place where he had stood in the LORD's
presence. **28** As he looked down toward Sodom
and Gomorrah and the whole region of the
Plain,* he saw dense smoke over the land rising
like fumes from a furnace.[f]

**29** Thus it came to pass: when God destroyed
the Cities of the Plain, he was mindful of Abraham by sending Lot away from the upheaval by
which God overthrew the cities where Lot had
been living.

**Moabites and Ammonites.*** **30** Since Lot
was afraid to stay in Zoar, he and his two daughters went up from Zoar and settled in the hill
country, where he lived with his two daughters
in a cave. **31** The older one said to the younger:
"Our father is getting old, and there is not a man
on earth to unite with us as was the custom
everywhere. **32** Come, let us ply our father
with wine and then lie with him, that we may
have offspring by our father." **33** So that night
they plied their father with wine, and the older
one went in and lay with her father; but he was
not aware of her lying down or her getting up.
**34** Next day the older one said to the younger:
"Last night it was I who lay with my father. Let
us ply him with wine again tonight, and then
you go in and lie with him, that we may both
have offspring by our father." **35** So that night,
too, they plied their father with wine, and then
the younger one went in and lay with him; but
again he was not aware of her lying down or her
getting up.

**36** Thus both of Lot's daughters became
pregnant by their father. **37** The older one gave

x 2 Pt 7, 9.
y Is 1, 7. 9; Zep 2, 9; Lk 17, 29.
z Wis 10, 6.
a Wis 10, 6.
b Pss 9, 6; 11, 6; 107, 34.
c Wis 10, 7; Is 1, 9; 13, 19; Lam 4, 6; 17, 29; 2 Pt 2, 6.
d Dt 29, 22; Jer 50, 40; Am 4, 11.
e Wis 10, 7; Lk 17, 32.
f Rv 9, 2; 14, 10f.
g Dt 2, 9.

*

19, 11: Blinding light: a preternatural flash that temporarily dazed the wicked men and revealed to Lot the true nature of his guests.

19, 12: Since Lot apparently had no sons, a glossator interpreted the term to mean sons-in-law.

19, 14: It is uncertain whether Lot's sons-in-law were fully married to his daughters or only "engaged" to them (Israelite "engagement" was the first part of the marriage ceremony), or even whether the daughters involved were the same as, or different from, the two daughters who were still in their father's house.

19, 20: A small place: the Hebrew word misar, literally "a little thing," has the same root consonants as the name of the town Zoar in v 22.

19, 25: Overthrew: the consistent use of this term, literally "turned upside down," to describe the destruction of the Cities of the Plain seems to imply that their upheaval (v 29) was caused primarily by an earthquake; this would naturally be accompanied by a disastrous fire, especially in a region containing bitumen (Gn 14, 10) and its accompanying gases.

19, 28f: From the height east of Hebron, Abraham could easily see the region at the southern end of the Dead Sea, where the Cities of the Plain were probably located.

19, 30–38: This Israelite tale about the origin of Israel's neighbors east of the Jordan and the Dead Sea was told partly to ridicule these racially related but rival nations and partly to give folk etymologies for their names.

19, 37: From my father: in Hebrew, meabi, similar in sound

birth to a son whom she named Moab, saying, "From my father."* He is the ancestor of the Moabites of today.[g] **38** The younger one, too, gave birth to a son, and she named him Ammon, saying, "The son of my kin."* He is the ancestor of the Ammonites of today.[h]

## CHAPTER 20

**Abraham at Gerar.*** **1** Abraham journeyed on to the region of the Negeb, where he settled between Kadesh and Shur. While he stayed in Gerar, **2** he said of his wife Sarah, "She is my sister." So Abimelech, king of Gerar, sent and took Sarah. **3** But God came to Abimelech in a dream one night and said to him, "You are about to die because of the woman you have taken, for she has a husband." **4** Abimelech, who had not approached her, said: "O Lord, would you slay a man even though he is innocent? **5** He himself told me, 'She is my sister,' and she herself also stated, 'He is my brother.' I did it in good faith and with clean hands." **6** God answered him in the dream: "Yes, I know you did it in good faith. In fact, it was I who kept you from sinning against me; that is why I did not let you touch her. **7** Therefore, return the man's wife—as a spokesman* he will intercede for you—that your life may be saved. If you do not return her, you can be sure that you and all who are yours will certainly die."

**8** Early the next morning Abimelech called all his court officials and informed them of everything that had happened, and the men were horrified. **9** Then Abimelech summoned Abraham and said to him: "How could you do this to us! What wrong did I do to you that you should have brought such monstrous guilt on me and my kingdom? You have treated me in an intolerable way. **10** What were you afraid of," he asked him, "that you should have done such a thing?" **11** "I was afraid," answered Abraham, "because I thought there would surely be no fear of God in this place, and so they would kill me on account of my wife. **12** Besides, she is in truth my sister, but only my father's daughter, not my mother's; and so she became my wife.[i] **13** When God sent me wandering from my father's house, I asked her: 'Would you do me this favor? In whatever place we come to, say that I am your brother.' "

**14** Then Abimelech took flocks and herds and male and female slaves and gave them to Abraham; and after he restored his wife Sarah to him, **15** he said, "Here, my land lies at your disposal; settle wherever you please." **16** To Sarah he said: "See, I have given your brother a thousand shekels of silver.* Let that serve you as a vindication before all who are with you; your honor has been preserved with everyone." **17** Abraham then interceded with God, and God restored health to Abimelech, that is, to his wife and his maidservants, so that they could bear children; **18** for God had tightly closed every womb in Abimelech's household on account of Abraham's wife Sarah.

## CHAPTER 21

**Birth of Isaac.** **1** The LORD took note of Sarah as he had said he would; he did for her as he had promised.[j] **2** Sarah became pregnant and bore Abraham a son in his old age, at the set time that God had stated.[k] **3** Abraham gave the name Isaac to this son of his whom Sarah bore him.[l] **4** When his son Isaac was eight days old, Abraham circumcised him, as God had commanded.[m] **5** Abraham was a hundred years old when his son Isaac was born to him. **6** Sarah then said, "God has given me cause to laugh, and all who hear of it will laugh with me.[n] **7** Who would have told Abraham," she added, "that Sarah would nurse children! Yet I have borne him a son in his old age." **8** Isaac grew, and on the day of the child's weaning Abraham held a great feast.

**9** *Sarah noticed the son whom Hagar the Egyptian had borne to Abraham playing with her son Isaac; **10** so she demanded of Abraham: "Drive out that slave and her son! No son of that slave is going to share the inheritance with my son Isaac!"[o] **11** Abraham was greatly distressed, especially on account of his son Ishmael. **12** But God said to Abraham: "Do not be distressed about the boy or about your slave woman. Heed the demands of Sarah, no matter what she is asking of you; for it is through Isaac that descendants shall bear your name.[p] **13** As for the son of the slave woman, I will make a great nation of him also, since he too is your offspring."

---

h Dt 2, 19.
i Gn 12, 13.
j Gn 17, 19; 18, 10.
k Gal 4, 23; Heb 11, 11.
l Mt 1, 2; Lk 3, 34.
m Gn 17, 10ff; Acts 7, 8.
n Gn 17, 17.
o Jgs 11, 2; Gal 4, 30.
p Rom 9, 7; Heb 11, 18.

---

* to the name "Moab."

19, 38: The son of my kin: in Hebrew, ben-ammi, similar in sound to the name "Ammonites."

20, 1–18: This story from the Elohist source (see note on Gn 4, 25) combines elements found in the two very similar but distinct stories of the Yahwist source in Gn 12, 10–20 and 26, 6–11.

20, 7: Spokesman: the Hebrew term nabi used here is regularly translated as "prophet," but it simply means "one who speaks on behalf of another," whether the latter is God, as in almost all cases, or another man, as in Ex 4, 16.

20, 16: A thousand shekels of silver: not a gift distinct from that of the animals and the slaves (v 14), but the monetary value of these.

21, 9–19: This story of Hagar's expulsion, in the Elohist source, is in general a duplicate of the one from the Yahwist source in Gn 16, 5–14; but the two stories differ greatly in detail.

**14** Early the next morning Abraham got
some bread and a skin of water and gave them
to Hagar. Then, placing the child on her back,*
he sent her away. As she roamed aimlessly in
the wilderness of Beer-sheba, **15** the water in
the skin was used up. So she put the child down
under a shrub, **16** and then went and sat down
opposite him, about a bowshot away; for she
said to herself, "Let me not watch to see the
child die." As she sat opposite him, he began
to cry. **17** God heard the boy's cry, and God's
messenger called to Hagar from heaven: "What
is the matter, Hagar? Don't be afraid; God has
heard the boy's cry in this plight of his.[q]
**18** Arise, lift up the boy and hold him by the
hand; for I will make of him a great nation."
**19** Then God opened her eyes, and she saw a
well of water. She went and filled the skin with
water, and then let the boy drink.

**20** God was with the boy as he grew up. He
lived in the wilderness and became an expert
bowman, **21** with his home in the wilderness of
Paran. His mother got a wife for him from the
land of Egypt.

**The Pact at Beer-sheba.** **22** About that
time Abimelech, accompanied by Phicol, the
commander of his army,* said to Abraham:
"God is with you in everything you do.
**23** Therefore, swear to me by God at this
place* that you will not deal falsely with me or
with my progeny and posterity, but will act as
loyally toward me and the land in which you
stay as I have acted toward you." **24** To this
Abraham replied, "I so swear."

**25** Abraham, however, reproached Abimelech about a well that Abimelech's men had
seized by force. **26** "I have no idea who did
that," Abimelech replied. "In fact, you never
told me about it, nor did I ever hear of it until
now."

**27** Then Abraham took sheep and cattle and
gave them to Abimelech and the two made a
pact. **28** Abraham also set apart seven ewe
lambs of the flock, **29** and Abimelech asked
him, "What is the purpose of these seven ewe
lambs that you have set apart?" **30** Abraham
answered, "The seven ewe lambs you shall accept from me that thus I may have your acknowledgment that the well was dug by me."
**31** This is why the place is called Beer-sheba;*
the two of them took an oath there. **32** When
they had thus made the pact in Beer-sheba,
Abimelech, along with Phicol, the commander
of his army, left and returned to the land of the
Philistines.

**33** Abraham planted a tamarisk at Beer-sheba, and there he invoked by name the LORD,
God the Eternal.* **34** Abraham resided in the
land of the Philistines for many years.

## CHAPTER 22

**The Testing of Abraham.** **1** Some time
after these events, God put Abraham to the
test.* He called to him, "Abraham!"
"Ready!" he replied.[r] **2** Then God said:
"Take your son Isaac, your only one,* whom
you love, and go to the land of Moriah. There
you shall offer him up as a holocaust on a height
that I will point out to you."[s] **3** Early the next
morning Abraham saddled his donkey, took
with him his son Isaac, and two of his servants
as well, and with the wood that he had cut for
the holocaust, set out for the place of which God
had told him.

**4** On the third day Abraham got sight of the
place from afar. **5** Then he said to his servants:
"Both of you stay here with the donkey, while
the boy and I go on over yonder. We will worship and then come back to you." **6** Thereupon
Abraham took the wood for the holocaust and
laid it on his son Isaac's shoulders, while he
himself carried the fire and the knife. **7** As the
two walked on together, Isaac spoke to his father Abraham: "Father!" he said. "Yes, son,"
he replied. Isaac continued, "Here are the fire
and the wood, but where is the sheep for the
holocaust?" **8** "Son," Abraham answered,
"God himself will provide the sheep for the
holocaust." Then the two continued going forward.

**9** When they came to the place of which God

q Gn 16, 7.
r Sir 44, 20.
s 2 Chr 3, 1; 1 Mc 2, 52; Heb 11, 17.
t Jas 2, 21.

*

21, 14: Placing the child on her back: the phrase is translated from an emended form of the Hebrew text. In the current faulty Hebrew text, Abraham put the bread and the waterskin on Hagar's back, while her son apparently walked beside her. This reading seems to be a scribal attempt at harmonizing the present passage with the data of the Priestly source, in which Ishmael would have been at least fourteen years old when Isaac was born; compare Gn 16, 16 with 21, 5; cf 17, 25. But in the present Elohist story Ishmael is obviously a little boy, not much older than Isaac; cf vv 15, 18.

21, 22: Here and in v 32 the Greek text has ". . . Abimelech, accompanied by Ahuzzath, his councilor, and Phicol . . ."; but this is probably a secondary harmonization with Gn 26, 26. Abimelech took Phicol with him in order to intimidate Abraham by a show of strength.

21, 23: This place: Beer-sheba (v 31). Abimelech had come from Gerar (Gn 20, 2), about thirty miles west of Beer-sheba.

21, 31: Beer-sheba: the Hebrew name really means "the well of the seven," i.e., the place where there are seven wells, alluded to in the episode of the seven ewe lambs, vv 28ff; but it can also be interpreted to mean "the well of the oath."

21, 33: God the Eternal: in Hebrew, el olam, perhaps the name of the deity of the pre-Israelite sanctuary at Beer-sheba, but used by Abraham merely as a title of Yahweh; cf Is 40, 28.

22, 1: God put Abraham to the test: to prove the firmness of Abraham's faith in God's promise that through Isaac all the nations of the earth would find blessing; cf Gn 18, 10. 18; 21, 12.

22, 2: Only one: uniquely precious, especially loved; therefore the same term is rendered in vv 12. 17 as "beloved."

had told him, Abraham built an altar there and
arranged the wood on it. Next he tied up his son
Isaac, and put him on top of the wood on the
altar.[t] **10** Then he reached out and took the
knife to slaughter his son.[u] **11** But the LORD's
messenger called to him from heaven, "Abraham, Abraham!" "Yes, Lord," he answered.
**12** "Do not lay your hand on the boy," said the
messenger. "Do not do the least thing to him.
I know now how devoted you are to God, since
you did not withhold from me your own beloved
son."[v] **13** As Abraham looked about, he spied
a ram caught by its horns in the thicket. So he
went and took the ram and offered it up as a
holocaust in place of his son. **14** Abraham
named the site Yahweh-yireh;* hence people
now say, "On the mountain the LORD will see."

**15** Again the LORD's messenger called to
Abraham from heaven **16** [w]and said: "I swear
by myself, declares the LORD, that because you
acted as you did in not withholding from me
your beloved son, **17** I will bless you abundantly and make your descendants as countless as
the stars of the sky and the sands of the seashore;
your descendants shall take possession of the
gates of their enemies,[x] **18** and in your descendants all the nations of the earth shall find
blessing—all this because you obeyed my command."[y]

**19** Abraham then returned to his servants,
and they set out together for Beer-sheba, where
Abraham made his home.

**Nahor's Descendants.*** **20** Some time afterward, the news came to Abraham: "Milcah
too has borne sons, to your brother Nahor:
**21** Uz, his first-born, his brother Buz, Kemuel
(the father of Aram), **22** Chesed, Hazo, Pil-
dash, Jidlaph and Bethuel." **23** Bethuel became the father of Rebekah. These eight Milcah
bore to Abraham's brother Nahor. **24** His concubine, whose name was Reumah, also bore
children: Tebah, Gaham, Tahash and Maacah.

## CHAPTER 23

**Purchase of a Burial Place.** **1** The span
of Sarah's life was one hundred and twenty-sev-
en years. **2** She died in Kiriatharba (that is,
Hebron) in the land of Canaan, and Abraham
performed the customary mourning rites for her.
**3** Then he left the side of his dead one and
addressed the Hittites:* **4** "Although I am a
resident alien* among you, sell me from your
holdings a piece of property for a burial ground,
that I may bury my dead wife."[z] **5** The Hittites
answered Abraham: "Please, sir, **6** listen to us!
You are an elect of God among us. Bury your
dead in the choicest of our burial sites. None of
us would deny you his burial ground for the
burial of your dead." **7** Abraham, however,
began to bow low before the local citizens, the
Hittites, **8** while he appealed to them: "If you
will allow me room for burial of my dead, listen
to me! Intercede for me with Ephron, son of
Zohar, asking him **9** to sell me the cave of
Machpelah that he owns; it is at the edge of his
field. Let him sell it to me in your presence, at
its full price, for a burial place."

**10** Now Ephron was present with the Hittites. So Ephron the Hittite replied to Abraham
in the hearing of the Hittites who sat on his town
council:* **11** "Please, sir, listen to me! I give
you both the field and the cave in it; in the
presence of my kinsmen I make this gift. Bury
your dead!" **12** But Abraham, after bowing
low before the local citizens, addressed Ephron
in the hearing of these men: **13** "Ah, if only
you would please listen to me! I will pay you the
price of the field. Accept it from me, that I may
bury my dead there." **14** Ephron replied to
Abraham, "Please, **15** sir, listen to me! A piece
of land worth four hundred shekels* of silver
—what is that between you and me, as long as
you can bury your dead?" **16** [a]Abraham accepted Ephron's terms; he weighed out to him
the silver that Ephron had stipulated in the hearing of the Hittites, four hundred shekels of silver
at the current market value.*

**17** [b]Thus Ephron's field in Machpelah, facing Mamre, together with its cave and all the
trees anywhere within its limits, was conveyed

u Wis 10, 5.
v Rom 8, 32; 1 Jn 4, 9.
w 16f: Gn 15, 5; Ex 32, 13; Lk 1, 73; Rom 4, 13; Heb 6, 13f; 11, 12.
x Gn 24, 60.
y Gn 12, 3; 18, 18; 26, 4; Sir 44, 21; Acts 3, 25; Gal 3, 16.
z Gn 33, 19; Acts 7, 16; Heb 11, 9.
a Acts 7, 16.
b 17f: Gn 49, 29f.

*

22, 14: Yahweh-yireh: a Hebrew expression meaning "the Lord will see"; the reference is to the words in v 8, "God himself will see to it."

22, 20–24: A list of Aramean tribes who lived to the east and northeast of Israel, twelve in number, like the twelve tribes of Israel (Gn 35, 23) and the twelve tribes of Ishmael (Gn 25, 12–16).

23, 3: The Hittites: a non-Semitic people in Canaan; their relationship to the well-known Hittites of Asia Minor is uncertain.

23, 4: A resident alien: literally "a sojourner and a settler," i.e., a long-term resident alien. Such a one would normally not have the right to own property. The importance of Abraham's purchase of the field in Machpelah, which is worded in technical legal terms, lies in the fact that it gave his descendants their first, though small, land rights in the country that God had promised the patriarch they would one day inherit as their own. Abraham therefore insists on purchasing the field and not receiving it as a gift.

23, 10: Who sat on his town council: probable meaning of the literal translation, "who came in at the gate of his city"; so also in v 18.

23, 15: Four hundred shekels: probably an exorbitant sum; Jeremiah (32, 9) paid only seventeen shekels for his field in Anathoth, though the Babylonian invasion no doubt helped to reduce the price.

23, 16: The current market values: the standard weight called a shekel varied according to time and place.

**18** to Abraham by purchase in the presence of all the Hittites who sat on Ephron's town council. **19** After this transaction, Abraham buried his wife Sarah in the cave of the field of Machpelah, facing Mamre (that is, Hebron) in the land of Canaan. **20** Thus the field with its cave was transferred from the Hittites to Abraham as a burial place.

## CHAPTER 24

**Isaac and Rebekah.** **1** Abraham had now reached a ripe old age, and the LORD had blessed him in every way. **2** [c]Abraham said to the senior servant of his household, who had charge of all his possessions: "Put your hand under my thigh,* **3** and I will make you swear by the LORD, the God of heaven and the God of earth, that you will not procure a wife for my son from the daughters of the Canaanites among whom I live,[d] **4** but that you will go to my own land and to my kindred to get a wife for my son Isaac." **5** The servant asked him: "What if the woman is unwilling to follow me to this land? Should I then take your son back to the land from which you migrated?" **6** "Never take my son back there for any reason," Abraham told him. **7** "The LORD, the God of heaven, who took me from my father's house and the land of my kin, and who confirmed by oath the promise he then made to me, 'I will give this land to your descendants,—he will send his messenger before you, and you will obtain a wife for my son there.[e] **8** If the woman is unwilling to follow you, you will be released from this oath. But never take my son back there!" **9** So the servant put his hand under the thigh of his master Abraham and swore to him in this undertaking.

**10** The servant then took ten of his master's camels, and bearing all kinds of gifts from his master, he made his way to the city of Nahor* in Aram Naharaim. **11** Near evening, at the time when women go out to draw water, he made the camels kneel by the well outside the city. **12** Then he prayed: "LORD, God of my master Abraham, let it turn out favorably for me* today and thus deal graciously with my master Abraham. **13** While I stand here at the spring and the daughters of the townsmen are coming out to draw water, **14** if I say to a girl, 'Please lower your jug, that I may drink,' and she answers, 'Take a drink, and let me give water to your camels, too,' let her be the one whom you have decided upon for your servant Isaac. In this way I shall know that you have dealt graciously with my master."

**15** [f]He had scarcely finished these words when Rebekah (who was born to Bethuel, son of Milcah, the wife of Abraham's brother Nahor) came out with a jug on her shoulder. **16** The girl was very beautiful, a virgin, untouched by man. She went down to the spring and filled her jug. As she came up, **17** the servant ran toward her and said, "Please give me a sip of water from your jug." **18** "Take a drink, sir," she replied, and quickly lowering the jug onto her hand, she gave him a drink. **19** When she had let him drink his fill, she said, "I will draw water for your camels, too, until they have drunk their fill." **20** With that, she quickly emptied her jug into the drinking trough and ran back to the well to draw more water, until she had drawn enough for all the camels. **21** The man watched her the whole time, silently waiting to learn whether or not the LORD had made his errand successful. **22** When the camels had finished drinking, the man took out a gold ring weighing half a shekel, which he fastened on her nose, and two gold bracelets weighing ten shekels, which he put on her wrists. **23** Then he asked her: "Whose daughter are you? Tell me, please. And is there room in your father's house for us to spend the night?" **24** She answered: "I am the daughter of Bethuel the son of Milcah, whom she bore to Nahor. **25** There is plenty of straw and fodder at our place," she added, "and room to spend the night." **26** The man then bowed down in worship to the LORD, **27** saying: "Blessed be the LORD, the God of my master Abraham, who has not let his constant kindness toward my master fail. As for myself also, the LORD has led me straight to the house of my master's brother."

**28** Then the girl ran off and told her mother's household about it. **29** [g]Now Rebekah had a brother named Laban. **30** As soon as he saw the ring and the bracelets on his sister Rebekah and heard her words about what the man had said to her, Laban rushed outside to the man at the spring. When he reached him, he was still standing by the camels at the spring. **31** So he said to him: "Come, blessed of the LORD! Why are you staying outside when I have made the house ready for you, as well as a place for the

c 2f: Gn 47, 29.
d Gn 24, 37; 28, 1f; Jgs 14, 3; Tb 4, 12.
e Gn 12, 7; Ex 6, 8; Tb 5, 17; Gal 3, 16.
f Gn 22, 23.
g Gn 27, 43.

*

24, 2: Put your hand under my thigh: the symbolism of this act was apparently connected with the Hebrew concept of children issuing from their father's "thigh" (Gn 46, 26; Ex 1, 5). Perhaps the man who took such an oath was thought to bring the curse of sterility on himself if he did not fulfill his sworn promise. Jacob made Joseph swear in the same way (Gn 47, 29). In both these instances, the oath was taken to carry out the last request of a man upon his death.

24, 10: Nahor: it is uncertain whether this is to be understood as the name of Abraham's brother (Gn 11, 27), Rebekah's grandfather (Gn 24, 15), or the city of the same name (as known from the Mari documents); Aram Naharaim, situated near Haran (Gn 11, 31) in northern Mesopotamia.

24, 12: Let it turn out favorably for me: let me have a favorable omen; cf end of v 14.

camels?'' 32 The man then went inside; and
while the camels were being unloaded and provided with straw and fodder, water was brought
to bathe his feet and the feet of the men who
were with him. 33 But when the table was set
for him, he said, ''I will not eat until I have told
my tale.'' ''Do so,'' they replied.

34 ''I am Abraham's servant,'' he began.
35 ''The LORD has blessed my master so abundantly that he has become a wealthy man; he has
given him flocks and herds, silver and gold,
male and female slaves, and camels and asses.
36 My master's wife Sarah bore a son to my
master in her old age, and he has given him
everything he owns. 37 My master put me under oath, saying: 'You shall not procure a wife
for my son among the daughters of the Canaanites in whose land I live; 38 instead, you shall
go to my father's house, to my own relatives,
to get a wife for my son.' 39 When I asked my
master, 'What if the woman will not follow
me?' 40 he replied: 'The LORD, in whose presence I have always walked, will send his messenger with you and make your errand successful, and so you will get a wife for my son from
my own kindred of my father's house.[h]
41 Then you shall be released from my ban. If
you visit my kindred and they refuse you, then,
too, you shall be released from my ban.'

42 ''When I came to the spring today, I
prayed: 'LORD, God of my master Abraham,
may it be your will to make successful the errand I am engaged on! 43 While I stand here at
the spring, if I say to a young woman who
comes out to draw water, Please give me a little
water from your jug, 44 and she answers, Not
only may you have a drink, but I will give water
to your camels, too—let her be the woman
whom the LORD has decided upon for my master's son.'

45 ''I had scarcely finished saying this
prayer to myself when Rebekah came out with
a jug on her shoulder. After she went down to
the spring and drew water, I said to her, 'Please
let me have a drink.' 46 She quickly lowered
the jug she was carrying and said, 'Take a drink,
and let me bring water for your camels, too.' So
I drank, and she watered the camels also.
47 When I asked her, 'Whose daughter are
you?' she answered, 'The daughter of Bethuel,
son of Nahor, born to Nahor by Milcah.' So I
put the ring on her nose and the bracelets on her
wrists. 48 Then I bowed down in worship to the
LORD, blessing the LORD, the God of my master
Abraham, who had led me on the right road to
obtain the daughter of my master's kinsman for
his son. 49 If, therefore, you have in mind to
show true loyalty to my master, let me know;
but if not, let me know that, too. I can then
proceed accordingly.''

50 [i]Laban and his household said in reply:
''This thing comes from the LORD; we can say
nothing to you either for or against it. 51 Here
is Rebekah, ready for you; take her with you,
that she may become the wife of your master's
son, as the LORD has said.'' 52 When Abraham's servant heard their answer, he bowed to
the ground before the LORD. 53 Then he
brought out objects of silver and gold and articles of clothing and presented them to Rebekah;
he also gave costly presents to her brother and
mother. 54 After he and the men with him had
eaten and drunk, they spent the night there.

When they were up the next morning, he
said, ''Give me leave to return to my master.''[j]
55 Her brother and mother replied, ''Let the
girl stay with us a short while, say ten days; after
that she may go.'' 56 But he said to them, ''Do
not detain me, now that the LORD has made my
errand successful; let me go back to my master.'' 57 They answered, ''Let us call the girl
and see what she herself has to say about it.''
58 So they called Rebekah and asked her, ''Do
you wish to go with this man?'' She answered,
''I do.'' 59 At this they allowed their sister
Rebekah and her nurse to take leave, along with
Abraham's servant and his men. 60 Invoking a
blessing on Rebekah, they said:

''Sister, may you grow
into thousands of myriads;
And may your descendants gain possession
of the gates of their enemies!''[k]

61 Then Rebekah and her maids started out;
they mounted their camels and followed the
man. So the servant took Rebekah and went on
his way.

62 Meanwhile Isaac had gone from Beer-lahai-roi and was living in the region of the
Negeb.[l] 63 One day toward evening he went
out . . .* in the field, and as he looked around,
he noticed that camels were approaching.
64 Rebekah, too, was looking about, and when
she saw him, she alighted from her camel
65 and asked the servant, ''Who is the man out
there, walking through the fields toward us?''
''That is my master,'' replied the servant. Then
she covered herself with her veil.

66 The servant recounted to Isaac all the
things he had done. 67 Then Isaac took Rebekah into his tent; he married her, and thus she
became his wife. In his love for her Isaac found
solace after the death of his mother Sarah.

h Tb 5, 17; 10, 13.
i 50f; Tb 7, 12.
j Tb 7, 14; 8, 20.
k Gn 22, 17.
l Gn 16, 13f; 25, 11.

* 24, 63: He went out: the meaning of the Hebrew term that follows this is obscure.

## CHAPTER 25

### Abraham's Sons by Keturah.

1 [m]*Abraham married another wife, whose
name was Keturah. 2 She bore him Zimran,
Jokshan, Medan, Midian, Ishbak and Shuah.
3 Jokshan became the father of Sheba and Dedan. The descendants of Dedan were the As-
shurim, the Letushim, and the Leummim.[n]
4 The descendants of Midian were Ephah,
Epher, Hanoch, Abida and Eldaah. All of these
were descendants of Keturah.

5 Abraham deeded everything that he owned
to his son Isaac. 6 To his sons by concubinage,
however, he made grants while he was still
living, as he sent them away eastward, to the
land of Kedem,* away from his son Isaac.

**Death of Abraham.** 7 The whole span of
Abraham's life was one hundred and seventy-
five years. 8 Then he breathed his last, dying at
a ripe old age, grown old after a full life; and
he was taken to his kinsmen. 9 [o]His sons Isaac
and Ishmael buried him in the cave of Machpelah, in the field of Ephron, son of Zohar the
Hittite, which faces Mamre, 10 the field that
Abraham had bought from the Hittites; there he
was buried next to his wife Sarah. 11 After the
death of Abraham, God blessed his son Isaac,
who made his home near Beer-lahai-roi.

**Descendants of Ishmael.** 12 These are
the descendants of Abraham's son Ishmael,
whom Hagar the Egyptian, Sarah's slave, bore
to Abraham. 13 [p]These are the names of Isma-
el's sons, listed in the order of their birth: Nebaioth (Ishmael's firstborn), Kedar, Adbeel, Mibsam,[q] 14 Mishma, Dumah, Massa, 15 Hadad,
Tema, Jetur, Naphish and Kedemah, 16 These
are the sons of Ishmael, their names by their
villages and encampments; twelve chieftains of
as many tribal groups.[r]

17 The span of Ishmael's life was one hundred and thirty-seven years. After he had
breathed his last and died, he was taken to his
kinsmen. 18 The Ishmaelites ranged from Hav-
ilah-by-Shur, which is on the border of Egypt,
all the way to Asshur; and each of them pitched
camp* in opposition to his various kinsmen.[s]

## *III: The Patriarchs Isaac and Jacob*

**Birth of Esau and Jacob.** 19 This is the
family history of Isaac, son of Abraham; Abraham had begotten Isaac. 20 Isaac was forty
years old when he married Rebekah, the daughter of Bethuel the Aramean of Paddan-aram and
the sister of Laban the Aramean.[t] 21 Isaac entreated the LORD on behalf of his wife, since she
was sterile. The LORD heard his entreaty, and
Rebekah became pregnant. 22 But the children
in her womb jostled each other so much that she
exclaimed, "If this is to be so, what good will
it do me!" She went to consult the LORD,
23 and he answered her:

"Two nations are in your womb,
two peoples are quarreling while still
within you;
But one shall surpass the other,
and the older shall serve the younger.[u]

24 When the time of her delivery came, there
were twins in her womb.[v] 25 The first to
emerge was reddish,* and his whole body was
like a hairy mantle; so they named him Esau.
26 His brother came out next, gripping Esau's
heel;* so they named him Jacob. Isaac was sixty
years old when they were born.[w]

27 As the boys grew up, Esau became a skillful hunter, a man who lived in the open; whereas
Jacob was a simple man, who kept to his tents.[x]
28 Isaac preferred Esau, because he was fond
of game; but Rebekah preferred Jacob.
29 Once, when Jacob was cooking a stew, Esau
came in from the open, famished. 30 He said to
Jacob, "Let me gulp down some of that red
stuff;* I'm starving." (That is why he was
called Edom.) 31 But Jacob replied, "First

m 1-4; 1 Chr 1, 32f.
n Is 21, 13.
o 9f: Gn 23, 3-20.
p 13-16: 1 Chr 1, 29ff.
q Is 60, 7.
r Gn 17, 20.
s Gn 16, 12.
t Gn 24, 66.
u Gn 27, 29; Nm 24, 18; Mal 1, 2-5; Rom 9, 11f.
v Hos 12, 3.
w Mt 1, 2
x Gn 27, 6f.
y Dt 21, 17.

*

25, 1-11: Though mentioned here, Abraham's marriage to a "concubine," or wife of secondary rank, and his death are not to be understood as happening chronologically after the events narrated in the preceding chapter.

25, 6: The land of Kedem: or "the country of the East," the region inhabited by the Kedemites or Easterners (Gn 29, 1; Jgs 6, 3. 33; Jb 1, 3; Is 11, 14). The names mentioned in vv 2ff, as far as they can be identified, are those of tribes in the Arabian desert.

25, 18: Pitched camp: literally "fell"; the same Hebrew verb is used in Jgs 7, 12 in regard to the hostile encampment of Bedouin tribes. The present passage shows the fulfillment of the prediction contained in Gn 16, 12.

25, 25: Reddish: in Hebrew, admoni, a reference to Edom, another name for Esau (v 30; 36, 1). Edom, however, was really the name of the country south of Moab where the descendants of Esau lived. It was called the "red" country because of its reddish sandstone. Hairy: in Hebrew, sear, a reference to Seir, another name for Edom (Gn 36, 8). One might expect the text to say, "So they named him Seir"; but Esau (esaw) also means "hairy."

25, 26: Esau's heel: the Hebrew is baaqeb esaw, a reference to the name Jacob; cf Gn 27, 36. Probably, however, the name Jacob has no true etymological connection with the Hebrew word for "heel" (aqeb), but is instead a shortened form of some such name as yaaqob-el ("may God protect").

25, 30: Red stuff: in Hebrew, adom; another play on the word Edom, the "red" land.

25, 31: Birthright: the privilege that entitled the first-born son to a position of honor in the family and to a double share in the possessions inherited from the father.

give me your birthright* in exchange for it."[y] **32** "Look," said Esau, "I'm on the point of dying. What good will any birthright do me?" **33** But Jacob insisted, "Swear to me first!" So he sold Jacob his birthright under oath.[z] **34** Jacob then gave him some bread and the lentil stew; and Esau ate, drank, got up, and went his way. Esau cared little for his birthright.

## CHAPTER 26

**Isaac and Abimelech.** **1** [a]There was a famine in the land (distinct from the earlier one that had occurred in the days of Abraham), and Isaac went down to Abimelech, king of the Philistines in Gerar.[b] **2** The LORD appeared to him and said: "Do not go down to Egypt, but continue to camp wherever in this land I tell you. **3** Stay in this land, and I will be with you and bless you; for to you and your descendants I will give all these lands, in fulfillment of the oath that I swore to your father Abraham.[c] **4** I will make your descendants as numerous as the stars in the sky and give them all these lands, and in your descendants all the nations of the earth shall find blessing—[d] **5** this because Abraham obeyed me, keeping my mandate (my commandments, my ordinances and my instructions)."

**6** *So Isaac settled in Gerar. **7** When the men of the place asked questions about his wife, he answered, "She is my sister." He was afraid, if he called her his wife, the men of the place would kill him on account of Rebekah, since she was very beautiful. **8** But when he had been there for a long time, Abimelech, king of the Philistines, happened to look out of a window and was surprised to see Isaac fondling his wife Rebekah. **9** He called for Isaac and said: "She must certainly be your wife! How could you have said, 'She is my sister'?" Isaac replied, "I thought I might lose my life on her account." **10** "How could you do this to us!" exclaimed Abimelech. "It would have taken very little for one of the men to lie with your wife, and you would have thus brought guilt upon us!" **11** Abimelech therefore gave this warning to all his men: "Anyone who molests this man or his wife shall forthwith be put to death."

**12** *Isaac sowed a crop in that region and reaped a hundredfold the same year. Since the LORD blessed him, **13** [e]he became richer and richer all the time, until he was very wealthy indeed. **14** He acquired such flocks and herds, and so many work animals, that the Philistines became envious of him. (**15** [f]The Philistines had stopped up and filled with dirt all the wells that his father's servants had dug back in the days of his father Abraham.) **16** So Abimelech said to Isaac, "Go away from us; you have become far too numerous for us." **17** Isaac left there and made the Wadi Gerar his regular campsite. (**18** Isaac reopened the wells which his father's servants had dug back in the days of his father Abraham and which the Philistines had stopped up after Abraham's death; he gave them the same names that his father had given them.) **19** But when Isaac's servants dug in the wadi and reached spring water in their well, **20** the shepherds of Gerar quarreled with Isaac's servants, saying, "The water belongs to us!" So the well was called Esek,* because they had challenged him there. **21** Then they dug another well, and they quarreled over that one too; so it was called Sitnah.* **22** When he had moved on from there, he dug still another well; but over this one they did not quarrel. It was called Rehoboth, because he said, "The LORD has now given us ample room, and we shall flourish in the land."

**23** From there Isaac went up to Beer-sheba. **24** The same night the LORD appeared to him and said: "I am the God of your father Abraham. You have no need to fear, since I am with you. I will bless you and multiply your descendants for the sake of my servant Abraham."[g] **25** So he built an altar there and invoked the LORD by name. After he had pitched his tent there, his servants began to dig a well nearby.

**26** [h]Abimelech had meanwhile come to him from Gerar, accompanied by Ahuzzath, his councilor, and Phicol, the general of his army. **27** Isaac asked them, "Why have you come to me, seeing that you hate me and have driven me away from you?" **28** They answered: "We are convinced that the LORD is with you, so we propose that there be a sworn agreement between our two sides—between you and us. Let us make a pact with you: **29** you shall not act unkindly toward us, just as we have not molested you, but have always acted kindly toward you and have let you depart in peace. Henceforth, 'The LORD's blessing be upon you!'" **30** Isaac then made a feast for them, and they ate and drank. **31** Early the next morning they

z Heb 12, 16.
a 1-14: Gn 12, 10-20.
b Gn 12, 1.
c Gn 12, 7; 15, 18; Ex 32, 13; Ps 105, 9; Sir 44, 22; Heb 11, 9.
d Gn 12, 3; 22, 17f; 28, 14; Ex 32, 13.
e 13f: Jb 1, 3.
f 15-24: Gn 21, 25-31.
g Gn 46, 3.
h 26-33: Gn 21, 22-31; Prv 16, 7.

*

26, 6–11: The Yahwist's version of the wife-sister episode at Gerar; the Elohist's version (Gn 20, 1–18) is connected with Abraham and Sarah.

26, 12–33: The Yahwist's version of the story about the wells at Beer-sheba; again, the Elohist's version (Gn 21, 22f) is connected with Abraham. A redactor joined the two accounts by means of the parenthetical verses 15 and 18.

26, 20: Esek: "challenge."

26, 21: Sitnah: "opposition"; one might expect the text to be continued by some such words as "because they were in opposition there."

exchanged oaths. Then Isaac bade them farewell, and they departed from him in peace.
**32** That same day Isaac's servants came and
brought him news about the well they had been
digging; they told him, "We have reached water!" **33** He called it Shibah;* hence the name
of the city, Beer-sheba, to this day.
**34** *When Esau was forty years old, he married Judith, daughter of Beeri the Hittite, and
Basemath, daughter of Elon the Hivite.[i] **35** But
they became a source of embitterment to Isaac
and Rebekah.

## CHAPTER 27

**Jacob's Deception.*** **1** When Isaac was so
old that his eyesight had failed him, he called his
older son Esau and said to him, "Son!" "Yes,
father!" he replied. **2** Isaac then said, "As you
can see, I am so old that I may now die at any
time. **3** Take your gear, therefore—your quiver
and bow—and go out into the country to hunt
some game for me. **4** With your catch prepare
an appetizing dish for me, such as I like, and
bring it to me to eat, so that I may give you my
special blessing* before I die."
**5** Rebekah had been listening while Isaac
was speaking to his son Esau. So when Esau
went out into the country to hunt some game for
his father,[j] **6** Rebekah said to her son Jacob,
"Listen! I overheard your father tell your brother Esau, **7** 'Bring me some game and with it
prepare an appetizing dish for me to eat, that I
may give you my blessing with the LORD's approval before I die.' **8** Now, son, listen carefully to what I tell you. **9** Go to the flock and get
me two choice kids. With these I will prepare
an appetizing dish for your father, such as he
likes. **10** Then bring it to your father to eat, that
he may bless you before he dies." **11** "But my
brother Esau is a hairy man," said Jacob to his
mother Rebekah, "and I am smooth-skinned![k]
**12** Suppose my father feels me? He will think
I am making sport of him, and I shall bring on
myself a curse instead of a blessing." **13** His
mother, however, replied: "Let any curse
against you, son, fall on me! Just do as I say.
Go and get me the kids."
**14** So Jacob went and got them and brought
them to his mother; and with them she prepared
an appetizing dish, such as his father liked.
**15** Rebekah then took the best clothes of her
older son Esau that she had in the house, and
gave them to her younger son Jacob to wear;
**16** and with the skins of the kids she covered up
his hands and the hairless parts of his neck.
**17** Then she handed her son Jacob the appetizing dish and the bread she had prepared.
**18** Bringing them to his father, Jacob said,
"Father!" "Yes?" replied Isaac. "Which of
my sons are you?" **19** Jacob answered his father: "I am Esau, your first-born. I did as you
told me. Please sit up and eat some of my game,
so that you may give me your special blessing."
**20** But Isaac asked, "How did you succeed
so quickly, son?" He answered, "The LORD,
your God, let things turn out well with me."
**21** Isaac then said to Jacob, "Come closer, son,
that I may feel you, to learn whether you really
are my son Esau or not." **22** So Jacob moved
up closer to his father. When Isaac felt him, he
said, "Although the voice is Jacob's, the hands
are Esau's." **23** (He failed to identify him because his hands were hairy, like those of his
brother Esau; so in the end he gave him his
blessing.) **24** Again he asked him, "Are you
really my son Esau?" "Certainly," he replied.
**25** Then Isaac said, "Serve me your game, son,
that I may eat of it and then give you my blessing." Jacob served it to him, and Isaac ate; he
brought him wine, and he drank. **26** Finally his
father Isaac said to him, "Come closer, son,
and kiss me." **27** As Jacob went up and kissed
him, Isaac smelled the fragrance of his clothes.
With that, he blessed him, saying,

"Ah, the fragrance of my son
is like the fragrance of a field
that the LORD has blessed![l]

**28** "May God give to you
of the dew of the heavens
And of the fertility of the earth
abundance of grain and wine.

**29** [m]"Let peoples serve you,
and nations pay you homage;
Be master of your brothers,

i 34f: Gn 27, 46.
j Gn 25, 28.
k Gn 25, 25.
l Gn 22, 17f; Heb 11, 20.
m Gn 25, 23; 49, 8; Nm 24, 9.

*

26, 33: Shibah: "seven," for the sake of a closer assonance with Beer-sheba; but the present version of the story says nothing about there being seven wells there as implied in Gn 21, 28–31. The Greek version understood the Hebrew text more logically as shebua, "oath," in keeping with the present story.

26, 34f: These verses from the Priestly source, which have no logical connection with the preceding stories, serve as an introduction to the following section on Esau's loss of his birthright by suggesting a motivation for this in Isaac's and Rebekah's dislike for Esau's Canaanite wives.

27, 1–45: What Jacob did in deceiving his father and thereby cheating Esau out of Isaac's deathbed blessing is condemned as blameworthy, not only by Hosea (12, 4) and Jeremiah (9, 3), but also, indirectly, by the Yahwist narrator of the present story, who makes the reader sympathize with Esau as the innocent victim of a cruel plot, and shows that Jacob and his mother, the instigator of the plot, paid for it by a lifelong separation from each other. The story was told because it was part of the mystery of God's ways in salvation history—his use of weak, sinful men to achieve his own ultimate purpose.

27, 4: My special blessing: "the blessing of my soul." The same expression is used also in vv 19. 25. 31. In the context it must mean something like a solemn deathbed blessing, believed to be especially efficacious.

and may your mother's sons bow down to
you.

Cursed be those who curse you,
and blessed be those who bless you."

**30** Jacob had scarcely left his father, just
after Isaac had finished blessing him, when his
brother Esau came back from his hunt. **31** Then
he too prepared an appetizing dish with his
game, and bringing it to his father, he said,
"Please, father, eat some of your son's game,
that you may then give me your special blessing." **32** "Who are you?" his father Isaac
asked him. "I am Esau," he replied, "your
first-born son." **33** With that, Isaac was seized
with a fit of uncontrollable trembling. "Who
was it, then," he asked, "that hunted game and
brought it to me? I finished eating it just before
you came, and I blessed him. Now he must
remain blessed!" **34** On hearing his father's
words, Esau burst into loud, bitter sobbing.
"Father, bless me too!" he begged. **35** When
Isaac explained, "Your brother came here by a
ruse and carried off your blessing," **36** Esau
exclaimed, "He has been well named Jacob! He
has now supplanted me* twice! First he took
away my birthright, and now he has taken away
my blessing." Then he pleaded, "Haven't you
saved a blessing for me?"[n] **37** Isaac replied: "I
have already appointed him your master, and I
have assigned to him all his kinsmen as his
slaves; besides, I have enriched him with grain
and wine. What then can I do for you, son?"
**38** But Esau urged his father, "Have you only
that one blessing, father? Bless me too!" Isaac,
however, made no reply; and Esau wept aloud.[o]
**39** Finally Isaac spoke again and said to him:

"Ah, far from the fertile earth
shall be your dwelling;
far from the dew of the heavens above![p]
**40** "By your sword you shall live,
and your brother you shall serve;
But when you become restive,
you shall throw off his yoke from your
neck."[q]

**41** Esau bore Jacob a grudge because of the
blessing his father had given him. He said to
himself, "When the time of mourning for my
father comes, I will kill my brother Jacob."[r]
**42** When Rebekah got news of what her older
son Esau had in mind, she called her younger
son Jacob and said to him: "Listen! Your brother Esau intends to settle accounts with you by
killing you. **43** Therefore, son, do what I tell
you: flee at once to my brother Laban in Haran,
**44** and stay with him a while until your brother's fury subsides **45** [until your brother's anger
against you subsides] and he forgets what you
did to him. Then I will send for you and bring
you back. Must I lose both of you in a single
day?"

**Jacob Sent to Laban.** **46** *Rebekah said
to Isaac: "I am disgusted with life because of
the Hittite women. If Jacob also should marry
a Hittite woman, a native of the land, like these
women, what good would life be to me?"[s]

## CHAPTER 28

**1** Isaac therefore called Jacob, greeted him
with a blessing, and charged him: "You shall
not marry a Canaanite woman![t] **2** Go now to
Paddan-aram, to the home of your mother's
father Bethuel, and there choose a wife for yourself from among the daughters of your uncle
Laban.[u] **3** May God Almighty bless you and
make you fertile, multiply you that you may
become an assembly of peoples. **4** May he extend to you and your descendants the blessing
he gave to Abraham, so that you may gain possession of the land where you are staying, which
he assigned to Abraham."[v] **5** Then Isaac sent
Jacob on his way; he went to Paddan-aram, to
Laban, son of Bethuel, the Aramean, and brother of Rebekah, the mother of Jacob and Esau.[w]
**6** Esau noted that Isaac had blessed Jacob
when he sent him to Paddan-aram to get himself
a wife there, charging him, as he gave him his
blessing, not to marry a Canaanite woman,
**7** and that Jacob had obeyed his father and
mother and gone to Paddan-aram. **8** Esau realized how displeasing the Canaanite women
were to his father Isaac, **9** so he went to Ishmael, and in addition to the wives he had, married
Mahalath, the daughter of Abraham's son Ishmael and sister of Nebaioth.[x]

**Jacob's Dream at Bethel.** **10** Jacob departed from Beer-sheba and proceeded toward
Haran. **11** When he came upon a certain

n Gn 25, 26. 29-34; Hos 12, 4.
o Heb 12, 17.
p Heb 11, 20.
q 2 Kgs 8, 20. 22; 2 Chr 21, 8.
r Wis 10, 10; Ob 1, 10.
s Gn 26, 34f.
t Gn 24, 3f; 26, 35.
u Gn 22, 22; 17, 1f. 4f.
v Ex 32, 13.
w Jdt 8, 26.
x Gn 36, 2f.

*

27, 36: He has now supplanted me: in Hebrew, wayyaqebeni, a wordplay on the name Jacob, yaaqob; see Jer 9, 3 and note, as well as Gn 25, 26. There is also a play between the Hebrew words bekora ("birthright") and beraka ("blessing").

27, 46—28, 9: This section, which is from the Priestly source and a direct sequel of Gn 26, 34f, presents a different, though not contradictory, reason for Jacob's going to Paddan-aram: namely, to preserve racial purity among the chosen people. The account of Esau's marriages is given for the purpose of explaining the racial mixture of the Edomites, who were descended in part from tribes related to Israel, in part from older peoples in Edom called Hittites, Horites or Hivites, and in part from the Ishmaelite (Arabian) tribes who later invaded the region.

28, 11: Shrine: literally "place," often used specifically of a

shrine,* as the sun had already set, he stopped
there for the night. Taking one of the stones at
the shrine, he put it under his head and lay down
to sleep at that spot. **12** Then he had a dream:
a stairway* rested on the ground, with its top
reaching to the heavens; and God's messengers
were going up and down on it.[y] **13** And there
was the LORD standing beside him and saying:
"I, the LORD, am the God of your forefather
Abraham and the God of Isaac; the land on
which you are lying I will give to you and your
descendants.[z] **14** These shall be as plentiful as
the dust of the earth, and through them you shall
spread out east and west, north and south. In
you and your descendants all the nations of the
earth shall find blessing.[a] **15** Know that I am
with you; I will protect you wherever you go,
and bring you back to this land. I will never
leave you until I have done what I promised
you."[b]

**16** When Jacob awoke from his sleep, he
exclaimed, "Truly, the LORD is in this spot,
although I did not know it!" **17** In solemn wonder he cried out: "How awesome is this shrine!
This* is nothing else but an abode of God, and
that is the gateway to heaven!" **18** Early the
next morning Jacob took the stone that he had
put under his head, set it up as a memorial
stone,* and poured oil on top if it.[c] **19** He
called that site Bethel,* whereas the former
name of the town had been Luz.[d]

**20** Jacob then made this vow: "If God remains with me, to protect me on this journey I
am making and to give me enough bread to eat
and clothing to wear, **21** and I come back safe
to my father's house, the LORD shall be my God.
**22** This stone that I have set up as a memorial
stone shall be God's abode. Of everything you
give me, I will faithfully return a tenth part to
you."

## CHAPTER 29

**Arrival in Haran.** **1** [e]After Jacob resumed
his journey, he came to the land of the Easterners.* **2** Looking about, he saw a well in the
open country, with three droves of sheep huddled near it, for droves were watered from that
well. A large stone covered the mouth of the
well.[f] **3** Only when all the shepherds were assembled there could they roll the stone away
from the mouth of the well and water the flocks.
Then they would put the stone back again over
the mouth of the well.

**4** Jacob said to them, "Friends, where are
you from?" "We are from Haran," they replied. **5** Then he asked them, "Do you know
Laban, son of Nahor?" "We do," they answered.[g] **6** He inquired further, "Is he well?"
"He is," they answered; "and here comes his
daughter Rachel with his flock." **7** Then he
said: "There is still much daylight left; it is
hardly the time to bring the animals home. Why
don't you water the flocks now, and then continue pasturing them?" **8** "We cannot," they replied, "until all the shepherds are here to roll the
stone away from the mouth of the well; only
then can we water the flocks."

**9** While he was still talking with them, Rachel arrived with her father's sheep; she was the
one who tended them. **10** As soon as Jacob saw
Rachel, the daughter of his uncle Laban, with
the sheep of his uncle Laban, he went up, rolled
the stone away from the mouth of the well, and
watered his uncle's sheep. **11** Then Jacob
kissed Rachel and burst into tears.* **12** He told
her that he was her father's relative, Rebekah's
son, and she ran to tell her father. **13** When
Laban heard the news about his sister's son
Jacob, he hurried out to meet him. After embracing and kissing him, he brought him to his
house. Jacob then recounted to Laban all that
had happened, **14** and Laban said to him, "You
are indeed my flesh and blood."*

**Marriage to Leah and Rachel.** After Jacob had stayed with him a full month, **15** Laban
said to him: "Should you serve me for nothing
just because you are a relative of mine? Tell me
what your wages should be." **16** Now Laban
had two daughters; the older was called Leah,
the younger Rachel. **17** Leah had lovely eyes,*

y Jn 1, 51.
z Dt 1, 8; Mi 7, 28.
a Gn 12, 3; 13, 14f; 15, 5f; 18, 18; 22, 17f; 26, 4; Dt 19, 8; Sir 44, 21.
b Gn 31, 3.
c Gn 31, 13; 35, 14f.
d Gn 35, 6; 48, 3; Jos 18, 13; Jgs 1, 23; Hos 12, 4.
e Wis 10, 10.
f Gn 24, 11f.
g Tb 7, 4.

* sacred site. Here the place was Bethel (v 19), a sacred site as early as the time of Abraham (Gn 12, 8).

28, 12: Stairway: in Hebrew, sullam, traditionally but inaccurately, translated as "ladder." The corresponding verb, sal-al, means "to heap up" something, such as dirt for a highway or ramp. The imagery in Jacob's dream is derived from the Babylonian ziggurat or temple tower, "with its top in the sky" (Gn 11, 4), and with brick steps leading up to a small temple at the top.

28, 17: This: the stone Jacob used as a headrest; cf v 22. That: the stairway Jacob saw in his dream.

28, 18: Memorial stone: in Hebrew, masseba, a stone which might vary in shape and size, set upright and usually intended for some religious purpose. Since the custom of erecting such "sacred pillars" in Palestine went back to its pre-Israelite period, their pagan associations were often retained; therefore, later Israelite religion forbade their erection (Lv 26, 1; Dt 16, 22) and ordered the destruction of those that were associated with paganism (Ex 34, 31; Dt 12, 3).

28, 19: Bethel: i.e., "house of God"; the reference is to the abode of God in v 17.

29, 1: Easterners: see note on Gn 25, 6.

29, 11: Burst into tears: literally "raised his voice and wept," i.e., for joy.

29, 14: Flesh and blood: literally "bone and flesh," i.e., a close relative; on the Hebrew idiom, see Gn 2, 23.

29, 17: Lovely eyes: The adjective modifying eyes is often translated as "weak," but "lovely" is the more probable word.

but Rachel was well formed and beautiful.
**18** Since Jacob had fallen in love with Rachel,
he answered Laban, "I will serve you seven
years for your younger daughter Rachel."*
**19** Laban replied, "I prefer to give her to you
rather than to an outsider. Stay with me."
**20** So Jacob served seven years for Rachel, yet
they seemed to him but a few days because of
his love for her.[h]

**21** Then Jacob said to Laban, "Give me my
wife, that I may consummate my marriage with
her, for my term is now completed." **22** So
Laban invited all the local inhabitants and gave
a feast. **23** At the nightfall he took his daughter
Leah and brought her to Jacob, and Jacob consummated the marriage with her. **24** (Laban
assigned his slave girl Zilpah to his daughter
Leah as her maidservant.) **25** In the morning
Jacob was amazed:* it was Leah! So he cried out
to Laban: "How could you do this to me! Was
it not for Rachel that I served you? Why did you
dupe me?" **26** "It is not the custom in our
country," Laban replied, "to marry off a younger daughter before an older one. **27** Finish the
bridal week* for this one, and then I will give
you the other too, in return for another seven
years of service with me."[i]

**28** Jacob agreed. He finished the bridal week
for Leah, and then Laban gave him his daughter
Rachel in marriage. **29** (Laban assigned his
slave girl Bilhah to his daughter Rachel as her
maidservant.) **30** Jacob then consummated his
marriage with Rachel also, and he loved her
more than Leah. Thus he remained in Laban's
service another seven years.[j]

**Jacob's Children.** **31** When the LORD saw
that Leah was unloved, he made her fruitful,
while Rachel remained barren. **32** Leah conceived and bore a son, and she named him Reuben;* for she said, "It means, 'The LORD saw
my misery; now my husband will love me.'"[k]
**33** She conceived again and bore a son, and
said, "It means, 'The LORD heard that I was
unloved,' and therefore he has given me this one
also"; so she named him Simeon.* **34** Again
she conceived and bore a son, and she said,
"Now at last my husband will become attached
to me, since I have now borne him three sons";
that is why she named him Levi.* **35** Once
more she conceived and bore a son, and she
said, "This time I will give grateful praise to the
LORD"; therefore she named him Judah.* Then
she stopped bearing children.[l]

## CHAPTER 30

**1** When Rachel saw that she failed to bear
children to Jacob, she became envious of her
sister. She said to Jacob, "Give me children or
I shall die!"[m] **2** In anger Jacob retorted, "Can
I take the place of God, who has denied you the
fruit of the womb?"[n] **3** She replied, "Here is
my maidservant Bilhah. Have intercourse with
her, and let her give birth on my knees,* so that
I too may have offspring, at least through
her."[o] **4** So she gave him her maidservant Bilhah as a consort,* and Jacob had intercourse
with her. **5** When Bilhah conceived and bore a
son, **6** Rachel said, "God has vindicated me;
indeed he has heeded my plea and given me a
son." Therefore she named him Dan.* **7** Rachel's maidservant Bilhah conceived again and
bore a second son, **8** and Rachel said, "I engaged in a fateful struggle with my sister, and
I prevailed." So she named him Naphtali.*

**9** When Leah saw that she had ceased to bear
children, she gave her maidservant Zilpah to
Jacob as a consort. **10** So Jacob had intercourse
with Zilpah, and she conceived and bore a son.
**11** Leah then said, "What good luck!" So she
named him Gad.* **12** Then Leah's maidservant
Zilpah bore a second son to Jacob; **13** and
Leah said, "What good fortune!"—meaning,
"Women call me fortunate." So she named him
Asher.*

---

h Hos 12, 13.
i Hos 12, 13.
j Dt 21, 15ff.
k Gn 49, 3.
l Mt 1, 2; Lk 3, 33.
m Prv 30, 16.
n 2 Kgs 5, 7.
o Gn 16, 2ff.

---

29, 18: Jacob offers to render service (Jos 15, 16f; 1 Sm 17, 25; 18, 17) in lieu of the customary bridal price (Ex 22, 16f; Dt 22, 29).

29, 25: Jacob was amazed: he had not recognized Leah because a bride was veiled when she was brought to her bridegroom; cf Gn 24, 65.

29, 27: The bridal week: an ancient wedding lasted for seven days of festivities; cf Jgs 14, 12.

29, 32: Reuben: The literal meaning of the Hebrew name is "look, a son!" But in this case, as also with the names of all the other sons of Jacob, a symbolic rather than an etymological interpretation of the name is given, because the name and the persons were regarded as closely interrelated. The symbolic interpretation of Reuben's name, according to the Yahwist source, is based on the similar-sounding, raa beonyi, "he saw my misery." In the Elohist source, the name is explained by the similar-sounding yeehabani, "he will love me."

29, 33: Simeon: in popular etymology, related to shama, "he heard."

29, 34: Levi: related to yillaweh, "he will become attached."

29, 35: Judah: related to odeh, "I will give grateful praise."

30, 3: On my knees: in the ancient Near East, a father would take a newborn child in his lap to signify that he acknowledged it as his own; Rachel uses the ceremony in order to adopt the child and establish her legal rights to it.

30, 4: Consort: the Hebrew word normally means "wife," but here it refers to a wife of secondary rank, who did not have the full legal rights of an ordinary wife.

30, 6: Dan: explained by the term dannanni, "he has vindicated me."

30, 8: Naphtali: explained by the phrase "naptule elohim niptalti, literally, "in a divine wrestling match I have wrestled," perhaps implying the concept of an ordeal; hence the above rendering, I engaged in a fateful struggle.

30, 11: Gad: explained by the Hebrew term begad, literally "in luck," i.e., what good luck!

30, 13: Asher: explained by the term beoshri, literally "in my good fortune," i.e., what good fortune, and by the term ishsheruni, "they call me fortunate."

**14** One day, during the wheat harvest, when
Reuben was out in the field, he came upon some
mandrakes* which he brought home to his
mother Leah. Rachel asked Leah, "Please let
me have some of your son's mandrakes."
**15** Leah replied, "Was it not enough for you to
take away my husband, that you must now take
my son's mandrakes too?" "Very well, then!"
Rachel answered. "In exchange for your son's
mandrakes, Jacob may lie with you tonight."
**16** That evening, when Jacob came home from
the fields, Leah went out to meet him. "You are
now to come in with me," she told him, "because I have paid for you with my son's mandrakes." So that night he slept with her, **17** and
God heard her prayer; she conceived and bore
a fifth son to Jacob. **18** Leah then said, "God
has given me my reward for having let my husband have my maidservant"; so she named him
Issachar.* **19** Leah conceived again and bore a
sixth son to Jacob; **20** and she said, "God has
brought me a precious gift. This time my husband will offer me presents, now that I have
borne him six sons"; so she named him Zebulun.* **21** Finally, she gave birth to a daughter,
and she named her Dinah.

**22** Then God remembered Rachel; he heard
her prayer and made her fruitful. **23** She conceived and bore a son, and she said, "God has
removed my disgrace."[p] **24** So she named him
Joseph,* meaning, "May the LORD add another
son to this one for me!"

**Jacob Outwits Laban.** **25** After Rachel
gave birth to Joseph, Jacob said to Laban:
"Give me leave to go to my homeland. **26** Let
me have my wives, for whom I served you, and
my children, too, that I may depart. You know
very well the service that I have rendered
you." **27** Laban answered him: "If you will
please. . . .

"I have learned through divination that it is
because of you that God has blessed me.
**28** So," he continued, "state what wages you
want from me, and I will pay them." **29** Jacob
replied: "You know what work I did for you and
how well your livestock fared under my care;
**30** the little you had before I came has grown
into very much, since the LORD's blessings
came upon you in my company. Therefore I
should now do something for my own household as well." **31** "What should I pay you?"
Laban asked. Jacob answered: "You do not
have to pay me anything outright. I will again
pasture and tend your flock, if you do this one
thing for me: **32** go through your whole flock
today and remove from it every dark animal
among the sheep and every spotted or speckled
one among the goats.* Only such animals shall
be my wages. **33** In the future, whenever you
check on these wages of mine, let my honesty
testify against me: any animal in my possession
that is not a speckled or spotted goat, or a dark
sheep, got there by theft!" **34** "Very well,"
agreed Laban. "Let it be as you say."

**35** That same day Laban removed the
streaked and spotted he-goats and all the speckled and spotted she-goats, all those with some
white on them, as well as the fully dark-colored
sheep; these he left . . . in charge of his sons.*
**36** Then he put a three days' journey between
himself and Jacob, while Jacob continued to
pasture the rest of Laban's flock.

**37** Jacob, however, got some fresh shoots of
poplar, almond and plane trees, and he made
white stripes in them by peeling off the bark
down to the white core of the shoots. **38** The
rods that he had thus peeled he then set upright
in the watering troughs, so that they would be
in front of the animals that drank from the
troughs. When the animals were in heat as they
came to drink, **39** *the goats mated by the rods,
and so they brought forth streaked, speckled and
spotted kids. **40** The sheep, on the other hand,
Jacob kept apart, and he set these animals to
face the streaked or fully dark-colored animals
of Laban. Thus he produced special flocks of his
own, which he did not put with Laban's flock.
**41** Moreover, whenever the hardier animals
were in heat, Jacob would set the rods in the
troughs in full view of these animals, so that
they mated by the rods; **42** but with the weaker
animals he would not put the rods there. So the
feeble animals would go to Laban, but the stur-

---

p Lk 1, 25.

---

30, 14: Mandrakes: an herb whose root was anciently thought to promote conception. The Hebrew word for mandrakes, dudaim, has erotic connotations, since it sounds like the words daddayim ("breasts") and dodim ("sexual pleasure").

30, 18: Issachar: explained by the terms, sekari, "my reward," and in v 16, sakor sekartika, literally "I have hired you," i.e., I have paid for you.

30, 20: Zebulun: related to the Akkadian word zubullum, "bridegroom's gift," is explained by the terms, zebadani . . . zebed tob, "he has brought me a precious gift," and yizbeleni, "he will offer me presents."

30, 24: Joseph: explained by the words yosep, "may he add," and in v 23, asap, "he has removed."

30, 32: Dark . . . sheep . . . spotted or speckled goats: In the Near East the normal color of sheep is light gray, whereas that of goats is uniform dark brown or black. Ordinarily, therefore, Jacob would have received but few animals.

30, 35: By giving the abnormally colored animals to his sons, Laban not only deprived Jacob of his first small wages, but he also designed to prevent in this way the future breeding of such animals in the part of his flock entrusted to Jacob.

30, 39–42: Jacob's stratagem was based on the widespread notion among simple people that visual stimuli can have prenatal effects on the offspring of breeding animals. Thus, the rods on which Jacob had whittled stripes or bands or chevron marks were thought to cause the female goats that looked at them to bear kids with lighter-colored marks on their dark hair, while the gray ewes were thought to bear lambs with dark marks on them simply by visual cross-breeding with the dark goats.

dy ones to Jacob. **43** Thus the man grew increasingly prosperous, and he came to own not
only large flocks but also male and female servants and camels and asses.

## CHAPTER 31

**Flight from Laban.** **1** Jacob learned that
Laban's sons were saying, "Jacob has taken
everything that belonged to our father, and he
has accumulated all this wealth of his by using
our father's property." **2** Jacob perceived, too,
that Laban's attitude toward him was not what
it had previously been. **3** Then the LORD said to
Jacob, "Return to the land of your fathers,
where you were born, and I will be with you."[q]

**4** So Jacob sent for Rachel and Leah to meet
him where he was in the field with his flock.
**5** There he said to them: "I have noticed that
your father's attitude toward me is not as it was
in the past; but the God of my father has been
with me. **6** You well know what effort I put into
serving your father; **7** yet your father cheated
me and changed my wages time after time. God,
however, did not let him do me any harm.[r]
**8** *Whenever your father said, 'The speckled
animals shall be your wages,' the entire flock
would bear speckled young; whenever he said,
'The streaked animals shall be your wages,' the
entire flock would bear streaked young. **9** Thus
God reclaimed your father's livestock and gave
it to me. **10** Once, in the breeding season, I had
a dream in which I saw mating he-goats that
were streaked, speckled and mottled. **11** In the
dream God's messenger called to me, 'Jacob!'
'Here!' I replied. **12** Then he said. 'Note well.
All the he-goats in the flock, as they mate, are
streaked, speckled and mottled, for I have seen
all the things that Laban has been doing to you.
**13** I am the God who appeared to you in Bethel,
where you anointed a memorial stone and made
a vow to me. Up, then! Leave this land and
return to the land of your birth.' "[s]

**14** Rachel and Leah answered him: "Have
we still an heir's portion in our father's house?
**15** Are we not regarded by him as outsiders?*
He not only sold us; he has even used up the
money that he got for us! **16** All the wealth that
God reclaimed from our father really belongs to
us and our children. Therefore, do just as God
has told you."[t] **17** Jacob proceeded to put his
children and wives on camels, **18** and he drove
off with all his livestock and all the property he
had acquired in Paddanaram, to go to his father
Isaac in the land of Canaan.

**19** Now Laban had gone away to shear his
sheep, and Rachel had meanwhile appropriated
her father's household idols.[u] * **20** Jacob had
hoodwinked* Laban the Aramean by not telling
him of his intended flight. **21** Thus he made his
escape with all that he had. Once he was across
the Euphrates, he headed for the highlands of
Gilead.

**22** On the third day, word came to Laban that
Jacob had fled. **23** Taking his kinsmen with
him, he pursued him for seven days* until he
caught up with him in the hill country of Gilead.
**24** But that night God appeared to Laban the
Aramean in a dream and warned him. "Take
care not to threaten Jacob with any harm."[v]

**Jacob and Laban in Gilead.** **25** When
Laban overtook Jacob, Jacob's tents were
pitched in the highlands; Laban also pitched his
tents there, on Mount Gilead. **26** "What do you
mean," Laban demanded of Jacob, "by hood-
winking me and carrying off my daughters like
war captives?* **27** Why did you dupe me by
stealing away secretly? You should have told
me, and I would have sent you off with merry
singing to the sound of tambourines and harps.
**28** You did not even allow me a parting kiss to
my daughters and grandchildren! What you
have now done is a senseless thing. **29** I have
it in my power to harm all of you; but last night
the God of your father said to me, 'Take care not
to threaten Jacob with any harm!' **30** Granted
that you had to leave because you were desper-
ately homesick for your father's house, why did
you steal my gods?" **31** "I was frightened,"
Jacob replied to Laban, "at the thought that you
might take your daughters away from me by
force. **32** But as for your gods, the one you find
them with shall not remain alive! If, with my
kinsmen looking on, you identify anything here
as belonging to you, take it." Jacob, of course,
had no idea that Rachel had stolen the idols.
**33** Laban then went in and searched Jacob's

q Gn 26, 3; 28, 15; 32, 10.
r Jdt 8, 26.
s Gn 28, 18.
t Wis 10, 10f.
u Gn 19, 34; 1 Sm 19, 13.
v Wis 10, 12.

*

31, 8–12: This Elohist account of the miraculous increase in Jacob's flock differs somewhat from the Yahwist account given in Gn 30, 32–42.

31, 15: Outsiders: literally "foreign women"; they lacked the favored legal status of native women. Used up: literally "eaten, consumed"; the bridal price that a man received for giving his daughter in marriage was legally reserved as her inalienable dowry.

31, 19: Household idols: in Hebrew, teraphim, figurines used in divination (Ez 21, 26; Zec 10, 2). Laban calls them his "gods" (v 30).

31, 20: Hoodwinked: literally "stolen the heart of," i.e., lulled the mind of. Aramean: The earliest extra-biblical references to the Arameans date from several centuries after the time of Jacob; to call Laban an Aramean and to have him speak Aramaic (v 47) would seem to be an anachronism.

31, 23: For seven days: literally "a way of seven days," a general term to designate a long distance; it would have taken a camel caravan many more days to travel from Haran to Gilead, the region east of the northern half of the Jordan.

31, 26: War captives: literally "women captured by the sword"; the women of a conquered people were treated as part of the victor's booty; cf 1 Sm 30, 2; 2 Kgs 5, 2.

tent and Leah's tent, as well as the tents of the
two maidservants; but he did not find the idols.
Leaving Leah's tent, he went into Rachel's.
**34** Now Rachel had taken the idols, put them
inside a camel cushion, and seated herself upon
them. When Laban had rummaged through the
rest of her tent without finding them,[w] **35** Rachel said to her father, "Let not my lord feel
offended that I cannot rise in your presence; a
woman's period is upon me." So, despite his
search, he did not find his idols.

**36** Jacob, now enraged, upbraided Laban.
"What crime or offense have I committed," he
demanded, "that you should hound me so
fiercely? **37** Now that you have ransacked all
my things, have you found a single object taken
from your belongings? If so, produce it here
before your kinsmen and mine, and let them
decide between us two.

**38** "In the twenty years that I was under you,
no ewe or she-goat of yours ever miscarried,
and I have never feasted on a ram of your flock.
**39** [x]I never brought you an animal torn by wild
beasts; I made good the loss myself. You held
me responsible for anything stolen by day or
night.* **40** How often the scorching heat ravaged me by day, and the frost by night, while
sleep fled from my eyes! **41** Of the twenty years
that I have now spent in your household, I
slaved fourteen years for your two daughters
and six years for your flock, while you changed
my wages time after time. **42** If my ancestral
God, the God of Abraham and the Awesome
One of Isaac, had not been on my side, you
would now have sent me away empty-handed.
But God saw my plight and the fruits of my toil,
and last night he gave judgment."[y]

**43** *Laban replied to Jacob: "The women
are mine, their children are mine, and the flocks
are mine; everything you see belongs to me. But
since these women are my daughters, I will now
do something for them and for the children they
have borne. **44** Come, then, we will make a
pact, you and I; the LORD shall be a witness
between us."

**45** Then Jacob took a stone and set it up as
a memorial stone.[z] **46** Jacob said to his kinsmen, "Gather some stones." So they got some
stones and made a mound; and they had a meal
there at the mound. **47** Laban called it Jegar-sahadutha,* but Jacob named it Galeed. **48** "This
mound," said Laban, "shall be a witness from
now on between you and me." That is why it
was named Galeed— **49** and also Mizpah,* for
he said: "May the LORD keep watch between
you and me when we are out of each other's
sight. **50** If you mistreat my daughters, or take
other wives besides my daughters, remember
that even though no one else is about, God will
be witness between you and me."

**51** Laban said further to Jacob: "Here is this
mound, and here is the memorial stone that I
have set up between you and me. **52** This
mound shall be witness, and this memorial
stone shall be witness, that, with hostile intent,
neither may I pass beyond this mound into your
territory nor may you pass beyond it into mine.
**53** May the God of Abraham and the god of
Nahor [their ancestral deities] maintain justice
between us!" Jacob took the oath by the Awesome One of Issac. **54** He then offered a sacrifice on the mountain and invited his kinsmen to
share in the meal. When they had eaten, they
passed the night on the mountain.

## CHAPTER 32

**1** Early the next morning, Laban kissed his
grandchildren and his daughters goodbye; then
he set out on his journey back home, **2** while
Jacob continued on his own way. Then God's
messengers encountered Jacob. **3** When he saw
them he said, "This is God's encampment." So
he named that place Mahanaim.*

**Embassy to Esau.** **4** Jacob sent messengers ahead to his brother Esau in the land of
Seir, the country of Edom,[a] **5** with this message: "Thus shall you say to my lord Esau:
'Your servant Jacob speaks as follows: I have
been staying with Laban and have been detained
there until now. **6** I own cattle, asses and sheep,
as well as male and female servants. I am sending my lord this information in the hope of
gaining your favor.'" **7** When the messengers
returned to Jacob, they said, "We reached your
brother Esau. He is now coming to meet you,
accompanied by four hundred men."

**8** Jacob was very much frightened. In his
anxiety, he divided the people who were with

w Gn 31, 19.
x Ex 22, 12.
y Gn 19, 24. 29.
z Gn 28, 18; 35, 14.
a Gn 36, 6.

*

31, 39: Laban's actions were contrary to the customs of the ancient Near East, as recorded in the Code of Hammurabi: "If in a sheepfold an act of god has occurred, or a lion has made a kill, the shepherd shall clear himself before the deity, and the owner of the fold must accept the loss" (par. 266); cf Ex 22, 12.

31, 43–54: In this account of the treaty between Laban and Jacob, the Yahwist and Elohist sources are closely interwoven. The mound or cairn of stones comes from the Yahwist source, the memorial stone or stele comes from the Elohist one.

31, 47: Jegar-sahadutha: an Aramaic term meaning "mound of witness." Galeed: in Hebrew, galed, with the same meaning; also offers an explanation of the regional name Gilead.

31, 49: Mizpah: a town in Gilead; cf Jgs. 10, 17; 11, 11. 34; Hos 5, 1. The Hebrew name mispa ("lookout") is allied to yisep yhwh ("may the Lord keep watch"), and also echoes the word masseba ("memorial pillar").

32, 3: Mahanaim: a town in Gilead (Jos 13, 26. 30; 21, 38; 2 Sm 2, 8; etc.). The Hebrew name means "two camps." There are other allusions to the name in vv 8. 11.

him, as well as his flocks, herds, and camels, into two camps. **9** "If Esau should attack and overwhelm one camp," he reasoned, "the remaining camp may still survive." **10** Then he prayed, "O God of my father Abraham and God of my father Isaac! You told me, O LORD, 'Go back to the land of your birth, and I will be good to you.'[b] **11** I am unworthy of all the acts of kindness that you have loyally performed for your servant: although I crossed the Jordan here with nothing but my staff, I have now grown into two companies. **12** Save me, I pray, from the hand of my brother Esau! Otherwise I fear that when he comes he will strike me down and slay the mothers and children.[c] **13** You yourself said, 'I will be very good to you, and I will make your descendants like the sands of the sea, which are too numerous to count.' "

**14** After passing the night there, Jacob selected from what he had with him the following presents for his brother Esau: **15** two hundred she-goats and twenty he-goats; two hundred ewes and twenty rams; **16** thirty milch camels and their young; forty cows and ten bulls; twenty she-asses and ten he-asses. **17** He put these animals in charge of his servants, in separate droves, and he told the servants, "Go on ahead of me, but keep a space between one drove and the next." **18** To the servant in the lead he gave this instruction: "When my brother Esau meets you, he may ask you, 'Whose man are you? Where are you going? To whom do these animals ahead of you belong?' **19** Then you shall answer, 'They belong to your brother Jacob, but they have been sent as a gift to my lord Esau; and Jacob himself is right behind us.' " **20** He gave similar instructions to the second servant and the third and to all the others who followed behind the droves, namely: "Thus and thus shall you say to Esau, when you reach him; **21** and be sure to add, 'Your servant Jacob is right behind us.' " For Jacob reasoned, "If I first appease him with gifts that precede me, then later, when I face him, perhaps he will forgive me." **22** So the gifts went on ahead of him, while he stayed that night in the camp.

**Struggle with the Angel.** **23** In the course of that night, however, Jacob arose, took his two wives, with the two maidservants and his eleven children, and crossed the ford of the Jabbok. **24** After he had taken them across the stream and had brought over all his possessions, **25** Jacob was left there alone. Then some man* wrestled with him until the break of dawn. **26** When the man saw that he could not prevail over him, he struck Jacob's hip at its socket, so that the hip socket was wrenched as they wrestled.[d] **27** The man then said, "Let me go, for it is daybreak." But Jacob said, "I will not let you go until you bless me." **28** "What is your name?" the man asked. He answered, "Jacob."[e] **29** Then the man said, "You shall no longer be spoken of as Jacob, but as Israel,* because you have contended with divine and human beings and have prevailed." **30** Jacob then asked him, "Do tell me your name, please." He answered, "Why should you want to know my name?" With that, he bade him farewell. **31** Jacob named the place Peniel,* "Because I have seen God face to face," he said, "yet my life has been spared."[f]

**32** At sunrise, as he left Penuel, Jacob limped along because of his hip. **33** That is why, to this day, the Israelites do not eat the sciatic muscle that is on the hip socket, inasmuch as Jacob's hip socket was struck at the sciatic muscle.

## CHAPTER 33

**Jacob and Esau Meet.** **1** Jacob looked up and saw Esau coming, accompanied by four hundred men. So he divided his children among Leah, Rachel and the two maidservants, **2** putting the maids and their children first, Leah and her children next, and Rachel and Joseph last. **3** He himself went on ahead of them, bowing to the ground seven times, until he reached his brother. **4** Esau ran to meet him, embraced him, and flinging himself on his neck, kissed him as he wept.

**5** When Esau looked about, he saw the women and children. "Who are these with you?" he asked. Jacob answered, "They are the children whom God has graciously bestowed on your servant." **6** Then the maidservants and their children came forward and bowed low; **7** next, Leah and her children came forward and bowed low; lastly, Rachel and her children came forward and bowed low. **8** Then Esau asked, "What did you intend with all those droves that I encountered?" Jacob answered, "It was to gain my lord's favor." **9** "I have plenty," replied Esau; "you should keep what is yours, brother." **10** "No, I beg you!" said Jacob. "If

b Gn 31, 3.
c Gn 28, 14; 48, 16; Ex 32, 13; Heb 11, 12.
d Hos 12, 4.
e Gn 35, 10; 1 Kgs 18, 31; 2 Kgs 17, 34.
f Jgs 13, 22.

*

32, 25: Some man: a messenger of the Lord in human form, as is clear from vv 29ff.

32, 29: Israel: the first part of the Hebrew name Yisrael is given a popular explanation in the word sarita, "you contended"; the second part is the first syllable of elohim, "divine beings." The present incident, with a similar allusion to the name Israel, is referred to in Hos 12, 5, where the mysterious wrestler is explicitly called an angel.

32, 31: Peniel: a variant of the word Penuel (v 32), the name of a town on the north bank of the Jabbok in Gilead (Jgs 8, 8f. 17; 1 Kgs 12, 25). The name is explained as meaning "the face of God," peni-el. Yet my life has been spared: see note on Gn 16, 13.

you will do me the favor, please accept this gift from me, since to come into your presence is for me like coming into the presence of God, now that you have received me so kindly. **11** Do accept the present I have brought you; God has been generous toward me, and I have an abundance." Since he so urged him, Esau accepted.

**12** Then Esau said, "Let us break camp and be on our way; I will travel alongside you." **13** But Jacob replied: "As my lord can see, the children are frail. Besides, I am encumbered with the flocks and herds, which now have sucklings; if overdriven for a single day, the whole flock will die. **14** Let my lord, then, go on ahead of me, while I proceed more slowly at the pace of the livestock before me and at the pace of my children, until I join my lord in Seir." **15** Esau replied, "Let me at least put at your disposal some of the men who are with me." But Jacob said, "For what reason? Please indulge me in this, my lord." **16** So on the same day that Esau began his journey back to Seir, **17** Jacob journeyed to Succoth. There he built a home for himself and made booths for his livestock. That is why the place was called Succoth.*

**18** Having thus come from Paddan-aram, Jacob arrived safely at the city of Shechem, which is in the land of Canaan, and he encamped in sight of the city.[g] **19** The plot of ground on which he had pitched his tent he bought for a hundred pieces of bullion* from the descendants of Hamor, the founder of Shechem.[h] **20** He set up a memorial stone there and invoked "El, the God of Israel."[i]

## CHAPTER 34

**The Rape of Dinah.** **1** *Dinah, the daughter whom Leah had borne to Jacob, went out to visit some of the women of the land. **2** When Shechem, son of Hamor the Hivite,* who was chief of the region, saw her, he seized her and lay with her by force. **3** Since he was strongly attracted to Dinah, daughter of Jacob, indeed was really in love with the girl, he endeavored to win her affection. **4** Shechem also asked his father Hamor, "Get me this girl for a wife."

**5** Meanwhile, Jacob heard that Shechem had defiled his daughter Dinah; but since his sons were out in the fields with his livestock, he held his peace until they came home. **6** Now Hamor, the father of Shechem, went out to discuss the matter with Jacob, **7** just as Jacob's sons were coming in from the fields. When they heard the news, the men were shocked and seethed with indignation. What Shechem had done was an outrage in Israel; such a thing could not be tolerated.[j]

**8** Hamor appealed to them, saying, "My son Shechem has his heart set on your daughter. Please give her to him in marriage. **9** Intermarry with us; give your daughters to us, and take our daughters for yourselves. **10** Thus you can live among us. The land is open before you; you can settle and move about freely in it, and acquire landed property here." **11** Then Shechem, too, appealed to Dinah's father and brothers: "Do me this favor, and I will pay whatever you demand of me. **12** No matter how high you set the bridal price, I will pay you whatever you ask; only give me the maiden in marriage."

**Revenge of Jacob's Sons.** **13** Jacob's sons replied to Shechem and his father Hamor with guile, speaking as they did because their sister Dinah had been defiled. **14** "We could not do such a thing," they said, "as to give our sister to an uncircumcised man; that would be a disgrace for us. **15** We will agree with you only on this condition, that you become like us by having every male among you circumcised. **16** Then we will give you our daughters and take yours in marriage; we will settle among you and become one kindred people with you. **17** But if you do not comply with our terms regarding circumcision, we will take our daughter and go away."

**18** Their proposal seemed fair to Hamor and his son Shechem. **19** The young man lost no time in acting in the matter, since he was deeply in love with Jacob's daughter. Moreover, he was more highly respected than anyone else in his clan. **20** So Hamor and his son Shechem went to their town council and thus presented the matter to their fellow townsmen: **21** "These men are friendly toward us. Let them settle in the land and move about in it freely; there is ample room in the country for them. We can marry their daughters and give our daughters to them in marriage. **22** But the men will agree to live with us and form one kindred people with

---

g Gn 12, 6; Jn 4, 6.
h Jos 24, 32; Jn 4. 5; Acts 7, 16.
i Jgs 6, 24.
j 2 Sm 13, 12.

---

33, 17: Succoth: an important town near the confluence of the Jabbok and the Jordan (Jos 13, 27; Jgs 8, 5–16; 1 Kgs 7, 46). Booths: in Hebrew, sukkot, of the same sound as the name of the town.

33, 19: Pieces of bullion: in Hebrew, kesita, a monetary unit of which the value is now unknown. Descendants of Hamor: Hamorites, "the men of Hamor"; cf Jgs 9, 28. Hamor was regarded as the eponymous ancestor of the pre-Israelite inhabitants of Shechem.

34, 1–31: Behind the story of the rape of Dinah and the revenge of Jacob's sons on the men of the city of Shechem there probably lies a dimly recollected historical event connected with an armed conflict between the earliest Israelite tribes invading central Canaan and the Hurrian inhabitants of the Shechem region.

34, 2: Hivite: The Greek text has "Horite"; the terms were apparently used indiscriminately to designate the Hurrian or other non-Semitic elements in Palestine.

us only on this condition, that every male
among us be circumcised as they themselves
are. 23 Would not the livestock they have acquired—all their animals—then be ours? Let us,
therefore, give in to them, so that they may
settle among us."

24 All the able-bodied men of the town*
agreed with Hamor and his son Shechem, and
all the males, including every able-bodied man
in the community, were circumcised. 25 On the
third day, while they were still in pain, Dinah's
full brothers Simeon and Levi, two of Jacob's
sons, took their swords, advanced against the
city without any trouble, and massacred all the
males.[k] 26 After they had put Hamor and his
son Shechem to the sword, they took Dinah
from Shechem's house and left.[l] 27 Then the
other sons of Jacob followed up the slaughter
and sacked the city in reprisal for their sister
Dinah's defilement. 28 They seized their
flocks, herds and asses, whatever was in the city
and in the country around. 29 They carried off
all their wealth, their women, and their children, and took for loot whatever was in the
houses.[m]

30 Jacob said to Simeon and Levi: "You
have brought trouble upon me by making me
loathsome to the inhabitants of the land, the
Canaanites and the Perizzites. I have so few
men that, if these people unite against me and
attack me, I and my family will be wiped out."
31 But they retorted, "Should our sister have
been treated like a harlot?"

## CHAPTER 35

**Bethel Revisited.** 1 God said to Jacob:
"Go up now to Bethel. Settle there and build an
altar there to the God who appeared to you while
you were fleeing from your brother Esau."[n]
2 So Jacob told his family and all the others
who were with him: "Get rid of the foreign
gods* that you have among you; then purify
yourselves and put on fresh clothes. 3 We are
now to go up to Bethel, and I will build an altar
there to the God who answered me in my hour
of distress and who has been with me wherever
I have gone." 4 They therefore handed over to
Jacob all the foreign gods in their possession
and also the rings* they had in their ears.
5 Then, as they set out, a terror from God fell
upon the towns round about, so that no one
pursued the sons of Jacob.

6 Thus Jacob and all the people who were
with him arrived in Luz [that is, Bethel] in the
land of Canaan.[o] 7 There he built an altar and
named the place Bethel, for it was there that
God had revealed himself to him when he was
fleeing from his brother.[p]

8 Death came to Rebekah's nurse Deborah;
she was buried under the oak below Bethel, and
so it was called Allonbacuth.*

9 On Jacob's arrival from Paddan-aram, God
appeared to him again and blessed him. 10 God
said to him:

"You whose name is Jacob
shall no longer be called Jacob,
but Israel shall be your name."[q]

Thus he was named Israel. 11 God also said
to him:

"I am God Almighty;
be fruitful and multiply.
A nation, indeed an assembly of nations,
shall stem from you,
and kings shall issue from your loins.
12 The land I once gave
to Abraham and Isaac
I now give to you;
And to your descendants after you
will I give this land."[r]

13 Then God departed from him. 14 On the
site where God had spoken with him, Jacob set
up a memorial stone, and upon it he made a
libation and poured out oil.[s] 15 Jacob named
the site Bethel, because God had spoken with
him there.

**Jacob's Family.** 16 Then they departed
from Bethel: but while they still had some distance to go on the way to Ephrath, Rachel began
to be in labor and to suffer great distress.
17 When her pangs were most severe, her midwife said to her, "Have no fear! This time, too,
you have a son." 18 With her last breath—for
she was at the point of death—she called him
Ben-oni;* his father, however, named him Ben-

k Gn 49, 6.
l Jdt 9, 2.
m Jdt 9, 3f.
n Gn 28, 12f.
o Gn 28, 19; Jos 18, 13; Jgs 1, 22f.
p Gn 28, 12f.
q 1 Kgs 18, 31; 2 Kgs 17, 34.
r Ex 32, 13; Heb 11, 9.
s Gn 28, 18; 31, 45.

*

34, 24: Every able-bodied man in the community: literally "all those who go out at the gate of the city," apparently meaning the men who go out to war. By temporarily crippling them through circumcision, Jacob's sons deprived the city of its defenders.

35, 2: Foreign gods: pagan images, including household idols (see note on Gn 31, 19), that Jacob's people brought with them from Paddan-aram.

35, 4: Rings: Earrings were often worn as amulets connected with pagan magic.

35, 8: This verse may have stood originally in some other context. Rebekah's nurse is spoken of without a name, in Gn 24, 59. Allon-bacuth: the Hebrew name means "oak of weeping."

35, 18: Ben-oni: means either "son of my vigor" or, more likely in the context, "son of affliction." Benjamin: "son of the right hand." This may be interpreted to signify a son who is his father's help and support, but more likely its original meaning was "southerner." In the Hebrew idiom, the south lies to one's right hand, and Benjamin was the southernmost of the Rachel tribes.

jamin. **19** [t]Thus Rachel died; and she was buried on the road to Ephrath [that is, Bethlehem].*
**20** Jacob set up a memorial stone on her grave,
and the same monument marks Rachel's grave
to this day.

**21** Israel moved on and pitched his tent beyond Migdal-eder. **22** While Israel was encamped in that region, Reuben went and lay
with Bilhah, his father's concubine. When Israel heard of it, he was greatly offended.[u]

The sons of Jacob were now twelve. **23** The
sons of Leah: Reuben, Jacob's first-born, Simeon, Levi, Judah, Issachar, and Zebulun;
**24** *the sons of Rachel: Joseph and Benjamin;
**25** the sons of Rachel's maid Bilhah: Dan and
Naphtali; **26** the sons of Leah's maid Zilpah:
Gad and Asher. These are the sons of Jacob who
were born to him in Paddan-aram.

**27** Jacob went home to his father Isaac at
Mamre, in Kiriath-arba [that is, Hebron], where
Abraham and Isaac had stayed. **28** The lifetime
of Isaac was one hundred and eighty years;
**29** then he breathed his last. After a full life, he
died as an old man and was taken to his kinsmen. His sons Esau and Jacob buried him.

## CHAPTER 36

**Edomite Lists.** **1** These are the descendants of Esau [that is, Edom]. **2** *Esau took his
wives from among the Canaanite women: Adah,
daughter of Elon the Hittite; Oholibamah,
granddaughter through Anah of Zibeon the Hivite;[v] **3** and Basemath, daughter of Ishmael and
sister of Nebaioth. **4** Adah bore Eliphaz to
Esau; Basemath bore Reuel;[w] **5** and Oholibamah bore Jeush, Jalam and Korah. These are the
sons of Esau who were born to him in the land
of Cannan.[x]

**6** Esau took his wives, his sons, his daughters, and all the members of his household, as
well as his livestock comprising various animals
and all the property he had acquired in the land
of Canaan, and went to the land of Seir, out of
the way of his brother Jacob.[y] **7** Their possessions had become too great for them to dwell
together, and the land in which they were staying could not support them because of their
livestock. **8** So Esau settled in the highlands of
Seir. [Esau is Edom.][z] **9** These are the descendants of Esau, ancestor of the Edomites, in the
highlands of Seir.

**10** These are the names of Esau's sons: Eliphaz, son of Esau's wife Adah; and Reuel, son
of Esau's wife Basemath. **11** [a]The sons of Eliphaz were Teman, Omar, Zepho, Gatam and
Kenaz. **12** (Esau's son Eliphaz had a concubine
Timna, and she bore Amalek to Eliphaz.) These
are the descendants of Esau's wife Adah.
**13** The sons of Reuel were Nahath, Zerah,
Shammah and Mizzah. These are the descendants of Esau's wife Basemath.[b] **14** The descendants of Esau's wife Oholibamah—granddaughter through Anah of Zibeon—whom she
bore to Esau were Jeush, Jalam and Korah.[c]

**15** The following are the clans of Esau's descendants. The descendants of Eliphaz, Esau's
first-born: the clans of Teman, Omar, Zepho,
Kenaz, **16** Korah, Gatam and Amalek. These
are the clans of Eliphaz in the land of Edom;
they are descended from Adah. **17** The descendants of Esau's son Reuel: the clans of Nahath, Zerah, Shammah and Mizzah. These are
the clans of Reuel in the land of Edom; they are
descended from Esau's wife Basemath. **18** The
descendants of Esau's wife Oholibamah: the
clans of Jeush, Jalam and Korah. These are the
clans of Esau's wife Oholibamah, daughter of
Anah. **19** Such are the descendants of Esau
[that is, Edom] according to their clans.

**20** The following are the descendants of Seir
the Horite,* the original settlers in the land:
Lotan, Shobal, Zibeon, Anah,[d] **21** Dishon,
Ezer and Dishan; they are the Horite clans descended from Seir, in the land of Edom.
**22** [e]Lotan's descendants were Hori and
Hemam, and Lotan's sister was Timna.
**23** Shobal's descendants were Alvan, Maha-
nath, Ebal, Shepho and Onam. **24** Zibeon's descendants were Aiah and Anah. (He is the Anah
who found water in the desert while he was
pasturing the asses of his father Zibeon.)
**25** The descendants of Anah were Dishon and
Oholibamah, daughter of Anah. **26** The descendants of Dishon were Hemdan, Eshban,
Ithran and Cheran. **27** The descendants of Ezer
were Bilhan, Zaavan and Akan. **28** The descendants of Dishan were Uz and Aran.
**29** These are the Horite clans: the clans of Lotan, Shobal, Zibeon, Anah, **30** Dishon, Ezer

t Gn 48, 7; 1 Sm 10, 2; Mi 5, 2.
u Gn 49, 4; 1 Chr 5, 1.
v Gn 26, 34.
w 1 Chr 1, 35.
x 1 Chr 1, 35.
y Gn 32, 4.
z Dt 2, 4f; Jos 24, 4.
a 11f: 1 Chr 1, 36.
b 1 Chr 1, 37.
c 1 Chr 1, 35.
d 20f: 1 Chr 1, 38.
e 22-28: 1 Chr 1, 39-42.

*

35, 19: Bethlehem: the gloss comes from a later tradition that identified the site with Bethlehem, also called Ephrath or Ephratha (Jos 15, 59; Ru 4, 11; Mi 5, 1). But Rachel's grave was actually near Ramah (Jer 31, 15), a few miles north of Jerusalem, in the territory of Benjamin (1 Sm 20, 2).

35, 24ff: Benjamin is here said to have been born in Paddanaram, either because all twelve sons of Jacob are considered as a unit, or because the Priestly source, from which vv 23–29 are taken, follows a tradition different from that of the Elohistic source found in vv 16–20.

36, 2–14: The names of Esau's wives and of their fathers given here differ considerably from their names cited from other old sources in Gn 26, 34 and 28, 9. Zibeon the Hivite: In v 20 he is called a "Horite"; see note on Gn 34, 2.

36, 20: Seir the Horite: According to Dt 2, 12, the highlands of Seir were inhabited by Horites before they were occupied by the Edomites.

and Dishan; they were the clans of the Horites,
clan by clan, in the land of Seir.
**31** [f]The following are the kings who reigned
in the land of Edom before any king reigned
over the Israelites.* **32** Bela, son of Beor, became king in Edom; the name of his city was
Dinhabah. **33** When Bela died, Jobab, son of
Zerah, from Bozrah, succeeded him as king.
**34** When Jobab died, Husham, from the land of
the Temanites, succeeded him as king. He defeated the Midianites in the country of Moab;
the name of his city was Avith. **35** When Husham died, Hadad, son of Bedad, succeeded
him as king. **36** When Hadad died, Samlah,
from Masrekah, succeeded him as king.
**37** When Samlah died, Shaul, from Reho-
both-on-the-River, succeeded him as king.
**38** When Shaul died, Baal-hanan, son of Achbor, succeeded him as king. **39** When Baal-Hanan died, Hadar succeeded him as king; the
name of his city was Pau. (His wife's name was
Mehetabel; she was the daughter of Matred, son
of Mezahab.)
**40** The following are the names of the clans
of Esau individually according to their subdivisions and localities: the clans of Timna, Alvah,
Jetheth, **41** Oholibamah, Elah, Pinon, **42** Kenaz, Teman, Mibzar, **43** Magdiel and Iram.
These are the clans of the Edomites, according
to their settlements in their territorial holdings.
[Esau was the father of the Edomites.]

## *IV.: Joseph and His Brothers*

### CHAPTER 37

**Joseph Sold into Egypt.** **1** Jacob settled
in the land where his father had stayed, the land
of Canaan. **2** This is his family history. When
Joseph was seventeen years old, he was tending
the flocks with his brothers; he was an assistant
to the sons of his father's wives Bilhah and
Zilpah, and he brought his father bad reports
about them.
**3** Israel loved Joseph best of all his sons, for
he was the child of his old age; and he had made
him a long tunic. **4** When his brothers saw that
their father loved him best of all his sons, they
hated him so much that they would not even
greet him.
**5** Once Joseph had a dream, which he told to
his brothers:[g] **6** "Listen to this dream I had.
**7** There we were, binding sheaves in the field,
when suddenly my sheaf rose to an upright position, and your sheaves formed a ring around my
sheaf and bowed down to it." **8** "Are you
really going to make yourself king over us?" his
brothers asked him. "Or impose your rule on
us?" So they hated him all the more because of
his talk about his dreams.[h]
**9** Then he had another dream, and this one,
too, he told to his brothers. "I had another
dream," he said; "this time, the sun and the
moon and eleven stars were bowing down to
me." **10** When he also told it to his father, his
father reproved him. "What is the meaning of
this dream of yours?" he asked, "Can it be that
I and your mother and your brothers are to come
and bow to the ground before you?" **11** So his
brothers were wrought up against him but his
father pondered the matter.
**12** One day, when his brothers had gone to
pasture their father's flocks at Shechem, **13** Israel said to Joseph, "Your brothers, you know,
are tending our flocks at Shechem. Get ready;
I will send you to them." "I am ready," Joseph
answered. **14** "Go then," he replied; "see if all
is well with your brothers and the flocks, and
bring back word." So he sent him off from the
valley of Hebron. When Joseph reached Shechem, **15** a man met him as he was wandering
about in the fields. "What are you looking
for?" the man asked him. **16** "I am looking for
my brothers," he answered. "Could you please
tell me where they are tending the flocks?"
**17** The man told him, "They have moved on
from here; in fact, I heard them say, 'Let us go
on to Dothan.'" So Joseph went after his brothers and caught up with them in Dothan.
**18** They noticed him from a distance, and before he came up to them, they plotted to kill
him. **19** They said to one another: "Here comes
that master dreamer! **20** Come on, let us kill
him and throw him into one of the cisterns here;
we could say that a wild beast devoured him.
We shall then see what comes of his dreams."[i]
**21** *When Reuben heard this, he tried to save
him from their hands, saying, "We must not
take his life. **22** Instead of shedding blood," he
continued, "just throw him into that cistern
there in the desert; but don't kill him outright."
His purpose was to rescue him from their hands
and restore him to his father.[j] **23** So when Joseph came up to them, they stripped him of the
long tunic he had on; **24** then they took him and

f 31-43: 1 Chr 1, 45-54.
g Gn 42, 9.
h Gn 50, 17.
i Gn 44, 28.
j Gn 42, 22.

*

36, 31: Before any king reigned over the Israelites: obviously this statement was written after the time of Saul, Israel's first king.

37, 21–36: The chapter thus far is from the Yahwist source, as are also vv 25–28a. But vv 21–24 and 28b–36 are from the Elohist source. In the latter, Reuben tries to rescue Joseph, who is taken in Reuben's absence by certain Midianites; in the Yahwist source, it is Judah who saves Joseph's life by having him sold to certain Ishmaelites. Although the two variant forms in which the story was handed down in early oral tradition differ in these minor points, they agree on the essential fact that Joseph was brought as a slave into Egypt because of the jealousy of his brothers.

threw him into the cistern, which was empty and
dry.
**25** They then sat down to their meal. Looking up, they saw a caravan of Ishmaelites coming from Gilead, their camels laden with gum,
balm and resin to be taken down to Egypt.[k]
**26** Judah said to his brothers: "What is to be
gained by killing our brother and concealing his
blood?[l] **27** Rather, let us sell him to these Ishmaelites, instead of doing away with him ourselves. After all, he is our brother, our own
flesh." His brothers agreed. **28** They sold Joseph to the Ishmaelites for twenty pieces of
silver.*

Some Midianite traders passed by, and they
pulled Joseph up out of the cistern and took him
to Egypt.[m] **29** When Reuben went back to the
cistern and saw that Joseph was not in it, he tore
his clothes, **30** and returning to his brothers, he
exclaimed: "The boy is gone! And I—where
can I turn?" **31** They took Joseph's tunic, and
after slaughtering a goat, dipped the tunic in its
blood. **32** They then sent someone to bring the
long tunic to their father, with the message:
"We found this. See whether it is your son's
tunic or not." **33** He recognized it and exclaimed: "My son's tunic! A wild beast has
devoured him! Joseph has been torn to
pieces!"[n] **34** Then Jacob rent his clothes, put
sackcloth on his loins, and mourned his son
many days. **35** Though his sons and daughters
tried to console him, he refused all consolation,
saying, "No, I will go down mourning to my
son in the nether world." Thus did his father
lament him.[o]

**36** The Midianites, meanwhile, sold Joseph
in Egypt to Potiphar, a courtier of Pharaoh and
his chief steward.[p]

## CHAPTER 38*

**Judah and Tamar.** **1** About that time Judah parted from his brothers and pitched his tent
near a certain Adullamite named Hirah.
**2** There he met the daughter of a Canaanite
named Shua, married her, and had relations
with her.[q] **3** She conceived and bore a son,
whom she named Er. **4** Again she conceived
and bore a son, whom she named Onan. **5** Then
she bore still another son, whom she named
Shelah. They were in Chezib* when he was
born.[r]

**6** Judah got a wife named Tamar for his
first-born, Er. **7** But Er, Judah's first-born,
greatly offended the LORD; so the LORD took his
life.[s] **8** [t]Then Judah said to Onan, "Unite with
your brother's widow, in fulfillment of your
duty as brother-in-law, and thus preserve your
brother's line."* **9** Onan, however, knew that
the descendants would not be counted as his; so
whenever he had relations with his brother's
widow, he wasted his seed on the ground, to
avoid contributing offspring for his brother.
**10** What he did greatly offended the LORD, and
the LORD took his life too. **11** Thereupon Judah
said to his daughter-in-law Tamar, "Stay as a
widow in your father's house until my son Shelah grows up"—for he feared that Shelah also
might die like his brothers. So Tamar went to
live in her father's house.

**12** Years passed, and Judah's wife, the
daughter of Shua, died. After Judah completed
the period of mourning, he went up to Timnah
for the shearing of his sheep, in company with
his friend Hirah the Adullamite. **13** When Tamar was told that her father-in-law was on his
way up to Timnah to shear his sheep, **14** she
took off her widow's garb, veiled her face by
covering herself with a shawl, and sat down at
the entrance to Enaim, which is on the way to
Timnah; for she was aware that, although Shelah was now grown up, she had not been given
to him in marriage.[u] **15** When Judah saw her,
he mistook her for a harlot, since she had covered her face. **16** So he went over to her at the
roadside, and not realizing that she was his
daughter-in-law, he said, "Come, let me have
intercourse with you." She replied, "What will
you pay me for letting you have intercourse with
me?" **17** He answered, "I will send you a kid
from the flock." "Very well," she said, "provided you leave a pledge until you send it."
**18** Judah asked, "What pledge am I to give
you?" She answered, "Your seal and cord,*

k Gn 43, 11.
l Jb 16, 18.
m Ps 105, 17; Wis 10, 13; Acts 7, 9.
n Gn 44, 28.
o Gn 42, 38.
p Ps 105, 17.
q 1 Chr 2, 3.
r 1 Chr 4, 21.
s 1 Chr 2, 3.
t Dt 25, 5; Mt 22, 24; Mk 12, 19; Lk 20, 28.
u Prv 7, 10.

*

37, 28: They sold Joseph . . . silver: in the Hebrew text, these words occur between out of the cistern and (they) took him to Egypt at the end of the verse.

38, 1–30: This chapter, from the Yahwist source, has nothing to do with the Joseph story in which Judah is still living with his father and brothers. The sacred author inserted this independent account from the life of Judah at this place to mark the long lapse of time during which Joseph's family knew nothing of his life in Egypt. This is apparently a personalized history of the early days of the tribe of Judah, which interbred with several Canaanite clans, though some of these soon became extinct.

38, 5: Chezib: a variant form of Achzib (Jos 15, 44; Mi 1, 14), a town in the Judean Shephelah.

38, 8: Preserve your brother's line: literally, "raise up seed for your brother." The ancient Israelites regarded as very important their law of levirate, or "brother-in-law" marriage; see notes on Dt 25, 5; Ru 2, 20. In the present story, it is primarily Onan's violation of this law, rather than the means he used to circumvent it, that brought on him God's displeasure (vv 9f).

38, 18: Seal and cord: the cylinder seal, through which a hole was bored lengthwise so that it could be worn from the neck by a cord, was a distinctive means of identification. Apparently a man's staff was also marked with his name (Nm 17, 16f) or other sign of identification.

and the staff you carry." So he gave them to her
and had intercourse with her, and she conceived
by him. **19** When she went away, she took off
her shawl and put on her widow's garb again.
**20** Judah sent the kid by his friend the Adullamite to recover the pledge from the woman;
but he could not find her. **21** So he asked the
men of the place, "Where is the temple prostitute,* the one by the roadside in Enaim?" But
they answered, "There has never been a temple
prostitute here." **22** He went back to Judah and
told him, "I could not find her; and besides, the
men of the place said there was no temple prostitute there." **23** "Let her keep the things," Judah replied; "otherwise we shall become a
laughingstock. After all, I did send her the kid,
even though you were unable to find her."
**24** About three months later, Judah was told
that his daughter-in-law Tamar had played the
harlot and was then with child from her harlotry.
"Bring her out," cried Judah; "she shall be
burned." **25** But as they were bringing her out,
she sent word to her father-in-law, "It is by the
man to whom these things belong that I am with
child. Please verify," she added, "whose seal
and cord and whose staff these are." **26** Judah
recognized them and said, "She is more in the
right than I am, since I did not give her to my
son Shelah." But he had no further relations
with her.
**27** When the time of her delivery came, she
was found to have twins in her womb.[v]
**28** While she was giving birth, one infant put
out his hand; and the midwife, taking a crimson
thread, tied it on his hand, to note that this one
came out first. **29** [w]But as he withdrew his
hand, his brother came out; and she said, "What
a breach you have made for yourself!" So he
was called Perez.* **30** Afterward his brother
came out; he was called Zerah.[x] *

## CHAPTER 39

**Joseph's Temptation.** **1** When Joseph
was taken down to Egypt, a certain Egyptian
(Potiphar, a courtier of Pharoah and his chief
steward*) bought him from the Ishmaelites who
had brought him there. **2** [y]But since the LORD
was with him, Joseph got on very well and was
assigned to the household of his Egyptian master. **3** When his master saw that the LORD was
with him and brought him success in whatever
he did, **4** he took a liking to Joseph and made
him his personal attendant; he put him in charge
of his household and entrusted to him all his
possessions.[z] **5** From the moment that he put
him in charge of his household and all his possessions, the LORD blessed the Egyptian's house
for Joseph's sake; in fact, the LORD's blessing
was on everything he owned, both inside the
house and out. **6** Having left everything he
owned in Joseph's charge, he gave no thought,
with Joseph there, to anything but the food he
ate.
Now Joseph was strikingly handsome in
countenance and body. **7** After a time, his master's wife began to look fondly at him and said,
"Lie with me." **8** But he refused. "As long as
I am here," he told her, "my master does not
concern himself with anything in the house, but
has entrusted to me all he owns. **9** He wields no
more authority in this house than I do, and he
has withheld from me nothing but yourself,
since you are his wife. How, then, could I commit so great a wrong and thus stand condemned
before God?" **10** Although she tried to entice
him day after day, he would not agree to lie
beside her, or even stay near her.[a]
**11** One such day, when Joseph came into the
house to do his work, and none of the household
servants were then in the house, **12** she laid
hold of him by his cloak, saying, "Lie with
me!" But leaving the cloak in her hand, he got
away from her and ran outside. **13** When she
saw that he had left his cloak in her hand as he
fled outside, **14** she screamed for her household
servants and told them, "Look! my husband has
brought in a Hebrew slave to make sport of us!
He came in here to lie with me, but I cried out
as loud as I could. **15** When he heard me
scream for help, he left his cloak beside me and
ran away outside."
**16** She kept the cloak with her until his master came home. **17** Then she told him the same
story: "The Hebrew slave whom you brought
here broke in on me, to make sport of me.
**18** But when I screamed for help, he left his
cloak beside me and fled outside." **19** As soon
as the master heard his wife's story about how
his slave had treated her, he became enraged.

v 1 Chr 2, 4.
w Rv 4, 12; Mt 1, 3; Lk 3, 33.
x Nm 26, 20; 1 Chr 2, 4; Mt 1, 3.
y 1 Sm 3, 19; 10, 7; 18, 14; 2 Sm 5, 10; 2 Kgs 18, 7; Acts 7, 9.
z Dn 1, 9.
a 1 Mc 2, 53.

*

38, 21: Temple prostitute: the Hebrew term qedesha, literally "consecrated woman," designates a woman who had ritual intercourse with men in pagan fertility rites; cf Dt 23, 18; Hos 4, 14, where the same Hebrew word is used. Hirah the Adullamite uses a word that refers to a higher social class than that designated by the term zona, common "harlot," used in vv 15. 24.

38, 29: He was called Perez: the Hebrew word means "breach."

38, 30: He was called Zerah: a name connected here by popular etymology with a Hebrew verb for the red light of dawn, alluding apparently to the crimson thread.

39, 1: (Potiphar . . . chief steward): These words in the text serve to harmonize ch 39 from the Yahwist source, with Gn 37, 36, and 40, 1–23, from the Elohist. In the former, the Ishmaelites who bought Joseph from his brothers (Gn 37, 28) sold him to the unnamed "Egyptian master" of ch 39. In the latter, the Midianites who kidnaped Joseph (Gn 37, 28; 40, 15) sold him to Potiphar, Paraoh's chief steward (Gn 37, 36), whose house was used as a royal prison (Gn 40, 2f).

**20** He seized Joseph and threw him into the jail where the royal prisoners were confined.[b]

But even while he was in prison, **21** the LORD remained with Joseph; he showed him kindness by making the chief jailer well-disposed toward him.[c] **22** The chief jailer put Joseph in charge of all the prisoners in the jail, and everything that had to be done there was done under his management. **23** The chief jailer did not concern himself with anything at all that was in Joseph's charge, since the LORD was with him and brought success to all he did.

## CHAPTER 40

**The Dreams Interpreted.** **1** Some time afterward, the royal cupbearer and baker gave offense to their lord, the king of Egypt. **2** Pharaoh was angry with his two courtiers, the chief cupbearer and the chief baker, **3** and he put them in custody in the house of the chief steward (the same jail where Joseph was confined). **4** The chief steward assigned Joseph to them, and he became their attendant.

After they had been in custody for some time, **5** the cupbearer and the baker of the king of Egypt who were confined in the jail both had dreams on the same night, each dream with its own meaning. **6** When Joseph came to them in the morning, he noticed that they looked disturbed. **7** So he asked Pharaoh's courtiers who were with him in custody in his master's house, "Why do you look so sad today?" **8** They answered him, "We have had dreams, but there is no one to interpret them for us." Joseph said to them, "Surely, interpretations come from God. Please tell the dreams to me."[d]

**9** Then the chief cupbearer told Joseph his dream. "In my dream," he said, "I saw a vine in front of me, **10** and on the vine were three branches. It had barely budded when its blossoms came out, and its clusters ripened into grapes. **11** Pharaoh's cup was in my hand; so I took the grapes, pressed them out into his cup, and put it in Pharaoh's hand." **12** Joseph said to him: "This is what it means. The three branches are three days; **13** within three days Pharaoh will lift up your head* and restore you to your post. You will be handing Pharaoh his cup as you formerly used to do when you were his cupbearer. **14** So if you will still remember, when all is well with you, that I was here with you, please do me the favor of mentioning me to Pharaoh, to get me out of this place. **15** The truth is that I was kidnaped from the land of the Hebrews, and here I have not done anything for which I should have been put into a dungeon."

**16** When the chief baker saw that Joseph had given this favorable interpretation, he said to him: "I too had a dream. In it I had three wicker baskets on my head; **17** in the top one were all kinds of bakery products for Pharaoh, but the birds were pecking at them out of the basket on my head." **18** Joseph said to him in reply: "This is what it means. The three baskets are three days; **19** within three days Pharaoh will lift up your head and have you impaled on a stake, and the birds will be pecking the flesh from your body."

**20** And in fact, on the third day, which was Pharaoh's birthday, when he gave a banquet to all his staff, with his courtiers around him, he lifted up the heads of the chief cupbearer and chief baker. **21** He restored the chief cupbearer to his office, so that he again handed the cup to Pharaoh; **22** but the chief baker he impaled—just as Joseph had told them in his interpretation. **23** Yet the chief cupbearer gave no thought to Joseph; he had forgotten him.

## CHAPTER 41

**Pharaoh's Dream.** **1** After a lapse of two years, Pharaoh had a dream. He saw himself standing by the Nile, **2** when up out of the Nile came seven cows, handsome and fat; they grazed in the reed grass. **3** Behind them seven other cows, ugly and gaunt, came up out of the Nile; and standing on the bank of the Nile beside the others, **4** the ugly, gaunt cows ate up the seven handsome, fat cows. Then Pharaoh woke up.

**5** He fell asleep again and had another dream. He saw seven ears of grain, fat and healthy, growing on a single stalk. **6** Behind them sprouted seven ears of grain, thin and blasted by the east wind; **7** and the seven thin ears swallowed up the seven fat, healthy ears. Then Pharaoh woke up, to find it was only a dream.

**8** Next morning his spirit was agitated. So he summoned all the magicians and sages of Egypt and recounted his dreams to them; but no one could interpret his dreams for him. **9** Then the chief cupbearer spoke up and said to Pharaoh: "On this occasion I am reminded of my negligence. **10** Once, when Pharaoh was angry, he put me and the chief baker in custody in the house of the chief steward. **11** Later, we both had dreams on the same night, and each of our dreams had its own meaning. **12** There with us was a Hebrew youth, a slave of the chief steward; and when we told him our dreams, he interpreted them for us and explained for each of us

b Ps 105, 18.
c Acts 7, 9f.
d Gn 41, 16.
e Dn 1, 17.

* 40, 13: Lift up your head: signifying "pardon you." In v 19 "to lift up the head" means "to behead"; and finally, in v 20, the same expression means "to review the case (of someone)." Joseph couches his interpretation of the dreams in equivocal terms.

the meaning of his dream.[e] **13** And it turned out just as he had told us: I was restored to my post, but the other man was impaled."

**14** Pharaoh therefore had Joseph summoned, and they hurriedly brought him from the dungeon. After he shaved and changed his clothes, he came into Pharaoh's presence.[f] **15** Pharaoh then said to him: "I had certain dreams that no one can interpret. But I hear it said of you that the moment you are told a dream you can interpret it." **16** "It is not I," Joseph replied to Pharaoh, "but God who will give Pharaoh the right answer."[g]

**17** Then Pharaoh said to Joseph: "In my dream, I was standing on the bank of the Nile, **18** when up from the Nile came seven cows, fat and well-formed; they grazed in the reed grass. **19** Behind them came seven other cows, scrawny, most ill-formed and gaunt. Never have I seen such ugly specimens as these in all the land of Egypt! **20** The gaunt, ugly cows ate up the first seven fat cows. **21** But when they had consumed them, no one could tell that they had done so, because they looked as ugly as before. Then I woke up. **22** In another dream, I saw seven ears of grain, fat and healthy, growing on a single stalk. **23** Behind them sprouted seven ears of grain, shriveled and thin and blasted by the east wind; **24** and the seven thin ears swallowed up the seven healthy ears. I have spoken to the magicians, but none of them can give me an explanation."

**25** Joseph said to Pharaoh: "Both of Pharaoh's dreams have the same meaning. God has thus foretold to Pharaoh what he is about to do. **26** The seven healthy cows are seven years, and the seven healthy ears are seven years—the same in each dream. **27** So also, the seven thin, ugly cows that came up after them are seven years, as are the seven thin, wind-blasted ears; they are seven years of famine. **28** It is just as I told Pharaoh: God has revealed to Pharaoh what he is about to do. **29** Seven years of great abundance are now coming throughout the land of Egypt; **30** but these will be followed by seven years of famine, when all the abundance in the land of Egypt will be forgotten. When the famine has ravaged the land, **31** no trace of the abundance will be found in the land because of the famine that follows it—so utterly severe will that famine be. **32** That Pharaoh had the same dream twice means that the matter has been reaffirmed by God and that God will soon bring it about.

**33** "Therefore, let Pharaoh seek out a wise and discerning man and put him in charge of the land of Egypt. **34** Pharaoh should also take action to appoint overseers, so as to regiment the land during the seven years of abundance. **35** They should husband all the food of the coming good years, collecting the grain under Pharaoh's authority, to be stored in the towns for food. **36** This food will serve as a reserve for the country against the seven years of famine that are to follow in the land of Egypt, so that the land may not perish in the famine."

**37** This advice pleased Pharaoh and all his officials.[h] **38** "Could we find another like him," Pharaoh asked his officials, "a man so endowed with the spirit of God?" **39** So Pharaoh said to Joseph: "Since God has made all this known to you, no one can be as wise and discerning as you are. **40** You shall be in charge of my palace, and all my people shall dart at your command. Only in respect to the throne shall I outrank you.[i] **41** Herewith," Pharaoh told Joseph, "I place you in charge of the whole land of Egypt." **42** With that, Pharaoh took off his signet ring* and put it on Joseph's finger. He had him dressed in robes of fine linen and put a gold chain about his neck. **43** He then had him ride in the chariot of his vizier, and they shouted "Abrek!"* before him.

Thus was Joseph installed over the whole land of Egypt. **44** "I, Pharaoh, proclaim," he told Joseph, "that without your approval no one shall move hand or foot in all the land of Egypt." **45** Pharaoh also bestowed the name of Zaphnath-paneah* on Joseph, and he gave him in marriage Asenath, the daughter of Potiphera, priest of Heliopolis. **46** Joseph was thirty years old when he entered the service of Pharaoh, king of Egypt.

After Joseph left Pharaoh's presence, he traveled throughout the land of Egypt. **47** During the seven years of plenty, when the land produced abundant crops, **48** he husbanded all the food of these years of plenty that the land of Egypt was enjoying and stored it in the towns, placing in each town the crops of the fields around it. **49** Joseph garnered grain in quantities like the sands of the sea, so vast that at last

f Ps 105, 20.
g Gn 40, 8.
h Acts 7, 10.
i Ps 105, 21; Wis 10, 14; 1 Mc 2, 53; Acts 7, 10.

*

41, 42: Signet ring: a finger ring in which was set a stamp seal, different from the cylinder seal such as Judah wore; see note on Gn 38, 18. This is an authentic detail. By receiving Pharaoh's signet ring, Joseph was made vizier of Egypt (v 43); the vizier was known as "seal-bearer of the king of Lower Egypt." Another authentic detail is the gold chain, a symbol of high office in ancient Egypt.

41, 43: Abrek: apparently a cry of homage, though the word's derivation and actual meaning are uncertain.

41, 45: Zaphenath-paneah: a Hebrew transcription of an Egyptian name meaning "the god speaks and he (the newborn child) lives." Asenath: means "belonging to (the Egyptian goddess) Neith." Potiphera: means "he whom Ra (the Egyptian god) gave"; a shorter form of the same name was borne by Joseph's master (Gn 37, 36). Heliopolis: in Hebrew, On, a city seven miles northeast of modern Cairo, site of the chief temple of the sun god; it is mentioned also in v 50; Gn 46, 20; Ez 30, 17.

he stopped measuring it, for it was beyond measure.
**50** Before the famine years set in, Joseph
became the father of two sons, born to him by
Asenath, daughter of Potiphera, priest of Heliopolis.[j] **51** He named his first-born Manasseh,* meaning, "God has made me forget entirely the sufferings I endured at the hands of my
family"; **52** and the second he named Ephraim,* meaning, "God has made me fruitful in
the land of my affliction."
**53** When the seven years of abundance enjoyed by the land of Egypt came to an end,
**54** the seven years of famine set in, just as
Joseph had predicted. Although there was famine in all the other countries, food was available
throughout the land of Egypt.[k] **55** When hunger came to be felt throughout the land of Egypt
and the people cried to Pharaoh for bread, Pharaoh directed all the Egyptians to go to Joseph
and do whatever he told them. **56** When the
famine had spread throughout the land, Joseph
opened all the cities that had grain and rationed
it to the Egyptians, since the famine had gripped
the land of Egypt. **57** In fact, all the world came
to Joseph to obtain rations of grain, for famine
had gripped the whole world.

## CHAPTER 42

### The Brothers' First Journey to Egypt.

**1** When Jacob learned that grain rations were
available in Egypt, he said to his sons: "Why
do you keep gaping at one another? **2** I hear,"
he went on, "that rations of grain are available
in Egypt. Go down there and buy some for us,
that we may stay alive rather than die of hunger."[l] **3** So ten of Joseph's brothers went down
to buy an emergency supply of grain from
Egypt. **4** It was only Joseph's full brother Benjamin that Jacob did not send with the rest, for
he thought some disaster might befall him.
**5** Thus, since there was famine in the land of
Canaan also, the sons of Israel were among
those who came to procure rations.[m]
**6** It was Joseph, as governor of the country,
who dispensed the rations to all the people.
When Joseph's brothers came and knelt down
before him with their faces to the ground,[n] **7** he
recognized them as soon as he saw them. But he
concealed his own identity from them and spoke
sternly to them. "Where do you come from?"
he asked them. They answered, "From the land
of Canaan, to procure food."
**8** When Joseph recognized his brothers, although they did not recognize him, **9** he was
reminded of the dreams he had about them. He
said to them: "You are spies.[o] You have come
to see the nakedness of the land."* **10** "No,
my lord," they replied. "On the contrary, your
servants have come to procure food. **11** All of
us are sons of the same man. We are honest
men; your servants have never been spies."
**12** But he answered them: "Not so! You have
come to see the nakedness of the land."
**13** "We your servants," they said, "were
twelve brothers, sons of a certain man in Canaan; but the youngest one is at present with our
father, and the other one is gone."[p] **14** "It is
just as I said," Joseph persisted; "you are spies.
**15** This is how you shall be tested: unless your
youngest brother comes here, I swear by the life
of Pharaoh that you shall not leave here. **16** So
send one of your number to get your brother,
while the rest of you stay here under arrest. Thus
shall your words be tested for their truth; if they
are untrue, as Pharaoh lives, you are spies!"
**17** With that, he locked them up in the guard-
house for three days.
**18** On the third day Joseph said to them: "Do
this, and you shall live; for I am a God-fearing
man. **19** If you have been honest, only one of
your brothers need be confined in this prison,
while the rest of you may go and take home
provisions for your starving families. **20** But
you must come back to me with your youngest
brother. Your words will thus be verified, and
you will not die." To this they agreed.[q] **21** To
one another, however, they said: "Alas, we are
being punished because of our brother. We saw
the anguish of his heart when he pleaded with
us, yet we paid no heed; that is why this anguish
has now come upon us."[r] **22** "Didn't I tell
you," broke in Reuben, "not to do wrong to the
boy? But you wouldn't listen! Now comes the
reckoning for his blood."[s] **23** They did not
know, of course, that Joseph understood what
they said, since he spoke with them through an
interpreter. **24** But turning away from them, he
wept. When he was able to speak to them again,
he had Simeon taken from them and bound before their eyes. **25** Then Joseph gave orders to
have their containers filled with grain, their
money replaced in each one's sack, and provisions given them for their journey. After this
had been done for them, **26** they loaded their
donkeys with the rations and departed.
**27** *At the night encampment, when one of

j Gn 46, 20; 48, 5.
k Ps 105, 16; Acts 7, 11.
l Acts 7, 12.
m Jdt 5, 10; Acts 7, 11.
n Ps 105, 21.
o Gn 37, 5.
p Gn 44, 20.
q Gn 43, 5.
r Gn 37, 18-27.
s Gn 37, 22.

*

41, 51: Manasseh: allusion to this name is in the Hebrew expression, nishshani, "he made me forget."

41, 52: Ephraim: related to the Hebrew expression hiphrani, "(God) has made me fruitful."

42, 9. 12: The nakedness of the land: the military weakness of the land, like human nakedness, should not be seen by strangers.

42, 27-28: These two verses are from the Yahwist source, whereas the rest of the chapter is from the Elohist source, in which the men find the money in their sacks (not "bags"—a

them opened his bag to give his donkey some fodder, he was surprised to see his money in the mouth of his bag. **28** "My money has been returned!" he cried out to his brothers. "Here it is in my bag!" At that their hearts sank. Trembling, they asked one another, "What is this that God has done to us?"

**29** When they got back to their father Jacob in the land of Canaan, they told him all that had happened to them. **30** "The man who is lord of the country," they said, "spoke to us sternly and put us in custody as if we were spying on the land. **31** But we said to him: 'We are honest men; we have never been spies. **32** There were twelve of us brothers, sons of the same father; but one is gone, and the youngest one is at present with our father in the land of Canaan.' **33** Then the man who is lord of the country said to us: 'This is how I shall know if you are honest men: leave one of your brothers with me, while the rest of you go home with rations for your starving families. **34** When you come back to me with your youngest brother, and I know that you are honest men and not spies, I will restore your brother to you, and you may move about freely in the land.' "

**35** When they were emptying their sacks, there in each one's sack was his moneybag! At the sight of their moneybags, they and their father were dismayed. **36** Their father Jacob said to them: "Must you make me childless? Joseph is gone, and Simeon is gone, and now you would take away Benjamin! Why must such things always happen to me!" **37** Then Reuben told his father: "Put him in my care, and I will bring him back to you. You may kill my own two sons if I do not return him to you." **38** But Jacob replied: "My son shall not go down with you. Now that his full brother is dead, he is the only one left. If some disaster should befall him on the journey you must make, you would send my white head down to the nether world in grief."[t]

## CHAPTER 43*

**The Second Journey to Egypt.** **1** Now the famine in the land grew more severe. **2** So when they had used up all the rations they had brought from Egypt, their father said to them, "Go back and procure us a little more food." **3** But Judah replied: "The man strictly warned us, 'You shall not appear in my presence unless your brother is with you.'[u] **4** If you are willing to let our brother go with us, we will go down to procure food for you. **5** But if you are not willing, we will not go down, because the man told us, 'You shall not appear in my presence unless your brother is with you.' "[v] **6** Israel demanded, "Why did you bring this trouble on me by telling the man that you had another brother?" **7** They answered: "The man kept asking about ourselves and our family: 'Is your father still living? Do you have another brother?' We had to answer his questions. How could we know that he would say, 'Bring your brother down here'?"

**8** Then Judah urged his father Israel: "Let the boy go with me, that we may be off and on our way if you and we and our children are to keep from starving to death.[w] **9** I myself will stand surety for him. You can hold me responsible for him. If I fail to bring him back, to set him in your presence, you can hold it against me forever.[x] **10** Had we not dilly-dallied, we could have been there and back twice by now!"

**11** Their father Israel then told them: "If it must be so, then do this: Put some of the land's best products in your baggage and take them down to the man as gifts: some balm and honey, gum and resin, and pistachios and almonds.[y] **12** Also take extra money along, for you must return the amount that was put back in the mouths of your bags; it may have been a mistake. **13** Take your brother, too, and be off on your way back to the man. **14** May God Almighty dispose the man to be merciful toward you, so that he may let your other brother go, as well as Benjamin. As for me, if I am to suffer bereavement, I shall suffer it."

**15** So the men got the gifts, took double the amount of money with them, and, accompanied by Benjamin, were off on their way down to Egypt to present themselves to Joseph. **16** When Joseph saw Benjamin with them, he told his head steward, "Take these men into the house, and have an animal slaughtered and prepared, for they are to dine with me at noon." **17** Doing as Joseph had ordered, the steward conducted the men to Joseph's house. **18** But on being led to his house, they became apprehensive. "It must be," they thought, "on account of the money put back in our bags the first time, that we are taken inside; they want to use it as a pretext to attack us and take our donkeys and seize us as slaves." **19** So they went up to Joseph's head steward and talked to him at the entrance of the house. **20** "If you please, sir," they said, "we came down here once before to procure food.[z] **21** But when we arrived at a night's encampment and opened our bags, there was each man's money in the mouth of his bag—our money in the full amount! We have

t Gn 37, 35.
u Gn 44, 23.
v Gn 42, 20.
w Gn 42, 37.
x Gn 44, 32.
y Gn 45, 23.
z Gn 42, 3.
a Gn 42, 27f.

* different Hebrew word) only when they arrive home (v 35); cf Gn 43, 21.

43, 1–34: This chapter and the following one are from the Yahwist source, in which Judah, not Reuben as in the Elohist source, volunteers to go surety for Benjamin.

now brought it back.[a] 22 We have brought other money to procure food with. We do not know
who put the first money in our bags." 23 "Be
at ease," he replied; "you have no need to fear.
Your God and the God of your father must have
put treasures in your bags for you. As for your
money, I received it." With that, he led Simeon
out to them.

24 The steward then brought the men inside
Joseph's house. He gave them water to bathe
their feet, and got fodder for their donkeys.
25 Then they set out their gifts to await Joseph's arrival at noon, for they had heard that
they were to dine there. 26 When Joseph came
home, they presented him with the gifts they
had brought inside, while they bowed down
before him to the ground. 27 After inquiring
how they were, he asked them, "And how is
your aged father, of whom you spoke? Is he still
in good health?"[b] 28 "Your servant our father
is thriving and still in good health," they said,
as they bowed respectfully. 29 When Joseph's
eye fell on his full brother Benjamin, he asked,
"Is this your youngest brother, of whom you
told me?" Then he said to him, "May God be
gracious to you, my boy!"[c] 30 With that, Joseph had to hurry out, for he was so overcome
with affection for his brother that he was on the
verge of tears. He went into a private room and
wept there.

31 After washing his face, he reappeared
and, now in control of himself, gave the order,
"Serve the meal." 32 It was served separately
to him,* to the brothers, and to the Egyptians
who partook of his board. (Egyptians may not
eat with Hebrews; that is abhorrent to them.)
33 When they were seated by his directions
according to their age, from the oldest to the
youngest, they looked at one another in amazement; 34 and as portions were brought to them
from Joseph's table, Benjamin's portion was
five times as large as* anyone else's. So they
drank freely and made merry with him.

## CHAPTER 44

**Final Test.** 1 *Then Joseph gave his head
steward these instructions: "Fill the men's bags
with as much food as they can carry, and put
each man's money in the mouth of his bag. 2 In
the mouth of the youngest one's bag put also my
silver goblet, together with the money for his
rations." The steward carried out Joseph's instructions. 3 At daybreak the men and their
donkeys were sent off. 4 They had not gone far
out of the city when Joseph said to his head
steward: "Go at once after the men! When you
overtake them, say to them, 'Why did you repay
good with evil? Why did you steal the silver
goblet from me? 5 It is the very one from which
my master drinks and which he uses for divination.* What you have done is wrong.' "

6 When the steward overtook them and repeated these words to them, 7 they remonstrated with him: "How can my lord say such
things? Far be it from your servants to do such
a thing! 8 We even brought back to you from
the land of Canaan the money that we found in
the mouths of our bags. Why, then, would we
steal silver or gold from your master's house?
9 If any of your servants is found to have the
goblet, he shall die, and as for the rest of us, we
shall become my lord's slaves." 10 But he replied, "Even though it ought to be as you propose, only the one who is found to have it shall
become my slave, and the rest of you shall be
exonerated." 11 Then each of them eagerly
lowered his bag to the ground and opened it;
12 and when a search was made, starting with
the oldest and ending with the youngest, the
goblet turned up in Benjamin's bag. 13 At this,
they tore their clothes. Then, when each man
had reloaded his donkey, they returned to the
city.

14 As Judah and his brothers reentered Joseph's house, he was still there; so they flung
themselves on the ground before him.
15 "How could you do such a thing?" Joseph
asked them. "You should have known that such
a man as I could discover by divination what
happened." 16 Judah replied: "What can we
say to my lord? How can we plead or how try
to prove our innocence? God has uncovered
your servant's guilt.* Here we are, then, the
slaves of my lord—the rest of us no less than the
one in whose possession the goblet was found."
17 "Far be it from me to act thus!" said Joseph. "Only the one in whose possession the
goblet was found shall become my slave; the
rest of you may go back safe and sound to your
father."

18 Judah then stepped up to him and said: "I
beg you, my lord, let your servant speak earnestly to my lord, and do not become angry with

b Tb 7, 4. c Gn 42, 13.

43, 32: Separately to him: that Joseph did not eat with the other Egyptians was apparently a matter of rank.

43, 34: Five times as large as: probably an idiomatic expression for "much larger than."

44, 1f: Replacement of the money in the men's bags is probably a redactional addition here, taken from the Yahwist account of the first visit. It is only the goblet in Benjamin's bag, not any replaced money, that plays a part in the rest of the chapter.

44, 5: Divination: seeking omens through liquids poured into a cup or bowl was a common practice in the ancient Near East; cf v 15. Even though divination was frowned on in later Israel (Lv 19, 31), it is in this place an authentic touch which the sacred author does not hesitate to ascribe to Joseph, the wisest man in Egypt.

44, 16: Guilt: in trying to do away with Joseph when he was young.

your servant, for you are the equal of Pharaoh.
**19** *My lord asked your servants, 'Have you a
father, or another brother?' **20** So we said to my
lord, 'We have an aged father, and a young
brother, the child of his old age. This one's full
brother is dead, and since he is the only one by
that mother who is left, his father dotes on
him.'[d] **21** Then you told your servants, 'Bring
him down to me that my eyes may look on him.'
**22** We replied to my lord, 'The boy cannot
leave his father; his father would die if he were
to leave him.' **23** But you told your servants,
'Unless your youngest brother comes back with
you, you shall not come into my presence
again.'[e] **24** When we returned to your servant
our father, we reported to him the words of my
lord.

**25** "Later, our father told us to come back
and buy some food for the family. **26** So we
reminded him, 'We cannot go down there; only
if our youngest brother is with us can we go, for
we may not see the man if our youngest brother
is not with us.' **27** Then your servant our father
said to us, 'As you know, my wife bore me two
sons. **28** One of them, however, disappeared,
and I had to conclude that he must have been
torn to pieces by wild beasts; I have not seen
him since.[f] **29** If you now take this one away
from me, too, and some disaster befalls him,
you will send my white head down to the nether
world in grief.'

**30** "If then the boy is not with us when I go
back to your servant my father, whose very life
is bound up with his, he will die as soon as he
sees that the boy is missing; **31** and your servants will thus send the white head of our father
down to the nether world in grief. **32** Besides,
I, your servant, got the boy from his father by
going surety for him, saying, 'If I fail to bring
him back to you, father, you can hold it against
me forever.'[g] **33** Let me, your servant, therefore, remain in place of the boy as the slave of
my lord, and let the boy go back with his brothers. **34** How could I go back to my father if the
boy were not with me? I could not bear to see
the anguish that would overcome my father."

## CHAPTER 45

**The Truth Revealed.** **1** Joseph could no
longer control himself in the presence of all his
attendants, so he cried out, "Have everyone
withdraw from me!" Thus no one else was
about when he made himself known to his
brothers. **2** But his sobs were so loud that the
Egyptians heard him, and so the news reached
Pharaoh's palace. **3** [h]"I am Joseph," he said to
his brothers. "Is my father still in good
health?" But his brothers could give him no
answer, so dumbfounded were they at him.

**4** "Come closer to me," he told his brothers.
When they had done so, he said: "I am your
brother Joseph, whom you once sold into
Egypt. **5** But now do not be distressed, and do
not reproach yourselves for having sold me
here. It was really for the sake of saving lives
that God sent me here ahead of you.[i] **6** For two
years now the famine has been in the land, and
for five more years tillage will yield no harvest.
**7** God, therefore, sent me on ahead of you to
ensure for you a remnant on earth and to save
your lives in an extraordinary deliverance. **8** So
it was not really you but God who had me come
here; and he has made of me a father to Pharaoh,* lord of all his household, and ruler over
the whole land of Egypt.

**9** *"Hurry back, then, to my father and tell
him: 'Thus says your son Joseph: God has made
me lord of all Egypt; come to me without delay.[j] **10** You will settle in the region of Goshen,* where you will be near me—you and
your children and grandchildren, your flocks
and herds, and everything that you own.
**11** Since five years of famine still lie ahead, I
will provide for you there, so that you and your
family and all that are yours may not suffer
want.' **12** Surely, you can see for yourselves,
and Benjamin can see for himself, that it is I,
Joseph, who am speaking to you. **13** Tell my
father all about my high position in Egypt and
what you have seen. But hurry and bring my
father down here." **14** Thereupon he flung
himself on the neck of his brother Benjamin and
wept, and Benjamin wept in his arms. **15** Joseph then kissed all his brothers, crying over
each of them; and only then were his brothers
able to talk with him.

**16** When the news reached Pharaoh's palace
that Joseph's brothers had come, Pharaoh and
his courtiers were pleased. **17** So Pharaoh told
Joseph: "Say to your brothers: 'This is what you
shall do: Load up your animals and go without
delay to the land of Canaan. **18** There get your
father and your families, and then come back
here to me; I will assign you the best land in
Egypt, where you will live off the fat of the

d Gn 42, 13.
e Gn 43, 3.
f Gn 37, 20. 33.
g Gn 43, 9.
h 3f: Acts 7, 13.
i Gn 50, 20; Sir 49, 15.
j Acts 7, 14.
k Acts 7, 14.

*

44, 19: My lord . . . your servants: such frequently repeated expressions in Judah's speech show the formal court style used by a subject in speaking to a high official.

45, 8: Father to Pharaoh: a term applied to a vizier in ancient Egypt.

45, 9–15: In these verses, as in Gn 46, 31–47, 5a, all from the Yahwist source, Joseph in his own name invites his father and brothers to come to Egypt. Only after their arrival is Pharaoh informed of the fact. On the other hand, in 45, 16–20 from the Elohist source, it is Pharaoh himself who invites Joseph's kinsmen to migrate to his domain.

45, 10: The region of Goshen: modern Wadi Tumilat in the eastern part of the Nile Delta.

land.'[k] **19** Instruct them further: 'Do this. Take wagons from the land of Egypt for your children and your wives and to transport your father on your way back here. **20** Do not be concerned about your belongings, for the best in the whole land of Egypt shall be yours.' "

**21** The sons of Israel acted accordingly. Joseph gave them the wagons, as Pharaoh had ordered, and he supplied them with provisions for the journey. **22** He also gave to each of them fresh clothing, but to Benjamin he gave three hundred shekels of silver and five sets of garments. **23** Moreover, what he sent to his father was ten jackasses loaded with the finest products of Egypt and ten jennies loaded with grain and bread and other provisions for his journey. **24** As he sent his brothers on their way, he told them, "Let there be no recriminations on the way."

**25** So they left Egypt and made their way to their father Jacob in the land of Canaan. **26** When they told him, "Joseph is still alive —in fact, it is he who is ruler of all the land of Egypt," he was dumbfounded; he could not believe them. **27** But when they recounted to him all that Joseph had told them, and when he saw the wagons that Joseph had sent for his transport, the spirit of their father Jacob revived. **28** "It is enough," said Israel. "My son Joseph is still alive! I must go and see him before I die."

## CHAPTER 46

**Migration to Egypt.** **1** Israel set out with all that was his. When he arrived at Beer-sheba, he offered sacrifices to the God of his father Isaac. **2** There God, speaking to Israel in a vision by night, called, "Jacob! Jacob!" "Here I am," he answered. **3** Then he said: "I am God,* the God of your father. Do not be afraid to go down to Egypt, for there I will make you a great nation. **4** Not only will I go down to Egypt with you; I will also bring you back here, after Joseph has closed your eyes."

**5** So Jacob departed from Beer-sheba, and the sons of Israel put their father and their wives and children on the wagons that Pharaoh had sent for his transport. **6** They took with them their livestock and the possessions they had acquired in the land of Canaan. Thus Jacob and all his descendants migrated to Egypt.[l] **7** His sons and his grandsons, his daughters and his granddaughters—all his descendants—he took with him to Egypt.

**8** These are the names of the Israelites, Jacob and his descendants, who migrated to Egypt. Reuben, Jacob's first-born,[m] **9** *and the sons of Reuben: Hanoch, Pallu, Hezron and Carmi.[n] **10** The sons of Simeon: Nemuel, Jamin, Ohad, Jachin, Zohar, and Shaul, son of a Canaanite woman.[o] **11** The sons of Levi: Gershon, Kohath and Merari.[p] **12** The sons of Judah: Er, Onan, Shelah, Perez and Zerah—but Er and Onan had died in the land of Canaan; and the sons of Perez were Hezron and Hamul.[q] **13** The sons of Issachar: Tola Puah, Jashub and Shimron.[r] **14** The sons of Zebulun: Sered, Elon and Jahleel.[s] **15** These were the sons whom Leah bore to Jacob in Paddan-aram, along with his daughter Dinah—thirty-three persons in all, male and female.

**16** The sons of Gad: Zephon, Haggi, Shuni, Ezbon, Eri, Arod and Areli.[t] **17** The sons of Asher: Imnah, Ishvah, Ishvi and Beriah, with their sister Serah; and the sons of Beriah: Heber and Malchiel.[u] **18** These were the descendants of Zilpah, whom Laban had given to his daughter Leah; these she bore to Jacob—sixteen persons in all.

**19** The sons of Jacob's wife Rachel: Joseph and Benjamin. **20** In the land of Egypt Joseph became the father of Manasseh and Ephraim, whom Asenath, daughter of Potiphera, priest of Heliopolis, bore to him.[v] **21** The sons of Benjamin: Bela, Becher, Ashbel, Gera, Naaman, Ahiram, Shupham, Hupham and Ard.[w] **22** These were the sons whom Rachel bore to Jacob—fourteen persons in all.

**23** The sons of Dan: Hushim.[x] **24** The sons of Naphtali: Jahzeel, Guni, Jezer and Shillem.[y] **25** These were the sons of Bilhah, whom Laban had given to his daughter Rachel; these she bore to Jacob—seven persons in all.

**26** Jacob's people who migrated to Egypt —his direct descendants, not counting the wives of Jacob's sons—numbered sixty-six persons in all.[z] **27** Together with Joseph's sons who were born to him in Egypt—two persons —all the people comprising Jacob's family who

l Ex 1, 1; Jos 24, 4; Jdt 5, 10; Acts 7, 15.
m Ex 1, 2.
n Ex 6, 14; Nm 26, 5; 1 Chr 5, 3.
o Ex 6, 15; Nm 26, 12; 1 Chr 4, 24.
p Ex 6, 16; Nm 3, 17; 26, 57; 1 Chr 6, 1.
q Gn 38, 3-10. 29f; Nm 26, 19; Rv 4, 18-22; 1 Chr 2, 5.
r Nm 26, 23f; 1 Chr 7, 1.
s Nm 26, 26.
t Nm 26, 15f.
u Nm 26, 44; 1 Chr 7, 30f.
v Gn 41, 50; Nm 26, 28. 35.
w Nm 26, 38; 1 Chr 7, 6; 8, 1-4.
x Nm 26, 42.
y Nm 26, 48f; 1 Chr 7, 13.
z Ex 1, 5.
a Ex 1, 5; Dt 10, 22; Acts 7, 14.

*

46, 3: I am God: more precisely according to the Hebrew text, "I am El." "El" is here a divine name, not the common noun "god."

46, 9–27: This genealogical list has here been inserted by a redactor who based it on the clan lists (Nm 26, 5–50) at the time of Moses. Therefore it includes some of Jacob's grandchildren, who would hardly have been born when Joseph was still a relatively young man. The number fourteen (v 22) is based on a garbled version of the genealogical list.

46, 27: Seventy persons: either to be understood as a round number, or arrived at by including Jacob and Joseph with the preceding persons, who add up to sixty-eight.

had come to Egypt amounted to seventy persons* in all.[a]

**28** Israel had sent Judah ahead to Joseph, so that he might meet him in Goshen. On his arrival in the region of Goshen, **29** Joseph hitched the horses to his chariot and rode to meet his father Israel in Goshen. As soon as he saw him, he flung himself on his neck and wept a long time in his arms. **30** And Israel said to Joseph, "At last I can die, now that I have seen for myself that Joseph is still alive."

**31** Joseph then said to his brothers and his father's household: "I will go and inform Pharaoh, telling him: 'My brothers and my father's household, whose home is in the land of Canaan, have come to me. **32** The men are shepherds, having long been keepers of livestock; and they have brought with them their flocks and herds, as well as everything else they own.' **33** So when Pharaoh summons you and asks what your occupation is, **34** you must answer. 'We your servants, like our ancestors, have been keepers of livestock from the beginning until now,' in order that you may stay in the region of Goshen, since all shepherds are abhorrent to the Egyptians."

## CHAPTER 47

**Settlement in Goshen.** **1** Joseph went and told Pharaoh, "My father and my brothers have come from the land of Canaan, with their flocks and herds and everything else they own; and they are now in the region of Goshen." **2** He then presented to Pharaoh five of his brothers whom he had selected from their full number. **3** When Pharaoh asked them what their occupation was, they answered, "We, your servants, like our ancestors, are shepherds. **4** We have come," they continued, "in order to stay in this country, for there is no pasture for your servants' flocks in the land of Canaan, so severe has the famine been there. Please, therefore, let your servants settle in the region of Goshen."[b] **5** Pharaoh said to Joseph, "They may settle in the region of Goshen; and if you know any of them to be qualified, you may put them in charge of my own livestock."

Thus, when Jacob and his sons came to Joseph in Egypt, and Pharaoh, king of Egypt, heard about it, Pharaoh said to Joseph, "Now that your father and brothers have come to you, **6** the land of Egypt is at your disposal; settle your father and brothers in the pick of the land." **7** Then Joseph brought his father Jacob and presented him to Pharaoh. After Jacob had paid his respects to Pharaoh, **8** Pharaoh asked him, "How many years have you lived?" **9** Jacob replied: "The years I have lived as a wayfarer amount to a hundred and thirty. Few and hard have been these years of my life, and they do not compare with the years that my ancestors lived as wayfarers."* **10** Then Jacob bade Pharaoh farewell and withdrew from his presence.

**11** As Pharaoh had ordered, Joseph settled his father and brothers and gave them holdings in Egypt on the pick of the land, in the region of Rameses.* **12** And Joseph sustained his father and brothers and his father's whole household, down to the youngest, with food.

**Joseph's Land Policy.** **13** Since there was no food in any country because of the extreme severity of the famine, and the lands of Egypt and Canaan were languishing from hunger, **14** Joseph gathered in, as payment for the rations that were being dispensed, all the money that was to be found in Egypt and Canaan, and he put it in Pharaoh's palace. **15** When all the money in Egypt and Canaan was spent, all the Egyptians came to Joseph, pleading, "Give us food or we shall perish under your eyes; for our money is gone." **16** "Since your money is gone," replied Joseph, "give me your livestock, and I will sell you bread in return for your livestock." **17** So they brought their livestock to Joseph, and he sold them food in return for their horses, their flocks of sheep and herds of cattle, and their donkeys. Thus he got them through that year with bread in exchange for all their livestock. **18** When that year ended, they came to him in the following one and said: "We cannot hide from my lord that, with our money spent and our livestock made over to my lord, there is nothing left to put at my lord's disposal except our bodies and our farm land. **19** Why should we and our land perish before your very eyes? Take us and our land in exchange for food, and we will become Pharaoh's slaves and our land his property; only give us seed, that we may survive and not perish, and that our land may not turn into a waste."

**20** Thus Joseph acquired all the farm land of Egypt for Pharaoh, since with the famine too much for them to bear, every Egyptian sold his field; so the land passed over to Pharaoh, **21** and the people were reduced to slavery, from one end of Egypt's territory to the other. **22** Only the priests' lands Joseph did not take over. Since the priests had a fixed allowance from Pharaoh and lived off the allowance Pharaoh had granted them, they did not have to sell their land.

---

b Ex 23, 9; Dt 23, 8.

*

47, 9: Wayfarer . . . wayfarers: man is merely a sojourner on earth; cf Ps 39, 13.

47, 11: The region of Rameses: same as the region of Goshen; see note on Gn 45, 10. The name Rameses, however, is an anachronism, since this royal name did not come into use before the end of the fourteenth century B.C., long after the time of Joseph.

**23** Joseph told the people: "Now that I have
acquired you and your land for Pharaoh, here is
your seed for sowing the land. **24** But when the
harvest is in, you must give a fifth of it to
Pharaoh, while you keep four-fifths as seed for
your fields, and as food for yourselves and your
families [and as food for your children]."
**25** "You have saved our lives!" they answered. "We are grateful to my lord that we can
be Pharaoh's slaves." **26** Thus Joseph made it
a law for the land in Egypt, which is still in
force, that a fifth of its produce should go to
Pharaoh. Only the land of the priests did not
pass over to Pharaoh.

**Jacob Blesses Ephraim and Manas-
seh.** **27** Thus Israel settled in the land of
Egypt, in the region of Goshen. There they
acquired property, were fertile, and increased
greatly.[c] **28** Jacob lived in the land of Egypt for
seventeen years; the span of his life came to a
hundred and forty-seven years. **29** When the
time approached for Israel to die, he called his
son Joseph and said to him: "If you really wish
to please me, put your hand under my thigh as
a sign of your constant loyalty to me; do not let
me be buried in Egypt. **30** When I lie down
with my ancestors, have me taken out of Egypt
and buried in their burial place."[d] **31** "I will
do as you say," he replied. But his father demanded, "Swear it to me!" So Joseph swore to
him. Then Israel bowed at the head of the bed.*

## CHAPTER 48

**1** Some time afterward, Joseph was informed, "Your father is failing." So he took
along with him his two sons, Manasseh and
Ephraim. **2** When Jacob was told, "Your son
Joseph has come to you," he rallied his strength
and sat up in bed.
**3** [e]Jacob then said to Joseph: "God Almighty appeared to me at Luz* in the land of
Canaan, and blessing me, **4** he said, 'I will
make you fertile and numerous and raise you
into an assembly of tribes, and I will give this
land to your descendants after you as a permanent possession.' **5** Your two sons, therefore,
who were born to you in the land of Egypt
before I joined you here, shall be mine; Ephraim
and Manasseh shall be mine as much as Reuben
and Simeon are mine. **6** Progeny born to you
after them shall remain yours; but their heritage
shall be recorded in the names of their two
brothers. **7** [f]I do this because, when I was returning from Paddan, your mother Rachel died,
to my sorrow, during the journey in Canaan,
while we were still a short distance from Ephrath; and I buried her there on the way to Ephrath [that is, Bethlehem]."*

**8** When Israel saw Joseph's sons, he asked,
"Who are these?" **9** "They are my sons," Joseph answered his father, "whom God has giv-
en me here." "Bring them to me," said his
father, "that I may bless them." **10** (Now Israel's eyes were dim from age, and he could not
see well.) When Joseph brought his sons close
to him, he kissed and embraced them. **11** Then
Israel said to Joseph, "I never expected to see
your face again, and now God has allowed me
to see your descendants as well!"
**12** Joseph removed them from his father's
knees and bowed down before him with his face
to the ground. **13** Then Joseph took the two,
Ephraim with his right hand, to Israel's left, and
Manasseh with his left hand, to Israel's right,
and led them to him. **14** But Israel, crossing his
hands, put out his right hand and laid it on the
head of Ephraim, although he was the younger,
and his left hand on the head of Manasseh,
although he was the first-born. **15** Then he
blessed them with these words:

"May the God in whose ways
  my fathers Abraham and Isaac walked,
The God who has been my shepherd
  from my birth to this day,[g]
**16** The Angel who has delivered me from all
    harm,
  bless these boys
That in them my name be recalled,
  and the names of my fathers, Abraham
    and Isaac,
And they may become teeming multitudes
  upon the earth!"

**17** When Joseph saw that his father had laid his
right hand on Ephraim's head, this seemed
wrong to him; so he took hold of his father's
hand, to remove it from Ephraim's head to Manasseh's, **18** saying, "That is not right, father;
the other one is the first-born; lay your right
hand on his head!" **19** But his father resisted.
"I know it, son," he said, "I know. That one
too shall become a tribe, and he too shall be
great. Nevertheless, his younger brother shall
surpass him, and his descendants shall become
a multitude of nations." **20** So when he blessed
them that day and said, "By you shall the people of Israel pronounce blessings; may they say,

c Ex 1, 7.
d Gn 50, 5.
e 3f: Gn 28, 12-15; 35, 6.
f Gn 35, 19.
g Heb 11, 21.
h Heb 11, 21.

*

47, 31: Israel bowed at the head of the bed: meaning perhaps that he gave a nod of assent and appreciation as he lay on his bed. By reading with different vowels the Hebrew word for "bed," the Greek version translated it as "staff," and understood the phrase to mean that he bowed in worship, leaning on the top of his staff; it is thus quoted in Heb 11, 21.

48, 3: Luz: an older name of Bethel (Gn 28, 19).

48, 7: Since her early death prevented Rachel from bearing more than two sons, Jacob feels justified in treating her two grandsons as if they were her own offspring.

'God make you like Ephraim and Manasseh,' "
he placed Ephraim before Manasseh.[h]
21 Then Israel said to Joseph: "I am about to
die. But God will be with you and will restore
you to the land of your fathers. 22 [i]As for me,
I give to you, as to the one above his brothers,
Shechem, which I captured from the Amorites
with my sword and bow."*

## CHAPTER 49

**Jacob's Testament.** 1 Jacob called his
sons and said: "Gather around, that I may tell
you what is to happen to you in days to come.

2 "Assemble and listen, sons of Jacob,
listen to Israel, your father.

3 "You, Reuben, my first-born,
my strength and the first fruit of my manhood,
excelling in rank and excelling in power!
4 Unruly as water, you shall no longer excel,
for you climbed into your father's bed
and defiled my couch to my sorrow.[j]

5 "Simeon and Levi, brothers indeed,
weapons of violence are their knives.*
6 Let not my soul enter their council,
or my spirit be joined with their company;
For in their fury they slew men,
in their willfulness they mained oxen.[k]
7 Cursed be their fury so fierce,
and their rage so cruel!
I will scatter them in Jacob,
disperse them throughout Israel.

8 "You, Judah, shall your brothers praise
—your hand on the neck of your enemies;
the sons of your father shall bow down to you.
9 Judah, like a lion's whelp,
you have grown up on prey, my son.
He crouches like a lion recumbent,
the king of beasts—who would dare rouse him?[l]
10 The scepter shall never depart from Judah,
or the mace from between his legs,
While tribute is brought to him,*
and he receives the people's homage.
11 He tethers his donkey to the vine,
his purebred ass to the choicest stem.
In wine he washes his garments,
his robe in the blood of grapes.*
12 His eyes are darker than wine,
and his teeth are whiter than milk.
13 "Zebulun shall dwell by the seashore
[This means a shore for ships],
and his flank shall be based on Sidon.

14 "Issachar is a rawboned ass,
crouching between the saddlebags.
15 When he saw how good a settled life was,
and how pleasant the country,
He bent his shoulder to the burden
and became a toiling serf.

16 "Dan shall achieve justice* for his kindred
like any other tribe of Israel.
17 Let Dan be a serpent by the roadside,
a horned viper by the path,
That bites the horse's heel,
so that the rider tumbles backward.

18 "[I long for your deliverance, O LORD!]

19 "Gad shall be raided by raiders,
but he shall raid at their heels.*

20 "Asher's produce is rich,
and he shall furnish dainties for kings.

21 "Naphtali is a hind let loose,
which brings forth lovely fawns.

22 "Joseph is a wild colt,
a wild colt by a spring,
a wild ass on a hillside.
23 Harrying and attacking,
the archers opposed him;
24 But each one's bow remained stiff,
as their arms were unsteady,
By the power of the Mighty One of Jacob,
because of the Shepherd, the Rock of Israel,
25 The God of your father, who helps you,*
God Almighty, who blesses you,
With the blessings of the heavens above,

i Jos 17, 14. 17f; Jn 4. 5.
j Gn 35, 22; 1 Chr 5, 1f.
k Gn 34, 25.
l 1 Chr 5, 2.

48, 22: Both the meaning of the Hebrew and the historical reference in this verse are obscure. By taking the Hebrew word for Shechem as a common noun meaning shoulder or mountain slope, some translators render the verse, "I give you one portion more than your brothers, which I captured . . ." The reference may be to the capture of Shechem by the sons of Jacob (Gn 34, 24–29). Shechem lay near the border separating the tribal territory of Manasseh from that of Ephraim (Jos 16, 4–9; 17, 1f. 7).

49, 5: Knives: if this is the meaning of the obscure Hebrew word here, the reference may be to the knives used in circumcising the men of Shechem (Gn 34, 24; cf Jos 5, 2).

49, 10: While tribute is brought to him: this translation is based on a slight change in the Hebrew text, which, as it stands would seem to mean, "until he comes to Shiloh." A somewhat different reading of the Hebrew text would be, "until he comes to whom it belongs." This last has been traditionally understood in a Messianic sense. In any case, the passage foretells the supremacy of the tribe of Judah, which found its fulfillment in the Davidic dynasty and ultimately in the Messianic Son of David, Jesus Christ.

49, 11: In Wine . . . the blood of grapes: Judah's clothes are poetically pictured as soaked with grape juice from trampling in the wine press, the rich vintage of his land; cf Is 63, 2.

49, 16: In Hebrew the verb for achieve justice is from the same root as the name Dan.

49, 19: In Hebrew there is a certain assonance between the name Gad and the words for "raided," raiders" and "raid."

49, 25f: A very similar description of the agricultural riches of the tribal land of Joseph is given in Dt 33, 13–16.

the blessings of the abyss that crouches
below,
The blessings of breasts and womb,
26 the blessings of fresh grain and blossoms,
The blessings of the everlasting mountains,
the delights of the eternal hills.
May they rest on the head of Joseph,
on the brow of the prince among his
brothers.

27 "Benjamin is a ravenous wolf;
mornings he devours the prey,
and evenings he distributes the spoils."

**Farewell and Death.** **28** All these are the
twelve tribes of Israel, and this is what their
father said about them, as he bade them farewell
and gave to each of them an appropriate message. **29** Then he gave them this charge: "Since
I am about to be taken to my kindred, bury me
with my fathers in the cave that lies in the field
of Ephron the Hittite, **30** the cave in the field
of Machpelah, facing on Mamre, in the land of
Canaan, the field that Abraham bought from
Ephron the Hittite for a burial ground.[m]
**31** There Abraham and his wife Sarah are buried, and so are Isaac and his wife Rebekah, and
there, too, I buried Leah— **32** the field and the
cave in it that had been purchased from the
Hittites."

**33** When Jacob had finished giving these instructions to his sons, he drew his feet into the
bed, breathed his last, and was taken to his
kindred.

## CHAPTER 50

**Jacob's Funeral.** **1** Joseph threw himself
on his father's face and wept over him as he
kissed him. **2** Then he ordered the physicians in
his service to embalm his father. When they
embalmed Israel, **3** they spent forty days at it,
for that is the full period of embalming; and the
Egyptians mourned him for seventy days.
**4** When that period of mourning was over, Joseph spoke to Pharaoh's courtiers. "Please do
me this favor," he said, "and convey to Pharaoh this request of mine. **5** Since my father, at
the point of death, made me promise on oath to
bury him in the tomb that he had prepared for
himself in the land of Canaan, may I go up there
to bury my father and then come back?"[n]
**6** Pharaoh replied, "Go and bury your father,
as he made you promise on oath."

**7** So Joseph left to bury his father; and with
him went all of Pharaoh's officials who were
senior members of his court and all the other
dignitaries of Egypt, **8** as well as Joseph's
whole household, his brothers, and his father's
household; only their children and their flocks
and herds were left in the region of Goshen.
**9** Chariots, too, and charioteers went up with
him; it was a very large retinue.

**10** When they arrived at Goren-ha-atad,*
which is beyond the Jordan, they held there a
very great and solemn memorial service; and
Joseph observed seven days of mourning for his
father. **11** When the Canaanites who inhabited
the land saw the mourning at Goren-ha-atad,
they said, "This is a solemn funeral the Egyptians are having." That is why the place was
named Abel-mizraim. It is beyond the Jordan.

**12** Thus Jacob's sons did for him as he had
instructed them. **13** They carried him to the
land of Canaan and buried him in the cave in the
field of Machpelah, facing on Mamre, the field
that Abraham had bought for a burial ground
from Ephron the Hittite.[o]

**14** After Joseph had buried his father he returned to Egypt, together with his brothers and
all who had gone up with him for the burial of
his father.

**Plea for Forgiveness.** **15** Now that their
father was dead, Joseph's brothers became fearful and thought, "Suppose Joseph has been
nursing a grudge against us and now plans to
pay us back in full for all the wrong we did
him!" **16** So they approached Joseph and said:
"Before your father died, he gave us these instructions: **17** 'You shall say to Joseph, Jacob
begs you to forgive the criminal wrongdoing of
your brothers, who treated you so cruelly.'
Please, therefore, forgive the crime that we, the
servants of your father's God, committed."
When they spoke these words to him, Joseph
broke into tears. **18** Then his brothers proceeded to fling themselves down before him and
said, "Let us be your slaves!" **19** But Joseph
replied to them: "Have no fear. Can I take the
place of God? **20** Even though you meant harm
to me, God meant it for good, to achieve his
present end, the survival of many people.[p]
**21** Therefore have no fear. I will provide for
you and for your children." By thus speaking
kindly to them, he reassured them.[q]

**22** Joseph remained in Egypt, together with
his father's family. He lived a hundred and ten
years. **23** He saw Ephraim's children to the

m Gn 23, 17.
n Gn 47, 30.
o Gn 23, 16; Acts 7, 16.
p Gn 45, 5; Sir 49, 15.
q Gn 47, 12.
r Nm 32, 39; Jos 17, 1.

*

50, 10f: Goren-ha-atad: "Threshing Floor of the Brambles." Abel-mizraim: although the name really means "watercourse of the Egyptians," it is understood here, by a play on the first part of the term, to mean "mourning of the Egyptians." The site has not been identified through either reading of the name. But it is difficult to see why the mourning rites should have been held in the land beyond the Jordan when the burial was at Hebron. Perhaps an earlier form of the story placed the mourning rites beyond the Wadi of Egypt, the traditional boundary between Canaan and Egypt (Nm 34, 5; Jos 15, 4. 47).

third generation, and the children of Manasseh's son Machir were also born on Joseph's knees.[r]

**Death of Joseph.** **24** Joseph said to his brothers: "I am about to die. God will surely take care of you and lead you out of this land to the land that he promised on oath to Abraham, Isaac and Jacob."[s] **25** Then, putting the sons of Israel under oath, he continued, "When God thus takes care of you, you must bring my bones up with you from this place."[t] **26** Joseph died at the age of a hundred and ten. He was embalmed and laid to rest in a coffin in Egypt.[u]

s Ex 3, 8; Jos 24, 32; Heb 11, 22.
t Ex 13, 19; Heb 11, 22.
u Sir 49, 15.

# The Book of
# EXODUS

*The second book of the Pentateuch is called Exodus from the Greek word for "departure," because the central event narrated in it is the departure of the Israelites from Egypt. It continues the history of the chosen people from the point where the Book of Genesis leaves off. It recounts the oppression by the Egyptians of the ever-increasing descendants of Jacob and their miraculous deliverance by God through Moses, who led them across the Red Sea to Mount Sinai where they entered into a special covenant with the Lord.*

*These events were of prime importance to the chosen people, for they became thereby an independent nation and enjoyed a unique relationship with God. Through Moses God gave to the Israelites at Mount Sinai the "law": the moral, civil and ritual legislation by which they were to become a holy people, in whom the promise of a Savior for all mankind would be fulfilled.*

*The principal divisions of Exodus are:*
*I. The Israelites in Egypt (Ex 1, 1—12, 36).*
*II. The Exodus from Egypt and the Journey to Sinai (Ex 12, 37—18, 27).*
*III. The Covenant at Mount Sinai (Ex 19, 1—24, 18).*
*IV. The Dwelling and Its Furnishings (Ex 25, 1—40, 38).*

## *I: The Israelites In Egypt*

### CHAPTER 1

**Jacob's Descendants in Egypt.** **1** These
are the names of the sons of Israel* who, accompanied by their households, migrated with Jacob
into Egypt: **2** *Reuben, Simeon, Levi and Judah; **3** Issachar, Zebulun and Benjamin; **4** Dan
and Naphtali; Gad and Asher. **5** The total number of the direct descendants* of Jacob was
seventy.[a] Joseph was already in Egypt.
**6** Now Joseph and all his brothers and that
whole generation died.[b] **7** But the Israelites
were fruitful and prolific. They became so numerous and strong that the land was filled with
them.

**The Oppression.** **8** Then a new king, who
knew nothing of Joseph,* came to power in
Egypt.[c] **9** He said to his subjects, "Look how
numerous and powerful the Israelite people are
growing, more so than we ourselves! **10** Come,
let us deal shrewdly with them to stop their
increase; otherwise, in time of war they too may
join our enemies to fight against us, and so leave
our country."
**11** Accordingly, taskmasters were set over
the Israelites to oppress them with forced labor.[d] Thus they had to build for Pharaoh* the
supply cities of Pithom and Raamses. **12** Yet
the more they were oppressed, the more they
multiplied and spread. The Egyptians, then,
dreaded the Israelites **13** and reduced them to
cruel slavery, **14** making life bitter for them
with hard work in mortar* and brick and all
kinds of field work—the whole cruel fate of
slaves.

**Command to the Midwives.** **15** The king
of Egypt told the Hebrew midwives, one of
whom was called Shiphrah and the other Puah,
**16** "When you act as midwives for the Hebrew
women and see them giving birth,* if it is a boy,
kill him; but if it is a girl, she may live."

a Gn 46, 27; Dt 10, 22; Acts 7, 14.
b Gn 50, 26.
c 8ff: Acts 7, 18.
d Dt 26, 6.

*

1, 1: Sons of Israel: here literally the first-generation sons of Jacob. Cf v 5. However, beginning with Ex 1, 7 the same Hebrew phrase refers to the more remote descendants of Jacob; hence, from there on, it is ordinarily rendered as "the Israelites." Households: the family in its fullest sense, including wives, children and servants.

1, 2: The sons of Jacob are listed here according to the respective mothers. Cf Gn 29, 31; 30, 30; 35, 16–26.

1, 5: Direct descendants: literally, persons coming from the loins of Jacob; hence, wives and servants are here excluded. Cf Gn 46, 26.

1, 8: Who knew nothing of Joseph: this king ignored the services that Joseph had rendered to Egypt.

1, 11: Pharaoh: not a personal name, but a title common to all the kings of Egypt.

1, 14: Mortar: either the wet clay with which the bricks were made, as in Na 3, 14, or the cement used between the bricks in building, as in Gn 11, 3.

1, 16: And see them giving birth: the Hebrew text is uncertain.

**17** The midwives, however, feared God; they
did not do as the king of Egypt had ordered
them, but let the boys live. **18** So the king
summoned the midwives and asked them,
"Why have you acted thus, allowing the boys
to live?" **19** The midwives answered Pharaoh,
"The Hebrew women are not like the Egyptian
women. They are robust and give birth before
the midwife arrives." **20** Therefore God dealt
well with the midwives. The people, too, increased and grew strong. **21** And because the
midwives feared God, he built up families for
them. **22** Pharaoh then commanded all his subjects, "Throw into the river* every boy that is
born to the Hebrews,[e] but you may let all the
girls live."

## CHAPTER 2

**Birth and Adoption of Moses.** **1** Now a
certain man of the house of Levi married a
Levite woman,[f] **2** who conceived and bore a
son. Seeing that he was a goodly child, she hid
him for three months.[g] **3** When she could hide
him no longer, she took a papyrus basket,*
daubed it with bitumen and pitch, and putting
the child in it, placed it among the reeds on the
river bank. **4** His sister stationed herself at a
distance to find out what would happen to him.

**5** Pharaoh's daughter came down to the river
to bathe, while her maids walked along the river
bank. Noticing the basket among the reeds, she
sent her handmaid to fetch it. **6** On opening it,
she looked, and lo, there was a baby boy, crying! She was moved with pity for him and said,
"It is one of the Hebrews' children." **7** Then
his sister asked Pharaoh's daughter, "Shall I go
and call one of the Hebrew women to nurse the
child for you?" **8** "Yes, do so," she answered.
So the maiden went and called the child's own
mother. **9** Pharaoh's daughter said to her,
"Take this child and nurse it for me, and I will
repay you." The woman therefore took the
child and nursed it. **10** When the child grew,*
she brought him to Pharaoh's daughter, who
adopted him as her son[h] and called him Moses;
for she said, "I drew him out of the water."

**Moses' Flight to Midian.** **11** On one occasion, after Moses had grown up,* when he visited his kinsmen[i] and witnessed their forced labor, he saw an Egyptian striking a Hebrew, one
of his own kinsmen. **12** Looking about and seeing no one, he slew the Egyptian and hid him
in the sand. **13** The next day he went out again,
and now two Hebrews were fighting! So he
asked the culprit, "Why are you striking your
fellow Hebrew?" **14** But he replied, "Who has
appointed you ruler and judge over us? Are you
thinking of killing me as you killed the Egyptian?" Then Moses became afraid and thought,
"The affair must certainly be known."

**15** Pharaoh, too, heard of the affair and
sought to put him to death. But Moses fled from
him and stayed in the land of Midian.[j] As he
was seated there by a well, **16** seven daughters
of a priest of Midian came to draw water and fill
the troughs to water their father's flock. **17** But
some shepherds came and drove them away.
Then Moses got up and defended them and watered their flock. **18** When they returned to their
father Reuel,* he said to them, "How is it you
have returned so soon today?" **19** They answered, "An Egyptian* saved us from the interference of the shepherds. He even drew water
for us and watered the flock!" **20** "Where is
the man?" he asked his daughters. "Why did
you leave him there? Invite him to have something to eat." **21** Moses agreed to live with
him, and the man gave him his daughter Zipporah in marriage. **22** She bore him a son, whom
he named Gershom;* for he said, "I am a
stranger in a foreign land."[k]

**The Burning Bush.** **23** A long time
passed, during which the king of Egypt died.
Still the Israelites groaned and cried out because
of their slavery. As their cry for release went up
to God,[l] **24** he heard their groaning and was
mindful of his covenant[m] with Abraham,
Isaac and Jacob. **25** He saw the Israelites and
knew. . . .

---

e Acts 7, 19.
f Ex 6, 20; Nm 26, 59.
g Acts 7, 20; Heb 11, 23.
h Acts 7, 21; Heb 11, 24.
i 11-14: Acts 7, 23-28.
j Acts 7, 29; Heb 11, 27.
k Ex 18, 3.
l Ex 3, 7. 9; Dt 26. 7.
m Ex 6, 5; Pss 105, 8f; 106, 44f.

---

*

1, 22: The river: the Nile, which was "the" river for the Egyptians.

2, 3: Basket: literally, "chest" or "ark"; the same Hebrew word is used in Gn 6, 14 for Noah's ark. Here, however, the chest was made of papyrus stalks.

2, 10: When the child grew: probably when he was weaned or a little later. Moses: in Hebrew, Mosheh; the Hebrew word for "draw out" is mashah. The explanation of the name is not intended as a scientific etymology but as a play on words. The name is probably derived from an Egyptian word for "has been born," referring the birth to a god thought to be its sponsor.

2, 11: After Moses had grown up: Acts 7, 23 indicates that this was after an interval of nearly forty years. Cf Ex 7, 7. Striking: probably in the sense of "flogging"; according to some, "slaying."

2, 18: Reuel: he was also called Jethro. Cf Ex 3, 1; 4, 18; 18, 1.

2, 19: An Egyptian: Moses was probably wearing Egyptian dress, or spoke Egyptian to Reuel's daughters.

2, 22: Gershom: the name is explained as if it came from the Hebrew word ger, "stranger," joined to the Hebrew word sham, "there." Some Greek and Latin manuscripts add here a passage taken from Ex 18, 4.

## CHAPTER 3

**1** Meanwhile Moses was tending the flock of
his father-in-law Jethro, the priest of Midian.
Leading the flock across the desert, he came to
Horeb, the mountain of God.* **2** There an angel
of the LORD* appeared to him in fire flaming out
of a bush.[n] As he looked on, he was surprised
to see that the bush, though on fire, was not
consumed. **3** So Moses decided, "I must go
over to look at this remarkable sight, and see
why the bush is not burned."

**The Call of Moses.** **4** When the LORD saw
him coming over to look at it more closely, God
called out to him from the bush, "Moses! Moses!" He answered, "Here I am." **5** God said,
"Come no nearer![o] Remove the sandals from
your feet, for the place where you stand is holy
ground. **6** [p]I am the God of your father," he
continued, "the God of Abraham, the God of
Isaac, the God of Jacob."* Moses hid his face,
for he was afraid to look at God. **7** But the LORD
said, "I have witnessed the affliction of my
people in Egypt and have heard their cry of
complaint against their slave drivers, so I know
well what they are suffering. **8** Therefore I have
come down* to rescue them from the hands of
the Egyptians and lead them out of that land into
a good and spacious land, a land flowing with
milk and honey, the country of the Canaanites,
Hittites, Amorites, Perizzites, Hivites and Jebusites.[q] **9** So indeed the cry of the Israelites has
reached me, and I have truly noted that the
Egyptians are oppressing them. **10** Come,
now! I will send you to Pharaoh to lead my
people, the Israelites, out of Egypt."

**11** But Moses said to God, "Who am I* that
I should go to Pharaoh and lead the Israelites out
of Egypt?" **12** He answered, "I will be with
you; and this shall be your proof that it is I who
have sent you: when you bring my people out
of Egypt, you will worship God on this very
mountain." **13** "But," said Moses to God,
"when I go to the Israelites and say to them,
'The God of your fathers has sent me to you,'
if they ask me, 'What is his name?' what am I
to tell them?" **14** God replied, "I am who
am."* Then he added, "This is what you shall
tell the Israelites: I AM sent me to you."

**15** God spoke further to Moses, "Thus shall
you say to the Israelites: The LORD, the God of
your fathers, the God of Abraham, the God of
Isaac, the God of Jacob, has sent me to you.

"This is my name forever;[r]
this is my title for all generations:

**16** "Go and assemble the elders* of the Israelites, and tell them: The LORD, the God of your
fathers, the God of Abraham, Isaac and Jacob,
has appeared to me and said: I am concerned
about you and about the way you are being
treated in Egypt; **17** so I have decided to lead
you up out of the misery of Egypt into the land
of the Canaanites, Hittites, Amorites, Perizzites, Hivites and Jebusites, a land flowing with
milk and honey.

**18** "Thus they will heed your message. Then
you and the elders of Israel shall go to the king
of Egypt and say to him:[s] The LORD, the God
of the Hebrews, has sent us word. Permit us,
then, to go a three-days' journey in the desert,
that we may offer sacrifice to the LORD, our
God.

**19** "Yet I know that the king of Egypt will
not allow you to go unless he is forced. **20** I will
stretch out my hand, therefore, and smite Egypt
by doing all kinds of wondrous deeds there.
After that he will send you away. **21** I will even
make the Egyptians so well-disposed toward
this people that, when you leave, you will not
go empty-handed. **22** [t]Every woman shall ask
her neighbor and her house guest for silver and
gold articles* and for clothing to put on your

n 2-10; Acts 7, 30-35.
o Jos 5, 15.
p Ex 4, 5; Mt 22, 32; Mk 12, 36; Lk 20, 37.
q 8f: Gn 15, 19ff.
r Ps 135, 13.
s Ex 5, 3.
t 21f: Ex 11, 2f; 12, 35f.

*

3, 1: The mountain of God: probably given this designation because of the divine apparitions which took place there, such as on this occasion and when the Israelites were there after the departure from Egypt.

3, 2: An angel of the Lord: the visual form under which God appeared and spoke to men is referred to indifferently in some Old Testament texts either as God's angel or as God himself. Cf Gn 16, 7. 13; Ex 14, 19. 24f; Nm 22, 22–35; Jgs 6, 11–18.

3, 6: The appearance of God caused fear of death, since it was believed that no one could see God and live; cf Gn 32, 30. The God of Abraham . . . Jacob: cited by Christ in proof of the resurrection since the patriarchs, long dead, live on in God who is the God of the living. Cf Mt 22, 32; Mk 12, 26; Lk 20, 37.

3, 8: I have come down: a figure of speech signifying an extraordinary divine intervention in human affairs. Cf Gn 11, 5. 7. Flowing with milk and honey: an expression denoting agricultural prosperity, which seems to have been proverbial in its application to Palestine. Cf Ex 13, 5; Nm 13, 27; Jos 5, 6; Jer 11, 5; 32, 22; Ez 20, 6. 15.

3, 11: Who am I: besides naturally shrinking from such a tremendous undertaking, Moses realized that, as a fugitive from Pharaoh, he could hardly hope to carry out a mission to him. Perhaps he also recalled that on one occasion even his own kinsmen questioned his authority. Cf Ex 2, 14.

3, 14: I am who am: apparently this utterance is the source of the word Yahweh, the proper personal name of the God of Israel. It is commonly explained in reference to God as the absolute and necessary Being. It may be understood of God as the Source of all created beings. Out of reverence for this name, the term Adonai, "my Lord," was later used as a substitute. The word Lord in the present version represents this traditional usage. The word "Jehovah" arose from a false reading of this name as it is written in the current Hebrew text.

3, 16: Elders: the Israelite leaders, who were usually older men. They were representatives of the people.

3, 22: Articles: probably jewelry. Despoil: this was permissible, that the Israelites might compensate themselves for their many years of servitude; besides, the Egyptians would give these things willingly. Cf Ex 12, 33–36.

sons and daughters. Thus you will despoil the
Egyptians.''

## CHAPTER 4

### Confirmation of Moses' Mission.

1 ''But,'' objected Moses, ''suppose they will
not believe me, nor listen to my plea? For they
may say, 'The LORD did not appear to you.' ''
2 The LORD therefore asked him, ''What is that
in your hand?'' ''A staff,'' he answered. 3 The
LORD then said, ''Throw it on the ground.''
When he threw it on the ground it was changed
into a serpent,[u] and Moses shied away from it.
4 ''Now, put out your hand,'' the LORD said to
him, ''and take hold of its tail.'' So he put out
his hand and laid hold of it, and it became a staff
in his hand. 5 ''This will take place so that they
may believe,'' he continued, ''that the LORD,
the God of their fathers, the God of Abraham,
the God of Isaac, the God of Jacob, did appear
to you.''

6 Again the LORD said to him, ''Put your
hand in your bosom.'' He put it in his bosom,
and when he withdrew it, to his surprise his
hand was leprous, like snow. 7 The LORD then
said, ''Now, put your hand back in your bosom.'' Moses put his hand back in his bosom,
and when he withdrew it, to his surprise it was
again like the rest of his body. 8 ''If they will
not believe you, nor heed the message of the
first sign, they should believe the message of the
second. 9 And if they will not believe even
these two signs, nor heed your plea, take some
water from the river and pour it on the dry land.
The water you take from the river will become
blood on the dry land.''[v]

**Aaron's Office as Assistant.** 10 Moses,
however, said to the LORD, ''If you please,
Lord, I have never been eloquent, neither in the
past, nor recently, nor now that you have spoken to your servant; but I am slow of speech and
tongue.''[w] 11 The LORD said to him, ''Who
gives one man speech and makes another deaf
and dumb? Or who gives sight to one and makes
another blind? Is it not I, the LORD? 12 Go,
then! It is I who will assist you in speaking and
will teach you what you are to say.'' 13 Yet he
insisted, ''If you please, Lord, send someone
else!''* 14 Then the LORD became angry with
Moses and said, ''Have you not your brother,
Aaron the Levite? I know that he is an eloquent
speaker. Besides, he is now on his way to meet
you. 15 When he sees you, his heart will be
glad. You are to speak to him, then, and put the
words in his mouth. I will assist both you and
him in speaking and will teach the two of you
what you are to do. 16 He shall speak to the
people for you: he shall be your spokesman,*
and you shall be as God to him.[x] 17 Take this
staff* in your hand; with it you are to perform
the signs.''

**Moses' Return to Egypt.** 18 After this
Moses returned to his father-in-law Jethro and
said to him, ''Let me go back, please, to my
kinsmen in Egypt, to see whether they are still
living.'' Jethro replied, ''Go in peace.''* 19 In
Midian[y] the LORD said to Moses, ''Go back to
Egypt, for all the men who sought your life are
dead.'' 20 So Moses took his wife and his sons,
and started back to the land of Egypt, with them
riding the ass. The staff of God he carried with
him. 21 The LORD said to him, ''On your return
to Egypt, see that you perform before Pharaoh
all the wonders I have put in your power. I will
make him obstinate,* however, so that he will
not let the people go. 22 [z]So you shall say to
Pharaoh: Thus says the LORD: Israel is my son,
my first-born. 23 Hence I tell you: Let my son
go, that he may serve me. If you refuse to let
him go, I warn you, I will kill your son, your
first-born.''[a]

24 *On the journey, at a place where they
spent the night, the Lord came upon Moses and
would have killed him. 25 [b]But Zipporah took
a piece of flint and cut off her son's foreskin
and, touching his person, she said, ''You are a
spouse of blood to me.'' 26 Then God let Moses go. At that time she said, ''A spouse of
blood,'' in regard to the circumcision.

27 The LORD said to Aaron, ''Go into the
desert to meet Moses.'' So he went, and when
they met at the mountain of God, Aaron kissed
him. 28 Moses informed him of all the LORD
had said in sending him, and of the various signs
he had enjoined upon him. 29 Then Moses and
Aaron went and assembled all the elders of the
Israelites. 30 Aaron told them everything the
LORD had said to Moses, and he performed the
signs before the people. 31 The people be-

---

u Ex 7, 10.
v Ex 7, 17. 19f.
w Ex 6, 12.
x 15f: Ex 7, 1.
y Ex 2, 15, 23.
z Sir 36, 11.
a Ex 11, 5; 12, 29.
b Is 6, 2; 7, 20.

---

*

4, 13: Send someone else: literally, "Send by means of him whom you will send," that is, "Send whom you will."

4, 16: Spokesman: literally, "mouth"; Aaron was to serve as a mouthpiece for Moses, as a prophet does for God; hence the relation between Moses and Aaron is compared to that between God and his prophet. Cf Ex 7, 1.

4, 17: This staff: probably the same as that of vv 2ff; but some understand it here of a new staff now given by God to Moses.

4, 18: Moses did not tell his father-in-law his main reason for returning to Egypt, but this secondary motive which he offered was also true.

4, 21: Make him obstinate: literally, "harden his heart." God permitted Pharaoh to be stubborn in his opposition to the departure of the Israelites. Cf Rom 9, 17f.

4, 24ff: Apparently God was angry with Moses for having failed to keep the divine command given to Abraham in Gn 17, 10ff. Moses' life is spared when his wife circumcises their son.

lieved, and when they heard that the LORD was concerned about them and had seen their affliction, they bowed down in worship.

## CHAPTER 5

**Pharaoh's Obduracy.** **1** After that, Moses and Aaron went to Pharaoh and said, "Thus says the LORD, the God of Israel: Let my people go, that they may celebrate a feast to me in the desert." **2** Pharaoh answered, "Who is the LORD, that I should heed his plea to let Israel go? I do not know the LORD; even if I did, I would not let Israel go." **3** They replied, "The God of the Hebrews has sent us word. Let us go a three days' journey in the desert, that we may offer sacrifice to the LORD, our God;[c] otherwise he will punish us with pestilence or the sword."

**4** The king of Egypt answered them, "What do you mean, Moses and Aaron, by taking the people away from their work? Off to your labor! **5** Look how numerous the people of the land are already," continued Pharaoh, "and yet you would give them rest from their labor!"

**6** That very day Pharaoh gave the taskmasters and foremen* of the people this order: **7** "You shall no longer supply the people with straw for their brickmaking* as you have previously done. Let them go and gather straw themselves! **8** Yet you shall levy upon them the same quota of bricks as they have previously made. Do not reduce it. They are lazy; that is why they are crying, 'Let us go to offer sacrifice to our God.' **9** Increase the work for the men, so that they keep their mind on it and pay no attention to lying words."

**10** So the taskmasters and foremen of the people went out and told them, "Thus says Pharaoh: I will not provide you with straw. **11** Go and gather the straw yourselves, wherever you can find it. Yet there must not be the slightest reduction in your work." **12** The people, then, scattered throughout the land of Egypt to gather stubble for straw, **13** while the taskmasters kept driving them on, saying, "Finish your work, the same daily amount as when your straw was supplied."

**Complaint of the Foremen.** **14** The foremen of the Israelites, whom the taskmasters of Pharaoh had placed over them, were beaten, and were asked, "Why have you not completed your prescribed amount of bricks yesterday and today, as before?"

**15** Then the Israelite foremen came and made this appeal to Pharaoh: "Why do you treat your servants in this manner? **16** No straw is supplied to your servants, and still we are told to make bricks. Look how your servants are beaten! It is you who are at fault." **17** Pharaoh answered, "It is just because you are lazy that you keep saying, 'Let us go and offer sacrifice to the LORD.' **18** Off to work, then! Straw shall not be provided for you, but you must still deliver your quota of bricks."

**19** The Israelite foremen knew they were in a sorry plight, having been told not to reduce the daily amount of bricks. **20** When, therefore, they left Pharaoh and came upon Moses and Aaron, who were waiting to meet them, **21** they said to them, "The LORD look upon you and judge! You have brought us into bad odor with Pharaoh and his servants and have put a sword in their hands to slay us."

**Renewal of God's Promise.** **22** Moses again had recourse to the LORD and said, "Lord, why do you treat this people so badly? And why did you send me on such a mission? **23** Ever since I went to Pharaoh to speak in your name, he has maltreated this people of yours, and you have done nothing to rescue them."

## CHAPTER 6

**1** Then the LORD answered Moses, "Now you shall see what I will do to Pharaoh. Forced by my mighty hand, he will send them away; compelled by my outstretched arm, he will drive them from his land."

**2** God also said to Moses, "I am the LORD. **3** As God the Almighty I appeared[d] to Abraham, Isaac and Jacob, but my name, LORD, I did not make known to them. **4** I also established my covenant with them, to give them the land of Canaan, the land in which they were living as aliens.[e] **5** And now that I have heard the groaning of the Israelites, whom the Egyptians are treating as slaves, I am mindful of my covenant.[f] **6** Therefore, say to the Israelites: I am the LORD. I will free you from the forced labor of the Egyptians and will deliver you from their slavery. I will rescue you by my outstretched arm and with mighty acts of judgment. **7** I will take you as my own people, and you shall have me as your God.[g] You will know that I, the LORD, am your God when I free you from the labor of the Egyptians **8** and bring you into the land which I swore to give to Abraham, Isaac and Jacob. I will give it to you as your own possession—I, the LORD!" **9** But when Moses told this to the Israelites, they would not listen to him because of their dejection and hard slavery.

c Ex 3, 18.
d Gn 17, 1; 35, 11.
e Gn 15, 18; 17, 4-8.
f Ex 2, 24.
g Lv 26, 12.

*

5, 6: The taskmasters and foremen: the former were higher officials and probably Egyptians; the latter were lower officials, chosen from the Israelites themselves. Cf v 14.

5, 7: Straw was mixed with the clay to give the sun-dried bricks greater consistency.

**10** Then the LORD said to Moses, **11** "Go and tell Pharaoh, king of Egypt, to let the Israelites leave his land." **12** But Moses protested to the LORD, "If the Israelites would not listen to me, how can it be that Pharaoh will listen to me, poor speaker[h] that I am!" **13** Still, the LORD, to bring the Israelites out of Egypt, spoke to Moses and Aaron and gave them his orders regarding both the Israelites and Pharaoh, king of Egypt.

### Genealogy of Moses and Aaron.

**14** These are the heads of the ancestral houses.* The sons of Reuben,[i] the first-born of Israel, were Hanoch, Pallu, Hezron and Carmi; these are the clans of Reuben. **15** The sons of Simeon[j] were Jemuel, Jamin, Ohad, Jachin, Zohar and Shaul, who was the son of a Canaanite woman; these are the clans of Simeon. **16** The names of the sons of Levi,[k] in their genealogical order, are Gershon, Kohath and Merari. Levi lived one hundred and thirty-seven years.

**17** The sons of Gershon,[l] as heads of clans, were Libni and Shimei. **18** The sons of Kohath[m] were Amram, Izhar, Hebron and Uzziel. Kohath lived one hundred and thirty-three years. **19** The sons of Merari[n] were Mahli and Mushi. These are the clans of Levi in their genealogical order.

**20** Amram married his aunt* Jochebed,[o] who bore him Aaron, Moses and Miriam. Amram lived one hundred and thirty-seven years. **21** The sons of Izhar were Korah, Nepheg and Zichri. **22** The sons of Uzziel were Mishael, Elzaphan and Sithri. **23** Aaron married Amminadab's[p] daughter, Elisheba, the sister of Nahshon; she bore him Nadab, Abihu, Eleazar and Ithamar. **24** The sons of Korah were Assir, Elkanah and Abiasaph. These are the clans of the Korahites. **25** Aaron's son, Eleazar, married one of Putiel's daughters, who bore him Phinehas. These are the heads of the ancestral clans of the Levites. **26** This is the Aaron and this the Moses to whom the LORD said, "Lead the Israelites from the land of Egypt, company by company." **27** These are the ones who spoke to Pharaoh, king of Egypt, to bring the Israelites out of Egypt—the same Moses and Aaron.

### Moses and Aaron before Pharaoh.

**28** On the day the LORD spoke to Moses in Egypt **29** he said, "I am the LORD. Repeat to Pharaoh, king of Egypt, all that I tell you." **30** But Moses protested to the LORD, "Since I am a poor speaker,[q] how can it be that Pharaoh will listen to me?"

## CHAPTER 7

**1** The LORD answered him, "See! I have made you as God to Pharaoh,[r] and Aaron your brother shall act as your prophet.* **2** You shall tell him all that I command you. In turn, your brother Aaron shall tell Pharaoh to let the Israelites leave his land. **3** Yet I will make Pharaoh so obstinate that, despite the many signs and wonders that I will work in the land of Egypt, **4** he will not listen to you. Therefore I will lay my hand on Egypt and by great acts of judgment I will bring the hosts of my people, the Israelites, out of the land of Egypt, **5** so that the Egyptians may learn that I am the LORD, as I stretch out my hand against Egypt and lead the Israelites out of their midst."

**6** Moses and Aaron did as the LORD had commanded them. **7** Moses was eighty years old and Aaron eighty-three when they spoke to Pharaoh.

**The Staff Turned into a Snake.** **8** The LORD told Moses and Aaron, **9** "If Pharaoh demands that you work a sign or wonder, you shall say to Aaron: Take your staff and throw it down before Pharaoh, and it will be changed into a snake."[s] **10** Then Moses and Aaron went to Pharaoh and did as the LORD had commanded. Aaron threw his staff down before Pharaoh and his servants, and it was changed into a snake. **11** Pharaoh, in turn, summoned wise men and sorcerers, and they also, the magicians[t] of Egypt, did likewise by their magic arts. **12** Each one threw down his staff, and it was changed into a snake. But Aaron's staff swallowed their staffs. **13** Pharaoh, however, was obstinate and would not listen to them, just as the LORD had foretold.

### First Plague: Water Turned into Blood.

**14** *Then the LORD said to Moses, "Pharaoh is obdurate in refusing to let the people go. **15** Tomorrow morning, when he sets out for the water, go and present yourself by the river bank,

h Ex 6, 30.
i Nm 26. 5f; 1 Chr 5, 3
j Nm 26, 12; 1 Chr 4, 24.
k Nm 3, 17; 1 Chr 6, 1. 16; 23, 6.
l Nm 3, 21; 1 Chr 6, 17; 23, 7.
m Nm 3, 27; 1 Chr 6, 2. 18.
n Nm 3, 20; 1 Chr 6, 19; 23, 21.
o Nm 26, 59.
p Ru 4, 19f; 1 Chr 2, 10.
q Ex 6, 12.
r Ex 4, 15f.
s Ex 4, 3.
t 2 Tm 3, 8.

*

6, 14: The purpose of the genealogy here is to give the line from which Moses and Aaron sprang. Reuben and Simeon are first mentioned because, as older brothers of Levi, their names occur before his in the genealogy.

6, 20: His aunt: more exactly, "his father's sister." Later on such a marriage was forbidden. Cf Lv 18, 12. Hence, the Greek and Latin versions render here, "his cousin."

7, 1: Just as God had his prophets to speak to men in his name, so Moses had Aaron as his "prophet" to speak to Pharaoh. Cf Ex 4, 16.

7, 14: Most of the ten plagues of Egypt seem to be similar to certain natural phenomena of that country; but they are represented as supernatural at least in their greater intensity and in their occurring exactly to Moses' commands.

holding in your hand the staff that turned into a serpent. **16** Say to him: The LORD, the God of the Hebrews, sent me to you with the message: Let my people go to worship me in the desert. But as yet you have not listened. **17** The LORD now says: This is how you shall know that I am the LORD. I will strike the water of the river with the staff I hold, and it shall be changed into blood.[u] **18** The fish in the river shall die, and the river itself shall become so polluted that the Egyptians will be unable to drink its water."

**19** The LORD then said to Moses, "Say to Aaron: Take your staff and stretch out your hand over the waters of Egypt—their streams and canals and pools, all their supplies of water—that they may become blood. Throughout the land of Egypt there shall be blood, even in the wooden pails and stone jars."

**20** Moses and Aaron did as the LORD had commanded. Aaron raised his staff and struck the waters of the river in full view of Pharaoh and his servants, and all the water of the river was changed into blood. **21** The fish in the river died, and the river itself became so polluted that the Egyptians could not drink its water. There was blood throughout the land of Egypt. **22** But the Egyptian magicians did the same by their magic arts. So Pharaoh remained obstinate and would not listen to Moses and Aaron, just as the LORD had foretold. **23** He turned away and went into his house, with no concern even for this. **24** All the Egyptians had to dig in the neighborhood of the river for drinking water, since they could not drink the river water.

**Second Plague: the Frogs.** **25** Seven days passed after the LORD had struck the river. **26** *Then the LORD said to Moses, "Go to Pharaoh and tell him:[v] Thus says the LORD: Let my people go to worship me. **27** If you refuse to let them go, I warn you, I will send a plague of frogs over all your territory. **28** The river will teem with frogs. They will come up into your palace and into your bedroom and onto your bed, into the houses of your servants, too, and your subjects, even into your ovens and your kneeding bowls. **29** The frogs will swarm all over you and your subjects and your servant."

## CHAPTER 8

**1** The LORD then told Moses, "Say to Aaron: Stretch out your hand and your staff over the streams and canals and pools, to make frogs overrun the land of Egypt." **2** Aaron stretched out his hand over the waters of Egypt, and the frogs came up and covered the land of Egypt. **3** But the magicians did the same by their magic arts. They, too, made frogs overrun the land of Egypt.

**4** Then Pharaoh summoned Moses and Aaron and said, "Pray the LORD to remove the frogs from me and my subjects, and I will let the people go to offer sacrifice to the LORD." **5** Moses answered Pharaoh, "Do me the favor of appointing the time when I am to pray for you and your servants and your subjects, that the frogs may be taken away from you and your houses and be left only in the river." **6** "Tomorrow," said Pharaoh. Then Moses replied, "It shall be as you have said, so that you may learn that there is none like the LORD, our God. **7** The frogs shall leave you and your houses, your servants and your subjects; only in the river shall they be left."

**8** After Moses and Aaron left Pharaoh's presence, Moses implored the LORD to fulfill the promise he had made to Pharaoh about the frogs; **9** and the LORD did as Moses had asked. The frogs in the houses and courtyards* and fields died off. **10** Heaps and heaps of them were gathered up, and there was a stench in the land. **11** But when Pharaoh saw that there was a respite, he became obdurate and would not listen to them, just as the LORD had foretold.

**Third Plague: the Gnats.** **12** Thereupon the LORD said to Moses, "Tell Aaron to stretch out his staff and strike the dust of the earth, that it may be turned into gnats[w] throughout the land of Egypt."* **13** They did so. Aaron stretched out his hand, and with his staff he struck the dust of the earth, and gnats came upon man and beast. The dust of the earth was turned into gnats throughout the land of Egypt. **14** Though the magicians tried to bring forth gnats by their magic arts, they could not do so.[x] As the gnats infested man and beast, **15** the magicians said to Pharaoh, "This is the finger of God."* Yet Pharaoh remained obstinate and would not listen to them, just as the LORD had foretold.

**Fourth Plague: the Flies.** **16** Again the LORD told Moses, "Early tomorrow morning present yourself to Pharaoh when he goes forth to the water, and say to him: Thus says the LORD: Let my people go to worship me. **17** If you will not let my people go, I warn you, I will loose swarms of flies upon you and your servants and your subjects and your houses. The houses of the Egyptians and the very ground on

u 17-21: Ex 4, 9; Pss 78, 44; 105, 29; Wis 11, 5-7.
v 26-29: Pss 78, 45; 105, 30.
w 12f: Ps 105, 31.
x Wis 17, 7.

7, 26—8, 28: This is Ex 8, 1–32 in the verse enumeration of the Vulgate.

8, 9: Courtyards: some render "farmhouses."

8, 12. 17: Gnats, flies: it is uncertain what species of troublesome insects are here meant.

8, 15: The finger of God: understood by the magicians as the staff mentioned in Ex 8, 13. Cf Lk 11, 20.

which they stand shall be filled with swarms of
flies. **18** But on that day I will make an exception of the land of Goshen: there shall be no flies
where my people dwell, that you may know that
I am the LORD in the midst of the earth. **19** I will
make this distinction between my people and
your people. This sign shall take place tomorrow." **20** This the LORD did. Thick swarms of
flies entered the house of Pharaoh and houses of
his servants; throughout Egypt the land was infested with flies.[y]

**21** Then Pharaoh summoned Moses and Aaron and said to them, "Go and offer sacrifice to
your God in this land." **22** But Moses replied,
"It is not right to do so, for the sacrifices we
offer to the LORD, our God, are an abomination
to the Egyptians.* If before their very eyes we
offer sacrifices which are an abomination to
them, will not the Egyptians stone us? **23** We
must go a three days' journey in the desert to
offer sacrifice to the LORD, our God, as he
commands us." **24** "Well, then," said Pharaoh, "I will let you go to offer sacrifice to the
LORD, your God, in the desert, provided that
you do not go too far away and that you pray for
me." **25** Moses answered, "As soon as I leave
your presence I will pray to the LORD that the
flies may depart tomorrow from Pharaoh and his
servants and his subjects. Pharaoh, however,
must not play false again by refusing to let the
people go to offer sacrifice to the LORD."
**26** When Moses left Pharaoh's presence, he
prayed to the LORD; **27** and the LORD did as
Moses had asked. He removed the flies from
Pharaoh and his servants and subjects. Not one
remained. **28** But once more Pharaoh became
obdurate and would not let the people go.

## CHAPTER 9

**Fifth Plague: the Pestilence.** **1** Then the
LORD said to Moses, "Go to Pharaoh and tell
him: Thus says the LORD, the God of the Hebrews: Let my people go to worship me. **2** If
you refuse to let them go and persist in holding
them, **3** I warn you, the LORD will afflict all
your livestock in the field—your horses, asses,
camels, herds and flocks—with a very severe
pestilence. **4** But the LORD will distinguish between the livestock of Israel and that of Egypt,
so that none belonging to the Israelites will
die." **5** And setting a definite time, the LORD
added, "Tomorrow the LORD shall do this in the
land." **6** And on the next day the LORD did so.
All the livestock of the Egyptians died,[z] but not
one beast belonging to the Israelites. **7** But
though Pharaoh's messengers informed him that
not even one beast belonging to the Israelites
had died, he still remained obdurate and would
not let the people go.

**Sixth Plague: the Boils.** **8** Then the LORD
said to Moses and Aaron, "Take a double handful of soot from a furnace, and in the presence
of Pharaoh let Moses scatter it toward the sky.
**9** It will then turn into fine dust over the whole
land of Egypt and cause festering boils on man
and beast throughout the land."

**10** So they took soot from a furnace and
stood in the presence of Pharaoh. Moses scattered it toward the sky, and it caused festering
boils on man and beast. **11** The magicians
could not stand in Moses' presence, for there
were boils on the magicians no less than on the
rest of the Egyptians. **12** But the LORD made
Pharaoh obstinate, and he would not listen to
them, just as the LORD had foretold to Moses.

**Seventh Plague: the Hail.** **13** Then the
LORD told Moses, "Early tomorrow morning
present yourself to Pharaoh and say to him:
Thus says the LORD, the God of the Hebrews:
Let my people go to worship me, **14** or this time
I will hurl all my blows upon you and your
servants and your subjects, that you may know
that there is none like me anywhere on earth.
**15** For by now I would have stretched out my
hand and struck you and your subjects with such
pestilence as would wipe you from the earth.
**16** But this is why I have spared you: to show
you* my power and to make my name resound
throughout the earth![a] **17** Will you still block
the way for my people by refusing to let them
go? **18** I warn you, then, tomorrow at this hour
I will rain down such fierce hail as there has
never been in Egypt from the day the nation was
founded up to the present. **19** Therefore, order
all your livestock and whatever else you have in
the open fields to be brought to a place of safety.
Whatever man or beast remains in the fields and
is not brought to shelter shall die when the hail
comes upon them." **20** Some of Pharaoh's servants feared the warning of the LORD and hurried their servants and livestock off to shelter.
**21** Others, however, did not take the warning
of the LORD to heart and left their servants and
livestock in the fields.

**22** The LORD then said to Moses, "Stretch
out your hand toward the sky, that hail may fall
upon the entire land of Egypt, on man and beast
and every growing thing in the land of Egypt."
**23** When Moses stretched out his staff toward
the sky, the LORD sent forth hail[b] and peals of
thunder. Lightning flashed toward the earth,

y Pss 78, 45; 105, 31; Wis 16, 9.
z Ps 78, 48.
a Rom 9, 17.
b 23f: Pss 78, 47; 105, 32f.

*

8, 22: The Egyptians would fiercely resent the sacrifice of any animal they considered sacred. Certain animals were worshiped in Egypt, at least as the symbols of various deities.

9, 16: To show you: some ancient versions read, "to show through you." Cf Rom 9, 17.

and the LORD rained down hail upon the land of
Egypt; **24** and lightning constantly flashed
through the hail, such fierce hail as had never
been seen in the land since Egypt became a
nation. **25** It struck down every man and beast
that was in the open throughout the land of
Egypt; it beat down every growing thing and
splintered every tree in the fields. **26** Only in
the land of Goshen, where the Israelites dwelt,
was there no hail.

**27** Then Pharaoh summoned Moses and Aaron and said to them, "I have sinned again! The
LORD is just; it is I and my subjects who are at
fault. **28** Pray to the LORD, for we have had
enough of God's thunder and hail. Then I will
let you go; you need stay no longer." **29** Moses
replied, "As soon as I leave the city I will
extend my hands to the LORD; the thunder will
cease, and there will be no more hail. Thus you
shall learn that the earth is the LORD's. **30** But
you and your servants, I know, do not yet fear
the LORD God."

**31** Now the flax and the barley were ruined,
because the barley was in ear and the flax in
bud. **32** But the wheat and the spelt were not
ruined, for they grow later.

**33** When Moses had left Pharaoh's presence
and had gone out of the city, he extended his
hands to the LORD. Then the thunder and the hail
ceased, and the rain no longer poured down
upon the earth. **34** But Pharaoh, seeing that the
rain and hail and thunder had ceased, sinned
again: he with his servants became obdurate,
**35** and in his obstinacy he would not let the
Israelites go, as the LORD had foretold through
Moses.

## CHAPTER 10

**Eighth Plague: the Locusts.** **1** Then the
LORD said to Moses, "Go to Pharaoh, for I have
made him and his servants obdurate in order that
I may perform these signs of mine among them
**2** and that you may recount to your son and
grandson how ruthlessly I dealt with the Egyptians and what signs I wrought among them, so
that you may know that I am the LORD."[c]

**3** So Moses and Aaron went to Pharaoh and
told him, "Thus says the LORD, the God of the
Hebrews: How long will you refuse to submit to
me? Let my people go to worship me. **4** If you
refuse to let my people go, I warn you, tomorrow I will bring locusts into your country.
**5** They shall cover the ground, so that the
ground itself will not be visible. They shall eat
up the remnant you saved unhurt from the hail,
as well as the foliage that has since sprouted in
your fields. **6** They shall fill your houses and
the houses of your servants and of all the Egyptians; such a sight your fathers or grandfathers
have not seen from the day they first settled on
this soil up to the present day." With that he
turned and left Pharaoh.

**7** But Pharaoh's servants said to him, "How
long must he be a menace to us? Let the men go
to worship the LORD, their God. Do you not yet
realize that Egypt is being destroyed?" **8** So
Moses and Aaron were brought back to Pharaoh, who said to them, "You may go and worship the LORD, your God. But how many of you
will go?" **9** "Young and old must go with us,"
Moses answered, "our sons and daughters as
well as our flocks and herds must accompany
us. That is what a feast of the LORD means to
us." **10** "The LORD help you,"* Pharaoh replied, "if I ever let your little ones go with you!
Clearly, you have some evil in mind. **11** No,
no! Just you men can go and worship the
LORD.* After all, that is what you want." With
that they were driven from Pharaoh's presence.

**12** The LORD then said to Moses, "Stretch
out your hand over the land of Egypt, that locusts[d] may swarm over it and eat up all the
vegetation and whatever the hail has left."
**13** So Moses stretched out his staff over the
land of Egypt, and the LORD sent an east wind*
blowing over the land all that day and all that
night. At dawn the east wind brought the locusts. **14** They swarmed over the whole land of
Egypt and settled down on every part of it.
Never before had there been such a fierce swarm
of locusts, nor will there ever be. **15** They covered the surface of the whole land, till it was
black with them. They ate up all the vegetation
in the land and the fruit of whatever trees the
hail had spared. Nothing green was left on any
tree or plant throughout the land of Egypt.

**16** Hastily Pharaoh summoned Moses and
Aaron and said, "I have sinned against the
LORD, your God, and against you. **17** But now,
do forgive me my sin once more, and pray the
LORD, your God, to take at least this deadly pest
from me." **18** When Moses left the presence of
Pharaoh, he prayed to the LORD, **19** and the
LORD changed the wind to a very strong west
wind, which took up the locusts and hurled them
into the Red Sea.* But though not a single locust
remained within the confines of Egypt, **20** the

c Dt 6, 20ff.
d 12ff: Pss 78, 46; 105, 34f.

*

10, 10: The Lord help you . . . : literally, "May the LORD be with you in the same way as I let you . . ."; a sarcastic blessing intended as a curse.

10, 11: Pharaoh realized that if the men alone went they would have to return to their families. He suspected that the Hebrews had no intention of returning.

10, 13: East wind: coming across the desert from Arabia, the strong east wind brings Egypt the burning sirocco and, at times, locusts. Cf Ex 14, 21.

10, 19: The Red Sea: according to the traditional translation, but the Hebrew is literally, "the Reed Sea"; hence the Red Sea of Exodus was probably a body of shallow water somewhat to the north of the present deep Red Sea.

LORD made Pharaoh obstinate, and he would not let the Israelites go.

**Ninth Plague: the Darkness.** **21** Then the LORD said to Moses, "Stretch out your hand toward the sky, that over the land of Egypt there may be such intense darkness* that one can feel it." **22** So Moses stretched out his hand toward the sky, and there was dense darkness[e] throughout the land of Egypt for three days. **23** Men could not see one another, nor could they move from where they were, for three days. But all the Israelites had light where they dwelt.

**24** Pharaoh then summoned Moses and Aaron and said, "Go and worship the LORD. Your little ones, too, may go with you. But your flocks and herds must remain." **25** Moses replied, "You must also grant us sacrifices and holocausts to offer up to the LORD, our God. **26** Hence, our livestock also must go with us. Not an animal must be left behind. Some of them we must sacrifice to the LORD, our God, but we ourselves shall not know which ones we must sacrifice to him until we arrive at the place itself." **27** But the LORD made Pharaoh obstinate, and he would not let them go. **28** "Leave my presence," Pharaoh said to him, "and see to it that you do not appear before me again! The day you appear before me you shall die!" **29** Moses replied, "Well said! I will never appear before you again."

## CHAPTER 11

**Tenth Plague: the Death of the First-born.** **1** Then the LORD told Moses, "One more plague will I bring upon Pharaoh and upon Egypt. After that he will let you depart. In fact, he will not merely let you go; he will drive you away. **2** Instruct your people that every man is to ask his neighbor, and every woman her neighbor, for silver and gold articles and for clothing."[f] **3** The LORD indeed made the Egyptians well-disposed toward the people; Moses himself was very highly regarded by Pharaoh's servants and the people in the land of Egypt.

**4** Moses then said, "Thus says the LORD: At midnight I will go forth through Egypt.[g] **5** Every first-born in this land shall die,[h] from the first-born of Pharaoh on the throne to the first-born of the slave-girl at the handmill, as well as all the first-born of the animals. **6** Then there shall be loud wailing throughout the land of Egypt, such as has never been, nor will ever be again. **7** But among the Israelites and their animals not even a dog shall growl, so that you may know how the LORD distinguishes between the Egyptians and the Israelites. **8** [i]All these servants of yours shall then come down to me, and prostrate before me, they shall beg me, 'Leave us, you and all your followers!' Only then will I depart." With that he left Pharaoh's presence in hot anger.

**9** The LORD said to Moses, "Pharaoh refuses to listen to you that my wonders may be multiplied in the land of Egypt." **10** Thus, although Moses and Aaron performed these various wonders in Pharaoh's presence, the LORD made Pharaoh obstinate, and he would not let the Israelites leave his land.

## CHAPTER 12

**The Passover Ritual Prescribed.** **1** The LORD said to Moses and Aaron in the land of Egypt, **2** "This month* shall stand at the head of your calendar; you shall reckon it the first month of the year.[j] **3** Tell the whole community of Israel: On the tenth of this month every one of your families must procure for itself a lamb, one apiece for each household. **4** If a family is too small for a whole lamb, it shall join the nearest household in procuring one and shall share in the lamb* in proportion to the number of persons who partake of it. **5** The lamb must be a year-old male and without blemish. You may take it from either the sheep or the goats. **6** You shall keep it until the fourteenth day of this month, and then, with the whole assembly of Israel present, it shall be slaughtered during the evening twilight. **7** They shall take some of its blood and apply it to the two doorposts and the lintel of every house in which they partake of the lamb. **8** That same night they shall eat its roasted flesh with unleavened bread and bitter herbs. **9** It shall not be eaten raw or boiled, but roasted whole, with its head and shanks and inner organs. **10** None of it must be kept beyond the next morning; whatever is left over in the morning shall be burned up.

**11** "This is how you are to eat it: with your loins girt, sandals on your feet and your staff in hand, you shall eat like those who are in flight. It is the Passover* of the LORD. **12** For on this

e Ps 105, 28.
f 2f: Ex 3, 21f; 12, 35f.
g Ex 12, 12.
h 5f: Ex 12, 29f.
i Ex 12, 31ff.
j 2-20: Lv 23, 5-8; Nm 9, 2-5; 28, 16ff; Dt 16, 1-8.

*

10, 21: Darkness: at times a storm from the south, called the khamsin, blackens the sky of Egypt with sand from the Sahara; the dust in the air is then so thick that the darkness can, in a sense, "be felt."

12, 2: This month: Abib, the month of "ripe grain." Cf Ex 13, 4; 23, 15; 34, 18; Dt 16, 1. It occurred near the vernal equinox, March-April. Later it was known by the Babylonian name of Nisan. Cf Neh 2, 1; Est 3, 7.

12, 4: Share in the lamb: probably, in the expenses of its purchase. Some explain, "reckon for the lamb the number of persons required to eat it." Cf Ex 12, 10.

12, 11: Passover: in Hebrew, pesach, in Aramaic, pascha. In the following verses the same root is used in the verb "to pass over." The word may be originally Egyptian, pesach, "the blow," i.e., the final plague which destroyed the Egyptian first-born.

same night I will go through Egypt, striking
down every first-born of the land, both man and
beast, and executing judgment on all the gods
of Egypt—I, the LORD! **13** But the blood will
mark the houses where you are. Seeing the
blood, I will pass over you; thus, when I strike
the land of Egypt, no destructive blow will
come upon you.[k]

**14** "This day shall be a memorial feast for
you, which all your generations shall celebrate
with pilgrimage to the LORD, as a perpetual
institution. **15** For seven days you must eat unleavened bread. From the very first day you
shall have your houses clear of all leaven. Whoever eats leavened bread from the first day to the
seventh shall be cut off from Israel. **16** On the
first day you shall hold a sacred assembly, and
likewise on the seventh. On these days you shall
not do any sort of work, except to prepare the
food that everyone needs.

**17** "Keep, then, this custom of the unleavened bread.[l] Since it was on this very day that
I brought your ranks out of the land of Egypt,
you must celebrate this day throughout your
generations as a perpetual institution. **18** From
the evening of the fourteenth day of the first
month until the evening of the twenty-first day
of this month you shall eat unleavened bread.
**19** For seven days no leaven may be found in
your houses. Anyone, be he a resident alien or
a native, who eats leavened food shall be cut off
from the community of Israel. **20** Nothing leavened may you eat; wherever you dwell you may
eat only unleavened bread."

**Promulgation of the Passover.** **21** Moses called all the elders of Israel and said to
them, "Go and procure lambs for your families,
and slaughter them as Passover victims.
**22** Then take a bunch of hyssop,* and dipping
it in the blood that is in the basin, sprinkle the
lintel and the two doorposts with this blood.[m]
But none of you shall go outdoors until morning. **23** For the LORD will go by, striking down
the Egyptians. Seeing the blood on the lintel and
the two doorposts, the LORD will pass over that
door and not let the destroyer come into your
houses to strike you down.

**24** "You shall observe this as a perpetual
ordinance for yourselves and your descendants.
**25** Thus, you must also observe this rite when
you have entered the land which the LORD will
give you as he promised. **26** When your children ask you, 'What does this rite of yours
mean?'[n] **27** you shall reply, 'This is the Passover sacrifice of the LORD, who passed over the
houses of the Israelites in Egypt; when he struck
down the Egyptians, he spared our houses.'"

Then the people bowed down in worship,
**28** and the Israelites went and did as the LORD
had commanded Moses and Aaron.

**Death of the First-born.** **29** At midnight
the LORD slew every first-born in the land of
Egypt,[o] from the first-born of Pharaoh on the
throne to the first-born of the prisoner in the
dungeon, as well as all the first-born of the
animals. **30** Pharaoh arose in the night, he and
all his servants and all the Egyptians; and there
was loud wailing throughout Egypt, for there
was not a house without its dead.

**Permission To Depart.** **31** During the
night Pharaoh summoned Moses and Aaron and
said, "Leave my people at once, you and the
Israelites with you! Go and worship the LORD as
you said. **32** Take your flocks, too, and your
herds, as you demanded, and begone; and you
will be doing me a favor."

**33** The Egyptians likewise urged the people
on, to hasten their departure from the land; they
thought that otherwise they would all die.
**34** The people, therefore, took their dough before it was leavened, in their kneading bowls
wrapped in their cloaks on their shoulders.
**35** The Israelites did as Moses had commanded: they asked the Egyptians for articles of silver
and gold and for clothing.[p] **36** The LORD indeed had made the Egyptians so well-disposed
toward the people that they let them have whatever they asked for. Thus did they despoil the
Egyptians.

## *II: The Exodus From Egypt and the Journey to Sinai*

**Departure from Egypt.** **37** The Israelites
set out from Rameses[q] for Succoth, about six
hundred thousand men on foot, not counting the
children. **38** A crowd of mixed ancestry* also
went up with them, besides their livestock, very
numerous flocks and herds. **39** Since the dough
they had brought out of Egypt was not leavened,
they baked it into unleavened loaves. They had
been rushed out of Egypt and had no opportunity even to prepare food for the journey.

**40** The time the Israelites had stayed in
Egypt* was four hundred and thirty years.[r]
**41** At the end of four hundred and thirty years,
all the hosts of the LORD left the land of Egypt

---

k Heb 11, 28.
l Ex 13, 3.
m 22f: Ex 12, 7. 13.
n 26f: Ex 13, 8. 14; Dt 6, 20f.
o 29f: Ex 11, 4ff; Pss 78, 51; 105, 36; 136, 10; Wis 18, 10-16.
p 35f: Ex 3, 21f; 11, 2f; Ps 105, 37f.
q Nm 33, 3ff.
r Gn 15, 13; Acts 7, 6; Gal 3, 17.

---

* 12, 22: Hyssop: a plant with many woody branchlets that make a convenient sprinkler.

12, 38: Mixed ancestry: half-Hebrew and half-Egyptian. Cf Nm 11, 4; Lv 24, 10f.

12, 40: In Egypt: according to some ancient sources, "in Canaan and Egypt," thus reckoning from the time of Abraham. Cf Gal 3, 17.

on this very date. **42** This was a night of vigil for the LORD, as he led them out of the land of Egypt; so on this same night all the Israelites must keep a vigil for the LORD throughout their generations.

**Passover Regulations.** **43** The LORD said to Moses and Aaron, "These are the regulations for the Passover. No foreigner may partake of it. **44** However, any slave who has been bought for money may partake of it, provided you have first circumcised him. **45** But no transient alien or hired servant may partake of it. **46** It must be eaten in one and the same house; you may not take any of its flesh outside the house.[s] You shall not break any of its bones.* **47** The whole community of Israel must keep this feast. **48** If any aliens[t] living among you wish to celebrate the Passover of the LORD, all the males among them must first be circumcised, and then they may join in its observance just like the natives. But no man who is uncircumcised may partake of it. **49** The law shall be the same for the resident alien as for the native."

**50** All the Israelites did just as the LORD had commanded Moses and Aaron. **51** On that same day the LORD brought the Israelites out of Egypt company by company.

## CHAPTER 13

**Consecration of First-born.** **1** The LORD spoke to Moses and said, **2** "Consecrate to me every first-born that opens the womb among the Israelites,[u] both of man and beast, for it belongs to me."

**3** Moses said to the people, "Remember this day on which you came out of Egypt, that place of slavery.[v] It was with a strong hand that the LORD brought you away. Nothing made with leaven must be eaten. **4** This day of your departure is in the month of Abib. **5** Therefore, it is in this month that you must celebrate this rite, after the LORD, your God, has brought you into the land of the Canaanites, Hittites, Amorites, Hivites and Jebusites, which he swore to your fathers he would give you, a land flowing with milk and honey. **6** For seven days you shall eat unleavened bread, and the seventh day shall also be a festival to the LORD. **7** Only unleavened bread may be eaten during the seven days; no leaven and nothing leavened may be found in all your territory. **8** On this day you shall explain to your son, 'This is because of what the LORD did for me when I came out of Egypt.' **9** It shall be as a sign on your hand and as a reminder on your forehead;[w] thus the law of the LORD will ever be on your lips, because with a strong hand the LORD brought you out of Egypt. **10** Therefore, you shall keep this prescribed rite at its appointed time from year to year.

**11** "When the LORD, your God, has brought you into the land of the Canaanites, which he swore to you and your fathers he would give you, **12** you shall dedicate to the LORD every son that opens the womb;[x] and all the male firstlings of your animals shall belong to the LORD. **13** Every first-born of an ass you shall redeem with a sheep. If you do not redeem it, you shall break its neck. Every first-born son you must redeem. **14** If your son should ask you later on, 'What does this mean?' you shall tell him, 'With a strong hand the LORD brought us out of Egypt, that place of slavery. **15** When Pharaoh stubbornly refused to let us go, the LORD killed every first-born in the land of Egypt, every first-born of man and of beast. This is why I sacrifice to the LORD everything of the male sex that opens the womb, and why I redeem every first-born of my sons.' **16** Let this, then, be as a sign on your hand and as a pendant on your forehead: with a strong hand the LORD brought us out of Egypt."[y]

**Toward the Red Sea.** **17** Now, when Pharaoh let the people go, God did not lead them by way of the Philistines' land,* though this was the nearest; for he thought, should the people see that they would have to fight, they might change their minds and return to Egypt. **18** Instead, he rerouted them toward the Red Sea by way of the desert road. In battle array the Israelites marched out of Egypt. **19** Moses also took Joseph's bones[z] along, for Joseph had made the Israelites swear solemnly that, when God should come to them, they would carry his bones away with them.

**20** Setting out from Succoth, they camped at Etham[a] near the edge of the desert.

**21** The Lord preceded them, in the daytime by means of a column of cloud to show them the way, and at night by means of a column of fire* to give them light.[b] Thus they could travel both day and night. **22** Neither the column of cloud

s Nm 9, 12; Jn 19, 36.
t 47f: Nm 9, 14.
u Ex 13, 12-15.
v 3-10: Ex 12, 2-20.
w Ex 13, 16; Dt 6, 8; 11, 18.
x 12-15; Ex 13, 2; 22, 29f; 34, 19f: Nm 3, 12f; 8, 16; 18, 15; Dt 15, 19.
y Ex 13, 9.
z Gn 50, 25; Jos 24, 32.
a Nm 33, 6.
b 21f: Ex 40, 38; Nm 9, 15-22; Dt 1, 33; Neh 9, 19; Pss 78, 14; 105, 39; Wis 10, 17.

*

12, 46: You shall not break any of its bones: the application of these words to our Lord on the cross shows that the Paschal lamb was a prophetic type of Christ, immolated to free men from the bondage of sin. Cf also 1 Cor 5, 7; 1 Pt 1, 19.

13, 17: By way of the Philistines' land: the most direct route from Egypt to Palestine, along the shore of the Mediterranean.

13, 21: A column of cloud . . . a column of fire: probably one and the same preternatural phenomenon, a central nucleus of fire surrounded by smoke; only at night was its luminous nature visible. Cf Ex 40, 38.

by day nor the column of fire by night ever left its place in front of the people.

## CHAPTER 14

**1** Then the LORD said to Moses, **2** *"Tell the Israelites to turn about and camp before Pi-hahiroth, between Migdol and the sea.[c] You shall camp in front of Baal-zephon, just opposite, by the sea. **3** Pharaoh will then say, 'The Israelites are wandering about aimlessly in the land. The desert has closed in on them.' **4** Thus will I make Pharaoh so obstinate that he will pursue them. Then I will receive glory through Pharaoh and all his army, and the Egyptians will know that I am the LORD."

This the Israelites did. **5** When it was reported to the king of Egypt that the people had fled, Pharaoh and his servants changed their minds about them. "What have we done!" they exclaimed. "Why, we have released Israel from our service!" **6** So Pharaoh made his chariots ready and mustered his soldiers— **7** six hundred first-class chariots and all the other chariots of Egypt, with warriors on them all. **8** So obstinate had the LORD made Pharaoh that he pursued[d] the Israelites even while they were marching away in triumph. **9** The Egyptians, then, pursued them; Pharaoh's whole army, his horses, chariots and charioteers, caught up with them as they lay encamped by the sea, at Pi-hahiroth, in front of Baal-zephon.

**Crossing of the Red Sea.** **10** Pharaoh was already near when the Israelites looked up and saw that the Egyptians were on the march in pursuit of them. In great fright they cried out to the LORD. **11** And they complained to Moses, "Were there no burial places in Egypt that you had to bring us out here to die in the desert? Why did you do this to us? Why did you bring us out of Egypt? **12** Did we not tell you this in Egypt, when we said, 'Leave us alone. Let us serve the Egyptians'? Far better for us to be the slaves of the Egyptians than to die in the desert." **13** But Moses answered the people, "Fear not! Stand your ground, and you will see the victory the LORD will win for you today. These Egyptians whom you see today you will never see again. **14** The LORD himself will fight for you; you have only to keep still."

**15** Then the LORD said to Moses, "Why are you crying out to me? Tell the Israelites to go forward. **16** And you, lift up your staff and, with hand outstretched over the sea, split the sea in two, that the Israelites may pass through it on dry land. **17** But I will make the Egyptians so obstinate that they will go in after them. Then I will receive glory through Pharaoh and all his army, his chariots and charioteers. **18** The Egyptians shall know that I am the LORD, when I receive glory through Pharaoh and his chariots and charioteers."

**19** The angel of God, who had been leading Israel's camp, now moved and went around behind them. The column of cloud also, leaving the front, took up its place behind them, **20** so that it came between the camp of the Egyptians and that of Israel. But the cloud now became dark,* and thus the night passed without the rival camps coming any closer together all night long. **21** Then Moses stretched out his hand over the sea, and the LORD swept the sea with a strong east wind throughout the night and so turned it into dry land.[e] When the water was thus divided, **22** the Israelites marched into the midst of the sea on dry land, with the water like a wall to their right and to their left.

**Destruction of the Egyptians.** **23** The Egyptians followed in pursuit; all Pharaoh's horses and chariots and charioteers went after them right into the midst of the sea. **24** In the night watch just before dawn the LORD cast through the column of the fiery cloud upon the Egyptian force a glance that threw it into panic; **25** and he so clogged their chariot wheels that they could hardly drive. With that the Egyptians sounded the retreat before Israel, because the LORD was fighting for them against the Egyptians.

**26** Then the LORD told Moses, "Stretch out your hand over the sea, that the water may flow back upon the Egyptians, upon their chariots and their charioteers." **27** So Moses stretched out his hand over the sea, and at dawn the sea flowed back to its normal depth. The Egyptians were fleeing head on toward the sea, when the LORD hurled them into its midst. **28** As the water flowed back, it covered the chariots and the charioteers of Pharaoh's whole army[f] which had followed the Israelites into the sea. Not a single one of them escaped. **29** But the Israelites had marched on dry land through the midst of the sea, with the water like a wall to their right and to their left. **30** Thus the LORD saved Israel on that day from the power of the Egyptians. When Israel saw the Egyptians lying dead

c Nm 33, 7f.
d 5-8: Wis 19, 3; 1 Mc 4, 9.
e 21f: Ex 15, 19; Pss 66, 6; 78, 13; 136, 13f; Wis 10, 18; 19, 7f; Is 63, 12f; Heb 11, 29.
f 28f: Dt 11, 4; Ps 106, 11.

*

14, 2: These places have not been definitively identified. Even the relative position of Pi-hahiroth and Baal-zephon is not clear; perhaps the former was on the west shore of the sea, where the Israelites were, and the latter on the opposite shore.

14, 20: The cloud now became dark: the light which it ordinarily cast at night would now have been a help to the Egyptians; its present obscurity serves as a shield for the Israelites. However, the reading of the original text here is not quite certain.

on the seashore 31 and beheld the great power
that the LORD had shown against the Egyptians,
they feared the LORD and believed in him[g] and
in his servant Moses.

## CHAPTER 15

1 Then Moses and the Israelites sang[h] this
song to the LORD:*

I will sing to the LORD, for he is gloriously
triumphant;
horse and chariot he has cast into the sea.
2 My strength and my courage is the LORD,
and he has been my savior.
He is my God, I praise him;
the God of my father, I extol him.[i]
3 The LORD is a warrior,
LORD is his name!
4 Pharaoh's chariots and army he hurled into
the sea;
the elite of his officers were submerged in
the Red Sea.

5 The flood waters covered them,
they sank into the depths like a stone.[j]

6 Your right hand, O LORD, magnificent in
power,
your right hand, O LORD, has shattered
the enemy.
7 In your great majesty you overthrew your
adversaries;
you loosed your wrath to consume them
like stubble.
8 At a breath of your anger the waters piled
up,
the flowing waters stood like a mound,
the flood waters congealed in the midst of
the sea.

9 The enemy boasted, "I will pursue and
overtake them;
I will divide the spoils and have my fill of
them;
I will draw my sword; my hand shall
despoil them!"
10 When your wind blew, the sea covered
them;
like lead they sank in the mighty waters.

11 Who is like to you among the gods, O
LORD?
Who is like to you, magnificent in
holiness?
O terrible in renown, worker of wonders,
12 when you stretched out your right hand,
the earth swallowed them!
13 In your mercy you led the people you
redeemed;
in your strength you guided them to your
holy dwelling.
14 The nations heard and quaked:
anguish gripped the dwellers in Philistia.
15 Then were the princes of Edom dismayed;
trembling seized the chieftains of Moab;
All the dwellers in Canaan melted away;
16 terror and dread fell upon them.[k]
By the might of your arm they were frozen
like stone,
while your people, O LORD, passed over,
while the people you had made your own
passed over.

17 And you brought them in and planted them
on the mountain of your inheritance—
the place where you made your seat, O
LORD,
the sanctuary, O LORD, which your hands
established.

18 The LORD shall reign forever and ever.

19 They sang thus because Pharaoh's horses
and chariots and charioteers had gone into the
sea, and the LORD made the waters of the sea
flow back upon them, though the Israelites had
marched on dry land through the midst of the
sea.[l] 20 The prophetess Miriam, Aaron's sister, took a tambourine in her hand, while all the
women went out after her with tambourines,
dancing; 21 and she led them* in the refrain:

Sing to the LORD, for he is gloriously
triumphant;
horse and chariot he has cast into the
sea.[m]

**At Marah and Elim.** 22 [n]Then Moses led
Israel forward from the Red Sea, and they
marched out to the desert of Shur. After traveling for three days through the desert without
finding water, 23 they arrived at Marah, where
they could not drink the water, because it was
too bitter. Hence this place was called Marah.
24 As the people grumbled against Moses, saying, "What are we to drink?" 25 he appealed
to the LORD, who pointed out to him a certain
piece of wood. When he threw this into the
water, the water became fresh.[o]

It was here that the LORD, in making rules and
regulations for them, put them to the test.
26 "If you really listen to the voice of the
LORD, your God," he told them, "and do what
is right in his eyes: if you heed his commandments and keep all his precepts, I will not afflict

g 31f: Ps 106, 12; Wis 10, 20.
h Ex 15, 21.
i Ps 118, 14; Is 12, 2.
j Neh 9, 11.
k 16f: Ps 78, 53ff.
l Ex 14, 21-29.
m Ex 15, 1.
n 22f: Nm 33, 8.
o Sir 38, 5.
p Dt 7, 15.

*

15, 1–21: This canticle (used in Christian liturgy) celebrates God's saving power, miraculously delivering his people from their enemies, and leading them to the victorious conquest of the Promised Land.

15, 21: She led them: Miriam's refrain re-echoes the first verse of this song and was probably sung as an antiphon after each verse.

you with any of the diseases with which I afflicted the Egyptians;[p] for I, the LORD, am your healer."

**27** Then they came to Elim, where there were twelve springs of water and seventy palm trees, and they camped there near the water.[q]

## CHAPTER 16

**The Desert of Sin.** **1** Having set out from Elim, the whole Israelite community came into the desert of Sin, which is between Elim and Sinai, on the fifteenth day of the second month* after their departure from the land of Egypt. **2** Here in the desert the whole Israelite community grumbled against Moses and Aaron. **3** The Israelites said to them, "Would that we had died at the LORD's hand in the land of Egypt, as we sat by our fleshpots and ate our fill of bread! But you had to lead us into this desert to make the whole community die of famine!"

**The Quail and Manna.** **4** Then the LORD said to Moses,[r] "I will now rain down bread from heaven* for you. Each day the people are to go out and gather their daily portion; thus will I test them, to see whether they follow my instructions or not. **5** On the sixth day, however, when they prepare what they bring in, let it be twice as much as they gather on the other days." **6** So Moses and Aaron told all the Israelites, "At evening you will know that it was the LORD who brought you out of the land of Egypt; **7** and in the morning you will see the glory of the LORD, as he heeds your grumbling against him.[s] But what are we that you should grumble against us? **8** When the LORD gives you flesh to eat in the evening," continued Moses, "and in the morning your fill of bread, as he heeds the grumbling you utter against him, what then are we? Your grumbling is not against us, but against the LORD."

**9** Then Moses said to Aaron, "Tell the whole Israelite community: Present yourselves before the LORD, for he has heard your grumbling." **10** When Aaron announced this to the whole Israelite community, they turned toward the desert, and lo, the glory of the LORD appeared in the cloud! **11** The LORD spoke to Moses and said, **12** "I have heard the grumbling of the Israelites. Tell them: In the evening twilight you shall eat flesh, and in the morning you shall have your fill of bread, so that you may know that I, the LORD, am your God."

**13** In the evening quail[t] came up and covered the camp. In the morning a dew lay all about the camp, **14** and when the dew evaporated, there on the surface of the desert were fine flakes like hoarfrost on the ground. **15** On seeing it, the Israelites asked one another, "What is this?"* for they did not know what it was. But Moses told them, "This is the bread which the LORD has given you to eat.[u]

**Regulations Regarding the Manna.** **16** "Now, this is what the LORD has commanded. So gather it that everyone has enough to eat, an omer for each person, as many of you as there are, each man providing for those of his own tent." **17** The Israelites did so. Some gathered a large and some a small amount. **18** *But when they measured it out by the omer, he who had gathered a large amount did not have too much, and he who had gathered a small amount did not have too little.[v] They so gathered that everyone had enough to eat. **19** Moses also told them, "Let no one keep any of it over until tomorrow morning." **20** But they would not listen to him. When some kept a part of it over until the following morning, it became wormy and rotten. Therefore Moses was displeased with them.

**21** Morning after morning they gathered it, till each had enough to eat; but when the sun grew hot, the manna melted away. **22** On the sixth day they gathered twice as much food, two omers for each person. When all the leaders of the community came and reported this to Moses, **23** he told them, "That is what the LORD prescribed. Tomorrow is a day of complete rest, the sabbath, sacred to the LORD. You may either bake or boil the manna, as you please; but whatever is left put away and keep for the morrow." **24** When they put it away for the morrow, as Moses commanded, it did not become rotten or wormy. **25** Moses then said, "Eat it today, for today is the sabbath of the LORD. On this day you will not find any of it on the ground. **26** On the other six days you can gather it, but on the seventh day, the sabbath, none of it will be there." **27** Still, on the seventh day some of the people went out to gather it, although they did

q Nm 33, 9.
r Pss 78, 24f; 105, 40; Jn 6, 31f; 1 Cor 10, 3.
s 6f: Ex 16, 12.
t Nm 11, 31; Ps 78, 27f.
u Dt 8, 3.
v 2 Cor 8, 15.

*

16, 1: On the fifteenth day of the second month: just one full month after their departure from Egypt. Cf Ex 12, 2. 51; Nm 33, 3f They encamped in the desert of Sin on a Friday; the murmuring (vv 2f) occurred on the sabbath, the arrival of the quail (v 13) the evening before Sunday, followed by six mornings (vv 14–27) of collecting manna before the next sabbath.

16, 4: Bread from heaven: as a gift from God, the manna is said to come down from the sky. Cf Ps 78, 25; Wis 16, 20. Perhaps it was similar to a natural substance that is still found in small quantities on the Sinai peninsula, but here it is, at least in part, clearly miraculous. Our Lord referred to the manna as a type of the Blessed Eucharist. Cf Jn 6, 32. 49–52.

16, 15: What is this: the original man hu is thus rendered by the ancient versions, which understood the phrase as a popular etymology of the Hebrew word man, "manna"; some render, "This is manna."

16, 18: St. Paul cites this passage as an example of equitable sharing. Cf 2 Cor 8, 15.

not find any. **28** Then the LORD said to Moses,
"How long will you refuse to keep my commandments and laws? **29** Take note! The LORD
has given you the sabbath. That is why on the
sixth day he gives you food for two days. On the
seventh day everyone is to stay home and no one
is to go out." **30** After that the people rested on
the seventh day.

**31** The Israelites called this food manna.[w] It
was like coriander seed,* but white, and it tasted like wafers made with honey.

**32** Moses said, "This is what the LORD has
commanded. Keep an omerful of manna for
your descendants, that they may see what food
I gave you to eat in the desert when I brought
you out of the land of Egypt." **33** Moses then
told Aaron, "Take an urn* and put an omer of
manna in it. Then place it before the LORD in
safekeeping for your descendants."[x] **34** So
Aaron placed it in front of the commandments*
for safekeeping, as the LORD had commanded
Moses.

**35** The Israelites ate this manna for forty
years, until they came to settled land;[y] they ate
manna until they reached the borders of Canaan.
**36** [An omer is one tenth of an ephah.]

## CHAPTER 17

**Water from the Rock.** **1** From the desert
of Sin the whole Israelite community journeyed
by stages, as the LORD directed, and encamped
at Rephidim.[z]

Here there was no water for the people to
drink. **2** They quarreled, therefore, with Moses
and said, "Give us water to drink."[a] Moses
replied, "Why do you quarrel with me? Why do
you put the LORD to a test?" **3** Here, then, in
their thirst for water, the people grumbled
against Moses, saying, "Why did you ever
make us leave Egypt? Was it just to have us die
here of thirst with our children and our livestock?" **4** So Moses cried out to the LORD,
"What shall I do with this people? A little more
and they will stone me!" **5** The LORD answered
Moses, "Go over there in front of the people,
along with some of the elders of Israel, holding
in your hand, as you go, the staff with which
you struck the river. **6** I will be standing there
in front of you on the rock in Horeb. Strike the
rock, and the water will flow from it for the
people to drink."[b] This Moses did, in the presence of the elders of Israel. **7** The place was
called Massah and Meribah,* because the Israelites quarreled there and tested the LORD, saying, "Is the LORD in our midst or not?"[c]

**Battle with Amalek.** **8** At Rephidim, Amalek* came and waged war against Israel.[d]
**9** Moses, therefore, said to Joshua, "Pick out
certain men, and tomorrow go out and engage
Amalek in battle. I will be standing on top of the
hill with the staff of God in my hand." **10** So
Joshua did as Moses told him: he engaged Amalek in battle after Moses had climbed to the top
of the hill with Aaron and Hur. **11** As long as
Moses kept his hands raised up, Israel had the
better of the fight, but when he let his hands
rest, Amalek had the better of the fight. **12** Moses' hands, however, grew tired; so they put a
rock in place for him to sit on. Meanwhile Aaron and Hur supported his hands, one on one side
and one on the other, so that his hands remained
steady till sunset. **13** And Joshua mowed down
Amalek and his people with the edge of the
sword.

**14** Then the LORD said to Moses, "Write this
down in a document as something to be remembered, and recite it in the ears of Joshua.[e] I will
completely blot out the memory of Amalek
from under the heavens." **15** Moses also built
an altar there, which he called Yahweh-nissi;*
**16** for he said, "The LORD takes in hand his
banner; the LORD will war against Amalek
through the centuries."

## CHAPTER 18

**Meeting with Jethro.** **1** Now Moses' father-in-law Jethro, the priest of Midian, heard
of all that God had done for Moses and for his
people Israel: how the LORD had brought Israel
out of Egypt. **2** So his father-in-law Jethro took
along Zipporah, Moses' wife, whom Moses had
sent back to him, **3** and her two sons. One of
these was called Gershom;[f] for he said, "I am
a stranger in a foreign land." **4** The other was
called Eliezer; for he said, "My father's God is
my helper; he has rescued me from Pharaoh's
sword." **5** Together with Moses' wife and
sons, then, his father-in-law Jethro came to him
in the desert where he was encamped near the
mountain of God, **6** and he sent word to Moses,
"I, Jethro, your father-in-law, am coming to

w Nm 11, 7.
x Heb 9, 4.
y Jos 5, 12.
z Nm 33, 12ff.
a 2-7: Nm 20, 2-13.
b 5f: Dt 8, 15; Pss 78, 15f; 105, 41; Wis 11, 4; Is 43, 20; 48, 21.
c Ps 95, 8f.
d Dt 25, 17; 1 Sm 15, 2.
e Nm 24, 20; 1 Sm 15, 3. 20.
f Ex 2, 22.

*

16, 31: Coriander seed: small, round, aromatic seeds of bright brown color; the comparison, therefore, refers merely to the size and shape, not to the taste or color of the manna.

16, 33: Urn: according to the Greek translation, which is followed in Heb 9, 4, this was a golden vessel.

16, 34: The commandments: the two tablets of the ten commandments, which were kept in the ark. Cf Ex 25, 16. 21f.

17, 7: Massah ... Meribah: Hebrew words meaning respectively, "the (place of the) test," and "the (place of the) quarreling."

17, 8: Amalek: the Amalekites were an aboriginal people of southern Palestine and the Sinai peninsula. Cf Nm 24, 20.

17, 15: Yahweh-nissi: meaning, "the LORD is my banner."

you, along with your wife and her two sons."
**7** Moses went out to meet his father-in-law,
bowed down before him, and kissed him. Having greeted each other, they went into the tent.
**8** Moses then told his father-in-law of all that
the LORD had done to Pharaoh and the Egyptians
for the sake of Israel, and of all the hardships
they had had to endure on their journey, and
how the LORD had come to their rescue. **9** Jethro rejoiced over all the goodness that the LORD
had shown Israel in rescuing them from the
hands of the Egyptians. **10** "Blessed be the
LORD," he said, "who has rescued his people
from the hands of Pharaoh and the Egyptians.
**11** Now I know that the LORD is a deity great
beyond any other; for he took occasion of their
being dealt with insolently to deliver the people
from the power of the Egyptians." **12** Then
Jethro, the father-in-law of Moses, brought a
holocaust and other sacrifices to God, and Aaron came with all the elders of Israel to participate with Moses' father-in-law in the meal before God.

**Appointment of Minor Judges.** **13** The
next day Moses sat in judgment for the people,
who waited about him from morning until evening. **14** When his father-in-law saw all that he
was doing for the people, he inquired, "What
sort of thing is this that you are doing for the
people? Why do you sit alone while all the
people have to stand about you from morning
till evening?" **15** Moses answered his father-
in-law, "The people come to me to consult
God. **16** Whenever they have a disagreement,
they come to me to have me settle the matter
between them and make known to them God's
decisions and regulations."
**17** "You are not acting wisely," his father-in-law replied. **18** "You will surely wear
yourself out, and not only yourself but also
these people with you. The task is too heavy for
you;[g] you cannot do it alone. **19** Now, listen to
me, and I will give you some advice, that God
may be with you. Act as the people's representative before God, bringing to him whatever
they have to say. **20** Enlighten them in regard
to the decisions and regulations, showing them
how they are to live and what they are to do.
**21** But you should also look among all the people for able and God-fearing men, trustworthy
men who hate dishonest gain, and set them as
officers over groups of thousands, of hundreds,
of fifties, and of tens.[h] **22** Let these men render
decisions for the people in all ordinary cases.
More important cases they should refer to you,
but all the lesser cases they can settle themselves. Thus, your burden will be lightened,
since they will bear it with you. **23** If you do
this, when God gives you orders you will be
able to stand the strain, and all these people will
go home satisfied."
**24** Moses followed the advice of his father-in-law and did all that he had suggested.
**25** He picked out able men from all Israel and
put them in charge of the people as officers over
groups of thousands, of hundreds, of fifties, and
of tens. **26** They rendered decisions for the people in all ordinary cases. The more difficult
cases they referred to Moses, but all the lesser
cases they settled themselves. **27** Then Moses
bade farewell to his father-in-law, who went off
to his own country.

## *III: The Covenant at Mount Sinai*

## CHAPTER 19

**Arrival at Sinai.** **1** [i]In the third month after
their departure from the land of Egypt, on its
first day, the Israelites came to the desert of
Sinai. **2** After the journey from Rephidim to the
desert of Sinai, they pitched camp.
While Israel was encamped here in front of
the mountain, **3** Moses went up the mountain to
God. Then the LORD called to him and said,
"Thus shall you say to the house of Jacob; **4** tell
the Israelites: You have seen for yourselves how
I treated the Egyptians and how I bore you up
on eagle wings and brought you here to myself.[j]
**5** Therefore, if you hearken to my voice and
keep my covenant, you shall be my special possession, dearer to me than all other people,[k]
though all the earth is mine. **6** You shall be to
me a kingdom of priests,* a holy nation.[l] That
is what you must tell the Israelites." **7** So Moses went and summoned the elders of the people. When he set before them all that the LORD
had ordered him to tell them, **8** the people all
answered together, "Everything the LORD has
said, we will do." Then Moses brought back to
the LORD the response of the people.
**9** The LORD also told him, "I am coming to
you in a dense cloud,[m] so that when the people
hear me speaking with you, they may always
have faith in you also." When Moses, then, had
reported to the LORD the response of the people,
**10** the LORD added, "Go to the people and have

g Nm 11, 14.
h 21. 25: Dt 1, 15; 16, 18.
i 1f: Nm 33, 15.
j Dt 32, 11.
k Dt 7, 6; 14, 2; 26, 18f; 32, 8f.
l 1 Pt 2, 9.
m Ex 20, 21; 24, 15-18.

*

19, 6: Kingdom of priests: inasmuch as the whole Israelite nation was consecrated to God in a special way, it formed a race of royal priests who participated in the liturgical sacrifices, even though the actual offering of the sacrifices was the exclusive prerogative of the Aaronic priesthood. The same condition exists in the New Dispensation as regards the whole Christian people and the Christian priesthood in the strict sense. Cf Is 61, 6; 1 Pt 2, 5. 9.

them sanctify themselves today and tomorrow. Make them wash their garments **11** and be ready for the third day; for on the third day the LORD will come down on Mount Sinai before the eyes of all the people. **12** Set limits for the people all around the mountain,[n] and tell them: Take care not to go up the mountain, or even to touch its base. If anyone touches the mountain he must be put to death. **13** No hand shall touch him; he must be stoned to death or killed with arrows. Such a one, man or beast, must not be allowed to live. Only when the ram's horn resounds may they go up to the mountain." **14** Then Moses came down from the mountain to the people and had them sanctify themselves and wash their garments. **15** He warned them, "Be ready for the third day. Have no intercourse with any woman."

**The Great Theophany.** **16** On the morning of the third day there were peals of thunder and lightning, and a heavy cloud over the mountain, and a very loud trumpet blast, so that all the people in the camp trembled. **17** But Moses let the people out of the camp to meet God, and they stationed themselves at the foot of the mountain.[o] **18** Mount Sinai was all wrapped in smoke, for the LORD came down upon it in fire. The smoke rose from it as though from a furnace, and the whole mountain trembled violently. **19** The trumpet blast grew louder and louder, while Moses was speaking and God answering him with thunder.

**20** When the LORD came down to the top of Mount Sinai, he summoned Moses to the top of the mountain, and Moses went up to him. **21** Then the LORD told Moses, "Go down and warn the people not to break through toward the LORD in order to see him; otherwise many of them will be struck down. **22** The priests, too, who approach the LORD must sanctify themselves; else he will vent his anger upon them." **23** Moses said to the LORD, "The people cannot go up to Mount Sinai, for you yourself warned us to set limits around the mountain to make it sacred." **24** The LORD repeated, "Go down now! Then come up again along with Aaron. But the priests and the people must not break through to come up to the LORD; else he will vent his anger upon them." **25** So Moses went down to the people and told them this.

## CHAPTER 20

**The Ten Commandments.** **1** Then God delivered all these commandments:*

**2** [p]"I, the LORD, am your God, who brought you out of the land of Egypt,[q] that place of slavery. **3** You shall not have other gods besides me. **4** You shall not carve idols[r] for yourselves in the shape of anything in the sky above or on the earth below or in the waters beneath the earth; **5** you shall not bow down before them or worship them.[s] For I, the LORD, your God, am a jealous* God, inflicting punishment for their fathers' wickedness on the children of those who hate me, down to the third and fourth generation; **6** but bestowing mercy down to the thousandth generation, on the children of those who love me and keep my commandments.

**7** "You shall not take the name of the LORD, your God, in vain.[t] For the LORD will not leave unpunished him who takes his name in vain.

**8** "Remember to keep holy the sabbath day. **9** Six days you may labor and do all your work, **10** but the seventh day is the sabbath of the LORD, your God.[u] No work may be done then either by you, or your son or daughter, or your male or female slave, or your beast, or by the alien who lives with you. **11** In six days the LORD made the heavens and the earth, the sea and all that is in them; but on the seventh day he rested.[v] That is why the LORD has blessed the sabbath day and made it holy.

**12** [w]"Honor your father and your mother, that you may have a long life in the land which the Lord, your God, is giving you.[x]

**13** "You shall not kill.[y]

**14** "You shall not commit adultery.[z]

**15** "You shall not steal.[a]

**16** "You shall not bear false witness against your neighbor.[b]

**17** "You shall not covet your neighbor's house. You shall not covet your neighbor's wife, nor his male or female slave, nor his ox or ass, nor anything else that belongs to him."[c]

**The Fear of God.** **18** When the people witnessed the thunder and lightning, the trumpet blast and the mountain smoking, they all feared and trembled.[d] So they took up a position much farther away **19** and said to Moses, "You speak to us, and we will listen; but let not God speak to us, or we shall die." **20** Moses answered the

n 12f: Ex 34, 3; Heb 12, 18f.
o 16ff: Dt 4, 10ff.
p 2-17: Dt 5, 6-21.
q Lv 26, 13; Ps 81, 10; Hos 13, 4.
r Ex 34, 17; Lv 26, 1; Dt 4, 15-19; 27, 15.
s Ex 34, 7. 14; Nm 14, 18; Dt 4, 24; 6, 15.
t Lv 19, 12; 24, 16.
u 8ff: Ex 23, 12; 31, 13-16; 34, 21; 35, 2; Lv 23, 3.
v Ex 31, 17; Gn 2, 2f.
w 12-16: Mt 19, 18f; Mk 10, 19; Lk 18, 20; Rom 13, 9.
x Mt 15, 4; Mk 7, 10; Eph 6, 2f.
y Mt 5, 21.
z Lv 18, 20; 20, 10; Dt 22, 22; Mt 5, 27.
a Lv 19, 11.
b Ex 23, 1; Dt 19, 16ff; Prv 19, 5. 9; 24, 28.
c Rom 7, 7.
d 18-21: Dt 4, 11; 5, 22-27; 18, 16; Heb 12, 18f.

*

20, 1–17: the precise division of these precepts into "ten commandments" is somewhat uncertain. Traditionally among Catholics vv 1–6 are considered as only one commandment, and v 17 as two. Cf Dt 5, 6–21.

20, 5: Jealous: demanding exclusive allegiance, such as a wife must have for her husband.

people, "Do not be afraid, for God has come to
you only to test you and put his fear upon you,
lest you should sin." **21** Still the people remained at a distance, while Moses approached
the cloud where God was.

**22** The LORD told Moses, "Thus shall you
speak to the Israelites: You have seen for yourselves that I have spoken to you from heaven.
**23** Do not make anything to rank with me; neither gods of silver nor gods of gold shall you
make for yourselves.[e]

**24** "An altar of earth you shall make for me,
and upon it you shall sacrifice your holocausts
and peace offerings, your sheep and your oxen.[f]
In whatever place I choose for the remembrance
of my name* I will come to you and bless you.
**25** If you make an altar of stone for me,[g] do not
build it of cut stone, for by putting a tool to it
you desecrate it. **26** You shall not go up by
steps to my altar, on which you must not be
indecently uncovered.

## CHAPTER 21

**Laws Regarding Slaves.** **1** "These are
the rules* you shall lay before them. **2** [h]When
you purchase a Hebrew slave, he is to serve you
for six years, but in the seventh year he shall be
given his freedom without cost. **3** If he comes
into service alone, he shall leave alone; if he
comes with a wife, his wife shall leave with
him. **4** But if his master gives him a wife and
she bears him sons or daughters, the woman and
her children shall remain the master's property
and the man shall leave alone. **5** If, however,
the slave declares, 'I am devoted to my master
and my wife and children; I will not go free,'
**6** his master shall bring him to God* and there,
at the door or doorpost, he shall pierce his ear
with an awl, thus keeping him as his slave forever.

**7** "When a man sells his daughter as a slave,
she shall not go free as male slaves do. **8** But
if her master, who had destined her* for himself, dislikes her, he shall let her be redeemed.
He has no right to sell her to a foreigner, since
he has broken faith with her. **9** If he destines her
for his son, he shall treat her like a daughter.
**10** If he takes another wife, he shall not withhold her food, her clothing, or her conjugal
rights. **11** If he does not grant her these three
things, she shall be given her freedom absolutely, without cost to her.

**Personal Injury.** **12** "Whoever strikes a
man a mortal blow must be put to death.[i]
**13** He, however, who did not hunt a man down,
but caused his death by an act of God, may flee
to a place which I will set apart for this purpose.
**14** But when a man kills another after maliciously scheming to do so, you must take him
even from my altar and put him to death.
**15** Whoever strikes his father or mother shall be
put to death.

**16** "A kidnaper, whether he sells his victim
or still has him when caught, shall be put to
death.[j]

**17** "Whoever curses his father or mother
shall be put to death.[k]

**18** "When men quarrel and one strikes the
other with a stone or with his fist, not mortally,
but enough to put him in bed, **19** the one who
struck the blow shall be acquitted, provided the
other can get up and walk around with the help
of his staff. Still, he must compensate him for
his enforced idleness and provide for his complete cure.

**20** "When a man strikes his male or female
slave with a rod so hard that the slave dies under
his hand, he shall be punished. **21** If, however,
the slave survives for a day or two, he is not to
be punished, since the slave is his own property.

**22** "When men have a fight and hurt a pregnant woman, so that she suffers a miscarriage,
but no further injury, the guilty one shall be
fined as much as the woman's husband demands
of him, and he shall pay in the presence of the
judges.[l] **23** *But if injury ensues, you shall
give life for life, **24** eye for eye, tooth for tooth,
hand for hand, foot for foot, **25** burn for burn,
wound for wound, stripe for stripe.

**26** "When a man strikes his male or female
slave in the eye and destroys the use of the eye,
he shall let the slave go free in compensation for
the eye. **27** If he knocks out a tooth of his male
or female slave, he shall let the slave go free in
compensation for the tooth.

**28** "When an ox gores a man or a woman to

---

e Ex 20, 3f.
f Dt 12, 5. 11; 14, 23; 16, 6.
g Dt 27, 5; Jos 8, 31.
h 2-6: Lv 25, 39ff; Dt 15, 12-18; Jer 34, 14.
i 12ff: Lv 24, 17; Nm 35, 15-29; Dt 4, 41f; 19, 2-5.
j Dt 24, 7.
k Lv 20, 9; Prv 20, 20; Mt 15, 4; Mk 7, 10.
l 22-25: Lv 24, 18-21; Dt 19, 21; Mt 5, 38.

---

*

20, 24: I choose for the remembrance of my name: literally, "where I make my name to be remembered": at the sacred site where God wishes to be worshiped and his name revered.

21, 1: Rules: judicial precedents to be used in settling questions of law and custom. This introductory phrase serves as the title of the following collection of civil and religious laws (chapters 21–23) which is called in Ex 24, 7, the book of the covenant.

21, 6: To God: to the sanctuary; or perhaps the phrase is to be rendered, "to the gods," in the sense of "to the judges." Cf Ps 82, 1. Since the expression "to have an open ear" meant to "obey," a pierced ear lobe was an ancient symbol of obedience. Cf Ps 40, 7.

21, 8: Destined her: intended her as a wife of second rank.

21, 23ff: This section is known as the lex talionis, the law of tit for tat. The purpose of this law was not merely the enforcement of rigorous justice, but also the prevention of greater penalties than would be just. Christ refers to this passage when he exhorts Christians to cede their lawful rights for the sake of charity. Cf Mt 5, 38ff.

death, the ox must be stoned; its flesh may not be eaten. The owner of the ox, however, shall go unpunished. **29** But if an ox was previously in the habit of goring people and its owner, though warned, would not keep it in; should it then kill a man or a woman, not only must the ox be stoned, but its owner also must be put to death. **30** If, however, a fine is imposed on him, he must pay in ransom for his life whatever amount is imposed on him. **31** This law applies if it is a boy or a girl that the ox gores. **32** But if it is a male or a female slave that it gores, he must pay the owner of the slave thirty shekels of silver, and the ox must be stoned.

**Property Damage.** **33** "When a man uncovers or digs a cistern and does not cover it over again, should an ox or an ass fall into it, **34** the owner of the cistern must make good by restoring the value of the animal to its owner; the dead animal, however, he may keep.

**35** "When one man's ox hurts another's ox so badly that it dies, they shall sell the live ox and divide this money as well as the dead animal equally between them. **36** But if it was known that the ox was previously in the habit of goring and its owner would not keep it in, he must make full restitution, an ox for an ox; but the dead animal he may keep.

**37** *"When a man steals an ox or a sheep and slaughters or sells it, he shall restore five oxen for the one ox, and four sheep for the one sheep.[m]

## CHAPTER 22

**1** "[If a thief is caught* in the act of housebreaking and beaten to death, there is no bloodguilt involved. **2** But if after sunrise he is thus beaten, there is bloodguilt.] He must make full restitution. If he has nothing, he shall be sold to pay for his theft. **3** If what he stole is found alive in his possession, be it an ox, an ass or a sheep, he shall restore two animals for each one stolen.

**4** *"When a man is burning over a field or a vineyard, if he lets the fires spread so that it burns in another's field, he must make restitution with the best produce of his own field or vineyard. **5** If the fire spreads further, and catches on to thorn bushes, so that shocked grain or standing grain or the field itself is burned up, the one who started the fire must make full restitution.

**Trusts and Loans.** **6** "When a man gives money or any article to another for safekeeping and it is stolen from the latter's house, the thief, if caught, must make twofold restitution. **7** If the thief is not caught, the owner of the house shall be brought to God,* to swear that he himself did not lay hands on his neighbor's property. **8** In every question of dishonest appropriation, whether it be about an ox, or an ass, or a sheep, or a garment, or anything else that has disappeared, where another claims that the thing is his, both parties shall present their case before God; the one whom God convicts must make two-fold restitution to the other.

**9** "When a man gives an ass, or an ox, or a sheep, or any other animal to another for safekeeping, if it dies, or is maimed or snatched away, without anyone witnessing the fact, **10** the custodian shall swear by the LORD that he did not lay hands on his neighbor's property; the owner must accept the oath, and no restitution is to be made. **11** But if the custodian is really guilty of theft, he must make restitution to the owner. **12** If it has been killed by a wild beast, let him bring it as evidence, and he need not make restitution for the mangled animal.[n]

**13** "When a man borrows an animal from his neighbor, if it is maimed or dies while the owner is not present, the man must make restitution. **14** But if the owner is present, he need not make restitution. If it was hired, this was covered by the price of its hire.

**Social Laws.** **15** "When a man seduces a virgin who is not betrothed, and lies with her, he shall pay her marriage price and marry her.[o] **16** If her father refuses to give her to him, he must still pay him the customary marriage price for virgins.*

**17** "You shall not let a sorceress live.[p]

**18** "Anyone who lies with an animal shall be put to death.[q]

**19** "Whoever sacrifices to any god, except to the LORD alone, shall be doomed.[r]

**20** "You shall not molest or oppress an alien, for you were once aliens yourselves in the land of Egypt.[s] **21** You shall not wrong any widow or orphan. **22** If ever you wrong them and they cry out to me, I will surely hear their cry. **23** My wrath will flare up, and I will kill

m 2 Sm 12, 6.
n Gn 31, 39.
o 15f: Dt 22, 28f.
p Lv 19, 26. 31; 20. 6. 27; Dt 18, 10f.
q Lv 18, 23; Dt 27, 21.
r Dt 13; 17, 2-7.
s 20-23: Ex 23, 9; Lv 19, 33f; Dt 10, 18f; 24, 17f; 27, 19; Zec 7, 10.

*

21, 37—22, 30: In the Vulgate, 22, 1–31.

22, 1f: If a thief is caught: this seems to be a fragment of what was once a longer law on housebreaking, which has been inserted here into the middle of a law on stealing animals. At night the householder would be justified in killing a burglar outright, but not so in the daytime, when the burglar could more easily be caught alive. He must make full restitution: this stood originally immediately after 21, 37.

22, 4: The Greek and Latin versions understood this verse as a prohibition against allowing one's cattle to graze in the field of another.

22, 7: Brought to God: see note on Ex 21, 6. Cf also Ex 22, 10.

22, 16: The customary marriage price for virgins: fifty shekels according to Dt 22, 29.

you with the sword; then your own wives will
be widows, and your children orphans.
24 [t]"If you lend money to one of your poor
neighbors among my people, you shall not act
like an extortioner toward him by demanding
interest from him. 25 If you take your neighbor's cloak as a pledge, you shall return it to him
before sunset; 26 for this cloak of his is the only
covering he has for his body. What else has he
to sleep in? If he cries out to me, I will hear him;
for I am compassionate.
27 "You shall not revile God,* nor curse a
prince of your people.[u]
28 "You shall not delay the offering of your
harvest and your press. You shall give me the
first-born of your sons. 29 You must do the
same with your oxen and your sheep; for seven
days the firstling may stay with its mother, but
on the eighth day you must give it to me.[v]
30 "You shall be men sacred to me. Flesh
torn to pieces in the field you shall not eat; throw
it to the dogs.[w]

## CHAPTER 23

1 "You shall not repeat a false report. Do not
join the wicked in putting your hand, as an
unjust witness, upon anyone.[x] 2 Neither shall
you allege the example of the many as an excuse
for doing wrong, nor shall you, when testifying
in a lawsuit, side with the many in perverting
justice. 3 You shall not favor a poor man in his
lawsuit.[y]
4 "When you come upon your enemy's ox or
ass going astray, see to it that it is returned to
him.[z] 5 When you notice the ass of one who
hates you lying prostrate under its burden, by no
means desert him; help him, rather, to raise it
up.
6 "You shall not deny one of your needy
fellow men his rights in his lawsuit. 7 You shall
keep away from anything dishonest. The innocent and the just you shall not put to death, nor
shall you acquit the guilty. 8 Never take a
bribe, for a bribe blinds even the most clear-
sighted and twists the words even of the just.[a]
9 You shall not oppress an alien; you well know
how it feels to be an alien, since you were once
aliens yourselves in the land of Egypt.[b]

**Religious Laws.** 10 [c]"For six years you
may sow your land and gather in its produce.
11 But the seventh year you shall let the land
lie untilled and unharvested, that the poor
among you may eat of it and the beasts of the
field may eat what the poor leave. So also shall
you do in regard to your vineyard and your olive
grove.
12 "For six days you may do your work, but
on the seventh day you must rest,[d] that your ox
and your ass may also have rest, and that the son
of your maidservant and the alien may be refreshed. 13 Give heed to all that I have told
you.
"Never mention the name of any other god;
it shall not be heard from your lips.
14 [e]"Three times a year you shall celebrate
a pilgrim feast to me.* 15 You shall keep the
feast of Unleavened Bread. As I have commanded you, you must eat unleavened bread for
seven days at the prescribed time in the month
of Abib, for it was then that you came out of
Egypt. No one shall appear before me* empty-handed. 16 You shall also keep the feast of
the grain harvest with the first of the crop that
you have sown in the field; and finally, the feast
at the fruit harvest at the end of the year, when
you gather in the produce from the fields.
17 Thrice a year shall all your men appear before the LORD God.
18 "You shall not offer the blood of my
sacrifice with leavened bread;[f] nor shall the fat
of my feast be kept overnight till the next day.
19 The choicest first fruits of your soil you shall
bring to the house of the LORD, your God.
"You shall not boil a kid in its mother's
milk.*

**Reward of Fidelity.** 20 "See, I am sending
an angel[g] before you, to guard you on the way
and bring you to the place I have prepared.
21 Be attentive to him and heed his voice. Do
not rebel against him, for he will not forgive
your sin. My authority resides in him.* 22 If
you heed his voice and carry out all I tell you,
I will be an enemy to your enemies and a foe to
your foes.
23 "My angel will go before you and bring
you to the Amorites, Hittites, Perizzites, Canaanites, Hivites and Jebusites; and I will wipe
them out. 24 Therefore, you shall not bow

---

t 24-26: Lv 25, 35-38; Dt 23, 19f; 24, 10-13; Ez 18, 7f. 17f.
u Acts 23, 5.
v Ex 13, 2; 34, 19; Lv 22, 27; Dt 15, 19.
w Lv 7, 24; 17, 15; 22, 8.
x 1f: Dt 19, 16ff.
y Lv 19, 15.
z Dt 22, 1ff.
a Dt 16, 19; 27, 25; Sir 20, 28.
b Ex 22, 21.
c 10f: Lv 25, 3-7.
d Ex 20, 8.
e 14-17: Ex 34, 18. 22ff; Lv 23; Dt 16, 1-17.
f 18f: Ex 34, 25f.
g Ex 14, 19; 32, 34; 33, 2.
h 23f: Ex 34, 10-16; Nm 33, 51f; Dt 7, 24ff.

---

22, 27: God: or perhaps "the gods," in the sense of "the judges," as the parallel with a price of your people suggests.

23, 14: These three feasts are elsewhere called the Passover, Pentecost and Booths. Cf Ex 34, 18–26; Lv 23; Dt 16.

23, 15: Appear before me: the original expression was "see my face"; so also in several other places, as Ex 23, 17; 34, 23f; Dt 16, 16; 31, 11.

23, 19: Boil a kid in its mother's milk: this was part of a Canaanite ritual; hence it is forbidden here as a pagan ceremony.

23, 21: My authority resides in him: literally, "My name is within him."

23, 24: Make anything like them: some render, "act according to their conduct." Sacred pillars: objects of religious veneration at Canaanite sanctuaries.

down in worship before their gods, nor shall you make anything like them;* rather, you must demolish them and smash their sacred pillars.[h] **25** The LORD, your God, you shall worship; then I will bless your food and drink, and I will remove all sickness from your midst; **26** no woman in your land will be barren or miscarry; and I will give you a full span of life.

**27** "I will have the fear of me precede you, so that I will throw into panic every nation you reach.[i] I will make all your enemies turn from you in flight, **28** and ahead of you I will send hornets* to drive the Hivites, Canaanites and Hittites out of your way. **29** But not in one year will I drive them all out before you; else the land will become so desolate that the wild beasts will multiply against you. **30** Instead, I will drive them out little by little before you, until you have grown numerous enough to take possession of the land. **31** [j]I will set your boundaries from the Red Sea to the sea of the Philistines,* and from the desert to the River; all who dwell in this land I will hand over to you to be driven out of your way. **32** You shall not make a covenant with them or their gods. **33** They must not abide in your land, lest they make you sin against me by ensnaring you into worshiping their gods."[k]

## CHAPTER 24

**Ratification of the Covenant.** **1** Moses himself was told, "Come up to the LORD, you and Aaron, with Nadab, Abihu, and seventy of the elders of Israel. You shall all worship at some distance, **2** but Moses alone is to come close to the LORD; the others shall not come too near, and the people shall not come up at all with Moses."

**3** When Moses came to the people and related all the words and ordinances of the LORD, they all answered with one voice, "We will do everything that the LORD has told us."[l] **4** Moses then wrote down all the words of the LORD and, rising early the next day, he erected at the foot of the mountain an altar and twelve pillars* for the twelve tribes of Israel. **5** Then, having sent certain young men of the Israelites to offer holocausts and sacrifice young bulls as peace offerings to the LORD, **6** Moses took half of the blood and put it in large bowls; the other half he splashed on the altar. **7** Taking the book of the covenant, he read it aloud to the people, who answered, "All that the LORD has said, we will heed and do." **8** Then he took the blood and sprinkled it on the people, saying, "This is the blood of the covenant which the LORD has made with you in accordance with all these words of his."[m]

**9** Moses then went up with Aaron, Nadab, Abihu, and seventy elders of Israel, **10** and they beheld the God of Israel. Under his feet there appeared to be sapphire tilework, as clear as the sky itself. **11** Yet he did not smite these chosen Israelites. After gazing on God,* they could still eat and drink.

**Moses on the Mountain.** **12** The LORD said to Moses, "Come up to me on the mountain and, while you are there, I will give you the stone tablets[n] on which I have written the commandments intended for their instruction." **13** So Moses set out with Joshua, his aide, and went up to the mountain of God. **14** The elders, however, had been told by him, "Wait here for us until we return to you. Aaron and Hur are staying with you. If anyone has a complaint, let him refer the matter to them." **15** After Moses had gone up, a cloud covered the mountain. **16** The glory of the LORD settled upon Mount Sinai. The cloud covered it for six days, and on the seventh day he called to Moses from the midst of the cloud.[o] **17** To the Israelites the glory of the LORD was seen as a consuming fire on the mountaintop.[p] **18** But Moses passed into the midst of the cloud as he went up on the mountain; and there he stayed for forty days and forty nights.[q]

# *IV: The Dwelling and Its Furnishings*

## CHAPTER 25

**Collection of Materials.** **1** This is what the LORD then said to Moses:[r] **2** "Tell the Israelites to take up a collection for me. From every man you shall accept the contribution that his heart prompts him to give me. **3** These are the contributions you shall accept from them: gold, silver and bronze;[s] **4** violet, purple and scarlet

i 27ff: Dt 2, 25; 7, 20ff.
j Gn 15, 18; Dt 11, 24; Jos 1, 4.
k 32f: Ex 34, 12-16; Dt 7, 2ff.
l Ex 19, 8.
m 5-8: Heb 9, 18ff.
n Ex 31, 18; 32, 15f; Dt 5, 22.
o Sir 45, 4.
p Ex 19, 18; Heb 12, 18.
q Ex 34, 28; Dt 9, 9.
r 1-7: Ex 35, 4-9. 20-29.
s Ex 35, 4-9.

*

23, 28: Hornets: some understand this figuratively of various troublesome afflictions; others translate the Hebrew word as "leprosy." Cf Dt 7, 20; Jos 24, 12; Wis 12, 8.

23, 31: The sea of the Philistines: the Mediterranean. The River: the Euphrates. Only in the time of David and Solomon did the territory of Israel come near to reaching such distant borders.

24, 4: Pillars: stone shafts or slabs, erected as symbols of the fact that each of the twelve tribes had entered into this covenant with God; not idolatrous as in Ex 23, 24, although the same Hebrew word is used in both passages. See note on Gn 28, 18.

24, 11: After gazing on God: the ancients thought that the sight of God would bring instantaneous death. Cf Ex 33, 20; Gn 16, 13; 32, 31; Jgs 6, 22f; 13, 22. Eat and drink: partake of the sacrificial meal.

yarn; fine linen and goat hair; **5** rams' skins dyed red, and tahash* skins; acacia wood; **6** oil for the light; spices for the anointing oil and for the fragrant incense; **7** onyx stones and other gems for mounting on the ephod and the breastpiece.

**8** "They shall make a sanctuary for me, that I may dwell in their midst.[t] **9** This Dwelling and all its furnishings you shall make exactly according to the pattern that I will now show you.[u]

**Plan of the Ark.** **10** "You shall make an ark of acacia wood,[v] two and a half cubits long, one and a half cubits wide, and one and a half cubits high. **11** Plate it inside and outside with pure gold, and put a molding of gold around the top of it. **12** Cast four gold rings and fasten them on the four supports of the ark, two rings on one side and two on the opposite side. **13** Then make poles of acacia wood and plate them with gold. **14** These poles you are to put through the rings on the sides of the ark, for carrying it; **15** they must remain in the rings of the ark and never be withdrawn. **16** In the ark you are to put the commandments which I will give you.

**17** "You shall then make a propitiatory* of pure gold, two cubits and a half long, and one and a half cubits wide. **18** Make two cherubim* of beaten gold for the two ends of the propitiatory, **19** fastening them so that one cherub springs direct from each end. **20** The cherubim shall have their wings spread out above, covering the propitiatory with them; they shall be turned toward each other, but with their faces looking toward the propitiatory. **21** This propitiatory you shall then place on top of the ark. In the ark itself you are to put the commandments which I will give you. **22** There I will meet you and there, from above the propitiatory, between the two cherubim on the ark of the commandments, I will tell you all the commands that I wish you to give the Israelites.

**The Table.** **23** "You shall also make a table of acacia[w] wood, two cubits long, a cubit wide, and a cubit and a half high. **24** Plate it with pure gold and make a molding of gold around it. **25** Surround it with a frame,* a hand-breadth high, with a molding of gold around the frame. **26** You shall also make four rings of gold for it and fasten them at the four corners, one at each leg, **27** on two opposite sides of the frame as holders for the poles to carry the table. **28** These poles for carrying the table you shall make of acacia wood and plate with gold. **29** Of pure gold you shall make its plates* and cups, as well as its pitchers and bowls for pouring libations. **30** On the table you shall always keep showbread set before me.[x]

**The Lampstand.** **31** "You shall make a lampstand of pure beaten gold[y]—its shaft and branches—with its cups and knobs and petals springing directly from it. **32** Six branches are to extend from the sides of the lampstand, three branches on one side, and three on the other. **33** *On one branch there are to be three cups, shaped like almond blossoms, each with its knob and petals; on the opposite branch there are to be three cups, shaped like almond blossoms, each with its knob and petals; and so for the six branches that extend from the lampstand. **34** On the shaft there are to be four cups,* shaped like almond blossoms, with their knobs and petals, **35** including a knob below each of the three pairs of branches that extend from the lampstand. **36** Their knobs and branches shall so spring from it that the whole will form but a single piece of pure beaten gold. **37** *You shall then make seven lamps[z] for it and so set up the lamps that they shed their light on the space in front of the lampstand. **38** These, as well as the trimming shears and trays,* must be of pure gold. **39** Use a talent of pure gold for the lampstand and all its appurtenances. **40** See that you make them according to the pattern shown you on the mountain.[a]

t 8f: Ex 26, 1-30; 36, 8-38.
u Acts 7, 44.
v 10-22: Ex 37, 1-9; Heb 9, 1-5.
w 23-30: Ex 37, 10-16.
x Lv 24, 5ff.
y 31-40: Ex 37, 17-24.
z Lv 24, 2ff; Nm 8, 2.
a Heb 8, 5.

*

25, 5: Tahash: perhaps the name of a marine animal, such as the dugong or the porpoise. The Greek and Latin versions took it for the color hyacinth.

25, 17: Propitiatory: this traditional rendering of the Hebrew term, which may mean merely "cover," is derived from its connection with the ceremony of the Day of Atonement whereby God was rendered "propitious." Cf Lv 16, 14ff.

25, 18ff: Cherubim: probably in the form of human-headed winged lions. The cherubim over the ark formed the throne for the invisible Lord. Cf Ps 80, 2. For a more detailed description of the somewhat different cherubim in the temple of Solomon, see 1 Kgs 6, 23–28; 2 Chr 3, 10–13.

25, 25: A frame: probably placed near the bottom of the legs to keep them steady. The golden table of Herod's temple is pictured thus on the Arch of Titus.

25, 29f: The plates held the showbread, that is, the holy bread which was placed upon the table every sabbath as an offering to God, and was later eaten by the priests. The cups held the incense which was strewn upon the bread. Cf Lv 24, 5–9. The libation wine was poured from the pitchers into the bowls. All these vessels were kept on the golden table.

25, 33: In keeping with the arrangement of the ornaments on the shaft, the three sets of ornaments on each branch were probably so placed that one was at the top and the other two equally spaced along the length of the branch. Knob: the cup-shaped seed capsule at the base of a flower.

25, 34f: Of the four ornaments on the shaft, one was at the top and one was below each of the three sets of side branches.

25, 37: The lamps were probably shaped like small boats, with the wick at one end; the end with the wick was turned toward the front of the lampstand.

25, 38: Trays: small receptacles for the burnt-out wicks.

## CHAPTER 26

**The Tent Cloth.** **1** "The Dwelling itself you shall make out of sheets* woven of fine linen twined and of violet, purple and scarlet yarn, with cherubim embroidered on them.[b] **2** The length of each shall be twenty-eight cubits, and the width four cubits; all the sheets shall be of the same size. **3** Five of the sheets are to be sewed together, edge to edge; and the same for the other five. **4** Make loops of violet yarn along the edge of the end sheet in one set, and the same along the edge of the end sheet in the other set. **5** There are to be fifty loops along the edge of the end sheet in the first set, and fifty loops along the edge of the corresponding sheet in the second set, and so placed that the loops are directly opposite each other. **6** Then make fifty clasps of gold, with which to join the two sets of sheets, so that the Dwelling forms one whole.

**7** "Also make sheets woven of goat hair, to be used as a tent covering* over the Dwelling. **8** Eleven such sheets are to be made; the length of each shall be thirty cubits, and the width four cubits: all eleven sheets shall be of the same size. **9** Sew five of the sheets, edge to edge, into one set, and the other six sheets into another set. Use the sixth sheet double at the front of the tent.* **10** Make fifty loops along the edge of the end sheet in one set, and fifty loops along the edge of the end sheet in the second set. **11** Also make fifty bronze clasps and put them into the loops, to join the tent into one whole. **12** There will be an extra half sheet of tent covering, which shall be allowed to hang down over the rear of the Dwelling. **13** Likewise, the sheets of the tent will have an extra cubit's length to be left hanging down on either side of the Dwelling to protect it. **14** Over the tent itself you shall make a covering of rams' skins dyed red, and above that, a covering of tahash skins.

**The Wooden Walls.** **15** [c]"You shall make boards of acacia wood as walls for the Dwelling. **16** The length of each board is to be ten cubits, and its width one and a half cubits. **17** Each board shall have two arms* that shall serve to fasten the boards in line. In this way all the boards of the Dwelling are to be made. **18** Set up the boards of the Dwelling as follows: twenty boards on the south side, **19** with forty silver pedestals under the twenty boards, so that there are two pedestals under each board, at its two arms; **20** twenty boards on the other side of the Dwelling, the north side, **21** with their forty silver pedestals, two under each board; **22** six boards for the rear of the Dwelling, to the west; **23** and two boards for the corners at the rear of the Dwelling. **24** These two shall be double at the bottom, and likewise double at the top, to the first ring. That is how both boards in the corners are to be made. **25** Thus, there shall be in the rear eight boards, with their sixteen silver pedestals, two pedestals under each board. **26** Also make bars of acacia wood: five for the boards on one side of the Dwelling, **27** five for those on the other side, and five for those at the rear, toward the west. **28** The center bar, at the middle of the boards, shall reach across from end to end. **29** Plate the boards with gold, and make gold rings on them as holders for the bars, which are also to be plated with gold. **30** You shall erect the Dwelling according to the pattern shown you on the mountain.

**The Veils.** **31** "You shall have a veil woven of violet, purple and scarlet yarn,[d] and of fine linen twined, with cherubim embroidered on it.[e] **32** It is to be hung on four gold-plated columns of acacia wood, which shall have hooks* of gold and shall rest on four silver pedestals. **33** Hang the veil from clasps. The ark of the commandments you shall bring inside, behind this veil which divides the holy place from the holy of holies. **34** Set the propitiatory on the ark of the commandments in the holy of holies.

**35** "Outside the veil you shall place the table and the lampstand, the latter on the south side of the Dwelling, opposite the table, which is to be put on the north side. **36** For the entrance of the tent make a variegated* curtain of violet, purple and scarlet yarn and of fine linen twined. **37** Make five columns of acacia wood for this curtain; have them plated with gold, with their hooks of gold; and cast five bronze pedestals for them.

## CHAPTER 27

**The Altar of Holocausts.** **1** "You shall make an altar[f] of acacia wood, on a square, five

b 1-14: Ex 36, 8-19.
c 15-30: Ex 36, 20-34.
d 2 Chr 3, 14.
e 31-37: Ex 36, 35-38.
f 1-8: Ex 38, 1-7.

*

26, 1: Sheets: strips of tapestry, woven of white linen, the colored threads being used for the cherubim which were embroidered on them. These sheets were stretched across the top of the Dwelling to form a roof, their free ends hanging down inside the boards which formed walls.

26, 7: Tent covering: the cloth made of sheets of goat hair to cover the Dwelling.

26, 9: Half the width of the end strip was folded back at the front of the Dwelling, thus leaving another half-strip to hang down at the rear. Cf v 12.

26, 17: Arms: literally, "hands." According to some, they served as "tongue and groove" to mortise the boards together; according to others, they were pegs at the bottom of the boards and fitted into sockets in the pedestals.

26, 32: Hooks: probably placed near the tops of the columns, to hold the rope from which the veils and curtains hung.

26, 36: Variegated: without definite designs such as the cherubim on the inner veil.

cubits long and five cubits wide; it shall be three
cubits high. **2** At the four corners there are to
be horns, so made that they spring directly from
the altar. You shall then plate it with bronze.
**3** Make pots for removing the ashes, as well as
shovels, basins, forks and fire pans, all of which
shall be of bronze. **4** Make a grating* of bronze
network for it; this to have four bronze rings,
one at each of its four corners. **5** Put it down
around the altar, on the ground. This network is
to be half as high as the altar. **6** You shall also
make poles of acacia wood for the altar, and
plate them with bronze. **7** These poles are to be
put through the rings, so that they are on either
side of the altar when it is carried. **8** Make the
altar itself in the form of a hollow* box, just as
it was shown you on the mountain.

**Court of the Dwelling.** **9** [g]"You shall also
make a court for the Dwelling. On the south side
the court shall have hangings a hundred cubits
long, woven of fine linen twined, **10** with twenty columns and twenty pedestals of bronze; the
hooks and bands on the columns shall be of
silver. **11** On the north side there shall be similar hangings, a hundred cubits long, with twenty
columns and twenty pedestals of bronze; the
hooks and bands on the columns shall be of
silver. **12** On the west side, across the width of
the court, there shall be hangings, fifty cubits
long, with ten columns and ten pedestals.
**13** The width of the court on the east side shall
be fifty cubits. **14** On one side there shall be
hangings to the extent of fifteen cubits, with
three columns and three pedestals; **15** On the
other side there shall be hangings to the extent
of fifteen cubits, with three columns and three
pedestals.

**16** "At the entrance of the court there shall
be a variegated curtain, twenty cubits long, woven of violet, purple and scarlet yarn and of fine
linen twined. It shall have four columns and
four pedestals.

**17** "All the columns around the court shall
have bands and hooks of silver, and pedestals of
bronze. **18** The enclosure of the court is to be
one hundred cubits long, fifty cubits wide, and
five cubits high. Fine linen twined must be
used, and the pedestals must be of bronze.

**19** All the fittings of the Dwelling, whatever
be their use, as well as all its tent pegs and all
the tent pegs of the court, must be of bronze.

**Oil for the Lamps.** **20** "You shall order the
Israelites to bring you clear oil of crushed olives, to be used for the light, so that you may
keep lamps burning regularly.[h] **21** From evening to morning Aaron and his sons shall maintain them before the LORD in the meeting tent,
outside the veil which hangs in front of the
commandments. This shall be a perpetual ordinance for the Israelites throughout their generations.

## CHAPTER 28

**The Priestly Vestments.** **1** [i]"From
among the Israelites have your brother Aaron,
together with his sons Nadab, Abihu, Eleazar
and Ithamar, brought to you, that they may be
my priests. **2** For the glorious adornment of
your brother Aaron you shall have sacred vestments made. **3** Therefore, to the various expert
workmen whom I have endowed with skill, you
shall give instructions to make such vestments
for Aaron as will set him apart for his sacred
service as my priest. **4** These are the vestments
they shall make: a breastpiece, an ephod, a
robe, a brocaded tunic, a miter and a sash. In
making these sacred vestments which your
brother Aaron and his sons are to wear in serving as my priests, **5** they shall use gold, violet,
purple and scarlet yarn and fine linen.

**The Ephod and Breastpiece.** **6** "The
ephod* they shall make of gold thread and of
violet, purple and scarlet yarn, embroidered on
cloth of fine linen twined.[j] **7** It shall have a pair
of shoulder straps joined to its two upper ends.
**8** The embroidered belt on the ephod shall extend out from it and, like it, be made of gold
thread, of violet, purple and scarlet yarn, and of
fine linen twined.

**9** "Get two onyx stones and engrave on them
the names of the sons of Israel: **10** six of their
names on one stone, and the other six on the
other stone, in the order of their birth. **11** As a
gem-cutter engraves a seal, so shall you have
the two stones engraved with the names of the
sons of Israel and then mounted in gold filigree
work. **12** Set these two stones on the shoulder
straps of the ephod as memorial stones of the
sons of Israel. Thus Aaron shall bear their
names on his shoulders as a reminder before the
LORD. **13** Make filigree rosettes of gold,[k]
**14** as well as two chains of pure gold, twisted

g 9-19: Ex 38, 9-20.
h 20f: Lv 24, 1-4.
i 1-5: Ex 39, 1; Sir 45, 7.
j 6-12: Ex 39, 2-7; Sir 45, 8-14.
k 13f: Ex 28, 22. 25; 39, 15. 18.

*

27, 4: Grating: it is not clear whether this was flush with the altar or at some small distance from it; in the latter case the space between the altar and the grating would be filled with stones and serve as a platform around the altar, which would otherwise be too high for the priest to reach conveniently.

27, 8: Hollow: probably filled with earth or stones when in use. Cf Ex 20, 24f.

28, 6: Ephod: this Hebrew word is retained in the translation because it is the technical term for a peculiar piece of the priestly vestments, the exact nature of which is uncertain. It seems to have been a sort of apron that hung from the shoulders of the priest by shoulder straps (v 7) and was tied around his waist by the loose ends of the attached belt (v 8).

like cords, and fasten the cordlike chains to the filigree rosettes.

15 [l]"The breastpiece* of decision you shall also have made, embroidered like the ephod with gold thread and violet, purple and scarlet yarn on cloth of fine linen twined. 16 It is to be square when folded double, a span high and a span wide. 17 *On it you shall mount four rows of precious stones: in the first row, a carnelian, a topaz and an emerald; 18 in the second row, a garnet, a sapphire and a beryl; 19 in the third row, a jacinth, an agate and an amethyst; 20 in the fourth row, a chrysolite, an onyx and a jasper. These stones are to be mounted in gold filigree work, 21 twelve of them to match the names of the sons of Israel, each stone engraved like a seal with the name of one of the twelve tribes.

22 "When the chains of pure gold, twisted like cords, have been made for the breastpiece, 23 you shall then make two rings of gold for it and fasten them to the two upper ends of the breastpiece. 24 The gold cords are then to be fastened to two rings at the upper ends of the breastpiece, 25 the other two ends of the cords being fastened in front to the two filigree rosettes which are attached to the shoulder straps of the ephod. 26 Make two other rings of gold and put them on the two lower ends of the breastpiece, on its edge that faces the ephod. 27 Then make two more rings of gold and fasten them to the bottom of the shoulder straps next to where they join the ephod in front, just above its embroidered belt. 28 Violet ribbons shall bind the rings of the breastpiece to the rings of the ephod, so that the breastpiece will stay right above the embroidered belt of the ephod and not swing loose from it.

29 "Whenever Aaron enters the sanctuary, he will thus bear the names of the sons of Israel on the breastpiece of decision over his heart as a constant reminder before the LORD. 30 In this breastpiece of decision[m] you shall put the Urim and Thummim,* that they may be over Aaron's heart whenever he enters the presence of the LORD. Thus he shall always bear the decisions for the Israelites over his heart in the LORD's presence.

**Other Vestments.** 31 "The robe of the ephod[n] you shall make entirely of violet material. 32 It shall have an opening for the head in the center, and around this opening there shall be a selvage, woven as at the opening of a shirt, to keep it from being torn. 33 All around the hem at the bottom you shall make pomegranates, woven of violet, purple and scarlet yarn and fine linen twined, with gold bells between them; 34 first a gold bell, then a pomegranate, and thus alternating all around the hem of the robe. 35 Aaron shall wear it when ministering, that its tinkling may be heard as he enters and leaves the LORD's presence in the sanctuary; else he will die.

36 "You shall also make a plate of pure gold and engrave on it, as on a seal engraving, "Sacred to the LORD." 37 This plate is to be tied over the miter with a violet ribbon in such a way that it rests on the front of the miter,[o] 38 over Aaron's forehead. Since Aaron bears whatever guilt the Israelites may incur in consecrating any of their sacred gifts, this plate must always be over his forehead, so that they may find favor with the LORD.

39 [p]"The tunic of fine linen shall be brocaded. The miter shall be made of fine linen. The sash shall be of variegated work.

40 "Likewise, for the glorious adornment of Aaron's sons you shall have tunics and sashes and turbans made. 41 With these you shall clothe your brother Aaron and his sons. Anoint and ordain them,* consecrating them as my priests. 42 You must also make linen drawers for them, to cover their naked flesh from their loins to their thighs.[q] 43 Aaron and his sons shall wear them whenever they go into the meeting tent or approach the altar to minister in the sanctuary, lest they incur guilt and die. This shall be a perpetual ordinance for him and for his descendants.

## CHAPTER 29

**Consecration of the Priests.** 1 "This is the rite you shall perform in consecrating them as my priests.[r] Procure a young bull and two unblemished rams. 2 With fine wheat flour make unleavened cakes mixed with oil, and unleavened wafers spread with oil, 3 and put them in a basket. Take the basket of them along with the bullock and the two rams. 4 Aaron and

l 15-21: Ex 39, 15-21.
m Lv 8, 8; Sir 45, 11.
n 31-35: Ex 39, 20ff; Lv 8, 9; Sir 45, 10.
o Ex 39, 31; Lv 8, 9.
p 39-43: Ex 39, 27ff.
q Ez 44, 18.
r 1-8: Lv 8, 1-9.

*

28, 15–30: Breastpiece: in shape like a modern altar burse, it was a pocketlike receptacle for holding the Urim and Thummim (v 30), and formed an integral part of the ephod, to which it was attached by an elaborate system of rings and chains. Both the ephod and its breastpiece were made of brocaded linen.

28, 17–20: The translation of the Hebrew names of some of these gems is quite conjectural.

28, 30: Urim and Thummim: both the meaning of these Hebrew words and the exact nature of the objects so designated are uncertain. They were apparently lots of some kind which were drawn or cast by the priest to ascertain God's decision in doubtful matters. Hence, the burse in which they were kept was called "the breastpiece of decision."

28, 41: Ordain them: literally, "fill their hands," a technical expression used solely for the installation of priests. The phrase probably originated in the custom of placing in the priests' hands the instruments or other symbols of the sacerdotal office.

his sons you shall also bring to the entrance of the meeting tent, and there wash them with water. **5** Take the vestments and clothe Aaron with the tunic, the robe of the ephod, the ephod itself, and the breastpiece, fastening the embroidered belt of the ephod around him. **6** Put the miter on his head, the sacred diadem on the miter. **7** Then take the anointing oil and anoint him with it, pouring it on his head. **8** Bring forward his sons also and clothe them with the tunics, **9** gird them with the sashes, and tie the turbans on them.[s] Thus shall the priesthood be theirs by perpetual law, and thus shall you ordain Aaron and his sons.

**Ordination Sacrifices.** **10** [t]"Now bring forward the bullock in front of the meeting tent. There Aaron and his sons shall lay their hands on its head. **11** Then slaughter the bullock before the LORD, at the entrance of the meeting tent. **12** Take some of its blood and with your finger put it on the horns of the altar. All the rest of the blood you shall pour out at the base of the altar. **13** All the fat that covers its inner organs, as well as the lobe of its liver and its two kidneys, together with the fat that is on them, you shall take and burn on the altar. **14** But the flesh and hide and offal of the bullock you must burn up outside the camp, since this is a sin offering.[u]

**15** "Then take one of the rams, and after Aaron and his sons have laid their hands on its head, **16** slaughter it. The blood you shall take and splash on all the sides of the altar. **17** Cut the ram into pieces; its inner organs and shanks you shall first wash, and then put them with the pieces and with the head. **18** The entire ram shall then be burned on the altar, since it is a holocaust, a sweet-smelling oblation to the LORD.

**19** "After this take the other ram, and when Aaron and his sons have laid their hands on its head, **20** slaughter it. Some of its blood you shall take and put on the tip of Aaron's right ear and on the tips of his sons' right ears and on the thumbs of their right hands and the great toes of their right feet. Splash the rest of the blood on all the sides of the altar. **21** Then take some of the blood that is on the altar, together with some of the anointing oil, and sprinkle this on Aaron and his vestments, as well as on his sons and their vestments, that his sons and their Vestments may be sacred.

**22** "Now, from this ram you shall take its fat: its fatty tail,* the fat that covers its inner organs, the lobe of its liver, its two kidneys with the fat that is on them, and its right thigh, since this is the ordination ram; **23** then, out of the basket of unleavened food that you have set before the LORD, you shall take one of the loaves of bread, one of the cakes made with oil, and one of the wafers. **24** All these things you shall put into the hands of Aaron and his sons, so that they may wave them as a wave offering* before the LORD. **25** After you have received them back from their hands, you shall burn them on top of the holocaust on the altar as a sweet-smelling oblation to the LORD. **26** Finally, take the breast of Aaron's ordination ram and wave it as a wave offering before the LORD; this is to be your own portion.

**27** *"Thus shall you set aside the breast of whatever wave offering is waved,[v] as well as the thigh of whatever raised offering is raised up, whether this be the ordination ram or anything else belonging to Aaron or to his sons. **28** Such things are due to Aaron and his sons from the Israelites by a perpetual ordinance as a contribution. From their peace offerings, too, the Israelites shall make a contribution, their contribution to the LORD.

**29** "The sacred vestments[w] of Aaron shall be passed down to his descendants, that in them they may be anointed and ordained. **30** The descendant who succeeds him as priest and who is to enter the meeting tent to minister in the sanctuary shall be clothed with them for seven days.

**31** [x]"You shall take the flesh of the ordination ram and boil it in a holy place. **32** At the entrance of the meeting tent Aaron and his sons shall eat the flesh of the ram and the bread that is in the basket. **33** They themselves are to eat of these things by which atonement was made at their ordination and consecration; but no layman may eat of them, since they are sacred. **34** If some of the flesh of the ordination sacrifice or some of the bread remains over on the next day, this remnant must be burned up; it is not to be eaten, since it is sacred. **35** Carry out all these orders in regard to Aaron and his sons just as I have given them to you.[y]

"Seven days you shall spend in ordaining them, **36** [z]sacrificing a bullock each day as a sin offering, to make atonement. Thus also shall you purge the altar* in making atonement for it;

s Lv 8, 13.
t 10-26: Lv 8, 14-30.
u Heb 13, 11.
v 27f: Lv 7, 31-34; 10, 14f; Nm 18, 18f; Dt 18, 3.
w Nm 20, 26. 28.
x 31-34: Lv 8, 31f.
y Lv 8, 36.
z 36f: Lv 8, 33ff.

29, 22: Fatty tail: the thick layer of fat surrounding the tails of sheep and rams bred in Palestine even today. It is regarded as a choice food. Cf Lv 3, 9.

29, 24-26: Wave offering: the portions of a peace offering, breast and right thigh, which the officiating priest moved to and fro (waved) in the presence of the Lord. They were reserved for Aaron and his sons.

29, 27-30: These verses are a parenthetical interruption of the ordination ritual; v 31 belongs logically immediately after v 26.

29, 36f: Purge the altar: the construction of an altar by profane hands rendered it impure. The anointing and consecration of the altar purified it and made it sacred.

you shall anoint it in order to consecrate it.
**37** Seven days you shall spend in making atonement for the altar and in consecrating it. Then
the altar will be most sacred, and whatever
touches it will become sacred.
**38** *"Now, this is what you shall offer on the
altar: two yearling lambs[a] as the sacrifice established for each day; **39** one lamb in the morning
and the other lamb at the evening twilight.
**40** With the first lamb there shall be a tenth of
an ephah of fine flour mixed with a fourth of a
hin of oil of crushed olives and, as its libation,
a fourth of a hin of wine. **41** The other lamb you
shall offer at the evening twilight, with the same
cereal offering and libation as in the morning.
You shall offer this as a sweet-smelling oblation
to the LORD. **42** Throughout your generations
this established holocaust shall be offered before the LORD at the entrance of the meeting
tent, where I will meet you and speak to you.
**43** "There, at the altar, I will meet the Israelites; hence, it will be made sacred by my glory.[b]
**44** Thus I will consecrate the meeting tent and
the altar, just as I also consecrate Aaron and his
sons to be my priests. **45** I will dwell in the
midst of the Israelites and will be their God.
**46** They shall know that I, the LORD, am their
God who brought them out of the land of Egypt,
so that I, the LORD, their God, might dwell
among them.

## CHAPTER 30

**Altar of Incense.** **1** "For burning incense
you shall make an altar of acacia wood,[c] **2** with
a square surface, a cubit long, a cubit wide, and
two cubits high, with horns that spring directly
from it. **3** Its grate on top, its walls on all four
sides, and its horns you shall plate with pure
gold. Put a gold molding around it. **4** Underneath the molding you shall put gold rings, two
on one side and two on the opposite side, as
holders for the poles used in carrying it. **5** Make
the poles, too, of acacia wood and plate them
with gold. **6** This altar you are to place in front
of the veil that hangs before the ark of the commandments where I will meet you.[d]
**7** "On it Aaron shall burn fragrant incense.
Morning after morning, when he prepares the
lamps, **8** and again in the evening twilight,
when he lights the lamps, he shall burn incense.
Throughout your generations this shall be the
established incense offering before the LORD.
**9** On this altar you shall not offer up any profane incense, or any holocaust or cereal offering; nor shall you pour out a libation upon it.
**10** Once a year Aaron shall perform the atonement rite on its horns.[e] Throughout your generations this atonement is to be made once a year
with the blood of the atoning sin offering. This
altar is most sacred to the LORD."

**Census Tax.** **11** The LORD also said to Moses, **12** "When you take a census[f] of the Israelites who are to be registered, each one, as he is
enrolled, shall give the LORD a forfeit for his
life, so that no plague may come upon them for
being registered. **13** Everyone who enters the
registered group must pay a half-shekel, according to the standard of the sanctuary shekel,
twenty gerahs to the shekel. This payment of a
half-shekel is a contribution to the LORD.[g]
**14** Everyone of twenty years or more who enters the registered group must give this contribution to the LORD. **15** The rich need not give
more, nor shall the poor give less, than a
half-shekel in this contribution to the LORD to
pay the forfeit for their lives. **16** [h]When you
receive this forfeit money from the Israelites,
you shall donate it to the service of the meeting
tent, that there it may be the Israelites' reminder, before the LORD, of the forfeit paid for their
lives."

**The Laver.** **17** The LORD said to Moses,
**18** "For ablutions you shall make a bronze laver with a bronze base. Place it between the
meeting tent and the altar, and put water in it.[i]
**19** Aaron and his sons shall use it in washing
their hands and feet.[j] **20** When they are about
to enter the meeting tent, they must wash with
water, lest they die. Likewise when they approach the altar in their ministry, to offer an
oblation to the LORD, **21** they must wash their
hands and feet, lest they die. This shall be a
perpetual ordinance for him and his descendants
throughout their generations."

**The Anointing Oil.** **22** The LORD said to
Moses, **23** "Take the finest spices: five hundred shekels of free-flowing myrrh; half that
amount, that is, two hundred and fifty shekels,
of fragrant cinnamon; two hundred and fifty
shekels of fragrant cane; **24** five hundred shekels of cassia—all according to the standard of
the sanctuary shekel; together with a hin of olive
oil; **25** and blend them into sacred anointing
oil,[k] perfumed ointment expertly prepared.
**26** [l]With this sacred anointing oil you shall
anoint the meeting tent and the ark of the commandments, **27** the table and all its appurtenances, the lampstand and its appurtenances,
the altar of incense **28** and the altar of holocausts with all its appurtenances, and the laver

a 38-42: Nm 28, 3-8.
b Ex 25, 22.
c 1-5; Ex 37, 25-28.
d Ex 40, 26.
e Lv 16, 18.
f Nm 1, 2f; 26, 2.
g Mt 17, 24-27.
h Ex 38, 25.
i Ex 38, 8; 40, 7. 30.
j 19ff: Ex 40, 31f.
k Ex 37, 29.
l 26-29: Ex 40, 9ff; Lv 8, 10; Nm 7, 1.

* 29, 38–42: A parenthesis inserted into the rubrics for consecrating the altar; v 43 belongs directly after v 37.

with its base. **29** When you have consecrated them, they shall be most sacred; whatever touches them shall be sacred. **30** Aaron and his sons you shall also anoint and consecrate as my priests.[m] **31** To the Israelites you shall say: As sacred anointing oil this shall belong to me throughout your generations. **32** It may not be used in any ordinary anointing of the body, nor may you make any other oil of a like mixture. It is sacred, and shall be treated as sacred by you. **33** Whoever prepares a perfume like this, or whoever puts any of this on a layman, shall be cut off from his kinsmen."

**The Incense.** **34** [n]The LORD told Moses, "Take these aromatic substances: storax and onycha and galbanum, these and pure frankincense in equal parts; **35** and blend them into incense. This fragrant powder, expertly prepared, is to be salted and so kept pure and sacred. **36** Grind some of it into fine dust and put this before the commandments in the meeting tent where I will meet you. This incense shall be treated as most sacred by you. **37** You may not make incense of a like mixture for yourselves; you must treat it as sacred to the LORD. **38** Whoever makes an incense like this for his own enjoyment of its fragrance, shall be cut off from his kinsmen."

## CHAPTER 31

**Choice of Artisans.** **1** [o]The LORD said to Moses, **2** "See, I have chosen Bezalel, son of Uri, son of Hur, of the tribe of Judah, **3** and I have filled him with a divine spirit of skill and understanding and knowledge in every craft: **4** in the production of embroidery, in making things of gold, silver or bronze, **5** in cutting and mounting precious stones, in carving wood, and in every other craft. **6** As his assistant I have appointed Oholiab, son of Ahisamach, of the tribe of Dan. I have also endowed all the experts with the necessary skill to make all the things I have ordered you to make: **7** [p]the meeting tent, the ark of the commandments with the propitiatory on top of it, all the furnishings of the tent, **8** the table with its appurtenances, the pure gold lampstand with all its appurtenances, the altar of incense, **9** the altar of holocausts with all its appurtenances, the laver with its base, **10** the service cloths,* the sacred vestments for Aaron the priest, the vestments for his sons in their ministry, **11** the anointing oil, and the fragrant incense for the sanctuary. All these things they shall make just as I have commanded you."

**Sabbath Laws.** **12** [q]The LORD said to Moses, **13** "You must also tell the Israelites: Take care to keep my sabbaths, for that is to be the token between you and me throughout the generations, to show that it is I, the LORD, who make you holy. **14** Therefore, you must keep the sabbath as something sacred. Whoever desecrates it shall be put to death. If anyone does work on that day, he must be rooted out of his people. **15** Six days there are for doing work, but the seventh day is the sabbath of complete rest, sacred to the LORD. Anyone who does work on the sabbath day shall be put to death. **16** So shall the Israelites observe the sabbath, keeping it throughout their generations as a perpetual covenant. **17** Between me and the Israelites it is to be an everlasting token; for in six days the LORD made the heavens and the earth, but on the seventh day he rested at his ease."

**18** When the LORD had finished speaking to Moses on Mount Sinai, he gave him the two tablets of the commandments, the stone tablets inscribed by God's own finger.[r]

## CHAPTER 32

**The Golden Calf.** **1** When the people became aware of Moses' delay in coming down from the mountain, they gathered around Aaron and said to him, "Come, make us a god who will be our leader; as for the man Moses who brought us out of the land of Egypt, we do not know what has happened to him."[s] **2** Aaron replied, "Have your wives and sons and daughters take off the golden earrings they are wearing, and bring them to me." **3** So all the people took off their earrings and brought them to Aaron, **4** who accepted their offering, and fashioning this gold with a graving tool, made a molten calf. Then they cried out, "This is your God, O Israel, who brought you out of the land of Egypt."[t] **5** On seeing this, Aaron built an altar before the calf and proclaimed, "Tomorrow is a feast of the LORD."* **6** Early the next day the people offered holocausts and brought peace offerings. Then they sat down to eat and drink, and rose up to revel.[u]

**7** With that, the LORD said to Moses, "Go down at once to your people, whom you brought out of the land of Egypt, for they have become depraved. **8** [v]They have soon turned aside from the way I pointed out to them, making for them-

m Ex 29, 7; Lv 8, 12.
n 34ff: Ex 25, 6; 37, 29.
o 1-6: Ex 35, 30-35.
p 7-11: Ex 35, 10-19.
q 12-17: Ex 20, 8-11; 35, 1-3.
r Ex 24, 12; 32, 15f; Dt 5, 22.
s Ex 32, 23; Acts 7, 40.
t Ex 32, 8; 1 Kgs 12, 28.
u 1 Cor 10, 7.
v 7f: Dt 9, 12. 16.

*

31, 10: The service cloths: so the Greek. They were perhaps the colored cloths mentioned in Nm 4, 4–15.

32, 5: The calf . . . a feast of the Lord: from this it is clear that the golden calf was intended as an image, not of a false god, but of the Lord himself, his strength being symbolized by the strength of a young bull. The Israelites, however, had been forbidden to represent the Lord under any visible form. Cf Ex 20, 4.

selves a molten calf and worshiping it, sacrificing to it and crying out, 'This is your God, O
Israel, who brought you out of the land of
Egypt!' **9** I see how stiff-necked this people
is,"[w] continued the LORD to Moses. **10** "Let
me alone, then, that my wrath may blaze up
against them to consume them. Then I will
make of you a great nation."

**11** But Moses implored the LORD, his God,
saying,[x] "Why, O LORD, should your wrath
blaze up against your own people, whom you
brought out of the land of Egypt with such great
power and with so strong a hand? **12** Why
should the Egyptians say, 'With evil intent he
brought them out, that he might kill them in the
mountains and exterminate them from the face
of the earth'? Let your blazing wrath die down;
relent in punishing your people. **13** Remember
your servants Abraham, Isaac and Israel, and
how you swore to them by your own self, saying,[y] 'I will make your descendants as numerous as the stars in the sky; and all this land that
I promised, I will give your descendants as their
perpetual heritage.' " **14** So the LORD relented
in the punishment he had threatened to inflict on
his people.

**15** Moses then turned and came down the
mountain with the two tablets of the commandments in his hands,[z] tablets that were written on
both sides, front and back; **16** tablets that were
made by God, having inscriptions on them that
were engraved by God himself.[a] **17** Now,
when Joshua heard the noise of the people
shouting, he said to Moses, "That sounds like
a battle in the camp." **18** But Moses answered,
"It does not sound like cries of victory, nor does
it sound like cries of defeat; the sounds that I
hear are cries of revelry." **19** As he drew near
the camp, he saw the calf and the dancing. With
that, Moses' wrath flared up, so that he threw
the tablets down and broke them on the base of
the mountain.[b] **20** Taking the calf they had
made, he fused it in the fire and then ground it
down to powder, which he scattered on the water* and made the Israelites drink.[c]

**21** Moses asked Aaron, "What did this people ever do to you that you should lead them into
so grave a sin?" Aaron replied, "Let not my
lord be angry. **22** You know well enough how
prone the people are to evil. **23** They said to
me, 'Make us a god to be our leader; as for the
man Moses who brought us out of the land of
Egypt, we do not know what has happened to
him.' **24** So I told them, 'Let anyone who has
gold jewelry take it off.' They gave it to me, and
I threw it into the fire, and this calf came out."

**25** When Moses realized that, to the scornful
joy of their foes, Aaron had let the people run
wild, **26** he stood at the gate of the camp and
cried, "Whoever is for the LORD, let him come
to me!" All the Levites[d] then rallied to him,
**27** and he told them, "Thus says the LORD, the
God of Israel: Put your sword on your hip, every
one of you! Now go up and down the camp,
from gate to gate, and slay your own kinsmen,*
your friends and neighbors!" **28** The Levites
carried out the command of Moses, and that day
there fell about three thousand of the people.
**29** Then Moses said, "Today you have been
dedicated to the LORD,* for you were against
your own sons and kinsmen, to bring a blessing
upon yourselves this day."

**The Atonement.** **30** On the next day Moses said to the people,[e] "You have committed
a grave sin. I will go up to the LORD, then;
perhaps I may be able to make atonement for
your sin." **31** So Moses went back to the LORD
and said, "Ah, this people has indeed committed a grave sin in making a god of gold for
themselves! **32** If you would only forgive their
sin! If you will not, then strike me out of the
book that you have written."* **33** The LORD
answered, "Him only who has sinned against
me will I strike out of my book. **34** Now, go
and lead the people whither I have told you. My
angel will go before you. When it is time for me
to punish, I will punish them for their sin."

**35** Thus the LORD smote the people for having had Aaron make the calf for them.

## CHAPTER 33

**1** The LORD told Moses, "You and the people whom you have brought up from the land of
Egypt, are to go up from here to the land which
I swore to Abraham, Isaac and Jacob I would
give to their descendants.[f] **2** Driving out the
Canaanites, Amorites, Hittites, Perizzites, Hivites and Jebusites, I will send an angel before
you[g] **3** to the land flowing with milk and honey. But I myself will not go up in your company, because you are a stiff-necked people; otherwise I might exterminate you on the way."
**4** When the people heard this bad news, they

w 9f: Dt 9, 13; Ps 106, 23.
x 11f: Nm 14, 13ff; Dt 9, 28.
y Gn 22, 16f.
z Dt 9, 15.
a Ex 31, 18.
b Dt 9, 16f.
c Dt 9, 21.
d 26-29: Dt 33, 8f.
e 30-34: Dt 9, 18ff.
f Gn 12, 7.
g Ex 23, 23.

*

32, 20: The water: the stream that flowed down Mount Sinai. Cf Dt 9, 21.

32, 27: Slay your own kinsmen: those who were especially guilty of the idolatry.

32, 29: Dedicated to the Lord: because of their zeal for the true worship of the Lord, the Levites were chosen to be special ministers of the ritual service. However, the meaning of the Hebrew here is somewhat disputed.

32, 32: The book that you have written: the list of God's intimate friends. In a similar sense St. Paul wished to be anathema from Christ for the sake of his brethren. Cf Rom 9, 3.

went into mourning, and no one wore his ornaments.
5 The LORD said to Moses, "Tell the Israelites: You are a stiff-necked people. Were I to go up in your company even for a moment, I would exterminate you. Take off your ornaments, therefore; I will then see what I am to do with you." 6 So, from Mount Horeb onward, the Israelites laid aside their ornaments.

**Moses' Intimacy with God.** 7 The tent,[h] which was called the meeting tent,* Moses used to pitch at some distance away, outside the camp. Anyone who wished to consult the LORD would go to this meeting tent outside the camp.
8 Whenever Moses went out to the tent, the people would all rise and stand at the entrance of their own tents, watching Moses until he entered the tent. 9 As Moses entered the tent, the column of cloud would come down and stand at its entrance while the LORD spoke with Moses. 10 On seeing the column of cloud stand at the entrance of the tent, all the people would rise and worship at the entrance of their own tents. 11 The LORD used to speak to Moses face to face,[i] as one man speaks to another. Moses would then return to the camp, but his young assistant, Joshua, son of Nun, would not move out of the tent.
12 Moses said to the LORD, "You, indeed, are telling me to lead this people on;[j] but you have not let me know whom you will send with me. Yet you have said, 'You are my intimate friend,' and also, 'You have found favor with me.' 13 Now, if I have found favor with you, do let me know your ways so that, in knowing you, I may continue to find favor with you. Then, too, this nation is, after all, your own people." 14 "I myself,"* the LORD answered, "will go along, to give you rest." 15 Moses replied, "If you are not going yourself, do not make us go up from here. 16 For how can it be known that we, your people and I, have found favor with you, except by your going with us? Then we, your people and I, will be singled out from every other people on the earth." 17 The LORD said to Moses, "This request, too, which you have just made, I will carry out, because you have found favor with me and you are my intimate friend."
18 Then Moses said, "Do let me see your glory!" 19 He answered, "I will make all my beauty pass before you, and in your presence I will pronounce my name, 'LORD'; I who show favors to whom I will, I who grant mercy to whom I will.[k] 20 But my face you cannot see,[l] for no man sees me and still lives. 21 Here," continued the LORD, "is a place near me where you shall station yourself on the rock. 22 When my glory passes I will set you in the hollow of the rock and will cover you with my hand until I have passed by. 23 Then I will remove my hand, so that you may see my back;* but my face is not to be seen."

## CHAPTER 34

**Renewal of the Tablets.** 1 The LORD said to Moses, "Cut two stone tablets like the former,[m] that I may write on them the commandments which were on the former tablets that you broke. 2 Get ready for tomorrow morning, when you are to go up Mount Sinai and there present yourself to me on the top of the mountain. 3 No one shall come up with you, and no one is even to be seen on any part of the mountain;[n] even the flocks and the herds are not to go grazing toward this mountain." 4 Moses then cut two stone tablets like the former, and early the next morning he went up Mount Sinai as the LORD had commanded him, taking along the two stone tablets.
5 Having come down in a cloud, the LORD stood with him there and proclaimed his name, "LORD." 6 Thus the LORD passed before him and cried out, "The LORD, the LORD, a merciful and gracious God, slow to anger and rich in kindness and fidelity, 7 continuing his kindness for a thousand generations, and forgiving wickedness and crime and sin; yet not declaring the guilty guiltless, but punishing children and grandchildren to the third and fourth generation for their fathers' wickedness!"[o] 8 Moses at once bowed down to the ground in worship.
9 Then he said, "If I find favor with you, O LORD, do come along in our company. This is indeed a stiff-necked people; yet pardon our wickedness and sins, and receive us as your own."

**Religious Laws.** 10 "Here, then," said the LORD, "is the covenant I will make. Before the eyes of all your people I will work such marvels as have never been wrought in any nation anywhere on earth, so that this people among whom you live may see how awe-inspiring are the deeds which I, the LORD, will do at

h Ex 29, 42f.
i Nm 12, 8; Dt 34, 10; Sir 45, 4-6.
j Ex 32, 34.
k Rom 9, 15.
l Jn 1, 18; 1 Tm 6, 16.
m Dt 10, 1f.
n Ex 19, 12f. 21.
o 6f: Ex 20, 5f; Nm 14, 18; Dt 5, 9f; Jer 32, 18.

33, 7–11: The meeting tent is mentioned here by anticipation; its actual construction is described in the following chapters.

33, 14: I myself: literally, "my face," that is, "my presence." To give you rest: in the Promised Land; some understand, "to put your mind at rest"; others, by a slight emendation in the text, render, "to lead you."

33, 23: You may see my back: man can see God's glory as reflected in creation, but his "face," that is, God as he is in himself, mortal man cannot behold. Cf 1 Cor 13, 12.

your side. **11** But you, on your part, must keep the commandments I am giving you today.[p]

"I will drive out before you the Amorites, Canaanites, Hittites, Perizzites, Hivites, and Jebusites. **12** [q]Take care, therefore, not to make a covenant with these inhabitants of the land that you are to enter; else they will become a snare among you. **13** Tear down their altars; smash their sacred pillars, and cut down their sacred poles.* **14** You shall not worship any other god, for the LORD is 'the Jealous One';* a jealous God is he. **15** Do not make a covenant with the inhabitants of that land; else, when they render their wanton worship to their gods and sacrifice to them, one of them may invite you and you may partake of his sacrifice. **16** Neither shall you take their daughters as wives for your sons; otherwise, when their daughters render their wanton worship to their gods, they will make your sons do the same.

**17** "You shall not make for yourselves molten gods.[r]

**18** "You shall keep the feast of Unleavened Bread.[s] For seven days at the prescribed time in the month of Abib you are to eat unleavened bread, as I commanded you; for in the month of Abib you came out of Egypt.

**19** "To me belongs every first-born male that opens the womb among all your livestock, whether in the herd or in the flock.[t] **20** The firstling of an ass you shall redeem with one of the flock; if you do not redeem it, you must break its neck. The first-born among your sons you shall redeem.

"No one shall appear before me empty-handed.

**21** "For six days you may work,[u] but on the seventh day you shall rest; on that day you must rest even during the seasons of plowing and harvesting.

**22** [v]"You shall keep the feast of Weeks* with the first of the wheat harvest; likewise, the feast at the fruit harvest at the close of the year. **23** Three times a year all your men shall appear before the Lord, the LORD God of Israel. **24** Since I will drive out the nations before you to give you a large territory, there will be no one to covet your land when you go up three times a year to appear before the LORD, your God.

**25** "You shall not offer me the blood of sacrifice with leavened bread, nor shall the sacrifice of the Passover feast be kept overnight for the next day.

**26** "The choicest first fruits of your soil you shall bring to the house of the LORD, your God.

"You shall not boil a kid in its mother's milk."[w]

### Radiance of Moses' Face.

**27** Then the LORD said to Moses, "Write down these words, for in accordance with them I have made a covenant with you and with Israel." **28** So Moses stayed there with the LORD for forty days and forty nights,[x] without eating any food or drinking any water, and he wrote on the tablets the words of the covenant, the ten commandments.

**29** As Moses came down from Mount Sinai with the two tablets of the commandments in his hands, he did not know that the skin of his face had become radiant while he conversed with the LORD. **30** When Aaron, then, and the other Israelites saw Moses and noticed how radiant the skin of his face had become, they were afraid to come near him. **31** Only after Moses called to them did Aaron and all the rulers of the community come back to him. Moses then spoke to them. **32** Later on, all the Israelites came up to him, and he enjoined on them all that the LORD had told him on Mount Sinai. **33** When he finished speaking with them, he put a veil over his face.* **34** Whenever Moses entered the presence of the LORD to converse with him, he removed the veil until he came out again.[y] On coming out, he would tell the Israelites all that had been commanded. **35** Then the Israelites would see that the skin of Moses' face was radiant; so he would again put the veil over his face until he went in to converse with the LORD.

## CHAPTER 35

### Sabbath Regulations.

**1** Moses assembled the whole Israelite community and said to them,[z] "This is what the LORD has commanded to be done. **2** On six days work may be done, but the seventh day shall be sacred to you as the sabbath of complete rest to the LORD. Anyone who does work on that day shall be put to death.

p Ex 13, 5; 33, 2.
q 12-16: Ex 23, 32f; Dt 7, 1-5; 12, 2f.
r Lv 19, 4; 5, 8f.
s Ex 12, 15ff; 13, 3f.
t 19f: Ex 13, 2. 12f; 23, 15.
u Ex 20, 9f.
v 22f: Ex 23, 16f; Dt 16, 10. 13. 16.
w 25f: Ex 23, 18f.
x Ex 24, 18; Dt 9, 9. 18; 10, 2. 4.
y 33f: 2 Cor 3, 13. 16.
z 1-3: Ex 31, 13-17.

*

34, 13: Sacred poles: "Ashera" was the name of a Canaanite goddess. In her honor wooden poles (asherot) were erected, just as stone pillars (massebot) were erected in honor of the god Baal. Both were placed near the altar in a Canaanite shrine.

34, 14: The Lord is "the Jealous One": see note on Ex 20, 5. Some, by a slight emendation, render, "The LORD is jealous for his name." Cf Ez 39, 25.

34, 22: Feast of Weeks: the festival of thanksgiving for the harvest, celebrated seven weeks or fifty days after the beginning of the harvest. It was also called Pentecost (fiftieth) and coincided with the giving of the law on Mount Sinai, fifty days after the offering of the first fruits; cf Lv 23 10f; Dt 16, 9.

34, 33: He put a veil over his face: St. Paul sees in this a symbol of the failure of the Jews to recognize Jesus as the promised Messiah. The true spiritual meaning of the writings of Moses and the prophets is still veiled from the unbelieving Jews. Cf 2 Cor 3, 7–18.

**3** You shall not even light a fire in any of your
dwellings on the sabbath day."

**Collection of Materials.** **4** Moses told the
whole Israelite community, "This is what the
LORD has commanded: **5** [a]Take up among you
a collection for the LORD. Everyone, as his heart
prompts him, shall bring, as a contribution to
the LORD, gold, silver and bronze; **6** violet,
purple and scarlet yarn; fine linen and goat hair;
**7** rams' skins dyed red, and tahash skins; acacia
wood; **8** oil for the light; spices for the anointing oil and for the fragrant incense; **9** onyx
stones and other gems for mounting on the
ephod and on the breastpiece.

**Call for Artisans.** **10** [b]"Let every expert
among you come and make all that the LORD has
commanded: **11** the Dwelling, with its tent, its
covering, its clasps, its boards, its bars, its columns and its pedestals; **12** the ark, with its
poles, the propitiatory, and the curtain veil;
**13** the table, with its poles and all its appurtenances, and the showbread; **14** the lampstand,
with its appurtenances, the lamps, and the oil
for the light; **15** the altar of incense, with its
poles; the anointing oil, and the fragrant incense; the entrance curtain for the entrance of
the Dwelling; **16** the altar of holocausts, with
its bronze grating, its poles, and all its appurtenances; the laver, with its base; **17** the hangings
of the court, with their columns and pedestals;
the curtain for the entrance of the court; **18** the
tent pegs for the Dwelling and for the court,
with their ropes; **19** the service cloths for use in
the sanctuary; the sacred vestments for Aaron,
the priest, and the vestments worn by his sons
in their ministry."

**The Contribution.** **20** When the whole Israelite community left Moses' presence, **21** everyone, as his heart suggested and his spirit
prompted, brought a contribution to the LORD
for the construction of the meeting tent, for all
its services, and for the sacred vestments.
**22** Both the men and the women, all as their
hearts prompted them, brought brooches, earrings, rings, necklaces and various other gold
articles.[c] Everyone who could presented an offering of gold to the LORD. **23** Everyone who
happened to have violet, purple or scarlet yarn,
fine linen or goat hair, rams' skins dyed red or
tahash skins, brought them. **24** Whoever could
make a contribution of silver or bronze offered
it to the LORD; and everyone who happened to
have acacia wood for any part of the work,
brought it. **25** All the women who were expert
spinners brought hand-spun violet, purple and
scarlet yarn and fine linen thread. **26** All the
women who possessed the skill, spun goat hair.
**27** The princes brought onyx stones and other
gems for mounting on the ephod and on the
breastpiece; **28** as well as spices, and oil for the
light, anointing oil, and fragrant incense.
**29** Every Israelite man and woman brought to
the LORD such voluntary offerings as they
thought best, for the various kinds of work
which the LORD had commanded Moses to have
done.

**The Artisans.** **30** Moses said to the Israelites,[d] "See, the LORD has chosen Bezalel, son
of Uri, son of Hur, of the tribe of Judah, **31** and
has filled him with a divine spirit of skill and
understanding and knowledge in every craft:
**32** in the production of embroidery, in making
things of gold, silver or bronze, **33** in cutting
and mounting precious stones, in carving wood,
and in every other craft. **34** He has also given
both him and Oholiab, son of Ahisamach, of the
tribe of Dan, the ability to teach others. **35** He
has endowed them with skill to execute all types
of work: engraving, embroidering, the making
of variegated cloth of violet, purple and scarlet
yarn and fine linen thread, weaving, and all
other arts and crafts.

## CHAPTER 36

**1** "Bezalel, therefore, will set to work with
Oholiab and with all the experts whom the LORD
has endowed with skill and understanding in
knowing how to execute all the work for the
service of the sanctuary, just as the LORD has
commanded."[e]

**2** Moses then called Bezalel and Oholiab and
all the other experts whom the LORD had endowed with skill, men whose hearts moved
them to come and take part in the work. **3** They
received from Moses all the contributions which
the Israelites had brought for establishing the
service of the sanctuary. Still, morning after
morning the people continued to bring their
voluntary offerings to Moses. **4** Thereupon the
experts who were executing the various kinds of
work for the sanctuary, all left the work they
were doing, **5** and told Moses, "The people are
bringing much more than is needed to carry out
the work which the LORD has commanded us to
do." **6** Moses, therefore, ordered a proclamation to be made throughout the camp: "Let neither man nor woman make any more contributions for the sanctuary." So the people stopped
bringing their offerings; **7** there was already
enough at hand, in fact, more than enough, to
complete the work to be done.

**The Tent Cloth and Coverings.** **8** [f]The
various experts who were executing the work,
made the Dwelling with its ten sheets woven of

a 5-9: Ex 25, 2-7.
b 10-19: Ex 31, 6-11.
c 22-28: Ex 25, 3-7.
d 30-35; Ex 31, 1-6.
e 1f: Ex 31, 1. 6.
f 8-19: Ex 26, 1-14.

fine linen twined, having cherubim embroidered on them with violet, purple and scarlet
yarn. **9** The length of each sheet was twenty-
eight cubits, and the width four cubits; all the
sheets were of the same size. **10** Five of the
sheets were sewed together, edge to edge; and
the same for the other five. **11** Loops of violet
yarn were made along the edge of the end sheet
in the first set, and the same along the edge of
the end sheet in the second set. **12** Fifty loops
were thus put on one inner sheet, and fifty loops
on the inner sheet in the other set, with the loops
directly opposite each other. **13** Then fifty
clasps of gold were made, with which the sheets
were joined so that the Dwelling formed one
whole.

**14** Sheets of goat hair were also woven as a
tent over the Dwelling. Eleven such sheets were
made. **15** The length of each sheet was thirty
cubits and the width four cubits; all eleven
sheets were of the same size. **16** Five of these
sheets were sewed edge to edge into one set; and
the other six sheets into another set. **17** Fifty
loops were made along the edge of the end sheet
in one set, and fifty loops along the edge of the
corresponding sheet in the other set. **18** Fifty
bronze clasps were made with which the tent
was joined so that it formed one whole. **19** A
covering for the tent was made of rams' skins
dyed red, and above that, a covering of tahash
skins.

**The Boards.** **20** [g]Boards of acacia wood
were made as walls for the Dwelling. **21** The
length of each board was ten cubits, and the
width one and a half cubits. **22** Each board had
two arms, fastening them in line. In this way all
the boards of the Dwelling were made. **23** They
were set up as follows: twenty boards on the
south side, **24** with forty silver pedestals under
the twenty boards, so that there were two pedestals under each board, at its two arms; **25** twenty boards on the other side of the Dwelling, the
north side, **26** with their forty silver pedestals,
two under each board; **27** six boards at the rear
of the Dwelling, to the west; **28** and two boards
at the corners in the rear of the Dwelling.
**29** These were double at the bottom, and likewise double at the top, to the first ring. That is
how both boards in the corners were made.
**30** Thus, there were in the rear eight boards,
with their sixteen silver pedestals, two pedestals
under each board. **31** Bars of acacia wood were
also made, five for the boards on one side of the
Dwelling, **32** five for those on the other side,
and five for those at the rear, to the west.
**33** The center bar, at the middle of the boards,
was made to reach across from end to end.
**34** The boards were plated with gold, and gold
rings were made on them as holders for the bars,
which were also plated with gold.

**The Veil.** **35** [h]The veil was woven of violet,
purple and scarlet yarn, and of fine linen
twined, with cherubim embroidered on it.
**36** Four gold-plated columns of acacia wood,
with gold hooks, were made for it, and four
silver pedestals were cast for them.

**37** The curtain for the entrance of the tent
was made of violet, purple and scarlet yarn, and
of fine linen twined, woven in a variegated manner. **38** Its five columns, with their hooks as
well as their capitals and bands, were plated
with gold; their five pedestals were of bronze.

## CHAPTER 37

**The Ark.** **1** Bezalel made the ark of acacia
wood, two and a half cubits long, one and a half
cubits wide, and one and a half cubits high.
**2** The inside and outside were plated with gold,
and a molding of gold was put around it. **3** Four
gold rings were cast and put on its four supports,
two rings for one side and two for the opposite
side. **4** Poles of acacia wood were made and
plated with gold; **5** these were put through the
rings on the sides of the ark, for carrying it.

**6** The propitiatory was made of pure gold,
two and a half cubits long and one and a half
cubits wide. **7** Two cherubim of beaten gold
were made for the two ends of the propitiatory,
**8** one cherub fastened at one end, the other at
the other end, springing directly from the
propitiatory at its two ends. **9** The cherubim
had their wings spread out above, covering the
propitiatory with them. They were turned toward each other, but with their faces looking
toward the propitiatory.[i]

**The Table.** **10** [j]The table was made of acacia wood, two cubits long, one cubit wide, and
one and a half cubits high. **11** It was plated with
pure gold, and a molding of gold was put around
it. **12** A frame a handbreadth high was also put
around it, with a molding of gold around the
frame. **13** Four rings of gold were cast for it and
fastened, one at each of the four corners.
**14** The rings were alongside the frame as holders for the poles to carry the table. **15** These
poles were made of acacia wood and plated with
gold. **16** The vessels that were set on the table,
its plates and cups, as well as its pitchers and
bowls for pouring libations, were of pure gold.

**The Lampstand.** **17** [k]The lampstand was
made of pure beaten gold—its shaft and
branches as well as its cups and knobs and petals
springing directly from it. **18** Six branches extended from its sides, three branches on one side
and three on the other. **19** On one branch there

g 20-34: Ex 26, 15-29.
h 35-38: Ex 26, 31-37.
i 1-9: Ex 25, 10-22.
j 10-16: Ex 25, 23-30.
k 17-24: Ex 25, 31-39.

were three cups, shaped like almond blossoms, each with its knob and petals; on the opposite branch there were three cups, shaped like almond blossoms, each with its knob and petals; and so for the six branches that extended from the lampstand. **20** On the shaft there were four cups, shaped like almond blossoms, with their knobs and petals, **21** including a knob below each of the three pairs of branches that extended from the lampstand. **22** The knobs and branches sprang so directly from it that the whole formed but a single piece of pure beaten gold. **23** Its seven lamps, as well as its trimming shears and trays, were made of pure gold. **24** A talent of pure gold was used for the lampstand and its various appurtenances.

**The Altar of Incense.** **25** [l]The altar of incense was made of acacia wood, on a square, a cubit long, a cubit wide, and two cubits high, having horns that sprang directly from it. **26** Its grate on top, its walls on all four sides, and its horns were plated with pure gold; and a molding of gold was put around it. **27** Underneath the molding gold rings were placed, two on one side and two on the opposite side, as holders for the poles to carry it. **28** The poles, too, were made of acacia wood and plated with gold.

**29** The sacred anointing oil and the fragrant incense were prepared in their pure form by a perfumer.[m]

## CHAPTER 38

**The Altar of Holocausts.** **1** The altar of holocausts[n] was made of acacia wood, on a square, five cubits long and five cubits wide; its height was three cubits. **2** At the four corners horns were made that sprang directly from the altar. The whole was plated with bronze. **3** All the utensils of the altar, the pots, shovels, basins, forks and fire pans, were likewise made of bronze. **4** A grating of bronze network was made for the altar and placed round it, on the ground, half as high as the altar itself. **5** Four rings were cast for the four corners of the bronze grating, as holders for the poles, **6** which were made of acacia wood and plated with bronze. **7** The poles were put through the rings on the sides of the altar for carrying it. The altar was made in the form of a hollow box.

**8** The bronze laver,[o] with its bronze base, was made from the mirrors of the women who served* at the entrance of the meeting tent.

**The Court.** **9** [p]The court was made as follows. On the south side of the court there were hangings, woven of fine linen twined, a hundred cubits long, **10** with twenty columns and twenty pedestals of bronze, the hooks and bands of the columns being of silver. **11** On the north side there were similar hangings, one hundred cubits long, with twenty columns and twenty pedestals of bronze, the hooks and bands of the columns being of silver. **12** On the west side there were hangings, fifty cubits long, with ten columns and ten pedestals, the hooks and bands of the columns being of silver. **13** On the east side the court was fifty cubits long. **14** Toward one side there were hangings to the extent of fifteen cubits, with three columns and three pedestals; **15** toward the other side, beyond the entrance of the court, there were likewise hangings to the extent of fifteen cubits, with three columns and three pedestals. **16** The hangings on all sides of the court were woven of fine linen twined. **17** The pedestals of the columns were of bronze, while the hooks and bands of the columns were of silver; the capitals were silver-plated, and all the columns of the court were banded with silver.

**18** At the entrance of the court there was a variegated curtain, woven of violet, purple and scarlet yarn and of fine linen twined, twenty cubits long and five cubits wide, in keeping with the hangings of the court. **19** There were four columns and four pedestals of bronze for it, while their hooks were of silver. **20** All the tent pegs for the Dwelling and for the court around it were of bronze.

**Amount of Metal Used.** **21** The following is an account of the various amounts used on the Dwelling, the Dwelling of the commandments, drawn up at the command of Moses by the Levites under the direction of Ithamar, son of Aaron the priest. **22** However, it was Bezalel, son of Uri,[q] son of Hur, of the tribe of Judah, who made all that the Lord commanded Moses, **23** and he was assisted by Oholiab, son of Ahisamach, of the tribe of Dan, who was an engraver, an embroiderer, and a weaver of variegated cloth of violet, purple and scarlet yarn and of fine linen.

**24** All the gold used in the entire construction of the sanctuary, having previously been given as an offering, amounted to twenty-nine talents and seven hundred and thirty shekels, according to the standard of the sanctuary shekel. **25** The amount of the silver received from the community was one hundred talents and one thousand seven hundred and seventy-five shekels, according to the standard of the sanctuary shekel; **26** one bekah apiece, that is, a half-shekel apiece, according to the standard of the

l 25-28: Ex 30, 1-5.
m Ex 30, 23ff. 34ff.
n 1-7: Ex 27, 1-8; 2 Chr 1, 5.
o Ex 30, 18-21.
p 9-20: Ex 27, 9-19.
q 22f: Ex 31, 2. 6; 35, 30. 34; 36, 1.
r Nm 1, 46.

*

38, 8: The reflecting surface of ancient mirrors was usually of polished bronze. The women who served: cf 1 Sm 2, 22.

sanctuary shekel, was received from every man
of twenty years or more who entered the registered group; the number of these was six hundred and three thousand five hundred and fifty
men.[r] **27** One hundred talents of silver were
used for casting the pedestals of the sanctuary
and the pedestals of the veil, one talent for each
pedestal, or one hundred talents for the one
hundred pedestals. **28** The remaining one thousand seven hundred and seventy-five shekels
were used for making the hooks on the columns,
for plating the capitals, and for banding them
with silver. **29** The bronze, given as an offering, amounted to seventy talents and two thousand four hundred shekels. **30** With this were
made the pedestals at the entrance of the meeting tent, the bronze altar with its bronze gratings
and all the appurtenances of the altar, **31** the
pedestals around the court, the pedestals at the
entrance of the court, and all the tent pegs for
the Dwelling and for the court around it.

## CHAPTER 39

**The Vestments.** **1** With violet, purple and
scarlet yarn were woven the service cloths for
use in the sanctuary, as well as the sacred vestments[s] for Aaron, as the LORD had commanded
Moses.

**2** [t]The ephod was woven of gold thread and
of violet, purple and scarlet yarn and of fine
linen twined. **3** Gold was first hammered into
gold leaf and then cut up into threads, which
were woven with the violet, purple and scarlet
yarn into an embroidered pattern on the fine
linen. **4** Shoulder straps were made for it and
joined to its two upper ends. **5** The embroidered
belt on the ephod extended out from it, and like
it, was made of gold thread, of violet, purple
and scarlet yarn, and of fine linen twined, as the
LORD had commanded Moses. **6** The onyx
stones were prepared and mounted in gold filigree work; they were engraved like seal engravings with the names of the sons of Israel.
**7** These stones were set on the shoulder straps
of the ephod as memorial stones of the sons of
Israel, just as the LORD had commanded Moses.

**8** [u]The breastpiece was embroidered like the
ephod, with gold thread and violet, purple and
scarlet yarn on cloth of fine linen twined. **9** It
was square and folded double, a span high and
a span wide in its folded form. **10** Four rows of
precious stones were mounted on it: in the first
row a carnelian, a topaz and an emerald; **11** in
the second row, a garnet, a sapphire and a beryl;
**12** in the third row a jacinth, an agate and an
amethyst; **13** in the fourth row a chrysolite, an
onyx and a jasper. They were mounted in gold
filigree work. **14** These stones were twelve, to
match the names of the sons of Israel, and each
stone was engraved like a seal with the name of
one of the twelve tribes.

**15** [v]Chains of pure gold, twisted like cords,
were made for the breastpiece, **16** together with
two gold filigree rosettes and two gold rings.
The two rings were fastened to the two upper
ends of the breastpiece. **17** The two gold chains
were then fastened to the two rings at the ends
of the breastpiece. **18** The other two ends of the
two chains were fastened in front to the two
filigree rosettes, which were attached to the
shoulder straps of the ephod. **19** Two other gold
rings were made and put on the two lower ends
of the breastpiece, on the edge facing the ephod.
**20** Two more gold rings were made and fastened to the bottom of the two shoulder straps
next to where they joined the ephod in front, just
above its embroidered belt. **21** Violet ribbons
bound the rings of the breastpiece to the rings
of the ephod, so that the breastpiece stayed right
above the embroidered belt of the ephod and did
not swing loose from it. All this was just as the
LORD had commanded Moses.

**The Other Vestments.** **22** The robe of the
ephod was woven entirely of violet yarn,
**23** with an opening in its center like the opening
of a shirt, with selvage around the opening to
keep it from being torn. **24** At the hem of the
robe pomegranates were made of violet, purple
and scarlet yarn and of fine linen twined;
**25** bells of pure gold were also made and put
between the pomegranates all around the hem of
the robe: **26** first a bell, then a pomegranate,
and thus alternating all around the hem of the
robe which was to be worn in performing the
ministry—all this, just as the LORD had commanded Moses.

**27** For Aaron and his sons there were also
woven tunics of fine linen;[w] **28** the miter of fine
linen; the ornate turbans of fine linen; drawers
of linen [of fine linen twined]; **29** and sashes of
variegated work made of fine linen twined and
of violet, purple and scarlet yarn, as the LORD
had commanded Moses. **30** The plate of the
sacred diadem was made of pure gold[x] and inscribed, as on a seal engraving: "Sacred to the
LORD." **31** It was tied over the miter with a
violet ribbon, as the LORD had commanded Moses.

**Presentation of the Work to Moses.**
**32** Thus the entire work of the Dwelling of the
meeting tent was completed. The Israelites did
the work just as the LORD had commanded Moses. **33** They then brought to Moses the Dwelling, the tent with all its appurtenances, the
clasps, the boards, the bars, the columns, the

s Ex 31, 10.
t 2-10: Ex 28, 6-12.
u 8-14: Ex 28, 15-21.
v 15-21: Ex 28, 31-35.
w 27ff: Ex 28, 39-42.
x 30f: Ex 28, 36f.

pedestals, **34** the covering of rams' skins dyed
red, the covering of tahash skins, the curtain
veil; **35** the ark of the commandments with its
poles, the propitiatory, **36** the table with all its
appurtenances and the showbread, **37** the pure
gold lampstand with its lamps set up on it and
with all its appurtenances, the oil for the light,
**38** the golden altar, the anointing oil, the fragrant incense; the curtain for the entrance of the
tent, **39** the altar of bronze with its bronze grating, its poles and all its appurtenances, the laver
with its base, **40** the hangings of the court with
their columns and pedestals, the curtain for the
entrance of the court with its ropes and tent
pegs, all the equipment for the service of the
Dwelling of the meeting tent; **41** the service
cloths for use in the sanctuary, the sacred vestments for Aaron the priest, and the vestments to
be worn by his sons in their ministry. **42** The
Israelites had carried out all the work just as the
LORD had commanded Moses. **43** So when Moses saw that all the work was done just as the
LORD had commanded, he blessed them.

## CHAPTER 40

**Erection of the Dwelling.** **1** Then the
LORD said to Moses, **2** [y]"On the first day of the
first month* you shall erect the Dwelling of the
meeting tent.[z] **3** Put the ark of the commandments in it, and screen off the ark with the veil.[a]
**4** Bring in the table and set it. Then bring in the
lampstand and set up the lamps on it. **5** Put the
golden altar of incense in front of the ark of the
commandments, and hang the curtain at the entrance of the Dwelling. **6** Put the altar of holocausts in front of the entrance of the Dwelling
of the meeting tent. **7** Place the laver between
the meeting tent and the altar, and put water in
it. **8** Set up the court round about, and put the
curtain at the entrance of the court.

**9** [b]"Take the anointing oil and anoint the
Dwelling and everything in it, consecrating it
and all its furnishings, so that it will be sacred.
**10** Anoint the altar of holocausts and all its
appurtenances, consecrating it, so that it will be
most sacred. **11** Likewise, anoint the laver with
its base, and thus consecrate it.

**12** [c]"Then bring Aaron and his sons to the
entrance of the meeting tent, and there wash
them with water. **13** Clothe Aaron with the sacred vestments and anoint him, thus consecrating him as my priest. **14** Bring forward his sons
also, and clothe them with the tunics. **15** As
you have anointed their father, anoint them also
as my priests. Thus, by being anointed, they
shall receive a perpetual priesthood throughout
all future generations."

**16** Moses did exactly as the LORD had commanded him. **17** On the first day of the first
month of the second year the Dwelling was
erected. **18** It was Moses who erected the
Dwelling. He placed its pedestals, set up its
boards, put in its bars, and set up its columns.
**19** He spread the tent over the Dwelling and put
the covering on top of the tent, as the LORD had
commanded him. **20** [d]He took the commandments and put them in the ark; he placed poles
alongside the ark and set the propitiatory upon
it. **21** He brought the ark into the Dwelling and
hung the curtain veil, thus screening off the ark
of the commandments, as the LORD had commanded him. **22** He put the table in the meeting
tent, on the north side of the Dwelling, outside
the veil, **23** and arranged the bread on it before
the LORD, as the LORD had commanded him.[e]
**24** He placed the lampstand in the meeting tent,
opposite the table, on the south side of the
Dwelling, **25** and he set up the lamps before the
LORD, as the LORD had commanded him. **26** He
placed the golden altar in the meeting tent, in
front of the veil, **27** and on it he burned fragrant
incense, as the LORD had commanded him.
**28** He hung the curtain at the entrance of the
Dwelling. **29** He put the altar of holocausts in
front of the entrance of the Dwelling of the
meeting tent, and offered holocausts and cereal
offerings on it, as the LORD had commanded
him. **30** [f]He placed the laver between the meeting tent and the altar, and put water in it for
washing. **31** Moses and Aaron and his sons
used to wash their hands and feet there, **32** for
they washed themselves whenever they went
into the meeting tent or approached the altar, as
the LORD commanded Moses. **33** Finally, he
set up the court around the Dwelling and the
altar and hung the curtain at the entrance of the
court. Thus Moses finished all the work.

**God's Presence in the Dwelling.**
**34** [g]Then the cloud covered the meeting tent,
and the glory of the LORD filled the Dwelling.
**35** Moses could not enter the meeting tent, because the cloud settled down upon it and the
glory of the LORD filled the Dwelling.
**36** Whenever the cloud rose from the Dwelling,
the Israelites would set out on their journey.
**37** But if the cloud did not lift, they would not
go forward; only when it lifted did they go
forward. **38** In the daytime the cloud of the
LORD was seen over the Dwelling; whereas at
night, fire was seen in the cloud by the whole
house of Israel in all the stages of their journey.

---

y 2-8: Ex 40, 16-33.
z Ex 26, 30.
a 3ff: Ex 26, 33ff.
b 9ff: Ex 30, 26-29.
c 12-15: Ex 28, 41; 29, 4-9; Lv 8, 1-13.
d 20ff: Ex 25, 16, 21; 26, 33ff.
e Ex 25, 30.
f 30ff: Ex 30, 18ff.
g 34-38; Nm 9, 15-22.

---

40, 2: On the first day of the first month: almost a year after the departure of the Israelites from Egypt, Cf v 17.

# The Book of
# LEVITICUS

*The name "Leviticus" was bestowed on the third book of the Pentateuch by the ancient Greek translators because a good part of this book consists of sacrificial and other ritual laws prescribed for the priests of the tribe of Levi.*

*Continuing the legislation given by God to Moses at Mount Sinai, Leviticus is almost entirely legislative in character; the rare narrative portions are subordinate to the main legislative theme. Generally speaking, the laws contained in this book serve to teach the Israelites that they should always keep themselves in a state of legal purity, or external sanctity, as a sign of their intimate union with the Lord. Accordingly, the central idea of Leviticus is contained in its oft-repeated injunction: "You shall be holy, because I, the* LORD*, am holy."*

*The main divisions of Leviticus are:*
- *I. Ritual of Sacrifices (Lv 1—7).*
- *II. Ceremony of Ordination (Lv 8—10).*
- *III. Laws regarding Legal Purity (Lv 11—16).*
- *IV. Code of Legal Holiness (Lv 17—26).*
- *V. Redemption of Offerings (Lv 27).*

## *I: Ritual of Sacrifices*

### CHAPTER 1

**Holocausts.** **1** The LORD called Moses,
and from the meeting tent gave him this message: **2** [a]"Speak to the Israelites and tell them:
When any one of you wishes to bring an animal
offering to the LORD, such an offering must be
from the herd or from the flock.*
**3** "If his holocaust* offering is from the
herd, it must be a male without blemish.[b] To
find favor with the LORD, he shall bring it to the
entrance of the meeting tent **4** and there lay his
hand on the head of the holocaust, so that it may
be acceptable to make atonement for him.[c]
**5** He shall then slaughter the bull before the
LORD, but Aaron's sons, the priests, shall offer
up its blood by splashing it on the sides of the
altar which is at the entrance of the meeting
tent.[d] **6** Then he shall skin the holocaust and
cut it up into pieces. **7** After Aaron's sons, the
priests, have put some burning embers on the
altar and laid some wood on them, **8** they shall
lay the pieces of meat, together with the head
and the suet, on top of the wood and embers on
the altar. **9** The inner organs and the shanks,
however, the offerer shall first wash with water.
The priest shall then burn the whole offering on
the altar as a holocaust, a sweet-smelling oblation to the LORD.[e]
**10** "If his holocaust offering is from the
flock, that is, a sheep or a goat, he must bring
a male without blemish. **11** This he shall
slaughter before the LORD at the north side of the
altar. Then Aaron's sons, the priests, shall
splash its blood on the sides of the altar.
**12** When the offerer has cut it up into pieces,
the priest shall lay these, together with the head
and suet, on top of the wood and the fire on the
altar. **13** The inner organs and the shanks, however, the offerer shall first wash with water. The
priest shall offer them up and then burn the
whole offering on the altar as a holocaust, a
sweet-smelling oblation to the LORD.
**14** "If he offers a bird as a holocaust to the
LORD, he shall choose a turtledove or a pigeon
as his offering.[f] **15** Having brought it to the
altar where it is to be burned, the priest shall
snap its head loose and squeeze out its blood
against the side of the altar.[g] **16** Its crop and
feathers shall be removed and thrown on the ash
heap at the east side of the altar. **17** Then, having split the bird down the middle without sepa-

---

a Lv 22, 18. 19.
b Ex 12, 5.
c Lv 3, 2. 8. 13; 4, 15; 8, 14. 22; 16, 21; Ex 29, 10. 15.
d Lv 3, 8.
e Lv 3, 5. 16; Ex 29, 18.
f Lv 5, 7; 12, 8; Lk 2, 24.
g Lv 5, 8.

---

1, 2: From the herd or from the flock: the only animals which could be used as sacrificial victims were either of the bovine class (bulls, cows and calves) or the ovine class (sheep and lambs, goats and kids). Excluded, therefore, were not only all wild animals, but also such "unclean" domestic animals as the camel and the ass. See note on Lv 11, 1ff.

1, 3: Holocaust: from the Greek word meaning "wholly burned," this is the technical term for the special type of sacrifice in which an entire animal except its hide was consumed in the fire on the altar. The primary purpose of this complete gift was to render glory and praise to God.

rating the halves, the priest shall burn it on the
altar, over the wood on the fire, as a holocaust,
a sweet-smelling oblation to the LORD.

## CHAPTER 2

**Cereal Offerings.** 1 "When anyone
wishes to bring a cereal offering to the LORD, his
offering must consist of fine flour. He shall pour
oil on it and put frankincense over it.[h] 2 When
he has brought it to Aaron's sons, the priests,
one of them shall take a handful of this fine flour
and oil, together with all the frankincense, and
this he shall burn on the altar as a token offering,* a sweet-smelling oblation to the LORD.[i]
3 The rest of the cereal offering belongs to Aaron and his sons. It is a most sacred oblation to
the LORD.[j]
4 "When the cereal offering you present is
baked in an oven, it must be in the form of
unleavened cakes made of fine flour mixed with
oil, or of unleavened wafers spread with oil.
5 If you present a cereal offering that is fried on
a griddle, it must be of fine flour mixed with oil
and unleavened.[k] 6 Such a cereal offering must
be broken into pieces, and oil must be poured
over it. 7 If you present a cereal offering that
is prepared in a pot, it must be of fine flour,
deep-fried in oil. 8 A cereal offering that is
made in any of these ways you shall bring to the
LORD, offering it to the priest, who shall take it
to the altar. 9 Its token offering the priest shall
then lift from the cereal offering and burn on the
altar as a sweet-smelling oblation to the LORD.
10 The rest of the cereal offering belongs to
Aaron and his sons. It is a most sacred oblation
to the LORD.
11 "Every cereal offering that you present to
the LORD shall be unleavened, for you shall not
burn any leaven or honey as an oblation to the
LORD.[l] 12 Such you may indeed present to the
LORD in the offering of first fruits, but they are
not to be placed on the altar for a pleasing odor.
13 However, every cereal offering that you
present to the LORD shall be seasoned with
salt.[m] Do not let the salt of the covenant of your
God* be lacking from your cereal offering. On
every offering you shall offer salt.
14 "If you present a cereal offering of first
fruits to the LORD, you shall offer it in the form
of fresh grits of new ears of grain, roasted by
fire. 15 On this cereal offering you shall put oil
and frankincense. 16 For its token offering the
priest shall then burn some of the grits and oil,
together with all the frankincense, as an oblation to the LORD.

## CHAPTER 3

**Peace Offerings.** 1 "If someone in presenting a peace offering* makes his offering
from the herd, he may offer before the LORD
either a male or a female animal, but it must be
without blemish.[n] 2 He shall lay his hand on
the head of his offering,[o] and then slaughter it
at the entrance of the meeting tent; but Aaron's
sons, the priests, shall splash its blood on the
sides of the altar. 3 From the peace offering he
shall offer as an oblation to the LORD the fatty
membrane over the inner organs, and all the fat
that adheres to them,[p] 4 as well as the two
kidneys, with the fat on them near the loins, and
the lobe of the liver,* which he shall sever
above the kidneys. 5 All this Aaron's sons shall
then burn on the altar with the holocaust,[q] on
the wood over the fire, as a sweet-smelling oblation to the LORD.
6 "If the peace offering he presents to the
LORD is from the flock, he may offer either a
male or a female animal, but it must be without
blemish. 7 If he presents a lamb as his offering,
he shall bring it before the LORD, 8 and after
laying his hand on the head of his offering, he
shall slaughter it before the meeting tent; but
Aaron's sons shall splash its blood on the sides
of the altar. 9 As an oblation to the LORD he
shall present the fat of the peace offering: the
whole fatty tail,* which he must sever close to
the spine, the fatty membrane over the inner
organs, and all the fat that adheres to them,[r]
10 as well as the two kidneys, with the fat on
them near the loins, and the lobe of the liver,
which he must sever above the kidneys. 11 All
this the priest shall burn on the altar as the food
of the LORD's oblation.
12 "If he presents a goat, he shall bring it
before the LORD, 13 and after laying his hand
on its head, he shall slaughter it before the meeting tent; but Aaron's sons shall splash its blood
on the sides of the altar. 14 From it he shall
offer as an oblation to the LORD the fatty mem-

h Nm 15, 4.
i Lv 6, 15.
j Lv 7, 9f; Sir 7, 31; 1 Cor 9, 13.
k 1 Chr 23, 29.
l Lv 6, 16f; Mt 16, 12; Mk 8, 15; Lk 12, 1; 1 Cor 5, 7; Gal 5, 9.
m Ez 43, 24.
n Lv 22, 21.
o Lv 1, 4.
p Ex 29, 13. 22.
q Lv 6, 12.
r Lv 9, 19.

*

2, 2: Token offering: literally, "reminder." Instead of burning the whole cereal offering, they burned only this part of it on the altar; it thus corresponded to the fat of the peace offering. See note on Lv 3, 1.

2, 13: The salt of the covenant of your God: the partaking in common of salt by those seated together at table was an ancient symbol of friendship and alliance. Cf Mk 9, 49 and Col 4, 6; and see note on Nm 18, 19.

3, 1: Peace offering: thus the ancient versions have rendered the Hebrew word, which perhaps means more exactly, "fulfillment sacrifice," offered up in fulfillment of a vow. Cf Prv 7, 14. Its characteristic feature was the sacred banquet at which the offerer and his guests partook of the meat of the sacrificed animal. Cf Lv 7, 11–21.

3, 4: The lobe of the liver: some render, "the fatty covering of the liver."

3, 9: The whole fatty tail: see note on Ex 29, 22.

brane over the inner organs, and all the fat that adheres to them, **15** as well as the two kidneys, with the fat on them near the loins, and the lobe of the liver, which he must sever above the kidneys. **16** All this the priest shall burn on the altar as the food of the sweet-smelling oblation. All the fat belongs to the LORD. **17** This shall be a perpetual ordinance for your descendants wherever they may dwell. You shall not partake of any fat* or any blood."[s]

## CHAPTER 4

**Sin Offerings: For Priests.** **1** The LORD said to Moses, **2** "Tell the Israelites: When a person inadvertently commits a sin* against some command of the LORD by doing one of the forbidden things,[t] **3** if it is the anointed priest* who thus sins and thereby makes the people also become guilty, he shall present to the LORD a young, unblemished bull as a sin offering for the sin he committed.[u] **4** Bringing the bullock to the entrance of the meeting tent, before the LORD, he shall lay his hand on its head and slaughter it before the LORD.[v] **5** The anointed priest shall then take some of the bullock's blood and bring it into the meeting tent, **6** where, dipping his finger in the blood, he shall sprinkle it seven times before the LORD, toward the veil of the sanctuary.[w] **7** The priest shall also put some of the blood on the horns of the altar[x] of fragrant incense which is before the LORD in the meeting tent. The rest of the bullock's blood he shall pour out at the base of the altar of holocausts which is at the entrance of the meeting tent. **8** From the sin-offering bullock he shall remove all the fat: the fatty membrane over the inner organs, and all the fat that adheres to them, **9** as well as the two kidneys, with the fat on them near the loins, and the lobe of the liver, which he must sever above the kidneys. **10** This is the same as is removed from the ox of the peace offering; and the priest shall burn it on the altar of holocausts. **11** The hide of the bullock and all its flesh, with its head, legs, inner organs and offal,[y] **12** in short, the whole bullock, shall be brought outside the camp to a clean place where the ashes are deposited and there be burned up in a wood fire. At the place of the ash heap, there it must be burned.

**For the Community.** **13** "If the whole community of Israel inadvertently and without even being aware of it does something that the LORD has forbidden and thus makes itself guilty,[z] **14** should it later on become known that the sin was committed, the community shall present a young bull as a sin offering. They shall bring it before the meeting tent, **15** and here, before the LORD, the elders of the community shall lay their hands on the bullock's head.[a] When the bullock has been slaughtered before the LORD, **16** the anointed priest shall bring some of its blood into the meeting tent, **17** and dipping his finger in the blood, he shall sprinkle it seven times before the LORD, toward the veil. **18** He shall also put some of the blood on the horns of the altar of fragrant incense which is before the LORD in the meeting tent. The rest of the blood he shall pour out at the base of the altar of holocausts which is at the entrance of the meeting tent. **19** All of its fat he shall take from it and burn on the altar, **20** doing with this bullock just as he did with the other sin-offering bullock. Thus the priest shall make atonement for them, and they will be forgiven. **21** This bullock must also be brought outside the camp and burned, just as has been prescribed for the other one. This is the sin offering for the community.

**For the Princes.** **22** "Should a prince commit a sin inadvertently by doing one of the things which are forbidden by some commandment of the LORD, his God, and thus become guilty, **23** if later on he learns of the sin he committed, he shall bring as his offering an unblemished male goat. **24** Having laid his hands on its head, he shall slaughter the goat as a sin offering before the LORD, in the place where the holocausts are slaughtered. **25** The priest shall then take some of the blood of the sin offering on his finger and put it on the horns of the altar of holocausts. The rest of the blood he shall pour out at the base of this altar. **26** All of the fat he shall burn on the altar like the fat of the peace offering.[b] Thus the priest shall make atonement for the prince's sin, and it will be forgiven.

**For Private Persons.** **27** "If a private person commits a sin inadvertently[c] by doing one of the things which are forbidden by the commandments of the LORD, and thus becomes guilty, **28** should he later on learn of the sin he committed, he shall bring an unblemished

s Lv 17, 10-14; Gn 9, 4; Dt 12, 16. 23; 15, 23.
t Lv 5, 15. 17; Nm 15, 22-29.
u Heb 7, 27.
v Lv 1, 3f.
w Lv 8, 11.
x Lv 8, 15; 9, 9; 16, 18; Ex 29, 12.
y Lv 8, 17; 9, 11; Ex 29, 14; Nm 19, 5.
z Lv 5, 2-4; Nm 15, 24-26.
a Lv 1, 4.
b Lv 3, 3-5.
c Nm 15, 27.

*

3, 17: Any fat: only the fat mentioned in vv 9f. 14f is meant; other fat could be eaten by the Israelites.

4, 2: A sin: not necessarily a moral fault; included are all the cases of ritual uncleanness which people necessarily incurred in certain unavoidable circumstances.

4, 3: The anointed priest: his violation of the ceremonial law brought a sort of collective guilt on all the people whom he represented before God. Sin offering: more exactly, "sacrifice for remitting sin"; sin is here understood as explained above.

she-goat as the offering for his sin. **29** Having
laid his hand on the head of the sin offering,[d]
he shall slaughter it at the place of the holocausts. **30** The priest shall then take some of its
blood on his finger and put it on the horns of the
altar of holocausts. The rest of the blood he shall
pour out at the base of the altar. **31** All the fat
shall be removed, just as the fat is removed from
the peace offering, and the priest shall burn it on
the altar for an odor pleasing to the LORD.[e] Thus
the priest shall make atonement for him, and he
will be forgiven.
**32** "If, however, for his sin offering he
presents a lamb, he shall bring an unblemished
female. **33** Having laid his hand on its head, he
shall slaughter this sin offering in the place
where the holocausts are slaughtered. **34** The
priest shall then take some of the blood of the
sin offering on his finger and put it on the horns
of the altar of holocausts. The rest of the blood
he shall pour out at the base of the altar. **35** All
the fat shall be removed, just as the fat is removed from the peace-offering lamb,[f] and the
priest shall burn it on the altar with the other
oblations of the LORD. Thus the priest shall
make atonement for the man's sin, and it will be
forgiven.

## CHAPTER 5

**For Special Cases.** **1** "If any person refuses to give the information which, as a witness
of something he has seen or learned, he has been
adjured to give, and thus commits a sin and has
guilt to bear;[g] **2** or if someone, without being
aware of it, touches any unclean thing, as the
carcass of an unclean wild animal,[h] or that of
an unclean domestic animal, or that of an unclean swarming creature, and thus becomes unclean and guilty; **3** or if someone, without being
aware of it, touches some human uncleanness,
whatever kind of uncleanness this may be, and
then recognizes his guilt; **4** or if someone, without being aware of it, rashly utters an oath[i] to
do good or evil, such as men are accustomed to
utter rashly, and then recognizes that he is guilty
of such an oath; **5** then whoever is guilty in any
of these cases shall confess the sin he has incurred,[j] **6** and as his sin offering for the sin he
has committed he shall bring to the LORD a
female animal from the flock, a ewe lamb or a
she-goat. The priest shall then make atonement
for his sin.
**7** "If, however, he cannot afford an animal
of the flock, he shall bring to the LORD as the
sin offering for his sin two turtledoves or two
pigeons, one for a sin offering and the other for
a holocaust.[k] **8** He shall bring them to the
priest, who shall offer the one for the sin offering first. Snapping its head loose at the neck, yet
without breaking it off completely,[l] **9** he shall
sprinkle some of the blood of the sin offering
against the side of the altar.[m] The rest of the
blood shall be squeezed out against the base of
the altar. Such is the offering for sin. **10** The
other bird shall be offered as a holocaust in the
usual way. Thus the priest shall make atonement for the sin the man committed, and it will
be forgiven.
**11** "If he is unable to afford even two turtledoves or two pigeons, he shall present as a sin
offering for his sin one tenth of an ephah of fine
flour. He shall not put oil or frankincense on it,
because it is a sin offering. **12** When he has
brought it to the priest, the latter shall take a
handful of this flour as a token offering, and this
he shall burn as a sin offering on the altar with
the other oblations of the LORD. **13** Thus the
priest shall make atonement for the sin that the
man committed in any of the above cases, and
it will be forgiven.[n] The rest of the flour, like
the cereal offerings, shall belong to the priest."

**Guilt Offerings.** **14** The LORD said to Moses, **15** "If someone commits a sin by inadvertently cheating* in the LORD's sacred dues, he
shall bring to the LORD as his guilt offering an
unblemished ram from the flock, valued at two
silver shekels according to the standard of the
sanctuary shekel. **16** He shall also restore what
he has sinfully withheld from the sanctuary,
adding to it a fifth of its value.[o] This is to be
given to the priest, who shall then make atonement for him with the guilt-offering ram, and he
will be forgiven.
**17** [p]"If someone, without being aware of
it,* commits such a sin by doing one of the
things which are forbidden by some commandment of the LORD, that he incurs guilt for which
he must answer, **18** he shall bring as a guilt
offering to the priest an unblemished ram of the
flock of the established value. The priest shall
then make atonement for the fault which was
unwittingly committed, and it will be forgiven.
**19** Such is the offering for guilt; the penalty of
the guilt must be paid to the LORD."

d Lv 1, 4.
e Lv 1, 9; 3, 3-5.
f Lv 3, 3. 9.
g Prv 29, 24.
h Lv 11, 24. 31. 39; 12; 13; 15.
i Jgs 11, 30f; 1 Sm 14, 24; Mk 6, 23; Acts 23, 12.
j Lv 26, 40; Nm 5, 7.
k Lv 12, 8; Lk 2, 24.
l Lv 1, 15. 17.
m Lv 1, 15.
n Lv 4, 26. 35.
o Lv 22, 14.
p Lv 4, 2.

*

5, 15: Cheating: not offering the full amount in tithes, first fruits, etc. Guilt offering: its characteristic was a certain additional penalty imposed as reparation for the injustice involved in the fault which was atoned for by this sacrifice. However, in certain passages, e.g., Lv 14, 12f; Nm 6, 12; Ezr 10, 19, the term "guilt offering" is used for more important cases of "sin offerings" where no apparent injustice is involved.

5, 17: Without being aware of it: the case naturally presupposes that later on the offender learns of his mistake. Cf Lv 4, 13f.

**20** The LORD said to Moses, **21** "If someone
commits a sin of dishonesty against the LORD by
denying his neighbor a deposit or a pledge for
a stolen article, or by otherwise retaining his
neighbor's goods unjustly, **22** or if, having
found a lost article, he denies the fact and
swears falsely about it with any of the sinful
oaths that men make in such cases, **23** he shall
therefore, since he has incurred guilt by his sin,
restore the thing that was stolen or unjustly retained by him or the deposit left with him or the
lost article he found **24** or whatever else he
swore falsely about; on the day of his guilt
offering he shall make full restitution of the
thing itself, and in addition, give the owner one
fifth of its value. **25** As his guilt offering he
shall bring to the LORD an unblemished ram of
the flock of the established value. When he has
presented this as his guilt offering to the priest,
**26** the latter shall make atonement for him before the LORD, and he will be forgiven whatever
guilt he may have incurred."

## CHAPTER 6

**The Daily Holocaust.** **1** The LORD said to
Moses, **2** "Give Aaron and his sons the following command: This is the ritual* for holocausts.
The holocaust is to remain on the hearth of the
altar all night until the next morning, and the fire
is to be kept burning on the altar. **3** The priest,
clothed in his linen robe and wearing linen
drawers on his body, shall take away the ashes
to which the fire has reduced the holocaust on
the altar, and lay them at the side of the altar.
**4** Then, having taken off these garments and
put on other garments, he shall carry the ashes
to a clean place outside the camp. **5** The fire on
the altar is to be kept burning; it must not go out.
Every morning the priest shall put firewood on
it. On this he shall lay out the holocaust and
burn the fat of the peace offerings. **6** The fire
is to be kept burning continuously on the altar;
it must not go out.

**Daily Cereal Offering.** **7** "This is the ritual of the cereal offering. One of Aaron's sons
shall first present it before the LORD, in front of
the altar. **8** Then he shall take from it a handful
of its fine flour and oil, together with all the
frankincense that is on it, and this he shall burn
on the altar as its token offering, a sweet-smelling oblation to the LORD. **9** The rest of it Aaron
and his sons may eat; but it must be eaten in the
form of unleavened cakes and in a sacred place:
in the court of the meeting tent they shall eat it.
**10** It shall not be baked with leaven. I have
given it to them as their portion from the oblations of the LORD; it is most sacred, like the sin
offering and the guilt offering. **11** All the male
descendants of Aaron may partake of it as their
rightful share in the oblations of the LORD per-
petually throughout your generations. Whatever
touches the oblations becomes sacred."
**12** *The LORD said to Moses, **13** "This is
the offering that Aaron and his sons shall
present to the LORD [on the day he is anointed]:
one tenth of a ephah of fine flour for the established cereal offering, half in the morning and
half in the evening. **14** It shall be well kneaded
and fried in oil on a griddle when you bring it
in. Having broken the offering into pieces, you
shall present it as a sweet-smelling oblation to
the LORD. **15** Aaron's descendant who succeeds him as the anointed priest shall do likewise. This is a perpetual ordinance: for the Lord
the whole offering shall be burned. **16** Every
cereal offering of a priest shall be a whole burnt
offering; it may not be eaten."

**Sin Offerings.** **17** The LORD said to Moses,
**18** "Tell Aaron and his sons: This is the ritual
for sin offerings. At the place where holocausts
are slaughtered, there also, before the LORD,
shall the sin offering be slaughtered.[q] It is most
sacred. **19** The priest who presents the sin offering may partake of it; but it must be eaten in
a sacred place,[r] in the court of the meeting tent.
**20** Whatever touches its flesh shall become sacred. If any of its blood is spilled on a garment,
the stained part must be washed in a sacred
place. **21** A clay vessel in which it has been
cooked shall thereafter be broken;[s] if it is
cooked in a bronze vessel, this shall be scoured
afterward and rinsed with water. **22** All the
males of the priestly line may partake of the sin
offering, since it is most sacred.[t] **23** But no one
may partake of any sin offering of which some
blood has been brought into the meeting tent[u]
to make atonement in the sanctuary; such an
offering must be burned up in the fire.

## CHAPTER 7

**Guilt Offerings.** **1** "This is the ritual for
guilt offerings, which are most sacred. **2** At the
place where the holocausts are slaughtered,
there also shall the guilt offering be slaughtered.[v] Its blood shall be splashed on the sides

q Lv 7, 2.
r Lv 10, 17.
s Lv 11, 33; 15, 12.
t Lv 7, 6; Nm 18, 10.
u Lv 4, 5; Heb 13, 11.
v Lv 6, 18.

*

6, 2: Ritual: literally, "law, instruction." Here, and in the following paragraphs, are given additional prescriptions for various kinds of sacrifices which were, in part, treated of in the preceding chapters.

6, 12–16: This is another law about the daily or "established" cereal offering. It differs in some respects from the preceding law (vv 7–11) and also from the law in Ex 29, 38–42. Hence, the words on the day he is anointed were probably added by some later scribe in order to avoid the difficulty of harmonizing this law with the other two laws on the same matter.

of the altar. **3** [w]All of its fat shall be taken from
it and offered up: the fatty tail, the fatty membrane over the inner organs, **4** as well as the two
kidneys with the fat on them near the loins, and
the lobe of the liver, which must be severed
above the kidneys. **5** All this the priest shall
burn on the altar as an oblation to the LORD.
This is the guilt offering. **6** All the males of the
priestly line may partake of it; but it must be
eaten in a sacred place, since it is most sacred.[x]

**7** "Because the sin offering and the guilt
offering are alike, both having the same ritual,
the guilt offering likewise belongs to the priest
who makes atonement with it. **8** Similarly, the
priest who offers a holocaust for someone may
keep for himself the hide of the holocaust that
he has offered. **9** [y]Also, every cereal offering
that is baked in an oven or deep-fried in a pot
or fried on a griddle shall belong to the priest
who offers it, **10** whereas all cereal offerings[z]
that are offered up dry or mixed with oil shall
belong to all of Aaron's sons without distinction.

**Peace Offerings.** **11** "This is the ritual for
the peace offerings that are presented to the
LORD. **12** When anyone makes a peace offering
in thanksgiving, together with his thanksgiving
sacrifice he shall offer unleavened cakes mixed
with oil, unleavened wafers spread with oil, and
cakes made of fine flour mixed with oil and well
kneaded. **13** His offering shall also include
loaves of leavened bread* along with the victim
of his peace offering for thanksgiving. **14** From
each of his offerings he shall present one portion
as a contribution to the LORD; this shall belong
to the priest who splashes the blood of the peace
offering.

**15** [a]"The flesh of the thanksgiving sacrifice
shall be eaten on the day it is offered; none of
it may be kept till the next day. **16** However,
if the sacrifice is a votive or a free-will offering,
it should indeed be eaten on the day the sacrifice
is offered, but what is left over may be eaten on
the next day. **17** Should any flesh from the
sacrifice be left over on the third day, it must be
burned up in the fire. **18** If, therefore, any of
the flesh of the peace offering is eaten on the
third day, it shall not win favor for him nor shall
it be reckoned to his credit; rather, it shall be
considered as refuse, and anyone who eats of it
shall have his guilt to bear. **19** Should the flesh
touch anything unclean, it may not be eaten, but
shall be burned up in the fire.

"All who are clean may partake of this flesh.
**20** If, however, someone while in a state of
uncleanness eats any of the flesh of a peace
offering belonging to the LORD, that person
shall be cut off from his people. **21** Likewise,
if someone touches anything unclean, whether
the uncleanness be of human or of animal origin
or from some loathsome crawling creature, and
then eats of a peace offering belonging to the
LORD, that person, too, shall be cut off from his
people."

**Prohibition against Blood and Fat.**
**22** The LORD said to Moses, **23** "Tell the Israelites: You shall not eat the fat* of any ox or
sheep or goat.[b] **24** Although the fat of an animal that has died a natural death or has been
killed by wild beasts may be put to any other
use, you may not eat it.[c] **25** If anyone eats the
fat of an animal from which an oblation is made
to the LORD, such a one shall be cut off from his
people. **26** Wherever you dwell, you shall not
partake of any blood, be it of bird or of animal.
**27** Every person who partakes of any blood
shall be cut off from his people."[d]

**The Portions for Priests.** **28** The LORD
said to Moses, **29** "Tell the Israelites: He who
presents a peace offering to the LORD shall bring
a part of it as his special offering to him, **30** carrying in with his own hands the oblations to the
LORD. The fat is to be brought in, together with
the breast, which is to be waved as a wave
offering* before the LORD. **31** The priest shall
burn the fat on the altar,[e] but the breast belongs
to Aaron and his sons. **32** Moreover, from your
peace offering you shall give to the priest the
right leg as a raised offering. **33** The descendant of Aaron who offers up the blood and fat of
the peace offering shall have the right leg as his
portion, **34** for from the peace offerings of the
Israelites I have taken the breast that is waved
and the leg that is raised up, and I have given
them to Aaron, the priest, and to his sons by a
perpetual ordinance as a contribution from the
Israelites."[f]

**35** This is the priestly share* from the oblations of the LORD, allotted to Aaron and his sons
on the day he called them to be the priests of the
LORD; **36** on the day he anointed them the LORD
ordered the Israelites to give them this share by

w 3-5: Lv 3, 4. 9f. 14-16; 4, 8f.
x Lv 6, 22.
y Lv 2, 3-10; Nm 18, 9; Ez 44, 29.
z Lv 2, 14f.
a 15-18: Lv 19, 6f.
b Lv 3, 17.
c Lv 22, 8.
d Lv 17, 10.
e Lv 3, 11, 16.
f Ex 29, 27f.

*

7, 13: Leavened bread: these loaves were not burned on the altar (cf Lv 2, 11), but were eaten at the "communion" meal which followed the sacrifice. See note on Lv 3, 1.

7, 23: The fat: only the particular portions specified in Lv 3, 9f. 14f are meant. Ox or sheep or goat: such animals as could be sacrificed; the fat of other clean animals could be eaten.

7, 30–34: A wave offering . . . a raised offering: these ceremonies are described in Ex 29, 24–28. The Hebrew word for "raised offering" is also rendered, in certain contexts, as "contribution."

7, 35: The priestly share: literally, "the anointed part."

a perpetual ordinance throughout their generations.
**37** This is the ritual for holocausts, cereal
offerings, sin offerings, guilt offerings, [ordina-
tion offerings] and peace offerings, **38** which
the LORD enjoined on Moses at Mount Sinai at
the time when he commanded the Israelites in
the wilderness of Sinai to bring their offerings
to the LORD.

## *II: Ceremony of Ordination*

### CHAPTER 8

**Ordination of Aaron and His Sons.**
**1** The LORD[g] said to Moses,* **2** "Take Aaron
and his sons, together with the vestments,* the
anointing oil, the bullock for a sin offering, the
two rams, and the basket of unleavened food.
**3** Then assemble the whole community at the
entrance of the meeting tent." **4** And Moses did
as the LORD had commanded. When the community had assembled at the entrance of the
meeting tent, **5** Moses told them what the LORD
had ordered to be done. **6** Bringing forward
Aaron and his sons, he first washed them with
water.[h] **7** Then he put the tunic on Aaron,[i]
girded him with the sash, clothed him with the
robe, placed the ephod on him, and girded him
with the embroidered belt of the ephod, fastening it around him. **8** [j]He then set the breastpiece
on him, with the Urim and Thummim* in it,
**9** [k]and put the miter on his head, attaching the
gold plate, the sacred diadem, over the front of
the miter, at his forehead, as the LORD had
commanded him to do.
**10** Taking the anointing oil, Moses anointed
and consecrated the Dwelling, with all that was
in it.[l] **11** Then he sprinkled some of this oil
seven times on the altar, and anointed the altar,
with all its appurtenances, and the laver, with its
base, thus consecrating them. **12** He also
poured some of the anointing oil on Aaron's
head, thus consecrating him.[m] **13** Moses likewise brought forward Aaron's sons, clothed
them with tunics, girded them with sashes, and
put turbans on them, as the LORD had commanded him to do.

**Ordination Sacrifices.** **14** When he had
brought forward the bullock for a sin offering,
Aaron and his sons laid their hands on its head.
**15** Then Moses slaughtered it, and taking some
of its blood, with his finger he put it on the horns
around the altar, thus purifying the altar. He
also made atonement for the altar by pouring out
the blood at its base when he consecrated it.[n]
**16** Taking all the fat that was over the inner
organs, as well as the lobe of the liver and the
two kidneys with their fat,[o] Moses burned them
on the altar. **17** The bullock, however, with its
hide and flesh and offal he burned in the fire
outside the camp, as the LORD had commanded
him to do.
**18** He next brought forward the holocaust
ram, and Aaron and his sons laid their hands on
its head. **19** When he had slaughtered it, Moses
splashed its blood on all sides of the altar.
**20** After cutting up the ram into pieces, he
burned the head, the cut-up pieces and the suet;
**21** then, having washed the inner organs and
the shanks with water, he also burned these
remaining parts of the ram on the altar as a
holocaust, a sweet-smelling oblation to the
LORD, as the LORD had commanded him to do.
**22** Then he brought forward the second ram,
the ordination ram, and Aaron and his sons laid
their hands on its head. **23** When he had slaughtered it, Moses took some of its blood and put
it on the tip of Aaron's right ear, on the thumb
of his right hand, and on the big toe of his right
foot.[p] **24** Moses had the sons of Aaron also
come forward, and he put some of the blood on
the tips of their right ears, on the thumbs of their
right hands, and on the big toes of their right
feet. The rest of the blood he splashed on the
sides of the altar. **25** He then took the fat: the
fatty tail and all the fat over the inner organs, the
lobe of the liver and the two kidneys with their
fat, and likewise the right leg; **26** from the basket of unleavened food that was set before the
LORD he took one unleavened cake, one loaf of
bread made with oil, and one wafer; these he
placed on top of the portions of fat and the right
leg. **27** He then put all these things into the
hands of Aaron and his sons, whom he had wave
them as a wave offering before the LORD.
**28** When he had received them back, Moses
burned them with the holocaust on the altar as
the ordination offering, a sweet-smelling oblation to the LORD. **29** He then took the breast and
waved it as a wave offering before the LORD;
this was Moses' own portion of the ordination
ram. All this was in keeping with the LORD's
command to Moses. **30** Taking some of the
anointing oil and some of the blood that was on
the altar, Moses sprinkled with it Aaron and his
vestments, as well as his sons and their vestments, thus consecrating both Aaron and his
vestments and his sons and their vestments.
**31** Finally, Moses said to Aaron and his
sons, "Boil the flesh at the entrance of the

g 1-36: cf Ex 29.
h 6f: Ex 40, 12f.
i 7ff: Sir 45, 8-13.
j Ex 28, 30.
k Ex 28, 36.
l Ex 30, 26.
m Sir 45, 15.
n Lv 4, 7; Heb 9, 22.
o 16f: Lv 3, 4; 4, 8-11.
p Lv 14, 14.

*

8, 1–9, 21: Though presented in the form of a narrative, this description of Aaron's ordination was intended to serve as a guide for all future ordinations.

8, 2: The vestments, etc.: already described in Ex 28–29.

8, 8: The Urim and Thummim: see note on Ex 28, 30.

meeting tent, and there eat it with the bread that is in the basket of the ordination offering, in keeping with the command I have received: 'Aaron and his sons shall eat of it.' **32** What is left over of the flesh and the bread you shall burn up in the fire. **33** Moreover, you are not to depart from the entrance of the meeting tent for seven days, until the days of your ordination are completed; for your ordination is to last for seven days. **34** *The LORD has commanded that what has been done today be done to make atonement for you. **35** Hence you must remain at the entrance of the meeting tent day and night for seven days, carrying out the prescriptions of the LORD; otherwise you shall die; for this is the command I have received." **36** So Aaron and his sons did all that the LORD had commanded through Moses.

## CHAPTER 9

**Octave of the Ordination.** **1** On the eighth day Moses summoned Aaron and his sons, together with the elders of Israel, **2** and said to Aaron, "Take a calf for a sin offering and a ram for a holocaust, both without blemish, and offer them before the LORD. **3** Tell the elders of Israel, too: Take a he-goat for a sin offering, a calf and a lamb, both unblemished yearlings, for a holocaust, **4** and an ox and a ram for a peace offering, to sacrifice them before the LORD, along with a cereal offering mixed with oil; for today he LORD will reveal himself to you." **5** So they brought what Moses had ordered. When the whole community had come forward and stood before the LORD, **6** Moses said, "This is what the LORD orders you to do, that the glory of the LORD may be revealed to you. **7** Come up to the altar," Moses then told Aaron, "and offer your sin offering and your holocaust in atonement for yourself and for your family; then present the offering of the people in atonement for them, as the LORD has commanded."

**8** Going up to the altar, Aaron first slaughtered the calf that was his own sin offering. **9** When his sons presented the blood to him, he dipped his finger in the blood and put it on the horns of the altar. The rest of the blood he poured out at the base of the altar. **10** He then burned on the altar the fat, the kidneys and the lobe of the liver that were taken from the sin offering, as the LORD had commanded Moses; **11** but the flesh and the hide he burned up in the fire outside the camp. **12** Then Aaron slaughtered his holocaust. When his sons brought him the blood, he splashed it on all sides of the altar. **13** They then brought him the pieces and the head of the holocaust, and he burned them on the altar. **14** Having washed the inner organs and the shanks, he burned these also with the holocaust on the altar.

**15** Thereupon he had the people's offering brought up. Taking the goat that was for the people's sin offering, he slaughtered it and offered it up for sin as before. **16** Then he brought forward the holocaust, other than the morning holocaust, and offered it in the usual manner. **17** He then presented the cereal offering; taking a handful of it, he burned it on the altar. **18** Finally he slaughtered the ox and the ram, the peace offering of the people. When his sons brought him the blood, Aaron splashed it on all sides of the altar. **19** The portions of fat from the ox and from the ram, the fatty tail, the fatty membrane over the inner organs, the two kidneys, with the fat that is on them, and the lobe of the liver,[q] **20** he placed on top of the breasts and burned them on the altar, **21** [r]having first waved the breasts and the right legs as a wave offering before the LORD, in keeping with the LORD's command to Moses.

**Revelation of the Lord Glory.** **22** Aaron then raised his hands over the people and blessed them. When he came down from offering the sin offering and holocaust and peace offering, **23** Moses and Aaron went into the meeting tent.[s] On coming out they again blessed the people. Then the glory of the LORD was revealed to all the people. **24** Fire came forth from the LORD's presence[t] and consumed the holocaust and the remnants of the fat on the altar. Seeing this, all the people cried out and fell prostrate.

## CHAPTER 10

**Nadab and Abihu.** **1** During this time Aaron's sons Nadab and Abihu* took their censers and, strewing incense on the fire they had put in them,[u] they offered up before the LORD profane fire, such as he had not authorized. **2** Fire* therefore came forth from the LORD's presence and consumed them,[v] so that they died in his presence. **3** Moses then said to Aaron, "This is as the LORD said:

q 19f: Lv 3, 3ff.
r Lv 7, 31f.
s Nm 6, 23-26.
t 1 Kgs 18, 38; 2 Chr 7, 1.
u Lv 16, 1; Nm 3, 4; 26, 61; 1 Chr 24, 2.
v Nm 16, 35.
w Lv 21, 17. 21.

*

8, 34: The sense is not quite clear. Either the verse gives merely the reason why God ordered this ceremony, or it contains God's command that the same ceremony be used in all future ordinations, or it decrees a repetition of the entire ceremony on each of the seven days. At least a sin offering for atonement was made on each of these days. Cf Ex 29, 29–36.

10, 1: Nadab and Abihu: the older sons of Aaron. Cf Ex 6, 23f.

10, 2: Fire: perhaps after the manner of lightning.

10, 3: I will manifest my sacredness: the presence of God

Through those who approach me I will
manifest my sacredness;*
In the sight of all the people I will reveal
my glory."[w]

But Aaron said nothing. **4** Then Moses summoned Mishael and Elzaphan, the sons of Aaron's uncle Uzziel, with the order, "Come, remove your kinsmen from the sanctuary and
carry them to a place outside the camp." **5** So
they went in and took them, in their tunics,*
outside the camp, as Moses had commanded.

**Conduct of the Priests.** **6** Moses said to
Aaron and his sons Eleazar and Ithamar, "Do
not bare your heads* or tear your garments,[x]
lest you bring not only death on yourselves but
God's wrath also on the whole community.
Your kinsmen, the rest of the house of Israel,
shall mourn for those whom the LORD's fire has
smitten; **7** but do not you go beyond the entry
of the meeting tent, else you shall die; for the
anointing oil of the LORD is upon you." So they
did as Moses told them.
**8** The LORD said to Aaron, **9** "When you are
to go to the meeting tent, you and your sons are
forbidden under pain of death, by a perpetual
ordinance throughout your generations, to drink
any wine or strong drink.[y] **10** You must be able
to distinguish between what is sacred and what
is profane, between what is clean and what is
unclean;[z] **11** you must teach the Israelites all
the laws that the LORD has given them through
Moses."[a]

**The Eating of the Priestly Portions.**
**12** Moses said to Aaron and his surviving sons,
Eleazar and Ithamar, "Take the cereal offering
left over from the oblations of the LORD, and eat
it beside the altar in the form of unleavened
cakes.[b] Since it is most sacred, **13** you must eat
it in a sacred place. This is your due from the
oblations of the LORD, and that of your sons;
such is the command I have received. **14** [c]With
your sons and daughters you shall also eat the
breast of the wave offering and the leg of the
raised offering, in a clean place; for these have
been assigned to you and your children as your
due from the peace offerings of the Israelites.
**15** The leg of the raised offering and the breast
of the wave offering shall first be brought in
with the oblations, the fatty portions, that are to
be waved as a wave offering before the LORD.
Then they shall belong to you and your children
by a perpetual ordinance, as the LORD has commanded."
**16** *When Moses inquired about the goat of
the sin offering, he discovered that it had all
been burned. So he was angry with the surviving sons of Aaron, Eleazar and Ithamar, and
said, **17** [d]"Why did you not eat the sin offering
in the sacred place, since it is most sacred? It has
been given to you that you might bear the guilt
of the community and make atonement for them
before the LORD. **18** If its blood was not
brought into the inmost part of the sanctuary,
you should certainly have eaten the offering in
the sanctuary, in keeping with the command I
had received." **19** Aaron answered Moses,
"Even though they presented their sin offering
and holocaust before the LORD today, yet this
misfortune has befallen me. Had I then eaten of
the sin offering today, would it have been pleasing to the LORD?" **20** On hearing this, Moses
was satisfied.

## *III: Laws Regarding Legal Purity*

## CHAPTER 11

**Clean and Unclean Food.** **1** The LORD
said to Moses and Aaron,* **2** "Speak to the
Israelites and tell them: Of all land animals these
are the ones you may eat: **3** any animal that has
hoofs you may eat, provided it is cloven-footed
and chews the cud. **4** But you shall not eat any
of the following that only chew the cud or only
have hoofs: the camel, which indeed chews the
cud, but does not have hoofs and is therefore
unclean for you; **5** the rock badger,* which indeed chews the cud, but does not have hoofs and
is therefore unclean for you; **6** the hare, which
indeed chews the cud, but does not have hoofs
and is therefore unclean for you; and the pig,

x Lv 21, 10.
y Ez 44, 21.
z Lv 11, 47; 20, 25; Ez 22, 26; 44, 23.
a Sir 45, 16.
b Lv 6, 16.
c 14f: Lv 7, 34.
d Lv 6, 18f.

* is so sacred that it strikes dead those who approach him without the proper holiness. Cf Nm 20, 13; Ez 28, 22.

10, 5: In their tunics: they were buried just as they were, with no shroud or funeral solemnities.

10, 6: Bare your heads: go without the customary head covering, as a sign of mourning. Some interpreters, however, understand it as the cutting off of one's hair, which ordinarily all the Israelites, men as well as women, let grow long. Cf Is 15, 2; Jer 7, 29. Still others understand the verb to mean "to let one's hair hang loose and wild." Cf Lv 13, 45; 21, 10, where the same phrase is used.

10, 16–19: Eleazar and Ithamar burned the entire goat of the sin offering (Lv 9, 15) instead of eating it in a sacred place (Lv 6, 19) to bear the guilt of the community. Aaron defends this action of his sons against Moses' displeasure by implying that they did not have sufficient sanctity to eat the flesh of the victim and thus perform the expiation of the people. They themselves still labored under the blow of the divine anger which struck their brothers Nadab and Abihu.

11, 1ff: These distinctions between edible and inedible meats were probably based on traditional ideas of hygiene, but they are here given a moral, religious basis: the inedible varieties are classified as "unclean" to remind the Israelites that they are to be a pure and holy people, dedicated to the Lord.

11, 5f: According to modern zoology, the rock badger (hyrax Syriacus) is classified as an ungulate, and the hare as a rodent; neither is a ruminant. They appear to chew their food as the true ruminants do, and it is upon this appearance that the classification in the text is based.

**7** which does indeed have hoofs and is cloven-footed, but does not chew the cud and is
therefore unclean for you. **8** Their flesh you
shall not eat, and their dead bodies you shall not
touch; they are unclean for you.

**9** "Of the various creatures that live in the
water, you may eat the following: whatever in
the seas or in river waters has both fins and
scales you may eat. **10** But of the various creatures that crawl or swim in the water, whether
in the sea or in the rivers, all those that lack
either fins or scales are loathsome for you,
**11** and you shall treat them as loathsome. Their
flesh you shall not eat, and their dead bodies you
shall loathe. **12** Every water creature that lacks
fins or scales is loathsome for you.

**13** "Of the birds, these you shall loathe and,
as loathsome, they shall not be eaten:* the eagle, the vulture, the osprey, **14** the kite, the
various species of falcons, **15** the various species of crows, **16** the ostrich, the nightjar, the
gull, the various species of hawks, **17** the owl,
the cormorant, the screech owl, **18** the barn
owl, the desert owl, the buzzard, **19** the stork,
the various species of herons, the hoopoe, and
the bat.*

**20** "The various winged insects that walk on
all fours are loathsome for you. **21** But of the
various winged insects that walk on all fours
you may eat those that have jointed legs for
leaping on the ground; **22** hence of these you
may eat the following: the various kinds of locusts,* the various kinds of grasshoppers, the
various kinds of katydids, and the various kinds
of crickets. **23** All other winged insects that
have four legs are loathsome for you.

**24** *"Such is the uncleanness that you contract, that everyone who touches their dead bodies shall be unclean until evening, **25** and everyone who picks up any part of their dead
bodies shall wash his garments and be unclean
until evening. **26** All hoofed animals that are
not cloven-footed* or do not chew the cud are
unclean for you; everyone who touches them
becomes unclean. **27** Of the various quad-
rupeds, all those that walk on paws* are unclean
for you; everyone who touches their dead bodies
shall be unclean until evening, **28** and everyone
who picks up their dead bodies shall wash his
garments and be unclean until evening. Such is
their uncleanness for you.

**29** "Of the creatures that swarm on the
ground, the following are unclean for you: the
rat, the mouse, the various kinds of lizards,
**30** the gecko, the chameleon, the agama, the
skink, and the mole. **31** Among the various
swarming creatures, these are unclean for you.
Everyone who touches them when they are dead
shall be unclean until evening. **32** Everything
on which one of them falls when dead becomes
unclean. Any such article that men use, whether
it be an article of wood, cloth, leather or goat
hair, must be put in water and remain unclean
until evening, when it again becomes clean.
**33** Should any of these creatures fall into a clay
vessel, everything in it becomes unclean, and
the vessel itself you must break. **34** Any solid
food that was in contact with water, and any
liquid that men drink, in any such vessel become unclean. **35** Any object on which one of
their dead bodies falls, becomes unclean; if it is
an oven or a jar-stand, this must be broken to
pieces; they are unclean and shall be treated as
unclean by you. **36** However, a spring or a
cistern for collecting water remains clean; but
whoever touches the dead body* becomes unclean. **37** Any sort of cultivated grain remains
clean even though one of their dead bodies falls
on it; **38** but if the grain has become moistened,
it becomes unclean when one of these falls on
it.

**39** "When one of the animals that you could
otherwise eat, dies of itself, anyone who
touches its dead body shall be unclean until
evening; **40** and anyone who eats of its dead
body shall wash his garments and be unclean
until evening;[e] so also, anyone who removes its
dead body shall wash his garments and be unclean until evening.

**41** "All the creatures that swarm on the
ground are loathsome and shall not be eaten.
**42** Whether it crawls on its belly, goes on all
fours, or has many legs, you shall eat no swarming creature: they are loathsome. **43** Do not
make yourselves loathsome or unclean with any
swarming creature through being contaminated
by them.[f] **44** For I, the LORD, am your God;
and you shall make and keep yourselves holy,
because I am holy.[g] You shall not make yourselves unclean, then, by any swarming creature
that crawls on the ground. **45** Since I, the
LORD, brought you up from the land of Egypt
that I might be your God, you shall be holy,
because I am holy.

**46** "This is the law for animals and birds and

---

e Lv 17, 15; 22, 8.
f 43f: Lv 20, 25f.
g Lv 19, 2; 20, 7. 26; Mt 5, 48; 1 Pt 1, 16.

---

11, 13–19. 30: The identification of the various Hebrew names for these birds and reptiles is in many cases uncertain.

11, 19: The bat: actually a mammal, but listed here with the birds because of its wings.

11, 22: The Hebrew distinguishes four classes of edible locust-like insects, but the difference between them is quite uncertain. Cf Mt 3, 4.

11, 24–28: This paragraph sharpens the prohibition against unclean animals: not only is their meat unfit for food, but contact with their dead bodies makes a person ritually unclean.

11, 26: All hoofed animals that are not cloven-footed: such as the horse and the ass.

11, 27: All those that walk on paws: such as dogs and cats.

11, 36: Whoever touches the dead body: to remove the dead insect from the water supply.

for all the creatures that move about in the water
or swarm on the ground, **47** that you may distinguish between the clean and the unclean, between creatures that may be eaten and those that
may not be eaten."[h]

## CHAPTER 12

**Uncleanness of Childbirth.** **1** The LORD
said to Moses, **2** "Tell the Israelites: When a
woman has conceived and gives birth to a boy,
she shall be unclean* for seven days, with the
same uncleanness as at her menstrual period.[i]
**3** On the eighth day, the flesh of the boy's
foreskin shall be circumcised,[j] **4** and then she
shall spend thirty-three days more in becoming
purified of her blood; she shall not touch anything sacred nor enter the sanctuary till the days
of her purification are fulfilled. **5** If she gives
birth to a girl, for fourteen days she shall be as
unclean as at her menstruation, after which she
shall spend sixty-six days in becoming purified
of her blood.

**6** "When the days of her purification for a
son or for a daughter are fulfilled,[k] she shall
bring to the priest at the entrance of the meeting
tent a yearling lamb for a holocaust and a pigeon
or a turtledove for a sin offering. **7** The priest
shall offer them up before the LORD to make
atonement for her, and thus she will be clean
again after her flow of blood. Such is the law for
the woman who gives birth to a boy or a girl
child. **8** *If, however, she cannot afford a
lamb, she may take two turtledoves or two pigeons,[l] the one for a holocaust and the other for
a sin offering. The priest shall make atonement
for her, and thus she will again be clean."

## CHAPTER 13

**Leprosy.** **1** The LORD said to Moses and
Aaron, **2** [m]"If someone has on his skin* a scab
or pustule or blotch which appears to be the sore
of leprosy, he shall be brought to Aaron, the
priest, or to one of the priests among his descendants, **3** who shall examine the sore on his
skin. If the hair on the sore has turned white and
the sore itself shows that it has penetrated below
the skin, it is indeed the sore of leprosy; the
priest, on seeing this, shall declare the man
unclean. **4** If, however, the blotch on the skin
is white, but does not seem to have penetrated
below the skin, nor has the hair turned white,
the priest shall quarantine the stricken man for
seven days. **5** On the seventh day the priest
shall again examine him. If he judges that the
sore has remained unchanged and has not spread
on the skin, the priest shall quarantine him for
another seven days, **6** and once more examine
him on the seventh day. If the sore is now dying
out and has not spread on the skin, the priest
shall declare the man clean; it was merely eczema. The man shall wash his garments and so
become clean. **7** But if, after he has shown
himself to the priest to be declared clean, the
eczema spreads at all on his skin, he shall once
more show himself to the priest. **8** Should the
priest, on examining it, find that the eczema has
indeed spread on the skin, he shall declare the
man unclean; it is leprosy.

**9** "When someone is stricken with leprosy,
he shall be brought to the priest. **10** Should the
priest, on examining him, find that there is a
white scab on the skin which has turned the hair
white and that there is raw flesh in it, **11** it is
skin leprosy that has long developed. The priest
shall declare the man unclean without first quar-
antining him, since he is certainly unclean.
**12** If leprosy breaks out on the skin* and, as far
as the priest can see, covers all the skin of the
stricken man from head to foot, **13** should the
priest then, on examining him, find that the
leprosy does cover his whole body, he shall
declare the stricken man clean; since it has all
turned white, the man is clean. **14** But as soon
as raw flesh appears on him, he is unclean;
**15** on observing the raw flesh, the priest shall
declare him unclean, because raw flesh is unclean; it is leprosy. **16** If, however, the raw
flesh again turns white, he shall return to the
priest; **17** should the latter, on examining him,
find that the sore has indeed turned white, he
shall declare the stricken man clean, and thus he
will be clean.

**18** "If a man who had a boil on his skin
which later healed, **19** should now in the place
of the boil have a white scab or a pink blotch,
he shall show himself to the priest. **20** If the
latter, on examination, sees that it is deeper than
the skin and that the hair has turned white, he
shall declare the man unclean: it is the sore of
leprosy that has broken out in the boil. **21** But
if the priest, on examining him, finds that there

h Lv 10, 10.
i Lv 15, 19.
j Gn 17, 12; Jn 7, 22.
k Lk 2, 22.
l Lv 1, 14; Lk 2, 24.
m Dt 24, 8.

*

12, 2f: The uncleanness of the woman was more serious during the first period, the seven days after the birth of a boy or the fourteen days after the birth of a girl; only during this period would the rules given in Lv 15, 19–24 apply.

12, 8: Forty days after the birth of Jesus, his Virgin Mother made this offering of the poor (Lk 2, 22. 24); since the holocaust was offered in thanksgiving for the birth of the child, this was most fittingly offered by Mary. However, because of her miraculous delivery, she was not really obliged to make the sin offering of purification.

13, 2ff: Various kinds of skin blemishes are treated here which were not contagious but simply disqualified their subjects from association with others, especially in public worship, until they were declared ritually clean. The Hebrew term used does not refer to Hansen's disease, currently called leprosy.

13, 12ff: If leprosy breaks out on the skin: the symptoms described here point to a form of skin disease which is merely on the surface and therefore easily cured.

is no white hair in it and that it is not deeper than the skin and is already dying out, the priest shall quarantine him for seven days. **22** If it has then spread on the skin, the priest shall declare him unclean; the man is stricken. **23** But if the blotch remains in its place without spreading, it is merely the scar of the boil; the priest shall therefore declare him clean.

**24** "If a man had a burn on his skin, and the proud flesh of the burn now becomes a pink or a white blotch, **25** the priest shall examine it. If the hair has turned white on the blotch and this seems to have penetrated below the skin, it is leprosy that has broken out in the burn; the priest shall therefore declare him unclean and stricken with leprosy. **26** But if the priest, on examining it, finds that there is no white hair on the blotch and that this is not deeper than the skin and is already dying out, the priest shall quarantine him for seven days. **27** Should the priest, when examining it on the seventh day, find that it has spread at all on the skin, he shall declare the man unclean and stricken with leprosy. **28** But if the blotch remains in its place without spreading on the skin and is already dying out, it is merely the scab of the burn; the priest shall therefore declare the man clean, since it is only the scar of the burn.

**29** "When a man or a woman has a sore on the head or cheek, **30** should the priest, on examining it, find that the sore has penetrated below the skin and that there is fine yellow hair on it, the priest shall declare the person unclean, for this is scall,* a leprous disease of the head or cheek. **31** But if the priest, on examining the scall sore, finds that it has not penetrated below the skin, though the hair on it may not be black, the priest shall quarantine the person with scall sore for seven days, **32** and on the seventh day again examine the sore. If the scall has not spread and has no yellow hair on it and does not seem to have penetrated below the skin, **33** the man shall shave himself, but not on the diseased spot. Then the priest shall quarantine him for another seven days. **34** If the priest, when examining the scall on the seventh day, finds that it has not spread on the skin and that it has not penetrated below the skin, he shall declare the man clean; the latter shall wash his garments, and thus he will be clean. **35** But if the scall spreads at all on his skin after he has been declared clean, **36** the priest shall again examine it. If the scall has indeed spread on the skin, he need not look for yellow hair; the man is surely unclean. **37** If, however, he judges that the scall has remained in its place and that black hair has grown on it, the disease has been healed; the man is clean, and the priest shall declare him clean.

**38** "When the skin of a man or a woman is spotted with white blotches, **39** the priest shall make an examination. If the blotches on the skin are white and already dying out, it is only tetter* that has broken out on the skin, and the person therefore is clean.

**40** "When a man loses the hair of his head, he is not unclean merely because of his bald crown. **41** So too, if he loses the hair on the front of his head, he is not unclean merely because of his bald forehead. **42** But when there is a pink sore on his bald crown or bald forehead, it is leprosy that is breaking out there. **43** The priest shall examine him; and if the scab on the sore of the bald spot has the same pink appearance as that of skin leprosy of the fleshy part of the body, **44** the man is leprous and unclean, and the priest shall declare him unclean by reason of the sore on his head.

**45** "The one who bears the sore of leprosy shall keep his garments rent and his head bare, and shall muffle his beard; he shall cry out, 'Unclean, unclean!' **46** As long as the sore is on him he shall declare himself unclean, since he is in fact unclean.[n] He shall dwell apart, making his abode outside the camp.

**Leprosy of Clothes.** **47** "When a leprous infection* is on a garment of wool or of linen, **48** or on woven or knitted material of linen or wool, or on a hide or anything made of leather, **49** if the infection on the garment or hide, or on the woven or knitted material, or on any leather article is greenish or reddish, the thing is indeed infected with leprosy and must be shown to the priest. **50** Having examined the infection, the priest shall quarantine the infected article for seven days.

**51** "On the seventh day the priest shall again examine the infection. If it has spread on the garment, or on the woven or knitted material, or on the leather, whatever be its use, the infection is malignant leprosy, and the article is unclean. **52** He shall therefore burn up the garment, or the woven or knitted material of wool or linen, or the leather article, whatever it may be, which is infected; since it has malignant leprosy, it must be destroyed by fire. **53** But if the priest, on examining the infection, finds that it has not spread on the garment, or on the woven or knitted material, or on the leather article, **54** he shall give orders to have the infected article washed and then quarantined for another seven days.

**55** "Then the priest shall again examine the infected article after it has been washed. If the

n Nm 5, 2; 12, 14f; 2 Kgs 15, 5; Lk 17, 12.

13, 30: Scall: a scabby or scaly eruption of the scalp. According to some, "ringworm."

13, 39: Tetter: vitiligo, a harmless form of skin disease.

13, 47: A leprous infection: some mold or fungus growth resembling human leprosy.

infection has not changed its appearance, even
though it may not have spread, the article is
unclean and shall be destroyed by fire. **56** But
if the priest, on examining the infection, finds
that it is dying out after the washing, he shall
tear the infected part out of the garment, or the
leather, or the woven or knitted material. **57** If,
however, the infection again appears on the garment, or on the woven or knitted material, or on
the leather article, it is still virulent and the thing
infected shall be destroyed by fire. **58** But if,
after the washing, the infection has left the garment, or the woven or knitted material, or the
leather article, the thing shall be washed a second time, and thus it will be clean. **59** This is
the law for leprous infection[o] on a garment of
wool or linen, or on woven or knitted material,
or on any leather article, to determine whether
it is clean or unclean."

## CHAPTER 14

**Purification after Leprosy.** 1 The LORD
said to Moses, **2** [p]"This is the law for the victim of leprosy at the time of his purification. He
shall be brought to the priest, **3** who is to go
outside the camp to examine him. If the priest
finds that the sore of leprosy has healed in the
leper, **4** he shall order the man who is to be
purified, to get two live, clean birds, as well as
some cedar wood, scarlet yarn,* and hyssop.
**5** The priest shall then order him to slay one of
the birds over an earthen vessel with spring
water* in it. **6** Taking the living bird with the
cedar wood, the scarlet yarn and the hyssop, the
priest shall dip them all in the blood of the bird
that was slain over the spring water, **7** and then
sprinkle seven times the man to be purified from
his leprosy. When he has thus purified him, he
shall let the living bird fly away over the countryside. **8** The man being purified shall then
wash his garments and shave off all his hair and
bathe in water; only when he is thus made clean
may he come inside the camp; but he shall still
remain outside his tent for seven days. **9** On the
seventh day he shall again shave off all the hair
of his head, his beard, his eyebrows, and any
other hair he may have, and also wash his garments and bathe his body in water; and so he
will be clean.

**Purification Sacrifices.** **10** "On the
eighth day he shall take two unblemished male
lambs, one unblemished yearling ewe lamb,
three tenths of an ephah of fine flour mixed with
oil for a cereal offering, and one log of oil.
**11** The priest who performs the purification
ceremony shall place the man who is being purified, as well as all these offerings, before the
LORD at the entrance of the meeting tent.
**12** Taking one of the male lambs, the priest
shall present it as a guilt offering, along with the
log of oil, waving them as a wave offering
before the LORD. **13** (This lamb he shall slaughter in the sacred place where the sin offering and
the holocaust are slaughtered; because, like the
sin offering, the guilt offering belongs to the
priest and is most sacred.) **14** Then the priest
shall take some of the blood of the guilt offering
and put it on the tip of the man's right ear, the
thumb of his right hand, and the big toe of his
right foot.[q] **15** The priest shall also take the log
of oil and pour some of it into the palm of his
own left hand; **16** then, dipping his right forefinger in it, he shall sprinkle it seven times
before the LORD. **17** Of the oil left in his hand
the priest shall put some on the tip of the man's
right ear, the thumb of his right hand, and the
big toe of his right foot, over the blood of the
guilt offering. **18** The rest of the oil in his hand
the priest shall put on the head of the man being
purified. Thus shall the priest make atonement
for him before the LORD. **19** Only after he has
offered the sin offering in atonement for the
man's uncleanness shall the priest slaughter the
holocaust **20** and offer it, together with the cereal offering, on the altar before the LORD.
When the priest has thus made atonement for
him, the man will be clean.

**Poor Leper's Sacrifice.** **21** "If a man is
poor and cannot afford so much, he shall take
one male lamb for a guilt offering, to be used
as a wave offering in atonement for himself, one
tenth of an ephah of fine flour mixed with oil for
a cereal offering, a log of oil, **22** and two turtledoves* or pigeons, which he can more easily
afford, the one as a sin offering and the other as
a holocaust. **23** On the eighth day of his purification he shall bring them to the priest, at the
entrance of the meeting tent before the LORD.
**24** Taking the guilt-offering lamb, along with
the log of oil, the priest shall wave them as a
wave offering before the LORD. **25** When he
has slaughtered the guilt-offering lamb, he shall
take some of its blood, and put it on the tip of
the right ear of the man being purified, on the
thumb of his right hand, and on the big toe of
his right foot. **26** The priest shall then pour
some of the oil into the palm of his own left hand
**27** and with his right forefinger sprinkle it sev-
en times before the LORD. **28** Some of the oil
in his hand the priest shall also put on the tip of

o Lv 14, 54.
p Mt 8, 4; Mk 1, 44; Lk 5, 14.
q Lv 8, 23f.

*

14, 4: Scarlet yarn: probably used for tying the hyssop sprig to the cedar branchlet.

14, 5: Spring water: literally, "living water," taken from some source of running water, not from a cistern.

14, 22: Two turtledoves: substitutes for the two additional lambs, similar to the offering of a poor woman after childbirth. Cf Lv 12, 8.

the man's right ear, the thumb of his right hand, and the big toe of his right foot, over the blood of the guilt offering. **29** The rest of the oil in his hand the priest shall put on the man's head. Thus shall he make atonement for him before the LORD. **30** Then, of the turtledoves or pigeons, such as the man can afford, **31** the priest shall offer up one as a sin offering and the other as a holocaust, along with the cereal offering. Thus shall the priest make atonement before the LORD for the man who is to be purified. **32** This is the law for one afflicted with leprosy who has insufficient means for his purification."

**Leprosy of Houses.** **33** The LORD said to Moses and Aaron, **34** "When you come into the land of Canaan, which I am giving you to possess, if I put a leprous infection on any house of the land you occupy, **35** the owner of the house shall come and report to the priest, 'It looks to me as if my house were infected.' **36** The priest shall then order the house to be cleared out before he goes in to examine the infection, lest everything in the house become unclean. Only after this is he to go in to examine the house. **37** If the priest, on examining it, finds that the infection on the walls of the house consists of greenish or reddish depressions which seem to go deeper than the surface of the wall, **38** he shall close the door of the house behind him and quarantine the house for seven days. **39** On the seventh day the priest shall return to examine the house again. If he finds that the infection has spread on the walls, **40** he shall order the infected stones to be pulled out and cast in an unclean place outside the city. **41** The whole inside of the house shall then be scraped, and the mortar that has been scraped off shall be dumped in an unclean place outside the city. **42** Then new stones shall be brought and put in the place of the old stones, and new mortar shall be made and plastered on the house.

**43** "If the infection breaks out once more after the stones have been pulled out and the house has been scraped and replastered, **44** the priest shall come again; and if he finds that the infection has spread in the house, it is corrosive leprosy, and the house is unclean. **45** It shall be pulled down, and all its stones, beams and mortar shall be hauled away to an unclean place outside the city. **46** Whoever enters a house while it is quarantined shall be unclean until evening. **47** Whoever sleeps or eats in such a house shall also wash his garments. **48** If the priest finds, when he comes to examine the house, that the infection has in fact not spread after the plastering, he shall declare the house clean, since the infection has been healed. **49** To purify the house, he shall take two birds, as well as cedar wood, scarlet yarn, and hyssop. **50** One of the birds he shall slay over an earthen vessel with spring water in it. **51** Then, taking the cedar wood, the hyssop and the scarlet yarn, together with the living bird, he shall dip them all in the blood of the slain bird and the spring water, and sprinkle the house seven times. **52** Thus shall he purify the house with the bird's blood and the spring water, along with the living bird, the cedar wood, the hyssop, and the scarlet yarn. **53** He shall then let the living bird fly away over the countryside outside the city. When he has thus made atonement for it, the house will be clean.

**54** "This is the law for every kind of human leprosy and scall, **55** [r]for leprosy of garments and houses, **56** as well as for scabs, pustules and blotches, **57** so that it may be manifest when there is a state of uncleanness and when a state of cleanness. This is the law for leprosy."

## CHAPTER 15

**Personal Uncleanness.** **1** The LORD said to Moses and Aaron, **2** "Speak to the Israelites and tell them: Every man who is afflicted with a chronic flow from his private parts is thereby unclean.[s] **3** Such is his uncleanness from this flow that it makes no difference whether the flow drains off or is blocked up; his uncleanness remains. **4** Any bed on which the man afflicted with the flow lies, is unclean, and any piece of furniture on which he sits, is unclean. **5** Anyone who touches his bed shall wash his garments, bathe in water, and be unclean until evening. **6** Whoever sits on a piece of furniture on which the afflicted man was sitting, shall wash his garments, bathe in water, and be unclean until evening. **7** Whoever touches the body of the afflicted man shall wash his garments, bathe in water, and be unclean until evening. **8** If the afflicted man spits on a clean man, the latter shall wash his garments, bathe in water, and be unclean until evening. **9** Any saddle on which the afflicted man rides, is unclean. **10** Whoever touches anything that was under him shall be unclean until evening; whoever lifts up any such thing shall wash his garments, bathe in water, and be unclean until evening. **11** Anyone whom the afflicted man touches with unrinsed hands shall wash his garments, bathe in water, and be unclean until evening. **12** Earthenware touched by the afflicted man shall be broken; and every wooden article shall be rinsed with water.

**13** "When a man who has been afflicted with a flow becomes free of his affliction, he shall wait seven days for his purification. Then he shall wash his garments and bathe his body in

r Lv 13, 47-58. s Nm 5, 2.

fresh water, and so he will be clean. **14** On the eighth day he shall take two turtledoves or two pigeons, and going before the LORD, to the entrance of the meeting tent, he shall give them to the priest, **15** who shall offer them up, the one as a sin offering and the other as a holocaust. Thus shall the priest make atonement before the LORD for the man's flow.

**16** "When a man has an emission of seed, he shall bathe his whole body in water and be unclean until evening. **17** Any piece of cloth or leather with seed on it shall be washed with water and be unclean until evening.

**18** "If a man lies carnally with a woman, they shall both bathe in water and be unclean until evening.

**19** "When a woman has her menstrual flow, she shall be in a state of impurity for seven days.[t] Anyone who touches her shall be unclean until evening. **20** Anything on which she lies or sits during her impurity shall be unclean. **21** Anyone who touches her bed shall wash his garments, bathe in water, and be unclean until evening. **22** Whoever touches any article of furniture on which she was sitting, shall wash his garments, bathe in water, and be unclean until evening. **23** *But if she is on the bed or on the seat when he touches it, he shall be unclean until evening. **24** If a man dares to lie with her, he contracts her impurity and shall be unclean for seven days;[u] every bed on which he then lies also becomes unclean.

**25** "When a woman is afflicted with a flow of blood for several days outside her menstrual period, or when her flow continues beyond the ordinary period,[v] as long as she suffers this unclean flow she shall be unclean, just as during her menstrual period. **26** Any bed on which she lies during such a flow becomes unclean, as it would during her menstruation, and any article of furniture on which she sits becomes unclean just as during her menstruation. **27** Anyone who touches them becomes unclean; he shall wash his garments, bathe in water, and be unclean until evening.

**28** "If she becomes freed from her affliction, she shall wait seven days, and only then is she to be purified. **29** On the eighth day she shall take two turtledoves or two pigeons and bring them to the priest at the entrance of the meeting tent. **30** The priest shall offer up one of them as a sin offering and the other as a holocaust. Thus shall the priest make atonement before the LORD for her unclean flow.

**31** "You shall warn the Israelites of their uncleanness, lest by defiling my Dwelling, which is in their midst, their uncleanness be the cause of their death.

**32** "This is the law for the man who is afflicted with a chronic flow, or who has an emission of seed, and thereby becomes unclean; **33** as well as for the woman who has her menstrual period, or who is afflicted with a chronic flow; the law for male and female; and also for the man who lies with an unclean woman."

## CHAPTER 16

**The Day of Atonement.** **1** After the death of Aaron's two sons, who died when they approached the LORD's presence, the LORD spoke to Moses **2** and said to him,[w] "Tell your brother Aaron that he is not to come whenever he pleases into the sanctuary, inside the veil,* in front of the propitiatory on the ark; otherwise, when I reveal myself in a cloud above the propitiatory, he will die. **3** Only in this way may Aaron enter the sanctuary. He shall bring a young bullock for a sin offering and a ram for a holocaust. **4** He shall wear the sacred linen tunic, with the linen drawers next his flesh, gird himself with the linen sash and put on the linen miter. But since these vestments are sacred, he shall not put them on until he has first bathed his body in water. **5** From the Israelite community he shall receive two male goats for a sin offering and one ram for a holocaust.[x]

**6** "Aaron shall bring in the bullock, his sin offering to atone for himself and for his household. **7** Taking the two male goats, and setting them before the LORD at the entrance of the meeting tent, **8** he shall cast lots to determine which one is for the LORD and which for Azazel.* **9** The goat that is determined by lot for the LORD, Aaron shall bring in and offer up as a sin offering. **10** But the goat determined by lot for Azazel he shall set alive before the LORD, so that with it he may make atonement by sending it off to Azazel in the desert.

**11** "Thus shall Aaron offer up the bullock, his sin offering, to atone for himself and for his family. When he has slaughtered it, **12** he shall take a censer full of glowing embers from the altar before the LORD, as well as a double handfull of finely ground fragrant incense, and bringing them inside the veil, **13** there before

t Lv 12, 2. 5.
u Lv 18, 19.
v Mt 9, 20; Mk 5, 25; Lk 8, 43.
w Heb 9, 6-12.
x Nm 29, 11.

*

15, 23: What is added to the legislation by this verse is uncertain in both the Hebrew and the Greek.

16, 2: The sanctuary, inside the veil: the innermost part of the sanctuary, known also as "the holy of holies." Cf Ex 26, 33f. Here the high priest was allowed to enter only once a year, on Yom Kippur, the Day of Atonement. In Heb 9, 3–12 this ceremony is applied to Christ's single act of Redemption, whereby he won for us an everlasting atonement, Propitiatory: see note on Ex 25, 17.

16, 8: Azazel: perhaps a name of Satan, used only in this chapter. The ancient versions translated this word as "the escaping goat," whence the English word "scapegoat."

16, 13: Else he will die: the smoke is to conceal the resplendent majesty of God, the sight of which would strike any man

the LORD he shall put incense on the fire, so that
a cloud of incense may cover the propitiatory
over the commandments; else he will die.*
**14** Taking some of the bullock's blood, he shall
sprinkle it with his finger on the fore part of the
propitiatory and likewise sprinkle some of the
blood with his finger seven times in front of the
propitiatory.[y]

**15** "Then he shall slaughter the people's
sin-offering goat, and bringing its blood inside
the veil, he shall do with it as he did with the
bullock's blood, sprinkling it on the propitiatory
and before it.[z] **16** Thus he shall make atonement for the sanctuary because of all the sinful
defilements and faults of the Israelites. He shall
do the same for the meeting tent, which is set
up among them in the midst of their uncleanness. **17** No one else may be in the meeting tent
from the time he enters the sanctuary to make
atonement until he departs. When he has made
atonement for himself and his household, as
well as for the whole Israelite community,
**18** he shall come out to the altar before the
LORD and make atonement for it also. Taking
some of the bullock's and the goat's blood, he
shall put it on the horns around the altar,[a]
**19** and with his finger sprinkle some of the
blood on it seven times. Thus he shall render it
clean and holy, purged of the defilements of the
Israelites.

**The Scapegoat.** **20** "When he has completed the atonement rite for the sanctuary, the
meeting tent and the altar, Aaron shall bring
forward the live goat. **21** Laying both hands on
its head, he shall confess over it all the sinful
faults and transgressions of the Israelites, and so
put them on the goat's head.[b] He shall then have
it led into the desert by an attendant. **22** Since
the goat is to carry off their iniquities to an
isolated region, it must be sent away into the
desert.[c]

**23** *"After Aaron has again gone into the
meeting tent, he shall strip off and leave in the
sanctuary the linen vestments he had put on
when he entered there. **24** After bathing his
body with water in a sacred place, he shall put
on his vestments, and then come out and offer
his own and the people's holocaust, in atonement for himself and for the people, **25** and also
burn the fat of the sin offering on the altar.

**26** "The man who has led away the goat for
Azazel shall wash his garments and bathe his
body in water; only then may he enter the camp.
**27** The sin-offering bullock and goat whose
blood was brought into the sanctuary to make
atonement, shall be taken outside the camp,[d]
where their hides and flesh and offal shall be
burned up in the fire. **28** The one who burns
them shall wash his garments and bathe his body
in water; only then may he enter the camp.

**The Fast.** **29** [e]"This shall be an everlasting
ordinance for you: on the tenth day of the seventh month every one of you, whether a native
or a resident alien, shall mortify himself* and
shall do no work. **30** Since on this day atonement is made for you to make you clean, so that
you may be cleansed of all your sins before the
LORD, **31** by everlasting ordinance it shall be a
most solemn sabbath for you, on which you
must mortify yourselves.

**32** "This atonement is to be made by the
priest who has been anointed and ordained to the
priesthood in succession to his father. He shall
wear the linen garments, the sacred vestments,
**33** and make atonement for the sacred sanctuary, the meeting tent and the altar, as well as for
the priests and all the people of the community.
**34** This, then, shall be an everlasting ordinance
for you: once a year atonement shall be made for
all the sins of the Israelites."[f]

Thus was it done, as the LORD had commanded Moses.

## *IV: Code of Legal Holiness*

## CHAPTER 17

**Sacredness of Blood.** **1** The LORD said to
Moses, **2** "Speak to Aaron and his sons, as
well as to all the Israelites, and tell them: This
is what the LORD has commanded. **3** *Any Israelite who slaughters an ox or a sheep or a goat,
whether in the camp or outside of it, **4** without
first bringing it to the entrance of the meeting
tent to present it as an offering to the LORD in
front of his Dwelling, shall be judged guilty of
bloodshed; and for this, such a man shall be cut
off from among his people. **5** Therefore, such
sacrifices as they used to offer up in the open
field the Israelites shall henceforth offer to the
LORD, bringing them to the priest at the entrance
of the meeting tent and sacrificing them there as

---

y Heb 9, 13. 25.
z Heb 5, 1; 6, 19.
a Ex 30, 12.
b Is 53, 6; 2 Cor 5, 21.
c Is 53, 11. 12; Jn 1, 29; 1 Pt 2, 24.
d Heb 13, 11.
e Lv 23, 27. 32; Nm 29, 7.
f Heb 9, 7. 25.

---

dead.

16, 23: This verse is best read after v 25. According to later Jewish practice the high priest again went into the holy of holies to remove the censer.

16, 29: Mortify himself: literally, "afflict his soul"; traditionally understood by the Jews as signifying abstinence from all food. This is the only fast day prescribed in the Mosaic law.

17, 3ff: The ancients considered blood the seat and sign of life, and therefore something sacred, even in animals. Cf Gn 9, 4f. Hence, even the ordinary butchering of an animal for meat was looked upon as having a sacrificial character, so that it should be performed at the sanctuary. This law, however, could not be carried out without great difficulty when the Israelites were scattered throughout Palestine, and so was modified in Dt 12, 20ff.

peace offerings to the LORD. **6** The priest shall
splash the blood on the altar of the LORD at the
entrance of the meeting tent and there burn the
fat for an odor pleasing to the LORD. **7** No
longer shall they offer their sacrifices to the
satyrs to whom they used to render their wanton
worship.[g] This shall be an everlasting ordinance for them and their descendants.

**8** "Tell them, therefore: Anyone, whether of
the house of Israel or of the aliens residing
among them, who offers a holocaust or sacrifice
**9** without bringing it to the entrance of the
meeting tent to offer it to the LORD, shall be cut
off from his kinsmen. **10** And if anyone,
whether of the house of Israel or of the aliens
residing among them, partakes of any blood, I
will set myself against that one who partakes of
blood and will cut him off from among his
people.[h] **11** [i]Since the life of a living body is
in its blood, I have made you put it on the altar,
so that atonement may thereby be made for your
own lives,* because it is the blood, as the seat
of life, that makes atonement. **12** That is why
I have told the Israelites: No one among you, not
even a resident alien, may partake of blood.

**13** "Anyone hunting, whether of the Israelites or of the aliens residing among them, who
catches an animal or a bird that may be eaten,
shall pour out its blood and cover it with earth.
**14** Since the life of every living body is its
blood, I have told the Israelites: You shall not
partake of the blood of any meat.[j] Since the life
of every living body is its blood, anyone who
partakes of it shall be cut off.

**15** [k]Everyone, whether a native or an alien,
who eats of an animal that died of itself or was
killed by a wild beast, shall wash his garments,
bathe in water, and be unclean until evening,
and then he will be clean. **16** If he does not
wash or does not bathe his body, he shall have
the guilt to bear."

## CHAPTER 18

**The Sanctity of Sex.** **1** The LORD said to
Moses, **2** "Speak to the Israelites and tell them:
I, the LORD, am your God. **3** You shall not do
as they do in the land of Egypt, where you once
lived, nor shall you do as they do in the land of
Canaan, where I am bringing you; do not conform to their customs. **4** My decrees you shall
carry out, and my statutes you shall take care to
follow. I, the LORD, am your God. **5** Keep,
then, my statutes and decrees, for the man who
carries them out will find life through them. I
am the LORD.[l]

**6** *"None of you shall approach a close relative to have sexual intercourse with her. I am the
LORD. **7** [m]You shall not disgrace your father by
having intercourse with your mother. Besides,
since she is your own mother, you shall not have
intercourse with her. **8** You shall not have intercourse with your father's wife,[n] for that would
be a disgrace to your father. **9** You shall not
have intercourse with your sister, your father's
daughter or your mother's daughter, whether
she was born in your own household or born
elsewhere. **10** You shall not have intercourse
with your son's daughter or with your daughter's daughter, for that would be a disgrace to
your own family. **11** You shall not have intercourse with the daughter whom your father's
wife bore to him, since she, too, is your sister.
**12** [o]You shall not have intercourse with your
father's sister, since she is your father's relative. **13** You shall not have intercourse with
your mother's sister, since she is your mother's
relative. **14** You shall not disgrace your father's
brother by being intimate with his wife,[p] since
she, too, is your aunt. **15** You shall not have
intercourse with your daughter-in-law; she is
your son's wife, and therefore you shall not
disgrace her. **16** You shall not have intercourse
with your brother's wife,* for that would be a
disgrace to your brother.[q] **17** You shall not
have intercourse with a woman and also with
her daughter, nor shall you marry and have
intercourse with her son's daughter or her
daughter's daughter; this would be shameful,
because they are related to her. **18** While your
wife is still living you shall not marry her sister
as her rival; for thus you would disgrace your
first wife.

**19** "You shall not approach a woman to have
intercourse with her while she is unclean from
menstruation. **20** You shall not have carnal relations with your neighbor's wife, defiling yourself with her. **21** [r]You shall not offer any of

g Ex 34, 15; Dt 32, 17; 2 Chr 11, 15; 1 Cor 10, 20.
h Lv 3, 17.
i Gn 9, 4.
j Lv 7, 26f.
k Lv 11, 39f; 22, 8.
l Gal 3, 12.
m 7-16: Lv 20, 11-21.
n Dt 23, 1; 27, 20; 1 Cor 5, 1.
o 12f: Lv 20, 19.
p Lv 20, 20.
q Lv 20, 21; Mt 14, 3f; Mk 6, 18.
r Lv 20, 2-5; Dt 18, 10; 2 Kgs 16, 3; 21, 6.

*

17, 11: That atonement may thereby be made for your own lives: hence, the sacrifice of an animal was a symbolic act which substituted the victim's life for the life of the offerer, who thus acknowledged that he deserved God's punishments for his sins. This idea of sacrifice is applied in Heb 9–10 to the death of Christ, inasmuch as "without the shedding of blood there is no forgiveness" (Heb 9, 22).

18, 6–18: These laws are formulated as directed to the male Israelites only, but naturally the same norms of consanguinity and affinity would apply to the women as well. Marriage, as well as casual intercourse, is here forbidden between men and women of the specified degrees of relationship.

18, 16: With your brother's wife: it was the violation of this law which aroused the wrath of John the Baptist against Herod Antipas. Cf Mk 6, 18. An exception to this law is made in Dt 25, 5.

18, 21: Immolated to Molech: the reference is to the Canaanite custom of sacrificing children to the god Molech. The little victims were first slain and then cremated. Cf Ez 16, 20ff;

your offspring to be immolated to Molech,*
thus profaning the name of your God. I am the
LORD. **22** You shall not lie with a male as with
a woman; such a thing is an abomination.[s]
**23** You shall not have carnal relations with an
animal, defiling yourself with it; nor shall a
woman set herself in front of an animal to mate
with it; such things are abhorrent.[t]
**24** "Do not defile yourselves by any of these
things by which the nations whom I am driving
out of your way have defiled themselves.
**25** Because their land has become defiled, I am
punishing it for its wickedness, by making it
vomit out its inhabitants. **26** You, however,
whether natives or resident aliens, must keep
my statutes and decrees forbidding all such
abominations **27** by which the previous inhabitants defiled the land; **28** otherwise the land will
vomit you out also for having defiled it, just as
it vomited out the nations before you. **29** Everyone who does any of these abominations
shall be cut off from among his people.
**30** Heed my charge, then, not to defile yourselves by observing the abominable customs
that have been observed before you.[u] I, the
LORD, am your God."

## CHAPTER 19

**Various Rules of Conduct.** **1** The LORD
said to Moses, **2** "Speak to the whole Israelite
community and tell them: Be holy, for I, the
LORD, your God, am holy.[v] **3** Revere your
mother and father,[w] and keep my sabbaths. I,
the LORD, am your God.
**4** "Do not turn aside to idols, nor make molten gods for yourselves.[x] I, the LORD, am your
God.
**5** "When you sacrifice your peace offering
to the LORD, if you wish it to be acceptable, **6** it
must be eaten on the very day of your sacrifice
or on the following day. Whatever is left over
until the third day shall be burned up in the fire.
**7** If any of it is eaten on the third day, the
sacrifice will be unacceptable as refuse;[y]
**8** whoever eats of it then shall pay the penalty
for having profaned what is sacred to the LORD.
Such a one shall be cut off from his people.
**9** "When you reap the harvest of your land,
you shall not be so thorough that you reap the
field to its very edge, nor shall you glean the
stray ears of grain.[z] **10** Likewise, you shall not
pick your vineyard bare, nor gather up the
grapes that have fallen. These things you shall
leave for the poor and the alien. I, the LORD, am
your God.
**11** "You shall not steal. You shall not lie or
speak falsely to one another.[a] **12** You shall not
swear falsely by my name, thus profaning the
name of your God.[b] I am the LORD.
**13** "You shall not defraud or rob your neighbor. You shall not withhold overnight the wages
of your day laborer.[c] **14** You shall not curse the
deaf, or put a stumbling block in front of the
blind, but you shall fear your God. I am the
LORD.
**15** "You shall not act dishonestly in rendering judgment. Show neither partiality to the
weak nor deference to the mighty, but judge
your fellow men justly.[d] **16** You shall not go
about spreading slander among your kinsmen;
nor shall you stand by idly when your neighbor's life is at stake. I am the LORD.
**17** "You shall not bear hatred for your brother in your heart.[e] Though you may have to
reprove your fellow man, do not incur sin because of him. **18** Take no revenge and cherish
no grudge against your fellow countrymen. You
shall love your neighbor as yourself.* I am the
LORD.[f]
**19** "Keep my statutes: do not breed any of
your domestic animals with others of a different
species; do not sow a field of yours with two
different kinds of seed; and do not put on a
garment woven with two different kinds of
thread.
**20** *"If a man has carnal relations with a
female slave who has already been living with
another man but has not yet been redeemed or
given her freedom, they shall be punished but
not put to death, because she is not free. **21** The
man, moreover, shall bring to the entrance of
the meeting tent a ram as his guilt offering to the
LORD. **22** With this ram the priest shall make
atonement before the LORD for the sin he has
committed, and it will be forgiven him.
**23** *"When you come into the land and plant
any fruit tree there, first look upon its fruit as if
it were uncircumcised. For three years, while its
fruit remains uncircumcised, it may not be eat-

s Lv 20, 13; Rom 1, 27; 1 Cor 6, 9f.
t Lv 20, 15f; Ex 22, 18.
u Lv 20, 23; Dt 18, 9.
v Lv 11, 44; Mt 5, 48; 1 Pt 1, 16.
w Ex 20, 12.
x Lv 26, 1; Ex 20, 3-5; 34, 17; Dt 27, 15.
y Lv 7, 18.
z Lv 23, 22; Dt 24, 19ff.
a Ex 20, 15f.
b Ex 20, 7; Mt 5, 33.
c Dt 24, 14f.
d Ex 23, 2f; Dt 1, 17; 16, 19; Ps 82, 2; Prv 24, 23.
e Mt 18, 15; Lk 17, 3; Gal 6, 1; 1 Jn 3, 14.
f Mt 5, 43; 19, 19; 22, 39; Mk 12, 31; Rom 13, 9; Gal 5, 14; Jas 2, 8.

*

20, 26. 31; 23, 37.

19, 18: You shall love your neighbor as yourself: cited by our Lord as the second of the two most important commandments of God. Cf Mt 22, 39; Mk 12, 31. Although in the present context the word "neighbor" is restricted to "fellow countrymen," in Lk 10, 29–37 Christ extends its meaning to embrace all men, even enemies. Cf also Mt 5. 43ff.

19, 20ff: This law seems out of its proper context here; perhaps it stood originally after Lv 20, 12. Female slave . . . given her freedom: reference is to the case treated of in Ex 21, 7–11.

19, 23ff: Uncircumcised: by analogy with a newborn boy, the newly planted tree was considered impure until "circumcised" by offering to the Lord all the fruit it bore in the fourth year.

en. **24** In the fourth year, however, all of its
fruit shall be sacred to the LORD as a thanksgiving feast to him. **25** Not until the fifth year may
you eat its fruit. Thus it will continue its yield
for you. I, the LORD, am your God.

**26** "Do not eat meat with the blood still in
it.[g] Do not practice divination or soothsaying.
**27** *Do not clip your hair at the temples, nor
trim the edges of your beard.[h] **28** Do not lacerate your bodies for the dead, and do not tattoo
yourselves. I am the LORD.

**29** "You shall not degrade your daughter by
making a prostitute of her; else the land will
become corrupt and full of lewdness. **30** Keep
my sabbaths, and reverence my sanctuary.[i] I am
the LORD.

**31** "Do not go to mediums or consult fortune-tellers, for you will be defiled by them.[j] I,
the LORD, am your God.

**32** "Stand up in the presence of the aged,
and show respect for the old; thus shall you fear
your God. I am the LORD.

**33** "When an alien resides with you in your
land, do not molest him.[k] **34** You shall treat the
alien who resides with you no differently than
the natives born among you; have the same love
for him as for yourself; for you too were once
aliens in the land of Egypt.[l] I, the LORD, am
your God.

**35** "Do not act dishonestly in using measures of length or weight or capacity. **36** You
shall have a true scale and true weights, an
honest ephah and an honest hin.[m] I, the LORD,
am your God, who brought you out of the land
of Egypt. **37** Be careful, then, to observe all my
statutes and decrees. I am the LORD."

## CHAPTER 20

**Penalties for Various Sins.** **1** The LORD
said to Moses, **2** "Tell the Israelites: Anyone,
whether an Israelite or an alien residing in Israel, who gives any of his offspring to Molech
shall be put to death.[n] Let his fellow citizens
stone him. **3** [o]I myself will turn against such a
man and cut him off from the body of his people; for in giving his offspring to Molech, he has
defiled my sanctuary and profaned my holy
name. **4** Even if his fellow citizens connive at
such a man's crime of giving his offspring to
Molech, and fail to put him to death, **5** I myself
will set my face against that man and his family
and will cut off from their people both him and
all who join him in his wanton worship of Molech. **6** Should anyone turn to mediums and
fortune-tellers and follow their wanton ways,[p]
I will turn against such a one and cut him off
from his people. **7** Sanctify yourselves, then,
and be holy; for I, the LORD, your God, am
holy.[q] **8** Be careful, therefore, to observe what
I, the LORD, who make you holy, have prescribed.

**9** "Anyone who curses his father or mother
shall be put to death;[r] since he has cursed his
father or mother, he has forfeited his life. **10** If
a man commits adultery with his neighbor's
wife, both the adulterer and the adulteress shall
be put to death.[s] **11** If a man disgraces his
father[t] by lying with his father's wife, both the
man and his stepmother shall be put to death;
they have forfeited their lives. **12** If a man lies
with his daughter-in-law,[u] both of them shall be
put to death; since they have committed an abhorrent deed, they have forfeited their lives.
**13** If a man lies with a male as with a woman,[v]
both of them shall be put to death for their
abominable deed; they have forfeited their lives.
**14** If a man marries a woman and her mother
also,[w] the man and the two women as well shall
be burned to death for their shameful conduct,
so that such shamefulness may not be found
among you. **15** If a man has carnal relations
with an animal, the man shall be put to death,[x]
and the animal shall be slain. **16** If a woman
goes up to any animal to mate with it,[y] the
woman and the animal shall be slain; let them
both be put to death; their lives are forfeit. **17** If
a man consummates marriage with his sister or
his half-sister,[z] they shall be publicly cut off
from their people for this shameful deed; the
man shall pay the penalty of having had intercourse with his own sister. **18** If a man lies in
sexual intercourse with a woman during her
menstrual period,[a] both of them shall be cut off
from their people, because they have laid bare
the flowing fountain of her blood. **19** You shall
not have intercourse with your mother's sister or
your father's sister;[b] whoever does so shall pay
the penalty of incest. **20** If a man disgraces his
uncle by having intercourse with his uncle's
wife, the man and his aunt shall pay the penalty
by dying childless. **21** If a man marries his
brother's wife and thus disgraces his brother,
they shall be childless because of this incest.

**22** "Be careful to observe all my statutes and
all my decrees; otherwise the land where I am
bringing you to dwell will vomit you out.

g Lv 3, 17; Dt 18, 10; 2 Kgs 17, 17; 21, 6; 2 Chr 33, 6.
h Lv 21, 5.
i Lv 26, 2; Ex 20, 8.
j Lv 20, 6. 27; Dt 18, 11; Is 8, 19.
k Ex 22, 20; 23, 9; Jer 22, 3; Mal 3, 5.
l Dt 10, 19.
m Dt 25, 13. 15; Prv 11, 1; 16, 11; 20, 10; Ez 45, 10.
n Lv 18, 21.
o Ez 23, 39.
p Lv 19, 31.
q Lv 11, 44; 19, 2; 1 Pt 1, 16.
r Ex 21, 17; Prv 20, 20; Mt 15, 4; Mk 7, 10.
s Lv 18, 20; Dt 22, 22; Jn 8, 5.
t Lv 18, 7f.
u Lv 18, 15.
v Lv 18, 22.
w Lv 18, 17; Dt 27, 23.
x Ex 22, 18; Dt 27, 21.
y Lv 18, 23.
z Lv 18, 9; Dt 27, 22.
a Lv 18, 19.
b Lv 18, 12f.

*19, 27: See note on Lv 21, 5.

**23** Do not conform, therefore, to the customs of the nations[c] whom I am driving out of your way, because all these things that they have done have filled me with disgust for them. **24** But to you I have said:[d] Their land shall be your possession, a land flowing with milk and honey. I am giving it to you as your own, I, the LORD, your God, who have set you apart from the other nations. **25** [e]You, too, must set apart, then, the clean animals from the unclean, and the clean birds from the unclean, so that you may not be contaminated with the uncleanness of any beast or bird or of any swarming creature in the land that I have set apart for you. **26** To me, therefore, you shall be sacred; for I, the LORD, am sacred,[f] I, who have set you apart from the other nations to be my own.

**27** *"A man or a woman who acts as a medium or fortune-teller[g] shall be put to death by stoning; they have no one but themselves to blame for their death."

## CHAPTER 21

**Sanctity of the Priesthood.** **1** The LORD said to Moses, "Speak to Aaron's sons, the priests, and tell them: None of you shall make himself unclean for any dead person* among his people,[h] **2** except for his nearest relatives, his mother or father, his son or daughter, his brother **3** or his maiden sister, who is of his own family while she remains unmarried; for these he may make himself unclean. **4** But for a sister who has married out of his family he shall not make himself unclean; this would be a profanation.

**5** *"The priests shall not make bare the crown of the head, nor shave the edges of the beard,[i] nor lacerate the body. **6** To their God they shall be sacred,* and not profane his name; since they offer up the oblations of the LORD, the food of their God, they must be holy.

**7** "A priest shall not marry a woman who has been a prostitute or has lost her honor, nor a woman who has been divorced by her husband; for the priest is sacred to his God.[j] **8** Honor him as sacred who offers up the food of your God; treat him as sacred, because I, the LORD, who have consecrated him, am sacred.

**9** "A priest's daughter who loses her honor by committing fornication and thereby dishonors her father also, shall be burned to death.

**10** "The most exalted of the priests, upon whose head the anointing oil has been poured and who has been ordained to wear the special vestments, shall not bare his head* or rend his garments, **11** nor shall he go near any dead person. Not even for his father or mother may he thus become unclean **12** or leave the sanctuary;[k] otherwise he will profane the sanctuary of his God, for with the anointing oil upon him, he is dedicated to his God, to me, the LORD.

**13** "The priest shall marry a virgin. **14** Not a widow or a woman who has been divorced or a woman who has lost her honor as a prostitute, but a virgin, taken from his own people, shall he marry;[l] **15** otherwise he will have base offspring among his people. I, the LORD, have made him sacred."

**Irregularities.** **16** The LORD said to Moses, **17** "Speak to Aaron and tell him: None of your descendants, of whatever generation, who has any defect shall come forward to offer up the food of his God. **18** Therefore, he who has any of the following defects may not come forward: he who is blind, or lame, or who has any disfigurement or malformation, **19** or a crippled foot or hand, **20** or who is hump-backed or weakly or walleyed, or who is afflicted with eczema, ringworm or hernia. **21** No descendant of Aaron the priest who has any such defect may draw near to offer up the oblations of the LORD; on account of his defect he may not draw near to offer up the food of his God. **22** He may, however, partake of the food of his God: of what is most sacred as well as of what is sacred. **23** Only, he may not approach the veil nor go up to the altar on account of his defect; he shall not profane these things that are sacred to me, for it is I, the LORD, who make them sacred."

**24** Moses, therefore, told this to Aaron and his sons and to all the Israelites.

## CHAPTER 22

**Sacrificial Banquets.** **1** The LORD said to Moses, **2** "Tell Aaron and his sons to respect the sacred offerings which the Israelites consecrate to me; else they will profane my holy name. I am the LORD.

**3** "Tell them: If any one of you, or of your descendants in any future generation, dares, while he is in a state of uncleanness, to draw

c Lv 18, 30.
d Ex 3, 8. 17; 6, 8.
e Lv 11, 2-47; Dt 14, 4-20.
f Lv 11, 44; Ex 19, 6; 1 Pt 1, 16.
g Lv 19, 31; Ex 22, 17; Dt 18, 11.
h Ez 44, 25.
i Ez 44, 20.
j Ez 44, 22.
k Lv 10, 7.
l Ez 44, 22.

*

20, 27: This verse is best read immediately after v 6.

21, 1: Unclean for any dead person: by preparing the corpse for burial. Cf Nm 6, 6; 19, 11–19.

21, 5: Such mourning customs of the Canaanites were forbidden to all the Israelites, but especially to the priests. Cf Lv 19, 27f.

21, 6: Sacred: the same Hebrew word has both the active meaning of "holy," that is, keeping oneself free from profane impurities, and the passive meaning of "sacred," that is, set apart from what is profane and therefore treated with religious reverence.

21, 10: Bare his head: see note on Lv 10, 6.

# Fathers of the Nation

### Abraham

God wanted to create a people who would have a special relationship with him, so that all other nations would be able to see how their trust in God brought them wholeness. God called Abraham, promising that his descendants would become a great nation. Through them, all people would see God's purposes and love. Abraham left Ur, on the river Euphrates, and eventually came to Canaan (Genesis 12:1-9), the Promised Land, and to Egypt (Genesis 12:10-20). He brought with him his wife, Sarah, and his nephew, Lot. Abraham's wife was a fine example of faith and prayerfulness.

### Isaac

Abraham had a son, Ishmael, by his servant Hagar. But in old age, Sarah, Abraham's wife, gave birth to a long-awaited son, Isaac, thus enabling the fulfilment of God's promise to make a great nation of Abraham's descendants (Genesis 18:1-15, 21:1-7).

***Above*: Abraham had large flocks of sheep and herds of cattle.**

### Jacob

Isaac married Rebekah, and had twin sons, Esau and Jacob. Jacob, the younger of the two, won the inheritance by deceiving his father (Genesis 27:1-40). He escaped his brother's vengeance by fleeing to Mesopotamia, where he married his uncle Laban's daughters, Leah and Rachel (Genesis 27:41-28:5, 29:15-30).

### Joseph

Jacob had twelve sons; his favorite, Joseph, was sold as a slave by his jealous brothers. After being wrongfully imprisoned in Egypt, Joseph rose to become chief minister of Pharaoh, bringing the rest of his family to Egypt when famine came (Genesis 37:1-36, 39:1-47:31).

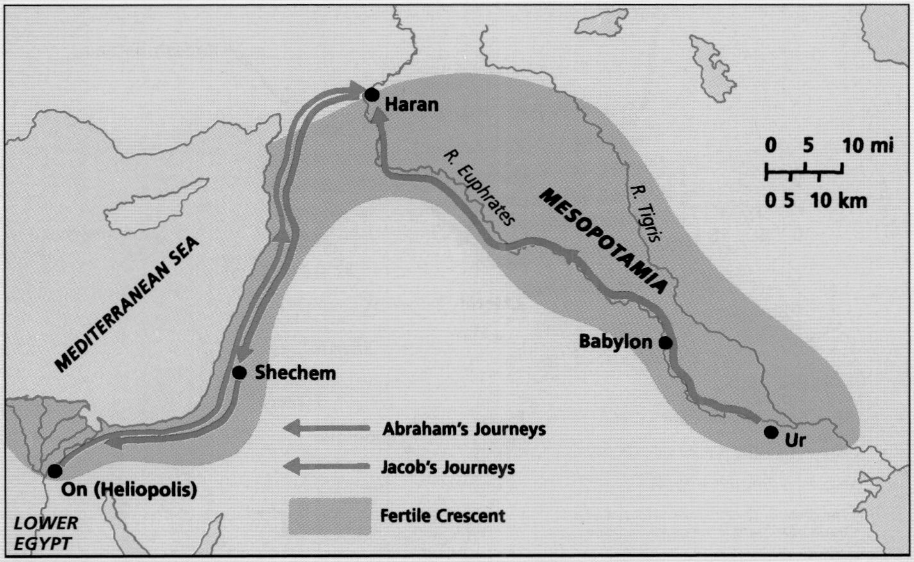

Haran
R. Euphrates
MESOPOTAMIA
R. Tigris
0 5 10 mi
0 5 10 km
MEDITERRANEAN SEA
Shechem
Babylon
Ur
On (Heliopolis)
LOWER EGYPT
Abraham's Journeys
Jacob's Journeys
Fertile Crescent

# Freedom
## MOSES AND THE EXODUS

### The Exodus

The Israelites, or Hebrews, remained in Egypt for four generations. In time they were no longer welcomed as visitors, but were pressed into slave labor (Exodus 1:1-22).

God sent Moses to set his people free, revealing himself to Moses as I AM (Exodus 3:14). It was only after Egypt had been struck with a series of terrible disasters that the Hebrews were able to leave (Exodus 7:14-12:42).

### The Ten Commandments

God now began to teach his people how he wanted them to be his special people. The message of Exodus is not only about freedom from oppression, but also about God's providing for his people's needs as he led them through the wilderness (Exodus 15:22-17:16).

At Mount Sinai God renewed the covenant he had made with Abraham, binding himself to all the Israelites. The Hebrews were also given a special code to live by, a code which included the Ten Commandments and many other rules and instructions (Exodus 19:1-24:18). God showed his people that they were to worship him alone and to live in a way pleasing to him.

### Wandering in the Desert

The Israelites spent 40 years in the wilderness, until the death of Moses. While they were wandering in the wilderness, the Israelites sent spies into Canaan. Most of the spies returned with dismaying reports, though the land was rich and fertile (Numbers 13:1-33).

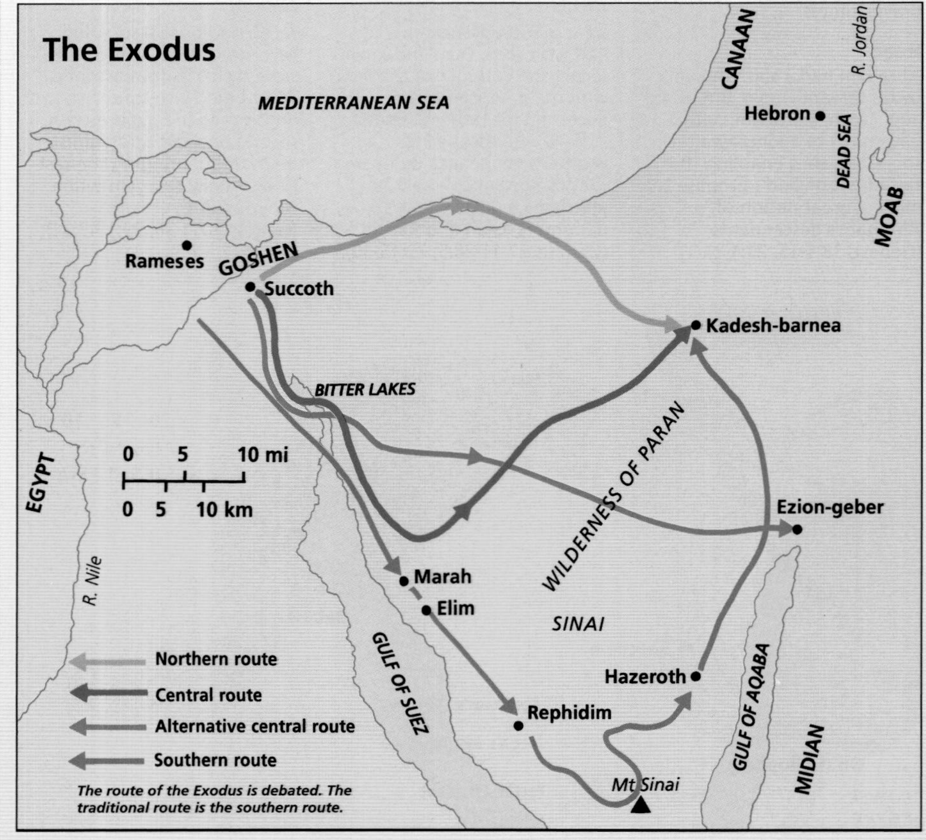

# The Promised Land



Not until Moses had died and Joshua had taken over as leader did the Israelites finally enter the Promised Land. According to the book of Joshua, they now had to conquer the land and settle it among the different tribes.

The book of Joshua records three campaigns: a central thrust through Jericho and Ai, a southern campaign, and a northern campaign (Joshua 5:13-8:29, 10:1-11:23).

Although the Israelites won many victories, the Philistines still controlled the coastal cities and the Canaanites many inland towns. After they entered the Promised Land, the Israelites faced the choice of serving God or the Canaanite gods.

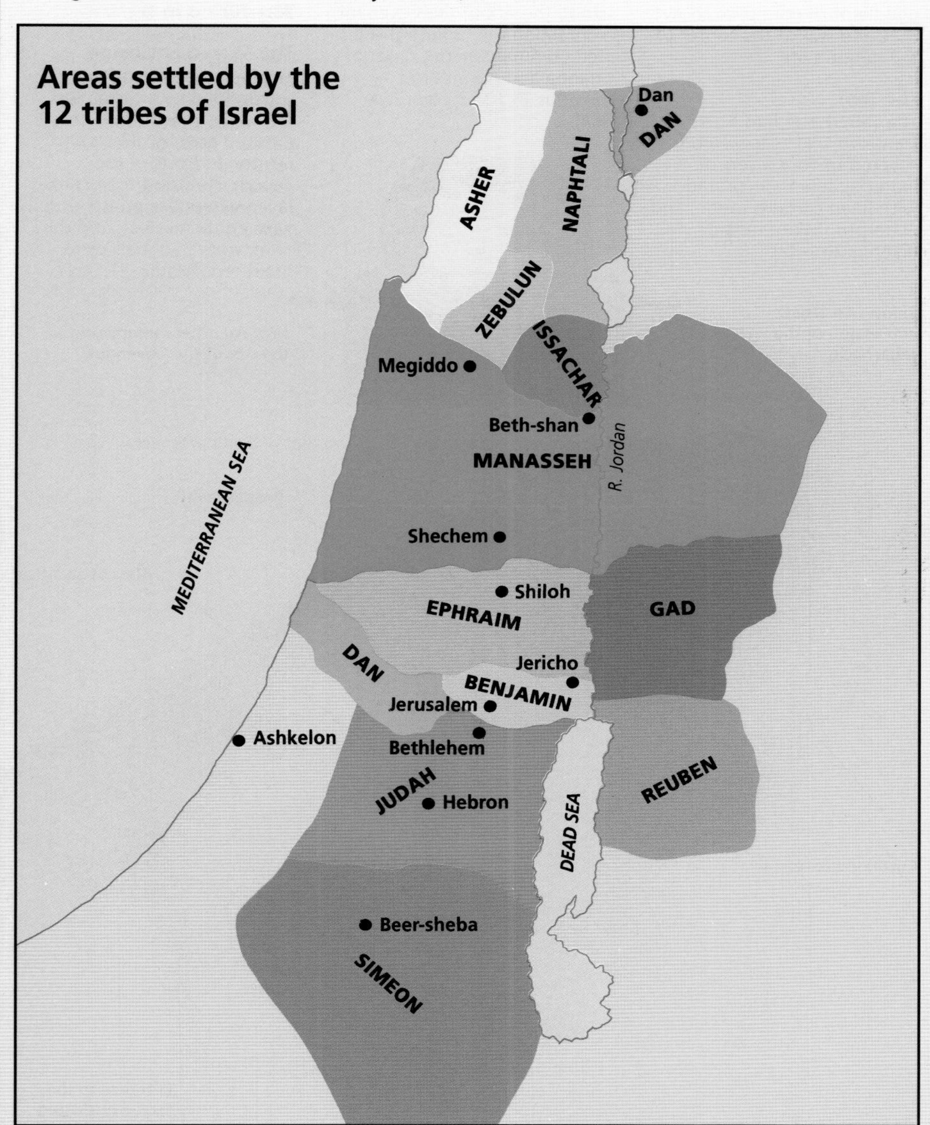

# The Tent
## OF GOD'S PRESENCE

While they were wandering in the desert, the Israelites built the Tabernacle, a special tent where they worshiped God. Each time they halted, they erected the Tabernacle in the middle of the camp, to show that God was at the center of the nation's life.

**The Tent**

The Tabernacle had a framework of acacia wood, covered by four layers of material. It was decorated with linen curtains inside, and waterproof skins outside (Exodus 26:1-37).

**Inside the Tent**

Inside the tent were two rooms. The small, inner room was the Holiest Place, and entered only by the high priest, only once a year. Here stood the Ark of the Covenant, containing the tablets of the Ten Commandments, a pot of manna and Aaron's rod (Exodus 25:10-22; Hebrews 9:4).

**The Holy Place**

In the outer room of the Holy Place stood the altar of incense, a seven-branched candlestick, and the table of showbread (Exodus 25:23-40, 30:1-10).

**The Sacred Enclosure**

The Tabernacle itself was surrounded by a curtained enclosure which could be entered only by priests and Levites. In front of the Tabernacle stood the bronze laver, where the priests ritually washed themselves, and the altar, where animals were sacrificed (Exodus 27:1-21).

***Below*: An artist's impression of the Tabernacle.**

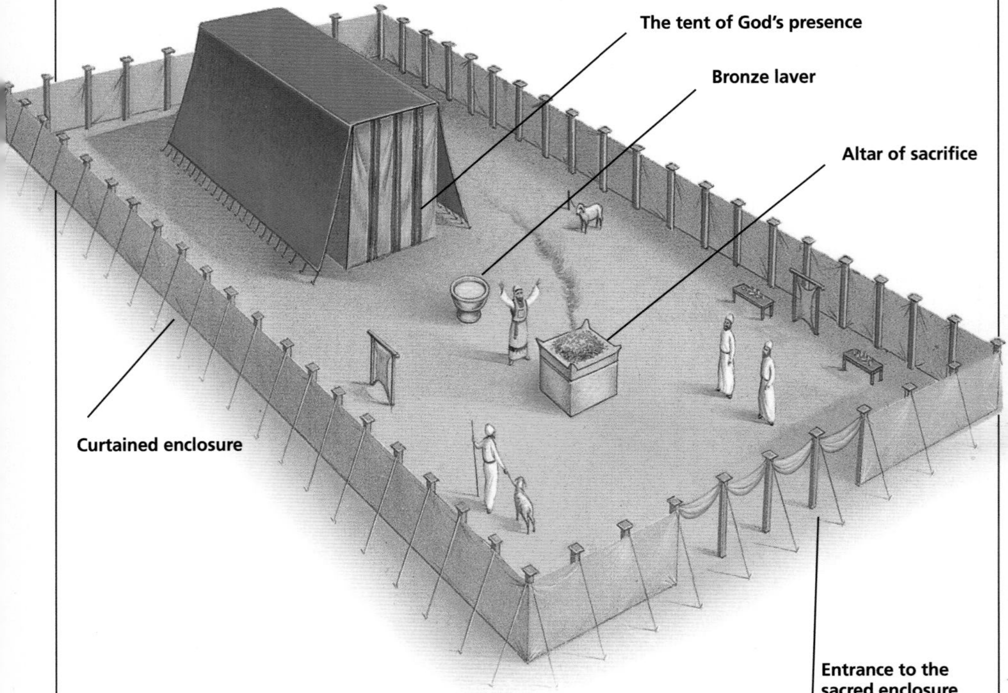

***Left*: An artist's impression of the Ark of the Covenant.**

**The tent of God's presence**

**Bronze laver**

**Altar of sacrifice**

**Curtained enclosure**

**Entrance to the sacred enclosure**

near the sacred offerings which the Israelites
consecrate to the LORD, such a one shall be cut
off from my presence. I am the LORD.
**4** "No descendant of Aaron who is stricken
with leprosy, or who suffers from a flow, may
eat of these sacred offerings, unless he again
becomes clean.[m] Moreover, if anyone touches
a person who has become unclean by contact
with a corpse, or if anyone has had an emission
of seed, **5** or if anyone touches[n] any swarming
creature or any man whose uncleanness, of
whatever kind it may be, is contagious, **6** the
one who touches such as these shall be unclean
until evening and may not eat of the sacred
portions until he has first bathed his body in
water;[o] **7** then, when the sun sets, he again
becomes clean. Only then may he eat of the
sacred offerings, which are his food. **8** He shall
not make himself unclean by eating of any animal that has died of itself or has been killed by
wild beasts.[p] I am the LORD.
**9** "They shall keep my charge and not do
wrong in this matter; else they will die for their
profanation. I am the LORD who have consecrated them.
**10** "Neither a lay person nor a priest's tenant
or hired servant may eat of any sacred offering.[q]
**11** But a slave whom a priest acquires by purchase or who is born in his house may eat of his
food. **12** A priest's daughter who is married to
a layman may not eat of the sacred contributions. **13** But if a priest's daughter is widowed
or divorced and, having no children, returns to
her father's house, she may then eat of her
father's food as in her youth. No layman, however, may eat of it. **14** [r]If such a one eats of a
sacred offering through inadvertence, he shall
make restitution to the priest for the sacred offering, with an increment of one fifth of the
amount. **15** The sacred offerings which the Israelites contribute to the LORD the priests shall
not allow to be profaned[s] **16** nor in the eating
of the sacred offering shall they bring down
guilt that must be punished; it is I, the LORD,
who make them sacred."

**Unacceptable Victims.** **17** The LORD said
to Moses, **18** "Speak to Aaron and his sons and
to all the Israelites, and tell them: When anyone
of the house of Israel, or any alien residing in
Israel, who wishes to offer a sacrifice, brings a
holocaust as a votive offering or as a free-will
offering to the LORD, **19** if it is to be acceptable,
the ox or sheep or goat that he offers must be
an unblemished male.[t] **20** You shall not offer
one that has any defect, for such a one would not
be acceptable for you.[u] **21** When anyone
presents a peace offering[v] to the LORD from the
herd or the flock in fulfillment of a vow, or as
a free-will offering, if it is to find acceptance,
it must be unblemished; it shall not have any
defect. **22** One that is blind or crippled or
maimed, or one that has a running sore or mange
or ringworm, you shall not offer to the LORD; do
not put such an animal on the altar as an oblation
to the LORD. **23** An ox or a sheep that is in any
way ill-proportioned or stunted you may indeed
present as a free-will offering, but it will not be
acceptable as a votive offering. **24** One that has
its testicles bruised or crushed or torn out or cut
off you shall not offer to the LORD. You shall
neither do this in your own land **25** nor receive
from a foreigner any such animals to offer up as
the food of your God; since they are deformed
or defective,[w] they will not be acceptable for
you."
**26** The LORD said to Moses, **27** "When an
ox or a lamb or a goat is born, it shall remain
with its mother for seven days; only from the
eighth day onward will it be acceptable, to be
offered as an oblation to the LORD.[x] **28** You
shall not slaughter an ox or a sheep on one and
the same day with its young. **29** Whenever you
offer a thanksgiving sacrifice to the LORD, so
offer it that it may be acceptable for you; **30** it
must, therefore, be eaten on the same day; none
of it shall be left over until the next day.[y] I am
the LORD.
**31** "Be careful to observe the commandments which I, the LORD, give you, **32** and do
not profane my holy name; in the midst of the
Israelites I, the LORD, must be held as sacred.
It is I who made you sacred **33** and led you out
of the land of Egypt, that I, the LORD, might be
your God."

## CHAPTER 23

**Holy Days.** **1** The LORD said to Moses,
**2** "Speak to the Israelites and tell them: The
following are the festivals of the LORD, my feast
days, which you shall celebrate with a sacred
assembly.
**3** "For six days work may be done; but the
seventh day is the sabbath rest, a day for sacred
assembly, on which you shall do no work. The
sabbath shall belong to the LORD wherever you
dwell.[z]

**Passover.** **4** "These, then, are the festivals
of the LORD which you shall celebrate at their
proper time with a sacred assembly.[a] **5** The
Passover of the LORD falls on the fourteenth day

m Lv 7, 20; 15, 16.
n Lv 11, 24. 43.
o Heb 10, 22.
p Lv 17, 15; Dt 14, 21; Ez 44, 31.
q 1 Sm 21, 6; Mt 12, 4.
r Lv 5, 16; 27, 13. 15. 19.
s Lv 19, 8; Nm 18, 32.
t Lv 1, 3. 10.
u Dt 15, 21; 17, 1; Mal 1, 8. 14.
v Lv 3, 1. 6.
w Mal 1, 14.
x Ex 22, 29.
y Lv 7, 15.
z Ex 20, 8-11; 23, 12; 31, 14f; 34, 21; Dt 5, 12-15; Lk 13, 14.
a Ex 23, 14-19.
b Nm 9, 2f; 28, 16.

of the first month, at the evening twilight.[b]
6 The fifteenth day of this month is the LORD's
feast of Unleavened Bread. For seven days you
shall eat unleavened bread.[c] 7 On the first of
these days you shall hold a sacred assembly and
do no sort of work.[d] 8 On each of the seven
days you shall offer an oblation to the LORD.
Then on the seventh day you shall again hold a
sacred assembly and do no sort of work."

9 The LORD said to Moses, 10 "Speak to the
Israelites and tell them: When you come into the
land which I am giving you, and reap your
harvest, you shall bring a sheaf of the first fruits
of your harvest to the priest, 11 who shall wave
the sheaf before the LORD that it may be acceptable for you. On the day after the sabbath* the
priest shall do this. 12 On this day, when your
sheaf is waved, you shall offer to the LORD for
a holocaust an unblemished yearling lamb.
13 Its cereal offering shall be two tenths of an
ephah of fine flour mixed with oil, as a
sweet-smelling oblation to the LORD; and its
libation shall be a fourth of a hin of wine.
14 Until this day, when you bring your God this
offering, you shall not eat any bread* or roasted
grain or fresh kernels. This shall be a perpetual
statute for you and your descendants wherever
you dwell.

**Pentecost.** 15 "Beginning with the day after the sabbath, the day on which you bring the
wave-offering sheaf, you shall count seven full
weeks,[e] 16 and then on the day after the seventh week, the fiftieth* day,[f] you shall present
the new cereal offering to the LORD. 17 For the
wave offering of your first fruits to the LORD,
you shall bring with you from wherever you live
two loaves of bread made of two tenths of an
ephah of fine flour and baked with leaven.
18 Besides the bread, you shall offer to the
LORD a holocaust of seven unblemished yearling lambs, one young bull, and two rams, along
with their cereal offering and libations, as a
sweet-smelling oblation to the LORD. 19 One
male goat shall be sacrificed as a sin offering,
and two yearling lambs as a peace offering.[g]
20 The priest shall wave the bread of the first
fruits and the two lambs as a wave offering
before the LORD; these shall be sacred to the
LORD and belong to the priest. 21 On this same
day you shall by proclamation have a sacred
assembly, and no sort of work may be done.
This shall be a perpetual statute for you and your
descendants wherever you dwell.

22 "When you reap the harvest of your land,
you shall not be so thorough that you reap the
field to its very edge, nor shall you glean the
stray ears of your grain. These things you shall
leave for the poor and the alien. I, the LORD, am
your God."

**New Year's Day.** 23 The LORD said to Moses, 24 "Tell the Israelites: On the first day of
the seventh month you shall keep a sabbath rest,
with a sacred assembly and with the trumpet
blasts as a reminder; 25 you shall then do no
sort of work, and you shall offer an oblation to
the LORD."

**The Day of Atonement.** 26 [h]The LORD
said to Moses, 27 "The tenth of this seventh
month is the Day of Atonement,[i] when you
shall hold a sacred assembly and mortify yourselves and offer an oblation to the LORD. 28 On
this day you shall not do any work, because it
is the Day of Atonement, when atonement is
made for you before the LORD, your God.
29 Anyone who does not mortify himself on
this day shall be cut off from his people; 30 and
if anyone does any work on this day, I will
remove him from the midst of his people.
31 This is a perpetual statute for you and your
descendants wherever you dwell: you shall do
no work, 32 but shall keep a sabbath of complete rest and mortify yourselves. Beginning on
the evening of the ninth of the month, you shall
keep this sabbath of yours from evening to evening."

**The Feast of Booths.** 33 The LORD said to
Moses, 34 "Tell the Israelites: The fifteenth
day of this seventh month[j] is the LORD's feast
of Booths,* which shall continue for seven
days. 35 On the first day there shall be a sacred
assembly, and you shall do no sort of work.
36 For seven days you shall offer an oblation to
the LORD, and on the eighth day you shall again
hold a sacred assembly and offer an oblation to

c Ex 12, 18; 13, 3. 10; 23, 15; 34, 18.
d Ex 12, 15; Nm 28, 18. 25.
e Ex 34, 22; Nm 28, 26; Dt 16, 9.
f Acts 2, 1.
g Nm 28, 30.
h Lv 25, 9.
i Lv 16, 29f; Nm 29, 7.
j Nm 29, 12; Dt 16, 13; 2 Mc 1, 9. 18; Jn 7, 2.

*

23, 11: The sabbath: according to the Jewish tradition this was the feast day itself, the fifteenth of Nisan, which was a special day of rest. Cf v 7. However, some understand here the Saturday of the Passover week, or even the Saturday following it; cf Jn 19, 31.

23, 14: Any bread: made from the new grain. The harvest had first to be sanctified for man's use by this offering to God.

23, 16: The fiftieth: from the Greek word for this we have the name "Pentecost." Cf 2 Mc 12, 31; Acts 2, 1. It was also called "the feast of the Seven Weeks," or simply "the feast of Weeks" (Nm 28, 26; Dt 16, 10; Tb 2, 1). The new cereal offering: of flour made from the new grain. Pentecost was the thanksgiving feast at the end of the grain harvest, which began after Passover. Later tradition made it a commemoration of the giving of the law at Sinai.

23, 34: Feast of Booths: the joyful observance of the vintage and fruit harvest. Cf Dt 16, 13. During the seven days of the feast the Israelites camped in booths of branches erected on the roofs of their houses or in the streets in commemoration of their wanderings in the desert, where they dwelt in booths.

the LORD. On that solemn closing you shall do
no sort of work.

**37** "These, therefore, are the festivals of the
LORD on which you shall proclaim a sacred
assembly, and offer as an oblation to the LORD
holocausts and cereal offerings, sacrifices and
libations, as prescribed for each day, **38** in addition to those of the LORD's sabbaths, your
donations, your various votive offerings and the
free-will offerings that you present to the LORD.

**39** "On the fifteenth day, then, of the seventh month, when you have gathered in the
produce of the land,[k] you shall celebrate a pilgrim feast of the LORD for a whole week. The
first and the eighth day shall be days of complete
rest. **40** On the first day you shall gather foliage* from majestic trees, branches of palms
and boughs of myrtles and of valley poplars,
and then for a week you shall make merry before
the LORD, your God. **41** By perpetual statute
for you and your descendants you shall keep this
pilgrim feast of the LORD for one whole week[l]
in the seventh month of the year. **42** During this
week every native Israelite among you shall
dwell in booths, **43** that your descendants[m]
may realize that, when I led the Israelites out of
the land of Egypt, I made them dwell in booths.
I, the LORD, am your God."

**44** Thus did Moses announce to the Israelites
the festivals of the LORD.

## CHAPTER 24

**The Sanctuary Light.** **1** The LORD said to
Moses, **2** "Order the Israelites to bring you
clear oil of crushed olives for the light, so that
you may keep lamps burning regularly.[n] **3** In
the meeting tent, outside the veil that hangs in
front of the commandments, Aaron shall set up
the lamps to burn before the LORD regularly,
from evening till morning. Thus, by a perpetual
statute for you and your descendants, **4** the
lamps shall be set up on the pure gold lampstand,[o] to burn regularly before the LORD.

**The Showbread.** **5** "You shall take fine
flour and bake it[p] into twelve cakes, using two
tenths of an ephah of flour for each cake.
**6** These you shall place in two piles, six in each
pile, on the pure gold table before the LORD.
**7** On each pile put some pure frankincense,
which shall serve as an oblation to the LORD, a
token offering for the bread. **8** Regularly on
each sabbath day this bread shall be set out
afresh[q] before the LORD, offered on the part of
the Israelites by an everlasting agreement. **9** It
shall belong to Aaron and his sons, who must
eat it in a sacred place, since, as something most
sacred among the various oblations to the LORD,
it is his by perpetual right."

**Punishment of Blasphemy.** **10** Among
the Israelites there was a man born of an Israelite
mother (Shelomith, daughter of Dibri, of the
tribe of Dan) and an Egyptian father. **11** This
man quarreled publicly with another Israelite
and cursed and blasphemed the LORD's name.
So the people brought him to Moses, **12** who
kept him in custody till a decision from the
LORD should settle the case for them. **13** The
LORD then said to Moses, **14** "Take the blasphemer outside the camp, and when all who
heard him have laid their hands on his head, let
the whole community stone him. **15** Tell the
Israelites: Anyone who curses his God shall
bear the penalty of his sin; **16** whoever blasphemes the name of the LORD shall be put to
death.[r] The whole community shall stone him;
alien and native alike must be put to death for
blaspheming the LORD's name.

**17** "Whoever takes the life of any human
being shall be put to death;[s] **18** whoever takes
the life of an animal shall make restitution of
another animal. A life for a life![t] **19** Anyone
who inflicts an injury on his neighbor shall receive the same in return. **20** Limb for limb, eye
for eye, tooth for tooth! The same injury that a
man gives another shall be inflicted on him in
return.[u] **21** Whoever slays an animal shall
make restitution, but whoever slays a man shall
be put to death. **22** You shall have but one rule,
for alien and native alike.[v] I, the LORD, am your
God."

**23** When Moses told this to the Israelites,
they took the blasphemer outside the camp and
stoned him;[w] they carried out the command that
the LORD had given Moses.

## CHAPTER 25

**The Sabbatical Year.** **1** The LORD said to
Moses on Mount Sinai, **2** "Speak to the Israelites and tell them: When you enter the land that
I am giving you, let the land, too, keep a sabbath for the LORD. **3** For six years you may sow
your field, and for six years prune your vineyard, gathering in their produce.[x] **4** But during

k Ex 23, 16; Dt 16, 13.
l Nm 29, 12-38.
m Dt 31, 10-13.
n Ex 27. 20f.
o Ex 25, 31.
p Ex 25, 30; 1 Kgs 7, 48; 2 Chr 4, 19; 13, 11; Heb 9, 2.
q 1 Chr 9, 32.
r 1 Kgs 21, 10. 13; Mt 26, 65f; Jn 10, 33.
s Gn 9, 5f; Ex 21, 12; Nm 35, 31; Dt 19, 11f.
t Ex 21, 33f.
u Dt 19, 21; Mt 5, 38.
v Lv 19, 34; Ex 12, 49; Nm 15, 16.
w Acts 7, 57f.
x Ex 23, 10f.
y 1 Mc 6, 49. 53.

* 23, 40: Foliage: literally, "fruit," but here probably used in the general sense of "produce, growth." These branches were used for constructing the "booths" or huts in which the people lived during the feast. Cf Neh 8, 15. However, from about the time of Christ on, the Jews have understood this of "fruit" in the strict sense; hence, branches of lemons and oranges were carried with the other branches in joyous procession.

the seventh year the land shall have a complete
rest, a sabbath for the LORD,[y] when you may
neither sow your field nor prune your vineyard.
**5** *The aftergrowth of your harvest you shall
not reap, nor shall you pick the grapes of your
untrimmed vines in this year of sabbath rest for
the land. **6** While the land has its sabbath, all
its produce will be food equally for you yourself
and for your male and female slaves, for your
hired help and the tenants who live with you,
**7** and likewise for your livestock and for the
wild animals on your land.

**The Jubilee Year.** **8** "Seven weeks of
years shall you count—seven times seven
years—so that the seven cycles amount to forty-nine years. **9** Then, on the tenth day of the
seventh month let the trumpet resound; on this,
the Day of Atonement, the trumpet blast shall
re-echo throughout your land. **10** This fiftieth
year* you shall make sacred by proclaiming
liberty in the land for all its inhabitants.[z] It shall
be a jubilee for you, when every one of you shall
return to his own property, every one to his own
family estate. **11** In this fiftieth year, your year
of jubilee, you shall not sow, nor shall you reap
the aftergrowth or pick the grapes from the untrimmed vines. **12** Since this is the jubilee,
which shall be sacred for you, you may not eat
of its produce, except as taken directly from the
field.

**13** "In this year of jubilee, then, every one
of you shall return to his own property.
**14** Therefore, when you sell any land to your
neighbor or buy any from him, do not deal
unfairly. **15** On the basis of the number of years
since the last jubilee shall you purchase the land
from him;[a] and so also, on the basis of the
number of years for crops, shall he sell it to you.
**16** When the years are many, the price shall be
so much the more; when the years are few, the
price shall be so much the less. For it is really
the number of crops that he sells you. **17** Do not
deal unfairly, then; but stand in fear of your god.
I, the LORD, am your God.

**18** "Observe my precepts and be careful to
keep my regulations, for then you will dwell
securely in the land. **19** The land will yield its
fruit and you will have food in abundance, so
that you may live there without worry.[b]
**20** Therefore, do not say, 'What shall we eat in
the seventh year, if we do not then sow or reap
our crop?'[c] **21** I will bestow such blessings on
you in the sixth year that there will then be crop
enough for three years. **22** When you sow in the
eighth year, you will continue to eat from the
old crop; and even into the ninth year, when the
crop comes in, you will still have the old to eat
from.[d]

**Redemption of Property.** **23** [e]"The land
shall not be sold in perpetuity; for the land is
mine, and you are but aliens who have become
my tenants. **24** Therefore, in every part of the
country that you occupy, you must permit the
land to be redeemed. **25** When one of your
countrymen is reduced to poverty and has to sell
some of his property, his closest relative, who
has the right to redeem it, may go and buy back
what his kinsman has sold.[f] **26** If, however, the
man has no relative to redeem his land, but later
on acquires sufficient means to buy it back in his
own name, **27** he shall make a deduction from
the price in proportion to the number of years
since the sale, and then pay back the balance to
the one to whom he sold it, so that he may thus
regain his own property. **28** But if he does not
acquire sufficient means to buy back his land,
what he has sold shall remain in the possession
of the purchaser until the jubilee, when it must
be released and returned to its original owner.[g]

**29** "When someone sells a dwelling in a
walled town, he has the right to buy it back
during the time of one full year from its sale.
**30** But if such a house in a walled town has not
been redeemed at the end of a full year, it shall
belong in perpetuity to the purchaser and his
descendants; nor shall it be released in the jubilee. **31** However, houses in villages that are not
encircled by walls shall be considered as belonging to the surrounding farm land; they may
be redeemed at any time, and in the jubilee they
must be released.

**32** "In levitical cities the Levites shall always have the right to redeem the town houses
that are their property. **33** Any town house of
the Levites in their cities that had been sold and
not redeemed, shall be released in the jubilee;
for the town houses of the Levites are their
hereditary property in the midst of the Israelites.
**34** Moreover, the pasture land belonging to
their cities shall not be sold at all;[h] it must
always remain their hereditary property.

**35** "When one of your fellow countrymen is

---

z Nm 36, 4; Is 61, 2; Ez 46, 17; Lk 4, 19.
a Lv 27, 18. 23.
b Lv 26, 5.
c Mt 6, 25. 31; Lk 12, 22. 29.
d Lv 26, 10.
e 1 Pt 2, 11.
f Ru 2, 20; 4, 4. 6; Jer 32, 7f.
g Lv 27, 24.
h Nm 35, 3.
i Dt 15, 7. 8.

---

25, 5ff: As long as the produce of the sabbatical year remains on the field, it remains available to everyone; cf v 12. In Ex 23, 10f the poor and the wild beasts that have no other source of nourishment are alone mentioned.

25, 10: Fiftieth year: to arrive at this number, the preceding year of jubilee is included in the count, and therefore this is more exactly the forty-ninth year, the seventh sabbatical year. Liberty: Israelite slaves were set free (v 50) and landed property was returned to its original owner (v 13): two important laws for preserving the social and economic equilibrium. Jubilee: derived from the Hebrew word yobel, "ram's horn," which was blown on this occasion.

reduced to poverty and is unable to hold out
beside you, extend to him the privileges of an
alien or a tenant, so that he may continue to live
with you.[i] **36** Do not exact interest from your
countryman either in money or in kind, but out
of fear of God let him live with you. **37** [j]You
are to lend him neither money at interest nor
food at a profit. **38** I, the LORD, am your God,
who brought you out of the land of Egypt to give
you the land of Canaan and to be your God.

**39** "When, then, your countryman becomes
so impoverished beside you that he sells you his
services, do not make him work as a slave.[k]
**40** Rather, let him be like a hired servant or like
your tenant, working with you until the jubilee
year, **41** when he, together with his children,
shall be released from your service and return to
his kindred and to the property of his ancestors.
**42** Since those whom I brought out of the land
of Egypt are servants of mine, they shall not be
sold as slaves to any man. **43** Do not lord it
over them harshly, but stand in fear of your
God.

**44** "Slaves, male and female, you may indeed possess, provided you buy them from
among the neighboring nations. **45** You may
also buy them from among the aliens who reside
with you and from their children who are born
and reared in your land. Such slaves you may
own as chattels, **46** and leave to your sons as
their hereditary property, making them perpetual slaves. But you shall not lord it harshly over
any of the Israelites, your kinsmen.[l]

**47** "When one of your countrymen is reduced to such poverty that he sells himself to a
wealthy alien who has a permanent or a temporary residence among you, or to one of the
descendants of an immigrant family, **48** even
after he has thus sold his services he still has the
right of redemption; he may be redeemed by one
of his own brothers, **49** or by his uncle or cousin, or by some other relative or fellow clansman;
or, if he acquires the means, he may redeem
himself. **50** With his purchaser he shall compute the years from the sale to the jubilee, distributing the sale price over these years as
though he had been hired as a day laborer.
**51** The more such years there are, the more of
the sale price he shall pay back as ransom;
**52** the fewer years there are left before the jubilee year, the more he has to his credit; in proportion to his years of service shall he pay his
ransom. **53** The alien shall treat him as a servant hired on an annual basis, and he shall not
lord it over him harshly under your very eyes.
**54** If he is not thus redeemed, he shall nevertheless be released, together with his children, in
the jubilee year.[m] **55** For to me the Israelites
belong as servants; they are servants of mine,
because I brought them out of the land of Egypt,
I, the LORD, your God.

## CHAPTER 26

**The Reward of Obedience.** **1** "Do not
make false gods for yourselves. You shall not
erect an idol or a sacred pillar for yourselves,
nor shall you set up a stone figure for worship
in your land;[n] for I, the LORD, am your God.
**2** Keep my sabbaths,[o] and reverence my sanctuary. I am the LORD.

**3** *"If you live in accordance with my precepts and are careful to observe my commandments, **4** I will give you rain in due season, so
that the land will bear its crops, and the trees
their fruit;[p] **5** your threshing will last till vintage time, and your vintage till the time for
sowing, and you will have food to eat in abundance, so that you may dwell securely in your
land. **6** I will establish peace in the land, that
you may lie down to rest without anxiety. I will
rid the country of ravenous beasts, and keep the
sword of war from sweeping across your land.
**7** You will rout your enemies and lay them low
with your sword. **8** Five of you will put a hundred of your foes to flight, and a hundred of you
will chase ten thousand of them, till they are cut
down by your sword. **9** I will look with favor
upon you, and make you fruitful and numerous,
as I carry out my covenant with you. **10** So
much of the old crops will you have stored up
for food that you will have to discard them to
make room for the new.[q] **11** [r]I will set my
Dwelling among you, and will not disdain you.
**12** Ever present in your midst, I will be your
God, and you will be my people; **13** for it is I,
the LORD, your God, who brought you out of the
land of the Egyptians and freed you from their
slavery, breaking the yoke they had laid upon
you and letting you walk erect.

**Punishment of Disobedience.** **14** "But
if you do not heed me and do not keep all these
commandments, **15** if you reject my precepts
and spurn my decrees, refusing to obey all my
commandments and breaking my covenant,
**16** then I, in turn, will give you your deserts.
I will punish you with terrible woes—with wasting and fever to dim the eyes and sap the life.
You will sow your seed in vain, for your enemies will consume the crop. **17** I will turn
against you, till you are beaten down before
your enemies and lorded over by your foes. You

j Dt 23, 19.
k 1 Kgs 9, 22.
l Is 14, 1f.
m Ex 21, 2f.
n Lv 19, 4; Ex 20, 4; Nm 33, 52; Dt 5, 8.
o Ex 20, 8.
p Ps 85, 13.
q Lv 25, 22.
r 11f: Ex 29, 45; Ez 39, 26ff; 2 Cor 6, 16.
s Dt 28, 25.

* 26, 3–45: Since God's covenant was with the Israelite nation as a whole, these promises and threats are made primarily to the entire community. The rewards and punishments are of a temporal nature because the community as such exists only here on earth, not in the hereafter.

will take to flight though no one pursues you.[s]
**18** "If even after this you do not obey me,
I will increase the chastisement for your sins
sevenfold, **19** to break your haughty confidence. I will make the sky above you as hard as
iron, and your soil as hard as bronze, **20** so that
your strength will be spent in vain; your land
will bear no crops, and its trees no fruit.
**21** "If then you become defiant in your un-
willingness to obey me, I will multiply my
blows another sevenfold, as your sins deserve.
**22** I will unleash the wild beasts against you, to
rob you of your children and wipe out your
livestock, till your population dwindles away
and your roads become deserted.
**23** "If, with all this, you still refuse to be
chastened by me and continue to defy me, **24** I,
too, will defy you and will smite you for your
sins seven times harder than before.[t] **25** I will
make the sword, the avenger of my covenant,
sweep over you. Though you then huddle together in your walled cities, I will send in pestilence among you, till you are forced to surrender to the enemy. **26** And as I cut off your
supply of bread, ten women will need but one
oven for baking all the bread they dole out to
you in rations[u] —not enough food to still your
hunger.
**27** "If, despite all this, you still persist in
disobeying and defying me, **28** I, also, will
meet you with fiery defiance and will chastise
you with sevenfold fiercer punishment for your
sins, **29** [v]till you begin to eat the flesh of your
own sons and daughters.* **30** I will demolish
your high places,[w] overthrow your incense
stands, and cast your corpses on those of your
idols. In my abhorrence of you, **31** I will lay
waste your cities and devastate your sanctuaries, refusing to accept your sweet-smelling offerings. **32** So devastated will I leave the land
that your very enemies who come to live there
will stand aghast at the sight of it.[x] **33** You
yourselves I will scatter among the nations[y] at
the point of my drawn sword, leaving your
countryside desolate and your cities deserted.
**34** Then shall the land retrieve its lost sabbaths
during all the time it lies waste, while you are
in the land of your enemies; then shall the land
have rest and make up for its sabbaths[z] **35** during all the time that it lies desolate, enjoying the
rest that you would not let it have on the sabbaths when you lived there.
**36** "Those of you who survive in the lands
of their enemies I will make so fainthearted that,
if leaves rustle behind them, they will flee headlong, as if from the sword, though no one pursues them; **37** stumbling over one another as if
to escape a weapon, while no one is after
them—so helpless will you be to take a stand
against your foes! **38** You will be lost among
the Gentiles, swallowed up in your enemies'
country. **39** Those of you who survive in the
lands of their enemies will waste away for their
own and their fathers' guilt.[a]
**40** "Thus they will have to confess that they
and their fathers were guilty of having rebelled
against me and of having defied me, **41** so that
I, too, had to defy them and bring them into
their enemies' land. Then, when their uncircumcised hearts are humbled and they make
amends for their guilt, **42** I will remember my
covenant with Jacob, my covenant with Isaac,
and my covenant with Abraham;[b] and of the
land, too, I will be mindful. **43** But the land
must first be rid of them, that in its desolation
it may make up its lost sabbaths, and that they,
too, may make good the debt of their guilt for
having spurned my precepts and abhorred my
statutes. **44** Yet even so, even while they are in
their enemies' land, I will not reject or spurn
them, lest, by wiping them out, I make void my
covenant with them; for I, the LORD, am their
God. **45** I will remember them because of the
covenant I made with their forefathers, whom I
brought out of the land of Egypt under the very
eyes of the Gentiles,[c] that I, the LORD, might
be their God."
**46** *These are the precepts, decrees and laws
which the LORD had Moses promulgate on
Mount Sinai in the pact between himself and the
Israelites.

## *V: Redemption of Offerings*

## CHAPTER 27

**Redemption of Votive Offerings.** **1** The
LORD said to Moses, **2** "Speak to the Israelites
and tell them: When anyone fulfills a vow of
offering one or more persons to the LORD, who
are to be ransomed at a fixed sum of money,
**3** for persons between the ages of twenty and
sixty, the fixed sum, in sanctuary shekels, shall
be fifty silver shekels for a man, **4** and thirty
shekels for a woman; **5** for persons between the
ages of five and twenty, the fixed sum shall be
twenty shekels for a youth, and ten for a maiden;
**6** for persons between the ages of one month

---

t 24f; Jer 2, 30; Ez 5, 17; 14, 17.
u Is 9, 19; Ez 4, 16; 5, 16; 14, 13; Mi 6, 14.
v Is 9, 18.
w 2 Chr 14, 5; 34, 3. 4. 7; Ez 6, 3-6.
x 1 Kgs 9, 8; Jer 9, 11; 18, 16; 19, 8; 25, 18; Ez 5, 15.
y Jer 9, 16; Zec 7, 14.
z Lv 25, 2; 2 Chr 36, 21.
a Ez 4, 17; 24, 23; 33, 10.
b Ex 6, 5; 2 Kgs 13, 23; Ps 106, 45; Ez 16, 60.
c Ex 12, 51.

---

26, 29: Eat the flesh of your own sons and daughters: extreme famine in cities under siege often forced their inhabitants to such dire means of subsistence. Cf Dt 28, 53; Jer 19, 9; Ez 5, 10; 2 Kgs 6, 28f.

26, 46: The Book of Leviticus seems originally to have ended here; the following chapter is an appendix.

and five years, the fixed sum shall be five silver shekels for a boy, and three for a girl; **7** for persons of sixty or more, the fixed sum shall be fifteen shekels for a man, and ten for a woman. **8** However, if the one who took the vow is too poor to meet the fixed sum, the person must be set before the priest, who shall determine the sum for his ransom in keeping with the means of the one who made the vow.

**9** "If the offering vowed to the LORD is an animal that may be sacrificed, every such animal, when vowed to the LORD, becomes sacred. **10** The offerer shall not present a substitute for it by exchanging either a better for a worse one or a worse for a better one. If he attempts to offer one animal in place of another, both the original and its substitute shall be treated as sacred. **11** If the animal vowed to the LORD is unclean and therefore unfit for sacrifice, it must be set before the priest, **12** who shall determine its value* in keeping with its good or bad qualities, and the value set by the priest shall stand. **13** If the offerer wishes to redeem the animal, he shall pay one fifth more than this valuation.[d]

**14** "When someone dedicates his house as sacred to the LORD, the priest shall determine its value in keeping with its good or bad points, and the value set by the priest shall stand. **15** If the one who dedicated his house wishes to redeem it, he shall pay one fifth more than the price thus established, and then it will again be his.

**16** "If the object which someone dedicates to the LORD is a piece of his hereditary land, its valuation shall be made according to the amount of seed required to sow it, the acreage sown with a homer of barley seed being valued at fifty silver shekels. **17** If the dedication of a field is made at the beginning of a jubilee period, the full valuation shall hold; **18** but if it is some time after this, the priest shall estimate its money value according to the number of years left until the next jubilee year, with a corresponding rebate on the valuation.[e] **19** If the one who dedicated his field wishes to redeem it, he shall pay one fifth more than the price thus established, and so reclaim it. **20** If, instead of redeeming such a field, he sells it to someone else, it may no longer be redeemed; **21** but at the jubilee it shall be released as sacred to the LORD; like a field that is doomed, it shall become priestly property.

**22** "If the field that some man dedicates to the LORD is one he had purchased and not a part of his hereditary property, **23** the priest shall compute its value in proportion to the number of years until the next jubilee, and on the same day the price thus established shall be given as sacred to the LORD; **24** at the jubilee,[f] however, the field shall revert to the hereditary owner of this land from whom it had been purchased.

**25** "Every valuation shall be made according to the standard of the sanctuary shekel. There are twenty gerahs to the shekel.

### Offerings Not To Be Redeemed.

**26** "Note that a first-born animal,[g] which as such already belongs to the LORD, may not be dedicated by vow to him. If it is an ox or a sheep, it shall be ceded to the LORD; **27** but if it is an unclean animal,* it may be redeemed by paying one fifth more than its fixed value. If it is not redeemed, it shall be sold at its fixed value.

**28** "Note, also, that any one of his possessions which a man vows as doomed to the LORD, whether it is a human being or an animal or a hereditary field, shall be neither sold nor ransomed; everything that is thus doomed becomes most sacred to the LORD.[h] **29** All human beings that are doomed* lose the right to be redeemed; they must be put to death.

**30** "All tithes of the land, whether in grain from the fields or in fruit from the trees, belong to the LORD, as sacred to him.[i] **31** If someone wishes to buy back any of his tithes, he shall pay one fifth more than their value. **32** The tithes of the herd and the flock shall be determined by ceding to the LORD as sacred every tenth animal as they are counted by the herdsman's rod. **33** It shall not matter whether good ones or bad ones are thus chosen, and no exchange may be made. If any exchange is attempted, both the original animal and its substitute shall be treated as sacred, without the right of being bought back."

**34** These are the commandments which the LORD gave Moses on Mount Sinai for the Israelites.

d Lv 22, 14.
e Lv 25, 15f.
f Lv 25, 10. 28. 41.
g Ex 13, 2.
h 1 Sm 15, 21.
i Nm 18, 21. 24; 2 Chr 31, 5f. 12; Mal 3, 8. 10.

*

27, 12: Determine its value: fix the price at which the animal may be sold to someone else. Only the original owner must pay the twenty percent tax, as a penalty for buying back what he had vowed to God. So also for houses and fields that are vowed to the Lord, as treated of in the following verses. The money from the sale or from the redemption of such vowed property naturally goes to the sanctuary.

27, 27: An unclean animal: such as the first-born of an ass, which was unfit for sacrifice. According to Ex 13, 13; 34, 20, a first-born ass was to be redeemed by offering a sheep in its stead, or was to have its neck broken. The present law is probably a later modification of the earlier one.

27, 29: All human beings that are doomed: according to some interpreters, this signifies the idolatrous Canaanites, who were doomed to destruction by divine authority; according to others, this drastic law was enacted for the purpose of discouraging private persons from rashly vowing their slaves or other dependents as offerings to God. Cf Ex 22, 19; Dt 13, 13–19.

# The Book of
# NUMBERS

*The Book of Numbers derives its name from the account of the two censuses of the Hebrew people taken, one near the beginning and the other toward the end of the journey in the desert (chapters 1 and 26). It continues the story of that journey, begun in Exodus, and describes briefly the experiences of the Israelites for a period of thirty-eight years, from the end of their encampment at Sinai to their arrival at the border of the Promised Land. Numerous legal ordinances are interspersed in the account, making the book a combination of law and history.*

*The various events described clearly indicate the action of God, who punishes the murmuring of the people by prolonging their stay in the desert, at the same time preparing them by this discipline to be his witnesses among the nations.*

*In the New Testament Christ and the Apostles derive useful lessons from such events in the Book of Numbers as the brazen serpent (Jn 3, 14f), the sedition of Korah and its consequences (1 Cor 10, 10), the prophecies of Balaam (2 Pt 2, 15f), and the water gushing from the rock (1 Cor 10, 4).*

*The chief divisions of the Book of Numbers are as follows:*
*I. Preparation for the Departure from Sinai (Nm 1, 1–10, 10).*
*II. From Sinai to the Plains of Moab (Nm 10, 11–22, 1).*
*III. On the Plains of Moab (Nm 22, 2–36, 13).*

## *I: Preparation for the Departure from Sinai*

### CHAPTER 1

**The Census.** 1 In the year following that of
the Israelites' departure from the land of Egypt,
on the first day of the second month, the LORD
said to Moses in the meeting tent in the desert
of Sinai: 2 *"Take a census of the whole community of the Israelites,[a] by clans and ancestral
houses, registering each male individually.
3 You and Aaron shall enroll in companies all
the men in Israel of twenty years or more who
are fit for military service.

**Moses' Assistants.** 4 "To assist you
there shall be a man from each tribe, the head
of his ancestral house. 5 [b]These are the names
of those who are to assist you:

from Reuben: Elizur, son of Shedeur;
6 from Simeon: Shelumiel, son of Zurishaddai;
7 from Judah: Nahshon, son of Amminadab;
8 from Issachar: Nethanel, son of Zuar;
9 from Zebulun: Eliab, son of Helon;
10 from Ephraim: Elishama, son of Ammihud,
and from Manasseh: Gamaliel, son of
Pedahzur, for the descendants of
Joseph;
11 from Benjamin: Abidan, son of Gideoni;
12 from Dan: Ahiezer, son of Ammishaddai;
13 from Asher: Pagiel, son of Ochran;
14 from Gad: Eliasaph, son of Reuel;
15 from Naphtali: Ahira, son of Enan."

16 [c]These were councilors of the community, princes of their ancestral tribes, chiefs of the
troops* of Israel. 17 So Moses and Aaron took
these men who had been designated, 18 and
assembled the whole community on the first day
of the second month. Every man of twenty years
or more then declared his name and lineage
according to clan and ancestral house, 19 as the
LORD had commanded Moses.

**Count of the Twelve Tribes.** This is their
census as taken in the desert of Sinai. 20 Of the
descendants of Reuben, the first-born of Israel,
registered by lineage in clans and ancestral
houses: when all the males of twenty years or
more who were fit for military service were
polled, 21 forty-six thousand five hundred
were enrolled in the tribe of Reuben.

22 Of the descendants of Simeon, registered
by lineage in clans and ancestral houses: when
all the males of twenty years or more who were

a 2f: Nm 14, 29; 26, 2-51.
b 5-15: Nm 10, 14-27.
c Ex 18, 21. 25.

*

1, 2: All Israel was divided into tribes, each tribe into clans, and each clan into ancestral houses.

1, 16: Troops: literally "thousands"; this division of the Israelites, with its subdivisions of "hundreds, fifties and tens," was primarily for military and judicial purposes. Cf Ex 18, 21: 2 Sm 18, 1.

fit for military service were polled, **23** fifty-
nine thousand three hundred were enrolled in
the tribe of Simeon.
**24** Of the descendants of Gad, registered by
lineage in clans and ancestral houses: when all
the males of twenty years or more who were fit
for military service were polled, **25** forty-five
thousand six hundred and fifty were enrolled in
the tribe of Gad.
**26** Of the descendants of Judah, registered
by lineage in clans and ancestral houses: when
all the males of twenty years or more who were
fit for military service were polled, **27** seventy-four thousand six hundred were enrolled in
the tribe of Judah.
**28** Of the descendants of Issachar, registered
by lineage in clans and ancestral houses: when
all the males of twenty years or more who were
fit for military service were polled, **29** fifty-
four thousand four hundred were enrolled in the
tribe of Issachar.
**30** Of the descendants of Zebulun, registered
by lineage in clans and ancestral houses: when
all the males of twenty years or more who were
fit for military service were polled, **31** fifty-
seven thousand four hundred were enrolled in
the tribe of Zebulun.
**32** Of the descendants of Joseph—
Of the descendants of Ephraim, registered by
lineage in clans and ancestral houses: when all
the males of twenty years or more who were fit
for military service were polled, **33** forty thousand five hundred were enrolled in the tribe of
Ephraim.
**34** Of the descendants of Manasseh, registered by lineage in clans and ancestral houses:
when all the males of twenty years or more who
were fit for military service were polled,
**35** thirty-two thousand two hundred were enrolled in the tribe of Manasseh.
**36** Of the descendants of Benjamin, registered by lineage in clans and ancestral houses:
when all the males of twenty years or more who
were fit for military service were polled,
**37** thirty-five thousand two hundred were enrolled in the tribe of Benjamin.
**38** Of the descendants of Dan, registered by
lineage in clans and ancestral houses: when all
the males of twenty years or more who were fit
for military service were polled, **39** sixty-two
thousand seven hundred were enrolled in the
tribe of Dan.
**40** Of the descendants of Asher, registered
by lineage in clans and ancestral houses: when
all the males of twenty years or more who were
fit for military service were polled, **41** forty-
one thousand five hundred were enrolled in the
tribe of Asher.
**42** Of the descendants of Naphtali, registered by lineage in clans and ancestral houses:
when all the males of twenty years or more who
were fit for military service were polled, **43** fifty-three thousand four hundred were enrolled in
the tribe of Naphtali.
**44** It was these who were registered, each
according to his ancestral house, in the census
taken by Moses and Aaron and the twelve
princes of Israel. **45** The total number of the
Israelites of twenty years or more who were fit
for military service, registered by ancestral
houses, **46** was six hundred and three thousand
five hundred and fifty.

**Levites Omitted in the Census.** **47** The
Levites, however, were not registered[d] by ancestral tribe with the others.* **48** For the LORD
had told Moses, **49** "The tribe of Levi alone
you shall not enroll nor include in the census
along with the other Israelites. **50** You are to
give the Levites charge of the Dwelling of the
commandments with all its equipment and all
that belongs to it. It is they who shall carry the
Dwelling with all its equipment and who shall
be its ministers.[e] They shall therefore camp
around the Dwelling. **51** When the Dwelling is
to move on, the Levites shall take it down; when
the Dwelling is to be pitched, it is the Levites
who shall set it up.[f] Any layman who comes
near it shall be put to death. **52** While the other
Israelites shall camp by companies, each in his
own division of the camp,[g] **53** the Levites shall
camp around the Dwelling of the commandments.[h] Otherwise God's wrath will strike the
Israelite community. The Levites, then, shall
have charge of the Dwelling of the commandments." **54** All this the Israelites fulfilled as the
LORD had commanded Moses.

## CHAPTER 2

**Arrangement of the Tribes.** **1** The LORD
said to Moses and Aaron: **2** "The Israelites
shall camp, each in his own division, under the
ensigns of their ancestral houses.[i] They shall
camp around the meeting tent, but at some distance from it.
**3** *"Encamped on the east side, toward the
sunrise, shall be the divisional camp of Judah,
arranged in companies. [The prince of the
Judahites was Nahshon, son of Amminadab,
**4** and his soldiers amounted in the census to

d Nm 2, 33; 3, 14-39; 26, 57-62.
e Nm 3, 7f; 4, 2-49; 1 Chr 6, 48.
f Nm 3, 10. 38; 18, 7; 2 Sm 6, 6f; 1 Chr 13, 10.
g Nm 2, 2. 34.
h Nm 3, 7f. 38; 8, 19; 18, 4f.
i Nm 1. 52.

*

1, 47: The Levites were not enrolled in this census, which was principally for military purposes, but a separate census was made of them. Cf Nm 3, 15f. 39.

2, 3–31: A similar arrangement of the tribes around the central sanctuary in the ideal Israelite state is given in Ez 48.

seventy-four thousand six hundred.] **5** With Judah shall camp the tribe of Issachar [their prince
was Nethanel, son of Zuar, **6** and his soldiers
amounted in the census to fifty-four thousand
four hundred] **7** and the tribe of Zebulun. [Their
prince was Eliab, son of Helon, **8** and his soldiers amounted in the census to fifty-seven
thousand four hundred. **9** The total number of
those registered by companies in the camp of
Judah was one hundred and eighty-six thousand
four hundred.] These shall be first on the march.

**10** "On the south side shall be the divisional
camp of Reuben, arranged in companies. [Their
prince was Elizur, son of Shedeur, **11** and his
soldiers amounted in the census to forty-six
thousand five hundred.] **12** Beside them shall
camp the tribe of Simeon [their prince was Shelumiel, son of Zurishaddai, **13** and his soldiers
amounted in the census to fifty-nine thousand
three hundred] **14** and next the tribe of Gad.
[Their prince was Eliasaph, son of Reuel,
**15** and his soldiers amounted in the census to
forty-five thousand six hundred and fifty.
**16** The total number of those registered by
companies in the camp of Reuben was one hundred and fifty-one thousand four hundred and
fifty.] These shall be second on the march.

**17** "Then the meeting tent and the camp of
the Levites shall set out in the middle of the line.
As in camp, so also on the march, every man
shall be in his proper place, with his own division.

**18** "On the west side shall be the divisional
camp of Ephraim, arranged in companies.
[Their prince was Elishama, son of Ammihud,
**19** and his soldiers amounted in the census to
forty thousand five hundred.] **20** Beside them
shall camp the tribe of Manasseh [their prince
was Gamaliel, son of Pedahzur, **21** and his soldiers amounted in the census to thirty-two thousand two hundred] **22** and the tribe of Benjamin. [Their prince was Abidan, son of Gideoni,
**23** and his soldiers amounted in the census to
thirty-five thousand four hundred. **24** The total
number of those registered by companies in the
camp of Ephraim was one hundred and eight
thousand one hundred.] These shall be third on
the march.

**25** "On the north side shall be the divisional
camp of Dan, arranged in companies. [Their
prince was Ahiezer, son of Ammishaddai,
**26** and his soldiers amounted in the census to
sixty-two thousand seven hundred.] **27** Beside
them shall camp the tribe of Asher [their prince
was Pagiel, son of Ochran, **28** and his soldiers
amounted in the census to forty-one thousand
five hundred] **29** and next the tribe of Naphtali.
[Their prince was Ahira, son of Enan, **30** and
his soldiers amounted in the census to fifty-three
thousand four hundred. **31** The total number of
those registered by companies in the camp of
Dan was one hundred and fifty-seven thousand
six hundred.] These shall be the last of the divisions on the march."

**32** [j]This was the census of the Israelites tak-
en by ancestral houses. The total number of
those registered by companies in the camps was
six hundred and three thousand five hundred
and fifty. **33** The Levites, however, were not
registered with the other Israelites, for so the
LORD had commanded Moses. **34** The Israelites did just as the LORD had commanded Moses; both in camp and on the march they were
in their own divisions, every man according to
his clan and his ancestral house.

## CHAPTER 3

**The Sons of Aaron.** **1** The following were
the descendants of Aaron and Moses at the time
that the LORD spoke to Moses on Mount Sinai.
**2** The sons of Aaron were Nadab his first-born,
Abihu, Eleazar, and Ithamar.[k] **3** These are the
names of the sons of Aaron, the anointed priests
who were ordained to exercise the priesthood.
**4** But when Nadab and Abihu offered profane
fire before the LORD in the desert of Sinai, they
met death[l] in the presence of the LORD, and left
no sons. Thereafter only Eleazar and Ithamar
performed the priestly functions under the direction of their father Aaron.

### Levites in Place of the First-born.

**5** Now the LORD said to Moses: **6** "Summon
the tribe of Levi and present them to Aaron the
priest, as his assistants.[m] **7** They shall discharge his obligations and those of the whole
community before the meeting tent[n] by serving
at the Dwelling. **8** They shall have custody of
all the furnishings of the meeting tent and discharge the duties of the Israelites in the service
of the Dwelling. **9** You shall give the Levites to
Aaron and his sons;[o] they have been set aside
from among the Israelites as dedicated to me.
**10** But only Aaron and his descendants shall
you appoint to have charge of the priestly functions.[p] Any layman who comes near shall be put
to death."

**11** The LORD said to Moses, **12** "It is I who
have chosen the Levites from the Israelites in
place of every first-born that opens the womb
among the Israelites.[q] The Levites, therefore,
are mine, **13** because every first-born is mine.
When I slew all the first-born in the land of
Egypt, I made all the first-born in Israel sacred
to me, both of man and of beast. They belong
to me; I am the LORD."

---

j 32-33: Nm 1, 46-49.
k Ex 6, 23.
l Nm 26, 61; Lv 10, 1f; 1 Chr 24, 2.
m Nm 18, 2.
n Nm 8, 24.
o Nm 8, 19.
p Nm 1, 51; 18, 7.
q 12f: Nm 3, 41; 8, 16f; Ex 13, 2. 12. 15.

**Census of the Levites.** 14 The LORD said
to Moses in the desert of Sinai, 15 "Take a
census of the Levites by ancestral houses and
clans, registering every male of a month or
more."[r] 16 Moses, therefore, took their census
in accordance with the command the LORD had
given him.

17 [s]The sons of Levi were named Gershon,
Kohath and Merari. 18 The descendants of
Gershon, by clans, were named Libni and
Shimei. 19 The descendants of Kohath, by
clans, were Amram, Izhar, Hebron and Uzziel.
20 The descendants of Merari, by clans, were
Mahli and Mushi. These were the clans of the
Levites by ancestral houses.

**Duties of the Levitical Clans.** 21 To Gershon belonged the clan of the Libnites and the
clan of the Shimeites; these were the clans of the
Gershonites. 22 When all their males of a
month or more were registered, they numbered
seven thousand five hundred. 23 The clans of
the Gershonites camped behind the Dwelling, to
the west. 24 The prince of their ancestral house
was Eliasaph, son of Lael. 25 [t]At the meeting
tent they had charge of whatever pertained to the
Dwelling,* the tent and its covering, the curtain
at the entrance of the meeting tent, 26 the hangings of the court, the curtain at the entrance of
the court enclosing both the Dwelling and the
altar, and the ropes.

27 To Kohath belonged the clans of the Amramites, the Izharites, the Hebronites, and the
Uzzielites; these were the clans of the Kohathites. 28 When all their males of a month or
more were registered, they numbered eight
thousand three hundred. They had charge of the
sanctuary. 29 The clans of the Kohathites
camped at the south side of the Dwelling.
30 The prince of their ancestral house was Elizaphan, son of Uzziel. 31 They had charge of
whatever pertained to the ark, the table, the
lampstand, the altars, the utensils with which
the ministry of the sanctuary was exercised, and
the veil.* 32 The chief prince of the Levites,
however, was Eleazar, son of Aaron the priest;
he was supervisor over those who had charge of
the sanctuary.

33 To Merari belonged the clans of the Mahlites and the Mushites; these were the clans of
Merari. 34 When all their males of a month or
more were registered, they numbered six thousand two hundred. 35 The prince of the ancestral house of the clans of Merari was Zuriel, son
of Abihail. They camped at the north side of the
Dwelling. 36 *The Merarites were charged
with the care of whatever pertained to the boards
of the Dwelling, its bars, columns, pedestals,
and all its fittings, 37 as well as the columns of
the surrounding court with their pedestals, pegs
and ropes.

38 East of the Dwelling, that is, in front of
the meeting tent, toward the sunrise, were
camped Moses and Aaron and the latter's sons.
They discharged the obligations of the sanctuary
for the Israelites. Any layman who came near
was to be put to death.

39 The total number of male Levites a month
old or more whom Moses had registered by
clans in keeping with the LORD's command,
was twenty-two thousand.

**Census and Ransom of First-born.**
40 The LORD then said to Moses, "Take a census of all the first-born males of the Israelites a
month old or more, and compute their total
number. 41 Then assign the Levites to me, the
LORD, in place of all the first-born of the Israelites, as well as their cattle in place of all the
first-born among the cattle of the Israelites."
42 So Moses took a census of all the first-born
of the Israelites, as the LORD had commanded
him. 43 When all the first-born males of a
month or more were registered, they numbered
twenty-two thousand two hundred and seventy-three.

44 The LORD said to Moses: 45 "Take the
Levites in place of all the first-born of the Israelites, and the Levites' cattle in place of their
cattle, that the Levites may belong to me. I am
the LORD. 46 As ransom for the two hundred
and seventy-three first-born of the Israelites
who outnumber the Levites, 47 you shall take
five shekels for each individual, according to
the standard of the sanctuary shekel, twenty
gerahs to the shekel.[u] 48 Give this silver to
Aaron and his sons as ransom for the extra
number." 49 So Moses took the silver as ransom from those who were left when the rest had
been redeemed by the Levites. 50 From the
first-born of the Israelites he received in silver
one thousand three hundred and sixty-five shekels according to the sanctuary standard. 51 He
then gave this ransom silver to Aaron and his
sons, as the LORD had commanded him.

r Nm 3, 39; 26, 62.
s 17-20: Nm 26, 57; Gn 46, 11; Ex 6, 16-19; 1 Chr 6, 1f. 16-19.
t 25-26: Ex 26, 7. 14. 36; 36, 14.
u Nm 18, 16; Ex 30, 13; Lv 27, 25; Ez 45, 12.

*

3, 25f: The Gershonites had two wagons for transporting these things; cf Nm 7, 7. For a description of the Dwelling, see Ex 26, 1–6; the tent, Ex 26, 7–13; its covering, Ex 26, 14; the curtain at the entrance, Ex 26, 36; the hangings of the court, Ex 27, 9–15; the curtain at the entrance of the court, Ex 27, 16; the ropes of the Dwelling, Ex 35, 18.

3, 31: The Kohathites had to carry these sacred objects on their shoulders; cf Nm 7, 9. For a description of the ark, see Ex 25, 10–22; the table, Ex 25, 23–30; the lampstand, Ex 25, 31–40; the altars, Ex 27, 1–8; 30, 1–10.

3, 36f: The Merarites had four wagons for transporting this heavy material; cf Nm 7, 8. For a description of the boards, bars, etc., of the Dwelling, see Ex 26, 15–30; the columns, pedestals, etc., of the court, Ex 27, 9–19.

## CHAPTER 4

**Duties Further Defined.** 1 The LORD said
to Moses and Aaron: 2 "Among the Levites
take a total of the Kohathites, by clans and
ancestral houses, all the men of the Kohathites
3 between thirty* and fifty years of age; these
are to undertake obligatory tasks in the meeting
tent.[v]

4 "The service of the Kohathites in the meeting tent concerns the most sacred objects. 5 In
breaking camp, Aaron and his sons shall go in
and take down the screening curtain* and cover
the ark of the commandments with it. 6 Over
these they shall put a cover of tahash skin, and
on top of this spread an all-violet cloth. They
shall then put the poles in place. 7 On the table
of the Presence they shall spread a violet cloth
and put on it the plates and cups, as well as the
bowls and pitchers for libations; the established
bread offering shall remain on the table. 8 Over
these they shall spread a scarlet cloth and cover
all this with tahash skin. They shall then put the
poles in place. 9 They shall use a violet cloth
to cover the lampstand with its lamps, trimming
shears, and trays, as well as the various containers of oil from which it is supplied. 10 The
lampstand with all its utensils they shall then
enclose in a covering of tahash skin, and place
on a litter. 11 Over the golden altar* they shall
spread a violet cloth, and cover this also with a
covering of tahash skin. They shall then put the
poles in place. 12 Taking the utensils of the
sanctuary service, they shall wrap them all in
violet cloth and cover them with tahash skin.
They shall then place them on a litter. 13 After
cleansing the altar* of its ashes, they shall
spread a purple cloth over it. 14 On this they
shall put all the utensils with which it is served:
the fire pans, forks,* shovels, basins, and all the
utensils of the altar. They shall then spread a
covering of tahash skin over this, and put the
poles in place.

15 "Only after Aaron and his sons have finished covering the sacred objects and all their
utensils on breaking camp, shall the Kohathites
enter to carry them. But they shall not touch the
sacred objects; if they do they will die.[w] These,
then, are the objects in the meeting tent that the
Kohathites shall carry.

16 "Eleazar, son of Aaron the priest, shall
be in charge of the oil for the light, the fragrant
incense, the established cereal offering, and the
anointing oil. He shall be in charge of the whole
Dwelling with all the sacred objects and utensils
that are in it."

17 The LORD said to Moses and Aaron:
18 "Do not let the group of Kohathite clans
perish from the body of the Levites. 19 That
they may live and not die when they approach
the most sacred objects, this is what you shall
do for them: Aaron and his sons shall go in and
assign to each of them his task and what he must
carry; 20 but the Kohathites shall not go in to
look upon the sacred objects, even for an instant; if they do, they will die."[x]

21 The LORD said to Moses, 22 "Take a
total among the Gershonites also, by ancestral
houses and clans, 23 of all the men between
thirty and fifty years of age; these are to undertake obligatory tasks in the meeting tent.
24 This is the task of the clans of the Gershonites, what they must do and what they must
carry: 25 they shall carry the sheets of the
Dwelling, the meeting tent with its covering and
the outer wrapping of tahash skin, the curtain at
the entrance of the meeting tent, 26 the hangings of the court, the curtain at the entrance of
the court that encloses both the Dwelling and the
altar, together with their ropes and all other
objects necessary in their use. Whatever is to be
done with these things shall be their task.
27 The service of the Gershonites shall be entirely under the direction of Aaron and his sons,
with regard to what they must do and what they
must carry; you shall make each man of them
responsible for what he is to carry. 28 This,
then, is the task of the Gershonites in the meeting tent; and they shall be under the supervision
of Ithamar, son of Aaron the priest.

29 "Among the Merarites, too, you shall enroll by clans and ancestral houses 30 all their
men between thirty and fifty years of age; these
are to undertake obligatory tasks in the meeting
tent. 31 [y]This is what they shall be responsible
for carrying, all the years of their service in the
meeting tent: the boards of the Dwelling with its
bars, columns and pedestals, 32 and the columns of the surrounding court with their pedestals, pegs and ropes. You shall designate for
each man of them all the objects connected with
his service, which he shall be responsible for
carrying. 33 This, then, is the task of the clans
of the Merarites during all their service in the
meeting tent under the supervision of Ithamar,
son of Aaron the priest."

v Nm 8, 24; 1 Chr 23, 24-27.
w 2 Sm 6, 6f; 1 Chr 13, 9f.
x 1 Sm 6, 19.
y Nm 3, 36f.

*

4, 3: Thirty: at a later period the Levites began to serve when they were twenty-five (Nm 8, 24) or even only twenty years old (1 Chr 23, 24. 27; 2 Chr 31, 17; Ezr 3, 8; but cf 1 Chr 23, 3).

4, 5: The screening curtain: the veil between the inner and the outer rooms of the sanctuary. Cf Ex 26, 31–33.

4, 11: The golden altar: the altar of incense. Cf Ex 30, 1–6.

4, 13: The altar: the bronze altar of holocausts. Cf Ex 27, 1–8.

4, 14: Forks: used in turning over the sacrificed animal on the fire of the altar. Basins: to receive the sacrificial blood; cf Zec 9, 15.

**Number of Adult Levites.** **34** So Moses
and Aaron and the princes of the community
made a registration among the Kohathites, by
clans and ancestral houses, **35** of all the men
between thirty and fifty years of age. These
were to undertake obligatory tasks in the meeting tent; **36** as registered by clans, they numbered two thousand seven hundred and fifty.
**37** Such was the census of all the men of the
Kohathite clans who were to serve in the meeting tent, which Moses took, together with Aaron, as the LORD bade him.

**38** The registration was then made among
the Gershonites, by clans and ancestral houses,
**39** of all the men between thirty and fifty years
of age. These were to undertake obligatory tasks
in the meeting tent; **40** as registered by clans
and ancestral houses, they numbered two thousand six hundred and thirty. **41** Such was the
census of all the men of the Gershonite clans
who were to serve in the meeting tent, which
Moses took, together with Aaron, at the LORD's
bidding.

**42** Then the registration was made among
the Merarites, by clans and ancestral houses,
**43** of all the men from thirty up to fifty years
of age. These were to undertake obligatory tasks
in the meeting tent; **44** as registered by clans,
they numbered three thousand two hundred.
**45** Such was the census of the men of the Merarite clans which Moses took, together with Aaron, as the LORD bade him.

**46** Therefore, when Moses and Aaron and
the Israelite princes had completed the registration among the Levites, by clans and ancestral
houses, **47** of all the men between thirty and
fifty years of age who were to undertake tasks
of service or transport of the meeting tent,
**48** the total number registered was eight thousand five hundred and eighty. **49** According to
the LORD's bidding to Moses, they gave them
their individual assignments for service and for
transport; so the LORD had commanded Moses.

## CHAPTER 5

**The Unclean Expelled.** **1** The LORD said
to Moses: **2** "Order the Israelites to expel from
camp every leper, and everyone suffering from
a discharge, and everyone who has become unclean by contact with a corpse.*[z] **3** Male and
female alike, you shall compel them to go out
of the camp; they are not to defile the camp in
which I dwell."[a] **4** The Israelites obeyed the
command that the LORD had given Moses; they
expelled them from the camp.

**Unjust Possession.** **5** *The LORD said to
Moses, **6** [b]"Tell the Israelites: If a man (or
woman) commits a fault against his fellow man
and wrongs him, thus breaking faith with the
LORD, **7** he shall confess the wrong he has
done, restore his ill-gotten goods in full, and in
addition give one fifth of their value to the one
he has wronged. **8** However, if the latter has no
next of kin* to whom restoration of the ill-gotten goods can be made, the goods to be restored
shall be the LORD's and shall fall to the priest;
this is apart from the atonement ram with which
the priest makes amends for the guilty man.
**9** Likewise, every sacred contribution that the
Israelites are bound to make shall fall to the
priest.[c] **10** Each Israelite man may dispose of
his own sacred contributions; they become the
property of the priest to whom he gives them."[d]

**Ordeal for a Suspected Adulteress.**
**11** The LORD said to Moses, **12** "Speak to the
Israelites and tell them: If a man's wife goes
astray and becomes unfaithful to him **13** by
having intercourse with another man,[e] though
her husband has not sufficient evidence of the
fact, so that her impurity remains unproved for
lack of a witness who might have caught her in
the act; **14** or if a man is overcome by a feeling
of jealousy that makes him suspect his wife,
whether she was actually impure or not: **15** he
shall bring his wife to the priest and shall take
along as an offering for her a tenth of an ephah
of barley meal. However, he shall not pour oil
on it nor put frankincense over it, since it is a
cereal offering of jealousy, a cereal offering for
an appeal in a question of guilt.

**16** "The priest shall first have the woman
come forward and stand before the LORD. **17** In
an earthen vessel he shall meanwhile put some
holy water,* as well as some dust that he has
taken from the floor of the Dwelling.[f] **18** Then,
as the woman stands before the LORD, the priest
shall uncover her head and place in her hands
the cereal offering of her appeal,* that is, the
cereal offering of jealousy, while he himself
shall hold the bitter water that brings a curse.
**19** Then he shall adjure the woman, saying to
her, 'If no other man has had intercourse with

z Nm 19, 11. 13; Lv 13, 46; 21, 1; 22, 4.
a Nm 35, 34.
b 6ff: Lv 5, 21-25.
c Dt 18, 3f; Ex 44, 29f.
d Lv 10, 12-15.
e Lv 18, 20; Jn 8, 4.
f Nm 19, 17.

*

5, 2: For the laws regarding victims of leprosy, see Lv 13–14; those suffering from a discharge, Lv 15; the unclean by contact with a corpse, Nm 19, 11–22; Lv 21, 1–4.

5, 5–10: The basic law on unjust possession is given in Lv 5, 14–26. The new item here concerns the case where the injured party has died and left no heirs, in which case the restitution must be made to the priest.

5, 8: Next of kin: literally, "redeemer," a technical term denoting the nearest relative, upon whom devolved the obligation of "redeeming" the family property, in order to keep it within the family. Cf Lv 25, 25; Ru 4, 1–6.

5, 17: Holy water: water from the laver that stood in the court of the Dwelling.

5, 18: Appeal: by which she invokes the Lord and refers her case to his decision.

you, and you have not gone astray by impurity
while under the authority of your husband, be
immune to the curse brought by this bitter water. **20** But if you have gone astray while under
the authority of your husband and have acted
impurely by letting a man other than your husband have intercourse with you'—; **21** so shall
the priest adjure the woman with this oath of
imprecation—'may the LORD make you an example of malediction and imprecation* among
your people by causing your thighs to waste
away and your belly to swell! **22** May this water, then, that brings a curse, enter your body to
make your belly swell and your thighs waste
away!'[g] And the woman shall say, 'Amen,
amen!'* **23** The priest shall put these imprecations in writing and shall then wash them off
into the bitter water, **24** which he is to have the
woman drink, so that it may go into her with all
its bitter curse. **25** But first he shall take the
cereal offering of jealousy from the woman's
hand, and having waved this offering before the
LORD, shall put it near the altar, **26** where he
shall take a handful of the cereal offering as its
token offering and burn it on the altar.[h] Only
then shall he have the woman drink the water.
**27** Once she has done so, if she has been impure and unfaithful to her husband, this bitter
water that brings a curse will go into her, and
her belly will swell and her thighs will waste
away, so that she will become an example of
imprecation among her people. **28** If, however,
the woman has not defiled herself, but is still
pure, she will be immune and will still be able
to bear children.

**29** "This, then, is the law for jealousy:
When a woman goes astray while under the
authority of her husband and acts impurely,
**30** or when such a feeling of jealousy comes
over a man that he becomes suspicious of his
wife, he shall have her stand before the LORD,
and the priest shall apply this law in full to her.
**31** The man shall be free from guilt,* but the
woman shall bear such guilt as she may have."

## CHAPTER 6

**Laws Concerning Nazirites.** **1** The LORD
said to Moses: **2** "Speak to the Israelites and
tell them: When a man (or a woman) solemnly
takes the nazirite* vow to dedicate himself to
the LORD, **3** he shall abstain from wine and
strong drink;[i] he may neither drink wine vinegar, other vinegar, or any kind of grape juice,
nor eat either fresh or dried grapes. **4** As long
as he is a nazirite he shall not eat anything of the
produce of the vine; not even unripe grapes or
grapeskins. **5** While he is under the nazirite
vow, no razar shall touch his hair.[j] Until the
period of his dedication to the LORD is over, he
shall be sacred, and shall let the hair of his head
grow freely. **6** As long as he is dedicated to the
LORD, he shall not enter where a dead person
is.[k] **7** Not even for his father or mother, his
sister or brother, should they die, may he become unclean, since his head bears his dedication to God. **8** As long as he is a nazirite he is
sacred to the LORD.

**9** "If someone dies very suddenly in his
presence, so that his dedicated head becomes
unclean, he shall shave his head on the day of
his purification, that is, on the seventh day.
**10** On the eighth day he shall bring two turtledoves or two pigeons to the priest at the entrance
of the meeting tent. **11** The priest shall offer up
the one as a sin offering and the other as a
holocaust, thus making atonement for him for
the sin he has committed by reason of the dead
person. On the same day he shall reconsecrate
his head **12** and begin anew the period of his
dedication to the LORD as a nazirite, bringing a
yearling lamb as a guilt offering. The previous
period is not valid, because his dedicated head
became unclean.

**13** "This is the ritual for the nazirite:[l] On the
day he completes the period of his dedication he
shall go to the entrance of the meeting tent,
**14** bringing as his offering to the LORD one
unblemished yearling lamb for a holocaust, one
unblemished yearling ewe lamb for a sin offering, one unblemished ram as a peace offering,
along with their cereal offerings and libations,
**15** and a basket of unleavened cakes of fine
flour mixed with oil and of unleavened wafers
spread with oil. **16** The priest shall present
them before the LORD, and shall offer up the sin
offering and the holocaust for him. **17** He shall
then offer up the ram as a peace offering to the
LORD, with its cereal offering and libation, and

g Ps 109, 18.
h Lv 5, 12.
i 3f: Jgs 13, 7. 14.
j Jgs 13, 5; 16, 17; 1 Sm 1, 11.
k Nm 19, 11. 16; Lv 21, 11.
l Acts 21, 24, 26.

*

5, 21: An example of malediction and imprecation: the woman's name would be used in curses and oaths to invoke a similar misfortune on another person or on oneself. Cf Is 65, 15; Jer 29, 22.

5, 22: Amen: a Hebrew word meaning, "certainly, truly," used to give assent to a statement, a curse, a blessing, a prayer, or the like; in this sense of "so be it," the Christian liturgy also uses it after prayers and blessings.

5, 31: Free from guilt: by fulfilling his obligation of obtaining a decision in the matter.

6, 1ff: Nazirite: from the Hebrew word nazir, meaning "set apart as sacred, dedicated, vowed." The nazirite vow could be either for a limited period or for life. Those bound by this vow had to abstain from all the products of the grapevine, from cutting or shaving their hair, and from contact with a corpse. They were regarded as men of God like the prophets; cf Am 2, 11f. Examples of lifelong nazirites were Samson (Jgs 13, 4f. 7; 16, 17), Samuel (1 Sm 1, 11), and John the Baptizer (Lk 1, 15). At the time of Christ the practice of taking the nazirite vow for a limited period seems to have been quite common, even among the early Christians; cf Acts 18, 18; 21, 23f. 26.

the basket of unleavened cakes. **18** Then at the
entrance of the meeting tent the nazirite shall
shave his dedicated head,[m] collect the hair, and
put it in the fire that is under the peace offering.
**19** After the nazirite has shaved off his dedicated hair, the priest shall take a boiled shoulder of
the ram, as well as one unleavened cake and one
unleavened wafer from the basket, and shall
place them in the hands of the nazirite. **20** The
priest shall then wave them as a wave offering
before the LORD. They become sacred and shall
belong to the priest, along with the breast of the
wave offering and the leg of the raised offering.
Only after this may the nazirite drink wine.

**21** "This, then, is the law for the nazarite;
this is the offering to the LORD which is included
in his vow of dedication apart from anything
else which his means may allow. Thus shall he
carry out the law of his dedication in keeping
with the vow he has taken."

**The Priestly Blessing.** **22** The LORD said
to Moses: **23** "Speak to Aaron and his sons and
tell them: This is how you shall bless the Israelites. Say to them:

**24** The LORD bless you and keep you!
**25** The LORD let his face shine* upon you, and
be gracious to you!
**26** The LORD look upon you kindly and give
you peace!*

**27** So shall they invoke my name upon the Israelites, and I will bless them."

## CHAPTER 7

**Offerings of Princes.** **1** Now, when Moses had completed the erection of the Dwelling
and had anointed and consecrated it with all its
equipment[n] (as well as the altar with all its
equipment), **2** an offering was made by the
princes of Israel, who were heads of ancestral
houses; the same princes of the tribes who su-
pervised the census. **3** The offering they
brought before the LORD consisted of six baggage wagons and twelve oxen, that is, a wagon
for every two princes, and an ox for every
prince. These they presented as their offering
before the Dwelling.

**4** The LORD then said to Moses, **5** "Accept
their offering, that these things may be put to
use in the service of the meeting tent. Assign
them to the Levites, to each group in proportion
to its duties." **6** So Moses accepted the wagons
and oxen, and assigned them to the Levites.
**7** He gave two wagons and four oxen to the
Gershonites[o] in proportion to their duties,
**8** and four wagons and eight oxen to the Merarites in proportion to their duties, under the
supervision of Ithamar, son of Aaron the priest.
**9** He gave none to the Kohathites, because they
had to carry on their shoulders the sacred objects
which were their charge.[p]

**10** For the dedication of the altar also, the
princes brought offerings before the altar on the
day it was anointed.[q] **11** But the LORD said to
Moses, "Let one prince a day present his offering for the dedication of the altar."

**12** *The one who presented his offering on
the first day was Nahshon, son of Amminadab,
prince of the tribe of Judah. **13** His offering
consisted of one silver plate weighing a hundred
and thirty shekels according to the sanctuary
standard and one silver basin weighing seventy
shekels, both filled with fine flour mixed with
oil for a cereal offering; **14** one gold cup of ten
shekels' weight filled with incense; **15** one
young bull, one ram, and one yearling lamb for
a holocaust; **16** one goat for a sin offering;
**17** and two oxen, five rams, five goats, and five
yearling lambs for a peace offering. This was
the offering of Nahshon, son of Amminadab.

**18** On the second day Nethanel, son of Zuar,
prince of Issachar, made his offering. **19** He
presented as his offering one silver plate weighing a hundred and thirty shekels according to the
sanctuary standard and one silver basin weighing seventy shekels, both filled with fine flour
mixed with oil for a cereal offering; **20** one gold
cup of ten shekels' weight filled with incense;
**21** one young bull, one ram, and one yearling
lamb for a holocaust; **22** one goat for a sin
offering; **23** and two oxen, five rams, five
goats, and five yearling lambs for a peace offering. This was the offering of Nethanel, son of
Zuar.

**24** On the third day it was the turn of Eliab,
son of Helon, prince of the Zebulunites. **25** His
offering consisted of one silver plate weighing
a hundred and thirty shekels according to the
sanctuary standard and one silver basin weighing seventy shekels, both filled with fine flour
mixed with oil for a cereal offering; **26** one gold
cup of ten shekels' weight filled with incense;
**27** one young bull, one ram, and one yearling
lamb for a holocaust; **28** one goat for a sin
offering; **29** and two oxen, five rams, five
goats, and five yearling lambs for a peace offering. This was the offering of Eliab, son of Helon.

**30** On the fourth day it was the turn of Elizur,
son of Shedeur, prince of the Reubenites.
**31** His offering consisted of one silver plate

---

m Acts 18, 18; 21, 24.
n Ex 40, 17.
o 7f: Nm 4, 24-33.
p Nm 3, 31; 4, 4-15.
q Nm 7, 84.

*

6, 25: Let his face shine: a Hebrew idiom for "smile."

6, 26: Peace: the Hebrew word includes the idea of "prosperity, happiness."

7, 12–88: The repetitious account of the same offerings brought by each of the twelve tribal princes and the summary of them are characteristic of an official registration.

weighing a hundred and thirty shekels according
to the sanctuary standard and one silver basin
weighing seventy shekels, both filled with fine
flour mixed with oil for a cereal offering;
**32** one gold cup of ten shekels' weight filled
with incense; **33** one young bull, one ram, and
one yearling lamb for a holocaust; **34** one goat
for a sin offering; **35** and two oxen, five rams,
five goats, and five yearling lambs for a peace
offering. This was the offering of Elizur, son of
Shedeur.

**36** On the fifth day it was the turn of Shelumiel, son of Zurishaddai, prince of the Simeonites. **37** His offering consisted of one silver
plate weighing a hundred and thirty shekels according to the sanctuary standard and one silver
basin weighing seventy shekels, both filled with
fine flour mixed with oil for a cereal offering;
**38** one gold cup of ten shekels' weight filled
with incense; **39** one young bull, one ram, and
one yearling lamb for a holocaust; **40** one goat
for a sin offering; **41** and two oxen, five rams,
five goats, and five yearling lambs for a peace
offering. This was the offering of Shelumiel,
son of Zurishaddai.

**42** On the sixth day it was the turn of Eliasaph, son of Reuel, prince of the Gadites.
**43** His offering consisted of one silver plate
weighing a hundred and thirty shekels according
to the sanctuary standard and one silver basin
weighing seventy shekels, both filled with fine
flour mixed with oil for a cereal offering;
**44** one gold cup of ten shekels' weight filled
with incense; **45** one young bull, one ram, and
one yearling lamb for a holocaust; **46** one goat
for a sin offering; **47** and two oxen, five rams,
five goats, and five yearling lambs for a peace
offering. This was the offering of Eliasaph, son
of Reuel.

**48** On the seventh day it was the turn of
Elishama, son of Ammihud, prince of the
Ephraimites. **49** His offering consisted of one
silver plate weighing a hundred and thirty shekels according to the sanctuary standard and one
silver basin weighing seventy shekels, both
filled with fine flour mixed with oil for a cereal
offering; **50** one gold cup of ten shekels' weight
filled with incense; **51** one young bull, one
ram, and one yearling lamb for a holocaust;
**52** one goat for a sin offering; **53** and two
oxen, five rams, five goats, and five yearling
lambs for a peace offering. This was the offering of Elishama, son of Ammihud.

**54** On the eighth day it was the turn of Gamaliel, son of Pedahzur, prince of the Manassehites. **55** His offering consisted of one silver
plate weighing a hundred and thirty shekels according to the sanctuary standard and one silver
basin weighing seventy shekels, both filled with
fine flour mixed with oil for a cereal offering;
**56** one gold cup of ten shekels' weight filled
with incense; **57** one young bull, one ram, and
one yearling lamb for a holocaust; **58** one goat
for a sin offering; **59** and two oxen, five rams,
five goats, and five yearling lambs for a peace
offering. This was the offering of Gamaliel, son
of Pedahzur.

**60** On the ninth day it was the turn of Abidan, son of Gideoni, prince of the Benjaminites.
**61** His offering consisted of one silver plate
weighing a hundred and thirty shekels according
to the sanctuary standard and one silver basin
weighing seventy shekels, both filled with fine
flour mixed with oil for a cereal offering;
**62** one gold cup of ten shekels' weight filled
with incense; **63** one young bull, one ram, and
one yearling lamb for a holocaust; **64** one goat
for a sin offering; **65** and two oxen, five rams,
five goats, and five yearling lambs for a peace
offering. This was the offering of Abidan, son
of Gideoni.

**66** On the tenth day it was the turn of Ahiezer, son of Ammishaddai, prince of the Danites.
**67** His offering consisted of one silver plate
weighing a hundred and thirty shekels according
to the sanctuary standard and one silver basin
weighing seventy shekels, both filled with fine
flour mixed with oil for a cereal offering;
**68** one gold cup of ten shekels' weight filled
with incense; **69** one young bull, one ram, and
one yearling lamb for a holocaust; **70** one goat
for a sin offering; **71** and two oxen, five rams,
five goats, and five yearling lambs for a peace
offering. This was the offering of Ahiezer, son
of Ammishaddai.

**72** On the eleventh day it was the turn of
Pagiel, son of Ochran, prince of the Asherites.
**73** His offering consisted of one silver plate
weighing a hundred and thirty shekels according
to the sanctuary standard and one silver basin
weighing seventy shekels, both filled with fine
flour mixed with oil for a cereal offering;
**74** one gold cup of ten shekels' weight filled
with incense; **75** one young bull, one ram, and
one yearling lamb for a holocaust; **76** one goat
for a sin offering; **77** and two oxen, five rams,
five goats, and five yearling lambs for a peace
offering. This was the offering of Pagiel, son of
Ochran.

**78** On the twelth day it was the turn of Ahira,
son of Enan, prince of the Naphtalites. **79** His
offering consisted of one silver plate weighing
a hundred and thirty shekels according to the
sanctuary standard and one silver basin weighing seventy shekels, both filled with fine flour
mixed with oil for a cereal offering; **80** one gold
cup of ten shekels' weight filled with incense;
**81** one young bull, one ram, and one yearling
lamb for a holocaust; **82** one goat for a sin
offering; **83** and two oxen, five rams, five
goats, and five yearling lambs for a peace offer-

ing. This was the offering of Ahira, son of Enan.

**84** These were the offerings for the dedication of the altar, given by the princes of Israel on the occasion of its anointing: twelve silver plates, twelve silver basins, and twelve gold cups. **85** Each silver plate weighed a hundred and thirty shekels, and each silver basin seventy, so that all the silver of these vessels amounted to two thousand four hundred shekels, according to the sanctuary standard. **86** The twelve gold cups that were filled with incense weighed ten shekels apiece, according to the sanctuary standard, so that all the gold of the cups amounted to one hundred and twenty shekels. **87** The animals for the holocausts were, in all, twelve young bulls, twelve rams, and twelve yearling lambs, with their cereal offerings; those for the sin offerings were twelve goats. **88** The animals for the peace offerings were, in all, twenty-four oxen, sixty rams, sixty goats, and sixty yearling lambs. These, then, were the offerings for the dedication of the altar after it was anointed.

**The Voice.** **89** When Moses entered the meeting tent to speak with him, he heard the voice addressing him from above the propitiatory[r] on the ark of the commandments, from between the two cherubim; and it spoke to him. . . .

## CHAPTER 8

**The Lamps Set Up.** **1** The LORD spoke to Moses, and said, **2** "Give Aaron this command: When you set up the seven lamps,[s] have them throw their light toward the front of the lampstand." **3** Aaron did so, setting up the lamps to face toward the front of the lampstand, just as the LORD had commanded Moses. **4** The lampstand was made of beaten gold[t] in both its shaft and its branches, according to the pattern which the LORD had shown Moses.

**Purification of the Levites.** **5** The LORD said to Moses: **6** "Take the Levites from among the Israelites and purify them.* **7** This is what you shall do to them to purify them. Sprinkle them with the water of remission;* then have them shave their whole bodies and wash their clothes, and so purify themselves. **8** They shall take a young bull, along with its cereal offering of fine flour mixed with oil; you shall take another young bull for a sin offering. **9** Then have the Levites come forward in front of the meeting tent, where you shall assemble also the whole community of the Israelites. **10** While the Levites are present before the LORD, the Israelites shall lay their hands upon them. **11** Let Aaron then offer the Levites before the LORD as a wave offering from the Israelites, thus devoting them to the service of the LORD. **12** The Levites in turn shall lay their hands on the heads of the bullocks, which shall then be immolated, the one as a sin offering and the other as a holocaust to the LORD, in atonement for the Levites. **13** Thus, then, shall you have the Levites stand before Aaron and his sons, to be offered as a wave offering to the LORD; **14** and thus shall you set aside the Levites from the rest of the Israelites, that they may be mine.[u]

**15** "Only then shall the Levites enter upon their service in the meeting tent. You shall purify them and offer them as a wave offering; **16** because they, among the Israelites, are strictly dedicated to me; I have taken them for myself in place of every first-born that opens the womb among the Israelites.[v] **17** Indeed, all the first-born among the Israelites, both of man and of beast, belong to me; I consecrated them to myself on the day I slew all the first-born in the land of Egypt.[w] **18** But in place of all the first-born Israelites I have taken the Levites; **19** and I have given these dedicated Israelites to Aaron and his sons[x] to discharge the duties of the Israelites in the meeting tent and to make atonement for them, so that no plague may strike among the Israelites should they come near the sanctuary."

**20** Thus, then, did Moses and Aaron and the whole community of the Israelites deal with the Levites, carrying out exactly the command which the LORD had given Moses concerning them. **21** When the Levites had cleansed themselves of sin* and washed their clothes, Aaron offered them as a wave offering before the LORD, and made atonement for them to purify them. **22** Only then did they enter upon their service in the meeting tent under the supervision of Aaron and his sons. The command which the LORD had given Moses concerning the Levites was carried out.

**Age Limits for Levitical Service.** **23** The LORD said to Moses: **24** "This is the rule for the Levites. Each from his twenty-fifth year onward shall perform the required service in the meeting tent.[y] **25** When he is fifty years old, he shall

r Ex 25, 22.
s Ex 25, 37.
t Ex 25, 31. 40.
u Nm 3, 45.
v Nm 3, 12. 45.
w Nm 3, 13; 13, 2; Lk 2, 23.
x Nm 3, 9f.
y Nm 4, 3. 23.

*

8, 6: Purify them: in the language of the Pentateuch only the priests were "consecrated," that is, made sacred or set aside for the Lord, in an elaborate ceremony described in Ex 29; Lv 8. The Levites were merely "purified," that is, made ritually clean for their special work.

8, 7: Water of remission: literally, "water of sin," that is, for the remission of sin.

8, 21: Cleansed themselves of sin: by having the "water of remission" sprinkled on them as prescribed in v 7.

retire from the required service and work no
longer. **26** His service with his fellow Levites
shall consist in sharing their responsibilities in
the meeting tent, but he shall not do the work.
This, then, is how you are to regulate the duties
of the Levites."

## CHAPTER 9

**Second Passover.** **1** In the first month of
the year following their departure from the land
of Egypt, the LORD said to Moses in the desert
of Sinai, **2** "Tell the Israelites to celebrate the
Passover at the prescribed time. **3** The evening
twilight of the fourteenth day of this month[z] is
the prescribed time when you shall celebrate it,
observing all its rules and regulations." **4** Moses, therefore, told the Israelites to celebrate the
Passover. **5** And they did so, celebrating the
Passover in the desert of Sinai during the evening twilight of the fourteenth day of the first
month, just as the LORD had commanded Moses.

**6** There were some, however, who were unclean because of a human corpse and so could
not keep the Passover that day. These men came
up to Moses and Aaron that same day **7** and
said, "Although we are unclean because of a
corpse, why should we be deprived of presenting the LORD's offering at its proper time along
with the other Israelites?" **8** Moses answered
them, "Wait until I learn what the LORD will
command in your regard."

**9** The LORD then said to Moses: **10** "Speak
to the Israelites and say: If any one of you or of
your descendants is unclean because of a
corpse, or if he is absent on a journey, he may
still keep the LORD's Passover. **11** But he shall
keep it in the second month,[a] during the evening twilight of the fourteenth day of that
month, eating it with unleavened bread and bitter herbs, **12** and not leaving any of it over till
morning, nor breaking any of its bones,[b] but
observing all the rules of the Passover.
**13** However, anyone who is clean and not away
on a journey, who yet fails to keep the Passover,
shall be cut off from his people, because he did
not present the LORD's offering at the prescribed
time. That man shall bear the consequences of
his sin.

**14** "If an alien* who lives among you wishes
to keep the LORD's Passover, he too shall observe the rules and regulations for the Passover.
You shall have the same law for the resident
alien as for the native of the land."[c]

**The Fiery Cloud.** **15** On the day when the
Dwelling was erected, the cloud* covered the
Dwelling, the tent of the commandments; but
from evening until morning it took on the appearance of fire over the Dwelling.[d] **16** It was
always so: during the day the Dwelling was
covered by the cloud, which at night had the
appearance of fire. **17** Whenever the cloud rose
from the tent, the Israelites would break camp;
wherever the cloud came to rest, they would
pitch camp.[e] **18** At the bidding of the LORD the
Israelites moved on, and at his bidding they
encamped.[f] As long as the cloud stayed over the
Dwelling, they remained in camp.

**19** Even when the cloud tarried many days
over the Dwelling, the Israelites obeyed the
LORD and would not move on; **20** yet sometimes the cloud was over the Dwelling only for
a few days. It was at the bidding of the LORD
that they stayed in camp, and it was at his bidding that they departed. **21** Sometimes the
cloud remained there only from evening until
morning; and when it rose in the morning, they
would depart. Or if the cloud lifted during the
day, or even at night, they would then set out.
**22** Whether the cloud tarried over the Dwelling
for two days or for a month or longer, the Israelites remained in camp and did not depart; but
when it lifted, they moved on. **23** Thus, it was
always at the bidding of the LORD that they
encamped, and at his bidding that they set out;
ever heeding the charge of the LORD, as he had
bidden them through Moses.

## CHAPTER 10

**The Silver Trumpets.** **1** The LORD said to
Moses: **2** "Make two trumpets of beaten silver,
which you shall use in assembling the community and in breaking camp. **3** When both are
blown, the whole community shall gather round
you at the entrance of the meeting tent; **4** but
when one of them is blown, only the princes, the
chiefs of the troops of Israel, shall gather round
you. **5** When you sound the first alarm, those
encamped on the east side shall set out; **6** when
you sound the second alarm, those encamped on
the south side shall set out; when you sound the
third alarm, those encamped on the West side
shall set out; when you sound the fourth alarm,
those encamped on the north side shall set out.
Thus shall the alarm be sounded for them to
depart. **7** But in calling forth an assembly you
are to blow an ordinary blast, without sounding
the alarm.

**8** "It is the sons of Aaron, the priests, who
shall blow the trumpets; and the use of them is
prescribed by perpetual statute for you and your

z Ex 12, 6; Lv 23, 5.
a 2 Chr 30, 2-15.
b Ex 12, 46; Jn 19, 36.
c Ex 12, 48f.
d Ex 13, 21.
e Wis 18, 3.
f 1 Cor 10, 1.

*

9, 14: An alien: this passage presupposes that he is already circumcised as prescribed in Ex 12, 48.

9, 15: The cloud: already mentioned at the departure from Egypt; cf Ex 13, 21f.

descendants. **9** [g]When in your own land you go
to war against an enemy that is attacking you,
you shall sound the alarm on the trumpets, and
the LORD, your God, will remember you and
save you from your foes. **10** On your days of
celebration,* your festivals, and your new-
moon feasts, you shall blow the trumpets over
your holocausts and your peace offerings;[h] this
will serve as a reminder of you before your God.
I, the LORD, am your God."

## *II: From Sinai to the Plains of Moab*

**Departure from Sinai.** **11** In the second
year, on the twentieth day of the second month,
the cloud rose from the Dwelling of the commandments. **12** The Israelites moved on from
the desert of Sinai by stages, until the cloud
came to rest in the desert of Paran.

**13** The first time that they broke camp at the
bidding of the LORD through Moses, **14** [i]the
camp of the Judahites, under its own standard
and arranged in companies, was the first to set
out. Nahshon, son of Amminadab, was over
their host, **15** and Nethanel, son of Zuar, over
the host of the tribe of Issachar, **16** and Eliab,
son of Helon, over the host of the tribe of Zebulun. **17** Then, after the Dwelling was disman-
tled, the clans of Gershon and Merari set out,
carrying the Dwelling. **18** The camp of the
Reubenites, under its own standard and arranged in companies, was the next to set out,
with Elizur, son of Shedeur, over their host,
**19** and Shelumiel, son of Zurishaddai, over the
host of the tribe of Simeon, **20** and Eliasaph,
son of Reuel, over the host of the tribe of Gad.
**21** The clan of Kohath then set out, carrying the
sacred objects for the Dwelling, which was to
be erected before their arrival. **22** The camp of
the Ephraimites next set out, under its own standard and arranged in companies, with Elishama,
son of Ammihud, over their host, **23** and Gamaliel, son of Pedahzur, over the host of the
tribe of Manasseh, **24** and Abidan, son of Gideoni, over the host of the tribe of Benjamin.
**25** Finally, as rear guard for all the camps, the
camp of the Danites set out, under its own standard and arranged in companies, with Ahiezer,
son of Amishaddai, over their host, **26** and Pagiel, son of Ochran, over the host of the tribe of
Asher, **27** and Ahira, son of Enan, over the host
of the tribe of Naphtali. **28** This was the order
of departure for the Israelites, company by company.

**Hobab as Guide.** As they were setting out,
**29** Moses said to his brother-in-law Hobab, son
of Reuel the Midianite, "We are setting out for
the place which the LORD has promised to give
us. Come with us, and we will be generous
toward you, for the LORD has promised, prosperity to Israel." **30** *But he answered, "No,
I will not come. I am going instead to my own
country and to my own kindred." **31** Moses
said, "Please, do not leave us; you know where
we can camp in the desert, and you will serve
as eyes for us. **32** If you come with us, we will
share with you the prosperity the LORD will
bestow on us."

**Into the Desert.** **33** [j]They moved on from
the mountain of the LORD,* a three days' journey, and the ark of the covenant of the LORD
which was to seek out their resting place went
the three days' journey with them. **34** And
when they set out from camp, the cloud of the
LORD was over them by day.

**35** Whenever the ark set out, Moses would
say,

"Arise, O LORD, that your enemies may be
scattered,
and those who hate you may flee before
you."

**36** And when it came to rest, he would say,
"Return, O LORD, you who ride upon the
clouds,
to the troops of Israel."

## CHAPTER 11

**Discontent of the People.** **1** Now the
people complained in the hearing of the LORD;[k]
and when he heard it his wrath flared up so that
the fire of the LORD burned among them and
consumed the outskirts of the camp. **2** But
when the people cried out to Moses, he prayed
to the LORD and the fire died out. **3** Hence that
place was called Taberah,* because there the
fire of the LORD burned among them.

**4** The foreign elements among them were so
greedy for meat that even the Israelites lamented
again,[l] "Would that we had meat for food!
**5** We remember the fish we used to eat without
cost in Egypt, and the cucumbers, the melons,
the leeks, the onions, and the garlic. **6** But now

g 2 Chr 13, 14.
h Nm 29, 1; 2 Chr 29, 26ff.
i 14ff: Nm 2, 3. 5. 7.
j Dt 1, 33.
k Dt 9, 22.
l Ps 78, 18.
m 5f: Nm 21, 5; Ex 16, 3; Acts 7, 39.

*

10, 10: Days of celebration: special holidays, such as the occasion of a victory. Festivals: the great annual feasts of the Passover, Pentecost and Booths described in Lv 23; Nm 28–29.

10, 30ff: Hobab wished to be coaxed before granting the favor. From Jgs 1, 16 it seems probable that he did accede to Moses' request.

10, 33: The mountain of the Lord: Sinai (Horeb), elsewhere always called "the mountain of God."

11, 3: Taberah: means "the burning."

we are famished; we see nothing before us but this manna."[m]

**7** [n]Manna was like coriander seed* and had the appearance of bdellium. **8** When they had gone about and gathered it up, the people would grind it between millstones or pound it in a mortar, then cook it in a pot and make it into loaves, which tasted like cakes made with oil. **9** At night, when the dew fell upon the camp, the manna also fell.[o]

**10** When Moses heard the people, family after family, crying at the entrance of their tents, so that the LORD became very angry, he was grieved. **11** "Why do you treat your servant so badly?" Moses asked the LORD. "Why are you so displeased with me that you burden me with all this people? **12** Was it I who conceived all this people? or was it I who gave them birth, that you tell me to carry them at my bosom, like a foster father carrying an infant, to the land you have promised under oath to their fathers? **13** Where can I get meat to give to all this people? For they are crying to me, 'Give us meat for our food.' **14** I cannot carry all this people by myself, for they are too heavy for me. **15** If this is the way you will deal with me, then please do me the favor of killing me at once, so that I need no longer face this distress."

**The Seventy Elders.** **16** Then the LORD said to Moses, "Assemble for me seventy of the elders of Israel, men you know for true elders and authorities among the people, and bring them to the meeting tent. When they are in place beside you, **17** I will come down and speak with you there. I will also take some of the spirit that is on you and will bestow it on them, that they may share the burden of the people with you. You will then not have to bear it by yourself.

**18** "To the people, however, you shall say: Sanctify yourselves for tomorrow, when you shall have meat to eat. For in the hearing of the LORD you have cried, 'Would that we had meat for food! Oh, how well off we were in Egypt!' Therefore the LORD will give you meat for food, **19** and you will eat it, not for one day, or two days, or five, or ten, or twenty days, **20** but for a whole month—until it comes out of your very nostrils and becomes loathsome to you. For you have spurned the LORD who is in your midst, and in his presence you have wailed, 'Why did we ever leave Egypt?' "

**21** But Moses said, "The people around me include six hundred thousand soldiers; yet you say, 'I will give them meat to eat for a whole month.' **22** Can enough sheep and cattle be slaughtered for them? If all the fish of the sea were caught for them, would they have enough?" **23** The LORD answered Moses, "Is this beyond the LORD's reach? You shall see now whether or not what I have promised you takes place."

**The Spirit on the Elders.** **24** So Moses went out and told the people what the LORD had said. Gathering seventy elders of the people, he had them stand around the tent. **25** The LORD then came down in the cloud and spoke to him. Taking some of the spirit that was on Moses, he bestowed it on the seventy elders; and as the spirit came to rest on them, they prophesied.*

**26** Now two men, one named Eldad and the other Medad, were not in the gathering but had been left in the camp. They too had been on the list, but had not gone out to the tent; yet the spirit came to rest on them also, and they prophesied in the camp. **27** So, when a young man quickly told Moses, "Eldad and Medad are prophesying in the camp," **28** Joshua, son on Nun, who from his youth had been Moses' aide, said, "Moses, my lord, stop them." **29** But Moses answered him, "Are you jealous for my sake? Would that all the people of the LORD were prophets! Would that the LORD might bestow his spirit on them all!" **30** Then Moses retired to the camp, along with the elders of Israel.

**The Quail.** **31** There arose a wind[p] sent by the LORD, that drove in quail from the sea and brought them down over the camp site at a height of two cubits from the ground* for a distance of a day's journey all around the camp. **32** [q]All that day, all night, and all the next day the people gathered in the quail. Even the one who got the least gathered ten homers of them. Then they spread them out* all around the camp. **33** But while the meat was still between their teeth, before it could be consumed, the LORD's wrath flared up against the people, and

n 7f: Ex 16, 14f. 31; Ps 78, 24; Wis 16, 20; Jn 6, 31.
o Ex 16, 14f.
p Ps 78, 26ff.
q 32f: 78, 26-31; 1 Cor 10, 6-7.

*

11, 7: Coriander seed: see note on Ex 16, 31. Bdellium: a transparent, amber-colored gum resin, which is also mentioned in Gn 2, 12.

11, 25: They prophesied: in the sense, not of foretelling the future, but of speaking in enraptured enthusiasm. Such manifestations of mystic exaltation occurred in the early days of Hebrew prophecy (1 Sm 10, 10ff; 19, 20ff) and in the first years of the Church (Acts 2, 6-II. 17; 19, 6; 1 Cor 12–14).

11, 31: At a height of two cubits from the ground: exhausted by the storm, the quail could take but short, low flights, so that they were easily captured. To give food to the hungry people, God may have used the natural phenomenon of the annual migration of quail across the Sinai Peninsula. In the spring large flocks of these birds cross the Gulf of Aqabah flying toward the west; in the fall they fly back eastward from the Mediterranean. The sea mentioned here probably refers to the former body of water.

11, 32: They spread them out: to cure by drying.

he struck them with a very great plague. 34 So
that place was named Kibroth-hattaavah,* because it was there that the greedy people were
buried.

35 From Kibroth-hattaavah the people set
out for Hazeroth.

## CHAPTER 12

**Jealousy of Aaron and Miriam.** While
they were in Hazeroth, 1 Miriam and Aaron
spoke against Moses on the pretext of the marriage he had contracted with a Cushite woman.*
2 They complained,* "Is it through Moses
alone that the LORD speaks? Does he not speak
through us also?" And the LORD heard this.
3 [r]Now, Moses himself was by far the meekest
man on the face of the earth. 4 So at once the
LORD said to Moses and Aaron and Miriam,
"Come out, you three, to the meeting tent."
And the three of them went. 5 Then the LORD
came down in the column of cloud, and standing
at the entrance of the tent, called Aaron and
Miriam. When both came forward, 6 he said,
"Now listen to the words of the LORD:

Should there be a prophet among you,
in visions will I reveal myself to him,
in dreams will I speak to him;
7 Not so with my Servant Moses!
Throughout my house he bears my trust:[s]
8 face to face I speak to him,[t]
plainly and not in riddles.
The presence of the LORD he beholds.

Why, then, did you not fear to speak against my
servant Moses?"

**Miriam's Leprosy.** 9 So angry was the
Lord against them that when he departed,
10 and the cloud withdrew from the tent, there
was Miriam,[u] a snow-white leper!* When Aaron turned and saw her a leper, 11 "Ah, my
lord!" he said to Moses, "please do not charge
us with the sin that we have foolishly committed! 12 Let her not thus be like the stillborn
babe that comes forth from its mother's womb
with its flesh half consumed." 13 Then Moses
cried to the LORD, "Please, not this! Pray, heal
her!" 14 But the LORD answered Moses, "Suppose her father had spit in her face, would she
not hide in shame for seven days? Let her be
confined outside the camp for seven days; only
then may she be brought back." 15 So Miriam
was confined outside the camp for seven days,
and the people did not start out again until she
was brought back.

16 After that the people set out from Hazeroth and encamped in the desert of Paran.

## CHAPTER 13

**The Twelve Scouts.** 1 The LORD said to
Moses, 2 "Send men to reconnoiter the land of
Canaan, which I am giving the Israelites. You
shall send one man from each ancestral tribe, all
of them princes." 3 [v]So Moses dispatched
them from the desert of Paran, as the LORD had
ordered. All of them were leaders among the
Israelites; 4 by name they were:

Shammua, son of Zaccur, of the tribe of Reuben;
5 Shaphat, son of Hori, of the tribe of Simeon;
6 Caleb, son of Jephunneh, of the tribe of Judah;
7 Igal [son of Joseph] of the tribe of Issachar;
10 Gaddiel, son of Sodi, of the tribe of Zebulun;
11 Gaddi, son of Susi, of the tribe of Manasseh, for the Josephites, with
8 Hoshea, son of Nun, of the tribe of Ephraim;
9 Palti, son of Raphu, of the tribe of Benjamin;
12 Ammiel, son of Gemalli, of the tribe of Dan;
13 Sethur, son of Michael, of the tribe of Asher;
14 Nahbi, son of Vophsi, of the tribe of Naphtali;
15 Geuel, son of Machi, of the tribe of Gad.

16 These are the names of the men whom Moses sent out to reconnoiter the land. But Hoshea,
son of Nun, Moses called Joshua.*

17 In sending them to reconnoiter the land of
Canaan, Moses said to them, "Go up here in the
Negeb, up into the highlands, 18 and see what
kind of land it is. Are the people living there
strong or weak, few or many? 19 Is the country
in which they live good or bad? Are the towns
in which they dwell open or fortified? 20 Is the
soil fertile or barren, wooded or clear? And do

r Sir 45, 1f.
s Sir 45, 3; Heb 3, 2. 5.
t Ex 33, 11; Dt 34, 10.
u Dt 24, 9.
v 3-33: Dt 1, 22-28.

*

11, 34: Kibroth-hattaavah: means "graves of greed."

12, 1: Cushite woman: apparently Zipporah, the Midianitess, is meant; cf Ex 2, 21. Perhaps the term is used here merely in the sense of "despised foreigner."

12, 2: The real reason for Miriam's quarrel with her brother Moses was her jealousy of his superior position; his Cushite wife served only as an occasion for the dispute. Aaron merely followed his sister in her rebellion; hence she alone was punished.

12, 10: A snow-white leper: afflicted with "white leprosy," a skin disease that generally is not serious or of long duration. Cf Lv 13, 3–6.

13, 16: Joshua: in Hebrew, "Jehoshua," which was later modified to "Jeshua," the Hebrew pronunciation of the name "Jesus." Hoshea and Joshua are variants of one original name meaning "the LORD saves." Cf Mt 1, 21.

your best to get some of the fruit of the land."
It was then the season for early grapes.
**21** So they went up and reconnoitered the
land from the desert of Zin* as far as where
Rehob adjoins Labo of Hamath. **22** [w]Going up
by way of the Negeb, they reached Hebron,
where Ahiman, Sheshai and Talmai, descendants of the Anakim,* were living. [Hebron had
been built seven years before Zoan in Egypt.]
**23** They also reached the Wadi Eshcol,* where
they cut down a branch with a single cluster of
grapes on it, which two of them carried on a
pole, as well as some pomegranates and figs.
**24** It was because of the cluster the Israelites
cut there that they called the place Wadi Eshcol.[x]

**Their Return.** **25** After reconnoitering the
land for forty days they returned, **26** [y]met Moses and Aaron and the whole community of the
Israelites in the desert of Paran at Kadesh, made
a report to them all, and showed them the fruit
of the country. **27** They told Moses: "We went
into the land to which you sent us. It does indeed
flow with milk and honey, and here is its fruit.
**28** However, the people who are living in the
land are fierce, and the towns are fortified and
very strong.[z] Besides, we saw descendants of
the Anakim there. **29** Amalekites live in the
region of the Negeb; Hittites, Jebusites and Amorites dwell in the highlands, and Canaanites
along the seacoast and the banks of the Jordan."
**30** Caleb, however, to quiet the people toward Moses, said, "We ought to go up and
seize the land, for we can certainly do so."
**31** But the men who had gone up with him said,
"We cannot attack these people; they are too
strong for us." **32** So they spread discouraging
reports[a] among the Israelites about the land they
had scouted, saying, "The land that we explored is a country and consumes its inhabitants. And all the people we saw there are huge
men, **33** [b]veritable giants* [the Anakim were a
race of giants]; we felt like mere grasshoppers,
and so we must have seemed to them."

## CHAPTER 14

**Threats of Revolt.** **1** At this, the whole
community broke out with loud cries, and even
in the night the people wailed. **2** [c]All the Israelites grumbled against Moses and Aaron, the
whole community saying to them, "Would that
we had died in the land of Egypt, or that here
in the desert we were dead! **3** Why is the LORD
bringing us into this land only to have us fall by
the sword? Our wives and little ones will be
taken as booty. Would it not be better for us to
return to Egypt?" **4** So they said to one another, "Let us appoint a leader and go back to
Egypt."

**5** But Moses and Aaron fell prostrate before
the whole assembled community of the Israelites; **6** while Joshua, son of Nun, and Caleb,
son of Jephunneh, who had been in the party
that scouted the land, tore their garments **7** and
said to the whole community of the Israelites,[d]
"The country which we went through and explored is a fine, rich land. **8** If the LORD is
pleased with us, he will bring us in and give us
that land, a land flowing with milk and honey.
**9** [e]But do not rebel against the LORD! You need
not be afraid of the people of that land; they are
but food for us!* Their defense has left them,
but the LORD is with us. Therefore, do not be
afraid of them." **10** In answer, the whole community threatened to stone them.

**The Lord's Sentence.** But then the glory
of the LORD appeared at the meeting tent to all
the Israelites. **11** And the LORD said to Moses,
"How long will this people spurn me? How
long will they refuse to believe in me, despite
all the signs I have performed among them?[f]
**12** I will strike them with pestilence and wipe
them out. Then I will make of you a nation
greater and mightier than they."[g]
**13** [h]But Moses said to the LORD: "Are the
Egyptians to hear of this? For by your power
you brought out this people from among them.
**14** And are they to tell of it to the inhabitants
of this land? It has been heard that you, O LORD,
are in the midst of this people; you, LORD, who
plainly reveal yourself! Your cloud stands over
them, and you go before them by day in a column of cloud and by night in a column of fire.[i]
**15** If now you slay this whole people, the nations who have heard such reports of you will

w Jos 11, 21f.
x Nm 32, 9; Dt 1, 24f.
y 26f: Ex 3, 8. 17.
z 28f: Dt 9, 1f.
a Nm 32, 9; Jos 14, 8.
b Dt 2, 10.
c Ex 16, 3; Ps 106, 25.
d 7f: Dt 1, 25.
e Dt 7, 18.
f Ps 78, 22. 32.
g Ex 32, 10.
h 13-16: Ex 32, 12; Dt 9, 26ff; Ps 106, 23.
i Ex 13, 21; Jos 2, 9f.

*

13, 21: The desert of Zin: north of Paran and southwest of the Dead Sea. It is quite distinct from "the desert of Sin" near the border of Egypt (Ex 16, 1; 17, 1; Nm 33, 11). Labo of Hamath: a town near Riblah (Jer 39, 5f) at the southern border of Hamath, an independent kingdom in southern Syria. David's conquests extended as far as Hamath (2 Sm 8, 9ff), and Labo thus formed the northern border of the ideal extent of Israel's possessions (Nm 34, 7ff; Ez 47, 15; 48, 1). Some commentators think that this verse is a later addition to the text; cf Dt 1, 24.

13, 22. 28: Anakim: an aboriginal race in southern Palestine, largely absorbed by the Canaanites before the Israelite invasion. Either because of their tall stature or because of the massive stone structures left by them the Israelites regarded them as giants.

13, 23: Eshcol: means "cluster."

13, 33: Giants: in Hebrew, "nephilim." Cf Gn 6, 4.

14, 9: They are but food for us: that is, "we can easily consume and destroy them." This is the answer to the pessimistic report that this land "consumes its inhabitants" (Nm 13, 32).

say, **16** 'The LORD was not able to bring this people into the land he swore to give them; that is why he slaughtered them in the desert.'[j] **17** Now then, let the power of my Lord be displayed in its greatness, even as you have said, **18** [k]'The LORD is slow to anger and rich in kindness, forgiving wickedness and crime; yet not declaring the guiltless guilty, but punishing children to the third and fourth generation for their fathers' wickedness.' **19** Pardon, then, the wickedness of this people in keeping with your great kindness, even as you have forgiven them from Egypt until now."[l]

**20** The LORD answered: "I pardon them as you have asked. **21** Yet, by my life and the LORD's glory that fills the whole earth, **22** of all the men who have seen my glory and the signs I worked in Egypt and in the desert,[m] and who nevertheless have put me to the test ten times already and have failed to heed my voice, **23** not one shall see the land which I promised on oath to their fathers. None of these who have spurned me shall see it. **24** But because my servant Caleb has a different spirit and follows me unreservedly,[n] I will bring him into the land where he has just been, and his descendants shall possess it. **25** But now, since the Amalekites and Canaanites are living in the valleys,* turn away tomorrow and set out in the desert on the Red Sea road."

**26** The LORD also said to Moses and Aaron: **27** "How long will this wicked community grumble against me?[o] I have heard the grumblings of the Israelites against me. **28** Tell them:* By my life, says the LORD, I will do to you just what I have heard you say. **29** Here in the desert[p] shall your dead bodies fall. Of all your men of twenty years or more, registered in the census, who grumbled against me, **30** not one shall enter the land where I solemnly swore to settle you, except Caleb, son of Jephunneh, and Joshua, son of Nun. **31** Your little ones, however, who you said would be taken as booty, I will bring in, and they shall appreciate the land you spurned.[q] **32** But as for you, your bodies shall fall here in the desert, **33** here where your children must wander for forty years, suffering for your faithlessness, till the last of you lies dead in the desert.[r] **34** Forty days you spent in scouting the land; forty years shall you suffer for your crimes: one year for each day. Thus you will realize what it means to oppose me. **35** I, the LORD, have sworn to do this to all this wicked community that conspired against me: here in the desert they shall die to the last man."

**36** And so it happened to the men whom Moses had sent to reconnoiter the land[s] and who on returning had set the whole community grumbling against him by spreading discouraging reports about the land; **37** these men who had given out the bad report about the land were struck down by the LORD had died. **38** Of all the men who had gone to reconnoiter the land, only Joshua, son of Nun, and Caleb, son of Jephunneh, survived.[t]

**Unsuccessful Invasion.** **39** When Moses repeated these words to all the Israelites, the people felt great remorse. **40** Early the next morning they started up into the foolhills, saying, "Here we are, ready to go up to the place that the LORD spoke of:[u] for we were indeed doing wrong." **41** But Moses said, "Why are you again disobeying the LORD's orders? This cannot succeed. **42** Do not go up, because the LORD is not in your midst; if you go, you will be beaten down before your enemies.[v] **43** For there the Amalekites and Canaanites face you, and you will fall by the sword. You have turned back from following the LORD; therefore the LORD will not be with you."

**44** Yet they dared to go up into the foothills,[w] even though neither the ark of the covenant of the LORD nor Moses left the camp. **45** And the Amalekites and Canaanites who dwelt in that hill country came down and defeated them, beating them back as far as Hormah.*

## CHAPTER 15

**Secondary Offerings.** **1** The LORD said to Moses, **2** *"Give the Israelites these instructions: When you have entered the land that I will give you for your homesteads, **3** if you make to the LORD a sweet-smelling oblation from the herd or from the flock, in holocaust, in fulfillment of a vow, or as a freewill offering, or for one of your festivals, **4** whoever does so shall also present to the LORD a cereal offering consisting of a tenth of an ephah of fine flour mixed with a fourth of a hin of oil, **5** as well as a

j Ex 32, 12; Dt 9, 28.
k Ex 20, 5; 34, 6f; Pss 103, 8; 145, 8.
l Ps 78, 38.
m 22f: Dt 1, 35.
n Jos 14, 8f.
o Ex 16, 7. 12.
p Dt 1, 35; Heb 3, 17.
q Dt 1, 39.
r 33f: Nm 13, 26; 32, 13; Ps 95, 10; Ez 4, 6.
s 36f: Nm 13, 17. 32f; 1 Cor 10, 10.
t Nm 26, 65.
u Nm 13, 18; Dt 1, 42.
v Dt 1, 42.
w Dt 1, 43.

*

14, 25: The valleys: the low-lying plains in the Negeb and along the seacoast and in the Jordan depression as well as the higher valleys in the mountains farther north; cf Nm 14, 45.

14, 28f: God punished the malcontents by giving them their wish; cf v 2. Their lack of faith and of confidence in God is cited in 1 Cor 10, 10, and Heb 3, 12–18, as a warning for Christians.

14, 45: Hormah: one of the Canaanite royal cities in southern Judea (Jos 12, 14), known at this time as "Zephath"; the origin of the later name is told in Nm 21, 3; Jgs 1, 17.

15, 2–16: These laws on sacrifice are complementary to those of Lv 1–3. Since the food of the Israelites consisted not only of meat but also of bread, oil and wine, so, besides the animal oblations, they offered flour, wine and oil in sacrifice to the Lord.

libation of a fourth of a hin of wine, with each
lamb sacrificed in holocaust or otherwise.
**6** With each sacrifice of a ram you shall present
a cereal offering of two tenths of an ephah of
fine flour mixed with a third of a hin of oil,
**7** and a libation of a third of a hin of wine, thus
making a sweet-smelling offering to the LORD.
**8** When you sacrifice an ox as a holocaust, or
in fulfillment of a vow, or as a peace offering
to the LORD, **9** with it you shall present a cereal
offering of three tenths of an ephah of fine flour
mixed with half a hin of oil, **10** and a libation
of half a hin of wine, as a sweet-smelling oblation to the LORD. **11** The same is to be done for
each ox, ram, lamb or goat. **12** Whatever the
number you offer, do the same for each of them.

**13** "All the native-born shall make these offerings in the same way, whenever they present
a sweet-smelling oblation to the LORD.
**14** Likewise, in any future generation, any
alien residing with you permanently or for a
time, who presents a sweet-smelling oblation to
the LORD, shall do as you do. **15** There is but
one rule for you and for the resident alien, a
perpetual rule for all your descendants. Before
the LORD you and the alien are alike, **16** with
the same law and the same application of it for
the alien residing among you as for yourselves."

**17** The LORD said to Moses, **18** "Speak to
the Israelites and tell them: When you enter the
land into which I will bring you **19** and begin
to eat of the food of that land, you shall offer
the LORD a contribution **20** consisting of a cake
of your first batch of dough.* You shall offer it
just as you offer a contribution from the threshing floor.[x] **21** Throughout your generations
you shall give a contribution to the LORD from
your first batch of dough.

**Sin Offerings.** **22** *"When through inadvertence you fail to carry out any of these commandments which the LORD gives to Moses,[y]
**23** and through Moses to you, from the time the
LORD first issues the commandment down
through your generations: **24** if the community
itself unwittingly becomes guilty of the fault of
inadvertence, the whole community shall offer
the holocaust of one young bull as a sweet-
smelling oblation pleasing to the LORD, along
with its prescribed cereal offering and libation,
as well as one he-goat as a sin offering.
**25** [z]Then the priest shall make atonement for
the whole Israelite community; thus they will be
forgiven the inadvertence for which they have
brought their holocaust as an oblation to the
LORD. **26** Not only the whole Israelite community, but also the aliens residing among you,
shall be forgiven, since the fault of inadvertence
affects all the people.

**27** "However, if it is an individual who sins
inadvertently,[a] he shall bring a yearling she-
goat as a sin offering, **28** and the priest shall
make atonement before the LORD for him who
sinned inadvertently; when atonement has been
made for him, he will be forgiven. **29** You shall
have but one law for him who sins inadvertently, whether he be a native Israelite or an alien
residing with you.

**30** "But anyone who sins defiantly,[b] whether he be a native or an alien, insults the LORD,
and shall be cut off from among his people.
**31** [c]Since he has despised the word of the LORD
and has broken his commandment, he must be
cut off. He has only himself to blame."

**The Sabbath-breaker.** **32** While the Israelites were in the desert, a man was discovered
gathering wood on the sabbath day. **33** Those
who caught him at it brought him to Moses and
Aaron and the whole assembly. **34** But they
kept him in custody, for there was no clear
decision* as to what should be done with him.[d]
**35** Then the LORD said to Moses, "This man
shall be put to death; let the whole community
stone him outside the camp." **36** So the whole
community led him outside the camp and stoned
him to death, as the LORD had commanded Moses.

**Tassels on the Cloak.** **37** The LORD said
to Moses, **38** "Speak to the Israelites and tell
them that they and their descendants must put
tassels* on the corners of their garments, fastening each corner tassel with a violet cord.[e]
**39** When you use these tassels, let the sight of
them remind you to keep all the commandments
of the LORD, without going wantonly astray
after the desires of your hearts and eyes.
**40** Thus you will remember to keep all my
commandments and be holy to your God. **41** I,
the LORD, am your God who, as God, brought
you out of Egypt that I, the LORD, may be your
God."[f]

x 19-20: Ez 44, 30.
y 22f: Lv 4, 13f.
z Lv 4, 20.
a 27f: Lv 4, 27f.
b Dt 17, 12.
c Prv 13, 13.
d Lv 24, 12.
e Dt 22, 12.
f Lv 22, 32f.

*

15, 20: Dough: some render, "barley grits." This word is used elsewhere only in Ez 44, 30 and Neh 10, 33; a related Hebrew word is used in Lv 2, 14.

15, 22ff: Although no moral guilt is incurred by an inadvertent violation of God's commandments, the sanctity of the law can require some reparation even for such violations.

15, 34: No clear decision: they already knew that a willful violation of the sabbath was a capital offense, but they did not yet know how the death penalty was to be inflicted.

15, 38: Tassels: at the time of Christ these tassels were worn by all pious Jews, including our Lord (Mt 9, 20f; Mk 6, 56); the Pharisees wore very large ones in ostentation of their zeal for the law (Mt 23, 5).

## CHAPTER 16

**Rebellion of Korah.** 1 Korah, son of Izhar, son of Kohath, son of Levi,* [and Dathan
and Abiram, sons of Eliab, son of Pallu, son of
Reuben] took 2 two hundred and fifty Israelites
who were leaders in the community, members of the council and men of note. They
stood before Moses, 3 and held an assembly
against Moses and Aaron, to whom they
said,[g] "Enough from you! The whole community, all of them, are holy; the LORD is in their
midst. Why then should you set yourselves over
the LORD's congregation?"

4 When Moses heard this, he fell prostrate.
5 Then he said to Korah and to all his band,
"May the LORD make known tomorrow morning who belongs to him and who is the holy one
and whom he will have draw near to him!
Whom he chooses, he will have draw near him.
6 Do this: take your censers [Korah and all his
band] 7 and put fire in them and place incense
in them before the LORD tomorrow. He whom
the LORD then chooses is the holy one. Enough
from you Levites!"

8 Moses also said to Korah, "Listen to me,
you Levites! 9 [h]Is it too little for you that the
God of Israel has singled you out from the community of Isreal, to have you draw near him for
the service of the LORD's Dwelling and to stand
before the community to minister for them?
10 He has allowed you and your kinsmen, the
descendants of Levi, to approach him, and yet
you now seek the priesthood too. 11 It is therefore against the LORD that you and all your band
are conspiring. For what has Aaron done that
you should grumble against him?"

**Rebellion of Dathan and Abiram.**
12 Moses summoned Dathan and Abiram, sons
of Eliab, but they answered, "We will not go.*
13 Are you not satisfied with having led us here
away from a land flowing with milk and honey,
to make us perish in the desert, that you must
now lord it over us? 14 Far from bringing us to
a land flowing with milk and honey, or giving
us fields and vineyards for our inheritance, will
you also gouge out our eyes?* No, we will not
go."

15 Then Moses became very angry and said
to the LORD, "Pay no heed to their offering. I
have never taken a single ass from them, nor
have I wronged any one of them."[i]

**Korah.** 16 Moses said to Korah, "You and
all your band shall appear before the LORD tomorrow—you and they and Aaron too. 17 Then
each of your two hundred and fifty followers
shall take his own censer, put incense in it, and
offer it to the LORD; and you and Aaron, each
with his own censer, shall do the same." 18 So
they all took their censers, and laying incense on
the fire they had put in them, they took their
stand by the entrance of the meeting tent along
with Moses and Aaron. 19 Then, when Korah
had assembled all his band against them at the
entrance of the meeting tent, the glory of the
LORD appeared to the entire community, 20 and
the LORD said to Moses and Aaron, 21 "Stand
apart from this band, that I may consume them
at once." 22 But they fell prostrate and cried
out, "O God, God of the spirits of all mankind,
will one man's sin make you angry with the
whole community?" 23 The LORD answered
Moses, 24 "Speak to the community and tell
them: Withdraw from the space around the
Dwelling" [of Korah, Dathan and Abiram].

**Punishment of Dathan and Abiram.**
25 Moses, followed by the elders of Israel,
arose and went to Dathan and Abiram.*
26 Then he warned the community, "Keep
away from the tents of these wicked men and do
not touch anything that is theirs: otherwise you
too will be swept away because of all their
sins." 27 When Dathan and Abiram had come
out and were standing at the entrances of their
tents with their wives and sons and little ones,
28 Moses said, "This is how you shall know
that it was the LORD who sent me to do all I have
done, and that it was not I who planned it: 29 if
these men die an ordinary death, merely suffering the fate common to all mankind, then it was
not the LORD who sent me. 30 But if the LORD
does something entirely new, and the ground
opens its mouth and swallows them alive down
into the nether world, with all belonging to
them, then you will know that these men have
defied the LORD." 31 [j]No sooner had he finished saying all this than the ground beneath

g Ps 106, 16ff; Sir 45, 19; 1 Cor 10, 10.
h Dt 10, 8.
i I Sm 12, 3.
j 31ff: Nm 26, 10; Lv 10, 2; Dt 11, 6; Ps 106, 7f.

*

16, 1ff: The evidence seems to show that there were two distinct rebellions: one of Korah and his band (Nm 27, 3) and the other of Dathan and Abiram (Dt 11, 6); cf Ps 106. The present account combines both events into one narrative; but even here it is rather easy to separate the two, once certain proper names (vv 1. 6. 24. 32. 35) have been identified as glosses. The rebellion of the Reubenites, Dathan and Abiram, was of a political nature, against Moses alone as the civil leader; these rebels were punished by being swallowed alive in an earthquake. The rebellion of Korah was of a religious nature, against the religious leadership of both Moses and Aaron; about two hundred and fifty malcontents joined Korah's band; they were punished by fire. The parts of the present section which refer to the rebellion of Dathan and Abiram are vv 12–15 and vv 25–34 of chapter 16; the rest of chapter 16 and all of chapter 17 concern the rebellion of Korah.

16, 12: We will not go: to appear before Moses' tribunal.

16, 14: Gouge out your eyes: blind us to the real state of affairs.

16, 25: Since Dathan and Abiram had refused to go to Moses (vv 12ff), he, with the elders as witnesses, was obliged to go to their tent.

them split open, **32** and the earth opened its
mouth and swallowed them and their families
[and all of Korah's men] and all their possessions. **33** They went down alive to the nether
world with all belonging to them; the earth
closed over them, and they perished from the
community. **34** But all the Israelites near them
fled at their shrieks, saying, "The earth might
swallow us too!"

**Punishment of Korah.** **35** So they withdrew from the space around the Dwelling [of
Korah,* Dathan and Abiram]. And fire from the
LORD came forth which consumed the two hundred and fifty men who were offering the incense.

## CHAPTER 17

**1** The LORD said to Moses, **2** "Tell Eleazar,
son of Aaron the priest, to remove the censers
from the embers; and scatter the fire some distance away, **3** *for these sinners have consecrated the censers at the cost of their lives. Have
them hammered into plates to cover the altar,
because in being presented before the LORD they
have become sacred. In this way they shall serve
as a sign to the Israelites." **4** So Eleazar the
priest had the bronze censers of those burned
during the offering hammered into a covering
for the altar, **5** in keeping with the orders which
the LORD had given him through Moses. This
cover was to be a reminder to the Israelites that
no layman, no one who was not a descendant of
Aaron, should approach the altar to offer incense before the LORD, lest he meet the fate of
Korah and his band.

**6** The next day the whole Israelite community grumbled against Moses and Aaron, saying,
"It is you who have slain the LORD's people."
**7** But while the community was deliberating
against them, Moses and Aaron turned toward
the meeting tent, and the cloud now covered it
and the glory of the LORD appeared. **8** Then
Moses and Aaron came to the front of the meeting tent, **9** and the LORD said to Moses and
Aaron, **10** "Depart from this community, that
I may consume them at once." But they fell
prostrate.

**11** Then Moses said to Aaron, "Take your
censer, put fire from the altar in it, lay incense
on it, and bring it quickly to the community to
make atonement for them; for wrath has come
forth from the LORD and the blow is falling."[k]
**12** Obeying the orders of Moses, Aaron took
his censer and ran in among the community,
where the blow was already falling on the people. Then, as he offered the incense and made
atonement for the people, **13** standing there between the living and the dead, the scourge was
checked. **14** Yet fourteen thousand seven hundred died from the scourge, in addition to those
who died because of Korah. **15** When the
scourge had been checked, Aaron returned to
Moses at the entrance of the meeting tent.

**Aaron's Staff.** **16** The LORD now said to
Moses, **17** "Speak to the Israelites and get one
staff* from them for each ancestral house,
twelve staffs in all, one from each of their tribal
princes. Mark each man's name on his staff;
**18** and mark Aaron's name on Levi's staff,* for
the head of Levi's ancestral house shall also
have a staff. **19** Then lay them down in the
meeting tent, in front of the commandments,
where I meet you. **20** There the staff of the man
of my choice shall sprout. Thus will I suppress
from my presence the Israelites' grumbling
against you."

**21** So Moses spoke to the Israelites, and their
princes gave him staffs, twelve in all, one from
each tribal prince; and Aaron's staff was with
them. **22** Then Moses laid the staffs down before the LORD in the tent of the commandments.
**23** The next day, when Moses entered the tent,
Aaron's staff, representing the house of Levi,
had sprouted and put forth not only shoots, but
blossoms as well, and even bore ripe almonds!
**24** Moses thereupon brought out all the staffs
from the LORD's presence to the Israelites. After
each prince identified his own staff and took it,
**25** the LORD said to Moses, "Put back Aaron's
staff in front of the commandments, to be kept
there as a warning to the rebellious, so that their
grumbling may cease before me; if it does not,
they will die." **26** And Moses did as the LORD
had commanded him.

**Charge of the Sacred Things.** **27** *Then
the Israelites cried out to Moses, "We are perishing; we are lost, we are all lost! **28** Every
time anyone approaches the Dwelling of the

k Wis 18, 20f.

*

16, 35: This verse continues v 24; the first sentence is transposed from v 27.

17, 3: Whatever was brought into intimate contact with something sacred shared in its sacredness. See note on Nm 19, 20.

17, 17: The staff was not merely an article of practical use, but also a symbol of authority; cf Gn 49, 10; Nm 24, 17; Jer 48, 17. Hence, the staff of a leader of a tribe was considered the emblem of his tribe; in fact, certain Hebrew words for "staff" also means "tribe." Perhaps for this reason, to avoid confusion, the author here uses the term "ancestral house" instead of the ordinary word for "tribe."

17, 18: Levi's staff: it is not clear whether this is considered as one of the twelve mentioned in the preceding verse, or as a thirteenth staff. Sometimes Levi is reckoned as one of the twelve tribes (e.g., Dt 27, 12f), but more often the number twelve is arrived at by counting the two sub-tribes of Joseph, i.e., Ephraim and Manasseh, as distinct tribes. In this passage also it seems probable that the tribe of Levi is considered apart from the other twelve.

17, 27f: Logically these two verses belong immediately after Nm 16, 35.

LORD, he dies! Are we to perish to the last
man?"

## CHAPTER 18

**1** The LORD said to Aaron,* "You and your
sons as well as the other members of your ancestral house shall be responsible for the sanctuary;
but the responsibility of the priesthood shall rest
on you and your sons alone. **2** Bring with you
also your other kinsmen of the tribe of Levi,
your ancestral tribe, as your associates* and
assistants, while you and your sons are in front
of the tent of the commandments. **3** They shall
look after your persons and the whole tent; however, they shall not come near the sacred vessels
or the altar, lest both they and you die. **4** As
your associates they shall have charge of all the
work connected with the meeting tent. But no
layman* shall come near you. **5** You shall have
charge of the sanctuary and of the altar, that
wrath may not fall again upon the Israelites.
**6** "Remember, it is I who have taken your
kinsmen, the Levites, from the body of the Israelites; they are a gift to you,[l] dedicated to the
LORD for the service of the meeting tent.
**7** [m]But only you and your sons are to have
charge of performing the priestly functions in
whatever concerns the altar and the room within
the veil.* I give you the priesthood as a gift.
Any layman who draws near shall be put to
death."

### The Priests' Share of the Sacrifices.
**8** The LORD said to Aaron,* "I myself have
given you charge of the contributions made to
me in the various sacred offerings of the Israelites;[n] by perpetual ordinance I have assigned
them to you and to your sons as your priestly
share. **9** You shall have the right to share in the
oblations that are most sacred, in whatever they
offer me as cereal offerings or sin offerings or
guilt offerings; these shares shall accrue to you
and to your sons. **10** In eating them you shall
treat them as most sacred; every male among
you may partake of them. As sacred, they belong to you.
**11** "You shall also have what is removed
from the gift in every wave offering* of the
Israelites; by perpetual ordinance I have assigned it to you and to your sons and daughters.[o] All in your family who are clean may
partake of it. **12** I have also assigned to you all
the best[p] of the new oil and of the new wine and
grain that they give to the LORD as their first
fruits; **13** and likewise, of whatever grows on
their land, the first products that they bring in
to the LORD shall be yours; all of your family
who are clean may partake of them. **14** Whatever is doomed* in Israel shall be yours. **15** Every living thing that opens the womb, whether
of man or of beast, such as are to be offered to
the LORD, shall be yours;[q] but you must let the
first-born of man, as well as of unclean animals,
be redeemed. **16** The ransom for a boy is to be
paid when he is a month old; it is fixed at five
silver shekels according to the sanctuary standard, twenty gerahs to the shekel. **17** But the
first-born of cattle, sheep or goats shall not be
redeemed; they are sacred. Their blood you
must splash on the altar and their fat you must
burn as a sweet-smelling oblation to the LORD.
**18** [r]Their meat, however, shall be yours, just
as the breast and the right leg of the wave offering belong to you. **19** By perpetual ordinance I
have assigned to you and to your sons and
daughters all the contributions from the sacred
gifts which the Israelites make to the LORD; this
is an inviolable covenant* to last forever before
the LORD, for you and for your descendants."
**20** [s]Then the LORD said to Aaron,* "You shall
not have any heritage in the land of the Israelites
nor hold any portion among them; I will be your
portion and your heritage among them.

### Tithes Due the Levites.
**21** "To the Le-
vites, however, I hereby assign all tithes in Israel as their heritage in recompense for the service
they perform in the meeting tent.[t] **22** The Israelites may no longer approach the meeting
tent; else they will incur guilt deserving death.

l Nm 3, 9; 8, 19.
m Nm 3, 10.
n Nm 5, 9.
o Ex 29, 27f; Lv 7, 34; 10, 14.
p 12f: Dt 18, 4; 26, 2.
q Ex 13, 2.
r Lv 7, 31-34.
s Dt 10, 9; 18, 1f; Jos 13, 33; Ez 44, 28.
t Heb 7, 5.

*

18, 1ff: This law, which kept unqualified persons from contact with sacred things, is the answer to the Israelites' cry in Nm 17, 28. It is followed by other laws concerning priests and Levites.

18, 2: Associates: in Hebrew this word alludes to the popular etymology of the name "Levi." Cf Gn 29, 34.

18, 4: Layman: here, "one who is not a Levite"; in v 7, "one who is not a priest."

18, 7: Veil: the outer veil, or "curtain," is probably meant.

18, 8ff: Two classes of offerings are here distinguished: the most sacred offering, which only the male members of the priestly families could eat (vv 8ff), and the other offerings, which even the women of the priestly families could eat (vv 11–19).

18, 11: Wave offering: this included the breast and right leg (v 18), the shoulder of the peace offering (Lv 7, 30–34), and portions of the nazirite sacrifice (Nm 6, 19f).

18, 14: Doomed: in Hebrew, herem, which means here "set aside from profane use and made sacred to the Lord." Cf Lv 27, 21. 28.

18, 19: An inviolable covenant: literally, "a covenant of salt." Cf 2 Chr 13, 5. The reference may perhaps be to the preservative power of salt (cf Mt 5, 13); but more likely the phrase refers to the custom of partaking of the same salt in common to render a contract unbreakable. See note on Lv 2, 13.

18, 20: The priests and Levites were forbidden to own hereditary land such as the other Israelites possessed; therefore in the allotment of the land they were not to receive any portion of it. Certain cities, however, were assigned to them for their residence; cf Nm 35, 1–8.

**23** Only the Levites are to perform the service
of the meeting tent, and they alone shall be held
responsible; this is a perpetual ordinance for all
your generations. The Levites, therefore, shall
not have any heritage among the Israelites,
**24** for I have assigned to them as their heritage
the tithes which the Israelites give as a contribution to the LORD. That is why I have ordered that
they are not to have any heritage among the
Israelites."

**Tithes Paid by the Levites.** **25** The LORD
said to Moses, **26** "Give the Levites these instructions: When you receive from the Israelites
the tithes I have assigned you from them as your
heritage, you are to make a contribution from
them to the LORD, a tithe of the tithes; **27** and
your contribution will be credited to you as if it
were grain from the threshing floor or new wine
from the press. **28** Thus you too shall make a
contribution from all the tithes you receive from
the Israelites, handing over to Aaron the priest
the part to be contributed to the LORD. **29** From
all the gifts that you receive, and from the best
parts, you are to consecrate to the LORD your
own full contribution.

**30** "Tell them also: Once you have made
your contribution from the best part, the rest of
the tithes will be credited to you Levites as if it
were produce of the threshing floor or of the
wine press. **31** Your families, as well as you,
may eat them anywhere, since they are your
recompense for service at the meeting tent.
**32** You will incur no guilt so long as you make
a contribution of the best part. Do not profane
the sacred gifts of the Israelites and so bring
death on yourselves."

## CHAPTER 19

**Ashes of the Red Heifer.** **1** The LORD
said to Moses and Aaron: **2** "This is the regulation which the law of the LORD prescribes. Tell
the Israelites to procure for you a red heifer that
is free from every blemish and defect and on
which no yoke has ever been laid. **3** This is to
be given to Eleazar the priest, to be led outside
the camp* and slaughtered in his presence.
**4** Eleazar the priest shall take some of its blood
on his finger and sprinkle it seven times toward
the front of the meeting tent.* **5** Then the heifer
shall be burned in his sight, with its hide and
flesh, its blood and offal; **6** and the priest shall
take some cedar wood, hyssop and scarlet yarn
and throw them into the fire in which the heifer
is being burned. **7** The priest shall then wash
his garments and bathe his body in water. He
remains unclean until the evening, and only
afterward may he return to the camp. **8** Likewise, he who burned the heifer shall wash his
garments, bathe his body in water, and be unclean until evening. **9** Finally, a man who is
clean shall gather up the ashes of the heifer and
deposit them in a clean place outside the camp.
There they are to be kept for preparing lustral
water for the Israelite community. The heifer is
a sin offering. **10** He who has gathered up the
ashes of the heifer shall also wash his garments
and be unclean until evening. This is a perpetual
ordinance, both for the Israelites and for the
aliens residing among them.

**Use of the Ashes.** **11** "Whoever touches
the dead body of any human being shall be
unclean for seven days; **12** he shall purify himself with the water on the third and on the seventh day, and then he will be clean again. But
if he fails to purify himself on the third and on
the seventh day, he will not become clean.
**13** [u]Everyone who fails to purify himself after
touching the body of any deceased person, defiles the Dwelling of the LORD and shall be cut
off from Israel. Since the lustral water has not
been splashed over him, he remains unclean; his
uncleanness still clings to him.

**14** "This is the law: When a man dies in a
tent, everyone who enters the tent, as well as
everyone already in it, shall be unclean for sev-
en days; **15** likewise, every vessel that is open,
or with its lid unfastened, shall be unclean.
**16** Moreover, everyone who in the open country touches a dead person, whether he was slain
by the sword or died naturally, or who touches
a human bone or a grave, shall be unclean for
seven days. **17** *For anyone who is thus unclean, ashes from the sin offering shall be put
in a vessel, and spring water shall be poured on
them. **18** Then a man who is clean shall take
some hyssop, dip it in this water, and sprinkle
it on the tent and on all the vessels and persons
that were in it, or on him who touched a bone,
a slain person or other dead body, or a grave.
**19** The clean man shall sprinkle the unclean on
the third and on the seventh day; thus purified
on the seventh day, he shall wash his garments
and bathe his body in water, and in the evening
he will be clean again. **20** *Any unclean man

---

u Lv 15, 31.

---

19, 3: Outside the camp: several Fathers of the Church saw in this a prefiguring of the sacrificial death of Christ outside the walls of Jerusalem; cf Jn 19, 20; Heb 13, 12; in the purifying water, into which the ashes of the red heifer were put, they saw a type of the water of Baptism.

19, 4: Toward the front of the meeting tent: since the tabernacle faced the east (Ex 26, 15–30), the killing of the heifer took place east of the camp; in later times it was done on the Mount of Olives, east of the Temple.

19, 17ff: "If . . . the sprinkled ashes of a heifer sanctify the unclean unto the cleansing of the flesh, how much more will the blood of Christ . . . cleanse your conscience from dead works?" (Heb 9, 13f).

19, 20: Ritual uncleanness is, as it were, contagious; so also sacredness; see note on Nm 17, 3.

who fails to have himself purified shall be cut off from the community, because he defiles the sanctuary of the LORD. As long as the lustral water has not been splashed over him, he remains unclean. **21** This shall be a perpetual ordinance for you.

"One who sprinkles the lustral water shall wash his garments, and anyone who comes in contact with this water shall be unclean until evening. **22** Moreover, whatever the unclean person touches becomes unclean itself, and anyone who touches it becomes unclean until evening."

## CHAPTER 20

**Death of Miriam.** **1** The whole Israelite community arrived in the desert of Zin in the first month,* and the people settled at Kadesh. It was here that Miriam died, and here that she was buried.

**Water Famine at Kadesh.** **2** As the community had no water, they held a council against Moses and Aaron. **3** The people contended with Moses, exclaiming, "Would that we too had perished with our kinsmen in the LORD's presence! **4** Why have you brought the LORD's community into this desert where we and our livestock are dying? **5** Why did you lead us out of Egypt, only to bring us to this wretched place which has neither grain nor figs nor vines nor pomegranates? Here there is not even water to drink!" **6** But Moses and Aaron went away from the assembly to the entrance of the meeting tent, where they fell prostrate.

**Sin of Moses and Aaron.** Then the glory of the LORD appeared to them, **7** and the LORD said to Moses, **8** "Take the staff and assemble the community, you and your brother Aaron, and in their presence order the rock to yield its waters. From the rock you shall bring forth water for the community and their livestock to drink." **9** So Moses took the staff from its place before the LORD, as he was ordered. **10** He and Aaron assembled the community in front of the rock, where he said to them,[v] "Listen to me, you rebels! Are we to bring water for you out of this rock?" **11** [w]Then, raising his hand, Moses struck the rock twice* with his staff, and water gushed out in abundance for the community and their livestock to drink. **12** *But the LORD said to Moses and Aaron, "Because you were not faithful to me in showing forth my sanctity before the Israelites, you shall not lead this community into the land I will give them."

**13** These are the waters of Meribah,[x] where the Israelites contended against the LORD, and where he revealed his sanctity among them.

**Edom's Refusal.** **14** From Kadesh Moses sent men to the king of Edom with the message: "Your brother Israel* has this to say: You know of all the hardships that have befallen us, **15** how our fathers went down to Egypt, where we stayed a long time, how the Egyptians maltreated us and our fathers, **16** and how, when we cried to the LORD,[y] he heard our cry and sent an angel who led us out of Egypt. Now here we are at the town of Kadesh at the edge of your territory. **17** Kindly let us pass through your country. We will not cross any fields or vineyards, nor drink any well water, but we will go straight along the royal road* without turning to the right or to the left, until we have passed through your territory."

**18** But Edom answered him, "You shall not pass through here; if you do, I will advance against you with the sword." **19** The Israelites insisted, "We want only to go up along the highway. If we or our livestock drink any of your water, we will pay for it. Surely there is no harm in merely letting us march through." **20** But Edom still said, "No, you shall not pass through,"[z] and advanced against them with a large and heavily armed force. **21** Therefore, since Edom refused to let them pass through their territory, Israel detoured around them.

**Death of Aaron.** **22** [a]Setting out from Kadesh, the whole Israelite community came to Mount Hor.* **23** There at Mount Hor, on the border of the land of Edom, the LORD said to

v Ex 17, 5f.
w Ps 78, 15f; Wis 11, 4; 1 Cor 10, 4.
x Nm 27, 14: Ex 17, 7.
y Ex 2, 23.
z Jgs 11, 17.
a 21f: Nm 33, 37.

*

20, 1: The first month: we would expect the mention also of the day and of the year (after the exodus) when this took place; cf similar dates in Nm 1, 1; 10, 11; 33, 38; Dt 1, 3. Here the full date seems to have been lost. Probably the Israelites arrived in Kadesh in the third year after the exodus. Cf Dt 1, 46. The desert of Zin: a barren region with a few good oases, southwest of the Dead Sea. See note on Nm 13, 21.

20, 11: Twice: perhaps because he had not sufficient faith to work the miracle with the first blow. Cf v 12.

20, 12f: The sin of Moses and Aaron consisted in doubting God's mercy toward the ever-rebellious people. In showing forth my sanctity: God's sacred power and glory: an allusion to the name of the place, Kadesh, which means "sanctified, sacred." Meribah means "contention." Cf Ex 17, 7.

20, 14: Your brother Israel: the Edomites were descended from Esau, the brother of Jacob. Their country, to the southeast of the Dead Sea, was also known as Seir; cf Gn 25, 24ff; 36, 1. 8f.

20, 17: The royal road: an important highway, running north and south along the plateau east of the Dead Sea. In ancient times it was much used by caravans and armies; later it was improved by the Romans, and large stretches of it are still clearly recognizable.

20, 22: Mount Hor: not definitively identified, but probably to be sought in the vicinity of Kadesh. According to Dt 10, 6, Aaron died at Moserah (cf "Moseroth" in Nm 33, 30f), which is apparently the name of the region in which Mount Hor is situated.

Moses and Aaron, **24** "Aaron is about to be
taken to his people; he shall not enter the land
I am giving to the Israelites, because you both
rebelled against my commandment at the waters
of Meribah. **25** Take Aaron and his son Eleazar
and bring them up on Mount Hor.[b] **26** Then
strip Aaron of his garments and put them on his
son Eleazar; for there Aaron shall be taken in
death."
**27** Moses did as the LORD commanded.
When they had climbed Mount Hor in view of
the whole community, **28** Moses stripped Aaron of his garments and put them on his son
Eleazar. Then Aaron died there on top of the
mountain.[c] When Moses and Eleazar came
down from the mountain, **29** all the community
understood that Aaron had passed away; and for
thirty days the whole house of Israel mourned
him.

## CHAPTER 21

**Victory over Arad.** **1** When the Canaanite
king of Arad,* who lived in the Negeb,[d] heard
that the Israelites were coming along the way of
Atharim, he engaged them in battle and took
some of them captive. **2** Israel then made this
vow to the LORD: "If you deliver this people
into my hand, I will doom their cities."[e] **3** Later, when the LORD heeded Israel's prayer and
delivered up the Canaanites,[f] they doomed
them and their cities. Hence that place was
named Hormah.*

**The Bronze Serpent.** **4** From Mount Hor
they set out on the Red Sea road, to bypass the
land of Edom. But with their patience worn out
by the journey, **5** the people complained[g]
against God and Moses, "Why have you
brought us up from Egypt to die in this desert,
where there is no food or water? We are disgusted with this wretched food!"*
**6** In punishment the LORD sent among the
people saraph* serpents, which bit[h] the people
so that many of them died. **7** Then the people
came to Moses and said, "We have sinned in
complaining against the LORD and you. Pray the
LORD to take the serpents from us." So Moses
prayed for the people, **8** and the LORD said to
Moses, "Make a saraph and mount it on a pole,
and if anyone who has been bitten looks at it,
he will recover."* **9** Moses accordingly made
a bronze serpent* and mounted it on a pole, and
whenever anyone who had been bitten by a
serpent looked at the bronze serpent, he recovered.[i]

**Journey around Moab.** **10** The Israelites
moved on and encamped in Oboth.[j] **11** Setting
out from Oboth, they encamped in Iyeabarim*
in the desert fronting Moab on the east. **12** Setting out from there, they encamped in the Wadi
Zered. **13** Setting out from there, they encamped on the other side of the Arnon, in the
desert that extends from the territory of the Amorites; for the Arnon forms Moab's boundary
with the Amorites. **14** Hence it is said in the
"Book of the Wars of the LORD"* :

"Waheb in Suphah and the wadies,
**15** Arnon and the wadi gorges
That reach back toward the site of Ar
and slant to the border of Moab."

**16** From there they went to Beer,* where
there was the well of which the LORD said to
Moses, "Bring the people together, and I will
give them water." **17** Then it was that Israel
sang this song:

"Spring up, O well!—so sing to it—
**18** The well that the princes sank,
that the nobles of the people dug,
with their scepters and their staffs."

From Beer they went to Mattanah, **19** from
Mattanah to Nahaliel, from Nahaliel to Bamoth,
**20** from Bamoth to the cleft in the plateau of
Moab at the headland of Pisgah that overlooks
Jeshimon.*

b 25f: Dt 32, 50.
c Nm 33, 38.
d Nm 33, 40.
e Jos 6, 17; Jgs 1, 17.
f Nm 14, 45.
g Nm 11, 6; Ex 16, 3.
h Dt 8, 15; Wis 16, 5; 1 Cor 10, 9.
i Wis 16, 6f. 10; Jn 3, 14f.
j Nm 33, 43f.

*

21, 1–3: The account of this episode seems to be a later insertion here, for Nm 21, 4, belongs logically immediately after Nm 20, 29. Perhaps this is the same event as that mentioned in Jgs 1, 16f.

21, 3: Hormah: related to the Hebrew word herem, meaning "doomed." See notes on Nm 14, 45; 18, 14.

21, 5: This wretched food: apparently the manna is meant.

21, 6: Saraph: the Hebrew name for a certain species of venomous snakes; the word probably signifies "the fiery one," these snakes being so called from the burning effect of their poisonous bite.

21, 8: If anyone who has been bitten looks at it, he will recover: "and as Moses lifted up the serpent in the desert, even so must the Son of Man be lifted up, that those who believe in him may not perish, but may have life everlasting" (Jn 3, 14f).

21, 9: King Hezekiah, in his efforts to abolish idolatry, "smashed the bronze serpent which Moses had made" (2 Kgs 18, 4).

21, 11: Iye-abarim: probably means "the ruins in the Abarim (Mountains)" See note on Nm 27, 12.

21, 14: The "Book of the Wars of the Lord": an ancient collection of Israelite songs, now lost. Waheb in Suphah: since neither place is mentioned elsewhere, it is quite uncertain whether these dubious Hebrew words are even to be considered as place names; some Hebrew words apparently lost must have preceded this phrase.

21, 16: Beer: means a well.

21, 20: Jeshimon: "the wasteland"; in 1 Sm 23, 19. 24, and 26, 1. 3, this is the desert of Judah, on the western side of the Dead Sea, but here and in Nm 23, 28, it seems to refer to the southern end of the Jordan valley where Beth-jeshimoth was situated.

**Victory over Sihon.** 21 Now Israel sent
men to Sihon, king of the Amorites, with the
message, 22 "Let us pass through your country. We will not turn aside into any field or
vineyard, nor will we drink any well water, but
we will go straight along the royal road until we
have passed through your territory." 23 Sihon,[k] however, would not let Israel pass
through his territory, but mustered all his forces
and advanced into the desert against Israel.
When he reached Jahaz, he engaged Israel in
battle. 24 But Israel defeated him at the point
of the sword, and took possession of his land
from the Arnon to the Jabbok and as far as the
country of the Ammonites, whose boundary
was at Jazer. 25 [l]Israel seized all the towns here
and settled in these towns of the Amorites, in
Heshbon and all its dependencies. 26 Now
Heshbon was the capital of Sihon, king of the
Amorites, who had fought against the former
king of Moab and had seized all his land from
Jazer to the Arnon. 27 That is why the poets
say:

"Come to Heshbon, let it be rebuilt,
let Sihon's capital be firmly constructed.
28 For fire went forth from Heshbon
and a blaze from the city of Sihon;
It consumed the cities of Moab
and swallowed up the high places of the
Arnon.
29 Woe to you, O Moab!
You are ruined, O people of Chemosh!*
He let his sons become fugitives
and his daughters be taken captive by the
Amorite king Sihon.
30 Their plowland is ruined from Heshbon to
Dibon;
Ar is laid waste; fires blaze as far as
Medeba."

31 When Israel had settled in the land of the
Amorites, 32 Moses sent spies to Jazer; Israel
then captured it with its dependencies and dispossessed the Amorites who were there.

**Victory over Og.** 33 [m]Then they turned
and went up along the road to Bashan. But Og,
king of Bashan, advanced against them with all
his people to give battle at Edrei. 34 The LORD,
however, said to Moses, "Do not be afraid of
him; for into your hand I will deliver him with
all his people and his land. Do to him as you did
to Sihon, king of the Amorites, who lived in
Heshbon."[n] 35 So they struck him down with
his sons and all his people, until not a survivor
was left to him, and they took possession of his
land.

## CHAPTER 22

1 Then the Israelites moved on and encamped in the plains of Moab* on the other side
of the Jericho stretch of the Jordan.

## *III: On the Plains of Moab*

**Balaam Summoned.** 2 Now Balak, son of
Zippor, saw all that Israel did to the Amorites.
3 Indeed, Moab feared the Israelites greatly because of their numbers, and detested them. 4 So
Moab said to the elders of Midian, "Soon this
horde will devour all the country around us as
an ox devours the grass of the field." And Balak, Zippor's son, who was king of Moab at that
time, 5 sent messengers to Balaam, son of
Beor, at Pethor on the Euphrates, in the land of
the Amawites, summoning him with these
words, "A people has come here from Egypt
who now cover the face of the earth and are
settling down opposite us! 6 Please come and
curse this people for us;* they are stronger than
we are. We may then be able to defeat them and
drive them out of the country. For I know that
whoever you bless is blessed and whoever you
curse is cursed." 7 Then the elders of Moab
and of Midian left with the divination fee in
hand and went to Balaam. When they had given
him Balak's message, 8 he said to them in reply, "Stay here overnight, and I will give you
whatever answer the LORD gives me." So the
princes of Moab lodged with Balaam.

9 Then God came to Balaam and said, "Who
are these men visiting you?" 10 Balaam answered God, "Balak, son of Zippor, king of
Moab, sent me the message: 11 'This people
that came here from Egypt now cover the face
of the earth. Please come and lay a curse on
them for us; we may then be able to give them
battle and drive them out.'" 12 But God said
to Balaam, "Do not go with them and do not
curse this people, for they are blessed." 13 The
next morning Balaam arose and told the princes
of Balak, "Go back to your own country, for the
LORD has refused to let me go with you." 14 So
the princes of Moab went back to Balak with the
report, "Balaam refused to come with us."

**Second Appeal to Balaam.** 15 Balak
again sent princes, who were more numerous
and more distinguished than the others. 16 On

k Dt 2, 32; Jgs 11, 20.
l 25f: Jos 21, 39; Jgs 11, 26.
m Dt 3, 1ff.
n Ps 136, 17ff.

*

21, 29: Chemosh: the chief god of the Moabites, and mentioned as such in the famous inscription of Mesha, king of Moab, who was the contemporary of the dynasty of Omri in Israel. Cf 1 Kgs 11, 7. 33; 2 Kgs 23, 13; Jer 48, 7. 13.

22, 1: The plains of Moab: the lowlands to the northeast of the Dead Sea, between the Jordan and the foothills below Mount Nebo. Here the Israelites remained until they crossed the Jordan, as told in Jos 1–4. Jericho lay to the west of the Jordan.

22, 6: Curse this people for us: Balak believed that if Balaam forecast an evil omen for Israel, this evil would come to pass, as if by magic. Balaam was a soothsayer or foreteller; cf Jos 13, 22.

coming to Balaam they told him, "This is what
Balak, son of Zippor, has to say: Please do not
refuse to come to me. **17** I will reward you very
handsomely and will do anything you ask of me.
Please come and lay a curse on this people for
me." **18** [o]But Balaam replied to Balak's officials, "Even if Balak gave me his house full of
silver and gold, I could not do anything, small
or great, contrary to the command of the LORD,
my God. **19** But, you too shall stay here overnight, till I learn what else the LORD may tell
me."

**20** That night God came to Balaam and said
to him, "If these men have come to summon
you, you may go with them; yet only on the
condition that you do exactly as I tell you."
**21** So the next morning when Balaam arose, he
saddled his ass, and went off with the princes of
Moab.

**The Talking Ass.** **22** But now the anger of
God flared up* at him for going, and the angel
of the LORD stationed himself on the road to
hinder him as he was riding along on his ass,
accompanied by two of his servants. **23** When
the ass saw the angel of the LORD standing on
the road with sword drawn, she turned off the
road and went into the field, and Balaam had to
beat her to bring her back on the road. **24** Then
the angel of the LORD took his stand in a narrow
lane between vineyards with a stone wall on
each side. **25** When the ass saw the angel of the
LORD there, she shrank against the wall; and
since she squeezed Balaam's leg against it, he
beat her again. **26** The angel of the LORD then
went ahead, and stopped next in a passage so
narrow that there was no room to move either
to the right or to the left. **27** When the ass saw
the angel of the LORD there, she cowered under
Balaam. So, in anger, he again beat the ass with
his stick.

**28** [p]But now the LORD opened the mouth of
the ass, and she asked Balaam, "What have I
done to you that you should beat me these three
times?" **29** "You have acted so willfully
against me," said Balaam to the ass, "that if I
but had a sword at hand, I would kill you here
and now." **30** But the ass said to Balaam, "Am
I not your own beast, and have you not always
ridden upon me until now? Have I been in the
habit of treating you this way before?" "No,"
replied Balaam.

**31** Then the LORD removed the veil from
Balaam's eyes, so that he too saw the angel of
the LORD standing on the road with sword
drawn; and he fell on his knees and bowed to the
ground. **32** But the angel of the LORD said to
him, "Why have you beaten your ass these
three times? It is I who have come armed to
hinder you because this rash journey of yours is
directly opposed to me. **33** When the ass saw
me, she turned away from me these three times.
If she had not turned away from me, I would
have killed you; her I would have spared."
**34** Then Balaam said to the angel of the LORD,
"I have sinned. Yet I did not know that you
stood against me to oppose my journey. Since
it has displeased you, I will go back home."
**35** But the angel of the LORD said to Balaam,
"Go with the men; but you may say only what
I tell you." So Balaam went on with the princes
of Balak.

**36** When Balak heard that Balaam was coming, he went out to meet him at the boundary
city Ir-Moab on the Arnon at the end of the
Moabite territory. **37** And he said to Balaam,
"I sent an urgent summons to you! Why did you
not come to me? Did you think I could not
reward you?" **38** Balaam answered him,
"Well, I have come to you after all. But what
power have I to say anything? I can speak only
what God puts in my mouth." **39** Then Balaam
went with Balak, and they came to Kiriath-hu-
zoth. **40** Here Balak slaughtered oxen and
sheep, and sent portions to Balaam and to the
princes who were with him.

**The First Oracle.** **41** The next morning Balak took Balaam up on Bamoth-baal, and from
there he saw some of the clans.

## CHAPTER 23

**1** Then Balaam said to Balak, "Build me
seven altars, and prepare seven bullocks and
seven rams for me here." **2** So he did as Balaam had ordered, offering a bullock and a ram
on each altar. And Balak said to him, "I have
erected the seven altars, and have offered a
bullock and a ram on each." **3** Balaam then
said to him, "Stand here by your holocaust
while I go over there. Perhaps the LORD will
meet me, and then I will tell you whatever he
lets me see." He went out on the barren height,
**4** and God met him. **5** When he had put an
utterance in Balaam's mouth, the LORD said to
him, "Go back to Balak, and speak accordingly." **6** So he went back to Balak, who was still
standing by his holocaust together with all the
princes of Moab. **7** Then Balaam gave voice to
his oracle:

---

o Nm 24, 13. q Nm 22, 6.
p 2 Pt 2, 16.

---

22, 22: The anger of God flared up: not merely because Balaam was going to Balak, for he had God's permission for the journey (v 20), but perhaps because he was tempted by avarice to curse Israel against God's command. "They have followed the way of Balaam, son of Bosor, who loved the wages of wrongdoing" (2 Pt 2, 15); "and have rushed on thoughtlessly into the error of Balaam for the sake of gain" (Jude 11). Cf v 32 and compare Ex 4, 18–26.

23, 7: Aram: the ancient name of the region later known as Syria. The Eastern Mountains: the low ranges in the Syrian

From Aram* has Balak brought me here,
 Moab's king, from the Eastern
 Mountains:[q]
''Come and lay a curse for me on Jacob,
 come and denounce Israel.''
8 How can I curse whom God has not cursed?
 How denounce whom the LORD has not
 denounced?
9 For from the top of the crags I see him,
 from the heights I behold him.
Here is a people that lives apart*
 and does not reckon itself among the
 nations.
10 Who has ever counted the dust of Jacob,
 or numbered Israel's wind-borne
 particles?*
May I die the death of the just,
 may my descendants be as many as theirs!

**11** ''What have you done to me?'' cried Balak to Balaam. ''It was to curse my foes that I
brought you here; instead, you have even
blessed them.'' **12** Balaam replied, ''Is it not
what the LORD puts in my mouth that I must
repeat with care?''

**The Second Oracle.** **13** Then Balak said
to him, ''Please come with me to another place*
from which you can see only some and not all
of them, and from there curse them for me.''
**14** So he brought him to the lookout field on the
top of Pisgah, where he built seven altars and
offered a bullock and a ram on each of them.
**15** Balaam then said to Balak, ''Stand here by
your holocaust, while I seek a meeting over
there.'' **16** Then the LORD met Balaam, and
having put an utterance in his mouth, he said to
him, ''Go back to Balak, and speak accordingly.'' **17** So he went back to Balak, who was still
standing by his holocaust together with the
princes of Moab. When Balak asked him,
''What did the LORD say?'' **18** Balaam gave
voice to his oracle:

Be aroused, O Balak, and hearken;
 give ear to my testimony, O son of
 Zippor!
19 God is not man that he should speak falsely,
 nor human, that he should change his
 mind.
Is he one to speak and not act,
 to decree and not fulfill?
20 It is a blessing I have been given to
 pronounce;
 a blessing which I cannot restrain.
21 Misfortune is not observed in Jacob,
 nor misery* seen in Israel.
The LORD, his God, is with him;
 with him is the triumph of his King.
22 It is God who brought him out of Egypt,[r]
 a wild bull of towering might.*
23 No, there is no sorcery against Jacob,
 nor omen against Israel.
It shall yet be said of Jacob,
 and of Israel, ''Behold what God has
 wrought!''
24 Here is a people that springs up like a
 lioness,
 and stalks forth like a lion;
It rests not till it has devoured its prey
 and has drunk the blood of the slain.[s]

**25** ''Even though you cannot curse them,''
said Balak to Balaam, ''at least do not bless
them.'' **26** But Balaam answered Balak, ''Did
I not warn you that I must do all that the LORD
tells me?''

**The Third Oracle.** **27** Then Balak said to
Balaam, ''Come, let me bring you to another
place; perhaps God will approve of your cursing
them for me from there.'' **28** So he took Balaam to the top of Peor, that overlooks Jeshimon. **29** Balaam then said to him, ''Here build
me seven altars; and here prepare for me seven
bullocks and seven rams.'' **30** And Balak did as
Balaam had ordered, offering a bullock and a
ram on each altar.

## CHAPTER 24

**1** Balaam, however, perceiving that the
LORD was pleased to bless Israel, did not go
aside as before to seek omens, but turned his
gaze toward the desert. **2** When he raised his
eyes and saw Israel encamped, tribe by tribe,
the spirit of God came upon him, **3** and he gave
voice to his oracle:

The utterance of Balaam, son of Beor,
 the utterance of the man whose eye is
 true,
4 The utterance of one who hears what God
 says,
 and knows what the Most High knows,
Of one who sees what the Almighty sees,
 enraptured, and with eyes unveiled:
5 How goodly are your tents, O Jacob;
 your encampments, O Israel!
6 They are like gardens beside a stream,
 like the cedars planted by the LORD.

r Nm 24, 8. s Nm 24, 9; Gn 49, 9.

*

desert near the Euphrates and Balaam's town of Pethor; cf Nm 22, 5.

23, 9: A people that lives apart: Israel, as the chosen people of God, occupied a unique place among the nations, from which they kept themselves aloof.

23, 10: The dust of Jacob . . . Israel's wind-borne particles: the Israelites will be as numerous as dust in a desert sandstorm. May I . . . as many as theirs: a formula by which Balaam swears he is speaking the truth; he sees the reward of virtue in having numerous descendants.

23, 13: To another place: Balak thought that if Balaam would view Israel from a different site, he could forecast a different kind of omen.

23, 21: Misfortune . . . misery: Balaam admits that he is unable to predict any evils for Israel.

23, 22: A wild bull of towering might: the reference is to Israel, rather than to God.

7 His wells shall yield free-flowing waters,
he shall have the sea within reach;
His king shall rise higher than. . . .
and his royalty shall be exalted.
8 It is God who brought him out of Egypt,
a wild bull of towering might.
He shall devour the nations like grass,
their bones he shall strip bare.[t]
9 He lies crouching like a lion,
or like a lioness; who shall arouse him?
Blessed is he who blesses you,
and cursed is he who curses you![u]

10 Balak beat his palms* together in a blaze
of anger at Balaam and said to him, "It was to
curse my foes that I summoned you here; yet
three times now you have even blessed them
instead![v] 11 Be off at once, then, to your home.
I promised to reward you richly, but the LORD
has withheld the reward from you!" 12 Balaam
replied to Balak, "Did I not warn the very messengers whom you sent to me, 13 'Even if Balak gave me his house full of silver and gold, I
could not of my own accord do anything, good
or evil, contrary to the command of the LORD'?
Whatever the LORD says I must repeat.[w]

**The Fourth Oracle.** 14 "But now that I am
about to go to my own people, let me first warn
you what this people will do to your people in
the days to come." 15 Then Balaam gave voice
to his oracle:

The utterance of Balaam, son of Beor,
the utterance of the man whose eye is
true,
16 The utterance of one who hears what God
says,
and knows what the Most High knows,
Of one who sees what the Almighty sees,
enraptured and with eyes unveiled.
17 I see him, though not now;
I behold him, though not near:
A star shall advance from Jacob,
and a staff* shall rise from Israel,
That shall smite the brows of Moab,[x]
and the skulls of all the Shuthites,
18 Till Edom is dispossessed,
and no fugitive is left in Seir.
Israel shall do valiantly,
19 and Jacob shall overcome his foes.

20 Upon seeing Amalek, Balaam gave voice to
his oracle:

First* of the peoples was Amalek,
but his end is to perish forever.[y]

21 Upon seeing the Kenites,* he gave voice to
his oracle:

Your abode is enduring, O smith,
and your nest is set on a cliff;
22 Yet destined for burning—
even as I watch—are your inhabitants.

23 Upon seeing . . . he gave voice to his oracle:

*Alas, who shall survive of Ishmael,
24 to deliver his people from the hands of
the Kittim?
When they have conquered Asshur and
conquered Eber,
He too shall perish forever.

25 Then Balaam set out on his journey home;
and Balak also went his way.

## CHAPTER 25

**Worship of Baal of Peor.** 1 While Israel
was living at Shittim,* the people degraded
themselves by having illicit relations with the
Moabite women.[z] 2 These then invited the people to the sacrifices of their god, and the people
ate of the sacrifices[a] and worshiped their god.
3 When Israel thus submitted to the rites of
Baal of Peor,[b] the LORD's anger flared up
against Israel, 4 [c]and he said to Moses, "Gather all the leaders of the people, and hold a public
execution* of the guilty ones before the LORD,
that his blazing wrath may be turned away from
Israel." 5 So Moses told the Israelite judges,
"Each of you shall kill those of his men who
have submitted to the rites of Baal of Peor."

t Nm 23, 22.
u Nm 23, 24; Gn 12, 3; 27, 29; 49, 9.
v Nm 23, 11.
w Nm 22, 18.
x 2 Sm 8, 2.
y Ex 17, 14; 1 Sm 15, 3.
z Nm 31, 16.
a Ex 34, 15f.
b Ps 106, 28; Hos 9, 10.
c Dt 4, 3.

*

24, 10: Balak beat his palms: a sign of disclaiming any responsibility for paying the promised reward.

24, 17: A star . . . a staff: many of the Fathers have understood this as a Messianic prophecy, although it is not referred to anywhere in the New Testament; in this sense the star is Christ himself, just as he is the staff from Israel; cf Is 11, 1. But it is doubtful whether this passage is to be connected with the "star of the Magi" in Mt 2, 1–12. The Shuthites: mentioned in other documents of this period as nomads on the borded of Palestine.

24, 20: First: literally "the beginning." Amalek was an aboriginal people in Palestine and therefore considered as of great antiquity. There is a deliberate contrast here between the words first and end.

24, 21: The Kenites lived in high strongholds in the mountains of southern Palestine and the Sinai Peninsula, and were skilled in working the various metals found in their territory. Their name is connected, at least by popular etymology, with the Hebrew word for "smith"; of similar sound is the Hebrew word for "nest"—hence the play on words in the present passage.

24, 23f: The translation of this short oracle is based on a reconstructed text and is rather uncertain. Ishmael: the survival of Ishmael is indicated in Gn 17, 20; 21, 13. 18.

25, 1: Shittim: the full name was Abel-shittim, a locality at the foot of the mountains in the northeastern corner of the plains of Moab (Nm 33, 49). Illicit relations: perhaps as part of the licentious worship of Baal of Peor.

25, 4: Hold a public execution: the same phrase occurs in 2 Sm 21, 6–14, where the context shows that at least a part of the penalty consisted in being denied honorable burial. In both passages, dismemberment as a punishment for the breaking of covenant pledges is a current understanding of the phrase.

**Zeal of Phinehas.** **6** Yet a certain Israelite came and brought in a Midianite woman* to his clansmen in the view of Moses and of the whole Israelite community, while they were weeping at the entrance of the meeting tent. **7** [d]When Phinehas, son of Eleazar, son of Aaron the priest, saw this, he left the assembly, and taking a lance in hand, **8** followed the Israelite into his retreat where he pierced the pair of them, the Israelite and the woman. Thus the slaughter of Israelites was checked; **9** but only after twenty-four thousand had died.

**10** Then the LORD said to Moses, **11** "Phinehas, son of Eleazar, son of Aaron the priest, has turned my anger from the Israelites by his zeal for my honor* among them; that is why I did not put an end to the Israelites for the offense to my honor. **12** [e]Announce, therefore, that I hereby give him my pledge of friendship, **13** which shall be for him and for his descendants after him the pledge of an everlasting priesthood, because he was zealous on behalf of his God and thus made amends for the Israelites."

**14** *The Israelite slain with the Midianite woman was Zimri, son of Salu, prince of an ancestral house of the Simeonites. **15** The slain Midianite woman was Cozbi, daughter of Zur, who was head of a clan, an ancestral house, in Midian.

**Vengeance on the Midianites.** **16** *The LORD then said to Moses, **17** [f]"Treat the Midianites as enemies and crush them, **18** for they have been your enemies by their wily dealings with you as regards Peor and as regards their kinswoman Cozbi, the daughter of the Midianite prince, who was killed at the time of the slaughter because of Peor."

## CHAPTER 26

**The Second Census.** **19** After the slaughter* **1** the LORD said to Moses and Eleazar, son of Aaron the priest, **2** "Take a census, by ancestral houses, throughout the community of the Israelites of all those of twenty years or more who are fit for military service in Israel."[g] **3** So on the plains of Moab along the Jericho stretch of the Jordan, Moses and the priest Eleazar registered **4** those of twenty years or more, as the LORD had commanded Moses.

The Israelites who came out of the land of Egypt were as follows:

**5** [h]Of Reuben, the first-born of Israel, the Reubenites by clans were: through Hanoch the clan of the Hanochites, through Pallu the clan of the Palluites, **6** through Hezron the clan of the Hezronites, through Carmi the clan of the Carmites. **7** These were the clans of the Reubenites, of whom forty-three thousand seven hundred and thirty men were registered.

**8** From Pallu descended Eliab, **9** and the descendants of Eliab were Dathan and Abiram[i]—the same Dathan and Abiram, councilors of the community, who revolted against Moses and Aaron [like Korah's band when it rebelled against the LORD]. **10** The earth opened its mouth and swallowed them as a warning [Korah too and the band that died when the fire consumed two hundred and fifty men. **11** The descendants of Korah, however, did not die out].

**12** The Simeonites by clans were: through Nemuel* the clan of the Nemuelites, through Jamin the clan of the Jaminites, through Jachin the clan of the Jachinites, **13** through Sohar the clan of the Soharites, through Shaul the clan of the Shaulites. **14** These were the clans of the Simeonites, of whom twenty-two thousand two hundred men were registered.

**15** The Gadites by clans were: through Zephon the clan of the Zephonites, through Haggi the clan of the Haggites, through Shuni the clan of the Shunites, **16** through Ozni the clan of the Oznites, through Eri the clan of the Erites, **17** through Arod the clan of the Arodites, through Areli the clan of the Arelites. **18** These were the clans of the Gadites, of whom forty thousand five hundred men were registered.

**19** The sons of Judah who died in the land of Canaan were Er and Onan.[j] **20** The Judahites by clans were: through Shelah the clan of the Shelahites, through Perez the clan of the Perezites, through Zerah the clan of the Zerahites. **21** The Perezites were: through Hezron the clan of the Hezronites, through Hamul the clan of the Hamulites. **22** These were the clans of Judah, of whom seventy-six thousand five hundred men were registered.

**23** The Issacharites by clans were: through

d Ps 106, 30.
e 12f: Sir 45, 23f; Ps 106, 31; 1 Mc 2, 26. 54.
f 17f: Nm 31, 2-12.
g Nm 1, 2f.
h 5f: 1 Chr 5, 3.
i 9f: Nm 16, 1. 32.
j Gn 38, 7. 10; 46, 12; 1 Chr 2, 3.

*

25, 6: Midianite woman: at this time the Midianites were leagued with the Moabites in opposing Israel; cf Nm 22, 4. 7. Balaam had induced both the Midianites (Nm 31, 16) and the Moabites (Rv 2, 14) to lure the Israelites to the obscene rites of Baal of Peor. They were weeping: on account of the plague that had struck them; cf v 8.

25, 11: For my honor: by taking vengeance on those who had made Baal of Peor a rival of the Lord.

25, 14f: The nobility of the slain couple is mentioned in order to stress the courage of Phinehas in punishing them. The zeal of Phinehas became proverbial; cf Ps 106, 30; Sir 45, 23; 1 Mc 2, 26. 54.

25, 16ff: The account of the execution of this command is given in Nm 31, 1–18.

26, 19: This is the last verse of Ch 25.

26, 12: Nemuel: so also in Gn 46, 10; 1 Chr 4, 24. In Ex 6, 15, the same man is called "Jemuel"; it is uncertain which form is correct.

Tola the clan of the Tolaites, through Puvah the
clan of the Puvahites, **24** through Jashub the
clan of the Jashubites, through Shimron the clan
of the Shimronites. **25** These were the clans of
Issachar, of whom sixty-four thousand three
hundred men were registered.

**26** The Zebulunites by clans were: through
Sered the clan of the Seredites, through Elon the
clan of the Elonites, through Jahleel the clan of
the Jahleelites. **27** These were the clans of the
Zebulunites, of whom sixty thousand five hundred men were registered.

**28** The sons of Joseph were Manasseh, and
Ephraim. **29** The Manassehites by clans were:
through Machir the clan of the Machirites,
through Gilead, a descendant of Machir, the
clan of the Gileadites. **30** The Gileadites were:
through Abiezer the clan of the Abiezrites,
through Helek the clan of the Helekites,
**31** through Asriel the clan of the Asrielites,
through Shechem the clan of the Shechemites,
**32** through Shemida the clan of the Shemida-
ites, through Hepher the clan of the Hepherites.
**33** [k]Zelophehad, son of Hepher, had no sons,
but only daughters, whose names were Mahlah,
Noah, Hoglah, Milcah and Tirzah. **34** These
were the clans of Manasseh, of whom fifty-
two thousand seven hundred men were registered.

**35** The Ephraimites by clans were: through
Shuthelah the clan of the Shuthelahites, through
Becher the clan of the Bechrites, through Tahan
the clan of the Tahanites. **36** The Shuthelahites
were: through Eran the clan of the Eranites.
**37** These were the clans of the Ephraimites, of
whom thirty-two thousand five hundred men
were registered.

These were the descendants of Joseph by
clans.

**38** The Benjaminites by clans were: through
Bela the clan of the Belaites, through Ashbel the
clan of the Ashbelites, through Ahiram the clan
of the Ahiramites, **39** through Shupham the
clan of the Shuphamites, through Hupham the
clan of the Huphamites. **40** The descendants of
Bela were Arad and Naaman: through Arad the
clan of the Aradites, through Naaman the clan
of the Naamanites. **41** These were the Benjaminites by clans, of whom forty-five thousand six
hundred men were registered.

**42** The Danites by clans were: through Shu-
ham the clan of the Shuhamites. These were the
clans of Dan, **43** of whom sixty-four thousand
four hundred men were registered.

**44** The Asherites by clans were: through Imnah the clan of the Imnites, through Ishvi the
clan of the Ishvites, through Beriah the clan of
the Beriites, **45** through Heber the clan of the
Heberites, through Malchiel the clan of the Mal-
chielites. **46** The name of Asher's daughter was
Serah. **47** These were the clans of Asher, of
whom fifty-three thousand four hundred men
were registered.

**48** The Naphtalites by clans were: through
Jahzeel the clan of the Jahzeelites, through Guni
the clan of the Gunites, **49** through Jezer the
clan of the Jezerites, through Shillem the clan
of the Shillemites. **50** These were the clans of
Naphtali, of whom forty-five thousand four
hundred men were registered.

**51** These six hundred and one thousand sev-
en hundred and thirty were the Israelites who
were registered.

**Allotment of the Land.** **52** *The LORD
said to Moses, **53** [l]"Among these groups the
land shall be divided as their heritage in keeping
with the number of individuals in each group.
**54** [m]To a large group you shall assign a large
heritage, to a small group a small heritage, each
group receiving its heritage in proportion to the
number of men registered in it. **55** But the land
shall be divided by lot, as the heritage of the
various ancestral tribes. **56** As the lot falls shall
each group, large or small, be assigned its heritage."

**Census of the Levites.** **57** The Levites
registered by clans were: through Gershon the
clan of the Gershonites, through Kohath the
clan of the Kohathites, through Merari the clan
of the Merarites. **58** These also were clans of
Levi: the clan of the Libnites, the clan of the
Hebronites, the clan of the Mahlites, the clan of
the Mushites, the clan of the Korahites.

Among the descendants of Kohath was Amram, **59** whose wife was named Jochebed. She
also was of the tribe of Levi, born to the tribe
in Egypt. To Amram she bore Aaron and Moses
and their sister Miriam. **60** To Aaron were born
Nadab and Abihu, Eleazar and Ithamar. **61** But
Nadab and Abihu died when they offered profane fire before the LORD.

**62** The total number of male Levites one
month or more of age, who were registered, was
twenty-three thousand.[n] They were not registered with the other Israelites, however, for no
heritage was given them among the Israelites.

**63** These, then, were the men registered by
Moses and the priest Eleazar in the census of the
Israelites taken on the plains of Moab along the

k Nm 27, 1; 36, 11; Jos 17, 3.
l Jos 11, 23.
m Nm 33, 54; 35, 8.
n Nm 3, 39.

* 26, 52–56: The division of Canaan among the various tribes and clans and families was determined partly by the size of each group and partly by lot. Perhaps the lots determined the respective locality of each tribal land and the section reserved for each clan, while the relative size of the allotted locality and section depended on the numerical strength of each group. The Hebrews considered the outcome of the drawing of lots as an expression of God's will; cf Acts 1, 23–26.

Jericho stretch of the Jordan. **64** Among them there was not a man of those who had been registered by Moses and the priest Aaron in the census of the Israelites taken in the desert of Sinai. **65** [o]For the LORD had told them that they would surely die in the desert, and not one of them was left except Caleb, son of Jephunneh, and Joshua, son of Nun.

## CHAPTER 27

**Zelophehad's Daughters.** **1** Zelophehad, son of Hepher, son of Gilead, son of Machir, son of Manasseh, son of Joseph, had daughters named Mahlah, Noah, Hoglah, Milcah and Tirzah.[p] They came forward, **2** and standing in the presence of Moses, the priest Eleazar, the princes, and the whole community at the entrance of the meeting tent, said: **3** "Our father died in the desert. Although he did not join those who banded together against the LORD* [in Korah's band], he died for his own sin without leaving any sons. **4** But why should our father's name be withdrawn from his clan merely because he had no son? Let us, therefore, have property among our father's kinsmen."

**Laws Concerning Heiresses.** **5** *When Moses laid their case before the LORD, **6** the LORD said to him, **7** "The plea of Zelophehad's daughters is just; you shall give them hereditary property among their father's kinsmen, letting their father's heritage pass on to them. **8** Therefore, tell the Israelites: If a man dies without leaving a son, you shall let his heritage pass on to his daughter; **9** if he has no daughter, you shall give his heritage to his brothers; **10** if he has no brothers, you shall give his heritage to his father's brothers; **11** if his father had no brothers, you shall give his heritage to his nearest relative in his clan, who shall then take possession of it." This is the legal norm for the Israelites, as the LORD commanded Moses.[q]

**Joshua To Succeed Moses.** **12** The LORD said to Moses, "Go up here into the Abarim Mountains* and view the land that I am giving to the Israelites.[r] **13** When you have viewed it, you too shall be taken to your people, as was your brother Aaron,[s] **14** because in the rebellion of the community in the desert of Zin you both rebelled against my order to manifest my sanctity to them by means of the water."[t] [This is the water of Meribah of Kadesh in the desert of Zin.]

**15** Then Moses said to the LORD, **16** "May the LORD, the God of the spirits of all mankind,* set over the community a man **17** who shall act as their leader in all things, to guide them in all their actions; that the LORD's community may not be like sheep without a shepherd." **18** And the LORD replied to Moses, "Take Joshua, son of Nun,[u] a man of spirit,* and lay your hand upon him. **19** Have him stand in the presence of the priest Eleazar and of the whole community, and commission him before their eyes. **20** Invest him with some of your own dignity, that the whole Israelite community may obey him. **21** He shall present himself to the priest Eleazar, to have him seek out for him the decisions of the Urim* in the LORD's presence; and as he directs, Joshua, all the Israelites with him, and the community as a whole shall perform all their actions."

**22** Moses did as the LORD had commanded him. Taking Joshua and having him stand in the presence of the priest Eleazar and of the whole community, **23** he laid his hands on him and gave him his commission, as the LORD had directed through Moses.

## CHAPTER 28

**General Sacrifices.** **1** The LORD said to Moses, **2** "Give the Israelites this commandment: At the times I have appointed, you shall be careful to present me the food offerings that are offered to me as sweet-smelling oblations.

**Each Morning and Evening.** **3** [v]"You shall tell them therefore: This is the oblation which you shall offer to the LORD: two unblem-

o Nm 14, 22ff. 29.
p Nm 26, 33; Jos 17, 3.
q Jer 32, 6-9.
r Dt 3, 27; 32, 49; 34, 1.
s 13f: Nm 20, 12. 24.
t Dt 32, 51.
u Dt 34, 9.
v 3-8: Ex 29, 38-42.

*

27, 3: He did not join . . . against the Lord: had he done so, he and his heirs could have rightly been deprived of the privilege of receiving a portion in the Promised Land.

27, 5–11: The purpose of this law, as also that of the related laws in Nm 36, 2–10 (heiresses to marry within the same tribe), Dt 25, 5–10 (levirate marriage), and Lv 25, 10 (return of property in the jubilee year), was to keep the landed property within the proper domain of each tribe.

27, 12: The Abarim Mountains: the range on the eastern side of the Dead Sea.

27, 16: The God of the spirits of all mankind: the sense is either that God knows the character and abilities of all men and therefore knows best whom to appoint (cf Acts 1, 24), or, more probably, that God is Master of life and death and therefore can call Moses from this world whenever he wishes; cf the same phrase in Nm 16, 22, where "spirit" evidently means "the life principle."

27, 18: A man of spirit: literally, "a man in whom there is spirit": one who has the qualities of a good leader—courage, prudence, and strength of will. Cf Gn 41, 38; Dt 34, 9.

27, 21: The Urim: certain sacred objects which the Hebrew priests employed to ascertain the divine will, probably by obtaining a positive or negative answer to a given question. The full expression was "the Urim and Thummim"; cf Ex 28, 30; Lv 8, 8; Dt 33, 8; Ezr 2, 63; Neh 7, 65. Joshua was ordinarily not to receive direct revelations from God as Moses had received them.

28, 3: The established holocaust: "the tamid holocaust," the technical term for the daily sacrifice.

ished yearling lambs each day as the established
holocaust,* **4** offering one lamb in the morning
and the other during the evening twilight,
**5** each with a cereal offering of one tenth of an
ephah of fine flour mixed with a fourth of a hin
of oil of crushed olives.* **6** This is the established holocaust that was offered at Mount Sinai
as a sweet-smelling oblation to the LORD.
**7** And as the libation for the first lamb, you
shall pour out to the LORD in the sanctuary* a
fourth of a hin of wine. **8** The other lamb, to be
offered during the evening twilight, you shall
offer with the same cereal offering and the same
libation as in the morning, as a sweet-smelling
oblation to the LORD.

**On the Sabbath.** **9** "On the sabbath day
you shall offer two unblemished yearling lambs,
with their cereal offering, two tenths of an
ephah of fine flour mixed with oil, and with
their libations. **10** Each sabbath there shall be
the sabbath holocaust in addition to the established holocaust and its libation.

**At the New Moon Feast.** **11** "On the first
of each month* you shall offer as a holocaust to
the LORD two bullocks, one ram, and seven
unblemished yearling lambs, **12** with three
tenths of an ephah of fine flour mixed with oil
as the cereal offering for each bullock, two
tenths of an ephah of fine flour mixed with oil
as the cereal offering for the ram, **13** and one
tenth of an ephah of fine flour mixed with oil as
the cereal offering for each lamb, that the holocaust may be a sweet-smelling oblation to the
LORD. **14** Their libations shall be half a hin of
wine for each bullock, a third of a hin for the
ram, and a fourth of a hin for each lamb. This
is the new moon holocaust for every new moon
of the year. **15** Moreover, one goat shall be
sacrificed as a sin offering to the LORD. These
are to be offered in addition to the established
holocaust and its libation.

**At the Passover.** **16** "On the fourteenth
day* of the first month falls the Passover of the
LORD,[w] **17** and the fifteenth day of this month
is the pilgrimage feast. For seven days unleavened bread is to be eaten. **18** On the first of
these days you shall hold a sacred assembly, and
do no sort of work.[x] **19** As an oblation you shall
offer a holocaust to the LORD, which shall consist of two bullocks, one ram, and seven yearling lambs that you are sure are unblemished,
**20** with their cereal offerings of fine flour
mixed with oil, offering three tenths of an ephah
for each bullock, two tenths for the ram, **21** and
one tenth for each of the seven lambs; **22** and
offer one goat as a sin offering in atonement for
yourselves. **23** These offerings you shall make
in addition to the established morning holocaust: **24** you shall make exactly the same offerings each day for seven days as food offerings, in addition to the established holocaust
with its libation, for a sweet-smelling oblation
to the LORD. **25** On the seventh day you shall
hold a sacred assembly, and do no sort of
work.[y]

**At Pentecost.** **26** "On the day of first
fruits,* on your feast of Weeks,[z] when you
present to the LORD the new cereal offering, you
shall hold a sacred assembly, and do no sort of
work. **27** You shall offer as a sweet-smelling
holocaust to the LORD two bullocks, one ram,
and seven yearling lambs that you are sure are
unblemished, **28** with their cereal offerings of
fine flour mixed with oil; offering three tenths
of an ephah for each bullock, two tenths for the
ram, **29** and one tenth for each of the seven
lambs. **30** Moreover, one goat shall be offered
as a sin offering in atonement for yourselves.
**31** You shall make these offerings, together
with their libations, in addition to the established holocaust with its cereal offering.

## CHAPTER 29

**On New Year's Day.** **1** "On the first day
of the seventh month* you shall hold a sacred
assembly, and do no sort of work; it shall be a
day on which you sound the trumpet.[a] **2** You
shall offer as a sweet-smelling holocaust to the
LORD one bullock, one ram, and seven unblemished yearling lambs, **3** with their cereal offerings of fine flour mixed with oil; offering three
tenths of an ephah for the bullock, two tenths for
the ram, **4** and one tenth for each of the seven
lambs. **5** Moreover, one goat shall be offered as
a sin offering in atonement for yourselves.
**6** These are to be offered in addition to the

w Ex 12, 18; Lv 23, 5; Dt 16, 1.
x Ex 12, 16; Lv 23, 7.
y Ex 12, 16; 13, 6; Lv 23, 8.
z Ex 34, 22.
a Nm 10, 10; Lv 23, 24.

*

28, 5: Oil of crushed olives: this oil, made in a mortar, was purer and more expensive than oil extracted in the olive press.

28, 7: In the sanctuary: according to Sir 50, 15, it was at the base of the altar.

28, 11: On the first of each month: literally, "at the new moons"; beginning on the evening when the crescent of the new moon first appeared.

28, 16: On the fourteenth day: toward evening at the end of this day; cf Ex 12, 6. 18.

28, 26: The day of first fruits: a unique term for this feast, which is usually called "the feast of Weeks"; it was celebrated as a thanksgiving for the wheat harvest seven weeks after the barley harvest (Passover). In the time of Christ it was commonly known by the Greek word "Pentecost," that is, "fiftieth" (day after the Passover); see note on Lv 23, 16.

29, 1: The first day of the seventh month: (about September-October) is now the Jewish New Year's Day. In the older calendar the year began with the first of Nisan (March-April); cf Ex 12, 2.

ordinary new moon holocaust with its cereal
offering, and in addition to the established holocaust with its cereal offering, together with the
libations prescribed for them, as a sweet-smelling oblation to the LORD.

**On the Day of Atonement.** 7 "On the
tenth day of this seventh month* you shall hold
a sacred assembly, and mortify yourselves, and
do no sort of work.[b] 8 You shall offer as a
sweet-smelling holocaust to the LORD one bullock, one ram, and seven yearling lambs that you
are sure are unblemished, 9 with their cereal
offerings of fine flour mixed with oil; offering
three tenths of an ephah for the bullock, two
tenths for the ram, 10 and one tenth for each of
the seven lambs. 11 Moreover, one goat shall
be sacrificed as a sin offering. These are to be
offered in addition to the atonement sin offering,* the established holocaust with its cereal
offering, and their libations.

**On the Feast of Booths.*** 12 "On the
fifteenth day of the seventh month you shall
hold a sacred assembly,[c] and do no sort of
work; then, for seven days following, you shall
celebrate a pilgrimage feast to the LORD.
13 You shall offer as a sweet-smelling holocaust to the LORD thirteen bullocks,* two rams,
and fourteen yearling lambs that are unblemished, 14 with their cereal offerings of fine
flour mixed with oil; offering three tenths of an
ephah for each of the thirteen bullocks, two
tenths for each of the two rams, 15 and one
tenth for each of the fourteen lambs. 16 Moreover, one goat shall be sacrificed as a sin offering. These are to be offered in addition to the
established holocaust with its cereal offering
and libation.
17 "On the second day you shall offer
twelve bullocks, two rams, and fourteen unblemished yearling lambs, 18 with their cereal
offerings and libations as prescribed for the
bullocks, rams and lambs in proportion to their
number, 19 as well as one goat for a sin offering, besides the established holocaust with its
cereal offering and libation.
20 "On the third day you shall offer eleven
bullocks, two rams, and fourteen unblemished
yearling lambs, 21 with their cereal offerings
and libations as prescribed for the bullocks,
rams and lambs in proportion to their number,
22 as well as one goat for a sin offering, besides
the established holocaust with its cereal offering
and libation.
23 "On the fourth day you shall offer ten
bullocks, two rams, and fourteen unblemished
yearling lambs, 24 with their cereal offerings
and libations as prescribed for the bullocks,
rams and lambs in proportion to their number,
25 as well as one goat for a sin offering, besides
the established holocaust with its cereal offering
and libation.
26 "On the fifth day you shall offer nine
bullocks, two rams, and fourteen unblemished
yearling lambs, 27 [d]with their cereal offerings
and libations as prescribed for the bullocks,
rams and lambs in proportion to their number,
28 as well as one goat for a sin offering, besides
the established holocaust with its cereal offering
and libation.
29 "On the sixth day you shall offer eight
bullocks, two rams, and fourteen unblemished
yearling lambs, 30 with their cereal offerings
and libations as prescribed for the bullocks,
rams and lambs in proportion to their number,
31 as well as one goat for a sin offering, besides
the established holocaust with its cereal offering
and libation.
32 "On the seventh day you shall offer seven
bullocks, two rams, and fourteen unblemished
yearling lambs, 33 with their cereal offerings
and libations as prescribed for the bullocks,
rams and lambs in proportion to their number,
34 as well as one goat for a sin offering, besides
the established holocaust with its cereal offering
and libation.
35 "On the eighth day[e] you shall hold a
solemn meeting,* and do no sort of work.
36 You shall offer up in holocaust as a
sweet-smelling oblation to the LORD one bullock, one ram, and seven unblemished yearling
lambs, 37 with their cereal offerings and libations as prescribed for the bullocks, rams and
lambs in proportion to their number, 38 as well
as one goat for a sin offering, besides the established holocaust with its cereal offering and libation.
39 "These are the offerings you shall make
to the LORD on your festivals, besides whatever
holocausts, cereal offerings, libations, and
peace offerings you present as your votive or
free-will offerings."

b Lv 16, 29; 23, 27f. 32.
c Lv 23, 34f.
d Nm 29, 30. 37.
e Lv 23, 36; Jn 7, 37.

*

29, 7: The tenth day of this seventh month: the Day of Atonement. Mortify yourselves: literally, "afflict your souls," that is, with fasting.

29, 11: The atonement sin offering: the bullock prescribed in Lv 16, 11f.

29, 12: This feast of Booths celebrating the vintage harvest was the most popular of all and therefore had the most elaborate ritual. See note on Lv 23, 34.

29, 13: Thirteen bullocks: the number of bullocks sacrificed before the octave day was seventy, arranged on a descending scale so that the number on the seventh day was the sacred number seven.

29, 35: A solemn meeting: the Hebrew word is the technical term for the closing celebration of the three major feasts of the Passover, Pentecost and Booths, or of other special feasts that lasted for a week. Cf Lv 23, 36; Dt 16, 8; 2 Chr 7, 9; Neh 8, 18.

## CHAPTER 30

**1** Moses then gave the Israelites these instructions, just as the LORD had ordered him.

**Validity and Annulment of Vows.** **2** Moses said to the heads of the Israelite tribes, "This is what the LORD has commanded: **3** When a man makes a vow to the LORD or binds himself under oath to a pledge* of abstinence, he shall not violate his word, but must fulfill exactly the promise he has uttered.[f]

**4** "When a woman, while still a maiden in her father's house, makes a vow to the LORD, or binds herself to a pledge, **5** if her father learns of her vow or the pledge to which she bound herself and says nothing to her about it, then any vow or any pledge she has made remains valid. **6** But if on the day he learns of it her father expresses to her his disapproval, then any vow or any pledge she has made becomes null and void; and the LORD releases her from it, since her father has expressed to her his disapproval.

**7** "If she marries while under a vow or under a rash pledge to which she bound herself, **8** and her husband learns of it, yet says nothing to her that day about it, then the vow or pledge she had made remains valid. **9** But if on the day he learns of it her husband expresses to her his disapproval, he thereby annuls the vow she had made or the rash pledge to which she had bound herself, and the LORD releases her from it. **10** The vow of a widow or of a divorced woman, or any pledge to which such a woman binds herself, is valid.

**11** "If it is in her husband's house* that she makes a vow or binds herself under oath to a pledge, **12** and her husband learns of it yet says nothing to express to her his disapproval, then any vow or any pledge she has made remains valid. **13** But if on the day he learns of them her husband annuls them, then whatever she has expressly promised in her vow or in her pledge becomes null and void; since her husband has annulled them, the LORD releases her from them.

**14** "Any vow or any pledge that she makes under oath to mortify herself, her husband can either allow to remain valid or render null and void. **15** But if her husband, day after day, says nothing at all to her about them, he thereby allows as valid any vow or any pledge she has made; he has allowed them to remain valid, because on the day he learned of them he said nothing to her about them. **16** If, however, he countermands them* some time after he first learned of them, he is responsible for her guilt."

**17** These are the statutes which the LORD prescribed through Moses concerning the relationship between a husband and his wife, as well as between a father and his daughter while she is still a maiden in her father's house.

## CHAPTER 31

**Extermination of the Midianites.** **1** The LORD said to Moses,* **2** "Avenge the Israelites on the Midianites, and then you shall be taken to your people." **3** So Moses told the people, "Select men from your midst and arm them for war, to attack the Midianites and execute the LORD's vengeance on them. **4** From each of the tribes of Israel you shall send a band of one thousand men to war." **5** From the clans of Israel, therefore, a thousand men of each tribe were levied, so that there were twelve thousand men armed for war. **6** Moses sent them out on the campaign, a thousand from each tribe, with Phinehas, son of Eleazar, the priest for the campaign, who had with him the sacred vessels and the trumpets for sounding the alarm. **7** They waged war against the Midianites, as the LORD had commanded Moses, and killed every male among them. **8** Besides those slain in battle, they killed the five Midianite kings:* Evi, Rekem, Zur, Hur and Reba; and they also executed Balaam, son of Beor, with the sword. **9** But the Israelites kept the women of the Midianites with their little ones as captives, and all their herds and flocks and wealth as spoil, **10** while they set on fire all the towns where they had settled and all their encampments. **11** Then they took all the booty, with the people and beasts they had captured, and brought the captives, together with the spoils and booty, **12** to Moses and the priest Eleazar and to the Israelite community at their camp on the plains of Moab, along the Jericho stretch of the Jordan.

**Treatment of the Captives.** **13** When Moses and the priest Eleazar, with all the princes of the community, went outside the camp to meet them, **14** Moses became angry with the officers of the army, the clan and company commanders, who were returning from combat. **15** "So you have spared all the women!" he exclaimed. **16** "Why, they are the very

f Dt 23, 22; Eccl 5, 3f. g 2 Pt 2, 15; Rv 2, 14.

*

30, 3: A vow . . . a pledge: here the former signifies the doing of some positive good deed, in particular the offering of some sacrifice; the latter signifies the abstaining from some otherwise licit action or pleasure; cf v 14.

30, 11: In her husband's house: after her marriage. This contrasts with the case given in vv 7ff.

30, 16: He countermands them: he prevents their fulfillment. Since he has first allowed the vows to remain valid, he can no longer annul them.

31, 1ff: The narrative of Israel's relations with Midian, which was interrupted after Nm 25, 18, is now resumed.

31, 8: The five Midianite kings: they are called "Midianite princes, Sihon's vassals" in Jos 13, 21.

ones who on Balaam's advice prompted the unfaithfulness of the Israelites toward the LORD in the Peor affair,[g] which began the slaughter of the LORD's community. **17** *Slay, therefore, every male child and every woman who has had intercourse with a man. **18** But you may spare and keep for yourselves all girls who had no intercourse with a man.

**Purification after Combat.** **19** "Moreover, you shall stay outside the camp for seven days, and those of you who have slain anyone or touched anyone slain in battle shall purify yourselves on the third and on the seventh day. This applies both to you and to your captives. **20** You shall also purify every article of cloth, leather, goats' hair, or wood."

**21** Eleazar the priest told the soldiers who had returned from combat: "This is what the law, as prescribed by the LORD to Moses, ordains: **22** Whatever can stand fire, such as gold, silver, bronze, iron, tin and lead, **23** you shall put into the fire, that it may become clean; however, it must also be purified with lustral water.* But whatever cannot stand fire you shall put into the water. **24** On the seventh day you shall wash your clothes, and then you will again be clean. After that you may enter the camp."

**Division of the Booty.** **25** The LORD said to Moses: **26** "With the help of the priest Eleazar and of the heads of the ancestral houses, count up all the human captives and the beasts that have been taken; **27** then divide them evenly,* giving half to those who took active part in the war by going out to combat, and half to the rest of the community. **28** You shall levy a tax for the LORD on the warriors who went out to combat: one out of every five hundred persons, oxen, asses and sheep **29** in their half of the spoil you shall turn over to the priest Eleazar as a contribution to the LORD. **30** From the Israelites' half you shall take one out of every fifty persons, and the same from the different beasts, oxen, asses and sheep, and give them to the Levites, who have charge of the LORD's Dwelling." **31** So Moses and the priest Eleazar did this, as the LORD had commanded Moses.

**Amount of Booty.** **32** This booty, what was left of the loot which the soldiers had taken, amounted to six hundred and seventy-five thousand sheep, **33** seventy-two thousand oxen, **34** sixty-one thousand asses, **35** and thirty-two thousand girls who were still virgins.

**36** The half that fell to those who had gone out to combat was: three hundred and thirty-seven thousand five hundred sheep, **37** of which six hundred and seventy-five fell as tax to the LORD; **38** thirty-six thousand oxen, of which seventy-two fell as tax to the LORD; **39** thirty thousand five hundred asses, of which sixty-one fell as tax to the LORD; **40** and sixteen thousand persons, of whom thirty-two fell as tax to the LORD. **41** The taxes contributed to the LORD, Moses gave to the priest Eleazar, as the LORD had commanded him.

**42** The half for the other Israelites, which fell to the community when Moses had taken it from the soldiers, was: **43** three hundred and thirty-seven thousand five hundred sheep, **44** thirty-six thousand oxen, **45** thirty thousand five hundred asses, **46** and sixteen thousand persons. **47** From this, the Israelites' share, Moses, as the LORD had ordered, took one out of every fifty, both of persons and of beasts, and gave them to the Levites, who had charge of the LORD's Dwelling.

**Gifts of the Officers.** **48** Then the officers who had been clan and company commanders of the army came up to Moses **49** and said to him, "Your servants have counted up the soldiers under our command, and not one is missing. **50** *So, to make atonement for ourselves before the LORD, each of us will bring as an offering to the LORD some gold article he has picked up, such as an anklet, a bracelet, a ring, an earring, or a necklace." **51** Moses and the priest Eleazar accepted this gold from them, all of it in well-wrought articles. **52** The gold that they gave as a contribution to the LORD amounted in all to sixteen thousand seven hundred and fifty shekels. This was from the clan and company commanders; **53** what the common soldiers had looted each one kept for himself. **54** Moses, then, and the priest Eleazar accepted the gold from the clan and company commanders, and put it in the meeting tent as a memorial for the Israelites before the LORD.

## CHAPTER 32

**Request of Gad and Reuben.** **1** Now the Reubenites and Gadites had a very large number of livestock. Noticing that the land of Jazer and

*

31, 17: There are later references to Midian in Jgs 6–8; 1 Kgs 11, 18; Is 60, 6. The present raid was only against those Midianites who were dwelling at this time near the encampment of the Israelites.

31, 23: Lustral water: water mixed with the ashes of the red heifer as prescribed in Nm 19, 9.

31, 27: Divide them evenly: for a similar division of the booty into two equal parts, between those who engaged in the fray and those who stayed with the baggage, cf 1 Sm 30, 24. But note that here the tax on the booty of the non-combatants is ten times as much as that on the soldier's booty.

31, 50: The precise nature and use of some of these articles of gold is not certain.

32, 1: Gilead: the name of the western part of the plateau east of the Jordan, sometimes signifying the whole region from the Yarmuk to the Jordan, sometimes only the northern part of this region, and sometimes, as here, only its southern part. Jazer lay to the east of southern Gilead.

of Gilead* was grazing country, **2** they came to Moses and the priest Eleazar and to the princes of the community and said, **3** *"The region of Ataroth, Dibon, Jazer, Nimrah, Heshbon, Elealeh, Sebam, Nebo and Baal-meon, **4** which the LORD has laid low before the community of Israel, is grazing country. Now, since your servants have livestock," **5** they continued, "if we find favor with you, let this land be given to your servants as their property. Do not make us cross the Jordan."

**Moses' Rebuke.** **6** But Moses answered the Gadites and Reubenites: "Are your kinsmen, then, to engage in war, while you remain here? **7** Why do you wish to discourage the Israelites from crossing to the land the LORD has given them? **8** That is just what your fathers did when I sent them from Kadesh-barnea to reconnoiter the land[h] **9** They went up to the Wadi Eshcol and reconnoitered the land, then so discouraged the Israelites that they would not enter the land the LORD had given them. **10** [i]At that time the wrath of the LORD flared up, and he swore, **11** 'Because they have not followed me unreservedly, none of these men of twenty years or more who have come up from Egypt shall ever see this country I promised under oath to Abraham and Isaac and Jacob, **12** [j]except the Kenizzite* Caleb, son of Jephunneh, and Joshua, son of Nun, who have followed the LORD unreservedly.' **13** So in his anger with the Israelites the LORD made them wander in the desert forty years, until the whole generation that had done evil in the sight of the LORD had died out. **14** And now here you are, a brood of sinners, rising up in your fathers' place to add still more to the LORD's blazing wrath against the Israelites. **15** If you turn away from following him, he will make them stay still longer in the desert, and so you will bring about the ruin of this whole nation."

**Counter Proposal.** **16** But they were insistent with him: "We wish only to build sheepfolds here for our flocks, and towns for our families; **17** but we ourselves will march as troops in the van of the Israelites,[k] until we have led them to their destination. Meanwhile our families can remain here in the fortified towns, safe from attack by the natives. **18** We will not return to our homes until every one of the Israelites has taken possession of his heritage, **19** [l]and will not claim any heritage with them once we cross the Jordan, so long as we receive a heritage for ourselves on this eastern side of the Jordan."

**Agreement Reached.** **20** *Moses said to them in reply: "If you keep your word to march as troops in the LORD's vanguard **21** and to cross the Jordan in full force before the LORD until he has driven his enemies out of his way **22** and the land is subdued before him, then you may return here, quit of every obligation to the LORD and to Israel, and this region shall be your possession before the LORD.[m] **23** But if you do not do this, you will sin against the LORD, and you can be sure that you will not escape the consequences of your sin. **24** Build the towns, then, for your families, and the folds for your flocks, but also fulfill your express promise."

**25** The Gadites and Reubenites answered Moses, "Your servants will do as you command, my lord. **26** [n]While our wives and children, our herds and other livestock remain in the towns of Gilead, **27** all your servants will go across as armed troops to battle before the LORD, just as your lordship says."

**28** Moses, therefore, gave this order in their regard to the priest Eleazar, to Joshua, son of Nun, and to the heads of the ancestral tribes of the Israelites: **29** "If all the Gadites and Reubenites cross the Jordan with you as combat troops before the LORD, you shall give them Gilead as their property when the land has been subdued before you. **30** But if they will not go across with you as combat troops before the LORD, you shall bring their wives and children and livestock across before you into Canaan, and they shall have their property with you in the land of Canaan."

**31** To this the Gadites and Reubenites replied, "We will do what the LORD has commanded us, your servants. **32** We ourselves will go across into the land of Canaan as troops before the LORD, but we will retain our hereditary property on this side of the Jordan." **33** So Moses gave them [* the Gadites and Reubenites, as well as half the tribe of Manasseh, son of Joseph, the kingdom of Sihon, king of the

h 8f: Nm 13, 31ff; Dt 1, 22.
i 10f: Dt 1, 34f.
j Nm 14, 24; Dt 1, 36.
k Jos 4, 12f.
l Jos 13, 8.
m Jos 1, 15.
n Jos 1, 14.
o Dt 3, 12; 29, 7; Jos 12, 6; 13, 8.

*

32, 3: The places named in this verse, as well as the additional ones given in vv 34–38, were all in the former kingdom of Sihon, that is, in the region between the Jabbok and the Arnon. Cf Nm 21, 23f; Jos 13, 19–21. 24–27.

32, 12: Kenizzite: a member of the clan of Kenaz, which, according to Gn 36, 11. 15. 42, was Edomitic; hence, although Caleb belonged to the tribe of Judah (Nm 13, 6; 34, 19), he must have had Edomite blood in his veins; cf also Jos 14, 6. 14.

32, 20ff: Since the ark of the Lord was borne into battle with the Israelite army, the vanguard was said to march before the Lord.

32, 33: The preceding is concerned solely with the two tribes of Gad and Reuben and with the land of the former kingdom of Sihon; hence it seems probable that the sudden reference here to the half-tribe of Manasseh and to their territory in Bashan, the former kingdom of Og, is a later addition to the text.

Amorites, and the kingdom of Og, king of Bashan,] the land with its towns and the districts
that surrounded them.[o]
**34** The Gadites rebuilt the fortified towns of
Dibon, Ataroth, Aroer, **35** Atroth-shophan, Jazer, Jogbehah, **36** Beth-nimrah and Beth-ha-
ran, and they built sheepfolds. **37** The Reubenites rebuilt Heshbon, Elealeh, Kiriathaim,
**38** Nebo, Baal-meon [names to be changed!],*
and Sibmah. These towns, which they rebuilt,
they called by their old names.

**Other Conquests.** **39** The descendants of
Machir, son of Manasseh, invaded Gilead and
captured it, driving out the Amorites who were
there. **40** [Moses gave Gilead to Machir,[p] son
of Manasseh, and he settled there.] **41** Jair,[q] a
Manassehite clan, campaigned against the tent
villages, captured them and called them Havvoth-jair. **42** Nobah also campaigned against
Kenath, captured it with its dependencies and
called it Nobah after his own name.

## CHAPTER 33

**Stages on the Journey.** **1** The following
are the stages by which the Israelites journeyed
up by companies from the land of Egypt under
the guidance of Moses and Aaron.* **2** By the
LORD's command Moses recorded the starting
places of the various stages. The starting places
of the successive stages were:

**3** *They set out from Rameses in the first
month,
on the fifteenth day of the first month.
On the Passover morrow the Israelites went
forth
in triumph, in view of all Egypt,
**4** While the Egyptians buried their first-born
all of whom the LORD had struck down;
on their gods, too, the LORD executed
judgments.[r]

**From Egypt to Sinai.** **5** Setting out from
Rameses, the Israelites camped at Succoth.
**6** Setting out from Succoth, they camped at
Etham near the edge of the desert. **7** Setting out
from Etham, they turned back to Pi-hahiroth,
which is opposite Baalzephon, and they camped
opposite Migdol.[s] **8** Setting out from Pi-hahiroth, they crossed over through the sea into the
desert,[t] and after a three days' journey in the
desert of Etham, they camped at Marah. **9** Setting out from Marah, they came to Elim, where
there were twelve springs of water and seventy
palm trees, and they camped there.[u] **10** Setting
out from Elim, they camped beside the Red Sea.
**11** Setting out from the Red Sea, they camped
in the desert of Sin. **12** Setting out from the
desert of Sin, they camped at Dophkah. **13** Setting out from Dophkah, they camped at Alush.
**14** Setting out from Alush, they camped at
Rephidim, where there was no water for the
people to drink.[v] **15** Setting out from Rephidim, they camped in the desert of Sinai.[w]

**From Sinai to Kadesh.** **16** Setting out
from the desert of Sinai, they camped at Kibroth-hattaavah. **17** Setting out from Kibroth-
hattaavah, they camped at Hazeroth.[x] **18** Setting out from Hazeroth, they camped at
Rithmah. **19** Setting out from Rithmah, they
camped at Rimmon-perez. **20** Setting out from
Rimmon-perez, they camped at Libnah.
**21** Setting out from Libnah, they camped at
Rissah. **22** Setting out from Rissah, they
camped at Kehelathah. **23** Setting out from Kehelathah, they camped at Mount Shepher.
**24** Setting out from Mount Shepher, they
camped at Haradah. **25** Setting out from Haradah, they camped at Makheloth. **26** Setting out
from Makheloth, they camped at Tahath.
**27** Setting out from Tahath, they camped at
Terah. **28** Setting out from Terah, they camped
at Mithkah. **29** Setting out from Mithkah, they
camped at Hashmonah. **30** *Setting out from
Hashmonah,—

**From Mount Hor to Ezion-geber.** They
camped at Moseroth. **31** Setting out from Moseroth, they camped at Bene-jaakan. **32** Setting
out from Bene-jaakan, they camped at Mount
Gidgad. **33** Setting out from Mount Gidgad,
they camped at Jotbathah. **34** Setting out from
Jotbathah, they camped at Abronah. **35** Setting

p Dt 3, 15.
q Dt 3, 14.
r 4f: Ex 12, 12. 29. 37.
s Ex 14, 2.
t Ex 15, 22.
u Ex 15, 27.
v Ex 17, 1.
w Ex 19, 2.
x 17f: Nm 11, 34f.

*

32, 38: The phrase in brackets is a gloss, warning the reader either to change the order of the preceding names, or, more probably, to read some other word, such as bosheth, "shame," for Baal. They called by their old names: literally, "they called by their names" (see Textual Notes); however, some understand the current Hebrew text to mean, "they called by new names."

33, 1ff: This list of camping sites was drawn up by Moses, as v 2 expressly states. However, in its present form it probably includes some glosses. Moreover, a comparison with the more detailed accounts of the journey as given elsewhere shows that this is not complete. It records just forty camping sites, not counting the starting place, Rameses, and the terminus, the plains of Moab. This number, which corresponds exactly to the forty years of wandering in the desert, is probably a schematic device. Besides, it seems that in its present form the order of some of these names has been disturbed. Several names listed here are not recorded elsewhere.

33, 3f: These two verses were probably borrowed from some ancient song celebrating the exodus from Egypt.

33, 30–36: Moseroth is mentioned in Dt 10, 6 (in the form of "Moserah"), as the place where Aaron died. It must therefore have been close to Mount Hor; cf Nm 20, 22ff. It seems very probable that the section vv 36b–41a stood originally immediately after v 30a.

out from Abronah, they camped at Ezion-geber.
**36** Setting out from Ezion-geber,—

**From Kadesh to Mount Hor.** They
camped in the desert of Zin, at Kadesh.[y]
**37** Setting out from Kadesh, they camped at
Mount Hor on the border of the land of Edom.
**38** [Aaron the priest ascended Mount Hor[z] at
the LORD's command, and there he died in the
fortieth year from the departure of the Israelites
from the land of Egypt, on the first day of the
fifth month. **39** Aaron was a hundred and twenty-three years old when he died on Mount Hor.
**40** *Now, when the Canaanite king of Arad,
who lived in the Negeb in the land of Canaan,
heard that the Israelites were coming. . . .]
**41** Setting out from Mount Hor,—

**From Ezion-geber to the Plains of Moab.*** They camped at Zalmonah. **42** Setting out from Zalmonah, they camped at Punon.
**43** Setting out from Punon, they camped at
Oboth. **44** Setting out from Oboth, they
camped at Iye-abarim on the border of Moab.
**45** Setting out from Iye-abarim, they camped at
Dibon-gad. **46** Setting out from Dibon-gad,
they camped at Almon-diblathaim. **47** Setting
out from Almon-diblathaim, they camped in the
Abarim Mountains opposite Nebo. **48** Setting
out from the Abarim Mountains, they camped
on the plains of Moab along the Jericho stretch
of the Jordan. **49** Their camp along the Jordan
on the plains of Moab extended from Beth-jeshimoth to Abel-shittim.

**Conquest and Division of Canaan.**
**50** The LORD spoke to Moses on the plains of
Moab beside the Jericho stretch of the Jordan
and said to him: **51** "Tell the Israelites: When
you go across the Jordan into the land of Canaan, **52** drive out all the inhabitants of the land
before you; destroy all their stone figures and
molten images, and demolish all their high
places.[a]

**53** "You shall take possession of the land
and settle in it, for I have given you the land as
your property. **54** You shall apportion the land
among yourselves by lot, clan by clan, assigning a large heritage to a large group and a small
heritage to a small group.[b] Wherever anyone's
lot falls, there shall his property be within the
heritage of his ancestral tribe.

**55** "But if you do not drive out the inhabitants of the land before you, those whom you
allow to remain will become as barbs in your
eyes and thorns in your sides, and they will
harass you in the country where you live,[c]
**56** and I will treat you as I had intended to treat
them."

## CHAPTER 34

**The Boundaries.** **1** The LORD said to Moses, **2** "Give the Israelites this order: When you
enter the land of Canaan, this is the territory that
shall fall to you as your heritage—the land of
Canaan with its boundaries:

**3** "Your southern boundary shall be at the
desert of Zin along the border of Edom;[d] on the
east it shall begin at the end of the Salt Sea,
**4** and turning south of the Akrabbim Pass, it
shall cross Zin, and extend south of Kadesh-barnea to Hazar-addar; thence it shall cross to Azmon,[e] **5** and turning from Azmon to the Wadi
of Egypt, shall terminate at the Sea.[f]

**6** "For your western boundary you shall
have the Great Sea* with its coast; this shall be
your western boundary.

**7** "The following shall be your boundary on
the north: from the Great Sea you shall draw a
line to Mount Hor,* **8** and shall continue it
from Mount Hor to Labo in the land of Hamath,
with the boundary extending through Zedad.
**9** Thence the boundary shall reach to Ziphron
and terminate at Hazar-enan. This shall be your
northern boundary.

**10** "For your eastern boundary you shall
draw a line from Hazar-enan to Shepham.
**11** From Shepham the boundary shall go down
to Ar-Baal, east of Ain, and descending further,
shall strike the ridge on the east side of the Sea
of Chinnereth; **12** thence the boundary shall
continue along the Jordan and terminate with
the Salt Sea.

"This is the land that shall be yours, with the
boundaries that surround it."

**13** Moses also gave this order to the Israelites: "This is the land, to be apportioned among
you by lot, which the LORD has commanded to
be given to the nine and one half tribes. **14** For
all the ancestral houses of the tribe of Reuben,
and the ancestral houses of the tribe of Gad, as
well as half of the tribe of Manasseh, have
already received their heritage; **15** these two
and one half tribes have received their heritage
on the eastern side of the Jericho stretch of the
Jordan, toward the sunrise."

---

y 36f: Nm 20, 1. 22.
z Nm 20, 25; Dt 32, 50.
a Ex 23, 31; 34, 13; Dt 7, 5; 12, 3.
b Nm 26, 53ff.
c Jos 23, 13; Jgs 2, 3.
d Jos 15, 1f.
e Jos 15, 3.
f Jos 15, 4.

---

33, 40: The verse begins the same account of the victory over Arad as is given in Nm 21, 1ff, where it also follows the account of Aaron's death.

33, 41b–49: It seems that this section stood originally immediately after v 36a.

34, 6: The Great Sea: the Mediterranean.

34, 7f: Mount Hor: different from the one where Aaron died; cf Nm 20, 22; 33, 37f.

**Supervisors of the Allotment.** 16 The
LORD said to Moses, 17 "These are the names
of the men who shall apportion the land among
you: Eleazar the priest, and Joshua, son of Nun,
18 [g]and one prince from each of the tribes
whom you shall designate for this task.
19 These shall be as follows:

from the tribe of Judah: Caleb, son of Jephunneh;
20 from the tribe of Simeon: Samuel, son of Ammihud;
21 from the tribe of Benjamin: Elidad, son of Chislon;
22 from the tribe of Dan: Bukki, son of Jogli;
23 from the tribe of Manasseh: Hanniel, son of Ephod; and
24 from the tribe of Ephraim: Kemuel, son of Shiphtan, for the descendants of Joseph;
25 from the tribe of Zebulun: Elizaphan, son of Parnach;
26 from the tribe of Issachar: Paltiel, son of Azzan;
27 from the tribe of Asher: Ahihud, son of Shelomi;
28 from the tribe of Naphtali: Pedahel, son of Ammihud."

29 These are they whom the LORD commanded
to assign the Israelites their heritage in the land
of Canaan.

## CHAPTER 35

**Cities for the Levites.** 1 The LORD gave
these instructions to Moses on the plains of
Moab beside the Jericho stretch of the Jordan:
2 [h]"Tell the Israelites that out of their hereditary property they shall give the Levites cities
for homes, as well as pasture lands around the
cities. 3 The cities shall serve them to dwell in,
and the pasture lands shall serve their herds and
flocks and other animals. 4 The pasture lands of
the cities to be assigned the Levites shall extend
a thousand cubits from the city walls in each
direction. 5 Thus you shall measure out two
thousand cubits outside the city along each
side—east, south, west and north—with the city
lying in the center. This shall serve them as the
pasture lands of their cities.

6 [i]"Now these are the cities you shall give
to the Levites: the six cities of asylum which you
must establish as places where a homicide can
take refuge, and in addition forty-two other cities— 7 a total of forty-eight cities with their
pasture lands to be assigned the Levites. 8 *In
assigning the cities from the property of the
Israelites, take more from a larger group and
fewer from a smaller one, so that each group
will cede cities to the Levites in proportion to its
own heritage."

**Cities of Asylum.** 9 The LORD said to Moses, 10 "Tell the Israelites: When you go
across the Jordan into the land of Canaan,
11 select for yourselves cities[j] to serve as cities
of asylum, where a homicide who has killed
someone unintentionally may take refuge.
12 These cities shall serve you as places of
asylum from the avenger of blood,* so that a
homicide shall not be put to death unless he is
first tried before the community. 13 Six cities
of asylum shall you assign: 14 three beyond the
Jordan, and three in the land of Canaan.
15 These six cities of asylum shall serve not
only the Israelites but all the resident or transient
aliens among them, so that anyone who has
killed another unintentionally may take refuge
there.

**Murder and Manslaughter.** 16 *"If a
man strikes another with an iron instrument and
causes his death, he is a murderer and shall be
put to death.[k] 17 If a man strikes another with
a death-dealing stone in his hand and causes his
death, he is a murderer and shall be put to death.
18 If a man strikes another with a death-dealing
club in his hand and causes his death, he is a
murdered and shall be put to death. 19 The
avenger of blood may execute the murderer,
putting him to death on sight.

20 "If a man pushes another out of hatred,
or after lying in wait for him throws something
at him, and causes his death,[l] 21 or if he strikes
another out of enmity and causes his death, he
shall be put to death as a murderer. The avenger
of blood may execute the murderer on sight.

22 [m]"However, if a man pushes another accidentally and not out of enmity, or if without
lying in wait for him he throws some object at
him, 23 or without seeing him throws a
death-dealing stone which strikes him and
causes his death, although he was not his enemy
nor seeking to harm him: 24 then the community, deciding the case between the slayer and the
avenger of blood in accordance with these
norms, 25 shall free the homicide from the
avenger of blood and shall remand him to the
city of asylum where he took refuge;[n] and he
shall stay there until the death of the high priest
who has been anointed with sacred oil. 26 If the

g Nm 1, 4.
h Jos 14, 3f; 21, 2.
i Dt 4, 41f; Jos 20, 2.
j 10ff: Dt 19, 2; Jos 20, 2ff.
k Ex 21, 12; Lv 24, 17.
l Ex 21, 14; Dt 19, 11.
m Jos 20, 3.
n Jos 20, 6.

*

35, 8: This provision was hardly observed in the actual assignment of the levitical cities as narrated in Jos 21.

35, 12: The avenger of blood: one of the close relatives of the slain (2 Sm 14, 7) who, as executor of public justice, had the right and duty to take the life of the murderer; cf Dt 19, 6. 12; Jos 20, 3. 5. 9.

35, 16–25: Here, as also in Dt 19, 1–13, there is a casuistic development of the original law as stated in Ex 21, 12ff.

homicide of his own accord leaves the bounds
of the city of asylum where he has taken refuge,
**27** and the avenger of blood finds him beyond
these bounds and kills him, the avenger incurs
no blood-guilt; **28** the homicide was bound to
stay in his city of asylum until the death of the
high priest. Only after the death of the high
priest may the homicide return to his own district.

**29** "These shall be norms for you and all
your descendants, wherever you live, for rendering judgment.

**Witnesses.** **30** "Whenever someone kills
another, the evidence of witnesses is required
for the execution of the murderer.[o] The evidence of a single witness is not sufficient for
putting a person to death.

**No Indemnity.** **31** "You shall not accept
indemnity in place of the life of a murderer who
deserves the death penalty; he must be put to
death. **32** Nor shall you accept indemnity to
allow a refugee to leave his city of asylum and
again dwell elsewhere in the land before the
death of the high priest. **33** You shall not desecrate the land where you live. Since bloodshed
desecrates the land, the land can have no atonement for the blood shed on it except through the
blood of him who shed it. **34** Do not defile the
land in which you live and in the midst of which
I dwell;[p] for I am the LORD who dwells; in the
midst of the Israelites."

## CHAPTER 36

**Property of Heiresses.** **1** The heads of the
ancestral houses in the clan of descendants of
Gilead, son of Machir, son of Manasseh—one
of the Josephite clans—came up and laid this
plea before Moses and the priest Eleazar and
before the princes who were the heads of the
ancestral houses of the other Israelites. **2** They
said: "The LORD commanded you, my lord, to
apportion the land by lot among the Israelites;[q]
and you, my lord, were also commanded by the
LORD to give the heritage of our kinsman Zelophehad to his daughters. **3** But if they marry
into one of the other Israelite tribes, their heritage will be withdrawn from our ancestral heritage and will be added to that of the tribe into
which they marry; thus the heritage that fell to
us by lot will be diminished. **4** When the Israelites celebrate the jubilee year,* the heritage of
these women will be permanently added to that
of the tribe into which they marry and will be
withdrawn from that of our ancestral tribe."

**5** *So Moses gave this regulation to the Israelites according to the instructions of the LORD:
"The tribe of the Josephites are right in what
they say. **6** This is what the LORD commands
with regard to the daughters of Zelophehad:
They may marry anyone they please, provided
they marry into a clan of their ancestral tribe,
**7** so that no heritage of the Israelites will pass
from one tribe to another, but all the Israelites
will retain their own ancestral heritage.
**8** Therefore, every daughter who inherits property in any of the Israelite tribes shall marry
someone belonging to a clan of her own ancestral tribe, in order that all the Israelites may
remain in possession of their own ancestral heritage. **9** Thus, no heritage can pass from one
tribe to another, but all the Israelite tribes will
retain their own ancestral heritage."

**10** The daughters of Zelophehad obeyed the
command which the LORD had given to Moses.
**11** Mahlah, Tirzah, Hoglah, Milcah and Noah,
Zelophehad's daughters, married relatives on
their father's side **12** within the clans of the
descendants of Manasseh, son of Joseph; hence
their heritage remained in the tribe of their father's clan.

**Conclusion.** **13** These are the commandments and decisions which the LORD prescribed
for the Israelites through Moses, on the plains
of Moab beside the Jericho stretch of the Jordan.

o Dt 17, 6; 19, 15; Jn 8, 17; 2 Cor 13, 1; 1 Tm 5, 19.
p Ex 29, 45.
q Nm 26, 55; 27, 6; Jos 17, 3f.

*

36, 4: Before the jubilee year various circumstances, such as divorce, could make such property revert to its original tribal owners; but in the jubilee year it became irrevocably attached to its new owners.

36, 5–9: This is a supplement to the law given in Nm 27, 5–11.

# The Book of
# DEUTERONOMY

*The fifth and last book of the Pentateuch is called Deuteronomy, meaning "second law." In reality, what it contains is not a new law but a partial repetition, completion and explanation of the law proclaimed on Mount Sinai. The historical portions of the book are also a résumé of what is related elsewhere in the Pentateuch. The chief characteristic of this book is its vigorous oratorical style. In a series of eloquent discourses Moses presents the theme of covenant renewal in a vital religious framework. He exhorts, corrects and threatens his people, appealing to their past glory, their historic mission and the promise of future triumph. His aim is to enforce among the Israelites the Lord's claim to their obedience, loyalty and love. The events contained in the Book of Deuteronomy took place in the plains of Moab (Dt 1, 5) between the end of the wanderings in the desert (Dt 1, 3) and the crossing of the Jordan River (Jos 4, 19), a period of no more than forty days. The Book of Deuteronomy, written after the Israelites had for centuries been resident in the Land of Promise, takes the form of a testament of Moses, the great leader and legislator, to his people on the eve of his death. At the time of our Lord's coming, it shared with the Psalms a preeminent religious influence among the Old Testament books. The Savior quoted passages of Deuteronomy in overcoming the threefold temptation of Satan in the desert (Mt 4; Dt 6, 13. 16; 8, 3; 10, 20), and in explaining to the lawyer the first and greatest commandment (Mt 22, 35–39; Dt 6, 4).*

*The book is divided as follows:*

*I. Historical Review and Exhortation (Dt 1, 1—4, 43).*
*II. God and His Covenant (Dt 4, 44—11, 32).*
*III. Exposition of the Law (Dt 12, 1—26, 19).*
*IV. Final Words of Moses (Dt 27, 1—34, 12).*

## I: *Historical Review and Exhortation*

### CHAPTER 1

**Introduction.** 1 These are the words which
Moses spoke to all Israel beyond the Jordan [*
in the desert, in the Arabah, opposite Suph,
between Paran and Tophel, Laban, Hazeroth
and Dizahab; 2 it is a journey of eleven days
from Horeb to Kadesh-barnea by way of the
highlands of Seir].
3 In the fortieth year, on the first day of the
eleventh month, Moses spoke to the Israelites
all the commands that the LORD had given him
in their regard. 4 After he had defeated Sihon,
king of the Amorites, who lived in Heshbon,[a]
and Og, king of Bashan, who lived in Ashtaroth
and in Edrei, 5 Moses began to explain the law
in the land of Moab beyond the Jordan, as follows:

**Departure from Horeb.** 6 "The LORD,
our God, said to us at Horeb, 'You have stayed
long enough at this mountain. 7 *Leave here
and go to the hill country of the Amorites and
to all the surrounding regions,[b] the land of the
Canaanites in the Arabah, the mountains, the
foothills, the Negeb and the seacoast; to Lebanon, and as far as the Great River [the Euphrates]. 8 I have given that land over to you.[c] Go
now and occupy the land I swore to your fathers,
Abraham, Isaac and Jacob, I would give to them
and to their descendants.'

**Appointment of Elders.** 9 "At that time
I said to you, 'Alone, I am unable to carry you.*
10 The LORD, your God, has so multiplied you

a Dt 3, 2; Nm 21, 21-35.
b Nm 13, 29.
c Gn 12, 7; 15, 18; 17, 7f; 28, 13f.
d Dt 10, 22; Gn 15, 5.

1, 1: The local setting of all these discourses is in the land of Moab beyond the Jordan (cf v 5), also known as the plains of Moab (Nm 36, 13).

1, 7: The Amorites and the Canaanites formed the principal part of the pre-Israelite population of Palestine. The foothills: the hills on the western slope of the Judean mountain range. The Arabah: the valley of the Jordan and the depression south of the Dead Sea. The Negeb: the arid land in southern Palestine.

1, 9: Carry you; cf v 31.

that you are now as numerous as the stars in the
sky.[d] **11** May the LORD, the God of your fathers, increase you a thousand times over, and
bless you as he promised! **12** But how can I
alone bear the crushing burden that you are,
along with your bickering? **13** [e]Choose wise,
intelligent and experienced men from each of
your tribes, that I may appoint them as your
leaders.' **14** You answered me, 'We agree to do
as you have proposed.' **15** So I took outstanding men of your tribes, wise and experienced,
and made them your leaders as officials over
thousands, over hundreds, over fifties and over
tens, and other tribal officers. **16** I charged your
judges at that time, 'Listen to complaints among
your kinsmen, and administer true justice to
both parties even if one of them is an alien.[f]
**17** In rendering judgment, do not consider who
a person is; give ear to the lowly and to the great
alike, fearing no man, for judgment is God's.
Refer to me any case that is too hard for you and
I will hear it.' **18** Thereupon I gave you all the
commands you were to fulfill.

**The Twelve Scouts.** **19** "Then, in obedience to the command of the LORD, our God, we
set out from Horeb and journeyed through the
whole desert, vast and fearful as you have
seen,[g] in the direction of the hill country of the
Amorites. We had reached Kadesh-barnea
**20** when I said to you, 'You have come to the
hill country of the Amorites, which the LORD,
our God, is giving us. **21** The LORD, your God,
has given this land over to you. Go up and
occupy it, as the LORD, the God of your fathers,
commands you. Do not fear or lose heart.'
**22** [h]Then all of you came up to me and said,
'Let us send men ahead to reconnoiter the land
for us and report to us on the road we must
follow and the cities we must take.' **23** Agreeing with the proposal, I chose twelve men from
your number, one from each tribe. **24** They set
out into the hill country as far as the Wadi
Eshcol, and explored it. **25** Then, taking along
some of the fruit of the land, they brought it
down to us and reported, 'The land which the
LORD, our God, gives us is good.'

**Threats of Revolt.** **26** "But you refused to
go up,[i] and after defying the command of the
LORD, your God, **27** you set to murmuring in
your tents,* 'Out of hatred for us the LORD has
brought us up out of the land of Egypt,[j] to
deliver us into the hands of the Amorites and
destroy us. **28** What shall we meet with up
there? Our kinsmen have made us fainthearted
by reporting that the people are stronger and
taller than we, and their cities are large and
fortified to the sky; besides, they saw the Anakim there.'[k]
**29** "But I said to you, 'Have no dread or fear
of them. **30** The LORD, your God, who goes
before you, will himself fight for you, just as he
took your part before your very eyes in Egypt,
**31** as well as in the desert, where you saw how
the LORD, your God, carried you, as a man
carries his child, all along your journey until
you arrived at this place.' **32** Despite this, you
would not trust the LORD, your God, **33** who
journeys before you to find you a resting
place—by day in the cloud, and by night in the
fire, to show the way you must go.[l] **34** When
the LORD heard your words, he was angry;
**35** and he swore, 'Not one man of this evil
generation shall look upon the good land I swore
to give to your fathers,[m] **36** except Caleb,* son
of Jephunneh; he shall see it. For to him and to
his sons I will give the land he trod upon, because he has followed the LORD unreservedly.'
**37** "The LORD was angered against me also
on your account, and said, 'Not even you shall
enter there,[n] **38** but your aide Joshua,[o] son of
Nun, shall enter. Encourage him, for he is to
give Israel its heritage. **39** Your little ones, who
you said would become booty, and your children, who as yet do not know good from bad
—they shall enter; to them I will give it, and
they shall occupy it.[p] **40** But as for yourselves:
turn about and proceed into the desert on the
Red Sea road.'

**Unsuccessful Invasion.** **41** [q]"In reply
you said to me, 'We have sinned against the
LORD. We will go up ourselves and fight, just
as the LORD, our God, commanded us.' And
each of you girded on his weapons, making light
of going up into the hill country. **42** But the
LORD said to me, 'Warn them: Do not go up and
fight, lest you be beaten down before your enemies, for I will not be in your midst.' **43** I gave
you this warning but you would not listen. In
defiance of the LORD's command you arrogantly
marched off into the hill country. **44** Then the
Amorites living there came out against you and,
like bees, chased you, cutting you down in Seir
as far as Hormah. **45** On your return you wept
before the LORD, but he did not listen to your cry
or give ear to you. **46** That is why you had to
stay as long as you did at Kadesh.

---

e 13ff: Ex 18, 21-25.
f 16f: Ex 18, 26; 2 Chr 19, 6f; Prv 24, 23; Jn 7, 24; Jas 2, 9.
g Dt 8, 15; 32, 10.
h 22-28: Nm 13, 2-34.
i Dt 9, 23.
j Dt 9, 28; Nm 14, 1-4; Ps 106, 25.
k Dt 9, 1f.
l Ex 13, 21; Nm 10, 33f; 14, 14.
m 34ff: Nm 14, 22f. 28-38; Jos 14, 9.
n Dt 4, 21; 34, 4; Nm 20, 12.
o Dt 31, 3. 7; Nm 27, 18ff; 34, 17.
p 39f: Nm 14, 31.
q 41-45: Nm 14, 40. 42-45.

---

1, 27: In your tents: among yourselves.

1, 36: Except Caleb: Joshua also was allowed to enter, but he is not referred to here because special mention is made of him in v 38 as the successor of Moses.

## CHAPTER 2

**Northward along Edom.** 1 "When we
did turn and proceed into the desert on the Red
Sea road,[r] as the LORD had commanded me, we
circled around the highlands of Seir for a long
time. 2 Finally the LORD said to me, 3 'You
have wandered round these highlands long
enough; turn and go north. 4 Give this order to
the people: You are now about to pass through
the territory of your kinsmen, the descendants
of Esau, who live in Seir. Though they are
afraid of you, be very careful 5 not to come in
conflict with them, for I will not give you so
much as a foot of their land, since I have already
given Esau possession of the highlands of Seir.
6 You shall purchase from them with silver the
food you eat and the well water you drink.
7 The LORD, your God, has blessed you in all
your undertakings; he has been concerned about
your journey through this vast desert. It is now
forty years that he has been with you, and you
have never been in want.'[s]

**Along Moab.** 8 "Then we left behind us the
Arabah route, Elath, Ezion-geber, and Seir,
where our kinsmen, the descendants of Esau,
live; and we went on toward the desert of
Moab.[t] 9 And the LORD said to me, 'Do not
show hostility to the Moabites or engage them
in battle, for I will not give you possession of
any of their land, since I have given Ar to the
descendants of Lot as their own.[u] 10 [Formerly
the Emim lived there, a people strong and numerous and tall like the Anakim;[v] 11 like them
they were considered Rephaim. It was the Moabites who called them Emim. 12 In Seir, however, the former inhabitants were the Horites;[w]
the descendants of Esau dispossessed them,
clearing them out of the way and taking their
place, just as the Israelites have done in the land
of their heritage which the LORD has given
them.] 13 Get ready, then, to cross the Wadi
Zered.'[x] So we crossed it. 14 Thirty-eight
years had elapsed between our departure from
Kadesh-barnea and that crossing; in the meantime the whole generation of soldiers had perished from the camp, as the LORD had sworn
they should.[y] 15 For it was the LORD's hand
that was against them, till he wiped them out of
the camp completely.

**Along Ammon.** 16 "When at length death
had put an end to all the soldiers among the
people, 17 the LORD said to me, 18 'You are
now about to leave Ar and the territory of Moab
behind. 19 As you come opposite the Ammonites,[z] do not show hostility or come in conflict
with them, for I will not give you possession of
any land of the Ammonites, since I have given
it to the descendants of Lot as their own.
20 [This also was considered a country of the
Rephaim from its former inhabitants, whom the
Ammonites called Zamzummim, 21 a people
strong and numerous and tall like the Anakim.
But these, too, the LORD cleared out of the way
for the Ammonites, who ousted them and took
their place. 22 He had done the same for the
descendants of Esau, who dwell in Seir, by
clearing the Horites out of their way, so that the
descendants of Esau have taken their place
down to the present. 23 So also the Caphtorim,* migrating from Caphtor, cleared away
the Avvim, who once dwelt in villages as far as
Gaza, and took their place.]

**Defeat of Sihon.** 24 " 'Advance now
across the Wadi Arnon.[a] I now deliver into your
hands Sihon, the Amorite king of Heshbon, and
his land. Begin the occupation; engage him in
battle. 25 This day I will begin to put a fear and
dread of you into every nation under the heavens, so that at the mention of your name they
will quake and tremble before you.'
26 "So I sent messengers from the desert of
Kedemoth to Sihon, king of Heshbon, with this
offer of Peace: 27 'Let me pass through your
country by the highway; I will go along it without turning aside to the right or to the left.
28 For the food I eat which you will supply, and
for the water you give me to drink, you shall be
paid in silver. Only let me march through, 29 as
the descendants of Esau who dwell in Seir[b] and
the Moabites who dwell in Ar have done, until
I cross the Jordan into the land which the LORD,
our God, is about to give us.' 30 But Sihon,
king of Heshbon, refused to let us pass through
his land, because the LORD, your God, made
him stubborn in mind and obstinate in heart that
he might deliver him up to you, as indeed he has
now done.
31 "Then the LORD said to me, 'Now that I
have already begun to hand over to you Sihon
and his land, begin the actual occupation.'
32 So Sihon and all his people advanced against
us to join battle at Jahaz; 33 but since the LORD,
our God, had delivered him to us, we defeated
him and his sons and all his people.[c] 34 At that
time we seized all his cities and doomed* them
all, with their men, women and children; we left

r Dt 1, 40; Nm 14, 25; 21, 4.
s Dt 8, 2ff.
t Jgs 11, 18.
u Gn 19, 36f.
v Dt 1, 28.
w Gn 36, 20f.
x Nm 21, 12.
y Nm 14, 29. 33. 35.
z Gn 19, 38.
a Nm 21, 13; Jgs 11, 19-22.
b Dt 2, 5. 8f; Jgs 11, 17.
c Dt 29, 7; Nm 21, 23-32.
d Dt 3, 6; 29, 7f.

*

2, 23: The Caphtorim: members of one of the groups of sea peoples who invaded the coast of Egypt and the southern part of Palestine about 1200 B.C. Caphtor: the ancient name of the island of Crete. Cf Am 9, 7.

2, 34: Doomed: see notes on Nm 18, 14; 21, 3.

no survivor.[d] **35** Our only booty was the livestock and the loot of the captured cities.
**36** From Aroer on the edge of the Wadi Arnon
and from the city in the wadi itself, as far as
Gilead,[e] no city was too well fortified for us to
whom the LORD had delivered them up.
**37** However, in obedience to the command of
the LORD, our God, you did not encroach upon
any of the Ammonite land, neither the region
bordering on the Wadi Jabbok, nor the cities of
the highlands.[f]

## CHAPTER 3

**Defeat of Og.** **1** "Then we turned and proceeded toward Bashan. But Og, king of Bashan,[g] advanced against us with all his people
to give battle at Edrei. **2** The LORD, however,
said to me,[h] 'Do not be afraid of him, for I have
delivered him into your hand with all his people
and his land. Do to him as you did to Sihon,
king of the Amorites, who lived in Heshbon.'
**3** And thus the LORD, our God, delivered into
our hands Og, king of Bashan, with all his
people. We defeated him so completely that we
left him no survivor. **4** At that time we captured
all his cities, none of them eluding our grasp,
the whole region of Argob, the kingdom of Og
in Bashan: sixty cities in all, **5** to say nothing
of the great number of unwalled towns. All the
cities were fortified with high walls and gates
and bars. **6** [i]As we had done to Sihon, king of
Heshbon, so also here we doomed all the cities,
with their men, women and children; **7** but all
the livestock and the loot of each city we took
as booty for ourselves.

**8** "And so at that time we took from the two
kings of the Amorites beyond the Jordan the
territory from the Wadi Arnon to Mount Hermon **9** [which is called Sirion by the Sidonians
and Senir by the Amorites], **10** comprising all
the cities of the plateau and all Gilead and all the
cities of the kingdom of Og in Bashan including
Salecah and Edrei. **11** [Og, king of Bashan,
was the last remaining survivor of the Rephaim.
He had a bed of iron,* nine regular cubits long
and four wide, which is still preserved in Rabbah of the Ammonites.]

**Allotment of the Conquered Lands.**
**12** [j]"When we occupied the land at that time,
I gave Reuben and Gad the territory from Aroer,
on the edge of the Wadi Arnon, halfway up into
the highlands of Gilead, with the cities therein.
**13** The rest of Gilead and all of Bashan, the
kingdom of Og, the whole Argob region, I gave
to the half-tribe of Manasseh. [All this region of
Bashan was once called a land of the Rephaim.
**14** Jair, a Manassehite clan,[k] took all the region
of Argob as far as the border of the Geshurites
and Maacathites, and called it after his own
name Bashan Havvoth-jair, the name it bears
today.] **15** To Machir I gave Gilead, **16** and to
Reuben and Gad the territory from Gilead to the
Wadi Arnon—including the wadi bed and its
banks—and to the Wadi Jabbok, which is the
border of the Ammonites, **17** as well as the
Arabah with the Jordan and its eastern banks
from Chinnereth to the Salt Sea of the Arabah,
under the slopes of Pisgah.[l]

**18** "At that time I charged them* as follows:
'The LORD, your God, has given you this land
as your own. But all you troops equipped for
battle must cross over in the vanguard of your
brother Israelites.[m] **19** Only your wives and
children, as well as your livestock, of which I
know you have a large number, shall remain
behind in the towns I have given you,[n] **20** until
the LORD has settled your kinsmen as well, and
they too possess the land which the LORD, your
God, will give them on the other side of the
Jordan.[o] Then you may all return to the possessions I have given you.'

**21** "It was then that I instructed Joshua,
'Your eyes have seen all that the LORD, your
God, has done to both these kings; so, too, will
the LORD do to all the kingdoms which you will
encounter over there. **22** Fear them not, for the
LORD, your God, will fight for you.'

**Refusal to Moses.** **23** "And it was then
that I besought the LORD, **24** 'O LORD God, you
have begun to show to your servant your greatness and might. For what god in heaven or on
earth can perform deeds as mighty as yours?
**25** Ah, let me cross over and see this good land
beyond the Jordan, this fine hill country, and the
Lebanon!' **26** But the LORD was angry with me
on your account and would not hear me.[p]
'Enough!' the LORD said to me. 'Speak to me
no more of this. **27** Go up to the top of Pisgah
and look out to the west, and to the north, and
to the south, and to the east. Look well, for you
shall not cross this Jordan.[q] **28** Commission
Joshua,[r] and encourage and strengthen him, for
he shall cross at the head of this people and shall
put them in possession of the land you are to
see.' **29** This was while we were in the ravine
opposite Beth-peor.

---

e Dt 3, 12; Jos 13, 9. 16; Jgs 11, 26.
f Nm 21, 24; Jos 12, 2.
g Dt 29, 6; Nm 21, 33.
h 2f: Nm 21, 34f.
i Ps 135, 10ff.
j 12f: Nm 32, 29. 32f; Jos 13, 8. 29.
k Nm 32, 41; Jos 13, 11. 13.
l Dt 4, 49; Jos 12, 3.
m Jos 1, 14; 4, 12.
n Nm 32, 1. 4; Jos 1, 14.
o Jos 22, 4.
p Dt 4, 21.
q Dt 34, 4; Nm 27, 12f.
r Dt 1, 38; 31, 7; Nm 27, 22f.

*

3, 11: Bed of iron: some translate, "a sarcophagus of basalt."

3, 18: I charged them: the words which follow were spoken to the men of Reuben and Gad (cf Nm 32).

## CHAPTER 4

**Advantages of Fidelity.** 1 "Now, Israel,
hear the statutes and decrees which I am teaching you to observe, that you may live, and may
enter in and take possession of the land which
the LORD, the God of your fathers, is giving
you. **2** In your observance of the commandments of the LORD, your God,[s] which I enjoin
upon you, you shall not add to what I command
you nor subtract from it. **3** You have seen with
your own eyes what the LORD did at Baal-peor:[t]
the LORD, your God, destroyed from your midst
everyone that followed the Baal of Peor; **4** but
you, who clung to the LORD, your God, are all
alive today. **5** Therefore, I teach you the statutes and decrees as the LORD, my God, has
commanded me, that you may observe them in
the land you are entering to occupy. **6** Observe
them carefully, for thus will you give evidence
of your wisdom and intelligence to the nations,
who will hear of all these statutes and say, 'This
great nation is truly a wise and intelligent people.' **7** [u]For what great nation is there that has
gods so close to it as the LORD, our God, is to
us whenever we call upon him? **8** Or what great
nation has statutes and decrees that are as just
as this whole law which I am setting before you
today?

**Revelation at Horeb.** 9 "However, take
care and be earnestly on your guard not to forget
the things which your own eyes have seen, nor
let them slip from your memory as long as you
live, but teach them to your children[v] and to
your children's children: **10** *There was the day
on which you stood before the LORD, your God,
at Horeb, and he said to me,[w] 'Assemble the
people for me; I will have them hear my words,
that they may learn to fear me as long as they
live in the land and may so teach their children.'
**11** You came near and stood at the foot of the
mountain,[x] which blazed to the very sky with
fire and was enveloped in a dense black cloud.
**12** Then the LORD spoke to you from the midst
of the fire.[y] You heard the sound of the words,
but saw no form; there was only a voice. **13** He
proclaimed to you his covenant, which he commanded you to keep: the ten commandments,
which he wrote on two tablets of stone. **14** The
LORD charged me at that time to teach you the
statutes and decrees which you are to observe
over in the land you will occupy.

**Danger of Idolatry.** 15 "You saw no form
at all on the day the LORD spoke to you at Horeb
from the midst of the fire.[z] Be strictly on your
guard, therefore, **16** not to degrade yourselves
by fashioning an idol to represent any figure,
whether it be the form of a man or of a woman,[a]
**17** of any animal on the earth or of any bird that
flies in the sky, **18** of anything that crawls on
the ground or of any fish in the waters under the
earth. **19** And when you look up to the heavens
and behold the sun or the moon or any star
among the heavenly hosts, do not be led astray
into adoring them and serving them.[b] These the
LORD, your God, has let fall to the lot of all
other nations under the heavens; **20** but you he
has taken and led out of that iron foundry,*
Egypt, that you might be his very own people,
as your are today.[c] **21** Since the LORD was
angered against me on your account[d] and swore
that I should not cross the Jordan nor enter the
good land which he is giving you as a heritage,
**22** I myself shall die in this country without
crossing the Jordan; but you will cross over and
take possession of that good land.[e] **23** Take
heed, therefore, lest, forgetting the covenant
which the LORD, your God, has made with you,
you fashion for yourselves against his command
an idol in any form whatsoever.[f] **24** For the
LORD, your God, is a consuming fire, a jealous
God.

**God's Fidelity.** 25 "When you have children and grandchildren, and have grown old* in
the land, should you then degrade yourselves by
fashioning an idol in any form and by this evil
done in his sight provoke the LORD, your God,
**26** I call heaven and earth this day to witness
against you, that you shall all quickly perish
from the land which you will occupy when you
cross the Jordan. You shall not live in it for any
length of time but shall be promptly wiped out.
**27** The LORD will scatter you among the nations, and there shall remain but a handful of
you among the nations to which the LORD will
lead you.[g] **28** There you shall serve gods fashioned by the hands of man out of wood and
stone, gods which can neither see nor hear,
neither eat nor smell.[h] **29** Yet there too you
shall seek the LORD, your God; and you shall
indeed find him when you search after him with

s Dt 13, 1.
t Nm 25, 3-9.
u 2 Sm 7, 23.
v Dt 11, 19; Ps 78, 3-6.
w Heb 12, 18f.
x Ex 19, 17f.
y Dt 4, 33. 36; 5, 4.
z Ex 24, 12; 31, 18; 34, 28.
a Dt 5, 8; Ex 20, 4.
b Dt 17, 3; Jb 31, 26ff.
c 1 Kgs 8, 51; Jer 11, 4.
d Dt 1, 37; 3, 26.
e Dt 3, 27.
f Dt 4, 16.
g 27f: Dt 28, 36. 62. 64.
h Ps 135, 15ff; Is 44, 9.
i Jer 29, 13.

*

4, 10: Beginning here and continuing on for several verses (at least to the end of v 14) is the "reminiscence," the account of the things that the Israelites should recall and teach their children.

4, 20: Egypt is called an iron foundry, or furnace for smelting iron, because God allowed the Israelites to be afflicted there for the sake of their spiritual purification; the same expression for Egypt occurs also in 1 Kgs 8, 51; Jer 11, 4; compare the expression, "the furnace of affliction," in Is 48, 10.

4, 25: Grown old: Israel will lose the freshness of its youthful fervor.

your whole heart and your whole soul.[i] **30** In
your distress, when all these things shall have
come upon you, you shall finally return to the
LORD, your God, and heed his voice. **31** Since
the LORD, your God, is a merciful God, he will
not abandon and destroy you, nor forget the
covenant which under oath he made with your
fathers.[j]

**Proofs of God's Love.** **32** "Ask now of
the days of old, before your time, ever since
God created man upon the earth; ask from one
end of the sky to the other: Did anything so great
ever happen before? Was it ever heard of?
**33** Did a people ever hear the voice of God
speaking from the midst of fire, as you did, and
live?[k] **34** Or did any god venture to go and take
a nation for himself from the midst of another
nation, by testings,* by signs and wonders,[l] by
war, with his strong hand and outstretched arm,
and by great terrors, all of which the LORD, your
God, did for you in Egypt before your very
eyes? **35** All this you were allowed to see that
you might know the LORD is God and there is
no other. **36** Out of the heavens he let you hear
his voice to discipline you; on earth he let you
see his great fire, and you heard him speaking
out of the fire. **37** For love of your fathers he
chose their descendants and personally led you
out of Egypt by his great power, **38** driving out
of your way nations greater and mightier than
you, so as to bring you in and to make their land
your heritage, as it is today. **39** This is why you
must now know, and fix in your heart, that the
LORD is God in the heavens above and on earth
below, and that there is no other.[m] **40** You
must keep his statutes and commandments
which I enjoin on you today, that you and your
children after you may prosper, and that you
may have long life on the land which the LORD,
your God, is giving you forever."[n]

**Cities of Refuge.** **41** [o]Then Moses set
apart three cities in the region east of the Jordan,
**42** that a homicide might take refuge there if he
unwittingly killed his neighbor to whom he had
previously borne no malice, and that he might
save his life by fleeing to one of these cities:
**43** Bezer in the desert, in the region of the
plateau, for the Reubenites; Ramoth in Gilead
for the Gadites; and Golan in Bashan for the
Manassehites.

## *II: God and His Covenant*

**Introduction.** **44** This is the law which Moses set before the Israelites. **45** These are the
ordinances, statutes and decrees which he proclaimed to them when they had come out of
Egypt **46** and were beyond the Jordan in the
ravine opposite Beth-peor, in the land of Sihon,
king of the Amorites, who dwelt in Hishbon and
whom Moses and the Israelites defeated after
coming out of Egypt. **47** They occupied his
land and the land of Og, king of Bashan, as
well—the land of these two kings of the Amorites in the region east of the Jordan: **48** from
Aroer on the edge of the Wadi Arnon to Mount
Sion* (that is, Hermon) **49** and all the Arabah
east of the Jordan, as far as the Arabah Sea
under the slopes of Pisgah.[p]

## CHAPTER 5

**The Covenant at Horeb.** **1** Moses summoned all Israel and said to them, "Hear, O
Israel, the statutes and decrees which I proclaim
in your hearing this day, that you may learn
them and take care to observe them. **2** The
LORD, our God, made a covenant with us at
Horeb;[q] **3** not with our fathers did he make this
covenant, but with us, all of us who are alive
here this day. **4** The LORD spoke with you face
to face on the mountain from the midst of the
fire. **5** [r]Since you were afraid of the fire and
would not go up the mountain, I stood between
the LORD and you at that time, to announce to
you these words of the LORD:

**The Decalogue.** **6** [s]'I, the LORD, am your
God, who brought you out of the land of Egypt,[t]
that place of slavery. **7** [u]You shall not have
other gods besides me. **8** You shall not carve
idols for yourselves[v] in the shape of anything in
the sky above or on the earth below or in the
waters beneath the earth; **9** *you shall not bow
down before them or worship them. For I, the
LORD, your God, am a jealous God,[w] inflicting
punishments for their fathers' wickedness on the
children of those who hate me, down to the third
and fourth generation **10** but bestowing mercy,
down to the thousandth generation,[x] on the children of those who love me and keep my commandments.

---

j Dt 31, 8.
k Dt 4, 36; 5, 24. 26; Ex 20, 19.
l Dt 7, 19; 26, 8; 29, 2; Ex 7, 3; 15, 3-10; Jer 32, 21.
m Dt 4, 35.
n Dt 6, 2f; 12, 28.
o 41ff: Dt 19, 2-13; Nm 35, 6-29; Jos 20, 8; 21, 27. 36f; 1 Chr 6, 71. 80.
p Dt 3, 17.
q Dt 28, 69.
r Ex 24, 2.
s 6-21: Ex 20, 2-17.
t Ps 81, 11.
u Ps 81, 10.
v Dt 27, 15; Lv 26, 1; Ps 97, 7.
w Ex 34, 14.
x Dt 7, 9; Ex 20, 6.

---

4, 34: Testings: the demonstrations of God's power as in the ten great plagues of Egypt; cf Dt 7, 19; 29, 2.

4, 48: Sion: another name for Mount Hermon, besides those mentioned in Dt 3, 9.

5, 9f: God does not punish us for another's sins, but because of the solidarity of human society, the good or evil deeds of one generation may make their effects felt even in later generations. Yet note how God's mercy allows the good effects of virtue to last much longer than the bad effects of vice: a thousand generations compared to three or four.

**11** 'You shall not take the name of the LORD,
your God, in vain.[y] For the LORD will not leave
unpunished him who takes his name in vain.
**12** 'Take care to keep holy the sabbath day
as the LORD, your God, commanded you.
**13** Six days you may labor and do all your
work; **14** but the seventh day is the sabbath of
the LORD, your God.[z] No work may be done
then, whether by you, or your son or daughter,
or your male or female slave, or your ox or ass
or any of your beasts, or the alien who lives with
you. Your male and female slave should rest as
you do. **15** For remember that you too were
once slaves in Egypt,[a] and the LORD, your God,
brought you from there with his strong hand and
outstretched arm. That is why the LORD, your
God, has commanded you to observe the sabbath day.

**16** [b]'Honor your father and your mother, as
the LORD, your God, has commanded you, that
you may have a long life and prosperity in the
land which the LORD, your God, is giving you.

**17** [c]'You shall not kill.

**18** 'You shall not commit adultery.

**19** 'You shall not steal.

**20** 'You shall not bear dishonest witness
against your neighbor.

**21** 'You shall not covet your neighbor's
wife.

'You shall not desire your neighbor's house
or field, nor his male or female slave, nor his ox
or ass, nor anything that belongs to him.'

**Moses as Mediator.** **22** "These words,
and nothing more, the LORD spoke with a loud
voice to your entire assembly on the mountain
from the midst of the fire and the dense cloud.
He wrote them upon two tablets of stone and
gave them to me. **23** But when you heard the
voice from the midst of the darkness, while the
mountain was ablaze with fire, you came to me
in the person of all your tribal heads and elders,
**24** and said, 'The LORD, our God, has indeed
let us see his glory and his majesty! We have
heard his voice from the midst of the fire[d] and
have found out today that a man can still live
after God has spoken with him. **25** But why
should we die now? Surely this great fire will
consume us. If we hear the voice of the LORD,
our God, any more, we shall die.[e] **26** For what
mortal has heard, as we have, the voice of the
living God speaking from the midst of fire, and
survived? **27** Go closer, you, and hear all that
the LORD, our God, will say, and then tell us
what the LORD, our God, tells you; we will
listen and obey.'[f]

**28** "The LORD heard your words as you were
speaking to me and said to me, 'I have heard the
words these people have spoken to you, which
are all well said.[g] **29** Would that they might
always be of such a mind, to fear me and to keep
all my commandments! Then they and their descendants
would prosper forever. **30** Go, tell
them to return to their tents. **31** Then you wait
here near me and I will give you all the commandments,
the statutes and decrees you must
teach them, that they may observe them in the
land which I am giving them to possess.'

**32** "Be careful, therefore, to do as the LORD,
your God, has commanded you, not turning
aside to the right or to the left, **33** but following
exactly the way prescribed for you by the LORD,
your God, that you may live and prosper, and
may have long life in the land which you are to
occupy.[h]

## CHAPTER 6

**1** "These then are the commandments, the
statutes and decrees[i] which the LORD, your
God, has ordered that you be taught to observe
in the land into which you are crossing for conquest,
**2** so that you and your son and your
grandson may fear the LORD, your God, and
keep, throughout the days of your lives, all his
statutes and commandments[j] which I enjoin on
you, and thus have long life. **3** Hear then, Israel,
and be careful to observe them, that you may
grow and prosper the more, in keeping with the
promise of the LORD, the God of your fathers,
to give you a land flowing with milk and honey.

**The Great Commandment.** **4** *"Hear, O
Israel! The LORD is our God, the LORD alone![k]
**5** Therefore, you shall love the LORD, your
God, with all your heart, and with all your soul,
and with all your strength.[l] **6** Take to heart
these words which I enjoin on you today.
**7** Drill them into your children.[m] Speak of
them at home and abroad, whether you are busy
or at rest. **8** Bind them at your wrist as a sign*
and let them be as a pendant on your forehead.[n]

---

y Mt 5, 33.
z Gn 2, 2; Ex 20, 8; 23, 12; Heb 4, 4.
a Dt 15, 15; 16, 12; 24, 18. 22.
b Sir 3, 2-16; Mt 15, 4; Mk 7, 10; Lk 18, 20; Eph 6, 2.
c 17-20: Mt 5, 21. 27; Lk 18, 20; Jas 2, 11.
d Dt 4, 33.
e Dt 18, 16.
f Ex 20, 19.
g Dt 18, 17.
h Dt 4, 40.
i Dt 4, 1; 5, 31; 12, 1.
j Dt 4, 40; 5, 29; 10, 12f.
k Mk 12, 29.
l Dt 10, 12; 11, 13; Mt 22, 37; Mk 12, 30; Lk 10, 27.
m 6f: Dt 4, 9; 11, 18; 32, 46.
n Dt 11, 18; Ex 13, 9. 16; Mt 23, 5.

---

6, 4f: This passage contains the basic principle of the whole Mosaic law, the keynote of the Book of Deuteronomy: since the Lord alone is God, we must love him with an undivided heart. Christ cited these words as "the greatest and the first commandment," embracing in itself the whole law of God (Mt 22, 37f and parallels).

6, 8: Bind them . . . as a sign: these injunctions were probably meant merely in a figurative sense; cf Ex 13, 9. 16. However, the later Jews understood them literally, and tied on their wrists and foreheads "phylacteries," boxes containing strips of parchment on which the words were inscribed; cf Mt 23, 5.

**9** Write them on the doorposts of your houses
and on your gates.[o]

**Fidelity in Prosperity.** **10** "When the
LORD, your God, brings you into the land which
he swore to your fathers, Abraham, Isaac and
Jacob, that he would give you, a land with fine,
large cities that you did not build,[p] **11** with
houses full of goods of all sorts that you did not
garner, with cisterns that you did not dig, with
vineyards and olive groves that you did not
plant; and when, therefore, you eat your fill,
**12** [q]take care not to forget the LORD, who
brought you out of the land of Egypt, that place
of slavery. **13** [r]The LORD, your God, shall you
fear; him shall you serve,* and by his name shall
you swear. **14** You shall not follow other gods,
such as those of the surrounding nations, **15** lest
the wrath of the LORD, your God, flare up
against you and he destroy you from the face of
the land;[s] for the LORD, your God, who is in
your midst, is a jealous God.

**16** [t]"You shall not put the LORD, your God,
to the test, as you did at Massah. **17** But keep
the commandments of the LORD, your God, and
the ordinances and statutes he has enjoined on
you. **18** Do what is right and good in the sight
of the LORD, that you may, according to his
word, prosper, and may enter in and possess the
good land which the LORD promised on oath to
your fathers, **19** thrusting all your enemies out
of your way.[u]

**Instruction to Children.** **20** "Later on,
when your son asks you what these ordinances,
statutes and decrees mean[v] which the LORD, our
God, has enjoined on you, **21** you shall say to
your son, 'We were once slaves of Pharaoh in
Egypt, but the LORD brought us out of Egypt
with his strong hand[w] **22** and wrought before
our eyes signs and wonders, great and dire,
against Egypt and against Pharaoh and his
whole house. **23** He brought us from there to
lead us into the land he promised on oath to our
fathers, and to give it to us. **24** Therefore, the
LORD commanded us to observe all these statutes in fear of the LORD, our God, that we may
always have as prosperous and happy a life as
we have today; **25** and our justice before the
LORD, our God, is to consist in carefully observing all these commandments he has enjoined on
us.'

## CHAPTER 7

**Destruction of Pagans.** **1** "When the
LORD, your God, brings you into the land which
you are to enter and occupy, and dislodges great
nations before you—the Hittites, Girgashites,
Amorites, Canaanites, Perizzites, Hivites and
Jebusites:[x] seven nations more numerous and
powerful than you— **2** and when the LORD,
your God, delivers them up to you and you
defeat them, you shall doom them. Make no
covenant with them[y] and show them no mercy.
**3** You shall not intermarry with them, neither
giving your daughters to their sons nor taking
their daughters for your sons.[z] **4** For they
would turn your sons from following me to
serving other gods, and then the wrath of the
LORD would flare up against you and quickly
destroy you.

**5** "But this is how you must deal with
them:[a] Tear down their altars, smash their sacred pillars, chop down their sacred poles,* and
destroy their idols by fire. **6** For you are a people sacred to the LORD, your God; he has chosen
you from all the nations on the face of the earth
to be a people peculiarly his own.[b] **7** It was not
because you are the largest of all nations that the
LORD set his heart on you and chose you, for
you are really the smallest of all nations. **8** It
was because the LORD loved you and because of
his fidelity to the oath he had sworn to your
fathers, that he brought you out with his strong
hand from the place of slavery, and ransomed
you from the hand of Pharaoh, king of Egypt.
**9** [c]Understand, then, that the LORD, your God,
is God indeed, the faithful God who keeps his
merciful covenant down to the thousandth generation toward those who love him and keep his
commandments, **10** but who repays with destruction the person who hates him; he does not
dally with such a one, but makes him personally
pay for it. **11** You shall therefore carefully observe the commandments, the statutes and the
decrees which I enjoin on you today.

**Blessings of Obedience.** **12** [d]"As your
reward for heeding these decrees and observing
them carefully, the LORD, your God, will keep
with you the merciful covenant which he promised on oath to your fathers. **13** He will love and
bless and multiply you; he will bless the fruit of
your womb and the produce of your soil, your
grain and wine and oil, the issue of your herds
and the young of your flocks, in the land which
he swore to your fathers he would give you.[e]
**14** You will be blessed above all peoples; no

o Dt 11, 20.
p 10f: Jos 24, 13.
q Dt 5, 6.
r Dt 10, 20; Mt 4, 10; Lk 4, 8.
s 14f: Dt 8, 19; 11, 16. 28.
t Nm 20, 1-13.
u Ex 23, 27; 34, 11.
v Ex 12, 26; 13, 14.
w Ex 20, 2.
x Ex 23, 23; 33, 2.
y Ex 34, 12.
z 3f: Ex 34, 16; 1 Kgs 11, 1f.
a Dt 12, 3; Ex 34, 13.
b Dt 14, 2; 26, 18; Ex 19, 6.
c 9f: Dt 5, 9f.
d 12-16: Dt 28, 1-14; Ex 23, 22-26; Lv 26, 3-13.
e Dt 30, 9.

*

6, 13: Him shall you serve: here, to "serve" God means especially to "worship" him; in this sense it is quoted by our Lord (Mt 4, 10) as an argument against worshiping the devil.

7, 5: Sacred pillars . . . poles: see note on Ex 34, 13.

man or woman among you shall be childless nor
shall your livestock be barren. **15** The LORD
will remove all sickness from you; he will not
afflict you with any of the malignant diseases
that you know from Egypt, but will leave them
with all your enemies.

**16** "You shall consume all the nations which
the LORD, your God, will deliver up to you. You
are not to look on them with pity, lest you be
ensnared into serving their gods. **17** Perhaps
you will say to yourselves,[f] 'These nations are
greater than we. How can we dispossess them?'
**18** But do not be afraid of them. Rather, call to
mind what the LORD, your God, did to Pharaoh
and to all Egypt: **19** the great testings which
your own eyes have seen, the signs and wonders, his strong hand and outstretched arm with
which the LORD, your God, brought you out.[g]
The same also will he do to all the nations of
whom you are now afraid. **20** Moreover, the
LORD, your God, will send hornets among
them, until the survivors who have hidden from
you are destroyed.[h] **21** Therefore, do not be
terrified by them, for the LORD, your God, who
is in your midst, is a great and awesome God.
**22** He will dislodge these nations before you
little by little. You cannot exterminate them all
at once, lest the wild beasts become too numerous for you.[i] **23** The LORD, your God, will
deliver them up to you and will rout them utterly
until they are annihilated.[j] **24** He will deliver
their kings into your hand, that you may make
their names perish from under the heavens. No
man will be able to stand up against you,[k] till
you have put an end to them. **25** The images of
their gods you shall destroy by fire. Do not
covet the silver or gold on them, nor take it for
yourselves, lest you be ensnared by it; for it is
an abomination to the LORD, your God. **26** You
shall not bring any abominable thing into your
house, lest you be doomed with it; loathe and
abhor it utterly as a thing that is doomed.

## CHAPTER 8

**God's Care.** **1** "Be careful to observe all
the commandments[l] I enjoin on you today, that
you may live and increase, and may enter in and
possess the land which the LORD promised on
oath to your fathers. **2** Remember how for forty
years now the LORD, your God, has directed all
your journeying in the desert,[m] so as to test you
by affliction and find out whether or not it was
your intention to keep his commandments.
**3** He therefore let you be afflicted with hunger,
and then fed you with manna,[n] a food unknown
to you and your fathers, in order to show you
that not by bread alone* does man live, but by
every word that comes forth from the mouth of
the LORD. **4** The clothing did not fall from you
in tatters, nor did your feet swell these forty
years.[o] **5** So you must realize that the LORD,
your God, disciplines you even as a man disciplines his son.

**Danger of Prosperity.** **6** "Therefore,
keep the commandments of the LORD, your
God, by walking in his ways and fearing him.
**7** For the LORD, your God, is bringing you into
a good country,[p] a land with streams of water,
with springs and fountains welling up in the hills
and valleys, **8** a land of wheat and barley, of
vines and fig trees and pomegranates, of olive
trees and of honey, **9** a land where you can eat
bread without stint and where you will lack
nothing, a land whose stones contain iron and
in whose hills you can mine cooper. **10** But
when you have eaten your fill, you must bless
the LORD, your God, for the good country he has
given you. **11** Be careful not to forget the
LORD, your God, by neglecting his commandments and decrees and statutes which I enjoin on
you today: **12** lest, when you have eaten your
fill, and have built fine houses and lived in
them, **13** and have increased your herds and
flocks, your silver and gold, and all your property, **14** you then become haughty of heart and
unmindful of the LORD, your God, who brought
you out of the land of Egypt, that place of
slavery; **15** who guided you through the vast
and terrible desert with its saraph serpents and
scorpions, its parched and waterless ground;
who brought forth water for you from the flinty
rock[q] **16** and fed you in the desert with manna,
a food unknown to your fathers, that he might
afflict you and test you, but also make you
prosperous in the end. **17** Otherwise, you might
say to yourselves,[r] 'It is my own power and the
strength of my own hand that has obtained for
me this wealth.' **18** Remember then, it is the
LORD, your God, who gives you the power to
acquire wealth, by fulfilling, as he has now
done, the covenant which he swore to your fathers. **19** But if you forget the LORD, your God,
and follow other gods, serving and worshiping
them,[s] I forewarn you this day that you will
perish utterly. **20** Like the nations which the
LORD destroys before you, so shall you too perish for not heeding the voice of the LORD, your
God.

f 17f: Dt 1, 28ff.
g Dt 4, 34.
h Ex 23, 28ff.
i Ex 23, 29f.
j Dt 7, 2.
k Dt 11, 25.
l Dt 4, 1; 6, 1.
m Dt 2, 7; 29, 4; Am 2, 10.
n Ex 16, 12-15. 35; Nm 11, 6-9; Mt 4, 4; Lk 4, 4.
o Dt 29, 4; Neh 9, 21.
p Dt 11, 10ff.
q Wis 11, 4.
r Dt 9, 4.
s Dt 4, 25f; 30, 18.

*

8, 3: Not by bread alone, etc.: quoted by our Lord in Mt 4, 4. The sense is: God takes care of those who love him even when natural means seem to fail them.

## CHAPTER 9

**Unmerited Success.** 1 "Hear, O Israel!
You are now about to cross the Jordan to enter
in and dispossess nations greater and stronger
than yourselves, having large cities fortified to
the sky,[t] **2** the Anakim, a people great and
tall.[u] You know of them and have heard it said
of them, 'Who can stand up against the Anakim?' **3** Understand, then, today that it is the
LORD, your God, who will cross over before
you as a consuming fire; he it is who will reduce
them to nothing and subdue them before you, so
that you can drive them out and destroy them
quickly, as the LORD promised you.[v] **4** After
the LORD, your God, has thrust them out of your
way, do not say to yourselves, 'It is because of
my merits that the LORD has brought me in to
possess this land';[w] for it is really because of the
wickedness of these nations that the LORD is
driving them out before you. **5** No, it is not
because of your merits or the integrity of your
heart that you are going in to take possession of
their land; but the LORD, your God, is driving
these nations out before you on account of their
wickedness and in order to keep the promise
which he made on oath to your fathers, Abraham, Isaac and Jacob. **6** Understand this, therefore: it is not because of your merits that the
LORD, your God, is giving you this good land
to possess, for you are a stiff-necked people.

**The Golden Calf.** 7 "Bear in mind and do
not forget how you angered the LORD, your
God, in the desert. From the day you left the
land of Egypt until you arrived in this place, you
have been rebellious toward the LORD.[x] **8** At
Horeb you so provoked the LORD that he was
angry enough to destroy you,[y] **9** when I had
gone up the mountain to receive the stone tablets
of the covenant which the LORD made with
you.[z] Meanwhile I stayed on the mountain forty
days and forty nights without eating or drinking,
**10** till the LORD gave me the two tablets of
stone inscribed, by God's own finger,[a] with a
copy of all the words that the LORD spoke to you
on the mountain from the midst of the fire on the
day of the assembly. **11** Then, at the end of the
forty days and forty nights, when the LORD had
given me the two stone tablets of the covenant,
**12** he said to me,[b] 'Go down from here now,
quickly, for your people whom you have
brought out of Egypt have become depraved;
they have already turned aside from the way I
pointed out to them and have made for themselves a molten idol. **13** I have seen how
stiff-necked this people is,' the LORD said to
me. **14** 'Let me be, that I may destroy them and
blot out their name from under the heavens. I
will then make of you a nation mightier and
greater than they.'

**15** "When I had come down again from the
blazing, fiery mountain, with the two tablets of
the covenant in both my hands,[c] **16** I saw how
you had sinned against the LORD, your God: you
had already turned aside from the way which the
LORD had pointed out to you by making for
yourselves a molten calf! **17** Raising the two
tablets with both hands I threw them from me
and broke them before your eyes.[d] **18** Then, as
before, I lay prostrate before the LORD for forty
days and forty nights without eating or drinking,
because of all the sin you had committed in the
sight of the LORD and the evil you had done to
provoke him.[e] **19** For I dreaded the fierce anger
of the LORD against you: his wrath would destroy you.[f] Yet once again the LORD listened to
me. **20** With Aaron, too, the LORD was deeply
angry, and would have killed him had I not
prayed for him also at that time. **21** Then, taking the calf, the sinful object you had made, and
fusing it with fire, I ground it down to powder
as fine as dust, which I threw into the wadi that
went down the mountainside.[g]

**22** "At Taberah, at Massah, and at Kibroth-hattaavah likewise, you provoked the
LORD to anger.[h] **23** And when he sent you up
from Kadesh-barnea to take possession of the
land he was giving you, you rebelled against
this command of the LORD, your God, and
would not trust or obey him.[i] **24** Ever since I
have known you, you have been rebels against
the LORD.

**25** "Those forty days, then, and forty nights,
I lay prostrate before the LORD, because he had
threatened to destroy you. **26** This was my
prayer to him: O Lord GOD, destroy not your
people, the heritage which your majesty has
ransomed and brought out of Egypt with your
strong hand. **27** Remember your servants,
Abraham, Isaac and Jacob. Look not upon the
stubbornness of this people nor upon their wickedness and sin, **28** lest the people from whose
land you have brought us say, 'The LORD was
not able to bring them into the land he promised
them'; or 'Out of hatred for them he brought
them out to slay them in the desert,'[j] **29** They
are, after all, your people and your heritage,
whom you have brought out by your great power and with your outstretched arm.[k]

---

t Dt 1, 28; 4, 38.
u Nm 13, 33.
v Dt 31, 3; Ex 23, 27.
w Dt 8, 17.
x Dt 31, 27; Ex 14, 11; Nm 14, 11.
y Ex 32, 4; Ps 106, 19.
z Ex 24, 12. 18; 34, 28.
a Ex 31, 18.
b 12ff: Ex 32, 7-10.
c Ex 32, 15.
d 16f: Ex 32, 19.
e Ex 32, 31; 34, 28.
f Dt 10, 10; Ex 32, 10.
g Ex 32, 20.
h Ex 17, 7; Nm 11, 1ff. 34.
i Nm 14, 1-4; Ps 106, 24f.
j Nm 14, 14ff.
k Dt 4, 20; Ex 6, 6f.

## CHAPTER 10

1 "At that time the LORD said to me, 'Cut
two tablets of stone like the former;[l] then come
up the mountain to me. Also make an ark of
wood. 2 I will write upon the tablets the commandments that were on the former tablets that
you broke, and you shall place them in the ark.'
3 So I made an ark of acacia wood, and cut two
tablets of stone like the former, and went up the
mountain carrying the two tablets.[m] 4 [n]The
LORD then wrote on them, as he had written
before, the ten commandments which he spoke
to you on the mountain from the midst of the fire
on the day of the assembly. After the LORD had
given them to me, 5 I turned and came down
the mountain, and placed the tablets in the ark
I had made.[o] There they have remained, in
keeping with the command the LORD gave me.

6 [The Israelites set out from Beeroth
Benejaakan[p] for Moserah, where Aaron died
and was buried, his son Eleazar succeeding him
in the priestly office. 7 From there they set out
for Gudgodah, and from Gudgodah for Jotbathah,[q] a region where there is water in the wadies.]

8 "At that time the LORD set apart the tribe
of Levi to carry the ark of the covenant of the
LORD,[r] to be in attendance before the LORD and
minister to him, and to give blessings in his
name, as they have done to this day. 9 For this
reason, Levi has no share in the heritage with his
brothers;[s] the LORD himself is his heritage, as
the LORD, your God, has told him.

10 "After I had spent these other forty days
and forty nights on the mountain, and the LORD
had once again heard me and decided not to
destroy you, 11 he said to me, 'Go now and set
out at the head of your people,[t] that they may
enter in and occupy the land which I swore to
their fathers I would give them.'

**The Lord's Majesty.** 12 "And now, Israel, what does the LORD, your God, ask of you
but to fear the LORD, your and follow his ways
exactly, to love and serve the LORD, your God,
with all your heart and all your soul,[u] 13 to
keep the commandments and statutes of the
LORD which I enjoin on you today for your own
good? 14 Think! The heavens, even the highest
heavens,* belong to the LORD, your God, as
well as the earth and everything on it.[v] 15 Yet
in his love for your fathers the LORD was so
attached to them as to choose you, their descendants, in preference to all other peoples, as
indeed he has now done.[w] 16 Circumcise your
hearts,* therefore, and be no longer stiff-
necked. 17 For the LORD, your God, is the God
of gods, the LORD of lords, the great God,
mighty and awesome, who has no favorites,
accepts no bribes;[x] 18 who executes justice for
the orphan and the widow, and befriends the
alien, feeding and clothing him. 19 So you too
must befriend the alien, for you were once
aliens yourselves in the land of Egypt.[y] 20 The
LORD, your God, shall you fear, and him shall
you serve; hold fast to him and swear by his
name.[z] 21 He is your glory, he, your God, who
has done for you those great and terrible things
which your own eyes have seen. 22 Your ancestors went down to Egypt seventy strong,[a]
and now the LORD, your God, has made you as
numerous as the stars of the sky.

## CHAPTER 11

**The Wonders of the Lord.** 1 "Love the
LORD, your God, therefore, and always heed his
charge: his statutes, decrees and commandments. 2 It is not your children, who have not
known it from experience, but you yourselves
who must now understand the discipline of the
LORD, your God; his majesty, his strong hand
and outstretched arm; 3 the signs and deeds he
wrought among the Egyptians, on Pharaoh,
king of Egypt, and on all his land;[b] 4 what he
did to the Egyptian army and to their horses and
chariots, engulfing them in the water of the Red
Sea as they pursued you,[c] and bringing ruin
upon them even to this day; 5 what he did for
you in the desert until you arrived in this place;
6 and what he did to the Reubenites Dathan and
Abiram, sons of Eliab, when the ground opened
its mouth and swallowed them up out of the
midst of Israel, with their families and tents and
every living thing that belonged to them.[d]
7 With your own eyes you have seen all these
great deeds that the LORD has done. 8 Keep all
the commandments, then, which I enjoin on you
today, that you may be strong enough to enter
in and take possession of the land into which
you are crossing, 9 and that you may have long
life on the land which the LORD swore to your

l Ex 34, 1.
m Ex 34, 4.
n Ex 20, 1-17; 34, 28.
o Ex 40, 20; 1 Kgs 8, 9.
p Nm 33, 31.
q Nm 33, 32f.
r Nm 3, 6; 6, 23-27; 16, 9.
s Nm 18, 20.
t Ex 32, 34; 33, 1.
u Dt 6, 2. 5.
v Neh 9, 6.
w Dt 7, 6ff.
x 2 Chr 19, 7; Jb 34, 19; Wis 6, 7; Acts 10, 34; Rom 2, 11; Gal 2, 6.
y Ex 22, 21; 23, 9; Lv 19, 33f.
z Dt 6, 13; Mt 4, 10; Lk 4, 8.
a Gn 46, 27; Ex 1, 5; Acts 7, 14.
b Dt 6, 22; Ps 78, 42-51.
c Ex 14, 26ff; 15, 9; Pss 78, 53; 106, 11.
d Nm 16, 31ff.

*

10, 14: Even the highest heavens: literally, "and the heavens of the heavens"; compare the phrase, "the third heaven," in 2 Cor 12, 2.

10, 16: Circumcise your hearts: cf Dt 30, 6; Jer 4, 4; Rom 2, 29. The "uncircumcised heart" (Lv 26, 41; Jer 9, 25; Ez 44, 7. 9) is closed and unreceptive to divine grace and guidance, just as "uncircumcised ears" (Jer 6, 10) are closed to sound, and "uncircumcised lips" (Ex 6, 12. 30) do not open well in speech.

fathers he would give to them and their descendants, a land flowing with milk and honey.

**The Gift of Rain.** **10** "For the land which
you are to enter and occupy is not like the land
of Egypt from which you have come, where you
would sow your seed and then water it by hand,
as in a vegetable garden. **11** [e]No, the land into
which you are crossing for conquest is a land of
hills and valleys that drinks in rain from the
heavens, **12** a land which the LORD, your God,
looks after; his eyes are upon it continually from
the beginning of the year to the end. **13** *If,
then, you truly heed my commandments which
I enjoin on you today, loving and serving the
LORD, your God, with all your heart and all your
soul,[f] **14** I will give the seasonal rain to your
land, the early rain* and the late rain, that you
may have your grain, wine and oil to gather in;
**15** and I will bring forth grass in your fields for
your animals.[g] Thus you may eat your fill.
**16** But be careful lest your heart be so lured
away that you serve other gods and worship
them.[h] **17** For then the wrath of the LORD will
flare up against you and he will close up the
heavens, so that no rain will fall, and the soil
will not yield its crops, and you will soon perish
from the good land he is giving you.

**Reward of Fidelity.** **18** [i]"Therefore, take
these words of mine into your heart and soul.
Bind them at your wrist as a sign, and let them
be a pendant on your forehead. **19** Teach them
to your children, speaking of them at home and
abroad, whether you are busy or at rest. **20** And
write them on the doorposts of your houses and
on your gates, **21** so that, as long as the heavens
are above the earth, you and your children may
live on in the land which the LORD swore to your
fathers he would give them.

**22** "For if you are careful to observe all
these commandments I enjoin on you, loving
the LORD, your God, and following his ways
exactly, and holding fast to him, **23** the LORD
will drive all these nations out of your way,[j] and
you will dispossess nations greater and mightier
than yourselves. **24** [k]Every place where you set
foot shall be yours: from the desert and from
Lebanon, from the Euphrates River to the Western Sea,* shall be your territory. **25** None shall
stand up against you; the LORD, your God, will
spread the fear and dread of you through any
land where you set foot, as he promised you.[l]

**A Blessing and a Curse.** **26** [m]"I set before you here, this day, a blessing and a curse:
**27** a blessing for obeying the commandments
of the LORD, your God, which I enjoin on you
today; **28** a curse if you do not obey the commandments of the LORD, your God, but turn
aside from the way I ordain for you today, to
follow other gods, whom you have not known.
**29** When the LORD, your God, brings you into
the land which you are to enter and occupy, then
you shall pronounce the blessing on Mount Gerizim,[n] the curse* on Mount Ebal. **30** [Are they
not beyond the Jordan, on the other side of the
western road in the country of the Canaanites
who live in the Arabah, opposite the Gilgal
beside the terebinth of Moreh?] **31** For you are
about to cross the Jordan to enter and occupy the
land which the LORD, your God, is giving you.
When therefore, you take possession of it and
settle there, **32** be careful to observe all the
statutes and decrees that I set before you today.

## *III: Exposition of the Law*

## CHAPTER 12

**One Sanctuary.** **1** "These are the statutes
and decrees which you must be careful to observe in the land which the LORD, the God of
your fathers, has given you to occupy, as long
as you live on its soil. **2** Destroy without fail
every place on the high mountains, on the hills,
and under every leafy tree where the nations you
are to dispossess worship their gods.[o] **3** Tear
down their altars, smash their sacred pillars,
destroy by fire their sacred poles, and shatter the
idols of their gods, that you may stamp out the
remembrance of them in any such place.

**4** "That is not how you are to worship the
LORD, your God. **5** Instead,[p] you shall resort to
the place which the LORD, your God, chooses
out of all your tribes and designates as his dwelling **6** and there you shall bring your holocausts
and sacrifices, your tithes and personal contributions, your votive and freewill offerings, and
the firstlings of your herds and flocks. **7** There,
too, before the LORD, your God, you and your
families shall eat and make merry over all your
undertakings, because the LORD, your God, has

e 11f: Dt 8, 7.
f 13f: Dt 10, 12; Lv 26, 4.
g Ps 104, 14.
h 16f: Dt 4, 25f; 6, 14.
i 18-21: Dt 6, 6-9.
j Dt 7, 1; 9, 1.
k Ex 23, 31.
l Dt 2, 25; 7, 24; Ex 23, 27.
m 26ff: Dt 28, 2-45; 30, 1. 15. 19.
n Dt 27, 12f.
o 2f: Dt 7, 5; Ex 23, 24; 34, 13.
p 5-7. 11f: Dt 14, 22-26; 15, 19f; 16, 2. 10f. 14f; 26, 2.

11, 13ff: As often in the Prophets, the discourse passes into the words of God himself. Cf Dt 7, 4; 17, 3; 28, 20; 29, 4f.

11, 14: The early rain: the rains which begin in October or November and continue intermittently throughout the winter. The late rain: the heavy showers of March and April. In Palestine the crops are sown in the autumn and reaped in the spring.

11, 24: The Western Sea: the Mediterranean.

11, 29: You shall pronounce the blessing . . . the curse: for the full ceremony, see chapters 27 and 28. Gerizim . . . Ebal: adjacent mountains in Samaria with a deep ravine between them. Their summits command an excellent view of the entire country.

blessed you. **8** You shall not do as we are now doing; here, everyone does what seems right to himself, **9** since you have not yet reached your resting place, the heritage which the LORD, your God, will give you. **10** But after you have crossed the Jordan and dwell in the land which the LORD, your God, is giving you as a heritage, when he has given you rest from all your enemies round about and you live there in security, **11** then to the place which the LORD, your God, chooses as the dwelling place for his name you shall bring all the offerings I command you: your holocausts and sacrifices, your tithes and personal contributions, and every special offering you have vowed to the LORD. **12** You shall make merry before the LORD, your God, with your sons and daughters, your male and female slaves, as well as with the Levite who belongs to your community but has no share of his own in your heritage. **13** Take care not to offer up your holocausts in any place you fancy, **14** but offer them up in the place which the LORD chooses from among your tribes; there you shall make whatever offerings I enjoin upon you.

**Profane and Sacred Meals.** **15** "However, in any of your communities you may slaughter and eat to your heart's desire as much meat as the LORD, your God, has blessed you with; and the unclean as well as the clean may eat it, as they do the gazelle or the deer. **16** Only, you shall not partake of the blood, but must pour it out on the ground like water.[q] **17** Moreover, you shall not, in your own communities, partake of your tithe of grain or wine or oil, of the first-born of your herd or flock, of any offering you have vowed, of your freewill offerings, or of your personal contributions. **18** These you must eat before the LORD, your God, in the place he chooses, along with your son and daughter, your male and female slave, and the Levite who belongs to your community; and there, before the LORD, you shall make merry over all your undertakings. **19** Take care, also, that you do not neglect the Levite as long as you live in the land.[r]

**20** "After the LORD, your God, has enlarged your territory, as he promised you,[s] when you wish meat for food,* you may eat it at will, to your heart's desire; **21** and if the place which the LORD, your God, chooses for the abode of his name is too far, you may slaughter in the manner I have told you any of your herd or flock that the LORD has given you, and eat it to your heart's desire in your own community. **22** You may eat it as you would the gazelle or the deer: the unclean and the clean eating it alike. **23** But make sure that you do not partake of the blood; for blood is life, and you shall not consume this seat of life with the flesh. **24** Do not partake of the blood, therefore, but pour it out on the ground like water. **25** Abstain from it, that you and your children after you may prosper for doing what is right in the sight of the LORD. **26** However, any sacred gifts or votive offerings that you may have, you shall bring with you to the place which the LORD chooses, **27** and there you must offer both the flesh and the blood of your holocausts on the altar of the LORD, your God; of your other sacrifices the blood indeed must be poured out against the altar of the LORD, your God,[t] but their flesh may be eaten. **28** Be careful to heed all these commandments I enjoin on you, that you and your descendants may always prosper for doing what is good and right in the sight of the LORD, your God.

**Pagan Rites.** **29** "When the LORD, your God, removes the nations from your way as you advance to dispossess them, be on your guard! Otherwise, once they have been wiped out before you and you have replaced them and are settled in their land, **30** you will be lured into following them. Do not inquire regarding their gods, 'How did these nations worship their gods? I, too, would do the same.' **31** You shall not thus worship the LORD, your God, because they offered to their gods every abomination that the LORD detests, even burning their sons and daughters to their gods.[u]

## CHAPTER 13

**Penalties for Idolatry.** **1** "Every command that I enjoin on you, you shall be careful to observe, neither adding to it nor subtracting from it.

**2** "If there arises among you a prophet or a dreamer* who promises you a sign or wonder, **3** urging you to follow other gods, whom you have not known, and to serve them: even though the sign or wonder he has foretold you comes to pass, **4** pay no attention to the words of that prophet or that dreamer; for the LORD, your God, is testing you to learn whether you really love him with all your heart and with all your soul. **5** The LORD, your God, shall you follow, and him shall you fear; his commandment shall you observe, and his voice shall you heed, serving him and holding fast to him alone. **6** [v]But

q Dt 15, 23; Gn 9, 4; Lv 3, 17.
r Dt 14, 27.
s Dt 19, 8; Gn 28, 14; Ex 34, 24.
t Lv 17, 11.
u Lv 18, 21: Jer 7, 31.
v 6-10. 14: Dt 6, 14; 17, 2-7.

*

12, 20: Meat for food: as on special feasts. Meat was not eaten every day in Israel, even by the wealthy.

13, 2. 4. 6: Dreamer: a false prophet who pretended to have received revelations from God in his dreams; of Jer 23, 25–32; Zec 10, 2. But dreams could also be a channel of true prophecy (Nm 12, 6; Jl 3, 1) and of genuine revelations (Gn 20, 3. 6; 31, 10. 24; 37, 5. 9; Mt 1, 20; 2, 12f. 19; etc.)

that prophet or that dreamer shall be put to
death, because, in order to lead you astray from
the way which the LORD, your God, has directed
you to take, he has preached apostasy from the
LORD, your God, who brought you out of the
land of Egypt and ransomed you from that place
of slavery. Thus shall you purge the evil from
your midst.
7 "If your own full brother, or your son or
daughter, or your beloved wife, or your intimate
friend, entices you secretly to serve other gods,
whom you and your fathers have not known,
8 gods of any other nation, near at hand or far
away, from one end of the earth to the other:
9 do not yield to him or listen to him, nor look
with pity upon him, to spare or shield him,
10 but kill him. Your hand shall be the first
raised to slay him; the rest of the people shall
join in with you. 11 You shall stone him to
death, because he sought to lead you astray from
the LORD, your God, who brought you out of the
land of Egypt, that place of slavery. 12 And all
Israel, hearing of it, shall fear and never again
do such evil as this in your midst.
13 "If, in any of the cities which the LORD,
your God, gives you to dwell in, you hear it said
14 that certain scoundrels have sprung up
among you and have led astray the inhabitants
of their city to serve other gods whom you have
not known, 15 you must inquire carefully into
the matter and investigate it thoroughly. If you
find that it is true and an established fact that this
abomination has been committed in your midst,
16 [w]you shall put the inhabitants of that city to
the sword, dooming the city and all life that is
in it, even its cattle, to the sword. 17 Having
heaped up all its spoils in the middle of its
square, you shall burn the city with all its spoils
as a whole burnt offering to the LORD, your
God. Let it be a heap of ruins forever, never to
be rebuilt. 18 You shall not retain anything that
is doomed, that the blazing wrath of the LORD
may die down and he may show you mercy and
in his mercy for you may multiply you as he
promised your fathers on oath; 19 because you
have heeded the voice of the LORD, your God,
keeping all his commandments which I enjoin
on you today, doing what is right in his sight.

## CHAPTER 14

**Pagan Mourning Rites.** 1 "You are children of the LORD, your God. You shall not gash
yourselves nor shave the hair above your foreheads for the dead.[x] 2 For you are a people
sacred to the LORD, your God, who has chosen
you from all the nations on the face of the earth
to be a people peculiarly his own.[y]

**Clean and Unclean Animals.** 3 "You
shall not eat any abominable thing.[z] 4 [a]These
are the animals you may eat: the ox, the sheep,
the goat, 5 the red deer, the gazelle, the roe
deer, the ibex, the addax, the oryx,* and the
mountain sheep. 6 Any animal that has hoofs
you may eat, provided it is cloven-footed and
chews the cud. 7 But you shall not eat any of
the following that only chew the cud or only
have cloven hoofs: the camel, the hare and the
rock badger, which indeed chew the cud, but do
not have hoofs and are therefore unclean for
you; 8 and the pig, which indeed has hoofs and
is cloven-footed, but does not chew the cud and
is therefore unclean for you. Their flesh you
shall not eat, and their dead bodies you shall not
touch.[b]
9 "Of the various creatures that live in the
water, whatever has both fins and scales you
may eat, 10 but all those that lack either fins or
scales you shall not eat; they are unclean for
you.
11 "You may eat all clean birds. 12 But you
shall not eat any of the following: the eagle, the
vulture, the osprey, 13 the various kites and
falcons, 14 all the various species of crows,
15 the ostrich, the nightjar, the gull, the various
species of hawks, 16 the owl, the screech owl,
the ibis, 17 the desert owl, the buzzard, the
cormorant, 18 the stork, the various species of
herons, the hoopoe, and the bat. 19 *All
winged insects, too, are unclean for you and
shall not be eaten. 20 But you may eat any
clean winged creatures.
21 "You must not eat any animal that has
died of itself, for you are a people sacred to the
LORD, your God.[c] But you may give it to an
alien who belongs to your community, and he
may eat it, or you may sell it to a foreigner.
"You shall not boil a kid in its mother's
milk.*

**Tithes.** 22 "Each year you shall tithe all the
produce that grows in the field you have sown;[d]
23 then in the place which the LORD, your God,
chooses as the dwelling place of his name[e] you
shall eat in his presence your tithe of the grain,
wine and oil, as well as the firstlings of your
herd and flock, that you may learn always to

w 16f: Jos 6, 18. 24; 7, 26; 8, 28.
x Lv 19, 28.
y Dt 7, 6.
z Ez 4, 14; Acts 10, 14.
a 4-20; Lv 11, 2-23.
b Lv 11, 26.
c Ex 22, 30; 23, 19; 34, 26.
d Lv 27, 30.
e 23f: Dt 12, 5ff.

*

14, 5: The gazelle, the addax, the oryx: species of antelopes. The ibex: a species of wild goat.

14, 19f: The apparent contradiction is to be resolved in the light of Lv 11, 20–23; the unclean winged insects are those that walk on the ground; the clean winged creatures are those that leap on the ground, such as certain species of locusts.

14, 21: Boil a kid in its mother's milk: see note on Ex 23, 19.

fear the LORD, your God. **24** If, however, the
journey is too much for you and you are not able
to bring your tithe, because the place which the
LORD, your God, chooses for the abode of his
name is too far for you, considering how the
LORD has blessed you,* **25** you may exchange
the tithe for money and, with the purse of money
in hand, go to the place which the LORD, your
God, chooses. **26** You may then exchange the
money for whatever you desire, oxen or sheep,
wine or strong drink, or anything else you
would enjoy, and there before the LORD, your
God, you shall partake of it and make merry
with your family. **27** But do not neglect the
Levite who belongs to your community, for he
has no share in the heritage with you.[f]

**28** "At the end of every third year you shall
bring out all the tithes of your produce for that
year and deposit them in community stores,
**29** that the Levite who has no share in the heritage with you, and also the alien, the orphan and
the widow who belong to your community, may
come and eat their fill;[g] so that the LORD, your
God, may bless you in all that you undertake.

## CHAPTER 15

**Debts and the Poor.** 1 "At the end of
every seven-year period* you shall have a relaxation of debts,[h] **2** which shall be observed as
follows. Every creditor shall relax his claim on
what he has loaned his neighbor; he must not
press his neighbor, his kinsman, because a
relaxation in honor of the LORD has been proclaimed. **3** You may press a foreigner, but you
shall relax the claim on your kinsman for what
is yours.[i] **4** Nay, more! since the LORD, your
God, will bless you abundantly in the land he
will give you to occupy as your heritage, there
should be no one of you in need. **5** If you but
heed the voice of the LORD, your God, and
carefully observe all these commandments
which I enjoin on you today, **6** you will lend to
many nations, and borrow from none;[j] you will
rule over many nations, and none will rule over
you, since the LORD, your God, will bless you
as he promised. **7** If one of your kinsmen in any
community is in need in the land which the
LORD, your God, is giving you, you shall not
harden your heart nor close your hand to him in
his need. **8** Instead, you shall open your hand
to him and freely lend him enough to meet his
need.[k] **9** Be on your guard lest, entertaining the
mean thought that the seventh year, the year of
relaxation, is near, you grudge help to your
needy kinsman and give him nothing; else he
will cry to the LORD against you and you will be
held guilty. **10** When you give to him, give
freely and not with ill will; for the LORD, your
God, will bless you for this in all your works
and undertakings. **11** The needy will never be
lacking* in the land; that is why I command you
to open your hand to your poor and needy kinsman in your country.[l]

**Hebrew Slaves.** 12 "If your kinsman, a
Hebrew man or woman, sells himself to you, he
is to serve you for six years, but in the seventh
year you shall dismiss him from your service,
a free man.[m] **13** When you do so, you shall not
send him away empty-handed, **14** but shall
weight him down with gifts from your flock and
threshing floor and wine press, in proportion to
the blessing the LORD, your God, has bestowed
on you. **15** For remember that you too were
once slaves in the land of Egypt, and the LORD,
your God, ransomed you. That is why I am
giving you this command today.[n] **16** If, however, he tells you that he does not wish to leave
you, because he is devoted to you and your
household, since he fares well with you, **17** you
shall take an awl and thrust it through his ear*
into the door, and he shall then be your slave
forever.[o] Your female slave, also, you shall
treat in the same way. **18** You must not be
reluctant to let your slave go free, since the
service he has given you for six years was worth
twice a hired man's salary; then also the LORD,
your God, will bless you in everything you do.

**Firstlings.** 19 [p]"You shall consecrate to
the LORD, your God, all the male firstlings of
your herd and of your flock. You shall not work
the firstlings of your cattle, nor shear the firstlings of your flock. **20** Year after year you and
your family shall eat them before the LORD,
your God, in the place he chooses.[q] **21** If, however, a firstling is lame or blind or has any other
serious defect, you shall not sacrifice it to the
LORD, your God, **22** but in your own communities you may eat it, the unclean and the clean
eating it alike, as you would a gazelle or a deer.
**23** Only, you shall not partake of its blood,

f Dt 12, 12. 19.
g 28f: Dt 26, 12.
h Neh 10, 31.
i Dt 23, 20.
j Dt 28, 12f.
k Lv 25, 35; Sir 29, 1f; Mt 5, 42.
l Dt 15, 8; Sir 29, 12.
m Ex 21, 2; Jer 34, 14.
n Dt 5, 15.
o 16f: Ex 21, 5f.
p Ex 13, 11.
q Dt 14, 23.
r 21ff: Dt 12, 15f; Lv 22, 20.

*

14, 24: Considering how the Lord has blessed you: should the Israelite farmer be blessed with an abundant harvest, a tenth of this would be too much to transport for a great distance.

15, 1: At the end of every seven-year period: in every seventh, or sabbatical, year Cf Dt 15, 9; 31, 10; and compare Jer 34, 14 with Dt 15, 12. A relaxation of debts: it is uncertain whether a full cancellation of debts is meant, or merely a suspension of payment on them or on their interest among the Israelites. Cf Ex 23, 11 where the same Hebrew root is used of a field that is "let lie fallow" in the sabbatical year.

15, 11: The needy will never be lacking: compare the words of Christ, "The poor you have always with you" (Mt 26, 11).

15, 17: His ear: cf Ex 21, 6 and the note there.

which must be poured out on the ground like water.[r]

## CHAPTER 16

**Feast of the Passover.** **1** "Observe the month of Abib* by keeping the Passover of the LORD, your God,[s] since it was in the month of Abib that he brought you by night out of Egypt. **2** You shall offer the Passover sacrifice from your flock or your herd to the LORD, your God, in the place which he chooses as the dwelling place of his name. **3** [t]You shall not eat leavened bread with it. For seven days you shall eat with it only unleavened bread, the bread of affliction, that you may remember as long as you live the day of your departure from the land of Egypt; for in frightened haste you left the land of Egypt. **4** Nothing leavened may be found in all your territory for seven days, and none of the meat which you sacrificed on the evening of the first day shall be kept overnight for the next day.

**5** "You may not sacrifice the Passover in any of the communities which the LORD, your God, gives you; **6** only at the place which he chooses as the dwelling place of his name, and in the evening at sunset, on the anniversary of your departure from Egypt, shall you sacrifice the Passover. **7** You shall cook and eat it at the place the LORD, your God, chooses; then in the morning you may return to your tents. **8** For six days you shall eat unleavened bread, and on the seventh there shall be a solemn meeting in honor of the LORD, your God; on that day you shall not do any sort of work.

**Feast of Weeks.** **9** [u]"You shall count off seven weeks, computing them from the day when the sickle is first put to the standing grain. **10** You shall then keep the feast of Weeks* in honor of the LORD, your God, and the measure of your own freewill offering shall be in proportion to the blessing the LORD, your God, has bestowed on you. **11** In the place which the LORD, your God, chooses as the dwelling place of his name,[v] you shall make merry in his presence together with your son and daughter, your male and female slave, and the Levite who belongs to your community, as well as the alien, the orphan and the widow among you. **12** Remember that you too were once slaves in Egypt, and carry out these statutes carefully.

**Feast of Booths.** **13** [w]"You shall celebrate the feast of Booths for seven days, when you have gathered in the produce from your threshing floor and wine press.* **14** You shall make merry at your feast,[x] together with your son and daughter, your male and female slave, and also the Levite, the alien, the orphan and the widow who belong to your community. **15** For seven days you shall celebrate this pilgrim feast in honor of the LORD, your God, in the place which he chooses; since the LORD, your God, has blessed you in all your crops and in all your undertakings, you shall do naught but make merry.

**16** "Three times a year,[y] then, every male among you shall appear before the LORD, your God, in the place which he chooses: at the feast of Unleavened Bread, at the feast of Weeks, and at the feast of Booths. No one shall appear before the LORD empty-handed, **17** but each of you with as much as he can give, in proportion to the blessings which the LORD, your God, has bestowed on you.

**Judges.** **18** "You shall appoint judges and officials throughout your tribes to administer true justice for the people in all the communities which the LORD, your God, is giving you. **19** You shall not distort justice; you must be impartial.[z] You shall not take a bribe; for a bribe blinds the eyes even of the wise and twists the words even of the just. **20** Justice and justice alone shall be your aim, that you may have life and may possess the land which the LORD, your God, is giving you.

**Pagan Worship.** **21** *"You shall not plant a sacred pole of any kind of wood beside the altar of the LORD, your God, which you will build;[a] **22** nor shall you erect a sacred pillar,* such as the LORD, your God, detests.

## CHAPTER 17

**1** "You shall not sacrifice to the LORD, your God, from the herd or from the flock an animal with any serious defect;[b] that would be an abomination to the LORD, your God.

**2** [c]"If there is found among you, in any one of the communities which the LORD, your God, gives you, a man or a woman who does evil in

s 1-8: Ex 12, 2-20; 23, 15; Nm 28, 16ff. 24f.
t 3f: Ex 13, 6f; 34, 18.
u 9-12: Lv 23, 15-21.
v Dt 12, 5. 7. 12. 18.
w 13-15: Ex 23, 16; Lv 23, 34-43; Nm 29, 12-38.
x Dt 16, 11.
y Ex 23, 14f. 17; 34, 23; 2 Chr 8, 13.
z Dt 1, 17; Ex 23, 8.
a 1 Kgs 14, 15; 2 Chr 33, 3.
b Lv 22, 20.
c 2-7: Dt 13, 6-15.

*16, 1: Abib: "ear of grain, ripe grain," the name of the month in which the barley harvest fell, corresponding to our March and April; at a later period this month received the Babylonian name of "Nisan."

16, 10: Feast of Weeks: later known more commonly as "Pentecost."

16, 13: See note on Lv 23, 34.

16, 21–17, 7: This section seems to be out of its proper place, since it interrupts the natural sequence of the laws for the judges (Dt 16, 18–20 and 17, 8–13). It probably belongs to the similar section, Dt 12, 29—14, 2.

16, 21f: Sacred pole . . . sacred pillar; see note on Ex 34, 13.

the sight of the LORD, your God, and transg-
resses his covenant, **3** by serving other gods, or
by worshiping the sun or the moon or any of the
host of the sky, against my command;[d] **4** and
if, on being informed of it, you find by careful
investigation that it is true and an established
fact that this abomination has been committed in
Israel; **5** you shall bring the man (or woman)
who had done the evil deed out to your city
gates* and stone him to death. **6** The testimony
of two or three witnesses is required for putting
a person to death;[e] no one shall be put to death
on the testimony of only one witness. **7** At the
execution, the witnesses are to be the first to
raise their hands against him; afterward all the
people are to join in.[f] Thus shall you purge the
evil from your midst.

**Judges.** **8** "If in your own community
there is a case at issue which proves too complicated for you to decide, in a matter of bloodshed
or of civil rights or of personal injury, you shall
then go up to the place which the LORD, your
God, chooses, **9** to the levitical priests or to the
judge who is in office at that time. They shall
study the case and then hand down to you their
decision.[g] **10** According to this decision that
they give you in the place which the LORD
chooses, you shall act, being careful to do exactly as they direct. **11** You shall carry out the
directions they give you and the verdict they
pronounce for you, without turning aside to the
right or to the left from the decision they hand
down to you. **12** Any man who has the insolence to refuse to listen to the priest* who offici-
ates there in the ministry of the LORD, your God,
or to the judge, shall die. Thus shall you purge
the evil from your midst. **13** And all the people,
on hearing of it, shall fear, and never again be
so insolent.

**The King.** **14** "When you have come into
the land which the LORD, your God, is giving
you, and have occupied it and settled in it,
should you then decide to have a king over you
like all the surrounding nations,[h] **15** you shall
set that man over you as your king whom the
LORD, your God, chooses.[i] He whom you set
over you as king must be your kinsman; a foreigner, who is no kin of yours, you may not set
over you. **16** But he shall not have a great number of horses;* nor shall he make his people go
back again to Egypt to acquire them, against the
LORD's warning that you must never go back
that way again.[j] **17** Neither shall he have a
great number of wives, lest his heart be estranged,[k] nor shall he accumulate a vast amount
of silver and gold. **18** When he is enthroned in
his kingdom, he shall have a copy of this law
made from the scroll that is in the custody of the
levitical priests.[l] **19** He shall keep it with him
and read it all the days of his life that he may
learn to fear the LORD, his God, and to heed and
fulfill all the words of this law and these statutes. **20** Let him not become estranged from his
countrymen through pride, nor turn aside to the
right or to the left from these commandments.
Then he and his descendants will enjoy a long
reign in Israel.

## CHAPTER 18

**Priests.** **1** "The whole priestly tribe of Levi
shall have no share in the heritage with Israel;
they shall live on the oblations of the LORD and
the portions due to him.[m] **2** Levi shall have no
heritage among his brothers; the LORD himself
is his heritage, as he has told him. **3** The priests
shall have a right to the following things from
the people: from those who are offering a sacrifice, whether the victim is from the herd or from
the flock, the priest shall receive the shoulder,
the jowls and the stomach. **4** You shall also
give him the first fruits of your grain and wine
and oil,[n] as well as the first fruits of the shearing
of your flock; **5** for the LORD, your God, has
chosen him and his sons out of all your tribes to
be always in attendance to minister in the name
of the LORD.

**6** "When a Levite goes from one of your
communities anywhere in Israel in which he
ordinarily resides, to visit, as his heart may
desire, the place which the LORD chooses, **7** he
may minister there in the name of the LORD, his
God, like all his fellow Levites who are in attendance there before the LORD, **8** He shall then
receive the same portions to eat as the rest,
along with his monetary offerings and heir-
looms.

**Prophets.** **9** "When you come into the land
which the LORD, your God, is giving you, you
shall not learn to imitate the abominations of the

d Dt 4, 19.
e Dt 19, 15; Nm 35, 30; Mt 18, 16; Jn 8, 17; 2 Cor 13, 1.
f Dt 13, 10.
g Dt 21, 5; 2 Chr 19, 8.
h 1 Sm 8, 5. 19f.
i 1 Sm 9, 16; 10, 24; 16, 12.
j Dt 28, 68; 1 Kgs 4, 26; 10, 26.
k 1 Kgs 11; 3f; Neh 13, 26.
l Dt 31, 9. 26.
m Nm 18, 8f. 20-24; 1 Cor 9, 13.
n Nm 18, 12; 2 Chr 31, 5.
o Dt 12, 29ff; Lv 18, 26-30.

*

17, 5: Out to your city gates: outside the gates in an unclean place; cf Lv 24, 14; Nm 15, 36; Acts 7, 58; Heb 13, 12.

17, 12: The priest: the high priest; the judge: a layman. The former presided over the court in cases which directly concerned religion, the latter in cases of a more secular nature; cf 2 Chr 19, 8–11.

17, 16: Horses: chariotry for war. The Lord's warning: the same warning is also referred to in Dt 28, 68, although it is not mentioned explicitly elsewhere in the Pentateuch. We know from other sources that Egypt used to export war horses to Palestine. The danger envisioned here is that some king might make Israel a vassal of Egypt for the sake of such military aid.

peoples there.[o] **10** Let there not be found
among you anyone who immolates his son or
daughter[p] in the fire,* nor a fortune-teller,
soothsayer, charmer, diviner, **11** or caster of
spells, nor one who consults ghosts and spirits
or seeks oracles from the dead. **12** Anyone who
does such things is an abomination to the LORD,
and because of such abominations the LORD,
your God, is driving these nations out of your
way.[q] **13** You, however, must be altogether
sincere toward the LORD, your God. **14** Though
these nations whom you are to dispossess listen
to their soothsayers and fortune-tellers, the
LORD, your God, will not permit you to do so.
**15** "A prophet like me* will the LORD, your
God, raise up for you from among your own
kinsmen; to him you shall listen.[r] **16** This is
exactly what you requested of the LORD, your
God, at Horeb on the day of the assembly, when
you said, 'Let us not again hear the voice of the
LORD, our God, nor see this great fire any more,
lest we die.'[s] **17** And the LORD said to me,
'This was well said. **18** I will raise up for them
a prophet like you from among their kinsmen,
and will put my words into his mouth; he shall
tell them all that I command him. **19** If any man
will not listen to my words which he speaks in
my name, I myself will make him answer for it.[t]
**20** But if a prophet presumes to speak in my
name[u] an oracle that I have not commanded him
to speak, or speaks in the name of other gods,
he shall die.'
**21** "If you say to yourselves, 'How can we
recognize an oracle which the LORD has spoken?', **22** know that, even though a prophet
speaks in the name of the LORD, if his oracle is
not fulfilled or verified, it is an oracle which the
LORD did not speak. The prophet has spoken it
presumptuously, and you shall have no fear of
him.

## CHAPTER 19

**Cities of Refuge.** **1** "When the LORD,
your God, removes the nations whose land he
is giving you, and you have taken their place
and are settled in their cities and houses, **2** [v]you
shall set apart three cities* in the land which the
LORD, your God, is giving you to occupy.
**3** You shall thereby divide into three regions
the land which the LORD, your God, will give
you as a heritage, and so arrange the routes that
every homicide will be able to find a refuge.
**4** "It is in the following case that a homicide
may take refuge in such a place to save his life:
when someone unwittingly kills his neighbor to
whom he had previously borne no malice.[w]
**5** For example, if he goes with his neighbor to
a forest to cut wood, and as he swings his ax to
fell a tree, its head flies off the handle and hits
his neighbor a mortal blow, he may take refuge
in one of these cities to save his life. **6** Should
the distance be too great, the avenger of blood*
may in the heat of his anger pursue the homicide
and overtake him and strike him dead, even
though he does not merit death since he had
previously borne the slain man no malice.
**7** That is why I order you to set apart three
cities.
**8** [x]"But if the LORD, your God, enlarges
your territory, as he swore to your fathers, and
gives you all the land he promised your fathers
he would give **9** in the event that you carefully
observe all these commandments which I enjoin
on you today, loving the LORD, your God, and
ever walking in his ways: then add three cities
to these three. **10** Thus, in the land which the
LORD, your God, is giving you as a heritage,
innocent blood will not be shed and you will not
become guilty of bloodshed.
**11** [y]"However, if someone lies in wait for
his neighbor out of hatred for him, and rising up
against him, strikes him mortally, and then
takes refuge in one of these cities, **12** the elders
of his own city shall send for him and have him
taken from there, and shall hand him over to be
slain by the avenger of blood. **13** Do not look
on him with pity, but purge from Israel the stain
of shedding innocent blood, that you may prosper.

**Removal of Landmarks.** **14** "You shall
not move your neighbor's landmarks erected by

---

p 10f: Lv 18, 21; 19, 31; 20, 27; 1 Sm 28, 7; 2 Kgs 17, 17; 21, 6.
q Dt 9, 4.
r Jn 1, 45; 6, 14; Acts 3, 22; 7, 37.
s Ex 20, 19.
t Acts 3, 23.
u 20. 22: Dt 13, 2ff.
v Dt 4, 41ff; Ex 21, 13; Nm 35, 10-15; Jos 20, 2. 8.
w Dt 4, 42; Nm 35, 15; Jos 20, 3. 5.
x Gn 15, 18-21; 28, 14; Ex 23, 31; 34, 24.
y 11ff: Ex 21, 12. 14; Nm 35, 20f.
z Dt 27, 17; Prv 23, 10; Hos 5, 10.

---

* 18, 10f: Immolates his son or daughter in the fire: to Molech. See note on Lv 18, 21. Such human sacrifices are classed here with other pagan superstitions because they were believed to possess magical powers for averting a calamity; cf 2 Kgs 3, 27. Three other forms of superstition are listed here: augury (by a fortune-teller, a soothsayer or a diviner); black magic (by a charmer . . . or caster of spells); and necromancy (by one who consults ghosts and spirits or seeks oracles from the dead).

18, 15: A prophet like me: from the context (opposition to the pagan soothsayers) it seems that Moses is referring in general to all the true prophets who were to succeed him. But since Christ is the Great Prophet in whom the prophetic office finds its fulfillment and completion, this passage was understood in a special Messianic sense both by the Jews (Jn 6, 14; 7, 40) and by the Apostles (Acts 3, 22; 7, 37).

19, 2: Set apart three cities: the Israelites were to have at least six cities of refuge, three in the land east of the Jordan and three in the land of Canaan west of the Jordan (Nm 35, 9–34); but since the three cities east of the Jordan had now been appointed (Dt 4, 41–43), reference is made here only to the three west of the Jordan. The execution of this command is narrated in Jos 20.

19, 6: The avenger of blood: see note on Nm 35, 12.

your forefathers in the heritage you receive in
the land which the LORD, your God, is giving
you to occupy.[z]

**False Witnesses.** 15 "One witness alone
shall not take the stand against a man in regard
to any crime or any offense of which he may be
guilty; a judicial fact shall be established only
on the testimony of two or three witnesses.[a]
16 "If an unjust witness takes the stand
against a man to accuse him of a defection from
the law, 17 the two parties in the dispute shall
appear before the LORD in the presence of the
priests or judges in office at that time;[b] 18 and
if after a thorough investigation the judges find
that the witness is a false witness and has accused his kinsman falsely, 19 you shall do to
him as he planned to do to his kinsman.[c] Thus
shall you purge the evil from your midst.
20 The rest, on hearing of it, shall fear, and
never again do a thing so evil among you.
21 Do not look on such a man with pity. Life
for life, eye for eye, tooth for tooth, hand for
hand, and foot for foot![d]

## CHAPTER 20

**Courage in War.** 1 "When you go out to
war against your enemies and you see horses
and chariots and an army greater than your own,
do not be afraid of them, for the LORD, your
God, who brought you up from the land of
Egypt, will be with you.
2 "When you are about to go into battle, the
priest shall come forward and say to the soldiers: 3 'Hear, O Israel! Today you are going
into battle against your enemies. Be not weak-
hearted or afraid; be neither alarmed nor frightened by them. 4 For it is the LORD, your God,
who goes with you to fight for you against your
enemies and give you victory.'[e]
5 "Then the officials shall say to the soldiers,[f] 'Is there anyone who has built a new
house and not yet had the housewarming? Let
him return home, lest he die in battle and another dedicate it. 6 Is there anyone who has planted a vineyard and never yet enjoyed its fruits?
Let him return home, lest he die in battle and
another enjoy its fruits in his stead. 7 Is there
anyone who has betrothed a woman and not yet
taken her as his wife? Let him return home, lest
he die in battle and another take her to wife.'[g]
8 In fine, the officials shall say to the soldiers,
'Is there anyone who is afraid and weakheart-
ed?[h] Let him return home, lest he make his
fellows as fainthearted as himself.'
9 "When the officials have finished speaking to the soldiers, military officers shall be
appointed over the army.

**Cities of the Enemy.** 10 "When you
march up to attack a city, first offer it terms of
peace. 11 If it agrees to your terms of peace and
opens its gates to you, all the people to be found
in it shall serve you in forced labor. 12 But if
it refuses to make peace with you and instead
offers you battle, lay siege to it, 13 and when
the LORD, your God, delivers it into your hand,
put every male in it to the sword; 14 but the
women and children and livestock and all else
in it that is worth plundering you may take as
your booty, and you may use this plunder of
your enemies which the LORD, your God, has
given you.[i]
15 "That is how you shall deal with any city
at a considerable distance from you, which does
not belong to the peoples of this land. 16 But
in the cities of those nations which the LORD,
your God, is giving you as your heritage, you
shall not leave a single soul alive. 17 You must
doom them all—the Hittites, Amorites, Canaanites, Perizzites, Hivites and Jebusites[j] —as
the LORD, your God, has commanded you,
18 lest they teach you to make any such abominable offerings as they make to their gods, and
you thus sin against the LORD, your God.

**Trees of a Besieged City.** 19 "When you
are at war with a city and have to lay siege to
it for a long time before you capture it, you shall
not destroy its trees by putting an ax to them.
You may eat their fruit, but you must not cut
down the trees. After all, are the trees of the
field men, that they should be included in your
siege? 20 However, those trees which you
know are not fruit trees you may destroy, cutting them down to build siegeworks with which
to reduce the city that is resisting you.

## CHAPTER 21

**Expiation of Untraced Murder.** 1 "If the
corpse of a slain man* is found lying in the open
on the land which the LORD, your God, is giving
you to occupy, and it is not known who killed
him, 2 your elders and judges shall go out and
measure the distances to the cities that are in the

a Dt 17, 6; Nm 35, 30; Mt 18, 16; Jn 8, 17; 2 Cor 13, 1.
b Dt 17, 8f.
c 18f: Dn 13, 61f.
d Ex 21, 23f; Lv 24, 20; Mt 5, 38.
e Dt 1, 30; 3, 22; Jos 23, 10.
f 5ff: 1 Mc 3, 56.
g Dt 24, 5.
h Jgs 7, 3.
i 13f: Nm 31, 7. 9. 11; Jos 22, 8.
j 16f: Dt 7, 1f; Jos 10, 40; 11, 14.

* 21, 1–9: This paragraph is best read immediately after Dt 19, 21. The slain man may not necessarily have been murdered; he may have been killed by a wild beast. But the blood of the slain cries out to God from the soil where it was shed; cf Gn 4, 10. Therefore a religious ceremony of propitiation is here prescribed in order to avert God's anger on the community.

neighborhood of the corpse. **3** When it is established which city is nearest the corpse, the elders of that city shall take a heifer that has never
been put to work as a draft animal under a yoke,
**4** and bringing it down to a wadi with an
ever-flowing stream at a place that has not been
plowed or sown, they shall cut the heifer's
throat there in the wadi.* **5** The priests, the
descendants of Levi, shall also be present, for
the LORD, your God, has chosen them to minister to him and to give blessings in his name, and
every case of dispute or violence must be settled
by their decision.[k] **6** Then all the elders of that
city nearest the corpse shall wash their hands*
over the heifer whose throat was cut in the wadi,
**7** and shall declare, 'Our hands did not shed
this blood,* and our eyes did not see the deed.
**8** Absolve, O LORD, your people Israel, whom
you have ransomed, and let not the guilt of
shedding innocent blood remain in the midst of
your people Israel.' Thus they shall be absolved
from the guilt of bloodshed, **9** and you shall
purge from your midst the guilt of innocent
blood, that you may prosper for doing what is
right in the sight of the LORD.

### Marriage with a Female Captive.

**10** "When you go out to war against your enemies and the LORD, your God, delivers them
into your hand, so that you take captives, **11** if
you see a comely woman among the captives
and become so enamored of her that you wish
to have her as wife, **12** you may take her home
to your house. But before she may live there,
she must shave her head* and pare her nails
**13** and lay aside her captive's garb. After she
has mourned her father and mother for a full
month, you may have relations with her, and
you shall be her husband and she shall be your
wife. **14** However, if later on you lose your
liking for her, you shall give her her freedom,
if she wishes it; but you shall not sell her or
enslave her, since she was married to you under
compulsion.

### Rights of the First-born.

**15** "If a man
with two wives loves one and dislikes the other;
and if both bear him sons, but the first-born is
of her whom he dislikes: **16** when he comes to
bequeath his property to his sons he may not
consider as his first-born the son of the wife he
loves, in preference to his true first-born, the
son of the wife whom he dislikes. **17** On the
contrary, he shall recognize as his first-born the
son of her whom he dislikes, giving him a double share of whatever he happens to own, since
he is the first fruits of his manhood, and to him
belong the rights of the first-born.

### The Incorrigible Son.

**18** "If a man has a
stubborn and unruly son who will not listen to
his father or mother, and will not obey them
even though they chastise him, **19** his father
and mother shall have him apprehended and
brought out to the elders at the gate* of his home
city, **20** where they shall say to those city elders, 'This son of ours is a stubborn and unruly
fellow who will not listen to us; he is a glutton
and a drunkard.' **21** Then all his fellow citizens
shall stone him to death. Thus shall you purge
the evil from your midst, and all Israel, on
hearing of it, shall fear.

### Corpse of a Criminal.

**22** "If a man guilty
of a capital offense is put to death and his corpse
hung on a tree,* **23** it shall not remain on the
tree overnight.[l] You shall bury it the same day;
otherwise, since God's curse rests on him who
hangs on a tree,* you will defile the land which
the LORD, your God, is giving you as an inheritance.

## CHAPTER 22

### Care for Lost Animals.

**1** "You shall not
see your kinsman's ox or sheep driven astray
without showing concern about it; see to it that
it is returned to your kinsman.[m] **2** If this kinsman does not live near you, or you do not know
who he may be, take it to your own place and
keep it with you until he claims it; then give it
back to him. **3** You shall do the same with his
ass, or his garment, or anything else which your
kinsman loses and you happen to find; you may
not be unconcerned about them. **4** You shall not
see your kinsman's ass or ox foundering on the

k Dt 19, 17.
l Gal 3, 13.
m 1-4: Ex 23, 4f.

*

21, 4: They shall cut the heifer's throat there in the wadi: its blood is to be carried away by the stream, signifying thereby the removal of the human blood from the soil. This is not a sacrifice but a symbolic action; the priests are present merely as official witnesses.

21, 6: Wash their hands: a symbolic gesture in protestation of one's own innocence when human blood is unjustly shed; cf Mt 27, 24.

21, 7: This blood: the blood of the slain man as symbolized by the heifer's blood.

21, 12f: Shave her head . . . : these symbolic actions are meant to signify the purification of the woman from her pagan defilement or perhaps the end of her period of mourning for her previous husband.

21, 19: The gate: in the city walls. This open space served as the forum for the administration of justice. Cf Dt 22, 15; 25, 7; Ru 4, 1f. 11; Is 29, 21; Am 5, 10. 12. 15.

21, 22: Hung on a tree: some understand, "impaled on a stake." In any case the hanging or impaling was not the means used to execute the criminal; he was first put to death by the ordinary means, stoning, and his corpse was then exposed on high as a salutary warning for others. Cf Jos 8, 29; 10, 26; 1 Sm 31, 10; 2 Sm 21, 9.

21, 23: God's curse rests on him who hangs on a tree: St. Paul quotes these words in Gal 3, 13, where he applies them to the crucified Savior, who "redeemed us from the curse of the law, becoming a curse for us."

road without showing concern about it; see to it
that you help him lift it up.

**Various Precepts.** 5 "A woman shall not
wear an article proper to a man, nor shall a man
put on a woman's dress; for anyone who does
such things is an abomination to the LORD, your
God.

6 "If, while walking along, you chance upon
a bird's nest with young birds or eggs in it, in
any tree or on the ground, and the mother bird
is sitting on them, you shall not take away the
mother bird along with her brood; 7 you shall
let her go, although you may take her brood
away. It is thus that you shall have prosperity
and a long life.

8 "When you build a new house, put a parapet around the roof; otherwise, if someone falls
off, you will bring blood-guilt upon your house.

9 [n]"You shall not sow your vineyard with
two different kinds of seed; if you do, its produce shall become forfeit,* both the crop you
have sown and the yield of the vineyard.
10 You shall not plow with an ox and an ass
harnessed together. 11 You shall not wear cloth
of two different kinds of thread, wool and linen,
woven together.

12 "You shall put twisted cords* on the four
corners of the cloak that you wrap around you.[o]

**Crimes against Marriage.** 13 "If a man,
after marrying a woman and having relations
with her, comes to dislike her, 14 and makes
monstrous charges against her and defames her
by saying, 'I married this woman, but when I
first had relations with her I did not find her a
virgin,' 15 the father and mother of the girl
shall take the evidence of her virginity* and
bring it to the elders at the city gate. 16 There
the father of the girl shall say to the elders, 'I
gave my daughter to this man in marriage, but
he has come to dislike her, 17 and now brings
monstrous charges against her, saying: I did not
find your daughter a virgin. But here is the
evidence of my daughter's virginity!' And they
shall spread out the cloth before the elders of the
city. 18 Then these city elders shall take the
man and chastise him,* 19 besides fining him
one hundred silver shekels, which they shall
give to the girl's father, because the man defamed a virgin in Israel. Moreover, she shall
remain his wife, and he may not divorce her as
long as he lives.

20 "But if this charge is true, and evidence
of the girl's virginity is not found, 21 they shall
bring the girl to the entrance of her father's
house and there her townsmen shall stone her to
death, because she committed a crime against
Israel by her unchasteness in her father's house.
Thus shall you purge the evil from your midst.

22 "If a man is discovered having relations
with a woman who is married to another, both
the man and the woman with whom he has had
relations shall die.[p] Thus shall you purge the
evil from your midst.

23 "If within the city a man comes upon a
maiden who is betrothed,* and has relations
with her, 24 you shall bring them both out to
the gate of the city and there stone them to
death: the girl because she did not cry out for
help though she was in the city, and the man
because he violated his neighbor's wife. Thus
shall you purge the evil from your midst.

25 "If, however, it is in the open fields that
a man comes upon such a betrothed maiden,
seizes her and has relations with her, the man
alone shall die. 26 You shall do nothing to the
maiden, since she is not guilty of a capital offense. This case is like that of a man who rises
up against his neighbor and murders him: 27 it
was in the open fields that he came upon her,
and though the betrothed maiden may have
cried out for help, there was no one to come to
her aid.

28 [q]"If a man comes upon a maiden that is
not betrothed, takes her and has relations with
her, and their deed is discovered, 29 the man
who had relations with her shall pay the girl's
father fifty silver shekels and take her as his
wife, because he has deflowered her. Moreover,
he may not divorce her as long as he lives.

## CHAPTER 23

1 "A man shall not marry his father's wife,*
nor shall he dishonor his father's bed.

**Membership in the Community.** 2 "No
one whose testicles have been crushed or whose
penis has been cut off, may be admitted into the
community of the Lord. 3 No child of an incestuous union may be admitted into the community of the LORD, nor any descendant of his even
to the tenth generation. 4 [r]No Ammonite or
Moabite may ever be admitted into the community of the LORD, nor any descendants of theirs
even to the tenth generation, 5 [s]because they
would not succor you with food and water on
your journey after you left Egypt, and because

n 9. 11: Lv 19, 19.
o Nm 15, 38; Mt 23, 5.
p Lv 20, 10; Jn 8, 4f.
q 28f: Ex 22, 16.
r Neh 13, 1f.
s Nm 24, 10.

22, 9: Become forfeit: to the sanctuary; cf Lv 19, 19; Jos 6, 19.

22, 12: Twisted cords: referred to as "tassels" on "violet cords" in Nm 15, 38. See note there.

22, 15: The evidence of her virginity: the bridal garment or sheet stained with a little blood from the first nuptial relations.

22, 18: Chastise him: flog him, as prescribed in Dt 25, 1-3.

22, 23: A maiden who is betrothed: a girl who is married but not yet brought to her husband's home and whose marriage is therefore still unconsummated.

23, 1: Father's wife: stepmother. Dishonor: cf Dt 27, 20.

Moab hired Balaam, son of Beor, from Pethor
in Aram Naharaim, to curse you; **6** though the
LORD, your God, would not listen to Balaam
and turned his curse into a blessing for you,
because he loves you. **7** Never promote their
peace and prosperity as long as you live. **8** [t]But
do not abhor the Edomite, since he is your
brother, nor the Egyptian, since you were an
alien in his country. **9** Children born to them
may in the third generation be admitted into the
community of the LORD.

**Cleanliness in Camp.** **10** "When you are
in camp during an expedition against your enemies, you shall keep yourselves from everything offensive. **11** If one of you becomes unclean because of a nocturnal emission, he shall
go outside the camp, and not return until, **12** toward evening, he has bathed in water; then,
when the sun has set, he may come back into the
camp. **13** Outside the camp you shall have a
place set aside to be used as a latrine. **14** You
shall also keep a trowel in your equipment and
with it, when you go outside to ease nature, you
shall first dig a hole and afterward cover up your
excrement. **15** Since the LORD, your God, journeys along within your camp to defend you and
to put your enemies at your mercy, your camp
must be holy; otherwise, if he sees anything
indecent in your midst, he will leave your company.

**Various Precepts.** **16** "You shall not
hand over to his master a slave who has taken
refuge from him with you. **17** Let him live with
you wherever he chooses, in any one of your
communities* that pleases him. Do not molest
him.

**18** *"There shall be no temple harlot among
the Israelite women, nor a temple prostitute
among the Israelite men.[u] **19** You shall not
offer a harlot's fee or a dog's price as any kind
of votive offering in the house of the LORD, your
God; both these things are an abomination to the
LORD, your God.

**20** "You shall not demand interest from your
countrymen on a loan of money or of food or of
anything else on which interest is usually demanded.[v] **21** You may demand interest from a
foreigner, but not from your countryman, so
that the LORD, your God, may bless you in all
your undertakings on the land you are to enter
and occupy.

**22** "When you make a vow to the LORD,
your God, you shall not delay in fulfilling it;
otherwise you will be held guilty, for the LORD,
your God, is strict in requiring it of you.
**23** Should you refrain from making a vow, you
will not be held guilty. **24** But you must keep
your solemn word and fulfill the votive offering
you have freely promised to the LORD.

**25** "When you go through your neighbor's
vineyard, you may eat as many of his grapes as
you wish, but do not put them in your basket.
**26** When you go through your neighbor's
grainfield, you may pluck some of the ears with
your hand, but do not put a sickle to your neighbor's grain.

## CHAPTER 24

**Marriage Laws.** **1** "When a man,* after
marrying a woman and having relations with
her, is later displeased with her because he finds
in her something indecent,* and therefore he
writes out a bill of divorce and hands it to her,
thus dismissing her from his house: **2** if on leaving his house she goes and becomes the wife of
another man, **3** and the second husband, too,
comes to dislike her and dismisses her from his
house by handing her a written bill of divorce;
**4** or if this second man who has married her,
dies; then her former husband, who dismissed
her, may not again take her as his wife after she
has become defiled. That would be an abomination before the LORD, and you shall not bring
such guilt upon the land which the LORD, your
God, is giving you as a heritage.

**5** [w]"When a man is newly wed, he need not
go out on a military expedition, nor shall any
public duty be imposed on him. He shall be
exempt for one year for the sake of his family,
to bring joy to the wife he has married.

**Justice, Equity and Charity.** **6** *"No one
shall take a hand mill or even its upper stone as

t Gn 25, 24ff.
u 1 Kgs 14, 24; 22, 46; 2 Kgs 23, 7.
v Ex 22, 25; Lv 25, 37; Lk 6, 34f.
w Dt 20, 7.

*

23, 17: In any one of your communities: from this it would seem that the slave in question is a fugitive from a foreign country.

23, 18f: The pagans believed that they could enter into special relationship with their gods and goddesses by having sexual relations with the pagan priests and priestesses who prostituted themselves for this purpose. The money paid for this was considered a sort of votive offering made to the pagan sanctuary. Such abominations were naturally forbidden in Israel. A dog's price: the money paid the pagan priest for his indecent service.

24, 1–4: This law is directly concerned only with forbidding divorced couples to remarry each other, and indirectly with checking hasty divorces, by demanding sufficient cause and certain legal formalities. Divorce itself is taken for granted and tolerated as an existing custom whose evils this law seeks to lessen. Cf Dt 22, 19. 29; Mal 2, 14ff. Christ gave the authentic interpretation of this law: "Moses, by reason of the hardness of your heart, permitted you to put away your wives; but it was not so from the beginning" (Mt 19, 8f).

24, 1: Something indecent: a rather indefinite phrase, meaning perhaps "immodest conduct." At the time of Christ the rabbis differed in opinion concerning the sufficient grounds for divorce; cf Mt 19, 3.

24, 6: Since the Israelites ground their grain into flour only in sufficient quantity for their current need, to deprive a debtor a pledge for debt, for he would be taking the debtor's sustenance as a pledge.

**7** "If a any man is caught kidnaping a fellow Israelite in order to enslave him and sell him, the kidnaper shall be put to death.[x] Thus shall you purge the evil from your midst.

**8** [y]"In an attack of leprosy you shall be careful to observe exactly and to carry out all the directions of the levitical priests. Take care to act in accordance with the instructions I have given them. **9** [z]Remember what the LORD, your God, did to Miriam on the journey after you left Egypt.

**10** *"When you make a loan of any kind to your neighbor, you shall not enter his house to receive a pledge from him, **11** but shall wait outside until the man to whom you are making the loan brings his pledge outside to you. **12** If he is a poor man, you shall not sleep in the mantle he gives as a pledge, **13** but shall return it to him at sunset that he himself may sleep in it.[a] Then he will bless you, and it will be a good deed of yours before the LORD, your God.

**14** "You shall not defraud a poor and needy hired servant, whether he be one of your own countrymen or one of the aliens who live in your communities. **15** You shall pay him each day's wages before sundown on the day itself, since he is poor and looks forward to them.[b] Otherwise he will cry to the LORD against you, and you will be held guilty.

**16** "Fathers shall not be put to death for their children, nor children for their fathers; only for his own guilt shall a man be put to death.[c]

**17** "You shall not violate the rights of the alien or of the orphan, nor take the clothing of a widow as a pledge.[d] **18** For, remember, you were once slaves in Egypt, and the LORD, your God, ransomed you from there; that is why I command you to observe this rule.

**19** [e]"When you reap the harvest in your field and overlook a sheaf there, you shall not go back to get it; let it be for the alien, the orphan or the widow, that the LORD, your God, may bless you in all your undertakings. **20** When you knock down the fruit of your olive trees, you shall not go over the branches a second time; let what remains be for the alien, the orphan and the widow. **21** When you pick your grapes, you shall not go over the vineyard a second time; let what remains be for the alien, the orphan, and the widow. **22** For remember that you were once slaves in Egypt; that is why I command you to observe this rule.

## CHAPTER 25

**1** "When men have a dispute and bring it to court, and a decision is handed down to them acquitting the innocent party and condemning the guilty party, **2** if the latter deserves stripes, the judge shall have him lie down and in his presence receive the number of stripes his guilt deserves. **3** Forty stripes* may be given him, but no more;[f] lest, if he were beaten with more stripes than these, your kinsman should be looked upon as disgraced because of the severity of the beating.

**4** *"You shall not muzzle an ox when it is treading out grain.[g]

**Levirate Marriage.** **5** "When brothers live together* and one of them dies without a son, the widow of the deceased shall not marry anyone outside the family; but her husband's brother shall go to her and perform the duty of a brother-in-law by marrying her.[h] **6** [i]The first-born son she bears shall continue the line of the deceased brother, that his name may not be blotted out from Israel. **7** If, however, a man does not care to marry his brother's wife, she shall go up to the elders at the gate and declare, 'My brother-in-law does not intend to perform his duty toward me and refuses to perpetuate his brother's name in Israel.' **8** Thereupon the elders of his city shall summon him and admonish him. If he persists in saying, 'I am not willing to marry her,' **9** *his sister-in-law, in the presence of the elders, shall go up to him and strip his sandal from his foot and spit in his face, saying publicly, 'This is how one should be treated who will not build up his brother's family!' **10** And his lineage shall be spoken of in Israel as 'the family of the man stripped of his sandal.'

x Ex 21, 16.
y Lv 13, 1-14.
z Nm 12, 10-15.
a Ex 22, 26.
b 14f: Lv 19, 13; Tb 4, 15; Sir 34, 25f; Jer 22, 13.
c 2 Kgs 14, 6; 2 Chr 25, 4; Ez 18, 20.
d Ex 22, 22; 23, 9.
e 19ff: Lv 19. 9f; 23, 22.
f 2 Cor 11, 24.
g 1 Cor 9, 9; 1 Tm 5, 18.
h Mt 22, 24; Mk 12, 19; Lk 20, 28.
i 6-9; Ru 4, 5-10.

* of his hand mill was virtually equivalent to condemning him to starve to death.

24, 10f: The debtor had the right to select the pledge that the creditor demanded as a guarantee for his loan.

25, 3: Forty stripes: a relatively mild punishment in ancient times. Later Jewish practice limited the number to thirty-nine; cf 2 Cor 11, 24.

25, 4: St Paul argues from this verse that a laborer has the right to live on the fruits of his labor; cf 1 Cor 9, 9; 1 Tm 5, 18.

25, 5: When brothers live together: when relatives of the same clan, though married, hold their property in common. It was only in this case that the present law was to be observed, since one of its purposes was to keep the property of the deceased within the same clan. Such a marriage of a widow with her brother-in-law is known as a "levirate" marriage from the Latin word levir, meaning "a husband's brother."

25, 9f: The penalty decreed for a man who refuses to comply with this law of family loyalty is public disgrace (the widow is to spit in his face) and the curse of poverty; sandals were proverbially a man's cheapest possession (cf Am 2, 6; 8, 6), and therefore "a man without sandals" was the poorest of the poor. Some commentators, however, connect this symbolic act with the ceremony mentioned in Ru 4, 7f.

**Various Precepts.** **11** "When two men are fighting and the wife of one intervenes to save her husband from the blows of his opponent, if she stretches out her hand and seizes the latter by his private parts, **12** you shall chop off her hand without pity.

**13** "You shall not keep two differing weights in your bag, one large and the other small;[j] **14** nor shall you keep two different measures in your house, one large and the other small. **15** But use a true and just weight, and a true and just measure, that you may have a long life on the land which the LORD, your God, is giving you. **16** Everyone who is dishonest in any of these matters is an abomination to the LORD, your God.

**17** *Bear in mind what Amalek did to you on the journey after you left Egypt,[k] **18** how without fear of any god he harassed you along the way, weak and weary as you were, and cut off at the rear all those who lagged behind. **19** Therefore, when the LORD, your God, gives you rest from all your enemies round about in the land which he is giving you to occupy as your heritage, you shall blot out the memory of Amalek from under the heavens.[l] Do not forget!

## CHAPTER 26

**Thanksgiving for the Harvest.** **1** "When you have come into the land which the LORD, your God, is giving you as a heritage, and have occupied it and settled in it, **2** you shall take some first fruits[m] of the various products of the soil which you harvest from the land which the LORD, your God, gives you, and putting them in a basket, you shall go to the place which the LORD, your God, chooses for the dwelling place of his name. **3** There you shall go to the priest in office at that time and say to him, 'Today I acknowledge to the LORD, my God, that I have indeed come into the land which he swore to our fathers he would give us.' **4** The priest shall then receive the basket from you and shall set it in front of the altar of the LORD, your God. **5** Then you shall declare before the LORD, your God, 'My father was a wandering Aramean* who went down to Egypt with a small household and lived there as an alien.[n] But there he became a nation great, strong and numerous. **6** [o]When the Egyptians maltreated and oppressed us, imposing hard labor upon us, **7** we cried to the LORD, the God of our fathers, and he heard our cry and saw our affliction, our toil and our oppression. **8** He brought us out of Egypt with his strong hand and outstretched arm, with terrifying power, with signs and wonders;[p] **9** and bringing us into this country, he gave us this land flowing with milk and honey.[q] **10** Therefore, I have now brought you the first fruits of the products of the soil which you, O LORD, have given me.' And having set them before the LORD, your God, you shall bow down in his presence. **11** Then you and your family, together with the Levite and the aliens who live among you, shall make merry over all these good things which the LORD, your God, has given you.[r]

**Prayer with the Tithes.** **12** "When you have finished setting aside all the tithes of your produce in the third year,[s] the year of the tithes, and you have given them to the Levite,* the alien, the orphan and the widow, that they may eat their fill in your own community, **13** you shall declare before the LORD, your God, 'I have purged my house of the sacred portion and I have given it to the Levite,* the alien, the orphan and the widow, just as you have commanded me. In this I have not broken or forgotten any of your commandments: **14** *I have not eaten any of the tithe as a mourner; I have not brought any of it out as one unclean; I have not offered any of it to the dead. I have thus hearkened to the voice of the LORD, my God, doing just as you have commanded me. **15** Look down, then, from heaven, your holy abode, and bless your people Israel and the soil you have given us in the land flowing with milk and honey which you promised on oath to our fathers.'

**The Covenant.** **16** "This day the LORD, your god, commands you to observe these statutes and decrees. Be careful, then, to observe them with all your heart and with all your soul. **17** Today you are making this agreement with the LORD: he is to be your God and you are to walk in his ways and observe his statutes, commandments and decrees, and to hearken to his voice.[t] **18** And today the LORD is making this agreement with you: you are to be a people peculiarly his own,[u] as he promised you; and provided you keep all his commandments, **19** he will then raise you high in praise and renown and glory above all other nations he has

j 13ff: Lv 19, 35f; Prv 16, 11; Ez 45, 10; Ml 6, 11.
k Ex 17, 8.
l Ex 17, 14; 1 Sm 15, 2f.
m Ex 23, 19; 34, 26.
n Gn 46, 6f; Acts 7, 14f.
o 6f: Ex 1, 8-22; 2, 23ff; 3, 9; Nm 20, 15f.
p Ex 12, 51.
q Ex 3, 8.
r Dt 12, 7. 12.
s Dt 14, 28f.
t Ex 24, 7.
u 18f: Dt 7, 6; 14, 2; 28, 1; Ex 19, 5.

*

25, 17–19: This attack on Israel by Amalek is not mentioned elsewhere in the Old Testament, although it probably was connected with the battle mentioned in Ex 17, 8. A campaign against Amalek was carried out by Saul; cf 1 Sm 15.

26, 5: Aramean: either in reference to the origin of the patriarchs from Aram Naharaim (cf Gn 24, 10; 25, 20; 28, 5; 31, 20. 24), or merely in the sense of "nomad," in the same way as "Arab" was later used; cf Jer 3, 2.

26, 12: And you have given them to the Levite . . . : as prescribed in Dt 14, 28f.

26, 14: These are allusions to pagan religious practices.

made, and you will be a people sacred to the
LORD, your God, as he promised."

## *IV: Final Words of Moses*

### CHAPTER 27

**Ceremonies.** **1** Then Moses, with the elders of Israel, gave the people this order: "Keep
all these commandments which I enjoin on you
today. **2** On the day you cross the Jordan into
the land which the LORD, your God, is giving
you, set up some large stones and coat them
with plaster. **3** Also write on them,[v] at the time
you cross, all the words of this law, that you
may thus enter into the land flowing with milk
and honey, which the LORD, your God, and the
God of your fathers, is giving you as he promised you. **4** When, moreover, you have crossed
the Jordan, besides setting up on Mount Ebal
these stones concerning which I command you
today, and coating them with plaster, **5** you
shall also build to the LORD, your God, an altar
made of stones that no iron tool has touched.[w]
**6** You shall make this altar of the LORD, your
God, with undressed stones, and shall offer on
it holocausts to the LORD, your God. **7** You
shall also sacrifice peace offerings and eat them
there, making merry before the LORD, your
God. **8** On the stones* you shall inscribe all the
words of this law very clearly."

**9** Moses, with the levitical priests, then said
to all Israel: "Be silent, O Israel, and listen!
This day you have become the people of the
LORD, your God.[x] **10** You shall therefore
hearken to the voice of the LORD, your God, and
keep his commandments and statutes which I
enjoin on you today."

**11** That same day Moses gave the people this
order: **12** "When you cross the Jordan, Simeon, Levi, Judah, Issachar, Joseph and Benjamin
shall stand on Mount Gerizim[y] to pronounce
blessings over the people, **13** while Reuben,
Gad, Asher, Zebulun, Dan and Naphtali shall
stand on Mount Ebal to pronounce curses.

**The Twelve Curses.** **14** "The Levites
shall proclaim aloud to all the men of Israel:
**15** 'Cursed be the man who makes a carved or
molten idol[z] —an abomination to the LORD, the
product of a craftsman's hands—and sets it up
in secret!' And all the people shall answer,
'Amen!'*

**16** 'Cursed be he who dishonors his father or
his mother!'[a] And all the people shall answer,
'Amen!'

**17** 'Cursed be he who moves his neighbor's
landmarks!'[b] And all the people shall answer,
'Amen!'

**18** 'Cursed be he who misleads a blind man
on his way!'[c] And all the people shall answer,
'Amen!'

**19** 'Cursed be he who violates the rights of
the alien, the orphan or the widow!'[d] And all
the people shall answer, 'Amen!'

**20** 'Cursed be he who has relations with his
father's wife, for he dishonors his father's
bed!'[e] And all the people shall answer, 'Amen!'

**21** 'Cursed be he who has relations with any
animal!'[f] And all the people shall answer,
'Amen!'

**22** 'Cursed be he who has relations with his
sister or his half-sister!'[g] And all the people
shall answer, 'Amen!'

**23** 'Cursed be he who has relations with his
mother-in-law!'[h] And all the people shall answer, 'Amen!'

**24** 'Cursed be he who slays his neighbor in
secret!'[i] And all the people shall answer,
'Amen!'

**25** 'Cursed be he who accepts payment for
slaying an innocent man!' And all the people
shall answer, 'Amen!'

**26** 'Cursed be he who fails to fulfill any of
the provisions of this law!'[j] And all the people
shall answer, 'Amen!'

### CHAPTER 28*

**Blessings for Obedience.** **1** "Thus,
then,[k] shall it be:[l] if you continue to heed the
voice of the LORD, your God, and are careful to
observe all his commandments which I enjoin
on you today, the LORD, your God, will raise
you high above all the nations of the earth.[m]
**2** When you hearken to the voice of the LORD,
your God, all these blessings will come upon
you and overwhelm you:

**3** "May you be blessed in the city,
and blessed in the country!
**4** "Blessed be the fruit of your womb,
the produce of your soil and the offspring
of your livestock,
the issue of your herds and the young of
your flocks![n]

---

v Jos 8, 32.
w Ex 20, 25; Jos 8, 31.
x Dt 26, 17ff.
y 12f: Dt 11, 29; Jos 8, 33f.
z Ex 20, 4. 23; Lv 19, 4; Wis 14, 8.
a Dt 21, 18-21; Ex 21, 17; Lv 20, 9.
b Dt 19, 14.
c Lv 19, 14.
d Dt 24, 17; Ex 22, 21f.
e Dt 22; 23, 1; Lv 18, 8; 20, 11.
f Ex 22, 18; Lv 18, 23; 20, 15.
g Lv 18, 9; 20, 17.
h Lv 18, 17; 20, 14.
i Ex 20, 13; 21, 12; Nm 35, 20f.
j Gal 3, 10.
k 1-68: Lv 26, 1-45.
l 1-14: Dt 7, 12-16.
m Dt 26, 19.
n Dt 7, 13; 30. 9.

---

27, 8: On the stones: cf vv 3f; not the stones of the altar.

27, 15-26: Amen: see note on Nm 5, 22.

28, 1-69: This chapter would read better immediately after chapter 26.

5 "Blessed be your grain bin and your
kneading bowl!
6 "May you be blessed in your coming in,
and blessed in your going out!*

**Victory and Prosperity.** 7 "The LORD
will beat down before you the enemies that rise
up against you; though they come out against
you from but one direction, they will flee before
you in seven.* 8 The LORD will affirm his
blessing upon you, on your barns and on all your
undertakings, blessing you in the land that the
LORD, your God, gives you. 9 Provided that
you keep the commandments of the LORD, your
God, and walk in his ways, he will establish you
as a people sacred to himself, as he swore to
you;[o] 10 so that, when all the nations of the
earth see you bearing the name of the LORD,*
they will stand in awe of you.[p] 11 The LORD
will increase in more than goodly measure the
fruit of your womb, the offspring of your livestock, and the produce of your soil, in the land
which he swore to your fathers he would give
you. 12 The LORD will open up for you his rich
treasure house of the heavens, to give your land
rain in due season, blessing all your undertakings, so that you will lend to many nations and
borrow from none.[q] 13 The LORD will make
you the head, not the tail,* and you will always
mount higher and not decline, as long as you
obey the commandments of the LORD, your
God, which I order you today to observe carefully; 14 not turning aside to the right or to the
left from any of the commandments which I
now give you, in order to follow other gods and
serve them.

**Curses for Disobedience.** 15 "But if
you do not hearken to the voice of the LORD,
your God,[r] and are not careful to observe all his
commandments which I enjoin on you today, all
these curses shall come upon you and overwhelm you:

16 "May you be cursed in the city,
and cursed in the country!

17 "Cursed be your grain bin and your
kneading bowl!

18 "Cursed be the fruit of your womb,
the produce of your soil and the offspring
of your livestock,
the issue of your herds and the young of
your flocks!

19 "May you be cursed in your coming in,
and cursed in your going out!

**Sickness and Defeat.** 20 "The LORD will
put a curse on you, defeat and frustration in
every enterprise you undertake, until your are
speedily destroyed and perish for the evil you
have done in forsaking me. 21 The LORD will
bring a pestilence upon you that will persist until
he has exterminated you from the land you are
entering to occupy. 22 The LORD will strike
you with wasting and fever, with scorching,
fiery drought, with blight and searing wind, that
will plague you until you perish. 23 The sky
over your heads will be like bronze and the earth
under your feet like iron.[s] 24 For rain the LORD
will give your land powdery dust, which will
come down upon you from the sky until you are
destroyed. 25 The LORD will let you be beaten
down before your enemies; though you advance
against them from one direction, you will flee
before them in seven, so that you will become
a terrifying example to all the kingdoms of the
earth.[t] 26 Your carcasses will become food for
all the birds of the air and for the beasts of the
field, with no one to frighten them off. 27 The
LORD will strike you with Egyptian boils[u] and
with tumors, eczema and the itch, until you
cannot be cured. 28 And the LORD will strike
you with madness, blindness and panic, 29 so
that even at midday you will grope like a blind
man in the dark, unable to find your way.

**Despoilment.** "You will be oppressed and
robbed continually, with no one to come to your
aid. 30 Though you betroth a wife, another man
will have her. Though you build a house, you
will not live in it. Though you plant a vineyard,
you will not enjoy its fruits. 31 Your ox will be
slaughtered before your eyes, and you will not
eat of its flesh. Your ass will be stolen in your
presence, but you will not recover it. Your
flocks will be given to your enemies, with no
one to come to your aid. 32 Your sons and
daughters will be given to a foreign nation while
you look on and grieve for them in constant
helplessness. 33 A people whom you do not
know will consume the fruit of your soil and of
all your labor, and you will be oppressed and
crushed at all times without surcease, 34 until
you are driven mad by what your eyes must look
upon. 35 *The LORD will strike you with malignant boils of which you cannot be cured, on

o Dt 26, 18; Ex 19, 5f.
p Dt 2, 25; 11, 25.
q Dt 15, 6.
r Bar 1, 20; Dn 9, 11; Mal 2, 2.
s 22f: Lv 26, 19.
t Lv 26, 17. 37.
u Ex 9, 9ff.

*

28, 6: In your coming in . . . in your going out: at the beginning and end of every action, or in all actions in general.

28, 7. 25: From but one direction . . . in seven: in one compact mass, contrasted with many scattered groups.

28, 10: You bearing the name of the Lord: literally, "The LORD'S name is called over you," an expression signifying ownership and protection. Cf 2 Sm 12, 28; 1 Kgs 8, 43; Is 4, 1; 63, 19; Jer 7, 10f; 14, 9; 15, 16; 25, 29; Am 9, 12.

28, 13: The head, not the tail: in the honorable position as leader. Cf Is 9, 14; 19, 15.

28, 35: This verse is best read with v 27.

your knees and legs, and from the soles of your
feet to the crown of your head.

**Exile.** **36** [v]"The LORD will bring you, and
your king whom you have set over you, to a
nation which you and your fathers have not
known, and there you will serve strange gods of
wood and stone, **37** and will call forth amazement, reproach and barbed scorn from all the
nations to which the LORD will lead you.

**Fruitless Labors.** **38** "Though you spend
much seed on your field, you will harvest but
little, for the locusts will devour the crop.[w]
**39** Though you plant and cultivate vineyards,
you will not drink or store up the wine, for the
grubs will eat the vines clean.[x] **40** Though you
have olive trees throughout your country, you
will have no oil for ointment, for your olives
will drop off unripe.[y] **41** Though you beget
sons and daughters, they will not remain with
you, but will go into captivity.[z] **42** Buzzing
insects will infest all your trees and the crops of
your soil. **43** The alien residing among you will
rise higher and higher above you, while you
sink lower and lower. **44** He will lend to you,
not you to him. He will become the head, you
the tail.

**45** "All these curses will come upon you,
pursuing you and overwhelming you, until you
are destroyed, because you would not hearken
to the voice of the LORD, your God, nor keep the
commandments and statutes he gave you.
**46** They will light on you and your descendants
as a sign and a wonder* for all time. **47** Since
you would not serve the LORD, your God, with
joy and gratitude for abundance of every kind,
**48** therefore in hunger and thirst, in nakedness
and utter poverty, you will serve the enemies
whom the LORD will send against you. He will
put an iron yoke on your neck, until he destroys
you.

**Invasion and Siege.** **49** [a]"The LORD will
raise up against you a nation from afar, from the
end of the earth, that swoops down like an eagle, a nation whose tongue you do not understand, **50** a nation of stern visage, that shows
neither respect for the aged nor pity for the
young. **51** They will consume the offspring of
your livestock and the produce of your soil,
until you are destroyed; they will leave you no
grain or wine or oil, no issue of your herds or
young of your flocks, until they have brought
about your ruin. **52** They will besiege you in
each of your communities, until the great, un-
scalable walls you trust in come tumbling down
all over your land. They will so besiege you in
every community throughout the land which the
LORD, your God, has given you, **53** that in the
distress of the siege to which your enemy subjects you, you will eat the fruit of your womb,
the flesh of your own sons and daughters[b]
whom the LORD, your God, has given you.
**54** The most refined and fastidious man among
you will begrudge his brother and his beloved
wife and his surviving children **55** any share in
the flesh of his children that he himself is using
for food when nothing else is left him in the
straits of the siege to which your enemy will
subject you in all your communities. **56** The
most refined and delicate woman among you, so
delicate and refined that she would not venture
to set the sole of her foot on the ground, will
begrudge her beloved husband and her son and
daughter **57** the afterbirth that issues from her
womb and the infant she brings forth when she
secretly uses them for food for want of anything
else, in the straits of the siege to which your
enemy will subject you in your communities.

**Plagues.** **58** "If you are not careful to observe every word of the law which is written in
this book, and to revere the glorious and awesome name of the LORD, your God, **59** he will
smite you and your descendants with severe and
constant blows, malignant and lasting maladies.
**60** He will again afflict you with all the diseases
of Egypt* which you dread, and they will persist
among you.[c] **61** Should there be any kind of
sickness or calamity not mentioned in this book
of the law, that too the LORD will bring upon
you until you are destroyed. **62** Of you who
were numerous as the stars in the sky,[d] only a
few will be left, because you would not hearken
to the voice of the LORD, your God.

**Exile.** **63** "Just as the LORD once took delight in making you grow and prosper,[e] so will
he now take delight in ruining and destroying
you, and you will be plucked out of the land you
are now entering to occupy. **64** The LORD will
scatter you among all the nations from one end
of the earth to the other,[f] and there you will
serve strange gods of wood and stone, such as
you and your fathers have not known.
**65** Among these nations you will find no repose, not a foot of ground to stand upon, for

v 1 Kgs 9, 7ff; 2 Chr 7, 20ff; 33, 11; 36, 6. 20.
w Mi 6, 15; Hg 1, 6.
x Zep 1, 13.
y Mi 6, 15.
z Lam 1, 5.
a 49-52: Jer 5, 15ff; Bar 4, 15f.
b Lv 26, 29; 2 Kgs 6, 28f; Jer 19, 9; Lam 4, 10; Bar 2. 3.
c Dt 28, 27.
d Dt 1, 10; Jer 42, 2.
e Dt 30, 9.
f Lv 26, 33.

*

28, 46: A sign and a wonder: an ominous example, attracting attention; cf Dt 29, 21–28.

28, 60: He will again afflict you with all the diseases of Egypt: such as the Lord had promised to remove from his people; cf Dt 7, 15.

28, 65: Wasted eyes: worn out and disappointed in their longing gaze.

there the LORD will give you an anguished heart
and wasted eyes* and a dismayed spirit.
**66** You will live in constant suspense and stand
in dread both day and night, never sure of your
existence. **67** In the morning you will say,
'Would that it were evening!' and in the evening
you will say, 'Would that it were morning!' for
the dread that your heart must feel and the sight
that your eyes must see. **68** The LORD will send
you back in galleys* to Egypt, to the region I
told you that you were never to see again;[g] and
there you will offer yourselves for sale to your
enemies as male and female slaves, but there
will be no buyer."

**69** These are the words of the covenant
which the LORD ordered Moses to make with the
Israelites in the land of Moab, in addition to the
covenant which he made with them at Horeb.

## CHAPTER 29

**Past Favors Recalled.** **1** Moses summoned all Israel and said to them, "You have
seen all that the LORD did in the land of Egypt
before your very eyes to Pharaoh and all his
servants and to all his land; **2** the great testings
your own eyes have seen, and those great signs
and wonders.[h] **3** But not even at the present day
has the LORD yet given you a mind to understand, or eyes to see, or ears to hear.* **4** 'I led
you for forty years in the desert.[i] Your clothes
did not fall from you in tatters nor your sandals
from your feet; **5** bread was not your food, nor
wine or beer your drink. Thus you should know
that I, the LORD, am your God.' **6** [j]When we
came to this place, Sihon, king of Heshbon, and
Og, king of Bashan, came out to engage us in
battle, but we defeated them **7** and took over
their land, which we then gave as a heritage to
the Reubenites, Gadites, and half the tribe of
Manasseh.[k] **8** Keep the terms of this covenant,
therefore, and fulfill them, that you may succeed in whatever you do.

**All Israel Bound to the Covenant.**
**9** "You are all now standing before the LORD,
your God—your chiefs and judges, your elders
and officials, and all of the men of Israel, **10** together with your wives and children and the
aliens who live in your camp, down to those
who hew wood and draw water for you—
**11** that you may enter into the covenant of the
LORD, your God, which he concluded with you
today under this sanction of a curse;* **12** so that
he may now establish you as his people and he
may be your God, as he promised you and as he
swore to your fathers Abraham, Isaac and Jacob. **13** But it is not with you alone that I am
making this covenant, under this sanction of a
curse; **14** it is just as much with those who are
not here among us* today as it is with those of
us who are now here present before the LORD,
our God.

**Warning against Idolatry.** **15** "You
know in what surroundings we lived in the land
of Egypt and what we passed by in the nations
we traversed, **16** and you saw the loathsome
idols of wood and stone, of gold and silver, that
they possess. **17** Let there be, then, no man or
woman, no clan or tribe among you, who would
now turn away their hearts from the LORD, our
God, to go and serve these pagan gods! Let there
be no root that would bear such poison and
wormwood among you! **18** If any such person,
upon hearing the words of this curse, should
beguile himself into thinking that he can safely
persist in his stubbornness of heart, as though to
sweep away both the watered soil and the
parched ground,* **19** the LORD will never consent to pardon him. Instead, the LORD's wrath
and jealousy will flare up against that man, and
every curse mentioned in this book will alight
on him. The LORD will blot out his name from
under the heavens **20** and will single him out
from all the tribes of Israel for doom, in keeping
with all the curses of the covenant inscribed in
this book of the law.

**Punishment for Infidelity.** **21** "Future
generations, your own descendants who will
rise up after you, as well as the foreigners who
will come here from far-off lands, when they
see the calamities of this land and the ills with
which the LORD has smitten it— **22** all its soil
being nothing but sulphur and salt, a burnt-out
waste, unsown and unfruitful, without a blade
of grass, destroyed like Sodom and Gomorrah,[l]
Admah and Zeboiim, which the LORD overthrew in his furious wrath— **23** they and all the
nations will ask, 'Why has the LORD dealt thus
with this land? Why this fierce outburst of
wrath?'[m] **24** And the answer will be, 'Because
they forsook the covenant which the LORD, the
God of their fathers, had made with them when
he brought them out of the land of Egypt,

---

g Hos 8, 13; 9, 3.
h Dt 4, 34; Ex 19, 4.
i Dt 8, 2. 4.
j Dt 2, 24. 32; 3, 1; Nm 21, 33ff.
k Dt 3, 16; Nm 32, 33.
l Gn 14, 10f; 19, 24f.
m 23f: 1 Kgs 9, 8f; Jer 22, 8f.

---

28, 68: In galleys: in the ships of the Phoenician slave traders (Ez 27, 13; Jl 4, 6; Am 1, 9), who also dealt with Egypt (Is 23, 3).

29, 3: Eyes to see ... ears to hear: with inner, spiritual discernment. Cf Mt 13, 43.

29, 11: Sanction of a curse: the present pact binds under penalty of the curses mentioned in this book. Cf v 20.

29, 14: Not here among us: this includes their descendants.

29, 18: To sweep away both the watered soil and the parched ground: apparently a proverb signifying that such an unfaithful Israelite will cause God to punish the good with the wicked, to root out the good plants growing in irrigated soil, together with the worthless plants growing in the dry ground.

**25** and they went and served other gods and
adored them, gods whom they did not know and
whom he had not let fall to their lot: **26** that is
why the LORD was angry with this land and
brought on it all the imprecations listed in this
book; **27** in his furious wrath and tremendous
anger the LORD uprooted them from their soil
and cast them out into a strange land,[n] where
they are today.' **28** [Both what is still hidden*
and what has already been revealed concern us
and our descendants forever, that we may carry
out all the words of this law.]

## CHAPTER 30

**Mercy for the Repentant.** **1** "When all
these things which I have set before you, the
blessings and the curses, are fulfilled in you,[o]
and from among whatever nations the LORD,
your God, may have dispersed you, you ponder
them in your heart: **2** then, provided that you
and your children return to the LORD, your God,
and heed his voice with all your heart and all
your soul,[p] just as I now command you, **3** the
LORD, your God, will change your lot; and taking pity on you, he will again gather you from
all the nations wherein he has scattered you.
**4** Though you may have been driven to the
farthest corner of the world, even from there
will the LORD, your God, gather you; even from
there will he bring you back. **5** The LORD, your
God, will then bring you into the land which
your fathers once occupied, that you too may
occupy it, and he will make you more prosperous and numerous than your fathers. **6** The
LORD, your God, will circumcise your hearts*
and the hearts of your descendants,[q] that you
may love the LORD, your God, with all your
heart and all your soul, and so may live. **7** But
all those curses the LORD, your God, will assign
to your enemies and the foes who persecuted
you. **8** You, however, must again heed the
LORD's voice and carry out all his commandments which I now enjoin on you. **9** Then the
LORD, your God, will increase in more than
goodly measure the returns from all your labors,
the fruit of your womb, the offspring of your
livestock, and the produce of your soil;[r] for the
LORD, your God, will again take delight in your
prosperity, even as he took delight in your fathers', **10** if only you heed the voice of the
LORD, your God, and keep his commandments
and statutes that are written in this book of the
law, when you return to the LORD, your God,
with all your heart and all your soul.

**God's Command Clear.** **11** *"For this
command which I enjoin on you today is not too
mysterious and remote for you. **12** It is not up
in the sky, that you should say, 'Who will go up
in the sky to get it for us and tell us of it, that
we may carry it out?' **13** Nor is it across the sea,
that you should say, 'Who will cross the sea to
get it for us and tell us of it, that we may carry
it out?' **14** No, it is something very near to you,
already in your mouths* and in your hearts; you
have only to carry it out.

**The Choice before Israel.** **15** "Here,
then, I have today set before you life and prosperity, death and doom. **16** If you obey the
commandments of the LORD, your God, which
I enjoin on you today, loving him, and walking
in his ways, and keeping his commandments,
statutes and decrees, you will live and grow
numerous, and the LORD, your God, will bless
you in the land you are entering to occupy.
**17** If, however, you turn away your hearts and
will not listen, but are led astray and adore and
serve other gods, **18** I tell you now that you will
certainly perish; you will not have a long life on
the land which you are crossing the Jordan to
enter and occupy. **19** I call heaven and earth
today to witness against you:[s] I have set before
you life and death, the blessing and the curse.[t]
Choose life, then, that you and your descendants may live, **20** by loving the LORD, your
God, heeding his voice, and holding fast to him.
For that will mean life for you, a long life for
you to live on the land which the LORD swore
he would give to your fathers Abraham, Isaac
and Jacob."

## CHAPTER 31

**The Lord's Leadership.** **1** When Moses
had finished speaking these words to all Israel,
**2** he said to them, "I am now one hundred and
twenty years old[u] and am no longer able to
move about freely; besides, the LORD has told
me that I shall not cross this Jordan. **3** It is the
LORD your God, who will cross before you; he
will destroy these nations before you, that you
may supplant them.[v] [It is Joshua who will
cross before you, as the LORD promised.]
**4** [w]The LORD will deal with them just as he

n Dn 9, 11-14.
o Dt 11, 26ff.
p 2f: Neh 1, 9.
q Dt 6, 5.
r Dt 28, 11.
s Dt 4, 26.
t Dt 11, 26ff; 28, 2. 15.
u Dt 34, 7; Nm 20, 12.
v Dt 9, 3.
w Nm 21, 21-35.

*

29, 28: What is still hidden: the events of the future. What has already been revealed: God's law and the punishments in store for those who break it. Leave the future to God; our business is to keep his law.

30, 6: Circumcise your hearts: see note on Dt 10, 16.

30, 11–14: God has revealed his will so clearly that ignorance of his law can be no excuse. St Paul in Rom 10, 6–10, applies these words to the ease with which we can come to faith and salvation in Christ.

30, 14: In your mouths: that you may readily talk about it; cf Dt 6, 7; 11, 19. And in your hearts: that you may easily remember it; cf Dt 6, 6; 11, 18.

dealt with Sihon and Og, the kings of the Amorites whom he destroyed, and with their country. **5** When, therefore, the LORD delivers them up to you, you must deal with them exactly as I have ordered you.[x] **6** Be brave and steadfast; have no fear or dread of them, for it is the LORD, your God, who marches with you; he will never fail you or forsake you."[y]

**Call of Joshua.** **7** Then Moses summoned Joshua and in the presence of all Israel said to him,[z] "Be brave and steadfast, for you must bring this people into the land which the LORD swore to their fathers he would give them; you must put them in possession of their heritage. **8** It is the LORD who marches before you; he will be with you and will never fail you or forsake you. So do not fear or be dismayed."

**The Reading of the Law.** **9** When Moses had written down this law, he entrusted it to the livitical priests who carry the ark of the covenant of the LORD, and to all the elders of Israel, **10** giving them this order: "On the feast of Booths,[a] at the prescribed time in the year of relaxation* which comes at the end of every seven-year period, **11** when all Israel goes to appear before the LORD, your God, in the place which he chooses, you shall read this law* aloud in the presence of all Israel. **12** Assemble the people—men, women and children, as well as the aliens who live in your communities—that they may hear it and learn it, and so fear the LORD, your God, and carefully observe all the words of this law. **13** Their children also, who do not know it yet, must hear it and learn it, that they too may fear the LORD, your God, as long as you live on the land which you will cross the Jordan to occupy."

**Commission of Joshua.** **14** The LORD said to Moses, "The time is now approaching for you to die. Summon Joshua, and present yourselves at the meeting tent that I may give him his commission." So Moses and Joshua went and presented themselves at the meeting tent.* **15** And the LORD appeared at the tent in a column of cloud, which stood still at the entrance of the tent.

**A Command to Moses.** **16** The LORD said to Moses, "Soon you will be at rest with your fathers, and then this people will take to rendering wanton worship to the strange gods among whom they will live in the land they are about to enter.[b] They will forsake me and break the covenant which I have made with them. **17** At that time my anger will flare up against them; I will forsake them and hide my face from them, so that they will become a prey to be devoured, and many evils and troubles will befall them. At that time they will indeed say, 'Is it not because our God is not among us that these evils have befallen us?' **18** Yet I will be hiding my face from them at that time only because of all the evil they have done in turning to other gods. **19** Write out this song,[c] then, for yourselves. Teach it to the Israelites and have them recite it, so that this song may be a witness for me against the Israelites. **20** For when I have brought them into the land flowing with milk and honey which I promised on oath to their fathers, and they have eaten their fill and grown fat, if they turn to other gods and serve them, despising me and breaking my covenant; **21** then, when many evils and troubles befall them, this song, which their descendants will not have forgotten to recite, will bear witness against them. For I know what they are inclined to do even at the present time, before I have brought them into the land which I promised on oath to their fathers." **22** So Moses wrote this song that same day, and he taught it to the Israelites.

**Commission of Joshua.** **23** Then the LORD commissioned Joshua, son of Nun, and said to him, "Be brave and steadfast, for it is you who must bring the Israelites into the land which I promised them on oath.[d] I myself will be with you."

**The Law Placed in the Ark.** **24** When Moses had finished writing out on a scroll the words of the law in their entirety, **25** he gave the Levites[e] who carry the ark of the covenant of the LORD this order: **26** "Take this scroll of the law and put it beside the ark of the covenant of the LORD, your God, that there it may be a witness against you. **27** For I already know how rebellious and stiff-necked you will be. Why, even now, while I am alive among you, you have been rebels against the LORD! How much more, then, after I am dead! **28** [f]Therefore, assemble all your tribal elders and your officials before me, that I may speak these words for them to hear, and so may call heaven and earth to witness against them. **29** [g]For I know that after my death you are sure to become corrupt and to turn aside from the way along which I directed you, so that evil will befall you in some future age because you have done evil in the

x Dt 7, 2.
y Dt 20, 3f.
z 7f: Jos 1, 6f. 9.
a 10f: Dt 16, 13ff.
b Jgs 2, 12. 17.
c Dt 31, 21; 32, 1-43.
d Dt 31, 7f; Jos 1, 5ff.
e 24f: Dt 31, 9.
f Dt 32, 1-43.
g Jgs 2, 19.

*

31, 10: The year of relaxation: cf Dt 15, 1ff and the note there.

31, 11ff: Reading the law not only instructed the people but also consoled them by the assurance of the divine goodness.

31, 14f. 23: V 23 is best read immediately after v 15; perhaps the original order was vv 7–8. 14–15. 23.

LORD's sight, and provoked him by your deeds.''

**The Song of Moses.** 30 Then Moses recited the words of this song from beginning to end, for the whole assembly of Israel to hear:

## CHAPTER 32

### A

1 Give ear, O heavens, while I speak;*
let the earth hearken to the words of my mouth!
2 May my instruction soak in like the rain,
and my discourse permeate like the dew,
Like a downpour upon the grass,
like a shower upon the crops:
3 For I will sing the LORD's renown.
Oh, proclaim the greatness of our God!
4 The Rock—how faultless are his deeds,
how right all his ways!
A faithful God, without deceit,
how just and upright he is![h]

5 Yet basely has he been treated by his degenerate children,
a perverse and crooked race![i]
6 Is the LORD to be thus repaid by you,
O stupid and foolish people?
Is he not your father who created you?
Has he not made you and established you?[j]

7 Think back on the days of old,
reflect on the years of age upon age.
Ask your father and he will inform you,
ask your elders and they will tell you:[k]
8 When the Most High assigned the nations their heritage,
when he parceled out the descendants of Adam,[l]
He set up the boundaries of the peoples
after the number of the sons of God;*
9 While the LORD's own portion was Jacob,
His hereditary share was Israel.[m]

10 He found them in a wilderness,
a wasteland of howling desert.
He shielded them and cared for them,
guarding them as the apple of his eye.[n]

11 As an eagle incites its nestlings forth
by hovering over its brood,
So he spread his wings to receive them
and bore them up on his pinions.[o]
12 The LORD alone was their leader,
no strange god was with him.
13 He had them ride triumphant over the summits of the land*
and live off the products of its fields,
Giving them honey to suck from its rocks
and olive oil from its hard, stony ground;
14 Butter from its cows and milk from its sheep,
with the fat of its lambs and rams;
Its Bashan* bulls and its goats,
with the cream of its finest wheat;
and the foaming blood of its grapes you drank.

### B

15 [So Jacob ate his fill,]
the darling* grew fat and frisky;
you became fat and gross and gorged.
They spurned the God who made them
and scorned their saving Rock.[p]
16 They provoked him with strange gods
and angered him with abominable idols.[q]

17 They offered sacrifice to demons, to "no-gods,"
to gods whom they had not known before,
To newcomers just arrived,
of whom their fathers had never stood in awe.
18 You were unmindful of the Rock that begot you,
You forgot the God who gave you birth.[r]
19 When the LORD saw this, he was filled with loathing
and anger toward his sons and daughters.
20 "I will hide my face from them," he said,
"and see what will then become of them.
What a fickle race they are,
sons with no loyalty in them![s]
21 "Since they have provoked me with their 'no god'
and angered me with their vain idols,
I will provoke them with a 'no-people';
with a foolish nation I will anger them.[t]

22 "'For by my wrath a fire is enkindled

h Ps 92, 15; Rv 15, 3.
i Dt 31, 29; Ps 78, 8; Lk 9, 41.
j Ex 4, 22; Is 63, 16; 64, 8; Jer 31, 9.
k Dt 4, 32; Ps 44, 2.
l Gn 10, 1-32; Acts 17, 26.
m Ex 19, 5; Ps 33, 12.
n Dt 8, 15; Jer 2, 6; Zec 2, 8.
o Ex 19, 4.
p Dt 31, 20.
q Nm 25, 2f; Ps 78, 58.
r Jer 2, 32.
s Dt 31, 17.
t Rom 10, 19.
u Lam 4, 11.

*

32, 1–43: In the style of the great prophets, the speaker is often God himself. The whole song is a poetic sermon, having for its theme God's benefits to Israel (vv 1–14) and Israel's ingratitude and idolatry in turning to the gods of the pagans, which sins will be punished by the pagans themselves (vv 15–29); in turn, the foolish pride of the pagans will be punished, and the Lord's honor will be vindicated (vv 30–43).

32, 8: The sons of God: the angels; cf Jb 1, 6; 2, 1; 38, 7; Ps 89, 7f. Here the various nations are portrayed as having their respective guardian angels. Cf Dn 10, 20f; 12, 1.

32, 13: The land: Canaan.

32, 14: Bashan: a fertile grazing land east of the Jordan, famous for its strong cattle. Cf Ps 22, 13; Ez 39, 18; Am 4, 1.

32, 15: The darling: a probable meaning of the Hebrew word yeshurun, a term of endearment for "Israel." Cf Dt 33, 5. 26; Is 44, 2.

that shall rage to the depths of the
netherworld,
Consuming the earth with its yield,
and licking with flames the roots of the
mountains.[u]
23 I will spend on them woe upon woe
and exhaust all my arrows against them:

24 "Emaciating hunger and consuming fever
and bitter pestilence,
And the teeth of wild beasts I will send
among them,
with the venom of reptiles gliding in the
dust.

25 "Snatched away by the sword in the street
and by sheer terror at home
Shall be the youth and the maiden alike,
the nursing babe as well as the hoary old
man.[v]

26 "I would have said, 'I will make an end of
them
and blot out their name from men's
memories,'
27 Had I not feared the insolence of their
enemies,
feared that these foes would mistakenly
boast,
'Our own hand won the victory;
the LORD had nothing to do with it.'"

28 For they are a people devoid of reason,*
having no understanding.
29 If they had insight they would realize what
happened,
they would understand their future and
say,

## C

30 "How could one man rout a thousand,
or two men put ten thousand to flight,
Unless it was because their Rock sold them
and the LORD delivered them up?"
31 Indeed, their "rock" is not like our Rock,
and our foes are under condemnation.

32 They are a branch of Sodom's vine-stock,
from the vineyards of Gomorrah.
Poisonous are their grapes and bitter their
clusters.
33 Their wine is the venom of dragons
and the cruel poison of cobras.

34 "Is not this preserved in my treasury,
sealed up in my storehouse,
35 Against the day of vengeance and requital,
against the time they lose their footing?"
Close at hand is the day of their disaster,
and their doom is rushing upon them!

36 Surely, the LORD shall do justice for his
people;
on his servants he shall have pity.
When he sees their strength failing,
and their protected and unprotected* alike
disappearing,[w]

37 He will say, "Where are their gods[x]
whom they relied on as their 'rock'?
38 Let those who ate the fat of your sacrifices
and drank the wine of your libations
Rise up now and help you!
Let them be your protection!

39 "Learn then that I, I alone, am God,
and there is no god beside me.
It is I who bring both death and life,
I who inflict wounds and heal them,
and from my hand there is no rescue.[y]

40 "To the heavens I raise my hand and swear:
As surely as I live forever,

41 I will sharpen my flashing sword,
and my hand shall lay hold of my quiver.

"With vengeance I will repay my foes
and require those who hate me.
42 I will make my arrows drunk with blood,
and my sword shall gorge itself with
flesh—
With the blood of the slain and the captured,
Flesh from the heads of the enemy
leaders."

43 Exult with him, you heavens,
glorify him, all you angels of God;
For he avenges the blood of his servants
and purges his people's land.

44 So Moses, together with Joshua, son of
Nun, went and recited all the words of this song
for the people to hear.

**Final Appeal.** 45 When Moses had finished
speaking all these words to all Israel, 46 he
said,[z] "Take to heart all the warning which I
have now given you and which you must impress on your children, that you may carry out
carefully every word of this law. 47 For this is
no trivial matter for you; rather, it means your
very life, since it is by this means that you are
to enjoy a long life on the land which you will
cross the Jordan to occupy."

**Moses to View Canaan.** 48 On that very
day the LORD said to Moses, 49 "Go up on

v Lv 26, 25.
w 2 Mc 7, 6.
x 37f: Jgs 10, 14; Jer 2, 28.
y Dt 4, 35; Tb 13, 2; Wis 16, 13.
z Dt 4, 9.
a Nm 27, 12; 33, 47f.

*

32, 28–35: The reference is to the pagan nations, not to Israel.

32, 36: Their protected and unprotected: the meaning of the Hebrew is uncertain; according to some, the idea is "slaves and freemen."

Mount Nebo, here in the Abarim Mountains [it
is in the land of Moab facing Jericho], and view
the land of Canaan, which I am giving to the
Israelites as their possession.[a] **50** Then you
shall die on the mountain you have climbed, and
shall be taken to your people, just as your brother Aaron died on Mount Hor and there was taken
to his people;[b] **51** because both of you broke
faith with me among the Israelites at the waters
of Meribath-kadesh in the desert of Zin by failing to manifest my sanctity among the Israelites.[c] **52** You may indeed view the land at a
distance, but you shall not enter that land which
I am giving to the Israelites."[d]

## CHAPTER 33

**Blessing upon the Tribes.** **1** This is the
blessing which Moses, the man of God, pronounced upon the Israelites before he died.
**2** He said:

"The LORD came from Sinai*
 and dawned on his people from Seir;
He shone forth from Mount Paran
 and advanced from Meribath-kadesh,
While at his right hand a fire blazed forth
 and his wrath devastated the nations.[e]

**3** But all his holy ones were in his hand;*
 they followed at his feet
 and he bore them up on his pinions.
**4** A law he gave to us;
 he made the community of Jacob his
  domain,[f]
**5** and he became king of his darling,*
When the chiefs of the people assembled
 and the tribes of Israel came together.
**6** "May Reuben live and not die out,[g]
 but let his men be few."*

**7** The following is for Judah. He said:
 "The LORD hears the cry of Judah;
 you will bring him to his people.*
His own hands defend his cause
 and you will be his help against his
  foes."[h]

**8** Of Levi he said:
 "To Levi belong your Thummim,
 to the man of your favor your Urim;*
For you put him to the test at Massah
 and you contended with him at the waters
  of Meribah.[i]
**9** He said of his father, 'I regard him not';
 his brothers he would not acknowledge,
 and his own children he refused to
  recognize.
Thus the Levites keep your words,
 and your covenant they uphold.*
**10** They promulgate your decisions to Jacob
 and your law to Israel.
They bring the smoke of sacrifice to your
  nostrils,
 and burnt offerings to your altar.[j]
**11** Bless, O LORD, his possessions
 and accept the ministry of his hands.
Break the backs of his adversaries
 and of his foes, that they may not rise."

**12** Of Benjamin he said:
 "Benjamin is the beloved of the LORD,
 who shelters him all the day,
 while he abides securely at his breast."[k]

**13** Of Joseph he said:[l]
 "Blessed by the LORD is his land
 with the best of the skies above
 and of the abyss crouching beneath;
**14** With the best of the produce of the year,
 and the choicest sheaves of the months;
**15** With the finest gifts of the age-old
  mountains
 and the best from the timeless hills;
**16** With the best of the earth and its fullness,
 and the favor of him who dwells in the
  bush.*
These shall come upon the head of Joseph
 and upon the brow of the prince among
  his brothers,
**17** The majestic bull, his father's first-born,
 whose horns are those of the wild ox
With which to gore the nations,
 even those at the ends of the earth."
[These are the myriads of Ephraim,
 and these the thousands of Manasseh.]

**18** Of Zebulun he said:[m]
"Rejoice, O Zebulun, in your pursuits,
 and you, Issachar, in your tents!
**19** You who invite the tribes to the mountains

---

b Nm 20, 24ff. 28; 27, 13; 33, 38.
c Nm 20, 12; 27, 14.
d Dt 3, 27; 34, 4.
e Ex 19, 18. 20; Jgs 5, 4f.
f Jn 1, 17; 7, 19.
g Gn 49, 3f.
h Gn 49, 8-12.
i Gn 49, 5; Ex 17, 7; 28, 30; Nm 20, 13.
j Ex 30, 7f.
k Gn 49, 27.
l 13-17: Gn 49, 22-26.
m 18f: Gn 49, 13ff.

---

*

33, 2–5. 26–29: These verses seem to form an independent hymn describing, in the form of a theophany, the conquest of Canaan. The first section of this hymn (vv 2–5) serves here as an introduction to the various "blessings"; the second section (vv 26–29), as their conclusion.

33, 3: His holy ones were in his hand: the Israelites were protected by the Lord.

33, 5. 26: The darling: see note on Dt 32, 15.

33, 6: In keeping with the other blessings, probably this verse was once introduced by the phrase, "Of Reuben he said." It is to be noted that there is no blessing here for Simeon.

33, 7: Bring him to his people: this probably refers to the isolated position of the tribe of Judah during the conquest of the Promised Land (cf Jgs 1, 17–19); according to some commentators the reference is to the divided kingdom.

33, 8: Thummim . . . Urim: see note on Ex 28, 30.

33, 9: The reference is probably to the Levites' slaughter of their brethren after the affair of the golden calf in the desert; cf Ex 32, 27–29.

33, 16: Him who dwells in the bush: a title given to the Lord because of his appearance to Moses in the burning bush; cf Ex 3.

33, 19: The abundance of the seas: perhaps the wealth that

where feasts are duly held,
Because you suck up the abundance of the seas*
and the hidden treasures of the sand."

20 Of Gad he said:[n]
"Blessed be he who has made Gad so vast!
He lies there like a lion
that has seized the arm and head of the prey.
21 He saw that the best should be his
when the princely portion* was assigned,
while the heads of the people were gathered.
He carried out the justice of the LORD
and his decrees respecting Israel."[o]

22 Of Dan he said:
"Dan is a lion's whelp,[p]
that springs forth from Bashan!"*

23 Of Naphtali he said:
"Naphtali is enriched with favors
and filled with the blessings of the LORD;
The lake* and south of it are his possession!"[q]

24 Of Asher he said:[r]
"More blessed than the other sons be Asher!
May he be the favorite among his brothers,
as the oil of his olive trees runs over his feet!*
25 May your bolts be of iron and bronze;
may your strength endure through all your days!"

26 "There is no god like the God of the darling,
who rides the heavens in his power,
and rides the skies in his majesty;
27 He spread out the primeval tent;
he extended the ancient canopy.
He drove the enemy out of your way
and the Amorite he destroyed.
28 Israel has dwelt securely,
and the fountain of Jacob has been undisturbed.
In a land of grain and wine,
where the heavens drip with dew.[s]
29 How fortunate you are, O Israel!
Where else is a nation victorious in the LORD?
The LORD is your saving shield,
and his sword is your glory.
Your enemies fawn upon you,
as you stride upon their heights."[t]

## CHAPTER 34

**Death and Burial of Moses.** 1 Then Mo-
ses went up from the plains of Moab to Mount
Nebo,[u] the headland of Pisgah which faces Jericho, and the LORD showed him all the land—
Gilead, and as far as Dan, 2 all Naphtali, the
land of Ephraim and Manasseh, all the land of
Judah as far as the Western Sea, 3 the Negeb,
the circuit of the Jordan with the lowlands at
Jericho, city of palms, and as far as Zoar. 4 The
LORD then said to him, "This is the land[v] which
I swore to Abraham, Isaac and Jacob that I
would give to their descendants. I have let you
feast your eyes upon it, but you shall not cross
over." 5 So there, in the land of Moab, Moses,
the servant of the LORD, died[w] as the LORD had
said; 6 and he was buried in the ravine opposite
Beth-peor in the land of Moab, but to this day
no one day no one knows the place of his burial.
7 Moses was one hundred and twenty years
old[x] when he died, yet his eyes were undimmed
and his vigor unabated. 8 For thirty days the
Israelites wept for Moses in the plains of Moab,
till they had completed the period of grief and
mourning for Moses.
9 Now Joshua, son of Nun,[y] was filled with
the spirit of wisdom, since Moses had laid his
hands upon him; and so the Israelites gave him
their obedience, thus carrying out the LORD's
command to Moses.
10 [z]Since then no prophet has arisen in Israel
like Moses, whom the LORD knew face to face.
11 [a]He had no equal in all the signs and wonders the LORD sent him to perform in the land
of Egypt against Pharaoh and all his servants
and against all his land, 12 and for the might
and the terrifying power that Moses exhibited in
the sight of all Israel.

---

n 20f: Gn 49, 19.
o Nm 32, 1. 5. 16-19. 31f; Jos 1, 12-15; 1 Chr 5, 18-22.
p Gn 49, 16f.
q Gn 49, 21; Jos 19, 32-39.
r 24f: Gn 49, 20.
s Gn 27, 28.
t Dt 4, 7f.
u Dt 3, 27.
v Dt 3, 27; 32, 52; Gn 12, 7; 15, 18.
w Dt 32, 50.
x Dt 31, 2.
y Nm 27, 18. 23; Jos 1, 17.
z Ex 33, 11.
a Dt 4, 34.

---

* comes from sea-borne trade or from fishing. The hidden treasures of the sand: possibly an allusion to the valuable purple dye extracted from certain marine shells found on the coast of northern Palestine.

33, 21: The princely portion: Moses gave the tribe of Gad their land on the east of the Jordan only on condition that they would help the other tribes conquer the land west of the river; cf Nm 32; Jos 22.

33, 22: The sense is, "May he leap up like a lion of Bashan"; the heavily wooded hills of Bashan were notorious for their lions, but the tribe of Dan was not settled in this region.

33, 23: The lake: the Lake of Gennesaret on which the land of this tribe bordered.

33, 24: The land of the tribe of Asher was covered with olive groves.

# The Book of JOSHUA

*The Book of Joshua derives its name from the successor of Moses, with whose deeds it is principally concerned. The purpose of the book is to demonstrate God's fidelity in giving to the Israelites the land he had promised them for an inheritance (Gn 15, 18ff; Jos 1, 2ff; 21, 41ff; 23, 14ff).*

*Their occupation of the country is begun with the crossing of the Jordan and the conquest of Jericho (ch 1–6), in both of which the Lord intervenes on their behalf. This is followed by a first foothold on the Palestinian mountain range, at Ai, Bethel and Gibeon (ch 7–9), and two sweeping campaigns against the city states in the south of the country (ch 10) and in the north (ch 11), with a summary in ch 12. The broad claim to total sovereignty thus established is spelled out by a combined list of tribal boundaries and of the towns contained within each area or administrative district (ch 13–19), including cities of asylum and cities for the Levites (ch 20, 21). The book closes with a narrative about the tribes east of the Jordan (ch 22), a warning speech by Joshua (ch 23), and a renewal at Shechem (ch 24) of the covenant with the Lord, already affirmed there near the beginning (8, 30–35) of the conquest.*

*Like the books which precede it, the Book of Joshua was built up by a long and complex process of editing traditional materials. Both Jewish and Christian believers have always regarded it as inspired.*

*The entire history of the conquest of the Promised Land is a prophecy of the spiritual conquest of the world through the church under the leadership of Jesus the Messiah.*

*The Book of Joshua may be divided as follows:*

*I. Conquest of Canaan (Jos 1, 1–12, 24).*
*II. Division of the Land (Jos 13, 1–21, 45).*
*III. Return of the Transjordan Tribes and Joshua's Farewell (Jos 22, 1–24, 33).*

## I: Conquest of Canaan

### CHAPTER 1

**Divine Promise of Assistance.** 1 After
Moses, the servant of the LORD, had died, the
LORD said to Moses' aid Joshua, son of Nun:
2 "My servant Moses is dead. So prepare to
cross the Jordan here, with all the people, into
the land I will give the Israelites. 3 As I promised Moses, I will deliver to you every place
where you set foot. 4 *Your domain is to be all
the land of the Hittites, from the desert and from
Lebanon east to the great river Euphrates and
west to the Great Sea.[a] 5 No one can withstand
you while you live. I will be with you as I was
with Moses:[b] I will not leave you nor forsake
you. 6 Be firm and steadfast, so that you may
give this people possession of the land which I
swore to their fathers I would give them.
7 Above all, be firm and steadfast, taking care
to observe the entire law which my servant Moses enjoined on you. Do not swerve from it
either to the right or to the left, that you may
succeed wherever you go. 8 Keep this book of
the law on your lips. Recite it by day and by
night, that you may observe carefully all that is
written in it; then you will successfully attain
your goal. 9 I command you: be firm and steadfast! Do not fear nor be dismayed, for the LORD,
your God, is with you wherever you go."[c]
10 So Joshua commanded the officers of the
people: 11 "Go through the camp and instruct
the people, 'Prepare your provisions, for three
days from now you shall cross the Jordan here,
to march in and take possession of the land
which the LORD, your God, is giving you.'"[d]

**The Transjordan Tribes.** 12 Joshua reminded the Reubenites, the Gadites, and the
half-tribe of Manasseh: 13 "Remember what
Moses, the servant of the LORD, commanded

a 3f: Jos 14, 9; Gn 15, 18; Dt 11, 24.
b Dt 31, 8; Heb 13, 5.
c 7. 9: Dt 31, 7f.
d Dt 11, 31.

* 1, 4: The ideal frontiers are given: in the south the desert of Sinai, in the north the Lebanon range, in the east the Euphrates, and in the west the Great Sea, the Mediterranean.

you when he said, The LORD, your God, will
permit you to settle in this land." **14** Your
wives, your children, and your livestock shall
remain in the land Moses gave you here beyond
the Jordan.[e] But all the warriors among you
must cross over armed ahead of your kinsmen
and you must help them **15** until the LORD has
settled your kinsmen, and they like you possess
the land which the LORD, your God, is giving
them. Afterward you may return and occupy
your own land, which Moses, the servant of the
LORD, has given you east of the Jordan."[f]
**16** "We will do all you have commanded us,"
they answered Joshua, "and we will go wherever you send us. We will obey you as completely as we obeyed Moses. **17** But may the
LORD, your God, be with you as he was with
Moses. **18** If anyone rebels against your orders
and does not obey every command you give
him, he shall be put to death. But be firm and
steadfast."

## CHAPTER 2

**Spies Saved by Rahab.** **1** Then Joshua,
son of Nun, secretly sent out two spies from
Shittim, saying, "Go, reconnoiter the land and
Jericho." When the two reached Jericho, they
went into the house of a harlot* named Rahab,[g]
where they lodged. **2** But a report was brought
to the king of Jericho that some Israelites had
come there that night to spy out the land. **3** So
the king of Jericho sent Rahab the order, "Put
out the visitors who have entered your house,
for they have come to spy out the entire land."
**4** The woman[h] had taken the two men and hidden them, so she said, "True, the men you
speak of came to me, but I did not know where
they came from. **5** At dark, when it was time
for the gate to be shut, they left, and I do not
know where they went. You will have to pursue
them immediately to overtake them." **6** Now,
she had led them to the roof, and hidden them
among her stalks of flax spread out* there.
**7** But the pursuers set out along the way to the
fords of the Jordan, and once they had left, the
gate was shut.

**8** Before the spies fell asleep, Rahab* came
to them on the roof **9** and said: "I know that
the LORD has given you the land, that a dread
of you had come upon us, and that all the inhabitants of the land are overcome with fear of
you.[i] **10** For we have heard how the LORD dried
up the waters of the Red Sea before you when
you came out of Egypt,[j] and how you dealt with
Sihon and Og, the two kings of the Amorites
beyond the Jordan, whom you doomed to destruction. **11** At these reports, we are disheartened; everyone is discouraged because of you,
since the LORD, your God, is God in heaven
above and on earth below.[k] **12** Now then,
swear to me by the LORD that, since I am showing kindness to you, you in turn will show kindness to my family;[l] and give me an unmistak-
able token **13** that you are to spare my father
and mother, brothers and sisters, and all their
kin, and save us from death." **14** "We pledge
our lives for yours," the men answered her. "If
you do not betray this errand of ours, we will be
faithful in showing kindness to you when the
LORD gives us the land."

**15** Then she let them down through the window with a rope; for she lived in a house built
into the city wall.* **16** "Go up into the hill
country," she suggested to them, "that your
pursuers may not find you. Hide there for three
days, until they return; then you may proceed on
your way." **17** The men answered her, "This
is how we will fulfill the oath you made us take:
**18** When we come into the land, tie this scarlet
cord in the window through which you are letting us down; and gather your father and mother, your brothers and all your family into your
house. **19** Should any of them pass outside the
doors of your house, he will be responsible for
his own death, and we shall be guiltless. But we
shall be responsible if anyone in the house with
you is harmed. **20** If, however, you betray this
errand of ours, we shall be quit of the oath you
have made us take." **21** "Let it be as you say,"
she replied, and bade them farewell. When they
were gone, she tied the scarlet cord in the window.

**22** They went up into the hills, where they
stayed three days until their pursuers, who had
sought them all along the road without finding
them, returned. **23** Then the two came back
down from the hills, crossed the Jordan to Joshua, son of Nun, and reported all that had befall-
en them. **24** They assured Joshua, "The LORD
has delivered all this land into our power; in-

e Nm 32, 26.
f Jos 22, 4; Dt 3, 20.
g Mt 1, 5; Jas 2, 25.
h Jos 6, 17.
i Ex 15, 15f; 23, 27.
j Jos 4, 23; Ex 14, 21; Nm 21, 23-26. 33ff.
k Dt 4, 39.
l Jos 2, 18; 6, 23. 25.

*

2, 1: Harlot: this is the regular equivalent of the Hebrew word, but perhaps it is used here of Rahab in the broader sense of a woman who kept a public house. Joshua's spies hoped to remain undetected at such an inn.

2, 6: Stalks of flax spread out: to dry in the sun, after they had been soaked in water, according to the ancient process of preparing flax for linen-making. In the Near East the flax harvest occurs near the time of the feast of the Passover (Jos 4, 19; 5, 10); cf Ex 9, 31.

2, 8–11: Rahab's faith and good works are praised in the New Testament; cf Heb 11, 31; Jas 2, 25.

2, 15: A house built into the city wall: such houses, which used the city wall for their own inner walls, have been found at ancient sites. The upper story of Rahab's house was evidently higher than the city wall. It was through the window of such a house that St. Paul escaped from Damascus; cf Acts 9, 25; 2 Cor 11, 33.

deed, all the inhabitants of the land are overcome with fear of us.''

## CHAPTER 3

### Preparations for Crossing the Jordan.

**1** Early the next morning, Joshua[m] moved with
all the Israelites from Shittim to the Jordan,
where they lodged before crossing over.
**2** Three days later the officers went through the
camp **3** and issued these instructions to the people: ''When you see the ark of the covenant of
the LORD, your God, which the levitical priests
will carry, you must also break camp and follow
it, **4** that you may know the way to take, for you
have not gone over this road before. But let
there be a space of two thousand cubits between
you and the ark. Do not come nearer to it.''
**5** Joshua also said to the people, ''Sanctify
yourselves, for tomorrow the LORD will perform
wonders among you.'' **6** And he directed the
priests to take up the ark of the covenant and go
on ahead of the people; and they did so.

**7** Then the LORD said to Joshua, ''Today I
will begin to exalt you in the sight of all Israel,
that they may know I am with you, as I was with
Moses.[n] **8** Now command the priests carrying
the ark of the covenant to come to a halt in the
Jordan when they reach the edge of the waters.''

**9** So Joshua said to the Israelites, ''Come
here and listen to the words of the LORD, your
God.'' **10** He continued: ''This is how you will
know that there is a living God in your midst,
who at your approach will dispossess the Canaanites, Hittites, Hivites, Perizzites, Girgashites, Amorites and Jebusites.[o] **11** The ark of
the covenant of the LORD of the whole earth will
precede you into the Jordan. **12** [Now choose
twelve men,[p] one from each of the tribes of
Israel.] **13** When the soles of the feet of the
priests carrying the ark of the LORD, the Lord of
the whole earth, touch the water of the Jordan,
it will cease to flow; for the water flowing down
from upstream will halt in a solid bank.''

### The Crossing Begun.

**14** The people
struck their tents to cross the Jordan, with the
priests carrying the ark of the covenant ahead of
them. **15** No sooner had these priestly bearers
of the ark waded into the waters at the edge of
the Jordan, which overflows all its banks during
the entire season of the harvest,* **16** than the
waters flowing from upstream halted, backing
up in a solid mass[q] for a very great distance
indeed, from Adam, a city in the direction of
Zarethan; while those flowing downstream toward the Salt Sea of the Arabah disappeared
entirely.* Thus the people crossed over opposite
Jericho. **17** While all Israel crossed over on dry
ground, the priests carrying the ark of the covenant of the LORD remained motionless on dry
ground in the bed of the Jordan[r] until the whole
nation had completed the passage.

## CHAPTER 4

### Memorial Stones.

**1** After the entire nation
had crossed the Jordan, the LORD said to Joshua,
**2** ''Choose twelve men[s] from the people, one
from each tribe, **3** and instruct them to take up
twelve stones from this spot in the bed of the
Jordan where the priests have been standing
motionless.[t] Carry them over with you, and
place them where you are to stay tonight.''

**4** Summoning the twelve men whom he had
selected from among the Israelites, one from
each tribe, **5** Joshua said to them: ''Go to the
bed of the Jordan in front of the ark of the LORD,
your God; lift to your shoulders one stone
apiece, so that they will equal in number the
tribes of the Israelites. **6** In the future, these are
to be a sign among you. When your children ask
you what these stones mean to you, **7** you shall
answer them, 'The waters of the Jordan ceased
to flow before the ark of the covenant of the
LORD when it crossed the Jordan.'[u] Thus these
stones are to serve as a perpetual memorial to
the Israelites.'' **8** The twelve Israelites did as
Joshua had commanded: they took up as many
stones from the bed of the Jordan as there were
tribes of the Israelites, and carried them along
to the camp site, where they placed them, according to the LORD's direction. **9** Josua also
had twelve stones set up in the bed of the Jordan
on the spot where the priests stood who were
carrying the ark of the covenant. They are there
to this day.

**10** *The priests carrying the ark remained in
the bed of the Jordan until everything had been
done that the LORD had commanded Joshua to
tell the people. The people crossed over quick-

---

m Jos 2, 1.
n Jos 1, 5; 4, 14.
o Ex 33, 2; Dt 7, 1.
p Jos 4, 2. 4.
q Ps 114, 3.
r Jos 4, 7. 22.
s Jos 3, 12.
t Jos 3, 13; 4, 8f; Dt 27, 2.
u Jos 3, 13. 16.

---

*

3, 15: Season of the harvest: toward the end of March and the beginning of April, when the grain and other crops that grew during the rainy season of winter were reaped. The crossing took place "on the tenth day of the first month" of the Hebrew year, which began with the first new moon after the spring equinox; cf Jos 4, 19. At this time of the year the Jordan would be swollen as a result of the winter rains and the melting snow of Mount Hermon.

3, 16: The sudden damming of the river could have been caused by a landslide, as has happened on other occasions. The miraculous character of this event would not thereby be removed because God, who foretold it (Jos 3, 13), also caused it to take place at precisely the right moment (Jos 3, 15), whether or not he used natural forces to accomplish his will.

4, 10–18: After the digression about the two sets of memorial stones, the author resumes the narrative by briefly repeating the story of the crossing, which he had already told in Jos 3, 14–17.

ly, **11** and when all had reached the other side,
the ark of the LORD, borne by the priests, also
crossed to its place in front of them. **12** The
Reubenites, Gadites, and half-tribe of Manasseh, armed, marched in the vanguard of the
Israelites, as Moses had ordered.[v] **13** About
forty thousand troops equipped for battle passed
over before the LORD to the plains of Jericho.

**14** That day the LORD exalted Joshua in the
sight of all Israel,[w] and thenceforth during his
whole life they respected him as they had respected Moses.

**15** Then the LORD said to Joshua, **16** "Command the priests carrying the ark of the commandments to come up from the Jordan."[x]
**17** Joshua did so, **18** and when the priests carrying the ark of the covenant of the LORD had
come up from the bed of the Jordan, as the soles
of their feet regained the dry ground, the waters
of the Jordan resumed their course and as before
overflowed all its banks.

**19** The people came up from the Jordan on
the tenth day of the first month, and camped in
Gilgal on the eastern limits of Jericho. **20** At
Gilgal Joshua set up the twelve stones which
had been taken from the Jordan, **21** saying to
the Israelites, "In the future, when the children
among you ask their fathers what these stones
mean, **22** you shall inform them, 'Israel
crossed the Jordan here on dry ground.' **23** For
the LORD, your God, dried up the waters of the
Jordan in front of you until you crossed over,
just as the LORD, your God, had done at the Red
Sea, which he dried up in front of us until we
crossed over;[y] **24** in order that all the peoples
of the earth may learn that the hand of the LORD
is mighty, and that you may fear the LORD, your
God, forever."

## CHAPTER 5

**Rites at Gilgal.** **1** When all the kings of
Amorites to the west of the Jordan and all the
kings of the Canaanites by the sea heard that the
LORD had dried up the waters of the Jordan
before the Israelites until they crossed over,
they were disheartened and lost courage at their
approach.

**2** On this occasion the LORD said to Joshua,
"Make flint knives and circumcise the Israelite
nation for the second time." **3** So Joshua made
flint knives and circumcised the Israelites at
Gibeath-haaraloth,* **4** under these circumstances: Of all the people who came out of
Egypt, every man of military age had died in the
desert[z] during the journey after they left Egypt.
**5** Though all the men who came out were circumcised, none of those born in the desert during the journey after the departure from Egypt
were circumcised. **6** Now the Israelites had
wandered forty years in the desert, until all the
warriors among the people that came forth from
Egypt died off because they had not obeyed the
command of the LORD.[a] For the LORD swore[b]
that he would not let them see the land flowing
with milk and honey which he had promised
their fathers he would give us. **7** [c]It was the
children whom he raised up in their stead whom
Joshua circumcised, for these were yet with
foreskins, not having been circumcised on the
journey. **8** When the rite had been performed,
the whole nation remained in camp where they
were, until they recovered. **9** Then the LORD
said to Joshua, "Today I have removed the
reproach of Egypt from you."[d] Therefore the
place is called Gilgal* to the present day.

**10** [e]While the Israelites were encamped at
Gilgal on the plains of Jericho, they celebrated
the Passover on the evening of the fourteenth of
the month.* **11** On the day after the Passover
they ate of the produce of the land in the form
of unleavened cakes and parched grain. On that
same day **12** after the Passover on which they
ate of the produce of the land, the manna
ceased. No longer was there manna for the Israelites, who that year ate of the yield of the land
of Canaan.[f]

**Siege at Jericho.** **13** *While Joshua was
near Jericho, he raised his eyes and saw one who
stood facing him, drawn sword in hand.[g] Joshua went up to him and asked, "Are you one of
us or of our enemies?" **14** He replied, "Neither. I am the captain of the host of the LORD
and I have just arrived." Then Joshua fell prostrate to the ground in worship, and said to him,
"What has my lord to say to his servant?"
**15** The captain of the host of the LORD replied
to Joshua, "Remove your sandals from your
feet, for the place on which you are standing is
holy."[h] And Joshua obeyed.

v Dt 3, 18.
w Jos 3, 7.
x Jos 3, 6.
y Ex 14, 21.
z Nm 14, 29; 26, 64f; Dt 2, 16; Ps 106, 26; 1 Cor 10, 5.
a Nm 14, 29.
b Heb 3, 11. 17.
c Dt 1, 39.
d Jos 4, 19.
e Ex 12, 6; Lv 23, 5; Nm 9, 3-5.
f Ex 16, 35.
g Ex 23, 20.
h Ex 3, 5; Acts 7, 33.

5, 3: Gibeath-haaraloth: "Hill of the Foreskins."

5, 9: The place is called Gilgal: by popular etymology, because of the similarity of sound with the Hebrew word gallothi, "I have removed." Gilgal probably means "(the place of) the circle of standing stones." Cf Jos 4, 4–8.

5, 10: The month: the first month of the year, later called Nisan; see note on Jos 3, 15. The crossing of the Jordan occurred, therefore, about the same time of the year as did the equally miraculous crossing of the Red Sea; cf Ex 12–14.

5, 13–6, 26: The account of the siege of Jericho embraces: (1) the command of the Lord, through his angel, to Joshua (Jos 5, 13–6, 5); (2) Joshua's instructions to the Israelites, with a brief summary of how these orders were carried out (Jos 6, 6–11); (3) a description of the action on each of the first six days (Jos 6, 12–14); (4) the events on the seventh day (Jos 6, 15–26).

## CHAPTER 6

**1** Now Jericho was in a state of siege because
of the presence of the Israelites, so that no one
left or entered. **2** And to Joshua the LORD said,
"I have delivered Jericho and its king into your
power. **3** Have all the soldiers circle the city,
marching once around it. Do this for six days,
**4** [i]with seven priests carrying ram's horns
ahead of the ark. On the seventh day march
around the city seven times, and have the priests
blow the horns. **5** When they give a long blast
on the ram's horns and you hear that signal, all
the people shall shout aloud. The wall of the city
will collapse, and they will be able to make a
frontal attack."

**6** Summoning the priests, Joshua, son of
Nun, then ordered them to take up the ark of the
covenant with seven of the priests carrying
ram's horns in front of the ark of the LORD.
**7** And he ordered the people to proceed in a
circle around the city, with the picked troops
marching ahead of the ark of the LORD. **8** At
this order they proceeded, with the seven priests
who carried the ram's horns before the LORD
blowing their horns, and the ark of the covenant
of the LORD following them. **9** In front of the
priests with the horns marched the picked
troops; the rear-guard followed the ark, and the
blowing of horns was kept up continually as
they marched. **10** But the people had been commanded by Joshua not to shout or make any
noise or outcry until he gave the word: only then
were they to shout. **11** So he had the ark of the
LORD circle the city, going once around it, after
which they returned to camp for the night.

**12** Early the next morning, Joshua had the
priests take up the ark of the LORD. **13** The
seven priests bearing the ram's horns marched
in front of the ark of the LORD, blowing their
horns. Ahead of these marched the picked
troops, while the rear guard followed the ark of
the LORD, and the blowing of horns was kept up
continually. **14** On this second day they again
marched around the city once before returning
to camp; and for six days in all they did the
same.

**15** On the seventh day, beginning at daybreak, they marched around the city seven times
in the same manner; on that day only did they
march around the city seven times. **16** The seventh time around, the priests blew the horns and
Joshua said to the people, "Now shout, for the
LORD has given you the city **17** and everything
in it.[j] It is under the LORD's ban. Only the harlot
Rahab and all who are in the house with her are
to be spared, because she hid the messengers we
sent. **18** [k]But be careful not to take, in your
greed, anything that is under the ban;* else you
will bring upon the camp of Israel this ban and
the misery of it. **19** All silver and gold, and the
articles of bronze or iron, are sacred to the
LORD. They shall be put in the treasury of the
LORD."

**The Fall of Jericho.** **20** As the horns blew,
the people began to shout. When they heard the
signal horn, they raised a tremendous shout.
The wall collapsed,* and the people stormed the
city in a frontal attack and took it.[l] **21** They
observed the ban by putting to the sword all
living creatures[m] in the city: men and women,
young and old, as well as oxen, sheep and asses.

**22** Joshua directed the two men who had
spied out the land, "Go into the harlot's house
and bring out the woman with all her kin, as you
swore to her you would do."[n] **23** The spies
entered and brought out Rahab, with her father,
mother, brothers, and all her kin.[o] Her entire
family they led forth and placed them outside
the camp of Israel. **24** The city itself they
burned with all that was in it,[p] except the silver,
gold, and articles of bronze and iron, which
were placed in the treasury of the house of the
LORD. **25** *Because Rahab the harlot had hidden the messengers whom Joshua had sent to
reconnoiter Jericho, Joshua spared her with her
family and all her kin, who continue in the midst
of Israel to this day.

**26** [q]On that occasion Joshua imposed the
oath: Cursed before the LORD be the man who
attempts to rebuild this city, Jericho. He shall
lose his first-born when he lays its foundation,
and he shall lose his youngest son when he sets
up its gates.*

**27** Thus the LORD was with Joshua so that his
fame spread throughout the land.[r]

## CHAPTER 7

**Defeat at Ai.** **1** But the Israelites violated
the ban; Achan, son of Carmi, son of Zerah, son
of Zara of the tribe of Judah, took goods that

i Nm 10, 8f.
j Jos 2, 4; Dt 20, 17; Heb 11, 31.
k Jos 7, 12. 25; Dt 13, 18.
l 2 Mc 12, 15; Heb 11, 30.
m Dt 7, 2.
n Jos 2, 14.
o Jos 2, 13; Heb 11, 31.
p Jos 8, 2.
q 1 Kgs 16, 34.
r Jos 1, 5.
s Jos 6, 18; 22, 20; 1 Chr 2, 7.

6, 18: That is under the ban: that is doomed to destruction; see notes on Lv 27, 29; Nm 18, 14; 21, 3.

6, 20: The wall collapsed: by the miraculous intervention of God. The blowing of the horns and the shouting of the people were a customary feature of ancient warfare, here intended by God as a test of the people's obedience and of their faith in his promise; cf Heb 11, 30.

6, 25: From Mt 1, 5, we learn that Rahab married Salmon of the tribe of Judah and thus became the great-great-grandmother of David, Christ's ancestor; cf Ru 4, 18–22.

6, 26: He shall lose his first-born . . . its gates: this curse was fulfilled when Hiel rebuilt Jericho as a fortified city during the reign of Ahab, king of Israel, cf 1 Kgs 16, 34. Till then Jericho was merely an unwalled village; cf Jos 18, 12. 21; Jgs 3, 13; 2 Sm 10, 5.

were under the ban,[s] and the anger of the LORD
flared up against the Israelites.
2 Joshua next sent men from Jericho to Ai,
which is near Bethel on its eastern side, with
instructions to go up and reconnoiter the land.
When they had explored Ai, 3 they returned to
Joshua and advised, "Do not send all the people
up; if only about two or three thousand go up,
they can overcome Ai. The enemy there are
few; you need not call for an effort from all the
people." 4 About three thousand of the people
made the attack, but they were defeated by those
at Ai, 5 who killed some thirty-six of them.
They pressed them back across the clearing in
front of the city gate till they broke ranks, and
defeated them finally on the descent, so that the
confidence of the people melted away like water.
6 Joshua, together with the elders of Israel,
rent his garments and lay prostrate before the
ark of the LORD until evening; and they threw
dust on their heads. 7 "Alas, O Lord GOD,"
Joshua prayed, "why did you ever allow this
people to pass over the Jordan, delivering us
into the power of the Amorites, that they might
destroy us? Would that we had been content to
dwell on the other side of the Jordan. 8 Pray,
Lord, what can I say, now that Israel has turned
its back to its enemies? 9 When the Canaanites
and the other inhabitants of the land hear of it,
they will close in around us and efface our name
from the earth. What will you do for your great
name?"
10 The LORD replied to Joshua: "Stand up.
Why are you lying prostrate? 11 [t]Israel has
sinned: they have violated the covenant which
I enjoined on them. They have stealthily taken
goods subject to the ban, and have deceitfully
put them in their baggage. 12 If the Israelites
cannot stand up to their enemies, but must turn
their back to them, it is because they are under
the ban.[u] I will not remain with you unless you
remove from among you whoever has incurred
the ban. 13 Rise, sanctify the people.[v] Tell
them to sanctify themselves before tomorrow,
for the LORD, the God of Israel, says: You are
under the ban, O Israel. You cannot stand up to
your enemies until you remove from among you
whoever has incurred the ban. 14 In the morning you must present yourselves by tribes. The
tribe which the LORD designates shall come forward by clans; the clan which the LORD designates shall come forward by families; the family
which the LORD designates shall come forward
one by one. 15 He who is designated as having
incurred the ban shall be destroyed by fire, with
all that is his, because he has violated the covenant of the LORD and has committed a shameful crime in Israel."

**Achan's Guilt and Punishment.** 16 Early the next morning Joshua had Israel come
forward by tribes, and the tribe of Judah was
designated.* 17 Then he had the clans of Judah
come forward, and the clan of Zerah was designated. He had the clan of Zerah[w] come forward
by families, and Zabdi was designated. 18 Finally he had that family come forward one by
one, and Achan, son of Carmi, son of Zabdi,
son of Zerah of the tribe of Judah, was designated. 19 Joshua said to Achan, "My son, give to
the LORD, the God of Israel, glory and honor by
telling me what you have done; do not hide it
from me." 20 Achan answered Joshua, "I
have indeed sinned against the LORD, the God
of Israel. This is what I have done: 21 Among
the spoils, I saw a beautiful Babylonian mantle,
two hundred shekels of silver, and a bar of gold
fifty shekels in weight; in my greed I took them.
They are now hidden in the ground inside my
tent, with the silver underneath." 22 The messengers whom Joshua sent hastened to the tent
and found them hidden there, with the silver
underneath. 23 They took them from the tent,
brought them to Joshua and all the Israelites,
and spread them out before the LORD.
24 Then Joshua and all Israel took Achan,
son of Zerah, with the silver, the mantle, and the
bar of gold, and with his sons and daughters, his
ox, his ass and his sheep, his tent, and all his
possessions, and led them off to the Valley of
Achor. 25 Joshua said, "The LORD bring upon
you today the misery with which you have afflicted us!"[x] And all Israel stoned him to death
26 and piled a great heap of stones over him,
which remains to the present day.[y] Then the
anger of the LORD relented. That is why the
place is called the Valley of Achor* to this day.

## CHAPTER 8

**Capture of Ai.** 1 The LORD then said to
Joshua, "Do not be afraid or dismayed. Take all
the army with you and prepare to attack Ai.[z] I
have delivered the king of Ai into your power,
with his people, city, and land. 2 Do to Ai and
its king what you did to Jericho and its king;
except that you may take its spoil and livestock
as booty.[a] Set an ambush behind the city."

t Jos 6, 17-19.
u Jos 6, 18.
v Jos 3, 5; Lv 20, 7; 1 Sm 16, 5.
w Nm 26, 20.
x Jos 6, 18; 22, 20; 1 Chr 2, 7.
y Jos 8, 29.
z Jos 2, 24.
a Jos 6, 21. 24; Dt 20, 14.

*

7, 16ff: Was designated: probably by means of the Urim and Thummim; cf 1 Sm 14, 38–42. See note on Ex 28, 30.

7, 26: Achor: "misery, affliction." The reference is to the saying of Joshua in v 25, with an allusion also to the similar-sounding name of Achan.

**3** So Joshua and all the soldiers prepared to
attack Ai. Picking out thirty thousand warriors,* Joshua sent them off by night **4** with
these orders: "See that you ambush the city
from the rear, at no great distance; then all of
you be on the watch. **5** The rest of the people
and I will come up to the city, and when they
make a sortie against us as they did the last time,
we will flee from them. **6** They will keep coming out after us until we have drawn them away
from the city, for they will think we are fleeing
from them as we did the last time. When this
occurs, **7** rise from ambush and take possession
of the city, which the LORD, your God, will
deliver into your power. **8** When you have tak-
en the city, set it afire in obedience to the
LORD's command. These are my orders to
you." **9** Then Joshua sent them away. They
went to the place of ambush, taking up their
position to the west of Ai, toward Bethel. Joshua, however, spent that night in the plain.

**10** Early the next morning Joshua mustered
the army and went up to Ai at its head, with the
elders of Israel. **11** When all the troops he led
were drawn up in position before the city, they
pitched camp north of Ai, on the other side of
the ravine. **12** [He took about five thousand
men and set them in ambush between Bethel and
Ai, west of the city.] **13** Thus the people took
up their stations, with the main body north of the
city and the ambush west of it, and Joshua waited overnight among his troops. **14** The king of
Ai saw this, and he and all his army came out
very early in the morning to engage Israel in
battle at the descent toward the Arabah, not
knowing that there was an ambush behind the
city. **15** Joshua and the main body of the Israelites fled in seeming defeat toward the desert,
**16** till the last of the soldiers in the city had been
called out to pursue them. **17** Since they were
drawn away from the city, with every man engaged in this pursuit of Joshua and the Israelites,
not a soldier remained in Ai [or Bethel], and the
city was open and unprotected.

**18** Then the LORD directed Joshua, "Stretch
out the javelin in your hand toward Ai, for I will
deliver it into your power." Joshua stretched
out the javelin in his hand toward the city,
**19** and as soon as he did so, the men in ambush
rose from their post, rushed in, captured the
city, and immediately set it on fire. **20** By the
time the men of Ai looked back, the smoke from
the city was already sky-high. Escape in any
direction was impossible, because the Israelites
retreating toward the desert now turned on their
pursuers; **21** for when Joshua and the main
body of Israelites saw that the city had been
taken from ambush and was going up in smoke,
they struck back at the men of Ai. **22** Since
those in the city came out to intercept them, the
men of Ai were hemmed in by Israelites on
either side, who cut them down without any
fugitives or survivors[b] **23** except the king,
whom they took alive and brought to Joshua.

**24** All the inhabitants of Ai who had pursued
the Israelites into the desert were slain by the
sword there in the open, down to the last man.
Then all Israel returned and put to the sword
those inside the city. **25** There fell that day a
total of twelve thousand men and women, the
entire population of Ai. **26** [c]Joshua kept the
javelin in his hand stretched out until he had
fulfilled the doom on all the inhabitants of Ai.
**27** However, the Israelites took for themselves
as booty the livestock and the spoil of that city,
according to the command of the LORD issued
to Joshua. **28** Then Joshua destroyed the place
by fire, reducing it to an everlasting mound of
ruins, as it remains today.[d] **29** He had the king
of Ai hanged on a tree until evening;[e] then at
sunset Joshua ordered the body removed from
the tree and cast at the entrance of the city gate,
where a great heap of stones was piled up over
it, which remains to the present day.

**Altar on Mount Ebal.** **30** *Later Joshua
built an altar to the LORD, the God of Israel, on
Mount Ebal, **31** of unhewn stones on which no
iron tool had been used,[f] in keeping with the
command to the Israelites of Moses, the servant
of the LORD, as recorded in the book of the law.
On this altar they offered holocausts and peace
offerings to the LORD. **32** There, in the presence of the Israelites, Joshua inscribed upon the
stones a copy of the law written by Moses.[g]
**33** And all Israel, stranger and native alike,
with their elders, officers and judges, stood on
either side of the ark facing the levitical priests
who were carrying the ark of the covenant of the
LORD.[h] Half of them were facing Mount Gerizim and half Mount Ebal, thus carrying out the
instructions of Moses, the servant of the LORD,
for the blessing of the people of Israel on this
first occasion. **34** [i]Then were read aloud all the
words of the law, the blessings and the curses,
exactly as written in the book of the law.
**35** [j]Every single word that Moses had commanded, Joshua read aloud to the entire com-

b Dt 7, 2.
c Ex 17, 11ff.
d Dt 13, 16.
e Jos 10, 26f; Dt 21, 22f; Jn 19, 31.
f Ex 20, 24f; Dt 27, 5f.
g Dt 27, 2. 8.
h Jos 3, 3; Dt 11, 27; 27, 12; 31, 9. 12.
i Dt 28, 2-68; 30, 19; 31, 11; Neh 8, 2f.
j Dt 31, 12.

*

8, 3: Thirty thousand warriors: this figure of the Hebrew text, which seems extremely high, may be due to a copyist's error; some manuscripts of the Septuagint have "three thousand," which is the number of the whole army in the first, unsuccessful attack (Jos 7, 4); the variant reading in v 12 mentions "five thousand."

8, 30–35: These ceremonies were prescribed in Dt 11, 29, and Dt 27, 2–26. See notes on those passages.

munity, including the women and children, and
the strangers who had accompanied Israel.

## CHAPTER 9

**Confederacy against Israel.** 1 When the
news reached the kings west of the Jordan, in
the mountain regions and in the foothills, and all
along the coast of the Great Sea as far as Lebanon: Hittites, Amorites, Canaanites, Perizzites,
Hivites and Jebusites,[k] 2 they all formed an
alliance to launch a common attack against
Joshua and Israel.

**The Gibeonite Deception.** 3 On learning
what Joshua had done to Jericho and Ai, the
inhabitants of Gibeon[l] 4 put into effect a device
of their own. They chose provisions for a journey, making use of old sacks for their asses, and
old wineskins, torn and mended. 5 They wore
old, patched sandals and shabby garments; and
all the bread they took was dry and crumbly.
6 Thus they journed to Joshua in the camp at
Gilgal, where they said to him and to the men
of Israel, "We have come from a distant land
to propose that you make an alliance with us."[m]
7 But the men of Israel replied to the Hivites,*
"You may be living in land that is ours. How,
then, can we make an alliance with you?"
8 But they answered Joshua, "We are your
servants." Then Joshua asked them, "Who are
you? Where do you come from?" 9 They answered him, "Your servants have come from a
far-off land, because of the fame of the LORD,
your God. For we have heard reports of all that
he did in Egypt[n] 10 and all that he did to the
two kings of the Amorites beyond the Jordan,[o]
Sihon, king of Heshbon, and Og, king of Bashan, who lived in Ashtaroth. 11 So our elders
and all the inhabitants of our country said to us,
'Take along provisions for the journey and go
to meet them. Say to them: We are your servants; we propose that you make an alliance
with us.' 12 This bread of ours was still warm
when we brought it from home as provisions the
day we left to come to you, but now it is dry and
crumbled. 13 Here are our wineskins, which
were new when we filled them, but now they are
torn. Look at our garments and sandals, which
are worn out from the very long journey."
14 Then the Israelite princes partook of their
provisions, without seeking the advice of the
LORD.[p] 15 So Joshua made an alliance with
them and entered into an agreement to spare
them,[q] which the princes of the community
sealed with an oath.

**Gibeonites Made Vassals.** 16 Three
days after the agreement was entered into, the
Israelites learned that these people were from
nearby, and would be living in Israel. 17 The
third day on the road, the Israelites came to their
cities of Gibeon, Chephirah, Beeroth and Kiriath-jearim, 18 but did not attack them, because
the princes of the community had sworn to them
by the LORD, the God of Israel. When the entire
community grumbled against the princes,
19 these all remonstrated with the people, "We
have sworn to them by the LORD, the God of
Israel, and so we cannot harm them. 20 Let us
therefore spare their lives and so deal with them
that we shall not be punished for the oath we
have sworn to them." 21 Thus the princes recommended that they be let live, as hewers of
wood and drawers of water* for the entire community; and the community did as the princes
advised them.
22 Joshua summoned the Gibeonites and
said to them, "Why did you lie to us and say
that you lived at a great distance from us, when
you will be living in our very midst? 23 For this
are you accursed: every one of you shall always
be a slave [hewers of wood and drawers of
water] for the house of my God." 24 They
answered Joshua, "Your servants were fully
informed of how the LORD, your God, commanded his servant Moses that you be given the
entire land and that all its inhabitants be destroyed before you. Since, therefore, at your
advance, we were in great fear for our lives, we
acted as we did.[r] 25 And now that we are in
your power, do with us what you think fit and
right." 26 *Joshua did what he had decided:
while he saved them from being killed by the
Israelites, 27 at the same time he made them,
as they still are, hewers of wood and drawers of
water for the community and for the altar of the
LORD, in the place of the LORD's choice.[s]

## CHAPTER 10

**The Siege of Gibeon.** 1 Now Adonizedek, king of Jerusalem, heard that, in the capture and destruction of Ai, Joshua had done to
that city and its king as he had done to Jericho
and its king.[t] He heard also that the inhabitants
of Gibeon had made their peace with Israel,

k Jos 3, 10; Ex 3, 8. 17; 23, 23; Dt 1, 7.
l Jos 6, 21. 24; 11, 19.
m Ex 23, 32; Dt 7, 2.
n Jos 2, 10.
o Nm 21, 25. 33.
p Nm 27, 21.
q Jos 11, 19; 2 Sm 21, 2.
r Ex 23, 27f; Dt 7, 1f.
s Dt 12, 5.
t Jos 9, 15; 6, 21. 24; 8, 26-29.

9, 7: The Hivites: apparently the Gibeonites belonged to this larger ethnic group (cf also Jos 11, 19), although in 2 Sm 21, 2 they are classed as Amorites; both groups are listed among the seven nations in Canaan whom the Israelites were to exterminate; cf Dt 7, 1f.

9, 21: Hewers of wood and drawers of water: proverbial terms for the lowest social class in the Israelite community; cf Dt 29, 10f.

9, 26f: Later on, Saul violated the immunity of the Gibeonites, but David vindicated it; cf 2 Sm 21, 1–9.

remaining among them, 2 and that there was
great fear abroad, because Gibeon was large
enough for a royal city, larger even than the city
of Ai, and all its men were brave. 3 So
Adonizedek, king of Jerusalem, sent for Ho-
ham, king of Hebron, Piram, king of Jarmuth,
Japhia, king of Lachish, and Debir, king of
Eglon, 4 to come to his aid for an attack on
Gibeon, since it had concluded peace with Joshua and the Israelites.[u] 5 The five Amorite
kings, of Jerusalem, Hebron, Jarmuth, Lachish
and Eglon,* united all their forces and marched
against Gibeon, where they took up siege positions. 6 Thereupon, the men of Gibeon sent an
appeal to Joshua in his camp at Gilgal: "Do not
abandon your servants. Come up here quickly
and save us. Help us, because all the Amorite
kings of the mountain country have joined
forces against us."[v]

**Joshua's Victory.** 7 So Joshua marched
up from Gilgal with his picked troops and the
rest of his soldiers. 8 Meanwhile the LORD said
to Joshua, "Do not fear them, for I have delivered them into your power. Not one of them will
be able to withstand you." 9 And when Joshua
made his surprise attack upon them after an
all-night march from Gilgal, 10 the LORD threw
them into disorder before him. The Israelites
inflicted a great slaughter on them at Gibeon and
pursued them down the Beth-horon slope,
harassing them as far as Azekah and Makkedah.

11 While they fled before Israel along the
descent from Beth-horon, the LORD hurled great
stones from the sky* above them all the way to
Azekah, killing many.[w] More died from these
hailstones than the Israelites slew with the
sword. 12 On this day, when the LORD delivered up the Amorites to the Israelites,

Joshua prayed to the LORD,
and said in the presence of Israel:
Stand still, O sun, at Gibeon,
O moon, in the valley of Aijalon!
13 And the sun stood still,
and the moon stayed,
while the nation took vengeance on its
foes.[x]

Is this not recorded* in the Book of Jashar? The
sun halted in the middle of the sky; not for a
whole day did it resume its swift course.
14 Never before or since was there a day like
this, when the LORD obeyed the voice of a man;
for the LORD fought for Israel. 15 [Then Joshua
and all Israel returned to the camp at Gilgal.]

**Execution of Amorite Kings.** 16 Meanwhile the five kings who had fled, hid in a cave
at Makkedah. 17 When Joshua was told that the
five kings had been discovered hiding in a cave
at Makkedah, 18 he said, "Roll large stones to
the mouth of the cave and post men over it to
guard them. 19 But do not remain there yourselves. Pursue your enemies, and harry them in
the rear. Do not allow them to escape to their
cities, for the LORD, your God, has delivered
them into your power."

20 Once Joshua and the Israelites had finally
inflicted the last blows in this very great slaughter, and the survivors had escaped from them
into the fortified cities, 21 all the army returned
safely to Joshua and the camp at Makkedah, no
man uttering a sound against the Israelites.
22 Then Joshua said, "Open the mouth of the
cave and bring out those five kings to me."
23 Obediently, they brought out to him from
the cave the five kings, of Jerusalem, Hebron,
Jarmuth, Lachish and Eglon. 24 When they had
done so, Joshua summoned all the men of Israel
and said to the commanders of the soldiers who
had marched with him, "Come forward and put
your feet on the necks of these kings." They
came forward and put their feet upon their
necks. 25 Then Joshua said to them, "Do not
be afraid or dismayed, be firm and steadfast.
This is what the LORD will do to all the enemies
against whom you fight." 26 [y]Thereupon Joshua struck and killed them, and hanged them on
five trees, where they remained hanging until
evening. 27 At sunset they were removed from
the trees at the command of Joshua and cast into
the cave where they had hidden; over the mouth
of the cave large stones were placed, which
remain until this very day.

**Conquest of Southern Canaan.**
28 [z]Makkedah, too, Joshua captured and put to
the sword at that time. He fulfilled the doom on
the city, on its king, and on every person in it,
leaving no survivors. Thus he did to the king of
Makkedah what he had done to the king of
Jericho. 29 Joshua then passed on with all Israel from Makkedah to Libnah, which he attacked. 30 Libnah also, with its king, the LORD

u Jos 9, 15.
v Jos 9, 6.
w Jb 38, 22.
x Sir 46, 4; Is 28, 21; Heb 3, 11.
y 26f: Jos 8, 29; Dt 21, 22f.
z Jos 6, 21.

*

10, 5: Hebron . . . Eglon: these four cities were to the south and southwest of Jerusalem.

10, 11: Great stones from the sky: the hailstones mentioned in the next sentence.

10, 13: Is this not recorded: the reference is to the preceding, poetic passage. Evidently the Book of Jashar, like the Book of the Wars of the Lord (Nm 21, 14), recounted in epic style the exploits of Israel's early heroes. The sun halted: though it is widely supposed that this passage describes in popular language and according to external appearances a miraculous lengthening of the day, it is equally probable that Joshua's prayer was rather for an abrupt obscuration of the sun, which would impede his enemies in their flight homeward and also prevent them from rallying their forces; this request would have been answered by the hailstorm (cf Sir 46, 5) and by a darkness relieved only twenty-four hours later, well into the next day.

delivered into the power of Israel. He put it to the sword with every person there, leaving no survivors. Thus he did to its king what he had done to the king of Jericho. **31** Joshua next passed on with all Israel from Libnah to Lachish, where they set up a camp during the attack. **32** The LORD delivered Lachish into the power of Israel, so that on the second day Joshua captured it and put it to the sword with every person in it, just as he had done to Libnah. **33** At that time Horam, king of Gezer, came up to help Lachish, but Joshua defeated him and his people, leaving him no survivors. **34** From Lachish, Joshua passed on with all Israel to Eglon; encamping near it, they attacked it **35** and captured it the same day, putting it to the sword. He fulfilled the doom that day on every person in it, just as he had done at Lachish. **36** From Eglon, Joshua went up with all Israel to Hebron, which they attacked **37** and captured. They put it to the sword with its king, all its towns, and every person there, leaving no survivors, just as Joshua had done to Eglon. He fulfilled the doom on it and on every person there. **38** Then Joshua and all Israel turned back to Debir and attacked it, **39** capturing it with its king and all its towns. They put them to the sword and fulfilled the doom on every person there, leaving no survivors. Thus was done to Debir and its king what had been done to Hebron, as well as to Libnah and its king.

**40** [a]Joshua conquered the entire country; the mountain regions, the Negeb, the foothills, and the mountain slopes, with all their kings. He left no survivors, but fulfilled the doom on all who lived there, just as the LORD, the God of Israel, had commanded. **41** Joshua conquered from Kadesh-barnea to Gaza, and all the land of Goshen* to Gibeon. **42** All these kings and their lands Joshua captured in a single campaign, for the LORD, the God of Israel, fought for Israel. **43** Thereupon Joshua with all Israel returned to the camp at Gilgal.

## CHAPTER 11

**Northern Confederacy.** **1** When Jabin, king of Hazor,* learned of this, he sent a message to Jobab, king of Madon, to the king of Shimron, to the king of Achshaph, **2** and to the northern kings in the mountain regions and in the Arabah near Chinneroth, in the foothills, and in Naphath-dor to the west.[b] **3** These were Canaanites to the east and west, Amorites, Hittites, Perizzites and Jebusites in the mountain regions, and Hivites at the foot of Hermon in the land of Mizpah. **4** They came out with all their troops, an army numerous as the sands on the seashore, and with a multitude of horses and chariots. **5** All these kings joined forces and marched to the waters of Merom,* where they encamped together to fight against Israel.

**6** The LORD said to Joshua, "Do not fear them, for by this time tomorrow I will stretch them slain before Israel. You must hamstring their horses and burn their chariots." **7** Joshua with his whole army came upon them at the waters of Merom in a surprise attack. **8** The LORD delivered them into the power of the Israelites, who defeated them and pursued them to Greater Sidon, to Misrephothmaim,[c] and eastward to the valley of Mizpeh. They struck them all down, leaving no survivors. **9** Joshua did to them as the LORD had commanded: he hamstrung their horses and burned their chariots.

**Conquest of Northern Canaan.** **10** At that time Joshua, turning back, captured Hazor and slew its king with the sword; for Hazor formerly was the chief of all those kingdoms. **11** He also fulfilled the doom by putting every person there to the sword, till none was left alive. Hazor itself he burned. **12** Joshua thus captured all those kings with their cities and put them to the sword, fulfilling the doom on them, as Moses, the servant of the LORD, had commanded.[d] **13** However, Israel did not destroy by fire any of the cities built on raised sites, except Hazor, which Joshua burned. **14** The Israelites took all the spoil and livestock of these cities as their booty; but the people they put to the sword, until they had exterminated the last of them, leaving none alive. **15** As the LORD had commanded his servant Moses, so Moses commanded Joshua, and Joshua acted accordingly.[e] He left nothing undone that the LORD had commanded Moses should be done.

**Survey of the Conquest.** **16** So Joshua captured all this land: the mountain regions, the entire Negeb, all the land of Goshen, the foothills, the Arabah, as well as the mountain regions and foothills of Israel,[f] **17** from Mount Halak that rises toward Seir[g] as far as Baalgad in the Lebanon valley at the foot of Mount Hermon. All their kings he captured and put to

a Dt 20, 16f.
b Jos 12, 3; Jgs 1, 27.
c Jos 13, 6.
d Dt 7, 2; 20, 16f.
e Dt 7, 2.
f Jos 10, 41; 12, 8.
g Jos 12, 7; Dt 7, 24.

*

10, 41: Goshen: a town and its surrounding district at the southern end of the Judean mountains (cf Jos 11, 16; 15, 51); not to be confused with the land of Goshen in northeastern Egypt (Gen 45, 10), although in the current Hebrew Bible both names are spelled the same.

11, 1ff: Hazor, Madon, Shimron, and Chinneroth: cities and their surrounding districts in eastern Galilee. Achshaph and Naphathdor: southwest of Galilee. The mountain regions: in central and northern Galilee.

11, 5: The waters of Merom: a stream in central Galilee that flows southeast to water the fertile Arabah, or plain of Chinneroth on the western shore of the lake of Gennesaret.

death. **18** Joshua waged war against all these
kings for a long time. **19** With the exception of
the Hivites who lived in Gibeon, no city made
peace with the Israelites; all were taken in battle.[h] **20** For it was the design of the LORD to
encourage them to wage war against Israel, that
they might be doomed to destruction and thus
receive no mercy, but be exterminated, as the
LORD had commanded Moses.[i]
**21** *At that time Joshua penetrated the
mountain regions and exterminated the Anakim
in Hebron,[j] Debir, Anab, the entire mountain
region of Judah, and the entire mountain region
of Israel. Joshua fulfilled the doom on them and
on their cities, **22** so that no Anakim were left
in the land of the Israelites. However, some
survived in Gaza, in Gath, and in Ashdod.
**23** [k]Thus Joshua captured the whole country,
just as the LORD had foretold to Moses. Joshua
gave it to Israel as their heritage, apportioning
it among the tribes. And the land enjoyed
peace.*

## CHAPTER 12*

**Lists of Conquered Kings.** **1** The kings
of the land east of the Jordan, from the River
Arnon to Mount Hermon, including all the eastern section of the Arabah, whom the Israelites
conquered and whose lands they occupied,
were: **2** [l]First, Sihon, king of the Amorites,
who lived in Heshbon. His domain extended
from Aroer, which is on the bank of the Wadi
Arnon, to include the wadi itself, and the land
northward through half of Gilead to the Wadi
Jabbok, **3** as well as the Arabah from the eastern side of the Sea of Chinnereth, as far south
as the eastern side of the Salt Sea of the Arabah
in the direction of Beth-jeshimoth,[m] to a point
under the slopes of Pisgah. **4** Secondly, Og,
king of Bashan, a survivor of the Rephaim, who
lived at Ashtaroth and Edrei.[n] **5** He ruled over
Mount Hermon, Salecah, and all Bashan as far
as the boundary of the Geshurites and Maacathites, and over half of Gilead as far as the
territory of Sihon, king of Heshbon. **6** After
Moses, the servant of the LORD, and the Israelites conquered them, he assigned their land to
the Reubenites, the Gadites, and the half-tribe
of Manasseh, as their property.[o]
**7** This is a list of the kings whom Joshua and
the Israelites conquered west of the Jordan and
whose land, from Baal-gad in the Lebanon valley to Mount Halak which rises toward Seir,
Joshua apportioned to the tribes of Israel. **8** It
included the mountain regions and foothills, the
Arabah, the slopes, the desert, and the Negeb,
belonging to the Hittites, Amorites, Canaanites,
Perizzites, Hivites and Jebusites. **9** They were
the kings of Jericho,[p] Ai (which is near Bethel),
**10** Jerusalem, Hebron, **11** Jarmuth, Lachish,[q]
**12** Eglon, Gezer,[r] **13** Debir, Geder,[s] **14** Hormah, Arad, **15** Libnah, Adullam,[t] **16** Makkedah, Bethel,[u] **17** Tappuah, Hepher,[v]
**18** Aphek, Lasharon,[w] **19** Madon, Hazor,[x]
**20** Shimron, Achshaph,[y] **21** Taanach, Megiddo,[z] **22** Kedesh, Jokneam (at Carmel),[a]
**23** and Dor (in Naphath-dor), the foreign king
at Gilgal,[b] **24** and the king of Tirzah, thirty-one
kings in all.

# *II: Division of the Land*

## CHAPTER 13

**Division of Land Commanded.** **1** When
Joshua was old and advanced in years, the LORD
said to him:[c] "Though now you are old and
advanced in years, a very large part of the land
still remains to be conquered. **2** This additional
land includes all Geshur* and all the districts of
the Philistines **3** (from the stream adjoining
Egypt to the boundary of Ekron in the north is
reckoned Canaanite territory, though held by
the five lords of the Philistines in Gaza, Ashdod, Ashkelon, Gath and Ekron); also where the
Avvim are in the south;[d] **4** all the land of the
Canaanites from Mearah of the Sidonians to
Aphek, and the boundaries of the Amorites;
**5** and the Gebalite territory; and all the Lebanon
on the east, from Baal-gad at the foot of Mount
Hermon to Labo in the land of Hamath. **6** At the
advance of the Israelites I will drive out all the
Sidonian inhabitants of the mountain regions
between Lebanon and Misrephoth-maim;[e] at

h Jos 9, 3. 7. 15.
i Dt 2, 30; 20, 16f.
j Jos 15, 13f; Nm 13, 22; Dt 1, 28.
k Jos 14, 1-19, 51; Nm 34, 2-12.
l 2-5: Nm 21, 21-26. 33ff.
m Jos 13, 20.
n Jos 13, 11f.
o Nm 32, 33; Dt 3, 12f.
p Jos 6, 2; 8, 23.
q 10f: Jos 10, 23.
r Jos 10, 23. 33.
s Jos 10, 38f; 15, 36.
t Jos 10, 29f; 15, 35.
u Jos 8, 17; 10, 28.
v Jos 15, 34.
w Jos 15, 53.
x Jos 11, 1. 10.
y Jos 11, 1.
z Jos 17, 11.
a Jos 19, 37.
b Jos 11, 2.
c Jos 23, 1.
d Jgs 3, 3.
e Jos 11, 8.

*

11, 21ff: Most of the land assigned to the tribe of Judah was not conquered by it till the early period of the Judges. See note on Jgs 1, 1–36.

11, 23: The land enjoyed peace: of a limited and temporary nature. Many of the individual tribes had still to fight against the remaining Canaanites; cf Jos 15, 13–17; 17, 12f. This verse forms the conclusion to the first part of the book. Cf note on Jos 12, 1–24.

12, 1–24: This chapter, inserted between the two principal parts of the book (chapters 1–11 and 13–21), resembles the lists of conquered cities which are inscribed on monuments of the Egyptian and Assyrian monarchs. Perhaps it was copied here from some such public Israelite record.

13, 2: Geshur: not to be confused with the large Aramaean district of the same name in Bashan (vv 11–13; Dt 3, 14); here it is a region to the south of the Philistine country, since vv 2–5 list the unconquered lands along the coast from south to north; cf also 1 Sm 27, 8.

least include these areas in the division of the Israelite heritage, just as I have commanded you. **7** Now, therefore, apportion among the nine tribes and the half-tribe of Manasseh the land which is to be their heritage."

**The Eastern Tribes.** **8** [f]Now the other half of the tribe of Manasseh, as well as the Reubenites and Gadites, had received their heritage which Moses, the servant of the LORD, had given them east of the Jordan: **9** from Aroer on the bank of the Wadi Arnon and the city in the wadi itself, through the tableland of Medeba and Dibon, **10** with the rest of the cities of Sihon, king of the Amorites, who reigned in Heshbon, to the boundary of the Ammonites; **11** also Gilead and the territory of the Geshurites and Maacathites, all Mount Hermon, and all Bashan as far as Salecah, **12** the entire kingdom in Bashan of Og, a survivor of the Rephaim, who reigned at Ashtaroth and Edrei. Though Moses conquered and occupied these territories, **13** the Israelites did not dislodge the Geshurites and Maacathites, so that Geshur and Maacath survive in the midst of Israel to this day. **14** [g]However, to the tribe of Levi Moses assigned no heritage since, as the LORD had promised them, the LORD, the God of Israel, is their heritage.

**Reuben.** **15** [h]What Moses gave to the Reubenite clans:[i] **16** Their territory reached from Aroer, on the bank of the Wadi Arnon, and the city in the wadi itself, through the tableland about Medeba, **17** to include Heshbon and all its towns which are on the tableland, Dibon, Bamoth-baal, Beth-baal-meon, **18** Jahaz, Kedemoth, Mephaath, **19** Kiriathaim, Sibmah, Zereth-shahar on the knoll within the valley, **20** Beth-peor, the slopes of Pisgah, Beth-jeshimoth, **21** and the other cities of the tableland and, generally, of the kingdom of Sihon. This Amorite king, who reigned in Heshbon, Moses had killed, with his vassals, the princes of Midian, who were settled in the land: Evi, Rekem, Zur, Hur and Reba;[j] **22** and among their slain followers the Israelites put to the sword also the soothsayer Balaam, son of Beor.[k] **23** The boundary of the Reubenites was the bank of the Jordan. These cities and their villages were the heritage of the clans of the Reubenites.

**Gad.** **24** [l]What Moses gave to the Gadite clans: **25** Their territory included Jazer, all the cities of Gilead, and half the land of the Ammonites as far as Aroer, toward Rabbah **26** (that is, from Heshbon to Ramath-mizpeh and Betonim, and from Mahanaim to the boundary of Lodebar); **27** and in the Jordan valley: Beth-haram, Beth-nimrah, Succoth, Zaphon, the other part of the kingdom of Sihon, king of Heshbon, with the bank of the Jordan to the southeastern tip of the Sea of Chinnereth. **28** These cities and their villages were the heritage of the clans of the Gadites.

**Manasseh.** **29** [m]What Moses gave to the clans of the half-tribe of Manasseh: **30** Their territory included Mahanaim, all of Bashan, the entire kingdom of Og, king of Bashan, and all the villages of Jair, which are sixty cities in Bashan[n] **31** Half of Gilead, with Ashtaroth and Edrei, once the royal cities of Og in Bashan, fell to the descendants of Machir, son of Manasseh, for half the clans descended from Machir.

**32** These are the portions which Moses gave when he was in the plains of Moab, beyond the Jordan east of Jericho. **33** However, Moses gave no heritage to the tribe of Levi, since the LORD himself, the God of Israel, is their heritage, as he promised.[o]

## CHAPTER 14

**The Western Tribes.** **1** Here follow the portions which the Israelites received in the land of Canaan.[p] Eleazar the priest, Joshua, son of Nun, and the heads of families in the tribes of the Israelites determined **2** their heritage by lot, in accordance with the instructions the LORD had given through Moses concerning the remaining nine and a half tribes.[q] **3** For to two and a half tribes Moses had already given a heritage beyond the Jordan; and though the Levites were given no heritage among the tribes,[r] **4** the descendants of Joseph formed two tribes, Manasseh and Ephraim. The Levites themselves received no share of the land except cities to live in, with their pasture lands for the cattle and flocks.[s]

**5** Thus, in apportioning the land, did the Israelites carry out the instructions of the LORD to Moses.

**Caleb's Portion.** **6** [t]When the Judahites came up to Joshua in Gilgal, the Kenizzite Caleb, son of Jephunneh, said to him: "You know what the LORD said to the man of God, Moses, about you and me in Kadesh-barnea. **7** [u]I was forty years old when the servant of the LORD, Moses, sent me from Kadesh-barnea to reconnoiter the land; and I brought back to him a

---

f Jos 12, 6; Nm 32, 33.
g Jos 14, 3f; Nm 18, 20-24.
h 15-31; Dt 3, 12-17.
i 15-23; Nm 21, 25-31; 32, 37f.
j Nm 21, 24; 31, 8; Dt 3, 10.
k Nm 31, 8.
l 24-28: Nm 32, 34ff.
m 29-31: Nm 32, 39ff.
n Nm 32, 41.
o Jos 18, 7; Nm 18, 20.
p Jos 17, 4; 21, 1; Nm 34, 17f.
q Nm 26, 55; 33, 54; 34, 13.
r Jos 13, 8. 14. 33.
s Jos 21, 3-40; Gn 48, 5.
t Nm 14, 24. 30; 32, 12; Dt 1, 36. 38.
u Nm 14, 6-9.

conscientious report. **8** [v]My fellow scouts who went up with me discouraged the people, but I was completely loyal to the LORD, my God. **9** On that occasion Moses swore this oath, "The land where you have set foot shall become your heritage and that of your descendants forever, because you have been completely loyal to the LORD, my God." **10** Now, as he promised, the LORD has preserved me while Israel was journeying through the desert, for the forty-five years since the LORD spoke thus to Moses; and although I am now eighty-five years old,[w] **11** I am still as strong today as I was the day Moses sent me forth, with no less vigor whether for war or for ordinary tasks.[x] **12** Give me, therefore, this mountain region which the LORD promised me that day, as you yourself heard. True, the Anakim are there, with large fortified cities, but if the LORD is with me I shall be able to drive them out, as the LORD promised."[y] **13** Joshua blessed Caleb, son of Jephunneh, and gave him Hebron as his heritage.[z] **14** Therefore Hebron remains the heritage of the Kenizzite Caleb, son of Jephunneh, to the present day, because he was completely loyal to the LORD, the God of Israel. **15** Hebron was formerly called Kiriatharba, for Arba, the greatest among the Anakim.[a] And the land enjoyed peace.

## CHAPTER 15

**Boundaries of Judah.** **1** The lot for the clans of the Judahite tribe fell in the extreme south toward the boundary of Edom, the desert of Zin in the Negeb.[b] **2** [c]The boundary there ran from the bay that forms the southern end of the Salt Sea, **3** southward below the pass of Akrabbim, across through Zin, up to a point south of Kadesh-barnea, across to Hezron, and up to Addar; from there, looping around Karka, **4** it crossed to Azmon and then joined the Wadi of Egypt before coming out at the sea. [This is your southern boundary.] **5** The eastern boundary was the Salt Sea as far as the mouth of the Jordan.

**6** [d]The northern boundary climbed from the bay where the Jordan meets the sea, up to Beth-hoglah, and ran north of Beth-arabah, up to Eben-Bohan-ben-Reuben. **7** Thence it climbed to Debir, north of the vale of Achor,[e] in the direction of the Gilgal that faces the pass of Adummim, on the south side of the wadi; from there it crossed to the waters of En-shemesh and emerged at En-rogel. **8** Climbing again to the Valley of Ben-Hinnom* on the southern flank of the Jebusites [that is, Jerusalem], the boundary rose to the top of the mountain at the northern end of the Valley of Rephaim,[f] which bounds the Valley of Hinnom on the west. **9** From the top of the mountain it ran to the fountain of waters of Nephtoah,[g] extended to the cities of Mount Ephron, and continued to Baalah, or Kiriath-jearim. **10** From Baalah the boundary curved westward to Mount Seir and passed north of the ridge of Mount Jearim (that is, Chesalon); thence it descended to Beth-shemesh, and ran across to Timnah. **11** It then extended along the northern flank of Ekron, continued through Shikkeron, and across to Mount Baalah, thence to include Jabneel, before it came out at the sea. **12** The western boundary was the Great Sea and its coast. This was the complete boundary of the clans of the Judahites.

**Conquest by Caleb.** **13** [h]As the LORD had commanded, Joshua gave Caleb, son of Jephunneh,[i] a portion among the Judahites, namely, Kiriath-arba (Arba was the father of Anak), that is, Hebron. **14** [j]And Caleb drove out from there the three Anakim, the descendants of Anak: Sheshai, Ahiman and Talmai. **15** From there he marched up against the inhabitants of Debir,[k] which was formerly called Kiriath-sepher. **16** Caleb said, "I will give my daughter Achsah in marriage to the one who attacks Kiriath-sepher and captures it." **17** *Othniel, son of Caleb's brother Kenaz, captured it, and so Caleb gave him his daughter Achsah in marriage. **18** On the day of her marriage to Othniel, she induced him to ask her father for some land. Then, as she alighted from the ass, Caleb asked her, "What is troubling you?" **19** She answered, "Give me an additional gift! Since you have assigned to me land in the Negeb, give me also pools of water." So he gave her the upper and the lower pools.

**Cities of Judah.** **20** *This is the heritage of the clans of the tribe of Judahites: **21** The cities

v Nm 13, 31ff; 14, 24; 32, 12; Dt 1, 36.
w Nm 14, 30.
x Sir 46, 1ff.
y Jos 11, 21.
z Jos 10, 36f; 15, 13-19; 21, 11f.
a Jgs 1, 10.
b Nm 34, 3.
c 2-4: Nm 34, 3ff.
d Jos 18, 18f. 22.
e Jos 7, 26; 18, 16ff: 2 Sm 17, 17.
f Jos 18, 16.
g Jos 18, 15.
h 13-19: Jgs 1, 10-15.
i Jos 14, 13ff.
j Nm 13, 22; Jgs 1, 20.
k Jos 10, 38.

*

15, 8: The Valley of Ben-hinnom: the southern limit of Jerusalem. Ben-hinnom means "son of Hinnom." The place was also called Valley of Hinnom, in Hebrew ge-hinnom, whence the word "Gehenna" is derived.

15, 17–19: The story of Othniel is told again in Jgs 1, 13–15; cf also Jgs 3, 9–11.

15, 20–62: This elaborate list of the cities of Judah was probably taken from a document made originally for administrative purposes; the cities are divided into four provincial districts, some of which have further subdivisions. For similar lists of the cities of Judah, cf Jos 19, 2–7; 1 Chr 4, 28–32; Neh 11, 25–30. This list has suffered in transmission, so that the totals given in vv 32 and 36 are not exact, and some of the names are probably misspelled; many of the cities cannot be identified.

of the tribe of the Judahites in the extreme southern district toward Edom were: Kabzeel, Eder,
Jagur, **22** Kinah, Dimonah, Adadah, **23** Kedesh, Hazor and Ithnan; **24** Ziph, Telem, Bea-
loth, **25** Hazor-hadattah, and Kerioth-hezron
(that is, Hazor); **26** Amam, Shema, Moladah, **27** Hazar-gaddah, Heshmon, Beth-pelet,
**28** Hazar-shual, Beer-sheba, and Biziothiah,
**29** Baalah, Iim, Ezem, **30** Elto-lad, Chesil,
Hormah, **31** Ziklag,[l] Madmannah, Sansannah,
**32** Lebaoth, Shilhim and En-rimmon; a total of
twenty-nine cities with their villages.

**33** In the foothills:* Eshtaol, Zorah, Ashnah, **34** Zanoah, Engannim, Tappuah,
Enam, **35** Jarmuth, Adullam, Socoh, Azekah,
**36** Shaaraim, Adithaim, Gederah, and Gedero-
thaim; fourteen cities and their villages. **37** Ze-
nan, Hadashah, Migdal-gad, **38** Dilean, Mizpeh, Joktheel, **39** Lachish, Bozkath, Eglon,
**40** Cabbon, Lahmam, Chitlish, **41** Gederoth,
Beth-dagon, Naamah and Makkedah; sixteen
cities and their villages. **42** Libnah, Ether,
Ashan, **43** Iphtah, Ashnah, Nezib, **44** Keilah,
Achzib and Mareshah; nine cities and their villages. **45** Ekron and its towns and villages;
**46** from Ekron to the sea, all the towns that lie
alongside Ashdod and their villages; **47** Ashdod and its towns and villages; Gaza and its
towns and villages, as far as the Wadi of Egypt
and the coast of the Great Sea.

**48** In the mountain regions: Shamir, Jattir,
Socoh, **49** Dannah, Kiriath-sannah (that is, Debir), **50** Anab, Eshtemoh, Anim, **51** Goshen,
Holon and Giloh; eleven cities and their villages. **52** Arab, Dumah, Eshan, **53** Janim,
Beth-tappuah, Aphekah, **54** Humtah, Kiriath-
arba (that is, Hebron), and Zior; nine cities and
their villages. **55** Maon, Carmel, Ziph, Juttah,
**56** Jezreel, Jokdeam, Zanoah, **57** Kain, Gib-
beah and Timnah; ten cities and their villages.
**58** Halhul, Beth-zur, Gedor, **59** Ma-arath,
Beth-anoth and Eltekon; six cities and their villages. Tekoa, Ephrathah (that is, Bethlehem),
Peor, Etam, Kulom, Tatam, Zores, Karim, Gallim, Bether and Manoko; eleven cities and their
villages. **60** Kiriath-baal (that is, Kiriath-jearim) and Rabbah: two cities and their villages.[m]

**61** In the desert:* Beth-arabah, Middin, Se-
cacah, **62** Nibshan, Ir-hamelah and Engedi; six
cities and their villages. **63** [But the Jebusites
who lived in Jerusalem the Judahites could not
drive out; so the Jebusites dwell in Jerusalem
beside the Judahites to the present day.[n]]

## CHAPTER 16

**The Joseph Tribes.** **1** The lot that fell to
the Josephites* extended from the Jordan at Jericho to the waters of Jericho east of the desert;
then the boundary went up from Jericho to the
heights at Bethel.* **2** Leaving Bethel for Luz,
it crossed the ridge to the border of the Archites
at Ataroth, **3** and descended westward to
the border of the Japhletites, to that of Lower
Beth-horon, and to Gezer, ending thence at the
sea.[o]

**Ephraim.** **4** Within the heritage of Manasseh and Ephraim, sons of Joseph, **5** the dividing
line* for the heritage of the clans of the Ephraimites ran from east of Ataroth-addar to Upper
Beth-horon[p] **6** and thence to the sea. From
Michmethath[q] on the north, their boundary
curved eastward around Taanath-shiloh, and
continued east of it to Janoah; **7** from there it
descended to Ataroth and Naarah, and skirting
Jericho, it ended at the Jordan. **8** From Tappuah[r] the boundary ran westward to the Wadi
Kanah and ended at the sea. This was the heritage of the clans of the Ephraimites, **9** including
the villages that belonged to each city set aside
for the Ephraimites within the territory of the
Manassehites.[s] **10** But they did not drive out
the Canaanites living in Gezer,[t] who live on
within Ephraim to the present day, though they
have been impressed as laborers.

## CHAPTER 17

**Manasseh.** **1** Now as for the lot that fell to
the tribe of Manasseh[u] as the first-born of Joseph: since his eldest son, Machir, the father of
Gilead, was a warrior, who had already obtained Gilead and Bashan, **2** [v]the allotment was
now made to the other descendants of Manasseh, the clans of Abiezer, Helek, Asriel, Shechem, Hepher and Shemida, the other male
children of Manasseh, son of Joseph.

**3** Furthermore, Zelophehad, son of Hepher,[w] son of Gilead, son of Machir, son of
Manasseh, had had no sons, but only daughters,
whose names were Mahlah, Noah, Hoglah,
Milcah, and Tirzah. **4** These presented them-

l 1 Sm 27, 6.
m Jos 18, 14.
n Jgs 1, 21; 2 Sm 5, 6.
o Jos 10, 10. 33.
p Jos 18, 13.
q Jos 17, 7.
r Jos 17, 7.
s Jos 17, 9.
t Jgs 1, 29.
u Gn 41, 51; 46, 20; 48, 18; 50, 23; Nm 26, 29; Dt 3, 13. 15.
v Nm 26, 29-32.
w Nm 26, 33; 27, 1; 36, 2.
x Nm 27, 6f; 36, 2.

*

15, 33: In the foothills: see note on Dt 1, 7.

15, 61: In the desert: in the Jordan rift near the Dead Sea.

16, 1–17, 18: The boundaries and cities of Judah, the most important tribe, having been given, the land of the next most important group, the two Josephite tribes of Ephraim and Manasseh, is now described, though it was separated from Judah by the territories of Benjamin (Jos 18, 11–20) and Dan (Jos 19, 40–48).

16, 1–3: This line formed the southern boundary of Ephraim and the northern boundaries of Benjamin and of Dan.

16, 5: The dividing line: separating Ephraim from Manasseh. Ephraim's northern border (v 5) is given in an east-to-west direction; its eastern border (v 6f) in a north-to-south direction.

selves to Eleazar the priest, to Joshua, son of
Nun, and to the princes, saying, "The LORD
commanded Moses to give us a heritage among
our kinsmen." So in obedience to the command
of the LORD a heritage was given to each of them
among their father's kinsmen.[x] **5** Thus ten
shares fell to Manasseh apart from the land of
Gilead and Bashan beyond the Jordan,[y] **6** since
these female descendants of Manasseh received
each a portion among his sons. The land of
Gilead fell to the rest of the Manassehites.
**7** Manasseh bordered on Asher.* From
Michmethath, near Shechem, another boundary
ran southward to include the natives of En-Tap-
puah, **8** because the district of Tappuah belonged to Manasseh, although Tappuah itself
was an Ephraimite city on the border of Manasseh. **9** This same boundary continued down to
the Wadi Kanah.[z] The cities that belonged to
Ephraim from among the cities of Manasseh
were those to the south of the wadi; thus the
territory of Manasseh ran north of the wadi and
ended at the sea. **10** The land on the south
belonged to Ephraim and that on the north to
Manasseh; with the sea as their common boundary, they reached Asher on the north and Issachar on the east.
**11** [a]Moreover, in Issachar and in Asher Manasseh was awarded Beth-shean[b] and its towns,
Ibleam and its towns, Dor and its towns and the
natives there, Endor and its towns and natives,
Taanach and its towns and natives, and Megiddo and its towns and natives [the third is Na-
phath-dor]. **12** Since the Manassehites could
not conquer these cities, the Canaanites persisted in this region. **13** When the Israelites grew
stronger they impressed the Canaanites as laborers, but they did not drive them out.

**Protest of Joseph Tribes.** **14** The descendants of Joseph said to Joshua, "Why have
you given us only one lot and one share as our
heritage?[c] Our people are too many, because of
the extent to which the LORD has blessed us."
**15** Joshua answered them, "If you are too
many, go up to the forest and clear out a place
for yourselves there in the land of the Perizzites
and Rephaim, since the mountain regions of
Ephraim are so narrow." **16** For the Josephites
said, "Our mountain regions are not enough for
us; on the other hand, the Canaanites living in
the valley region all have iron chariots, in particular those in Beth-shean and its towns, and
those in the valley of Jezreel."[d] **17** Joshua
therefore said to Ephraim and Manasseh, the
house of Joseph, "You are a numerous people
and very strong. You shall have not merely one
share, **18** for the mountain region which is now
forest shall be yours when you clear it. Its adjacent land shall also be yours if, despite their
strength and iron chariots, you drive out the
Canaanites."

## CHAPTER 18

**1** After they had subdued the land, the whole
community of the Israelites assembled at Shiloh, where they set up the meeting tent.[e]

**The Seven Remaining Portions.** **2** Sev-
en tribes among the Israelites had not yet received their heritage. **3** Joshua therefore said to
the Israelites, "How much longer will you put
off taking steps to possess the land which the
LORD, the God of your fathers, has given you?
**4** Choose three men from each of your tribes;
I will commission them to begin a survey of the
land, which they shall describe for purposes of
inheritance. When they return to me, **5** you
shall divide it into seven parts. Judah is to retain
its territory in the south,[f] and the house of Joseph its territory in the north. **6** You shall bring
here to me the description of the land in seven
sections. I will then cast lots for you here before
the LORD, our God. **7** For the Levites have no
share among you,[g] because the priesthood of
the LORD is their heritage; while Gad, Reuben,
and the half-tribe of Manasseh have already
received the heritage east of the Jordan which
Moses, the servant of the LORD, gave them."
**8** When those who were to map out the land
were ready for the journey, Joshua instructed
them to survey the land, prepare a description
of it, and return to him; then he would cast lots
for them there before the LORD in Shiloh. **9** So
they went through the land, listed its cities in
writing in seven sections, and returned to Joshua in the camp at Shiloh. **10** Joshua then divided up the land for the Israelites into their separate shares, casting lots for them before the
LORD in Shiloh.

**Benjamin.** **11** One lot fell to the clans of the
tribe of Benjaminites. The territory allotted
them lay between the descendants of Judah and
those of Joseph. **12** [h]Their northern boundary*

y Jos 13, 30f.
z Jos 16, 8f.
a 1 Chr 7, 29.
b 11ff: Jgs 1, 27f.
c Jos 16, 4; Gn 48, 19f. 22.
d Jgs 6, 33.
e Jos 19, 51.
f Jos 15, 1—17, 18.
g Jos 13, 8. 33.
h Jos 16, 1.

*

17, 7: Manasseh bordered on Asher: only at the extreme northwestern section of Manasseh's territory. The boundary given in the following sentences (vv 7–10) is a more detailed description of the one already mentioned in Jos 16, 5ff, as separating Manasseh from Ephraim.

18, 12–20: Benjamin's northern boundary (vv 12f) corresponded to part of the southern boundary of Ephraim (Jos 16, 1f). Their western border (v 14) was the eastern border of Dan (cf Jos 19, 40–47). Their southern boundary (vv 15–19) corresponded to part of the northern boundary of Judah (Jos 15, 6–9).

began at the Jordan and went over the northern
flank of Jericho, up westward into the mountains, till it reached the desert of Beth-aven.
**13** From there it crossed over to the southern
flank of Luz (that is, Bethel). Then it ran down
to Ataroth-addar, on the mountaintop south of
Lower Beth-horon.[i] **14** For the western border,
the boundary line swung south from the mountaintop opposite Beth-horon till it reached Kiriath-baal (that is, Kiriath-jearim), which city belonged to the Judahites. This was the western
boundary. **15** The southern boundary began at
the limits of Kiriath-jearim and projected to the
spring at Nephtoah. **16** It went down to the
edge of the mountain on the north of the Valley
of Rephaim, where it faces the Valley of Ben-
hinnom; and continuing down the Valley of
Hinnom along the southern flank of the Jebusites, reached En-rogel.[j] **17** Inclining to the
north, it extended to En-shemesh, and thence to
Geliloth, opposite the pass of Adummim.
Then it dropped to Eben-Bohan-ben-Reuben,
**18** across the northern flank of the Arabah overlook, down into the Arabah.[k] **19** From there the
boundary continued across the northern flank of
Beth-hoglah and extended to the northern tip of
the Salt Sea, at the southern end of the Jordan.
This was the southern boundary. **20** The Jordan
bounded it on the east. This was how the heritage of the clans of the Benjaminites was bounded on all sides.

**21** Now the cities belonging to the clans
of the tribe of the Benjaminites were: Jericho, Beth-hoglah, Emek-keziz, **22** Beth-arabah, Zemaraim, Bethel, **23** Avvim, Parah,
Ophra, **24** Chepharammoni, Ophni and Geba;
twelve cities and their villages. **25** Also Gibeon, Ramah, Beeroth, **26** Mizpeh, Chephirah,
Mozah, **27** Rekem, Irpeel, Taralah, **28** Zela,
Haeleph, the Jebusite city (that is, Jerusalem),
Gibeah and Kiriath; fourteen cities and their
villages. This was the heritage of the clans of
Benjaminites.

## CHAPTER 19

**Simeon.** **1** The second lot fell to Simeon.
The heritage of the clans of the tribe of Simeonites lay within that of the Judahites. **2** [l]For their
heritage they received Beer-sheba, Shema,
Moladah, **3** Hazar-shual, Balah, Ezem, **4** Elto-
lad, Bethul, Hormah, **5** Ziklag, Beth-mar-
caboth, Hazar-susah, **6** Beth-lebaoth and Sha-
ruhen; thirteen cities and their villages. **7** Also
En-rimmon, Ether and Ashan; four cities and
their villages, **8** besides all the villages around
these cities as far as Baalath-beer (that is, Ra-
moth-negeb). This was the heritage of the clans
of the tribe of the Simeonites. **9** This heritage
of the Simeonites was within the confines of the
Judahites; for since the portion of the latter was
too large for them, the Simeonites obtained their
heritage within it.

**Zebulun.** **10** *The third lot fell to the clans
of the Zebulunites. The limit of their heritage
was at Sarid. **11** Their boundary went up
west . . . and through Mareal, reaching Dabbe-
sheth and the wadi that is near Jokneam.
**12** From Sarid eastward it ran to the district of
Chisloth-tabor, on to Daberath, and up to Japhia. **13** From there it continued eastward to
Gath-hepher and to Eth-kazin, extended to Rimmon, and turned to Neah. **14** Skirting north of
Hannathon, the boundary ended at the valley of
Iphtahel. **15** Thus, with Kattath, Nahalal,
Shimron, Idalah and Bethlehem, there were
twelve cities and their villages **16** to comprise
the heritage of the clans of the Zebulunites.

**Issachar.** **17** *The fourth lot fell to Issachar. The territory of the clans of the Issacharites **18** included Jezreel, Chesulloth, Shunem,
**19** Hapharaim, Shion, Anaharath, **20** Rabbith,
Kishion, Ebez, **21** Remeth, En-gannim, En-
haddah and Beth-pazzez. **22** The boundary
reached Tabor, Shahazumah and Beth-shemesh, ending at the Jordan. These sixteen cities
and their villages **23** were the heritage of the
clans of the Issacharites.

**Asher.** **24** *The fifth lot fell to the clans of
the tribe of the Asherites. **25** Their territory
include Helkath, Hali, Beten, Achshaph,
**26** Allammelech, Amad and Mishal, and
reached Carmel on the west, and Shihor-lib-
nath. **27** In the other direction, it ran eastward
of Beth-dagon, reached Zebulun and the valley
of Iphtahel; then north of Beth-emek and Neiel,
it extended to Cabul, **28** Mishal, Abdon, Rehob,[m] Hammon and Kanah, near Greater Sidon. **29** Then the boundary turned back to Ramah and to the fortress city of Tyre; thence it cut

i Jos 16, 2f. 5; Gn 28, 19.
j Jos 15, 7f.
k Jos 15, 6.
l 2-8: 1 Chr 4, 28-33.
m 28f: Jgs 1, 31.

*

19, 10–16: Zebulun's territory was in the central section of the Plain of Esdraelon and of southern Galilee; it was bounded on the south by Manasseh, on the southeast by Issachar, on the northeast and north by Naphtali, and on the west by Asher. The site of the later city of Nazareth was within its borders. Bethlehem of Zebulun was, of course, distinct from the city of the same name in Judah. Twelve cities: apparently seven of the names are missing from v 15, unless some of the places mentioned in vv 12–14 are to be included in the number.

19, 17–23: Issachar's land was on the eastern watershed of the Plain of Esdraelon, but also included the southeastern end of the Galilean mountains. It was surrounded by Manasseh on the south and east, by Naphtali on the north, and by Zebulun on the west. Jezreel (v 18) dominated the plain to which it gave its name, the later form of which was Esdraelon.

19, 24–31: Asher inherited the western slope of the Galilean hills as far as the sea, with Manasseh to the south, Zebulun and Naphtali to the east, and Phoenicia to the north.

back to Hosah and ended at the sea. Thus, with Mahalab, Achzib, **30** Ummah, Acco, Aphek and Rehob, there were twenty-two cities and their villages **31** to comprise the heritage of the clans of the tribe of the Asherites.

**Naphtali.** **32** *The sixth lot fell to the Naphtalites. The boundary of the clans of the Naphtalites **33** extended from Heleph, from the oak at Zaanannim to Lakkum, including Adami-nekeb and Jabneel, and ended at the Jordan. **34** In the opposite direction, westerly, it ran through Aznoth-tabor and from there extended to Hukkok; it touched Zebulun on the south, Asher on the west, and the Jordan on the east. **35** The fortified cities were Ziddim, Zer, Hammath, Rakkath, Chinnereth, **36** Adamah, Ramah, Hazor, **37** Kedesh, Edrei, En-hazor, **38** Yiron, Migdal-el, Horem, Beth-anath and Beth-shemesh;[n] nineteen cities and their villages, **39** to comprise the heritage of the clans of the tribe of the Naphtalites.

**Dan.** **40** *The seventh lot fell to the clans of the tribe of Danites. **41** Their heritage was the territory of Zorah, Eshtaol, Ir-shemesh, **42** Shaalabbin, Aijalon, Ithlah,[o] **43** Elon, Timnah, Ekron, **44** Eltekoh, Gibbethon, Baalath, **45** Jehud, Bene-berak, Gath-rimmon, **46** Me-jarkon and Rakkon, with the coast at Joppa. **47** [p]But the territory of the Danites was too small for them; so the Danites marched up and attacked Leshem,* which they captured and put to the sword. Once they had taken possession of Leshem, they renamed the settlement after their ancestor Dan. **48** These cities and their villages were the heritage of the clans of the tribe of the Danites.

**Joshua's City.** **49** When the last of them had received the portions of the land they were to inherit, the Israelites assigned a heritage in their midst to Joshua, son of Nun. **50** In obedience to the command of the LORD, they gave him the city which he requested, Timnah-serah[q] in the mountain region of Ephraim. He rebuilt the city and made it his home.

**51** These are the final portions into which Eleazar the priest, Joshua, son of Nun, and the heads of families in the tribes of the Israelites divided the land by lot in the presence of the LORD, at the door of the meeting tent in Shiloh.

## CHAPTER 20

**Cities of Asylum.** **1** The LORD said to Joshuah:* **2** "Tell the Israelites to designate the cities of which I spoke to them through Moses,[r] **3** to which one guilty of accidental and unintended homicide may flee for asylum from the avenger of blood. **4** To one of these cities the killer shall flee, and standing at the entrance of the city gate, he shall plead his case before the elders, who must receive him and assign him a place in which to live among them. **5** Though the avenger of blood pursues him, they are not to deliver up the homicide who slew his fellow man unintentionally and not out of previous hatred. **6** Once he has stood judgment before the community, he shall live on in that city till the death of the high priest who is in office at the time. Then the killer may go back home to his own city from which he fled."[s]

**List of Cities.** **7** So they set apart Kedesh in Galilee in the mountain region of Naphtali, Shechem in the mountain region of Ephraim, and Kiriath-arba (that is, Hebron) in the mountain region of Judah.[t] **8** And beyond the Jordan east of Jericho they designated Bezer on the open tableland in the tribe of Reuben, Ramoth in Gilead in the tribe of Gad, and Golan in Bashan in the tribe of Manasseh.[u] **9** These were the designated cities[v] to which any Israelite or stranger living among them who had killed a person accidentally might flee to escape death at the hand of the avenger of blood, until he could appear before the community.

## CHAPTER 21

**Levitical Cities.** **1** The heads of the Levite families* came up to Eleazar the priest, to Joshua, son of Nun, and to the heads of families of the other tribes of the Israelites[w] **2** at Shiloh in the land of Canaan, and said to them, "The LORD commanded, through Moses, that cities

n Jgs 1, 33.
o Jgs 1, 35.
p Jgs 18, 27-29.
q Jos 24, 30; Jgs 2, 9.
r Ex 21, 13; Nm 35, 10-14; Dt 4, 41-43; 19, 2-9.
s Nm 35, 12. 24f.
t Jos 15, 13; 19, 37; 21, 21.
u Jos 21, 27. 36f.
v Nm 35, 15.
w Ex 6, 16-19; Nm 3, 17-20.
x Nm 35, 2.

*

19, 32–39: Naphtali received eastern Galilee; Asher was to the west and Zebulun and Issachar were to the south, while the upper Jordan and Mount Hermon formed the eastern border. Part of the tribe of Dan later on occupied the northern extremity of Naphtali's lands, at the sources of the Jordan (v 47).

19, 40–46: The original territory of Dan was a small enclave between Judah, Benjamin, Ephraim and the Philistines.

19, 47: Leshem: called Laish in Jgs 18, where the story of the migration of the Danites is told at greater length.

20, 1–9: The laws concerning the cities of refuge are given in Nm 35, 9–28; Dt 19, 1–13; see notes on Nm 35, 16–25; Dt 19, 2.

21, 1: The order to establish special cities for the Levites is given in Nm 35, 1–8. The forty-eight cities listed here were hardly the exclusive possession of the Levites; at least the more important of them, such as Hebron, Shechem and Ramoth in Gilead, were certainly peopled for the most part by the tribe in whose territory they were situated. But in all these cities the Levites had special property rights which they did not possess in other cities; cf Lv 25, 32ff.

be given us to dwell in, with pasture lands for our livestock."[x] **3** Out of their own heritage, in obedience to this command of the LORD, the Israelites gave the Levites the following cities with their pasture lands.

**4** When the first lot among the Levites fell to the clans of the Kohathites, the descendants of Aaron the priest obtained thirteen cities by lot from the tribes of Judah, Simeon and Benjamin. **5** The rest of the Kohathites obtained ten cities by lot from the clans of the tribe of Ephraim, from the tribe of Dan, and from the half-tribe of Manasseh. **6** The Gershonites obtained thirteen cities by lot from the clans of the tribe of Issachar, from the tribe of Asher, from the tribe of Naphtali, and from the half-tribe of Manasseh. **7** The clans of the Merarites obtained twelve cities from the tribes of Reuben, Gad and Zebulun. **8** These cities with their pasture lands the Israelites allotted to the Levites in obedience to the LORD's command through Moses.[y]

**Cities of the Priests.** **9** [z]From the tribes of the Judahites and Simeonites they designated the following cities, **10** and assigned them to the descendants of Aaron in the Kohathite clan of the Levites, since the first lot fell to them: **11** first, Kiriatharba (Arba was the father of Anak), that is, Hebron, in the mountain region of Judah, with the adjacent pasture lands, **12** although the open country and villages belonging to the city had been given to Caleb, son of Jephunneh, as his property.[a] **13** Thus to the descendants of Aaron the priest were given the city of asylum for homicides at Hebron, with its pasture lands; also, Libnah with its pasture lands, **14** Jattir with its pasture lands, Eshtemoa with its pasture lands, **15** Holon with its pasture lands, Debir with its pasture lands, **16** Ashan with its pasture lands, Juttah with its pasture lands, and Bethshemesh with its pasture lands: nine cities from the two tribes mentioned. **17** From the tribe of Benjamin they obtained the four cities of Gibeon with its pasture lands, Geba with its pasture lands, **18** Anathoth[b] with its pasture lands, and Almon with its pasture lands. **19** These cities which with their pasture lands belonged to the priestly descendants of Aaron, were thirteen in all.

**Cities of the Other Kohathites.** **20** [c]The rest of the Kohathite clans among the Levites obtained by lot, from the tribe of Ephraim, four cities. **21** They were assigned, with its pasture lands, the city of asylum for homicides at Shechem in the mountain region of Ephraim; also Gezer with its pasture lands, **22** Kibzaim with its pasture lands, and Beth-horon with its pasture lands. **23** From the tribe of Dan they obtained the four cities of Elteke with its pasture lands, Gibbethon with its pasture lands, **24** Aijalon with its pasture lands, and Gath-rimmon with its pasture lands; **25** and from the half-tribe of Manasseh the two cities of Taanach with its pasture lands and Ibleam with its pasture lands. **26** These cities which with their pasture lands belonged to the rest of the Kohathite clans were ten in all.

**Cities of the Gershonites.** **27** [d]The Gershonite clan of the Levites received from the half-tribe of Manasseh two cities: the city of asylum for homicides at Golan with its pasture lands; and also Beth-Astharoth with its pasture lands. **28** From the tribe of Issachar they obtained the four cities of Kishion with its pasture lands, Daberath with its pasture lands, **29** Jarmuth with its pasture lands, and Engannim with its pasture lands; **30** from the tribe of Asher, the four cities of Mishal with its pasture lands, Abdon with its pasture lands, **31** Helkath with its pasture lands, and Rehob with its pasture lands; **32** and from the tribe of Naphtali, three cities: the city of asylum for homicides at Kedesh in Galilee, with its pasture lands; also Hammath with its pasture lands, and Rakkath with its pasture lands. **33** These cities which with their pasture lands belonged to the Gershonite clans were thirteen in all.

**Cities of the Merarites.** **34** [e]The Merarite clans, the last of the Levites, received from the tribe of Zebulun the four cities of Jokneam with its pasture lands, Kartah with its pasture lands, **35** Rimmon with its pasture lands, and Nahalal with its pasture lands; **36** also, across the Jordan, from the tribe of Reuben, four cities: the city of asylum for homicides at Bezer with its pasture lands, Jahaz with its pasture lands, **37** Kedemoth with its pasture lands, and Mephaath with its pasture lands; **38** and from the tribe of Gad a total of four cities: the city of asylum for homicides at Ramoth in Gilead with its pasture lands, also Mahanaim with its pasture lands, **39** Heshbon with its pasture lands, and Jazer with its pasture lands. **40** The cities which were allotted to the Merarite clans, the last of the Levites, were therefore twelve in all.

**41** Thus the total number of cities[f] within the territory of the Israelites which, with their pasture lands, belonged to the Levites, was forty-eight. **42** With each and every one of these cities went the pasture lands round about it.

**43** And so the LORD gave Israel all the land he had sworn to their fathers he would give them.[g] Once they had conquered and occupied it, **44** the LORD gave them peace on every side, just as he had promised their fathers. Not one of

y Nm 35, 2.
z 9-19: 1 Chr 6, 54-60.
a Jos 14, 14; 15, 13.
b Jer 1, 1.
c 20-26: 1 Chr 6, 66-70.
d 27-33: 1 Chr 6, 71-76.
e 34-38: 1 Chr 6. 77-81.
f Nm 35, 7.
g Gn 12, 7; 13, 15; 15, 18; 26, 3; 28, 4. 13.

their enemies could withstand them; the LORD
brought all their enemies under their power.
45 Not a single promise[h] that the LORD made
to the house of Israel was broken; every one was
fulfilled.

## *III.: Return of the Transjordan Tribes and Joshua's Farewell*

## CHAPTER 22

**The Eastern Tribes Dismissed.** 1 At
that time Joshua summoned the Reubenites, the
Gadites, and the half-tribe of Manasseh 2 and
said to them:[i] "You have done all that Moses,
the servant of the LORD, commanded you, and
have obeyed every command I gave you. 3 For
many years now you have not once abandoned
your kinsmen, but have faithfully carried out the
commands of the LORD, your God. 4 Since,
therefore, the LORD, your God, has settled your
kinsmen as he promised them, you may now
return to your tents beyond the Jordan; to your
own land, which Moses, the servant of the
LORD, gave you.[j] 5 But be very careful to observe the precept and law which Moses, the
servant of the LORD, enjoined upon you: love
the LORD, your God;[k] follow him faithfully;
keep his commandments; remain loyal to him;
and serve him with your whole heart and soul."
6 Joshua then blessed them and sent them away
to their own tents.

7 (For, to half the tribe of Manasseh Moses
had assigned land in Bashan;[l] and to the other
half Joshuah had given a portion along with
their kinsmen west of the Jordan.) What Joshua
said to them when he sent them off to their tents
with his blessing was, 8 "Now that you are
returning to your own tents with great wealth,
with very numerous livestock, with silver, gold,
bronze and iron, and with a very large supply of
clothing, divide these spoils of your enemies
with your kinsmen there."[m] 9 So the Reubenites, the Gadites, and the half-tribe of Manasseh
left the other Israelites at Shiloh in the land of
Canaan and returned to the land of Gilead, their
own property, which they had received according to the LORD's command through Moses.[n]

**The Altar beside the Jordan.** 10 When
the Reubenites, the Gadites, and the half-tribe
of Manasseh came to the region of the Jordan in
the land of Canaan, they built there at the Jordan
a conspicuously large altar. 11 The other Israelites heard the report[o] that the Reubenites, the
Gadites, and the half-tribe of Manasseh had
built an altar in the region of the Jordan facing
the land of Canaan,* across from them, 12 and
therefore they assembled their whole community at Shiloh to declare war on them.*

**Accusation of the Western Tribes.**
13 First, however, they sent to the Reubenites,
the Gadites, and the half-tribe of Manasseh in
the land of Gilead an embassy consisting of
Phinehas, son of Eleazar the priest,[p] 14 and ten
princes, one from every tribe of Israel, each one
being both prince and military leader of his
ancestral house. 15 When these came to the
Reubenites, the Gadites, and the half-tribe of
Manasseh in the land of Gilead, they said to
them: 16 [q]"The whole community of the LORD
sends this message: What act of treachery is this
you have committed against the God of Israel?
You have seceded from the LORD this day, and
rebelled against him by building an altar of your
own! 17 For the sin of Peor, a plague came
upon the community of the LORD.[r] 18 We are
still not free of that; must you now add to it?
You are rebelling against the LORD today and by
tomorrow he will be angry with the whole community of Israel! 19 If you consider the land
you now possess unclean,* cross over to the
land the LORD possesses, where the Dwelling of
the LORD stands,[s] and share that with us. But do
not rebel against the LORD, nor involve us in
rebellion, by building an altar of your own in
addition to the altar of the LORD, our God.
20 When Achan, son of Zerah,[t] violated the
ban, did not wrath fall upon the entire community of Israel? Though he was but a single man,
he did not perish alone* for his guilt!"

**Reply of the Eastern Tribes.** 21 The
Reubenites, the Gadites, and the half-tribe of
Manasseh replied to the military leaders of the
Israelites: "The LORD is the God of gods.
22 The LORD, the God of gods,* knows and

h Jos 23, 14f.
i Jos 1, 16f; Nm 32, 20ff; Dt 3, 18ff.
j Jos 1, 13; 13, 8; Nm 32, 33.
k Dt 6, 5f. 17; 10, 12; 11, 1. 13. 22.
l Jos 17, 5.
m Nm 31, 27.
n Jos 18, 1; Nm 32, 1. 26. 29.
o Dt 13, 13ff.
p Ex 6, 25; Sir 45, 28.
q Lv 17, 8f.
r Nm 25, 3f; Dt 4, 3.
s Jos 18, 1.
t Jos 7, 1. 5.

*

22, 11: In the region of the Jordan facing the land of Canaan: on the eastern side of the Jordan valley. The river itself formed the boundary between these eastern tribes and the rest of the tribes who lived in what was formerly Canaan—though the term Canaan could also be used of both sides of the Jordan valley (cf v 10). The Transjordan tribes naturally built their altar in their own territory.

22, 12: To declare war on them: the western Israelites considered this altar, which seemed to violate the customary unity of the sanctuary (cf Lv 17, 1–9; Dt 12, 4–14), as a sign of secession and dangerous to national unity. The motives for the war were political as well as religious.

22, 19: Unclean: not sanctified by the Dwelling of the Lord.

22, 20: Achan . . . did not perish alone: his guilt caused the failure of the first attack on Ai (Jos 7, 4–23); this fact is adduced as an argument for the solidarity and mutual responsibility of all the Israelites.

22, 22: The Lord, the God of gods: the Hebrew, which cannot be adequately rendered in English here, adds to the

Israel shall know. If now we have acted out of
rebellion or treachery against the LORD, our
God, **23** and if we have built an altar of our own
to secede from the LORD, or to offer holocausts,
grain offerings or peace offerings upon it, the
LORD himself will exact the penalty. **24** We did
it rather out of our anxious concern lest in the
future your children should say to our children:
'What have you to do with the LORD, the God
of Israel? **25** For the LORD has placed the Jordan as a boundary between you and us. You
descendants of Reuben and Gad have no share
in the LORD.' Thus your children would prevent
ours from revering the LORD. **26** So we decided
to guard our interests by building this altar of
our own: not for holocausts or for sacrifices,
**27** [u]but as evidence for you on behalf of ourselves and our descendants, that we have the
right to worship the LORD in his presence with
our holocausts, sacrifices, and peace offerings.
Now in the future your children cannot say to
our children, "You have no share in the LORD."
**28** Our thought was, that if in the future they
should speak thus to us or to our descendants,
we could answer: 'Look at the model of the altar
of the LORD which our fathers made, not for
holocausts or for sacrifices, but to witness* between you and us.' **29** Far be it from us to rebel
against the LORD or to secede now from the
LORD by building an altar for holocaust, grain
offering, or sacrifice in addition to the altar of
the LORD, our God, which stands before his
Dwelling."

**30** When Phinehas the priest and the princes
of the community, the military leaders of the
Israelites, heard what the Reubenites, the Gadites and the Manassehites had to say, they were
satisfied. **31** Phinehas, son of Eleazar the
priest, said to the Reubenites, the Gadites and
the Manassehites, "Now we know that the
LORD is with us. Since you have not committed
this act of treachery against the LORD, you have
kept the Israelites free from punishment by the
LORD."

**32** Phinehas, son of Eleazar the priest, and
the princes returned from the Reubenites and the
Gadites in the land of Gilead to the Israelites in
the land of Canaan, and reported the matter to
them. **33** The report satisfied the Israelites,
who blessed God and decided against declaring
war on the Reubenites and Gadites or ravaging
the land they occupied.

**34** The Reubenites and the Gadites gave the
altar its name* as a witness among them that the
LORD is God.

## CHAPTER 23

**Joshua's Final Plea.** **1** Many years later,
after the LORD had given the Israelites rest from
all their enemies round about them, and when
Joshua was old and advanced in years,[v] **2** he
summoned all Israel (including their elders,
leaders, judges and officers) and said to them:
"I am old and advanced in years. **3** You have
seen all that the LORD, your God, has done for
you against all these nations; for it has been the
LORD, your God, himself who fought for you.
**4** [w]Bear in mind that I have apportioned among
your tribes as their heritage the nations that
survive [as well as those I destroyed] between
the Jordan and the Great Sea in the west. **5** The
LORD, your God, will drive them out and dislodge them at your approach, so that you will
take possession of their land as the LORD, your
God, promised you. **6** Therefore strive hard to
observe and carry out all that is written in the
book of the law of Moses, not straying from it
in any way,[x] **7** or mingling with these nations
while they survive among you. You must not
invoke their gods, or swear by them, or serve
them, or worship them,[y] **8** but you must remain
loyal to the LORD, your God, as you have been
to this day. **9** At your approach the LORD has
driven out large and strong nations, and to this
day no one has withstood you. **10** One of you
puts to flight a thousand, because it is the LORD,
your God, himself who fights for you,[z] as he
promised you. **11** Take great care, however, to
love the LORD, your God. **12** For if you ever
abandon him and ally yourselves with the remnant of these nations while they survive among
you, by intermarrying and intermingling with
them,[a] **13** know for certain that the LORD, your
God, will no longer drive these nations out of
your way. Instead they will be a snare and a trap
for you, a scourge for your sides and thorns for
your eyes, until you perish from this good land
which the LORD, your God, has given you.

**14** "Today, as you see, I am going the way
of all men.* So now acknowledge with your
whole heart and soul that not one of all the
promises the LORD, your God, made to you has
remained unfulfilled. Every promise has been
fulfilled for you, with not one single exception.
**15** [b]But just as every promise the LORD, your

u Dt 12, 5f. 17f.
v Jos 13, 1.
w Jos 13, 2-7; 14, 2; 18, 10; Ps 78, 55.
x Jos 1, 7.
y Dt 7, 2ff.
z Ex 14, 14; Lv 26, 8; Dt 3, 22.
a Ex 34, 16; Dt 7, 3.
b Lv 26, 14-39; Dt 28, 15-68.

*

divine name Yahweh ("the LORD") two synonymous words for "God," el and elohim. The repetition of these three sacred words adds force to the protestations of fidelity and innocence.

22, 28: To witness: far from being destined to form a rival sanctuary, the model of the altar was intended by the eastern tribes solely as a means of teaching their children to be faithful to the one true sanctuary beyond the Jordan.

22, 34: The name of this altar was the Hebrew word for "witness," [c] ed.

23, 14: Going the way of all men: drawing near to death, the inevitable goal of all; cf 1 Kgs 2, 1f.

23, 15: Every threat: mentioned especially in Dt 28, 15–68.

God, made to you as has been fulfilled for you,
so will he fulfill every threat,* even so far as to
exterminate you from this good land which the
LORD, your God, has given you. **16** If you
transgress the covenant of the LORD, your God,
which he enjoined on you, serve other gods and
worship them, the anger of the LORD will flare
up against you and you will quickly perish from
the good land which he has given you."

## CHAPTER 24

### Reminder of the Divine Goodness.

**1** Joshua gathered together all the tribes of Israel at Shechem, summoning their elders, their
leaders, their judges and their officers. When
they stood in ranks before God, **2** Joshua addressed all the people: "Thus says the LORD, the
God of Israel: In times past your fathers, down
to Terah,[c] father of Abraham and Nahor, dwelt
beyond the River* and served other gods. **3** But
I brought your father Abraham from the region
beyond the River and led him through the entire
land of Canaan.[d] I made his descendants numerous, and gave him Isaac. **4** To Isaac I gave
Jacob and Esau.[e] To Esau I assigned the mountain region of Seir in which to settle, while
Jacob and his children went down to Egypt.

**5** "Then I sent Moses and Aaron, and smote
Egypt with the prodigies which I wrought in her
midst.[f] **6** Afterward I led you out of Egypt, and
when you reached the sea, the Egyptians pursued your fathers to the Red Sea with chariots
and horsemen.[g] **7** Because they cried out to the
LORD,[h] he put darkness between your people
and the Egyptians, upon whom he brought the
sea so that it engulfed them. After you witnessed what I did to Egypt, and dwelt a long
time in the desert, **8** [i]I brought you into the land
of the Amorites who lived east of the Jordan.
They fought against you, but I delivered them
into your power. You took possesion of their
land, and I destroyed them [the two kings of the
Amorites] before you. **9** [j]Then Balak, son of
Zippor, king of Moab, prepared to war against
Israel. He summoned Balaam, son of Beor, to
curse you; **10** [k]but I would not listen to Balaam.
On the contrary, he had to bless you, and I saved
you from him. **11** Once you crossed the Jordan[l]
and came to Jericho, the men of Jericho fought
against you, but I delivered them also into your
power. **12** And I sent the hornets* ahead of you
which drove them [the Amorites, Perizzites,
Canaanites, Hittites, Girgashites, Hivites and
Jebusites] out of your way; it was not your
sword or your bow.[m]

**13** "I gave you a land which you had not
tilled and cities which you had not built, to
dwell in; you have eaten of vineyards and olive
groves which you did not plant.[n]

**14** [o]"Now, therefore, fear the LORD and
serve him completely and sincerely. Cast out
the gods your fathers served beyond the River
and in Egypt, and serve the LORD. **15** [p]If it does
not please you to serve the LORD, decide today
whom you will serve, the gods your fathers
served* beyond the River or the gods of the
Amorites in whose country you are dwelling.
As for me and my household, we will serve the
LORD."

**Renewal of the Covenant.** **16** But the
people answered, "Far be it from us to forsake
the LORD for the service of other gods. **17** For
it was the LORD, our God, who brought us and
our fathers up out of the land of Egypt, out of
a state of slavery. He performed those great
miracles before our very eyes and protected us
along our entire journey and among all the peoples through whom we passed. **18** At our approach the LORD drove out [all the peoples,
including] the Amorites who dwelt in the land.
Therefore we also will serve the LORD, for he
is our God."

**19** Joshua in turn said to the people, "You
may not be able* to serve the LORD, for he is
a holy God; he is a jealous God[q] who will not
forgive your transgressions or your sins. **20** If,
after the good he has done for you, you forsake
the LORD and serve strange gods, he will do evil
to you and destroy you."

**21** But the people answered Joshua, "We
will still serve the LORD." **22** Joshua therefore
said to the people, "You are your own witnesses that you have chosen to serve the LORD."
They replied, "We are, indeed!" **23** "Now,
therefore, put away the strange gods that are
among you and turn your hearts to the LORD, the
God of Israel." **24** Then the people promised
Joshua, "We will serve the LORD, our God, and
obey his voice."

**25** So Joshua made a covenant with the people that day and made statutes and ordinances
for them at Shechem, **26** which he recorded in
the book of the law of God. Then he took a large

c Gn 11, 26. 31; 31, 53.
d Gn 12, 1; Acts 7, 2-4.
e Gn 25, 24ff; 36, 8; 46, 1. 6; Acts 7, 15.
f Ex 3, 10; 7, 14-12, 30.
g Ex 12, 37. 51; 14, 9.
h Ex 14, 10. 20. 27f.
i Nm 21, 21-35.
j Nm 22, 2-5.
k Nm 23, 1-24, 25.
l Jos 3, 14; 6, 1.
m Jos 11, 20; Ex 23, 28; Dt 7, 20.
n Dt 6, 10f.
o Dt 10, 12; 1 Sm 7, 3; 12, 24; Tb 14, 9.
p Dt 30, 15-19.
q Ex 20, 5; 23, 21; 34, 14; Lv 19, 2.
r Gn 28, 18; 31, 45; Jgs 9, 6.

24, 2: Beyond the River: east of the Euphrates; cf Gn 11, 28–31.

24, 12: the hornets: see note on Ex 23, 28.

24, 15: The gods your fathers served: Abraham's ancestors were polytheists.

24, 19: You may not be able: fidelity to God's service is not easy, and therefore those who take such solemn obligations on themselves must be ever vigilant against human weakness.

stone and set it up there under the oak that was
in the sanctuary of the LORD.[r] 27 And Joshua
said to all the people, "This stone shall be our
witness,[s] for it has heard all the words which the
LORD spoke to us. It shall be a witness against
you, should you wish to deny your God."
28 Then Joshua dismissed the people, each to
his own heritage.[t]

**Death of Joshua.** 29 [u]After these events,
Joshua, son of Nun, servant of the LORD, died
at the age of a hundred and ten. 30 He was
buried within the limits of his heritage at Tim-
nath-serah[v] in the mountain region of Ephraim
north of Mount Gaash. 31 Israel served the
LORD during the entire lifetime of Joshua and
that of the elders who outlived Joshua and knew
all that the LORD had done for Israel. 32 [w]The
bones of Joseph,* which the Israelites had
brought up from Egypt, were buried in Shechem
in the plot of ground Jacob had bought from the
sons of Hamor, father of Shechem, for a hundred pieces of money. This was a heritage of the
descendants of Joseph. 33 When Eleazar, son
of Aaron, also died, he was buried on the hill
which had been given to his son Phinehas[x] in
the mountain region of Ephraim.

s Gn 31, 48. 52; Dt 31, 19. 21. 26.
t Jgs 2, 6.
u 29ff: Jgs 2, 7ff.
v Jos 19, 50: Jgs 2, 9.
w Gn 33, 19; 50, 24; Ex 13, 19.
x Jos 22, 13.

*24, 32: The bones of Joseph: the mummified body of Joseph (Gn 50, 25f), which the Israelites took with them as they left Egypt (Ex 13, 19), was fittingly buried at the ancient city of Shechem, near the border between the two Josephite tribes of Ephraim and Manasseh.

# The Book of
# JUDGES

*The Book of Judges derives its title from the twelve heroes of Israel whose deeds it records. They were not magistrates, but military leaders sent by God to aid and to relieve his people in time of external danger. They exercised their activities in the interval of time between the death of Joshua and the institution of the monarchy in Israel. Six of them—Othniel, Ehud, Barak, Gideon, Jephtah and Samson—are treated in some detail and have accordingly been styled the Major Judges. The other six, of whose activities this book preserves but a summary record, are called the Minor Judges. There were two other judges, whose judgeships are described in 1 Samuel—Eli and Samuel, who seem to have ruled the entire nation of Israel just before the institution of the monarchy. The twelve judges of the present book, however, very probably exercised their authority, sometimes simultaneously, over one or another tribe of Israel, never over the entire nation.*

*The purpose of the book is to show that the fortunes of Israel depended upon the obedience or disobedience of the people to God's law. Whenever they rebelled against him, they were oppressed by pagan nations; when they repented, he raised up judges to deliver them (cf Jgs 2, 10–23).*

*The accounts of various events, whether written shortly after their occurrence or orally transmitted, were later skillfully unified according to the moral purpose of the redactor sometime during the Israelite monarchy.*

*The book is divided as follows:*

*I. Palestine after the Death of Joshua (Jgs 1, 1–3, 6).*
*II. Stories of the Judges (Jgs 3, 7–16, 31).*
*III. The Tribes of Dan and Benjamin in the Days of the Judges (Jgs 17, 1–21, 25).*

## *I: Palestine After the Death of Joshua*

### CHAPTER 1

**Pagan Survivors in Palestine.** **1** After
the death of Joshua* the Israelites consulted the
LORD, asking, "Who shall be first among us to
attack the Canaanites and to do battle with
them?"[a] **2** The LORD answered, "Judah shall
attack: I have delivered the land into his power." **3** Judah then said to his brother Simeon,
"Come up with me into the territory allotted to
me, and let us engage the Canaanites in battle.
I will likewise accompany you into the territory
allotted to you." So Simeon went with him.
**4** When the forces of Judah attacked, the
LORD delivered the Canaanites and Perizzites
into their power, and they slew ten thousand of
them in Bezek. **5** It was in Bezek that they came
upon Adonibezek and fought against him.
When they defeated the Canaanites and Perizzites, **6** Adonibezek fled. They set out in pursuit, and when they caught him, cut off his
thumbs and his big toes. **7** At this Adonibezek
said, "Seventy kings, with their thumbs and big
toes cut off, used to pick up scraps under my
table. As I have done, so has God repaid me."
He was brought to Jerusalem, and there he died.
**8** [The Judahites fought against Jerusalem and
captured it, putting it to the sword; then they
destroyed the city by fire.]
**9** [b]Afterward the Judahites went down to
fight against the Canaanites who lived in the
mountain region, in the Negeb, and in the foothills, **10** [c]Judah also marched against the Canaanites who dwelt in Hebron, which war formerly called Kiriath-arba, and defeated
Sheshai, Ahiman and Talmai.[d] **11** From there
they marched against the inhabitants of Debir,
which was formerly called Kiriath-sepher.
**12** And Caleb said, "I will give my daughter
Achsah in marriage to the one who attacks Kiriath-sepher and captures it." **13** [e]Othniel, son

a Jgs 20, 18: Nm 27, 21.
b Jos 10, 40; 11, 16; 12, 8.
c Jos 15, 13-19.
d Nm 13, 22; Jos 14, 15.
e Jgs 3, 9.

* 1, 1–36: This chapter summarizes events most of which occurred shortly after the death of Joshua. Perhaps because they were planned and inaugurated by him, they are also attributed to him in the last half of the preceding book (Jos 14—22).

of Caleb's younger brother Kenaz, captured it; so Caleb gave him his daughter Achsah in marriage. **14** On the day of her marriage to Othniel she induced him to ask her father for some land. Then, as she alighted from the ass, Caleb asked her, "What is troubling you?" **15** "Give me an additional gift," she answered. "Since you have assigned land in the Negeb to me, give me also pools of water." So Caleb gave her the upper and the lower pool. **16** The descendants of the Kenite, Moses' father-in-law,* came up with the Judahites from the city of palms to the desert at Arad [which is in the Negeb]. But they later left and settled among the Amalekites.[f]

**17** [g]Judah then went with his brother Simeon, and they defeated the Canaanites who dwelt in Zephath. After having doomed the city to destruction, they renamed it Hormah. **18** [h]Judah, however, did not occupy Gaza with its territory, Ashkelon with its territory, or Ekron with its territory. **19** [i]Since the LORD was with Judah, he gained possession of the mountain region. Yet he could not dislodge those who lived on the plain, because they had iron chariots. **20** As Moses had commanded, Hebron was given to Caleb, who then drove from it the three sons of Anak.[j]

**21** *The Benjaminites did not dislodge the Jebusites who dwelt in Jerusalem, with the result that the Jebusites live in Jerusalem beside the Benjaminites to the present day.[k]

**22** The house of Joseph, too, marched up against Bethel, and the LORD was with them. **23** The house of Joseph had a reconnaissance made of Bethel, which formerly was called Luz.[l] **24** The scouts saw a man coming out of the city and said to him, "Show us a way into the city, and we will spare you." **25** He showed them a way into the city, which they then put to the sword; but they let the man and his whole clan go free. **26** He then went to the land of the Hittites, where he built a city and called it Luz, as it is still called.

**27** Manasseh did not take possession of Beth-shean with its towns or of Taanach with its towns. Neither did he dislodge the inhabitants of Dor and its towns, those of Ibleam and its towns, or those of Megiddo and its towns.[m] The Canaanites kept their hold in this district. **28** When the Israelites grew stronger, they impressed the Canaanites as laborers, but did not drive them out. **29** Similarly, the Ephraimites did not drive out the Canaanites living in Gezer, and so the Canaanites live in Gezer in their midst.[n]

**30** Zebulun did not dislodge the inhabitants of Kitron or those of Nahalol; the Canaanites live among them, but have become forced laborers.

**31** [o]Nor did Asher drive out the inhabitants of Acco or those of Sidon, or take possession of Mahaleb, Achzib, Helbah, Aphik or Rehob. **32** The Asherites live among the Canaanite natives of the land, whom they have not dislodged.

**33** [p]Naphtali did not drive out the inhabitants of Beth-shemesh or those of Beth-anath, and so they live among the Canaanite natives of the land. However, the inhabitants of Beth-shemesh and Beth-anath have become forced laborers for them.

**34** The Amorites hemmed in the Danites in the mountain region, not permitting them to go down into the plain.[q] **35** The Amorites had a firm hold in Harheres, Aijalon and Shaalbim, but as the house of Joseph gained the upper hand, they were impressed as laborers.

**36** The territory of the Amorites extended from the Akrabbim pass to Sela and beyond.

## CHAPTER 2

**Infidelities of the Israelites.** **1** [r]An angel of the LORD went up from Gilgal to Bochim and said, "It was I who brought you up from Egypt and led you into the land which I promised on oath to your fathers. I said that I would never break my covenant with you, **2** but that you were not to make a pact with the inhabitants of this land, and you were to pull down their altars. Yet you have not obeyed me.[s] What did you mean by this? **3** For now I tell you, I will not clear them out of your way; they shall oppose you and their gods shall become a snare for you."[t]

**4** When the angel of the LORD had made these threats to all the Israelites, the people wept aloud; **5** and so that place came to be called Bochim.* They offered sacrifice there to the LORD.

**6** [u]When Joshua dismissed the people, each Israelite went to take possession of his own hereditary land. **7** The people served the LORD during the entire lifetime of Joshua, and of those elders who outlived Joshua and who had seen all the great work which the LORD had done for

f Jgs 4, 11; Nm 10, 29-32.
g Nm 21, 3.
h Jos 11, 22.
i Jos 17, 16ff.
j Jos 14, 9. 13: 15, 14.
k Jos 15, 63.
l Gn 28, 19; 35, 6; 48, 3; Jos 18, 13.
m 27f: Jos 17, 11ff.
n Jos 16, 10.
o 31f: Jos 19, 24-31.
p Jos 19, 32-39.
q Jos 19, 47f.
r 1ff: Jgs 6, 8ff.
s Ex 34, 12f. 15; Dt 7, 2. 5; 21, 2f.
t Nm 33, 55; Jos 23, 13.
u 6-9: Jos 24, 28-31.

*

1, 16: Moses' father-in-law: Reuel; cf Nm 10, 29–32 and note. City of palms: Jericho (cf Dt 34, 3), or a town in the Negeb.

1, 21: According to Jos 18, 16, Jerusalem was assigned to the tribe of Benjamin. But it was not actually taken from the Jebusites until David captured it (2 Sm 5, 6–9) and made it his capital, outside the tribal organization.

2, 5: Bochim: the Hebrew word for "weepers."

Israel. **8** Joshua, son of Nun, the servant of the
LORD, was a hundred and ten years old when he
died; **9** and they buried him within the borders
of his heritage at Timnath-heres in the mountain
region of Ephraim north of Mount Gaash.[v]

**10** But once the rest of that generation were
gathered to their fathers, and a later generation
arose that did not know the LORD, or what he
had done for Israel, **11** the Israelites offended
the LORD by serving the Baals.*[w] **12** Abandoning the LORD, the God of their fathers, who had
led them out of the land of Egypt, they followed
the other gods of the various nations around
them, and by their worship of these gods provoked the LORD.

**13** Because they had thus abandoned him
and served Baal and the Ashtaroth,* **14** the anger of the LORD flared up against Israel, and he
delivered them over to plunderers who despoiled them. He allowed them to fall into the
power of their enemies round about whom they
were no longer able to withstand. **15** Whatever
they undertook, the LORD turned into disaster
for them, as in his warning he had sworn he
would do, till they were in great distress.[x]
**16** Even when the LORD raised up judges to
deliver them from the power of their despoilers,
**17** they did not listen to their judges, but abandoned themselves to the worship of other gods.
They were quick to stray from the way their
fathers had taken, and did not follow their example of obedience to the commandments of the
LORD. **18** Whenever the LORD raised up judges
for them, he would be with the judge and save
them from the power of their enemies as long as
the judge lived; it was thus the LORD took pity
on their distressful cries of affliction under their
oppressors. **19** But when the judge died, they
would relapse and do worse than their fathers,
following other gods in service and worship,
relinquishing none of their evil practices or
stubborn conduct.[y]

**20** [z]In his anger toward Israel the LORD said,
"Inasmuch as this nation has violated my covenant which I enjoined on their fathers, and has
disobeyed me, **21** I for my part will not clear
away for them any more of the nations which
Joshua left when he died." **22** Through these
nations the Israelites were to be made to prove
whether or not they would keep to the way of
the LORD and continue in it as their fathers had
done; **23** therefore the LORD allowed them to
remain instead of expelling them immediately,
or delivering them into the power of Israel.

## CHAPTER 3

**1** The following are the nations which the LORD
allowed to remain, so that through them he
might try all those Israelites who had no experience of the battles with Canaan **2** [just to instruct, by training them in battle, those generations only of the Israelites who would not have
had that previous experience]: **3** [a]the five lords
of the Philistines;* and all the Canaanites, the
Sidonians, and the Hivites who dwell in the
mountain region of Lebanon between Baal-hermon and the entrance to Hamath. **4** These
served to put Israel to the test, to determine
whether they would obey the commandments
the LORD had enjoined on their fathers through
Moses. **5** Besides, the Israelites were living
among the Canaanites, Hittites, Amorites, Perizzites, Hivites and Jebusites. **6** In fact, they
took their daughters in marriage, and gave their
own daughters to their sons in marriage, and
served their gods.

## *II: Stories of the Judges*

**Othniel.** **7** [b]Because the Israelites had offended the LORD by forgetting the LORD, their
God, and serving the Baals and the Asherahs,*
**8** the anger of the LORD flared up against them,
and he allowed them to fall into the power of
Cushan-rishathaim, king of Aram Naharaim,
whom they served for eight years. **9** But when
the Israelites cried out to the LORD, he raised up
for them a savior, Othniel, son of Caleb's younger brother Kenaz, who rescued them. **10** The
spirit of the LORD came upon him, and he
judged Israel.[c] When he went out to war, the
LORD delivered Cushan-risha-thaim, king of
Aram, into his power, so that he made him
subject. **11** The land then was at rest for forty
years,[d] until Othniel, son of Kenaz, died.

**Ehud.** **12** Again the Israelites offended the
LORD, who because of this offense strengthened
Eglon, king of Moab, against Israel. **13** In alliance with the Ammonites and Amalekites, he
attacked and defeated Israel, taking possession
of the city of palms. **14** The Israelites then
served Eglon, king of Moab, for eighteen years.

v Jos 19, 50.
w 11. 14; Jgs 3, 7f; 4, 1f; 6, 1; 10, 6f; 13, 1.
x Dt 28, 15-68.
y Jgs 3, 12; 4, 1; 6, 1; 8, 33.
z 20f: Jos 23, 16.
a Jos 13, 2-6.
b Jgs 2, 11ff.
c Jgs 6, 34; 11, 29; 13, 25; 14, 6. 19; 15, 14.
d Jgs 5, 31; 8, 28.

*

2, 11: Baals: the chief god of the Canaanites and the Phoenicians was called "Baal," a word meaning "lord." He was honored by various titles, hence the plural form here, equivalent to "the pagan gods."

2, 13: Ashtaroth: the Canaanite Phoenician goddess of love and fertility was Astarte. The plural form used here refers to her various titles and images and is equivalent to "goddesses."

3, 3: The Philistines; non-Semitic invaders, who gave their name to all Palestine, although they occupied only its southwestern plains. Their confederation embraced the five leading cities of Gaza, Ashkelon, Ashdod, Gath and Ekron.

3, 7: Asherahs: elsewhere rendered "sacred poles." See note on Ex 34, 13 and on Dt 7, 5. Here the word seems to mean "goddesses."

**15** But when the Israelites cried out to the LORD, he raised up for them a savior, the Benjaminite Ehud, son of Gera, who was left-handed. It was by him that the Israelites sent their tribute to Eglon, king of Moab. **16** Ehud made himself a two-edged dagger a foot long, and wore it under his clothes over his right thigh. **17** He presented the tribute to Eglon, king of Moab, who was very fat, **18** and after the presentation went off with the tribute bearers. **19** He returned, however, from where the idols are, near Gilgal, and said, "I have a private message for you, O king." And the king said, "Silence!" Then when all his attendants had left his presence, **20** and Ehud went in to him where he sat alone in his cool upper room, Ehud said, "I have a message from God for you." So the king rose from his chair, **21** and then Ehud with his left hand drew the dagger from his right thigh, and thrust it into Eglon's belly. **22** The hilt also went in after the blade, and the fat closed over the blade because he did not withdraw the dagger from his body.

**23** Then Ehud went out into the hall, shutting the doors of the upper room on him and locking them. **24** When Ehud had left and the servants came, they saw that the doors of the upper room were locked, and thought, "He must be easing himself in the cool chamber." **25** They waited until they finally grew suspicious. Since he did not open the doors of the upper room, they took the key and opened them. There on the floor, dead, lay their lord!

**26** During their delay Ehud made good his escape and, passing the idols, took refuge in Seirah. **27** On his arrival he sounded the horn in the mountain region of Ephraim, and the Israelites went down from the mountains with him as their leader. **28** "Follow me," he said to them, "for the LORD has delivered your enemies the Moabites into your power." So they followed him down and seized the fords of the Jordan leading to Moab, permitting no one to cross.[e] **29** On that occasion they slew about ten thousand Moabites, all of them strong and valiant men. Not a man escaped. **30** Thus was Moab brought under the power of Israel at that time; and the land had rest for eighty years.

**Shamgar.** **31** After him there was Shamgar, son of Anath, who slew six hundred Philistines with an oxgoad. He, too, rescued Israel.

## CHAPTER 4

**Deborah and Barak.** **1** After Ehud's death, however, the Israelites again offended the LORD. **2** So the LORD allowed them to fall into the power of the Canaanite king, Jabin, who reigned in Hazor.[f] The general of his army was Sisera, who dwelt in Harosheth-ha-goiim. **3** But the Israelites cried out to the LORD; for with his nine hundred iron chariots he sorely oppressed the Israelites for twenty years.

**4** At this time the prophetess Deborah, wife of Lappidoth, was judging Israel. **5** She used to sit under Deborah's palm tree, situated between Ramah and Bethel in the mountain region of Ephraim, and there the Israelites came up to her for judgment. **6** She sent and summoned Barak, son of Abinoam,[g] from Kedesh of Naphtali. "This is what the LORD, the God of Israel, commands," she said to him; "go, march on Mount Tabor, and take with you ten thousand Naphtalites and Zebulunites. **7** I will lead Sisera, the general of Jabin's army, out to you at the Wadi Kishon,[h] together with his chariots and troops, and will deliver them into your power." **8** But Barak answered her, "If you come with me, I will go; if you do not come with me, I will not go." **9** "I will certainly go with you," she replied, "but you shall not gain the glory in the expedition on which you are setting out, for the LORD will have Sisera fall into the power of a woman." So Deborah joined Barak and journeyed with him to Kedesh.

**10** Barak summoned Zebulun and Naphtali to Kedesh, and ten thousand men followed him. Deborah also went up with him.[i] **11** *Now the Kenite Heber had detached himself from his own people, the descendants of Hobab, Moses' brother-in-law,[j] and had pitched his tent by the tere-binth of Zaanannim, which was near Kedesh.

**12** It was reported to Sisera that Barak, son of Abinoam, had gone up to Mount Tabor. **13** So Sisera assembled from Harosheth-hagoiim at the Wadi Kishon all nine hundred of his iron chariots and all his forces. **14** Deborah then said to Barak, "Be off, for this is the day on which the LORD has delivered Sisera into your power. The LORD marches before you." So Barak went down Mount Tabor, followed by his ten thousand men. **15** And the LORD put Sisera[k] and all his chariots and all his forces to rout before Barak. Sisera himself dismounted from his chariot and fled on foot. **16** Barak, however, pursued the chariots and the army as far as Harosheth-ha-goiim. The entire army of Sisera fell beneath the sword, not even one man surviving.

**17** *Sisera, in the meantime, had fled on foot

e Jgs 4, 7. 14; 7, 9. 15.
f Jos 11, 1. 10; Ps 83, 10; 1 Sm 12, 9.
g Heb 11, 32.
h Jgs 5, 21; Ps 83, 10.
i Jgs 5, 18.
j Nm 10, 29.
k Ps 83, 10.

*

4, 11: Most of the Kenites occupied a district in the southern part of Judah (Jgs 1, 16). A group of them, however, had detached themselves and settled in lower Galilee.

4, 17–22: It is to be noted that the sacred author merely records the fact of the murder of Sisera. We must not construe this as approval of Jael's action.

to the tent of Jael, wife of the Kenite Heber,
since Jabin, king of Hazor, and the family of the
Kenite Heber were at peace with one another.
**18** Jael went out to meet Sisera and said to him,
"Come in, my lord, come in with me; do not be
afraid." So he went into her tent, and she covered him with a rug. **19** He said to her, "Please
give me a little water to drink. I am thirsty."
But she opened a jug of milk for him to drink,
and then covered him over.[l] **20** "Stand at the
entrance of the tent," he said to her. "If anyone
comes and asks, 'Is there someone here?' say,
'No!' " **21** Instead Jael, wife of Heber, got a
tent peg and took a mallet in her hand. While
Sisera was sound asleep, she stealthily approached him and drove the peg through his
temple down into the ground, so that he perished in death.[m] **22** Then when Barak came in
pursuit of Sisera, Jael went out to meet him and
said to him, "Come, I will show you the man
you seek." So he went in with her, and there lay
Sisera dead, with the tent peg through his temple.
**23** Thus on that day God humbled the Canaanite king, Jabin, before the Israelites;
**24** their power weighed ever heavier upon him,
till at length they destroyed the Canaanite king
Jabin.

## CHAPTER 5

**Canticle of Deborah.** **1** On that day Deborah [and Barak, son of Abinoam] sang this
song:

**2** Of chiefs who took the lead in Israel,*
of noble deeds by the people who bless the LORD,
**3** Hear, O kings! Give ear, O princes!
I to the LORD will sing my song,
my hymn to the LORD, the God of Israel.

**4** O LORD, when you went out from Seir,
when you marched from the land of Edom,
The earth quaked and the heavens were shaken,
while the clouds sent down showers.
**5** Mountains trembled
in the presence of the LORD, the One of Sinai,[n]
in the presence of the LORD, the God of Israel.[o]

**6** In the days of Shamgar, son of Anath,[p]
in the days of slavery caravans ceased;
Those who traveled the roads
went by roundabout paths.
**7** Gone was freedom beyond the walls
gone indeed from Israel.

When I, Deborah, rose,
when I rose, a mother in Israel,
**8** New gods* were their choice;
then the war was at their gates.
Not a shield could be seen, nor a lance,
among forty thousand in Israel!

**9** My heart is with the leaders of Israel,
nobles of the people who bless the LORD;
**10** They who ride on white asses,
seated on saddlecloths as they go their way;
**11** Sing of them to the strains of the harpers at the wells,
where men recount the just deeds of the LORD,
his just deeds that brought freedom to Israel.

**12** Awake, awake, Deborah!
awake, awake, strike up a song.
Strength! arise, Barak,
make despoilers your spoil, son of Abinoam.
**13** Then down came the fugitives with the mighty,
the people of the LORD came down for me as warriors.

**14** From Ephraim, princes were in the valley;*
behind you was Benjamin, among your troops.
From Machir came down commanders,
from Zebulun wielders of the marshal's staff.

**15** With Deborah were the princes of Issachar;
Barak, too, was in the valley, his course unchecked.

Among the clans of Reuben
great were the searchings of heart.[q]
**16** Why do you stay beside your hearths
listening to the lowing of the herds?
Among the clans of Reuben
great were the searchings of heart!

**17** Gilead, beyond the Jordan, rests;
why does Dan spend his time in ships?
Asher, who dwells along the shore,

l Jgs 5, 25.
m Jgs 5, 26.
n Dt 33, 2; 2 Sm 22, 8; Pss 18, 8; 68, 9.
o Ex 19, 16; Dt 4, 11; Ps 97, 5.
p Jgs 3, 31.
q Jgs 4, 14.

*

5, 2–31: This canticle is an excellent example of early Hebrew poetry, even though some of its verses are now obscure.

5, 8: New gods: pagan deities; cf Dt 32, 16–18. God punished the idolatry of the Israelites by leaving them relatively unarmed before the attacks of their enemies, who had better weapons, made of iron; cf 1 Sm 13, 19–22.

5, 14–22: Praise for the tribes which formed the Israelite league against Sisera: Ephraim, Benjamin, Manasseh (represented by Machir), Zebulun, Issachar, and Naphtali (led by Barak), The tribes of Reuben, Gad (Gilead), Dan, and Asher are chided for their lack of co-operation. The more distant tribes of Judah and Simeon are not mentioned.

is resting in his coves.
**18** Zebulum is the people defying death;
Naphtali, too, on the open heights![r]

**19** The kings came and fought;
then they fought, those kings of Canaan,
At Taanach by the waters of Megiddo;
no silver booty did they take.[s]
**20** From the heavens the stars, too, fought;*
from their courses they fought against
Sisera.

**21** The Wadi Kishon swept them away;
a wadi . . . , the Kishon.[u]
**22** Then the hoofs of the horses pounded,
with the dashing, dashing of his steeds.

**23** "Curse Meroz,"* says the LORD,
"hurl a curse at its inhabitants!
For they came not to my help,
as warriors to the help of the LORD."

**24** Blessed among women be Jael,
blessed among tent-dwelling women.[v]
**25** He asked for water, she gave him milk;[w]
in a princely bowl she offered curds.
**26** With her left hand she reached for the peg,
with her right, for the workman's mallet.

She hammered Sisera, crushed his head;
she smashed, stove in his temple.
**27** At her feet he sank down, fell, lay still;
down at her feet he sank and fell;
where he sank down, there he fell, slain.

**28** From the window peered down and wailed
the mother of Sisera, from the lattice:
"Why is his chariot so long in coming?
why are the hoofbeats of his chariots
delayed?"
**29** The wisest of her princesses answers her,
and she, too, keeps answering herself:
**30** They must be dividing the spoil they took:
there must be a damsel or two for each
man,
Spoils of dyed cloth as Sisera's spoil,
an ornate shawl or two for me in the
spoil."
**31** May all your enemies perish thus, O LORD![x]
but your friends be as the sun rising in its
might!

And the land was at rest for forty years.

## CHAPTER 6

**The Call of Gideon.** **1** The Israelites offended the LORD, who therefore delivered them
into the power of Midian for seven years, **2** so
that Midian held Israel subject. For fear of Midian the Israelites established the fire signals on
the mountains, the caves for refuge, and the
strongholds. **3** And it used to be that when the
Israelites had completed their sowing, Midian,
Amalek and the Kedemites would come up,[y]
**4** encamp opposite them, and destroy the produce of the land as far as the outskirts of Gaza,
leaving no sustenance in Israel, nor sheep, oxen
or asses. **5** For they would come up with their
livestock, and their tents would become as numerous as locusts; and neither they nor their
camels could be numbered, when they came
into the land to lay it waste. **6** Thus was Israel
reduced to misery by Midian, and so the Israelites cried out to the LORD.

**7** When Israel cried out to the LORD because
of Midian, **8** [z]he sent a prophet to the Israelites
who said to them, "The LORD, the God of Israel, says: I led you up from Egypt; I brought you
out of the place of slavery. **9** I rescued you from
the power of Egypt and of all your other oppressors. I drove them out before you and gave you
their land. **10** And I said to you: I, the LORD,
am your God; you shall not venerate the gods of
the Amorites in whose land you are dwelling.
But you did not obey me."

**11** Then the angel of the LORD came and sat
under the terebinth in Ophrah that belonged to
Joash the Abiezrite. While his son Gideon was
beating out wheat in the wine press to save it
from the Midianites, **12** the angel of the LORD
appeared to him and said, "The LORD is with
you, O champion!" **13** "My LORD," Gideon
said to him, "if the LORD is with us, why has
all this happened to us? Where are his wondrous
deeds of which our fathers told us when they
said, 'Did not the LORD bring us up from
Egypt?' For now the LORD has abandoned us
and has delivered us into the power of Midian."
**14** The LORD turned to him and said, "Go with
the strength you have and save Israel from the
power of Midian. It is I who send you." **15** But
he answered him, "Please, my lord, how can I
save Israel? My family is the meanest in Manasseh, and I am the most insignificant in my father's house." **16** "I shall be with you," the
LORD said to him, "and you will cut down
Midian to the last man." **17** He answered him,
"If I find favor with you, give me a sign that
you are speaking with me. **18** Do not depart
from here, I pray you, until I come back to you
and bring out my offering and set it before
you." He answered, "I will await your return."

r Jgs 4, 10.
s Jgs 1, 27; Jos 17, 11.
t Jgs 4, 15; Jos 10, 14.
u Jgs 4, 7. 13.
v Jgs 4, 17; Jdt 13, 17; Lk 1, 28. 42.
w 25f: Jgs 4, 19. 21.
x Ps 83, 10-19.
y 3f: Jgs 7, 12; Dt 28, 30ff.
z 8ff: Jgs 2, 1f; 10, 11-14.

*

5, 20f: It would seem that nature aided the Hebrews in some way. Perhaps the torrential rains swelled the waters of Kishon, which then overwhelmed the Canaanites.

5, 23: Meroz: an unknown locality in which Hebrews probably resided, since its inhabitants are cursed for their failure to proffer aid.

**19** So Gideon went off and prepared a kid
and an ephah of flour in the form of unleavened
cakes. Putting the meat in a basket and the broth
in a pot, he brought them out to him under the
terebinth and presented them. **20** The angel of
God said to him, "Take the meat and unleavened cakes and lay them on this rock; then pour
out the broth."[a] When he had done so, **21** the
angel of the LORD stretched out the tip of the
staff he held, and touched the meat and unleavened cakes. Thereupon a fire came up from the
rock which consumed the meat and unleavened
cakes, and the angel of the LORD disappeared
from sight. **22** [b]Gideon, now aware that it had
been the angel of the LORD, said, "Alas, Lord,
GOD, that I have seen the angel of the LORD face
to face!" **23** The LORD answered him, "Be
calm, do not fear. You shall not die." **24** So
Gideon built there an altar to the LORD and
called it Yahweh-shalom.* To this day it is still
in Ophrah of the Abiezrites.

**25** That same night the LORD said to him,
"Take the seven-year-old spare bullock and destroy your father's altar to Baal and cut down the
sacred pole* that is by it. **26** You shall build,
instead, the proper kind of altar to the LORD,
your God, on top of this stronghold. Then take
the spare bullock and offer it as a holocaust on
the wood from the sacred pole you have cut
down." **27** So Gideon took ten of his servants
and did as the LORD had commanded him. But
through fear of his family and of the townspeople, he would not do it by day, but did it at night.
**28** Early the next morning the townspeople
found that the altar of Baal had been destroyed,
the sacred pole near it cut down, and the spare
bullock offered on the altar that was built.
**29** They asked one another, "Who did this?"
Their inquiry led them to the conclusion that
Gideon, son of Joash, had done it. **30** So the
townspeople said to Joash, "Bring out your son
that he may die, for he was destroyed the altar
of Baal and has cut down the sacred pole that
was near it." **31** But Joash replied to all who
were standing around him, "Do you intend to
act in Baal's stead, or be his champion? If anyone acts for him, he shall be put to death by
morning. If he whose altar has been destroyed
is a god, let him act for himself!" **32** So on that
day Gideon was called Jerubbaal,* because of
the words, "Let Baal take action against him,
since he destroyed his altar."[c]

**33** Then all Midian and Amalek and the
Kedemites mustered and crossed over into the
valley of Jezreel, where they encamped.
**34** The spirit of the LORD enveloped Gideon; he
blew the horn that summoned Abiezer to follow
him. **35** He sent messengers, too, throughout
Manasseh, which also obeyed his summons;
through Asher, Zebulun and Naphtali, likewise,
he sent messengers and these tribes advanced to
meet the others. **36** Gideon said to God, "If
indeed you are going to save Israel through me,
as you promised, **37** I am putting this woolen
fleece on the threshing floor. If dew comes on
the fleece alone, while all the ground is dry, I
shall know that you will save Israel through me,
as you promised." **38** That is what took place.
Early the next morning he wrung the dew from
the fleece, squeezing out of it a bowlful of water. **39** Gideon then said to God, "Do not be
angry with me if I speak once more. Let me
make just one more test with the fleece. Let the
fleece alone be dry, but let there be dew on all
the ground." **40** That night God did so; the
fleece alone was dry, but there was dew on all
the ground.

## CHAPTER 7

**Defeat of Midian.** **1** Early the next morning
Jerubbaal[d] (that is, Gideon) encamped by Enharod with all his soldiers. The camp of Midian
was in the valley north of Gibeath-hammoreh.
**2** The LORD said to Gideon, "You have too
many soldiers with you for me to deliver Midian
into their power, lest Israel vaunt itself against
me and say, 'My own power brought me the
victory.' **3** Now proclaim to all the soldiers, 'If
anyone is afraid or fearful, let him leave.' "[e]
When Gideon put them to this test on the mountain, twenty-two thousand of the soldiers left,
but ten thousand remained. **4** The LORD said to
Gideon, "There are still too many soldiers.
Lead them down to the water and I will test them
for you there. If I tell you that a certain man is
to go with you, he must go with you. But no one
is to go if I tell you he must not." **5** *When
Gideon led the soldiers down to the water, the
LORD said to him, "You shall set to one side
everyone who laps up the water as a dog does
with its tongue; to the other, everyone who
kneels down to drink." **6** Those who lapped up
the water raised to their mouths by hand numbered three hundred, but all the rest of the soldiers knelt down to drink the water. **7** The
LORD said to Gideon, "By means of the three
hundred who lapped up the water I will save you

a Jgs 13, 19.
b 22f: Gn 32, 31; Dt 5, 24ff.
c 1 Sm 12, 11.
d Jgs 6, 32.
e Dt 20, 8.

*

6, 24: Yahweh-shalom: Hebrew for "the LORD is peace," a reference to the Lord's words, "Be calm," literally, "Peace be to you!"

6, 25: The sacred pole: see note on Ex 34, 13.

6, 32: Jerubbaal: similar in sound to the Hebrew words meaning, "Let Baal take action."

7, 5: The Lord desired not numerous but reliable soldiers. Those who drank from their hands were alert, standing ready to resist attack, whereas the others were careless and undependable. The cowardly soldiers had already been dismissed (v 3); cf Dt 20, 8.

and will deliver Midian into your power. So let
all the other soldiers go home." **8** Their horns,
and such supplies as the soldiers had with them,
were taken up, and Gideon ordered the rest of
the Israelites to their tents, but kept the three
hundred men. Now the camp of Midian was
beneath him in the valley.

**9** That night the LORD said to Gideon, "Go,
descend on the camp, for I have delivered it up
to you. **10** If you are afraid to attack, go down
to the camp with your aide Purah. **11** When you
hear what they are saying, you will have the
courage to descend on the camp." So he went
down with his aide Purah to the outposts of the
camp. **12** The Midianites, Amalekites, and all
the Kedemites lay in the valley, as numerous as
locusts. Nor could their camels be counted, for
these were as many as the sands on the seashore.
**13** *When Gideon arrived, one man was telling
another about a dream. "I had a dream," he
said, "that a round loaf of barley bread was
rolling into the camp of Midian. It came to our
tent and struck it, and as it fell it turned the tent
upside down." **14** "This can only be the sword
of the Israelite Gideon, son of Joash," the other
replied. "God has delivered Midian and all the
camp into his power." **15** When Gideon heard
the description and explanation of the dream, he
prostrated himself. Then returning to the camp
of Israel, he said, "Arise, for the LORD has
delivered the camp of Midian into your power."

**16** He divided the three hundred men into
three companies, and provided them all with
horns and with empty jars and torches inside the
jars. **17** "Watch me and follow my lead," he
told them. "I shall go to the edge of the camp,
and as I do, you must do also. **18** When I and
those with me blow horns, you too must blow
horns all around the camp and cry out, 'For the
LORD and for Gideon!' " **19** So Gideon and the
hundred men who were with him came to the
edge of the camp at the beginning of the middle
watch,* just after the posting of the guards.
They blew the horns and broke the jars they
were holding. **20** All three companies blew
horns and broke their jars. They held the torches
in their left hands, and in their right the horns
they were blowing, and cried out, "A sword for
the LORD and Gideon!" **21** They all remained
standing in place around the camp, while the
whole camp fell to running and shouting and
fleeing. **22** But the three hundred men kept
blowing the horns, and throughout the camp the
LORD set the sword of one against another.[f] The
army fled as far as Beth-shittah in the direction
of Zarethan, near the border of Abel-meholah at
Tabbath.

**23** The Israelites were called to arms from
Naphtali, from Asher, and from all Manasseh,
and they pursued Midian. **24** Gideon also sent
messengers throughout the mountain region of
Ephraim to say, "Go down to confront Midian,
and seize the water courses against them as far
as Beth-barah, as well as the Jordan." So all the
Ephraimites were called to arms, and they
seized the water courses as far as Beth-barah,
and the Jordan as well. **25** [g]They captured the
two princes of Midian, Oreb and Zeeb, killing
Oreb at the rock of Oreb and Zeeb at the wine
press of Zeeb. Then they pursued Midian and
carried the heads of Oreb and Zeeb to Gideon
beyond the Jordan.

## CHAPTER 8

**1** But the Ephraimites said to him, "What
have you done to us, not calling us when you
went to fight against Midian?" And they quar-
relled bitterly with him. **2** "What have I accomplished now in comparison with you?" he
answered them. "Is not the gleaning of Ephraim
better than the vintage of Abiezer?[h] **3** Into your
power God delivered the princes of Midian,
Oreb and Zeeb. What have I been able to do in
comparison with you?" When he said this, their
anger against him subsided.

**4** When Gideon reached the Jordan and
crossed it with his three hundred men, they were
exhausted and famished. **5** So he said to the
men of Succoth, "Will you give my followers
some loaves of bread? They are exhausted, and
I am pursuing Zebah and Zalmunna, kings of
Midian." **6** But the princes of Succoth replied,
"Are the hands of Zebah and Zalmunna already
in your possession, that we should give food to
your army?"* **7** Gideon said, "Very well;
when the LORD has delivered Zebah and Zalmunna into my power, I will grind your flesh in
with the thorns and briers of the desert." **8** He
went up from there to Penuel and made the same
request of them, but the men of Penuel answered him as had the men of Succoth. **9** So to
the men of Penuel, too, he said, "When I return
in triumph, I will demolish this tower."

**10** Now Zebah and Zalmunna were in Kar-
kor with their force of about fifteen thousand
men; these were all who were left of the whole
Kedemite army, a hundred and twenty thousand
swordsmen having fallen. **11** Gideon went up

f 22f: Ps 83, 10; Is 9, 4.
g Jgs 8, 3; Ps 83, 12; Is 10, 26.
h Jg 6, 34.

*

7, 13: The barley loaf represents the agricultural Hebrews while the tent refers to the nomadic Midianites. The overthrow of the tent indicates the victory of the Hebrews over their Midianite oppressors.

7, 19: At the beginning of the middle watch: about two hours before midnight. The ancient Hebrews divided the night into three watches of about four hours each. At the beginning of a watch the sentinels were changed.

8, 6: Are the hands . . . in your possession . . .?: i.e., can you already boast of victory? The hands as well as the heads of slain enemies were cut off and counted as trophies; cf 2 Sm 4, 8; 2 Kgs 10, 7f; and the Ugaritic Anath Epic, V AB, II 10ff.

the route of the nomads east of Nobah and Jogbehah, and attacked the camp when it felt secure. **12** Zebah and Zalmunna fled. He pursued them and took the two kings of Midian, Zebah and Zalmunna, captive, throwing the entire army into panic.

**13** Then Gideon, son of Joash, returned from battle by the pass of Heres. **14** He captured a young man of Succoth, who upon being questioned listed for him the seventy-seven princes and elders of Succoth. **15** So he went to the men of Succoth and said, "Here are Zebah and Zalmunna, with whom you taunted me, 'Are the hands of Zebah and Zalmunna already in your possession, that we should give food to your weary followers?' " **16** He took the elders of the city, and thorns and briers of the desert, and ground these men of Succoth into them. **17** He also demolished the tower of Penuel and slew the men of the city.

**18** Then he said to Zebah and Zalmunna, "Where now are the men you killed at Tabor?" "They all resembled you," they replied. "They appeared to be princes." **19** "They were my brothers, my mother's sons," he said. "As the LORD lives, if you had spared their lives, I should not kill you." **20** Then he said to his first-born, Jether, "Go, kill them." Since Jether was still a boy, he was afraid and did not draw his sword. **21** Zebah and Zalmunna said, "Come, kill us yourself, for a man's strength is like the man." So Gideon stepped forward and killed Zebah and Zalmunna. He also took the crescents that were on the necks of their camels.

**22** The Israelites then said to Gideon, "Rule over us—you, your son, and your son's son—for you rescued us from the power of Midian." **23** But Gideon answered them, "I will not rule over you, nor shall my son rule over you. The LORD must rule over you."

**24** Gideon went on to say, "I should like to make a request of you. Will each of you give me a ring from his booty?" (For being Ishmaelites,* the enemy had gold rings.) **25** "We will gladly give them," they replied, and spread out a cloak into which everyone threw a ring from his booty. **26** The gold rings that he requested weighed seventeen hundred gold shekels, in addition to the crescents and pendants, the purple garments worn by the kings of Midian, and the trappings that were on the necks of their camels. **27** Gideon made an ephod out of the gold and placed it in his city Ophrah. However, all Israel paid idolatrous homage to it there, and caused the ruin of Gideon and his family.

**28** Thus was Midian brought into subjection by the Israelites; no longer did they hold their heads high. And the land had rest for forty years, during the lifetime of Gideon.

**Gideon's Son Abimelech.** **29** Then Jerubbaal, son of Joash, went back home to stay. **30** [i]Now Gideon had seventy sons, his direct descendants, for he had many wives. **31** His concubine* who lived in Shechem also bore him a son, whom he named Abimelech. **32** At a good old age Gideon, son of Joash, died and was buried in the tomb of his father Joash in Ophrah of the Abiezrites. **33** But after Gideon was dead, the Israelites again abandoned themselves to the Baals, making Baal of Berith* their god **34** and forgetting the LORD, their God, who had delivered them from the power of their enemies all around them. **35** Nor were they grateful to the family of Jerubbaal [Gideon] for all the good he had done for Israel.

## CHAPTER 9

**1** Abimelech, son of Jerubbaal, went to his mother's kinsmen in Shechem,[j] and said to them and to the whole clan to which his mother's family belonged, **2** "Put this question to all the citizens of Shechem: 'Which is better for you: that seventy men, or all Jerubbaal's sons, rule over you, or that one man rule over you?' You must remember that I am your own flesh and bone." **3** When his mother's kin repeated these words to them on his behalf, all the citizens of Shechem sympathized with Abimelech, thinking, "He is our kinsman." **4** They also gave him seventy silver shekels from the temple of Baal of Berith, with which Abimelech hired shiftless men and ruffians as his followers. **5** He then went to his ancestral house in Ophrah, and slew his brothers, the seventy sons of Jerubbaal, on one stone. Only the youngest son of Jerubbaal, Jotham, escaped, for he was hidden. **6** Then all the citizens of Shechem and all Beth-millo came together and proceeded to make Abimelech king by the terebinth at the memorial pillar in Shechem.

**7** When this was reported to him, Jotham went to the top of Mount Gerizim, and standing there, cried out to them in a loud voice: "Hear me, citizens of Shechem, that God may then hear you! **8** Once the trees went to anoint a king over themselves. So they said to the olive tree, 'Reign over us.'[k] **9** But the olive tree answered

i Jgs 9, 2. 5.
j Jgs 8, 31.
k Jgs 8, 22f.

*

8, 24: Ishmaelites: here as in Gn 37, 25–28, the designation is not ethnic; it refers rather to their status as nomads.

8, 31: Concubine: a wife of secondary rank.

8, 33: Baal of Berith: one of the titles of Baal as worshiped by the Canaanites of Shechem, meaning "the lord of the covenant."

9, 9: Whereby men and gods are honored: oil was used in the worship both of the true God and of false gods; it was prescribed in the worship of Yahweh (Lv 2, 1. 6. 15; 24, 2). It was also used to consecrate prophets, priests and kings (Ex 30, 25. 30; 1 Sm 10, 1; 16, 13).

them, 'Must I give up my rich oil, whereby men
and gods are honored,* and go to wave over the
trees?' **10** Then the trees said to the fig tree,
'Come; you reign over us!' **11** But the fig tree
answered them, 'Must I give up my sweetness
and my good fruit, and go to wave over the
trees?' **12** Then the trees said to the vine,
'Come you, and reign over us.' **13** But the vine
answered them, 'Must I give up my wine that
cheers gods* and men, and go to wave over the
trees?' **14** Then all the trees said to the buckthorn, 'Come; you reign over us!' **15** But the
buckthorn replied to the trees, 'If you wish to
anoint me king over you in good faith, come and
take refuge in my shadow. Otherwise, let fire
come from the buckthorn and devour the cedars
of Lebanon.'

**16** *"Now then, if you have acted in good
faith and honorably in appointing Abimelech
your king, if you have dealt well with Jerubbaal
and with his family, and if you have treated him
as he deserved— **17** for my father fought for
you at the risk of his life when he saved you
from the power of Midian; **18** but you have
risen against his family this day and have killed
his seventy sons upon one stone, and have made
Abimelech, the son of his handmaid,[l] king over
the citizens of Shechem, because he is your
kinsman— **19** if, then, you have acted in good
faith and with honor toward Jerubbaal and his
family this day, rejoice in Abimelech and may
he in turn rejoice in you. **20** But if not, let fire
come forth from Abimelech to devour the citizens of Shechem and Beth-millo, and let fire
come forth from the citizens and from Beth-millo to devour Abimelech." **21** Then Jotham
went in flight to Beer, where he remained for
fear of his brother Abimelech.

**22** When Abimelech had ruled Israel for
three years, **23** God put bad feelings between
Abimelech and the citizens of Shechem, who
rebelled against Abimelech. **24** This was to repay the violence done to the seventy sons of
Jerubbaal and to avenge their blood upon their
brother Abimelech, who killed them, and upon
the citizens of Shechem, who encouraged him
to kill his brothers. **25** The citizens of Shechem
then set men in ambush for him on the mountaintops, and these robbed all who passed them
on the road. But it was reported to Abimelech.

**26** Now Gaal, son of Ebed, came over to
Shechem with his kinsmen. The citizens of Shechem put their trust in him, **27** and went out
into the fields, harvested their grapes and trod
them out. Then they held a festival and went to
the temple of their god, where they ate and
drank and cursed Abimelech. **28** Gaal, son of
Ebed, said, "Who is Abimelech? And why
should we of Shechem serve him? Were not the
son of Jerubbaal and his lieutenant Zebul once
subject to the men of Hamor, father of Shechem?[m] Why should we serve him? **29** Would
that this people were entrusted to my command!
I would depose Abimelech. I would say to
Abimelech, 'Get a larger army and come
out!' "

**30** At the news of what Gaal, son of Ebed,
had said, Zebul, the ruler of the city, was angry
**31** and sent messengers to Abimelech in Arumah with the information: "Gaal, son of Ebed,
and his kinsmen have come to Shechem and are
stirring up the city against you. **32** Now rouse
yourself; set an ambush tonight in the fields,
you and the men who are with you. **33** Promptly at sunrise tomorrow morning, make a raid on
the city. When he and his followers come out
against you, deal with him as best you can."

**34** During the night Abimelech advanced
with all his soldiers and set up an ambush for
Shechem in four companies. **35** Gaal, son of
Ebed, went out and stood at the entrance of the
city gate. When Abimelech and his soldiers rose
from their place of ambush, **36** Gaal saw them
and said to Zebul, "There are men coming
down from the hilltops!" But Zebul answered
him, "You see the shadow of the hills as men."
**37** But Gaal went on to say, "Men are coming
down from the region of Tabbur-Haares, and
one company is coming by way of Elon-Meone-
nim." **38** Zebul said to him, "Where now is
the boast you uttered, 'Who is Abimelech that
we should serve him?' Are these not the men for
whom you expressed contempt? Go out now
and fight with them." **39** So Gaal went out at
the head of the citizens of Shechem and fought
against Abimelech. **40** But Abimelech routed
him, and he fled before him; and many fell slain
right up to the entrance of the gate. **41** Abimelech returned to Arumah, but Zebul drove Gaal
and his kinsmen from Shechem, which they had
occupied.

**42** The next day, when the people were taking the field, it was reported to Abimelech,
**43** who divided the men he had into three companies, and set up an ambush in the fields. He
watched till he saw the people leave the city,
and then rose against them for the attack.
**44** Abimelech and the company with him
dashed in and stood by the entrance of the city
gate, while the other two companies rushed
upon all who were in the field and attacked
them. **45** That entire day Abimelech fought

l Jgs 8, 31. m Gn 34, 2. 6.

*

9, 13: Cheers gods: wine was used in the libations both of the Temple of Jerusalem and of pagan temples.

9, 16: Just as the noble trees refused the honor of royalty and were made subject to a mean plant, so did Abimelech of less noble birth than the seventy sons of Gideon now tyrannize over the people.

9, 45: Sowing the site with salt: a severe measure, which was a symbol of desolation, and even more, since it actually rendered the ground barren and useless.

against the city, and captured it. He then killed
its inhabitants and demolished the city, sowing
the site with salt.*
46 When they heard of this, all the citizens
of Migdal-shechem went into the crypt of the
temple of El-berith. 47 It was reported to
Abimelech that all the citizens of Migdal-shechem were gathered together. 48 So he went up
Mount Zalmon with all his soldiers, took his ax
in his hand, and cut down some brushwood.
This he lifted to his shoulder, then said to the
men with him, "Hurry! Do just as you have
seen me do." 49 So all the men likewise cut
down brushwood, and following Abimelech,
placed it against the crypt. Then they set the
crypt on fire over their heads, so that every one
of the citizens of Migdal-shechem, about a
thousand men and women, perished.
50 Abimelech proceeded to Thebez, which
he invested and captured. 51 Now there was a
strong tower in the middle of the city, and all the
men and women, in a word all the citizens of the
city, fled there, shutting themselves in and going up to the roof of the tower. 52 Abimelech
came up to the tower and fought against it,
advancing to the very entrance of the tower to
set it on fire. 53 But a certain woman cast the
upper part of a millstone down on Abimelech's
head, and it fractured his skull.[n] 54 He immediately called his armor-bearer and said to him,
"Draw your sword and dispatch me, lest they
say of me that a woman killed me."[o] So his
attendant ran him through and he died.
55 When the Israelites saw that Abimelech was
dead, they all left for their homes.
56 Thus did God requite the evil Abimelech
had done to his father in killing his seventy
brothers. 57 God also brought all their wickedness home to the Shechemites, for the curse of
Jotham, son of Jerubbaal, overtook them.

## CHAPTER 10

**Tola.** 1 After Abimelech there rose to save
Israel the Issacharite Tola, son of Puah, son of
Dodo, a resident of Shamir in the mountain
region of Ephraim. 2 When he had judged Isra-
el twenty-three years, he died and was buried in
Shamir.

**Jair.** 3 Jair the Gileadite came after him and
judged Israel twenty-two years. 4 He had thirty
sons who rode on thirty saddle-asses* and possessed thirty cities in the land of Gilead; these
are called Havvoth-jair to the present day.[p]
5 Jair died and was buried in Kamon.

**Oppression by the Ammonites.** 6 The
Israelites again offended the LORD, serving the
Baals and Ashtaroths, the gods of Aram, the
gods of Sidon, the gods of Moab, the gods of
the Ammonites, and the gods of the Philistines.
Since they had abandoned the LORD and would
not serve him, 7 the LORD became angry with
Israel and allowed them to fall into the power of
[the Philistines and] the Ammonites. 8 For
eighteen years they afflicted and oppressed the
Israelites in Bashan, and all the Israelites in the
Amorite land beyond the Jordan in Gilead.
9 The Ammonites also crossed the Jordan to
fight against Judah, Benjamin, and the house of
Ephraim, so that Israel was in great distress.
10 Then the Israelites cried out to the LORD,
"We have sinned against you; we have forsaken
our God and have served the Baals." 11 [q]The
LORD answered the Israelites: "Did not the
Egyptians, the Amorites,[r] the Ammonites, the
Philistines, 12 the Sidonians, the Amalekites,
and the Midianites oppress you?[s] Yet when you
cried out to me, and I saved you from their
grasp, 13 you still forsook me and worshiped
other gods. Therefore I will save you no more.
14 Go and cry out to the gods you have chosen;
let them save you now that you are in distress."
15 But the Israelites said to the LORD, "We
have sinned. Do to us whatever you please.
Only save us this day." 16 And they cast out
the foreign gods from their midst and served the
LORD, so that he grieved over the misery of
Israel.
17 The Ammonites had gathered for war and
encamped in Gilead, while the Israelites assembled and encamped in Mizpah.[t] 18 And among
the people the princes of Gilead said to one
another, "The one who begins the war against
the Ammonites shall be leader of all the inhabitants of Gilead."[u]

## CHAPTER 11

**Jephthah.** 1 There was a chieftain, the Gileadite Jephthah, born to Gilead of a harlot.
2 Gilead's wife had also borne him sons, and
on growing up the sons of the wife had driven
Jephthah away, saying to him, "You shall inherit nothing in our family, for you are the son
of another woman." 3 So Jephthah had fled
from his brothers and had taken up residence in
the land of Tob. A rabble had joined company
with him, and went out with him on raids.
4 Some time later, the Ammonites warred on
Israel. 5 When this occurred the elders of Gilead went to bring Jephthah from the land of Tob.
6 "Come," they said to Jephthah, "be our

n 2 Sm 11, 21.
o 1 Sm 31, 4; 1 Chr 10, 4.
p Dt 3, 14.
q 11-14: Jgs 2, 1ff; 6, 8ff.
r Nm 21, 21-32.
s Jgs 6, 3.
t Jgs 11, 29.
u Jgs 11, 5-11.

*

10, 4: Saddle-asses: a sign of rank and wealth; cf Jgs 5, 10; 12, 14.

commander that we may be able to fight the Ammonites.'' **7** ''Are you not the ones who hated me and drove me from my father's house?'' Jephthah replied to the elders of Gilead. ''Why do you come to me now, when you are in distress?'' **8** The elders of Gilead said to Jephthah, ''In any case, we have now come back to you; if you go with us to fight against the Ammonites, you shall be the leader of all of us who dwell in Gilead.'' **9** Jephthah answered the elders of Gilead, ''If you bring me back to fight against the Ammonites and the LORD delivers them up to me, I shall be your leader.'' **10** The elders of Gilead said to Jephthah, ''The LORD is witness between us that we will do as you say.''

**11** So Jephthah went with the elders of Gilead, and the people made him their leader and commander.[v] In Mizpah, Jephthah settled all his affairs before the LORD. **12** Then he sent messengers to the king of the Ammonites to say, ''What have you against me that you come to fight with me in my land?'' **13** He answered the messengers of Jephthah, ''Israel took away my land from the Arnon to the Jabbok and the Jordan when they came up from Egypt.[w] Now restore the same peaceably.''

**14** Again Jephthah sent messengers to the king of the Ammonites, **15** saying to him, ''This is what Jephthah says: Israel did not take the land of Moab or the land of the Ammonites.[x] **16** For when they came up from Egypt, Israel went through the desert to the Red Sea and came to Kadesh. **17** Israel then sent messengers to the king of Edom saying, 'Let me pass through your land.' But the king of Edom did not give consent. They also sent to the king of Moab, but he too was unwilling. So Israel remained in Kadesh.[y] **18** Then they went through the desert, and by-passing the land of Edom and the land of Moab, went east of the land of Moab and encamped across the Arnon.[z] Thus they did not go through the territory of Moab, for the Arnon is the boundary of Moab. **19** [a]Then Israel sent messengers to Sihon, king of the Amorites, king of Heshbon. Israel said to him, 'Let me pass through your land to my own place.' **20** But Sihon refused to let Israel pass through his territory. On the contrary, he gathered all his soldiers, who encamped at Jahaz and fought Israel. **21** But the LORD, the God of Israel, delivered Sihon and all his men into the power of Israel, who defeated them and occupied all the land of the Amorites dwelling in that region, **22** the whole territory from the Arnon to the Jabbok, from the desert to the Jordan. **23** If now the LORD, the God of Israel, has cleared the Amorites out of the way of his people, are you to dislodge Israel? **24** Should you not possess that which your god Chemosh* gave you to possess, and should we not possess all that the LORD, our God, has cleared out for us?[b] **25** Again, are you any better than Balak, son of Zippor, king of Moab? Did he ever quarrel with Israel, or did he war against them[c] **26** when Israel occupied Heshbon and its villages, Aroer and its villages, and all the cities on the banks of the Arnon?[d] Three hundred years have passed; why did you not recover them during that time? **27** I have not sinned against you, but you wrong me by warring against me. Let the LORD, who is judge, decide this day between the Israelites and the Ammonites!'' **28** But the king of the Ammonites paid no heed to the message Jephthah sent him.

**Jephthah's Vow.** **29** The spirit of the LORD came upon Jephthah. He passed through Gilead and Manasseh, and through Mizpah-Gilead as well, and from there he went on to the Ammonites. **30** *Jephthah made a vow to the LORD. ''If you deliver the Ammonites into my power,'' he said, **31** ''whoever comes out of the doors of my house to meet me when I return in triumph from the Ammonites shall belong to the LORD. I shall offer him up as a holocaust.''

**32** Jephthah then went on to the Ammonites to fight against them, and the LORD delivered them into his power, **33** so that he inflicted a severe defeat on them, from Aroer to the approach of Minnith (twenty cities in all) and as far as Abel-keramim. Thus were the Ammonites brought into subjection by the Israelites. **34** When Jephthah returned to his house in Mizpah, it was his daughter who came forth, playing the tambourines and dancing. She was an only child: he had neither son nor daughter besides her. **35** When he saw her, he rent his garments and said, ''Alas, daughter, you have struck me down and brought calamity upon me. For I have made a vow to the LORD and I cannot retract.''[e] **36** ''Father,'' she replied, ''you have made a vow to the LORD. Do with me as you have vowed, because the LORD has wrought

v Jgs 10, 18.
w Nm 21, 13. 24ff.
x Dt 2, 9. 19.
y Nm 20, 1. 14. 18-21; Dt 1, 46.
z Nm 21, 4. 11. 13; 22, 36; Dt 2, 8.
a 19-22: Nm 21, 21-26; Dt 2, 26-36.
b Nm 21, 29; 1 Kgs 11, 7.
c Nm 22, 2; Jos 24, 9; Mi 6, 5.
d Nm 21, 25; Dt 2, 36.
e Nm 30, 3.

*

11, 24: Chemosh: the chief god of the Moabites—not of the Ammonites, whose leading deity was called Molech or Milcom; cf Nm 21, 29; 1 Kgs 11, 7; 2 Kgs 23, 13. The error is probably due to an ancient copyist. Jephthah argues from the viewpoint of his adversaries, the Ammonites, that they were entitled to all the land they had conquered with the aid of their god. It does not necessarily follow that Jephthah himself believed in the actual existence of this pagan god.

11, 30–40: The text clearly implies that Jephthah vowed a human sacrifice, according to the custom of his pagan neighbors; cf 2 Kgs 3, 27. The inspired author merely records the fact; he does not approve of the action.

vengeance for you on your enemies the Ammonites.'' **37** Then she said to her father, ''Let
me have this favor. Spare me for two months,
that I may go off down the mountains to
mourn my virginity* with my companions.''
**38** ''Go,'' he replied, and sent her away for two
months. So she departed with her companions
and mourned her virginity on the mountains.
**39** At the end of the two months she returned
to her father, who did to her as he had vowed.
She had not been intimate with man. It then
became a custom in Israel **40** for Israelite wom-
en to go yearly to mourn the daughter of Jephthah the Gileadite for four days of the year.

## CHAPTER 12

**The Shibboleth Incident.** **1** The men of
Ephraim gathered together and crossed over to
Zaphon. They said to Jephthah, ''Why do you
go on to fight with the Ammonites without calling us to go with you? We will burn your house
over you.''[f] **2** Jephthah answered them, ''My
soldiers and I were engaged in a critical contest
with the Ammonites. I summoned you, but you
did not rescue me from their power. **3** When I
saw that you would not effect a rescue, I took
my life in my own hand and went on to the
Ammonites, and the LORD delivered them into
my power. Why, then, do you come up against
me this day to fight with me?''

**4** Then Jephthah called together all the men
of Gilead and fought against Ephraim, whom
they defeated; for the Ephraimites had said,
''You of Gilead are Ephraimite fugitives in territory belonging to Ephraim and Manasseh.''
**5** The Gileadites took the fords of the Jordan
toward Ephraim. When any of the fleeing
Ephraimites said, ''Let me pass,'' the men of
Gilead would say to him, ''Are you an Ephraimite?'' If he answered, ''No!'' **6** they would ask
him to say ''Shibboleth.''* If he said ''Sibbo-
leth,'' not being able to give the proper pronunciation, they would seize him and kill him at the
fords of the Jordan. Thus forty-two thousand
Ephraimites fell at that time.

**7** After having judged Israel for six years,
Jephthah the Gileadite died and was buried in
his city in Gilead.

**Ibzan.** **8** After him Ibzan of Bethlehem
judged Israel. **9** He had thirty sons. He also had
thirty daughters married outside the family, and
he brought in as wives for his sons thirty young
women from outside the family. After having
judged Israel for seven years, **10** Ibzan died and
was buried in Bethlehem.

**Elon.** **11** After him the Zebulunite Elon
judged Israel. When he had judged Israel for ten
years, **12** the Zebulunite Elon died and was
buried in Elon in the land of Zebulun.

**Abdon.** **13** After him the Pirathonite Abdon, son of Hillel, judged Israel. **14** He had
forty sons and thirty grandsons who rode on
seventy saddle-asses. After having judged Israel
for eight years, **15** the Pirathonite Abdon, son
of Hillel, died and was buried in Pirathon in the
land of Ephraim on the mountain of the Amalekites.

## CHAPTER 13

**The Birth of Samson.** **1** The Israelites
again offended the LORD, who therefore delivered them into the power of the Philistines for
forty years.[g]

**2** There was a certain man from Zorah, of the
clan of the Danites, whose name was Manoah.
His wife was barren and had borne no children.
**3** An angel of the LORD appeared to the woman
and said to her, ''Though you are barren and
have had no children, yet you will conceive and
bear a son.[h] **4** Now, then, be careful to take no
wine or strong drink and to eat nothing unclean.
**5** As for the son you will conceive and bear, no
razor shall touch his head,[i] for this boy is to be
consecrated* to God from the womb. It is he
who will begin the deliverance of Israel from the
power of the Philistines.''

**6** The woman went and told her husband, ''A
man of God came to me; he had the appearance
of an angel of God, terrible indeed. I did not ask
him where he came from, nor did he tell me his
name. **7** But he said to me, 'You will be with
child and will bear a son. So take neither wine
nor strong drink, and eat nothing unclean. For
the boy shall be consecrated to God from the
womb, until the day of his death.' '' **8** Manoah
then prayed to the LORD. ''O LORD, I beseech
you,'' he said, ''may the man of God whom you
sent, return to us to teach us what to do for the
boy who will be born.''

**9** God heard the prayer of Manoah, and the

---

f Jgs 8, 1.
g Jgs 10, 6.
h 3f: 1 Sm 1, 20; Lk 1, 31.
i Nm 6, 5.

---

11, 37: Mourn my virginity: to bear children was woman's greatest pride; to be childless was regarded as a great misfortune. Hence Jephthah's daughter asks permission to mourn the fact that she will be put to death before she can bear children.

12, 6: Shibboleth: "an ear of grain." But this Hebrew word can also mean "flood water" as in Ps 69, 3. 16. Apparently the Gileadites engaged the Ephraimites in conversation about the "flood water" of the Jordan. Differences in enunciating the initial sibilant of the Hebrew word betrayed different tribal affinities.

13, 5: Consecrated: In Hebrew, nazir. Samson therefore was for life to be under the nazirite vow, which obliged him to abstain from drinking wine or having his hair cut; cf Nm 6, 2–8.

angel of God came again to the woman as she
was sitting in the field. Since her husband Manoah was not with her, **10** the woman ran in
haste and told her husband. "The man who
came to me the other day has appeared to me,"
she said to him; **11** so Manoah got up and followed his wife. When he reached the man, he
said to him, "Are you the one who spoke to my
wife?" "Yes," he answered. **12** Then Manoah
asked, "Now, when that which you say comes
true, what are we expected to do for the boy?"
**13** The angel of the LORD answered Manoah,
"Your wife is to abstain from all the things of
which I spoke to her. **14** She must not eat anything that comes from the vine, nor take wine
or strong drink, nor eat anything unclean. Let
her observe all that I have commanded her."
**15** Then Manoah said to the angel of the LORD,
"Can we persuade you to stay, while we prepare a kid for you?" **16** But the angel of the
LORD answered Manoah, "Although you press
me, I will not partake of your food. But if you
will, you may offer a holocaust to the LORD."
Not knowing that it was the angel of the LORD,
**17** Manoah said to him, "What is your name,
that we may honor you when your words come
true?" **18** The angel of the LORD answered
him,[j] "Why do you ask my name, which is
mysterious?"* **19** [k]Then Manoah took the kid
with a cereal offering and offered it on the rock
to the LORD, whose works are mysteries. While
Manoah and his wife were looking on, **20** as the
flame rose to the sky from the altar, the angel
of the LORD ascended in the flame of the altar.
When Manoah and his wife saw this, they fell
prostrate to the ground; **21** but the angel of the
LORD was seen no more by Manoah and his
wife. Then Manoah, realizing that it was the
angel of the LORD, **22** said to his wife, "We
will certainly die, for we have seen God."[l]
**23** But his wife pointed out to him, "If the
LORD had meant to kill us, he would not have
accepted a holocaust and cereal offering from
our hands! Nor would he have let us see all this
just now, or hear what we have heard."

**24** The woman bore a son and named him
Samson.[m] The boy grew up and the LORD
blessed him; **25** the spirit of the LORD first
stirred him in Mahaneh-dan, which is between
Zorah and Eshtaol.

## CHAPTER 14

**Marriage of Samson.** **1** Samson went
down to Timnah and saw there one of the Philistine women.* **2** On his return he told his father
and mother, "There is a Philistine woman I saw
in Timnah whom I wish you to get as a wife for
me." **3** His father and mother said to him,
"Can you find no wife among your kinsfolk or
among all our people, that you must go and take
a wife from the uncircumcised Philistines?" But
Samson answered his father, "Get her for me,
for she pleases me." **4** [n]Now his father and
mother did not know that this had been brought
about by the LORD, who was providing an opportunity against the Philistines; for at that time
they had dominion over Israel.

**5** *So Samson went down to Timnah with his
father and mother. When they had come to the
vineyards of Timnah, a young lion came roaring
to meet him. **6** But the spirit of the LORD came
upon Samson, and although he had no weapons,
he tore the lion in pieces as one tears a kid.
**7** However, on the journey to speak for the
woman, he did not mention to his father or
mother what he had done. **8** Later, when he
returned to marry the woman who pleased him,
he stepped aside to look at the remains of the
lion and found a swarm of bees and honey in the
lion's carcass. **9** So he scooped the honey out
into his palms and ate it as he went along. When
he came to his father and mother, he gave them
some to eat, without telling them that he had
scooped the honey from the lion's carcass.

**10** His father also went down to the woman,
and Samson gave a banquet there, since it was
customary for the young men to do this.
**11** When they met him, they brought thirty men
to be his companions.* **12** Samson said to
them, "Let me propose a riddle to you. If within
the seven days of the feast you solve it for me
successfully, I will give you thirty linen tunics
and thirty sets of garments. **13** But if you cannot answer it for me, you must give me thirty
tunics and thirty sets of garments." "Propose
your riddle," they responded; "we will listen to
it." **14** So he said to them,

"Out of the eater came forth food,
and out of the strong came forth
sweetness."

After three days' failure to answer the riddle,
**15** they said on the fourth day to Samson's

j Gn 32, 29.
k 19f: Jgs 6, 19ff.
l 21f: Jgs 6, 22f.
m Heb 11, 32.
n Jgs 15, 11.

*

13, 18: Mysterious: incomprehensible, above human understanding. Hence, the angel speaks in the name of the Lord himself, to whom Manoah at once offers a sacrifice.

14, 1–3: Marriages were arranged by the parents of the bridegroom as well as of the bride; cf Gn 24, 2–8; 34, 3–6. The Mosaic law specified only seven pagan nations, not including the Philistines, in the prohibition against mixed marriages; cf Dt 7, 1–4. But national and religious sentiment was against any marriage with a non-Israelite; cf Gn 28, 1f; 1 Kgs 11, 1–10.

14, 5ff: Although Samson was accompanied by his parents on the journey to Timnah, v 7 implies that he was not near them when he tore the lion in pieces.

14, 11: Companions: known at a later period as "the friends of the bridegroom" (1 Mc 9, 39; Mk 2, 19), the best man and his fellows. Here they are Philistines (v 16), appointed by the family of the bride, who would also have several bridesmaids; cf Mt 25, 1–13.

wife, "Coax your husband to answer the riddle
for us, or we will burn you and your family. Did
you invite us here to reduce us to poverty?"
**16** At Samson's side, his wife wept and said,
"You must hate me; you do not love me, for
you have proposed a riddle to my countrymen,
but have not told me the answer." He said to
her, "If I have not told it even to my father or
my mother, must I tell it to you?" **17** But she
wept beside him during the seven days the feast
lasted. On the seventh day, since she importuned him, he told her the answer, and she
explained the riddle to her countrymen.
**18** On the seventh day, before the sun set,
the men of the city said to him,

> "What is sweeter than honey,
> and what is stronger than a lion?"

He replied to them,

> "If you had not plowed with my heifer,
> you would not have solved my riddle."

**19** The spirit of the LORD came upon him,
and he went down to Ashkelon, where he killed
thirty of their men and despoiled them; he gave
their garments to those who had answered the
riddle. Then he went off to his own family in
anger, **20** and Samson's wife was married to
the one who had been best man at his wedding.[o]

## CHAPTER 15

**Samson Defeats the Philistines.** **1** After some time, in the season of the wheat harvest, Samson visited his wife, bringing a kid.
But when he said, "Let me be with my wife in
private," her father would not let him enter,
**2** saying, "I thought it certain you wished to
repudiate her; so I gave her to your best man.
Her younger sister is more beautiful than she;
you may have her instead." **3** Samson said to
them, "This time the Philistines cannot blame
me if I harm them." **4** So Samson left and
caught three hundred foxes. Turning them tail to
tail, he tied between each pair of tails one of the
torches he had at hand. **5** He then kindled the
torches and set the foxes loose in the standing
grain of the Philistines, thus burning both the
shocks and the standing grain, and the vineyards
and olive orchards as well.
**6** [p]When the Philistines asked who had done
this, they were told, "Samson, the son-in-law
of the Timnite, because his wife was taken and
given to his best man." So the Philistines went
up and destroyed her and her family by fire.
**7** Samson said to them, "If this is how you act,
I will not stop until I have taken revenge on
you." **8** And with repeated blows, he inflicted
a great slaughter on them. Then he went down
and remained in a cavern of the cliff of Etam.
**9** The Philistines went up and, from a camp
in Judah, deployed against Lehi. **10** When the
men of Judah asked, "Why have you come up
against us?" they answered, "To take Samson
prisoner; to do to him as he has done to us."
**11** Three thousand men of Judah went down to
the cavern in the cliff of Etam and said to Samson, "Do you not know that the Philistines are
our rulers? Why, then, have you done this to
us?" He answered them, "As they have done
to me, so have I done to them." **12** They said
to him, "We have come to take you prisoner,
to deliver you over to the Philistines." Samson
said to them, "Swear to me that you will not kill
me yourselves." **13** "No," they replied, "we
will certainly not kill you but will only bind you
and deliver you over to them."[q] So they bound
him with two new ropes and brought him up
from the cliff. **14** When he reached Lehi, and
the Philistines came shouting to meet him, the
spirit of the LORD came upon him: the ropes
around his arms became as flax that is consumed
by fire and his bonds melted away from his
hands. **15** Near him was the fresh jawbone of
an ass; he reached out, grasped it, and with it
killed a thousand men. **16** Then Samson said,

> "With the jawbone of an ass
> I have piled them in a heap;
> With the jawbone of an ass
> I have slain a thousand men."

**17** As he finished speaking he threw the jawbone from him; and so that place was named
Ramath-lehi.* **18** Being very thirsty, he cried
to the LORD and said, "You have granted this
great victory by the hand of your servant. Must
I now die of thirst or fall into the hands of the
uncircumcised?" **19** Then God split the cavity
in Lehi, and water issued from it, which Samson
drank till his spirit returned and he revived.
Hence that spring in Lehi is called En-hakkore*
to this day.
**20** Samson judged Israel for twenty years in
the days of the Philistines.[r]

## CHAPTER 16

**1** Once Samson went to Gaza, where he saw
a harlot and visited her. **2** Informed that Samson had come there, the men of Gaza surrounded him with an ambush at the city gate all night
long. And all the night they waited, saying,
"Tomorrow morning we will kill him."
**3** Samson rested there until midnight. Then he
rose, seized the doors of the city gate and the
two gateposts, and tore them loose, bar and all.
He hoisted them on his shoulders and carried

o Jgs 15, 2. 6.
p Jgs 14, 20.
q Jgs 16, 11f.
r Jgs 16, 31.

*

15, 17: Ramath-lehi: "heights of the jawbone."
15, 19: En-hakkore: "the spring of him who cries out," an allusion to Samson's cry in v 18.

them to the top of the ridge opposite Hebron.

**Samson and Delilah.** 4 After that he fell
in love with a woman in the Wadi Sorek whose
name was Delilah. 5 The lords of the Philistines
came to her and said, "Beguile him and find out
the secret of his great strength, and how we may
overcome and bind him so as to keep him helpless. We will each give you eleven hundred
shekels of silver."

6 So Delilah said to Samson, "Tell me the
secret of your great strength and how you may
be bound so as to be kept helpless." 7 "If they
bind me with seven fresh bowstrings which
have not dried," Samson answered her, "I shall
be as weak as any other man." 8 So the lords
of the Philistines brought her seven fresh bowstrings which had not dried, and she bound him
with them. 9 She had men lying in wait in the
chamber and so she said to him, "The Philistines are upon you, Samson!" But he snapped
the strings as a thread of tow is severed by a
whiff of flame;[s] and the secret of his strength
remained unknown.

10 Delilah said to Samson, "You have
mocked me and told me lies. Now tell me how
you may be bound." 11 "If they bind me tight
with new ropes, with which no work has been
done," he answered her, "I shall be as weak as
any other man."[t] 12 So Delilah took new ropes
and bound him with them. Then she said to him,
"The Philistines are upon you, Samson!" For
there were men lying in wait in the chamber.
But he snapped them off his arms like thread.

13 Delilah said to Samson again, "Up to
now you have mocked me and told me lies. Tell
me how you may be bound." He said to her, "If
you weave my seven locks of hair into the web
and fasten them with the pin, I shall be as weak
as any other man." 14 So while he slept, Delilah wove his seven locks of hair into the web,
and fastened them in with the pin. Then she
said, "The Philistines are upon you, Samson!"
Awakening from his sleep, he pulled out both
the weaver's pin and the web.

15 Then she said to him, "How can you say
that you love me when you do not confide in
me? Three times already you have mocked me,
and not told me the secret of your great
strength!" 16 She importuned him continually
and vexed him with her complaints till he was
deathly weary of them. 17 So he took her completely into his confidence and told her, "No
razor has touched my head,[u] for I have been
consecrated to God from my mother's womb. If
I am shaved, my strength will leave me, and I
shall be as weak as any other man!" 18 When
Delilah saw that he had taken her completely
into his confidence, she summoned the lords of
the Philistines, saying, "Come up this time, for
he has opened his heart to me." So the lords of
the Philistines came and brought up the money
with them. 19 She had him sleep on her lap,
and called for a man who shaved off his seven
locks of hair. Then she began to mistreat him,
for his strength had left him. 20 When she said,
"The Philistines are upon you, Samson!", and
he woke from his sleep, he thought he could
make good his escape as he had done time and
again, for he did not realize that the LORD had
left him. 21 But the Philistines seized him and
gouged out his eyes. Then they brought him
down to Gaza and bound him with bronze fetters, and he was put to grinding in the prison.
22 But the hair of his head began to grow as
soon as it was shaved off.

**The Death of Samson.** 23 [v]The lords of
the Philistines assembled to offer a great sacrifice to their god Dagon* and to make merry.
They said,

"Our god has delivered into our power
Samson our enemy."

25 When their spirits were high, they said,
"Call Samson that he may amuse us." So they
called Samson from the prison, and he played
the buffoon before them. 24 When the people
saw him, they praised their god. For they said,

"Our god has delivered into our power
our enemy, the ravager of our land,
the one who has multiplied our slain."

Then they stationed him between the columns. 26 Samson said to the attendant who was
holding his hand, "Put me where I may touch
the columns that support the temple and may
rest against them." 27 The temple was full of
men and women: all the lords of the Philistines
were there, and from the roof about three thousand men and women looked on as Samson
provided amusement. 28 Samson cried out to
the LORD and said, "O Lord GOD, remember
me! Strengthen me, O God, this last time that
for my two eyes I may avenge myself once and
for all on the Philistines." 29 Samson grasped
the two middle columns on which the temple
rested and braced himself against them, one at
his right hand, the other at his left. 30 And
Samson said, "Let me die with the Philistines!"
He pushed hard, and the temple fell upon the
lords and all the people who were in it. Those
he killed at his death were more than those he
had killed during his lifetime.

31 All his family and kinsmen went down
and bore him up for burial in the grave of his

s Jgs 15, 14.
t Jgs 15, 13.
u Jgs 13, 5.
v 1 Sm 5, 2-5.
w Jgs 15, 20.

* 16, 23: Dagon was originally a Mesopotamian deity, whom the Philistines came to worship as their own god of grain.

father Manoah between Zorah and Eshtaol. He had judged Israel for twenty years.[w]

## III: The Tribes of Dan and Benjamin in the Days of the Judges

### CHAPTER 17

**Micah and the Levite.** **1** There was a man in the mountain region of Ephraim whose name was Micah. **2** He said to his mother, "The eleven hundred shekels of silver over which you pronounced a curse in my hearing when they were taken from you, are in my possession. It was I who took them; so now I will restore them to you." **3** When he restored the eleven hundred shekels of silver to his mother, she took two hundred of them and gave them to the silversmith, who made of them a carved idol* overlaid with silver.[x] **4** Then his mother said, "May the LORD bless my son! I have consecrated the silver to the LORD as my gift in favor of my son, by making a carved idol overlaid with silver." It remained in the house of Micah. **5** Thus the layman Micah had a sanctuary. He also made an ephod and household idols,[y] and consecrated one of his sons, who became his priest. **6** In those days there was no king in Israel; everyone did what he thought best.[z]

**7** There was a young Levite who had resided within the tribe of Judah at Bethlehem of Judah. **8** From that city he set out to find another place of residence. On his journey he came to the house of Micah in the mountain region of Ephraim. **9** Micah said to him, "Where do you come from?" He answered him, "I am a Levite from Bethlehem in Judah, and am on my way to find some other place of residence." **10** "Stay with me," Micah said to him. "Be father and priest to me,[a] and I will give you ten silver shekels a year, a set of garments, and your food." **11** So the young Levite decided to stay with the man, to whom he became as one of his own sons. **12** *Micah consecrated the young Levite, who became his priest, remaining in his house. **13** Therefore Micah said, "Now I know that the LORD will prosper me, since the Levite has become my priest."

### CHAPTER 18

**Migration of the Danites.** **1** At that time there was no king in Israel.[b] Moreover the tribe of Danites were in search of a district to dwell in, for up to that time they had received no heritage among the tribes of Israel.*

**2** So the Danites sent from their clan a detail of five valiant men of Zorah and Eshtaol, to reconnoiter the land and scout it. With their instructions to go and scout the land, they traveled as far as the house of Micah in the mountain region of Ephraim, where they passed the night. **3** Near the house of Micah, they recognized the voice* of the young Levite[c] and turned in that direction. "Who brought you here and what are you doing here?" they asked him. "What is your interest here?" **4** "This is how Micah treats me," he replied to them. "He pays me a salary and I am his priest."[d] **5** They said to him, "Consult God, that we may know whether the undertaking we are engaged in will succeed." **6** The priest said to them, "Go and prosper: the LORD is favorable to the undertaking you are engaged in."

**7** So the five men went on and came to Laish. They saw that the people dwelling there lived securely after the manner of the Sidonians, quiet and trusting, with no lack of any natural resources. They were distant from the Sidonians and had no contact with other people. **8** When the five returned to their kinsmen in Zorah and Eshtaol and were asked for a report, **9** they replied, "Come, let us attack them, for we have seen the land and it is very good. Are you going to hesitate? Do not be slothful about beginning your expedition to possess the land. **10** Those against whom you go are a trusting people, and the land is ample. God has indeed given it into your power: a place where no natural resource is lacking."

**11** So six hundred men of the clan of the Danites, fully armed with weapons of war, set out from where they were in Zorah and Eshtaol, **12** and camped in Judah, up near Kiriath-jearim; hence to this day the place, which lies west of Kiriath-jearim, is called Mahaneh-dan.[e]

**13** From there they went on to the mountain region of Ephraim and came to the house of Micah. **14** The five men who had gone to reconnoiter the land of Laish said to their kinsmen, "Do you know that in these houses there are an ephod, household idols, and a carved idol overlaid with silver?[f] Now decide what you must do!" **15** So turning in that direction, they went to the house of the young Levite at the home of Micah and greeted him. **16** The six

x Ex 20, 4; Lv 19, 4.
y Jgs 18, 14. 17.
z Jgs 18, 1; 21, 25.
a Jgs 18, 19.
b Jos 19, 40-48.
c Jgs 17, 7.
d Jgs 17, 10.
e Jgs 13, 25.
f Jgs 17, 4f.

*

17, 3: Idol: an image, not of a pagan god, but of the Lord. The Mosaic law forbade the making of an image even of the true God.

17, 12f: According to Nm 18, 1–7 only those Levites who were descended from Aaron could be consecrated as priests.

18, 1: The tribe of Dan had been assigned a territory with definite limits in central Palestine. However they were unable to gain possession of the better portion of their land (Jgs 1, 34). So they now seek territory elsewhere in Palestine.

18, 3: Recognized the voice: perhaps they noticed the peculiar pronunciation of his south Hebrew dialect.

hundred men girt with weapons of war, who
were Danites, stood by the entrance of the gate,
and the priest stood there also. **17** Meanwhile
the five men who had gone to reconnoiter the
land went up and entered the house of Micah.
**18** When they had gone in and taken the ephod,
the household idols, and the carved idol overlaid with silver, the priest said to them, "What
are you doing?" **19** They said to him, "Be still:
put your hand over your mouth. Come with us
and be our father and priest.[g] Is it better for you
to be priest for the family of one man or to be
priest for a tribe and a clan in Israel?" **20** The
priest, agreeing, took the ephod, household
idols, and carved idol and went off in the midst
of the band. **21** As they turned to depart, they
placed their little ones, their livestock, and their
goods at the head of the column.

**22** The Danites had already gone some distance, when those in the houses near that of
Micah took up arms and overtook them.
**23** They called to the Danites, who turned
about and said to Micah, "What do you want,
that you have taken up arms?" **24** "You have
taken my god, which I made, and have gone off
with my priest as well," he answered. "What
is left for me? How, then, can you ask me what
I want?" **25** The Danites said to him, "Let us
hear no further sound from you, lest fierce men
fall upon you and you and your family lose your
lives." **26** The Danites then went on their way,
and Micah, seeing that they were stronger than
he, returned home.

**27** Having taken what Micah had made, and
the priest he had had, they attacked Laish, a
quiet and trusting people; they put them to the
sword and destroyed their city by fire. **28** No
one came to their aid, since the city was far from
Sidon and they had no contact with other people. The Danites then rebuilt the city, which was
in the valley that belongs to Beth-rehob, and
lived there. **29** They named it Dan after their
ancestor Dan, son of Israel. However, the name
of the city was formerly Laish. **30** The Danites
set up the carved idol for themselves, and Jonathan, son of Gershom, son of Moses, and his
descendants were priests for the tribe of the
Danites until the time of the captivity of the
land.* **31** They maintained the carved idol Micah had made as long as the house of God was
in Shiloh.

## CHAPTER 19

**The Levite from Ephraim.** **1** At that time,
when there was no king in Israel,[h] there was a
Levite residing in remote parts of the mountain
region of Ephraim who had taken for himself a
concubine from Bethlehem of Judah. **2** His
concubine was unfaithful to him and left him for
her father's house in Bethlehem of Judah, where
she stayed for some four months. **3** Her husband then set out with his servant and a pair of
asses, and went after her to forgive her and take
her back. She brought him into her father's
house, and on seeing him, the girl's father joyfully made him welcome. **4** He was detained by
the girl's father, and so he spent three days with
this father-in-law of his, eating and drinking and
passing the night there. **5** *On the fourth day
they rose early in the morning and he prepared
to go. But the girl's father said to his son-in-law,
"Fortify yourself with a little food; you can go
later on." **6** So they stayed and the two men ate
and drank together. Then the girl's father said
to the husband, "Why not decide to spend the
night here and enjoy yourself?" **7** The man still
made a move to go, but when his father-in-law
pressed him he went back and spent the night
there.

**8** On the fifth morning he rose early to depart, but the girl's father said, "Fortify yourself
and tarry until the afternoon." When he and his
father-in-law had eaten, **9** and the husband was
ready to go with his concubine and servant, the
girl's father said to him, "It is already growing
dusk. Stay for the night. See, the day is coming
to an end. Spend the night here and enjoy yourself. Early tomorrow you can start your journey
home." **10** The man, however, refused to stay
another night; he and his concubine set out with
a pair of saddled asses, and traveled till they
came opposite Jebus, which is Jerusalem.
**11** Since they were near Jebus with the day far
gone, the servant said to his master, "Come, let
us turn off to this city of the Jebusites and spend
the night in it." **12** But his master said to him,
"We will not turn off to a city of foreigners,
who are not Israelites, but will go on to Gibeah.[i]
**13** Come," he said to his servant, "let us make
for some other place, either Gibeah or Ramah,
to spend the night."[j] **14** So they continued on
their way till the sun set on them when they were
abreast of Gibeah of Benjamin.

**15** *There they turned off to enter Gibeah for
the night.[k] The man waited in the public square
of the city he had entered, but no one offered
them the shelter of his home for the night. **16** In
the evening, however, an old man came from
his work in the field; he was from the mountain
region of Ephraim, though he lived among the

g Jgs 17, 10.
h Jgs 17, 6.
i Jgs 1, 21.
j Jos 18, 25.
k Jgs 20, 4.

*

18, 30: Until . . . land: about the year 734 B.C., when the Assyrian emperor Tiglath-pileser III subjected northern Palestine.

19, 5–9: Such importuning of guests to prolong their stay at the home of their host is characteristic of Oriental hospitality.

19, 15: Private hospitality was the customary means of providing comfort to travelers where public facilities were so rare.

Benjaminite townspeople of Gibeah. **17** When
he noticed the traveler in the public square of the
city, the old man asked where he was going, and
whence he had come. **18** He said to him, "We
are traveling from Bethlehem of Judah far up
into the mountain region of Ephraim, where I
belong. I have been to Bethlehem of Judah and
am now going back home; but no one has offered us the shelter of his house. **19** We have
straw and fodder for our asses, and bread and
wine for the woman and myself and for our
servant; there is nothing else we need."
**20** "You are welcome," the old man said to
him, "but let me provide for all your needs, and
do not spend the night in the public square."
**21** So he led them to his house and provided
fodder for the asses. Then they washed their
feet, and ate and drank.[l]

**The Outrage at Gibeah.** **22** [m]While they
were enjoying themselves, the men of the city,
who were corrupt,* surrounded the house and
beat on the door. They said to the old man
whose house it was, "Bring out your guest, that
we may abuse him." **23** The owner of the
house went out to them and said, "No, my
brothers; do not be so wicked. Since this man
is my guest, do not commit this crime. **24** Rather let me bring out my maiden daughter or his
concubine. Ravish them, or do whatever you
want with them; but against the man you must
not commit this wanton crime." **25** When the
men would not listen to his host, the husband
seized his concubine and thrust her outside to
them. They had relations with her and abused
her all night until the following dawn, when
they let her go. **26** Then at daybreak the woman
came and collapsed at the entrance of the house
in which her husband was a guest, where she lay
until the morning. **27** When her husband rose
that day and opened the door of the house to
start out again on his journey, there lay the
woman, his concubine, at the entrance of the
house with her hands on the threshold. **28** He
said to her, "Come, let us go"; but there was
no answer. So the man placed her on an ass and
started out again for home.

**29** *On reaching home, he took a knife to the
body of his concubine, cut her into twelve
pieces, and sent them throughout the territory of
Israel. **30** [n]Everyone who saw this said,
"Nothing like this has been done or seen from
the day the Israelites came up from the land of
Egypt to this day. Take note of it, and state what
you propose to do."

## CHAPTER 20

**Assembly of Israelites.** **1** So all the Israelites came out as one man: from Dan to
Beer-she-ba,* and from the land of Gilead, the
community was gathered to the LORD at Mizpah. **2** The leaders of all the people and all the
tribesmen of Israel, four hundred thousand foot
soldiers who were swordsmen, presented themselves in the assembly of the people of God.
**3** Meanwhile, the Benjaminites heard that the
Israelites had gone up to Mizpah. The Israelites
asked to be told how the crime had taken place,
**4** and the Levite, the husband of the murdered
woman, testified: "My concubine and I went
into Gibeah of Benjamin[o] for the night. **5** [p]But
the citizens of Gibeah rose up against me by
night and surrounded the house in which I was.
Me they attempted to kill, and my concubine
they abused so that she died. **6** [q]So I took my
concubine and cut her up and sent her through
every part of the territory of Israel, because of
the monstrous crime they had committed in Israel. **7** *Now that you are all here, O Israelites,
state what you propose to do."[r] **8** All the people rose as one man to say, "None of us is to
leave for his tent or return to his home. **9** Now
as for Gibeah, this is what we will do: We will
proceed against it by lot, **10** taking from all the
tribes of Israel ten men for every hundred, a
hundred for every thousand, a thousand for every ten thousand, and procuring supplies for the
soldiers who will go to deal fully and suitably
with Gibeah of Benjamin for the crime it committed in Israel."

**11** When, therefore, all the men of Israel
without exception were leagued together against
the city, **12** *the tribes of Israel sent men
throughout the tribe of Benjamin to say, "What
is this evil which has occurred among you?
**13** Now give up these corrupt men of Gibeah,
that we may put them to death and thus purge
the evil from Israel." But the Benjaminites refused to accede to the demand of their brothers,
the Israelites. **14** Instead, the Benjaminites assembled from their other cities to Gibeah, to do
battle with the Israelites. **15** The number of the

l Gn 18, 4; 24, 32; 43, 24.
m 22-25: Gn 19, 4-9.
n Hos 9, 9; 10, 9.
o Jgs 19, 14f.
p Jgs 19, 22-27.
q Jgs 19, 29.
r Jgs 19, 30.

*

19, 22: Who were corrupt: literally "sons of Belial," indicating extreme perversion; cf Gn 19, 4–8. This crime and its punishment made the name Gibeah proverbial as a place of shameful wickedness; cf Hos 9, 9; 10, 9.

19, 29: A drastic means for arousing the tribes to avenge the unheard of crime of the Benjaminites.

20, 1: From Dan to Beer-sheba: from north to south. The land of Gilead: all the territory east of the Jordan.

20, 7: The Israelites were asked to decide at once what action to take concerning this crime; cf 2 Sm 16, 20. The Levite undoubtedly addressed the tribal heads who would speak in behalf of the multitude.

20, 12: Before the crime at Gibeah was punished, the Benjaminites were invited to join their brethren, the Israelites, in punishing the crime. Since they failed to respond, special messengers were sent asking them to deliver up the guilty ones. They replied by gathering their forces for combat.

Benjaminite swordsmen from the other cities on
that occasion was twenty-six thousand, in addition to the inhabitants of Gibeah. **16** Included
in this total were seven hundred picked men
who were left-handed, every one of them able
to sling a stone at a hair without missing.
**17** Meanwhile the other Israelites who, without
Benjamin, mustered four hundred thousand
swordsmen ready for battle, **18** moved on to
Bethel and consulted God. When the Israelites
asked who should go first in the attack on the
Benjaminites,[s] the LORD said, "Judah shall go
first."* **19** The next day the Israelites advanced
on Gibeah with their forces.

**War with Benjamin.** **20** On the day the
Israelites drew up in battle array at Gibeah for
the combat with Benjamin, **21** the Benjaminites came out of the city and felled twenty-two
thousand men of Israel. **23** Then the Israelites
went up and wept before the LORD until evening. "Shall I again engage my brother Benjamin in battle?" they asked the LORD; and the
LORD answered that they should. **22** But though
the Israelite soldiers took courage and again
drew up for combat in the same place as on the
previous day, **24** when they met the Benjaminites for the second time, **25** once again the
Benjaminites who came out of Gibeah against
them felled eighteen thousand Israelites, all of
them swordsmen. **26** So the entire Israelite
army went up to Bethel, where they wept and
remained fasting before the LORD until evening
of that day, besides offering holocausts and
peace offerings before the LORD. **27** [t]When the
Israelites consulted the LORD (for the ark of the
covenant of God was there in those days,
**28** and Phinehas, son of Eleazar, son of Aaron,
was ministering to him in those days), and
asked, "Shall I go out again to battle with Benjamin, my brother, or shall I desist?" the LORD
said, "Attack! for tomorrow I will deliver him
into your power." **29** [u]So Israel set men in
ambush around Gibeah.*

**30** The Israelites went up against the Benjaminites for the third time and formed their line
of battle at Gibeah as on other occasions.
**31** The Benjaminites went out to meet them,
and in the beginning they killed off about thirty
of the Israelite soldiers in the open field, just as
on the other occasions. **32** Therefore the Benjaminites thought, "We are defeating them as
before"; not realizing that disaster was about to
overtake them. The Israelites, however, had
planned the flight so as to draw them away from
the city onto the highways. They were drawn
away from the city onto the highways, of which
the one led to Bethel, the other to Gibeon.
**33** And then all the men of Israel rose from their
places. They re-formed their ranks at Baal-ta-
mar, and the Israelites in ambush rushed from
their place west of Gibeah, **34** ten thousand
picked men from all Israel, and advanced
against the city itself. In a fierce battle, **35** the
LORD defeated Benjamin before Israel; and on
that day the Israelites killed twenty-five thousand one hundred men of Benjamin, all of them
swordsmen.

**36** To the Benjaminites it had looked as
though the enemy were defeated, for the men of
Israel gave ground to Benjamin, trusting in the
ambush they had set at Gibeah. **37** But then the
men in ambush made a sudden dash into Gibeah, overran it, and put the whole city to the
sword. **38** Now, the other Israelites had agreed
with the men in ambush on a smoke signal they
were to send up from the city. **39** And though
the men of Benjamin had begun by killing off
some thirty of the men of Israel, under the impression that they were defeating them as surely
as in the earlier fighting, the Israelites wheeled
about to resist **40** as the smoke of the signal
column began to rise up from the city. It was
when Benjamin looked back and saw the whole
city in flames against the sky **41** that the men
of Israel wheeled about. Therefore the men of
Benjamin were thrown into confusion, for they
realized the disaster that had overtaken them.
**42** They retreated before the men of Israel in
the direction of the desert, with the fight being
pressed against them. In their very midst, meanwhile, those who had been in the city were
spreading destruction. **43** The men of Benjamin had been surrounded, and were now pursued to a point east of Gibeah, **44** while eighteen thousand of them fell, warriors to a man.
**45** The rest turned and fled through the desert
to the rock Rimmon.[v] But on the highways the
Israelites picked off five thousand men among
them, and chasing them up to Gidom, killed
another two thousand of them there. **46** Those
of Benjamin who fell on that day were in all
twenty-five thousand swordsmen, warriors to a
man. **47** But six hundred others who turned and
fled through the desert reached the rock Rimmon, where they remained for four months.
**48** The men of Israel withdrew through the
territory of the Benjaminites, putting to the
sword the inhabitants of the cities, the livestock,
and all they chanced upon. Moreover they de-

s Jgs 1, 1f.
t 1 Sm 4, 3f.
u 29-46: Jos 8, 4-24.
v Jgs 21, 13.

*

20, 18: Judah shall go first: the same response as in Jgs 1, 1f, but without the assurance of immediate success. Only after the Israelites were punished at the hands of the Benjaminites for their own grossness, and had performed penance, did they succeed in punishing the latter for their part in the crime of rape and murder, by gaining the victory over them.

20, 29–46: This stratagem proved more useful to the Israelites than force, as in the siege of Ai (Jos 8, 3–21). In the parallel accounts the first (vv 29–35) is a summary of the second (vv 36–46).

stroyed by fire all the cities they came upon.

## CHAPTER 21

**Wives for the Survivors.** **1** Now the men of Israel* had sworn at Mizpah that none of them would give his daughter in marriage to anyone from Benjamin. **2** So the people went to Bethel and remained there before God until evening, raising their voices in bitter lament.[w] **3** They said, "LORD, God of Israel, why has it come to pass in Israel that today one tribe of Israel should be lacking?" **4** Early the next day the people built an altar there and offered holocausts and peace offerings. **5** Then the Israelites asked, "Are there any among all the tribes of Israel who did not come up to the LORD for the assembly?" For they had taken a solemn oath that anyone who did not go up to the LORD at Mizpah should be put to death without fail.[x]

**6** *The Israelites were disconsolate over their brother Benjamin and said, "Today one of the tribes of Israel has been cut off. **7** What can we do about wives for the survivors, since we have sworn by the LORD not to give them any of our daughters in marriage?" **8** And when they asked whether anyone among the tribes of Israel had not come up to the LORD in Mizpah, they found that none of the men of Jabesh-gilead had come to the encampment for the assembly. **9** A roll call of the army established that none of the inhabitants of that city were present. **10** The community, therefore, sent twelve thousand warriors with orders to go to Jabesh-gilead and put those who lived there to the sword, including the women and children. **11** They were told to include under the ban* all males and every woman who was not still a virgin.[y] **12** Finding among the inhabitants of Jabesh-gilead four hundred young virgins, who had had no relations with men, they brought them to the camp at Shiloh in the land of Canaan. **13** [z]Then the whole community sent a message to the Benjaminites at the rock Rimmon, offering them peace. **14** When Benjamin returned at that time, they gave them as wives the women of Jabesh-gilead whom they had spared; but these proved to be not enough for them.

**15** The people were still disconsolate over Benjamin because the LORD had made a breach* among the tribes of Israel. **16** And the elders of the community said, "What shall we do for wives for the survivors? For every woman in Benjamin has been put to death." **17** They said, "Those of Benjamin who survive must have heirs, else one of the Israelite tribes will be wiped out. **18** *Yet we cannot give them any of our daughters in marriage, because the Israelites have sworn, 'Cursed be he who gives a woman to Benjamin!' " **19** Then they thought of the yearly feast of the LORD at Shiloh, north of Bethel, east of the highway that goes up from Bethel to Shechem, and south of Lebonah. **20** And they instructed the Benjaminites, "Go and lie in wait in the vineyards. **21** When you see the girls of Shiloh come out to do their dancing, leave the vineyards and each of you seize one of the girls of Shiloh for a wife, and go to the land of Benjamin. **22** When their fathers or their brothers come to complain to us, we shall say to them, 'Release them to us as a kindness, since we did not take a woman apiece in the war. Had you yourselves given them these wives, you would now be guilty.' "

**23** The Benjaminites did this; they carried off a wife for each of them from their raid on the dancers, and went back to their own territory, where they rebuilt and occupied the cities. **24** Also at that time the Israelites dispersed; each of them left for his own heritage in his own clan and tribe.

**25** *In those days there was no king in Israel; everyone did what he thought best.[a]

w Jgs 20, 26.
x Jgs 20, 8ff.
y Nm 31, 17.
z Jgs 20, 47.
a Jgs 17, 6; 18, 1; 19, 1.

*

21, 1–3: The anger of the Israelites led them to destroy their brethren, the Benjaminites. Having realized their goal, however, they were soon filled with dismay, and sought to restore the tribe they had all but exterminated.

21, 6–9: This account is summarized in the parallel passage in vv 2–5.

21, 11: Under the ban: see note on Nm 21, 3.

21, 15: Had made a breach: what is here attributed to God was in reality the free and deliberate act of the Israelites and happened only by the permissive will of God. The ancients attributed to the first primary cause what is more directly due to secondary causes.

21, 18: Regardless of the serious consequences of their vow, the Israelites considered themselves obliged to fulfill it; cf Jgs 11, 31. 35f. 39.

21, 25: Cf Jgs 17, 6; 18, 1; 19, 1. The verse gives the reason why the lawlessness of the period of judges, and the events described herein, were possible.

# The Book of
# RUTH

*The Book of Ruth is named after the Moabite woman who was joined to the Israelite people by her marriage with the influential Boaz of Bethlehem.*

*The book contains a beautiful example of filial piety, pleasing to the Hebrews especially because of its connection with King David, and useful both to Hebrews and to Gentiles. Its aim is to demonstrate the divine reward for such piety even when practiced by a stranger. Ruth's piety (Ru 2, 11), her spirit of self-sacrifice, and her moral integrity were favored by God with the gift of faith and an illustrious marriage whereby she became the ancestress of David and of Christ. In this, the universality of the messianic salvation is foreshadowed.*

*In the Greek and Latin canons the Book of Ruth is placed just after Judges, to which it is closely related because of the time of its action, and just before Samuel, for which it is an excellent introduction, since it traces the ancestry of the Davidic dynasty. One might characterize the literary form of this book as dramatic, since about two-thirds of it is in dialogue. Yet there is every indication that, as tradition has always held, it contains true history.*

*There is no certainty about the author of the book. It was written long after the events had passed (Ru 4, 7), which took place "in the time of the judges" (Ru 1, 1).*

## CHAPTER 1

**Naomi in Moab.** **1** Once in the time of the judges* there was a famine in the land; so a man from Bethlehem of Judah departed with his wife and two sons to reside on the plateau of Moab. **2** The man was named Elimelech, his wife Naomi, and his sons Mahlon and Chilion; they were Ephrathites from Bethlehem of Judah. Some time after their arrival on the Moabite plateau, **3** Elimelech, the husband of Naomi, died, and she was left with her two sons, **4** who married Moabite women, one named Orpah, the other Ruth. When they had lived there about ten years, **5** both Mahlon and Chilion died also, and the woman was left with neither her two sons nor her husband. **6** She then made ready to go back from the plateau of Moab because word reached her there that the LORD had visited his people and given them food.

**7** She and her two daughters-in-law left the place where they had been living. Then as they were on the road back to the land of Judah, **8** Naomi said to her two daughters-in-law, "Go back, each of you, to your mother's house!* May the LORD be kind to you as you were to the departed and to me! **9** May the LORD grant each of you a husband and a home in which you will find rest." She kissed them good-by, but they wept with loud sobs, **10** and told her they would return with her to her people. **11** "Go back, my daughters!" said Naomi. "Why should you come with me? Have I other sons in my womb who may become your husbands?* **12** Go back, my daughters! Go, for I am too old to marry again. And even if I could offer any hopes, or if tonight I had a husband or had borne sons, **13** would you then wait and deprive yourselves of husbands until those sons grew up? No, my daughters! my lot is too bitter for you, because the LORD has extended his hand against me." **14** Again they sobbed aloud and wept; and Orpah kissed her mother-in-law good-by, but Ruth stayed with her.

**15** "See now!" she said, "your sister-in-law has gone back to her people and her god. Go back after your sister-in-law!" **16** *But Ruth said, "Do not ask me to abandon or forsake you! for wherever you go I will go, wherever you lodge I will lodge, your people shall be my people, and your God my God. **17** Wherever

*

---

1, 1f: In the time of the judges: three generations before the end of the period of Judges; cf Ru 4, 21f. Bethlehem of Judah: to distinguish it from the town of the same name in the tribe of Zebulun (Jos 19, 15). Ephrathites from Bethlehem: belonging to a Judean clan which settled in Bethlehem; cf 1 Sm 17, 12; 1 Chr 2, 50f; 4, 4.

1, 8: Mother's house: the women's part of the dwelling; cf Jgs 4, 17; Song 3, 4.

1, 11: Have I other sons . . . husbands?: Naomi insisted that her daughters-in-law remain in their own country only for the sake of posterity. If she had had other sons, the levirate law would have obliged them to marry the widows of her deceased sons to perpetuate the names of the deceased; cf Gn 38, 8; Dt 25, 5f.

1, 16f: An example of heroic fidelity and piety. Ruth's decision, confirmed with an oath, to adhere to her mother-in-law impelled her to abandon her country and its pagan worship.

you die I will die, and there be buried. May the
LORD do so and so to me, and more besides, if
aught but death separates me from you!"
18 Naomi then ceased to urge her, for she saw
she was determined to go with her.

**The Return to Bethlehem.** 19 So they
went on together till they reached Bethlehem.
On their arrival there, the whole city was astir
over them, and the women asked, "Can this be
Naomi?" 20 [a]But she said to them, "Do not
call me Naomi.* Call me Mara, for the Almighty has made it very bitter for me. 21 I went
away with an abundance, but the LORD has
brought me back destitute. Why should you call
me Naomi, since the LORD has pronounced
against me and the Almighty has brought evil
upon me?" 22 Thus it was that Naomi returned
with the Moabite daughter-in-law, Ruth, who
accompanied her back from the plateau of
Moab. They arrived in Bethlehem at the beginning of the barley harvest.*

## CHAPTER 2

**The Meeting.** 1 Naomi had a prominent
kinsman named Boaz,[b] of the clan of her husband Elimelech. 2 Ruth the Moabite said to
Naomi, "Let me go and glean ears of grain* in
the field of anyone who will allow me that favor."[c] Naomi said to her, "Go, my daughter,"
3 and she went. The field she entered to glean
after the harvesters happened to be the section
belonging to Boaz of the clan of Elimelech.
4 Boaz himself came from Bethlehem and said
to the harvesters, "The LORD be with you!"*
and they replied, "The LORD bless you!"
5 Boaz asked the overseer of his harvesters,
"Whose girl is this?" 6 The overseer of the
harvesters answered, "She is the Moabite girl
who returned from the plateau of Moab with
Naomi.[d] 7 She asked leave to gather the gleanings into sheaves after the harvesters; and ever
since she came this morning she has remained
here until now, with scarcely a moment's rest."
8 Boaz said to Ruth, "Listen, my daughter!
Do not go to glean in anyone else's field; you
are not to leave here. Stay here with my women
servants. 9 Watch to see which field is to be
harvested, and follow them; I have commanded
the young men to do you no harm. When you
are thirsty, you may go and drink from the
vessels the young men have filled." 10 Casting
herself prostrate upon the ground, she said to
him, "Why should I, a foreigner, be favored
with your notice?" 11 [e]Boaz answered her: "I
have had a complete account of what you have
done for your mother-in-law after your husband's death; you have left your father and your
mother and the land of your birth, and have
come to a people whom you did not know previously. 12 May the LORD reward what you have
done! May you receive a full reward from the
LORD, the God of Israel, under whose wings
you have come for refuge." 13 She said, "May
I prove worthy of your kindness, my lord: you
have comforted me, your servant, with your
consoling words; would indeed that I were a
servant of yours!" 14 At mealtime Boaz said to
her, "Come here and have some food; dip your
bread in the sauce." Then as she sat near the
reapers, he handed her some roasted grain and
she ate her fill and had some left over. 15 She
rose to glean, and Boaz instructed his servants
to let her glean among the sheaves themselves
without scolding her, 16 and even to let drop
some handfuls and leave them for her to glean
without being rebuked.
17 She gleaned in the field until evening, and
when she beat out what she had gleaned it came
to about an ephah of barley, 18 which she took
into the city and showed to her mother-in-law.
Next she brought out and gave her what she had
left over from lunch. 19 So her mother-in-law
said to her, "Where did you glean today?
Where did you go to work? May he who took
notice of you be blessed!" Then she told her
mother-in-law with whom she had worked.
"The man at whose place I worked today is
named Boaz," she said. 20 [f]"May he be
blessed by the LORD, who is ever merciful to the
living and to the dead," Naomi exclaimed to her
daughter-in-law; and she continued, "He is a
relative of ours, one of our next of kin."*
21 "He even told me," added Ruth the Moabite, "that I should stay with his servants until
they complete his entire harvest." 22 "You
would do well, my dear," Naomi rejoined, "to
go out with his servants; for in someone else's
field you might be insulted." 23 So she stayed

a Ex 15, 23.
b Ru 3, 2. 12; 4, 21; Mt 1, 5.
c Dt 24, 19.
d Ru 1, 22.
e Ru 1, 14-17.
f Ru 3, 9.

*

1, 20f: Naomi: means "amiable" or "pleasant," suggesting God's favor toward her. The Almighty has brought evil upon me: the ancients regarded adversity as a punishment from God for personal sin, as if good and evil were always repaid in a temporal and material manner.

1, 22: Barley harvest: early April. This circumstance favored the events of the narrative that follow.

2, 2: Let me go and glean . . . grain: even the poor, the widow, the stranger, and the orphan had a right to glean at harvest time; cf Lv 19, 9f, 23, 22; Dt 24, 19–22.

2, 4: The Lord be with you: courtesy and religious feeling characterize the salutations of the Hebrews. This greeting is used in the Christian liturgy.

2, 20: One of our next of kin: literally "our redeemer," a near relative of the same clan who had the right and duty to restore the land which an impoverished kinsman had alienated (Lv 25, 25–28), and to marry the widow of a relative who had died without male offspring so as to raise up posterity to his name (Dt 25, 5–10).

gleaning with the servants of Boaz until the end
of the barley and wheat harvests.

## CHAPTER 3

**Ruth Again Presents Herself.** When she
was back with her mother-in-law, **1** Naomi said
to her, "My daughter, I must seek a home for
you that will please you. **2** [g]Now is not Boaz,
with whose servants you were, a relative of
ours? This evening he will be winnowing barley
at the threshing floor. **3** So bathe and anoint
yourself; then put on your best attire and go
down to the threshing floor. Do not make yourself known to the man before he has finished
eating and drinking. **4** But when he lies down,
take note of the place where he does so. Then
go, uncover a place at his feet,* and lie down.
He will tell you what to do." **5** "I will do
whatever you advise," Ruth replied. **6** So she
went down to the threshing floor and did just as
her mother-in-law had instructed her.
**7** Boaz ate and drank to his heart's content.
Then when he went and lay down at the edge of
the sheaves, she stole up, uncovered a place at
his feet, and lay down. **8** In the middle of the
night, however, the man gave a start and turned
around to find a woman lying at his feet. **9** He
asked, "Who are you?" And she replied, "I am
your servant Ruth. Spread the corner of your
cloak over me,* for you are my next of kin."
**10** He said, "May the LORD bless you, my
daughter! You have been even more loyal now
than before in not going after the young men,
whether poor or rich.[h] **11** So be assured,
daughter, I will do for you whatever you say; all
my townspeople know you for a worthy woman. **12** [i]Now, though indeed I am closely related to you, you have another relative still closer.* **13** Stay as you are for tonight, and
tomorrow, if he wishes to claim you, good! let
him do so. But if he does not wish to claim you,
as the LORD lives, I will claim you myself. Lie
there until morning."[j] **14** So she lay at his feet
until morning, but rose before men could recognize one another. Boaz said, "Let it not be
known that this woman came to the threshing
floor." **15** Then he said to her, "Take off your
cloak and hold it out." When she did so, he
poured out six measures of barley, helped her
lift the bundle,[k] and left for the city.
**16** Ruth went home to her mother-in-law,
who asked, "How have you fared, my daughter?" So she told her all the man had done for
her, **17** and concluded, "He gave me these six
measures of barley because he did not wish me
to come back to my mother-in-law empty-handed!" **18** Naomi then said, "Wait here, my
daughter, until you learn what happens, for the
man will not rest, but will settle the matter
today."

## CHAPTER 4

**Boaz Marries Ruth.** **1** Boaz went and took
a seat at the gate;* and when he saw the closer
relative[l] of whom he had spoken come along,
he called to him by name, "Come and sit beside
me!" And he did so. **2** Then Boaz picked out
ten of the elders* of the city and asked them to
sit nearby. When they had done this, **3** he said
to the near relative: "Naomi, who has come
back from the Moabite plateau, is putting up for
sale the piece of land that belonged to our kinsman Elimelech. **4** *So I thought I would inform
you, bidding you before those here present, including the elders of my people, to put in your
claim for it if you wish to acquire it as next of
kin.[m] But if you do not wish to claim it, tell me
so, that I may be guided accordingly, for no one
has a prior claim to yours, and mine is next."
He answered, "I will put in my claim."
**5** *Boaz continued, "Once you acquire the
field from Naomi, you must take also Ruth the
Moabite,[n] the widow of the late heir, and raise
up a family for the departed on his estate."
**6** The near relative replied, "I cannot exercise
my claim lest I depreciate my own estate. Put
in a claim yourself in my stead, for I cannot
exercise my claim." **7** Now it used to be the
custom in Israel that, to make binding a contract
of redemption or exchange, one party would
take off his sandal* and give it to the other. This
was the form of attestation in Israel. **8** So the
near relative, in saying to Boaz, "Acquire it for
yourself," drew off his sandal. **9** Boaz then

g Ru 1.
h Dt 25, 5.
i Ru 4, 1.
j Ru 4, 5; Dt 25, 5.
k Ru 2, 17.
l Ru 3, 12.
m Lv 25, 25.
n Ru 3, 13; Dt 25, 5.

*

3, 4: Uncover a place at his feet . . . : confident of the virtue of Ruth and Boaz, Naomi advises this unusual expedient to her daughter-in-law for the purpose of introducing her claim.

3, 9: Spread the corner of your cloak over me: be my protector by marrying me according to the duty of a near kinsman; cf Dt 25, 5; Ez 16, 8.

3, 12: Relative still closer: who had a prior right and duty to marry Ruth.

4, 1: Took a seat at the gate: i.e., of the city, where business affairs were settled.

4, 2: Ten of the elders: to serve as judges in legal matters as well as witnesses of the settlement of business affairs; cf Dt 25, 7–9.

4, 4: Poverty had obliged Naomi to sell the land of her deceased husband. The law permitted the nearest kinsman to redeem the land and thus preserve the family patrimony; cf Lv 25, 25.

4, 5f: The heir of Elimelech's field had died without children (Ru 1, 5). The nearest of kin could now redeem the land but he must also take Ruth, the widow of the late heir, to wife to perpetuate the family of the deceased; cf Dt 25, 5f. The first male child of such a marriage would be the legal son of Mahlon and grandson of Elimelech.

4, 7: Take off his sandal . . . : by this act the near relative renounced his legal right, both to the field of Elimelech and to the marriage with Ruth. The custom mentioned in Dt 25, 6 is somewhat different.

said to the elders and to all the people, "You are
witnesses today that I have acquired from Naomi all the holdings of Elimelech, Chilion and
Mahlon. **10** I also take Ruth the Moabite, the
widow of Mahlon, as my wife, in order to raise
up a family for her late husband on his estate,
so that the name of the departed may not perish
among his kinsmen and fellow citizens. Do you
witness this today?" **11** [o]All those at the gate,
including the elders, said, "We do so. May the
LORD make this wife come into your house like
Rachel and Leah, who between them built up
the house of Israel. May you do well in Ephrathah and win fame in Bethlehem. **12** [p]With the
offspring the LORD will give you from this girl,
may your house become like the house of Perez,
who Tamar bore to Judah."*
**13** Boaz took Ruth. When they came together as man and wife, the LORD enabled her to
conceive and she bore a son. **14** Then the wom-
en said to Naomi, "Blessed is the LORD who has
not failed to provide you today with an heir!
May he become famous in Israel! **15** He will be
your comfort and the support of your old age,
for his mother is the daughter-in-law who loves
you. She is worth more to you than seven
sons!" **16** Naomi took the child, placed him on
her lap,* and became his nurse. **17** And the
neighbor women gave him his name,[q] at the
news that a grandson had been born to Naomi.
They called him Obed. He was the father of
Jesse, the father of David.*
**18** [r]These are the descendants of Perez: Perez was the father of Hezron,[s] **19** Hezron was
the father of Ram, Ram was the father of Amminadab, **20** [t]Amminadab was the father of
Nahshon, Nahshon was the father of Salmon,
**21** Salmon was the father of Boaz, Boaz was
the father of Obed, **22** [u]Obed was the father of
Jesse, and Jesse became the father of David.

---

o Gn 29, 31-30, 24; 35, 19.
p Gn 38, 29.
q Lk 1, 58.
r 18-22: 1 Chr 2, 4-15; Mt 1, 3-6.
s Gn 46, 12; 1 Chr 4, 1.
t Ex 6, 23; Nm 1, 7.
u 1 Sm 16, 10-13.

---

*

4, 12: Perez, whom Tamar bore to Judah: the right which Judah unwittingly satisfied for his daughter-in-law Tamar (Gn 38), Boaz willingly rendered to Ruth.

4, 16: Placed him on her lap: took him as her own; cf Gn 30, 3; 48, 12; Nm 11, 12.

4, 17: The father of Jesse, the father of David: indicating the place of Obed, Jesse and David in the line of Judah and the ancestry of Christ, the Messiah; cf Mt 1, 5f.

# THE HISTORICAL BOOKS

*The historical books include 1 and 2 Samuel, 1 and 2 Kings, 1 and 2 Chronicles, Ezra, Nehemiah, 1 and 2 Maccabees. To these are added the special literary group of Tobit, Judith and Esther.*

*The books of Tobit, Judith, and 1 and 2 Maccabees, as well as parts of Esther, are called deuterocanonical: they are not contained in the Hebrew canon but have been accepted by the Catholic Church as canonical and inspired.*

*By means of a series of episodes involving the persons of Samuel, Saul, and David, a century of history unfolds in 1 and 2 Samuel from the close of the period of Judges to the rise and establishment of the monarchy in Israel. Most important is God's promise to David of a lasting dynasty (2 Sm 7), from which royal messianism in the Bible developed.*

*In 1 and 2 Kings the religious history of Israel extends another four centuries, from the last days of David to the Babylonian captivity and the destruction of Jerusalem (587 B.C.). The various sources for these books are woven into a uniform pattern based on the principle of fidelity to Yahweh for rulers and people alike. The sequence of regnal chronicles in both books is interrupted by a cycle of traditions surrounding the prophets Elijah (1 Kgs) and Elisha (2 Kgs).*

*Chronicles, Ezra and Nehemiah form a historical work, uniform in style and basic ideas. Chronicles records the long period from the reign of Saul to the return from exile, not so much with exactitude of detail as with concern for the meaning of the facts which demonstrate God's intervention in history. The Ezra-Nehemiah chronicle constitutes the most important source for the formation of the Jewish religious community after the Babylonian exile; the two persons most responsible for the reorganization of Jewish life were Ezra and Nehemiah.*

*1 and 2 Maccabees contain independent accounts of partially identical events which accompanied the attempted suppression of Judaism in Palestine in the second century B.C. Vigorous reaction to this attempt established for a time the religious and political independence of the Jews. 1 Maccabees portrays God as the eternal benefactor of the Jews and their unfailing source of help. The people are required to be devoted to his exclusive worship and to observe exactly the law he has given them. 2 Maccabees, besides supplementing the former volume, gives a theological interpretation of the history of the period and contains teaching on the resurrection from the dead, intercession of the saints, and suffrages for the dead.*

*Tobit, Judith, and Esther are examples of free composition—the religious novel used for purposes of edification and instruction. Interest in whatever historical data these books may contain is merely intensified by the addition of vivid details. Judith is a lesson in Providence: a pious reflection on the annual Passover observance to convey the reassurance that God is still the master of history who saves Israel from her enemies. Esther's purpose is the glorification of the Jewish people and the explanation of the origin, significance, and date of the feast of Purim. It is a literary development of the principle of reversal of fortune through punishment of the prosperous rich and reward for the virtuous who are oppressed.*

Samuel to Maccabees *demonstrates that before as well as during the millennium of history with which it is concerned, Israel was a covenanted people, bound to Yahweh, Lord of the universe, by the ties of faith and obedience. This required observance of the law and worship in his temple, the consequent rewards of which were divine favor and protection. In this way these books anticipate and prepare for the coming of him who would bring type and prophecy to fulfillment, history to term, and holiness to perfection: Christ, the Son of David and the promised Messiah.*

# The Books of
# SAMUEL

*Originally but one book, the scroll of Samuel was early divided into two. The Greek translators called these the first and second Books of Kingdoms, a title St. Jerome later modified to "Kings." The Hebrew title, "Samuel," alludes to the leading figure in the first book, who was responsible for the enthronement of David. It is David's history that the second book recounts.*

*This sacred work thus comprises the history of about a century, describing the close of the age of the Judges and the beginnings of monarchy in Israel under Saul and David. It is not a complete and continuous history, nor a systematic account of the period, but rather a series of episodes centered around the persons of Samuel, Saul and David, the principal figures leading up to the establishment of the royal dynasty of David.*

*The final editor is unknown, nor are we certain of the time at which the various strands of the narrative were put together, though one may think of the period, perhaps late in the seventh century B.C., when the other volumes of the "Former Prophets," from Joshua through Kings, were built into a more or less continuous historical corpus. The Samuel-Saul-David narratives clearly depend on several written sources: a Samuel cycle, two sets of stories about Saul and David, and a family history of David. This last (2 Sm 9–20; 1 Kgs 1–2), one of the most vivid historical narratives surviving from ancient times, probably originated early in the reign of Solomon.*

*One of the most significant theological contributions of the Old Testament is found in 2 Samuel 7, the oracle of Nathan. David is here promised an eternal dynasty, and this becomes the basis for the development of royal messianism throughout the Bible. With this promise to David one should compare 1 Chr 17; Pss 89, 20–38 and 132, 11ff; Acts 2, 30; and Heb 1, 5.*

*The contents of this work may be divided as follows:*

*I. History of the Last Judges, Eli and Samuel (1 Sm 1, 1–7, 17).*
*II. Establishment of the Monarchy in Israel (1 Sm 8, 1–12, 25).*
*III. Saul and David (1 Sm 13, 1–2 Sm 2, 7).*
*IV. The Reign of David (2 Sm 2, 8–20, 26).*
*V. Appendixes (2 Sm 21, 1–24, 25).*

# THE FIRST BOOK OF SAMUEL

## *I: History of the Last Judges, Eli and Samuel*

### CHAPTER 1

#### Elkanah and His Family at Shiloh.

**1** There was a certain man from Rama-thaim,
Elkanah by name, a Zuphite from the hill country of Ephraim. He was the son of Jeroham, son
of Elihu, son of Tohu, son of Zuph, an Ephraimite.[a] **2** He had two wives, one named Hannah,
the other Peninnah; Peninnah had children, but
Hannah was childless. **3** This man regularly
went on pilgrimage from his city to worship the
LORD of hosts and to sacrifice to him at Shiloh,
where the two sons of Eli, Hophni and Phinehas, were ministering as priests of the LORD.[b]
**4** When the day came for Elkanah to offer sacrifice, he used to give a portion each to his wife
Peninnah and to all her sons and daughters,
**5** but a double portion to Hannah because he
loved her, though the LORD had made her barren.[c] **6** Her rival, to upset her, turned it into a
constant reproach to her that the LORD had left
her barren.[d] **7** This went on year after year;
each time they made their pilgrimage to the
sanctuary of the LORD, Peninnah would approach her, and Hannah would weep and refuse
to eat. **8** Her husband Elkanah used to ask her:

a 1 Chr 6, 19f.
b Ex 23, 14-17; 34, 23; Dt 16, 16; Jgs 21, 19.
c Dt 21, 15ff.
d Gn 16, 4f.
e Ru 4, 15.

"Hannah, why do you weep, and why do you
refuse to eat? Why do you grieve? Am I not
more to you than ten sons?"[e]

**Hannah's Prayer.** 9 Hannah rose after one
such meal at Shiloh, and presented herself before the LORD; at the time, Eli the priest was
sitting on a chair near the doorpost of the LORD's
temple. 10 In her bitterness she prayed to the
LORD, weeping copiously, 11 and she made a
vow, promising: "O LORD of hosts, if you look
with pity on the misery of your handmaid, if you
remember me and do not forget me, if you give
your handmaid a male child, I will give him to
the LORD* for as long as he lives; neither wine
nor liquor shall he drink, and no razor shall ever
touch his head."[f] 12 As she remained long at
prayer before the LORD, Eli watched her mouth,
13 for Hannah was praying silently; though her
lips were moving, her voice could not be heard.
Eli, thinking her drunk, 14 said to her, "How
long will you make a drunken show of yourself?
Sober up from your wine!" 15 "It isn't that,
my lord," Hannah answered. "I am an unhappy
woman. I have had neither wine nor liquor; I
was only pouring out my troubles to the LORD.
16 Do not think your handmaid a ne'er-do-
well; my prayer has been prompted by my deep
sorrow and misery." 17 Eli said, "Go in
peace, and may the God of Israel grant you what
you have asked of him." 18 She replied,
"Think kindly of your maidservant," and left.
She went to her quarters, ate and drank with her
husband, and no longer appeared downcast.
19 Early the next morning they worshiped before the LORD, and then returned to their home
in Ramah.

**Hannah Bears a Son.** When Elkanah had
relations with his wife Hannah, the LORD remembered her. 20 She conceived, and at the
end of her term bore a son whom she called
Samuel, since she had asked* the LORD for him.
21 The next time her husband Elkanah was going up with the rest of his household to offer the
customary sacrifice to the LORD and to fulfill his
vows, 22 Hannah did not go, explaining to her
husband, "Once the child is weaned, I will take
him to appear before the LORD and to remain
there forever; I will offer him as a perpetual
nazirite." 23 Her husband Elkanah answered
her: "Do what you think best; wait until you
have weaned him. Only, may the LORD bring
your resolve to fulfillment!" And so she remained at home and nursed her son until she had
weaned him.

**Samuel is Offered to God.** 24 Once he
was weaned, she brought him up with her, along
with a three-year-old bull, an ephah* of flour,
and a skin of wine, and presented him at the
temple of the LORD in Shiloh. 25 After the
boy's father had sacrificed the young bull, Hannah, his mother, approached Eli 26 and said:
"Pardon, my lord! As you live, my lord, I am
the woman who stood near you here, praying to
the LORD. 27 I prayed for this child, and the
LORD granted my request. 28 Now I, in turn,
give him to the LORD; as long as he lives, he
shall be dedicated to the LORD." She left him
there;* 1 and as she worshiped the LORD, she
said:

## CHAPTER 2

"My heart exults in the LORD,*
my horn* is exalted in my God.
I have swallowed up my enemies;
I rejoice in my victory.[g]
2 There is no Holy One like the LORD;
there is no Rock like our God.[h]

3 "Speak boastfully no longer,
nor let arrogance issue from your
mouths.*
For an all-knowing God is the LORD,
a God who judges deeds.[i]
4 The bows of the mighty are broken,
while the tottering gird on strength.[j]
5 The well-fed hire themselves out for bread,
while the hungry batten on spoil.
The barren wife bears seven sons,
while the mother of many languishes.
6 "The LORD puts to death and gives life;
he casts down to the nether world; he
raises up again.[k]
7 The LORD makes poor and makes rich,
he humbles, he also exalts.
8 He raises the needy from the dust;
from the ash heap he lifts up the poor,
To seat them with nobles

f Nm 6, 1-5; Jgs 13, 2-5; 16, 17; Lk 1, 15.
g Dt 33, 17; 2 Sm 22, 3; Ps 18, 2; Is 61, 10; Lk 1, 47. 69
h 2 Sm 22, 3; Ps 18, 2.
i Ps 75, 4.
j Is 40, 29.
k Dt 32, 39; Tb 4, 19; Jb 5, 11; Ps 30, 4; Wis 16, 13; Lk 1, 52.
l Jb 9, 6; 38, 6; Ps 104, 5; 121, 3.

*

1, 11: Give him to the Lord: some ancient texts call Samuel a nazir in this context; see note on Nm 6, 1ff.

1, 20: Since she had asked: this explanation would be more directly appropriate for the name Saul, which means "asked"; Samuel means "name of God."

1, 24: An ephah: a little more than a bushel.

1, 1: And ... said: this belongs to ch 2.

2, 1–10: A hymn attributed to Hannah, the mother of Samuel, as her thanksgiving to God because she has borne a son despite her previous sterility. She praises God as the helper of the weak (1ff), who casts down the mighty and raises up the lowly (3ff), and who alone is the source of true strength (8ff); the hymn ends with a prayer for the king (v 10). This canticle has several points of resemblance with our Lady's Magnificat.

2, 1: Horn: the symbol of strength; cf Pss 18, 3; 75, 5; 89, 18; 112, 9.

2, 3: Speak ... mouths: addressed to the enemies mentioned in v 1.

and make a glorious throne their
heritage.[l]
He gives to the vower his vow,
and blesses the sleep of the just.

"For the pillars of the earth are the LORD's,
and he has set the world upon them.
9 He will guard the footsteps of his faithful
ones,
but the wicked shall perish in the
darkness.
For not by strength does man prevail;
10 the LORD's foes shall be shattered.
The Most High in heaven thunders;
The LORD judges the ends of the earth.
Now may he give strength to his king
and exalt the horn of his anointed!"[m]

11 When Elkanah returned home to Ramah,
the child remained in the service of the LORD
under the priest Eli.

**Wickedness of Eli's Sons.** 12 Now the
sons of Eli were wicked; they had respect neither for the LORD 13 nor for the priests' duties
toward the people. When someone offered a
sacrifice, the priest's servant would come with
a three-pronged fork, while the meat was still
boiling,[n] 14 and would thrust it into the basin,
kettle, caldron, or pot. Whatever the fork
brought up, the priest would keep. That is how
all the Israelites were treated who came to the
sanctuary at Shiloh. 15 In fact, even before the
fat was burned, the priest's servant would come
and say to the man offering the sacrifice, "Give
me some meat to roast for the priest. He will not
accept boiled meat from you, only raw meat."
16 And if the man protested to him, "Let the
fat be burned first as is the custom, then take
whatever you wish," he would reply, "No,
give it to me now, or else I will take it by
force."[o] 17 Thus the young men sinned grievously in the presence of the LORD; they treated
the offerings to the LORD with disdain.

**The Lord Rewards Hannah.** 18 Meanwhile the boy Samuel, girt with a linen apron,*
was serving in the presence of the LORD. 19 His
mother used to make a little garment for him,
which she would bring him each time she went
up with her husband to offer the customary sacrifice. 20 And Eli would bless Elkanah and his
wife, as they were leaving for home. He would
say, "May the LORD repay you with children
from this woman for the gift she has made to the
LORD!" 21 The LORD favored Hannah so that
she conceived and gave birth to three more sons
and two daughters, while young Samuel grew
up in the service of the LORD.[p]

**Eli's Futile Rebuke.** 22 When Eli was
very old, he heard repeatedly how his sons were
treating all Israel [and that they were having
relations with the women serving at the entry of
the meeting tent.]* 23 So he said to them:
"Why are you doing such things? 24 No, my
sons, you must not do these things! It is not a
good report that I hear the people of the LORD
spreading about you. 25 If a man sins against
another man, one can intercede for him with the
LORD; but if a man sins against the LORD, who
can intercede for him?" But they disregarded
their father's warning, since the LORD had decided on their death. 26 Meanwhile, young
Samuel was growing in stature and in worth in
the estimation of the LORD and of men.[q]

**Doom of Eli's House.*** 27 A man of God
came to Eli and said to him: "This is what the
LORD says: 'I went so far as to reveal myself to
your father's family when they were in Egypt as
slaves to the house of Pharaoh. 28 I chose them
out of all the tribes of Israel to be my priests,
to go up to my altar, to burn incense, and to
wear the ephod* before me; and I assigned all
the oblations of the Israelites to your father's
family.[r] 29 Why do you keep a greedy eye on
my sacrifices and on the offerings which I have
prescribed? And why do you honor your sons in
preference to me, fattening yourselves with the
choicest part of every offering of my people
Israel?' 30 [s]This, therefore, is the oracle of the
LORD, the God of Israel: 'I said in the past that
your family and your father's family should
minister in my presence forever. But now,' the
LORD declares, 'away with this! for I will honor
those who honor me, but those who spurn me
shall be accursed. 31 Yes, the time is coming
when I will break your strength and the strength
of your father's family, so that no man in your
family shall reach old age. 32 You shall witness

m Ps 98, 9.
n 13-15: Ex 29, 27f; Lv 7, 29-36; Dt 18, 3.
o Lv 3, 3ff.
p 1 Sm 3, 19.
q Lk 2, 52.
r 1 Sm 23, 9; 30, 7f; Jgs 17, 5.
s 30f: 2 Sm 22, 26; 1 Kgs 2, 27; Ps 18, 25.

*

2, 18: Linen apron: called in Hebrew "ephod," but not the same as the high priest's ephod (Ex 28, 6–14) or the ephod used in divination (v 28). Samuel wore a simple apron such as was worn by the priests (1 Sm 22, 18), and on one occasion also by David (2 Sm 6, 14).

2, 22: The bracketed words, which recall Ex 38, 8, are a gloss in the received text; they are lacking in the oldest Greek translation, and in a Hebrew manuscript from Qumran.

2, 27–36: These verses propose the punishment of Eli from a point of view contemporary with the reform of Josiah (2 Kgs 23, 9; cf v 36); they hint at the events recorded in 1 Sm 22, 18–23 and 1 Kgs 2, 27. The older story of this divine warning is that in 1 Sm 3, 11–14.

2, 28: Ephod: a portable container, presumably of cloth, for the lots used in ritual consultation of God during the days of the Judges (Jgs 17, 5; 18, 14–15) and down into the time of David (1 Sm 14, 3ff; 23, 6ff; 30, 7f). The ephod of the high priest described in Ex 28, 6ff becomes a garment upon which a breastpiece of decision symbolizes, but no longer serves for, such consultation. The Exodus text codifies a later form of the tradition.

as a disappointed rival all the benefits enjoyed by Israel, but there shall never be an old man in your family. **33** I will permit some of your family to remain at my altar, to wear out their eyes in consuming greed; but the rest of the men of your family shall die by the sword. **34** You shall have a sign in what will happen to your two sons, Hophni and Phinehas: both shall die on the same day.[t] **35** I will choose a faithful priest who shall do what I have in heart and mind. I will establish a lasting house for him which shall function in the presence of my anointed forever. **36** Then whoever is left of your family will come to grovel before him for a piece of silver or a loaf of bread, and will say: Appoint me, I beg you, to a priestly function, that I may have a morsel of bread to eat.' "[u]

## CHAPTER 3

**Revelation to Samuel.** **1** During the time young Samuel was minister to the LORD under Eli, a revelation of the LORD was uncommon* and vision infrequent. **2** One day Eli was asleep in his usual place. His eyes had lately grown so weak that he could not see. **3** The lamp of God was not yet extinguished, and Samuel was sleeping in the temple of the LORD where the ark of God was.[v] **4** The LORD called to Samuel, who answered, "Here I am." **5** He ran to Eli and said, "Here I am. You called me." "I did not call you," Eli said. "Go back to sleep." So he went back to sleep. **6** Again the LORD called Samuel, who rose and went to Eli. "Here I am," he said. "You called me." But he answered, "I did not call you, my son. Go back to sleep."

**7** At that time Samuel was not familiar with the LORD, because the LORD had not revealed anything to him as yet. **8** The LORD called Samuel again, for the third time. Getting up and going to Eli, he said, "Here I am. You called me." Then Eli understood that the LORD was calling the youth. **9** So he said to Samuel, "Go to sleep, and if you are called, reply, 'Speak, LORD, for your servant is listening.' " When Samuel went to sleep in his place, **10** the LORD came and revealed his presence, calling out as before, "Samuel, Samuel!" Samuel answered, "Speak, for your servant is listening." **11** The LORD said to Samuel: "I am about to do something in Israel that will cause the ears of everyone who hears it to ring. **12** On that day I will carry out in full against Eli everything I threatened against his family. **13** I announce to him that I am condemning his family once and for all, because of this crime: though he knew his sons were blaspheming God, he did not reprove them.[w] **14** Therefore, I swear to the family of Eli that no sacrifice or offering will ever expiate its crime." **15** Samuel then slept until morning, when he got up early and opened the doors of the temple of the LORD. He feared to tell Eli the vision, **16** but Eli called to him, "Samuel, my son!" He replied, "Here I am." **17** Then Eli asked, "What did he say to you? Hide nothing from me! May God do thus and so to you* if you hide a single thing he told you." **18** So Samuel told him everything, and held nothing back. Eli answered, "He is the LORD. He will do what he judges best."

**Samuel Acknowledged as Prophet.** **19** Samuel grew up, and the LORD was with him, not permitting any word of his to be without effect.[x] **20** [y]Thus all Israel from Dan to Beer-sheba came to know that Samuel was an accredited prophet of the LORD. **21** The LORD continued to appear at Shiloh; he manifested himself to Samuel at Shiloh through his word, **1** *and Samuel spoke to all Israel.

## CHAPTER 4

**Defeat of the Israelites.** At that time, the Philistines gathered for an attack on Israel. Israel went out to engage them in battle and camped at Ebenezer, while the Philistines camped at Aphek. **2** The Philistines then drew up in battle formation against Israel. After a fierce struggle Israel was defeated by the Philistines, who slew about four thousand men on the battlefield. **3** When the troops retired to the camp, the elders of Israel said, "Why has the LORD permitted us to be defeated today by the Philistines? Let us fetch the ark of the LORD from Shiloh that it may go into battle among us and save us from the grasp of our enemies."

**Loss of the Ark.** **4** So the people sent to Shiloh and brought from there the ark of the LORD of hosts, who is enthroned upon the cherubim.* The two sons of Eli, Hophni and Phinehas, were with the ark of God.[z] **5** When the ark of the LORD arrived in the camp, all Israel shouted so loudly that the earth resounded. **6** The Philistines, hearing the noise of shouting, asked, "What can this loud shouting in the

t 1 Sm 4, 11.
u 2 Kgs 23, 9.
v Ex 25, 22; 27, 20f; Lv 24, 2. 4; 2 Chr 13, 11.
w 1 Sm 2, 27-36.
x 1 Sm 2, 21.
y Jgs 20, 1.
z Ex 25, 22.

*

3, 1: Uncommon: prophetic communications from God were almost unknown.

3, 17: May God do thus and so to you: the Biblical writers avoid repeating for us the specific terms of a curse as the speaker would have uttered it.

3, 1: And . . . Israel: this belongs to ch 4.

4, 4: Enthroned upon the cherubim: this title of the Lord seems to have originated in the sanctuary at Shiloh; it represents the divine Majesty as seated upon a throne on which he can be borne through the heavens by winged creatures somewhat as in the visions of Ez 1 and 10.

camp of the Hebrews mean?'' On learning that
the ark of the LORD had come into the camp,
7 the Philistines were frightened. They said,
"Gods have come to their camp." They said
also, "Woe to us! This has never happened
before. 8 Woe to us! Who can deliver us from
the power of these mighty gods?* These are the
gods that struck the Egyptians with various
plagues and with pestilence. 9 Take courage
and be manly, Philistines; otherwise you will
become slaves to the Hebrews, as they were
your slaves. So fight manfully!" 10 The Philistines fought and Israel was defeated; every man
fled to his own tent. It was a disastrous defeat,
in which Israel lost thirty thousand foot soldiers.[a] 11 The ark of God was captured, and
Eli's two sons, Hophni and Phinehas, were
among the dead.[b]

**Death of Eli.** 12 A Benjaminite fled from
the battlefield and reached Shiloh that same
day, with his clothes torn and his head covered
with dirt.[c] 13 When he arrived, Eli was sitting
in his chair beside the gate, watching the road,
for he was troubled at heart about the ark of
God. The man, however, went into the city to
divulge his news, which put the whole city in an
uproar. 14 Hearing the outcry of the men standing near him, Eli inquired, "What does this
commotion mean?" 15 (Eli was ninety-eight
years old, and his eyes would not focus, so that
he could not see.) 16 The man quickly came up
to Eli and said, "It is I who have come from the
battlefield; I fled from there today." He asked,
"What happened, my son?" 17 And the messenger answered: "Israel fled from the Philistines; in fact, the troops suffered heavy losses.
Your two sons, Hophni and Phinehas, are
among the dead, and the ark of God has been
captured." 18 At this mention of the ark of
God, Eli fell backward from his chair into the
gateway; since he was an old man and heavy,
he died of a broken neck. He had judged Israel
for forty years.

19 His daughter-in-law, the wife of Phinehas, was with child and at the point of giving
birth. When she heard the news concerning the
capture of the ark and the deaths of her father-in-law and her husband, she was seized
with the pangs of labor, and gave birth. 20 She
was about to die when the women standing
around her said to her, "Never fear! You have
given birth to a son." Yet she neither answered
nor paid any attention.[d] 21 [She named the
child Ichabod, saying, "Gone is the glory from
Israel," with reference to the capture of the ark
of God and to her father-in-law and her husband.] 22 She said, "Gone is the glory from
Israel," because the ark of God had been captured.[e]

## CHAPTER 5

**The Ark in the Temple of Dagon.** 1 [f]The
Philistines, having captured the ark of God,
transferred it from Ebenezer to Ashdod. 2 They
then took the ark of God and brought it into the
temple of Dagon, placing it beside Dagon.
3 When the people of Ashdod rose early the
next morning, Dagon was lying prone on the
ground before the ark of the LORD. So they
picked Dagon up and replaced him. 4 But the
next morning early, when they arose, Dagon lay
prone on the ground before the ark of the LORD,
his head and hands broken off and lying on the
threshold, his trunk alone intact. 5 For this reason, neither the priests of Dagon nor any others
who enter the temple of Dagon tread on the
threshold of Dagon in Ashdod to this very day;
they always step over it.

**The Ark is Carried About.** 6 Now the
LORD dealt severely with the people of Ashdod.
He ravaged and afflicted the city and its vicinity
with hemorrhoids; he brought upon the city a
great and deadly plague of mice* that swarmed
in their ships and overran their fields.[g] 7 On
seeing how matters stood, the men of Ashdod
decided, "The ark of the God of Israel must not
remain with us, for he is handling us and our
god Dagon severely." 8 So they summoned all
the Philistine lords and inquired of them,
"What shall we do with the ark of the God of
Israel?" The men of Gath replied, "Let them
move the ark of the God of Israel on to us."
9 So they moved the ark of the God of Israel to
Gath! But after it had been brought there, the
LORD threw the city into utter turmoil: he afflicted its inhabitants, young and old, and hemorrhoids broke out on them. 10 The ark of God was
next sent to Ekron; but as it entered that city, the
people there cried out, "Why have they brought
the ark of the God of Israel here to kill us and
our kindred?" 11 Then they, too, sent a summons to all the Philistine lords and pleaded:
"Send away the ark of God of Israel. Let it
return to its own place, that it may not kill us
and our kindred." A deadly panic had seized the
whole city, since the hand of God had been very
heavy upon it. 12 Those who escaped death

a Ps 78, 61.
b 1 Sm 2, 34.
c Jos 7, 6; 2 Sm 1, 2; Jer 7, 12.
d 1 Sm 14, 3; Gn 35, 16ff.
e Ps 78, 61.
f 1-5: Jgs 16, 23-30; Is 45, 5f. 20f.
g Ps 78, 66.

*

4, 8: These mighty gods: the Philistines, who were polytheists, are represented as supposing the Israelites honored several gods.

5, 6: Hemorrhoids . . . mice: a double calamity fell upon them—a plague of mice or rats, and a severe epidemic of pestilential tumors, probably the bubonic plague.

were afflicted with hemorrhoids, and the outcry from the city went up to the heavens.

## CHAPTER 6

**The Ark To Be Returned.** **1** The ark of the LORD had been in the land of the Philistines seven months **2** when they summoned priests and fortune-tellers to ask, "What shall we do with the ark of the LORD? Tell us what we should send back with it." **3** They replied: "If you intend to send away the ark of the God of Israel, you must not send it alone, but must, by all means, make amends to him through a guilt offering.* Then you will be healed, and will learn why he continues to afflict you." **4** When asked further, "What guilt offering should be our amends to him?", they replied:

"Five golden hemorrhoids and five golden mice to correspond to the number of Philistine lords, since the same plague has struck all of you and your lords. **5** Therefore, make images of the hemorrhoids and of the mice that are infesting your land and give them as a tribute to the God of Israel. Perhaps then he will cease to afflict you, your gods, and your land. **6** Why should you become stubborn, as the Egyptians and Pharaoh were stubborn? Was it not after he had dealt ruthlessly with them that the Israelites were released and departed?[h] **7** So now set to work and make a new cart. Then take two milch cows that have not borne the yoke; hitch them to the cart, but drive their calves indoors away from them.[i] **8** You shall next take the ark of the LORD and place it on the cart, putting in a box beside it the golden articles that you are offering, as amends for your guilt. Start it on its way, and let it go. **9** Then watch! If it goes up to Beth-shemesh along the route to his own territory, he has brought this great calamity upon us; if not, we will know it was not he who struck us, but that an accident happened to us."

**The Ark in Beth-shemesh.** **10** They acted upon this advice. Taking two milch cows, they hitched them to the cart but shut up their calves indoors. **11** Then they placed the ark of the LORD on the cart, along with the box containing the golden mice and the images of the hemorrhoids. **12** The cows went straight for the route to Beth-shemesh and continued along this road, mooing as they went, without turning right or left. The Philistine lords followed them as far as the border of Beth-shemesh. **13** The people of Beth-shemesh were harvesting the wheat in the valley. When they looked up and spied the ark, they greeted it with rejoicing. **14** The cart came to the field of Joshua the Beth-shemite and stopped there. At a large stone in the field, the wood of the cart was split up and the cows were offered as a holocaust to the LORD.[j] **15** The Levites, meanwhile, had taken down the ark of God and the box beside it, in which the golden articles were, and had placed them on the great stone. The men of Beth-shemesh also offered other holocausts and sacrifices to the LORD that day. **16** After witnessing this, the five Philistine lords returned to Ekron the same day.

**Guilt Offering.** **17** The golden hemorrhoids the Philistines sent back as a guilt offering to the LORD were as follows: one for Ashdod, one for Gaza, one for Ashkelon, one for Gath, and one for Ekron. **18** The golden mice, however, corresponded to the number of all the cities of the Philistines belonging to the five lords, including fortified cities and open villages. The large stone on which the ark of the LORD was placed is still in the field of Joshua the Beth-shemite at the present time.

**Penalty for Irreverence.** **19** The descendants of Jeconiah did not join in the celebration with the inhabitants of Beth-shemesh when they greeted the ark of the LORD, and seventy of them were struck down. The people went into mourning at this great calamity with which the LORD had afflicted them. **20** The men of Beth-shemesh asked, "Who can stand in the presence of this Holy One? To whom shall he go from us?" **21** They then sent messengers to the inhabitants of Kiriath-jearim, saying, "The Philistines have returned the ark of the LORD; come down and get it."

## CHAPTER 7

**1** So the inhabitants of Kiriath-jearim came for the ark of the LORD and brought it into the house of Abinadab on the hill, appointing his son Eleazar as guardian of the ark of the LORD.

**Religious Reform.** **2** From the day the ark came to rest in Kiriath-jearim a long time, twenty years, elapsed, and the whole Israelite population turned to the LORD. **3** Samuel said to them: "If you wish with your whole heart to return to the LORD, put away your foreign gods and your Ashtaroth, devote yourselves to the LORD, and worship him alone. Then he will deliver you from the power of the Philistines."[k] **4** So the Israelites put away their Baals and Ashtaroth, and worshiped the LORD alone. **5** Samuel then gave orders, "Gather all Israel

h Ex 7, 14; 8, 15; 9, 34.
i Nm 19, 2; Dt 21, 3; 2 Sm 6, 3.
j 2 Sm 24, 21ff.
k 1 Sm 12, 10. 20. 24; Jos 24, 23; Jgs 6, 6-10; 10, 10-16.
l 1 Sm 10, 17; Jgs 20, 1.

*

6, 3: A guilt offering: a propitiatory offering customary after unwitting transgression of the ordinances of God regarding holy things or property rights; cf Lv 6, 1ff.

to Mizpah, that I may pray to the LORD for
you."[l] **6** When they were gathered at Mizpah,
they drew water and poured it out on the
ground* before the LORD, and they fasted that
day, confessing, "We have sinned against the
LORD." It was at Mizpah that Samuel began to
judge the Israelites.[m]

**Rout of the Philistines.** **7** When the Philistines heard that the Israelites had gathered at
Mizpah, their lords went up against Israel.
Hearing this, the Israelites became afraid of the
Philistines **8** and said to Samuel, "Implore the
LORD our God unceasingly for us, to save us
from the clutches of the Philistines."[n] **9** Samuel therefore took an unweaned lamb and offered
it entire as a holocaust to the LORD.[o] He implored the LORD for Israel, and the LORD heard
him. **10** While Samuel was offering the holocaust, the Philistines advanced to join battle
with Israel. That day, however, the LORD thundered loudly against the Philistines, and threw
them into such confusion that they were defeated by Israel. **11** Thereupon the Israelites sallied
forth from Mizpah and pursued the Philistines,
harrying them down beyond Bethcar. **12** Samuel then took a stone and placed it between Mizpah and Jeshanah; he named it Ebenezer,* explaining, "To this point has the LORD helped
us." **13** Thus were the Philistines subdued,
never again to enter the territory of Israel, for
the LORD was severe with them as long as Samuel lived.[p] **14** The cities from Ekron to Gath
which the Philistines had taken from Israel were
restored to them. Israel also freed the territory
of these cities from the dominion of the Philistines. Moreover there was peace between Israel
and the Amorites.
**15** Samuel judged Israel as long as he lived.
**16** He made a yearly journey, passing through
Bethel, Gilgal and Mizpah and judging Israel at
each of these sanctuaries. **17** Then he used to
return to Ramah, for that was his home. There,
too, he judged Israel and built an altar to the
LORD.[q]

## *II: Establishment of the Monarchy in Israel*

### CHAPTER 8*

**Request for a King.** **1** In his old age Samuel appointed his sons judges over Israel. **2** His
first-born was named Joel, his second son, Abijah; they judged at Beer-sheba. **3** His sons did
not follow his example but sought illicit gain
and accepted bribes, perverting justice.[r]
**4** Therefore all the elders of Israel came in a
body to Samuel at Ramah **5** and said to him,
"Now that you are old, and your sons do not
follow your example, appoint a king over us, as
other nations have, to judge us."[s]

**God Grants the Request.** **6** Samuel was
displeased when they asked for a king to judge
them. He prayed to the LORD, however, **7** who
said in answer: "Grant the people's every request. It is not you they reject, they are rejecting
me as their king.[t] **8** As they have treated me
constantly from the day I brought them up from
Egypt to this day, deserting me and worshiping
strange gods, so do they treat you too. **9** Now
grant their request; but at the same time, warn
them solemnly and inform them of the rights of
the king who will rule them."

**The Rights of a King.** **10** Samuel delivered the message of the LORD in full to those
who were asking him for a king. **11** He told
them: "The rights of the king who will rule you
will be as follows: He will take your sons and
assign them to his chariots and horses, and they
will run before his chariot.[u] **12** He will also
appoint from among them his commanders of
groups of a thousand and of a hundred soldiers.
He will set them to do his plowing and his
harvesting, and to make his implements of war
and the equipment of his chariots.[v] **13** He will
use your daughters as ointment-makers, as
cooks, and as bakers. **14** He will take the best
of your fields, vineyards, and olive groves, and
give them to his officials.[w] **15** He will tithe
your crops and your vineyards, and give the
revenue to his eunuchs and his slaves. **16** He
will take your male and female servants, as well
as your best oxen and your asses, and use them
to do his work. **17** He will tithe your flocks and
you yourselves will become his slaves.[x]
**18** When this takes place, you will complain

m Jgs 20, 26; Ps 22, 14; Lam 2, 19.
n Ex 17, 9-13.
o 9f: 2 Sm 22, 14f; Sir 46, 16ff.
p Jgs 3, 30; 8, 28; 11, 33.
q 1 Sm 9, 12; 14, 35.
r Ex 23, 8; Dt 16, 19; Prv 17, 23.
s 5f: Dt 17, 14f; Hos 13, 10; Acts 13, 21.
t 7f: 1 Sm 12, 1. 12f; Jgs 8, 22f; 10, 13; 1 Kgs 9, 9.
u 1 Sm 10, 25; Dt 17, 14-20; 1 Kgs 12.
v 2 Sm 15, 1; 1 Kgs 1, 5.
w 1 Sm 22, 7; 1 Kgs 21, 1-24; Ez 46, 18.
x 1 Kgs 12, 4.

*

7, 6: Poured it out on the ground: for the symbolism, cf 2 Sm 14, 14.

7, 12: Ebenezer: or eben ha-ezer, means "stone of help."

8, 1: From this chapter on, the First Book of Samuel gives us two and sometimes three viewpoints on most of the events with which it is concerned, such as the appointment of Saul as king, the reasons for his downfall, his relationship with David, even the circumstances of Saul's death (1 Sm 31; 2 Sm 1). The choice of Saul as king is seen, in ch 8, followed by 10, 17–27 and ch 12, as motivated by the people's defection from the proper service of God; this later editorial approach incorporates not only narratives with which it is consistent, but also early traditions (9, 1–10. 16; ch 11) which portray the events and their motivation quite differently.

against the king whom you have chosen, but on
that day the LORD will not answer you."

**Persistent Demand.** **19** The people, however, refused to listen to Samuel's warning and
said, "Not so! There must be a king over us.[y]
**20** We too must be like other nations, with a
king to rule us and to lead us in warfare and fight
our battles." **21** When Samuel had listened to
all the people had to say, he repeated it to the
LORD, **22** *who then said to him, "Grant their
request and appoint a king to rule them." Samuel thereupon said to the men of Israel, "Each of
you go to his own city."

## CHAPTER 9

**1** There was a stalwart man from Benjamin
named Kish, who was the son of Abiel, son of
Zeror, son of Becorath, son of Aphiah, a Benjaminite.[z] **2** He had a son named Saul, who was
a handsome young man. There was no other
Israelite handsomer than Saul; he stood head
and shoulders above the people.[a]

**The Lost Asses.** **3** Now the asses of Saul's
father, Kish, had wandered off. Kish said to his
son Saul, "Take one of the servants with you
and go out and hunt for the asses." **4** Accordingly they went through the hill country of
Ephraim, and through the land of Shalishah.
Not finding them there, they continued through
the land of Shaalim without success. They also
went through the land of Benjamin, but they
failed to find the animals. **5** When they came to
the land of Zuph, Saul said to the servant who
was with him, "Come, let us turn back, lest my
father forget about the asses and become anxious about us." **6** The servant replied, "Listen!
There is a man of God in this city, a man held
in high esteem; all that he says is sure to come
true. Let us go there now! Perhaps he can tell
us how to accomplish our errand." **7** [b]But Saul
said to his servant, "If we go, what can we offer
the man? There is no bread in our bags, and we
have no present to give the man of God. What
have we?" **8** Again the servant answered Saul,
"I have a quarter of a silver shekel.* If I give
that to the man of God, he will tell us our way."
**10** Saul then said to his servant, "Well said!
Come on, let us go!" And they went to the city
where the man of God lived.

**Quest for Samuel's Aid.** **11** [c]As they
were going up the ascent to the city, they met
some girls coming out to draw water and inquired of them, "Is the seer in town?" **9** [d](In
former times in Israel, anyone who sent to consult God used to say, "Come, let us go to the
seer." For he who is now called prophet was
formerly called seer.)* **12** [e]The girls answered,
"Yes, there—straight ahead. Hurry now; just
today he came to the city, because the people
have a sacrifice today on the high place.*
**13** When you enter the city, you may reach him
before he goes up to the high place to eat. The
people will not eat until he arrives; only after he
blesses the sacrifice will the invited guests eat.
Go up immediately, for you should find him
right now."

**Samuel's Revelation about Saul.** **14** So
they went up to the city. As they entered it,
Samuel was coming toward them on his way to
the high place. **15** The day before Saul's arrival, the LORD had given Samuel the revelation:[f]
**16** "At this time tomorrow I will send you a
man from the land of Benjamin whom you are
to anoint as commander of my people Israel. He
shall save my people from the clutches of the
Philistines, for I have witnessed their misery
and accepted their cry for help."[g] **17** When
Samuel caught sight of Saul, the LORD assured
him, "This is the man of whom I told you; he
is to govern my people." **18** Saul met Samuel
in the gateway and said, "Please tell me where
the seer lives." **19** Samuel answered Saul: "I
am the seer. Go up ahead of me to the high place
and eat with me today. In the morning, before
dismissing you, I will tell you whatever you
wish. **20** As for the asses you lost three days
ago, do not worry about them, for they have
been found. Whom does Israel desire ardently
if not you and your father's family?" **21** Saul
replied: "Am I not a Benjaminite, of one of the
smallest tribes of Israel, and is not my clan the
least among the clans of the tribe of Benjamin?
Why say such things to me?"[h]
**22** Samuel then took Saul and his servant and
brought them to the room, where he placed them
at the head of the guests, of whom there were
about thirty. **23** He said to the cook, "Bring the
portion I gave you and told you to put aside."
**24** So the cook took up the leg and what went

y 1 Sm 10, 19.
z 1 Sm 14, 51; 1 Chr 8, 33.
a 1 Sm 10, 23.
b 7f: Nm 22, 7; 1 Kgs 14, 3; 2 Kgs 4, 42; 5, 15; 8, 8f.
c Gn 24, 11ff; Ex 2, 16.
d Sir 46, 15.
e 1 Sm 7, 17; 16, 2. 5; 20, 6. 29; Dt 12, 13; 1 Kgs 3, 2. 4.
f Acts 13, 21.
g 1 Sm 10, 1.
h 1 Sm 15, 17.

*

9, 8: A quarter of a silver shekel: about a tenth of an ounce of silver.

9, 9: This verse is a later explanation of the term seer, first used in the text in 1 Sm 9, 11.

9, 12: On the high place: the local sanctuary on the top of a hill, where the sacrifice was offered and the sacrificial meal eaten.

9, 24: And what went with it: a slight change would give "and the fatty tail" as perhaps the original reading. Sheep in the Near East are exceptionally fat-tailed, and such a portion would be thought a special delicacy by the Hebrews. However, the ritual legislation as we know it (Lv 3, 9) would require that the fat tail be burned on the altar. If this general rule was later than the time of Samuel, the present text may have been

with it,* and placed it before Saul. Samuel said:
"This is a reserved portion that has been set
before you. Eat, for it was kept for you until
your arrival; I explained that I was inviting some
guests." Thus Saul dined with Samuel that day.
**25** When they came down from the high place
into the city, a mattress was spread for Saul on
the roof, **26** and he slept there.

**Saul's Anointing.** At daybreak Samuel
called to Saul on the roof, "Get up, and I will
start you on your journey." Saul rose, and he
and Samuel went outside the city together.
**27** As they were approaching the edge of the
town, Samuel said to Saul, "Tell the servant to
go on ahead of us, but stay here yourself for the
moment, that I may give you a message from
God."

## CHAPTER 10

**1** Then, from a flask he had with him, Samuel poured oil on Saul's head; he also kissed him,
saying: "The LORD anoints you commander
over his heritage. You are to govern the LORD's
people Israel, and to save them from the grasp
of their enemies roundabout.[i]

"This will be the sign for you that the LORD
has anointed you commander over his heritage:
**2** When you leave me today, you will meet two
men near Rachel's tomb* at Zelah in the territory of Benjamin, who will say to you, 'The asses
you went to look for have been found. Your
father is no longer worried about the asses, but
is anxious about you and says, What shall I do
about my son?'[j] **3** Farther on, when you arrive
at the terebinth of Tabor, you will be met by
three men going up to God at Bethel; one will
be bringing three kids, another three loaves of
bread, and the third a skin of wine. **4** They will
greet you and offer you two wave offerings of
bread, which you will take from them. **5** [k]After
that you will come to Gibeath-elohim, where
there is a garrison of the Philistines.* As you
enter that city, you will meet a band of prophets,
in a prophetic state, coming down from the high
place, preceded by lyres, tambourines, flutes
and harps. **6** The spirit of the LORD will rush
upon you, and you will join them in their prophetic state and will be changed into another
man.[l] **7** When you see these signs fulfilled, do
whatever you judge feasible, because God is
with you. **8** [m]Now go down ahead of me to
Gilgal, for I shall come down to you, to offer
holocausts and to sacrifice peace offerings.
Wait seven days until I come to you; I shall then
tell you what you must do."*

**Fulfillment of the Signs.** **9** As Saul turned
to leave Samuel, God gave him another heart.
That very day all these signs came to pass. . . .
**10** *When they were going from there to Gibeah, a band of prophets met him, and the spirit
of God rushed upon him, so that he joined them
in their prophetic state.[n] **11** When all who had
known him previously saw him in a prophetic
state among the prophets, they said to one another, "What has happened to the son of Kish?
Is Saul also among the prophets?"[o] **12** And
someone from that district added, "And who is
their father?" Thus the proverb arose, "Is Saul
also among the prophets?" **13** When he came
out of the prophetic state, he went home.

**Silence about the Kingship.** **14** Saul's
uncle inquired of him and his servant, "Where
have you been?" Saul replied, "To look for the
asses. When we could not find them, we went
to Samuel." **15** Then Saul's uncle said, "Tell
me, then, what Samuel said to you." **16** Saul
said to his uncle, "He assured us that the asses
had been found." But he mentioned nothing to
him of what Samuel had said about the kingship.

**Saul Chosen King by Lot.** **17** Samuel
called the people together to the LORD at Mizpah[p] **18** and addressed the Israelites: "Thus
says the LORD, the God of Israel, 'It was I who
brought Israel up from Egypt and delivered you
from the power of the Egyptians and from the
power of all the kingdoms that oppressed you.'[q]
**19** But today you have rejected your God, who
delivers you from all your evils and calamities,
by saying to him, 'Not so, but you must appoint
a king over us.' Now, therefore, take your stand
before the LORD according to tribes and families."[r] **20** So Samuel had had all the tribes of
Israel come forward, and the tribe of Benjamin
was chosen. **21** Next he had the tribe of Benja-

i 1 Sm 9, 16f; 24, 7; Jgs 9, 9; 1 Kgs 1, 39; Acts 13, 21.
j Jer 31, 15; Mk 14, 13.
k 5f: 1 Sm 13, 3; 16, 13; 19, 20f.
l 1 Sm 11, 6; 16, 13; Jgs 14, 6. 19; 15, 14; 2 Kgs 3, 15.
m 1 Sm 13, 8; Lv 3, 1.
n 1 Sm 19, 20-24; Nm 11, 25.
o 1 Sm 19, 24.
p 1 Sm 7, 5.
q Ex 20, 2; Lv 11, 45; 25, 38; Nm 15, 41; Dt 5, 6; Jgs 6, 8f.
r 1 Sm 8, 19.

*

retouched so as not to seem to contravene it. A Qumran text has "the festive (leg)" here.

10, 2: Here, as in Jer 31, 15, Rachel's tomb is placed north of Jerusalem. Later tradition understood Gn 35, 19f in the sense given by Mt 2, 16ff, and placed the tomb at Bethlehem, farther south.

10, 5: A garrison of the Philistines: the Hebrew word for "garrison" has been explained alternatively to mean a pillar erected to mark the Philistine occupation, or an inspector or officer for the collection of taxes. In a prophetic state: in an ecstatic condition due to strong feelings of religious enthusiasm induced by a communal observance, possibly accompanied by music and dancing.

10, 8: By inserting this verse, with its seven days, an editor has prepared for one narrative of the rejection of Saul (1 Sm 13, 8–15) in the very context of Saul's anointing.

10, 10: The story has here been abridged by omitting the fulfillment of the first two signs given by Samuel (1 Sm 10, 2ff).

min come forward in clans, and the clan of
Matri was chosen, and finally Saul, son of Kish,
was chosen. But they looked for him in vain.
**22** [s]Again they consulted the LORD, "Has he
come here?" The LORD answered, "He is hiding among the baggage." **23** They ran to bring
him from there; and when he stood among the
people, he was head and shoulders above all the
crowd.[t] **24** Samuel said to all the people, "Do
you see the man whom the LORD has chosen?
There is none like him among all the people!"
Then all the people shouted, "Long live the
king!"[u]

**25** Samuel next explained to the people the
law of royalty* and wrote it in a book, which he
placed in the presence of the LORD. This done,
Samuel dismissed the people, each to his own
place.[v] **26** Saul also went home to Gibeah, accompanied by warriors whose hearts the LORD
had touched. **27** But certain worthless men
said, "How can this fellow save us?" They
despised him and brought him no present.[w]

## CHAPTER 11

**Defeat of the Ammonites.** **1** About a
month later,* Nahash the Ammonite went up
and laid siege to Jabesh-gilead. All the men of
Jabesh begged Nahash, "Make a treaty with us,
and we will be your subjects."[x] **2** But Nahash
the Ammonite replied, "This is my condition
for a treaty with you: I must gouge out every
man's right eye, that I may thus bring ignominy
on all Israel." **3** The elders of Jabesh said to
him: "Give us seven days to send messengers
throughout the territory of Israel. If no one rescues us, we will surrender to you." **4** When the
messengers arrived at Gibeah of Saul, they related the news to the people, all of whom wept
aloud. **5** Just then Saul came in from the field,
behind his oxen. "Why are the people weeping?" he asked. The message of the inhabitants
of Jabesh was repeated to him. **6** As he listened
to this report, the spirit of God rushed upon him
and he became very angry.[y] **7** Taking a yoke of
oxen, he cut them into pieces, which he sent
throughout the territory of Israel by couriers
with the message, "If anyone does not come out
to follow Saul [and Samuel], the same as this
will be done to his oxen!" In dread of the LORD,
the people turned out to a man.[z] **8** When he
reviewed them in Bezek, there were three hundred thousand Israelites and seventy thousand
Judahites.

**9** To the messengers who had come he said,
"Tell the inhabitants of Jabesh-gilead that tomorrow, while the sun is hot, they will be rescued." The messengers came and reported this
to the inhabitants of Jabesh, who were jubilant,
**10** and said to Nahash, "Tomorrow we will
surrender to you, and you may do whatever you
please with us." **11** On the appointed day, Saul
arranged his troops in three companies and invaded the camp during the dawn watch. They
slaughtered Ammonites until the heat of the
day; by then the survivors were so scattered that
no two were left together.

**Saul Accepted as King.** **12** *The people
then said to Samuel: "Who questioned whether
Saul should rule over us? Hand over the men
and we will put them to death."[a] **13** But Saul
broke in to say, "No man is to be put to death
this day, for today the LORD has saved Israel."[b]
**14** Samuel said to the people, "Come, let us go
to Gilgal to inaugurate the kingdom there."
**15** So all the people went to Gilgal, where, in
the presence of the LORD, they made Saul king.
They also sacrificed peace offerings there before the LORD, and Saul and all the Israelites
celebrated the occasion with great joy.

## CHAPTER 12

**Samuel's Integrity.** **1** Samuel addressed
all Israel: "I have granted your request in every
respect," he said. "I have set a king over you[c]
**2** and now the king is your leader. As for me,
I am old and gray, and have sons among you.
I have lived with you from my youth to the
present day. **3** Here I stand! Answer me in the
presence of the LORD and of his anointed.
Whose ox have I taken? Whose ass have I tak-
en? Whom have I cheated? Whom have I oppressed? From whom have I accepted a bribe
and overlooked his guilt? I will make restitution
to you."[d] **4** They replied, "You have neither
cheated us, nor oppressed us, nor accepted anything from anyone." **5** So he said to them,
"The LORD is witness against you this day, and
his anointed as well, that you have found nothing in my possession." "He is witness," they
agreed.

s 1 Sm 30, 24.
t 1 Sm 9, 2; 16, 7.
u 2 Sm 16, 16; 1 Kgs 1, 25; 2 Kgs 11, 12.
v 1 Sm 8, 11; Dt 17, 14-20.
w 1 Sm 11, 12.
x 1 Sm 12, 12; 31, 11.
y 1 Sm 16, 13; Jgs 14, 6. 19.
z 1 Kgs 11, 30; 2 Kgs 13, 18.
a 1 Sm 10, 27.
b 2 Sm 19, 23.
c 1 Sm 8, 7. 9. 22.
d Ex 20, 17; 23, 8; Nm 16, 15; Dt 16, 19; Sir 46, 19.

*

10, 25: The law of royalty: the charter defining the rights of the king.

11, 1: About a month later: there is ancient evidence for a longer introduction to this campaign. The time indication here may refer to its earlier stages rather than to the events of ch 10.

11, 12–14: With these verses, an editor has harmonized the account of the acknowledgment of Saul as king at Mizpah (1 Sm 10, 17–24) with the public acclamation at Gilgal (1 Sm 11, 15) after the defeat of the Ammonites (1 Sm 11, 1–11). The Greek text of 1 Sm 11, 15 reads "and Samuel anointed Saul as king," instead of they made Saul king.

**Samuel Upbraids the People.** 6 Continuing, Samuel said to the people: "The LORD is
witness, who appointed Moses and Aaron, and
who brought your fathers up from the land of
Egypt.[e] 7 Now, therefore, take your stand, and
I shall arraign you before the LORD, and shall
recount for you all the acts of mercy the LORD
has done for you and your fathers. 8 When
Jacob and his sons went to Egypt and the Egyptians oppressed them, your fathers appealed to
the LORD, who sent Moses and Aaron to bring
them out of Egypt, and he gave them this place
to live in.[f] 9 But they forgot the LORD their
God; and he allowed them to fall into the
clutches of Sisera, the captain of the army of
Jabin, king of Hazor, into the grasp of the Philistines, and into the grip of the king of Moab,
who made war against them.[g] 10 Each time
they appealed to the LORD and said, 'We have
sinned in forsaking the LORD and worshiping
Baals and Ashtaroth; but deliver us now from
the power of our enemies, and we will worship
you.'[h] 11 Accordingly, the LORD sent Jerubbaal, Barak, Jephthah, and Samson; he delivered
you from the power of your enemies on every
side, so that you were able to live in security.[i]
12 Yet, when you saw Nahash, king of the
Ammonites, advancing against you, you said to
me, 'Not so, but a king must rule us,' even
though the LORD your God is your king.[j]

**Warnings for People and King.**
13 "Now you have the king you want, a king
the LORD has given you.[k] 14 If you fear the
LORD and worship him, if you are obedient to
him and do not rebel against the LORD's command, if both you and the king who rules you
follow the LORD your God—well and good.
15 But if you do not obey the LORD and if you
rebel against his command, the LORD will deal
severely with you and your king, and destroy
you. 16 Now then, stand ready to witness the
great marvel the LORD is about to accomplish
before your eyes. 17 Are we not in the harvest
time for wheat? Yet I shall call to the LORD, and
he will send thunder and rain. Thus you will see
and understand how greatly the LORD is displeased that you have asked for a king."[l]
18 Samuel then called to the LORD, and the
LORD sent thunder and rain that day.

**Assistance Promised.** As a result, all the
people dreaded the LORD and Samuel. 19 They
said to Samuel, "Pray to the LORD your God for
us, your servants, that we may not die for having added to all our other sins the evil of asking
for a king." 20 "Do not fear," Samuel answered them. "It is true you have committed all
this evil; still, you must not turn from the LORD,
but must worship him with your whole heart.
21 Do not turn to meaningless idols which can
neither profit nor save; they are nothing.[m]
22 For the sake of his own great name the LORD
will not abandon his people, since the LORD
himself chose to make you his people.[n] 23 As
for me, far be it from me to sin against the LORD
by ceasing to pray for you and to teach you the
good and right way.[o] 24 But you must fear the
LORD and worship him faithfully with your
whole heart; keep in mind the great things he has
done among you. 25 If instead you continue to
do evil, both you and your king shall perish."

## III: *Saul and David*

### CHAPTER 13

1 [Saul was . . . years old when he became
king and he reigned . . . (two) years over Israel.]*

**Saul Offers Sacrifice.** 2 Saul chose three
thousand men of Israel, of whom two thousand
remained with him in Michmash and in the hill
country of Bethel, and one thousand were with
Jonathan in Gibeah of Benjamin. He sent the
rest of the people back to their tents. 3 Now
Jonathan overcame the Philistine garrison*
which was in Gibeah, and the Philistines got
word of it. Then Saul sounded the horn throughout the land, with a proclamation, "Let the
Hebrews hear!"[p] 4 Thus all Israel learned that
Saul had overcome the garrison of the Philistines and that Israel had brought disgrace upon
the Philistines; and the soldiers were called up
to Saul in Gilgal. 5 The Philistines also assembled for battle, with three thousand chariots, six
thousand horsemen, and foot soldiers as numerous as the sands of the seashore. Moving up
against Israel, they encamped in Michmash,
east of Beth-aven. 6 Some Israelites, aware of
the danger and of the difficult situation, hid
themselves in caves, in thickets, among rocks,

e Mi 6, 4.
f Gn 46, 5; Ex 1, 11; 2, 23ff.
g Jgs 3, 12ff; 4, 2f; 10, 7; 13, 1.
h 1 Sm 7, 3f.
i Jgs 6, 14. 32; 11, 1.
j 1 Sm 8, 6f. 19; 11, 1f; Jgs 8, 23.
k 1 Sm 8, 7.
l Ex 9, 23. 28ff; 1 Kgs 18, 1.
m Dt 32, 37ff.
n Jer 14, 21; Ex 20, 9; Dn 3, 34.
o Ex 32, 11.
p 1 Sm 14, 1-15; Jgs 3, 27; 6, 34; 2 Sm 20, 1f.
q 1 Sm 14, 22.

*

13, 1: A formula like that of 2 Sm 5, 4 was introduced here at some time; but the age of Saul when he became king remains a blank, and the two years assigned for his reign in the received text cannot be correct. Tradition (Acts 13, 21) offers the round number, "forty years."

13, 3–4: The Philistine garrison: see note on 1 Sm 10, 5. Let the Hebrews hear: a different reading of these verses, based on the Greek, would yield: "And the Philistines heard that the Hebrews (or: the slaves) had revolted. Saul in the meantime sounded the trumpet throughout all the land (v 4), and all Israel heard that Saul. . . ."

in caverns, and in cisterns,[q] **7** and other Hebrews passed over the Jordan into the land of Gad and Gilead. Saul, however, held out at Gilgal, although all his followers were seized with fear.* **8** He waited seven days—the time Samuel had determined. When Samuel did not arrive at Gilgal, the men began to slip away from Saul.[r] **9** He then said, "Bring me the holocaust and peace offerings," and he offered up the holocaust.

**King Saul Reproved.** **10** He had just finished this offering when Samuel arrived. Saul went out to greet him, **11** and Samuel asked him, "What have you done?" Saul replied: "When I saw that the men were slipping away from me, since you had not come by the specified time, and with the Philistines assembled at Michmash, **12** I said to myself, 'Now the Philistines will come down against me at Gilbal, and I have not yet sought the LORD's blessing.' So in my anxiety I offered up the holocaust." **13** Samuel's response was: "You have been foolish! Had you kept the command the LORD your God gave you, the LORD would now establish your kingship in Israel as lasting; **14** but as things are, your kingdom shall not endure. The LORD has sought out a man after his own heart and has appointed him commander of his people, because you broke the LORD's command."[s]

**Philistine Invasion.** **15** Then Samuel set out from Gilgal and went his own way; but the rest of the people went up after Saul to meet the soldiers, going from Gilgal to Gibeah of Benjamin. Saul then numbered the soldiers he had with him, who were about six hundred.[t] **16** Saul, his son Jonathan, and the soldiers they had with them were now occupying Geba of Benjamin, and the Philistines were encamped at Michmash. **17** Meanwhile, raiders left the camp of the Philistines in three bands.[u] One band took the Ophrah road toward the district of Shual; **18** another turned in the direction of Beth-horon; and the third took the road for Geba that overlooks the Valley of the Hyenas toward the desert.

**Disarmament of Israel.** **19** Not a single smith was to be found in the whole land of Israel, for the Philistines had said, "Otherwise the Hebrews will make swords or spears."[v] **20** All Israel, therefore, had to go down to the Philistines to sharpen their plowshares, mattocks, axes, and sickles. **21** The price for the plowshares and mattocks was two-thirds of a shekel, and a third of a shekel for sharpening the axes and for setting the ox-goads. **22** And so on the day of battle neither sword nor spear could be found in the possession of any of the soldiers with Saul or Jonathan. Only Saul and his son Jonathan had them.

**Jonathan's Exploit.** **23** An outpost of the Philistines had pushed forward to the pass of Michmash.[w]

## CHAPTER 14

**1** One day Jonathan, son of Saul, said to his armor-bearer, "Come, let us go over to the Philistine outpost on the other side." But he did not inform his father.[x] **2** (Saul's command post was under the pomegranate tree near the threshing floor on the outskirts of Geba; those with him numbered about six hundred men. **3** Ahijah, son of Ahitub, brother of Ichabod, who was the son of Phinehas, son of Eli, the priest of the LORD at Shiloh, was wearing the ephod.) Nor did the soldiers know that Jonathan had gone.[y] **4** Flanking the ravine through which Jonathan intended to get over to the Philistine outpost there was a rocky crag on each side, one called Bozez, the other Seneh. **5** One crag was to the north, toward Michmash, the other to the south, toward Geba. **6** Jonathan said to his armor-bearer: "Come, let us go over to that outpost of the uncircumcised. Perhaps the LORD will help us, because it is no more difficult for the LORD to grant victory through a few than through many."[z] **7** His armor-bearer replied, "Do whatever you are inclined to do; I will match your resolve." **8** Jonathan continued: "We shall go over to those men and show ourselves to them. **9** If they say to us, "Stay there until we can come to you,' we shall stop where we are; we shall not go up to them. **10** But if they say, 'Come up to us,' we shall go up, because the LORD has delivered them into our grasp. That will be our sign." **11** Accordingly, the two of them appeared before the outpost of the Philistines, who said, "Look, some Hebrews are coming out of the holes where they have been hiding." **12** The men of the outpost called to Jonathan and his armor-bearer. "Come up here," they said, "and we will teach you a lesson." So Jonathan said to his armor-bearer, "Climb up after me, for the LORD has delivered them into the grasp of Israel." **13** Jonathan clambered up with his armor-bearer behind him; as the Philistines turned to flee him, he cut them down, and his armor-bearer followed him and

r 1 Sm 10, 8.
s 1 Sm 25, 30; 2 Sm 7, 15f; Ps 78, 70; Acts 13, 22.
t 1 Sm 14, 2.
u 1 Sm 14, 15.
v Jgs 5, 8.
w 1 Sm 14, 15.
x 1 Sm 13, 3.
y 1 Sm 2, 28; 4, 21; 14, 18; 23, 9; 30, 7.
z 1 Sm 17, 26. 36. 47; Sir 39, 18; 1 Mc 3, 19.

* 13, 7–15: These verses, like 1 Sm 10, 8, anticipate the rejection of Saul; a different occasion and motivation for this are given in ch 15, resumed in 1 Sm 28, 17f.

finished them off. **14** In this first exploit Jonathan and his armor-bearer slew about twenty
men within half a furlong. **15** Then panic
spread to the army and to the countryside, and
all the soldiers, including the outpost and the
raiding parties, were terror-stricken. The earth
also shook, so that the panic was beyond human
endurance.

**Rout of the Philistines.** **16** The lookouts
of Saul in Geba of Benjamin saw that the enemy
camp had scattered and were running about in
all directions. **17** Saul said to those around him,
"Count the troops and find out if any of us are
missing." When they had investigated, they
found Jonathan and his armor-bearer missing.
**18** Saul then said to Ahijah, "Bring the ephod*
here." (Ahijah was wearing the ephod in front
of the Israelites at that time.) **19** While Saul
was speaking to the priest, the tumult in the
Philistine camp kept increasing. So he said to
the priest, "Withdraw your hand." **20** And
Saul and all his men shouted and rushed into the
fight, where the Philistines, wholly confused,
were thrusting swords at one another.[a] **21** In
addition, the Hebrews who had previously sided
with the Philistines and had gone up with them
to the camp, turned to join the Israelites under
Saul and Jonathan.[b] **22** Likewise, all the Israelites who were hiding in the hill country of
Ephraim, on hearing that the Philistines were
fleeing, pursued them in the rout.[c] **23** Thus the
LORD saved Israel that day.

**Saul's Oath.** The battle continued past
Beth-horon;* **24** the whole people, about ten
thousand combatants, were with Saul, and there
was scattered fighting in every town in the hill
country of Ephraim. And Saul swore a very rash
oath that day, putting the people under this ban:
"Cursed be the man who takes food before
evening, before I am able to avenge myself on
my enemies." So none of the people tasted
food. **25** Indeed, there was a honeycomb lying
on the ground, **26** and when the soldiers came
to the comb the swarm had left it; yet no one
would raise a hand to his mouth from it, because
the people feared the oath.

**Violation of the Oath.** **27** Jonathan, who
had not heard that his father had put the people
under oath, thrust out the end of the staff he was
holding and dipped it into the honey. Then he
raised it to his mouth and his eyes lit up. **28** At
this one of the soldiers spoke up: "Your father
put the people under a strict oath, saying,
'Cursed be the man who takes food this day!' As
a result the people are weak." **29** Jonathan replied: "My father brings trouble to the land.
Look how bright my eyes are from this small
taste of honey I have had. **30** What is more, if
the people had eaten freely today of their enemy's booty when they came across it, would not
the slaughter of the Philistines by now have
been the greater for it?"

**Use of Flesh with Blood Forbidden.**
**31** After the Philistines were routed that day
from Michmash to Aijalon, the people were
completely exhausted. **32** So they pounced
upon the spoil and took sheep, oxen and calves,
slaughtering them on the ground and eating the
flesh with blood.[d] **33** Informed that the people
were sinning against the LORD by eating the
flesh with blood, Saul said: "You have broken
faith. Roll a large stone here for me." **34** He
continued: "Mingle with the people and tell
each of them to bring his ox or his sheep to me.
Slaughter it here and then eat, but you must not
sin against the LORD by eating the flesh with
blood." So everyone brought to the LORD whatever ox he had seized, and they slaughtered
them there; **35** and Saul built an altar to the
LORD—this was the first time he built an altar
to the LORD.[e]

**Jonathan in Danger of Death.** **36** Then
Saul said, "Let us go down in pursuit of the
Philistines by night, to plunder among them
until daybreak and to kill them all off." They
replied, "Do what you think best." But the
priest said, "Let us consult God." **37** So Saul
inquired of God: "Shall I go down in pursuit of
the Philistines? Will you deliver them into the
power of Israel?" But he received no answer on
this occasion.[f] **38** Saul then said, "Come here,
all officers of the army. We must investigate
and find out how this sin was committed today.
**39** As the LORD lives who has given victory to
Israel, even if my son Jonathan has committed
it, he shall surely die!" But none of the people
answered him. **40** So he said to all Israel,
"Stand on one side, and I and my son Jonathan
will stand on the other." The people responded,
"Do what you think best."[g] **41** And Saul said

a Jgs 7, 22.
b 1 Sm 29, 4.
c 1 Sm 13, 6.
d 1 Sm 15, 19. 21; Lv 3, 17; 7, 26f; 17, 10-14; Acts 15, 20. 29.
e 1 Sm 7, 17; Jgs 6, 24.
f 1 Sm 28, 6. 15.
g Jos 7, 13ff.
h 1 Sm 28, 6; Ex 28, 30; Dt 33, 8.

*

14, 18: Ephod: to be used in consulting God; see note on v 41, and that on 1 Sm 2, 28, above.

14, 23: Past Beth-horon: this is a textual correction influenced by 1 Sm 13, 18; the received Hebrew text refers to Bethel (Bethaven), but the effect of the victory would seem to have been that the main ridge of mountains in the territories of Benjamin and Ephraim was cleared of Philistines.

14, 41: The Urim and Thummim, or sacred lots, were a device for ascertaining the will of God; they ceased to be used after the time of David. The material and the shape of these objects, and the manner in which they were used, are unknown. They gave a "yes" or "no" answer to specific questions.

to the LORD, the God of Israel: "Why did you
not answer your servant this time? If the blame
for this resides in me or my son Jonathan, LORD,
God of Israel, respond with Urim; but if this
guilt is in your people Israel, respond with
Thummim."* Jonathan and Saul were designated, and the people went free.[h] **42** Saul then
said, "Cast lots between me and my son Jonathan." And Jonathan was designated. **43** Saul
said to Jonathan, "Tell me what you have
done." Jonathan replied, "I only tasted a little
honey from the end of the staff I was holding.
Am I to die for this?" **44** Saul said, "May God
do thus and so to me if you do not indeed die,
Jonathan!"[i]

**Rescue of Jonathan.** **45** But the army
said to Saul: "Is Jonathan to die, though it was
he who brought Israel this great victory? This
must not be! As the LORD lives, not a single hair
of his head shall fall to the ground, for God was
with him in what he did today!" Thus the soldiers were able to rescue* Jonathan from death.[j]
**46** After that Saul gave up the pursuit of the
Philistines, who returned to their own territory.

**Wars and Victories.** **47** After taking over
the kingship of Israel, Saul waged war on all
their surrounding enemies—Moab, the Ammonites, Aram, Bethrehob, the king of Zobah,
and the Philistines. Wherever he turned, he was
successful[k] **48** and fought bravely. He defeated
Amalek and delivered Israel from the hands of
those who were plundering them.

**Saul's Family.** **49** The sons of Saul were
Jonathan, Ishvi,* and Malchishua; his two
daughters were named, the elder, Merob, and
the younger, Michal.[l] **50** Saul's wife, who was
named Ahinoam, was the daughter of Ahimaaz.
The name of his general was Abner, son of
Saul's uncle, Ner; **51** Kish, Saul's father, and
Ner, Abner's father, were sons of Abiel.[m]

**52** An unremitting war was waged against
the Philistines during Saul's lifetime. When
Saul saw any strong or brave man, he took him
into his service.

## CHAPTER 15

**1** Samuel said to Saul: "It was I the LORD
sent to anoint you king over his people Israel.
Now, therefore, listen to the message of the
LORD. **2** This is what the LORD of hosts has to
say: 'I will punish what Amalek did to Israel
when he barred his way as he was coming up
from Egypt.[n] **3** Go, now, attack Amalek, and
deal with him and all that he has under the ban.*
Do not spare him, but kill men and women,
children and infants, oxen and sheep, camels
and asses.' "[o]

**Disobedience of Saul.** **4** Saul alerted the
soldiers, and at Telaim reviewed two hundred
thousand foot soldiers and ten thousand men of
Judah.* **5** Saul went to the city of Amalek, and
after setting an ambush in the wadi, **6** [p]warned
the Kenites: "Come! Leave Amalek and withdraw, that I may not have to destroy you with
them, for you were kind to the Israelites when
they came up from Egypt." After the Kenites
left, **7** Saul routed Amalek from Havilah to the
approaches of Shur, on the frontier of Egypt.[q]
**8** He took Agag, king of Amalek, alive, but on
the rest of the people he put into effect the ban
of destruction by the sword. **9** He and his troops
spared Agag and the best of the fat sheep and
oxen, and the lambs. They refused to carry out
the doom on anything that was worthwhile,
dooming only what was worthless and of no
account.

**Saul Is Reproved.** **10** Then the LORD
spoke to Samuel: **11** "I regret* having made
Saul king, for he has turned from me and has not
kept my command." At this Samuel grew angry
and cried out to the LORD all night. **12** Early in
the morning he went to meet Saul, but was
informed that Saul had gone to Carmel, where
he erected a trophy in his own honor, and that
on his return he had passed on and gone down
to Gilgal. **13** When Samuel came to him, Saul
greeted him: "The LORD bless you! I have kept
the command of the LORD." **14** But Samuel
asked, "What, then, is the meaning of this
bleating of sheep that comes to my ears, and the
lowing of oxen that I hear?" **15** Saul replied:
"They were brought from Amalek. The men
spared the best sheep and oxen to sacrifice to the
LORD, your God; but we have carried out the
ban on the rest." **16** Samuel said to Saul:
"Stop! Let me tell you what the LORD said to

i 1 Sm 3, 17; Ru 1, 17.
j 2 Sm 14, 11; 1 Kgs 1, 52.
k 2 Sm 1, 22; 8, 2-5.
l 1 Sm 18, 20. 25; 31, 2; 1 Chr 8, 33; 9, 39; 10, 2.
m 1 Sm 9, 1.
n Ex 17, 8-10. 16; Dt 25, 17ff.
o 1 Sm 27, 8; 30, 17; Ex 17, 16; Nm 24, 20.
p Nm 24, 21.
q 1 Sm 27, 8.

*

14, 45: Rescue: the Hebrew word used is that for the "redemption" of the first-born (Ex 13, 13ff).

14, 49: Ishvi: known also as Ishbaal, in 2 Sm 2, 8 and elsewhere. The name may once have read "Ishyo" here.

15, 3: Under the ban: in such wars of extermination, all things (men, cities, beasts, etc.) were to be blotted out; nothing could be reserved for private use. The interpretation of God's will here attributed to Samuel is in keeping with the abhorrent practices of blood revenge prevalent among pastoral, seminomadic peoples such as the Hebrews had recently been. The slaughter of the innocent has never been in conformity with the will of God.

15, 4: The numbers here are not realistic; compare 1 Sm 14, 24 above.

15, 11: I regret: God manifests "regret" when, offended by men, he takes away his benefits, graces and favors. It is not God, but men, who change, to their own detriment.

me last night." "Speak!" he replied. **17** Samuel then said: "Though little in your own esteem,
are you not leader of the tribes of Israel? The
LORD anointed you king of Israel[r] **18** and sent
you on a mission, saying, 'Go and put the sinful
Amalekites under a ban of destruction. Fight
against them until you have exterminated
them.'[s] **19** Why then have you disobeyed the
LORD? You have pounced on the spoil, thus
displeasing the LORD."[t] **20** Saul answered
Samuel: "I did indeed obey the LORD and fulfill
the mission on which the LORD sent me. I have
brought back Agag, and I have destroyed Amalek under the ban. **21** But from the spoil the
men took sheep and oxen, the best of what had
been banned, to sacrifice to the LORD their God
in Gilgal."[u] **22** [v]But Samuel said:

"Does the LORD so delight in holocausts and sacrifices
as in obedience to the command of the LORD?
Obedience is better than sacrifice,
and submission than the fat of rams.*
**23** For a sin like divination is rebellion,
and presumption is the crime of idolatry.
Because you have rejected the command of the LORD,
he, too, has rejected you as a ruler."

## Saul Asks Forgiveness.

**24** Saul replied
to Samuel: "I have sinned, for I have disobeyed
the command of the LORD and your instructions.
In my fear of the people, I did what they said.[w]
**25** Now forgive my sin, and return with me,
that I may worship the LORD." **26** But Samuel
said to Saul, "I will not return with you, because you rejected the command of the LORD
and the LORD rejects you as king of Israel."[x]
**27** As Samuel turned to go, Saul seized a loose
end of his mantle, and it tore off.[y] **28** So Samuel said to him: "The LORD has torn the kingdom
of Israel from you this day, and has given it to
a neighbor of yours, who is better than you.[z]
**29** The Glory of Israel neither retracts nor repents, for he is not man that he should repent."[a]
**30** But he answered: "I have sinned, yet honor
me now before the elders of my people and
before Israel. Return with me that I may worship the LORD your God." **31** And so Samuel
returned with him, and Saul worshiped the
LORD.

## Agag Is Cut Down.

**32** Afterward Samuel
commanded, "Bring Agag, king of Amalek, to
me." Agag came to him struggling and saying,
"So it is bitter death!" **33** And Samuel said,

"As your sword has made women childless,
so shall your mother be childless among women."

Then he cut Agag down before the LORD in
Gilgal.[b]
**34** Samuel departed for Ramah, while Saul
went up to his home in Gibeah of Saul. **35** Never again, as long as he lived, did Samuel see
Saul. Yet he grieved over Saul, because the
LORD regretted having made him king of Israel.[c]

# CHAPTER 16

## Samuel Sent to Bethlehem.

**1** [d]The
LORD said to Samuel: "How long will you
grieve for Saul, whom I have rejected as king
of Israel? Fill your horn with oil, and be on your
way. I am sending you to Jesse of Bethlehem,
for I have chosen my king from among his
sons."* **2** But Samuel replied: "How can I go?
Saul will hear of it and kill me." To this the
LORD answered: "Take a heifer along and say,
'I have come to sacrifice to the LORD.' **3** Invite
Jesse to the sacrifice, and I myself will tell you
what to do; you are to anoint for me the one I
point out to you."
**4** Samuel did as the LORD had commanded
him. When he entered Bethlehem, the elders of
the city came trembling to meet him and inquired, "Is your visit peaceful, O seer?" **5** He
replied: "Yes! I have come to sacrifice to the
LORD. So cleanse yourselves and join me today
for the banquet." He also had Jesse and his sons
cleanse themselves and invited them to the sacrifice.[e] **6** As they came, he looked at Eliab and
thought, "Surely the LORD's anointed is here
before him." **7** But the LORD said to Samuel:
"Do not judge from his appearance or from his
lofty stature, because I have rejected him. Not
as man sees does God see, because man sees the
appearance but the LORD looks into the heart."[f]
**8** [g]Then Jesse called Abinadab and presented
him before Samuel, who said, "The LORD has
not chosen him." **9** Next Jesse presented
Shammah, but Samuel said, "The LORD has not
chosen this one either." **10** In the same way

r 1 Sm 9, 21.
s 1 Sm 28, 18.
t 1 Sm 14, 32.
u Lv 27, 28.
v Prv 21, 3; Hos 6, 6; Am 5, 21-25; Zec 10, 2; Mt 9, 13; 12, 7; Heb 10, 9.
w 1 Sm 26, 21.
x 1 Kgs 11, 11. 30f.
y 1 Sm 24, 6.
z 1 Sm 28, 17; 2 Sm 7, 15f.
a Nm 23, 19.
b Ex 21, 23.
c Gn 6, 6.
d 1 Kgs 1, 39; Ru 4, 17-22; 1 Chr 11, 3; Is 11, 1; Lk 2, 4.
e 1 Sm 9, 12f; 20, 26; Ex 19, 10; Jb 1, 5.
f 1 Sm 10, 23f; 1 Chr 28, 9; Prv 15, 11; Jer 17, 10; 20, 12; Lk 16, 15; Acts 1, 24.
g 8ff: 1 Sm 17, 12f; 1 Chr 2, 13ff.

*

15, 22: Samuel is disapproving, not of sacrifices in general, but of merely external sacrifices offered in defiance of God's commandment and without heartfelt obedience.

16, 1: The anointing here prepared for is unknown to David's brother Eliab in the next chapter (1 Sm 17, 28), and David is twice anointed after Saul's death (2 Sm 2, 4; 5, 3).

Jesse presented seven sons before Samuel, but Samuel said to Jesse, "The LORD has not chosen any one of these." **11** Then Samuel asked Jesse, "Are these all the sons you have?" Jesse replied, "There is still the youngest, who is tending the sheep." Samuel said to Jesse, "Send for him; we will not begin the sacrificial banquet until he arrives here."[h] **12** Jesse sent and had the young man brought to them. He was ruddy, a youth handsome to behold and making a splendid appearance. The LORD said, "There—anoint him, for this is he!"[i] **13** Then Samuel, with the horn of oil in hand, anointed him in the midst of his brothers; and from that day on, the spirit of the LORD rushed upon David. When Samuel took his leave, he went to Ramah.[j]

**Saul's Spirit of Melancholy.** **14** [k]The spirit of the LORD had departed from Saul, and he was tormented by an evil spirit sent by the LORD.* **15** So the servants of Saul said to him: "Please! An evil spirit from God is tormenting you. **16** If your lordship will order it, we, your servants here in attendance on you, will look for a man skilled in playing the harp. When the evil spirit from God comes over you, he will play and you will feel better." **17** Saul then told his servants, "Find me a skillful harpist and bring him to me." **18** [l]A servant spoke up to say: "I have observed that one of the sons of Jesse of Bethlehem is a skillful harpist. He is also a stalwart soldier, besides being an able speaker, and handsome. Moreover, the LORD is with him."*

**David Made Armor-Bearer.** **19** Accordingly, Saul dispatched messengers to ask Jesse to send him his son David, who was with the flock. **20** Then Jesse took five loaves of bread, a skin of wine, and a kid, and sent them to Saul by his son David.[m] **21** Thus David came to Saul and entered his service. Saul became very fond of him, made him his armor-bearer,[n] **22** and sent Jesse the message, "Allow David to remain in my service, for he meets with my approval." **23** Whenever the spirit from God seized Saul, David would take the harp and play, and Saul would be relieved and feel better, for the evil spirit would leave him.

## CHAPTER 17

**The Challenge of Goliath.** **1** The Philistines rallied their forces for battle at Socoh in Judah and camped between Socoh and Azekah at Ephes-dammim. **2** Saul and the Israelites also gathered and camped in the Vale of the Terebinth, drawing up their battle line to meet the Philistines. **3** The Philistines were stationed on one hill and the Israelites on an opposite hill, with a valley between them.

**4** A champion named Goliath of Gath came out from the Philistine camp; he was six and a half feet tall. **5** He had a bronze helmet on his head and wore a bronze corselet of scale armor weighing five thousand shekels, **6** and bronze greaves, and had a bronze scimitar* slung from a baldric. **7** The shaft of his javelin was like a weaver's heddle-bar, and its iron head weighed six hundred shekels.* His shield-bearer went before him.[o] **8** He stood and shouted to the ranks of Israel: "Why come out in battle formation? I am a Philistine, and you are Saul's servants. Choose one of your men, and have him come down to me. **9** If he beats me in combat and kills me, we will be your vassals; but if I beat him and kill him, you shall be our vassals and serve us." **10** The Philistine continued: "I defy the ranks of Israel today. Give me a man and let us fight together." **11** Saul and all the men of Israel, when they heard this challenge of the Philistine, were dismayed and terror-stricken.

**David Comes to the Camp.*** **12** [David was the son of an Ephrathite named Jesse, who was from Bethlehem in Judah. He had eight sons, and in the days of Saul was old and well on in years.[p] **13** The three oldest sons of Jesse had followed Saul to war; these three sons who had gone off to war were named, the first-born Eliab, the second son Abinadab, and the third Shammah. **14** David was the youngest. While the three oldest had joined Saul, **15** David would go and come from Saul to tend his father's sheep at Bethlehem.[q]

h 1 Sm 17, 15. 28. 34; 2 Sm 7, 8.
i 1 Sm 9, 2.
j 1 Sm 10, 6; 11, 6; Jgs 3, 10; 9, 9; Sir 46, 13.
k 1 Sm 18, 10f.
l 2 Sm 17, 8.
m 1 Sm 9, 7f; 10, 4. 27; 16, 1; 17, 27ff.
n 1 Sm 18, 2.
o 2 Sm 21, 19; 1 Chr 11, 23; 20, 5.
p 1 Sm 16, 1. 10; Ru 1, 2.
q 1 Sm 18, 2; 2 Sm 7, 8.

*

16, 14: An evil spirit sent by the Lord: the Lord permitted Saul to be tormented with violent fits of rage.

16, 18: Of the two traditions which describe the coming of David into Saul's service, the oldest Greek translation retains only the one comprised in 1 Sm 16, 14–23; 17, 1–11. 32–54. This effort at consistency is not in accord with the character of the rest of the book; see note on 1 Sm 8, 1. Though square brackets are used in this edition to indicate the passages lacking in the oldest translation, this is meant only to help the reader follow one account at a time. Both are equally a part of the inspired text, as are also the various amplifications and retouchings of the narrative given within brackets in chs 18 and 19.

17, 6: Scimitar: the Hebrew word for this is rather rare, and the nature of the weapon was in doubt until recent years. It is not the same as the sword of v 45.

17, 7: Six hundred shekels: over 15 pounds.

17, 12–31: An alternative account of how David came to undertake the combat with the Philistine is here inserted; it is continued in 1 Sm 17, 55—18, 6. See note on 1 Sm 16, 18.

16 [Meanwhile the Philistine came forward
and took his stand morning and evening for
forty days.

17 [Now Jesse said to his son David: "Take
this ephah of roasted grain and these ten loaves
for your brothers, and bring them quickly to
your brothers in the camp. 18 Also take these
ten cheeses for the field officer. Greet your
brothers and bring home some token from them.
19 Saul, and they, and all Israel are fighting
against the Philistines in the Vale of the Terebinth." 20 Early the next morning, having left
the flock with a shepherd, David set out on his
errand, as Jesse had commanded him. He
reached the barricade of the camp just as the
army, on their way to the battleground, were
shouting their battle cry.[r] 21 The Israelites and
the Philistines drew up opposite each other in
battle array. 22 David entrusted what he had
brought to the keeper of the baggage and hastened to the battle line where he greeted his
brothers.[s] 23 While he was talking with them,
the Philistine champion, by name Goliath of
Gath, came up from the ranks of the Philistines
and spoke as before, and David listened.
24 When the Israelites saw the man, they all
retreated before him, very much afraid. 25 The
Israelites had been saying: "Do you see this
man coming up? He comes up to insult Israel.
If anyone should kill him, the king would give
him great wealth, and his daughter as well, and
would grant exemption to his father's family in
Israel."[t] 26 David now said to the men standing by: "What will be done for the man who
kills this Philistine and frees Israel of the disgrace? Who is this uncircumcised Philistine in
any case, that he should insult the armies of the
living God?"[u] 27 They repeated the same
words to him and said, "That is how the man
who kills him will be rewarded." 28 When
Eliab, his oldest brother, heard him speaking
with the men, he grew angry with David and
said: "Why did you come down? With whom
have you left those sheep in the desert meanwhile? I know your arrogance and your evil
intent. You came down to enjoy the battle!"
29 David replied, "What have I done now?—I
was only talking." 30 Yet he turned from him
to another and asked the same question; and
everyone gave him the same answer as before.
31 The words that David had spoken were overheard and reported to Saul, who sent for him.]

**David Fights Goliath.** 32 Then David
spoke to Saul: "Let your majesty not lose courage. I am at your service to go and fight this
Philistine." 33 But Saul answered David,
"You cannot go up against this Philistine and
fight with him, for you are only a youth, while
he has been a warrior from his youth."
34 [v]Then David told Saul: "Your servant used
to tend his father's sheep, and whenever a lion
or bear came to carry off a sheep from the flock,
35 I would go after it and attack it and rescue
the prey from its mouth. If it attacked me, I
would seize it by the jaw, strike it, and kill it.
36 Your servant has killed both a lion and a
bear, and this uncircumcised Philistine will be
as one of them, because he has insulted the
armies of the living God."

37 David continued: "The LORD, who delivered me from the claws of the lion and the bear,
will also keep me safe from the clutches of this
Philistine." Saul answered David, "Go! the
LORD will be with you."[w]

**Preparation for the Encounter.** 38 Then
Saul clothed David in his own tunic, putting a
bronze helmet on his head and arming him with
a coat of mail. 39 David also girded himself
with Saul's sword over the tunic. He walked
with difficulty, however, since he had never
tried armor before. He said to Saul, "I cannot
go in these, because I have never tried them
before." So he took them off. 40 Then, staff in
hand, David selected five smooth stones from
the wadi and put them in the pocket of his
shepherd's bag. With his sling also ready to
hand, he approached the Philistine.

**David's Victory.** 41 With his shield-bearer
marching before him, the Philistine also advanced closer and closer to David. 42 When he
had sized David up, and seen that he was youthful, and ruddy, and handsome in appearance, he
held him in contempt. 43 The Philistine said to
David, "Am I a dog that you come against me
with a staff?" Then the Philistine cursed David
by his gods 44 and said to him, "Come here to
me, and I will leave your flesh for the birds of
the air and the beasts of the field."[x] 45 David
answered him: "You come against me with
sword and spear and scimitar, but I come
against you in the name of the LORD of hosts,
the God of the armies of Israel that you have
insulted. 46 Today the LORD shall deliver you
into my hand; I will strike you down and cut off
your head. This very day I will leave your
corpse and the corpses of the Philistine army for
the birds of the air and the beasts of the field;
thus the whole land shall learn that Israel has a
God. 47 All this multitude, too, shall learn that
it is not by sword or spear that the LORD saves.
For the battle is the LORD's, and he shall deliver
you into our hands."[y]

48 The Philistine then moved to meet David

r 1 Sm 26, 5.
s 1 Sm 25, 13.
t 1 Sm 18, 17; Jos 15, 16.
u 1 Sm 18, 25; Jgs 15, 18; 2 Kgs 19, 4; Is 37, 4.
v 34f: Jgs 14, 6; Sir 47, 3.
w Prv 28, 1.
x Dt 28, 26; Is 18, 6; Jer 15, 3.
y 1 Sm 14, 6; Ps 33, 16.

at close quarters, while David ran quickly toward the battle line in the direction of the Philistine. **49** David put his hand into the bag and
took out a stone, hurled it with the sling, and
struck the Philistine on the forehead. The stone
embedded itself in his brow, and he fell prostrate on the ground. **50** [Thus David overcame
the Philistine with sling and stone; he struck the
Philistine mortally, and did it without a
sword.][z] **51** Then David ran and stood over
him; with the Philistine's own sword [which he
drew from its sheath] he dispatched him and cut
off his head.[a]

**Flight of the Philistines.** When they saw
that their hero was dead, the Philistines took to
flight. **52** Then the men of Israel and Judah,
with loud shouts, went in pursuit of the Philistines to the approaches of Gath and to the gates
of Ekron, and Philistines fell wounded along the
road from Shaaraim as far as Gath and Ekron.
**53** On their return from the pursuit of the Philistines, the Israelites looted their camp.
**54** [b]David took the head of the Philistine and
brought it to Jerusalem; but he kept Goliath's
armor in his own tent.*

**David Presented to Saul.** **55** [When Saul
saw David go out to meet the Philistine, he
asked his general Abner, "Abner, whose son is
that youth?" Abner replied, "As truly as your
majesty is alive, I have no idea." **56** And the
king said, "Find out whose son the lad is."
**57** So when David returned from slaying the
Philistine, Abner took him and presented him to
Saul. David was still holding the Philistine's
head. **58** Saul then asked him, "Whose son are
you, young man?" David replied, "I am the son
of your servant Jesse of Bethlehem."

## CHAPTER 18

**David and Jonathan.** **1** [By the time David finished speaking with Saul, Jonathan had
become as fond of David as if his life depended
on him; he loved him as he loved himself.[c]
**2** Saul laid claim to David that day and did not
allow him to return to his father's house.[d]
**3** And Jonathan entered into a bond with David,
because he loved him as himself. **4** Jonathan
divested himself of the mantle he was wearing
and gave it to David, along with his military
dress, and his sword, his bow and his belt.[e]
**5** David then carried out successfully every
mission on which Saul sent him. So Saul put
him in charge of his soldiers, and this was agreeable to the whole army, even to Saul's own
officers.]

**Saul's Jealousy.** **6** At the approach of
Saul and David (on David's return after slaying
the Philistine), women came out from each of
the cities of Israel to meet King Saul, singing
and dancing, with tambourines, joyful songs,
and sistrums.[f] **7** The women played and sang:

"Saul has slain his thousands,
and David his ten thousands."[g]

**8** Saul was very angry and resentful of the
song, for he thought: "They give David ten
thousands, but only thousands to me. All that
remains for him is the kingship." **9** [And from
that day on, Saul was jealous of David.

**10** [[h] The next day an evil spirit from God
came over Saul, and he raged in his house.
David was in attendance, playing the harp as at
other times, while Saul was holding his spear.
**11** Saul poised the spear, thinking to nail David
to the wall, but twice David escaped him.]
**12** Saul then began to fear David, [because the
LORD was with him, but had departed from Saul
himself.] **13** Accordingly, Saul removed him
from his presence by appointing him a field
officer. So David led the people on their military expeditions, **14** and prospered in all his
enterprises, for the LORD was with him. **15** Seeing how successful he was, Saul conceived a
fear of David; **16** on the other hand, all Israel
and Judah loved him, since he led them on their
expeditions.[i]

**17** [Saul said to David, "There is my older
daughter, Merob, whom I will give you in marriage if you become my champion and fight the
battles of the LORD." Saul had in mind, "I shall
not touch him; let the Philistines strike him."[j]
**18** But David answered Saul: "Who am I? And
who are my kin or my father's clan in Israel that
I should become the king's son-in-law?"
**19** However, when it was time for Saul's
daughter Merob to be given to David, she was
given in marriage to Adriel the Meholathite instead.][k]

**20** Now Saul's daughter Michal loved David, and it was reported to Saul, who was
pleased at this,[l] **21** for he thought, "I will offer
her to him to become a snare for him, so that the
Philistines may strike him." [Thus for the second time Saul said to David, "You shall become my son-in-law today." ] **22** Saul then
ordered his servants to speak to David privately

z Sir 47, 4; 1 Mc 4, 30.
a 1 Sm 21, 10.
b 1 Sm 31, 9.
c 1 Sm 19, 1-7; 20, 17; 23, 16; 2 Sm 1, 26; 9, 1.
d 1 Sm 16, 21; 17, 15.
e 2 Sm 1, 22.
f Ex 15, 20f; Jgs 11, 34; Jdt 15, 12.
g 1 Sm 21, 12; 29, 5; Sir 47, 6f.
h 10f: 1 Sm 16, 14; 19, 9f; 20, 33; 22, 6; 26, 8.
i 2 Sm 5, 2.
j 1 Sm 14, 49; 17, 25.
k 1 Sm 21, 8; 24, 16.
l 1 Sm 14, 49; 25, 44; 26, 23; 2 Sm 3, 13.

* 17, 54: At the time supposed by this narrative, Jerusalem was still Jebusite, and David had no military tent of his own; the verse is a later gloss.

and to say: "The king is fond of you, and all his
officers love you. You should become the
king's son-in-law." **23** But when Saul's servants mentioned this to David, he said: "Do you
think it easy to become the king's son-in-law?
I am poor and insignificant." **24** When his servants reported to him the nature of David's answer, **25** Saul commanded them to say this to
David: "The king desires no other price for the
bride than the foreskins of one hundred Philistines, that he may thus take vengeance on his
enemies." Saul intended in this way to bring
about David's death through the Philistines.[m]
**26** When the servants reported this offer to David, he was pleased with the prospect of becoming the king's son-in-law. [Before the year was
up,] **27** David made preparations and sallied
forth with his men and slew two hundred Philistines. He brought back their foreskins and
counted them out before the king, that he might
thus become the king's son-in-law. So Saul
gave him his daughter Michal in marriage.
**28** Saul thus came to recognize that the LORD
was with David; besides, his own daughter Michal loved David. **29** Therefore Saul feared David all the more [and was his enemy ever after].

**30** [The Philistine chiefs continued to make
forays, but each time they took the field, David
was more successful against them than any other of Saul's officers, and as a result acquired
great fame.]

## CHAPTER 19

**Persecution of David.** **1** Saul discussed
his intention of killing David with his son Jonathan and with all his servants. But Saul's son
Jonathan, who was very fond of David,[n] **2** told
him: "My father Saul is trying to kill you.
Therefore, please be on your guard tomorrow
morning; get out of sight and remain in hiding.
**3** I, however, will go out and stand beside my
father in the countryside where you are, and will
speak to him about you. If I learn anything, I
will let you know."

**4** Jonathan then spoke well of David to his
father Saul, saying to him: "Let not your majesty sin against his servant David, for he has
committed no offense against you, but has
helped you very much by his deeds. **5** When he
took his life in his hands and slew the Philistine,
and the LORD brought about a great victory for
all Israel through him, you were glad to see it.
Why, then, should you become guilty of shedding innocent blood by killing David without
cause?"[o] **6** Saul heeded Jonathan's plea and
swore, "As the LORD lives, he shall not be
killed." **7** So Jonathan summoned David and
repeated the whole conversation to him. Jonathan then brought David to Saul, and David
served him as before.

**8** When war broke out again, David went out
to fight against the Philistines and inflicted a
great defeat upon them, putting them to flight.
**9** [p]Then an evil spirit from the LORD came upon
Saul as he was sitting in his house with spear in
hand and David was playing the harp nearby.
**10** Saul tried to nail David to the wall with the
spear, but David eluded Saul, so that the spear
struck only the wall, and David got away safe.

**11** The same night, Saul sent messengers to
David's house to guard it, that he might kill him
in the morning. David's wife Michal informed
him, "Unless you save yourself tonight, tomorrow you will be killed."* **12** Then Michal let
David down through a window, and he made his
escape in safety.[q] **13** Michal took the household idol and laid it in the bed, putting a net of
goat's hair at its head and covering it with a
spread.[r] **14** When Saul sent messengers to arrest David, she said, "He is sick." **15** Saul,
however, sent the messengers back to see David
and commanded them, "Bring him up to me in
the bed, that I may kill him." **16** But when the
messengers entered, they found the household
idol in the bed, with the net of goat's hair at its
head. **17** Saul therefore asked Michal: "Why
did you play this trick on me? You have helped
my enemy to get away!" Michal answered Saul:
"He threatened me, 'Let me go or I will kill
you.'"

**David and Samuel in Ramah.** **18** Thus
David got safely away; he went to Samuel in
Ramah, informing him of all that Saul had done
to him. Then he and Samuel went to stay in the
sheds. **19** When Saul was told that David was
in the sheds near Ramah, **20** he sent messengers
to arrest David. But when they saw the band of
prophets, presided over by Samuel, in a prophetic frenzy, they too fell into the prophetic
state.[s] **21** Informed of this, Saul sent other
messengers, who also fell into the prophetic
state. For the third time Saul sent messengers,
but they too fell into the prophetic state.

**Saul among the Prophets.** **22** Saul then
went to Ramah himself. Arriving at the cistern
of the threshing floor on the bare hilltop, he
inquired, "Where are Samuel and David?",
and was told, "At the sheds near Ramah."
**23** As he set out from the hilltop toward the
sheds, the spirit of God came upon him also,

m 1 Sm 17, 26; Gn 34, 12.
n 1 Sm 18, 1; 20, 1ff.
o Dt 19, 10; Ps 119, 109.
p 9f: 1 Sm 16, 14; 18, 10f.
q Jos 2, 15; Acts 9, 25; 2 Cor 11, 33.
r Gn 31, 19; Jos 17, 5; 18, 14, 18. 20.
s 1 Sm 10, 5f. 10; Nm 11, 25.

* 19, 11: This story in all probability originally followed 1 Sm 18, 29, placing the episode of David's escape on the night of his marriage with Michal.

and he continued on in a prophetic condition
until he reached the spot. At the sheds near
Ramah **24** he, too, stripped himself of his garments and he, too, remained in the prophetic
state in the presence of Samuel; all that day and
night he lay naked. That is why they say, "Is
Saul also among the prophets?"[t]

## CHAPTER 20

**David Consults with Jonathan.** **1** David
fled from the sheds near Ramah, and went to
Jonathan. "What have I done?" he asked him.
"What crime or what offense does your father
hold against me that he seeks my life?"[u] **2** Jonathan answered him: "Heaven forbid that you
should die! My father does nothing, great or
small, without disclosing it to me. Why, then,
should my father conceal this from me? This
cannot be so!" **3** But David replied: "Your
father is well aware that I am favored with your
friendship, so he has decided, 'Jonathan must
not know of this lest he be grieved.' Nevertheless, as the LORD lives and as you live, there is
but a step between me and death." **4** Jonathan
then said to David, "I will do whatever you
wish." **5** David answered: "Tomorrow is the
new moon, which I should in fact dine with the
king. Let me go and hide in the open country
until evening.[v] **6** If it turns out that your father
misses me, say, 'David urged me to let him go
on short notice to his city Bethlehem, because
his whole clan is holding its seasonal sacrifice
there.' **7** If he says, 'Very well,' your servant
is safe. But if he becomes quite angry, you can
be sure he has planned some harm. **8** [w]Do this
kindness for your servant because of the LORD's
bond between us, into which you brought me:
if I am guilty, kill me yourself! Why should you
give me up to your father?" **9** But Jonathan
answered: "Not I! If ever I find out that my
father is determined to inflict injury upon you,
I will certainly let you know." **10** David then
asked Jonathan, "Who will tell me if your father gives you a harsh answer?"

**Mutual Agreement.** **11** [Jonathan replied
to David, "Come, let us go out into the field."
When they were out in the open country together, **12** Jonathan said to David: "As the LORD,
the God of Israel, lives, I will sound out my
father about this time tomorrow. Whether he is
well disposed toward David or not, I will send
you the information. **13** [x]Should it please my
father to bring any injury upon you, may the
LORD do thus and so to Jonathan if I do not
apprise you of it and send you on your way in
peace. May the LORD be with you even as he
was with my father. **14** Only this: if I am still
alive, may you show me the kindness of the
LORD. But if I die, **15** never withdraw your
kindness from my house. And when the LORD
exterminates all the enemies of David from the
surface of the earth, **16** the name of Jonathan
must never be allowed by the family of David
to die out from among you, or the LORD will
make you answer for it." **17** And in his love for
David, Jonathan renewed his oath to him, because he loved him as his very self.]
**18** Jonathan then said to him: "Tomorrow is
the new moon; and you will be missed, since
your place will be vacant. **19** On the following
day you will be missed all the more. Go to the
spot where you hid on the other occasion and
wait near the mound there.[y] **20** On the third day
of the month I will shoot arrows, as though
aiming at a target. **21** I will then send my attendant to go and recover the arrows. If in fact I say
to him, 'Look, the arrow is this side of you; pick
it up,' come, for you are safe. As the LORD
lives, there will be nothing to fear. **22** But if I
say to the boy, 'Look, the arrow is beyond you,'
go, for the LORD sends you away. **23** However,
in the matter which you and I have discussed,
the LORD shall be between you and me forever." **24** So David hid in the open country.
On the day of the new moon, when the king
sat at table to dine, **25** taking his usual place
against the wall, Jonathan sat facing him, while
Abner sat at the king's side, and David's place
was vacant. **26** [z]Saul, however, said nothing
that day, for he thought, "He must have become
unclean by accident, and not yet have been
cleansed."* **27** On the next day, the second
day of the month, David's place was vacant.
Saul inquired of his son Jonathan, "Why has the
son of Jesse not come to table yesterday or
today?" **28** Jonathan answered Saul: "David
urgently asked me to let him go to his city,
Bethlehem. **29** 'Please let me go,' he begged,
'for we are to have a clan sacrifice in our city,
and my brothers insist on my presence. Now,
therefore, if you think well of me, give me leave
to visit my brothers.' That is why he has not
come to the king's table." **30** But Saul was
extremely angry with Jonathan and said to him:
"Son of a rebellious woman, do I not know that,
to your own shame and to the disclosure of your
mother's shame, you are the companion of Jesse's son? **31** Why, as long as the son of Jesse
lives upon the earth, you cannot make good
your claim to the kingship! So send for him, and
bring him to me, for he is doomed."[a] **32** But
Jonathan asked his father Saul: "Why should he

t 1 Sm 10, 10ff.
u 1 Sm 19, 1-7, 11-17
v Nm 10, 10; 28, 11-15.
w 8f: 1 Sm 23, 17f.
x 13-16: 1 Sm 24, 22f; 2 Sm 9, 1-13; 21, 7.
y 1 Sm 19, 1-7.
z 1 Sm 16, 5; Lv 7, 20f; 15, 1ff.
a 2 Sm 12, 5.

* 20, 26: The meal on the first day of the month would have religious overtones, and a ritual impurity (Lv 15, 16; Dt 23, 10ff) would bar David from sharing in it.

die? What has he done?'' **33** At this Saul brandished his spear to strike him, and thus Jonathan
learned that his father was resolved to kill David.[b] **34** Jonathan sprang up from the table in
great anger and took no food that second day of
the month, for he was grieved on David's account, since his father had railed against him.

**Jonathan's Farewell.** **35** The next morning Jonathan went out into the field with a little
boy for his appointment with David. **36** There
he said to the boy, "Run and fetch the arrow."
And as the boy ran, he shot an arrow beyond
him in the direction of the city. **37** When the
boy made for the spot where Jonathan had shot
the arrow, Jonathan called after him, "The arrow is farther on!" **38** Again he called to his
lad, "Hurry, be quick, don't delay!" Jonathan's boy picked up the arrow and brought it
to his master. **39** The boy knew nothing; only
Jonathan and David knew what was meant.
**40** Then Jonathan gave his weapons to this boy
of his and said to him, "Go, take them to the
city." **41** When the boy had left, David rose
from beside the mound and prostrated himself
on the ground three times before Jonathan in
homage. They kissed each other and wept aloud
together. **42** [c]At length Jonathan said to David,
"Go in peace, in keeping with what we two
have sworn by the name of the LORD; 'The LORD
shall be between you and me, and between your
posterity and mine forever.' "

## CHAPTER 21

**1** Then David departed on his way, while
Jonathan went back into the city.

**The Holy Bread.** **2** David went to Ahimelech, the priest of Nob, who came trembling to
meet him and asked, "Why are you alone? Is
there no one with you?"[d] **3** David answered the
priest: "The king gave me a commission and
told me to let no one know anything about the
business on which he sent me or the commission
he gave me. For that reason I have arranged a
meeting place with my men. **4** [e]Now what have
you on hand? Give me five loaves, or whatever
you can find." **5** But the priest replied to David, "I have no ordinary bread on hand, only
holy bread; if the men have abstained from
women, you may eat some of that."* **6** David
answered the priest: "We have indeed been
segregated from women as on previous occasions. Whenever I go on a journey, all the young
men are consecrated—even for a secular journey. All the more so today, when they are consecrated at arms!" **7** So the priest gave him
holy bread, for no other bread was on hand
except the showbread which had been removed
from the LORD's presence and replaced by fresh
bread when it was taken away.[f] **8** One of Saul's
servants was there that day, detained before the
LORD; his name was Doeg the Edomite, and he
was Saul's chief henchman.

**The Sword of Goliath.** **9** David then asked
Ahimelech: "Do you have a spear or a sword on
hand? I brought along neither my sword nor my
weapons, because the king's business was urgent." **10** The priest replied: "The sword of
Goliath the Philistine, whom you killed in the
Vale of the Terebinth, is here [wrapped in a
mantle] behind an ephod. If you wish to take
that, take it; there is no sword here except that
one." David said: "There is none to match it.
Give it to me!"[g]

**David a Fugitive.** **11** That same day David
took to flight from Saul, going to Achish, king
of Gath.[h] **12** But the servants of Achish said,
"Is this not David, the king of the land? During
their dances do they not sing,

'Saul has slain his thousands,
but David his ten thousands'?"[i]

**13** David took note of these remarks and became very much afraid of Achish, king of Gath.
**14** So, as they watched, he feigned insanity and
acted like a madman in their hands, drumming
on the doors of the gate and drooling onto his
beard. **15** Finally Achish said to his servants:
"You see the man is mad. Why did you bring
him to me? **16** Do I not have enough madmen,
that you bring in this one to carry on in my
presence? Should this fellow come into my
house?"

## CHAPTER 22

**1** David left Gath and escaped to the cave of
Adullam. When his brothers and the rest of his
family heard about it, they came down to him
there.[j] **2** He was joined by all those who were
in difficulties or in debt, or who were embittered, and he became their leader. About four
hundred men were with him.

**3** From there David went to Mizpeh of Moab
and said to the king of Moab, "Let my father
and mother stay with you, until I learn what God
will do for me." **4** He left them with the king

b 1 Sm 18, 11.
c 2 Sm 9, 1; 21, 7.
d Is 10, 32; Mk 2, 26.
e Lv 24, 5. 9.
f 1 Sm 22, 9; Lv 24, 5-9; Mt 12, 3f; Mk 2, 26; Lk 6, 3ff.
g 1 Sm 17, 51, 54.
h 1 Sm 27, 2; 29, 5.
i 1 Sm 18, 7; 29, 5.
j 2 Sm 23, 13; Ps 63; Mi 1, 15.

*

21, 5f: From women: the high priest, willing to distribute the holy bread to David and his men, requires that they be free from ritual uncleanness, associated in Old Testament times (Lv 15, 18) with the marriage act. David's answer supposes the discipline of a military campaign under the conditions of "holy war" (Dt 23, 10).

22, 4–5: Refuge: seemingly connected with the cave complex spoken of in v 1.

of Moab, and they stayed with him as long as
David remained in the refuge.*

**5** But the prophet Gad said to David: "Do
not remain in the refuge. Leave, and go to the
land of Judah." And so David left and went to
the forest of Hereth.

**Doeg Betrays Ahimelech.** **6** Now Saul
heard that David and his men had been located.
At the time he was sitting in Gibeah under a
tamarisk tree on the high place, holding his
spear, while all his servants were standing by.[k]
**7** So he said to them: "Listen, men of Benjamin! Will the son of Jesse give all of you fields
and vineyards? Will he make each of you an
officer over a thousand or a hundred men,[l]
**8** that you have all conspired against me and no
one tells me that my son has made an agreement
with the son of Jesse? None of you shows sympathy for me or discloses to me that my son has
stirred up my servant to be an enemy against
me, as is the case today." **9** [m]Then Doeg the
Edomite, who was standing with the officers of
Saul, spoke up: "I saw the son of Jesse come
to Ahimelech, son of Ahitub, in Nob. **10** He
consulted the LORD for him and gave him supplies, and the sword of Goliath the Philistine as
well."

**Slaughter of the Priests.** **11** At this the
king sent a summons to Ahimelech the priest,
son of Ahitub, and to all his family who were
priests in Nob; and they all came to the king.
**12** Then Saul said, "Listen, son of Ahitub!"
He replied, "Yes, my lord." **13** Saul asked
him, "Why did you conspire against me with
the son of Jesse by giving him food and a sword
and by consulting God for him, that he might
rebel against me and become my enemy, as is
the case today?" **14** Ahimelech answered the
king: "And who among all your servants is as
loyal as David, the king's son-in-law, captain of
your bodyguard, and honored in your own
house? **15** Is this the first time I have consulted
God for him? No indeed! Let not the king accuse
his servant or anyone in my family of such a
thing. Your servant knows nothing at all, great
or small, about the whole matter." **16** But the
king said, "You shall die, Ahimelech, with all
your family." **17** The king then commanded
his henchmen standing by: "Make the rounds
and kill the priests of the LORD, for they assisted
David. They knew he was a fugitive and yet
failed to inform me." But the king's servants
refused to lift a hand to strike the priests of the
LORD.[n]

**18** The king therefore commanded Doeg,
"You make the rounds and kill the priests!" So
Doeg the Edomite went from one to the next and
killed the priests himself, slaying on that day
eighty-five who wore the linen ephod. **19** Saul
also put the priestly city of Nob to the sword,
including men and women, children and infants, and oxen, asses and sheep.

**Abiathar Escapes.** **20** One son of Ahimelech, son of Ahitub, named Abiathar, escaped
and fled to David.[o] **21** When Abiathar told David that Saul had slain the priests of the LORD,
**22** David said to him: "I knew that day, when
Doeg the Edomite was there, that he would
surely tell Saul. I am responsible for the death
of all your family. **23** Stay with me. Fear nothing; he that seeks your life must seek my life
also. You are under my protection."

## CHAPTER 23

**Keilah Liberated.** **1** David received information that the Philistines were attacking Keilah
and plundering the threshing floors.[p] **2** So he
consulted the LORD, inquiring, "Shall I go and
defeat these Philistines?" The LORD answered,
"Go, for you will defeat the Philistines and
rescue Keilah."[q] **3** But David's men said to
him: "We are afraid here in Judah. How much
more so if we go to Keilah against the forces of
the Philistines!" **4** Again David consulted the
LORD, who answered, "Go down to Keilah, for
I will deliver the Philistines into your power."
**5** David then went with his men to Keilah and
fought with the Philistines. He drove off their
cattle and inflicted a severe defeat on them, and
thus rescued the inhabitants of Keilah.

**6** Abiathar, son of Ahimelech, who had fled
to David, went down with David to Keilah,
taking the ephod with him.[r]

**Flight from Keilah.** **7** When Saul was told
that David had entered Keilah, he said: "God
has put him in my grip. Now he has shut himself
in, for he has entered a city with gates and
bars." **8** Saul then called all the people to war,
in order to go down to Keilah and besiege David
and his men. **9** When David found out that Saul
was planning to harm him, he said to the priest
Abiathar, "Bring forward the ephod."[s] **10** David then said: "O LORD God of Israel, your
servant has heard a report that Saul plans to
come to Keilah, to destroy the city on my account. **11** Will they hand me over? And now:
will Saul come down as your servant has heard?
O LORD God of Israel, tell your servant." The
LORD answered, "He will come down."
**12** David then asked, "Will the citizens of Keilah deliver me and my men into the grasp of
Saul?" And the LORD answered, "Yes." **13** So

k Ps 52.
l 1 Sm 8, 14.
m 9f: 1 Sm 21, 2-10.
n 1 Sm 2, 31. 33; 21, 7.
o 1 Sm 23, 6; 30, 7; 1 Kgs 2, 28f.
p Jos 15, 44.
q 1 Sm 28, 6.
r 1 Sm 22, 20; 30, 7.
s 1 Sm 2, 28.

David and his men, about six hundred in number, left Keilah and wandered from place to place. When Saul was informed that David had escaped from Keilah, he abandoned the expedition.

**David and Jonathan in Horesh.** **14** David now lived in the refuges in the desert, or in the barren hill country near Ziph. Though Saul sought him continually, the LORD did not deliver David into his grasp. **15** David was apprehensive because Saul had come out to seek his life; but while he was at Horesh in the barrens near Ziph, **16** Saul's son, Jonathan, came down there to David and strengthened his resolve in the LORD.[t] **17** He said to him: "Have no fear, my father Saul shall not lay a hand to you. You shall be king of Israel and I shall be second to you. Even my father Saul knows this." **18** They made a joint agreement before the LORD in Horesh, where David remained, while Jonathan returned to his home.[u]

**Treachery of the Ziphites.** **19** Some of the Ziphites went up to Saul in Gibeah and said, "David is hiding among us, now in the refuges, and again at Horesh, or on the hill of Hachilah, south of the wasteland.[v] **20** Therefore, whenever the king wishes to come down, let him do so. It will be our task to deliver him into the king's grasp." **21** Saul replied: "The LORD bless you for your sympathy toward me.[w] **22** Go now and make sure once more! Take note of the place where he sets foot" (for he thought, perhaps they are playing some trick on me). **23** "Look around and learn in which of all the various hiding places he is holding out. Then come back to me with sure information, and I will go with you. If he is in the region, I will search him out among all the families of Judah." **24** So they went off to Ziph ahead of Saul. At this time David and his men were in the desert below Maon, in the Arabah south of the wasteland.[x]

**Escape from Saul.** **25** When Saul and his men came looking for him, David got word of it and went down to the gorge in the desert below Maon. Saul heard of this and pursued David into the desert below Maon. **26** As Saul moved along one rim of the gorge, David and his men took to the other. David was in anxious flight to escape Saul, and Saul and his men were attempting to outflank David and his men in order to capture them, **27** when a messenger came to Saul, saying, "Come quickly, because the Philistines have invaded the land." **28** Saul interrupted his pursuit of David and went to meet the Philistines. This is how that place came to be called the Gorge of Divisions.

## CHAPTER 24

**David Spares Saul.** **1** David then went up from there and stayed in the refuges behind Engedi. **2** And when Saul returned from the pursuit of the Philistines, he was told that David was in the desert near Engedi. **3** So Saul took three thousand picked men from all Israel and went in search of David and his men in the direction of the wild goat crags. **4** When he came to the sheepfolds along the way, he found a cave, which he entered to ease nature. David and his men were occupying the inmost recesses of the cave.[y]

**5** David's servants said to him, "This is the day of which the LORD said to you, 'I will deliver your enemy into your grasp; do with him as you see fit.'" So David moved up and stealthily cut off an end of Saul's mantle. **6** Afterward, however, David regretted that he had cut off an end of Saul's mantle.[z] **7** He said to his men, "The LORD forbid that I should do such a thing to my master, the LORD's anointed, as to lay a hand on him, for he is the LORD's anointed."[a] **8** With these words David restrained his men and would not permit them to attack Saul. Saul then left the cave and went on his way. **9** David also stepped out of the cave, calling to Saul, "My lord the king!" When Saul looked back, David bowed to the ground in homage **10** and asked Saul: "Why do you listen to those who say, 'David is trying to harm you'? **11** You see for yourself today that the LORD just now delivered you into my grasp in the cave. I had some thought of killing you, but I took pity on you instead. I decided, 'I will not raise a hand against my lord, for he is the LORD's anointed and a father to me.' **12** Look here at this end of your mantle which I hold. Since I cut off an end of your mantle and did not kill you, see and be convinced that I plan no harm and no rebellion. I have done you no wrong, though you are hunting me down to take my life.[b] **13** The LORD will judge between me and you, and the LORD will exact justice from you in my case. I shall not touch you. **14** The old proverb says, 'From the wicked comes forth wickedness.' So I will take no action against you. **15** Against whom are you on campaign, O king of Israel? Whom are you pursuing? A dead dog, or a single flea! **16** The LORD will be the judge; he will decide between me and you. May he see this, and take my part, and grant me justice beyond your reach!"[c]

t 1 Sm 18, 1.
u 1 Sm 18, 3; 20, 8.
v 1 Sm 26, 1-3; Ps 54.
w 2 Sm 2, 5.
x 1 Sm 25, 2.
y Ps 57.
z 1 Sm 15, 27.
a 1 Sm 10, 1; 31, 4; 2 Sm 1, 14.
b Rom 12, 19.
c 1 Sm 18, 19. 31; 26, 19; Pss 35, 1ff; 43, 1.

**Saul's Remorse.** **17** When David finished saying these things to Saul, Saul answered, "Is that your voice, my son David?" And he wept aloud. **18** Saul then said to David: "You are in the right rather than I; you have treated me generously, while I have done you harm. **19** Great is the generosity you showed me today, when the LORD delivered me into your grasp and you did not kill me. **20** For if a man meets his enemy, does he send him away unharmed? May the LORD reward you generously for what you have done this day. **21** And now, since I know that you shall surely be king and that sovereignty over Israel shall come into your possession,[d] **22** swear to me by the LORD that you will not destroy my descendants and that you will not blot out my name and family."[e] **23** David gave Saul his oath and Saul returned home, while David and his men went up to the refuge.

## CHAPTER 25

**Death of Samuel.** **1** Samuel died, and all Israel gathered to mourn him; they buried him at his home in Ramah.[f]

**Nabal and Abigail.** **2** Then David went down to the desert of Maon. There was a man of Maon who had property in Carmel; he was very wealthy, owning three thousand sheep and a thousand goats. At this time he was present for the shearing of his flock in Carmel.[g] **3** The man was named Nabal, his wife, Abigail. The woman was intelligent and attractive, but Nabal himself, a Calebite, was harsh and ungenerous in his behavior.[h] **4** When David heard in the desert that Nabal was shearing his flock, **5** he sent ten young men, instructing them: "Go up to Carmel. Pay Nabal a visit and greet him in my name. **6** Say to him, 'Peace be with you, my brother, and with your family, and with all who belong to you. **7** I have just heard that shearers are with you. Now, when your shepherds were with us, we did them no injury, neither did they miss anything all the while they were in Carmel. **8** Ask your servants and they will tell you so. Look kindly on these young men, since we come at a festival time. Please give your servants and your son David whatever you can manage.' "

**9** When David's young men arrived, they delivered this message fully to Nabal in David's name, and then waited. **10** But Nabal answered the servants of David: "Who is David? Who is the son of Jesse? Nowadays there are many servants who run away from their masters. **11** Must I take my bread, my wine, my meat that I have slaughtered for my own shearers, and give them to men who come from I know not where?" **12** So David's young men retraced their steps and on their return reported to him all that had been said. **13** Thereupon David said to his men, "Let everyone gird on his sword." And so everyone, David included, girded on his sword. About four hundred men went up after David, while two hundred remained with the baggage.

**14** But Nabal's wife Abigail was informed of this by one of the servants, who said: "David sent messengers from the desert to greet our master, but he flew at them screaming. **15** Yet these men were very good to us. We were done no injury, neither did we miss anything all the while we were living among them during our stay in the open country. **16** For us they were like a rampart night and day the whole time we were pasturing the sheep near them. **17** Now, see what you can do, for you must realize that otherwise evil is in store for our master and for his whole family. He is so mean that no one can talk to him." **18** Abigail quickly got together two hundred loaves, two skins of wine, five dressed sheep, five seahs of roasted grain, a hundred cakes of pressed raisins, and two hundred cakes of pressed figs, and loaded them on asses. **19** She then said to her servants, "Go on ahead; I will follow you." But she did not tell her husband Nabal.

**20** As she came down through a mountain defile riding on an ass, David and his men were also coming down from the opposite direction. When she met them, **21** David had just been saying: "Indeed, it was in vain that I guarded all this man's possessions in the desert, so that he missed nothing. He has repaid good with evil. **22** May God do thus and so to David, if by morning I leave a single male alive among all those who belong to him."[i] **23** As soon as Abigail saw David, she dismounted quickly from the ass and, falling prostrate on the ground before David, did him homage. **24** As she fell at his feet she said: "My lord, let the blame be mine. Please let your handmaid speak to you, and listen to the words of your handmaid. **25** Let not my lord pay attention to that worthless man Nabal, for he is just like his name. Fool is his name,* and he acts the fool. I, your handmaid, did not see the young men whom my lord sent. **26** Now, therefore, my lord, as the LORD lives, and as you live, it is the LORD who has kept you from shedding blood and from avenging yourself personally. May your enemies and those who seek to harm my lord become as

d 1 Sm 26, 25.
e 2 Sm 9, 1ff.
f 1 Sm 28, 3; Sir 46, 13-20.
g 1 Sm 23, 24; Jos 15, 55.
h 1 Sm 27, 3; Jos 14, 6; 1 Chr 2, 42. 45.
i 1 Kgs 16, 11; 21, 21; 2 Kgs 9, 8.

*

25, 25: Fool is his name: Nabal in Hebrew means "a fool."

25, 26: Abigail anticipates that some misfortune will shortly overtake Nabal, as in fact it does (vv 37–38).

Nabal!* 27 Accept this present, then, which
your maidservant has brought for my lord, and
let it be given to the young men who follow my
lord. 28 Please forgive the transgression of
your handmaid, for the LORD shall certainly
establish a lasting dynasty for my lord, because
your lordship is fighting the battles of the LORD,
and there is no evil to be found in you your
whole life long. 29 If anyone rises to pursue
you and to seek your life, may the life of my lord
be bound in the bundle of the living* in the care
of the LORD your God; but may he hurl out the
lives of your enemies as from the hollow of a
sling.[j] 30 And when the LORD carries out for
my lord the promise of success he has made
concerning you, and appoints you as commander over Israel,[k] 31 you shall not have this as a
qualm or burden on your conscience, my lord,
for having shed innocent blood or for having
avenged yourself personally. When the LORD
confers this benefit on your lordship, remember
your handmaid." 32 David said to Abigail:
"Blessed be the LORD, the God of Israel, who
sent you to meet me today. 33 Blessed be your
good judgment and blessed be you yourself,
who this day have prevented me from shedding
blood and from avenging myself personally.
34 Otherwise, as the LORD, the God of Israel,
lives, who has restrained me from harming you,
if you had not come so promptly to meet me, by
dawn Nabal would not have had a single man or
boy left alive." 35 David then took from her
what she had brought him and said to her: "Go
up to your home in peace! See, I have granted
your request as a personal favor."

**Nabal's Death.** 36 When Abigail came to
Nabal, there was a drinking party in his house
like that of a king, and Nabal was merry because
he was very drunk. So she told him nothing at
all before daybreak the next morning. 37 But
then, when Nabal had become sober, his wife
told him what had happened. At this his courage
died within him, and he became like a stone.
38 About ten days later the LORD struck him
and he died. 39 On hearing that Nabal was
dead, David said: "Blessed be the LORD, who
has requited the insult I received at the hand of
Nabal, and who restrained his servant from doing evil, but has punished Nabal for his own evil
deeds."

**David Marries Abigail and Ahinoam.**
David then sent a proposal of marriage to Abigail. 40 When David's servants came to Abigail in Carmel, they said to her, "David has sent
us to you that he may take you as his wife."
41 Rising and bowing to the ground, she answered, "Your handmaid would become a slave
to wash the feet of my lord's servants." 42 She
got up immediately, mounted an ass, and followed David's messengers, with her five maids
following in attendance upon her. She became
his wife, 43 [l]and David also married Ahinoam
of Jezreel. Thus both of them were his wives;
but Saul gave David's wife Michal, Saul's own
daughter, to Palti, son of Laish, who was from
Gallim.[m]

## CHAPTER 26

**Saul's Life Again Spared.** 1 [n]Men from
Ziph came to Saul in Gibeah, reporting that
David was hiding on the hill of Hachilah at the
edge of the wasteland. 2 So Saul went off down
to the desert of Ziph with three thousand picked
men of Israel, to search for David in the desert
of Ziph. 3 Saul camped beside the road on the
hill of Hachilah, at the edge of the wasteland.
David, who was living in the desert, saw that
Saul had come into the desert after him 4 and
sent out scouts, who confirmed Saul's arrival.
5 David himself then went to the place where
Saul was encamped and examined the spot
where Saul and Abner, son of Ner, the general,
had their sleeping quarters. Saul's were within
the barricade, and all his soldiers were camped
around him.[o] 6 David asked Ahimelech the
Hittite, and Abishai, son of Zeruiah and brother
of Joab, "Who will go down into the camp with
me to Saul?" Abishai replied, "I will."[p] 7 So
David and Abishai went among Saul's soldiers
by night and found Saul lying asleep within the
barricade, with his spear thrust into the ground
at his head and Abner and his men sleeping
around him.

8 Abishai whispered to David: "God has delivered your enemy into your grasp this day. Let
me nail him to the ground with one thrust of the
spear; I will not need a second thrust!"[q] 9 But
David said to Abishai, "Do not harm him, for
who can lay hands on the LORD's anointed and
remain unpunished? 10 As the LORD lives,"
David continued, "it must be the LORD himself
who will strike him, whether the time comes for
him to die, or he goes out and perishes in battle.
11 But the LORD forbid that I touch his anointed! Now take the spear which is at his head and
the water jug, and let us be on our way." 12 So
David took the spear and the water jug from

j Ps 69, 28.
k 1 Sm 13, 14; 2 Sm 3, 10.
l 1 Sm 27, 3.
m 1 Sm 18, 20; 27, 3; 30, 5; 2 Sm 3, 2. 13ff; 1 Chr 3, 1.
n 1f: 1 Sm 23, 19f; Ps 54.
o 1 Sm 17, 20.
p 1 Chr 2, 16.
q 1 Sm 18, 11; 19, 10.

*

25, 29: The bundle of the living: the figure is perhaps taken from the practice of tying up valuables in a kerchief or bag for safekeeping. Abigail desires that David enjoy permanent peace and security, but that his enemies be subject to constant agitation and humiliation like a stone whirled about, cast out of the sling, and thereafter disregarded.

their place at Saul's head, and they got away without anyone's seeing or knowing or awakening. All remained asleep, because the LORD had put them into a deep slumber.

**David Taunts Abner.** **13** Going across to an opposite slope, David stood on a remote hilltop at a great distance from Abner, son of Ner, and the troops. **14** He then shouted, "Will you not answer, Abner?" And Abner answered, "Who is it that calls me?" **15** David said no to Abner: "Are you not a man whose like does not exist in Israel? Why, then, have you not guarded your lord the king when one of his subjects went to kill the king, your lord? **16** This is no creditable service you have performed. As the LORD lives, you people deserve death because you have not guarded your lord, the LORD's anointed. Go, look: where are the king's spear and the water jug that was at his head?"

**Saul Admits His Guilt.** **17** Saul recognized David's voice and asked, "Is that your voice, my son David?" David answered, "Yes, my lord the king." **18** He continued: "Why does my lord pursue his servant? What have I done? What evil do I plan? **19** Please, now, let my lord the king listen to the words of his servant. If the LORD has incited you against me, let an offering appease him; but if men, may they be cursed before the LORD, because they have exiled me so that this day I have no share in the LORD's inheritance,* but am told: 'Go, serve other gods!'[r] **20** Do not let my blood flow to the ground far from the presence of the LORD. For the king of Israel has come out to seek a single flea as if he were hunting partridge in the mountains." **21** Then Saul said: "I have done wrong. Come back, my son David, I will not harm you again, because you have held my life precious today. Indeed, I have been a fool and have made a serious mistake." **22** But David answered: "Here is the king's spear. Let an attendant come over to get it. **23** The LORD will reward each man for his justice and faithfulness. Today, though the LORD delivered you into my grasp, I would not harm the LORD's anointed.[s] **24** As I valued your life highly today, so may the LORD value my life highly and deliver me from all difficulties." **25** Then Saul said to David: "Blessed are you, my son David! You shall certainly succeed in whatever you undertake." David went his way, and Saul returned to his home.[t]

## CHAPTER 27

**Refuge among Philistines.** **1** But David said to himself: "I shall perish some day at the hand of Saul. I have no choice but to escape to the land of the Philistines; then Saul will give up his continuous search for me throughout the land of Israel, and I shall be out of his reach." **2** Accordingly, David departed with his six hundred men and went over to Achish, son of Maoch, king of Gath.[u] **3** David and his men lived in Gath with Achish; each one had his family, and David had his two wives, Ahinoam from Jezreel and Abigail, the widow of Nabal from Carmel.[v] **4** When Saul was told that David had fled to Gath, he no longer searched for him.

**In Ziklag.** **5** David said to Achish: "If I meet with your approval, let me have a place to live in one of the country towns. Why should your servant live with you in the royal city?" **6** That same day Achish gave him Ziklag, which has, therefore, belonged to the kings of Judah* up to the present time.[w] **7** In all, David lived a year and four months in the country of the Philistines.[x]

**Raids on Israel's Foes.** **8** David and his men went up and made raids on the Geshurites, Girzites, and Amalekites—peoples living in the land between Telam, on the approach to Shur, and the land of Egypt.[y] **9** In attacking the land David would not leave a man or woman alive, but would carry off sheep, oxen, asses, camels, and clothes. On his return he brought these to Achish, **10** who asked, "Whom did you raid this time?" And David answered, "The Negeb of Judah," or "The Negeb of Jarahmeel," or "The Negeb of the Kenites."[z] **11** But David would not leave a man or woman alive to be brought to Gath, fearing that they would betray him by saying, "This is what David did." This was his custom as long as he lived in the country of the Philistines. **12** And Achish trusted David, thinking, "He must certainly be detested by his people Israel. I shall have him as my vassal forever."

## CHAPTER 28

**1** In those days the Philistines mustered their military forces to fight against Israel. So Achish said to David, "You realize, of course, that you and your men must go out on campaign with me to Jezreel." **2** David answered Achish, "Good! Now you shall learn what your servant

r 1 Sm 24, 16.
s 1 Sm 18, 20.
t 1 Sm 24, 21.
u 1 Sm 21, 11-16.
v 1 Sm 25, 3. 44; 30, 3ff; 2 Sm 2, 3.
w 1 Sm 30, 1.
x 1 Sm 29, 3.
y 1 Sm 15, 3, 7.
z 1 Sm 30, 14, 29; 1 Chr 2, 9. 25. 42.

*

26, 19: The Lord's inheritance; the land of Israel (Dt 32, 8f), under the Lord's special protection, where he could be freely worshiped.

27, 6: Has . . . belonged to the kings of Judah: as a personal holding, outside the system of tribal lands; Jerusalem, when taken by David, had a similar status (2 Sm 5, 7–9).

can do.'' Then Achish said to David, ''I shall
appoint you my permanent bodyguard.''
**3** Now Samuel had died and, after being
mourned by all Israel, was buried in his city,
Ramah. Meanwhile Saul had driven mediums
and fortune-tellers out of the land.[a]

**Saul in Dismay.** **4** The Philistine levies advanced to Shunem and encamped. Saul, too,
mustered all Israel; they camped on Gilboa.
**5** When Saul saw the camp of the Philistines,
he was dismayed and lost heart completely.
**6** He therefore consulted the LORD; but the
LORD gave no answer, whether in dreams or by
the Urim or through prophets.[b] **7** Then Saul
said to his servants, ''Find me a woman who is
a medium, to whom I can go to seek counsel
through her.'' His servants answered him,
''There is a woman in Endor who is a medium.''[c]

**The Witch of Endor.** **8** So he disguised
himself, putting on other clothes, and set out
with two companions. They came to the woman
by night, and Saul said to her, ''Tell my fortune
through a ghost; conjure up for me the one I ask
you to.''[d] **9** But the woman answered him,
''You are surely aware of what Saul has done,
in driving the mediums and fortune-tellers out
of the land. Why, then, are you laying snares for
my life, to have me killed?'' **10** But Saul swore
to her by the LORD, ''As the LORD lives, you
shall incur no blame for this.'' **11** Then the
woman asked him, ''Whom do you want me to
conjure up?'' and he answered, ''Samuel.''

**Samuel Appears.** **12** When the woman
saw Samuel, she shrieked at the top of her voice
and said to Saul, ''Why have you deceived me?
You are Saul!''* **13** But the king said to her,
''Have no fear. What do you see?'' The woman
answered Saul, ''I see a preternatural being rising from the earth.'' **14** ''What does he look
like?'' asked Saul. And she replied, ''It is an old
man who is rising, clothed in a mantle.'' Saul
knew that it was Samuel, and so he bowed face
to the ground in homage.

**Saul's Doom.** **15** Samuel then said to Saul,
''Why do you disturb me by conjuring me up?''
Saul replied: ''I am in great straits, for the Philistines are waging war against me and God has
abandoned me. Since he no longer answers me
through prophets or in dreams, I have called you
to tell me what I should do.''[e] **16** To this Samuel said: ''But why do you ask me, if the LORD
has abandoned you and is with your neighbor?[f]
**17** The LORD has done to you what he foretold
through me: he has torn the kingdom from your
grasp and has given it to your neighbor David.
**18** ''Because you disobeyed the LORD's directive and would not carry out his fierce anger
against Amalek, the LORD has done this to you
today.[g] **19** Moreover, the LORD will deliver
Israel, and you as well, into the clutches of the
Philistines. By tomorrow you and your sons will
be with me, and the LORD will have delivered
the army of Israel into the hands of the Philistines.''[h]

**Saul's Despair.** **20** Immediately Saul fell
full length on the ground, for he was badly
shaken by Samuel's message. Moreover, he had
no bodily strength left, since he had eaten nothing all that day and night. **21** Then the woman
came to Saul, and seeing that he was quite terror-stricken, said to him: ''Remember, your
maidservant obeyed you: I took my life in my
hands and fulfilled the request you made of me.
**22** Now you, in turn, please listen to your
maidservant. Let me set something before you
to eat, so that you may have strength when you
go on your way.'' **23** But he refused, saying,
''I will not eat.'' However, when his servants
joined the woman in urging him, he listened to
their entreaties, got up from the ground, and sat
on a couch. **24** The woman had a stall-fed calf
in the house, which she now quickly slaughtered. Then taking flour, she kneaded it and
baked unleavened bread. **25** She set the meal
before Saul and his servants, and they ate. Then
they stood up and left the same night.

## CHAPTER 29

**David's Aid Rejected.** **1** Now the Philistines had mustered all their forces in Aphek, and
the Israelites were encamped at the spring of
Harod near Jezreel.[i] **2** As the Philistine lords
were marching their groups of a hundred and a
thousand, David and his men were marching in
the rear guard with Achish. **3** The Philistine
chiefs asked, ''What are those Hebrews doing
here?'' And Achish answered them: ''Why, that
is David, the officer of Saul, king of Israel. He
has been with me now for a year or two, and I
have no fault to find with him from the day he

a 1 Sm 25, 1; Sir 46, 20.
b 1 Sm 14, 37. 41; Ex 28, 30; Lv 8, 8.
c Lv 19, 31; 20, 27; Dt 18, 10ff; 1 Chr 10, 13f; Acts 16, 16.
d 1 Kgs 14, 2.
e Sir 46, 20.
f 1 Sm 15, 27f.
g 1 Sm 15, 18f. 26.
h 1 Sm 31, 2-6; Sir 46, 20.
i 1 Sm 4, 1.
j 1 Sm 27, 7.

* 28, 12: Human beings cannot communicate at will with the souls of the dead. God may, however, permit a departed soul to appear to the living and even to disclose things unknown to them. Saul's own prohibition of necromancy and divination (v 3) was in keeping with the consistent teaching of the Old Testament. If we are to credit the reality of the apparition to Saul, it was due, not to the summons of the witch, but to God's will; the woman merely furnished the occasion.

came over to me until the present.''[j] **4** But the
Philistine chiefs were angered at this and said to
him: ''Send that man back! Let him return to the
place you picked out for him. He must not go
down into battle with us, lest during the battle
he become our enemy. For how else can he win
back his master's favor, if not with the heads of
these men of ours?[k] **5** Is this not the David of
whom they sing during their dances,

'Saul has slain his thousands,
 but David his ten thousands'?''[l]

**6** So Achish summoned David and said to him:
''As the LORD lives, you are honest, and I
should be pleased to have you active with me in
the camp, for I have found nothing wrong with
you from the day of your arrival to this day. But
you are not welcome to the lords. **7** Withdraw
peaceably, now, and do nothing that might displease the Philistine lords.'' **8** But David said
to Achish: ''What have I done? Or what have
you against your servant from the first day I
have been with you to this day, that I cannot go
to fight against the enemies of my lord the
king?'' **9** ''You know,'' Achish answered David, ''that you are acceptable to me. But the
Philistine chiefs have determined you are not to
go up with us to battle. **10** So the first thing
tomorow, you and your lord's servants who
came with you, go to the place I picked out for
you. Do not decide to take umbrage at this; you
are as acceptable to me as an angel of God. But
make an early morning start, as soon as it grows
light, and be on your way.'' **11** So David and
his men left early in the morning to return to the
land of the Philistines. The Philistines, however, went on up to Jezreel.

## CHAPTER 30

**Ziklag in Ruins.** **1** Before David and his
men reached Ziklag on the third day, the Amalekites had raided the Negeb and Ziklag, had
stormed the city, and had set it on fire.[m] **2** They
had taken captive the women and all who were
in the city, young and old, killing no one; they
had carried them off when they left. **3** David
and his men arrived at the city to find it burned
to the ground and their wives, sons and daughters taken captive. **4** Then David and those who
were with him wept aloud until they could weep
no more. **5** David's two wives, Ahinoam of
Jezreel and Abigail, the widow of Nabal from
Carmel, had also been carried off with the rest.[n]
**6** Now David found himself in great difficulty,
for the men spoke of stoning him, so bitter were
they over the fate of their sons and daughters.
But with renewed trust in the LORD his God,
**7** [o]David said to Abiathar, the priest, son of
Ahimelech, ''Bring me the ephod!'' When Abiathar brought him the ephod, **8** David inquired
of the LORD, ''Shall I pursue these raiders? Can
I overtake them?'' The LORD answered him,
''Go in pursuit, for you shall surely overtake
them and effect a rescue.''

**Raid of the Amalekites.** **9** So David went
off with his six hundred men and came as far as
the Wadi Besor, where those who were to remain behind halted. **10** David continued the
pursuit with four hundred men, but two hundred
were too exhausted to cross the Wadi Besor and
remained behind. **11** An Egyptian was found in
the open country and brought to David. He was
provided with food, which he ate, and given
water to drink; **12** a cake of pressed figs and
two cakes of pressed raisins were also offered
to him. When he had eaten, he revived; he had
not taken food nor drunk water for three days
and three nights. **13** Then David asked him,
''To whom do you belong, and where do you
come from?'' He replied: ''I am an Egyptian,
the slave of an Amalekite. My master abandoned me because I fell sick three days ago
today. **14** We raided the Negeb of the Cherethites, the territory of Judah, and the Negeb of
Caleb; and we set Ziklag on fire.''[p] **15** David
then asked him, ''Will you lead me down to this
raiding party?'' He answered, ''Swear to me by
God that you will not kill me or deliver me to
my master, and I will lead you to the raiding
party.'' **16** He did lead them, and there were
the Amalekites scattered all over the ground,
eating, drinking, and in a festive mood because
of all the rich booty they had taken from the land
of the Philistines and from the land of Judah.

**The Booty Recovered.** **17** From dawn to
sundown David attacked them, putting them
under the ban so that none escaped except four
hundred young men, who mounted their camels
and fled.[q] **18** David recovered everything the
Amalekites had taken, and rescued his two
wives. **19** Nothing was missing, small or great,
booty or sons or daughters, of all that the Amalekites had taken. David brought back everything. **20** Moreover, David took all the sheep
and oxen, and as they drove them before him,
they shouted, ''This is David's spoil.''

**Division of the Spoils.** **21** When David
came to the two hundred men who had been too
exhausted to follow him, and whom he had left
behind at the Wadi Besor, they came out to meet
David and the men with him. On nearing them
David greeted them. **22** But all the stingy and
worthless men among those who had accompa-

k 1 Chr 12, 19f.
l 1 Sm 18, 6f; 21, 11.
m 1 Sm 27, 6. 10; 1 Chr 12, 21.
n 1 Sm 25, 42; 27, 3; 30, 5.
o 7f: 1 Sm 2, 28; 23, 6; Ex 28, 30.
p 1 Sm 27, 10; Ez 25, 16.
q 1 Sm 15, 3; Jos 6, 17; Jgs 7, 12.

nied David spoke up to say, "Since they did not
accompany us, we will not give them anything
from the booty, except to each man his wife and
children. Let them take those along and be on
their way." 23 But David said: "You must not
do this, my brothers, after what the LORD has
given us. He has protected us and delivered into
our grip the band that came against us. 24 Who
could agree with this proposal of yours? Rather,
the share of the one who goes down to battle and
that of the one who remains with the baggage
shall be the same; they shall share alike."[r]
25 And from that day forward he made it a law
and a custom in Israel, as it still is today.[s]

**David's Gifts to Judah.** 26 When David
came to Ziklag, he sent part of the spoil to the
elders of Judah, city by city, saying, "This is
a gift to you from the spoil of the enemies of the
LORD": 27 to those in Bethel, to those in Ra-
moth-negeb, to those in Jattir, 28 to those in
Aroer, to those in Siphmoth, to those in Eshtemoa, 29 to those in Racal, to those in the Jerah-
meelite cities, to those in the Kenite cities,[t]
30 to those in Hormah, to those in Borashan, to
those in Athach, 31 to those in Hebron, and to
all the places frequented by David and his men.

## CHAPTER 31

**Death of Saul and His Sons.** 1 [u]As they
pressed their attack on Israel, with the Israelites
fleeing before them and falling mortally wounded on Mount Gilboa, 2 the Philistines pursued
Saul and his sons closely, and slew Jonathan,
Abinadab, and Malchishua, sons of Saul.[v]
3 The battle raged around Saul, and the archers
hit him; he was pierced through the abdomen.
4 Then Saul said to his armor-bearer, "Draw
your sword and run me through, lest these uncircumcised come and make sport of me." But his
armor-bearer, badly frightened, refused to do it.
So Saul took his own sword and fell upon it.[w]
5 [x]When the armor-bearer saw that Saul was
dead, he too fell upon his sword and died with
him.* 6 Thus Saul, his three sons, and his armor-bearer died together on that same day.
7 When the Israelites on the slope of the
valley and those along the Jordan saw that the
men of Israel had fled and that Saul and his sons
were dead, they too abandoned their cities and
fled. Then the Philistines came and lived in
those cities.
8 The day after the battle the Philistines came
to strip the slain, and found Saul and his three
sons lying on Mount Gilboa. 9 They cut off
Saul's head and stripped him of his armor, and
then sent the good news throughout the land of
the Philistines to their idols and to the people.[y]
10 They put his armor in the temple of Astarte,
but impaled his body on the wall of Bethshan.

**Burial of Saul.** 11 [z]When the inhabitants of
Jabesh-gilead heard what the Philistines had
done to Saul, 12 all their warriors set out, and
after marching throughout the night, removed
the bodies of Saul and his sons from the wall of
Beth-shan, and brought them to Jabesh, where
they cremated them.* 13 Then they took their
bones and buried them under the tamarisk tree
in Jabesh, and fasted for seven days.

r 1 Sm 17, 22; 25, 13.
s Nm 31, 27.
t 1 Sm 27, 10.
u 1-13: 1 Chr 10, 1-12; 2 Sm 1, 1-16; 4, 4.
v 1 Sm 14, 49; 28, 19; 1 Chr 10, 2f.
w 1 Sm 24, 7; Jgs 9, 54; 1 Chr 10, 4.
x 1 Sm 10, 1; 26, 9; 2 Mc 14, 42.
y 1 Sm 17, 54; 2 Sm 1, 20; 2 Mc 15, 35.
z 11ff: 1 Sm 11, 1-11; 2 Sm 2, 4-7.

*

31, 5: This report of the suicidal act of Saul is presented as a part of his downfall, to be judged accordingly.

31, 12: Cremated them: cremation was not normally practiced in Israel, though it was known in the country from pre-Israelite times.

# The Second Book of SAMUEL

## CHAPTER 1

**Report of Saul's Death.** 1 After the death
of Saul, David returned from his defeat of the
Amalekites and spent two days in Ziklag.[a]
2 On the third day a man came from Saul's
camp, with his clothes torn and dirt on his head.
Going to David, he fell to the ground in homage. 3 David asked him, "Where do you come
from?" He replied, "I have escaped from the
Israelite camp." 4 "Tell me what happened,"
David bade him. He answered that the soldiers
had fled the battle and that many of them had
fallen and were dead, among them Saul and his
son Jonathan. 5 Then David said to the youth
who was reporting to him, "How do you know
that Saul and his son Jonathan are dead?"
6 [b]The youthful informant replied: "It was by
chance that I found myself on Mount Gilboa and
saw Saul leaning on his spear, with chariots and
horsemen closing in on him. 7 He turned
around and, seeing me, called me to him. When
I said, 'Here I am,' 8 he asked me, 'Who are
you?' and I replied, 'An Amalekite.' 9 Then he
said to me, 'Stand up to me, please, and finish
me off, for I am in great suffering, yet fully
alive.' 10 So I stood up to him and dispatched
him, for I knew that he could not survive his
wound. I removed the crown from his head and
the armlet from his arm and brought them here
to my lord."

11 David seized his garments and rent them,
and all the men who were with him did likewise.[c] 12 They mourned and wept and fasted
until evening for Saul and his son Jonathan, and
for the soldiers of the LORD of the clans of
Israel, because they had fallen by the sword.[d]
13 Then David said to the young man who had
brought him the information, "Where are you
from?" He replied, "I am the son of an Amalekite immigrant." 14 David said to him,
"How is it that you were not afraid to put forth
your hand to desecrate the LORD's anointed?"[e]
15 David then called one of the attendants and
said to him, "Come, strike him down"; and the
youth struck him a mortal blow. 16 Meanwhile
David said to him, "You are responsible for
your own death, for you testified against yourself when you said, 'I dispatched the LORD's
anointed.' "

**Elegy for Saul and Jonathan.** 17 Then
David chanted this elegy for Saul and his son
Jonathan, 18 which is recorded in the Book of
Jashar to be taught to the Judahites. He sang:[f]

19 "Alas! the glory of Israel, Saul,
slain upon your heights;
how can the warriors have fallen!

20 "Tell it not in Gath,
herald it not in the streets of Ashkelon,
Lest the Philistine maidens rejoice,
lest the daughters of the strangers exult![g]
21 Mountains of Gilboa,
may there be neither dew nor rain upon
you,
nor upsurgings of the deeps!*
Upon you lie begrimed the warriors' shields,
the shield of Saul, no longer anointed
with oil.[h]

22 "From the blood of the slain,
from the bodies of the valiant,
The bow of Jonathan did not turn back,
or the sword of Saul return unstained.[i]
23 Saul and Jonathan, beloved and cherished,
separated neither in life nor in death,
swifter than eagles, stronger than lions!
24 Women of Israel, weep over Saul,
who clothed you in scarlet and in finery,
who decked your attire with ornaments of
gold.

25 "How can the warriors have fallen—
in the thick of the battle,
slain upon your heights!
26 "I grieve for you, Jonathan my brother!
most dear have you been to me;
More precious have I held love for you
than love for women.[j]

27 "How can the warriors have fallen,
the weapons of war have perished!"

a 1 Sm 30, 17-20; 31, 1-13.
b 6-10: 2 Sm 4, 10; 1 Sm 31, 1-4; 1 Chr 10, 1-4.
c 2 Sm 13, 31.
d 1 Sm 31, 13.
e 1 Sm 10, 1; 24, 7; Ps. 105, 15.
f Jos 10, 13.
g Jgs 16, 23; 1 Sm 31, 9; Mi 1, 10.
h Gn 27, 28.
i 1 Sm 14, 47.
j 1 Sm 18, 1; 1 Mc 9, 21.

* 1, 21: Upsurgings of the deeps: this reading attempts to recover from an unintelligible Hebrew phrase the poetic parallel to dew and rain. The sense would be a wish that the mountain should have neither moisture from above nor water from springs or wells.

## CHAPTER 2

**David Anointed King.** **1** After this David inquired of the LORD, "Shall I go up into one of the cities of Judah?" The LORD replied to him, "Yes." Then David asked, "Where shall I go?" He replied, "To Hebron." **2** So David went up there accompanied by his two wives, Ahinoam of Jezreel and Abigail, the widow of Nabal of Carmel.[k] **3** David also brought up his men with their families, and they dwelt in the cities near Hebron. **4** Then the men of Judah came there and anointed David king of the Judahites.[l]

A report reached David that the men of Jabesh-gilead had buried Saul. **5** So David sent messengers to the men of Jabesh-gilead and said to them: "May you be blessed by the LORD for having done this kindness to your lord Saul in burying him. **6** And now may the LORD be kind and faithful to you. I, too, will be generous to you for having done this. **7** Take courage, therefore, and prove yourselves valiant men, for though your lord Saul is dead, the Judahites have anointed me their king."

# *IV: The Reign of David*

**Ishbaal King of Israel.** **8** Abner, son of Ner, Saul's general, took Ishbaal, son of Saul, and brought him over to Mahanaim,[m] **9** where he made him king over Gilead, the Ashurites, Jezreel, Ephraim, Benjamin, and the rest of Israel. **10** Ishbaal, son of Saul, was forty years old when he became king over Israel, and he reigned for two years. The Judahites alone followed David. **11** In all, David spent seven years and six months in Hebron as king of the Judahites.[n]

**Combat near Gibeon.** **12** Now Abner, son of Ner, and the servants of Ishbaal, Saul's son, left Mahanaim for Gibeon. **13** Joab, son of Zeruiah, and David's servants also set out and met them at the pool of Gibeon. And they sat down, one group on one side of the pool and the other on the opposite side. **14** Then Abner said to Joab, "Let the young men rise and perform for us." Joab replied, "All right!" **15** So they rose and were counted off: twelve of the Benjaminites of Ishbaal, son of Saul, and twelve of David's servants. **16** Then each one grasped his opponent's head and thrust his sword into his opponent's side, and all fell down together.* And so that place, which is in Gibeon, was named the Field of the Sides.

**Death of Asahel.** **17** After a very fierce battle that day, Abner and the men of Israel were defeated by David's servants. **18** The three sons of Zeruiah were there—Joab, Abishai, and Asahel. Asahel, who was as fleet of foot as a gazelle in the open field,[o] **19** set out after Abner, turning neither right nor left in his pursuit.[p] **20** Abner turned around and said, "Is that you, Asahel?" He replied, "Yes." **21** Abner said to him, "Turn right or left; seize one of the young men and take what you can strip from him." But Asahel would not desist from his pursuit. **22** Once more Abner said to Asahel: "Stop pursuing me! Why must I strike you to the ground? How could I face your brother Joab?"[q] **23** Still he refused to stop. So Abner struck him in the abdomen with the heel of his javelin, and the weapon protruded from his back. He fell there and died on the spot. And all who came to the place where Asahel had fallen and died, came to a halt. **24** Joab and Abishai, however, continued the pursuit of Abner. The sun had gone down when they came to the hill of Ammah which lies east of the valley toward the desert near Geba.

**Truce between Joab and Abner.** **25** Here the Benjaminites rallied around Abner, forming a single group, and made a stand on the hilltop. **26** Then Abner called to Joab and said: "Must the sword destroy to the utmost? Do you not know that afterward there will be bitterness? How much longer will you refrain from ordering the people to stop the pursuit of their brothers?" **27** Joab replied, "As God lives, if you had not spoken, the soldiers would not have been withdrawn from the pursuit of their brothers until morning." **28** Joab then sounded the horn, and all the soldiers came to a halt, pursuing Israel no farther and fighting no more. **29** Abner and his men marched all night long through the Arabah, crossed the Jordan, marched all through the morning, and came to Mahanaim. **30** Joab, after interrupting the pursuit of Abner, assembled all the men. Besides Asahel, nineteen other servants of David were missing. **31** But David's servants had fatally wounded three hundred and sixty men of Benjamin, followers of Abner. **32** They took up Asahel and buried him in his father's tomb in Bethlehem. Joab and his men made an all-night march, and dawn found them in Hebron.

## CHAPTER 3

**1** There followed a long war between the house of Saul and that of David, in which David grew stronger, but the house of Saul weaker.

k 1 Sm 25, 42f.
l 1 Sm 31, 11ff.
m 1 Sm 14, 50.
n 2 Sm 5, 5; 1 Kgs 2, 11.
o 2 Sm 23, 24: 1 Chr 2, 16.
p 1 Chr 27, 7.
q 2 Sm 3, 27f. 30.

*

2, 16: The nature of this gruesome game is not clear, and the place name is variously given in the older texts.

**Sons Born in Hebron.** 2 [r]Sons were born
to David in Hebron: his first-born, Amnon, of
Ahinoam from Jezreel; 3 the second, Chileab,
of Abigail the widow of Nabal of Carmel; the
third, Absalom, son of Maacah the daughter of
Talmai, king of Geshur;[s] 4 the fourth, Adonijah, son of Haggith; the fifth, Shephatiah, son
of Abital;[t] 5 and the sixth, Ithream, of David's
wife Eglah. These were born to David in Hebron.

**Ishbaal and Abner Quarrel.** 6 During the
war between the house of Saul and of David,
Abner was gaining power in the house of Saul.
7 Now Saul had had a concubine, Rizpah, the
daughter of Aiah. And Ishbaal, son of Saul, said
to Abner, "Why have you been intimate with
my father's concubine?"[u] 8 Enraged at the
words of Ishbaal, Abner said, "Am I a dog's
head in Judah? At present I am doing a kindness
to the house of your father Saul, to his brothers
and his friends, by keeping you out of David's
clutches; yet this day you charge me with a
crime involving a woman! 9 May God do thus
and so to Abner if I do not carry out for David
what the LORD swore to him[v] — 10 that is, take
away the kingdom from the house of Saul and
establish the throne of David over Israel and
over Judah from Dan to Beersheba."[w] 11 In
his fear of Abner, Ishbaal was no longer able to
say a word to him.

**Abner and David Reconciled.** 12 Then
Abner sent messengers to David in Telam,
where he was at the moment, to say, "Make an
agreement with me, and I will aid you by bringing all Israel over to you." 13 He replied,
"Very well, I will make an agreement with you.
But one thing I require of you. You must not
appear before me unless you bring back Michal,
Saul's daughter, when you come to present
yourself to me."[x] 14 At the same time David
sent messengers to Ishbaal, son of Saul, to say,
"Give me my wife Michal, whom I espoused by
paying a hundred Philistine foreskins."
15 Ishbaal sent for her and took her away from
her husband Paltiel, son of Laish,[y] 16 who followed her weeping as far as Bahurim. But Abner said to him, "Go back!" And he turned
back.

17 Abner then said in discussion with the
elders of Israel: "For a long time you have been
seeking David as your king. 18 Now take action, for the LORD has said of David, 'By my
servant David I will save my people Israel from
the grasp of the Philistines and from the grasp
of all their enemies.'" 19 Abner also spoke
personally to Benjamin, and then went to make
his own report to David in Hebron concerning
all that would be agreeable to Israel and to the
whole house of Benjamin. 20 When Abner, accompanied by twenty men, came to David in
Hebron, David prepared a feast for Abner and
for the men who were with him. 21 Then Abner
said to David, "I will now go to assemble all
Israel for my lord the king, that they may make
an agreement with you; you will then be king
over all whom you wish to rule." So David bade
Abner farewell, and he went away in peace.

**Death of Abner.** 22 Just then David's servants and Joab were coming in from an expedition, bringing much plunder with them. Abner,
having been dismissed by David, was no longer
with him in Hebron but had gone his way in
peace. 23 When Joab and the whole force he
had with him arrived, he was informed, "Abner, son of Ner, came to David; he has been sent
on his way in peace." 24 So Joab went to the
king and said: "What have you done? Abner
came to you. Why did you let him go peacefully
on his way? 25 Are you not aware that Abner
came to deceive you and to learn the ins and outs
of all that you are doing?" 26 Joab then left
David, and without David's knowledge sent
messengers after Abner, who brought him back
from the cistern of Sirah. 27 When Abner returned to Hebron, Joab took him aside within
the city gate as though to speak with him privately. There he stabbed him in the abdomen,
and he died in revenge for the killing of Joab's
brother Asahel.[z] 28 Later David heard of it and
said: "Before the LORD, I and my kingdom are
forever innocent.[a] 29 May the full responsibility for the death of Abner, son of Ner, be laid to
Joab and to all his family. May the men of
Joab's family never be without one suffering
from a discharge, or a leper, or one unmanly,
one falling by the sword, or one in need of
bread!" 30 [Joab and his brother Abishai had
lain in wait for Abner because he killed their
brother Asahel in battle at Gibeon.]

**David Mourns Abner.** 31 Then David said
to Joab and to all the people who were with him,
"Rend your garments, gird yourselves with
sackcloth, and mourn over Abner." King David
himself followed the bier.[b] 32 When they had
buried Abner in Hebron, the king wept aloud at
the grave of Abner, and the people also wept.
33 And the king sang this elegy over Abner:

"Would Abner have died like a fool?
34 Your hands were not bound with chains,
nor your feet placed in fetters;
As men fall before the wicked, you fell."

And all the people continued to weep for him.

---

r 2-5: 1 Chr 3, 14.
s 2 Sm 13, 37; 15, 8.
t 1 Kgs 1, 5.
u 2 Sm 21, 8ff.
v Ru 1, 17.
w 2 Sm 5, 2; 1 Sm 25, 30.
x 1 Sm 18, 20-27.
y 1 Sm 25, 44.
z 1 Kgs 2, 5. 32.
a 28. 30: 2 Sm 2, 22f.
b 2 Sm 21, 10.

**35** Then they went to console David with food
while it was still day. But David swore, "May
God do thus and so to me if I eat bread or
anything else before sunset."[c] **36** All the people noted this with approval, just as they were
pleased with everything that the king did. **37** So
on that day all the people and all Israel came to
know that the king had no part in the killing of
Abner, son of Ner. **38** The king then said to his
servants: "You must recognize that a great general has fallen today in Israel. **39** Although I am
the anointed king, I am weak this day, and these
men, the sons of Zeruiah, are too ruthless for
me. May the LORD requite the evildoer in accordance with his evil deed."[d]

## CHAPTER 4

**Death of Ishbaal.** **1** When Ishbaal, son of
Saul, heard that Abner had died in Hebron, he
ceased to resist and all Israel was alarmed.
**2** Ishbaal, son of Saul, had two company leaders named Baanah and Rechab, sons of Rimmon
the Beerothite, of the tribe of Benjamin. [Bee-
roth, too, was ascribed to Benjamin:[e] **3** the Be-
erothites fled to Gittaim, where they have been
resident aliens to this day.[f] **4** Jonathan, son of
Saul, had a son named Meribbaal* with crippled
feet. He was five years old when the news about
Saul and Jonathan came from Jezreel, and his
nurse took him up and fled. But in their hasty
flight, he fell and became lame.][g] **5** The sons
of Rimmon the Beerothite, Rechab and Baanah,
came into the house of Ishbaal during the heat
of the day, while he was taking his siesta. **6** The
portress of the house had dozed off while sifting
wheat, and was asleep. So Rechab and his
brother Baanah slipped past **7** and entered the
house while Ishbaal was lying asleep in his bedroom. They struck and killed him, and cut off
his head. Then, taking the head, they traveled
on the Arabah road all night long.

**The Murder Avenged.** **8** They brought the
head of Ishbaal to David in Hebron and said to
the king: "This is the head of Ishbaal, son of
your enemy Saul, who sought your life. Thus
has the LORD this day avenged my lord the king
on Saul and his posterity." **9** But David replied
to Rechab and his brother Baanah, sons of Rimmon the Beerothite: "As the LORD lives, who
rescued me from all difficulty, **10** in Ziklag I
seized and put to death the man who informed
me of Saul's death, thinking himself the bearer
of good news for which I ought to give him a
reward.[h] **11** How much more now, when wicked men have slain an innocent man in bed at
home, must I hold you responsible for his death
and destroy you from the earth!" **12** So at a
command from David, the young men killed
them and cut off their hands and feet, hanging
them up near the pool in Hebron. But he took
the head of Ishbaal and buried it in Abner's
grave in Hebron.[i]

## CHAPTER 5

**David King of Israel.** **1** [j]All the tribes of
Israel came to David in Hebron and said: "Here
we are, your bone and your flesh. **2** In days
past, when Saul was our king, it was you who
led the Israelites out and brought them back.
And the LORD said to you, 'You shall shepherd
my people Israel and shall be commander of
Israel.'"[k] **3** When all the elders of Israel came
to David in Hebron, King David made an agreement with them there before the LORD, and they
anointed him king of Israel. **4** David was thirty
years old when he became king, and he reigned
for forty years: **5** seven years and six months in
Hebron over Judah, and thirty-three years in
Jerusalem over all Israel and Judah.[l]

**Capture of Zion.*** **6** [m]Then the king and
his men set out for Jerusalem against the Jebusites who inhabited the region. David was told,
"You cannot enter here: the blind and the lame
will drive you away!" which was their way of
saying, "David cannot enter here."[n] **7** But David did take the stronghold of Zion, which is the
City of David. **8** On that day David said: "All
who wish to attack the Jebusites must strike at
them through the water shaft. The lame and the
blind shall be the personal enemies of David."
That is why it is said, "The blind and the lame
shall not enter the palace."[o] **9** David then
dwelt in the stronghold, which was called the
City of David; he built up the area from Millo
to the palace.[p] **10** David grew steadily more
powerful, for the LORD of hosts was with him.[q]
**11** [r]Hiram, king of Tyre, sent ambassadors to
David; he furnished cedar wood, as well as
carpenters and masons, who built a palace for
David.[s] **12** And David knew that the LORD had

---

c Ru 1, 17.
d Ps 28, 4; Is 3, 11.
e 2 Sm 9, 3; Jos 9, 17f.
f Jos 18, 25.
g 2 Sm 9, 3; 19, 25.
h 2 Sm 1, 6-10. 14. 16.
i Dt 21, 22f; 1 Sm 31, 10.
j 1ff: 1 Chr 11, 1ff.
k 2 Sm 3, 10; Dt 17, 15; 1 Sm 18, 16.
l 2 Sm 2, 11; 1 Kgs 2, 11; 1 Chr 3, 4.
m 6-10: 1 Chr 11, 4-9.
n Jos 15, 63; Jgs 1, 19. 21; Is 29, 3.
o Lv 21, 18; Mt 21, 14f.
p 1 Kgs 3, 1; 11, 27.
q Pss 78, 70ff. 89; 132, 13.
r 11-25: 1 Chr 14, 1-16.
s 11f: 1 Kgs 5, 15; 1 Chr 14, 1f.

---

*4, 4: Saul's grandson Meribbaal is the subject of ch 9 below. The text of this verse may owe its present place to the fact that pre-Christian copies of the Books of Samuel tended to confuse his name with that of his uncle Ishbaal, Saul's son and successor, a principal figure in chapters 2–4.

5, 6–12: David's most important military exploit, the taking of Jerusalem, is here presented before his battles with the Philistines, vv 17–25, which were earlier in time. The sense of vv 6 and 8 is in doubt.

established him as king of Israel and had exalted
his rule for the sake of his people Israel.

**David's Family in Jerusalem.** 13 [t]David
took more concubines and wives in Jerusalem
after he had come from Hebron, and more sons
and daughters were born to him in Jerusalem.
14 These are the names of those who were born
to him in Jerusalem: Shammua, Shobab, Nathan, Solomon, 15 Ibhar, Elishua, Nepheg, Japhia, 16 Elishama, Baaliada, and Eliphelet.

**Rout of the Philistines.** 17 When the
Philistines heard that David had been anointed
king of Israel, they all took the field in search
of him. On hearing this, David went down to the
refuge.* 18 The Philistines came and overran
the valley of Rephaim.* 19 David inquired of
the LORD, "Shall I attack the Philistines—will
you deliver them into my grip?" The LORD
replied to David, "Attack, for I will surely deliver the Philistines into your grip." 20 David
then went to Baal-perazim,* where he defeated
them. He said, "The LORD has scattered my
enemies before me like waters that have broken
free." That is why the place is called Baal-perazim. 21 They abandoned their gods there, and
David and his men carried them away. 22 But
the Philistines came up again and overran the
valley of Rephaim. 23 So David inquired of the
LORD, who replied: "You must not attack fron-
tally, but circle their rear and meet them before
the mastic trees. 24 When you hear a sound of
marching* in the tops of the mastic trees, act
decisively, for the LORD will have gone forth
before you to attack the camp of the Philistines." 25 David obeyed the LORD's command
and routed the Philistines from Gibeon as far as
Gezer.

## CHAPTER 6

### The Ark Brought to Jerusalem.

1 [u]David again assembled all the picked men of
Israel, thirty thousand in number. 2 Then David and all the people who were with him set out
for Baala of Judah to bring up from there the ark
of God, which bears the name of the LORD of
hosts enthroned above the cherubim.[v] 3 The
ark of God was placed on a new cart and taken
away from the house of Abinadab on the hill.
Uzzah and Ahio, sons of Abinadab, guided the
cart,[w] 4 with Ahio walking before it, 5 while
David and all the Israelites made merry before
the LORD with all their strength, with singing
and with citharas, harps, tambourines, sistrums
and cymbals.[x] 6 When they came to the threshing floor of Nodan, Uzzah reached out his hand
to the ark of God and steadied it, for the oxen
were making it tip. 7 But the LORD was angry
with Uzzah; God struck him on that spot, and
he died there before God. 8 David was disturbed because the LORD had vented his anger
on Uzzah. (The place has been called Perez-uz-
zah down to the present day.)[y] 9 David feared
the LORD that day and said, "How can the ark
of the LORD come to me?" 10 So David would
not have the ark of the LORD brought to him in
the City of David, but diverted it to the house
of Obededom the Gittite.

11 The ark of the LORD remained in the
house of Obededom the Gittite for three
months, and the LORD blessed Obededom and
his whole house.[z] 12 [a]When it was reported to
King David that the LORD had blessed the family of Obededom and all that belonged to him,
David went to bring up the ark of God from the
house of Obededom into the City of David amid
festivities. 13 As soon as the bearers of the ark
of the LORD had advanced six steps, he sacrificed an ox and a fatling. 14 Then David, girt
with a linen apron, came dancing before the
LORD with abandon,[b] 15 as he and all the Israelites were bringing up the ark of the LORD with
shouts of joy and to the sound of the horn.
16 As the ark of the LORD was entering the City
of David, Saul's daughter Michal looked down
through the window and saw King David leaping and dancing before the LORD, and she despised him in her heart. 17 [c]The ark of the
LORD was brought in and set in its place within
the tent David had pitched for it. Then David
offered holocausts and peace offerings before
the LORD. 18 When he finished making these
offerings, he blessed the people in the name of
the LORD of hosts. 19 He then distributed
among all the people, to each man and each
woman in the entire multitude of Israel, a loaf
of bread, a cut of roast meat, and a raisin cake.
With this, all the people left for their homes.

20 When David returned to bless his own
family, Saul's daughter Michal came out to
meet him and said, "How the king of Israel has
honored himself today, exposing himself to the
view of the slave girls of his followers, as a

t 13-16: 1 Chr 3, 5-8; 14, 3-7.
u 1-11: 1 Chr 13, 1-14.
v Ex 25, 10; Jos 15, 9; Ps 132, 8ff; 1 Chr 1, 4.
w 1 Sm 4, 3f; 6, 7f; 7, 1; Dn 3, 55.
x Pss 68, 25f; 150, 3. 5.
y 1 Kgs 8, 1.
z 1 Chr 26. 4.
a 12-23: 1 Chr 15, 1-29; Ps 24, 7-10.
b 1 Sm 2, 18.
c 17ff: Lv 1, 1-17; 3, 1-17; 1 Chr 16, 1ff.
d 1 Chr 16, 43.

*

5, 17: Refuge: probably near Adullam (1 Sm 22, 1–5).

5, 18–25: The successive defeats of the Philistines in the valley of Rephaim southwest of Jerusalem had the effect of blocking their access to the mountain ridge near Gibeon, and confining them to their holdings on the coast and in the foothills beyond Gezer to the west and south.

5, 20: Baal-perazim: means approximately "the lord of scatterings."

5, 24: Sound of marching: the wind in the treetops suggestive of the Lord's footsteps.

commoner might do!"[d] **21** But David replied to Michal: "I was dancing before the LORD. As the LORD lives, who preferred me to your father and his whole family when he appointed me commander of the LORD's people, Israel, not only will I make merry before the LORD,[e] **22** but I will demean myself even more. I will be lowly in your esteem, but in the esteem of the slave girls you spoke of I will be honored." **23** And so Saul's daughter Michal was childless to the day of her death.

## CHAPTER 7

**David's Concern for the Ark.** **1** [f]When King David was settled in his palace, and the LORD had given him rest from his enemies on every side,[g] **2** he said to Nathan the prophet, "Here I am living in a house of cedar, while the ark of God dwells in a tent!"[h] **3** Nathan answered the king, "Go, do whatever you have in mind, for the LORD is with you."[i] **4** But that night the LORD spoke to Nathan and said: **5** "Go, tell my servant David, 'Thus says the LORD: Should you build me a house to dwell in?[j] **6** I have not dwelt in a house from the day on which I led the Israelites out of Egypt to the present, but I have been going about in a tent under cloth. **7** In all my wanderings everywhere among the Israelites, did I ever utter a word to any one of the judges whom I charged to tend my people Israel, to ask: Why have you not built me a house of cedar?'

**The Lord's Promises.** **8** "Now then, speak thus to my servant David, 'The LORD of hosts has this to say:* It was I who took you from the pasture and from the care of the flock to be commander of my people Israel.[k] **9** I have been with you wherever you went, and I have destroyed all your enemies before you. And I will make you famous like the great ones of the earth.[l] **10** I will fix a place for my people Israel; I will plant them so that they may dwell in their place without further disturbance. Neither shall the wicked continue to afflict them as they did of old, **11** since the time I first appointed judges over my people Israel. I will give you rest from all your enemies. The LORD also reveals to you that he will establish a house for you.[m] **12** [n]And when your time comes and you rest with your ancestors, I will raise up your heir after you, sprung from your loins, and I will make his kingdom firm. **13** It is he who shall build a house for my name. And I will make his royal throne firm forever. **14** I will be a father to him, and he shall be a son to me. And if he does wrong, I will correct him with the rod of men and with human chastisements; **15** but I will not withdraw my favor from him as I withdrew it from your predecessor Saul, whom I removed from my presence.[o] **16** Your house and your kingdom shall endure forever before me; your throne shall stand firm forever.' "[p] **17** Nathan reported all these words and this entire vision to David.

**King David's Prayer.** **18** Then King David went in and sat before the LORD and said, "Who am I, Lord GOD, and who are the members of my house, that you have brought me to this point?[q] **19** Yet even this you see as too little, Lord GOD; you have also spoken of the house of your servant for a long time to come: this too you have shown to man,* Lord GOD! **20** What more can David say to you? You know your servant, Lord GOD! **21** For your servant's sake and as you have had at heart, you have brought about this entire magnificent disclosure to your servant. **22** And so—

"Great are you, Lord GOD! There is none like you and there is no God but you, just as we have heard it told.[r] **23** What other nation on earth is there like your people Israel, which God has led, redeeming it as his people; so that you have made yourself renowned by doing this magnificent deed, and by doing awe-inspiring things as you have cleared nations and their gods out of the way of your people, which you redeemed for yourself from Egypt?[s] **24** [t]You have established for yourself your people Israel as yours forever, and you, LORD, have become their God. **25** And now, LORD God, confirm for all time the prophecy you have made concerning your servant and his house, and do as you have promised. **26** Your name will be forever great,

e 1 Sm 13, 14; 15, 28.
f 1-29: 1 Chr 17, 1-27.
g 1 Kgs 5, 4.
h Dt 12, 10; 25, 19.
i Ps 132, 1-5.
j 1 Kgs 5, 17; 8, 16. 27; 1 Chr 22, 8; 28, 3; Is 66, 1; Acts 7, 48.
k 1 Sm 16, 13; 17, 15-20; Ps 78, 70f; Am 7, 14.
l Ps 89, 27.
m 2 Sm 23, 5; 1 Kgs 2, 4-24.
n 12ff: 1 Kgs 5, 19, 8, 19; 1 Chr 22, 10; 2 Chr 7, 18; Ps 89, 5, 27f. 30. 37f; Lk 1, 32; Heb 1, 5.
o 2 Sm 23, 5; 1 Sm 13, 14; 15, 26. 28; 2 Kgs 19, 34; 1 Chr 17, 11-14; Ps 89, 34.
p 2 Sm 23, 5; Dn 2, 45; 1 Mc 2, 57; Mk 11, 10; Lk 1, 32f; Heb 1, 8.
q 1 Chr 17, 16.
r Ex 15, 11; Is 45, 5.
s Dt 4, 7. 34.
t 24f: Ex 6, 7; Dt 7, 6; 26, 17; 29, 12.

*

7, 8–16: The prophecy to David contained in these verses is cited again, in poetic form, in Ps 89, 20–38, and alluded to in Ps 132. The promise regarding the people of Israel, vv 10–11, is a part of the promise to David at least as old as the composition of this chapter of Samuel, where it is anticipated in vv 6–7, and alluded to in David's thanksgiving, vv 23–24; it applies to the people an expression used of David in Ps 89, 23. The prophecy to David is the basis for Jewish expectation of a messiah, son of David, which Jesus Christ fulfilled in a transcendent way; cf Acts 2, 30; Heb 1, 5.

7, 19: This too you have shown to man: the text as transmitted has, rather, "and this is instruction for (or: the law of) mankind." The author of Chronicles (1 Chr 17, 17) saw approximately the same phrase, which he endeavored to fit into the context in a quite different sense. The above is conjectural; cf Dt 5, 24.

when men say, 'The LORD of hosts is God of
Israel,' and the house of your servant David
stands firm before you. **27** It is you, LORD of
hosts, God of Israel, who said in a revelation to
your servant, 'I will build a house for you.'
Therefore your servant now finds the courage to
make this prayer to you. **28** And now, Lord
GOD, you are God and your words are truth; you
have made this generous promise to your servant.[u] **29** Do, then, bless the house of your
servant that it may be before you forever; for
you, Lord GOD, have promised, and by your
blessing the house of your servant shall be
blessed forever."

## CHAPTER 8

**Summary of David's Wars.** **1** [v]After this
David attacked the Philistines and conquered
them, wresting . . .* from the Philistines. **2** He
also defeated Moab and then measured them
with a line, making them lie down on the
ground. He told off two lengths of line for execution, and a full length* to be spared. Thus the
Moabites became tributary to David. **3** [w]Next
David defeated Hadadezer, son of Rehob, king
of Zobah, when he went to reestablish his dominion at the Euphrates River.[x] **4** David captured from him one thousand seven hundred
horsemen and twenty thousand foot soldiers.
And he hamstrung all the chariot horses, preserving only enough for a hundred chariots.[y]
**5** When the Arameans of Damascus came to the
aid of Hadadezer, king of Zobah, David slew
twenty-two thousand of them. **6** David then
placed garrisons in Aram of Damascus, and the
Arameans became subjects, tributary to David.
The LORD brought David victory in all his undertakings. **7** David also took away the golden
shields used by Hadadezer's servants and
brought them to Jerusalem. [These Shishak,
king of Egypt, took away when he came to
Jerusalem in the days of Rehoboam, son of
Solomon.] **8** From Tebah and Berothai, towns
of Hadadezer, King David removed a very large
quantity of bronze. **9** When Toi, king of Hamath, heard that David had defeated all the
forces of Hadadezer, **10** he sent his son Hadoram to King David to greet him and to congratulate him for his victory over Hadadezer in battle,
because Toi had been in many battles with Hadadezer. Hadoram also brought with him articles
of silver, gold, and bronze. **11** These, too,
King David consecrated to the LORD, together
with the silver and gold he had taken from every
nation he had conquered: **12** from Edom and
Moab, from the Ammonites, from the Philistines, from the Amalekites, and from the plunder of Hadadezer, son of Rehob, king of Zobah.
**13** On his return,* David became famous for
having slain eighteen thousand Edomites in the
Salt Valley;[z] **14** after which he placed garrisons
in Edom. Thus all the Edomites became David's
subjects, and the LORD brought David victory in
all his undertakings.

**David's Officials.** **15** [a]David reigned over
all Israel, judging and administering justice to
all his people. **16** Joab, son of Zeruiah, was in
command of the army. Jehoshaphat, son of Ahilud, was chancellor. **17** Zadok, son of Ahitub,
and Ahimelech, son of Abiathar, were priests.
Shawsha was scribe. **18** Benaiah, son of Jehoiada, was in command of the Cherethites and
Pelethites. And David's sons were priests.[b]

## CHAPTER 9

**David and Meribbaal.** **1** David asked, "Is
there any survivor of Saul's house to whom I
may show kindness for the sake of Jonathan?"[c]
**2** Now there was a servant of the family of Saul
named Ziba. He was summoned to David, and
the king asked him, "Are you Ziba?" He replied, "Your servant."[d] **3** Then the king inquired, "Is there any survivor of Saul's house
to whom I may show God's kindness?" Ziba
answered the king, "There is still Jonathan's
son, whose feet are crippled."[e] **4** The king said
to him, "Where is he?" and Ziba answered,
"He is in the house of Machir, son of Ammiel,
in Lodebar."[f] **5** So King David sent for him
and had him brought from the house of Machir,
son of Ammiel, in Lodebar. **6** When Meribbaal, son of Jonathan, son of Saul, came to David, he fell prostrate in homage. David said,
"Meribbaal," and he answered, "Your servant." **7** "Fear not," David said to him, "I
will surely be kind to you for the sake of your
father Jonathan. I will restore to you all the
lands of your grandfather Saul, and you shall
always eat at my table." **8** Bowing low, he
answered, "What is your servant that you

u Nm 23, 19; Jn 17, 17.
v 1-18: 1 Chr 18, 1-17.
w 3-8: 2 Sm 10, 15-19.
x 2 Sm 10, 6; 1 Kgs 11, 23.
y Jos 11, 6. 9.
z 2 Kgs 14, 7.
a 15-18: 2 Sm 20, 23-26; 1 Kgs 4, 1-6; 1 Chr 18, 14-17.
b 2 Sm 15, 18; 20, 7. 23; 23, 20.
c 2 Sm 21, 7; 1 Sm 18, 1-4; 20, 8ff. 15f. 42.
d 2 Sm 16, 1-4; 19, 27.
e 2 Sm 4, 4.
f 2 Sm 17, 27.
g 1 Sm 24, 15.

*

8, 1: Wresting . . .: the Hebrew text here gives "the bridle of the cubit"; 1 Chr 18, 1 understood "Gath and its dependent villages"; others implausibly read "dominion of the capital city."

8, 2: Two lengths . . . a full length: usually taken to mean that two-thirds of them were executed; but it could mean that two-thirds were spared, if the line was used full length in their case but doubled on itself to make "two lines" for those to be put to death.

8, 13: On his return: possibly to Jerusalem, after the revolt of Absalom, a circumstance which this catalogue of victories would avoid mentioning. 1 Chr 18, 13 attributes the defeat of the Edomites to Abishai.

should pay attention to a dead dog like me?''[g] **9** The king then called Ziba, Saul's attendant, and said to him: "I am giving your lord's son all that belonged to Saul and to all his family. **10** You and your sons and servants must till the land for him. You shall bring in the produce, which shall be food for your lord's family to eat. But Meribbaal, your lord's son, shall always eat at my table.'' Ziba, who had fifteen sons and twenty servants, **11** said to the king, "Your servant shall do just as my lord the king has commanded him.'' And so Meribbaal ate at David's table like one of the king's sons.[h] **12** Meribbaal had a young son whose name was Mica; and all the tenants of Ziba's family worked for Meribbaal.[i] **13** But Meribbaal lived in Jerusalem, because he always ate at the king's table. He was lame in both feet.[j]

## CHAPTER 10

**Insult of the Ammonites.** **1** [k]Some time later* the king of the Ammonites died, and his son Hanun succeeded him as king. **2** David thought, "I will be kind to Hanun, son of Nahash, as his father was kind to me.'' So David sent his servants with condolences to Hanun for the loss of his father. But when David's servants entered the country of the Ammonites, **3** the Ammonite princes said to their lord Hanun: "Do you think that David is honoring your father by sending men with condolences? Is it not rather to explore the city, to spy on it, and to overthrow it, that David has sent his messengers to you?'' **4** Hanun, therefore, seized David's servants and, after shaving off half their beards and cutting away the lower halves of their garments at the buttocks, sent them away.[l] **5** When he was told of it, King David sent out word to them, since the men were quite ashamed. "Stay in Jericho until your beards grow,'' he said, "and then come back.''

**Ammonites Defeated.** **6** *In view of the offense they had given to David, the Ammonites sent for and hired twenty thousand Aramean foot soldiers from Beth-rehob and Zobah, as well as the king of Maacah with one thousand men, and twelve thousand men from Tob.[m] **7** On learning this, David sent out Joab with the entire levy of trained soldiers.[n] **8** The Ammonites came out and drew up in battle formation at the entrance of their city gate, while the Arameans of Zobah and Rehob and the men of Tob and Maacah remained apart in the open country. **9** When Joab saw the battle lines drawn up against him, both front and rear, he made a selection from all the picked troops of Israel and arrayed them against the Arameans. **10** He placed the rest of the soldiers under the command of his brother Abishai, who arrayed them against the Ammonites. **11** Joab said, "If the Arameans are stronger than I, you shall help me. But if the Ammonites are stronger than you, I will come to help you. **12** Be brave; let us prove our valor for the sake of our people and the cities of our God; the LORD will do what he judges best.'' **13** When Joab and the soldiers who were with him approached the Arameans for battle, they fled before him. **14** The Ammonites, seeing that the Arameans had fled, also fled from Abishai and withdrew into the city. Joab then ceased his attack on the Ammonites and returned to Jerusalem.

**Arameans Defeated.** **15** [o]Then the Arameans responded to their defeat by Israel with a full mustering of troops; **16** Hadadezer sent for and enlisted Arameans from beyond the Euphrates. They came to Helam, with Shobach, general of Hadadezer's army, at their head. **17** On receiving this news, David assembled all Israel, crossed the Jordan, and went to Helam. The Arameans drew up in formation against David and fought with him. **18** But the Arameans gave way before Israel, and David's men killed seven hundred charioteers and forty thousand of the Aramean foot soldiers. Shobach, general of the army, was struck down and died on the field. **19** All of Hadadezer's vassal kings, in view of their defeat by Israel, then made peace with the Israelites and became their subjects. And the Arameans were afraid to give further aid to the Ammonites.

## CHAPTER 11

**David's Sin.** **1** At the turn of the year,* when kings go out on campaign, David sent out Joab along with his officers and the army of Israel, and they ravaged the Ammonites and besieged Rabbah. David, however, remained in Jerusalem.[p] **2** One evening David rose from his siesta and strolled about on the roof of the palace. From the roof he saw a woman bathing, who was very beautiful. **3** David had inquiries made about the woman and was told, "She is

h 2 Sm 19, 29.
i 1 Chr 8, 34.
j 2 Sm 21, 7.
k 1-19: 1 Chr 19, 1-19.
l Is 20, 4.
m 2 Sm 8, 3; 1 Sm 14, 47.
n 2 Sm 11, 1.
o 15-19: 2 Sm 8, 3-8; 1 Chr 9, 16-19.
p 2 Sm 10, 7; 1 Chr 20, 1.
q 2 Sm 23, 39.

*

10, 1: Some time later: early in the reign of David, since Hanun's father had been ruling in Ammon at the beginning of Saul's reign (1 Sm 11) and Solomon was as yet unborn (2 Sm 11, 1; 12, 24).

10, 6–9: A Hebrew text from Qumran (4Q Sam*) comes closer in these verses to what is given in 1 Chr 19, 6–9. The scene of the conflict is more likely Rabbath-Ammon, with Josephus (Ant., vii, 123), than Madeba, as in 1 Chr; compare ch 11.

11, 1: At the turn of the year: in the spring.

Bathsheba, daughter of Eliam, and wife of
[Joab's armor-bearer] Uriah the Hittite."[q]
**4** Then David sent messengers and took her.
When she came to him, he had relations with
her, at a time when she was just purified after
her monthly period. She then returned to her
house.[r] **5** But the woman had conceived, and
sent the information to David, "I am with
child."

**6** David therefore sent a message to Joab,
"Send me Uriah the Hittite." So Joab sent Uriah to David. **7** When he came, David questioned him about Joab, the soldiers, and how the
war was going, and Uriah answered that all was
well. **8** David then said to Uriah, "Go down to
your house and bathe your feet." Uriah left the
palace, and a portion was sent out after him
from the king's table. **9** But Uriah slept at the
entrance of the royal palace with the other officers of his lord, and did not go down to his own
house. **10** David was told that Uriah had not
gone home. So he said to Uriah, "Have you not
come from a journey? Why, then, did you not
go down to your house?" **11** Uriah answered
David, "The ark and Israel and Judah are
lodged in tents, and my lord Joab and your
majesty's servants are encamped in the open
field. Can I go home to eat and to drink and to
sleep with my wife? As the LORD lives and as
you live, I will do no such thing."[s] **12** Then
David said to Uriah, "Stay here today also, I
shall dismiss you tomorrow." So Uriah remained in Jerusalem that day. On the day following, **13** David summoned him, and he ate
and drank with David, who made him drunk.
But in the evening he went out to sleep on his
bed among his lord's servants, and did not go
down to his home. **14** The next morning David
wrote a letter to Joab which he sent by Uriah.
**15** In it he directed: "Place Uriah up front,
where the fighting is fierce. Then pull back and
leave him to be struck down dead." **16** So
while Joab was besieging the city, he assigned
Uriah to a place where he knew the defenders
were strong. **17** When the men of the city made
a sortie against Joab, some officers of David's
army fell, and among them Uriah the Hittite
died.

**18** Then Joab sent David a report of all the
details of the battle, **19** instructing the messenger, "When you have finished giving the king
all the details of the battle, **20** the king may
become angry and say to you: 'Why did you go
near the city to fight? Did you not know that
they would shoot from the wall above? **21** Who
killed Abimelech, son of Jerubbaal? Was it not
a woman who threw a millstone down on him
from the wall above, so that he died in Thebez?
Why did you go near the wall?' Then you in turn
shall say, 'Your servant Uriah the Hittite is also
dead.' "[t] **22** The messenger set out, and on his
arrival he relayed to David all the details as Joab
had instructed him.* **23** He told David: "The
men had us at a disadvantage and came out into
the open against us, but we pushed them back
to the entrance of the city gate. **24** Then the
archers shot at your servants from the wall
above, and some of the king's servants died,
among them your servant Uriah." **25** David
said to the messenger: "This is what you shall
convey to Joab: 'Do not be chagrined at this, for
the sword devours now here and now there.
Strengthen your attack on the city and destroy
it.' Encourage him."

**26** When the wife of Uriah heard that her
husband had died, she mourned her lord.
**27** But once the mourning was over, David sent
for her and brought her into his house. She
became his wife and bore him a son. But the
LORD was displeased with what David had
done.

## CHAPTER 12

**Nathan's Parable.** **1** *The LORD sent Nathan to David, and when he came to him, he
said: "Judge this case for me! In a certain town
there were two men, one rich, the other poor.[u]
**2** The rich man had flocks and herds in great
numbers. **3** But the poor man had nothing at all
except one little ewe lamb that he had bought.
He nourished her, and she grew up with him and
his children. She shared the little food he had
and drank from his cup and slept in his bosom.
She was like a daughter to him. **4** Now, the rich
man received a visitor, but he would not take
from his own flocks and herds to prepare a meal
for the wayfarer who had come to him. Instead
he took the poor man's ewe lamb and made a
meal of it for his visitor." **5** David grew very
angry with that man and said to Nathan: "As the
LORD lives, the man who has done this merits
death! **6** He shall restore the ewe lamb four-fold
because he has done this and has had no pity."[v]

**David's Punishment.** **7** Then Nathan said
to David: "You are the man! Thus says the
LORD God of Israel: 'I anointed you king of
Israel. I rescued you from the hand of Saul.[w]
**8** I gave you your lord's house and your lord's
wives for your own. I gave you the house of
Israel and of Judah. And if this were not

r Lv 15, 19.
s 1 Sm 4, 3f.
t Jgs 9, 50-54.
u Sir 47, 1.
v Ex 21, 37; Lk 19, 8.
w 1 Sm 16, 13.

*

11, 22: After this verse, the Greek text, which is here the older form, has David, angry with Joab, repeat exactly the questions Joab had foreseen in vv 20ff. In v 24 of our oldest Greek text, the messenger specifies that about eighteen men were killed.

12, 1–4: This utterance of Nathan is in regular lines in Hebrew, resembling English blank verse.

enough, I could count up for you still more.
**9** Why have you spurned the LORD and done
evil in his sight? You have cut down Uriah the
Hittite with the sword; you took his wife as your
own, and him you killed with the sword of the
Ammonites. **10** Now, therefore, the sword
shall never depart from your house, because you
have despised me and have taken the wife of
Uriah to be your wife.'[x] **11** Thus says the
LORD: 'I will bring evil upon you out of your
own house. I will take your wives while you live
to see it, and will give them to your neighbor.
He shall lie with your wives in broad daylight.[y]
**12** You have done this deed in secret, but I will
bring it about in the presence of all Israel, and
with the sun looking down.' "

**David's Repentance.** **13** Then David said
to Nathan, "I have sinned against the LORD."
Nathan answered David: "The LORD on his part
has forgiven your sin: you shall not die.[z] **14** But
since you have utterly spurned the LORD by this
deed, the child born to you must surely die."
**15** Then Nathan returned to his house.

The LORD struck the child that the wife of
Uriah had borne to David, and it became desper-
ately ill. **16** David besought God for the child.
He kept a fast, retiring for the night to lie on the
ground clothed in sackcloth. **17** The elders of
his house stood beside him urging him to rise
from the ground; but he would not, nor would
he take food with them. **18** On the seventh day,
the child died. David's servants, however, were
afraid to tell him that the child was dead, for
they said: "When the child was alive, we spoke
to him, but he would not listen to what we said.
How can we tell him the child is dead? He may
do some harm!" **19** But David noticed his servants whispering among themselves and realized that the child was dead. He asked his servants, "Is the child dead?" They replied,
"Yes, he is." **20** Rising from the ground, David washed and anointed himself, and changed
his clothes. Then he went to the house of the
LORD and worshiped. He returned to his own
house, where at his request food was set before
him, and he ate. **21** His servants said to him:
"What is this you are doing? While the child
was living, you fasted and wept and kept vigil;
now that the child is dead, you rise and take
food." **22** He replied: "While the child was
living, I fasted and wept, thinking, 'Perhaps the
LORD will grant me the child's life.' **23** But
now he is dead. Why should I fast? Can I bring
him back again? I shall go to him, but he will
not return to me."[a] **24** Then David comforted
his wife Bathsheba. He went and slept with her;
and she conceived and bore him a son, who was
named Solomon. The LORD loved him **25** and
sent the prophet Nathan to name him Jedidiah,
on behalf of the LORD.

**Ammonite War Ends.** **26** [b]Joab fought
against Rabbah of the Ammonites and captured
this royal city. **27** He sent messengers to David
with the word: "I have fought against Rabbah
and have taken the water-city. **28** Therefore,
assemble the rest of the soldiers, join the siege
against the city and capture it, lest it be I that
capture the city and it be credited to me." **29** So
David assembled the rest of the soldiers and
went to Rabbah. When he had fought against it
and captured it, **30** he took the crown from
Milcom's head. It weighed a talent,* of gold
and precious stones; it was placed on David's
head. He brought out immense booty from the
city, **31** and also led away the inhabitants,
whom he assigned to work with saws, iron
picks, and iron axes, or put to work at the brick-
mold. This is what he did to all the Ammonite
cities. David and all the soldiers then returned
to Jerusalem.

## CHAPTER 13

**The Crime of Amnon.** **1** Some time later
the following incident occurred. David's son
Absalom had a beautiful sister named Tamar,
and David's son Amnon loved her.[c] **2** He was
in such straits over his sister Tamar that he
became sick; since she was a virgin, Amnon
thought it impossible to carry out his designs
toward her. **3** Now Amnon had a friend named
Jonadab, son of David's brother Shimeah, who
was very clever.[d] **4** He asked him, "Prince,
why are you so dejected morning after morning?
Why not tell me?" So Amnon said to him, "I
am in love with Tamar, my brother Absalom's
sister." **5** Then Jonadab replied, "Lie down on
your bed and pretend to be sick. When your
father comes to visit you, say to him, 'Please let
my sister Tamar come and encourage me to take
food. If she prepares something appetizing in
my presence, for me to see, I will eat it from her
hand.' " **6** So Amnon lay down and pretended
to be sick. When the king came to visit him,
Amnon said to the king, "Please let my sister
Tamar come and prepare some fried cakes before my eyes, that I may take nourishment from
her hand."

**7** David then sent home a message to Tamar,
"Please go to the house of your brother Amnon
and prepare some nourishment for him." **8** Tamar went to the house of her brother Amnon,
who was in bed. Taking dough and kneading it,

x 2 Sm 13, 28f; 18, 14.
y 2 Sm 16, 11. 22.
z 1 Kgs 21, 29; Pss 32, 5; 50, 6; Sir 47, 11.
a Jb 7, 9.
b 26-31: 1 Chr 20, 1-3.
c 2 Sm 3, 2f; 1 Chr 3, 9.
d 1 Sm 21, 21.

* 12, 30: Weighed a talent: since this would be more than 75 pounds, some commentators picture the idol's crown as displaying a single precious stone of large size, which David took to wear; but the text does not say this.

she twisted it into cakes before his eyes and fried the cakes. **9** Then she took the pan and set out the cakes before him. But Amnon would not eat; he said, "Have everyone leave me." When they had all left him, **10** Amnon said to Tamar, "Bring the nourishment into the bedroom, that I may have it from your hand." So Tamar picked up the cakes she had prepared and brought them to her brother Amnon in the bedroom. **11** But when she brought them to him to eat, he seized her and said to her, "Come! Lie with me, my sister!" **12** But she answered him, "No, my brother! Do not shame me! That is an intolerable crime in Israel. Do not commit this insensate deed.[e] **13** Where would I take my shame? And you would be a discredited man in Israel. So please, speak to the king; he will not keep me from you."[f]

**14** Not heeding her plea, he overpowered her; he shamed her and had relations with her. **15** Then Amnon conceived an intense hatred for her, which far surpassed the love he had had for her. "Get up and leave," he said to her. **16** She replied, "No, brother, because to drive me out would be far worse than the first injury you have done me." He would not listen to her, **17** but called the youth who was his attendant and said, "Put her outside, away from me, and bar the door after her." **18** Now she had on a long tunic, for that is how maiden princesses dressed in olden days. When his attendant put her out and barred the door after her, **19** Tamar put ashes on her head and tore the long tunic in which she was clothed. Then, putting her hands to her head, she went away crying loudly. **20** Her brother Absalom said to her: "Has your brother Amnon been with you? Be still now, my sister; he is your brother. Do not take this affair to heart." But Tamar remained grief-stricken and forlorn in the house of her brother Absalom. **21** King David, who got word of the whole affair, became very angry. He did not, however, spark the resentment of his son Amnon, whom he favored because he was his firstborn. **22** Absalom, moreover, said nothing at all to Amnon, although he hated him for having shamed his sister Tamar.

**Absalom's Plot.** **23** After a period of two years Absalom had shearers in Baalhazor near Ephraim, and he invited all the princes. **24** Absalom went to the king and said: "Your servant is having shearers. Please, your majesty, come with all your retainers to your servant." **25** But the king said to Absalom, "No, my son, all of us should not go lest we be a burden to you." And though Absalom urged him, he refused to go and began to bid him goodbye. **26** Absalom then said, "If you will not come yourself, please let my brother Amnon come to us." The king asked him, "Why should he go to you?" **27** At Absalom's urging, however, he sent Amnon and all the other princes with him. Absalom prepared a banquet fit for royalty. **28** [g]But he had instructed his servants: "Now watch! When Amnon is merry with wine and I say to you, 'Kill Amnon,' put him to death. Do not be afraid, for it is I who order you to do it. Be resolute and act manfully."

**Death of Amnon.** **29** When the servants did to Amnon as Absalom had commanded, all the other princes rose, mounted their mules, and fled. **30** While they were still on the road, a report reached David that Absalom had killed all the princes and that not one of them had survived. **31** The king stood up, rent his garments, and then lay on the ground. All his servants standing by him also rent their garments.[h] **32** But Jonadab, son of David's brother Shimeah, spoke up: "Let not my lord think that all the young princes have been killed! Amnon alone is dead, for Absalom was determined on this ever since Amnon shamed his sister Tamar. **33** So let not my lord the king put faith in the report that all the princes are dead. Amnon alone is dead." **34** Meanwhile, Absalom had taken flight. Then the servant on watch looked about and saw a large group coming down the slope from the direction of Bahurim. He came in and reported this, telling the king that he had seen some men coming down the mountainside from the direction of Bahurim. **35** So Jonadab said to the king: "There! The princes have come. It is as your servant said." **36** No sooner had he finished speaking than the princes came in, weeping aloud. The king, too, and all his servants wept very bitterly. **37** But Absalom, who had taken flight, went to Talmai, son of Ammihud, king of Geshur,[i] **38** and stayed in Geshur for three years.

**Efforts for Absalom's Return.** **39** The king continued during all that time to mourn over his son; but his longing reached out for Absalom as he became reconciled to the death of Amnon.

## CHAPTER 14

**1** When Joab, son of Zeruiah, observed how the king felt toward Absalom, **2** he sent to Tekoa and brought from there a gifted woman, to whom he said: "Pretend to be in mourning. Put on mourning apparel and do not anoint yourself with oil, that you may appear to be a woman who has been long in mourning for a departed one. **3** Then go to the king and speak to him in this manner." And Joab instructed her what to say.

e Lv 18, 9; 20, 17; Dt 27, 22.
f Gn 34, 7.
g 28f: 2 Sm 12, 10.
h 2 Sm 1, 11.
i 2 Sm 3, 3; 15, 8.

4 So the woman of Tekoa went to the king
and fell prostrate to the ground in homage, saying, "Help, your majesty!" 5 [j]The king said to
her, "What do you want?" She replied: "Alas,
I am a widow; my husband is dead. 6 Your
servant had two sons, who quarreled in the
field. There being no one to part them, one of
them struck his brother and killed him. 7 Then
the whole clan confronted your servant and demanded: 'Give up the one who killed his brother. We must put him to death for the life of his
brother whom he has slain; we must extinguish
the heir also.' Thus they will quench my remaining hope* and leave my husband neither
name nor posterity upon the earth."[k] 8 The
king then said to the woman: "Go home. I will
issue a command on your behalf." 9 The woman of Tekoa answered him, "Let me and my
family be to blame, my lord king; you and your
throne are innocent." 10 Then the king said,
"If anyone says a word to you, have him
brought to me, and he shall not touch you
again." 11 But she went on to say, "Please,
your majesty, keep in mind the LORD your God,
that the avenger of blood may not go too far in
destruction and that my son may not be done
away with." He replied, "As the LORD lives,
not a hair of your son shall fall to the ground."

12 The woman continued, "Please let your
servant say still another word to my lord the
king." He replied, "Speak." 13 So the woman
said: "Why, then, do you think of this same
kind of thing against the people of God? In
pronouncing as he has, the king shows himself
guilty, for not bringing back his own banished
son. 14 We must indeed die; we are then like
water that is poured out on the ground and cannot be gathered up. Yet, though God does not
bring back life, he does take thought how not to
banish* anyone from him.[l] 15 And now, if I
have presumed to speak of this matter to your
majesty, it is because the people have given me
cause to fear. And so your servant thought: 'Let
me speak to the king. Perhaps he will grant the
petition of his maidservant. 16 For the king
must surely consent to free his servant from the
grasp of one who would seek to destroy me and
my son as well from God's inheritance.' "
17 And the woman concluded: "Let the word
of my lord the king provide a resting place;*
indeed, my lord the king is like an angel of God,
evaluating good and bad. The LORD your God
be with you."[m]

18 The king answered the woman, "Now do
not conceal from me anything I may ask you!"
The woman said, "Let my lord the king
speak." 19 So the king asked, "Is Joab involved with you in all this?" And the woman
answered: "As you live, my lord the king, it is
just as your majesty has said, and not otherwise.
It was your servant Joab who instructed me and
told your servant all these things she was to say.
20 Your servant Joab did this to come at the
issue in a roundabout way. But my lord is as
wise as an angel of God, so that he knows all
things on earth."

**Absalom's Return.** 21 Then the king said
to Joab: "I hereby grant this request. Go, therefore, and bring back young Absalom." 22 Falling prostrate to the ground in homage and blessing the king, Joab said, "This day I know that
I am in good favor with you, my lord the king,
since the king has granted the request of his
servant." 23 Joab then went off to Geshur and
brought Absalom to Jerusalem. 24 But the king
said, "Let him go to his own house; he shall not
appear before me." So Absalom went off to his
house and did not appear before the king.

25 In all Israel there was not a man who
could so be praised for his beauty as Absalom,
who was without blemish from the sole of his
foot to the crown of his head. 26 When he
shaved his head—which he used to do at the end
of every year, because his hair became too
heavy for him—the hair weighed two hundred
shekels according to the royal standard. 27 Absalom had three sons born to him, besides a
daughter named Tamar, who was a beautiful
woman.[n]

**Absalom Is Pardoned.** 28 Absalom lived
in Jerusalem for two years without appearing
before the king. 29 Then he summoned Joab to
send him to the king, but Joab would not come
to him. Although he summoned him a second
time, Joab refused to come. 30 He therefore
instructed his servants: "You see Joab's field
that borders mine, on which he has barley. Go,
set it on fire." And so Absalom's servants set
the field on fire.[o] Joab's farmhands came to him
with torn garments and reported to him what had
been done. 31 At this, Joab went to Absalom in
his house and asked him, "Why have your servants set my field on fire?" 32 Absalom answered Joab: "I was summoning you to come
here, that I may send you to the king to say:
'Why did I come back from Geshur? I would be
better off if I were still there!' Now, let me
appear before the king. If I am guilty, let him

j 5f: 2 Kgs 6, 26f.
k Nm 35, 19.
l Jb 7, 9; 14, 7-12; Ps 88, 5, 11ff.
m 17. 20: 1 Sm 29, 9.
n 2 Sm 18, 18.
o Jgs 15, 4f.

*

14, 7: Hope: literally, "glowing coal." The image is similar to that of the lighted lamp, e.g., Ps 89, 17, to keep alive the ancestral name.

14, 14: How not to banish: a possible allusion to the religious institution of cities of refuge for involuntary murderers; see Nm 35, 9–15.

14, 17: A resting place: cf Ps 95, 11; Heb 3, 7—4, 11. The reference here is to a return home for Absalom to Israel.

put me to death." **33** Joab went to the king and reported this. The king then called Absalom, who came to him and in homage fell on his face to the ground before the king. Then the king kissed him.

## CHAPTER 15

**Absalom's Plot.** **1** After this Absalom provided himself with chariots, horses, and fifty henchmen.[p] **2** Moreover, Absalom used to rise early and stand alongside the road leading to the gate. If someone had a lawsuit to be decided by the king, Absalom would call to him and say, "From what city are you?" And when he replied, "Your servant is of such and such a tribe of Israel," **3** Absalom would say to him, "Your suit is good and just, but there is no one to hear you in the king's name." **4** And he would continue: "If only I could be appointed judge in the land! Then everyone who has a lawsuit to be decided might come to me and I would render him justice." **5** Whenever a man approached him to show homage, he would extend his hand, hold him, and kiss him. **6** By behaving in this way toward all the Israelites who came to the king for judgment, Absalom was stealing away the loyalties of the men of Israel.

**Conspiracy in Hebron.** **7** After a period of four years, Absalom said to the king: "Allow me to go to Hebron and fulfill a vow I made to the LORD. **8** For while living in Geshur in Aram, your servant made this vow: 'If the LORD ever brings me back to Jerusalem, I will worship him in Hebron.' "[q] **9** The king wished him a safe journey, and he went off to Hebron. **10** Then Absalom sent spies throughout the tribes of Israel to say, "When you hear the sound of the horn, declare Absalom king in Hebron." **11** Two hundred men had accompanied Absalom from Jerusalem. They had been invited and went in good faith, knowing nothing of the plan. **12** Absalom also sent to Ahithophel the Gilonite, David's counselor, an invitation to come from his town, Giloh, for the sacrifices he was about to offer. So the conspiracy gained strength, and the people with Absalom increased in numbers.[r]

**David Flees Jerusalem.** **13** An informant came to David with the report, "The Israelites have transferred their loyalty to Absalom."[s] **14** At this, David said to all his servants who were with him in Jerusalem: "Up! Let us take flight, or none of us will escape from Absalom. Leave quickly, lest he hurry and overtake us, then visit disaster upon us and put the city to the sword." **15** The king's officers answered him, "Your servants are ready, whatever our lord the king chooses to do." **16** Then the king set out, accompanied by his entire household, except for ten concubines whom he left behind to take care of the palace.[t] **17** As the king left the city, with all his officers accompanying him, they halted opposite the ascent of the Mount of Olives, at a distance, **18** while the whole army marched past him.[u]

**David and Ittai.** As all the Cherethites and Pelethites, and the six hundred men of Gath who had accompanied him from that city, were passing in review before the king, **19** he said to Ittai the Gittite: "Why should you also go with us? Go back and stay with the king, for you are a foreigner and you, too, are an exile from your own country. **20** You came only yesterday, and shall I have you wander about with us today, wherever I have to go? Return and take your brothers with you, and may the LORD be kind and faithful to you." **21** But Ittai answered the king, "As the LORD lives, and as my lord the king lives, your servant shall be wherever my lord the king may be, whether for death or for life."[v] **22** So the king said to Ittai, "Go, then, march on." And Ittai the Gittite, with all his men and all the dependents that were with him, marched on. **23** Everyone in the countryside wept aloud as the last of the soldiers went by, and the king crossed the Kidron Valley with all the soldiers moving on ahead of him by way of the Mount of Olives, toward the desert.

**David and the Priests.** **24** Zadok, too [with all the Levite bearers of the ark of the covenant of God], and Abiathar brought the ark of God to a halt until the soldiers had marched out of the city. **25** Then the king said to Zadok: "Take the ark of God back to the city. If I find favor with the LORD, he will bring me back and permit me to see it and its lodging. **26** But if he should say, 'I am not pleased with you,' I am ready; let him do to me as he sees fit."[w] **27** The king also said to the priest Zadok: "See to it that you and Abiathar return to the city in peace, and both your sons with you, your own son Ahimaaz, and Abiathar's son Jonathan. **28** Remember, I shall be waiting at the fords near the desert until I receive information from you." **29** So Zadok and Abiathar took the ark of God back to Jerusalem and remained there.

**30** As David went up the Mount of Olives, he wept without ceasing. His head was covered, and he was walking barefoot. All those who were with him also had their heads covered and were weeping as they went.[x] **31** When David

p 1 Sm 8, 11; 1 Kgs 1, 5.
q 2 Sm 3, 3; 13, 37.
r 2 Sm 16, 23.
s Ps 3.
t 2 Sm 16, 21f; 20, 3.
u 2 Sm 8, 18.
v Ru 1, 16.
w 2 Sm 16, 10.
x 2 Sm 19, 5; Mi 1, 8.
y 2 Sm 16, 23; 17, 14. 23.

was informed that Ahithophel was among the conspirators with Absalom, he said, "O LORD, turn the counsel of Ahithophel to folly!"[y]

**David and Hushai.** **32** When David reached the top, where men used to worship God, Hushai the Archite was there to meet him, with rent garments and dirt upon his head.[z] **33** David said to him: "If you come with me, you will be a burden to me. **34** But if you return to the city and say to Absalom, 'Let me be your servant, O king; I was formerly your father's servant, but now I will be yours,' you will undo for me the counsel of Ahithophel.[a] **35** You will have the priests Zadok and Abiathar there with you. If you hear anything from the royal palace, you shall report it to the priests Zadok and Abiathar, **36** who have there with them both Zadok's son Ahimaaz and Abiathar's son Jonathan. Through them you shall send on to me whatever you hear." **37** So David's friend Hushai went into the city of Jerusalem as Absalom was about to enter it.

## CHAPTER 16

**David and Ziba.** **1** David had gone a little beyond the top when Ziba, the servant of Meribbaal, met him with saddled asses laden with two hundred loaves of bread, an ephah of cakes of pressed raisins, an ephah of summer fruits, and a skin of wine.[b] **2** The king said to Ziba, "What do you plan to do with these?" Ziba replied: "The asses are for the king's household to ride on. The bread and summer fruits are for your servants to eat, and the wine for those to drink who are weary in the desert." **3** Then the king said, "And where is your lord's son?" Ziba answered the king, "He is staying in Jerusalem, for he said, 'Now the Israelites will restore to me my father's kingdom.' "[c] **4** The king therefore said to Ziba, "So! Everything Meribbaal had is yours." Then Ziba said: "I pay you homage, my lord the king. May I find favor with you!"[d]

**David and Shimei.** **5** As David was approaching Bahurim, a man named Shimei, the son of Gera of the same clan as Saul's family, was coming out of the place, cursing as he came.[e] **6** He threw stones at David and at all the king's officers, even though all the soldiers, including the royal guard, were on David's right and on his left. **7** Shimei was saying as he cursed: "Away, away, you murderous and wicked man! **8** The LORD has requited you for all the bloodshed in the family of Saul,* in whose stead you became king, and the LORD has given over the kingdom to your son Absalom. And now you suffer ruin because you are a murderer." **9** Abishai, son of Zeruiah, said to the king: "Why should this dead dog curse my lord the king? Let me go over, please, and lop off his head."[f] **10** But the king replied: "What business is it of mine or of yours, sons of Zeruiah, that he curses? Suppose the LORD has told him to curse David; who then will dare to say, 'Why are you doing this?' "[g] **11** Then the king said to Abishai and to all his servants: "If my own son, who came forth from my loins, is seeking my life, how much more might this Benjaminite do so? Let him alone and let him curse, for the LORD has told him to.[h] **12** Perhaps the LORD will look upon my affliction and make it up to me with benefits for the curses he is uttering this day." **13** David and his men continued on the road, while Shimei kept abreast of them on the hillside, all the while cursing and throwing stones and dirt as he went.[i] **14** The king and all the soldiers with him arrived at the Jordan tired out, and stopped there for a rest.

**Absalom's Counselors.** **15** In the meantime Absalom, accompanied by Ahithophel, entered Jerusalem with all the Israelites. **16** When David's friend Hushai the Archite came to Absalom, he said to him: "Long live the king! Long live the king!"[j] **17** But Absalom asked Hushai: "Is this your devotion to your friend? Why did you not go with your friend?" **18** Hushai replied to Absalom: "On the contrary, I am his whom the LORD and all this people and all Israel have chosen, and with him I will stay. **19** Furthermore, as I was in attendance upon your father, so will I be before you. Whom should I serve, if not his son?"[k] **20** Then Absalom said to Ahithophel, "Offer your counsel on what we should do." **21** Ahithophel replied to Absalom: "Have relations with your father's concubines, whom he left behind to take care of the palace. When all Israel hears how odious you have made yourself to your father, all your partisans will take courage."[l] **22** So a tent was pitched on the roof for Absalom, and he visited his father's concubines in view of all Israel.[m]

**Counsel of Ahithophel.** **23** Now the counsel given by Ahithophel at that time was as though one had sought divine revelation. Such

z 2 Sm 16, 16.
a 2 Sm 16, 19.
b 2 Sm 4, 4; 9, 1-13; 19, 18. 25.
c 2 Sm 19, 26f.
d 2 Sm 19, 30.
e 2 Sm 3, 16; 19, 17. 22f; 1 Kgs 2, 8.
f 2 Sm 19, 23. 29; 1 Sm 24, 15; 26, 6.
g 2 Sm 15, 25f; 19, 23.
h 2 Sm 12, 11.
i 2 Sm 19, 19-24.
j 2 Sm 15, 32-37.
k 2 Sm 15, 34.
l 2 Sm 15, 16; 20, 3.
m 2 Sm 12, 11f.
n 2 Sm 15, 12. 31; 17, 23.

* 16, 8: Bloodshed . . . Saul: refers to the episode recounted in 2 Sm 21, 1–14.

was all his counsel both to David and to Absalom.[n]

## CHAPTER 17

**1** Ahithophel went on to say to Absalom: "Please let me choose twelve thousand men, and be off in pursuit of David tonight. **2** If I come upon him when he is weary and discouraged, I shall cause him to panic. When all the people with him flee, I shall strike down the king alone. **3** Then I can bring back the rest of the people to you, as a bride returns to her husband. It is the death of only one man you are seeking; then all the people will be at peace." **4** This plan was agreeable to Absalom and to all the elders of Israel.

**Counsel of Hushai.** **5** Then Absalom said, "Now call Hushai the Archite also; let us hear what he too has to say." **6** When Hushai came to Absalom, Absalom said to him: "This is what Ahithophel proposed. Shall we follow his proposal? If not, speak up." **7** Hushai replied to Absalom, "This time Ahithophel has not given good counsel." **8** And he went on to say: "You know that your father and his men are warriors, and that they are as fierce as a bear in the wild robbed of her cubs. Moreover, since your father is skilled in warfare, he will not spend the night with the people.[o] **9** Even now he lies hidden in one of the caves or in some other place. And if some of our soldiers should fall at the first attack, whoever hears of it will say, 'Absalom's followers have been slaughtered.' **10** Then even the brave man with the heart of a lion will lose courage. For all Israel knows that your father is a warrior and that those who are with him are brave.

**11** "This is what I counsel: Let all Israel from Dan to Beer-sheba, who are as numerous as the sands by the sea, be called up for combat; and go with them yourself. **12** We can then attack him wherever we find him, settling down upon him as dew alights on the ground. None shall survive—neither he nor any of his followers. **13** And if he retires into a city, all Israel shall bring ropes to that city and we can drag it into the gorge, so that not even a pebble of it can be found." **14** Then Absalom and all the Israelites pronounced the counsel of Hushai the Archite better than that of Ahithophel. For the LORD had decided to undo Ahithophel's good counsel, in order thus to bring Absalom to ruin.[p]

**David Told of the Plan.** **15** Then Hushai said to the priests Zadok and Abiathar: "This is the counsel Ahithophel gave Absalom and the elders of Israel, and this is what I counseled. **16** So send a warning to David immediately, not to spend the night at the fords near the desert, but to cross over without fail. Otherwise the king and all the people with him will be destroyed." **17** Now Jonathan and Ahimaaz were staying at En-rogel, since they could not risk being seen entering the city. A maidservant was to come with information for them, and they in turn were to go and report to King David. **18** But an attendant saw them and informed Absalom. They sped on their way and reached the house of a man in Bahurim who had a cistern in his courtyard. They let themselves down into this, **19** and the housewife took the cover and spread it over the cistern, strewing ground grain on the cover so that nothing could be noticed. **20** When Absalom's servants came to the woman at the house, they asked, "Where are Ahimaaz and Jonathan?" The woman replied, "They went by a short while ago toward the water." They searched, but found no one, and so returned to Jerusalem. **21** As soon as they left, Ahimaaz and Jonathan came up out of the cistern and went on to inform King David. They said to him: "Leave! Cross the water at once, for Ahithophel has given the following counsel in regard to you." **22** So David and all his people moved on and crossed the Jordan. By daybreak, there was no one left who had not crossed.

**23** When Ahithophel saw that his counsel was not acted upon, he saddled his ass and departed, going to his home in his own city. Then, having left orders concerning his family, he hanged himself. And so he died and was buried in his father's tomb.[q]

**24** Now David had gone to Mahanaim when Absalom crossed the Jordan accompanied by all the Israelites. **25** Absalom had put Amasa in command of the army in Joab's place. Amasa was the son of an Ishmaelite named Ithra, who had married Abigail, daughter of Jesse and sister of Joab's mother Zeruiah.[r] **26** Israel and Absalom encamped in the territory of Gilead.

**27** When David came to Mahanaim, Shobi, son of Nahash from Rabbah of the Ammonites, Machir, son of Ammiel from Lodebar, and Barzillai, the Gileadite from Rogelim,[s] **28** brought couches, coverlets, basins and earthenware, as well as wheat, barley, flour, roasted grain, beans, lentils,[t] **29** honey, butter and cheese from the flocks and herds, for David and those who were with him to eat; for they said, "The people have been hungry and tired and thirsty in the desert."

## CHAPTER 18

**Preparation for Battle.** **1** After mustering the troops he had with him, David placed offi-

o Hos 13, 8.
p 2 Sm 15, 31.
q 2 Sm 15, 31; 16, 23.
r 2 Sm 19, 14; 20, 4-13.
s 2 Sm 9, 4; 19, 32; 1 Kgs 2, 7.
t 2 Sm 19, 32; Ezr 2, 61.

cers in command of groups of a thousand and
groups of a hundred. **2** David then put a third
part of the soldiers under Joab's command, a
third under command of Abishai, son of Zeruiah
and brother of Joab, and a third under command
of Ittai the Gittite. The king then said to the
soldiers, "I intend to go out with you myself."
**3** But they replied: "You must not come out
with us. For if we should flee, we shall not
count; even if half of us should die, we shall not
count. You are equal to ten thousand of us.
Therefore it is better that we have you to help
us from the city." **4** So the king said to them,
"I will do what you think best"; and he stood
by the gate as all the soldiers marched out in
units of a hundred and of a thousand. **5** But the
king gave this command to Joab, Abishai and
Ittai: "Be gentle with young Absalom for my
sake." All the soldiers heard the king instruct
the various leaders with regard to Absalom.

**Defeat of Absalom.** **6** David's army then
took the field against Israel, and a battle was
fought in the forest near Mahanaim. **7** The
forces of Israel were defeated by David's servants, and the casualties there that day were
heavy—twenty thousand men. **8** The battle
spread out over that entire region, and the thickets consumed more combatants that day than did
the sword.

**Death of Absalom.** **9** Absalom unexpectedly came up against David's servants. He was
mounted on a mule, and, as the mule passed
under the branches of a large terebinth, his hair
caught fast in the tree. He hung between heaven
and earth while the mule he had been riding ran
off. **10** Someone saw this and reported to Joab
that he had seen Absalom hanging from a terebinth. **11** Joab said to his informant: "If you
saw him, why did you not strike him to the
ground on the spot? Then it would have been my
duty to give you fifty pieces of silver and a
belt." **12** But the man replied to Joab: "Even
if I already held a thousand pieces of silver in
my two hands, I would not harm the king's son,
for the king charged you and Abishai and Ittai
in our hearing to protect the youth Absalom for
his sake. **13** Had I been disloyal and killed him,
the whole matter would have come to the attention of the king, and you would stand aloof."
**14** Joab replied, "I will not waste time with
you in this way." And taking three pikes in
hand, he thrust for the heart of Absalom, still
hanging from the tree alive.[u] **15** Next, ten of
Joab's young armor-bearers closed in on Absalom, and killed him with further blows. **16** Joab
then sounded the horn, and the soldiers turned
back from the pursuit of the Israelites, because
Joab called on them to halt.[v] **17** Absalom was
taken up and cast into a deep pit in the forest,
and a very large mound of stones was erected
over him. And all the Israelites fled to their own
tents.[w]

**18** During his lifetime Absalom had taken a
pillar and erected it for himself in the King's
Valley, for he said, "I have no son to perpetuate
my name." The pillar which he named for himself is called Yad-abshalom to the present day.[x]

### David Told of Absalom's Death.

**19** Then Ahimaaz, son of Zadok, said, "Let me
run to take the good news to the king that the
LORD has set him free from the grasp of his
enemies." **20** But Joab said to him: "You are
not the man to bring the news today. On some
other day you may take the good news, but
today you would not be bringing good news, for
in fact the king's son is dead." **21** Then Joab
said to a Cushite, "Go, tell the king what you
have seen." The Cushite bowed to Joab and
sped away. **22** But Ahimaaz, son of Zadok,
said to Joab again, "Come what may, permit
me also to run after the Cushite." Joab replied:
"Why do you want to run, my son? You will
receive no reward." **23** But he insisted,
"Come what may, I want to run." Joab said to
him, "Very well." Ahimaaz sped off by way of
the Jordan plain and outran the Cushite.

**24** Now David was sitting between the two
gates, and a lookout mounted to the roof of the
gate above the city wall, where he looked about
and saw a man running all alone. **25** The lookout shouted to inform the king, who said, "If he
is alone, he has good news to report." As he
kept coming nearer, **26** the lookout spied another runner. From his place atop the gate he
cried out, "There is another man running by
himself." And the king responded, "He, too, is
bringing good news." **27** Then the lookout
said, "I notice that the first one runs like Ahimaaz, son of Zadok." The king replied, "He is
a good man; he comes with good news."[y]
**28** Then Ahimaaz called out and greeted the
king. With face to the ground he paid homage
to the king and said, "Blessed be the LORD your
God, who has delivered up the men who rebelled against my lord the king." **29** But the
king asked, "Is the youth Absalom safe?" And
Ahimaaz replied, "I saw a great disturbance
when the king's servant Joab sent your servant
on, but I do not know what it was." **30** The
king said, "Step aside and remain in attendance
here." So he stepped aside and remained there.
**31** When the Cushite came in, he said, "Let my
lord the king receive the good news that this day
the LORD has taken your part, freeing you from
the grasp of all who rebelled against you."
**32** But the king asked the Cushite, "Is young

u 2 Sm 12, 10; 13, 28f.
v 2 Sm 20, 23-26.
w Jos 7, 26; 8, 29; 10, 27.
x 2 Sm 14, 27.
y 2 Kgs 9, 20.

Absalom safe?'' The Cushite replied, ''May the
enemies of my lord the king and all who rebel
against you with evil intent be as that young
man!''

## CHAPTER 19

**1** The king was shaken, and went up to the
room over the city gate to weep. He said as he
wept, ''My son Absalom! My son, my son Absalom! If only I had died instead of you, Absalom, my son, my son!''

**Joab Reproves David.** **2** Joab was told
that the king was weeping and mourning for
Absalom; **3** and that day's victory was turned
into mourning for the whole army when they
heard that the king was grieving for his son.
**4** The soldiers stole into the city that day like
men shamed by flight in battle. **5** Meanwhile
the king covered his face and cried out in a loud
voice, ''My son Absalom! Absalom! My son,
my son!''[z] **6** Then Joab went to his residence
and said: ''Though they saved your life and your
sons' and daughters' lives, also the lives of your
wives and those of your concubines, you have
put all your servants to shame today **7** by loving
those who hate you and hating those who love
you. For you have shown today that officers and
servants mean nothing to you. Indeed I am now
certain that if Absalom were alive today and all
of us dead, you would think that more suitable.
**8** Now then, get up! Go out and speak kindly
to your servants. I swear by the LORD that if you
do not go out, not a single man will remain with
you overnight, and this will be a far greater
disaster for you than any that has afflicted you
from your youth until now.'' **9** So the king
stepped out and sat at the gate. When all the
people were informed that the king was sitting
at the gate, they came into his presence.

**The Reconciliation.** Now the Israelites had
fled to their separate tents, **10** but throughout
the tribes of Israel all the people were arguing
among themselves, saying to one another: ''The
king delivered us from the clutches of our enemies, and it was he who rescued us from the grip
of the Philistines. But now he has fled from the
country before Absalom, **11** and Absalom,
whom we anointed over us, died in battle. Why,
then, should you remain silent about restoring
the king to his palace?'' When the talk of all
Israel reached the king, **12** David sent word to
the priests Zadok and Abiathar: ''Say to the
elders of Judah: 'Why should you be last to
restore the king to his palace? **13** You are my
brothers, you are my bone and flesh. Why
should you be last to restore the king?' **14** Also
say to Amasa: 'Are you not my bone and flesh?
May God do thus and so to me, if you do not
become my general permanently in place of
Joab.' ''[a] **15** He won over all the Judahites as
one man, and so they summoned the king to
return, with all his servants.

**David and Shimei.** **16** When the king, on
his return, reached the Jordan, Judah had come
to Gilgal to meet him and to escort him across
the Jordan. **17** Shimei, son of Gera, the Benjaminite from Bahurim, hurried down with the
Judahites to meet King David,[b] **18** accompanied by a thousand men from Benjamin. Ziba,
too, the servant of the house of Saul, accompanied by his fifteen sons and twenty servants,
hastened to the Jordan before the king.[c]
**19** [d]They crossed over the ford to bring the
king's household over and to do whatever he
wished. When Shimei, son of Gera, crossed the
Jordan, he fell down before the king **20** and
said to him: ''May my lord not hold me guilty,
and may he not remember and take to heart the
wrong that your servant did the day my lord the
king left Jerusalem. **21** For your servant knows
that he has done wrong. Yet realize that I have
been the first of the whole house of Joseph to
come down today to meet my lord the king.''
**22** But Abishai, son of Zeruiah, countered:
''Shimei must be put to death for this. He cursed
the LORD's anointed.'' **23** David replied:
''What has come between you and me, sons of
Zeruiah, that you would create enmity for me
this day? Should anyone die today in Israel? Am
I not aware that today I am king of Israel?''[e]
**24** Then the king said to Shimei, ''You shall
not die.'' And the king gave him his oath.

**David and Meribbaal.** **25** Meribbaal, son
of Saul, also went down to meet the king. He
had not washed his feet nor trimmed his mus-
tache nor washed his clothes from the day the
king left until he returned safely. **26** When he
came from Jerusalem to meet the king, the king
asked him, ''Why did you not go with me,
Meribbaal?''[f] **27** He replied: ''My lord the
king, my servant betrayed me. For your servant,
who is lame, said to him, 'Saddle the ass for me,
that I may ride on it and go with the king.'[g]
**28** But he slandered your servant before my
lord the king. But my lord the king is like an
angel of God. Do what you judge best. **29** For
though my father's entire house deserved only
death from my lord the king, yet you placed
your servant among the guests at your table.
What right do I still have to make further appeal
to the king?''[h] **30** But the king said to him:
''Why do you go on talking? I say, 'You and

z 2 Sm 15, 30.
a 2 Sm 17, 25; 20, 4.
b 2 Sm 16, 5-13.
c 2 Sm 16, 1-4; 19, 25-31.
d 19ff: 2 Sm 16, 13; Ex 22, 27; 1 Kgs 2, 8.
e 2 Sm 16, 9f; 1 Sm 11, 13; 1 Kgs 2, 8. 38. 46.
f 2 Sm 16, 3.
g 2 Sm 9, 2-13; Dt 21, 12f.
h 2 Sm 9, 9ff.
i 2 Sm 16, 4.

Ziba shall divide the property.' "[i] **31** Meribbaal answered the king, "Indeed let him have it
all, now that my lord the king has returned
safely to his palace."

**David and Barzillai.** **32** Barzillai the Gileadite also came down from Rogelim and escorted the king to the Jordan for his crossing, taking
leave of him there.[j] **33** It was Barzillai, a very
old man of eighty and very wealthy besides,
who had provisioned the king during his stay in
Mahanaim. **34** The king said to Barzillai,
"Cross over with me, and I will provide for
your old age as my guest in Jerusalem." **35** But
Barzillai answered the king: "How much longer
have I to live, that I should go up to Jerusalem
with the king? **36** I am now eighty years old.
Can I distinguish between good and bad? Can
your servant taste what he eats and drinks, or
still appreciate the voices of singers and song-
stresses? Why should your servant be any further burden to my lord the king? **37** In escorting
the king across the Jordan, your servant is doing
little enough! Why should the king give me this
reward? **38** Please let your servant go back to
die in his own city by the tomb of his father and
mother. Here is your servant Chimham. Let him
cross over with my lord the king. Do for him
whatever you will." **39** Then the king said to
him, "Chimham shall come over with me, and
I will do for him as you would wish. And anything else you would like me to do for you, I will
do." **40** Then all the people crossed over the
Jordan, but the king remained; he kissed Barzillai and bade him Godspeed as he returned to his
own district. **41** Finally the king crossed over to
Gilgal, accompanied by Chimham.

**Israel and Judah Quarrel.** All the people
of Judah and half of the people of Israel had
escorted the king across. **42** But all these Israelites began coming to the king and saying, "Why
did our brothers the Judahites steal you away
and escort the king and his household across the
Jordan, along with all David's men?" **43** All
the Judahites replied to the men of Israel: "Because the king is our relative. Why are you
angry over this affair? Have we had anything to
eat at the king's expense? Or have portions from
his table been given to us?" **44** The Israelites
answered the Judahites: "We have ten shares in
the king. Also, we are the first-born rather than
you. Why do you slight us? Were we not first
to speak of restoring the king?" Then the Judahites in turn spoke even more fiercely than the
Israelites.[k]

## CHAPTER 20

**Sheba's Rebellion.** **1** Now a rebellious individual from Benjamin named Sheba, the son
of Bichri, happened to be there. He sounded the
horn and cried out,

> "We have no portion in David,
> nor any share in the son of Jesse.
> Every man to his tent, O Israel!"[l]

**2** So all the Israelites left David for Sheba, son
of Bichri. But from the Jordan to Jerusalem the
Judahites remained loyal to their king. **3** When
King David came to his palace in Jerusalem, he
took the ten concubines whom he had left behind to take care of the palace and placed them
in confinement. He provided for them, but had
no further relations with them. And so they
remained in confinement to the day of their
death, lifelong widows.[m]

**Amasa's Death.** **4** Then the king said to
Amasa: "Summon the Judahites for me within
three days. Then present yourself here."[n]
**5** Accordingly Amasa set out to summon Judah, but delayed beyond the time set for him by
David. **6** Then David said to Abishai: "Sheba,
son of Bichri, may now do us more harm than
Absalom did. Take your lord's servants and
pursue him, lest he find fortified cities and take
shelter while we look on." **7** So Joab and the
Cherethites and Pelethites and all the warriors
marched out behind Abishai from Jerusalem to
campaign in pursuit of Sheba, son of Bichri.[o]
**8** *They were at the great stone in Gibeon when
Amasa met them. Now Joab had a belt over his
tunic, from which was slung, in its sheath near
his thigh, a sword that could be drawn with a
downward movement.[p] **9** And Joab asked Amasa, "How are you, my brother?" With his
right hand Joab held Amasa's beard as if to kiss
him. **10** And since Amasa was not on his guard
against the sword in Joab's other hand, Joab
stabbed him in the abdomen with it, so that his
entrails burst forth to the ground, and he died
without receiving a second thrust. Then Joab
and his brother Abishai pursued Sheba, son of
Bichri.[q] **11** One of Joab's attendants stood by
Amasa and said, "Let him who favors Joab and
is for David follow Joab." **12** Amasa lay covered with blood in the middle of the highroad,
and the man noticed that all the soldiers were
stopping. So he removed Amasa from the road
to the field and placed a garment over him,
because all who came up to him were stopping.
**13** When he had been removed from the road,
everyone went on after Joab in pursuit of Sheba,
son of Bichri.

---

j 2 Sm 17, 27ff; 1 Kgs 2, 7; Ezr 2, 61.
k 1 Kgs 11, 31.
l 1 Kgs 12, 16.
m 2 Sm 15, 16; 16, 20ff.
n 2 Sm 17, 25; 19, 14.
o 2 Sm 8, 18.
p 2 Sm 2, 13.
q 1 Kgs 2, 5.

---

* 20, 8: The text of this verse is quite uncertain.

**Joab Pursues Sheba.** **14** Sheba passed through all the tribes of Israel to Abel Beth-maacah. Then all the Bichrites assembled and they too entered the city after him. **15** So David's servants came and besieged him in Abel Beth-maacah. They threw up a mound against the city, and all the soldiers who were with Joab began battering the wall to throw it down. **16** Then a wise woman from the city stood on the outworks and called out, "Listen, listen! Tell Joab to come here, that I may speak with him." **17** When Joab had come near her, the woman said, "Are you Joab?" And he replied, "Yes." She said to him, "Listen to what your maidservant has to say." He replied, "I am listening." **18** Then she went on to say: "There is an ancient saying,* 'Let them ask if they will in Abel[r] **19** or in Dan whether loyalty is finished or ended in Israel.' You are seeking to beat down a city that is a mother in Israel. Why do you wish to destroy the inheritance of the LORD?" **20** Joab answered, "Not at all, not at all! I do not wish to destroy or to ruin anything. **21** That is not the case at all. A man named Sheba, son of Bichri, from the hill country of Ephraim has rebelled against King David. Surrender him alone, and I will withdraw from the city." Then the woman said to Joab, "His head shall be thrown to you across the wall." **22** She went to all the people with her advice, and they cut off the head of Sheba, son of Bichri, and threw it out to Joab. He then sounded the horn, and they scattered from the city to their own tents, while Joab returned to Jerusalem to the king.

**David's Officials.** **23** Joab was in command of the whole army of Israel. Banaiah, son of Jehoiada, was in command of the Cherethites and Pelethites.[s] **24** Adoram was in charge of the forced labor. Jehoshaphat, son of Ahilud, was the chancellor. **25** Shawsha was the scribe. Zadok and Abiathar were priests.[t] **26** Ira the Jairite was also David's priest.

## *V: APPENDIXES*

### CHAPTER 21

**Gibeonite Vengeance.** **1** During David's reign there was a famine for three successive years. David had recourse to the LORD, who said, "There is bloodguilt on Saul and his family because he put the Gibeonites to death."[u] **2** So the king called the Gibeonites and spoke to them. (Now the Gibeonites were not Israelites, but survivors of the Amorites; and although the Israelites had given them their oath, Saul had attempted to kill them off in his zeal for the men of Israel and Judah.)[v] **3** David said to the Gibeonites, "What must I do for you and how must I make atonement, that you may bless the inheritance of the LORD?" **4** The Gibeonites answered him, "We have no claim against Saul and his house for silver or gold, nor is it our place to put any man to death in Israel." Then he said, "I will do for you whatever you propose." **5** They said to the king, "As for the man who was exterminating us and who intended to destroy us that we might have no place in all the territory of Israel, **6** let seven men from among his descendants be given to us, that we may dismember them before the LORD in Gibeon, on the LORD's mountain." The king replied, "I will give them up." **7** The king, however, spared Meribbaal, son of Jonathan, son of Saul, because of the LORD's oath that formed a bond between David and Saul's son Jonathan.[w] **8** But the king took Armoni and Meribbaal, the two sons that Aiah's daughter Rizpah had borne to Saul, and the five sons of Saul's daughter Merob that she had borne to Adriel, son of Barzillai the Meholathite,[x] **9** and surrendered them to the Gibeonites. They then dismembered them on the mountain before the LORD. The seven fell at the one time; they were put to death during the first days of the harvest—that is, at the beginning of the barley harvest.

**10** Then Rizpah, Aiah's daughter, took sackcloth and spread it out for herself on the rock from the beginning of the harvest until rain came down on them from the sky, fending off the birds of the sky from settling on them by day, and the wild animals by night.[y] **11** When David was informed of what Rizpah, Aiah's daughter, the concubine of Saul, had done, **12** he went and obtained the bones of Saul and of his son Jonathan from the citizens of Jabesh-gilead, who had carried them off secretly from the public square of Beth-shan, where the Philistines had hanged them at the time they killed Saul on Gilboa.[z] **13** When he had brought up from there the bones of Saul and of his son Jonathan, the bones of those who had been dismembered were also gathered up. **14** Then the bones of Saul and of his son Jonathan were buried in the tomb of his father Kish at Zela in the territory of Benjamin. After all that the king commanded had been carried out, God granted relief to the land.[a]

**Exploits in Philistine Wars.** **15** There was another battle between the Philistines and Israel. David went down with his servants and

r Gn 49, 16.
s 2 Sm 8, 16ff; 23, 20.
t 2 Sm 8, 17f.
u 2 Sm 24, 13.
v Jos 9, 3-27.
w 2 Sm 9, 13; 1 Sm 18, 3; 20, 8ff. 15f. 42.
x 2 Sm 3, 7.
y 2 Sm 3, 31; 12, 16.
z 1 Sm 31, 10-13.
a 2 Sm 24, 25.

* 20, 18f: The proverbial expression here has been poorly transmitted, and its sense is doubtful.

fought the Philistines, but David grew tired.
16 Dadu, one of the Rephaim, whose bronze
spear weighed three hundred shekels, was about
to take him captive. Dadu was girt with a new
sword and planned to kill David, 17 but Abishai, son of Zeruiah, came to his assistance and
struck and killed the Philistine. Then David's
men swore to him, "You must not go out to
battle with us again, lest you quench the lamp
of Israel."[b]

18 [c]After this there was another battle with
the Philistines in Gob. On that occasion Sibbecai, from Husha, killed Saph, one of the Rephaim.[d] 19 [e]There was another battle with the
Philistines in Gob, in which Elhanan, son of Jair
from Bethlehem, killed Goliath of Gath, who
had a spear with a shaft like a weaver's heddle-bar. 20 There was another battle at Gath in
which there was a man of large stature with six
fingers on each hand and six toes on each
foot—twenty-four in all. He too was one of the
Rephaim. 21 And when he insulted Israel, Jonathan, son of David's brother Shimei, killed
him.[f] 22 These four were Rephaim in Gath,
and they fell at the hands of David and his
servants.

## CHAPTER 22

**Song of Thanksgiving.*** 1 David sang the
words of this song to the LORD when the LORD
had rescued him from the grasp of all his enemies and from the hand of Saul.[g] 2 This is what
he sang:[h]

### A

I

"O LORD, my rock, my fortress, my deliverer,
3 my God, my rock of refuge!
My shield, the horn of my salvation,*
my stronghold, my refuge,
my savior, from violence you keep me safe.[i]
4 'Praised be the LORD,' I exclaim,
and I am safe from my enemies.

II

5 "The breakers of death surged round about me,*
the floods of perdition overwhelmed me;
6 The cords of the nether world enmeshed me,
the snares of death overtook me.
7 In my distress I called upon the LORD
and cried out to my God;
From his temple* he heard my voice,
and my cry reached his ears.

III

8 "The earth swayed and quaked;*
the foundations of the heavens trembled
and shook when his wrath flared up.
9 Smoke rose from his nostrils,
and a devouring fire from his mouth;
he kindled coals into flame.
10 He inclined the heavens and came down,
with dark clouds under his feet.[j]
11 He mounted a cherub* and flew,
borne on the wings of the wind.[k]
12 He made darkness the shelter about him,
with spattering rain and thickening clouds.
13 From the brightness of his presence
coals were kindled to flame.

14 "The LORD thundered from heaven;
the Most High gave forth his voice.
15 He sent forth arrows to put them to flight;
he flashed lightning and routed them.[l]
16 Then the wellsprings of the sea appeared,
the foundations of the earth were laid bare,
At the rebuke of the LORD,
at the blast of the wind of his wrath.

17 "He reached out from on high and grasped me;
he drew me out of the deep waters.[m]
18 He rescued me from my mighty enemy,
from my foes, who were too powerful for me.
19 They attacked me on my day of calamity,
but the LORD came to my support.

b 1 Kgs 11, 36; 15, 4; 2 Kgs 8, 19.
c 18-22: 1 Chr 20, 4-8.
d 2 Sm 23, 27.
e 19f: 1 Sm 17, 4. 7.
f 2 Sm 13, 3.
g Ps 18, 1.
h 2-51: Ps 18, 3-51.
i 1 Sm 2, 1f.
j Ps 144, 5.
k Ex 25, 18.
l Ps 144, 6.
m Ps 144, 7.

*

22, 1–51: This song of thanksgiving is also given, with a few small variants, in Ps 18. In both places it is attributed to David. Two main sections can be distinguished. In the first part, after an introductory stanza of praise to God (2–4), David describes the peril he was in (5–7), and then poetically depicts, under the form of a theophany, God's intervention in his behalf (8–20), concluding with an acknowledgment of God's justice (21–31). In the second part, God is praised for having prepared the psalmist for war (32–35), given him victory over his enemies (36–39), whom he put to flight (40–43), and bestowed on him dominion over many peoples (44–46). The entire song ends with paean of grateful praise (47–51).

22, 3: The horn of my salvation: my strong savior. The horn, the dreadful weapon of an enraged bull, was a symbol of strength; cf Lk 1, 69.

22, 5f: These verses are to be understood figuratively.

22, 7: His temple: his heavenly abode.

22, 8ff: God's intervention is graphically portrayed under the figures of an earthquake (vv 8. 16) and a thunderstorm (vv 9–15); cf Jgs 5, 4f; Pss 29; 97, 2–6; Hb 3.

22, 11: He mounted a cherub: since God makes the winds his messengers, or "angels" (Ps 104, 4), he is spoken of poetically as riding on the clouds, or on the angelic creatures called "cherubim." His earthly throne above the ark of the covenant was likewise associated with two winged cherubim; cf Ex 37, 7ff. In both senses the Lord is enthroned upon the cherubim; cf Pss 79, 2; 99, 1.

20 He set me free in the open,
and rescued me, because he loves me.

IV

21 "The LORD rewarded me according to my justice;
according to the cleanness of my hands he requited me.
22 For I kept the ways of the LORD
and was not disloyal to my God.
23 For his ordinances were all present to me,
and his statutes I put not from me;
24 But I was wholehearted toward him,
and I was on my guard against guilt.
25 And the LORD requited me according to my justice,
according to my innocence in his sight.

26 [n]"Toward the faithful you are faithful;*
toward the wholehearted you are wholehearted;
27 Toward the sincere you are sincere;
but toward the crooked you are astute.
28 You save lowly people,
though on the lofty your eyes look down.
29 You are my lamp,* O LORD!
O my God, you brighten the darkness about me.
30 For with your aid I run against an armed band,
and by the help of my God I leap over a wall.
31 God's way is unerring;
the promise of the LORD is fire-tried;
he is a shield to all who take refuge in him."[o]

## B

I

32 "For who is God except the LORD?
Who is a rock save our God?
33 The God who girded me with strength
and kept my way unerring;
34 Who made my feet swift as those of hinds
and set me on the heights;*
35 Who trained my hands for war
till my arms could bend a bow of brass.

II

36 "You have given me your saving shield,
and your help has made me great.
37 You made room for my steps;
unwavering was my stride.
38 I pursued my enemies and destroyed them,
nor did I turn again till I made an end of them.
39 I smote them and they did not rise;
they fell beneath my feet.

III

40 "You girded me with strength for war;
you subdued my adversaries beneath me.
41 My enemies you put to flight before me
and those who hated me I destroyed.
42 They cried for help—but no one saved them;
to the LORD—but he answered them not.
43 I ground them fine as the dust of the earth;
like the mud in the streets I trampled them down.

IV

44 "You rescued me from the strife of my people;
you made me head over nations.
A people I had not known became my slaves;
45 as soon as they heard me, they obeyed.
46 The foreigners fawned and cringed before me;
they staggered forth from their fortresses."

## C

47 "The LORD live! And blessed be my Rock!
Extolled be my God, Rock of my salvation.
48 O God, who granted me vengeance,
who made peoples subject to me
49 and helped me escape from my enemies,
Above my adversaries you exalt me
and from the violent man you rescue me.
50 Therefore will I proclaim you, O LORD,
among the nations,
and I will sing praise to your name,[p]
51 You who gave great victories to your king
and showed kindness to your anointed,
to David and his posterity forever."

# CHAPTER 23

## The Last Words of David*

1 These are the last words of David:
"The utterance of David, son of Jesse;
the utterance of the man God raised up,
Anointed of the God of Jacob,
favorite of the Mighty One of Israel.[q]
2 The spirit of the LORD spoke through me;
his word was on my tongue.[r]
3 The God of Israel spoke;
of me the Rock of Israel said,
'He that rules over men in justice,

n 26f: 1 Sm 2, 30.
o Prv 30, 5.
p Ps 22, 23; Rom 15, 9.
q 1 Kgs 2, 3-9; Sir 47, 8.
r Is 59, 21; Jer 1, 9.
s Ps 72, 1-4.

22, 26f: Men are treated by God in the same way they treat him and their fellow men.

22, 29: My lamp: a figure of life and happiness; cf 1 Kgs 11, 36.

22, 34: The heights: a natural stronghold safe from attack; cf Ps 62, 3; Hb 3, 19.

23, 1–7: The text of this short composition in the spirit of the wisdom writers (Prv 30, 1–6) is difficult in places; it views David's career in retrospect.

that rules in the fear of God,[s]
**4** Is like the morning light at sunrise
on a cloudless morning,
making the greensward sparkle after
rain.'[t]
**5** Is not my house firm before God?
He has made an eternal covenant with me,
set forth in detail and secured.[u]
Will he not bring to fruition
all my salvation and my every desire?
**6** But the wicked are all like thorns to be cast
away;
they cannot be taken up by hand.[v]
**7** He who wishes to touch them
must arm himself with iron and the shaft
of a spear,
and they must be consumed by fire."

**David's Warriors.** **8** These are the names
of David's warriors.* Ishbaal, son of Hachamoni, was the first of the Three. It was he
who brandished his battle-ax over eight hundred
slain in a single encounter.[w] **9** Next to him,
among the Three warriors, was Eleazar, son of
Dodo the Ahohite. He was with David at Ephes-
dammim when the Philistines assembled there
for battle. The Israelites had retreated,[x] **10** but
he stood his ground and fought the Philistines
until his hand grew tired and became cramped,
holding fast to the sword. The LORD brought
about a great victory on that day; the soldiers
turned back after Eleazar, but only to strip the
slain. **11** Next to him was Shammah, son of
Agee the Hararite. The Philistines had assembled at Lehi, where there was a plot of land full
of lentils. When the soldiers fled from the Philistines,[y] **12** he took his stand in the middle of
the plot and defended it. He slew the Philistines,
and the LORD brought about a great victory.
Such were the deeds of the Three warriors.

**13** During the harvest three of the Thirty
went down to David in the cave of Adullam,
while a Philistine clan was encamped in the
Vale of Rephaim.[z] **14** At that time David was
in the refuge, and there was a garrison of Philistines in Bethlehem. **15** Now David had a strong
craving and said, "Oh, that someone would
give me a drink of water from the cistern that is
by the gate of Bethlehem!" **16** So the Three
warriors broke through the Philistine camp and
drew water from the cistern that is by the gate
of Bethlehem. But when they brought it to David he refused to drink it, and instead poured it
out to the LORD, **17** saying: "The LORD forbid
that I do this! Can I drink the blood of these men
who went at the risk of their lives?" So he
refused to drink it.

**18** Abishai, brother of Joab, son of Zeruiah,
was at the head of the Thirty. It was he who
brandished his spear over three hundred slain.
He was listed among the Thirty **19** and commanded greater respect than the Thirty, becoming their leader. However, he did not attain to
the Three.

**20** Benaiah, son of Jehoiada, a stalwart from
Kabzeel, was a man of great achievements. It
was he who slew the two lions in Moab. He also
went down and killed the lion in the cistern at
the time of the snow.[a] **21** It was he, too, who
slew an Egyptian of large stature. Although the
Egyptian was armed with a spear, he went
against him with a club and wrested the spear
from the Egyptian's hand, then killed him with
his own spear. **22** Such were the deeds performed by Benaiah, son of Jehoiada. He was
listed among the Thirty warriors **23** and commanded greater respect than the Thirty. However, he did not attain to the Three. David put him
in command of his bodyguard.[b] **24** Asahel,*
brother of Joab. . . .[c]

Among the Thirty were: Elhanan, son of
Dodo, from Bethlehem; **25** Shammah from
En-harod; Elika from En-harod; **26** Helez from
Beth-pelet; Ira, son of Ikkesh, from Tekoa;
**27** Abiezer from Anathoth; Sibbekai from Hu-
shah;[d] **28** Zalmon from Ahoh; Maharai from
Netophah; **29** Heled, son of Baanath, from Netophah; Ittai, son of Ribai, from Gibeah of the
Benjaminites; **30** Benaiah from Pirathon; Hid-
dai from Nahale-gaash; **31** Abibaal from
Beth-arabah; Azmaveth from Bahurim; **32** Eliahba from Shaalbon; Jashen the Gunite; Jonathan, **33** son of Shammah the Hararite; Ahiam,
son of Sharar the Hararite; **34** Eliphelet, son of
Ahasbai, from Beth-maacah; Eliam, son of
Ahithophel, from Gilo; **35** Hezrai from Carmel; Paarai the Arbite; **36** Igal, son of Nathan,
from Zobah; Bani the Gadite; **37** Zelek the Ammonite; Naharai from Beeroth, armor-bearer of
Joab, son of Zeruiah; **38** Ira from Jattir; Gareb
from Jattir; **39** Uriah the Hittite—thirty-seven
in all.[e]

t Jgs 5, 31; Ps 72, 6.
u 2 Sm 7, 11. 15f; Ps 89, 30; Is 55, 3.
v Dt 13, 14.
w 8-39: 1 Chr 11, 41; 27, 1-15.
x 1 Sm 17, 1.
y Jgs 15, 9.
z 1 Sm 22, 1; Mi 1, 15.
a 2 Sm 8, 18; 20, 23; Jgs 14, 6; 1 Kgs 2, 29f.
b 1 Sm 22, 14.
c 2 Sm 2, 18-23.
d 2 Sm 21, 18.
e 2 Sm 11, 3f.

*

23, 8ff: There are thirty-seven warriors in all mentioned in this list. First there are the Three warriors most noted for singlehanded exploits (vv 8–12). Then comes the story of a daring adventure by three unnamed members of the larger group (vv 13–17). Next come the commanders of the king's bodyguard, Abishai (vv 18–19) and Benaiah (vv 20–23), with whom must be counted Asahel (v 24) and Joab (vv 18. 24. 37), and finally the group of the Thirty (vv 24–39).

23, 24: A more complete notice about Asahel, who died early in his career (2 Sm 2, 16–23), is to be presumed lost at this point. Elhanan is the first of the Thirty.

## CHAPTER 24

**Census of the People.** **1** *The LORD's anger against Israel flared again,[f] and he incited David against the Israelites by prompting him to number Israel and Judah. **2** Accordingly the king said to Joab and the leaders of the army who were with him, "Tour all the tribes in Israel from Dan to Beer-sheba and register the people, that I may know their number." **3** But Joab said to the king: "May the LORD your God increase the number of people a hundredfold for your royal majesty to see it with his own eyes. But why does it please my lord the king to order a thing of this kind?" **4** The king, however, overruled Joab and the leaders of the army, so they left the king's presence in order to register the people of Israel. **5** Crossing the Jordan, they began near Aroer, south of the city in the wadi, and went in the direction of Gad, toward Jazer. **6** They continued on to Gilead and to the district below Mount Hermon. Then they proceeded to Dan; from there they turned toward Sidon, **7** going to the fortress of Tyre and to all the cities of the Hivites and Canaanites, and ending up at Beer-sheba in the Negeb of Judah. **8** Thus they toured the whole country, reaching Jerusalem again after nine months and twenty days. **9** Joab then reported to the king the number of people registered: in Israel, eight hundred thousand men fit for military service; in Judah, five hundred thousand.

**The Pestilence.** **10** Afterward, however, David regretted having numbered the people, and said to the LORD: "I have sinned grievously in what I have done.[g] But now, LORD, forgive the guilt of your servant, for I have been very foolish."* **11** When David rose in the morning, the LORD had spoken to the prophet Gad, David's seer, saying: **12** "Go and say to David, 'This is what the LORD says: I offer you three alternatives; choose one of them, and I will inflict it on you.' " **13** Gad then went to David to inform him. He asked: "Do you want a three years' famine to come upon your land, or to flee from your enemy three months while he pursues you, or to have a three days' pestilence in your land? Now consider and decide what I must reply to him who sent me."[h] **14** David answered Gad: "I am in very serious difficulty. Let us fall by the hand of God, for he is most merciful; but let me not fall by the hand of man." **15** Thus David chose the pestilence. Now it was the time of the wheat harvest when the plague broke out among the people. [The LORD then sent a pestilence over Israel from morning until the time appointed, and seventy thousand of the people from Dan to Beer-sheba died.] **16** But when the angel stretched forth his hand toward Jerusalem to destroy it, the LORD regretted the calamity and said to the angel causing the destruction among the people, "Enough now! Stay your hand." The angel of the LORD was then standing at the threshing floor of Araunah the Jebusite.[i] **17** When David saw the angel who was striking the people, he said to the LORD: "It is I who have sinned; it is I, the shepherd, who have done wrong. But these are sheep; what have they done? Punish me and my kindred."*

**Sacrifice of Atonement.** **18** On the same day Gad went to David and said to him, "Go up and build an altar to the LORD on the threshing floor of Araunah the Jebusite." **19** Following Gad's bidding, David went up as the LORD had commanded. **20** Now Araunah looked down and noticed the king and his servants coming toward him while he was threshing wheat. So he went out and paid homage to the king, with face to the ground. **21** Then Araunah asked, "Why does my lord the king come to his servant?" David replied, "To buy the threshing floor from you, to build an altar to the LORD, that the plague may be checked among the people." **22** [j]But Araunah said to David: "Let my lord the king take and offer up whatever he may wish. Here are oxen for holocausts, and threshing sledges and the yokes of the oxen for wood. **23** All this does Araunah give to the king." Araunah then said to the king, "May the LORD your God accept your offering." **24** The king, however, replied to Araunah, "No, I must pay you for it, for I cannot offer to the LORD my God holocausts that cost nothing." So David bought the threshing floor and the oxen for fifty silver shekels. **25** Then David built an altar there to the LORD, and offered holocausts and peace offerings. The LORD granted relief to the country, and the plague was checked in Israel.

f 1-25: 1 Chr 21, 1-27.
g 1 Sm 24, 6; 1 Chr 21, 7.
h 2 Sm 21, 1.
i Ex 12, 23; 2 Kgs 19, 35.
j 22f: 1 Sm 6, 14; 1 Kgs 19, 21.

*

24, 1ff: This story was probably joined at one time to 2 Sm 21, 1–14.

24, 10: The narrative supposes that since the people belonged to the Lord rather than to the king, only the Lord should know their exact number.

24, 17: Before this verse a Qumran manuscript (4Q Sam$^{a}$) gives the fuller text of 1 Chr 21, 16, an alternative to the words "When David saw the angel who was striking the people."

# The Books of
# KINGS

*The two Books of Kings were originally, like 1 and 2 Samuel, a single historical work. In conjunction with the Books of Samuel, they extend the consecutive history of Israel from the birth of Samuel to the destruction of Jerusalem in 587 B.C. This combined work is designed as a religious history; hence in Kings the temple, which is the chosen site for the worship of Yahweh, occupies the center of attention.*

*The Books of Kings show clearly the theological bent of a Deuteronomic editor. In them, as already in Judges, material from various sources, such as the "book of the acts of Solomon" (1 Kgs 11, 41) and the "book of the chronicles of the kings of Israel" (1 Kgs 14, 19), is forged into structural unity by an editor whose principal interest is in the fidelity to Yahweh of rulers and people. The reigns of individual kings are adapted to an editorial framework consisting of a presentation and an obituary notice for each, in stereotyped formulas. In between, the achievements of the king are reported—above all, his fidelity or lack of fidelity to Yahweh. The faithful prosper; the unfaithful pay for their defections. Since this is basically a narrative of sin and retribution, it would not be inappropriate to entitle the Books of Kings "The Rise and Fall of the Israelite Monarchy."*

*Without minimizing the complexity of the process by which this material was transmitted for many centuries, one may speak of two editions of the Books: the first at some time between 621 B.C. and 597 B.C. and the second, final edition during the Exile; probably shortly after Jehoiachin was released from his Babylonian Prison (561 B.C.)*

*1 Kings carries the history of Israel from the last days and death of David to the accession in Samaria of Ahaziah, son of Ahab, near the end of the reign of Jehoshaphat, king of Judah. Judgment is passed on Ahaziah's reign but the details are given only later, in 2 Kings. We should note the two large cycles of traditions which grew up around the great prophetic figures of Elijah and Elisha, the former in 1 Kings and the latter chiefly in 2 Kings. These cycles, which interrupt the sequence of regnal chronicles, were very probably preserved and transmitted by the prophetic communities to which there are references in the same traditions. The Elijah cycle is the more important since it dramatically underscores Israel's critical struggle with the religion of Canaan.*

*The principal divisions of the Books of Kings are:*

*I. The Reign of Solomon (1 Kgs 1, 1–11, 43).*
*II. Judah and Israel to the Time of Ahab (1 Kgs 12, 1–16, 34).*
*III. Stories of the Prophets (1 Kgs 17, 1–22, 54).*
*IV. The Kingdoms of Israel and Judah (2 Kgs 1, 1–17, 41).*
*V. The Kingdom of Judah after 721 B.C. (2 Kgs 18, 1–25, 30).*

# THE FIRST BOOK OF KINGS

## I: The Reign of Solomon

### CHAPTER 1

**1** When King David was old and advanced in years, though they spread covers over him he could not keep warm. **2** His servants therefore said to him, "Let a young virgin be sought to attend you, lord king, and to nurse you. If she sleeps with your royal majesty, you will be kept warm." **3** So they sought for a beautiful girl throughout the territory of Israel, and found Abishag the Shunamite, whom they brought to the king. **4** The maiden, who was very beautiful, nursed the king and cared for him, but the king did not have relations with her.

**Ambition of Adonijah.** **5** Adonijah, son of Haggith, began to display his ambition to be king. He acquired chariots, drivers, and fifty henchmen. **6** Yet his father never rebuked him or asked why he was doing this. Adonijah was also very handsome, and next in age to Absalom by the same mother. **7** He conferred with Joab, son of Zeruiah, and with Abiathar the priest, and they supported him. **8** However, Zadok the priest, Benaiah, son of Jehoiada, Nathan the prophet, and Shimei and his companions, the pick of David's army, did not side with Adonijah. **9** When he slaughtered sheep, oxen, and fatlings at the stone Zoheleth, near En-rogel,* Adonijah invited all his brothers, the king's sons, and all the royal officials of Judah. **10** But he did not invite the prophet Nathan, or Benaiah, or the pick of the army, or his brother Solomon.

**Solomon Proclaimed King.** **11** Then Nathan said to Bathsheba, Solomon's mother: "Have you not heard that Adonijah, son of Haggith, has become king without the knowledge of our lord David? **12** Come now, let me advise you so that you may save your life and that of your son Solomon. **13** Go, visit King David, and say to him, 'Did you not, lord king, swear to your handmaid: Your son Solomon shall be king after me and shall sit upon my throne? Why, then, has Adonijah become king?' **14** And while you are still there speaking to the king, I will come in after you and confirm what you have said."

**15** So Bathsheba visited the king in his room, while Abishag the Shunamite was attending him because of his advanced age. **16** Bathsheba bowed in homage to the king, who said to her, "What do you wish?" **17** She answered him: "My lord, you swore to me your handmaid by the LORD, your God, that my son Solomon should reign after you and sit upon your throne. **18** But now Adonijah has become king, and you, my lord king, do not know it. **19** He has slaughtered oxen, fatlings, and sheep in great numbers; he has invited all the king's sons, Abiathar the priest, and Joab, the general of the army, but not your servant Solomon. **20** Now, my lord king, all Israel is waiting for you to make known to them who is to sit on the throne after your royal majesty.* **21** If this is not done, when my lord the king sleeps with his fathers, I and my son Solomon will be considered criminals."

**22** While she was still speaking to the king, the prophet Nathan came in. **23** When he had been announced, the prophet entered the king's presence and, bowing to the floor, did him homage. **24** Then Nathan said: "Have you decided, my lord king, that Adonijah is to reign after you and sit on your throne? **25** He went down today and slaughtered oxen, fatlings, and sheep in great numbers; he invited all the king's sons, the commanders of the army, and Abiathar the priest, and they are eating and drinking in his company and saying, 'Long live King Adonijah!' **26** But me, your servant, he did not invite; nor Zadok the priest, nor Benaiah, son of Jehoiada, nor your servant Solomon. **27** Was this done by my royal master's order without my being told who was to succeed to your majesty's kingly throne?"

**28** King David answered, "Call Bathsheba here." When she re-entered the king's presence and stood before him, **29** the king swore, "As the LORD lives, who has delivered me from all distress, **30** this very day I will fulfill the oath I swore to you by the LORD, the God of Israel, that your son Solomon should reign after me and should sit upon my throne in my place." **31** Bowing to the floor in homage to the king, Bathsheba said, "May my lord, King David, live forever!" **32** Then King David summoned Zadok the priest, Nathan the prophet, and Benaiah, son of Jehoiada. When they had entered the king's presence, **33** he said to them: "Take with you the royal attendants. Mount my son Solomon upon my own mule and escort him down to Gihon. **34** There Zadok the priest and Nathan the prophet are to anoint him king of Israel, and you shall blow the horn and cry, 'Long live King Solomon!' **35** When you come back in his train, he is to go and sit upon my throne and reign in my place. I designate him ruler of Israel and of Judah." **36** In answer to the king, Benaiah, son of Jehoiada, said: "So be it! May the LORD, the God of my lord the king, so decree! **37** As the LORD has been with your royal majesty, so may he be with Solomon, and exalt his throne even more than that of my lord, King David!"

**38** So Zadok the priest, Nathan the prophet, Benaiah, son of Jehoiada, and the Cherethites and Pelethites* went down, and mounting Solomon on King David's mule, escorted him to Gihon. **39** Then Zadok the priest took the horn of oil from the tent and anointed Solomon. They blew the horn and all the people shouted, "Long live King Solomon!" **40** Then all the people went up after him, playing flutes and rejoicing so much as to split open the earth with their shouting.

**41** Adonijah and all the guests who were with him heard it, just as they ended their banquet. When Joab heard the sound of the horn, he asked, "What does this uproar in the city mean?" **42** As he was speaking, Jonathan, son

*

1, 9: En-rogel: the modern Job's Well southeast of Jerusalem. It marked the ancient boundary between the tribes of Benjamin and Judah (Jos 15, 7; 18, 16). Here David's men sought information about Absalom's revolt (2 Sm 17, 17).

1, 20: At this time, neither law nor the right of primogeniture, but the will of the ruling monarch, determined succession to the throne.

1, 38: Cherethites and Pelethites: mercenaries in David's bodyguard. They became part of his retinue after he defeated the Philistines and established himself in Jerusalem; cf 2 Sm 8, 18; 15, 18; 20, 23.

of Abiathar the priest, arrived. "Come," said
Adonijah, "you are a man of worth and must
bring good news." **43** "On the contrary!" Jonathan answered him. "Our lord, King David,
has made Solomon king. **44** The king sent with
him Zadok the priest, Nathan the prophet, Benaiah, son of Jehoiada, and the Cherethites and
Pelethites, and they mounted him upon the
king's own mule. **45** Zadok the priest and Nathan the prophet anointed him king at Gihon,
and they went up from there rejoicing, so that
the city is in an uproar. That is the noise you
heard. **46** Besides, Solomon took his seat on
the royal throne, **47** and the king's servants
went in and paid their respects to our lord, King
David, saying, 'May God make Solomon more
famous than you and exalt his throne more than
your own!' And the king in his bed worshiped
God, **48** and this is what he said: 'Blessed be
the LORD, the God of Israel, who has this day
seated one of my sons upon my throne, so that
I see it with my own eyes.' "

**49** All the guests of Adonijah left in terror,
each going his own way. **50** Adonijah, in fear
of Solomon, also left; he went and seized the
horns of the altar.* **51** It was reported to Solomon that Adonijah, in his fear of King Solomon, had seized the horns of the altar and said,
"Let King Solomon first swear that he will not
kill me, his servant, with the sword." **52** Solomon answered, "If he proves himself worthy,
not a hair shall fall from his head. But if he is
found guilty of crime, he shall die." **53** King
Solomon sent to have him brought down from
the altar, and he came and paid homage to the
king. Solomon then said to him, "Go to your
home."

## CHAPTER 2

### David's Last Instructions and Death.

**1** When the time of David's death drew near,*
he gave these instructions to his son Solomon:
**2** "I am going the way of all mankind. Take
courage and be a man. **3** Keep the mandate of
the Lord, your God, following his ways and
observing his statutes, commands, ordinances,
and decrees as they are written in the law of
Moses, that you may succeed in whatever you
do, wherever you turn,[a] **4** and the LORD may
fulfill the promise he made on my behalf when
he said, 'If your sons so conduct themselves that
they remain faithful to me with their whole heart
and with their whole soul, you shall always have
someone of your line on the throne of Israel.'[b]
**5** You yourself know what Joab, son of Zeruiah, did to me when he slew the two generals of
Israel's armies, Abner, son of Ner, and Amasa,
son of Jether. He took revenge for the blood of
war in a time of peace, and put blood shed
without provocation on the belt about my waist
and on the sandal on my foot.[c] **6** Act with the
wisdom you possess; you must not allow him to
go down to the grave in peaceful old age.

**7** "But be kind to the sons of Barzillai the
Gileadite, and have them eat at your table. For
they received me kindly when I was fleeing your
brother Absalom.[d]

**8** "You also have with you Shimei, son of
Gera, the Benjaminite of Bahurim, who cursed
me balefully when I was going to Mahanaim.
Because he came down to meet me at the Jordan, I swore to him by the LORD that I would
not put him to the sword.[e] **9** But you must not
let him go unpunished. You are a prudent man
and will know how to deal with him to send
down his hoary head in blood to the grave."

**10** David rested with his ancestors and was
buried in the City of David.[f] **11** The length of
David's reign over Israel was forty years: he
reigned seven years in Hebron and thirty-three
years in Jerusalem.[g]

**The Kingdom Made Secure.** **12** When
Solomon was seated on the throne of his father
David, with his sovereignty firmly established,
**13** Adonijah, son of Haggith, went to Bathsheba, the mother of Solomon. "Do you come as
a friend?" she asked. "Yes," he answered,
**14** and added, "I have something to say to
you." She replied, "Say it." **15** So he said:
"You know that the kingdom was mine, and all
Israel expected me to be king. But the kingdom
escaped me and became my brother's, for the
LORD gave it to him. **16** But now there is one
favor I would ask of you. Do not refuse me."
And she said, "Speak on." **17** He said,
"Please ask King Solomon, who will not refuse
you, to give me Abishag the Shunamite for my
wife."* **18** "Very well," replied Bathsheba,
"I will speak to the king for you."

**19** Then Bathsheba went to King Solomon to
speak to him for Adonijah, and the king stood

a Dt 17, 19.
b 2 Sm 7, 11-16; Ps 132, 11f.
c 2 Sm 3, 27; 20, 10.
d 2 Sm 19, 33ff.
e 2 Sm 16, 5; 19, 19.
f Acts 2, 29.
g 1 Chr 29, 27.

*

1, 50: Horns of the altar: the protuberances on each of the four corners of the altar were surrounded with a special degree of holiness (Ex 27, 2; 29, 12), and constituted a place of asylum for transgressors of the law (Ex 21, 13f; 1 Kgs 2, 28).

2, 1–6. 8–9: Solomon is expected to remove from his father's family the imputation of blood guilt brought upon it by Joab in the unwarranted killings of Abner (2 Sm 3, 27–29) and Amasa (2 Sm 19, 9–10); and likewise to punish Shimei for his curse, the effects of which David had pledged himself not to avenge in person (2 Sm 19, 21–23). The standards of morality presumed in these verses are far from the Christian ones.

2, 17. 22–25: Abishag had been the concubine of King David (1 Kgs 1, 4). His successor, Solomon, inherited his father's harem. When Adonijah requested Abishag as his wife, he was subtly undermining the security of Solomon's throne and exposing himself to the suspicion of insurrection that would cost him his life; cf 2 Sm 3, 6–11; 16, 22.

up to meet her and paid her homage. Then he sat down upon his throne, and a throne was provided for the king's mother, who sat at his right. **20** "There is one small favor I would ask of you," she said. "Do not refuse me." "Ask it, my mother," the king said to her, "for I will not refuse you." **21** So she said, "Let Abishag the Shunamite be given to your brother Adonijah for his wife." **22** "And why do you ask Abishag the Shunamite for Adonijah?" King Solomon answered his mother. "Ask the kingdom for him as well, for he is my elder brother and has with him Abiathar the priest and Joab, son of Zeruiah." **23** And King Solomon swore by the LORD: "May God do thus and so to me, and more besides, if Adonijah has not proposed this at the cost of his life. **24** And now, as the LORD lives, who has seated me firmly on the throne of my father David and made of me a dynasty as he promised, this day shall Adonijah be put to death." **25** Then King Solomon sent Benaiah, son of Jehoiada, who struck him dead.

**26** The king said to Abiathar the priest: "Go to your land in Anathoth. Though you deserve to die, I will not put you to death this time, because you carried the ark of the Lord GOD before my father David and shared in all the hardships my father endured." **27** So Solomon deposed Abiathar from his office of priest of the LORD, thus fulfilling the prophecy which the LORD had made in Shiloh about the house of Eli.[h]

**28** When the news came to Joab, who had sided with Adonijah, though not with Absalom, he fled to the tent of the LORD and seized the horns of the altar. **29** King Solomon was told that Joab had fled to the tent of the LORD and was at the altar. He sent Benaiah, son of Jehoiada, with the order, "Go, strike him down." **30** Benaiah went to the tent of the LORD and said to him, "The king says, 'Come out.'" But he answered, "No! I will die here." Benaiah reported to the king, "This is what Joab said to me in reply." **31** The king answered him: "Do as he has said. Strike him down and bury him, and you will remove from me and from my family the blood which Joab shed without provocation. **32** The LORD will hold him responsible for his own blood, because he struck down two men better and more just than himself, and slew them with the sword without my father David's knowledge: Abner, son of Ner, general of Israel's army, and Amasa, son of Jether, general of Judah's army.[i] **33** Joab and his descendants shall be responsible forever for their blood. But there shall be the peace of the LORD forever for David, and his descendants, and his house, and his throne." **34** Benaiah, son of Jehoiada, went back, struck him down and killed him; he was buried in his house in the desert. **35** The king appointed Benaiah, son of Jehoiada, over the army in his place, and put Zadok the priest in place of Abiathar.

**36** Then the king summoned Shimei and said to him: "Build yourself a house in Jerusalem and live there. Do not go anywhere else. **37** For if you leave, and cross the Kidron Valley, be certain you shall die without fail. You shall be responsible for your own blood." **38** Shimei answered the king: "I accept. Your servant will do just as the king's majesty has said." So Shimei stayed in Jerusalem for a long time. **39** But three years later, two of Shimei's servants ran away to Achish, son of Maacah, king of Gath, and Shimei was informed that his servants were in Gath. **40** So Shimei rose, saddled his ass, and went to Achish in Gath in search of his servants, whom he brought back. **41** When Solomon was informed that Shimei had gone from Jerusalem to Gath, and had returned, **42** the king summoned Shimei and said to him: "Did I not have you swear by the LORD to your clear understanding of my warning that, if you left and went anywhere else, you should die without fail? And you answered, 'I accept and obey.' **43** Why, then, have you not kept the oath of the LORD and the command that I gave you?" **44** And the king said to Shimei: "You know in your heart the evil that you did to my father David. Now the LORD requites you for your own wickedness. **45** But King Solomon shall be blessed, and David's throne shall endure before the LORD forever." **46** The king then gave the order to Benaiah, son of Jehoiada, who struck him dead as he left.

## CHAPTER 3

**Wisdom of Solomon.** **1** With the royal power firmly in his grasp, Solomon allied himself by marriage with Pharaoh, king of Egypt. The daughter of Pharaoh, whom he married, he brought to the City of David, until he should finish building his palace, and the temple of the LORD, and the wall around Jerusalem.[j]

**2** However, the people were sacrificing on the high places, for up to that time no temple had been built to the name of the LORD. **3** Solomon loved the LORD, and obeyed the statutes of his father David; yet he offered sacrifice and burned incense on the high places.

**4** The king went to Gibeon to sacrifice there, because that was the most renowned high place. Upon its altar Solomon offered a thousand holocausts. **5** In Gibeon the LORD appeared to Solomon in a dream at night. God said, "Ask something of me and I will give it to you." **6** Solomon answered: "You have shown great favor to your servant, my father David, because

h 1 Sm 2, 31.
i 2 Sm 3, 27; 20, 10.
j 1 Kgs 7, 8; 2 Chr 1, 1.

he behaved faithfully toward you, with justice
and an upright heart; and you have continued
this great favor toward him, even today, seating
a son of his on his throne. **7** O LORD, my God,
you have made me, your servant, king to succeed my father David; but I am a mere youth,
not knowing at all how to act. **8** I serve you in
the midst of the people whom you have chosen,
a people so vast that it cannot be numbered or
counted. **9** Give your servant, therefore, an understanding heart to judge your people and to
distinguish right from wrong. For who is able to
govern this vast people of yours?"[k]

**10** The LORD was pleased that Solomon
made this request. **11** So God said to him: "Because you have asked for this—not for a long
life for yourself, nor for riches, nor for the life
of your enemies, but for understanding so that
you may know what is right— **12** I do as you
requested. I give you a heart so wise and understanding that there has never been anyone like
you up to now, and after you there will come no
one to equal you. **13** In addition, I give you
what you have not asked for, such riches and
glory that among kings there is not your like.[l]
**14** And if you follow me by keeping my statutes and commandments, as your father David
did, I will give you a long life."

**15** When Solomon awoke from his dream,
he went to Jerusalem, stood before the ark of the
covenant of the LORD, offered holocausts and
peace offerings, and gave a banquet for all his
servants.

**Solomon's Judgment.** **16** Later, two harlots came to the king and stood before him.
**17** One woman said: "By your leave, my lord,
this woman and I live in the same house, and I
gave birth in the house while she was present.
**18** On the third day after I gave birth, this woman also gave birth. We were alone in the house;
there was no one there but us two. **19** This
woman's son died during the night; she smoth-
ered him by lying on him. **20** Later that night
she got up and took my son from my side, as I,
your handmaid, was sleeping. Then she laid
him in her bosom, after she had laid her dead
child in my bosom. **21** I rose in the morning to
nurse my child, and I found him dead. But when
I examined him in the morning light, I saw it
was not the son whom I had borne."

**22** The other woman answered, "It is not so!
The living one is my son, the dead one is
yours." But the first kept saying, "No, the dead
one is your child, the living one is mine!" Thus
they argued before the king.

**23** Then the king said: "One woman claims,
'This, the living one, is my child, and the dead
one is yours.' The other answers, 'No! The dead
one is your child; the living one is mine.' "
**24** The king continued, "Get me a sword."
When they brought the sword before him, **25** he
said, "Cut the living child in two, and give half
to one woman and half to the other." **26** The
woman whose son it was, in the anguish she felt
for it, said to the king, "Please, my lord, give
her the living child—please do not kill it!" The
other, however, said, "It shall be neither mine
nor yours. Divide it!" **27** The king then answered, "Give the first one the living child! By
no means kill it, for she is the mother."

**28** When all Israel heard the judgment the
king had given, they were in awe of him, because they saw that the king had in him the
wisdom of God for giving judgment.

## CHAPTER 4

**Chief Officers of the Kingdom.** **1** Solomon was king over all Israel, **2** and these were
the officials he had in his service:

Azariah, son of Zadok, priest;
**3** Elihoreph and Ahijah, sons of Shisha, scribes;
Jehoshaphat, son of Ahilud, chancellor;
**4** [Benaiah, son of Jehoiada, commander of the army;
Zadok and Abiathar, priests;]
**5** Azariah, son of Nathan, chief of the commissaries;
Zabud, son of Nathan, companion to the king;
**6** Ahishar, major-domo of the palace; and
Adoniram, son of Abda, superintendent of the forced labor.

**Solomon's Royal State.** **7** *Solomon had
twelve commissaries for all Israel who supplied
food for the king and his household, each having to provide for one month in the year.
**8** Their names were:

the son of Hur in the hill country of Ephraim;
**9** the son of Deker in Makaz, Shaalbim, Beth-shemesh, Elon and Beth-hanan;
**10** the son of Hesed in Arubboth, as well as in Socoh and the whole region of Hepher;
**11** the son of Abinadab, who was married to Solomon's daughter Taphath, in all the Naphath-dor;
**12** Baana, son of Ahilud, in Taanach and Megiddo, and beyond Jokmeam, and in all Bethshean, and in the country around Zarethan below Jezreel from Beth-shean to Abelmeholah;
**13** the son of Geber in Ramoth-Gilead, having charge of the villages of Jair, son of

k 2 Chr 1, 10. l Wis 7, 11; Mt 6, 29.

*

4, 7–19: The administration of the kingdom thus initiated by Solomon continued in its main features for the duration of the monarchy in Israel and Judah.

Manasseh, in Gilead; and of the district
of Argob in Bashan—sixty large walled
cities with gates barred with bronze;
14 Ahinadab, son of Iddo, in Mahanaim;
15 Ahimaaz, who was married to Basemath,
another daughter of Solomon, in
Naphtali;
16 Baana, son of Hushai, in Asher and along
the rocky coast;
17 Jehoshaphat, son of Paruah, in Issachar;
18 Shimei, son of Ela, in Benjamin;
19 Geber, son of Uri, in the land of Gilead, the
land of Sihon, king of the Amorites,
and of Og, king of Bashan.

There was one prefect besides, in the king's
own land.*

## CHAPTER 5

7 These commissaries, one for each month,
provided food for King Solomon and for all the
guests at the royal table. They left nothing un-
provided. 8 For the chariot horses and draft
animals also, each brought his quota of barley
and straw to the required place.

20 *Judah and Israel were as numerous as the
sands by the sea; they ate and drank and made
merry. 1 Solomon ruled over all the kingdoms
from the River to the land of the Philistines,
down to the border of Egypt; they paid Solomon
tribute and were his vassals as long as he lived.[m]

2 Solomon's supplies for each day were thirty kors of fine flour, sixty kors of meal, 3 ten
fatted oxen, twenty pasture-fed oxen, and a
hundred sheep, not counting harts, gazelles,
roebucks, and fatted fowl.

4 He ruled over all the land west of the Euphrates, from Tiphsah to Gaza, and over all its
kings, and he had peace on all his borders round
about. 5 Thus Judah and Israel lived in security, every man under his vine or under his fig tree
from Dan to Beer-sheba, as long as Solomon
lived.

6 Solomon had four thousand stalls for his
twelve thousand chariot horses.[n]

9 [o]Moreover, God gave Solomon wisdom
and exceptional understanding and knowledge,
as vast as the sand on the seashore. 10 Solomon
surpassed all the Cedemites and all the Egyptians in wisdom. 11 He was wiser than all other
men—than Ethan the Ezrahite, or Heman,
Chalcol, and Darda, the musicians—and his
fame spread throughout the neighboring nations. 12 Solomon also uttered three thousand
proverbs, and his songs numbered a thousand
and five.[p] 13 He discussed plants, from the
cedar on Lebanon to the hyssop growing out of
the wall, and he spoke about beasts, birds, reptiles, and fishes. 14 Men came to hear Solomon's wisdom from all nations, sent by all the
kings of the earth who had heard of his wisdom.

**Preparations for the Temple.** 15 When
Hiram, king of Tyre, heard that Solomon had
been anointed king in place of his father, he sent
an embassy to him; for Hiram had always been
David's friend. 16 Solomon sent back this message to Hiram: 17 "You know that my father
David, because of the enemies surrounding him
on all sides, could not build a temple in honor
of the LORD, his God, until such a time as the
LORD should put these enemies under the soles
of his feet. 18 But now the LORD, my God, has
given me peace on all sides. There is no enemy
or threat of danger. 19 So I propose to build a
temple in honor of the LORD, my God, as the
LORD predicted to my father David when he
said: 'It is your son whom I will put upon your
throne in your place who shall build the temple
in my honor.'[q] 20 Give orders, then, to have
cedars from the Lebanon cut down for me. My
servants shall accompany yours, since you
know that there is no one among us who is
skilled in cutting timber like the Sidonians, and
I will pay you whatever you say for your servants' salary."

21 When he had heard the words of Solomon, Hiram was pleased and said, "Blessed be
the LORD this day, who has given David a wise
son to rule this numerous people." 22 Hiram
then sent word to Solomon, "I agree to the
proposal you sent me, and I will provide all the
cedars and fir trees you wish. 23 My servants
shall bring them down from the Lebanon to the
sea, and I will arrange them into rafts in the sea
and bring them wherever you say. There I will
break up the rafts, and you shall take the lum-
ber. You, for your part, shall furnish the provisions I desire for my household."

24 So Hiram continued to provide Solomon
with all the cedars and fir trees he wished;
25 while Solomon every year gave Hiram
twenty thousand kors of wheat to provide for his
household, and twenty thousand measures of
pure oil. 26 The LORD, moreover, gave Solomon wisdom as he promised him, and there was
peace between Hiram and Solomon, since they
were parties to a treaty.

27 King Solomon conscripted thirty thousand workmen from all Israel. 28 He sent them
to the Lebanon each month in relays of ten
thousand, so that they spent one month in the
Lebanon and two months at home. Adoniram

m Sir 47, 15f; 2 Chr 9, 26.
n 2 Chr 9, 25f.
o 9-14; Sir 47, 16f.
p 1 Kgs 3, 12.
q 2 Sm 7, 13; 1 Chr 22, 10.

*

4, 19: One prefect . . . in the king's own land: the royal territory of Judah had its own peculiar administration different from that of the twelve districts which had to supply the king and his household with a month's provisions of food each year (v 7).

5, 20: This verse belongs to ch 4.

was in charge of the draft. **29** Solomon had
seventy thousand carriers and eighty thousand
stonecutters in the mountain, **30** in addition to
three thousand three hundred overseers, answerable to Solomon's prefects for the work,
directing the people engaged in the work.
**31** By order of the king, fine, large blocks were
quarried to give the temple a foundation of hewn
stone. **32** Solomon's and Hiram's builders,
along with the Gebalites, hewed them out, and
prepared the wood and stones for building the
temple.

## CHAPTER 6

**Building of the Temple.** **1** In the four hundred and eightieth year from the departure of the
Israelites from the land of Egypt, in the fourth
year of Solomon's reign over Israel, in the
month of Ziv, which is the second month, the
construction of the temple of the LORD* was
begun.[r]
**2** The temple which King Solomon built for
the LORD was sixty cubits long, twenty wide,
and twenty-five high. **3** The porch in front of
the temple was twenty cubits from side to side,
along the width of the nave, and ten cubits deep
in front of the temple. **4** Splayed windows with
trellises were made for the temple, **5** and adjoining the wall of the temple, which enclosed
the nave and the sanctuary, an annex of several
stories was built. **6** Its lowest story was five
cubits wide, the middle one six cubits wide, the
third seven cubits wide, because there were offsets along the outside of the temple so that the
beams would not be fastened into the walls of
the temple. **7** (The temple was built of stone
dressed at the quarry, so that no hammer, axe,
or iron tool was to be heard in the temple during
its construction.) **8** The entrance to the lowest
floor of the annex was at the right side of the
temple, and stairs with intermediate landings
led up to the middle story and from the middle
story to the third. **9** When the temple was built
to its full height, it was roofed in with rafters
and boards of cedar. **10** The annex, with its
lowest story five cubits high, was built all along
the outside of the temple, to which it was joined
by cedar beams.
**11** This word of the LORD* came to Solomon: **12** "As to this temple you are building
—if you observe my statutes, carry out my ordinances, keep and obey all my commands, I will
fulfill toward you the promise I made to your
father David.[s] **13** [t]I will dwell in the midst of
the Israelites and will not forsake my people
Israel."
**14** When Solomon finished building the temple, **15** its walls were lined from floor to ceiling
beams with cedar paneling, and its floor was
laid with fir planking. **16** At the rear of the
temple a space of twenty cubits was set off by
cedar partitions from the floor to the rafters,
enclosing the sanctuary, the holy of holies.
**17** The nave, or part of the temple in front of
the sanctuary, was forty cubits long. **18** The
cedar in the interior of the temple was carved in
the form of gourds and open flowers; all was of
cedar, and no stone was to be seen.
**19** In the innermost part of the temple* was
located the sanctuary to house the ark of the
LORD's covenant, **20** twenty cubits long, twenty wide, and twenty high.* **21** Solomon overlaid the interior of the temple with pure gold. He
made in front of the sanctuary a cedar altar,
overlaid it with gold, and looped it with golden
chains. **22** The entire temple was overlaid with
gold so that it was completely covered with it;
the whole altar before the sanctuary was also
overlaid with gold. **23** In the sanctuary were
two cherubim, each ten cubits high, made of
olive wood. **24** Each wing of a cherub measured five cubits so that the space from wing tip
to wing tip of each was ten cubits. **25** The cherubim were identical in size and shape, **26** and
each was exactly ten cubits high. **27** The cherubim were placed in the inmost part of the temple, with their wings spread wide, so that one
wing of each cherub touched a side wall while
the other wing, pointing toward the middle of
the room, touched the corresponding wing of
the second cherub. **28** The cherubim, too, were
overlaid with gold.
**29** The walls on all sides of both the inner
and the outer rooms had carved figures of cherubim, palm trees, and open flowers. **30** The
floor of both the inner and the outer rooms was
overlaid with gold. **31** At the entrance of the
sanctuary, doors of olive wood were made; the

r 2 Chr 3, 1.
s 2 Sm 7, 13.
t 1 Chr 22, 9f.

*

6, 1: Construction of the temple of the Lord is here paralleled in importance with the founding of the nation after the departure from Egypt. In both, God is the central figure who chose Israel as his people, and now chooses the place where his temple should be built (Dt 12, 4–18. 26). The year is given in a round number, 480, which corresponds to twelve generations. The fourth year of Solomon's reign: c. 968 B.C.

6, 11ff: The word of the Lord . . . my people Israel: the oracle, which came as a climax at the completion of the work, was an expression of God's acceptance and approval. Nevertheless the fulfillment of God's promises to David and his royal descendants will depend on their observance of his ordinances and commands.

6, 19: The innermost part of the temple: the sanctuary or holy of holies reserved exclusively for the Lord. Here through his presence he dwelt as on a throne between the cherubim above the ark of the covenant (2 Kgs 6, 23–28; 2 Chr 3, 10–13). See note on Ex 25, 18ff.

6, 20: Twenty (cubits) high: it is usually supposed that the holy of holies was of this height because it had a raised floor, five cubits above the floor level of the nave, rather than a dropped ceiling. The building was twenty-five cubits high (v 2) according to the reading here followed.

doorframes had beveled posts. **32** The two doors were of olive wood, with carved figures of cherubim, palm trees, and open flowers. The doors were overlaid with gold, which was also molded to the cherubim and the palm trees. **33** The same was done at the entrance to the nave, where the doorposts of olive wood were rectangular. **34** The two doors were of fir wood; each door was banded by a metal strap, front and back, **35** and had carved cherubim, palm trees, and open flowers, over which gold was evenly applied.

**36** The inner court was walled off by means of three courses of hewn stones and one course of cedar beams.

**37** The foundations of the LORD's temple were laid in the month of Ziv **38** in the fourth year, and it was completed in all particulars, exactly according to plan, in the month of Bul, the eighth month, in the eleventh year. Thus it took Solomon seven years to build it.

## CHAPTER 7

**Building of the Palace.** **1** His own palace Solomon completed after thirteen years of construction.[u] **2** He built the hall called the Forest of Lebanon one hundred cubits long, fifty wide, and thirty high; it was supported by four rows of cedar columns, with cedar capitals upon the columns. **3** Moreover, it had a ceiling of cedar above the beams resting on the columns; these beams numbered forty-five, fifteen to a row. **4** There were three window frames at either end, with windows in strict alignment. **5** The posts of all the doorways were rectangular, and the doorways faced each other, three at either end. **6** The porch of the columned hall he made fifty cubits long and thirty wide. The porch extended the width of the columned hall, and there was a canopy in front. **7** He also built the vestibule of the throne where he gave judgment—that is, the tribunal; it was paneled with cedar from floor to ceiling beams. **8** His living quarters were in another court, set in deeper than the tribunal and of the same construction. A palace like this tribunal was built for Pharaoh's daughter, whom Solomon had married.[v]

**9** All these buildings were of fine stones, hewn to size and trimmed front and back with a saw, from the foundation to the bonding course. **10** (The foundation was made of fine, large blocks, some ten cubits and some eight cubits. **11** Above were fine stones hewn to size, and cedar wood.) **12** The great court was enclosed by three courses of hewn stones and a bonding course of cedar beams. So also were the inner court of the temple of the LORD and the temple porch.

**Furnishing of the Temple.** **13** King Solomon had Hiram brought from Tyre. **14** He was a bronze worker, the son of a widow from the tribe of Naphtali; his father had been from Tyre. He was endowed with skill, understanding, and knowledge of how to produce any work in bronze. He came to King Solomon and did all his metal work.

**15** Two hollow bronze columns* were cast, each eighteen cubits high and twelve cubits in circumference; their metal was of four fingers' thickness.[w] **16** There were also two capitals cast in bronze, to place on top of the columns, each of them five cubits high. **17** Two pieces of network with a chainlike mesh were made to cover the (nodes of the) capitals on top of the columns, one for each capital. **18** Four hundred pomegranates were also cast; two hundred of them in a double row encircled the piece of network on each of the two capitals. **19** The capitals on top of the columns were finished wholly in a lotus pattern **20** above the level of the nodes and their enveloping network. **21** The columns were then erected adjacent to the porch of the temple, one to the right, called Jachin, and the other to the left, called Boaz. **22** Thus the work on the columns was completed.

**23** *The sea was then cast; it was made with a circular rim, and measured ten cubit across, five in height, and thirty in circumference.[x] **24** Under the brim, gourds encircled it, ten to the cubit all the way around; the gourds were in two rows and were cast in one mold with the sea. **25** This rested on twelve oxen, three facing north, three facing west, three facing south, and three facing east, with their haunches all toward the center, where the sea was set upon them. **26** It was a handbreadth thick, and its brim resembled that of a cup, being lily-shaped. Its capacity was two thousand measures.

**27** Ten stands were also made of bronze, each four cubits long, four wide, and three high. **28** When these stands were constructed, panels were set within the framework. **29** On the panels between the frames there were lions, oxen, and cherubim; and on the frames likewise, above and below the lions and oxen, there were wreaths in relief.

**30** Each stand had four bronze wheels and bronze axles. **32** The four wheels were below the paneling, and the axle-trees of the wheels and the stand were of one piece. Each wheel was

u 1 Kgs 9, 10.
v 1 Kgs 3, 1.
w Jer 52, 21.
x 2 Chr 4, 2.

* 7, 15–21: The two hollow bronze columns, Jachin and Boaz (2 Chr 3, 17), stood free to the right and left of the temple porch. The names are related to God's power (Boaz) founding (Jachin) the temple and his people.

7, 23–26: The sea . . . rested on twelve oxen: this was a large circular tank containing about twelve thousand gallons of water.

a cubit and a half high. **33** The wheels were
constructed like chariot wheels; their axles, fel-
lies, spokes, and hubs were all cast.

The four legs of each stand had cast braces,
which were under the basin; they had wreaths on
each side. **34** These four braces, extending to
the corners of each stand, were of one piece with
the stand.

**35** On top of the stand there was a raised
collar half a cubit high, with supports and panels
which were of one piece with the top of the
stand. **31** This was surmounted by a crown one
cubit high within which was a rounded opening
to provide a receptacle a cubit and a half in
depth. There was carved work at the opening,
on panels that were angular, not curved. **36** On
the surfaces of the supports and on the panels,
wherever there was a clear space, cherubim,
lions, and palm trees were carved, as well as
wreaths all around. **37** This was how the ten
stands were made, all of the same casting, the
same size, the same shape. **38** Ten bronze basins were then made, each four cubits in diameter with a capacity of forty measures, one basin
for the top of each of the ten stands. **39** The
stands were placed, five on the south side of the
temple and five on the north. The sea was placed
off to the southeast from the south side of the
temple.

**40** When Hiram made the pots, shovels, and
bowls, he therewith completed all his work for
King Solomon in the temple of the LORD:
**41** two columns, two nodes for the capitals on
top of the columns, two pieces of network covering the nodes for the capitals on top of the
columns, **42** four hundred pomegranates in
double rows on both pieces of network that
covered the two nodes of the capitals where they
met the columns, **43** ten stands, ten basins on
the stands, **44** one sea, twelve oxen supporting
the sea, **45** pots, shovels, and bowls. All these
articles which Hiram made for King Solomon in
the temple of the LORD were of burnished
bronze. **46** The king had them cast in the neighborhood of the Jordan, in the clayey ground
between Succoth and Zarethan. **47** Solomon
did not weigh all the articles because they were
so numerous; the weight of the bronze, therefore, was not determined.

**48** Solomon had all the articles made for the
interior of the temple of the LORD: the golden
altar; the golden table on which the showbread
lay; **49** the lampstands of pure gold, five to the
right and five to the left before the sanctuary,
with their flowers, lamps, and tongs of gold;
**50** basins, snuffers, bowls, cups, and fire pans
of pure gold; and hinges of gold for the doors
of the inner room, or holy of holies, and for the
doors of the outer room, the nave.

**51** When all the work undertaken by King
Solomon in the temple of the LORD was completed, he brought in the dedicated offerings of
his father David, putting the silver, gold, and
other articles in the treasuries of the temple of
the LORD.[y]

## CHAPTER 8

**Dedication of the Temple.** **1** At the order
of Solomon, the elders of Israel and all the
leaders of the tribes, the princes in the ancestral
houses of the Israelites, came to King Solomon
in Jerusalem, to bring up the ark of the LORD's
covenant from the City of David [which is
Zion].[z] **2** All the men of Israel assembled before King Solomon during the festival in the
month of Ethanim (the seventh month).
**3** When all the elders of Israel had arrived, the
priests took up the ark; **4** they carried the ark of
the LORD and the meeting tent with all the sacred
vessels that were in the tent. (The priests and
Levites carried them.)

**5** King Solomon and the entire community of
Israel present for the occasion sacrificed before
the ark sheep and oxen too many to number or
count. **6** *The priests brought the ark of the
covenant of the LORD to its place beneath the
wings of the cherubim in the sanctuary, the holy
of holies of the temple. **7** The cherubim had
their wings spread out over the place of the ark,
sheltering the ark and its poles from above.
**8** The poles were so long that their ends could
be seen from that part of the holy place adjoining the sanctuary; however, they could not be
seen beyond. (They have remained there to this
day.) **9** There was nothing in the ark but the two
stone tablets which Moses had put there at Horeb, when the LORD made a covenant with the
Israelites at their departure from the land of
Egypt.[a]

**10** When the priests left the holy place, the
cloud filled the temple of the LORD **11** so that
the priests could no longer minister because of
the cloud, since the LORD's glory had filled the
temple of the LORD. **12** Then Solomon said,
"The LORD intends to dwell in the dark cloud;[b]
**13** I have truly built you a princely house, a
dwelling where you may abide forever."

**14** The king turned and greeted the whole
community of Israel as they stood. **15** He said
to them: "Blessed be the LORD, the God of

---

y 2 Chr 5, 1. z 2 Chr 5, 2. a Ex 34, 27; Heb 9, 4. b 2 Chr 6, 1.

---

* 8, 6–9: The transfer of the ark of the covenant into the newly constructed temple building, and the oracle of God's acceptance (1 Kgs 9, 3–9), and his act of possession (1 Kgs 8, 10–13), constituted the temple's solemn dedication, and made of it the abiding dwelling of God among his people for which David had hoped (2 Sm 6, 12–15; 7, 1–3). The concurrence of the feast of Booths marks an appropriate transition of God's dwelling among nomadic tribes to his permanent abode among a settled people.

Israel, who with his own mouth made a promise
to my father David and by his hand has brought
it to fulfillment. It was he who said, 16 'Since
the day I brought my people Israel out of Egypt,
I have not chosen a city out of any tribe of Israel
for the building of a temple to my honor; but I
choose David to rule my people Israel.'
17 When my father David wished to build a
temple to the honor of the LORD, the God of
Israel,[c] 18 the Lord said to him, 'In wishing to
build a temple to my honor, you do well. 19 It
will not be you, however, who will build the
temple; but the son who will spring from you,
he shall build the temple to my honor.' 20 And
now the LORD has fulfilled the promise that he
made: I have succeeded my father David and sit
on the throne of Israel, as the LORD foretold, and
I have built this temple to honor the LORD, the
God of Israel. 21 I have provided in it a place
for the ark in which is the covenant of the LORD,
which he made with our fathers when he
brought them out of the land of Egypt.''

**Solomon's Prayer.** 22 Solomon stood before the altar of the LORD in the presence of the
whole community of Israel, and stretching forth
his hands toward heaven, 23 he said, ''LORD,
God of Israel, there is no God like you in heaven
above or on earth below; you keep your covenant of kindness with your servants who are
faithful to you with their whole heart. 24 You
have kept the promise you made to my father
David, your servant. You who spoke that promise, have this day, by your own power, brought
it to fulfillment. 25 Now, therefore, LORD, God
of Israel, keep the further promise you made to
my father David, your servant, saying, 'You
shall always have someone from your line to sit
before me on the throne of Israel, provided only
that your descendants look to their conduct so
that they live in my presence, as you have lived
in my presence.'[d] 26 Now, LORD, God of Israel, may this promise which you made to my
father David, your servant, be confirmed.

27 ''Can it indeed be that God dwells among
men on earth? If the heavens and the highest
heavens cannot contain you, how much less this
temple which I have built! 28 Look kindly on
the prayer and petition of your servant, O LORD,
my God, and listen to the cry of supplication
which I, your servant, utter before you this day.
29 May your eyes watch night and day over this
temple, the place where you have decreed you
shall be honored; may you heed the prayer
which I, your servant, offer in this place.
30 Listen to the petitions of your servant and of
your people Israel which they offer in this place.
Listen from your heavenly dwelling and grant
pardon.

31 ''If a man sins against his neighbor and is
required to take an oath sanctioned by a curse,
when he comes and takes the oath before your
altar in this temple, 32 listen in heaven; take
action and pass judgment on your servants.
Condemn the wicked and punish him for his
conduct, but acquit the just and establish his
innocence.

33 *''If your people Israel sin against you
and are defeated by an enemy, and if then they
return to you, praise your name, pray to you,
and entreat you in this temple, 34 listen in
heaven and forgive the sin of your people Israel,
and bring them back to the land you gave their
fathers.

35 ''If the sky is closed, so that there is no
rain, because they have sinned against you and
you afflict them, and if then they repent of their
sin, and pray, and praise your name in this
place, 36 listen in heaven and forgive the sin of
your servant and of your people Israel, teaching
them the right way to live and sending rain upon
this land of yours which you have given to your
people as their heritage.

37 ''If there is famine in the land or pestilence; or if blight comes, or mildew, or a locust
swarm, or devouring insects; if an enemy of
your people besieges them in one of their cities;
whatever plague or sickness there may be, 38 if
then any one [of your entire people Israel] has
remorse of conscience and offers some prayer or
petition, stretching out his hands toward this
temple, 39 listen from your heavenly dwelling
place and forgive. You who alone know the
hearts of all men, render to each one of them
according to his conduct; knowing their hearts,
so treat them 40 that they may fear you as long
as they live on the land you gave our fathers.

41 ''To the foreigner, likewise, who is not of
your people Israel, but comes from a distant
land to honor you 42 (since men will learn of
your great name and your mighty hand and your
outstretched arm), when he comes and prays
toward this temple, 43 listen from your heavenly dwelling. Do all that the foreigner asks of
you, that all the peoples of the earth may know
your name, may fear you as do your people
Israel, and may acknowledge that this temple
which I have built is dedicated to your honor.

44 ''Whatever the direction in which you
may send your people forth to war against their
enemies, if they pray to you, O LORD, toward
the city you have chosen and the temple I have
built in your honor, 45 listen in heaven to their
prayer and petition, and defend their cause.

46 ''When they sin against you (for there is
no man who does not sin), and in your anger

c 2 Sm 7, 5.
d 2 Sm 7, 12.
e 2 Chr 6, 36; Eccl 7, 20; 1 Jn 1, 8.

* 8, 33–34. 46–53: These references to deportation of Israelites to a hostile land are an expansion of Solomon's prayer dating from the Babylonian exile four centuries later.

against them you deliver them to the enemy, so
that their captors deport them to a hostile land,
far or near,[e] **47** may they repent in the land of
their captivity and be converted. If then they
entreat you in the land of their captors and say,
'We have sinned and done wrong; we have been
wicked'; **48** if with their whole heart and soul
they turn back to you in the land of the enemies
who took them captive, pray to you toward the
land you gave their fathers, the city you have
chosen, and the temple I have built in your
honor, **49** listen from your heavenly dwelling.
**50** Forgive your people their sins and all the
offenses they have committed against you, and
grant them mercy before their captors, so that
these will be merciful to them. **51** For they are
your people and your inheritance, whom you
brought out of Egypt, from the midst of an iron
furnace.

**52** "Thus may your eyes be open to the petition of your servant and to the petition of your
people Israel. Hear them whenever they call
upon you, **53** because you have set them apart
among all the peoples of the earth for your
inheritance, as you declared through your servant Moses when you brought our fathers out of
Egypt, O Lord GOD."

**54** When Solomon finished offering this entire prayer of petition to the LORD, he rose from
before the altar of the LORD, where he had been
kneeling with his hands outstretched toward
heaven. **55** He stood and blessed the whole
community of Israel, saying in a loud voice:
**56** "Blessed be the LORD who has given rest to
his people Israel, just as he promised. Not a
single word has gone unfulfilled of the entire
generous promise he made through his servant
Moses. **57** May the LORD, our God, be with us
as he was with our fathers and may he not
forsake us nor cast us off. **58** May he draw our
hearts to himself, that we may follow him in
everything and keep the commands, statutes,
and ordinances which he enjoined on our fathers. **59** May this prayer I have offered to the
LORD, our God, be present to him day and night,
that he may uphold the cause of his servant and
of his people Israel as each day requires, **60** that
all the peoples of the earth may know the LORD
is God and there is no other. **61** You must be
wholly devoted to the LORD, our God, observing his statutes and keeping his commandments,
as on this day."

**62** The king and all Israel with him offered
sacrifices before the LORD. **63** Solomon offered
as peace offerings to the LORD twenty-two thousand oxen and one hundred twenty thousand
sheep. Thus the king and all the Israelites dedicated the temple of the LORD. **64** On that day
the king consecrated the middle of the court
facing the temple of the LORD; he offered there
the holocausts, the cereal offerings, and the fat
of the peace offerings, because the bronze altar
before the LORD was too small to hold these
offerings.

**65** On this occasion Solomon and all the Israelites, who had assembled in large numbers
from Labo of Hamath to the wadi of Egypt,
celebrated the festival before the LORD, our
God, for seven days. **66** On the eighth day he
dismissed the people, who bade the king farewell and went to their homes, rejoicing and
happy over all the blessings the LORD had given
to his servant David and to his people Israel.

## CHAPTER 9

### Promise and Warning to Solomon.

**1** After Solomon finished building the temple
of the LORD, the royal palace, and everything
else that he had planned, **2** the LORD appeared
to him a second time, as he had appeared to him
in Gibeon.[f] **3** The LORD said to him: "I have
heard the prayer of petition which you offered
in my presence. I have consecrated this temple
which you have built; I confer my name upon
it forever, and my eyes and my heart shall be
there always. **4** As for you, if you live in my
presence as your father David lived, sincerely
and uprightly, doing just as I have commanded
you, keeping my statutes and decrees, **5** I will
establish your throne of sovereignty over Israel
forever, as I promised your father David when
I said, 'You shall always have someone from
your line on the throne of Israel.'[g] **6** But if you
and your descendants ever withdraw from me,
fail to keep the commandments and statutes
which I set before you, and proceed to venerate
and worship strange gods, **7** I will cut off Israel
from the land I gave them and repudiate the
temple I have consecrated to my honor. Israel
shall become a proverb and a byword among all
nations, **8** and this temple shall become a heap
of ruins. Every passerby shall catch his breath
in amazement, and ask, 'Why has the LORD
done this to the land and to this temple?'[h]
**9** Men will answer: 'They forsook the LORD,
their God, who brought their fathers out of the
land of Egypt; they adopted strange gods which
they worshiped and served. That is why the
LORD has brought down upon them all this
evil.' "

### Other Acts of the King.

**10** After the
twenty years during which Solomon built the
two houses, the temple of the LORD and the
palace of the king— **11** Hiram, king of Tyre,
supplying Solomon with all the cedar wood, fir
wood, and gold he wished—King Solomon
gave Hiram twenty cities in the land of Galilee.

f 1 Kgs 3, 5; 11, 9; 2 Chr 7, 12.
g 2 Sm 7, 12-16.
h Dt 29, 23; Jer 22, 8.

**12** Hiram left Tyre to see the cities Solomon had given him, but was not satisfied with them. **13** So he said, "What are these cities you have given me, my brother?" And he called them the land of Cabul, as they are called to this day. **14** Hiram, however, had sent King Solomon one hundred and twenty talents of gold.*

**15** This is an account of the forced labor which King Solomon levied in order to build the temple of the LORD, his palace, Millo,* the wall of Jerusalem, Hazor, Megiddo, Gezer **16** (Pharaoh king of Egypt, had come up and taken Gezer and, after destroying it by fire and slaying all the Canaanites living in the city, had given it as dowry to his daughter, Solomon's wife; **17** Solomon then rebuilt Gezer), Lower Beth-horon, **18** Baalath, Tamar in the desert of Judah, **19** all his cities for supplies, cities for chariots and for horses, and whatever else Solomon decided should be built in Jerusalem, in Lebanon, and in the entire land under his dominion. **20** All the non-Israelite people who remained in the land, descendants of the Amorites, Hittites, Perizzites, Hivites, and Jebusites **21** whose doom the Israelites had been unable to accomplish, Solomon conscripted as forced laborers, as they are to this day. **22** But Solomon enslaved none of the Israelites, for they were his fighting force, his ministers, commanders, adjutants, chariot officers, and charioteers. **23** The supervisors of Solomon's works who policed the people engaged in the work numbered five hundred and fifty.

**24** As soon as Pharaoh's daughter went up from the City of David to her palace, which he had built for her, Solomon built Millo.

**25** Three times a year Solomon used to offer holocausts and peace offerings on the altar which he had built to the LORD, and to burn incense before the LORD; and he kept the temple in repair.

**26** King Solomon also built a fleet at Ezion-geber, which is near Elath on the shore of the Red Sea in the land of Edom.* **27** In this fleet Hiram placed his own expert seamen with the servants of Solomon. **28** They went to Ophir, and brought back four hundred and twenty talents of gold to King Solomon.

## CHAPTER 10

**Visit of the Queen of Sheba.** **1** The queen of Sheba,* having heard of Solomon's fame, came to test him with subtle questions.[i] **2** She arrived in Jerusalem with a very numerous retinue, and with camels bearing spices, a large amount of gold, and precious stones. She came to Solomon and questioned him on every subject in which she was interested. **3** King Solomon explained everything she asked about, and there remained nothing hidden from him that he could not explain to her.

**4** When the queen of Sheba witnessed Solomon's great wisdom, the palace he had built, **5** the food at his table, the seating of his ministers, the attendance and garb of his waiters, his banquet service, and the holocausts he offered in the temple of the LORD, she was breathless. **6** "The report I heard in my country about your deeds and your wisdom is true," she told the king. **7** "Though I did not believe the report until I came and saw with my own eyes, I have discovered that they were not telling me the half. Your wisdom and prosperity surpass the report I heard. **8** Happy are your men, happy these servants of yours, who stand before you always and listen to your wisdom. **9** Blessed be the LORD, your God, whom it has pleased to place you on the throne of Israel. In his enduring love for Israel, the LORD has made you king to carry out judgment and justice." **10** Then she gave the king one hundred and twenty gold talents, a very large quantity of spices, and precious stones. Never again did anyone bring such an abundance of spices as the queen of Sheba gave to King Solomon.

**11** Hiram's fleet, which used to bring gold from Ophir, also brought from there a large quantity of cabinet* wood and precious stones. **12** With the wood the king made supports for the temple of the LORD and for the palace of the king, and harps and lyres for the chanters. No more such wood was brought or seen to the present day.

**13** King Solomon gave the queen of Sheba everything she desired and asked for, besides such presents as were given her from Solomon's royal bounty. Then she returned with her servants to her own country.

**Solomon's Wealth.** **14** The gold that Solomon received every year weighed six hundred and sixty-six gold talents, **15** in addition to what came from the Tarshish fleet, from the traffic of merchants, and from all the kings of Arabia and the governors of the country.

i 2 Chr 9, 1; Mt 12, 42; Lk 11, 31.

*

9, 14: One hundred and twenty talents of gold: approximately three million six hundred thousand dollars.

9, 15: Millo: probably means a filling, and may refer to an artificial earthwork or platform of stamped ground south of the temple area. It was begun by David (2 Sm 5, 9); cf 1 Kgs 9, 24; 11, 27.

9, 26: Ezion-geber . . . Edom: the first mention of maritime commerce in the Israelite kingdom (to which the land of Edom was subject after its conquest by King David; cf 2 Sm 8, 14).

10, 1: Queen of Sheba: women rulers among the Arabs are recorded in eighth-century-B.C. Assyrian inscriptions. Sheba was for centuries the leading principality in what is now the Yemen.

10, 11f: Cabinet: an unknown wood, probably fragrant.

# God's Anointed
## SAUL, DAVID & SOLOMON

### King Saul
Although God had given his people a land of their own, they turned their backs on God and tried to become like the surrounding nations. The Israelites thought that if, instead of relying on God's rule, they had a king they could see, they would conquer their enemies. King Saul was anointed by Samuel to be the first king of Israel. But he openly disobeyed God and died at the battle of Gilboa (1 Samuel 9:1-31:13).

### King David
Samuel also anointed David, Jesse's youngest son. God promised that a descendant of David would be a king who reigned forever. David failed many times, but always loved God and returned to him (1 Samuel 16:1-30:31; 2 Samuel 1:1-24:25).

### King Solomon
Under David's son, Solomon, the kingdom prospered. Solomon became renowned for his wisdom, and during his reign the great Temple was finally built in Jerusalem. Yet Solomon, too, turned away from God and built temples to foreign gods (1 Kings 1:1-11:43).

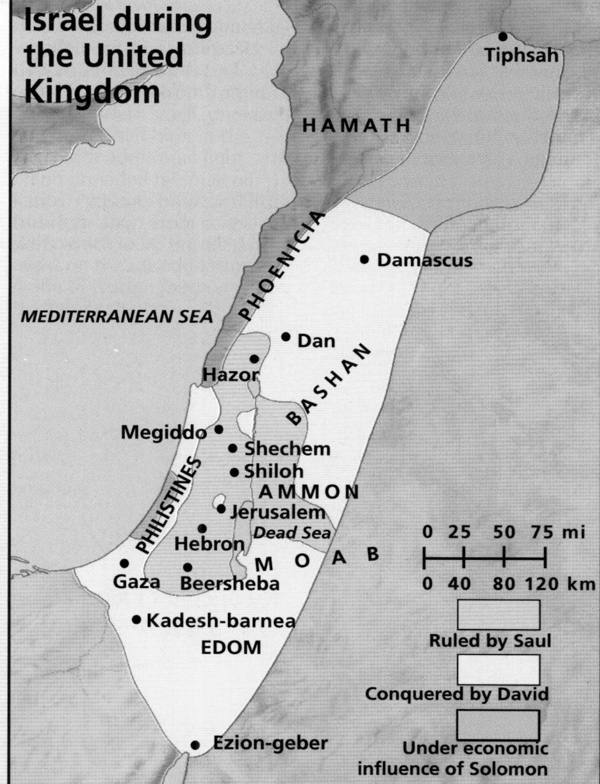


*Below*: Diagram of the water-shaft by which David captured Jerusalem (2 Samuel 5:6-9.)

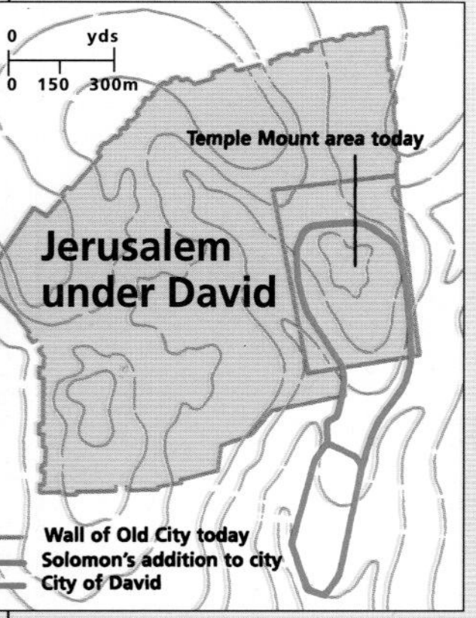


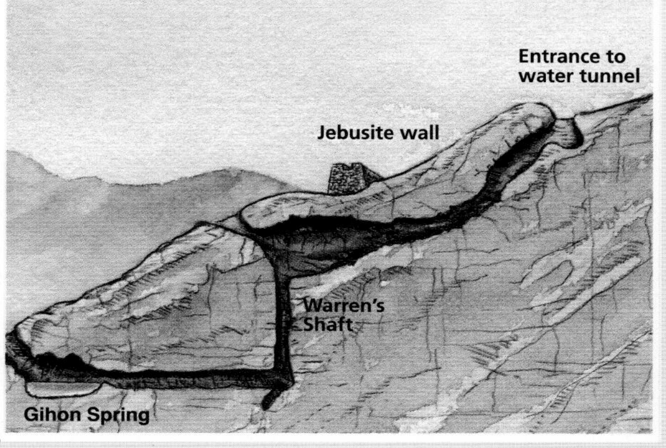

# The Divided Kingdom

**Israel**

After Solomon's death, the ten northern tribes rebelled and set up a separate kingdom of Israel, ruled by Jeroboam, with its capital at Shechem and worship centers at Dan and Bethel (1 Kings 12:1-33). Omri, a ninth-century king of Israel, founded a new capital called Samaria (1 Kings 16:24). Omri was succeeded by such kings as Ahab and Jehu (1 Kings 15:25-22:40, 22:51-53; 2 Kings 1:1-8:15, 9:1-13:25, 14:23-29, 15:8-31, 17:1-6).

**Judah**

David's successors continued to rule the southern kingdom of Judah from the capital, Jerusalem (1 Kings 14:21-31, 15:1-24, 22:41-50; 2 Kings 8:16-29, 11:1-12:21, 14:1-22,15:1-7, 15:32-16:20, 18:1-25:30). This division continued until the Exile.

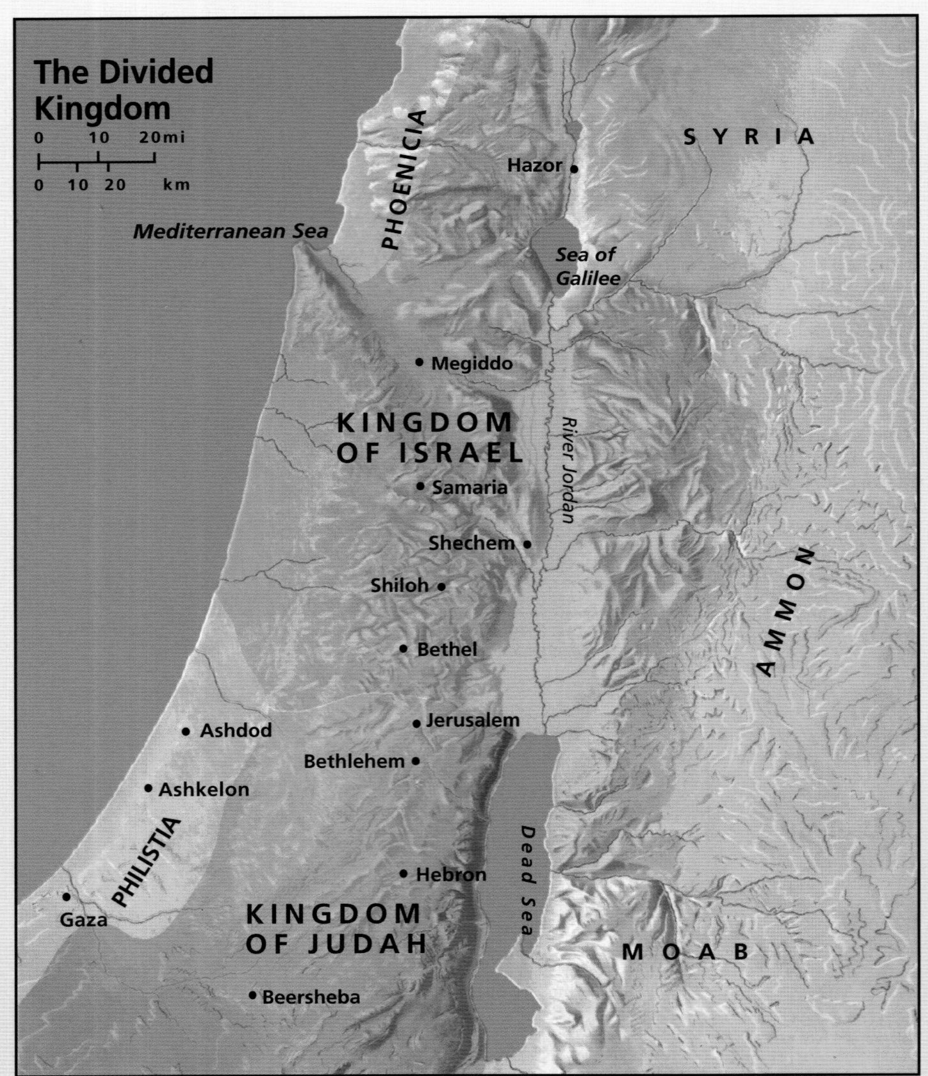

# Kings and Prophets

During the period of the Divided Kingdom, a number of prophets brought God's message to Israel and Judah, condemning social evils, faulty foreign policy and the kings who promoted the worship of pagan gods. This time-chart shows the years of ministry of these prophets and the reigns of the kings of Judah and Israel (1 Kings 12:1-22-22:53; 2 Kings).

| | ***Judah*** | ***Israel*** | |
|---|---|---|---|
| ***Prophets*** | ***Kings*** | ***Kings*** | ***Prophets*** |
| *Shemaiah* | **• Rehoboam 931-913** | **• Jeroboam I 931-910** | *Ahijah* |
| | **• Abijam 913-911** | | |
| | **• Asa 911-870** | **• Nadab 910-909** | *Iddo* |
| | | **• Baasha 909-886** | |
| | | **• Elah 886-885** | |
| *Azariah* | | **• Zimri 885-884** | |
| *Hanani* | | **• (Tibni 885-880*)** | |
| | | **• Omri 885-874** | |
| | **• Jehoshaphat 870-848** | **• Ahab 874-853** | *Jehu* |
| | | **• Ahaziah 853-852** | *Elijah* |
| *Jahaziel* | **• Jehoram 848-841** | **• Jehoram 852-841** | *Elisha* |
| | **• Ahaziah 841** | **• Jehu 841-814** | |
| *Joel* | **• Athaliah 841-835** | | |
| | **• Joash 835-796** | **• Jehoahaz 814-798** | |
| | | **• Joash 798-782** | |
| | **• Amaziah 796-767** | **• Jeroboam II 782-753** | |
| | **• Uzziah 767-740** | **• Zechariah 753-752** | |
| *Isaiah* | | **• Shallum 752** | |
| *Micah* | | **• Menahem 752-742** | |
| | **• Jotham 740-732** | **• Pekahiah 742-740** | |
| | | **• Pekah 740-732** | *Amos* |
| | **• Ahaz 732-716** | **• Hoshea 732-722** | *Hosea* |
| | **• Hezekiah 715-687** | ***Fall of Samaria 722 Israel in captivity – no kings*** | |
| | **• Manasseh 687-642** | | |
| | **• Amon 642-40** | | |
| *Zephaniah* | **• Josiah 640-609** | | |
| *Huldah* | **• Jehoahaz 609** | | |
| *Habakkuk* | **• Jehoiakim 609-598** | | |
| *Jeremiah* | **• Jehoiachin 598- 597** | | |
| *Ezekiel* | **• Zedekiah 597-587** | | |
| | ***Fall of Jerusalem 587*** | | |

* *See 1 Kings 16:21-22*

# God's House
## KING SOLOMON'S TEMPLE

Following the conquest of Canaan, the Israelites stopped carrying the Tabernacle wherever they went. Finally, when the monarchy was established, King David brought the Ark of the Covenant to Jerusalem, planning to build a temple there (2 Samuel 6:1-19). But it was his son Solomon who actually built the first Temple.

### Like the Tabernacle

Built of stone, the Temple was similar in its ground-plan to the Tabernacle, but much larger. It was panelled inside with cedarwood imported from Lebanon. Like the Tabernacle, the Temple housed the altar of incense, the table of showbread, lampstands and, in the Holiest Place, the Ark of the Covenant (1 Kings 5:1-6:38, 7:13-8:11).

### Not a Church

The Temple was not a meeting-place for God's people, like a modern church; only priests were permitted inside it to perform the ritual sacrifices and other duties.

Solomon's Temple was destroyed when the Babylonians captured Jerusalem in 587 B.C. (2 Chronicles 36:15-19).

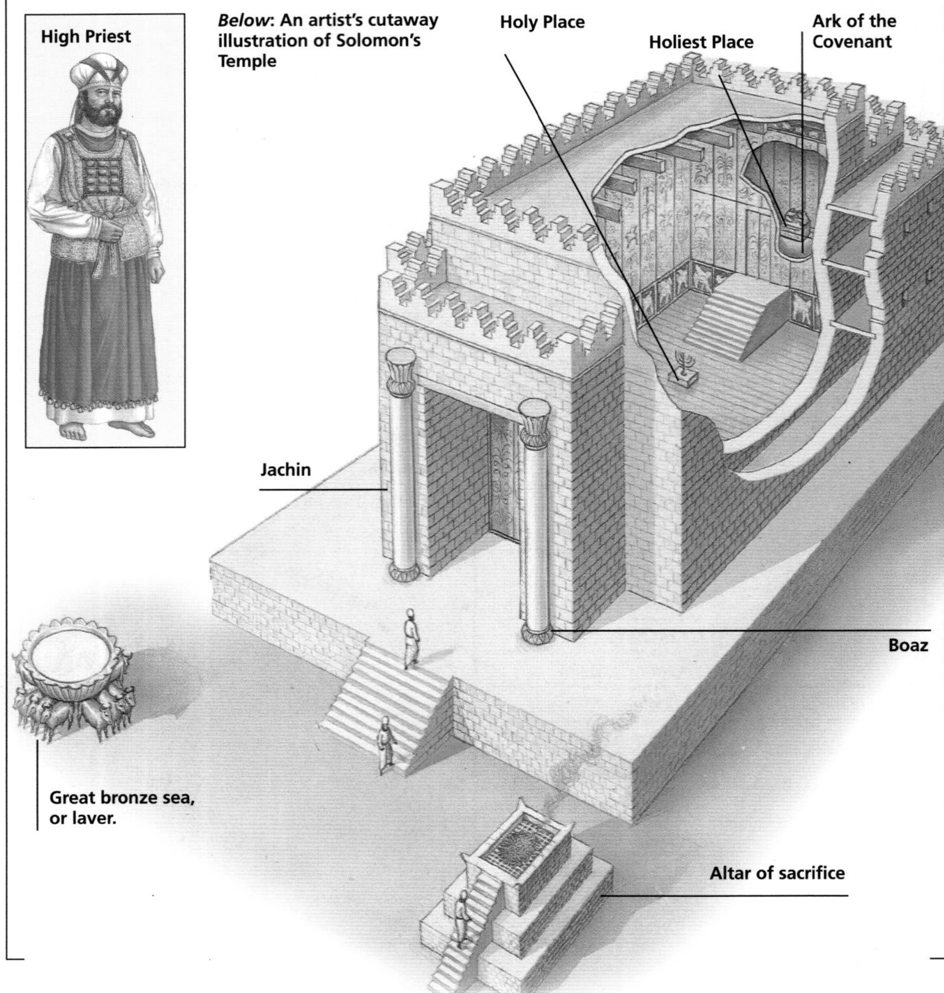


***Below*: An artist's cutaway illustration of Solomon's Temple**

**16** Moreover, King Solomon made two hundred shields of beaten gold (six hundred gold
shekels went into each shield)[j] **17** and three
hundred bucklers of beaten gold (three minas of
gold went into each buckler); and he put them
in the hall of the Forest of Lebanon. **18** The
king also had a large ivory throne made, and
overlaid it with refined gold. **19** The throne had
six steps, a back with a round top, and an arm
on each side of the seat. Next to each arm stood
a lion; **20** and twelve other lions stood on the
steps, two to a step, one on either side of each
step. Nothing like this was produced in any
other kingdom. **21** In addition, all King Solomon's drinking vessels were of gold, and all the
utensils in the hall of the Forest of Lebanon were
of pure gold. There was no silver, for in Solomon's time it was considered worthless. **22** The
king had a fleet of Tarshish ships* at sea with
Hiram's fleet. Once every three years the fleet
of Tarshish ships would come with a cargo of
gold, silver, ivory, apes, and monkeys.
**23** Thus King Solomon surpassed in riches and
wisdom all the kings of the earth. **24** And the
whole world sought audience with Solomon, to
hear from him the wisdom which God had put
in his heart. **25** Each one brought his yearly
tribute: silver or gold articles, garments, weapons, spices, horses and mules.

**26** Solomon collected chariots and drivers;
he had one thousand four hundred chariots and
twelve thousand drivers; these he allocated
among the chariot cities and to the king's service in Jerusalem.[k] **27** The king made silver as
common in Jerusalem as stones, and cedars as
numerous as the sycamores of the foothills.
**28** Solomon's horses were imported from Cilicia, where the king's agents purchased them.
**29** A chariot imported from Egypt cost six hundred shekels, a horse one hundred and fifty
shekels; they were exported at these rates to all
the Hittite and Aramean kings.

## CHAPTER 11

**The Sins of Solomon.** **1** *King Solomon
loved many foreign women besides the daughter
of Pharaoh (Moabites, Ammonites, Edomites,
Sidonians, and Hittites),[l] **2** from nations with
which the LORD had forbidden the Israelites to
intermarry, "because," he said, "they will turn
your hearts to their gods."[m] **3** But Solomon fell
in love with them. He had seven hundred wives
of princely rank and three hundred concubines,
and his wives turned his heart.

**4** When Solomon was old his wives had
turned his heart to strange gods, and his heart
was not entirely with the LORD, his God, as the
heart of his father David had been. **5** By adoring Astarte, the goddess of the Sidonians, and
Milcom, the idol of the Ammonites, **6** Solomon
did evil in the sight of the LORD; he did not
follow him unreservedly as his father David had
done. **7** Solomon then built a high place to Chemosh, the idol of Moab, and to Molech, the idol
of the Ammonites, on the hill opposite Jerusalem. **8** He did the same for all his foreign wives
who burned incense and sacrificed to their gods.
**9** The LORD, therefore, became angry with Solomon, because his heart was turned away from
the LORD, the God of Israel, who had appeared
to him twice[n] **10** (for though the LORD had
forbidden him this very act of following strange
gods, Solomon had not obeyed him).

**11** So the LORD said to Solomon: "Since this
is what you want, and you have not kept my
covenant and my statutes which I enjoined on
you, I will deprive you of the kingdom and give
it to your servant. **12** I will not do this during
your lifetime, however, for the sake of your
father David; it is your son whom I will deprive.[o] **13** Nor will I take away the whole kingdom. I will leave your son one tribe for the sake
of my servant David and of Jerusalem, which I
have chosen."

**14** The LORD then raised up an adversary to
Solomon: Hadad the Edomite, who was of the
royal line in Edom. **15** Earlier, when David had
conquered Edom, Joab, the general of the army,
while going to bury the slain, put to death every
male in Edom.[p] **16** Joab and all Israel remained
there six months until they had killed off every
male in Edom. **17** Meanwhile, Hadad, who
was only a boy, fled toward Egypt with some
Edomite servants of his father. **18** They left
Midian and passing through Paran, where they
picked up additional men, they went into Egypt
to Pharaoh, king of Egypt, who gave Hadad a
house, appointed him rations, and assigned him
land.

**19** Hadad won great favor with Pharaoh, so

j 1 Kgs 14, 26.
k 2 Chr 1, 14.
l Dt 17, 17; Sir 47, 19f.
m Ex 34, 16.
n 1 Kgs 9, 2.
o 1 Kgs 12, 15.
p 2 Sm 8, 14.

*

10, 22: Tarshish ships: large, strong vessels for long voyages. Tarshish was the ancient Tartessus, a Phoenician colony in southern Spain, the name of which denotes a center for smelting metallic ore.

11, 1–3. 7: The glorious rise of Solomon, his piety and wisdom, administrative skill and wealth, the extension of his kingdom, his prestige among neighboring rulers, his reign of peace, above all his friendship with God—these are now eclipsed by his sins of intermarriage with great numbers of pagan wives and the consequent forbidden worship of their gods (Ex 34, 11–16; Dt 7, 1–5). His construction of temples in their honor merited the punishment of loss of a united kingdom to his posterity, and the opposition of adversaries to himself (vv 14. 23–27). Hadad the Edomite rebelled against Solomon at the beginning of his reign (v 25). Rezon of Syria established a new kingdom in Dàmascus; Jeroboam of Israel constituted the greatest threat because of his revolt from within. This threefold threat culminated in the breakup of Solomon's kingdom.

that he gave him in marriage the sister of Queen
Tahpenes, his own wife. **20** Tahpenes' sister
bore Hadad a son, Genubath. After his weaning, the queen kept him in Pharaoh's palace,
where he then lived with Pharaoh's own sons.
**21** When Hadad in Egypt heard that David rested with his ancestors and that Joab, the general
of the army, was dead, he said to Pharaoh,
"Give me leave to return to my own country."
**22** Pharaoh said to him, "What do you lack
with me, that you are seeking to return to your
own country?" "Nothing," he said, "but
please let me go!"

**23** God raised up against Solomon another
adversary, in Rezon, the son of Eliada, who had
fled from his lord, Hadadezer, king of Zobah,
**24** when David defeated them with slaughter.
Rezon gathered men about him and became
leader of a band, went to Damascus, settled
there, and became king in Damascus. **25** He
was an enemy of Israel as long as Solomon
lived; this added to the harm done by Hadad,
who made a rift in Israel by becoming king over
Edom.

**26** Solomon's servant Jeroboam, son of Nebat, an Ephraimite from Zeredah with a widowed mother, Zeruah, also rebelled against the
king.[q] **27** This is why he rebelled. King Solomon was building Millo, closing up the breach
of his father's City of David. **28** Jeroboam was
a man of means, and when Solomon saw that he
was also an industrious young man, he put him
in charge of the entire labor force of the house
of Joseph. **29** At that time Jeroboam left Jerusalem, and the prophet Ahijah the Shilonite met
him on the road. The two were alone in the area,
and the prophet was wearing a new cloak.[r]
**30** Ahijah took off his new cloak, tore it into
twelve pieces, **31** and said to Jeroboam:

"Take ten pieces for yourself; the LORD, the
God of Israel, says: 'I will tear away the kingdom from Solomon's grasp and will give you
ten of the tribes.[s] **32** One tribe shall remain to
him for the sake of David my servant, and of
Jerusalem, the city I have chosen out of all the
tribes of Israel. **33** The ten I will give you because he has forsaken me and has worshiped
Astarte, goddess of the Sidonians, Chemosh,
god of Moab, and Milcom, god of the Ammonites; he has not followed my ways or done what
is pleasing to me according to my statutes and
my decrees, as his father David did. **34** Yet I
will not take any of the kingdom from Solomon
himself, but will keep him a prince as long as
he lives for the sake of my servant David, whom
I chose, who kept my commandments and statutes. **35** But I will take the kingdom from his
son and will give it to you—that is, the ten
tribes. **36** I will give his son one tribe, that my
servant David may always have a lamp before
me in Jerusalem, the city in which I choose to
be honored. **37** I will take you; you shall reign
over all that you desire and shall become king
of Israel. **38** If, then, you heed all that I command you, follow my ways, and please me by
keeping my statutes and my commandments
like my servant David, I will be with you. I will
establish for you, as I did for David, a lasting
dynasty; I will give Israel to you. **39** I will
punish David's line for this, but not forever.' "

**40** When Solomon tried to have Jeroboam
killed for his rebellion, he escaped to King Shishak, in Egypt, where he remained until Solomon's death.

**41** The rest of the acts of Solomon, with all
his deeds and his wisdom, are recorded in the
book of the chronicles of Solomon. **42** The time
that Solomon reigned in Jerusalem over all Israel was forty years. **43** Solomon rested with his
ancestors; he was buried in his father's City of
David, and his son Rehoboam succeeded him as
king.

## *II: Judah and Israel to the Time of Ahab*

## CHAPTER 12

**Secession of Israel.** **1** Rehoboam went to
Shechem,* where all Israel had come to proclaim him king.[t] **3** They said to Rehoboam:
**4** "Your father put on us a heavy yoke. If you
now lighten the harsh service and the heavy
yoke your father imposed on us, we will serve
you." **5** "Come back to me in three days," he
answered them. When the people had departed,
**6** King Rehoboam consulted the elders who had
been in his father's service while he was alive,
and asked, "What answer do you advise me to
give this people?" **7** They replied, "If today
you will be the servant of this people and submit
to them, giving them a favorable answer, they
will be your servants forever." **8** But he ignored the advice the elders had given him, and
consulted the young men who had grown up
with him and were in his service. **9** He said to
them, "What answer do you advise me to give
this people, who have asked me to lighten the
yoke my father imposed on them?" **10** The
young men who had grown up with him replied,
"This is what you must say to this people who
have asked you to lighten the yoke your father
put on them: 'My little finger is thicker than my
father's body. **11** Whereas my father put a

q 2 Chr 13, 6.
r 1 Kgs 14, 2; 2 Chr 10, 15
s 1 Kgs 12, 15.
t 2 Chr 10, 1.

* 12, 1: Shechem: chief city of the northern tribes, where a covenant of fidelity had previously been made between the Lord and his people and a stone of witness had been erected in memory of the event (Jos 24, 25ff).

heavy yoke on you, I will make it heavier. My father beat you with whips, but I will beat you with scorpions.' "

**12** On the third day all Israel came back to King Rehoboam, as he had instructed them to do. **13** Ignoring the advice the elders had given him, the king gave the people a harsh answer. **14** He said to them, as the young men had advised: "My father put on you a heavy yoke, but I will make it heavier. My father beat you with whips, but I will beat you with scorpions." **15** The king did not listen to the people, for the LORD brought this about to fulfill the prophecy he had uttered to Jeroboam, son of Nebat, through Ahijah the Shilonite.[u]

**16** When all Israel saw that the king did not listen to them, the people answered the king:

"What share have we in David?*
We have no heritage in the son of Jesse.
To your tents, O Israel!
Now look to your own house, David."

So Israel went off to their tents, **17** but Rehoboam reigned over the Israelites who lived in the cities of Judah. **18** King Rehoboam then sent out Adoram, superintendent of the forced labor, but all Israel stoned him to death. Rehoboam managed to mount his chariot to flee to Jerusalem, **19** and Israel went into rebellion against David's house to this day. **2** Jeroboam, son of Nebat, who was still in Egypt, where he had fled from King Solomon, returned from Egypt as soon as he learned this. **20** When all Israel heard that Jeroboam had returned, they summoned him to an assembly and made him king over all Israel. None remained loyal to David's house except the tribe of Judah alone.

**21** On his arrival in Jerusalem, Rehoboam gathered together all the house of Judah and the tribe of Benjamin—one hundred eighty thousand seasoned warriors—to fight against the house of Israel, to restore the kingdom to Rehoboam, son of Solomon. **22** [v]However, the LORD spoke to Shemaiah, a man of God: **23** "Say to Rehoboam, son of Solomon, king of Judah, and to the house of Judah and to Benjamin, and to the rest of the people: **24** 'Thus says the LORD: You must not march out to fight against your brother Israelites. Let every man return home, for I have brought this about.' " They accepted this message of the LORD and gave up the expedition accordingly.

**25** Jeroboam built up Shechem in the hill country of Ephraim and lived there. Then he left it and built up Penuel.

## Religious Rebellion.*

**26** Jeroboam thought to himself: "The kingdom will return to David's house. **27** If now this people go up to offer sacrifices in the temple of the LORD in Jerusalem, the hearts of this people will return to their master, Rehoboam, king of Judah, and they will kill me." **28** After taking counsel, the king made two calves of gold and said to the people: "You have been going up to Jerusalem long enough. Here is your God, O Israel, who brought you up from the land of Egypt."[w] **29** And he put one in Bethel, the other in Dan.* **30** This led to sin, because the people frequented these calves in Bethel and in Dan. **31** He also built temples on the high places and made priests from among the people who were not Levites.[x] **32** Jeroboam established a feast in the eighth month on the fifteenth day of the month to duplicate in Bethel the pilgrimage feast of Judah, with sacrifices to the calves he had made; and he stationed in Bethel priests of the high places he had built.

## Message of the Prophet from Judah.

**33** Jeroboam ascended the altar he built in Bethel on the fifteenth day of the eighth month, the month in which he arbitrarily chose to establish a feast for the Israelites; he was going to offer sacrifice.

## CHAPTER 13

**1** A man of God came from Judah to Bethel by the word of the LORD, while Jeroboam was standing at the altar to offer sacrifice. **2** He cried out against the altar the word of the LORD: "O altar, altar, the LORD says, 'A child shall be born to the house of David, Josiah by name, who shall slaughter upon you the priests of the high places who offer sacrifice upon you, and he shall burn human bones upon you.' "[y] **3** He gave a sign that same day and said: "This is the sign that the LORD has spoken: The altar shall break up and the ashes on it shall be strewn about."

**4** When King Jeroboam heard what the man of God was crying out against the altar, he

u 1 Kgs 11, 12. 31.
v 22-24; 2 Chr 11, 2ff.
w Tb 1, 5; Ex 32, 8.
x 2 Chr 11, 15.
y 2 Kgs 23, 16.

*

12, 16: What share have we in David: even in David's time the northern tribes seemed ready to withdraw from Judah (2 Sm 20, 1). The unreasonable attitude of Rehoboam toward them intensified the discontent caused by the oppression of Solomon (v 4) and thus precipitated the establishment of a rival monarchy (v 20).

12, 26–32: Jeroboam feared reunification of the divided kingdom through worship in the single temple in Jerusalem. To prevent this he encouraged shrines on the high places, and appointed false priests to supplement those of levitical descent. The golden bullocks he installed in two of his sanctuaries, though probably intended as bearers of the invisible Divine Majesty, quickly became occasions for idolatry. Thus Jeroboam caused Israel to sin, and sealed his doom and that of his royal house (1 Kgs 13, 34; 14, 7–14).

12, 29: Bethel and Dan: at the southern and northern boundaries of the separate kingdom of Israel, where sanctuaries had existed in the past (Gn 12, 8; 13, 3; 18, 10–22; 25, 1–16; Jgs 18, 1–31).

stretched forth his hand from the altar and said,
"Seize him!" But the hand he stretched forth
against him withered, so that he could not draw
it back. **5** Moreover, the altar broke up and the
ashes from it were strewn about—the sign the
man of God had given as the word of the LORD.
**6** Then the king appealed to the man of God.
"Entreat the LORD, your God," he said, "and
intercede for me that I may be able to withdraw
my hand." So the man of God entreated the
LORD, and the king recovered the normal use of
his hand. **7** "Come home with me for some
refreshment," the king invited the man of God,
"and I will give you a present." **8** "If you gave
me half your kingdom," the man of God said
to the king, "I would not go with you, nor eat
bread or drink water in this place. **9** For I was
instructed by the word of the LORD not to eat
bread or drink water and not to return by the way
I came." **10** So he departed by another road
and did not go back the way he had come to
Bethel.

**11** There was an old prophet living in the
city, whose sons came and told him all that the
man of God had done that day in Bethel. When
they repeated to their father the words he had
spoken to the king, **12** the father asked them,
"Which way did he go?" And his sons pointed
out to him the road taken by the man of God who
had come from Judah. **13** Then he said to his
sons, "Saddle the ass for me." When they had
saddled it, he mounted **14** and followed the
man of God, whom he found seated under a
terebinth. When he asked him, "Are you the
man of God who came from Judah?" he answered, "Yes." **15** Then he said, "Come
home with me and have some bread." **16** "I
cannot go back with you, and I cannot eat bread
or drink water with you in this place," he answered, **17** "for I was told by the word of the
LORD neither to eat bread nor drink water here,
and not to go back the way I came." **18** But he
said to him, "I, too, am a prophet like you, and
an angel told me in the word of the LORD to
bring you back with me to my house and to have
you eat bread and drink water." He was lying
to him, however.

**19** So he went back with him, and ate bread
and drank water in his house. **20** But while they
were sitting at table, the LORD spoke to the
prophet who had brought him back, **21** and he
cried out to the man of God who had come from
Judah: "The LORD says, 'Because you rebelled
against the command of the LORD and did not
keep the command which the LORD, your God,
gave you, **22** but returned and ate bread and
drank water in the place where he told you to do
neither, your corpse shall not be brought to the
grave of your ancestors.' "

**23** After he had eaten bread and drunk water,
the ass was saddled for him, and he again **24** set
out. But a lion met him on the road, and killed
him. His corpse lay sprawled on the road, and
the ass remained standing by it, and so did the
lion. **25** Some passersby saw the body lying in
the road, with the lion standing beside it, and
carried the news to the city where the old prophet lived. **26** On hearing it, the prophet who had
brought him back from his journey said: "It is
the man of God who rebelled against the command of the LORD. He has delivered him to a
lion, which mangled and killed him, as the
LORD predicted to him." **27** Then he said to his
sons, "Saddle the ass for me." When they had
saddled it, **28** he went off and found the body
lying in the road with the ass and the lion standing beside it. The lion had not eaten the body
nor had it harmed the ass. **29** The prophet lifted
up the body of the man of God and put it on the
ass, and brought it back to the city to mourn
over it and to bury it. **30** He laid the man's body
in his own grave, and they mourned over it:
"Alas, my brother!" **31** After he had buried
him, he said to his sons, "When I die, bury me
in the grave where the man of God is buried.
Lay my remains beside his. **32** For the word of
the LORD which he proclaimed against the altar
in Bethel and against all the shrines on the high
places in the cities of Samaria shall certainly
come to pass."

**33** Jeroboam did not give up his evil ways
after this event, but again made priests for the
high places from among the common people.
Whoever desired it was consecrated and became
a priest of the high places. **34** This was a sin on
the part of the house of Jeroboam for which it
was to be cut off and destroyed from the earth.

## CHAPTER 14

**Death of Abijah.** **1** At that time Abijah, son
of Jeroboam, took sick. **2** So Jeroboam said to
his wife, "Get ready and disguise yourself so
that none will recognize you as Jeroboam's
wife. Then go to Shiloh, where you will find the
prophet Ahijah. It is he who predicted my reign
over this people.[z] **3** Take along ten loaves,
some cakes, and a jar of preserves, and go to
him. He will tell you what will happen to the
child." **4** The wife of Jeroboam obeyed. She
made the journey to Shiloh and entered the
house of Ahijah who could not see because age
had dimmed his sight.

**5** The LORD had said to Ahijah: "Jeroboam's
wife is coming to consult you about her son, for
he is sick. This is what you must tell her. When
she comes, she will be in disguise." **6** So Ahijah, hearing the sound of her footsteps as she
entered the door, said, "Come in, wife of Jeroboam. Why are you in disguise? I have been

z 1 Kgs 11, 29.

commissioned to give you bitter news. **7** Go,
tell Jeroboam, 'This is what the LORD, the God
of Israel, says: I exalted you from among the
people and made you ruler of my people Israel.
**8** I deprived the house of David of the kingdom
and gave it to you. Yet you have not been like
my servant David, who kept my commandments and followed me with his whole heart,
doing only what pleased me. **9** You have done
worse than all who preceded you: you have gone
and made for yourself strange gods and molten
images to provoke me; but me you have cast
behind your back. **10** Therefore, I am bringing
evil upon the house of Jeroboam: I will cut off
every male in Jeroboam's line, whether slave or
freeman in Israel, and will burn up the house of
Jeroboam completely, as though dung were being burned.[a] **11** When one of Jeroboam's line
dies in the city, dogs will devour him; when one
of them dies in the field, he will be devoured by
the birds of the sky. For the LORD has spoken!'[b]
**12** So leave; go home! As you step inside the
city, the child will die, **13** and all Israel will
mourn him and bury him, for he alone of Jeroboam's line will be laid in the grave, since in
him alone of Jeroboam's house has something
pleasing to the LORD, the God of Israel, been
found. **14** Today, at this very moment, the
LORD will raise up for himself a king of Israel
who will destroy the house of Jeroboam.
**15** The LORD will strike Israel like a reed tossed
about in the water and will pluck out Israel from
this good land which he gave their fathers, scattering them beyond the River, because they
made sacred poles for themselves and thus provoked the LORD. **16** He will give up Israel because of the sins Jeroboam has committed and
caused Israel to commit."

**17** So Jeroboam's wife started back; when
she reached Tirzah and crossed the threshold of
her house, the child died. **18** He was buried
with all Israel mourning him, as the LORD had
prophesied through his servant the prophet Ahijah.

**19** The rest of the acts of Jeroboam, with his
warfare and his reign, are recorded in the book
of the chronicles of the kings of Israel. **20** The
length of Jeroboam's reign was twenty-two
years. He rested with his ancestors, and his son
Nadab succeeded him as king.

**Reign of Rehoboam.** **21** Rehoboam, son
of Solomon, reigned in Judah. He was forty-one
years old when he became king, and he reigned
seventeen years in Jerusalem, the city in which,
out of all the tribes of Israel, the LORD chose to
be honored. His mother was the Ammonite
named Naamah.[c]

**22** Judah did evil in the sight of the LORD,
and by their sins angered him even more than
their fathers had done. **23** They, too, built for
themselves high places, pillars, and sacred
poles, upon every high hill and under every
green tree. **24** There were also cult prostitutes
in the land. Judah imitated all the abominable
practices of the nations whom the LORD had
cleared out of the Israelites' way.

**25** In the fifth year of King Rehoboam, Shishak, king of Egypt, attacked Jerusalem.*
**26** He took everything, including the treasures
of the temple of the LORD and those of the royal
palace, as well as all the gold shields made
under Solomon.[d] **27** To replace them, King
Rehoboam had bronze shields made, which he
entrusted to the officers of the guard on duty at
the entrance of the royal palace. **28** Whenever
the king visited the temple of the LORD, those
on duty would carry the shields, and then return
them to the guardroom.

**29** The rest of the acts of Rehoboam, with all
that he did, are recorded in the book of the
chronicles of the kings of Judah. **30** There was
constant warfare between Rehoboam and Jeroboam. **31** Rehoboam rested with his ancestors;
he was buried with them in the City of David.
His mother was the Ammonite named Naamah.
His son Abijam succeeded him as king.

## CHAPTER 15

**Reign of Abijam.** **1** In the eighteenth year
of King Jeroboam, son of Nebat, Abijam became king of Judah;[e] **2** he reigned three years
in Jerusalem. His mother's name was Maacah,
daughter of Abishalom. **3** He imitated all the
sins his father had committed before him, and
his heart was not entirely with the LORD, his
God, like the heart of his grandfather David.
**4** Yet for David's sake the LORD, his God, gave
him a lamp in Jerusalem, raising up his son after
him and permitting Jerusalem to endure; **5** because David had pleased the LORD and did not
disobey any of his commands as long as he
lived, except in the case of Uriah the Hittite.[f]

**7** The rest of Abijam's acts, with all that he
did, are written in the book of the chronicles of
the kings of Judah.[g] **6** There was war between
Abijam and Jeroboam. **8** Abijam rested with
his ancestors; he was buried in the City of Da-

a 1 Kgs 15, 29.
b 1 Kgs 16, 4.
c 2 Chr 12, 13.
d 1 Kgs 10, 16.
e 2 Chr 13, 1f.
f 2 Sm 11, 4.
g 2 Chr 13, 2.

*

14, 25: In the fifth year . . . Shishak, king of Egypt, attacked Jerusalem: c. 926 B.C. According to 2 Chr 12, 1–12, the repentance of King Rehoboam and of the princes of Israel after the warning of the prophet Shemaiah diverted the actual attack on Jerusalem. Shishak, however, carried off the treasures of the temple of the Lord and of the king's palace (2 Chr 12, 9). A bas-relief of this Pharaoh in the temple of Aman at Karnak commemorates his conquest of some hundred and fifty Palestinian and Trans-Jordanian cities and towns.

vid, and his son Asa succeeded him as king.

**Reign of Asa.** **9** In the twentieth year of
Jeroboam, king of Israel, Asa, king of Judah,
began to reign; **10** he reigned forty-one years in
Jerusalem. His grandmother's name was Maacah, daughter of Abishalom. **11** Asa pleased
the LORD like his forefather David, **12** banish-
ing the temple prostitutes from the land and
removing all the idols his father had made.
**13** He also deposed his grandmother Maacah
from her position as queen mother, because she
had made an outrageous object for Asherah.
Asa cut down this object and burned it in the
Kidron Valley. **14** The high places did not disappear; yet Asa's heart was entirely with the
LORD as long as he lived. **15** He brought into
the temple of the LORD his father's and his own
votive offerings of silver, gold, and various
utensils.

**16** There was war between Asa and Baasha,
king of Israel, as long as they both reigned.
**17** Baasha, king of Israel, attacked Judah and
fortified Ramah to prevent communication with
Asa, king of Judah.[h] **18** Asa then took all the
silver and gold remaining in the treasuries of the
temple of the LORD and of the royal palace.
Entrusting them to his ministers, King Asa sent
them to Ben-hadad, son of Tabrimmon, son of
Hezion, king of Aram,* resident in Damascus.
He said: **19** "There is a treaty between you and
me, as there was between your father and my
father. I am sending you a present of silver and
gold. Go, break your treaty with Baasha, king
of Israel, that he may withdraw from me."
**20** Ben-hadad agreed with King Asa and sent
the leaders of his troops against the cities of
Israel. They attacked Ijon, Dan, Abel-beth-maacah, and all Chinnereth, besides all the land of
Naphtali. **21** When Baasha heard of it, he left
off fortifying Ramah, and stayed in Tirzah.
**22** Then King Asa summoned all Judah without
exception, and they carried away the stones and
beams with which Baasha was fortifying Ramah. With them King Asa built Geba of Benjamin and Mizpeh.

**23** The rest of the acts of Asa, with all his
valor and accomplishments, and the cities he
built, are written in the book of the chronicles
of the kings of Judah. In his old age, Asa had
an infirmity in his feet. **24** He rested with his
ancestors; he was buried in his forefather's City
of David, and his son Jehoshaphat succeeded
him as king.[i]

**Reign of Nadab.** **25** In the second year of
Asa, king of Judah, Nadab, son of Jeroboam,
became king of Israel; he reigned over Israel
two years. **26** He did evil in the LORD's sight,
imitating his father's conduct and the sin which
he had caused Israel to commit. **27** Baasha, son
of Ahijah, of the house of Issachar, plotted
against him and struck him down at Gibbethon
of the Philistines, which Nadab and all Israel
were besieging. **28** Baasha killed him in the
third year of Asa, king of Judah, and reigned in
his stead. **29** Once he was king, he killed off the
entire house of Jeroboam, not leaving a single
soul to Jeroboam but destroying him utterly,
according to the warning which the LORD had
pronounced through his servant, Ahijah the Shilonite,[j] **30** because of the sins Jeroboam committed and caused Israel to commit, by which he
provoked the LORD, the God of Israel, to anger.
**31** The rest of the acts of Nadab, with all that
he did, are written in the book of the chronicles
of the kings of Israel. **32** [There was war between Asa and Baasha, king of Israel, as long
as they lived.]

**Reign of Baasha.** **33** In the third year of
Asa, king of Judah, Baasha, son of Ahijah,
began his twenty-four-year reign over Israel in
Tirzah. **34** He did evil in the LORD's sight,
imitating the conduct of Jeroboam and the sin he
had caused Israel to commit.

## CHAPTER 16

**1** The LORD spoke against Baasha to Jehu,
son of Hanani, and said: **2** "Inasmuch as I lifted you up from the dust and made you ruler of
my people Israel, but you have imitated the
conduct of Jeroboam and have caused my people Israel to sin, provoking me to anger by their
sins, **3** I will destroy you, Baasha, and your
house;[k] **4** I will make your house like that of
Jeroboam, son of Nebat. If anyone of Baasha's
line dies in the city, dogs shall devour him; if
he dies in the field, he shall be devoured by the
birds of the sky."[l]
**5** The rest of the acts of Baasha, with all his
valor and accomplishments, are written in the
book of the chronicles of the kings of Israel.[m]
**6** Baasha rested with his ancestors; he was buried in Tirzah, and his son Elah succeeded him
as king. **7** [Through the prophet Jehu, son of
Hanani, the LORD had threatened Baasha and
his house, because of all the evil Baasha did in
the sight of the LORD, provoking him to anger
by his evil deeds, so that he became like the
house of Jeroboam; and because he killed Nadab.]

---

h 2 Chr 16, 1.
i 2 Chr 17, 1.
j 1 Kgs 14, 10; 21, 22.
k 1 Kgs 21, 22.
l 1 Kgs 14, 11.
m 2 Chr 16, 1.

*

15, 18: Ben-hadad . . . king of Aram: Ben-hadad I, third successor of Rezon, who had thrown off the yoke of the Israelites during the reign of Solomon and become king of Aram (11, 23f).

**Reign of Elah.** **8** In the twenty-sixth year of
Asa, king of Judah, Elah, son of Baasha, began
his two-year reign over Israel in Tirzah. **9** His
servant Zimri, commander of half his chariots,
plotted against him. As he was in Tirzah, drinking to excess in the house of Arza, superintendent of his palace in Tirzah, **10** Zimri entered;
he struck and killed him in the twenty-seventh
year of Asa, king of Judah, and reigned in his
place.[n] **11** Once he was seated on the royal
throne, he killed off the whole house of Baasha,
not sparing a single male relative or friend of
his. **12** Zimri destroyed the entire house of Baasha, as the LORD had prophesied to Baasha
through the prophet Jehu, **13** because of all the
sins which Baasha and his son Elah committed
and caused Israel to commit, provoking the
LORD, the God of Israel, to anger by their idols.
**14** The rest of the acts of Elah, with all that
he did, are written in the book of the chronicles
of the kings of Israel.

**Reign of Zimri.** **15** In the twenty-seventh
year of Asa, king of Judah, Zimri reigned seven
days in Tirzah. The army was besieging Gibbethon of the Philistines **16** when they heard that
Zimri had formed a conspiracy and had killed
the king. So that day in the camp all Israel
proclaimed Omri, general of the army, king of
Israel. **17** Omri marched up from Gibbethon,
accompanied by all Israel, and laid siege to
Tirzah. **18** When Zimri saw the city was captured, he entered the citadel of the royal palace
and burned down the palace over him. He died
**19** because of the sins he had committed, doing
evil in the sight of the LORD by imitating the
sinful conduct of Jeroboam, thus causing Israel
to sin.
**20** The rest of the acts of Zimri, with the
conspiracy he carried out, are written in the
book of the chronicles of the kings of Israel.
**21** At that time the people of Israel were
divided, half following Tibni, son of Ginath, to
make him king, and half for Omri. **22** The partisans of Omri prevailed over those of Tibni, son
of Ginath. Tibni died and Omri became king.

**Reign of Omri.** **23** In the thirty-first year of
Asa, king of Judah, Omri became king; he
reigned over Israel twelve years, the first six of
them in Tirzah. **24** He then bought the hill of
Samaria from Shemer for two silver talents and
built upon the hill, naming the city he built
Samaria after Shemer, the former owner.
**25** But Omri did evil in the LORD's sight beyond any of his predecessors. **26** He closely
imitated the sinful conduct of Jeroboam, son of
Nebat, causing Israel to sin and to provoke the
LORD, the God of Israel, to anger by their idols.
**27** The rest of the acts of Omri, with all his
valor and accomplishments, are written in the
book of the chronicles of the kings of Israel.
**28** Omri rested with his ancestors; he was buried in Samaria, and his son Ahab succeeded him
as king.

**Reign of Ahab.** **29** In the thirty-eighth year
of Asa, king of Judah, Ahab, son of Omri,
became king of Israel; he reigned over Israel in
Samaria for twenty-two years. **30** Ahab, son of
Omri, did evil in the sight of the LORD more
than any of his predecessors. **31** It was not
enough for him to imitate the sins of Jeroboam,
son of Nebat. He even married Jezebel, daughter of Ethbaal, king of the Sidonians, and went
over to the veneration and worship of Baal.
**32** Ahab erected an altar to Baal in the temple
of Baal which he built in Samaria, **33** and also
made a sacred pole. He did more to anger the
LORD, the God of Israel, than any of the kings
of Israel before him.
**34** [o]During his reign, Hiel from Bethel rebuilt Jericho. He lost his first-born son, Abiram,
when he laid the foundation, and his youngest
son, Segub, when he set up the gates, as the
LORD had foretold through Joshua, son of Nun.

## *III: Stories of the Prophets*

### CHAPTER 17

**Drought Predicted by Elijah.** **1** Elijah
the Tishbite,* from Tishbe in Gilead, said to
Ahab: "As the LORD, the God of Israel, lives,
whom I serve, during these years there shall be
no dew or rain except at my word."[p] **2** The
LORD then said to Elijah: **3** "Leave here, go
east and hide in the Wadi Cherith, east of the
Jordan. **4** You shall drink of the stream, and I
have commanded ravens to feed you there."
**5** So he left and did as the LORD had commanded. He went and remained by the Wadi Cherith,
east of the Jordan. **6** Ravens brought him bread
and meat in the morning, and bread and meat in
the evening, and he drank from the stream.

**Elijah and the Widow.** **7** After some time,
however, the brook ran dry, because no rain had
fallen in the land. **8** So the LORD said to him:
**9** "Move on to Zarephath of Sidon and stay

n 2 Kgs 9, 31.
o Jos 6, 26.
p Sir 48, 3; Jas 5, 17.

*

17, 1: Elijah the Tishbite: one of the most important figures in Old Testament history. As his name indicates ("Yahweh is my God"), Elijah was the successful leader in the struggle to preserve the knowledge and worship of Yahweh against the encroaching worship of Baal introduced into Israel by Jezebel, the Tyrian wife of Ahab. The Elijah cycle of narratives includes, besides the above struggle, miracle stories, denunciations of kings, and a preparation for the prophet's role as eschatological forerunner of the "great day of the Lord"; cf Mal 3, 23–24; Mt 17, 10–13; Lk 1, 17.

there. I have designated a widow there to provide for you." 10 He left and went to Zarephath. As he arrived at the entrance of the city,
a widow was gathering sticks there; he called
out to her, "Please bring me a small cupful of
water to drink."[q] 11 She left to get it, and he
called out after her, "Please bring along a bit of
bread." 12 "As the LORD, your God, lives,"
she answered, "I have nothing baked; there is
only a handful of flour in my jar and a little oil
in my jug. Just now I was collecting a couple of
sticks, to go in and prepare something for myself and my son; when we have eaten it, we shall
die." 13 "Do not be afraid," Elijah said to her.
"Go and do as you propose. But first make me
a little cake and bring it to me. Then you can
prepare something for yourself and your son.
14 For the LORD, the God of Israel, says, 'The
jar of flour shall not go empty, nor the jug of oil
run dry, until the day when the LORD sends rain
upon the earth.' " 15 She left and did as Elijah
had said. She was able to eat for a year, and he
and her son as well; 16 the jar of flour did not
go empty, nor the jug of oil run dry, as the LORD
had foretold through Elijah.

17 Some time later the son of the mistress of
the house fell sick, and his sickness grew more
severe until he stopped breathing. 18 So she
said to Elijah, "Why have you done this to me,
O man of God? Have you come to me to call
attention to my guilt and to kill my son?"
19 "Give me your son," Elijah said to her.
Taking him from her lap, he carried him to the
upper room where he was staying, and laid him
on his own bed. 20 He called out to the LORD:
"O LORD, my God, will you afflict even the
widow with whom I am staying by killing her
son?" 21 Then he stretched himself out upon
the child three times and called out to the LORD:
"O LORD, my God, let the life breath return to
the body of this child." 22 The LORD heard the
prayer of Elijah; the life breath returned to the
child's body and he revived. 23 Taking the
child, Elijah brought him down into the house
from the upper room and gave him to his mother. "See!" Elijah said to her, "your son is
alive." 24 "Now indeed I know that you are a
man of God," the woman replied to Elijah.
"The word of the LORD comes truly from your
mouth."

## CHAPTER 18

**Elijah and the Prophets of Baal.** 1 Long
afterward, in the third year, the LORD spoke to
Elijah. "Go, present yourself to Ahab," he
said, "that I may send rain upon the earth."
2 So Elijah went to present himself to Ahab.

3 Now the famine in Samaria was bitter,
4 and Ahab had summoned Obadiah, his vizier,
who was a zealous follower of the LORD. When
Jezebel was murdering the prophets of the
LORD, Obadiah took a hundred prophets, hid
them away fifty each in two caves, and supplied
them with food and drink. 5 Ahab said to Obadiah, "Come, let us go through the land to all
sources of water and to all the streams. We may
find grass and save the horses and mules, so that
we shall not have to slaughter any of the
beasts." 6 Dividing the land to explore between them, Ahab went one way by himself,
Obadiah another way by himself.

7 As Obadiah was on his way, Elijah met
him. Recognizing him, Obadiah fell prostrate
and asked, "Is it you, my lord Elijah?"
8 "Yes," he answered. "Go tell your master,
'Elijah is here!' " 9 But Obadiah said, "What
sin have I committed, that you are handing me
over to Ahab to have me killed? 10 As the
LORD, your God, lives, there is no nation or
kingdom where my master has not sent in search
of you. When they replied, 'He is not here,' he
made each kingdom and nation swear they
could not find you. 11 And now you say, 'Go
tell your master: Elijah is here!' 12 After I leave
you, the spirit of the LORD will carry you to
some place I do not know, and when I go to
inform Ahab and he does not find you, he will
kill me. Your servant has revered the LORD from
his youth. 13 Have you not been told, my lord,
what I did when Jezebel was murdering the
prophets of the LORD—that I hid a hundred of
the prophets of the LORD, fifty each in two
caves, and supplied them with food and drink?
14 And now you say, 'Go tell your master:
Elijah is here!' He will kill me!" 15 Elijah
answered, "As the LORD of hosts lives, whom
I serve, I will present myself to him today."

16 So Obadiah went to meet Ahab and informed him. Ahab came to meet Elijah, 17 and
when he saw Elijah, said to him, "Is it you, you
disturber of Israel?" 18 "It is not I who disturb
Israel," he answered, "but you and your family, by forsaking the commands of the LORD and
following the Baals. 19 Now summon all Israel
to me on Mount Carmel, as well as the four
hundred and fifty prophets of Baal and the four
hundred prophets of Asherah who eat at Jezebel's table." 20 So Ahab sent to all the Israelites and had the prophets assemble on Mount
Carmel.

21 Elijah appealed to all the people and said,
"How long will you straddle the issue? If the
LORD is God, follow him; if Baal, follow him."
The people, however, did not answer him.
22 So Elijah said to the people, "I am the only
surviving prophet of the LORD, and there are
four hundred and fifty prophets of Baal.
23 Give us two young bulls. Let them choose
one, cut it into pieces, and place it on the wood,

q Lk 4, 26.

but start no fire. I shall prepare the other and
place it on the wood, but shall start no fire.
**24** You shall call on your gods, and I will call
on the LORD. The God who answers with fire is
God.'' All the people answered, ''Agreed!''
**25** Elijah then said to the prophets of Baal,
''Choose one young bull and prepare it first, for
there are more of you. Call upon your gods, but
do not start the fire.'' **26** Taking the young bull
that was turned over to them, they prepared it
and called on Baal from morning to noon, saying, ''Answer us, Baal!'' But there was no
sound, and no one answering. And they hopped
around the altar they had prepared. **27** When it
was noon, Elijah taunted them: ''Call louder,
for he is a god and may be meditating, or may
have retired, or may be on a journey. Perhaps
he is asleep and must be awakened.'' **28** They
called out louder and slashed themselves with
swords and spears, as was their custom, until
blood gushed over them. **29** Noon passed and
they remained in a prophetic state until the time
for offering sacrifice. But there was not a sound;
no one answered, and no one was listening.
**30** Then Elijah said to all the people, ''Come
here to me.'' When they had done so, he repaired the altar of the LORD which had been
destroyed. **31** He took twelve stones, for the
number of tribes of the sons of Jacob, to whom
the LORD had said, ''Your name shall be Israel.'' **32** He built an altar in honor of the LORD
with the stones, and made a trench around the
altar large enough for two seahs of grain.
**33** When he had arranged the wood, he cut up
the young bull and laid it on the wood. **34** ''Fill
four jars with water,'' he said, ''and pour it over
the holocaust and over the wood.'' ''Do it
again,'' he said, and they did it again. ''Do it
a third time,'' he said, and they did it a third
time. **35** The water flowed around the altar, and
the trench was filled with the water.
**36** At the time for offering sacrifice, the
prophet Elijah came forward and said, ''LORD,
God of Abraham, Isaac, and Israel, let it be
known this day that you are God in Israel and
that I am your servant and have done all these
things by your command. **37** Answer me,
LORD! Answer me, that this people may know
that you, LORD, are God and that you have
brought them back to their senses.'' **38** The
LORD's fire came down and consumed the holocaust, wood, stones, and dust, and it lapped up
the water in the trench. **39** Seeing this, all the
people fell prostrate and said, ''The LORD is
God! The LORD is God!'' **40** Then Elijah said
to them, ''Seize the prophets of Baal. Let none
of them escape!'' They were seized, and Elijah
had them brought down to the brook Kishon and
there he slit their throats.
**41** Elijah then said to Ahab, ''Go up, eat and
drink, for there is the sound of a heavy rain.''
**42** So Ahab went up to eat and drink, while
Elijah climbed to the top of Carmel, crouched
down to the earth, and put his head between his
knees. **43** ''Climb up and look out to sea,'' he
directed his servant, who went up and looked,
but reported, ''There is nothing.'' Seven times
he said, ''Go, look again!'' **44** And the seventh
time the youth reported, ''There is a cloud as
small as a man's hand rising from the sea.''
Elijah said, ''Go and say to Ahab, 'Harness up
and leave the mountain before the rain stops
you.' '' **45** In a trice, the sky grew dark with
clouds and wind, and a heavy rain fell. Ahab
mounted his chariot and made for Jezreel.
**46** But the hand of the LORD was on Elijah, who
girded up his clothing and ran before Ahab as
far as the approaches to Jezreel.

## CHAPTER 19

**Flight to Horeb.** **1** Ahab told Jezebel all
that Elijah had done—that he had put all the
prophets to the sword. **2** Jezebel then sent a
messenger to Elijah and said, ''May the gods do
thus and so to me if by this time tomorrow I have
not done with your life what was done to each
of them.'' **3** Elijah was afraid and fled for his
life, going to Beer-sheba of Judah. He left his
servant there **4** and went a day's journey into
the desert, until he came to a broom tree and sat
beneath it. He prayed for death: ''This is
enough, O LORD! Take my life, for I am no
better than my fathers.'' **5** He lay down and fell
asleep under the broom tree, but then an angel
touched him and ordered him to get up and eat.
**6** He looked and there at his head was a hearth
cake and a jug of water. After he ate and drank,
he lay down again, **7** but the angel of the LORD
came back a second time, touched him, and
ordered, ''Get up and eat, else the journey will
be too long for you!'' **8** He got up, ate and
drank; then strengthened by that food, he
walked forty days and forty nights to the mountain of God, Horeb.
**9** There he came to a cave, where he took
shelter. But the word of the LORD came to him,
''Why are you here, Elijah?'' **10** He answered:
''I have been most zealous for the LORD, the
God of hosts, but the Israelites have forsaken
your covenant, torn down your altars, and put
your prophets to the sword. I alone am left, and
they seek to take my life.'' **11** *Then the LORD

---

19, 11ff: Compare these divine manifestations to Elijah with those to Moses (Ex 19, 1–23; 33, 21ff; 34, 5) on the same Mount Horeb (Sinai) (Dt 4, 10–15). Though various phenomena, such as wind, storms, earthquakes, fire (Ex 19, 18f), herald the divine presence, they do not constitute the presence itself which, like the tiny whispering sound, is imperceptible and bespeaks the spirituality of God. It was fitting that Elijah, whose mission it was to reestablish the covenant and restore the pure faith, should have returned to Horeb where the covenant was

said, "Go outside and stand on the mountain
before the LORD; the LORD will be passing by."
A strong and heavy wind was rending the mountains and crushing rocks before the LORD—but
the LORD was not in the wind. After the wind
there was an earthquake—but the LORD was not
in the earthquake. **12** After the earthquake there
was fire—but the LORD was not in the fire. After
the fire there was a tiny whispering sound.
**13** When he heard this, Elijah hid his face in his
cloak and went and stood at the entrance of the
cave. A voice said to him, "Elijah, why are you
here?" **14** He replied, "I have been most zealous for the LORD, the God of hosts. But the
Israelites have forsaken your covenant, torn
down your altars, and put your prophets to the
sword. I alone am left, and they seek to take my
life."[r] **15** *"Go, take the road back to the
desert near Damascus," the LORD said to him.
"When you arrive, you shall anoint Hazael as
king of Aram. **16** Then you shall anoint Jehu,
son of Nimshi, as king of Israel, and Elisha, son
of Shaphat of Abel-meholah, as prophet to succeed you.[s] **17** If anyone escapes the sword of
Hazael, Jehu will kill him. If he escapes the
sword of Jehu, Elisha will kill him. **18** Yet I
will leave seven thousand men in Israel—all
those who have not knelt to Baal or kissed
him."[t]

**Call of Elisha.*** **19** Elijah set out, and came
upon Elisha, son of Shaphat, as he was plowing
with twelve yoke of oxen; he was following the
twelfth. Elijah went over to him and threw his
cloak over him. **20** Elisha left the oxen, ran
after Elijah, and said, "Please, let me kiss my
father and mother goodbye, and I will follow
you." "Go back!" Elijah answered. "Have I
done anything to you?" **21** Elisha left him and,
taking the yoke of oxen, slaughtered them; he
used the plowing equipment for fuel to boil their
flesh, and gave it to his people to eat. Then he
left and followed Elijah as his attendant.

## CHAPTER 20

### Ahab's Victories over Ben-hadad.

**1** Ben-hadad, king of Aram, gathered all his
forces, and accompanied by thirty-two kings
with horses and chariotry, proceeded to invest
and attack Samaria. **2** He sent couriers to Ahab,
king of Israel, within the city, **3** and said to
him, "This is Ben-hadad's message: 'Your silver and gold are mine, and your wives and your
promising sons are mine.' " **4** The king of Israel answered, "As you say, my lord king, I and
all I have are yours." **5** But the couriers came
again and said, "This is Ben-hadad's message:
'I sent you word to give me your silver and gold,
your wives and your sons. **6** Now, however, at
this time tomorrow I will send my servants to
you, and they shall ransack your house and the
houses of your servants. They shall seize and
take away whatever they consider valuable.' "
**7** The king of Israel then summoned all the
elders of the land and said: "Understand clearly
that this man wants to ruin us. When he sent to
me for my wives and sons, my silver and my
gold, I did not refuse him." **8** All the elders and
all the people said to him, "Do not listen. Do
not give in." **9** Accordingly he directed the
couriers of Ben-hadad, "Say to my lord the
king, 'I will do all that you demanded of your
servant the first time. But this I cannot do.' "
The couriers left and reported this. **10** Ben-hadad then sent him the message, "May the gods
do thus and so to me if there is enough dust in
Samaria to make handfuls for all my followers." **11** The king of Israel replied, "Tell him,
'It is not for the man who is buckling his armor
to boast as though he were taking it off.' "
**12** Ben-hadad was drinking in the pavilions
with the kings when he heard this reply. "Prepare the assault," he commanded his servants;
and they made ready to storm the city.

**13** Then a prophet came up to Ahab, king of
Israel, and said: "The LORD says, 'Do you see
all this huge army? When I deliver it up to you
today, you will know that I am the LORD.' "
**14** But Ahab asked, "Through whom will it be
delivered up?" He answered, "The LORD says,
'Through the retainers of the governors of the
provinces.' " Then Ahab asked, "Who is to
attack?" He replied, "You are." **15** So Ahab
called up the retainers of the governors of the
provinces, two hundred thirty-two of them. Behind them he mustered all the Israelite soldiery,
who numbered seven thousand. **16** They
marched out at noon, while Ben-hadad was
drinking heavily in the pavilions with the thirty-two kings who were his allies. **17** When the
retainers of the governors of the provinces
marched out first, Ben-hadad received word that
some men had marched out of Samaria. **18** He
answered, "Whether they have come out for
peace or for war, in any case take them alive."
**19** But when these had come out of the city

r Rom 11, 3. t Rom 11, 4.
s 2 Kgs 9, 2.

* revealed to Moses and through him to the Israelite people (Ex 3, 1–4. 17; 33, 18—34, 9). Moses and Elijah appeared with Christ at the time of his transfiguration (Mt 17, 1–9; Mk 9, 1–7; Lk 9, 28–36).

19, 15–17: Elijah himself carried out only the third of the commissions entrusted to him (vv 19–21); Elisha was deputed to perform the first in person (2 Kgs 8, 7–19), and the second through one of his followers (2 Kgs 9, 1–10).

19, 19–21: Elijah's act of throwing his mantle over the shoulders of Elisha expressed the divine call to share the prophetic mission. Elisha's prompt response through destruction of his plow and oxen is an example of total obedience and detachment from his former manner of living in order to promote the glory of God.

—the soldiers of the governors of the provinces with the army following them— **20** each of them struck down his man. The Arameans fled with Israel pursuing them, while Ben-hadad, king of Aram, escaped on a chariot steed. **21** The king of Israel went out, took the horses and chariots, and inflicted a severe defeat on Aram.

**22** Then the prophet went up to the king of Israel and said to him: "Go, regroup your forces. Mark well what you do, for at the beginning of the year* the king of Aram will attack you." **23** On the other hand, the servants of the king of Aram said to him: "Their gods are gods of mountains. That is why they defeated us. But if we fight them on level ground, we shall be sure to defeat them. **24** This is what you must do: Take the kings from their posts and put prefects in their places. **25** Mobilize an army as large as the army that has deserted you, horse for horse, chariot for chariot. Let us fight them on level ground, and we shall surely defeat them." He took their advice and did this.

**26** At the beginning of the year, Ben-hadad mobilized Aram and went up to Aphek to fight against Israel. **27** The Israelites, too, were called to arms and supplied with provisions; then they went out to engage the foe. The Israelites, encamped opposite them, seemed like a couple of small flocks of goats, while Aram covered the countryside. **28** A man of God came up and said to the king of Israel: "The LORD says, 'Because Aram has said the LORD is a god of mountains, not a god of plains, I will deliver up to you all this large army, that you may know I am the LORD.' " **29** They were encamped opposite each other for seven days. On the seventh day battle was joined, and the Israelites struck down one hundred thousand foot soldiers of Aram in one day. **30** The survivors, twenty-seven thousand of them, fled into the city of Aphek, and there the wall collapsed. Ben-hadad, too, fled, and took refuge within the city, in an inside room.

**31** His servants said to him: "We have heard that the kings of the land of Israel are merciful kings. Allow us, therefore, to garb ourselves in sackcloth, with cords around our heads, and go out to the king of Israel. Perhaps he will spare your life." **32** So they dressed in sackcloth girded at the waist, and wearing cords around their heads, they went to the king of Israel. "Your servant Ben-hadad pleads for his life," they said. "Is he still alive?" the king asked. "He is my brother." **33** Hearing this as a good omen, the men quickly took him at his word and said, "Ben-hadad is your brother." He answered, "Go and get him." When Ben-hadad came out to him, the king had him mount his chariot. **34** Ben-hadad said to him, "I will restore the cities which my father took from your father, and you may make yourself bazaars in Damascus, as my father did in Samaria." "On these terms," Ahab replied, "I will set you free." So he made an agreement with him and then set him free.

**35** One of the guild prophets was prompted by the LORD to say to his companion, "Strike me." But he refused to strike him. **36** Then he said to him, "Since you did not obey the voice of the LORD, a lion will kill you when you leave me." When they parted company, a lion came upon him and killed him. **37** The prophet met another man and said, "Strike me." The man struck him a blow and wounded him. **38** The prophet went on and waited for the king on the road, having disguised himself with a bandage over his eyes. **39** As the king was passing, he called out to the king and said, "Your servant went into the thick of the battle, and suddenly someone turned and brought me a man and said, 'Guard this man. If he is missing, you shall have to pay for his life with your life or pay out a talent of silver.' **40** But while your servant was looking here and there, the man disappeared." The king of Israel said to him, "That is your sentence. You have decided it yourself." **41** He immediately removed the bandage from his eyes, and the king of Israel recognized him as one of the prophets. **42** He said to him: "The LORD says, 'Because you have set free the man I doomed to destruction, your life shall pay for his life, your people for his people.' " Disturbed and angry, the king of Israel went off homeward and entered Samaria.[u]

## CHAPTER 21

**Seizure of Naboth's Vineyard.** **1** Some time after this, as Naboth the Jezreelite had a vineyard in Jezreel next to the palace of Ahab, king of Samaria, **2** Ahab said to Naboth, "Give me your vineyard to be my vegetable garden, since it is close by, next to my house. I will give you a better vineyard in exchange, or, if you prefer, I will give you its value in money." **3** "The LORD forbid," Naboth answered him, "that I should give you my ancestral heritage." **4** Ahab went home disturbed and angry at the answer Naboth the Jezreelite had made to him: "I will not give you my ancestral heritage." Lying down on his bed, he turned away from food and would not eat.

**5** His wife Jezebel came to him and said to him, "Why are you so angry that you will not eat?" **6** He answered her, "Because I spoke to Naboth the Jezreelite and said to him, 'Sell me your vineyard, or, if you prefer, I will give you

u 1 Kgs 22, 35.

* 20, 22: At the beginning of the year: in the spring.

a vineyard in exchange.' But he refused to let
me have his vineyard." **7** "A fine ruler over
Israel you are indeed!" his wife Jezebel said to
him. "Get up. Eat and be cheerful. I will obtain
the vineyard of Naboth the Jezreelite for you."
**8** So she wrote letters in Ahab's name and,
having sealed them with his seal, sent them to
the elders and to the nobles who lived in the
same city with Naboth. **9** This is what she
wrote in the letters: "Proclaim a fast and set
Naboth at the head of the people. **10** Next, get
two scoundrels to face him and accuse him of
having cursed God and king. Then take him out
and stone him to death." **11** His fellow citizens—the elders and the nobles who dwelt in his
city—did as Jezebel had ordered them in writing, through the letters she had sent them.
**12** They proclaimed a fast and placed Naboth at
the head of the people. **13** Two scoundrels
came in and confronted him with the accusation, "Naboth has cursed God and king." And
they led him out of the city and stoned him to
death. **14** Then they sent the information to
Jezebel that Naboth had been stoned to death.
**15** When Jezebel learned that Naboth had
been stoned to death, she said to Ahab, "Go on,
take possession of the vineyard of Naboth the
Jezreelite which he refused to sell you, because
Naboth is not alive, but dead." **16** On hearing
that Naboth was dead, Ahab started off on his
way down to the vineyard of Naboth the Jezreelite, to take possession of it.
**17** But the LORD said to Elijah the Tishbite:
**18** "Start down to meet Ahab, king of Israel,
who rules in Samaria. He will be in the vineyard
of Naboth, of which he has come to take possession. **19** *[v] This is what you shall tell him, 'The
LORD says: After murdering, do you also take
possession? For this, the LORD says: In the place
where the dogs licked up the blood of Naboth,
the dogs shall lick up your blood, too.'"
**20** *"Have you found me out, my enemy?"
Ahab said to Elijah. "Yes," he answered. "Because you have given yourself up to doing evil
in the LORD's sight, **21** I am bringing evil upon
you: I will destroy you and will cut off every
male in Ahab's line, whether slave or freeman,
in Israel.[w] **22** I will make your house like that
of Jeroboam, son of Nebat, and like that of
Baasha, son of Ahijah, because of how you
have provoked me by leading Israel into sin."[x]
**23** (Against Jezebel, too, the LORD declared,
"The dogs shall devour Jezebel in the district of
Jezreel.")[y] **24** "When one of Ahab's line dies
in the city, dogs will devour him; when one of
them dies in the field, the birds of the sky will
devour him." **25** Indeed, no one gave himself
up to the doing of evil in the sight of the LORD
as did Ahab, urged on by his wife Jezebel.
**26** He became completely abominable by following idols, just as the Amorites had done,
whom the LORD drove out before the Israelites.
**27** When Ahab heard these words, he tore his
garments and put on sackcloth over his bare
flesh. He fasted, slept in the sackcloth, and went
about subdued. **28** Then the LORD said to Elijah
the Tishbite, **29** "Have you seen that Ahab has
humbled himself before me? Since he has humbled himself before me, I will not bring the evil
in his time. I will bring the evil upon his house
during the reign of his son."[z]

## CHAPTER 22

### Campaign against Ramoth-gilead.

**1** Three years passed without war between
Aram and Israel.[a] **2** In the third year, however,
King Jehoshaphat of Judah came down to the
king of Israel, **3** who said to his servants, "Do
you not know that Ramoth-gilead is ours and we
are doing nothing to take it from the king of
Aram?" **4** He asked Jehoshaphat, "Will you
come with me to fight against Ramoth-gilead?"
Jehoshaphat answered the king of Israel, "You
and I are as one, and your people and my people, your horses and my horses as well." **5** Jehoshaphat also said to the king of Israel, "Seek
the word of the LORD at once."
**6** The king of Israel gathered together the
prophets, about four hundred of them, and
asked, "Shall I go to attack Ramoth-gilead or
shall I refrain?" "Go up," they answered.
"The LORD will deliver it over to the king."
**7** But Jehoshaphat said, "Is there no other
prophet of the LORD here whom we may consult?" **8** The king of Israel answered, "There
is one other through whom we might consult the
LORD, Micaiah, son of Imlah; but I hate him
because he prophesies not good but evil about
me." Jehoshaphat said, "Let not your majesty
speak of evil against you."
**9** So the king of Israel called an official and
said to him, "Get Micaiah, son of Imlah, at
once." **10** The king of Israel and King Jehoshaphat of Judah were seated, each on his throne,

---

v 1 Kgs 22, 38.
w 2 Kgs 9, 8.
x 1 Kgs 15, 29; 16, 3.
y 2 Kgs 9, 36.
z 2 Kgs 9, 26.
a 2 Chr 18, 1.

---

*

21, 19: The response of Ahab to this divine judgment is described in v 27, and the consequences are given in vv 28–29, and in 2 Kgs 9, 21–26.

21, 20–26: In these verses the Judean editor of the Books of Kings substitutes, for the message of Elijah prepared for in v 19, a sweeping and definitive judgment against the whole family of Ahab in the same terms as were used against the families of Jeroboam I (1 Kgs 14, 9–11) and Baasha (1 Kgs 16, 2–4). This judgment is the fruit of later theological reflection; it is not occasioned directly by the crime against Naboth, but by the idolatry of Ahab and Jezebel. The judgment on Jezebel herself (v 23) may have been uttered by Elijah during the Naboth episode; it finds its fulfillment in 2 Kgs 9, 36–37. Still another theological explanation for the death of Ahab is given by the north Israelite writer of 1 Kgs 20, 35–42 above.

clothed in their robes of state on a threshing
floor at the entrance of the gate of Samaria, and
all the prophets were prophesying before them.
**11** Zedekiah, son of Chenaanah, made himself
horns of iron and said, "The LORD says, 'With
these you shall gore Aram until you have destroyed them.' " **12** The other prophets prophesied in a similar vein, saying: "Go up to Ramoth-gilead; you shall succeed. The LORD will
deliver it over to the king."

**13** The messenger who had gone to call Micaiah said to him, "Look now, the prophets are
unanimously predicting good for the king. Let
your word be the same as any of theirs; predict
good." **14** "As the LORD lives," Micaiah answered, "I shall say whatever the LORD tells
me."

**15** When he came to the king, the king said
to him, "Micaiah, shall we go to fight against
Ramoth-gilead, or shall we refrain?" "Go up,"
he answered, "you shall succeed! The LORD
will deliver it over to the king." **16** But the king
answered him, "How many times must I adjure
you to tell me nothing but the truth in the name
of the LORD?" **17** So Micaiah said:

"I see all Israel
scattered on the mountains,
like sheep without a shepherd,
and the LORD saying, 'These have no
master!
Let each of them go back home in peace.' "

**18** The king of Israel said to Jehoshaphat, "Did
I not tell you he prophesies not good but evil
about me?" **19** *Micaiah continued: "Therefore hear the word of the LORD: I saw the LORD
seated on his throne, with the whole host of
heaven standing by to his right and to his left.
**20** The LORD asked, 'Who will deceive Ahab,
so that he will go up and fall at Ramoth-gilead?'
And one said this, another that, **21** until one of
the spirits came forth and presented himself to
the LORD, saying, 'I will deceive him.' The
LORD asked, 'How?' **22** He answered, 'I will
go forth and become a lying spirit in the mouths
of all his prophets.' The LORD replied, 'You
shall succeed in deceiving him. Go forth and do
this.' **23** So now, the LORD has put a lying spirit
in the mouths of all these prophets of yours, but
the LORD himself has decreed evil against you."

**24** Thereupon Zedekiah, son of Chenaanah,
came up and slapped Micaiah on the cheek,
saying, "Has the spirit of the LORD, then, left
me to speak with you?" **25** "You shall find
out," Micaiah replied, "on that day when you
retreat into an inside room to hide." **26** The
king of Israel then said, "Seize Micaiah and
take him back to Amon, prefect of the city, and
to Joash, the king's son, **27** and say, 'This is the
king's order: Put this man in prison and feed him
scanty rations of bread and water until I return
in safety.' " **28** But Micaiah said, "If ever you
return in safety, the LORD has not spoken
through me."*

**29** The king of Israel and King Jehoshaphat
of Judah went up to Ramoth-gilead, **30** and the
king of Israel said to Jehoshaphat, "I will disguise myself and go into battle, but you put on
your own clothes." So the king of Israel disguised himself and entered the fray. **31** In the
meantime the king of Aram had given his thirty-two chariot commanders the order, "Do not
fight with anyone at all except the king of Israel." **32** When the chariot commanders saw Jehoshaphat, they cried out, "That must be the
king of Israel!" and shifted to fight him. But
Jehoshaphat shouted his battle cry, **33** and the
chariot commanders, aware that he was not the
king of Israel, gave up pursuit of him.
**34** Someone, however, drew his bow at random, and hit the king of Israel between the
joints of his breast-plate. He ordered his charioteer, "Rein about and take me out of the ranks,
for I am disabled." **35** The battle grew fierce
during the day, and the king, who was propped
up in his chariot facing the Arameans, died in
the evening. The blood from his wound flowed
to the bottom of the chariot.[b] **36** At sunset a cry
went through the army, "Every man to his city,
every man to his land, **37** for the king is dead!"
So they went to Samaria, where they buried the
king. **38** When the chariot was washed at the
pool of Samaria, the dogs licked up his blood
and harlots bathed there, as the LORD had prophesied.[c]

**39** The rest of the acts of Ahab, with all that
he did, including the ivory palace and all the
cities he built, are recorded in the book of the
chronicles of the kings of Israel. **40** Ahab rested
with his ancestors, and his son Ahaziah succeeded him as king.

**Reign of Jehoshaphat.** **41** Jehoshaphat,
son of Asa, began to reign over Judah in the
fourth year of Ahab, king of Israel. **42** Jehoshaphat was thirty-five years old when he began to
reign, and reigned twenty-five years in Jerusalem. His mother's name was Azubah, daughter
of Shilhi. **43** He followed all the ways of his
father Asa unswervingly, doing what was right
in the LORD's sight. **44** Nevertheless, the high
places did not disappear, and the people continued to sacrifice and to burn incense on the high

b 1 Kgs 20, 42. c 1 Kgs 21, 19.

*

22, 19–23: The prophet Micaiah uses as a last resort to deter Ahab from his foolhardy design of fighting against Ramoth-gilead the literary device of describing false prophets as messengers of a lying spirit which God, after holding counsel with his angels, permits to deceive them.

22, 28: A note in the Hebrew text after this verse attributes to Micaiah ben Imlah the first words of the book of a different Micaiah, the minor prophet of Moreshet.

places. 45 Jehoshaphat also made peace with
the king of Israel. 46 The rest of the acts of
Jehoshaphat, with his prowess, what he did and
how he fought, are recorded in the book of the
chronicles of the kings of Judah.

47 He removed from the land the rest of the
cult prostitutes who had remained in the reign
of his father Asa. 48 There was no king in
Edom, but an appointed regent. 49 Jehoshaphat
made Tarshish ships to go to Ophir for gold; but
in fact the ships did not go, because they were
wrecked at Ezion-geber. 50 Then Ahaziah, son
of Ahab, said to Jehoshaphat, "Let my servants
accompany your servants in the ships." But
Jehoshaphat would not agree. 51 Jehoshaphat
rested with his ancestors; he was buried in his
forefathers' City of David. His son Jehoram
succeeded him as king.

**Reign of Ahaziah.** 52 Ahaziah, son of
Ahab, began to reign over Israel in Samaria in
the seventeenth year* of Jehoshaphat, king of
Judah; he reigned two years over Israel. 53 He
did evil in the sight of the LORD, behaving like
his father, his mother, and Jeroboam, son of
Nebat, who caused Israel to sin. 54 He served
and worshiped Baal, thus provoking the LORD,
the God of Israel, just as his father had done.

*

22, 52: Seventeenth year: so the present Hebrew text. More consistent with 2 Kgs 1, 17 would be a date in the twenty-fourth year of Jehoshaphat for Ahab's death; see note on 2 Kgs 1, 1.

The Second Book of

# KINGS

## I: *The Kingdoms of Israel and Judah*

### CHAPTER 1

**Ahaziah Consults Baalzebub.** 1 After
Ahab's death, Moab rebelled against Israel.[a]
2 Ahaziah had fallen through the lattice of his
roof terrace at Samaria and had been injured. So
he sent out messengers with the instructions:
"Go and inquire of Baalzebub,* the god of
Ekron, whether I shall recover from this injury."
3 Meanwhile, the angel of the LORD said to
Elijah the Tishbite: "Go, intercept the messengers of Samaria's king, and ask them, 'Is it
because there is no God in Israel that you are
going to inquire of Baalzebub, the god of Ekron?' 4 For this, the LORD says: 'You shall not
leave the bed upon which you lie; instead, you
shall die.' " And with that, Elijah departed.
5 The messengers then returned to Ahaziah,
who asked them, "Why have you returned?"
6 "A man came up to us," they answered,
"who said to us, 'Go back to the king who sent
you and tell him: The LORD says, Is it because
there is no God in Israel that you are sending to
inquire of Baalzebub, the god of Ekron? For this
you shall not leave the bed upon which you lie;
instead, you shall die.' " 7 The king asked
them, "What was the man like who came up to
you and said these things to you?" 8 "Wearing
a hairy garment,"* they replied, "with a leather
girdle about his loins." "It is Elijah the Tishbite!" he exclaimed.[b]

**Death of Two Captains.** 9 Then the king
sent a captain with his company of fifty men
after Elijah. The prophet was seated on a hilltop
when he found him. "Man of God," he ordered, "the king commands you to come
down." 10 "If I am a man of God," Elijah
answered the captain, "may fire come down
from heaven and consume you and your fifty
men." And fire came down from heaven and
consumed him and his fifty men.[c] 11 Ahaziah
sent another captain with his company of fifty
men after Elijah. "Man of God," he called out
to Elijah, "the king commands you to come
down immediately." 12 "If I am a man of
God," Elijah answered him, "May fire come
down from heaven and consume you and your
fifty men." And divine fire* came down from
heaven, consuming him and his fifty men.

**Death of the King.** 13 Again, for the third
time, Ahaziah sent a captain with his company
of fifty men. When the third captain arrived, he
fell to his knees before Elijah, pleading with
him. "Man of God," he implored him, "let my
life and the lives of these fifty men, your servants, count for something in your sight! 14 Already fire has come down from heaven, consuming two captains with their companies of
fifty men. But now, let my life mean something
to you!" 15 Then the angel of the LORD said to
Elijah, "Go down with him; you need not be
afraid of him."
16 So Elijah left and went down with him
and stated to the king: "Thus says the LORD:
'Because you sent messengers to inquire of
Baalzebub, the god of Ekron, you shall not
leave the bed upon which you lie; instead you
shall die.' "[d]
17 Ahaziah died in fulfillment of the prophecy of the LORD spoken by Elijah. Since he had
no son, his brother Joram* succeeded him as
king, in the second year of Jehoram, son of
Jehoshaphat, king of Judah. 18 The rest of the
acts of Ahaziah are recorded in the book of
chronicles of the kings of Israel.

---

a 2 Kgs 3, 4-27.
b Zec 13, 4.
c Lv 10, 2; Sir 48, 3f; Lk 9, 54f.
d Sir 48, 6.

---

*

1, 2: Baalzebub: in this form, "Baal of flies." The name in the Hebrew text is a derisive alteration of Baalzebul, "Prince Baal." The best New Testament evidence supports the latter form in Mt. 10, 25; Lk 11, 15. Later associations with Aramaic beeldebaba, "enemy," gave the ancient name its connotation of "devil."

1, 8: Hairy garment: a sign of ascetical and prophetic calling, imitated by John the Baptizer; see Mt 3, 4; Mk 1, 6.

1, 12: Divine fire: literally, "fire of God," which in Hebrew sounds quite like man of God. The play on words is the basis for Elijah's alleged retort. This story was told among the people to enhance the dignity of the prophet and to reflect the power of God whom he served. The mercy which God extends even to the wicked is described in Wis 11, 17–12, 22, and the prophet Elijah was well aware of it (1 Kgs 21, 28f).

1, 17: Joram: in the Second Book of Kings the name Joram (yoram), alternately Jehoram (yehoram), appears in numerous passages to designate both the king of Judah, son and successor of Jehoshaphat (848–841 B.C.), and the contemporary king of Israel, son of Ahab (852–841 B.C.). For the convenience of the reader in distinguishing these two kings, the longer form, Jehoram, is used to designate the king of Judah and the shorter form, Joram, to designate the king of Israel. See note on 2 Kgs 3, 1.

## CHAPTER 2

**Elijah and Elisha.** **1** When the LORD was
about to take Elijah up to heaven in a whirlwind,
he and Elisha were on their way from Gilgal.*
**2** "Stay here, please," Elijah said to Elisha.
"The LORD has sent me on to Bethel." "As the
LORD lives, and as you yourself live," Elisha
replied, "I will not leave you." So they went
down to Bethel, **3** where the guild prophets
went out to Elisha and asked him, "Do you
know that the LORD will take your master from
over you today?" "Yes, I know it," he replied.
"Keep still."

**4** Then Elijah said to him, "Stay here,
please, Elisha, for the LORD has sent me on to
Jericho." "As the LORD lives, and as you yourself live," Elisha replied, "I will not leave
you." **5** They went on to Jericho, where the
guild prophets approached Elisha and asked
him, "Do you know that the LORD will take
your master from over you today?" "Yes, I
know it," he replied. "Keep still."

**6** Elijah said to Elisha, "Please stay here; the
LORD has sent me on to the Jordan." "As the
LORD lives, and as you yourself live," Elisha
replied, "I will not leave you." And so the two
went on together. **7** Fifty of the guild prophets
followed, and when the two stopped at the Jordan, stood facing them at a distance. **8** Elijah
took his mantle, rolled it up and struck the water, which divided, and both crossed over on dry
ground.[e]

**Elisha Succeeds Elijah.** **9** When they had
crossed over, Elijah said to Elisha, "Ask for
whatever I may do for you, before I am taken
from you." Elisha answered, "May I receive a
double portion of your spirit."* **10** "You have
asked something that is not easy," he replied.
"Still, if you see me taken up from you, your
wish will be granted; otherwise not."[f] **11** As
they walked on conversing, a flaming chariot
and flaming horses came between them, and
Elijah went up to heaven in a whirlwind.[g]
**12** When Elisha saw it happen he cried out,
"My father!* my father! Israel's chariots and
drivers!" But when he could no longer see him,
Elisha gripped his own garment and tore it in
two.[h]

**13** Then he picked up Elijah's mantle which
had fallen from him, and went back and stood
at the bank of the Jordan.[i] **14** Wielding the
mantle which had fallen from Elijah, he struck
the water in his turn and said, "Where is the
LORD, the God of Elijah?" When Elisha struck
the water it divided and he crossed over.

**15** The guild prophets in Jericho, who were
on the other side, saw him and said, "The spirit
of Elijah rests on Elisha." They went to meet
him, bowing to the ground before him.
**16** "Among your servants are fifty brave
men," they said. "Let them go in search of your
master. Perhaps the spirit of the LORD has carried him away to some mountain or some valley." "Do not send them," he answered.[j]
**17** However, they kept urging him, until he was
embarrassed and said, "Send them." So they
sent the fifty men, who searched for three days
without finding him. **18** When they returned to
Elisha in Jericho, where he was staying, he said
to them, "Did I not tell you not to go?"

**Healing of the Water.** **19** Once the inhabitants of the city complained to Elisha, "The
site of the city is fine indeed, as my lord can see,
but the water is bad and the land unfruitful."
**20** "Bring me a new bowl," Elisha said, "and
put salt into it." When they had brought it to
him, **21** he went out to the spring and threw salt
into it, saying, "Thus says the LORD, 'I have
purified this water. Never again shall death or
miscarriage spring from it.' " **22** And the water
has stayed pure even to this day, just as Elisha
prophesied.

**The Prophet's Curse.** **23** *From there
Elisha went up to Bethel. While he was on the
way, some small boys came out of the city and
jeered at him. "Go up, baldhead," they shouted, "go up, baldhead!" **24** The prophet turned
and saw them, and he cursed them in the name
of the LORD. Then two she-bears came out of the
woods and tore forty-two of the children to
pieces. **25** From there he went to Mount Carmel, and thence he returned to Samaria.

---

e Ex 14, 16. 22.
f Nm 11, 17. 25.
g Gn 5, 24; 1 Mc 2, 58; Acts 1, 9.
h 2 Kgs 13, 14; Sir 48, 9. 12.
i 1 Kgs 19, 19.
j 1 Kgs 18, 12.

*

2, 1: Gilgal: commonly identified with Jiljulieh, about seven miles north of Bethel, and different from the Gilgal in Dt 11, 30 near Shechem, and that in Jos 4 and 5, passim, near Jericho.

2, 9: Double portion of your spirit: as the first-born son inherited a double portion of his father's property (Dt 21, 17), so Elisha asks to inherit from Elijah his spirit of prophecy in the degree befitting his principal disciple. In Nm 11, 17. 25, God bestows some of the spirit of Moses on others.

2, 12: My father: a religious title accorded prophetic leaders; cf 2 Kgs 6, 21; 8, 9. Israel's chariots and drivers: Elijah was worth more than a whole army in defending Israel and the true religion. King Joash of Israel uses the same phrase of Elisha himself (2 Kgs 13, 14).

2, 23f: This story, like the one about Elijah and the captains (ch 1), is preserved for us in Scripture to convey a popular understanding of the dignity of the prophet. Told in popular vein, it becomes a caricature, in which neither Elisha nor the bears behave in character. See note on 2 Kgs 1, 12 and the contrasting narrative in ch 4.

## CHAPTER 3

### Campaign of Joram against Moab.

**1** Joram, son of Ahab, became king of Israel in
Samaria [in the eighteenth year of Jehoshaphat,
king of Judah, and he reigned for twelve
years].* **2** He did evil in the LORD's sight,
though not as much as his father and mother. He
did away with the pillar of Baal, which his
father had made, **3** but he still clung to the sin
to which Jeroboam, son of Nebat, had lured
Israel; this he did not give up.

**4** Now Mesha, king of Moab, who raised
sheep, used to pay the king of Israel as tribute
a hundred thousand lambs and the wool of a
hundred thousand rams. **5** But when Ahab
died, the king of Moab had rebelled against the
king of Israel. **6** Joram as king mustered all
Israel, and when he set out on a campaign from
Samaria, **7** he sent the king of Judah the message: "The king of Moab is in rebellion against
me. Will you join me in battle against Moab?"
"I will," he replied. "You and I shall be as
one, your people and mine, and your horses and
mine as well."[k] **8** They discussed the route for
their attack, and settled upon the route through
the desert of Edom.

**9** So the king of Israel set out, accompanied
by the king of Judah and the king of Edom.
After their roundabout journey of seven days the
water gave out for the army and for the animals
with them. **10** "Alas!" exclaimed the king of
Israel. "The LORD has called together these
three kings to put them in the grasp of Moab."
**11** But the king of Judah asked, "Is there no
prophet of the LORD here through whom we may
inquire of the LORD?" One of the officers of the
king of Israel replied, "Elisha, son of Shaphat,
who poured water on the hands of Elijah, is
here."[l] **12** "He has the word of the LORD," the
king of Judah agreed. So the kings of Israel,
Judah, and Edom went down to Elisha.
**13** "What do you want with me?" Elisha asked
the king of Israel. "Go to the prophets of your
father and to the prophets of your mother."
"No," the king of Israel replied. "The LORD
has called these three kings together to put them
in the grasp of Moab." **14** Then Elisha said,
"As the LORD of hosts lives, whom I serve,
were it not that I respect the king of Judah, I
should neither look at you nor notice you at
all.[m] **15** Now get me a minstrel."

When the minstrel played, the power of the
LORD came upon Elisha **16** and he announced:
"Thus says the LORD, 'Provide many catch basins in this wadi.' **17** For the LORD says,
'Though you will see neither wind nor rain, yet
this wadi will be filled with water for you, your
livestock, and your pack animals to drink.'
**18** And since the LORD does not consider this
enough, he will also deliver Moab into your
grasp. **19** You shall destroy every fortified city,
fell every fruit tree, stop up all the springs, and
ruin every fertile field with stones."[n]

**20** In the morning, at the time of the sacrifice, water came from the direction of Edom and
filled the land.[o] **21** Meanwhile, all Moab heard
that the kings had come to give them battle;
every man capable of bearing arms was called
up and stationed at the border. **22** Early that
morning, when the sun shone on the water, the
Moabites saw the water at a distance as red as
blood.* **23** "This is blood!" they exclaimed.
"The kings have fought among themselves and
killed one another. Quick! To the spoils, Moabites!" **24** But when they reached the camp of
Israel, the Israelites rose up and attacked the
Moabites, who fled from them. They ranged
through the countryside striking down the Moabites, and **25** destroying the cities; each of
them cast stones onto every fertile field till they
had loaded it down; all the springs they stopped
up and every useful tree they felled. Finally only
Kir-hareseth* was left behind its stone walls,
and the slingers had surrounded it and were
attacking it.[p] **26** When he saw that he was losing the battle, the king of Moab took seven
hundred swordsmen to break through to the king
of Aram, but he failed. **27** So he took his
first-born, his heir apparent, and offered him as
a holocaust upon the wall. The wrath against

k 1 Kgs 22, 4.
l 1 Kgs 22, 7.
m 1 Kgs 18, 15.
n Dt 20, 19.
o 1 Kgs 18, 29.
p Jb 5, 23.
q Jgs 11, 30f.

*

3, 1: The sequence of the reigns between Ahab and Jehu of Israel may be reconstructed as follows: Jehoshaphat of Judah outlived Ahab by a short time, so that Ahaziah of Israel was his contemporary. Jehoram of Judah succeeded his father Jehoshaphat while Ahaziah of Israel was still alive. Jehoram (Joram) of Israel became king, following his brother Ahaziah, in the second year of Jehoram of Judah (2 Kgs 1, 17); this is one datum on which the earliest Greek evidence and the standard Hebrew text are in agreement.

The two Jehorams were contemporary for much of their reigns; Jehoram of Judah was succeeded by Ahaziah something more than a year before Jehu did away with the rulers of both kingdoms (2 Kgs 9, 1–29).

The Moabite campaign of 2 Kgs 3, 4–27 is thus best placed under the two Kings Jehoram, before the Edomite rebellion mentioned in 2 Kgs 8, 20. In the received Hebrew text, Jehoshaphat has been made the Judahite protagonist in the campaign against Moab as a tribute to his piety; this assimilates the story of 2 Kgs 3 to that of 1 Kgs 22, but creates difficulties in the chronology which the extant data leave party unresolved. An older practice for stories of the Israelite kings was to leave them and their fellow kings without identification by name; cf 2 Kgs 6, 8—7, 20. The name of Jehoshaphat has been omitted from a number of places in 2 Kgs 3—8, in this translation; cf 1 Kgs 22, 51.

3, 22: Red as blood: possibly caused by the red sandstone of the Wadi Zered (Dt 2, 13), south of Moab.

3, 25: Kir-hareseth: modern Kerak, east of the Dead Sea; cf Is 16, 7. 11; Jer 48, 31. 36.

3, 27: The wrath against Israel: probably the wrath of Chemosh, the Moabite god to whom the child was offered. He was feared by the Israelites who lost heart on foreign soil.

Israel* was so great that they gave up the siege and returned to their own land.[q]

## CHAPTER 4

**The Widow's Oil.** **1** [r]A certain woman, the widow of one of the guild prophets, complained to Elisha: "My husband, your servant, is dead. You know that he was a God-fearing man, yet now his creditor has come to take my two children as his slaves."* **2** "How can I help you?" Elisha answered her. "Tell me what you have in the house." "This servant of yours has nothing in the house but a jug of oil," she replied. **3** "Go out," he said, "borrow vessels from all your neighbors—as many empty vessels as you can. **4** Then come back and close the door on yourself and your children; pour the oil into all the vessels, and as each is filled, set it aside." **5** She went and did so, closing the door on herself and her children. As they handed her the vessels, she would pour in oil. **6** When all the vessels were filled, she said to her son, "Bring me another vessel." "There is none left," he answered her. And then the oil stopped. **7** She went and told the man of God, who said, "Go and sell the oil to pay off your creditor; with what remains, you and your children can live."

**Elisha and the Shunammite.** **8** One day Elisha came to Shunem, where there was a woman of influence, who urged him to dine with her. Afterward, whenever he passed by, he used to stop there to dine. **9** So she said to her husband, "I know that he is a holy man of God. Since he visits us often, **10** let us arrange a little room on the roof and furnish it for him with a bed, table, chair, and lamp, so that when he comes to us he can stay there." **11** Some time later Elisha arrived and stayed in the room overnight. **12** Then he said to his servant Gehazi, "Call this Shunammite woman." He did so, and when she stood before Elisha, **13** he told Gehazi, "Say to her, 'You have lavished all this care on us; what can we do for you? Can we say a good word for you to the king or to the commander of the army?' " She replied, "I am living among my own people." **14** Later Elisha asked, "Can something be done for her?" "Yes!" Gehazi answered. "She has no son, and her husband is getting on in years." **15** "Call her," said Elisha. When she had been called, and stood at the door, **16** Elisha promised, "This time next year you will be fondling a baby son." "Please, my lord," she protested, "you are a man of God; do not deceive your servant."[s] **17** Yet the woman conceived, and by the same time the following year she had given birth to a son, as Elisha promised.

**18** The day came when the child was old enough to go out to his father among the reapers.[t] **19** "My head hurts!" he complained to his father. "Carry him to his mother," the father said to a servant. **20** The servant picked him up and carried him to his mother; he stayed with her until noon, when he died in her lap. **21** The mother took him upstairs and laid him on the bed of the man of God. Closing the door on him, she went out **22** and called to her husband, "Let me have a servant and a donkey. I must go quickly to the man of God, and I will be back." **23** "Why are you going to him today?" he asked. "It is neither the new moon nor the sabbath." But she bade him good-bye, **24** and when the donkey was saddled, said to her servant: "Lead on! Do not stop my donkey unless I tell you to." **25** She kept going till she reached the man of God on Mount Carmel. When he spied her at a distance, the man of God said to his servant Gehazi: "There is the Shunammite! **26** Hurry to meet her, and ask if all is well with her, with her husband, and with the boy." "Greetings,"* she replied. **27** But when she reached the man of God on the mountain, she clasped his feet. Gehazi came near to push her away, but the man of God said: "Let her alone, she is in bitter anguish; the LORD hid it from me and did not let me know." **28** "Did I ask my lord for a son?" she cried out. "Did I not beg you not to deceive me?" **29** "Gird your loins," Elisha said to Gehazi, "take my staff with you and be off; if you meet anyone, do not greet him,* and if anyone greets you, do not answer. Lay my staff upon the boy." **30** But the boy's mother cried out: "As the LORD lives and as you yourself live, I will not release you." So he started to go back with her.

**31** [u]Meanwhile, Gehazi had gone on ahead and had laid the staff upon the boy, but there was no sound or sign of life. He returned to meet Elisha and informed him that the boy had not awakened. **32** When Elisha reached the house, he found the boy lying dead. **33** He went in, closed the door on them both, and prayed to the LORD.[v] **34** Then he lay upon the child on the bed, placing his mouth upon the child's mouth, his eyes upon the eyes, and his hands upon the hands. As Elisha stretched himself over the child, the body became warm. **35** He arose, paced up and down the room, and then once

r 1 Kgs 17, 8-16.
s Gn 18, 10.
t 1 Kgs 17, 17-24.
u 31-36; Acts 20, 10ff.
v 1 Kgs 17, 21-23.
w Heb 11, 35.

*

4, 1: His creditor . . . slaves: Hebrew law permitted the selling of wife and children as chattels for debt; cf. Ex 21, 7; Am 2, 6; 8, 6; Is 50.

4, 26: Greetings: the conventional answer to Gehazi's question, which tells him nothing.

4, 29: Do not greet him: the profuse exchange of compliments among Orientals meeting and greeting one another consumed time. Urgency necessitated their omission, as our Lord counseled his disciples (Lk 10, 4).

more lay down upon the boy, who now sneezed
seven times and opened his eyes.[w] **36** Elisha
summoned Gehazi and said, "Call the Shunammite." She came at his call, and Elisha said to
her, "Take your son." **37** She came in and fell
at his feet in gratitude; then she took her son and
left the room.

**The Poisoned Stew.** **38** When Elisha returned to Gilgal, there was a famine in the land.
Once, when the guild prophets were seated before him, he said to his servant, "Put the large
pot on, and make some vegetable stew for the
guild prophets." **39** Someone went out into the
field to gather herbs and found a wild vine, from
which he picked a clothful of wild gourds. On
his return he cut them up into the pot of vegetable stew without anybody's knowing it. **40** The
stew was poured out for the men to eat, but
when they began to eat it, they exclaimed,
"Man of God, there is poison in the pot!" And
they could not eat it. **41** "Bring some meal,"
Elisha said. He threw it into the pot and said,
"Serve it to the people to eat." And there was
no longer anything harmful in the pot.

**Multiplication of Loaves.** **42** A man
came from Baal-shalishah bringing the man of
God twenty barley loaves made from the
first-fruits, and fresh grain in the ear. "Give it
to the people to eat," Elisha said. **43** But his
servant objected, "How can I set this before a
hundred men?" "Give it to the people to eat,"
Elisha insisted. "For thus says the LORD, 'They
shall eat and there shall be some left over.' "
**44** And when they had eaten, there was some
left over, as the LORD had said.

## CHAPTER 5

**Cure of Naaman.** **1** Naaman, the army
commander of the king of Aram, was highly
esteemed and respected by his master, for
through him the LORD had brought victory to
Aram. But valiant as he was, the man was a
leper. **2** Now the Arameans had captured from
the land of Israel in a raid a little girl, who
became the servant of Naaman's wife. **3** "If
only my master would present himself to the
prophet in Samaria," she said to her mistress,
"he would cure him of his leprosy." **4** Naaman
went and told his lord just what the slave girl
from the land of Israel had said. **5** "Go," said
the king of Aram. "I will send along a letter to
the king of Israel." So Naaman set out, taking
along ten silver talents, six thousand gold
pieces, and ten festal garments. **6** To the king
of Israel he brought the letter, which read:
"With this letter I am sending my servant Naaman to you, that you may cure him of his leprosy."

**7** When he read the letter, the king of Israel
tore his garments and exclaimed: "Am I a god
with power over life and death, that this man
should send someone to me to be cured of leprosy? Take note! You can see he is only looking
for a quarrel with me!"[x] **8** When Elisha, the
man of God, heard that the king of Israel had
torn his garments, he sent word to the king:
"Why have you torn your garments? Let him
come to me and find out that there is a prophet
in Israel."

**9** Naaman came with his horses and chariots
and stopped at the door of Elisha's house.
**10** The prophet sent him the message: "Go and
wash seven times in the Jordan, and your flesh
will heal, and you will be clean."[y] **11** But Naaman went away angry, saying, "I thought that
he would surely come out and stand there to
invoke the LORD his God, and would move his
hand over the spot, and thus cure the leprosy.
**12** Are not the rivers of Damascus, the Abana
and the Pharpar, better than all the waters of
Israel? Could I not wash in them and be
cleansed?"* With this, he turned about in anger
and left.

**13** But his servants came up and reasoned
with him. "My father," they said, "if the
prophet had told you to do something extraordinary, would you not have done it? All the more
now, since he said to you, 'Wash and be clean,'
should you do as he said." **14** So Naaman went
down and plunged into the Jordan seven times
at the word of the man of God. His flesh became
again like the flesh of a little child, and he was
clean.[z]

**15** He returned with his whole retinue to the
man of God. On his arrival he stood before him
and said, "Now I know that there is no God in
all the earth, except in Israel. Please accept a
gift from your servant."

**16** "As the LORD lives whom I serve, I will
not take it," Elisha replied; and despite Naaman's urging, he still refused. **17** Naaman said:
"If you will not accept, please let me, your
servant, have two mule-loads of earth,* for I
will no longer offer holocaust or sacrifice to any
other god except to the LORD. **18** But I trust the
LORD will forgive your servant this: when my
master enters the temple of Rimmon to worship
there, then I, too, as his adjutant, must bow
down in the temple of Rimmon. May the LORD

---

x Gn 30, 2; 1 Sm 2, 6; Jn 5, 21.
y Jn 9, 7.
z Lk 4, 27.

---

5, 12: Wash in them and be cleansed: typical of the ambiguity in ritual healing or cleanliness. The muddy waters of the Jordan are no match hygienically for the mountain spring waters of Damascus; ritually, it is the other way around.

5, 17: Two mule-loads of earth: Israelite earth on which to erect in Aram an altar to the God of Israel.

forgive your servant this." 19 "Go in
peace,"* Elisha said to him.
20 Naaman had gone some distance when
Gehazi, the servant of Elisha, the man of God,
thought to himself: "My master was too easy
with this Aramean Naaman, not accepting what
he brought. As the LORD lives, I will run after
him and get something out of him." 21 So
Gehazi hurried after Naaman. Aware that someone was running after him, Naaman alighted
from his chariot to wait for him. "Is everything
all right?" he asked. 22 "Yes," Gehazi replied, "but my master sent me to say, 'Two
young men have just come to me, guild prophets
from the hill country of Ephraim. Please give
them a talent of silver and two festal garments.' " 23 "Please take two talents," Naaman said, and pressed them upon him. He tied
up these silver talents in bags and gave them,
with the two festal garments, to two of his servants, who carried them before Gehazi.
24 When they reached the hill, Gehazi took
what they had, carried it into the house, and sent
the men on their way.
25 He went in and stood before Elisha his
master, who asked him, "Where have you
been, Gehazi?" He answered, "Your servant
has not gone anywhere." 26 But Elisha said to
him: "Was I not present in spirit when the man
alighted from his chariot to wait for you? Is this
a time to take money or to take garments, olive
orchards or vineyards, sheep or cattle, male or
female servants? 27 The leprosy of Naaman
shall cling to you and your descendants forever." And Gehazi left Elisha, a leper white as
snow.[a]

## CHAPTER 6

**Recovery of the Lost Ax.** 1 The guild
prophets once said to Elisha: "There is not
enough room for us to continue to live here with
you. 2 Let us go to the Jordan, where by getting
one beam apiece we can build ourselves a place
to live." "Go," Elisha said. 3 "Please agree
to accompany your servants," one of them requested. "Yes, I will come," he replied.
4 So he went with them, and when they arrived at the Jordan they began to fell trees.
5 While one of them was felling a tree trunk,
the iron axhead slipped into the water. "O master," he cried out, "it was borrowed!"
6 "Where did it fall?" asked the man of God.
When he pointed out the spot, Elisha cut off a
stick, threw it into the water, and brought the
iron to the surface. 7 "Pick it up," he said.
And the man reached down and grasped it.

**Aramean Ambush.** 8 When the king of
Aram was waging war on Israel, he would make
plans with his servants to attack a particular
place. 9 But the man of God would send word
to the king of Israel, "Be careful! Do not pass
by this place, for Aram will attack there."
10 So the king of Israel would send word to the
place which the man of God had indicated, and
alert it; then they would be on guard. This happened several times.
11 Greatly disturbed over this, the king of
Aram called together his officers. "Will you not
tell me," he asked them, "who among us is for
the king of Israel?" 12 "No one, my lord
king," answered one of the officers. "The Israelite prophet Elisha can tell the king of Israel the
very words you speak in your bedroom."
13 "Go, find out where he is," he said, "so
that I may take him captive."

**Blinded Aramean Soldiers.** Informed
that Elisha was in Dothan, 14 he sent there a
strong force with horses and chariots. They arrived by night and surrounded the city. 15 Early
the next morning, when the attendant of the man
of God arose and went out, he saw the force
with its horses and chariots surrounding the
city. "Alas!" he said to Elisha. "What shall we
do, my lord?" 16 "Do not be afraid," Elisha
answered. "Our side outnumbers theirs."
17 Then he prayed, "O LORD, open his eyes,
that he may see." And the LORD opened the
eyes of the servant, so that he saw the mountainside filled with horses and fiery chariots around
Elisha.[b]
18 When the Arameans came down to get
him, Elisha prayed to the LORD, "Strike this
people blind, I pray you." And in answer to the
prophet's prayer the LORD struck them blind.
19 Then Elisha said to them: "This is the
wrong road, and this is the wrong city. Follow
me! I will take you to the man you want." And
he led them to Samaria. 20 When they entered
Samaria, Elisha prayed, "O LORD, open their
eyes that they may see." The LORD opened their
eyes, and they saw that they were inside Samaria. 21 When the king of Israel saw them, he
asked, "Shall I kill them, my father?"
22 "You must not kill them," replied Elisha.
"Do you slay those whom you have taken captive with your sword or bow?* Serve them bread
and water. Let them eat and drink, and then go
back to their master." 23 The king spread a
great feast for them. When they had eaten and

a Ex 4, 6; Nm 12, 10. b 2 Kgs 7, 6; Ps 67, 18.

*

5, 19: Go in peace: Elisha understands and approves the situation of Naaman who, though a proselyte as regards belief in and worship of the God of Israel, is required by his office to assist his master, the king, worshiping in the pagan temple of Rimmon.

6, 22: With your sword or bow: since the king would not slay prisoners who had surrendered to his power, much less should he slay prisoners captured by God's power. By Oriental custom they became guests within Samaria's walls.

drunk he sent them away, and they went back
to their master. No more Aramean raiders came
into the land of Israel.

**Siege of Samaria.** **24** After this, Ben-hadad, king of Aram, mustered his whole army
and laid siege to Samaria. **25** Because of the
siege the famine in Samaria was so severe that
an ass's head sold for eighty pieces of silver,
and a fourth of a kab of wild onion for five
pieces of silver.

**26** One day, as the king of Israel was walking on the city wall, a woman cried out to him,
"Help, my lord king!" **27** "No," he replied,
"the LORD help you! Where could I find help for
you: from the threshing floor or the winepress?" **28** Then the king asked her, "What is
your trouble?" She replied: "This woman said
to me, 'Give up your son that we may eat him
today; then tomorrow we will eat my son.'[c]
**29** So we boiled my son and ate him. The next
day I said to her, 'Now give up your son that we
may eat him.' But she hid her son." **30** When
the king heard the woman's words, he tore his
garments. And as he was walking on the wall,
the people saw that he was wearing sackcloth
underneath, next to his skin.[d]

**31** "May God do thus and so to me," the
king exclaimed, "if the head of Elisha, son of
Shaphat, stays on him today!" **32** Meanwhile,
Elisha was sitting in his house in conference
with the elders. The king had sent a man ahead
before he himself should come to him. Elisha
had said to the elders: "Do you know that this
son of a murderer is sending someone to cut off
my head? When the messenger comes, see that
you close the door and hold it fast against him.
His master's footsteps are echoing behind
him." **33** While Elisha was still speaking, the
king came down to him and said, "This evil is
from the LORD. Why should I trust in the LORD
any longer?"

## CHAPTER 7

**1** Elisha said: "Hear the word of the LORD!
Thus says the LORD, 'At this time tomorrow a
seah of fine flour will sell for a shekel, and two
seahs of barley for a shekel, in the market* of
Samaria.' " **2** But the adjutant on whose arm
the king leaned, answered the man of God,
"Even if the LORD were to make windows in
heaven, how could this happen?" "You shall
see it with your own eyes," Elisha said, "but
you shall not eat of it."[e]

**The Lepers at the Gate.** **3** At the city gate
were four lepers who were deliberating, "Why
should we sit here until we die?[f] **4** If we decide
to go into the city, we shall die there, for there
is famine in the city. If we remain here, we shall
die too. Come, let us desert to the camp of the
Arameans. If they spare us, we live; if they kill
us, we die." **5** At twilight they left for the
Arameans; but when they reached the edge of
the camp, no one was there. **6** [g]The LORD had
caused the army of the Arameans to hear the
sound of chariots and horses, the din of a large
army, and they had reasoned among themselves, "The king of Israel has hired the kings
of the Hittites and the kings of the borderlands*
to fight us." **7** Then in the twilight they fled,
abandoning their tents, their horses, and their
asses, the whole camp just as it was, and fleeing
for their lives.

**8** After the lepers reached the edge of the
camp, they went first into one tent, ate and
drank, and took silver, gold, and clothing from
it, and went out and hid them. Back they came
into another tent, took things from it, and again
went out and hid them. **9** Then they said to one
another: "We are not doing right. This is a day
of good news, and we are keeping silent. If we
wait until morning breaks, we shall be blamed.
Come, let us go and inform the palace."

**10** They came and summoned the city gatekeepers. "We went to the camp of the Arameans," they said, "but no one was there—not a
human voice, only the horses and asses tethered, and the tents just as they were left."
**11** The gatekeepers announced this and it was
reported within the palace. **12** Though it was
night, the king got up; he said to his servants:
"Let me tell you what the Arameans have done
to us. Knowing that we are in famine, they have
left their camp to hide in the field, hoping to
take us alive and enter our city when we leave
it." **13** One of his servants, however, suggested: "Since those who are left in the city are not
better off than all the throng that has perished,
let some of us take five of the abandoned horses
and send scouts to investigate."

**End of the Siege.** **14** They took two chariots, and horses, and the king sent them to reconnoiter the Aramean army. "Go and find out,"
he ordered. **15** They followed the Arameans as
far as the Jordan, and the whole route was
strewn with garments and other objects that the
Arameans had thrown away in their haste. The
messengers returned and told the king.

**16** The people went out and plundered the
camp of the Arameans; and then a seah of fine
flour sold for a shekel and two seahs of barley
for a shekel, as the LORD had said.

c Dt 28, 53-57.
d 1 Kgs 20, 31; 21, 27.
e 2 Kgs 7, 17; Ps 78, 23; Is 24, 18.
f Lv 13, 46.
g 6f: 2 Kgs 6, 17; 19, 35f; 2 Sm 5. 24.

*

7, 1: Market: literally "gate," the principal place of trading in ancient walled cities in time of peace.

7, 6: Kings of the borderlands: from Musur in Anatolia rather than Egypt.

**17** The king put in charge of the gate the officer who was his adjutant; but the people trampled him to death at the gate, just as the man of God had predicted when the king visited him. **18** Thus was fulfilled the prophecy of the man of God to the king, "Two seahs of barley will sell for a shekel, and one seah of fine flour for a shekel at this time tomorrow at the gate of Samaria." **19** The adjutant had answered the man of God, "Even if the LORD were to make windows in heaven, how could this happen?" And Elisha has replied, "You shall see it with your own eyes, but you shall not eat of it." **20** And that is what happened to him, for the people trampled him to death at the gate.

## CHAPTER 8

**Prediction of Famine.** **1** Elisha once said to the woman whose son he had restored to life: "Get ready! Leave with your family and settle wherever you can, because the LORD has decreed a seven-year famine which is coming upon the land."[h] **2** The woman got ready and did as the man of God said, setting out with her family and settling in the land of the Philistines for seven years. **3** At the end of the seven years, the woman returned from the land of the Philistines and went out to the king to claim her house and her field. **4** The king was talking with Gehazi, the servant of the man of God. "Tell me," he said, "all the great things that Elisha has done." **5** Just as he was relating to the king how his master had restored a dead person to life, the very woman whose son Elisha had restored to life came to the king to claim her house and field. "My lord king," Gehazi said, "this is the woman, and this is that son of hers whom Elisha restored to life." **6** The king questioned the woman, and she told him her story. With that the king placed an official* at her disposal, saying, "Restore all her property to her, with all that the field produced from the day she left the land until now."

**Death of Ben-hadad Foretold.** **7** Elisha came to Damascus at a time when Ben-hadad, king of Aram, lay sick. When he was told that the man of God had come there, **8** the king said to Hazael, "Take a gift with you and go call on the man of God. Have him consult the LORD as to whether I shall recover from this sickness." **9** Hazael went to visit him, carrying a present, and with forty camel loads of the best goods of Damascus. On his arrival, he stood before the prophet and said, "Your son Ben-hadad, king of Aram, has sent me to ask you whether he will recover from his sickness." **10** "Go and tell him," Elisha answered, "that he will surely recover. However, the LORD has showed me that he will in fact die." **11** Then he stared him down until Hazael became ill at ease. The man of God wept, **12** and Hazael asked, "Why are you weeping, my lord?" Elisha replied, "Because I know the evil that you will inflict upon the Israelites. You will burn their fortresses, you will slay their youth with the sword, you will dash their little children to pieces, you will rip open their pregnant women."[i]

**13** Hazael exclaimed, "How can a dog like me, your servant,* do anything so important?" "The LORD has showed you to me as king over Aram," replied Elisha.[j]

**14** Hazael left Elisha and returned to his master. "What did Elisha tell you?" asked Ben-hadad. "He told me that you would surely recover," replied Hazael. **15** The next day, however, Hazael took a cloth, dipped it in water, and spread it over the king's face, so that he died. And Hazael reigned in his stead.

**Reign of Jehoram of Judah.** **16** In the fifth year of Joram, son of Ahab, king of Israel, Jehoram,* son of Jehoshaphat, king of Judah, became king. **17** [k]He was thirty-two years old when he began to reign, and he reigned eight years in Jerusalem. **18** He conducted himself like the kings of Israel of the line of Ahab, since the sister of Ahab was his wife; and he did evil in the LORD's sight. **19** Even so, the LORD was unwilling to destroy Judah, because of his servant David. For he had promised David that he would leave him a lamp in the LORD's presence for all time.[l] **20** During Jehoram's reign, Edom revolted against the sovereignty of Judah and chose a king of its own. **21** Thereupon Jehoram with all his chariots crossed over to Zair. He arose by night and broke through the Edomites when they had surrounded him and the commanders of his chariots. Then his army fled homeward. **22** To this day Edom has been in revolt against the rule of Judah. Libnah also revolted at that time.[m] **23** The rest of the acts of Jehoram, with all that he did, are recorded in the book of the chronicles of the kings of Judah. **24** Jehoram rested with his ancestors and was buried with them in the City of David. His son Ahaziah succeeded him as king.

---

h 2 Kgs 4, 36.
i 2 Kgs 13, 7.
j 2 Kgs 15, 16; 1 Kgs 19, 15.
k 17ff: 2 Chr 21, 5ff.
l 2 Sm 7, 11-16; 21, 17; 1 Kgs 11, 36; 15, 4; 2 Chr 21, 7.
m Gn 27, 40; 2 Chr 21, 8ff.

---

8, 6: An official: Literally "eunuch," and perhaps actually so in this instance.

8, 13: A dog . . . your servant: Hazael feigns humility (1 Sm 24, 14; 2 Sm 9, 8), without attending to the crimes he would commit after usurping the royal power as the prophet predicts. Anything so important: literally "a great deed" for a patriotic Syrian.

8, 16: Jehoram of Judah succeeded his father Jehoshaphat during the reign of Ahaziah of Israel. See note on 2 Kgs 3, 1.

**Accession of Ahaziah.** **25** Ahaziah, son
of Jehoram, king of Judah, became king in the
twelfth year of Joram,* son of Ahab, king of
Israel. **26** He was twenty-two years old when
he began his reign, and he reigned one year in
Jerusalem. His mother's name was Athaliah;
she was the daughter of Omri, king of Israel.
**27** He conducted himself like the house of
Ahab, doing evil in the LORD's sight as they did,
since he was related to them by marriage.
**28** He joined Joram, son of Ahab, in battle
against Hazael, king of Aram, at Ramoth-gilead, where the Arameans wounded Joram.[n]
**29** King Joram returned to Jezreel to be healed
of the wounds which the Arameans had inflicted
on him at Ramah in his battle against Hazael,
king of Aram. Then Ahaziah, son of Jehoram,
king of Judah, went down to Jezreel to visit him
there in his illness.

## CHAPTER 9

**Anointing of Jehu.** **1** The prophet Elisha
called one of the guild prophets and said to him:
"Gird your loins, take this flask of oil with you,
and go to Ramoth-gilead.[o] **2** When you get
there, look for Jehu, son of Jehoshaphat, son of
Nimshi. Enter and take him away from his companions into an inner chamber.[p] **3** From the
flask you have, pour oil on his head, and say,
'Thus says the LORD: I anoint you king over
Israel.' Then open the door and flee without
delay."[q] **4** The young man (the guild prophet)
went to Ramoth-gilead. **5** When he arrived, the
commanders of the army were in session. "I
have a message for you, commander," he said.
"For which one of us?" asked Jehu. "For you,
commander," he answered. **6** Jehu got up and
went into the house. Then the young man
poured the oil on his head and said, "Thus says
the LORD, the God of Israel: 'I anoint you king
over the people of the LORD, over Israel.
**7** *You shall destroy the house of Ahab your
master; thus will I avenge the blood of my servants the prophets, and the blood of all the other
servants of the LORD shed by Jezebel, **8** [r]and by
all the rest of the family of Ahab. I will cut off
every male in Ahab's line, whether slave or
freeman in Israel. **9** I will deal with the house
of Ahab as I dealt with the house of Jeroboam,
son of Nebat, and with the house of Baasha, son
of Ahijah. **10** Dogs shall devour Jezebel at the
confines of Jezreel, so that no one can bury
her.' " Then he opened the door and fled.

**11** When Jehu rejoined his master's servants, they asked him, "Is all well? Why did
that madman come to you?" "You know that
kind of man and his talk," he replied. **12** But
they said, "Not at all! Come, tell us." So he
told them what the young man had said to him,
and finally, "Thus says the LORD: 'I anoint you
king over Israel.' " **13** At once each took his
garment, spread it under Jehu on the bare steps,
blew the trumpet, and cried out, "Jehu is
king!"[s]

**14** [t]Thus Jehu, son of Jehoshaphat, son of
Nimshi, formed a conspiracy against Joram.
Joram, with all Israel, had been besieging Ramoth-gilead against Hazael, king of Aram,
**15** but had returned to Jezreel to be healed of
the wounds the Arameans had inflicted on him
in the battle against Hazael, king of Aram.

**Murder of Joram.** "If you are truly with
me," Jehu said, "see that no one escapes from
the city to report in Jezreel." **16** Then Jehu
mounted his chariot and drove to Jezreel, where
Joram lay ill and Ahaziah, king of Judah, had
come to visit him.

**17** The watchman standing on the tower in
Jezreel saw the troop of Jehu coming and reported, "I see chariots." "Get a driver," Joram
said, "and send him to meet them and to ask
whether all is well." **18** So a driver went out to
meet him and said, "The king asks whether all
is well." "What does it matter to you how
things are?" Jehu said. "Get behind me." The
watchman reported to the king, "The messenger has reached them, but is not returning."

**19** Joram sent a second driver, who went to
them and said, "The king asks whether all is
well." "What does it matter to you how things
are?" Jehu replied. "Get behind me."

**20** The watchman reported, "The messenger
has reached them, but is not returning. The
driving is like that of Jehu, son of Nimshi, in its
fury." **21** "Prepare my chariot," said Joram.
When they had done so, Joram, king of Israel,
and Ahaziah, king of Judah, set out, each in his
own chariot, to meet Jehu. They reached him
near the field of Naboth the Jezreelite. **22** When
Joram recognized Jehu, he asked, "Is all well,
Jehu?" "How can all be well," Jehu replied,
"as long as the many fornications and witchcrafts* of your mother Jezebel continue?"
**23** Joram reined about and fled, crying to Ahaziah, "Treason, Ahaziah!" **24** But Jehu drew
his bow and shot Joram between the shoulders,
so that the arrow went through his heart and he

n 2 Kgs 9, 14f.
o 1 Kgs 21, 29; Hos 1, 4.
p 1 Kgs 19, 16;
q 1 Kgs 19, 16.
r 8ff: 1 Kgs 14, 10f; 16, 3f: 21, 21-24.
s Mt 21, 8.
t 14f: 2 Kgs 8, 28f; 1 Kgs 22, 3f.

*

8, 25: Twelfth year of Joram: i.e., of Israel, who probably reigned only eight years.

9, 7–10: The editors of the Books of Kings have here added to the prophet's message the same type of indictment and sanctions against the family of Ahab as were invoked against the dynasties of Jeroboam (1 Kgs 14, 10f), Baasha (1 Kgs 16, 3f), and Ahab on a previous occasion (1 Kgs 21, 21–24).

9, 22: Fornications and witchcrafts: the worship of foreign gods.

collapsed in his chariot. **25** [u]Then Jehu said to his adjutant Bidkar, "Take him and throw him into the field of Naboth the Jezreelite. For I remember that when we were driving teams behind his father Ahab, the LORD delivered this oracle against him: **26** 'As surely as I saw yesterday the blood of Naboth and the blood of his sons,' says the LORD, 'I will repay you for it in that very plot of ground, says the LORD.' So now take him into this plot of ground, in keeping with the word of the LORD."

**Death of Ahaziah.** **27** [v]Seeing what was happening, Ahaziah, king of Judah, fled toward Beth-haggan. Jehu pursued him, shouting, "Kill him too!" And they pierced him as he rode through the pass of Gur near Ibleam. He continued his fight as far as Megiddo and died there. **28** His servants brought him in a chariot to Jerusalem and buried him in the tomb of his ancestors in the City of David. **29** Ahaziah had become king of Judah in the eleventh year of Joram, son of Ahab.

**Death of Jezebel.** **30** When Jezebel learned that Jehu had arrived in Jezreel, she shadowed her eyes, adorned her hair, and looked down from her window. **31** As Jehu came through the gate, she cried out, "Is all well, Zimri, murderer of your master?"[w] **32** Jehu looked up to the window and shouted, "Who is on my side? Anyone?" At this, two or three eunuchs looked down toward him. **33** "Throw her down," he ordered. They threw her down, and some of her blood spurted against the wall and against the horses. Jehu rode in over her body **34** and, after eating and drinking, he said: "Attend to that accursed woman and bury her; after all, she was a king's daughter." **35** But when they went to bury her, they found nothing of her but the skull, the feet, and the hands. **36** They returned to Jehu, and when they told him, he said, "This is the sentence which the LORD pronounced through his servant Elijah the Tishbite: 'In the confines of Jezreel dogs shall eat the flesh of Jezebel.[x] **37** The corpse of Jezebel shall be like dung in the field in the confines of Jezreel, so that no one can say: This was Jezebel.' "

## CHAPTER 10

**Killing of Ahab's Descendants.** **1** Ahab had seventy descendants in Samaria. Jehu prepared letters and sent them to the city rulers, to the elders, and to the guardians of Ahab's descendants in Samaria.[y] **2** "Since your master's sons are with you," he wrote, "and you have the chariots, the horses, a fortified city, and the weapons, when this letter reaches you **3** decide which is the best and the fittest of your master's offspring, place him on his father's throne, and fight for your master's house." **4** They were overcome with fright and said, "If two kings could not withstand him, how can we?" **5** So the vizier and the ruler of the city, along with the elders and the guardians, sent this message to Jehu: "We are your servants, and we will do everything you tell us. We will proclaim no one king; do whatever you think best." **6** So Jehu wrote them a second letter: "If you are on my side and will obey me, count the heads of your master's sons and come to me in Jezreel at this time tomorrow." [The seventy princes were in the care of prominent men of the city, who were rearing them.]

**7** When the letter arrived, they took the princes and slew all seventy of them, put their heads in baskets, and sent them to Jehu in Jezreel. **8** "They have brought the heads of the princes," a messenger came in and told him. "Pile them in two heaps at the entrance of the city until morning," he ordered. **9** Going out in the morning, he stopped and said to all the people: "You are not responsible, and although I conspired against my lord and slew him, yet who killed all these? **10** Know that not a single word which the LORD has spoken against the house of Ahab shall go unfulfilled. The LORD has accomplished all that he foretold through his servant Elijah."[z] **11** Thereupon Jehu slew all who were left of the family of Ahab in Jezreel, as well as all his powerful supporters, intimates, and priests, leaving him no survivor.[a]

**Ahaziah's Kinsmen.** **12** [b]Then he set out for Samaria, and at Beth-eked-haroim on the way, **13** he came across kinsmen of Ahaziah, king of Judah. "Who are you?" he asked. "We are kinsmen of Ahaziah," they replied. "We are going down to visit the princes and the family of the queen mother." **14** "Take them alive," Jehu ordered. They were taken alive, forty-two in number, then slain at the pit of Beth-eked. Not one of them was spared.

**Jehu in Samaria.** **15** When he had left there, Jehu met Jehonadab, son of Rechab, on the road. He greeted him and asked, "Are you sincerely disposed toward me, as I am toward you?" "Yes," replied Jehonadab. "If you are," continued Jehu, "give me your hand." Jehonadab gave him his hand, and Jehu drew him up into his chariot.[c] **16** "Come with me," he said, "and see my zeal for the LORD." And he took him along in his own chariot.

**17** When he arrived in Samaria, Jehu slew all

u 25f: 1 Kgs 21, 9-16.
v 27ff: 2 Chr 22, 7ff.
w 1 Kgs 16, 9ff.
x 1 Kgs 21, 23.
y Jgs 9, 5; 1 Kgs 15, 29; 16, 11.
z 1 Kgs 21, 17-24. 29.
a Hos 1, 4.
b 12ff: 2 Chr 22, 8f.
c 1 Chr 2, 55; Jer 35, 1-11.

who remained there of Ahab's line, doing away
with them completely and thus fulfilling the
prophecy which the LORD had spoken to Elijah.

**Baal's Temple Destroyed.** **18** Jehu gathered all the people together and said to them:
"Ahab served Baal to some extent, but Jehu
will serve him yet more.[d] **19** Now summon for
me all Baal's prophets, all his worshipers, and
all his priests. See that no one is absent, for I
have a great sacrifice for Baal. Whoever is absent shall not live." This Jehu did as a ruse, so
that he might destroy the worshipers of Baal.
**20** Jehu said further, "Proclaim a solemn assembly in honor of Baal." They did so, **21** and
Jehu sent word of it throughout the land of
Israel. All the worshipers of Baal without exception came into the temple of Baal, which was
filled to capacity. **22** Then Jehu said to the custodian of the wardrobe, "Bring out the garments for all the worshipers of Baal." When he
had brought out the garments for them,[e]
**23** Jehu, with Jehonadab, son of Rechab, entered the temple of Baal and said to the worshipers of Baal, "Search and be sure that there is no
worshiper of the LORD here with you, but only
worshipers of Baal." **24** Then they proceeded
to offer sacrifices and holocausts. Now Jehu had
stationed eighty men outside with this warning,
"If one of you lets anyone escape of those
whom I shall deliver into your hands, he shall
pay life for life." **25** As soon as he finished
offering the holocaust, Jehu said to the guards
and officers, "Go in and slay them. Let no one
escape." So the guards and officers put them to
the sword and cast them out. Afterward they
went into the inner shrine of the temple of Baal,
**26** took out the stele of Baal, and burned the
shrine. **27** Then they smashed the stele of Baal,
tore down the building, and turned it into a
latrine, as it remains today.

**28** Thus Jehu rooted out the worship of Baal
from Israel. **29** However, he did not desist from
the sins which Jeroboam, son of Nebat, had
caused Israel to commit, as regards the golden
calves at Bethel and at Dan.[f] **30** The LORD said
to Jehu, "Because you have done well what I
deem right, and have treated the house of Ahab
as I desire, your sons to the fourth generation
shall sit upon the throne of Israel."[g] **31** But
Jehu was not careful to observe wholeheartedly
the law of the LORD, the God of Israel, since he
did not desist from the sins which Jeroboam
caused Israel to commit.

**32** [h]At that time the LORD began to dismember Israel. Hazael defeated the Israelites
throughout their territory **33** east of the Jordan
(all the land of Gilead, of the Gadites, Reubenites and Manassehites), from Aroer on the river
Arnon up through Gilead and Bashan.

**34** The rest of the acts of Jehu, his valor and
all his accomplishments, are written in the book
of the chronicles of the kings of Israel. **35** Jehu
rested with his ancestors and was buried in Samaria. His son Jehoahaz succeeded him as king.
**36** The length of Jehu's reign over Israel in
Samaria was twenty-eight years.

## CHAPTER 11

**Rule of Athaliah.** **1** When Athaliah, the
mother of Ahaziah, saw that her son was dead,
she began to kill off the whole royal family.[i]
**2** But Jehosheba,* daughter of King Jehoram
and sister of Ahaziah, took Joash, his son, and
spirited him away, along with his nurse, from
the bedroom where the princes were about to be
slain. She concealed him from Athaliah, and so
he did not die. **3** For six years he remained
hidden in the temple of the LORD, while Athaliah ruled the land.

**4** [j]But in the seventh year, Jehoiada summoned the captains of the Carians and of the
guards. He had them come to him in the temple
of the LORD, exacted from them a sworn commitment, and then showed them the king's son.
**5** He gave them these orders: "This is what you
must do: the third of you who come on duty on
the sabbath shall guard the king's palace; **6** another third shall be at the gate Sur; and the last
third shall be at the gate behind the guards.
**7** The two of your divisions who are going off
duty that week shall keep guard over the temple
of the LORD for the king. **8** You shall surround
the king, each with drawn weapons, and if anyone tries to approach the cordon, kill him; stay
with the king, whatever he may do."

**9** [k]The captains did just as Jehoiada the
priest commanded. Each one with his men, both
those going on duty for the sabbath and those
going off duty that week, came to Jehoiada the
priest. **10** [l]He gave the captains King David's
spears and shields, which were in the temple of
the LORD. **11** And the guards, with drawn
weapons, lined up from the southern to the
northern limit of the enclosure, surrounding the
altar and the temple on the king's behalf.
**12** Then Jehoiada led out the king's son and put
the crown and the insignia upon him. They proclaimed him king and anointed him, clapping
their hands and shouting, "Long live the
king!"[m]

**13** [n]Athaliah heard the noise made by the
people, and appeared before them in the temple

d 1 Kgs 16, 30ff.
e 1 Kgs 16, 32.
f 1 Kgs 12, 28f.
g 2 Kgs 15, 12ff.
h Am 1, 3.
i Jgs 9, 5.
j 4-8: 2 Chr 23, 1-7.
k 9-12: 2 Chr 23, 8-11.
l 10ff: 2 Sm 8, 7; 1 Kgs 1, 33f.
m 2 Sm 1, 10.
n 13-16: 2 Chr 23, 12-15.

* 11, 2: Jehosheba was the wife of Jehoida, the high priest; cf 2 Chr 22, 11.

of the LORD. **14** When she saw the king standing by the pillar,* as was the custom, and the captains and trumpeters near him, with all the people of the land rejoicing and blowing trumpets, she tore her garments and cried out, "Treason, treason!" **15** Then Jehoiada the priest instructed the captains in command of the force: "Bring her outside through the ranks. If anyone follows her," he added, "let him die by the sword." He had given orders that she should not be slain in the temple of the LORD. **16** She was led out forcibly to the horse gate of the royal palace, where she was put to death.

**17** [o]Then Jehoiada made a covenant between the LORD as one party and the king and the people as the other, by which they would be the LORD's people; and another covenant, between the king and the people. **18** Thereupon all the people of the land went to the temple of Baal and demolished it. They shattered its altars and images completely, and slew Mattan, the priest of Baal, before the altars. After appointing a detachment for the temple of the LORD, Jehoiada **19** with the captains, the Carians, the guards, and all the people of the land, led the king down from the temple of the LORD through the guards' gate to the palace, where Joash took his seat on the royal throne. **20** All the people of the land rejoiced and the city was quiet, now that Athaliah had been slain with the sword at the royal palace.

## CHAPTER 12

**Reign of Joash.** **1** Joash was seven years old when he became king.[p] **2** Joash began to reign in the seventh year of Jehu, and he reigned forty years in Jerusalem. His mother, who was named Zibiah, was from Beer-sheba. **3** Joash did what was pleasing to the LORD as long as he lived, because the priest Jehoiada guided him. **4** Still, the high places did not disappear; the people continued to sacrifice and to burn incense there.

**5** [q]For the priests Joash made this rule: "All the funds for sacred purposes that are brought to the temple of the LORD—the census tax, personal redemption money, and whatever funds are freely brought to the temple of the LORD— **6** the priests may take for themselves, each from his own clients. However, they must make whatever repairs on the temple may prove necessary." **7** Nevertheless, as late as the twenty-third year of the reign of King Joash, the priests had not made needed repairs on the temple. **8** Accordingly, King Joash summoned the priest Jehoiada and the other priests. "Why do you not repair the temple?" he asked them. "You must no longer take funds from your clients, but you shall turn them over for the repairs." **9** [r]So the priests agreed that they would neither take funds from the people nor make the repairs on the temple.

**10** The priest Jehoiada then took a chest, bored a hole in its lid, and set it beside the stele, on the right as one entered the temple of the LORD. The priests who guarded the entry would put into it all the funds that were brought to the temple of the LORD. **11** When they noticed that there was a large amount of silver in the chest, the royal scribe [and the priest] would come up, and they would melt down all the funds that were in the temple of the LORD, and weigh them. **12** The amount thus realized they turned over to the master workmen in the temple of the LORD. They in turn would give it to the carpenters and builders working in the temple of the LORD, **13** and to the lumbermen and stone cutters, and for the purchase of the wood and hewn stone used in repairing the breaches, and for any other expenses that were necessary to repair the temple. **14** None of the funds brought to the temple of the LORD were used there to make silver cups, snuffers, basins, trumpets, or any gold or silver article. **15** Instead, they were given to the workmen, and with them they repaired the temple of the LORD. **16** Moreover, no reckoning was asked of the men who were provided with the funds to give to the workmen, because they held positions of trust. **17** The funds from guilt-offerings and from sin-offerings, however, were not brought to the temple of the LORD; they belonged to the priests.

**18** [s]Then King Hazael of Aram mounted a siege against Gath. When he had taken it, Hazael decided to go on to attack Jerusalem.[t] **19** But King Jehoash of Judah took all the dedicated offerings presented by his forebears, Jehoshaphat, Jehoram, and Ahaziah, kings of Judah, as well as his own, and all the gold there was in the treasuries of the temple and the palace, and sent them to King Hazael of Aram, who then led his forces away from Jerusalem. **20** The rest of the acts of Joash, with all that he did, are recorded in the book of the chronicles of the kings of Judah. **21** Certain of his officials entered into a plot against him and killed him at Beth-millo. **22** Jozacar, son of Shimeath, and Jehozabad, son of Shomer, were the officials who killed him. He was buried in his forefathers' City of David, and his son Amaziah succeeded him as king.

## CHAPTER 13

**Reign of Jehoahaz of Israel.** **1** In the twenty-third year of Joash, son of Ahaziah, king

o 17-20: 2 Chr 23, 16-21.
p 1f: 2 Chr 24, 1f.
q 5-8: 2 Chr 24, 5-10.
r 9-16: 2 Chr 24, 11-14.
s 2 Kgs 8, 12.
t 18-22: 2 Chr 24, 23-27.

* 11, 14: By the pillar: see note on 2 Chr 23, 13.

of Judah, Jehoahaz, son of Jehu, began his sev-
enteen-year reign over Israel in Samaria. **2** He
did evil in the LORD's sight, conducting himself
like Jeroboam, son of Nebat, and not renouncing the sin he had caused Israel to commit.
**3** The LORD was angry with Israel and for a
long time left them in the power of Hazael, king
of Aram, and of Ben-hadad, son of Hazael.
**4** Then Jehoahaz entreated the LORD, who
heard him, since he saw the oppression to which
the king of Aram had subjected Israel.[u] **5** So
the LORD gave Israel a savior,* and the Israelites, freed from the power of Aram, dwelt in
their own homes as formerly. **6** Nevertheless,
they did not desist from the sins which the house
of Jeroboam had caused Israel to commit, but
persisted in them. The sacred pole* also remained standing in Samaria.[v] **7** No soldiers
were left to Jehoahaz, except fifty horsemen
with ten chariots and ten thousand foot soldiers,
since the king of Aram had destroyed them and
trampled them like dust. **8** The rest of the acts
of Jehoahaz, with all his valor and accomplishments, are recorded in the book of the chronicles of the kings of Israel. **9** Jehoahaz rested
with his ancestors and was buried in Samaria.
His son Joash succeeded him as king.

**Reign of Joash of Israel.** **10** In the thirty-seventh year of Joash, king of Judah, Jehoash, son of Jehoahaz, began his sixteen-year
reign over Israel in Samaria. **11** He did evil in
the sight of the LORD; he did not desist from any
of the sins which Jeroboam, son of Nebat, had
caused Israel to commit, but persisted in them.
**12** *[The rest of the acts of Joash, the valor with
which he fought against Amaziah, king of Judah, and all his accomplishments, are recorded
in the book of the chronicles of the kings of
Israel.[w] **13** Joash rested with his ancestors, and
Jeroboam occupied the throne. Joash was buried
with the kings of Israel in Samaria.]
**14** When Elisha was suffering from the sickness of which he was to die, King Joash of Israel
went down to visit him. "My father, my father!"* he exclaimed, weeping over him. "Israel's chariots and horsemen!"[x] **15** "Take a
bow and some arrows," Elisha said to him.
When he had done so, **16** *Elisha said to the
king of Israel, "Put your hand on the bow." As
the king held the bow, Elisha placed his hands
over the king's hands **17** and said, "Open the
window toward the east." He opened it, Elisha
said, "Shoot," and he shot. The prophet exclaimed, "The LORD's arrow of victory! The
arrow of victory over Aram! You will completely conquer Aram at Aphec."
**18** Then he said to the king of Israel, "Take
the arrows," which he did. Elisha said to him,
"Strike the ground!" He struck the ground
three times and stopped. **19** Angry with him,
the man of God said: "You should have struck
five or six times; you would have defeated Aram
completely. Now, you will defeat Aram only
three times."
**20** Elisha died and was buried. At the time,
bands of Moabites used to raid the land each
year. **21** Once some people were burying a
man, when suddenly they spied such a raiding
band. So they cast the dead man into grave of
Elisha, and everyone went off. But when the
man came in contact with the bones of Elisha,
he came back to life and rose to his feet.[y]
**22** King Hazael of Aram oppressed Israel
during the entire reign of Jehoahaz. **23** But the
LORD was merciful with Israel and looked on
them with compassion because of his covenant
with Abraham, Isaac, and Jacob. He was unwilling to destroy them or to cast them out from
his presence.[z] **24** So when King Hazael of
Aram died and his son Ben-hadad succeeded
him as king, **25** Joash, son of Jehoahaz, took
back from Ben-hadad, son of Hazael, the cities
which Hazael had taken in battle from his father
Jehoahaz. Joash defeated Ben-hadad three
times, and thus recovered the cities of Israel.

## CHAPTER 14

**Amaziah of Judah.*** **1** In the second year
of Joash, son of Jehoahaz, king of Israel, Amaziah, son of Joash, king of Judah, began to
reign. **2** [a]He was twenty-five years old when he
became king, and he reigned twenty-nine years
in Jerusalem. His mother, whose name was Je-
hoaddin, was from Jerusalem. **3** He pleased the
LORD, yet not like his forefather David, since he
did just as his father Joash had done. **4** Thus the
high places did not disappear, but the people

u 2 Kgs 14, 26f.
v Ex 34, 13.
w 2 Kgs 14, 8-16.
x 2 Kgs 2, 12.
y Sir 48, 14.
z Dt 9, 27.
a 2f: 2 Chr 25, 1f.

*

13, 5: A savior: by this language, typical of the Book of Judges (Jgs 3, 9, 15), Jeroboam II of Israel is meant; cf 2 Kgs 14, 27.

13, 6: Sacred pole: see note on Ex 34, 13.

13, 12f: The conclusion to the reign of Joash is given again in 2 Kgs 14, 15f, where it is more appropriate.

13, 14: My father, my father: the king expresses here the same sentiments as those with which Elisha addressed Elijah.

13, 16–19: Symbolic acts similar to these are seen in Ex 17, 8ff; Jos 8, 18ff; Ez 4, 1ff.

14, 1f: In the second year . . . twenty-nine years in Jerusalem: the reigns of the kings of Judah between Athaliah and Ahaz are assigned too many years in all to correspond to the reigns in Israel from Jehu to the fall of Samaria. It seems probable that Amaziah was murdered as soon as his son Azaiah was old enough to rule, and that Amaziah's reign was nearer nineteen than twenty-nine years. The correlation, in 2 Kgs 15, 1, of the beginning of Azariah's reign with the 27th year of Jeroboam II can hardly be correct; and the sixteen-year reign of Joatham of Judah (2 Kgs 15, 33) consisted for the most part of a regency during the illness of his father (2 Kgs 15, 5).

continued to sacrifice and to burn incense on them. **5** [b]When Amaziah had the kingdom firmly in hand, he slew the officials who had murdered the king, his father. **6** But the children of the murderers he did not put to death, obeying the LORD's command written in the book of the law of Moses, "Fathers shall not be put to death for their children, nor shall children be put to death for their fathers; each one shall die for his own sin."[c]

**7** Amaziah slew ten thousand Edomites in the Salt Valley, and took Sela in battle. He renamed it Joktheel, the name it has to this day.[d]

**8** Then Amaziah sent messengers to Jehoash, son of Jehoahaz, son of Jehu, king of Israel, with this challenge, "Come, let us meet face to face."[e] **9** King Jehoash of Israel sent this reply to the king of Judah: "The thistle of Lebanon sent word to the cedar of Lebanon, 'Give your daughter to my son in marriage,' but an animal of Lebanon passed by and trampled the thistle underfoot. **10** You have indeed conquered Edom, and you have become ambitious. Enjoy your glory, but stay at home! Why involve yourself and Judah with you in misfortune and failure?"

**11** But Amaziah would not listen. King Jehoash of Israel then advanced, and he and King Amaziah of Judah met in battle at Beth-shemesh of Judah. **12** Judah was defeated by Israel, and all the Judean soldiery fled homeward. **13** King Jehoash of Israel captured Amaziah, son of Jehoash, son of Ahaziah, king of Judah, at Beth-shemesh. He went on to Jerusalem where he tore down four hundred cubits of the city wall, from the Gate of Ephraim to the Corner Gate. **14** He took all the gold and silver and all the utensils there were in the temple of the LORD and in the treasuries of the palace, and hostages as well. Then he returned to Samaria. **15** The rest of the acts of Jehoash, his valor, and how he fought Amaziah, king of Judah, are recorded in the book of the chronicles of the kings of Israel.[f] **16** Jehoash rested with his ancestors; he was buried in Samaria with the kings of Israel. His son Jeroboam succeeded him as king.

**17** Amaziah, son of Joash, king of Judah, survived Jehoash, son of Jehoahaz, king of Israel, by fifteen years.* **18** The rest of the acts of Amaziah are written in the book of the chronicles of the kings of Judah. **19** When a conspiracy was formed against him in Jerusalem, he fled to Lachish. But he was pursued to Lachish and killed there. **20** He was brought back on horses and buried with his ancestors in the City of David in Jerusalem. **21** Thereupon all the people of Judah took the sixteen-year-old Azariah* and proclaimed him king to succeed his father Amaziah.[g] **22** It was Azariah who rebuilt Elath and restored it to Judah, after King Amaziah rested with his ancestors.

**Jeroboam II of Israel.** **23** In the fifteenth year of Amaziah, son of Joash, king of Judah, Jeroboam, son of Joash, king of Israel, began his forty-one-year reign in Samaria. **24** He did evil in the sight of the LORD; he did not desist from any of the sins which Jeroboam, son of Nebat, had caused Israel to commit. **25** He restored the boundaries of Israel from Labo-of-Hamath to the sea of the Arabah,* just as the LORD, the God of Israel, had prophesied through his servant, the prophet Jonah, son of Amittai, from Gath-hepher. **26** For the LORD saw the very bitter affliction of Israel, where there was neither slave nor freeman, no one at all to help Israel.[h] **27** Since the LORD had not determined to blot out the name of Israel from under the heavens, he saved them through Jeroboam, son of Joash. **28** The rest of the acts of Jeroboam, his valor and all his accomplishments, how he fought with Damascus and turned back Hamath from Israel, are recorded in the book of the chronicles of the kings of Israel. **29** Jeroboam rested with his ancestors, the kings of Israel, and his son Zechariah succeeded him as king.

## CHAPTER 15

**Azariah of Judah.** **1** [i]Azariah, son of Amaziah, king of Judah, became king in the twenty-seventh year* of Jeroboam, king of Israel. **2** He was sixteen years old when he began to reign, and he reigned fifty-two years in Jerusalem. His mother, whose name was Jecholiah, was from Jerusalem. **3** He pleased the LORD just as his father Amaziah had done. **4** Yet the high places did not disappear; the people continued to sacrifice and to burn incense on them. **5** [j]The LORD afflicted the king, and he was a leper to the day of his death. He lived in a house apart, while Jotham, the king's son, was vizier and regent for the people of the land. **6** The rest of the acts of Azariah, and all his accomplishments, are recorded in the book of the chronicles of the kings of Judah. **7** Azariah rested with his ancestors, and was buried with them in

b 5f: 2 Chr 25, 3f.
c Dt 24, 16; Ez 18, 20.
d 2 Sm 8, 13f; 2 Chr 25, 11.
e 2 Kgs 13, 12; Jgs 9, 8-15.
f 2 Kgs 13, 12f.
g 2 Chr 26, 1f.
h 2 Kgs 13, 4f; 1 Kgs 14, 10.
i 1ff: 2 Chr 26, 3f.
j 5ff: 2 Chr 26, 21ff.

*

14, 17: See note on 2 Kgs 14, 1f.

14, 21: Azariah: also called Uzziah in many texts.

14, 25: Sea of the Arabah: the Dead Sea. Jonah: see note on Jon 1, 1.

15, 1: Twenty-seventh year: see note on 2 Kgs 14, 1f.

the City of David. His son Jotham succeeded
him as king.

**Zechariah of Israel.** 8 In the thirty-eighth
year of Azariah, king of Judah, Zechariah, son
of Jeroboam, was king of Israel in Samaria for
six months. 9 He did evil in the sight of the
LORD as his fathers had done, and did not desist
from the sins which Jeroboam, son of Nebat,
had caused Israel to commit. 10 Shallum, son
of Jabesh, conspired against Zechariah, attacked and killed him at Ibleam, and reigned in
his place. 11 The rest of the acts of Zechariah
are recorded in the book of the chronicles of the
kings of Israel. 12 Thus the LORD's promise to
Jehu, "Your descendants to the fourth generation shall sit upon the throne of Israel," was
fulfilled.[k]

**Shallum of Israel.** 13 Shallum, son of Jabesh, became king in the thirty-ninth year of
Uzziah, king of Judah; he reigned one month in
Samaria. 14 Menahem, son of Gadi, came up
from Tirzah to Samaria, where he attacked and
killed Shallum, son of Jabesh, and reigned in his
place. 15 The rest of the acts of Shallum, and
the fact of his conspiracy, are recorded in the
book of the chronicles of the kings of Israel.
16 At that time, Menahem punished Tappuah,
all the inhabitants of the town and of its whole
district, because on his way from Tirzah they
did not let him in. He punished them even to
ripping open all the pregnant women.

**Menahem of Israel.** 17 In the thirty-ninth
year of Azariah, king of Judah, Menahem, son
of Gadi, began his ten-year reign over Samaria.
18 He did evil in the sight of the LORD, not
desisting from the sins which Jeroboam, son of
Nebat, had caused Israel to commit. During his
reign, 19 Pul,* king of Assyria, invaded the
land, and Menahem gave him a thousand talents
of silver to have his assistance in strengthening
his hold on the kingdom. 20 Menahem secured
the money to give to the king of Assyria by
exacting it from all the men of substance in the
country, fifty silver shekels from each. The king
of Assyria did not remain in the country but
withdrew. 21 The rest of the acts of Menahem,
and all his accomplishments, are recorded in the
book of the chronicles of the kings of Israel.
22 Menahem rested with his ancestors, and his
son Pekahiah succeeded him as king.

**Pekahiah of Israel.** 23 In the fiftieth year
of Azariah, king of Judah, Pekahiah, son of
Menahem, began his two-year reign over Israel
in Samaria. 24 He did evil in the sight of the
LORD, not desisting from the sins which Jeroboam, son of Nebat, had caused Israel to commit.
25 His adjutant Pekah, son of Remaliah, who
had with him fifty men from Gilead, conspired
against him, killed him within the palace stronghold in Samaria, and reigned in his place.
26 The rest of the acts of Pekahiah, and all his
accomplishments, are recorded in the book of
the chronicles of the kings of Israel.

**Pekah of Israel.** 27 In the fifty-second year
of Azariah, king of Judah, Pekah, son of Remaliah, began his twenty-year reign over Israel in
Samaria.* 28 He did evil in the sight of the
LORD, not desisting from the sins which Jeroboam, son of Nebat, had caused Israel to commit.
29 During the reign of Pekah, king of Israel,
Tiglath-pileser, king of Assyria, came and took
Ijon, Abel-beth-maacah, Janoah, Kedesh, Hazor, all the territory of Naphtali, Gilead, and
Galilee, deporting the inhabitants to Assyria.
30 Hoshea, son of Elah, conspired against Pekah, son of Remaliah; he attacked and killed
him, and reigned in his place [in the twentieth
year of Jotham, son of Uzziah]. 31 The rest of
the acts of Pekah, and all his accomplishments,
are recorded in the book of the chronicles of the
kings of Israel.

**Jotham of Judah.** 32 [l]In the second year
of Pekah, son of Remaliah, king of Israel, Jotham, son of Uzziah, king of Judah, began to
reign. 33 He was twenty-five years old when he
became king, and he reigned sixteen years in
Jerusalem. His mother's name was Jerusha,
daughter of Zadok. 34 He pleased the LORD,
just as his father Uzziah had done. 35 Nevertheless the high places did not disappear and the
people continued to sacrifice and to burn incense on them. It was he who built the Upper
Gate* of the temple of the LORD. 36 The rest
of the acts of Jotham, and all his accomplishments, are recorded in the book of the chronicles of the kings of Judah. 37 It was at that time
that the LORD first loosed Rezin, king of Aram,
and Pekah, son of Remaliah, against Judah.
38 Jotham rested with his ancestors and was
buried with them in his forefather's City of David. His son Ahaz succeeded him as king.

---

k 2 Kgs 10, 30. 7-9.
l 32-38: 2 Chr 27, 1-4.

*

15, 19: Pul: the Babylonian throne name of the Assyrian Tiglathpileser III; cf 2 Kgs 15, 29.

15, 27: The twenty years here ascribed to Pekah are an impossibility; the calculation which made his reign, of five years at most, appear so long may have been based on the attempt to give Jotham of Judah a full sixteen-year reign independently of his regency. See 2 Kgs 16, 1 and the note on 2 Kgs 14, 1f.

15, 35: The Upper Gate: also the Gate of Benjamin; cf Jer 20, 2; Ez 9, 2.

## CHAPTER 16

**Ahaz of Judah.** **1** [m]In the seventeenth year of Pekah, son of Remaliah, Ahaz, son of Jotham, king of Judah, began to reign. **2** Ahaz was twenty years old when he became king, and he reigned sixteen years in Jerusalem. He did not please the LORD, his God, like his forefather David, **3** but conducted himself like the kings of Israel, and even immolated his son by fire, in accordance with the abominable practice of the nations whom the LORD had cleared out of the way of the Israelites.[n] **4** Further, he sacrificed and burned incense on the high places, on hills, and under every leafy tree.[o]

**5** Then Rezin, king of Aram, and Pekah, son of Remaliah, king of Israel, came up to Jerusalem to attack it. Although they besieged Ahaz, they were unable to conquer him.[p] **6** At the same time the king of Edom recovered Elath for Edom, driving the Judeans out of it. The Edomites then entered Elath, which they have occupied until the present.[q]

**7** Meanwhile, Ahaz sent messengers to Tiglath-pileser, king of Assyria, with the plea: "I am your servant and your son. Come up and rescue me from the clutches of the king of Aram and the king of Israel, who are attacking me."[r] **8** Ahaz took the silver and gold that were in the temple of the LORD and in the palace treasuries and sent them as a present to the king of Assyria,[s] **9** who listened to him and moved against Damascus, which he captured. He deported its inhabitants to Kir and put Rezin to death.*

**10** King Ahaz went to Damascus to meet Tiglath-pileser, king of Assyria. When he saw the altar in Damascus, King Ahaz sent to Uriah the priest a model of the altar and a detailed design of its construction. **11** Uriah the priest built an altar according to the plans which King Ahaz sent him from Damascus, and had it completed by the time the king returned home. **12** On his arrival from Damascus, the king inspected this altar, then went up to it and offered sacrifice on it, **13** burning his holocaust and cereal-offering, pouring out his libation, and sprinkling the blood of his peace-offerings on the altar.[t] **14** The bronze altar that stood before the LORD he brought from the front of the temple—that is, from the space between the new altar and the temple of the Lord—and set it on the north side of his altar. **15** [u]"Upon the large altar," King Ahaz commanded Uriah the priest, "burn the morning holocaust and the evening cereal-offering, the royal holocaust and cereal-offering, as well as the holocausts, cereal-offerings, and libations of the people. You must also sprinkle on it all the blood of holocausts and sacrifices. But the old bronze altar shall be mine for consultation."* **16** Uriah the priest did just as King Ahaz had commanded. **17** King Ahaz detached the frames from the bases and removed the lavers from them; he also took down the bronze sea from the bronze oxen that supported it, and set it on a stone pavement.[v] **18** In deference to the king of Assyria he removed from the temple of the LORD the emplacement which had been built in the temple for a throne, and the outer entrance for the king.* **19** The rest of the acts of Ahaz are recorded in the book of the chronicles of the kings of Judah.[w] **20** Ahaz rested with his ancestors and was buried with them in the City of David. His son Hezekiah succeeded him as king.

## CHAPTER 17

**Hoshea of Israel.** **1** In the twelfth year of Ahaz, king of Judah, Hoshea, son of Elah, began his nine-year reign over Israel in Samaria. **2** He did evil in the sight of the LORD, yet not to the extent of the kings of Israel before him. **3** Shalmaneser,* king of Assyria, advanced against him, and Hoshea became his vassal and paid him tribute.[x] **4** But the king of Assyria found Hoshea guilty of conspiracy for sending envoys to the king of Egypt at Sais, and for failure to pay the annual tribute to his Assyrian overlord. **5** For this, the king of Assyria arrested and imprisoned Hoshea; he then occupied the whole land and attacked Samaria, which he besieged for three years. **6** In the ninth year of Hoshea, the king of Assyria* took Samaria, and deported the Israelites to Assyria, settling them in Halah, at the Habor, a river of Gozan, and in the cities of the Medes.[y]

**7** This came about because the Israelites

m 1-4: 2 Chr 28, 1-4.
n Lv 18, 21.
o Dt 12, 2.
p 2 Chr 28, 5f.
q 2 Chr 28, 17.
r 2 Chr 28, 16.
s 2 Chr 28, 21.
t 2 Chr 28, 23.
u Ex 29, 38f; Nm 28, 3f.
v 2 Chr 28, 24.
w 2 Chr 28, 26f.
x 2 Kgs 18, 9; Tb 1, 2.
y 2 Kgs 18, 10f.

*

16, 9: Firmly dated events bearing on chapters 16 through 20 are: the fall of Damascus (16, 9) in 732 B.C., the fall of Samaria (18, 9–11) in 721 B.C., and Sennacherib's invasion of Judah (18, 13) in 701 B.C., which is equated both in Kgs and in Is 36, 1 with the 14th year of Hezekiah. These data make it necessary to credit Ahaz with at least a twenty-year reign, between 735 and c. 715 B.C., and to exclude the correlations between Hoshea of Israel and Hezekiah in chapter 18.

If the 14th-year correspondence for 701 B.C. is given up, other arrangements are possible. The alleged ages of Jotham (15, 33), Ahaz (16, 2), and Hezekiah (18, 2) at their successive accessions to the throne do not argue for an early date for Hezekiah; but one or more of these may be artificial. Azariah (15, 1–7; Is 6, 1) was still on the throne of Judah in 743 B.C.

16, 15: For consultation: perhaps the introduction into Judah of the Babylonian practice of omen sacrifices; cf Ez 21, 16.

16, 18: Emplacement . . . for a throne, and the outer entrance for the king: signs of sovereignty for the Hebrew kings.

17, 3: Shalmaneser: son and successor of Tiglath-pileser.

17, 6: The king of Assyria: Shalmaneser's successor and usurper, Sargon II.

sinned against the LORD, their God, who had
brought them up from the land of Egypt, from
under the domination of Pharaoh, king of
Egypt, and because they venerated other gods.
**8** They followed the rites of the nations whom
the LORD had cleared out of the way of the
Israelites [and the kings of Israel whom they set
up]. **9** They adopted unlawful practices toward
the LORD, their God. They built high places in
all their settlements, the watchtowers as well as
the walled cities. **10** They set up pillars and
sacred poles for themselves on every high hill
and under every leafy tree.[z] **11** There, on all the
high places, they burned incense like the nations
whom the LORD had sent into exile at their
coming. They did evil things that provoked the
LORD, **12** and served idols, although the LORD
had told them, "You must not do this."

**13** And though the LORD warned Israel and
Judah by every prophet and seer, "Give up your
evil ways and keep my commandments and statutes, in accordance with the entire law which I
enjoined on your fathers and which I sent you
by my servants the prophets," **14** [a]they did not
listen, but were as stiff-necked as their fathers,
who had not believed in the LORD, their God.
**15** They rejected his statutes, the covenant
which he had made with their fathers, and the
warnings which he had given them. The vanity
they pursued, they themselves became: they followed the surrounding nations whom the LORD
had commanded them not to imitate.[b] **16** They
disregarded all the commandments of the LORD,
their God, and made for themselves two molten
calves; they also made a sacred pole and worshiped all the host of heaven, and served Baal.[c]
**17** [d]They immolated their sons and daughters
by fire, practiced fortune-telling and divination,
and sold themselves into evildoing in the
LORD's sight, provoking him **18** till, in his great
anger against Israel, the LORD put them away
out of his sight. Only the tribe of Judah was left.

**19** Even the people of Judah, however, did
not keep the commandments of the LORD, their
God, but followed the rites practiced by Israel.
**20** So the LORD rejected the whole race of Israel. He afflicted them and delivered them over to
plunderers, finally casting them out from before
him. **21** When he tore Israel away from the
house of David, they made Jeroboam, son of
Nebat, king: he drove the Israelites away from
the LORD, causing them to commit a great sin.[e]
**22** The Israelites imitated Jeroboam in all the
sins he committed, nor would they desist from
them. **23** Finally, the LORD put Israel away out
of his sight as he had foretold through all his
servants, the prophets; and Israel went into exile
from their native soil to Assyria, an exile lasting
to the present.[f]

**24** The king of Assyria brought people from
Babylon, Cuthah, Avva, Hamath, and Sepharvaim, and settled them in the cities of Samaria
in place of the Israelites. They took possession
of Samaria and dwelt in its cities. **25** When they
first settled there, they did not venerate the
LORD, so he sent lions among them that killed
some of their number. **26** A report reached the
king of Assyria: "The nations whom you deported and settled in the cities of Samaria do not
know how to worship the God of the land, and
he has sent lions among them that are killing
them, since they do not know how to worship
the God of the land." **27** The king of Assyria
gave the order, "Send back one of the priests
whom I deported, to go there and settle, to teach
them how to worship the God of the land."
**28** So one of the priests who had been deported
from Samaria returned and settled in Bethel,
and taught them how to venerate the LORD.

**29** But these peoples began to make their
own gods in the various cities in which they
were living; in the shrines on the high places
which the Samarians had made, each people set
up gods.[g] **30** Thus the Babylonians made Marduk and his consort; the men of Cuth made
Nergal; the men of Hamath made Ashima;
**31** the men of Avva made Nibhaz and Tartak;
and the men of Sepharvaim immolated their
children by fire to their city gods, King Hadad
and his consort Anath. **32** They also venerated
the LORD, choosing from their number priests
for the high places, who officiated for them in
the shrines on the high places.[h] **33** But, while
venerating the LORD, they served their own
gods, following the worship of the nations from
among whom they had been deported.

**34** To this day they worship according to
their ancient rites.* [They did not venerate the
LORD nor observe the statutes and regulations,
the law and commandments, which the LORD
enjoined on the descendants of Jacob, whom he
had named Israel.[i] **35** When he made a covenant with them, he commanded them: "You
must not venerate other gods, nor worship
them, nor serve them, nor offer sacrifice to
them.[j] **36** The LORD, who brought you up from
the land of Egypt with great power and outstretched arm: him shall you venerate, him shall
you worship, and to him shall you sacrifice.
**37** You must be careful to observe forever the
statutes and regulations, the law and command-

z Ex 23, 24; 34, 13; Dt 12, 2.
a Jer 25, 5; Dt 9, 13.
b Jer 2, 5.
c 1 Kgs 12, 28; Ex 34, 13; Dt 4, 19; 17, 2f.
d Lv 18, 21; Dt 18, 10.
e 1 Kgs 12, 19f; 12, 26-33.
f Jer 25, 9.
g Jn 4, 9.
h 1 Kgs 12, 31.
i Gn 32, 29.
j Ex 20, 3ff.

*

17, 34–40: They did not . . . earlier manner: this passage is an adaptation of language denouncing the Israelites to make it applicable to the later Samaritan sect of post-exilic times. The original bearing of the discourse (vv 13–15) can be seen by reading it between vv 22 and 23. Cf also 2 Kgs 18, 12.

ment, which he wrote for you, and you must not venerate other gods. **38** The covenant which I made with you, you must not forget; you must not venerate other gods. **39** But the LORD, your God, you must venerate; it is he who will deliver you from the power of all your enemies." **40** They did not listen, however, but continued in their earlier manner.] **41** Thus these nations venerated the LORD, but also served their idols. And their sons and grandsons, to this day, are doing as their fathers did.

## *II: The Kingdom of Judah after 721 B.C.*

### CHAPTER 18

**Hezekiah.** **1** [k]In the third year of Hoshea, son of Elah, king of Israel, Hezekiah, son of Ahaz, king of Judah, began to reign. **2** He was twenty-five years old when he became king, and he reigned twenty-nine years in Jerusalem. His mother's name was Abi, daughter of Zechariah. **3** He pleased the LORD, just as his forefather David had done. **4** It was he who removed the high places, shattered the pillars, and cut down the sacred poles. He smashed the bronze serpent called Nehushtan which Moses had made, because up to that time the Israelites were burning incense to it.[l] **5** He put his trust in the LORD, the God of Israel; and neither before him nor after him was there anyone like him among all the kings of Judah. **6** Loyal to the LORD, Hezekiah never turned away from him, but observed the commandments which the LORD had given Moses. **7** The LORD was with him, and he prospered in all that he set out to do. He rebelled against the king of Assyria and did not serve him. **8** He also subjugated the watchtowers and walled cities of the Philistines, all the way to Gaza and its territory.

**9** In the fourth year of King Hezekiah, which was the seventh year of Hoshea, son of Elah, king of Israel, Shalmaneser, king of Assyria, attacked Samaria, laid siege to it,* **10** [m]and after three years captured it. In the sixth year of Hezekiah, the ninth year of Hoshea, king of Israel, Samaria was taken. **11** The king of Assyria then deported the Israelites to Assyria and settled them in Halah, at the Habor, a river of Gozan, and in the cities of the Medes. **12** This came about because they had not heeded the warning of the LORD, their God, but violated his covenant, not heeding and not fulfilling the commandments of Moses, the servant of the LORD.[n]

**Invasion of Sennacherib.** **13** *In the fourteenth year of King Hezekiah, Sennacherib,* king of Assyria, went on an expedition against all the fortified cities of Judah and captured them.[o] **14** Hezekiah, king of Judah, sent this message to the king of Assyria at Lachish: "I have done wrong. Leave me, and I will pay whatever tribute you impose on me." The king of Assyria exacted three hundred talents of silver and thirty talents of gold from Hezekiah, king of Judah. **15** Hezekiah paid him all the funds there were in the temple of the LORD and in the palace treasuries. **16** He broke up the door panels and the uprights of the temple of the LORD which he himself had ordered to be overlaid with gold, and gave the gold to the king of Assyria.[p]

**17** The king of Assyria sent the general, the lord chamberlain, and the commander* from Lachish with a great army to King Hezekiah at Jerusalem. They went up, and on their arrival in Jerusalem, stopped at the conduit of the upper pool on the highway of the fuller's field.[q] **18** They called for the king, who sent out to them Eliakim, son of Hilkiah, the master of the palace; Shebnah the scribe; and the herald Joah, son of Asaph.[r] **19** The commander said to them, "Tell Hezekiah, 'Thus says the great king, the king of Assyria: On what do you base this confidence of yours? **20** Do you think mere words substitute for strategy and might in war? On whom, then, do you rely, that you rebel against me? **21** This Egypt, the staff on which you rely, is in fact a broken reed which pierces the hand of anyone who leans on it. That is what Pharaoh, king of Egypt, is to all who rely on him.[s] **22** But if you say to me, We rely on the LORD, our God, is not he the one whose high places and altars Hezekiah has removed, commanding Judah and Jerusalem to worship before this altar in Jerusalem?'

**23** "Now, make a wager with my lord, the king of Assyria: I will give you two thousand horses if you can put riders on them. **24** How then can you repulse even one of the least servants of my lord, relying as you do on Egypt for chariots and horsemen? **25** Was it without the LORD's will that I have come up to destroy this

k 1ff: 2 Chr 28, 27; 29, 1f.
l Ex 23, 24; 34, 13; Nm 21, 9; Dt 12, 2; 2 Chr 31, 1; Wis 16, 6; Jn 3, 14.
m 10f: 2 Kgs 17. 6; Tb 1, 2.
n 2 Kgs 17, 7-18.
o 2 Chr 32, 1ff; Sir 48, 18; Is 36, 1.
p 1 Kgs 6, 20-22.
q 2 Chr 32, 9; Is 36, 1ff.
r Is 22, 13-25.
s Is 30, 1-7; 31, 1-3; Ez 29, 6-7.

*

18, 9: See note on 2 Kgs 16, 9.

18, 13—20, 11: Duplication of Is 36, 1—38, 8. 21. 22.

18, 13: Sennacherib succeeded Sargon II as king of Assyria. His Judean campaign was waged in 701 B.C. See note on 2 Kgs 16, 9.

18, 17: General, the lord chamberlain . . . commander: the text lists three major functionaries by their Assyrian titles, of which only the first, more nearly "lord lieutenant," is military in origin; the commander was technically the king's chief butler.

place? The LORD said to me, 'Go up and destroy that land!' "

**26** Then Eliakim, son of Hilkiah, and Shebnah and Joah said to the commander: "Please speak to your servants in Aramaic; we understand it. Do not speak to us in Judean within earshot of the people who are on the wall."

**27** But the commander replied: "Was it to your master and to you that my lord sent me to speak these words? Was it not rather to the men sitting on the wall, who, with you, will have to eat their own excrement and drink their urine?" **28** Then the commander stepped forward and cried out in a loud voice in Judean, "Listen to the words of the great king, the king of Assyria. **29** Thus says the king: 'Do not let Hezekiah deceive you, since he cannot deliver you out of my hand. **30** Let not Hezekiah induce you to rely on the LORD, saying, The LORD will surely save us; this city will not be handed over to the king of Assyria. **31** Do not listen to Hezekiah, for the king of Assyria says: Make peace with me and surrender! Then each of you will eat of his own vine and of his own fig-tree, and drink the water of his own cistern, **32** until I come to take you to a land like your own, a land of grain and wine, of bread and orchards, of olives, oil and fruit syrup. Choose life, not death. Do not listen to Hezekiah when he would seduce you by saying, The LORD will rescue us. **33** Has any of the gods of the nations ever rescued his land from the hand of the king of Assyria? **34** Where are the gods of Hamath and Arpad? Where are the gods of Sepharvaim, Hena, and Avva? Where are the gods of the land of Samaria?[t] **35** Which of the gods for all these lands ever rescued his land from my hand? Will the LORD then rescue Jerusalem from my hand?' " **36** But the people remained silent and did not answer him one word, for the king had ordered them not to answer him.

**37** Then the master of the palace, Eliakim, son of Hilkiah, Shebnah the scribe, and the herald Joah, son of Asaph, came to Hezekiah with their garments torn, and reported to him what the commander had said.

## CHAPTER 19

**Hezekiah and Isaiah.** **1** [u]When King Hezekiah heard this, he tore his garments, wrapped himself in sackcloth, and went into the temple of the LORD. **2** He sent Eliakim, the master of the palace, Shebnah the scribe, and the elders of the priests, wrapped in sackcloth, to tell the prophet Isaiah, son of Amoz, **3** "Thus says Hezekiah: 'This is a day of distress, of rebuke, and of disgrace. Children are at the point of birth, but there is no strength to bring them forth.* **4** Perhaps the LORD, your God, will hear all the words of the commander, whom his master, the king of Assyria, sent to taunt the living God, and will rebuke him for the words which the LORD, your God, has heard. So send up a prayer for the remnant that is here.' " **5** When the servants of King Hezekiah had come to Isaiah, **6** he said to them, "Tell this to your master: 'Thus says the LORD: Do not be frightened by the words you have heard, with which the servants of the king of Assyria have blasphemed me.[v] **7** I am about to put in him such a spirit that, when he hears a certain report, he will return to his own land, and there I will cause him to fall by the sword.' "

**8** When the commander, on his return, heard that the king of Assyria had withdrawn from Lachish, he found him besieging Libnah. **9** The king of Assyria heard a report that Tirhakah, king of Ethiopia, had come out to fight against him. Again he sent envoys to Hezekiah with this message: **10** "Thus shall you say to Hezekiah, king of Judah: 'Do not let your God on whom you rely deceive you by saying that Jerusalem will not be handed over to the king of Assyria. **11** You have heard what the kings of Assyria have done to all other countries: they doomed them! Will you, then, be saved? **12** Did the gods of the nations whom my fathers destroyed save them? Gozan, Haran, Rezeph, or the Edenites in Telassar?[w] **13** Where are the king of Hamath, the king of Arpad, or the kings of the cities Sepharvaim, Hena and Avva?' "[x]

**14** [y]Hezekiah took the letter from the hand of the messengers and read it; then he went up to the temple of the LORD, and spreading it out before him, **15** he prayed in the LORD's presence: "O LORD, God of Israel, enthroned upon the cherubim! You alone are God over all the kingdoms of the earth. You have made the heavens and the earth.[z] **16** Incline your ear, O LORD, and listen! Open your eyes, O LORD, and see! Hear the words of Sennacherib which he sent to taunt the living God. **17** Truly, O LORD, the kings of Assyria have laid waste the nations and their lands, **18** and cast their gods into the fire; they destroyed them because they were not gods, but the work of human hands, wood and stone.[a] **19** Therefore, O LORD, our God, save us from the power of this man, that all the kingdoms of the earth may know that you alone, O LORD, are God."[b]

**Punishment of Sennacherib.** **20** Then Isaiah, son of Amoz, sent this message to Hezekiah: "Thus says the LORD, the God of Israel,

t 2 Kgs 17, 24.
u 1-7: Is 37, 1-7.
v Is 10, 5-19.
w 2 Kgs 17, 6.
x 2 Kgs 18, 34.
y 14-19: 2 Chr 32, 20; Is 37, 14-20.
z Ex 25, 18.
a Jer 10, 3.
b 1 Kgs 18, 24.

* 19, 3: See note on Is 37, 3.

in answer to your prayer for help against Sennacherib, king of Assyria: I have listened!
**21** This is the word the LORD has spoken concerning him:*

" 'She despises you, laughs you to scorn,
the virgin daughter Zion!
Behind you she wags her head,
daughter Jerusalem.
**22** Whom have you insulted and blasphemed,
against whom have you raised your voice
And lifted up your eyes on high?
Against the Holy One of Israel!
**23** Through your servants you have insulted the
LORD.
You said: With my many chariots
I climbed the mountain heights,
the recesses of Lebanon;
I cut down its lofty cedars,
its choice cypresses;
I reached the remotest heights,
its forest park.
**24** I dug wells and drank water in foreign
lands;
I dried up with the soles of my feet
all the rivers of Egypt.

**25** " 'Have you not heard?
Long ago I prepared it,
From days of old I planned it.
Now I have brought it to pass:
That you should reduce fortified cities
into heaps of ruins,
**26** While their inhabitants, shorn of power,
are dismayed and ashamed,
Becoming like the plants of the field, like
the green growth,
like the scorched grass on the housetops.
**27** I am aware whether you stand or sit;
I know whether you come or go,[c]
**28** and also your rage against me.
Because of your rage against me
and your fury which has reached my ears,
I will put my hook in your nose
and my bit in your mouth,
and make you return the way you came.

**29** " 'This shall be a sign for you:
this year you shall eat the aftergrowth,
next year, what grows of itself;
But in the third year, sow and reap,
plant vineyards and eat their fruit!
**30** The remaining survivors of the house of
Judah
shall again strike root below
and bear fruit above.
**31** For out of Jerusalem shall come a remnant,
and from Mount Zion, survivors.
The zeal of the LORD of hosts shall do
this.'

**32** "Therefore, thus says the LORD concerning the king of Assyria: 'He shall not reach this
city, nor shoot an arrow at it, nor come before
it with a shield, nor cast up siege-works against
it. **33** He shall return by the same way he came,
without entering the city, says the LORD. **34** I
will shield and save this city for my own sake,
and for the sake of my servant David.' "[d]

**35** That night the angel of the LORD went
forth and struck down one hundred and
eighty-five thousand men in the Assyrian camp.
Early the next morning, there they were, all the
corpses of the dead.[e] **36** So Sennacherib, the
king of Assyria, broke camp, and went back
home to Nineveh.

**37** When he was worshiping in the temple of
his god Nisroch, his sons Adram-melech and
Sharezer slew him with the sword and fled into
the land of Ararat. His son Esar-haddon reigned
in his stead.

## CHAPTER 20

**Hezekiah's Illness.** **1** [f]In those days,
when Hezekiah was mortally ill, the prophet
Isaiah, son of Amoz, came and said to him:
"Thus says the LORD: 'Put your house in order,
for you are about to die; you shall not recover.' " **2** He turned his face to the wall and
prayed to the LORD: **3** "O LORD, remember
how faithfully and wholeheartedly I conducted
myself in your presence, doing what was pleasing to you!" And Hezekiah wept bitterly.

**4** Before Isaiah had left the central courtyard, the word of the LORD came to him: **5** "Go
back and tell Hezekiah, the leader of my people:
'Thus says the LORD, the God of your forefather
David: I have heard your prayer and seen your
tears. I will heal you. In three days you shall go
up to the LORD's temple; **6** I will add fifteen
years to your life. I will rescue you and this city
from the hand of the king of Assyria; I will be
a shield to this city for my own sake, and for the
sake of my servant David.' "

**7** Isaiah then ordered a poultice of figs to be
brought and applied to the boil, that he might
recover. **8** Then Hezekiah asked Isaiah, "What
is the sign that the LORD will heal me and that
I shall go up to the temple of the LORD on the
third day?" **9** Isaiah replied, "This will be the
sign for you from the LORD that he will do what
he has promised: Shall the shadow go forward
or back ten steps?"

**10** "It is easy for the shadow to advance ten
steps," Hezekiah answered. "Rather, let it go
back ten steps." **11** So the prophet Isaiah invoked the LORD, who made the shadow retreat

c Ps 139, 2f.
d 2 Sm 7, 12; Hos 1, 7.
e Sir 48, 21; 2 Chr 32, 21f; Is 37, 36-38; 1 Mc 7, 41; 2 Mc 8, 19.
f 1-9: 2 Chr 32, 24; Is 38, 1-8.

* 19, 21–31: vv 21–28 are addressed to Sennacherib, vv 29–31 to Judah.

the ten steps it had descended on the staircase
to the terrace of Ahaz.
**12** *At that time, when Merodach-baladan,
son of Baladan, king of Babylon, heard that
Hezekiah had been ill, he sent letters and gifts
to him.[g] **13** Hezekiah was pleased at this, and
therefore showed the messengers his whole treasury, his silver, gold, spices and fine oil, his
armory, and all that was in his storerooms; there
was nothing in his house or in all his realm that
Hezekiah did not show them.
**14** Then Isaiah the prophet came to King
Hezekiah and asked him: "What did these men
say to you? Where did they come from?"
"They came from a distant land, from Babylon," replied Hezekiah. **15** "What did they
see in your house?" the prophet asked. "They
saw everything in my house," answered Hezekiah. "There is nothing in my storerooms that
I did not show them."
**16** Then Isaiah said to Hezekiah: "Hear the
word of the LORD: **17** The time is coming when
all that is in your house, and everything that
your fathers have stored up until this day, shall
be carried off to Babylon; nothing shall be left,
says the LORD. **18** Some of your own bodily
descendants shall be taken and made servants in
the palace of the king of Babylon."
**19** Hezekiah replied to Isaiah, "The word of
the LORD which you have spoken is favorable."
For he thought, "There will be peace and security in my lifetime."
**20** The rest of the acts of Hezekiah, all his
valor, and his construction of the pool and conduit* by which water was brought into the city,
are written in the book of the chronicles of the
kings of Judah.[h] **21** Hezekiah rested with his
ancestors and his son Manasseh succeeded him
as king.

## CHAPTER 21

**Reign of Manasseh.** **1** [i]Manasseh was
twelve years old when he began to reign, and he
reigned fifty-five years in Jerusalem. His mother's name was Hephzibah. **2** He did evil in the
sight of the LORD, following the abominable
practices of the nations whom the LORD had
cleared out of the way of the Israelites. **3** He
rebuilt the high places which his father Hezekiah had destroyed. He erected altars to Baal, and
also set up a sacred pole, as Ahab, king of
Israel, had done. He worshiped and served the
whole host of heaven.[j] **4** He built altars in the
temple of the LORD, about which the LORD had
said, "I will establish my name in Jerusalem"— **5** altars for the whole host of heaven,
in the two courts of the temple.[k]
**6** He immolated his son by fire. He practiced
soothsaying and divination, and reintroduced
the consulting of ghosts and spirits. He did
much evil in the LORD's sight and provoked him
to anger.
**7** The Asherah idol he had made, he set up
in the temple, of which the LORD had said to
David and to his son Solomon: "In this temple
and in Jerusalem, which I have chosen out of all
the tribes of Israel, I shall place my name forever.[l] **8** I will not in future allow Israel to be
driven off the land I gave their fathers, provided
that they are careful to observe all I have commanded them, the entire law which my servant
Moses enjoined upon them." **9** But they did not
listen, and Manasseh misled them into doing
even greater evil than the nations whom the
LORD had destroyed at the coming of the Israelites.
**10** Then the LORD spoke through his servants
the prophets: **11** "Because Manasseh, king of
Judah, has practiced these abominations and has
done greater evil than all that was done by the
Amorites before him, and has led Judah into sin
by his idols,[m] **12** therefore thus says the LORD,
the God of Israel: 'I will bring such evil on
Jerusalem and Judah that, whenever anyone
hears of it, his ears shall ring. **13** I will measure
Jerusalem with the same cord as I did Samaria,
and with the plummet I used for the house of
Ahab. I will wipe Jerusalem clean as one wipes
a dish, wiping it inside and out.[n] **14** I will cast
off the survivors of my inheritance and deliver
them into enemy hands, to become a prey and
a booty for all their enemies, **15** because they
have done evil in my sight and provoked me
from the day their fathers came forth from Egypt
until today.' "
**16** In addition to the sin which he caused
Judah to commit, Manasseh did evil in the sight
of the LORD, shedding so much innocent blood
as to fill the length and breadth of Jerusalem.
**17** The rest of the acts of Manasseh, the sin he
committed and all that he did, are written in the
book of the chronicles of the kings of Judah.[o]
**18** Manasseh rested with his ancestors and was
buried in his palace garden, the garden of Uzza.
His son Amon succeeded him as king.

**Reign of Amon.** **19** [p]Amon was twenty-
two years old when he began to reign, and he
reigned two years in Jerusalem. His mother's
name was Meshullemeth, daughter of Haruz of
Jotbah. **20** He did evil in the sight of the LORD,

g 12f: Is 39, 1f; 2 Chr 32, 27ff.
h 2 Chr 32, 30; Sir 48, 17.
i 1-10: 2 Chr 33, 1-10.
j 2 Kgs 17, 16; 1 Kgs 18, 4; 16, 32f.
k Lv 18, 21.
l 2 Sm 7, 13; 1 Kgs 8, 16: 9, 3.
m 1 Kgs 21, 26; Jer 15, 4.
n Is 34, 11; Am 7, 7-9; Lam 2, 8.
o 2 Chr 33, 18ff.
p 19-26: 2 Chr 33, 21-25.

*

20, 12–19: Duplication of Is 39, 1–8.

20, 20: Pool and conduit: Hezekiah's tunnel; cf 2 Chr 32, 30.

as his father Manasseh had done. 21 He followed exactly the path his father had trod, serving and worshiping the idols his father had
served. 22 He abandoned the LORD, the God of
his fathers, and did not follow the path of the
LORD. 23 Subjects of Amon conspired against
him and slew the king in his palace, 24 but the
people of the land then slew all who had conspired against King Amon, and proclaimed his
son Josiah king in his stead. 25 The rest of the
acts that Amon did are written in the book of the
chronicles of the kings of Judah. 26 He was
buried in his own grave in the garden of Uzza,
and his son Josiah succeeded him as king.

## CHAPTER 22

**Reign of Josiah.** 1 [q]Josiah was eight years
old when he began to reign, and he reigned
thirty-one years in Jerusalem. His mother's
name was Jedidah, daughter of Adaiah of Bozkath. 2 He pleased the LORD and conducted
himself unswervingly just as his ancestor David
had done.

3 [r]In his eighteenth year, King Josiah sent
the scribe Shaphan,* son of Azaliah, son of
Meshullam, to the temple of the LORD with
orders to 4 [s]go to the high priest Hilkiah and
have him smelt down the precious metals that
had been donated to the temple of the Lord,
which the doorkeepers had collected from the
people. 5 They were to be consigned to the
master workmen in the temple of the LORD, who
should then pay them out to the carpenters,
builders, and lumbermen making repairs on the
temple, 6 and for the purchase of wood and
hewn stone for the temple repairs. 7 No reckoning was asked of them regarding the funds consigned to them, because they held positions of
trust.

**The Book of the Law.** 8 The high priest
Hilkiah informed the scribe Shaphan, "I have
found the book of the law in the temple of the
LORD." Hilkiah gave the book to Shaphan, who
read it. 9 Then the scribe Shaphan went to the
king and reported, "Your servants have smelted
down the metals available in the temple and
have consigned them to the master workmen in
the temple of the LORD." 10 The scribe Shaphan also informed the king that the priest Hilkiah had given him a book, and then read it aloud
to the king. 11 When the king had heard the
contents of the book of the law, he tore his
garments[t] 12 and issued this command to Hilkiah the priest, Ahikam, son of Shaphan, Achbor, son of Micaiah, the scribe Shaphan, and the
king's servant Asaiah: 13 "Go, consult the
LORD for me, for the people, for all Judah, about
the stipulations of this book that has been found,
for the anger of the LORD has been set furiously
ablaze against us, because our fathers did not
obey the stipulations of this book, nor fulfill our
written obligations."

14 So Hilkiah the priest, Ahikam, Achbor,
Shaphan, and Asaiah betook themselves to the
Second Quarter in Jerusalem, where the prophetess Huldah resided. She was the wife of Shallum, son of Tikvah, son of Harhas, keeper of the
wardrobe. When they had spoken to her, 15 she
said to them, "Thus says the LORD, the God of
Israel: 'Say to the man who sent you to me,
16 Thus says the LORD: I will bring upon this
place and upon its inhabitants all the evil that is
threatened in the book which the king of Judah
has read. 17 Because they have forsaken me
and have burned incense to other gods, provoking me by everything to which they turn their
hands, my anger is ablaze against this place and
it cannot be extinguished.'

18 "But to the king of Judah who sent you
to consult the LORD, give this response: 'Thus
says the LORD, the God of Israel: As for the
threats you have heard, 19 because you were
heartsick and have humbled yourself before the
LORD when you heard my threats that this place
and its inhabitants would become a desolation
and a curse; because you tore your garments and
wept before me; I in turn have listened, says the
LORD. 20 I will therefore gather you to your
ancestors; you shall go to your grave in peace,
and your eyes shall not see all the evil I will
bring upon this place.' " This they reported to
the king.

## CHAPTER 23

1 [u]The king then had all the elders of Judah
and of Jerusalem summoned together before
him. 2 The king went up to the temple of the
LORD with all the men of Judah and all the
inhabitants of Jerusalem: priests, prophets, and
all the people, small and great. He had the entire
contents of the book of the covenant that had
been found in the temple of the LORD, read out
to them. 3 Standing by the column, the king
made a covenant before the LORD that they
would follow him and observe his ordinances,
statutes and decrees with their whole hearts and
souls, thus reviving the terms of the covenant
which were written in this book. And all the
people stood as participants in the covenant.
4 Then the king commanded the high priest
Hilkiah, his vicar, and the doorkeepers to re-

q 1f: 2 Chr 34, 1f.
r 3-13: 2 Chr 34, 8-21.
s 4-7: 2 Kgs 12, 11-16.
t 11-20: 2 Chr 34, 19-28.
u 1-5: 2 Chr 34, 29-33.
v 2 Chr 34, 3-5; Sir 49, 3.

*

22, 3: Shaphan: head of a prominent family in the reign of Josiah, secretary to the king, bearer and reader of the new-found book of the law (vv 3–13; 2 Chr 34, 8f. 15–20). He and his sons favored the reform of King Josiah and supported the prophet Jeremiah; cf Jer 26, 24.

move from the temple of the LORD all the objects that had been made for Baal, Asherah, and
the whole host of heaven. He had these burned
outside Jerusalem on the slopes of the Kidron
and their ashes carried to Bethel.[v] **5** He also put
an end to the pseudo-priests whom the kings of
Judah had appointed to burn incense on the high
places in the cities of Judah and in the vicinity
of Jerusalem, as well as those who burned incense to Baal, to the sun, moon, and signs of the
Zodiac, and to the whole host of heaven.[w]
**6** From the temple of the LORD he also removed
the sacred pole, to the Kidron Valley, outside
Jerusalem; there he had it burned and beaten to
dust, which was then scattered over the common graveyard.[x] **7** He tore down the apartments of the cult prostitutes* which were in the
temple of the LORD, and in which the women
wove garments for the Asherah.[y]

**8** He brought in all the priests from the cities
of Judah, and then defiled, from Geba to
Beer-sheba, the high places where they had offered incense. He also tore down the high place
of the satyrs, which was at the entrance of the
Gate of Joshua, governor of the city, to the left
as one enters the city gate.[z] **9** The priests of the
high places could not function at the altar of the
LORD in Jerusalem; but they, along with their
relatives, ate the unleavened bread.

**10** The king also defiled Topheth in the Valley of Ben-hinnom, so that there would no longer be any immolation of sons or daughters by
fire* in honor of Molech.[a] **11** He did away with
the horses which the kings of Judah had dedicated to the sun; these were at the entrance of the
temple of the LORD, near the chamber of Na-
than-melech the eunuch, which was in the large
building.* The chariots of the sun he destroyed
by fire. **12** He also demolished the altars made
by the kings of Judah on the roof (the roof
terrace of Ahaz), and the altars made by Manasseh in the two courts of the temple of the LORD.
He pulverized them and threw the dust into the
Kidron Valley.[b] **13** The king defiled the high
places east of Jerusalem, south of the Mount of
Misconduct,* which Solomon, king of Israel,
had built in honor of Astarte, the Sidonian horror, of Chemosh, the Moabite horror, and of
Milcom, the idol of the Ammonites.[c] **14** He
broke to pieces the pillars, cut down the sacred
poles, and filled the places where they had been
with human bones.[d] **15** Likewise the altar
which was at Bethel, the high place built by
Jeroboam, son of Nebat, who caused Israel to
sin—this same altar and high place he tore
down, breaking up the stones and grinding them
to powder, and burning the Asherah.[e]

**16** When Josiah turned and saw the graves
there on the mountainside, he ordered the bones
taken from the graves and burned on the altar,
and thus defiled it in fulfillment of the word of
the LORD which the man of God had proclaimed
as Jeroboam was standing by the altar on the
feast day. When the king looked up and saw the
grave of the man of God who had proclaimed
these words, **17** he asked, "What is that tomb-
stone I see?" The men of the city replied, "It
is the grave of the man of God who came from
Judah and predicted the very things you have
done to the altar of Bethel." **18** [f]"Let him be,"
he said, "let no one move his bones." So they
left his bones undisturbed together with the
bones of the prophet who had come from Samaria.*

**19** Josiah also removed all the shrines on the
high places near the cities of Samaria which the
kings of Israel had erected, thereby provoking
the LORD; he did the very same to them as he
had done in Bethel.[g] **20** He slaughtered upon
the altars all the priests of the high places that
were at the shrines, and burned human bones
upon them. Then he returned to Jerusalem.

**21** The king issued a command to all the
people to observe the Passover of the LORD,
their God, as it was prescribed in that book of
the covenant.[h] **22** No Passover such as this had
been observed during the period when the
Judges ruled Israel, or during the entire period
of the kings of Israel and the kings of Judah,
**23** until the eighteenth year of King Josiah,
when this Passover of the LORD was kept in
Jerusalem.

**24** Further, Josiah did away with the consultation of ghosts and spirits, with the household
gods, idols,* and all the other horrors to be seen
in the land of Judah and in Jerusalem, so that he
might carry out the stipulations of the law written in the book that the priest Helkiah had found
in the temple of the LORD.[i]

**25** Before him there had been no king who
turned to the LORD as he did, with his whole

w Dt 17, 3ff.
x Dt 16, 21; 1 Kgs 14, 23.
y 1 Kgs 14, 24; Dt 23, 18f.
z Dt 12, 2f.
a Lv 18, 21.
b 2 Kgs 21, 5.
c 1 Kgs 11, 7.
d Dt 16, 21f; 1 Kgs 14, 23.
e 1 Kgs 12, 31f; 13, 32.
f 1 Kgs 13, 31.
g 2 Chr 34, 6f.
h Dt 16, 1-8; 2 Chr 35, 1ff. 18f.
i 2 Kgs 21, 6; Gn 31, 19; Dt 18, 11; Jgs 18, 14.
j Dt 6, 5.

*

23, 7: Cult prostitutes: of both sexes; cf 1 Kgs 14, 24.

23, 10: Topheth . . . by fire: condemned by Deuteronomic law and denounced by Jeremiah (Dt 12, 31; Jer 7, 29ff; Jer 19).

23, 11: Large building: to the west of the temple area (1 Chr 26, 18), named in the Hebrew by an Egyptian name for a similar construction.

23, 13: Mount of Misconduct: a paranomasia on "Mount of Olives" (in Hebrew Maschit/mischcheh) as suggested by the Targum. Cf Vulgate, "Mount of Offense." Horror . . . idol: in all three phrases here the Hebrew uses a pejorative designation meaning "abomination."

23, 18: From Samaria: more narrowly, from Bethel; cf 1 Kgs 13, 31f.

23, 24: Household gods . . . idols: teraphim. See note on Gn 31, 19.

heart, his whole soul, and his whole strength, in accord with the entire law of Moses; nor could any after him compare with him.[j]

**26** Yet, because of all the provocations that Manasseh had given, the LORD did not desist from his fiercely burning anger against Judah. **27** The LORD said: "Even Judah will I put out of my sight as I did Israel. I will reject this city, Jerusalem, which I chose, and the temple of which I said, 'There shall my name be.' "[k]

**28** The rest of the acts of Josiah, with all that he did, are written in the book of the chronicles of the kings of Judah.[l] **29** In his time Pharaoh Neco, king of Egypt, went up toward the river Euphrates to the king of Assyria. King Josiah set out to confront him, but was slain at Megiddo at the first encounter.[m] **30** His servants brought his body on a chariot from Megiddo to Jerusalem, where they buried him in his own grave. Then the people of the land* took Jehoahaz, son of Josiah, anointed him, and proclaimed him king to succeed his father.

**Reign of Jehoahaz.** **31** Jehoahaz was twenty-three years old when he began to reign, and he reigned three months in Jerusalem. His mother, whose name was Hamutal, daughter of Jeremiah, was from Libnah.[n] **32** He did evil in the sight of the LORD, just as his forebears had done. **33** Pharaoh Neco took him prisoner at Riblah in the land of Hamath, thus ending his reign in Jerusalem. He imposed a fine upon the land of a hundred talents of silver and a talent of gold.* **34** Pharaoh Neco then appointed Eliakim, son of Josiah, king in place of his father Josiah; he changed his name to Jehoiakim. Jehoahaz he took away with him to Egypt, where he died. **35** Jehoiakim gave the silver and gold to Pharaoh, but taxed the land to raise the amount Pharaoh demanded. He exacted the silver and gold from the people of the land, from each proportionately, to pay Pharaoh Neco.

**Reign of Jehoiakim.** **36** [o]Jehoiakim was twenty-five years old when he began to reign, and he reigned eleven years in Jerusalem. His mother's name was Zebidah, daughter of Pedaiah, from Rumah. **37** He did evil in the sight of the LORD, just as his forebears had done.

## CHAPTER 24

**1** [p]During his reign Nebuchadnezzar, king of Babylon, moved against him, and Jehoiakim became his vassal for three years. Then Jehoiakim turned and rebelled against him. **2** The LORD loosed against him bands of Chaldeans, Arameans, Moabites, and Ammonites; he loosed them against Judah to destroy it, as the LORD had threatened through his servants the prophets.[q] **3** This befell Judah because the LORD had stated that he would inexorably put them out of his sight for the sins Manasseh had committed in all that he did; **4** and especially because of the innocent blood he shed, with which he filled Jerusalem, the LORD would not forgive.[r]

**5** The rest of the acts of Jehoiakim, with all that he did, are written in the book of the chronicles of the kings of Judah.[s] **6** Jehoiakim rested with his ancestors, and his son Jehoiachin succeeded him as king. **7** The king of Egypt did not again leave his own land, for the king of Babylon had taken all that belonged to the king of Egypt from the wadi of Egypt to the Euphrates River.

**Reign of Jehoiachin.** **8** Jehoiachin was eighteen years old when he began to reign, and he reigned three months* in Jerusalem. His mother's name was Nehushta, daughter of Elnathan of Jerusalem. **9** He did evil in the sight of the LORD, just as his forebears had done.

**10** At that time the officials of Nebuchadnezzar, king of Babylon, attacked Jerusalem, and the city came under siege.[t] **11** Nebuchadnezzar, king of Babylon, himself arrived at the city while his servants were besieging it. **12** Then Jehoiachin, king of Judah, together with his mother, his ministers, officers, and functionaries, surrendered to the king of Babylon, who, in the eighth year of his reign, took him captive. **13** He carried off all the treasures of the temple of the LORD and those of the palace, and broke up all the gold utensils that Solomon, king of Israel, had provided in the temple of the LORD, as the LORD had foretold.[u] **14** He deported all Jerusalem: all the officers and men of the army, ten thousand in number, and all the craftsmen and smiths. None were left among the people of the land except the poor. **15** He deported Jehoiachin to Babylon, and also led captive from Jerusalem to Babylon the king's mother and wives, his functionaries, and the chief men of the land.[v] **16** The king of Babylon also led captive to Babylon all seven thousand men of the army, and a thousand craftsmen and smiths, all of them trained soldiers. **17** In place of Jehoiachin, the king of Babylon appointed his uncle Mattaniah king, and changed his name to Zedekiah.

k 2 Kgs 24, 2.
l 2 Chr 35, 26f.
m 2 Chr 35, 20-24.
n 2 Chr 36, 2f.
o 36f: 2 Chr 36, 4f.
p 1-5: 2 Chr 36, 6ff.
q 2 Kgs 23, 27.
r 2 Kgs 21, 16.
s 2 Chr 36, 8.
t 2 Chr 36, 10; Dn 1, 1f.
u 2 Kgs 20, 17; Is 39, 6.
v Est A, 3; 2, 6.

*

23, 30, 35: People of the land: in this period, the phrase referred to "landed gentry"; in later times it meant "the poor." Cf 2 Kgs 24, 14.

23, 33: A talent of gold: some manuscripts of the Greek and Syriac texts have "ten talents."

24, 8: He reigned three months: in the year 597 B.C.

**Reign of Zedekiah.** **18** Zedekiah was twenty-one years old when he became king, and he reigned eleven years in Jerusalem. His mother's name was Hamutal, daughter of Jeremiah of Libnah.[w] **19** He also did evil in the sight of the LORD, just as Jehoiakim had done. **20** The LORD's anger befell Jerusalem and Judah till he cast them out from his presence. Thus Zedekiah rebelled against the king of Babylon.[x]

## CHAPTER 25

**1** *[y] In the tenth month of the ninth year of Zedekiah's reign, on the tenth day of the month, Nebuchadnezzar, king of Babylon, and his whole army advanced against Jerusalem, encamped around it, and built siege walls on every side. **2** The siege of the city continued until the eleventh year of Zedekiah. **3** On the ninth day of the fourth month, when famine had gripped the city, and the people had no more bread, **4** the city walls were breached. Then the king and all the soldiers left the city by night through the gate between the two walls which was near the king's garden. Since the Chaldeans had the city surrounded, they went in the direction of the Arabah. **5** But the Chaldean army pursued the king and overtook him in the desert near Jericho, abandoned by his whole army.

**6** The king was therefore arrested and brought to Riblah to the king of Babylon, who pronounced sentence on him. **7** He had Zedekiah's sons slain before his eyes. Then he blinded Zedekiah, bound him with fetters, and had him brought to Babylon.

**8** On the seventh day of the fifth month (this was in the nineteenth year of Nebuchadnezzar, king of Babylon), Nebuzaradan, captain of the bodyguard, came to Jerusalem as the representative of the king of Babylon. **9** He burned the house of the LORD, the palace of the king, and all the houses of Jerusalem; every large building was destroyed by fire.[z] **10** Then the Chaldean troops who were with the captain of the guard tore down the walls that surrounded Jerusalem.

**11** Then Nebuzaradan, captain of the guard, led into exile the last of the people remaining in the city, and those who had deserted* to the king of Babylon, and the last of the artisans. **12** But some of the country's poor, Nebuzaradan, captain of the guard, left behind as vinedressers and farmers.

**13** The bronze pillars that belonged to the house of the LORD, and the wheeled carts and the bronze sea in the house of the LORD, the Chaldeans broke into pieces; they carried away the bronze to Babylon.[a] **14** They took also the pots, the shovels, the snuffers, the bowls, the pans and all the bronze vessels used for service.[b] **15** The fire-holders and the bowls which were of gold or silver the captain of the guard also carried off. **16** The weight in bronze of the two pillars, the bronze sea, and the wheeled carts, all of them furnishings which Solomon had made for the house of the LORD, was never calculated. **17** Each of the pillars was eighteen cubits high; a bronze capital five cubits high surmounted each pillar, and a network with pomegranates encircled the capital, all of bronze; and so for the other pillar, as regards the network.[c]

**18** The captain of the guard also took Seraiah the high priest, Zephaniah the second priest, and the three keepers of the entry. **19** And from the city he took one courtier, a commander of soldiers, five men in the personal service of the king who were still in the city, the scribe of the army commander, who mustered the people of the land, and sixty of the common people still remaining in the city. **20** The captain of the guard, Nebuzaradan, arrested these and brought them to the king of Babylon at Riblah; **21** the king had them struck down and put to death in Riblah, in the land of Hamath. Thus was Judah exiled from her land.

**Governorship of Gedaliah.** **22** [d]As for the people whom he had allowed to remain in the land of Judah, Nebuchadnezzar, king of Babylon, appointed as their governor Gedaliah, son of Ahikam, son of Shaphan. **23** Hearing that the king of Babylon had appointed Gedaliah governor, all the army commanders with their men came to him at Mizpah: Ishmael, son of Nethaniah, Johanan, son of Kareah, Seraiah, son of Tanhumeth the Netophathite, and Jaazaniah, from Beth-maacah. **24** Gedaliah gave the commanders and their men his oath. "Do not be afraid of the Chaldean officials," he said to them. "Remain in the country and serve the king of Babylon, and all will be well with you."

**25** But in the seventh month Ishmael, son of Nethaniah, son of Elishama, of royal descent, came with ten men, attacked Gedaliah and killed him, along with the Jews and Chaldeans who were in Mizpah with him. **26** Then all the people, great and small, left with the army commanders and went to Egypt for fear of the Chaldeans.

**Release of Jehoiachin.** **27** [e]In the thirty-seventh year of the exile of Jehoiachin, king

w 2 Chr 36, 9; Jer 37, 1f; 52, 1ff.
x 2 Kgs 22, 17; 23, 27.
y 1-21: Jer 39, 1-10; 52, 4-28.
z 2 Chr 36, 19; Ps 74, 7.
a 2 Kgs 16, 17; 1 Kgs 7, 15-39; 2 Chr 3, 15; 36, 18; Jer 27, 19.
b 1 Kgs 7, 48ff.
c 1 Kgs 7, 15; Jer 52, 21ff.
d 22-26: Jer 40, 5. 7-41, 1-3.
e 27-30: Jer 52, 31-34.

*

25, 1–30: This chapter parallels Jer 39 and 52; see notes to those parts of Jeremiah.

25, 11: Those who had deserted: perhaps on the advice of Jeremiah; cf Jer 38, 2f.

of Judah, on the twenty-seventh day of the
twelfth month, Evil-merodach, king of Babylon, in the inaugural year of his own reign,
raised up Jehoiachin, king of Judah, from prison. **28** He spoke kindly to him and gave him a
throne higher than that of the other kings who
were with him in Babylon. **29** Jehoiachin took
off his prison garb and ate at the king's table as
long as he lived. **30** The allowance granted him
by the king was a perpetual allowance, in fixed
daily amounts, for as long as he lived.

# The First Book of

# CHRONICLES

*Originally the two books of Chronicles formed, with the Books of Ezra and Nehemiah, a single historical work, uniform in style and basic ideas. The Greek title,* paraleipomena, *means "things omitted, or passed over (in Samuel and Kings)." The Books of Chronicles, however, are more than a supplement to Samuel and Kings; a comparison of the two histories discloses striking differences in scope and purpose. The Books of Chronicles record in some detail the lengthy span from the reign of Saul to the return from the Exile. Unlike the exact science of history today, wherein factual accuracy and impartiality of judgment are the standards for estimating what is of permanent worth, ancient biblical history, with rare exceptions, was less concerned with reporting in precise detail all the facts of a situation than with explaining the meaning of those facts. Such history was primarily interpretative and, in the Old Testament, its purpose was to disclose the action of the living God in the affairs of men. For this reason we speak of it as "sacred history"; its writer's first concern was to bring out the divine or supernatural dimension in history.*

*This is apparent when we examine the primary objective of the Chronicler in compiling his work. In view of the situation which confronted the Jewish people at this time (the end of the fifth century B.C.), the Chronicler realized that Israel's political greatness was a thing of the past. It would be a people under God, or nothing. Yet Israel's past held the key to her future. The Chronicler proposed to establish and defend the legitimate claims of the Davidic monarchy in Israel's history, and to underscore the place of Jerusalem and its divinely established temple worship as the center of religious life for the Jewish community of his day. If Judaism was to survive and prosper, it would have to heed the lessons of the past and devoutly serve Yahweh in the place where he had chosen to dwell, the temple of Jerusalem. From the Chronicler's point of view, David's reign was the ideal to which all subsequent rule in Judah must aspire.*

*The Chronicler was much more interested in David's religious and cultic influence than in his political power. There is little of royal messianism in his book. He apparently regarded as something of the distant past the prophet Zechariah's abortive attempt to have the Davidic kingdom reestablished in the time of Zerubbabel at the end of the sixth century B.C. (Zec 6, 9–15). He saw David's primary importance as deriving from the establishment of Jerusalem and its temple as the center of the true worship of the Lord. Furthermore, he presented David as the one who had authorized the elaborate ritual (which, in point of fact, only gradually evolved in the temple built by Zerubbabel) and who had also appointed Levites to supervise the liturgical services there.*

*There are good reasons for believing that originally the Books of Ezra and Nehemiah formed the last part of a single literary work that began with 1 and 2 Chronicles. Some authors even regard Ezra himself as having been the anonymous Chronicler. In any case, the Chronicler's Hebrew as well as his religious and political outlook points to c. 400 B.C. as the time of composition of this work.*

*The Chronicler used sources in writing his history. Besides the canonical Books of Genesis, Exodus, Numbers, Joshua and Ruth, and especially the Books of Samuel and Kings, he cites the titles of many other works no longer extant. "The books of the kings of Israel," or "the books of the kings of Israel and Judah," "the history of Samuel the seer," "the history of Nathan the prophet," "the history of Gad the seer," "the commentary of the Books of Kings," are some of the documents mentioned as historical sources.*

*In addition, the Chronicler's work contains early preexilic material not found in the Books of Kings. At one time scholars discounted the value of this material, but modern research has shown that, even though the Chronicler may have at times treated the material rather freely, he derived it from authentic and reliable sources.*

*The principal divisions of 1 Chronicles are as follows:*
*I. Genealogical Tables (1, 1—9, 34).*
*II. The History of David (9, 35—29, 30).*

## *I: Genealogical Tables*

### CHAPTER 1

**From Adam to Abraham.** **1** [a]* Adam, Seth, Enosh, **2** [b]Kenan, Mahalalel, Jared, **3** Enoch, Methuselah, Lamech,[c] **4** Noah, Shem, Ham, and Japheth.[d] **5** [e]The descendants of Japheth were Gomer, Magog, Madai, Javan, Tubal, Meshech, and Tiras. **6** The descendants of Gomer were Ashkenaz, Riphath, and Togarmah. **7** The descendants of Javan were Elishah, Tarshis, the Kittim, and the Rodanim.

**8** [f]The descendants of Ham were Cush, Mesraim, Put, and Canaan. **9** The descendants of Cush were Seba, Havilah, Sabta, Raama, and Sabteca. The descendants of Raama were Sheba and Dedan. **10** Cush became the father of Nimrod, who was the first to be a conqueror on the earth. **11** [g]Mesraim became the father of the Ludim, Anamim, Lehabim, Naphtuhim, **12** Pathrusim, Casluhim, and Caphtorim, from whom the Philistines sprang. **13** Canaan became the father of Sidon, his first-born, and Heth, **14** and the Jebusite, the Amorite, the Girgashite, **15** the Hivite, the Arkite, the Sinite, **16** the Arvadite, the Zemarite, and the Hamathite.

**17** [h]The descendants of Shem were Elam, Asshur, Arpachshad, Lud, and Aram. The descendants of Aram were Uz, Hul, Gether, and Mash. **18** Arpachshad became the father of Shelah, and Shelah became the father of Eber. **19** Two sons were born to Eber; the first was named Peleg (for in his time the world was divided), and his brother was Joktan. **20** Joktan became the father of Almodad, Sheleph, Hazarmaveth, Jerah, **21** Hadoram, Uzal, Diklah, **22** Ebal, Abimael, Sheba, **23** Ophir, Havilah, and Jobab; all these were the sons of Joktan.

**24** [i]Shem, Arpachshad, Shelah, **25** Eber, Peleg, Reu, **26** Serug, Nahor, Terah, **27** Abram, who was Abraham.[j]

**From Abraham to Jacob.** **28** The sons of Abraham were Isaac and Ishmael.[k] **29** These were their descendants:[l]

Nebaioth, the first-born of Ishmael, then Kedar, Adbeel, Mibsam, **30** Mishma, Dumah, Massa, Hadad, Tema, **31** Jetur, Naphish, and Kedemah. These were the descendants of Ishmael.

**32** [m]The descendants of Keturah, Abraham's concubine: she bore Zimran, Jokshan, Medan, Midian, Ishbak, and Shuah. The sons of Jokshan were Sheba and Dedan. **33** The descendants of Midian were Ephah, Epher, Hanoch, Abida, and Eldaah. All these were the descendants of Keturah.

**34** Abraham became the father of Isaac. The sons of Isaac were Esau and Israel.[n]

**35** [o]The sons of Esau were Eliphaz, Reuel, Jeush, Jalam, and Korah. **36** The sons of Eliphaz were Teman, Omar, Zephi, Gatam, Kenaz, [Timna,] and Amalek. **37** The sons of Reuel were Nahath, Zerah, Shammah, and Mizzah.

**38** [p]The descendants of Seir* were Lotan, Shobal, Zibeon, Anah, Dishon, Ezer, and Dishan. **39** The sons of Lotan were Hori and Homam; Timna was the sister of Lotan. **40** The sons of Shobal were Alian, Manahath, Ebal, Shephi, and Onam. The sons of Zibeon were Aiah and Anah. **41** The sons of Anah: Dishon. The sons of Dishon were Hemdan, Eshban, Ithran, and Cheran. **42** The sons of Ezer were Bilhan, Zaavan, and Jaakan. The sons of Dishan were Uz and Aran.

**43** [q]The kings who reigned in the land of Edom before they had Israelite kings were the following: Bela, son of Beor, the name of whose city was Ninhabah. **44** When Bela died, Jobab, son of Zerah, from Bozrah, succeeded him.[r] **45** When Jobab died, Husham, from the land of the Temanites, succeeded him.[s] **46** Husham died and Hadad, son of Bedad, succeeded him. He overthrew the Midianites on the Moabite plateau, and the name of his city was Avith. **47** Hadad died and Samlah of Masrekah suc-

a 1 Chr 4, 25f; Gn 5, 3. 6. 9.
b 2ff: Gn 5, 9-32; 10, 2ff.
c Gn 4, 25.
d Gn 5, 32; 6, 10; 9, 18.
e 5ff: Gn 10, 2ff.
f Gn 10, 8.
g 11-16: Gn 10, 13-18.
h 17-23: Gn 10, 22-29; 11, 10-18.
i 24-27: Gn 11, 10-26; Lk 3, 34ff.
j Gn 17, 5; Neh 9, 7.
k Gn 16, 11. 15; 21, 2f; Gal 4, 22f; Heb 11, 11.
l 29ff: Gn 25, 13-16.
m 32f: Gn 25, 1-4.
n Gn 21, 2f; 25, 19. 25f: 32, 28f; Mt 1, 2; Lk 3, 34.
o 35ff: Gn 36, 4f. 10-13. 15ff.
p 38-42; Gn 36, 20-28.
q 43-54: Gn 36, 31-43.
r Is 34, 6; 63, 1; Jer 49, 13. 22.
s Gn 36, 11; Jb 2, 11; Jer 49, 7. 20.

*

1, 1–9, 34: The Chronicler set as his task the retelling, from his particular viewpoint, of the story of God's people from the beginning to his own day. Since his primary interest was the history of David and the Davidic dynasty of Judah, he presents through mere genealogical lists a summary of what preceded the reign of Saul, David's predecessor in the kingdom. The sources for these genealogies are mostly the canonical Hebrew Scriptures that were already in their present form in his time. The cross references in this book indicate in each case the scriptural sources used.

1, 38: Seir: another name for Esau (v 35) or Edom (v 43).

ceeded him. **48** Samlah died and Shaul from
Rehoboth-han-nahar succeeded him. **49** When
Shaul died, Baalhanan, son of Achbor, succeeded him. **50** Baalhanan died and Hadad succeeded him. The name of his city was Pai, and his
wife's name was Mehetabel. She was the
daughter of Matred, who was the daughter of
Mezahab. **51** [t]After Hadad died. . . .

These were the chiefs of Edom: the chiefs of
Timna, Aliah, Jetheth, **52** Oholibamah, Elah,
Pinon, **53** Kenaz, Teman, Mibzar, **54** Magdi-
el, and Iram were the chiefs of Edom.

## CHAPTER 2

**1** These were the sons of Israel: Reuben,
Simeon, Levi, Judah, Issachar, Zebulun,[u]
**2** Dan, Joseph, Benjamin, Naphtali, Gad, and
Asher.[v]

**Judah.** **3** The sons of Judah* were: Er,
Onan, and Shelah; these three were born to him
of Bathshua, a Canaanite woman. But Judah's
first-born, Er, was wicked in the sight of the
LORD, so he killed him.[w] **4** Judah's daughter-in-law Tamar bore him Perez and Zerah, so
that he had five sons in all.[x]

**5** The sons of Perez were Hezron and Hamul.[y] **6** The sons of Zerah were Zimri, Ethan,
Heman, Calcol, and Darda—five in all.[z] **7** The
sons of Zimri: Carmi. The sons of Carmi:
Achar, who brought trouble upon Israel by violating the ban.[a] **8** The sons of Ethan: Azariah.
**9** The sons born to Hezron were Jerahmeel,
Ram, and Chelubai.[b] *

**10** *Ram became the father of Ammina 'ab,
and Amminadab became the father of Nahshon,
a prince of the Judahites.[c] **11** [d]Nahshon became the father of Salma. Salma became the
father of Boaz. **12** Boaz became the father of
Obed. Obed became the father of Jesse.
**13** [e]Jesse became the father of Eliab, his
first-born, of Abinadab, the second son, Shimea, the third,[f] **14** Nethanel, the fourth, Raddai,
the fifth, **15** Ozem, the sixth, and David, the
seventh. **16** Their sisters were Zeruiah and Abigail. Zeruiah had three sons: Abishai, Joab, and
Asahel.[g] **17** Abigail bore Amasa, whose father
was Jether the Ishmaelite.[h]

**18** *By his wife Azubah, Caleb, son of Hezron, became the father of a daughter, Jerioth.
Her sons were Jesher, Shobab, and Ardon.[i]
**19** When Azubah died, Caleb married Ephrath,
who bore him Hur.[j] **20** Hur became the father
of Uri, and Uri became the father of Bezalel.[k]
**21** Then Hezron had relations with the daughter
of Machir, the father of Gilead, having married
her when he was sixty years old. She bore him
Segub.[l] **22** Segub became the father of Jair,[m]
who possessed twenty-three cities in the land of
Gilead. **23** Geshur and Aram took from them
the villages of Jair, that is, Kenath and its
towns, sixty cities in all, which had belonged to
the sons of Machir, the father of Gilead.[n]
**24** After the death of Hezron, Caleb had relations with Ephrathah, the widow of his father
Hezron, and she bore him Ashhur, the father of
Tekoa.[o]

**25** The sons of Jerahmeel,* the first-born of
Hezron, were Ram, the first-born, then Bunah,
Oren, and Ozem, his brothers.[p] **26** Jerahmeel
also had another wife, Atarah by name, who
was the mother of Onam. **27** The sons of Ram,
the first-born of Jerahmeel, were Maaz, Jamin,
and Eker. **28** The sons of Onam were Shammai
and Jada. The sons of Shammai were Nadab and
Abishur. **29** Abishur's wife, who was named
Abihail, bore him Ahban and Molid. **30** The
sons of Nadab were Seled and Appaim. Seled
died without sons. **31** The sons of Appaim:
Ishi. The sons of Ishi: Sheshan. The sons of
Sheshan: Ahlai.[q] **32** The sons of Jada, the
brother of Shammai, were Jether and Jonathan.
Jether died without sons. **33** The sons of Jonathan were Peleth and Zaza. These were the descendants of Jerahmeel. **34** Sheshan, who had
no sons, only daughters, had an Egyptian slave
named Jarha. **35** Sheshan gave his daughter in
marriage to his slave Jarha, and she bore him
Attai. **36** Attai became the father of Nathan.
Nathan became the father of Zabad. **37** Zabad
became the father of Ephlal. Ephlal became the

t 51-54: Gn 36, 40-43.
u Gn 29, 32-35; 30, 18. 20; 35, 23.
v Gn 30, 6. 8. 11. 13. 24; 35, 18. 24ff.
w 1 Chr 4, 21; Gn 38, 1-5; 46, 12.
x Gn 38, 7. 13-30; 46, 12; Rv 4, 12. 18; Mt 1, 3.
y Gn 46, 12.
z 1 Kgs 5, 11.
a Jos 7, 1. 18ff. 24f; 22, 20.
b Rv 4, 19; Mt 1, 3.
c Rv 4, 19; Mt 1, 4.
d 11f: Nm 1, 7; Rv 4, 20f; Mt 1, 4f.
e 13ff: 1 Sm 16, 6-13; 17, 13f.
f 2 Chr 11, 18.
g 2 Sm 2, 18.
h 2 Sm 17, 25; 19, 14; 20, 4-13.
i 1 Chr 2, 24.
j 1 Chr 2, 24.
k Ex 24, 14; 31, 2; 35, 30; 2 Chr 1, 5.
l Nm 26, 29; 27, 1; 32, 32; Jos 13, 31; Jgs 5, 14.
m Nm 32, 41; 1 Kgs 4, 13.
n Dt 3, 14; Jos 13, 30; Jgs 10, 4.
o 1 Chr 2, 19; 2 Sm 14, 2; 2 Chr 11, 6.
p 1 Sm 27, 10; 30, 29; Jb 32, 2.
q 1 Chr 4, 20.

*

2, 3—4, 23: For two reasons, the Chronicler places the genealogy of the tribe of Judah before that of the other tribes, giving it also at greater length than the others: because of his interest in David and because in the Chronicler's time the people of God were almost exclusively Jews. Both David and the Jews were of the tribe of Judah.

2, 9: Chelubai: a variant form of the name Caleb (vv 18. 42), distinct from Chelub of 1 Chr 4, 11.

2, 10–17: Immediate ancestors of David. A similar list is given in Ru 4, 19–22; each list, independent of the other, derives from a common source.

2, 18–24: Descendants of Caleb. In 1 Chr 4, 15, as is often the case in the Pentateuch (Nm 13, 6; 14, 6, 30; 26, 65; etc.), Caleb is called son of Jephunneh. Here he is called son of Hezron, perhaps because the Calebites were reckoned as part of the clan of the Hezronites.

2, 25–41: The Jerahmeelites were a clan in the Negeb of Judah.

father of Obed. **38** Obed became the father of
Jehu. Jehu became the father of Azariah.
**39** Azariah became the father of Helez. Helez
became the father of Eleasah. **40** Eleasah became the father of Sismai. Sismai became the
father of Shallum. **41** Shallum became the father of Jekamiah. Jekamiah became the father of
Elishama.

**42** The descendants of Caleb,* the brother of
Jerahmeel: [Mesha] his first-born, who was the
father of Ziph. Then the sons of Mareshah, who
was the father of Hebron. **43** The sons of Hebron were Korah, Tappuah, Rekem, and Shema. **44** Shema became the father of Raham,
who was the father of Jorkeam. Rekem became
the father of Shammai. **45** The sons of Shammai: Maon, who was the father of Beth-zur.
**46** Ephah, Caleb's concubine, bore Haran,
Moza, and Gazez. Haran became the father of
Gazez. **47** The sons of Jahdai were Regem,
Jotham, Geshan, Pelet, Ephah, and Shaaph.
**48** Maacah, Caleb's concubine, bore Sheber
and Tirhanah. **49** She also bore Shaaph, the
father of Madmannah, Sheva, the father of
Mach-benah, and the father of Gibea. Achsah
was Caleb's daughter.[r]

**50** These were descendants of Caleb, sons of
Hur,* the first-born of Ephrathah: Shobal, the
father of Kiriath-jearim, **51** Salma, the father of
Bethlehem, and Hareph, the father of Bethgad-
er. **52** The sons of Shobal, the father of Kiriath-jearim, were Reaiah, half the Manahathites,
**53** and the clans of Kiriath-jearim: the Ithrites,
the Puthites, the Shumathites, and the Mishra-
ites. From these the people of Zorah and the
Eshtaolites derived.[s] **54** The descendants of
Salma were Bethlehem, the Netophathites, At-
roth-beth-Joab, half the Manahathites, and the
Zorites. **55** [t]The clans of the Sopherim dwelling in Jabez were the Tirathites, the Shimeath-
ites, and the Sucathites. They were the Kenites,
who came from Hammath of the ancestor of the
Rechabites.

## CHAPTER 3

**1** [u]The following* were the sons of David
who were born to him in Hebron: the first-born,
Amnon, by Ahinoam of Jezreel; the second,
Daniel,* by Abigail of Carmel; **2** the third, Absalom, son of Maacah, who was the daughter of
Talmai, king of Geshur; the fourth, Adonijah,
son of Haggith; **3** the fifth, Shephatiah, by Abital; the sixth, Ithream, by his wife Eglah. **4** Six
in all were born to him in Hebron, where he
reigned seven years and six months. Then he
reigned thirty-three years in Jerusalem,[v]
**5** [w]where the following were born to him:
Shimea,* Shobab, Nathan, Solomon—four by
Bathsheba, the daughter of Ammiel,[x] **6** Ibhar,
Elishua, Eliphelet, **7** Nogah, Nepheg, Japhia,
**8** Elishama, Eliada, and Eliphelet—nine. **9** All
these were sons of David, in addition to other
sons by concubines; and Tamar was their sister.[y]

**10** [z]* The son of Solomon was Rehoboam,
whose son was Abijah, whose son was Asa,
whose son was Jehoshaphat,[a] **11** whose son
was Joram, whose son was Ahaziah, whose son
was Joash,[b] **12** whose son was Amaziah,
whose son was Azariah, whose son was Jotham,[c] **13** whose son was Ahaz, whose son was
Hezekiah, whose son was Manasseh,[d]
**14** whose son was Amon, whose son was Josiah.[e] **15** The sons of Josiah were: the first-born,
Johanan; the second, Jehoiakim; the third, Zedekiah; the fourth, Shallum.*[f] **16** The sons of
Jehoiakim were: Jeconiah, his son; Zedekiah,
his son.[g]

**17** The sons of Jeconiah* the captive were:
Shealtiel,[h] **18** Malchiram, Pedaiah, Shenazzar,* Jekamiah, Shama, and Nedabiah. **19** The
sons of Pedaiah were Zerubbabel* and Shimei.
The sons of Zerubbabel were Meshullam and
Hananiah; Shelomith was their sister. **20** The
sons of Meshullam were Hashubah, Ohel, Bere-

---

r Jos 15, 16; Jgs 1, 12.
s Jgs 18, 2.
t Nm 24, 21; Jgs 1, 16; 4, 11; 1 Sm 15, 6.
u 1-4: 2 Sm 3, 2-5.
v 2 Sm 2, 11; 5, 5.
w 5-8: 2 Sm 5, 14ff.
x 2 Sm 5, 5.
y 2 Sm 13, 1f.
z 10-17: Mt 1, 7-12.
a 1 Kgs 11, 43; 14, 31; 15, 1. 8. 24; 2 Chr 9, 31; 12, 16; 13, 23; 17, 1.
b 1 Kgs 22, 51; 2 Chr 21, 1; 22, 1; 24, 1. 27.
c 2 Kgs 12, 21; 14, 21; 15, 7; 2 Chr 25, 1; 26, 1. 23; 27, 1.
d 2 Kgs 15, 38; 16, 20; 20, 21; 2 Chr 28, 1. 27; 32, 33.
e 2 Kgs 21, 18. 26; 2 Chr 33, 20. 25.
f 2 Kgs 23, 34; 24, 17; 2 Chr 36, 4. 10.
g 2 Kgs 24, 6. 17; 2 Chr 36, 8. 10.
h 17. 19; Ezr 2, 2; 3, 2. 8; 5, 2; Sir 49, 11; Hg 1, 1. 12. 14; Mt 1, 12f; Lk 3, 27.

---

*

2, 42–49: Another list, dating from preexilic times, of the Calebites, a clan that inhabited the south of Judah.

2, 50–55: The Hurites, a clan dwelling to the south and west of Jerusalem and related to the Calebites.

3, 1–9: David's sons.

3, 1: Daniel: called Chileab in 2 Sm 3, 3.

3, 5: Shimea: called Shammua in 2 Sm 5, 14. Ammiel: called Eliam in 2 Sm 11, 3.

3, 10–16: The kings of Judah from Solomon to the destruction of Jerusalem by the Babylonians.

3, 15: Shallum: the same as Jehoahaz, Josiah's successor; cf Jer 22, 11.

3, 17–24: The descendants of King Jechoniah up to the time of the Chronicler. If twenty-five years are allowed to each generation, the ten generations between Jechoniah and Anani (the last name on the list) would bring the birth of the latter to about 405 B.C.—an important item in establishing the approximate date of the Chronicler.

3, 18: Shenazzar: presumably the same as Sheshbazzar of Ezr 1, 8. 11; 5, 14ff, the prince of Judah who was the first Jewish governor of Judah after the exile. Both forms of the name probably go back to the Babylonian name Sin-ab-ussar signifying, "O [god] Sin, protect [our] father!"

3, 19: Zerubbabel: here called the son of Pedaiah, though elsewhere (Hg 1, 12. 14; 2, 2. 23; Ezr 3, 2. 8; 5, 2; Neh 12, 1) called son of Shealtiel. The latter term may merely mean that Zerubbabel succeeded Shealtiel as head of the house of David.

chiah, Hasadiah, Jushabhesed—five. **21** The sons of Hananiah were Pelatiah, Jeshaiah, Rephaiah, Arnan, Obadiah, and Shecaniah. **22** [i]The sons of Shecaniah were Shemiah, Hattush, Igal, Bariah, Neariah, Shaphat—six. **23** The sons of Neariah were Elioenai, Hizkiah, and Azrikam—three. **24** The sons of Elioenai were Hodaviah, Eliashib, Pelaiah, Akkub, Johanan, Delaiah, and Anani—seven.

## CHAPTER 4

**1** *The descendants of Judah were: Perez, Hezron, Carmi, Hur, and Shobal.[j] **2** Reaiah, the son of Shobal, became the father of Jahath, and Jahath became the father of Ahumai and Lahad. These were the clans of the Zorathites.

**3** These were the descendants of Hareph, the father of Etam: Jezreel, Ishma, and Idbash; their sister was named Hazzelelponi. **4** Penuel was the father of Gedor, and Ezer the father of Hushah. These were the descendants of Hur, the first-born of Ephrathah, the father of Bethlehem.

**5** Ashhur, the father of Tekoa, had two wives, Helah and Naarah.[k] **6** Naarah bore him Ahuzzam, Hepher, the Temenites and the Ahashtarites. These were the descendants of Naarah. **7** The sons of Helah were Zereth, Izhar, Ethnan, and Koz. **8** Koz became the father of Anub and Zobebah, as well as of the clans of Aharhel, son of Harum. **9** Jabez was the most distinguished of the brothers. His mother had named him Jabez, saying, "I bore him with pain." **10** Jabez prayed to the God of Israel: "Oh, that you may truly bless me and extend my boundaries! Help me and make me free of misfortune, without pain!" And God granted his prayer.

**11** Chelub, the brother of Shuhah, became the father of Mehir, who was the father of Eshton. **12** Eshton became the father of Beth-rapha, Paseah, and Tehinnah, the father of the city of Nahash. These were the men of Recah.

**13** The sons of Kenaz were Othniel and Seraiah. The sons of Othniel were Hathath and Meonothai;[l] **14** Meonothai became the father of Ophrah. Seraiah became the father of Joab, the father of Geharashim, so called because they were craftsmen. **15** The sons of Caleb, son of Jephunneh, were Ir, Elah, and Naam. The sons of Elah were . . . and Kenaz.[m] **16** The sons of Jehallelel were Ziph, Ziphah, Tiria, and Asarel. **17** The sons of Ezrah were Jether, Mered, Epher, and Jalon. Jether became the father of Miriam, Shammai, and Ishbah, the father of Eshtemoa. [. . . . . . . .][n] **18** His (Mered's) Egyptian wife bore Jared, the father of Gedor, Heber, the father of Soco, and Jekuthiel, the father of Zanoah. These were the sons of Bithiah, the daughter of Pharaoh, whom Mered married. **19** The sons of his Jewish wife, the sister of Naham, the father of Keilah, were Shimon the Garmite and Ishi the Maacathite. **20** The sons of Shimon were Amnon, Rinnah, Benhanan, and Tilon. The son of Ishi was Zoheth and the son of Zoheth. . . .

**21** The descendants of Shelah, son of Judah, were: Er, the father of Lecah; Laadah, the father of Mareshah; the clans of the linen weavers' guild in Bethashbea;[o] **22** Jokim; the men of Cozeba; and Joash and Saraph, who held property in Moab, but returned to Bethlehem. [These are events of old.] **23** They were potters and inhabitants of Netaim and Gederah, where they lived in the king's service.

**Simeon.** **24** The sons of Simeon were Nemuel, Jamin, Jachin, Zerah, and Shaul,[p] **25** whose son was Shallum, whose son was Mibsam, whose son was Mishma. **26** The descendants of Mishma were his son Hammuel, whose son was Zaccur, whose son was Shimei. **27** Shimei had sixteen sons and six daughters. His brothers, however, did not have many sons, and as a result all their clans did not equal the number of the Judahites.

**28** [q]They dwelt in Beer-sheba, Moladah, Hazar-shual, **29** Bilhah, Ezem, Tolad, **30** Bethuel, Hormah, Ziklag, **31** Bethmarcaboth, Hazar-susim, Bethbiri, and Shaaraim. Until David came to reign, these were their cities **32** and their villages. Etam, also, and Ain, Rimmon, Tochen, and Ashan—five cities, **33** together with all their outlying villages as far as Baal. Here is where they dwelt, and so it was inscribed of them in their family records.

**34** Meshobab, Jamlech, Joshah, son of Amaziah, **35** Joel, Jehu, son of Joshibiah, son of Seraiah, son of Asiel, **36** Elioenai, Jaakobath, Jeshohaiah, Asaiah, Adiel, Jesimiel, Benaiah, **37** Ziza, son of Shiphi, son of Allon, son of Jedaiah, son of Shimri, son of Shemaiah— **38** these just named were princes in their clans, and their ancestral houses spread out to such an extent[r] **39** that they went to the approaches of Gedor,* east of the valley, seeking pasture for their flocks. **40** They found abundant and good pastures, and the land was spacious, quiet, and peaceful. **41** They who have just been listed by name set out during the reign of Hezekiah, king of Judah, and attacked the tents of Ham (for Hamites dwelt there formerly) and also the Me-

i Neh 3, 29.
j 1 Chr 2, 4f. 7. 9. 50; Gn 38, 29; 46, 12; Mt 1, 3.
k 1 Chr 2, 24.
l Jos 15, 17; Jgs 1, 13; 3, 9. 11.
m Nm 13, 6; 14, 6; 32, 12; Jos 14, 6. 14.
n 1 Sm 30, 28.
o 1 Chr 2, 3; Gn 38, 5; 46, 12; Nm 26, 20.
p Gn 46, 10; Ex 6, 15; Nm 26, 12f.
q 28-32: Jos 19, 2-8.
r Nm 1, 2.
s 2 Kgs 18, 1f; 2 Chr 29, 1.

* 4, 1-43: The southern tribes.
4, 39: Gedor: in the Greek, Gerar, no doubt correct.

unites who were there. They pronounced
against them the ban that is still in force and
dwelt in their place because they found pasture
there for their flocks.[s]

**42** Five hundred of them (the Simeonites)
went to Mount Seir under the leadership of Pelatiah, Neariah, Rephaiah, and Uzziel, sons of
Ishi. **43** They attacked the surviving Amalekites who had escaped, and have resided there to
the present day.[t]

## CHAPTER 5

**Reuben.** **1** *The sons of Reuben, the
first-born of Israel. (He was indeed the first-
born, but because he disgraced the couch of his
father his birthright was given to the sons of
Joseph, son of Israel, so that he is not listed in
the family records according to birthright.[u]
**2** Judah, in fact, became powerful among his
brothers, so that the ruler came from him,
though the birthright had been Joseph's.)[v]
**3** The sons of Reuben, the first-born of Israel,
were Hanoch, Pallu, Hezron, and Carmi.[w]
**4** His son was Joel, whose son was Shemaiah,
whose son was Gog, whose son was Shimei,
**5** whose son was Micah, whose son was Reaiah, whose son was Baal, **6** whose son was
Beerah, whom Tiglath-pileser, the king of Assyria, took into exile; he was a prince of the
Reubenites.[x] **7** His brothers who belonged to
his clans, when they were listed in the family
records according to their descendants, were:
Jeiel, the chief, and Zechariah, **8** and Bela, son
of Azaz, son of Shema, son of Joel. The Reubenites lived in Aroer and as far as Nebo and
Baalmeon;[y] **9** toward the east they dwelt as far
as the desert which extends from the Euphrates
River, for they had much livestock in the land
of Gilead.[z] **10** During the reign of Saul they
waged war with the Hagrites, and when they
had defeated them they occupied their tents
throughout the region east of Gilead.[a]

**Gad.** **11** The Gadites lived alongside them in
the land of Bashan as far as Salecah.[b] **12** Joel
was chief, Shapham was second in command,
and Janai was judge in Bashan.[c] **13** Their
brothers, corresponding to their ancestral
houses, were: Michael, Meshullam, Sheba, Jo-
rai, Jacan, Zia, and Eber—seven. **14** These
were the sons of Abihail, son of Huri, son of
Jaroah, son of Gilead, son of Michael, son of
Jeshishai, son of Jahdo, son of Buz. **15** Ahi son
of Abdiel, son of Guni, was the head of their
ancestral houses. **16** They dwelt in Gilead, in
Bashan and its towns, and in all the pasture
lands of Sirion to the borders. **17** All were listed in the family records in the time of Jotham,
king of Judah, and of Jeroboam, king of Israel.
**18** The Reubenites, Gadites, and half-tribe
of Manasseh were warriors, men who bore
shield and sword and who drew the bow, trained
in warfare—forty-four thousand seven hundred
and sixty men fit for military service. **19** When
they waged war against the Hagrites and against
Jetur, Naphish, and Nodab,[d] **20** they received
help so that they mastered the Hagrites and all
who were with them. For during the battle they
called on God, and he heard them because they
had put their trust in him.[e] **21** Along with one
hundred thousand men they also captured their
livestock: fifty thousand camels, two hundred
fifty thousand camels, two hundred fifty thousand sheep, and two thousand asses. **22** Many
had fallen in battle, for victory is from God; and
they took over their dwelling place until the time
of the exile.[f]

**East Manasseh.** **23** The numerous members of the half-tribe of Manasseh lived in the
land of Bashan as far as Baal-hermon, Senir,
and Mount Hermon. **24** The following were the
heads of their ancestral houses: Epher, Ishi,
Eliel, Azriel, Jeremiah, Hodaviah, and Jahdi-
el—men who were warriors, famous men, and
heads over their ancestral houses.

**25** However, they offended the God of their
fathers by lusting after the gods of the natives
of the land, whom God had cleared out of their
way.[g] **26** Therefore the God of Israel incited
against them the anger of Pul,* king of Assyria,
and of Tiglath-pileser, king of Assyria, who
deported the Reubenites, the Gadites, and the
half-tribe of Manasseh and brought them to Halah, Habor, and Hara, and to the river Gozan,
where they have remained to this day.[h]

**Levi.*** **27** The sons of Levi were Gershon,
Kohath, and Merari.[i] **28** The sons of Kohath
were Amram, Izhar, Hebron, and Uzziel.[j]
**29** The children of Amram were Aaron, Moses,
and Miriam. The sons of Aaron were Nadab,

t Ex 17, 8. 14; Dt 25, 17ff; 1 Sm 14, 48; 15, 3. 7f; 2 Sm 8, 12.
u Gn 35, 22; 48, 5. 15-22; 49, 3f; Dt 33, 6.
v 1 Chr 28, 4; Gn 49, 8ff.
w Gn 46, 9; Ex 6, 14; Nm 26, 5f.
x 2 Kgs 15, 29.
y Jos 13, 9. 16f; Nm 32, 3. 38.
z Jos 22, 9.
a Ps 83, 6.
b Jos 13, 11. 24-28.
c Gn 46, 16.
d 1 Chr 1, 31; 5, 10; Gn 25, 15; Ps 83, 6.
e Dt 33, 20f.
f Nm 32, 39; Dt 3, 8ff; Jgs 3, 3.
g Ex 34, 14ff; 2 Kgs 17, 7.
h 2 Kgs 15, 9. 29; 17, 6.
i 1 Chr 6, 1; 23, 6; Gn 46, 11; Ex 6, 16; Nm 26, 57.
j 1 Chr 6, 3; Ex 6, 18.
k Ex 6, 20; Nm 26, 59f.

*

5, 1–26: The Transjordan tribes.

5, 26: Pul: the name which the Assyrian king Tiglath-pileser III (745–727 B.C.) took as king of Babylon.

5, 27—6, 66: The tribe of Levi. The list gives special prominence to Levi's son Kohath, from whom were descended both the Aaronite priests (1 Chr 5, 28–41) and the leading group of temple singers (1 Chr 6, 18–23).

Abihu, Eleazar, and Ithamar.[k] **30** *Eleazar, became the father of Phinehas. Phinehas became
the father of Abishua. **31** Abishua became the
father of Bukki. Bukki became the father of
Uzzi. **32** Uzzi became the father of Zerahiah.
Zerahiah became the father of Meraioth.
**33** Meraioth became the father of Amariah.
Amariah became the father of Ahitub. **34** Ahitub became the father of Zadok. Zadok became
the father of Ahimaaz. **35** Ahimaaz became the
father of Azariah. Azariah became the father of
Johanan. **36** Johanan became the father of Azariah, who served as priest in the temple Solomon built in Jerusalem. **37** Azariah became the
father of Amariah. Amariah became the father
of Ahitub. **38** Ahitub became the father of Zadok. Zadok became the father of Shallum.
**39** Shallum became the father of Hilkiah. Hilkiah became the father of Azariah. **40** Azariah
became the father of Seraiah. Seraiah became
the father of Jehozadak. **41** Jehozadak was one
of those who went into the exile which the LORD
inflicted on Judah and Jerusalem through Nebuchadnezzar.

## CHAPTER 6

**1** The sons of Levi were Gershon, Kohath,
and Merari.[l] **2** The sons of Gershon were
named Libni and Shimei.[m] **3** The sons of Kohath were Amram, Izhar, Hebron, and Uzziel.[n]
**4** [o]The sons of Merari were Mahli and Mushi.
The following were the clans of Levi, distributed according to their ancestors: **5** of Gershon:
his son Libni, whose son was Jahath, whose son
was Zimmah, **6** whose son was Joah, whose
son was Iddo, whose son was Zerah, whose son
was Jetherai.
**7** The descendants of Kohath were: his son
Amminadab, whose son was Korah, whose son
was Assir, **8** whose son was Elkanah, whose
son was Ebiasaph, whose son was Assir,
**9** whose son was Tahath, whose son was Uriel,
whose son was Uzziah, whose son was Shaul.
**10** The sons of Elkanah were Amasai and Ahi-
moth, **11** whose son was Elkanah, whose son
was Zophai, whose son was Nahath, **12** whose
son was Eliab, whose son was Jeroham, whose
son was Elkanah, whose son was Samuel.
**13** The sons of Samuel were Joel, the first-
born, and Abijah, the second.
**14** The descendants of Merari were Mahli,
whose son was Libni, whose son was Shimei,
whose son was Uzzah,[p] **15** whose son was
Shimea, whose son was Haggiah, whose son
was Asaiah.
**16** The following were entrusted by David
with the choir services* in the LORD's house
from the time when the ark had obtained a permanent resting place. **17** They served as singers
before the Dwelling of the meeting tent until
Solomon built the temple of the LORD in Jerusalem, and they performed their services in an
order prescribed for them. **18** Those who so
performed are the following, together with their
descendants.
Among the Kohathites: Heman, the chanter,
son of Joel, son of Samuel, **19** son of Elkanah,
son of Jeroham, son of Eliel, son of Toah,
**20** son of Zuth, son of Elkanah, son of Mahath,
son of Amasi, **21** son of Elkanah, son of Joel,
son of Azariah, son of Zephaniah, **22** son of
Tahath, son of Assir, son of Ebiasaph, son of
Korah,[q] **23** son of Izhar, son of Kohath, son of
Levi, son of Israel.
**24** His brother Asaph stood at his right hand.
Asaph was the son of Berechiah, son of Shimea,
**25** son of Michael, son of Baaseiah, son of
Malchijah, **26** son of Ethni, son of Zerah, son
of Adaiah, **27** son of Ethan, son of Zimmah,[r]
son of Shimei, **28** son of Jahath, son of Gershon, son of Levi.
**29** Their brothers, the Merarites, stood at the
left: Ethan, son of Kishi, son of Abdi, son of
Malluch, **30** son of Hashabiah, son of Amaziah, son of Hilkiah, **31** son of Amzi, son of
Bani, son of Shemer, **32** son of Mahli, son of
Mushi, son of Merari, son of Levi.[s]
**33** Their brother Levites were appointed to
all other services of the Dwelling of the house
of God.[t] **34** However, it was Aaron and his
descendants who burnt the offerings on the altar
of holocausts and on the altar of incense; they
alone had charge of the holy of holies and of
making atonement for Israel, as Moses, the servant of God, had ordained.[u]
**35** These were the descendants of Aaron: his
son Eleazer, whose son was Phinehas, whose
son was Abishua, **36** whose son was Bukki,
whose son was Uzzi, whose son was Zerahiah,
**37** whose son was Meraioth, whose son was
Amariah, whose son was Ahitub, **38** whose son
was Zadok, whose son was Ahimaaz.
**39** *The following were their dwelling
places to which their encampment was limited.
To the descendants of Aaron who belonged to
the clan of the Kohathites, since the first lot fell

l 1 Chr 5, 27; 23, 6; Gn 46, 11; Ex 6, 16; Nm 26, 57.
m Ex 6, 17.
n Ex 6, 18; Nm 3, 19; 26, 59.
o 1 Chr 6, 14; Ex 6, 19; Nm 3, 20; 26, 58.
p 1 Chr 6, 4; Ex 6, 19; Nm 3, 20; 26, 58.
q Ex 6, 24.
r 1 Chr 6, 2. 5.
s Ex 6, 19; Nm 26, 58.
t 1 Chr 15, 17. 19; 16, 41f; 2 Chr 5, 12.
u 1 Chr 16, 39f.

*

5, 30–41: The line of preexilic priests. The list seems to be confused in vv 36ff, which repeat the names, mostly in inverse order, that occur in vv 34f. A similar but shorter list is given, with variations, in Ezr 7, 1–5.

6, 16–32: The origin of the choir services performed by the levitical families in the postexilic temple at the time of the Chronicler is here attributed to David, somewhat as all the laws in the Pentateuch are attributed to Moses.

6, 39–66: Regarding the nature of the rights of Levites in the cities assigned to them, see note on Jos 21, 1.

to them, **40** was assigned Hebron with its adjacent pasture lands in the land of Judah, **41** although the open country and the villages belonging to the city had been given to Caleb, the
son of Jephunneh. **42** There were assigned to
the descendants of Aaron: Hebron, a city of
asylum, Libnah with its pasture lands, Jattir
with its pasture lands, Eshtemoa with its pasture
lands, **43** Holon with its pasture lands, Debir
with its pasture lands, **44** Ashan with its pasture
lands, Jetta with its pasture lands, and Beth-shemesh with its pasture lands. **45** Also from the
tribe of Benjamin: Gibeon with its pasture
lands, Geba with its pasture lands, Almon with
its pasture lands, Anathoth with its pasture
lands. In all, they had thirteen cities with their
pasture lands. **49** The Israelites assigned these
cities with their pasture lands to the Levites,
**50** designating them by name and assigning
them by lot from the tribes of the Judahites,
Simeonites, and Benjaminites.

**46** The other Kohathites obtained ten cities
by lot for their clans from the tribe of Ephraim,
from the tribe of Dan, and from the half-tribe of
Manasseh. **47** The clans of the Gershonites obtained thirteen cities from the tribes of Issachar,
Asher, and Naphtali, and from the half-tribe of
Manasseh in Bashan. **48** The clans of the Merarites obtained twelve cities by lot from the tribes
of Reuben, Gad, and Zebulun.

**51** The clans of the Kohathites obtained cities by lot from the tribe of Ephraim. **52** They
were assigned: Shechem in the mountain region
of Ephraim, a city of asylum, with its pasture
lands, Gezer with its pasture lands, **53** Kibzaim
with its pasture lands, and Beth-horon with its
pasture lands. **54** From the tribe of Dan: Elteke
with its pasture lands, Gibbethon with its pasture lands, Aijalon with its pasture lands, and
Gath-rimmon with its pasture lands. **55** From
the half-tribe of Manasseh: Taanach with its
pasture lands and Ibleam with its pasture lands.
These belonged to the rest of the Kohathite clan.

**56** The clans of the Gershonites received
from the half-tribe of Manasseh: Golan in Bashan with its pasture lands and Ashtaroth with
its pasture lands. **57** From the tribe of Issachar:
Kedesh with its pasture lands, Daberath with its
pasture lands, **58** Ramoth with its pasture
lands, and Engannim with its pasture lands.
**59** From the tribe of Asher: Mashal with its
pasture lands, Abdon with its pasture lands,
**60** Hilkath with its pasture lands, and Rehob
with its pasture lands. **61** From the tribe of
Naphtali: Kedesh in Galilee with its pasture
lands, Hammon with its pasture lands, and Kiriathaim with its pasture lands.

**62** The rest of the Merarites received from
the tribe of Zebulun: Jokneam with its pasture
lands, Kartah with its pasture lands, Rimmon
with its pasture lands, and Tabor with its pasture
lands. **63** Across the Jordan at Jericho [that is,
east of the Jordan] they received from the tribe
of Reuben: Bezer in the desert with its pasture
lands, Jahzah with its pasture lands, **64** Kedemoth with its pasture lands, and Mephaath with
its pasture lands. **65** From the tribe of Gad:
Ramoth in Gilead with its pasture lands, Mahanaim with its pasture lands, **66** Heshbon with
its pasture lands, and Jazer with its pasture
lands.

## CHAPTER 7

**Issachar.*** **1** The sons of Issachar were
Tola, Puah, Jashub, and Shimron: four.[v] **2** The
sons of Tola were Uzzi, Rephaiah, Jeriel, Jah-
mai, Ibsam, and Shemuel, warrior heads of the
ancestral houses of Tola. Their kindred numbered twenty-two thousand six hundred in the
time of David.[w] **3** The sons of Uzzi: Izarahiah.
The sons of Izarahiah were Michael, Obadiah,
Joel, and Isshiah. All five of these were chiefs.
**4** Their kindred, by ancestral houses, numbered thirty-six thousand men in organized military troops, since they had more wives and sons
**5** than their fellow tribesmen. In all the clans of
Issachar there was a total of eighty-seven thousand warriors in their family records.

**Benjamin.** **6** The sons of Benjamin were
Bela, Becher, and Jediael—three.[x] **7** The sons
of Bela were Ezbon, Uzzi, Uzziel, Jerimoth,
and Iri—five. They were heads of their ancestral houses and warriors. Their family records
listed twenty-two thousand and thirty-four.
**8** The sons of Becher were Zemirah, Joash,
Eliezer, Elioenai, Omri, Jeremoth, Abijah, Anathoth, and Alemeth—all these were sons of
Becher.[y] **9** Their family records listed twenty
thousand two hundred of their kindred who
were heads of their ancestral houses and warriors. **10** The sons of Jediael: Bilhan. The sons
of Bilhan were Jeush, Benjamin, Ehud,
Chenaanah, Zethan, Tarshish, and Ahishahar.
**11** All these were descendants of Jediael, heads
of ancestral houses and warriors. They numbered seventeen thousand two hundred men fit
for military service . . . Shupham and Hupham.[z]

**Dan, Naphtali and Manasseh.** **12** [a]The
sons of Dan: Hushim. **13** The sons of Naphtali
were Jahziel, Guni, Jezer, and Shallum. These
were descendants of Bilhah. **14** The sons of

v Gn 46, 13.
w Nm 26, 23f; Jgs 10, 1.
x 1 Chr 7, 6; Gn 46, 21; Nm 26, 38.
y 1 Chr 7, 8.
z Nm 26, 39.
a 12f: Gn 46, 24; Nm 26, 48f.
b 14-19: Nm 26, 29-32.
c Nm 26, 29; Jos 17, 1.

* 7, 1–40: The northern tribes.

Manasseh, whom his Aramean concubine
bore:[b] she bore Machir, the father of Gilead.[c]
15 Machir took a wife whose name was Maacah; his sister's name was Molecheth. Manasseh's second son was named Zelophehad, but to
Zelophehad only daughters were born.[d]
16 Maacah, Machir's wife, bore a son whom
she named Peresh. He had a brother named
Sheresh, whose sons were Ulam and Rakem.
17 The sons of Ulam: Bedan. These were the
descendants of Gilead, the son of Machir, the
son of Manasseh. 18 His sister Molecheth bore
Ishhod, Abiezer, and Mahlah. 19 The sons of
Shemida were Ahian, Shechem, Likhi, and
Aniam.

**Ephraim.** 20 [e]The sons of Ephraim: Shuthelah, whose son was Bered, whose son was
Tahath, whose son was Eleadah, whose son was
Tahath, 21 whose son was Zabad, Ephraim's
son Shuthelah, and Ezer and Elead, who were
born in the land, were slain by the inhabitants
of Gath because they had gone down to take
away their livestock. 22 Their father Ephraim
mourned a long time, but after his kinsmen had
come and comforted him, 23 he visited his
wife, who conceived and bore a son whom he
named Beriah, since evil had befallen his
house.[f] 24 He had a daughter, Sheerah, who
built lower and upper Beth-horon and Uzzen-
sheerah. 25 Zabad's son was Rephah, whose
son was Resheph, whose son was Telah, whose
son was Tahan, 26 whose son was Ladan,
whose son was Ammihud, whose son was
Elishama,[g] 27 whose son was Nun, whose son
was Joshua.

28 Their property and their dwellings were in
Bethel and its towns, Naaran to the east, Gezer
and its towns to the west, and also Shechem and
its towns as far as Ayyah and its towns.[h]
29 Manasseh, however, had possession of
Beth-shean and its towns, Taanach and its
towns, Megiddo and its towns, and Dor and its
towns. In these dwelt the descendants of Joseph, the son of Israel.[i]

**Asher.** 30 The sons of Asher were Imnah,
Iishvah, Ishvi, and Beriah; their sister was Serah.[j] 31 Beriah's sons were Heber and Malchiel, who was the father of Birzaith. 32 Heber
became the father of Japhlet, Shomer, Hotham,
and their sister Shua. 33 The sons of Japhlet
were Pasach, Bimhal, and Ashvath; these were
the sons of Japhlet. 34 The sons of Shomer
were Ahi, Rohgah, Jehubbah, and Aram.
35 The sons of his brother Hotham were Zophah, Imna, Shelesh, and Amal. 36 The sons of
Zophah were Suah, Harnepher, Shual, Beri,
Imrah, 37 Bezer, Hod, Shamma, Shilshah, Ithran, and Beera. 38 The sons of Jether were
Jephunneh, Pispa, and Ara. 39 The sons of Ulla
were Arah, Hanniel, and Rizia. 40 All these
were descendants of Asher, heads of ancestral
houses, distinguished men, warriors, and chiefs
among the princes. Their family records numbered twenty-six thousand men fit for military
service.

## CHAPTER 8

**Benjamin.*** 1 Benjamin became the father
of Bela, his first-born, Ashbel, the second son,
Aharah, the third,[k] 2 Nohah, the fourth, and
Rapha, the fifth. 3 The sons of Bela were Addar and Gera, the father of Ehud. 4 The sons of
Ehud were Abishua, Naaman, Ahoah,[l] 5 Gera,
Shephuphan, and Huram. 6 These were the
sons of Ehud, family heads over those who
dwelt in Geba and were deported to Manahath.
7 Also Naaman, Ahijah, and Gera. The last,
who led them into exile, became the father of
Uzza and Ahihud. 8 Shaharaim became a father
on the Moabite plateau after he had put away his
wives Hushim and Baara. 9 By his wife Hodesh
he became the father of Jobab, Zibia, Mesha,
Malcam, 10 Jeuz, Sachia, and Mirmah. These
were his sons, family heads. 11 By Hushim he
became the father of Abitub and Elpaal. 12 The
sons of Elpaal were Eber, Misham, Shemed,
who built Ono and Lod with its nearby towns,[m]
13 Beriah, and Shema. They were family heads
of those who dwelt in Aijalon, and they put the
inhabitants of Gath to flight. 14 Their brethren
were Elpaal, Shashak, and Jeremoth. 15 Zebadiah, Arad, Eder, 16 Michael, Ishpah, and
Joha were the sons of Beriah. 17 Zebadiah,
Meshullam, Hizki, Heber, 18 Ishmerai, Izliah,
and Jobab were the sons of Elpaal. 19 Jakim,
Zichri, Zabdi, 20 Elienai, Zillethai, Eliel,
21 Adaiah, Beraiah, and Shimrath were the
sons of Shimei. 22 Ishpan, Eber, Eliel, 23 Abdon, Zichri, Hanan, 24 Hananiah, Elam, An-
thothijah, 25 Iphdeiah, and Penuel were the
sons of Shashak. 26 Shamsherai, Shehariah,
Athaliah, 27 Jaareshiah, Elijah, and Zichri
were the sons of Jeroham. 28 These were family heads over their kindred, chiefs who dwelt in
Jerusalem.

29 [n]In Gibeon dwelt Jeiel, the founder of
Gibeon, whose wife's name was Maacah;
30 also his first-born son, Abdon, and Zur,
Kish, Baal, Ner, Nadab, 31 Gedor, Ahio,
Zecher, and Mikloth. 32 Mikloth became the

d Nm 26, 33; Jos 17, 3.
e Nm 26, 35.
f 1 Chr 8, 13.
g Nm 1, 10; 2, 18; 7, 48; 10, 22.
h Gn 12, 8; 1 Kgs 9, 16.
i Jos 17, 11.
j Gn 46, 17; Nm 26, 44ff.
k 1 Chr 7, 6; Gn 46, 21; Nm 26, 38ff.
l Jgs 3, 15.
m Neh 11, 35.
n 29-32: 1 Chr 9, 35-38.

* 8, 1–40: A second, variant list of the Benjaminites, with special prominence given to Saul's family (vv 33–40).

father of Shimeah. These, too, dwelt with their relatives in Jerusalem, opposite their fellow tribesmen. **33** [o]Ner became the father of Kish, and Kish became the father of Saul. Saul became the father of Jonathan, Malchishua, Abinadab, and Eshbaal.[p] **34** The son of Jonathan was Meribbaal, and Meribbaal became the father of Micah.[q] **35** The sons of Micah were Pithon, Melech, Tarea, and Ahaz. **36** Ahaz became the father of Jehoaddah, and Jehoaddah became the father of Alemeth, Azmaveth, and Zimri. Zimri became the father of Moza.[r] **37** Moza became the father of Binea, whose son was Raphah, whose son was Eleasah, whose son was Azel.[s] **38** Azel had six sons, whose names were Azrikam, his first-born, Ishmael, Sheariah, Azariah, Obadiah, and Hanan; all these were the sons of Azel. **39** The sons of Eshek, his brother, were Ulam, his first-born, Jeush, the second son, and Eliphelet, the third. **40** The sons of Ulam were combat archers, and many were their sons and grandsons: one hundred and fifty. All these were the descendants of Benjamin.

## CHAPTER 9

**1** Thus all Israel was inscribed in its family records which are recorded in the book of the kings of Israel.[t]

Now Judah had been carried in captivity to Babylon because of its rebellion. **2** [u]*The first to settle again in their cities and dwell there were certain lay Israelites, the priests, the Levites, and the temple slaves.[v]

**Jerusalemites.** **3** In Jerusalem lived Judahites and Benjaminites; also Ephraimites and Manassehites. **4** Among the Judahites was Uthai, son of Ammihud, son of Omri, son of Imri, son of Bani, one of the descendants of Perez, son of Judah. **5** Among the Shelanites were Asaiah, the first-born, and his sons. **6** Among the Zerahites were Jeuel and six hundred and ninety of their brethren. **7** Among the Benjaminites were Sallu, son of Meshullam, son of Hodaviah, son of Hassenuah; **8** Ibneiah, son of Jeroham; Elah, son of Uzzi, son of Michri; Meshullam, son of Shephatiah, son of Reuel, son of Ibnijah. **9** Their kindred of various families were nine hundred and fifty-six. All those named were heads of their ancestral houses.

**10** Among the priests were Jedaiah; Jehoiarib; Jachin; **11** Azariah, son of Hilkiah, son of Meshullam, son of Zadok, son of Meraioth, son of Ahitub, the ruler of the house of God; **12** Adaiah, son of Jeroham, son of Pashhur, son of Malchijah; Maasai, son of Adiel, son of Jahzerah, son of Meshullam, son of Meshillemith, son of Immer. **13** Their brethren, heads of their ancestral houses, were one thousand seven hundred and sixty, valiant for the work of the service of the house of God.

**14** Among the Levites were Shemaiah, son of Hasshub, son of Azrikam, son of Hashabiah, one of the descendants of Merari; **15** Bakbakkar; Heresh; Galal; Mattaniah, son of Mica, son of Zichri, a descendant of Asaph; **16** Obadiah, son of Shemaiah, son of Galal, a descendant of Jeduthun; and Berechiah, son of Asa, son of Elkanah, whose family lived in the villages of the Netophathites.

**17** The gatekeepers were Shallum, Akkub, Talmon, Ahiman, and their brethren; Shallum was the chief. **18** Previously they had stood guard at the king's gate on the east side; now they became gatekeepers for the encampments of the Levites. **19** Shallum, son of Kore, son of Ebiasaph, a descendant of Korah, and his brethren of the same ancestral house of the Korahites had as their assigned task the guarding of the threshold of the tent, just as their fathers had guarded the entrance to the encampment of the LORD. **20** Phinehas, son of Eleazar, had been their chief in times past—the LORD be with him![w] **21** Zechariah, son of Meshelemiah, guarded the gate of the meeting tent.[x] **22** In all, those who were chosen for gatekeepers at the threshold were two hundred and twelve. They were inscribed in the family records of their villages. David and Samuel the seer had established them in their position of trust. **23** Thus they and their sons kept guard over the gates of the house of the LORD, the house which was then a tent. **24** The gatekeepers were stationed at the four sides, to the east, the west, the north, and the south.[y] **25** Their kinsmen who lived in their own villages took turns in assisting them for seven-day periods,[z] **26** while the four chief gatekeepers were on constant duty. These were the Levites who also had charge of the chambers and treasures of the house of God. **27** At night they lodged about the house of God, for it was in their charge and they had the duty of opening it each morning.

**28** Some of them had charge of the liturgical equipment, tallying it as it was brought in and taken out. **29** Others were appointed to take care of the utensils and all the sacred vessels, as well as the fine flour, the wine, the oil, the

o 33-38: 1 Chr 9, 39-44.
p 1 Chr 10, 2; 1 Sm 9, 1; 14, 49. 51; 31, 2.
q 2 Sm 4, 4; 9, 6. 10. 12.
r 1 Chr 9, 42.
s 1 Chr 9, 43.
t 2 Chr 16, 11; 20, 34; 25, 26; 27, 7; 33, 18; 36, 8.
u 2-22: Neh 11, 3-19.
v Ezr 2, 70; 7, 7; Neh 11, 3.
w Ex 6, 25; Nm 25, 7. 11; Jgs 20, 28.
x 1 Chr 26, 2. 14.
y 1 Chr 26, 13.
z 2 Chr 23, 4f.

* 9, 2-34: The inhabitants of Jerusalem after the exile. A similar list, with many variants in the names, is given in Neh 11, 3-24.

frankincense, and the spices. **30** It was the sons
of priests, however, who mixed the spiced ointments.[a] **31** [b]Mattithiah, one of the Levites, the
first-born of Shallum the Koreite, was entrusted
with preparing the cakes. **32** Benaiah the Kohathite, one of their brethren, was in charge of
setting out the showbread each sabbath.[c]

**33** These were the chanters and the gatekeepers, family heads over the Levites. They stayed
in the chambers when free of duty, for day and
night they had to be ready for service. **34** These
were the levitical family heads over their kindred, chiefs who dwelt in Jerusalem.

## *II: The History of David*

**Genealogy of Saul.** **35** [d]In Gibeon dwelt
Jeiel, the founder of Gibeon, whose wife's
name was Maacah. **36** His first-born son was
Abdon; then came Zur, Kish, Baal, Ner, Nadab, **37** Gedor, Ahio, Zechariah, and Mikloth.
**38** Mikloth became the father of Shimeam.
These, too, with their brethren, dwelt opposite
their brethren in Jerusalem. **39** Ner became the
father of Kish, and Kish became the father of
Saul. Saul became the father of Jonathan, Malchishua, Abinadab, and Eshbaal. **40** The son of
Jonathan was Meribbaal, and Meribbaal became the father of Micah. **41** The sons of Micah were Pithon, Melech, Tahrea, and Ahaz.
**42** Ahaz became the father of Jehoaddah, and
Jehoaddah became the father of Alemeth, Azmaveth, and Zimri. Zimri became the father of
Moza. **43** Moza became the father of Binea,
whose son was Rephaiah, whose son was Eleasah, whose son was Azel. **44** Azel had six sons,
whose names were Azrikam, his first-born, Ishmael, Sheariah, Azariah, Obadiah, and Hanan;
these were the sons of Azel.

### CHAPTER 10

**His Death and Burial.** **1** [e]Now the Philistines were at war with Israel; the Israelites fled
before the Philistines, and a number of them
fell, slain on Mount Gilboa. **2** The Philistines
pressed hard after Saul and his sons. When the
Philistines had killed Jonathan, Abinadab, and
Malchishua, sons of Saul, **3** the whole fury of
the battle descended upon Saul. Then the archers found him, and wounded him with their
arrows.

**4** Saul said to his armor-bearer, "Draw your
sword and thrust me through with it, that these
uncircumcised may not come and maltreat me."
But the armor-bearer, in great fear, refused. So
Saul took his own sword and fell on it; **5** and
seeing him dead, the armor-bearer also fell on
his sword and died. **6** Thus, with Saul and his
three sons, his whole house died at one time.
**7** When all the Israelites who were in the valley
saw that Saul and his sons had died in the rout,
they left their cities and fled; thereupon the Philistines came and occupied them.

**8** On the following day, when the Philistines
came to strip the slain, they found Saul and his
sons where they had fallen on Mount Gilboa.
**9** They stripped him, cut off his head, and took
his armor; these they sent throughout the land of
the Philistines to convey the good news to their
idols and their people. **10** His armor they put in
the house of their gods, but his skull they impaled on the temple of Dagon.

**11** When all the inhabitants of Jabesh-gilead
had heard what the Philistines had done to Saul,
**12** its warriors rose to a man, recovered the
bodies of Saul and his sons, and brought them
to Jabesh. They buried their bones under the oak
of Jabesh, and fasted seven days.[f]

**13** *Thus Saul died because of his rebellion
against the LORD in disobeying his command,
and also because he had sought counsel of a
necromancer,[g] **14** and had not rather inquired
of the LORD. Therefore the LORD slew him, and
transferred his kingdom to David, the son of
Jesse.[h]

### CHAPTER 11

**David Is Made King.** **1** [i]Then all Israel
gathered about David in Hebron, and they said:
"Surely, we are of the same bone and flesh as
you. **2** Even formerly, when Saul was still the
king, it was you who led Israel in all its battles.
And now the LORD, your God, has said to you,
'You shall shepherd my people Israel and be
ruler over them.' "[j] **3** Then all the elders of
Israel came to the king at Hebron, and there
David made a covenant with them in the presence of the LORD; and they anointed him king
over Israel, in accordance with the word of the
LORD as revealed through Samuel.[k]

**Jerusalem Captured.** **4** Then David and
all Israel went to Jerusalem, that is, Jebus,
where the natives of the land were called Jebusites.[l] **5** The inhabitants of Jebus said to David,
"You shall not enter here." David nevertheless
captured the fortress of Sion, which is the City

a Ex 30, 22-33.
b 31f: 1 Chr 23, 29; Lv 2, 1ff; 6, 13ff; 7, 11.
c Ex 25, 30; Lv 24, 5-8.
d 35-44: 1 Chr 8, 29-38.
e 1-12: 1 Sm 31, 1-13.
f 2 Sm 2, 5.
g Dt 18, 10ff; 1 Sm 13, 13f; 15, 3. 11. 26.
h 1 Sm 15, 28; 2 Sm 3, 9f.
i 1-9: 2 Sm 5, 1-10.
j 1 Sm 18, 5. 13-16. 30; 19, 8.
k 1 Sm 16, 1. 13; 2 Sm 2, 4.
l Jos 15, 8; Jgs 1, 21; 19, 10f.

*

10, 13f: The Chronicler's comment on why Saul met his tragic end: he had disobeyed the Lord's command given through the prophet Samuel (1 Sm 15, 3–9), and had sought counsel of a necromancer (1 Sm 28, 6–19), contrary to the Mosaic law against necromancy (Dt 18, 10f).

of David. **6** David said, "Whoever strikes the Jebusites first shall be made the chief commander." Joab, the son of Zeruiah, was the first to go up; and so he became chief.[m] **7** David took up his residence in the fortress, which thenceforth was called the City of David. **8** He rebuilt the city on all sides, from the Millo all the way around, while Joab restored the rest of the city.[n] **9** David became more and more powerful, for the LORD of hosts was with him.

**David's Warriors.** **10** [o]These were David's chief warriors who, together with all Israel, supported him in his reign in order to make him true king, even as the LORD had commanded concerning Israel. **11** Here is the list of David's warriors:

Ishbaal, the son of Hachamoni, chief of the Three.* He brandished his spear against three hundred, whom he slew in a single encounter.

**12** Next to him Eleazar, the son of Dodo the Ahohite, one of the Three warriors.[p] **13** He was with David at Pasdammim, where the Philistines had massed for battle. The plowland was fully planted with barley, but its defenders were retreating before the Philistines.[q] **14** He made a stand on the sown ground, kept it safe, and cut down the Philistines. Thus the LORD brought about a great victory.

**15** Three of the Thirty chiefs went down to the rock, to David, who was in the cave of Adullam while the Philistines were encamped in the valley of Rephaim.[r] **16** David was then in the stronghold, and a Philistine garrison was at Bethlehem. **17** David expressed a desire: "Oh, that someone would give me a drink from the cistern that is by the gate at Bethlehem!" **18** Thereupon the Three broke through the encampment of the Philistines, drew water from the cistern by the gate at Bethlehem, and carried it back to David. But David refused to drink it. Instead, he poured it out as a libation to the LORD, **19** saying, "God forbid that I should do such a thing! Could I drink the blood of these men who risked their lives?" For at the risk of their lives they brought it; and so he refused to drink it. Such deeds as these the Three warriors performed.

**20** [s]Abishai, the brother of Joab. He was the chief of the Thirty;* he brandished his spear against three hundred, and slew them. Thus he had a reputation like that of the Three.[t] **21** He was twice as famous as any of the Thirty and became their commander, but he did not attain to the Three.

**22** Benaiah, the son of Jehoiada, a valiant man of mighty deeds, from Kabzeel. He killed the two sons of Ariel of Moab, and also, on a snowy day, he went down and killed the lion in the cistern. **23** He likewise slew the Egyptian, a huge man five cubits tall. The Egyptian carried a spear that was like a weaver's heddle-bar, but he came against him with a staff, wrested the spear from the Egyptian's hand, and killed him with his own spear. **24** Such deeds as these of Benaiah, the son of Jehoiada, gave him a reputation like that of the Three. **25** He was more famous than any of the Thirty, but he did not attain to the Three. David put him in charge of his bodyguard.[u]

**26** Also these warriors: Asahel, the brother of Joab; Elhanan, son of Dodo, from Bethlehem;[v] **27** Shammoth, from En-harod; Helez, from Palti; **28** Ira, son of Ikkesh, from Tekoa; Abiezer, from Anathoth; **29** Sibbecai, from Husha; Ilai, from Ahoh;[w] **30** Maharai, from Netophah; Heled, son of Baanah, from Netophah;[x] **31** Ithai, son of Ribai, from Gibeah of Benjamin; Benaiah, from Pirathon;[y] **32** Hurai, from the valley of Gaash; Abiel, from Betharabah; **33** Azmaveth, from Bahurim; Eliahba, from Shaalbon; **34** Jashen the Gunite; Jonathan, son of Shagee, from Enharod; **35** Ahiam, son of Sachar, from Enharod; Elipheleth, son of **36** Ahasabi, from Bethmaacah; Ahijah, from Gilo; **37** Hezro, from Carmel; Naarai, the son of Ezbai; **38** Joel, brother of Nathan, from Rehob, the Gadite; **39** Zelek the Ammonite; Naharai, from Beeroth, the armor-bearer of Joab, son of Zeruiah; **40** Ira, from Jattir; Gareb, from Jattir; **41** Uriah the Hittite; Zabad, son of Ahlai, **42** and, in addition to the Thirty, Adina, son of Shiza, the Reubenite, chief of the tribe of Reuben; **43** Hanan, from Beth-maacah; Joshaphat the Mithnite; **44** Uzzia, from Ashterath; Shama and Jeiel, sons of Hotham, from Aroer; **45** Jediael, son of Shimri, and Joha, his brother, the Tizite; **46** Eliel the Mahavite; Jeribai and Joshaviah, sons of Elnaam; Ithmah, from Moab; **47** Eliel, Obed, and Jaasiel the Mezobian.

## CHAPTER 12

**David's Early Followers.** **1** The following men came to David in Ziklag while he was still under banishment from Saul, son of Kish; they, too, were among the warriors who helped him in his battles.[z] **2** They were archers who

m 2 Sm 2, 13ff; 8, 16.
n 1 Kgs 9, 15. 24; 11, 27; 2 Chr 32, 5.
o 10-41: 2 Sm 23, 8-39.
p 1 Chr 27, 4.
q 1 Sm 17, 1.
r 1 Chr 14, 9; 2 Sm 5, 18. 22.
s 20f: 2 Sm 23, 18f.
t 1 Chr 18, 12; 1 Sm 26, 6ff; 2 Sm 16, 9; 18, 2; 21, 17.
u 2 Sm 8, 18; 20, 23.
v 1 Chr 2, 16; 27, 7.
w 1 Chr 27, 11.
x 1 Chr 27, 13.
y 1 Chr 27, 14.
z 1 Sm 27, 1-7.

*11, 11f: The Three: the Chronicler names only two of them: Ishbaal and Eleazar. According to 2 Sm 23, 8–12, the Three were Ishbaal, Eleazar, and Shammah.

11, 20: The Thirty: listed by name in vv 26–47. The list given in 2 Sm 23, 8–39 often differs in names and spellings; for the numbers, see the note there.

could use either the right or the left hand, both
in slinging stones and in shooting arrows with
the bow. They were some of Saul's kinsmen,
from Benjamin. **3** Ahiezer was their chief,
along with Joash, both sons of Shemaah of Gibeah; also Jeziel and Pelet, sons of Azmaveth;
Beracah; Jehu, from Anathoth;[a] **4** Ishmaiah the
Gibeonite, a warrior on the level of the Thirty,
and in addition to their number: **5** Jeremiah;
Jahaziel; Johanan; Jozabad, from Gederah;
**6** Eluzai; Jerimoth; Bealiah; Shemariah; Shephatiah the Haruphite; **7** Elkanah, Isshiah, Azarel, Joezer, and Ishbaal, who were Korahites;
**8** Joelah, finally, and Zebadiah, sons of Jeroham, from Gedor.

**9** Some of the Gadites also went over to David when he was at the stronghold in the wilderness. They were valiant warriors, experienced
soldiers equipped with shield and spear, who
bore themselves like lions, and were as swift as
the gazelles on the mountains.[b] **10** Ezer was
their chief, Obadiah was second, Eliab third,
**11** Mishmannah fourth, Jeremiah fifth, **12** Attai sixth, Eliel seventh, **13** Johanan eighth, Elzabad ninth, **14** Jeremiah tenth, and Machban-
nai eleventh. **15** These Gadites were army
commanders, the lesser placed over hundreds
and the greater over thousands. **16** It was they
who crossed over the Jordan when it was overflowing both its banks in the first month, and
dispersed all who were in the valleys to the east
and to the west.

**17** Some Benjaminites and Judahites also
came to David at the stronghold. **18** David went
out to meet them and addressed them in these
words: "If you come peacefully, to help me, I
am of a mind to have you join me. But if you
have come to betray me to my enemies though
my hands have done no wrong, may the God of
our fathers see and punish you."

**19** Then spirit enveloped Amasai, the chief
of the Thirty, who spoke:

"We are yours, O David,
we are with you, O son of Jesse.
Peace, peace to you,
and peace to him who helps you;
your God it is who helps you."

So David received them and placed them among
the leaders of his troops.

**20** Men from Manasseh also deserted to David when he came with the Philistines to battle
against Saul. However, he did not help the Philistines, for their lords took counsel and sent him
home, saying, "At the cost of our heads he will
desert to his master Saul." **21** As he was returning to Ziklag, therefore, these deserted to
him from Manasseh: Adnah, Jozabad, Jediael,
Michael, Jozabad, Elihu, and Zillethai, chiefs
of thousands of Manasseh. **22** They helped David by taking charge of his troops, for they were
all warriors and became commanders of his
army. **23** And from day to day men kept coming to David's help until there was a vast encampment, like an encampment of angels.

**The Assembly at Hebron.** **24** This is the
muster of the detachments of armed troops that
came to David at Hebron to transfer to him
Saul's kingdom, as the LORD had ordained.
**25** *Judahites bearing shields and spears: six
thousand eight hundred armed troops. **26** Of
the Simeonites, warriors fit for battle: seven
thousand one hundred. **27** Of the Levites: four
thousand six hundred, **28** along with Jehoiada,
leader of the line of Aaron, with another three
thousand seven hundred, **29** and Zadok, a
young warrior, with twenty-two princes of his
father's house. **30** Of the Benjaminites, the
brethren of Saul: three thousand—until this
time, most of them had held their allegiance to
the house of Saul. **31** Of the Ephraimites: twenty thousand eight hundred warriors, men renowned in their ancestral houses. **32** Of the
half-tribe of Manasseh: eighteen thousand, designated by name to come and make David king.
**33** Of the Issacharites, their chiefs who were
endowed with an understanding of the times and
who knew what Israel had to do: two hundred
chiefs, together with all their brethren under
their command. **34** From Zebulun, men fit for
military service, set in battle array with every
kind of weapon for war: fifty thousand men
rallying with a single purpose. **35** From Naphtali: one thousand captains, and with them,
armed with shield and lance, thirty-seven thousand men. **36** Of the Danites, set in battle array:
twenty-eight thousand six hundred. **37** From
Asher, fit for military service and set in battle
array: forty thousand. **38** From the other side of
the Jordan, of the Reubenites, Gadites, and the
half-tribe of Manasseh, men equipped with every kind of weapon of war: one hundred and
twenty thousand.

**39** All these soldiers, drawn up in battle order, came to Hebron with the resolute intention
of making David king over all Israel. The rest
of Israel was likewise of one mind to make
David king. **40** They remained with David for
three days, feasting and drinking, for their
brethren had prepared for them. **41** Moreover,
their neighbors from as far as Issachar, Zebulun, and Naphtali came bringing food on asses,

a 1 Chr 27, 12. b Dt 33, 20.

* 12, 25–38: The Chronicler fills out the pageantry of joyous occasions in keeping with his much later appreciation of the significance of the event in the history of God's people: the numbers in attendance at David's crowning in Hebron (cf 2 Sm 5, 1ff) are recounted in the same spirit of enthusiasm which in v 23 compares David's band of desert freebooters to a numerous encampment of angels.

camels, mules, and oxen—provisions in great
quantity of meal, pressed figs, raisins, wine,
oil, oxen, and sheep. For there was rejoicing in
Israel.

## CHAPTER 13

**Transfer of the Ark.** 1 [c]After David had
taken counsel with his commanders of thousands and of hundreds, that is to say, with every
one of his leaders, 2 he said to the whole assembly of Israel: "If it seems good to you, and is
so decreed by the LORD our God, let us summon
the rest of our brethren from all the districts of
Israel, and also the priests and the Levites from
their cities with pasture lands, that they may join
us;[d] 3 and let us bring the ark of our God here
among us, for in the days of Saul we did not visit
it." 4 And the whole assembly agreed to do
this, for the idea was pleasing to all the people.
5 Then David assembled all Israel, from Shihor of Egypt* to Labo of Hamath, to bring the
ark of God from Kiriath-jearim.[e] 6 David and
all Israel went up to Baalah, that is, to Kiriath-jearim, of Judah, to bring back the ark of
God, which was known by the name "LORD
enthroned upon the cherubim."[f] 7 They transported the ark of God on a new cart from the
house of Abinadab; Uzzah and Ahio were guiding the cart, 8 while David and all Israel danced
before God with great enthusiasm, amid songs
and music on lyres, harps, tambourines, cymbals, and trumpets.
9 As they reached the threshing floor of Chidon,* Uzzah stretched out his hand to steady the
ark, for the oxen were upsetting it. 10 Then the
LORD became angry with Uzzah and struck him;
he died there in God's presence, because he had
laid his hand on the ark. 11 David was disturbed because the LORD's anger had broken out
against Uzzah. Therefore that place has been
called Perez-uzza* even to this day.
12 David was now afraid of God, and he
said, "How can I bring the ark of God with
me?" 13 Therefore he did not take the ark back
with him to the City of David, but he took it
instead to the house of Obed-edom the Gittite.
14 The ark of God remained in the house of
Obed-edom with his family for three months,
and the LORD blessed Obed-edom's household
and all that he possessed.[g]

## CHAPTER 14

**David in Jerusalem.** 1 [h]Hiram, king of
Tyre, sent envoys to David along with masons
and carpenters, and cedar wood to build him a
house.[i] 2 David now understood that the LORD
had truly confirmed him as king over Israel, for
his kingdom was greatly exalted for the sake of
his people Israel. 3 [j]David took other wives in
Jerusalem and became the father of more sons
and daughters. 4 These are the names of those
who were born to him in Jerusalem: Shammua,
Shobab, Nathan, Solomon, 5 Ibhar, Elishua,
Elpelet, 6 Nogah, Nepheg, Japhia, 7 Elishama, Beeliada, and Eliphelet.

**The Philistine Wars.** 8 When the Philistines had heard that David was anointed king
over all Israel, they went up in unison to seek
him out. But when David heard of this, he
marched out against them. 9 Meanwhile the
Philistines had come and raided the valley of
Rephaim.[k] 10 David inquired of God, "Shall I
advance against the Philistines, and will you
deliver them into my power?" The LORD answered him, "Advance, for I will deliver them
into your power." 11 They advanced, therefore, to Baal-perazim, and David defeated them
there. Then David said, "God has used me to
break through my enemies just as water breaks
through a dam." Therefore that place was
called Baal-perazim. 12 The Philistines had left
their gods there, and David ordered them to be
burnt.[l]
13 Once again the Philistines raided the valley, 14 and again David inquired of God. But
God answered him: "Do not try to pursue them,
but go around them and come upon them from
the direction of the mastic trees. 15 When you
hear the sound of marching in the tops of the
mastic trees, then go forth to battle, for God has
already gone before you to strike the army of the
Philistines." 16 David did as God commanded
him, and they routed the Philistine army from
Gibeon to Gezer.
17 Thus David's fame was spread abroad
through every land, and the LORD made all the
nations fear him.

## CHAPTER 15

**The Ark Brought to Jerusalem.** 1 David
built houses for himself in the City of David and
prepared a place for the ark of God, pitching a
tent for it there. 2 At that time he said, "No one
may carry the ark of God except the Levites, for
the LORD chose them to carry the ark of the

c 1-14: 2 Sm 6, 1-11.
d Nm 35, 1ff; Jos 14, 4; 21, 2ff.
e 1 Chr 15, 3; Jos 13, 3. 5; 1 Sm 6, 21; 7, 1f; 2 Sm 6, 1-11.
f Jos 15, 9; 18, 14; 1 Sm 4, 4; 7, 1.
g 1 Chr 26, 4f.
h 1-16: 2 Sm 5, 11-25.
i 1 Kgs 5, 1; 2 Chr 2, 3.
j 3-7: 1 Chr 3, 5-8; 2 Sm 5, 13-16.
k 1 Chr 11, 15.
l Dt 7, 5. 25.
m Nm 1, 50; 7, 9; Dt 10, 8; 31, 25; 1 Sm 6, 15; Jos 3, 8.

*

13, 5: Shihor of Egypt: the eastern branch of the Nile delta. Labo of Hamath: in southern Syria.

13, 9: Chidon: in 2 Sm 6, 6, Nodan.

13, 11: Perez-uzza: A Hebrew term meaning "the breaking out against Uzza."

LORD and to minister to him forever."[m] 3 Then David assembled all Israel in Jerusalem to bring the ark of the LORD to the place which he had prepared for it.[n] 4 David also called together the sons of Aaron and the Levites: 5 of the sons of Kohath, Uriel, their chief, and one hundred and twenty of his brethren; 6 of the sons of Merari, Asaiah, their chief, and two hundred and twenty of his brethren; 7 of the sons of Gershon, Joel, their chief, and one hundred and thirty of his brethren; 8 of the sons of Elizaphan, Shemaiah, their chief, and two hundred of his brethren; 9 of the sons of Hebron, Eliel, their chief, and eighty of his brethren; 10 of the sons of Uzziel, Amminadab, their chief, and one hundred and twelve of his brethren.

11 David summoned the priests Zadok and Abiathar, and the Levites Uriel, Asaiah, Joel, Shemaiah, Eliel, and Amminadab,[o] 12 and said to them: "You, the heads of the levitical families, must sanctify yourselves along with your brethren and bring the ark of the LORD, the God of Israel, to the place which I have prepared for it.[p] 13 Because you were not with us the first time, the wrath of the LORD our God burst upon us, for we did not seek him aright."[q] 14 Accordingly, the priests and the Levites sanctified themselves to bring up the ark of the LORD, the God of Israel. 15 The Levites bore the ark of God on their shoulders with poles, as Moses had ordained according to the word of the LORD[r]. 16 David commanded the chiefs of the Levites to appoint their brethren as chanters, to play on musical instruments, harps, lyres, and cymbals, to make a loud sound of rejoicing.[s] 17 Therefore the Levites appointed Heman, son of Joel, and, among his brethren, Asaph, son of Berechiah; and among the sons of Merari, their brethren, Ethan, son of Kushaiah;[t] 18 and, together with these, their brethren of the second rank: the gatekeepers Zechariah, Uzziel, Shemiramoth, Jehiel, Unni, Eliab, Benaiah, Maaseiah, Mattithiah, Eliphelehu, Mikneiah, Obededom, and Jeiel. 19 The chanters, Heman, Asaph, and Ethan, sounded brass cymbals. 20 Zechariah, Uzziel, Shemiramoth, Jehiel, Unni, Eliab, Maaseiah, and Benaiah played on harps set to "Alamoth."* 21 But Mattithiah, Eliphelehu, Mikneiah, Obed-edom, and Jeiel led the chant on lyres set to "the eighth." 22 Chenaniah was the chief of the Levites in the chanting; he directed the chanting, for he was skillful.[u] 23 Berechiah and Elkanah were gatekeepers before the ark. 24 The priests, Shebaniah, Joshaphat, Nethanel, Amasai, Zechariah, Benaiah, and Eliezer, sounded the trumpets before the ark of God. Obed-edom and Jeiel were also gatekeepers before the ark.[v]

25 [w]Thus David, the elders of Israel, and the commanders of thousands went to bring up the ark of the covenant of the LORD with joy from the house of Obed-edom. 26 While the Levites, with God's help, were bearing the ark of the covenant of the LORD, seven bulls and seven rams were sacrificed.[x] 27 David was clothed in a robe of fine linen, as were all the Levites who carried the ark, the singers, and Chenaniah, the leader of the chant; David was also wearing a linen ephod.[y] 28 Thus all Israel brought back the ark of the covenant of the LORD with joyful shouting, and to the sound of horns, trumpets, and cymbals, and the music of harps and lyres. 29 But as the ark of the covenant of the LORD was entering the City of David, Michal, daughter of Saul, looked down from her window, and when she saw King David leaping and dancing, she despised him in her heart.[z]

## CHAPTER 16

1 [a]They brought in the ark of God and set it within the tent which David had pitched for it. Then they offered up holocausts and peace offerings to God.[b] 2 When David had finished offering up the holocausts and peace offerings, he blessed the people in the name of the LORD, 3 and distributed to every Israelite, to every man and to every woman, a loaf of bread, a piece of meat, and a raisin cake.

**The Ministering Levites.** 4 He now appointed certain Levites to minister before the ark of the LORD, to celebrate, thank, and praise the LORD, the God of Israel.[c] 5 Asaph was their chief, and second to him were Zechariah, Uzziel, Shemira-moth, Jehiel, Mattithiah, Eliab, Benaiah, Obed-edom, and Jeiel. These were to play on harps and lyres, while Asaph was to sound the cymbals, 6 and the priests Benaiah and Jahaziel were to be the regular trumpeters before the ark of the covenant of God.

7 Then, on that same day, David appointed Asaph and his brethren to sing for the first time these praises of the LORD:

8 *Give thanks to the LORD, invoke his
name;[d]

n 1 Chr 13, 5; 2 Sm 6, 15. 17.
o 1 Chr 16, 39; 2 Sm 8, 17; 15, 29. 35.
p 2 Chr 29, 5. 15. 34; 30, 3. 15. 24.
q 1 Chr 13, 3.
r Ex 25, 13ff; Nm 1, 50; 7, 9; 2 Chr 35, 3.
s 1 Chr 13, 8; 16, 5; 2 Chr 5, 12; 29, 25; Neh 12, 27.
t 1 Chr 6, 31-47; 25, 1-8.
u 1 Chr 26, 29.
v Nm 10, 8; Jos 6, 4ff.
w 25-29: 2 Sm 6, 12-16.
x 2 Sm 6, 17; 2 Chr 29, 21.
y 1 Sm 2, 18; 2 Sm 6, 14.
z 2 Sm 6, 20ff.
a 1-3: 2 Sm 6, 17ff.
b 1 Chr 15, 1.
c Sir 47, 9.
d 8-22: Ps 105, 1-15.

15, 20: Alamoth: a musical term (literally, "young women") of uncertain meaning, occurring also in Ps 46, 1, where it is rendered as virgins. Perhaps it may mean something like "soprano," whereas the term "eighth" (Hebrew sheminith, v 21) may then mean "bass"; cf Pss 6, 1; 12, 1.

16, 8–36: A hymn composed of parts, with textual variants,

make known among the nations his deeds.
9 Sing to him, sing his praise,
proclaim all his wondrous deeds.
10 Glory in his holy name;
rejoice, O hearts that seek the LORD!
11 Look to the LORD in his strength;
seek to serve him constantly.
12 Recall the wondrous deeds that he has
wrought,
his portents, and the judgments he has
uttered,
13 You descendants of Israel, his servants,
sons of Jacob, his chosen ones!

14 He, the LORD, is our God;
throughout the earth his judgments
prevail.
15 He remembers forever his covenant
which he made binding for a thousand
generations—
16 Which he entered into with Abraham
and by his oath to Isaac;
17 Which he established for Jacob by statute,
for Israel as an everlasting covenant,
18 Saying, "To you will I give the land of
Canaan
as your alloted inheritance."

19 When they were few in number,
a handful, and strangers there,
20 Wandering from nation to nation,
from one kingdom to another people,
21 He let no one oppress them,
and for their sake he rebuked kings:
22 "Touch not my anointed,
and to my prophets do no harm."

23 [e]Sing to the LORD, all the earth,
announce his salvation, day after day.
24 Tell his glory among the nations;
among all peoples, his wondrous deeds.
25 For great is the LORD and highly to be
praised;
and awesome is he, beyond all gods.
26 For all the gods of the nations are things of
nought,
but the LORD made the heavens.
27 Splendor and majesty go before him;
praise and joy are in his holy place.

28 Give to the LORD, you families of nations,
give to the LORD glory and praise;
29 Give to the LORD the glory due his name!
Bring gifts, and enter his presence;
worship the LORD in holy attire.
30 Tremble before him, all the earth;
he has made the world firm, not to be
moved.

31 Let the heavens be glad and the earth
rejoice;
let them say among the nations: The LORD
is king.
32 Let the sea and what fills it resound;
let the plains rejoice and all that is in
them!
33 Then shall all the trees of the forest exult
before the LORD, for he comes:
he comes to rule the earth.

34 [f]Give thanks to the LORD, for he is good,
for his kindness endures forever;
35 And say, "Save us, O God, our savior,
gather us and deliver us from the nations,
That we may give thanks to your holy name
and glory in praising you."
36 Blessed be the LORD, the God of Israel,
through all eternity!
Let all the people say, Amen! Alleluia.

37 Then David left Asaph and his brethren
there before the ark of the covenant of the LORD
to minister before the ark regularly according to
the daily ritual; 38 he also left there Obed-edom
and sixty-eight of his brethren, including
Obed-edom, son of Jeduthun, and Hosah, to be
gatekeepers.[g]
39 But the priest Zadok and his priestly
brethren he left before the Dwelling of the LORD
on the high place at Gibeon,[h] 40 to offer holocausts to the LORD on the altar of holocausts
regularly, morning and evening, and to do all
that is written in the law of the LORD which he
has decreed for Israel.[i] 41 With them were Heman and Jeduthun and the others who were
chosen and designated by name to give thanks
to the LORD, "because his kindness endures
forever,"[j] 42 with trumpets and cymbals for
accompaniment, and instruments for the sacred
chant. The sons of Jeduthun kept the gate.[k]
43 Then all the people departed, each to his
own home, and David returned to bless his
household.[l]

## CHAPTER 17

**The Oracle of Nathan.** 1 [m]After David
had taken up residence in his house, he said to
Nathan the prophet, "See, I am living in a house
of cedar, but the ark of the covenant of the LORD
dwells under tentcloth."[n] 2 Nathan replied to
David, "Do, therefore, whatever you desire,
for God is with you."
3 But that same night the word of God came
to Nathan: 4 "Go and tell my servant David,
Thus says the LORD: It is not you who are to
build a house for me to dwell in.[o] 5 For I have

e 23-33: Ps 96, 1-13.
f 34ff: Ps 106, 1. 47f.
g 1 Chr 15, 24.
h 1 Kgs 3, 4.
i Ex 29, 38-42; Lv 6, 9; Nm 28, 3. 6; 2 Chr 13, 11.
j 2 Chr 5, 12; 7, 3. 6; 20, 21; Ezr 3, 11.
k 2 Chr 29, 27.
l 2 Sm 6, 19f.
m 1-27: 2 Sm 7, 1-29.
n 1 Chr 15, 1; 2 Sm 5, 11.
o 1 Chr 28, 3; 1 Kgs 8, 19.

* from several Psalms; vv 8–22 = Ps 105, 1–15; vv 23–33 = Ps 96, 1–13; vv 34–36 = Ps 106, 1. 47f.

never dwelt in a house, from the time when I led
Israel onward, even to this day, but I have been
lodging in tent or pavilion **6** as long as I have
wandered about with all of Israel. Did I ever say
a word to any of the judges of Israel whom I
commanded to guide my people, such as, 'Why
have you not built me a house of cedar?'
**7** Therefore, tell my servant David, Thus says
the LORD of hosts: I took you from the pasture,
from following the sheep, that you might become ruler over my people Israel.[p] **8** I was with
you wherever you went, and I cut down all your
enemies before you. I will make your name
great like that of the greatest on the earth. **9** I
will assign a place for my people Israel and I
will plant them in it to dwell there henceforth
undisturbed; nor shall wicked men ever again
oppress them, as they did at first, **10** and during
all the time when I appointed judges over my
people Israel. And I will subdue all your enemies. Moreover, I declare to you that I, the
LORD, will build you a house; **11** so that when
your days have been completed and you must
join your fathers, I will raise up your offspring
after you who will be one of your own sons, and
I will establish his kingdom.[q] **12** He it is who
shall build me a house, and I will establish his
throne forever.[r] **13** I will be a father to him,
and he shall be a son to me, and I will not
withdraw my favor from him as I withdrew it
from him who preceded you;[s] **14** but I will
maintain him in my house and in my kingdom
forever, and his throne shall be firmly established forever.''

**15** All these words and this whole vision Nathan related exactly to David.

**David's Thanksgiving.** **16** Then David
came in and sat in the LORD's presence, saying:
''Who am I, O LORD God, and what is my
family, that you should have brought me as far
as I have come? **17** And yet, even this you now
consider too little, O God! For you have made
a promise regarding your servant's family
reaching into the distant future, and you have
looked on me as henceforth the most notable of
men, O LORD God.[t] **18** What more can David
say to you? You know your servant. **19** O
LORD, for your servant's sake and in keeping
with your purpose, you have done this great
thing. **20** O LORD, there is no one like you and
there is no God but you, just as we have always
understood.[u]

**21** ''Is there, like your people Israel, whom
you redeemed from Egypt, another nation on
earth whom a god went to redeem as his people?
You won for yourself a name for great and
awesome deeds by driving out the nations before your people.[v] **22** You made your people
Israel your own forever, and you, O LORD,
became their God. **23** Therefore, O LORD, may
the promise that you have uttered concerning
your servant and his house remain firm forever.
Bring about what you have promised, **24** that
your renown as LORD of hosts, God of Israel,
may be great and abide forever, while the house
of David, your servant, is established in your
presence.

**25** ''Because you, O my God, have revealed
to your servant that you will build him a house,
your servant has made bold to pray before you.[w]
**26** Since you, O LORD, are truly God and have
promised this good thing to your servant,
**27** and since you have deigned to bless the
house of your servant, so that it will remain
forever—since it is you, O LORD, who blessed
it, it is blessed forever.''[x]

## CHAPTER 18

**David's Victories.** **1** [y]After this, David defeated the Philistines and subdued them; and he
took Gath and its towns away from the control
of the Philistines. **2** He also defeated Moab,
and the Moabites became his subjects, paying
tribute.

**3** David then defeated Hadadezer, king of
Zobah toward Hamath, when the latter was on
his way to set up his victory stele at the river
Euphrates. **4** David took from him twenty thousand foot soldiers, one thousand chariots, and
seven thousand horsemen. Of the chariot
horses, David hamstrung all but one hundred.[z]
**5** The Arameans of Damascus came to the aid
of Hadadezer, king of Zobah, but David also
slew twenty-two thousand of their men. **6** Then
David set up garrisons in the Damascus region
of Aram, and the Arameans became his subjects, paying tribute. Thus the LORD made David victorious in all his campaigns.

**7** David took the golden shields that were
carried by Hadadezer's attendants and brought
them to Jerusalem. **8** He likewise took away
from Tibhath and Cun, cities of Hadadezer,
large quantities of bronze, which Solomon later
used to make the bronze sea and the pillars and
the vessels of bronze.[a]

**9** When Tou, king of Hamath, heard that
David had defeated the entire army of Hadadezer, king of Zobah, **10** he sent his son Hadoram
to wish King David well and to congratulate him
on having waged a victorious war against Hadadezer; for Hadadezer had been at war with
Tou. He also sent David gold, silver and bronze
utensils of every sort.[b] **11** These also King Da-

p 1 Sm 16, 11.
q 2 Sm 7, 12f.
r 1 Chr 22, 10; 28, 6. 10.
s 2 Sm 7, 14.
t 2 Sm 7, 19.
u Sir 36, 4.
v Dt 4, 7; 2 Sm 7, 23.
w 2 Sm 7, 27.
x Nm 22, 6.
y 1-13: 2 Sm 8, 1-14.
z 2 Sm 8, 14; Jos 11, 6. 9.
a 2 Sm 8, 8; 1 Kgs 7, 15. 23. 27.
b 2 Sm 8, 10.

vid consecrated to the LORD along with all the
silver and gold that he had taken from the nations: from Edom, Moab, the Ammonites, the
Philistines, and Amalek.
**12** Abishai, the son of Zeruiah, also slew
eighteen thousand Edomites in the Valley of
Salt.[c] **13** He set up garrisons in Edom, and all
the Edomites became David's subjects. Thus
the LORD made David victorious in all his campaigns.

**David's Officials.** **14** [d]David reigned over
all Israel and dispensed justice and right to all
his people. **15** Joab, son of Zeruiah, was in
command of the army; Jehoshaphat, son of Ahilud, was herald;[e] **16** Zadok, son of Ahitub, and
Ahimelech, son of Abiathar, were priests;*
Shavsha was scribe;[f] **17** Benaiah, son of Jehoiada, was in command of the Cherethites and the
Pelethites; and David's sons were the chief assistants to the king.*[g]

## CHAPTER 19

### Campaigns against Ammon.

**1** [h]Afterward Nahash, king of the Ammonites,
died and his son succeeded him as king. **2** David said, "I will show kindness to Hanun, the
son of Nahash, for his father treated me with
kindness." Therefore he sent envoys to him to
comfort him over the death of his father. But
when David's servants had entered the land of
the Ammonites to comfort Hanun, **3** the Ammonite princes said to Hanun, "Do you think
David is doing this—sending you these consol-
ers—to honor your father? Have not his servants
rather come to you to explore the land, spying
it out for its overthrow?" **4** Thereupon Hanun
seized David's servants and had them shaved
and their garments cut off half-way at the hips.
Then he sent them away. **5** When David was
informed of what had happened to his men, he
sent messengers to meet them, for the men had
been greatly disgraced. "Remain at Jericho,"
the king told them, "until your beards have
grown again; and then you may come back
here."
**6** When the Ammonites realized that they
had put themselves in bad odor with David,
Hanun and the Ammonites sent a thousand talents of silver to hire chariots and horsemen from
Aram Naharaim, from Aram-maacah, and from
Zobah. **7** They hired thirty-two thousand chariots along with the king of Maacah and his army,
who came and encamped before Medeba. The
Ammonites also assembled from their cities and
came out for war.
**8** When David heard of this, he sent Joab and
his whole army of warriors against them. **9** The
Ammonites marched out and lined up for battle
at the gate of the city, while the kings who had
come to their help remained apart in the open
field. **10** When Joab saw that there was a battle
line both in front of and behind him, he chose
some of the best fighters among the Israelites
and set them in array against the Arameans;[i]
**11** the rest of the army, which he placed under
the command of his brother Abishai, then lined
up to oppose the Ammonites.[j] **12** And he said:
"If the Arameans prove too strong for me, you
must come to my help; and if the Ammonites
prove too strong for you, I will save you.
**13** Hold steadfast and let us show ourselves
courageous for the sake of our people and the
cities of our God; then may the LORD do what
seems best to him." **14** Joab therefore advanced with his men to engage the Arameans in
battle; but they fled before him. **15** And when
the Ammonites saw that the Arameans had fled,
they also took to flight before his brother Abishai, and reentered the city. Joab then returned to
Jerusalem.
**16** Seeing themselves vanquished by Israel,
the Arameans sent messengers to bring out the
Arameans from the other side of the River, with
Shophach, the general of Hadadezer's army, at
their head. **17** When this was reported to David, he gathered all Israel together, crossed the
Jordan, and met them. With the army of David
drawn up to fight the Arameans, they gave battle. **18** But the Arameans fled before Israel, and
David slew seven thousand of their chariot
fighters and forty thousand of their foot soldiers;
he also killed Shophach, the general of the
army. **19** When the vassals of Hadadezer saw
themselves vanquished by Israel, they made
peace with David and became his subjects. After this, the Arameans refused to come to the aid
of the Ammonites.

---

c 2 Sm 8, 13; 2 Kgs 14, 7.
d 14-17: 2 Sm 8, 15-18.
e 1 Chr 11, 6; 2 Sm 8, 16; 1 Kgs 4, 3.
f 1 Chr 24, 3. 6. 31; 2 Sm 8, 17.
g 1 Chr 11, 22; 2 Sm 8, 18; 1 Kgs 1, 38. 44.
h 1-19: 2 Sm 10, 1-19.
i 1 Chr 20, 23; 1 Kgs 2, 28. 34.
j 1 Chr 23, 18f.

---

* 18, 16: Zadok . . . and Ahimelech, son of Abiathar, were priests: as in the Chronicler's source, 2 Sm 8, 17. But according to 2 Sm 15, 24. 29. 35; 17, 15; 19, 11; 20, 25, and even 1 Chr 15, 11, it was Abiathar who shared the priestly office with Zadok, and he remained in this office even during the early years of Solomon's reign (1 Kgs 2, 26; 4, 4). Moreover, according to 1 Sm 22, 20; 23, 6; 30, 7, Ahimelech was the father, not the son, of Abiathar. If the text Ahimelech, son of Abiathar, is not due to a scribal change, one must assume that Abiathar had a son who was named after his grandfather and who shared the priestly office with his father during the last years of David's reign.

18, 17: David's sons were the chief assistants to the king: in the parallel passage, 2 Sm 8, 18, which was the Chronicler's source, David's sons were priests. The change is characteristic of the Chronicler, for whom only Aaron's descendants could be priests.

## CHAPTER 20

1 At the beginning of the following year, the
time when kings go to war, Joab led the army
out in force, laid waste the land of the Ammonites, and went on to besiege Rabbah, while David himself remained in Jerusalem. When Joab
had attacked Rabbah and destroyed it, 2 [k]David
took the crown of Milcom from the idol's head.
It was found to weigh a talent of gold; and it
contained precious stones, which David wore
on his own head. He also brought out a great
amount of booty from the city. 3 He deported
the people of the city and set them to work with
saws, iron picks, and axes. Thus David dealt
with all the cities of the Ammonites. Then he
and his whole army returned to Jerusalem.

### Victories over the Philistines.

4 [l]Afterward there was another battle with the
Philistines, at Gezer. At that time, Sibbecai the
Hushathite slew Sippai, one of the descendants
of the Raphaim, and the Philistines were subdued.[m] 5 Once again there was war with the
Philistines, and Elhanan, the son of Jair, slew
Lahmi, the brother of Goliath* of Gath, whose
spear shaft was like a weaver's heddle-bar.[n]
6 In still another battle, at Gath, they encountered a giant, also a descendant of the Raphaim, who had six fingers to each hand and six
toes to each foot; twenty-four in all. 7 He defied Israel, and Jonathan, the son of Shimea,
David's brother, slew him. 8 These were the
descendants of the Raphaim of Gath who died
at the hands of David and his servants.

## CHAPTER 21

**David's Census; the Plague.** 1 [o]A satan* rose up against Israel, and he enticed David
into taking a census of Israel.[p] 2 David therefore said to Joab and to the other generals of the
army, "Go, find out the number of the Israelites
from Beer-sheba to Dan, and report back to me
that I may know their number." 3 But Joab
replied: "May the LORD increase his people a
hundredfold! My lord king, are not all of them
my lord's subjects? Why does my lord seek to
do this thing? Why will he bring guilt upon
Israel?" 4 However, the king's command prevailed over Joab, who departed and traversed all
of Israel, and then returned to Jerusalem.
5 Joab reported the result of the census to David: of men capable of wielding a sword, there
were in all Israel one million one hundred thousand, and in Judah four hundred and seventy
thousand. 6 Levi and Benjamin, however, he
did not include in the census, for the king's
command was repugnant to Joab.[q] 7 This command displeased God, who began to punish Israel. 8 Then David said to God, "I have sinned
greatly in doing this thing. Take away your
servant's guilt, for I have acted very foolishly."
9 Then the LORD spoke to Gad, David's seer,
in these words:[r] 10 "Go, tell David: Thus says
the LORD: I offer you three alternatives; choose
one of them, and I will inflict it on you."
11 Accordingly, Gad went to David and said to
him: "Thus says the LORD: Decide now—
12 will it be three years of famine; or three
months of fleeing your enemies, with the sword
of your foes ever at your back; or three days of
the LORD's own sword, a pestilence in the land,
with the LORD's destroying angel in every part
of Israel? Therefore choose: What answer am I
to give him who sent me?" 13 Then David said
to Gad: "I am in dire straits. But I prefer to fall
into the hand of the LORD, whose mercy is very
great, than into the hands of men."
14 Therefore the LORD sent pestilence upon
Israel, and seventy thousand men of Israel died.
15 God also sent an angel to destroy Jerusalem;
but as he was on the point of destroying it, the
LORD saw and decided against the calamity, and
said to the destroying angel, "Enough now!
Stay your hand!"[s]

**Ornan's Threshing Floor.** The angel of
the LORD was then standing by the threshing
floor of Ornan the Jebusite. 16 When David
raised his eyes, he saw the angel of the LORD
standing between earth and heaven, with a naked sword in his hand stretched out against Jerusalem. David and the elders, clothed in sackcloth, prostrated themselves face to the ground,
17 and David prayed to God: "Was it not I who
ordered the census of the people? I am the one
who sinned, I did this wicked thing. But these
sheep, what have they done? O LORD, my God,
strike me and my father's family, but do not
afflict your people with this plague!"
18 Then the angel of the LORD commanded
Gad to tell David to go up and erect an altar to
the LORD on the threshing floor of Ornan the

k 2f: 2 Sm 12, 30f.
l 4-8: 2 Sm 21, 18-22.
m 1 Chr 11, 29; 27, 11.
n 1 Chr 11, 26; 1 Sm 17, 4. 23.
o 1-7: 2 Sm 24, 1-25.
p Zec 3, 1f.
q 1 Chr 27, 24; Nm 1, 49.
r 1 Chr 29, 29; 1 Sm 9, 9; 2 Chr 29, 25.
s Gn 6, 6; Ex 32, 14; 2 Sm 24, 16; Jon 3, 10.
t 2 Chr 3, 1.

*

20, 5: Elhanan . . . slew Lahmi, the brother of Goliath: the Chronicler thus solves the difficulty of the apparent contradiction between 1 Sm 17, 49ff (David killed Goliath) and 2 Sm 21, 19 (Elhanan killed Goliath).

21, 1: A satan: in the parallel passage of 2 Sm 24, 1, the Lord's anger. The change in the term reflects the changed theological outlook of postexilic Israel, when evil could no longer be attributed directly to God. At an earlier period the Hebrew word satan ("adversary," or, especially in a court of law, "accuser"), when not used of men, designated an angel who accused men before God (Jb 1, 6–12; 2, 1–7; Zec 3, 1f). Here, as in later Judaism (Wis 2, 24) and in the New Testament, satan, or the "devil" (from the Greek translation of the word), designates an evil spirit who tempts men to wrongdoing.

Jebusite.[t] **19** David went up at Gad's command, given in the name of the LORD. **20** While
Ornan was threshing wheat, he turned around
and saw the king, and his four sons who were
with him, without recognizing them. **21** But as
David came on toward him, he looked up and
saw that it was David. Then he left the threshing
floor and bowed down before David, his face to
the ground. **22** David said to Ornan: "Sell me
the ground of this threshing floor, that I may
build on it an altar to the LORD. Sell it to me at
its full price, that the plague may be stayed from
the people." **23** But Ornan said to David:
"Take it as your own, and let my lord the king
do what seems best to him. See, I also give you
the oxen for the holocausts, the threshing
sledges for the wood, and the wheat for the
cereal offering. I give it all to you." **24** But
King David replied to Ornan: "No! I will buy
it from you properly, at its full price. I will not
take what is yours for the LORD, nor offer up
holocausts that cost me nothing." **25** So David
paid Ornan six hundred shekels of gold* for the
place.

**Altar of Holocausts.** **26** David then built
an altar there to the LORD, and offered up holocausts and peace offerings. When he called
upon the LORD, he answered him by sending
down fire from heaven upon the altar of holocausts.[u] **27** Then the LORD gave orders to the
angel to return his sword to its sheath.

**28** Once David saw that the LORD had heard
him on the threshing floor of Ornan the Jebusite,
he continued to offer sacrifices there. **29** The
Dwelling of the LORD, which Moses had built
in the desert, and the altar of holocausts were at
that time on the high place at Gibeon.[v] **30** But
David could not go there to worship God, for he
was fearful of the sword of the angel of the
LORD. **1** Therefore David said, "This is the
house of the LORD God, and this is the altar of
holocausts for Israel."*[w]

## CHAPTER 22

**Material for the Temple.** **2** *David then
ordered that all the aliens who lived in the land
of Israel be brought together, and he appointed
them stonecutters to hew out stone blocks for
building the house of God.[x] **3** He also laid up
large stores of iron to make nails for the doors
of the gates, and clamps, together with so much
bronze that it could not be weighed,[y] **4** and
cedar trees without number. The Sidonians and
Tyrians brought great stores of cedar logs to
David,[z] **5** who said: "My son Solomon is
young and immature; but the house that is to be
built for the LORD must be made so magnificent
that it will be renowned and glorious in all countries. Therefore I will make preparations for it."
Thus before his death David laid up materials in
abundance.[a]

**Charge to Solomon.** **6** Then he called for
his son Solomon and commanded him to build
a house for the LORD, the God of Israel.
**7** [b]David said to Solomon: "My son, it was my
purpose to build a house myself for the honor of
the LORD, my God. **8** But this word of the LORD
came to me: 'You have shed much blood, and
you have waged great wars. You may not build
a house in my honor, because you have shed too
much blood upon the earth in my sight. **9** However, a son is to be born to you. He will be a
peaceful man, and I will give him rest from all
his enemies on every side. For Solomon shall be
his name, and in his time I will bestow peace*
and tranquility on Israel.[c] **10** It is he who shall
build a house in my honor; he shall be a son to
me, and I will be a father to him, and I will
establish the throne of his kingship over Israel
forever.'[d] **11** Now, my son, the LORD be with
you, and may you succeed in building the house
of the LORD your God, as he has said you shall.
**12** May the LORD give you prudence and discernment when he brings you to rule over Israel,
so that you keep the law of the LORD, your God.
**13** Only then shall you succeed, if you are careful to observe the precepts and decrees which
the LORD gave Moses for Israel. Be brave and
steadfast; do not fear or lose heart.[e] **14** See,

u Lv 9, 24; Jgs 6, 21; 1 Kgs 18. 38; 2 Chr 7, 1; 2 Mc 2, 10ff.
v 1 Chr 16, 39; 1 Kgs 8, 4; 2 Chr 1, 8.
w 1 Chr 21, 18. 26. 28; 2 Chr 3, 1.
x 1 Kgs 5, 31f; 9, 20f; 2 Chr 2, 16f.
y 1 Chr 18, 8; 1 Kgs 7, 47.
z 1 Chr 10, 27; Ezr 3, 7.
a 1 Chr 29, 1.
b 7-10: 1 Chr 17, 1-14; 28, 2-7; 2 Sm 7, 1-16; 1 Kgs 5, 3ff; 8, 17-21.
c 2 Sm 12, 24.
d Heb 1, 5.
e 1 Chr 28, 7. 20; Dt 31, 6. 23; Jos 1, 6f. 9; 1 Kgs 2, 2f.
f 1 Chr 29, 2ff.

*

21, 25: Six hundred shekels of gold: about 10,000 dollars. According to 2 Sm 24, 24, David paid 50 shekels of silver, about 20 dollars, for Ornan's threshing floor; but for the Chronicler the site of the temple was much more precious than that.

21, 1: This belongs to ch 22.

22, 2ff: According to 1 Kgs 5, 15–32, it was Solomon who made the material preparations for building the temple, even though David had wished to do so (1 Kgs 5, 17ff). The Chronicler, however, sought to have David, who was Israel's ideal king, more closely connected with Israel's most sacred sanctuary, the temple of Jerusalem.

22, 9: The Hebrew word for peace, shalom, is reflected in the name Solomon, in Hebrew, Shelomo. A contrast is drawn here between Solomon, the peaceful man, and David, who waged great wars (v 8). David was prevented from building the temple, not only because all his time was taken up in waging war (1 Kgs 5, 17), but also because he shed much blood (v 8), and in the eyes of the Chronicler this made him ritually unfit for the task.

22, 14: A hundred thousand talents of gold: about 3,775 tons of gold. A million talents of silver: about 37,750 tons of silver. The fantastically exaggerated figures are intended merely to stress the inestimable value of the temple as the center of Israelite worship. More modest figures are given in

with great effort I have laid up for the house of the LORD a hundred thousand talents of gold,* a million talents of silver, and bronze and iron in such great quantities that they cannot be weighed. I have also stored up wood and stones, to which you must add.[f] **15** Moreover, you have available an unlimited supply of workmen, stonecutters, masons, carpenters, and every kind of craftsman **16** skilled in gold, silver, bronze, and iron. Set to work, therefore, and the LORD be with you!"

**Charge to the Leaders.** **17** David also commanded all of Israel's leaders to help his son Solomon: **18** "Is not the LORD your God with you? Has he not given you rest on every side? Indeed, he has delivered the occupants of the land into my power, and the land is subdued before the LORD and his people.[g] **19** Therefore, devote your hearts and souls to seeking the LORD your God. Proceed to build the sanctuary of the LORD God, that the ark of the covenant of the LORD and God's sacred vessels may be brought into the house built in honor of the LORD."[h]

## CHAPTER 23

**The Levitical Classes.** **1** When David had grown old and was near the end of his days, he made his son Solomon king over Israel.[i] **2** He then gathered together all the leaders of Israel, together with the priests and the Levites.

**3** The Levites thirty years old and above were counted, and their total number was found to be thirty-eight thousand men.[j] **4** Of these, twenty-four thousand were to direct the service of the house of the LORD, six thousand were to be officials and judges, **5** four thousand were to be gatekeepers, and four thousand were to praise the LORD with the instruments which David had devised for praise.[k] **6** David divided them into classes according to the sons of Levi: Gershon, Kohath, and Merari.[l]

**7** To the Gershonites belonged Ladan and Shimei. **8** The sons of Ladan: Jehiel the chief, then Zetham and Joel; three in all.[m] **9** The sons of Shimei were Shelomoth, Haziel, and Haran; three. These were the heads of the families of Ladan. **10** The sons of Shimei were Jahath, Zizah, Jeush, and Beriah; these were the sons of Shimei, four in all. **11** Jahath was the chief and Zizah was second to him; but Jeush and Beriah had not many sons, and therefore they were classed as a single family, fulfilling a single office.

**12** The sons of Kohath: Amram, Izhar, Hebron, and Uzziel; four in all.[n] **13** The sons of Amran were Aaron and Moses. Aaron was set apart to be consecrated as most holy, he and his sons forever, to offer sacrifice before the LORD, to minister to him, and to bless his name forever.[o] **14** As for Moses, however, the man of God, his sons were counted as part of the tribe of Levi. **15** The sons of Moses were Gershon and Eliezer.[p] **16** The sons of Gershon: Shubael the chief.[q] **17** The sons of Eliezer were Rehabiah the chief—Eliezer had no other sons, but the sons of Rehabiah were very numerous. **18** The sons of Izhar: Shelomith the chief. **19** The sons of Hebron: Jeriah, the chief, Amariah, the second, Jahaziel, the third, and Jekameam, the fourth.[r] **20** The sons of Uzziel: Micah, the chief, and Isshiah, the second.[s]

**21** The sons of Merari: Mahli and Mushi. The sons of Mahli: Eleazar and Kish.[t] **22** Eleazar died leaving no sons, only daughters; the sons of Kish, their kinsmen, married them.[u] **23** The sons of Mushi: Mahli, Eder, and Jeremoth; three in all.[v]

**24** These were the sons of Levi according to their ancestral houses, the family heads as they were enrolled one by one according to their names. They performed the work of the service of the house of the LORD from twenty years of age upward,[w] **27** for David's final orders were to enlist the Levites from the time they were twenty years old.

**25** David said: "The LORD, the God of Israel, has given rest to his people, and has taken up his dwelling in Jerusalem.[x] **26** Henceforth the Levites need not carry the Dwelling or any of its furnishings or equipment.[y] **28** Rather, their duty shall be to assist the sons of Aaron in the service of the house of the LORD, having charge of the courts, the chambers, and the preservation of everything holy: they shall take part in the service of the house of God. **29** They shall also have charge of the showbread, of the fine flour for the cereal offering, of the wafers of unleavened bread, and of the baking and mixing, and of all measures of quantity and size.[z] **30** They must be present every morning to offer thanks and to praise the LORD, and likewise in the evening;[a] **31** and at every offering of holocausts to the LORD on sabbaths, new

g 1 Chr 23, 25; Jos 21, 44; 23, 1; 2 Sm 7, 1.
h 1 Kgs 8, 6. 21; 2 Chr 5, 7; 6, 11.
i 1 Chr 28, 5; 1 Kgs 1, 30.
j Nm 4, 3. 23. 30. 35. 39. 43. 47; 8, 23-26; 2 Chr 31, 17.
k 1 Chr 9, 22.
l 1 Chr 6, 1. 16-30; 26, 1-19; Ex 6, 16; Nm 3, 17; 26, 57.
m 1 Chr 26, 21f; 29, 8.
n 1 Chr 26, 23; Ex 6, 18; Nm 3, 19; 26, 23ff.
o 1 Chr 6, 49; Ex 6, 20; 28, 1; Nm 6, 23.
p Ex 2, 22; 18, 3f.
q 1 Chr 26, 24.
r 1 Chr 24, 23.
s 1 Chr 24, 24f.
t 1 Chr 6, 29; 24, 26. 28f; Ex 6, 19; Nm 3, 20. 33.
u 1 Chr 24, 28f.
v 1 Chr 6, 47; 24, 30.
w 2 Chr 31, 17; Ezr 3, 8.
x 1 Chr 22, 18; Ps 132, 13.
y 1 Chr 15, 15; 2 Chr 35, 3.
z 1 Chr 9, 29. 31f; Lv 2, 1. 4f; 24, 5-8.
a Nm 28, 3-8.
b Nm 28, 2-29. 39.

* 1 Kgs 9, 14. 28; 10, 10. 14.

moons, and feast days, in such numbers as are prescribed, they must always be present before the LORD.[b] **32** They shall observe what is prescribed for them concerning the meeting tent, the sanctuary, and the sons of Aaron, their brethren, in the service of the house of the LORD."[c]

## CHAPTER 24

**The Priestly Classes.** **1** The descendants of Aaron also were divided into classes. The sons of Aaron were Nadab, Abihu, Eleazar, and Ithamar.[d] **2** Nadab and Abihu died before their father, leaving no sons; therefore only Eleazar and Ithamar served as priests.[e] **3** David, with Zadok, a descendant of Eleazar, and Ahimelech, a descendant of Ithamar, assigned the functions for the priestly service.[f] **4** But since the descendants of Eleazar were found to be more numerous than those of Ithamar, the former were divided into sixteen groups, and the latter into eight groups, each under its family head. **5** Their functions were assigned impartially by lot, for there were officers of the holy place, and officers of the divine presence, descended both from Eleazar and from Ithamar. **6** The scribe Shemaiah, son of Nethanel, a Levite, made a record of it in the presence of the king, and of the leaders, of Zadok the priest, and of Ahimelech, son of Abiathar,* and of the heads of the ancestral houses of the priests and of the Levites, listing two successive family groups from Eleazar before each one from Ithamar.[g]

**7** [h]The first lot fell to Jehoiarib, the second to Jedaiah, **8** the third to Harim, the fourth to Seorim, **9** the fifth to Malchijah, the sixth to Mijamin, **10** the seventh to Hakkoz, the eighth to Abijah,[i] **11** the ninth to Jeshua, the tenth to Shecaniah, **12** the eleventh to Eliashib, the twelfth to Jakim, **13** the thirteenth to Huppah, the fourteenth to Ishbaal, **14** the fifteenth to Bilgah, the sixteenth to Immer, **15** the seventeenth to Hezir, the eighteenth to Happizzez, **16** the nineteenth to Pethahiah, the twentieth to Jehezkel, **17** the twenty-first to Jachin, the twenty-second to Gamul, **18** the twenty-third to Delaiah, the twenty-fourth to Maaziah. **19** This was the appointed order of their service when they functioned in the house of the LORD in keeping with the precepts given them by Aaron, their father, as the LORD, the God of Israel, had commanded him.[j]

**Other Levites.** **20** [k]Of the remaining Levites, there were Shubael, of the descendants of Amram, and Jehdeiah, of the descendants of Shubael; **21** Isshiah, the chief, of the descendants of Rehabiah; **22** Shelomith of the Izharites, and Jahath of the descendants of Shelomith. **23** The descendants of Hebron were Jeriah, the chief, Amariah, the second, Jahaziel, the third, Jekameam, the fourth. **24** The descendants of Uzziel were Micah; Shamir, of the descendants of Micah; **25** Isshiah, the brother of Micah; and Zechariah, a descendant of Isshiah. **26** The descendants of Merari were Mahli, Mushi, and the descendants of his son Uzziah. **27** The descendants of Merari through his son Uzziah: Shoham, Zaccur, and Ibri. **28** Descendants of Mahli were Eleazar, who had no sons, **29** and Jerahmeel, of the descendants of Kish. **30** The descendants of Mushi were Mahli, Eder, and Jerimoth.

These were the descendants of the Levites according to their ancestral houses. **31** They too, in the same manner as their relatives, the descendants of Aaron, cast lots in the presence of King David, Zadok, Ahimelech, and the heads of the priestly and levitical families; the more important family did so in the same way as the less important one.[l]

## CHAPTER 25

**The Singers.** **1** David and the leaders of the liturgical cult set apart for service the descendants of Asaph, Heman, and Jeduthun, as singers of inspired song to the accompaniment of lyres and harps and cymbals.[m]

This is the list of those who performed this service: **2** *Of the sons of Asaph: Zaccur, Joseph, Nethaniah, and Asharelah, sons of Asaph, under the direction of Asaph, who sang inspired songs under the guidance of the king. **3** Of Jeduthun, these sons of Jeduthun: Gedaliah, Zeri, Jeshaiah, Shimei, Hashabiah, and Mattithiah; six, under the direction of their father Jeduthun, who sang inspired songs to the accompaniment of a lyre, to give thanks and praise to the LORD. **4** Of Heman, these sons of Heman: Bukkiah, Mattaniah, Uzziel, Shubael, and Jerimoth; Hananiah, Hanani, Eliathah, Giddal-

---

c Nm 3, 6-9; 18, 2-5.
d Ex 6, 23; Nm 3, 2ff; 26, 60.
e Lv 10, 1-7. 12; Nm 3, 2. 4.
f 1 Chr 18, 16; 2 Sm 8, 17; 2 Chr 8, 14.
g 1 Chr 18, 16; 2 Sm 8, 17.
h 7-10: 1 Chr 9, 10ff; Ezr 2, 36ff; Neh 7, 39ff; 11, 10ff.
i Lk 1, 5.
j 2 Chr 23, 8.
k 20-31: 1 Chr 23, 7-23.
l 1 Chr 25, 8; 26, 13.
m 1 Chr 6, 31ff; 15, 16f. 19; 16, 37; 2 Chr 5, 12; 35, 15; Neh 12, 27. 45.

---

* 24, 6: Ahimelech, son of Abiathar: see note on 1 Chr 18, 16.

25, 2–31: This list of twenty-four classes of temple singers balances the list of the twenty-four classes of priests (1 Chr 24, 4–19). The last nine names in 1 Chr 25, 4, which seem to form a special group, appear to have been originally fragments or incipits of hymns. With some slight changes in the vocalization, the names would mean: "Have mercy on me, O Lord," "Have mercy on me," "You are my God," "I magnify," "I extol the help of . . . ," "Sitting in adversity," "I have fulfilled," "He made abundant," and "Visions."

ti, Romamti-ezer, Joshbekashah, Mallothi, Hothir, and Mahazioth. **5** All these were the sons
of Heman, the king's seer in divine matters; to
enhance his prestige, God gave Heman fourteen
sons and three daughters.[n] **6** All these, whether
of Asaph, Jeduthun, or Heman, were under
their fathers' direction in the singing in the
house of the LORD to the accompaniment of
cymbals, harps and lyres, serving in the house
of God, under the guidance of the king.[o]
**7** Their number, together with that of their
brethren who were trained in singing to the
LORD, all of them skilled men, was two hundred
and eighty-eight. **8** They cast lots for their functions equally, young and old, master and pupil
alike.[p]

**9** The first lot fell to Asaph, the family of
Joseph; he and his sons and his brethren were
twelve. Gedaliah was the second; he and his
brethren and his sons were twelve. **10** The third
was Zaccur, his sons and his brethren: twelve.
**11** The fourth fell to Izri, his sons, and his
brethren: twelve. **12** The fifth was Nethaniah,
his sons, and his brethren: twelve. **13** The sixth
was Bukkiah, his sons, and his brethren:
twelve. **14** The seventh was Jesarelah, his sons,
and his brethren: twelve. **15** The eighth was
Jeshaiah, his sons, and his brethren: twelve.
**16** The ninth was Mattaniah, his sons, and his
brethren: twelve. **17** The tenth was Shimei, his
sons, and his brethren: twelve. **18** The eleventh
was Uzziel, his sons, and his brethren: twelve.
**19** The twelfth fell to Hashabiah, his sons, and
his brethren: twelve. **20** The thirteenth was
Shubael, his sons, and his brethren: twelve.
**21** The fourteenth was Mattithiah, his sons, and
his brethren: twelve. **22** The fifteenth fell to
Jeremoth, his sons, and his brethren: twelve.
**23** The sixteenth fell to Hananiah, his sons, and
his brethren: twelve. **24** The seventeenth fell to
Joshbekashah, his sons, and his brethren:
twelve. **25** The eighteenth fell to Hanani, his
sons, and his brethren: twelve. **26** The nineteenth fell to Mallothi, his sons, and his brethren: twelve. **27** The twentieth fell to Eliathah,
his sons, and his brethren: twelve. **28** The
twenty-first fell to Hothir, his sons, and his
brethren: twelve. **29** The twenty-second fell to
Giddalti, his sons, and his brethren: twelve.
**30** The twenty-third fell to Mahazioth, his
sons, and his brethren: twelve. **31** The twenty-fourth fell to Romamti-ezer, his sons, and his
brethren: twelve.

## CHAPTER 26

**Classes of Gatekeepers.** **1** [q]As for the
classes of gatekeepers. Of the Korahites was
Meshelemiah, the son of Kore, one of the sons
of Abiasaph. **2** Meshelemiah's sons: Zechariah, the first-born, Jediael, the second son, Zebadiah, the third, Jathniel, the fourth, **3** Elam,
the fifth, Jehohanan, the sixth, Eliehoenai, the
seventh. **4** Obed-edom's sons: Shemaiah, the
first-born, Jehozabad, a second son, Joah, the
third, Sachar, the fourth, Nethanel, the fifth,
**5** Ammiel, the sixth, Issachar, the seventh, Pe-
ullethai, the eighth, for God blessed him. **6** To
his son Shemaiah were born sons who ruled
over their family, for they were warriors. **7** The
sons of Shemaiah were Othni, Rephael, Obed,
and Elzabad; also his brethren who were men of
might, Elihu and Semachiah. **8** All these were
of the sons of Obed-edom, who, together with
their sons and their brethren, were mighty men,
fit for the service. Of Obed-edom, sixty-two.
**9** Of Meshelemiah, eighteen sons and brethren,
mighty men.

**10** Hosah, a descendant of Merari, had these
sons: Shimri, the chief (for though he was not
the first-born, his father made him chief),[r]
**11** Hilkiah, the second son, Tebaliah, the third,
Zechariah, the fourth. All the sons and brethren
of Hosah were thirteen.

**12** To these classes of gatekeepers, under
their chief men, were assigned watches in the
service of the house of the LORD, for each group
in the same way. **13** They cast lots for each
gate, the small and the large families alike.
**14** When the lot was cast for the east side, it fell
to Meshelemiah. Then they cast lots for his son
Zechariah, a prudent counselor, and the north
side fell to his lot.[s] **15** To Obededom fell the
south side, and to his sons the storehouse.
**16** To Hosah fell the west side with the Shal-
lecheth gate at the ascending highway. For each
family, watches were established. **17** On the
east, six watched each day, on the north, four
each day, on the south, four each day, and at the
storehouse they were two and two; **18** as for the
large building* on the west, there were four at
the highway and two at the large building.
**19** These were the classes of the gatekeepers,
descendants of Kore and Merari.

**Treasurers.** **20** Their brother Levites superintended the stores for the house of God and
the stores of votive offerings.[t] **21** Among the
descendants of Ladan the Gershonite, the family
heads were descendants of Jehiel: the descendants of Jehiel,[u] **22** [v]Zetham and his brother
Joel, who superintended the treasures of the
house of the LORD. **23** From the Amramites,

n 2 Chr 35, 15.
o 1 Chr 15, 16.
p 1 Chr 24, 31.
q 1 Chr 9, 19; 2 Chr 8, 14; 23, 19; 35, 15; Neh 12, 45.
r 1 Chr 16, 38.
s 1 Chr 9, 24.
t 1 Chr 28, 12; 1 Kgs 7, 51.
u 1 Chr 23, 7f; 29, 8.
v 22ff: 1 Chr 23, 8. 12. 16.

* 26, 18: The large building (in the Hebrew text Parbar): see note on 2 Kgs 23, 11.

Izharites, Hebronites, and Uzzielites, **24** Shubael, son of Gershon, son of Moses, was chief superintendent over the treasures. **25** [w]His associate pertained to Eliezer, whose son was Rehabiah, whose son was Jeshaiah, whose son was Joram, whose son was Zichri, whose son was Shelomith. **26** This Shelomith and his brethren superintended all the stores of the votive offerings dedicated by King David, the heads of the families, the commanders of thousands and of hundreds, and the commanders of the army,[x] **27** from the booty they had taken in the wars, for the enhancement of the house of the LORD. **28** Also, whatever Samuel the seer, Saul, son of Kish, Abner, son of Ner, Joab, son of Zeruiah, and all others had consecrated, was under the charge of Shelomith and his brethren.

**Magistrates.** **29** Among the Izharites, Chananiah and his sons were in charge of Israel's civil affairs as officials and judges.[y] **30** Among the Hebronites, Hashabiah and his brethren, one thousand seven hundred police officers, had the administration of Israel on the western side of the Jordan in all the work of the LORD and in the service of the king.[z] **31** Among the Hebronites, Jerijah was their chief according to their family records. In the fortieth year of David's reign search was made, and there were found among them outstanding officers at Jazer of Gilead.[a] **32** His brethren were also police officers, two thousand seven hundred heads of families. King David appointed them to the administration of the Reubenites, the Gadites, and the half-tribe of Manasseh in everything pertaining to God and to the king.

## CHAPTER 27

**Army Commanders.*** **1** This is the list of the Israelite family heads, commanders of thousands and of hundreds, and other officers who served the king in all that pertained to the divisions, of twenty-four thousand men each, that came and went month by month throughout the year.

**2** Over the first division for the first month was Ishbaal, son of Zabdiel, and in his division were twenty-four thousand men; **3** a descendant of Perez, he was chief over all the commanders of the army for the first month. **4** Over the division of the second month was Eleazar, son of Dodo, from Ahoh, and in his division were twenty-four thousand men.[b] **5** [c]The third army commander, chief for the third month, was Benaiah, son of Jehoiada the priest, and in his division were twenty-four thousand men. **6** This Benaiah was a warrior among the Thirty and over the Thirty. His son Ammizabad was over his division. **7** Fourth, for the fourth month, was Asahel, brother of Joab, and after him his son Zebadiah, and in his division were twenty-four thousand men.[d] **8** Fifth, for the fifth month, was the commander Shamhuth, a descendant of Zerah, and in his division were twenty-four thousand men. **9** Sixth, for the sixth month, was Ira, son of Ikkesh, from Tekoa, and in his division were twenty-four thousand men. **10** Seventh, for the seventh month, was Helles, from Beth-pheleth, of the sons of Ephraim, and in his division were twenty-four thousand men. **11** Eighth, for the eighth month, was Sibbecai the Hushathite, a descendant of Zerah, and in his division were twenty-four thousand men.[e] **12** Ninth, for the ninth month, was Abiezer from Anathoth, of Benjamin, and in his division were twenty-four thousand men. **13** Tenth, for the tenth month, was Maharai from Netophah, a descendant of Zerah, and in his division were twenty-four thousand men. **14** Eleventh, for the eleventh month, was Benaiah the Pirathonite, of Ephraim, and in his division were twenty-four thousand men. **15** Twelfth, for the twelfth month, was Heldai the Netophathite, of the family of Othniel, and in his division were twenty-four thousand men.

**Tribal Heads.** **16** Over the tribes of Israel, for the Reubenites the leader was Eliezer, son of Zichri; for the Simeonites, Shephatiah, son of Maacah; **17** for Levi, Hashabiah, son of Kemuel; for Aaron, Zadok; **18** for Judah, Eliab, one of David's brothers; for Issachar, Omri, son of Michael;[f] **19** for Zebulun, Ishmaiah, son of Obadiah; for Naphtali, Jeremoth, son of Azriel; **20** for the sons of Ephraim, Hoshea, son of Azaziah; for the half-tribe of Manasseh, Joel, son of Pedaiah; **21** for the half-tribe of Manasseh in Gilead, Iddo, son of Zechariah; for Benjamin, Jaasiel, son of Abner; **22** for Dan, Azarel, son of Jeroham. These were the commanders of the tribes of Israel.

**23** David did not count those who were twenty years of age or younger, for the LORD had promised to multiply Israel like the stars of the heavens.[g] **24** Joab, son of Zeruiah, began to take the census, but he did not complete it, for because of it wrath fell upon Israel. Therefore

w 1 Chr 23, 17f; 24, 21.
x 2 Sm 8, 11.
y 1 Chr 23, 4.
z 1 Chr 27, 17; Neh 11, 15f.
a 1 Chr 23, 19; 29, 27; Jos 13, 25.
b 1 Chr 9, 37; 11, 12; 2 Sm 23, 9.
c 5f: 1 Chr 11, 22ff; 18, 17; 2 Sm 23, 20ff.
d 2 Sm 2, 18; 23, 24.
e 1 Chr 11, 29; 20, 4; 2 Sm 21, 18.
f 1 Chr 2, 13.
g 1 Chr 22, 17.
h 2 Sm 24, 10.

* 27, 1–15: This list of army commanders is similar to, but distinct from, the list of David's warriors as given in 1 Chr 11, 10–47. The schematic enumeration of the soldiers as presented here is, no doubt, artificial and grossly exaggerated (12 × 24,000 = 288,000 men!), unless the Hebrew word (eleph) for thousand is understood as designating a military unit of much smaller size; see note on 1 Chr 12, 25–38.

the number did not enter into the book of chronicles of King David.[h]

**Overseers.** **25** Over the treasures of the
king was Azmaveth, the son of Adiel. Over the
stores in the country, the cities, the villages, and
the towers was Jonathan, son of Uzziah.[i]
**26** Over the farm workers who tilled the soil
was Ezri, son of Chelub. **27** Over the vineyards
was Shimei from Ramah, and over their produce for the wine cellars was Zabdi the Shiph-
mite. **28** Over the olive trees and sycamores of
the foothills was Baalhanan the Gederite, and
over the stores of oil was Joash. **29** Over the
cattle that grazed in Sharon was Shitrai the Shar-
onite, and over the cattle in the valleys was
Shaphat, the son of Adlai; **30** over the camels
was Obil the Ishmaelite; over the she-asses was
Jehdeiah the Meronothite; **31** and over the
flocks was Jaziz the Hagrite. All these were the
overseers of King David's possessions.

**David's Court.** **32** Jonathan, David's uncle
and a man of intelligence, was counselor and
scribe; he and Jehiel, the son of Hachmoni,
were tutors of the king's sons. **33** Ahithophel
was also the king's counselor, and Hushai the
Archite was the king's confidant.[j] **34** After
Ahithophel* came Jehoiada, the son of Benaiah, and Abiathar. The commander of the king's
army was Joab.

## CHAPTER 28

**The Assembly at Jerusalem.** **1** David
assembled at Jerusalem all the leaders of Israel,
the heads of the tribes, the commanders of the
divisions who were in the service of the king,
the commanders of thousands and of hundreds,
the overseers of all the king's estates and possessions, and his sons, together with the courtiers, the warriors, and every important man.[k]
**2** [l]King David rose to his feet and said: "Hear
me, my brethren and my people. It was my
purpose to build a house of repose myself for the
ark of the covenant of the LORD, the footstool
for the feet of our God;* and I was preparing to
build it. **3** But God said to me, 'You may not
build a house in my honor, for you are a man
who fought wars and shed blood.' **4** However,
the LORD, the God of Israel, chose me from all
my father's family to be king over Israel forever. For he chose Judah as leader, then one family of Judah, that of my father; and finally,
among all the sons of my father, it pleased him
to make me king over all Israel.[m] **5** And of all
my sons—for the LORD has given me many
sons—he has chosen my son Solomon to sit on
the LORD's royal throne over Israel.[n] **6** For he
said to me: 'It is your son Solomon who shall
build my house and my courts, for I have chosen
him for my son, and I will be a father to him.[o]
**7** I will establish his kingdom forever, if he
perseveres in keeping my commandments and
decrees as he keeps them now.' **8** Therefore in
the presence of all Israel, the assembly of the
LORD, and in the hearing of our God, I exhort
you to keep and to carry out all the commandments of the LORD, your God, that you may
continue to possess this good land and afterward
leave it as an inheritance to your children forever.[p]
**9** "As for you, Solomon, my son, know the
God of your father and serve him with a perfect
heart and a willing soul, for the LORD searches
all hearts and understands all the mind's
thoughts. If you seek him, he will let himself be
found by you; but if you abandon him, he will
cast you off forever.[q] **10** See, then! The LORD
has chosen you to build a house as his sanctuary.
Take courage and set to work."

**Temple Plans Given to Solomon.**
**11** Then David gave to his son Solomon the
pattern of the portico and of the building itself,
with its storerooms, its upper rooms and inner
chambers, and the room with the propitiatory.[r]
**12** He provided also the pattern for all else that
he had in mind by way of courts for the house
of the LORD, with the surrounding compartments for the stores for the house of God and the
stores of the votive offerings, **13** as well as for
the divisions of the priests and Levites, for all
the work of the service of the house of the LORD,
and for all the liturgical vessels of the house of
the LORD. **14** He specified the weight of gold to
be used in the golden vessels for the various
services and the weight of silver to be used in
the silver vessels for the various services;
**15** likewise for the golden lampstands and their
lamps he specified the weight of gold for each
lampstand and its lamps, and for the silver

i 2 Sm 23, 31.
j 2 Sm 15, 12. 32-37; 16, 16-19. 23; 17, 5-16. 23.
k 1 Chr 27, 2-22. 25-31; 11, 10ff.
l 2f: 1 Chr 17, 4; 22, 7ff; 2 Sm 7, 5; 1 Kgs 5, 3; Ps 132, 3-7.
m 1 Chr 17, 23; Gn 49, 8ff; 1 Sm 16, 6-13.
n 1 Chr 3, 1-9; 14, 3-7; 22, 9; 23, 1; Wis 9, 7.
o 1 Chr 17, 11ff; 22, 9f; 2 Sm 7, 12f.
p Dt 4, 5.
q 1 Chr 29, 17; 2 Chr 15, 2; 1 Kgs 8, 61.
r Ex 25, 9. 40; 26, 30.
s Ex 25, 31-37.

*

27, 34: After Ahithophel: after his suicide (2 Sm 17, 23). Jehoiada then succeeded him as the king's counselor. Abiathar: the priest. The Chronicler does not mention his office because he regards only the Zadokites as legitimate high priests.

28, 2: The ark . . . the footstool . . . of our God: the Lord, who was invisibly enthroned upon the cherubim that were associated with the ark of the covenant at Shiloh and later in the Jerusalem temple, had the ark as his footstool; cf Pss 99, 5; 132, 7. The propitiatory (1 Chr 28, 11) and the chariot throne (1 Chr 28, 18) reflect the different circumstances of the postexilic community, for whom only the place of the ark was a focal point of worship, though the ark itself was no longer present.

lampstands he specified the weight of silver for
each lampstand and its lamps, depending on the
use to which each lampstand was to be put.[s]
**16** He specified the weight of gold for each
table to hold the showbread, and the silver for
the silver tables; **17** the pure gold to be used for
the forks and pitchers; the amount of gold for
each golden bowl and the silver for each silver
bowl; **18** the refined gold, and its weight, to be
used for the altar of incense; and, finally, gold
for what would suggest a chariot throne:* the
cherubim that spread their wings and covered
the ark of the covenant of the LORD.[t] **19** He had
successfully committed to writing the exact
specifications of the pattern, because the hand
of the LORD was upon him.
**20** Then David said to his son Solomon: "Be
firm and steadfast; go to work without fear or
discouragement, for the LORD God, my God, is
with you. He will not fail you or abandon you
before you have completed all the work for the
service of the house of the LORD.[u] **21** The
classes of the priests and Levites are ready for
all the service of the house of God; they will
help you in all your work with all those who are
eager to show their skill in every kind of crafts-
manship. Also the leaders and all the people will
do everything that you command."[v]

## CHAPTER 29

**Offerings for the Temple.** **1** King David
then said to the whole assembly: "My son Solomon, whom alone God has chosen, is still
young and immature; the work, however, is
great, for this castle is not intended for man, but
for the LORD God.[w] **2** For this reason I have
stored up for the house of my God, as far as I
was able, gold for what will be made of gold,
silver for what will be made of silver, bronze for
what will be made of bronze, iron for what will
be made of iron, wood for what will be made of
wood, onyz stones and settings for them, carnelian and mosaic stones, every other kind of precious stone, and great quantities of marble.[x]
**3** But now, because of the delight I take in the
house of my God, in addition to all that I stored
up for the holy house, I give to the house of my
God my personal fortune in gold and silver:
**4** three thousand talents of Ophir gold, and sev-
en thousand talents of refined silver, for over-
laying the walls of the rooms,[y] **5** for the various
utensils to be made of gold and silver, and for
every work that is to be done by artisans. Now,
who else is willing to contribute generously this
day to the LORD?"[z]
**6** Then the heads of the families, the leaders
of the tribes of Israel, the commanders of thousands and of hundreds, and the overseers of the
king's affairs came forward willingly[a] **7** and
contributed for the service of the house of God
five thousand talents and ten thousand darics of
gold, ten thousand talents of silver, eighteen
thousand talents of bronze, and one hundred
thousand talents of iron.[b] **8** Those who had
precious stones gave them into the keeping of
Jehiel the Gershonite for the treasury of the
house of the LORD.[c] **9** The people rejoiced over
these free-will offerings, which had been contributed to the LORD wholeheartedly. King David also rejoiced greatly.[d]

**David's Prayer.** **10** Then David blessed the
LORD in the presence of the whole assembly,
praying in these words:

"Blessed may you be, O LORD,
God of Israel our father,
from eternity to eternity.

**11** "Yours, O LORD, are grandeur and power,
majesty, splendor, and glory.
For all in heaven and on earth is yours;
yours, O LORD, is the sovereignty;
you are exalted as head over all.

**12** "Riches and honor are from you,
and you have dominion over all.
In your hand are power and might;
it is yours to give grandeur and strength
to all.[e]
**13** Therefore, our God, we give you thanks
and we praise the majesty of your name."

**14** "But who am I, and who are my people, that
we should have the means to contribute so freely? For everything is from you, and we only
give you what we have received from you.
**15** For we stand before you as aliens: we are
only your guests, like all our fathers. Our life on
earth is like a shadow that does not abide.[f] **16** O
LORD our God, all this wealth that we have
brought together to build you a house in honor
of your holy name comes from you and is entirely yours. **17** I know, O my God, that you put
hearts to the test and that you take pleasure in
uprightness. With a sincere heart I have willingly given all these things, and now with joy I
have seen your people here present also giving
to you generously. **18** O LORD, God of our
fathers Abraham, Isaac, and Israel, keep such
thoughts in the hearts and minds of your people

t Ex 25, 18-22; 30, 1-10; 1 Kgs 6, 23-28.
u 1 Chr 22, 13. 16; Jos 1, 5.
v Ex 36, 1-5.
w 1 Chr 22, 5; 28, 5.
x 1 Chr 22, 14.
y 2 Chr 9, 10; 1 Kgs 9, 28; 10, 11.
z Ex 25, 2; 35, 5f.
a 1 Chr 27, 1. 25-31; 28, 1.
b Ezr 2, 69; 8, 27; Neh 7, 70ff.
c 1 Chr 23, 8; 26, 21.
d 2 Kgs 12, 4.
e 2 Chr 20, 6; Wis 6, 3.
f Lv 25, 23; Wis 2, 5; 5, 9.
g Ex 3, 6. 15f; 4. 5; 1 Kgs 18, 36.

* 28, 18: Chariot throne: probably suggested by Ez 1, 4–24; 10, 1–22.

forever, and direct their hearts toward you.[g]
19 Give to my son Solomon a wholehearted
desire to keep your commandments, precepts,
and statutes, that he may carry out all these
plans and build the castle for which I have made
preparation."
20 Then David besought the whole assembly, "Now bless the LORD your God!" And the
whole assembly blessed the LORD, the God of
their fathers, bowing down and prostrating
themselves before the LORD and before the
king. 21 On the following day they offered sacrifices and holocausts to the LORD, a thousand
bulls, a thousand rams, and a thousand lambs,
together with their libations and many other
sacrifices for all Israel; 22 and on that day they
ate and drank in the LORD's presence with great
rejoicing.

**Solomon Anointed.** Then for a second
time* they proclaimed David's son Solomon
king, and they anointed him as the LORD's
prince, and Zadok as priest. 23 Thereafter Solomon sat on the throne of the LORD as king in
place of his father David; he prospered, and all
Israel obeyed him.[h] 24 All the leaders and warriors, and also all the other sons of King David,
swore allegiance to King Solomon. 25 And the
LORD exalted Solomon greatly in the eyes of all
Israel, giving him a glorious reign such as had
not been enjoyed by any king over Israel before
him.[i]

**Death of David.** 26 Thus David, the son of
Jesse, had reigned over all Israel. 27 The time
that he reigned over Israel was forty years: in
Hebron he reigned seven years, and in Jerusalem thirty-three.[j] 28 He died at a ripe old age,
rich in years and wealth and glory, and his son
Solomon succeeded him as king.[k]
29 Now the deeds of King David, first and
last, can be found written in the history of Samuel the seer, the history of Nathan the prophet,
and the history of Gad the seer,[l] 30 together
with the particulars of his reign and valor, and
of the events that affected him and all Israel and
all the kingdoms of the surrounding lands.

h 1 Chr 28, 5; 2 Chr 9, 8; 1 Kgs 2, 10ff.
i 2 Chr 1, 12; 1 Kgs 3, 13.
j 2 Sm 5, 5; 1 Kgs 2, 11.
k 1 Chr 23, 1.
l 1 Chr 21, 9; 1 Sm 22, 5.

* 29, 22: For a second time: the first time is referred to in 1 Chr 23, 1. Here there is a solemn public ratification of David's earlier appointment of Solomon as his successor.

# The Second Book of
# CHRONICLES

*The Second Book of Chronicles takes up the history of the monarchy where the First Book breaks off. It begins with the account of the reign of Solomon from the special viewpoint of the Chronicler. The portrait of Solomon is an idealized one; he appears as second only to David. The great achievement of the building of the temple and the magnificence of Solomon's court are described in detail while the serious defects of his reign are passed over without comment. All this is in keeping with the Chronicler's purpose of stressing the supreme importance of the temple and its worship. He wishes to impress on his readers the splendor of God's dwelling and the magnificence of the liturgy of sacrifice, prayer and praise offered there. Judah's kings are judged by their attitude toward the temple and its cult. To this ideal of one people, united in the worship of the one true God at the temple of Jerusalem founded by David and Solomon, the restored community would have to conform.*

*In treating the period of divided monarchy, the Chronicler gives practically all his attention to the kingdom of Judah. His omission of the northern Israelite kings is significant. In his view, the northern tribes of Israel were in religious schism as long as they worshiped Yahweh in a place other than the temple of Jerusalem. The Chronicler makes no mention of the important sanctuaries of Yahweh at Dan and Bethel—as though they had never existed. Nevertheless he retains the ancient ideal of "all Israel" (a phrase occurring forty-one times in Chronicles) as the people of God. The condition he places for a united people is that "the whole congregation of Israel" worship the Lord only in his temple at Jerusalem. This explains his praise of Kings Hezekiah and Josiah for striving, after the fall of Samaria, to unite the remnants of the northern tribes of Israel into the kingdom of Judah.*

*At the end of the fifth century B.C., during the Chronicler's own time, "the people of the land" were the descendants of the people of all the tribes (including Judah) who had not gone into exile. These had become intermingled with aliens and had evolved a religion of Yahweh very different from the Judaism that developed during the Babylonian exile. Thus, religious and political cooperation between the returned exiles and these "people of the land" was out of the question for the Chronicler. This he clearly shows in the last part of his work, the Books of Ezra and Nehemiah.*

*The Second Book of Chronicles is divided as follows:*

*I. The Reign of Solomon (1, 1–9, 31).*
*II. The Monarchy before Hezekiah (10, 1–27, 9).*
*III. Reforms of Hezekiah and Josiah (28, 1–36, 1).*
*IV. End of the Kingdom (36, 2–23).*

## I: The Reign of Solomon

### CHAPTER 1

**Solomon at Gibeon.** 1 Solomon, son of
David, strengthened his hold on the kingdom,
for the LORD, his God, was with him, constantly
making him more renowned. 2 He sent a summons to all Israel, to the commanders of thousands and of hundreds, the judges, the princes
of all Israel, and the family heads; 3 [a]and, accompanied by the whole assembly, he went to
the high place at Gibeon, because the meeting
tent of God, made in the desert by Moses, the
LORD's servant, was there. 4 (The ark of God,
however, David had brought up from Kiriath-
jearim to Jerusalem, where he had provided a
place and pitched a tent for it.) 5 The bronze

a 3-12: 1 Kgs 3, 4-15; 1 Chr 21, 29.
b Ex 27, 1f; 31, 2; 1 Chr 2, 20.

*

1, 5: The bronze altar . . . the Lord's Dwelling: the Chronicler justifies Solomon's worship at the high place of Gibeon. He pictures the Lord's Dwelling, i.e., the Mosaic meeting tent,

altar made by Bezalel, son of Uri, son of Hur,
he put in front of the LORD's Dwelling* on the
high place. There Solomon and the assembly
consulted the LORD,[b] 6 and Solomon offered
sacrifice in the LORD's presence on the bronze
altar at the meeting tent; he offered a thousand
holocausts upon it.

7 That night God appeared to Solomon and
said to him, "Make a request of me, and I will
grant it to you." 8 Solomon answered God:
"You have shown great favor to my father David, and you have allowed me to succeed him
as king. 9 Now, LORD God, may your promise
to my father David be fulfilled, for you have
made me king over a people as numerous as the
dust of the earth. 10 Give me, therefore, wisdom and knowledge to lead this people, for
otherwise who could rule this great people of
yours?" 11 God then replied to Solomon:
"Since this has been your wish and you have not
asked for riches, treasures and glory, nor for the
life of those who hate you, nor even for a long
life for yourself, but have asked for wisdom and
knowledge in order to rule my people over
whom I have made you king, 12 wisdom and
knowledge are given you; but I will also give
you riches, treasures and glory, such as kings
before you never had, nor will those have them
who come after you."

**Solomon's Wealth.** 13 Solomon returned
to Jerusalem from the high place at Gibeon,
from the meeting tent, and became king over
Israel. 14 He gathered together chariots and
drivers, so that he had one thousand four hundred chariots and twelve thousand drivers he
could station in the chariot cities and with the
king in Jerusalem.[c] 15 The king made silver
and gold as common in Jerusalem as stones,
while cedars became as numerous as the sycamores of the foothills.[d] 16 Solomon also imported horses from Egypt and Cilicia.[e] The
king's agents would acquire them by purchase
from Cilicia,* 17 and would then bring up chariots from Egypt and export them at six hundred
silver shekels, with the horses going for a hundred and fifty shekels. At these rates they served
as middlemen for all the Hittite and Aramean
kings.[f]

**Preparations for the Temple.** 18 Solomon gave orders for the building of a house to
honor the LORD and also of a house for his own
royal estate.

## CHAPTER 2

1 He conscripted seventy thousand men to
carry stone and eighty thousand to cut the stone
in the mountains, and over these he placed three
thousand six hundred overseers.[g]
2 [h]Moreover, Solomon sent this message to
Huram, king of Tyre: "As you dealt with my
father David, sending him cedars to build a
house for his dwelling, so deal with me. 3 I
intend to build a house for the honor of the
LORD, my God, and to consecrate it to him, for
the burning of fragrant incense in his presence,
for the perpetual display of the showbread, for
holocausts morning and evening, and for the
sabbaths, new moons, and festivals of the
LORD, our God: such is Israel's perpetual obligation.[i] 4 And the house I intend to build must
be large, for our God is greater than all other
gods. 5 Yet who is really able to build him a
house, since the heavens and even the highest
heavens cannot contain him? And who am I that
I should build him a house, unless it be to offer
incense in his presence?[j] 6 Now, send me men
skilled at work in gold, silver, bronze and iron,
in purple, crimson, and violet fabrics, and who
know how to do engraved work, to join the
craftsmen who are with me in Judah and Jerusalem, whom my father David appointed. 7 Also
send me boards of cedar, cypress and cabinet
wood from Lebanon, for I realize that your servants know how to cut the wood of the Lebanon.
My servants will labor with yours 8 in order to
prepare for me a great quantity of wood, since
the house I intend to build must be lofty and
wonderful. 9 I will furnish as food for your
servants, the hewers who cut the wood, twenty
thousand kors of wheat, twenty thousand kors
of barley, twenty thousand measures of wine,
and twenty thousand measures of oil."[k]

10 Huram, king of Tyre, wrote an answer
which he sent to Solomon: "Because the LORD
loves his people, he has placed you over them
as king." 11 He added: "Blessed be the LORD,
the God of Israel, who made heaven and earth,
for having given King David a wise son of
intelligence and understanding, who will build
a house for the LORD and also a house for his
royal estate.[l] 12 I am now sending you a crafts-

---

c 2 Chr 9, 25; 10, 26-29.
d 1 Kgs 10, 27.
e 1 Kgs 10, 28.
f 1 Kgs 10, 29.
g 2 Chr 2, 17; 5, 29f.
h 2-9: 1 Kgs 5, 15-20; 1 Chr 14, 1.
i Lv 24, 5-8; Nm 28-29.
j 2 Chr 6, 18.
k 1 Kgs 5, 25; Ezr 3, 7.
l 1 Kgs 5, 21.
m 12f: 1 Kgs 7, 13f; Ex 31, 1-5.

---

* and the bronze altar made at Moses' command (Ex 31, 1–9) as still at Gibeon after David had removed the ark of the covenant from there to a new tent in Jerusalem (1 Chr 15, 1. 25; 16, 1). The altar made by Bezalel is described as being of acacia wood plated with bronze (Ex 27, 1f). Solomon later made an all-bronze altar for the temple in Jerusalem (2 Chr 4, 1).

1, 16f: Egypt . . . Cilicia: it seems likely that the horses came from Cilicia and the chariots from Egypt. Some read the source of these data in 1 Kgs 10, 28f as containing the name (Musur) of a mountain district north of Cilicia, rather than of Egypt; but the author of Chronicles surely understood Egypt; cf 2 Chr 9, 28.

man of great skill, Huramabi,[m] **13** son of a
Danite woman* and of a father from Tyre; he
knows how to work with gold, silver, bronze
and iron, with stone and wood, with purple,
violet, fine linen and crimson, and also how to
do all kinds of engraved work and to devise
every type of artistic work that may be given
him and your craftsmen and the craftsmen of my
lord David your father. **14** [n]And now, let my
lord send to his servants the wheat, barley, oil
and wine which he has promised. **15** For our
part, we will cut trees on Lebanon, as many as
you need, and float them down to you at the port
of Joppa, whence you may take them up to
Jerusalem."[o]

**16** [p]Thereupon Solomon took a census of all
the alien men who were in the land of Israel
(following the census David his father had taken
of them), who were found to number one hundred fifty-three thousand six hundred. **17** Of
these he made seventy thousand carriers and
eighty thousand cutters in the mountains, and
three thousand six hundred overseers to keep the
people working.[q]

## CHAPTER 3

**Building of the Temple.** **1** [r]Then Solomon began to build the house of the LORD in
Jerusalem on Mount Moriah,* which had been
pointed out to his father David, on the spot
which David had selected, the threshing-floor of
Ornan the Jebusite. **2** He began to build in the
second month of the fourth year of his reign.
**3** These were the specifications laid down by
Solomon for building the house of God: the
length was sixty cubits according to the old
measure, and the width was twenty cubits;[s]
**4** the porch which lay before the nave along the
width of the house was also twenty cubits, and
it was twenty cubits high.* He overlaid its interior with pure gold.[t] **5** The nave he overlaid
with cypress wood which he covered with fine
gold, embossing on it palms and chains.[u] **6** He
also decorated the building with precious
stones. **7** The house; its beams and thresholds,
as well as its walls and its doors, he overlaid
with gold, and he engraved cherubim upon the
walls. (The gold was from Parvaim.) **8** He also
made the room of the holy of holies. Its length
corresponded to the width of the house, twenty
cubits, and its width was also twenty cubits. He
overlaid it with fine gold to the amount of six
hundred talents.[v] **9** The weight of the nails was
fifty gold shekels. The upper chambers he likewise covered with gold.

**10** [w]For the room of the holy of holies he
made two cherubim of carved workmanship,
which were then overlaid with gold. **11** The
wings of the cherubim spanned twenty cubits:
**12** one wing of each cherub, five cubits in
length, extended to a wall of the building, while
the other wing, also five cubits in length,
touched the corresponding wing of the second
cherub. **13** The combined wingspread of the
two cherubim was thus twenty cubits. They
stood upon their own feet, facing toward the
nave. **14** He made the veil* of violet, purple,
crimson and fine linen, and had cherubim embroidered upon it.[x]

**15** [y]In front of the building he set two columns thirty-five cubits high; the capital topping
each was of five cubits. **16** He worked out
chains in the form of a collar with which he
encircled the capitals of the columns, and he
made a hundred pomegranates which he set on
the chains. **17** He set up the columns to correspond with the nave, one for the right side and
the other for the left, and he called the one to
the right Jachin and the one to the left Boaz.

## CHAPTER 4

**1** Then he made a bronze altar twenty cubits
long, twenty cubits wide and ten cubits high.[z]
**2** [a]He also made the molten sea. It was perfectly round, ten cubits in diameter, five in depth,
and thirty in circumference; **3** below the rim a
ring of figures of oxen* encircled the sea, ten to
the cubit, all the way around; there were two
rows of these cast in the same mold with the sea.
**4** It rested on twelve oxen, three facing north,
three west, three south, and three east, with
their haunches all toward the center; the sea

n 14f: 1 Kgs 5, 22-26.
o Ezr 3, 7.
p 16f: 1 Chr 22, 2.
q 2 Chr 2, 1.
r 1f: Gn 22, 2; 1 Kgs 6, 1; 1 Chr 21, 22-26.
s 1 Kgs 6, 2; Ez 40, 5.
t 1 Kgs 6, 3; Ez 40, 48.
u 1 Kgs 6, 15; Ez 41, 1.
v 1 Kgs 6, 16f. 20; Ez 41, 3.
w 10-13: 1 Kgs 6, 23-27.
x Mt 27, 51.
y 15ff: 1 Kgs 7, 15-22; Ez 40, 49.
z Ez 43, 13-17.
a 2-5: 1 Kgs 7, 23-26; Ez 43, 13.

*

2, 13: A Danite woman: a widow of the tribe of Naphtali (1 Kgs 7, 14). The Danites had settled in the northern section of Naphtali's territory (Jgs 18, 27ff). Bezalel's fellow craftsman was of the tribe of Dan (Ex 31, 6).

3, 1: Mount Moriah: the height in the land of Moriah (Gn 22, 2). This is the only place in the Bible where the temple mount is identified with the site where Abraham was to sacrifice Isaac.

3, 4: The porch . . . twenty cubits high: this measurement, not given in the Books of Kings, is here based on a variant Greek text that may be a later revision. The received Hebrew text says, "one hundred and twenty cubits high." The height of the two freestanding columns adjacent to the porch (1 Kgs 7, 15–16) is nearly doubled by the Chronicler (2 Chr 3, 15).

3, 14: The veil: at the entrance of the holy of holies, as also in the Mosaic meeting tent (Ex 26, 31f). Solomon's temple had doors at this place (1 Kgs 6, 31). Apparently there was a veil here in the temple of the Chronicler's time as there was also in Herod's temple (Mt 27, 51; Mk 15, 38; Lk 23, 45).

4, 3: Oxen: in 1 Kgs 7, 24 this double row of ornaments is described as being gourds. The text of Kings available to the Chronicler may have been faulty on this point as the words are similar in sound. In 2 Chr 4, 16 the forks correspond in a similar way to bowls in the text of 1 Kings (7, 40).

rested on their backs. **5** It was a handbreadth thick, and its brim was made like that of a cup, being lily-shaped. It had a capacity of three thousand measures.*

**6** Then he made ten basins for washing, placing five of them to the right and five to the left. Here were cleansed the victims for the holocausts; but the sea was for the priests to wash in.[b]

**7** He made the lampstands of gold, ten of them as was prescribed, and placed them in the nave, five to the right and five to the left.[c] **8** He made ten tables and had them set in the nave, five to the right and five to the left; and he made a hundred golden bowls.[d] **9** He made the court of the priests and the great courtyard and the gates of the courtyard; the gates he overlaid with bronze.[e] **10** The sea was placed off to the southeast from the right side of the temple.[f]

**11** [g]Huram also made the pots, the shovels and the bowls. Huram thus completed the work he had to do for King Solomon in the house of God: **12** two columns, two nodes for the capitals topping these two columns, and two networks covering the nodes of the capitals topping the columns; **13** also four hundred pomegranates for the two networks, with two rows of pomegranates to each network, to cover the two nodes of the capitals topping the columns. **14** He made the stands, and the basins on the stands; **15** one sea, and the twelve oxen under it; **16** likewise the pots, the shovels and the forks. Huram-abi made all these articles for King Solomon from polished bronze for the house of the LORD. **17** The king had them cast in the Jordan region, in the clayey ground between Succoth and Zeredah. **18** Solomon made all these vessels, so many in number that the weight of the bronze was not ascertained.

**19** Solomon had all these articles made for the house of God: the golden altar, the tables on which the showbread lay, **20** the lampstands and their lamps of pure gold which were to burn according to prescription before the sanctuary, **21** flowers, lamps and gold tongs [this was the purest gold], **22** snuffers, bowls, cups and firepans of pure gold. As for the entry to the house, its inner doors to the holy of holies, as well as the doors to the nave, were of gold.

## CHAPTER 5

**Dedication of the Temple.** **1** [h]When all the work undertaken by Solomon for the temple of the LORD had been completed, he brought in the dedicated offerings of his father David, putting the silver, the gold and all the other articles in the treasuries of the house of God. **2** At Solomon's order the elders of Israel and all the leaders of the tribes, the princes of the Israelite ancestral houses, came to Jerusalem to bring up the ark of the LORD's covenant from the City of David (which is Zion). **3** All the men of Israel assembled before the king during the festival of the seventh month. **4** [i]When all the elders of Israel had arrived, the Levites* took up the ark, **5** and they carried the ark and the meeting tent with all the sacred vessels that were in the tent; it was the levitical priests who carried them.

**6** King Solomon and the entire community of Israel gathered about him before the ark were sacrificing sheep and oxen so numerous that they could not be counted or numbered. **7** The priests brought the ark of the covenant of the LORD to its place beneath the wings of the cherubim in the sanctuary, the holy of holies of the temple. **8** The cherubim had their wings spread out over the place of the ark, sheltering the ark and its poles from above. **9** The poles were long enough so that their ends could be seen from that part of the holy place nearest the sanctuary; however, they could not be seen beyond. The ark has remained there to this day.* **10** There was nothing in it but the two tablets which Moses put there on Horeb, the tablets of the covenant which the LORD made with the Israelites at their departure from Egypt.

**11** When the priests came out of the holy place (all the priests who were present had purified themselves without reference to the rotation of their various classes), **12** the Levites who were singers, all who belonged to Asaph, Heman, Jeduthun, and their sons and brothers, clothed in fine linen, with cymbals, harps and lyres, stood east of the altar, and with them a hundred and twenty priests blowing trumpets.

**13** When the trumpeters and singers were heard as a single voice praising and giving thanks to the LORD, and when they raised the sound of the trumpets, cymbals and other musical instruments to "give thanks to the LORD, for he is good, for his mercy endures forever," the building of the LORD's temple was filled with a cloud. **14** The priests could not continue to minister because of the cloud, since the LORD's glory filled the house of God.[j]

b 1 Kgs 7, 38f; Ez 40, 38.
c 1 Kgs 7, 49.
d 1 Kgs 7, 50; 1 Chr 28, 16.
e 1 Kgs 7, 12.
f 1 Kgs 7, 39.
g 11-22; 1 Kgs 7, 40-51.
h 1-14: 1 Kgs 7, 51-8, 13.
i 4f: 2 Chr 35, 3.
j 2 Chr 7, 2; 1 Kgs 8, 10f.

*

4, 5: Three thousand measures: according to 1 Kgs 7, 26, "two thousand measures."

5, 4: The Levites: The parallel passage in 1 Kgs 8, 3 has the priests; but see 2 Chr 5, 5, where the Deuteronomic term levitical priests is used, as also in 2 Chr 23, 18; 30, 27.

5, 9: The ark has remained there to this day: the Chronicler must have copied this from his source (1 Kgs 8, 8) without reflecting that the ark was lost in the Babylonian destruction of Jerusalem; cf 2 Mc 2, 4–8.

## CHAPTER 6

**1** [k]Then Solomon said: "The LORD intends to dwell in the dark cloud. **2** I have truly built you a princely house and dwelling, where you may abide forever." **3** [l]Turning about, the king greeted the whole community of Israel as they stood. **4** He said: "Blessed be the LORD, the God of Israel, who with his own mouth made a promise to my father David and by his own hands brought it to fulfillment. He said: **5** 'Since the day I brought my people out of the land of Egypt, I have not chosen any city from among all the tribes of Israel for the building of a temple to my honor, nor have I chosen any man to be commander of my people Israel; **6** but now I choose Jerusalem, where I shall be honored, and I choose David to rule my people Israel.' **7** My father David wished to build a temple to the honor of the LORD, the God of Israel, **8** but the LORD said to him: 'In wishing to build a temple to my honor, you do well. **9** However, you shall not build the temple; rather, your son whom you will beget shall build the temple to my honor.'

**10** "Now the LORD has fulfilled the promise that he made. I have succeeded my father David and have taken my seat on the throne of Israel, as the LORD foretold, and I have built the temple to the honor of the LORD, the God of Israel. **11** And I have placed there the ark, in which abides the covenant of the LORD which he made with the Israelites."

**Solomon's Prayer.** **12** [m]Solomon then took his place before the altar of the LORD in the presence of the whole community of Israel and stretched forth his hands. **13** He had made a bronze platform five cubits long, five cubits wide, and three cubits high, which he had placed in the middle of the courtyard. Having ascended it, Solomon knelt in the presence of the whole of Israel and stretched forth his hands toward heaven.* **14** Thus he prayed: "LORD, God of Israel, there is no god like you in heaven or on earth; you keep your covenant and show kindness to your servants who are wholeheartedly faithful to you. **15** You have kept the promise you made to my father David, your servant. With your own mouth you spoke it, and by your own hand you have brought it to fulfillment this day. **16** Now, therefore, LORD, God of Israel, keep the further promise you made to my father David, your servant, when you said, 'You shall always have someone from your line to sit before me on the throne of Israel, provided only that your descendants look to their conduct so as always to live according to my law, even as you have lived in my presence.' **17** Now, LORD, God of Israel, may this promise which you made to your servant David be confirmed.

**18** "Can it indeed be that God dwells with mankind on earth? If the heavens and the highest heavens cannot contain you, how much less this temple which I have built! **19** Look kindly on the prayer and petition of your servant, O LORD, my God, and listen to the cry of supplication your servant makes before you. **20** May your eyes watch day and night over this temple, the place where you have decreed you shall be honored; may you heed the prayer which I your servant offer toward this place. **21** Listen to the petitions of your servant and of your people Israel which they direct toward this place. Listen from your heavenly dwelling, and when you have heard, pardon.

**22** "When any man sins against his neighbor and is required to take an oath of execration against himself, and when he comes for the oath before your altar in this temple, **23** listen from heaven: take action and pass judgment on your servants, requiting the wicked man and holding him responsible for his conduct, but absolving the innocent and rewarding him according to his virtue. **24** When your people Israel have sinned against you and are defeated by the enemy, but afterward they return and praise your name, and they pray to you and entreat you in this temple, **25** listen from heaven and forgive the sin of your people Israel, and bring them back to the land which you gave them and their fathers. **26** When the sky is closed so that there is no rain, because they have sinned against you, but then they pray toward this place and praise your name, and they withdraw from sin because you afflict them, **27** listen in heaven and forgive the sin of your servants and of your people Israel. But teach them the right way to live, and send rain upon your land which you gave your people as their heritage. **28** When there is famine in the land, when there is pestilence, or blight, or mildew, or locusts, or caterpillars; when their enemies besiege them at any of their gates; whenever there is a plague or sickness of any kind; **29** when any Israelite of all your people offers a prayer or petition of any kind, and in awareness of his affliction and pain, stretches out his hands toward this temple, **30** listen from your heavenly dwelling place, and forgive. Knowing his heart, render to everyone according to his conduct, for you alone know the hearts of men. **31** So may they fear you and walk in your ways as long as they live on the land you gave our fathers.

**32** "For the foreigner, too, who is not of your people Israel, when he comes from a dis-

k 1f: 1 Kgs 8, 12f. m 12-41: 1 Kgs 8, 22-53.
l 3-11: 1 Kgs 8, 14-21.

* 6, 13: This verse is not found in the Chronicler's source; cf 1 Kgs 8, 22f. He has Solomon praying on a bronze platform . . . in the middle of the courtyard because at the time of the Chronicler only the priests prayed before the alter.

tant land to honor your great name, your mighty
power, and your outstretched arm, when they
come in prayer to this temple, **33** listen from
your heavenly dwelling place, and do whatever
the foreigner entreats you, that all the peoples
of the earth may know your name, fearing you
as do your people Israel, and knowing that this
house which I have built is dedicated to your
honor.

**34** "When your people go forth to war
against their enemies, wherever you send them,
and pray to you in the direction of this city and
of the house I have built to your honor, **35** listen
from heaven to their prayer and petition, and
defend their cause. **36** When they sin against
you (for there is no man who does not sin), and
in your anger against them you deliver them to
the enemy, so that their captors deport them to
another land, far or near, **37** when they repent
in the land where they are captive and are converted, when they entreat you in the land of their
captivity and say, 'We have sinned and done
wrong; we have been wicked,' **38** and with
their whole heart and with their whole soul they
turn back to you in the land of those who hold
them captive, when they pray in the direction of
their land which you gave their fathers, and of
the city you have chosen, and of the house
which I have built to your honor, **39** listen from
your heavenly dwelling place, hear their prayer
and petitions, and uphold their cause. Forgive
your people who have sinned against you.
**40** My God, may your eyes be open and your
ears attentive to the prayer of this place. **41** And
now,

"Advance, LORD God, to your resting place,
you and the ark of your majesty.
May your priests, LORD God, be clothed
with salvation,
may your faithful ones rejoice in good
things.
**42** LORD God, reject not the plea of your
anointed,
remember the devotion of David, your
servant."

## CHAPTER 7

**1** [n]When Solomon had ended his prayer, fire
came down from heaven and consumed the
holocaust and the sacrifices, and the glory of the
LORD filled the house. **2** But the priests could
not enter the house of the LORD, for the glory
of the LORD had filled the house of the LORD.[o]
**3** All the Israelites looked on while the fire
came down and the glory of the LORD was upon
the house, and they fell down upon the pavement with their faces to the earth and adored,
praising the LORD, "for he is good, for his
mercy endures forever." **4** The king and all the
people were offering sacrifices before the
LORD.[p] **5** King Solomon offered as sacrifice
twenty-two thousand oxen, and one hundred
twenty thousand sheep.[q]

**End of the Dedication.** **6** Thus the king
and all the people dedicated the house of God.
The priests were standing at their stations, as
were the Levites, with the musical instruments
of the LORD which King David had made for
"praising the LORD, for his mercy endures forever," when David used them to accompany the
hymns. Across from them the priests blew the
trumpets and all Israel stood.[r]

**7** Then Solomon consecrated the middle part
of the court which lay before the house of the
LORD; there he offered the holocausts and the fat
of the peace offerings, since the bronze altar
which Solomon had made could not hold the
holocausts, the cereal offerings and the fat.[s]

**8** On this occasion Solomon and with him all
Israel, who had assembled in very large numbers from Labo of Hamath to the Wadi of Egypt,
celebrated the festival for seven days.[t] **9** [u]On
the eighth day they held a special meeting, for
they had celebrated the dedication of the altar
for seven days and the feast* for seven days.
**10** On the twenty-third day of the seventh
month he sent the people back to their tents,
rejoicing and glad at heart at the good things the
LORD had done for David, for Solomon, and for
his people Israel. **11** [v]Solomon completed the
house of the LORD and the royal palace; he
successfully accomplished everything he had
planned to do in regard to the house of the LORD
and his own house.

**God's Promise to Solomon.** **12** The
LORD appeared to Solomon during the night and
said to him: "I have heard your prayer, and I
have chosen this place for my house of sacrifice.
**13** If I close heaven so that there is no rain, if
I command the locust to devour the land, if I
send pestilence among my people, **14** and if my
people, upon whom my name has been pronounced, humble themselves and pray, and seek
my presence and turn from their evil ways, I will
hear them from heaven and pardon their sins and
revive their land. **15** Now my eyes shall be

n 1-10: 1 Kgs 8, 54-66; Jgs 6, 21; 1 Chr 21, 26; 2 Mc 2, 10.
o 2 Chr 5, 14; Ex 24, 16; 1 Kgs 8, 10f.
p 2 Chr 5, 13; 1 Kgs 8, 62; Ps 136, 1.
q 1 Kgs 8, 62f.
r Nm 10, 8. 10; Ps 136, 1.
s 1 Kgs 8, 64.
t 1 Kgs 8, 65.
u 9f: 1 Kgs 8, 66.
v 11-22: 1 Kgs 9, 1-9.

* 7, 9f: The feast: of Booths, celebrated on the fifteenth day of the seventh month and followed by a solemn octave lasting through the twenty-second day (Lv 23, 33-36; Nm 29, 12-35); the people are therefore sent home on the twenty-third day (v 10). The festival (v 8) for the dedication of the altar and of the temple lasted for seven days before the feast of Booths, from the seventh to the fourteenth day. According to 1 Kgs 8, 65f, the people are dismissed at the end of these seven days.

open and my ears attentive to the prayer of this place. **16** And now I have chosen and consecrated this house that my name may be there forever; my eyes and my heart also shall be there always.

**17** "As for you, if you live in my presence as your father David did, doing all that I have commanded you and keeping my statutes and ordinances, **18** I will establish your royal throne as I covenanted with your father David when I said, 'There shall never be lacking someone of yours as ruler in Israel.' **19** But if you turn away and forsake my statutes and commands which I placed before you, if you proceed to venerate and worship strange gods, **20** then I will uproot the people from the land I gave them; I will cast from my sight this house which I have consecrated to my honor, and I will make it a proverb and a byword among all peoples. **21** This temple which is so exalted —everyone passing by it will be amazed and ask: 'Why has the LORD done this to this land and to this house?' **22** And men will answer: 'They forsook the LORD, the God of their fathers, who brought them out of the land of Egypt, and they adopted strange gods and worshiped them and served them. That is why he has brought down upon them all this evil.' "

## CHAPTER 8

**Public Works.** **1** [w]After the twenty years during which Solomon built the house of the LORD and his own house, **2** he built up the cities which Huram had given him,* and settled Israelites there. **3** Then Solomon went to Hamath of Zoba and conquered it. **4** He built Tadmor* in the desert region and all the supply cities, which he built in Hamath. **5** [x]He built Upper Beth-horon and Lower Beth-horon, fortified cities with walls, gates and bars; **6** also Baalath, all the supply cities belonging to Solomon, and all the cities for the chariots, the cities for the horsemen, and whatever else Solomon decided should be built in Jerusalem, in the Lebanon, and in the entire land under his dominion. **7** All the people that remained of the Hittites, Amorites, Perizzites, Hivites, and Jebusites, who were not of Israel— **8** that is, their descendants remaining in the land, whom the Israelites had not destroyed—Solomon subjected to forced labor, as they continue to this day. **9** But Solomon did not enslave the Israelites for his works. They became soldiers, commanders of his warriors, and commanders of his chariots and his horsemen. **10** They were also King Solomon's two hundred and fifty overseers who had charge of the people.

**Solomon's Piety.** **11** Solomon brought the daughter of Pharaoh up from the City of David to the palace which he had built for her, for he said, "No wife of mine shall dwell in the house of David, king of Israel, for the places where the ark of the LORD has come are holy."

**12** In those times Solomon offered holocausts to the LORD upon the altar of the LORD which he had built in front of the porch, **13** as was required day by day according to the command of Moses, and in particular on the sabbaths, at the new moons, and on the fixed festivals three times a year: on the feast of the Unleavened Bread, the feast of Weeks and the feast of Booths.[y]

**14** And according to the ordinance of his father David he appointed the various classes of the priests for their service, and the Levites according to their functions of praise and ministry alongside the priests, as the daily duty required. The gatekeepers of the various classes stood guard at each gate, since such was the command of David, the man of God.[z] **15** There was no deviation from the king's command in any respect relating to the priests and Levites or the treasuries. **16** All of Solomon's work was carried out successfully from the day the foundation of the house of the LORD was laid until the house of the LORD had been completed in every detail.

**Glories of the Court.** **17** In those times Solomon went to Ezion-geber and to Elath on the seashore of the land of Edom.[a] **18** Huram, through his servants, sent him ships and crewmen acquainted with the sea, who accompanied Solomon's servants to Ophir and brought back from there four hundred and fifty talents of gold to King Solomon.[b]

## CHAPTER 9

**1** When the queen of Sheba heard of Solomon's fame, she came to Jerusalem to test him with subtle questions, accompanied by a very numerous retinue and by camels bearing spices, much gold, and precious stones. She came to Solomon and questioned him on every subject in which she was interested.[c] **2** Solomon explained to her everything she asked about, and

w 1f: 1 Kgs 9, 10f.
x 5-12: 1 Kgs 9, 18-25.
y 1 Kgs 9, 25; Ex 23, 14; Nm 28—29.
z 1 Chr 23—26; Neh 12, 46.
a 1 Kgs 9, 26; Mt 12, 42; Lk 11, 31.
b 1 Kgs 9, 27f.
c 1 Kgs 10, 1f; Mt 12, 42; Lk 11, 31.

*

8, 2: The cities which Huram had given him: according to 1 Kgs 9, 10–14, Solomon had ceded the cities as payment for the timber and gold received from Tyre. But since Huram was dissatisfied, he may have returned the cities to Solomon.

8, 4: Tadmor: later known as Palmyra, an important caravan city in the Syrian desert. The parallel passage in 1 Kgs 9, 18 has Tamar, in southern Judah; cf Ez 47, 19; 48, 28. But Solomon may well have fortified Tadmor against the Arameans.

there remained nothing hidden from Solomon
that he could not explain to her.
**3** When the queen of Sheba witnessed Solomon's wisdom, the palace he had built, **4** the
food at his table, the seating of his ministers, the
attendance of his servants and their dress, his
cupbearers and their dress, and the holocausts
he offered in the house of the LORD, it took her
breath away. **5** "The account I heard in my
country about your deeds and your wisdom is
true," she told the king. **6** "Yet I did not believe the report until I came and saw with my
own eyes. I have discovered that they did not
tell me the half of your great wisdom; you have
surpassed the stories I heard. **7** Happy are your
men, happy these servants of yours, who stand
before you always and listen to your wisdom.
**8** Blessed be the LORD, your God, who has
been so pleased with you as to place you on his
throne as king for the LORD, your God. Because
your God has so loved Israel as to will to make
it last forever, he has appointed you over them
as king to administer right and justice." **9** Then
she gave the king one hundred and twenty gold
talents and a very large quantity of spices, as
well as precious stones. There was no other
spice like that which the queen of Sheba gave
to King Solomon.
**10** The servants of Huram and of Solomon
who brought gold from Ophir also brought cabinet wood and precious stones. **11** With the
cabinet wood the king made stairs for the temple
of the LORD and the palace of the king; also lyres
and harps for the chanters. The like of these had
not been seen before in the land of Judah.
**12** King Solomon gave the queen of Sheba
everything she desired and asked him for, more
than she had brought to the king. Then she
returned to her own country with her servants.
**13** [d]The gold that Solomon received each
year weighed six hundred and sixty-six gold
talents, **14** in addition to what was collected
from travelers and what the merchants brought.
All the kings of Arabia also, and the governors
of the country, brought gold and silver to Solomon.
**15** Moreover, King Solomon made two hundred large shields of beaten gold, six hundred
shekels of beaten gold going into each shield,
**16** and three hundred bucklers of beaten gold,
three hundred shekels of gold going into each
buckler; these the king put in the hall of the
Forest of Lebanon.
**17** King Solomon also made a large ivory
throne which he overlaid with fine gold. **18** The
throne had six steps; a footstool of gold was
fastened to it, and there was an arm on each side
of the seat, with two lions standing beside the
arms. **19** Twelve other lions also stood there,
one on either side of each step. Nothing like this
had ever been produced in any other kingdom.
**20** Furthermore, all of King Solomon's drinking vessels were of gold, and all the utensils in
the hall of the Forest of Lebanon were of pure
gold; silver was not considered of value in Solomon's time. **21** For the king had ships that went
to Tarshish with the servants of Huram. Once
every three years the fleet of Tarshish would
return with a cargo of gold and silver, ivory,
apes and monkeys. **22** Thus King Solomon surpassed all the other kings of the earth in riches
as well as in wisdom.
**23** All the kings of the earth sought audience
with Solomon, to hear from him the wisdom
which God had put in his heart. **24** Year in and
year out, each one would bring his tribute—silver and gold articles, garments, weapons,
spices, horses and mules. **25** Solomon also had
four thousand stalls of horses, chariots, and
twelve thousand horsemen, which he assigned
to the chariot cities and to the king in Jerusalem.
**26** He was ruler over all the kings from the
River to the land of the Philistines and down to
the border of Egypt. **27** The king made silver as
common in Jerusalem as stones, while cedars
became as numerous as the sycamores of the
foothills. **28** Horses were imported for Solomon from Egypt and from all the lands.*

**The Death of Solomon.** **29** [e]The rest of
the acts of Solomon, first and last, are written,
as is well known, in the acts of Nathan the
prophet, in the prophecy of Ahijah the Shilonite, and in the visions of Iddo the seer which
concern Jeroboam, son of Nebat. **30** Solomon
reigned in Jerusalem over all Israel for forty
years. **31** He rested with his ancestors; he was
buried in his father's City of David, and his son
Rehoboam succeeded him as king.

# *II: The Monarchy before Hezekiah*

## CHAPTER 10

**Division of the Kingdom.** **1** [f]Rehoboam
went to Shechem, for all Israel* had come to
Shechem to proclaim him king. **2** When Jeroboam, son of Nebat, heard of this in Egypt
where he had fled from King Solomon, he returned from Egypt. **3** Jeroboam was summoned
to the assembly, and he and all Israel said to
Rehoboam: **4** "Your father laid a heavy yoke
upon us. If you now lighten the harsh service

d 13-28: 1 Kgs 10, 14-28. f 1-14: 1 Kgs 12, 1-14.
e 29ff: 1 Kgs 11, 41ff.

*

9, 28: See note on 2 Chr 1, 16f.

10, 1: All Israel: as in the original source (1 Kgs 12, 1), the northern tribes, distinct from Judah and Benjamin. Contrast the Chronicler's own terms, those Israelites who lived in the cities of Judah (v 17), and all the Israelites [literally, all Israel] in Judah and Benjamin (2 Chr 11, 3).

and the heavy yoke that your father imposed on us, we will serve you.'' **5** ''In three days,'' he answered them, ''come back to me.''

When the people had departed, **6** King Rehoboam consulted the elders who had been in the service of his father during Solomon's lifetime, asking, ''What answer do you advise me to give this people?'' **7** They replied, ''If you will deal kindly with this people and give in to them, acceding to their request, they will be your servants forever.'' **8** But he ignored the advice the elders had given him and consulted the young men who had grown up with him and were in his service. **9** He said to them, ''What answer do you advise me to give this people, who have asked me to lighten the yoke my father imposed on them?'' **10** The young men who had grown up with him replied: ''This is the answer you should give to this people who have said to you, 'Your father laid a heavy yoke upon us, but do you lighten our yoke'; this you should say to them: 'My little finger is thicker than my father's body. **11** Whereas my father put a heavy yoke on you, I will make it heavier! My father beat you with whips, but I will beat you with scorpions!' ''

**12** On the third day, Jeroboam and all the people came back to King Rehoboam as he had instructed them to do. **13** Ignoring the advice the elders had given him, the king gave them a harsh answer, **14** speaking to them according to the advice of the young men: ''My father laid a heavy yoke on you, but I will make it heavier. My father beat you with whips, but I will beat you with scorpions.'' **15** The king would not listen to the people, for this turn of events was divinely ordained to fulfill the prophecy the LORD had uttered to Jeroboam, the son of Nebat, through Ahijah the Shilonite.[g]

**16** [h]When all Israel saw that the king would not listen to them, the people answered the king,

''What share have we in David?
  We have no heritage in the son of Jesse.
Everyone to your tents, O Israel!
  Now look to your own house, David!''

So all Israel went off to their tents. **17** Rehoboam, therefore, reigned over only those Israelites who lived in the cities of Judah. **18** King Rehoboam then sent out Hadoram, who was superintendent of the forced labor, but the Israelites stoned him to death. Rehoboam himself managed to mount his chariot and flee to Jerusalem. **19** Thus Israel has been in rebellion against David's house to this day.

## CHAPTER 11

**1** [i]On his arrival in Jerusalem Rehoboam gathered together the house of Judah and Benjamin, a hundred and eighty thousand seasoned warriors, to have them fight against Israel and restore the kingdom to him. **2** However, the word of the LORD came to Shemiah, a man of God: **3** ''Say to Rehoboam, son of Solomon, king of Judah, and to all the Israelites in Judah and Benjamin: **4** 'Thus says the LORD: You must not march out to fight against your brothers. Let every man return home, for what has occurred I have brought about.' '' They obeyed this message of the LORD and gave up the expedition against Jeroboam.

**Rehoboam's Works.*** **5** Rehoboam took up residence in Jerusalem and built fortified cities in Judah. **6** He built up Bethlehem, Etam, Tekoa, **7** Beth-zur, Soco, Adullam, **8** Gath, Mareshah, Ziph, **9** Adoraim, Lachish, Azekah, **10** Zorah, Aijalon, and Hebron; these were fortified cities in Judah and Benjamin. **11** Then he strengthened the fortifications and put commanders in them, with supplies of food, oil and wine. **12** In every city were shields and spears, and he made them very strong. Thus Judah and Benjamin remained his.

**Refugees from the North.** **13** Now the priests and Levites throughout Israel presented themselves to him from all parts of their land, **14** for the Levites left their assigned pasture lands and their holdings and came to Judah and Jerusalem, because Jeroboam and his sons repudiated them as priests of the LORD.[j] **15** In their place, he himself appointed priests for the high places and satyrs and calves he had made.[k] **16** After them, all those of the Israelite tribes who firmly desired to seek the LORD, the God of Israel, came to Jerusalem to sacrifice to the LORD, the God of their fathers. **17** Thus they strengthened the kingdom of Judah and made Rehoboam, son of Solomon, prevail for three years; for they walked in the way of David and Solomon three years.

**Rehoboam's Family.** **18** Rehoboam took to himself as wife Mahalath, daughter of Jerimoth, son of David and of Abihail, daughter of Eliab, son of Jesse. **19** She bore him sons: Jehush, Shemariah and Zaham. **20** After her, he married Maacah, daughter of Absalom, who bore him Abijah, Attai, Ziza and Shelomith.[l] **21** Rehoboam loved Maacah, daughter of Absalom, more than all his other wives and concubines; he had taken eighteen wives and sixty concubines, and he fathered twenty-eight sons and sixty daughters. **22** Rehoboam constituted

g 1 Kgs 11, 29-39; 12, 15.
h 16-19: 1 Kgs 12, 16-19.
i 1-4: 1 Kgs 12, 21-24.
j 1 Kgs 12, 32.
k 1 Kgs 12, 32; Lv 17, 7.
l 1 Kgs 15, 2.

* 11, 5-12: These verses, though not found in 1 Kgs, are apparently based on a reliable, ancient source.

Abijah, son of Maacah, commander among his
brothers, for he intended to make him king.
**23** He acted prudently, distributing various of
his sons throughout all the districts of Judah and
Benjamin, in all the fortified cities; and he furnished them with copious provisions and sought
an abundance of wives for them.

## CHAPTER 12

**His Apostasy.** **1** After Rehoboam had consolidated his rule and had become powerful, he
abandoned the law of the LORD, he and all Israel
with him.[m] **2** Thus it happened that in the fifth
year of King Rehoboam, Shishak, king of
Egypt, attacked Jerusalem, for they had been
unfaithful to the LORD.[n] **3** He came up with
twelve hundred chariots and sixty thousand
horsemen, and there was no counting the army
that came with him from Egypt—Libyans, Sukkites* and Ethiopians. **4** They captured the fortified cities of Judah and came as far as Jerusalem. **5** Then Shemaiah the prophet came to
Rehoboam and the commanders of Judah who
had gathered at Jerusalem because of Shishak,
and said to them: "Thus says the LORD: 'You
have abandoned me, and therefore I have abandoned you to the power of Shishak.' "[o]

**6** However, the commanders of Israel and
the king humbled themselves, saying, "The
LORD is just." **7** When the LORD saw that they
had humbled themselves, the word of the LORD
came to Shemaiah: "Because they have humbled themselves, I will not destroy them; I will
give them some deliverance, and my wrath shall
not be poured out upon Jerusalem through Shishak. **8** But they shall be his servants, that they
may know what it is to serve me and what it is
to serve earthly kingdoms." **9** [p]Therefore Shishak, king of Egypt, attacked Jerusalem and
carried off the treasures of the temple of the
LORD and of the king's palace. He took everything, including the gold bucklers that Solomon
had made. **10** (To replace them, King Rehoboam made bronze bucklers, which he entrusted to
the officers of the guard on duty at the entrance
of the royal palace. **11** Whenever the king visited the temple of the LORD, the troops would
come bearing them, and then they would return
them to the guardroom.) **12** Because he had
humbled himself, the anger of the LORD turned
from him so that it did not destroy him completely; and in Judah, moreover, good deeds
were found.

**13** King Rehoboam consolidated his power
in Jerusalem and continued to rule; he was forty-one years old when he became king, and he
reigned seventeen years in Jerusalem, the city in
which, out of all the tribes of Israel, the LORD
chose to be honored. Rehoboam's mother was
named Naamah, an Ammonite.[q] **14** He did
evil, for he had not truly resolved to seek the
LORD. **15** [r]The acts of Rehoboam, first and
last, are written, as is well known, in the history
of Shemaiah the prophet and of Iddo the seer
[his family record]. There was war continually
between Rehoboam and Jeroboam. **16** Rehoboam rested with his ancestors; he was buried in
the City of David. His son Abijah succeeded
him as king.

## CHAPTER 13

**War between Abijah and Jeroboam.**
**1** [s]In the eighteenth year of King Jeroboam,
Abijah became king of Judah; **2** he reigned
three years in Jerusalem. His mother was named
Michaiah, daughter of Uriel of Gibeah. There
was war between Abijah and Jeroboam.

**3** Abijah joined battle with a force of four
hundred thousand picked warriors, while Jeroboam lined up against him in battle with eight
hundred thousand picked and valiant warriors.
**4** *Abijah stood on Mount Zemaraim, which is
in the highlands of Ephraim, and said: "Listen
to me, Jeroboam and all Israel! **5** Do you not
know that the LORD, the God of Israel, has given
the kingdom of Israel to David forever, to him
and to his sons, by a covenant made in salt?
**6** Yet Jeroboam, son of Nebat, the servant of
Solomon, son of David, has stood up and rebelled against his lord![t] **7** Worthless men,
scoundrels, joined him and overcame Rehoboam, son of Solomon, when Rehoboam was
young and unthinking, and no match for them.
**8** But now, do you think you are a match for the
kingdom of the LORD commanded by the sons
of David, simply because you are a huge multitude and have with you the golden calves which
Jeroboam made you for gods?

**9** "Have you not expelled the priests of the
LORD, the sons of Aaron, and the Levites, and
made for yourselves priests like the peoples of
foreign lands? Everyone who comes to consecrate himself with a young bull and seven rams
becomes a priest of no-gods. **10** But as for us,
the LORD is our God, and we have not forsaken
him. The priests ministering to the LORD are
sons of Aaron, and the Levites also have their
offices. **11** They burn holocausts to the LORD
and fragrant incense morning after morning and
evening after evening; they display the showbread on the pure table, and the lamps of the
golden lampstand burn evening after evening;

m 1 Kgs 11, 4; 14, 22.
n 1 Kgs 14, 25.
o 2 Chr 11, 2.
p 9ff: 1 Kgs 14, 25-28.
q 1 Kgs 14, 21.
r 15f: 1 Kgs 14, 29ff.
s 1f: 1 Kgs 15, 1f.
t 1 Kgs 11, 26.

* 12, 3: Sukkites: foreign mercenaries in the Egyptian army.

13, 4–12: This is a free composition of the Chronicler to show that this was a religious, rather than a political, war.

for we observe our duties to the LORD, our God,
but you have abandoned him. **12** See, God is
with us, at our head, and his priests are here
with trumpets to sound the attack against you.
Do not battle against the LORD, the God of your
fathers, O Israelites, for you will not succeed!"
**13** But Jeroboam had an ambush go around
them to come at them from the rear; so that
while his army faced Judah, his ambush lay
behind them. **14** When Judah turned and saw
that they had to battle on both fronts, they cried
out to the LORD and the priests sounded the
trumpets. **15** Then the men of Judah shouted;
and when they did so, God defeated Jeroboam
and all Israel before Abijah and Judah. **16** The
Israelites fled before Judah, and God delivered
them into their hands. **17** Abijah and his people
inflicted a severe defeat upon them; five hundred thousand picked men of Israel fell slain.
**18** The Israelites were subdued on that occasion
and the Judahites were victorious because they
relied on the LORD, the God of their fathers.
**19** Abijah pursued Jeroboam and took cities
from him: Bethel and its dependencies, Jeshanah and its dependencies, and Ephron and its
dependencies. **20** Jeroboam did not regain
power during the time of Abijah; the LORD
struck him down and he died, **21** while Abijah
continued to grow stronger. He took to himself
fourteen wives and fathered twenty-two sons
and sixteen daughters.

**Death of Abijah.** **22** [u]The rest of Abijah's
acts, his deeds and his words, are written in the
midrash of the prophet Iddo. **23** Abijah rested
with his ancestors; they buried him in the City
of David. His son Asa succeeded him as king.
During his time, ten years of peace began in the
land.

## CHAPTER 14

**Asa the Reformer.** **1** [v]Asa did what was
good and pleasing to the LORD, his God, **2** removing the heathen altars and the high places,
breaking to pieces the sacred pillars, and cutting
down the sacred poles. **3** He commanded Judah
to seek the LORD, the God of their fathers, and
to observe the law and its commands. **4** He
removed the high places and incense stands
from all the cities of Judah, and under him the
kingdom had peace. **5** He built fortified cities
in Judah, for the land had peace and no war was
waged against him during these years, because
the LORD had given him peace. **6** He said to
Judah: "Let us build these cities and surround
them with walls, towers, gates and bars. The
land is still ours, for we have sought the LORD,
our God; we sought him, and he has given us
rest on every side." So they built and prospered.

**The Ethiopian Invasion.*** **7** Asa had an
army of three hundred thousand shield and lan-
cebearers from Judah, and two hundred and
eighty thousand from Benjamin who carried
bucklers and were archers, all of them valiant
warriors. **8** Zerah the Ethiopian moved against
them with a force of one million men and three
hundred chariots, and he came as far as Mareshah.[w] **9** Asa went out to meet him and set
himself in battle array in the valley of Zepha-
thah, near Mareshah. **10** Asa called upon the
LORD, his God, praying: "O LORD, there is
none like you to help the powerless against the
strong. Help us, O LORD, our God, for we rely
on you, and in your name we have come against
this multitude. You are the LORD, our God; let
no man prevail against you."[x] **11** And so the
LORD defeated the Ethiopians before Asa and
Judah, and they fled.[y] **12** Asa and those with
him pursued them as far as Gerar, and the Ethiopians fell until there were no survivors, for they
were crushed before the LORD and his army,
which carried away enormous spoils. **13** Then
the Judahites conquered all the cities around
Gerar, for the fear of the LORD was upon them;
they despoiled all the cities, for there was much
booty in them. **14** They attacked also the tents
of the cattle-herders and carried off a great number of sheep and camels. Then they returned to
Jerusalem.

## CHAPTER 15

**Cult Reform.** **1** Upon Azariah, son of
Oded, came the spirit of God. **2** He went forth
to meet Asa and said to him: "Hear me, Asa and
all Judah and Benjamin! The LORD is with you
when you are with him, and if you seek him he
will be present to you; but if you abandon him,
he will abandon you.[z] **3** For a long time Israel
had no true God, no priest-teacher and no law,
**4** but when in their distress they turned to the
LORD, the God of Israel, and sought him, he was
present to them.[a] **5** In that former time there
was no place for anyone to go or come, but there
were many terrors upon the inhabitants of the
lands. **6** Nation crushed nation and city crushed
city, for God destroyed them by every kind of
adversity.[b] **7** But as for you, be strong and do
not relax, for your work shall be rewarded."[c]

u 22f: 2 Chr 12, 15; 1 Kgs 7ff.
v 1f: 2 Chr 33, 15; Ex 23, 24; 34, 13; 1 Kgs 15, 11f.
w 2 Chr 16, 8.
x 2 Chr 32, 8.
y Pss 20, 7f; 60, 11f.
z Jer 29, 13f; Hos 3, 4f.
a Dt 4, 29f.
b Is 19, 2.
c Is 7, 4; Jer 31, 16.

* 14, 7–14: An Ethiopian invasion of Judah is mentioned only in 1 Chronicles. This account may be a legend contrived to show how the pious King Asa was rewarded through divine assistance. There may, however, have been an incursion of nomads from the Negeb at this time; cf vv 13f.

**8** When Asa heard these words and the prophecy [Oded the prophet], he was encouraged to remove the detestable idols from the whole land of Judah and Benjamin and from the cities he had taken in the highlands of Ephraim, and to restore the altar of the LORD which was before the vestibule of the LORD. **9** Then he convened all Judah and Benjamin, together with those of Ephraim, Manasseh and Simeon who sojourned with them; for many had fled to him from Israel when they saw that the LORD, his God, was with him. **10** *They gathered at Jerusalem in the third month of the fifteenth year of Asa's reign, **11** and sacrificed to the LORD at that time seven hundred oxen and seven thousand sheep of the booty they had brought. **12** They entered into a covenant to seek the LORD, the God of their fathers, with all their heart and soul; **13** and everyone who would not seek the LORD, the God of Israel, was to be put to death, whether small or great, whether man or woman.[d] **14** They swore to the LORD with a loud voice, with shouting and with trumpets and horns. **15** All Judah rejoiced over the oath, for they had sworn with their whole heart and sought him with complete desire, so that he was present to them. And the LORD gave them rest on every side.[e]

**16** [f]Maacah, the mother of King Asa, he deposed as queen mother because she had made an outrageous object for Asherah; Asa cut this down, smashed it, and burnt it in the Kidron Valley. **17** Although the high places did not disappear from Israel, yet Asa's heart was undivided as long as he lived. **18** He brought into the house of God his father's votive offerings and his own: silver, gold, and various utensils. **19** There was no war until the thirty-fifth year of Asa's reign.

## CHAPTER 16

**Asa's Infidelity.** **1** [g]In the thirty-sixth year of Asa's reign, Baasha, king of Israel, attacked Judah and fortified Ramah to prevent any communication with Asa, king of Judah. **2** Asa then brought out silver and gold from the treasuries of the temple of the LORD and of the royal palace and sent them to Ben-hadad, king of Aram, who lived in Damascus, with this message: **3** "There is a treaty between you and me, as there was between your father and my father. See, I am sending you silver and gold. Go, break your treaty with Baasha, king of Israel, that he may withdraw from me." **4** Ben-hadad agreed to King Asa's request and sent the leaders of his troops against the cities of Israel. They attacked Ijon, Dan, Abelmaim, and all the store cities of Naphtali. **5** When Baasha heard of it, he left off fortifying Ramah; he stopped his work. **6** Then King Asa commandeered all of Judah to carry away the stone and wood with which Baasha had been fortifying Ramah, and with them he fortified Geba and Mizpah.

**7** At that time Hanani the seer came to Asa, king of Judah, and said to him: "Because you relied on the king of Aram and did not rely on the LORD, your God, the army of the king of Aram has escaped* your hand. **8** Were not the Ethiopians and Libyans a vast army, with great numbers of chariots and drivers? And yet, because you relied on the LORD, he delivered them into your power.[h] **9** The eyes of the LORD roam over the whole earth, to encourage those who are devoted to him wholeheartedly. You have acted foolishly in this matter, for from now on you will have wars."[i] **10** But Asa became angry with the seer and imprisoned him in the stocks, so greatly was he enraged at him over this. Asa also oppressed some of his people at this time.

**11** [j]Now the acts of Asa, first and last, can be found recorded in the book of the kings of Judah and Israel. **12** In the thirty-ninth year of his reign, Asa contracted a serious disease in his feet. But even in his sickness he did not seek the LORD, but only the physicians. **13** Asa rested with his ancestors; he died in the forty-first year of his reign. **14** They buried him in the tomb he had hewn for himself in the City of David, having laid him upon a couch which was filled with spices and various kinds of aromatics compounded into an ointment. They also burned a very great funeral pyre for him.

## CHAPTER 17

**Zeal of Jehoshaphat for the Law.** **1** His son Jehoshaphat succeeded him as king and strengthened his hold against Israel.[k] **2** He placed armed forces in all the fortified cities of Judah, and put garrisons in the land of Judah and in the cities of Ephraim which his father Asa had taken. **3** The LORD was with Jehoshaphat,* for he walked in the ways his father had pursued in the beginning, and he did not consult the Baals.

d Neh 10, 30.
e Dt 4, 29.
f 16ff: 1 Kgs 15, 13ff.
g 1-6: 1 Kgs 15, 16-21.
h 2 Chr 14, 8-14.
i Ps 33, 13ff.
j 11-14: 1 Kgs 15, 23f.
k 1 Kgs 15, 24.

*

15, 10ff: With this description of a covenant ceremony in the third month of a year beginning in the spring, the Chronicler lays a foundation for celebrating the ancient feast of Pentecost (Weeks) as the time for a solemn renewal of the people's covenant with God on Mount Sinai; see Ex 19, 1ff; Lv 23, 16 and the note there. This is also the background for Pentecost as the "birthday of the Church."

16, 7: The king of Aram ... escaped: according to the Lucianic recension, "the king of Israel escaped": this may well be the original reading; Asa was friendly with Aram.

17, 3: The Lord was with Jehoshaphat: along with Hezekiah and Josiah, Jehoshaphat was one of the Chronicler's favorite kings.

**4** Rather, he sought the God of his father and
observed his commands, and not the practices
of Israel. **5** As a result, the LORD made his
kingdom secure, and all Judah gave Jehoshaphat gifts, so that he enjoyed great wealth and
glory. **6** Thus he was encouraged to follow the
LORD's ways, and again he removed the high
places and the sacred poles from Judah.[l]
**7** In the third year of his reign he sent his
leading men, Ben-hail, Obadiah, Zechariah,
Nethanel and Micaiah, to teach in the cities of
Judah. **8** With them he sent the Levites Shemaiah, Nethaniah, Zebadiah, Asahel, Shemira-
moth, Jehonathan, Adonijah and Tobijah, together with the priests Elishama and Jehoram.[m]
**9** They taught in Judah, having with them the
book containing the law of the LORD; they traveled through all the cities of Judah and taught
among the people.[n]

**His Power.** **10** Now the fear of the LORD
was upon all the kingdoms of the countries surrounding Judah, so that they did not war against
Jehoshaphat. **11** Some of the Philistines
brought Jehoshaphat gifts and a tribute of silver;
and the Arabs also brought him a flock of seven
thousand seven hundred rams and seven thousand seven hundred he-goats.
**12** Jehoshaphat grew steadily greater. He
built strongholds and store cities in Judah.
**13** He carried out many works in the cities of
Judah, and he had soldiers, valiant warriors, in
Jerusalem. **14** This was their mustering according to their ancestral houses. Of Judah, the commanders of thousands: Adnah the commander,
and with him three hundred thousand valiant
warriors. **15** Next to him, Jehohanan the commander, and with him two hundred eighty thousand. **16** Next to him, Amasiah, son of Zichri,
who offered himself to the LORD, and with him
two hundred thousand valiant warriors.
**17** From Benjamin: Eliada, a valiant warrior,
and with him two hundred thousand armed with
bow and buckler. **18** Next to him, Jozabad, and
with him one hundred and eighty thousand
equipped for war. **19** These were at the service
of the king; in addition were those whom the
king had placed in the fortified cities throughout
all Judah.

## CHAPTER 18

**Alliance with Israel.** **1** [o]Jehoshaphat
therefore had wealth and glory in abundance;
but he became related to Ahab by marriage.
**2** After some years he went down to Ahab at
Samaria; Ahab offered numerous sheep and
oxen for him and the people with him, and
persuaded him to go up against Ramoth-gilead.
**3** Ahab, king of Israel, asked Jehoshaphat, king
of Judah, "Will you come with me to Ramoth-gilead?" "You and I are as one," was his
answer; "your people and my people as well.
We will be with you in the battle." **4** But Jehoshaphat also said to the king of Israel, "Seek
the word of the LORD at once."

**The Prophets.** **5** The king of Israel gathered his prophets, four hundred in number, and
asked them, "Shall we go to attack Ramoth-gilead, or shall I refrain?" "Go up," they answered. "God will deliver it over to the king."
**6** But Jehoshaphat said, "Is there no other
prophet of the LORD here whom we may consult?" **7** The king of Israel answered Jehoshaphat, "There is still another through whom we
may consult the LORD, but I hate him, for he
prophesies not good but always evil about me.
That is Micaiah, son of Imlah." Jehoshaphat
said, "Let not your Majesty speak of evil
against you." **8** So the king of Israel called an
official, to whom he said, "Get Micaiah, son of
Imlah, at once." **9** The king of Israel and King
Jehoshaphat of Judah were seated each on his
throne, clothed in their robes of state on a
threshing floor at the entrance of the gate of
Samaria, and all the prophets were prophesying
before them.
**10** Zedekiah, son of Chenaanah, made iron
horns for himself and said: "The LORD says,
'With these you shall gore Aram until you have
destroyed them.' " **11** The other prophets
prophesied in the same vein, saying: "Go up to
Ramoth-gilead. You shall succeed; the LORD
will deliver it over to the king." **12** *The messenger who had gone to call Micaiah said to
him: "Look now, the prophets unanimously
predict good for the king. Let your word, like
each of theirs, predict good." **13** "As the LORD
lives," Micaiah answered, "I will say what my
God tells me."
**14** When he came to the king, the king said
to him, "Micaiah, shall we go to fight against
Ramoth-gilead, or shall I refrain?" "Go up,"
he answered, "and succeed; they will be delivered into your power." **15** But the king said to
him, "How many times must I adjure you to tell
me nothing but the truth in the name of the
LORD?" **16** Then Micaiah answered:

"I see all Israel
scattered on the mountains,
like sheep without a shepherd,
and the LORD saying, 'These have no
master!
Let each of them go back home in peace.' "

**17** The king of Israel said to Jehoshaphat, "Did
I not tell you that he prophesies no good about

l 2 Chr 20, 33; Ex 34, 13.
m 2 Chr 19, 8.
n Ezr 7, 25.
o 1-34: 1 Kgs 22, 1-35.

* 18, 12–22: See note on 1 Kgs 22, 19–23.

me, but only evil?'' **18** But Micaiah continued:
''Therefore hear the word of the LORD: I saw the
LORD seated on his throne, with the whole host
of heaven standing by to his right and to his left.
**19** The LORD asked, 'Who will deceive Ahab,
king of Israel, so that he will go up and fall at
Ramoth-gilead?' And one said this, another
that, **20** until a spirit came forward and presented himself to the LORD, saying, 'I will deceive
him,' The LORD asked, 'How?' **21** He answered, 'I will go forth and become a lying
spirit in the mouths of all his prophets.' The
LORD agreed: 'You shall succeed in deceiving
him. Go forth and do this.' **22** So now the LORD
himself has put a lying spirit in the mouths of
these your prophets, but the LORD himself has
decreed evil against you.''

**23** Thereupon Zedekiah, son of Chenaanah,
came up and slapped Micaiah on the cheek,
saying, ''Which way did the spirit of the LORD
go when he left me to speak to you?'' **24** ''You
shall find out,'' Micaiah replied, ''on that day
when you enter an innermost chamber to hide.''
**25** The king of Israel then said: ''Seize Micaiah
and take him back to Amon, prefect of the city,
and to Joash the king's son, **26** and say, 'This
is the king's order: Put this man in prison and
feed him scanty rations of bread and water until
I return in safety!' '' **27** But Micaiah said, ''If
ever you return in safety, the LORD has not
spoken through me.'' And he said, ''Hear, O
peoples, all of you!''*

**Ahab's Death.** **28** The king of Israel and
King Jehoshaphat of Judah went up to Ramoth-gilead **29** and the king of Israel said to
Jehoshaphat, ''I will go into battle disguised,
but you put on your own clothes.'' So the king
of Israel disguised himself and they entered the
fray. **30** Meanwhile, the king of Aram had giv-
en his chariot commanders the order, ''Fight
with no one, small or great, except the king of
Israel.'' **31** When the commanders saw Jehoshaphat, they exclaimed, ''That must be the king
of Israel!'' and shifted to fight him. But Jehoshaphat cried out and the LORD helped him; God
induced them to leave him. **32** The chariot
commanders became aware that he was not the
king of Israel and gave up their pursuit of him.
**33** Someone, however, drew his bow at random and hit the king of Israel between the joints
of his breastplate. He ordered his charioteer,
''Rein about and take me out of the ranks, for
I am disabled.''[p] **34** The battle grew fierce during the day, and the king of Israel braced himself up on his chariot facing the Arameans until
evening. He died as the sun was setting.

## CHAPTER 19

**Jehoshaphat Rebuked.** **1** King Jehoshaphat of Judah returned in safety to his house in
Jerusalem. **2** Jehu the seer, son of Hanani,* met
King Jehoshaphat and said to him: ''Should you
help the wicked and love those who hate the
LORD? For this reason, wrath is upon you from
the LORD. **3** Yet some good things are to be
found in you, since you have removed the sacred poles from the land and have been determined to seek God.''

**Judges Appointed.** **4** Jehoshaphat dwelt
in Jerusalem; but he went out again among the
people from Beer-sheba to the highlands of
Ephraim and brought them back to the LORD,
the God of their fathers. **5** He appointed judges
in the land, in all the fortified cities of Judah,
city by city, **6** and he said to them: ''Take care
what you do, for you are judging, not on behalf
of man, but on behalf of the LORD; he judges
with you.[q] **7** And now, let the fear of the LORD
be upon you. Act carefully, for with the LORD,
our God, there is no injustice, no partiality, no
bribe-taking.''[r] **8** In Jerusalem also, Jehoshaphat appointed some Levites and priests and
some of the family heads of Israel to judge in the
name of the LORD and to settle quarrels among
the inhabitants of Jerusalem.[s] **9** He gave them
this command: ''You shall act faithfully and
wholeheartedly in the fear of the LORD. **10** And
in every dispute that your brethren living in their
cities bring to you, whether it concerns blood-
guilt or questions of law, command, statutes, or
judgments, warn them lest they become guilty
before the LORD and his wrath come upon you
and your brethren. Do that and you shall be
guiltless.[t] **11** See now, Amariah is high priest
over you in everything that pertains to the LORD,
and Zebadiah, son of Ishmael, is leader of the
house of Judah in all that pertains to the king;
and the Levites will be your officials. Act firmly, and the LORD will be with the good.''

## CHAPTER 20

**Invasion from Edom.*** **1** After this the
Moabites, the Ammonites, and with them some

p 2 Chr 35, 23; 1 Kgs 22, 34.
q Dt 1, 16ff; 16, 19f.
r Dt 10, 17.
s 2 Chr 17, 8f; Dt 17, 8-13; Ps 122, 3ff.
t Nm 35, 19.

*

18, 27: "Hear, O peoples, all of you!": this quotation, which appears in some texts of 1 Kgs 22, 28, ascribes to the prophets Micaiah ben Imlah the opening words of the prophetic utterance of Micah of Moresheth (Mi 1, 2), a century later.

19, 2: Jehu the seer, son of Hanani: hardly the same seer as Jehu, son of Hanani, who prophesied against Baasha almost 50 years earlier (1 Kgs 16–1).

20, 1–30: Although the account here seems to be a free composition of the Chronicler, there is probably a basis in fact

Meunites came to fight against Jehoshaphat.
**2** The message was brought to Jehoshaphat: "A
great multitude is coming against you from
across the sea, from Edom; they are already in
Hazazontamar" (which is En-gedi). **3** Jehoshaphat was frightened, and he hastened to consult
the LORD. He proclaimed a fast for all Judah.
**4** Then Judah gathered to seek help from the
LORD; from every one of the cities of Judah they
came to seek the LORD.[u]

**Prayer of Jehoshaphat.** **5** Jehoshaphat
stood up in the assembly of Judah and Jerusalem
in the house of the LORD before the new court,
**6** and he said: "LORD, God of our fathers, are
you not the God in heaven, and do you not rule
over all the kingdoms of the nations? In your
hand is power and might, and no one can withstand you.[v] **7** Was it not you, our God, who
drove out the inhabitants of this land before your
people Israel and gave it forever to the descendants of Abraham, your friend?[w] **8** They have
dwelt in it and they built in it a sanctuary to your
honor, saying, **9** 'When evil comes upon us,
the sword of judgment, or pestilence, or famine,
we will stand before this house and before you,
for your name is in this house, and we will cry
out to you in our affliction, and you will hear
and save!' **10** And now, see the Ammonites,
Moabites, and those of Mount Seir whom you
did not allow Israel to invade when they came
from the land of Egypt, but instead they passed
them by and did not destroy them.[x] **11** See how
they are now repaying us by coming to drive us
out of the possession you have given us. **12** O
our God, will you not pass judgment on them?
We are powerless before this vast multitude that
comes against us. We are at a loss what to do,
hence our eyes are turned toward you."

**Victory Prophesied.** **13** All Judah was
standing before the LORD, with their little ones,
their wives, and their young sons. **14** And the
spirit of the LORD came upon Jahaziel, son of
Zechariah, son of Benaiah, son of Jeiel, son of
Mattaniah, a Levite of the clan of Asaph, in the
midst of the assembly, **15** and he said: "Listen,
all of Judah, inhabitants of Jerusalem, and King
Jehoshaphat! The LORD says to you: 'Do not
fear or lose heart at the sight of this vast multitude, for the battle is not yours but God's.
**16** Go down against them tomorrow. You will
see them coming up by the ascent of Ziz, and
you will come upon them at the end of the wadi
which opens on the wilderness of Jeruel.
**17** You will not have to fight in this encounter.
Take your places, stand firm, and see how the
LORD will be with you to deliver you, Judah and
Jerusalem. Do not fear or lose heart. Tomorrow
go out to meet them, and the LORD will be with
you.' "[y] **18** Then Jehoshaphat knelt down with
his face to the ground, and all Judah and the
inhabitants of Jerusalem fell down before the
LORD in worship. **19** Levites from among the
Kohathites and Korahites rose to sing the
praises of the LORD, the God of Israel, in a
resounding chorus.

**The Invaders Destroyed.** **20** In the early
morning they hastened out to the wilderness of
Tekoa. As they were going out, Jehoshaphat
halted and said: "Listen to me, Judah and inhabitants of Jerusalem! Trust in the LORD, your
God, and you will be found firm. Trust in his
prophets and you will succeed."[z] **21** After consulting with the people, he appointed some to
sing to the LORD and some to praise the holy
Appearance* as it went forth at the head of the
army. They sang: "Give thanks to the LORD, for
his mercy endures forever."[a] **22** At the moment they began their jubilant hymn, the LORD
laid an ambush against the Ammonites, Moabites, and those of Mount Seir who were coming
against Judah, so that they were vanquished.
**23** For the Ammonites and Moabites set upon
the inhabitants of Mount Seir and completely
exterminated them. And when they had finished
with the inhabitants of Seir, they began to destroy each other.[b]
**24** When Judah came to the watchtower of
the desert and looked toward the throng, they
saw only corpses fallen on the ground, with no
survivors. **25** Jehoshaphat and his people came
to take plunder, and they found an abundance of
cattle and personal property, garments and precious vessels. They took so much that they were
unable to carry it all; they were three days taking
the spoil, so great was it. **26** On the fourth day
they held an assembly in the Valley of Beracah—for there they blessed the LORD; therefore
that place has ever since been called the Valley
of Beracah.* **27** Then all the men of Judah and
Jerusalem, with Jehoshaphat at their head,
turned back toward Jerusalem celebrating the
joyful victory the LORD had given them over
their enemies. **28** They came to Jerusalem, to
the house of the LORD, with harps, lyres and
trumpets. **29** And the fear of God came upon all
the kingdoms of the surrounding lands when
they heard how the LORD had fought against the

---

u Jer 36, 6; Jb 1, 14.
v 2 Chr 32, 7; Dt 4, 39.
w Dn 3, 35.
x Dt 2, 4f. 9f. 18f.
y Is 8, 10.
z Is 7, 9.
a Ps 136, 1.
b Jos 6, 17; Ez 38, 21.

---

* for it; there could well have been a raid of nomads against Judah in the reign of Jehoshaphat, similar to Zerah's attack on Asa (2 Chr 14, 8–14). The story may also, in some way, be connected with the campaign of Israel and Judah against Moab through the territory of Edom (2 Kgs 3, 4–27).

20, 21: Holy Appearance: the Lord, who is with the Israelite army (v 17), manifests himself (the same language is in Ps 29, 2) in bringing Israel the victory (Ex 14, 14. 24).

20, 26: Beracah: the Hebrew word for "blessing."

enemies of Israel. **30** Thereafter Jehoshaphat's
kingdom enjoyed peace, for his God gave him
rest on every side.

**Jehoshaphat's Other Deeds.** **31** [c]Thus
Jehoshaphat reigned over Judah. He was thirty-five years old when he became king, and he
reigned twenty-five years in Jerusalem. His
mother was named Azubah, daughter of Shilhi.
**32** He followed the path of his father Asa unswervingly, doing what was right in the LORD's
sight. **33** But the high places were not removed,
nor as yet had the people fixed their hearts on
the God of their fathers.

**34** The rest of the acts of Jehoshaphat, first
and last, can be found written in the chronicle
of Jehu, son of Hanani, which is inserted in the
book of the kings of Israel. **35** After this, King
Jehoshaphat of Judah allied himself with King
Ahaziah of Israel, who did evil. **36** [d]He joined
with him in building ships to sail to Tarshish; the
fleet was built at Ezion-geber. **37** But Eliezer,
son of Dodavahu from Mareshah, prophesied
against Jehoshaphat, saying, "Because you
have joined with Ahaziah, the LORD will shatter
your work." And the ships were wrecked and
were unable to sail to Tarshish.

## CHAPTER 21

**1** Jehoshaphat rested with his ancestors; he
was buried with them in the City of David.
Jehoram, his son, succeeded him as king.[e]
**2** His brothers, sons of Jehoshaphat, were Azariah, Jehiel, Zechariah, Azariah, Michael and
Shephatiah; all these were sons of King Jehoshaphat of Judah. **3** Their father gave them numerous gifts of silver, gold and precious objects, together with fortified cities in Judah, but
the kingship he gave to Jehoram because he was
the first-born.

**Evil Deeds of Jehoram.** **4** When Jehoram
had come into his father's kingdom and had
consolidated his power, he put to the sword all
his brothers and also some of the princes of
Israel. **5** [f]Jehoram was thirty-two years old
when he became king, and he reigned eight
years in Jerusalem. **6** He conducted himself
like the kings of Israel of the line of Ahab,
because one of Ahab's daughters* was his wife.
He did evil in the sight of the LORD, **7** but the
LORD would not destroy the house of David
because of the covenant he had made with David and because of his promise to give him and
his sons a lamp for all time.[g]

**8** [h]During his time Edom revolted against
the soveriegnty of Judah; they chose a king of
their own. **9** Thereupon Jehoram crossed over
with his officers and all the chariots he had. He
arose by night and broke through the Edomites
when they had surrounded him and the commanders of his chariots. **10** However, Edom
has continued in revolt against the sovereignty
of Judah down to the present time. Libnah also
revolted at that time against Jehoram's sovereignty because he had forsaken the LORD, the
God of his fathers. **11** He also set up high
places in the mountains of Judah; he led the
inhabitants of Jerusalem into idolatry and seduced Judah.

**Retribution.** **12** He received a letter from
the prophet Elijah* with this message: Thus
says the LORD, the God of your ancestor David:
'Because you have not followed the path of your
father Jehoshaphat, nor of Asa, king of Judah,
**13** but instead have walked in the way of the
kings of Israel and have led Judah and the inhabitants of Jerusalem into idolatry, as did the
house of Ahab, and also because you have murdered your brothers of your father's house who
were better than you, **14** the LORD will strike
your people, your children, your wives, and all
that is yours with a great plague; **15** and you
shall have severe pains from a disease in your
bowels, while your bowels issue forth because
of the disease, day after day.' "

**16** Then the LORD stirred up against Jehoram
the animosity of the Philistines and of the Arabs
who bordered on the Ethiopians. **17** They came
up against Judah, invaded it, and carried away
all the wealth found in the king's palace, along
with his sons and his wives; there was left to him
only one son, Jehoahaz, his youngest. **18** After
these events, the LORD afflicted him with an
incurable disease of the bowels. **19** As time
went on until a period of two years had elapsed,
his bowels issued forth because of the disease
and he died in great pain. His people did not
make a pyre for him like that of his fathers.
**20** He was thirty-two years old when he became
king, and he reigned eight years in Jerusalem.
He departed unloved and was buried in the City
of David, but not in the tombs of the kings.[i]

## CHAPTER 22

**Ahaziah.** **1** [j]Then the inhabitants of Jerusalem made Ahaziah, his youngest son, king in his
stead, since all the older sons had been slain by

c 31-34: 1 Kgs 22, 41-45.
d 36f: 1 Kgs 22, 48f.
e 1 Kgs 22, 51.
f 5ff: 2 Kgs 8, 17ff.
g 1 Kgs 11, 36; 2 Kgs 8, 19.
h 8ff: Gn 27, 40; 2 Kgs 8, 20ff.
i 2 Kgs 8, 24.
j 1-6: 2 Kgs 8, 24-29.

*

21, 6: One of Ahab's daughters: Athaliah. In 2 Chr 22, 2 (and its source, 2 Kgs 8, 26) she is called Omri's daughter; but this should probably be understood in the sense of granddaughter.

21, 12: Elijah: the only mention by the Chronicler of this prophet of the northern kingdom of Israel. It is doubtful that Elijah was still living in the reign of Jehoram of Judah; in any case, the attribution of the letter to him is most likely an imaginative filling out of the narration.

the band that had come into the fort with the
Arabs. Thus Ahaziah, son of Jehoram, reigned
as king of Judah. **2** He was twenty-two years
old when he became king, and he reigned one
year in Jerusalem. His mother was named Athaliah, daughter of Omri. **3** He, too, followed the
ways of the house of Ahab, because his mother
counseled him to act sinfully. **4** To his own
destruction, he did evil in the sight of the LORD,
as did the house of Ahab, since they were his
counselors after the death of his father.

**5** He was also following their counsel when
he accompanied Jehoram, son of Ahab, king of
Israel, to battle against Hazael, king of Aram,
at Ramoth-gilead. There Jehoram was wounded
by the Arameans. **6** He returned to Jezreel to be
healed of the wounds he had received at Rama
in his battle against Hazael, king of Aram. Because of this illness, Ahaziah, son of Jehoram,
king of Judah, went down to visit Jehoram, son
of Ahab, in Jezreel. **7** Now it was willed by
God for Ahaziah's downfall that he should join
Jehoram, for after his arrival he rode out with
Jehoram to Jehu, son of Nimshi, whom the
LORD had anointed to cut down the house of
Ahab.[k] **8** While Jehu was executing judgment
on the house of Ahab, he also encountered the
princes of Judah and the nephews of Ahaziah
who were his attendants, and he slew them.[l]
**9** Then he looked for Ahaziah himself. They
caught him where he was hiding in Samaria and
brought him to Jehu, who put him to death.
They buried him, for they said, "He was the
grandson of Jehoshaphat, who sought the LORD
with his whole heart."[m] There remained in
Ahaziah's house no one powerful enough to
wield the kingship.*

**Usurpation of Athaliah.** **10** [n]When Athaliah, mother of Ahaziah, learned that her son
was dead, she proceeded to kill off all the royal
offspring of the house of Judah. **11** But Jehosheba, a royal princess, secretly took Ahaziah's
son Joash from among the king's sons who were
about to be slain, and put him and his nurse in
a bedroom. In this way Jehosheba, who was the
daughter of King Jehoram, a sister of Ahaziah,
and wife of Jehoiada the priest, hid the child
from Athaliah's sight, so that she did not put
him to death. **12** For six years he remained
hidden with them in the house of God, while
Athaliah ruled over the land.

## CHAPTER 23

**Athaliah Overthrown.** **1** [o]In the seventh
year, Jehoiada took courage and entered a conspiracy with certain captains: Azariah, son of
Jehoram; Ishmael, son of Jehohanan; Azariah,
son of Obed; Masseiah, son of Adaiah; and
Elishaphat, son of Zichri. **2** They journeyed
about Judah, gathering the Levites from all the
cities of Judah and also the heads of the Israelite
families. When they had come to Jerusalem,
**3** the whole assembly made a covenant with the
king in the house of God. Jehoiada said to them:
"Here is the king's son who must reign, as the
LORD promised concerning the sons of David.
**4** This is what you must do: a third of your
number, both priests and Levites, who come in
on the sabbath must guard the thresholds, **5** another third must be at the king's palace, and the
final third at the Foundation Gate, when all the
people will be in the courts of the LORD's temple. **6** Let no one enter the LORD's house except
the priests and those Levites who are ministering. They may enter because they are holy; but
all the other people must observe the prescriptions of the LORD. **7** The Levites shall surround
the king on all sides, each with his weapon
drawn. Whoever tries to enter the house must be
slain. Stay with the king wherever he goes."

**8** The Levites and all Judah did just as Jehoiada the priest commanded. Each brought his
men, those who were to come in on the sabbath
as well as those who were to depart on the
sabbath, since Jehoiada the priest had not dismissed any of the divisions.[p] **9** Jehoiada the
priest gave the captains the spears, shields and
bucklers of King David which were in the house
of God. **10** He stationed all the people, each
with his spear in hand, from the southern to the
northern extremity of the enclosure, around the
altar and the temple on the king's behalf.
**11** Then they brought out the king's son, set the
crown and the insignia upon him, and made him
king. Jehoiada and his sons anointed him, and
they cried, "Long live the king!"

**12** When Athaliah heard the din of the people
running and acclaiming the king, she went to the
people in the temple of the LORD. **13** She
looked, and there was the king standing beside
his pillar* at the entrance, the officers and the
trumpeters around him, and all the people of the
land rejoicing and blowing trumpets, while the
singers with their musical instruments were
leading the acclaim. Athaliah tore her garments
and cried out, "Treason! treason!" **14** Then
Jehoiada the priest sent out the captains who
were in command of the army; he said to them:

---

k 2 Kgs 9, 21; 10, 12ff.
l 2 Kgs 10, 12ff.
m 2 Kgs 9, 27f.
n 10ff: 2 Kgs 11, 1ff.
o 1-17. 19ff: 2 Kgs 11, 4-20.
p 2 Kgs 11, 9; 1 Chr 24, 19.

---

22, 9: This account of the death of Ahaziah of Judah is not derived from 2 Kgs 9, 27f, with which it is at variance.

23, 13: Beside his pillar: the king had a special place in the eastern gateway of the temple court that contained the altar of holocausts. He occupied this place on feasts and sabbaths at the time of the statutory offerings, or when he made freewill offerings of his own; cf 2 Kgs 11, 4 and also Ez 46, 1–8 for a later reflection of this.

"Take her outside through the ranks, and if anyone tries to follow her, let him die by the sword. For," the priest continued, "you must not put her to death in the LORD's temple."
15 So they seized her, and when she arrived at the entrance to the Horse Gate of the palace, they put her to death there.

16 Then Jehoiada made a covenant between himself and all the people and the king, that they should be the LORD's people. 17 And all the
people went to the temple of Baal and tore it down. They smashed its altars and images, and they slew Mattan, the priest of Baal, before the
altars. 18 Then Jehoiada gave the charge of the LORD's temple into the hands of the levitical priests, to whom David had assigned turns in the temple for offering the holocausts of the LORD, as is written in the law of Moses, with rejoicing and song, as David had provided.[q] 19 Moreover, he stationed guards at the gates of the LORD's temple, so that no one unclean in any respect might enter. 20 Then he took the cap-
tains, the nobles, the rulers among the people, and all the people of the land, and led the king out of the LORD's house. When they had come within the upper gate of the king's house, they seated the king upon the royal throne. 21 All
the people of the land rejoiced and the city was quiet, now that Athaliah had been put to death by the sword.

## CHAPTER 24

**The Temple Restored.** 1 [r]Joash was sev-
en years old when he became king, and he reigned forty years in Jerusalem. His mother, named Zibiah, was from Beer-sheba. 2 Joash
did what was pleasing to the LORD as long as Jehoiada the priest lived. 3 Jehoiada provided
him with two wives, and he became the father of sons and daughters.

4 After some time, Joash decided to restore
the LORD's temple. 5 He called together the priests and Levites and said to them: "Go out to all the cities of Judah and collect money* from all Israel that you may repair the house of your God over the years. You must hasten this affair." But the Levites did not hasten. 6 Then
the king summoned Jehoiada, who was in charge, and said to him: "Why have you not required the Levites to bring in from Judah and Jerusalem the tax levied by Moses, the servant of the LORD, and by the assembly of Israel, for the tent of the testimony?"[s] 7 For the wicked
Athaliah and her sons had damaged the house of God and had even turned over to the Baals the dedicated resources of the LORD's temple.

8 At the king's command, therefore, they
made a chest, which they put outside the gate of the LORD's temple.[t] 9 They had it proclaimed
throughout Judah and Jerusalem that the tax which Moses, the servant of God, had imposed on Israel in the desert should be brought to the LORD.[u] 10 All the princes and the people rejoiced; they brought what was asked and cast it into the chest until it was filled. 11 Whenever
the chest was brought to the royal officials by the Levites and they saw that it contained much money, the royal scribe and an overseer for the high priest came, emptied the chest, then took it back and returned it to its place. This they did day after day until they had collected a large sum of money. 12 Then the king and Jehoiada
gave it to the workmen in charge of the labor on the LORD's temple, who hired masons and car-penters to restore the temple, and also iron- and bronze-smiths to repair it. 13 The workmen la-
bored, and the task of restoration progressed under their hands. They restored the house of God according to its original form, and rein-forced it. 14 After they had finished, they
brought the rest of the money to the king and to Jehoiada, who had it made into utensils for the LORD's temple, utensils for the service and the holocausts, and basins and other gold and silver utensils. They offered holocausts in the LORD's temple continually throughout the lifetime of Jehoiada. 15 Jehoiada lived to a ripe old age; he
was a hundred and thirty years old when he died. 16 He was buried in the City of David
with the kings, because he had done good in Israel, in particular with respect to God and his temple.

**Apostasy of King Joash.** 17 After the
death of Jehoiada, the princes of Judah came and paid homage to the king, and the king then listened to them. 18 They forsook the temple of
the LORD, the God of their fathers, and began to serve the sacred poles and the idols; and because of this crime of theirs, wrath came upon Judah and Jerusalem.[v] 19 Although prophets
were sent to them to convert them to the LORD, the people would not listen to their warnings.
20 Then the spirit of God possessed Zechariah,
son of Jehoiada the priest. He took his stand above the people and said to them: "God says, 'Why are you transgressing the LORD's com-mands, so that you cannot prosper? Because you have abandoned the LORD, he has aban-doned you.' " 21 But they conspired against
him, and at the king's order they stoned him to death in the court of the LORD's temple.

q 1 Chr 23, 13.
r 1-14: 2 Kgs 12, 1-13.
s Ex 25, 1-9; Neh 10, 33.
t 2 Chr 34, 9.
u Ex 30, 13.
v Ex 34, 13.

*

24, 5: Collect money: according to 2 Kgs 12, 5, the people themselves brought the money to the temple; it consisted, at least in part, of voluntary contributions. At the time of the Chronicler (see Neh 10, 32) there was a fixed head tax for the upkeep of the temple (2 Chr 34, 9), based on Ex 30, 12–16. This was still in force in New Testament times (Mt 17, 24f).

**22** Thus King Joash was unmindful of the devotion shown him by Jehoiada, Zechariah's father,
and slew his son. And as he was dying, he said,
"May the LORD see and avenge."

**Retribution.** **23** At the turn of the year a
force of Arameans came up against Joash. They
invaded Judah and Jerusalem, did away with all
the princes of the people, and sent all their spoil
to the king of Damascus.[w] **24** Though the Aramean force came with few men, the LORD surrendered a very large force into their power,
because Judah had abandoned the LORD, the
God of their fathers. So punishment was meted
out to Joash.[x] **25** [y]After the Arameans had departed from him, leaving him in grievous suffering, his servants conspired against him because
of the murder of the son of Jehoiada the priest.
They killed him on his sickbed. He was buried
in the City of David, but not in the tombs of the
kings.

**26** These conspired against him: Zabad, son
of Shimeath from Ammon, and Jehozabad, son
of Shimrith from Moab. **27** Of his sons, and the
great tribute imposed on him, and of his rebuilding of the house of God, there is a written account in the midrash of the book of the kings.
His son Amaziah succeeded him as king.[z]

## CHAPTER 25

**Campaign in Edom.** **1** [a]Amaziah was
twenty-five years old when he became king, and
he reigned twenty-nine years in Jerusalem. His
mother, named Jehoaddan, was from Jerusalem. **2** He did what was pleasing in the sight of
the LORD, though not wholeheartedly. **3** After
he had strengthened his hold on the kingdom, he
slew those of his servants who had killed the
king, his father; **4** but he did not put their children to death, for he acted according to what is
written in the law, in the Book of Moses, as the
LORD commanded: "Fathers shall not be put to
death for their children, nor children for their
fathers; but only for his own guilt shall a man
be put to death."[b]

**5** Amaziah mustered Judah and placed them,
out of all Judah and Benjamin according to their
ancestral houses, under leaders of thousands
and of hundreds. When he had counted those of
twenty years and over, he found them to be three
hundred thousand picked men fit for war, capable of handling lance and shield. **6** He also
hired a hundred thousand valiant warriors from
Israel for a hundred talents of silver. **7** But a
man of God came to him and said: "O king, let
not the army of Israel go with you, for the LORD
is not with Israel, with any Ephraimite. **8** Instead, go on your own, strongly prepared for the
conflict; otherwise the LORD will defeat you in
the face of the enemy. It is God who has the
power to reinforce or to defeat." **9** Amaziah
answered the man of God, "But what is to be
done about the hundred talents that I paid for the
troops of Israel?" The man of God replied,
"The LORD can give you much more than that."
**10** Amaziah then disbanded the troops that had
come to him from Ephraim, and sent them
home. They, however, became furiously angry
with Judah, and returned home blazing with
resentment.

**11** Amaziah now assumed command of his
army. They proceeded to the Valley of Salt, and
there they killed ten thousand men of Seir.[c]
**12** The Judahites also brought back another ten
thousand alive, whom they led to the summit of
the Rock and then cast down, so that they were
all crushed. **13** Meanwhile, the mercenaries
whom Amaziah had dismissed from battle service with him raided the cities of Judah from
Samaria to Beth-horon. They killed three thousand of the inhabitants and took away much
booty.

**Infidelity of Amaziah.** **14** When Amaziah
returned from his conquest of the Edomites he
brought back with him the gods of the people of
Seir, which he set up as his own gods; he bowed
down before them and offered sacrifice to them.
**15** Then the anger of the LORD blazed out
against Amaziah, and he sent a prophet to him
who said: "Why have you had recourse to this
people's gods that could not save their own
people from your hand?" **16** While he was still
speaking, however, the king said to him: "Have
you been made the king's counselor? Be silent!
Why should it be necessary to kill you?" Therefore the prophet desisted. "I know, however,"
he said, "that God has let you take counsel to
your own destruction, because you have done
this thing and have refused to hear my counsel."

**Retribution.** **17** [d]Having taken counsel,
King Amaziah of Judah sent messengers to Joash, son of Jehoahaz, son of Jehu, the king of
Israel, saying, "Come, let us meet each other
face to face." **18** King Joash of Israel sent this
reply to King Amaziah of Judah: "The thistle of
the Lebanon sent a message to the cedar of the
Lebanon, saying, 'Give your daughter to my
son for his wife.' But the wild beasts of the
Lebanon passed by and trampled the thistle
down.[e] **19** You are thinking, 'See, I have beat-
en Edom!,' and thus ambition makes you proud.
Remain at home. Why involve yourself, and
Judah with you, in misfortune and failure?"

---

w 2 Kgs 12, 17f.
x Dt 32, 30.
y 25f: 2 Kgs 12, 21f.
z 2 Kgs 12, 19. 22.
a 1-4: 2 Kgs 14, 1-6.
b Dt 24, 16; 2 Kgs 14, 5f; Ez 18, 20.
c 2 Kgs 14, 7.
d 17-24: 2 Kgs 14, 8-14.
e Jgs 9, 7-15; 2 Kgs 14, 9.

**20** But Amaziah would not listen, for God had determined to hand them over because they had had recourse to the gods of Edom.

**21** Therefore King Joash of Israel advanced and he and King Amaziah met in battle at Beth-shemesh of Judah. **22** There Judah was defeated by Israel, and all the Judean soldiers fled homeward. **23** King Joash of Israel captured Amaziah, king of Judah, son of Joash, son of Jehoahaz, at Beth-shemesh and brought him to Jerusalem. Then he tore down the wall of Jerusalem from the Ephraim Gate to the Corner Gate, a distance of four hundred cubits. **24** He took away all the gold and silver and all the vessels he found in the house of God with Obed-edom,* together with the treasures of the palace, and hostages as well. Then he returned to Samaria.

**25** [f]Amaziah, son of Joash, king of Judah, survived Joash, son of Jehoahaz, king of Israel, by fifteen years. **26** The rest of the acts of Amaziah, first and last, can be found written, as is well known, in the book of the kings of Judah and Israel. **27** Now from the time that Amaziah ceased to follow the LORD, a conspiracy was formed against him in Jerusalem; hence he fled to Lachish. But they pursued him to Lachish and put him to death there. **28** They brought him back on horses and buried him with his ancestors in the City of Judah.*

## CHAPTER 26

**The Works of Uzziah.** **1** [g]All the people of Judah chose Uzziah, though he was but sixteen years of age, and proclaimed him king to succeed his father Amaziah. **2** He rebuilt Elath and restored it to Judah; this was after King Amaziah had gone to rest with his ancestors. **3** Uzziah was sixteen years old when he became king, and he reigned fifty-two years in Jerusalem. His mother, named Jecoliah, was from Jerusalem. **4** He pleased the LORD, just as his father Amaziah had done.

**5** He was prepared to seek God as long as Zechariah* lived, who taught him to fear God; and as long as he sought the LORD, God made him prosper.[h] **6** He went out and fought the Philistines and razed the walls of Gath, Jabneh and Ashdod [and built cities in the district of Ashdod and in Philistia].[i] **7** God helped him against the Philistines, against the Arabs who dwelt in Gurbaal, and against the Meunites. **8** The Ammonites paid tribute to Uzziah and his fame spread as far as Egypt, for he grew stronger and stronger. **9** Moreover, Uzziah built towers in Jerusalem at the Corner Gate, at the Valley Gate, and at the Angle, and he fortified them. **10** He built towers in the desert and dug numerous cisterns, for he had many cattle. He had plowmen in the foothills and the plains, and vinedressers in the highlands and the garden land. He was a lover of the soil.

**11** Uzziah also had a standing army of fit soldiers divided into bands according to the number in which they were mustered by Jeiel the scribe and Maaseiah the recorder, under the command of Hananiah, one of the king's officials. **12** The entire number of family heads over these valiant warriors was two thousand six hundred, **13** and at their disposal was a mighty army of three hundred seven thousand five hundred fighting men of great valor to help the king against his enemies. **14** Uzziah provided for them—for the entire army—bucklers, lances, helmets, breastplates, bows and slingstones. **15** He also built machines in Jerusalem, devices contrived to stand on the towers and at the angles of the walls to shoot arrows and cast large stones. His fame spread far and wide, and his power was ascribed to the marvelous help he had received.

**Pride and Fall.** **16** But after he had become strong, he became proud to his own destruction and broke faith with the LORD, his God. He entered the temple of the LORD to make an offering on the altar of incense. **17** But Azariah the priest, and with him eighty other priests of the LORD, courageous men, followed him. **18** They opposed King Uzziah, saying to him: "It is not for you, Uzziah, to burn incense to the LORD, but for the priests, the sons of Aaron, who have been consecrated for this purpose. Leave the sanctuary, for you have broken faith and no longer have a part in the glory that comes from the LORD God."[j] **19** Uzziah, who was holding a censer for burning the incense, became angry, but at the moment he showed his anger to the priests, while they were looking at him in the house of the LORD beside the altar of incense, leprosy broke out on his forehead.[k] **20** Azariah the chief priest and all the other priests examined him, and when they saw that his forehead was leprous, they expelled him from the temple. He himself fled willingly, for the LORD had afflicted him. **21** [l]King Uzziah remained a leper to the day of his death. As a leper he dwelt in a segregated house, for he was

f 25-28: 2 Kgs 14, 17-20.
g 1-4: 2 Kgs 14, 21f; 15, 1ff.
h 2 Chr 24, 2.
i Am 1, 8.
j Ex 30, 7.
k Nm 12, 10.
l 21ff: 2 Kgs 15, 5ff; Lv 13, 46; Nm 19, 20.

*

25, 24: With Obed-edom: possibly a reference to the priest of an Edomite false worship (cf v 14), if not to a levitical family of gatekeepers; cf 1 Chr 15, 18; 26, 12–15.

25, 28: The city of Judah: in the parallel passage of 2 Kgs 14, 20, the City of David. The Chronicler is referring, by this term, to the capital of Judah, Jerusalem.

26, 5: Zechariah: this person, not otherwise identified, is referred to in language suggesting a pious layman rather than a priest or prophet; cf 2 Chr 29, 1.

excluded from the house of the LORD. Therefore his son Jotham was regent of the palace and ruled the people of the land.

**22** The prophet Isaiah, son of Amos, wrote the rest of the acts of Uzziah, first and last. **23** Uzziah rested with his ancestors; he was buried with them in the field adjoining the royal cemetery, for they said, "He was a leper." His son Jotham succeeded him as king.

## CHAPTER 27

**Jotham.** **1** [m]Jotham was twenty-five years old when he became king, and he reigned sixteen years in Jerusalem. His mother was named Jerusa, daughter of Zadok. **2** He pleased the LORD just as his father Uzziah had done, though he did not enter the temple of the LORD; the people, however, continued to act sinfully.

**3** He built the upper gate of the LORD's house and had much construction done on the wall of Ophel. **4** Moreover, he built cities in the hill country of Judah, and in the forest land he set up fortresses and towers. **5** He fought with the king of the Ammonites and conquered them. That year the Ammonites paid him one hundred talents of silver, together with ten thousand kors of wheat and ten thousand of barley. They brought the same to him also in the second and in the third year. **6** Thus Jotham continued to grow strong because he lived resolutely in the presence of the LORD, his God. **7** [n]The rest of the acts of Jotham, his wars and his activities, can be found written in the book of the kings of Israel and Judah. **8** He was twenty-five years old when he became king, and he reigned sixteen years in Jerusalem. **9** Jotham rested with his ancestors and was buried in the City of David, and his son Ahaz succeeded him as king.

# *III: Reforms of Hezekiah and Josiah*

## CHAPTER 28

**Impiety of Ahaz.** **1** [o]Ahaz was twenty years old when he became king, and he reigned sixteen years in Jerusalem. He did not please the LORD as his forefather David had done, **2** but conducted himself like the kings of Israel and even made molten idols of the Baals. **3** Moreover, he offered sacrifice in the Valley of Ben-hinnom, and immolated his sons by fire according to the abominable practice of the nations which the LORD had cleared out before the Israelites.[p] **4** He offered sacrifice and incense on the high places, on hills, and under every leafy tree.

**Retribution.** **5** Therefore the LORD, his God, delivered him into the power of the king of Aram. The Arameans defeated him and carried away captive a large number of his people, whom they brought to Damascus. He was also delivered into the power of the king of Israel, who defeated him with great slaughter.[q] **6** For Pekah, son of Remaliah, slew one hundred and twenty thousand of Judah in a single day, all of them valiant men, because they had abandoned the LORD, the God of their fathers. **7** Zichri, an Ephraimite warrior, killed Maaseiah, the king's son, and Azrikam, the master of the palace, and also Elkanah, who was second to the king. **8** The Israelites took away as captives two hundred thousand of their brethren's wives, sons and daughters; they also took from them much plunder, which they brought to Samaria.

**The Prophecy of Oded.** **9** In Samaria there was a prophet of the LORD by the name of Oded. He went out to meet the army returning to Samaria and said to them: "It was because the LORD, the God of your fathers, was angry with Judah that he delivered them into your hands. You, however, have slaughtered them with a fury that has reached up to heaven. **10** And now you are planning to make the children of Judah and Jerusalem your slaves and bondwomen. Are not you yourselves, therefore, guilty of a crime against the LORD, your God? **11** Now listen to me: send back the captives you have carried off from among your brethren, for the burning anger of the LORD is upon you."

**12** At this, some of the Ephraimite leaders, Azariah, son of Johanan, Berechiah, son of Meshillemoth, Jehizkiah, son of Shallum, and Amasa, son of Hadlai, themselves stood up in opposition to those who had returned from the war. **13** They said to them: "Do not bring the captives here, for what you propose will make us guilty before the LORD and increase our sins and our guilt. Our guilt is already great, and there is a burning anger upon Israel." **14** Therefore the soldiers left their captives and the plunder before the princes and the whole assembly. **15** Then the men just named proceeded to help the captives. All of them who were naked they clothed from the booty; they clothed them, put sandals on their feet, gave them food and drink, anointed them, and all who were weak they set on asses. They brought them to Jericho, the city of palms, to their brethren. Then they returned to Samaria.[r]

**Further Sins of Ahaz.** **16** At that time King Ahaz sent an appeal for help to the kings

m 1-3; 2 Kgs 15, 32-35.
n 7-9: 2 Kgs 15, 36ff.
o 1-4: 2 Kgs 16, 1-4.
p 2 Kgs 16, 3; Lv 18, 21.
q 2 Kgs 16, 5; Is 7, 1-9.
r Lk 10, 25-37.
s 2 Kgs 16, 7.

of Assyria.[s] **17** The Edomites had returned,
attacked Judah, and carried off captives.[t]
**18** The Philistines too had raided the cities of
the foothills and the Negeb of Judah; they captured Beth-shemesh, Aijalon, Gederoth, Soco
and its dependencies, Timnah and its dependencies, and Gimzo and its dependencies, and occupied them. **19** For the LORD had brought Judah low because of Ahaz, king of Israel,* who
let Judah go its own way and proved utterly
faithless to the LORD. **20** Tilgath-pilneser, king
of Assyria, did indeed come to him, but to
oppress him rather than to help him.[u]
**21** Though Ahaz plundered the LORD's house
and the houses of the king and the princes to
make payment to the king of Assyria, it availed
him nothing.[v]

**22** While he was already in distress, the same
King Ahaz became even more unfaithful to the
LORD. **23** He sacrificed to the gods of Damascus who had defeated him, saying, "Since it
was the gods of the kings of Aram who helped
them, I will sacrifice to them that they may help
me also." However, they only caused further
disaster to him and to all Israel.[w] **24** Ahaz gathered up the utensils of God's house and broke
them in pieces. He closed the doors of the
LORD's house and had altars made for himself
in every corner of Jerusalem.[x] **25** In every city
throughout Judah he set up high places to offer
sacrifice to other gods. Thus he angered the
LORD, the God of his fathers.

**26** [y]The rest of his deeds and his activities,
first and last, can be found written in the book
of the kings of Judah and Israel. **27** Ahaz rested
with his ancestors and was buried in Jerusalem—in the city, for they did not bring him to
the tombs of the kings of Israel. His son Hezekiah succeeded him as king.

## CHAPTER 29

**Reforms of Hezekiah.** **1** [z]Hezekiah was
twenty-five years old when he became king, and
he reigned twenty-nine years in Jerusalem. His
mother was named Abia, daughter of Zechariah. **2** He pleased the LORD just as his forefather
David had done. **3** It was he who, in the first
month of the first year of his reign, opened the
doors of the LORD's house and repaired them.[a]
**4** He summoned the priests and Levites, gathered them in the open space to the east, **5** and
said to them: "Listen to me, you Levites! Sanctify yourselves now and sanctify the house of
the LORD, the God of your fathers, and clean out
the filth from the sanctuary. **6** Our fathers acted
faithlessly and did evil in the eyes of the LORD,
our God. They abandoned him, turned away
their faces from the LORD's dwelling, and
turned their backs on him. **7** They also closed
the doors of the vestibule, extinguished the
lamps, and refused to burn incense and offer
holocausts in the sanctuary to the honor of the
God of Israel.[b] **8** [c]Therefore the anger of the
LORD has come upon Judah and Jerusalem; he
has made them an object of terror, astonishment
and mockery, as you see with your own eyes.
**9** For our fathers, as you know, fell by the
sword, and our sons, our daughters and our
wives have been taken captive because of this.
**10** Now, I intend to make a covenant with the
LORD, the God of Israel, that his burning anger
may withdraw from us. **11** My sons, be not
negligent any longer, for it is you whom the
LORD has chosen to stand before him, to minister to him, to be his ministers and to offer incense."

**12** Then the Levites arose: Mahath, son of
Amasai, and Joel, son of Azariah, descendants
of the Kohathites; of the sons of Merari: Kish,
son of Abdi, and Azariah, son of Jehallel; of the
Gershonites: Joah, son of Zimmah, and Eden,
son of Joah; **13** of the sons of Elizaphan: Shimri
and Jeuel; of the sons of Asaph: Zechariah and
Mattaniah; **14** of the sons of Heman: Jehuel and
Shimei; of the sons of Jeduthun: Shemiah and
Uzziel. **15** They gathered their brethren together and sanctified themselves; then they came as
the king had ordered, to cleanse the LORD's
house in keeping with his words.

**16** The priests entered the interior of the
LORD's house to cleanse it; and whatever they
found in the LORD's temple that was unclean
they brought out to the court of the LORD's
house, where the Levites took it from them and
carried it out to the Kidron Valley. **17** They
began the work of consecration on the first day
of the first month, and on the eighth day of the
month they arrived at the vestibule of the LORD;
they consecrated the LORD's house during eight
days, and on the sixteenth day of the first
month, they had finished.

**18** Then they went inside to King Hezekiah
and said: "We have cleansed the entire house of
the LORD, the altar of holocausts with all its
utensils, and the table for the showbread with all
its utensils. **19** All the articles which King Ahaz
during his reign had thrown away because of his
apostasy, we have restored and consecrated,
and they are now before the LORD's altar."

---

t 2 Kgs 16, 6.
u 2 Kgs 16, 10; Is 7, 17-20; 8, 5-8.
v 2 Kgs 16, 8.
w 2 Kgs 16, 12f; Is 10, 20.
x 2 Chr 29, 3; 30, 14; 2 Kgs 16, 17.
y 26f: 2 Kgs 16, 19f.
z 1ff: 2 Kgs 18, 1ff.
a 2 Chr 28, 24.
b 2 Kgs 16, 15.
c 8f: Lv 26, 32f; Dt 28, 25; Jer 25, 18.

---

* 28, 19: Ahaz, king of Israel: in the period of the divided kingdom the term king of Israel would elsewhere mean "king of the northern Kingdom of Israel."

**The Rite of Expiation.** **20** Then King Hezekiah hastened to convoke the princes of the city
and went up to the LORD's house. **21** Seven
bulls, seven rams, seven lambs and seven he-
goats were brought for a sin offering for the
kingdom, for the sanctuary, and for Judah, and
he ordered the sons of Aaron, the priests, to
offer them on the altar of the LORD. **22** They
slaughtered the bulls, and the priests collected
the blood and cast it on the altar. Then they
slaughtered the rams and cast the blood on the
altar; then they slaughtered the lambs and cast
the blood on the altar. **23** Then the he-goats for
the sin offering were led before the king and the
assembly, who laid their hands upon them.
**24** The priests then slaughtered them and offered their blood on the altar to atone for the sin
of all Israel; for "The holocaust and the sin
offering," the king had said, "is for all Israel."

**25** He stationed the Levites in the LORD's
house with cymbals, harps and lyres according
to the prescriptions of David, of Gad the king's
seer, and of Nathan the prophet; for the prescriptions were from the LORD through his
prophets. **26** The Levites were stationed with
the instruments of David, and the priests with
the trumpets. **27** Then Hezekiah ordered the
holocaust to be sacrificed on the altar, and in the
same instant that the holocaust began, they also
began the song of the LORD, to the accompaniment of the trumpets and the instruments of
David, king of Israel. **28** The entire assembly
prostrated itself, and they continued to sing the
song and to sound the trumpets until the holocaust had been completed. **29** As the holocaust
was completed, the king and all who were with
him knelt and prostrated themselves. **30** King
Hezekiah and the princes then commanded the
Levites to sing the praises of the LORD in the
words of David and of Asaph the seer. They
sang praises till their joy was full, then fell down
and prostrated themselves.

**31** Hezekiah now spoke out this command:
"You have undertaken a work for the LORD.
Approach, and bring forward the sacrifices and
thank offerings for the house of the LORD."
Then the assembly brought forward the sacrifices and thank offerings and all the holocausts
which were free-will offerings. **32** The number
of holocausts that the assembly brought forward
was seventy oxen, one hundred rams, and two
hundred lambs: all of these as a holocaust to the
LORD. **33** As consecrated gifts there were six
hundred oxen and three thousand sheep.
**34** Since the priests were too few in number to
be able to skin all the victims for the holocausts,
their brethren the Levites assisted them until the
task was completed and the priests had sanctified themselves; the Levites, in fact, were more
willing than the priests to sanctify themselves.[d]
**35** Also, the holocausts were many, along with
the fat of the peace offerings and the libations
for the holocausts. Thus the service of the house
of the LORD was reestablished. **36** Hezekiah
and all the people rejoiced over what God had
reestablished for the people, and at how suddenly this had been done.

## CHAPTER 30

**Invitation to the Passover.** **1** Hezekiah
sent a message to all Israel and Judah, and even
wrote letters to Ephraim and Manasseh saying
that they should come to the house of the LORD
in Jerusalem to celebrate the Passover in honor
of the LORD, the God of Israel.[e] **2** [f]The king,
his princes, and the entire assembly in Jerusalem had agreed to celebrate the Passover during
the second month, **3** for they could not celebrate it at the time of the restoration: the priests
had not sanctified themselves in sufficient numbers, and the people were not gathered at Jerusalem. **4** When this proposal had been approved
by the king and the entire assembly, **5** they
issued a decree to be proclaimed throughout all
Israel from Beer-sheba to Dan, that everyone
should come to Jerusalem to celebrate the Passover in honor of the LORD, the God of Israel; for
not many had kept it in the manner prescribed.
**6** Accordingly the couriers, with the letters
written by the king and his princes, traversed all
Israel and Judah, and at the king's command
they said: "Israelites, return to the LORD, the
God of Abraham, Isaac and Israel, that he may
return to you, the remnant left from the hands
of the Assyrian kings. **7** Be not like your fathers
and your brethren who proved faithless to the
LORD, the God of their fathers, so that he delivered them over to desolation, as you yourselves
now see.[g] **8** Be not obstinate, as your fathers
were; extend your hands to the LORD and come
to his sanctuary that he has consecrated forever,
and serve the LORD, your God, that he may turn
away his burning anger from you. **9** For when
you return to the LORD, your brethren and your
children will find mercy with their captors and
return to this land; for merciful and compassionate is the LORD, your God, and he will not turn
away his face from you if you return to him."[h]

**10** So the couriers passed from city to city in
the land of Ephraim and Manasseh and as far as
Zebulun, but they were derided and scoffed at.
**11** Nevertheless, some from Asher, Manasseh
and Zebulun humbled themselves and came to
Jerusalem. **12** In Judah, however, the power of
God brought it about that the people were of one
mind to carry out the command of the king and
the princes in accordance with the word of the
LORD. **13** Thus many people gathered in Jeru-

d 1 Chr 15, 12.
e Ex 12, 1-28.
f 2ff: Nm 9, 6-13.
g Acts 7, 51.
h 1 Kgs 8, 50.

salem to celebrate the feast of Unleavened Bread in the second month; it was a very great assembly.

**The Passover Celebrated.** **14** They proceeded to take down the altars that were in Jerusalem; also they removed all the altars of incense and cast them into the Kidron Valley.[i] **15** They slaughtered the Passover on the fourteenth day of the second month. The priests and Levites, touched with shame, sanctified themselves and brought holocausts into the house of the LORD. **16** They stood in the places prescribed for them according to the law of Moses, the man of God. The priests sprinkled the blood given them by the Levites; **17** for many in the assembly had not sanctified themselves, and the Levites were in charge of slaughtering the Passover victims for all who were unclean and therefore could not consecrate them to the LORD.[j] **18** The greater part of the people, in fact, chiefly from Ephraim, Manasseh, Issachar and Zebulun, had not cleansed themselves. Nevertheless they ate the Passover, contrary to the prescription; for Hezekiah prayed for them, saying, "May the LORD, who is good, grant pardon to **19** everyone who has resolved to seek God, the LORD, the God of his fathers, though he be not clean as holiness requires." **20** The LORD heard Hezekiah and spared the people.

**21** Thus the Israelites who were in Jerusalem celebrated the feast of Unleavened Bread with great rejoicing for seven days, and the Levites and the priests sang the praises of the LORD day after day with all their strength. **22** Hezekiah spoke encouragingly to all the Levites who had shown themselves well skilled in the service of the LORD. And when they had completed the seven days of festival, slaying peace offerings and singing praises to the LORD, the God of their fathers, **23** the whole assembly agreed to celebrate another seven days. With joy, therefore, they continued the festivity seven days longer. **24** King Hezekiah of Judah had contributed a thousand bulls and seven thousand sheep to the assembly, and the princes had contributed to the assembly a thousand bulls and ten thousand sheep. The priests sanctified themselves in great numbers, **25** and the whole assembly of Judah rejoiced, together with the priests and Levites and the rest of the assembly that had come from Israel, as well as the sojourners from the land of Israel and those that lived in Judah. **26** There was great rejoicing in Jerusalem, for since the days of Solomon, son of David, king of Israel, there had not been the like in the city. **27** Then the levitical priests rose and blessed the people; their voice was heard and their prayer reached heaven, God's holy dwelling.

## CHAPTER 31

**Liturgical Reform.** **1** After all this was over, those Israelites who had been present went forth to the cities of Judah and smashed the sacred pillars, cut down the sacred poles, and tore down the high places and altars throughout Judah, Benjamin, Ephraim and Manasseh, until all were destroyed. Then the Israelites returned to their various cities, each to his own possession.[k]

**2** Hezekiah reestablished the classes of the priests and the Levites according to their former classification, assigning to each priest and Levite his proper service, whether in regard to holocausts or peace offerings, thanksgiving or praise, or ministering in the gates of the encampment of the LORD. **3** From his own wealth the king allotted a portion for holocausts, those of morning and evening and those on sabbaths, new moons and festivals, as prescribed in the law of the LORD.[l] **4** He also commanded the people living in Jerusalem to provide the support of the priests and Levites, that they might devote themselves entirely to the law of the LORD.

**5** As soon as the order was promulgated, the Israelites brought, in great quantities, the best of their grain, wine, oil and honey, and all the produce of the fields; they gave a generous tithe of everything.[m] **6** Israelites and Judahites living in other cities of Judah also brought in tithes of oxen, sheep, and things that had been consecrated to the LORD, their God; these they brought in and set out in heaps.[n] **7** It was in the third month that they began to establish these heaps, and they completed them in the seventh month.* **8** When Hezekiah and the princes had come and seen the heaps, they blessed the LORD and his people Israel. **9** Then Hezekiah questioned the priests and the Levites concerning the heaps, **10** and the priest Azariah, head of the house of Zadoc, answered him, "Since they began to bring the offerings to the house of the LORD, we have eaten to the full and have had much left over, for the LORD has blessed his people. This great supply is what was left over."[o]

**11** Hezekiah then gave orders that chambers should be constructed in the house of the LORD. When this had been done, **12** the offerings,

---

i 2 Chr 28, 42f.
j 2 Chr 35, 6.
k 2 Chr 34, 3f; 2 Kgs 18, 4.
l 1 Chr 29, 3; Ez 45, 17; Nm 28—29.
m Nm 18, 8-24; Dt 14, 22f.
n Nm 12, 44-47; 13, 10-13.
o Lv 25, 19-22.

---

* 31, 7: Third month . . . seventh month: between the feast of Pentecost and that of Booths, an interval without rain in Palestine, at the end of which the problem of storage (v 11) would become more urgent.

tithes and consecrated things were deposited there in safekeeping. The overseer of these things was Conaniah the Levite, and his brother Shimei was second in charge. **13** Jehiel, Azaziah, Nathan, Asahel, Jerimoth, Jozabad, Eliel, Ismachiah, Mahath and Benaiah were supervisors subject to Conaniah and his brother Shimei by appointment of King Hezekiah and of Azariah, the prefect of the house of God. **14** Kore, the son of Imnah, a Levite and the keeper of the eastern gate, was in charge of the free-will gifts made to God; he distributed the offerings made to the LORD and the most holy of the consecrated things. **15** Under him in the priestly cities were Eden, Miniamin, Jeshua, Shemaiah, Amariah and Shecaniah, who faithfully made the distribution to their brethren, great and small alike, according to their classes.

**16** There was also a register by ancestral houses of males thirty years of age and over, for all priests who were eligible to enter the house of the LORD according to the daily rule to fulfill their service in the order of their classes.[p] **17** The priests were inscribed in their family records according to their ancestral houses, and the Levites of twenty years and over according to their various offices and classes.[q] **18** A distribution was also made to all who were inscribed in the family records, for their little ones, wives, sons and daughters—thus for the entire assembly, since they were to sanctify themselves by sharing faithfully in the consecrated things. **19** The sons of Aaron, the priests who lived on the lands attached to their cities, had in every city men designated by name to distribute portions to every male among the priests and to every Levite listed in the family records.

**20** This Hezekiah did in all Judah. He did what was good, upright and faithful before the LORD, his God. **21** Everything that he undertook, for the service of the house of God or for the law and the commandments, was to do the will of his God. He did this wholeheartedly, and he prospered.[r]

## CHAPTER 32

**Invasion of Sennacherib.** **1** But after he had proved his fidelity by such deeds, Sennacherib, king of Assyria, came. He invaded Judah, besieged the fortified cities, and proposed to take them by storm.[s] **2** When Hezekiah saw that 'Sennacherib was coming with the intention of attacking Jerusalem, **3** he decided in counsel with his princes and warriors to stop the waters of the springs outside the city. When they had pledged him their support, **4** [t]a large crowd was gathered which stopped all the springs and also the running stream in the valley nearby. For they said, "Why should the kings of Assyria come and find an abundance of water?" **5** He then looked to his defenses: he rebuilt the wall where it was broken down, raised towers upon it, and built another wall outside. He strengthened the Millo of the City of David and had a great number of spears and shields prepared.[u] **6** Then he appointed army commanders over the people. He gathered them together in his presence in the open space at the gate of the city and encouraged them with these words: **7** "Be brave and steadfast; do not be afraid or dismayed because of the king of Assyria and all the throng that is coming with him, for there is more with us than with him.[v] **8** For he has only an arm of flesh, but we have the LORD, our God, to help us and to fight our battles." And the people took confidence from the words of King Hezekiah of Judah.[w]

**Threat of Sennacherib.** **9** [x]After this, while Sennacherib, king of Assyria, himself remained at Lachish with all his forces, he sent his officials to Jerusalem with this message for King Hezekiah of Judah, and all the Judahites who were in Jerusalem: **10** "King Sennacherib of Assyria has this to say: On what are you relying, while you remain under siege in Jerusalem? **11** Has not Hezekiah deceived you, delivering you over to a death of famine and thirst, by his claim that 'the LORD, our God, will save us from the grasp of the king of Assyria'? **12** Has not this same Hezekiah removed his high places and altars and commanded Judah and Jerusalem, 'You shall prostrate yourselves before one altar only, and on it alone you shall offer incense'? **13** Do you not know what my fathers and I have done to all the peoples of other lands? Were the gods of the nations in those lands able to save their lands from my hand? **14** Who among all the gods of those nations which my fathers put under the ban was able to save his people from my hand? Will your god, then, be able to save you from my hand? **15** Let not Hezekiah mislead you further and deceive you in any such way. Do not believe him! Since no other god of any other nation or kingdom has been able to save his people from my hand or the hands of my fathers, how much the less shall your god save you from my hand!"

**16** His officials said still more against the LORD God and against his servant Hezekiah, **17** for he had written letters to deride the LORD, the God of Israel, speaking of him in these terms: "As the gods of the nations in other lands have not saved their people from my hand, neither shall Hezekiah's god save his people from

p 1 Chr 23, 3f.
q 1 Chr 23, 6-24.
r Ps 119, 2f.
s 2 Kgs 18, 13.
t Is 22, 9. 11.
u Neh 2, 17f.
v 2 Chr 14, 10; 20, 6-12.
w Is 31, 3.
x 9-20: 2 Kgs 18, 17-37; Is 36, 1-22.
y 2 Kgs 19, 9-13; Is 37, 9-13.

my hand."[y] **18** In a loud voice they shouted in
the Judean language to the people of Jerusalem
who were on the wall, to frighten and terrify
them so that they might capture their city.
**19** They spoke of the God of Israel as though
he were one of the gods of the other peoples of
the earth, a work of human hands. **20** But because of this, King Hezekiah and the prophet
Isaiah, son of Amos, prayed and called out to
heaven.[z]

**Defeat of Sennacherib.** **21** Then the
LORD sent an angel, who destroyed every valiant warrior, leader and commander in the camp
of the Assyrian king, so that he had to return
shamefaced to his own country. And when he
entered the temple of his god, some of his own
offspring struck him down there with the
sword.[a] **22** Thus the LORD saved Hezekiah and
the inhabitants of Jerusalem from the hand of
Sennacherib, king of Assyria, as from every
other power; he gave them rest on every side.
**23** Many brought gifts for the LORD to Jerusalem and costly objects for King Hezekiah of
Judah, who thereafter was exalted in the eyes of
all the nations.[b]

**Hezekiah's Other Deeds.** **24** In those
days Hezekiah became mortally ill. He prayed
to the LORD, who answered him by giving him
a sign.[c] **25** Hezekiah, however, did not then
discharge his debt of gratitude, for he had become proud. Therefore anger descended upon
him and upon Judah and Jerusalem. **26** [d]But
then Hezekiah humbled himself for his pride
—both he and the inhabitants of Jerusalem; and
therefore the LORD did not vent his anger on
them during the time of Hezekiah.

**27** [e]Hezekiah possessed very great wealth
and glory. He had treasuries made for his silver,
gold, precious stones, spices, jewels, and other
precious things of all kinds; **28** also storehouses
for the harvest of grain, for wine and oil, and
barns for the various kinds of cattle and for the
flocks. **29** He built cities for himself, and he
acquired sheep and oxen in great numbers, for
God gave him very great riches. **30** This same
Hezekiah stopped the upper outflow of water
from Gihon and led it underground westward to
the City of David. Hezekiah prospered in all his
undertakings.[f] **31** Nevertheless, in respect to
the ambassadors [princes] sent to him from Babylon to investigate the sign that had occurred in
the land, God forsook him to test him, that he
might know all that was in his heart.

**32** The rest of Hezekiah's acts, including his
pious works, can be found written in the Vision
of the Prophet Isaiah, son of Amos, and in the
book of the kings of Judah and Israel. **33** Hezekiah rested with his ancestors; he was buried at
the approach to the tombs* of the descendants
of David. All Judah and the inhabitants of Jerusalem paid him honor at his death. His son
Manasseh succeeded him as king.

## CHAPTER 33

**Impiety of Manasseh.** **1** [g]Manasseh was
twelve years old when he became king, and he
reigned fifty-five years in Jerusalem. **2** He did
evil in the sight of the LORD, following the
abominable practices of the nations whom the
LORD had cleared out of the way of the Israelites. **3** He rebuilt the high places which his
father Hezekiah had torn down, erected altars
for the Baals, made sacred poles, and prostrated
himself before the whole host of heaven and
worshiped them. **4** He even built altars in the
temple of the LORD, of which the LORD had
said, "In Jerusalem shall my name be forever":
**5** he built altars to the whole host of heaven in
the two courts of the LORD's house. **6** It was he,
too, who immolated his sons by fire in the Valley of Ben-hin-nom. He practiced augury, divination and magic, and appointed necromancers
and diviners of spirits, so that he provoked the
LORD with the great evil that he did in his sight.
**7** He placed an idol that he had carved in the
house of God, of which God had said to David
and his son Solomon: "In this house and in
Jerusalem which I have chosen from all the
tribes of Israel I shall place my name forever.
**8** I will not again allow Israel's feet to leave the
land which I assigned to your fathers, provided
they are careful to observe all that I commanded
them, keeping the whole law and the statutes
and the ordinances given by Moses." **9** Manasseh misled Judah and the inhabitants of Jerusalem into doing even greater evil than the nations
which the LORD had destroyed at the coming of
the Israelites. **10** The LORD spoke to Manasseh
and his people, but they paid no attention.

**His Conversion.** **11** [h]Therefore the LORD
brought against them the army commanders of
the Assyrian king; they took Manasseh with
hooks, shackled him with chains, and trans-

---

z 2 Kgs 19, 14-19; Is 37, 14-20.
a 2 Kgs 19, 35ff; Is 37, 36ff.
b 2 Chr 14, 6.
c 2 Kgs 20, 1-11; Is 38, 1-8.
d 26. 31: 2 Kgs 20, 12-19; Is 39, 1-8.
e 27f: 2 Kgs 20, 13; Is 39, 2.
f 2 Kgs 20, 20f.
g 1-10: 2 Kgs 21, 1-9.
h Jb 36, 7f; Ez 19, 9.

---

* 32, 33: The approach to the tombs: literally, "the ascent of the tombs," which may mean "the upper section of the tombs," their most prominent and honored place.

33, 11: There is no evidence elsewhere for an imprisonment of King Manasseh in Babylon. However, according to the Assyrian inscriptions, he paid tribute to the Assyrian kings Esarhaddon (680–669 B.C.) and Asshurbanipal (668–627 B.C.). He may well have been obliged to go to Nineveh to take the oath of allegiance as vassal to the king of Assyria.

ported him to Babylon.* **12** In this distress, he
began to appease the LORD, his God. He humbled himself abjectly before the God of his fathers **13** and prayed to him.* The LORD let himself be won over: he heard his prayer and
restored him to his kingdom in Jerusalem. Then
Manasseh understood that the LORD is indeed
God.

**14** Afterward he built an outer wall for the
City of David to the west of Gihon in the valley,
extending to the Fish Gate and encircling Ophel;
he built it very high. He stationed army officers
in all the fortified cities of Judah. **15** He removed the foreign gods and the idol from the
LORD's house and all the altars he had built on
the mount of the LORD's house and in Jerusalem, and he cast them outside the city.[i] **16** He
restored the altar of the LORD, and sacrificed on
it peace offerings and thank offerings, and commanded Judah to serve the LORD, the God of
Israel. **17** Though the people continued to sacrifice on the high places, they now did so to the
LORD, their God.

**18** [j]The rest of the acts of Manasseh, his
prayer to his God, and the words of the seers
who spoke to him in the name of the LORD, the
God of Israel, can be found written in the chronicles of the kings of Israel. **19** His prayer and
how his supplication was heard, all his sins and
his infidelity, the sites where he built high
places and erected sacred poles and carved images before he humbled himself, all can be
found written down in the history of his seers.
**20** Manasseh rested with his ancestors and was
buried in his own palace. His son Amon succeeded him as king.

**Amon.** **21** [k]Amon was twenty-two years old
when he became king, and he reigned two years
in Jerusalem. **22** He did evil in the sight of the
LORD, just as his father Manasseh had done.
Amon offered sacrifice to all the idols which his
father Manasseh had made, and worshiped
them. **23** Moreover, he did not humble himself
before the LORD as his father Manasseh had
done; on the contrary, Amon only increased his
guilt. **24** His servants conspired against him
and put him to death in his own house. **25** But
the people of the land slew all those who had
conspired against King Amon, and then they,
the people of the land, made his son Josiah king
in his stead.

## CHAPTER 34

**Reforms of Josiah.** **1** [l]Josiah was eight
years old when he became king, and he reigned
thirty-one years in Jerusalem. **2** He pleased the
LORD, following the path of his ancestor David.
**3** [m]In the eighth year of his reign, while he was
still a youth, he began to seek after the God of
his forefather David, and in his twelfth year* he
began to purge Judah and Jerusalem of the high
places, the sacred poles and the carved and molten images. **4** In his presence, the altars of the
Baals were destroyed; the incense stands erected
above them were torn down; the sacred poles
and the carved and molten images were shattered and beaten into dust, which was strewn
over the tombs of those who had sacrificed to
them; **5** and the bones of the priests he burned
upon their altars. Thus he purged Judah and
Jerusalem. **6** He did likewise in the cities of
Manasseh, Ephraim, Simeon, and in the ruined
villages of the surrounding country as far as
Naphtali; **7** he destroyed the altars, broke up the
sacred poles and carved images and beat them
into dust, and tore down the incense stands
throughout the land of Israel. Then he returned
to Jerusalem.

**The Temple Restored.** **8** [n]In the eighteenth year of his reign, in order to cleanse the
temple as well as the land, he sent Shaphan, son
of Azaliah, Maaseiah, the ruler of the city, and
Joah, son of Joahaz, the chamberlain, to restore
the house of the LORD, his God. **9** They came
to Hilkiah the high priest and turned over the
money brought to the house of God which the
Levites, the guardians of the threshold, had collected from Manasseh, Ephraim, and all the
remnant of Israel, as well as from all of Judah,
Benjamin, and the inhabitants of Jerusalem.[o]
**10** They turned it over to the master workmen
in the house of the LORD, and these in turn used
it to pay the workmen in the LORD's house who
were restoring and repairing the temple.
**11** They also gave it to the carpenters and the
masons to buy hewn stone and timber for the tie
beams and rafters of the buildings which the
kings of Judah had allowed to fall into ruin.
**12** The men worked faithfully at their tasks;
their overseers were Jahath and Obadiah, Levites of the line of Merari, and Zechariah and
Meshullam, of the Kohathites, who directed
them. All those Levites who were skillful with

i 2 Chr 14, 2.
j 18. 20: 2 Kgs 21, 17f.
k 21-25: 2 Kgs 21, 19-26.
l 1f: 2 Kgs 22, 1f.
m 3-7: 2 Chr 14, 1-4; 31, 1; 2 Kgs 23, 4-20.
n 8-13: 2 Kgs 22, 3-7.
o 2 Chr 24, 8f.

*

33, 13: And prayed to him: these words led an unknown writer to compose the apocryphal "Prayer of Manasseh," which is added as an appendix to many editions of the Vulgate Bible and is used in the public prayers of the church.

34, 3: In his twelfth year: c. 628 B.C., the year after Asshurbanipal's death, when Judah could free itself from Assyrian domination. From 2 Kgs 22, 1—23, 25 alone, one might think that Josiah's reform began only after the discovery of the book of the law in the temple, in the eighteenth year of his reign. But the Chronicler is no doubt right in placing the beginning of the reform at an earlier period. The very repair of the temple, which led to the finding of the book of the law, must have been occasioned by a cultic reform.

musical instruments **13** were in charge of the
men who carried the burdens, and they directed
all the workers in every kind of labor. Some of
the other Levites were scribes, officials and
gatekeepers.

**The Finding of the Law.** **14** [p]When they
brought out the money that had been deposited
in the house of the LORD, Hilkiah the priest
found the book of the law of the LORD given
through Moses. **15** He reported this to Shaphan
the scribe, saying, "I have found the book of the
law in the house of the LORD." Hilkiah gave the
book to Shaphan, **16** who brought it to the king
at the same time that he was making his report
to him. He said, "Your servants are doing everything that has been entrusted to them;
**17** they have turned into bullion the metals deposited in the LORD's house and have handed it
over to the overseers and the workmen."
**18** Then Shaphan the scribe announced to the
king, "Hilkiah the priest has given me a book."
And Shaphan read from it before the king.

**19** When the king heard the words of the
law, he tore his garments **20** and issued this
command to Hilkiah, to Ahikam, son of Shaphan, to Abdon, son of Michah, to Shaphan the
scribe, and to Asaiah, the king's servant:
**21** "On behalf of myself and those who are left
in Israel and Judah, go, consult the LORD concerning the words of the book that has been
found. For the anger of the LORD has been set
furiously ablaze against us, since our fathers
have not kept the word of the LORD and have not
done all that is written in this book." **22** Then
Hilkiah and the other men from the king went
to the prophetess Huldah, the wife of Shallum,
son of Tokhath, son of Hasrah, the guardian of
the wardrobe; she dwelt in Jerusalem, in the
new quarter. They spoke to her as they had been
instructed, **23** and she said to them: "Thus says
the LORD, the God of Israel: 'Tell the one who
sent you to me, **24** The LORD says: I am prepared to bring evil upon this place and upon its
inhabitants, all the curses written in the book
that has been read before the king of Judah.
**25** Because they have abandoned me and have
offered incense to other gods, provoking me by
every deed that they have performed, my anger
is ablaze against this place and cannot be extinguished.'

**26** "But to the king of Judah who sent you
to consult the LORD, give this response: 'Thus
says the LORD, the God of Israel, concerning the
threats you have heard: **27** Because you were
heartsick and have humbled yourself before
God on hearing his words spoken against this
place and its inhabitants; because you have
humbled yourself before me, have torn your
garments, and have wept before me, I in turn
have listened—so declares the LORD. **28** I will
gather you to your ancestors and you shall be
taken to your grave in peace. Your eyes shall not
see all the evil I will bring upon this place and
upon its inhabitants.' "

They brought back this message to the king.

**Renewal of the Covenant.** **29** [q]The king
now convened all the elders of Judah and Jerusalem. **30** He went up to the house of the LORD
with all the men of Judah and the inhabitants of
Jerusalem, the priests, the Levites, and all the
people, great and small; and he had read aloud
to them the entire text of the book of the covenant that had been found in the house of the
LORD. **31** Standing at his post,* the king made
a covenant before the LORD to follow the LORD
and to keep his commandments, decrees, and
statutes with his whole heart and soul, thus observing the terms of the covenant written in this
book. **32** He thereby committed all who were of
Jerusalem and Benjamin, and the inhabitants of
Jerusalem conformed themselves to the covenant of God, the God of their fathers. **33** Josiah removed every abominable thing from all the
territory belonging to the Israelites, and he
obliged all who were in Israel to serve the LORD,
their God. During his lifetime they did not
desert the LORD, the God of their fathers.[r]

## CHAPTER 35

**The Passover.** **1** [s]Josiah celebrated in Jerusalem a Passover to honor the LORD; the Passover sacrifice was slaughtered on the fourteenth
day of the first month.[t] **2** He reappointed the
priests to their duties and encouraged them in
the service of the LORD's house. **3** He said to
the Levites who were to instruct all Israel, and
who were consecrated to the LORD: "Put the
holy ark in the house built by Solomon, son of
David, king of Israel. It shall no longer be a
burden on your shoulders. Serve now the LORD,
your God, and his people Israel.[u] **4** Prepare
yourselves in your ancestral houses and your
classes according to the prescriptions of King
David of Israel and his son Solomon. **5** Stand
in the sanctuary according to the divisions of the
ancestral houses of your brethren, the common
people, so that the distribution of the Levites
and the families may be the same.[v] **6** Slay the
Passover sacrifice, sanctify yourselves, and be
at the disposition of your brethren, that all may
be carried out according to the word of the LORD
given through Moses."[w]

p 14-28: 2 Kgs 22, 8-20.
q 29-32: 2 Kgs 23, 1ff.
r 2 Kgs 23, 4-20.
s 1-19: 2 Kgs 23, 21ff.
t Ex 12, 1-28; 2 Kgs 23, 21.
u 2 Chr 5, 4; 1 Chr 15, 12. 15.
v 1 Chr 24—26.
w 2 Chr 30, 17.

* 34, 31: Standing at his post: see note on 2 Chr 23, 13.

**7** Josiah contributed to the common people a
flock of lambs and kids, thirty thousand in number, each to serve as a Passover victim for any
who were present, and also three thousand
oxen; these were from the king's property.[x]
**8** His princes also gave a free-will gift to the
people, the priests and the Levites. Hilkiah,
Zechariah and Jehiel, prefects of the house of
God, gave to the priests two thousand six hundred Passover victims together with three hundred oxen.[y] **9** Conaniah and his brothers Shemaiah, Nethanel, Hashabiah, Jehiel and
Jozabad, the rulers of the Levites, contributed to
the Levites five thousand Passover victims, together with five hundred oxen.

**10** When the service had been arranged, the
priests took their places, as did the Levites in
their classes according to the king's command.
**11** The Passover sacrifice was slaughtered,
whereupon the priests sprinkled some of the
blood and the Levites proceeded to the skin-
ning. **12** They separated what was destined for
the holocaust and gave it to various groups of
the ancestral houses of the common people to
offer to the LORD, as is prescribed in the book
of Moses. They did the same with the oxen.
**13** They cooked the Passover on the fire as
prescribed, and also cooked the sacred meals in
pots, cauldrons and pans, then brought them
quickly to all the common people.[z] **14** Afterward they prepared the Passover for themselves
and for the priests. Indeed the priests, the sons
of Aaron, were busy offering holocausts and the
fatty portions until night; therefore the Levites
prepared for themselves and for the priests, the
sons of Aaron. **15** The singers, the sons of
Asaph, were at their posts as prescribed by David: Asaph, Heman and Jeduthun, the king's
seer. The gatekeepers were at every gate; there
was no need for them to leave their stations, for
their brethren, the Levites, prepared for them.
**16** Thus the entire service of the Lord was arranged that day so that the Passover could be
celebrated and the holocausts offered on the
altar of the Lord, as King Josiah had commanded. **17** The Israelites who were present on that
occasion kept the Passover and the feast of the
Unleavened Bread for seven days. **18** [a]No such
Passover had been observed in Israel since the
time of the prophet Samuel, nor had any king of
Israel kept a Passover like that of Josiah, the
priests and Levites, all of Judah and Israel that
were present, and the inhabitants of Jerusalem.
**19** It was in the eighteenth year of Josiah's
reign that this Passover was observed.

**Josiah's Reign Ends.** **20** After Josiah had
done all this to restore the temple, Neco, king
of Egypt, came up to fight at Carchemish on the
Euphrates, and Josiah went out to intercept him.
**21** Neco sent messengers to him, saying:
"What quarrel is between us, king of Judah? I
have not come against you this day, for my war
is with another kingdom, and God has told me
to hasten. Do not interfere with God who is with
me, as otherwise he will destroy you." **22** But
Josiah would not withdraw from him, for he had
sought a pretext for fighting with him. Therefore he would not listen to the words of Neco
that came from the mouth of God, but went out
to fight in the plain of Megiddo. **23** Then the
archers shot King Josiah, who said to his servants, "Take me away, for I am seriously
wounded."[b] **24** His servants removed him
from his own chariot, placed him in another he
had in reserve, and brought him to Jerusalem,
where he died. He was buried in the tombs of
his ancestors, and all Judah and Jerusalem
mourned him. **25** Jeremiah also composed a
lamentation over Josiah,* which is recited to
this day by all the male and female singers in
their lamentations over Josiah. These have been
made obligatory for Israel, and can be found
written in the Lamentations.

**26** [c]The rest of the chronicle of Josiah, his
pious deeds in regard to what is written in the
law of the LORD, and his acts, first and last, can
be found written in the book of the kings of
Israel and Judah.

## CHAPTER 36

**1** [d]The people of the land took Jehoahaz, son
of Josiah, and made him king in Jerusalem in his
father's stead.

### *IV: End of the Kingdom*

**Jehoahaz.** **2** Jehoahaz was twenty-three
years old when he became king, and he reigned
three months in Jerusalem. **3** The king of Egypt
deposed him in Jerusalem and fined the land one
hundred talents of silver and a talent of gold.
**4** Then the king of Egypt made his brother Eliakim king over Judah and Jerusalem, and
changed his name to Jehoiakim. Neco took his
brother Jehoahaz away and brought him to
Egypt.

**Jehoiakim.** **5** Jehoiakim was twenty-five
years old when he became king, and he reigned eleven years in Jerusalem. He did evil
in the sight of the LORD, his God.[e]

---

x Ex 12, 5.
y Nm 7, 1-83.
z Nm 12, 8f.
a 18f: 2 Kgs 23, 22f.
b 2 Chr 18, 33f.
c 2 Kgs 23, 28.
d 1-4: 2 Kgs 23, 30-34; 1 Chr 3, 15f.
e 2 Kgs 23, 36f; Jer 22, 18f.

---

* 35, 25: The reference to a lamentation over Josiah composed by Jeremiah is not found either in 2 Kgs or Jer; but see note on Zec 12, 11. Their lamentations: probably a reference to the canonical Book of Lamentations.

6 [f]Nebuchadnezzar, king of Babylon, came up
against him and bound him with chains to take
him to Babylon.* 7 Nebuchadnezzar also carried away to Babylon some of the vessels of the
house of the LORD and put them in his palace in
Babylon. 8 The rest of the acts of Jehoiakim,
the abominable things that he did, and what
therefore happened to him, can be found written
in the book of the kings of Israel and Judah. His
son Jehoiachin succeeded him as king.[g]

**Jehoiachin.** 9 Jehoiachin was eighteen
years old when he became king, and he reigned
three months [and ten days] in Jerusalem. He
did evil in the sight of the LORD.[h] 10 At the turn
of the year, King Nebuchadnezzar sent for him
and had him brought to Babylon, along with
precious vessels from the temple of the LORD.
He made his brother Zedekiah* king over Judah
and Jerusalem.[i]

**Zedekiah.** 11 Zedekiah was twenty-one
years old when he became king, and he reigned
eleven years in Jerusalem.[j] 12 He did evil in
the sight of the LORD, his God, and he did not
humble himself before the prophet Jeremiah,
who spoke the word of the Lord.[k] 13 He also
rebelled against King Nebuchadnezzar, who
had made him swear by God. He became stiff-
necked and hardened his heart rather than return
to the LORD, the God of Israel.[l] 14 Likewise all
the princes of Judah, the priests and the people
added infidelity to infidelity, practicing all the
abominations of the nations and polluting the
LORD's temple which he had consecrated in Jerusalem.

**Dissolution of Judah.** 15 Early and often
did the LORD, the God of their fathers, send his
messengers to them, for he had compassion on
his people and his dwelling place.[m] 16 But they
mocked the messengers of God, despised his
warnings, and scoffed at his prophets, until the
anger of the LORD against his people was so
inflamed that there was no remedy.[n] 17 Then
he brought up against them the king of the Chaldeans, who slew their young men in their own
sanctuary building, sparing neither young man
nor maiden, neither the aged nor the decrepit; he
delivered all of them over into his grip.[o] 18 All
the utensils of the house of God, the large and
the small, and the treasures of the LORD's house
and of the king and his princes, all these he
brought to Babylon.[p] 19 They burnt the house
of God, tore down the walls of Jerusalem, set
all its palaces afire, and destroyed all its precious objects.[q] 20 Those who escaped the
sword he carried captive to Babylon, where they
became his and his sons' servants until the kingdom of the Persians came to power. 21 All this
was to fulfill the word of the LORD spoken by
Jeremiah: "Until the land has retrieved its lost
sabbaths, during all the time it lies waste it shall
have rest while seventy years are fulfilled."

**Decree of Cyrus.** 22 *In the first year of
Cyrus, king of Persia, in order to fulfill the word
of the LORD spoken by Jeremiah, the LORD inspired King Cyrus of Persia to issue this proclamation throughout his kingdom, both by word
of mouth and in writing:[r] 23 "Thus says Cyrus, king of Persia: 'All the kingdoms of the
earth the LORD, the God of heaven, has given
to me, and he has also charged me to build him
a house in Jerusalem, which is in Judah. Whoever, therefore, among you belongs to any part
of his people, let him go up, and may his God
be with him!' "

---

f 2 Kgs 24, 1f.
g 2 Kgs 24, 5.
h 2 Kgs 24, 8f.
i 2 Kgs 24, 10-16.
j 2 Kgs 24, 18ff; Jer 52, 1ff.
k Jer 37, 1ff.
l 2 Kgs 25, 1; Jer 52, 4; Ex 17, 13-16.
m Jer 7, 25; Heb 1, 1.
n Mt 23, 34ff.
o Lam 1, 15; 5, 11-14.
p 2 Kgs 25, 14f.
q 2 Kgs 25, 9f; Lam 2, 8.
r Ezr 1, 1ff.

---

36, 6: Nebuchadnezzar . . . bound him with chains to take him to Babylon: the Chronicler does not say that Jehoiakim was actually taken to Babylon. According to 2 Kgs 24, 1–6, Jehoiakim revolted after being Nebuchadnezzar's vassal for three years; he died in Jerusalem before the Babylonian king could reach the city. However, Dn 1, 1f, apparently based on 2 Chr 36, 6f, speaks of Jehoiakim's deportation to Babylon.

36, 10: His brother Zedekiah: Zedekiah was actually the brother of Jehoiakim and the uncle of Jehoiachin (2 Kgs 24, 17; Jer 37, 1), though scarcely older than his nephew (2 Kgs 24, 8. 18; 2 Chr 36, 9. 11).

36, 22f: The words of these verses are identical with those of Ezr 1, 1–3a. Originally Ezra-Nehemiah formed the last part of the single work of the Chronicler, of which 1 and 2 Chronicles formed the first part. But when Ezra-Nehemiah was regarded as a natural sequence to the Books of Samuel and of Kings, it was separated from 1 and 2 Chronicles and placed before them. Thus, 1 and 2 Chronicles became the last part of the Hebrew Bible. To prevent this work from ending on a note of doom, Ezr 1, 1–3a was repeated as 2 Chr 36, 22f.

# The Book of
# EZRA

*The last four books of the Hebrew canon are Ezra, Nehemiah, 1 and 2 Chronicles, in that order. Originally, however, Ezra and Nehemiah followed the Books of Chronicles, and formed with them a unified historical work so homogeneous in spirit that one usually speaks of a single author for the four books. He is called "the Chronicler." The treatment of Ezra-Nehemiah as a single book by the earliest chroniclers was undoubtedly due to the fact that in ancient times the two books were put under the one name—Ezra. The combined work Ezra-Nehemiah is our most important literary source for the formation of the Jewish religious community after the Babylonian exile. This is known as the period of the Restoration, and the two men most responsible for the reorganization of Jewish life at this time were Ezra and Nehemiah.*

*In the present state of the Ezra-Nehemiah text, there are several dislocations of large sections so that the chronological or logical sequence is disrupted. The major instances are pointed out in the footnotes. Although Ezra appears before Nehemiah in this work, it seems probable that Nehemiah's activity preceded his.*

*What is known of Ezra and his work is due almost exclusively to Ezra 7–10 (the "Ezra Memoirs") and to Neh 8–9. Strictly speaking, the term "Ezra Memoirs" should be used only of that section in which Ezra speaks in the first person, i.e., 7, 27–9, 15. Compare the "Nehemiah Memoirs" in Neh 1, 1–7, 72a; 11, 1f; 12, 27–43; 13, 4–31. The Chronicler combined this material with other sources at his disposal. The personality of Ezra is less known than that of Nehemiah. Ben Sirach, in his praise of the fathers, makes no mention of Ezra. The genealogy of Ezra (7, 1–5) traces his priesthood back to Aaron, brother of Moses. This was the accepted way of establishing the legality of one's priestly office. He is also called* a scribe, well-versed in the law of Moses *(7, 6), indicating Ezra's dedication to the study of the Torah, which he sought to make the basic rule of life in the restored community. It was in religious and cultic reform rather than in political affairs that Ezra made his mark as a postexilic leader. Jewish tradition holds him in great honor; the Talmud even regards him as a second Moses, claiming that the Torah would have been given to Israel through Ezra had not Moses preceded him.*

*Ezra is sometimes accused of having been a mere legalist who gave excessive attention to the letter of the law. His work, however, should be seen and judged within a specific historical context. He gave to his people a cohesion and spiritual unity which prevented the disintegration of the small Jewish community. Had it not been for the intransigence of Ezra and of those who adopted his ideal, it is doubtful that Judaism would have so effectively resisted Hellenism, then or in later centuries. Ezra set the tone of the postexilic community, and it was characterized by fidelity to the Torah, Judaism's authentic way of life. It is in this light that we can judge most fairly the work of Ezra during the Restoration.*

*The Book of Ezra is divided as follows:*
*I. The Return from Exile (1, 1–6, 22).*
*II. The Deeds of Ezra (7, 1–10, 44).*

The following list of the kings of Persia, with the dates of their reigns, will be useful for dating the events mentioned in Ezra-Nehemiah:

| | |
|---|---|
| Cyrus | 538–529 B.C. |
| Cambyses | 529–521 B.C. |
| Darius I | 521–485 B.C. |
| Xerxes | 485–464 B.C. |
| Artaxerxes I | 464–423 B.C. |
| Darius II | 423–404 B.C. |
| Artaxerxes II | 404–358 B.C. |

Artaxerxes III ............................................358–337 B.C.
End of the Persian Empire (Defeat of Darius III) ..................331 B.C.

## I: The Return from Exile

### CHAPTER 1

**The Decree of Cyrus.** 1 [a]In the first year
of Cyrus,* king of Persia, in order to fulfill the
word of the LORD spoken by Jeremiah, the LORD
inspired King Cyrus of Persia to issue this proclamation throughout his kingdom, both by word
of mouth and in writing: 2 "Thus says Cyrus,
king of Persia: 'All the kingdoms of the earth the
LORD, the God of heaven, has given to me, and
he has also charged me to build him a house in
Jerusalem, which is in Judah. 3 Whoever,
therefore, among you belongs to any part of his
people, let him go up, and may his God be with
him! 4 Let everyone who has survived, in whatever place he may have dwelt, be assisted by the
people of that place with silver, gold, goods,
and cattle, together with free will offerings for
the house of God in Jerusalem.' "

5 Then the family heads of Judah and Benjamin and the priests and Levites—everyone, that
is, whom God had inspired to do so—prepared
to go up to build the house of the LORD in
Jerusalem. 6 All their neighbors gave them
help in every way, with silver, gold, goods, and
cattle, and with many precious gifts besides all
their free-will offerings.[b] 7 King Cyrus, too,
had the utensils of the house of the LORD
brought forth which Nebuchadnezzar had taken
away from Jerusalem and placed in the house of
his god. 8 Cyrus, king of Persia, had them
brought forth by the treasurer Mithredath, and
counted out to Sheshbazzar,* the prince of Judah. 9 This was the inventory: sacks of gold-
ware, thirty; sacks of silverware, one thousand
and twenty-nine; 10 golden bowls, thirty; silver
bowls, four hundred and ten; other ware, one
thousand pieces. 11 Total of the gold- and silverware: five thousand four hundred pieces.*
All these Sheshbazzar took with him when the
exiles were brought back from Babylon to Jerusalem.

### CHAPTER 2

**Census of the Province.** 1 *These are the
inhabitants of the province who returned from
the captivity of the exiles, whom Nebuchadnezzar, king of Babylon, had carried away to Babylon,[c] and who came back to Jerusalem and
Judah, each man in his own city* 2 (those who
returned with Zerubbabel, Jeshua, Nehemiah,
Seraiah, Reelaiah, Mordecai, Bilshan, Mispereth, Bigvai, Rehum, and Baanah):

The census of the men of Israel: 3 sons of
Parosh, two thousand one hundred and seventy-two; 4 sons of Shephatiah, three hundred
and seventy-two; 5 sons of Arah, seven hundred and seventy-five; 6 sons of Pahath-moab,
who were sons of Jeshua and Joab, two thousand eight hundred and twelve; 7 sons of Elam,
one thousand two hundred and fifty-four;
8 sons of Zattu, nine hundred and forty-five;
9 sons of Zaccai, seven hundred and sixty;
10 sons of Bani, six hundred and forty-two;
11 sons of Bebai, six hundred and twenty-
three; 12 sons of Azgad, one thousand two hundred and twenty-two; 13 sons of Adonikam, six
hundred and sixty-six; 14 sons of Bigvai, two
thousand and fifty-six; 15 sons of Adin, four
hundred and fifty-four; 16 sons of Ater, who
were sons of Hezekiah, ninety-eight; 17 sons of
Bezai, three hundred and twenty-three; 18 sons
of Jorah, one hundred and twelve; 19 sons of
Hashum, two hundred and twenty-three;
20 sons of Gibeon, ninety-five; 21 sons of
Bethlehem, one hundred and twenty-three;
22 men of Netophah, fifty-six; 23 men of Anathoth, one hundred and twenty-eight; 24 men of
Beth-azmaveth, forty-two; 25 men of Kiriath-
jearim, Chephirah, and Beeroth, seven hundred
and forty-three; 26 men of Ramah and Geba,
six hundred and twenty-one; 27 men of Michmas, one hundred and twenty-two; 28 men of
Bethel and Ai, two hundred and twenty-three;
29 sons of Nebo, fifty-two; 30 sons of Mag-
bish, one hundred and fifty-six; 31 sons of the
other Elam, one thousand two hundred and fifty-four; 32 sons of Harim, three hundred and
twenty; 33 sons of Lod, Hadid, and Ono, seven
hundred and twenty-five; 34 sons of Jericho,
three hundred and forty-five; 35 sons of Senaah, three thousand six hundred and thirty.

36 The priests: sons of Jedaiah, who were of
the house of Jeshua, nine hundred and seven-

a 1ff: Ezr 36, 22f; Jer 25, 11f; 29, 10; Zec 1, 12.
b Ex 3, 22; 11, 2; 12, 35.
c Neh 7, 6-67.

*

1, 1: In the first year of Cyrus: as sovereign over the world empire which began with his conquest of Babylon; that is, 538 B.C.

1, 8: Sheshbazzar: very probably the fourth son of Jehoiachin, king of Judah, taken captive to Babylon in 598 B.C., listed in 1 Chr 3, 18 as Senneser; if so, he was the uncle of Zerubbabel (Ezr 3, 2ff); see note on 1 Chr 3, 18.

1, 11: Total . . . five thousand four hundred pieces: either this figure or the figures given for one or more of the items listed (vv 9f) have been corrupted in the transmission of the text.

2, 1–67: As it now stands, this list is an expanded form of the lists of returned captives from the sixth century B.C.; see Neh 7, 6–72, where it reappears.

ty-three; **37** sons of Immer, one thousand and
fifty-two; **38** sons of Pashhur, one thousand
two hundred and forty-seven; **39** sons of Harim, one thousand and seventeen.

**40** The Levites: sons of Jeshua, Kadmiel,
Binnui, and Hodaviah, seventy-four.[d]

**41** The singers: sons of Asaph, one hundred
and twenty-eight.

**42** The gatekeepers: sons of Shallum, sons of
Ater, sons of Talmon, sons of Akkub, sons of
Hatita, sons of Shobai, one hundred and thir-
ty-nine in all.

**43** The temple slaves: sons of Ziha, sons of
Hasupha, sons of Tabbaoth, **44** sons of Keros,
sons of Siaha, sons of Padon, **45** sons of Leba-
nah, sons of Hagabah, sons of Akkub, **46** sons
of Hagab, sons of Shamlai, sons of Hanan,
**47** sons of Giddel, sons of Gahar, sons of Reaiah, **48** sons of Rezin, sons of Nekoda, sons of
Gazzam, **49** sons of Uzza, sons of Paseah, sons
of Besai, **50** sons of Asnah, sons of the Meunites, sons of the Nephusites, **51** sons of Bakbuk, sons of Hakupha, sons of Harhur, **52** sons
of Bazluth, sons of Mehida, sons of Harsha,
**53** sons of Barkos, sons of Sisera, sons of Te-
mah, **54** sons of Neziah, sons of Hatipha.

**55** Descendants of the slaves of Solomon:
sons of Sotai, sons of Hassophereth, sons of
Peruda, **56** sons of Jaalah, sons of Darkon, sons
of Giddel, **57** sons of Shephatiah, sons of Hattil, sons of Pochereth-hazzebaim, sons of Ami.
**58** The total of the temple slaves and the descendants of the slaves of Solomon was three
hundred and ninety-two.

**59** The following who returned from Tel-
melah, Tel-harsha, Cherub, Addan, and Immer
were unable to prove that their ancestral houses
and their descent were Israelite: **60** sons of Delaiah, sons of Tobiah, sons of Nekoda, six hundred and fifty-two. **61** Also, of the priests: sons
of Habaiah, sons of Hakkoz, sons of Barzillai
(he had married one of the daughters of Barzillai
the Gileadite and became known by his name).[e]
**62** These men searched their family records,
but their names could not be found written there;
hence they were degraded from the priesthood,
**63** and His Excellency* ordered them not to
partake of the most holy foods until there should
be a priest bearing the Urim and Thummim.

**64** The entire assembly taken together came
to forty-two thousand three hundred and sixty,
**65** not counting their male and female slaves,
who were seven thousand three hundred and
thirty-seven. They also had two hundred male
and female singers. **66** Their horses were seven
hundred and thirty-six, their mules two hundred
and forty-five, **67** their camels four hundred
and thirty-five, their asses six thousand seven
hundred and twenty.

**68** When they arrived at the house of the
LORD in Jerusalem, some of the family heads
made free-will offerings for the house of God,
to rebuild it in its place. **69** According to their
means they contributed to the treasury for the
temple service: sixty-one thousand drachmas of
gold, five thousand minas of silver, and one
hundred garments for the priests. **70** The
priests, the Levites, and some of the common
people took up residence in Jerusalem; but the
singers, the gatekeepers, and the temple slaves
dwelt in their cities. Thus all the Israelites dwelt
in their cities.

## CHAPTER 3

**Restoration of the Altar.** **1** Now when the
seventh month* came, after the Israelites had
settled in their cities, the people gathered at
Jerusalem as one man.[f] **2** Then Jeshua, son of
Jozadak, together with his brethren the priests,
and Zerrubbabel, son of Shealtiel, together with
his brethren, set about rebuilding the altar of the
God of Israel in order to offer on it the holocausts prescribed in the law of Moses, the man
of God. **3** Despite their fear of the peoples of
the land, they replaced the altar on its foundations and offered holocausts to the LORD on it,
both morning and evening.[g] **4** They also kept
the feast of Booths in the manner prescribed,
and they offered the daily holocausts in the
proper number required for each day.[h] **5** Thereafter they offered the established holocaust, the
sacrifices prescribed for the new moons and all
the festivals sacred to the LORD, and those
which anyone might offer as a free-will gift to
the LORD. **6** From the first day of the seventh
month they began to offer holocausts to the
LORD, though the foundation of the temple of
the LORD had not yet been laid.

**Founding of the Temple.** **7** Then they
hired stonecutters and carpenters, and sent food
and drink and oil to the Sidonians and Tyrians

d Neh 12, 24.
e 2 Sm 17, 27; 19, 32f; 1 Kgs 2, 7.
f Neh 7, 73—8, 1.
g 1 Kgs 8, 64; Dn 9, 25.
h Ex 23, 16; Nm 28, 3-8.
i 1 Chr 22, 4; 2 Chr 2, 9.

*

2, 63: His Excellency: the deputy of the Persian government; from the context, he was one of the Jewish exile leaders. Nehemiah as governor receives the same title (Neh 8, 9; 10, 2). Urim and Thummim: see note on Ex 28, 30.

3, 1f: The seventh month: Tishri (September–October), apparently of 538 B.C.; cf Ezr 1, 1; 4, 5. In this case, it was Sheshbazzar who erected the first altar, since he began the work on the foundations of the temple in Jerusalem; cf Ezr 5, 16. It was in the second year of Darius I, i.e., in 520 B.C., that Jeshua and Zerubbabel resumed the work on the temple that had been temporarily interrupted (Ezr 4, 24—5, 1; Hg 1, 1; 2, 1). The Chronicler or a later editor of the text here attributes to them the beginning of the work which, in reality, they merely completed. Shealtiel: the oldest son of King Jehoiachin of Judah and the brother of Sheshbazzar (1 Chr 3, 18f); Zerubbabel was therefore the grandson of Jehoiachin; see note on Ezr 1, 8.

that they might ship cedar trees from the Lebanon to the port of Joppa, as Cyrus, king of Persia, had authorized.[i] **8** In the year after their coming to the house of God in Jerusalem, in the second month, Zerubbabel, son of Shealtiel, and Jeshua, son of Jozadak, together with the rest of their brethren, the priests and Levites and all who had come from the captivity to Jerusalem, began by appointing the Levites twenty years of age and over to supervise the work on the house of the LORD. **9** Jeshua and his sons and brethren, with Kadmiel and Binnui, son of Henadad, and their sons and their brethren, the Levites, stood as one man to supervise those who were engaged in the work on the house of God. **10** When the builders had laid the foundation of the LORD's temple, the vested priests with the trumpets and the Levites, sons of Asaph, were stationed there with the cymbals to praise the LORD in the manner laid down by David, king of Israel.[j] **11** They alternated in songs of praise and thanksgiving to the LORD, "for he is good, for his kindness to Israel endures forever"; and all the people raised a great shout of joy, praising the LORD because the foundation of the LORD's house had been laid.[k] **12** Many of the priests, Levites, and family heads, the old men who had seen the former house, cried out in sorrow as they watched the foundation of the present house being laid.[l] Many others, however, lifted up their voices in shouts of joy, **13** and no one could distinguish the sound of the joyful shouting from the sound of those who were weeping; for the people raised a mighty clamor which was heard afar off.[m]

## CHAPTER 4

**Samaritan Interference.** **1** When the enemies of Judah and Benjamin heard that the exiles were building a temple for the LORD, the God of Israel, **2** they approached Zerubbabel and the family heads and said to them, "Let us build with you, for we seek your God just as you do, and we have sacrificed to him since the days of Esarhaddon, king of Assyria, who had us brought here." **3** But Zerubbabel, Jeshua, and the rest of the family heads of Israel answered them, "It is not your responsibility to build with us a house for our God, but we alone must build it for the LORD, the God of Israel, as King Cyrus of Persia has commanded us." **4** Thereupon the people of the land set out to intimidate and dishearten the people of Judah so as to keep them from building. **5** They also suborned counselors to work against them and thwart their plans during the remaining years of Cyrus, king of Persia, and until the reign of Darius,* king of Persia.

**Later Hostility.** **6** Also at the beginning of the reign of Ahashuerus they prepared a written accusation against the inhabitants of Judah and Jerusalem.

**7** Again, in the time of Artaxerxes, Mithredath wrote in concert with Tabeel and the rest of his fellow officials to Artaxerxes, king of Persia. The document was written in Aramaic* and was accompanied by a translation. [Aramaic:]

**8** *Then Rehum, the governor, and Shimshai, the scribe, wrote the following letter against Jerusalem to King Artaxerxes: **9** "Rehum, the governor, Shimshai, the scribe, and their fellow judges, officials, and agents from among the Persian, Urukian, Babylonian, Susian (that is, Elamite), **10** and the other peoples whom the great and illustrious Assurbanipal transported and settled in the city of Samaria and elsewhere in the province West-of-Euphrates, as follows. . . ." **11** This is a copy of the letter that they sent to him:

"To King Artaxerxes, your servants, the men of West-of-Euphrates, as follows: **12** Let it be known to the king that the Jews who came up from you to us have arrived at Jerusalem and are now rebuilding this rebellious and evil city. They are raising up its walls, and the foundations have already been laid. **13** Now let it be known to the king that if this city is rebuilt and its walls are raised up again, they will no longer pay taxes, tributes, or tolls; thus it can only result in harm to the throne. **14** Now, since we partake of the salt of the palace, we ought not simply to look on while the king is being dishonored. Therefore we have sent this message to inform you, O king, **15** so that inquiry may be made in the historical records of your fathers. In the historical records you can discover and verify that this city is a rebellious city which has proved fatal to kings and provinces, and that sedition has been fostered there since ancient times. For that reason this city was destroyed.

j Ezr 2, 41.
k Pss 100, 5; 136; Jer 33, 11.
l Hg 2, 3.
m Tb 14, 5.

*

4, 5: Darius: Darius I (521–485 B.C.). The temple-building narrative continues in Ezr 4, 24. In between (Ezr 4, 6–23) is a series of notes about the opposition to the returned exiles voiced at the Persian court in the early fifth century B.C., after the temple had been reestablished.

4, 7: Aramaic: this word in the original text seems to be a note indicating a change of language from Hebrew to Aramaic, which in fact takes place here. The Aramaic section ends with Ezr 6, 18, but again in Ezr 7, 12–26 a royal letter is cited in Aramaic.

4, 8–23: The central question here is the rebuilding of the fortification walls of Jerusalem, not the building of the temple. The interruption of work on the city wall some time before 445 B.C. was the occasion for the coming of Nehemiah to Palestine (Neh 1, 1–4; 2, 1–5). Artaxerxes: Artaxerxes I (464–423 B.C.).

**16** We inform you, O king, that if this city is
rebuilt and its walls are raised up again, by that
very fact you will no longer own any part of
West-of-Euphrates.''

**17** The king sent this answer: ''To Rehum,
the governor, Shimshai, the scribe, and their
fellow officials living in Samaria and elsewhere
in the province West-of-Euphrates, greetings
and the following: **18** The communication
which you sent us has been read plainly in my
presence. **19** When at my command inquiry
was made, it was verified that from ancient
times this city has risen up against kings and that
rebellion and sedition have been fostered there.
**20** Powerful kings were once in Jerusalem who
ruled over all West-of-Euphrates, and taxes,
tributes, and tolls were paid to them. **21** Give
orders, therefore, that will stop the work of
these men. This city may not be rebuilt until a
further decree has been issued by me. **22** Take
care that you do not neglect this matter, lest the
evil grow to the detriment of the throne.''

**23** As soon as a copy of King Artaxerxes'
letter had been read before Rehum, the governor, Shimshai, the scribe, and their fellow officials, they went in all haste to the Jews in Jerusalem and stopped their work by force of arms.[n]

**Rebuilding of the Temple.** **24** Thus it
was that the work on the house of God in Jerusalem was halted. This inaction lasted until the
second year of the reign of Darius,* king of
Persia.

## CHAPTER 5

**1** Then the prophets Haggai and Zechariah,*
son of Iddo, began to prophesy to the Jews in
Judah and Jerusalem in the name of the God of
Israel.[o] **2** Thereupon Zerubbabel, son of Shealtiel, and Jeshua, son of Jozadak, began again to
build the house of God in Jerusalem, with the
prophets of God giving them support. **3** At that
time there came to them Tattenai, governor of
West-of-Euphrates, and Shethar-bozenai, and
their fellow officials, who asked of them: ''Who
issued the decree for you to build this house and
raise this edifice? **4** What are the names of the
men who are building this structure?'' **5** But
their God watched over the elders of the Jews
so that they were not hindered, until a report
could go to Darius and then a written order be
sent back concerning this matter.

**6** A copy of the letter sent to King Darius by
Tattenai, governor of West-of-Euphrates, and
Shethar-bozenai, and their fellow officials from
West-of-Euphrates; **7** they sent him a report in
which was written the following:

''To King Darius, all good wishes! **8** Let it
be known to the king that we have visited the
province of Judah and the house of the great
God: it is being rebuilt of cut stone and the walls
are being reinforced with timber; the work is
being carried on diligently and is making good
progress under their hands. **9** We then questioned the elders, addressing to them the following words: 'Who issued the decree for you to
build this house and raise this edifice?' **10** We
also asked them their names, to report them to
you in a list of the men who are their leaders.
**11** This was their answer to us: 'We are the
servants of the God of heaven and earth, and we
are rebuilding the house built here long years
ago, which a great king of Israel built and finished. **12** But because our fathers provoked the
wrath of the God of heaven, he delivered them
into the power of the Chaldean, Nebuchadnezzar, king of Babylon, who destroyed this house
and led the people captive to Babylon. **13** However, in the first year of Cyrus, king of Babylon,
King Cyrus issued a decree for the rebuilding of
this house of God. **14** Moreover, the gold and
silver utensils of the house of God which Nebuchadnezzar had taken from the temple in Jerusalem and carried off to the temple in Babylon,
King Cyrus ordered to be removed from the
temple in Babylon and consigned to a certain
Sheshbazzar, whom he named governor.
**15** And he commanded him: Take these utensils and deposit them in the temple of Jerusalem,
and let the house of God be rebuilt on its former
site. **16** Then this same Sheshbazzar came and
laid the foundations of the house of God in
Jerusalem. Since that time the building has been
going on, and it is not yet completed.' **17** Now,
if it please the king, let a search be made in the
royal archives of Babylon to discover whether
a decree really was issued by King Cyrus for the
rebuilding of this house of God in Jerusalem.
And may the king's pleasure in this matter be
communicated to us.''

## CHAPTER 6

**The Decree of Darius.** **1** Thereupon King
Darius issued an order to search the archives in
which the Babylonian records were stored
away; **2** [p]and in Ecbatana, the stronghold in the
province of Media, a scroll was found containing the following text: ''Memorandum. **3** In the
first year of King Cyrus, King Cyrus issued a
decree: The house of God in Jerusalem. The
house is to be rebuilt as a place for offering

n Neh 1, 3.
o Hg 1, 14—2, 9; Zec 4, 9.
p 2-12; Ezr 1, 4-11.

*

4, 24: The second year . . . of Darius: 520 B.C.; it marks the beginning of the successful restoration of the temple, which was accomplished within the five years following (Ezr 5, 1—6, 18).

5, 1: The prophets Haggai and Zechariah: two of the Minor Prophets, whose books record their role in the encouragement of this work.

sacrifices and bringing burnt offerings. Its height is to be sixty cubits and its width sixty cubits. **4** It shall have three courses of cut stone for each one of timber. The costs are to be borne by the royal palace. **5** Also, the gold and silver utensils of the house of God which Nebuchadnezzar took from the temple of Jerusalem and brought to Babylon are to be sent back: to be returned to their place in the temple of Jerusalem and deposited in the house of God.

**6** "Now, therefore, Tattenai, governor of West-of-Euphrates, and Shethar-bozenai, and you, their fellow officials in West-of-Euphrates, do not interfere in that place. **7** Let the governor and the elders of the Jews continue the work on that house of God; they are to rebuild it on its former site. **8** I also issue this decree concerning your dealing with these elders of the Jews in the rebuilding of that house of God: From the royal revenue, the taxes of West-of-Euphrates, let these men be repaid for their expenses, in full and without delay. **9** Whatever else is required—young bulls, rams, and lambs for holocausts to the God of heaven, wheat, salt, wine, and oil, according to the requirements of the priests who are in Jerusalem—is to be delivered to them day by day without fail, **10** that they may continue to offer sacrifices of pleasing odor to the God of heaven and pray for the life of the king and his sons. **11** I also issue this decree: If any man violates this edict, a beam is to be taken from his house, and he is to be lifted up and impaled on it; and his house is to be reduced to rubble for this offense. **12** And may the God who causes his name to dwell there overthrow every king or people who may undertake to alter this or to destroy this house of God in Jerusalem. I, Darius, have issued this decree; let it be carefully executed."

**13** Then Tattenai, the governor of West-of-Euphrates, and Shethar-bozenai, and their fellow officials carried out fully the instructions King Darius had sent them. **14** The elders of the Jews continued to make progress in the building, supported by the message of the prophets, Haggai and Zechariah, son of Iddo. They finished the building according to the command of the God of Israel and the decrees of Cyrus and Darius [and of Artaxerxes, king of Persia]. **15** They completed this house on the third day of the month Adar, in the sixth year of the reign of King Darius. **16** The Israelites—priests, Levites, and the other returned exiles—celebrated the dedication of this house of God with joy. **17** For the dedication of this house of God, they offered one hundred bulls, two hundred rams, and four hundred lambs, together with twelve he-goats as a sin-offering for all Israel, in keeping with the number of the tribes of Israel. **18** Finally, they set up the priests in their classes and the Levites in their divisions for the service of God in Jerusalem, as is prescribed in the book of Moses.

**The Passover.** **19** [q]The exiles kept the Passover on the fourteenth day of the first month. **20** The Levites, every one of whom had purified himself for the occasion, sacrificed the Passover for the rest of the exiles, for their brethren the priests, and for themselves. **21** The Israelites who had returned from the exile partook of it together with all those who had separated themselves from the uncleanness of the peoples of the land to join them in seeking the LORD, the God of Israel.[r] **22** They joyfully kept the feast of Unleavened Bread for seven days, for the LORD had filled them with joy by making the king of Assyria* favorable to them, so that he gave them help in their work on the house of God, the God of Israel.

## *II: The Deeds of Ezra*

### CHAPTER 7

**Ezra the Scribe.** **1** After these events,* during the reign of Artaxerxes, king of Persia, Ezra, son of Seraiah, son of Azariah, son of Hilkiah, **2** son of Shallum, son of Zadok, son of Ahitub, **3** son of Amariah, son of Azariah, son of Meraioth, **4** son of Zerahiah, son of Uzzi, son of Bukki, **5** son of Abishua, son of Phinehas, son of Eleazar, son of the high priest Aaron— **6** this Ezra came up from Babylon. He was a scribe, well-versed in the law of Moses which was given by the LORD, the God of Israel. Because the hand of the LORD, his God, was upon him, the king granted him all that he requested.[s]

**7** Some of the Israelites and some priests, Levites, singers, gatekeepers, and temple slaves also came up to Jerusalem in the seventh year of King Artaxerxes. **8** Ezra came to Jerusalem in the fifth month of that seventh year of the king. **9** On the first day of the first month he resolved on the journey up from Babylon, and on the first day of the fifth month he arrived at

q 19-22; Ex 12, 1-20.
r Ps 47, 9.
s Ezr 7, 28; 8, 18; Neh 2, 8. 18.

*

6, 22: Assyria: used here in a broad sense for the Persian Empire.

7, 1–8: The date of Ezra's journey to Palestine is not known with certainty. The seventh year of King Artaxerxes I would be 458 B.C., and the present order of the text suggests that date. The narratives of Ezra and Nehemiah make it seem to many, however, that the arrival of Nehemiah in 445 B.C. should precede that of Ezra. If so, Ezra may be thought to have come in 398 B.C., the seventh year of King Artaxerxes II. Others argue for the thirty-seventh year of Artaxerxes I, that is, 428 B.C.; this would suppose that the date given in the text has suffered in transmission.

Jerusalem, for the favoring hand of his God was upon him. **10** Ezra had set his heart on the study and practice of the law of the LORD and on teaching statutes and ordinances in Israel.[t]

**The Decree of Artaxerxes.** **11** This is a copy of the rescript which King Artaxerxes gave to Ezra the priest-scribe, the scribe of the text of the LORD's commandments and statutes for Israel:

**12** [u]"Artaxerxes, king of kings, to Ezra the priest, scribe of the law of the God of heaven (then, after greetings): **13** I have issued this decree, that anyone in my kingdom belonging to the people of Israel, its priests or Levites, who is minded to go up to Jerusalem with you, may do so. **14** You are the envoy from the king and his seven counselors to supervise Judah and Jerusalem in respect of the law of your God which is in your possession, **15** and to bring with you the silver and gold which the king and his counselors have freely contributed to the God of Israel, whose dwelling is in Jerusalem, **16** as well as all the silver and gold which you may receive throughout the province of Babylon, together with the free-will offerings which the people and priests freely contribute for the house of their God in Jerusalem. **17** You must take care, therefore, to use this money to buy bulls, rams, lambs, and the cereal offerings and libations proper to these, and offer them on the altar of the house of your God in Jerusalem. **18** You and your brethren may do whatever seems best to you with the remainder of the silver and gold, conformably to the will of your God. **19** The utensils consigned to you for the service of the house of your God you are to deposit before the God of Jerusalem. **20** Whatever else you may be required to supply for the needs of the house of your God, you may draw from the royal treasury. **21** I, Artaxerxes the king, issue this decree to all the treasurers of West-of-Euphrates: Whatever Ezra the priest, scribe of the law of the God of heaven, requests of you, dispense to him accurately, **22** within these limits: silver, one hundred talents; wheat, one hundred kors; wine, one hundred baths; oil, one hundred baths; salt, without limit. **23** Let everything that is ordered by the God of heaven be carried out exactly for the house of the God of heaven, that wrath may not come upon the realm of the king and his sons. **24** We also inform you that it is not permitted to impose taxes, tributes, or tolls on any priest, Levite, singer, gatekeeper, temple slave, or any other servant of that house of God.

**25** "As for you, Ezra, in accordance with the wisdom of your God* which is in your possession, appoint magistrates and judges to administer justice to all the people in West-of-Euphrates, to all, that is, who know the laws of your God. Instruct those who do not know these laws.[v] **26** Whoever does not obey the law of your God and the law of the king, let strict judgment be executed upon him, whether death, or corporal punishment, or a fine on his goods, or imprisonment."

**Ezra and His Companions.** **27** Blessed be the LORD, the God of our fathers, who thus disposed the mind of the king to glorify the house of the LORD in Jerusalem, **28** and who let me find favor with the king, with his counselors, and with all the most influential royal officials. I herefore took courage and, with the hand of the LORD, my God, upon me, I gathered together Israelite family heads to make the return journey with me.[w]

## CHAPTER 8

**1** This is the list of the family heads who returned with me from Babylon during the reign of King Artaxerxes:

**2** Of the sons of Phinehas, Gershon; of the sons of Ithamar, Daniel; of the sons of David, Hattush, **3** son of Shecaniah; of the sons of Parosh, Zechariah, and with him one hundred and fifty males were enrolled; **4** of the sons of Pahath-moab, Eliehoenai, son of Zerahiah, and with him two hundred males; **5** of the sons of Zattu, Shecaniah, son of Jahaziel, and with him three hundred males; **6** of the sons of Adin, Ebed, son of Jonathan, and with him fifty males; **7** of the sons of Elam, Jeshaiah, son of Athaliah, and with him seventy males; **8** of the sons of Shephatiah, Zebadiah, son of Michael, and with him eighty males; **9** of the sons of Joab, Obadiah, son of Jehiel, and with him two hundred and eighteen males; **10** of the sons of Bani, Shelomith, son of Josiphiah, and with him one hundred and sixty males; **11** of the sons of Bebai, Zechariah, son of Bebai, and with him twenty-eight males; **12** of the sons of Azgad, Johanan, son of Hakkatan, and with him one hundred and ten males; **13** of the sons of Adonikam, younger sons, whose names were Eliphelet, Jeiel, and Shemaiah, and with them sixty males; **14** of the sons of Bigvai, Uthai, son of Zakkur, and with him seventy males.

**The Journey to Jerusalem.** **15** I had them assemble by the river that flows toward Ahava,* where we made camp for three days. There I perceived that both laymen and priests were present, but I could not discover a single

t Ps 119, 45.
u 12-17: Ezr 1, 2ff.
v 2 Chr 17, 9.
w Ezr 7, 6.

*

7, 25: The wisdom of your God: the Mosaic law; cf vv 6, 14.

8, 15: Ahava: a town at an unidentified site in Babylonia. The river that flowed toward it was probably a branch or canal of the Euphrates.

Levite. **16** Therefore I sent Eliezer, Ariel, Shemaiah, Jarib, Elnathan, Nathan, Zechariah, and
Meshullam, wise leaders, **17** with a command
for Iddo, the leader in the place Casiphia, instructing them what to say to Iddo and his brethren, and to the temple slaves in Casiphia, in
order to procure for us ministers for the house
of our God. **18** They sent to us—for the favoring hand of our God was upon us—a well-in-
structed man, one of the sons of Mahli, son of
Levi, son of Israel, namely Sherebiah, with his
sons and brethren, eighteen men.[x] **19** They also
sent us Hashabiah, and with him Jeshaiah, sons
of Merari, and their brethren and their sons,
twenty men. **20** Of the temple slaves (those
whom David and the princes appointed to serve
the Levites) there were two hundred and twenty.
All these men were enrolled by name.[y]

**21** Then I proclaimed a fast, there by the
river of Ahava, that we might humble ourselves
before our God to petition from him a safe journey for ourselves, our children, and all our possessions. **22** For I would have been ashamed to
ask the king for troops and horsemen to protect
us against enemies along the way, since we had
said to the king, "The favoring hand of our God
is upon all who seek him, but his mighty wrath
is against all who forsake him."[z] **23** So we
fasted, and prayed to our God for this, and our
petition was granted. **24** Next I selected twelve
of the priestly leaders along with Sherebiah,
Hashabiah, and ten of their brethren, **25** and I
weighed out before them the silver and the gold
and the utensils offered for the house of our God
by the king, his counselors, his officials, and all
the Israelites of that region. I consigned it to
them in these amounts: **26** silver, six hundred
and fifty talents; silver utensils, one hundred;
gold, one hundred talents; **27** twenty golden
bowls valued at a thousand darics; two vases of
excellent polished bronze, as precious as gold.
**28** I addressed them in these words: "You are
consecrated to the LORD, and the utensils are
also consecrated; the silver and the gold are a
free-will offering to the LORD, the God of your
fathers. **29** Keep good watch over them till you
weigh them out in Jerusalem in the presence of
the chief priests and Levites and the family leaders of Israel, in the chambers of the house of the
LORD." **30** The priests and the Levites then
took over the silver, the gold, and the utensils
that had been weighted out, to bring them to
Jerusalem, to the house of our God.

**31** We set out for Jerusalem from the river of
Ahava on the twelfth day of the first month. The
hand of our God remained upon us, and he
protected us from enemies and bandits along the
way. **32** Thus we arrived at Jerusalem, where
we first rested for three days. **33** On the fourth
day, the silver, the gold, and the utensils were
weighed out in the house of our God and consigned to the priest Meremoth, son of Uriah,
who was assisted by Eleazar, son of Phinehas;
they were assisted by the Levites Jozabad, son
of Jeshua, and Noadiah, son of Binnui. **34** Everything was in order as to number and weight,
and the total weight was registered. At that same
time, **35** those who had returned from the captivity, the exiles, offered as holocausts to the
God of Israel twelve bulls for all Israel, ninety-six rams, seventy-seven lambs, and twelve
goats as sin-offerings: all these as a holocaust to
the LORD. **36** Finally, the orders of the king
were presented to the king's satraps and to the
governors in West-of-Euphrates, who gave their
support to the people and to the house of God.*

## CHAPTER 9

### Denunciation of Mixed Marriages.
**1** [a]When these matters had been concluded, the
leaders approached me with this report: "Neither the Israelite laymen nor the priests nor the
Levites have kept themselves aloof from the
peoples of the land and their abominations [Ca-
naanites, Hittites, Perizzites, Jebusites, Ammonites, Moabites, Egyptians, and Amorites];
**2** for they have taken some of their daughters as
wives for themselves and their sons, and thus
they have desecrated the holy race with the peoples of the land. Furthermore, the leaders and
rulers have taken a leading part in this apostasy!"

**Ezra's Exhortation.** **3** When I had heard
this thing, I tore my cloak and my mantle,
plucked hair from my head and beard, and sat
there stupefied.[b] **4** Around me gathered all who
were in dread of the sentence of the God of
Israel on this apostasy of the exiles, while I
remained motionless until the evening sacrifice.[c] **5** Then, at the time of the evening sacrifice, I rose in my wretchedness, and with cloak
and mantle torn I fell on my knees, stretching
out my hands to the LORD, my God.

**6** I said: "My God, I am too ashamed and
confounded to raise my face to you, O my God,
for our wicked deeds are heaped up above our
heads and our guilt reaches up to heaven.[d]
**7** *From the time of our fathers even to this day
great has been our guilt, and for our wicked
deeds we have been delivered over, we and our

x Ezr 7, 6.
y Ezr 2, 43.
z Neh 2, 9.
a 1f: Dt 7, 1; Neh 9, 2.
b Ps 119, 136.
c Is 66, 2.
d Ps 38, 4.

*

8, 36: The story of Ezra's mission is seemingly continued from this point by Neh 7, 72b—8, 18, which may be read before Ezr 9, 1.

9, 7: After this verse, the next part of the prayer attributed to Ezra is perhaps to be found in Neh 9, 6–37, which may be read as leading up to Ezr 9, 8–15.

kings and our priests, to the will of the kings of
foreign lands, to the sword, to captivity, to pillage, and to disgrace, as is the case today.
**8** "And now, but a short time ago, mercy
came to us from the LORD, our God, who left
us a remnant and gave us a stake in his holy
place; thus our God has brightened our eyes and
given us relief in our servitude.[e] **9** For slaves
we are, but in our servitude our God has not
abandoned us; rather, he has turned the good
will of the kings of Persia toward us. Thus he
has given us new life to raise again the house of
our God and restore its ruins, and has granted
us a fence in Judah and Jerusalem.[f] **10** But
now, O our God, what can we say after all this?
For we have abandoned your commandments,
**11** which you gave through your servants the
prophets: the land which you are entering to take
as your possession is a land unclean with the
filth of the peoples of the land, with the abominations with which they have filled it from one
end to the other in their uncleanness.[g] **12** Do
not, then, give your daughters to their sons in
marriage, and do not take their daughters for
your sons. Never promote their peace and prosperity; thus you will grow strong, enjoy the
produce of the land, and leave it as an inheritance to your children forever.[h]
**13** "After all that has come upon us for our
evil deeds and our great guilt—though you, our
God, have made less of our sinfulness than it
deserved and have allowed us to survive as we
do— **14** shall we again violate your commandments by intermarrying with these abominable
peoples? Would you not become so angered
with us as to destroy us without remnant or
survivor? **15** O LORD, God of Israel, you are
just; yet we have been spared, the remnant we
are today. Here we are before you in our sins.
Because of all this, we can no longer stand in
your presence."

## CHAPTER 10

**The People's Response.** **1** While Ezra
prayed and acknowledged their guilt, weeping
and prostrate before the house of God, a very
large assembly of Israelites gathered about him,
men, women, and children; and the people wept
profusely. **2** Then Shecaniah, the son of Jehiel,
one of the sons of Elam, made this appeal to
Ezra: "We have indeed betrayed our God by
taking as wives foreign women of the peoples
of the land. Yet even now there remains a hope
for Israel. **3** Let us therefore enter into a covenant before our God to dismiss all our foreign
wives and the children born of them, in keeping
with what you, my lord, advise, and those who
fear the commandments of our God. Let the law
be observed! **4** Rise, then, for this is your duty!
We will stand by you, so have courage and take
action!"
**5** Ezra rose to his feet and demanded an oath
from the chiefs of the priests, from the Levites
and from all Israel that they would do as had
been proposed; and they swore it. **6** Then Ezra
retired from his place before the house of God
and entered the chamber of Johanan, son of
Eliashib,* where he spent the night neither eating food nor drinking water, for he was in
mourning over the betrayal by the exiles. **7** A
proclamation was made throughout Judah and
Jerusalem that all the exiles should gather together in Jerusalem, **8** and that whoever failed
to appear within three days would, according to
the judgment of the leaders and elders, suffer
the confiscation of all his possessions, and himself be excluded from the assembly of the exiles.
**9** All the men of Judah and Benjamin gathered together in Jerusalem within the three-day
period: it was in the ninth month,* on the twentieth day of the month. All the people, standing
in the open place before the house of God, were
trembling both over the matter at hand and because it was raining. **10** Then Ezra, the priest,
stood up and said to them: "Your unfaithfulness
in taking foreign women as wives has added to
Israel's guilt. **11** But now, give praise to the
LORD, the God of your fathers, and do his will:
separate yourselves from the peoples of the land
and from these foreign women."[i] **12** In answer, the whole assembly cried out with a loud
voice: "Yes, it is our duty to do as you say!
**13** But the people are numerous and it is the
rainy season, so that we cannot remain out-
of-doors; besides, this is not a task that can be
performed in a single day or even two, for those
of us who have sinned in this regard are many.
**14** Let our leaders represent the whole assembly; then let all those in our cities who have
taken foreign women for wives appear at appointed times, accompanied by the elders and
magistrates of each city in question, till we have
turned away from us our God's burning anger
over this affair." **15** Only Jonathan, son of Asahel, and Jahzeiah, son of Tikvah, were against

e Is 4, 3.
f Ps 106, 46.
g Lv 18, 24f; Ez 36, 17.
h Dt 7, 3.
i Neh 9, 2.

*

10, 6: Johanan, son of Eliashib: actually, the grandson of Eliashib; the father of Johanan was Eliashib's son Joiada (Neh 12, 10f, 22). Since Eliashib was high priest at the time of Nehemiah (Neh 3, 1. 20f; 13, 4. 7) and Johanan, if not yet high priest, was at least old enough to have his own separate quarters (chamber) in the temple at the time of Ezra, it is practically certain that Nehemiah's activity in Jerusalem must have preceded that of Ezra.

10, 9: Ninth month: Chislev (November–December), during the "early rains" in Palestine. Since the assembly took place in the open . . . all the people . . . were trembling . . . because it was raining.

this proposal, with Meshullam and Shabbethai
the Levite supporting them.

**The Guilty.** **16** *The exiles did as agreed.
Ezra appointed as his assistants men who were
family heads, one for each family, all of them
designated by name. They held sessions to examine the matter, beginning with the first day
of the tenth month. **17** By the first day of the
first month they had passed judgment on all the
men who had taken foreign women for wives.
**18** Among the priests, the following were
found to have taken foreign women for wives:
Of the sons of Jeshua, son of Jozadak, and his
brethren: Maaseiah, Eliezer, Jarib, and Gedaliah. **19** They pledged themselves to dismiss
their wives, and as a guilt-offering for their guilt
they gave a ram from the flock. **20** Of the sons
of Immer: Hanani and Zebadiah; **21** of the sons
of Harim: Maaseiah, Elijah, Shemaiah, Jehiel,
and Uzziah; **22** of the sons of Pashhur: Elioenai, Maaseiah, Ishmael, Nethanel, Jozabad,
and Elasah.
**23** Of the Levites: Jozabad, Shemei, Kelaiah
(also called Kelita), Pethahiah, Judah, and Eliezer.[j]
**24** Of the singers: Eliashib and Zakkur; of
the gatekeepers: Shallum, Telem, and Uri.
**25** Among the other Israelites: Of the sons of
Parosh: Ramiah, Izziah, Malchijah, Mijamin,
Eleazar, Malchijah, and Benaiah; **26** of the
sons of Elam: Mattaniah, Zechariah, Jehiel,
Abdi, Jeremoth, and Elijah; **27** of the sons of
Zattu: Elioenai, Eliashib, Mattaniah, Jeremoth,
Zabad, and Aziza; **28** of the sons of Bebai:
Jehohanan, Hananiah, Zabbai, and Athlai;
**29** of the sons of Bani: Meshullam, Malluch,
Adaiah, Jashub, Sheal, and Jeremoth; **30** of the
sons of Pahath-moab: Adna, Chelal, Benaiah,
Maaseiah, Mattaniah, Bezalel, Binnui, and Manasseh; **31** of the sons of Harim: Eliezer, Is-
shijah, Malchijah, Shemaiah, Shimeon,
**32** Benjamin, Malluch, Shemariah; **33** of the
sons of Hashum: Mattenai, Mattattah, Zabad,
Eliphelet, Jeremai, Manasseh, Shimei; **34** of
the sons of Begui: Maadai, Amram, Uel,
**35** Benaiah, Bedeiah, Cheluhi, **36** Vaniah,
Meremoth, Eliashib, **37** Mattaniah, Mattenai,
and Jaasu; **38** of the sons of Binnui: Shimei,
**39** Shelemiah, Nathan, and Adaiah; **40** of the
sons of Zachai: Shashai, Sharai, **41** Azarel,
Shelemiah, Shemariah, **42** Shallum, Amariah,
Joseph; **43** of the sons of Nebo: Jeiel, Mattithiah, Zabad, Zebina, Jaddai, Joel, Benaiah.
**44** All these had taken foreign wives; but
they sent them away, both the women and their
children.*

j Neh 8, 7; 10, 11.

*

10, 16f: The work of the committee lasted three months, from the first day of the tenth month, Tebet (December–January), to the first day of the first month, Nisan (March–April), of the following Jewish year.

10, 44: The account of the problem of mixed marriages at the time of Ezra is continued in Neh 9, 1–5; this may be read immediately after Ezr 10, 44, though the date given in Neh 9, 1 fits more precisely after Ezr 10, 15; cf Hg 2, 10–14.

# The Book of

# NEHEMIAH

*Problems common to the combined Books Ezra-Nehemiah have been pointed out in the Introduction to the Book of Ezra. The achievements of the two men were complementary; each helped to make it possible for Judaism to maintain its identity during the difficult days of the Restoration. Nehemiah was the man of action who rebuilt the walls of Jerusalem and introduced necessary administrative reforms. Ezra in turn was the great religious reformer who succeeded in establishing the Torah as the constitution of the returned community.*

*The biblical sources for Nehemiah's life and work are the autobiographical portions scattered through the book. They are called the "Memoirs of Nehemiah," and have been used more extensively and effectively by "the Chronicler" than the "Memoirs of Ezra." No competent scholar questions the authenticity of Nehemiah's memoirs. From these and other sources, the picture emerges of a man dedicated to the single purpose of the welfare of his people. Despite temperamental shortcomings, Nehemiah was a man of good practical sense combined with deep faith in God. In view of his selfless service to a community capable of severely testing any leader, we can be indulgent toward his numerous appeals to God to credit him with the work he had done. Nehemiah was a layman, and his generous dedication of talents to the service of God and of God's people remains an example of undiminished force for laymen today.*

*The Book of Nehemiah is divided as follows:*
*I. The Deeds of Nehemiah (1, 1—7, 72).*
*II. Promulgation of the Law (8, 1—13, 31).*

## I: The Deeds of Nehemiah

### CHAPTER 1

**Nehemiah's Vocation.** 1 The words of
Nehemiah, the son of Hacaliah.*
In the month Chislev of the twentieth year, I
was in the citadel of Susa 2 when Hanani, one
of my brothers, came with other men from Judah. I asked them about the Jews, the remnant
preserved after the captivity, and about Jerusalem, 3 and they answered me: "The survivors
of the captivity there in the province are in great
distress and under reproach. Also, the wall of
Jerusalem lies breached, and its gates have been
gutted with fire." 4 When I heard this report,
I began to weep and continued mourning for
several days; I fasted and prayed before the God
of heaven.

5 I prayed: "O LORD, God of heaven, great
and awesome God, you who preserve your covenant of mercy toward those who love you and
keep your commandments,[a] 6 may your ear be
attentive, and your eyes open, to heed the prayer
which I, your servant, now offer in your presence day and night for your servants the Israelites, confessing the sins which we of Israel have
committed against you, I and my father's house
included.[b] 7 Grievously have we offended
you, not keeping the commandments, the statutes, and the ordinances which you committed
to your servant Moses.[c] 8 But remember, I
pray, the promise which you gave through Moses, your servant, when you said:[d] 'Should you
prove faithless, I will scatter you among the
nations; 9 but should you return to me and carefully keep my commandments, even though
your outcasts have been driven to the farthest
corner of the world, I will gather them from
there, and bring them back to the place which
I have chosen as the dwelling place for my
name.' 10 They are your servants, your people,
whom you freed by your great might and your
strong hand.[e] 11 O LORD, may your ear be
attentive to my prayer and that of all your will-

a Dt 7, 9. 12; Dn 9, 4.
b 2 Chr 6, 40.
c Dn 3, 29f.
d 8f: Dt 30, 1-5.
e Dt 9, 29.
f Ps 118, 25.

*

1, 1: The first mission of Nehemiah, from the twentieth year of Artaxerxes I, lasted from the spring (Neh 2, 1) of 445 B.C. until 433 B.C. (Neh 5, 14). It is recounted in Neh 1, 1—6, 15; 12, 27–43; 6, 16—7, 5; 11, 1–21, which may be read in that order.

1, 11: Cupbearer to the king: an important official in the royal household. Because Nehemiah could appear in the queen's presence (Neh 2, 6), it is commonly presumed that he was a eunuch; but this is not necessarily so.

ing servants who revere your name. Grant success to your servant this day, and let him find
favor with this man"—for I was cupbearer to
the king.*[f]

## CHAPTER 2

**Appointment by the King.** **1** In the month
Nisan of the twentieth year of King Artaxerxes,
when the wine was in my charge, I took some
and offered it to the king. As I had never before
been sad in his presence, **2** the king asked me,
"Why do you look sad? If you are not sick, you
must be sad at heart." Though I was seized with
great fear, **3** I answered the king: "May the
king live forever! How could I not look sad
when the city where my ancestors are buried lies
in ruins, and its gates have been eaten out by
fire?" **4** The king asked me, "What is it, then,
that you wish?" I prayed to the God of heaven
**5** and then answered the king: "If it please the
king, and if your servant is deserving of your
favor, send me to Judah, to the city of my
ancestors' graves, to rebuild it." **6** Then the
king, and the queen seated beside him, asked
me how long my journey would take and when
I would return. I set a date that was acceptable
to him, and the king agreed that I might go.
**7** I asked the king further: "If it please the
king, let letters be given to me for the governors
of West-of-Euphrates, that they may afford me
safe-conduct till I arrive in Judah; **8** also a letter
for Asaph, the keeper of the royal park, that he
may give me wood for timbering the gates of the
temple-citadel and for the city wall and the
house that I shall occupy." The king granted my
requests, for the favoring hand of my God was
upon me.[g] **9** Thus I proceeded to the governors
of West-of-Euphrates and presented the king's
letters to them. The king also sent with me army
officers and cavalry.[h]
**10** When Sanballat the Horonite* and Tobiah the Ammonite slave had heard of this, they
were very much displeased that someone had
come to seek the welfare of the Israelites.

**Circuit of the City.** **11** When I had arrived
in Jerusalem, I first rested there for three days.
**12** Then I set out by night with only a few other
men (for I had not told anyone what my God had
inspired me to do for Jerusalem) and with no
other animals but my own mount. **13** *I rode
out at night by the Valley Gate, passed by the
Dragon Spring, and came to the Dung Gate,
observing how the walls of Jerusalem lay in
ruins and its gates had been eaten out by fire.
**14** Then I passed over to the Spring Gate and
to the King's Pool. Since there was no room
here for my mount to pass with me astride, **15** I
continued on foot up the wadi by night, inspecting the wall all the while till I once more reached
the Valley Gate, by which I went back in.
**16** The magistrates knew nothing of where I
had gone or what I was doing, for as yet I had
disclosed nothing to the Jews, neither to the
priests, nor to the nobles, nor to the magistrates,
nor to the others who would be concerned about
the matter.

**Rebuilding Jerusalem's Walls.** **17** Afterward I said to them: "You see the evil plight
in which we stand: how Jerusalem lies in ruins
and its gates have been gutted by fire. Come, let
us rebuild the wall of Jerusalem, so that we may
no longer be an object of derision!" **18** Then I
explained to them how the favoring hand of my
God had rested upon me, and what the king had
said to me. They replied, "Let us be up and
building!" And they undertook the good work
with vigor.[i]
**19** On hearing of this, Sanballat the Horonite, Tobiah the Ammonite slave, and Geshem
the Arab mocked us and ridiculed us. "What is
this that you are about?" they asked. "Are you
rebelling against the king?" **20** My answer to
them was this: "It is the God of heaven who will
grant us success. We, his servants, shall set
about the rebuilding; but for you there is to be
neither share nor claim nor memorial* in Jerusalem."

---

g Ezr 7, 6.
h Ezr 8, 22.
i Ezr 7, 6.

---

2, 10: Sanballat the Horonite: the governor of the province of Samaria (Neh 3, 33f), apparently a native of one of the Bethhorons. A letter from the Jews living at Elephantine in southern Egypt, dated 408–407 B.C., mentions "Delayah and Shelemyah, the sons of Sanballat, the governor of Samaria." Although his own name was Babylonian—Sin-uballit, i.e., "Sin (the moon god) has given life"—two sons had names referring to Yahweh. Tobiah, the Ammonite slave: the governor of the province of Ammon in Transjordan. His honorary title, "servant" (in Hebrew, ebed), i.e., of the king, could also be understood as slave, and Nehemiah no doubt meant it in this derogatory sense. The Tobiads remained a powerful family even in Maccabean times (2 Mc 3, 11). Sanballat and Tobiah together with Geshem the Arab (Neh 2, 19; 6, 1f), who was probably in charge of Edom and the regions to the south and southeast of Judah, opposed the rebuilding of Jerusalem's walls on policital grounds; the city was the capital of a rival province.

2, 13ff: Nehemiah left Jerusalem by the Valley Gate near the northwestern end of the old City of David and went south down the Tyropoean Valley toward the Dragon Spring (or the En-rogel of Jos 15, 7; 18, 16; 2 Sm 17, 17; 1 Kgs 1, 9, now known as Job's Well) at the juncture of the Valley of Hinnom and the Kidron Valley; he then turned north at the Dung Gate (or the Potsherd Gate of Jer 19, 2) at the southern end of the city and proceeded up the wadi, that is, the Kidron Valley, passing the Spring Gate (at the Spring of Gihon) and the King's Pool (unidentified); finally he turned west and then south to his starting point.

2, 20: Neither share nor claim nor memorial: although Sanballat and Tobiah were Yahwist, Nehemiah would not let them participate in any of the rights of the religious community in Jerusalem.

## CHAPTER 3

**List of Workers.*** 1 Eliashib the high priest
and his priestly brethren took up the task of
rebuilding the Sheep Gate. They timbered it and
set up its doors, its bolts, and its bars, then
continued the rebuilding to the Tower of Hananel.[j] 2 At their side the men of Jericho were
rebuilding, and next to them was Zaccur, son of
Imri. 3 The Fish Gate was rebuilt by the sons
of Hassenaah; they timbered it and set up its
doors, its bolts, and its bars.[k] 4 At their side
Meremoth, son of Uriah, son of Hakkoz, carried out the work of repair; next to him was
Meshullam, son of Berechiah, son of Meshezabel; and next to him was Zadok, son of Baana.
5 Next to him the Tekoites carried out the work
of repair; however, some of their outstanding
men would not submit to the labor asked by their
lords. 6 The New City Gate was repaired by
Joiada, son of Paseah; and Meshullam, son of
Besodeiah; they timbered it and set up its doors,
its bolts, and its bars. 7 At their side were Mela-
tiah the Gibeonite, Jadon the Meronothite, and
the men of Gibeon and of Mizpah, who were
under the jurisdiction of the governor of
West-of-Euphrates. 8 Next to them the work of
repair was carried out by Uzziel, son of Harha-
iah, a member of the goldsmiths' guild, and at
his side was Hananiah, one of the perfumers'
guild. They restored Jerusalem as far as the wall
of the public square.* 9 Next to them the work
of repair was carried out by Rephaiah, son of
Hur, leader of half the district of Jerusalem,
10 and at his side was Jedaiah, son of Haru-
maph, who repaired opposite his own house.
Next to him Hattush, son of Hashabneiah, carried out the work of repair. 11 The adjoining
sector, as far as the Oven Tower, was repaired
by Malchijah, son of Harim, and Hasshub, of
Pahathmoab. 12 At their side the work of repair
was carried out by Shallum, son of Halohesh,
leader of half the district of Jerusalem, by himself and his daughters. 13 The Valley Gate was
repaired by Hanun and the inhabitants of Zanoah; they rebuilt it and set up its doors, its bolts,
and its bars. They also repaired a thousand cubits of the wall up to the Dung Gate. 14 The
Dung Gate was repaired by Malchijah, son of
Rechab, leader of the district of Beth-haccherem; he rebuilt it and set up its doors, its
bolts, and its bars. 15 The Spring Gate was
repaired by Shallum, son of Colhozeh, leader of
the district of Mizpah; he rebuilt it, roofed it
over, and set up its doors, its bolts, and its bars.
He also repaired the wall of the Aqueduct Pool
near the king's garden as far as the steps that
lead down from the City of David. 16 After
him, the work of repair was carried out by Nehemiah, son of Azbuk, leader of half the district
of Beth-zur, to a place opposite the tombs of
David, as far as the artificial pool and the bar-
racks.

17 After him, the Levites carried out the
work of repair: Rehum, son of Bani. Next to
him, for his own district, was Hashabiah, leader
of half the district of Keilah. 18 After him, their
brethren carried out the work of repair: Binnui,
son of Henadad, leader of half the district of
Keilah; 19 next to him Ezer, son of Jeshua,
leader of Mizpah, who repaired the adjoining
sector, the Corner, opposite the ascent to the
arsenal. 20 After him, Baruch, son of Zabbai,
repaired the adjoining sector from the Corner to
the entrance of the house of Eliashib, the high
priest. 21 After him, Meremoth, son of Uriah,
son of Hakkoz, repaired the adjoining sector
from the entrance of Eliashib's house to the end
of the house.

22 After him, the work of repair was carried
out by the priests, men of the surrounding country. 23 After them, Benjamin and Hasshub carried out the repair in front of their houses; after
them, Azariah, son of Maaseiah, son of Ananiah, made the repairs alongside his house.
24 After him, Binnui, son of Henadad, repaired
the adjoining sector from the house of Azariah
to the Corner [that is, to the Angle]. 25 After
him, Palal, son of Uzai, carried out the work of
repair opposite the Corner and the tower projecting from the Upper Palace at the quarters of
the guard. After him, Pedaiah, son of Parosh,
carried out the work of repair 26 to a point
opposite the Water Gate on the east, and the
projecting tower. 27 After him, the Tekoites
repaired the adjoining sector opposite the great
projecting tower, to the wall of Ophel [the temple slaves were dwelling on Ophel].

28 Above the Horse Gate the priests carried
out the work of repair, each before his own
house. 29 After them Zadok, son of Immer,
carried out the repair before his house, and after
him the repair was carried out by Shemaiah, son
of Shecaniah, keeper of the East Gate.[l] 30 After him, Hananiah, son of Shelemiah, and Hanun, the sixth son of Zalaph, repaired the adjoining sector; after them, Meshullam, son of
Berechiah, repaired the place opposite his own
lodging. 31 After him, Malchijah, a member of
the goldsmiths' guild, carried out the work of
repair as far as the quarters of the temple slaves
and the merchants, before the Gate of Inspec-

j Jer 31, 38.
k Ezr 2, 35; Zep 1, 10.
l Ezr 40, 6.

*

3, 1–32: The construction work on the gates and walls of the city is described in counterclockwise direction, beginning and ending at the Sheep Gate (to the north of the temple). The exact sites of many of the topographical points mentioned are uncertain.

3, 8: Wall of the public square: that is, the section of wall bounding the place of assembly outside the Gate of Ephraim, or New City Gate; cf Neh 3, 6; 8, 16.

tion and as far as the upper chamber of the
Angle. **32** Between the upper chamber of the
Angle and the Sheep Gate, the goldsmiths and
the merchants carried out the work of repair.

### Opposition from Judah's Foes.

**33** When Sanballat heard that we were rebuilding the wall, it roused his anger and he became
very much incensed. He ridiculed the Jews,
**34** saying in the presence of his brethren and
the troops of Samaria: "What are these miserable Jews trying to do? Will they complete their
restoration in a single day? Will they recover
these stones, burnt as they are, from the heaps
of dust?" **35** Tobiah the Ammonite was beside
him, and he said: "It is a rubble heap they are
building. Any fox that attacked it would breach
their wall of stones!" **36** Take note, O our God,
how we were mocked! Turn back their derision
upon their own heads and let them be carried
away to a land of captivity! **37** Hide not their
crime and let not their sin be blotted out in your
sight, for they insulted the builders to their
face![m] **38** We, however, continued to build the
wall, which was soon filled in and completed up
to half its height. The people worked with a
will.

## CHAPTER 4

**1** When Sanballat, Tobiah, the Arabs, the
Ammonites, and the Ashdodites heard that the
restoration of the walls of Jerusalem was progressing—for the gaps were beginning to be
closed up—they became extremely angry.
**2** Thereupon they all plotted together to come
and fight against Jerusalem and thus to throw us
into confusion. **3** We prayed to our God and
posted a watch against them day and night for
fear of what they might do. **4** Meanwhile the
Judahites were saying:

"Slackened is the bearers' strength,
there is no end to the rubbish;
Never shall we be able
the wall to rebuild."

**5** Our enemies thought, "Before they are aware
of it or see us, we shall come into their midst,
kill them, and put an end to the work."

**6** When the Jews who lived near them had
come to us from one place after another, and had
told us ten times over that they were about to
attack us, **7** I stationed guards down below,
behind the wall, near the exposed points, assigning them by family groups with their
swords, their spears, and their bows. **8** I made
an inspection, then addressed these words to the
nobles, the magistrates, and the rest of the people: "Have no fear of them! Keep in mind the
LORD, who is great and to be feared, and fight
for your brethren, your sons and daughters,
your wives and your homes." **9** When our enemies became aware that we had been warned
and that God had upset their plan, we all went
back, each to his own task at the wall.

**10** From that time on, however, only half my
able men took a hand in the work, while the
other half, armed with spears, bucklers, bows,
and breastplates, stood guard behind the whole
house of Judah[n] **11** as they rebuilt the wall. The
load carriers, too, were armed; each did his
work with one hand and held a weapon with the
other. **12** Every builder, while he worked, had
his sword girt at his side. Also, a trumpeter
stood beside me, **13** for I had said to the nobles,
the magistrates, and the rest of the people: "Our
work is scattered and extensive, and we are
widely separated from one another along the
wall; **14** wherever you hear the trumpet sound,
join us there; our God will fight with us."
**15** Thus we went on with the work, half of the
men with spears at the ready, from daybreak till
the stars came out.

**16** At the same time I told the people to
spend the nights inside Jerusalem, each man
with his own attendant, so that they might serve
as a guard by night and a working force by day.
**17** Neither I, nor my kinsmen, nor any of my
attendants, nor any of the bodyguard that accompanied me took off his clothes; everyone
kept his weapon at his right hand.

## CHAPTER 5

**Antisocial Conduct.** **1** [o]Then there rose a
great outcry of the common people and their
wives against certain of their fellow Jews.
**2** Some said: "We are forced to pawn our sons
and daughters in order to get grain to eat that we
may live." **3** Others said: "We are forced to
pawn our fields, our vineyards, and our houses,
that we may have grain during the famine."
**4** Still others said: "To pay the king's tax we
have borrowed money on our fields and our
vineyards. **5** And though these are our own
kinsmen and our children are as good as theirs,
we have had to reduce our sons and daughters
to slavery, and violence has been done to some
of our daughters! Yet we can do nothing about
it, for our fields and our vineyards belong to
others."[p]

**Nehemiah's Action.** **6** I was extremely
angry when I heard the reasons they had for
complaint. **7** After some deliberation, I called
the nobles and magistrates to account, saying to
them, "You are exacting interest from your
own kinsmen!"* I then rebuked them severely,

m Jer 18, 23.
n Ps 149, 6.
o 1f: Jer 34, 8-22.
p Ez 21, 7; Lv 25, 39.

* 5, 7: You are exacting interest from your own kinsmen!: contrary to the Mosaic law (Dt 23, 20).

**8** saying to them: "As far as we were able, we
bought back our fellow Jews who had been sold
to Gentiles; you, however, are selling your own
brothers, to have them bought back by us."
They remained silent, for they could find no
answer.[q] **9** I continued: "What you are doing
is not good. Should you not walk in the fear of
our God, and put an end to the derision of our
Gentile enemies? **10** I myself, my kinsmen,
and my attendants have lent the people money
and grain without charge. Let us put an end to
this usury! **11** I ask that you return to them this
very day their fields, their vineyards, their olive
groves, and their houses, together with the interest on the money, the grain, the wine, and the
oil that you have lent them." **12** They answered: "We will return everything and exact
nothing further from them. We will do just what
you ask." Then I called for the priests and had
them administer an oath to these men that they
would do as they had promised. **13** I also shook
out the folds of my garment, saying, "Thus may
God shake from his home and his fortune every
man who fails to keep this promise, and may he
thus be shaken out and emptied!" And the
whole assembly answered, "Amen," and
praised the LORD. Then the people did as they
had promised.

### Nehemiah's Lack of Self-Interest.

**14** Moreover, from the time that King Artaxerxes appointed me governor in the land of Judah, from his twentieth to his thirty-second
year—during these twelve years neither I nor
my brethren lived from the governor's allowance. **15** The earlier governors, my predecessors, had laid a heavy burden on people, taking
from them each day forty silver shekels for their
food; then too, their men oppressed the people.
But I, because I feared God, did not act thus.
**16** Moreover, though I had acquired no land of
my own, I did my part in this work on the wall,
and all my men were gathered there for the
work. **17** Though I set my table for a hundred
and fifty persons, Jews and magistrates, as well
as those who came to us from the nations round
about, **18** and though the daily preparations
were made at my expense—one beef, six choice
muttons, poultry—besides all kinds of wine in
abundance every ten days, despite this I did not
claim the governor's allowance, for the labor
lay heavy upon this people. **19** Keep in mind,
O my God, in my favor all that I did for this
people.

## CHAPTER 6

### Plots against Nehemiah.

**1** When it had
been reported to Sanballat, Tobiah, Geshem the
Arab, and our other enemies that I had rebuilt
the wall and that there was no breach left in it
(though up to that time I had not yet set up the
doors in the gates), **2** Sanballat and Geshem
sent me this message: "Come, let us hold council together at Caphirim in the plain of Ono."
They were planning to do me harm. **3** However, I sent messengers to them with this reply: "I
am engaged in a great enterprise and am unable
to come down; why should the work stop, while
I leave it to come down to you?" **4** Four times
they sent me this same proposal, and each time
I gave the same reply. **5** Then, the fifth time,
Sanballat sent me the same message by one of
his servants, who bore an unsealed letter **6** containing this text: "Among the nations it has been
reported—Geshem is witness to this—that you
and the Jews are planning a rebellion; that for
this reason you are rebuilding the wall; and that
you are to be their king"—and so on. **7** "Also,
that you have set up prophets in Jerusalem to
proclaim you king of Judah. Now, since matters
like these must reach the ear of the king, come,
let us hold council together." **8** I sent him this
answer: "Nothing of what you report has taken
place; rather, it is the invention of your own
mind." **9** They were all trying to frighten us,
thinking, "Their hands will slacken in the
work, and it will never be completed." But
instead, I now redoubled my efforts.

**10** I went to the house of Shemaiah, son of
Delaiah, son of Mehetabel, who was unable to
go about, and he said:

"Let us meet in the house of God,
inside the temple building;
let us lock the doors of the temple.
For men are coming to kill you;
by night they are coming coming to kill
you."

**11** My answer was: "A man like me take
flight? Can a man like me enter the temple to
save his life? I will not go!" **12** For on consideration it was plain to me that God had not sent
him; rather, because Tobiah and Sanballat had
bribed him, he voiced this prophecy concerning
me **13** that I might act on it out of fear and
commit this sin. Then they would have had a
shameful story with which to discredit me.
**14** Keep in mind Tobiah and Sanballat, O my
God, because of these things they did; keep in
mind as well Noadiah the prophetess and the
other prophets who were trying to frighten me.[r]

### Conclusion of the Work.

**15** The wall
was finished on the twenty-fifth day of Elul;* it
had taken fifty-two days. **16** When all our ene-

q Lv 25, 48. s Ps 118, 22f; 127, 1.
r Jer 23, 9-40; Zec 13, 3.

*

6, 15: Elul: the sixth month (August–September). Fifty-two days: according to Josephus (Antiquities XI, v 8), the rebuilding of the walls of Jerusalem by Nehemiah took two years and four months, which seems more probable.

mies had heard of this, and all the nations round
about had taken note of it, our enemies lost
much face in the eyes of the nations, for they
knew that it was with our God's help that this
work had been completed.[s] **17** *At that same
time, however, many letters were going to Tobiah from the nobles of Judah, and Tobiah's
letters were reaching them, **18** for many in Judah were in league with him, since he was the
son-in-law of Shecaniah, son of Arah, and his
son Jehohanan had married the daughter of Meshullam, son of Berechiah. **19** Thus they would
praise his good deeds in my presence and relate
to him whatever I said; and Tobiah sent letters
trying to frighten me.

## CHAPTER 7

**1** When the wall had been rebuilt, I had the
doors set up, and the gatekeepers [and the singers and the Levites] were put in charge of them.
**2** Over Jerusalem I placed Hanani, my brother,
and Hananiah, the commander of the citadel,
who was a more trustworthy and God-fearing
man than most. **3** I said to them: "The gates of
Jerusalem are not to be opened until the sun is
hot, and while the sun is still shining they shall
shut and bar the doors. Appoint as watchmen
the inhabitants of Jerusalem, some at their
watch posts, and others before their own
houses."

**Census of the Province.** **4** Now the city
was quite wide and spacious, but its population
was small, and none of the houses had been
rebuilt. **5** When my God had put it into my
mind to gather together the nobles, the magistrates, and the common people, and to examine
their family records, I came upon the family list
of those who had returned in the earliest period.
There I found the following written:

**6** [t]* These are the inhabitants of the province
who returned from the captivity of the exiles
whom Nebuchadnezzar, king of Babylon, had
carried away, and who came back to Jerusalem
and Judah, each man to his own city **7** (those
who returned with Zerubbabel, Jeshua, Nehemiah, Azariah, Raamiah, Nahamani, Mordecai, Bilshan, Mispereth, Bigvai, Nehum, and
Baanah).

The census of the men of Israel: **8** sons of
Parosh, two thousand one hundred and seventy-two; **9** sons of Shephatiah, three hundred
and seventy-two; **10** sons of Arah, six hundred
and fifty-two; **11** sons of Pahath-moab who
were sons of Jeshua and Joab, two thousand
eight hundred and eighteen; **12** sons of Elam,
one thousand two hundred and fifty-four;
**13** sons of Zattu, eight hundred and forty-five;
**14** sons of Zaccai, seven hundred and sixty;
**15** sons of Binnui, six hundred and forty-eight;
**16** sons of Bebai, six hundred and twenty-
eight; **17** sons of Azgad, two thousand three
hundred and twenty-two; **18** sons of Adonikam, six hundred and sixty-seven; **19** sons of
Bigvai, two thousand and sixty-seven; **20** sons
of Adin, six hundred and fifty-five; **21** sons of
Ater who were sons of Hezekiah, ninety-eight;
**22** sons of Hashum, three hundred and twenty-eight; **23** sons of Bezai, three hundred and
twenty-four; **24** sons of Hariph, one hundred
and twelve; **25** sons of Gibeon, ninety-five;
**26** men of Bethlehem and Netophah, one hundred and eighty-eight; **27** men of Anathoth, one
hundred and twenty-eight; **28** men of Beth-azmaveth, forty-two; **29** men of Kiriath-jearim,
Chephirah, and Beeroth, seven hundred and forty-three; **30** men of Ramah and Geba, six hundred and twenty-one; **31** men of Michmas, one
hundred and twenty-two; **32** men of Bethel and
Ai, one hundred and twenty-three; **33** men of
Nebo, fifty-two; **34** sons of another Elam, one
thousand two hundred and fifty-four; **35** sons of
Harim, three hundred and twenty; **36** sons of
Jericho, three hundred and forty-five; **37** sons
of Lod, Hadid, and Ono, seven hundred and
twenty-one; **38** sons of Senaah, three thousand
nine hundred and thirty.

**39** The priests: sons of Jedaiah who were of
the house of Jeshua, nine hundred and seventy-three; **40** sons of Immer, one thousand and
fifty-two; **41** sons of Pashhur, one thousand
two hundred and forty-seven; **42** sons of Harim, one thousand and seventeen.

**43** The Levites: sons of Jeshua, Kadmiel,
Binnui, Hodeviah, seventy-four.

**44** The singers: sons of Asaph, one hundred
and forty-eight.

**45** The gatekeepers: sons of Shallum, sons of
Ater, sons of Talmon, sons of Akkub, sons of
Hatita, sons of Shobai, one hundred and thir-
ty-eight.

**46** The temple slaves: sons of Ziha, sons of
Hasupha, sons of Tabbaoth, **47** sons of Keros,
sons of Sia, sons of Padon, **48** sons of Lebana,
sons of Hagaba, sons of Shalmai, **49** sons of
Hanan, sons of Giddel, sons of Gahar, **50** sons
of Reaiah, sons of Rezin, sons of Nekoda,
**51** sons of Gazzam, sons of Uzza, sons of Paseah, **52** sons of Besai, sons of the Meunites,
sons of the Nephusites, **53** sons of Bakbuk,
sons of Hakupha, sons of Harhur, **54** sons of
Bazlith, sons of Mehida, sons of Harsha,
**55** sons of Barkos, sons of Sisera, sons of Te-
mah, **56** sons of Neziah, sons of Hatipha.

**57** Descendants of the slaves of Solomon:
sons of Sotai, sons of Sophereth, sons of Perida,
**58** sons of Jaala, sons of Darkon, sons of Gid-

t 6-72: Ezr 2, 1-70.

*

6, 17ff: These verses should be read immediately after v 14.

7, 6–72a: See note on Ezr 2, 1–67.

del, **59** sons of Shephatiah, sons of Hattil, sons
of Pochereth-hazzebaim, sons of Amon.
**60** The total of the temple slaves and the descendants of the slaves of Solomon was three
hundred and ninety-two.

**61** The following who returned from Tel-
melah, Tel-harsha, Cherub, Addon, and Immer
were unable to prove that their ancestral houses
and their descent were Israelite: **62** sons of Delaiah, sons of Tobiah, sons of Nekoda, six hundred and forty-two. **63** Also, of the priests: sons
of Hobaiah, sons of Hakkoz, sons of Barzillai
(he had married one of the daughters of Barzillai
the Gileadite and became known by his name).
**64** These men searched their family records,
but their names could not be found written there;
hence they were degraded from the priesthood,
**65** and His Excellency* ordered them not to
partake of the most holy foods until there should
be a priest bearing the Urim and Thummim.

**66** The entire assembly taken together came
to forty-two thousand three hundred and sixty,
**67** not counting their male and female slaves,
who were seven thousand three hundred and
thirty-seven. They also had two hundred male
and female singers. Their horses were seven
hundred and thirty-six, their mules two hundred
and forty-five, **68** their camels four hundred
and thirty-five, their asses six thousand seven
hundred and twenty.

**69** Certain of the family heads contributed to
the service. His Excellency put into the treasury
one thousand drachmas of gold, fifty basins,
thirty garments for priests, and five hundred
minas of silver. **70** Some of the family heads
contributed to the treasury for the temple service: twenty thousand drachmas of gold and two
thousand two hundred minas of silver. **71** The
contributions of the rest of the people amounted
to twenty thousand drachmas of gold, two thousand minas of silver, and sixty-seven garments
for priests.

**72** The priests, the Levites, the gatekeepers,
the singers, the temple slaves, and all Israel took
up residence in their cities.

## *II: Promulgation of the Law*

## CHAPTER 8

**Ezra Reads the Law.*** Now when the seventh month came, **1** the whole people gathered
as one man in the open space before the Water
Gate, and they called upon Ezra the scribe to
bring forth the book of the law of Moses which
the LORD prescribed for Israel.[u] **2** On the first
day of the seventh month, therefore, Ezra the
priest brought the law before the assembly,
which consisted of men, women, and those children old enough to understand. **3** Standing at
one end of the open place that was before the
Water Gate, he read out of the book from daybreak till midday, in the presence of the men,
the women, and those children old enough to
understand; and all the people listened attentively to the book of the law. **4** Ezra the scribe stood
on a wooden platform that had been made for
the occasion; at his right side stood Mattithiah,
Shema, Anaiah, Uriah, Hilkiah, and Maaseiah,
and on his left Pedaiah, Mishael, Malchijah,
Hashum, Hash-baddanah, Zechariah, Meshullam. **5** Ezra opened the scroll so that all the
people might see it (for he was standing higher
up than any of the people); and, as he opened
it, all the people rose. **6** Ezra blessed the LORD,
the great God, and all the people, their hands
raised high, answered, "Amen, amen!" Then
they bowed down and prostrated themselves before the LORD, their faces to the ground. **7** [The
Levites Jeshua, Bani, Sherebiah, Jamin, Akkub, Shabbethai, Hodiah, Maaseiah, Kelita,
Azariah, Jozabad, Hanan, and Pelaiah explained the law to the people, who remained in
their places.][v] **8** Ezra read plainly from the
book of the law of God, interpreting it so that
all could understand what was read.[w] **9** Then
[Nehemiah, that is, His Excellency, and] Ezra
the priest-scribe [and the Levites who were instructing the people] said to all the people: "Today is holy to the LORD your God. Do not be
sad, and do not weep"—for all the people were
weeping as they heard the words of the law.
**10** He said further: "Go, eat rich foods and
drink sweet drinks, and allot portions to those
who had nothing prepared; for today is holy to
our LORD. Do not be saddened this day, for
rejoicing in the LORD must be your strength!"[x]
**11** [And the Levites quieted all the people, saying, "Hush, for today is holy, and you must not
be saddened."] **12** Then all the people went to
eat and drink, to distribute portions, and to celebrate with great joy, for they understood the
words that had been expounded to them.

**The Feast of Booths.** **13** On the second
day, the family heads of the whole people and
also the priests and the Levites gathered around
Ezra the scribe and examined the words of the
law more closely. **14** They found it written in
the law prescribed by the LORD through Moses
that the Israelites must dwell in booths during

u Ezr 3, 1.
v Neh 10, 11.
w Ezr 7, 6.
x Est 9, 19.
y Ex 23, 14; Lv 23, 33-36.

*

7, 65. 69: His Excellency: see note on Ezr 2, 63.

7, 72b—8, 18: to be read after Ezr 8, 36. The gloss mentioning Nehemiah in v 9 was inserted in this Ezra section after the dislocation of several parts of Ezra-Nehemiah had occurred. There is no clear evidence of a simultaneous presence of Nehemiah and Ezra in Jerusalem; Neh. 12, 26 and 12, 36 are also scribal glasses.

the feast of the seventh month;[y] **15** and that
they should have this proclamation made
throughout their cities and in Jerusalem: "Go
out into the hill country and bring in branches
of olive trees, oleasters, myrtle, palm, and other
leafy trees, to make booths, as the law prescribes."[z] **16** The people went out and brought
in branches with which they made booths for
themselves, on the roofs of their houses, in their
courtyards, in the courts of the house of God,
and in the open spaces of the Water Gate and the
Gate of Ephraim. **17** Thus the entire assembly
of the returned exiles made booths and dwelt in
them. Now the Israelites had done nothing of
this sort from the days of Jeshua, son of Nun,
until this occasion; therefore there was very
great joy. **18** Ezra read from the book of the law
of God day after day, from the first day to the
last. They kept the feast for seven days, and the
solemn assembly on the eighth day, as was required.

## CHAPTER 9

**Confession of the People.** **1** [a]* On the
twenty-fourth day of this month, the Israelites
gathered together fasting and in sackcloth, their
heads covered with dust. **2** Those of Israelite
descent separated themselves from all who were
of foreign extraction, then stood forward and
confessed their sins and the guilty deeds of their
fathers.[b] **3** When they had taken their places,
they read from the book of the law of the LORD
their God, for a fourth part of the day, and
during another fourth part they made their confession and prostrated themselves before the
LORD their God. **4** Standing on the platform of
the Levites were Jeshua, Binnui, Kadmiel,
Shebaniah, Bunni, Sherebiah, Bani, and
Chenani, who cried out to the LORD their God
with a loud voice. **5** The Levites Jeshua, Kadmiel, Bani, Hashabneiah, Sherebiah, Hodiah,
Shebaniah, and Pethahiah said,

"Arise, bless the LORD, your God,
from eternity to eternity!"

The Israelites answered with the blessing,

"Blessed is your glorious name,
and exalted above all blessing and
praise."[c]

**6** *Then Ezra said: "It is you, O LORD, you
are the only one; you made the heavens, the
highest heavens and all their host, the earth and
all that is upon it, the seas and all that is in them.
To all of them you give life, and the heavenly
hosts bow down before you.
**7** "You, O LORD, are the God who chose
Abram, who brought him out from Ur of the
Chaldees, and named him Abraham.[d] **8** When
you had found his heart faithful in your sight,
you made the covenant with him to give to him
and his posterity the land of the Canaanites,
Hittites, Amorites, Perizzites, Jebusites, and
Girgashites. These promises of yours you fulfilled, for you are just.[e]

**9** "You saw the affliction of our fathers in
Egypt,
you heard their cry by the Red Sea;[f]
**10** You worked signs and wonders against
Pharoah,
against all his servants and the people of
his land,
Because you knew of their insolence toward
them;
thus you made for yourself a name even
to this day.[g]
**11** The sea you divided before them,
on dry ground they passed through the
midst of the sea;
Their pursuers you hurled into the depths,
like a stone into the mighty waters.[h]
**12** With a column of cloud you led them by
day,
and by night with a column of fire,
To light the way of their journey,
the way in which they must travel.[i]
**13** On Mount Sinai you came down,
you spoke with them from heaven;
You gave them just ordinances, firm laws,
good statutes, and commandments;[j]
**14** Your holy sabbath you made known to
them,
commandments, statutes, and law you
prescribed for them,
by the hand of Moses your servant.[k]
**15** Food from heaven you gave them in their
hunger,
water from a rock you sent them in their
thirst.
You bade them enter and occupy the land
which you had sworn with upraised hand
to give them.[l]

**16** "But they, our fathers, proved to be insolent; they held their necks stiff and would not
obey your commandments. **17** They refused to
obey and no longer remembered the miracles
you had worked for them. They stiffened their
necks and turned their heads to return to their
slavery in Egypt. But you are a God of pardons,
gracious and compassionate, slow to anger and

z Ps 118, 27.
a Dn 9, 3.
b Ezr 9, 1f; 10, 11.
c Dn 2, 20; 3, 52.
d Gn 12, 1; 17, 5.
e Gn 15, 18f.
f Ex 2, 23f.
g Ex 7—11; 14.
h Ex 15, 5. 10.
i Ex 13, 21f.
j Ex 19—20.
k Ex 20, 8.
l Ex 16, 4; 17, 1f.
m Nm 14, 1-4; Ex 34, 6; Dn 9, 9.

*

9, 1–5: This is a continuation of the account concerning the problem of mixed marriages at the time of Ezra; it should be read immediately after Ezr 10, 44.

9, 6–37: The prayer of Ezra which began in Ezr 9, 6f is here continued; see note on Ezr 9, 7.

rich in mercy; you did not forsake them.[m]
**18** Though they made for themselves a molten
calf, and proclaimed, 'Here is your God who
brought you up out of Egypt,' and were guilty
of great effronteries,[n] **19** yet in your great mercy you did not forsake them in the desert. The
column of cloud did not cease to lead them by
day on their journey, nor did the column of fire
by night cease to light for them the way by
which they were to travel.

**20** "Your good spirit you bestowed on them,
to give them understanding; your manna you did
not withhold from their mouths, and you gave
them water in their thirst.[o] **21** Forty years in the
desert you sustained them: they did not want;
their garments did not become worn, and their
feet did not become swollen.[p] **22** You gave
them kingdoms and peoples, which you divided
up among them as border lands. They possessed
the land of Sihon, king of Heshbon, and the land
of Og, king of Bashan.[q]

**23** "You made their children as numerous as
the stars of the heavens, and you brought them
into the land which you had commanded their
fathers to enter and possess.[r] **24** The sons went
in to take possession of the land, and you humbled before them the Canaanite inhabitants of
the land and delivered them over into their power, their kings as well as the peoples of the land,
to do with them as they would. **25** They captured fortified cities and fertile land; they took
possession of houses filled with all good things,
cisterns already dug, vineyards, olive groves,
and fruit trees in abundance. They could eat and
have their fill, fatten and feast themselves on
your immense good gifts.[s]

**26** "But they were contemptuous and rebellious: they cast your law behind their backs,
they slew your prophets who bore witness
against them in order to bring them back to you,
and they were guilty of great effronteries.[t]
**27** Therefore you delivered them into the power
of their enemies, who oppressed them. But in
the time of their oppression they would cry out
to you, and you would hear them from heaven,
and according to your great mercy give them
saviors to deliver them from the power of their
enemies.[u]

**28** "As soon as they had relief, they would
go back to doing evil in your sight. Then again
you abandoned them to the power of their enemies, who crushed them. Then they cried out to
you, and you heard them from heaven and delivered them according to your mercy, many times
over. **29** You bore witness against them, in order to bring them back to your law. But they
were insolent and would not obey your commandments; they sinned against your ordinances, from which men draw life when they
practice them. They turned stubborn backs,
stiffened their necks, and would not obey.[v]
**30** You were patient with them for many years,
bearing witness against them through your spirit, by means of your prophets; still they would
not listen. Thus you delivered them over into the
power of the peoples of the lands. **31** Yet in
your great mercy you did not completely destroy them and you did not forsake them, for
you are a kind and merciful God.

**32** "Now, therefore, O our God, great,
mighty, and awesome God, you who in your
mercy preserve the covenant, take into account
all the disasters that have befallen us, our kings,
our princes, our priests, our prophets, our fathers, and your entire people, from the time of
the kings of Assyria until this day![w] **33** In all
that has come upon us you have been just, for
you kept faith while we have done evil.[x]
**34** Yes, our kings, our princes, our priests, and
our fathers have not kept your law; they paid no
attention to your commandments and the obligations of which you reminded them. **35** While
they were yet in their kingdom, in the midst of
the many good things that you had given them
and in the wide and fertile land that you had
spread out before them, they did not serve you
nor did they turn away from their evil deeds.
**36** But, see, we today are slaves; and as for the
land which you gave our fathers that they might
eat its fruits and good things—see, we have
become slaves upon it! **37** Its rich produce goes
to the kings whom you set over us because of
our sins, who rule over our bodies and our cattle
as they please. We are in great distress!"

## CHAPTER 10

**Agreement of the People.** **1** *In view of
all this, we are entering into a firm pact, which
we are putting into writing. On the sealed document appear the names of our princes, our Levites, and our priests.[y]

**2** On the sealed document: His Excellency
Nehemiah, son of Hacaliah, and Zedekiah.

**3** Seraiah, Azariah, Jeremiah, **4** Pashhur,
Amariah, Malchijah, **5** Hattush, Shebaniah,
Malluch, **6** Harim, Meremoth, Obadiah,
**7** Daniel, Ginnethon, Baruch, **8** Meshullam,
Abijah, Mijamin, **9** Maaziah, Bilgai, Shema-
iah: these are the priests.

**10** The Levites: Jeshua, son of Azaniah; Bin-

n Ex 32, 4.
o Dt 2, 7.
p Dt 8, 4.
q Nm 21, 21—35; Dt 1, 4; 2, 26-3, 11.
r Dt 1, 10.
s Dt 3, 5; 6, 10f; 11, 11; 32, 15.
t Wis 2, 10-20.
u Dn 9, 19.
v Lv 18, 5; 30. 16; 32, 47.
w Lam 5.
x Dn 3, 27; 9, 14.
y Neh 12, 12-26.

* 10, 1–40: This section belongs to the Nehemiah narrative rather than to that of Ezra. It is best read after Neh 13, 31. In view of all this; considering the situation described in Neh 13, 4–31.

nui, of the sons of Henadad; Kadmiel; **11** and
their brethren Shebaniah, Hodiah, Kelita, Pelaiah, Hanan,[z] **12** Mica, Rehob, Hashabiah,
**13** Zaccur, Sherebiah, Shebaniah, **14** Hodiah,
Bani, Beninu.

**15** The leaders of the people: Parosh, Pahath-moab, Elam, Zattu, Bani, **16** Bunni, Azgad, Bebai, **17** Adonijah, Bigvai, Adin,
**18** Ater, Hezekiah, Azzur, **19** Hodiah, Hashum, Bezai, **20** Hariph, Anathoth, Nebai,
**21** Magpiash, Meshullam, Hazir, **22** Meshezabel, Zadok, Jaddua, **23** Pelatiah, Hanan, Anaiah, **24** Hoshea, Hananiah, Hasshub, **25** Hallo-
hesh, Pilha, Shobek, **26** Rehum, Hashabnah,
Maaseiah, **27** Ahiah, Hanan, Anan, **28** Malluch, Harim, Baanah.

**Provisions of the Pact.** **29** The rest of the
people, priests, Levites, gatekeepers, singers,
temple slaves, and all others who have separated themselves from the peoples of the lands in
favor of the law of God, with their wives, their
sons, their daughters, all who are of the age of
discretion, **30** join with their brethren who are
their princes, and with the sanction of a curse
take this oath to follow the law of God which
was given through Moses, the servant of God,
and to observe carefully all the commandments
of the LORD, our LORD, his ordinances and his
statutes.[a]

**31** Agreed, that we will not marry our daughters to the peoples of the land, and that we will
not take their daughters for our sons.[b]

**32** When the peoples of the land bring in
merchandise or any kind of grain for sale on the
sabbath day, we will not buy from them on the
sabbath or on any other holyday. We will forgo
the seventh year, as well as every kind of debt.[c]

**33** We impose these commandments on ourselves: to give a third of a shekel each year for
the service of the house of our God,[d] **34** for the
showbread, for the daily cereal offering, for the
daily holocaust, for the sabbaths, new moons,
and festivals, for the holy offerings, for sin
offerings to make atonement for Israel, and for
every service of the house of our God. **35** We,
priests, Levites, and people, have determined
by lot concerning the procurement of wood: it
is to be brought to the house of our God by each
of our family houses at stated times each year,
to be burnt on the altar of the LORD, our God,
as the law prescribes.[e] **36** [f]We have agreed to
bring each year to the house of the LORD the first
fruits of our fields and of our fruit trees, of
whatever kind; **37** also, as is prescribed in the
law, to bring to the house of our God, to the
priests who serve in the house of our God, the
first-born of our children and our animals, including the first-born of our flocks and herds.
**38** The first batch of our dough, and our offerings of the fruit of every tree, of wine and of oil,
we will bring to the priests, to the chambers of
the house of our God. The tithe of our fields we
will bring to the Levites; they, the Levites, shall
take the tithe in all the cities of our service.[g]
**39** An Aaronite priest shall be with the Levites
when they take the tithe, and the Levites shall
bring the tithe of the tithes to the house of our
God, to the chambers of the treasury. **40** For to
these chambers the Israelites and Levites bring
the offerings of grain, wine, and oil; there also
are housed the utensils of the sanctuary, and the
ministering priests, the gatekeepers, and the
singers. We will not neglect the house of our
God.

## CHAPTER 11

**Repeopling of Jerusalem.** **1** *The leaders of the people took up residence in Jerusalem,
and the rest of the people cast lots to bring one
man in ten to reside in Jerusalem, the holy city,
while the other nine would remain in the other
cities.[h] **2** The people applauded all those men
who willingly agreed to take up residence in
Jerusalem.

**The Residents of Jerusalem.** **3** [i]These
are the heads of the province who took up residence in Jerusalem. (In the cities of Judah dwelt
lay Israelites, priests, Levites, temple slaves,
and the descendants of the slaves of Solomon,
each man on the property he owned in his own
city.)

**4** In Jerusalem dwelt both Judahites and Benjaminites. Of the Judahites: Athaiah, son of Uzziah, son of Zechariah, son of Amariah, son of
Shephatiah, son of Mehallalel, of the sons of
Perez; **5** Maaseiah, son of Baruch, son of Colhozeh, son of Hazaiah, son of Adaiah, son of
Joiarib, son of Zechariah, a son of the Shelanites. **6** The total of the sons of Perez who dwelt
in Jerusalem was four hundred and sixty-eight
valiant men.

**7** These were the Benjaminites: Sallu, son of
Meshullam, son of Joed, son of Pedaiah, son of
Kolaiah, son of Maaseiah, son of Ithiel, son of
Jeshaiah, **8** and his brethren, warriors, nine
hundred and twenty-eight in number. **9** Joel,
son of Zichri, was their commander, and Judah,

z Ezr 10, 23.
a Neh 13, 23-27.
b Neh 13, 15-22.
c Neh 5, 1-13; Ex 20, 8; Lv 25, 2-7.
d 2 Chr 24, 6, 9f; Lv 24, 5-9.
e Neh 13, 31.
f 36f: Ex 13, 1. 11ff; Dt 26, 1.
g Neh 13, 10-14; Nm 18, 21. 24ff.
h Neh 7, 4.
i 3-19: 1 Chr 9, 2-34.

* 11, 1–19: This list of the family heads who lived in Jerusalem at the time of Nehemiah is best read after Neh 7, 72a. It is basically the same as that given in 1 Chr 9, 2–17, but there are many differences between the two lists.

son of Hassenuah, was second in charge of the
city.
**10** Among the priests were: Jedaiah; Joiarib;
Jachin; **11** Seraiah, son of Hilkiah, son of Meshullam, son of Zadok, son of Meraioth, son of
Ahitub, the ruler of the house of God, **12** and
their brethren who carried out the temple service, eight hundred and twenty-two; Adaiah,
son of Jeroham, son of Pelaliah, son of Amzi,
son of Zechariah, son of Pashhur, son of Malchijah, **13** and his brethren, family heads, two
hundred and forty-two; and Amasai, son of Azarel, son of Ahzai, son of Meshillemoth, son of
Immer, **14** and his brethren, warriors, one hundred and twenty-eight. Their commander was
Zabdiel, son of Haggadol.
**15** Among the Levites were Shemaiah, son
of Hasshub, son of Azrikam, son of Hashabiah,
son of Bunni; **16** Shabbethai and Jozabad, levitical chiefs who were placed over the external
affairs of the house of God; **17** Mattaniah, son
of Micah, son of Zabdi, son of Asaph, director
of the psalms, who led the thanksgiving at
prayer; Bakbukiah, second in rank among his
brethren; and Abda, son of Shammua, son of
Galal, son of Jeduthun. **18** The total of the Levites in the holy city was two hundred and
eighty-four.
**19** The gatekeepers were Akkub, Talmon,
and their brethren, who kept watch over the
gates; one hundred and seventy-two in number.
**20** The rest of Israel, including priests and
Levites, were in all the other cities of Judah,
each man in his inheritance.
**21** The temple slaves lived on Ophel. Ziha
and Gishpa were in charge of the temple slaves.
**22** The prefect of the Levites in Jerusalem
was Uzzi, son of Bani, son of Hashabiah, son
of Mattaniah, son of Mica; he was one of the
sons of Asaph, the singers appointed to the service of the house of God[j] — **23** for they had
been appointed by royal decree, and there was
a fixed schedule for the singers assigning them
their daily duties.
**24** Pethahiah, son of Meshezabel, a descendant of Zerah, son of Judah, was royal deputy in
all affairs that concerned the people.

**The Other Cities.** **25** As concerns their villages in the country: Judahites lived in Kiriatharba and its dependencies, in Dibon and its
dependencies, in Jekabzeel and its villages,
**26** in Jeshua, Moladah, Beth-pelet, **27** in Hazar-shual, in Beer-sheba and its dependencies,
**28** in Ziklag, in Meconah and its dependencies,
**29** in En-rimmon, Zorah, Jarmuth, **30** Zanoah,
Adullam, and their villages, Lachish and its
countryside, Azekah and its dependencies.
They were settled from Beer-sheba to Ge-hinnom.
**31** Benjaminites were in Geba, Mich-mash,
Aija, Bethel and its dependencies, **32** Anathoth, Nob, Ananiah, **33** Hazor, Ramah, Gittaim, **34** Hadid, Zeboim, Neballat, **35** Lod,
Ono, and the Valley of the Artisans.
**36** Some sections of the Levites from Judah
settled in Benjamin.

## CHAPTER 12

**Priests and Levites under Zerubbabel.**
**1** [k]The following are the priests and Levites
who returned with Zerubbabel, son of Shealtiel,
and Jeshua: Seraiah, Jeremiah, Ezra, **2** Amariah, Malluch, Hattush, **3** Shecaniah, Rehum,
Meremoth, **4** Iddo, Ginnethon, Abijah, **5** Mijamin, Maadiah, Bilgah, **6** Shemaiah, and Joiarib, Jedaiah, **7** Sallu, Amok, Hilkiah, Jedaiah.
These were the priestly heads and their brethren
in the days of Jeshua.
**8** The Levites were Jeshua, Binnui, Kadmiel, Sherebiah, Judah, Mattaniah; the last-men-
tioned, together with his brethren, was in charge
of the hymns, **9** while Bakbukiah and Unno and
their brethren ministered opposite them by
turns.

**High Priests.*** **10** Jeshua became the father
of Joiakim, Joiakim became the father of Eliashib, and Eliashib became the father of Joiada.
**11** Joiada became the father of Johanan, and
Johanan became the father of Jaddua.

**Priests and Levites under Joiakim.**
**12** [l]In the days of Joiakim these were the priest-
ly family heads: for Seraiah, Meraiah; for Jere-
miah, Hananiah; **13** for Ezra, Meshullam; for
Amariah, Jehohanan; **14** for Malluch, Jona-
than; for Shebaniah, Joseph; **15** for Harim,
Adna; for Meremoth, Helkai; **16** for Iddo,
Zechariah; for Ginnethon, Meshullam; **17** for
Abijah, Zichri; for Miamin, . . . ; for Maadiah,
Piltai; **18** for Bilgah, Shammua; for Shemaiah,
Jehonathan; **19** and for Joiarib, Mattenai; for
Jedaiah, Uzzi; **20** for Sallu, Kallai; for Amok,

j 2 Chr 20, 14.
k 1-6; Neh 12, 12-22.
l 12-22: Neh 10, 3-9; 12, 1-6.

*

12, 10f: Jeshua, the high priest when Zerubbabel was governor, i.e., the last decades of the sixth century B.C. (Hg 1, 1. 12. 14; 2, 2. 4). He was the grandfather of Eliashib, the high priest at least in the early period of Nehemiah's governorship, i.e., 445–433 B.C. (Ezr 10, 6; Neh 3, 1. 20f; 13, 4. 7). Eliashib, in turn, was the grandfather of Johanan, a grown man, if not yet a high priest, at the time of Ezra, i.e., c. 400 B.C. (Ezr 10, 6, and note). According to Josephus (Antiquities XI, v), whose testimony here is doubtful, Jaddua, son of Johanan, died as an old man about the same time that Alexander the Great died, i.e., 323 B.C. If this list of the postexilic high priests, at least as far as Johanan, comes, as seems probable (cf v 23), from the Chronicler himself and not from a later scribe, it is of prime importance for dating the Chronicler's work in the first decades of the fourth century B.C.

Eber; **21** for Hilkiah, Hashabiah; for Jedaiah, Nethanel.

**22** In the time of Eliashib, Joiada, Johanan, and Jaddua, the family heads of the priests were written down in the Book of Chronicles, up until the reign of Darius the Persian. **23** The sons of Levi: the family heads were written down in the Book of Chronicles, up until the time of Johanan, the son of Eliashib.

**24** The heads of the Levites were Hashabiah, Sherebiah, Jeshua, Binnui, Kadmiel. Their brethren who stood opposite them to sing praises and thanksgiving in fulfillment of the command of David, the man of God, one section opposite the other,[m] **25** were Mattaniah, Bakbukiah, Obadiah.

Meshullam, Talmon, and Akkub were gatekeepers. They kept watch over the storerooms at the gates.[n]

**26** All these lived in the time of Joiakim, son of Jeshua, son of Jozadak [and in the time of Nehemiah the governor and of Ezra the priest-scribe].

**Dedication of the City Wall.** 27 *At the dedication of the wall of Jerusalem, the Levites were sought out wherever they lived and were brought to Jerusalem to celebrate a joyful dedication with thanksgiving hymns and the music of cymbals, harps, and lyres. **28** The levitical singers gathered together from the region about Jerusalem, from the villages of the Netophathites, **29** from Beth-gilgal, and from the plains of Geba and Azmaveth (for the singers had built themselves settlements about Jerusalem). **30** The priests and Levites first purified themselves, then they purified the people, the gates, and the wall.

**31** I had the princes of Judah mount the wall, and I arranged two great choirs. The first of these proceeded to the right, along the top of the wall, in the direction of the Dung Gate, **32** followed by Hoshaiah and half the princes of Judah, **33** along with Azariah, Ezra, Meshullam, **34** Judah, Benjamin, Shemaiah, and Jeremiah, **35** priests with the trumpets, and also Zechariah, son of Jonathan, son of Shemaiah, son of Mattaniah, son of Micaiah, son of Zaccur, son of Asaph, **36** and his brethren Shemaiah, Azarel, Milalai, Gilalai, Maai, Nethanel, Judah, and Hanani, with the musical instruments of David, the man of God. [Ezra the scribe was at their head.] **37** At the Spring Gate they went straight up by the steps of the City of David and continued along the top of the wall above the house of David until they came to the Water Gate on the east.

**38** The second choir proceeded to the left, followed by myself and the other half of the princes of the people, along the top of the wall past the Oven Tower as far as the Broad Wall, **39** then past the Ephraim Gate [the New City Gate], the Fish Gate, the Tower of Hananel, and the Hundred Tower, as far as the Sheep Gate [and they came to a halt at the Prison Gate].

**40** The two choirs took up a position in the house of God; I, too, who had with me half the magistrates, **41** the priests Eliakim, Maaseiah, Minjamin, Micaiah, Elioenai, Zechariah, Hananiah, with the trumpets, **42** and Maaseiah, Shemaiah, Eleazar, Uzzi, Jehohanan, Malchijah, Elam, and Ezer. The singers were heard under the leadership of Jezrahiah. **43** Great sacrifices were offered on that day, and there was rejoicing over the great feast of the LORD in which they shared. The women and the children joined in, and the rejoicing at Jerusalem could be heard from afar off.

**Offerings for Priests and Levites.***
**44** [o]At that time men were appointed over the chambers set aside for stores, offerings, first fruits, and tithes; in them they were to collect from the fields of the various cities the portions legally assigned to the priests and Levites. For Judah rejoiced in its appointed priests and Levites **45** who carried out the ministry of their God and the ministry of purification (as did the singers and the gatekeepers) in accordance with the prescriptions of David and of Solomon, his son. **46** For the heads of the families of the singers and the hymns of praise and thanksgiving to God came down from the days of David and Asaph in times of old.[p] **47** Thus all Israel, in the days of Zerubbabel [and in the days of Nehemiah], gave the singers and the gatekeepers their portions, according to their daily needs. They made their consecrated offering to the Levites, and the Levites made theirs to the sons of Aaron.[q]

## CHAPTER 13

**Separation from Aliens.** 1 [r]* At that time, when there was reading from the book of

m Ezr 2, 40.
n Neh 11, 17.
o 44f: 1 Chr 23—26; 2 Chr 8, 14.
p 2 Chr 29, 30; 35, 15.
q Neh 13, 10f; 10, 39; Nm 18, 26.
r 1ff: Dt 23, 3-6.

*

12, 27–43: The dedication of the wall of Jerusalem took place, no doubt, soon after the restoration of the wall and its gates had been completed. Therefore, this section is best read after Neh 6, 15.

12, 44–47: This account of the provisions made for the temple services is apparently a composition of the Chronicler. At that time: a mere connective; no particular time is meant, but the account fits best after that of the restoration of the temple (Ezr 6, 13–18) in the days of Zerubbabel (v 47). The gloss mentioning Nehemiah is not in the ancient Greek version.

13, 1ff: These verses were composed by the Chronicler to serve as an introduction to the reforms that Nehemiah instituted during his second mission in Jerusalem (vv 4–31). The part of the book of Moses read to the people is freely quoted here

Moses in the hearing of the people, it was found
written there that "no Ammonite or Moabite
may ever be admitted into the assembly of God;
**2** for they would not succor the Israelites with
food and water, but they hired Balaam to curse
them, though our God turned the curse into a
blessing."[s] **3** When they had heard the law,
they separated from Israel every foreign element.[t]

**Reform in the Temple.** **4** *Before this, the
priest Eliashib, who had been placed in charge
of the chambers of the house of our God and
who was an associate of Tobiah, **5** had set aside
for the latter's use a large chamber in which had
previously been stored the cereal offerings, incense and utensils, the tithes in grain, wine, and
oil allotted to the Levites, singers, and gatekeepers, and the offerings due the priests.[u]
**6** During all this time I had not been in Jerusalem, for in the thirty-second year of Artaxerxes,
king of Babylon, I had gone back to the king.
After due time,* however, I asked leave of the
king **7** and returned to Jerusalem, where I discovered the evil thing that Eliashib had done for
Tobiah, in setting aside for him a chamber in the
courts of the house of God. **8** This displeased
me very much, and I had all of Tobiah's household goods thrown outside the chamber. **9** Then
I gave orders to purify the chambers, and I had
them replace there the utensils of the house of
God, the cereal offerings, and the incense.

**10** I learned, too, that the portions due the
Levites were no longer being given, so that the
Levites and the singers who should have been
carrying out the services had deserted, each man
to his own field. **11** I took the magistrates to
task, demanding, "Why is the house of God
abandoned?" Then I brought the Levites together and had them resume their stations. **12** All
Judah once more brought in the tithes of grain,
wine, and oil to the storerooms;[v] **13** and in
charge of the storerooms I appointed the priest
Shelemiah, Zadok the scribe, and Pedaiah, one
of the Levites, together with Hanan, son of
Zaccur, son of Mattaniah, as their assistant; for
these men were held to be trustworthy. It was
their duty to make the distribution to their brethren. **14** Remember this to my credit, O my
God! Let not the devotion which I showed for
the house of my God and its services be forgotten!

**Sabbath Observance.** **15** In those days I
perceived that men in Judah were treading the
winepresses on the sabbath; that they were
bringing in sheaves of grain, loading them on
their asses, together with wine, grapes, figs,
and every other kind of burden, and bringing
them to Jerusalem on the sabbath day. I warned
them to sell none of these victuals.[w] **16** In Jerusalem itself the Tyrians who were resident there
were importing fish and every other kind of
merchandise and selling it to the Judahites on
the sabbath. **17** I took the nobles of Judah to
task, demanding of them: "What is this evil
thing that you are doing, profaning the sabbath
day? **18** Did not your fathers act in this same
way, with the result that our God has brought all
this evil upon us and upon this city? Would you
add to the wrath against Israel by once more
profaning the sabbath?"

**19** When the shadows were falling on the
gates of Jerusalem before the sabbath, I ordered
the doors to be closed and forbade them to be
reopened till after the sabbath. I posted some of
my own men at the gates so that no burden
might enter on the sabbath day. **20** The merchants and sellers of various kinds of merchandise spent the night once or twice outside Jerusalem, **21** but then I warned them, saying to
them: "Why do you spend the night alongside
the wall? If you keep this up, I will lay hands
on you!" From that time on, they did not return
on the sabbath. **22** Then I ordered the Levites
to purify themselves and to go and watch the
gates, so that the sabbath day might be kept
holy. This, too, remember in my favor, O my
God, and have mercy on me in accordance with
your great mercy!

**Mixed Marriages.** **23** Also in those days I
saw Jews who had married Ashdodite, Ammonite, or Moabite wives.[x] **24** Of their children,
half spoke Ashdodite,* and none of them knew
how to speak Jewish; and so it was in regard to
the languages of the various other peoples. **25** I
took them to task and cursed them; I had some
of them beaten and their hair pulled out; and I
adjured them by God: "You shall not marry
your daughters to their sons nor take any of their
daughters for your sons or for yourselves!
**26** Did not Solomon, the king of Israel, sin
because of them? Though among the many nations there was no king like him, and though he
was beloved of his God and God had made him
king over all Israel, yet even he was made to sin
by foreign women.[y] **27** Must it also be heard of

s Nm 22—24.
t Neh 13, 23-28.
u Neh 12, 44.
v Neh 10, 38f; 12, 44f. 47; 2 Chr 31, 6.
w Neh 10, 32; Ex 20, 8.
x Neh 10, 31; 13, 1ff; Dt 23, 3.
y 1 Kgs 11, 1-13.

* from Dt 23, 3–6.

13, 4–31: This is part of the "Memoirs of Nehemiah"; it is continued in Neh 10, 1–40.

13, 6: After due time: It is not known when Nehemiah returned to Jerusalem or how long his second period of activity there lasted, but it probably ended before Ezra came to Palestine; see note on Ezr 7, 1–8.

13, 24: Ashdodite: the language spoken at Ashdod, more likely an Aramaic rather than a Philistine dialect. Jewish: Hebrew as spoken in postexilic Judah.

you that you have done this same very great
evil, betraying our God by marrying foreign
women?''
**28** One of the sons of Joiada, son of Eliashib
the high priest, was the son-in-law of Sanballat
the Horonite! I drove him from my presence.[z]
**29** Remember against them, O my God, how
they defiled the priesthood and the covenant of
the priesthood and the Levites!
**30** Thus I cleansed them of all foreign contamination. I established the various functions
for the priests and Levites, so that each had his
appointed task. **31** I also provided for the procurement of wood at stated times and for the
first fruits. Remember this in my favor, O my
God![a]

z Neh 2, 10; 13, 4f. 7ff. a Neh 10, 35f.

# The Book of
# TOBIT

*The Book of Tobit, named after its principal hero, combines specifically Jewish piety and morality with oriental folklore in a fascinating story that has enjoyed wide popularity in both Jewish and Christian circles. Prayers, psalms, and words of wisdom, as well as the skillfully constructed story itself, provide valuable insights into the faith and the religious milieu of its unknown author. The book was probably written early in the second century B.C.; it is not known where.*

*Tobit, a devout and wealthy Israelite living among the captives deported to Nineveh, from the northern kingdom of Israel in 721 B.C., suffers severe reverses and is finally blinded. Because of his misfortunes he begs the Lord to let him die. But recalling the large sum he had formerly deposited in far-off Media, he sends his son Tobiah there to bring back the money. In Media, at this same time, a young woman, Sarah, also prays for death, because she has lost seven husbands, each killed in turn on his wedding night by the demon Asmodeus. God hears the prayers of Tobit and Sarah, and sends the angel Raphael in disguise to aid them both.*

*Raphael makes the trip to Media with Tobiah. When Tobiah is attacked by a large fish as he bathes, Raphael orders him to seize it and to remove its gall, heart, and liver because they make "useful medicines." Later, at Raphael's urging, Tobiah marries Sarah, and uses the fish's heart and liver to drive Asmodeus from the bridal chamber. Returning to Nineveh with his wife and his father's money, Tobiah rubs the fish's gall into his father's eyes and cures them. Finally, Raphael reveals his true identity and returns to heaven. Tobit then utters his beautiful hymn of praise. Before dying, Tobit tells his son to leave Nineveh because God will destroy that wicked city. After Tobiah buries his father and mother, he and his family depart for Media, where he later learns that the destruction of Nineveh has taken place.*

*The inspired author of the book used the literary form of religious novel (as in Jonah and Judith) for the purpose of instruction and edification. There may have been a historical nucleus around which the story was composed, but this possibility has nothing to do with the teaching of the book. The seemingly historical data—names of kings, cities, etc.—are used merely as vivid details to create interest and charm.*

*Although the Book of Tobit is usually listed with the historical books, it more correctly stands midway between them and the wisdom literature. It contains numerous maxims like those found in the wisdom books (cf 4, 3–19, 21; 12, 6–10; 14, 7.9) as well as the customary sapiential themes: fidelity to the law, the intercessory function of angels, piety toward parents, the purity of marriage, reverence for the dead, and the value of almsgiving, prayer, and fasting. The book makes Tobit a relative of* Ahiqar, *a hero of ancient Near Eastern folklore.*

*Written in Aramaic, the original of the book was lost for centuries. The Greek translation, existing in three different recensions, is our primary source. In 1955, fragments of the book in Aramaic and in Hebrew were recovered from Cave IV at Qumran. These texts are in substantial agreement with the Greek recension that has served as the basis for the present translation.*

*The divisions of the Book of Tobit are:*

*I. Tobit's Ordeals (1, 3—3, 6).*
*II. Sarah's Plight (3, 7–17).*
*III. Tobiah's Journey and Marriage to Sarah (4, 1—9, 6).*
*IV. Tobiah's Return; Cure of Tobit's Blindness (10, 1—11, 18).*
*V. Raphael Reveals His Identity (12, 1–22).*
*VI. Tobit's Song of Praise (13, 1–18).*
*VII. Epilogue (14, 1–15).*

## CHAPTER 1

**Tobit.** 1 This book tells the story of Tobit,* son of Tobiel, son of Hananiel, son of Aduel, son of Gabael of the family of Asiel, of the tribe of Naphtali, 2 who during the reign of Shalmaneser,* king of Assyria, was taken captive from Thisbe, which is south of Kedesh Naphtali in upper Galilee, above and to the west of Asser, north of Phogor.[a]

## I: *Tobit's Ordeals*

**His Virtue.** 3 I, Tobit, have walked all the days of my life on the paths of truth and righteousness. I performed many charitable works for my kinsmen and my people who had been deported with me to Nineveh, in Assyria.
4 When I lived as a young man in my own country, Israel, the entire tribe of my forefather Naphtali had broken away from the house of David and from Jerusalem. This city had been singled out of all Israel's tribes, so that they all might offer sacrifice in the place where the temple, God's dwelling, had been built and consecrated for all generations to come. 5 [b]All my kinsmen, like the rest of the tribe of my forefather Naphtali, used to offer sacrifice on all the mountains of Galilee as well as to the young bull which Jeroboam, king of Israel, had made in Dan.*

6 [c]I, for my part, would often make the pilgrimage alone to Jerusalem for the festivals, as is prescribed for all Israel by perpetual decree.* Bringing with me the first fruits of the field and the firstlings of the flock, together with a tenth of my income and the first shearings of the sheep,[d] I would hasten to Jerusalem 7 [e]and present them to the priests, Aaron's sons, at the altar. To the Levites who were doing service in Jerusalem I would give the tithe of grain, wine, olive oil, pomegranates, figs, and other fruits. And except for sabbatical years, I used to give a second tithe in money, which each year I would go and disburse in Jerusalem. 8 The third tithe I gave to orphans and widows, and to converts who were living with the Israelites. Every third year I would bring them this offering, and we ate it in keeping with the decree of the Mosaic law and the commands of Deborah, the mother of my father Tobiel; for when my father died, he left me an orphan.

9 When I reached manhood, I married Anna, a woman of our own lineage. By her I had a son whom I named Tobiah. 10 Now after I had been deported to Nineveh, all my brothers and relatives ate the food of heathens,[f] 11 but I refrained from eating that kind of food. 12 Because of this wholehearted service of God, 13 the Most High granted me favor and status with Shalmaneser, so that I became purchasing agent for all his needs.[g] 14 Every now and then until his death I would go to Media to buy goods for him. I also deposited several pouches containing a great sum of money* with my kinsman Gabael, son of Gabri, who lived at Rages, in Media. 15 But when Shalmaneser died and his son Sennacherib* succeeded him as king, the roads to Media became unsafe, so I could no longer go there.

**Courage in Burying the Dead.** 16 During Shalmaneser's reign I performed many charitable works for my kinsmen and my people. 17 [h]I would give my bread to the hungry and my clothing to the naked. If I saw one of my people who had died and been thrown outside the walls of Nineveh, I would bury him.*
18 I also buried anyone whom Sennacherib slew when he returned as a fugitive from Judea during the days of judgment decreed against him by the heavenly King because of the blasphemies he had uttered. In his rage he killed many Israelites, but I used to take their bodies by stealth and bury them; so when Sennacherib looked for them, he could not find them. 19 But a certain citizen of Nineveh informed the king

a 2 Kgs 17, 3; 18, 9ff.
b 1 Kgs 12, 26-32.
c Ex 23, 14f. 17; 34, 23.
d Dt 16, 16.
e 7f: Nm 18, 12f. 24; Dt 14, 22-29; 18, 4f.
f Lv 11: Dt 14, 3-21; Acts 15, 29; 1 Cor 8, 7ff.
g Dn 2, 48f.
h Jb 31, 16-20.

*

1, 1: Tobit: in the fragments of the book found at Qumran, is given as Tobi, an abbreviated form of Tobiyah (v 9; Ezr 2, 60) or of Tobiyabu (2 Chr 17, 8), a name which means "Yahweh is good." Tobiel, "God is good"; Hananiel, "God is merciful." The book abounds in theophoric names.

1, 2: Shalmaneser V (727–722 B.C.): began the siege of Samaria; the inhabitants of the northern kingdom were taken into captivity by his successor, Sargon II (722–705). Thisbe and Phogor: towns of Galilee that have not been identified; Thisbe in Gilead was perhaps the birthplace of Elijah. Kedesh: cf Jos 20, 7. Asser: Hazor (Jos 11, 1).

1, 5: Jeroboam established sanctuaries in Dan and Bethel so that the people would no longer go to Jerusalem for the festivals. The gold statues of bulls which he placed in the sanctuaries were considered the throne of Yahweh; but the people soon came to worship the images themselves. Jeroboam also encouraged the high places or hilltop shrines (1 Kgs 12, 26–33).

1, 6ff: Perpetual decree: Dt 12, 11. 13–14. Refusing to worship at Jeroboam's shrines, the faithful Tobit continued to bring his offerings to Jerusalem; see 2 Chr 11, 16. For the various tithes, cf Nm 18, 20–32; 2 Chr 31, 4–6; Dt 14, 22–29; 26, 12f.

1, 14: A great sum of money; literally, "ten silver talents," about ten thousand dollars. Rages: modern Rai, about five miles southeast of Teheran. Media: the northwestern part of modern Iran.

1, 15: Sennacherib (705–681 B.C.): the son of Sargon (722–705 B.C.); neither was descended from Shalmaneser. Inconsistencies such as this point to the fact that the Book of Tobit is a religious novel (see Introduction; also notes on 5, 6 and 14, 15).

1, 17–18: Tobit risked his own life to bury the dead. Deprivation of burial was viewed with horror by the Jews. Cf Tb 4, 3–4; 6, 15; 14, 12–13.

that it was I who buried the dead. When I found out that the king knew all about me and wanted to put me to death, I went into hiding; then in my fear I took to flight. **20** Afterward, all my property was confiscated; I was left with nothing. All that I had was taken to the king's palace, except for my wife Anna and my son Tobiah.

**21** But less than forty days later the king was assassinated by two of his sons, who then escaped into the mountains of Ararat. His son Esarhaddon,* who succeeded him as king, placed Ahiqar, my brother Anael's son, in charge of all the accounts of his kingdom, so that he took control over the entire administration.[i] **22** Then Ahiqar interceded on my behalf, and I was able to return to Nineveh. For under Sennacherib, king of Assyria, Ahiqar had been chief cupbearer, keeper of the seal, administrator, and treasurer; and Esarhaddon reappointed him. He was a close relative—in fact, my nephew.

## CHAPTER 2

**1** Thus under King Esarhaddon I returned to my home, and my wife Anna and my son Tobiah were restored to me. Then on our festival of Pentocost, the feast of Weeks,* a fine dinner was prepared for me, and I reclined to eat.[j] **2** The table was set for me, and when many different dishes were placed before me, I said to my son Tobiah: "My son, go out and try to find a poor man from among our kinsmen exiled here in Nineveh. If he is a sincere worshiper of God, bring him back with you, so that he can share this meal with me. Indeed, son, I shall wait for you to come back."*

**3** Tobiah went out to look for some poor kinsman of ours. When he returned he exclaimed, "Father!" I said to him, "What is it, son?" He answered, "Father, one of our people has been murdered! His body lies in the market place where he was just strangled!" **4** I sprang to my feet, leaving the dinner untouched; and I carried the dead man from the street and put him in one of the rooms, so that I might bury him after sunset. **5** Returning to my own quarters, I washed myself* and ate my food in sorrow.[k] **6** I was reminded of the oracle pronounced by the prophet Amos against Bethel:[l]

"Your festivals shall be returned into
mourning,
And all your songs into lamentation."

**7** And I wept. Then at sunset I went out, dug a grave, and buried him.

**8** The neighbors mocked me, saying to one another: "Will this man never learn! Once before he was hunted down for execution because of this very thing; yet now that he has escaped, here he is again burying the dead!"

**Tobit's Blindness.** **9** That same night I bathed, and went to sleep next to the wall of my courtyard. Because of the heat I left my face uncovered. **10** I did not know there were birds perched on the wall above me, till their warm droppings settled in my eyes, causing cataracts.* I went to see some doctors for a cure, but the more they anointed my eyes with various salves, the worse the cataracts became, until I could see no more. For four years I was deprived of eyesight, and all my kinsmen were grieved at my condition. Ahiqar, however, took care of me for two years, until he left for Elymais.

**11** At that time my wife Anna worked for hire at weaving cloth, the kind of work women do. **12** When she sent back the goods to their owners, they would pay her. Late in winter* she finished the cloth and sent it back to the owners. They paid her the full salary, and also gave her a young goat for the table. **13** On entering my house the goat began to bleat. I called to my wife and said: "Where did this goat come from? Perhaps it was stolen! Give it back to its owners; we have no right to eat stolen food! **14** [m]But she said to me, "It was given to me as a bonus over and above my wages." Yet I would not believe her; and told her to give it back to its owners. I became very angry with her over this. So she retorted: "Where are your charitable deeds now? Where are your virtuous acts? See! Your true character is finally showing itself!"*

i 2 Kgs 19, 37; 2 Chr 32, 21; Sir 48, 21; Is 37, 38; 2 Mc 8, 19.
j Lv 23, 15-21; Nm 28, 26-31; Dt 16, 9-12.
k Nm 19, 11-22.
l Am 8, 10; 1 Mc 1, 39.
m Jb 2, 9.

*

1, 21: Esarhaddon: 681–669 B.C. Ahiqar: a hero of ancient folklore, known for his outstanding wisdom. The Story (or Wisdom) of Ahiqar was very popular in antiquity and is extant in many different forms: Aramaic, Syriac, Armenian, Arabic (Arabian Nights), Greek (Aesop's Fables), Slavonic, Ethiopic, and Romanian. The sacred author makes Tobit the uncle of the famous Ahiqar in order to enhance Tobit's own prestige. See note on Tb 14, 10.

2, 1: The feast of Weeks: also called by its Greek name Pentecost, was celebrated fifty days after the Passover. Cf Lv 23, 15–21; Dt 16, 9–12.

2, 2: Almsgiving and charity to the poor are important virtues taught by the book (Tb 4, 7–11. 16f; 12, 8f; 14, 10f).

2, 5: I washed myself: because of ritual defilement from touching a corpse (Nm 19, 11–13).

2, 10: Cataracts: literally, "white scales, or films." Elymais: the Greek name of ancient Elam, a district northeast of the head of the Persian Gulf.

2, 12: Late in winter: literally, "seventh of Dystros," the Macedonian month which corresponds to the Jewish month of Shebat (January–February). For the table: literally, "for the hearth"; the gift had probably been made in view of some springtime festival like the Jewish Purim.

2, 14: Anna's sharp rebuke calls to mind the words of Job's wife (Jb 2, 9).

## CHAPTER 3

1 Grief-stricken in spirit, I groaned and wept
aloud. Then with sobs I began to pray:

### Tobit's Prayer for Death

2 "You are righteous, O Lord,
and all your deeds are just;
All your ways are mercy and truth;
you are the judge of the world.[n]
3 And now, O Lord, may you be mindful of
me,
and look with favor upon me.
Punish me not for my sins,
nor for my inadvertent offenses,
nor for those of my fathers.[o]

"They sinned against you,
4 and disobeyed your commandments.
So you handed us over to plundering, exile,
and death,
till we were an object lesson, a byword, a
reproach
in all the nations among whom you
scattered us.[p]

5 "Yes, your judgments are many and true
in dealing with me as my sins
and those of my fathers deserve.
For we have not kept your commandments,
nor have we trodden the paths of truth
before you.

6 "So now, deal with me as you please,
and command my life breath to be taken
from me,
that I may go from the face of the earth
into dust.
It is better for me to die than to live,*
because I have heard insulting calumnies,
and I am overwhelmed with grief.[q]

"Lord, command me to be delivered from
such anguish;
let me go to the everlasting abode;
Lord, refuse me not.
For it is better for me to die
than to endure so much misery in life,
and to hear these insults!"

## II: *Sarah's Plight*

**Sarah Falsely Accused.** 7 *On the same
day, at Ecbatana in Media, it so happened that
Raguel's daughter Sarah also had to listen to
abuse, from one of her father's maids. 8 For
she had been married to seven husbands, but the
wicked demon Asmodeus* killed them off before they could have intercourse with her, as it
is prescribed for wives. So the maid said to her:
"You are the one who strangles your husbands!
Look at you! You have already been married
seven times, but you have had no joy with any
one of your husbands. 9 Why do you beat us?
Because your husbands are dead? Then why not
join them! May we never see a son or daughter
of yours!"
10 That day she was deeply grieved in spirit.
She went in tears to an upstairs room in her
father's house with the intention of hanging herself. But she reconsidered, saying to herself:
"No! People would level this insult against my
father: 'You had only one beloved daughter, but
she hanged herself because of ill fortune!' And
thus would I cause my father in his old age to
go down to the nether world laden with sorrow.
It is far better for me not to hang myself, but to
beg the Lord to have me die, so that I need no
longer live to hear such insults."[r]
11 At that time, then, she spread out her
hands, and facing the window,* poured out this
prayer:

### Sarah's Prayer for Death

"Blessed are you, O Lord, merciful God!
Forever blessed and honored is your holy
name;
may all your works forever bless you.[s]
12 And now, O Lord, to you I turn my face
and raise my eyes.
13 Bid me to depart from the earth,
never again to hear such insults.

14 "You know, O Master, that I am innocent
of any impure act with a man,
15 And that I have never defiled my own name
or my father's name in the land of my
exile.

"I am my father's only daughter,

---

n Pss 25, 10; 119, 137; Dn 3, 27.
o Ex 34, 7.
p Dt 28, 15; Bar 1, 16-22; 2, 4f; 3, 8; Dn 9, 5f.
q Nm 11, 15; 1 Kgs 19, 4; Jb 7, 15; Jon 4, 3.
r Tb 6, 15; Gn 37, 35; 42, 38; 44, 29. 31.
s 1 Kgs 8, 44, 48; Pss 28, 2; 134, 2; Dn 6, 11.

---

3, 6: It is better for me to die than to live: in his distress Tobit uses the words of the petulant Jonah (Jon 4, 3. 8), who wished to die because God did not destroy the hated Ninevites. In similar circumstances, Moses (Nm 11, 15), Elijah (1 Kgs 19, 4), and Job (Jb 7, 15) also prayed for death. Everlasting abode: a reference to Sheol, the dismal abode of the dead from which no one returns (Jb 7, 9–10; 14, 12; Is 26, 14). The revelation of a blessed immortality had not yet been made. See note on Tb 4, 6.

3, 7: From here on, the story is told in the third person. V 7 relates one of the several marvelous coincidences which the story-teller uses to heighten interest; see also vv 16. 17; 4, 1; 5, 4. Ecbatana: Hamadan in modern Iran; this was the capital of ancient Media. Raguel: "friend of God."

3, 8: Asmodeus: in Persian aeshma daeva, "demon of wrath," adopted into Aramaic with the sense of "the Destroyer." He will be subdued (Tb 8, 3) by Raphael (v 17), "God heals."

3, 11: Facing the window: that is, looking toward Jerusalem; cf Dn 6, 11: Blessed are you and "Blessed be God" are traditional openings of Jewish prayers (Tb 8, 5, 15; 11, 14; 13, 1).

and he has no other child to make his
heir,
Nor does he have a close kinsman or other
relative
whom I might bide my time to marry.
I have already lost seven husbands;
why then should I live any longer?
But if it please you, Lord, not to slay me,
look favorably upon me and have pity on
me;
never again let me hear these insults!"

**An Answer to Prayer.** 16 At that very
time, the prayer of these two suppliants was
heard in the glorious presence of Almighty God.
17 [t]So Raphael was sent to heal them both: to
remove the cataracts from Tobit's eyes, so that
he might again see God's sunlight; and to marry
Raguel's daughter Sarah to Tobit's son Tobiah,
and then drive the wicked demon Asmodeus
from her. For Tobiah had the right* to claim her
before any other who might wish to marry her.
In the very moment that Tobit returned from
the courtyard to his house, Raguel's daughter
Sarah came downstairs from her room.*

## III: Tobiah's Journey and Marriage to Sarah

### CHAPTER 4

**A Father's Instruction.** 1 That same day
Tobit remembered the money he had deposited
with Gabael at Rages in Media, and he thought,
2 "Now that I have asked for death, why
should I not call my son Tobiah and let him
know about this money before I die?" 3 So he
called his son Tobiah; and when he came, he
said to him:* "My son, when I die, give me a
decent burial. Honor your mother, and do not
abandon her as long as she lives. Do whatever
pleases her, and do not grieve her spirit in any
way.[u] 4 Remember, my son, that she went
through many trials for your sake while you
were in her womb. And when she dies, bury her
in the same grave with me.
5 "Through all your days, my son, keep the
Lord in mind, and suppress every desire to sin
or to break his commandments. Perform good
works all the days of your life, and do not tread
the paths of wrongdoing. 6 [v]For if you are
steadfast in your service, your good works will
bring success, not only to you, but also to all
those who live uprightly.*
7 "Give alms from your possessions. Do not
turn your face away from any of the poor, and
God's face will not be turned away from you.[w]
8 Son, give alms in proportion to what you
own. If you have great wealth, give alms out of
your abundance; if you have but little, distribute
even some of that. But do not hesitate to give
alms; 9 you will be storing up a goodly treasure
for yourself against the day of adversity.[x]
10 Almsgiving frees one from death, and keeps
one from going into the dark abode. 11 Alms
are a worthy offering in the sight of the Most
High for all who give them.[y]
12 "Be on your guard, son, against every
form of immorality, and above all, marry a
woman of the lineage of your forefathers. Do
not marry a stranger who is not of your father's
tribe, because we are sons of the prophets. My
boy, keep in mind Noah, Abraham, Isaac, and
Jacob, our fathers from of old; all of them took
wives from among their own kinsmen and were
blessed in their children. Remember that their
posterity shall inherit the land.[z] 13 Therefore,
my son, love your kinsmen. Do not be so proud-
hearted toward your kinsmen, the sons and
daughters of your people, as to refuse to take a
wife for yourself from among them. For in such
arrogance there is ruin and great disorder. Likewise, in worthlessness there is decay and dire
poverty, for worthlessness is the mother of famine.
14 "Do not keep with you overnight the
wages of any man who works for you, but pay
him immediately. If you thus behave as God's
servant, you will receive your reward. Keep a
close watch on yourself, my son, in everything
you do, and discipline yourself in all your conduct.[a] 15 Do to no one what you yourself dislike. Do not drink wine till you become drunk,
nor let drunkenness accompany you on your
way.[b]
16 [c]"Give to the hungry some of your bread,
and to the naked some of your clothing. Whatever you have left over, give away as alms; and
do not begrudge the alms you give. 17 [d]Be

t Tb 4, 12f; 6, 12f; Gn 24, 3f.
u Ex 20, 12; Prv 23, 22; Sir 7, 27.
v Tb 13, 6; Jn 3, 21; Eph 4, 15.
w 7f: Tb 12, 8ff; Dt 15, 7f. 11; Prv 19, 17; Sir 4, 1-6; 14, 13; Lk 14, 13; 1 Jn 3, 17.
x Mt 6, 20f.
y Sir 3, 30; 29, 12.
z Tb 3, 15. 17; 6, 12; Gn 11, 29. 31; 25, 20; 28, 1-4; 29, 15-30; Ex 34, 16; Dt 7, 3; Jgs 14, 3.
a Lv 19, 13; Dt 24, 15.
b Mt 7, 12; Lk 6, 31.
c Dt 15, 10; Is 58, 7; Mt 25, 35f; 2 Cor 9, 7.
d Jer 16, 7; Lk 14, 13.

*

3, 17: Tobiah had the right: according to the patriarchal custom of marriage within the family group. Tobiah was Sarah's closest eligible relative (Tb 6, 12). Cf Tb 4, 12–13; Gn 24.

4, 3–19: A collection of maxims which parallel those in the wisdom literature, especially Prv and Sir (see Introduction): duties toward parents (3–4); cf also Tb 14, 13; perseverance in virtue and avoidance of evil (5–6. 14b); necessity and value of almsgiving and charity (7–11. 16–17); marriage to a kinsman (12–13a); industry (13b); prompt payment of wages (14a); the golden rule (15a); temperance (15b); docility (18); prayer (19).

4, 6: Before the revelation of retribution for all men in the afterlife—a doctrine taught in the Book of Wisdom—Old Testament man believed that virtue guaranteed earthly prosperity, and sin earthly disaster (cf Dt 28).

4, 17: Tobit counsels his son either to give alms in honor

lavish with your bread and wine at the burial of the virtuous, but do not share them with sinners.*

**18** "Seek counsel from every wise man, and do not think lightly of any advice that can be useful. **19** [e]At all times bless the Lord God, and ask him to make all your paths straight and to grant success to all your endeavors and plans. For no pagan nation possesses good counsel, but the Lord himself gives all good things. If the Lord chooses, he raises a man up; but if he should decide otherwise, he casts him down to the deepest recesses of the nether world. So now, my son, keep in mind my commandments, and never let him be erased from your heart.*

**20** "And now, son, I wish to inform you that I have deposited a great sum of money with Gabri's son Gabael at Rages in Media. **21** Do not be discouraged, my child, because of our poverty. You will be a rich man if you fear God, avoid all sin, and do what is right before the Lord your God."[f]

## CHAPTER 5

**The Angel Raphael.** **1** Then Tobiah replied to his father Tobit: "Everything that you have commanded me, father, I will do. **2** But how shall I be able to obtain the money from him, since he does not know me nor do I know him? What can I show him to make him recognize me and trust me, so that he will give me the money? I do not even know which roads to take for the journey into Media!" **3** Tobit answered his son Tobiah: "We exchanged signatures on a document* written in duplicate; I divided it into two parts, and each of us kept one; his copy I put with the money. Think of it, twenty years have already passed since I deposited that money! So now, my son, find yourself a trustworthy man who will make the journey with you. We will, of course, give him a salary when you return; but get back that money from Gabael."

**4** Tobiah went to look for someone acquainted with the roads who would travel with him to Media. As soon as he went out, he found the angel Raphael standing before him, though he did not know* that this was an angel of God.[g] **5** Tobiah said to him, "Who are you, young man?" He replied, "I am an Israelite, one of your kinsmen. I have come here to work." Tobiah said, "Do you know the way to Media?" **6** The other replied: "Yes, I have been there many times. I know the place well and I know all the routes. I have often traveled to Media; I used to stay with our kinsman Gabael, who lives at Rages in Media. It is a good two days' travel from Ecbatana to Rages,* for Rages is situated at the mountains, Ecbatana out on the plateau." **7** Tobiah said to him, "Wait for me, young man, till I go back and tell my father; for I need you to make the journey with me. I will, of course, pay you."[h] **8** Raphael replied, "Very well, I will wait for you; but do not be long."

**9** Tobiah went back to tell his father Tobit what had happened. He said to him, "I have just found a man who is one of our own Israelite kinsmen!" Tobit said, "Call the man, so that I may find out what family and tribe he comes from, and whether he is trustworthy enough to travel with you, son." Tobiah went out to summon the man saying, "Young man, my father would like to see you."

**10** When Raphael entered the house, Tobit greeted him first. Raphael said, "Hearty greetings* to you!" Tobit replied: "What joy is left for me any more? Here I am, a blind man who cannot see God's sunlight, but must remain in darkness, like the dead who no longer see the light! Though alive, I am among the dead. I can hear a man's voice, but I cannot see him." Raphael said, "Take courage! God has healing in store for you; so take courage!" Tobit then said: "My son Tobiah wants to go to Media. Can you go with him to show him the way? I will of course pay you, brother." Raphael answered: "Yes, I can go with him, for I know all the routes. I have often traveled to Media and crossed all its plains and mountains; so I know every road well." **11** Tobit asked, "Brother, tell me, please, what family and tribe are you from?" **12** Raphael said: "Why? Do you need a tribe and a family? Or are you looking for a hired man to travel with your son?" Tobit replied, "I wish to know truthfully whose son you are, brother, and what your name is."[i]

**13** Raphael answered, "I am Azariah,* son

e Dt 4, 6; Ps 119, 10.
f 1 Tm 6, 6ff.
g Heb 13, 2.
h Tb 12, 2.
i Jgs 13, 17f.

*

of the dead, or, more probably, to give the "bread of consolation" to the family of the deceased. Cf Jer 16, 7; Ez 24, 17.

4, 19: Prayer is the foundation of a moral life.

5, 3: Document: in Greek cheirographon. In the Middle Ages, notably in England, a deed and its duplicate were written on one piece of parchment, with the Latin word chirographum inscribed across the top of the sheet or between the two copies of the text. The document was then cut in two in either a straight or a wavy line, the parts being given to the persons concerned. Perhaps this procedure derived from the present verse of Tobit. Duplicate documents, usually one open and the other sealed, are well known from the ancient Near East.

5, 4: He did not know: the theme of an angel in disguise occurs frequently in folklore as well as in the Old Testament (Gn 18; cf Heb 13, 2).

5, 6: It is a good two days' travel from Echatana to Rages: Alexander's army took eleven days in forced marches to cover this distance, about 180 miles. The author is merely using popular impressions about faraway places; he is not teaching geography. (See notes on Tb 1, 15; 3, 7 and Introduction.)

5, 10: Hearty greetings and what joy form a wordplay on the Greek verb chairein, "to greet" and "to be joyful."

5, 13–14: Azariah, "Yahweh helps"; Hananiah, "Yahweh is merciful"; Nathaniah, "Yahweh gives"; Shemaiah, "Yahweh hears."

of Hananiah the elder, one of your own kinsmen.” **14** Tobit exclaimed: “Welcome! God
save you, brother! Do not be provoked with me,
brother, for wanting to learn the truth about your
family. So it turns out that you are a kinsman,
and from a noble and good line! I knew Hananiah and Nathaniah, the two sons of Shemaiah the
elder; with me they used to make the pilgrimage
to Jerusalem, where we would worship together. No, they did not stray from the right path;
your kinsmen are good men. You are certainly
of good lineage, and welcome!”
**15** Then he added: “For each day you are
away I will give you the normal wages,* plus
expenses for you and for my son. If you go with
my son, **16** I will even add a bonus to your
wages!” Raphael replied: “I will go with him;
have no fear. In good health we shall leave you,
and in good health we shall return to you, for the
way is safe.” **17** Tobit said, “God bless you,
brother.” Then he called his son and said to
him: “My son, prepare whatever you need for
the journey, and set out with your kinsman.
May God in heaven protect you on the way and
bring you back to me safe and sound; and may
his angel accompany you for safety, my son.”
Before setting out on his journey, Tobiah
kissed his father and mother. Tobit said to him,
“Have a safe journey.” **18** But his mother began to weep. She said to Tobit: “Why have you
decided to send my child away? Is he not the
staff to which we cling, ever there with us in all
that we do? **19** I hope more money is not your
chief concern! Rather let it be a ransom for our
son! **20** What the Lord has given us to live on
is certainly enough for us.” **21** Tobit reassured
her. “Have no such thought. Our son will leave
in good health and come back to us in good
health. Your own eyes will see the day when he
returns to you safe and sound. **22** So, no such
thought; do not worry about them, my love.*
For a good angel will go with him, his journey
will be successful, and he will return unharmed.” **1** Then she stopped weeping.*

## CHAPTER 6

**Journey to Rages.** **2** When the boy left
home, accompanied by the angel, the dog followed Tobiah out of the house and went with
him. The travelers walked till nightfall, and
made camp beside the Tigris River. **3** Now
when the boy went down to wash his feet in the
river, a large fish suddenly leaped out of the
water and tried to swallow his foot. He shouted
in alarm. **4** But the angel said to him, “Take
hold of the fish and don't let it get away!” The
boy seized the fish and hauled it up on the shore.
**5** The angel then told him: “Cut the fish open
and take out its gall, heart, and liver, and keep
them with you; but throw away the entrails. Its
gall, heart, and liver make useful medicines.”*
**6** After the lad had cut the fish open, he put
aside the gall, heart, and liver. Then he broiled
and ate part of the fish; the rest he salted and
kept for the journey.

**Raphael's Instructions.** **7** Afterward
they traveled on together till they were near
Media. The boy asked the angel this question:
“Brother Azariah, what medicinal value is there
in the fish's heart, liver, and gall?” **8** He answered: “As regards the fish's heart and liver,
if you burn them so that the smoke surrounds a
man or a woman who is afflicted by a demon or
evil spirit, the affliction will leave him completely, and no demons will ever return to him
again. **9** And as for the gall, if you rub it on the
eyes of a man who has cataracts, blowing into
his eyes right on the cataracts, his sight will be
restored.”
**10** When they had entered Media and were
getting close to Ecbatana, **11** Raphael said to
the boy, “Brother Tobiah!” He answered,
“Yes, what is it?” Raphael continued: “Tonight we must stay with Raguel, who is a relative of yours. He has a daughter named Sarah,
**12** but no other child. Since you are Sarah's
closest relative, you before all other men have
the right to marry her. Also, her father's estate
is rightfully yours to inherit. Now the girl is
sensible, courageous, and very beautiful; and
her father loves her dearly.”[j] **13** He continued:
“Since you have the right to marry her, listen
to me, brother. Tonight I will ask the girl's
father to let us have her as your bride. When we
return from Rages, we will hold the wedding
feast for her. I know that Raguel cannot keep her
from you or let her become engaged to another
man; that would be a capital crime according to
the decree in the Book of Moses,* and he knows
that it is your right, before all other men, to
marry his daughter. So heed my words, brother;
tonight we must speak for the girl, so that we
may have her engaged to you. And when we
return from Rages, we will take her and bring
her back with us to your house.”
**14** Tobiah objected, however: “Brother Az-

j Tb 4, 12f; Nm 36, 8.

*

5, 15: The normal wages: literally, “a drachma,” about seventeen cents, a day's wage for a workingman.

5, 22: My love: literally, “sister,” a term of endearment applied to one's wife; cf Tb 7, 11. 15; 8, 4. 21; 10, 6. 13; Song 4, 9. 10. 12; 5, 1f. A good angel: a reference to the guardian angel, though Tobit does not know, of course, that Raphael himself, disguised as Azariah, is the good angel in this case.

5, 1: Then . . . weeping: this verse belongs to ch 6.

6, 5: Its gall . . . medicines: belief in the healing power of these organs was common among the physicians of antiquity.

6, 13: Raguel . . . Book of Moses: Nm 36, 6–8 prescribed marriage within the ancestral tribe, but no death penalty is mentioned.

ariah, I have heard that this woman has already been married seven times, and that her husbands died in their bridal chambers. On the very night they approached her, they dropped dead. And I have heard it said that it was a demon who killed them. **15** So now I too am afraid of this demon. Because he loves her, he does not harm her; but he does slay any man who wishes to come close to her. I am my father's only child. If I should die, I would bring my father and mother down to their grave in sorrow over me. And they have no other son to bury them!''[k]

**16** Raphael said to him: ''Do you not remember your father's orders? He commanded you to marry a woman from your own family. So now listen to me, brother; do not give another thought to this demon, but marry Sarah. I know that tonight you shall have her for your wife! **17** When you go into the bridal chamber, take the fish's liver and heart, and place them on the embers for the incense. **18** As soon as the demon smells the odor they give off, he will flee and never again show himself near her. Then when you are about to have intercourse with her, both of you first rise up to pray.* Beg the Lord of heaven to show you mercy and grant you deliverance. But do not be afraid, for she was set apart for you before the world existed. You will save her, and she will go with you. And I suppose that you will have children by her, who will take the place of brothers for you. So do not worry.''

When Tobiah heard Raphael say that she was his kinswoman, of his own family's lineage, he fell deeply in love with her, and his heart became set on her.

## CHAPTER 7

**At the House of Raguel.** **1** When they entered Ecbatana, Tobiah said, ''Brother Azariah, lead me straight to our kinsman Raguel.'' So he brought him to the house of Raguel, whom they found seated by his courtyard gate. They greeted him first. He said to them, ''Greetings to you too, brothers! Good health to you, and welcome!'' When he brought them into his home, **2** he said to his wife Edna, ''This young man looks just like my kinsman Tobit!'' **3** So Edna asked them, ''Who are you, brothers?'' They answered, ''We are of the exiles from Naphtali at Nineveh.'' **4** She said, ''Do you know our kinsman Tobit?'' They answered, ''Indeed we do!'' She asked, ''Is he well?'' **5** They answered, ''Yes, he is alive and well.'' Then Tobiah exclaimed, ''He is my father!'' **6** Raguel sprang up and kissed him, shedding tears of joy. **7** But when he heard that Tobit had lost his eyesight, he was grieved and wept aloud. He said to Tobiah: ''My child, God bless you! You are the son of a noble and good father. But what a terrible misfortune that such a righteous and charitable man should be afflicted with blindness!'' He continued to weep in the arms of his kinsman Tobiah. **8** His wife Edna also wept for Tobit; and even their daughter Sarah began to weep.

**Marriage of Tobiah and Sarah.** **9** Afterward, Raguel slaughtered a ram from the flock and gave them a cordial reception. When they had bathed and reclined to eat, Tobiah said to Raphael, ''Brother Azariah, ask Raguel to let me marry my kinswoman Sarah.'' **10** Raguel overheard the words; so he said to the boy: ''Eat and drink and be merry tonight, for no man is more entitled to marry my daughter Sarah than you, brother. Besides, not even I have the right to give her to anyone but you, because you are my closest relative. But I will explain the situation to you very frankly. **11** I have given her in marriage to seven men, all of whom were kinsmen of ours, and all died on the very night they approached her. But now, son, eat and drink. I am sure the Lord will look after you both.'' Tobiah answered, ''I will eat or drink nothing until you set aside what belongs to me.''

Raguel said to him: ''I will do it. She is yours according to the decree of the Book of Moses. Your marriage to her has been decided in heaven! Take your kinswoman; from now on you are her love, and she is your beloved. She is yours today and ever after. And tonight, son, may the Lord of heaven prosper you both. May he grant you mercy and peace.'' **12** Then Raguel called his daughter Sarah, and she came to him. He took her by the hand and gave her to Tobiah with the words: ''Take her according to the law. According to the decree written in the Book of Moses she is your wife. Take her and bring her back safely to your father. And may the God of heaven grant both of you peace and prosperity.''[l] **13** He then called her mother and told her to bring a scroll, so that he might draw up a marriage contract stating that he gave Sarah to Tobiah as his wife according to the decree of the Mosaic law. Her mother brought the scroll, and he drew up the contract, to which they affixed their seals.[m]

**14** Afterward they began to eat and drink. **15** Later Raguel called his wife Edna and said, ''My love, prepare the other bedroom and bring the girl there.'' **16** She went and made the bed in the room, as she was told, and brought the girl there. After she had cried over her, she wiped away the tears and said: **17** ''Be brave, my daughter. May the Lord of heaven grant you

k Tb 3, 10.
l Gn 24, 50f.
m Tb 6, 12.

* 6, 18: Rise up to pray: prayer is needed to drive out the demon.

joy in place of your grief. Courage, my daughter." Then she left.

## CHAPTER 8

**Expulsion of the Demon.** 1 When they
had finished eating and drinking, the girl's parents wanted to retire. They brought the young
man out of the dining room and led him into the
bedroom. 2 At this point Tobiah, mindful of
Raphael's instructions, took the fish's liver and
heart from the bag which he had with him, and
placed them on the embers for the incense.*
3 The demon, repelled by the odor of the fish,
fled into Upper Egypt;* Raphael pursued him
there and bound him hand and foot. Then Raphael returned immediately. 4 When the girl's
parents left the bedroom and closed the door
behind them, Tobiah arose from bed and said to
his wife, "My love, get up. Let us pray and beg
our Lord to have mercy on us and to grant us
deliverance." 5 She got up, and they started to
pray and beg that deliverance might be theirs.
He began with these words:

"Blessed are you, O God of our fathers;
praised be your name forever and ever.
Let the heavens and all your creation
praise you forever.[n]
6 You made Adam and you gave him his wife
Eve
to be his help and support;
and from these two the human race
descended.
You said, 'It is not good for the man to be
alone;
let us make him a partner like himself.'[o]
7 Now, Lord, you know that I take this wife
of mine
not because of lust,
but for a noble purpose.
Call down your mercy on me and on her,
and allow us to live together to a happy
old age."

8 They said together, "Amen, amen," 9 and
went to bed for the night.
But Raguel got up and summoned his servants. With him they went out to dig a grave,
10 for he said, "I must do this, because if Tobiah should die, we would be subjected to ridicule
and insult." 11 When they had finished digging the grave, Raguel went back into the house
and called his wife, 12 saying, "Send one of
the maids in to see whether Tobiah is alive or
dead, so that if necessary we may bury him
without anyone's knowing about it." 13 She
sent the maid, who lit a lamp, opened the bedroom door, went in, and found them sound
asleep together. 14 The maid went out and told
the girl's parents that Tobiah was alive, and that
there was nothing wrong. 15 Then Raguel
praised the God of heaven in these words:

"Blessed are you, O God, with every holy
and pure blessing!
Let all your chosen ones praise you;
let them bless you forever!
16 Blessed are you, who have made me glad;
what I feared did not happen.
Rather you have dealt with us
according to your great mercy.
17 Blessed are you, for you were merciful
toward two only children.
Grant them, Master, mercy and deliverance,
and bring their lives to fulfillment
with happiness and mercy."

18 Then he told his servants to fill in the grave
before dawn.

**Wedding Feast.** 19 He asked his wife to
bake many loaves of bread; he himself went out
to the herd and picked out two steers and four
rams which he ordered to be slaughtered. So the
servants began to prepare the feast. 20 He summoned Tobiah and made an oath in his presence, saying: "For fourteen days* you shall not
stir from here, but shall remain here eating and
drinking with me; and you shall bring joy to my
daughter's sorrowing spirit. 21 Take, to begin
with, half of whatever I own when you go back
in good health to your father; the other half will
be yours when I and my wife die. Be of good
cheer, my son! I am your father, and Edna is
your mother; and we belong to you and to your
beloved now and forever. So be happy, son!"

## CHAPTER 9

**The Money Recovered.** 1 Then Tobiah
called Raphael and said to him: 2 "Brother Azariah, take along with you four servants and two
camels and travel to Rages. Go to Gabael's
house and give him this bond. Get the money
and then bring him along with you to the wedding celebration. 4 For you know that my father
is counting the days. If I should delay my return
by a single day, I would cause him intense grief.
3 You witnessed the oath that Raguel has
sworn; I cannot violate his oath." 5 So Raphael, together with the four servants and two camels, traveled to Rages in Media, where they

n Dn 3, 26. o Gn 2, 18-23.

*

8, 2f: The manner of coping with demonic influences among the ancients seems quaint to us. However, the fish here is part of the story, and not a recipe for exorcism. It is clear that the author places primary emphasis on the value of prayer to God (Tb 6, 18; 8, 4–8), on the role of the angel as God's agent, and on the pious dispositions of Tobiah.

8, 3: Into Upper Egypt: to the desert there. The desert was considered the dwelling place of demons. Cf Is 13, 21; 34, 14; Mt 4, 1; 12, 43.

8, 20: For fourteen days: because of the happy, and unexpected, turn of events, Raguel doubles the time of the wedding feast. When Tobiah returns home, the usual seven-day feast is held (Tb 11, 18). Cf Jgs 14, 12.

stayed at Gabael's house. Raphael gave Gabael
his bond and told him about Tobit's son Tobiah,
and that he had married and was inviting him to
the wedding celebration. Gabael promptly
checked over the sealed moneybags, and they
placed them on the camels.
**6** The following morning they got an early
start and traveled to the wedding celebration.
When they entered Raguel's house, they found
Tobiah reclining at table. He sprang up and
greeted Gabael, who wept and blessed him,
exclaiming: "O noble and good child, son of a
noble and good, upright and charitable man,
may the Lord grant heavenly blessing to you and
to your wife, and to your wife's father and
mother. Blessed be God, because I have seen
the very image of my cousin Tobit!"

## *IV: Tobiah's Return; Cure of Tobit's Blindness*

### CHAPTER 10

**Anxiety of the Parents.** **1** Meanwhile,
day by day, Tobit was keeping track of the time
Tobiah would need to go and to return. When
the number of days was reached and his son did
not appear, **2** he said, "I wonder what has happened. Perhaps he has been detained there; or
perhaps Gabael is dead, and there is no one to
give him the money." **3** And he began to worry. **4** His wife Anna said, "My son has perished and is no longer among the living!" And
she began to weep aloud and to wail over her
son: **5** "Alas, my child, light of my eyes, that
I let you make this journey!" **6** But Tobit kept
telling her: "Hush, do not think about it, my
love; he is safe! Probably they have to take care
of some unexpected business there. The man
who is traveling with him is trustworthy, and is
one of our own kinsmen. So do not worry over
him, my love. He will be here soon." **7** But she
retorted, "Stop it, and do not lie to me! My
child has perished!" She would go out and keep
watch all day at the road her son had taken, and
she ate nothing. At sunset she would go back
home to wail and cry the whole night through,
getting no sleep at all.[p]

**Departure from Ecbatana.** Now at the
end of the fourteen-day wedding celebration
which Raguel had sworn to hold for his daughter, Tobiah went to him and said: "Please let me
go, for I know that my father and mother do not
believe they will ever see me again. So I beg
you, father, let me go back to my father. I have
already told you how I left him." **8** Raguel said
to Tobiah: "Stay, my child, stay with me. I am
sending messengers to your father Tobit, and
they will give him news of you." **9** But Tobiah
insisted, "No, I beg you to let me go back to
my father."
**10** Raguel then promptly handed over to Tobiah Sarah his wife, together with half of all his
property: male and female slaves, oxen and
sheep, asses and camels, clothing, money, and
household goods. **11** Bidding them farewell, he
let them go. He embraced Tobiah and said to
him: "Good-bye, my son. Have a safe journey.
May the Lord of heaven grant prosperity to you
and to your wife Sarah. And may I see children
of yours before I die!" **12** Then he kissed his
daughter Sarah and said to her: "My daughter,
honor your father-in-law and your mother-in-
law, because from now on they are as much
your parents as the ones who brought you into
the world. Go in peace, my daughter; let me
hear good reports about you as long as I live."
Finally he said goodbye to them and sent them
away.
**13** Then Edna said to Tobiah: "My child and
beloved kinsman, may the Lord bring you back
safely, and may I live long enough to see children of you and of my daughter Sarah before I
die. Before the Lord, I entrust my daughter to
your care. Never cause her grief at any time in
your life. Go in peace, my child. From now on
I am your mother, and Sarah is your beloved.
May all of us be prosperous all the days of our
lives." She kissed them both and sent them
away in peace.
**14** When Tobiah left Raguel, he was full of
happiness and joy, and he blessed the Lord of
heaven and earth, the King of all, for making his
journey so successful. Finally he said goodbye
to Raguel and his wife Edna, and added, "May
I honor you all the days of my life!"

### CHAPTER 11

**Homeward Journey.** **1** Then they left and
began their return journey. When they were
near Kaserin, just before Nineveh, **2** Raphael
said: "You know how we left your father. **3** Let
us hurry on ahead of your wife to prepare the
house while the rest of the party are still on the
way." **4** So they both went on ahead and Raphael said to Tobiah, "Have the gall in your
hand!" And the dog ran along behind them.
**5** Meanwhile, Anna sat watching the road by
which her son was to come. **6** When she saw
him coming, she exclaimed to his father, "Tobit, your son is coming, and the man who traveled with him!"
**7** Raphael said to Tobiah before he reached
his father: "I am certain that his eyes will be
opened. **8** Smear the fish gall on them. This
medicine will make the cataracts shrink and peel

p Gn 45, 26.

off from his eyes; then your father will again be
able to see the light of day."

**Sight Restored.** 9 Then Anna ran up to her
son, threw her arms around him, and said to
him, "Now that I have seen you again, son, I
am ready to die!" And she sobbed aloud.[q]
10 Tobit got up and stumbled out through the
courtyard gate. Tobiah went up to him 11 with
the fish gall in his hand, and holding him firmly,
blew into his eyes. "Courage, father," he said.
12 Next he smeared the medicine on his eyes,
13 and it made them smart. Then, beginning at
the corners of Tobit's eyes, Tobiah used both
hands to peel off the cataracts. When Tobit saw
his son, he threw his arms around him 14 and
wept. He exclaimed, "I can see you, son, the
light of my eyes!" Then he said:

"Blessed be God,
  and praised be his great name,
  and blessed be all his holy angels.
May his holy name be praised
  throughout all the ages,
15 Because it was he who scourged me,
  and it is he who has had mercy on me.
  Behold, I now see my son Tobiah!"

Then Tobit went back in, rejoicing and praising
God with full voice. Tobiah told his father that
his journey had been a success; that he had
brought back the money; and that he had married Raguel's daughter Sarah, who would arrive
shortly, for she was approaching the gate of
Nineveh.[r]
16 Rejoicing and praising God, Tobit went
out to the gate of Nineveh to meet his daughter-in-law. When the people of Nineveh saw
him walking along briskly, with no one leading
him by the hand, they were amazed. 17 Before
them all Tobit proclaimed how God had mercifully restored sight to his eyes. When Tobit
reached Sarah, the wife of his son Tobiah, he
greeted her: "Welcome, my daughter! Blessed
be your God for bringing you to us, daughter!
Blessed are your father and your mother.
Blessed is my son Tobiah, and blessed are you,
daughter! Welcome to your home with blessing
and joy. Come in, daughter!" That day there
was joy for all the Jews who lived in Nineveh.
18 Ahiqar and his nephew Nadab also came to
rejoice with Tobit. They celebrated Tobiah's
wedding feast for seven happy days, and he
received many gifts.

## *V: Raphael Reveals His Identity*

### CHAPTER 12

**Raphael's Wages.*** 1 When the wedding
celebration came to an end, Tobit called his son
Tobiah and said to him, "Son, see to it that you
give what is due to the man who made the
journey with you; give him a bonus too." 2 Tobiah said: "Father, how much shall I pay him?
It would not hurt me at all to give him half of
all the wealth he brought back with me.[s] 3 He
led me back safe and sound; he cured my wife;
he brought the money back with me; and he
cured you. How much of a bonus should I give
him?" 4 Tobit answered, "It is only fair, son,
that he should receive half of all that he brought
back." 5 So Tobiah called Raphael and said,
"Take as your wages half of all that you have
brought back, and go in peace."

**Exhortation.*** 6 Raphael called the two
men aside privately and said to them: "Thank
God! Give him the praise and the glory. Before
all the living, acknowledge the many good
things he has done for you, by blessing and
extolling his name in song. Before all men,
honor and proclaim God's deeds, and do not be
slack in praising him.* 7 A king's secret it is
prudent to keep, but the works of God are to be
declared and made known. Praise them with due
honor. Do good, and evil will not find its way
to you. 8 Prayer and fasting are good, but better
than either is almsgiving accompanied by righteousness.* A little with righteousness is better
than abundance with wickedness. It is better to
give alms than to store up gold;[t] 9 for almsgiving saves one from death and expiates every sin.
Those who regularly give alms shall enjoy a full
life;[u] 10 but those habitually guilty of sin are
their own worst enemies.

**Raphael's Identity.** 11 "I will now tell
you the whole truth; I will conceal nothing at all
from you. I have already said to you, 'A king's
secret it is prudent to keep, but the works of God
are to be made known with due honor.' 12 [v]I
can now tell you that when you, Tobit, and

q Gn 33, 4; 45, 14; 46, 29f; Lk 15, 20.
r Tb 13, 2; Dt 32, 39; 1 Sm 2, 6.
s Tb 5, 3. 7. 15f.
t Tb 4, 7-11; Sir 29, 8-13.
u Dn 4, 24.
v Jb 33, 23f; Acts 10, 4; Rv 8, 3f.

*

12, 1–5: Tobit and his son generously agree to give Azariah far more than the wages agreed upon in Tb 5, 15–16.

12, 6–10: In the fashion of a wisdom teacher, Raphael gives the two men a short exhortation similar to the one Tobit gave his son in Tb 4, 3–19.

12, 6f: The Jews considered the duty of praising God their most esteemed privilege. Without praise of God, life was meaningless. Cf Is 38, 16–20.

12, 8: Prayer . . . fasting . . . almsgiving . . . righteousness: these, together with the proper attitude toward wealth, are treated in great detail by Christ our Lord in the Sermon on the Mount (Mt 6).

12, 12. 15: Raphael is one of the seven specially designated intercessors who present man's prayers to God. Angelology was developing in this period. The names of two other angels are given in the Bible: Gabriel (Dn 8, 16; 9, 21; Lk 1, 19. 26) and Michael (Dn 10, 13. 21; 12, 1; Jude 9; Rv 12, 7).

Sarah prayed, it was I who presented and read
the record of your prayer before the Glory of the
Lord; and I did the same thing when you used
to bury the dead.* **13** When you did not hesitate
to get up and leave your dinner in order to go
and bury the dead, **14** I was sent to put you to
the test.* At the same time, however, God commissioned me to heal you and your daughter-
in-law Sarah. **15** I am Raphael, one of the sev-
en angels who enter and serve before the Glory
of the Lord."[w]

**16** Stricken with fear, the two men fell to the
ground. **17** But Raphael said to them: "No
need to fear; you are safe. Thank God now and
forever. **18** As for me, when I came to you it
was not out of any favor on my part, but because
it was God's will. So continue to thank him
every day; praise him with song. **19** Even
though you watched me eat and drink, I did not
really do so; what you were seeing was a vision.
**20** So now get up from the ground and praise
God. Behold, I am about to ascend to him who
sent me; write down all these things that have
happened to you."[x] **21** When Raphael ascended, they rose to their feet and could no longer
see him. **22** They kept thanking God and singing his praises; and they continued to acknowledge these marvelous deeds which he had done
when the angel of God appeared to them.

## *VI: Tobit's Song of Praise*

## CHAPTER 13

**1** Then Tobit composed this joyful prayer:*
Blessed be God who lives forever,
because his kingdom lasts for all ages.[y]
**2** For he scourges and then has mercy;
he casts down to the depths of the netherworld,
and he brings up from the great abyss.
No one can escape his hand.[z]

**3** Praise him, you Israelites, before the Gentiles,
for though he has scattered you among them,
**4** he has shown you his greatness even there.
Exalt him before every living being,
because he is the Lord our God,
our Father and God forever.
**5** He scourged you for your iniquities,
but will again have mercy on you all.
He will gather you from all the Gentiles
among whom you have been scattered.[a]

**6** When you turn back to him with all your heart,
to do what is right before him,
Then he will turn back to you,
and no longer hide his face from you.[b]
So now consider what he has done for you,
and praise him with full voice.
Bless the Lord of righteousness,
and exalt the King of the ages.

In the land of my exile I praise him,
and show his power and majesty to a sinful nation.
"Turn back, you sinners! do the right before him:
perhaps he may look with favor upon you
and show you mercy.

**7** "As for me, I exalt my God,
and my spirit rejoices in the King of heaven.
**8** Let all men speak of his majesty,
and sing his praises in Jerusalem."

**9** O Jerusalem, holy city,
he scourged you for the works of your hands,*
but will again pity the children of the righteous.[c]
**10** Praise the Lord for his goodness,
and bless the King of the ages,
so that his tent may be rebuilt in you with joy.
May he gladden within you all who were captives;
all who were ravaged may he cherish within you
for all generations to come.[d]

**11** A bright light will shine to all parts of the earth;
many nations shall come to you from afar,
And the inhabitants of all the limits of the earth,
drawn to you by the name of the Lord God,
Bearing in their hands their gifts for the King of heaven.
Every generation shall give joyful praise in you,
and shall call you the chosen one,
through all ages forever.[e]

w Lk 1, 19; Rv 8, 2.
x Jgs 13, 20.
y Tb 3, 11; 8, 5. 15; 1 Chr 29, 10; Dn 3, 26.
z Tb 11, 15; 13, 9; Dt 32, 39; 1 Sm 2, 6; Wis 16, 13.
a Dt 30, 3; Neh 1, 9.
b Dt 30, 2.
c Tb 11, 15; Mi 7, 19; Rv 21.
d Is 44, 26, 28; Am 9, 11; Zec 1, 16.
e Is 2, 3f; 9, 1; 49, 6; 60, 1; Mi 4, 2; Zec 8, 22.

*

12, 14: I was sent . . . test: God often sends trials to purify his faithful servants further. Cf Jb 1—2.

13, 1–18: Tobit's hymn of praise (cf Ex 15, 1–18; Jdt 16, 1–17) is divided into two parts. The first part (vv 1–8) is a song of praise that echoes themes from the hymns and psalms of the kingdom; the second (vv 9–18) is addressed to Jerusalem in the style of the prophets who spoke of a new and ideal Jerusalem (Is 60); cf Rv 21.

, of your hands: idols.

12 Accursed are all who speak a harsh word
against you;
accursed are all who destroy you
and pull down your walls,
And all who overthrow your towers
and set fire to your homes;
but forever blessed are all those who build
you up.[f]

13 Go, then, rejoice over the children of the
righteous,
who shall all be gathered together
and shall bless the Lord of the ages.
14 Happy are those who love you,
and happy those who rejoice in your
prosperity.

Happy are all the men who shall grieve over
you,
over all your chastisements,
For they shall rejoice in you
as they behold all your joy forever.[g]

15 My spirit blesses the Lord, the great King;
16 Jerusalem shall be rebuilt as his home
forever.
Happy for me if a remnant of my offspring
survive
to see your glory and to praise the King
of heaven!

The gates of Jerusalem shall be built with
sapphire and emerald,
and all your walls with precious stones.
The towers of Jerusalem shall be built with
gold,
and their battlements with pure gold.[h]
17 The streets of Jerusalem shall be paved
with rubies and stones of Ophir;
18 The gates of Jerusalem shall sing hymns of
gladness,
and all her houses shall cry out,
"Alleluia!"

"Blessed be God who has raised you up!
may he be blessed for all ages!"
For in you they shall praise his holy name
forever.

The end of Tobit's hymn of praise.

## *VII: Epilogue*

## CHAPTER 14

**Parting Advice.** 1 Tobit died peacefully at
the age of a hundred and twelve, and received
an honorable burial in Nineveh. 2 He was sixty-two years old when he lost his eyesight, and
after he recovered it he lived in prosperity, giving alms and continually blessing God and
praising the divine Majesty.
3 Just before he died, he called his son Tobiah and Tobiah's seven sons, and gave him this
command: "Son, take your children[i] 4 and flee
into Media, for I believe God's word which was
spoken by Nahum* against Nineveh. It shall all
happen, and shall overtake Assyria and Nineveh; indeed, whatever was said by Israel's
prophets, whom God commissioned, shall occur. Not one of all the oracles shall remain
unfulfilled, but everything shall take place in
the time appointed for it. So it will be safer in
Media than in Assyria or Babylon. For I know
and believe that whatever God has spoken will
be accomplished. It shall happen, and not a
single word of the prophecies shall prove false.
"As for our kinsmen who dwell in Israel,
they shall all be scattered and led away into exile
from the Good Land. The entire country of Israel shall become desolate; even Samaria and Jerusalem shall become desolate! God's temple
there shall be burnt to the ground and shall be
desolate for a while.[j] 5 But God will again have
mercy on them and bring them back to the land
of Israel. They shall rebuild the temple, but it
will not be like the first one, until the era when
the appointed times shall be completed.* Afterward all of them shall return from their exile,
and they shall rebuild Jerusalem with splendor.
In her the temple of God shall also be rebuilt;
yes, it will be rebuilt for all generations to come,
just as the prophets of Israel said of her.[k] 6 [l]All
the nations of the world shall be converted and
shall offer God true worship; all shall abandon
their idols which have deceitfully led them into
error,* 7 and shall bless the God of the ages in
righteousness. Because all the Israelites who are
to be saved in those days will truly be mindful
of God, they shall be gathered together and go
to Jerusalem; in security shall they dwell forever
in the land of Abraham, which will be given
over to them. Those who sincerely love God
shall rejoice, but those who become guilty of sin
shall completely disappear from the land.[m]
9 "Now, children, I give you this command:

f Bar 4, 31f.
g Ps 122, 6; Is 66, 10.
h Tb 14, 5; Is 54, 11-13; 62, 2; Rv 21, 10-21.
i Gn 47, 29f.
j Na 2, 2—3, 19.
k Neh 12, 27; Jer 31, 38.
l Tb 45, 14; Is 60, 1-4.
m Is 60, 21; Jer 32, 37; Ex 34, 28; 37, 25; 39, 26.

*

14, 4f: Nahum: one of the minor prophets, whose book contains oracles of doom against Nineveh. Here, in keeping with the period to which he assigns his story, the sacred author makes Tobit speak as if the punishment of Nineveh, the destruction of Jerusalem (587 B.C.), the exile from Judah and the return, would all take place in the future. The technique of using the facts of past history as seemingly future predictions, is a frequent device of apocalyptic writers. The Good Land: a favorite name for the promised land. Cf Dt 1, 35; 3, 25; 4, 21. 22.

14, 5: Until the era . . . completed: a reference to the advent of messianic times, in which a new, more perfect temple was to be expected. Cf Heb 9, 1–14.

14, 6: Conversion of the Gentiles is also to come in the messianic era.

serve God faithfully and do what is right before
him; you must tell your children to do what is
upright and to give alms, to be mindful of God
and at all times to bless his name sincerely and
with all their strength.
**8** "Now, as for you, my son, depart from
Nineveh; do not remain here. **10** The day you
bury your mother next to me, do not even stay
overnight within the confines of the city. For I
see that people here shamelessly commit all
sorts of wickedness and treachery. Think, my
son, of all that Nadab* did to Ahiqar, the very
one who brought him up: Ahiqar went down
alive into the earth! Yet God made Nadab's
disgraceful crime rebound against him. Ahiqar
came out again into the light, but Nadab went
into the everlasting darkness, for he had tried to
kill Ahiqar. Because Ahiqar had given alms to
me, he escaped from the deadly trap Nadab had
set for him. But Nadab himself fell into the
deadly trap, and it destroyed him.[n] **11** So, my
children, note well what almsgiving does, and
also what wickedness does—it kills! But now
my spirit is about to leave me."

**Death of Tobit and Tobiah.** **12** They
placed him on his bed and he died; and he
received an honorable burial. When Tobiah's
mother died, he buried her next to his father. He
then departed with his wife and children for
Media, where he settled in Ecbatana with his
father-in-law Raguel.[o] **13** He took respectful
care of his aging father-in-law and mother-in-
law; and he buried them at Ecbatana in Media.
Then he inherited Raguel's estate as well as that
of his father Tobit. **14** He died at the venerable
age of a hundred and seventeen. **15** But before
he died, he heard of the destruction of Nineveh
and saw its effects. He witnessed the exile of the
city's inhabitants when Cyaxares,* king of Media, led them captive into Media. Tobiah
praised God for all that he had done against the
citizens of Nineveh and Assyria. Before dying
he rejoiced over Nineveh's destruction, and he
blessed the Lord God forever and ever. Amen.

n Tb 1, 21f. o Tb 4, 4.

*

14, 10: Nadab: In the story of Ahiqar, the hero Ahiqar, chancellor under the Assyrian kings Sennacherib and Esarhaddon, adopts his nephew Nadab and prepares him to become his successor. But Nadab treacherously plots to have his uncle put to death. Ahiqar hides in a friend's house, and is finally vindicated (came out again into the light) when Nadab's scheme is discovered. Thereupon Nadab is thrown into a dungeon where he dies (went into everlasting darkness). It was Ahiqar's almsgiving that delivered him from death; see note on Tb 2, 2.

14, 15: Cyaxares: Nabopolassar, king of Babylon, and Cyaxares conquered and destroyed Nineveh in 612 B.C.; see note on Tb 1, 15.

# The Book of
# JUDITH

*The Book of Judith is a vivid story relating how, in a grave crisis, God delivered the Jewish people through the instrumentality of a woman. The unknown author composed this edifying narrative of divine providence at the end of the second or the beginning of the first century B.C. The original was almost certainly written in Hebrew, but the Greek text shows so much freedom in adapting from the Septuagint the language of older biblical books that it must be regarded as having a literary character of its own. It is this Greek form of the book, accepted as canonical by the Catholic Church, which is translated here. St. Jerome, who prepared (with some reluctance) a Latin text of Judith, based his work on a secondary Aramaic text available to him in Palestine, combined with an older Latin rendering from the Greek. The long hymn of chapter 16 he took in its entirety from that earlier Latin text.*

*Since it is no longer possible to determine with any precision the underlying events which may have given rise to this narrative, it is enough to note that the author sought to strengthen the faith of his people in God's abiding presence among them. The Book of Judith is a tract for difficult times; the reader, it was hoped, would take to heart the lesson that God was still the Master of history, who could save Israel from her enemies. Note the parallel with the time of the Exodus: as God had delivered his people by the hand of Moses, so he could deliver them by the hand of the pious widow Judith (see note on 2, 12).*

*The story can be divided into two parts. In the first (cc 1–7), Holofernes, commander-in-chief of the armies of Nebuchadnezzar, leads an overwhelming Assyrian force in a punitive campaign against the vassals who refused to help in the Assyrian war against the Medes. The Jewish people stubbornly resist the enemy at Bethulia, guarding the route of access to Jerusalem. Despite the warning of Achior that the Jews cannot be conquered unless they sin against God, the proud general lays siege to the town and cuts off its water supply. After a siege of thirty-four days, the exhausted defenders are desperate and ready to surrender.*

*At this point, the climax of the story, Judith (the name means "Jewess") appears and promises to defeat the Assyrians. The rest of the story is too well known to repeat in detail. Having fasted and prayed, Judith dresses in her finest garments and proceeds to the Assyrian camp, where she succeeds in killing Holofernes while he lies in a drunken stupor. The Assyrians panic when they discover this, and the Jews are able to rout and slaughter them. The beautiful hymn of the people honoring Judith (15, 9–10) is often applied to Mary in the liturgy.*

*Any attempt to read the book directly against the backdrop of Jewish history in relation to the empires of the ancient world is bound to fail. The story was written as a pious reflection on the meaning of the yearly Passover observance. It draws its inspiration from the Exodus narrative (especially Ex 14, 31) and from the texts of Isaiah and the Psalms portraying the special intervention of God for the preservation of Jerusalem. The theme of God's hand as the agent of this providential activity, reflected of old in the hand of Moses and now in the hand of Judith, is again exemplified at a later time in Jewish synagogue art. God's hand reaching down from heaven appears as part of the scene at Dura-Europos (before A.D. 256) in paintings of the Exodus, of the sacrifice of Isaac (Gn 22), and of Ezekiel's valley of dry bones (Ez 37).*

*The Book of Judith is divided as follows:*
*I. Peril of the Jews (1, 1—7, 32).*
*II. Deliverance of the Jews (8, 1—14, 10).*
*III. Victory (14, 11—16, 25).*

## I: Peril of the Jews

### CHAPTER 1

**War against the Medes.** 1 It was the
twelfth year of the reign of Nebuchadnezzar,
king of the Assyrians in the great city of Nineveh. At that time Arphaxad ruled over the
Medes in Ecbatana. 2 Around this city he built
a wall of blocks of stone, each three cubits in
height and six in length. He made the wall seventy cubits high and fifty thick. 3 At the gates
he raised towers of a hundred cubits, with a
thickness of sixty cubits at the base. 4 The gateway he built to a height of seventy cubits, with
an opening forty cubits wide for the passage of
his chariot forces and the marshaling of his infantry. 5 Then King Nebuchadnezzar waged
war against King Arphaxad in the vast plain, in
the district of Ragae. 6 To him there rallied all
the inhabitants of the mountain region, all who
dwelt along the Euphrates, the Tigris, and the
Hydaspes, and King Arioch of the Elamites, in
the plain. Thus many nations came together to
resist the people of Cheleoud.*

**Ultimatum to the West.** 7 Now Nebuchadnezzar, king of the Assyrians, sent messengers to all the inhabitants of Persia, and to all
those who dwelt in the West: to the inhabitants
of Cilicia and Damascus, Lebanon and Anti-
Lebanon, to all who dwelt along the seacoast,
8 to the peoples of Carmel, Gilead, Upper Galilee, and the vast plain of Esdraelon, 9 to all
those in Samaria and its cities, and west of the
Jordan as far as Jerusalem, Bethany, Chelous,
Kadesh, and the River of Egypt; to Tahpanhes,
Raamses, all the land of Goshen, 10 Tanis,
Memphis and beyond, and to all the inhabitants
of Egypt as far as the borders of Ethiopia.

11 But the inhabitants of all that land disregarded the summons of Nebuchadnezzar, king
of the Assyrians, and would not go with him to
the war. They were not afraid of him but regarded him as a lone individual opposed to them,
and turned away his envoys emptyhanded, in
disgrace. 12 Then Nebuchadnezzar fell into a
violent rage against all that land, and swore by
his throne and his kingdom that he would
avenge himself on all the territories of Cilicia
and Damascus and Syria, and also destroy with
his sword all the inhabitants of Moab, Ammon,
the whole of Judea, and those living anywhere
in Egypt as far as the borders of the two seas.*

**Defeat of Arphaxad.** 13 In the seventeenth year he proceeded with his army against
King Arphaxad, and was victorious in his campaign. He routed the whole force of Arphaxad,
his entire cavalry and all his chariots, 14 and
took possession of his cities. He pressed on to
Ecbatana and took its towers, sacked its marketplaces, and turned its glory into shame. 15 Arphaxad himself he overtook in the mountains of
Ragae, ran him through with spears, and utterly
destroyed him. 16 Then he returned home with
all his numerous, motley horde of warriors; and
there he and his army relaxed and feasted for a
hundred and twenty days.[a]

### CHAPTER 2

**Council of War against the West.** 1 In
the eighteenth year, on the twenty-second day
of the first month, there was a discussion in the
palace of Nebuchadnezzar, king of the Assyrians, about taking revenge on the whole world,
as he had threatened. 2 He summoned all his
ministers and nobles, laid before them his secret
plan, and urged the total destruction of those
countries. 3 They decided to do away with all
those who had refused to comply with the order
he had issued.

4 When he had completed his plan, Nebuchadnezzar, king of the Assyrians, summoned
Holofernes, general in chief of his forces, second to himself in command, and said to him:
5 [b]"Thus says the great king, the lord of all the
earth: Go forth from my presence, take with you
men of proven valor, a hundred and twenty
thousand infantry and twelve thousand cavalry,
6 and proceed against all the land of the West,
because they did not comply with the order I
issued. 7 Tell them to have earth and water*
ready, for I will come against them in my wrath;
I will cover all the land with the feet of my
soldiers, to whom I will deliver them as spoils.
8 Their slain shall fill their ravines and wadies,
the swelling torrent shall be choked with their
dead; 9 and I will deport them as exiles to the
very ends of the earth.

10 "You go before me and take possession
of all their territories for me. If they surrender
to you, guard them for me till the day of their
punishment. 11 As for those who resist, show
them no quarter, but deliver them up to slaughter and plunder in each country you occupy.
12 For as I live,* and by the strength of my

---

a Est 1, 3f. b 5f: Est 3, 8f.

---

1, 6: Cheleoud: probably the Chaldeans are meant.

1, 12: The two seas: the ancient rulers in Mesopotamia often designated the limits of their realm as extending from the Upper Sea (the Mediterranean) to the Lower Sea (the Persian Gulf).

2, 7: Earth and water: in the Persian period, the offering of these to a conqueror was a symbolic gesture of unconditional surrender.

2, 12: As I live: in the Old Testament, an oath proper to divinity; cf Dt 32, 40. Nebuchadnezzar is making himself equal to God; see Jdt 6, 2. By my power: literally "by my hand." The hand of Nebuchadnezzar raised in opposition to God and to his people is the occasion for Judith's intervention by a wom-

kingdom, what I have spoken I will accomplish
by my power. **13** Do not disobey a single one
of the orders of your lord; fulfill them exactly
as I have commanded you, and do it without
delay."

**Campaign of Holofernes.** **14** So Holofernes left the presence of his lord, and summoned all the princes, and the generals and
officers of the Assyrian army. **15** He mustered
a hundred and twenty thousand picked troops,
as his lord had commanded, and twelve thousand mounted archers, **16** and grouped them
into a complete combat force. **17** He took along
a very large number of camels, asses, and mules
for their baggage; innumerable sheep, cattle,
and goats for their food supply; **18** abundant
provisions for each man, and much gold and
silver from the royal palace.

**19** Then he and his whole army proceeded on
their expedition in advance of King Nebuchadnezzar, to cover all the western region with their
chariots and cavalry and regular infantry. **20** A
huge, irregular force, too many to count, like
locusts or the dust of the earth, went along with
them.[c]

**21** After a three-day march from Nineveh,
they reached the plain of Bectileth, and from
Bectileth they next encamped near the mountains to the north of Upper Cilicia. **22** From
there Holofernes took his whole force, the infantry, calvary, and chariots, and marched into
the mountain region. **23** He devastated Put and
Lud,* and plundered all the Rassisites and the
Ishmaelites on the border of the desert toward
the south of Chaldea.

**24** Then, following the Euphrates, he went
through Mesopotamia, and battered down every
fortified city along the Wadi Abron, until he
reached the sea. **25** He seized the territory of
Cilicia, and cut down everyone who resisted
him. Then he proceeded to the southern borders
of Japheth, toward Arabia. **26** He surrounded
all the Midianites, burned their tents, and plundered their sheepfolds. **27** Descending to the
plain of Damascus at the time of the wheat
harvest, he set fire to all their fields, destroyed
their flocks and herds, despoiled their cities,
devastated their plains, and put all their youths
to the sword.

**28** The fear and dread of him fell upon all the
inhabitants of the coastland, upon those in Sidon and Tyre, and those who dwelt in Sur and
Ocina, and the inhabitants of Jamnia. Those in
Azotus and Ascalon also feared him greatly.

## CHAPTER 3

**Submission of the West.** **1** They therefore sent messengers to him to sue for peace in
these words: **2** "We, the servants of Nebuchadnezzar the great king, lie prostrate before you;
do with us as you will. **3** Our dwellings and all
our wheat fields, our flocks and herds, and all
our encampments are at your disposal; make use
of them as you please. **4** Our cities and their
inhabitants are also at your service; come and
deal with them as you see fit."

**5** After the spokesmen had reached Holofernes and given him this message, **6** he went
down with his army to the seacoast, and stationed garrisons in the fortified cities; from
them he impressed picked troops as auxiliaries.
**7** The people of these cities and all the inhabitants of the countryside received him with garlands and dancing to the sound of timbrels.
**8** Nevertheless, he devastated their whole territory and cut down their sacred groves, for he
had been commissioned to destroy all the gods
of the earth, so that every nation might worship
Nebuchadnezzar alone, and every people and
tribe invoke him as a god.[d] **9** At length Holofernes reached Esdraelon in the neighborhood of
Dothan, the approach to the main ridge of the
Judean mountains; **10** he set up his camp between Geba* and Scythopolis, and stayed there
a whole month to refurbish all the equipment of
his army.

## CHAPTER 4

**Israelite Defense.** **1** When the Israelites
who dwelt in Judea heard of all that Holofernes,
commander in chief of Nebuchadnezzar, king of
the Assyrians, had done to the nations, and how
he had despoiled all their temples and destroyed
them, **2** they were in extreme dread of him, and
greatly alarmed for Jerusalem and the temple of
the LORD, their God. **3** Now, they had lately
returned from exile, and only recently had all
the people of Judea been gathered together, and
the vessels, the altar, and the temple been purified from profanation.* **4** So they sent word to
the whole region of Samaria, to Kona, Beth-horon, Belmain, and Jericho, to Choba and
Aesora, and to the valley of Salem. **5** The people there posted guards on all the summits of the
high mountains, fortified their villages, and

c Jgs 7, 12. d Ex 34, 13.

an's hand; cf Jdt 9, 9f; Is 10, 5–14.

2, 23: Put and Lud: the same as the "Put and Lud" mentioned in Ez 30, 5 as allies of Egypt, and in Ez 27, 10 as supplying mercenary soldiers to Tyre. Here they seem inserted to embellish the narrative with assonance and prophetic associations rather than to indicate definite localities.

3, 10: Geba: perhaps originally "Gelboe," the mountain range near the eastern end of which lay Scythopolis, the Greek name for ancient Beth-shean (Jos 17, 11).

4, 3: Returned from exile . . . profanation: these allusions are variously attributed—to the Persian period (538–323 B.C.), or even to a condition in the days of Antiochur Epiphanes (175–164 B.C.).

since their fields had recently been harvested,
stored up provisions in preparation for war.
**6** Joakim, who was high priest* in Jerusalem
in those days, wrote to the inhabitants of Bethulia [and Betomesthaim], which is on the way
to Esdraelon, facing the plain near Dothan,
**7** and instructed them to keep firm hold of the
mountain passes, since these offered access to
Judea. It would be easy to ward off the attacking
forces, as the defile was only wide enough for
two abreast. **8** The Israelites carried out the
orders given them by Joakim, the high priest,
and the senate of the whole people of Israel,
which met in Jerusalem.*

**Prayer and Penance.** **9** All the men of
Israel cried to God with great fervor and did
penance— **10** [e]they, along with their wives,
and children, and domestic animals.* All their
resident aliens, hired laborers, and slaves also
girded themselves with sackcloth. **11** And all
the Israelite men, women, and children who
lived in Jerusalem prostrated themselves in front
of the temple building,* with ashes strewn on
their heads, displaying their sackcloth covering
before the LORD. **12** The altar, too, they draped
in sackcloth; and with one accord they cried out
fervently to the God of Israel not to allow their
children to be seized, their wives to be taken
captive, the cities of their inheritance to be ruined, or the sanctuary to be profaned and
mocked for the nations to gloat over.[f]

**13** The LORD heard their cry and had regard
for their distress. For the people observed a fast
of many days' duration throughout Judea, and
before the sanctuary of the LORD Almighty in
Jerusalem.[g] **14** The high priest Joakim, and all
the priests in attendance on the LORD who
served his altar, were also girded with sackcloth
as they offered the daily holocaust, the votive
offerings, and the free-will offerings of the people. **15** With ashes upon their turbans, they
cried to the LORD with all their strength to look
with favor on the whole house of Israel.

## CHAPTER 5

**Council against the Israelites.** **1** It was
reported to Holofernes, commander in chief of
the Assyrian army, that the Israelites were ready
for battle, and had blocked the mountain passes,
fortified the summits of all the higher peaks, and
placed roadblocks in the plains. **2** In great anger
he summoned all the rulers of the Moabites, the
generals of the Ammonites, and all the satraps
of the seacoast **3** and said to them: "Now tell
me, you Canaanites, what sort of people is this
that dwells in the mountains? Which cities do
they inhabit? How large is their army? In what
does their power and strength consist? Who has
set himself up as their king and the leader of
their army? **4** Why have they refused to come
out to meet me along with all the other inhabitants of the West?"

**Achior's Speech.** **5** Then Achior, the
leader of all the Ammonites, said to him: "My
lord, hear this account from your servant; I will
tell you the truth about this people that lives near
you [that inhabits this mountain region]; no lie
shall escape your servant's lips.[h]

**6** *"These people are descendants of the
Chaldeans. **7** They formerly dwelt in Mesopotamia, for they did not wish to follow the gods
of their forefathers who were born in the land of
the Chaldeans.[i] **8** Since they abandoned the
way of their ancestors, and acknowledged with
divine worship the God of heaven, their forefathers expelled them from the presence of their
gods. So they fled to Mesopotamia and dwelt
there a long time. **9** Their God bade them leave
their abode and proceed to the land of Canaan.
Here they settled, and grew very rich in gold,
silver, and a great abundance of livestock.[j]
**10** Later, when famine had gripped the whole
land of Canaan, they went down into Egypt.
They stayed there as long as they found sustenance, and grew into such a great multitude that
the number of their race could not be counted.[k]
**11** [l]The king of Egypt, however, rose up
against them, shrewdly forced them to labor at
brickmaking, oppressed and enslaved them.
**12** But they cried to their God, and he struck the
land of Egypt with plagues for which there was
no remedy. When the Egyptians expelled them,
**13** [m]God dried up the Red Sea before them,
**14** and led them along the route to Sinai and
Kadesh-barnea. First they drove out all the inhabitants of the desert; **15** then they settled in
the land of the Amorites, destroyed all the Hesh-
bonites by main force, crossed the Jordan, and
took possession of the whole mountain region.[n]

e 10f: Jon 3, 7f.
f Est 4, 1f.
g Est 4, 16.
h Jdt 11, 9-19.
i Gn 11, 31.
j Gn 11, 31—12, 5.
k Gn 42, 1-5; 46, 1-7; Ex 1, 7.
l 11f: Ex 5, 4-21; 7, 1-9.
m 13f: Ex 14, 21f. 29.
n Nm 21, 21-32; Jos 2, 10.

*

4, 6: Joakim, who was high priest: see Bar 1, 7 and the footnote on Bar 1, 8f; this name for a high priest cannot be used in dating the events in Jdt.

4, 8: The organization of the Jewish nation as subject to a high priest and a senate, or council of elders, was proper to the Greek period (after 323 B.C.), and is reflected in the coinage of John Hyrcanus (135–104 B.C.).

4, 10: Domestic animals: see note on Jon 3, 8.

4, 11: Prostrated themselves in front of the temple building: for a parallel to this ceremony of entreaty, see Jl 1, 13f; 2, 15ff, and the note on Jl 2, 17.

5, 6–9: Achior outlines the early history of the Hebrews, whose forefather, Abraham, first lived in Ur of the Chaldeans (Gn 11, 28) and then migrated to Haran (Gn 11, 31) in Aram Naharaim (Gn 24, 10), which was called Mesopotamia by the Greeks. The gods of their forefathers were the pagan deities worshiped by Abraham's relatives (Jos 24, 2).

**16** They expelled the Canaanites, the Perizzites, the Jebusites, the Shechemites, and all the Gergesites; and they lived in these mountains a long time.[o]

**17** [p]"As long as the Israelites did not sin in the sight of their God, they prospered, for their God, who hates wickedness, was with them. **18** But when they deviated from the way he prescribed for them, they were ground down steadily, more and more, by frequent wars, and finally taken as captives into foreign lands. The temple of their God was razed to the ground, and their cities were occupied by their enemies.[q] **19** But now that they have returned to their God, they have come back from the Dispersion wherein they were scattered, and have repossessed Jerusalem, where their sanctuary is, and have settled again in the mountain region which was unoccupied.

**20** [r]"So now, my lord and master, if these people are at fault, and are sinning against their God, and if we verify this offense of theirs, then we shall be able to go up and conquer them. **21** But if they are not a guilty nation, then your lordship should keep his distance; otherwise their LORD and God will shield them, and we shall become the laughingstock of the whole world."

**22** Now when Achior had concluded his recommendation, all the people standing round about the tent murmured; and the officers of Holofernes and all the inhabitants of the seacoast and of Moab alike said he should be cut to pieces. **23** "We are not afraid of the Israelites," they said, "for they are a powerless people, incapable of a strong defense. **24** Let us therefore attack them; your great army, Lord Holofernes, will swallow them up."[s]

## CHAPTER 6

**Holofernes' Answer.** **1** When the noise of the crowd surrounding the council had subsided, Holofernes, commander in chief of the Assyrian army, said to Achior, in the presence of the whole throng of coast-land peoples, of the Moabites, and of the Ammonite mercenaries: **2** "Who are you, Achior, to prophesy among us as you have done today, and to tell us not to fight against the Israelites because their God protects them? What god is there beside Nebuchadnezzar? He will send his force and destroy them from the face of the earth. Their God will not save them;[t] **3** but we, the servants of Nebuchadnezzar, will strike them down as one man, for they will be unable to withstand the force of our cavalry.[u] **4** We will overwhelm them with it, and the mountains shall be drunk with their blood, and their plains filled with their corpses. Not a trace of them shall survive our attack: they shall utterly perish, says King Nebuchadnezzar, lord of all the earth; for he has spoken, and his words shall not remain unfulfilled.[v] **5** As for you, Achior, you Ammonite mercenary, for saying these things in a moment of perversity you shall not see my face after today, until I have taken revenge on this race of people from Egypt. **6** Then at my return, the sword of my army or the spear of my servants will pierce your sides, and you shall fall among their slain.[w] **7** My servants will now conduct you to the mountain region, and leave you at one of the towns along the ascent. **8** You shall not die till you are destroyed together with them. **9** If you still cherish the hope that they will not be taken, then there is no need for you to be downcast. I have spoken, and my words shall not prove false in any respect."

**Achior in Bethulia.** **10** Then Holofernes ordered the servants who were standing by in his tent to seize Achior, conduct him to Bethulia, and hand him over to the Israelites. **11** So the servants took him in custody and brought him out of the camp into the plain. From there they led him into the mountain region till they reached the springs below Bethulia. **12** When the men of the city saw them, they seized their weapons and ran out of the city to the crest of the ridge; and all the slingers blocked the ascent of Holofernes' servants by hurling stones upon them. **13** So they took cover below the mountain, where they bound Achior and left him lying at the foot of the mountain; then they returned to their lord.

**14** The Israelites came down to him from their city, loosed him, and brought him into Bethulia. They haled him before the rulers of the city, **15** who in those days were Uzziah, son of Micah of the tribe of Simeon, Chabris, son of Gothoniel, and Charmis, son of Melchiel. **16** They then convened all the elders of the city; and all their young men, as well as the women, gathered in haste at the place of assembly. They placed Achior in the center of the throng, and Uzziah questioned him about what had happened. **17** He replied by giving them an account of what was said in the council of Holofernes, and of all his own words among the Assyrian officers, and of all the boasting threats of Holofernes against the house of Israel.

**18** At this the people fell prostrate and worshiped God; and they cried out: **19** "LORD, God

o Dt 7, 1.
p 17f: Dt 28—30; Ps 106, 40-46; Is 59, 7.
q 2 Kgs 25.
r 20f: Jdt 8, 18ff; 11, 10.
s Jdt 6, 2; 9, 7; 16, 2.
t Jdt 3, 8; 9, 7.
u Is 36, 18ff.
v Jdt 6, 17.
w Jdt 5, 22.

*

6, 19: The Latin Vulgate (6, 15) has a longer form of this prayer: "Lord, God of heaven and earth, behold their arrogance; regard our lowliness and look with favor on your holy ones; show that you do not abandon those who trust in you,

of heaven, behold their arrogance! Have pity on
the lowliness of our people, and look with favor
this day on those who are consecrated to you."*
**20** Then they reassured Achior and praised him
highly. **21** Uzziah brought him from the assembly to his home, where he gave a banquet for the
elders. That whole night they called upon the
God of Israel for help.

## CHAPTER 7

**Siege of Bethulia.** **1** The following day
Holofernes ordered his whole army, and all the
allied troops that had come to his support, to
move against Bethulia, seize the mountain
passes, and engage the Israelites in battle.
**2** That same day all their fighting men went into
action. Their forces numbered a hundred and
seventy thousand infantry and twelve thousand
horsemen, not counting the baggage train or the
men who accompanied it on foot—a very great
army. **3** They encamped at the spring in the
valley near Bethulia, and spread out in breadth
toward Dothan as far as Balbaim, and in length
from Bethulia to Cyamon, which faces Esdraelon.

**4** When the Israelites saw how many there
were, they said to one another in great dismay:
"Soon they will devour the whole country. Neither the high mountains nor the valleys and hills
can support the mass of them." **5** Yet they all
seized their weapons, lighted fires on their bastions,* and kept watch throughout the night.

**6** On the second day Holofernes led out all
his cavalry in the sight of the Israelites who were
in Bethulia. **7** He reconnoitered the approaches
to their city and located their sources of water;
these he seized, stationing armed detachments
around them, while he himself returned to his
troops.

**8** All the commanders of the Edomites and
all the leaders of the Ammonites, together with
the generals of the seacoast, came to Holofernes
and said: **9** "Sir, listen to what we have to say,
that there may be no losses among your troops.
**10** These Israelites do not rely on their spears,
but on the height of the mountains where they
dwell; it is not easy to reach the summit of their
mountains.[x] **11** Therefore, sir, do not attack
them in regular formation; thus not a single one
of your troops will fall. **12** Stay in your camp,
and spare all your soldiers. Have some of your
servants keep control of the source of water that
flows out at the base of the mountain, **13** for
that is where the inhabitants of Bethulia get their
water. Then thirst will begin to carry them off,
and they will surrender their city. Meanwhile,
we and our men will go up to the summits of the
nearby mountains, and encamp there to guard
against anyone's leaving the city.[y] **14** They and
their wives and children will languish with hunger, and even before the sword strikes them they
will be laid low in the streets of their city.
**15** Thus you will render them dire punishment
for their rebellion and their refusal to meet you
peacefully."

**16** Their words pleased Holofernes and all
his ministers, and he ordered their proposal to
be carried out. **17** Thereupon the Moabites
moved camp, together with five thousand Assyrians. They encamped in the valley, and held
the water supply and the springs of the Israelites. **18** The Edomites and the Ammonites went
up and encamped in the mountain region opposite Dothan; and they sent some of their men to
the south and to the east opposite Egrebel, near
Chusi, which is on Wadi Mochmur. The rest of
the Assyrian army was encamped in the plain,
covering the whole countryside. Their enormous store of tents and equipment was spread
out in profusion everywhere.

**19** The Israelites cried to the LORD, their
God, for they were disheartened, since all their
enemies had them surrounded, and there was no
way of slipping through their lines.[z] **20** The
whole Assyrian camp, infantry, chariots, and
cavalry, kept them thus surrounded for thirty-
four days. All the reservoirs of water failed the
inhabitants of Bethulia, **21** and the cisterns ran
dry, so that on no day did they have enough to
drink, but their drinking water was rationed.
**22** Their children fainted away, and the women
and youths were consumed with thirst and were
collapsing in the streets and gateways of the
city, with no strength left in them.

**23** All the people, therefore, including
youths, women, and children, went in a crowd
to Uzziah and the rulers of the city. They set up
a great clamor and said before the elders:
**24** "God judge between you and us! You have
done us grave injustice in not making peace with
the Assyrians. **25** There is no help for us now!
Instead, God has sold us into their power by
laying us prostrate before them in thirst and utter
exhaustion. **26** Therefore, summon them and
deliver the whole city as booty to the troops of
Holofernes and to all his forces; **27** we would
be better off to become their prey. We should
indeed be made slaves, but at least should live,
and not have to behold our little ones dying
before our eyes and our wives and children
breathing out their souls. **28** We adjure you by
heaven and earth, and by our God, the LORD of

x 1 Kgs 20, 23. 28.
y Ex 5, 21.
z Ps 106, 6.

* but that you humble those who trust in themselves and glory in their own strength."

7, 5: Lighted fires on their bastions: to serve as signals for alerting the neighboring towns. Reference to fire signals in time of siege is made in the Lachish ostraca at the beginning of the sixth century B.C. Kept watch throughout the night: to prevent a surprise attack.

our forefathers, who is punishing us for our sins
and those of our forefathers, to do as we have
proposed, this very day.''
**29** All in the assembly with one accord broke
into shrill wailing and loud cries to the LORD
their God. **30** But Uzziah said to them, ''Courage, my brothers! Let us wait five days more for
the LORD our God, to show his mercy toward us;
he will not utterly forsake us. **31** But if those
days pass without help coming to us, I will do
as you say.'' **32** Then he dispersed the men to
their posts, and they returned to the walls and
towers of the city; the women and children he
sent to their homes. Throughout the city they
were in great misery.

## *II: Deliverance of the Jews*

### CHAPTER 8

**Judith.** **1** Now in those days Judith, daughter of Merari, son of Joseph, son of Oziel, son
of Elkiah, son of Ananias, son of Gideon, son
of Raphain, son of Ahitob, son of Elijah, son of
Hilkiah, son of Eliab, son of Nathanael, son of
Salamiel, son of Sarasadai,* son of Simeon, son
of Israel, heard of this. **2** Her husband, Manasseh, of her own tribe and clan, had died at the
time of the barley harvest. **3** While he was in
the field supervising those who bound the
sheaves, he suffered sunstroke; and he died of
this illness in Bethulia, his native city. He was
buried with his forefathers in the field between
Dothan and Balamon. **4** The widowed Judith
remained three years and four months at home,
**5** where she set up a tent* for herself on the roof
of her house. She put sackcloth about her loins
and wore widow's weeds. **6** She fasted all the
days of her widowhood, except sabbath eves
and sabbaths, new moon eves and new moons,
feastdays and holidays of the house of Israel.[a]
**7** She was beautifully formed and lovely to behold. Her husband, Manasseh, had left her gold
and silver, servants and maids, livestock and
fields, which she was maintaining. **8** No one
had a bad word to say about her, for she was a
very God-fearing woman.

**Her Words to the Elders.** **9** When Judith,
therefore, heard of the harsh words which the
people, discouraged by their lack of water, had
spoken against their ruler, and of all that Uzziah
had said to them in reply, swearing that he
would hand over the city to the Assyrians at the
end of five days, **10** she sent the maid who was
in charge of all her things to ask Uzziah, Chabris, and Charmis, the elders of the city, to visit
her. **11** When they came, she said to them:
''Listen to me, you rulers of the people of Bethulia. What you said to the people today is not
proper. When you promised to hand over the
city to our enemies at the end of five days unless
within that time the LORD comes to our aid, you
interposed between God and yourselves this
oath which you took. **12** Who are you, then,
that you should have put God to the test this day,
setting yourselves in the place of God in human
affairs?[b] **13** It is the LORD Almighty for whom
you are laying down conditions; will you never
understand anything? **14** You cannot plumb the
depths of the human heart or grasp the workings
of the human mind; how then can you fathom
God, who has made all these things, discern his
mind, and understand his plan?[c]
''No, my brothers, do not anger the LORD our
God. **15** For if he does not wish to come to our
aid within the five days, he has it equally within
his power to protect us at such time as he
pleases, or to destroy us in the face of our enemies. **16** It is not for you to make the LORD our
God give surety for his plans.

''God is not man that he should be moved
by threats,
nor human, that he may be given an
ultimatum.

**17** ''So while we wait for the salvation that
comes from him, let us call upon him to help us,
and he will hear our cry if it is his good pleasure.
**18** For there has not risen among us in recent
generations, nor does there exist today, any
tribe, or clan, or town, or city of ours that
worships gods made by hands, as happened in
former days.[d] **19** It was for such conduct that
our forefathers were handed over to the sword
and to pillage, and fell with great destruction
before our enemies.[e] **20** But since we acknowledge no other god but the LORD, we hope that
he will not disdain us or any of our people. **21** If
we are taken, all Judea will fall, our sanctuary
will be plundered, and God will make us pay for
its profanation with our life's blood. **22** For the
slaughter of our kinsmen, for the taking of exiles from the land, and for the devastation of our
inheritance, he will lay the guilt on our heads.
Wherever we shall be enslaved among the nations, we shall be a mockery and a reproach in
the eyes of our masters. **23** Our enslavement
will not be turned to our benefit, but the LORD
our God will maintain it to our disgrace.
**24** ''Therefore, my brothers, let us set an
example for our kinsmen. Their lives depend on

---

a Lk 2, 37.
b Jb 38, 2; 40, 2. 7f; 42, 3.
c Jb 41, 3; Prv 14, 10; Wis 9, 13; Is 40, 13; Rom 11, 33f; 1 Cor 2, 11
d Jdt 5, 20f; 11, 10.
e Pss 78, 56f; 106, 13f; Jer 7, 16-20; 14, 7.

---

* 8, 1: Salamiel, son of Sarasadai: head of the tribe of Simeon during the wanderings of the Israelites in the desert (Nm 1, 6).

8, 5: A tent: erected by Judith on the roof of her house (v 5); it was here that the elders came to confer with her (v 11).

us, and the defense of the sanctuary, the temple,
and the altar rests with us. **25** [f]Besides all this,
we should be grateful to the LORD our God, for
putting us to the test, as he did our forefathers.
**26** Recall how he dealt with Abraham, and how
he tried Isaac, and all that happened to Jacob in
Syrian Mesopotamia while he was tending the
flocks of Laban, his mother's brother. **27** Not
for vengeance did the LORD put them in the
crucible to try their hearts, nor has he done so
with us. It is by way of admonition that he
chastises those who are close to him."[g]

**Uzziah's Response.** **28** Then Uzziah said
to her: "All that you have said was spoken with
good sense, and no one can gainsay your words.
**29** Not today only is your wisdom made evident, but from your earliest years all the people
have recognized your prudence, which corresponds to the worthy dispositions of your heart.
**30** The people, however, were so tortured with
thirst that they forced us to speak to them as we
did, and to bind ourselves by an oath that we
cannot break. **31** But now, God-fearing woman
that you are, pray for us that the LORD may send
rain to fill up our cisterns, lest we be weakened
still further."

**32** Then Judith said to them: "Listen to me!
I will do something that will go down from
generation to generation among the descendants
of our race. **33** Stand at the gate tonight to let
me pass through with my maid; and within the
days you have specified before you will surrender the city to our enemies, the LORD will rescue
Israel by my hand. **34** You must not inquire
into what I am doing, for I will not tell you until
my plan has been accomplished." **35** Uzziah
and the rulers said to her, "Go in peace, and
may the LORD God go before you to take vengeance upon our enemies!" **36** Then they withdrew from the tent and returned to their posts.

## CHAPTER 9

**The Prayer of Judith.** **1** Judith threw herself down prostrate, with ashes strewn upon her
head, and wearing nothing over her sackcloth.
While the incense was being offered in the temple of God in Jerusalem that evening, Judith
prayed to the LORD with a loud voice:[h]
**2** "LORD, God of my forefather Simeon! You
put a sword into his hand to take revenge upon
the foreigners who had immodestly loosened the
maiden's* girdle, shamefully exposed her
thighs, and disgracefully violated her body.
This they did, though you forbade it.[i] **3** Therefore you had their rulers slaughtered; and you
covered with their blood the bed in which they
lay deceived, the same bed that had felt the
shame of their own deceiving. You smote the
slaves together with their princes, and the
princes together with their servants.* **4** Their
wives you handed over to plunder, and their
daughters to captivity; and all the spoils you
divided among your favored sons, who burned
with zeal for you, and in their abhorrence of the
defilement of their kinswoman, called on you
for help.
**5** "O God, my God, hear me also, a widow.
It is you who were the author of those events and
of what preceded and followed them. The
present, also, and the future you have planned.
Whatever you devise comes into being;[j] **6** the
things you decide on come forward and say,
'Here we are!' All your ways are in readiness,
and your judgment is made with foreknowledge.[k]
**7** [l]"Here are the Assyrians, a vast force,
priding themselves on horse and rider, boasting
of the power of their infantry, trusting in shield
and spear, bow and sling. They do not know that

**8** " 'You, the LORD, crush warfare;
Lord is your name.'

"Shatter their strength in your might, and crush
their force in your wrath; for they have resolved
to profane your sanctuary, to defile the tent
where your glorious name resides, and to overthrow with iron the horns of your altar. **9** See
their pride, and send forth your wrath upon their
heads. Give me, a widow, the strong hand to
execute my plan.[m] **10** With the guile of my
lips, smite the slave together with the ruler, the
ruler together with his servant; crush their pride
by the hand of a woman.
**11** "Your strength is not in numbers, nor
does your power depend upon stalwart men; but
you are the God of the lowly, the helper of the
oppressed, the supporter of the weak, the protector of the forsaken, the savior of those without hope.
**12** "Please, please, God of my forefather,
God of the heritage of Israel, LORD of heaven
and earth, Creator of the waters, King of all you
have created, hear my prayer! **13** Let my guile-
ful speech bring wound and wale on those who
have planned dire things against your covenant,
your holy temple, Mount Zion, and the homes
your children have inherited.[n] **14** Let your
whole nation and all the tribes know clearly that

f 25f: Gn 22, 1-12; 29, 22-30.
g Dt 4, 7.
h Ex 30, 7f; Ps 141, 2.
i Gn 34.
j Is 44, 7.
k Jb 38, 35; Is 46, 9-13; Bar 3, 35.
l 7f: Jdt 5, 23; 6, 2; 16, 2.
m Ps 33, 16.
n Jdt 10, 4; 11, 20. 23; 16, 6. 9.

*

9, 2: The maiden: Dinah, Jacob's daughter, who was violated by Shechem, the Hivite (Gn 34, 2).

9, 3: Because Shechem had deceived and violated Dinah, her brothers, Simeon and Levi, tricked Shechem and the men of his city into being circumcised, and then slew them while they were confined to bed from the circumcision; cf Gn 34, 13–29.

you are the God of all power and might, and that there is no other who protects the people of Israel but you alone."

## CHAPTER 10

**Judith's Departure.** 1 As soon as Judith had thus concluded, and ceased her invocation to the God of Israel, 2 she rose from the ground. She called her maid and they went down into the house, which she used only on sabbaths and feast days. 3 She took off the sackcloth she had on, laid aside the garments of her widowhood, washed her body with water, and anointed it with rich ointment. She arranged her hair and bound it with a fillet, and put on the festive attire she had worn while her husband, Manasseh, was living.[o] 4 She chose sandals for her feet, and put on her anklets, bracelets, rings, earrings, and all her other jewelry. Thus she made herself very beautiful, to captivate the eyes of all the men who should see her.[p]

5 She gave her maid a leather flask of wine and a cruse of oil. She filled a bag with roasted grain, fig cakes, bread and cheese; all these provisions she wrapped up and gave to the maid to carry.[q]

6 Then they went out to the gate of the city of Bethulia and found Uzziah and the elders of the city, Chabris and Charmis, standing there. 7 When these men saw Judith transformed in looks and differently dressed, they were very much astounded at her beauty and said to her, 8 "May the God of our fathers bring you to favor, and make your undertaking a success, for the glory of the Israelites and the exaltation of Jerusalem."

Judith bowed down to God. Then she said to them, 9 "Order the gate of the city opened for me, that I may go to carry out the business we discussed." So they ordered the youths to open the gate for her as she requested. 10 When they did so, Judith and her maid went out. The men of the city kept her in view as she went down the mountain and crossed the valley; then they lost sight of her.

**Judith Captured.** 11 As Judith and her maid walked directly across the valley, they encountered the Assyrian outpost. 12 The men took her in custody and asked her, "To what people do you belong? Where do you come from, and where are you going?" She replied: "I am a daughter of the Hebrews, and I am fleeing from them, because they are about to be delivered up to you as prey.* 13 I have come to see Holofernes, the general in chief of your forces, to give him a trustworthy report; I will show him the route by which he can ascend and take possession of the whole mountain district without a single one of his men suffering injury or loss of life."[r]

14 When the men heard her words and gazed upon her face, which appeared wondrously beautiful to them, they said to her, 15 "By coming down thus promptly to see our master, you have saved your life. Now go to his tent; some of our men will accompany you to present you to him. 16 When you stand before him, have no fear in your heart; give him the report you speak of, and he will treat you well." 17 So they detailed a hundred of their men as an escort for her and her maid, and these conducted them to the tent of Holofernes.

18 When the news of her arrival spread among the tents, a crowd gathered in the camp. They came and stood around her as she waited outside the tent of Holofernes, while he was being informed about her. 19 They marveled at her beauty, regarding the Israelites with wonder because of her, and they said to one another, "Who can despise this people that has such women among them? It is not wise to leave one man of them alive, for if any were to be spared they could beguile the whole world."

**Judith Meets Holofernes.** 20 The guard of Holofernes and all his servants came out and ushered her into the tent. 21 Now Holofernes was reclining on his bed under a canopy with a netting of crimson and gold, emeralds and other precious stones. 22 When they announced her to him, he came out to the antechamber, preceded by silver lamps; 23 and when Holofernes and his servants beheld Judith, they all marveled at the beauty of her face. She threw herself down prostrate before him, but his servants raised her up.

## CHAPTER 11

1 Then Holofernes said to her: "Take courage, lady; have no fear in your heart! Never have I harmed anyone who chose to serve Nebuchadnezzar, king of all the earth. 2 Nor, would I have raised my spear against your people who dwell in the mountain region, had they not despised me and brought this upon themselves. 3 But now tell me why you fled from them and came to us. In any case, you have come to safety. Take courage! Your life is spared tonight and for the future. 4 No one at all will harm you. Rather, you will be well treated, as are all the servants of my lord, King Nebuchadnezzar."

o Jdt 8, 6ff.
p Jdt 9, 13.
q Jdt 12, 2.
r Jdt 11, 5f.

* 10, 12f: The deceitful means used by Judith against Holofernes, here and in Jdt 11, 5–19, are to be judged in the light of the moral concepts of Old Testament times; cf Gn 27, 1–25; 34, 13–29; 37, 32ff; Jos 2, 1–7; Jgs 4, 17–22.

**5** [s]Judith answered him: "Listen to the
words of your servant, and let your handmaid
speak in your presence! I will tell no lie to my
lord this night, **6** and if you follow out the
words of your handmaid, God will give you
complete success, and my lord will not fail in
any of his undertakings. **7** By the life of Nebuchadnezzar, king of all the earth, and by the
power of him who has sent you to set all creatures aright! not only do men serve him through
you; but even the wild beasts and the cattle and
the birds of the air, because of your strength,
will live for Nebuchadnezzar and his whole
house.[t] **8** Indeed, we have heard of your wisdom and sagacity, and all the world is aware that
throughout the kingdom you alone are competent, rich in experience, and distinguished in
military strategy.

**9** [u]"As for Achior's speech in your council,
we have heard of it. When the men of Bethulia
spared him, he told them all he had said to you.
**10** So then, my lord and master, do not disregard his word, but bear it in mind, for it is true.
For our people are not punished, nor does the
sword prevail against them, except when they
sin against their God.[v] **11** But now their guilt
has caught up with them by which they bring the
wrath of their God upon them whenever they do
wrong; so that my lord will not be repulsed and
fail, but death will overtake them. **12** Since
their food gave out and all their water ran low,
they decided to kill their animals, and determined to consume all the things which God in
his laws forbade them to eat. **13** They decreed
that they would use up the first fruits of grain
and the tithes of wine and oil which they had
sanctified and reserved for the priests who minister in the presence of our God in Jerusalem:
things which no layman should even touch with
his hands. **14** They have sent messengers to
Jerusalem to bring back to them authorization
from the council of the elders; for the inhabitants there have also done these things. **15** On
the very day when the response reaches them
and they act upon it, they will be handed over
to you for destruction.

**16** "As soon as I, your handmaid, learned all
this, I fled from them. God has sent me to
perform with you such deeds that people
throughout the world will be astonished on hearing of them. **17** Your handmaid is, indeed, a
God-fearing woman, serving the God of heaven
night and day. Now I will remain with you, my
lord; but each night your handmaid will go out
to the ravine and pray to God. He will tell me
when the Israelites have committed their
crimes. **18** Then I will come and let you know,
so that you may go out with your whole force,
and not one of them will be able to withstand
you. **19** I will lead you through Judea, till you
come to Jerusalem, and there I will set up your
judgment seat. You will drive them like sheep
that have no shepherd, and not even a dog will
growl at you. This was told me, and announced
to me in advance, and I in turn have been sent
to tell you."

**20** Her words pleased Holofernes and all his
servants; they marveled at her wisdom and exclaimed,[w] **21** "No other woman from one end
of the world to the other looks so beautiful and
speaks so wisely!" **22** Then Holofernes said to
her: "God has done well in sending you ahead
of your people, to bring victory to our arms, and
destruction to those who have despised my lord.
**23** You are fair to behold, and your words are
well spoken. If you do as you have said, your
God will be my God; you shall dwell in the
palace of King Nebuchadnezzar, and shall be
renowned throughout the earth."[x]

## CHAPTER 12

**Judith's Conduct.** **1** Then he ordered
them to lead her into the room where his silverware was kept, and bade them set a table for her
with his own delicacies to eat and his own wine
to drink. **2** But Judith said, "I will not partake
of them, lest it be an occasion of sin; but I shall
be amply supplied from the things I brought
with me."[y] **3** Holofernes asked her: "But if
your provisions give out, where shall we get
more of the same to provide for you? None of
your people are with us." **4** Judith answered
him, "As surely as you, my lord, live, your
handmaid will not use up her supplies till the
LORD accomplishes by my hand what he has
determined."

**5** Then the servants of Holofernes led her
into the tent, where she slept till midnight. In the
night watch just before dawn, she rose **6** and
sent this message to Holofernes, "Give orders,
my lord, to let your handmaid go out for
prayer." **7** So Holofernes ordered his bodyguard not to hinder her. Thus she stayed in the
camp three days. Each night she went out to the
ravine of Bethulia, where she washed herself at
the spring of the camp. **8** After bathing, she
besought the LORD, the God of Israel, to direct
her way for the triumph of his people. **9** Then
she returned purified to the tent, and remained
there until her food was brought to her toward
evening.

**Holofernes' Banquet.** **10** On the fourth
day Holofernes gave a banquet for his servants

---

s 5f: Jdt 10, 13.
t Jer 27, 6; Bar 3, 16f; Dn 2, 38.
u 9f: Jdt 5, 5.
v Jdt 5, 21; 8, 18.
w Jdt 9, 13.
x Jdt 9, 13.
y Jdt 10, 5; Dn 1, 8.

---

12, 10: Banquet for his servants alone . . . officers: Holofernes invited the officials of his household, but not the officers

alone, to which he did not invite any of the
officers.* **11** And he said to Bagoas, the eunuch in charge of his household: "Go and persuade this Hebrew woman in your care to come
and to eat and drink with us. **12** It would be a
disgrace for us to have such a woman with us
without enjoying her company. If we do not
entice her, she will laugh us to scorn."

**13** So Bagoas left the presence of Holofernes, and came to Judith and said, "So fair a
maiden should not be reluctant to come to my
lord to be honored by him, to enjoy drinking
wine with us, and to be like one of the Assyrian
women who live in the palace of Nebuchadnezzar." **14** She replied, "Who am I to refuse my
lord? Whatever is pleasing to him I will promptly do. This will be a joy for me till the day of
my death."

**15** Thereupon she proceeded to put on her
festive garments and all her feminine adornments. Meanwhile her maid went ahead and
spread out on the ground for her in front of
Holofernes the fleece Bagoas had furnished for
her daily use in reclining at her dinner. **16** Then
Judith came in and reclined on it. The heart of
Holofernes was in rapture over her, and his
spirit was shaken. He was burning with the
desire to possess her, for he had been biding his
time to seduce her from the day he saw her.
**17** Holofernes said to her, "Drink and be merry
with us!" **18** Judith replied, "I will gladly
drink, my lord, for at no time since I was born
have I ever enjoyed life as much as I do today."
**19** She then took the things her maid had prepared, and ate and drank in his presence.
**20** Holofernes, charmed by her, drank a great
quantity of wine, more than he had ever drunk
on one single day in his life.

## CHAPTER 13

**1** When it grew late, his servants quickly
withdrew. Bagoas closed the tent from the outside and excluded the attendants from their master's presence. They went off to their beds, for
they were all tired from the prolonged banquet.
**2** Judith was left alone in the tent with Holofernes, who lay prostrate on his bed, for he was
sodden with wine. **3** She had ordered her maid
to stand outside the bedroom and wait, as on the
other days, for her to come out; she said she
would be going out for her prayer. To Bagoas
she had said this also.

**Beheading of Holofernes.** **4** When all
had departed, and no one, small or great, was
left in the bedroom, Judith stood by Holofernes'
bed and said within herself: "O LORD, God of
all might, in this hour look graciously on my
undertaking for the exaltation of Jerusalem;
**5** now is the time for aiding your heritage and
for carrying out my design to shatter the enemies who have risen against us." **6** She went to
the bedpost near the head of Holofernes, and
taking his sword from it, **7** drew close to the
bed, grasped the hair of his head, and said,
"Strengthen me this day, O God of Israel!"
**8** Then with all her might she struck him twice
in the neck and cut off his head.[z] **9** She rolled
his body off the bed and took the canopy from
its supports. Soon afterward, she came out and
handed over the head of Holofernes to her maid,
**10** who put it into her food pouch; and the two
went off together as they were accustomed to do
for prayer.

**The Return to Bethulia.** They passed
through the camp, and skirting the ravine,
reached Bethulia on the mountain. As they approached its gates, **11** Judith shouted to the
guards from a distance: "Open! Open the gate!
God, our God, is with us. Once more he has
made manifest his strength in Israel and his
power against our enemies; he has done it this
very day." **12** When the citizens heard her
voice, they quickly descended to their city gate
and summoned the city elders. **13** All the people, from the least to the greatest, hurriedly
assembled, for her return seemed unbelievable.
They opened the gate and welcomed the two
women. They made a fire for light; and when
they gathered around the two, **14** Judith urged
them with a loud voice: "Praise God, praise
him! Praise God, who has not withdrawn his
mercy from the house of Israel, but has shattered our enemies by my hand this very night."
**15** Then she took the head out of the pouch,
showed it to them, and said: "Here is the head
of Holofernes, general in charge of the Assyrian
army, and here is the canopy under which he lay
in his drunkenness. The LORD struck him down
by the hand of a woman.[a] **16** As the LORD
lives, who has protected me in the path I have
followed, I swear that it was my face that seduced Holofernes to his ruin, and that he did not
sin with me to my defilement or disgrace."

**17** All the people were greatly astonished.
They bowed down and worshiped God, saying
with one accord, "Blessed are you, our God,
who today have brought to nought the enemies
of your people." **18** Then Uzziah said to her:
"Blessed are you, daughter, by the Most High
God, above all the women on earth; and blessed
be the LORD God, the creator of heaven and
earth, who guided your blow at the head of the
chief of our enemies.[b] **19** Your deed of hope
will never be forgotten by those who tell of the
might of God. **20** May God make this redound
to your everlasting honor, rewarding you with

z Jgs 4, 21.
a Jdt 14, 18.
b Jgs 5, 24; Lk 1, 28. 42.

* of his army who were needed for military duty.

blessings, because you risked your life when
your people were being oppressed, and you
averted our disaster, walking uprightly before
our God." And all the people answered,
"Amen! Amen!"

## CHAPTER 14

**Judith's Counsel.** 1 Then Judith said to
them: "Listen to me, my brothers. Take this
head and hang it on the parapet of your wall.
2 At daybreak, when the sun rises on the earth,
let each of you seize his weapons, and let all the
able-bodied men rush out of the city under command of a captain, as if about to go down into
the plain against the advance guard of the Assyrians, but without going down. 3 They will seize
their armor and hurry to their camp to awaken
the generals of the Assyrian army. When they
run to the tent of Holofernes and do not find
him, panic will seize them, and they will flee
before you. 4 Then you and all the other inhabitants of the whole territory of Israel will pursue
them and strike them down in their tracks.
5 But before doing this, summon for me Achior
the Ammonite, that he may see and recognize
the one who despised the house of Israel and
sent him here to meet his death."

**Achior Summoned.*** 6 So they called
Achior from the house of Uzziah. When he
came and saw the head of Holofernes in the
hand of one of the men in the assembly of the
people, he fell forward in a faint. 7 Then, after
they lifted him up, he threw himself at the feet
of Judith in homage, saying: "Blessed are you
in every tent of Judah; and in every foreign
nation, all who hear of you will be struck with
terror. 8 But now, tell me all that you did during these days." So Judith told him, in the
presence of the people, all that she had been
doing from the day she left till the time she
began speaking to them. 9 When she finished
her account, the people cheered loudly, and
their city resounded with shouts of joy. 10 Now
Achior, seeing all that the God of Israel had
done, believed firmly in him. He had the flesh
of his foreskin circumcised, and he has been
united with the house of Israel to the present
day.

## *III: Victory*

**Consternation in the Camp.** 11 At daybreak they hung the head of Holofernes on the
wall. Then all the Israelite men took up their
arms and went to the slopes of the mountain.
12 When the Assyrians saw them, they notified
their captains; these, in turn, went to the generals and division leaders and all their other commanders. 13 They came to the tent of Holofernes and said to the one in charge of all his
things, "Waken our master, for the slaves have
dared come down to give us battle, to their utter
destruction." 14 Bagoas went in, and knocked
at the entry of the tent, presuming that he was
sleeping with Judith. 15 As no one answered,
he parted the curtains, entered the bedroom, and
found him lying on the floor, a headless corpse.
16 He broke into a loud clamor of weeping,
groaning, and howling, and rent his garments.
17 Then he entered the tent where Judith had
her quarters; and, not finding her, he rushed out
to the troops and cried: 18 "The slaves have
duped us! A single Hebrew woman has brought
disgrace on the house of King Nebuchadnezzar.
Here is Holofernes headless on the ground!"[c]
19 When the commanders of the Assyrian
army heard these words, they rent their tunics
and were seized with consternation. Loud
screaming and howling arose in the camp.

## CHAPTER 15

1 On hearing what had happened, those still
in their tents were amazed, 2 and overcome
with fear and trembling. No one kept ranks any
longer; they scattered in all directions, and fled
along every road, both through the valley and in
the mountains. 3 Those also who were stationed in the mountain district around Bethulia
took to flight. Then all the Israelite warriors
overwhelmed them.

**Pursuit.** 4 Uzziah sent messengers to Beto-
masthaim, to Choba and Kona, and to the whole
country of Israel to report what had happened,
that all might fall upon the enemy and destroy
them. 5 On hearing this, all the Israelites, with
one accord, attacked them and cut them down
as far as Choba. Even those from Jerusalem and
the rest of the mountain region took part in this,
for they too had been notified of the happenings
in the camp of their enemies. The Gileadites and
the Galileans struck the enemy's flanks with
great slaughter, even beyond Damascus and its
territory. 6 The remaining inhabitants of Bethulia swept down on the camp of the Assyrians,
plundered it, and acquired great riches. 7 The
Israelites who returned from the slaughter took
possession of what was left, till the towns and
villages in the mountains and on the plain were
crammed with the enormous quantity of booty
they had seized.[d]
8 The high priest Joakim and the elders of the
Israelites, who dwelt in Jerusalem, came to see

c Jdt 13, 15; 16, 5-9; Jgs 9, 54.
d Est 9, 5. 16.
e Est 9, 10.

* 14, 6–10: In recognizing the head of Holofernes, whom he had known personally, Achior was so overcome with the evidence of the Lord's power exerted through a woman that he believed in the God of Israel.

for themselves the good things that the LORD
had done for Israel, and to meet and congratulate Judith.[e] 9 When they had visited her, all
with one accord blessed her, saying:

"You are the glory of Jerusalem,
the surpassing joy of Israel;
You are the splendid boast of our
people.*
10 With your own hand you have done all this;
You have done good to Israel,
and God is pleased with what you have
wrought.
May you be blessed by the LORD Almighty
forever and ever!"

And all the people answered, "Amen!"
11 For thirty days the whole populace plundered the camp, giving Judith the tent of Holofernes, with all his silver, his couches, his
dishes, and all his furniture, which she accepted. She harnessed her mules, hitched her wagons to them, and loaded these things on them.
12 All the women of Israel gathered to see
her; and they blessed her and performed a dance
in her honor. She took branches in her hands and
distributed them to the women around her.[f]
13 and she and the other women crowned themselves with garlands of olive leaves. At the head
of all the people, she led the women in the
dance, while the men of Israel followed in their
armor, wearing garlands and singing hymns.

**Hymn of Praise.** 14 Judith led all Israel in
this song of thanksgiving, and the people
swelled this hymn of praise:

## CHAPTER 16

1 "Strike up the instruments,
a song to my God with timbrels,
chant to the LORD with cymbals;
Sing to him a new song,
exalt and acclaim his name.[g]
2 For the LORD is God; he crushes warfare,
and sets his encampment among his
people;
he snatched me from the hands of my
persecutors.[h]

3 "The Assyrian came from the mountains of
the north,
with the myriads of his forces he came;
Their numbers blocked the torrents, their
horses covered the hills.
4 He threatened to burn my land,
put my youths to the sword,
Dash my babes to the ground,
make my children a prey,
and seize my virgins as spoil.

5 "But the LORD Almighty thwarted them,
by a woman's hand he confounded them.[i]
6 Not by youths was their mighty one struck
down,
nor did titans bring him low,
nor huge giants attack him;
But Judith, the daughter of Merari,
by the beauty of her countenance disabled
him.[j]
7 She took off her widow's garb
to raise up the afflicted in Israel.
She anointed her face with fragrant oil;
8 with a fillet she fastened her tresses
and put on a linen robe to beguile him.
9 Her sandals caught his eyes,
and her beauty captivated his mind.
The sword cut through his neck.[k]

10 "The Persians were dismayed at her daring,
the Medes appalled at her boldness.
11 When my lowly ones shouted, they were
terrified;
when my weaklings cried out, they
trembled;
at the sound of their war cry, they took to
flight.
12 The sons of slave girls pierced them
through;
the supposed sons of rebel mothers cut
them down;
they perished before the ranks of my
LORD.

13 "A new hymn I will sing to my God.
O LORD, great are you and glorious,
wonderful in power and unsurpassable.[l]
14 Let your every creature serve you;
for you spoke, and they were made,
You sent forth your spirit, and they were
created;
no one can resist your word.[m]
15 The mountains to their bases, and the seas,
are shaken;
the rocks, like wax, melt before your
glance.[n]

"But to those who fear you,
you are very merciful.
16 Though the sweet odor of every sacrifice is
a trifle,
and the fat of all holocausts but little in
your sight,
one who fears the LORD is forever great.[o]

f Ex 15, 20f; Jgs 11, 34; 1 Sm 18, 6; Jer 31, 4. 13.
g Pss 81, 2f; 135, 1ff; 149, 1ff.
h Jdt 5, 23; 6, 2; 9. 7f; Ex 15, 3; Ps 46, 10.
i Jdt 14, 8.
j Jdt 9, 13.
k Jdt 9, 13.
l Ps 144, 9.
m Pss 33, 9; 104, 30; 148, 5.
n Jgs 5, 5; Ps 97, 5.
o Ps 86, 11; Sir 34, 13-17.

* 15, 9: You are the glory of Jerusalem, the surpassing joy of Israel; you are the splendid boast of our people: these words are used in the liturgy of the Church in regard to the Blessed Virgin Mary.

17 "Woe to the nations that rise against my
people!
the LORD Almighty will requite them;
in the day of judgment he will punish
them:
He will send fire and worms into their
flesh,*
and they shall burn and suffer forever."[p]

**Thanksgiving.** 18 The people then went to
Jerusalem to worship God; when they were purified, they offered their holocausts, free-will
offerings, and gifts. 19 Judith dedicated, as a
votive offering to God, all the things of Holofernes that the people had given her, as well as
the canopy that she herself had taken from his
bedroom.[q] 20 For three months the people continued their celebration in Jerusalem before the
sanctuary, and Judith remained with them.

**Judith's Renown.** 21 When those days
were over, each one returned to his inheritance.
Judith went back to Bethulia and remained on
her estate. For the rest of her life she was renowned throughout the land. 22 Many wished
to marry her, but she gave herself to no man all
the days of her life from the time of the death
and burial of her husband, Manasseh. 23 She
lived to be very old in the house of her husband,
reaching the advanced age of a hundred and
five. She died in Bethulia, where they buried
her in the tomb of her husband, Manasseh;[r]
24 and the house of Israel mourned her for sev-
en days. Before she died, she distributed her
goods to the relatives of her husband, Manasseh, and to her own relatives; and to the maid
she gave her freedom.

25 [s]During the life of Judith and for a long
time after her death, no one again disturbed the
Israelites.*

---

p Is 66, 24.
q Nm 31, 48-54; Dt 13, 13-18; Jos 6, 18f.
r Gn 23, 19; 49, 29-32.
s Jgs 3, 11. 30; 5, 31; 8, 28.

---

16, 17: Fire and worms into their flesh: see footnote on Is 66, 24.

16, 25: The Vulgate adds: "The feast day of this victory was adopted by the Hebrews into the calendar of their holy days, and has been celebrated by the Jews from that time to the present." However, there is no other evidence of such a festivity; and it is the ancient feast of Passover to which the narrative is especially suited.

# The Book of
# ESTHER

*The Book of Esther is named after its Jewish heroine. It tells the story of the plot of Haman the Agagite, jealous and powerful vizier of King Xerxes (Ahasuerus) of Persia (485–464 B.C.), to destroy in a single day all the Jews living in the Persian Empire. He is moved to this out of hatred for the Jewish servant Mordecai, who for religious motives refuses to render him homage. The day of the proposed massacre is determined by lot. Meanwhile Esther, niece and adopted daughter of Mordecai, is chosen queen by King Xerxes in place of Vashti. She averts the pogrom planned against her people and has the royal decree of extermination reversed against Haman and the enemies of the Jews. Mordecai replaces Haman, and together with Esther, works for the welfare of their people. The event is celebrated with feasting and great joy, and the memory of it is to be perpetuated by the annual observance of the feast of Purim (lots), when the lot of destruction for the Jews was reversed for one of deliverance and triumph by Queen Esther and her uncle Mordecai.*

*The purpose of the book is didactic: the glorification of the Jewish people and the explanation of the origin, significance and date of the feast of Purim on the fourteenth and fifteenth of Adar (February–March). The book was intended as a consolation for Israel, a reminder that God's providence continually watches over them, never abandoning them when they serve him faithfully or turn to him in sincere repentance. There is no justification for interpreting the story in mythological or cultic terms, as though Mordecai and Esther represented Marduk and Ishtar in their mythological triumph over two Elamite deities.*

*The Hebrew text of Esther is found in the Hebrew Bible, where it is the last of the five* megilloth *(scrolls) read on special feasts of the Jewish liturgical year.*

*The book is a free composition—not a historical document, despite the Achaemenian coloring of the narrative. Its time of composition may well have been at the end of the Persian Empire, toward the close of the fourth century B.C. The author shows skill in developing his story and in using the art of contrast for instruction and edification. The solution to the difficulties of the book is to be found in its literary presentation rather than in a forced attempt to square detailed data of the narrative with facts. The evident literary motif of the reversal of fortune of the prosperous wicked and the oppressed virtuous through eventual punishment of the former and triumph of the latter finds parallels in the story of Joseph (Gn 37; 39—45) and of Judith (8—16). The book is vindictive, but it should be remembered that the precept of love of enemies had not yet been taught by the word and example of Christ.*

*The text of Esther, written originally in Hebrew, was transmitted in two forms: a short Hebrew form and a longer Greek version. The latter contains 107 additional verses, inserted at appropriate places within the Hebrew form of the text. A few of these seem to have a Hebrew origin while the rest are Greek in original composition. It is possible that the Hebrew form of the text is original throughout. If it systematically omits reference to God and his Providence over Israel, this is perhaps due to fear of irreverent response (see note on 4, 14). The Greek text with the above-mentioned additions is probably a later literary paraphrase in which the author seeks to have the reader share his sentiments. This standard Greek text is pre-Christian in origin. The church has accepted the additions as equally inspired with the rest of the book.*

*In the present translation, the portions preceded by the letters A through F indicate the underlying Greek additions referred to above. The regular chapter numbers apply to the Hebrew text.*

*The book may be divided as follows:*

*I. Prologue (A, 1–17).*
*II. Elevation of Esther (1, 1—2, 23).*

*III. Haman's Plot against the Jews (3, 1–13; B, 1–7; 3, 14—4, 8; B, 8; 4, 9–16; C, 1—D, 16; 5, 1–14).*
*IV. Vindication of the Jews (6, 1—8, 12; E, 1–24; 8, 13—10, 3).*
*V. Epilogue (F, 1–11).*

*The order of the Vulgate text in relation to the order of the Greek text is as follows:*

*Vulg. 11, 2—12, 6 = A, 1–17 at the beginning of the book.*
*13, 1–7 = B, 1—7 after 3, 13.*
*13, 8—15, 3–19 = C, 1—D, 16 after 4, 16.*
*15, 1–2 = B, 8.9 after 4, 8.*
*16, 1–24 = E 1–24 after 8, 12.*
*10, 4—10, 13 = F 1–10 after 10, 3.*

## I: Prologue

### CHAPTER A

**Dream of Mordecai.** **1** In the second year
of the reign of the great King Ahasuerus,* on
the first day of Nisan, Mordecai, son of Jair, son
of Shimei, son of Kish, of the tribe of Benjamin,
had a dream.[a] **2** He was a Jew residing in the
city of Susa, a prominent man who served at the
king's court, **3** and one of the captives whom
Nebuchadnezzar, king of Babylon, had taken
from Jerusalem with Jeconiah, king of Judah.[b]
**4** [c]This was his dream.* There was noise and
tumult, thunder and earthquake—confusion
upon the earth. **5** Two great dragons came on,
both poised for combat. They uttered a mighty
cry, **6** and at their cry every nation prepared for
war, to fight against the race of the just. **7** It was
a dark and gloomy day. Tribulation and distress, evil and great confusion, lay upon the
earth. **8** The whole race of the just were dismayed with fear of the evils to come upon them,
and were at the point of destruction. **9** [d]Then
they cried out to God, and as they cried, there
appeared to come forth a great river, a flood of
water from a little spring. **10** The light of the
sun broke forth; the lowly were exalted and they
devoured the nobles.
**11** Having seen this dream and what God
intended to do, Mordecai awoke. He kept it in
mind, and tried in every way, until night, to
understand its meaning.

**The Plot Discovered.** **12** [e]Mordecai
lodged at the court with Bagathan and Thares,
two eunuchs of the king who were court guards.
**13** He overheard them plotting, investigated
their plans, and discovered that they were preparing to lay hands on King Ahasuerus. So he
informed the king about them, **14** and the king
had the two eunuchs questioned and, upon their
confession, put to death. **15** Then the king had
these things recorded; Mordecai, too, put them
into writing. **16** The king also appointed Mordecai to serve at the court, and rewarded him*
for his actions.[f]
**17** Haman, however, son of Hammedatha
the Agagite,* who was in high honor with the
king, sought to harm Mordecai and his people
because of the two eunuchs of the king.[g]

## II: Elevation of Esther

### CHAPTER 1

**The Banquet of Ahasuerus.** **1** During
the reign of Ahasuerus—this was the Ahasuerus
who ruled over a hundred and twenty-seven
provinces from India to Ethiopia *—**2** while he

a Est 2, 5.
b Est 2, 6; 2 Kgs 24, 15; 2 Chr 36, 9f; Jer 22, 24ff; 24, 1; 29, 1f.
c 4ff: Est F, 2. 4ff.
d gf: Est F, 3.
e 12-15: Est 2, 21ff; 6, 1ff.
f Est 6, 3.
g Est 3, 1-15; B, 1-7; E, 13.

*

A, 1: King Ahasuerus: Xerxes I (485–464 B.C.). Mordecai: a Babylonian name, after the God Marduk. The genealogy of Mordecai is designed to reflect opposition to Israel's enemy, as narrated in 1 Sm 15, 7ff, where Saul (whose father's name was Kish, of the Tribe of Benjamin) conquered Agag the Amalekite; in A, 17 Haman is said to be the son of an Agagite. Further emphasis on the Benjaminite-Agagite opposition can be seen in Shimei, the Benjaminite who reviled David (2 Sm 16, 5ff). Jair appears to be the minor Judge, a Transjordan Manassehite (Jgs 10, 3). The chronology of the book would make Mordecai well over one hundred years old, since he was deported with Jehoiachin about 598 B.C., cf Est 2, 5f.

A, 4: The interpretation of this dream is given in Est F, 1–6.

A, 16: Rewarded him: this reward comes only later; see the sequence of events from the Hebrew text of Esther at 2, 22f, and 6, 3, below.

A, 17: Haman . . . the Agagite: opposed Mordecai the Benjaminite, by whom, however, he was overcome (Est 9, 9f), just as King Agag the Amalekite, was conquered by King Saul ancestor of Mordecai (1 Sm 15, 7ff).

1, 1: From India to Ethiopia: from western India to Upper Egypt, the greatest extent of the Persian Empire achieved under Darius the Great, father of Ahasuerus.

1, 2: Susa: ancient capital of Elam (Gn 14, 1); under the Achamenid kings, one of the two capitals of the Persian Empire. The other was Persepolis, the summer palace of the kings.

was occupying the royal throne in the stronghold of Susa,* **3** in the third year of his reign,
he presided over a feast for all his officers and
ministers: the Persian and Median aristocracy,
the nobles, and the governors of the provinces.[h]
**4** For as many as a hundred and eighty days, he
displayed the glorious riches of his kingdom and
the resplendent wealth of his royal estate.

**5** At the end of this time the king gave a feast
of seven days in the garden court of the royal
palace for all the people, great and small, who
were in the stronghold of Susa. **6** There were
white cotton draperies and violet hangings, held
by cords of crimson byssus from silver rings on
marble pillars. Gold and silver couches were on
the pavement, which was of porphyry, marble,
mother-of-pearl, and colored stones. **7** Liquor
was served in a variety of golden cups, and the
royal wine flowed freely, as befitted the king's
munificence. **8** By ordinance of the king the
drinking was unstinted, for he had instructed all
the stewards of his household to comply with
the good pleasure of everyone.

**9** Queen Vashti* also gave a feast for the
women inside the royal palace of King Ahasuerus.

**Deposal of Vashti.** **10** On the seventh day,
when the king was merry with wine, he instructed Mehuman, Biztha, Harbona, Bigtha, Abag-
tha, Zethar, and Carkas, the seven eunuchs who
attended King Ahasuerus,[i] **11** to bring Queen
Vashti into his presence wearing the royal
crown, that he might display her beauty to the
populace and the officials, for she was lovely to
behold. **12** But Queen Vashti refused to come
at the royal order issued through the eunuchs. At
this the king's wrath flared up, and he burned
with fury. **13** He conferred with the wise men
versed in the law, because the king's business
was conducted in general consultation with law-
yers and jurists. **14** He summoned Carshena,
Shethar, Admatha, Tarshish, Meres, Marsena
and Memucan, the seven Persian and Median
officials who were in the king's personal service
and held first rank in the realm,[j] **15** and asked
them, "What is to be done by law with Queen
Vashti for disobeying the order of King Ahasuerus issued through the eunuchs?"

**16** In the presence of the king and of the
officials, Memucan answered: "Queen Vashti
has not wronged the king alone, but all the
officials and the populace throughout the provinces of King Ahasuerus. **17** For the queen's
conduct will become known to all the women,
and they will look with disdain upon their husbands when it is reported, 'King Ahasuerus
commanded that Queen Vashti be ushered into
his presence, but she would not come.' **18** This
very day the Persian and Median ladies who
hear of the queen's conduct will rebel against all
the royal officials, with corresponding disdain
and rancor. **19** If it please the king, let an irrevocable royal decree* be issued by him and
inscribed among the laws of the Persians and
Medes, forbidding Vashti to come into the presence of King Ahasuerus and authorizing the
king to give her royal dignity to one more worthy than she.[k] **20** Thus, when the decree which
the king will issue is published throughout his
realm, vast as it is, all wives will honor their
husbands, from the greatest to the least."

**21** This proposal found acceptance with the
king and the officials, and the king acted on the
advice of Memucan. **22** He sent letters to all the
royal provinces, to each province in its own
script and to each people in its own language,*
to the effect that every man should be lord in his
own home.

## CHAPTER 2

**Esther Made Queen.** **1** After this, when
King Ahasuerus' wrath had cooled, he thought
over what Vashti had done and what had been
decreed against her. **2** Then the king's personal
attendants suggested: "Let beautiful young virgins be sought for the king. **3** Let the king
appoint commissaries in all the provinces of his
realm to bring together all beautiful young virgins to the harem in the stronghold of Susa.
Under the care of the royal eunuch Hegai, custodian of the women, let cosmetics be given
them. **4** Then the girl who pleases the king shall
reign in place of Vashti." This suggestion
pleased the king, and he acted accordingly.

**5** There was in the stronghold of Susa a certain Jew named Mordecai, son of Jair, son of
Shimei, son of Kish, a Benjaminite, **6** who had
been exiled from Jerusalem with the captives
taken with Jeconiah, king of Judah, whom Nebuchadnezzar, king of Babylon, had deported.[l]
**7** He was foster father to Hadassah,* that is,
Esther, his cousin; for she had lost both father

h Jdt 1, 16.
i Dn 5, 1.
j Ezr 7, 14.
k Est 8, 5. 8; Dn 6, 8f.
l Est A, 3; 2 Kgs 24, 15; 2 Chr 36, 9f; Jer 22, 24ff; 24, 1; 29, 1f.
m Est 2, 15.

*

1, 9: Queen Vashti: Herodotus (Histories 7, 61) relates that the wife of Ahasuerus was Amestris.

1, 19: Irrevocable royal decree: the historian Siculus indicates that such a concept of irrevocable laws existed in the time of Darius III (335–331 B.C.), the last of the Persian kings, cf Est 8, 8.

1, 22: To each province . . . script and to each people . . . language: many languages were spoken in the Persian Empire, the principal ones being Persian, Elamite, Babylonian, Aramaic, Phoenician, Egyptian, and Greek. Each of them had its own script.

2, 7: Hadassah (the feminine form of hadas, myrtle), was the name by which this woman would be known among her Jewish compatriots. Esther is a variant of the name of the Babylonian goddess Ishtar.

and mother. The girl was beautifully formed
and lovely to behold. On the death of her father
and mother, Mordecai had taken her as his own
daughter.[m]
**8** When the king's order and decree had been
obeyed and many maidens brought together to
the stronghold of Susa under the care of Hegai,
Esther also was brought in to the royal palace
under the care of Hegai, custodian of the wom-
en. **9** The girl pleased him and won his favor.
So he promptly furnished her with cosmetics
and provisions. Then picking out seven maids
for her from the royal palace, he transferred
both her and her maids to the best place in the
harem. **10** Esther did not reveal her nationality
or family, for Mordecai had commanded her not
to do so.
**11** Day by day Mordecai would walk about
in front of the court of the harem, to learn how
Esther was faring and what was to become of
her.
**12** Each girl went in turn to visit King
Ahasuerus after the twelve months' preparation
decreed for the women. Of this period of beautifying treatment, six months were spent with oil
of myrrh, and the other six months with perfumes and cosmetics. **13** Then, when the girl
was to visit the king, she was allowed to take
with her from the harem to the royal palace
whatever she chose. **14** She would go in the
evening and return in the morning to a second
harem under the care of the royal eunuch Sha-
ashgaz, custodian of the concubines. She could
not return to the king unless he was pleased with
her and had her summoned by name.[n]
**15** As for Esther, daughter of Abihail and
adopted daughter of his nephew Mordecai,
when her turn came to visit the king, she did not
ask for anything but what the royal eunuch Hegai, custodian of the women, suggested. Yet she
won the admiration of all who saw her. **16** Esther was led to King Ahasuerus in his palace in
the tenth month, Tebeth, in the seventh year of
his reign. **17** The king loved Esther more than
all other women, and of all the virgins she won
his favor and benevolence. So he placed the
royal diadem on her head and made her queen
in place of Vashti. **18** Then the king gave a
great feast in honor of Esther to all his officials
and ministers, granting a holiday* to the provinces and bestowing gifts with royal bounty.

**The Plot Discovered.*** **19** [o][To resume:
From the time the virgins had been brought
together, and while Mordecai was passing his
time at the king's gate, **20** Esther had not revealed her family or nationality, because Mordecai had told her not to; and Esther continued
to follow Mordecai's instructions, just as she
had when she was being brought up by him.
**21** [p]And during the time that Mordecai spent at
the king's gate,* Bagathan and Thares, two of
the royal eunuchs who guarded the entrance,
had plotted in anger to lay hands on King
Ahasuerus. **22** When the plot became known to
Mordecai, he told Queen Esther, who in turn
informed the king for Mordecai. **23** The matter
was investigated and verified, and both of them
were hanged on a gibbet.* This was written in
the annals for the king's use.]

## *III: Haman's Plot Against the Jews*

## CHAPTER 3

### Mordecai Refuses to Honor Haman.

**1** After these events King Ahasuerus raised Haman, son of Hammedatha the Agagite, to high
rank, seating him above all his fellow officials.[q]
**2** All the king's servants who were at the royal
gate would kneel and bow down to Haman, for
that is what the king had ordered in his regard.[r]
Mordecai, however, would not kneel and bow
down.* **3** The king's servants who were at the
royal gate said to Mordecai, "Why do you disobey the king's order?"[s] **4** When they had reminded him day after day and he would not
listen to them, they informed Haman, to see
whether Mordecai's explanation was acceptable, since he had told them that he was a Jew.

**Haman's Reprisal.** **5** When Haman observed that Mordecai would not kneel and bow
down to him, he was filled with anger. **6** Moreover, he thought it was not enough to lay hands
on Mordecai alone. Since they had told Haman
of Mordecai's nationality, he sought to destroy
all the Jews, Mordecai's people, throughout the
realm of King Ahasuerus. **7** In the first month,
Nisan, in the twelfth year of King Ahasuerus,
the ***pur,**** or lot, was cast in Haman's presence,
to determine the day and the month for the
destruction of Mordecai's people on a single

n Est 2, 19f; 4, 11. 16.
o 19f: Est 2, 14.
p 21ff: Est A, 12-15; 6, 1ff.
q Est B, 3; 5, 11; E, 11.
r Est C, 5; 5, 9. 13; 6, 10. 12.
s Est 4, 16.
t Est 9, 24ff; F, 10.

*

2, 18: A holiday: or perhaps, "a remission of taxes."

2, 19–23: This is a resumption, in a slightly different form, of the story already told in Est A, 12–15.

2, 21: Mordecai . . . at the king's gate: to exercise watchful care for Esther. Some understand this to mean that Mordecai was stationed at the gate to render royal service; cf Est A, 2.

2, 23: Hanged on a gibbet: impaled, perhaps, after the Babylonian manner.

3, 2: Mordecai . . . would not kneel and bow down: in order not to render to man, the homage which he regarded as belonging to God alone; cf Est C, 5ff.

3, 7: Pur: a Babylonian word which the Hebrew translates as goral, "lot." This word is preserved in the text because its plural, purim, became the name of the feast of Purim commemorating the deliverance of the Jews; cf Est 9, 24. 26.

day, and the lot fell on the thirteenth day of the
twelfth month, Adar.[t]

**Decree against the Jews.** 8 Then Haman
said to King Ahasuerus: "Dispersed among the
nations throughout the provinces of your kingdom, there is a certain people living apart, with
laws differing from those of every other people.
They do not obey the laws of the king, and so
it is not proper for the king to tolerate them.[u]
9 If it please the king, let a decree be issued to
destroy them; and I will deliver to the procurators ten thousand silver talents for deposit in the
royal treasury."[v] 10 The king took the signet
ring* from his hand and gave it to Haman, son
of Hammedatha the Agagite, the enemy of the
Jews.[w] 11 "The silver you may keep," the
king said to Haman, "but as for this people, do
with them whatever you please."
12 So the royal scribes were summoned; and
on the thirteenth day of the first month they
wrote, at the dictation of Haman, an order to the
royal satraps, the governors of every province,
and the officials of every people, to each province in its own script and to each people in its
own language. It was written in the name of
King Ahasuerus and sealed with the royal signet
ring. 13 Letters were sent by couriers to all the
royal provinces, that all the Jews, young and
old, including women and children, should be
killed, destroyed, wiped out in one day, the
thirteenth day of the twelfth month, Adar, and
that their goods should be seized as spoil.[x]

## CHAPTER B

1 This is a copy of the letter:
"The great King Ahasuerus writes to the satraps of the hundred and twenty-seven provinces
from India to Ethiopia, and the governors subordinate to them, as follows: 2 When I came to
rule many peoples and to hold sway over the
whole world, I determined not to be carried
away with the sense of power, but always to
deal fairly and with clemency; to provide for my
subjects a life of complete tranquillity; and by
making my government humane and effective
as far as the borders, to restore the peace desired
by all men.[y] 3 When I consulted my counselors
as to how this might be accomplished, Haman,
who excels among us in wisdom, who is outstanding for constant devotion and steadfast loyalty, and who has gained the second rank in the
kingdom,[z] 4 brought it to our attention that,
mixed in with all the races throughout the
world, there is one people of bad will, which by
its laws is opposed to every other people and
continually disregards the decrees of kings, so
that the unity of empire blamelessly designed by
us cannot be established.[a]
5 "Having noted, therefore, that this most
singular people is continually at variance with
all men, lives by divergent and alien laws, is
inimical to our interests, and commits the worst
crimes, so that stability of government cannot
be obtained, 6 we hereby decree that all those
who are indicated to you in the letters of Haman,
who is in charge of the administration and is a
second father to us, shall, together with their
wives and children, be utterly destroyed by the
swords of their enemies, without any pity or
mercy, on the fourteenth day* of the twelfth
month, Adar, of the current year;[b] 7 so that
when these people, whose present ill will is of
long standing, have gone down into the nether
world by a violent death on one same day, they
may at last leave our affairs stable and undisturbed for the future."

## CHAPTER 3

14 A copy of the decree to be promulgated as
law in every province was published to all the
peoples, that they might be prepared for that
day. 15 The couriers set out in haste at the
king's command; meanwhile, the decree was
promulgated in the stronghold of Susa. The king
and Haman then sat down to feast, but the city
of Susa was thrown into confusion.

## CHAPTER 4

**Esther's Aid Sought by Mordecai.**
1 When Mordecai learned all that was happening, he tore his garments, put on sackcloth
and ashes, and walked through the city, crying
out loudly and bitterly,[c] 2 till he came before
the royal gate, which no one clothed in sackcloth might enter. 3 (Likewise in each of the
provinces, wherever the king's legal enactment
reached, the Jews went into deep mourning,
with fasting, weeping, and lament; they all slept
on sackcloth and ashes.)
4 Queen Esther's maids and eunuchs came
and told her. Overwhelmed with anguish, she
sent garments for Mordecai to put on, so that he
might take off his sackcloth; but he refused.
5 Esther then summoned Hathach, one of the
king's eunuchs whom he had placed at her service, and commanded him to find out what this

u Est 3, 13; B, 4; E, 24; Dn 3, 8-12; Wis 2, 14f.
v Est 7, 4.
w Gn 41, 42.
x Est B, 6; 7, 4.
y Est E, 8f.
z Est 3, 1; 5, 11; E, 11.
a Est 3, 8; E, 24.
b Est 3, 13; 7, 4; E, 11ff.
c Jdt 4, 12.

3, 10: Signet ring: a ring containing a seal which was impressed on documents to authenticate them. By giving this ring to Haman, the king bestowed on him the power to authenticate royal decrees.

B, 6: Fourteenth day: the Hebrew text, as in Est 2, 13 above, and the Greek text here translated do not agree on the day of the month specified by the king; in fact, a two-day celebration is decreed in chapter 9, and the 13th, 14th and 15th of Adar are all mentioned; see Est 9, 15. 18.

action of Mordecai meant and the reason for it. **6** So Hathach went out to Mordecai in the public square in front of the royal gate, **7** and Mordecai told him all that had happened, as well as the exact amount of silver Haman had promised to pay to the royal treasury for the slaughter of the Jews. **8** He also gave him a copy of the written decree for their destruction which had been promulgated in Susa, to show and explain to Esther. He was to instruct her to go to the king; she was to plead and intercede with him in behalf of her people. **B, 8** "Remember the days of your lowly estate," Mordecai had him say, "when you were brought up in my charge; for Haman, who is second to the king, has asked for our death. **B, 9** Invoke the LORD and speak to the king for us; save us from death."

**9** Hathach returned to Esther and told her what Mordecai had said. **10** Then Esther replied to Hathach and gave him this message for Mordecai: **11** "All the servants of the king and the people of his provinces know that any man or woman who goes to the king in the inner court without being summoned, suffers the automatic penalty of death, unless the king extends to him the golden scepter, thus sparing his life. Now as for me, I have not been summoned to the king for thirty days."[d]

**12** When Esther's words were reported to Mordecai, **13** he had this reply brought to her: "Do not imagine that because you are in the king's palace, you alone of all the Jews will escape. **14** Even if you now remain silent, relief and deliverance will come to the Jews from another source;* but you and your father's house will perish. Who knows but that it was for a time like this that you obtained the royal dignity?"

**15** Esther sent back to Mordecai the response: **16** "Go and assemble all the Jews who are in Susa; fast on my behalf, all of you, not eating or drinking, night or day, for three days. I and my maids will also fast in the same way. Thus prepared, I will go to the king, contrary to the law. If I perish, I perish!"[e]

## CHAPTER C

**Prayer of Mordecai.** Mordecai went away and did exactly as Esther had commanded. **1** Recalling all that the LORD had done, he prayed to him **2** and said: "O Lord God, almighty King, all things are in your power, and there is no one to oppose you in your will to save Israel. **3** You made heaven and earth and every wonderful thing under the heavens. **4** You are LORD of all, and there is no one who can resist you, LORD. **5** [f]You know all things. You know, O LORD, that it was not out of insolence or pride or desire for fame that I acted thus in not bowing down to the proud Haman. **6** Gladly would I have kissed the soles of his feet for the salvation of Israel. **7** But I acted as I did so as not to place the honor of man above that of God. I will not bow down to anyone but you, my LORD. It is not out of pride that I am acting thus. **8** And now, LORD God, King, God of Abraham, spare your people, for our enemies plan our ruin and are bent upon destroying the inheritance that was yours from the beginning. **9** Do not spurn your portion, which you redeemed for yourself out of Egypt. **10** Hear my prayer; have pity on your inheritance and turn our sorrow into joy: thus we shall live to sing praise to your name, O LORD. Do not silence those who praise you."

**11** All Israel, too, cried out with all their strength, for death was staring them in the face.

**Prayer of Esther.** **12** [g]Queen Esther, seized with mortal anguish, likewise had recourse to the LORD. **13** Taking off her splendid garments, she put on garments of distress and mourning. In place of her precious ointments she covered her head with dirt and ashes. She afflicted her body severely; all her festive adornments were put aside, and her hair was wholly disheveled.

**14** Then she prayed to the LORD, the God of Israel, saying: "My LORD, our King, you alone are God. Help me, who am alone and have no help but you, **15** for I am taking my life in my hand.[h] **16** As a child I was wont to hear from the people of the land of my fore-fathers that you, O LORD, chose Israel from among all peoples, and our fathers from among all their ancestors, as a lasting heritage, and that you fulfilled all your promises to them.[i] **17** But now we have sinned in your sight, and you have delivered us into the hands of our enemies, **18** because we worshiped their gods. You are just, O LORD. **19** But now they are not satisfied with our bitter servitude, but have undertaken **20** to do away with the decree you have pronounced, and to destroy your heritage; to close the mouths of those who praise you, and to extinguish the glory of your temple and your altar; **21** to open the mouths of the heathen to acclaim their false gods, and to extol an earthly king forever.

**22** "O LORD, do not relinquish your scepter to those that are nought. Let them not gloat over our ruin, but turn their own counsel against them and make an example of our chief enemy. **23** Be mindful of us, O LORD. Manifest yourself in the time of our distress and give me courage, King of gods and Ruler of every pow-

d Est 2, 14; 4, 12; D, 12.
e Est C, 12f.
f 5ff: Est 3, 2; 5, 9.
g 12f: Est 4, 16.
h Est 4, 16.
i Dt 4, 20; 7, 6; 9, 29; 14, 2; 26, 18; 32, 9.

* 4, 14: From another source: very probably Mordecai refers to divine aid; the Greek additions (C) are explicit about this.

er. **24** Put in my mouth persuasive words in the
presence of the lion and turn his heart to hatred
for our enemy, so that he and those who are in
league with him may perish. **25** Save us by
your power, and help me, who am alone and
have no one but you, O LORD.

"You know all things. **26** You know that I
hate the glory of the pagans, and abhor the bed
of the uncircumcised or of any foreigner.
**27** You know that I am under constraint, that I
abhor the sign of grandeur which rests on my
head when I appear in public; abhor it like a
polluted rag, and do not wear it in private. **28** I,
your handmaid, have never eaten at the table of
Haman, nor have I graced the banquet of the
king or drunk the wine of libations.* **29** From
the day I was brought here till now, your handmaid has had no joy except in you, O LORD,
God of Abraham. **30** O God, more powerful
than all, hear the voice of those in despair. Save
us from the power of the wicked, and deliver me
from my fear."

## CHAPTER D

**Esther Is Received by the King.** **1** On
the third day, putting an end to her prayers, she
took off her penitential garments and arrayed
herself in her royal attire. **2** In making her state
appearance, after invoking the all-seeing God
and savior, she took with her two maids; **3** on
the one she leaned gently for support, **4** while
the other followed her, bearing her train. **5** She
glowed with the perfection of her beauty and her
countenance was as joyous as it was lovely,
though her heart was shrunk with fear. **6** She
passed through all the portals till she stood face
to face with the king, who was seated on his
royal throne, clothed in full robes of state, and
covered with gold and precious stones, so that
he inspired great awe. **7** As he looked up, his
features ablaze with the height of majestic anger, the queen staggered, changed color, and
leaned weakly against the head of the maid in
front of her. **8** But God changed the king's
anger to gentleness. In great anxiety he sprang
from his throne, held her in his arms until she
recovered, and comforted her with reassuring
words. **9** "What is it, Esther?" he said to her.
"I am your brother. Take courage! **10** You
shall not die because of this general decree of
ours. **11** Come near!" **12** Raising the golden
scepter, he touched her neck with it, embraced
her, and said, "Speak to me."[j]

**13** She replied: "I saw you, my lord, as an
angel of God, and my heart was troubled with
fear of your majesty. **14** For you are awesome,
my lord, though your glance is full of kindness." **15** As she said this, she fainted. **16** The
king became troubled and all his attendants tried
to revive her.

## CHAPTER 5

**1** *[Now on the third day, Esther put on her
royal garments and stood in the inner courtyard,
looking toward the royal palace, while the king
was seated on his royal throne in the audience
chamber, facing the palace doorway. **2** He saw
Queen Esther standing in the courtyard, and
made her welcome by extending toward her the
golden staff which he held. She came up to him,
and touched the top of the staff.]

**3** Then the king said to her, "What is it,
Queen Esther? What is your request? Even if it
is half of my kingdom, it shall be granted
you."[k] **4** "If it please your majesty," Esther
replied, "come today with Haman to a banquet
I have prepared." **5** And the king ordered,
"Have Haman make haste to fulfill the wish of
Esther."

**First Banquet of Esther.** So the king went
with Haman to the banquet Esther had prepared.
**6** During the drinking of the wine, the king said
to Esther, "Whatever you ask for shall be granted, and whatever request you make shall be
honored, even if it is for half my kingdom."[l]
**7** Esther replied: "This is my petition and request: **8** if I have found favor with the king and
if it pleases your majesty to grant my petition
and honor my request, come with Haman tomorrow to a banquet which I shall prepare for
you; and then I will do as you ask."

**Haman's Plot against Mordecai.** **9** That
day Haman left happy and in good spirits. But
when he saw that Mordecai at the royal gate did
not rise, and showed no fear of him, he was
filled with anger toward him.[m] **10** Haman restrained himself, however, and went home,
where he summoned his friends and his wife
Zeresh. **11** He recounted the greatness of his
riches, the large number of his sons, and just
how the king had promoted him and placed him
above the officials and royal servants.[n]
**12** "Moreover," Haman added, "Queen Esther invited no one but me to the banquet with
the king; again tomorrow I am to be her guest,
with the king. **13** Yet none of this satisfies me
as long as I continue to see the Jew Mordecai
sitting at the royal gate."[o] **14** His wife Zeresh
and all his friends said to him, "Have a gibbet
set up, fifty cubits in height, and in the morning
ask the king to have Mordecai hanged on it.
Then go to the banquet with the king in good

j Est 4, 11.
k Est 5, 6; 7, 2; 9, 12.
l Est 5, 3.
m Est 3, 2f; C, 5ff; 6, 10. 12.
n Est 3, 1; B, 3; E, 11; 9, 6-10.
o Est 3, 2f; 6, 10, 12.
p Est 6, 4; 7, 9f.

* C, 28: Wine of libations: offered in sacrifice to the gods.
5, 1f: The Hebrew text here translated is a short form of the account already given in Greek.

cheer." This suggestion pleased Haman, and he
had the gibbet erected.[p]

## *IV: Vindication of the Jews*

## CHAPTER 6

**Mordecai's Reward from the King.**
**1** That night the king, unable to sleep, asked
that the chronicle of notable events be brought
in. While this was being read to him, **2** the
passage occurred in which Mordecai reported
Bagathan and Teresh, two of the royal eunuchs
who guarded the entrance, for seeking to lay
hands on King Ahasuerus.[q] **3** The king asked,
"What was done to reward and honor Mordecai
for this?" The king's attendants replied, "Nothing was done for him."[r]
**4** "Who is in the court?" the king asked.
Now Haman had entered the outer court of the
king's palace to suggest to the king that Mordecai should be hanged on the gibbet he had raised
for him.[s] **5** The king's servants answered him,
"Haman is waiting in the court." "Let him
come in," the king said. **6** When Haman entered, the king said to him, "What should be
done for the man whom the king wishes to
reward?" Now Haman thought to himself,
"Whom would the king more probably wish to
reward than me?" **7** So he replied to the king:
"For the man whom the king wishes to reward
**8** there should be brought the royal robe which
the king wore and the horse on which the king
rode when the royal crown was placed on his
head. **9** The robe and the horse should be consigned to one of the noblest of the king's officials, who must clothe the man the king wishes
to reward, have him ride on the horse in the
public square of the city, and cry out before
him, 'This is what is done for the man whom the
king wishes to reward.' "[t] **10** Then the king
said to Haman: "Hurry! Take the robe and horse
as you have proposed, and do this for the Jew
Mordecai, who is sitting at the royal gate. Do
not omit anything you proposed."[u] **11** So Haman took the robe and horse, clothed Mordecai,
had him ride in the public square of the city, and
cried out before him, "This is what is done for
the man whom the king wishes to reward."
**12** Mordecai then returned to the royal gate,
while Haman hurried home, his head covered in
grief.[v] **13** When he told his wife Zeresh and all
his friends everything that had happened to him,
his advisers and his wife Zeresh said to him, "If
Mordecai, before whom you are beginning to
decline, is of the Jewish race, you will not prevail against him, but will surely be defeated by
him."

**Esther's Second Banquet.** **14** While
they were speaking with him, the king's eunuchs arrived and hurried Haman off to the
banquet Esther had prepared.

## CHAPTER 7

**1** So the king of Haman went to the banquet
with Queen Esther. **2** Again, on this second
day, during the drinking of the wine, the king
said to Esther, "Whatever you ask, Queen Esther, shall be granted you. Whatever request
you make shall be honored, even for half the
kingdom."[w] **3** Queen Esther replied: "If I have
found favor with you, O king, and if it pleases
your majesty, I ask that my life be spared, and
I beg that you spare the lives of my people.
**4** For my people and I have been delivered to
destruction, slaughter, and extinction. If we
were to be sold into slavery I would remain
silent, but as it is, the enemy will be unable to
compensate for the harm done to the king."[x]
**5** "Who and where," said King Ahasuerus to
Queen Esther, "is the man who has dared to do
this?"[y] **6** Esther replied, "The enemy oppressing us is this wicked Haman." At this, Haman
was seized with dread of the king and queen.
**7** The king left the banquet in anger and went
into the garden of the palace, but Haman stayed
to beg Queen Esther for his life, since he saw
that the king had decided on his doom. **8** When
the king returned from the garden of the palace
to the banquet hall, Haman had thrown himself
on the couch on which Esther was reclining; and
the king exclaimed, "Will he also violate the
queen while she is with me in my own house!"
Scarcely had the king spoken, when the face of
Haman was covered over.

**Punishment of Haman.** **9** [z]Harbona, one
of the eunuchs who attended the king, said, "At
the house of Haman stands a gibbet fifty cubits
high. Haman prepared it for Mordecai, who
gave the report that benefited the king." The
king answered, "Hang him on it." **10** So they
hanged Haman on the gibbet which he had made
ready for Mordecai, and the anger of the king
abated.

## CHAPTER 8

**1** That day King Ahasuerus gave the house of
Haman, enemy of the Jews, to Queen Esther;
and Mordecai was admitted to the king's presence, for Esther had revealed his relationship to
her.[a] **2** The king removed his signet ring from
Haman, and transferred it into the keeping of

q Est A, 12ff; 2, 21ff.
r Est A, 16.
s Est 5, 14; 7, 9f.
t Gn 41, 42f; 1 Kgs 1, 33; Dn 5, 29.
u Est 2, 21; 3, 2f; 5, 9. 13.
v Est 2, 21; 3, 2f; 5, 9. 13.
w Est 5, 3.
x Est 3, 13; B, 6.
y Est 3, 8f.
z 9f: Est 5, 14; 6, 4.
a Est 9, 1; Prv 11, 8; 26, 27; Mt 7, 2.
b Prv 13, 22; Dn 2, 48f.

Mordecai; and Esther put Mordecai in charge of
the house of Haman.[b]

**The Second Royal Decree.** 3 In another
audience with the king, Esther fell at his feet and
tearfully implored him to revoke the harm done
by Haman the Agagite, and the plan he had
devised against the Jews. **4** The king stretched
forth the golden scepter to Esther. So she rose
and, standing in his presence, **5** said: "If it
pleases your majesty and seems proper to you,
and if I have found favor with you and you love
me, let a document be issued to revoke the
letters which that schemer Haman, son of Hammedatha the Agagite, wrote for the destruction
of the Jews in all the royal provinces.[c] **6** For
how can I witness the evil that is to befall my
people, and how can I behold the destruction of
my race?"

**7** King Ahasuerus then said to Queen Esther
and to the Jew Mordecai: "Now that I have
given Esther the house of Haman, and they have
hanged him on the gibbet because he attacked
the Jews, **8** [d]you in turn may write in the king's
name what you see fit concerning the Jews and
seal the letter with the royal signet ring." For
whatever is written in the name of the king and
sealed with the royal signet ring cannot be revoked.*

**9** At that time, on the twenty-third day of the
third month, Sivan, the royal scribes were summoned. Exactly as Mordecai dictated, they
wrote to the Jews and to the satraps, governors,
and officials of the hundred and twenty-seven
provinces from India to Ethiopia: to each province in its own script and to each people in its
own language, and to the Jews in their own
script and language. **10** These letters, which he
wrote in the name of King Ahasuerus and sealed
with the royal signet ring, he sent by mounted
couriers riding thoroughbred royal steeds.
**11** [e]In these letters the king authorized the Jews
in each and every city to group together and
defend their lives, and to kill, destroy, wipe out,
along with their wives and children, every
armed group of any nation or province which
should attack them, and to seize their goods as
spoil **12** throughout the provinces of King
Ahasuerus, on a single day, the thirteenth of the
twelfth month, Adar.

## CHAPTER E

**1** The following is a copy of the letter:
"King Ahasuerus the Great to the governors
of the provinces in the hundred and twenty-sev-
en satrapies from India to Ethiopia, and to those
responsible for our interests: Greetings!

**2** "Many have become the more ambitious
the more they were showered with honors
through the bountiful generosity of their patrons. **3** Not only do they seek to do harm to our
subjects; incapable of bearing such greatness,
they even begin plotting against their own benefactors. **4** Not only do they drive out gratitude
from among men; with the arrogant boastfulness
of those to whom goodness has no meaning,
they suppose they will escape the vindictive
judgment of the all-seeing God.

**5** "Often, too, the fair speech of friends entrusted with the administration of affairs has
induced many placed in authority to become
accomplices in the shedding of innocent blood,
and has involved them in irreparable calamities
**6** by deceiving with malicious slander the sincere good will of rulers. **7** This can be verified
in the ancient stories that have been handed
down to us, but more fully when one considers
the wicked deeds perpetrated in your midst by
the pestilential influence of those undeserving
of authority. **8** [f]We must provide for the future,
so as to render the kingdom undisturbed and
peaceful for all men, **9** taking advantage of
changing conditions and deciding always with
equitable treatment matters coming to our attention.

**10** "For instance, Haman, son of Hammedatha, a Macedonian,* certainly not of Persian
blood, and very different from us in generosity,
was hospitably received by us. **11** He so far
enjoyed the good will which we have toward all
peoples that he was proclaimed 'father of the
king,' before whom everyone was to bow down;
he attained the rank second to the royal throne.[g]
**12** But, unequal to this dignity, he strove to
deprive us of kingdom and of life; **13** and by
weaving intricate webs of deceit, he demanded
the destruction of Mordecai, our savior and constant benefactor, and of Esther, our blameless
royal consort, together with their whole race.[h]
**14** For by such measures he hoped to catch us
defenseless and to transfer the rule of the Persians to the Macedonians. **15** But we find that
the Jews, who were doomed to extinction by
this arch-criminal, are not evildoers, but rather
are governed by very just laws **16** and are the
children of the Most High, the living God of
majesty, who has maintained the kingdom in a

c Est 1, 19.
d Est 1, 19.
e 11f: Est 9, 1-4.
f 8f: Est B, 2.
g Est B, 3. 6.
h Est A, 17.

*

8, 8: Whatever is written . . . cannot be revoked: the king cannot directly grant Esther's request (v 5) to revoke the previous decree against the Jews because of the irrevocable character of the laws of the Medes and Persians (Est 1, 19; Dn 6, 9); but he empowers Esther to issue a new decree in his name which renders the earlier decree without effect; cf Est 3, 12f.

E, 10: Macedonian: a redactor of the book in the Hellenistic period used the designation Macedonian, here and in v 14, to express, after Macedonia's conquest of Persia, the most odious kind of man that a Persian ruler could be supposed to think of; the Hebrew text, for a similar reason, called Haman an Agagite. See note on Est A, 17.

flourishing condition for us and for our forebears.
**17** "You will do well, then, to ignore the
letter sent by Haman, son of Hammedatha,
**18** for he who composed it has been hanged,
together with his entire household, before the
gates of Susa. Thus swiftly has God, who governs all, brought just punishment upon him.[i]
**19** "You shall exhibit a copy of this letter
publicly in every place, to certify that the Jews
may follow their own laws, **20** and that you
may help them on the day set for their ruin, the
thirteenth day of the twelfth month, Adar, to
defend themselves against those who attack
them. **21** For God, the ruler of all, has turned
that day for them from one of destruction of the
chosen race into one of joy. **22** Therefore, you
too must celebrate this memorable day among
your designated feasts with all rejoicing, **23** so
that both now and in the future it may be, for
us and for loyal Persians, a celebration of victory, and for those who plot against us a reminder
of destruction.
**24** "Every city and province, without exception, that does not observe this decree shall be
ruthlessly destroyed with fire and sword, so that
it will be left not merely untrodden by men, but
even shunned by wild beasts and birds forever."[j]

## CHAPTER 8

**13** A copy of the letter to be promulgated as
law in each and every province was published
among all the peoples, so that the Jews might be
prepared on that day to avenge themselves on
their enemies.* **14** Couriers mounted on royal
steeds sped forth in haste at the king's order, and
the decree was promulgated in the stronghold of
Susa.
**15** Mordecai left the king's presence clothed
in a royal robe of violet and of white cotton,
with a large crown of gold and a cloak of crimson byssus. The city of Susa shouted with joy,[k]
**16** and there was splendor and merriment for
the Jews, exultation and triumph. **17** In each
and every province and in each and every city,
wherever the king's order arrived, there was
merriment and exultation, banqueting and feasting for the Jews. And many of the peoples of the
land embraced Judaism, for they were seized
with a fear of the Jews.[l]

## CHAPTER 9

**Victory of the Jews.** **1** [m]When the day
arrived on which the order decreed by the king
was to be carried out, the thirteenth day of the
twelfth month, Adar, on which the enemies of
the Jews had expected to become masters of
them, the situation was reversed: the Jews became masters of their enemies. **2** The Jews
mustered in their cities throughout the provinces
of King Ahasuerus to attack those who sought
to do them harm, and no one could withstand
them, but all peoples were seized with a fear of
them. **3** Moreover, all the officials of the provinces, the satraps, governors, and royal procurators supported the Jews from fear of Mordecai;
**4** for Mordecai was powerful in the royal palace, and the report was spreading through all the
provinces that he was continually growing in
power.
**5** The Jews struck down all their enemies
with the sword, killing and destroying them;
they did to their enemies as they pleased.[n]
**6** [o]In the stronghold of Susa, the Jews killed
and destroyed five hundred men. **7** They also
killed Parshandatha, Dalphon, Aspatha,
**8** Porathai, Adalia, Aridatha, **9** Parmashta,
Arisai, Aridai, and Vaizatha, **10** [p]the ten sons
of Haman, son of Hammedatha, the foe of the
Jews. However, they did not engage in plundering.*
**11** On the same day, when the number of
those killed in the stronghold of Susa was reported to the king, **12** he said to Queen Esther:
"In the stronghold of Susa the Jews have killed
and destroyed five hundred men, as well as the
ten sons of Haman. What must they have done
in the other royal provinces! You shall again be
granted whatever you ask, and whatever you
request shall be honored." **13** So Esther said,
"If it pleases your majesty, let the Jews in Susa
be permitted again tomorrow to act according to
today's decree, and let the ten sons of Haman
be hanged on gibbets." **14** The king then gave
an order to this effect, and the decree was published in Susa. So the ten sons of Haman were
hanged,[q] **15** and the Jews in Susa mustered
again on the fourteenth of the month of Adar and
killed three hundred men in Susa.* However,
they did not engage in plundering.[r]
**16** The other Jews, who dwelt in the royal
provinces, also mustered and defended themselves, and obtained rest from their enemies.
They killed seventy-five thousand* of their

i Est 7, 10; 9, 14.
j Est 3, 8f; B, 4.
k Dn 5, 7.
l Est 9, 27.
m 1f: Est 8, 11f.
n Jdt 15, 6.
o 6-10: Est 5, 11; B, 3; E, 11.
p Est 9, 15; Jdt 15, 7. 11.
q Est 7, 10; E, 18.
r Est 9, 10.
s Jdt 15, 6.

*

8, 13: Avenge themselves on their enemies: partly in self-defense (Est E, 20), and partly to express the fact that the extreme cruelty designed against the Jews by their enemies now recoiled upon the latter as a punishment. Cf 9, 1f.

9, 10: They did not engage in plundering: in contrast to the Israelites who fought Agag (1 Sm 15, 9); cf also vv 15f.

9, 15: This second slaughter explains the two dates (13th and 14th) of the Purim celebration by Jews in Susa (v 18).

9, 16: Seventy-five thousand: according to the Greek text this number was fifteen thousand.

foes, without engaging in plunder,[s] **17** on the
thirteenth day of the month of Adar. On the
fourteenth of the month they rested, and made
it a day of feasting and rejoicing.

**18** (The Jews in Susa, however, mustered on
the thirteenth and fourteenth of the month. But
on the fifteenth they rested, and made it a day
of feasting and rejoicing.) **19** That is why the
rural Jews, who dwell in villages, celebrate the
fourteenth of the month of Adar as a day of
rejoicing and feasting, a holiday on which they
send gifts of food to one another.

**The Feast of Purim.** **20** Mordecai recorded these events and sent letters to all the Jews,
both near and far, in all the provinces of King
Ahasuerus. **21** He ordered them to celebrate
every year both the fourteenth and the fifteenth
of the month of Adar **22** as the day on which the
Jews obtained rest from their enemies and as the
month which was turned for them from sorrow
into joy, from mourning into festivity. They
were to observe these days with feasting and
gladness, sending food to one another and gifts
to the poor. **23** The Jews took upon themselves
for the future this observance which they instituted at the written direction of Mordecai.[t]

**24** [u]Haman, son of Hammedatha the Agagite, the foe of all the Jews, had planned to
destroy them and had cast the ***pur,*** or lot, for the
time of their defeat and destruction. **25** Yet,
when Esther entered the royal presence, the
king ordered in writing that the wicked plan
Haman had devised against the Jews should
instead be turned against Haman and that he and
his sons should be hanged on gibbets.[v] **26** And
so these days have been named Purim after the
word ***pur.***

Thus, because of all that was contained in this
letter, and because of what they had witnessed
and experienced in this affair, **27** the Jews established and took upon themselves, their descendants, and all who should join them, the
inviolable obligation of celebrating these two
days every year in the manner prescribed by this
letter, and at the time appointed.[w] **28** These
days were to be commemorated and kept in
every generation, by every clan, in every province, and in every city. These days of Purim
were never to fall into disuse among the Jews,
nor into oblivion among their descendants.

**29** Queen Esther, daughter of Abihail and of
Mordecai* the Jew, wrote to confirm with full
authority this second letter about Purim,
**30** when Mordecai sent documents concerning
peace and security to all the Jews in the hundred
and twenty-seven provinces of Ahasuerus'
kingdom.[x] **31** Thus were established, for their
appointed time, these days of Purim which Mordecai the Jew and Queen Esther had designated
for the Jews, just as they had previously enjoined upon themselves and upon their race the
duty of fasting and supplication.* **32** The command of Esther confirmed these prescriptions
for Purim and was recorded in the book.

## CHAPTER 10

**1** King Ahasuerus laid tribute on the land and
on the islands of the sea. **2** All the acts of his
power and valor, as well as a detailed account
of the greatness of Mordecai, whom the king
promoted, are recorded in the chronicles of the
kings of Media and Persia. **3** The Jew Mordecai
was next in rank to King Ahasuerus, in high
standing among the Jews, and was regarded
with favor by his many brethren, as the promoter of his people's welfare and the herald of
peace for his whole race.[y]

# *V: Epilogue*

## CHAPTER F

**Mordecai's Dream Fulfilled.** **1** [z]Then
Mordecai said: "This is the work of God. **2** I
recall the dream I had about these very things,
and not a single detail has been left unfulfilled—
**3** the tiny spring that grew into a river, the light
of the sun, the many waters. The river is Esther,
whom the king married and made queen. **4** The
two dragons are myself and Haman. **5** The nations are those who assembled to destroy the
name of the Jews, **6** but my people is Israel,
who cried to God and was saved.

"The LORD saved his people and delivered us
from all these evils. God worked signs and great
wonders, such as have not occurred among the
nations. **7** For this purpose he arranged two
lots:* one for the people of God, the second for
all the other nations. **8** These two lots were
fulfilled in the hour, the time, and the day of
judgment before God and among all the nations.

t Est 9, 29.
u 24ff: Est 3, 7; F, 10.
v Est 6, 5-13.
w Est 8, 12. 17.
x Est 9, 23-26.
y 2 Mc 15, 14.
z 1-6: Est A, 4-10.

*

9, 29: Queen Esther, daughter of Abihail and of Mordecai: the natural offspring of Abihail and adopted daughter of Mordecai; cf Est 2, 15. This second letter: for the burden of this letter see Est 9, 20ff. It was endorsed by Queen Esther. The first letter, written in the king's name, is referred to in Est 8, 9.

9, 31: Fasting and supplication: as the Jews had previously undertaken the duty of fasting and supplication to prevent the impending disaster, they now observe days of festival to commemorate their deliverance—in both cases (cf Est 4, 3. 15f) at the request of Mordecai and Esther.

F, 7: Two lots: in this passage of the Greek text, which gives a more religious interpretation of the feast, the two lots are drawn by God to determine, respectively, the destiny of Israel and that of the nations. In Est 3, 7 above, translated from the Hebrew text, the feast is called Purim because of the lots which Aman cast to determine the day for the extinction of the Jews.

9 God remembered his people and rendered
justice to his inheritance.[a]
10 "Gathering together with joy and happiness before God, they shall celebrate these days on the fourteenth and fifteenth of the month Adar throughout all future generations of his people Israel."*

a Est 3, 7; 9, 17f. 21. 24-28.

*

F, 10: The Greek text of Esther contains a postscript as follows: In the fourth year of the reign of Ptolemy and Cleopatra, Dositheus, who said he was a priest and Levite, and his son Ptolemy brought the present letter of Purim, saying that it was genuine and that Lysimachus, son of Ptolemy, of the community of Jerusalem, had translated it. The date referred to in this postscript is most probably 78–77 B.C., in the reign of Ptolemy XII and Cleopatra V.

# The First Book of
# MACCABEES

*The name Maccabee, probably meaning "hammer," is actually applied in the Books of Maccabees to only one man, Judas, third son of the priest Mattathias and first leader of the revolt against the Seleucid kings who persecuted the Jews (1 Mc 2, 4. 66; 2 Mc 8, 5. 16; 10, 1. 16). Traditionally the name has come to be applied to the brothers of Judas, his supporters, and even to other Jewish heroes of the period, such as the seven brothers (2 Mc 7).*

*The two Books of Maccabees, placed last in the Douai version of the Old Testament, contain independent accounts of events in part identical which accompanied the attempted suppression of Judaism in Palestine in the second century B.C. The vigorous reaction to this attempt established for a time the religious and political independence of the Jews.*

*1 Maccabees was written about 100 B.C., in Hebrew, but the original has not come down to us. Instead, we have an early, pre-Christian, Greek translation full of Hebrew idioms. The author, probably a Palestinian Jew, is unknown. He was familiar with the traditions and sacred books of his people and had access to much reliable information on their recent history (from 175 to 134 B.C.). He may well have played some part in it himself in his youth. His purpose in writing is to record the salvation of Israel which God worked through the family of Mattathias (5, 62)—especially through his three sons, Judas, Jonathan, and Simon, and his grandson, John Hyrcanus. Implicitly the writer compares their virtues and their exploits with those of the ancient heroes, the Judges, Samuel, and David.*

*There are seven poetic sections in the book which imitate the style of classical Hebrew poetry: four laments (1, 25–28. 36–40; 2, 8–13; 3, 45), and three hymns of praise of "our fathers" (2, 51–64), of Judas (3, 3–9), and of Simon (14, 4–15).*

*The doctrine expressed in the book is the customary belief of Israel, without the new developments which appear in 2 Maccabees and Daniel. The people of Israel have been specially chosen by the one true God as his covenant-partner, and they alone are privileged to know him and worship him. He is their eternal benefactor and their unfailing source of help. The people, in turn, must be loyal to his exclusive worship and must observe exactly the precepts of the law he has given them.*

*There is no doctrine of individual immortality except in the survival of one's name and fame, nor does the book express any messianic expectation, though messianic images are applied historically to "the days of Simon" (14, 4–17). In true deuteronomic tradition, the author insists on fidelity to the law as the expression of Israel's love for God. The contest which he describes is a struggle, not simply between Jew and Gentile, but between those who would uphold the law and those, Jews or Gentiles, who would destroy it. His severest condemnation goes, not to the Seleucid politicians, but to the lawless apostates among his own people, adversaries of Judas and his brothers, who are models of faith and loyalty.*

*1 Maccabees has importance also for the New Testament. Salvation is paralleled with Jewish national aspirations (1 Mc 4, 46—14, 41), in contrast to the universal reign of God taught by Christ in the Gospel (Mt 13, 47–50; 22, 1–14). Also, destruction of the wall of the temple separating Jew from Gentile is an act of desecration in 1 Mc 9, 54, but in Eph 2, 14, an act of redemption and unification of both through Christ. On the other hand, association, in 1 Mc 2, 52, of Abraham's offering up of Isaac (Gn 22) with his justification by God (Gn 15, 6) is reflected in Jn 2, 21f, just as the Scriptures are regarded as a source of consolation in 1 Mc 12, 9 and in Rom 15, 4.*

*The Books of Maccabees, though regarded by Jews and Protestants as apocryphal, i.e., not inspired Scripture, because not contained in the Palestinian Canon or list of books drawn up at the end of the first century A.D., have nevertheless always been accepted by the Catholic Church as inspired, on the basis of apostolic tradition.*

*1 Maccabees is divided as follows:*
*I. Introduction: Hellenism in Asia Minor (1, 1–9).*
*II. The Maccabean Revolt (1, 10—2, 70).*
*III. Leadership of Judas Maccabeus (3, 1—9, 22).*
*IV. Leadership of Jonathan (9, 23—12, 54).*
*V. Simon, High Priest and Ethnarch (13, 1—16, 24).*

# *I: Introduction: Hellenism In Asia Minor*

## CHAPTER 1

### Conquests and Death of Alexander.

**1** [a]After Alexander the Macedonian, Philip's son, who came from the land of Kittim,* had defeated Darius, king of the Persians and Medes, he became king in his place, having first ruled in Greece. **2** He fought many campaigns, captured fortresses, and put kings to death. **3** He advanced to the ends of the earth, gathering plunder from many nations; the earth fell silent before him, and his heart became proud and arrogant. **4** He collected a very strong army and conquered provinces, nations, and rulers, and they became his tributaries. **5** But after all this he took to his bed, realizing that he was going to die. **6** He therefore summoned his officers, the nobles, who had been brought up with him from his youth, to divide his kingdom among them while he was still alive. **7** Alexander had reigned twelve years* when he died.

**8** So his officers took over his kingdom, each in his own territory, **9** and after his death they all put on royal crowns, and so did their sons after them for many years, causing much distress over the earth.

# *II: The Maccabean Revolt*

### Pact between Jews and Gentiles.

**10** There sprang from these a sinful offshoot, Antiochus Epiphanes, son of King Antiochus, once a hostage at Rome. He became king in the year one hundred and thirty-seven* of the kingdom of the Greeks.[b]

**11** In those days there appeared in Israel men who were breakers of the law, and they seduced many people, saying: "Let us go and make an alliance with the Gentiles all around us; since we separated from them, many evils have come upon us."[c] **12** The proposal was agreeable; **13** [d]some from among the people promptly went to the king, and he authorized them to introduce the way of living of the Gentiles. **14** Thereupon they built a gymnasium* in Jerusalem according to the Gentile custom. **15** They covered over the mark of their circumcision and abandoned the holy covenant; they allied themselves with the Gentiles and sold themselves to wrongdoing.[e]

### Egyptian Campaign of Antiochus.

**16** When his kingdom seemed secure, Antiochus proposed to become king of Egypt, so as to rule over both kingdoms. **17** He invaded Egypt with a strong force, with chariots and elephants,* and with a large fleet,[f] **18** to make war on Ptolemy, king of Egypt. Ptolemy was frightened at his presence and fled, leaving many casualties. **19** The fortified cities in the land of Egypt were captured, and Antiochus plundered the land of Egypt.

**Persecution of the Jews.** **20** [g]After Antiochus had defeated Egypt in the year one hundred and forty-three,* he returned and went up to Israel and to Jerusalem with a strong force. **21** He insolently invaded the sanctuary and took away the golden altar, the lampstand for the light with all its fixtures, **22** the offering table, the cups and the bowls, the golden cen-

a 1-10: Dn 8, 20ff; 11, 3f. 21.
b 2 Mc 4, 7.
c 2 Mc 4, 9-17.
d 13ff: 2 Mc 4, 7-17.
e 1 Cor 7, 18.
f 2 Mc 5, 1; Dn 11, 25-28.
g 20-24: 2 Mc 5, 11-21.

*

1, 1: Land of Kittim: Greece. The name referred originally to inhabitants of Kiti, capital of the isle of Cyprus, then to any Cypriots (Is 23, 1; Jer 2, 10), later to Greeks in general, and finally even to Romans. See note on Dn 11, 30. Darius: Darius III, Codoman (336–331 B.C.).

1, 7: Twelve years: 336–323 B.C.

1, 10: The year one hundred and thirty-seven: Antiochus IV seized the throne in September, 175 B.C. Dates are given in this book according to the Seleucid era, which however was reckoned in two different ways. Antiochians considered this date to be October, 312 B.C. (Syrian calendar), while Babylonians and Jewish priests accepted April, 311 B.C. as the commencement of the era (temple calendar). The author of 1 Mc dates political events by the Syrian calendar but religious events by the temple calendar. Accordingly, the civil New Year occurred variously in September or October, the religious New Year in March or April.

1, 14: Gymnasium: symbol and center of athletic and intellectual life, it was the chief instrument of Hellenistic propaganda. Jewish youth were attracted by sports and encouraged to join youth clubs. They received training in military skills and in the duties of citizens. Through participation in the intellectual life, many were gradually won over to paganism.

1, 17: Elephants: an important part of Seleucid armament. About 300 B.C. Seleucus I, founder of the dynasty, procured five hundred of them from India; cf 1 Mc 6, 34–37.

1, 20: Defeated Egypt in the year one hundred and forty-three: 169 B.C. No mention is made in 1 Mc of the second expedition to Egypt a year later, described in 2 Mc 5, 1. 11. Dn 11, 25. 29 records both.

sers, the curtain, the crowns, and the golden
ornament on the façade of the temple. He
stripped off everything, **23** and took away the
gold and silver and the precious vessels; he also
took all the hidden treasures he could find.
**24** Taking all this, he went back to his own
country, after he had spoken with great arrogance and shed much blood.

**25** And there was great mourning for Israel, in
  every place where they dwelt,
**26** and the rulers and the elders groaned.
Virgins and young men languished,
  and the beauty of the women was
    disfigured.
**27** Every bridegroom took up lamentation,
  she who sat in the bridal chamber
    mourned,
**28** And the land was shaken on account of its
    inhabitants,
  and all the house of Jacob was covered
    with shame.

**29** [h]Two years later, the king sent the Mysian commander to the cities of Judah, and he
came to Jerusalem with a strong force. **30** He
spoke to them deceitfully in peaceful terms, and
won their trust. Then he attacked the city suddenly, in a great onslaught, and destroyed many
of the people in Israel. **31** He plundered the city
and set fire to it, demolished its houses and its
surrounding walls, **32** took captive the women
and children, and seized the cattle. **33** Then
they built up the City of David* with a high,
massive wall and strong towers, and it became
their citadel.[i] **34** There they installed a sinful
race, perverse men, who fortified themselves
inside it, **35** storing up weapons and provisions, and depositing there the plunder they had
collected from Jerusalem. And they became a
great threat.

**36** The citadel became an ambush against the
    sanctuary,
  and a wicked adversary to Israel at all
    times.
**37** And they shed innocent blood around the
    sanctuary;
  they defiled the sanctuary.
**38** Because of them the inhabitants of Jerusalem
    fled away,
  and she became the abode of strangers.
She became a stranger to her own offspring,
  and her children forsook her.
**39** Her sanctuary was as desolate as a
    wilderness;[j]
  her feasts were turned into mourning,
Her sabbaths to shame,
  her honor to contempt.
**40** Her dishonor was as great as her glory had
    been,
  and her exaltation was turned into
    mourning.

**Prohibitions against Religion.** **41** Then
the king wrote to his whole kingdom that all
should be one people, **42** each abandoning his
particular customs. All the Gentiles conformed
to the command of the king, **43** and many Israelites were in favor of his religion; they sacrificed to idols and profaned the sabbath.

**44** [k]The king sent messengers with letters to
Jerusalem and to the cities of Judah, ordering
them to follow customs foreign to their land:
**45** to prohibit holocausts, sacrifices, and libations in the sanctuary, to profane the sabbaths
and feast days, **46** [l]to desecrate the sanctuary
and the sacred ministers, to build pagan altars
and temples and shrines, **47** to sacrifice swine
and unclean animals, **48** to leave their sons uncircumcised, and to let themselves be defiled
with every kind of impurity and abomination,
**49** so that they might forget the law and change
all their observances. **50** Whoever refused to
act according to the command of the king should
be put to death.[m]

**51** Such were the orders he published
throughout his kingdom. He appointed inspec-
tors over all the people, and he ordered the cities
of Judah to offer sacrifices, each city in turn.
**52** Many of the people, those who abandoned
the law, joined them and committed evil in the
land. **53** Israel was driven into hiding, wherever places of refuge could be found.

**54** On the fifteenth day of the month Chislev,
in the year one hundred and forty-five,* the king
erected the horrible abomination upon the altar
of holocausts, and in the surrounding cities of
Judah they built pagan altars.[n] **55** They also
burnt incense at the doors of houses and in the
streets. **56** Any scrolls of the law* which they
found they tore up and burnt. **57** Whoever was
found with a scroll of the covenant, and whoever observed the law, was condemned to death by
royal decree.[o] **58** So they used their power
against Israel, against those who were caught,
each month, in the cities. **59** On the twenty-

h 29-32: 2 Mc 5, 24ff.
i 1 Mc 6, 18.
j 39f: Tb 2, 6; Am 8, 10.
k 44-63: 2 Mc 6, 1-11.
l 2 Mc 6, 2; Dn 9, 27.
m 2 Mc 6, 18—7, 41.
n 1 Mc 6, 7; Dn 9, 27; 11, 31.
o 2 Mc 2, 14.

*

1, 33: City of David: not Mount Zion on the eastern hill of Jerusalem, which David captured from the Jebusites (2 Sm 5, 7), but a new fortress built on the western hill and overlooking the temple and its courts on Mount Zion. It was occupied for twenty-six years by the Syro-Macedonian garrison, together with apostate Jews, and was a continual threat to the temple and the Jewish people (v 36); cf 1 Mc 13, 49ff.

1, 54: Fifteenth day of the month Chislev in the year one hundred and forty-five: early December, 167 B.C. Horrible abomination: in the original Hebrew, a contemptuous pun on the title "Lord of heaven" given to the god Zeus Olympios, to whom an image or perhaps an altar was erected upon the altar of holocausts in the temple of Jerusalem; cf Dn 9, 27; 11, 31.

1, 56f: Scrolls of the law: one or more of the first five books of the Old Testament.

fifth day of each month they sacrificed on the
altar erected over the altar of holocausts.
**60** [p]Women who had had their children circumcised were put to death, in keeping with the
decree, **61** with the babies hung from their
necks; their families also and those who had
circumcised them were killed. **62** But many in
Israel were determined and resolved in their
hearts not to eat anything unclean; **63** they preferred to die rather than to be defiled with unclean food or to profane the holy covenant; and
they did die. Terrible affliction was upon Israel.[q]

## CHAPTER 2

**Mattathias and His Sons.** **1** In those days
Mattathias, son of John, son of Simeon, a priest
of the family of Joarib, left Jerusalem and settled in Modein.* **2** He had five sons: John, who
was called Gaddi;[r] **3** Simon, who was called
Thassi; **4** Judas, who was called Maccabeus;
**5** Eleazar, who was called Avaran; and Jonathan, who was called Apphus. **6** When he saw
the sacrileges that were being committed in Judah and in Jerusalem, **7** he said: "Woe is me!
Why was I born to see the ruin of my people and
the ruin of the holy city, and to sit idle while it
is given into the hands of enemies, and the
sanctuary into the hands of strangers?

**8** "Her temple has become like a man
disgraced,
**9** her glorious ornaments have been carried
off as spoils,
Her infants have been murdered in her
streets,
her young men by the sword of the
enemy.[s]
**10** What nation has not taken its share of her
realm,
and laid its hand on her possessions?
**11** All her adornment has been taken away.
From being free, she has become a slave.
**12** We see our sanctuary and our beauty
and our glory laid waste,
And the Gentiles have defiled them!
**13** Why are we still alive?"

**14** Then Mattathias and his sons tore their garments, put on sackcloth, and mourned bitterly.

**Pagan Worship Refused.** **15** The officers
of the king in charge of enforcing the apostasy
came to the city of Modein to organize the sacrifices. **16** Many of Israel joined them, but Mattathias and his sons gathered in a group apart.
**17** Then the officers of the king addressed Mattathias: "You are a leader, an honorable and
great man in this city, supported by sons and
kinsmen. **18** Come now, be the first to obey the
king's command, as all the Gentiles and the men
of Judah and those who are left in Jerusalem
have done. Then you and your sons shall be
numbered among the King's Friends,* and shall
be enriched with silver and gold and many
gifts." **19** But Mattathias answered in a loud
voice: "Although all the Gentiles in the king's
realm obey him, so that each forsakes the religion of his fathers and consents to the king's
orders, **20** yet I and my sons and my kinsmen
will keep to the covenant of our fathers. **21** God
forbid that we should forsake the law and the
commandments. **22** We will not obey the
words of the king nor depart from our religion
in the slightest degree."

**23** As he finished saying these words, a certain Jew came forward in the sight of all to offer
sacrifice on the altar in Modein according to the
king's order. **24** When Mattathias saw him, he
was filled with zeal; his heart was moved and his
just fury was aroused; he sprang forward and
killed him upon the altar. **25** At the same time,
he also killed the messenger of the king who was
forcing them to sacrifice, and he tore down the
altar. **26** Thus he showed his zeal for the law,
just as Phinehas did with Zimri, son of Salu.[t]

**27** Then Mattathias went through the city
shouting, "Let everyone who is zealous for the
law and who stands by the covenant follow after
me!" **28** Thereupon he fled to the mountains
with his sons, leaving behind in the city all their
possessions.[u] **29** Many who sought to live according to righteousness and religious custom
went out into the desert* to settle there, **30** they
and their sons, their wives and their cattle, because misfortunes pressed so hard on them.

**31** It was reported to the officers and soldiers
of the king who were in the City of David, in
Jerusalem, that certain men who had flouted the
king's order had gone out to the hiding places
in the desert. **32** [v]Many hurried out after them,
and having caught up with them, camped opposite and prepared to attack them on the sabbath.
**33** "Enough of this!" the pursuers said to
them. "Come out and obey the king's command, and your lives will be spared." **34** But
they replied, "We will not come out, nor will
we obey the king's command to profane the
sabbath." **35** Then the enemy attacked them at
once; **36** but they did not retaliate; they neither
threw stones, nor blocked up their own hiding

p 60f: 2 Mc 6, 10.
q 2 Mc 6, 10.
r 1 Chr 24, 7.
s Lam 2, 11, 21.
t 1 Mc 2, 54; Nm 25, 6-14.
u 2 Mc 5, 27.
v 32-38: 2 Mc 6, 11.

*

2, 1: Modein: a village twenty miles northwest of Jerusalem.

2, 18: The King's Friends: a regular order of nobility at Hellenistic courts. The various grades are frequently mentioned in this book: Friends, Chief Friends, Kinsmen.

2, 29: The desert: the sparsely inhabited mountain country southward from Jerusalem and west of the Dead Sea. It was an arid region with some perennial springs and a fair amount of rain in winter.

places. **37** They said, "Let us all die without
reproach; heaven and earth are our witnesses
that you destroy us unjustly." **38** So the officers and soldiers attacked them on the sabbath,
and they died with their wives, their children
and their cattle, to the number of a thousand
persons.

**39** When Mattathias and his friends heard of
it, they mourned deeply for them. **40** "If we all
do as our kinsmen have done," they said to one
another, "and do not fight against the Gentiles
for our lives and our traditions, they will soon
destroy us from the earth." **41** On that day they
came to this decision: "Let us fight against
anyone who attacks us on the sabbath, so that
we may not all die as our kinsmen died in the
hiding places."

**42** Then they were joined by a group of Hasideans,* valiant Israelites, all of them devout
followers of the law. **43** And all those who
were fleeing from the disaster joined them and
supported them. **44** They gathered an army and
struck down sinners in their anger and lawbreakers in their wrath, and the survivors fled to
the Gentiles for safety.[w] **45** Mattathias and his
friends went about and tore down the pagan
altars; **46** they also forcibly circumcised any
uncircumcised boys whom they found in the
territory of Israel. **47** They put to flight the
arrogant, and the work prospered in their hands.
**48** They saved the law from the hands of the
Gentiles and of the kings and did not let the
sinner triumph.

**Death of Mattathias.** **49** When the time
came for Mattathias to die, he said to his sons:
"Arrogance and scorn have now grown strong;
it is a time of disaster and violent anger.
**50** Therefore, my sons, be zealous for the law
and give your lives for the covenant of our
fathers.

**51** "Remember the deeds that our fathers did in
their times,
and you shall win great glory and an
everlasting name.
**52** Was not Abraham found faithful in trial,
and it was reputed to him as uprightness?[x]
**53** Joseph, when in distress, kept the
commandment,
and he became master of Egypt.[y]
**54** Phinehas our father, for his burning zeal,
received the covenant of an everlasting
priesthood.[z]
**55** Joshua, for executing his commission,
became a judge in Israel.[a]
**56** Caleb, for bearing witness before the
assembly,
received an inheritance in the land.[b]
**57** David, for his piety,
received as a heritage a throne of
everlasting royalty.[c]
**58** Elijah, for his burning zeal for the law,
was taken up to heaven.[d]
**59** Hananiah, Azariah and Mishael, for their
faith,
were saved from the fire.[e]
**60** Daniel, for his innocence,
was delivered from the jaws of lions.[f]
**61** And so, consider this from generation to
generation,
that none who hope in him shall fail in
strength.
**62** Do not fear the words of a sinful man,
for his glory ends in corruption and
worms.
**63** Today he is exalted, and tomorrow he is not
to be found,
because he has returned to his dust,
and his schemes have perished.
**64** Children! be courageous and strong in
keeping the law,
for by it you shall be glorified.

**65** "Here is your brother Simeon who I know
is a wise man; listen to him always, and he will
be a father to you. **66** And Judas Maccabeus, a
warrior from his youth, shall be the leader of
your army and direct the war against the nations. **67** You shall also gather about you all
who observe the law, and you shall avenge the
wrongs of your people. **68** Pay back the Gentiles what they deserve, and observe the precepts of the law."

**69** Then he blessed them, and he was united
with his fathers. **70** He died in the year one
hundred and forty-six,* and was buried in the
tombs of his fathers in Modein, and all Israel
mourned him greatly.

## *III: Leadership of Judas Maccabeus*

## CHAPTER 3

**Defeat of Apollonius and Seron.** **1** Then
his son Judas, who was called Maccabeus, took
his place. **2** All his brothers and all who had
joined his father supported him, and they carried on Israel's war joyfully.

**3** He spread abroad the glory of his people,
and put on his breastplate like a giant.
He armed himself with weapons of war;

---

w Is 63, 3.
x Gn 15, 6; 22, 1ff.
y Gn 39, 7-10; 41, 39-43.
z Nm 25, 10-13; Sir 45, 24; Jos 14, 14.
28ff.
a Jos 1, 2, 5.
b Nm 13, 30; 14, 6-9.
c 2 Sm 2, 4; 7, 16.
d 1 Kgs 19, 10. 14; 2 Kgs 2, 11.
e Dn 3, 50.
f Dn 6, 23; 14, 31-42.
g 2 Mc 8, 5.

---

* 2, 42: Hasideans: in Hebrew hasidim, "pious ones," a religious group devoted to the strict observance of the law. They were the forerunners of both the Pharisees and the Essenes. They first supported the Maccabean movement, but subsequently opposed it, regarding it as too political.

2, 70: In the year one hundred and forty-six: 166 B.C.

he planned battles and protected the camp
with his sword.[g]
4 In his actions he was like a lion,
like a young lion roaring for prey.
5 He pursued the wicked, hunting them out,
and those who troubled his people he
destroyed by fire.
6 The lawbreakers were cowed by fear of him,
and all evildoers were dismayed.
By his hand redemption was happily
achieved,
7 and he afflicted many kings;
He made Jacob glad by his deeds,
and his memory is blessed forever.
8 He went about the cities of Judah
destroying the impious there.
He turned away wrath from Israel
9 and was renowned to the ends of the
earth;
he gathered together those who were
perishing.

**10** Then Apollonius* gathered the Gentiles,
together with a large army from Samaria, to
fight against Israel. **11** When Judas learned of
it, he went out to meet him and defeated and
killed him. Many fell wounded, and the rest
fled. **12** Their possessions were seized and the
sword of Apollonius was taken by Judas, who
fought with it the rest of his life.

**13** But Seron, commander of the Syrian
army, heard that Judas had gathered many about
him, an assembly of faithful men ready for war.
**14** So he said, "I will make a name for myself
and win glory in the kingdom by defeating Judas
and his followers, who have despised the king's
command." **15** And again a large company of
renegades advanced with him to help him take
revenge on the Israelites. **16** When he reached
the ascent of Beth-horon,* Judas went out to
meet him with a few men. **17** But when they
saw the army coming against them, they said to
Judas: "How can we, few as we are, fight such
a mighty host as this? Besides, we are weak
today from fasting." **18** But Judas said: "It is
easy for many to be overcome by a few; in the
sight of Heaven there is no difference between
deliverance by many or by few; **19** for victory
in war does not depend upon the size of the
army, but on strength that comes from Heav-
en.[h] **20** With great presumption and lawlessness they come against us to destroy us and our
wives and children and to despoil us; **21** but we
are fighting for our lives and our laws. **22** He
himself* will crush them before us; so do not be
afraid of them." **23** When he finished speaking, he rushed suddenly upon Seron and his
army, who were crushed before him. **24** He
pursued Seron down the descent of Beth-horon
into the plain. About eight hundred* of their
men fell, and the rest fled to the country of the
Philistines.[i] **25** Then Judas and his brothers began to be feared, and dread fell upon the Gentiles about them. **26** His fame reached the king,
and all the Gentiles talked about the battles of
Judas.

**Regency of Lysias.** **27** When Antiochus
heard about these events, he was angry; so he
ordered a muster of all the forces of his kingdom, a very strong army. **28** He opened his
treasure chests, gave his soldiers a year's pay,
and commanded them to be prepared for anything. **29** He then found that this exhausted the
money in his treasury; moreover the income
from the province was small, because of the
dissension and distress he had brought upon the
land by abolishing the laws which had been in
effect from of old. **30** He feared that, as had
happened more than once, he would not have
enough for his expenses and for the gifts that he
had previously given with a more liberal hand
than the preceding kings. **31** Greatly perplexed, he decided to go to Persia and levy
tribute on those provinces, and so raise a large
sum of money. **32** He left Lysias, a nobleman
of royal blood, in charge of the king's affairs
from the Euphrates River to the frontier of
Egypt, **33** and commissioned him to take care
of his son Antiochus until his own return.
**34** He entrusted to him half of the army, and the
elephants, and gave him instructions concerning
everything he wanted done. As for the inhabitants of Judea and Jerusalem, **35** Lysias was to
send an army against them to crush and destroy
the power of Israel and the remnant of Jerusalem
and efface their memory from the land. **36** He
was to settle foreigners in all their territory and
distribute their land by lot.

**37** The king took the remaining half of the
army and set out from Antioch, his capital, in
the year one hundred and forty-seven; he
crossed the Euphrates River and advanced inland.*

h 1 Sm 14, 16. i Jos 10, 10.

*

3, 10: Apollonius: the Mysian commander mentioned in 1 Mc 1, 29 and in 2 Mc 5, 24.

3, 16: Beth-horon: the famous pass leading up from the coastal plain to the Judean hill country. Here Joshua won an important battle (Jos 10, 10f), and in 66 A.D. a Roman force under Cestius was trapped and massacred.

3, 22: He himself: out of reverence for God, the author of 1 Mc prefers to use this and other expressions, such as "Heaven," instead of the divine name. Cf 1 Mc 3, 50.

3, 24: About eight hundred: the figures given in this book for strength of armies and number of casualties are not to be taken literally. In accordance with biblical usage, they indicate rather the importance of the battle described or the greatness of the victory.

3, 37: This expedition, in the spring of 165 B.C., resulted in failure; cf ch 6.

**The Victories of Judas.** **38** [j]Lysias chose
Ptolemy, son of Dorymenes, and Nicanor* and
Gorgias, capable men among the King's
Friends,[k] **39** and with them he sent forty thousand men and seven thousand cavalry to invade
the land of Judah and ravage it according to the
king's orders. **40** Setting out with all their
forces, they came and pitched their camp near
Emmaus* in the plain. **41** When the merchants
of the country heard of their fame, they came to
the camp, bringing fetters and a large sum of
silver and gold, to buy the Israelites as slaves.
A force from Idumea and from Philistia joined
with them.

**42** Judas and his brothers saw that the situation had become critical now that armies were
encamped within their territory; they knew of
the orders which the king had given to destroy
and utterly wipe out the people. **43** So they said
to one another, "Let us restore our people from
their ruined estate, and fight for our people and
our sanctuary!"

**44** The assembly gathered together to prepare for battle and to pray and implore mercy
and compassion.

**45** Jerusalem was uninhabited, like a desert;
not one of her children entered or came
out.
The sanctuary was trampled on,
and foreigners were in the citadel;
it was a habitation of Gentiles.
Joy had disappeared from Jacob,
and the flute and the harp were silent.

**46** [l]Thus they assembled and went to Mizpah
near Jerusalem, because there was formerly at
Mizpah a place of prayer for Israel.* **47** That
day they fasted and wore sackcloth; they sprinkled ashes on their heads and tore their clothes.
**48** They unrolled the scroll of the law, to learn
about the things for which the Gentiles consulted the images of their idols.* **49** They brought
with them the priestly vestments, the first fruits,
and the tithes; and they brought forward the
nazirites* who had completed the time of their
vows.[m] **50** And they cried aloud to Heaven:
"What shall we do with these men, and where
shall we take them? **51** For your sanctuary has
been trampled on and profaned, and your priests
are in mourning and humiliation. **52** Now the
Gentiles are gathered together against us to destroy us. You know what they plot against us.
**53** How shall we be able to resist them unless
you help us?" **54** Then they blew the trumpets
and cried out loudly.

**55** After this Judas appointed officers among
the people, over thousands, over hundreds, over
fifties, and over tens. **56** He proclaimed that
those who were building houses, or were just
married, or were planting vineyards, and those
who were afraid, could each return to his home,
according to the law.[n] **57** Then the army moved
off, and they camped to the south of Emmaus.
**58** Judas said: "Arm yourselves and be brave;
in the morning be ready to fight these Gentiles
who have assembled against us to destroy us and
our sanctuary. **59** It is better for us to die in
battle than to witness the ruin of our nation and
our sanctuary. Whatever Heaven wills, he will
do."[o]

## CHAPTER 4

**1** Now Gorgias took five thousand infantry
and a thousand picked cavalry, and this detachment set out at night **2** in order to attack the
camp of the Jews and take them by surprise.
Some men from the citadel were their guides.
**3** Judas heard of it, and himself set out with his
soldiers to attack the king's army at Emmaus,
**4** while the latter's forces were still scattered
away from the camp. **5** During the night
Gorgias came into the camp of Judas, and found
no one there; so he began to hunt for them in the
mountains, saying, "They are fleeing from
us."

**6** But at daybreak Judas appeared in the plain
with three thousand men, who lacked such armor and swords as they would have wished.
**7** They saw the army of the Gentiles, strong and
breastplated, flanked with cavalry, and made up
of expert soldiers. **8** Judas said to the men with
him: "Do not be afraid of their numbers or
dread their attack. **9** Remember how our fathers
were saved in the Red Sea, when Pharaoh pursued them with an army.[p] **10** So now let us cry
to Heaven in the hope that he will favor us,
remember his covenant with our fathers, and
destroy this army before us today.[q] **11** All the
Gentiles shall know that there is One who redeems and delivers Israel."

**12** When the foreigners looked up and saw
them marching toward them, **13** they came out
of their camp for battle, and the men with Judas
blew the trumpet. **14** The battle was joined and

j 38-44: 2 Mc 8, 8-15.
k 38f: 1 Mc 7, 26; 2 Mc 4, 45; 8, 8f; 10, 14.
l 46ff: 1 Sm 7, 5f; 2 Mc 8, 16-23.
m Nm 6, 2-5.
n Dt 20, 5-8; Jgs 7, 3.
o 1 Mc 2, 21f.
p Ex 14, 21ff.
q 1 Mc 2, 21.

3, 38: Nicanor: the leader of another attack against the Jews four years later. He was finally killed by Judas; cf 1 Mc 7, 26–46.

3, 40: Emmaus: probably not the village mentioned in Lk 24, 13, but a settlement about twenty miles west of Jerusalem at the edge of the hill country.

3, 46: . . . Mizpah a place of prayer for Israel: a holy place established of old eight miles north and slightly west of Jerusalem. It was here that Samuel began to judge the Israelites (1 Sm 7, 5–11; 10, 17).

3, 48: To learn . . . idols: favorable omens for the coming battle. A contrast is intended between the idol worship of the pagans and the consultation of the word of God by the Jews; cf 2 Mc 8, 23.

3, 49: Nazirites: see note on Nm 6, 1ff.

the Gentiles were defeated and fled toward the plain. **15** Their whole rearguard fell by the sword, and they were pursued as far as Gazara* and the plains of Judea, to Azotus and Jamnia. About three thousand of their men fell.

**16** When Judas and the army returned from the pursuit, **17** he said to the people: "Do not be greedy for the plunder, for there is a fight ahead of us, **18** and Gorgias and his army are near us on the mountain. But now stand firm against our enemies and overthrow them. Afterward you can freely take the plunder."

**19** As Judas was finishing this speech, a detachment appeared, looking down from the mountain. **20** They saw that their army had been put to flight and their camp was being burned. The smoke that could be seen indicated what had happened. **21** When they realized this, they were terrified; and when they also saw the army of Judas in the plain ready to attack, **22** they all fled to Philistine territory.*

**23** Then Judas went back to plunder the camp, and his men collected much gold and silver, violet and crimson cloth, and great treasure. **24** As they returned, they were singing hymns and glorifying Heaven, "for he is good, for his mercy endures forever."[r] **25** Thus Israel had a great deliverance that day.

**Victory over Lysias.** **26** [s]But those of the foreigners who had escaped went and told Lysias all that had occurred. **27** When he heard it he was disturbed and discouraged, because things in Israel had not turned out as he intended and as the king had ordered.

**28** So the following year he gathered together sixty thousand picked men and five thousand cavalry, to subdue them. **29** They came into Idumea and camped at Beth-zur,* and Judas met them with ten thousand men. **30** Seeing that the army was strong, he prayed thus:

"Blessed are you, O Savior of Israel, who broke the rush of the mighty one by the hand of your servant David and delivered the camp of the Philistines into the hand of Jonathan, the son of Saul, and his armor-bearer.[t] **31** Give this army into the hands of your people Israel; make them ashamed of their troops and their cavalry. **32** Strike them with fear, weaken the boldness of their strength, and let them tremble at their own destruction. **33** Strike them down by the sword of those who love you, that all who know your name may hymn your praise."

**34** Then they engaged in battle, and about five thousand of Lysias' men fell in hand-to-hand fighting. **35** When Lysias saw his ranks beginning to give way, and the increased boldness of Judas, whose men were ready either to live or to die bravely, he withdrew to Antioch and began to recruit mercenaries so as to return to Judea with greater numbers.*

**Purification of the Temple.** **36** [u]Then Judas and his brothers said, "Now that our enemies have been crushed, let us go up to purify the sanctuary* and rededicate it." **37** So the whole army assembled, and went up to Mount Zion. **38** They found the sanctuary desolate, the altar desecrated, the gates burnt, weeds growing in the courts as in a forest or on some mountain, and the priests' chambers demolished.[v] **39** Then they tore their clothes and made great lamentation; they sprinkled their heads with ashes **40** and fell with their faces to the ground. And when the signal was given with trumpets, they cried out to Heaven.

**41** Judas appointed men to attack those in the citadel, while he purified the sanctuary. **42** He chose blameless priests, devoted to the law; **43** these purified the sanctuary and carried away the stones of the Abomination to an unclean place. **44** They deliberated what ought to be done with the altar of holocausts that had been desecrated.[w] **45** The happy thought came to them to tear it down, lest it be a lasting shame to them that the Gentiles had defiled it; so they tore down the altar.[x] **46** They stored the stones in a suitable place on the temple hill, until a prophet should come and decide what to do with them. **47** Then they took uncut stones, according to the law, and built a new altar like the former one.[y] **48** They also repaired the sanctuary and the interior of the temple and purified the courts. **49** They made new sacred vessels and brought the lampstand, the altar of incense, and the table into the temple.[z] **50** Then they burned incense on the altar and lighted the lamps on the lampstand, and these illuminated the temple.[a] **51** They also put loaves on the table and hung up the curtains. Thus they finished all the work they had undertaken.

**52** Early in the morning on the twenty-fifth

r Ps 118, 1ff. 29.
s 26-35: 2 Mc 11, 1-12.
t 1 Sm 17, 48ff.
u 36-59: 2 Mc 10, 1-8.
v Ps 74, 2-7.
w 1 Kgs 8, 64.
x 1 Mc 6, 7.
y Ex 20, 25.
z Ex 25, 23-39; 30, 1-6.
a Ex 30, 7ff.

*

4, 15: Gazara: Gezer of the Hebrew Bible, five miles northwest of Emmaus: Azotus, Hebrew Ashdod, lay to the southwest; and Jamnia, Hebrew Jabneel (Jos 15, 11) or Jabneh (2 Chr 26, 6), to the west of Gazara.

4, 22: Philistine territory: the coastal cities of southern Palestine, traditionally hostile to Jerusalem. Jamnia in particular was an important base for the Seleucid power.

4, 29: Beth-zur: an important frontier city in the mountain area, fifteen miles southwest of Jerusalem. Its inhabitants were sympathetic to the Maccabees and refused to receive Lysias.

4, 35: According to 2 Mc 11, 13–15, peace negotiations followed between Lysias and Judas.

4, 36: The sanctuary: the whole temple area with its walls, courts and outbuildings, to be distinguished from the temple proper, the oblong edifice with porch, main room and inner shrine.

4, 52: Twenty-fifth day of the ninth month . . . in the year one hundred and forty-eight: December 14, 164 B.C.

day of the ninth month, that is, the month of Chislev, in the year one hundred and forty-eight,* **53** they arose and offered sacrifice according to the law on the new altar of holocausts that they had made.[b] **54** On the anniversary of the day on which the Gentiles had defiled it, on that very day it was reconsecrated with songs, harps, flutes, and cymbals. **55** All the people prostrated themselves and adored and praised Heaven, who had given them success.

**56** For eight days they celebrated the dedication of the altar and joyfully offered holocausts and sacrifices of deliverance and praise. **57** They ornamented the façade of the temple with gold crowns and shields; they repaired the gates and the priests' chambers and furnished them with doors. **58** There was great joy among the people now that the disgrace of the Gentiles was removed. **59** Then Judas and his brothers and the entire congregation of Israel decreed that the days of the dedication* of the altar should be observed with joy and gladness on the anniversary every year for eight days, from the twenty-fifth day of the month Chislev.[c]

**60** At that time they built high walls and strong towers around Mount Zion, to prevent the Gentiles from coming and trampling over it as they had done before. **61** Judas also placed a garrison there to protect it, and likewise fortified Beth-zur, that the people might have a stronghold facing Idumea.

## CHAPTER 5

**Punishment of Hostile Acts.** **1** [d]When the Gentiles round about heard that the altar had been rebuilt and the sanctuary consecrated as before, they were very angry.* **2** So they decided to destroy the descendants of Jacob who were among them, and they began to massacre and persecute the people. **3** [e]Then Judas attacked the sons of Esau at Akrabattene* in Idumea, because they were blockading Israel; he defeated them heavily, overcame and despoiled them. **4** He also remembered the malice of the sons of Baean,* who had become a snare and a stumblingblock to the people by ambushing them along the roads. **5** He forced them to take refuge in towers, which he besieged; he vowed their annihilation and burned down the towers along with all the persons in them. **6** *Then he crossed over to the Ammonites, where he found a strong army and a large body of people with Timothy as their leader. **7** He fought many battles with them, routed them, and struck them down. **8** After seizing Jazer and its villages, he returned to Judea.

**Liberation of Galilean Jews.** **9** The Gentiles in Gilead assembled to attack and destroy the Israelites who were in their territory; these then fled to the stronghold of Dathema. **10** They sent a letter to Judas and his brothers saying: "The Gentiles around us have combined against us to destroy us, **11** and they are preparing to come and seize this stronghold to which we have fled. Timothy is the leader of their army. **12** Come at once and rescue us from them, for many of us have fallen. **13** All our kinsmen who were among the Tobiads have been killed; the Gentiles have carried away their wives and children and their goods, and they have slain there about a thousand men."[f]

**14** While they were reading this letter, suddenly other messengers, in torn clothes, arrived from Galilee to deliver a similar message: **15** that the inhabitants of Ptolemais,* Tyre, and Sidon, and the whole of Gentile Galilee had joined forces to destroy them. **16** When Judas and the people heard this, a great assembly convened to consider what they should do for their unfortunate kinsmen who were being attacked by enemies.

**17** Judas said to his brother Simon: "Choose men for yourself, and go, rescue your kinsmen in Galilee; I and my brother Jonathan will go to Gilead."

**18** In Judea he left Joseph, son of Zechariah, and Azariah, leader of the people, with the rest of the army to guard it. **19** "Take charge of these people," he commanded them, "but do not fight against the Gentiles until we return." **20** Three thousand men were allotted to Simon, to go into Galilee, and eight thousand men to Judas, for Gilead.

**21** Simon went into Galilee and fought many battles with the Gentiles. They were crushed before him, **22** and he pursued them to the very gate of Ptolemais. About three thousand men of the Gentiles fell, and he gathered their spoils. **23** He took with him the Jews who were in Galilee and in Arbatta, with their wives and children and all that they had, and brought them to Judea with great rejoicing.

---

b 53. 56: Ex 30, 10; Ez 43, 18-27.
c Jn 10, 22.
d 1f: 1 Mc 13, 6.
e 3ff: 2 Mc 10, 15-23.
f 2 Mc 12, 17.

---

4, 59: Days of the dedication . . . Chislev: institution of the feast of Hannukah, also called the feast of Dedication (Jn 10, 22). Josephus Flavius calls it the feast of Lights.

5, 1: The events of this chapter occurred within the year 163 B.C.

5, 3: Akrabattene: a district southwest of the Dead Sea.

5, 4: Sons of Baean: 2 Mc 10, 15–23 calls them simply Idumeans.

5, 6ff: This summary anticipates the order of events and would fit better between vv 36 and 37. It corresponds to 2 Mc 12, 17–23. The action was probably a reprisal for the massacre referred to in v 13. Timothy was the Seleucid governor of Transjordan. Jazer: a town on the road from the Jordan to Amman.

5, 15: Ptolemais: Hebrew Acco (Jgs 1, 31), modern Acre, on the coast north of Haifa.

**Rescue in Gilead.** **24** [g]Judas Maccabeus
and his brother Jonathan crossed the Jordan and
marched for three days through the desert.
**25** There they met some Nabateans,* who received them peacefully and told them all that
had happened to the Jews in Gilead: **26** "Many
of them have been imprisoned in Bozrah, in
Bosor near Alema, in Chaspho, Maked, and
Carnaim"—all of these are large, fortified cities— **27** "and some have been imprisoned in
the other cities of Gilead. Tomorrow their enemies plan to attack the strongholds and to seize
and destroy all these people in one day."

**28** Thereupon Judas suddenly changed direction with his army, marched across the desert to
Bozrah, and captured the city. He slaughtered
all the male population, took all their possessions, and set fire to the city. **29** He led his
army from that place by night, and they
marched toward the stronghold of Dathema.
**30** When morning came, they looked ahead and
saw a countless multitude of people, with lad-
ders and devices for capturing the stronghold,
and beginning to attack the people within.
**31** When Judas perceived that the struggle had
begun and that the noise of the battle was resounding to heaven with trumpet blasts and loud
shouting, **32** he said to the men of his army,
"Fight for our kinsmen today."

**33** He came up behind them with three columns blowing their trumpets and shouting in
prayer. **34** When the army of Timothy realized
that it was Maccabeus, they fell back before
him, and he inflicted on them a crushing defeat.
About eight thousand of their men fell that day.
**35** Then he turned toward Alema and attacked
and captured it; he killed all the male population, plundered the place, and burned it down.
**36** From there he moved on and took Chaspho,
Maked, Bosor, and the other cities of Gilead.

**37** [h]After these events Timothy assembled
another army and camped opposite Raphon, on
the other side of the stream. **38** Judas sent men
to spy on the camp, and they reported to him:
"All the Gentiles around us have rallied to him,
making a very large force; **39** they have also
hired Arabs to help them, and have camped
beyond the stream, ready to attack you." So
Judas went forward to attack them.

**40** As Judas and his army were approaching
the running stream, Timothy said to the officers
of his army: "If he crosses over to us first, we
shall not be able to resist him; he will certainly
defeat us.[i] **41** But if he is afraid and camps on
the other side of the river, we will cross over to
him and defeat him."

**42** But when Judas reached the running
stream, he stationed the officers of the people
beside the stream and gave them this order: "Do
not allow any man to pitch a tent; all must go
into battle." **43** He was the first to cross to the
attack, with all the people behind him, and the
Gentiles were crushed before them; they threw
away their arms and fled to the temple enclosure
at Carnaim. **44** The Jews captured that city and
burnt the enclosure with all who were in it. So
Carnaim was subdued, and Judas met with no
more resistance.[j]

**45** Then he assembled all the Israelites, great
and small, who were in Gilead, with their wives
and children and their goods, a great crowd of
people, to go into the land of Judah. **46** [k]When
they reached Ephron,* a large and strongly fortified city along the way, they found it impossible to encircle it on either the right or the left;
they would have to march right through it.
**47** But the men in the city shut them out and
blocked up the gates with stones.[l] **48** Then Judas sent them his peaceful message: "We wish
to cross your territory in order to reach our own;
no one will harm you; we will only march
through." But they would not open to him.

**49** So Judas ordered a proclamation to be
made in the camp that everyone make an attack
from the place where he was. **50** When the men
of the army took up their positions, he assaulted
the city all that day and night, and it was delivered to him. **51** He slaughtered every male,
razed and plundered the city, and passed
through it over the slain.

**52** Then they crossed the Jordan to the great
plain in front of Beth-shan; **53** and Judas kept
rounding up the stragglers and encouraging the
people the whole way, until he reached the land
of Judah. **54** They ascended Mount Zion in joy
and gladness and offered holocausts, because
not one of them had fallen; they returned in
safety.

**Joseph and Azariah Defeated.** **55** During the time that Judas and Jonathan were in the
land of Gilead, and Simon his brother was in
Galilee opposite Ptolemais, **56** Joseph, son of
Zechariah, and Azariah, the leaders of the
army, heard about the brave deeds and the fighting that they were doing. **57** They said, "Let us
also make a name for ourselves by going out and
fighting against the Gentiles around us."

**58** They gave orders to the men of their army
who were with them, and marched toward

g 24-36: 2 Mc 12, 10ff.
h 37-44; 2 Mc 12, 20-26.
i 1 Sm 14, 9f.
j 2 Mc 12, 21.
k 46-54; 2 Mc 12, 27-31.
l Nm 20, 17-21; 21, 21-25.

*

5, 25: Nabateans: an Arab people who acquired wealth and power as caravan merchants in the final two centuries B.C. They settled down, established Petra as their capital, and for a time controlled all of Transjordan, even as far as Damascus. It was from a Nabatean governor that St. Paul escaped about 38 A.D. (2 Cor 11, 32f).

5, 46: Ephron: a city in Trans-Jordan opposite Bethshan, about five miles east of the Jordan River. Situated on a height, it dominated the valleys of the two tributaries of the Jordan.

Jamnia. **59** But Gorgias and his men came out
of the city to meet them in battle. **60** Joseph and
Azariah were beaten, and were pursued to the
frontiers of Judea, and about two thousand Israelites fell that day. **61** It was a bad defeat for the
people, because they had not obeyed Judas and
his brothers, thinking that they would do brave
deeds. **62** But they did not belong to the family
of those men to whom it was granted to achieve
Israel's salvation. **63** The valiant Judas and his
brothers were greatly renowned in all Israel and
among all the Gentiles, wherever their name
was heard; **64** and men gathered about them
and praised them.

**65** Then Judas and his brothers went out and
attacked the sons of Esau* in the country toward
the south; he took Hebron and its villages, and
he destroyed its strongholds and burned the towers around it. **66** He then set out for the land of
the Philistines and passed through Marisa.
**67** At that time some priests fell in battle who
had gone out rashly to fight in their desire to
distinguish themselves. **68** Judas then turned
toward Azotus in the land of the Philistines. He
destroyed their altars and burned the statues of
their gods; and after plundering their cities he
returned to the land of Judah.

## CHAPTER 6

### Defeat and Death of Antiochus IV.

**1** [m]As King Antiochus was traversing the inland provinces, he heard that in Persia there was
a city called Elymais,* famous for its wealth in
silver and gold, **2** and that its temple was very
rich, containing gold helmets, breastplates, and
weapons left there by Alexander, son of Philip,
king of Macedon, the first king of the Greeks.
**3** He went therefore and tried to capture and
pillage the city. But he could not do so, because
his plan became known to the people of the city
**4** who rose up in battle against him. So he
retreated and in great dismay withdrew from
there to return to Babylon.

**5** While he was in Persia, a messenger
brought him news that the armies sent into the
land of Judah had been put to flight; **6** that
Lysias had gone at first with a strong army and
been driven back by the Israelites; that they had
grown strong by reason of the arms, men, and
abundant possessions taken from the armies
they had destroyed; **7** that they had pulled down
the Abomination which he had built upon the
altar in Jerusalem; and that they had surrounded
with high walls both the sanctuary, as it had
been before, and his city of Beth-zur.[n]

**8** When the king heard this news, he was
struck with fear and very much shaken. Sick
with grief because his designs had failed, he
took to his bed. **9** There he remained many
days, overwhelmed with sorrow, for he knew he
was going to die.

**10** So he called in all his Friends and said to
them: "Sleep has departed from my eyes, for
my heart is sinking with anxiety. **11** I said to
myself: 'Into what tribulation have I come, and
in what floods of sorrow am I now! **12** Yet I
was kindly and beloved in my rule.' But I now
recall the evils I did in Jerusalem, when I carried
away all the vessels of gold and silver that were
in it, and for no cause gave orders that the
inhabitants of Judah be destroyed. **13** I know
that this is why these evils have overtaken me;
and now I am dying, in bitter grief, in a foreign
land."

**14** Then he summoned Philip, one of his
Friends, and put him in charge of his whole
kingdom. **15** He gave him his crown, his robe,
and his signet ring, so that he might guide the
king's son Antiochus and bring him up to be
king. **16** King Antiochus died in Persia in the
year one hundred and forty-nine.*

**The Citadel Besieged.** **17** When Lysias
learned that the king was dead, he set up the
king's son Antiochus,* whom he had reared as
a child, to be king in his place; and he gave him
the title Eupator.[o]

**18** The men in the citadel were hemming in
Israel around the sanctuary, continually trying
to harm them and to strengthen the Gentiles.[p]
**19** But Judas planned to destroy them, and
called all the people together to besiege them.
**20** So in the year one hundred and fifty* they
assembled and stormed the citadel, for which
purpose he constructed catapults and other devices. **21** Some of the besieged escaped, joined
by impious Israelites; **22** they went to the king
and said:

"How long will you fail to do justice and
avenge our kinsmen? **23** We agreed to serve
your father and to follow his orders and obey his
edicts. **24** And for this the sons of our people
have become our enemies; they have put to

m 1-13: 2 Mc 1, 12-17; 9, 1-29.
n 1 Mc 1, 54; 4, 41ff.60f.
o 2 Mc 10, 10f.
p 1 Mc 1, 33ff.

* 5, 65: Sons of Esau: Idumeans.

6, 1: Elymais: the mountainous region of Elam, north of the Persian Gulf. This section continues the story from 1 Mc 3, 37 and pertains to events preceding those in 1 Mc 4, 37ff.

6, 16: The year one hundred and forty-nine: September 22, 164, to October 9, 163 B.C. A Babylonian list of the Seleucid kings indicates that Antiochus died in November or early December of 164.

6, 17: The king's son Antiochus: Antiochus V Eupator, then about nine years old. He was in Antioch, still in the charge of Lysias, who proceeded to govern and wage wars in his name. Both were put to death two years later, when Demetrius, brother of Antiochus IV, arrived to claim the kingship; cf 1 Mc 7, 1ff.

6, 20: The year one hundred and fifty: October, 163, to September, 162 B.C.

death as many of us as they could find and have plundered our estates. **25** They have acted aggressively not only against us, but throughout their whole territory. **26** Look! They have now besieged the citadel in Jerusalem in order to capture it, and they have fortified the sanctuary and Beth-zur. **27** Unless you quickly forestall them, they will do even worse things than these, and you will not be able to stop them.''

**Campaign against Judas.** **28** [q]When the king heard this he was angry, and he called together all his Friends, the officers of his army, and the commanders of the cavalry.[r] **29** Mercenary forces also came to him from other kingdoms and from the islands of the seas. **30** His army numbered a hundred thousand foot-soldiers, twenty thousand cavalry, and thirty-two elephants trained for war. **31** They passed through Idumea and camped before Beth-zur. For many days they attacked it; they constructed siege-devices, but the besieged made a sortie and burned these, and they fought bravely.

**32** Then Judas marched away from the citadel and moved his camp to Beth-zechariah, on the way to the king's camp. **33** The king, rising before dawn, moved his force hastily along the road to Beth-zechariah; and the armies prepared for battle, while the trumpets sounded. **34** They made the elephants drunk on grape and mulberry wine to provoke them to fight. **35** The beasts were distributed along the phalanxes, each elephant having assigned to it a thousand men in coats of mail, with bronze helmets, and five hundred picked cavalry. **36** These anticipated the beast wherever it was; and wherever it moved, they moved too and never left it. **37** A strong wooden tower covering each elephant, and fastened to it by a harness, held, besides the Indian mahout, three soldiers who fought from it. **38** The remaining cavalry were stationed on one or the other of the two flanks of the army, to harass the enemy and to be protected from the phalanxes. **39** When the sun shone on the gold and bronze shields, the mountains gleamed with their brightness and blazed like flaming torches. **40** Part of the king's army extended over the heights, while some were on low ground, but they marched forward steadily and in good order. **41** All who heard the noise of their numbers, the tramp of their marching, and the clashing of the arms, trembled; for the army was very great and strong.

**42** Judas with his army advanced to fight, and six hundred men of the king's army fell. **43** Eleazar, called Avaran, saw one of the beasts bigger than any of the others and covered with royal armor, and he thought the king must be on it.[s] **44** So he gave up his life to save his people and win an everlasting name for himself. **45** He dashed up to it in the middle of the phalanx, killing men right and left, so that they fell back from him on both sides. **46** He ran right under the elephant and stabbed it in the belly, killing it. The beast fell to the ground on top of him, and he died there.

**47** When the Jews saw the strength of the royal army and the ardor of its forces, they retreated from them. **48** [t]A part of the king's army went up to Jerusalem to attack them, and the king established camps in Judea and at Mount Zion. **49** [u]He made peace with the men of Beth-zur, and they evacuated the city, because they had no food there to enable them to stand a siege, for that was a sabbath year in the land.* **50** The king took Beth-zur and stationed a garrison there to hold it. **51** For many days he besieged the sanctuary, setting up artillery and machines, fire-throwers, catapults and mechanical bows for shooting arrows and slingstones. **52** The Jews countered by setting up machines of their own, and kept up the fight a long time. **53** But there were no provisions in the storerooms, because it was the seventh year, and the tide-over provisions had been eaten up by those who had been rescued from the Gentiles and brought to Judea. **54** Few men remained in the sanctuary; the rest scattered, each to his own home, for the famine was too much for them.

**Peace Treaty.** **55** [v]Lysias heard that Philip, whom King Antiochus, before his death, had appointed to train his son Antiochus to be king, **56** had returned from Persia and Media with the army that accompanied the king, and that he was seeking to take over the government. **57** So he hastily resolved to withdraw. He said to the king, the leaders of the army, and the soldiers: ''We are growing weaker every day, our provisions are scanty, the place we are besieging is strong, and it is our duty to take care of the affairs of the kingdom.[w] **58** Therefore let us now come to terms with these men, and make peace with them and all their nation. **59** Let us grant them freedom to live according to their own laws as formerly; it was on account of their laws, which we abolished, that they became angry and did all these things.''

**60** The proposal found favor with the king and the leaders; he sent peace terms to the Jews, and they accepted. **61** So the king and the leaders swore an oath to them, and on these terms they evacuated the fortification. **62** But when

q 28-54: 2 Mc 13, 1-23.
r 28ff: 2 Mc 13, 1f.
s 2 Mc 13, 15.
t 48f: 2 Mc 13, 22-23.
u Lv 25, 2.
v 55-63: 2 Mc 13, 23-26.
w 2 Mc 11, 13ff.

* 6, 49: A sabbath year in the land: when sowing and reaping were prohibited (Ex 23, 10f; Lv 25, 2–7). The year without a harvest (autumn of 164 to autumn of 163) was followed by a food shortage.

the king entered Mount Zion and saw how the
place was fortified, he broke the oath he had
sworn and gave orders for the encircling wall to
be destroyed. **63** Then he departed in haste and
returned to Antioch, where he found Philip in
possession of the city. He fought against him
and took the city by force.

## CHAPTER 7

### Expedition of Bacchides and Alcimus.

**1** [x]In the year one hundred and fifty-one,* Demetrius, son of Seleucus, set out from Rome,
arrived with a few men in a city on the seacoast,
and began to rule there. **2** As he was preparing
to enter the royal palace of his ancestors, the
soldiers seized Antiochus and Lysias to bring
them to him. **3** When he was informed of this,
he said, "Do not show me their faces." **4** So
the soldiers killed them, and Demetrius sat on
the royal throne.

**5** Then all the lawless and impious men of
Israel came to him. They were led by Alcimus,*
who desired to be high priest. **6** They made this
accusation to the king against the people: "Judas and his brothers have destroyed all your
friends and have driven us out of our country.
**7** So now, send a man whom you trust to go and
see all the havoc Judas has done to us and to the
king's land, and let him punish them and all
their supporters."

**8** Then the king chose Bacchides, one of the
King's Friends, governor of West-of-Euphrates, a great man in the kingdom, and faithful to
the king. **9** [y]He sent him and the impious Alcimus, to whom he granted the high priesthood,
with orders to take revenge on the Israelites.
**10** They set out and, on arriving in the land of
Judah with a great army, sent messengers who
spoke deceitfully to Judas and his brothers in
peaceful terms. **11** But these paid no attention
to their words, seeing that they had come with
a great army. **12** A group of scribes, however,
gathered about Alcimus and Bacchides to ask
for a just agreement. **13** [z]The Hasideans were
the first among the Israelites to seek peace with
them, **14** for they said, "A priest of the line of
Aaron has come with the army, and he will not
do us any wrong." **15** He spoke with them
peacefully and swore to them, "We will not try
to injure you or your friends." **16** So they trusted him. But he arrested sixty of them and killed
them in one day, according to the text of Scripture:

**17** "The flesh of your saints they have strewn,
and their blood they have shed round
about Jerusalem,
and there was no one to bury them.[a]

**18** Then fear and dread of them came upon all
the people, who said: "There is no truth or
justice among them; they violated the agreement
and the oath that they swore."

**19** Bacchides withdrew from Jerusalem and
pitched his camp in Beth-zaith.* He had many
of the men arrested who deserted him, throwing
them into the great pit. **20** He handed the province over to Alcimus, leaving troops to help
him, while he himself returned to the king.

**21** Alcimus spared no pains to maintain his
high priesthood, **22** and all those who were disturbing their people gathered about him. They
took possession of the land of Judah and caused
great distress in Israel. **23** When Judas saw all
the evils that Alcimus and his men were bringing upon the Israelites, more than even the Gentiles had done, **24** he went about all the borders
of Judea and took revenge on the men who had
deserted, preventing them from going out into
the country. **25** But when Alcimus saw that
Judas and his followers were gaining strength
and realized that he could not oppose them, he
returned to the king and accused them of grave
crimes.

**Defeat of Nicanor.** **26** [b]Then the king sent
Nicanor, one of his famous officers, who was
a bitter enemy of Israel, with orders to destroy
the people. **27** Nicanor came to Jerusalem with
a large force and deceitfully sent to Judas* and
his brothers this peaceable message: **28** "Let
there be no fight between me and you. I will
come with a few men to meet you peaceably."

**29** So he came to Judas, and they greeted one
another peaceably. But Judas' enemies were
prepared to seize him. **30** When he became
aware that Nicanor had come to him with
treachery in mind, Judas was afraid and would
not meet him again.[c] **31** When Nicanor saw

x 1-7: 2 Mc 14, 1-11.
y 9ff: 2 Mc 14, 46.
z 13f: 1 Mc 2, 42.
a Ps 79, 1ff.
b 26f: 1 Mc 3, 38; 2 Mc 8, 9; 14, 12f.
c 2 Mc 14, 30.

*

7, 1ff: The year one hundred and fifty-one: the spring of 161 B.C. Demetrius, son of Seleucus, was the lawful heir to the kingdom; but when only nine years old, he was taken as a hostage at Rome in place of his uncle, who ruled as Antiochus IV Epiphanes. At the age of twenty-five Demetrius fled secretly from Rome and, with the support of the Syrians, overcame his rival Antiochus V and put him to death. The royal palace: at Antioch.

7, 5f: Alcimus: a renegade Jew hostile to the Maccabees, who became high priest after the death of Menelaus (2 Mc 14, 3). He received confirmation in his office from the new King Demetrius (v 9), and brought malicious charges against Judas and his brothers and the people (v 6). He wrought more evils on the Israelites than the Gentiles had done (v 23).

7, 19: Beth-zaith: about three miles north of Beth-zur and twelve miles south of Jerusalem.

7, 27: Nicanor . . . deceitfully sent to Judas: a more favorable picture of Nicanor, as an honest man who became a personal friend of Judas, is given in 2 Mc 14, 17–25. Their friendship was broken by the intrigues of Alcimus (2 Mc 14, 26–30).

7, 31: Caphar-salama: a village seven miles north-north-

that his plan had been discovered, he went out
to fight Judas near Caphar-salama.* **32** About
five hundred men of Nicanor's army fell; the
rest fled to the City of David.

**33** [d]After this, Nicanor went up to Mount
Zion. Some of the priests from the sanctuary
and some of the elders of the people came out
to greet him peaceably and to show him the
holocaust that was being offered for the king.
**34** But he mocked and ridiculed them, defiled
them,* and spoke disdainfully. **35** In a rage he
swore: "If Judas and his army are not delivered
to me at once, when I return victorious I will
burn this temple down." He went away in great
anger. **36** The priests, however, went in and
stood before the altar and the sanctuary.[e] They
wept and said: **37** "You have chosen this house
to bear your name, to be a house of prayer and
petition for your people. **38** Take revenge on
this man and his army, and let them fall by the
sword. Remember their blasphemies, and do
not let them continue."

**39** Nicanor left Jerusalem and pitched his
camp at Beth-horon, where the Syrian army
joined him. **40** But Judas camped in Adasa*
with three thousand men. Here Judas uttered
this prayer: **41** "When they who were sent by
the king blasphemed, your angel went out and
killed a hundred and eighty-five thousand of
them.[f] **42** In the same way, crush this army
before us today, and let the rest know that Nicanor spoke wickedly against your sanctuary;
judge him according to his wickedness."[g]

**43** The armies met in battle on the thirteenth
day of the month Adar. Nicanor's army was
crushed, and he himself was the first to fall in
the battle.[h] **44** When his army saw that Nicanor
was dead, they threw down their arms and fled.
**45** The Jews pursued them a day's journey,
from Adasa to near Gazara, blowing the trumpets behind them as signals. **46** From all the
surrounding villages of Judea people came out
and closed in on them. They hemmed them in,
and all the enemies fell by the sword; not a
single one escaped.

**47** Then the Jews collected the spoils and the
booty; they cut off Nicanor's head and his right
arm, which he had lifted up so arrogantly. These
they brought to Jerusalem and displayed there.
**48** The people rejoiced greatly, and observed
that day as a great festival. **49** They decreed
that it should be observed every year on the
thirteenth of Adar.* **50** And for a short time*
the land of Judah was quiet.

## CHAPTER 8

**Treaty with the Romans.*** **1** Judas had
heard of the reputation of the Romans. They
were valiant fighters and acted amiably to all
who took their side. They established a friendly
alliance with all who applied to them. **2** He was
also told of their battles and the brave deeds that
they had performed against the Gauls,* conquering them and forcing them to pay tribute.
**3** They had gotten possession of the silver and
gold mines in Spain, **4** and by planning and
persistence had conquered the whole country,
although it was very remote from their own.
They had crushed the kings who had come
against them from the far corners of the earth
and had inflicted on them severe defeat, and the
rest paid tribute to them every year. **5** Philip*
and Perseus, king of the Macedonians, and the
others who opposed them in battle had been
overwhelmed and subjugated. **6** Antiochus*
the Great, king of Asia, who had fought against
them with a hundred and twenty elephants and
with cavalry and chariots and a very great army,
had been defeated by them. **7** They had taken
him alive and obliged him and the kings who
succeeded him to pay a heavy tribute, to give
hostages and a section of **8** Lycia, Mysia,* and

d 33-38: 2 Mc 14, 31-36.
e Jl 2, 17.
f 41f: 2 Mc 8, 19; 15, 22ff.
g Is 37, 36ff.
h 2 Mc 15, 25-35.

* west of Jerusalem, on the road leading to Beth-horon.

7, 34: Defiled them: spitting on the priests caused them to become legally defiled.

7, 40: Adasa: a village southeast of Caphar-salama.

7, 49: The thirteenth of Adar: March 27, 160 B.C. This day in the Jewish calendar was called the "Day of Nicanor" (2 Mc 15, 36); but it was not long celebrated by the Jews.

7, 50: A short time: about one month following the death of Nicanor. After that began the attack of Bacchides resulting in the death of Judas (1 Mc 9, 1–18).

8, 1: This chapter contains the account of the embassy which Judas sent to Rome, probably before the death of Nicanor, to conclude a treaty of alliance between Rome and the Jewish nation. Without precise chronology, the pertinent data are gathered into a unified theme.

The image of the Roman Republic greatly impressed the smaller Eastern peoples seeking support against their overlords (1–16), because of Roman success in war (2–11) and effective aid to their allies (12–13). Numerous interventions by Rome in the politics of the Near East bear witness to its power and prestige in the second century B.C. Cf 1 Mc 1, 10; 7, 2; 12, 3; 15, 15–24; 2 Mc 11, 34. With the Roman control of Palestine in 63 B.C., the Republic and later the Empire became heartily detested. The eulogy of Rome in this chapter is one of the reasons why 1 Maccabees was not preserved by the Palestinian Jews of the century that followed.

8, 2: Gauls: probably the Celts of northern Italy and southern France, subdued by the Romans in 222 B.C., and again in 200–191 B.C.; but perhaps also those in Asia Minor (the Galatians), whom the Romans defeated in 189 B.C.

8, 5: Philip: Philip V of Macedonia, defeated by a Graeco-Roman alliance at Cynoscephalae in 197 B.C. Perseus, his son, was defeated at Pydna in 168 B.C., and died a prisoner. With this, the kingdom of Macedonia came to an end.

8, 6: Antiochus: Antiochus III, greatest of the Seleucid kings. He was defeated at Magnesia in 190 B.C. By the Treaty of Apamea in 189, he was obliged to pay Rome a crushing indemnity of 15,000 talents. It was the weakening of Antiochene power and the growing military and economic influence of Rome that led Antiochus IV to adopt the policy of political, religious and cultural unification of Syria and Palestine.

8, 8: Lycia, Mysia: regions in western Asia Minor. These

Lydia from among their best provinces. The
Romans took these from him and gave them to
King Eumenes. **9** *When the men of Greece
had planned to come and destroy them, **10** the
Romans discovered it, and sent against the
Greeks a single general who made war on them.
Many were wounded and fell, and the Romans
took their wives and children captive. They
plundered them, took possession of their land,
tore down their strongholds and reduced them to
slavery even to this day. **11** All the other kingdoms and islands that had ever opposed them
they destroyed and enslaved; **12** with their
friends, however, and those who relied on
them, they maintained friendship. They had
conquered kings both far and near, and all who
heard of their fame were afraid of them. **13** In
truth, those whom they desired to help to a
kingdom became kings, and those whom they
wished to depose they deposed; and they were
greatly exalted. **14** Yet with all this, none of
them put on a crown or wore purple as a display
of grandeur. **15** They had made for themselves
a senate house, and every day three hundred and
twenty men took counsel, deliberating on all
that concerned the people and their well-being.
**16** They entrusted their government to one
man* every year, to rule over their entire country, and they all obeyed that one, and there was
no envy or jealousy among them.

**17** So Judas chose Eupolemus, son of John,
son of Accos, and Jason, son of Eleazar, and
sent them to Rome to establish an alliance of
friendship with them.[i] **18** He did this to get rid
of the yoke, for it was obvious that the kingdom
of the Greeks was subjecting Israel to slavery.
**19** After making a very long journey to Rome,
the envoys entered the senate and spoke as follows: **20** "Judas, called Maccabeus, and his
brothers, with the Jewish people, have sent us
to you to make a peaceful alliance with you, and
to enroll ourselves among your allies and
friends." **21** The proposal pleased the Romans,
**22** and this is a copy of the reply they inscribed
on bronze tablets and sent to Jerusalem,* to
remain there with the Jews as a record of peace
and alliance:[j]

**23** "May it be well with the Romans and the
Jewish nation at sea and on land forever; may
sword and enemy be far from them. **24** But if
war is first made on Rome, or any of its allies
in any of their dominions, **25** the Jewish nation
will help them wholeheartedly, as the occasion
shall demand; **26** and to those who wage war
they shall not give nor provide grain, arms,
money, or ships; this is Rome's decision. They
shall fulfill their obligations without receiving
any recompense. **27** In the same way, if war is
made first on the Jewish nation, the Romans
will help them willingly, as the occasion shall
demand, **28** and to those who are attacking
them there shall not be given grain, arms, money, or ships; this is Rome's decision. They shall
fulfill their obligations without deception.
**29** On these terms the Romans have made an
agreement with the Jewish people. **30** But if
both parties hereafter decide to add or take away
anything, they shall do as they choose, and
whatever they shall add or take away shall be
valid.

**31** "Moreover, concerning the wrongs that
King Demetrius has done to them, we have
written to him thus: 'Why have you made your
yoke heavy upon our friends and allies the
Jews? **32** If they complain about you again, we
will do them justice and make war on you by
land and sea.' "

## CHAPTER 9

**Invasion of Judah.** **1** When Demetrius
heard that Nicanor and his army had fallen in
battle, he again sent Bacchides and Alcimus
into the land of Judah, along with the right wing
of his army. **2** They took the road to Galilee,
and camping opposite the ascent at Arbela, they
captured it* and killed many people. **3** In the
first month of the year one hundred and fifty-
two,* they encamped against Jerusalem.
**4** Then they set out for Berea with twenty thousand men and two thousand cavalry. **5** Judas,
with three thousand picked men, had camped at
Elasa. **6** When his men saw the great number of

---

i 1 Mc 12, 1f; 15, 15-22. j 1 Mc 14, 18.

---

* names are restored here by conjectural emendation: the Greek text has "India, Media," most likely through scribal error. Eumenes: Eumenes II (197–158), king of Pergamum, an ally of Rome who benefited greatly from Antiochus' losses.

8, 9f: The revolt of the Achaean League, inserted here, occurred in 146 B.C., after Judas' time. It was crushed by the Roman consul Lucius Mummius and marked the end of Greek independence. The author regards all Greeks as the enemies of God.

8, 16: They entrusted their government to one man: actually the Roman Republic always had two consuls as joint heads of the government. Presumably, a single one dealt with embassies and answered letters, hence the impression the Jews received; cf 1 Mc 15, 16.

8, 22: The reply . . . on bronze tablets and sent to Jerusalem: the decree of the Senate would be inscribed on bronze and kept in the Roman Capitol, with only a copy in letter form sent to Jerusalem. The translation of the decree into Hebrew and then into Greek, as found here in 1 Mc, may have occasioned this error.

9, 2: They took the road . . . Arbela, they captured it: this passage is restored, in part, by conjectural emendation. The present Greek text could be translated, "They took the road to Gilgal, and camping opposite Mesaloth at Arbela, they captured it." But Arbela (modern Khirbet Irbid) was in Galilee—on a high hill overlooking the western shore of the Sea of Galilee. Gilgal, on the contrary, was in the Jordan valley near Jericho. "Mesaloth" is probably a corrupt form of a Hebrew word meaning "steps, ascent."

9, 3: The first month of the year one hundred and fifty-two: April/May 160 B.C., by the temple calendar.

the troops, they were very much afraid, and
many slipped away from the camp, until only
eight hundred men remained.
**7** As Judas saw that his army was melting
away just when the battle was imminent, he was
panic-stricken, because he had no time to gather
them together. **8** But in spite of his discouragement, he said to those who remained: "Let us
go forward to meet our enemies; perhaps we can
put up a good fight against them." **9** They tried
to dissuade him, saying: "We certainly cannot.
Let us save our lives now, and come back with
our kinsmen, and then fight against them. Now
we are too few." **10** But Judas said: "Far be it
from me to do such a thing as to flee from them!
If our time has come, let us die bravely for our
kinsmen and not leave a stain upon our glory!"

**Death of Judas.** **11** Then the army of Bacchides moved out of camp and took its position
for combat. The cavalry were divided into two
squadrons, and the slingers and the archers
came on ahead of the army, and all the valiant
men were in the front line. **12** Bacchides was
on the right wing. Flanked by the two squadrons, the phalanx attacked as they blew their
trumpets. Those who were on Judas' side also
blew their trumpets. **13** The earth shook with
the noise of the armies, and the battle raged
from morning until evening. **14** Seeing that
Bacchides was on the right, with the main force
of his army, Judas, with all the most stouthearted rallying to him, **15** drove back the right wing
and pursued them as far as the mountain
slopes.* **16** But when the men on the left wing
saw that the right wing was driven back, they
turned and followed Judas and his men, taking
them in the rear. **17** The battle was fought des-
perately, and many on both sides fell wounded.
**18** Then Judas fell, and the rest fled.
**19** Jonathan and Simon took their brother
Judas and buried him in the tomb of their fathers
at Modein. **20** All Israel bewailed him in great
grief. They mourned for him many days, and
they said, **21** "How the mighty one has fallen,
the savior of Israel!"[k] **22** The other acts of
Judas, his battles, the brave deeds he performed, and his greatness have not been recorded; but they were very many.

## *IV: Leadership of Jonathan*

**Bacchides and Jonathan.** **23** After the
death of Judas, the transgressors of the law
raised their heads in every part of Israel, and all
kinds of evildoers appeared. **24** In those days
there was a very great famine, and the country
deserted to them. **25** Bacchides chose impious
men and made them masters of the country.
**26** These sought out and hunted down the
friends of Judas and brought them to Bacchides,
who punished and derided them. **27** There had
not been such great distress in Israel since the
time prophets ceased to appear among the people.
**28** Then all the friends of Judas came together and said to Jonathan: **29** "Since your brother
Judas died, there has been no one like him to
oppose our enemies, Bacchides and those who
are hostile to our nation. **30** Now therefore we
have chosen you today to be our ruler and leader
in his place, and to fight our battle." **31** From
that moment Jonathan accepted the leadership,
and took the place of Judas his brother.
**32** When Bacchides learned of it, he sought
to kill him. **33** But Jonathan and his brother
Simon and all the men with him discovered this,
and they fled to the desert of Tekoa* and
camped by the waters of the pool of Asphar.*
**35** Jonathan sent his brother* as leader of the
convoy to ask permission of his friends, the
Nabateans, to deposit with them their great
quantity of baggage.[l] **36** But the sons of Jambri
from Medaba* made a raid and seized and carried off John and everything he had. **37** After
this, word was brought to Jonathan and his
brother Simon: "The sons of Jambri are celebrating a great wedding, and with a large escort
they are bringing the bride, the daughter of one
of the great princes of Canaan, from Nada-
bath." **38** Remembering the blood of John their
brother, they went up and hid themselves under
cover of the mountain. **39** They watched, and
suddenly saw a noisy crowd with baggage; the
bridegroom and his friends and kinsmen had
come out to meet the bride's party with tambourines and musicians and much equipment.
**40** The Jews rose up against them from their
ambush and killed them. Many fell wounded,
and after the survivors fled toward the mountain, all their spoils were taken. **41** Thus the
wedding was turned into mourning, and the
sound of music into lamentation. **42** Having
taken their revenge for the blood of their brother, the Jews returned to the marshes of the Jordan.
**43** When Bacchides heard of it, he came on
the sabbath to the banks of the Jordan with a
large force. **44** Then Jonathan said to his companions, "Let us get up now and fight for our
lives, for today is not like yesterday and the day

k 2 Sam 1, 27. l 1 Mc 5, 25.

*

9, 15: As far as the mountain slopes: conjectural emendation. The Greek text has "as far as Mount Azotus"; this is most unlikely. Apparently the Greek translator mistook the Hebrew word ashdot, "slopes," for asdod, "Azotus."

9, 33: Tekoa: Home of the prophet Amos in the wild country above the Dead Sea, southeast of Jerusalem.

9, 34: Omitted, it is a dittography of verse 43.

9, 35: Jonathan sent his brother: this was John who was called Gaddi (1 Mc 2, 2; cf 9, 36. 38).

9, 36: Medaba: northeast of the Dead Sea.

before. **45** The battle is before us, and behind
us are the waters of the Jordan on one side,
marsh and thickets on the other, and there is no
way of escape.* **46** Cry out now to Heaven for
deliverance from our enemies.'' **47** When they
joined battle, Jonathan raised his arm to strike
Bacchides, but Bacchides backed away from
him. **48** Jonathan and his men jumped into the
Jordan and swam across to the other side, but
the enemy did not pursue them across the Jordan. **49** A thousand men on Bacchides' side fell
that day.

**50** On returning to Jerusalem, Bacchides
built strongholds in Judea: the Jericho fortress,
as well as Emmaus, Beth-horon, Bethel, Tim-
nath, Pharathon, and Tephon, with high walls
and gates and bars.* **51** In each he put a garrison to oppose Israel. **52** He fortified the city of
Beth-zur, Gazara and the citadel, and put soldiers in them and stores of provisions. **53** He
took as hostages the sons of the leaders of the
country and put them in custody in the citadel
at Jerusalem.[m]

**54** In the year one hundred and fifty-three, in
the second month,* Alcimus ordered the wall of
the inner court of the sanctuary to be torn down,
thus destroying the work of the prophets. But he
only began to tear it down. **55** Just at that time
he had a stroke, and his work was interrupted;
his mouth was closed and he was paralyzed, so
that he could no longer utter a word to give
orders concerning his house. **56** Finally he died
in great agony. **57** Seeing that Alcimus was
dead, Bacchides returned to the king, and the
land of Judah was quiet for two years.

**58** Then all the transgressors of the law held
a council and said: ''Jonathan and his companions are living in peace and security. Now then,
let us have Bacchides return, and he will capture
all of them in a single night.'' **59** So they went
and took counsel with him. **60** When Bacchides
was setting out with a large force, he sent letters
secretly to all his allies in Judea, telling them to
seize Jonathan and his companions. They were
not able to do this, however, because their plot
became known. **61** In fact, Jonathan's men
seized about fifty of the men of the country who
were ring-leaders in the mischief and put them
to death. **62** Then Jonathan and Simon and their
companions withdrew to Bethbasi* in the
desert; they rebuilt and strengthened its fortifications that had been demolished. **63** When
Bacchides learned of this, he gathered together
his whole force and sent word to those who were
in Judea. **64** He came and pitched his camp
before Bethbasi, and constructing siege-ma-
chines, he fought against it for many days.

**65** Leaving his brother Simon in the city,
Jonathan, accompanied by a small group of
men, went out into the field. **66** He struck down
Odomera and his kinsmen and the sons of Phasi-
ron in their encampment; these men had set out
to go up to the siege with their forces. **67** Simon
and his men then sallied forth from the city and
set fire to the machines. **68** They fought against
Bacchides, and he was beaten. This caused him
great distress. Because the enterprise he had
planned came to naught, **69** he was angry with
the lawless men who had advised him to invade
the province. He killed many of them and resolved to return to his own country.

**70** Jonathan learned of this and sent ambassadors to make peace with him and to obtain the
release of the prisoners. **71** He agreed to do as
Jonathan had asked. He swore an oath to him
that he would never try to injure him for the rest
of his life; **72** and he released the prisoners he
had previously taken from the land of Judah. He
returned to his own country and never came into
their territory again.

**73** Then the sword ceased in Israel. Jonathan
settled in Michmash; he began to judge* the
people, and he destroyed the impious in Israel.

## CHAPTER 10

**Revolt of Alexander.** **1** In the year one
hundred and sixty,* Alexander, who was called
Epiphanes, son of Antiochus, came up and took
Ptolemais. He was accepted and began to reign
there. **2** When King Demetrius heard of it, he
mustered a very large army and marched out to
engage him in combat. **3** Demetrius sent a letter
to Jonathan written in peaceful terms, to pay
him honor; **4** for he said: ''Let us be the first to
make peace with him, before he makes peace
with Alexander against us, **5** since he will remember all the wrongs we have done to him, his
brothers, and his nation.''

**6** So Demetrius authorized Jonathan, as his
ally, to gather an army and procure arms; and
he ordered that the hostages in the citadel be
released to him. **7** Accordingly Jonathan went

---

m 1 Mc 10, 9.

*

9, 45: Jonathan's force was apparently trapped in one of the many oxbows of the lower Jordan. Bacchides had crossed and caught them still on the east bank.

9, 50: These sites constitute a ring on the edges of the province of Judea.

9, 54: In the year . . . second month: May 159 B.C.

9, 62: Bethbasi: two miles east of Bethlehem, and six miles north of Tekoa.

9, 73: Began to judge: exercise the governing authority as in the book of Judges. With Jerusalem and the garrison towns (v 50) firmly in Seleucid hands, Jonathan's freedom of action was greatly restricted. Michmash, southeast of Bethel, famous for the exploit of the former Jonathan, son of Saul; cf 1 Sm 14.

10, 1: The year one hundred and sixty: 152 B.C. Alexander . . . Antiochus: Alexander Balas claimed to be a son of Antiochus IV. He had the backing of the Romans, who had never forgiven Demetrius for becoming king without their permission. The latter meanwhile had become unpopular with his own people as well as with the Jews.

up to Jerusalem and read the letter to all the
people. The men in the citadel **8** were struck
with fear when they heard that the king had
given him authority to gather an army. **9** They
released the hostages to Jonathan, and he gave
them back to their parents.[n] **10** Thereafter Jonathan dwelt in Jerusalem, and began to build
and restore the city. **11** He ordered the workmen to build the walls and encircle Mount Zion
with square stones for its fortification, which
they did. **12** The foreigners in the strongholds
that Bacchides had built, took flight; **13** each
one of them left his place and returned to his
own country. **14** Only in Beth-zur did some
remain of those who had abandoned the law and
the commandments, for they used it as a place
of refuge.

**Jonathan Supports Alexander.** **15** King
Alexander heard of the promises that Demetrius
had made to Jonathan; he was also told of the
battles and valiant deeds of Jonathan and his
brothers and the troubles that they had endured.
**16** He said, "Shall we ever find another man
like him? Let us now make him our friend and
ally." **17** So he sent Jonathan a letter written in
these terms: **18** "King Alexander sends greetings to his brother Jonathan. **19** We have heard
of you, that you are a mighty warrior and worthy
to be our friend. **20** We have therefore appointed you today to be high priest of your nation;
you are to be called the King's Friend, and you
are to look after our interests and preserve amity
with us." He also sent him a purple robe and a
crown of gold.[o]

**21** Jonathan put on the sacred vestments in
the seventh month of the year one hundred and
sixty at the feast of Booths,* and he gathered an
army and procured many arms. **22** When Demetrius heard of these things, he was distressed
and said: **23** Why have we allowed Alexander
to get ahead of us by gaining the friendship of
the Jews and thus strengthening himself? **24** I
too will write them conciliatory words and offer
dignities and gifts, so that they may be an aid
to me."

**25** So he sent them this message: "King Demetrius sends greetings to the Jewish nation.
**26** We have heard how you have kept the treaty
with us and continued in our friendship and not
gone over to our enemies, and we are glad.
**27** Continue, therefore, to keep faith with us,
and we will reward you with favors in return for
what you do in our behalf. **28** We will grant you
many exemptions and will bestow gifts on you.

**29** "I now free you, as I also exempt all the
Jews, from the tribute, the salt tax, and the
crown levies.[p] **30** [q]Instead of collecting the
third of the grain and the half of the fruit of the
trees that should be my share, I renounce the
right from this day forward. Neither now nor in
the future will I collect them from the land of
Judah or from the three districts annexed from
Samaria.* **31** Let Jerusalem and her territory,
her tithes and her tolls, be sacred and free from
tax. **32** I also yield my authority over the citadel
in Jerusalem, and I transfer it to the high priest,
that he may put in it such men as he shall choose
to guard it. **33** Every one of the Jews who has
been carried into captivity from the land of Judah into any part of my kingdom I set at liberty
without ransom; and let all their taxes, even
those on their cattle, be canceled. **34** Let all
feast days, sabbaths, new moon festivals, appointed days, and the three days that precede
each feast day, and the three days that follow,
be days of immunity and exemption for every
Jew in my kingdom. **35** Let no man have authority to exact payment from them or to molest
any of them in any matter.

**36** "Let thirty thousand Jews be enrolled in
the king's army and allowances be given them,
as is due to all the king's soldiers. **37** Let some
of them be stationed in the king's principal
strongholds, and of these let some be given
positions of trust in the affairs of the kingdom.
Let their superiors and their rulers be taken from
among them, and let them follow their own
laws, as the king has commanded in the land of
Judah.

**38** "Let the three districts that have been
added to Judea from the province of Samaria be
incorporated with Judea so that they may be
under one man and obey no other authority than
the high priest. **39** Ptolemais and its confines I
give as a present to the sanctuary in Jerusalem
for the necessary expenses of the sanctuary.
**40** I make a yearly personal grant of fifteen
thousand silver shekels out of the royal revenues, from appropriate places. **41** All the additional funds that the officials did not hand over
as they had done in the first years, shall henceforth be handed over for the services of the
temple. **42** Moreover, the dues of five thousand
silver shekels that used to be taken from the
revenue of the sanctuary every year shall be
canceled, since these funds belong to the priests
who perform the services. **43** Whoever takes
refuge in the temple of Jerusalem or in any of

---

n 1 Mc 9, 53.
o 1 Mc 2, 18.
p 1 Mc 11, 28f. 35.
q 1 Mc 11, 28, 34.

---

10, 21: Jonathan . . . feast of Booths: Jonathan began to discharge the office of high priest October 23–30, 152 B.C. For seven years after the death of Alcimus there had been no high priest in Jerusalem. It was taken for granted that the king, though a Gentile, had the power to appoint one. The Maccabees, though a priestly family, were not of the line of Zadok, and some in Israel regarded Jonathan's tenure as a usurpation.

10, 30: The three districts annexed from Samaria: mentioned by name in 1 Mc 11, 34. The present Greek text, by a scribal error, has added "and Galilee" after "Samaria."

its precincts, because of money he owes the
king, or because of any other debt, shall be
released, together with all the goods he possesses in my kingdom. **44** The cost of rebuilding and restoring the structures of the sanctuary
shall be covered out of the royal revenue.
**45** Likewise the cost of building the walls of
Jerusalem and fortifying it all around, and of
building walls in Judea, shall be donated from
the royal revenue."

**46** When Jonathan and the people heard
these words, they neither believed nor accepted
them, for they remembered the great evil that
Demetrius had done in Israel, and how sorely he
had afflicted them. **47** They therefore decided
in favor of Alexander, for he had been the first
to address them peaceably, and they remained
his allies for the rest of his life.

**48** King Alexander gathered together a large
army and encamped opposite Demetrius.
**49** The two kings joined battle, and when the
army of Demetrius fled, Alexander pursued
him, and overpowered his soldiers. **50** He
pressed the battle hard until sunset, and Demetrius fell that day.

## Treaty of Ptolemy and Alexander.

**51** Alexander sent ambassadors to Ptolemy,
king of Egypt, with this message: **52** "Now
that I have returned to my realm, taken my seat
on the throne of my fathers, and established my
rule by crushing Demetrius and gaining control
of my country— **53** for I engaged him in battle,
defeated him and his army, and recovered the
royal throne— **54** let us now establish friendship with each other. Give me your daughter for
my wife; and as your son-in-law, I will give to
you and to her gifts worthy of you."

**55** King Ptolemy answered in these words:
"Happy the day on which you returned to the
land of your fathers and took your seat on their
royal throne! **56** I will do for you what you have
written; but meet me in Ptolemais, so that we
may see each other, and I will become your
father-in-law as you have proposed."

**57** So Ptolemy with his daughter Cleopatra*
set out from Egypt and came to Ptolemais in the
year one hundred and sixty-two. **58** There King
Alexander met him, and Ptolemy gave him his
daughter Cleopatra in marriage. Their wedding
was celebrated at Ptolemais with great splendor
according to the custom of kings.

**59** King Alexander also wrote to Jonathan to
come and meet him. **60** So he went with pomp
to Ptolemais, where he met the two kings and
gave them and their friends silver and gold and
many gifts and thus won their favor.[r] **61** Some
pestilent Israelites, transgressors of the law,
united against him to accuse him, but the king
paid no heed to them. **62** He ordered Jonathan
to be divested of his ordinary garments and to
be clothed in royal purple; and so it was done.
**63** The king also had him seated at his side. He
said to his magistrates: "Go with him to the
center of the city and make a proclamation that
no one is to bring charges against him on any
grounds or be troublesome to him in any way."

**64** [s]When his accusers saw the honor paid to
him in the proclamation, and the purple with
which he was clothed, they all fled. **65** The
king also honored him by numbering him
among his Chief Friends and made him military
commander and governor of the province.
**66** So Jonathan returned in peace and happiness
to Jerusalem.

## Victory over Apollonius.

**67** In the year
one hundred and sixty-five,* Demetrius, son of
Demetrius, came from Crete to the land of his
fathers. **68** When King Alexander heard of it he
was greatly troubled, and returned to Antioch.
**69** Demetrius appointed Apollonius governor
of Coelesyria. Having gathered a large army,
Apollonius pitched his camp at Jamnia. From
there he sent this message to Jonathan the high
priest:

**70** "You are the only one who resists us. I
am laughed at and put to shame on your account. Why are you displaying power against us
in the mountains? **71** If you have confidence in
your forces, come down now to us in the plain,
and let us test each other's strength there; the
city forces are on my side. **72** Inquire and learn
who I am and who the others are who are helping me. Men say that you cannot make a stand
against us because your fathers were twice put
to flight in their own land. **73** Now you too will
be unable to withstand our cavalry and such a
force as this in the plain, where there is not a
stone or a pebble or a place to flee."

**74** When Jonathan heard the message of
Apollonius, he was roused. Choosing ten thousand men, he set out from Jerusalem, and Simon
his brother joined him to help him. **75** He
pitched camp near Joppa, but the men in the city
shut him out because Apollonius had a garrison
there. When the Jews besieged it, **76** the men
of the city became afraid and opened the gates,
and so Jonathan took possession of Joppa.*

**77** When Apollonius heard of it, he drew up
three thousand horsemen and an innumerable
infantry. He marched on Azotus as though he

r 1 Mc 2, 18.  s 64f: 1 Mc 2, 18; 11, 27.

*

10, 57: Cleopatra: Cleopatra Thea, then about fifteen years old. She later married Demetrius II, and later still, his brother Antiochus VII. The year one hundred and sixty-two. 151/150 B.C.

10, 67: The year one hundred and sixty-five: 147 B.C. Demetrius: Demetrius II Nicator.

10, 76: Joppa: about forty miles northwest of Jerusalem. For the first time the Maccabees took possession of a seaport; nominally it was on behalf of King Alexander.

were going on through the country, but at the
same time he advanced into the plain, because
he had such a large number of horsemen to rely
on. **78** Jonathan followed him to Azotus, and
they engaged in battle. **79** Apollonius, however, had left a thousand cavalry in hiding behind
them. **80** When Jonathan discovered that there
was an ambush behind him, his army was surrounded. From morning until evening they
showered his men with arrows. **81** But his men
held their ground, as Jonathan had commanded,
whereas the enemy's horses became tired out.
**82** When the horsemen were exhausted, Simon
attacked the phalanx, overwhelmed it and put it
to flight. **83** The horsemen too were scattered
over the plain. The enemy fled to Azotus and
entered Beth-dagon, the temple of their idol, to
save themselves. **84** But Jonathan burned and
plundered Azotus with its neighboring towns,
and destroyed by fire both the temple of Dagon
and the men who had taken refuge in it.[t]
**85** Those who fell by the sword, together with
those who were burned alive, came to about
eight thousand men. **86** Then Jonathan left
there and pitched his camp at Ashkalon, and the
people of that city came out to meet him with
great pomp. **87** He and his men then returned
to Jerusalem, laden with much booty. **88** When
King Alexander heard of these events, he accorded new honors to Jonathan. **89** He sent him
a gold buckle, such as is usually given to King's
Kinsmen;* he also gave him Ekron and all its
territory as a possession.

## CHAPTER 11

### Alliance of Demetrius and Ptolemy.

**1** The king of Egypt gathered his forces, as
numerous as the sands of the seashore, and
many ships; and he sought by deceit to take
Alexander's kingdom and add it to his own.
**2** He entered Syria with peaceful words, and
the people in the cities opened their gates to
welcome him, as King Alexander had ordered
them to do, since Ptolemy was his father-in-
law. **3** But when Ptolemy entered the cities, he
stationed garrison troops in each one. **4** When
he reached Azotus, he was shown the temple of
Dagon destroyed by fire, Azotus and its suburbs
demolished, corpses lying about, and the
charred bodies of those burned by Jonathan in
the war and stacked up along his route.[u] **5** To
prejudice the king against Jonathan, he was told
what the latter had done; but the king said nothing. **6** Jonathan met the king with pomp at Joppa, and they greeted each other and spent the
night there. **7** Jonathan accompanied the king
as far as the river called Eleutherus* and then
returned to Jerusalem.

**8** Plotting evil against Alexander, King
Ptolemy took possession of the cities along the
seacoast as far as Seleucia-by-the-Sea.* **9** He
sent ambassadors to King Demetrius, saying:
"Come, let us make a pact with each other; I
will give you my daughter whom Alexander has
married, and you shall reign over your father's
kingdom. **10** I regret that I gave him my daughter, for he has sought to kill me."* **11** His real
reason for accusing Alexander, however, was
that he coveted Alexander's kingdom. **12** After
taking his daughter away and giving her to Demetrius, Ptolemy broke with Alexander; their
enmity became open. **13** Then Ptolemy entered
Antioch and assumed the crown of Asia; he thus
wore two crowns on his head, that of Egypt and
that of Asia.

### Deaths of Alexander and Ptolemy.

**14** King Alexander was in Cilicia at that time,
because the people of that region had revolted.
**15** When Alexander heard the news, he came to
challenge Ptolemy in battle. Ptolemy marched
out and met him with a strong force and put him
to flight. **16** Alexander fled to Arabia to seek
protection. King Ptolemy's triumph was complete **17** when the Arab Zabdiel cut off Alexander's head and sent it to Ptolemy. **18** But three
days later King Ptolemy himself died, and his
men in the fortified cities were killed by the
inhabitants of the strongholds. **19** Thus Demetrius became king in the year one hundred and
sixty-seven.*

**Pact with Demetrius.** **20** At that time Jonathan gathered together the men of Judea to
attack the citadel in Jerusalem, and they set up
many machines against it. **21** Some transgressors of the law, enemies of their own nation,
went to the king and informed him that Jonathan
was besieging the citadel. **22** When Demetrius
heard this, he was furious, and set out immediately for Ptolemais. He wrote to Jonathan to
discontinue the siege and to meet him for a
conference at Ptolemais as soon as possible.

**23** On hearing this, Jonathan ordered the
siege to continue. He selected some elders and
priests of Israel and exposed himself to danger
**24** by going to the king at Ptolemais. He

t 1 Mc 11, 4; 1 Sm 5, 2-5. u 1 Mc 10, 84.

*

10, 89: Kinsmen: a class higher than Chief Friends:

11, 7: Eleutherus: modern Nahr el-Kebir, the northern border of modern Lebanon; in the second century B.C. the northern limit of Coelesyria.

11, 8: Seleucia-by-the-Sea: at the mouth of the Orontes, the port city of Antioch.

11, 10: I regret . . . to kill me: according to Josephus, Ammonius, a friend of Alexander, had tried to assassinate Ptolemy, and the latter claimed that Alexander was the instigator, thus calumniating him to gain his kingdom (v 11).

11, 19: The year one hundred and sixty-seven: 146/145 B.C. The two deaths (vv 17–18) occurred in the summer of 145 B.C.

brought with him silver, gold apparel, and many
other presents, and found favor with the king.
**25** Although some impious men of his own nation brought charges against him, **26** the king
treated him just as his predecessors had done
and showed him great honor in the presence of
all his Friends. **27** He confirmed him in the
high priesthood and in all the honors he had
previously held, and had him enrolled among
his Chief Friends.

**28** Jonathan asked the king to exempt Judea
and the three districts of Samaria from tribute,
promising him in return three hundred talents.[v]
**29** The king agreed and wrote the following
letter to Jonathan about all these matters:

**30** [w]"King Demetrius sends greetings to his
brother* Jonathan and to the Jewish nation.
**31** We are sending you, for your information,
a copy of the letter that we wrote to Lasthenes*
our kinsman concerning you. **32** 'King Demetrius sends greetings to his father Lasthenes.
**33** Because of the good will they show us, we
have decided to bestow benefits on the Jewish
nation, who are our friends and who observe
their obligations to us. **34** [x]Therefore we confirm their possession, not only of the territory of
Judea, but also of the three districts of
Aphairema,* Lydda, and Ramathaim. These
districts, together with all their dependencies,
were transferred from Samaria to Judea in favor
of all those who offer sacrifices for us in Jerusalem instead of paying the royal taxes that formerly the king received from them each year
from the produce of the soil and the fruit of the
trees. **35** From this day on we grant them release from payment of all other things that
would henceforth be due to us, that is, of tithes
and tribute and of the tax on the salt pans and
the crown tax. **36** Henceforth none of these
provisions shall ever be revoked. **37** Be sure,
therefore, to have a copy of these instructions
made and given to Jonathan, that it may be
displayed in a conspicuous place on the holy
hill.' "

**The Intrigue of Trypho.** **38** When King
Demetrius saw that the land was peaceful under
his rule and that he had no opposition, he dismissed his entire army, every man to his home,
except the foreign troops which he had hired
from the islands of the nations. So all the soldiers who had served under his predecessors
hated him. **39** When a certain Trypho, who had
previously belonged to Alexander's party, saw
that all the troops were grumbling at Demetrius,
he went to Imalkue the Arab, who was bringing
up Alexander's young son Antiochus.[y] **40** Trypho kept urging Imalkue to hand over the boy
to him, that he might make him king in his
father's place. During his stay there of many
days, he told him of all that Demetrius had done
and of the hatred that his soldiers had for him.

**Jonathan Aids Demetrius.** **41** Meanwhile Jonathan sent the request to King Demetrius to withdraw his troops from the citadel of
Jerusalem and from the other strongholds, for
they were constantly hostile to Israel. **42** Demetrius, in turn, sent this word to Jonathan: "I
will not only do this for you and your nation, but
I will greatly honor you and your nation when
I find the opportunity. **43** Do me the favor,
therefore, of sending men to fight for me, because all my troops have revolted."

**44** So Jonathan sent three thousand good
fighting men to him at Antioch. When they
came to the king, he was delighted over their
arrival, **45** for the populace, one hundred and
twenty thousand strong, had massed in the center of the city in an attempt to kill him. **46** But
he took refuge in the palace, while the populace
gained control of the main streets and began to
fight. **47** So the king called the Jews to his aid.
They all rallied around him and spread out
through the city. On that day they killed about
a hundred thousand men in the city, **48** which,
at the same time, they set on fire and plundered
on a large scale. Thus they saved the king's life.
**49** When the populace saw that the Jews held
the city at their mercy, they lost courage and
cried out to the king in supplication, **50** "Give
us your terms and let the Jews stop attacking us
and our city." So they threw down their arms
and made peace. **51** The Jews thus gained glory
in the eyes of the king and all his subjects, and
they became renowned throughout his kingdom. Finally they returned to Jerusalem with
much spoil.

**52** But when King Demetrius was sure of his
royal throne, and the land was peaceful under
his rule, **53** he broke all his promises and became estranged from Jonathan. Instead of rewarding Jonathan for all the favors he had received from him, he caused him much trouble.

---

v 1 Mc 10, 29; 11, 34. 28.
w 30-37: 1 Mc 10, 26-45. y 1 Mc 12, 39.
x 34f: 1 Mc 10, 29; 11,

---

11, 30: Brother: this title and father in v 32 are honorific titles used of the Kinsmen.

11, 31: Lasthenes: leader of the mercenary troops who had come with Demetrius from Crete. He was now the young king's chief minister and was apparently responsible for the disastrous policy (v 38) of disbanding the national army.

11, 34: Aphairema: the Ophrah of Jos 18, 23; 1 Sm 23, 6; the Ephron of 2 Chr 13, 19; and the Ephraim of Jn 11, 54—modern et-Taiyibeh, five miles northeast of Bethel. Lydda: the Lod of the postexilic Jews (Ez 2, 33; Neh 11, 35) and the hometown of Aeneas, who was cured by Peter (Acts 9, 32ff). It is ten miles southeast of Joppa. Ramathaim: the Ramathaim-zophim of 1 Sm 1, 1, and the Arimathea of Mt 27, 57—modern Rentis, nine miles northeast of Lydda.

**Alliance with Trypho.** 54 After this, Trypho returned and brought with him the young
boy Antiochus, who became king and wore the
royal crown.[z] 55 All the soldiers whom Demetrius had discharged rallied around Antiochus
and fought against Demetrius, who was routed
and fled. 56 Trypho captured the elephants and
occupied Antioch. 57 Then young Antiochus
wrote to Jonathan: "I confirm you in the high
priesthood and appoint you ruler over the four
districts and wish you to be one of the King's
Friends." 58 He also sent him gold dishes and
a dinner service, gave him the right to drink
from gold cups, to dress in royal purple, and to
wear a gold buckle.[a] 59 Likewise, he made
Jonathan's brother Simon governor of the region from the Ladder of Tyre* to the frontier of
Egypt.

60 Jonathan set out and traveled through
West-of-Euphrates* and its cities, and all the
forces of Syria espoused his cause as allies.
When he arrived at Ashkalon, the citizens welcomed him with pomp. 61 But when he set out
for Gaza, the people of Gaza locked their gates
against him. So he besieged it and burned and
plundered its suburbs. 62 Then the people of
Gaza appealed to him for mercy, and he granted
them peace. He took the sons of their chief men
as hostages and sent them to Jerusalem. He then
traveled on through the province as far as Damascus.

**War with Demetrius.** 63 Jonathan heard
that the generals of Demetrius had come with a
strong force to Kadesh in Galilee, intending to
remove him from office. 64 So he went to meet
them, leaving his brother Simon in the province. 65 Simon besieged Beth-zur, attacked it
for many days, and blockaded the inhabitants.
66 When they sued for peace, he granted it to
them. He expelled them from the city, took
possession of it, and put a garrison there.

67 Meanwhile, Jonathan and his army
pitched their camp near the waters of Gennesaret, and at daybreak they went to the plain of
Hazor.* 68 There, in front of him on the plain,
was the army of the foreigners. This army attacked him in the open, having first detached an
ambush against him in the mountains. 69 Then
the men in ambush rose out of their places and
joined in the battle. 70 All of Jonathan's men
fled; no one stayed except the army commanders Mattathias, son of Absalom, and Judas, son
of Chalphi. 71 Jonathan tore his clothes, threw
earth on his head, and prayed. 72 Then he went
back to the combat and so overwhelmed the
enemy that they took to flight. 73 Those of his
men who were running away saw it and returned
to him; and with him they pursued the enemy as
far as their camp in Kadesh, where they pitched
their own camp. 74 Three thousand of the foreign troops fell on that day. Then Jonathan returned to Jerusalem.

## CHAPTER 12

**Alliances with Rome and Sparta.**
1 When Jonathan saw that the times favored
him, he sent selected men to Rome to confirm
and renew his friendship with the Romans.[b]
2 He also sent letters to Sparta and other places
for the same purpose.

3 After reaching Rome, the men entered the
senate chamber and said, "The high priest Jonathan and the Jewish people have sent us to renew
the earlier friendship and alliance between you
and them." 4 The Romans gave them letters
addressed to the authorities in the various
places, requesting them to provide the envoys
with safe conduct to the land of Judah.

5 This is a copy of the letter that Jonathan
wrote to the Spartans: 6 "Jonathan the high
priest, the senate of the nation, the priests, and
the rest of the Jewish people send greetings to
their brothers the Spartans. 7 Long ago a letter
was sent to the high priest Onias* from Arius,
who then reigned over you, stating that you are
our brothers, as the attached copy shows.[c]
8 Onias welcomed the envoy with honor and
received the letter, which clearly referred to
alliance and friendship. 9 [d]Though we have no
need of these things, since we have for our
encouragement the sacred books that are in our
possession,* 10 we have ventured to send word
to you for the renewal of brotherhood and
friendship, so as not to become strangers to you
altogether; a long time has passed since your
mission to us. 11 We, on our part, have never
ceased to remember you in the sacrifices and
prayers that we offer on our feasts and other
appropriate days, as it is right and proper to
remember brothers. 12 We likewise rejoice in
your renown. 13 But many hardships and wars
have beset us, and the kings around us have
attacked us. 14 We did not wish to be trouble-

z 1 Mc 11, 39; 12, 39.
a 1 Mc 2, 18.
b 1 Mc 8, 17.
c 1 Mc 12, 20-23.
d Rom 15, 4.

*

11, 59: Laddir of Tyre: modern Ras en-Naquurah, on the border between Lebanon and Israel, where the mountains reach the sea, so that the coastal road must ascend in a series of steps.

11, 60: West-of-Euphrates: refers here to the territory of Palestine and Coelesyria, but not Upper Syria; cf 1 Mc 3, 32; 7, 8.

11, 67: Plain of Hazor: the site of the ancient Canaanite city (Jos 11, 10), ten miles north of the Lake of Gennesaret.

12, 7: Onias: Onias I, high priest from 323–300 or 290 B.C. Arius: Arius I, king from 309 to 265 B.C. The letter was sent long ago, i.e., a century and a half before.

12, 9: The sacred books . . . in our possession: a reference to "the law, the prophets and other books," as mentioned in the Prologue to Sirach (v 1), after 132 B.C.

some to you and to the rest of our allies and friends in these wars; **15** with the help of Heaven for our support, we have been saved from our enemies, and they have been humbled. **16** So we have chosen Numenius, son of Antiochus, and Antipater, son of Jason, and we have sent them to the Romans to renew our former friendship and alliance with them.[e] **17** We have also ordered them to come to you and greet you, and to deliver to you our letter about the renewal of our brotherhood. **18** Therefore kindly send us an answer on this matter."

**19** This is a copy of the letter that was sent to Onias: **20** [f]"Arius, king of the Spartans, sends greetings to Onias the high priest. **21** A document has been found stating that the Spartans and the Jews are brothers; both nations descended from Abraham. **22** Now that we have learned this, kindly write to us about your welfare. **23** We, on our part, are informing you that your cattle and your possessions are ours, and ours are yours. We have, therefore, given orders that you should be told of this."

**Demetrius Repelled.** **24** Jonathan heard that the generals of Demetrius had returned to attack him with a stronger army than before. **25** He set out from Jerusalem and went into the country of Hamath* to meet them, giving them no time to enter his province. **26** The spies he had sent into their camp came back and reported that the enemy had made ready to attack the Jews that very night. **27** Therefore, when the sun set, Jonathan ordered his men to be on guard and to remain armed, ready for combat, throughout the night. He also set outposts all around the camp. **28** When the enemy heard that Jonathan and his men were ready for battle, their hearts sank with fear and dread. They lighted fires and then withdrew. **29** But because Jonathan and his men were watching the lights burning, they did not know what had happened until morning. **30** Then Jonathan pursued them, but he could not overtake them, for they had crossed the river Eleutherus. **31** So Jonathan turned aside against the Arabs who are called Zabadeans, overwhelming and plundering them. **32** Then he marched on to Damascus and traversed that whole region.

**33** Simon also set out and went as far as Ashkalon and its neighboring strongholds. He then turned to Joppa and occupied it, **34** for he heard that its men had intended to hand over this stronghold to the supporters of Demetrius. He left a garrison there to guard it.

**35** When Jonathan returned, he assembled the elders of the people, and with them he made plans for building strongholds in Judea, **36** for making the walls of Jerusalem still higher, and for erecting a high barrier between the citadel and the city, that would isolate the citadel and so prevent its garrison from commerce with the city. **37** The people therefore worked together on building up the city, for part of the east wall above the ravine had collapsed. The quarter called Chaphenatha was also repaired. **38** Simon likewise built up Adida in the Shephelah, and strengthened its fortifications by providing them with gates and bars.

**Capture of Jonathan.** **39** Trypho was determined to become king of Asia, assume the crown, and do away with King Antiochus.[g] **40** But he was afraid that Jonathan would not permit him, but would fight against him. Looking for a way to seize and kill him, he set out and reached Beth-shan. **41** Jonathan marched out against him with forty thousand picked fighting men and came to Beth-shan. **42** But when Trypho saw that Jonathan had arrived with a large army, he was afraid to offer him violence. **43** Instead, he received him with honor, introduced him to all his friends, and gave him presents. He also ordered his friends and soldiers to obey him as they would himself. **44** Then he said to Jonathan: "Why have you put all your soldiers to so much trouble when we are not at war? **45** Pick out a few men to stay with you, send the rest back home, and then come with me to Ptolemais. I will hand it over to you together with other strongholds and their garrisons, as well as the officials, then I will leave and go home. That is why I came here."

**46** Jonathan believed him and did as he said. He dismissed his troops, and they returned to the land of Judah. **47** But he kept with him three thousand men, of whom he sent two thousand to Galilee while one thousand accompanied him. **48** Then as soon as Jonathan had entered Ptolemais, the men of the city closed the gates and seized him; all who had entered with him, they killed with the sword.

**49** Trypho sent soldiers and cavalry to Galilee and the Great Plain* to destroy all Jonathan's men. **50** These, upon learning that Jonathan had been captured and his companions killed, encouraged one another and went out in compact body ready to fight. **51** As their pursuers saw that they were ready to fight for their lives, they turned back. **52** Thus all these men of Jonathan came safely into the land of Judah. They mourned over Jonathan and his men, and

e 1 Mc 14, 22; 15, 15.
f 20-23: 1 Mc 12, 6f.
g 1 Mc 11, 39f. 54f.

*

12, 25: Country of Hamath: the Seleucid territory of Upper Syria northeast of Coelesyria and separated from it by the Eleutherus River. The latter territory was under the command of Jonathan (1 Mc 11, 59f).

12, 49: The Great Plain: of Beth-shan (v 41), where Jonathan's disbanded troops remained.

were in great fear, and all Israel fell into deep mourning.

**53** All the nations round about sought to destroy them. They said, "Now that they have no leader to help them, let us make war on them and wipe out their memory from among men."[h]

## *V: Simon, High Priest and Ethnarch*

### CHAPTER 13

**Simon, Leader of the Jews.** **1** When Simon heard that Trypho was gathering a large army to invade and ravage the land of Judah, **2** and saw that the people were in dread and terror, he went up to Jerusalem. There he assembled the people **3** and exhorted them in these words: "You know what I, my brothers, and my father's house have done for the laws and the sanctuary; what battles and disasters we have been through. **4** It was for the sake of these, for the sake of Israel, that all my brothers have perished, and I alone am left. **5** Far be it from me, then, to save my own life in any time of distress, for I am not better than my brothers. **6** Rather will I avenge my nation and the sanctuary, as well as your wives and children, for all the nations out of hatred have united to destroy us."[i]

**7** As the people heard these words, their spirit was rekindled. **8** They shouted in reply: "You are our leader in place of your brothers Judas and Jonathan. **9** Fight our battles, and we will do everything that you tell us." **10** So Simon mustered all the men able to fight, and quickly completing the walls of Jerusalem, fortified it on every side. **11** He sent Jonathan, son of Absalom, to Joppa with a large force; Jonathan drove out the occupants and remained there.

**Deceit and Treachery of Trypho.** **12** Then Trypho moved from Ptolemais with a large army to invade the land of Judah, bringing Jonathan with him as prisoner. **13** But Simon pitched his camp at Adida, facing the plain. **14** When Trypho learned that Simon had succeeded his brother Jonathan, and that he intended to fight him, he sent envoys to him with this message: **15** "We have detained your brother Jonathan on account of the money that he owed the royal treasury in connection with the offices that he held. **16** Therefore, if you send us a hundred talents of silver, and two of his sons as hostages to guarantee that when he is set free he will not revolt against us, we will release him."

**17** Although Simon knew that they were speaking deceitfully to him, he gave orders to get the money and the boys, for fear of provoking much hostility among the people, who might say **18** that Jonathan perished because Simon would not send Trypho the money and the boys. **19** So he sent the boys and the hundred talents; but Trypho broke his promise and would not let Jonathan go. **20** *Next he began to invade and ravage the country. His troops went around by the road that leads to Adora, but Simon and his army moved along opposite him everywhere he went. **21** The men in the citadel sent messengers to Trypho, urging him to come to them by way of the desert, and to send them provisions. **22** Although Trypho got all his cavalry ready to go, there was a heavy fall of snow that night, and he could not go. So he left for Gilead. **23** When he was approaching Baskama,* he had Jonathan killed and buried there. **24** Then Trypho returned to his own country.

**Jonathan's Tomb.** **25** Simon sent for the remains of his brother Jonathan, and buried him in Modein, the city of his fathers. **26** All Israel bewailed him with solemn lamentation, mourning over him for many days. **27** Then Simon erected over the tomb of his father and his brothers a monument of stones, polished front and back, and raised high enough to be seen at a distance. **28** He set up seven pyramids facing one another for his father and his mother and his four brothers. **29** For the pyramids he devised a setting of big columns, on which he carved suits of armor as a perpetual memorial, and next to the armor he placed carved ships, which could be seen by all who sailed the sea. **30** This tomb which he built at Modein is there to the present day.

**Pact between Simon and Demetrius.** **31** Trypho dealt treacherously with the young King Antiochus. He killed him **32** and assumed the kingship in his place, putting on the crown of Asia. Thus he brought much evil on the land. **33** Simon, on his part, built up the strongholds of Judea, strengthening their fortifications with high towers, thick walls, and gates with bars, and he stored up provisions in the fortresses. **34** Simon also sent chosen men to King Demetrius with the request that he grant the land a release from taxation, for all that Trypho did was to plunder the land. **35** In reply, King Demetrius sent him the following letter:

**36** "King Demetrius sends greetings to Simon the high priest, the friend of kings, and to

h 1 Mc 5, 2; 13, 6. i 1 Mc 5, 2; 12, 53.

*

13, 20f: The invaders made a wide flanking movement to invade Judea from the south. Adora was a few miles southwest of Bethzur. They would avoid Beth-zur itself and other strongholds of the Maccabees by following the way of the desert.

13, 23: Baskama: northeast of the Sea of Galilee.

the elders and the Jewish people. **37** We have
received the gold crown and the palm branch
that you sent. We are willing to be on most
peaceful terms with you and to write to our
official to grant you release from tribute.
**38** Whatever we have guaranteed to you remains in force, and the strongholds that you
have built shall remain yours. **39** We remit any
oversights and defaults incurred up to now, as
well as the crown tax that you owe. Any other
tax that may have been collected in Jerusalem
shall no longer be collected there. **40** If any of
you are qualified for enrollment in our service,
let them be enrolled. Let there be peace between
us.''

**41** Thus in the year one hundred and seventy,* the yoke of the Gentiles was removed from
Israel, **42** and the people began to write in their
records and contracts, ''In the first year of Simon, high priest, governor, and leader of the
Jews.''

### Capture of Gazara and the Citadel.

**43** In those days Simon besieged Gazara* and
surrounded it with troops. He made a siege machine, pushed it up against the city, and attacked
and captured one of the towers.[j] **44** The men
who had been on the siege machine jumped
down into the city and caused a great tumult
there. **45** The men of the city, joined by their
wives and children, went up on the wall, with
their garments rent, and cried out in loud voices,
begging Simon to grant them peace. **46** ''Do
not treat us according to our evil deeds,'' they
said, ''but according to your mercy.''

**47** So Simon came to terms with them and
did not destroy them. He made them leave the
city, however, and he purified the houses in
which there were idols. Then he entered the city
with hymns and songs of praise. **48** After removing from it everything that was impure, he
settled there men who observed the law. He
improved its fortifications and built himself a
residence.

**49** The men in the citadel in Jerusalem were
prevented from going out into the country and
back for the purchase of food; they suffered
greatly from hunger, and many of them died of
starvation. **50** They finally cried out to Simon
for peace, and he gave them peace. He expelled
them from the citadel and cleansed it of impurities. **51** On the twenty-third day of the second
month,* in the year one hundred and seventy-one, the Jews entered the citadel with shouts
of jubilation, waving of palm branches, the music of harps and cymbals and lyres, and the
singing of hymns and canticles, because a great
enemy of Israel had been destroyed.[k] **52** Simon
decreed that this day should be celebrated every
year with rejoicing. He also strengthened the
fortifications of the temple hill alongside the
citadel, and he and his companions dwelt there.
**53** Seeing that his son John* was now a grown
man, Simon made him commander of all his
soldiers, with his residence in Gazara.

## CHAPTER 14

### Capture of Demetrius.

**1** In the year one
hundred and seventy-two,* King Demetrius assembled his army and marched into Media to
obtain help so that he could fight Trypho.
**2** When Arsaces,* king of Persia and Media,
heard that Demetrius had invaded his territory,
he sent one of his generals to take him alive.
**3** The general went forth and defeated the army
of Demetrius; he captured him and brought him
to Arsaces, who put him in prison. Glory of
Simon

**4** The land was at rest all the days of Simon,
who sought the good of his nation.
His people were delighted with his power
and his magnificence throughout his
reign.[l]
**5** As his crowning glory he captured the port
of Joppa
and made it a gateway to the isles of the
sea.
**6** He enlarged the borders of his nation
and gained control of the country.[m]
**7** He took many enemies prisoners of war
and made himself master of Gazara,
Beth-zur, and the citadel.

He cleansed the citadel of its impurities;
there was no one to withstand him.
**8** The people cultivated their land in peace;
the land yielded its produce
and the trees of the field their fruit.[n]
**9** Old men sat in the squares,
all talking about the good times,
while the young men wore the glorious
apparel of war.[o]
**10** He supplied the cities with food
and equipped them with means of
defense,

---

j 2 Mc 10, 32-38.
k 1 Mc 1, 36.
l 1 Mc 3, 3-9.
m Ex 34, 24.
n Zec 8, 12.
o Zec 8, 4f.

---

*

13, 41: The year one hundred and seventy: March, 142, to April, 141 B.C., by the temple calendar.

13, 43: Gazara: a key position in the Shephelah, fortified by Bacchides in 160 B.C.; cf 1 Mc 9, 52.

13, 51: The twenty-third day of the second month: June 3, 141 B.C.

13, 53: John: John Hyrcanus, who was to succeed his father as ruler and high priest; cf 1 Mc 16, 23f.

14, 1: The year one hundred and seventy-two: 141–140 B.C. The expedition began most probably in the spring of 140.

14, 2: Arsaces: Arsaces VI, also called Mithridates I, the Parthian king (171–138 B.C.). Parthians had overrun Persia and now held Babylonia, both of which had hitherto belonged to the Seleucid empire. The Greeks and Macedonians in these countries had appealed to Demetrius for help.

till his glorious name reached the ends of
the earth.
11 He brought peace to the land,
and Israel was filled with happiness.[p]
12 Every man sat under his vine and his fig
tree,
with no one to disturb him.[q]
13 No one was left to attack them in their land;
the kings in those days were crushed.
14 He strengthened all the lowly among his
people
and was zealous for the law;
he suppressed all the lawless and the
wicked.
15 He made the temple splendid
and enriched its equipment.

**Alliance with Rome and Sparta.**
16 When people heard in Rome and even in
Sparta that Jonathan had died, they were deeply
grieved.* 17 But when the Romans heard that
his brother Simon had been made high priest in
his place and was master of the country and the
cities, 18 they sent him inscribed tablets of
bronze to renew with him the friendship and
alliance that they had established with his brothers Judas and Jonathan.[r] 19 These were read
before the assembly in Jerusalem.
20 This is a copy of the letter that the Spartans sent: "The rulers and the citizens of Sparta
send greetings to Simon the high priest, the
elders, the priests, and the rest of the Jewish
people, our brothers. 21 The envoys you sent to
our people have informed us of your glory and
fame, and we were happy that they came. 22 In
accordance with what they said we have recorded the following in the public decrees: Since
Numenius, son of Antiochus, and Antipater,
son of Jason, envoys of the Jews, have come to
us to renew their friendship with us,[s] 23 the
people have voted to receive the men with hon-
or, and to deposit a copy of their words in the
public archives, so that the people of Sparta may
have a record of them. A copy of this decree has
been made for Simon the high priest."
24 After this, Simon sent Numenius to Rome
with a great gold shield weighing a thousand
minas, to confirm the alliance with the Romans.[t]

**Decree of Honor.** 25 When the people
heard of these things, they said, "How can we
thank Simon and his sons? 26 He and his brothers and his father's house have stood firm and
repulsed Israel's enemies. They have thus preserved its liberty." So they made an inscription
on bronze tablets, which they affixed to pillars
on Mount Zion. 27 The following is a copy of
the inscription:
"On the eighteenth day of Elul,* in the year
one hundred and seventy-two, that is, the third
year under Simon the high priest in Asaramel,
28 in a great assembly of priests, people, rulers
of the nation, and elders of the country, the
following proclamation was made:
29 " 'Since there have often been wars in
our country, Simon, son of the priest Mattathias, descendant of Joarib, and his brothers have
put themselves in danger and resisted the enemies of their nation, so that their sanctuary and
law might be maintained, and they have thus
brought great glory to their nation. 30 After
Jonathan had rallied his nation and become their
high priest, he was gathered to his kinsmen.
31 When the enemies of the Jews sought to
invade and devastate their country and to lay
hands on their temple, 32 Simon rose up and
fought for his nation, spending large sums of his
own money to equip the men of his nation's
armed forces and giving them their pay. 33 He
fortified the cities of Judea, especially the frontier city of Beth-zur, where he stationed a garrison of Jewish soldiers, and where previously the
enemy's arms had been stored. 34 He also fortified Joppa by the sea and Gazara on the border
of Azotus, a place previously occupied by the
enemy; these cities he resettled with Jews, and
furnished them with all that was necessary for
their restoration. 35 When the Jewish people
saw Simon's loyalty and the glory he planned to
bring to his nation, they made him their leader
and high priest because of all he had accomplished and the loyalty and justice he had shown
his nation. In every way he sought to exalt his
people.
36 " 'In his time and under his guidance they
succeeded in driving the Gentiles out of their
country, especially those in the City of David in
Jerusalem, who had built for themselves a citadel from which they used to sally forth to defile
the environs of the temple and inflict grave injury on its purity. 37 In this citadel he stationed
Jewish soldiers, and he strengthened its fortifications for the defense of the land and the city,
while he also raised the wall of Jerusalem to a
greater height. 38 Consequently, King Demetrius confirmed him in the high priesthood,
39 [u]made him one of his Friends, and conferred
the highest honors on him. 40 He had indeed
heard that the Romans had addressed the Jews
as friends, allies, and brothers and that they had
received Simon's envoys with honor.
41 " 'The Jewish people and their priest

p Lv 26, 6.
q Mi 4, 4; Zec 3, 10.
r Mc 8, 22.
s 1 Mc 12, 16; 15, 15.
t 1 Mc 12, 16; 15, 15.
u 39f: 1 Mc 2, 18.

*

14, 16: The embassy to Rome and Sparta was sent soon after Simon's accession to power, and the replies were received before Demetrius' expedition (vv 1–3)—probably in 142 B.C.

14, 27: Eighteenth day of Elul: September 13, 140 B.C. Asaramel: a Hebrew name meaning "court of the people of God."

have, therefore, made the following decisions. Simon shall be their permanent leader and high priest until a true prophet arises. **42** He shall act as governor general over them, and shall have charge of the temple, to make regulations concerning its functions and concerning the country, its weapons and strongholds; **43** he shall be obeyed by all. All contracts made in the country shall be dated by his name. He shall have the right to wear royal purple and gold ornaments. **44** It shall not be lawful for any of the people or priests to nullify any of these decisions, or to contradict the orders given by him, or to convene an assembly in the country without his consent, to be clothed in royal purple or wear an official gold brooch. **45** Whoever acts otherwise or violates any of these prescriptions shall be liable to punishment.

**46** "'All the people approved of granting Simon the right to act in accord with these decisions, **47** and Simon accepted and agreed to act as high priest, governor general, and ethnarch* of the Jewish people and priests and to exercise supreme authority over all.'"

**48** It was decreed that this inscription should be engraved on bronze tablets, to be set up in a conspicuous place in the precincts of the temple, **49** and that copies of it should be deposited in the treasury, where they would be available to Simon and his sons.

## CHAPTER 15

**Letter of Antiochus.** **1** Antiochus,* son of King Demetrius, sent a letter from the islands of the sea to Simon, the priest and ethnarch of the Jews, and to all the nation, **2** which read as follows:

"King Antiochus sends greetings to Simon, the priest and ethnarch, and to the Jewish nation. **3** Whereas certain villains have gained control of the kingdom of my ancestors, I intend to reclaim it, that I may restore it to its former state. I have recruited a large number of mercenary troops and equipped warships **4** to make a landing in my country and take revenge on those who have ruined it and laid waste many cities in my realm.

**5** "Now, therefore, I confirm to you all the tax exemptions that the kings before me granted you and whatever other privileges they conferred on you. **6** I authorize you to coin your own money, as legal tender in your country. **7** Jerusalem and its temple shall be free. All the weapons you have prepared and all the strongholds you have built and now occupy shall remain in your possession. **8** All debts, present or future, due to the royal treasury shall be canceled for you, now and for all time. **9** When we recover our kingdom, we will greatly honor you and your nation and the temple, so that your glory will be manifest in all the earth."

**10** In the year one hundred and seventy-four,* Antiochus invaded the land of his ancestors, and all the troops rallied to him, so that few were left with Trypho. **11** Pursued by Antiochus, Trypho fled to Dor, by the sea,* **12** realizing what a mass of troubles had come upon him now that his soldiers had deserted him. **13** Antiochus encamped before Dor with a hundred and twenty thousand infantry and eight thousand horsemen. **14** While he invested the city, his ships closed in along the coast, so that he blockaded it by land and sea and let no one go in or out.

**Roman Alliance Renewed.** **15** Meanwhile, Numenius and his companions left Rome with letters such as this addressed to various kings and countries:[v]

**16** "Lucius,* Consul of the Romans, sends greetings to King Ptolemy. **17** Certain envoys of the Jews, our friends and allies, have come to us to renew their earlier alliance of friendship. They had been sent by Simon the high priest and the Jewish people, **18** and they brought with them a gold shield worth a thousand minas.[w] **19** Therefore we have decided to write to various kings and countries, that they are not to harm them, or wage war against them or their cities or their country, and are not to assist those who fight against them. **20** We have also decided to accept the shield from them. **21** If, then, any troublemakers from their country take refuge with you, hand them over to Simon the high priest, so that he may punish them according to their law."

**22** The consul sent similar letters to Kings Demetrius, Attalus,* Ariarthes and Arsaces; **23** to all the countries—Sampsames, Sparta, Delos, Myndos, Sicyon, Caria, Samos, Pamphylia, Lycia, Halicarnassus, Rhodes, Phaselis, Cos, Side, Aradus, Gortyna, Cnidus, Cyprus,

v 1 Mc 8, 17; 12, 16; 14, 22, 24. w 1 Mc 14, 24.

14, 47: Ethnarch: a subaltern ruler over a racial group whose office needed confirmation by a higher authority within the empire.

15, 1: Antiochus: Antiochus VII Sidetes, son of Demetrius I, and younger brother of Demetrius II, now a prisoner of the Parthians. At the age of twenty he set out from the island of Rhodes to take his brother's place and drive out the usurper Trypho.

15, 10: The year one hundred and seventy-four: 138 B.C.

15, 11: Dor, by the sea: a fortress on the Palestinian coast, fifteen miles south of Carmel.

15, 16: Lucius: perhaps Lucius Caecilius Metellus, consul in 142 B.C., or Lucius Calpurnicus Piso, consul in 140–139 B.C. This document pertains to Simon's first year as leader.

15, 22: Attalus: Attalus II of Pergamum, reigned 159–138 B.C. Ariarthes: Ariarthes V of Cappadocia, reigned 162–130 B.C. Arsaces: see note on 1 Mc 14, 2.

and Cyrene. **24** A copy of the letter was also sent to Simon the high priest.

**Hostility of Antiochus.** **25** When King Antiochus was encamped before Dor, he assaulted it continuously both with troops and with the siege machines he had made. He blockaded Trypho by preventing anyone from going in or out. **26** Simon sent to Antiochus' support two thousand elite troops, together with gold and silver and much equipment. **27** But he refused to accept the aid; in fact, he broke all the agreements he had previously made with Simon and became hostile toward him.

**28** He sent Athenobius, one of his Friends, to confer with Simon and say: "You are occupying Joppa and Gazara and the citadel of Jerusalem; these are cities of my kingdom. **29** You have laid waste their territories, done great harm to the land, and taken possession of many districts in my realm. **30** Therefore, give up the cities you have seized and the tribute money of the districts outside the territory of Judea of which you have taken possession; **31** or instead, pay me five hundred talents of silver for the devastation you have caused and five hundred talents more for the tribute money of the cities. If you do not do this, we will come and make war on you."

**32** So Athenobius, the king's Friend, came to Jerusalem, and on seeing the splendor of Simon's court, the gold and silver plate on the sideboard, and the rest of his rich display, he was amazed. When he gave him the king's message, **33** Simon said to him in reply:

"We have not seized any foreign land; what we took is not the property of others, but our ancestral heritage which for a time had been unjustly held by our enemies. **34** Now that we have the opportunity, we are holding on to the heritage of our ancestors. **35** As for Joppa and Gazara, which you demand, the men of these cities were doing great harm to our people and laying waste our country; however, we are willing to pay you a hundred talents for these cities."

**36** Athenobius made no reply, but returned to the king in anger. When he told him of Simon's words, of his splendor, and of all he had seen, the king fell into a violent rage.

**Victory over Cendebeus.** **37** Trypho had gotten aboard a ship and escaped to Orthosia.* **38** Then the king appointed Cendebeus commander in chief of the seacoast, and gave him infantry and cavalry forces. **39** He ordered him to move his troops against Judea and to fortify Kedron* and strengthen its gates, so that he could launch attacks against the Jewish people. Meanwhile the king went in pursuit of Trypho. **40** When Cendebeus came to Jamnia, he began to harass the people and to make incursions into Judea, where he took people captive or massacred them. **41** As the king ordered, he fortified Kedron and stationed horsemen and infantry there, so that they could go out and patrol the roads of Judea.

## CHAPTER 16

**1** John then went up from Gazara and told his father Simon what Cendebeus was doing. **2** Simon called his two oldest sons, Judas and John, and said to them: "I and my brothers and my father's house have fought the battles of Israel from our youth until today, and many times we succeeded in saving Israel. **3** I have now grown old, but you, by the mercy of Heaven, have come to man's estate. Take my place and my brother's, and go out and fight for our nation; and may the help of Heaven be with you!"

**4** John then mustered in the land twenty thousand warriors and horsemen. Setting out against Cendebeus, they spent the night at Modein, **5** rose early, and marched into the plain. There, facing them, was an immense army of foot soldiers and horsemen, and between the two armies was a stream. **6** John and his men took their position against the enemy. Seeing that his men were afraid to cross the stream, John crossed first. When his men saw this, they crossed over after him. **7** Then he divided his infantry into two corps and put his cavalry between them, for the enemy's horsemen were very numerous. **8** They blew the trumpets, and Cendebeus and his army were put to flight; many of them fell wounded, and the rest fled toward the stronghold. **9** It was then that John's brother Judas fell wounded; but John pursued them until Cendebeus reached Kidron, which he had fortified. **10** Some took refuge in the towers on the plain of Azotus, but John set fire to these, and about two thousand of the enemy perished. He then returned to Judea in peace.

**Murder of Simon and His Sons.** **11** Ptolemy, son of Abubus, had been appointed governor of the plain of Jericho, and he had much silver and gold, **12** being the son-in-law of the high priest. **13** But he became ambitious and sought to get control of the country. So he made treacherous plans to do away with Simon and his sons. **14** As Simon was inspecting the cities of the country and providing for their needs, he and his sons Mattathias and Judas went down to Jericho in the year one hundred
*

15, 37: Orthosia: a port between Tripoli and the Eleutherus River.

15, 39: Kedron: a few miles southeast of Jamnia and facing the fortress of Gazara held by John Hyrcanus.

16, 14: In the year one hundred and seventy-seven, in the eleventh month: January-February, 134 B.C., by the temple calendar.

and seventy-seven, in the eleventh month* (that
is, the month Shebat). **15** The son of Abubus
gave them a deceitful welcome in the little
stronghold called Dok* which he had built.
While serving them a sumptuous banquet, he
had his men hidden there. **16** Then, when Simon and his sons had drunk freely, Ptolemy and
his men sprang up, weapons in hand, rushed
upon Simon in the banquet hall, and killed him,
his two sons, and some of his servants. **17** By
this vicious act of treason he repaid good with
evil.

**18** Then Ptolemy wrote an account of this
and sent it to the king, asking that troops be sent
to help him and that the country be turned over
to him. **19** He sent other men to Gazara to do
away with John. To the army officers he sent
letters inviting them to come to him so that he
might present them with silver, gold, and gifts.
**20** He also sent others to seize Jerusalem and
the mount of the temple. **21** But someone ran
ahead and brought word to John at Gazara that
his father and his brothers had perished, and that
Ptolemy had sent men to kill him also. **22** On
hearing this, John was utterly astounded. When
the men came to kill him, he had them arrested
and put to death, for he knew what they meant
to do. **23** *Now the rest of the history of John,
his wars and the brave deeds he performed, his
rebuilding of the walls, and his other achievements— **24** these things are recorded in the
chronicle of his pontificate, from the time that
he succeeded his father as high priest.

---

16, 15: Dok: a fortress built on a cliff three miles northwest of Jericho, near modern Ain Duq.

16, 23f: John Hyrcanus was ruler and high priest from 134 B.C. till his death in 104 B.C. These verses suggest that the book was written, or at least completed, only after he died.

# The Second Book of
# MACCABEES

*Although this book, like the preceding one, receives its title from its protagonist, Judas Maccabee (or Maccabeus), it is not a sequel to 1 Maccabees. The two differ in many respects. Whereas the first covers the period from the beginning of the reign of Antiochus IV (175 B.C.) to the accession of John Hyrcanus I (134 B.C.), this present book treats of the events in Jewish history from the time of the high priest Onias III and King Seleucus IV (c. 180 B.C.) to the defeat of Nicanor's army (161 B.C.).*

*The author of 2 Maccabees states (2, 23) that his one-volume work is an abridgment of a certain five-volume work by Jason of Cyrene; but since this latter has not survived, it is difficult to determine its relationship to the present epitome. One does not know how freely the anonymous epitomizer may have rewritten his shorter composition, or how closely he may have followed the wording of the original in the excerpts he made. Some parts of the text here, clearly not derived from Jason's work, are the Preface (2, 19–32), the Epilogue (15, 37–39), and probably also certain moralizing reflections (e.g., 5, 17–20; 6, 12–17). It is certain, however, that both works were written in Greek, which explains why the Second Book of Maccabees was not included in the canon of the Hebrew Bible.*

*The book is not without genuine historical value in supplementing 1 Maccabees, and it contains some apparently authentic documents (11, 16–38). Its purpose, whether intended by Jason himself or read into it by the compiler, is to give a theological interpretation to the history of the period. There is less interest, therefore, in the actual exploits of Judas Maccabeus than in God's marvelous interventions. These direct the course of events, both to punish the sacrilegious and blasphemous pagans, and to purify God's holy temple and restore it to his faithful people. The author sometimes effects his purpose by transferring events from their proper chronological order, and giving exaggerated figures for the size of armies and the numbers killed in battle; he also places long, edifying discourses and prayers in the mouths of his heroes, and inclines to elaborate descriptions of celestial apparitions (3, 24–34; 5, 2ff; 10, 29f; 15, 11–16). He is the earliest known composer of stories that glorify God's holy martyrs (6, 18–7, 42; 14, 37–46).*

*Of theological importance are the author's teachings on the resurrection of the just on the last day (7, 9. 11. 14. 23; 14, 46), the intercession of the saints in heaven for people living on earth (15, 11–16), and the power of the living to offer prayers and sacrifices for the dead (12, 39–46).*

*The beginning of 2 Maccabees consists of two letters sent by the Jews of Jerusalem to their coreligionists in Egypt. They deal with the observance of the feast commemorating the central event of the book, the purification of the temple. It is uncertain whether the author or a later scribe prefixed these letters to the narrative proper. If the author is responsible for their insertion, he must have written his book some time after 124 B.C., the date of the more recent of the two letters. In any case, Jason's five-volume work very likely continued the history of the Jews well into the Hasmonean period, so that 2 Maccabees would probably not have been produced much before the end of the second century B.C.*

*The main divisions of 2 Maccabees are:*

*I. Letters to the Jews in Egypt (1, 1—2, 18).*
*II. Author's Preface (2, 19–32).*
*III. Heliodorus' Attempt To Profane the Temple (3, 1–40).*
*IV. Profanation and Persecution (4, 1—7, 42).*
*V. Victories of Judas and Purification of the Temple (8, 1—10, 8).*
*VI. Renewed Persecution (10, 9—15, 36).*
*VII. Epilogue (15, 37–39).*

## *I: Letters to the Jews In Egypt*

### CHAPTER 1

**First Letter 124 B.C.** **1** The Jews in Jerusalem and in the land of Judea send greetings to
their brethren, the Jews in Egypt, and wish them
true peace! **2** May God bless you and remember
his covenant with his faithful servants, Abraham, Isaac and Jacob. **3** May he give to all of
you a heart to worship him and to do his will
readily and generously. **4** May he open your
heart to his law and his commandments and
grant you peace. **5** May he hear your prayers,
and be reconciled to you, and never forsake you
in time of adversity. **6** Even now we are praying for you here.

**7** In the reign of Demetrius,* the year one
hundred and sixty-nine, we Jews wrote to you
during the trouble and violence that overtook us
in those years after Jason and his followers had
revolted against the holy land and the kingdom,[a] **8** setting fire to the gatehouse and shedding innocent blood. But we prayed to the
LORD, and our prayer was heard;* we offered
sacrifices and fine flour; we lighted the lamps
and set out the loaves of bread.[b] **9** We are now
reminding you to celebrate the feast of Booths
in the month of Chislev.* **10** Dated in the year
one hundred and eighty-eight.*

**Festival Letter 164 B.C.** The people of
Jerusalem and Judea, the senate, and Judas send
greetings and good wishes to Aristobulus, counselor of King Ptolemy and member of the family
of the anointed priests, and to the Jews in Egypt.
**11** Since we have been saved by God from
grave dangers, we give him great thanks for
having fought on our side against the king;*
**12** [c]it was he who drove out those who fought
against the holy city. **13** When their leader arrived in Persia with his seemingly irresistible
army, they were cut to pieces in the temple of
the goddess Nanea* through a deceitful stratagem employed by Nanea's priests. **14** *On the
pretext of marrying the goddess, Antiochus with
his Friends had come to the place to get its great
treasures by way of dowry. **15** When the priests
of the Nanaeon had displayed the treasures, Antiochus with a few attendants came to the temple
precincts. As soon as he entered the temple, the
priests locked the doors. **16** Then they opened
a hidden trapdoor in the ceiling, hurled stones
at the leader and his companions and struck
them down. They dismembered the bodies, cut
off their heads and tossed them to the people
outside. **17** Forever blessed be our God, who
has thus punished the wicked!

**18** *We shall be celebrating the purification
of the temple on the twenty-fifth day of the
month Chislev, so we thought it right to inform
you that you too may celebrate the feast of
Booths and of the fire that appeared when Nehemiah, the rebuilder of the temple* and the altar,
offered sacrifices. **19** When our fathers were
being exiled to Persia,* devout priests of the
time took some of the fire from the altar and hid
it secretly in the hollow of a dry cistern, making
sure that the place would be unknown to anyone. **20** Many years later, when it so pleased
God, Nehemiah, commissioned by the king of
Persia, sent the descendants of the priests who
had hidden the fire to look for it. **21** When they
informed us that they could not find any fire, but
only muddy water, he ordered them to scoop
some out and bring it. After the material for the
sacrifices had been prepared, Nehemiah ordered
the priests to sprinkle with the water the wood
and what lay on it. **22** When this was done and
in time the sun, which had been clouded over,
began to shine, a great fire blazed up, so that
everyone marveled. **23** While the sacrifice was
being burned, the priests recited a prayer, and
all present joined in with them, Jonathan leading and the rest responding with Nehemiah.

**24** The prayer was as follows: "LORD, LORD
God, creator of all things, awesome and strong,
just and merciful, the only king and benefactor,
**25** who alone are gracious, just, almighty, and

---

a 2 Mc 4, 7-20.
b 1 Mc 4, 38.
c 12-17: 2 Mc 9, 1-29; 1 Mc 6, 1-13.

---

*

1, 7: Demetrius: Demetrius II, king of Syria (145–139, 129–125 B.C.). The year one hundred and sixty-nine of the Seleucid era, 143 B.C. Regarding the dates in 1 and 2 Mc, see note on 1 Mc 1, 10. On the troubles caused by Jason and his revolt against the kingdom, i.e., the rule of the legitimate high priest, see 2 Mc 4, 7–22.

1, 8: Our prayer was heard: in the ultimate victory of the Maccabees.

1, 9: Feast of Booths in the month of Chislev: really the feast of the Dedication of the temple (2 Mc 10, 1–8), celebrated on the twenty-fifth of Chislev (Nov.-Dec.). Its solemnity resembles that of the true feast of Booths (Lv 23, 33–43), celebrated on the fifteenth of Tishri (Sept.-Oct.); cf 2 Mc 1, 18.

1, 10: 124 B.C. The date pertains to the preceding, not the following letter. King Ptolemy: Ptolemy VI Philometor, ruler of Egypt from 180 to 145 B.C.; he is mentioned also in 1 Mc 1, 18; 10, 51–59.

1, 11f: The king: Antiochus IV of Syria, the bitter persecutor of the Jews, who, as leader of the Syrian army that invaded Persia, perished there in 164 B.C.

1, 13: Nanea: an oriental goddess comparable to Artemis of the Greeks.

1, 14–17: A different account of the death of Antiochus IV is given in 2 Mc 9, 1–29, and another variant account in 1 Mc 6, 1–16. The writer of this letter had probably heard a distorted rumor of the king's death. This fact and other indications show that the letter was written very soon after Antiochus IV died, hence in 164 B.C.

1, 18–36: This purely legendary account of Nehemiah's miraculous fire is incorporated in the letter because of its connection with the temple and its rededication.

1, 18: Nehemiah, the rebuilder of the temple: he rebuilt the walls of Jerusalem, but the temple had been rebuilt by Zerubbabel almost a century before.

1, 19: Persia: actually Babylonia, which later became part of the Persian Empire.

eternal, Israel's savior from all evil, who chose our forefathers and sanctified them: **26** accept this sacrifice on behalf of all your people Israel and guard and sanctify your heritage. **27** Gather together our scattered people, free those who are the slaves of the Gentiles, look kindly on those who are despised and detested, and let the Gentiles know that you are our God. **28** Punish those who tyrannize over us and arrogantly mistreat us. **29** Plant your people in your holy place, as Moses promised."[d]

**30** Then the priests began to sing hymns. **31** After the sacrifice was burned, Nehemiah ordered the rest of the liquid to be poured upon large stones. **32** As soon as this was done, a flame blazed up, but its light was lost in the brilliance cast from a light on the altar. **33** When the event became known and the king of the Persians was told that, in the very place where the exiled priests had hidden the fire, a liquid was found with which Nehemiah and his people had burned the sacrifices, **34** the king, after verifying the fact, fenced the place off and declared it sacred. **35** To those on whom the king wished to bestow favors he distributed the large revenues he received there. **36** Nehemiah and his companions called the liquid nephthar, meaning purification, but most people name it naphtha.*

## CHAPTER 2

**1** *You will find in the records, not only that Jeremiah the prophet ordered the deportees to take some of the aforementioned fire with them, **2** but also that the prophet, in giving them the law, admonished them not to forget the commandments of the LORD or be led astray in their thoughts, when seeing the gold and silver idols and their ornaments.[e] **3** With other similar words he urged them not to let the law depart from their hearts. **4** [f]The same document also tells how the prophet, following a divine revelation, ordered that the tent and the ark should accompany him and how he went off to the mountain* which Moses climbed to see God's inheritance. **5** When Jeremiah arrived there, he found a room in a cave in which he put the tent, the ark, and the altar of incense; then he blocked up the entrance. **6** Some of those who followed him came up intending to mark the path, but they could not find it. **7** When Jeremiah heard of this, he reproved them: "The place is to remain unknown until God gathers his people together again and shows them mercy. **8** Then the LORD will disclose these things, and the glory of the LORD will be seen in the cloud, just as it appeared in the time of Moses and when Solomon prayed that the Place* might be gloriously sanctified."[g]

**9** It is also related how Solomon in his wisdom offered a sacrifice at the dedication and the completion of the temple. **10** Just as Moses prayed to the LORD and fire descended from the sky and consumed the sacrifices, so Solomon also prayed and fire came down and burned up the holocausts.[h] **11** Moses had said,[i] "Because it had not been eaten, the sin offering was burned up."* **12** Solomon also celebrated the feast in the same way for eight days.

**13** Besides these things, it is also told in the records and in Nehemiah's Memoirs* how he collected the books about the kings, the writings of the prophets and of David, and the royal letters about sacred offerings. **14** In like manner Judas also collected for us the books that had been scattered because of the war, and we now have them in our possession.[j] **15** If you need them, send messengers to get them for you.

**16** As we are about to celebrate the feast of the purification of the temple, we are writing to you requesting you also to please celebrate the feast. **17** It is God who has saved all his people and has restored to all of them their heritage, the kingdom, the priesthood, and the sacred rites, **18** as he promised through the law. We trust in God, that he will soon have mercy on us and gather us together from everywhere under the heavens to his holy Place, for he has rescued us from great perils and has purified his Place.[k]

## *II: Author's Preface*

**19** This is the story of Judas Maccabeus and his brothers, of the purification of the great temple, the dedication of the altar, **20** the campaigns against Antiochus Epiphanes and his son Eupator,* **21** and of the heavenly manifestations accorded to the heroes who fought bravely for Judaism, so that, few as they were, they seized the whole land, put to flight the barbarian hordes, **22** regained possession of the world-famous temple, liberated the city, and reestab-

---

d 2 Mc 2, 18; Dt 30, 3ff.
e Bar 6, 3-72.
f 4f: Dt 32, 49; 34, 1; Rv 11, 19.
g 1 Kgs 8, 11.
h Lv 9, 23f; 2 Chr 7, 1.
i Lv 10, 16-20.
j 1 Mc 1, 57.
k Dt 30, 3ff.

---

*

1, 36: By a play on words, the Greek term naphtha (petroleum) is assimilated to some Semitic word, perhaps nephthar, meaning "loosened."

2, 1–8: This legendary account of how Jeremiah hid the sacred tent (which was not mentioned after the time of Solomon!), the ark and the altar is given for the purpose of explaining why the postexilic temple was the legitimate place of worship even without these sacred objects.

2, 4: The mountain: Nebo; cf Dt 34, 1.

2, 8: The place: the temple of Jerusalem.

2, 11: The statement attributed here to Moses seems to be based on Lv 10, 16–20.

2, 13: Nehemiah's Memoirs: a lost apocryphal work.

2, 20: For the account of the campaigns against Antiochus IV Epiphanes, see 2 Mc 4, 7—10, 9; and for the account of those against his son Antiochus V Eupator, see 2 Mc 10, 10—13, 26.

lished the laws that were in danger of being abolished, while the LORD favored them with all his generous assistance. **23** All this, which Jason of Cyrene set forth in detail in five volumes, we will try to condense into a single book.

**Purpose and Method.** **24** In view of the flood of statistics, and the difficulties encountered by those who wish to plunge into historical narratives where the material is abundant, **25** we have aimed to please those who prefer simple reading, as well as to make it easy for the studious who wish to commit things to memory, and to be helpful to all. **26** For us who have taken upon ourselves the labor of making this digest, the task, far from being easy, is one of sweat and of sleepless nights, **27** just as the preparation of a festive banquet is no light matter for one who thus seeks to give enjoyment to others. Similarly, to win the gratitude of many we will gladly endure these inconveniences, **28** while we leave the responsibility for exact details to the original author, and confine our efforts to giving only a summary outline. **29** As the architect of a new house must give his attention to the whole structure, while the man who undertakes the decoration and the frescoes has only to concern himself with what is needed for ornamentation, so I think it is with us. **30** To enter into questions and examine them thoroughly from all sides is the task of the professional historian; **31** but the man who is making an adaptation should be allowed to aim at brevity of expression and to omit detailed treatment of the matter. **32** Here, then, we shall begin our account without further ado; it would be nonsense to write a long preface to a story and then abbreviate the story itself.

## *III: Heliodorus' Attempt to Profane the Temple**

### CHAPTER 3

**Treachery of Simon.** **1** [l]While the holy city lived in perfect peace and the laws were strictly observed because of the piety of the high priest Onias* and his hatred of evil, **2** the kings themselves honored the Place and glorified the temple with the most magnificent gifts. **3** Thus Seleucus,* king of Asia, defrayed from his own revenues all the expenses necessary for the sacrificial services. **4** But a certain Simon, of the priestly course of Bilgah,* who had been appointed superintendent of the temple, had a quarrel with the high priest about the supervision of the city market.[m] **5** Since he could not prevail against Onias, he went to Apollonius of Tarsus, who at that time was governor of Coelesyria and Phoenicia, **6** and reported to him that the treasury in Jerusalem was so full of untold riches that the total sum of money was incalculable and out of all proportion to the cost of the sacrifices, and that it would be possible to bring it all under the control of the king.

**Mission of Heliodorus.** **7** When Apollonius had an audience with the king, he informed him about the riches that had been reported to him. The king chose his minister Heliodorus and sent him with instructions to expropriate the aforesaid wealth. **8** So Heliodorus immediately set out on his journey, ostensibly to visit the cities of Coelesyria and Phoenicia, but in reality to carry out the king's purpose. **9** When he arrived in Jerusalem and had been graciously received by the high priest of the city, he told him about the information that had been given, and explained the reason for his presence, and he asked if these things were really true. **10** The high priest explained that part of the money was a care fund for widows and orphans,[n] **11** and a part was the property of Hyrcanus, son of Tobias,* a man who occupied a very high position. Contrary to the calumnies of the impious Simon, the total amounted to four hundred talents of silver and two hundred of gold. **12** He added that it was utterly unthinkable to defraud those who had placed their trust in the sanctity of the Place and in the sacred inviolability of a temple venerated all over the world. **13** But because of the orders he had from the king, Heliodorus said that in any case the money must be confiscated for the royal treasury. **14** So on the day he had set he went in to take an inventory of the funds.

**Anguish of the Faithful.** There was great distress throughout the city. **15** Priests prostrated themselves in their priestly robes before the altar, and loudly begged him in heaven who had given the law about deposits to keep the deposits safe for those who had made them. **16** Whoever saw the appearance of the high priest was pierced to the heart, for the changed color of his face manifested the anguish of his soul. **17** The

l 1ff: 2 Mc 5, 19f; 15, 12. n Dt 14, 29.
m 2 Mc 4, 23.

*

3, 1–40: This legendary episode about Heliodorus is recounted here for the purpose of stressing the inviolability of the temple of Jerusalem; its later profanation was allowed by God because of the people's sins; cf 2 Mc 5, 17f.

3, 1: The high priest Onias: Onias III, who was priest from 196 to 175 B.C., and died in 171 B.C. He was the son of Simon, whose praises are sung in Sir 50, 1–21.

3, 3: Seleucus: Seleucus IV Philopator, who reigned from 187 to 175 B.C.

3, 4: Bilgah: a priestly family mentioned in Neh 12, 5. 18.

3, 11: Son of Tobias: a member of the Tobiad family of Transjordan (Neh 2, 10; 6, 17ff; 13, 4–8). Hyrcanus' father was Joseph, whose mother was the sister of the high priest Onias II.

terror and bodily trembling that had come over
the man clearly showed those who saw him the
pain that lodged in his heart. **18** People rushed
out of their houses in crowds to make public
supplication, because the Place was in danger of
being profaned. **19** Women, girded with sackcloth below their breasts, filled the streets;
maidens secluded indoors ran together, some to
the gates, some to the walls, others peered
through the windows, **20** all of them with hands
raised toward heaven, making supplication.
**21** It was pitiful to see the populace variously
prostrated in prayer and the high priest full of
dread and anguish.

**Divine Intervention.** **22** While they were
imploring the almighty LORD to keep the deposits safe and secure for those who had placed
them in trust, **23** Heliodorus went on with his
plan. **24** But just as he was approaching the
treasury with his bodyguards, the LORD of spirits who holds all power manifested himself in so
striking a way that those who had been bold
enough to follow Heliodorus were panic-strick-
en at God's power and fainted away in terror.
**25** There appeared to them a richly caparisoned
horse, mounted by a dreadful rider. Charging
furiously, the horse attacked Heliodorus with its
front hoofs. The rider was seen to be wearing
golden armor. **26** Then two other young men,
remarkably strong, strikingly beautiful, and
splendidly attired, appeared before him. Standing on each side of him, they flogged him unceasingly until they had given him innumerable
blows. **27** Suddenly he fell to the ground, enveloped in great darkness. Men picked him up
and laid him on a stretcher. **28** The man who a
moment before had entered that treasury with a
great retinue and his whole bodyguard was carried away helpless, having dearly experienced
the sovereign power of God. **29** While he lay
speechless and deprived of all hope of aid, due
to an act of God's power, **30** the Jews praised
the LORD who had marvelously glorified his
holy Place; and the temple, charged so shortly
before with fear and commotion, was filled with
joy and gladness, now that the almighty LORD
had manifested himself.

**31** Soon some of the companions of Heliodorus begged Onias to invoke the Most High,
praying that the life of the man who was about
to expire might be spared. **32** Fearing that the
king might think that Heliodorus had suffered
some foul play at the hands of the Jews, the high
priest offered a sacrifice for the man's recovery.
**33** While the high priest was offering the sacrifice of atonement, the same young men in the
same clothing again appeared and stood before
Heliodorus. "Be very grateful to the high priest
Onias," they told him. "It is for his sake that
the LORD has spared your life. **34** Since you
have been scourged by Heaven, proclaim to all
men the majesty of God's power." When they
had said this, they disappeared.

**Testimony of Heliodorus.** **35** After Heliodorus had offered a sacrifice to the LORD and
made most solemn vows to him who had spared
his life, he bade Onias farewell, and returned
with his soldiers to the king. **36** Before all men
he gave witness to the deeds of the most high
God that he had seen with his own eyes.
**37** When the king asked Heliodorus who would
be a suitable man to be sent to Jerusalem next,
he answered: **38** "If you have an enemy or a
plotter against the government, send him there,
and you will receive him back well-flogged, if
indeed he survives at all; for there is certainly
some special divine power about the Place.
**39** He who has his dwelling in heaven watches
over that Place and protects it, and he strikes
down and destroys those who come to harm it."
**40** This was how the matter concerning Heliodorus and the preservation of the treasury
turned out.

## *IV: Profanation and Persecution*

## CHAPTER 4

**Onias Appeals to the King.** **1** The Simon
mentioned above as the informer about the
funds against his own country, made false accusations that it was Onias who threatened Heliodorus and instigated the whole miserable affair. **2** He dared to brand as a plotter against the
government the man who was a benefactor of
the city, a protector of his compatriots, and a
zealous defender of the laws. **3** When Simon's
hostility reached such a point that murders were
being committed by one of his henchmen,
**4** Onias saw that the opposition was serious and
that Apollonius, son of Menestheus, the governor of Coelesyria and Phoenicia, was abetting
Simon's wickedness. **5** So he had recourse to
the king, not as an accuser of his countrymen,
but as a man looking to the general and particular good of all the people. **6** He saw that, unless
the king intervened, it would be impossible to
have a peaceful government, and that Simon
would not desist from his folly.

**Jews Led by Jason To Apostatize.**
**7** But Seleucus died,* and when Antiochus surnamed Epiphanes succeeded him on the throne,

o 2 Mc 1, 7; 1 Mc 1, 10.

*

4, 7: Seleucus died: he was murdered by Heliodorus. Antiochus Epiphanes was his younger brother. Onias' brother showed his love for the Greek way of live (v 10) by changing his Hebrew name Joshua, or Jesus, to the Greek name Jason.

Onias' brother Jason obtained the high priesthood by corrupt means:[o] **8** in an interview, he
promised the king three hundred and sixty talents of silver, as well as eighty talents from
another source of income. **9** Besides this he
agreed to pay a hundred and fifty more, if he
were given authority to establish a gymnasium
and a youth club* for it and to enroll men in
Jerusalem as Antiochians.

**10** When Jason received the king's approval
and came into office, he immediately initiated
his countrymen into the Greek way of life.
**11** He set aside the royal concessions granted to
the Jews through the mediation of John, father
of Eupolemus* (that Eupolemus who would later go on an embassy to the Romans to establish
a treaty of friendship with them); he abrogated
the lawful institutions and introduced customs
contrary to the law.[p] **12** He quickly established
a gymnasium* at the very foot of the acropolis,
where he induced the noblest young men to
wear the Greek hat.[q] **13** The craze for Hellenism and foreign customs reached such a pitch,
through the outrageous wickedness of the ungodly pseudo-highpriest Jason, **14** that the
priests no longer cared about the service of the
altar. Disdaining the temple and neglecting the
sacrifices, they hastened, at the signal for the
discus-throwing, to take part in the unlawful
exercises on the athletic field. **15** They despised what their ancestors had regarded as honors, while they highly prized what the Greeks
esteemed as glory. **16** Precisely because of this,
they found themselves in serious trouble: the
very people whose manner of life they emulat-
ed, and whom they desired to imitate in everything, became their enemies and oppressors.
**17** It is no light matter to flout the laws of God,
as the following period will show.

**18** When the quinquennial games were held
at Tyre in the presence of the king, **19** the vile
Jason sent envoys as representatives of the Antiochians of Jerusalem, to bring there three hundred silver drachmas for the sacrifice to Hercules. But the bearers themselves decided that
the money should not be spent on a sacrifice, as
that was not right, but should be used for some
other purpose. **20** So the contribution destined
by the sender for the sacrifice to Hercules was
in fact applied, by those who brought it, to the
construction of triremes.*

**21** When Apollonius, son of Menestheus,
was sent to Egypt for the coronation of King
Philometor,* Antiochus learned that the king
was opposed to his policies; so he took measures
for his own security. **22** After going to Joppa,
he proceeded to Jerusalem. There he was received with great pomp by Jason and the people
of the city, who escorted him with torchlights
and acclamations; following this, he led his
army into Phoenicia.

**Menelaus Supplants Jason.** **23** Three
years later Jason sent Menelaus,* brother of the
aforementioned Simon, to deliver the money to
the king, and to obtain decisions on some important matters. **24** When he had been introduced to the king, he flattered him with such an
air of authority that he secured the high priesthood for himself, outbidding Jason by three
hundred talents of silver. **25** He returned with
the royal commission, but with nothing that
made him worthy of the high priesthood; he had
the temper of a cruel tyrant and the rage of a
wild beast. **26** Then Jason, who had cheated his
own brother and now saw himself cheated by
another man, was driven out as a fugitive to the
country of the Ammonites.

**27** Although Menelaus had obtained the office, he did not make any payments of the money he had promised to the king, **28** in spite of
the demand of Sostratus, the commandant of the
citadel, whose duty it was to collect the taxes.
For this reason, both were summoned before the
king. **29** Menelaus left his brother Lysimachus
as his substitute in the high priesthood, while
Sostratus left Crates, commander of the Cypriots, as his substitute.

**Murder of Onias.** **30** While these things
were taking place, the people of Tarsus and
Mallus* rose in revolt, because their cities had
been given as a gift to Antiochis, the king's
mistress. **31** The king, therefore, went off in
haste to settle the affair, leaving Andronicus,
one of his nobles, as his deputy. **32** Then
Menelaus, thinking this a good opportunity,
stole some gold vessels from the temple and
presented them to Andronicus; he had already
sold some other vessels in Tyre and in the neighboring cities. **33** When Onias had clear evidence of the facts, he made a public protest,
after withdrawing to the inviolable sanctuary at

p 1 Mc 8, 17. q 1 Mc 1, 14.

*

4, 9: Youth club: an educational institution in which young men were trained both in Greek intellectual culture and in physical fitness. Antiochians: honorary citizens of Antioch, a Hellenistic city of the Seleucid Kingdom that had a corporation of such Antiochians, who enjoyed certain political and commercial privileges.

4, 11: Eupolemus: one of the two envoys sent to Rome by Judas Maccabeus (1 Mc 8, 17).

4, 12: Since the gymnasium, where the youth exercised naked (Greek gymnos), lay in the Tyropoeon Valley to the east of the citadel, it was directly next to the temple on its eastern side. The Greek hat: a wide-brimmed hat, traditional headgear of Hermes, the patron god of athletic contests; it formed part of the distinctive costume of the members of the "youth club."

4, 20: Triremes: war vessels with three banks of oars.

4, 21: Philometor: Ptolemy VI, king of Egypt, c. 172 to c. 145 B.C.

4, 23: Menelaus: Jewish high priest from c. 172 to his execution in 162 B.C. (2 Mc 13, 3–8).

4, 30: Mallus: a city of Cilicia (v 36) in southeastern Asia Minor, about thirty miles east of Tarsus.

Daphne, near Antioch. **34** Thereupon Menelaus approached Andronicus privately and asked him to lay hands on Onias. So Andronicus went to Onias, and by treacherously reassuring him through sworn pledges with right hands joined, persuaded him, in spite of his suspicions, to leave the sanctuary. Then, without any regard for justice, he immediately put him to death.

**35** As a result, not only the Jews, but many people of other nations as well, were indignant and angry over the unjust murder of the man. **36** When the king returned from the region of Cilicia, the Jews of the city,* together with the Greeks who detested the crime, went to see him about the murder of Onias. **37** Antiochus was deeply grieved and full of pity; he wept as he recalled the prudence and noble conduct of the deceased. **38** Inflamed with anger, he immediately stripped Andronicus of his purple robe, tore off his other garments, and had him led through the whole city to the very place where he had committed the outrage against Onias; and there he put the murderer to death. Thus the LORD rendered him the punishment he deserved.

**Riot against Lysimachus.** **39** Many sacrilegious thefts had been committed by Lysimachus in the city* with the connivance of Menelaus. When word was spread that a large number of gold vessels had been stolen, the people assembled in protest against Lysimachus. **40** As the crowds, now thoroughly enraged, began to riot, Lysimachus launched an unjustified attack against them with about three thousand armed men under the leadership of Auranus, a man as advanced in folly as he was in years. **41** Reacting against Lysimachus' attack, the people picked up stones or pieces of wood or handfuls of the ashes lying there and threw them in wild confusion at Lysimachus and his men. **42** As a result, they wounded many of them and even killed a few, while they put all the rest to flight. The sacrilegious thief himself they slew near the treasury.

**43** Charges about this affair were brought against Menelaus. **44** When the king came to Tyre, three men sent by the senate* presented to him the justice of their cause. **45** But Menelaus, seeing himself on the losing side, promised Ptolemy, son of Dorymenes, a substantial sum of money if he would win the king over.[r] **46** So Ptolemy retired with the king under a colonnade, as if to get some fresh air, and persuaded him to change his mind. **47** Menelaus, who was the cause of all the trouble, the king acquitted of the charges, while he condemned to death those poor men who would have been declared innocent even if they had pleaded their case before Scythians. **48** Thus, those who had prosecuted the case for the city, for the people, and for the sacred vessels, quickly suffered unjust punishment. **49** For this reason, even some Tyrians were indignant over the crime and provided sumptuously for their burial. **50** But Menelaus, thanks to the covetousness of the men in power, remained in office, where he grew in wickedness and became the chief plotter against his fellow citizens.

## CHAPTER 5

**Sedition and Death of Jason.** **1** About this time Antiochus sent his second expedition* into Egypt.[s] **2** [t]It then happened that all over the city, for nearly forty days, there appeared horsemen charging in midair, clad in garments interwoven with gold—companies fully armed with lances **3** and drawn swords; squadrons of cavalry in battle array, charges and countercharges on this side and that, with brandished shields and bristling spears, flights of arrows and flashes of gold ornaments, together with armor of every sort. **4** Therefore all prayed that this vision might be a good omen.

**5** But when a false rumor circulated that Antiochus was dead, Jason* gathered fully a thousand men and suddenly attacked the city. As the defenders on the walls were forced back and the city was finally being taken, Menelaus took refuge in the citadel. **6** Jason then slaughtered his fellow citizens without mercy, not realizing that triumph over one's own kindred was the greatest failure, but imagining that he was winning a victory over his enemies, not his fellow countrymen. **7** Even so, he did not gain control of the government, but in the end received only disgrace for his treachery, and once again took refuge in the country of the Ammonites. **8** At length he met a miserable end. Called to account before Aretas,* king of the Arabs, he fled from city to city, hunted by all men, hated as a trans-

r 2 Mc 8, 8; 1 Mc 3, 38.
s 1 Mc 1, 17.
t 2f: 2 Mc 3, 24ff; 10, 29f; 11, 8.

*

4, 36: The city: Antioch. But some understand the Greek to mean "each city."

4, 39: The city: Jerusalem. Menelaus was still in Syria.

4, 44: The senate: the council of Jewish elders at Jerusalem; cf 1 Mc 12, 6.

5, 1: Second expedition: the first invasion of Egypt by Antiochus in 169 B.C. (1 Mc 1, 16–20) is not mentioned in 2 Mc, unless the coming of the Syrian army to Palestine (2 Mc 4, 21f) is regarded as the first invasion. The author of 2 Mc apparently combines the first pillage of Jerusalem in 169 B.C. after Antiochus' first invasion of Egypt (1 Mc 1, 20–28; cf 2 Mc 5, 5ff) with the second pillage of the city two years later (167 B.C.), following the king's second invasion of Egypt in 168 B.C. (1 Mc 1, 29–35; cf 2 Mc 5, 24ff).

5, 5: Jason: brother of Onias III, was claimant of the high priesthood (2 Mc 4, 7–10). Later he was supplanted by Menelaus who drove him into Transjordan (2 Mc 4, 26).

5, 8: Aretas: King Aretas I of the Nabateans; cf 1 Mc 5, 25.

gressor of the laws, abhorred as the butcher of his country and his countrymen. After being driven into Egypt, **9** he crossed the sea to the Spartans, among whom he hoped to find protection because of his relations with them. There he who had exiled so many from their country perished in exile; **10** and he who had cast out so many to lie unburied went unmourned himself with no funeral of any kind or any place in the tomb of his ancestors.

**The City Ravaged.** **11** [u]When these happenings were reported to the king, he thought that Judea was in revolt. Raging like a wild animal, he set out from Egypt and took Jerusalem by storm. **12** He ordered his soldiers to cut down without mercy those whom they met and to slay those who took refuge in their houses. **13** There was a massacre of young and old, a killing of women and children, a slaughter of virgins and infants. **14** In the space of three days, eighty thousand were lost, forty thousand meeting a violent death, and the same number being sold into slavery. **15** Not satisfied with this, the king dared to enter the holiest temple in the world; Menelaus, that traitor both to the laws and to his country, served as guide. **16** He laid his impure hands on the sacred vessels and gathered up with profane hands the votive offerings made by other kings for the advancement, the glory, and the honor of the Place. **17** Puffed up in spirit, Antiochus did not realize that it was because of the sins of the city's inhabitants that the LORD was angry for a little while and hence disregarded the holy Place.[v] **18** If they had not become entangled in so many sins, this man, like Heliodorus, who was sent by King Seleucus to inspect the treasury, would have been flogged and turned back from his presumptuous action as soon as he approached. **19** [w]The LORD, however, had not chosen the people for the sake of the Place, but the Place for the sake of the people.* **20** Therefore, the Place itself, having shared in the people's misfortunes, afterward participated in their good fortune; and what the Almighty had forsaken in his anger was restored in all its glory, once the great Sovereign became reconciled.

**21** Antiochus carried off eighteen hundred talents from the temple, and hurried back to Antioch. In his arrogance he planned to make the land navigable and the sea passable on foot, so carried away was he with pride.[x] **22** But he left governors to harass the nation: at Jerusalem, Philip, a Phrygian by birth,* and in character more cruel than the man who appointed him; **23** at Mount Gerizim,* Andronicus; and besides these, Menelaus, who lorded it over his fellow citizens worse than the others did. Out of hatred for the Jewish citizens, **24** [y]the king sent Apollonius,* commander of the Mysians, at the head of an army of twenty-two thousand men, with orders to kill all the grown men and sell the women and young men into slavery. **25** When this man arrived in Jerusalem, he pretended to be peacefully disposed and waited until the holy day of the sabbath; then, finding the Jews refraining from work, he ordered his men to parade fully armed. **26** All those who came out to watch, he massacred, and running through the city with armed men, he cut down a large number of people.

**27** But Judas Maccabeus with about nine others withdrew to the wilderness where he and his companions lived like wild animals in the hills, continuing to eat what grew wild to avoid sharing the defilement.[z]

## CHAPTER 6

**The Temple Desecrated.** **1** [a]Not long after this the king sent an Athenian senator to force the Jews to abandon the customs of their ancestors and live no longer by the laws of God; **2** also to profane the temple in Jerusalem and dedicate it to Olympian Zeus,* and that on Mount Gerizim to Zeus the Hospitable, as the inhabitants of the place requested.[b] **3** This intensified the evil in an intolerable and utterly disgusting way. **4** The Gentiles filled the temple with debauchery and revelry; they amused themselves with prostitutes* and had intercourse with women even in the sacred court. They also brought into the temple things that were forbidden, **5** so that the altar was covered with abominable offerings prohibited by the laws.

**Abolition of the Law.** **6** A man could not keep the sabbath or celebrate the traditional feasts, nor even admit that he was a Jew. **7** Moreover, at the monthly celebration of the

u 11-21: 1 Mc 1, 20-24.
v 2 Mc 6, 12-16; 7, 16-19. 32-38.
w 19ff: 2 Mc 3, 1ff; 1 Chr 17, 9; Mk 2, 27.
x 1 Mc 1, 23f.
y 24ff: 1 Mc 1, 29f.
z 1 Mc 2, 28.
a 1-11: 1 Mc 1, 44-63.
b 1 Mc 1, 46; Dn 9, 27.

*

5, 19: Man is more important than even the most sacred institutions; cf Mk 2, 27.

5, 22: Philip, a Phrygian by birth: the Philip of 2 Mc 6, 11 and 8, 8, but probably not the same as Philip the regent of 2 Mc 9, 29 and 1 Mc 6, 14.

5, 23: Mount Gerizim: the sacred mountain of the Samaritans at Shechem; cf 2 Mc 6, 2.

5, 24: Apollonius: the Mysian commander of 1 Mc 1, 29; mentioned also in 2 Mc 3, 5; 4, 4.

6, 2: Olympain Zeus: equated with the Syrian Baal shomem ("the lord of the heavens"), a term which the Jews rendered as "Shiqqus shomem," horrible abomination (Dn 9, 27; 11, 31; 12, 11; 1 Mc 1, 54).

6, 4: Amused themselves with prostitutes: as in the fertility cults of the ancient Near East; see notes on Bar 6, 10. 42f.

6, 7: Dionysus: called also Bacchus the god of the grape harvest and of wine; ivy was one of his symbols.

king's birthday the Jews had, from bitter necessity, to partake of the sacrifices, and when the
festival of Dionysus* was celebrated, they were
compelled to march in his procession, wearing
wreaths of ivy.
**8** At the suggestion of the citizens of Ptolemais, a decree was issued ordering the neighboring Greek cities to act in the same way
against the Jews: oblige them to partake of the
sacrifices, **9** and put to death those who would
not consent to adopt the customs of the Greeks.
It was obvious, therefore, that disaster was im-
pended. **10** Thus, two women who were arrested for having circumcised their children were
publicly paraded about the city with their babies
hanging at their breasts and then thrown down
from the top of the city wall.[c] **11** Others, who
had assembled in nearby caves to observe the
sabbath in secret, were betrayed to Philip and all
burned to death. In their respect for the holiness
of that day, they had scruples about defending
themselves.[d]

**Purpose of Divine Judgment.** **12** [e]Now
I beg those who read this book not to be disheartened by these misfortunes, but to consider
that these chastisements were meant not for the
ruin but for the correction of our nation. **13** It
is, in fact, a sign of great kindness to punish
sinners promptly instead of letting them go for
long. **14** [f]Thus, in dealing with other nations,
the LORD patiently waits until they reach the full
measure of their sins before he punishes them;
but with us he has decided to deal differently,
**15** in order that he may not have to punish us
more severely later, when our sins have reached
their fullness. **16** He never withdraws his mercy from us. Although he disciplines us with
misfortunes, he does not abandon his own people. **17** Let these words suffice for recalling this
truth. Without further ado we must go on with
our story.

**Martyrdom of Eleazar.*** **18** Eleazar, one
of the foremost scribes, a man of advanced age
and noble appearance, was being forced to open
his mouth to eat pork.[g] **19** But preferring a
glorious death to a life of defilement, he spat out
the meat, and went forward of his own accord
to the instrument of torture, **20** as men ought to
do who have the courage to reject the food
which it is unlawful to taste even for love of life.
**21** Those in charge of that unlawful ritual meal
took the man aside privately, because of their
long acquaintance with him, and urged him to
bring meat of his own providing, such as he
could legitimately eat, and to pretend to be eating some of the meat of the sacrifice prescribed
by the king; **22** in this way he would escape the
death penalty, and be treated kindly because of
their old friendship with him. **23** But he made
up his mind in a noble manner, worthy of his
years, the dignity of his advanced age, the merited distinction of his gray hair, and of the admirable life he had lived from childhood; and so
he declared that above all he would be loyal to
the holy laws given by God.
He told them to send him at once to the abode
of the dead, explaining: **24** "At our age it
would be unbecoming to make such a pretense;
many young men would think the ninety-
year-old Eleazar had gone over to an alien religion. **25** Should I thus dissimulate for the sake
of a brief moment of life, they would be led
astray by me, while I would bring shame and
dishonor on my old age. **26** Even if, for the
time being, I avoid the punishment of men, I
shall never, whether alive or dead, escape the
hands of the Almighty. **27** Therefore, by manfully giving up my life now, I will prove myself
worthy of my old age, **28** and I will leave to the
young a noble example of how to die willingly
and generously for the revered and holy laws."
He spoke thus, and went immediately to the
instrument of torture. **29** Those who shortly before had been kindly disposed, now became
hostile toward him because what he had said
seemed to them utter madness. **30** When he was
about to die under the blows, he groaned and
said: "The LORD in his holy knowledge knows
full well that, although I could have escaped
death, I am not only enduring terrible pain in my
body from this scourging, but also suffering it
with joy in my soul because of my devotion to
him." **31** This is how he died, leaving in his
death a model of courage and an unforgettable
example of virtue not only for the young but for
the whole nation.

## CHAPTER 7

**Martyrdom of a Mother and Her Sons.**
**1** It also happened that seven brothers with their
mother were arrested and tortured with whips
and scourges by the king, to force them to eat
pork in violation of God's law.[h] **2** One of the
brothers, speaking for the others, said: "What
do you expect to achieve by questioning us? We
are ready to die rather than transgress the laws
of our ancestors." **3** At that the king, in a fury,
gave orders to have pans and caldrons heated.

c 1 Mc 1, 60f.
d 1 Mc 2, 32-38.
e 12-16: 2 Mc 5, 17; 7, 16-19. 32-38.
f Wis 11, 9f; 12, 2, 22.
g Lv 11, 7f; Heb 11, 35.
h Jer 15, 9.

*

6, 18–7, 42: The stories of Eleazar and of the mother and her seven sons, among the earliest models of "martyrology," were understandably popular among the Christians of the early centuries. Written originally to encourage God's people in times of persecution, they add gruesome details to the record of tortures, and place long speeches in the mouths of the martyrs.

**4** While they were being quickly heated, he
commanded his executioners to cut out the
tongue of the one who had spoken for the others,
to scalp him and cut off his hands and feet,
while the rest of his brothers and his mother
looked on. **5** When he was completely maimed
but still breathing, the king ordered them to
carry him to the fire and fry him. As a cloud of
smoke spread from the pan, the brothers and
their mother encouraged one another to die
bravely, saying such words as these: **6** "The
LORD God is looking on, and he truly has compassion on us, as Moses declared in his canticle,
when he protested openly with the words, 'And
he will have pity on his servants.' "[i]

**7** When the first brother had died in this manner, they brought the second to be made sport
of. After tearing off the skin and hair of his
head, they asked him, "Will you eat the pork
rather than have your body tortured limb by
limb?" **8** Answering in the language of his
forefathers, he said, "Never!" So he too in turn
suffered the same tortures as the first. **9** At the
point of death he said: "You accursed fiend,
you are depriving us of this present life, but the
King of the world will raise us up* to live again
forever. It is for his laws that we are dying."[j]

**10** After him the third suffered their cruel
sport. He put out his tongue at once when told
to do so, and bravely held out his hands, **11** as
he spoke these noble words: "It was from Heav-
en that I received these; for the sake of his laws
I disdain them; from him I hope to receive them
again."[k] **12** Even the king and his attendants
marveled at the young man's courage, because
he regarded his sufferings as nothing.

**13** After he had died, they tortured and maltreated the fourth brother in the same way.
**14** When he was near death, he said, "It is my
choice to die at the hands of men with the
God-given hope of being restored to life by him;
but for you, there will be no resurrection to
life."

**15** They next brought forward the fifth brother and maltreated him. **16** Looking at the king,
he said:[l] "Since you have power among men,
mortal though you are, do what you please. But
do not think that our nation is forsaken by God.
**17** Only wait, and you will see how his great
power will torment you and your descendants."

**18** After him they brought the sixth brother.
When he was about to die, he said: "Have no
vain illusions. We suffer these things on our
own account, because we have sinned against
our God; that is why such astonishing things
have happened to us. **19** Do not think, then,
that you will go unpunished for having dared to
fight against God."[m]

**20** Most admirable and worthy of everlasting
remembrance was the mother, who saw her sev-
en sons perish in a single day, yet bore it courageously because of her hope in the LORD.
**21** Filled with a noble spirit that stirred her
womanly heart with manly courage, she exhorted each of them in the language of their forefathers with these words: **22** "I do not know how
you came into existence in my womb; it was not
I who gave you the breath of life, nor was it I
who set in order the elements of which each of
you is composed. **23** Therefore, since it is the
Creator of the universe who shapes each man's
beginning, as he brings about the origin of everything, he, in his mercy, will give you back
both breath and life, because you now disregard
yourselves for the sake of his law."

**24** Antiochus, suspecting insult in her
words, thought he was being ridiculed. As the
youngest brother was still alive, the king appealed to him, not with mere words, but with
promises on oath, to make him rich and happy
if he would abandon his ancestral customs: he
would make him his Friend and entrust him with
high office. **25** When the youth paid no attention to him at all, the king appealed to the mother, urging her to advise her boy to save his life.
**26** After he had urged her for a long time, she
went through the motions of persuading her son.
**27** In derision of the cruel tyrant, she leaned
over close to her son and said in their native
language: "Son, have pity on me, who carried
you in my womb for nine months, nursed you
for three years, brought you up, educated and
supported you to your present age. **28** I beg
you, child, to look at the heavens and the earth
and see all that is in them; then you will know
that God did not make them out of existing
things;* and in the same way the human race
came into existence. **29** Do not be afraid of this
executioner, but be worthy of your brothers and
accept death, so that in the time of mercy I may
receive you again with them."

**30** She had scarcely finished speaking when
the youth said: "What are you waiting for? I
will not obey the king's command. I obey the
command of the law given to our forefathers
through Moses. **31** But you, who have contrived every kind of affliction for the Hebrews,
will not escape the hands of God. **32** [n]We,
indeed, are suffering because of our sins.
**33** Though our living LORD treats us harshly for
a little while to correct us with chastisements,

---

i Dt 32, 36.
j 2 Mc 12, 44; 14, 46.
k 2 Mc 12, 43ff.
l 16-19: 2 Mc 5, 17; 6, 12-16.
m Acts 5, 39.
n 32. 38: 2 Mc 5, 17; 6, 12-16; 17, 16-19.

---

* 7, 9: The King of the world will raise us up; here, and in vv 11. 14. 23. 29. 36, belief in the future resurrection of the body, at least for the just, is clearly stated; cf also 2 Mc 12, 44; 14, 46; Dn 12, 2.

7, 28: God did not make them out of existing things: that is, God made all things solely by his omnipotent will and his creative word; cf Heb 11, 3.

he will again be reconciled with his servants.
**34** But you, wretch, vilest of all men! do not,
in your insolence, concern yourself with un-
founded hopes, as you raise your hand against
the children of Heaven. **35** You have not yet
escaped the judgment of the almighty and all-
seeing God. **36** My brothers, after enduring
brief pain, have drunk of never-failing life, under God's covenant, but you, by the judgment
of God, shall receive just punishments for your
arrogance. **37** Like my brothers, I offer up my
body and my life for our ancestral laws, imploring God to show mercy soon to our nation, and
by afflictions and blows to make you confess
that he alone is God. **38** Through me and my
brothers, may there be an end to the wrath of the
Almighty that has justly fallen on our whole
nation." **39** At that, the king became enraged
and treated him even worse than the others,
since he bitterly resented the boy's contempt.
**40** [o]Thus he too died undefiled, putting all his
trust in the LORD. **41** The mother was last to
die, after her sons.

**42** Enough has been said about the sacrificial
meals and the excessive cruelties.

## *V: Victories of Judas and Purification of the Temple*

### CHAPTER 8

**Judas Maccabeus.** **1** [p]Judas Maccabeus
and his companions entered the villages secretly, summoned their kinsmen, and by also enlist-
ing others who remained faithful to Judaism,
assembled about six thousand men. **2** They implored the LORD to look kindly upon his people,
who were being oppressed on all sides; to have
pity on the temple, which was profaned by godless men; **3** to have mercy on the city, which
was being destroyed and about to be leveled to
the ground; to hearken to the blood that cried out
to him; **4** to remember the criminal slaughter of
innocent children and the blasphemies uttered
against his name; and to manifest his hatred of
evil. **5** [q]Once Maccabeus got his men organized, the Gentiles could not withstand him, for
the LORD's wrath had now changed to mercy.
**6** Coming unexpectedly upon towns and villages, he would set them on fire. He captured
strategic positions, and put to flight a large number of the enemy. **7** He preferred the nights as
being especially helpful for such attacks. Soon
the fame of his valor spread everywhere.

**First Victory over Nicanor.*** **8** When
Philip saw that Judas was gaining ground little
by little and that his successful advances were
becoming more frequent, he wrote to Ptolemy,
governor of Coelesyria and Phoenicia, to come
to the aid of the king's government.[r] **9** Ptolemy
promptly selected Nicanor, son of Patroclus,
one of the Chief Friends, and sent him at the
head of at least twenty thousand armed men of
various nations to wipe out the entire Jewish
race. With him he associated Gorgias, a professional military commander, well-versed in the
art of war.[s] **10** Nicanor planned to raise the two
thousand talents of tribute owed by the king to
the Romans by selling captured Jews into slavery. **11** So he immediately sent word to the
coastal cities, inviting them to buy Jewish
slaves and promising to deliver ninety slaves for
a talent—little did he dream of the punishment
that was to fall upon him from the Almighty.

**12** When Judas learned of Nicanor's advance
and informed his companions about the approach of the army, **13** the cowardly and those
who lacked faith in God's justice deserted and
got away. **14** But the others sold everything
they had left, and at the same time besought the
LORD to deliver those whom the ungodly Nicanor had sold before even meeting them.
**15** They begged the LORD to do this, if not for
their sake, at least for the sake of the covenants
made with their forefathers, and because they
themselves bore his holy, glorious name.
**16** Maccabeus assembled his men, six thousand strong, and exhorted them not be panic-
stricken before the enemy, nor to fear the large
number of the Gentiles attacking them unjustly,
but to fight courageously, **17** keeping before
their eyes the lawless outrage perpetrated by the
Gentiles against the holy Place and the affliction
of the humiliated city, as well as the subversion
of their ancestral way of life. **18** "They trust in
weapons and acts of daring," he said, "but we
trust in almighty God, who can by a mere nod
destroy not only those who attack us, but the
whole world." **19** He went on to tell them of
the times when help had been given their ancestors: both the time of Sennacherib, when a hundred and eighty-five thousand of his men were
destroyed,[t] **20** and the time of the battle in Babylonia against the Galatians, when only eight
thousand Jews fought along with four thousand
Macedonians; yet when the Macedonians were
hard pressed, the eight thousand routed one
hundred and twenty thousand and took a great
quantity of booty, because of the help they received from Heaven. **21** With such words he
encouraged them and made them ready to die
for their laws and their country.

o 40f: Heb 11, 35.
p 1-7: 2 Mc 5, 27; 1 Mc 3, 10-26.
q 5ff: 1 Mc 3, 3-9.
r 2 Mc 4, 45; 1 Mc 3, 38.
s 1 Mc 7, 26.
t 2 Mc 15, 22; 2 Kgs 19, 35; Is 37, 36.

* 8, 8–29, 34ff: This account of the campaign of Nicanor and Gorgias against Judas is paralleled, with certain differences, in 1 Mc 3, 38–4, 24.

Then Judas divided his army into four,
**22** placing his brothers, Simon, Joseph,* and
Jonathan, each over a division, assigning to
each fifteen hundred men. **23** (There was also
Eleazar.) After reading to them from the holy
book and giving them the watchword, "The
Help of God," he himself took charge of the
first division and joined in battle with Nicanor.[u]
**24** With the Almighty as their ally, they killed
more than nine thousand of the enemy, wounded and disabled the greater part of Nicanor's
army, and put all of them to flight. **25** They also
seized the money of those who had come to buy
them as slaves. When they had pursued the
enemy for some time, **26** they were obliged to
return by reason of the late hour. It was the day
before the sabbath, and for that reason they
could not continue the pursuit. **27** They collected the enemy's arms and stripped them of their
spoils, and then observed the sabbath with fervent praise and thanks to the LORD who kept
them safe for that day on which he let descend
on them the first dew of his mercy. **28** After the
sabbath, they gave a share of the booty to the
persecuted and to widows and orphans; the rest
they divided among themselves and their children. **29** When this was done, they made supplication in common, imploring the merciful
LORD to be completely reconciled with his servants.

### Timothy and Bacchides Defeated.

**30** They also challenged the forces of Timothy
and Bacchides, killed more than twenty thousand of them, and captured some very high
fortresses. They divided the enormous plunder,
allotting half to themselves and the rest to the
persecuted, to orphans, widows, and the aged.
**31** They collected the enemies' weapons and
carefully stored them in suitable places; the rest
of the spoils they carried to Jerusalem. **32** They
also killed the commander of Timothy's forces,
a most wicked man, who had done great harm
to the Jews. **33** While celebrating the victory in
their ancestral city, they burned both those who
had set fire to the sacred gates and Callisthenes,
who had taken refuge in a little house; so he
received the reward his wicked deeds deserved.

### Humiliation of Nicanor.

**34** [v]The ac-
cursed Nicanor, who had brought the thousand
slave dealers to buy the Jews, **35** after being
humbled through the LORD's help by those
whom he had thought of no account, laid aside
his fine clothes and fled alone across country
like a runaway slave, until he reached Antioch.
He was eminently successful in destroying his
own army. **36** So he who had promised to provide tribute for the Romans by the capture of the
people of Jerusalem testified that the Jews had
a champion, and that they were invulnerable for
the very reason that they followed the laws laid
down by him.

## CHAPTER 9

### Punishment and Death of Antiochus.*

**1** [w]About that time Antiochus retreated in disgrace from the region of Persia. **2** He had entered the city called Persepolis and attempted to
rob the temple and gain control of the city.
Thereupon the people had swift recourse to
arms, and Antiochus' men were routed, so that
in the end Antiochus was put to flight by the
natives and forced to beat a shameful retreat.
**3** On his arrival in Ecbatana, he learned what
had happened to Nicanor and to Timothy's
forces. **4** Overcome with anger, he planned to
make the Jews suffer for the injury done by
those who had put him to flight. Therefore he
ordered his charioteer to drive without stopping
until he finished the journey.

Yet the condemnation of Heaven rode with
him, since he said in his arrogance, "I will
make Jerusalem the common graveyard of the
Jews as soon as I arrive there." **5** So the all-seeing LORD, the God of Israel, struck him down
with an unseen but incurable blow; for scarcely
had he uttered those words when he was seized
with excruciating pains in his bowels and sharp
internal torment,[x] **6** a fit punishment for him
who had tortured the bowels of others with
many barbarous torments. **7** Far from giving up
his insolence, he was all the more filled with
arrogance. Breathing fire in his rage against the
Jews, he gave orders to drive even faster. As a
result he hurtled from the dashing chariot, and
every part of his body was racked by the violent
fall. **8** [y]Thus he who previously, in his superhuman presumption, thought he could command the waves of the sea, and imagined he
could weigh the mountaintops in his scales, was
now thrown to the ground and had to be carried
on a litter, clearly manifesting to all the power
of God. **9** [z]The body of this impious man

u 1 Mc 3, 48.
v 34f: 2 Mc 8, 23f; 1 Mc 7, 26.
w 1-29: 2 Mc 1, 12-17; 1 Mc 6, 1-13.
x Acts 12, 20-23.
y Jb 38, 8-11; Ps 65, 6f; Is 40, 12.
z Acts 12, 23.

*

8, 22: Joseph: called John in 1 Mc 2, 2, 9, 36. 38. This paragraph interrupts the story of Nicanor's defeat, which is resumed in v 34. The purpose of the author apparently is to group together the defeats suffered by the Syrians on various occasions. Battles against Timothy are recounted in 1 Mc 5, 37–44 and 2 Mc 12, 10–25; against Bacchides in 1 Mc 7, 8–20.

9, 1–28: In order to keep together the various accounts of God's punishment of the persecutors of his people, the author places here the stories of Antiochus' illness and death (in actuality the king died only after the purification of the temple; cf 1 Mc 4, 36–59; 6, 1–16; 2 Mc 10, 1–8); of Judas' campaigns in Idumea and Transjordan (cf 2 Mc 5, 1–51; 2 Mc 10, 14–38); and of the first expedition of Lysias (1 Mc 4, 26–35; 2 Mc 11, 1–15).

swarmed with worms, and while he was still
alive in hideous torments, his flesh rotted off,
so that the entire army was sickened by the
stench of his corruption. **10** Shortly before, he
had thought that he could reach the stars of
heaven, and now, no one could endure to transport the man because of this intolerable stench.

**11** At last, broken in spirit, he began to give
up his excessive arrogance, and to gain some
understanding, under the scourge of God, for he
was racked with pain unceasingly. **12** When he
could no longer bear his own stench, he said,
"It is right to be subject to God, and not to think
one's mortal self divine." **13** Then this vile
man vowed to the LORD, who would no longer
have mercy on him, **14** that he would set free
the holy city, toward which he had been hurrying with the intention of leveling it to the ground
and making it a common graveyard; **15** he
would put on perfect equality with the Athenians all the Jews, whom he had judged not even
worthy of burial, but fit only to be thrown out
with their children to be eaten by vultures and
wild animals; **16** he would adorn with the finest
offerings the holy temple which he had previously despoiled; he would restore all the sacred
vessels many times over; and would provide
from his own revenues the expenses required for
the sacrifices. **17** Besides all this, he would
become a Jew himself and visit every inhabited
place to proclaim there the power of God.
**18** But since God's punishment had justly come
upon him, his sufferings were not lessened, so
he lost hope for himself and wrote the following
letter to the Jews in the form of a supplication.
It read thus:

**19** *"To my esteemed Jewish citizens, Antiochus, their king and general, sends hearty
greetings and best wishes for their health and
happiness. **20** If you and your children are well
and your affairs are going as you wish, I thank
God very much, for my hopes are in heaven.
**21** Now that I am ill, I recall with affection the
esteem and good will you bear me. On returning
from the regions of Persia, I fell victim to a
troublesome illness; so I thought it necessary to
form plans for the general welfare of all. **22** Actually, I do not despair about my health, since
I have great hopes of recovering from my illness. **23** Nevertheless, I know that my father,
whenever he went on campaigns in the hinter-
land, would name his successor, **24** so that, if
anything unexpected happened or any unwelcome news came, the people throughout the
realm would know to whom the government had
been entrusted, and so not be disturbed. **25** I am
also bearing in mind that the neighboring rulers,
especially those on the borders of our kingdom,
are on the watch for opportunities and waiting
to see what will happen. I have therefore appointed as king my son Antiochus, whom I have
often before entrusted and commended to most
of you, when I made hurried visits to the outlying provinces. I have written to him the letter
copied below.* **26** Therefore I beg and entreat
each of you to remember the general and individual benefits you have received, and to continue to show good will toward me and my son.
**27** I am confident that, following my policy, he
will treat you with mildness and kindness in his
relations with you."

**28** So this murderer and blasphemer, after
extreme sufferings, such as he had inflicted on
others, died a miserable death in the mountains
of a foreign land. **29** His foster brother Philip
brought the body home; but fearing Antiochus'
son, he later withdrew into Egypt, to Ptolemy
Philometor.

## CHAPTER 10

### Purification of Temple and City.

**1** [a]When Maccabeus and his companions, under the LORD's leadership, had recovered the
temple and the city, **2** they destroyed the altars
erected by the Gentiles in the marketplace and
the sacred enclosures. **3** After purifying the
temple, they made a new altar. Then, with fire
struck from flint, they offered sacrifice for the
first time in two years,* burned incense, and
lighted lamps. They also set out the showbread.
**4** When they had done this, they prostrated
themselves and begged the LORD that they
might never again fall into such misfortunes,
and that if they should sin at any time, he might
chastise them with moderation and not hand
them over to blasphemous and barbarous Gentiles. **5** On the anniversary of the day on which
the temple had been profaned by the Gentiles,
that is, the twenty-fifth of the same month Chislev, the purification of the temple took place.
**6** The Jews celebrated joyfully for eight days as
on the feast of Booths, remembering how, a
little while before, they had spent the feast of
Booths living like wild animals in caves on the
mountains. **7** Carrying rods entwined with
leaves, green branches and palms, they sang
hymns of grateful praise to him who had
brought about the purification of his own Place.
**8** By public edict and decree they prescribed

---

a 1-8: 1 Mc 4, 36-59.

---

*

9, 19–27: Despite the statement in v 18, this letter is not really a supplication. It is rather a notification to all the king's subjects of the appointment of his son as his successor and a request that they be loyal to the new king. Apparently the same letter, which has every appearance of being authentic, was sent to the various peoples throughout the kingdom, with only a few words of address changed for each group.

9, 25: The letter copied below: not included in the text of 2 Mc.

10, 3: Two years: three years according to 1 Mc 1, 54 and 4, 52.

that the whole Jewish nation should celebrate these days every year.

## *VI: Renewed Persecution*

**Death of Ptolemy.** **9** Such was the end of Antiochus surnamed Epiphanes.[b] **10** Now we shall relate what happened under Antiochus Eupator, the son of that godless man, and shall give a summary of the chief evils caused by the wars. **11** When Eupator succeeded to the kingdom, he put a certain Lysias in charge of the government as commander in chief of Coelesyria and Phoenicia. **12** Ptolemy, surnamed Macron,* had taken the lead in treating the Jews fairly because of the previous injustice that had been done them, and he endeavored to have peaceful relations with them. **13** As a result, he was accused before Eupator by the King's Friends. In fact, on all sides he heard himself called a traitor for having abandoned Cyprus, which Philometor had entrusted to him, and for having gone over to Antiochus Epiphanes. Since he could not command the respect due to his high office, he ended his life by taking poison.

**Victory over the Idumeans.*** **14** When Gorgias became governor of the region, he employed foreign troops and used every opportunity to attack the Jews. **15** [c]At the same time the Idumeans, who held some important strongholds, were harassing the Jews; they welcomed fugitives from Jerusalem and endeavored to continue the war. **16** Maccabeus and his companions, after public prayers asking God to be their ally, moved quickly against the strongholds of the Idumeans. **17** Attacking vigorously, they gained control of the places, drove back all who manned the walls, and cut down those who opposed them, killing as many as twenty thousand men. **18** When at least nine thousand took refuge in two very strong towers, containing everything necessary to sustain a siege, **19** Maccabeus left Simon and Joseph, along with Zacchaeus and his men, in sufficient numbers to besiege them, while he himself went off to places where he was more urgently needed. **20** But some of the men in Simon's force who were money lovers let themselves be bribed by some of the men in the towers; on receiving seventy thousand drachmas, they allowed a number of them to escape. **21** When Maccabeus was told what had happened, he assembled the rulers of the people and accused those men of having sold their kinsmen for money by setting their enemies free to fight against them. **22** So he put them to death as traitors, and without delay captured the two towers. **23** As he was successful at arms in all his undertakings, he destroyed more than twenty thousand men in the two strongholds.

**Victory over Timothy.** **24** Timothy, who had previously been defeated by the Jews,* gathered a tremendous force of foreign troops and collected a large number of cavalry from Asia; then he appeared in Judea, ready to conquer it by force. **25** At his approach, Maccabeus and his men made supplication to God, sprinkling earth upon their heads and girding their loins in sackcloth. **26** Lying prostrate at the foot of the altar, they begged him to be gracious to them, and to be an enemy to their enemies, and a foe to their foes, as the law declares.[d]

**27** After the prayer, they took up their arms and advanced a considerable distance from the city, halting when they were close to the enemy. **28** As soon as dawn broke,* the armies joined battle, the one having as pledge of success and victory not only their valor but also their reliance on the LORD, and the other taking fury as their leader in the fight.

**29** [e]In the midst of the fierce battle, there appeared to the enemy from the heavens five majestic men riding on golden-bridled horses, who led the Jews on. **30** They surrounded Maccabeus, and shielding him with their own armor, kept him from being wounded. They shot arrows and hurled thunderbolts at the enemy, who were bewildered and blinded, thrown into confusion and routed. **31** Twenty-five hundred of their foot soldiers and six hundred of their horsemen were slain. **32** Timothy, however, fled to a well-fortified stronghold called Gazara, where Chaereas was in command.[f] **33** For four days Maccabeus and his men eagerly besieged the fortress. **34** Those inside, relying on the strength of the place, kept repeating outrageous blasphemies and uttering abominable words. **35** When the fifth day dawned, twenty young men in the army of Maccabeus, angered over such blasphemies, bravely stormed the wall and with savage fury cut down everyone they encountered. **36** Others who climbed up the same way swung around on the defenders, taking the besieged in the rear; they put the towers to the torch, spread the fire and burned the blasphemers alive. Still others broke down the gates and

b 2 Mc 2, 21; 1 Mc 6, 17.
c 15-23: 1 Mc 5, 3ff.
d Ex 23, 22.
e 29f: 2 Mc 3, 24ff; 5, 2f: 10, 29f; 11, 8.
f 1 Mc 13, 43-48.

*

10, 12: Ptolemy Macron: son of Dorymenes (2 Mc 4, 45); was formerly hostile to the Jews (2 Mc 6, 8).

10, 14–23: Probably the same campaign of Judas against the Idumeans that is mentioned in 1 Mc 5, 1–3.

10, 24: Timothy . . . previously . . . defeated by the Jews: as recounted in 2 Mc 8, 30ff.

10, 28: As soon as dawn broke: the same battle at dawn as in 1 Mc 5, 30–34.

let in the rest of the troops, who took possession
of the city. **37** Timothy had hidden in a cistern,
but they killed* him, along with his brother
Chaereas, and Apollophanes. **38** On completing these exploits, they blessed, with hymns of
grateful praise, the LORD who shows great kindness to Israel and grants them victory.

## CHAPTER 11

**Defeat of Lysias.*** **1** [g]Very soon afterward, Lysias, guardian and kinsman of the king
and head of the government, being greatly displeased at what had happened, **2** mustered
about eighty thousand infantry and all his cavalry and marched against the Jews. His plan was
to make Jerusalem a Greek settlement; **3** to levy
tribute on the temple, as he did on the sanctuaries of the other nations; and to put the high
priesthood up for sale every year. **4** He did not
take God's power into account at all, but felt
exultant confidence in his myriads of foot soldiers, his thousands of horsemen, and his eighty
elephants. **5** So he invaded Judea, and when he
reached Beth-zur, a fortified place about twenty
miles from Jerusalem, launched a strong attack
against it. **6** When Maccabeus and his men
learned that Lysias was besieging the strongholds, they and all the people begged the LORD
with lamentations and tears to send a good angel
to save Israel.[h] **7** Maccabeus himself was the
first to take up arms, and he exhorted the others
to join him in risking their lives to help their
kinsmen. Then they resolutely set out together.
**8** Suddenly, while they were still near Jerusalem, a horseman appeared at their head, clothed
in white garments and brandishing gold weapons.[i] **9** Then all of them together thanked God
for his mercy, and their hearts were filled with
such courage that they were ready to assault not
only men, but the most savage beasts, yes, even
walls of iron. **10** Now that the LORD had shown
his mercy toward them, they advanced in battle
order with the aid of their heavenly ally.
**11** Hurling themselves upon the enemy like lions, they laid low eleven thousand foot soldiers
and sixteen hundred horsemen, and put all the
rest to flight. **12** Most of those who got away
were wounded and stripped of their arms, while
Lysias himself escaped only by shameful flight.

**Peace with the Syrians.** **13** [j]But Lysias
was not a stupid man. He reflected on the defeat
he had suffered, and came to realize that the
Hebrews were invincible because the mighty
God was their ally. He therefore sent a message
**14** persuading them to settle everything on just
terms, and promising to persuade the king also,
and to induce him to become their friend.
**15** Maccabeus, solicitous for the common
good, agreed to all that Lysias proposed; and the
king, on his part, granted in behalf of the Jews
all the written requests of Maccabeus to Lysias.

**Official Letters.** **16** These are the terms of
the letter which Lysias wrote to the Jews: "Lysias sends greetings to the Jewish people.
**17** John and Absalom, your envoys, have presented your signed communication and asked
about the matters contained in it. **18** Whatever
had to be referred to the king I called to his
attention, and the things that were acceptable he
has granted. **19** If you maintain your loyalty to
the government, I will endeavor to further your
interests in the future. **20** On the details of these
matters I have authorized my representatives, as
well as your envoys, to confer with you.
**21** Farewell." The year one hundred and forty-eight,* the twenty-fourth of Dioscorinthius.
**22** The king's letter read thus: "King Antiochus sends greetings to his brother Lysias.
**23** Now that our father has taken his place
among the gods, we wish the subjects of our
kingdom to be undisturbed in conducting their
own affairs. **24** We understand that the Jews do
not agree with our father's policy concerning
Greek customs but prefer their own way of life.
They are petitioning us to let them retain their
own customs. **25** Since we desire that this people too should be undisturbed, our decision is
that their temple be restored to them and that
they live in keeping with the customs of their
ancestors. **26** Accordingly, please send them
messengers to give them our assurances of
friendship, so that, when they learn of our decision, they may have nothing to worry about but
may contentedly go about their own business."
**27** The king's letter to the people was as
follows: "King Antiochus sends greetings to the
Jewish senate and to the rest of the Jews. **28** If
you are well, it is what we desire. We too are
in good health. **29** Menelaus has told us of your
wish to return home and attend to your own
affairs. **30** Therefore, those who return by the
thirtieth of Xanthicus will have our assurance of
full permission **31** to observe their dietary laws
and other laws, just as before, and none of the
Jews shall be molested in any way for faults
committed through ignorance. **32** I have also

g 1-12: 1 Mc 4, 26-35.
h Ex 23, 20.
i 2 Mc 3, 24ff; 5, 2f; 10, 29f.
j 13-33: 1 Mc 6, 57-61.

*

10, 37: Timothy . . . they killed: apparently, the same Timothy is still alive in 2 Mc 12, 2. 18–25. The present passage is not in chronological order, Gazara, v 32 (Gezer) was not captured by the Jews until much later (cf 1 Mc 9, 50ff; 13, 53).

11, 1–12: The defeat of Lysias at Beth-zur probably occurred before the purification of the temple; cf 1 Mc 4, 26–35.

11, 21: The year one hundred and forty-eight: 164 B.C. The reading of the name of the month and its position in the calendar are uncertain.

sent Menelaus to reassure you. **33** Farewell.''
In the year one hundred and forty-eight, the
fifteenth of Xanthicus.*
**34** The Romans also sent them a letter as
follows: ''Quintus Memmius and Titus Manius,
legates of the Romans, send greetings to the
Jewish people. **35** Whatever Lysias, kinsman
of the king, has granted you, we also approve.
**36** But the matters on which he passed judgment should be submitted to the king. As soon
as you have considered them, send someone to
us with your decisions so that we may present
them to your advantage, for we are on our way
to Antioch. **37** Make haste, then, to send us
those who can inform us of your intentions.
**38** Farewell.'' In the year one hundred and forty-eight, the fifteenth of Xanthicus.*

## CHAPTER 12

**Persecution Renewed.** 1 After these
agreements were made, Lysias returned to the
king, and the Jews went about their farming.
**2** But some of the local governors, Timothy and
Apollonius, son of Gennaeus,* as also Hierony-
mus and Demophon, to say nothing of Nicanor,
the commander of the Cyprians, would not allow them to live in peace.
**3** Some people of Joppa also committed this
outrage: they invited the Jews who lived among
them, together with their wives and children, to
embark on boats which they had provided.
There was no hint of enmity toward them: **4** this
was done by public vote of the city. When the
Jews, not suspecting treachery and wishing to
live on friendly terms, accepted the invitation,
the people of Joppa took them out to sea and
drowned at least two hundred of them.

**Activity of Judas.** 5 As soon as Judas
heard of the barbarous deed perpetrated against
his countrymen, he summoned his men; **6** and
after calling upon God, the just judge, he
marched against the murderers of his kinsmen.
In a night attack he set the harbor on fire, burnt
the boats, and put to the sword those who had
taken refuge there. **7** When the gates of the
town were shut, he withdrew, intending to come
back later and wipe out the entire population of
Joppa.
**8** On hearing that the men of Jamnia planned
to give like treatment to the Jews who lived
among them, **9** he attacked the Jamnian populace by night, setting fire to the harbor and the
fleet, so that the glow of the flames was visible
as far as Jerusalem, thirty miles away.
**10** [k]When the Jews had gone about a mile
from there* in the campaign against Timothy,
they were attacked by Arabs numbering at least
five thousand foot soldiers, and five hundred
horsemen. **11** After a hard fight, Judas and his
companions, with God's help, were victorious.
The defeated nomads begged Judas to make
friends with them and promised to supply the
Jews with cattle and to help them in every other
way. **12** Realizing that they could indeed be
useful in many respects, Judas agreed to make
peace with them. After the pledge of friendship
had been exchanged, the Arabs withdrew to
their tents.
**13** He also attacked a certain city called Cas-
pin, fortified with earthworks and ramparts and
inhabited by a mixed population of Gentiles.
**14** Relying on the strength of their walls and
their supply of provisions, the besieged treated
Judas and his men with contempt, insulting
them and even uttering blasphemies and
profanity. **15** But Judas and his men invoked
the aid of the great Sovereign of the world, who,
in the day of Joshua, overthrew Jericho without
battering-ram or siege machine; then they furiously stormed the ramparts.[l] **16** Capturing the
city by the will of God, they inflicted such
indescribable slaughter on it that the adjacent
pool, which was about a quarter of a mile wide,
seemed to be filled with the blood that flowed
into it.
**17** [m]When they had gone on some ninety
miles, they reached Charax,[n] where there were
certain Jews known as Toubiani.* **18** But they
did not find Timothy in that region, for he had
already departed from there without having
done anything except to leave behind in one
place a very strong garrison. **19** But Dositheus
and Sosipater, two of Maccabeus' captains,
marched out and destroyed the force of more
than ten thousand men that Timothy had left in
the stronghold. **20** Meanwhile, Maccabeus divided his army into cohorts, with a commander
over each cohort, and went in pursuit of Timothy, who had a force of a hundred and twenty
thousand foot soldiers and twenty-five hundred
horsemen. **21** When Timothy learned of the approach of Judas, he sent on ahead of him the
women and children, as well as the baggage, to

k 10-16: 1 Mc 5, 24-36.
l Jos 6, 1-21.
m 17-26: 1 Mc 5, 37-44.
n 1 Mc 5, 13.

*

11, 33: The date, which is the same as the date of the Romans' letter (v 38) cannot be correct. The king's letter must be connected with the peace treaty of the year 149 of the Seleucid era, i.e., 163 B.C. Perhaps the mention of the month of Xanthicus in the body of the letter (v 30) caused the date of the Romans' letter to be transferred to this one.

11, 38: The date is April 12, 164 B.C.

12, 2: Apollonius, son of Gennaeus: not the Apollonius who was the son of Menestheus (2 Mc 4, 21). Nicanor: probably distinct from the Nicanor of 2 Mc 14, 2.

12, 10: From there: not from the aforesaid Jamnia (vv 8f) or Joppa (vv 3–7), but from a place in Transjordan; vv 10–26 parallel the account given in 1 Mc 5, 9–13. 24–54 of Judas' campaign in northern Transjordan.

12, 17: Certain Jews known as Toubiani: because they lived "in the land of Tob" (1 Mc 5, 13).

a place called Karnion, which was hard to besiege and even hard to reach because of the difficult terrain of that region. 22 But when Judas' first cohort appeared, the enemy was overwhelmed with fear and terror at the manifestation of the All-seeing. Scattering in every direction, they rushed away in such headlong flight that in many cases they wounded one another, pierced by the swords of their own men. 23 Judas pressed the pursuit vigorously, putting the sinners to the sword and destroying as many as thirty thousand men.

24 Timothy himself fell into the hands of the men under Dositheus and Sosipater; but with great cunning, he asked them to spare his life and let him go, because he had in his power the parents and relatives of many of them, and could make these suffer. 25 When he had fully confirmed his solemn pledge to restore them unharmed, they let him go for the sake of saving their brethren.

**Further Successes.** 26 Judas then marched to Karnion and the shrine of Atargatis,* where he killed twenty-five thousand people. 27 [o]After the defeat and destruction of these, he moved his army to Ephron, a fortified city inhabited by people of many nationalities. Robust young men took up their posts in defense of the walls, from which they fought valiantly; inside were large supplies of machines and missiles. 28 But the Jews, invoking the Sovereign who forcibly shatters the might of his enemies, got possession of the city and slaughtered twenty-five thousand of the people in it. 29 Then they set out from there and hastened on to Scythopolis,* seventy-five miles from Jerusalem. 30 But when the Jews who lived there testified to the good will shown by the Scythopolitans and to their kind treatment even in times of adversity, 31 Judas and his men thanked them and exhorted them to be well disposed to their race in the future also. Finally they arrived in Jerusalem, shortly before the feast of Weeks.

32 After this feast called Pentecost, they lost no time in marching against Gorgias, governor of Idumea, 33 who opposed them with three thousand foot soldiers and four hundred horsemen. 34 In the ensuing battle, a few of the Jews were slain. 35 A man called Dositheus, a powerful horseman and one of Bacenor's men,* caught hold of Gorgias, grasped his military cloak and dragged him along by main strength, intending to capture the vile wretch alive, when a Thracian horseman attacked Dositheus and cut off his arm at the shoulder. Then Gorgias fled to Marisa. 36 After Esdris and his men had been fighting for a long time and were weary, Judas called upon the LORD to show himself their ally and leader in the battle. 37 Then, raising a battle cry in his ancestral language, and with songs, he charged Gorgias' men when they were not expecting it and put them to flight.

**Expiation for the Dead.** 38 Judas rallied his army and went to the city of Adullam. As the week was ending, they purified themselves according to custom and kept the sabbath there. 39 On the following day, since the task had now become urgent, Judas and his men went to gather up the bodies of the slain and bury them with their kinsmen in their ancestral tombs. 40 But under the tunic of each of the dead they found amulets sacred to the idols of Jamnia, which the law forbids the Jews to wear. So it was clear to all that this was why these men had been slain.[p] 41 They all therefore praised the ways of the LORD, the just judge who brings to light the things that are hidden. 42 *Turning to supplication, they prayed that the sinful deed might be fully blotted out. The noble Judas warned the soldiers to keep themselves free from sin, for they had seen with their own eyes what had happened because of the sin of those who had fallen. 43 He then took up a collection among all his soldiers, amounting to two thousand silver drachmas, which he sent to Jerusalem to provide for an expiatory sacrifice. In doing this he acted in a very excellent and noble way, inasmuch as he had the resurrection of the dead in view; 44 for if he were not expecting the fallen to rise again, it would have been useless and foolish to pray for them in death. 45 But if he did this with a view to the splendid reward that awaits those who had gone to rest in godliness, it was a holy and pious thought. 46 Thus he made atonement for the dead that they might be freed from this sin.

## CHAPTER 13

**The Syrians Invade Judea.** 1 In the year one hundred and forty-nine,* Judas and his men learned that Antiochus Eupator was invading

---

o 27-31: 2 Mc 5, 45-54. p Dt 7, 25.

---

12, 26: Atargatis: a Syrian goddess, represented by the body of a fish.

12, 29: Scythopolis: the Greek name of the city of Bethshan; cf 1 Mc 5, 52.

12, 35: One of Bacenor's men: certain ancient witnesses to the text have "one of the Toubiani"; cf v 17.

12, 42–46: This is the earliest statement of the doctrine that prayers (v 42) and sacrifices (v 43) for the dead are beneficial. The statement is made here, however, only for the purpose of proving that Judas believed in the resurrection of the just (2 Mc 7, 9. 14. 23. 36). That is, he believed that expiation could be made for certain sins of otherwise good men—soldiers who had given their lives for God's cause. Thus, they could share in the resurrection. His belief was similar to, but not quite the same as, the Catholic doctrine of purgatory.

13, 1: In the year one hundred and forty-nine: 163–162 B.C.

Judea with a large force, **2** and that with him
was Lysias, his guardian, who was in charge of
the government. They led* a Greek army of one
hundred and ten thousand foot soldiers, fifty-
three hundred horsemen, twenty-two elephants,
and three hundred chariots armed with
scythes.[q]

**Death of Menelaus.** **3** Menelaus also
joined them, and with great duplicity kept
urging Antiochus on, not for the welfare of his
country, but in the hope of being established in
office. **4** But the King of kings aroused the
anger of Antiochus against the scoundrel. When
the king was shown by Lysias that Menelaus
was to blame for all the trouble, he ordered him
to be taken to Beroea* and executed there in the
customary local method.[r] **5** There is at that
place a tower seventy-five feet high, full of
ashes,* with a circular rim sloping down steeply
on all sides toward the ashes. **6** A man guilty
of sacrilege or notorious for certain other crimes
is brought up there and then hurled down to
destruction. **7** In such a manner was Menelaus,
the transgressor of the law, fated to die; he was
deprived even of decent burial. **8** It was altogether just that he who had committed so many
sins against the altar with its pure fire and ashes
should meet his death in ashes.

**Skirmish near Modein.** **9** The king was
advancing, his mind full of savage plans for
inflicting on the Jews worse things than those
they suffered in his father's time. **10** When Judas learned of this, he urged the people to call
upon the LORD night and day, to help them now,
if ever, **11** when they were about to be deprived
of their law, their country, and their holy temple; and not to allow this nation, which had just
begun to revive, to be subjected again to blasphemous Gentiles. **12** When they had all joined
in doing this, and had implored the merciful
LORD continuously with weeping and fasting
and prostrations for three days, Judas encouraged them and told them to stand ready. **13** After a private meeting with the elders, he decided
that, before the king's army could invade Judea
and take possession of the city, the Jews should
march out and settle the matter with God's help.
**14** Leaving the outcome to the Creator of the
world, and exhorting his followers to fight nobly to death for the laws, the temple, the city,
the country, and the government, he pitched his
camp near Modein. **15** Giving his men the battle cry "God's Victory," he made a night attack
on the king's pavilion with a picked force of the
bravest young men and killed about two thousand in the camp. They also slew* the lead
elephant and its rider.[s] **16** Finally they withdrew in triumph,* having filled the camp with
terror and confusion. **17** Day was just breaking
when this was accomplished with the help and
protection of the LORD.

**Treaty with Antiochus V.** **18** [t]The king,
having had a taste of the Jews' daring, tried to
take their positions by a stratagem. **19** So he
marched against Beth-zur, a strong fortress of
the Jews; but he was driven back, checked, and
defeated. **20** Judas then sent supplies to the men
inside, **21** but Rhodocus, of the Jewish army,
betrayed military secrets* to the enemy. He was
found out, arrested, and imprisoned. **22** The
king made a second attempt by negotiating with
the men of Beth-zur. After giving them his
pledge and receiving theirs, he withdrew
**23** and attacked Judas and his men. But he was
defeated. Next he heard that Philip, who was
left in charge of the government in Antioch, had
rebelled. Dismayed, he parleyed with the Jews,
submitted to their terms, and swore to observe
their rights. Having come to this agreement, he
offered a sacrifice, and honored the temple with
a generous donation. **24** He approved of Maccabeus and left him as military and civil governor of the territory from Ptolemais to the region
of the Gerrenes.* **25** When he came to Ptolemais, the people of that city were angered by the
peace treaty; in fact they were so indignant that
they wanted to annul its provisions. **26** But
Lysias took the platform, defended the treaty as
well as he could, and won them over by persuasion. After calming them and gaining their good
will, he returned to Antioch.

That is how the king's attack and withdrawal
went.

## CHAPTER 14

**Antagonism of Alcimus.** **1** [u]Three years
later,* Judas and his men learned that Demetri-

q 1 Mc 6, 30.
r 1 Tm 6, 15; Rv 17, 14; 19, 16.
s 1 Mc 6, 43-46.
t 18-23: 1 Mc 6, 48-53.
u 1-11: 1 Mc 7, 1-7.

*

13, 2: They led: the Greek means literally "Each (of them) led," but it is unlikely that the author meant the already immense numbers to be doubled; the numbers are similar to those in 1 Mc 6, 30.

13, 4: Beroea: the Greek name of Aleppo.

13, 5: Ashes: probably smoldering ashes; the tower resembles the ancient Persian fire towers.

13, 15: Slew: literally "stabbed"; the deed was done by Eleazar (1 Mc 6, 43–46).

13, 16: They withdrew in triumph: according to 1 Mc 6, 47 they fled.

13, 21: Military secrets: probably about the lack of provisions in the besieged city; cf 1 Mc 6, 49.

13, 24: The Greek text is uncertain and may be rendered: "He approved of Maccabeus, then left Hegemonides as governor of the territory . . ." Gerrenes: probably the inhabitants of Gerar, southeast of Gaza.

14, 1: Three years later: actually, Demetrius (I Soter), son of Seleucus (IV), landed at Tripolis in the year 151 of the Seleucid era (v 4), i.e., 162–161 B.C.; cf 1 Mc 7, 1–7.

us, son of Seleucus, had sailed into the port of
Tripolis with a powerful army and a fleet, **2** and
that he had occupied the country, after doing
away with Antiochus and his guardian Lysias.
**3** A certain Alcimus, a former high priest,
who had willfully incurred defilement at the
time of the revolt, realized that there was no way
for him to salvage his position and regain access
to the holy altar. **4** So he went to King Demetrius in the year one hundred and fifty-one and
presented him with a gold crown and a palm
branch, as well as some of the customary olive
branches from the temple. On that occasion he
kept quiet.[v] **5** But he found an opportunity to
further his mad scheme when he was invited to
the council by Demetrius and questioned about
the dispositions and intentions of the Jews. He
replied: **6** "Those Jews called Hasideans, led
by Judas Maccabeus, are warmongers, who stir
up sedition and keep the kingdom from enjoying
peace and quiet. **7** For this reason, now that I
am deprived of my ancestral dignity, that is to
say, the high priesthood, I have come here—
**8** first, out of my genuine concern for the king's
interests, and secondly, out of consideration for
my own countrymen, since our entire nation is
suffering great affliction from the unreasonable
conduct of the people just mentioned. **9** When
you have informed yourself in detail on these
matters, O king, act in the interest of our country and its hard-pressed people with the same
gracious consideration that you show toward
all. **10** As long as Judas is around, it is impossible for the state to enjoy peace." **11** When he
had said this, the other Friends who were hostile
to Judas quickly added fuel to Demetrius' indignation.

**Dealings with Nicanor.** **12** [w]The king immediately chose Nicanor, who had been in command of the elephants, and appointed him governor of Judea. He sent him off **13** with orders
to put Judas to death, to disperse his followers,
and to set up Alcimus as high priest of the great
temple. **14** The Gentiles from Judea, who
would have banished Judas,* came flocking to
Nicanor, thinking that the misfortunes and calamities of the Jews would mean prosperity for
themselves. **15** [x]When the Jews heard of Nicanor's coming, and that the Gentiles were rallying to him, they sprinkled themselves with earth
and prayed to him who established his people
forever, and who always comes to the aid of his
heritage. **16** At their leader's command, they
set out at once and came upon the enemy at the
village of Adasa. **17** Judas' brother Simon had
engaged Nicanor, but because of the sudden
appearance of the enemy suffered a slight repulse. **18** However, when Nicanor heard of the
valor of Judas and his men, and the great courage with which they fought for their country, he
shrank from deciding the issue by bloodshed.
**19** So he sent Posidonius, Theodotus and Mattathias to arrange an agreement. **20** After a long
discussion of the terms, each leader communicated them to his troops; and when general
agreement was expressed, they assented to the
treaty. **21** A day was set on which the leaders
would meet by themselves. From each side a
chariot came forward and thrones were set in
place. **22** Judas had posted armed men in readiness at suitable points for fear that the enemy
might suddenly carry out some treacherous
plan. But the conference was held in the proper
way. **23** Nicanor stayed on in Jerusalem, where
he did nothing out of place. He got rid of the
throngs of ordinary people who gathered around
him; **24** but he always kept Judas in his company, for he had a cordial affection for the man.
**25** He urged him to marry and have children; so
Judas married, settled down, and shared the
common life.

**Threats against Judas.** **26** When Alcimus saw their friendship for each other, he
took the treaty that had been made, went to
Demetrius, and said that Nicanor was plotting
against the state, and that he had appointed Judas, the conspirator against the kingdom, to be
his successor. **27** Stirred up by the villain's
calumnies, the king became enraged. He wrote
to Nicanor, stating that he was displeased with
the treaty, and ordering him to send Maccabeus
as a prisoner to Antioch without delay.
**28** When this message reached Nicanor he was
dismayed, for he hated to break his agreement
with a man who had done no wrong. **29** However, there was no way of opposing the king, so
he watched for an opportunity to carry out this
order by a stratagem. **30** But Maccabeus noticed that Nicanor was becoming cool in his
dealings with him, and acting with unaccus-
tomed rudeness when they met; he concluded
that this coldness betokened no good. So he
gathered together a large number of his men,
and went into hiding from Nicanor.
**31** [y]When Nicanor realized that he had been
disgracefully outwitted by the man, he went to
the great and holy temple, at a time when the
priests were offering the customary sacrifices,
and ordered them to surrender Judas. **32** As
they declared under oath that they did not know
where the wanted man was, **33** he raised his
right hand toward the temple and swore this
oath: "If you do not hand Judas over to me as

v 1 Mc 7, 7. 25.
w 12f: 2 Mc 8, 9; 1 Mc 3, 38f.
x 15-19: 1 Mc 7, 26-32.
y 31-36: 1 Mc 7, 33-38.

* 14, 14: Who would have banished Judas: the meaning of the Greek is uncertain; some render it: "who had fled before Judas."

prisoner, I will level this shrine of God to the
ground; I will tear down the altar, and erect here
a splendid temple to Dionysus.'' **34** With these
words he went away. The priests stretched out
their hands toward heaven, calling upon the
unfailing defender of our nation in these words:
**35** ''LORD of all, though you are in need of
nothing, you have approved of a temple for your
dwelling place among us.[z] **36** Therefore, O
holy One, LORD of all holiness, preserve forever
undefiled this house, which has been so recently
purified.''

**The Story of Razis.*** **37** A certain Razis,
one of the elders of Jerusalem, was denounced
to Nicanor as a patriot. A man highly regarded,
he was called a father of the Jews because of his
love for them. **38** In the early days of the revolt,
he had been convicted of Judaism, and had
risked body and life in his ardent zeal for it.
**39** Nicanor, to show his detestation of the Jews,
sent more than five hundred soldiers to arrest
him. **40** He thought that by arresting such a
man he would deal the Jews a hard blow.
**41** But when these troops, on the point of capturing the tower, were forcing the outer gate and
calling for fire to set the door ablaze, Razis, now
caught on all sides, turned his sword against
himself, **42** preferring to die nobly rather than
fall into the hands of vile men and suffer out-
rages unworthy of his noble birth. **43** In the
excitement of the struggle he failed to strike
exactly. So while the troops rushed in through
the doors, he gallantly ran up to the top of the
wall and with manly courage threw himself
down into the crowd. **44** But as they quickly
drew back and left an opening, he fell into the
middle of the empty space. **45** Still breathing,
and inflamed with anger, he got up and ran
through the crowd, with blood gushing from his
frightful wounds. **46** Then, standing on a steep
rock, as he lost the last of his blood, he tore out
his entrails and flung them with both hands into
the crowd, calling upon the LORD of life and of
spirit to give these back to him again. Such was
the manner of his death.[a]

## CHAPTER 15

**Nicanor's Blasphemy.** **1** When Nicanor
learned that Judas and his companions were in
the territory of Samaria, he decided to attack
them in all safety on the day of rest. **2** The Jews
who were forced to follow him pleaded, ''Do
not massacre them in that way, like a savage
barbarian, but show respect for the day which
the All-seeing has exalted with holiness above
all other days.'' **3** At this the thrice-sinful
wretch asked if there was a ruler in heaven who
prescribed the keeping of the sabbath day.[b]
**4** When they replied that there was indeed such
a ruler in heaven, the living LORD himself, who
commanded the observance of the sabbath day,
**5** he said, ''I, on my part, am ruler on earth,
and my orders are that you take up arms and
carry out the king's business.'' Nevertheless he
did not succeed in carrying out his cruel plan.

**Fresh Hope.** **6** In his utter boastfulness and
arrogance Nicanor had determined to erect a
public monument of victory* over Judas and his
men. **7** But Maccabeus remained confident,
fully convinced that he would receive help from
the LORD. **8** He urged his men not to fear the
enemy, but mindful of the help they had received from Heaven in the past, to expect that
now, too, victory would be given them by the
Almighty. **9** By encouraging them with words
from the law and the prophets,* and by reminding them of the battles they had already won, he
filled them with fresh enthusiasm. **10** Having
stirred up their courage, he gave his orders and
pointed out at the same time the perfidy of the
Gentiles and their violation of oaths. **11** When
he had armed each of them, not so much with
the safety of shield and spear as with the encouragement of noble words, he cheered them all by
relating a dream, a kind of vision, worthy of
belief.

**12** What he saw was this: Onias, the former
high priest,* a good and virtuous man, modest
in appearance, gentle in manners, distinguished
in speech, and trained from childhood in every
virtuous practice, was praying with outstretched
arms for the whole Jewish community.[c]
**13** Then in the same way another man appeared, distinguished by his white hair and dignity, and with an air about him of extraordinary,
majestic authority. **14** Onias then said of him,
''This is God's prophet Jeremiah,* who loves
his brethren and fervently prays for his people
and their holy city.'' **15** Stretching out his right
hand, Jeremiah presented a gold sword to Judas.
As he gave it to him he said, **16** ''Accept this
holy sword as a gift from God; with it you shall
crush your adversaries.''

z Acts 17, 25.
a 2 Mc 7, 9ff.
b 1 Mc 7, 34.
c 2 Mc 3, 1ff.

*

14, 37–46: The story of Razis belongs to the "martyrology" class of literature; it is similar to the stores in 2 Mc 6, 18–7, 42.

15, 6: Public monument of victory: a heap of stones covered with the arms and armor of the fallen enemy.

15, 9: The law and the prophets: the first of the three parts of the Hebrew Scriptures, called the sacred books (1 Mc 12, 9).

15, 12: Onias, the former high priest: Onias III (2 Mc 3, 1–40). Evidently the author believed that the departed just were in some way alive even before the resurrection.

15, 14: Jeremiah: regarded by the postexilic Jews as one of the greatest figures in their history; cf 2 Mc 2, 1; Mt 16, 14. Who . . . prays for his people: a clear belief in the intercession of the saints.

**Defeat and Death of Nicanor.** **17** Encouraged by Judas' noble words, which had
power to instill valor and stir young hearts to
courage, the Jews determined not to delay, but
to charge gallantly and decide the issue by
hand-to-hand combat with the utmost courage,
since their city and its temple with the sacred
vessels were in danger. **18** They were not so
much concerned about their wives and children
or their brothers and kinsmen; their first and
foremost fear was for the consecrated sanctuary.[d] **19** Those who remained in the city suffered a like agony, anxious as they were about
the battle in the open country.

**20** Everyone now awaited the decisive moment. The enemy were already drawing near
with their troops drawn up in battle line, their
elephants placed in strategic positions, and their
cavalry stationed on the flanks. **21** Maccabeus,
contemplating the hosts before him, their elaborate equipment, and the fierceness of their elephants, stretched out his hands toward heaven
and called upon the LORD who works miracles;
for he knew that it is not through arms but
through the LORD's decision that victory is won
by those who deserve it. **22** [e]He prayed to him
thus: "You, O LORD, sent your angel in the days
of King Hezekiah of Judea, and he slew a hundred and eighty-five thousand men of Sennacherib's army. **23** Sovereign of the heavens, send
a good angel now to spread fear and dread before us. **24** By the might of your arm may those
be struck down who have blasphemously come
against your holy people!" With this he ended
his prayer.

**25** [f]Nicanor and his men advanced to the
sound of trumpets and battle songs. **26** But Judas and his men met the army with supplication
and prayers. **27** Fighting with their hands and
praying to God with their hearts, they laid low
at least thirty-five thousand, and rejoiced greatly over this manifestation of God's power.
**28** When the battle was over and they were
joyfully departing, they discovered Nicanor lying there in all his armor; **29** so they raised
tumultuous shouts in their native tongue in
praise of the divine Sovereign.

**30** Then Judas, who was ever in body and
soul the chief defender of his fellow citizens,
and had maintained from youth his affection for
his countrymen, ordered Nicanor's head and
whole right arm to be cut off and taken to Jerusalem. **31** When he arrived there, he assembled
his countrymen, stationed the priests before the
altar, and sent for those in the citadel.* **32** He
showed them the vile Nicanor's head and the
wretched blasphemer's arm that had been boastfully stretched out against the holy dwelling of
the Almighty. **33** He cut out the tongue of the
godless Nicanor, saying he would feed it piece-
meal to the birds and would hang up the other
wages of his folly opposite the temple. **34** At
this, everyone looked toward heaven and
praised the LORD who manifests his divine power, saying, "Blessed be he who has kept his own
Place undefiled!"

**35** Judas hung up Nicanor's head on the wall
of the citadel, a clear and evident proof to all of
the Lord's help.[g] **36** By public vote it was
unanimously decreed never to let this day pass
unobserved,[h] but to celebrate it on the thirteenth
day of the twelfth month, called Adar in Aramaic, the eve of Mordecai's Day.*

## *VII: Epilogue*

**Author's Apology.** **37** Since Nicanor's
doings ended in this way, with the city remaining in possession of the Hebrews from that time
on, I will bring my own story to an end here too.
**38** If it is well written and to the point, that is
what I wanted; if it is poorly done and mediocre,
that is the best I could do. **39** Just as it is harmful to drink wine alone or water alone, whereas
mixing wine with water makes a more pleasant
drink that increases delight, so a skillfully composed story delights the ears of those who read
the work. Let this, then, be the end.

d 1 Mc 4, 36.
e 22f: 2 Mc 8, 19; 2 Kgs 19, 35; Is 37, 36; 1 Mc 7, 40f.
f 25-36: 2 Mc 8, 39-50.
g 1 Sm 31, 9f.
h 1 Mc 7, 49.

*

15, 31: Those in the citadel: presumably Jewish soldiers; actually, the citadel was still in the possession of the Syrians.

15, 36: Mordecai's Day: the feast of Purim, celebrated on the fourteenth and fifteenth days of Adar (Est 9, 17–22).

# THE WISDOM BOOKS

*The Books of Job, Psalms, Proverbs, Ecclesiastes, the Song of Songs, Wisdom, and Sirach, are all versified by the skillful use of parallelism, that is, of the balanced and symmetrical phrases peculiar to Hebrew poetry. With the exception of the Psalms, the majority of which are devotional lyrics, and the Song of Songs, a nuptial hymn, these books belong to the general class of wisdom or didactic literature, strictly so called because their chief purpose is instruction.*

*The widom literature of the Bible is the fruit of a movement among ancient oriental people to gather, preserve and express, usually in aphoristic style, the results of human experience as an aid toward understanding and solving the problems of life. In Israel especially, the movement concerned itself with such basic and vital problems as man's origin and destiny, his quest for happiness, the problem of suffering, of good and evil in human conduct, of death, and the state beyond the grave. Originating with oral tradition, these formulations found their way into the historical books of the Old Testament in the shape of proverbs, odes, chants, epigrams, and also into those psalms intended for instruction.*

*The developed compositions of this literature form the sapiential books. The Book of Proverbs is a collection of sentences or practical norms for moral conduct. The Book of Job is an artistic dialogue skillfully handling the problem of suffering though only from the standpoint of temporal life. Ecclesiastes examines a wide range of human experience only to conclude that all things are vanity except the fear of the Lord and observance of his commandments, and that God requites man in his own good time. Sirach gathers and presents the fruits of past experience, thus preparing for the Book of Wisdom, which sees for the just man seeking happiness the full hope of immortality (Wis 3, 4).*

*Those who cultivated wisdom were called sages. Men of letters, scribes, skilled in the affairs of government, and counselors to rulers, they were instructors of the people, especially of youth (Sir 51, 13–30). In times of crisis they guided the people by revaluating tradition, thus helping to preserve unity, peace and good will. The most illustrious of the sages, and the originator of wisdom literature in Israel, was Solomon. Because of his fame, some of the wisdom books of which he was not the author bear his name.*

*Despite numerous resemblances, sometimes exaggerated, between the sapiential literature of pagan nations and the wisdom books of the Bible, the former are often replete with vagaries and abound in polytheistic conceptions; the latter remained profoundly human, universal, fundamentally moral, and essentially religious and monotheistic. Under the influence of the law and the prophets, wisdom became piety and virtue; impiety and vice were folly. The teachers of wisdom were regarded as men of God, and their books were placed beside the law and the prophets. The highest wisdom became identified with the spirit of God through which the world was created and preserved (Prv 8, 22–31), and mankind was enlightened.*

*The limitations of Old Testament wisdom served to crystallize the problems of human life and destiny, thus preparing for their solution through New Testament revelation. Ecclesiastes' vain search for success and happiness on earth ends when the Savior assures these things to his followers, not in this world but in the bliss of heaven. The anxiety in the Book of Job over reconciling God's justice and wisdom with the suffering of the innocent is relieved by the account of the crucified and risen Redeemer in the gospel. By fulfilling all that the Psalms foretold concerning him, Jesus makes the Psalter his prayer book and that of the church for all time. The love of God for the chosen people which underlies the Song of Songs is perfected in the union of Christ with his church. The personification of the wisdom of Proverbs, Wisdom and Sirach shines forth in resplendent reality in the Word who was with God, and who was God, and who became incarnate to dwell among us; cf Jn 1, 2. 14.*

# The Book of
# JOB

*The Book of Job, named after its protagonist, is an exquisite dramatic poem which treats of the problem of the suffering of the innocent, and of retribution. The contents of the book, together with its artistic structure and elegant style, place it among the literary masterpieces of all time.*

*Job, an oriental chieftain, pious and upright, richly endowed in his own person and in domestic prosperity, suffers a sudden and complete reversal of fortune. He loses his property and his children; a loathsome disease afflicts his body; and sorrow oppresses his soul. Nevertheless, Job does not complain against God. When some friends visit him to condole with him, Job protests his innocence and does not understand why he is afflicted. He curses the day of his birth and longs for death to bring an end to his sufferings. The debate which ensues consists of three cycles of speeches. Job's friends insist that his plight can only be a punishment for personal wrongdoing and an invitation from God to repentance. Job rejects their inadequate explanation and calls for a response from God himself. At this point the speeches of a youth named Elihu (ch 32–37) interrupt the development.*

*In response to Job's plea that he be allowed to see God and hear from him the cause of his suffering, God answers, not by justifying his action before men, but by referring to his own omniscience and almighty power. Job is content with this. He recovers his attitude of humility and trust in God, which is deepened now and strengthened by his experience of suffering.*

*The author of the book is not known; it was composed some time between the 7th and 5th centuries B.C. Its literary form, with speeches, prologue and epilogue disposed according to a studied plan, indicates that the purpose of the writing is didactic. The lesson is that even the just may suffer here, and their sufferings are a test of their fidelity. They shall be rewarded in the end. Man's finite mind cannot probe the depths of the divine omniscience that governs the world. The problems we encounter can be solved by a broader and deeper awareness of God's power, presence (42, 5) and wisdom.*

*The divisions of the Book of Job are as follows:*


*I. Prologue (1, 1—2, 13).*
*II. First Cycle of Speeches (3, 1—14, 22).*
*III. Second Cycle of Speeches (15, 1—21, 34).*
*IV. Third Cycle of Speeches (22, 1—28, 28).*
*V. Job's Final Summary of His Cause (29, 1—31, 37)*
*VI. Elihu's Speeches (32, 1—37, 24).*
*VII. The Lord's Speech (38, 1—42, 6).*
*VIII. Epilogue (42, 7—17).*


## *I: Prologue*

### CHAPTER 1

**Job's Wealth and Piety.** **1** In the land of
Uz* there was a blameless and upright man
named Job,[a] who feared God and avoided evil.
**2** *Seven sons and three daughters were born to
him; **3** and he had seven thousand sheep, three
thousand camels, five hundred yoke of oxen,
five hundred she-asses, and a great number of
work animals, so that he was greater than any
of the men of the East.* **4** His sons used to take
turns giving feasts, sending invitations to their
three sisters to eat and drink with them. **5** And
when each feast had run its course, Job would
send for them and sanctify them, rising early
and offering holocausts for every one of them.
For Job said, "It may be that my sons have

a Jb 2, 3.

*

1, 1: Uz: somewhere in Edom or Arabia. Job: a not uncommon name in ancient Semitic circles; its original meaning was "enemy."

1, 2f: The numbers mentioned here indicate Job's great wealth and happiness, external proof of God's friendship.

1, 3: Men of the East: that is, east of Palestine.

sinned and blasphemed God in their hearts."
This Job did habitually.
**6** [b]One day, when the sons of God* came to
present themselves before the LORD, Satan also
came among them.[c] **7** And the LORD said to
Satan, "Whence do you come?" Then Satan
answered the LORD and said,[d] "From roaming
the earth and patrolling it." **8** And the LORD
said to Satan, "Have you noticed my servant
Job, and that there is no one on earth like him,
blameless and upright, fearing God and avoiding evil?" **9** But Satan answered the LORD and
said, "Is it for nothing that Job is God-fearing?
**10** Have you not surrounded him and his family
and all that he has with your protection? You
have blessed the work of his hands, and his
livestock are spread over the land. **11** [e]But now
put forth your hand and touch anything that he
has, and surely he will blaspheme you to your
face." **12** And the LORD said to Satan, "Behold, all that he has is in your power; only do
not lay a hand upon his person." So Satan went
forth from the presence of the LORD.

**The First Trial.** **13** And so one day, while
his sons and his daughters were eating and
drinking wine in the house of their eldest brother, **14** a messenger came to Job and said, "The
oxen were plowing and the asses grazing beside
them, **15** and the Sabeans* carried them off in
a raid. They put the herdsmen to the sword, and
I alone have escaped to tell you." **16** While he
was yet speaking, another came and said,
"Lightning* has fallen from heaven and struck
the sheep and their shepherds and consumed
them; and I alone have escaped to tell you."
**17** While he was yet speaking, another came
and said, "The Chaldeans formed three columns, seized the camels, carried them off, and
put those tending them to the sword, and I alone
have escaped to tell you." **18** While he was yet
speaking, another came and said, "Your sons
and daughters were eating and drinking wine in
the house of their eldest brother, **19** when suddenly a great wind came across the desert and
smote the four corners of the house. It fell upon
the young people and they are dead; and I alone
have escaped to tell you." **20** Then Job began
to tear his cloak and cut off his hair. He cast
himself prostrate upon the ground, **21** and said,

"Naked I came forth from my mother's
womb,[f]
and naked shall I go back again.*
The LORD gave and the LORD has taken
away;
blessed be the name of the LORD!"

**22** In all this Job did not sin,[g] nor did he say
anything disrespectful of God.

## CHAPTER 2

**The Second Trial.** **1** Once again the sons
of God[h] came to present themselves before the
LORD, and Satan also came with them. **2** And
the LORD said to Satan, "Whence do you
come?" And Satan answered the LORD and
said, "From roaming the earth and patrolling
it." **3** And the LORD said to Satan, "Have you
noticed my servant Job, and that there is no one
on earth like him, faultless and upright, fearing
God and avoiding evil?[i] He still holds fast to his
innocence although you incited me against him
to ruin him without cause." **4** And Satan answered the LORD and said, "Skin for skin!* All
that a man has will he give for his life. **5** [j]But
now put forth your hand and touch his bone and
his flesh, and surely he will blaspheme you to
your face." **6** And the LORD said to Satan, "He
is in your power; only spare his life." **7** So
Satan went forth from the presence of the LORD
and smote Job with severe boils from the soles
of his feet to the crown of his head. **8** And he
took a potsherd to scrape himself, as he sat
among the ashes. **9** Then his wife said to him,[k]
"Are you still holding to your innocence? Curse
God and die."* **10** But he said to her, "Are
even you going to speak as senseless women
do? We accept good things from God; and
should we not accept evil?" Through all this,
Job said nothing sinful.[l]

**Job's Three Friends.** **11** Now when three
of Job's friends heard of all the misfortune that
had come upon him, they set out each one from
his own place: Eliphaz from Teman, Bildad
from Shuh, and Zophar from Naamath.* They
met and journeyed together to give him sympathy and comfort. **12** But when, at a distance,
they lifted up their eyes and did not recognize
him, they began to weep aloud; they tore their
cloaks and threw dust upon their heads.
**13** Then they sat down upon the ground with

b 6ff: Jb 2, 1ff.
c Gn 6, 2, 4; Zec 3, 1; Lk 22, 31; Rv 12, 9.
d 1 Pt 5, 8.
e Jb 2, 5.
f Eccl 5, 14; 1 Tm 6, 7.
g Jb 2, 10; Jas 5, 11.
h Jb 1, 6.
i Jb 1, 1.
j Jb 1, 11.
k Jb 19, 17.
l Jb 1, 22; Sir 2, 4; Jas 5, 11.

*

1, 6: Sons of God: angels. Satan: literally, "adversary."

1, 15: Sabeans: from southern Arabia.

1, 16: Lightning: literally, "God's fire."

1, 21: Go back again: to the earth; cf Gn 2, 7; Sir 40, 1.

2, 4: Skin for skin: an expression which, as applied to Job, means that he has borne his suffering patiently thus far only because he seeks to avoid greater suffering and to receive greater favors from God.

2, 9: Curse God and die: you have nothing to hope for from God and therefore nothing to live for.

2, 11: The names of Job's friends suggest Edomite origin. The Edomites (Ob 8f) and more specifically the Temanites (Jer 49, 7) enjoyed a reputation for wisdom.

him seven days and seven nights, but none of them spoke a word to him; for they saw how great was his suffering.

## *II: First Cycle of Speeches*

### CHAPTER 3

**Job's Plaint.** 1 After this, Job opened his mouth and cursed his day. 2 Job spoke out and said:

**3** Perish the day on which I was born,[m]
the night when they said, "The child is a boy!"
**4** May that day be darkness:
let not God above call for it, nor light shine upon it!
**5** May darkness and gloom claim it,
clouds settle upon it, the blackness of night affright it!
**6** May obscurity seize that day;
let it not occur among the days of the year, nor enter into the count of the months!
**7** May that night be barren;
let no joyful outcry greet it!
**8** Let them curse it who curse the sea,
the appointed disturbers of Leviathan!*
**9** May the stars of its twilight be darkened;
may it look for daylight, but have none,
nor gaze on the eyes of the dawn,
**10** Because it kept not shut the doors of the womb
to shield my eyes from trouble!
**11** Why did I not perish at birth,[n]
come forth from the womb and expire?
**16** Or why was I not buried away like an untimely birth,*
like babes that have never seen the light?
**12** Wherefore did the knees receive me?
or why did I suck at the breasts?
**13** For then I should have lain down and been tranquil;
had I slept, I should then have been at rest
**14** With kings and counselors of the earth
who built where now there are ruins
**15** Or with princes who had gold
and filled their houses with silver.
**17** There* the wicked cease from troubling,
there the weary are at rest.
**18** There the captives are at ease together,
and hear not the voice of the slave driver.
**19** Small and great are there the same,
and the servant is free from his master.
**20** Why is light given to the toilers,
and life to the bitter in spirit?
**21** They wait for death and it comes not;
they search for it rather than for hidden treasures,
**22** Rejoice in it exultingly,
and are glad when they reach the grave:
**23** Men whose path is hidden from them,
and whom God has hemmed in!
**24** For sighing comes more readily to me than food,
and my groans well forth like water.
**25** For what I fear overtakes me,
and what I shrink from comes upon me.
**26** I have no peace nor ease;
I have no rest, for trouble comes!

### CHAPTER 4

**Eliphaz's First Speech.** 1 Then spoke Eliphaz the Temanite, who said:

**2** If someone attempts a word with you, will you mind?
For how can anyone refrain from speaking?
**3** Behold, you have instructed many,
and have made firm their feeble hands.
**4** Your words have upheld the stumbler;
you have strengthened his faltering knees.
**5** But now that it comes to you, you are impatient;
when it touches yourself, you are dismayed.
**6** Is not your piety a source of confidence,
and your integrity of life your hope?
**7** Reflect now, what innocent person perishes?[o]
Since when are the upright destroyed?
**8** As I see it, those who plow for mischief
and sow trouble, reap the same.
**9** By the breath of God they perish,[p]
and by the blast of his wrath they are consumed.
**10** Though the lion* roars, though the king of beasts cries out,
yet the teeth of the young lions are broken;
**11** The old lion perishes for lack of prey,
and the cubs of the lioness are scattered.
**12** For a word was stealthily brought to me,*
and my ear caught a whisper of it.

m Jer 20, 14.
n Jb 10, 18f.
o Ps 37, 25.
p Ps 18, 16; Is 11, 4; 2; Thes 2, 8.

*

3, 8: Leviathan: in Jb 40, 25, the crocodile; here the reference is probably to a mythological sea monster symbolizing primeval chaos. Cf Jb 9, 13; 26, 13; Pss 74, 13f; 104, 26; Is 27, 1.

3, 16: This verse has been placed between vv 11 and 12 where it probably stood originally. There is reason to believe that here, as well as in several other places in Job, the original order of the poetic lines was accidentally disturbed in the early transmission of the text; so in chapters 12–15; 19–21; 24–31; 34; 36; 38–42. The verse numbers given in such cases are always those of the current Hebrew text, though the arrangement may differ. The footnotes will advise the reader of the difficulties and provide him with further indications for following the progress of thought in the book.

3, 17: There: in death.

4, 10: The lion: used figuratively here for the violent, rapacious sinner who cannot prevail against God.

4, 12–21: A dramatic presentation of the idea of man's nothingness in contrast to God's greatness.

13 In my thoughts during visions of the night,[q]
when deep sleep falls on men,
14 Fear came upon me, and shuddering,
that terrified me to the bones.
15 Then a spirit passed before me,
and the hair of my flesh stood up.
16 It paused, but its likeness I could not discern;
a figure was before my eyes, and I heard a still voice:
17 "Can a man be righteous as against God?[r]
Can a mortal be blameless against his Maker?
18 Lo, he puts no trust in his servants,[s]
and with his angels he can find fault.
19 How much more with those that dwell in houses of clay,
whose foundation is in the dust,
who are crushed more easily than the moth!
20 Morning or evening they may be shattered;
with no heed paid to it, they perish forever.
21 The pegs of their tent are plucked up;
they die without knowing wisdom."

## CHAPTER 5

1 Call now! Will anyone respond to you?
To which of the holy ones will you appeal?
2 Nay, impatience kills the fool
and indignation slays the simpleton.
3 I have seen a fool spreading his roots,[t]
but his household suddenly decayed.
4 His children shall be far from safety;
they shall be crushed at the gate* without a rescuer.
5 What they have reaped the hungry shall eat up;
[or God shall take it away by blight;]
and the thirsty shall swallow their substance.
6 For mischief comes not out of the earth,
nor does trouble spring out of the ground;
7 But man himself begets mischief,
as sparks* fly upward.
8 In your place, I would appeal to God, and to God I would state my plea.*
10 He gives rain upon the earth
and sends water upon the fields;
11 [u]He sets up on high the lowly,
and those who mourn he exalts to safety.
12 He frustrates the plans of the cunning,
so that their hands achieve no success;
13 He catches the wise in their own ruses,[v]
and the designs of the crafty are routed.
14 They meet with darkness in the daytime,
and at noonday they grope as though it were night.
15 But the poor from the edge of the sword
and from the hand of the mighty, he saves.
16 Thus the unfortunate have hope,
and iniquity closes her mouth.
17 Happy is the man whom God reproves!
The Almighty's chastening do not reject.
18 For he wounds, but he binds up;[w]
he smites, but his hands give healing.
19 Out of six troubles he will deliver you,
and at the seventh* no evil shall touch you.
20 In famine he will deliver you from death,
and in war from the threat of the sword;
21 From the scourge of the tongue you shall be hidden,
and shall not fear approaching ruin.
22 At destruction and want you shall laugh;
the beasts of the earth you need not dread.
23 You shall be in league with the stones of the field,
and the wild beasts shall be at peace with you.
24 And you shall know that your tent is secure;
taking stock of your household, you shall miss nothing.
25 You shall know that your descendants are many,
and your offspring as the grass of the earth.
26 You shall approach the grave in full vigor,
as a shock of grain comes in at its season.
27 Lo, this we have searched out; so it is!
This we have heard, and you should know.

## CHAPTER 6

**Job's First Reply.** 1 Then Job answered and said:

2 Ah, could my anguish but be measured
and my calamity laid with it in the scales,
3 They would now outweigh the sands of the sea!
Because of this I speak without restraint.
4 For the arrows of the Almighty pierce me,[x]
and my spirit drinks in their poison;
the terrors of God are arrayed against me.
5 Does the wild ass bray when he has grass?*
Does the ox low over his fodder?
6 Can a thing insipid be eaten without salt?

q Jb 33, 15.
r Jb 9, 2; 15, 14ff; 25, 4; Pss 130, 3; 143, 2.
s Jb 15, 15; 2 Pt 2, 4; Jude 6.
t Ps 37, 35f.
u 1 Sm 2, 7f; Ps 113, 7; Lk 1, 52.
v 1 Cor 3, 19.
w Hos 6, 1f.
x Ps 88, 17.

*

5, 4: At the gate: of the city, where justice was administered.

5, 7: Sparks: in Hebrew, "sons of resheph," which the ancient versions took as the name of a bird.

5, 9: Omitted here; it is a duplicate of Jb 9, 10.

5, 19: Six . . . the seventh: proverbial expression for any large number; cf Prv 24, 16; Lk 17, 4.

6, 5f: Job would not complain if his life were as pleasant to him as fodder to a hungry animal; but his life is as disagreeable as insipid food. White of an egg: thus the obscure Hebrew has been understood in Jewish tradition; some render it "mallow juice."

Is there flavor in the white of an egg?
7 I refuse to touch them;
they are loathsome food to me.
8 Oh, that I might have my request,
and that God would grant what I long for:
9 Even that God would decide to crush me,
that he would put forth his hand and cut me off!
10 Then I should still have consolation
and could exult through unremitting pain,
because I have not transgressed the commands of the Holy One.
11 What strength have I that I should endure,
and what is my limit that I should be patient?
12 Have I the strength of stones,
or is my flesh of bronze?
13 Have I no helper,[y]
and has advice deserted me?
14 A friend owes kindness to one in despair,
though he have forsaken the fear of the Almighty.
15 My brethren are undependable as a brook,
as watercourses that run dry in the wadies;
16 Though they may be black with ice,
and with snow heaped upon them,
17 Yet once they flow, they cease to be;
in the heat, they disappear from their place.
18 Caravans turn aside from their routes;
they go into the desert and perish.
19 The caravans of Tema* search,
the companies of Sheba have hopes;
20 They are disappointed, though they were confident;
they come there and are frustrated.
21 It is thus that you have now become for me;
you see a terrifying thing and are afraid.
22 Have I asked you to give me anything,
to offer a gift for me from your possessions,
23 Or to deliver me from the enemy,
or to redeem me from oppressors?
24 Teach me, and I will be silent;
prove to me wherein I have erred.
25 How agreeable are honest words;
yet how unconvincing is your argument!
26 Do you consider your words as proof,
but the sayings of a desperate man as wind?
27 You would even cast lots for the orphan,
and would barter away your friend!
28 Come, now, give me your attention;
surely I will not lie to your face.
29 Think it over; let there be no injustice.
Think it over; I still am right.
30 Is there insincerity on my tongue,
or cannot my taste discern falsehood?

## CHAPTER 7

1 [z] Is not man's life on earth a drudgery?*
Are not his days those of a hireling?
2 He is a slave who longs for the shade,
a hireling who waits for his wages.
3 So I have been assigned months of misery,
and troubled nights have been told off for me.
4 If in bed I say, "When shall I arise?"
Then the night drags on;
I am filled with restlessness until the dawn.
5 My flesh is clothed with worms and scabs;[a]
my skin cracks and festers;
6 My days are swifter than a weaver's shuttle;
they come to an end without hope.
7 Remember that my life is like the wind; [b]
I shall not see happiness again.
8 The eye that now sees me shall no more behold me;
as you look at me, I shall be gone.
9 As a cloud dissolves and vanishes,[c]
so he who goes down to the nether world shall come up no more.
10 He shall not again return to his house;
his place shall know him no more.
11 My own utterance I will not restrain;
I will speak in the anguish of my spirit;
I will complain in the bitterness of my soul.
12 *Am I the sea, or a monster of the deep,
that you place a watch over me?*
Why have you set me up as an object of attack?
or why should I be a target for you?
13 When I say, "My bed shall comfort me,
my couch shall ease my complaint,"
14 Then you affright me with dreams
and with visions terrify me,
15 So that I should prefer choking
and death rather than my pains.
16 I waste away: I cannot live forever;[d]
let me alone, for my days are but a breath.
17 What is man, that you make much of him,
or pay him any heed?
18 You observe him with each new day[e]
and try him at every moment!
19 How long will it be before you look away from me,
and let me alone long enough to swallow my spittle?
20 Though I have sinned, what can I do to you,
O watcher of men?
21 Why do you not pardon my offense,
or take away my guilt?
For soon I shall lie down in the dust;
and should you seek me I shall then be gone.

y Jb 19, 14f.
z Jb 14, 14.
a Jb 2, 7f.
b Pss 8, 5; 144, 3.
c 9f: Jb 10. 21; 14, 10ff; 2 Sm 12, 23; 14, 14; Wis 2, 1.
d Jb 14, 1ff, 5.
e Ps 17, 3.

*

6, 19: Tema: in northwest Arabia. Sheba: see note on Jb 1, 15.

7, 1: Drudgery: taken by some to refer to military service; cf also Jb 14, 14.

7, 12: An allusion in poetic imagery to primeval chaos as a monstrous ocean vanquished by God at the world's creation.

7, 12-21: Job now speaks, not to his friends, but to God.

## CHAPTER 8

**Bildad's First Speech.** 1 Bildad the Shuhite spoke out and said:

2 How long will you utter such things?
The words from your mouth are like a mighty wind!
3 Does God pervert judgment,[f]
and does the Almighty distort justice?
4 If your children have sinned against him
and he has left them in the grip of their guilt,
5 Still, if you yourself have recourse to God
and make supplication to the Almighty,
6 Should you be blameless and upright,
surely now he will awake for you
and restore your rightful domain;
7 Your former state will be of little moment,
for in time to come you will flourish indeed.
8 If you inquire of the former generations,
and give heed to the experience of the fathers[g]
9 (As we are but of yesterday and have no knowledge,
because our days on earth are but a shadow),[h]
10 Will they not teach you and tell you
and utter their words of understanding?
11 Can the papyrus grow up without mire?*
Can the reed grass flourish without water?
12 While it is yet green and uncut,
it withers quicker than any grass.
13 So is the end of everyone who forgets God,
and so shall the hope of the godless man perish.
14 His confidence is but a gossamer thread and
his trust is a spider's web.
15 He shall rely upon his family, but it shall not last;
he shall cling to it, but it shall not endure.
16 He is full of sap before sunrise,
and beyond his garden his shoots go forth;
17 About a heap of stones are his roots entwined;
among the rocks he takes hold.
18 Yet if one tears him from his place,
it will disown him: "I have never seen you!"
19 There he lies rotting beside the road,
and out of the soil another sprouts.
20 Behold, God will not cast away the upright;
neither will he take the hand of the wicked.
21 Once more will he fill your mouth with laughter,
and your lips with rejoicing.
22 They that hate you shall be clothed with shame,
and the tent of the wicked shall be no more.

## CHAPTER 9

**Job's Second Reply.** 1 Then Job answered and said:

2 I know well that it is so;
but how can a man be justified before God?
3 Should one wish to contend with him,
he could not answer him once in a thousand times.
4 God is wise in heart and mighty in strength;
who has withstood him and remained unscathed?
5 He removes the mountains before they know it;
he overturns them in his anger.
6 He shakes the earth out of its place,[i]
and the pillars beneath it tremble.
7 He commands the sun, and it rises not;
he seals up the stars.
8 He alone stretches out the heavens[j]
and treads upon the crests of the sea.
9 He made the Bear and Orion,
the Pleiades and the constellations of the south;
10 He does great things past finding out,
marvelous things beyond reckoning.
11 Should he come near me, I see him not;
should he pass by, I am not aware of him;
12 Should he seize me forcibly, who can say him nay?
Who can say to him, "What are you doing?"
13 He is God and he does not relent;
the helpers of Rahab* bow beneath him.
14 How much less shall I give him any answer,
or choose out arguments against him!
15 Even though I were right, I could not answer him,[k]
but should rather beg for what was due me.
16 If I appealed to him and he answered my call,
I could not believe that he would hearken to my words;
17 With a tempest he might overwhelm me,
and multiply my wounds without cause;
18 He need not suffer me to draw breath,
but might fill me with bitter griefs.
19 If it be a question of strength, he is mighty;
and if of judgment, who will call him to account?
20 Though I were right, my own mouth might condemn me;[l]

---

f Jb 34, 10ff.
g Dt 4, 32; 32, 7.
h Jb 14, 2; Pss 102, 12; 109, 23; 144, 4; Wis 2, 5.
i Jb 26, 11.
j Ps 104, 2; Is 40, 22.
k Jb 10, 15.
l Jb 15, 6.

---

* 8, 11ff: As marsh plants need water, so man needs God. These verses are taken by some as a quotation from the teaching of the forefathers; cf v 10.

9, 13: Rahab: cf Jb 26, 12. See note on Ps 89, 11.

were I innocent, he might put me in the
wrong.
21 Though I am innocent, I myself cannot
know it;
I despise my life.
22 It is all one! therefore I say:
Both the innocent and the wicked he
destroys.[m]
23 When the scourge slays suddenly,
he laughs at the despair of the innocent.
24 The earth is given into the hands of the
wicked;
he covers the faces of its judges.
If it is not he, who then is it?
25 My days are swifter than a runner,
they flee away; they see no happiness;[n]
26 They shoot by like skiffs of reed,
like an eagle swooping upon its prey.
27 If I say: I will forget my complaining,
I will lay aside my sadness and be of
good cheer,
28 Then I am in dread of all my pains;
I know that you* will not hold me
innocent.
29 If I must be accounted guilty,
why then should I strive in vain?
30 If I should wash myself with snow
and cleanse my hands with lye,
31 Yet you would plunge me in the ditch,
so that my garments would abhor me.
32 For he is not a man like myself, that I
should answer him,
that we should come together in
judgment.
33 Would that there were an arbiter between us,
who could lay his hand upon us both
34 and withdraw his rod from me.
Would that his terrors did not frighten me;
35 that I might speak without being afraid of
him.
Since this is not the case with me,
10, 1 *I loathe my life.[o]
I will give myself up to complaint;
I will speak from the bitterness of my
soul.
2 I will say to God: Do not put me in the
wrong!
Let me know why you oppose me.
3 Is it a pleasure for you to oppress,
to spurn the work of your hands,
and smile on the plan of the wicked?
4 Have you eyes of flesh?
Do you see as man sees?
5 Are your days as the days of a mortal,[p]
and are your years as a man's lifetime,
6 That you seek for guilt in me
and search after my sins,
7 Even though you know that I am not
wicked,[q]
and that none can deliver me out of your
hand?
8 Your hands have formed me and fashioned
me;
will you then turn and destroy me?
9 Oh, remember that you fashioned me from
clay![r]
Will you then bring me down to dust
again?
10 Did you not pour me out as milk,
and thicken me like cheese?
11 With skin and flesh you clothed me,
with bones and sinews knit me together.
12 Grace and favor you granted me,
and your providence has preserved my
spirit.
13 Yet these things you have hidden in your
heart;
I know that they are your purpose:
14 If I should sin, you would keep a watch
against me,
and from my guilt you would not absolve
me.
15 If I should be wicked, alas for me!
if righteous, I dare not hold up my head,
filled with ignominy and sodden with
affliction!
16 Should it lift up, you hunt me like a lion:
repeatedly you show your wondrous
power against me,
17 You renew your attack upon me
and multiply your harassment of me;
in waves your troops come against me.
18 Why then did you bring me forth from the
womb?[s]
I should have died and no eye have seen
me.
19 I should be as though I had never lived;
I should have been taken from the womb
to the grave.
20 Are not the days of my life few?
Let me alone, that I may recover a little
21 Before I go whence I shall not return,[t]
to the land of darkness and of gloom,
22 The black, disordered land
where darkness is the only light.

## CHAPTER 11

**Zophar's First Speech.** 1 And Zophar the
Naamathite spoke out and said:

2 Should not the man of many words be
answered,
or must the garrulous man necessarily be
right?
3 Shall your babblings keep men silent,
and shall you deride and no one give
rebuke?
4 Shall you say: "My teaching is pure,
and I am clean in your sight"?
5 But oh, that God would speak,

m Eccl 9, 2.
n Jb 7, 6.
o Jb 9, 21.
p Jb 36, 26.
q Jb 2, 3. 9; Dt 32, 39; Wis 16, 15.
r Jb 4, 19; 33, 6; Gn 2, 7; 3, 19; Ps 146, 4.
s Jb 3, 3, 11.
t Jb 7, 9f; 16, 22.

* 9, 28–31: You: refers to God.

10, 1: I loathe my life: this is the first verse of ch 10.

and open his lips against you,
6 And tell you that the secrets of wisdom
are twice as effective:
So you might learn that God
will make you answer for your guilt.
7 Can you penetrate the designs of God?[u]
Dare you vie with the perfection of the Almighty?
8 It is higher than the heavens; what can you do?
It is deeper than the nether world; what can you know?
9 It is longer than the earth in measure,
and broader than the sea.
10 If he seize and imprison
or call to judgment, who then can say him nay?
11 For he knows the worthlessness of men
and sees iniquity; will he then ignore it?
12 Will empty man then gain understanding,
and the wild jackass[v] be made docile?
13 If you set your heart aright
and stretch out your hands toward him,
14 If you remove all iniquity from your conduct,
and let not injustice dwell in your tent,
15 Surely then you may lift up your face in innocence;
you may stand firm and unafraid.
16 For then you shall forget your misery,
or recall it like waters that have ebbed away.
17 Then your life shall be brighter than the noonday;
its gloom shall become as the morning,
18 And you shall be secure, because there is hope;
you shall look round you and lie down in safety,[w]
19 and you shall take your rest with none to disturb.
Many shall entreat your favor,
20 but the wicked, looking on, shall be consumed with envy.
Escape shall be cut off from them,
they shall wait to expire.

## CHAPTER 12

**Job's Third Reply.** 1 Then Job replied and said:

2 No doubt you are the intelligent folk,
and with you wisdom shall die!
3 But I have intelligence as well as you;[x]
for who does not know such things as these?
4 I have become the sport of my neighbors:*
"The one whom God answers when he calls upon him,
The just, the perfect man," is a laughing-stock;[y]
5 The undisturbed esteem my downfall a disgrace
such as awaits unsteady feet;
6 Yet the tents of robbers are prosperous,
and those who provoke God are secure.
7 But now ask the beasts to teach you,
and the birds of the air to tell you;
8 Or the reptiles on earth to instruct you,
and the fish of the sea to inform you.
9 Which of all these does not know
that the hand of God has done this?
10 In this hand is the soul of every living thing,[z]
and the life breath of all mankind.
11 Does not the ear judge words
as the mouth tastes food?[a]
12 So with old age is wisdom,[b] and with length of days understanding.
13 With him are wisdom and might;
his are counsel and understanding.
14 If he breaks a thing down, there is no rebuilding;[c]
if he imprisons a man, there is no release.
15 He holds back the waters and there is drought;[d]
he sends them forth and they overwhelm the land.
18 He loosens the bonds imposed by kings
and leaves but a waistcloth to bind the king's own loins.*
21 He breaks down the barriers of the streams
19 and lets their never-failing waters flow away.
16 With him are strength and prudence;
the misled and the misleaders are his.
17 He sends counselors away barefoot,
and of judges he makes fools.
20 He silences the trusted adviser,
and takes discretion from the aged.
22 The recesses of the darkness he discloses,
and brings the gloom forth to the light.
23 He makes nations great and he destroys them;
he spreads peoples abroad and he abandons them.
24 He takes understanding from the leaders of the land,
25 till they grope in the darkness without light;
he makes them stagger like drunken men.

## CHAPTER 13

1 Lo, all this my eye has seen;
my ear has heard and perceived it.
2 What you know, I also know;[e]
I fall not short of you.

u Rom 11, 33.
v Jb 39, 5-8.
w Lv 26, 6; Ps 4, 9.
x Jb 13, 2; 15, 9.
y Jb 21, 3; 30, 1.
z Acts 17, 28.
a Jb 34, 3.
b Jb 32, 7.
c Rv 3, 7.
d Gn 7, 11-24.
e Jb 12, 3; 15, 9.

12, 4f: The Hebrew is somewhat obscure, but the general sense is that the wicked mock at the pious when the latter appear to be abandoned by God; cf Ps 22, 7ff; Mt 27, 39–43.

12, 18: Waistcloth . . . loins: he reduces kings to the condition of slaves, who wear only a cloth wrapped about the waist.

**3** But I would speak with the Almighty;[f]
I wish to reason with God.
**4** You are glossing over falsehoods
and offering vain remedies, every one of you!
**5** Oh, that you would be altogether silent!
This for you would be wisdom.
**6** Hear now the rebuke I shall utter
and listen to the reproof from my lips.
**7** Is it for God that you speak falsehood?
Is it for him that you utter deceit?
**8** Is it for him that you show partiality?
Do you play advocate on behalf of God?
**9** Will it be well when he shall search you out?
Would you impose on him as one does on men?
**10** He will openly rebuke you
if even in secret you show partiality.
**11** Surely will his majesty affright you
and the dread of him fall upon you.
**12** Your reminders are ashy maxims,
your fabrications are mounds of clay.
**13** Be silent, let me alone! that I may speak
and give vent to my feelings.
**14** I will carry my flesh between my teeth,
and take my life in my hand.*
**15** Slay me though he might,[g] I will wait for him;
I will defend my conduct before him.
**16** And this shall be my salvation,
that no impious man can come into his presence.
**17** Pay careful heed to my speech,
and give my statement a hearing.
**18** Behold, I have prepared my case,[h]
I know that I am in the right.
**19** If anyone can make a case against me,
then I shall be silent and die.
**20** These things only do not use against me,*
then from your presence I need not hide:
**21** Withdraw your hand far from me,
and let not the terror of you frighten me.
**22** Then call me, and I will respond;
or let me speak first, and answer me.
**23** What are my faults and my sins?
My misdeeds and my sins make known to me!
**24** Why do you hide your face[i]
and consider me your enemy?
**25** Will you harass a wind-driven leaf,
or pursue a withered straw?
**26** For you draw up bitter indictments against me,
and punish in me the faults of my youth.
**27** You put my feet in the stocks;
you watch all my paths
and trace out all my footsteps.

## CHAPTER 14

**1** Man born of woman
is short-lived and full of trouble,[j]
**2** Like a flower that springs up and fades,[k]
swift as a shadow that does not abide.
**3** Upon such a one will you cast your eyes
so as to bring him into judgment before you,
**13, 28** Though he wears out like a leather bottle,
like a garment that the moth has consumed?*
**4** Can a man be found who is clean of defilement?[l]
There is none, **5** however short his days.
You know the number of his months;
you have fixed the limit which he cannot pass.
**6** Look away from him and let him be,
while, like a hireling, he completes his day.
**7** For a tree there is hope,
if it be cut down, that it will sprout again
and that its tender shoots will not cease.
**8** Even though its root grow old in the earth,
and its stump die in the dust,
**9** Yet at the first whiff of water it may flourish again
and put forth branches like a young plant.
**10** But when a man dies, all vigor leaves him;[m]
when man expires, where then is he?
**11** As when the waters of a lake fail,
or a stream grows dry and parches,
**12** So men lie down and rise not again.
Till the heavens are no more, they shall not awake,
nor be roused out of their sleep.[n]
**13** Oh, that you would hide me in the nether world
and keep me sheltered till your wrath is past;
would fix a time for me, and then remember me!
**14** When a man has died, were he to live again,
all the days of my drudgery I would wait,[o]
until my relief should come.
**15** You would call, and I would answer you;
you would esteem the work of your hands.
**16** Surely then you would count my steps,[p]
and not keep watch for sin in me.

f Jb 23, 4.
g Jb 27, 5.
h Jb 33, 9.
i Jb 19, 11; 33, 10.
j Jb 10, 20; 15, 14; Pss 39, 5f; 89, 46; Wis 2, 1.
k Jb 8, 9; Pss 90:6; 102, 12; 103, 15; 109, 23; 144, 4; Is 40, 6f; Jas 1, 10.
l Ps 51, 4, 7.
m Jb 20, 7.
n Jb 7, 10.
o Jb 7, 1.
p Jb 31, 4; 34, 21.

*

13, 14: The second half of the verse is a common biblical expression for risking one's life; cf Jgs 12, 3; 1 Sm 19, 5; 28, 21; Ps 119, 109; the first half of the verse must have a similar meaning. Job is so confident of his innocence that he is willing to risk his life by going to judgment with God.

13, 20: From here to the end of chapter 14, Job pleads his case, addressing God rather than his three friends.

13, 28: This verse has been transposed from ch 13.

17 My misdeeds would be sealed up in a
pouch,*
and you would cover over my guilt.
18 But as a mountain falls at last
and its rock is moved from its place,
19 As waters wear away the stones
and floods wash away the soil of the land,
so you destroy the hope of man.
20 You prevail once for all against him and he
passes on;
with changed appearance you send him
away.
21 If his sons are honored, he is not aware of
it;
if they are in disgrace, he does not know
about them.
22 Only his own flesh pains him, and his soul
grieves for him.

## *III: Second Cycle of Speeches*

### CHAPTER 15

**Second Speech of Eliphaz.** 1 Then Eliphaz the Temanite spoke and said:

2 Should a wise man answer with airy
opinions,
or puff himself up with wind?
3 Should he argue in speech which does not
avail,
and in words which are to no profit?
4 You in fact do away with piety,
and you lessen devotion toward God,
5 Because your wickedness instructs your
mouth,
and you choose to speak like the crafty.
6 Your own mouth condemns you, not I;[q]
your own lips refute you.
7 Are you indeed the first-born of mankind,
or were you brought forth before the hills?
8 Are you privy to the counsels of God,[r]
and do you restrict wisdom to yourself?
9 What do you know that we do not know?[s]
What intelligence have you which we
have not?
10 There are gray-haired old men among us
more advanced in years than your father.
11 Are the consolations of God not enough for
you,
and speech that deals gently with you?
12 Why do your notions carry you away,
and why do your eyes blink,
13 So that you turn your anger against God
and let such words escape your mouth!
14 What is a man that he should be blameless,[t]
one born of woman that he should be
righteous?[u]
15 If in his holy ones God places no
confidence,[v]
and if the heavens are not clean in his
sight,
16 How much less so is the abominable, the
corrupt:
man, who drinks in iniquity like water!
17 I will show you, if you listen to me;
what I have seen I will tell—
18 What wise men relate
and have not contradicted since the days
of their fathers,
19 To whom alone the land was given,
when no foreigner moved among them.
20 The wicked man is in torment all his days,
and limited years are in store for the
tyrant;
21 The sound of terrors is in his ears;
when all is prosperous, the spoiler comes
upon him.
22 He despairs of escaping the darkness,
and looks ever for the sword;
23 A wanderer, food for the vultures,
he knows that his destruction is imminent.
24 By day the darkness fills him with dread;
distress and anguish overpower him.
25 Because he has stretched out his hand
against God
and bade defiance to the Almighty,
26 One shall rush sternly upon him
with the stout bosses of his shield,
like a king prepared for the charge.
27 Because he has blinded himself with his
crassness,
padding his loins with fat,
28 He shall dwell in ruinous cities,
in houses that are deserted,
That are crumbling into clay
29 with no shadow to lengthen over the
ground.
He shall not be rich, and his possessions
shall not endure;
31 for vain shall be his bartering.
30 A flame shall wither him up in his early
growth,
and with the wind his blossoms shall
disappear.
32 His stalk shall wither before its time,
and his branches shall be green no more.
33 He shall be like a vine that sheds its grapes
unripened,
and like an olive tree casting off its
bloom.
34 For the breed of the impious shall be
sterile,[w]
and fire shall consume the tents of
extortioners.
35 They conceive malice and bring forth
emptiness;[x]
they give birth to failure.*

q Jb 9, 20.
r Jb 11, 7; Wis 9, 13; Jer 23, 18; Rom 11, 34; 1 Cor 2, 11, 16.
s Jb 12, 3; 13, 2.
t 14ff: Jb 25, 4ff.
u Jb 14, 4.
v Jb 4, 18f.
w Wis 3, 11, 18.
x Ps 7, 15; Is 59, 4.

*

14, 17: Sealed up in a pouch: hidden away and forgotten.
15, 35: They give birth to failure: their wicked plans yield nothing but futile results. Cf Ps 7, 15; Is 59, 4.

## CHAPTER 16

**Job's Fourth Reply.** 1 Then Job answered and said:

2 I have heard this sort of thing many times.[y]
Wearisome comforters are you all!
3 Is there no end to windy words?
Or what sickness have you that you speak on?
4 I also could talk as you do, were you in my place.
I could declaim over you, or wag my head at you;
5 I could strengthen you with talk,
or shake my head with silent lips.
6 If I speak, this pain I have will not be checked;
if I leave off, it will not depart from me.
7 But now that I am exhausted and stunned,
all my company has closed in on me.
8 As a witness there rises up
my traducer, speaking openly against me;
9 I am the prey his wrath assails,
he gnashes his teeth against me.
My enemies lord it over me;
10 their mouths are agape to bite me.
They smite me on the cheek insultingly;
they are all enlisted against me.
11 God has given me over to the impious;
into the clutches of the wicked he has cast me.
12 I was in peace, but he dislodged me;
he seized me by the neck and dashed me to pieces.
He has set me up for a target;
13 his arrows strike me from all directions,
He pierces my sides without mercy,
he pours out my gall upon the ground.
14 He pierces me with thrust upon thrust;
he attacks me like a warrior.
15 I have fastened sackcloth over my skin,
and have laid my brow in the dust.
16 My face is inflamed with weeping
and there is darkness over my eyes,
17 Although my hands are free from violence,
and my prayer is sincere.
18 O earth, cover not my blood,
nor let my outcry come to rest!*
19 Even now, behold, my witness* is in heaven,
and my spokesman is on high.
20 My friends it is who wrong me;
before God my eyes drop tears,
21 That he may do justice for a mortal in his presence
and decide between a man and his neighbor.
22 For my years are numbered now,
and I am on a journey from which I shall not return.
17, 1 My spirit is broken, my lamp of life extinguished;
my burial is at hand.
2 I am indeed mocked,
and, as their provocation mounts, my eyes grow dim.
3 Grant me one to offer you a pledge on my behalf:*
who is there that will give surety for me?
4 You darken their minds to knowledge;
therefore they do not understand.
5 My lot is described as evil,
6 and I am made a byword of the people;[z]
their object lesson I have become.
7 My eye has grown blind with anguish,
and all my frame is shrunken to a shadow.
8 Upright men are astonished at this,
and the innocent aroused against the wicked.
9 Yet the righteous shall hold to his way,
and he who has clean hands increase in strength.
10 But turn now, and come on again;
for I shall not find a wise man among you!
11 My days are passed away, my plans are at an end,
the cherished purposes of my heart.
12 Such men change the night into day;
where there is darkness they talk of approaching light.
13 If I look for the nether world as my dwelling,
if I spread my couch in the darkness,
14 If I must call corruption "my father,"
and the maggot "my mother" and "my sister,"
15 Where then is my hope,
and my prosperity, who shall see?
16 Will they descend with me into the nether world?
Shall we go down together into the dust?

## CHAPTER 18

**Bildad's Second Speech.** 1 Then Bildad the Shuhite replied and said:

2 When will you put an end to words?
Reflect, and then we can have discussion.
3 Why are we accounted like the beasts,
their equals in your sight?
4 You who tear yourself in your anger,*
shall the earth be neglected on your account
[or the rock be moved out of its place]?

y Jb 12, 3. z Jb 30, 9.

*

16, 18: As the blood of those who were unjustly slain cries to heaven for vengeance (Gn 4, 10; Ez 24, 6–9), so Job's sufferings demand redress.

16, 19: Witness: refers either to God or, more probably, to Job's prayer.

17, 3: Addressed to God; v 10 to Job's friends.

18, 4: Job himself is portrayed as having the heedless rage of wild beasts, despite which God does not forsake the usual course of Divine Providence.

5 Truly, the light of the wicked is extinguished;
no flame brightens his hearth.
6 The light is darkened in his tent;
in spite of him, his lamp goes out.[a]
7 His vigorous steps are hemmed in,
and his own counsel casts him down.
8 For he rushes headlong into a net,
and he wanders into a pitfall.
9 A trap seizes him by the heel,
and a snare lays hold of him.
10 A noose for him is hid on the ground,
and the toils for him on the way.
11 On every side terrors affright him;[b]
they harry him at each step.
12 Disaster is ready at his side,
13 the first-born of death* consumes his limbs.
14 Fiery destruction lodges in his tent,
and marches him off to the king of terrors.*
He is plucked from the security of his tent;
15 over his abode brimstone is scattered.
16 Below, his roots dry up,
and above, his branches wither.
17 His memory perishes from the land,[c]
and he has no name on the earth.
18 He is driven from light into darkness,
and banished out of the world.
19 He has neither son nor grandson among his people,
nor any survivor where once he dwelt.
20 They who come after shall be appalled at his fate;
they who went before are struck with horror.
21 So is it then with the dwelling of the impious man,
and such is the place of him who knows not God!

## CHAPTER 19

**Job's Fifth Reply.** 1 Then Job answered and said:

2 How long will you vex my soul,
grind me down with words?
3 These ten times you have reviled me,
have assailed me without shame!
4 Be it indeed that I am at fault
and that my fault remains with me.
5 Even so, if you would vaunt yourselves against me
and cast up to me my reproach,
6 Know then that God has dealt unfairly with me,
and compassed me round with his net.
7 If I cry out "Injustice!" I am not heard.[d]
I cry for help, but there is no redress.
8 He has barred my way and I cannot pass;
he has veiled my path in darkness;
9 He has stripped me of my glory,
and taken the diadem from my brow.
10 He breaks me down on every side, and I am gone;
my hope he has uprooted like a tree.
11 His wrath he has kindled against me;
he counts me among his enemies.[e]
12 His troops advance as one man;
they build up their road to attack me,
and they encamp around my tent.
13 My brethren have withdrawn from me,[f]
and my friends are wholly estranged.
14 My kinsfolk and companions neglect me,
and my guests have forgotten me.
15 Even my handmaids treat me as a stranger;
I am an alien in their sight.
16 I call my servant, but he gives no answer,
though in my speech I plead with him.
17 My breath is abhorred by my wife;[g]
I am loathsome to the men of my family.
18 The young children, too, despise me;
when I appear, they speak against me.
19 All my intimate friends hold me in horror;
those whom I loved have turned against me![h]
20 My bones cleave to my skin,
and I have escaped with my flesh between my teeth.*
21 Pity me, pity me, O you my friends,
for the hand of God has struck me!
22 Why do you hound me as though you were divine,*
and insatiably prey upon me?
23 Oh, would that my words were written down![i]
Would that they were inscribed in a record:*
24 That with an iron chisel and with lead
they were cut in the rock forever!
25 But as for me, I know that my Vindicator lives,*
and that he will at last stand forth upon the dust;[j]

a Jb 21, 17; Prv 13, 9; 24, 20.
b Jb 15, 20-24; 27, 20.
c Ps 34, 17; Prv 2, 22; 10, 7.
d Jb 30, 20.
e Jb 13, 24; 33, 10.
f Jb 6, 13.
g Jb 2, 9.
h Sir 6, 8.
i Jb 31, 35.
j 25ff: Phil 3, 20; Ti 2, 13.

*

18, 13: First-born of death: that is, disease, plague.

18, 14: The king of terrors: of the nether world, death; however, the Hebrew is obscure.

19, 20: With my flesh between my teeth: meaning perhaps that Job has been reduced to such an extremity that he scarcely has thin lips over his teeth. But the current Hebrew text of this line is probably corrupt.

19, 22: Divine: possessing God's attributes of judgment and authority to punish.

19, 23f: Job regards what he is about to say as so important that he wishes it recorded in a permanent manner.

19, 25. 27: The meaning of this passage is obscure because the original text has been poorly preserved and the ancient versions do not agree among themselves. It is certain that Job expresses his belief in a future vindication by God (called here in the Hebrew "Goel"), but the time and manner of this vindication are undefined. In the Vulgate Job is made to indicate a belief in physical resurrection after death, but the Hebrew and the other ancient versions are less specific.

27 Whom I myself shall see:
my own eyes, not another's, shall behold him,
26 And from my flesh I shall see God;
my inmost being is consumed with longing.
28 But you who say, "How shall we persecute him,
seeing that the root of the matter is found in him?"
29 Be afraid of the sword for yourselves,
for these crimes deserve the sword;
that you may know that there is a judgment.

## CHAPTER 20

**Zophar's Second Speech.** 1 Then Zophar the Naamathite spoke and said:

3 A rebuke which puts me to shame I hear,
2 and because of this I am disturbed.
So now my thoughts provide me with an answer,
and from my understanding a spirit gives me a reply.
4 Do you not know this from olden time,
since man was placed upon the earth,
5 That the triumph of the wicked is short
and the joy of the impious but for a moment?[k]
6 Though his pride mount up to the heavens
and his head reach to the clouds,
7 Yet he perishes forever like the fuel of his fire,
and the onlookers say, "Where is he?"[l]
8 Like a dream he takes flight and is not found again;
he fades away like a vision of the night.
9 The eye which saw him does so no more;
nor shall his dwelling again behold him.
11 Though his frame is full of youthful vigor,
this shall lie with him in the dust.
12 Though wickedness is sweet in his mouth,
and he hides it under his tongue,
13 Though he retains it and will not let it go
but keeps it still within his mouth,
14 Yet in his stomach the food shall turn;
it shall be venom of asps inside him.
15 The riches he swallowed he shall disgorge;
God shall compel his belly to disown them.
16 The poison of asps he shall drink in;
the viper's fangs shall slay him.
17 He shall see no streams of oil,*
no torrents of honey or milk.
18 Restoring his gains, he shall not enjoy them;
though his wealth increases, he shall not rejoice.
19 Because he has oppressed the poor,
and stolen a patrimony he had not built up,
21 Therefore his prosperity shall not endure,
10 and his hands shall yield up his riches.[m]
20 Though he has known no quiet in his greed,
his treasures shall not save him.[n]
22 [o]When he abounds to overflowing, he shall be brought into straits,
and nought shall be left of his goods.
23 God shall send against him the fury of his wrath
and rain down his missiles of war upon him.
24 Should he escape the iron weapon,
the bow of bronze shall pierce him through;
25 The dart shall come out of his back;
terrors shall fall upon him.
26 Complete darkness is in store for him;
the fire which shall consume him needs not to be fanned.[p]
27 The heavens shall reveal his guilt,
and the earth shall rise up against him.
28 The flood shall sweep away his house
with the waters that run off in the day of God's anger.
29 This is the portion of a wicked man,
and the heritage appointed him by God.[q]

## CHAPTER 21

**Job's Sixth Reply.** 1 Then Job said in reply:

2 At least listen to my words,[r]
and let that be the consolation you offer.
3 Bear with me while I speak;
and after I have spoken, you can mock!
4 Is my complaint toward man?
And why should I not be impatient?
5 Look at me and be astonished,
put your hands over your mouths.
6 When I think of it, I am dismayed,
and horror takes hold on my flesh.

7 Why do the wicked survive,
grow old, become mighty in power?[s]
8 Their progeny is secure in their sight;
they see before them their kinsfolk and their offspring.
9 Their homes are safe and without fear,
nor is the scourge of God upon them.
10 Their bulls gender without fail;
their cows calve and do not miscarry.
11 These folk have infants numerous as lambs,
and their children dance.
12 They sing to the timbrel and harp,
and make merry to the sound of the flute.
13 They live out their days in prosperity,

---

k Jb 21, 13; Ps 37, 35f.
l Jb 14, 10; Ps 37, 10, 36.
m Jb 27, 14.
n Eccl 5, 9; Lk 12, 20.
o Jb 15, 20-35.
p Dt 32, 22.
q Jb 27, 13.
r Jb 13, 17.
s Jb 12, 6; Pss 37, 35; 73, 3; Eccl 8, 14; Jer 12, 1f; Mal 3, 14f.
t Jb 34, 20.

---

* 20, 17: Oil: olive oil, one of the main agricultural products of Palestine, a land proverbially rich in honey and milk.

and tranquilly go down to the nether
world.[t]
14 Yet they say to God, "Depart from us,[u]
for we have no wish to learn your ways!
15 What is the Almighty that we should serve
him?
And what gain shall we have if we pray
to him?"[v]
16 If their happiness is not in their own hands
and if the counsel of the wicked is
repulsive to God,[w]
17 How often is the lamp of the wicked put
out?
How often does destruction come upon
them,
the portion he allots in his anger?

18 Let them be like straw before the wind,
and like chaff which the storm snatches
away!
19 May God not store up the man's misery for
his children;
let him requite the man himself so that he
feels it,
20 Let his own eyes see the calamity,
and the wrath of the Almighty let him
drink!
21 For what interest has he in his family after
him,
when the number of his months is
finished?

23 One dies in his full vigor,
wholly at ease and content;
24 His figure is full and nourished,
and his bones are rich in marrow.
25 Another dies in bitterness of soul,
having never tasted happiness.
26 Alike they lie down in the dust,
and worms cover them both.

27 Behold, I know your thoughts,
and the arguments you rehearse against
me.
28 For you say, "Where is the house of the
magnate,
and where the dwelling place of the
wicked?"
29 Have you not asked the wayfarers
and do you not recognize their
monuments?
30 Nay, the evil man is spared calamity when it
comes;
32 and on the day he is carried to the grave
31 Who will charge him with his conduct to his
face,
and for what he has done who will repay
him?
33 Sweet to him are the clods of the valley,
and over him the funeral mound keeps
watch,
While all the line of mankind follows him,
and the countless others who have gone
before.
34 How then can you offer me vain comfort,
while in your answers perfidy remains?

## *IV: Third Cycle of Speeches*

## CHAPTER 22

**Eliphaz's Third Speech.** 1 Then Eliphaz
the Temanite answered and said:

2 Can a man be profitable to God?[x]
Though to himself a wise man be
profitable!
21, 22 Can anyone teach God knowledge,
seeing that he judges those on high?*
3 Is it of advantage to the Almighty if you are
just?[y]
Or is it a gain to him if you make your
ways perfect?
4 Is it because of your piety that he reproves
you—
that he enters with you into judgment?
5 Is not your wickedness manifold?
Are not your iniquities endless?

6 You have unjustly kept your kinsmen's
goods in pawn,*
left them stripped naked of their
clothing.[z]
7 To the thirsty you have given no water to
drink,
and from the hungry you have withheld
bread;
8 As if the land belonged to the man of might,
and only the privileged were to dwell in
it.
9 You have sent widows away emptyhanded,
and the resources of orphans you have
destroyed.[a]
10 Therefore snares are round about you,[b]
and a sudden terror causes you dismay,
11 Or darkness, in which you cannot see;
a deluge of waters covers you.

12 Does not God, in the heights of the
heavens,[c]
behold the stars, high though they are?
13 Yet you say, "What does God know?[d]
Can he judge through the thick darkness?
14 Clouds hide him so that he cannot see;
he walks upon the vault of the heavens!"

u Jb 22, 17.
v Mal 3, 14.
w Jb 22, 18.
x Jb 9, 2.
y Jb 35, 7.
z Jb 24, 3; Dt 24, 6, 17; Ez 18, 12, 16.
a Dt 24, 17; 27, 19.
b Jb 18, 8ff.
c Jb 11, 8.
d 13f: Pss 10, 11; 73, 11; 94, 7; Is 29, 15; Ez 8, 12: 9, 9.

*

21, 22: Those on high: the angels. (This verse has been transposed from ch 21.)

22, 6ff: This criticism of Job by Eliphaz is altogether untrue, but it is made to dramatize the latter's argument that God always acts justly when he causes someone to suffer. Verse 8 is misplaced.

15 Do you indeed keep to the ancient way
trodden by worthless men,
16 Who were snatched away before their time;
whose foundations a flood swept away?
17 These men said to God, "Depart from us!"
and, "What can the Almighty do to us?"
18 [Yet he had filled their houses with good
things![e]
But far be from me the mind of the
impious!]*
19 The just look on and are gladdened,
and the innocent deride them:[f]
20 "Truly these have been destroyed where
they stood,
and such as were left, fire has
consumed!"

21 Come to terms with him to be at peace.
In this shall good come to you:
22 Receive instruction from his mouth,
and lay up his words in your heart.
23 If you return to the Almighty, you will be
restored;
if you put iniquity far from your tent,
24 And treat raw gold like dust,
and the fine gold of Ophir* as pebbles
from the brook,
25 Then the Almighty himself shall be your
gold
and your sparkling silver.

26 For then you shall delight in the Almighty
and you shall lift up your face toward
God.
27 You shall entreat him and he will hear you,[g]
and your vows you shall fulfill.
28 When you make a decision, it shall succeed
for you,
and upon your ways the light shall shine.
29 For he brings down the pride of the
haughty,
but the man of humble mien he saves.[h]
30 God delivers him who is innocent;
you shall be delivered through cleanness
of hands.[i]

## CHAPTER 23

**Job's Seventh Reply.** 1 Again Job answered and said:

2 Though I know my complaint is bitter,
his hand is heavy upon me in my
groanings.
3 Oh, that today I might find him,
that I might come to his judgment seat!
4 I would set out my cause before him,
and fill my mouth with arguments;
5 I would learn the words with which he
would answer,
and understand what he would reply to
me.
6 Even should he contend against me with his
great power,
yet, would that he himself might heed me!
7 There the upright man might reason with
him,
and I should once and for all preserve my
rights.

8 But if I go to the east, he is not there;
or to the west, I cannot perceive him;
9 Where the north enfolds him, I behold him
not;
by the south he is veiled, and I see him
not.
10 Yet he knows my way;
if he proved me, I should come forth as
gold.[j]
11 My foot has always walked in his steps;
his way I have kept and have not turned
aside.
12 From the commands of his lips I have not
departed;
the words of his mouth I have treasured in
my heart.
13 But he has decided, and who can say him
nay?
What he desires, that he does.[k]
14 For he will carry out what is appointed for
me;
and many such things may yet be in his
mind.

15 Therefore am I dismayed before him;
when I take thought, I fear him.
16 Indeed God has made my courage fail;
the Almighty has put me in dismay.
17 Yes, would that I had vanished in darkness,
and that thick gloom were before me to
conceal me.

## CHAPTER 24

1 Why are not times set by the Almighty,
and why do his friends not see his days?*
2 The wicked remove landmarks;
they steal away herds and pasture them.
3 The asses of orphans they drive away;
they take the widow's ox for a pledge.
4 They force the needy off the road;
all the poor of the land are driven into
hiding.
5 Like wild asses in the desert, these go forth
to their task of seeking food;
The steppe provides food for the young
among them;
6 they harvest at night in the untilled land.

e Jb 21, 16.
f Ps 107, 42.
g Jb 33, 26.
h Ps 138, 6; Prv 29, 23; Mt 23, 12; Lk 1, 52; Jas 4, 10; 1 Pt 5, 5.
i Jb 17.9; Ps 18, 21, 25.
j Ps 66, 10; Prv 17, 3; Mal 3, 3; 1 Pt 1, 7.
k Jb 42, 2; Pss 115, 3; 135, 6.

*

22, 18: A gloss, taken partly from Jb 21, 16.

22, 24: Ophir: cf note to Ps 45, 10.

24, 1: Why does not God favor his friends by the speedy punishment of his enemies? (The text and order of verses in this chapter are not certain; note the omission of v 9 which duplicates words of vv 2–4.)

**7** They pass the night naked, without clothing,
for they have no covering against the cold;
**8** They are drenched with the rain of the mountains,
and for want of shelter they cling to the rock.
**11** Between the rows they press out the oil;
they glean in the vineyard of the wicked.
They tread the wine presses, yet suffer thirst,
**10** and famished are those who carry the sheaves.

**12** From the dust the dying groan,
and the souls of the wounded cry out
[yet God does not treat it as unseemly].
**13** There are those who are rebels against the light;[l]
they know not its ways;
they abide not in its paths.
**14** When there is no light the murderer rises,
to kill the poor and needy.
**15** The eye of the adulterer watches for the twilight;[m]
he says, "No eye will see me."
In the night the thief roams about,
and he puts a mask over his face;
**16** in the dark he breaks into houses.
By day they shut themselves in;
none of them know the light,
**17** for daylight they regard as darkness.*

* * *

**18** Their portion in the land is accursed,
**20** and wickedness is splintered like wood.
**19. 21.** . . . . . . . . . . . . . . . . . . . . . . . . . . . .
**22** To him who rises without assurance of his life
**23** he gives safety and support.
He sustains the mighty by his strength,
and his eyes are on their ways.
**24** They are exalted for a while, and then they are gone;
they are laid low and, like all others, are gathered up;
like ears of grain they shrivel.

**25** If this be not so, who will confute me,
and reduce my argument to nought?

## CHAPTER 25

**Bildad's Third Speech.** **1** Then Bildad the Shuhite answered and said:

**2** Dominion and awesomeness are his
who brings about harmony in his heavens.
**3** Is there any numbering of his troops?*
Yet to which of them does not his light extend?
**4** How can a man be just in God's sight,[n]
or how can any woman's child be innocent?
**5** Behold, even the moon is not bright
and the stars are not clear in his sight.
**6** How much less man, who is but a maggot,
the son of man, who is only a worm?[o]

## CHAPTER 26

**Job's Reply.** **1** Then Job spoke again and said:*

**2** What help you give to the powerless,
what strength to the feeble arm!
**3** How you counsel, as though he had no wisdom;
how profuse is the advice you offer!
**4** With whose help have you uttered those words,
and whose is the breath that comes forth from you?[p]
**5** The shades* beneath writhe in terror,[q]
the waters, and their inhabitants.
**6** Naked before him is the nether world,*
and Abaddon has no covering.[r]
**7** He stretches out the North* over empty space,
and suspends the earth over nothing at all;
**8** He binds up the waters in his clouds,
yet the cloud is not rent by their weight;
**9** He holds back the appearance of the full moon
by spreading his clouds before it.

**10** He has marked out a circle* on the surface

l Jn 3, 19f.
m Prv 7, 9f.
n Jb 4, 17ff; 9, 2.
o Jb 4, 19; 15, 16.
p Gn 2, 7.
q Prv 9, 18.
r Ps 139, 7-12.
s Jb 38, 8-11; Prv 8, 29.

*

24, 17: The asterisks which follow this verse mark off a passage (vv 18–24) which cannot be ascribed to Job with certainty. Vv 17–24 are in general poorly preserved; and much of vv 18–21 has not been translated because these verses are obscure. St. Jerome renders them as follows: (18) "He is light upon the face of the water, cursed be his portion on the earth; let him not walk by the way of vineyards. (19) Let him pass from the snow waters to excessive heat, and his sin even to hell. (20) Let mercy forget him; may worms be his sweetness; let him be remembered no more, but be broken in pieces as an unfruitful tree. (21) For he has fed the barren that bears not, and to the widow he has done no good."

25, 3: His troops: the heavenly hosts, the stars or the angels. His light: compare the wording in Jb 24, 13: those who are rebels against the light.

26, 1–14: Probably to be read as Job's reply to Bildad's short speech. Some, however, would make it the reply to Zophar (Jb 27, 13–21); it would thus lead up to the poem of ch 28.

26, 5: Shades: the dead in Sheol, the nether world; cf Pss 6, 6; 88, 11.

26, 6: Nether world: cf note to Ps 6, 6. Abaddon: Hebrew for "(place of) destruction," a synonym for nether world: cf Jb 28, 22; Rv 9, 11.

26, 7: The North: used here as a synonym for the firmament, the heavens; cf Is 14, 13.

26, 10: Circle: the horizon of the ocean which serves as the boundary for the activity of light and darkness.

of the deep[s]
as the boundary of light and darkness.
11 The pillars of the heavens tremble[t]
and are stunned at his thunderous rebuke;
12 By his power he stirs up the sea,
and by his might he crushes Rahab;*
13 With his angry breath he scatters the water,
and he hurls the lightning against it
relentlessly;
His hand pierces the fugitive dragon*
as from his hand it strives to flee.[u]
14 Lo, these are but the outlines of his ways,
and how faint is the word we hear!

## CHAPTER 27

### Job's Reply

11 I will teach you the manner of God's
dealings,
and the way of the Almighty I will not
conceal.
2 As God lives,* who withholds my deserts,[v]
the Almighty, who has made bitter my
soul,
3 So long as I still have life in me
and the breath of God is in my nostrils,
4 My lips shall not speak falsehood,
nor my tongue utter deceit!
5 Far be it from me to account you right;
till I die I will not renounce my
innocence.[w]
6 My justice I maintain and I will not
relinquish it;
my heart does not reproach me for any of
my days.
7 Let my enemy be as the wicked
and my adversary as the unjust!
8 For what can the impious man expect when
he is cut off,
when God requires his life?
9 Will God then attend to his cry
when calamity comes upon him?
10 Will he then delight in the Almighty
and call upon him constantly?
12 Behold, you yourselves have all seen it;
why then do you spend yourselves in idle
words!

* * *

13 *This is the portion of a wicked man from
God,
the inheritance an oppressor receives from
the Almighty:[x]
14 Though his children be many, the sword is
their destiny.
His offspring shall not be filled with
bread.
15 His survivors, when they die, shall have no
burial,
and their widows shall not be mourned.
16 Though he heap up silver like dust
and store away mounds of clothing,
17 What he has stored the just man shall wear,
and the innocent shall divide the silver.
18 He builds his house as of cobwebs,
or like a booth put up by the vinekeeper.
19 He lies down a rich man, one last time;
he opens his eyes and nothing remains to
him.[y]
20 Terrors rush upon him by day;
at night the tempest carries him off.
21 The storm wind seizes him and he
disappears;
it sweeps him out of his place.*

* * *

## CHAPTER 28

### The Inaccessibility of Wisdom

1 There is indeed a mine for silver,*
and a place for gold which men refine.
2 Iron is taken from the earth,
and copper is melted out of stone.
4 . . . . . . . . . . . . . . . . . . . . . . . . .
. . .
5 The earth, though out of it comes forth
bread,
is in fiery upheaval underneath.
6 Its stones are the source of sapphires,
and there is gold in its dust.

12 But whence can wisdom be obtained,
and where is the place of understanding?[z]
13 Man knows nothing to equal it,
nor is it to be had in the land of the
living.
15 Solid gold cannot purchase it,
nor can its price be paid with silver.[a]

t Jb 9, 6.
u Is 27, 1.
v Jb 34, 5.
w Jb 2, 3, 9; 13, 15; 33, 9.
x Jb 20, 4-29.
y Pss 49, 18; 76, 6.
z Eccl 7, 24f; Bar 3, 14f. 29-33.
a Prv 3, 14; 8, 10f, 19; 16, 16; Wis 7, 7-11.

*

26, 12: Rahab: cf Jb 9, 13; see note on Ps 89, 11.

26, 13: The fugitive dragon: the same term occurs in Is 27, 1 in apposition to Leviathan; see note on Jb 3, 8. This is actually Jb 27, 22.

27, 2-12: This is probably to be read as Job's reply to Zophar's speech of Jb 27, 13–21. In the current Hebrew text the heading for this chapter (Jb 27, 1, here omitted) is identical with Jb 29, 1; we should expect rather such a heading as is Jb 21, 1; 23, 1; 26, 1.

27, 13–21: This is probably to be read as Zophar's third speech. The asterisks are present to indicate it is not likely that the sacred writer intended these words to be ascribed to Job.

27, 21: The Hebrew has two more verses: v 22 (read above with Jb 26, 13); and v 23, which is a variant form of v 21.

28, 1–28: Note the changed order of verses; v 4 is uncertain.

This chapter contains a beautifully vivid description of that Wisdom which is beyond the attainment of creatures; known only to God, it is reflected in the order and majesty of his creation. Man, however, can, in a way, participate in this Wisdom by fearing the Lord and avoiding evil. Scholars are not agreed regarding the authorship of this poem, though it is altogether worthy of the author of the Book of Job. Used here as a counterpoise to ch 3 at the beginning of the dialogue, it may have been first conceived as an independent poem.

16 It cannot be bought with gold of Ophir,*
with the precious onyx or the sapphire.
17 Gold or crystal cannot equal it,
nor can golden vessels reach its worth.
18 Neither coral nor jasper should be thought of;
it surpasses pearls and 19 Arabian topaz.

20 Whence, then, comes wisdom,
and where is the place of understanding?
21 It is hid from the eyes of any beast;
from the birds of the air it is concealed.
7 The path to it no bird of prey knows,
nor has the hawk's eye seen that path.
8 The proud beasts have not trodden it,
nor has the lion gone that way.
14 The abyss declares, "It is not in me";
and the sea says, "I have it not."
22 Abaddon* and Death say,
"Only by rumor have we heard of it."

23 God knows the way to it;[b]
it is he who is familiar with its place.[c]
24 For he beholds the ends of the earth
and sees all that is under the heavens.
3 He has set a boundary for the darkness;
to the farthest confines he penetrates.
9 He sets his hand to the flinty rock,
and overturns the mountains at their foundations.
10 He splits channels in the rocks;
his eyes behold all that is precious.
11 He probes the wellsprings of the streams,
and brings hidden things to light.
25 He has weighed out the wind,
and fixed the scope of the waters;
26 When he made rules for the rain
and a path for the thunderbolts,[d]
27 Then he saw wisdom and appraised it,
gave it its setting, knew it through and through.
28 And to man he said:
Behold, the fear of the LORD is wisdom;
and avoiding evil is understanding.[e]

## *V: Job's Final Summary of His Cause*

### CHAPTER 29

1 Job took up his theme anew and said:
2 Oh, that I were as in the months past!
as in the days when God watched over me,[f]
3 While he kept his lamp shining above my head,
and by his light I walked through darkness;
4 As I was in my flourishing days,
when God sheltered my tent;
5 When the Almighty was yet with me,
and my children were round about me;
6 When my footsteps were bathed in milk,
and the rock flowed with streams of oil;*
7 When I went forth to the gate of the city
and set up my seat in the square—
8 Then the young men saw me and withdrew,
while the elders rose up and stood;
9 The chief men refrained from speaking
and covered their mouths with their hands;[g]
10 The voice of the princes was silenced,
and their tongues stuck to the roofs of their mouths.

21 For me they listened and waited;
they were silent for my counsel.
22 Once I spoke, they said no more,
but received my pronouncement drop by drop.
23 They waited for me as for the rain;
they drank in my words like the spring rains.

24 When I smiled on them they were reassured;
25 mourners took comfort from my cheerful glance.
I chose out their way and presided;
I took a king's place in the armed forces.
11 Whoever heard of me blessed me;
those who saw me commended me.

12 For I rescued the poor who cried out for help,
the orphans, and the unassisted;
13 The blessing of those in extremity came upon me,
and the heart of the widow I made joyful.
14 I wore my honesty like a garment;
justice was my robe and my turban.
15 I was eyes to the blind,
and feet to the lame was I;
16 I was a father to the needy;
the rights of the stranger I studied,
17 And I broke the jaws of the wicked man;
from his teeth I forced the prey.

18 Then I said: "In my own nest I shall grow old;
I shall multiply years like the phoenix.*
19 My root is spread out to the waters;
the dew rests by night on my branches.
20 My glory is fresh within me,
and my bow is renewed in my hand!"

b 23-27: Prv 8, 22-31.
c Prv 2, 6; Sir 1, 1; Jas 1, 5.
d Jb 38, 25; Prv 3, 20.
e Ps 111, 10; Prv 1, 7; 9, 10; Sir 1, 16.
f Jb 1, 10.
g Wis 8, 10ff.

*

28, 16: Ophir: cf note to Ps 45, 10.

28, 22: Abaddon: cf note to Jb 26, 6.

29, 6: Hyperbole to express abundance; see note on Jb 20, 17.

29, 18: Phoenix: a legendary bird which, after several centuries of life, consumed itself in fire, then rose from its ashes in youthful freshness. This meaning, originally intended in the Greek, later came to mean "palm tree." Some render the Hebrew as "sand."

## CHAPTER 30

1 But now they hold me in derision who are
younger in years than I;[h]
Whose fathers I should have disdained to
rank with the dogs of my flock.
2 Such strength as they had, to me meant
nought;
they were utterly destitute.

3 In want and hunger was their lot,[i]
they who fled to the parched wastelands:
4 They plucked saltwort* and shrubs;
the roots of the broom plant were their
food.
5 They were banished from among men,
with an outcry like that against a thief—
6 To dwell on the slopes of the wadies,
in caves of sand and stone;
7 Among the bushes they raised their raucous
cry;
under the nettles they huddled together.
8 Irresponsible, nameless men,
they were driven out of the land.

9 Yet now they sing of me in mockery;
I am become a byword among them.[j]
10 They abhor me, they stand aloof from me,
they do not hesitate to spit in my face!
11 Indeed, they have loosed their bonds; they
lord it over me,
and have thrown off restraint in my
presence.

12 To subvert my paths they rise up;
they build their approaches for my ruin.
13 To destroy me, they attack with none to stay
them;
14 as through a wide breach they advance.
Amid the uproar they come on in waves;
15 over me rolls the terror.
My dignity is borne off on the wind,
and my welfare vanishes like a cloud.
18 One with great power lays hold of my
clothing;*
by the collar of my tunic he seizes me:
19 He has cast me into the mire;
I am leveled with the dust and ashes.

20 I cry to you, but you do not answer me;[k]
you stand off and look at me,
21 Then you turn upon me without mercy
and with your strong hand you buffet me.
22 You raise me up and drive me before the
wind;
I am tossed about by the tempest.
23 Indeed I know you will turn me back in
death
to the destined place of everyone alive.[l]
24 Yet should not a hand be held out
to help a wretched man in his calamity?
25 Or have I not wept for the hardships of
others;
was not my soul grieved for the
destitute?[m]
26 Yet when I looked for good, then evil came;
when I expected light, then came
darkness.
16 My soul ebbs away from me;
27 days of affliction have overtaken me.
17 My frame takes no rest by night;
my inward parts seethe and will not be
stilled.
28 I go about in gloom, without the sun;
I rise up in public to voice my grief.

29 I have become the brother of jackals,
companion to the ostrich.
30 My blackened skin falls away from me;
the heat scorches my very frame.
31 My harp is turned to mourning,
and my reed pipe to sounds of weeping.

## CHAPTER 31

2 But what is man's lot from God above,
his inheritance from the Almighty on
high?
3 Is it not calamity for the unrighteous,
and woe for evildoers?
4 Does he not see my ways,
and number all my steps?[n]
6 Let God weigh me in the scales of justice;
thus will he know my innocence![o]

5 If I have walked in falsehood*
and my foot has hastened to deceit;
7 If my steps have turned out of the way,
and my heart has followed my eyes,
or any stain clings to my hands,
8 Then may I sow, but another eat of it,
or may my planting be rooted up!

38 If my land has cried out against me
till its very furrows complained;
39 If I have eaten its produce without payment
and grieved the hearts of its tenants;
40 Then let the thistles grow instead of wheat
and noxious weeds instead of barley!
1 If I have made an agreement with my eyes*
and entertained any thoughts against a
maiden;
9 If my heart has been enticed toward a
woman,
and I have lain in wait at my neighbor's
door;

h Jb 12, 4; 19, 18.
i 3-8: Jb 24, 5f.
j Jb 17, 6.
k Jb 19, 7.
l Heb 9, 27.
m Jb 29, 12-16.
n Jb 14, 16; 34, 21; Ps 139, 3; Prv 5, 21.
o Jb 23, 10.

*

30, 4: Saltwort: found in salt marshes and very sour to the taste; eaten by the extremely poor as a cooked vegetable. Broom plant: the juniper or brushwood; cf Ps 120, 4; a figure of bitterness and poverty, because of its bitter-tasting roots which are practically inedible.

30, 18–23: Job here refers to God's stern treatment of him.

31, 5–34: Job's final protestation of his innocence.

31, 1. 9: Note the gradation: avoidance of sinful glances and thoughts against a maiden; desire for another's wife.

**10** Then may my wife grind for another,
and may others cohabit with her!

**11** For that would be heinous,
a crime to be condemned;[p]
**12** A fire that should burn down to the abyss
till it consumed all my possessions to the roots.[q]
**13** Had I refused justice to my manservant
or to my maid, when they had a claim against me,
**14** What then should I do when God rose up;
what could I answer when he demanded an account?
**15** Did not he who made me in the womb make him?
Did not the same One fashion us before our birth?

**16** If I have denied anything to the poor,[r]
or allowed the eyes of the widow to languish
**17** While I ate my portion alone,
with no share in it for the fatherless,
**18** Though like a father God has reared me from my youth,
guiding me even from my mother's womb—
**19** If I have seen a wanderer without clothing,
or a poor man without covering,
**20** Whose limbs have not blessed me
when warmed with the fleece of my sheep;
**21** If I have raised my hand against the innocent
because I saw that I had supporters at the gate—*
**22** Then may my arm fall from the shoulder,
my forearm be broken at the elbow!
**23** For the dread of God will be upon me,
and his majesty will overpower me.
**24** Had I put my trust in gold
or called fine gold my security;
**25** Or had I rejoiced that my wealth was great,
or that my hand had acquired abundance—
**26** Had I looked upon the sun as it shone,[s]
or the moon in the splendor of its progress,*
**27** And had my heart been secretly enticed
to waft them a kiss with my hand;
**28** This too would be a crime for condemnation,
for I should have denied God above.[t]

**29** Had I rejoiced at the destruction of my enemy
or exulted when evil fell upon him,[u]
**30** Even though I had not suffered my mouth to sin
by uttering a curse against his life—

**31** Had not the men of my tent exclaimed,
"Who has not been fed with his meat!"*
**32** Because no stranger lodged in the street,
but I opened my door to wayfarers—

**33** Had I, out of human weakness, hidden my sins
and buried my guilt in my bosom*
**34** Because I feared the noisy multitude
and the scorn of the tribes terrified me—
then I should have remained silent, and not come out of doors!

**35** Oh, that I had one to hear my case,
and that my accuser would write out his indictment![v]
**36** Surely, I should wear it on my shoulder*
or put it on me like a diadem;
**37** Of all my steps I should give him an account;
like a prince* I should present myself before him.

This is my final plea; let the Almighty answer me!
The words of Job are ended.

## *VI: Elihu's Speeches*

## CHAPTER 32

**1** Then the three men ceased to answer Job,
because he was righteous[w] in his own eyes.
**2** [x]But the anger of Elihu,* son of Barachel the
Buzite, of the family of Ram, was kindled. He
was angry with Job for considering himself rather than God to be in the right. **3** [y]He was angry
also with the three friends because they had not
found a good answer and had not condemned
Job. **4** But since these men were older than he,
Elihu bided his time before addressing Job.

p Ex 20, 14; Lv 20, 10; Dt 22, 22.
q Sir 9, 8f.
r 16-23: Jb 29, 12-16.
s 26f: Dt 4, 19.
t Dt 17, 2-7.
u Prv 24, 17.
v Jb 19, 23; 23, 3-7.
w Jb 33, 9.
x Jb 13, 18; 27, 6; 34, 5; 35, 2.
y Jb 22, 5.

31, 21: Gate: cf notes on Jb 5, 4; Ru 4, 1.

31, 26ff: Job never sinned by worshiping the sun or the moon; waft them a kiss: an act of idolatrous worship.

31, 31: The members of his household will testify to his hospitality.

31, 33f: Job's present protest is made, not in spite of hidden sins which he had been unwilling to disclose, but out of genuine innocence.

31, 36: On my shoulder: i.e., boldly, proudly.

31, 37: Like a prince: not as a frightened criminal. Final plea: literally, "tau," the last letter of the Hebrew alphabet; in the current Hebrew text this line is in v 35, while the following one ends v 40.

32, 2: Elihu means "My God is he." This speaker was from Buz, which, according to Jer 25, 23, was near Tema and Dedan. A young man, he impetuously and impatiently upbraids Job for his boldness toward God, and the three friends for not successfully answering Job. He undertakes to defend God's absolute justice and to explain more clearly why there is suffering. While fundamentally his position is the same as that of the three friends, he does locate more definitely, though not perfectly, the place of suffering in the divine plan.

5 When, however, Elihu saw that there was no
reply in the mouths of the three men, his wrath
was inflamed. 6 So Elihu, son of Barachel the
Buzite, spoke out and said:

I am young and you are very old;
therefore I held back and was afraid to declare to you my knowledge.
7 Days should speak, I thought,
and many years teach wisdom![z]
8 But it is a spirit in man,[a]
the breath of the Almighty, that gives him understanding.
9 It is not those of many days who are wise,
nor the aged who understand the right.
10 Therefore I say, hearken to me;
let me too set forth my knowledge!

11 Behold, I have waited for your discourses,
and have given ear to your arguments.
12 Yes, I followed you attentively
as you searched out what to say;
And behold, there is none who has convicted Job,
not one of you who could refute his statements.
13 Yet do not say, "We have met wisdom.*
God may vanquish him but not man!"
14 For had he addressed his words to me,
I should not then have answered him as you have done.

15 They are dismayed, they make no more reply;
words fail them.
16 Must I wait? Now that they speak no more,
and have ceased to make reply,
17 I too will speak my part;
I also will show my knowledge!

18 For I am full of matters to utter;
the spirit within me compels me.
19 Like a new wineskin with wine under pressure,
my bosom is ready to burst.
20 Let me speak and obtain relief;
let me open my lips, and make reply.
21 I would not be partial to anyone,
nor give flattering titles to any.
22 For I know nought of flattery;
if I did, my Maker would soon take me away.

## CHAPTER 33

1 Therefore, O Job, hear my discourse,
and hearken to all my words.
2 Behold, now I open my mouth;
my tongue and my voice form words.
3 I will state directly what is in my mind,
my lips shall utter knowledge sincerely;
4 For the spirit of God has made me,
the breath of the Almighty keeps me alive.[b]
5 If you are able, refute me;
draw up your arguments and stand forth.
6 Behold I, like yourself, have been taken
from the same clay by God.[c]
7 Therefore no fear of me should dismay you,
nor should my presence weigh heavily upon you.

8 But you have said in my hearing,
as I listened to the sound of your words:
9 "I am clean and without transgression;
I am innocent; there is no guilt in me.[d]
10 Yet he invents pretexts against me
and reckons me as his enemy.[e]
11 He puts my feet in the stocks;
he watches all my ways!"[f]

12 In this you are not just, let me tell you;
for God is greater than man.
13 Why, then, do you make complaint against him
that he gives no account of his doings?[g]
14 For God does speak, perhaps once,
or even twice, though one perceive it not.

15 In a dream, in a vision of the night,
[when deep sleep falls upon men]
as they slumber in their beds,
16 It is then he opens the ears of men
and as a warning to them, terrifies them;
17 By turning man from evil
and keeping pride away from him,
18 He withholds his soul from the pit
and his life from passing to the grave.

19 Or a man is chastened on his bed by pain
and unceasing suffering within his frame,
20 So that to his appetite food becomes repulsive,
and his senses reject the choicest nourishment.[h]
21 His flesh is wasted so that it cannot be seen,
and his bones, once invisible, appear;
22 His soul draws near to the pit,
his life to the place of the dead.

23 If then there be for him an angel,*
one out of a thousand, a mediator,
To show him what is right for him
and bring the man back to justice,
24 He will take pity on him and say,
"Deliver him from going down to the pit;
I have found him a ransom."

25 Then his flesh shall become soft as a boy's;

z Jb 12, 12.
a Jb 33, 4.
b Jb 32, 8.
c Jb 31, 15.
d Jb 10, 7; 13, 18; 27, 5f; 29, 14; 32, 1; 34, 5.
e Jb 13, 24; 19, 11.
f Jb 13, 27; 31, 4.
g Jb 31, 35.
h Jb 6, 7.

*

32, 13: Met wisdom: in Job's arguments.

33, 23: Angel: one of the thousands who stand between God and man as intermediaries, reminding man of his duties and giving God an account of their fulfillment.

he shall be again as in the days of his
youth.
**26** He shall pray and God will favor him;
he shall see God's face with rejoicing.[i]
**27** He shall sing before men and say,
"I sinned and did wrong,
yet he has not punished me accordingly.
**28** He delivered my soul from passing to the
pit,
and I behold the light of life."
**29** Lo, all these things God does,
twice, or thrice, for a man,
**30** Bringing back his soul from the pit
to the light, in the land of the living.
**31** Be attentive, O Job; listen to me!
Be silent and I will speak.
**32** If you have aught to say, then answer me.
Speak out! I should like to see you
justified.
**33** If not, then do you listen to me;
be silent while I teach you wisdom.

## CHAPTER 34

**1** Then Elihu continued and said:

**2** Hear, O wise men, my discourse,
and you that have knowledge, hear me!
**3** For the ear tests words,
as the taste does food.[j]
**4** Let us discern for ourselves what is right;
let us learn between us what is good.
**5** For Job has said, "I am innocent,
but God has taken what is my due.[k]
**6** Notwithstanding my right I am set at nought;
in my wound the arrow rankles, sinless
though I am."[l]

**7** What man is like Job?
He drinks in blasphemies like water,
**8** Keeps company with evildoers
and goes along with wicked men,
**9** When he says, "It profits a man nought
that he is pleasing to God."[m]

**10** Therefore, men of understanding, hearken to
me:
far be it from God to do wickedness;
far from the Almighty to do wrong![n]
**11** Rather, he requites men for their conduct,
and brings home to a man his way of
life.[o]
**12** Surely, God cannot act wickedly,
the Almighty cannot violate justice.[p]
**13** Who gave him government over the earth,
or who else set all the land in its place?[q]
**14** If he were to take back his spirit to himself,
withdraw to himself his breath,
**15** All flesh would perish together,
and man would return to the dust.[r]

**16** Now, do you, O Job, hear this!
Hearken to the words I speak!
**17** Can an enemy of justice indeed be in
control,
or will you condemn the supreme Just
One,
**18** Who says to a king, "You are worthless!"
and to nobles, "You are wicked!"
**19** Who neither favors the person of princes,
nor respects the rich more than the poor?
For they are all the work of his hands;[s]
**20** in a moment they die, even at midnight.[t]
He brings on nobles, and takes them away,
removing the powerful without lifting a
hand;
**21** For his eyes are upon the ways of man,
and he beholds all his steps.

**22** There is no darkness so dense
that evildoers can hide in it.
**25** Therefore he discerns their works;
he turns at night and crushes them.
**23** For he forewarns no man of his time
to come before God in judgment.
**24** Without a trial he breaks the mighty,[u]
and sets others in their stead,
**27** Because they turned away from him
and heeded none of his ways,
**28** But caused the cries of the poor to reach
him,
so that he heard the plea of the afflicted.

**29** If he remains tranquil, who then can
condemn?*
If he hides his face, who then can behold
him?
**30** . . . . . . . . . . . . . . . . . . . . . . . . . . . . . .
. . .
**31** When anyone says to God,
"I was misguided; I will offend no more.
**32** Teach me wherein I have sinned;
if I have done wrong, I will do so no
more,"
**33** Would you then say that God must punish,
since you reject what he is doing?
It is you who must choose, not I;
speak, therefore, what you know.

**34** Men of understanding will say to me,
every wise man who hears my views:
**35** "Job speaks without intelligence,
and his words are without sense."[v]
**36** Let Job be tried to the limit,
since his answers are those of the
impious;
**37** For he is adding rebellion to his sin

---

i Jb 22, 26-29.
j Jb 12, 11.
k Jb 33, 9f.
l Jb 9, 20.
m Jb 9, 22f. 30f; 21, 15; 35, 3.
n Jb 36, 23.
o Ps 62, 13; Prv 24, 12; Mt 16, 27; Rom 2, 6; 2 Cor 5, 10; Rv 22, 12.
p Jb 8, 3.
q Jb 38, 4-7.
r Jb 10, 9.
s Dt 10, 17; 2 Chr 19, 7; Wis 6, 7; Acts 10, 34; Rom 2, 11; Eph 6, 9; Col 3, 25; 1 Pt 1, 17.
t Jb 21, 3.
u Ps 2, 9.
v Jb 35, 16; 38, 2; 42, 3.

---

* 34, 26. 29f: The extant Hebrew text of these verses contains several added phrases which either represent duplication or are very obscure.

by brushing off our arguments
and addressing many words to God.

## CHAPTER 35

1 Then Elihu proceeded and said:
2 Do you think it right to say,
"I am just rather than God"?[w]
3 To say, "What does it profit me;
what advantage have I more than if
I had sinned?"[x]
4 I have words for a reply to you*
and your three companions as well.
5 Look up to the skies and behold;
regard the heavens high above you.
6 If you sin, what injury do you do to God?
Even if your offenses are many, how do
you hurt him?
7 If you are righteous, what do you give him,
or what does he receive from your hand?[y]
8 Your wickedness can affect only a man like
yourself;
and your justice only a fellow human
being.

9 In great oppression men cry out;
they call for help because of the power of
the mighty,
10 Saying, "Where is God, my Maker,
who has given visions in the night,
11 Taught us rather than the beasts of the earth,
and made us wise rather than the birds of
the heavens?"
12 Though thus they cry out, he answers not
against the pride of the wicked.
13 But it is idle to say God does not hear
or that the Almighty does not take notice.
14 Even though you say that you see him not,*
the case is before him; with trembling
should you wait upon him.
15 But now that you have done otherwise,
God's anger punishes,
nor does he show concern that a man will
die.
16 Yet Job to no purpose opens his mouth,
and without knowledge multiplies words.[z]

## CHAPTER 36

1 Elihu proceeded further and said:

2 Wait yet a little and I will instruct you,
for there are still words to be said on
God's behalf.
3 I will bring my knowledge from afar,
and to my Maker I will accord the right.
4 For indeed, my theme cannot fail me:
the one perfect in knowledge I set before
you.
5 Behold, God rejects the obstinate in heart;*
he preserves not the life of the wicked,
6 He withholds not the just man's rights,
but grants vindication to the oppressed[a]
7 And with kings upon thrones
he sets them, exalted forever.[b]
8 Or if they are bound with fetters
and held fast by bonds of affliction,
9 Then he makes known to them what they
have done
and their sins of boastful pride.
10 He opens their ears to correction
and exhorts them to turn back from evil.

11 If they obey and serve him,
they spend their days in prosperity,
their years in happiness.
12 But if they obey not, they perish;
they die for lack of knowledge.*

13 The impious in heart lay up anger for
themselves;
they cry not for help when he enchains
them;
14 Therefore they expire in youth,
and perish among the reprobate.*
15 But he saves the unfortunate through their
affliction,
and instructs them through distress.
16-20 . . . . . . . . . . . . . . . . . . . . . . . .
. . .*
21 Take heed, turn not to evil;
for you have preferred carousal to
affliction.

22 Behold, God is sublime in his power.
What teacher is there like him?
23 Who prescribes for him his conduct,
or who can say, "You have done
wrong"?[c]
24 Remember, you should extol his work,
which men have praised in song.
25 All men contemplate it;
man beholds it from afar.

26 Lo, God is great beyond our knowledge;

w Jb 32, 2.
x Jb 34, 9.
y Jb 22, 3; 41, 2; Lk 17, 10; Rom 11, 35.
z Jb 34, 35; 38, 2; 42, 3.
a Ps 72, 4. 12f.
b Ps 113, 7f.
c Jb 34, 10; Is 40, 13.

*

35, 4: A reply to you: Elihu refers to Job's statement that the innocent suffer as much as the wicked, and especially to Eliphaz's words in Jb 22, 2f.

35, 14f: The text here is uncertain. It seems to indicate that Job should have realized God's indifference is only apparent, and that, because he has not done so, God will punish him.

36, 5–21: Perhaps this section should be read between vv 6 and 7 of chapter 34.

36, 12: Knowledge: practical wisdom in serving God, which they lack because they refused it when warned (cf v 10).

36, 14: Reprobate: cf Dt 23, 18f.

36, 16–20: The Hebrew text here is in disorder. The Vulgate has: "(16) Therefore he will give you most ample salvation from the narrow mouth which has no foundations beneath it; but the repose of your table will be filled with fatness. (17) Your case has been judged as that of the wicked; case and judgment you will receive. (18) Let no wrath, then, overcome you, that you oppress anyone; nor let numerous gifts mislead you. (19) Lay down your greatness without tribulation, and all who are mighty in strength. (20) Do not draw out the night, that people may go in place of them."

the number of his years is past searching
out.
**27** He holds in check the waterdrops
that filter in rain through his mists,
**28** Till the skies run with them
and the showers rain down on mankind.
**31** For by these* he nourishes the nations,
and gives them food in abundance.
**29. 30** Lo! he spreads the clouds in layers
as the carpeting of his tent.*
**32** In his hands he holds the lightning,
and he commands it to strike the mark.
**33** His thunder speaks for him
and incites the fury of the storm.

## CHAPTER 37

**1** At this my heart trembles
and leaps out of its place,
**2** To hear his angry voice*
as it rumbles forth from his mouth!
**3** Everywhere under the heavens he sends it,
with his lightning, to the ends of the
earth.
**4** Again his voice roars—
the majestic sound of his thunder.
**5** He does great things beyond our knowing;
wonders past our searching out.
**6** For he says to the snow, "Fall to the
earth";
likewise to his heavy, drenching rain.
**7** He shuts up all mankind indoors;
**8** the wild beasts take to cover
and remain quietly in their dens.

**9** Out of its chamber* comes forth the
tempest;
from the north winds, the cold.
**10** With his breath God brings the frost,
and the broad waters become congealed.[d]
**11** With hail, also, the clouds are laden,
as they scatter their flashes of light.
**12** He it is who changes their rounds,*
according to his plans,
in their task upon the surface of the earth,
**13** whether for punishment or mercy, as he
commands.

**14** Hearken to this, O Job!
Stand and consider the wondrous works of
God!
**15** Do you know how God lays his commands
upon them,
and makes the light shine forth from his
clouds?
**16** Do you know how the clouds are banked,
the wondrous work of him who is perfect
in knowledge?
**17** You, whom the streams of water fail
when a calm from the south comes over
the land,
**18** Do you spread out with him the firmament
of the skies,
hard as a brazen mirror?*
**19** Teach us then what we shall say to him;
we cannot, for the darkness, make our
plea.
**20** Will he be told about it when I speak,
or when a man says he is being
destroyed?*
**21** Nay, rather, it is as the light which men see
not
while it is obscured among the clouds,
till the wind comes by and sweeps the
clouds away.*

**22** From the North the splendor comes,*
surrounding God's awesome majesty!
**23** The Almighty! we cannot discover him,
pre-eminent in power and judgment;
his great justice owes no one an
accounting.
**24** Therefore men revere him,
though none can see him, however wise
their hearts.

# *VII: The Lord's Speech*

## CHAPTER 38

**1** Then the LORD* addressed Job out of the
storm and said:

**2** Who is this that obscures divine plans with
words of ignorance?
**3** Gird up your loins* now, like a man;
I will question you, and you tell me the
answers![e]

d Ps 148, 17. e Jb 40, 1

*

36, 31: These: refers to the showers of v 28, if the verse order indicated above is correct.

36, 29f: Because of the uncertainty of the text, no translation of these verses has received unanimous approval from exegetes.

37, 2: Voice: the thunder.

37, 9: Chamber: where it was popularly believed storms were kept enclosed.

37, 12: Their rounds: of rain (Jb 36, 27), of clouds (Jb 36, 29f), of lightning and thunder (Jb 36, 32f), of snow (Jb 37, 6), of winds (Jb 37, 9).

37, 18: The firmament . . . mirror: the ancients thought of the sky as a ceiling above which were the "upper waters" (cf Gn 1, 6f; 7, 11); when this ceiling became as hard as metal, the usual rain failed to fall on the earth (cf Lv 26, 19; Dt 28, 23).

37, 20: Will an angel bring this to God's attention?

37, 21: Even though God seems not to know our circumstances, he does know them, just as surely as the sun shines, unseen by man, behind the clouds.

37, 22: Now the storms of doubt and ignorance disappear, and from the North, used here as a symbol for God's mysterious abode, comes the splendor of the manifestation of God's majestic ways.

38, 1: Now the Lord enters the debate and addresses two discourses (38—39 and 40—41) to Job, in which he speaks of his wisdom and power, which are altogether beyond the capacity of Job, who therefore should never dare to demand a reason for the divine actions. Out of the storm: frequently the background of the appearances of the Lord in the Old Testament; cf Pss 18; 50; Na 1, 3; Hb 3.

38, 3: Gird up your loins: prepare for combat—figuratively, be ready to defend yourself in debate.

**4** Where were you when I founded the earth?
Tell me, if you have understanding.
**5** Who determined its size; do you know?
Who stretched out the measuring line for it?
**6** Into what were its pedestals sunk,
and who laid the cornerstone,
**7** While the morning stars sang in chorus
and all the sons of God* shouted for joy?

**8** And who shut within doors the sea,
when it burst forth from the womb;[f]
**9** When I made the clouds its garment
and thick darkness its swaddling bands?
**10** When I set limits for it
and fastened the bar of its door,
**11** And said: Thus far shall you come but no farther,
and here shall your proud waves be stilled!

**12** Have you ever in your lifetime commanded the morning
and shown the dawn its place
**13** For taking hold of the ends of the earth,
till the wicked are shaken from its surface?
**14** The earth is changed as is clay by the seal,
and dyed as though it were a garment;
**15** But from the wicked the light is withheld,
and the arm of pride is shattered.

**16** Have you entered into the sources of the sea,
or walked about in the depths of the abyss?
**17** Have the gates of death been shown to you,
or have you seen the gates of darkness?
**18** Have you comprehended the breadth of the earth?
Tell me, if you know all:
**19** Which is the way to the dwelling place of light,
and where is the abode of darkness,
**20** That you may take them to their boundaries
and set them on their homeward paths?
**21** You know, because you were born before them,
and the number of your years is great!*
**22** Have you entered the storehouse of the snow,
and seen the treasury of the hail
**23** Which I have reserved for times of stress,
for the days of war* and of battle?
**24** Which way to the parting of the winds,
whence the east wind spreads over the earth?
**25** Who has laid out a channel for the downpour
and for the thunderstorm a path
**26** To bring rain to no man's land,
the unpeopled wilderness;
**27** To enrich the waste and desolate ground
till the desert blooms with verdure?
**28** Has the rain a father;
or who has begotten the drops of dew?
**29** Out of whose womb comes the ice,
and who gives the hoarfrost its birth in the skies,
**30** When the waters lie covered as though with stone
that holds captive the surface of the deep?

**31** Have you fitted a curb to the Pleiades,*
or loosened the bonds of Orion?
**32** Can you bring forth the Mazzaroth in their season,
or guide the Bear with its train?
**33** Do you know the ordinances of the heavens;
can you put into effect their plan on the earth?

**34** Can you raise your voice among the clouds,
or veil yourself in the waters of the storm?*
**35** Can you send forth the lightnings on their way,
or will they say to you, "Here we are"?*
**37** Who counts the clouds in his wisdom?
Or who tilts the water jars of heaven
**38** So that the dust of earth is fused into a mass
and its clods made solid?
**39** Do you hunt the prey for the lioness
or appease the hunger of her cubs,
**40** While they crouch in their dens,
or lie in wait in the thicket?
**36** Who puts wisdom in the heart,
and gives the cock its understanding?*
**41** Who provides nourishment for the ravens
when their young ones cry out to God,[g]
and they rove abroad without food?

## CHAPTER 39

**1** Do you know about the birth of the mountain goats,
watch for the birth pangs of the hinds,
**2** Number the months that they must fulfill,
and fix the time of their bringing forth?
**3** They crouch down and bear their young;
they deliver their progeny in the desert.
**4** When their offspring thrive and grow,
they leave and do not return.
**5** Who has given the wild ass his freedom,
and who has loosed him from bonds?
**6** I have made the wilderness his home

f Gn 1, 9. g Ps 147, 9.

*

38, 7: Sons of God: angels; cf Jb 1, 6.

38, 21: Divine irony.

38, 22f: Hail . . . of war: thus God used a hailstorm to rout Joshua's foes in the battle of Gibeon; cf Jos 10, 11; Sir 46, 5.

38, 31f: Pleiades . . . Orion . . . Bear: cf Jb 9, 9. Mazzaroth: it is uncertain what astronomical group is meant by this Hebrew word; perhaps a southern constellation (cf Jb 9, 9).

38, 34: Veil yourself . . . storm: wrap yourself in a cloud, as God comes in a theophany; cf Ps 18, 12.

38, 35: Here we are: at your service.

38, 36: Understanding: the reflection of divine Wisdom discernible in the created animal instincts of the cock.

and the salt flats his dwelling.
7 He scoffs at the uproar of the city,
and hears no shouts of a driver.
8 He ranges the mountains for pasture,
and seeks out every patch of green.

9 Will the wild ox consent to serve you,
and to pass the nights by your manger?
10 Will a rope bind him in the furrow,
and will he harrow the valleys after you?
11 Will you trust him for his great strength
and leave to him the fruits of your toil?
12 Can you rely on him to thresh out your grain
and gather in the yield of your threshing floor?
13 The wings of the ostrich* beat idly;
her plumage is lacking in pinions.
14 When she leaves her eggs on the ground*
and deposits them in the sand,
15 Unmindful that a foot may crush them,
that the wild beasts may trample them,
16 She cruelly disowns her young
and ruthlessly makes nought of her brood;
17 For God has withheld wisdom from her
and has given her no share in understanding.
18 Yet in her swiftness of foot
she makes sport of the horse and his rider.

19 Do you give the horse his strength,*
and endow his neck with splendor?
20 Do you make the steed to quiver
while his thunderous snorting spreads terror?
21 He jubilantly paws the plain
and rushes in his might against the weapons.
22 He laughs at fear and cannot be deterred;
he turns not back from the sword.
23 Around him rattles the quiver,
flashes the spear and the javelin.
24 Frenzied and trembling he devours the ground;
he holds not back at the sound of the trumpet,
25 but at each blast he cries, "Aha!"
Even from afar he scents the battle,
the roar of the chiefs and the shouting.

26 Is it by your discernment that the hawk soars,
that he spreads his wings toward the south?
27 Does the eagle fly up at your command
to build his nest aloft?
28 On the cliff he dwells and spends the night,
on a spur of the cliff or the fortress.
29 From thence he watches for his prey;
his eyes behold it afar off.
30 His young ones greedily drink blood;
where the slain are, there is he.[h]

## CHAPTER 40

1 The LORD then said to Job:
2 Will we have arguing with the Almighty by the critic?
Let him who would correct God give answer![i]

3 Then Job answered the LORD and said:
4 Behold, I am of little account; what can I answer you?
I put my hand over my mouth.
5 Though I have spoken once, I will not do so again;
though twice, I will do so no more.

6 Then the LORD addressed Job out of the
storm and said:
7 Gird up your loins now, like a man.
I will question you, and you tell me the answers!
8 Would you refuse to acknowledge my right?
Would you condemn me that you may be justified?

9 Have you an arm like that of God,
or can you thunder with a voice like his?
10 Adorn yourself with grandeur and majesty,
and array yourself with glory and splendor.
11 Let loose the fury of your wrath;
12 tear down the wicked and shatter them.
Bring down the haughty with a glance;
13 bury them in the dust together;
in the hidden world imprison them.
14 Then will I too acknowledge
that your own right hand can save you.

15 See, besides you I made Behemoth,*
that feeds on grass like an ox.
16 Behold the strength in his loins,
and his vigor in the sinews of his belly.
17 He carries his tail like a cedar;
the sinews of his thighs are like cables.
18 His bones are like tubes of bronze;
his frame is like iron rods.
19 He came at the beginning of God's ways,
and was made the taskmaster of his fellows;
20 For the produce of the mountains is brought to him,
and of all wild animals he makes sport.
21 Under the lotus trees he lies,
in coverts of the reedy swamp.
22 The lotus trees cover him with their shade;

h Mt 24, 28; Lk 17, 37. i Jb 38, 3.

*

39, 13: The wings of the ostrich cannot raise her from the ground, but they help her to run swiftly.

39, 14ff: It was popularly believed that, because the ostrich laid her eggs on the sand, she was thereby cruelly abandoning them; cf Lam 4, 3.

39, 19–25: The famous description of a war horse.

40, 15: Behemoth: the hippopotamus.

all about him are the poplars on the bank.
23 If the river grows violent, he is not
disturbed;
he is tranquil though the torrent surges
about his mouth.
24 Who can capture him by his eyes,
or pierce his nose* with a trap?

25 Can you lead about Leviathan* with a hook,
or curb his tongue with a bit?
26 Can you put a rope into his nose,
or pierce through his cheek with a gaff?
27 Will he then plead with you, time after
time,
or address you with tender words?
28 Will he make an agreement with you
that you may have him as a slave forever?
29 Can you play with him, as with a bird?
Can you put him in leash for your
maidens?
30 Will the traders bargain for him?
Will the merchants* divide him up?
31 Can you fill his hide with barbs,
or his head with fish spears?
32 Once you but lay a hand upon him,
no need to recall any other conflict!
41, 2 Is he not relentless when aroused;
who then dares stand before him?*
1 Whoever might vainly hope to do so
need only see him to be overthrown.
3 Who has assailed him and come off safe—
Who under all the heavens?

4 I need hardly mention his limbs,
his strength, and the fitness of his armor.
5 Who can strip off his outer garment,
or penetrate his double corselet?
6 Who can force open the doors of his mouth,
close to his terrible teeth?
7 Rows of scales are on his back,
tightly sealed together;
8 They are fitted each so close to the next
that no space intervenes;
9 So joined one to another
that they hold fast and cannot be parted.

10 When he sneezes, light flashes forth;
his eyes are like those of the dawn.
11 Out of his mouth go forth firebrands;
sparks of fire leap forth.
12 From his nostrils issues steam,
as from a seething pot or bowl.
13 His breath sets coals afire;
a flame pours from his mouth.
14 Strength abides in his neck,
and terror leaps before him.

15. 16 His heart is hard as stone:
his flesh, as the lower millstone.
17 When he rises up, the mighty are afraid;
the waves of the sea fall back.*
18 Should the sword reach him, it will not
avail;
nor will the spear, nor the dart, nor the
javelin.
19 He regards iron as straw,
and bronze as rotten wood.
20 The arrow will not put him to flight;
slingstones used against him are but
straws.
21 Clubs he esteems as splinters;
he laughs at the crash of the spear.

22 His belly is sharp as pottery fragments;
he spreads like a threshing sledge upon
the mire.
23 He makes the depths boil like a pot;
the sea he churns like perfume in a kettle.
24 Behind him he leaves a shining path;
you would think the deep had the hoary
head of age.
25 Upon the earth there is not his like,
intrepid he was made.36
26 All, however lofty, fear him;
he is king over all proud beasts.

## CHAPTER 42

1 Then Job answered the LORD and said:

2 I know that you can do all things,*
and that no purpose of yours can be
hindered.
3 I have dealt with great things that I do not
understand;
things too wonderful for me, which I
cannot know.[j]
5 I had heard of you by word of mouth,
but now my eye has seen you.
6 Therefore I disown what I have said,
and repent in dust and ashes.

## VIII: Epilogue

**Job's Restoration.** 7 And it came to pass
after the LORD had spoken these words to Job,
that the LORD said to Eliphaz the Temanite, "I
am angry with you and with your two friends;*
for you have not spoken rightly concerning me,
as has my servant Job. 8 Now, therefore, take

j Jb 34, 35; 35, 16; 38, 2.

*

40, 24: Eyes . . . nose: the only exposed parts of the submerged beast.

40, 25: Leviathan here is the crocodile. But cf Jb 3, 8.

40, 30: Merchants: literally, "Canaanites," whose reputation for trading was so widespread that their name came to be used for merchants; cf Prv 31, 24. The meaning of this verse is that the crocodile is too powerful a creature to be sold like common fish.

41, 2: Before him: some read, "before me," i.e., God; also in v 3.

41, 17: The text here is uncertain.

42, 2–6: In the current Hebrew text, this final utterance of Job is interrupted by words ascribed to God (vv 3f) which are in large part a duplication of Jb 38, 2f.

42, 7: The three friends of Job (Elihu is ignored in the Epilogue) are criticized by the Lord because they had (even though in good faith) leveled false charges against him.

42, 8: Job becomes the intercessor for his friends, as were other great Old Testament characters, e.g., Abraham and Mo-

seven bullocks and seven rams, and go to my
servant Job, and offer up a holocaust for yourselves; and let my servant Job pray for you;* for
his prayer I will accept, not to punish you severely. For you have not spoken rightly concerning me, as has my servant Job.'' **9** Then
Eliphaz the Temanite, and Bildad the Shuhite,
and Zophar the Naamathite, went and did as the
LORD had commanded them. And the LORD
accepted the intercession of Job.

**10** Also, the LORD restored the prosperity of
Job, after he had prayed for his friends; the
LORD even gave to Job twice as much as he had
before. **11** Then all his brethren and his sisters
came to him, and all his former acquaintances,
and they dined with him in his house. They
condoled with him and comforted him for all the
evil which the LORD had brought upon him; and
each one gave him a piece of money* and a gold
ring.

**12** [k]Thus the LORD blessed the latter days of
Job more than his earlier ones. For he had fourteen thousand sheep, six thousand camels, a
thousand yoke of oxen, and a thousand she-
asses. **13** And he had seven sons and three
daughters, **14** of whom* he called the first Jemimah, the second Keziah, and the third Ker-
en-happuch. **15** In all the land no other women
were as beautiful as the daughters of Job; and
their father gave them an inheritance* among
their brethren. **16** After this, Job lived a hundred and forty years;* and he saw his children,
his grandchildren, and even his great-grandchil-
dren.[l] **17** Then Job died, old and full of years.

---

k Jb 1, 3. l Jb 5, 25f.

---

* ses, and as our Lord would be, whom he prefigured. Seven: a symbolic number.

42, 11: A piece of money: the term is the same as that used in Gn 33, 19; Jos 24, 32. Gold ring: for the nose or ear.

42, 14: Job's daughters had names symbolic of their charms: Jemimah, dove; Keziah, precious perfume (cf Ps 45, 9); Kerenhappuch, cosmetic jar—more precisely, a container for a black powder that was used like modern mascara.

42, 15: Ordinarily daughters did not inherit property unless there were no sons; cf Nm 27, 1–11.

42, 16: As his other rewards were twice as much as he had before (v 10), so Job's hundred and forty years were double the expected span of human life; cf Ps 90, 10.

# The Book of PSALMS

*The Hebrew Psalter numbers 150 songs. The corresponding number in the LXX differs because of a different division of certain psalms. Hence the numbering in the Greek Psalter (which was followed by the Latin Vulgate) is usually one digit behind the Hebrew. In the New American Bible the numbering of the verses follows the Hebrew numbering; many of the traditional English translations are often a verse number behind the Hebrew because they do not count the superscriptions as a verse.*

*The superscriptions derive from pre-Christian Jewish tradition, and they contain technical terms, many of them apparently liturgical, which are no longer known to us. Seventy-three psalms are attributed to David, but there is no sure way of dating any psalm. Some are pre-exilic (before 587 B.C.), and others are post-exilic (after 539 B.C.), but not as late as the Maccabean period (ca. 165 B.C.). The psalms are the product of many individual collections (e.g., Songs of Ascents, Pss 120–134), which were eventually combined into the present work in which one can detect five "books," because of the doxologies which occur at 41:14; 72:18-19; 89:53; 106:48.*

*Two important features of the psalms deserve special notice. First, the majority were composed originally precisely for liturgical worship. This is shown by the frequent indication of liturgical leaders interacting with the community (e.g., 118:1–4). Secondly, they follow certain distinct patterns or literary forms. Thus, the hymn is a song of praise, in which a community is urged joyfully to sing out the praise of God. Various reasons are given for this praise (often introduced by "for" or "because"): the divine work of creation and sustenance (Pss 8, 104), or the divine acts in Israel's favor (Pss 135:1–12; 136). Some of the hymns have received a more specific classification, based on content. The "Songs of Zion" are so called because they exalt Zion, the city in which God dwells among the people (Pss 46, 48). Others are termed "enthronement" psalms because they re-enact or re-present in the liturgy the kingship of the Lord (Pss 47; 96–99). Characteristic of the songs of praise is the joyful summons to get involved in the activity; Ps 104 is an exception to this, although it remains universal in its thrust.*

*Another type of psalm is similar to the hymn: the thanksgiving psalm. This too is a song of praise acknowledging the Lord as the rescuer of the psalmist from a desperate situation. Very often the psalmist will give a flash-back, recounting the past distress, and the plea that was uttered (Pss 30; 116). The setting for such prayers seems to have been the offering of a* todah *(a "praise" sacrifice) with friends in the Temple.*

*There are more psalms of lament than of any other type. They may be individual (e.g., Pss 3–7; 22) or communal (e.g., Ps 44). Although they usually begin with a cry for help, they develop in various ways. The description of the distress is couched in the broad imagery typical of the Bible (one is in Sheol, the Pit, or is afflicted by enemies or wild beasts, etc.)—in such a way that one cannot pinpoint the exact nature of the psalmist's plight. However, Ps 51 (cf. also Ps 130) seems to refer clearly to deliverance from sin. Several laments end on a note of certainty that the Lord has heard the prayer (cf. Ps 7, but contrast Ps 88), and the Psalter has been characterized as a movement from lament to praise. If this is somewhat of an exaggeration, it serves at least to emphasize the frequent expressions of trust which characterize the lament. In some cases it would seem as if the theme of trust has been lifted out to form a literary type all its own; cf. Pss 23, 62, 91. Among the communal laments can be counted Pss 74 and 79. They complain to the Lord about some national disaster, and try to motivate God to intervene in favor of the suffering people.*

*Other psalms are clearly classified on account of content, and they may be in themselves laments or psalms of thanksgiving. Among the "royal" psalms, that deal directly with the currently reigning king, are Pss 20, 21, and 72. Many of the royal psalms were given a messianic interpretation by Christians. In Jewish tradition they were preserved, even after kingship had disappeared, because they were read in the light of the Davidic covenant reported in 2 Samuel 7. Certain psalms are called wisdom psalms because they seem to betray the influence of the concerns of the sages (cf. Pss 37, 49), but there is no general agreement as to the number of these prayers. Somewhat related to the wisdom psalms are the "torah" psalms, in which the* torah *(instruction or law) of the Lord is glorified (Pss 1, 19:8–14; 119). Pss 78, 105 and 106 can be considered as "historical" psalms. Although the majority of the psalms have a liturgical setting, there are certain prayers that may be termed "liturgies," so clearly does their structure reflect a liturgical incident (e.g., Pss 15, 24).*

*It is obvious that not all of the psalms can be pigeon-holed into neat classifications, but even a brief sketch of these types help us to catch the structure and spirit of the psalms we read. It has been rightly said that the psalms are "a school of prayer." They not only provide us with models to follow, but inspire us to voice our own deepest feelings and aspirations.*

# *FIRST BOOK — PSALMS 1–41*

## PSALM 1*

### True Happiness in God's Law

I

1 Happy those* who do not follow
the counsel of the wicked,
Nor go the way* of sinners,
nor sit in company with scoffers.[a]
2 Rather, the law of the LORD* is their joy;
God's law they study day and night.[b]
3 They are like a tree[c]
planted near streams of water,
that yields its fruit in season;
Its leaves never wither;
whatever they do prospers.

II

4 But not the wicked!*
They are like chaff driven by the wind.[d]
5 Therefore the wicked will not survive
judgment,
nor will sinners in the assembly of the
just.
6 The LORD watches over the way of the
just,[e]
but the way of the wicked leads to ruin.

## PSALM 2*

### A Psalm for a Royal Coronation

1 Why do the nations protest
and the peoples grumble in vain?[f]
2 Kings on earth rise up
and princes plot together
against the LORD and his anointed:[g]*
3 "Let us break their shackles
and cast off their chains"[h]
4 The one enthroned in heaven laughs;
the Lord derides them,[i]
5 Then speaks to them in anger,
terrifies them in wrath:
6 "I myself have installed my king
on Zion, my holy mountain."
7 I will proclaim the decree of the LORD,
who said to me, "You are my son;
today I am your father.[j]
8 Only ask it of me,
and I will make your inheritance the
nations,
your possession the ends of the earth.
9 With an iron rod you shall shepherd them,
like a clay pot you will shatter them."[k]
10 And now, kings, give heed;
take warning, rulers on earth.
11 Serve the LORD with fear;
with trembling bow down in homage,
Lest God be angry and you perish from the
way
in a sudden blaze of anger.
Happy are all who take refuge in God![l]

## PSALM 3*

### Threatened but Trusting

1 *A psalm of David, when he fled from his son Absalom.*[m]*

I

2 How many are my foes, LORD!
How many rise against me!

a Pss 26,4-5; 40,5.
b Jos 1,8; Ps 119; Sir 39,1.
c Pss 52,10; 92,13-15; Jer 17,8.
d Pss 35,5; 83,14-16; Jb 21,18.
e Ps 37,18.
f Rv 11,18.
g Ps 83,6.
h Ps 149,8.
i Pss 37,13; 59,9; Wis 4,18.
j Pss 89,27; 110,2-3; Is 49,1.
k Rv 2,27; 12,5; 19,15.
l Pss 34,9; 146,5; Prv 16,20.
m 2 Sm 15,13ff.

*

Ps 1: A preface to the whole Book of Psalms, contrasting with striking similes the destiny of the good and the wicked. The psalm views life as activity, as choosing either the good or the bad. Each "way" brings its inevitable consequences. The wise through their good actions will experience rootedness and life, and the wicked, rootlessness and death.

1, 1: *Those*: literally, "the man." That word is used here and in many of the Psalms as typical, and therefore is translated "they."

1, 1: *The way*: a common biblical term for manner of living or moral conduct (Pss 32, 8; 101, 2, 6; Prv 2, 20; 1 Kgs 8, 36).

1, 2: *The law of the LORD*: either the Torah, the first five books of the Bible, or, more probably, divine teaching or instruction.

1, 4: *The wicked*: those who by their actions distance themselves from God's life-giving presence.

Ps 2: A royal psalm. To rebellious kings (1–3) God responds vigorously (4–6). A speaker proclaims the divine decree (in the legal adoption language of the day), making the Israelite king the earthly representative of God (7–9) and warning kings to obey (10–11). The psalm has a messianic meaning for the Church; the New Testament understands it of Christ (Acts 4, 25–27; 13, 33; Heb 1, 5).

2, 2: *Anointed*: in Hebrew *mashiah*, "anointed"; in Greek *christos*, whence English Messiah and Christ. In Israel kings (Jgs 9, 8; 1 Sm 9, 16; 16, 12–13) and high priests (Lv 8, 12; Nm 3, 3) received the power of their office through anointing.

Ps 3: An individual lament complaining of enemies who deny that God will come to the rescue (2–3). Despite such taunts the psalmist hopes for God's protection even in sleep

3 How many say of me,
"God will not save that one."[n] *Selah**
4 But you, LORD, are a shield around me;
my glory, you keep my head high.[o]

II
5 Whenever I cried out to the LORD,
I was answered from the holy mountain.
*Selah**
6 Whenever I lay down and slept,
the LORD preserved me to rise again.[p]
7 I do not fear, then, thousands of people
arrayed against me on every side.

III
8 Arise, LORD! Save me, my God!
You will shatter the jaws of all my foes;
you will break the teeth of the wicked.[q]
9 Safety comes from the LORD!
Your blessing for your people![r] *Selah**

## PSALM 4*

## Trust in God

1 *For the leader;* with stringed instruments. A psalm of David.*

I
2 Answer when I call, my saving God.
In my troubles, you cleared a way;
show me favor; hear my prayer.[s]

II
3 How long will you people mock my honor,
love what is worthless, chase after lies?[t]
*Selah*
4 Know that the LORD works wonders for the
faithful;
the LORD hears when I call out.
5 Tremble* and do not sin;
upon your beds ponder in silence.[u]
6 Offer fitting sacrifice
and trust in the LORD.[v]

III
7 Many say, "May we see better times!
LORD, show us the light of your face!"[w]
*Selah*
8 But you have given my heart more joy
than they have when grain and wine
abound.
9 In peace I shall both lie down and sleep,[x]
for you alone, LORD, make me secure.

## PSALM 5*

## Prayer for Divine Help

1 *For the leader; with wind instruments. A psalm of David.*

I
2 Hear my words, O LORD;
listen to my sighing.[y]
3 Hear my cry for help,
my king, my God!
To you I pray, O LORD;
4 at dawn you will hear my cry;
at dawn I will plead before you and
wait.[z]

II
5 You are not a god who delights in evil;
no wicked person finds refuge with you;
6 the arrogant cannot stand before you.
You hate all who do evil;
7 you destroy all who speak falsely.[a]
Murderers and deceivers
the LORD abhors.

III
8 But I can enter your house
because of your great love.
I can worship in your holy temple
because of my reverence for you, LORD.[b]
9 Guide me in your justice because of my
foes;
make straight your way before me.[c]

IV
10 For there is no sincerity in their mouths;
their hearts are corrupt.
Their throats* are open graves;[d]
on their tongues are subtle lies.
11 Declare them guilty, God;
make them fall by their own devices.[e]

---

n Ps 71,11.
o Pss 7,11; 18,3; 62, 7-8; Dt 33,29; Is 60, 19.
p Ps 4,9; Prv 3,24.
q Ps 58,7.
r Ps 28,9; Jon 2,10.
s Ps 118,5.
t Ps 62,4.
u Eph 4,26.
v Ps 51,19.
w Pss 31,17; 44,4; 67,1; 80,4; Jb 13,24; Nm 6, 25; Dn 9,17.
x Ps 3,6.
y Pss 86,6; 130,1-2.
z Wis 16,28.
a Ps 101,7; Wis 14,9; Hb 1,13.
b Ps 138,2; Jon 2,5.
c Ps 23,3; Prv 4,11; Is 26,7.
d Rom 3,13.
e Ps 141,10.

---

(4–7). The psalm prays for an end to the enemies' power to speak maliciously (8) and closes peacefully with an expression of trust (9).

3, 1: The superscription, added later, relates the psalm to an incident in the life of David.

3, 3. 5. 9: *Selah*: the term is generally considered a direction to the cantor or musicians but its exact meaning is not known. It occurs 71 times in 39 psalms.

Ps 4: A individual lament emphasizing trust in God. The petition is based upon the psalmist's vivid experience of God as savior (2). That experience of God is the basis for the warning to the wicked: revere God who intervenes on the side of the faithful (3–6). The faithful psalmist exemplifies the blessings given to the just (7–9).

4, 1: *For the leader*: many psalm headings contain this rubric. Its exact meaning is unknown but may signify that such psalms once stood together in a collection of "the choirmaster." Cf 1 Chr 15, 21.

4, 5: *Tremble*: be moved deeply with religious awe. The Greek translation understood the emotion to be anger, and it is so cited in Eph 4, 26.

Ps 5: A lament contrasting the security of the house of God (8–9. 12–13) with the danger of the company of evildoers (5–7. 10–11). The psalmist therefore prays that God will hear (2–4) and grant the protection and joy of the temple.

5, 10: *Their throats*: their speech brings harm to their hearers (cf Jer 5, 16). The verse mentions four parts of the body, each a source of evil to the innocent.

Drive them out for their many sins;
they have rebelled against you.

V

12 Then all who take refuge in you will be glad
and forever shout for joy.[f]
Protect them that you may be the joy
of those who love your name.
13 For you, LORD, bless the just;
you surround them with favor like a
shield.

## PSALM 6*

## Prayer in Distress

1 *For the leader; with stringed instruments, "upon the eighth."* A psalm of David.*

I

2 Do not reprove me in your anger, LORD,
nor punish me in your wrath.[g]
3 Have pity on me, LORD, for I am weak;
heal me, LORD, for my bones are
trembling.[h]
4 In utter terror is my soul—
and you, LORD, how long . . . ?[i]*
5 Turn, LORD, save my life;
in your mercy* rescue me.
6 For who among the dead remembers you?
Who praises you in Sheol?[j]*

II

7 I am wearied with sighing;
all night long tears drench my bed;
my couch is soaked with weeping.
8 My eyes are dimmed with sorrow,
worn out because of all my foes.[k]

III

9 Away from me, all who do evil![l]
The LORD has heard my weeping.
10 The LORD has heard my prayer;
the LORD takes up my plea.
11 My foes will be terrified and disgraced;
all will fall back in sudden shame.[m]

## PSALM 7*

## God the Vindicator

1 *A plaintive song of David, which he sang to the LORD concerning Cush, the Benjaminite.*

I

2 LORD my God, in you I take refuge;
rescue me; save me from all who pursue
me,[n]
3 Lest they maul me like lions,
tear me to pieces with none to save.

II

4 LORD my God, if I am at fault in this,*
if there is guilt on my hands,
5 If I have repaid my friend with evil—
I spared even those who hated me without
cause—
6 Then let my enemy pursue and overtake me,
trample my life to the ground,
and leave me dishonored in the dust.[o]
*Selah*

III

7 Rise up, LORD, in your anger;
rise against the fury of my foes.[p]
Wake to judge as you have decreed.
8 Have the assembly of the peoples gather
about you;
sit on your throne high above them,
9 O LORD, judge of the nations.
Grant me justice, LORD, for I am blameless,
free of any guilt.
10 Bring the malice of the wicked to an end;
uphold the innocent,
O God of justice,
who tries hearts and minds.[q]

f Ps 64,11.
g Ps 38,2.
h Jer 17,14-15.
i Pss 13,2-3; 74,10; 89, 47.
j Pss 30,10; 88,11; 115,17; Is 38,18.
k Pss 31,10; 38,11; 40, 13.
l Ps 119,115; Mt 7,23; Lk 13,27.
m Pss 35,4. 26; 40,15; 71,13.
n Pss 6,5; 22,21.
o Ps 143,3.
p Pss 9,4; 19,20.
q Pss 17,3; 26,2; 35,24; 43,1; 139,23; Jer 17, 10; 20,12.

*

Ps 6: The first of the seven Penitential Psalms (Pss 6, 32, 38, 51, 102, 130, 143), a designation dating from the seventh century A.D. for psalms suitable to express repentance. The psalmist does not, as in many laments, claim to be innocent but appeals to God's mercy (5). Sin here, as often in the Bible, is both the sinful act and its injurious consequences; here it is physical sickness (3–4. 7–8) and the attacks of enemies (8. 9. 11). The psalmist prays that the effects of personal and social sin be taken away.

6, 1: *Upon the eighth*: apparently a musical notation, now lost.

6, 4: *How long?*: elliptical for "How long will it be before you answer my prayer?" Cf Ps 13, 2–3.

6, 5: *Mercy*: Hebrew *hesed*, translated as "mercy" or "love," describes God's affectionate fidelity to human beings, which is rooted in divine and not human integrity.

6, 6: A motive for God to preserve the psalmist from death: in the shadowy world of the dead no one offers you praise. Sheol is the biblical term for the underworld where the insubstantial souls of dead human beings dwelt. It was similar to the Hades of Greek and Latin literature. In the second century B.C., biblical books begin to speak positively of life with God after death (Dn 12, 1–3; Wis 3).

Ps 7: An individual lament. The psalmist flees to God's presence in the sanctuary for justice and protection (2–3) and takes an oath that only the innocent can swear (4–6). The innocent psalmist can thus hope for the just God's protection (7–14) and be confident that the actions of the wicked will come back upon their own heads (15–17). The justice of God leads the psalmist to praise (18).

7, 4: *At fault in this*: in the accusation the enemies have made against the psalmist.

IV
11 A shield before me is God
who saves the honest heart.[r]
12 God is a just judge,
who rebukes in anger every day.
13 If sinners do not repent,
God sharpens his sword,
strings and readies the bow,[s]
14 Prepares his deadly shafts,
makes arrows blazing thunderbolts.[t]

V
15 Sinners conceive iniquity;
pregnant with mischief,
they give birth to failure.[u]
16 They open a hole and dig it deep,
but fall into the pit they have dug.[v]
17 Their mischief comes back upon themselves;
their violence falls on their own heads.

VI
18 I praise the justice of the LORD;
I celebrate the name of the LORD Most
High.[w]

## PSALM 8*

## Divine Majesty and Human Dignity

1 *For the leader; "upon the* gittith.*"* A psalm of David.*

2 O LORD, our Lord,
how awesome is your name through all
the earth!
You have set your majesty above the
heavens!
3 Out of the mouths of babes[x] and infants*
you have drawn a defense against your
foes,
to silence enemy and avenger.
4 When I see your heavens, the work of your
fingers,
the moon and stars that you set in
place—
5 What are humans that you are mindful of
them,[y]
mere mortals* that you care for them?[z]
6 Yet you have made them little less than a
god,*
crowned them with glory and honor.
7 You have given them rule over the works of
your hands,[a]
put all things at their feet:
8 All sheep and oxen,
even the beasts of the field,
9 The birds of the air, the fish of the sea,
and whatever swims the paths of the
seas.
10 O LORD, our Lord,
how awesome is your name through all
the earth!

## PSALM 9–10*

## Thanksgiving for Victory and Prayer for Justice

1 *For the leader; according to* Muth Labben.* *A psalm of David.*

### A

I
2 I will praise you, LORD, with all my heart;
I will declare all your wondrous deeds.
3 I will delight and rejoice in you;
I will sing hymns to your name, Most
High.
4 For my enemies turn back;
they stumble and perish before you.

II
5 You upheld my right and my cause,
seated on your throne, judging justly.
6 You rebuked the nations, you destroyed the
wicked;

r Ps 3,4.
s Ps 11,2.
t Is 50,11.
u Jb 15,35; Is 59,4.
v Pss 9,16; 35,8; 57,7; Prv 26,27; Eccl 10,8; Sir 27,26.
w Pss 18,50; 30,5; 135, 3; 146,2.
x Mt 21,16; Wis 10,21.
y Ps 144,3; Jb 7,17.
z Heb 2,6ff.
a 7ff: Gn 1,26. 28; Wis 9,2; 1 Cor 15,27.

*

Ps 8: While marvelling at the limitless grandeur of God (2–3), the psalmist is struck first by the smallness of human beings in creation (4–5), and then by the royal dignity and power that God has graciously bestowed upon them (6–10).

8, 1: *Upon the gittith*: probably the title of the melody to which the psalm was to be sung or a musical instrument.

8, 3: *Babes and infants*: the text is obscure. Some join this line to the last line of 2 (itself obscure) to read: "(you) whose majesty is exalted above the heavens / by the mouths of babes and infants." *Drawn a defense*: some prefer the Septuagint's "fashioned praise," which is quoted in Mt 21, 16. *Enemy and avenger*: probably cosmic enemies. The primeval powers of watery chaos are often personified in poetic texts (Pss 74, 13–14; 89, 11; Jb 9, 13; 26, 12–13; Is 51, 9).

8, 5: *Humans . . . mere mortals*: literally, "(mortal) person" . . . "son of man (in sense of a human being, Hebrew *'adam*)." The emphasis is on the fragility and mortality of human beings to whom God has given great dignity.

8, 6: *Little less than a god*: Hebrew *'elohim*, the ordinary word for "God" or "the gods" or members of the heavenly court. The Greek version translated *'elohim* by "angel, messenger"; several ancient and modern versions so translate. The meaning seems to be that God created human beings almost at the level of the beings in the heavenly world. Heb 2, 9 finds the eminent fulfillment of this verse in Jesus Christ, who was humbled before being glorified. Cf also 1 Cor 15, 27, where St. Paul applies to Christ the closing words of v 7.

Pss 9–10: Pss 9 and 10 in the Hebrew text have been transmitted as separate poems but they actually form a single acrostic poem and are so transmitted in the Greek and Latin tradition. Each verse of the two psalms begins with a successive letter of the Hebrew alphabet (though several letters have no corresponding stanza). The psalm states loosely connected themes: the rescue of the helpless poor from their enemies, God's worldwide judgment and rule over the nations, the psalmist's own concern for rescue (14–15).

9, 1: *Muth Labben*: probably the melodic accompaniment of the psalm, now lost.

their name you blotted out for all time.[b]
7 The enemies have been ruined forever;
you destroyed their cities;
their memory has perished.

III
8 The LORD rules forever,
has set up a throne for judgment.
9 It is God who governs the world with justice,[c]
who judges the peoples with fairness.
10 The LORD is a stronghold for the oppressed,
a stronghold in times of trouble.[d]
11 Those who honor your name trust in you;
you never forsake those who seek you, LORD.

IV
12 Sing hymns to the LORD enthroned on Zion;
proclaim God's deeds among the nations!
13 For the avenger of bloodshed remembers,
does not forget the cry of the afflicted.[e]

V
14 Have mercy on me, LORD;
see how my foes afflict me!
You alone can raise me from the gates of death.[f]
15 Then I will declare all your praises,
sing joyously of your salvation
in the gates of daughter Zion.*

VI
16 The nations fall into the pit they dig;
in the snare they hide, their own foot is caught.
17 The LORD is revealed in this divine rule:*
by the deeds they do the wicked are trapped.[g] *Higgaion. Selah*

VII
18 To Sheol the wicked will depart,
all the nations that forget God.
19 The needy will never be forgotten,
nor will the hope of the afflicted ever fade.[h]
20 Arise, LORD, let no mortal prevail;
let the nations be judged in your presence.
21 Strike them with terror, LORD;
show the nations they are mere mortals.
*Selah*

## B

I
1 Why, LORD, do you stand at a distance
and pay no heed to these troubled times?
2 Arrogant scoundrels pursue the poor;
they trap them by their cunning schemes.[i]

II
3 The wicked even boast of their greed;
these robbers curse and scorn the LORD.[j]
4 In their insolence the wicked boast:
"God doesn't care, doesn't even exist."[k]
5 Yet their affairs always succeed;
they ignore your judgment on high;
they sneer at all who oppose them.
6 They say in their hearts, "We will never fall;
never will we see misfortune."
7 Their mouths are full of oaths, violence, and lies;
discord and evil are under their tongues.[l]
8 They wait in ambush near towns;
their eyes watch for the helpless,
to murder the innocent in secret.[m]
9 They lurk in ambush like lions in a thicket,
hide there to trap the poor,
snare them and close the net.[n]
10 The helpless are crushed, laid low;
they fall into the power of the wicked,
11 Who say in their hearts, "God pays no attention,
shows no concern, never bothers to look."[o]

III
12 Rise up, LORD God! Raise your arm!
Do not forget the poor!
13 Why should the wicked scorn God,
say in their hearts, "God doesn't care"?
14 But you do see;
you do observe this misery and sorrow;[p]
you take the matter in hand.
To you the helpless can entrust their cause;
you are the defender of orphans.[q]
15 Break the arms of the wicked and depraved;
make them account for their crimes;
let none of them survive.

IV
16 The LORD is king forever;[r]
the nations have vanished from God's land.
17 You listen, LORD, to the needs of the poor;
you encourage them and hear their prayers.
18 You win justice for the orphaned and oppressed;[s]
no one on earth will cause terror again.

b Jb 18,17.
c Pss 96,10; 98,9.
d Ps 37,39; Is 25,4.
e Jb 16,18.
f Wis 16,13.
g Sir 27,26.
h Prv 23,18.
i Is 32,7.
j Ps 36,2.
k Ps 14,1; Jb 22,13; Is 29,15; Jer 5,12; Zep 1,12.
l Is 32,7; Rom 3,14.
m Ps 11,2; Jb 24,14.
n Ps 17,12; Prv 1,11; Jer 5,26.
o Pss 44,25; 64,6; 73,11; 94,7; Ez 9,9.
p Pss 31,8; 56,9; 2 Kgs 20,5; Is 25,8; Rv 7,17.
q Ex 22,21-22.
r Ps 145,13; Jer 10,10.
s Dt 10,18.

* 9, 15: *Daughter Zion*: an ancient Near Eastern city could sometimes be personified as a woman or a queen, the spouse of the god of the city.

9, 17: *The Lord is revealed in this divine rule*: God has so made the universe that the wicked are punished by the very actions they perform.

## PSALM 11*

### Confidence in the Presence of God

1 *For the leader. Of David.*

I
In the LORD I take refuge;
how can you say to me,
"Flee like a bird to the mountains![t]
2 See how the wicked string their bows,
fit their arrows to the string
to shoot from the shadows at the upright.[u]
3 When foundations* are being destroyed,
what can the upright do?"

II
4 The LORD is in his holy temple;
the LORD's throne is in heaven.[v]
God's eyes keep careful watch;
they test all peoples.
5 The LORD tests the good and the bad,
hates those who love violence,
6 And rains upon the wicked
fiery coals and brimstone,
a scorching wind their allotted cup.[w]*
7 The LORD is just and loves just deeds;
the upright shall see his face.

## PSALM 12*

### Prayer against Evil Tongues

1 *For the leader; "upon the eighth." A psalm of David.*

I
2 Help, LORD, for no one loyal remains;
the faithful have vanished from the human race.[x]
3 Those who tell lies to one another
speak with deceiving lips and a double heart.[y]

II
4 May the LORD cut off all deceiving lips,
and every boastful tongue,
5 Those who say, "By our tongues we prevail;
when our lips speak, who can lord it over us?"[z]

III
6 "Because they rob the weak, and the needy groan,
I will now arise," says the LORD;
"I will grant safety to whoever longs for it."[a]

IV
7 The promises of the LORD are sure,
silver refined in a crucible,*
silver purified seven times.[b]
8 LORD, protect us always;
preserve us from this generation.
9 On every side the wicked strut;
the shameless are extolled by all.

## PSALM 13*

### Prayer in Time of Illness

1 *For the leader. A psalm of David.*

I
2 How long, LORD? Will you utterly forget me?
How long will you hide your face from me?[c]
3 How long must I carry sorrow in my soul,
grief in my heart day after day?
How long will my enemy triumph over me?

II
4 Look upon me, answer me, LORD, my God!
Give light to my eyes lest I sleep in death,
5 Lest my enemy say, "I have prevailed,"
lest my foes rejoice at my downfall.[d]

III
6 I trust in your faithfulness.
Grant my heart joy in your help,
That I may sing of the LORD,
"How good our God has been to me!"[e]

t Pss 55,7; 91,4.
u Pss 7,13; 37,14; 57,5; 64,4.
v Pss 14,2; 102,20; Hb 2,20; Dt 26,15; Is 66, 1; Mt 5,34.
w Pss 120,4; 140,11; Prv 16,27; Ez 38,22; Rv 8,5; 20,10.
x Pss 14,3; 116,11; Is 59,15; Mi 7,2.
y Pss 28,3; 55,22; Is 59,3-4; Jer 9,7.
z Sir 5,3.
a Is 33,10.
b Pss 18,31; 19,8; Prv 30,5.
c Pss 6,4; 44,25; 77,8; 79,5; 89,47; 94,3; Lam 5,20.
d Ps 38,17.
e Ps 116,7.

*

Ps 11: A song of trust. Though friends counsel flight to the mountain country (a traditional hideout) to escape trouble (1–3), the innocent psalmist reaffirms confidence in God, who protects those who seek asylum in the temple (4–7).

11, 3: *Foundations*: usually understood of public order. Cf Ps 82, 5.

11, 6: *Their allotted cup*: the cup that God gives people to drink is a common figure for their destiny. Cf Pss 16, 5; 75, 9; Mt 20, 22; 26, 39; Rv 14, 10.

Ps 12: A lament. The psalmist, thrown into a world where lying and violent people persecute the just (2–3), prays that the wicked be punished (4–5). The prayer is not simply for vengeance but arises from a desire to see God's justice appear on earth. V 6 preserves the word of assurance spoken by the priest to the lamenter; it is not usually transmitted in such psalms. In vv 7–9 the psalmist affirms the intention to live by the word of assurance.

12, 7: *A crucible*: literally "in a crucible in the ground." The crucible was placed in the ground for support.

Ps 13: A lament in which the psalmist, seriously ill (4), expresses fear that enemies will interpret his or her death as a divine judgment. Hence the heartfelt prayer (2–3) is for healing that will signal to those enemies that the psalmist enjoys God's favor (4–5). The poem ends with a confession of trust in God and a statement of praise (6).

## PSALM 14*

### A Lament over Widespread Corruption

1 *For the leader. Of David.*

I
Fools* say in their hearts,
"There is no God."[f]
Their deeds are loathsome and corrupt;
not one does what is right.
2 The LORD looks down from heaven
upon the human race,[g]
To see if even one is wise,[h]
if even one seeks God.
3 All have gone astray;
all alike are perverse.
Not one does what is right,
not even one.[i]

II
4 Will these evildoers never learn?
They devour my people as they devour bread;[j]
they do not call upon the LORD.[k]
5 They have good reason, then, to fear;
God is with the company of the just.
6 They would crush the hopes of the poor,
but the poor have the LORD as their refuge.

III
7 Oh, that from Zion might come
the deliverance of Israel,
That Jacob may rejoice, and Israel be glad
when the LORD restores his people![l]*

## PSALM 15*

### The Righteous Israelite

1 *A psalm of David.*

I
LORD, who may abide in your tent?
Who may dwell on your holy mountain?[m]*

II
2 Whoever walks without blame,[n]
doing what is right,
speaking truth from the heart;
3 Who does not slander a neighbor,
does no harm to another,
never defames a friend;
4 Who disdains the wicked,
but honors those who fear the LORD;
Who keeps an oath despite the cost,
5 lends no money at interest,*
accepts no bribe against the innocent.[o]

III
Whoever acts like this
shall never be shaken.

## PSALM 16*

### God the Supreme Good

1 A miktam* *of David.*

I
Keep me safe, O God;
in you I take refuge.[p]
2 I say to the LORD,
you are my Lord,
you are my only good.
3 Worthless are all the false gods of the land.
Accursed are all who delight in them.
4 They multiply their sorrows
who court other gods.
Blood libations to them I will not pour out,
nor will I take their names* upon my lips.
5 LORD, my allotted portion and my cup,
you have made my destiny secure.[q]
6 Pleasant places were measured out for me;*
fair to me indeed is my inheritance.

II
7 I bless the LORD who counsels me;
even at night my heart exhorts me.

---

f Pss 10,4; 36,2; Is 32, 6; Jer 5,12.
g Pss 11,4; 102,20.
h 2b-3: Rom 3,11-12.
i Ps 12,1.
j Ps 27,2; Is 9,11.
k Ps 79,6.
l Ps 85,2.
m Is 56,7.
n Ps 119,1.
o Ex 22,24; 23,8.
p Ps 25,20.
q Pss 23,5; 73,26; Nm 18,20; Lam 3,24.

---

Ps 14: The lament (duplicated in Ps 53) depicts the world as consisting of two types of people: "the fools" (= the wicked, 1–3) and "the company of the just" (4–6; also called "my people," and "the poor"). The wicked persecute the just, but the psalm expresses the hope that God will punish the wicked and reward the good.

14, 1: *Fools*: literally, "the fool." The singular is used typically, hence the plural translation.

14, 7: *Israel . . . Jacob . . . his people*: the righteous poor are identified with God's people.

Ps 15: The psalm records a liturgical scrutiny at the entrance to the temple court (cf Ps 24, 3–6; Is 33, 14b–16). The Israelite wishing to be admitted had to ask the temple official what conduct was appropriate to God's precincts. Note the emphasis on virtues relating to one's neighbor.

15, 1: *Your tent . . . your holy mountain*: the temple could be referred to as "tent" (Ps 61, 5; Is 33, 20), a reference to the tent of the wilderness period and the tent of David (2 Sm 6, 17; 7, 2), predecessors of the temple. *Holy mountain*: a venerable designation of the divine abode (Pss 2, 6; 3, 5; 43, 3; 48, 2, etc.).

15, 5: *Lends no money at interest*: lending money in the Old Testament was often seen as assistance to the poor in their distress, not as an investment; making money off the poor by charging interest was thus forbidden (Ex 22, 24; Lv 25, 36–37; Dt 23, 20).

Ps 16: In the first section, the psalmist rejects the futile worship of false gods (2–5), preferring Israel's God (1), the giver of the land (6). The second section reflects on the wise and life-giving presence of God (7–11).

16, 1: *Miktam*: a term occurring six times in psalm0al superscriptions, always with "David." Its meaning is unknown.

16, 4: *Take their names*: to use the gods' names in oaths and hence to affirm them as one's own gods.

16, 6: *Pleasant places were measured out for me*: the psalmist is pleased with the plot of land measured out to the family, which was to be passed on to succeeding generations ("my inheritance").

8 I keep the LORD always before me;
with the Lord at my right, I shall never be shaken.[r]
9 Therefore my heart is glad, my soul rejoices;
my body also dwells secure,
10 For you will not abandon me to Sheol,
nor let your faithful servant see the pit.[s]*
11 You will show me the path to life,
abounding joy in your presence,
the delights at your right hand forever.

## PSALM 17*

## Prayer for Rescue from Persecutors

1 *A prayer of David.*

I
Hear, LORD, my plea for justice;
pay heed to my cry;
Listen to my prayer
spoken without guile.
2 From you let my vindication come;
your eyes see what is right.
3 You have tested my heart,
searched it in the night.[t]
You have tried me by fire,
but find no malice in me.
My mouth has not transgressed
4 as humans always do.
As your lips have instructed me,
I have kept the way of the law.
5 My steps have kept to your paths;
my feet have not faltered.[u]

II
6 I call upon you; answer me, O God.
Turn your ear to me; hear my prayer.
7 Show your wonderful love,
you who deliver with your right arm
those who seek refuge from their foes.
8 Keep me as the apple of your eye;
hide me in the shadow of your wings*
9 from the violence of the wicked.[v]

III
My ravenous enemies press upon me;[w]
10 *they close their hearts,
they fill their mouths with proud roaring.
11 Their steps even now encircle me;
they watch closely, keeping low to the ground,
12 Like lions eager for prey,
like young lions lurking in ambush.
13 Rise, O LORD, confront and cast them down;
rescue me so from the wicked.
14 Slay them with your sword;
with your hand, LORD, slay them;
snatch them from the world in their prime.
Their bellies are being filled with your friends;
their children are satisfied too,
for they share what is left with their young.
15 I am just—let me see your face;
when I awake,* let me be filled with your presence.[x]

## PSALM 18*

## A King's Thanksgiving for Victory

1 *For the leader. Of David, the servant of the LORD, who sang to the LORD the words of this song after the LORD had rescued him from the clutches of all his enemies and from the hand of Saul.* 2 *He said:*

I
I love you, LORD, my strength,
3 LORD, my rock, my fortress, my deliverer,[y]
My God, my rock of refuge,
my shield, my saving horn,* my stronghold![z]
4 Praised be the LORD, I exclaim!
I have been delivered from my enemies.

II
5 The breakers of death surged round about me;
the menacing floods terrified me.

---

r Pss 73,23; 121,5. 8-12; Acts 2,25-28.
s Pss 28,1; 30,4; 49,16; 86,13; Jon 2,7; Acts 13,35.
t Pss 26,2; 139,23.
u Ps 18,36; Jb 23, 11-12.
v Pss 36,8; 57,2; 61,5; 63,8; 91,4; Dt 32,10; Ru 2,12; Zec 2,12; Mt 23,37.
w 9b-12: Pss 10,9; 22, 14. 22; 35,17; 58,7; Jb 4,10-11.
x Pss 4,7; 31,17; 67,2; 80,4; Nm 6,25; Dn 9, 17.
y 2-51: 2 Sm 22,2-51.
z Pss 3,4; 31,3-4; 42, 10; Gn 49,24; Dt 32, 4.

---

16, 10: *Nor let your faithful servant see the pit*: Hebrew *shahath* means here the pit, a synonym for Sheol, the underworld. The Greek translation derives the word here and elsewhere from the verb *shahath*, "to be corrupt." On the basis of the Greek, Acts 2, 25–32 and 13, 35–37 apply the verse to Christ's resurrection, "Nor will you suffer your holy one to see corruption."

Ps 17: A lament of an individual unjustly attacked who has taken refuge in the temple. Confident of being found innocent, the psalmist cries out for God's just judgment (1–5) and requests divine help against enemies (6–9a). Those ravenous lions (9b–12) should be punished (13–14). The psalm ends with a serene statement of praise (15). The Hebrew text of vv 3–4 and 14 is uncertain.

17, 8: *Apple of your eye . . . shadow of your wings*: images of God's special care. Cf Dt 32, 10; Prv 7, 2; Is 49, 2.

17, 10–12. 14: An extended metaphor: the enemies are lions.

17, 15: *When I awake*: probably the psalmist has spent the night in the sanctuary (cf 3) and hopes to wake to an oracle assuring God's protective presence.

Ps 18: A royal thanksgiving for a military victory, duplicated in 2 Sm 22. Thanksgiving psalms are in essence reports of divine rescue. The psalm has two parallel reports of rescue, the first told from a heavenly perspective (5–20), and the second from an earthly perspective (36–46). The first report adapts old mythic language of a cosmic battle between sea and rainstorm in order to depict God's rescue of the Israelite king from his enemies. Each report has a short hymnic introduction (2–4. 32–35) and conclusion (21–31. 47–51).

18, 3: *My saving horn*: my strong savior. The horn referred to is the weapon of a bull and the symbol of fertility. Cf 1 Sm 2, 10; Ps 132, 17; Lk 1, 69.

6 The cords* of Sheol tightened;
the snares of death lay in wait for me.[a]
7 In my distress I called out: LORD!
I cried out to my God.[b]
From his temple* he heard my voice;
my cry to him reached his ears.
8 *The earth rocked and shook;
the foundations of the mountains
trembled;
they shook as his wrath flared up.[c]
9 Smoke rose in his nostrils,
a devouring fire poured from his mouth;
it kindled coals into flame.
10 He parted the heavens and came down,
a dark cloud under his feet.[d]
11 Mounted on a cherub* he flew,
borne along on the wings of the wind.
12 He made darkness the cover about him;
his canopy, heavy thunderheads.
13 Before him scudded his clouds,
hail and lightning too.[e]
14 The LORD thundered from heaven;
the Most High made his voice resound.[f]
15 He let fly his arrows* and scattered them;
shot his lightning bolts and dispersed
them.[g]
16 Then the bed of the sea appeared;
the world's foundations lay bare,[h]
At the roar of the LORD,
at the storming breath of his nostrils.
17 He reached down from on high and seized
me;
drew me out of the deep waters.[i]
18 He rescued me from my mighty enemy,
from foes too powerful for me.
19 They attacked me on a day of distress,
but the LORD came to my support.
20 He set me free in the open;
he rescued me because he loves me.

III

21 The LORD acknowledged my righteousness,
rewarded my clean hands.[j]
22 For I kept the ways of the LORD;
I was not disloyal to my God.
23 His laws were all before me,
his decrees I did not cast aside.
24 I was honest toward him;
I was on guard against sin.
25 So the LORD rewarded my righteousness,
the cleanness of my hands in his sight.
26 Toward the faithful you are faithful;
to the honest you are honest;[k]
27 Toward the sincere, sincere;
but to the perverse you are devious.
28 Humble people you save;
haughty eyes you bring low.[l]
29 You, LORD, give light to my lamp;
my God brightens the darkness about
me.[m]
30 With you I can rush an armed band,
with my God to help I can leap a wall.
31 God's way is unerring;
the LORD's promise is tried and true;
he is a shield for all who trust in him.[n]

IV

32 Truly, who is God except the LORD?
Who but our God is the rock?[o]
33 This God who girded me with might,
kept my way unerring,
34 Who made my feet swift as a deer's,
set me safe on the heights,[p]
35 Who trained my hands for war,
my arms to bend even a bow of bronze.[q]*

V

36 You have given me your protecting shield;
your right hand has upheld me;
you stooped to make me great.
37 You gave me room to stride;
my feet never stumbled.[r]
38 I pursued my enemies and overtook them;
I did not turn back till I destroyed them.
39 I struck them down; they could not rise;
they fell dead at my feet.
40 You girded me with strength for war,
subdued adversaries at my feet.
41 My foes you put to flight before me;
those who hated me I destroyed.
42 They cried for help, but no one saved them;
cried to the LORD but got no answer.
43 I ground them fine as dust in the wind;
like mud in the streets I trampled them
down.
44 You rescued me from the strife of peoples;
you made me head over nations.
A people I had not known became my
slaves;
45 as soon as they heard of me they obeyed.
Foreigners cringed before me;
46 their courage failed;
they came trembling from their
fortresses.[s]

---

a Pss 88,8; 93,3-4; 116, 3-4.
b Jon 2,3.
c Pss 97,3-4; 99,1; Jgs 5,4-5; Is 64,1; Hab 3, 9-11.
d Pss 104,3; 144,5; Is 63,19.
e Ex 13,21; 19,16.
f Pss 29; 77,19; Ex 19, 19; Jb 37,3-4.
g Ps 144,6; Wis 5,21.
h Ps 77,17; Zec 9,14.
i Ps 144,7.
j Ps 26; 1 Sm 26,23.
k Ps 125,4.
l Jb 22,29; Prv 3,34.
m Pss 27,1; 36,10; 43,3; 119,105; Jb 29,3; Mi 7,8.
n Pss 12,6; 77,13; Prv 30,5.
o Is 44,8; 45,21.
p Hb 3,19.
q Ps 144,1.
r Ps 17,5.
s Mi 7,17.

---

18, 6: *Cords*: hunting imagery, the cords of a snare.

18, 7: *His temple*: his heavenly abode.

18, 8–16: God appears in the storm, which in Palestine comes from the west. The introduction to the theophany (vv 8–9) is probably a description of a violent, hot, and dry east-wind storm. In the fall transition period from the rainless summer to the rainy winter such storms regularly precede the rains. Cf Ex 14, 21–22.

18, 11: *Cherub*: a winged creature, derived from myth, in the service of the deity (Gn 3, 24; Ex 25, 18–20; 37, 6–9). Cherubim were the throne bearers of the deity (Pss 80, 2; 99, 1; 1 Kgs 6, 23–28; 8, 6–8).

18, 15: *Arrows*: lightning.

18, 35: *Bow of bronze*: hyperbole for a bow difficult to bend and therefore capable of propelling an arrow with great force.

VI
47 The LORD lives! Blessed be my rock![t]
Exalted be God, my savior!
48 O God who granted me vindication,
made peoples subject to me,[u]
49 and preserved me from my enemies,
Truly you have exalted me above my adversaries,
from the violent you have rescued me.
50 Thus I will proclaim you, LORD, among the nations;
I will sing the praises of your name.[v]
51 You have given great victories to your king,
and shown kindness to your anointed,
to David and his posterity forever.[w]

## PSALM 19*

## God's Glory in the Heavens and in the Law

1 *For the leader. A psalm of David.*

I
2 The heavens declare the glory of God;
the sky proclaims its builder's craft.[x]
3 One day to the next conveys that message;
one night to the next imparts that knowledge.
4 There is no word or sound;*
no voice is heard;
5 Yet their report goes forth through all the earth,
their message, to the ends of the world.
God has pitched there a tent for the sun;*
6 it comes forth like a bridegroom from his chamber,
and like an athlete joyfully runs its course.
7 From one end of the heavens it comes forth;
its course runs through to the other;
nothing escapes its heat.

II
8 The law of the LORD is perfect,
refreshing the soul.
The decree of the LORD is trustworthy,
giving wisdom to the simple.[y]
9 The precepts of the LORD are right,
rejoicing the heart.
The command of the LORD is clear,
enlightening the eye.
10 The fear of the LORD is pure,
enduring forever.
The statutes of the LORD are true,
all of them just;
11 More desirable than gold,
than a hoard of purest gold,
Sweeter also than honey
or drippings from the comb.[z]
12 By them your servant is instructed;*
obeying them brings much reward.

III
13 Who can detect heedless failings?
Cleanse me from my unknown faults.
14 But from willful sins keep your servant;
let them never control me.
Then shall I be blameless,
innocent of grave sin.
15 Let the words of my mouth meet with your favor,
keep the thoughts of my heart before you,
LORD, my rock and my redeemer.

## PSALM 20*

## Prayer for the King in Time of War

1 *For the leader. A psalm of David.*

I
2 The LORD answer you in time of distress;
the name of the God of Jacob defend you!
3 May God send you help from the temple,
from Zion be your support.[a]
4 May God remember* your every offering,
graciously accept your holocaust, *Selah*
5 Grant what is in your heart,
fulfill your every plan.
6 May we shout for joy at your victory,*
raise the banners in the name of our God.
The LORD grant your every prayer!

II
7 Now I know victory is given
to the anointed of the LORD.[b]

t Ps 144,1.
u Ps 144,2.
v Pss 7,18; 30,5; 57,9; 135,3; 146,2; Rom 15, 9.
w Pss 89,28-37; 144,10; 1 Sm 2,10.
x Pss 8,1; 50,6; 97,6.
y Pss 12,7; 119.
z Sir 24,19.
a Pss 128,5; 134,3.
b Pss 18,51; 144,10; 1 Sm 2,10.

*

Ps 19: The heavenly elements of the world, now beautifully arranged, bespeak the power and wisdom of their creator (2–7). The creator's wisdom is available to human beings in the law (8–11), toward which the psalmist prays to be open (12–15). The themes of light and speech unify the poem.

19, 4: *No word or sound*: the regular functioning of the heavens and the alternation of day and night inform humans without words of the creator's power and wisdom.

19, 5: *The sun*: in other religious literature the sun is a judge and lawgiver since it sees all in its daily course; 5b–7 form a transition to the law in 8–11. The six synonyms for God's revelation (8–11) are applied to the sun in comparable literature.

19, 12: *Instructed*: the Hebrew verb means both to shine and to teach. Cf Dn 12, 3.

Ps 20: The people pray for the king before battle. The people ask for divine help (2–6) and express confidence that such help will be given (7–10). A solemn assurance of divine help may well have been given between the two sections in the liturgy, something like the promises of Pss 12, 6 and 21, 9–13. The final verse (10) echoes the opening verse.

20, 4: *Remember*: God's remembering implies readiness to act. Cf Gn 8, 1; Ex 2, 24.

20, 6: *Victory*: the Hebrew root is often translated "salvation," "to save," but in military contexts it can have the specific meaning of "victory."

God will answer him from the holy heavens
with a strong arm that brings victory.
8 Some rely on chariots, others on horses,
but we on the name of the LORD our God.[c]
9 They collapse and fall,
but we stand strong and firm.[d]
10 LORD, grant victory to the king;
answer when we call upon you.

## PSALM 21*

## Thanksgiving and Assurances for the King

1 *For the leader. A psalm of David.*

I

2 LORD, the king finds joy in your power;[e]
in your victory how greatly he rejoices!
3 You have granted him his heart's desire;
you did not refuse the prayer of his lips.
*Selah*
4 For you welcomed him with goodly blessings;
you placed on his head a crown of pure gold.
5 He asked life of you;
you gave it to him,
length of days forever.[f]
6 Great is his glory in your victory;
majesty and splendor you confer upon him.
7 You make him the pattern of blessings forever,
you gladden him with the joy of your presence.
8 For the king trusts in the LORD,
stands firm through the love of the Most High.

II

9 Your hand will reach all your enemies;
your right hand will reach your foes!
10 At the time of your coming
you will drive them into a furnace.
Then the LORD's anger will consume them,
devour them with fire.
11 Even their descendants you will wipe out from the earth,
their offspring from the human race.
12 Though they intend evil against you,
devising plots, they will not succeed,
13 For you will put them to flight;
you will aim at them with your bow.

III

14 Arise, LORD, in your power![g]
We will sing and chant the praise of your might.

## PSALM 22*

## The Prayer of an Innocent Person

1 *For the leader; according to "The deer of the dawn."* A psalm of David.*

I

2 My God, my God, why have you abandoned me?
Why so far from my call for help,
from my cries of anguish?[h]
3 My God, I call by day, but you do not answer;
by night, but I have no relief.[i]
4 Yet you are enthroned as the Holy One;
you are the glory of Israel.[j]
5 In you our ancestors trusted;
they trusted and you rescued them.
6 To you they cried out and they escaped;
in you they trusted and were not disappointed.[k]
7 But I am a worm, hardly human,*
scorned by everyone, despised by the people.[l]
8 All who see me mock me;
they curl their lips and jeer;
they shake their heads at me:[m]
9 "You relied on the LORD—let him deliver you;
if he loves you, let him rescue you."[n]
10 Yet you drew me forth from the womb,
made me safe at my mother's breast.
11 Upon you I was thrust from the womb;
since birth you are my God.[o]
12 Do not stay far from me,
for trouble is near,

c Ps 147,10-11; 2 Chr 14,10; Prv 21,31; 1 Sm 17,45; Is 31,1; 36,9.
d Is 40,30.
e Ps 63,12.
f 1 Kgs 3,14.
g Nm 10,35.
h Is 49,14; 54,7; Mt 27, 46; Mk 15,34.
i Sir 2,10.
j Is 6,3.
k Ps 25,3; Is 49,23; Dn 3,40.
l Is 53,3.
m Ps 109,25; Mt 27,39; Mk 15,29; Lk 23,35.
n Ps 71,11; Wis 2, 18-20; Mt 27,43.
o Ps 71,6; Is 44,2; 46,3.

*

Ps 21: The first part of this royal psalm is a thanksgiving (2–8), and the second is a promise that the king will triumph over his enemies (9–14). The king's confident prayer (3. 5) and trust in God (8) enable him to receive the divine gifts of vitality, peace, and military success. V 14 reprises v 1. When kings ceased in Israel after the sixth century B.C., the psalm was sung of a future Davidic king.

Ps 22: A lament unusual in structure and in intensity of feeling. The psalmist's present distress is contrasted with God's past mercy in vv 2–12. In vv 13–22 enemies surround the psalmist. The last third is an invitation to praise God (23–27), becoming a universal chorus of praise (28–32). The psalm is important in the New Testament. Its opening words occur on the lips of the crucified Jesus (Mk 15, 34; Mt 27, 46), and several other verses are quoted, or at least alluded to, in the accounts of Jesus' passion (Mt 27, 35. 43; Jn 19, 24).

22, 1: *The deer of the dawn*: apparently the title of the melody.

22, 7: *I am a worm, hardly human*: the psalmist's sense of isolation and dehumanization, an important motif of Ps 22, is vividly portrayed here.

and there is no one to help.[p]

II

13 Many bulls* surround me;
fierce bulls of Bashan encircle me.
14 They open their mouths against me,
lions that rend and roar.[q]
15 Like water my life drains away;
all my bones grow soft.
My heart has become like wax,
it melts away within me.
16 As dry as a potsherd is my throat;
my tongue sticks to my palate;
you lay me in the dust of death.*
17 Many dogs surround me;
a pack of evildoers closes in on me.
So wasted are my hands and feet
18 that I can count all my bones.[r]
They stare at me and gloat;
19 they divide my garments among them;
for my clothing they cast lots.[s]
20 But you, LORD, do not stay far off;
my strength, come quickly to help me.
21 Deliver me from the sword,
my forlorn life from the teeth of the dog.
22 Save me from the lion's mouth,
my poor life from the horns of wild
bulls.[t]

III

23 Then I will proclaim your name to the
assembly;
in the community I will praise you:[u]*
24 "You who fear the LORD, give praise!
All descendants of Jacob, give honor;
show reverence, all descendants of Israel!
25 For God has not spurned or disdained
the misery of this poor wretch,
Did not turn away* from me,
but heard me when I cried out.
26 I will offer praise in the great assembly;
my vows I will fulfill before those who
fear him.
27 The poor* will eat their fill;
those who seek the LORD will offer praise.
May your hearts enjoy life forever!"[v]

IV

28 All the ends of the earth
will worship and turn to the LORD;
All the families of nations
will bow low before you.[w]
29 For kingship belongs to the LORD,
the ruler over the nations.[x]
30 *All who sleep in the earth
will bow low before God;
All who have gone down into the dust
will kneel in homage.
31 And I will live for the LORD;
my descendants will serve you.
32 The generation to come will be told of the
Lord,
that they may proclaim to a people yet
unborn
the deliverance you have brought.[y]

# PSALM 23*

## The Lord, Shepherd and Host

1 *A psalm of David.*

I

The LORD is my shepherd;*
there is nothing I lack.[z]
2 In green pastures you let me graze;
to safe waters you lead me;
3 you restore my strength.
You guide me along the right path*
for the sake of your name.[a]
4 Even when I walk through a dark valley,[b]*
I fear no harm for you are at my side;
your rod and staff give me courage.

II

5 You set a table before me*
as my enemies watch;

p Pss 35,22; 38,22; 71,12.
q Ps 17,12; Jb 4,10; 1 Pt 5,8.
r Ps 109,24.
s Mt 27,35; Mk 15,24; Lk 23,34; Jn 19,24.
t Pss 7,2-3; 17,12; 35,17; 57,5; 58,7; 2 Tm 4,17.
u Pss 26,12; 35,18; 40,10; 109,30; 149,1; 2 Sm 22,50; Heb 2,12.
v Pss 23,5; 69,33.
w Ps 86,9; Tb 13,11; Is 45,22; 52,10; Zec 14,16.
x Ps 103,19; Ob 21; Zec 14,9.
y Pss 48,14-15; 71,18; 78,6; 102,19; Is 53,10.
z Pss 80,2; 95,7; 100,3; Dt 2,7.
a Prv 4,11.
b Jb 10,21-22; Is 50,10.

*

22, 13–14: *Bulls*: the enemies of the psalmist are also portrayed in less-than-human form, as wild animals (cf 17. 21–22). *Bashan*: a grazing land east of the Jordan, famed for its cattle. Cf Dt 32, 14; Ez 39, 18; Am 4, 1.

22, 16: *The dust of death*: the netherworld, the domain of the dead.

22, 23: *In the community I will praise you*: the person who offered a thanksgiving sacrifice in the temple recounted to the other worshipers the favor received from God and invited them to share in the sacrificial banquet. The final section (24–32) may be a summary or a citation of the psalmist's poem of praise.

22, 25: *Turn away*: literally, "hides his face from me," an important metaphor for God withdrawing from someone, e.g., Mi 3, 4; Is 8, 17; Pss 27, 9; 69, 18; 88, 15.

22, 27: *The poor*: originally the poor, who were dependent on God; the term (*'anawim*) came to include the religious sense of "humble, pious, devout."

22, 30: Hebrew unclear. The translation assumes that all on earth (28–29) and under the earth (30) will worship God.

Ps 23: God's loving care for the psalmist is portrayed under the figures of a shepherd for the flock (1–4) and a host's generosity toward a guest (5–6). The imagery of both sections is drawn from traditions of the exodus (Is 40, 11; 49, 10; Jer 31, 10).

23, 1: *My shepherd*: God as good shepherd is common in both the Old Testament and the New Testament (Ez 34, 11–16 and Jn 10, 11–18).

23, 3: *The right path*: connotes "right way" and "way of righteousness."

23, 4: *A dark valley*: a different division of the Hebrew consonants yields the translation "the valley of the shadow of death."

23, 5: *You set a table before me*: this expression occurs in an exodus context in Ps 78, 19. *As my enemies watch*: my enemies see that I am God's friend and guest.

23, 5: *Oil*: a perfumed ointment made from olive oil, used especially at banquets (Ps 104, 15; Mt 26, 7; Lk 7, 37. 46; Jn

You anoint my head with oil;[c]*
my cup overflows.[d]
6 Only goodness and love* will pursue me
all the days of my life;
I will dwell in the house of the LORD[e]
for years to come.

## PSALM 24*

## The Glory of God in Procession to Zion

1 *A psalm of David.*

I
The earth is the LORD's and all it holds,[f]
the world and those who live there.
2 For God founded it on the seas,
established it over the rivers.[g]

II
3 Who may go up the mountain of the LORD?[h]
Who can stand in his holy place?
4 *"The clean of hand and pure of heart,
who are not devoted to idols,
who have not sworn falsely.
5 They will receive blessings from the LORD,
and justice from their saving God.
6 Such are the people that love the LORD,
that seek the face of the God of Jacob."
*Selah*

III
7 Lift up your heads, O gates;
rise up, you ancient portals,*
that the king of glory may enter.
8 Who is this king of glory?
The LORD, a mighty warrior,
the LORD, mighty in battle.
9 Lift up your heads, O gates;
rise up, you ancient portals,
that the king of glory may enter.
10 Who is this king of glory?
The LORD of hosts is the king of glory.
*Selah*

## PSALM 25*

## Confident Prayer for Forgiveness and Guidance

1 *Of David.*

I
I wait for you, O LORD;
I lift up my soul
2 to my God.[j]
In you I trust; do not let me be disgraced;[k]
do not let my enemies gloat over me.
3 No one is disgraced who waits for you,[l]
but only those who lightly break faith.
4 Make known to me your ways, LORD;
teach me your paths.[m]
5 Guide me in your truth and teach me,
for you are God my savior.
For you I wait all the long day,
because of your goodness, LORD.*
6 Remember your compassion and love,
O LORD;
for they are ages old.[n]
7 Remember no more the sins of my youth;[o]
remember me only in light of your love.

II
8 Good and upright is the LORD,
who shows sinners the way,
9 Guides the humble rightly,
and teaches the humble the way.
10 All the paths of the LORD are faithful love
toward those who honor the covenant
demands.
11 For the sake of your name, LORD,
pardon my guilt, though it is great.
12 Who are those who fear the LORD?
God shows them the way to choose.[p]
13 They live well and prosper,
and their descendants inherit the land.[q]
14 The counsel of the LORD belongs to the
faithful;
the covenant instructs them.
15 My eyes are ever upon the LORD,
who frees my feet from the snare.[r]

III
16 Look upon me, have pity on me,
for I am alone and afflicted.[s]
17 Relieve the troubles of my heart;
bring me out of my distress.

c Ps 92,11.
d Ps 16,5.
e Ps 27,4.
f Pss 50,12; 89,12; Dt 10,14; 1 Cor 10,26.
g Ps 136,6; Is 42,5.
h Ps 15,1.
i Ps 118,19-20.
j Pss 86,4; 143,8.
k Ps 71,1.
l Ps 22,6; Is 49,23; Dn 3,40.
m Pss 27,11; 86,11; 119,12. 35; 143,8. 10.
n Sir 51,8.
o Jb 13,26; Is 64,8.
p Prv 19,23.
q Ps 37,9. 29.
r Pss 123,1. 2; 141,8.
s Pss 86,16; 119,132.

12, 2).

23, 6: *Goodness and love*: the blessings of God's covenant with Israel.

Ps 24: The psalm apparently accompanied a ceremony of the entry of God (invisibly enthroned upon the ark), followed by the people, into the temple. The temple commemorated the creation of the world (1–2). The people had to affirm their fidelity before being admitted into the sanctuary (3–6; cf Ps 15). A choir identifies the approaching God and invites the very temple gates to bow down in obeisance (7–10).

24, 4–5: Literally, "the one whose hands are clean." The singular is used for the entire class of worshipers, hence the plural translation.

24, 7. 9: *Lift up your heads, O gates . . . you ancient portals*: the literal meaning is impossible since the portcullis (a gate that moves up and down) was unknown in the ancient world. Extra-biblical parallels suggest a full personification of the circle of gate towers: they are like a council of elders, bowed down and anxious, awaiting the return of the army and the Great Warrior gone to battle.

Ps 25: A lament. Each verse begins with a successive letter of the Hebrew alphabet. Such acrostic psalms are often a series of statements only loosely connected. The psalmist mixes ardent pleas (1–2. 16–22) with expressions of confidence in God who forgives and guides.

25, 5: *Because of your goodness, LORD*: these words have been transposed from the end of 7 to preserve the pattern of two lines per letter of the Hebrew alphabet in the acrostic poem.

18 Put an end to my affliction and suffering;
take away all my sins.
19 See how many are my enemies,
see how fiercely they hate me.
20 Preserve my life and rescue me;
do not let me be disgraced, for I trust in
you.
21 Let honesty and virtue preserve me;
I wait for you, O LORD.
22 *Redeem Israel, God,
from all its distress!

## PSALM 26*

## Prayer of Innocence

1 *Of David.*

I
Grant me justice, LORD!
I have walked without blame.[t]
In the LORD I have trusted;
I have not faltered.
2 Test me, LORD, and try me;
search my heart and mind.[u]
3 Your love is before my eyes;
I walk guided by your faithfulness.[v]

II
4 I do not sit with deceivers,
nor with hypocrites do I mingle.
5 I hate the company of evildoers;
with the wicked I do not sit.
6 I will wash my hands* in innocence[w]
and walk round your altar, LORD,
7 Lifting my voice in thanks,
recounting all your wondrous deeds.
8 LORD, I love the house where you dwell,
the tenting-place of your glory.[x]

III
9 Do not take me away with sinners,
nor my life with the violent.[y]
10 Their hands carry out their schemes;
their right hands are full of bribes.
11 But I walk without blame;[z]
redeem me, be gracious to me![a]
12 My foot stands on level ground;*
in assemblies I will bless the LORD.[b]

## PSALM 27*

## Trust in God

1 *Of David*

### A

I
The LORD is my light and my salvation;[c]
whom do I fear?
The LORD is my life's refuge;
of whom am I afraid?
2 When evildoers come at me
to devour my flesh,[d]*
These my enemies and foes
themselves stumble and fall.
3 Though an army encamp against me,
my heart does not fear;
Though war be waged against me,
even then do I trust.

II
4 One thing I ask of the LORD;
this I seek:
To dwell in the LORD's house
all the days of my life,
To gaze on the LORD's beauty,
to visit his temple.[e]
5 For God will hide me in his shelter
in time of trouble,[f]
Will conceal me in the cover of his tent;
and set me high upon a rock.
6 Even now my head is held high
above my enemies on every side!
I will offer in his tent
sacrifices with shouts of joy;
I will sing and chant praise to the LORD.

### B

I
7 Hear my voice, LORD, when I call;
have mercy on me and answer me.
8 "Come," says my heart, "seek God's face";*
your face, LORD, do I seek![g]

t Ps 7,9.
u Pss 17,3; 139,23.
v Ps 86,11.
w Ps 73,13.
x Pss 29,9; 63,3; Ex 24, 16; 25,8.
y Ps 28,3.
z Ps 101,6.
a Ps 25,16.
b Pss 22,23; 35,18; 149,1.
c Pss 18,29; 36,10; 43, 3; Is 10,17; Mi 7,8.
d Ps 14,4.
e Pss 23,6; 61,5.
f Ps 31,21.
g Ps 24,6; Hos 5,15.

*

25, 22: A final verse beginning with the Hebrew letter *pe* is added to the normal 22-letter alphabet. Thus the letters *aleph, lamed,* and *pe* open the first, middle (v 11), and last lines of the psalm. Together, they spell *aleph*, the first letter of the alphabet.

Ps 26: Like a priest washing before approaching the altar (Ex 30, 17–21), the psalmist seeks God's protection upon entering the temple. 1–3, matched by 11–12, remind God of past integrity while asking for purification; 4–5, matched by 9–10, pray for inclusion among the just; 6–8, the center of the poem, express the joy in God at the heart of all ritual.

26, 6: *I will wash my hands*: the washing of hands was a liturgical act (Ex 30, 19. 21; 40, 31–32), symbolic of inner as well as outer cleanness. Cf Is 1, 16.

26, 12: *On level ground*: in safety, where there is no danger of tripping and falling. *In assemblies*: at the temple. Having walked around the altar, the symbol of God's presence, the psalmist blesses God.

Ps 27: Tradition has handed down the two sections of the psalm (1–6 and 7–14) as one psalm, though each part could be understood as complete in itself. Asserting boundless hope that God will bring rescue (1–3), the psalmist longs for the presence of God in the temple, protection from all enemies (4–6). In part B there is a clear shift in tone (7–12); the climax of the poem comes with "I believe" (13), echoing "I trust" (3).

27, 2: *To devour my flesh*: the psalmist's enemies are rapacious beasts (Pss 7, 3; 17, 12; 22, 14. 17).

27, 8: *Seek God's face* (literally: "to seek his face"): to commune with God in the temple. The idiom is derived from the practice of journeying to sacred places. Cf Hos 5, 15; 2 Sm 21, 1; Ps 24, 6.

9 Do not hide your face from me;
do not repel your servant in anger.
You are my help; do not cast me off;
do not forsake me, God my savior!
10 Even if my father and mother forsake me,
the LORD will take me in.[h]

II
11 LORD, show me your way;
lead me on a level path
because of my enemies.[i]
12 Do not abandon me to the will of my foes;
malicious and lying witnesses have risen
against me.
13 But I believe I shall enjoy the LORD's
goodness
in the land of the living.[j]*
14 Wait for the LORD, take courage;
be stouthearted, wait for the LORD!

## PSALM 28*

### Petition and Thanksgiving

1 *Of David.*

I
To you, LORD, I call;
my Rock, do not be deaf to me.[k]
If you fail to answer me,
I will join those who go down to the
pit.[l]*
2 Hear the sound of my pleading when I cry
to you,
lifting my hands toward your holy
place.[m]*
3 Do not drag me off with the wicked,
with those who do wrong,[n]
Who speak peace to their neighbors
though evil is in their hearts.[o]
4 Repay them for their deeds,
for the evil that they do.
For the work of their hands repay them;
give them what they deserve.[p]
5 They pay no heed to the LORD's works,
to the deeds of God's hands.[q]
God will tear them down,
never to be rebuilt.

II
6 *Blessed be the LORD,
who has heard the sound of my pleading.
7 The LORD is my strength and my shield,
in whom my heart trusted and found help.
So my heart rejoices;
with my song I praise my God.

III
8 LORD, you are the strength of your people,
the saving refuge of your anointed king.*
9 Save your people, bless your inheritance;
feed and sustain them forever!

## PSALM 29*

### The Lord of Majesty Acclaimed as King of the World

1 *A psalm of David.*

I
Give to the LORD, you heavenly beings,*
give to the LORD glory and might;
2 Give to the LORD the glory due God's name.
Bow down before the LORD's holy
splendor![r]

II
3 The voice of the LORD* is over the waters;
the God of glory thunders,
the LORD, over the mighty waters.
4 The voice of the LORD is power;
the voice of the LORD is splendor.[s]
5 The voice of the LORD cracks the cedars;
the LORD splinters the cedars of Lebanon,
6 Makes Lebanon leap like a calf,
and Sirion* like a young bull.

---

h Is 49,15.
i Pss 25,4; 86,11.
j Ps 116,9; Is 38,11.
k Ps 18,2.
l Pss 30,4; 88,5; 143,7; Prv 1,12.
m Ps 134,2.
n Ps 26,9.
o Pss 12,2; 55,22; 62,5; Prv 26,24-28.
p 2 Sm 3,39.
q Is 5,12.
r Pss 68,35; 96,7-9.
s Pss 46,7; 77,18-19; Jb 37,4; Is 30,30.

---

27, 13: *In the land of the living*: or "in the land of life," an epithet of the Jerusalem temple (Pss 52, 7; 116, 9; Is 38, 11), where the faithful had access to the life-giving presence of God.

Ps 28: A lament asking that the psalmist, who has taken refuge in the temple (2), not be punished with the wicked, who are headed inevitably toward destruction (1. 3–5). The statement of praise is exceptionally lengthy and vigorous (6–7). The psalm ends with a prayer (8–9).

28, 1: *The pit*: a synonym for Sheol, the shadowy place of the dead.

28, 2: *Your holy place*: the innermost part of the temple, the holy of holies, containing the ark. Cf 1 Kgs 6, 16. 19–23; 8, 6–8.

28, 6: The psalmist shifts to fervent thanksgiving, probably responding to a priestly or prophetic oracle in 5cd (not usually transmitted) assuring the worshiper that the prayer has been heard.

28, 8: *Your people ... your anointed king*: salvation is more than individual, affecting all the people and their God-given leader.

Ps 29: The hymn invites the members of the heavenly court to acknowledge God's supremacy by ascribing glory and might to God alone (1–2a. 9b). Divine glory and might are dramatically visible in the storm (3–9a). The storm apparently comes from the Mediterranean onto the coast of Syria-Palestine and then moves inland. In 10 the divine beings acclaim God's eternal kingship. The psalm concludes with a prayer that God will impart the power just displayed to the Israelite king and through the king to Israel.

29, 1: *You heavenly beings*: literally "sons of God," i.e., members of the heavenly court who served Israel's God in a variety of capacities.

29, 3: *The voice of the LORD*: the sevenfold repetition of the phrase imitates the sound of crashing thunder and may allude to God's primordial slaying of Leviathan, the seven-headed sea monster of Canaanite mythology.

29, 6: *Sirion*: the Phoenician name for Mount Hermon. Cf Dt 3, 9.

7 The voice of the LORD strikes with fiery flame;
8 the voice of the LORD rocks the desert;
the LORD rocks the desert of Kadesh.*
9 *The voice of the LORD twists the oaks
and strips the forests bare.
All in his palace say, "Glory!"

III
10 The LORD sits enthroned above the flood![t]*
The LORD reigns as king forever!
11 May the LORD give might to his people;*
may the LORD bless his people with peace![u]

## PSALM 30*

## Thanksgiving for Deliverance

1 *A psalm. A song for the dedication of the temple.* Of David.*

I
2 I praise you, LORD, for you raised me up
and did not let my enemies rejoice over me.
3 O LORD, my God,
I cried out to you and you healed* me.
4 LORD, you brought me up from Sheol;
you kept me from going down to the pit.[v]*

II
5 Sing praise to the LORD, you faithful;
give thanks to God's holy name.
6 For divine anger lasts but a moment;
divine favor lasts a lifetime.
At dusk weeping comes for the night;
but at dawn there is rejoicing.

III
7 Complacent,* I once said,
"I shall never be shaken."
8 LORD, when you showed me favor
I stood like the mighty mountains.
But when you hid your face
I was struck with terror.[w]
9 To you, LORD, I cried out;
with the Lord I pleaded for mercy:
10 *"What gain is there from my lifeblood,
from my going down to the grave?
Does dust give you thanks
or declare your faithfulness?
11 Hear, O LORD, have mercy on me;
LORD, be my helper."

IV
12 You changed my mourning into dancing;
you took off my sackcloth
and clothed me with gladness.[x]
13 With my whole being I sing
endless praise to you.
O LORD, my God,
forever will I give you thanks.

## PSALM 31*

## Prayer in Distress and Thanksgiving for Escape

1 *For the leader. A psalm of David.*

I
2 In you, LORD, I take refuge;[y]
let me never be put to shame.
In your justice deliver me;
3 incline your ear to me;
make haste to rescue me!
Be my rock of refuge,
a stronghold to save me.
4 You are my rock and my fortress;[z]
for your name's sake lead and guide me.
5 Free me from the net they have set for me,
for you are my refuge.
6 Into your hands I commend my spirit;[a]*
you will redeem me, LORD, faithful God.
7 You hate those who serve worthless idols,
but I trust in the LORD.
8 I will rejoice and be glad in your love,
once you have seen my misery,
observed my distress.[b]

t Bar 3,3.
u Ps 68,36.
v Ps 28,1; Jon 2,7.
w Ps 104,29.
x Is 61,3; Jer 31,13.
y 2-4: Ps 71,1-3.
z Ps 18,2.
a Lk 23,46; Acts 7,59.
b Ps 10,14.

*

29, 8: *The desert of Kadesh*: probably north of Palestine in the neighborhood of Lebanon and Hermon.

29, 9b–10: Having witnessed God's supreme power (3–9a), the gods acknowledge the glory that befits the king of the divine and human world.

29, 10: *The flood*: God defeated the primordial waters and made them part of the universe. Cf Pss 89, 10–13 and 93, 3–4.

29, 11: *His people*: God's people, Israel.

Ps 30: An individual thanksgiving in four parts: praise and thanks for deliverance and restoration (2–4); an invitation to others to join in (5–6); a flashback to the time before deliverance (7–11); a return to praise and thanks (12–13). Two sets of images recur: 1) going down, death, silence; 2) coming up, life, praising. God has delivered the psalmist from one state to the other.

30, 1: *For the dedication of the temple*: a later adaptation of the psalm to celebrate the purification of the temple in 164 B.C. during the Maccabean Revolt.

30, 3: *Healed*: for God as healer, see also Pss 103, 3; 107, 20; Hos 6, 1; 7, 1; 11, 3; 14, 5.

30, 4: *Sheol . . . pit*: the shadowy underworld residence of the spirits of the dead, here a metaphor for near death.

30, 7: *Complacent*: untroubled existence is often seen as a source of temptation to forget God. Cf Dt 8, 10–18; Hos 13, 6; Prv 30, 9.

30, 10: In the stillness of Sheol no one gives you praise; let me live and be among your worshipers. Cf Pss 6, 6; 88, 11–13; 115, 17; Is 38, 18.

Ps 31: A lament (2–19) with a strong emphasis on trust (4. 6. 15–16), ending with an anticipatory thanksgiving (20–25). As is usual in laments, the affliction is couched in general terms. The psalmist feels overwhelmed by evil people but trusts in the "faithful God" (6).

31, 6: *Into your hands I commend my spirit*: in Lk 23, 46 Jesus breathes his last with this psalm verse. Stephen in Acts 7, 59 alludes to these words as he is attacked by enemies. The verse is used as an antiphon in the Divine Office at Compline, the last prayer of the day.

9 You will not abandon me into enemy hands,
but will set my feet in a free and open space.

II

10 Be gracious to me, LORD, for I am in distress;
with grief my eyes are wasted,
my soul and body spent.
11 My life is worn out by sorrow,
my years by sighing.
My strength fails in affliction;
my bones are consumed.[c]
12 To all my foes I am a thing of scorn,
to my neighbors, a dreaded sight,
a horror to my friends.
When they see me in the street,
they quickly shy away.[d]
13 I am forgotten, out of mind like the dead;
I am like a shattered dish.*
14 I hear the whispers of the crowd;
terrors are all around* me.
They conspire against me;
they plot to take my life.
15 But I trust in you, LORD;
I say, "You are my God."[e]
16 My times are in your hands;
rescue me from my enemies,
from the hands of my pursuers.
17 Let your face shine on your servant;[f]
save me in your kindness.
18 Do not let me be put to shame,
for I have called to you, LORD.
Put the wicked to shame;
reduce them to silence in Sheol.
19 Strike dumb their lying lips,
proud lips that attack the just
in contempt and scorn.[g]

III

20 How great is your goodness, LORD,
stored up for those who fear you.
You display it for those who trust you,
in the sight of all the people.
21 You hide them in the shelter of your presence,
safe from scheming enemies.
You keep them in your abode,
safe from plotting tongues.[h]
22 Blessed be the LORD,
who has shown me wondrous love,
and been for me a city most secure.
23 Once I said in my anguish,
"I am shut out from your sight."[i]
Yet you heard my plea,
when I cried out to you.
24 Love the LORD, all you faithful.
The LORD protects the loyal,
but repays the arrogant in full.
25 Be strong and take heart,
all you who hope in the LORD.

## PSALM 32*

### Remission of Sin

1 *Of David. A maskil.*

I

Happy the sinner whose fault is removed,
whose sin is forgiven.[j]
2 Happy those to whom the LORD imputes no guilt,
in whose spirit is no deceit.

II

3 As long as I kept silent,* my bones wasted away;
I groaned all the day.[k]
4 For day and night your hand was heavy upon me;
my strength withered as in dry summer heat. *Selah*
5 Then I declared my sin to you;
my guilt I did not hide.[l]
I said, "I confess my faults to the LORD,"
and you took away the guilt of my sin. *Selah*
6 Thus should all your faithful pray
in time of distress.
Though flood waters* threaten,
they will never reach them.[m]
7 You are my shelter; from distress you keep me;
with safety you ring me round. *Selah*

III

8 I will instruct you and show you the way you should walk,
give you counsel and watch over you.
9 Do not be senseless like horses or mules;
with bit and bridle their temper is curbed,
else they will not come to you.

---

c Pss 32,3; 38,10-11.
d Jb 19,13-19.
e Ps 140,7; Is 25,1.
f Ps 67,1; Nm 6,24.
g Ps 12,4.
h Ps 27,5.
i Jon 2,5.
j Is 1,18; Ps 65,3; Rom 4,7-8.
k Ps 31,11.
l Pss 38,19; 51,5.
m Ps 18,5.

---

31, 13: *Like a shattered dish*: a common comparison for something ruined and useless. Cf Is 30, 14; Jer 19, 11; 22, 28.

31, 14: *Terrors are all around*: a cry used in inescapable danger. Cf Jer 6, 25; 20, 10; 46, 5; 49, 29.

Ps 32: An individual thanksgiving and the second of the seven Penitential Psalms (cf Ps 6). The opening declaration—the forgiven are blessed (1–2)—arises from the psalmist's own experience. At one time the psalmist was stubborn and closed, a victim of sin's power (3–4), and then became open to the forgiving God (5–7). Sin here, as often in the Bible, is not only the personal act of rebellion against God but also the consequences of that act—frustration and waning of vitality. Having been rescued, the psalmist can teach others the joys of justice and the folly of sin (8–11).

32, 3: *I kept silent*: did not confess the sin before God.

32, 6: *Flood waters*: the untamed waters surrounding the earth, a metaphor for danger.

IV
10 Many are the sorrows of the wicked,
but love surrounds those who trust in the LORD.
11 Be glad in the LORD and rejoice, you just;
exult, all you upright of heart.[n]

## PSALM 33*

## Praise of God's Power and Providence

I
1 Rejoice, you just, in the LORD;
praise from the upright is fitting.[o]
2 Give thanks to the LORD on the harp;
on the ten-stringed lyre offer praise.[p]
3 Sing to God a new song;
skillfully play with joyful chant.
4 For the LORD's word is true;
all his works are trustworthy.
5 The LORD loves justice and right
and fills the earth with goodness.[q]

II
6 By the LORD's word the heavens were made;
by the breath of his mouth all their host.[r]*
7 The waters of the sea were gathered as in a bowl;*
in cellars the deep was confined.[s]

III
8 Let all the earth fear the LORD;
let all who dwell in the world show reverence.
9 For he spoke, and it came to be,
commanded, and it stood in place.[t]
10 The LORD foils the plan of nations,
frustrates the designs of peoples.
11 But the plan of the LORD stands forever,
wise designs through all generations.[u]
12 Happy the nation whose God is the LORD,
the people chosen as his very own.[v]

IV
13 From heaven the LORD looks down
and observes the whole human race,[w]
14 Surveying from the royal throne
all who dwell on earth.
15 The one who fashioned the hearts of them all
knows all their works.

V
16 A king is not saved by a mighty army,
nor a warrior delivered by great strength.
17 Useless is the horse for safety;
its great strength, no sure escape.
18 But the LORD's eyes are upon the reverent,
upon those who hope for his gracious help,
19 Delivering them from death,
keeping them alive in times of famine.

VI
20 Our soul waits for the LORD,
who is our help and shield.[x]
21 For in God our hearts rejoice;
in your holy name we trust.
22 May your kindness, LORD, be upon us;
we have put our hope in you.

## PSALM 34*

## Thanksgiving to God Who Delivers the Just

1 *Of David, when he feigned madness before Abimelech,* who forced him to depart.*

I
2 I will bless the LORD at all times;
praise shall be always in my mouth.[y]
3 My soul will glory in the LORD
that the poor may hear and be glad.
4 Magnify the LORD with me;
let us exalt his name together.

II
5 I sought the LORD, who answered me,
delivered me from all my fears.
6 Look to God that you may be radiant with joy
and your faces may not blush for shame.
7 In my misfortune I called,
the LORD heard and saved me from all distress.
8 The angel of the LORD, who encamps with them,
delivers all who fear God.[z]

n Ps 33,1.
o Pss 32,11; 147,1.
p Pss 92,4; 144,9.
q Ps 119,64.
r Gn 2,1.
s Ps 78,13; Gn 1,9-10; Ex 15,8.
t Ps 148,5; Gn 1,3f; Jdt 16,14.
u Prv 19,21; Is 40,8.
v Ps 144,15; Ex 19,6; Dt 7,6.
w Jb 34,21; Sir 15,19; Jer 16,17; 32,19.
x Ps 115,9.
y Ps 145,2.
z Ex 14,19.

*

Ps 33: A hymn in which the just are invited (1–3) to praise God, who by a mere word (4–5) created the three-tiered universe of the heavens, the cosmic waters, and the earth (6–9). Human words, in contrast, effect nothing (10–11). The greatness of human beings consists in God's choosing them as a special people and their faithful response (12–22).

33, 6: *All their host*: the stars of the sky are commonly viewed as a vast army, e.g., Neh 9, 6; Is 40, 26; 45, 12; Jer 33, 22.

33, 7: *The waters . . . as in a bowl*: ancients sometimes attributed the power keeping the seas from overwhelming land to a primordial victory of the storm-god over personified Sea. God confines the seas as easily as one puts water in a bowl.

Ps 34: A thanksgiving in acrostic form, each line beginning with a successive letter of the Hebrew alphabet. In this psalm one letter is missing and two are in reverse order. The psalmist, fresh from the experience of being rescued (5. 7), can teach the "poor," those who are defenseless, to trust in God alone (4. 12). God will make them powerful (5–11) and give them protection (12–23).

34, 1: *Abimelech*: a scribal error for Achish. In 1 Sm 21, 13–16, David feigned madness before Achish, not Abimelech.

**9** Learn to savor how good the LORD is;
happy are those who take refuge in him.[a]
**10** Fear the LORD, you holy ones;
nothing is lacking to those who fear him.[b]
**11** The powerful* grow poor and hungry,
but those who seek the LORD lack no
good thing.

III
**12** Come, children,* listen to me;[c]
I will teach you the fear of the LORD.
**13** Who among you loves life,[d]
takes delight in prosperous days?
**14** Keep your tongue from evil,
your lips from speaking lies.
**15** Turn from evil and do good;[e]
seek peace and pursue it.
**16** The LORD has eyes for the just[f]
and ears for their cry.
**17** The LORD's face is against evildoers
to wipe out their memory from the earth.
**18** When the just cry out, the LORD hears
and rescues them from all distress.
**19** The LORD is close to the brokenhearted,
saves those whose spirit is crushed.
**20** Many are the troubles of the just,
but the LORD delivers from them all.
**21** God watches over all their bones;
not a one shall be broken.[g]
**22** Evil will slay the wicked;
those who hate the just are condemned.
**23** The LORD redeems loyal servants;
no one is condemned whose refuge is
God.

## PSALM 35*

## Prayer for Help against Unjust Enemies

**1*** *Of David.*

I
Oppose, LORD, those who oppose me;
war upon those who make war upon me.
**2** Take up the shield and buckler;
rise up in my defense.
**3** Brandish lance and battle-ax
against my pursuers.
Say to my heart,
"I am your salvation."
**4** Let those who seek my life
be put to shame and disgrace.
Let those who plot evil against me[h]
be turned back and confounded.
**5** Make them like chaff before the wind,[i]
with the angel of the LORD driving them
on.
**6** Make their way slippery and dark,
with the angel of the LORD pursuing them.

II
**7** Without cause they set their snare for me;
without cause they dug a pit for me.
**8** Let ruin overtake them unawares;
let the snare they have set catch them;
let them fall into the pit they have dug.[j]
**9** Then I will rejoice in the LORD,
exult in God's salvation.
**10** My very bones shall say,
"O LORD, who is like you,[k]
Who rescue the afflicted from the powerful,
the afflicted and needy from the
despoiler?"

III
**11** Malicious witnesses come forward,
accuse me of things I do not know.
**12** They repay me evil for good
and I am all alone.[l]
**13** *Yet I, when they were ill, put on
sackcloth,
afflicted myself with fasting,
sobbed my prayers upon my bosom.
**14** I went about in grief as for my brother,
bent in mourning as for my mother.
**15** Yet when I stumbled they gathered with
glee,
gathered against me like strangers.
They slandered me without ceasing;
**16** without respect they mocked me,
gnashed their teeth against me.

IV
**17** Lord, how long will you look on?
Save me from roaring beasts,
my precious life from lions![m]
**18** Then I will thank you in the great assembly;
I will praise you before the mighty
throng.[n]
**19** Do not let lying foes smirk at me,
my undeserved enemies wink knowingly.[o]
**20** They speak no words of peace,

a Ps 2,12.
b Prv 3,7.
c Prv 1,8; 4,1.
d 13-17: 1 Pt 3,10-12.
e Ps 37,27.
f Ps 33,18.
g Jn 19,36.
h Pss 40,15; 71,13.
i Pss 1,4; 83,14; Jb 21,18.
j Pss 7,16; 9,16; 57,7; Prv 26,27; Eccl 10,8; Sir 27,26.
k Ps 86,8; 89,7. 9; Ex 15,11.
l Pss 27,12; 38,20-21; 109,5; Jer 18,20.
m Pss 17,12; 22,22; 58,7.
n Pss 22,23; 26,12; 35,18; 40,10; 149,1.
o Ps 38,17.

34, 11: *The powerful*: literally, "lions." Fierce animals were sometimes metaphors for influential people.

34, 12: *Children*: the customary term for students in Wisdom literature.

Ps 35: A lament of a person betrayed by friends. The psalmist prays that the evildoers be publicly exposed as unjust (1–8), and gives thanks in anticipation of vindication (9–10). Old friends are the enemies (11–16). May their punishment come quickly (17–21)! The last part (22–26) echoes the opening in praying for the destruction of the psalmist's persecutors. The psalm may appear vindictive, but one must keep in mind that the psalmist is praying for *public* redress now of a *public* injustice. There is at this time no belief in an afterlife in which justice will be redressed.

35, 1–6: The mixture of judicial, martial, and hunting images shows that the language is figurative. The actual injustice is false accusation of serious crimes (11. 15. 20–21). The psalmist seeks lost honor through a trial before God.

35, 13. 15–17: The Hebrew is obscure.

but against the quiet in the land
they fashion deceitful speech.[p]
21 They open wide their mouths against me.
They say, "Aha! Good!
Our eyes relish the sight!"[q]
22 You see this, LORD; do not be silent;[r]
Lord, do not withdraw from me.
23 Awake, be vigilant in my defense,
in my cause, my God and my Lord.
24 Defend me because you are just, LORD;
my God, do not let them gloat over me.
25 Do not let them say in their hearts,
"Aha! Just what we wanted!"
Do not let them say,
"We have devoured that one!"
26 Put to shame and confound
all who relish my misfortune.
Clothe with shame and disgrace
those who lord it over me.
27 But let those who favor my just cause
shout for joy and be glad.
May they ever say, "Exalted be the LORD
who delights in the peace of his loyal
servant."
28 Then my tongue shall recount your justice,
declare your praise, all the day long.[s]

## PSALM 36*

## Human Wickedness and Divine Providence

1 *For the leader. Of David, the servant of the* LORD.

I

2 Sin directs the heart of the wicked;
their eyes are closed to the fear of God.[t]
3 For they live with the delusion:
their guilt will not be known and hated.*
4 Empty and false are the words of their
mouth;
they have ceased to be wise and do good.
5 In their beds they hatch plots;
they set out on a wicked way;
they do not reject evil.[u]

II

6 LORD, your love reaches to heaven;
your fidelity, to the clouds.[v]
7 Your justice is like the highest mountains;
your judgments,* like the mighty deep;
all living creatures you sustain, LORD.
8 How precious is your love, O God!
We take refuge in the shadow of your
wings.[w]*
9 We feast on the rich food of your house;
from your delightful stream[x] you give us
drink.
10 For with you is the fountain of life,[y]
and in your light we see light.[z]
11 Continue your kindness toward your friends,
your just defense of the honest heart.
12 Do not let the foot of the proud overtake
me,
nor the hand of the wicked disturb me.
13 There make the evildoers fall;
thrust them down, never to rise.

## PSALM 37*

## The Fate of Sinners and the Reward of the Just

1 *Of David.*

### Aleph

Do not be provoked by evildoers;
do not envy those who do wrong.[a]
2 Like grass they wither quickly;
like green plants they wilt away.[b]

### Beth

3 Trust in the LORD and do good
that you may dwell in the land* and live
secure.[c]
4 Find your delight in the LORD
who will give you your heart's desire.[d]

p Ps 120,6-7.
q Ps 40,16; Lam 2,16.
r Pss 22,12; 38,21; 109,1.
s Ps 71,15-16.
t Rom 3,18.
u Mi 2,1.
v Pss 57,11; 71,19.
w Ps 17,8.
x Gn 2,8. 10.
y Is 55,1; Jn 4,14.
z Ps 80,4. 8. 20.
a Prv 3,31; 23,17; 24,1. 19.
b Pss 90,5-6; 102,12; 103,15-16; Jb 14,2; Is 40,7.
c Ps 128,2.
d Prv 10,24.

Ps 36: A psalm with elements of wisdom (2–5), the hymn (6–10), and the lament (11–13). The rule of sin over the wicked (2–5) is contrasted with the rule of divine love and mercy over God's friends (6–10). The psalm ends with a prayer that God's guidance never cease (11–13).

36, 3: *Hated*: punished by God.

36, 6–7: *Love . . . judgments*: God actively controls the entire world.

36, 8: *The shadow of your wings*: metaphor for divine protection. It probably refers to the winged cherubim in the holy of holies in the temple. Cf 1 Kgs 6, 23–28. 32; 2 Chr 3, 10–13; Ez 1, 4–9.

Ps 37: The psalm responds to the problem of evil, which the Old Testament often expresses as a question: Why do the wicked prosper and the good suffer? The psalm answers that the situation is only temporary. God will reverse things, rewarding the good and punishing the wicked here on earth. The perspective is concrete and earthbound: people's very actions place them among the ranks of the good or wicked. Each group or "way" has its own inherent dynamism — eventual frustration for the wicked, eventual reward for the just. The psalm is an acrostic, i.e., each section begins with a successive letter of the Hebrew alphabet. Each section has its own imagery and logic.

37, 3. 9. 11. 22. 27. 29. 34: *The land*: the promised land, Israel, which became for later interpreters a type or figure of heaven. Cf Heb 11, 9–10. 13–16. The New Testament Beatitudes (Mt 5, 3–12; Lk 6, 20–26) have been influenced by the psalm, especially their total reversal of the present and their interpretation of the happy future as possession of the land.

**Gimel**

5 Commit your way to the LORD;
trust that God will act[e]
6 And make your integrity shine like the dawn,
your vindication like noonday.[f]

**Daleth**

7 Be still before the LORD;
wait for God.
Do not be provoked by the prosperous,
nor by malicious schemers.

**He**

8 Give up your anger, abandon your wrath;
do not be provoked; it brings only harm.
9 Those who do evil will be cut off,
but those who wait for the LORD will possess the land.[g]*

**Waw**

10 Wait a little, and the wicked will be no more;
look for them and they will not be there.
11 But the poor will possess the land,[h]*
will delight in great prosperity.

**Zayin**

12 The wicked plot against the just
and grind their teeth at them;
13 But the LORD laughs at them,[i]
knowing their day is coming.

**Heth**

14 The wicked draw their swords;
they string their bows
To fell the poor and oppressed,
to slaughter those whose way is honest.[j]
15 Their swords will pierce their own hearts;
their bows will be broken.

**Teth**

16 Better the poverty of the just
than the great wealth of the wicked.[k]
17 The arms of the wicked will be broken;
the LORD will sustain the just.

**Yodh**

18 The LORD watches over the days of the blameless;
their heritage lasts forever.
19 They will not be disgraced when times are hard;
in days of famine they will have plenty.

**Kaph**

20 The wicked perish,
the enemies of the LORD;
Like the beauty of meadows they vanish;
like smoke they disappear.[l]

**Lamedh**

21 The wicked borrow but do not repay;
the just are generous in giving.
22 For those blessed by the Lord will possess the land,*
but those accursed will be cut off.

**Mem**

23 Those whose steps are guided by the LORD;[m]
whose way God approves,
24 May stumble, but they will never fall,
for the LORD holds their hand.

**Nun**

25 Neither in my youth, nor now in old age
have I ever seen the just abandoned[n]
or their children begging bread.
26 The just always lend generously,
and their children become a blessing.

**Samekh**

27 Turn from evil and do good,
that you may inhabit the land* forever.[o]
28 For the LORD loves justice
and does not abandon the faithful.

**Ayin**

When the unjust are destroyed,
and the children of the wicked cut off,
29 The just will possess the land*
and live in it forever.[p]

**Pe**

30 The mouths of the just utter wisdom;[q]
their tongues speak what is right.
31 God's teaching is in their hearts;[r]
their steps do not falter.

**Sadhe**

32 The wicked spy on the just
and seek to kill them.
33 But the LORD does not leave the just in their power,
nor let them be condemned when tried.

---

e Ps 55,23; Prv 3,5; 16,3.
f Wis 5,6; Is 58,10.
g Ps 25,13; Prv 2,21; Is 57,13.
h Mt 5,4.
i Pss 2,4; 59,9; Wis 4,18.
j Pss 11,2; 57,5; 64,4.
k Prv 15,16; 16,8.
l Wis 5,14.
m Prv 20,24.
n Jb 4,7; Sir 2,10.
o Ps 34,14-15; Am 5,14.
p Ps 25,13; Prv 2,21; Is 57,13.
q Prv 10,31.
r Ps 40,9; Dt 6,6; Is 51,7; Jer 31,33.

### Qoph

34 Wait eagerly for the LORD,
and keep to the way;[s]
God will raise you to possess the land;*
you will gloat when the wicked are cut off.

### Resh

35 I have seen ruthless scoundrels,
strong as flourishing cedars.[t]
36 When I passed by again, they were gone;
though I searched, they could not be found.

### Shin

37 Observe the honest, mark the upright;
those at peace with God have a future.[u]
38 But all sinners will be destroyed;
the future of the wicked will be cut off.

### Taw

39 The salvation of the just is from the LORD,
their refuge in time of distress.[v]
40 The LORD helps and rescues them,
rescues and saves them from the wicked,
because in God they take refuge.

## PSALM 38*

## Prayer of an Afflicted Sinner

1 *A psalm of David. For remembrance.*

I

2 LORD, punish me no more in your anger;
in your wrath do not chastise me![w]
3 Your arrows have sunk deep in me;[x]
your hand has come down upon me.
4 My flesh is afflicted because of your anger;
my frame aches because of my sin.[y]
5 My iniquities overwhelm me,
a burden beyond my strength.[z]

II

6 Foul and festering are my sores
because of my folly.
7 I am stooped and deeply bowed;[a]
all day I go about mourning.
8 My loins burn with fever;
my flesh is afflicted.
9 I am numb and utterly crushed;
I wail with anguish of heart.[b]
10 My Lord, my deepest yearning is before you;
my groaning is not hidden from you.
11 My heart shudders, my strength forsakes me;
the very light of my eyes has failed.[c]
12 Friends and companions shun my pain;
my neighbors stand far off.
13 Those who seek my life lay snares for me;
they seek my misfortune, they speak of ruin;
they plot treachery all the day.

III

14 But I am like the deaf, hearing nothing,
like the dumb, saying nothing,
15 Like someone who does not hear,
who has no answer ready.
16 LORD, I wait for you;
O Lord, my God, answer me.[d]
17 For I fear they will gloat,
exult over me if I stumble.

IV

18 I am very near to falling;
my pain is with me always.
19 I acknowledge my guilt
and grieve over my sin.[e]
20 But many are my foes without cause,
a multitude of enemies without reason,
21 Repaying me evil for good,
harassing me for pursuing good.[f]
22 Forsake me not, O LORD;
my God, be not far from me![g]
23 Come quickly to help me,[h]
my Lord and my salvation!

## PSALM 39*

## The Vanity of Life

1 *For the leader, for Jeduthun.*[i] *A psalm of David.*

I

2 I said, "I will watch my ways,
lest I sin with my tongue;
I will set a curb on my mouth."
3 Dumb and silent before the wicked,
I refrained from any speech.
But my sorrow increased;
4 my heart smoldered within me.[j]
In my thoughts a fire blazed up,
and I broke into speech:

s Ps 31,24.
t Ps 92,8-9; Is 2,13; Ez 31,10-11.
u Prv 23,18; 24,14.
v Ps 9,10; Is 25,4.
w Ps 6,2.
x Jb 6,4; Lam 3,12; Pss 31,11; 64,7.
y Is 1,5-6.
z Ps 40,13; Ezr 9,6.
a Ps 35,14.
b Ps 102,4-6.
c Pss 6,8; 31,10.
d Ps 13,4.
e Pss 32,5; 51,5.
f Ps 109,5.
g Pss 22,2.12. 20; 35,22.
h Ps 40,14.
i 1 Chr 16,41; Pss 62,1; 77,1.
j Jer 20,9.

*

Ps 38: In this lament, one of the Penitential Psalms (cf Ps 6), the psalmist acknowledges the sin that has brought physical and mental sickness and social ostracism. There is no one to turn to for help; only God can undo the past and restore the psalmist.

Ps 39: The lament of a mortally ill person who at first had resolved to remain silently submissive (2–4). But the grief was too much and now the psalmist laments the brevity and vanity of life (5–7), yet remaining hopeful (8–10). The psalmist continues to express both acceptance of the illness and hope for healing in 11–14.

II

5 LORD, let me know my end, the number of
my days,
that I may learn how frail I am.
6 You have given my days a very short span;
my life is as nothing before you.
All mortals are but a breath.[k] *Selah*
7 Mere phantoms, we go our way;
mere vapor, our restless pursuits;
we heap up stores without knowing for
whom.
8 And now, Lord, what future do I have?
You are my only hope.
9 From all my sins deliver me;
let me not be the taunt of fools.

III

10 I was silent and did not open my mouth
because you were the one who did this.
11 Take your plague away from me;
I am ravaged by the touch of your hand.
12 You rebuke our guilt and chasten us;
you dissolve all we prize like a cobweb.
All mortals are but a breath. *Selah*
13 Listen to my prayer, LORD, hear my cry;
do not be deaf to my weeping!
I sojourn with you like a passing stranger,
a guest, like all my ancestors.[l]
14 Turn your gaze from me, that I may find
peace
before I depart to be no more.

## PSALM 40*

## Gratitude and Prayer for Help

1 *For the leader. A psalm of David.*

### A

I

2 I waited, waited for the LORD;
who bent down and heard my cry,[m]
3 Drew me out of the pit of destruction,
out of the mud of the swamp,[n]
Set my feet upon rock,
steadied my steps,
4 And put a new song* in my mouth,[o]
a hymn to our God.
Many shall look on in awe
and they shall trust in the LORD.

II

5 Happy those whose trust is the LORD,
who turn not to idolatry
or to those who stray after falsehood.[p]
6 How numerous, O LORD, my God,
you have made your wondrous deeds!
And in your plans for us
there is none to equal you.[q]
Should I wish to declare or tell them,
too many are they to recount.[r]

III

7 *Sacrifice and offering you do not want;[s]
but ears open to obedience you gave me.
Holocausts and sin-offerings you do not
require;
8 so I said, "Here I am;
your commands for me are written in the
scroll.
9 To do your will is my delight;
my God, your law is in my heart!"[t]
10 I announced your deed to a great assembly;
I did not restrain my lips;
you, LORD, are my witness.[u]
11 Your deed I did not hide within my heart;
your loyal deliverance I have proclaimed.
I made no secret of your enduring kindness
to a great assembly.

### B

I

12 LORD, do not withhold your compassion
from me;
may your enduring kindness ever preserve
me.[v]
13 For all about me are evils beyond count;
my sins so overcome me I cannot see.
They are more than the hairs of my head;
my courage fails me.[w]

II

14 LORD, graciously rescue me![x]
Come quickly to help me, LORD!
15 Put to shame and confound
all who seek to take my life.
Turn back in disgrace
those who desire my ruin.[y]

---

k Pss 62,10; 90,9-10; 144,4; Jb 7,6. 16; 14, 1. 5; Eccl 6,12; Wis 2, 5.
l Ps 119,19; Gn 23,4; Heb 11,13; 1 Pt 2,11.
m Lam 3,25.
n Pss 28,1; 30,4; 69,3. 15-16; 88,5; Prv 1,12; Jon 2,7.
o Ps 33,3.
p Ps 1,1; Prv 16,20; Jer 17,7.
q Ps 35,10.
r Pss 71,15; 139,17-18.
s 7-9: Heb 10,5-7; Ps 51,18-19; Am 5,22; Hos 6,6; Is 1,11-15.
t Ps 37,31.
u Pss 22,23; 26,12; 35, 18; 149,1.
v Ps 89,34.
w Ps 38,5. 11; Ezr 9,6.
x 14-18: Pss 70,2-6; 71, 12.
y Ps 35,4. 26.

---

Ps 40: A thanksgiving (2–13) has been combined with a lament (14–18), that appears also in Ps 70. The psalmist describes the rescue in spatial terms—being raised up from the swampy underworld to firm earth where one can praise God (2–4). All who trust God will experience like protection (5–6)! The psalm stipulates the precise mode of thanksgiving: not animal sacrifice but open and enthusiastic proclamation of the salvation just experienced (7–11). A prayer for protection concludes (12–18).

40, 4: *A new song*: a song in response to the new action of God (cf Pss 33, 3; 96, 1; 144, 9; 149, 1; Is 42, 10). Giving thanks is not purely a human response but is itself a divine gift.

40, 7–9: Obedience is better than sacrifice (cf 1 Sm 15, 22; Is 1, 10–20; Hos 6, 6; Am 5, 22–25; Mi 6, 6–8; Acts 7, 42–43 [quoting Am 5, 25–26 LXX]). Heb 10, 5–9 quotes the somewhat different Greek version and interprets it as Christ's self-oblation.

16 Let those who say "Aha!"[z]
know dismay and shame.
17 But may all who seek you
rejoice and be glad in you.
May those who long for your help
always say, "The LORD be glorified."[a]
18 Though I am afflicted and poor,
the Lord keeps me in mind.
You are my help and deliverer;
my God, do not delay!

## PSALM 41*

### Thanksgiving after Sickness

1 *For the leader. A psalm of David.*

I
2 Happy those concerned for the lowly and poor;*
when misfortune strikes, the LORD delivers them.[b]
3 The LORD keeps and preserves them,
makes them happy in the land,
and does not betray them to their enemies.
4 The LORD sustains them on their sickbed,
allays the malady when they are ill.

II
5 Once I prayed, "LORD, have mercy on me;
heal me, I have sinned against you.
6 My enemies say the worst of me:
'When will that one die and be forgotten?'
7 When people come to visit me,
they speak without sincerity.
Their hearts store up malice;
they leave and spread their vicious lies.[c]
8 My foes all whisper against me;
they imagine the worst about me:
9 I have a deadly disease, they say;
I will never rise from my sickbed.
10 Even the friend who had my trust,
who shared my table, has scorned me.[d]*
11 But you, LORD, have mercy and raise me up
that I may repay them as they deserve."*

III
12 By this I know you are pleased with me,
that my enemy no longer jeers at me.
13 For my integrity you have supported me
and let me stand in your presence forever.

* * *

14 *Blessed be the LORD, the God of Israel,
from all eternity and forever.
Amen. Amen.[e]

## SECOND BOOK — PSALMS 42–72

## PSALM 42–43*

### Longing for God's Presence in the Temple

1 *For the leader. A* maskil *of the Korahites.**

I
2 As the deer longs for streams of water,[f]
so my soul longs for you, O God.
3 My being thirsts for God, the living God.
When can I go and see the face of God?[g]*
4 My tears have been my food day and night,[h]
as they ask daily, "Where is your God?"[i]
5 Those times I recall
as I pour out my soul,[j]
When I went in procession with the crowd,
I went with them to the house of God,
Amid loud cries of thanksgiving,
with the multitude keeping festival.[k]
6 Why are you downcast, my soul;
why do you groan within me?

z Ps 35,21. 25.
a Ps 35,27.
b Tb 4,7-11.
c Pss 31,12; 38,12-13; 88,8; Jb 19,13-19; Jer 20,10.
d Ps 55,14-15; Jn 13, 18.
e Neh 9,5.
f 2-3: Pss 63,2; 84,3; 143,6; Is 26,9.
g Ps 27,4.
h Pss 80,6; 102,10.
i Ps 79,10; Jl 2,17.
j Lam 3,20.
k Ps 122,5.

*

Ps 41: A thanksgiving for rescue from illness (4. 5. 9). Many people, even friends, have interpreted the illness as a divine punishment for sin and have ostracized the psalmist (5–11). The healing shows the return of God's favor and rebukes the psalmist's detractors (12–13).

41, 2: *Happy those concerned for the lowly and poor*: other psalms use the same formula ("Happy those") for those whom God favors. Cf Pss 32, 1–2; 34, 9; 40, 5; 65, 5. The psalmist's statement about God's love of the poor is based on the experience of being rescued (1–3).

41, 10: *Even the friend . . . has scorned me:* Jn 13, 18 cites this verse to characterize Judas as a false friend. *Scorned me*: an interpretation of the unclear Hebrew, "made great the heel against me."

41, 11: *That I may repay them as they deserve*: the healing itself is an act of judgment through which God decides for the psalmist and against the false friends. The prayer is not necessarily for strength to punish enemies.

41, 14: The doxology, not part of the psalm, marks the end of the first of the five books of the Psalter. Compare Pss 72, 18–20; 89, 53; 106, 48.

Pss 42–43: Pss 42–43 form a single lament of three sections, each section ending in an identical refrain (42, 6. 12; 43, 5). The psalmist is in the extreme north of Israel, far from Jerusalem, and longs for the divine presence that Israel experienced in the temple liturgy. Despite sadness, the psalmist hopes once again to join the worshiping crowds.

42, 1: *The Korahites:* a major guild of temple singers (2 Chr 20, 19) whose name appears in the superscriptions of Pss 42; 44–49; 84–85; 87–88.

42, 3: *See the face of God*: "face" designates a personal presence (Gn 33, 10; Ex 10, 28–29; 2 Sm 17, 11). The expressions "see God/God's face" occur elsewhere (Pss 11, 7; 17, 15; 63, 3; cf Ex 24, 10; 33, 7–11; Jb 33, 26) for the presence of God in the temple.

Wait for God, whom I shall praise again,
my savior and my God.

II

7 My soul is downcast within me;
therefore I will remember you
From the land of the Jordan* and Hermon,
from the land of Mount Mizar.[l]
8 Here deep calls to deep* in the roar of your torrents.
All your waves and breakers sweep over me.[m]
9 At dawn may the LORD bestow faithful love
that I may sing praise through the night,
praise to the God of my life.
10 I say to God, "My rock,
why do you forget me?[n]
Why must I go about mourning
with the enemy oppressing me?"
11 It shatters my bones, when my adversaries reproach me.
They say to me daily: "Where is your God?"
12 Why are you downcast, my soul,
why do you groan within me?
Wait for God, whom I shall praise again,
my savior and my God.

III

1 Grant me justice, God;
defend me from a faithless people;
from the deceitful and unjust rescue me.[o]
2 You, God, are my strength.
Why then do you spurn me?
Why must I go about mourning,
with the enemy oppressing me?
3 Send your light and fidelity,*
that they may be my guide[p]
And bring me to your holy mountain,
to the place of your dwelling,[q]
4 That I may come to the altar of God,
to God, my joy, my delight.
Then I will praise you with the harp,
O God, my God.
5 Why are you downcast, my soul?
Why do you groan within me?
Wait for God, whom I shall praise again,
my savior and my God.

## PSALM 44*

## God's Past Favor and Israel's Present Need

1 *For the leader*. A maskil *of the Korahites*.

I

2 O God, we have heard with our own ears;
our ancestors have told us[r]
The deeds you did in their days,
with your own hand in days of old:
3 You rooted out nations to plant them,[s]
crushed peoples to make room for them.
4 Not with their own swords did they conquer the land,[t]
nor did their own arms bring victory;
It was your right hand, your own arm,
the light of your face, for you favored them.[u]
5 You are my king and my God,[v]
who bestows victories on Jacob.
6 Through you we batter our foes;
through your name, trample our adversaries.
7 Not in my bow do I trust,
nor does my sword bring me victory.
8 You have brought us victory over our enemies,
shamed those who hate us.
9 In God we have boasted all the day long;
your name we will praise forever. *Selah*

II

10 But now you have rejected and disgraced us;[w]
you do not march out with our armies.[x]
11 You make us retreat* before the foe;
those who hate us plunder us at will.[y]
12 You hand us over like sheep to be slaughtered,
scatter us among the nations.[z]
13 You sell your people for nothing;
you make no profit from their sale.[a]
14 You make us the reproach of our neighbors,[b]
the mockery and scorn of those around us.
15 You make us a byword among the nations;
the peoples shake their heads at us.
16 All day long my disgrace is before me;
shame has covered my face
17 At the sound of those who taunt and revile,
at the sight of the spiteful enemy.

l Ps 43,3.
m Pss 18,5; 32,6; 69,2; 88,8; Jon 2,4.
n Pss 18,2; 31,3-4.
o Ps 119,154.
p Pss 18,29; 27,1; 36,10; Mi 7,8.
q Ps 122,1.
r Ps 78,3.
s Pss 78,55; 80,9f.
t Dt 8,17f; Jos 24,12.
u Pss 4,7; 31,17; 67,2; 80,4; Nm 6,25; Dn 9,17.
v Ps 145,1.
w 10-27: Ps 89,39-52.
x Ps 60,12.
y Lv 26,17; Dt 28,25.
z Lv 26,33; Dt 28,64.
a Dt 32,30; Is 52,3.
b 14-17: Pss 79,4; 80,7; 123,3-4; Jb 12,4; Dn 9,16.

42, 7: *From the land of the Jordan*: the sources of the Jordan are in the foothills of Mount Hermon in present-day southern Lebanon. Mount Mizar is presumed to be a mountain in the same range.

42, 8: *Here deep calls to deep*: to the psalmist, the waters arising in the north are overwhelming and far from God's presence, like the waters of chaos (Pss 18, 5; 69, 2–3. 15; Jon 2, 3–6).

43, 3: *Your light and fidelity*: a pair of divine attributes personified as guides for the pilgrimage. The psalmist seeks divine protection for the journey to Jerusalem.

Ps 44: In this lament the community reminds God of past favors which it has always acknowledged (2–9). But now God has abandoned Israel to defeat and humiliation (10–17), though the people are not conscious of any sin against the covenant (18–23). They struggle with being God's special people amid divine silence; yet they continue to pray (24–27).

44, 11: *You make us retreat*: the corollary of v 4. Defeat, like victory, is God's doing; neither Israel nor its enemies can claim credit (23).

III

18 All this has come upon us,
though we have not forgotten you,
nor been disloyal to your covenant.
19 Our hearts have not turned back,*
nor have our steps strayed from your path.
20 Yet you have left us crushed,
desolate in a place of jackals;[c]*
you have covered us with darkness.
21 If we had forgotten the name of our God,
stretched out our hands to another god,
22 Would not God have discovered this,
God who knows the secrets of the heart?
23 For you we are slain all the day long,
considered only as sheep to be
slaughtered.[d]

IV

24 Awake! Why do you sleep, O Lord?
Rise up! Do not reject us forever![e]
25 Why do you hide your face;[f]
why forget our pain and misery?
26 We are bowed down to the ground;[g]
our bodies are pressed to the earth.
27 Rise up, help us!
Redeem us as your love demands.

## PSALM 45*

## Song for a Royal Wedding

1 *For the leader; according to "Lilies." A maskil of the Korahites. A love song.*

I

2 My heart is stirred by a noble theme,
as I sing my ode to the king.
My tongue is the pen of a nimble scribe.

II

3 You are the most handsome of men;
fair speech has graced your lips,
for God has blessed you forever.[h]
4 Gird your sword upon your hip, mighty
warrior!
In splendor and majesty ride on
triumphant![i]
5 In the cause of truth and justice
may your right hand show you wondrous
deeds.
6 Your arrows are sharp;
peoples will cower at your feet;
the king's enemies will lose heart.
7 Your throne, O god,* stands forever;[j]
your royal scepter is a scepter for justice.
8 You love justice and hate wrongdoing;
therefore God, your God, has anointed
you
with the oil of gladness above your fellow
kings.
9 With myrrh, aloes, and cassia
your robes are fragrant.
From ivory-paneled palaces*
stringed instruments bring you joy.
10 Daughters of kings are your lovely wives;
a princess arrayed in Ophir's gold*
comes to stand at your right hand.

III

11 Listen, my daughter, and understand;
pay me careful heed.
Forget your people and your father's house,*
12 that the king might desire your beauty.
He is your lord;
13 honor him, daughter of Tyre.
Then the richest of the people
will seek your favor with gifts.[k]
14 All glorious is the king's daughter as she
enters,[l]
her raiment threaded with gold;
15 In embroidered apparel she is led to the
king.
The maids of her train are presented to
the king.
16 They are led in with glad and joyous
acclaim;
they enter the palace of the king.

IV

17 The throne of your fathers your sons will
have;
you shall make them princes through all
the land.[m]
18 I will make your name renowned through all
generations;
thus nations shall praise you forever.[n]

---

c Jer 9,10.
d Rom 8,36.
e Pss 10,1; 74,1; 77,8; 79,5; 83,2.
f Pss 10,11; 89,47; Jb 13,24.
g Ps 119,25.
h Song 5,10-16.
i Ps 21,5.
j 7-8: Heb 1,8-9.
k Ps 72,10-11; Is 60,5f.
l 14-16: Ez 16,10-13.
m Gn 17,6.
n Is 60,15.

---

*

44, 19: *Our hearts have not turned back*: Israel's defeat was not caused by its lack of fidelity.

44, 20: *A place of jackals*: following Israel's defeat and exile (11–12), the land lies desolate, inhabited only by jackals. Cf Is 13, 22; Jer 9, 10; 10, 22. Others take *tannim* as "sea monster" (cf Ez 29, 3; 32, 2) and render: "you crushed us as you did the sea monster."

Ps 45: A song for the Davidic king's marriage to a foreign princess from Tyre in Phoenicia. The court poet sings (2. 18) of God's choice of the king (3. 8), of his role in establishing divine rule (4–8), and of his splendor as he waits for his bride (9–10). The woman is to forget her own house when she becomes wife to the king (11–13). Her majestic beauty today is a sign of the future prosperity of the royal house (14–18). The psalm was retained in the collection when there was no reigning king, and came to be applied to the king who was to come, the messiah.

45, 7: *O god*: the king, in courtly language, is called "god," i.e., more than human, representing God to the people. Heb 1, 8–9 applies 7–8 to Christ.

45, 9: *Ivory-paneled palaces*: literally, "palaces of ivory." Ivory paneling and furniture decoration have been found in Samaria and other ancient Near Eastern cities. Cf Am 3, 15.

45, 10: *Ophir's gold*: uncertain location, possibly a region on the coast of southern Arabia or eastern Africa, famous for its gold. Cf 1 Kgs 9, 28; 10, 11; Jb 22, 24.

45, 11: *Forget your people and your father's house*: the bride should no longer consider herself a daughter of her father's house, but the wife of the king—the queen.

## PSALM 46*

## God, the Protector of Zion

1 *For the leader. A song of the Korahites. According to* alamoth.*

I
2 God is our refuge and our strength,
an ever-present help in distress.[o]
3 *Thus we do not fear, though earth be shaken
and mountains quake to the depths of the sea,
4 Though its waters rage and foam
and mountains totter at its surging.[p]
The LORD of hosts is with us;*
our stronghold is the God of Jacob. *Selah*

II
5 *Streams of the river gladden the city of God,
the holy dwelling of the Most High.[q]
6 God is in its midst; it shall not be shaken;
God will help it at break of day.[r]
7 Though nations rage and kingdoms totter,
God's voice thunders and the earth trembles.[s]
8 The LORD of hosts is with us;*
our stronghold is the God of Jacob. *Selah*

III
9 Come and see the works of the LORD,
who has done fearsome deeds on earth;[t]
10 Who stops wars to the ends of the earth,
breaks the bow, splinters the spear,
and burns the shields with fire;[u]
11 Who says:
"Be still and confess that I am God!
I am exalted among the nations,
exalted on the earth."[v]
12 The LORD of hosts is with us;*
our stronghold is the God of Jacob. *Selah*

## PSALM 47*

## The Ruler of All the Nations

1 *For the leader. A psalm of the Korahites.*

I
2 All you peoples, clap your hands;
shout to God with joyful cries.[w]
3 For the LORD, the Most High, inspires awe,
the great king over all the earth,[x]
4 Who made people subject to us,
brought nations under our feet,[y]
5 Who chose a land for our heritage,
the glory* of Jacob, the beloved.[z] *Selah*

II
6 God mounts the throne* amid shouts of joy;
the LORD, amid trumpet blasts.[a]
7 Sing praise to God, sing praise;
sing praise to our king, sing praise.

III
8 God is king over all the earth;[b]
sing hymns of praise.
9 God rules over the nations;
God sits upon his holy throne.
10 The princes of the peoples assemble
with the people of the God of Abraham.
For the rulers of the earth belong to God,
who is enthroned on high.[c]

## PSALM 48*

## The Splendor of the Invincible City

1 *A psalm of the Korahites.* A song.*

I
2 Great is the LORD and highly praised
in the city of our God:[d]
The holy mountain, 3 fairest of heights,
the joy of all the earth,[e]

o Ps 48,4; Is 33,2.
p Ps 93,3-4; Jb 9,5-6; Is 24,18-20; 54,10.
q Pss 48,2-3; 76,3.
r Is 7,14.
s Pss 2,1-5; 48,5-8; 76, 7-9; Is 17,12-14.
t Ps 48,9-10.
u Ps 76,4.
v Ps 48,11.
w Ps 89,16; Zep 3,14.
x Ps 95,3; Ex 15,18; Is 24,23; 52,7.
y Ps 2,8.
z Is 58,14.
a Pss 24,8. 10; 68, 18-19; 98,6.
b 8-9: Pss 72,11; 93,1; 96,10; 97,1; 99,1; Jer 10,7.
c Ps 89,19; Ex 3,6; Is 2,2-4.
d Pss 96,4; 145,3.
e Ps 50,2; Lam 2,15.

*

Ps 46: A song of confidence in God's protection of Zion with close parallels to Ps 48. The dominant note in Ps 46 is sounded by the refrain, *The LORD of hosts is with us* (4. 8. 12). The first strophe (2–4) sings of the security of God's presence even in utter chaos; the second (5–8), of divine protection of the city from its enemies; the third (9–12), of God's imposition of imperial peace.

46, 1: *Alamoth:* the melody of the psalm, now lost.

46, 3–4: Figurative ancient Near Eastern language to describe social and political upheavals.

46, 4b: The first line of the refrain is similar in structure and meaning to Isaiah's name for the royal child, Immanuel, *With us is God* (Is 7, 14; 8, 8. 10).

46, 5: Jerusalem is not situated on a river. This description derives from mythological descriptions of the divine abode and symbolizes the divine presence as the source of all life (cf Is 33, 21; Ez 47, 1–12; Jl 4, 18; Zec 14, 8; Rv 22, 1–2).

Ps 47: A hymn calling on the nations to acknowledge the universal rule of Israel's God (2–5) who is enthroned as king over Israel and the nations (6–10).

47, 5: *Our heritage . . . the glory*: the land of Israel (cf Is 58, 14), which God has given Israel in an act of sovereignty.

47, 6: *God mounts the throne*: "has gone up to the throne," according to the context (9). Christian liturgical tradition has applied the verse to the ascension of Christ.

Ps 48: A Zion hymn, praising the holy city as the invincible dwelling place of God. Unconquerable, it is an apt symbol of God who has defeated all enemies. After seven epithets describing the city (2–3), the psalm describes the victory by the Divine Warrior over hostile kings (4–8). The second half proclaims the dominion of the God of Zion over all the earth (9–12) and invites pilgrims to announce that God is eternally invincible like Zion itself (13–15).

48, 1: *Korahites:* see note on Ps 42, 1.

48, 3: *The heights of Zaphon*: the mountain abode of the Canaanite storm-god Baal in comparable texts. To speak of Zion as if it were Zaphon was to claim for Israel's God what Canaanites claimed for Baal. Though topographically speak-

Mount Zion, the heights of Zaphon,[f]*
the city of the great king.

II

4 God is its citadel,
renowned as a stronghold.
5 See! The kings assembled,
together they invaded.
6 When they looked* they were astounded;
terrified, they were put to flight![g]
7 Trembling seized them there,
anguish, like a woman's labor,[h]
8 As when the east wind wrecks
the ships of Tarshish!*

III

9 What we had heard we now see*
in the city of the LORD of hosts,
In the city of our God,
founded to last forever. *Selah*
10 O God, within your temple
we ponder your steadfast love.
11 Like your name, O God,
your praise reaches the ends of the earth.[i]
Your right hand is fully victorious.
12 Mount Zion is glad!
The cities of Judah rejoice
because of your saving deeds![j]

IV

13 Go about Zion, walk all around it,
note the number of its towers.
14 Consider the ramparts, examine its citadels,
that you may tell future generations:[k]
15 "Yes, so mighty is God,*
our God who leads us always!"

## PSALM 49*

## Confidence in God rather than in Riches

1 *For the leader. A psalm of the Korahites.**

2 Hear this, all you peoples!
Give ear, all who inhabit the world,
3 You of lowly birth or high estate,
rich and poor alike.
4 My mouth shall speak wisdom,
my heart shall offer insight.[l]
5 I will turn my attention to a problem,*
expound my question to the music of a lyre.

I

6 Why should I fear in evil days,
when my wicked pursuers ring me round,
7 Those who trust in their wealth
and boast of their abundant riches?[m]
8 One cannot redeem oneself,*
pay to God a ransom.[n]
9 Too high the price to redeem a life;
one would never have enough
10 To stay alive forever
and never see the pit.
11 Anyone can see that the wisest die,
the fool and the senseless pass away too,[o]
and must leave their wealth to others.[p]
12 Tombs are their homes forever,
their dwellings through all generations,
though they gave their names to their lands.
13 For all their riches
mortals do not abide;
they perish like the beasts.[q]

II

14 This is the destiny of those who trust in folly,
the end of those so pleased with their wealth. *Selah*
15 Like sheep they are herded into Sheol,
where death will be their shepherd.
Straight to the grave they descend,
where their form will waste away,
Sheol will be their palace.
16 But God will redeem my life, *Selah*
will take me* from the power of Sheol.[r]
17 Do not fear when others become rich,

f Is 14,13.
g Jgs 5,19.
h Ex 15,14; Jer 4,31.
i Mal 1,11.
j Ps 97,8.
k Pss 22,31-32; 71,18.
l Ps 78,2; Mt 13,35.
m Jb 31,24.
n Prv 10,15; 11,4; Ez 7,19; Mt 16,26.
o Eccl 2,16.
p Ps 39,7; Sir 11,18-19.
q Eccl 3,18-21.
r Pss 16,10; 86,13; 103,4; 116,8.

* ing Zion is only a hill, viewed religiously it towers over other mountains as the home of the supreme God (cf Ps 68, 16–17).

48, 6: *When they looked*: the kings are stunned by the sight of Zion, touched by divine splendor. The language is that of holy war, in which the enemy panics and flees at the sight of divine glory.

48, 8: *The ships of Tarshish*: large ships, named after the distant land or port of Tarshish, probably ancient Tartessus in southern Spain, although other identifications have been proposed. Cf Is 2, 16; 60, 9; Jon 1, 3.

48, 9: *What we had heard we now see*: the glorious things that new pilgrims had heard about the holy city—its beauty and awesomeness—they now see with their own eyes. The seeing here contrasts with the seeing of the hostile kings in 6.

48, 15: *So mighty is God*: Israel's God is like Zion in being eternal and invincible. The holy city is therefore a kind of "sacrament" of God.

Ps 49: The psalm affirms confidence in God (cf Pss 23; 27, 1–6; 62) in the face of the apparent good fortune of the unjust rich. Cf Pss 37; 73. Reliance on wealth is misplaced (8–10) for it is of no avail in the face of death (18–20). After inviting all to listen to this axiom of faith (2–5), the psalmist depicts the self-delusion of the ungodly (6–13), whose destiny is to die like ignorant beasts (13. 18; cf Prv 7, 21–23). Their wealth should occasion no alarm, for they will come to nought, whereas God will save the just (14–21).

49, 1: *Korahites*: see note on Ps 42, 1.

49, 5: *Problem*: the psalmist's personal solution to the perennial biblical problem of the prosperity of the wicked. *Question*: parallel in meaning to *problem*; in Wisdom literature it means the mysterious way of how the world works.

49, 8: *One cannot redeem oneself*: an axiom. For the practice of redemption, cf Jb 6, 21–23. A play on the first Hebrew word of v 8 and v 16 relates the two verses.

49, 16: *Will take me*: the same Hebrew verb is used of God "taking up" a favored servant: Enoch in Gn 5,24; Elijah in 2 Kgs 2, 11–12; the righteous person in Ps 73, 24. The verse apparently states the hope that God will rescue the faithful psalmist in the same manner.

when the wealth of their houses grows great.
18 When they die they will take nothing with them,
their wealth will not follow them down.[s]
19 When living, they congratulate themselves and say:
"All praise you, you do so well."
20 But they will join the company of their forebears,
never again to see the light.[t]
21 For all their riches,
if mortals do not have wisdom,
they perish like the beasts.

## PSALM 50*

## The Acceptable Sacrifice

1 *A psalm of Asaph.*

I
The LORD, the God of gods,
has spoken and summoned the earth
from the rising of the sun to its setting.[u]
2 From Zion God shines forth,[v]
perfect in beauty.
3 Our God comes and will not be silent!
Devouring fire precedes,
storming fiercely round about.[w]
4 God summons the heavens above
and the earth to the judgment of his people:
5 "Gather my faithful ones before me,
those who made a covenant with me by sacrifice."
6 The heavens proclaim divine justice,
for God alone is the judge.[x] *Selah*

II
7 "Listen, my people, I will speak;
Israel, I will testify against you;
God, your God, am I.
8 Not for your sacrifices do I rebuke you,
nor for your holocausts, set before me daily.
9 I need no bullock from your house,
no goats from your fold.[y]
10 For every animal of the forest is mine,
beasts by the thousands on my mountains.
11 I know every bird of the heavens;
the creatures of the field belong to me.
12 Were I hungry, I would not tell you,
for mine is the world and all that fills it.[z]
13 Do I eat the flesh of bulls
or drink the blood of goats?
14 Offer praise as your sacrifice to God;[a]
fulfill your vows to the Most High.
15 Then call on me in time of distress;[b]
I will rescue you, and you shall honor me."

III
16 But to the wicked God says:
"Why do you recite my commandments
and profess my covenant with your lips?
17 You hate discipline;
you cast my words behind you!
18 When you see thieves, you befriend them;
with adulterers you throw in your lot.
19 You give your mouth free rein for evil;
you harness your tongue to deceit.
20 You sit maligning your own kin,
slandering the child of your own mother.
21 When you do these things should I be silent?
Or do you think that I am like you?
I accuse you, I lay the charge before you."

IV
22 "Understand this, you who forget God,
lest I attack you with no one to rescue.
23 Those who offer praise as a sacrifice honor me;
to the obedient I will show the salvation of God."[c]

## PSALM 51*

## The Miserere: Prayer of Repentance

1 *For the leader. A psalm of David,* **(2)** *when Nathan the prophet came to him after his affair with Bathsheba.*[d]

I
3 Have mercy on me, God, in your goodness;
in your abundant compassion blot out my offense.
4 Wash away all my guilt;
from my sin cleanse me.

s Sir 11,18-19; Eccl 5, 15; 1 Tm 6,7.
t Jb 10,21-22.
u Dt 10,17; Jos 22,22.
v Ps 48,2.
w Ps 97,3; Dn 7,10.
x Pss 19,2; 97,6.
y Ps 69,32; Am 5, 21-22.
z Pss 24,1; 89,12; Dt 10,14; 1 Cor 10,26.
a Heb 13,15.
b Ps 77,3.
c Ps 91,16.
d 2 Sm 12.

Ps 50: A covenant lawsuit stating that the sacrifice God really wants is the sacrifice of praise accompanied by genuine obedience (cf Mi 6, 1–8). It begins with a theophany and the summoning of the court (1–6). Then in direct address God explains what is required of the faithful (7–15), rebukes the hypocritical worshiper (16–21), and concludes with a threat and a promise (22–23; cf Is 1, 19–20).

Ps 51: A lament, the most famous of the seven Penitential Psalms, prays for the removal of the personal and social disorders that sin has brought. The poem has two parts of approximately equal length: 3–10 and 11–19, and a conclusion in 20–21. The two parts interlock by repetition of "blot out" in the first verse of each section (3. 11), of "wash (away)" just after the first verse of each section (4) and just before the last verse (9) of the first section, and of "heart," "God," and "spirit" in 12 and 19. The first part (3- 10) asks deliverance from sin, which is not just a past act but its emotional, physical, and social consequences. The second part (11–19) seeks something more profound than wiping the slate clean: nearness to God, living by the spirit of God (12–13), like the relation between God and people described in Jer 31, 33–34. Nearness to God brings joy and the authority to teach sinners (15–16). Such proclamation is better than offering sacrifice (17–19). The last two verses ask for the rebuilding of Jerusalem (20–21).

5 For I know my offense;
my sin is always before me.[e]
6 Against you alone have I sinned;
I have done such evil in your sight
That you are just in your sentence,
blameless when you condemn.[f]
7 True, I was born guilty,
a sinner, even as my mother conceived
me.[g]*
8 Still, you insist on sincerity of heart;
in my inmost being teach me wisdom.
9 Cleanse me with hyssop,* that I may be
pure;
wash me, make me whiter than snow.[h]
10 Let me hear sounds of joy and gladness;
let the bones you have crushed rejoice.

II
11 Turn away your face from my sins;
blot out all my guilt.
12 A clean heart create for me, God;
renew in me a steadfast spirit.[i]
13 Do not drive me from your presence,
nor take from me your holy spirit.[j]
14 Restore my joy in your salvation;
sustain in me a willing spirit.
15 I will teach the wicked your ways,
that sinners may return to you.
16 Rescue me from death, God, my saving
God,
that my tongue may praise your healing
power.[k]
17 Lord, open my lips;
my mouth will proclaim your praise.
18 For you do not desire sacrifice;*
a burnt offering you would not accept.[l]
19 My sacrifice, God, is a broken spirit;
God, do not spurn a broken, humbled
heart.

III
20 *Make Zion prosper in your good pleasure;
rebuild the walls of Jerusalem.[m]
21 Then you will be pleased with proper
sacrifice,
burnt offerings and holocausts;
then bullocks will be offered on your
altar.

## PSALM 52*

## The Deceitful Tongue

1 *For the leader. A maskil of David,* (2) *when Doeg the Edomite went and told Saul, "David went to the house of Ahimelech."*[n]

I
3 Why do you glory in evil,
you scandalous liar?
All day long (4) you plot destruction;
your tongue is like a sharpened razor,
you skillful deceiver.[o]
5 You love evil rather than good,
lies rather than honest speech.[p] *Selah*
6 You love any word that destroys,
you deceitful tongue.[q]

II
7 Now God will strike you down,
leave you crushed forever,
Pluck you from your tent,
uproot you from the land of the living.[r]
*Selah*
8 The righteous will look on with awe;
they will jeer and say:[s]
9 "That one did not take God as a refuge,
but trusted in great wealth,
relied on devious plots."[t]

III
10 But I, like an olive tree* in the house of
God,[u]
trust in God's faithful love forever.
11 I will praise you always
for what you have done.
I will proclaim before the faithful[v]
that your name is good.

e Pss 32,5; 38,19; Is 59,12.
f Rom 3,4.
g Jb 14,4.
h Jb 9,30; Is 1,18; Ez 36,25.
i Ez 11,19.
j Wis 1,5; 9,17; Is 63, 11; Hg 2,5; Rom 8,9.
k Ps 30,10.
l Pss 40,7; 50,8; Am 5, 21-22; Hos 6,6; Is 1, 11-15; Heb 10,5-7.
m Jer 31,4; Ez 36,33.
n 1 Sm 21,8; 22,6ff.
o Pss 12,3; 59,8; 120, 2-3; Sir 51,3.
p Jer 4,22; Jn 3,19-20.
q Jer 9,4.
r Pss 27,13; 28,5; 56, 14; Jb 18,14; Prv 2, 22; Is 38,11.
s Pss 44,14; 64,9.
t Jb 31,24; Prv 11,28.
u Pss 1,3; 92,12-14; Jer 11,16; 17,8.
v Pss 22,23; 26,12; 35, 18; 149,1.

*

51, 7: *A sinner, even as my mother conceived me*: literally, "In iniquity was I conceived," an instance of hyperbole: at no time was the psalmist ever without sin. Cf Ps 88, 16, "I am mortally afflicted since youth," i.e., I have always been afflicted. The verse does not imply that the sexual act of conception is sinful.

51, 9: *Hyssop*: a small bush whose many woody twigs make a natural sprinkler. It was prescribed in the Mosaic law as an instrument for sprinkling sacrificial blood or lustral water for cleansing. Cf Ex 12, 22; Lv 14, 4; Nm 19, 18.

51, 18: *For you do not desire sacrifice*: the mere offering of the ritual sacrifice apart from good dispositions is not acceptable to God. Cf Ps 50.

51, 20–21: Most scholars think that these verses were added to the psalm some time after the destruction of the temple in 587 B.C. The verses assume that the rebuilt temple will be an ideal site for national reconciliation.

Ps 52: A condemnation of the powerful and arrogant (3–6), who bring down upon themselves God's judgment (7). The just, those who trust in God alone, are gladdened and strengthened by the downfall of their traditional enemies (8–11).

52, 10: *Like a green olive tree*: the righteous will flourish in the house of God like a well-watered olive tree. Cf Pss 92, 14; 128, 3.

## PSALM 53*

## A Lament over Widespread Corruption

1 *For the leader; according to* Mahalath. *A* maskil *of David*.

I

2 Fools say in their hearts,[w]
"There is no God."[x]
Their deeds are loathsome and corrupt;
not one does what is right.
3 God looks down from heaven
upon the human race,[y]
To see if even one is wise,[z]
if even one seeks God.
4 All have gone astray;
all alike are perverse.
Not one does what is right, not even one.[a]

II

5 Will these evildoers never learn?
They devour my people as they devour bread;[b]
they do not call upon God.[c]
6 They have good reason to fear,
though now they do not fear.
For God will certainly scatter
the bones of the godless.
They will surely be put to shame,
for God has rejected them.

III

7 Oh, that from Zion might come
the deliverance of Israel,
That Jacob may rejoice and Israel be glad[d]
when God restores the people!

## PSALM 54*

## Confident Prayer in Great Peril

1 *For the leader. On stringed instruments. A* maskil *of David,* (2) when the Ziphites came and said to Saul, "David is hiding among us."[e]

I

3 O God, by your name* save me.
By your strength defend my cause.
4 O God, hear my prayer.
Listen to the words of my mouth.
5 The arrogant have risen against me;
the ruthless seek my life;
they do not keep God before them.[f] *Selah*

II

6 God is present as my helper;[g]
the Lord sustains my life.
7 Turn back the evil upon my foes;
in your faithfulness, destroy them.[h]
8 Then I will offer you generous sacrifice
and praise your gracious name, LORD,
9 Because it has rescued me from every trouble,
and my eyes look down on my foes.[i]

## PSALM 55*

## A Lament over Betrayal

1 *For the leader. On stringed instruments. A* maskil *of David.*

I

2 Listen, God, to my prayer;[j]
do not hide from my pleading;
3 hear me and give answer.
I rock with grief; I groan
4 at the uproar of the enemy,
the clamor of the wicked.
They heap trouble upon me,
savagely accuse me.
5 My heart pounds within me;
death's terrors fall upon me.
6 Fear and trembling overwhelm me;
shuddering sweeps over me.
7 I say, "If only I had wings like a dove
that I might fly away and find rest.[k]
8 Far away I would flee;
I would stay in the desert.[l] *Selah*
9 I would soon find a shelter
from the raging wind and storm."

II

10 Lord, check and confuse their scheming.
I see violence and strife in the city
11 making rounds on its walls day and night.
Within are mischief and evil;
12 treachery is there as well;
oppression and fraud never leave its streets.[m]
13 If an enemy had reviled me,

w 2-6a: Ps 14,1-5a.
x Pss 10,4; 36,2; Is 32, 6; Jer 5,12.
y Pss 11,4; 102,20.
z 2b-3: Rom 3,11-12.
a Ps 12,2.
b Ps 27,2; Is 9,11.
c Ps 79,6.
d Ps 85,2.
e 1 Sm 23,19; 26,1.
f Ps 86,14.
g Ps 118,7.
h Ps 143,12.
i Pss 59,11; 91,8; 92, 12.
j 2-3: Pss 5,2-3; 55, 2-3; 86,6; 130,1-2; Lam 3,56; Jon 2,3.
k Ps 11,1.
l Jer 9,1; Rv 12,6.
m Jer 5,1; 6,6; Ez 22,2; Hb 1,3; Zep 3,1.

*

Ps 53: A lament of an individual, duplicated in Ps 14, except that "God" is used for "the LORD," and v 6 is different. See under Ps 14.

Ps 54: A lament in which the person under attack calls directly upon God for help (3–5). Refusing to despair, the psalmist hopes in God, who is active in history and just (6–7). The psalm ends with a serene promise to return thanks (8–9).

54, 3: *By your name*: one is present in one's name, hence God as revealed to humans.

Ps 55: The psalmist, betrayed by intimate friends (14–15, 21–22), prays that God punish those oath breakers and thus be acknowledged as the protector of the wronged. The sufferings of the psalmist include both ostracism (4) and mental turmoil (5–6), culminating in the wish to flee society (7–9). The wish for a sudden death for one's enemies (16) occurs elsewhere in the psalms; an example of such a death is the earth opening under the wicked Dathan and Abiram (Nm 16, 31–32). The psalmist, confident of vindication, exhorts others to a like trust in the God of justice (23–24). The psalm is not so much for personal vengeance as for a public vindication of God's righteousness now. There was no belief in an afterlife where such vindication could take place.

that I could bear;
If my foe had viewed me with contempt,
from that I could hide.
14 But it was you, my other self,
my comrade and friend,[n]
15 You, whose company I enjoyed,
at whose side I walked
in procession in the house of God.

III
16 Let death take them by surprise;
let them go down alive to Sheol,[o]
for evil is in their homes and hearts.
17 But I will call upon God,
and the LORD will save me.
18 At dusk, dawn, and noon
I will grieve and complain,
and my prayer will be heard.[p]
19 God will give me freedom and peace
from those who war against me,
though there are many who oppose me.
20 God, who sits enthroned forever,[q]
will hear me and humble them.
For they will not mend their ways;
they have no fear of God.
21 They strike out at friends
and go back on their promises.
22 Softer than butter is their speech,
but war is in their hearts.
Smoother than oil are their words,
but they are unsheathed swords.[r]
23 Cast your care upon the LORD,
who will give you support.
God will never allow
the righteous to stumble.[s]
24 But you, God, will bring them down
to the pit of destruction.[t]
These bloodthirsty liars
will not live half their days,
but I put my trust in you.[u]

## PSALM 56*

## Trust in God

1 *For the director. According to* Yonath elem rehoqim.* *A miktam of David, when the Philistines seized him at Gath.*[v]

I
2 Have mercy on me, God,
for I am treated harshly;
attackers press me all the day.
3 My foes treat me harshly all the day;
yes, many are my attackers.
O Most High, (4) when I am afraid,
in you I place my trust.
5 God, I praise your promise;
in you I trust, I do not fear.[w]
What can mere flesh do to me?[x]

II
6 All the day they foil my plans;
their every thought is of evil against me.
7 They hide together in ambush;
they watch my every step;
they lie in wait for my life.[y]
8 They are evil; watch them, God!
Cast the nations down in your anger!
9 My wanderings you have noted;
are my tears not stored in your vial,*
recorded in your book?[z]
10 My foes turn back when I call on you.
This I know: God is on my side.
11 God, I praise your promise;
12 in you I trust, I do not fear.
What can mere mortals do to me?

III
13 I have made vows to you, God;
with offerings I will fulfill them,[a]
14 Once you have snatched me from death,
kept my feet from stumbling,
That I may walk before God
in the light of the living.

## PSALM 57*

## Confident Prayer for Deliverance

1 *For the director. Do not destroy.** A miktam *of David, when he fled from Saul into a cave.*[b]

I
2 Have mercy on me, God,
have mercy on me.
In you I seek shelter.
In the shadow of your wings* I seek shelter
till harm pass by.[c]
3 I call to God Most High,
to God who provides for me.

n Ps 41,10; Jer 9,3; Mt 26,21-24 par.
o Ps 49,15; Nm 16,33; Prv 1,2; Is 5,14.
p Dn 6,11.
q Pss 29,10; 93,2; Bar 3,3.
r Pss 12,3; 28,3; 57,5; 62,5; 64,4; Prv 26, 24-28; Jer 9,7.
s Ps 37,5; Prv 3,5; 16, 3; 1 Pt 5,7.
t Pss 28,1; 30,4; 40,3; 88,5; 143,7; Prv 1,12; Jon 2,7.
u Pss 25,2; 56,4; 130,5.
v 1 Sm 21,10.
w Ps 130,5.
x Ps 118,6; Heb 13,6.
y Ps 140,5-6.
z Ps 10,14; 2 Kgs 20,5; Is 25,8; Rv 7,17.
a Nm 30,3.
b 1 Sm 22,1.
c Pss 17,8; 36,8.

*

Ps 56: Beset physically (2–3) and psychologically (6–7), the psalmist maintains a firm confidence in God (5. 9–10). Nothing will prevent the psalmist from keeping the vow to give thanks for God's gift of life (13–14). A refrain (5. 11–12) divides the psalm in two equal parts.

56, 1: *Yonath elem rehoqim*: Hebrew words probably designating the melody to which the psalm was to be sung.

56, 9: *Are my tears not stored in your vial*: a unique saying in the Old Testament. The context suggests that the tears are saved because they are precious; God puts a high value on each of the psalmist's troubles.

Ps 57: Each of the two equal strophes contains a prayer for rescue from enemies, accompanied by joyful trust in God (2–5, 7–11). The refrain prays that God be manifested as saving (6, 12). Ps 108 is nearly identical to part of this psalm (57, 8–12 = 108, 2–6).

57, 1: *Do not destroy*: Probably the title of the melody to which the psalm was to be sung.

57, 2: *The shadow of your wings*: probably refers to the wings of the cherubim (powerful winged animals) whose wings spread over the ark in the inner chamber of the temple (1 Kgs 6, 23–28).

4 May God send help from heaven to save
me,
shame those who trample upon me.
May God send fidelity and love. *Selah*
5 I must lie down in the midst of lions
hungry for human prey.[d]
Their teeth are spears and arrows;
their tongue, a sharpened sword.[e]
6 Show yourself over the heavens, God;
may your glory appear above all the
earth.[f]

II

7 They have set a trap for my feet;
my soul is bowed down;
They have dug a pit before me.
May they fall into it themselves![g] *Selah*
8 My heart is steadfast, God,
my heart is steadfast.
I will sing and chant praise.[h]
9 Awake, my soul;
awake, lyre and harp!
I will wake the dawn.[i]*
10 I will praise you among the peoples, Lord;
I will chant your praise among the
nations.[j]
11 For your love towers to the heavens;
your faithfulness, to the skies.[k]
12 Show yourself over the heavens, God;
may your glory appear above all the earth.

## PSALM 58*

### The Dethroning of Unjust Rulers

1 *For the leader. Do not destroy.** A miktam *of David.*

I

2 Do you indeed pronounce justice, O gods;*
do you judge mortals fairly?[l]
3 No, you freely engage in crime;
your hands dispense violence to the earth.

II

4 The wicked have been corrupt since birth;
liars from the womb, they have gone
astray.
5 *Their poison is like the poison of a snake,
like that of a serpent stopping its ears,[m]
6 So as not to hear the voice of the charmer
who casts such cunning spells.

III

7 O God, smash the teeth in their mouths;
break the jaw-teeth of these lions, LORD![n]
8 Make them vanish like water flowing
away;[o]
trodden down, let them wither like grass.[p]
9 Let them dissolve like a snail that oozes
away,*
like an untimely birth that never sees the
sun.[q]
10 Suddenly, like brambles or thistles,
have the whirlwind snatch them away.[r]
11 Then the just shall rejoice to see the
vengeance
and bathe their feet in the blood of the
wicked.[s]
12 Then it will be said:
"Truly there is a reward for the just;
there is a God who is judge on earth!"

## PSALM 59*

### Complaint Against Bloodthirsty Enemies

1 *For the director. Do not destroy.** A miktam *of David, when Saul sent people to watch his house and kill him.*[t]

I

2 Rescue me from my enemies, my God;
lift me out of reach of my foes.
3 Deliver me from evildoers;
from the bloodthirsty save me.
4 They have set an ambush for my life;
the powerful conspire against me.
For no offense or misdeed of mine, LORD,
5 for no fault they hurry to take up arms.
Come near and see my plight!
6 You, LORD of hosts, are the God of
Israel!

d Pss 17,11-12; 22,22; 58,7.
e Pss 11,2; 64,4.
f Ps 72,19; Nm 14,21.
g Pss 7,15; 140,5-6.
h Ps 108,2.
i Jb 38,12.
j Pss 9,12; 18,50.
k Pss 36,6; 71,19.
l Ps 82,2; Dt 16,19.
m Pss 64,4; 140,3; Rom 3,13.
n Ps 3,7.
o Wis 16,29.
p Ps 37,2.
q Jb 3,16.
r Jb 21,18; Hos 13,3; Na 1,10.
s Ps 68,24; Is 63,1-6.
t 1 Sm 19,11.

* 57, 9: *I will wake the dawn*: by a bold figure the psalmist imagines the sound of music and singing will waken a new day.

Ps 58: A lament expressing trust in God's power to dethrone all powers obstructing divine rule of the world. First condemned are "the gods," the powers that were popularly imagined to control human destinies (2–3), then "the wicked," the human instruments of these forces (4–6). The psalmist prays God to prevent them from harming the just (7–10). The manifestation of justice will gladden the just; they will see that their God is with them (11–12). The psalm is less concerned with personal vengeance than with public vindication of God's justice now.

58, 1: *Do not destroy*: probably the title of the melody to which the psalm was to be sung.

58, 2: *Gods*: the Bible sometimes understands pagan gods to be lesser divine beings who are assigned by Israel's God to rule the foreign nations. Here they are accused of injustice, permitting the human judges under their patronage to abuse the righteous. Cf Ps 82.

58, 5–6: The image is that of a poisonous snake that is controlled by the voice or piping of its trainer.

58, 9: *A snail that oozes away*: empty shells suggested to ancients that snails melted away as they left a slimy trail.

Ps 59: A lament in two parts (2–9, 11b–17), each ending in a refrain (10, 18). Both parts alternate prayer for vindication (2–3, 5b–6; 11b–14) with vivid depictions of the psalmist's enemies (4–5a. 7–8. 15–16). The near curse in 12–13 is not a crude desire for revenge but a wish that God's just rule over human affairs be recognized now.

59, 1: *Do not destroy*: probably the title of the melody to which the psalm was to be sung.

Awake! Punish all the nations.
Have no mercy on these worthless traitors. *Selah*
**7** Each evening they return,
growling like dogs, prowling the city.[u]
**8** Their mouths pour out insult;
sharp words are on their lips.
They say: "Who is there to hear?"*
**9** You, LORD, laugh at them;
you deride all the nations.[v]
**10** My strength, for you I watch;
you, God, are my fortress, (11) my loving God.

II
May God go before me,
and show me my fallen foes.
**12** Slay them, God,
lest they deceive my people.
Shake them by your power;
Lord, our shield, bring them down.
**13** For the sinful words of their mouths and lips
let them be caught in their pride.
For the lies they have told under oath[w]
**14** destroy them in anger,
destroy till they are no more.
Then people will know God rules over Jacob,
yes, even to the ends of the earth.[x] *Selah*
**15** Each evening they return,
growling like dogs, prowling the city.
**16** They roam about as scavengers;
if they are not filled, they howl.

III
**17** But I shall sing of your strength,
extol your love at dawn,
For you are my fortress,
my refuge in time of trouble.
**18** My strength, your praise I will sing;
you, God, are my fortress, my loving God.

## PSALM 60*

### Lament after Defeat in Battle

**1** *For the leader; according to "The Lily of . . . ." A* miktam *of David (for teaching),* **(2)** *when he fought against Aram-Naharaim and Aram-Zobah; and Joab, coming back, killed twelve thousand Edomites in the Valley of Salt.*[y]

I
**3** O God, you rejected us, broke our defenses;
you were angry but now revive us.
**4** You rocked the earth, split it open;[z]
repair the cracks for it totters.
**5** You made your people go through hardship,
made us stagger from the wine you gave us.[a]
**6** Raise up a flag for those who revere you,
a refuge for them out of bowshot. *Selah*
**7** *Help with your right hand and answer us
that your loved ones may escape.

II
**8** In the sanctuary God promised:
"I will exult, will apportion Shechem;
the valley of Succoth I will measure out.*
**9** Gilead is mine, mine is Manasseh;
Ephraim is the helmet for my head,
Judah, my own scepter.*
**10** Moab is my washbowl;*
upon Edom I cast my sandal.[b]
I will triumph over Philistia."

III
**11** Who will bring me to the fortified city?*
Who will lead me into Edom?
**12** Was it not you who rejected us, God?
Do you no longer march with our armies?[c]
**13** Give us aid against the foe;
worthless is human help.
**14** We will triumph with the help of God,
who will trample down our foes.

## PSALM 61*

### Prayer of the King in Time of Danger

**1** *For the leader; with stringed instruments. Of David.*

I
**2** Hear my cry, O God,
listen to my prayer!
**3** From the brink of Sheol* I call;

---

u Ps 55,11.
v Pss 2,4; 37,13; Wis 4, 18.
w Prv 12,13; 18,7.
x Ps 83,18-19; Ez 5,13.
y 2 Sm 8,2. 3. 13; 1 Chr 18,2. 3. 12.
z Ps 75,4; Is 24,19.
a Ps 75,9; Is 51,17. 21-22; Jer 25,15.
b Ru 4,7-8.
c Ps 44,10.

---

59, 8: *Who is there to hear?*: a sample of the enemies' godless reflection. The answer is that God hears their blasphemies.

Ps 60: The community complains that God has let the enemy win the battle (3–5) and asks for an assurance of victory (6–7). In the oracle God affirms ownership of the land; the invasion of other nations is not permanent and will be reversed ultimately (8–10). With renewed confidence, the community resolves to fight again (11). The opening lament is picked up again (12–14), but this time with new awareness of God's power and human limitation.

60, 7–14: These verses occur again as the second half of Ps 108.

60, 8: *I will apportion . . . measure out*: God lays claim to these places. *The valley of Succoth*: probably the lower stretch of the Jabbok valley.

60, 9: *Judah, my own scepter*: an allusion to the Testament of Jacob, Gn 49, 10.

60, 10: *Moab is my washbowl*: Moab borders the Dead Sea, hence a metaphor for the country. *Upon Edom I cast my sandal*: an ancient legal gesture of taking possession of land.

60, 11: *The fortified city*: perhaps Bozrah, the fortified capital of Edom. Cf Is 34, 6; 63, 1; Am 1, 12.

Ps 61: A lament of the king who feels himself at the brink of death (3) and cries out for the strong and saving presence of God (3b–5). The king cites the prayer being made for him (7–8), and promises to give thanks to God.

61, 3: *Brink of Sheol*: literally, "edge of the earth," "earth" being taken in its occasional meaning "the underworld." Cf Jon 2, 3.

my heart grows faint.
Raise me up, set me on a rock,
4 for you are my refuge,
a tower of strength against the foe.[d]
5 Then I will ever dwell in your tent,
take refuge in the shelter of your wings.[e]
*Selah*

II
6 O God, when you accept my vows
and hear the plea of those
who revere your name in prayer:*
7 "Add to the days of the king's life;
may his years be many generations;[f]
8 May he reign before God forever;[g]
may your love and fidelity preserve
him"—[h]
9 Then* I will sing your name forever,
fulfill my vows day after day.

## PSALM 62*

## Trust in God Alone

1 *For the leader;* ʿal Jeduthun.* *A psalm of David.*

I
2 My soul rests in God alone,[i]
from whom comes my salvation.
3 God alone is my rock and salvation,
my secure height; I shall never fall.
4 How long will you set upon people,
all of you beating them down,
As though they were a sagging fence
or a battered wall?
5 Even from my place on high
they plot to dislodge me.
They delight in lies;
they bless with their mouths,
but inwardly they curse.[j] *Selah*

II
6 My soul, be at rest in God alone,
from whom comes my hope.
7 God alone is my rock and my salvation,
my secure height; I shall not fall.
8 My safety and glory are with God,[k]
my strong rock and refuge.
9 Trust God at all times, my people!
Pour out your hearts to God our refuge!
*Selah*

III
10 Mortals are a mere breath,
the powerful but an illusion;[l]
On a balance they rise;*
together they are lighter than air.
11 Do not trust in extortion;
in plunder put no empty hope.
Though wealth increase,
do not set your heart upon it.[m]
12 One thing God has said;
two things* I have heard:[n]
Power belongs to God;
13 so too, Lord, does kindness,
And you render to each of us
according to our deeds.[o]

## PSALM 63*

## Ardent Longing for God

1 *A psalm of David, when he was in the wilderness of Judah.*[p]

I
2 O God, you are my God—
for you I long!
For you my body yearns;
for you my soul thirsts,
Like a land parched, lifeless,
and without water.[q]
3 So I look to you in the sanctuary
to see your power and glory.
4 For your love is better than life;*
my lips offer you worship!

II
5 I will bless you as long as I live;
I will lift up my hands, calling on your
name.
6 My soul shall savor the rich banquet of
praise,
with joyous lips my mouth shall honor
you!
7 When I think of you upon my bed,

d Ps 46,2.
e Pss 17,8; 36,8; 57,2.
f Ps 21,5.
g Pss 72,5; 89,5. 30. 37.
h Pss 85,11; 89,15. 25; Prv 20,28.
i 2-3. 6-7: Pss 18,3; 31,3-4; 42,10; 118,8; 146,3.
j Pss 12,3; 28,3; 55,22; Prv 26,24-25.
k Ps 3,3; Is 26,4; 60,19.
l Pss 39,6-7; 144,4; Jb 7,16; Wis 2,5.
m Jb 31,25; Eccl 5,9; Jer 17,11; Mt 6,19-21. 24.
n Jb 40,5.
o Pss 28,4; 31,24; 2 Sm 3,39; Jb 34,11; Jer 17,10; Mt 16,27; Rom 2,6; 2 Tm 4,14.
p 1 Sm 24.
q Pss 42,2; 143,6; Is 26,9.

*

61, 6: *In prayer*: added for sense. Vv 7–8 express *the plea* of v 6.

61, 9: *Then*: Hebrew "just as," i.e., in accord with the vows referred to in v 6.

Ps 62: A song of trust displaying serenity from experiencing God's power (the refrains of 2–3 and 6–7) and anger toward unjust enemies (4–5). From the experience of being rescued, the psalmist can teach others to trust in God (10–13).

62, 1: *ʿAl Jeduthun*: apparently the Hebrew name for the melody.

62, 10: *On a balance they rise*: precious objects were weighed by balancing two pans suspended from a beam. The lighter pan rises.

62, 12: *One thing . . . two things*: parallelism of numbers for the sake of variation, a common device in Semitic poetry. One should not literally add up the numbers. Cf Am 1, 3; Prv 6, 16–19; 30, 15. 18. 21.

Ps 63: A psalm expressing the intimate relationship between God and the worshiper. Separated from God (2), the psalmist longs for the divine life given in the temple (3–6), which is based on a close relationship with God (7–9). May all my enemies be destroyed and God's true worshipers continue in giving praise (10–12)!

63, 4: *For your love is better than life*: only here in the Old Testament is anything prized above life—in this case God's love.

through the night watches I will recall
8 That you indeed are my help,
and in the shadow of your wings I shout for joy.[r]
9 My soul clings fast to you;
your right hand upholds me.

III
10 But those who seek my life will come to ruin;
they shall go down to the depths of the earth!
11 They shall be handed over to the sword
and become the prey of jackals!
12 But the king shall rejoice in God;
all who swear by the Lord* shall exult,
for the mouths of liars will be shut![s]

## PSALM 64*

## Treacherous Conspirators Punished by God

1 *For the leader. A psalm of David.*

I
2 O God, hear my anguished voice;
from the foes I dread protect my life.
3 Hide me from the malicious crowd,
the mob of evildoers.
4 They sharpen their tongues like swords,
ready their bows for arrows of poison words.[t]
5 They shoot at the innocent from ambush,
shoot without risk, catch them unawares.*
6 They resolve on their wicked plan;
they conspire to set snares;
they say: "Who will see us?"
7 They devise wicked schemes,
conceal the schemes they devise;
the designs of their hearts are hidden.[u]

II
8 But God will shoot arrows at them
and strike them unawares.[v]
9 They will be brought down by their own tongues;
all who see them will shake their heads.[w]
10 Then all will fear and proclaim God's deed,
pondering what has been done.
11 The just will rejoice and take refuge in the LORD;
all the upright will glory in their God.[x]

## PSALM 65*

## Thanksgiving for God's Blessings

1 *For the leader. A psalm of David. A song.*

I
2 To you we owe our hymn of praise,
O God on Zion;
To you our vows* must be fulfilled,
3 you who hear our prayers.
To you all flesh must come[y]*
4 with its burden of wicked deeds.*
We are overcome by our sins;
only you can pardon them.[z]
5 Happy the chosen ones you bring
to dwell in your courts.
May we be filled with the good things of your house,
the blessings of your holy temple!

II
6 You answer us with awesome deeds* of justice,
O God our savior,
The hope of all the ends of the earth
and of far distant islands.[a]
7 You are robed in power,
you set up the mountains by your might.
8 You still the roaring of the seas,[b]
the roaring of their waves,
the tumult of the peoples.[c]
9 Distant peoples stand in awe of your marvels;
east and west you make resound with joy.
10 *You visit the earth and water it,
make it abundantly fertile.[d]
God's stream* is filled with water;
with it you supply the world with grain.
Thus do you prepare the earth:
11 you drench plowed furrows,
and level their ridges.
With showers you keep the ground soft,
blessing its young sprouts.

r Pss 17,8; 36,8.
s Ps 107,42.
t Pss 11,2; 37,14; 55, 22; 57,5.
u Ps 140,3; Prv 6,14.
v Pss 7,13-14; 38,3; Dt 32,42.
w Pss 5,11; 44,14; 52,6.
x Pss 36,8; 57,2.
y Is 66,23.
z Pss 32,1-2; 78,38; Is 1,18.
a Is 66,19.
b Pss 89,10; 107,29; Jb 38,11; Mt 8,26.
c Is 17,12.
d Lv 26,4; Is 30,23. 25; Jl 2,22-23.

*

63, 12: *All who swear by the Lord*: to swear by a particular god meant that one was a worshiper of that god (Is 45, 23; 48, 1; Zep 1, 5).

Ps 64: A lament of a person overwhelmed by the malice of the wicked who are depicted in the psalms as the enemies of the righteous (2–7). When people see God bringing upon the wicked the evil they intended against others, they will know who is the true ruler of the world (8–10). The final verse is a vow of praise (11).

64, 5: *Catch them unawares*: literally, "suddenly," i.e., "unexpectedly."

Ps 65: The community, aware of its unworthiness (3–4), gives thanks for divine bounty (5), a bounty resulting from God's creation victory (6–9). At God's touch the earth comes alive with vegetation and flocks (10–14).

65, 2: *Vows*: the Israelites were accustomed to promising sacrifices in the temple if their prayers were heard.

65, 3: *To you all flesh must come*: all must have recourse to God's mercy.

65, 6: *Awesome deeds*: the acts of creating—installing mountains, taming seas, restraining nations (7–8)—that are visible worldwide (6. 9).

65, 10–14: Apparently a description of the agricultural year, beginning with the first fall rains that soften the hard sun-baked soil (10–11).

65, 10: *God's stream*: the fertile waters of the earth derive from God's fertile waters in the heavenly world.

12 You adorn the year with your bounty;
your paths* drip with fruitful rain.
13 The untilled meadows also drip;
the hills are robed with joy.
14 The pastures are clothed with flocks,
the valleys blanketed with grain;
they cheer and sing for joy.[e]

## PSALM 66*

### Praise of God, Israel's Deliverer

1 *For the leader. A song; a psalm.*

I

Shout joyfully to God, all you on earth;
2 sing of his glorious name;
give him glorious praise.[f]
3 Say to God: "How awesome your deeds!
Before your great strength your enemies cringe.
4 All on earth fall in worship before you;[g]
they sing of you, sing of your name!" *Selah*

II

5 *Come and see the works of God,
awesome in the deeds done for us.
6 He changed the sea to dry land;
through the river they passed on foot.[h]
Therefore let us rejoice in him,
7 who rules by might forever,
Whose eyes are fixed upon the nations.
Let no rebel rise to challenge! *Selah*
8 Bless our God, you peoples;
loudly sound his praise,
9 Who has kept us alive
and not allowed our feet to slip.[i]
10 You tested us, O God,
tried us as silver tried by fire.[j]
11 You led us into a snare;
you bound us at the waist as captives.
12 You let captors set foot on our neck;*
we went through fire and water;
then you led us out to freedom.[k]

III

13 I will bring holocausts* to your house;
to you I will fulfill my vows,
14 The vows my lips pronounced
and my mouth spoke in distress.
15 Holocausts of fatlings I will offer you
and burnt offerings of rams;
I will sacrifice oxen and goats. *Selah*
16 Come and hear, all you who fear God,
while I recount what has been done for me.
17 I called to the Lord with my mouth;
praise was upon my tongue.
18 Had I cherished evil in my heart,
the Lord would not have heard.
19 But God did hear
and listened to my voice in prayer.
20 Blessed be God, who did not refuse me
the kindness I sought in prayer.

## PSALM 67*

### Harvest Thanks and Petition

1 *For the leader; with stringed instruments. A psalm; a song.*

I

2 May God be gracious to us* and bless us;
may God's face shine upon us.[l] *Selah*
3 So shall your rule be known upon the earth,
your saving power among all the nations.[m]
4 May the peoples praise you, God;
may all the peoples praise you!

II

5 May the nations be glad and shout for joy;
for you govern the peoples justly,
you guide the nations upon the earth.[n] *Selah*
6 May the peoples praise you, God;
may all the peoples praise you!

III

7 The earth has yielded its harvest;
God, our God, blesses us.[o]
8 May God bless us still;
that the ends of the earth may revere our God.

---

e Is 44,23.
f Ps 65,14; Is 44,23.
g 3-4: Ps 18,45; Mi 7, 17.
h Pss 74,15; 114,3; Ex 14,21f; Jos 3,14ff; Is 44,27; 50,2.
i Pss 91,12; 121,3; 1 Sm 2,9; Prv 3,23.
j Is 48,10.
k Is 43,2.
l Pss 4,7; 31,17; 44,4; 80,4; Dn 9,17.
m Jer 33,9.
n Ps 98,9.
o Ps 85,13; Lv 26,4; Ez 34,27; Hos 2,23-24.

---

* 65, 12: *Paths*: probably the tracks of God's storm chariot dropping rain upon earth.

Ps 66: In the first part (1–12), the community praises God for powerful acts for Israel, both in the past (the exodus from Egypt and the entry into the land [6]) and in the present (deliverance from a recent but unspecified calamity [8–12]). In the second part (13–20), an individual from the rescued community fulfills a vow to offer a sacrifice of thanksgiving. As often in thanksgivings, the rescued person steps forward to teach the community what God has done (16–20).

66, 5–6: Cf the events described in Ex 14, 1–15, 21; Jos 3, 11–4, 24, and Ps 114.

66, 12: *You let captors set foot on our neck*: literally, "you let men mount our head." Conquerors placed their feet on the neck of their enemies as a sign of complete defeat. Cf Jos 10, 24. A ceremonial footstool of the Egyptian king Tutankhamen portrays bound and prostrate bodies of enemies ready for the king's feet on their heads, and one of Tutankhamen's ceremonial chariots depicts the king as a sphinx standing with paw atop the neck of an enemy.

66, 13: *Holocausts*: wholly burnt offerings. Cf Lv 1, 3–13; 6, 1–4; 22, 17–20.

Ps 67: A petition for a bountiful harvest (7), made in the awareness that Israel's prosperity will persuade the nations to worship its God.

67, 2: *May God be gracious to us*: the people's petition echoes the blessing pronounced upon them by the priests. Cf Nm 6, 22–27.

## PSALM 68*

## The Exodus and Conquest, Pledge of Future Help

1 *For the leader. A psalm of David, a song.*

I
2 *God will arise for battle;
the enemy will be scattered;
those who hate God will flee.[p]
3 The wind will disperse them like smoke;
as wax is melted by fire,
so the wicked will perish before God.[q]
4 Then the just will be glad;
they will rejoice before God;
they will celebrate with great joy.

II
5 Sing to God, praise the divine name;
exalt the rider of the clouds.*
Rejoice before this God
whose name is the LORD.[r]
6 Father of the fatherless, defender of
widows[s] —
this is the God whose abode is holy,
7 Who gives a home to the forsaken,
who leads prisoners out to prosperity,
while rebels live in the desert.*

III
8 God, when you went forth before your
people,[t]
when you marched through the desert,
*Selah*
9 The earth quaked, the heavens shook,
before God, the One of Sinai,
before God, the God of Israel.
10 You claimed a land as your own, O God;
11 your people settled there.
There you poured abundant rains, God,
graciously given to the poor in their need.

IV
12a *The Lord announced the news of victory:
13a "The kings and their armies are in
desperate flight.[u]
12b All you people so numerous,
14a will you stay by the sheepfolds?[v]
13b Every household will share the booty,
14b perhaps a dove sheathed with silver,
14c its wings covered with yellow gold."
15 When the Almighty routed the kings there,
the spoils were scattered like snow on
Zalmon.*

V
16 You high mountains of Bashan,
you rugged mountains of Bashan,
17 You rugged mountains, why look with envy
at the mountain* where God has chosen to
dwell,
where the LORD resides forever?[w]
18 God's chariots were myriad, thousands upon
thousands;
from Sinai the Lord entered the holy
place.
19 You went up to its lofty height;
you took captives, received slaves as
tribute.[x]
No rebels can live in the presence of God.

VI
20 Blessed be the Lord day by day,
God, our salvation, who carries us.[y]
*Selah*
21 Our God is a God who saves;
escape from death is in the LORD God's
hands.
22 God will crush the skulls of the enemy,

p Nm 10,35.
q Ps 97,5; Jdt 16,15; Wis 5,14; Mi 1,4.
r Pss 18,10; 104,3; Dt 33,26; Is 19,1.
s 6-7: Pss 103,6; 146,7. 9; Ex 22,20-22; Bar 6, 37.
t 8-9: Pss 44,10; 114,4. 7; Jgs 5,4-5; Heb 12, 26.
u Jgs 5,19. 22.
v Jgs 5,16.
w Ps 132,13-14; Ez 43, 7.
x Ps 47,8; Eph 4,8-10.
y Pss 34,2; 145,2; Is 46,3-4; 63,9.
z Dt 32,42.

*

Ps 68: The psalm is extremely difficult because the Hebrew text is badly preserved and the ceremony that it describes is uncertain. The translation assumes the psalm accompanied the early autumn Feast of Tabernacles (Sukkoth), which included a procession of the tribes (25–28). Israel was being oppressed by a foreign power, perhaps Egypt (31–32) — unless Egypt stands for any oppressor. The psalm may have been composed from segments of ancient poems, which would explain why the transitions are implied rather than explicitly stated. At any rate, v 2 is based on Nm 10, 35–36, and vv 8–9 are derived from Jgs 5, 4–5.

The argument develops in nine stanzas (each of three to five poetic lines): 1) confidence that God will destroy Israel's enemies (2–4); 2) call to praise God as savior (5–7); 3) God's initial rescue of Israel from Egypt (8), the Sinai encounter (9), and the settlement in Canaan (10–11); 4) the defeat of the Canaanite kings (12–15); 5) the taking of Jerusalem, where Israel's God will rule the world (16–19); 6) praise for God's past help and for the future interventions that will be modeled on the ancient exodus-conquest (20–24); 7) procession at the Feast of Tabernacles (25–28); 8) prayer that the defeated enemies bring tribute to the temple (29–32); 9) invitation for all kingdoms to praise Israel's God (33–36).

68, 2: The opening line alluding to Nm 10, 35 makes clear that God's assistance in the period of the exodus and conquest is the model and assurance of all future divine help.

68, 5: *Exalt the rider of the clouds*: God's intervention is in the imagery of Canaanite myth in which the storm-god mounted the storm clouds to ride to battle. Such theophanies occur throughout the psalm: 2–3. 8–10. 12–15. 18–19. 22–24. 29–32. 34–35. See Dt 33, 26; Ps 18, 8–16; Is 19, 1.

68, 7: *While rebels live in the desert*: rebels must live in the arid desert, whereas God's people will live in the well-watered land (vv 8–11).

68, 12–15: The Hebrew text upon which the translation is based has apparently suffered dislocation and has been substantially rearranged for sense. The version of the defeat of the kings differs from that in the Book of Joshua, where the people play a significant role. Here God alone is responsible for the victory (though the actual battle is not described); Israel only gathers the spoils. God alone is the source of Israel's success; human effort is not important.

68, 15: *Zalmon*: generally taken as the name of a mountain where snow is visible in winter, perhaps to be located in the Golan Heights or in the mountains of Bashan or Hauran east of the Sea of Galilee.

68, 17: *The mountain*: Mount Zion, the site of the temple.

the hairy heads of those who walk in sin.[z]
23 The Lord has said:
"Even from Bashan I will fetch them,
fetch them even from the depths of the sea.*
24 You will wash your feet in your enemy's blood;
the tongues of your dogs will lap it up."[a]

VII
25 Your procession* comes into view, O God,
your procession into the holy place, my God and king.
26 The singers go first, the harpists follow;
in their midst girls sound the timbrels.[b]
27 In your choirs, bless God;
bless the LORD, you from Israel's assemblies.
28 In the lead is Benjamin, few in number;
there the princes of Judah, a large throng,
the princes of Zebulun, the princes of Naphtali, too.[c]

VIII
29 Summon again, O God, your power,
the divine power you once showed for us.
30 Show it from your temple on behalf of Jerusalem,
that kings may bring you tribute.
31 Roar at the wild beast of the reeds,*
the herd of mighty bulls, the lords of nations;
scatter the nations that delight in war.
32 Exact rich tribute from lower Egypt,[d]*
from upper Egypt, gold and silver;
make Ethiopia extend its hands to God.[e]

IX
33 You kingdoms of the earth, sing to God;[f]
chant the praises of the Lord, *Selah*
34 Who rides the heights of the ancient heavens,
whose voice is thunder, mighty thunder.
35 Confess the power of God,
whose majesty protects Israel,
whose power is in the sky.
36 Awesome is God in his holy place,
the God of Israel,
who gives power and strength to his people.[g]
Blessed be God!

## PSALM 69*

## A Cry of Anguish in Great Distress

1 *For the leader; according to "Lilies."* Of David.*

I
2 Save me, God,
for the waters* have reached my neck.[h]
3 I have sunk into the mire of the deep,
where there is no foothold.
I have gone down to the watery depths;
the flood overwhelms me.[i]
4 I am weary with crying out;
my throat is parched.
My eyes have failed,
looking for my God.[j]
5 More numerous than the hairs of my head
are those who hate me without cause.[k]
Too many for my strength
are my treacherous enemies.
Must I now restore
what I did not steal?*

II
6 God, you know my folly;
my faults are not hidden from you.
7 Let those who wait for you, LORD of hosts,
not be shamed through me.
Let those who seek you, God of Israel,[l]
not be disgraced through me.
8 For your sake I bear insult,
shame covers my face.[m]
9 I have become an outcast to my kin,
a stranger to my mother's children.[n]
10 Because zeal for your house consumes me,*
I am scorned by those who scorn you.[o]

a Pss 58,11; 1 Kgs 21, 19; 22,38; Is 63,1-6.
b Pss 81,2-3; 87,7; 149, 3; 150,3-5; 2 Sm 6,5.
c Is 8,23.
d Ez 29,2ff,
e Is 18,7; 45,14.
f Ps 138,4.
g Pss 28,8; 29,11.
h Pss 18,5; 93,3-4; Jb 22,11.
i Pss 40,2; 124,4-5.
j Pss 25,15; 119,82; 123,2; 141,8; Is 38, 14.
k Ps 40,13; Lam 3,52; Jn 15,25.
l Ps 40,17.
m Jer 15,15.
n Jb 19,13-15.
o Ps 119,139; Jn 2,17; Rom 15,3.

*

68, 23: *Even from Bashan . . . from the depths of the sea*: the heights and the depths, the farthest places where enemies might flee.

68, 25–28: *Your procession*: the procession renews God's original taking up of residence on Zion, described in 16–19.

68, 31: *The wild beast of the reeds*: probably the Nile crocodile, a symbol for Egypt: see 32 and Ez 29, 2–5.

68, 31–32: *Lower Egypt* is the delta area north of Cairo. *Upper Egypt* is the Nile Valley from Cairo to Aswan. *Ethiopia* is still further south.

Ps 69: A lament complaining of suffering in language both metaphorical (2–3 and 15–16, the waters of chaos) and literal (4. 5. 9. 11–13, exhaustion, alienation from family and community, false accusation). In the second part the psalmist prays with special emphasis that the enemies be punished for all to see (23–29). Despite the pain, the psalmist does not lose hope that all be set right, and promises public praise (30–37). The psalm, which depicts the suffering of the innocent just person vividly, is cited often by the New Testament especially in the passion accounts, e.g., v 5 in Jn 15, 25; v 22 in Mk 15, 23. 36 and parallels and in Jn 19, 29. The psalm prays not so much for personal vengeance as for public vindication of God's justice. There was, at this time, no belief in an afterlife where such vindication could take place. Redress had to take place now, in the sight of all.

69, 1: *"Lilies"*: apparently the name of the melody.

69, 2: *Waters*: the waters of chaos from which God created the world are a common metaphor for extreme distress. Cf Pss 18, 5; 42, 8; 88, 8; Jon 2, 3–6.

69, 5: *What I did not steal*: the psalmist, falsely accused of theft, is being forced to make restitution.

69, 10: *Zeal for your house consumes me*: the psalmist's commitment to God's cause brings only opposition. Cf Jn 2, 17. *I am scorned by those who scorn you*: Rom 15, 3 uses the verse as an example of Jesus' unselfishness.

11 I have wept and fasted,[p]
but this led only to scorn.
12 I clothed myself in sackcloth;
I became a byword for them.
13 They who sit at the gate gossip about me;
drunkards make me the butt of their songs.

III
14 But I pray to you, LORD,
for the time of your favor.
God, in your great kindness answer me
with your constant help.[q]
15 Rescue me from the mire;[r]
do not let me sink.
Rescue me from my enemies
and from the watery depths.
16 Do not let the floodwaters overwhelm me,
nor the deep swallow me,
nor the mouth of the pit close over me.
17 Answer me, LORD, in your generous love;
in your great mercy turn to me.
18 Do not hide your face from your servant;
in my distress hasten to answer me.[s]
19 Come and ransom my life;
because of my enemies redeem me.
20 You know my reproach, my shame, my disgrace;
before you stand all my foes.
21 Insult has broken my heart, and I am weak;
I looked for compassion, but there was none,
for comforters, but found none.[t]
22 Instead they put gall in my food;
for my thirst they gave me vinegar.[u]

IV
23 Make their own table a snare for them,
a trap for their friends.[v]
24 Make their eyes so dim they cannot see;
keep their backs ever feeble.
25 Pour out your wrath upon them;
let the fury of your anger overtake them.
26 Make their camp desolate,
with none to dwell in their tents.[w]
27 For they pursued the one you struck,
added to the pain of the one you wounded.
28 Add that to their crimes;
let them not attain to your reward.
29 Strike them from the book of the living;
do not count them among the just![x]

V
30 But I am afflicted and in pain;
let your saving help protect me, God,
31 That I may praise God's name in song*
and glorify it with thanksgiving.
32 My song will please the LORD more than oxen,
more than bullocks with horns and hooves:[y]
33 "See, you lowly ones, and be glad;
you who seek God, take heart![z]
34 For the LORD hears the poor,
does not spurn those in bondage.
35 Let the heavens and the earth sing praise,
the seas and whatever moves in them!"

VI
36 God will rescue Zion,
rebuild the cities of Judah.[a]
God's servants shall dwell in the land and possess it;
37 it shall be the heritage of their descendants;
those who love God's name shall dwell there.[b]

## PSALM 70*

## Prayer for Divine Help

1 *For the leader; of David. For remembrance.*

2 Graciously rescue me, God![c]
Come quickly to help me, LORD![d]
3 Confound and put to shame
those who seek my life.[e]
Turn back in disgrace
those who desire my ruin.
4 Let those who say "Aha!"[f]
turn back in their shame.
5 But may all who seek you
rejoice and be glad in you.
May those who long for your help
always say, "God be glorified!"[g]
6 Here I am, afflicted and poor.
God, come quickly!
You are my help and deliverer.
LORD, do not delay!

## PSALM 71*

## Prayer in Time of Old Age

I
1 In you, LORD, I take refuge;[h]
let me never be put to shame.[i]

p 11-13: Ps 109,24-25; Jb 30,9; Lam 3,14.
q Is 49,8.
r 15-16: Pss 28,1; 30,4; 32,6; 40,3; 88,5; Prv 1,12.
s Pss 102,3; 143,7.
t Lam 1,2.
u Lam 3,15; Mt 27,34. 48; Mk 15,23.
v Rom 11,9-10.
w Acts 1,20.
x Ps 139,16; Ex 32,32; Is 4,3; Dn 12,1; Mal 3,16; Rv 3,5.
y Pss 40,7; 50,8-9. 14; 51,18; Is 1,11-15; Hos 6,6; Am 5,21-22; Heb 10,5-8.
z Pss 22,27; 35,27; 70, 5.
a Is 44,26; Ez 36,10.
b Ps 102,29; Is 65,9.
c 2-6: Ps 40,14-18.
d Ps 71,12.
e Ps 35,4. 26.
f Ps 35,21. 25.
g Ps 35,27.
h 1-3: Ps 31,2-4.
i Ps 25,2.

* 69, 31: *That I may praise God's name in song*: the actual song is cited in 33–35, the word "praise" in 35 referring back to "praise" in 31.

Ps 70: A lament of a poor and afflicted person (6) who has no resource except God, and who cries out to be saved from the enemy. The psalm is almost identical to Ps 40, 14–18.

Ps 71: A lament of an old person (9. 18) whose afflictions are interpreted by enemies as a divine judgment (11). The first part of the psalm pleads for help (1–4) on the basis of a hope learned from a lifetime's experience of God; the second part describes the menace (9–13) yet remains buoyant (14–16);

**2** In your justice rescue and deliver me;
listen to me and save me!
**3** Be my rock and refuge,
my secure stronghold;
for you are my rock and fortress.[j]
**4** My God, rescue me from the power of the wicked,
from the clutches of the violent.[k]
**5** You are my hope, Lord;
my trust, GOD, from my youth.
**6** On you I depend since birth;
from my mother's womb you are my strength;[l]
my hope in you never wavers.
**7** I have become a portent to many,*
but you are my strong refuge!
**8** My mouth shall be filled with your praise,
shall sing your glory every day.

II

**9** Do not cast me aside in my old age;
as my strength fails, do not forsake me.
**10** For my enemies speak against me;
they watch and plot against me.[m]
**11** They say, "God has abandoned that one.
Pursue, seize the wretch!
No one will come to the rescue!"
**12** God, do not stand far from me;
my God, hasten to help me.[n]
**13** Bring to a shameful end
those who attack me;
Cover with contempt and scorn
those who seek my ruin.[o]
**14** I will always hope in you
and add to all your praise.
**15** My mouth shall proclaim your just deeds,
day after day your acts of deliverance,
though I cannot number them all.[p]
**16** I will speak of the mighty works of the Lord;
O GOD, I will tell of your singular justice.

III

**17** God, you have taught me from my youth;
to this day I proclaim your wondrous deeds.
**18** Now that I am old and gray,[q]
do not forsake me, God,
That I may proclaim your might
to all generations yet to come,[r]
Your power **19** and justice, God,
to the highest heaven.
You have done great things;[s]
O God, who is your equal?[t]
**20** You have sent me many bitter afflictions,
but once more revive me.
From the watery depths of the earth
once more raise me up.
**21** Restore my honor;
turn and comfort me,
**22** That I may praise you with the lyre
for your faithfulness, my God,
And sing to you with the harp,
O Holy One of Israel!
**23** My lips will shout for joy as I sing your praise;
my soul, too, which you have redeemed.
**24** Yes, my tongue shall recount
your justice day by day.
For those who sought my ruin
will have been shamed and disgraced.

## PSALM 72*

## A Prayer for the King

**1** *Of Solomon.*

I

O God, give your judgment to the king;
your justice to the son of kings;[u]*
**2** That he may govern your people with justice,
your oppressed with right judgment,[v]
**3** That the mountains may yield their bounty for the people,
and the hills great abundance,[w]
**4** That he may defend the oppressed among the people,
save the poor and crush the oppressor.

II

**5** May he live as long as the sun endures,
like the moon, through all generations.[x]
**6** May he be like rain coming down upon the fields,
like showers watering the earth,[y]
**7** That abundance may flourish in his days,
great bounty, till the moon be no more.

III

**8** May he rule from sea to sea,
from the river to the ends of the earth.[z]*

j Ps 18,3.
k Ps 140,2.
l Ps 22,11.
m Pss 3,2; 22,8.
n Ps 22,20.
o Pss 35,4; 40,15; 70,3.
p Ps 35,28.
q Is 46,3-4.
r Pss 22,31-32; 48, 14-15; 145,4.
s Ps 72,18.
t Ps 86,8.
u Ps 99,4; Jer 23,5.
v Prv 31,8-9.
w Is 52,7; 55,12.
x Ps 89,37-38; Jer 31, 35.
y Dt 32,2; Is 45,8; Hos 6,3.
z Dt 11,24; Zec 9,10.

* the third develops the theme of hope and praise.

71, 7: *A portent to many*: the afflictions of the sufferer are taken as a manifestation of God's anger. Cf Dt 28, 46; Ps 31, 12.

Ps 72: A royal psalm in which the Israelite king, as the representative of God, is the instrument of divine justice (1–4. 12–14) and blessing (5–7. 15–17) for the whole world. The king is human, giving only what he has received from God. Hence intercession must be made for him. The extravagant language is typical of oriental royal courts.

72, 1: *The king . . . the son of kings*: the crown prince is the king's son; the prayer envisages the dynasty.

72, 8: *From sea to sea . . . the ends of the earth*: the boundaries of the civilized world known at the time: from the Mediterranean Sea (the western sea) to the Persian Gulf (the eastern sea), and from the Euphrates (the river) to the islands and lands of southwestern Europe, "the ends of the earth." The words may also have a mythic nuance—the earth surrounded by cosmic waters, hence everywhere.

**9** May his foes kneel before him,
his enemies lick the dust.[a]
**10** May the kings of Tarshish and the islands*
bring tribute,
the kings of Arabia and Seba offer gifts.[b]
**11** May all kings bow before him,
all nations serve him.[c]
**12** For he rescues the poor when they cry out,
the oppressed who have no one to help.
**13** He shows pity to the needy and the poor[d]
and saves the lives of the poor.
**14** From extortion and violence he frees them,
for precious is their blood* in his sight.

IV

**15** Long may he live, receiving gold from
Arabia,
prayed for without cease, blessed day by
day.
**16** *May wheat abound in the land,
flourish even on the mountain heights.
May his fruit increase like Lebanon's,
his wheat like the grasses of the land.[e]
**17** May his name be blessed forever;
as long as the sun, may his name endure.[f]
May the tribes of the earth give blessings
with his name;*
may all the nations regard him as
favored.[g]

* * *

**18** *Blessed be the LORD, the God of Israel,
who alone does wonderful deeds.[h]
**19** Blessed be his glorious name forever;
may all the earth be filled with the
LORD's glory.[i]
Amen and amen.
**20** The end of the psalms of David, son of
Jesse.

# *THIRD BOOK — PSALMS 73–89*

## PSALM 73*

## The Trial of the Just

**1** *A psalm of Asaph.*
How good God is to the upright,
the Lord, to those who are clean of heart!

I

**2** But, as for me, I lost my balance;
my feet all but slipped,
**3** Because I was envious of the arrogant
when I saw the prosperity of the wicked.[j]
**4** For they suffer no pain;
their bodies are healthy and sleek.
**5** They are free of the burdens of life;
they are not afflicted like others.
**6** Thus pride adorns them as a necklace;
violence clothes them as a robe.
**7** Out of their stupidity comes sin;
evil thoughts flood their hearts.[k]
**8** They scoff and spout their malice;
from on high they utter threats.[l]
**9** They set their mouths against the heavens,*
their tongues roam the earth.
**10** *So my people turn to them
and drink deeply of their words.
**11** They say, "Does God really know?"
"Does the Most High have any
knowledge?"[m]
**12** Such, then, are the wicked,
always carefree, increasing their wealth.

II

**13** Is it in vain that I have kept my heart clean,
washed my hands in innocence?[n]
**14** For I am afflicted day after day,
chastised every morning.
**15** Had I thought, "I will speak as they do,"
I would have betrayed your people.
**16** Though I tried to understand all this,
it was too difficult for me,
**17** Till I entered the sanctuary of God
and came to understand their end.*

III

**18** You set them, indeed, on a slippery road;
you hurl them down to ruin.
**19** How suddenly they are devastated;
undone by disasters forever!
**20** They are like a dream after waking, Lord,
dismissed like shadows when you arise.[o]

a Is 49,23; Mi 7,17.
b Ps 68,30; Is 60,5-6; 1 Kgs 10,1ff.
c Pss 47,8.
d Prv 31,9.
e Is 27,6; Hos 14,6-8; Am 9,13.
f Ps 21,7.
g Gn 12,3; Zec 8,13.
h Pss 41,14; 89,53; 106,48; 136,4.
i Ps 57,5; Nm 14,21.
j Ps 37,1; Jb 21,13.
k Jb 15,27.
l Ps 17,10.
m Ps 10,11; Jb 22,13.
n Ps 26,6; Mal 3,14.
o Jb 20,8.

*

72, 10: *Tarshish and the islands*: the far west (Ps 48, 6); *Arabia and Seba*: the far south (1 Kgs 10, 1).

72, 14: *Their blood*: cf Ps 116, 15.

72, 16: The translation of the difficult Hebrew is tentative.

72, 17: *May the tribes of the earth give blessing with his name*: an echo of the promise to the ancestors (Gn 12, 3; 26, 4; 28, 14), suggesting that the monarchy in Israel fulfilled the promise to Abraham, Isaac, and Jacob.

72, 18–19: A doxology marking the end of Book II of the Psalter.

Ps 73: The opening verse of this probing poem (cf Pss 37, 49) is actually the psalmist's hard-won conclusion from personal experience: God is just and good! The psalmist describes near loss of faith (2–3), occasioned by observing the wicked who blasphemed God with seeming impunity (4–12). Feeling abandoned despite personal righteousness, the psalmist could not bear the injustice until an experience of God's nearness in the temple made clear how deluded the wicked were. Their sudden destruction shows their impermanence (13–20). The just can thus be confident, for, as the psalmist now knows, their security is from God (1. 23–28).

73, 9: *They set their mouths against the heavens*: in an image probably derived from mythic stories of half-divine giants, the monstrous speech of the wicked is likened to enormous jaws gaping wide, devouring everything in sight.

73, 10: The Hebrew is obscure.

73, 17: *And came to understand their end*: the psalmist receives a double revelation in the temple: 1) the end of the wicked comes unexpectedly (18–20); 2) God is with me.

IV

**21** Since my heart was embittered
and my soul deeply wounded,
**22** I was stupid and could not understand;
I was like a brute beast in your presence.
**23** Yet I am always with you;
you take hold of my right hand.[p]
**24** With your counsel you guide me,
and at the end receive me with honor.*
**25** Whom else have I in the heavens?
None beside you delights me on earth.
**26** Though my flesh and my heart fail,
God is the rock of my heart, my portion forever.
**27** But those who are far from you perish;
you destroy those unfaithful to you.
**28** As for me, to be near God is my good,
to make the Lord GOD my refuge.
I shall declare all your works
in the gates of daughter Zion.

## PSALM 74*

## Prayer at the Destruction of the Temple

**1** *A maskil of Asaph.*

I

Why, God, have you cast us off forever?[q]*
Why does your anger burn against the sheep of your pasture?[r]
**2** Remember your flock that you gathered of old,
the tribe you redeemed as your very own.
Remember Mount Zion where you dwell.[s]
**3** Turn your steps toward the utter ruins,
toward the sanctuary devastated by the enemy.
**4** Your foes roared triumphantly in your shrine;
they set up their own tokens of victory.
**5** They hacked away like foresters gathering boughs,
swinging their axes in a thicket of trees.
**6** They smashed all your engraved work,
pounded it with hammer and pick.
**7** They set your sanctuary on fire;
the abode of your name they razed and profaned.[t]
**8** They said in their hearts, "Destroy them all!
Burn all the shrines of God in the land!"
**9** Now we see no signs,*
we have no prophets,[u]
no one who knows how long.
**10** How long, O God, shall the enemy jeer?[v]
Shall the foe revile your name forever?
**11** Why draw back your right hand,
why keep it idle beneath your cloak?

II

**12** *Yet you, God, are my king from of old,
winning victories throughout the earth.
**13** You stirred up the sea in your might;[w]
you smashed the heads of the dragons on the waters.[x]
**14** You crushed the heads of Leviathan,[y]
tossed him for food to the sharks.
**15** You opened up springs and torrents,
brought dry land out of the primeval waters.
**16** Yours the day and yours the night;
you set the moon and sun in place.
**17** You fixed all the limits of the earth;
summer and winter you made.[z]
**18** Remember how the enemy has jeered, O LORD,
how a foolish people has reviled your name.
**19** Do not surrender to beasts those who praise you;
do not forget forever the life of your afflicted.
**20** Look to your covenant,
for the land is filled with gloom;
the pastures, with violence.
**21** Let not the oppressed turn back in shame;
may the poor and needy praise your name.
**22** Arise, God, defend your cause;
remember the constant jeers of the fools.

p Ps 121,5.
q Pss 10,1; 44,24; 77,8.
r Ps 80,5.
s Pss 68,17; 132,13; Ex 15,17; Jer 10,16; 51, 19.
t Is 64,10; Ps 79,1.
u Lam 2,9.
v Ps 89,47.
w Ps 89,10.
x Is 51,9-10.
y Jb 3,8; 40,25; Is 27,1.
z 16-17: Gn 1.

*

73, 24: *And at the end receive me with honor*: a perhaps deliberately enigmatic verse. It is understood by some commentators as reception into heavenly glory, hence the traditional translation, "receive me into glory." The Hebrew verb can indeed refer to mysterious divine elevation of a righteous person into God's domain: Enoch in Gn 5, 24; Elijah in 2 Kgs 2, 11–12; the righteous psalmist in Ps 49, 16. Personal resurrection in the Old Testament, however, is clearly attested only in the second century B.C. The verse is perhaps best left unspecified as a reference to God's nearness and protection.

Ps 74: A communal lament sung when the enemy invaded the temple; it would be especially appropriate at the destruction of Jerusalem in 587 B.C. Israel's God is urged to look upon the ruined sanctuary and remember the congregation who worshiped there (1–11). People and sanctuary are bound together; an attack on Zion is an attack on Israel. In the second half of the poem, the community brings before God the story of their origins—their creation (12–17)—in order to move God to reenact that deed of creation now. Will God allow a lesser power to destroy the divine project (18–23)?

74, 1: *Forever*: the word implies that the disaster is already of long duration. Cf 74, 9 and note.

74, 9: *Now we see no signs*: ancients often asked prophets to say for how long a divine punishment was to last. Cf 2 Sm 24, 13. Here no prophet has arisen to indicate the duration.

74, 12–17: Comparable Canaanite literature describes the storm-god's victory over all-encompassing Sea and its allies (dragons and Leviathan) and the subsequent peaceful arrangement of the universe, sometimes through the placement of paired cosmic elements (day and night, sun and moon). Cf Ps 89, 12–13. The psalm apparently equates the enemies attacking the temple with the destructive cosmic forces already tamed by God. Why then are those forces now raging untamed against your own people?

23 Do not ignore the clamor of your foes,
the unceasing uproar of your enemies.

## PSALM 75*

## God the Judge of the World

1 *For the leader. Do not destroy! A psalm of Asaph; a song.*

I

2 We thank you, God, we give thanks;
we call upon your name,
declare your wonderful deeds.
You said:*
3 "I will choose the time;
I will judge fairly.
4 The earth and all its inhabitants will quake,
but I have firmly set its pillars."[a] *Selah*

II

5 So I say to the boastful: "Do not boast!"[b]
to the wicked: "Do not raise your horns!*
6 Do not raise your horns against heaven!
Do not speak arrogantly against the Rock!"[c]
7 For judgment comes not from east or from west,
not from the desert or from the mountains,[d]
8 But from God who decides,
who brings some low and raises others high.[e]
9 Yes, a cup* is in the LORD's hand,
foaming wine, fully spiced.
When God pours it out,
they will drain it even to the dregs;
all the wicked of the earth must drink.[f]
10 But I will rejoice forever;
I will sing praise to the God of Jacob,
11 Who has said:
"I will break off all the horns of the wicked,
but the horns of the just shall be lifted up."[g]

## PSALM 76*

## God Defends Zion

1 *For the leader; a psalm with stringed instruments. A song of Asaph.*

I

2 Renowned in Judah is God,[h]
whose name is great in Israel.
3 On Salem* is God's tent, a shelter on Zion.
4 There the flashing arrows were shattered,
shield, sword, and weapons of war.[i] *Selah*

II

5 Terrible and awesome are you,
stronger than the ancient mountains.*
6 Despoiled are the bold warriors;
they sleep their final sleep;
the hands of all the mighty have failed.[j]
7 At your roar, O God of Jacob,
chariots and steeds lay still.
8 So terrible and awesome are you;
who can stand before you and your great anger?[k]
9 From the heavens you pronounced sentence;
the earth was terrified and reduced to silence,
10 When you arose, O God, for judgment
to deliver the afflicted of the land. *Selah*
11 Even wrathful Edom praises you;
the remnant of Hamath* keeps your feast.

III

12 Make and keep vows to the LORD your God.[l]
May all present bring gifts to this awesome God,
13 Who checks the pride of princes,
inspires awe among the kings of earth.

## PSALM 77*

## Confidence in God during National Distress

1 *For the leader;* 'al Jeduthun. *A psalm of Asaph.*

I

2 I cry aloud to God,
cry to God to hear me.

a Pss 46,3; 60,4; 93,1; 96,10; 104,5; 1 Sm 2, 8; Is 24,19.
b 1 Sm 2,3; Zec 2,1-4.
c Jb 15,25.
d Mt 24,23-27.
e Jb 5,11; 1 Sm 2,7.
f Ps 60,5; Jb 21,20; Is 51,17. 21-22; Jer 25, 15ff; Hb 2,16.
g Ps 92,11.
h Hb 3,2.
i Pss 46,10; 122,6-9.
j 2 Kgs 19,35; Jer 51, 39; Na 3,18.
k Dt 7,21; 1 Sm 6,20; Na 1,6; Mal 3,2.
l Nm 30,3.

*

Ps 75: The psalmist gives thanks and rejoices (2. 10) for the direct intervention of God, which is promised in two oracles (3–4. 11). Expecting that divine intervention, the psalmist warns evildoers to repent (5–9).

75, 2: *You said*: supplied for clarity here and in v 11. The translation assumes in both places that the psalmist is citing an oracle of God.

75, 5: *Do not raise your horns!*: the horn is the symbol of strength; to raise one's horn is to exalt one's own power as v 6 explains.

75, 9: *A cup*: "the cup of God's wrath" is the punishment inflicted on the wicked. Cf Is 51, 17; Jer 25, 15–29; 49, 12; Ez 23, 31–33. *Spiced*: literally, "a mixed drink"; spices or drugs were added to wine. Cf Prv 9, 2. 5.

Ps 76: A song glorifying Zion, the mountain of Jerusalem where God destroyed Israel's enemies. Zion is thus the appropriate site to celebrate the victory (3–4), a victory described in parallel scenes (5–7. 8–11). Israel is invited to worship its powerful patron deity (12–13).

76, 3: *Salem*: an ancient name for Jerusalem, used here perhaps on account of its allusion to the Hebrew word for peace, *shalom*. Cf Gn 14, 18; Heb 7, 1–3.

76, 5: *Ancient mountains*: conjectural translation of a difficult Hebrew phrase on the basis of Gn 49, 26. The mountains are part of the structure of the universe (Ps 89, 12–13).

76, 11: *Edom . . . Hamath*: conjectural translation. Israel's neighbors to the southeast and north.

Ps 77: A community lament in which the speaker ("I") describes the anguish of Israel at God's silence when its very existence is at stake (2–11). In response the speaker recites

**3** On the day of my distress I seek the Lord;
by night my hands are raised
unceasingly;[m]
I refuse to be consoled.
**4** When I think of God, I groan;
as I ponder, my spirit grows faint.[n] *Selah*
**5** My eyes cannot close in sleep;
I am troubled and cannot speak.
**6** I consider the days of old;
the years long past (7) I remember.[o]
In the night I meditate in my heart;
I ponder and my spirit broods:
**8** "Will the Lord reject us forever,[p]
never again show favor?
**9** Has God's love ceased forever?
Has the promise failed for all ages?
**10** Has God forgotten mercy,
in anger withheld compassion?" *Selah*
**11** I conclude:* "My sorrow is this,
the right hand of the Most High has left
us."[q]

II

**12** I will remember* the deeds of the LORD;
yes, your wonders of old I will
remember.[r]
**13** I will recite all your works;
your exploits I will tell.
**14** Your way, O God, is holy;
what god is as great as our God?[s]
**15** You alone are the God who did wonders;
among the peoples you revealed your
might.[t]
**16** With your arm you redeemed your people,
the descendants of Jacob and Joseph.[u]
*Selah*
**17** The waters saw you, God;
the waters saw you and lashed about,
trembled even to their depths.[v]
**18** The clouds poured down their rains;
the thunderheads rumbled;
your arrows flashed back and forth.[w]
**19** The thunder of your chariot wheels
resounded;
your lightning lit up the world;
the earth trembled and quaked.[x]
**20** Through the sea was your path;
your way, through the mighty waters,
though your footsteps were unseen.[y]
**21** You led your people like a flock
under the care of Moses and Aaron.[z]

## PSALM 78*

## A New Beginning in Zion and David

**1** *A maskil of Asaph.*

I

Attend, my people, to my teaching;
listen to the words of my mouth.
**2** I will open my mouth in story,*
drawing lessons from of old.[a]
**3** We have heard them, we know them;
our ancestors have recited them to us.[b]
**4** We do not keep them from our children;
we recite them to the next generation,
The praiseworthy and mighty deeds of the
LORD,
the wonders that he performed.[c]
**5** God set up a decree in Jacob,
established a law in Israel:[d]
What he commanded our ancestors,
they were to teach their children;
**6** That the next generation might come to
know,
children yet to be born.[e]
In turn they were to recite them to their
children,
**7** that they too might put their trust in God,
And not forget the works of God,
keeping his commandments.
**8** They were not to be like their ancestors,
a rebellious and defiant generation,[f]
A generation whose heart was not constant,[g]
whose spirit was not faithful to God,
**9** Like the ranks of Ephraimite archers,*

m Pss 50,15; 88,2.
n Jon 2,8.
o Ps 143,5; Dt 32,7.
p 8-10: Pss 13,2; 44,24; 74,1; 80,5; 89,47; Lam 3,31.
q Ex 15,6. 12; Pss 17,7; 18,36.
r Ps 143,5.
s Ps 18,31; Ex 15,11.
t Pss 86,10; 89,6.
u Gn 46,26-27; Neh 1, 10.
v Pss 18,16; 114,3; Na 1,4.
w Pss 18,14-15; 29; 144,6; Jb 37,3-4; Wis 5,21; Hb 3,10-11; Zec 9,14.
x Pss 18,8; 97,4; 99,1; Ex 19,16; Jgs 5,4-5.
y Neh 9,11; Wis 14,3; Is 51,10; Hb 3,15.
z Ps 78,52; Is 63,11-14; Hos 12,14; Mi 6,4.
a Ps 49,5; Mt 13,35.
b Ps 44,2.
c Ex 10,2; Dt 4,9; Jb 8, 8.
d Ps 147,19; Dt 33,4.
e Ps 22,31-32; Dt 4,9; 6,7.
f Dt 31,27; 32,5.
g Ps 95,10.

*

the story of how God brought the people into existence (12–21). The question is thus posed to God: Will you allow the people you created to be destroyed?

77, 11: *I conclude*: literally, "I said." The psalmist, after pondering the present distress and God's promises to Israel, has decided that God has forgotten the people.

77, 12: *I will remember*: the verb sometimes means to make present the great deeds of Israel's past by reciting them. Cf Pss 78, 42; 105, 5; 106, 7.

Ps 78: A recital of history to show that past generations did not respond to God's gracious deeds and were punished by God making the gift into a punishment. Will Israel now fail to appreciate God's new act – the choosing of Zion and of David? The tripartite introduction invites Israel to learn the lessons hidden in its traditions (1–4. 5–7. 8–11); each section ends with the mention of God's acts. There are two distinct narratives of approximately equal length: the wilderness events (12–39) and the movement from Egypt to Canaan (40–72). The structure of both is parallel: gracious act (12–16. 40–55), rebellion (17–20. 56–58), divine punishment (21–31. 59–64), God's readiness to forgive and begin anew (32–39. 65–72). The psalm may reflect the reunification program of either King Hezekiah (late eighth century) or King Josiah (late seventh century) in that the Northern Kingdom (Ephraim, Joseph) is especially invited to accept Zion and the Davidic king.

78, 2: *Story*: Hebrew *mashal* literally means "comparison" and can signify a story with a hidden meaning. Mt 13, 35 cites the verse to explain Jesus' use of parables.

78, 9: *Ephraimite archers*: Ephraim was the most important tribe of the Northern Kingdom. Its military defeat (here unspecified) demonstrates its infidelity to God, who otherwise would have protected it.

who retreated on the day of battle.
**10** They did not keep God's covenant;
they refused to walk by his law.
**11** They forgot his works,
the wondrous deeds he had shown them.

II

## A

**12** In the sight of their ancestors God did wonders,
in the land of Egypt, the plain of Zoan.[h]*
**13** He split the sea and led them across,[i]
piling up the waters rigid as walls.[j]
**14** God led them with a cloud by day,
all night with the light of fire.[k]
**15** He split rock in the desert,
gave water to drink, abounding as the deep.[l]
**16** He made streams flow from crags,
drew out rivers of water.

## B

**17** But they went on sinning against him,
rebelling against the Most High in the desert.[m]
**18** They tested God in their hearts,
demanding the food they craved.[n]
**19** They spoke against God, and said,
"Can God spread a table in the desert?[o]
**20** True, when he struck the rock,
water gushed forth,
the wadis flooded.
But can he also provide bread,
give meat to his people?"

## C

**21** The LORD heard and grew angry;[p]
fire blazed up against Jacob;
anger flared up against Israel.
**22** For they did not believe in God,
did not trust in his saving power.
**23** *So he commanded the skies above;
the doors of heaven he opened.
**24** God rained manna upon them for food;
bread from heaven he gave them.[q]
**25** All ate a meal fit for heroes;
food he sent in abundance.
**26** He stirred up the east wind in the heavens;
by his power God brought on the south wind.
**27** He rained meat upon them like dust,
winged fowl like the sands of the sea,
**28** Brought them down in the midst of the camp,
round about their tents.
**29** They ate and were well filled;
he gave them what they had craved.
**30** But while they still wanted more,
and the food was still in their mouths,
**31** God's anger attacked them,
killed their best warriors,
laid low the youth of Israel.[r]
**32** In spite of all this they went on sinning,
they did not believe in his wonders.

## D

**33** God ended their days abruptly,
their years in sudden death.
**34** When he slew them, they began to seek him;
they again inquired of their God.[s]
**35** They remembered* that God was their rock,
God Most High, their redeemer.
**36** But they deceived him with their mouths,
lied to him with their tongues.
**37** Their hearts were not constant toward him;
they were not faithful to his covenant.[t]
**38** *But God is merciful and forgave their sin;
he did not utterly destroy them.
Time and again he turned back his anger,
unwilling to unleash all his rage.[u]
**39** He was mindful that they were flesh,
a breath that passes and does not return.

III

## A

**40** How often they rebelled against God in the desert,
grieved him in the wasteland.
**41** Again and again they tested God,
provoked the Holy One of Israel.
**42** They did not remember his power,
the day he redeemed them from the foe,[v]
**43** *When he displayed his wonders in Egypt,
his marvels in the plain of Zoan.[w]
**44** God changed their rivers to blood;
their streams they could not drink.
**45** He sent insects that devoured them,[x]
frogs that destroyed them.
**46** He gave their harvest to the caterpillar,
the fruits of their labor to the locust.
**47** He killed their vines with hail,[y]
their sycamores with frost.

h Ps 106,7.
i 13-14: Ex 14-15; Ps 136,13.
j Ex 14,22; 15,8.
k Ps 105,39; Ex 13,21; Wis 18,3.
l Pss 105,41; 114,8; Ex 17,1-7; Nm 20,2-13; Dt 8,15; Wis 11,4; Is 48,21.
m Dt 9,7; Ez 20,13.
n Ps 106,14; Ex 16, 2-36.
o Ps 23,5.
p 21f: Nm 11; Dt 32,22.
q Ps 105,40; Ex 16,4. 14; Dt 8,3; Wis 16,20; Jn 6,31.
r Nm 14,29.
s Dt 32,15. 18; Is 26, 16.
t Ps 95,10; Is 29,13.
u Ps 85,4; Ex 32,14; Is 48,9; Ez 20,22.
v Ps 106,21.
w 43f: Pss 105,27-36; 135,9; Ex 7,14-11,10; 12,29-36; Wis 16-18.
x Ex 8,17.
y Wis 16,16.

*

78, 12. 43: *Zoan*: a city on the arm of the Nile, a former capital of Egypt.

78, 23–31: On the manna and the quail, see Ex 16 and Nm 11. Unlike Ex 16, here both manna and quail are instruments of punishment, showing that a divine gift can become deadly because of Israel's apostasy.

78, 35: *Remembered*: invoked God publicly in worship. Their words were insincere (36).

78, 38: God is always ready to forgive and begin anew, as in choosing Zion and David (65–72).

78, 43–55: Ex 7–12 records ten plagues. Here there are six divine attacks upon Egypt; the seventh climactic act is God's bringing Israel to the holy land.

**48** He exposed their flocks to deadly hail,
their cattle to lightning.[z]
**49** He unleashed against them his fiery breath,
roar, fury, and distress,
storming messengers of death.
**50** He cleared a path for his anger;
he did not spare them from death;
he delivered their beasts to the plague.
**51** He struck all the firstborn of Egypt,[a]
love's first child in the tents of Ham.
**52** God led forth his people like sheep;
he guided them through the desert like a flock.[b]
**53** He led them on secure and unafraid,
but the sea enveloped their enemies.[c]
**54** He brought them to his holy land,
the mountain his right hand had won.[d]
**55** God drove out the nations before them,
apportioned them a heritage by lot,
settled the tribes of Israel in their tents.

### B

**56** But they tested, rebelled against God Most High,
his decrees they did not observe.
**57** They turned back, deceitful like their ancestors;
they proved false like a bow with no tension.
**58** They enraged him with their high places;
with their idols they goaded him.[e]

### C

**59** God heard and grew angry;
he rejected Israel completely.
**60** He forsook the shrine at Shiloh,[f]*
the tent where he dwelt with humans.
**61** He gave up his might into captivity,
his glorious ark into the hands of the foe.[g]
**62** God abandoned his people to the sword;
he was enraged against his heritage.
**63** Fire consumed their young men;
their young women heard no wedding songs.[h]
**64** Their priests fell by the sword;
their widows made no lamentation.

### D

**65** Then the Lord awoke as from sleep,
like a warrior from the effects of wine.
**66** He put his enemies to flight;
everlasting shame he dealt them.
**67** He rejected the tent of Joseph,
chose not the tribe of Ephraim.
**68** *God chose the tribe of Judah,
Mount Zion which he favored.[i]
**69** He built his shrine like the heavens,
like the earth which he founded forever.
**70** He chose David his servant,
took him from the sheepfold.[j]
**71** From tending sheep God brought him,
to shepherd Jacob, his people,
Israel, his heritage.[k]
**72** He shepherded them with a pure heart;
with skilled hands he guided them.

## PSALM 79*

## A Prayer for Jerusalem

**1** *A psalm of Asaph.*

I

O God, the nations have invaded your heritage;
they have defiled your holy temple,
have laid Jerusalem in ruins.[l]
**2** They have left the corpses of your servants
as food for the birds of the heavens,
the flesh of your faithful for the beasts of the earth.[m]
**3** They have spilled their blood like water
all around Jerusalem,
and no one is left to bury them.[n]
**4** We have become the reproach of our neighbors,
the scorn and derision of those around us.[o]

II

**5** How long, LORD? Will you be angry forever?
Will your rage keep burning like fire?[p]
**6** Pour out your wrath on nations that reject you,
on kingdoms that do not call on your name,[q]
**7** For they have devoured Jacob,
laid waste his home.
**8** Do not hold past iniquities against us;
may your compassion come quickly,
for we have been brought very low.[r]

z Ex 9,3.
a Pss 105,36; 136,10; Ex 12,29.
b Ps 77,21.
c Ex 14,26-28.
d Ex 15,17.
e Dt 32,16. 21.
f Jos 18,1; 1 Sm 1,3; Jer 7,12; 26,6.
g 1 Sm 4,11. 22.
h Dt 32,25; Jer 7,34.
i Pss 48,2; 50,2; Lam 2,15.
j Ps 89,21; Ez 34,23; 37,24; 2 Chr 6,6.
k 1 Sm 16,11-13; 2 Sm 7,8.
l 2 Kgs 25,9-10; Lam 1, 10.
m Jer 7,33.
n 1 Mc 7,17; Jer 14,16.
o Pss 44,14; 80,7; 123, 3-4; Jb 12,4; Dn 9,16; Zep 2,8.
p Pss 13,2; 44,24; 89, 47; Dt 4,24.
q Ps 14,4; Jer 10,25.
r Ps 142,7.

*

78, 60: *Shiloh*: an important shrine in the north prior to Jerusalem. Despite its holy status, it was destroyed (60–64; cf Jer 7, 12. 14).

78, 68. 70: God's ultimate offer of mercy to the sinful helpless people is Zion and the Davidic king.

Ps 79: A communal lament complaining that the nations have defiled the temple and murdered the holy people, leaving their corpses unburied (1–4). The occasion is probably the destruction of Jerusalem by the Babylonian army in 587 B.C. The people ask how long the withdrawal of divine favor will last (5), pray for action now (6–7), and admit that their own sins have brought about the catastrophe (8–9). They seek to persuade God to act for reasons of honor: the nations who do not call upon the Name are running amok (6); the divine honor is compromised (1. 10. 12); God's own servants suffer (2–4. 11).

III

9 Help us, God our savior,
for the glory of your name.
Deliver us, pardon our sins
for your name's sake.[s]
10 Why should the nations say,
"Where is their God?"[t]
Before our eyes make clear to the nations
that you avenge the blood of your
servants.[u]

IV

11 Let the groans of prisoners come before you;
by your great power free those doomed to
death.[v]
12 Lord, inflict on our neighbors sevenfold
the disgrace they inflicted on you.[w]
13 Then we, your people, the sheep of your
pasture,
will give thanks to you forever;
through all ages we will declare your
praise.

## PSALM 80*

## Prayer to Restore God's Vineyard

1 *For the leader; according to "Lilies."* Eduth.*
*A psalm of Asaph.*

I

2 Shepherd of Israel, listen,
guide of the flock of Joseph!
From your throne upon the cherubim reveal
yourself[x]
3 to Ephraim, Benjamin, and Manasseh.
Stir up your power, come to save us.
4 O LORD of hosts, restore us;
Let your face shine upon us,
that we may be saved.[y]

II

5 LORD of hosts,
how long will you burn with anger
while your people pray?[z]
6 You have fed them the bread of tears,
made them drink tears in abundance.[a]
7 You have left us to be fought over by our
neighbors;
our enemies deride us.[b]
8 O LORD of hosts, restore us;
let your face shine upon us,
that we may be saved.

III

9 You brought a vine* out of Egypt;
you drove away the nations and planted it.
10 You cleared the ground;
it took root and filled the land.
11 The mountains were covered by its shadow,
the cedars of God by its branches.
12 It sent out boughs as far as the sea,*
shoots as far as the river.
13 Why have you broken down the walls,
so that all who pass by pluck its fruit?[c]
14 The boar from the forest strips the vine;
the beast of the field feeds upon it.[d]
15 Turn again, LORD of hosts;
look down from heaven and see;
Attend to this vine,
16 the shoot your right hand has planted.
17 Those who would burn or cut it down—
may they perish at your rebuke.
18 May your help be with the man at your right
hand,
with the one* whom you once made
strong.
19 Then we will not withdraw from you;
revive us, and we will call on your name.
20 LORD of hosts, restore us;
let your face shine upon us,
that we may be saved.

## PSALM 81*

## An Admonition to Fidelity

1 *For the leader; "upon the* gittith."* *Of Asaph.*

I

2 Sing joyfully to God our strength;[e]
shout in triumph to the God of Jacob!
3 Take up a melody, sound the timbrel,
the sweet-sounding harp and lyre.
4 Blow the trumpet at the new moon,
at the full moon,* on our solemn feast.[f]

s Ez 20,44; 36,22.
t Pss 42,4; 115,2; Jl 2, 17.
u Jl 4,21.
v Ps 102,21.
w Ps 89,51-52.
x Pss 23,1-3; 95,7; 100, 3; Gn 48,15; Ex 25, 22; 1 Sm 4,4; 2 Sm 6, 2; Mi 7,14.
y 4. 8. 20: Pss 4,7; 31, 17; 67,2; 85,5; Nm 6, 25; Dn 9,17.
z Pss 13,2; 44,24; 74,1; 79,5; 89,47; Dt 4,24.
a Pss 42,4; 102,10.
b Pss 44,14; 79,4; 123, 3-4; Jb 12,4; Dn 9,16; Zep 2,8.
c Ps 89,41.
d Hos 2,14.
e Pss43,4; 68,26; 149, 3; 150,3-4; Jdt 16,1.
f Lev23,24; Nm 29,1.

*

Ps 80: A community lament in time of military defeat. Using the familiar image of Israel as a vineyard, the people complain that God has broken down the wall protecting the once splendid vine brought from Egypt (9–14). They pray that God will again turn to them and use the Davidic king to lead them to victory (15–20).

80, 1: *Lilies . . . . Eduth*: the first term is probably the title of the melody to which the psalm was to be sung; the second is unexplained.

80, 9: *A vine*: a frequent metaphor for Israel. Cf Is 5, 1–7; 27, 2–5; Jer 2, 21; Hos 10, 1; Mt 21, 33.

80, 12: *The sea*: the Mediterranean. *The river*: the Euphrates. Cf Gn 15, 18; 1 Kgs 5, 1. The terms may also have a mythic nuance—the seas that surround the earth; sea and river are sometimes paralleled in poetry.

80, 18: *The man at your right hand . . . the one*: the Davidic king who will lead the army in battle.

Ps 81: At a pilgrimage feast, probably harvest in the fall, the people assemble in the temple in accord with the Sinai ordinances (2–6a). They hear a divine word (mediated by a temple speaker) telling how God rescued them from slavery in Egypt (7–9), gave them the fundamental commandment of fidelity (9–11), which would bring punishment if they refused to obey (12–13). But if Israel repents, God will be with them once again, bestowing protection and fertility (14–17).

81, 1: *Upon the gittith*: probably the title of the melody to which the psalm was to be sung or a muscial instrument.

81, 4: *New moon . . . full moon*: the pilgrimage feast of harvest began with a great assembly (Lv 23, 24; Nm 29, 1),

5 For this is a law in Israel,
an edict of the God of Jacob,[g]
6 Who made it a decree for Joseph
when he came out of the land of Egypt.

II
I hear a new oracle:*
7 "I relieved their shoulders of the burden;*
their hands put down the basket.[h]
8 In distress you called and I rescued you;
unseen, I spoke to you in thunder;
At the waters of Meribah* I tested you and
said:[i] *Selah*
9 'Listen, my people, I give you warning!
If only you will obey me, Israel![j]
10 There must be no foreign god among you;[k]*
you must not worship an alien god.
11 I, the LORD, am your God,
who brought you up from the land of
Egypt.
Open wide your mouth that I may fill it.'
12 But my people did not listen to my words;
Israel did not obey me.
13 So I gave them over to hardness of heart;
they followed their own designs.[l]
14 But even now if my people would listen,
if Israel would walk in my paths,[m]
15 In a moment I would subdue their foes,
against their enemies unleash my hand.[n]
16 Those who hate the LORD would tremble,
their doom sealed forever.
17 But Israel I would feed with the finest
wheat,
satisfy them with honey from the rock."[o]

## PSALM 82*

## The Downfall of Unjust Gods

1 *A psalm of Asaph.*

I
God rises in the divine council,
gives judgment in the midst of the gods.[p]
2 "How long will you judge unjustly
and favor the cause of the wicked?[q] *Selah*
3 Defend the lowly and fatherless;
render justice to the afflicted and needy.
4 Rescue the lowly and poor;
deliver them from the hand of the
wicked."[r]

II
5 *The gods neither know nor understand,
wandering about in darkness,
and all the world's foundations shake.
6 I declare: "Gods though you be,*
offspring of the Most High all of you,
7 Yet like any mortal you shall die;
like any prince you shall fall."
8 Arise, O God, judge the earth,*
for yours are all the nations.

## PSALM 83*

## Prayer against a Hostile Alliance

1 *A song; a psalm of Asaph.*

I
2 God, do not be silent;
God, be not still and unmoved![s]
3 See how your enemies rage;
your foes proudly raise their heads.
4 They conspire against your people,
plot against those you protect.[t]
5 They say, "Come, let us wipe out their nation;
let Israel's name be mentioned no more!"
6 They scheme with one mind,
in league against you:[u]
7 The tents of Ishmael and Edom,
the people of Moab and Hagar,[v]*

g Ex 23,14ff.
h Ex 1,14; 6,6.
i Ps 95,8; ex 2,23ff; 17, 7; 19,16; Nm 20,13; 27,14.
j Ex 1,14; 6,6.
k 10-11: Ex 20,2-6; Dt 5,6-10.
l Jer 3,17; 7,24.
m Is 48,18.
n Lv 26,7-8.
o Ps 147,14; Dt 32, 13-14.
p Is 3,13-14.
q Ps 58,2.
r Dt 1,17.
s Pss 10,1; 44,24; 109, 1.
t Jer 11,9.
u Ps 2,2.
v Nm 20,23; 1 Chr 5,10. 19.

*

used the new moon as a sign (Nm 29, 6), and included trumpets (Lv 23, 24).

81, 6: *I hear a new oracle*: literally, "a tongue I do not know I hear." A temple official speaks the word of God (6b–17), which is authoritative and unlike merely human words (cf Nm 24, 4. 16).

81, 7: *I relieved their shoulders of the burden*: literally, "his [Israel's] shoulder," hence the plural translation. A reference to the liberation of Israel from salvery in Egypt. *The basket*: for carrying clay to make bricks. Cf Ex 1, 14.

81, 8: *Meribah*: place of rebellion in the wilderness; cf Ex 17, 7; Nm 20, 13.

81, 10: *There must be no foreign god among you*: as in Pss 50 and 95, Israel is challenged to obey the first commandment of fidelity to God after the proclamation of the exodus.

Ps 82: As in Ps 58, the pagan gods are seen as subordinate divine beings to whom Israel's God had delegated oversight of the foreign countries in the beginning (Dt 32, 8–9 LXX). Now God arises in the heavenly assembly (1) to rebuke the unjust "gods" (2–4), who are stripped of divine status and reduced in rank to mortals (5–7). They are accused of misruling the earth by not upholding the poor. A short prayer for universal justice concludes the psalm (8).

82, 5: The gods are blind and unable to declare what is right. Their misrule shakes earth's foundations (cf Pss 11, 3; 75, 4), which God made firm in creation (Ps 96, 10).

82, 6: *I declare: "Gods though you be"*: in Jn 10, 34 Jesus uses the verse to prove that those to whom the word of God is addressed can fittingly be called "gods."

82, 8: *Judge the earth*: according to Dt 32, 8–9 LXX, Israel's God had originally assigned jurisdiction over the foreign nations to the subordinate deities, keeping Israel as a personal possession. Now God will directly take over the rulership of the whole world.

Ps 83: The community lament complains to God of the nations' attempts to wipe out the name of Israel (2–9). The psalmist sees all Israel's enemies throughout its history united in a conspiracy (3–9). May God destroy the current crop of enemies as the enemies of old were destroyed (10–13), and may they be pursued until they acknowledge the name of Israel's God (14–19).

83, 7–9: Apart from the Assyrians, all the nations listed

8 Gebal, Ammon, and Amalek,[w]
Philistia and the inhabitants of Tyre.[x]
9 Assyria, too, in league with them
gives aid to the descendants of Lot. *Selah*

II
10 *Deal with them as with Midian;
as with Sisera and Jabin at the torrent
Kishon,[y]
11 Those destroyed at Endor,
who became dung for the ground.[z]
12 Make their nobles like Oreb and Zeeb,
all their princes like Zebah and Zalmunna,
13 Who made a plan together,
"Let us seize the pastures of God."
14 My God, turn them into withered grass,
into chaff flying before the wind.[a]
15 As a fire raging through a forest,
a flame setting mountains ablaze,[b]
16 Pursue them with your tempest;
terrify them with your storm.[c]
17 Cover their faces with shame,
till they pay you homage, LORD.
18 Let them be dismayed and shamed forever;
let them perish in disgrace.
19 Show them you alone are the LORD,
the Most High over all the earth.[d]

## PSALM 84*

### Prayer of a Pilgrim to Jerusalem

1 *For the leader; "upon the* gittith." *A psalm of the Korahites.*

I
2 How lovely your dwelling,
O LORD of hosts![e]
3 My soul yearns and pines
for the courts of the LORD.[f]
My heart and flesh cry out
for the living God.
4 *As the sparrow finds a home
and the swallow a nest to settle her
young,
My home is by your altars,
LORD of hosts, my king and my God![g]
5 Happy are those who dwell in your house!
They never cease to praise you. *Selah*

II
6 Happy are those who find refuge in you,
whose hearts are set on pilgrim roads.
7 As they pass through the Baca valley,*
they find spring water to drink.
Also from pools the Lord provides water
for those who lose their way.
8 They pass through outer and inner wall
and see the God of gods on Zion.

III
9 LORD of hosts, hear my prayer;
listen, God of Jacob. *Selah*
10 O God, look kindly on our shield;
look upon the face of your anointed.[h]*

IV
11 Better one day in your courts
than a thousand elsewhere.
Better the threshold of the house of my God
than a home in the tents of the wicked.
12 For a sun and shield is the LORD God,
bestowing all grace and glory.
The LORD withholds no good thing
from those who walk without reproach.
13 O LORD of hosts,
happy are those who trust in you!

## PSALM 85*

### Prayer for Divine Favor

1 *For the leader. A psalm of the Korahites.*

I
2 You once favored, LORD, your land,
restored the good fortune of Jacob.[i]
3 You forgave the guilt of your people,
pardoned all their sins. *Selah*
4 You withdrew all your wrath,
turned back your burning anger.[j]

II
5 Restore us once more, God our savior;
abandon your wrath against us.[k]
6 Will you be angry with us forever,
drag out your anger for all generations?[l]
7 Please give us life again,

w Ex 17,8.
x Jos 13,2.
y Ex 2,15; Is 9,3; 10,26.
z Jer 8,2.
a Pss 1,4; 35,5; 58,10; Is 5,24; 10,17; 17,13; 29,5; Ez 21,3.
b Ps 50,3.
c Jb 25,32; 27,21.
d Ps 97,9; Dt 4,39; Dn 3,45.
e Pss 43,3-4; 122,1.
f Pss 42,2-3; 63,2-3; 143,6; Is 26,9.
g Ps 5,3.
h Ps 89,19.
i Pss 14,7; 126,4.
j Ps 78,38; Ex 32,14; Is 48,9.
k Ps 80,4.
l Pss 79,5; 89,47.

*

here were neighbors of Israel. *The people of . . . Hagar*: a tribe of the desert regions east of *Ammon* and *Moab* (1 Chr 5, 10. 19–22). *Gebal* is the Phoenician city of Byblos or perhaps a mountain region south of the Dead Sea. *The descendants of Lot* are Moab and Edom (Gn 19, 36–38 and Dt 2, 9). These nations were never united against Israel in the same period; the psalm has lumped them all together.

83, 10–13: For the historical events, see Jgs 4–8.

Ps 84: Israelites celebrated three pilgrimage feasts in Jerusalem annually. The psalm expresses the sentiments of the pilgrims eager to enjoy the divine presence.

84, 4: The desire of a restless bird for a secure home is an image of the desire of a pilgrim for the secure house of God. Cf Ps 42, 2–3, where the image for the desire of the pilgrim is the thirst of the deer for water.

84, 7: *Baca valley*: Hebrew obscure; probably a valley on the way to Jerusalem.

84, 10: *Our shield . . . your anointed*: the king had a role in the liturgical celebration. For the king as shield, cf Ps 89, 19.

Ps 85: A national lament reminding God of past favors and forgiveness (2–4) and begging for forgiveness and grace now (5–8). A speaker represents the people who wait humbly with open hearts (9–10): God will be active on their behalf (11–14). The situation suggests the conditions of Judea during the early postexilic period, the fifth century B.C.; the thoughts are similar to those of postexilic prophets (Hg 1, 5–11; 2, 6–9).

that your people may rejoice in you.
8 Show us, LORD, your love;
grant us your salvation.

III
9 *I will listen for the word of God;
surely the LORD will proclaim peace
To his people, to the faithful,
to those who trust in him.
10 Near indeed is salvation for the loyal;
prosperity will fill our land.
11 *Love and truth will meet;
justice and peace will kiss.[m]
12 Truth will spring from the earth;
justice will look down from heaven.[n]
13 The LORD will surely grant abundance;
our land will yield its increase.[o]
14 Prosperity will march before the Lord,
and good fortune will follow behind.

## PSALM 86*

### Prayer in Time of Distress

1 *A prayer of David.*

I
Hear me, LORD, and answer me,
for I am poor and oppressed.
2 Preserve my life, for I am loyal;
save your servant who trusts in you.
3 You are my God; pity me, Lord;
to you I call all the day.
4 Gladden the soul of your servant;
to you, Lord, I lift up my soul.[p]
5 Lord, you are kind and forgiving,
most loving to all who call on you.[q]
6 LORD, hear my prayer;
listen to my cry for help.[r]
7 In this time of trouble I call,
for you will answer me.

II
8 None among the gods can equal you, O
Lord;
nor can their deeds compare to yours.[s]
9 All the nations you have made shall come
to bow before you, Lord,
and give honor to your name.[t]
10 For you are great and do wondrous deeds;
and you alone are God.

III
11 Teach me, LORD, your way
that I may walk in your truth,[u]
single-hearted and revering your name.
12 I will praise you with all my heart,
glorify your name forever, Lord my God.
13 Your love for me is great;
you have rescued me from the depths of
Sheol.[v]
14 O God, the arrogant have risen against me;
a ruthless band has sought my life;
to you they pay no heed.
15 But you, Lord, are a merciful and gracious
God,
slow to anger, most loving and true.[w]
16 Turn to me, have pity on me;
give your strength to your servant;
save this child of your handmaid.[x]
17 Give me a sign of your favor:
make my enemies see, to their confusion,
that you, LORD, help and comfort me.

## PSALM 87*

### Zion the True Birthplace of Diaspora Pilgrims

1 *A psalm of the Korahites. A song.*

I
The LORD loves the city[y]
founded on holy mountains,
2 Loves the gates* of Zion
more than any dwelling in Jacob.
3 Glorious things are said of you,
O city of God! *Selah*

II
4 From Babylon and Egypt I count
those who acknowledge the LORD.
Philistia, Ethiopia, Tyre,
of them it can be said:
"This one was born there."
5 *But of Zion it must be said:
"They all were born here."[z]
The Most High confirms this;[a]
6 the LORD notes in the register of the
peoples:
"This one was born here."[b] *Selah*

m Pss 89,15; 97,2.
n Is 45,8.
o Ps 67,7; Lv 26,4; Ez 34,27; Hos 2,23-24; Zec 8,12.
p Pss 25,1; 143,8.
q Jl 2,13.
r Pss 5,2; 130,1-2.
s Pss 35,10; 89,9; Ex 15,11; Dt 3,24; Jer 10,6.
t Ps 22,28; Zec 14,16; Rv 15,4.
u Pss 25,4; 26,3; 27,11; 119,12. 35; 143,8. 10.
v Pss 30,4; 40,3; Jon 2, 7.
w Pss 103,8; 130,7; 145,8; Ex 34,6.
x Pss 25,16; 116,16; Wis 9,5.
y 1-2: Pss 76,2-3; 78, 68-69.
z Gal 4,26.
a Ps 48,9.
b Is 4,3.

*

85, 9: The prophet listens to God's revelation. Cf Hb 2, 1.

85, 11-14: Divine activity is personified as pairs of virtues.

Ps 86: An individual lament. The psalmist, "poor and oppressed" (1), "devoted" (2), "your servant" (2. 4. 16), "rescued from the depths of Sheol" (13), attacked by the ruthless (14), desires only God's protection (1-7. 11-17).

Ps 87: A song of Zion, like Psalms 46, 48, 76, and 132. After the exile of the sixth century B.C., diaspora Jews from all over the world (4) made the long pilgrimage to Jerusalem, the city of God (1-3). Such Jews may have hailed from distant lands, but the psalm sees them as children of Zion (5-7). The original occasion may have been Pentecost, which always attracted a large number of diaspora Jews.

87, 2: *The gates*: the city itself, a common Hebrew idiom.

87, 5-6: The bond between the exile and the holy city was so strong as to override the exile's citizenship of lesser cities.

**7** So all sing in their festive dance:
"Within you is my true home."[c]

## PSALM 88*

### A Despairing Lament

**1** *A song; a psalm of the Korahites. For the leader; according to* Mahalath. *For singing; a* maskil *of Heman the Ezrahite.*

I
**2** LORD, my God, I call out by day;
at night I cry aloud in your presence.[d]
**3** Let my prayer come before you;
incline your ear to my cry.[e]
**4** *For my soul is filled with troubles;[f]
my life draws near to Sheol.
**5** I am reckoned with those who go down to the pit;
I am weak, without strength.
**6** My couch is among the dead,
with the slain who lie in the grave.
You remember them no more;
they are cut off from your care.
**7** You plunged me into the bottom of the pit;
into the darkness of the abyss.
**8** Your wrath lies heavy upon me;
all your waves crash over me.[g] *Selah*
**9** Because of you my friends shun me;
you make me loathsome to them;[h]
Caged in, I cannot escape;
**10** my eyes grow dim from trouble.

II
All day I call on you, LORD;
I stretch out my hands to you.
**11** *Do you work wonders for the dead?
Do the shades arise and praise you?[i] *Selah*
**12** Is your love proclaimed in the grave,
your fidelity in the tomb?
**13** Are your marvels declared in the darkness,
your righteous deeds in the land of oblivion?

III
**14** But I cry out to you, LORD;
in the morning my prayer comes before you.
**15** Why do you reject me, LORD?
Why hide your face from me?
**16** I am mortally afflicted since youth;
lifeless, I suffer your terrible blows.
**17** Your wrath has swept over me;
your terrors have reduced me to silence.[j]
**18** All the day they surge round like a flood;
from every side they close in on me.
**19** Because of you companions shun me;[k]
my only friend is darkness.

## PSALM 89*

### A Lament over God's Promise to David

**1** *A* maskil *of Ethan the Ezrahite.*

I
**2** The promises of the LORD I will sing forever,[l]
proclaim your loyalty through all ages.
**3** *For you said, "My love is established forever;
my loyalty will stand as long as the heavens.
**4** I have made a covenant with my chosen one;
I have sworn to David my servant:
**5** I will make your dynasty stand forever
and establish your throne through all ages."[m] *Selah*

II
**6** The heavens praise your marvels, LORD,
your loyalty in the assembly of the holy ones.[n]
**7** Who in the skies ranks with the LORD?
Who is like the LORD among the gods?[o]*
**8** A God dreaded in the council of the holy ones,
greater and more awesome than all who sit there!
**9** LORD, God of hosts, who is like you?
Mighty LORD, your loyalty is always present.

c Pss 68,26; 149,3.
d Ps 77,3.
e Ps 119,170.
f 4-7: Pss 28,1; 30,4; 40,3; 86,13; 143,7; Nm 16,33; Jb 17,1; Jon 2,7.
g Pss 18,5; 32,6; 42,8; 69,2; Jon 2,4.
h Pss 38,12; 79,4; 80,7; 123,3-4; 142,8; Jb 12, 4; 19,13; Lam 3,7; Dn 9,16.
i Pss 6,6; 30,10; 38,18; 115,17.
j Jb 6,4; 20,25.
k Jb 19,13.
l Is 63,7.
m Pss 61,7-8; 132,11; 2 Sm 7,8-16.
n Pss 29,1; 82,1; Jb 1, 6; 5,1.
o 7-9: Pss 35,10; 86,8; 113,5; Ex 15,11; Jer 10,6.

*

Ps 88: A lament in which the psalmist prays for rescue from the alienation of approaching death. Each of the three stanzas begins with a call to God (2. 10b. 14) and complains of the death that separates one from God. The tone is persistently grim.

88, 4–8: In imagination the psalmist already experiences the alienation of Sheol.

88, 11–13: The psalmist seeks to persuade God to act out of concern for divine honor: the shades give you no worship, so keep me alive to offer you praise.

Ps 89: The community laments the defeat of the Davidic king, to whom God promised kingship as enduring as the heavens (2–5). The psalm narrates how God became king of the divine beings (6–9) and how the Davidic king became king of earthly kings (20–38). Since the defeat of the king calls into question God's promise, the community ardently prays God to be faithful to the original promise to David (39–52).

89, 3–5: David's dynasty is to be as long-lasting as the heavens, a statement reinforced by using the same verbs (establish, stand) both of the divine love and loyalty and of the Davidic dynasty and throne. Cf 29–30.

89, 7: *The gods*: literally, "the sons of gods," "the holy ones" and "courtiers" of 6 and 8. These heavenly spirits are members of God's court.

**10** You rule the raging sea;[p]
you still its swelling waves.
**11** You crushed Rahab* with a mortal blow;
your strong arm scattered your foes.
**12** Yours are the heavens, yours the earth;
you founded the world and everything in it.[q]
**13** Zaphon and Amanus* you created;
Tabor and Hermon rejoice in your name.
**14** Mighty your arm, strong your hand,
your right hand is ever exalted.
**15** Justice and judgment are the foundation of your throne;
love and loyalty march before you.[r]
**16** Happy the people who know you, LORD,
who walk in the radiance of your face.
**17** In your name they sing joyfully all the day;
at your victory they raise the festal shout.[s]
**18** You are their majestic strength;
by your favor our horn* is exalted.[t]
**19** Truly the LORD is our shield,
the Holy One of Israel, our king![u]

III

**20** Once you spoke in vision;[v]
to your faithful ones you said:
"I have set a leader over the warriors;
I have raised up a hero from the army.
**21** I have chosen David, my servant;
with my holy oil I have anointed him.
**22** My hand will be with him;[w]
my arm will make him strong.
**23** No enemy shall outwit him,
nor shall the wicked defeat him.
**24** I will crush his foes before him,
strike down those who hate him.
**25** My loyalty and love will be with him;
through my name his horn will be exalted.
**26** I will set his hand upon the sea,
his right hand upon the rivers.*
**27** He shall cry to me, 'You are my father,[x]
my God, the Rock that brings me victory!'
**28** I myself make him firstborn,
Most High* over the kings of the earth.
**29** Forever I will maintain my love for him;[y]
my covenant with him stands firm.
**30** I will establish his dynasty forever,
his throne as the days of the heavens.
**31** If his descendants forsake my law,[z]
do not follow my decrees,
**32** If they fail to observe my statutes,
do not keep my commandments,
**33** I will punish their crime with a rod
and their guilt with lashes.
**34** But I will not take my love from him,
nor will I betray my bond of loyalty.[a]
**35** I will not violate my covenant;
the promise of my lips I will not alter.[b]
**36** By my holiness I swore once for all:[c]
I will never be false to David.
**37** His dynasty will continue forever,[d]
his throne, like the sun before me.
**38** Like the moon it will stand eternal,
forever firm like the sky!"* *Selah*

IV

**39** But now you have rejected and spurned,[e]
been enraged at your anointed.
**40** You renounced the covenant with your servant,
defiled his crown in the dust.
**41** You broke down all his defenses,[f]
left his strongholds in ruins.
**42** All who pass through seize plunder;
his neighbors deride him.
**43** You have exalted the right hand of his foes,
have gladdened all his enemies.[g]
**44** You turned back his sharp sword,
did not support him in battle.
**45** You brought to an end his splendor,
hurled his throne to the ground.
**46** You cut short the days of his youth,
covered him with shame. *Selah*
**47** How long, LORD?
Will you stay hidden forever?
Must your wrath smolder like fire?[h]
**48** Remember how brief is my life,
how frail the race you created![i]
**49** What mortal can live and not see death?
Who can escape the power of Sheol?[j] *Selah*
**50** Where are your promises of old, Lord,
the loyalty sworn to David?
**51** Remember, Lord, the insults to your servants,

p 10-11: Pss 65,8; 74, 13-15; 107,29; Jb 7, 12; Is 51,9-10.
q Pss 24,1-2; 50,12; Dt 10,14; 1 Cor 10,26.
r Pss 85,11-12; 97,2.
s Ps 47,2; Zep 3,14.
t Pss 112,9; 148,14.
u Pss 47,9; 96,10; 97,1; 99,1; Is 6,3.
v 20-21: Pss 78,70; 132,11-12; 2 Sm 7,4. 8-16; 1 Chr 17,3. 7-14; Is 42,1; Acts 13, 22
w 22-25: 1 Sm 2,9-10.
x 27-28: Pss 2,7; 110, 2-3; 2 Sm 7,9. 14; Col 1,15. 18; Rv 1,5.
y 29-30: Pss 18,51; 61, 8; 144,10; 2 Sm 7,11; Is 55,3.
z 31-33: Lv 26,14-33.
a Ps 40,12; Sir 47,22.
b Jer 33,20-21.
c Am 4,2.
d 37-38: Pss 61,8; 72,5; Sir 43,6.
e 39-47: Ps 44,10-25.
f 41-42: Ps 80,13-14.
g Lam 1,5.
h Pss 13,2; 44,25; 74, 10; 79,5; Dt 4,24.
i Pss 39,5-6; 62,10; 90, 9-10; 144,4; Jb 7,6. 16; 14,1. 5; Eccl 6,12; Wis 2,5.
j Ps 90,3.

*

89, 11: *Rahab*: a mythological sea monster whose name is used in the Bible mainly as a personification of primeval chaos. Cf Jb 9, 13; 26, 12; Ps 74, 13–14; Is 51, 9.

89, 13: *Zaphon and Amanus*: two sacred mountains in northern Syria. *Tabor*: a high hill in the valley of Jezreel in northern Israel. *Hermon*: a mountain in Lebanon, forming the southern spur of the Anti-Lebanon range.

89, 18. 25: *Horn*: a concrete noun for an abstract quality; horn is a symbol of strength.

89, 26: *The sea . . . the rivers*: geographically the limits of the Davidic Empire (the Mediterranean and the Euphrates); mythologically, the traditional forces of chaos. See note on v 11.

89, 28: *Most High*: a divine title, which is here extended to David as God's own king. Cf Ps 2, 7–9; Is 9, 5. As God rules over the members of the heavenly council (6–9), so David, God's surrogate, rules over earthly kings.

89, 37–38: *Like the sun before me . . . like the sky*: as enduring as the heavenly lights. Cf 2–5 and Ps 72, 5. 17.

how I bear all the slanders of the
nations.[k]
52 Your enemies, LORD, insult your anointed;
they insult my every endeavor.

* * *

53 *Blessed be the LORD forever! Amen and
amen![l]

## FOURTH BOOK — PSALMS 90–106

### PSALM 90*

### God's Eternity and Human Frailty

1 *A prayer of Moses, the man of God.*

I
Lord, you have been our refuge
through all generations.
2 Before the mountains were born,
the earth and the world brought forth,
from eternity to eternity you are God.[m]
4 A thousand years in your eyes
are merely a yesterday,[n]
3 But humans you return* to dust,
saying, "Return, you mortals!"[o]
4c Before a watch passes in the night,*
5 you have brought them to their end;[p]*
They disappear like sleep at dawn;
they are like grass that dies.
6 It sprouts green in the morning;
by evening it is dry and withered.[q]*

II
7 Truly we are consumed by your anger,
filled with terror by your wrath.
8 You have kept our faults before you,
our hidden sins exposed to your sight.[r]
9 Our life ebbs away under your wrath;[s]
our years end like a sigh.
10 Seventy is the sum of our years,
or eighty, if we are strong;
Most of them are sorrow and toil;
they pass quickly, we are all but gone.
11 Who comprehends your terrible anger?
Your wrath matches the fear it inspires.
12 Teach us to count our days aright,
that we may gain wisdom of heart.
13 Relent, O LORD! How long?
Have pity on your servants!
14 Fill us at daybreak with your love,[t]
that all our days we may sing for joy.
15 Make us glad as many days as you humbled
us,
for as many years as we have seen
trouble.[u]
16 Show your deeds to your servants,
your glory to their children.
17 May the favor of the Lord our God be
ours.[v]
Prosper the work of our hands!
Prosper the work of our hands!

### PSALM 91*

### Security Under God's Protection

I
1 You who dwell in the shelter of the Most
High,*
who abide in the shadow of the Almighty,
2 Say to the LORD, "My refuge and fortress,
my God in whom I trust."[w]
3 God will rescue you from the fowler's snare,
from the destroying plague,
4 Will shelter you with pinions,
spread wings that you may take refuge;[x]
God's faithfulness is a protecting shield.
5 You shall not fear the terror of the night
nor the arrow that flies by day,[y]
6 Nor the pestilence that roams in darkness,
nor the plague that ravages at noon.[z]
7 Though a thousand fall at your side,
ten thousand at your right hand,
near you it shall not come.
8 You need simply watch;

k Ps 79,12.
l Pss 41,14; 72,18; 106,48.
m Pss 48,15; 55,20; 93, 2; 102,13; Hb 1,12.
n 2 Pt 3,8.
o Pss 103,14; 104,29; 146,4; Gn 3,19; 1 Mc 2,63; Jb 34,14-15; Eccl 3,20; 12,7; Sir 40,11.
p Ps 89,48.
q Pss 37,2; 102,11; 103,15-16; Jb 14,1-2; Is 40,6-8.
r Ps 109,14-15; Hos 7, 2.
s 9-10: Pss 39,5-7; 62, 10; 102,24-25; 144,4; Gn 6,3; Jb 7,6. 16; 14,5; Prv 10,27; Eccl 6,12; Wis 2,5; Sir 18, 8; Is 65,20.
t Ps 17,15.
u Nm 14,34; Jer 31,13.
v Ps 33,22.
w Pss 18,3; 31,3-4; 42, 10; 142,6; 2 Sm 22,3.
x Pss 17,8; 36,8; 57,2; 63,8; Dt 32,11; Ru 2, 12; Mt 23,37.
y Prv 3,25; Song 3,8.
z Dt 32,24.

*

89, 53: The doxology at the end of the third book of the Psalms; it is not part of Ps 89.

Ps 90: A communal lament that describes only in general terms the cause of the community's distress. After confidently invoking God (1), the psalm turns to a complaint contrasting God's eternity with the brevity of human life (2–6) and sees in human suffering the punishment for sin (7–12). The psalm concludes with a plea for God's intervention (13–17).

90, 3: *Return*: one word of God is enough to return mortals to the dust from which they were created. Humans were created from earth in Gn 2, 7; 3, 19.

90, 4: The translation reverses the order of the difficult Hebrew verses 3 and 4 to get the probable original order. *A watch in the night*: the night was divided into three sentry periods or watches. Cf Jgs 7, 19.

90, 5: *You have brought them to their end*: an interpretation of the unclear Hebrew.

90, 6: *It is dry and withered*: the transitory nature of the grass under the scorching sun was proverbial. Cf Ps 129, 6; Is 40, 6–8.

Ps 91: A prayer of someone who has taken refuge in the security of the temple (1–2). The psalmist is confident that God's presence will protect the people in every dangerous situation (3–13). The final verses are an oracle of salvation promising salvation to those who trust in God (14–16).

91, 1: *The shelter of the Most High*: basically "hiding place" but in the psalms a designation for the protected temple precincts. Cf Pss 27, 5; 31, 21; 61, 5. *The shadow of the Almighty*: literally, "the shadow of the wings of the Almighty." Cf Pss 17, 8; 36, 8; 57, 2; 63, 8. V 4 makes clear that the shadow is an image of the safety afforded by the outstretched wings of the cherubim in the holy of holies.

the punishment of the wicked you will
see.[a]
9 You have the LORD for your refuge;
you have made the Most High your
stronghold.
10 No evil shall befall you,
no affliction come near your tent.[b]
11 *For God commands the angels[c]
to guard you in all your ways.[d]
12 With their hands they shall support you,
lest you strike your foot against a stone.[e]
13 You shall tread upon the asp and the viper,
trample the lion and the dragon.[f]

II
14 Whoever clings to me I will deliver;
whoever knows my name I will set on
high.[g]
15 All who call upon me I will answer;[h]
I will be with them in distress;[i]
I will deliver them and give them honor.
16 With length of days I will satisfy them
and show them my saving power.[j]

## PSALM 92*

### A Hymn of Thanksgiving for God's Fidelity

1 *A psalm. A sabbath song.*

I
2 It is good to give thanks to the LORD,
to sing praise to your name, Most High,[k]
3 To proclaim your love in the morning,
your faithfulness in the night,
4 With the ten-stringed harp,
with melody upon the lyre.[l]
5 For you make me jubilant, LORD, by your
deeds;
at the works of your hands I shout for
joy.

II
6 How great are your works, LORD![m]
How profound your purpose!
7 A senseless person cannot know this;
a fool cannot comprehend.
8 Though the wicked flourish like grass
and all sinners thrive,[n]
They are destined for eternal destruction;
9 for you, LORD, are forever on high.
10 Indeed your enemies, LORD,
indeed your enemies shall perish;
all sinners shall be scattered.[o]

III
11 You have given me the strength of a wild
bull;[p]
you have poured rich oil upon me.[q]
12 My eyes look with glee on my wicked
enemies;
my ears delight in the fall of my foes.[r]
13 The just shall flourish like the palm tree,
shall grow like a cedar of Lebanon.[s]
14 Planted* in the house of the LORD,
they shall flourish in the courts of our
God.
15 They shall bear fruit even in old age,
always vigorous and sturdy,
16 As they proclaim: "The LORD is just;
our rock, in whom there is no wrong."[t]

## PSALM 93*

### God is a Mighty King

1 The LORD is king,* robed with majesty;
the LORD is robed, girded with might.[u]
The world will surely stand in place,
never to be moved.[v]
2 Your throne stands firm from of old;
you are from everlasting, LORD.[w]
3 The flood* has raised up, LORD;
the flood has raised up its roar;
the flood has raised its pounding waves.
4 More powerful than the roar of many
waters,
more powerful than the breakers of the
sea,
powerful in the heavens is the LORD.
5 Your decrees are firmly established;
holiness belongs to your house, LORD,
for all the length of days.

a Ps 92,12.
b Prv 12,21; Dt 7,15.
c 11-12: Mt 4,6; Lk 4,10f.
d Heb 1,14.
e Ps 121,3; Prv 3,23.
f Is 11,8; Lk 10,19.
g Pss 9,11; 119,132.
h Jer 33,3; Zec 13,9.
i Is 43,2.
j Prv 3,2.
k Pss 33,1; 147,1.
l Pss 33,2; 144,9.
m 6-7: Pss 131,1; 139,6. 17; Wis 13,1; 17,1.
n Ps 37,35.
o Pss 68,1-2; 125,5.
p Ps 75,10; Dt 33,17.
q Ps 23,5.
r Ps 91,8.
s Pss 1,3; 52,10; Jer 17,8.
t Dt 32,4.
u Pss 47,8; 96,10; 97,1; 99,1.
v Pss 75,2-3; 104,5.
w Pss 55,20; 90,2; 102,13; Hb 1,12.

*

91, 11–12: The words are cited in Mt 4, 6; Lk 4, 10–11, as part of Satan's challenge to Jesus in the desert.

Ps 92: A hymn of praise and thanks for God's faithful deeds (2–5). The wicked, deluded by their prosperity (6–9), are punished (10), whereas the psalmist has already experienced God's protection (11–16).

92, 14: *Planted*: the just are likened to trees growing in the sacred precincts of the temple, which is often seen as the source of life and fertility because of God's presence. Cf Ps 36, 9. 10; Ez 47, 1–12.

Ps 93: A hymn celebrating the kingship of God, who created the world (1–2) by defeating the sea (3–4). In the ancient myth that is alluded to here, Sea completely covered the land, making it impossible for the human community to live. Sea, or Flood, roars in anger against God, who is personified in the storm. God's utterances or decrees are given authority by the victory over Sea (5).

93, 1: *The LORD is king*: literally, "the LORD reigns." This psalm, and Pss 47 and 96–99, are sometimes called enthronement psalms. They may have been used in a special liturgy during which God's ascent to the throne was ritually reenacted. They have also been interpreted eschatologically, pointing to the coming of God as king at the end-time.

93, 3: *The flood*: the primordial sea was tamed by God in the act of creation. It is a figure of chaos and rebellion. Cf Ps 46, 4.

## PSALM 94*

### A Prayer for Deliverance from the Wicked

I

1 LORD, avenging God,
avenging God, shine forth![x]
2 Rise up, judge of the earth;
give the proud what they deserve.[y]

II

3 How long, LORD, shall the wicked,
how long shall the wicked glory?[z]
4 How long will they mouth haughty speeches,
go on boasting, all these evildoers?[a]
5 They crush your people, LORD,
torment your very own.
6 They kill the widow and alien;
the fatherless they murder.[b]
7 They say, "The LORD does not see;
the God of Jacob takes no notice."[c]

III

8 Understand, you stupid people!
You fools, when will you be wise?[d]
9 Does the one who shaped the ear not hear?
The one who formed the eye not see?[e]
10 Does the one who guides nations not rebuke?
The one who teaches humans not have knowledge?
11 The LORD does know human plans;
they are only puffs of air.[f]

IV

12 Happy those whom you guide, LORD,[g]
whom you teach by your instruction.
13 You give them rest from evil days,
while a pit is being dug for the wicked.
14 You, LORD, will not forsake your people,
nor abandon your very own.[h]
15 Judgment shall again be just,
and all the upright of heart will follow it.

V

16 Who will rise up for me against the wicked?
Who will stand up for me against evildoers?
17 If the LORD were not my help,
I would long have been silent in the grave.[i]
18 When I say, "My foot is slipping,"
your love, LORD, holds me up.[j]
19 When cares increase within me,
your comfort gives me joy.

VI

20 Can unjust judges be your allies,
those who create burdens in the name of law,
21 Those who conspire against the just
and condemn the innocent to death?
22 No, the LORD is my secure height,
my God, the rock where I find refuge,
23 Who will turn back their evil upon them[k]
and destroy them for their wickedness.
Surely the LORD our God will destroy them![l]

## PSALM 95*

### A Call to Praise and Obedience

I

1 Come, let us sing joyfully to the LORD;
cry out to the rock of our salvation.[m]
2 Let us greet him with a song of praise,
joyfully sing out our psalms.
3 For the LORD is the great God,
the great king over all gods,[n]
4 Whose hand holds the depths of the earth;
who owns the tops of the mountains.
5 The sea and dry land belong to God,
who made them, formed them by hand.[o]

II

6 Enter, let us bow down in worship;
let us kneel before the LORD who made us.
7 For this is our God,
whose people we are,
God's well-tended flock.[p]

III

Oh, that today you would hear his voice:[q]
8 Do not harden your hearts as at Meribah,*
as on the day of Massah in the desert.
9 There your ancestors tested me;
they tried me though they had seen my works.[r]

---

x Na 1,2.
y Jer 51,56; Lam 3,64.
z Pss 13,2; 75,5; Jer 12,1.
a Ps 73; Mal 2,17; 3,14.
b Ex 22,21-22; Dt 24, 17-22.
c Pss 10,11; 64,6; 73, 11; Jb 22,13-14; Ez 9, 9.
d Prv 1,22; 8,5.
e Ex 4,11; Prv 20,12.
f Ps 33,15; 1 Cor 3,20.
g Ps 119,71; Jb 5,17.
h 1 Sm 12,22; Sir 47, 22.
i Ps 115,17.
j Ps 145,14.
k Pss 7,16; 9,16; 35,8; 57,7; Prv 26,27; Eccl 10,8; Sir 27,26.
l Ps 107,42.
m Dt 32,15.
n Pss 47,2; 135,5.
o Ps 24,1-2.
p Pss 23,1-3; 100,3; Mi 7,14.
q 7c-11: Pss 81,8; 106, 32; Heb 3,7-11. 15; 4, 3. 5. 7.
r Nm 14,22; 20,2-13; Dt 6,16; 33,8.

---

Ps 94: A lament of an individual who is threatened by wicked people. The danger affects the whole community. Calling upon God as judge (1–2), the psalm complains about oppression of the holy community by people within (3–7). Bold declarations of faith follow: denunciation of evildoers (8–11) and assurance to the just (12–15). The psalm continues with further lament (16–19) and ends with strong confidence in God's response (20–23).

Ps 95: Twice the psalm calls the people to praise and worship God (1–2. 6), the king of all creatures (3–5) and shepherd of the flock (7ab). The last strophe warns the people to be more faithful than were their ancestors in the journey to the promised land (7c–11). This invitation to praise God regularly opens the Church's official prayer, the Liturgy of the Hours.

95, 8: *Meribah*: literally, "contention"; the place where the Israelites quarreled with God. *Massah*: "testing," the place where they put God to the trial. Cf Ex 17, 7; Nm 20, 13.

10 Forty years I loathed that generation;
I said: "This people's heart goes astray;
they do not know my ways."[s]
11 Therefore I swore in my anger:
"They shall never enter my rest."*

## PSALM 96*
## God of the Universe

I
1 Sing to the LORD a new song;[t]
sing to the LORD, all the earth.
2 Sing to the LORD, bless his name;
announce his salvation day after day.
3 Tell God's glory among the nations;
among all peoples, God's marvelous
deeds.[u]

II
4 *For great is the LORD and highly to be
praised,
to be feared above all gods.[v]
5 For the gods of the nations all do nothing,
but the LORD made the heavens.[w]
6 Splendor and power go before him;
power and grandeur are in his holy place.

III
7 Give to the LORD, you families of nations,
give to the LORD glory and might;
8 give to the LORD the glory due his name![x]
Bring gifts and enter his courts;
9 bow down to the LORD, splendid in
holiness.
Tremble before God, all the earth;
10 say among the nations: The LORD is
king.[y]
The world will surely stand fast, never to be
moved.
God rules the peoples with fairness.

IV
11 Let the heavens be glad and the earth
rejoice;
let the sea and what fills it resound;[z]
12 let the plains be joyful and all that is in
them.
Then let all the trees of the forest rejoice
13 before the LORD who comes,
who comes to govern the earth,[a]
To govern the world with justice
and the peoples with faithfulness.

## PSALM 97*
## The Divine Ruler of All

I
1 The LORD is king; let the earth rejoice;
let the many islands be glad.[b]
2 Cloud and darkness surround the Lord;
justice and right are the foundation of his
throne.[c]
3 Fire goes before him;
everywhere it consumes the foes.
4 Lightning illumines the world;
the earth sees and trembles.[d]
5 The mountains melt like wax before the
LORD,
before the Lord of all the earth.[e]
6 The heavens proclaim God's justice;
all peoples see his glory.[f]

II
7 All who serve idols are put to shame,
who glory in worthless things;
all gods* bow down before you.[g]
8 Zion hears and is glad,
and the cities of Judah rejoice
because of your judgments, O LORD.[h]
9 You, LORD, are the Most High over all the
earth,[i]
exalted far above all gods.
10 The LORD loves those who hate evil,
protects the lives of the faithful,[j]
rescues them from the hand of the
wicked.
11 Light dawns for the just;
gladness, for the honest of heart.[k]
12 Rejoice in the LORD, you just,
and praise his holy name.[l]

## PSALM 98*
## The Coming of God

1 *A psalm.*

I
Sing a new song to the LORD,
who has done marvelous deeds,[m]

---

s Ps 78,8; Nm 14,34; Dt 32,5.
t Ps 98,1; Is 42,10.
u Pss 98,4; 105,1.
v Pss 48,2; 95,3; 145,3.
w Ps 97,7; Is 40,17; 1 Cor 8,4.
x Ps 29,2.
y Pss 75,4; 93,1.
z Ps 98,7.
a Ps 98,9.
b Pss 75,4; 93,1; 96,10.
c Pss 85,11; 89,15; Ex 19,6; Dt 4,11; 5,22; 1 Kgs 8,12.
d Pss 18,8; 50,3; 77,18; 99,1; Jgs 5,4-5.
e Jdt 16,15; Mi l,4.
f Ps 50,6.
g Ps 96,5.
h Ps 48,12.
i Ps 83,19.
j Ps 121,7.
k Ps 112,4.
l Ps 30,5.
m Ps 96,1; Is 42,10.

---

95, 11: *My rest*: the promised land as in Dt 12, 9. Heb 4 applies the verse to the eternal rest of heaven.

Ps 96: A hymn inviting all humanity to praise the glories of Israel's God (1–3), who is the sole God (4–6). To the just ruler of all belongs worship (7–10); even inanimate creation is to offer praise (11–13). This psalm has numerous verbal and thematic contacts with Is 40–55, as does Ps 98. Another version of the psalm is 1 Chr 16, 23–33.

96, 4: For references to other gods, see comments on Pss 58 and 82.

Ps 97: The hymn begins with God appearing in a storm, a traditional picture of some ancient Near Eastern gods (1–6); cf Ps 18, 8–16; Mi 1, 3–4; Hb 3, 3–15. Israel rejoices in the overthrowing of idol worshipers and their gods (7–9) and the rewarding of the faithful righteous (10–12).

97, 7: *All gods*: divine beings thoroughly subordinate to Israel's God. The Greek translates "angels," an interpretation adopted by Heb 1, 6.

Ps 98: A hymn, similar to Ps 96, extolling God for Israel's victory (1–3). All nations (4–6) and even inanimate nature

Whose right hand and holy arm
have won the victory.[n]*
2 The LORD has made his victory known;
has revealed his triumph for the nations to see,
3 Has remembered faithful love
toward the house of Israel.
All the ends of the earth have seen
the victory of our God.

II
4 Shout with joy to the LORD, all the earth;
break into song; sing praise.
5 Sing praise to the LORD with the harp,
with the harp and melodious song.
6 With trumpets and the sound of the horn
shout with joy to the King, the LORD.[o]

III
7 Let the sea and what fills it resound,[p]
the world and those who dwell there.
8 Let the rivers clap their hands,
the mountains shout with them for joy,[q]
9 Before the LORD who comes,
who comes to govern the earth,[r]
To govern the world with justice
and the peoples with fairness.[s]

## PSALM 99*

## The Holy King

I
1 The LORD is king, the peoples tremble;
God is enthroned on the cherubim,* the earth quakes.[t]
2 The LORD is great on Zion,
exalted above all the peoples.
3 Let them praise your great and awesome name:
holy is God![u]

II
4 O mighty king, lover of justice,
you alone have established fairness;
you have created just rule in Jacob.[v]
5 Exalt the LORD, our God;
bow down before his footstool;[w]*
holy is God!

III
6 Moses and Aaron were among his priests,
Samuel among those who called on God's name;
they called on the LORD, who answered them.[x]
7 From the pillar of cloud God spoke to them;
they kept the decrees, the law they received.[y]
8 O LORD, our God, you answered them;
you were a forgiving God,
though you punished their offenses.[z]
9 Exalt the LORD, our God;
bow down before his holy mountain;
holy is the LORD, our God.

## PSALM 100*

## Communal Thanks in the Temple

1 *A psalm of thanksgiving.*

Shout joyfully to the LORD, all you lands;
2 worship the LORD with cries of gladness;
come before him with joyful song.
3 *Know that the LORD is God,
our maker to whom we belong,
whose people we are, God's well-tended flock.[a]
4 Enter the temple gates with praise,
its courts with thanksgiving.
Give thanks to God, bless his name;[b]
5 good indeed is the LORD,
Whose love endures forever,
whose faithfulness lasts through every age.

## PSALM 101*

## Norm of Life for Rulers

1 *A psalm of David.*

I
I sing of love and justice;
to you, LORD, I sing praise.

---

n Is 59,16; 63,5.
o Ps 47,6-7.
p Ps 96,11.
q Is 44,23; 55,12.
r Ps 96,13.
s Ps 67,5.
t Pss 18,8-11; 80,2; 93, 1; Ex 25,22; 1 Sm 4, 4; 2 Sm 6,2.
u Is 6,3.
v Pss 72,1; 99,4; Jer 23,5.
w Ps 132,7.
x Jer 15,1.
y Ex 33,9; Nm 12,5.
z Ex 32,11; Nm 20,12.
a Pss 23,1; 95,7; Mi 7, 14; Is 64,7.
b 4-5: Pss 106,1; 107,1; 118,1; 136,1; 138,8; Jer 33,11.

---

(7–8) are summoned to welcome God's coming to rule over the world (9).

98, 1: *Marvelous deeds ... victory*: the conquest of all threats to the peaceful existence of Israel, depicted in the psalms variously as a cosmic force such as Sea, or nations bent on Israel's destruction, or evildoers seemingly triumphant. *Whose right hand and holy arm*: God is pictured as a powerful warrior.

Ps 99: A hymn to God as the king whose grandeur is most clearly seen on Mount Zion (2) and in the laws given to Israel (4). Israel is special because of God's word of justice, which was mediated by the revered speakers, Moses, Aaron, and Samuel (6–8). The poem is structured by the threefold statement that God is holy (3. 5. 9) and by the twice-repeated command to praise (5. 9).

99, 1: *Enthroned on the cherubim*: cherubim were composite beings with animal and human features, common in ancient Near Eastern art. Two cherubim were placed on the ark (or box) of the covenant in the holy of holies. Upon them God was believed to dwell invisibly. Cf Ex 25, 20–22; 1 Sm 4, 4; 2 Sm 6, 2; Ps 80, 2.

99, 5: *Footstool*: a reference to the ark. Cf 1 Chr 28, 2; Ps 132, 7.

Ps 100: A hymn inviting the people to enter the temple courts with thank offerings for the God who created them.

100, 3: Although the people call on all the nations of the world to join in their hymn, they are conscious of being the chosen people of God.

Ps 101: The king, grateful at being God's chosen (1), promises to be a ruler after God's own heart (2–3), allowing into the royal service only the God-fearing (3–8).

2 I follow the way of integrity;[c]
when will you come to me?
I act with integrity of heart
within my royal court.[d]*
3 I do not allow into my presence
anyone who speaks perversely.
Whoever acts shamefully I hate;
no such person can be my friend.[e]
4 I shun the devious of heart;
the wicked I do not tolerate.
5 Whoever slanders another in secret
I reduce to silence.[f]
Haughty eyes and arrogant hearts[g]
I cannot endure.

II
6 I look to the faithful of the land;*
they alone can be my companions.
Those who follow the way of integrity,[h]
they alone can enter my service.
7 No one who practices deceit
can hold a post in my court.
No one who speaks falsely
can be among my advisors.[i]
8 Each morning* I clear the wicked from the land,
and rid the LORD's city of all evildoers.

## PSALM 102*

## Prayer in Time of Distress

1 *The prayer of one afflicted and wasting away whose anguish is poured out before the LORD.*

I
2 LORD, hear my prayer;
let my cry come to you.
3 Do not hide your face from me
now that I am in distress.[j]
Turn your ear to me;
when I call, answer me quickly.
4 For my days vanish like smoke;[k]
my bones burn away as in a furnace.
5 I am withered, dried up like grass,
too wasted to eat my food.
6 From my loud groaning
I become just skin and bones.
7 I am like a desert owl,
like an owl among the ruins.
8 I lie awake and moan,
like a lone sparrow on the roof.
9 All day long my enemies taunt me;
in their rage, they make my name a curse.*
10 I eat ashes like bread,
mingle my drink with tears.[l]
11 Because of your furious wrath,
you lifted me up just to cast me down.
12 My days are like a lengthening shadow;[m]
I wither like the grass.[n]

II
13 But you, LORD, are enthroned forever;
your renown is for all generations.[o]
14 You will again show mercy to Zion;
now is the time for pity;
the appointed time has come.
15 Its stones are dear to your servants;
its dust moves them to pity.
16 The nations shall revere your name, LORD,
all the kings of the earth, your glory,[p]
17 Once the LORD has rebuilt Zion
and appeared in glory,
18 Heeding the plea of the lowly,
not scorning their prayer.
19 Let this be written for the next generation,
for a people not yet born,
that they may praise the LORD:[q]
20 *"The LORD looked down from the holy heights,
viewed the earth from heaven,[r]
21 To attend to the groaning of the prisoners,
to release those doomed to die."[s]
22 Then the LORD's name will be declared on Zion,
the praise of God in Jerusalem,
23 When all peoples and kingdoms gather
to worship the LORD.[t]

III
24 God has shattered my strength in mid-course,
has cut short my days.
25 I plead, O my God,
do not take me in the midst of my days.[u]*
Your years last through all generations.
26 Of old you laid the earth's foundations;[v]

c Ps 26,11.
d 1 Kgs 9,4; Is 33,15.
e Prv 11,20.
f Prv 17,20; 30,10.
g Prv 21,4.
h Ps 26,11; Prv 20,7.
i Ps 5,5; Prv 25,5.
j Pss 69,18; 143,7.
k 4-6: Ps 38,7-9.
l Pss 42,4; 80,6.
m Pss 109,23; 144,4; Jb 8,9; 14,2; Eccl 6,12; Wis 2,5.
n Ps 90,5-6.
o Pss 55,20; 90,2; 93,2; 102,13; 135,13; 145, 13; Lam 5,19; Hb 1, 12.
p Is 59,19; 66,18.
q Ps 22,31-32.
r Pss 11,4; 14,2.
s Ps 79,11.
t Is 60,3-4; Zec 2,15; 8, 22.
u Pss 39,5; 90,10; Jb 14,5.
v 26-28: Heb 1,10-12.

*

101, 2: *Within my royal court*: the king promises to make his own household a model for Israel, banning all officials who abuse their power.

101, 6: *I look to the faithful of the land*: the king seeks companions only among those faithful to God.

101, 8: *Each morning*: the normal time for the administration of justice (2 Sm 15, 2; Jer 21, 12) and for the arrival of divine aid (Pss 59, 17; 143, 8; Is 33, 2). *I clear the wicked from the land*: the king, as God's servant, is responsible for seeing that divine justice is carried out.

Ps 102: A lament, one of the Penitential Psalms. The psalmist, experiencing psychic and bodily disintegration (4–12), cries out to God (1–3). In the temple precincts where God has promised to be present, the psalmist recalls God's venerable promises to save the poor (13–23). The final part (24–29) restates the original complaint and prayer, and emphasizes God's eternity.

102, 9: *They make my name a curse*: enemies use the psalmist's name in phrases such as, "May you be as wretched as this person!"

102, 20–23: Both 20–21 and 22–23 depend on 19.

102, 25: *In the midst of my days*: when the normal span of life is but half completed. Cf Is 38, 10; Jer 17, 11.

the heavens are the work of your hands.
27 They perish, but you remain;
they all wear out like a garment;
Like clothing you change them and they are changed,
28 but you are the same, your years have no end.
29 May the children of your servants live on;
may their descendants live in your presence.[w]

## PSALM 103*
## Praise of Divine Goodness

1 *Of David.*

I
Bless the LORD, my soul;
all my being, bless his holy name!
2 Bless the LORD, my soul;
do not forget all the gifts of God,
3 Who pardons all your sins,
heals all your ills,
4 Delivers your life from the pit,[x]
surrounds you with love and compassion,
5 Fills your days with good things;
your youth is renewed like the eagle's.*

II
6 The LORD does righteous deeds,
brings justice to all the oppressed.[y]
7 His ways were revealed to Moses,
mighty deeds to the people of Israel.
8 Merciful and gracious is the LORD,
slow to anger, abounding in kindness.[z]
9 God does not always rebuke,
nurses no lasting anger,
10 Has not dealt with us as our sins merit,
nor requited us as our deeds deserve.

III
11 As the heavens tower over the earth,
so God's love towers over the faithful.[a]
12 As far as the east is from the west,
so far have our sins been removed from us.
13 As a father has compassion on his children,
so the LORD has compassion on the faithful.
14 For he knows how we are formed,
remembers that we are dust.[b]
15 Our days are like the grass;
like flowers of the field we blossom.[c]
16 The wind sweeps over us and we are gone;
our place knows us no more.
17 But the LORD's kindness is forever,
toward the faithful from age to age.
He favors the children's children
18 of those who keep his covenant,
who take care to fulfill its precepts.

IV
19 The LORD's throne is established in heaven;
God's royal power rules over all.
20 Bless the LORD, all you angels,[d]
mighty in strength and attentive,
obedient to every command.
21 Bless the LORD, all you hosts,
ministers who do God's will.
22 Bless the LORD, all creatures,
everywhere in God's domain.
Bless the LORD, my soul!

## PSALM 104*
## Praise of God the Creator

I
1 Bless the LORD, my soul!
LORD, my God, you are great indeed!
You are clothed with majesty and glory,
2 robed in light as with a cloak.
You spread out the heavens like a tent;[e]
3 you raised your palace upon the waters.*
You make the clouds your chariot;
you travel on the wings of the wind.
4 You make the winds your messengers;
flaming fire, your ministers.[f]

II
5 *You fixed the earth on its foundation,
never to be moved.
6 The ocean covered it like a garment;
above the mountains stood the waters.
7 At your roar they took flight;
at the sound of your thunder they fled.[g]
8 They rushed up the mountains, down the valleys
to the place you had fixed for them.

w Ps 69,36-37.
x Pss 28,1; 30,4; 40,3; 69,16; 88,5; 143,7; Prv 1,12; Jon 2,7.
y Ps 146,6-7.
z Pss 86,15; 145,8; Ex 34,6-7; Nm 14,18; Jer 3,12; Jl 2,13; Jon 4,2.
a Is 55,9.
b Ps 90,3.
c Pss 37,2; 90,5-6; Is 40,7.
d Ps 148,2; Dn 3,58.
e Prv 8,27-28; Jb 9,8; Is 40,22; Gn 1,6-7; Am 9,6.
f Heb 1,7.
g Ps 29,3.

*

Ps 103: The speaker in this hymn begins by praising God for personal benefits (1–5), then moves on to God's mercy toward all the people (6–18). Even sin cannot destroy that mercy (11–13), for the eternal God is well aware of the people's human fragility (14–18). The psalmist invites the heavenly beings to join in praise (19–22).

103, 5: *Your youth is renewed like the eagle's*: because of the eagle's long life it was a symbol of perennial youth and vigor. Cf Is 40, 31.

Ps 104: A hymn praising God who easily and skillfully made rampaging waters and primordial night into a world vibrant with life. The psalmist describes God's splendor in the heavens (1–4), how the chaotic waters were tamed to fertilize and feed the world (5–18), and how primordial night was made into a gentle time of refreshment (19–23). The picture is like Gn 1, 1–2: a dark and watery chaos is made dry and lighted so that creatures might live. The psalmist reacts to the beauty of creation with awe (24–34). May sin not deface God's work (35)!

104, 3: *Your palace upon the waters*: God's heavenly dwelling above the upper waters of the sky. Cf Gn 1, 6–7; Ps 29, 10.

104, 5–9: God places the gigantic disk of the earth securely on its foundation and then, as a warrior, chases away the enveloping waters and confines them under, above, and around the earth.

9 You set a limit they cannot pass;
never again will they cover the earth.[h]

III
10 You made springs flow into channels
that wind among the mountains.
11 They give drink to every beast of the field;[i]
here wild asses quench their thirst.
12 Beside them the birds of heaven nest;
among the branches they sing.
13 You water the mountains from your palace;
by your labor the earth abounds.
14 You raise grass for the cattle
and plants for our beasts of burden.
You bring bread from the earth,
15 and wine to gladden our hearts,
Oil to make our faces gleam,
food to build our strength.
16 *The trees of the LORD drink their fill,
the cedars of Lebanon, which you
planted.
17 There the birds build their nests;
junipers are the home of the stork.[j]
18 The high mountains are for wild goats;
the rocky cliffs, a refuge for badgers.

IV
19 You made the moon to mark the seasons,[k]
the sun that knows the hour of its setting.
20 You bring darkness and night falls,
then all the beasts of the forest roam
abroad.
21 Young lions roar for prey;
they seek their food from God.[l]
22 When the sun rises, they steal away
and rest in their dens.
23 People go forth to their work,
to their labor till evening falls.

V
24 How varied are your works, LORD!
In wisdom you have wrought them all;
the earth is full of your creatures.[m]
25 Look at the sea, great and wide!
It teems with countless beings,
living things both large and small.[n]
26 Here ships ply their course;
here Leviathan,* your creature, plays.[o]

VI
27 All of these look to you
to give them food in due time.[p]
28 When you give to them, they gather;
when you open your hand, they are well
filled.
29 *When you hide your face, they are lost.
When you take away their breath, they
perish
and return to the dust from which they
came.[q]
30 When you send forth your breath, they are
created,
and you renew the face of the earth.

VII
31 May the glory of the LORD endure forever;
may the LORD be glad in these works!
32 If God glares at the earth, it trembles,
If God touches the mountains, they
smoke![r]
33 I will sing to the LORD all my life;
I will sing praise to my God while I live.[s]
34 May my theme be pleasing to God;
I will rejoice in the LORD.
35 May sinners vanish from the earth,
and the wicked be no more.
Bless the LORD, my soul! Hallelujah!*

## PSALM 105*

### God's Fidelity to the Promise

I
1 Give thanks to the LORD, invoke his name;[t]
make known among the peoples his
deeds![u]
2 Sing praise, play music;
proclaim all his wondrous deeds!
3 Glory in his holy name;
rejoice, O hearts that seek the LORD!
4 Rely on the mighty LORD;
constantly seek his face.[v]
5 Recall the wondrous deeds he has done,
his signs and his words of judgment,
6 You descendants of Abraham his servant,
offspring of Jacob the chosen one!

II
7 The LORD is our God,
who rules the whole earth.
8 He remembers forever his covenant,

h Jer 5,22; Gn 9,11-15.
i 11-14: Ps 147,8-9.
j Ez 31,6.
k Sir 43,6.
l Jb 38,39.
m Ps 92,6; Sir 39,16.
n Sir 43,26.
o Jb 3,8; 40,25.
p Pss 136,25; 145, 15-16.
q Jb 34,14-15; Eccl 3, 20; Ps 90,3.
r Ps 144,5.
s Ps 146,2.
t 1-15: 1 Chr 16,8-22.
u Pss 18,50; 96,3; 145, 5; Is 12,4-5.
v Pss 24,6; 27,8.

*

104, 16–18: Even the exotic flora and fauna of the high mountains of the Lebanon range receive adequate water.

104, 26: *Leviathan*: a sea monster symbolizing primeval chaos. Cf Ps 74, 14; Is 27, 1; Jb 40, 25. God does not destroy chaos but makes it part of the created order.

104, 29–30: On one level, the spirit (or wind) of God is the fall and winter rains that provide food for all creatures. On another, it is the breath (or spirit) of God that makes beings live.

104, 35: *Hallelujah*: a frequent word in the last third of the Psalter. The word combines the plural imperative of praise (*hallelu*) with an abbreviated form of the divine name Yah(weh).

Ps 105: A hymn to God who promised the land of Canaan to the holy people. Cf Pss 78; 106; 136. Israel is invited to praise and seek the presence of God (1–6), who is faithful to the promise of land to the ancestors (7–11). In every phase of the national story—the ancestors in the land of Canaan (12–15), Joseph in Egypt (16–22), Israel in Egypt (23–38), Israel in the desert on the way to Canaan (39–45)—God remained faithful, reiterating the promise of the land to successive servants.

the pact imposed for a thousand
generations,
9 Which was made with Abraham,
confirmed by oath to Isaac,[w]
10 And ratified as binding for Jacob,
an everlasting covenant for Israel:
11 "To you I give the land of Canaan,
your own allotted heritage."[x]

III
12 When they were few in number,[y]
a handful, and strangers there,
13 Wandering from nation to nation,
from one kingdom to another,
14 He let no one oppress them;
for their sake he rebuked kings:*
15 "Do not touch my anointed,
to my prophets* do no harm."

IV
16 Then he called down a famine on the land,
destroyed the grain that sustained them.[z]
17 He had sent a man ahead of them,
Joseph, sold as a slave.[a]
18 They shackled his feet with chains;
collared his neck in iron,[b]
19 Till his prediction came to pass,
and the word of the LORD proved him true.[c]
20 The king sent and released him;
the ruler of peoples set him free.[d]
21 He made him lord over his palace,
ruler over all his possessions,[e]
22 To instruct his princes by his word,
to teach his elders wisdom.

V
23 Then Israel entered Egypt;[f]
Jacob lived in the land of Ham.*
24 God greatly increased his people,
made them too many for their foes.[g]
25 He turned their hearts to hate his people,
to treat his servants unfairly.[h]
26 He sent his servant Moses,
Aaron whom he had chosen.[i]
27 They worked his signs in Egypt[j]
and wonders in the land of Ham.*
28 He sent darkness and it grew dark,
but they rebelled against his word.
29 He turned their waters into blood
and killed all their fish.
30 Their land swarmed with frogs,
even the chambers of their kings.
31 He spoke and there came swarms of flies,
gnats through all their country.
32 For rain he gave them hail,
flashes of lightning throughout their land.
33 He struck down their vines and fig trees,
shattered the trees of their country.
34 He spoke and the locusts came,
grasshoppers without number.[k]
35 They devoured every plant in the land;
they ravaged the crops of their fields.
36 He struck down every firstborn in the land,
the first fruits of all their vigor.
37 He brought his people out,
laden with silver and gold;[l]
no stragglers among the tribes.
38 Egypt rejoiced when they left,
for panic had seized them.

VI
39 He spread a cloud as a cover,
and made a fire to light up the night.[m]
40 They asked and he brought them quail;
with bread from heaven he filled them.[n]
41 He split the rock and water gushed forth;
it flowed through the desert like a river.[o]
42 For he remembered his sacred word
to Abraham his servant.
43 He brought his people out with joy,
his chosen ones with shouts of triumph.
44 He gave them the lands of the nations,
the wealth of the peoples to own,[p]
45 That they might keep his laws
and observe his teachings.[q]
Hallelujah!

## PSALM 106*

## Israel's Confession of Sin

1 *Hallelujah!*

### A

Give thanks to the LORD, who is good,
whose love endures forever.[r]

---

w Gn 15,1ff; 26,3.
x Gn 12,7; 15,18.
y 12-13: Dt 4,27; 26,5.
z Gn 41,54. 57.
a Gn 37,28. 36; 45,5.
b Gn 39,20.
c Gn 40-41.
d Gn 41,14.
e Gn 41,41-44.
f Gn 46,1-47,12; Acts 7,15.
g Ex 1,7; Acts 7,17.
h Ex 1,8-14.
i Ex 3,10; 4,27.
j 27-36: Ps 78,43-51; Ex 7-12.
k Jl 1,4.
l Ex 12,33-36.
m Ps 78,14; Ex 13, 21-22; Wis 18,3.
n Ps 78,24-28; Ex 16, 13-15; Nm 11,31ff; Wis 16,20.
o Ps 78,15-16; Ex 17, 1-7; Nm 20,11.
p Dt 4,37-40.
q Dt 6,20-25; 7,8-11.
r Pss 100,5; 107,1; 1 Chr 16,34; Jer 33, 11; Dn 3,89.

---

105, 14: *Kings*: Pharaoh and Abimelech of Gerar. Cf Gn 12, 17; 20, 6–7.

105, 15: *My anointed . . . my prophets*: the patriarchs Abraham, Isaac, and Jacob, who were "anointed" in the sense of being consecrated and recipients of God's revelation.

105, 23. 27: *The land of Ham*: a synonym for Egypt. Cf Gn 10, 6.

105, 27–38: This psalm and Ps 78, 43–51 have an account of the plagues differing in number or in order from Ex 7, 14–12, 30. Several versions of the exodus story were current.

Ps 106: Israel is invited to praise the God whose mercy has always tempered judgment of Israel (1–3). The speaker, on behalf of all, seeks solidarity with the people, who can always count on God's fidelity despite their sin (4–5). Confident of God's mercy, the speaker invites national repentance (6) by reciting from Israel's history eight instances of sin, judgment, and forgiveness. The sins are the rebellion at the Red Sea (6–12; see Ex 14–15), the craving for meat in the desert (13–15; see Nm 11), the challenge to Moses' authority (16–18; see Nm 16), the golden calf episode (19–23; see Ex 32–34), the refusal to take Canaan by the southern route (24–27; see Nm 13–14 and Dt 1–2), the rebellion at Baal-Peor (28–31; see Nm 25, 1–10), the anger of Moses (32–33; see Nm 20, 1–13), and mingling with the nations (34–47). The last, as suggested by its length and generalized language, may be

**2** Who can tell the mighty deeds of the LORD,
proclaim in full God's praise?
**3** Happy those who do what is right,
whose deeds are always just.[s]
**4** Remember me, LORD, as you favor your people;
come to me with your saving help,[t]
**5** That I may see the prosperity of your chosen,
rejoice in the joy of your people,
and glory with your heritage.

## B

**6** We have sinned like our ancestors;[u]
we have done wrong and are guilty.

I
**7** Our ancestors in Egypt
did not attend to your wonders.
They did not remember your great love;
they defied the Most High at the Red Sea.
**8** Yet he saved them for his name's sake
to make his power known.[v]
**9** He roared at the Red Sea and it dried up.
He led them through the deep as through a desert.[w]
**10** He rescued them from hostile hands,
freed them from the power of the enemy.
**11** The waters covered their oppressors;
not one of them survived.
**12** Then they believed his words
and sang songs of praise.[x]

II
**13** But they soon forgot all he had done;
they had no patience for his plan.
**14** In the desert they gave way to their cravings,
tempted God in the wasteland.[y]
**15** So he gave them what they asked
and sent among them a wasting disease.[z]

III
**16** In the camp they challenged Moses[a]
and Aaron, the holy one of the LORD.
**17** The earth opened and swallowed Dathan,
it closed on the followers of Abiram.
**18** Against that company the fire blazed;
flames consumed the wicked.

IV
**19** At Horeb they fashioned a calf,[b]
worshiped a metal statue.
**20** They exchanged their glorious God
for the image of a grass-eating bull.
**21** They forgot the God who saved them,
who did great deeds in Egypt,[c]
**22** Amazing deeds in the land of Ham,
fearsome deeds at the Red Sea.
**23** He would have decreed their destruction,
had not Moses, the chosen leader,
Withstood him in the breach*
to turn back his destroying anger.[d]

V
**24** Next they despised the beautiful land;[e]
they did not believe the promise.
**25** In their tents they complained;
they did not obey the LORD.
**26** So with raised hand he swore
to destroy them in the desert,
**27** To scatter their descendants among the nations,
disperse them in foreign lands.

VI
**28** They joined in the rites of Baal of Peor,[f]
ate food sacrificed to dead gods.
**29** They provoked him by their actions,
and a plague broke out among them.
**30** Then Phinehas rose to intervene,
and the plague was brought to a halt.
**31** This was counted for him as a righteous deed
for all generations to come.

VII
**32** At the waters of Meribah they angered God,[g]
and Moses suffered because of them.*
**33** They so embittered his spirit
that rash words crossed his lips.

VIII
**34** They did not destroy the peoples
as the LORD had commanded them,[h]
**35** But mingled with the nations
and imitated their ways.[i]
**36** They worshiped their idols
and were ensnared by them.[j]
**37** They sacrificed to the gods*

---

s Is 56,1-2.
t Ps 25,7; Neh 5,19.
u 6-7: Ps 78,11-17; Ex 14,11; Lv 26,40; 1 Kgs 8,47; Bar 2,12; Dn 9,5.
v Ez 36,20-22.
w Ex 14,21-31; Is 50,2; 63,11-14; Na 1,4.
x Ex 15,1-21.
y Ps 78,18; Ex 15,24; 16,3; Nm 11,1-6.
z Ps 78,26-31; Nm 11, 33.
a 16-18: Nm 16; Dt 11, 6; Is 26,11.
b 19-20: Ex 32; Dt 9, 8-21; Jer 2,11; Acts 7, 41; Rom 1,23.
c Ps 78,42-58; Dt 32, 18; Jer 2,32.
d Ex 32,11; Dt 9,25; Ez 22,30.
e 24-27: Lv 26,33; Nm 14; Dt 1,25-36; Ez 20, 15. 23.
f 28-31: Nm 25; Dt 26, 14; Sir 45,23-24.
g 32-33: Ps 95,8-9; Ex 17,1-7; Nm 20,2-13; Dt 6,16; 33,8.
h Dt 7,1; Jgs 2,1-5.
i Lv 18,3; Jgs 1,27-35; 3,5.
j 36-38: Lv 18,21; Nm 35,33; Dt 32,17; Jgs 2,11-13. 17. 19; 2 Kgs 16,3; Bar 4,7; 1 Cor 10,20.

---

the sin that invites the repentance of the present generation. The text gives the site of each sin: Egypt (7), the desert (14), the camp (16), Horeb (19), in their tents (25), Baal-Peor (28), the waters of Meribah (32), Canaan (38).

106, 23: *Withstood him in the breach*: the image is that of Moses standing in a narrow break made in the wall to keep anyone from entering.

106, 32: *Moses suffered because of them*: Moses was not allowed to enter the promised land because of his rash words (Nm 20, 12). According to Dt 1, 37, Moses was not allowed to cross because of the people's sin, not his own.

106, 37: *The gods*: Hebrew *shedim*, customarily translated "demons," occurs in parallelism with "gods" in an important

their own sons and daughters,
38 Shedding innocent blood,
the blood of their own sons and daughters,
Whom they sacrificed to the idols of Canaan,
desecrating the land with bloodshed.
39 They defiled themselves by their actions,
became adulterers by their conduct.
40 So the LORD grew angry with his people,
abhorred his own heritage.
41 He handed them over to the nations,
and their adversaries ruled them.[k]
42 Their enemies oppressed them,
kept them under subjection.
43 Many times did he rescue them,
but they kept rebelling and scheming
and were brought low by their own guilt.[l]
44 Still God had regard for their affliction
when he heard their wailing.
45 For their sake he remembered his covenant
and relented in his abundant love,[m]
46 Winning for them compassion
from all who held them captive.

C

47 Save us, LORD, our God;
gather us from among the nations
That we may give thanks to your holy name
and glory in praising you.[n]

* * *

48 *Blessed be the LORD, the God of Israel,
from everlasting to everlasting!
Let all the people say, Amen![o]
Hallelujah!

## *FIFTH BOOK — PSALMS 107–150*

## PSALM 107*

### God the Savior of Those in Distress

1 "Give thanks to the LORD who is good,
whose love endures forever!"[p]
2 Let that be the prayer of the LORD's redeemed,
those redeemed from the hand of the foe,[q]
3 Those gathered from foreign lands,
from east and west, from north and south.[r]

I

4 Some had lost their way in a barren desert;
found no path toward a city to live in.
5 They were hungry and thirsty;
their life was ebbing away.[s]
6 In their distress they cried to the LORD,
who rescued them in their peril,
7 Guided them by a direct path[t]
so they reached a city to live in.[u]
8 Let them thank the LORD for such kindness,
such wondrous deeds for mere mortals.
9 For he satisfied the thirsty,
filled the hungry with good things.[v]

II

10 Some lived in darkness and gloom,
in prison, bound with chains,
11 Because they rebelled against God's word,
scorned the counsel of the Most High,[w]
12 Who humbled their hearts through hardship;
they stumbled with no one to help.[x]
13 In their distress they cried to the LORD,
who saved them in their peril,
14 Led them forth from darkness and gloom
and broke their chains asunder.[y]
15 Let them thank the LORD for such kindness,
such wondrous deeds for mere mortals.
16 For he broke down the gates of bronze
and snapped the bars of iron.

III

17 Some fell sick from their wicked ways,
afflicted because of their sins.
18 They loathed all manner of food;[z]
they were at the gates of death.
19 In their distress they cried to the LORD,
who saved them in their peril,
20 Sent forth the word to heal them,[a]
snatched them from the grave.
21 Let them thank the LORD for such kindness,
such wondrous deeds for mere mortals.
22 Let them offer a sacrifice in thanks,
declare his works with shouts of joy.

IV

23 Some went off to sea in ships,
plied their trade on the deep waters.[b]
24 They saw the works of the LORD,
the wonders of God in the deep.
25 He spoke and roused a storm wind;
it tossed the waves on high.[c]

k Jgs 2,14-23.
l Is 63,7-9.
m Lv 26,42.
n 1 Chr 16,35.
o Pss 41,14; 72,18; 89,53; 1 Chr 16,36; Neh 9,5.
p Pss 100,4-5; 106,1; Jer 33,11.
q Is 63,12.
r Is 43,5-6; 49,12; Zec 8,7.
s Dt 8,15; 32,10; Is 49,10.
t Is 35,8; 40,3; 43,19.
u Dt 6,10.
v Lk 1,53.
w Is 42,7. 22; Jb 36,8-9; Prv 1,25.
x Ps 106,43.
y Is 42,7; 49,9; 51,14.
z Jb 6,6-7; 33,20.
a Ps 147,15; Wis 16,12; Is 55,11; Mt 8,8.
b Sir 43,25.
c Jon 1,4.

* inscription from Transjordan and hence is translated "gods."
106, 48: A doxology ending Book IV of the Psalter. It is not part of the psalm.
Ps 107: A hymn inviting those who have been rescued by God to give praise (1–3). Four archetypal divine rescues are described, each ending in thanksgiving: from the sterile desert (4–9), from imprisonment in gloom (10–16), from mortal illness (17–22), and from the angry sea (23–32). The number four connotes totality, all the possible varieties of rescue. The same saving activity of God is shown in Israel's history (33–41); whenever the people were endangered God rescued them. The last verses invite people to ponder the persistent saving acts of God (42–43).

**26** They rose up to the heavens, sank to the depths;
their hearts trembled at the danger.
**27** They reeled, staggered like drunkards;
their skill was of no avail.[d]
**28** In their distress they cried to the LORD,
who brought them out of their peril,
**29** Hushed the storm to a murmur;
the waves of the sea were stilled.[e]
**30** They rejoiced that the sea grew calm,
that God brought them to the harbor they longed for.
**31** Let them thank the LORD for such kindness,
such wondrous deeds for mere mortal.
**32** Let them praise him in the assembly of the people,
give thanks in the council of the elders.

V

**33** *God changed rivers into desert,
springs of water into thirsty ground,[f]
**34** Fruitful land into a salty waste,
because of the wickedness of its people.[g]
**35** He changed the desert into pools of water,
arid land into springs of water,[h]
**36** And settled the hungry there;
they built a city to live in.[i]
**37** They sowed fields and planted vineyards,
brought in an abundant harvest.[j]
**38** God blessed them, they became very many,
and their livestock did not decrease.[k]
**40** But he poured out contempt on princes,
made them wander the trackless wastes,[l]
**39** Where they were diminished and brought low
through misery and cruel oppression,
**41** While the poor were released from their affliction;
their families increased like their flocks.[m]
**42** The upright saw this and rejoiced;[n]
all wickedness shut its mouth.
**43** Whoever is wise will take note of these things,[o]
will ponder the merciful deeds of the LORD.

## PSALM 108*

## Prayer for Victory

**1** *A song; a psalm of David.*

I

**2** My heart is steadfast, God;[p]
my heart is steadfast.
I will sing and chant praise.
**3** Awake, my soul; awake, lyre and harp!
I will wake the dawn.[q]
**4** I will praise you among the peoples, LORD;
I will chant your praise among the nations.[r]
**5** For your love towers to the heavens;
your faithfulness, to the skies.[s]
**6** Appear on high over the heavens, God;
may your glory appear above all the earth.
**7** Help with your right hand and answer us
that your loved ones may escape.

II

**8** God promised in the sanctuary:[t]
"I will exult, I will apportion Shechem;
the valley of Succoth I will measure out.
**9** Gilead is mine, mine is Manasseh;
Ephraim is the helmet for my head,
Judah, my own scepter.
**10** Moab is my washbowl;
upon Edom I cast my sandal;[u]
I will triumph over Philistia."

III

**11** Who will bring me to the fortified city?
Who will lead me into Edom?
**12** Was it not you who rejected us, God?
Do you no longer march with our armies?[v]
**13** Give us aid against the foe;
worthless is human help.
**14** We will triumph with the help of God,
who will trample down our foes.

## PSALM 109*

## Prayer of a Person Falsely Accused

**1** *For the leader. A psalm of David.*

I

O God, whom I praise, do not be silent,[w]
**2** for wicked and treacherous mouths attack me.
They speak against me with lying tongues;
**3** with hateful words they surround me,

d Is 29,9.
e Pss 65,8; 89,10; Mt 8, 26 par.
f Is 35,7; 42,15; 50,2.
g Gn 19,23-28; Dt 29, 22; Sir 39,23.
h Ps 114,8; Is 41,8.
i Ez 36,35.
j Is 65,21; Jer 31,5.
k Dt 7,13-14.
l Jb 12,23-25.
m Ps 113,7.
n Pss 58,11; 63,12.
o Hos 14,10.
p 2-6: Ps 57,8-12.
q Jb 38,12.
r Pss 9,12; 18,50; 148, 13.
s Pss 36,6; 71,19.
t 8-14: Ps 60,8-14.
u Ru 4,7-8.
v Ps 44,10.
w Pss 35,22; 83,1.

* 107, 33–41: God destroyed Sodom and Gomorrah in Gn 18–19, which the psalm sees as the destruction of the wicked inhabitants of Canaan to prepare the way for Israel (33–34). God then led Israel through the desert to give them a fertile land (35–38) and protected them from every danger (39–41).

Ps 108: A prayer compiled from two other psalms: 2–6 are virtually the same as Ps 57, 8–12; 7–14 are the same as Ps 60, 7–14. An old promise of salvation (8–10) is combined with a confident assurance (1–6. 14) and petition (7. 12–13).

Ps 109: A lament notable for the length and vehemence of its prayer against evildoers (6–20); the cry to God (1) and the complaint (22–25) are brief in comparison. The psalmist is apparently the victim of a slander campaign, potentially devastating in a society where reputation and honor are paramount. In the emotional perspective of the psalm, there are only two types of people: the wicked and their poor victims. The psalmist is a poor victim (22. 31) and by that fact a friend of God and enemy of the wicked. The psalmist seeks vindication not on the basis of personal virtue but because of God's promise to protect the poor.

attacking me without cause.
4 In return for my love they slander me,
even though I prayed for them.
5 They repay me evil for good,
hatred for my love.[x]

II
My enemies say of me:
6 "Find a lying witness,
an accuser* to stand by his right hand,
7 That he may be judged and found guilty,
that his plea may be in vain.
8 May his days be few;
may another take his office.[y]
9 May his children be fatherless,
his wife, a widow.[z]
10 May his children be vagrant beggars,
driven from their hovels.
11 May the usurer snare all he owns,
strangers plunder all he earns.
12 May no one treat him kindly
or pity his fatherless children.
13 May his posterity be destroyed,[a]
his name cease in the next generation.
14 May the LORD remember his fathers' guilt;
his mother's sin not be canceled.[b]
15 May their guilt be always before the LORD,[c]
till their memory is banished from the
earth,[d]
16 For he did not remember to show kindness,
but hounded the wretched poor
and brought death to the brokenhearted.
17 He loved cursing; may it come upon him;
he hated blessing; may none come to him.
18 May cursing clothe him like a robe;
may it enter his belly like water,
seep into his bones like oil.
19 May it be near as the clothes he wears,
as the belt always around him."

III
20 May the LORD bring all this* upon my
accusers,
upon those who speak evil against me.
21 But you, LORD, my God,
deal kindly with me for your name's sake;
in your great mercy rescue me.
22 For I am sorely in need;
my heart is pierced within me.
23 Like a lengthening shadow I near my end,
all but swept away like the locust.
24 My knees totter from fasting;[e]
my flesh has wasted away.
25 I have become a mockery to them;
when they see me, they shake their heads.
26 Help me, LORD, my God;
save me in your kindness.
27 Make them know this is your hand,
that you, LORD, have acted.
28 Though they curse, may you bless;
shame my foes, that your servant may
rejoice.
29 Clothe my accusers with disgrace;
make them wear shame like a mantle.
30 I will give fervent thanks to the LORD;
before all I will praise my God.[f]
31 For God stands at the right hand of the poor
to defend them against unjust accusers.

## PSALM 110*

## God Appoints the King both King and Priest

1 *A psalm of David.*

The LORD says to you, my lord:*
"Take your throne at my right hand,
while I make your enemies your
footstool."[g]
2 The scepter of your sovereign might
the LORD will extend from Zion.
The LORD says: "Rule over your enemies!
3 Yours is princely power from the day of
your birth.
In holy splendor before the daystar,
like the dew I begot you."[h]*
4 The LORD has sworn and will not waver:
"Like Melchizedek* you are a priest
forever."[i]
5 At your right hand is the Lord,
who crushes kings on the day of wrath,[j]
6 Who, robed in splendor, judges nations,
crushes heads across the wide earth,
7 Who drinks from the brook by the wayside*

x Pss 35,12; 38,21; Prv 17,13; Jer 18,20.
y Acts 1,20.
z Ex 22,23; Jer 18,21.
a Ps 21,11; Prv 10,7.
b Ex 20,5.
c Ps 90,8.
d Ps 34,16.
e 24-25: Ps 69,11-13.
f Ps 111,1.
g Mt 22,44; Acts 2, 34-35; 1 Cor 15,25; Heb 1,13; 8,1; 10, 12-13; 1 Pt 3,22.
h Pss 2,7; 89,27; Is 49, 1.
i Pss 89,35; 132,11; Gn 14,18; Heb 5,6; 7, 21.
j Ps 2,9; Rv 2,27; 12,5; 19,15.

*

109, 6: *An accuser*: Hebrew *satan*, a word occurring in Jb 1–2 and Zec 3, 1–2. In the latter passage Satan stands at the right hand of the high priest to bring false accusations against him before God. Here the accuser is human.

109, 20: *May the LORD bring all this*: the psalmist prays that God ratify the curses of 6–19 and bring them upon the wicked.

Ps 110: A royal psalm in which a court singer recites three oracles in which God assures the king that his enemies are conquered (1–2), makes the king "son" in traditional adoption language (3), gives priestly status to the king and promises to be with him in future military ventures (4–7).

110, 1: *The LORD says to you, my lord*: literally, "The LORD says to my lord," a polite form of address of an inferior to a superior. Cf 1 Sm 25, 25; 2 Sm 1, 10. The court singer refers to the king. Jesus in the synoptic gospels (Mt 22, 41–46 and parallels) takes the psalmist to be David and hence "my lord" refers to the messiah, who must be someone greater than David. *Your footstool*: in ancient times victorious kings put their feet on the prostrate bodies of their enemies.

110, 3: *Before the daystar*: possibly an expression for before the world began (Prv 8, 22). *Like the dew I begot you*: an adoption formula as in Pss 2, 7; 89, 27–28.

110, 4: *Like Melchizedek*: Melchizedek was the ancient king of Salem (Jerusalem) who blessed Abraham (Gn 14, 18–20); like other kings of the time he performed priestly functions. Heb 7 sees in Melchizedek a type of Christ.

110, 7: *Who drinks from the brook by the wayside*: the meaning is uncertain. Some see an allusion to a rite of royal

and thus holds high the head.[k]

## PSALM 111*

## Praise of God for Goodness to Israel

1 *Hallelujah!*

I will praise the LORD with all my heart[l]
in the assembled congregation of the upright.*
2 Great are the works of the LORD,
to be treasured for all their delights.
3 Majestic and glorious is your* work,
your wise design endures forever.
4 You won renown for your wondrous deeds;
gracious and merciful is the LORD.[m]
5 You gave food to those who fear you,*
mindful of your covenant forever.
6 You showed powerful deeds to your people,
giving them the lands* of the nations.
7 The works of your hands are right and true,
reliable all your decrees,
8 Established forever and ever,
to be observed with loyalty and care.
9 You sent deliverance to your people,
ratified your covenant forever;
holy and awesome is your name.
10 The fear of the LORD* is the beginning of wisdom;[n]
prudent are all who live by it.
Your praise endures forever.

## PSALM 112*

## The Blessings of the Just

1 *Hallelujah!*

Happy are those* who fear the LORD,
who greatly delight in God's commands.[o]
2 Their descendants shall be mighty in the land,
a generation upright and blessed.
3 Wealth and riches shall be in their homes;
their prosperity* shall endure forever.
4 They shine through the darkness, a light for the upright;[p]
they are gracious, merciful, and just.
5 All goes well for those gracious in lending,
who conduct their affairs with justice.
6 They shall never be shaken;
the just shall be remembered forever.[q]
7 They shall not fear an ill report;
their hearts are steadfast, trusting the LORD.
8 Their hearts are tranquil, without fear,
till at last they look down on their foes.
9 Lavishly they give to the poor;
their prosperity shall endure forever;[r]
their horn* shall be exalted in honor.
10 The wicked shall be angry to see this;
they will gnash their teeth and waste away;
the desires of the wicked come to nothing.

## PSALM 113*

## Praise of God's Care of the Poor

1 *Hallelujah!*

I

Praise, you servants of the LORD,
praise the name of the LORD.[s]
2 Blessed be the name of the LORD
both now and forever.
3 From the rising of the sun to its setting
let the name of the LORD be praised.

II

4 High above all nations is the LORD;
above the heavens God's glory.[t]
5 Who is like the LORD,
our God enthroned on high,
6 looking down on heaven and earth?[u]
7 The LORD raises the needy from the dust,
lifts the poor from the ash heap,[v]
8 Seats them with princes,
the princes of the people,
9 Gives the childless wife a home,

k Ps 3,4.
l Ps 138,1.
m Ps 103,8; 112,4.
n Prv 1,7; 9,10; Sir 1, 16.
o Pss 1,1-2; 119,1-2; 128,1.
p Pss 37,6; 97,11; Prv 13,9; Is 58,10.
q Prv 10,7; Wis 8,13.
r Prv 22,9; 2 Cor 9,9.
s Ps 135,1.
t Ps 148,13.
u Ps 89,7-9.
v Ps 107,41; 1 Sm 2, 7-8.

*

consecration at the Gihon spring (cf 1 Kgs 1, 33. 38). Others find here an image of the divine warrior (or king) pursuing enemies so relentlessly that he does not stop long enough to eat and drink.

Ps 111: A temple singer (1) tells how God is revealed in Israel's history (2–10). The deeds reveal God's very self, powerful, merciful, faithful. The poem is an acrostic, each verse beginning with a successive letter of the Hebrew alphabet.

111, 1: *In the assembled congregation of the upright*: in the temple. Cf Ps 149, 1.

111, 3: *Your*: the psalm refers to God in the third person throughout; the shift to the second person is for the sake of inclusive language.

111, 5: *Food to those who fear you*: probably a reference to the manna in the desert, which elsewhere is seen as a type of the Eucharist. Cf Jn 6, 31–33. 49–51.

111, 6: *Lands*: literally, "inheritance, heritage."

111, 10: *The fear of the LORD*: reverence for God, the Hebrew term for religion.

Ps 112: An acrostic poem detailing the blessings received by those who remain close to God by obedience to the commandments. Among their blessings are children (2), wealth that enables them to be magnanimous (3. 5. 9), and virtue by which they encourage others (4). The just person is an affront to the wicked, whose hopes remain unfulfilled (10). The logic resembles Pss 1 and 111.

112, 1: *Happy are those*: literally, "Happy the person." "Person" is used typically, hence the plural translation.

112, 3: *Prosperity*: literally, "justice." In the Second Temple Period the word acquired the nuance of liberality and almsgiving. Cf Sir 3, 30; 7, 10; Mt 6, 1–4.

112, 9: *Their horn*: the symbol for vitality and honor.

Ps 113: A hymn exhorting the congregation to praise God's name, i.e., the way in which God is present in the world; the name is mentioned three times in 1–3. The divine name is especially honored in the temple (1) but its recognition is not limited by time (2) and space (3), for God is everywhere active (4–5) especially in rescuing the lowly faithful (7–9).

the joyful mother of children.[w]
Hallelujah!

## PSALM 114*

## The Lord's Wonders at the Exodus

1 When Israel came forth from Egypt,
the house of Jacob from an alien people,
2 Judah became God's holy place,
Israel, God's domain.[x]
3 *The sea beheld and fled;
the Jordan turned back.[y]
4 The mountains skipped like rams;
the hills, like lambs of the flock.[z]
5 Why was it, sea, that you fled?
Jordan, that you turned back?
6 You mountains, that you skipped like rams?
You hills, like lambs of the flock?
7 Tremble, earth, before the Lord,[a]
before the God of Jacob,
8 *Who turned rock into pools of water,
stone into flowing springs.[b]

## PSALM 115*

## The Greatness of the True God

I
1 Not to us, LORD, not to us
but to your name give glory
because of your faithfulness and love.[c]
2 Why should the nations say,
"Where is their God?"[d]*
3 Our God is in heaven;
whatever God wills is done.[e]

II
4 Their idols are silver and gold,[f]
the work of human hands.[g]
5 They have mouths but do not speak,
eyes but do not see.
6 They have ears but do not hear,
noses but do not smell.
7 They have hands but do not feel,
feet but do not walk,
and no sound rises from their throats.
8 Their makers shall be like them,
all who trust in them.

III
9 The house of Israel trusts in the LORD,[h]*
who is their help and shield.[i]
10 The house of Aaron trusts in the LORD,
who is their help and shield.
11 Those who fear the LORD* trust in the LORD,
who is their help and shield.
12 The LORD remembers us and will bless us,
will bless the house of Israel,
will bless the house of Aaron,
13 Will bless those who fear the LORD,
small and great alike.
14 May the LORD increase your number,
you and your descendants.
15 May you be blessed by the LORD,
who made heaven and earth.
16 The heavens* belong to the LORD,
but the earth is given to us.[j]
17 *The dead do not praise the LORD,
all those gone down into silence.[k]
18 It is we who bless the LORD,
both now and forever.
Hallelujah!

## PSALM 116*

## Thanksgiving to God Who Saves from Death

I
1 I love the LORD, who listened
to my voice in supplication,
2 Who turned an ear to me
on the day I called.

w 1 Sm 2,5; Is 54,1.
x Ex 19,6.
y Ex 14,21f; Jos 3,14ff; Pss 66,6; 74,15.
z Ps 29,6; Wis 19,9.
a Ps 68,9.
b Ex 17,6; Nm 20,11.
c Ez 36,22-23.
d Ps 79,10.
e Ps 135,6.
f 4-10: Ps 135,15-19; Wis 15,15-16; Is 44, 9f; Jer 10,1-5.
g Is 40,19.
h Ps 118,2-4.
i Ps 33,20.
j Gn 1,28.
k Pss 6,6; 88,11ff; Sir 17,22f; Is 38,18.

*

Ps 114: A hymn celebrating Israel's escape from Egypt, journey through the wilderness, and entry into the promised land, and the miracles of nature that bore witness to God's presence in their midst. In the perspective of the psalm, the people proceed directly from Egypt into the promised land (1–2). Sea and Jordan, which stood like soldiers barring the people from their land, flee before the mighty God as the earth recoils from the battle (3–4). The poet taunts the natural elements as one taunts defeated enemies (5–6).

114, 3–4: Pairs of cosmic elements such as sea and rivers, mountains and hills, are sometimes mentioned in creation accounts. Personified here as warriors, the pairs tremble in fear before the Divine Warrior. The quaking also recalls the divine appearance in the storm at Sinai (Ex 19, 16–19) and elsewhere (Jgs 5, 4–5; Ps 18, 8–16).

114, 8: The miracles of giving drink to the people in the arid desert. Cf Ex 17, 1–7; Is 41, 17–18.

Ps 115: A response to the enemy taunt, "Where is your God?" This hymn to the glory of Israel's God (1–3) ridicules the lifeless idols of the nations (4–8), expresses in a litany the trust of the various classes of the people in God (9–11), invokes God's blessing on them as they invoke the divine name (12–15), and concludes as it began with praise of God. Ps 135, 15–18 similarly mocks the Gentile gods and has a similar litany and hymn (Ps 135, 19–21).

115, 2: *Where is their God?*: implies that God cannot help them.

115, 9–11: *The house of Israel . . . the house of Aaron . . . those fear the LORD*: the laity of Israelite birth, the priests, and the converts to Judaism. Cf Pss 118, 2–4; 135, 19–21. In the New Testament likewise "those who fear the Lord" means converts to Judaism (cf Act 10, 2. 22. 35; 13, 16. 26).

115, 16: *The heavens*: literally "the heaven of heavens" or "the highest heavens," i.e., above the firmament. See note on Ps 148, 4.

115, 17: See note on Ps 6, 6.

Ps 116: A thanksgiving in which the psalmist responds to divine rescue from mortal danger (3–4) and from near despair (10–11) with vows and temple sacrifices (13–14. 17–19). The Greek and Latin versions divide the psalm into two parts: 1–9 and 10–19, corresponding to its two major divisions.

3 I was caught by the cords of death;[l]*
the snares of Sheol had seized me;
I felt agony and dread.
4 Then I called on the name of the LORD,
"O LORD, save my life!"

II
5 Gracious is the LORD and just;
yes, our God is merciful.[m]
6 The LORD protects the simple;
I was helpless, but God saved me.
7 Return, my soul, to your rest;
the LORD has been good to you.[n]
8 For my soul has been freed from death,
my eyes from tears, my feet from
stumbling.[o]
9 I shall walk before the LORD
in the land of the living.[p]*

III
10 I kept faith, even when I said,*
"I am greatly afflicted!"[q]
11 I said in my alarm,
"No one can be trusted!"[r]
12 How can I repay the LORD
for all the good done for me?
13 I will raise the cup of salvation*
and call on the name of the LORD.
14 I will pay my vows to the LORD
in the presence of all his people.
15 Too costly in the eyes of the LORD*
is the death of his faithful.[s]
16 LORD, I am your servant,
your servant, the child of your
maidservant;[t]
you have loosed my bonds.
17 I will offer a sacrifice of thanksgiving
and call on the name of the LORD.[u]
18 I will pay my vows to the LORD[v]
in the presence of all his people,
19 In the courts of the house of the LORD,
in your midst, O Jerusalem.
Hallelujah!

## PSALM 117*

## The Nations Called to Praise

1 Praise the LORD, all you nations!
Give glory, all you peoples![w]
2 The LORD's love for us is strong;
the LORD is faithful forever.
Hallelujah!

## PSALM 118*

## Hymn of Thanksgiving

I
1 Give thanks to the LORD, who is good,[x]
whose love endures forever.
2 Let the house of Israel say:
God's love endures forever.
3 Let the house of Aaron say,
God's love endures forever.
4 Let those who fear the LORD say,[y]
God's love endures forever.

II
5 In danger I called on the LORD;
the LORD answered me and set me free.
6 The LORD is with me; I am not afraid;
what can mortals do against me?[z]
7 The LORD is with me as my helper;
I shall look in triumph on my foes.
8 Better to take refuge in the LORD[a]
than to put one's trust in mortals.
9 Better to take refuge in the LORD
than to put one's trust in princes.

III
10 All the nations surrounded me;
in the LORD's name I crushed them.
11 They surrounded me on every side;
in the LORD's name I crushed them.
12 They surrounded me like bees;[b]
they blazed like fire among thorns;
in the LORD's name I crushed them.
13 I was hard pressed and falling,
but the LORD came to my help.[c]
14 The LORD, my strength and might,
came to me as savior.[d]

l Ps 18,5; Jon 2,3.
m Ex 34,6.
n Ps 13,6.
o Ps 56,14; Is 25,8; Rv 21,4.
p Pss 27,13; 56,14; Is 38,11.
q 2 Cor 4,13.
r Ps 12,2.
s Ps 72,14; Is 43,4.
t Pss 86,16; 143,12; Wis 9,5.
u Lv 7,12ff.
v Jon 2,10.
w Rom 15,11.
x Pss 100,5; 136,1f.
y Ps 115,9-11.
z Ps 27,1; Heb 13,6.
a 8f: Ps 146,3.
b Dt 1,44.
c Ps 129,1-2.
d Ex 15,2; Is 12,2.

116, 3: *The cords of death*: death is personified here; it attempts to capture the psalmist with snares and nets. Cf Ps 18, 6.

116, 9: *The land of the living*: the phrase elsewhere is an epithet of the Jerusalem temple (cf Pss 27, 13; 52, 7; Is 38, 11). Hence the psalmist probably refers to being present to God in the temple.

116, 10: *I kept faith, even when I said*: even in the days of despair, the psalmist did not lose all hope.

116, 13: *The cup of salvation*: probably the libation of wine poured out in gratitude for rescue. Cf Ex 25, 29; Nm 15, 5. 7. 10.

116, 15: *Too costly in the eyes of the LORD*: the meaning is that the death of God's faithful is grievous to God, not that God is pleased with the death. Cf Ps 72, 14. In Wis 3, 5–6 God accepts the death of the righteous as a sacrificial burnt offering.75

Ps 117: This shortest of hymns calls on the nations to acknowledge God's supremacy. The supremacy of Israel's God has been demonstrated to them by the people's secure existence, which is owed entirely to God's gracious fidelity.

Ps 118: A thanksgiving liturgy accompanying a victory procession of the king and the people into the temple precincts. After an invocation in the form of a litany (1–4), the psalmist (very likely speaking in the name of the community) describes how the people confidently implored God's help (5–9) when hostile peoples threatened its life (10–14); vividly God's rescue is recounted (15–18). Then follows a dialogue at the temple gates between the priests and the psalmist as the latter enters to offer the thanksgiving sacrifice (19–25). Finally, the priests impart their blessing (26–27), and the psalmist sings in gratitude (28–29).

IV

15 The joyful shout of deliverance
is heard in the tents of the victors:
"The LORD's right hand strikes with power;
16 the LORD's right hand is raised;
the LORD's right hand strikes with
power."
17 I shall not die but live
and declare the deeds of the LORD.
18 The LORD chastised me harshly,
but did not hand me over to death.

V

19 Open the gates of victory;
I will enter and thank the LORD.[e]
20 This is the LORD's own gate,
where the victors enter.*
21 I thank you for you answered me;
you have been my savior.
22 The stone the builders rejected*
has become the cornerstone.[f]
23 By the LORD has this been done;
it is wonderful in our eyes.
24 This is the day the LORD has made;
let us rejoice in it and be glad.
25 LORD, grant salvation!*
LORD, grant good fortune!

VI

26 Blessed is he
who comes in the name of the LORD.[g]
We bless you from the LORD's house.
27 The LORD is God and has given us light.
Join in procession with leafy branches
up to the horns of the altar.

VII

28 You are my God, I give you thanks;
my God, I offer you praise.
29 Give thanks to the LORD, who is good,
whose love endures forever.

## PSALM 119*

## A Prayer to God, the Lawgiver

### Aleph

1 Happy those whose way is blameless,
who walk by the teaching of the LORD.[h]
2 Happy those who observe God's decrees,
who seek the LORD with all their heart.[i]
3 They do no wrong;
they walk in God's ways.
4 You have given them the command
to keep your precepts with care.
5 May my ways be firm
in the observance of your laws!
6 Then I will not be ashamed
to ponder all your commands.
7 I will praise you with sincere heart
as I study your just edicts.
8 I will keep your laws;
do not leave me all alone.

### Beth

9 How can the young walk without fault?
Only by keeping your words.
10 With all my heart I seek you;
do not let me stray from your commands.
11 In my heart I treasure your promise,
that I may not sin against you.
12 Blessed are you, O LORD;
teach me your laws.[j]
13 With my lips I recite
all the edicts you have spoken.
14 I find joy in the way of your decrees
more than in all riches.
15 I will ponder your precepts
and consider your paths.
16 In your laws I take delight;
I will never forget your word.

### Gimel

17 Be kind to your servant that I may live,
that I may keep your word.
18 Open my eyes to see clearly
the wonders of your teachings.
19 I am a sojourner in the land;[k]*

e Is 26,2.
f Mt 21,42; Lk 20,17; Acts 4,11; Rom 9,33; 1 Pt 2,7.
g Mt 21,9; 23,39.
h Pss 1,1-2; 15,2; 112,1.
i Dt 4,29.
j Pss 25,4; 27,11; 86,11; 143,8. 10.
k Ps 39,13.

118, 20: *Where the victors enter*: their victory has demonstrated that God favors them; they are "just" in the biblical sense.

118, 22: *The stone the builders rejected*: a proverb: what is insignificant to human beings has become great through divine election. The "stone" may originally have meant the foundation stone or capstone of the temple. The New Testament interpreted the verse as referring to the death and resurrection of Christ (Mt 21, 42; Acts 4, 11; cf Is 28, 16 and Rom 9, 33; 1 Pt 2, 7).

118, 25: *Grant salvation*: the Hebrew for this cry has come into English as "Hosanna." This cry and the words in 26 were used in the gospels to welcome Jesus entering the temple on Palm Sunday (Mk 11, 9–10).

Ps 119: This psalm, the longest by far in the psalter, praises God for giving such splendid laws and instruction for people to live by. The author glorifies and thanks God for the Torah, prays for protection from sinners enraged by others' fidelity to the law, laments the cost of obedience, delights in the law's consolations, begs for wisdom to understand the precepts, and asks for the rewards of keeping them. Several expected elements do not appear in the psalm: Mount Sinai with its story of God's revelation and gift to Israel of instruction and commandments, the temple and other institutions related to revelation and laws (frequent in other psalms). The psalm is fascinated with God's word directing and guiding human life.

The poem is an acrostic; its twenty-two stanzas (of eight verses each) are in the order of the Hebrew alphabet. Each of the eight verses within a stanza begins with the same letter. Each verse contains one word for "instruction." The translation here given attempts to translate each Hebrew word for "instruction" with the same English word. There are, however, nine words for "instruction," not eight, so the principle of a different word for "instruction" in each verse cannot be maintained with perfect consistency. The nine words for "instruction" in the translation are: law, edict, command, precept, word, utterance, way, decree, and teaching.

119, 19: *A sojourner in the land*: like someone without the

do not hide your commands from me.
**20** At all times my soul is stirred
with longing for your edicts.
**21** With a curse you rebuke the proud
who stray from your commands.
**22** Free me from disgrace and contempt,
for I observe your decrees.
**23** Though princes meet and talk against me,
your servant studies your laws.
**24** Your decrees are my delight;
they are my counselors.

### Daleth

**25** I lie prostrate in the dust;[l]
give me life in accord with your word.
**26** I disclosed my ways and you answered me;
teach me your laws.
**27** Make me understand the way of your precepts;
I will ponder your wondrous deeds.
**28** I weep in bitter pain;
in accord with your word to strengthen me.
**29** Lead me from the way of deceit;
favor me with your teaching.
**30** The way of loyalty I have chosen;
I have set your edicts before me.
**31** I cling to your decrees, LORD;
do not let me come to shame.
**32** I will run the way of your commands,
for you open my docile heart.*

### He

**33** LORD, teach me the way of your laws;
I shall observe them with care.[m]
**34** Give me insight to observe your teaching,
to keep it with all my heart.
**35** Lead me in the path of your commands,[n]
for that is my delight.
**36** Direct my heart toward your decrees
and away from unjust gain.
**37** Avert my eyes from what is worthless;
by your way give me life.
**38** For your servant fulfill your promise
made to those who fear you.
**39** Turn away from me the taunts I dread,
for your edicts bring good.
**40** See how I long for your precepts;
in your justice give me life.

### Waw

**41** Let your love come to me, LORD,
salvation in accord with your promise.
**42** Let me answer my taunters with a word,
for I trust in your word.
**43** Do not take the word of truth from my mouth,
for in your edicts is my hope.
**44** I will keep your teachings always,
for all time and forever.
**45** I will walk freely in an open space
because I cherish your precepts.
**46** I will speak openly of your decrees
without fear even before kings.
**47** I delight in your commands,
which I dearly love.
**48** I lift up my hands to your commands;*
I study your laws, which I love.

### Zayin

**49** Remember your word to your servant
by which you give me hope.
**50** This is my comfort in affliction,
your promise that gives me life.
**51** Though the arrogant utterly scorn me,
I do not turn from your teaching.
**52** When I recite your edicts of old
I am comforted, LORD.
**53** Rage seizes me because of the wicked;
they forsake your teaching.
**54** Your laws become my songs
wherever I make my home.
**55** Even at night I remember your name
in observance of your teaching, LORD.
**56** This is my good fortune,
for I have observed your precepts.

### Heth

**57** My portion is the LORD;
I promise to keep your words.
**58** I entreat you with all my heart:
have mercy on me in accord with your promise.
**59** I have examined my ways
and turned my steps to your decrees.
**60** I am prompt, I do not hesitate
in keeping your commands.
**61** Though the snares of the wicked surround me,
your teaching I do not forget.
**62** At midnight I rise to praise you
because your edicts are just.
**63** I am the friend of all who fear you,
of all who keep your precepts.
**64** The earth, LORD, is filled with your love;[o]
teach me your laws.

### Teth

**65** You have treated your servant well,
according to your word, O LORD.
**66** Teach me wisdom and knowledge,
for in your commands I trust.
**67** Before I was afflicted I went astray,
but now I hold to your promise.
**68** You are good and do what is good;

l Ps 44,26.
m Ps 19,12.
n Pss 25,4; 27,11; 86, 11; 143,8. 10.
o Ps 33,5.

* legal protection of a native inhabitant, the psalmist has a special need for the guidance of God's teaching.

119, 32: *For you open my docile heart*: literally, "you make broad my heart."

119, 48: *I lift up my hands to your commands*: to lift up the hands was an ancient gesture of reverence to God. Here the picture is applied to God's law.

teach me your laws.
69 The arrogant smear me with lies,
but I observe your precepts with all my heart.
70 Their hearts are gross and fat;[p]
as for me, your teaching is my delight.
71 It was good for me to be afflicted,
in order to learn your laws.
72 Teaching from your lips is more precious to me
than heaps of silver and gold.

### Yodh

73 Your hands made me and fashioned me;
give me insight to learn your commands.
74 Those who fear you rejoice to see me,
because I hope in your word.
75 I know, LORD, that your edicts are just;
though you afflict me, you are faithful.
76 May your love comfort me
in accord with your promise to your servant.
77 Show me compassion that I may live,
for your teaching is my delight.
78 Shame the proud for oppressing me unjustly,
that I may study your precepts.
79 Let those who fear you turn to me,
those who acknowledge your decrees.
80 May I be wholehearted toward your laws,
that I may not be put to shame.

### Kaph

81 My soul longs for your salvation;
I put my hope in your word.[q]
82 My eyes long to see your promise.[r]
When will you comfort me?
83 I am like a wineskin shriveled by smoke,[s]
but I have not forgotten your laws.
84 How long can your servant survive?
When will your edict doom my foes?
85 The arrogant have dug pits for me;
defying your teaching.
86 All your commands are steadfast.
Help me! I am pursued without cause.
87 They have almost ended my life on earth,
but I do not forsake your precepts.
88 In your kindness give me life,
to keep the decrees you have spoken.

### Lamedh

89 *Your word, LORD, stands forever;[t]
it is firm as the heavens.
90 Through all generations your truth endures;
fixed to stand firm like the earth.
91 By your edicts they stand firm to this day,
for all things are your servants.
92 Had your teaching not been my delight,
I would have perished in my affliction.
93 I will never forget your precepts;
through them you give me life.
94 I am yours; save me,
for I cherish your precepts.
95 The wicked hope to destroy me,
but I pay heed to your decrees.
96 I have seen the limits of all perfection,
but your command is without bounds.

### Mem

97 How I love your teaching, LORD!
I study it all day long.
98 Your command makes me wiser than my foes,
for it is always with me.
99 I have more understanding than all my teachers,
because I ponder your decrees.
100 I have more insight than my elders,
because I observe your precepts.[u]
101 I keep my steps from every evil path,
that I may obey your word.
102 From your edicts I do not turn,
for you have taught them to me.
103 How sweet to my tongue is your promise,
sweeter than honey to my mouth![v]
104 Through your precepts I gain insight;
therefore I hate all false ways.

### Nun

105 Your word is a lamp for my feet,
a light for my path.[w]
106 I make a solemn vow
to keep your just edicts.
107 I am very much afflicted, LORD;
give me life in accord with your word.
108 Accept my freely offered praise;[x]
LORD, teach me your decrees.
109 My life is always at risk,
but I do not forget your teaching.
110 The wicked have set snares for me,
but from your precepts I do not stray.
111 Your decrees are my heritage forever;
they are the joy of my heart.
112 My heart is set on fulfilling your laws;
they are my reward forever.

### Samekh

113 I hate every hypocrite;
your teaching I love.
114 You are my refuge and shield;
in your word I hope.
115 Depart from me, you wicked,[y]
that I may observe the commands of my God.
116 Sustain me by your promise that I may live;
do not disappoint me in my hope.

p Pss 17,10; 73,7; Jb 15,27.
q Ps 130,6.
r Pss 25,15; 123,1-2; 141,8.
s Jb 30,30.
t Is 40,8.
u Jb 32,6; Wis 4,8-9.
v Ps 19,11.
w Ps 18,29; Prv 6,23.
x Ps 50,14. 23; Heb 13, 15.
y Pss 6,9; 139,19; Jb 21,14.

* 119, 89–91: God's word creates the world, which manifests that word by its permanence and reliability.

117 Strengthen me that I may be safe,
ever to contemplate your laws.
118 You reject all who stray from your laws,
for vain is their deceit.
119 Like dross you regard all the wicked on earth;
therefore I love your decrees.
120 My flesh shudders with dread of you;
I hold your edicts in awe.

### Ayin

121 I have fulfilled your just edict;
do not abandon me to my oppressors.
122 Guarantee your servant's welfare;
do not let the arrogant oppress me.
123 My eyes long to see your salvation
and the justice of your promise.
124 Act with kindness toward your servant;
teach me your laws.
125 I am your servant; give me discernment
that I may know your decrees.
126 It is time for the LORD to act;
they have disobeyed your teaching.
127 Truly I love your commands
more than the finest gold.
128 Thus I follow all your precepts;
every wrong way I hate.

### Pe

129 Wonderful are your decrees;
therefore I observe them.
130 The revelation of your words sheds light,
gives understanding to the simple.
131 I sigh with open mouth,
yearning for your commands.
132 Turn to me and be gracious,[z]
your edict for lovers of your name.
133 Steady my feet in accord with your promise;
do not let iniquity lead me.
134 Free me from human oppression,
that I may keep your precepts.
135 Let your face shine upon your servant;
teach me your laws.
136 My eyes shed streams of tears
because your teaching is not followed.

### Sadhe

137 You are righteous, LORD,
and just are your edicts.[a]
138 You have issued your decrees in justice
and in surpassing faithfulness.
139 I am consumed with rage,
because my foes forget your words.
140 Your servant loves your promise;
it has been proved by fire.
141 Though belittled and despised,
I do not forget your precepts.
142 Your justice is forever right,
your teaching forever true.
143 Though distress and anguish come upon me,
your commands are my delight.
144 Your decrees are forever just;
give me discernment that I may live.

### Qoph

145 I call with all my heart, O LORD;
answer me that I may observe your laws.
146 I call to you to save me
that I may keep your decrees.
147 I rise before dawn and cry out;
I put my hope in your words.
148 My eyes greet the night watches
as I meditate on your promise.[b]
149 Hear my voice in your love, O LORD;
by your edict give me life.
150 Malicious persecutors draw near me;
they are far from your teaching.
151 You are near, O LORD;
reliable are all your commands.
152 Long have I known from your decrees
that you have established them forever.

### Resh

153 Look at my affliction and rescue me,
for I have not forgotten your teaching.
154 Take up my cause and redeem me;[c]
for the sake of your promise give me life.
155 Salvation is far from sinners
because they do not cherish your laws.
156 Your compassion is great, O LORD;
in accord with your edicts give me life.
157 Though my persecutors and foes are many
I do not turn from your decrees.
158 I view the faithless with loathing,[d]
because they do not heed your promise.
159 See how I love your precepts, LORD;
in your kindness give me life.
160 Your every word is enduring;
all your just edicts are forever.

### Shin

161 Princes persecute me without reason,
but my heart reveres only your word.
162 I rejoice at your promise,
as one who has found rich spoil.
163 Falsehood I hate and abhor;
your teaching I love.
164 Seven times a day I praise you
because your edicts are just.
165 Lovers of your teaching have much peace;[e]
for them there is no stumbling block.
166 I look for your salvation, LORD,
and I fulfill your commands.
167 I observe your decrees;
I love them very much.
168 I observe your precepts and decrees;
all my ways are before you.

z Pss 25,16; 86,16.
a Tb 3,2.
b Pss 63,7; 77,7.
c Ps 43,1.
d Ps 139,22.
e Ps 72,7.

### Taw

169 Let my cry come before you, LORD;[f]
in keeping with your word give me discernment.
170 Let my prayer come before you;
rescue me according to your promise.
171 May my lips pour forth your praise,
because you teach me your laws.
172 May my tongue sing of your promise,
for all your commands are just.
173 Keep your hand ready to help me,
for I have chosen your precepts.
174 I long for your salvation, LORD;
your teaching is my delight.
175 Let me live to praise you;
may your edicts give me help.
176 I have wandered like a lost sheep;
seek out your servant,
for I do not forget your commands.[g]

## PSALM 120*

## Prayer of a Returned Exile

1 *A song of ascents.**

I

The LORD answered me
when I called in my distress:[h]
2 LORD, deliver me from lying lips,
from treacherous tongues.[i]

II

3 What will the Lord inflict on you,
O treacherous tongue,
and what more besides?*
4 A warrior's sharpened arrows
and fiery coals of brushwood![j]*

III

5 Alas, I was an alien in Meshech,*
I lived near the tents of Kedar!
6 Too long did I live
among those who hated peace.
7 When I spoke of peace,
they were for war.[k]

## PSALM 121*

## The Lord My Guardian

1 *A song of ascents.*

I

I raise my eyes toward the mountains.*
From where will my help come?[l]
2 My help comes from the LORD,
the maker of heaven and earth.[m]

II

3 God will not allow your foot to slip;[n]
your guardian does not sleep.
4 Truly, the guardian of Israel
never slumbers nor sleeps.
5 *The LORD is your guardian;
the LORD is your shade
at your right hand.[o]
6 By day the sun cannot harm you,
nor the moon by night.[p]
7 The LORD will guard you from all evil,
will always guard your life.[q]
8 The LORD will guard your coming and going
both now and forever.[r]

## PSALM 122*

## A Pilgrim's Prayer for Jerusalem

1 *A song of ascents. Of David.*

I

I rejoiced when they said to me,
"Let us go to the house of the LORD."[s]

f Ps 88,3.
g Is 53,6; Jer 50,6; Lk 15,1-7.
h Jon 2,3.
i Ps 12,3-5; Sir 51,3.
j Pss 11,6; 140,11; Prv 16,27.
k Pss 35,20; 140,3-4.
l Jer 3,23.
m Pss 124,8; 146,6.
n Pss 66,9; 91,12; 1 Sm 2,9; Prv 3,23.
o Pss 16,8; 73,23.
p Wis 18,3; Is 25,4; 49, 10.
q Ps 97,10.
r Dt 28,6.
s Pss 43,3-4; 84,2-5.

*

Ps 120: A thanksgiving, reporting divine rescue (1) yet with fervent prayer for further protection against lying attackers (2–4). The psalmist is acutely conscious of living away from God's own land where divine peace prevails (5–7).

120, 1: *Song of ascents*: Pss 120–134 all begin with this superscription. Most probably these fifteen psalms once formed a collection of psalms sung when pilgrims went to Jerusalem, since one "ascended" to Jerusalem (1 Kgs 12, 28; Pss 24, 3; 122, 4; Lk 2, 42) or to the house of God or to an altar (1 Kgs 12, 33; 2 Kgs 23, 2; Ps 24, 3). Less probable is the explanation that these psalms were sung by the exiles when they "ascended" to Jerusalem from Babylonia (cf Ezr 7, 9). The idea, found in the Mishnah, that the fifteen steps on which the Levites sang corresponded to these fifteen psalms (*Middot* 2, 5) must underlie the Vulgate translation *canticum graduum*, "song of the steps" or "gradual song."

120, 3: *More besides*: a common curse formula in Hebrew was "May the Lord do such and such evils to you [the evils being specified], and add *still more* to them." Cf 1 Sm 3, 17; 14, 44; 25, 22. Here the psalmist is at a loss for a suitable malediction.

120, 4: *Coals of brushwood*: coals made from the stalk of the broom plant burn with intense heat. The psalmist thinks of lighted coals cast at his enemies.

120, 5: *Meshech* was in the far north (Gn 10, 2) and *Kedar* was a tribe of the north Arabian desert (Gn 25, 13). The psalmist may be thinking generally of all aliens living among inhospitable peoples.

Ps 121: A blessing given to someone embarking on a dangerous journey, whether a soldier going on a campaign or a pilgrim returning home from the temple. People look anxiously at the wooded hills. Will God protect them on their journey (1)? The speaker declares that God is not confined to a place or a time (2), that every step is guarded (3–4); night and day (5–6) God watches over their every movement (7–8).

121, 1: *The mountains*: possibly Mount Zion, the site of the temple and hence of safety, but more probably mountains as a place of dangers, causing anxiety to the psalmist.

121, 5–6: The image of shade, a symbol of protection, is apt: God as shade protects from the harmful effects that ancients believed were caused by the sun and moon.

Ps 122: A song of Zion, sung by pilgrims obeying the law to visit Jerusalem three times on a journey. The singer anticipates joining the procession into the city (1–3). Jerusalem is a place of encounter, where the people praise God (4) and hear the divine justice mediated by the king (5). The very build-

2 And now our feet are standing
within your gates, Jerusalem.
3 Jerusalem, built as a city,
walled round about.[t]*
4 Here the tribes have come,
the tribes of the LORD,
As it was decreed for Israel,
to give thanks to the name of the LORD.[u]
5 Here are the thrones of justice,
the thrones of the house of David.

II
6 For the peace of Jerusalem pray:
"May those who love you prosper!
7 May peace be within your ramparts,
prosperity within your towers."[v]
8 For family and friends I say,
"May peace be yours."
9 For the house of the LORD, our God, I pray,
"May blessings be yours."

## PSALM 123*

### Reliance on the Lord

1 *A song of ascents.*

To you I raise my eyes,
to you enthroned in heaven.[w]
2 Yes, like the eyes of a servant
on the hand of his master,
Like the eyes of a maid
on the hand of her mistress,
So our eyes are on the LORD our God,
till we are shown favor.
3 Show us favor, LORD, show us favor,
for we have our fill of contempt.[x]
4 We have our fill of insult from the insolent,
of disdain from the arrogant.

## PSALM 124*

### God, the Rescuer of the People

1 *A song of ascents. Of David.*

I
Had not the LORD been with us,
let Israel say,[y]
2 Had not the LORD been with us,
when people rose against us,
3 They would have swallowed us alive,[z]
for their fury blazed against us.
4 The waters would have engulfed us,
the torrent overwhelmed us;[a]
5 seething waters would have drowned us.

II
6 Blessed be the LORD, who did not leave us
to be torn by their fangs.
7 We escaped with our lives
like a bird from the fowler's snare;
the snare was broken and we escaped.
8 Our help is the name* of the LORD,
the maker of heaven and earth.[b]

## PSALM 125*

### Israel's Protector

1 *A song of ascents.*

I
Like Mount Zion are they
who trust in the LORD,
unshakable, forever enduring.[c]
2 As mountains surround Jerusalem,
the LORD surrounds his people
both now and forever.[d]

II
3 The scepter of the wicked will not prevail
in the land given to the just,*
Lest the just themselves
turn their hands to evil.

III
4 Do good, LORD, to the good,
to those who are upright of heart.[e]
5 But those who turn aside to crooked ways
may the LORD send down with the
wicked.[f]
Peace upon Israel![g]

t Ps 48,13-14.
u Dt 16,16.
v Ps 128,5.
w Pss 25,15; 119,82; 141,8.
x Ps 44,13-14; Jb 12,4.
y Ps 129,1.
z Prv 1,12.
a Pss 18,5; 69,2.
b Pss 121,2; 146,6.
c Prv 10,25.
d Dt 32,11.
e Ps 18,25ff.
f Prv 3,32.
g Ps 128,6.

ings bespeak God's power (cf Ps 48, 13–15). May the grace of this place transform the people's lives (6–9)!

122, 3: *Walled round about*: literally, "which is joined to it," probably referring both to the density of the buildings and to the dense population.

Ps 123: A lament that begins as a prayer of an individual (1), who expresses by a touching comparison exemplary confidence in God (2). The psalm ends in prayer that God relieve the people's humiliation at the hands of the arrogant (3–4).

Ps 124: A thanksgiving which teaches that Israel's very existence is owed to God who rescues them. In the first part Israel's enemies are compared to the mythic sea dragon (2b–3a; cf Jer 51, 34) and Flood (3b–5; cf Is 51, 9–10). The psalm heightens the malice of human enemies by linking them to the primordial enemies of God's creation. Israel is a bird freed from the trapper's snare (6–8)—freed originally from Pharaoh and now from the current danger.

124, 8: *Our help is the name*: for the idiom, see Ex 18, 4.

Ps 125: In response to exilic anxieties about the ancient promises of restoration, the psalm expresses confidence that God will surround the people as the mountains surround Zion (1–2). The just will not be contaminated by the wicked (3). May God judge between the two groups (4–5).

125, 3: *The land given to the just*: literally, "the lot of the just." The promised land was divided among the tribes of Israel by lot (Nm 26, 55; Jos 18). *The just* are the members of the people who are obedient to God. If the domination of the wicked were to continue in the land, even the just would be infected by their evil attitudes.

## PSALM 126*

### The Reversal of Zion's Fortunes

1 *A song of ascents.*

I

When the LORD restored the fortunes of
Zion,[h]
then we thought we were dreaming.
2 Our mouths were filled with laughter;
our tongues sang for joy.[i]
Then it was said among the nations,
"The LORD has done great things for
them."
3 The LORD had done great things for us;
Oh, how happy we were!
4 Restore again our fortunes, LORD,
like the dry stream beds of the Negeb.*

II

5 Those who sow in tears
will reap with cries of joy.[j]
6 Those who go forth weeping,
carrying sacks of seed,
Will return with cries of joy,
carrying their bundled sheaves.

## PSALM 127*

### The Need of God's Blessing

1 *A song of ascents. Of Solomon.*

I

Unless the LORD build the house,
they labor in vain who build.
Unless the LORD guard the city,
in vain does the guard keep watch.
2 It is vain for you to rise early
and put off your rest at night,
To eat bread earned by hard toil—
all this God gives to his beloved in
sleep.[k]

II

3 Children too are a gift from the LORD,
the fruit of the womb, a reward.[l]
4 Like arrows in the hand of a warrior
are the children born in one's youth.
5 Blessed are they whose quivers are full.
They will never be shamed
contending with foes at the gate.*

## PSALM 128*

### The Happy Home of the Just

*1* A song of ascents.

I

Happy are all who fear the LORD,*
who walk in the ways of God.[m]
2 What your hands provide you will enjoy;
you will be happy and prosper:[n]
3 Like a fruitful vine
your wife within your home,
Like olive plants
your children around your table.[o]
4 Just so will they be blessed
who fear the LORD.

II

5 May the LORD bless you from Zion,
all the days of your life[p]
That you may share Jerusalem's joy
6 and live to see your children's children.[q]
Peace upon Israel![r]

## PSALM 129*

### Against Israel's Enemies

1 *A song of ascents.*

I

Much have they oppressed me from my
youth,
now let Israel say.[s]
2 Much have they oppressed me from my
youth,[t]
yet they have not prevailed.
3 Upon my back the plowers plowed,
as they traced their long furrows.[u]

h Ps 14,7.
i Jb 8,21.
j Bar 4,23; Is 65,19.
k Eccl 2,24.
l Pss 115,14; 128,3; Dt 28,11; Prv 17,6.
m Ps 112,1.
n Ps 112,3.
o Jb 29,5; Ps 144,12.
p Pss 20,3; 134,3.
q Jb 42,16; Prv 17,6.
r Ps 125,5.
s Ps 124,1.
t Ps 118,13.
u Is 51,23.

*

Ps 126: A lament probably sung shortly after Israel's return from exile. The people rejoice that they are in Zion (1–3) but mere presence in the holy city is not enough; they must pray for the prosperity and the fertility of the land (4). The last verses are probably an oracle of promise: the painful work of sowing will be crowned with life (5–6).

126, 4: *Like the dry stream beds of the Negeb*: the psalmist prays for rain in such abundance that the dry riverbeds will run.

Ps 127: The psalm puts together two proverbs (1–2 and 3–5) on God establishing "houses" or families. The prosperity of human groups is not the work of humans but the gift of God.

127, 5: *At the gate*: the reference is not to enemies besieging the walls of a city but to adversaries in litigation. Lawcourts functioned in the open area near the main city gate. The more adult sons a man had, the more forceful he would appear in disputes. Cf Prv 31, 23.

Ps 128: A statement that the ever-reliable God will bless the reverent (1). God's blessing is concrete: satisfaction and prosperity, a fertile spouse and abundant children (2–4). The perspective is that of the adult male, ordinarily the ruler and representative of the household to the community. The last verses extend the blessing to all the people for generations to come (5–6).

128, 1: *All who fear the LORD*: literally, singular: "the one fearing," is used in a typical sense and so is translated by the plural.

Ps 129: A psalm giving thanks for God's many rescues of Israel over the long course of their history (1–4); the people pray that their oppressors never know the joy of harvest (5–8).

4 But the just LORD cut me free
from the ropes of the yoke of the wicked.*

II
5 May they be scattered in disgrace,
all who hate Zion.
6 May they be like grass on the rooftops*
withered in early growth,[v]
7 Never to fill the reaper's hands,
nor the arms of the binders of sheaves,
8 With none passing by to call out:
"The blessing of the LORD be upon you!*
We bless you in the name of the LORD!"[w]

## PSALM 130*

## Prayer for Pardon and Mercy

1 *A song of ascents.*

I
Out of the depths* I call to you, LORD;
2 Lord, hear my cry!
May your ears be attentive
to my cry for mercy.[x]
3 If you, LORD, mark our sins,
Lord, who can stand?[y]
4 But with you is forgiveness
and so you are revered.*

II
5 I wait with longing for the LORD,
my soul waits for his word.[z]
6 My soul looks for the Lord
more than sentinels for daybreak.[a]
More than sentinels for daybreak,
7 let Israel look for the LORD,
For with the LORD is kindness,
with him is full redemption,[b]
8 And God will redeem Israel
from all their sins.[c]

## PSALM 131*

## Humble Trust in God

1 *A song of ascents. Of David.*

LORD, my heart is not proud;
nor are my eyes haughty.
I do not busy myself with great matters,
with things too sublime for me.[d]
2 Rather, I have stilled my soul,
hushed it like a weaned child.
Like a weaned child on its mother's lap,
so is my soul within me.[e]
3 Israel, hope in the LORD,
now and forever.

## PSALM 132*

## The Covenant between David and God

1 *A song of ascents.*

I
LORD, remember David
and all his anxious care;*
2 How he swore an oath to the LORD,
vowed to the Mighty One of Jacob:*
3 "I will not enter the house where I live,[f]
nor lie on the couch where I sleep;
4 I will give my eyes no sleep,
my eyelids no rest,
5 Till I find a home for the LORD,
a dwelling for the Mighty One of Jacob."

6 "We have heard of it in Ephrathah;*
we have found it in the fields of Jaar.
7 Let us enter God's dwelling;
let us worship at God's footstool."[g]

8 "Arise, LORD, come to your resting place,[h]

v Is 37,27.
w Ps 118,26.
x Pss 5,2-3; 55,2-3; 86, 6; Lam 3,55-56; Jon 2,3.
y Na 1,6.
z Ps 119,81.
a Is 21,11; 26,9.
b Pss 86,15; 100,5; 103,8.
c Ps 25,22; Mt 1,21.
d Ps 139,6.
e Is 66,12-13.
f 2 Sm 7; 1 Chr 28,2.
g Ps 99,5.
h 8-10: Pss 2,2; 89,21; 95,11; Nm 10,35; 2 Chr 6,41-42; Sir 24, 7.

129, 4: *The ropes of the yoke of the wicked*: usually understood as the rope for yoking animals to the plow. If it is severed, the plowing (cf 3) comes to a halt.

129, 6: *Like grass on the rooftops*: after the spring rains, grass would sprout from the coat of mud with which the flat roofs of simple houses were covered, but when the dry summer began there was no moisture in the thin roof-covering to sustain the grass.

129, 8: *The blessing of the LORD be upon you*: harvesters greeted one another with such blessings. Cf Ru 2, 4.

Ps 130: This lament, a Penitential Psalm, is the *De profundis* used in liturgical prayers for the faithful departed. In deep sorrow the psalmist cries to God (1–2), asking for mercy (3–4). The psalmist's trust (5–6) becomes a model for the people (7–8).

130, 1: *The depths*: Sheol here is a metaphor of total misery. Deep anguish makes the psalmist feel "like those descending to the pit" (Ps 143, 7).

130, 4: *And so you are revered*: the experience of God's mercy leads one to a greater sense of God.

Ps 131: A song of trust, in which the psalmist gives up self-sufficiency (1), like a babe enjoying the comfort of its mother's lap (2), thus providing a model for Israel's faith (3).

Ps 132: A song for a liturgical ceremony in which the ark, the throne of Israel's God, was carried in procession to the temple. The singer asks that David's care for the proper housing of the ark be regarded with favor (1–5), and tells how it was brought to Jerusalem (6–10). There follows God's promise of favor to the Davidic dynasty (11–12) and to Zion (13–17). The transfer of the ark to the tent in Jerusalem is described in 2 Sm 6.

132, 1: *All his anxious care*: to build the temple. Cf 2 Sm 7, 1–17 and 1 Kgs 8, 17.

132, 2. 5: *Mighty One of Jacob*: one of the titles of Israel's God. Cf Gn 49, 24; Is 49, 26; 60, 16.

132, 6: *Ephrathah*: the homeland of David. Cf Ru 4, 11. *The fields of Jaar*: poetic for Kiriath-jearim, a town west of Jerusalem, where the ark remained for several generations. Cf 1 Sm 7, 1–2 ; 2 Sm 6, 2; 1 Chr 13, 5–6.

you and your majestic ark.
9 Your priests will be clothed with justice;
your faithful will shout for joy."
10 For the sake of David your servant,
do not reject your anointed.

II
11 The LORD swore an oath to David,
a pledge never to be broken:[i]
"Your own offspring[j] I will set upon your throne.
12 If your sons observe my covenant,
the laws I shall teach them,
Their sons, in turn,
shall sit forever on your throne."
13 Yes, the LORD has chosen Zion,
desired it for a dwelling:
14 "This is my resting place forever;
here I will dwell, for I desire it.
15 I will bless Zion with meat;
its poor I will fill with bread.
16 I will clothe its priests with blessing;
its faithful shall shout for joy.[k]
17 There I will make a horn sprout for David's line;[l]*
I will set a lamp for my anointed.
18 His foes I will clothe with shame,
but on him my crown shall gleam."

## PSALM 133*

## A Vision of a Blessed Community

1 *A song of ascents. Of David.*

How good it is, how pleasant,
where the people* dwell as one!
2 Like precious ointment* on the head,[m]
running down upon the beard,
Upon the beard of Aaron,
upon the collar of his robe.
3 Like dew* of Hermon coming down
upon the mountains of Zion.[n]
There the LORD has lavished blessings,
life for evermore![o]

## PSALM 134*

## Exhortation to the Night Watch to Bless God

1 *A song of ascents.*

Come, bless the LORD,
all you servants of the LORD*
Who stand in the house of the LORD
through the long hours of night.[p]
2 Lift up your hands toward the sanctuary,[q]
and bless the LORD.
3 May the LORD who made heaven and earth[r]
bless you from Zion.

## PSALM 135*

## Praise of God, the Ruler and Benefactor of Israel

1 *Hallelujah!*

I
Praise the name of the LORD!
Praise, you servants of the LORD,[s]
2 Who stand in the house of the LORD,
in the courts of the house of our God![t]
3 Praise the LORD; the LORD is good!
Sing to God's name; it is gracious!
4 *For the LORD has chosen Jacob,
Israel as a treasured possession.[u]

II
5 I know that the LORD is great,
our Lord is greater than all gods.[v]
6 Whatever the LORD wishes
he does in heaven and on earth,
in the seas and in all the deeps.[w]

i Ps 110,4; 2 Sm 7,12.
j 11-14: Ps 68,17; 1 Kgs 8,13; Sir 24,7.
k 2 Chr 6,41; Is 61,10.
l Is 11,1; Jer 33,15; Ez 29,21; Zec 3,8; Lk 1, 69.
m Ex 30,25. 30.
n Hos 14,6.
o Dt 28,8; 30,20.
p Ps 135,1-2; 1 Chr 9, 33.
q Pss 28,2; 141,2.
r Pss 20,3; 128,5; Nm 6,24.
s Ps 113,1.
t Ps 134,1.
u Pss 33,12; 144,15; Ex 19,6; Dt 7,6.
v Ps 95,3; Ex 18,11.
w Ps 115,3.

*

132, 17: *A horn sprout for David's line*: the image of the horn, a symbol of strength, is combined with that of a "sprout," a term used for the Davidic descendant (cf Jer 23, 5; 33, 15; Zec 3, 8; 6, 12). Early Christians referred the latter designation to Christ as son of David (Lk 1, 69).

Ps 133: A benediction over a peaceful community, most probably the people Israel, but appropriate too for Israelite families (1). The history of Israel, whether of its ancestors in the book of Genesis or of later periods, was a history of distinct groups struggling to live in unity. Here that unity is declared blessed, like the holy oils upon the priest Aaron or the dew of the rainless summer that waters the crops (2–3).

133, 1: *The people*: literally, "brothers," i.e., male and female members of a kin group or people—most probably, the people Israel.

133, 2: *Ointment*: oil was used at the consecration of the high priest (Ex 30, 22–33).

133, 3: *Dew*: dew was an important source of moisture in the dry climate (Gn 27, 28; Hos 14, 6). *Hermon*: the majestic snow-capped mountain visible in the north of Palestine.

Ps 134: A brief liturgy exhorting the temple singers to acknowledge the great deeds of God at a night service (cf Is 30, 29). Mount Zion is the place from which blessings affect the lives of humans, for there Israel's God dwells.

134, 1: *Servants of the LORD*: priests and Levites. Cf Dt 10, 8; Pss 113, 1; 135, 1; Dn 3, 84–85.

Ps 135: The hymn begins and ends with an invitation to praise God (1–3, 19–20) for the great act of choosing Israel (4). The story of Israel's emergence as a people is told in 5–14; God created and redeemed the people, easily conquering all opposition. God's defeat of hostile powers means that the powers themselves and their images are useless (15–18). The last three verses appear also in Ps 115, 4–8.

135, 4: Though all nations are God's, Israel has a special status as God's "treasured" people: Ex 19, 5; Dt 7, 6; 14, 2; 26, 18; Mal 3, 17.

7 He raises storm clouds from the end of the earth,
makes lightning and rain,
brings forth wind from the storehouse.[x]

III
8 He struck down Egypt's firstborn,[y]
human and beast alike,
9 And sent signs and portents against you, Egypt,
against Pharaoh and all his servants.
10 The Lord struck down many nations,[z]
slew mighty kings—
11 Sihon, king of the Amorites,
Og, king of Bashan,
all the kings of Canaan—
12 And made their land a heritage,
a heritage for Israel his people.
13 O LORD, your name is forever,
your renown, from age to age![a]
14 For the LORD defends his people,
shows mercy to his servants.[b]

IV
15 The idols of the nations are silver and gold,[c]
the work of human hands.
16 They have mouths but speak not;
they have eyes but see not;
17 They have ears but hear not;
no breath is in their mouths.
18 Their makers shall be like them,
all who trust in them.

V
19 House of Israel, bless the LORD![d]
House of Aaron, bless the LORD!
20 House of Levi, bless the LORD!
You who fear the LORD, bless the LORD!
21 Blessed from Zion be the LORD,
who dwells in Jerusalem!
Hallelujah!

## PSALM 136*

## Hymn of Thanksgiving for God's Everlasting Love

I
1 Praise the LORD, who is so good;[e]
God's love endures forever;
2 Praise the God of gods;
God's love endures forever;
3 Praise the Lord of lords;
God's love endures forever;

II
4 Who alone has done great wonders,[f]
God's love endures forever;
5 Who skillfully made the heavens,[g]
God's love endures forever;
6 Who spread the earth upon the waters,[h]
God's love endures forever;
7 Who made the great lights,
God's love endures forever;
8 The sun to rule the day,
God's love endures forever;
9 The moon and stars to rule the night,[i]
God's love endures forever;

III
10 Who struck down the firstborn of Egypt,[j]
God's love endures forever;
11 And led Israel from their midst,
God's love endures forever;
12 With mighty hand and outstretched arm,[k]
God's love endures forever;
13 Who split in two the Red Sea
God's love endures forever;
14 And led Israel through,
God's love endures forever;
15 But swept Pharaoh and his army into the Red Sea,[l]
God's love endures forever;
16 Who led the people through the desert,[m]
God's love endures forever;

IV
17 Who struck down great kings,[n]
God's love endures forever;
18 Slew powerful kings,
God's love endures forever;
19 Sihon, king of the Amorites,
God's love endures forever;
20 Og, king of Bashan,
God's love endures forever;
21 And made their lands a heritage,
God's love endures forever;
22 A heritage for Israel,* God's servant,
God's love endures forever.

V
23 The LORD remembered us in our misery,
God's love endures forever;
24 Freed us from our foes,
God's love endures forever;
25 And gives food to all flesh,
God's love endures forever.

x Ps 148,8; Jer 10,13; 51,16; Jb 37,9.
y 8-9: Pss 78,51; 105, 27. 36; 136,10; Ex 12, 29.
z 10-12: Nm 21,21-35; Dt 2,24-3,17; Ps 136, 17-22.
a Ps 102,13; Ex 3,15.
b Dt 32,36.
c 15-18: Ps 115,4-6. 8.
d 19-20: Ps 118,2-4.
e Pss 100,5; 118,1.
f Ps 72,18.
g Gn 1,9-19.
h Ps 24,2.
i Jer 31,35.
j Ex 12,29. 51; 14,22. 27; 15,22; Pss 78, 51-52; 135,8.
k Dt 4,34.
l Ex 14,21f.
m Dt 8,2. 15.
n 17-22: Ps 135,10-12.

*

Ps 136: The hymn praises Israel's God ("the God of gods," 2), who has created the world in which Israel lives. The refrain occurring after every line suggests that a speaker and chorus sang the psalm in antiphonal fashion. A single act of God is described in 4–25: God arranges the heavens and the earth as the environment for human community, and then creates the community by freeing them and giving them land. In the final section (23–25) God, who created the people and gave them land, continues to protect and nurture them.

136, 22: *A heritage for Israel*: the land was given to Israel by God to be handed on to future generations.

# Jewish Festivals

God gave the Jewish people numerous feast days, or festivals, to celebrate different events through the year. Many of the feasts were originally farming festivals. The **Feast of Passover**, the **Feast of Weeks** and the **Feast of Tabernacles** were the three major festivals.

**Feast of Passover** (***Pesach***) celebrated Israel's deliverance from slavery in Egypt. On 14 Nisan each Jewish family ate their own Passover meal (*Seder*), re-enacting the first Passover (Exodus 12:1-49).

**Feast of Unleavened Bread** was the seven days following Passover, when Jewish families ate unleavened bread, (Bread of Affliction) to remember the 40 years wandering in the wilderness (Leviticus 23:5-8).

**Feast of Weeks** (**Harvest** or **Pentecost**) started seven full weeks (50 days) after Passover and was to give thanks for God's blessing on the harvest (Leviticus 23:15-22).

**Feast of Trumpets, *Rosh Hashanah* – New Year's Day** (Leviticus 23:23-25), recalled God's creation of the world and was celebrated on 1 Tishri.

**Day of Atonement** (***Yom Kippur***) was the most solemn holy day of national confession of sins, on 10 Tishri, when the high priest went into the Holiest Place of the Temple to sprinkle blood of the sacrifice (Leviticus 23:26-32).

**Feast of Tabernacles** (***Sukkoth***, **Booths**, or **Ingathering**), a week's celebration of the harvest, 15-21 Tishri, when the Jews lived in temporary shelters of branches (booths) to remember God's care for the Hebrews during their journey from Egypt to Canaan (Leviticus 23:33-43).

***Chanukkah*** or **Feast of Lights** was the Feast of Dedication, on 25 Kislev, to celebrate Judas Maccabeus' victory and the rededication of the Temple in 165/4 B.C. Known as the Feast of Lights because an eight-branched candlestick is used, with an extra light to light the others on each of the eight days of the feast, it recalls the miraculous provision of oil at the first celebration (John 10:22).

**Purim** is celebrated during 13-15 Adar and marks the deliverance of the Jews through Esther (Esther 9:1-32).

**New Moon**
The Jews celebrated the beginning of each month (Numbers 28:11).

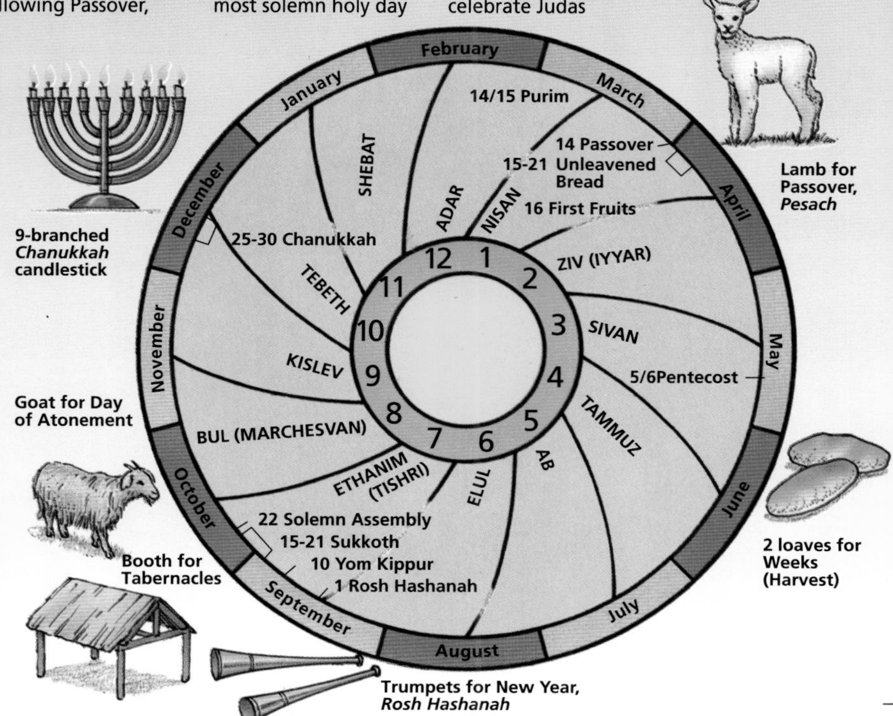

# Clothing

Most people living in Bible times wore simple clothing. The basic male garment was a loin-cloth. Over this, most men wore an inner and an outer garment. The inner garment was normally made of linen or wool and had long sleeves. It was fastened with a belt and fell to the knees or ankles.

The outer garment, worn on top of this, was normally a square cloak made of animal skin or wool. It was worn draped over one or both shoulders. A man was regarded as naked without it. He could also use it at night to sleep in. Wealthy men often wore beautifully embroidered outer garments of fine linen.

**Women's Clothing**

Women, too, wore a simple under-garment, though it was usually higher at the neck and often reached right down to the ankles. Women's clothes were usually white in color, though some women wore black or blue. Rich women, like their men-folk, wore fine linen, dyed purple and red, and decorated with jewels, gold, silver, and elaborate embroidery.

Women also wore simple head-coverings rather like modern prayer shawls.

***Above*: A pair of leather sandals from Bible times.**

# Daily Life



Ordinary peoples' homes were very simple and usually built of mud, or lath and plaster. Although houses sometimes consisted of only one or two rooms, in villages small houses were often built with four rooms around a central courtyard, where the animals could be sheltered. In the cities the houses were built close together, but were sometimes two stories high. Houses had flat roofs, often only 6 feet (1.8 meters) from the floor. On the roof, constructed from brushwood, earth and clay, the family could rest, sleep and work.

**Inside the House**

Doors were low and framed by wooden or stone doorposts; they rotated inwards and could be barred from within. Windows were small, unglazed and positioned high in the wall, with additional light being provided by small oil-lamps. Peasants possessed little furniture apart from coarse skins which were unrolled at night on the raised platform made of beaten mud on which the family slept.

**Housework**

The woman of the house did housework – cooking, cleaning, spinning, weaving and sewing. She would also help sometimes in the fields and vineyards, and teach her children in their early years.

There were normally just two meals each day: a breakfast of bread, fruit and cheese; and a larger supper of meat, vegetables and wine. Bread was baked fresh each day in an oven or on a hearth in the house or in the courtyard.

***Below*: An artist's cutaway illustration of a typical peasant house of Bible times.**

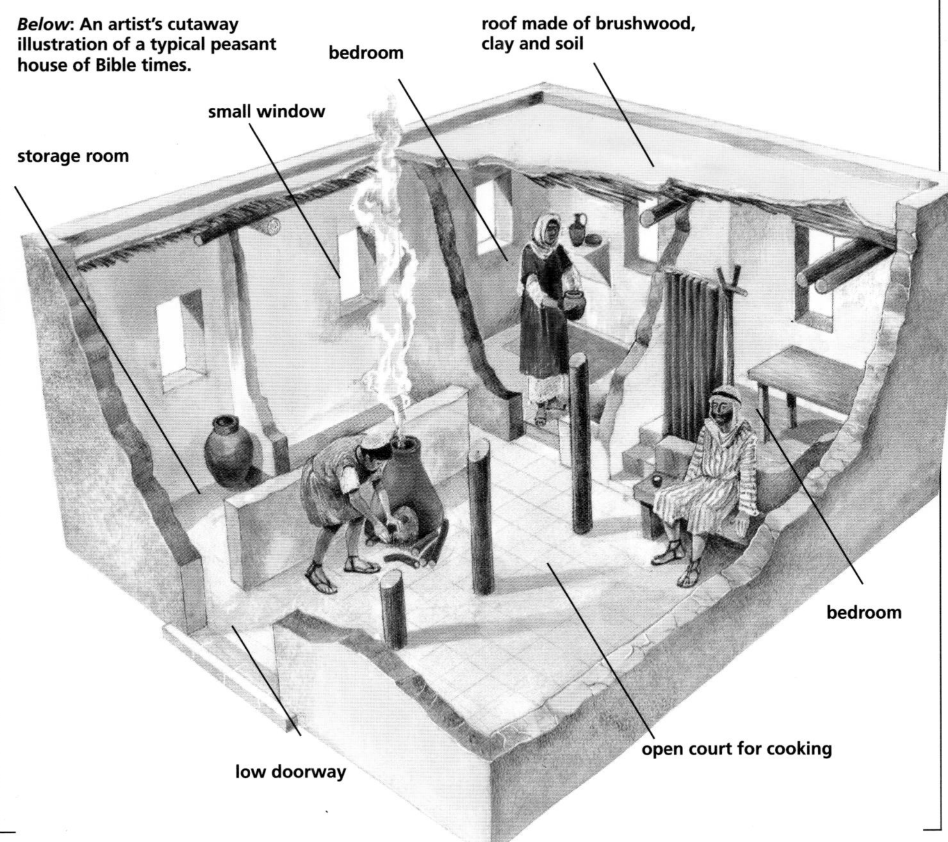

# Writing

People did not write on paper in Bible times, but on clay tablets, pieces of pot, waxed boards and even bits of wood. People also started writing on parchment, made from sheepskin, and on papyrus, a type of paper made from papyrus reed, which grows near the river Nile.

People used different tools to write on the different surfaces. To write on wax or on wood, they used a sharp-pointed stylus; to write on papyrus or parchment, they used a reed brush or quill pen.

In Old Testament times, pages of writing were often joined together by their edges and rolled up to make a scroll. But by New Testament times, people had begun sewing pages together at their edges to make hinged books like ours.

**Language**

The Old Testament was originally written in Hebrew. Hebrew has 22 consonants in its alphabet, but no vowels. The characters of the alphabet are different from ours, and Hebrew is read from right to left instead of left to right.

Some parts of the Bible were written in Aramaic, which was closely related to Hebrew. Most ordinary people in Palestine spoke Aramaic in Jesus' time.

The New Testament was first written in the Greek of ordinary people, which is called Koine Greek. The Greek alphabet had 24 letters, which look different from the letters in our alphabet.

**Above**: **In Bible times, official records, histories and inscriptions were often made on stone tablets such as this.**

***Above*: People often wrote short messages in ink or with a sharp point on pieces of broken pottery, called *ostraca*.**

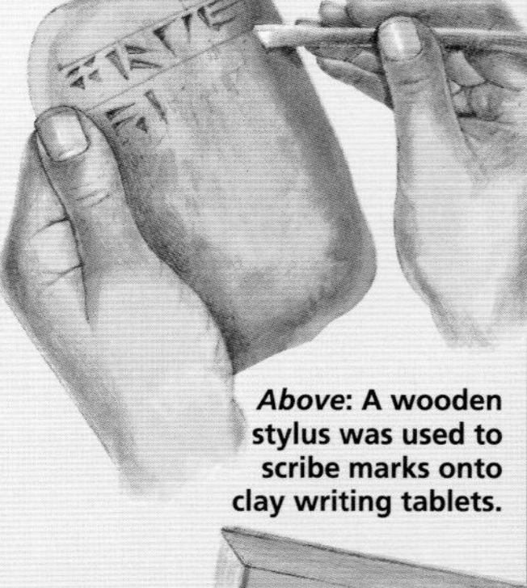

***Above*: A wooden stylus was used to scribe marks onto clay writing tablets.**

***Right*: A simple waxed writing tablet such as school children used in New Testament times.**

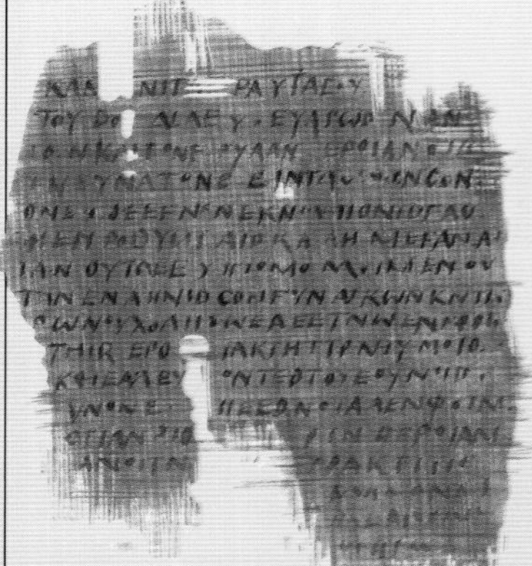

***Above*: This papyrus document contains verses from the book of Acts.**

***Below*: Part of the Isaiah Scroll found at Qumran among the Dead Sea Scrolls.**

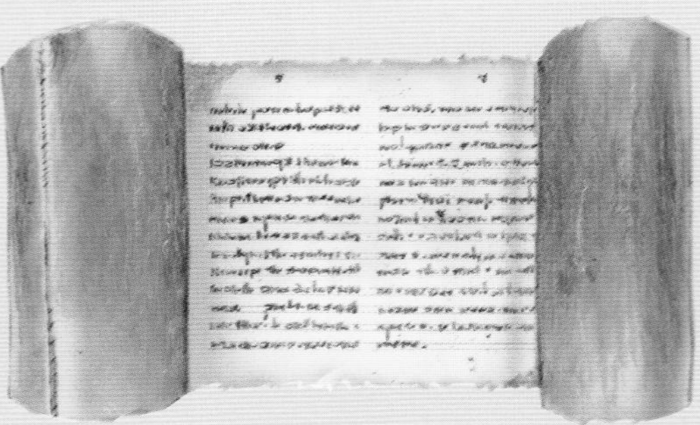

VI
26 Praise the God of heaven,
God's love endures forever.

## PSALM 137*

## Sorrow and Hope in Exile

I
1 By the rivers of Babylon
we sat mourning and weeping
when we remembered Zion.[o]
2 On the poplars* of that land
we hung up our harps.[p]
3 There our captors asked us
for the words of a song;
Our tormentors, for a joyful song:
"Sing for us a song of Zion!"
4 But how could we sing a song of the LORD
in a foreign land?

II
5 If I forget you, Jerusalem,
may my right hand wither.[q]
6 May my tongue stick to my palate
if I do not remember you,
If I do not exalt Jerusalem
beyond all my delights.

III
7 Remember, LORD, against Edom
that day at Jerusalem.
They said: "Level it, level it
down to its foundations!"[r]
8 Fair Babylon, you destroyer,
happy those who pay you back
the evil you have done us![s]
9 Happy those who seize your children
and smash them against a rock.[t]*

## PSALM 138*

## Hymn of a Grateful Heart

1 *Of David*.

I
I thank you, LORD, with all my heart;[u]
before the gods* to you I sing.
2 I bow low toward your holy temple;
I praise your name for your fidelity and love.
For you have exalted over all
your name and your promise.
3 When I cried out, you answered;
you strengthened my spirit.

II
4 All the kings of earth will praise you, LORD,
when they hear the words of your mouth.
5 They will sing of the ways of the LORD:
"How great is the glory of the LORD!"
6 The LORD is on high, but cares for the lowly[v]
and knows the proud from afar.
7 Though I walk in the midst of dangers,
you guard my life when my enemies rage.
You stretch out your hand;
your right hand saves me.
8 The LORD is with me to the end.
LORD, your love endures forever.
Never forsake the work of your hands!

## PSALM 139*

## The All-knowing and Ever-present God

1 *For the leader. A psalm of David.*

I
LORD, you have probed me, you know me:
2 you know when I sit and stand;[w]*
you understand my thoughts from afar.
3 My travels and my rest you mark;
with all my ways you are familiar.
4 Even before a word is on my tongue,
LORD, you know it all.
5 Behind and before you encircle me
and rest your hand upon me.
6 Such knowledge is beyond me,
far too lofty for me to reach.[x]

II
7 Where can I hide from your spirit?
From your presence, where can I flee?
8 If I ascend to the heavens, you are there;
if I lie down in Sheol, you are there too.[y]

---

o Ez 3,15; Lam 3,48.
p Is 24,8; Lam 5,14.
q Jer 51,50.
r Jer 49,7; Lam 4, 21-22; Ez 25,12-14.
s Is 47,1-3; Jer 50-51.
t Hos 14,1.
u Ps 9,1.
v Lk 1,51-52.
w 2 Kgs 19,27; Jb 12,3.
x Ps 131,1.
y Jb 23,8-9; Jer 23, 23-24.

---

*

Ps 137: A temple singer refuses to sing the people's sacred songs in an alien land despite demands from Babylonian captors (1–4). The singer swears an oath by what is most dear to a musician—hands and tongue—to exalt Jerusalem always (5–6). The psalm ends with a prayer that the old enemies of Jerusalem, Edom and Babylon, be destroyed (7–9).

137, 2: *Poplars*: sometimes incorrectly translated "willow." The Euphrates poplar is a high tree common on riverbanks in the Orient.

137, 9: *Happy those who seize your children and smash them against a rock*: the infants represent the future generations, and so must be destroyed if the enemy is truly to be eradicated.

Ps 138: A thanksgiving to God, who came to the rescue of the psalmist. Divine rescue was not the result of the psalmist's virtues but of God's loving fidelity (1–3). The act is not a private transaction but a public act that stirs the surrounding nations to praise God's greatness and care for the people (4–6). The psalmist, having experienced salvation, trusts that God will always be there in moments of danger (7–8).

138, 1: *Before the gods*: i.e., heavenly beings, who were completely subordinate to Israel's God. The earthly temple represents the heavenly palace of God.

Ps 139: A hymnic meditation on God's omnipresence and omniscience. The psalmist is keenly aware of God's all-knowing gaze (1–6), of God's presence in every part of the universe (7–12), and of God's control over the psalmist's very self (13–16). Summing up 1–16, 17–18 express wonder. There is only one place hostile to God's rule—wicked people. The psalmist prays to be removed from their company (19–24).

139, 2: *When I sit and stand*: in all my physical movement.

9 If I fly with the wings of dawn*
and alight beyond the sea,
10 Even there your hand will guide me,
your right hand hold me fast.
11 If I say, "Surely darkness shall hide me,
and night shall be my light"—*
12 Darkness is not dark for you,
and night shines as the day.
Darkness and light are but one.[z]

III
13 You formed my inmost being;
you knit me in my mother's womb.[a]
14 I praise you, so wonderfully you made me;
wonderful are your works!
My very self you knew;
15 my bones were not hidden from you,
When I was being made in secret,
fashioned as in the depths of the earth.*
16 Your eyes foresaw my actions;
in your book all are written down;[b]
my days were shaped, before one came to be.

IV
17 How precious to me are your designs, O God;
how vast the sum of them!
18 Were I to count, they would outnumber the sands;
to finish, I would need eternity.[c]
19 If only you would destroy the wicked, O God,
and the bloodthirsty would depart from me![d]
20 Deceitfully they invoke your name;
your foes swear faithless oaths.
21 Do I not hate, LORD, those who hate you?
Those who rise against you, do I not loathe?[e]
22 With fierce hatred I hate them,
enemies I count as my own.

V
23 Probe me, God, know my heart;
try me, know my concerns.[f]
24 See if my way is crooked,
then lead me in the ancient paths.*

## PSALM 140*

### Prayer for Deliverance from the Wicked

1 *For the leader. A psalm of David.*

I
2 Deliver me, LORD, from the wicked;
preserve me from the violent,[g]
3 From those who plan evil in their hearts,
who stir up conflicts every day,
4 *Who sharpen their tongues like serpents,
venom of asps upon their lips.[h] *Selah*

II
5 Keep me, LORD, from the clutches of the wicked;
preserve me from the violent,
who plot to trip me up.[i]
6 The arrogant have set a trap for me;
villains have spread a net,*
laid snares for me by the wayside. *Selah*
7 I say to the LORD: You are my God;[j]
listen, LORD, to the words of my prayer,
8 My revered LORD, my strong helper,
my helmet on the day of battle.
9 LORD, do not grant the desires of the wicked;
do not let their plots succeed. *Selah*
10 Around me they raise their proud heads;
may the mischief they threaten overwhelm them.
11 May God rain burning coals upon them,[k]
cast them into the grave never more to rise.

III
12 Slanderers will not survive on earth;
evil will quickly entrap the violent.
13 For I know the LORD will secure
justice for the needy, rights for the poor.
14 Then the just will give thanks to your name;
the upright will dwell in your presence.[l]

## PSALM 141*

### Prayer for Deliverance from the Wicked

1 *A psalm of David.*

LORD, I call to you;
come quickly to help me;

z Jb 12,22.
a Wis 7,1; Eccl 11,5; Jb 1,21.
b Mal 3,16.
c Jb 11,7.
d Jb 21,14.
e Ps 119,158.
f Pss 17,3; 26,2.
g Ps 71,4.
h Ps 64,4; Rom 3,13.
i Jer 18,22; Pss 56,7; 57,7.
j Ps 31,15.
k Pss 11,6; 120,4; Gn 19,24.
l Pss 11,7; 16,11; 17, 15.

*

139, 9: *Fly with the wings of dawn*: go to the extremities of the east. *Beyond the sea*: uttermost bounds of the west; the sea is the Mediterranean.

139, 11: *Night shall be my light*: night to me is what day is to others.

139, 15: *The depths of the earth*: figurative language for the womb, stressing the hidden and mysterious operations that occur there.

139, 24: *My way . . . the ancient paths*: the manner of living of our ancestors, who were faithful to God's will. Cf Jer 6, 16.

Ps 140: A lament seeking rescue from violent and treacherous foes (2–6). The psalmist remains trusting (7–8), vigorously praying that the plans of the wicked recoil upon themselves (9–12). A serene statement of praise ends the psalm (13–14). The psalmist is content to be known as one of "the needy," "the poor," "the just," "the upright" (13–14), a class of people expecting divine protection.

140, 4: Similar metaphors for a wicked tongue are used in Pss 52, 4; 55, 22; 58, 5.

140, 6: *Have set a trap . . . have spread a net*: the same figure, of hunters setting traps, occurs in Pss 9, 16; 31, 5; 35, 7; 64, 6. Cf Mt 22, 15; Lk 11, 54.

Ps 141: A lament of an individual (1–2) who is keenly aware that only the righteous can worship God properly and

listen to my plea when I call.
2 Let my prayer be incense* before you;
my uplifted hands an evening sacrifice.[m]
3 Set a guard, LORD, before my mouth,
a gatekeeper at my lips.[n]
4 Do not let my heart incline to evil,
or yield to any sin.
I will never feast upon
the fine food of evildoers.
5 *Let the just strike me; that is kindness;
let them rebuke me; that is oil for my
head.[o]
All this I shall not refuse,
but will pray despite these trials.
6 When their leaders are cast over the
cliff,
all will learn that my prayers were
heard.
7 As when a farmer plows a field into
broken clods,
so their bones will be strewn at the mouth
of Sheol.
8 My eyes are upon you, O GOD, my Lord;[p]
in you I take refuge; do not strip me of
life.
9 Guard me from the trap they have set for
me,
from the snares of evildoers.[q]

10 Into their own nets let all the wicked
fall,
while I make good my own escape.

## PSALM 142*

### A Prayer in Time of Trouble

1 *A* maskil *of David, when he was in the cave.**
*A prayer.*

2 With full voice I cry to the LORD;
with full voice I beseech the LORD.
3 Before God I pour out my complaint,
lay bare my distress.
4 My spirit is faint within me,[r]
but you know my path.[s]
Along the way I walk
they have hidden a trap for me.[t]
5 I look to my right hand,[u]
but no friend is there.
There is no escape for me;
no one cares for me.
6 I cry out to you, LORD,
I say, You are my refuge,[v]
my portion in the land of the living.[w]
7 Listen to my cry for help,
for I am brought very low.[x]
Rescue me from my pursuers,
for they are too strong for me.
8 Lead me out of my prison,
that I may give thanks to your name.
Then the just shall gather around me*
because you have been good to me.

## PSALM 143*

### A Prayer in Distress

1 *A psalm of David.*

LORD, hear my prayer;
in your faithfulness listen to my pleading;
answer me in your justice.
2 Do not enter into judgment with your
servant;
before you no living being can be just.[y]
3 The enemy has pursued me;
they have crushed* my life to the
ground.[z]
They have left me in darkness
like those long dead.[a]
4 My spirit is faint within me;
my heart is dismayed.[b]
5 I remember the days of old;
I ponder all your deeds;
the works of your hands I recall.[c]
6 I stretch out my hands to you;
I thirst for you like a parched land.[d]
*Selah*
7 Hasten to answer me, LORD;
for my spirit fails me.
Do not hide your face from me,
lest I become like those descending to the
pit.[e]

---

m Ps 134,2; Ex 30,8.
n Sir 22,27.
o Prv 9,8; 25,12.
p Pss 25,15; 123,1-2.
q Ps 142,4.
r Ps 143,4.
s Ps 139,24.
t Ps 141,9.
u Pss 16,8; 73,23; 121, 5.
v Ps 91,2. 9.
w Pss 16,5; 27,13; 116, 9; Is 38,11.
x Ps 79,8.
y Ecc 7,20; Jb 4,17; Rom 3,20.
z Ps 7,6.
a Lam 3,6.
b Ps 142,4; Jb 17,1.
c Ps 77,6. 12.
d Pss 42,2; 63,2.
e Pss 28,1; 30,4; 88,5; Prv 1,12.

---

who therefore prays to be protected from the doomed wicked (3–10).

141, 2: *Incense*: literally, "smoke," i.e., the fragrant fumes arising from the altar at the burning of sacrificial animals or of aromatic spices; also used in Rv 5, 8 as a symbol of prayer. *My uplifted hands*: the gesture of supplication. Cf Pss 28, 2; 63, 5; 88, 10; 119, 48; 134, 2; 143, 6.

141, 5–7: The Hebrew text is obscure.

Ps 142: In this lament imploring God for help (2–4b), the psalmist tells how enemies have set a trap (4c–5), and prays for rescue (6–8). The speaker feels utterly alone (5), exhausted (7), and may even be imprisoned (8a). Prison is possibly a metaphor for general distress. The last two verses are the vow of praise, made after receiving an assurance of divine help (8cd).

142, 1: *In the cave*: cf 1 Sm 22, 1; 24, 1–3; Ps 57, 1.

142, 8: *Then the just shall gather around me*: in the temple, when the psalmist offers a thanksgiving sacrifice.

Ps 143: One of the Church's seven Penitential Psalms, this lament is a prayer to be freed from death-dealing enemies. The psalmist addresses God, aware that there is no equality between God and humans; salvation is a gift (1–2). Victimized by evil people (3–4), the psalmist recites ("remembers") God's past actions on behalf of the innocent (5–6). The psalm continues with fervent prayer (7–9) and a strong desire for guidance and protection (10–12).

143, 3: *They have crushed*: literally, "he crushed"; the singular is used typically, hence the plural translation.

8 At dawn let me hear of your kindness,
for in you I trust.
Show me the path I should walk,
for to you I entrust my life.[f]
9 Rescue me, LORD, from my foes,
for in you I hope.
10 Teach me to do your will,
for you are my God.
May your kind spirit guide me
on ground that is level.
11 For your name's sake, LORD, give me life;
in your justice lead me out of distress.
12 In your kindness put an end to my foes;
destroy all who attack me,
for I am your servant.[g]

## PSALM 144*

### A Prayer for Victory and Prosperity

1 *Of David.*

I
*Blessed be the LORD, my rock,
who trains my hands for battle,
my fingers for war;
2 My safeguard and my fortress,
my stronghold, my deliverer,
My shield, in whom I trust,
who subdues peoples under me.

II
3 *LORD, what are mortals that you notice
them;
human beings, that you take thought of
them?[h]
4 *They are but a breath;
their days are like a passing shadow.[i]
5 *LORD, incline your heavens and come;
touch the mountains and make them
smoke.[j]
6 Flash forth lightning and scatter my foes;
shoot your arrows and rout them.
7 Reach out your hand from on high;
deliver me from the many waters;
rescue me from the hands of foreign foes.
8 Their mouths speak untruth;
their right hands are raised in lying
oaths.*
9 O God, a new song I will sing to you;
on a ten-stringed lyre I will play for you.[k]
10 You give victory to kings;
you delivered David your servant.[l]
From the menacing sword 11 deliver me;
rescue me from the hands of foreign foes.
Their mouths speak untruth;
their right hands are raised in lying
oaths.*

III
12 May our sons be like plants[m]
well nurtured from their youth,
Our daughters, like carved columns,
shapely as those of the temple.
13 May our barns be full
with every kind of store.
May our sheep increase by thousands,
by tens of thousands in our fields;
may our oxen be well fattened.
14 May there be no breach in the walls,
no exile, no outcry in our streets.[n]
15 Happy the people so blessed;
happy the people whose God is the
LORD.[o]

## PSALM 145*

### The Greatness and Goodness of God

1 *Praise. Of David.*

I will extol you, my God and king;
I will bless your name forever.
2 Every day I will bless you;
I will praise your name forever.[p]
3 Great is the LORD and worthy of high
praise;[q]
God's grandeur is beyond understanding.
4 One generation praises your deeds to the
next
and proclaims your mighty works.[r]
5 They speak of the splendor of your majestic
glory,
tell of your wonderful deeds.[s]
6 They speak of your fearsome power
and attest to your great deeds.[t]

f Pss 25,4; 27,11; 86, 11; 119,12. 35.
g Ps 116,16.
h Jb 7,17.
i Pss 62,10; 90,9-10; Jb 7,16; Eccl 6,12; Wis 2,5.
j Is 63,19.
k Ps 33,2-3.
l Ps 18,51.
m Ps 128,3.
n Is 65,19.
o Ps 33,12.
p Ps 34,2.
q Pss 48,2; 95,3; 96,4; Jb 36,26.
r Pss 22,31-32; 48, 14-15; 71,18; 78,4; Ex 10,2; Dt 4,9.
s Pss 96,3; 105,2.
t Ps 66,3.

*

Ps 144: The psalm may reflect a ceremony in which the king, as leader of the army, asked God's help (1–8). In 9 the poem shifts abruptly from pleading to thanksgiving, and (except for 11) shifts again to prayer for the people. The first section (1–2) is a prayer of thanks for victory; the second (3–7a), a humble acknowledgment of human nothingness and a supplication that God show forth saving power; the third (9–11), a promise of future thanksgiving; the fourth (12–15), a wish for prosperity and peace. A prayer for deliverance from treacherous foes serves as a refrain after the second and third sections (7b–8. 11). Except for its final section, the psalm is made up almost entirely of verses from other psalms.

144, 1–2: Composed of phrases from Ps 18, 3. 35. 47–48.

144, 3: Similar to Ps 8, 5.

144, 4: Composed of phrases from Pss 39, 6; 102, 12.

144, 5–7: Adapted in large part from Pss 18, 10. 15. 17; 104, 32.

144, 8b. 11b: *Their right hands are raised in lying oaths*: the psalmist's enemies give false testimony.

Ps 145: A hymn in acrostic form; every verse begins with a successive letter of the Hebrew alphabet. Acrostic poems usually do not develop ideas but consist rather of loosely connected statements. The singer invites all to praise God (1–3. 21). The "works of God" make God present and invite human praise (4–7); they climax in a confession (8–9). God's mighty acts show forth divine kingship (10–20), a major theme in the literature of early Judaism and in Christianity.

7 They publish the renown of your abounding goodness
and joyfully sing of your justice.
8 The LORD is gracious and merciful,
slow to anger and abounding in love.[u]
9 The LORD is good to all,
compassionate to every creature.[v]
10 All your works give you thanks, O LORD
and your faithful bless you.[w]
11 They speak of the glory of your reign
and tell of your great works,
12 Making known to all your power,
the glorious splendor of your rule.
13 Your reign is a reign for all ages,
your dominion for all generations.[x]
The LORD is trustworthy in every word,
and faithful in every work.
14 The LORD supports all who are falling
and raises up all who are bowed down.[y]
15 The eyes of all look hopefully to you;
you give them their food in due season.[z]
16 You open wide your hand
and satisfy the desire of every living thing.
17 You, LORD, are just in all your ways,
faithful in all your works.[a]
18 You, LORD, are near to all who call upon you,
to all who call upon you in truth.[b]
19 You satisfy the desire of those who fear you;
you hear their cry and save them.[c]
20 You, LORD, watch over all who love you,
but all the wicked you destroy.[d]
21 My mouth will speak your praises, LORD;
all flesh will bless your holy name forever.[e]

## PSALM 146*

### Trust in God the Creator and Redeemer

1 *Hallelujah!*
2 Praise the LORD, my soul;
I shall praise the LORD all my life,
sing praise to my God while I live.[f]

I
3 Put no trust in princes,
in mere mortals powerless to save.[g]
4 When they breathe their last, they return to the earth;
that day all their planning comes to nothing.[h]

II
5 Happy those whose help is Jacob's God,
whose hope is in the LORD, their God,
6 The maker of heaven and earth,
the seas and all that is in them,[i]
Who keeps faith forever,
7 secures justice for the oppressed,[j]
gives food to the hungry.
The LORD sets prisoners free;[k]
8 the LORD gives sight to the blind.
The LORD raises up those who are bowed down;[l]
the LORD loves the righteous.
9 The LORD protects the stranger,
sustains the orphan and the widow,[m]
but thwarts the way of the wicked.
10 The LORD shall reign forever,
your God, Zion, through all generations![n]
Hallelujah!

## PSALM 147*

### God's Word Restores Jerusalem

1 *Hallelujah!*

I
How good to celebrate our God in song;
how sweet to give fitting praise.[o]
2 The LORD rebuilds Jerusalem,
gathers the dispersed of Israel,[p]
3 Heals the brokenhearted,
binds up their wounds,[q]
4 Numbers all the stars,
calls each of them by name.[r]
5 Great is our Lord, vast in power,
with wisdom beyond measure.[s]
6 The LORD sustains the poor,
but casts the wicked to the ground.[t]

II
7 Sing to the LORD with thanksgiving;
with the lyre celebrate our God,[u]
8 *Who covers the heavens with clouds,

u Pss 86,5. 15; 103,8; Ex 34,6; Sir 2,11.
v Pss 103,13; Wis 11,24.
w Dn 3,57.
x Pss 10,16; 102,13; 146,10; Lam 5,19; Dn 3,100; Rv 11,15.
y Pss 94,18; 146,8.
z Pss 136,25; 104, 27-28; Mt 6,25-26.
a Dt 32,4.
b Dt 4,7; Is 55,6; 58,9.
c Ps 34,18.
d Jgs 5,31.
e Sir 40,35.
f Pss 103,1; 104,33.
g Ps 118,8-9.
h Pss 90,3; 104,29; 1 Mc 2,63; Jb 34, 14-15; Eccl 3,20; 12, 7; Sir 40,11; Is 2,22.
i Ex 20,11; Pss 121,2; 124,8; Acts 14,15; Rv 14,7.
j Ps 103,6.
k Ps 68,7; Is 49,9; 61,1.
l Ps 145,14.
m Ps 68,6; Dt 10,18.
n Pss 145,13; Lam 5,19.
o Pss 33,1; 92,2.
p Is 11,12; 56,8; Jer 31, 10.
q Jb 5,18; Is 30,26; 61, 1; Jer 33,6.
r Is 40,26.
s Jdt 16,13; Jer 51,15.
t Ps 146,9; 1 Sm 2,7-8.
u Ps 71,22.

*

Ps 146: A hymn of someone who has learned there is no other source of strength except the merciful God. Only God, not mortal humans (3–4), can help vulnerable and oppressed people (5–9). The first of the five hymns that conclude the Psalter.

Ps 147: The hymn is divided into three sections by the calls to praise in 1, 7, and 12. The first section praises the powerful creator who restores exiled Judah (1–6); the second section, the creator who provides food to animals and humans; the third and climactic section exhorts the holy city to recognize it has been re-created and made the place of disclosure for God's word, a word as life-giving as water.

147, 8–9: God clothes the fields and feeds the birds. Cf Mt 6, 26. 30.

provides rain for the earth,
makes grass sprout on the mountains,[v]
9 Who gives animals their food
and ravens what they cry for.[w]
10 *God takes no delight in the strength of horses,
no pleasure in the runner's stride.[x]
11 Rather the LORD takes pleasure in the devout,
those who await his faithful care.

III
12 Glorify the LORD, Jerusalem;
Zion, offer praise to your God,
13 Who has strengthened the bars of your gates,
blessed your children within you,[y]
14 Brought peace to your borders,
and filled you with finest wheat.[z]
15 *The LORD sends a command to earth;
his word runs swiftly![a]
16 Thus snow is spread like wool,
frost is scattered like ash,[b]
17 Hail is dispersed like crumbs;
before such cold the waters freeze.
18 Again he sends his word and they melt;
the wind is unleashed and the waters flow.
19 The LORD also proclaims his word to Jacob,
decrees and laws to Israel.[c]
20 God has not done this for other nations;
of such laws they know nothing.
Hallelujah!

## PSALM 148*

## All Creation Summoned to Praise

1 *Hallelujah!*

I
Praise the LORD from the heavens;
give praise in the heights.
2 Praise him, all you angels;
give praise, all you hosts.[d]
3 Praise him, sun and moon;
give praise, all shining stars.
4 Praise him, highest heavens,*
you waters above the heavens.
5 Let them all praise the LORD's name;
for the LORD commanded and they were created,[e]
6 Assigned them duties forever,
gave them tasks that will never change.

II
7 Praise the LORD from the earth,
you sea monsters and all deep waters;[f]
8 You lightning and hail, snow and clouds,
storm winds that fulfill his command;
9 You mountains and all hills,
fruit trees and all cedars;[g]
10 You animals wild and tame,
you creatures that crawl and fly;[h]
11 You kings of the earth and all peoples,
princes and all who govern on earth;
12 Young men and women too,
old and young alike.
13 Let them all praise the LORD's name,
for his name alone is exalted,
majestic above earth and heaven.[i]
14 The LORD has lifted high the horn of his people,*
to the glory of all the faithful,
of Israel, the people near to their God.
Hallelujah!

## PSALM 149*

## Praise God with Song and Sword

1 *Hallelujah!*

Sing to the LORD a new song,
a hymn in the assembly of the faithful.[j]
2 Let Israel be glad in their maker,
the people of Zion rejoice in their king.
3 Let them praise his name in festive dance,
make music with tambourine and lyre.[k]*
4 For the LORD takes delight in his people,
honors the poor with victory.
5 Let the faithful rejoice in their glory,
cry out for joy at their banquet,*
6 With the praise of God in their mouths,
and a two-edged sword in their hands,[l]

v Ps 104,13f; Jb 5,10; Jer 14,22; Jl 2,23.
w Jb 38,41; Mt 6,26.
x Pss 20,8; 33,16-18.
y Ps 48,14.
z Ps 81,17.
a Ps 33,9.
b Jb 6,16; 37,10; 38,22.
c Ps 78,5; Bar 3,37; Dt 4,7-8.
d Dn 3,58-63; Ps 103, 20f.
e Ps 33,9; Gn 1,3f; Jdt 16,14.
f Gn 1,21; Ps 135,6.
g Is 44,23.
h Gn 1,21. 24f; Ps 30,5. Dt 4,7.
i Ps 30,5; Dt 4,7.
j Pss 22,23; 26,12; 35, 18; 40,10; Jdt 16,1.
k Pss 68,26; 81,2-3; 87, 7; 150,3-4.
l Neh 4,10-12; 2 Mc 15, 27.

*

147, 10–11: Acknowledging one's dependence upon God rather than claiming self-sufficiency pleases God. Cf Pss 20, 8; 33, 16–19.

147, 15–19: God speaks through the thunder of nature and the word of revealed law. Cf Is 55, 10–11. The weather phenomena are well known in Jerusalem: a blizzard of snow and hail followed by a thunderstorm that melts the ice.

Ps 148: A hymn inviting the beings of heaven (1–6) and of earth (7–14) to praise God. The hymn does not distinguish between inanimate and animate (and rational) nature.

148, 4: *Highest heavens*: literally, "the heavens of the heavens," i.e., the space above the firmament, where the "upper waters" are stored. Cf Gn 1, 6–7; Dt 10, 14; 1 Kgs 8, 27; Ps 104, 3. 13.

148, 14: *The LORD has lifted high the horn of his people*: horn = strength, the concrete noun for the abstract. Of all peoples God has chosen Israel to return praise and thanks in a special way.

Ps 149: A hymn inviting the people of Israel to celebrate their God in song and festive dance (1–3. 5) because God has chosen them and given them victory (4). The exodus and conquest are the defining acts of Israel; the people must be ready to do again those acts in the future at the divine command (6–9).

149, 3: *Make music with tambourine and lyre*: the verse recalls the great exodus hymn of Ex 15, 20.

149, 5: *At their banquet*: literally, "upon their couches." The people reclined to banquet.

7 To bring retribution on the nations,
punishment on the peoples,[m]
8 To bind their kings with chains,
shackle their nobles with irons,
9 To execute the judgments decreed for them—
such is the glory* of all God's faithful.
Hallelujah!

## PSALM 150*
## Final Doxology

1 *Hallelujah!*

Praise God in his holy sanctuary;[n]*
give praise in the mighty dome of heaven.
2 Give praise for his mighty deeds,[o]
praise him for his great majesty.
3 Give praise with blasts upon the horn,[p]
praise him with harp and lyre.
4 Give praise with tambourines and dance,
praise him with flutes and strings.[q]
5 Give praise with crashing cymbals,
praise him with sounding cymbals.
6 Let everything that has breath
give praise to the LORD![r]
Hallelujah!

m Wis 3,8.
n Dn 3,53.
o Dt 3,24.
p 3ff: Pss 81,3-4; 149,3; 2 Sm 6,5; 1 Chr 13,8; 16,5. 42; 2 Chr 5, 12-13; 7,6.
q Ps 68,26; Ex 15,20.
r Rv 5,13.

*

149, 9: *The glory*: what brings honor to the people is their readiness to carry out the divine will, here conceived as punishing injustice done by the nations.

Ps 150: The psalm is a closing doxology both for the fifth book of the Psalms (107–149) and for the Psalter as a whole. Temple musicians and dancers are called to lead all beings on earth and in heaven in praise of God. The psalm proclaims to whom praise shall be given, and where (1); what praise shall be given, and why (2); how praise shall be given (3–5), and by whom (6).

150, 1: *His holy sanctuary*: God's temple on earth. *The mighty dome of the heavens*: literally, "[God's] strong vault"; heaven is here imagined as a giant plate separating the inhabited world from the waters of the heavens.

# The Book of

# PROVERBS

*The first word of this book, MISHLE, has provided the title by which it is generally designated in Jewish and Christian circles. The name "Proverbs," while not an exact equivalent of MISHLE, describes the main contents satisfactorily, even though it is hardly an adequate designation for such parts as 1, 1—9, 18 or 31, 10–31. Among some early Christian writers the book was also known by the name of "Wisdom," and in the Roman Missal it was for many centuries referred to as a "Book of Wisdom."*

*The Book of Proverbs is an anthology of didactic poetry forming part of the sapiential literature of the Old Testament. Its primary purpose, indicated in the first sentence (1, 2f), is to teach wisdom. It is thus directed particularly to the young and inexperienced (1, 4); but also to those who desire advanced training in wisdom (1, 5f). The wisdom which the book teaches, covers a wide field of human and divine activity, ranging from matters purely secular to most lofty moral and religious truths, such as God's omniscience (5, 21; 15, 3–11), power (19, 21; 21, 30), providence (20, 1-24), goodness (15, 29), and the joy and strength resulting from abandonment to him (3, 5; 16, 20; 18, 10). The teaching of the entire book is placed on a firm religious foundation by the principle that "the fear of the Lord is the beginning of knowledge" (1, 7; cf 9, 10).*

*To Solomon are explicitly ascribed parts II and V of the book; he is the patron of Hebrew wisdom. Of Agur (part VI) and Lemuel (part VIII), nothing further is known. Parts III and IV are attributed to "the wise." The remaining parts are anonymous.*

*The manner of compilation is conjectural. Parts II and V may have circulated first as independent collections, compiled before the fall of Jerusalem, as the references to Solomon (10, 1) and Hezekiah (25, 1) suggest. Parts III, IV and VII would seem to belong together as a third collection of a similar kind. The author of the first nine chapters, a religious sage familiar with the earlier sacred books, was the editor of the whole as we have it, probably in the early part of the fifth century B.C.*

*Christ and the Apostles often expressly quoted the Proverbs (Jn 7, 38; Rom 12, 20; Jas 4, 6) or repeated their teaching; compare Lk 10, 14, and Prv 25, 7; 1 Pt 4, 8; Jas 5, 20 and Prv 10, 12. The book has an important place in the Latin and Greek liturgies.*

*On the basis of titles, subject matter, and poetic structure the Book of Proverbs may be divided as follows:*

- *I. Introduction: The Value of Wisdom (1, 1—9, 18).*
- *II. First Collection of the Proverbs of Solomon (10, 1—22, 16).*
- *III. Sayings of the Wise (22, 17—24, 22).*
- *IV. Other Sayings of the Wise (24, 23–34).*
- *V. Second Collection of the Proverbs of Solomon (25, 1—29, 27).*
- *VI. The Words of Agur (30, 1–6).*
- *VII. Numerical Proverbs (30, 7–33).*
- *VIII. The Words of Lemuel (31, 1–9). The Ideal Wife (31, 10–31).*

## *I: Introduction: The Value of Wisdom*

## CHAPTER 1

### Purpose of the Proverbs of Solomon*

1 The proverbs of Solomon,[a] the son of
David,
king of Israel:
2 That men may appreciate wisdom and
discipline,*
may understand words of intelligence;
3 May receive training in wise conduct,
in what is right, just and honest;
4 That resourcefulness may be imparted to the
simple,*
to the young man knowledge and
discretion.
5 A wise man by hearing them will advance in
learning,
an intelligent man will gain sound
guidance,
6 That he may comprehend proverb and
parable,
the words of the wise and their riddles.

7 The fear of the LORD* is the beginning of
knowledge;[b]
wisdom and instruction fools despise.

### The Path of the Wicked: Greed and Violence*

8 Hear, my son, your father's instruction,
and reject not your mother's teaching;
9 A graceful diadem will they be for your
head;
a torque for your neck.
10 My son, should sinners entice you, 11 and
say,
"Come along with us!
Let us lie in wait for the honest man,
let us, unprovoked, set a trap for the
innocent;
12 Let us swallow them up, as the nether world
does, alive,
in the prime of life, like those who go
down to the pit!
13 All kinds of precious wealth shall we gain,
we shall fill our houses with booty;
14 Cast in your lot with us,
we shall all have one purse!"—

15 My son, walk not in the way with them,
hold back your foot from their path!
16 [For their feet run to evil,
they hasten to shed blood.[c]]
17 It is in vain that a net is spread*
before the eyes of any bird—
18 These men lie in wait for their own blood,
they set a trap for their own lives.
19 This is the fate of everyone greedy of loot:
unlawful gain takes away the life of him
who acquires it.

### Wisdom in Person Gives Warning*

20 Wisdom cries aloud in the street,
in the open squares she raises her voice;[d]
21 Down the crowded ways she calls out,
at the city gates she utters her words:
22 "How long, you simple ones, will you love
inanity,
23 how long will you turn away at my
reproof?
Lo! I will pour out to you my spirit,
I will acquaint you with my words.

24 "Because I called and you refused,
I extended my hand and no one took
notice;[e]
25 Because you disdained all my counsel,
and my reproof you ignored—
26 I, in my turn, will laugh at your doom;
I will mock when terror overtakes you;
27 When terror comes upon you like a storm,
and your doom approaches like a
whirlwind;
when distress and anguish befall you.

28 "Then they call me, but I answer not;
they seek me, but find me not;*
29 Because they hated knowledge,
and chose not the fear of the LORD;
30 They ignored my counsel,
they spurned all my reproof;
And in their arrogance they preferred
arrogance,
and like fools they hated knowledge:

---

a Prv 10, 1; 25, 1; 1 Kgs 4, 32.
b Prv 9, 10; Jb 28, 28; Ps 111, 10; Sir 1, 16.
c Is 59, 7.
d Prv 8, 1-3; 9, 3.
e Is 65, 2. 12; 66, 4; Jer 7, 13.

*

---

1, 1–6: This prologue explains the purpose of the book: to educate the inexperienced in knowledge and right conduct, and to increase the learning of the wise man by proverbs, parables and riddles.

1, 2: Discipline: education or formation which dispels ignorance and corrects vice.

1, 4: Simple: immature and inexperienced, hence easily influenced for good or evil.

1, 7: Fear of the Lord; reverential fear and respect for God on account of his sovereignty, goodness and justice toward men. This is the foundation of religion.

1, 8–19: A warning against association with the greedy and the violent who seek to destroy the honest man and to steal his possessions (11–14). The trap which the wicked set for the innocent (11), in the end (19) takes away the life of the wicked themselves.

1, 17: Instructed by the wise man, the youth (of v 4) will recognize the invitation of the wicked (11–14) as a net spread before him, and he will thus, like the bird, be protected against falling into it.

1, 20–33: Wisdom is here personified: with divine authority she sets forth and proclaims the moral order, instructing and threatening (24–33) the multitudes in the streets and places of assembly.

1, 28: Overtaken by doom, the foolish seek wisdom, but in vain because they do so too late. Cf Jn 7, 34; 8, 21.

31 "Now they must eat the fruit of their own way,
and with their own devices be glutted.*
32 For the self-will of the simple kills them,
the smugness of fools destroys them.
33 But he who obeys me dwells in security,
in peace, without fear of harm."[f]

## CHAPTER 2*

### The Blessings of Wisdom*

1 My son, if you receive my words
and treasure my commands,
2 Turning your ear to wisdom,*
inclining your heart to understanding;
3 Yes, if you call to intelligence,
and to understanding raise your voice;
4 If you seek her like silver,
and like hidden treasures search her out:

5 Then will you understand the fear of the LORD;
the knowledge of God you will find;
6 For the LORD gives wisdom,
from his mouth come knowledge and understanding;[g]
7 He has counsel in store for the upright,
he is the shield of those who walk honestly,
8 Guarding the paths of justice,
protecting the way of his pious ones.

9 Then you will understand rectitude and justice,
honesty, every good path;
10 For wisdom will enter your heart,
knowledge will please your soul,
11 Discretion will watch over you,
understanding will guard you;

12 Saving you from the way of evil men,
from men of perverse speech,
13 Who leave the straight paths
to walk in ways of darkness,
14 Who delight in doing evil,
rejoice in perversity;
15 Whose ways are crooked,
and devious their paths;

16 Saving you from the wife of another,
from the adulteress with her smooth words,[h]
17 Who forsakes the companion of her youth
and forgets the pact with her God;
18 For her path sinks down to death,
and her footsteps lead to the shades;[i]
19 None who enter thereon come back again,
or gain the paths of life.

20 Thus you may walk in the way of good men,
and keep to the paths of the just.
21 For the upright will dwell in the land,[j]
the honest will remain in it;
22 But the wicked will be cut off from the land,
the faithless will be rooted out of it.

## CHAPTER 3

### Attitude toward the Lord*

1 My son, forget not my teaching,
keep in mind my commands;
2 For many days, and years of life,[k]
and peace, will they bring you.

3 Let not kindness and fidelity leave you;
bind them around your neck;
4 Then will you win favor and good esteem
before God and man.

5 Trust in the LORD with all your heart,
on your own intelligence rely not;
6 In all your ways be mindful of him,
and he will make straight your paths.

7 Be not wise in your own eyes,[l]
fear the LORD and turn away from evil;
8 This will mean health for your flesh
and vigor for your bones.

9 Honor the LORD with your wealth,
with first fruits of all your produce;[m]
10 Then will your barns be filled with grain,
with new wine your vats will overflow.
11 The discipline of the LORD, my son, disdain not;[n]
spurn not his reproof;
12 For whom the LORD loves he reproves,
and he chastises the son he favors.[o]

f Prv 8, 33f.
g Jb 32, 8; Wis 7, 25; Sir 1, 1; Jas 1, 5.
h Prv 5, 3. 20; 6, 24; 7, 5; 22, 14.
i Prv 5, 5f; 7, 27.
j 21f: Prv 10, 7. 30; Jb 18, 17; Pss 21, 9-13; 37, 22. 28.
k Prv 4, 10; 9, 11; 10, 27.
l Rom 11, 25; 12, 16.
m Ex 34, 26; Lv 27, 30; Dt 26, 2; Sir 7, 31; 35, 7.
n Heb 12, 5f.
o Jdt 8, 27; Rv 3, 19.

*

1, 31: Sinners are punished by the bad fruits which their sins produce. Cf Wis 11, 16.

2—7: These chapters form an ordered discourse in seven "columns" of twenty-two verses each. Chapter 2 introduces the four topics about which the sage instructs his pupil: the service of God (3, 1–12. 25–34), the search for wisdom (3, 13–24. 35; 4, 1–9), the avoidance of evil companions among men (4, 10–27; 5, 21–23), and among women (5, 1–20; 6, 20—7, 27). The last topic is treated at a length equal to the first three because the discourse is meant especially for youths (cf Prv 1, 4).

2, 1–22: The search for wisdom (1–4) leads to the protection of God (5–8) and of wisdom herself (9ff; cf Prv 1, 20–33) and to deliverance from evil men (12–15) and evil women (16–19), and so to lasting happiness (20ff).

2, 2f: Wisdom, understanding, intelligence: various names or aspects of the same gift.

3, 1–12: Many are the rewards for fidelity and trust in God, and for diffidence of self (1–8). Cf Dt 30, 20; Is 38, 19. The offering of material things for divine worship is blessed by an increase of such goods (9f). Even correction and chastisement are a mark of God's love and favor (11f).

### The Value of Wisdom*

13 Happy the man who finds wisdom,
the man who gains understanding![p]
14 For her profit is better than profit in silver,
and better than gold is her revenue;
15 She is more precious than corals,*
and none of your choice possessions can compare with her.[q]

16 Long life is in her right hand,
in her left are riches and honor;
17 Her ways are pleasant ways,
and all her paths are peace;
18 She is a tree of life* to those who grasp her,[r]
and he is happy who holds her fast.

19 The LORD by wisdom founded the earth,
established the heavens by understanding;
20 By his knowledge the depths break open,
and the clouds drop down dew.*
21 My son, let not these slip out of your sight:
keep advice and counsel in view;
22 So will they be life to your soul,
and an adornment for your neck.
23 Then you may securely go your way;
your foot will never stumble;
24 When you lie down, you need not be afraid,
when you rest, your sleep will be sweet.
35 Honor is the possession of wise men,
but fools inherit shame.

### Attitude toward Fellow Men*

25 Be not afraid of sudden terror,
of the ruin of the wicked* when it comes;
26 For the LORD will be your confidence,
and will keep your foot from the snare.

27 Refuse no one the good on which he has a claim
when it is in your power to do it for him.
28 Say not to your neighbor, "Go, and come again,
tomorrow I will give," when you can give at once.

29 Plot no evil against your neighbor,
against him who lives at peace with you.
30 Quarrel not with a man without cause,
with one who has done you no harm.
31 Envy not the lawless man
and choose none of his ways:[s]
32 To the LORD the perverse man is an abomination,
but with the upright is his friendship.

33 The curse of the LORD is on the house of the wicked,
but the dwelling of the just he blesses;
34 When he is dealing with the arrogant, he is stern,[t]
but to the humble he shows kindness.

## CHAPTER 4

### Wisdom: the Supreme Guide of Men*

1 Hear, O children, a father's instruction,
be attentive, that you may gain understanding!
2 Yes, excellent advice I give you;
my teaching do not forsake.
3 When I was my father's child,
frail, yet the darling of my mother,
4 He taught me, and said to me:
"Let your heart hold fast my words:[u]
keep my commands, that you may live!

5 "Get wisdom, get understanding!
Do not forget or turn aside from the words I utter.
6 Forsake her not, and she will preserve you;
love her, and she will safeguard you;
7 The beginning of wisdom is: get wisdom;
at the cost of all you have, get understanding.
8 Extol her, and she will exalt you;
she will bring you honors if you embrace her;
9 She will put on your head a graceful diadem;
a glorious crown will she bestow on you."

### The Good and the Evil Way*

10 Hear, my son, and receive my words,
and the years of your life shall be many.[v]
11 On the way of wisdom I direct you,
I lead you on straightforward paths.

p Prv 8, 34f.
q Prv 8, 11. 19; Wis 7, 8-11.
r Prv 4, 13; 8, 35; 11, 30; Gn 2, 9; 3, 22.
s Prv 23, 17; 24, 1. 19; Ps 37, 1.
t Prv 1, 26.
u 1 Kgs 2, 2ff.
v Prv 3, 2.

*

3, 13–24: Wisdom, or understanding, is more valuable than silver and gold. Its fruit is long life, riches, honor and happiness (13–18). Even the creation of the universe and its adornment (Gn 1) were not done without wisdom (19f). It is the life of the soul and gives security in work and in repose (21–24).

3, 15: Corals: some precious stone may be intended.

3, 18: A tree of life: cf Prv 11, 30; 13, 12; Gn 2, 9.

3, 20: For the Hebrews, the depths enclosed the great subterranean ocean; the rain and dew descended from the celestial ocean above the firmament; cf Gn 1, 6–10; Jb 26, 8. 12; Pss 18, 16; 24, 2.

3, 25–34: Serving God with confidence in him (25f) requires serving one's neighbor through kindness (27f), peace with the good (29ff), no envy of the wicked (31), because the Lord's friendship and kindness are with the just; his curse is with the wicked.

3, 25: The ruin of the wicked: i.e., the ruin that comes upon the wicked.

4, 1–9: The sage speaks as a father admonishing his children to secure wisdom at any cost.

4, 10–27: The way of wisdom leads directly to life (10–13); it is a light that grows brighter (18). The wise man is bound to shun (14–17) the dark and violent path of the wicked (19). Singleness of purpose and right conduct proceed from the heart of a wise man as from the source of life (23–26); they save him from destruction on evil paths (4, 27; 5, 21ff).

12 When you walk, your step will not be
impeded,
and should you run, you will not stumble.
13 Hold fast to instruction, never let her go;
keep her, for she is your life.

14 The path of the wicked enter not,
walk not on the way of evil men;
15 Shun it, cross it not,
turn aside from it, and pass on.
16 For they cannot rest unless they have done
evil;
to have made no one stumble steals away
their sleep.
17 For they eat the bread of wickedness
and drink the wine of violence.
19 The way of the wicked is like darkness;
they know not on what they stumble.
18 But the path of the just is like shining light,
that grows in brilliance till perfect day.*

20 My son, to my words be attentive,
to my sayings incline your ear;
21 Let them not slip out of your sight,
keep them within your heart;
22 For they are life to those who find them,[w]
to man's whole being they are health.

23 With closest custody, guard your heart,
for in it are the sources of life.
24 Put away from you dishonest talk,
deceitful speech put far from you.
25 Let your eyes look straight ahead
and your glance be directly forward.
26 Survey the path for your feet,
and let all your ways be sure.
27 Turn neither to right nor to left,
keep your foot far from evil.

## CHAPTER 5

### Warning against Adultery*

1 My son, to my wisdom be attentive,
to my knowledge incline your ear,
2 That discretion may watch over you,
and understanding may guard you.
3 The lips of an adulteress drip with honey,
and her mouth is smoother than oil;[x]
4 But in the end she is as bitter as wormwood,
as sharp as a two-edged sword.
5 Her feet go down to death,
to the nether world her steps attain;[y]
6 Lest you see before you the road to life,
her paths will ramble, you know not
where.

7 So now, O children, listen to me,
go not astray from the words of my
mouth.
8 Keep your way far from her,[z]
approach not the door of her house,
9 Lest you give your honor* to others,[a]
and your years to a merciless one;
10 Lest strangers have their fill of your wealth,
your hard-won earnings go to an alien's
house;
11 And you groan in the end,
when your flesh and your body are
consumed;
12 And you say, "Oh, why did I hate
instruction,
and my heart spurn reproof!
13 Why did I not listen to the voice of my
teachers,
nor to my instructors incline my ear!
14 I have all but come to utter ruin,
condemned by the public assembly!"

15 Drink water from your own cistern,
running water from your own well.
16 How may your water sources be dispersed
abroad,
streams of water in the streets?
17 Let your fountain be yours alone,
not one shared with strangers;
18 And have joy of the wife of your youth,
19 your lovely hind, your graceful doe.*
Her love will invigorate you always,
through her love you will flourish
continually,
6, 22 When you lie down she will watch over
you,
and when you wake, she will share your
concerns;
wherever you turn, she will guide you.*
20 Why then, my son, should you go astray for
another's wife
and accept the embraces of an adulteress?

21 For each man's ways are plain to the LORD's
sight;*
all their paths he surveys;[b]
22 By his own iniquities the wicked man will
be caught,
in the meshes of his own sin he will be
held fast;
23 He will die from lack of discipline,
through the greatness of his folly he will
be lost.

w Prv 8, 35.
x Prv 7, 5.
y Prv 2, 18; 7, 27.
z Prv 7, 25.
a 9f: Sir 9, 6.
b Jb 14, 16; 31, 4; 34, 21.

4, 18: Till perfect day: literally, "till the day is established"; this may refer to full daylight or to noonday.

5, 1–20: Understanding and discretion guard a man against the wiles of an adulteress, which lead astray and beget bitterness, bloodshed and death (1–6). They destroy honor, waste the years of life, despoil hard-earned wealth, consume the flesh, and bring remorse in the end (7–14). Conjugal fidelity and love for one wife only bring happiness and security (15–20). Cf Prv 6, 20—7, 27.

5, 9: Honor: the words "life" and "wealth" have also been read in this place. A merciless one: the offended husband; cf Prv 6, 34f.

5, 19: Lovely hind . . . graceful doe: oriental symbols of feminine beauty and charm; cf Song 2, 7. 9. 17.

6, 22: This is transposed from chapter 6, 22.

5, 21–23: These verses are best read after Prv 4, 27.

## CHAPTER 6

### Miscellaneous Proverbs*

1 My son, if you have become surety to your
neighbor,[c]
given your hand in pledge* to another,
2 You have been snared by the utterance of
your lips,
caught by the words of your mouth;
3 So do this, my son, to free yourself,
since you have fallen into your neighbor's
power:
Go, hurry, stir up your neighbor!
4 Give no sleep to your eyes,
nor slumber to your eyelids;
5 Free yourself as a gazelle from the snare,
or as a bird from the hand of the fowler.

6 Go to the ant,[d] O sluggard,
study her ways and learn wisdom;
7 For though she has no chief,
no commander or ruler,
8 She procures her food in the summer,
stores up her provisions in the harvest.
9 How long, O sluggard, will you rest?
when will you rise from your sleep?
10 A little sleep, a little slumber,
a little folding of the arms to rest—*
11 Then will poverty come upon you like a
highwayman,
and want like an armed man.

12 A scoundrel, a villain, is he
who deals in crooked talk.
13 He winks his eyes,
shuffles his feet,
makes signs with his fingers;
14 He has perversity in his heart,
is always plotting evil,
sows discord.
15 Therefore suddenly ruin comes upon him;
in an instant he is crushed beyond cure.

16 There are six things the LORD hates,
yes, seven are an abomination to him;*
17 Haughty eyes, a lying tongue,
and hands that shed innocent blood;
18 A heart that plots wicked schemes,
feet that run swiftly to evil,
19 The false witness who utters lies,
and he who sows discord among brothers.

### Warning against Adultery*

20 Observe, my son, your father's bidding,
and reject not your mother's teaching;
21 Keep them fastened over your heart always,
put them around your neck;
23 For the bidding is a lamp, and the teaching
a light,
and a way to life are the reproofs of
discipline;
24 To keep you from your neighbor's wife,
from the smooth tongue of the
adulteress.[e]
25 Lust not in your heart after her beauty,
let her not captivate you with her glance![f]
26 For the price of a loose woman
may be scarcely a loaf of bread,
But if she is married,
she is a trap for your precious life.*
27 Can a man take fire to his bosom,
and his garments not be burned?
28 Or can a man walk on live coals,
and his feet not be scorched?
29 So with him who goes in to his neighbor's
wife—
none who touches her shall go
unpunished.[g]

30 Men despise not the thief if he steals
to satisfy his appetite when he is hungry;
31 Yet if he be caught he must pay back
sevenfold;
all the wealth of his house he may yield
up.
32 But he who commits adultery is a fool;
he who would destroy himself does it.
33 A degrading beating will he get,
and his disgrace will not be wiped away;
34 For vindictive is the husband's wrath,
he will have no pity on the day of
vengeance;
35 He will not consider any restitution,
nor be satisfied with the greatest gifts.

## CHAPTER 7

1 My son, keep my words,
and treasure my commands.
2 Keep my commands and live,
my teaching as the apple of your eye;
3 Bind them on your fingers,
write them on the tablet of your heart.[h]
4 Say to Wisdom, "You are my sister!"
call Understanding, "Friend!"

---

c 1f: Prv 11, 15; 22, 26; Sir 8, 13; 29, 19.
d Prv 30, 25.
e Prv 2, 16; 7, 5.
f Ex 20, 17; Dt 5, 21; Sir 9, 8; 25, 20; Mt 5, 28.
g Sir 9, 9.
h Dt 6, 8.

*

6, 1–19: These verses interrupt the discourse of chapters 2—7, which should be read apart from them; they contain four shorter proverbs akin to those in chapter 30.

6, 1: Given your hand in pledge: literally, "struck your hands"; this was probably the legal method for closing a contract.

6, 10: This verse may be regarded as the sluggard's reply or as a continuation of the remonstrance.

6, 16–19: The seven vices symbolized for the most part by bodily organs are pride, lying, murder, intrigue, readiness to do evil, false witness, and the stirring up of discord.

6, 20—7, 27: Parental training and the love of wisdom are an invaluable and constant help for the young (6, 20–23; 7, 1–4). They are the best defense against adultery (6, 24; 7, 5. 24f), which involves the guilty in many dangers and punishments (6, 26–35; 7, 6–27). Cf Prv 5, 1–20.

6, 26: Some interpret the verse in a progressive sense, i.e., to satisfy the increasing demands of a courtesan a man is reduced to poverty; if the woman is married, even his very life is endangered.

5 That they may keep you from another's wife,
from the adulteress with her smooth words.[i]
6 For at the window of my house,
through my lattice I looked out—

7 And I saw among the simple ones,
I observed among the young men,
a youth with no sense,
8 Going along the street near the corner,
then walking in the direction of her house—
9 In the twilight, at dusk of day,
at the time of the dark of night.
10 And lo! the woman comes to meet him,
robed like a harlot, with secret designs—
11 She is fickle and unruly,
in her home her feet cannot rest;
12 Now she is in the streets, now in the open squares,
and at every corner she lurks in ambush—
13 When she seizes him, she kisses him,
and with an impudent look says to him:

14 "I owed peace offerings,
and today I have fulfilled my vows;*
15 So I came out to meet you,
to look for you, and I have found you!
16 With coverlets I have spread my couch,
with brocaded cloths of Egyptian linen;
17 I have sprinkled my bed with myrrh,
with aloes, and with cinnamon.

18 "Come, let us drink our fill of love,
until morning, let us feast on love!
19 For my husband is not at home,
he has gone on a long journey;
20 A bag of money he took with him,
not till the full moon will he return home."

21 She wins him over by her repeated urging,
with her smooth lips she leads him astray;[j]
22 He follows her stupidly,
like an ox that is led to slaughter;
Like a stag that minces toward the net,
23 till an arrow pierces its liver;
Like a bird that rushes into a snare,
unaware that its life is at stake.

24 So now, O children, listen to me,
be attentive to the words of my mouth!
25 Let not your heart turn to her ways,
go not astray in her paths;
26 For many are those she has struck down dead,
numerous, those she has slain.
27 Her house is made up of ways to the nether world,
leading down into the chambers of death.[k]

## CHAPTER 8

### The Discourse of Wisdom*

1 Does not Wisdom call,
and Understanding raise her voice?[l]
2 On the top of the heights along the road,
at the crossroads she takes her stand;
3 By the gates at the approaches of the city,
in the entryways she cries aloud:
4 "To you, O men, I call;
my appeal is to the children of men.
5 You simple ones, gain resource,
you fools,* gain sense.
6 "Give heed! for noble things I speak;
honesty opens my lips.
7 Yes, the truth my mouth recounts,*
but wickedness my lips abhor.
8 Sincere are all the words of my mouth,
no one of them is wily or crooked;
9 All of them are plain to the man of intelligence,
and right to those who attain knowledge.
10 Receive my instruction in preference to silver,
and knowledge rather than choice gold.
11 [For Wisdom is better than corals,
and no choice possession can compare with her.[m] ]

12 "I, Wisdom, dwell with experience,
and judicious knowledge I attain.
13 [The fear of the LORD is to hate evil;]
Pride, arrogance, the evil way,
and the perverse mouth I hate.[n]
14 Mine are counsel and advice;
Mine is strength; I am understanding.*
15 By me kings reign,
and lawgivers establish justice;
16 By me princes govern,
and nobles; all the rulers of earth.

17 "Those who love me I also love,
and those who seek me find me.

i Prv 2, 16; 6, 24.
j Prv 5, 3; 6, 24.
k Prv 2, 18f; 5, 5.
l Prv 1, 20f; 9, 3.
m Prv 3, 15; Wis 7, 8.
n Prv 6, 16f; 16, 5.

*

7, 14: "Peace offerings . . . vows": a portion of the sacrifice reverted to the donor and had to be eaten on the same day at a family festival (Lv 7, 11–15). In this figure, the adulteress offers to share with the foolish young man the deadly feast of her sensuality.

8, 1–36: Wisdom is here personified as in Prv 1, 20–33, to confirm the words of the teacher of wisdom. She exalts her grandeur and origin, and invites all (1–11) to be attentive to her salutary influence in human society (12–21), for she was privileged to be present at the creation of the world (22–31). Finally, she promises life and the favor of God to those who find her, death to those who despise her.

8, 5: Simple ones . . . fools: see note on Prv 1, 4.

8, 7f: The truth and sincerity of wisdom are absolute because they are divine. They can neither deceive nor tolerate deception. An intelligent man understands and accepts them.

8, 14: What is here predicated of wisdom is elsewhere attributed to God (Jb 12, 13–16).

18 With me are riches and honor,[o]
enduring wealth and prosperity.
19 My fruit is better than gold, yes, than pure
gold,
and my revenue than choice silver.[p]
20 On the way of duty I walk,
along the paths of justice,
21 Granting wealth to those who love me,
and filling their treasuries.

22 "The LORD begot me, the firstborn of his
ways,*
the forerunner of his prodigies of long
ago;[q]
23 From of old I was poured forth,*
at the first, before the earth.[r]
24 When there were no depths I was brought
forth,*
when there were no fountains or springs
of water;
25 Before the mountains were settled into
place,
before the hills, I was brought forth;
26 While as yet the earth and the fields were
not made,
nor the first clods of the world.

27 "When he established the heavens I was
there,[s]
when he marked out the vault over the
face of the deep;
28 When he made firm the skies above,
when he fixed fast the foundations of the
earth;
29 When he set for the sea its limit,
so that the waters should not transgress
his command;
30 Then was I beside him as his craftsman,*
and I was his delight day by day,[t]
Playing before him all the while,
31 playing on the surface of his earth;
and I found delight in the sons of men.

32 "So now, O children, listen to me;
33 instruction and wisdom do not reject!
Happy the man who obeys me,
and happy those who keep my ways,
34 Happy the man watching daily at my gates,
waiting at my doorposts;
35 For he who finds me finds life,[u]
and wins favor from the LORD;
36 But he who misses me harms himself;
all who hate me love death."

## CHAPTER 9

### The Two Banquets*

1 Wisdom has built her house,
she has set up her seven columns;
2 She has dressed her meat, mixed her wine,
yes, she has spread her table.
3 She has sent out her maidens; she calls*
from the heights out over the city:[v]
4 "Let whoever is simple turn in here;
to him who lacks understanding, I say,
5 Come, eat of my food,
and drink of the wine I have mixed!
6 Forsake foolishness that you may live;
advance in the way of understanding.
11 For by me your days will be multiplied
and the years of your life increased."[w]

7 He who corrects an arrogant man earns
insult;
and he who reproves a wicked man incurs
opprobrium.
8 Reprove not an arrogant man, lest he hate
you;
reprove a wise man, and he will love
you.[x]
9 Instruct a wise man, and he becomes still
wiser;
teach a just man, and he advances in
learning.

10 The beginning of wisdom is the fear of the
LORD,
and knowledge of the Holy One is
understanding.[y]
12 If you are wise, it is to your own advantage;
and if you are arrogant, you alone shall
bear it.

13 The woman Folly is fickle,[z]
she is inane, and knows nothing.
14 She sits at the door of her house
upon a seat on the city heights,
15 Calling to passers-by

o Prv 3, 16.
p Prv 3, 14.
q Wis 9, 9; Sir 1, 1; 24, 9.
r Sir 1, 4.
s Prv 3, 19; Sir 24, 4f.
t Wis 9, 9.
u Prv 3, 13-18; 4, 22.
v Prv 8, 1f.
w Prv 3, 2. 16; 4, 10; 10, 27.
x Sir 10, 27.
y Prv 1, 7; Jb 28, 28; Ps 111, 10; Sir 1, 16.
z 13-18; Prv, 7, 7-27.

*

8, 22–31: Wisdom is of divine origin. It is here represented as a being which existed before all things (22–26) and concurred with God when he planned and executed the creation of the universe, adorned it with beauty and variety, and established its wonderful order (27–30). Here that plurality of divine Persons is foreshadowed which was afterward to be fully revealed when Wisdom in the Person of Jesus Christ became incarnate.

8, 23: Poured forth: the exact meaning of the Hebrew is uncertain; the expression must imply the equivalent of "born." The Hebrews likened the movement of air and of spirit to that of liquids.

8, 24–26: The formless mass from which God created the heavens and the earth; cf Gn 1, 1f; 2, 4ff.

8, 30: His craftsman: furnishing God with the plan, as it were, for the creation of all things; cf Jb 38, 1f; Wis 7, 22—8, 1. I was his delight: the ever-present object of God's complacency.

9, 1–6. 13–18: Wisdom and folly are represented as matrons, each inviting people to her banquet. Wisdom offers the food and drink of divine doctrine and virtue which give life (1–6). Unstable and senseless folly furnishes the stolen bread and water of deceit and vice which bring death to her guests.

9, 3: She calls: i.e., indirectly, through her maidens; but the text could also mean that wisdom herself publicly proclaims her invitation.

as they go on their straight way:
16 "Let whoever is simple turn in here,
or who lacks understanding; for to him I say,
17 Stolen water is sweet,
and bread gotten secretly is pleasing!"*
18 Little he knows that the shades are there,
that in the depths of the nether world are her guests!*

## II: *First Collection of the Proverbs of Solomon**

### CHAPTER 10

1 The Proverbs of Solomon:
A wise son makes his father glad,
but a foolish son is a grief to his mother.[a]

2 Ill-gotten treasures profit nothing,
but virtue saves from death.[b]

3 The LORD permits not the just to hunger,
but the craving of the wicked he thwarts.

4 The slack hand impoverishes,
but the hand of the diligent enriches.[c]

5 A son who fills the granaries in summer is a credit;
a son who slumbers during harvest, a disgrace.

6 Blessings are for the head of the just,
but a rod for the back of the fool.

7 The memory of the just will be blessed,
but the name of the wicked will rot.

8 A wise man heeds commands,
but a prating fool will be overthrown.

9 He who walks honestly walks securely,
but he whose ways are crooked will fare badly.

10 He who winks at a fault causes trouble,
but he who frankly reproves promotes peace.

11 A fountain of life is the mouth of the just,
but the mouth of the wicked conceals violence.

12 Hatred stirs up disputes,
[d]but love covers all offenses.*

13 On the lips of the intelligent is found wisdom,
[but the mouth of the wicked conceals violence].

14 Wise men store up knowledge,
but the mouth of a fool is imminent ruin.

15 The rich man's wealth is his strong city;
the ruination of the lowly is their poverty.*

16 The just man's recompense leads to life,
the gains of the wicked, to sin.[e]

17 A path to life is his who heeds admonition,
but he who disregards reproof goes astray.[f]

18 It is the lips of the liar that conceal hostility;
but he who spreads accusations is a fool.

19 Where words are many, sin is not wanting;
but he who restrains his lips does well.[g]

20 Like choice silver is the just man's tongue;
the heart of the wicked is of little worth.

21 The just man's lips nourish many,
but fools die for want of sense.

22 It is the LORD's blessing that brings wealth,[h]
and no effort can substitute for it.*

23 Crime is the entertainment of the fool;
so is wisdom for the man of sense.

24 What the wicked man fears will befall him,
but the desire of the just will be granted.

25 When the tempest passes, the wicked man is no more;
but the just man is established forever.

26 As vinegar to the teeth, and smoke to the eyes,
is the sluggard to those who use him as a messenger.

a Prv 1, 1; 15, 20; 17, 25; 19, 13; 25, 1; 29, 15.
b Prv 11, 4. 6.
c Prv 6, 11; 12, 24; 13, 4; 20, 13; 28, 19.
d 1 Cor 13, 4-7; 1 Pt 4, 8.
e Prv 11, 18f.
f Prv 15, 10.
g Prv 17, 27; Sir 20, 17; Jas 1, 19.
h Sir 11, 22.

*

9, 17: The secrecy implies wrongdoing.

9, 18: The banquet chamber of folly is a tomb from which no one who enters it is released.

10, 1—22, 16: The varied contents of this first collection of Solomon's proverbs apply mostly to individual life. Each of its three hundred and seventy-five proverbs is meant to be distinct from the others, developing one idea through contrasting parallelism in chapters 10—15, and a climactic treatment in 16—22.

10, 12: Love covers all offenses: a favorite maxim of the Apostles; cf 1 Cor 13, 7; Jas 5, 20; 1 Pt 4, 8; also Prv 17, 9.

10, 15: The inspired author reflects upon the reality of the power of money and the defeat of poverty, without approving these things.

10, 22: The blessing of God rather than our own industry crowns our efforts with success; cf Ps 127, 1f; Mt 6, 25–34.

27 The fear of the LORD prolongs life,
but the years of the wicked are brief.[i]

28 The hope of the just brings them joy,
but the expectation of the wicked comes to nought.

29 The LORD is a stronghold to him who walks honestly,
but to evildoers, their downfall.

30 The just man will never be disturbed,
but the wicked will not abide in the land.

31 The mouth of the just yields wisdom,
but the perverse tongue will be cut off.

32 The lips of the just know how to please,
but the mouth of the wicked, how to pervert.

## CHAPTER 11

1 False scales are an abomination to the LORD,
but a full weight is his delight.[j]

2 When pride comes, disgrace comes;
but with the humble is wisdom.

3 The honesty of the upright guides them;
the faithless are ruined by their duplicity.

4 Wealth is useless on the day of wrath,[k]
but virtue saves from death.*

5 The honest man's virtue makes his way straight,
but by his wickedness the wicked man falls.[l]

6 The virtue of the upright saves them,
but the faithless are caught in their own intrigue.

7 When a wicked man dies his hope perishes,[m]
and what is expected from strength comes to nought.

8 The just man escapes trouble,
and the wicked man falls into it in his stead.

9 With his mouth the impious man would ruin his neighbor,[n]
but through their knowledge the just make their escape.

10 When the just prosper, the city rejoices;[o]
and when the wicked perish, there is jubilation.

11 Through the blessing of the righteous the city is exalted,
but through the mouth of the wicked it is overthrown.

12 He who reviles his neighbor has no sense,
but the intelligent man keeps silent.

13 A newsmonger reveals secrets,[p]
but a trustworthy man keeps a confidence.

14 For lack of guidance a people falls;
security lies in many counselors.[q]

15 He is in a bad way who becomes surety for another,[r]
but he who hates giving pledges is safe.

16 A gracious woman wins esteem,
but she who hates virtue is covered with shame.

[The slothful become impoverished,
but the diligent gain wealth.]

17 A kindly man benefits himself,
but a merciless man harms himself.

18 The wicked man makes empty profits,
but he who sows virtue has a sure reward.[s]

19 Virtue directs toward life,
but he who pursues evil does so to his death.

20 The depraved in heart are an abomination to the LORD,
but those who walk blamelessly are his delight.

21 Truly the evil man shall not go unpunished,
but those who are just shall escape.

22 Like a golden ring in a swine's snout
is a beautiful woman with a rebellious disposition.

23 The desire of the just ends only in good;
the expectation of the wicked is wrath.

24 One man is lavish yet grows still richer;
another is too sparing, yet is the poorer.

25 He who confers benefits will be amply enriched,

i Prv 3, 2; 4, 10; 9, 11; 14, 27.
j Prv 16, 11; 20, 10; Lv 19, 35f.
k Prv 10, 2.
l Prv 28, 18.
m Prv 10, 28; Wis 3, 18.
n Prv 29, 5.
o Prv 28, 12; 29, 2.
p Prv 20, 19.
q Prv 15, 22; 20, 18; 24, 6.
r Prv 6, 1f.
s Prv 10, 16.

*

11, 4: Wealth . . . death: not what a man is worth but what he is, counts before God.

and he who refreshes others will himself
be refreshed.

26 Him who monopolizes grain, the people
curse—
but blessings upon the head of him who
distributes it!

27 He who seeks the good commands favor,
but he who pursues evil will have evil
befall him.

28 He who trusts in his riches will fall,
but like green leaves the just flourish.[t]

29 He who upsets his household has empty air
for a heritage;
and the fool will become slave to the wise
man.

30 The fruit of virtue is a tree of life,
but violence takes lives away.

31 If the just man is punished on earth,
how much more the wicked and the
sinner![u]

## CHAPTER 12

1 He who loves correction loves knowledge,
but he who hates reproof is stupid.[v]

2 The good man wins favor from the LORD,
but the schemer is condemned by him.

3 No man is built up by wickedness,
but the root of the just will never be
disturbed.

4 A worthy wife is the crown of her
husband,[w]
but a disgraceful one is like rot in his
bones.

5 The plans of the just are legitimate;
the designs of the wicked are deceitful.

6 The words of the wicked are a deadly
ambush,
but the speech of the upright saves them.

7 The wicked are overthrown and are no
more,
but the house of the just stands firm.

8 According to his good sense a man is
praised,
but one with a warped mind is despised.

9 Better a lowly man who supports himself
than one of assumed importance who
lacks bread.[x]

10 The just man takes care of his beast,
but the heart of the wicked is merciless.

11 He who tills his own land has food in
plenty,
but he who follows idle pursuits is a
fool.[y]

12 The stronghold of evil men will be
demolished,
but the root of the just is enduring.

13 In the sin of his lips the evil man is
ensnared,
but the just comes free of trouble.

14 From the fruit of his words a man has his
fill of good things,[z]
and the work of his hands comes back to
reward him.*

15 The way of the fool seems right in his own
eyes,
but he who listens to advice is wise.

16 The fool immediately shows his anger,
but the shrewd man passes over an insult.

17 He tells the truth who states what he is sure
of,
but a lying witness speaks deceitfully.[a]

18 The prating of some men is like sword
thrusts,
but the tongue of the wise is healing.

19 Truthful lips endure forever,
the lying tongue, for only a moment.

20 Deceit is in the hands of those who plot
evil,
but those who counsel peace have joy.

21 No harm befalls the just,
but the wicked are overwhelmed with
misfortune.

22 Lying lips are an abomination to the LORD,[b]
but those who are truthful are his delight.

23 A shrewd man conceals his knowledge,
but the hearts of fools gush forth folly.

24 The diligent hand will govern,
but the slothful will be enslaved.[c]

25 Anxiety in a man's heart depresses it,

t Ps 52, 9f.
u 1 Pt 4, 18.
v Prv 15, 5. 10; 29, 1; Sir 19, 5; 21, 6.
w Sir 26, 1. 16.
x Sir 10, 26.
y Prv 28, 19; Sir 20, 27.
z Prv 13, 2; 18, 20.
a Prv 14, 5.
b Prv 6, 17.
c Prv 10, 4; 13, 4.
d Prv 15, 13; 17, 22.

* 12, 14: Cf Mt 7, 17; Gal 6, 8.

but a kindly word makes it glad.[d]

26 The just man surpasses his neighbor,
but the way of the wicked leads them astray.

27 The slothful man catches not his prey,
but the wealth of the diligent man is great.

28 In the path of justice there is life,
but the abominable way leads to death.

## CHAPTER 13

1 A wise son loves correction,
but the senseless one heeds no rebuke.

2 From the fruit of his words a man eats good things,[e]
but the treacherous one craves violence.

3 He who guards his mouth protects his life;
to open wide one's lips brings downfall.[f]

4 The soul of the sluggard craves in vain,
but the diligent soul is amply satisfied.

5 Anything deceitful the just man hates,
but the wicked brings shame and disgrace.

6 Virtue guards one who walks honestly,
but the downfall of the wicked is sin.[g]

7 One man pretends to be rich, yet has nothing;
another pretends to be poor, yet has great wealth.

8 A man's riches serve as ransom for his life,
but the poor man heeds no rebuke.

9 The light of the just shines gaily,
but the lamp* of the wicked goes out.[h]

10 The stupid man sows discord by his insolence,
but with those who take counsel is wisdom.

11 Wealth quickly gotten dwindles away,
but amassed little by little, it grows.[i]

12 Hope deferred makes the heart sick,
but a wish fulfilled is a tree of life.

13 He who despises the word* must pay for it,
but he who reveres the commandment will be rewarded.

14 The teaching of the wise is a fountain of life,
that a man may avoid the snares of death.

15 Good sense brings favor,
but the way of the faithless is their ruin.

16 The shrewd man does everything with prudence,
but the fool peddles folly.

17 A wicked messenger brings on disaster,
but a trustworthy envoy is a healing remedy.

18 Poverty and shame befall the man who disregards correction,
but he who heeds reproof is honored.

19 Lust indulged starves the soul,
but fools hate to turn from evil.

20 Walk with wise men and you will become wise,
but the companion of fools will fare badly.[j]

21 Misfortune pursues sinners,
but the just shall be recompensed with good.

22 The good man leaves an inheritance to his children's children,
but the wealth of the sinner is stored up for the just.

23 A lawsuit devours the tillage of the poor,
but some men perish for lack of a law court.

24 He who spares his rod hates his son,
but he who loves him takes care to chastise him.[k]

25 When the just man eats, his hunger is appeased;
but the belly of the wicked suffers want.

## CHAPTER 14

1 Wisdom builds her house,
but Folly tears hers down with her own hands.

2 He who walks uprightly fears the LORD,
but he who is devious in his ways spurns him.

3 In the mouth of the fool is a rod for his back,

e Prv 12, 14; 18, 20.
f Prv 18, 7; 21, 23.
g Prv 11, 3. 5f.
h Prv 24, 20.
i Prv 28, 20. 22.
j Sir 6, 34; 8, 8. 17.
k Prv 19, 18; 22, 15; 23, 13f; 29, 15; Sir 30, 1. 8-13.

*

13, 9: Light . . . lamp: symbols of life and prosperity; cf Prv 4, 18f.
13, 13: Word: advice, or God's law.

but the lips of the wise preserve them.

4 Where there are no oxen, the crib remains empty;
but large crops come through the strength of the bull.

5 A truthful witness does not lie,
but a false witness utters lies.[l]

6 The senseless man seeks in vain for wisdom,
but knowledge is easy to the man of intelligence.

7 To avoid the foolish man, take steps!
But knowing lips one meets with by surprise.

8 The shrewd man's wisdom gives him knowledge of his way,
but the folly of fools is their deception.

9 Guilt lodges in the tents of the arrogant,
but favor in the house of the just.

10 The heart knows its own bitterness,
and in its joy no one else shares.

11 The house of the wicked will be destroyed,
but the tent of the upright will flourish.[m]

12 Sometimes a way seems right to a man,
but the end of it leads to death![n]

13 Even in laughter the heart may be sad
and the end of joy may be sorrow.

14 The scoundrel suffers the consequences of his ways,
and the good man reaps the fruit of his paths.

15 The simpleton believes everything,
but the shrewd man measures his steps.

16 The wise man is cautious and shuns evil;
the fool is reckless and sure of himself.

17 The quick-tempered man makes a fool of himself,
but the prudent man is at peace.

18 The adornment of simpletons is folly,
but shrewd men gain the crown of knowledge.

19 Evil men must bow down before the good,
and the wicked, at the gates of the just.

20 Even by his neighbor the poor man is hated,
but the friends of the rich are many.[o]

21 He sins who despises the hungry;
but happy is he who is kind to the poor!

22 Do not those who plot evil go astray?
But those intent on good gain kindness and constancy.

23 In all labor there is profit,
but mere talk tends only to penury.

24 The crown of the wise is resourcefulness;
the diadem of fools is folly.

25 The truthful witness saves lives,
but he who utters lies is a betrayer.

26 In the fear of the LORD is a strong defense;
even for one's children he will be a refuge.

27 The fear of the LORD is a fountain of life,
that a man may avoid the snares of death.

28 In many subjects lies the glory of the king;
but if his people are few, it is the prince's ruin.

29 The patient man shows much good sense,
but the quick-tempered man displays folly at its height.[p]

30 A tranquil mind gives life to the body,
but jealousy rots the bones.

31 He who oppresses the poor blasphemes his Maker,
but he who is kind to the needy glorifies him.[q]

32 The wicked man is overthrown by his wickedness,
but the just man finds a refuge in his honesty.

33 In the heart of the intelligent wisdom abides,
but in the bosom of fools it is unknown.

34 Virtue exalts a nation,
but sin is a people's disgrace.

35 The king favors the intelligent servant,
but the worthless one incurs his wrath.

## CHAPTER 15

1 A mild answer calms wrath,[r]
but a harsh word stirs up anger.

2 The tongue of the wise pours out knowledge,
but the mouth of fools spurts forth folly.

3 The eyes of the LORD are in every place,

l Prv 12. 17.
m Prv 3, 33; 12, 7; 15, 25.
n Prv 16, 25.
o Prv 19, 4. 7; Sir 6, 8, 12.
p Prv 16, 32; 19, 11; Jas 1, 19.
q Prv 17, 5.
r Prv 25, 15; Sir 6, 5.

keeping watch on the evil and the good.

4 A soothing tongue is a tree of life,
but a perverse one crushes the spirit.

5 The fool spurns his father's admonition,
but prudent is he who heeds reproof.[s]

6 In the house of the just there are ample resources,
but the earnings of the wicked are in turmoil.

7 The lips of the wise disseminate knowledge,
but the heart of fools is perverted.

8 The sacrifice of the wicked is an abomination to the LORD,[t]
but the prayer of the upright is his delight.

9 The way of the wicked is an abomination to the LORD,
but he loves the man who pursues virtue.[u]

10 Severe punishment is in store for the man who goes astray;
he who hates reproof will die.

11 The nether world and the abyss* lie open before the LORD;
how much more the hearts of men!

12 The senseless man loves not to be reproved;
to wise men he will not go.

13 A glad heart lights up the face,
but by mental anguish the spirit is broken.[v]

14 The mind of the intelligent man seeks knowledge,
but the mouth of fools feeds on folly.

15 Every day is miserable for the depressed,
but a lighthearted man has a continual feast.

16 Better a little with fear of the LORD*
than a great fortune with anxiety.

17 Better a dish of herbs where love is
than a fatted ox and hatred with it.

18 An ill-tempered man stirs up strife,[w]
but a patient man allays discord.

19 The way of the sluggard is hemmed in as with thorns,
but the path of the diligent is a highway.

20 A wise son makes his father glad,
but a fool of a man despises his mother.[x]

21 Folly is joy to the senseless man,
but the man of understanding goes the straight way.

22 Plans fail when there is no counsel,
but they succeed when counselors are many.[y]

23 There is joy for a man in his utterance;
a word in season, how good it is![z]

24 The path of life leads the prudent man upward,
that he may avoid the nether world below.

25 The LORD overturns the house of the proud,
but he preserves intact the widow's landmark.

26 The wicked man's schemes are an abomination to the LORD,[a]
but the pure speak what is pleasing to him.

27 He who is greedy of gain brings ruin on his own house,
but he who hates bribes will live.

28 The just man weighs well his utterance,
but the mouth of the wicked pours out evil.

29 The LORD is far from the wicked,
but the prayer of the just he hears.

30 A cheerful glance brings joy to the heart;
good news invigorates the bones.

31 He who listens to salutary reproof[b]
will abide among the wise.

32 He who rejects admonition despises his own soul,
but he who heeds reproof gains understanding.

33 The fear of the LORD is training for wisdom,
and humility goes before honors.[c]

s Prv 12, 1; 13, 18.
t Prv 21, 27; Eccl 4, 17; Sir 34, 18ff; Is 1, 11-15.
u Prv 11, 20; 21, 21.
v Prv 12, 25; 17, 22; Sir 30, 22.
w Prv 26, 21; 29, 22; Sir 28, 11.
x Prv 10, 1; 29, 3.
y Prv 11, 14.
z Prv 25, 11; Sir 20, 6.
a Prv 6, 18.
b Prv 25, 12.
c Prv 1, 7; Sir 1, 24.

15, 11: Nether world . . . abyss: the abode of the dead, signifying the profound obscurity which is open nevertheless to the sight and power of God.

15, 16f: Not the amount of temporal goods but the virtue of their possessor makes them a source of happiness.

## CHAPTER 16

**1** Man may make plans in his heart,
but what the tongue utters is from the LORD.*

**2** All the ways of a man may be pure in his own eyes,
but it is the LORD who proves the spirit.[d]

**3** Entrust your works to the LORD,
and your plans will succeed.

**4** The LORD has made everything for his own ends,
even the wicked for the evil day.*

**5** Every proud man is an abomination to the LORD;[e]
I assure you that he will not go unpunished.

**6** By kindness and piety guilt is expiated,
and by the fear of the LORD man avoids evil.

**7** When the LORD is pleased with a man's ways,
he makes even his enemies be at peace with him.

**8** Better a little with virtue,
than a large income with injustice.

**9** In his mind a man plans his course,
but the LORD directs his steps.[f]

**10** The king's lips are an oracle;
no judgment he pronounces is false.*

**11** Balance and scales belong to the LORD;
all the weights used with them are his concern.[g]

**12** Kings have a horror of wrongdoing,
for by righteousness the throne endures.[h]

**13** The king takes delight in honest lips,
and the man who speaks what is right he loves.[i]

**14** The king's wrath is like messengers of death,[j]
but a wise man can pacify it.

**15** In the light of the king's countenance is life,
and his favor is like a rain cloud in spring.

**16** How much better to acquire wisdom than gold!
To acquire understanding is more desirable than silver.[k]

**17** The path of the upright avoids misfortune;
he who pays attention to his way safeguards his life.

**18** Pride goes before disaster,
and a haughty spirit before a fall.

**19** It is better to be humble with the meek than to share plunder with the proud.[l]

**20** He who plans a thing will be successful;
happy is he who trusts in the LORD!

**21** The wise man is esteemed for his discernment,
yet pleasing speech increases his persuasiveness.

**22** Good sense is a fountain of life to its possessor,
but folly brings chastisement on fools.

**23** The mind of the wise man makes him eloquent,
and augments the persuasiveness of his lips.

**24** Pleasing words are a honeycomb,
sweet to the taste and healthful to the body.

**25** Sometimes a way seems right to a man,
but the end of it leads to death![m]

**26** The laborer's appetite labors for him,
for his mouth urges him on.[n]

**27** A scoundrel is a furnace of evil,
and on his lips there is a scorching fire.

**28** An intriguer sows discord,
and a talebearer separates bosom friends.[o]

**29** A lawless man allures his neighbor,
and leads him into a way that is not good.

**30** He who winks his eye is plotting trickery;
he who compresses his lips has mischief ready.

**31** Gray hair is a crown of glory;[p]

d Prv 21, 2.
e Prv 6, 16f; 8, 13.
f Prv 19, 21; 20, 24.
g Prv 11, 1.
h Prv 25, 5.
i Prv 14, 35; 22, 11.
j Prv 19, 12; 20, 2.
k Prv 8, 10f. 19.
l Prv 11, 2.
m Prv 14, 12.
n Prv 10, 4.
o Prv 6, 14. 19; 17, 9; 26, 22; Sir 28, 15.
p Prv 20, 29.

*

16, 1: Words, like actions, often produce results different from those which were planned.

16, 4: Even the wicked, in their punishment, cannot escape glorifying God's justice.

16, 10: Decisions of supreme judicial authority were presumed disinterested and correct.

it is gained by virtuous living.

32 A patient man is better than a warrior,
and he who rules his temper, than he who takes a city.[q]

33 When the lot is cast into the lap,
its decision depends entirely on the LORD.*

## CHAPTER 17

1 Better a dry crust with peace
than a house full of feasting with strife.

2 An intelligent servant will rule over a worthless son,
and will share the inheritance with the brothers.*

3 The crucible for silver, and the furnace for gold,
but the tester of hearts is the LORD.

4 The evil man gives heed to wicked lips,
and listens to falsehood from a mischievous tongue.*

5 He who mocks the poor blasphemes his Maker;[r]
he who is glad at calamity will not go unpunished.

6 Grandchildren are the crown of old men,
and the glory of children is their parentage.

7 Fine words are out of place in a fool;
how much more, lying words in a noble!

8 A man who has a bribe to offer rates it a magic stone;
at every turn it brings him success.

9 He who covers up a misdeed fosters friendship,
but he who gossips about it separates friends.

10 A single reprimand does more for a man of intelligence
than a hundred lashes for a fool.

11 On rebellion alone is the wicked man bent,
but a merciless messenger will be sent against him.

12 Face a bear robbed of her cubs,
but never a fool in his folly!

13 If a man returns evil for good,
from his house evil will not depart.[s]

14 The start of strife is like the opening of a dam;
therefore, check a quarrel before it begins!

15 He who condones the wicked,[t] he who condemns the just,
are both an abomination to the LORD.

16 Of what use in the fool's hand are the means
to buy wisdom, since he has no mind for it?

17 He who is a friend is always a friend,
and a brother is born for the time of stress.[u]

18 Senseless is the man who gives his hand in pledge,
who becomes surety for his neighbor.[v]

19 He who loves strife loves guilt;[w]
he who builds his gate high* courts disaster.

20 He who is perverse in heart finds no good,
and a double-tongued man falls into trouble.

21 To be a fool's parent is grief for a man;
the father of a numskull has no joy.

22 A joyful heart is the health of the body,
but a depressed spirit dries up the bones.[x]

23 The wicked man accepts a concealed bribe
to pervert the course of justice.

24 The man of intelligence fixes his gaze on wisdom,[y]
but the eyes of a fool are on the ends of the earth.

25 A foolish son is vexation to his father,
and bitter sorrow to her who bore him.[z]

26 It is wrong to fine an innocent man,
but beyond reason to scourge princes.

---

q Prv 14, 29.
r Prv 14, 31.
s Mt 5, 39; Rom 12, 17; 1 Thes 5, 15; 1 Pt 3, 9.
t Prv 24, 24; Is 5, 23.
u Prv 18, 24.
v Prv 6, 1f; 11, 15.
w Prv 15, 18.
x Prv 12, 25; 15, 13.
y Eccl 8, 1.
z Prv 10, 1; 29, 15.

---

*

16, 33: The favorable or unfavorable result of chance depends on God. Deciding strifes and doubts by lot was practiced by the ancient Hebrews; cf Ex 28, 15–30; Lv 16, 8; Jos 7, 14; 1 Sm 10, 20f.

17, 2: Intelligence and ability are esteemed more highly than nobility of blood.

17, 4: To justify his own evil ways, a wicked man judges evil of others. Cf Mt 7, 1–5.

17, 19: Builds . . . high: a symbol of arrogance.

27 He who spares his words is truly wise,
and he who is chary of speech is a man of intelligence.[a]

28 Even a fool, if he keeps silent, is considered wise;
if he closes his lips, intelligent.

## CHAPTER 18

1 In estrangement one seeks pretexts:
with all persistence he picks a quarrel.

2 The fool takes no delight in understanding,
but rather in displaying what he thinks.

3 With wickedness comes contempt,
and with disgrace comes scorn.

4 The words from a man's mouth are deep waters,
but the source of wisdom is a flowing brook.[b]

5 It is not good to be partial to the guilty,
and so to reject a rightful claim.[c]

6 The fool's lips lead him into strife,
and his mouth provokes a beating.

7 The fool's mouth is his ruin;
his lips are a snare to his life.[d]

8 The words of a talebearer are like dainty morsels
that sink into one's inmost being.[e]

9 The man who is slack in his work
is own brother to the man who is destructive.

10 The name of the LORD is a strong tower;*
the just man runs to it and is safe.

11 The rich man's wealth is his strong city;[f]
he fancies it a high wall.

12 Before his downfall a man's heart is haughty,[g]
but humility goes before honors.*

13 He who answers before he hears[h] —
his is the folly and the shame.*

14 A man's spirit sustains him in infirmity—
but a broken spirit who can bear?

15 The mind of the intelligent gains knowledge,
and the ear of the wise seeks knowledge.

16 A man's gift clears the way for him,
and gains him access to great men.[i]

17 The man who pleads his case first seems to be in the right;
then his opponent comes and puts him to the test.

18 The lot puts an end to disputes,
and is decisive in a controversy between the mighty.*

19 A brother is a better defense than a strong city,
and a friend is like the bars of a castle.

20 From the fruit of his mouth a man has his fill;*
with the yield of his lips he sates himself.[j]

21 Death and life are in the power of the tongue;[k]
those who make it a friend shall eat its fruit.

22 He who finds a wife finds happiness;
it is a favor he receives from the LORD.[l]

23 The poor man implores,
but the rich man answers harshly.

24 Some friends bring ruin on us,
but a true friend is more loyal than a brother.[m]

## CHAPTER 19

1 Better a poor man who walks in his integrity
than he who is crooked in his ways and rich.[n]

2 Without knowledge even zeal is not good;
and he who acts hastily, blunders.

3 A man's own folly upsets his way,
but his heart is resentful against the LORD.

a Prv 10, 19; Sir 1, 21; Jas 1, 19.
b Prv 20, 5; Jn 7, 38.
c Prv 24, 23; 28, 21.
d Prv 10, 14; 12, 13; 13, 3; Eccl 10, 12.
e Prv 26, 22.
f Prv 10, 15.
g Prv 11, 2; 16, 18; Sir 10, 15.
h Sir 11, 8.
i Prv 21, 14.
j Prv 12, 14; 13, 2.
k Sir 37, 18.
l Prv 12, 4; 19, 14; Sir 7, 26.
m Prv 17, 17.
n Prv 28, 6.

*

18, 10f: Religion is a strong support and sure refuge in the struggle of life. The rich foolishly rely on their wealth for such support.

18, 12: Compare the Savior's words: "Whoever exalts himself shall be humbled, but whoever humbles himself shall be exalted" (Mt 23, 12).

18, 13: To speak without first listening is characteristic of a fool; cf Prv 10, 14; Sir 11, 8.

18, 18: See note on Prv 16, 33.

18, 20f: Everyone must accept the consequences, of benefit or harm to himself, which his words produce.

4 Wealth adds many friends,
but the friend of the poor man deserts him.[o]

5 The false witness will not go unpunished,
and he who utters lies will not escape.[p]

6 Many curry favor with a noble;
all are friends of the man who has something to give.

7 All the poor man's brothers hate him;
how much more do his friends shun him!

8 He who gains intelligence is his own best friend;
he who keeps understanding will be successful.

9 The false witness will not go unpunished,
and he who utters lies will perish.

10 Luxury is not befitting a fool;
much less should a slave rule over princes.

11 It is good sense in a man to be slow to anger,
and it is his glory to overlook an offense.

12 The king's wrath is like the roaring of a lion,
but his favor, like dew on the grass.[q]

13 The foolish son is ruin to his father,[r]
and the nagging of a wife is a persistent leak.

14 Home and possessions are an inheritance from parents,
but a prudent wife is from the LORD.[s]

15 Laziness plunges a man into deep sleep,
and the sluggard must go hungry.[t]

16 He who keeps the precept keeps his life,
but the despiser of the word will die.[u]

17 He who has compassion on the poor lends to the LORD,[v]
and he will repay him for his good deed.*

18 Chastise your son, for in this there is hope;
but do not desire his death.[w]

19 The man of violent temper pays the penalty;
even if you rescue him, you will have it to do again.

20 Listen to counsel and receive instruction,
that you may eventually become wise.

21 Many are the plans in a man's heart,
but it is the decision of the LORD that endures.[x]

22 From a man's greed comes his shame;
rather be a poor man than a liar.

23 The fear of the LORD is an aid to life;
one eats and sleeps without being visited by misfortune.

24 The sluggard loses his hand in the dish;
he will not even lift it to his mouth.[y]

25 If you beat an arrogant man, the simple learn a lesson;
if you rebuke an intelligent man, he gains knowledge.[z]

26 He who mistreats his father, or drives away his mother,
is a worthless and disgraceful son.[a]

27 If a son ceases to hear instruction,
he wanders from words of knowledge.

28 An unprincipled witness perverts justice,
and the mouth of the wicked pours out iniquity.

29 Rods are prepared for the arrogant,
and blows for the backs of fools.[b]

## CHAPTER 20

1 Wine is arrogant, strong drink is riotous;
none who goes astray for it is wise.[c]

2 The dread of the king is as when a lion roars;[d]
he who incurs his anger forfeits his life.

3 It is honorable for a man to shun strife,
while every fool starts a quarrel.

4 In seedtime the sluggard plows not;
when he looks for the harvest, it is not there.

5 The intention in the human heart is like water far below the surface,
but the man of intelligence draws it forth.[e]

o Prv 14, 20; Sir 13, 20ff.
p Dt 19, 16-20; Dn 13, 61.
q Prv 20, 2.
r Prv 10, 1; 17, 25.
s Prv 18, 22.
t Prv 6, 9ff.
u Prv 13, 13; 16, 17.
v Prv 14, 21; 22, 9; 28, 27.
w Prv 13, 24; 23, 13f.
x Prv 16, 9.
y Prv 26, 15.
z Prv 17, 10; 21, 11.
a Sir 3, 16.
b Prv 26, 3.
c Prv 23, 29-35.
d Prv 19, 12.
e Prv 18, 4.

* 19, 17: Cf Mt 25, 34-40.

**6** Many are declared to be men of virtue:
but who can find one worthy of trust?

**7** When a man walks in integrity and justice,
happy are his children after him!

**8** A king seated on the throne of judgment
dispels all evil with his glance.

**9** Who can say, "I have made my heart clean,[f]
I am cleansed of my sin"?*

**10** Varying weights, varying measures,
are both an abomination to the LORD.[g]

**11** Even by his manners the child betrays
whether his conduct is innocent and right.

**12** The ear that hears, and the eye that sees—
the LORD has made them both.

**13** Love not sleep, lest you be reduced to poverty;
eyes wide open mean abundant food.

**14** "Bad, bad!" says the buyer;
but once he has gone his way, he boasts.*

**15** Like gold or a wealth of corals,
wise lips are a precious ornament.

**16** Take his garment who becomes surety for another,[h]
and for strangers yield it up!*

**17** The bread of deceit is sweet to a man,
but afterward his mouth will be filled with gravel.

**18** Plans made after advice succeed;
so with wise guidance wage your war.

**19** A newsmonger reveals secrets;
so have nothing to do with a babbler!

**20** If one curses his father or mother,
his lamp will go out* at the coming of darkness.[i]

**21** Possessions gained hastily at the outset
will in the end not be blessed.

**22** Say not, "I will repay evil!"
Trust in the LORD and he will help you.[j]

**23** Varying weights are an abomination to the LORD,
and false scales are not good.[k]

**24** Man's steps are from the LORD;[l]
how, then, can a man understand his way?*

**25** Rashly to pledge a sacred gift is a trap for a man,
or to regret a vow once made.*

**26** A wise king winnows the wicked,
and threshes them under the cartwheel.

**27** A lamp from the LORD is the breath of man;
it searches through all his inmost being.

**28** Kindness and piety safeguard the king,
and he upholds his throne by justice.[m]

**29** The glory of young men is their strength,
and the dignity of old men is gray hair.[n]

**30** Evil is cleansed away by bloody lashes,
and a scourging to the inmost being.

## CHAPTER 21

**1** Like a stream is the king's heart in the hand of the Lord;
wherever it pleases him, he directs it.

**2** All the ways of a man may be right in his own eyes,
but it is the LORD who proves hearts.[o]

**3** To do what is right and just[p]
is more acceptable to the LORD than sacrifice.*

**4** Haughty eyes and a proud heart—
the tillage of the wicked is sin.

**5** The plans of the diligent are sure of profit,
but all rash haste leads certainly to poverty.

f 1 Kgs 8, 46; 2 Chr 6, 36; Eccl 7, 20; 1 Jn 1, 8.
g Prv 11, 1; 20, 23.
h Prv 27, 13.
i Prv 30, 11. 17; Ex 21, 17; Lv 20, 9; Mt 15, 4.
j Prv 24, 29; Sir 28, 1; Mt 5, 39; Rom 12, 17. 19; 1 Thes 5, 15; 1 Pt 3, 9.
k Prv 11, 1; 20, 10.
l Prv 16, 9.
m Prv 16, 12.
n Prv 16, 31.
o Prv 16, 2.
p 1 Sm 15, 22; Hos 6, 6.

*

20, 9: Man can be free of sin only by the power of God. Cf 1 Kgs 8, 46ff; Jb 4, 17; 14, 4; Pss 51, 2ff; 130, 3f; Rom 3, 23f; 1 Jn 1, 8.

20, 14: What one wishes to buy is valued cheaply in order that it may be obtained at a low price; once purchased, it is deemed more valuable.

20, 16: Caution is again advised in the matter of becoming surety; cf Prv 6, 1ff.

20, 20: His lamp will go out: misfortune, even death, awaits him; cf Prv 13, 9; Ex 21, 17.

20, 24: Man is dependent upon God and cannot fully foresee his own course.

20, 25: This verse cautions against making vows without proper reflection; cf Dt 23, 22ff; Eccl 5, 4f.

21, 3: External rites or sacrifices do not please God unless accompanied by internal worship and right moral conduct; cf Prv 15, 8; 21, 27; Is 1, 11–15; Am 5, 22; Mal 1, 12.

**6** He who makes a fortune by a lying tongue
is chasing a bubble over deadly snares.

**7** The oppression of the wicked will sweep them away,
because they refuse to do what is right.

**8** The way of the culprit is crooked,
but the conduct of the innocent is right.

**9** It is better to dwell in a corner of the housetop
than in a roomy house with a quarrelsome woman.[q]

**10** The soul of the wicked man desires evil;
his neighbor finds no pity in his eyes.

**11** When the arrogant man is punished, the simple are the wiser;
when the wise man is instructed, he gains knowledge.[r]

**12** The just man appraises the house of the wicked:
there is one who brings down the wicked to ruin.

**13** He who shuts his ear to the cry of the poor
will himself also call and not be heard.

**14** A secret gift allays anger,
and a concealed present, violent wrath.

**15** To practice justice is a joy for the just,
but terror for evildoers.[s]

**16** The man who strays from the way of good sense
will abide in the assembly of the shades.*

**17** He who loves pleasure will suffer want;
he who loves wine and perfume will not be rich.

**18** The wicked man serves as ransom for the just,*
and the faithless man for the righteous.[t]

**19** It is better to dwell in a wilderness
than with a quarrelsome and vexatious wife.

**20** Precious treasure remains in the house of the wise,
but the fool consumes it.

**21** He who pursues justice and kindness
will find life and honor.

**22** The wise man storms a city of the mighty,
and overthrows the stronghold in which it trusts.

**23** He who guards his mouth and his tongue
keeps himself from trouble.[u]

**24** Arrogant is the name for the man of overbearing pride
who acts with scornful effrontery.

**25** The sluggard's propensity slays him,
for his hands refuse to work.

**26** Some are consumed with avarice all the day,
but the just man gives unsparingly.

**27** The sacrifice of the wicked is an abomination,
the more so when they offer it with a bad intention.[v]

**28** The false witness will perish,[w]
but he who listens will finally have his say.

**29** The wicked man is brazenfaced,
but the upright man pays heed to his ways.

**30** There is no wisdom, no understanding,
no counsel, against the LORD.

**31** The horse is equipped for the day of battle,
but victory is the LORD's.

## CHAPTER 22

**1** A good name is more desirable than great riches,
and high esteem, than gold and silver.[x]

**2** Rich and poor have a common bond:
the LORD is the maker of them all.[y]

**3** The shrewd man perceives evil and hides,
while simpletons continue on and suffer the penalty.[z]

**4** The reward of humility and fear of the LORD
is riches, honor and life.

**5** Thorns and snares are on the path of the crooked;

q Prv 21, 19; 25, 24; 27, 15; Sir 25, 23.
r Prv 19, 25.
s Prv 10, 29.
t Prv 11, 8.
u Prv 13, 3.
v Prv 15, 8; Sir 34, 18ff.
w Prv 19, 5. 9.
x Eccl 7, 1.
y Prv 29, 13.
z Prv 27, 12.

*

21, 16: Assembly of the shades: cf note on Jb 26, 5.

21, 18: Wicked . . . ransom for the just: exemplified in the history of God's chosen people whom he ransomed from Egypt at the cost of the life of Pharaoh and his army (Ex 14, 23–31), and from Babylon by giving to Cyrus, the Persian conqueror, Egypt, Ethiopia and Seba, the richest lands of the world (Is 43, 1ff).

he who would safeguard his life will shun
them.

6 Train a boy in the way he should go;
even when he is old, he will not swerve
from it.

7 The rich rule over the poor,
and the borrower is the slave of the
lender.

8 He who sows iniquity reaps calamity,[a]
and the rod destroys his labors.

9 The kindly man will be blessed,
for he gives of his sustenance to the poor.

10 Expel the arrogant man and discord goes
out;
strife and insult cease.

11 The LORD loves the pure of heart;[b]
the man of winning speech has the king
for his friend.

12 The eyes of the LORD safeguard knowledge,
but he defeats the projects of the faithless.

13 The sluggard says, "A lion is outside;[c]
in the streets I might be slain."*

14 The mouth of the adulteress is a deep pit;[d]
he with whom the LORD is angry will fall
into it.

15 Folly is close to the heart of a child,
but the rod of discipline will drive it far
from him.

16 He who oppresses the poor to enrich himself
will yield up his gains to the rich as sheer
loss.*

## III: *Sayings of the Wise**

17 The sayings of the wise:*

Incline your ear, and hear my words,[e]
and apply your heart to my doctrine;
18 For it will be well if you keep them in your
bosom,
if they all are ready on your lips.
19 That your trust may be in the LORD,
I make known to you the words of
Amen-em-Ope.*
20 Have I not written for you the "Thirty,"
with counsels and knowledge,
21 To teach you truly
how to give a dependable report to one
who sends you?

22 Injure not the poor because they are poor,
nor crush the needy at the gate;
23 For the LORD will defend their cause,[f]
and will plunder the lives of those who
plunder them.

24 Be not friendly with a hotheaded man,
nor the companion of a wrathful man,
25 Lest you learn his ways,
and get yourself into a snare.

26 Be not one of those who give their hand in
pledge,
of those who become surety for debts;[g]
27 For if you have not the means to pay,
your bed will be taken from under you.

28 Remove not the ancient landmark
which your fathers set up.[h]

29 You see a man skilled at his work?
He will stand in the presence of kings;
he will not stand in the presence of
obscure men.

## CHAPTER 23

1 When you sit down to dine with a ruler,
keep in mind who is before you;
2 And put a knife to your throat*
if you have a ravenous appetite.
3 Do not desire his delicacies;
they are deceitful food.
4 Toil not to gain wealth,
cease to be concerned about it;
5 While your glance flits to it, it is gone!
for assuredly it grows wings,
like the eagle that flies toward heaven.

6 Do not take food with a grudging man,

a Jb 4, 8; Sir 7, 3; Hos 8, 7.
b Mt 5, 8.
c Prv 26, 13.
d Prv 23, 27.
e Prv 5, 1.
f Prv 23, 11.
g Prv 6, 1f; 11, 15; 17, 18.
h Prv 23, 10; Dt 19, 14; 27, 17.

22, 13: To avoid the effort required for doing good, the sluggard exaggerates the difficulties that must be overcome.

22, 16: Money gained by exploiting the poor is in turn lost to those who are more wealthy.

22, 17—24, 22: This collection of proverbs, introduced as sayings of the wise, is given in the more intimate and personal form of an address to a pupil called the son and is arranged in strophes instead of couplets.

22, 17—23, 35: The maxims warn against: oppression of the poor and defenseless (22, 22f), anger (24f), giving surety for debts (26f), bad manners at a king's table (23, 1f), anxiety for riches (4f), a grudging host (6ff), intemperance in food and drink (19ff. 29–35), and adultery (26ff). They exhort to: careful workmanship (22, 29), respect for the rights of orphans (23, 10f), correction of the young (13f), filial piety (15f. 22–25), and fear of the Lord (17f).

22, 19f: Amen-em-Ope: an Egyptian scribe to whom is attributed a collection of maxims in Thirty chapters (v 20) composed for the instruction of his children and addressed to a young man who wishes to enter upon a career. The inspired editor of Proverbs does not translate these, but uses their materials in constructing a similar collection of proverbs.

23, 2: Put a knife to your throat: a proverbial metaphor for self-restraint.

and do not desire his dainties;
7 For in his greed he is like a storm.
''Eat and drink,'' he says to you,
though his heart is not with you;
8 The little you have eaten you will vomit up,
and you will have wasted your agreeable words.
9 Speak not for the fool's hearing;
he will despise the wisdom of your words.[i]

10 Remove not the ancient landmark,[j]
nor invade the fields of orphans;
11 For their redeemer is strong;
he will defend their cause against you.[k]

12 Apply your heart to instruction,
and your ears to words of knowledge.

13 Withhold not chastisement from a boy;
if you beat him with the rod, he will not die.[l]
14 Beat him with the rod,[m]
and you will save him from the nether world.

15 My son, if your heart be wise,
my own heart also will rejoice;
16 And my inmost being will exult,
when your lips speak what is right.

17 Let not your heart emulate sinners,[n]
but be zealous for the fear of the LORD always;
18 For you will surely have a future,
and your hope will not be cut off.[o]

19 Hear, my son, and be wise,
and guide your heart in the right way.
20 Consort not with winebibbers,
nor with those who eat meat to excess;
21 For the drunkard and the glutton come to poverty,
and torpor clothes a man in rags.

22 Listen to your father who begot you,
and despise not your mother when she is old.
23 Get the truth, and sell it not—
wisdom, instruction and understanding.
24 The father of a just man will exult with glee;
he who begets a wise son will have joy in him.[p]
25 Let your father and mother have joy;
let her who bore you exult.

26 My son, give me your heart,
and let your eyes keep to my ways.
27 For the harlot is a deep ditch,
and the adulteress a narrow pit;
28 Yes, she lies in wait like a robber,[q]
and increases the faithless among men.
29 Who scream? Who shriek?*
Who have strife? Who have anxiety?
Who have wounds for nothing?
Who have black eyes?
30 Those who linger long over wine,
those who engage in trials of blended wine.[r]
31 Look not on the wine when it is red,
when it sparkles in the glass.
It goes down smoothly;
32 but in the end it bites like a serpent,
or like a poisonous adder.
33 Your eyes behold strange sights,
and your heart utters disordered thoughts;
34 You are like one now lying in the depths of the sea,
now sprawled at the top of the mast.
35 ''They struck me, but it pained me not;
they beat me, but I felt it not;
When shall I awake
to seek wine once again?''*

## CHAPTER 24

1 Be not emulous of evil men,*
and desire not to be with them;[s]
2 For their hearts plot violence,
and their lips speak of foul play.

3 By wisdom is a house built,
by understanding is it made firm;
4 And by knowledge are its rooms filled
with every precious and pleasing possession.
5 A wise man is more powerful than a strong man,
and a man of knowledge than a man of might;[t]
6 For it is by wise guidance that you wage your war,
and the victory is due to a wealth of counselors.[u]

7 For a fool, to be silent is wisdom;[v]
not to open his mouth at the gate.*
8 He who plots evil doing—

i Prv 9, 7.
j Prv 22, 28.
k Prv 22, 23.
l Prv 13, 24; 19, 18; Sir 30, 1.
m Prv 29, 15. 17.
n Prv 3, 31; 24, 1.19.
o Prv 24, 14.
p Prv 10, 1.
q Prv 7, 10-27.
r Prv 20, 1; Sir 19, 2; Hos 4, 11.
s Prv 3, 31; 23, 17.
t Prv 21, 22.
u Prv 20, 18.
v Sir 6, 21.

*

23, 29–35: A vivid description of the evil effects, physical and psychological, of drunkenness.

23, 35: Wine makes the drunkard insensible to bodily and moral harm. His one desire is to indulge again.

24, 1–22: These verses continue an exhortation to wisdom (vv 3–7. 13f), and against: violence (1f), pride and intrigue (8f), callousness (10–12), injustice (15f), joy in the failure of others (17f) or scandal at their success (19f), and rebellion against authority (21f).

24, 7: At the gate: of the city, where justice was administered and public affairs discussed; see note on Ru 4, 1. Cf also Pss 69, 13; 127, 5; Prv 22, 22; 31, 23. 31.

men call him an intriguer.
**9** Beyond intrigue and folly and sin,
it is arrogance that men find abominable.

**10** If you remain indifferent* in time of adversity,
your strength will depart from you.
**11** Rescue those who are being dragged to death,*
and from those tottering to execution withdraw not.
**12** If you say, "I know not this man!"
does not he who tests hearts perceive it?
He who guards your life knows it,
and he will repay each one according to his deeds.[w]

**13** If you eat honey, my son, because it is good,
if virgin honey is sweet to your taste;
**14** Such, you must know, is wisdom to your soul.
If you find it, you will have a future,
and your hope will not be cut off.[x]

**15** Lie not in wait against the home of the just man,
ravage not his dwelling place;
**16** For the just man* falls seven times and rises again,
but the wicked stumble to ruin.

**17** Rejoice not when your enemy falls,
and when he stumbles, let not your heart exult,
**18** Lest the LORD see it, be displeased with you,
and withdraw his wrath from your enemy.

**19** Be not provoked with evildoers,
nor envious of the wicked;
**20** For the evil man has no future,
the lamp of the wicked will be put out.[y]

**21** My son, fear the LORD and the king;*
have nothing to do with those who rebel against them;
**22** For suddenly arises the destruction they send,
and the ruin from either one, who can measure?

## IV: *Other Sayings of the Wise**

**23** These also are sayings of the wise:

To show partiality in judgment is not good.[z]
**24** He who says to the wicked man, "You are just"—
men will curse him, people will denounce him;
**25** But those who convict the evildoer will fare well,
and on them will come the blessing of prosperity.
**26** He gives a kiss on the lips*
who makes an honest reply.

**27** Complete your outdoor tasks,
and arrange your work in the field;
afterward you can establish your house.*

**28** Be not a witness against your neighbor without just cause,[a]
thus committing folly with your lips.
**29** Say not, "As he did to me, so will I do to him;[b]
I will repay the man according to his deeds."*

**30** I passed by the field of the sluggard,
by the vineyard of the man without sense;
**31** And behold! it was all overgrown with thistles;
its surface was covered with nettles,
and its stone wall broken down.
**32** And as I gazed at it, I reflected;
I saw and learned the lesson:
**33** A little sleep, a little slumber,[c]
a little folding of the arms to rest—
**34** Then will poverty come upon you like a highwayman,
and want like an armed man.

## V: *Second Collection of the Proverbs of Solomon*

## CHAPTER 25

**1** These also are proverbs of Solomon.[d] The men of Hezekiah,* king of Judah, transmitted them.

w Ps 62, 13; Sir 16, 12; Mt 16, 27; Rom 2, 6.
x Prv 23, 18.
y Prv 13, 9.
z Prv 18, 5; 28, 21; Lv 19, 15; Dt 1, 17; 16, 19.
a Prv 19, 5; 25, 18.
b Prv 20, 22.
c 33f: Prv 6, 10f.
d Prv 1, 1.

24, 10: Indifferent: to those who suffer unjustly.
24, 11: Rescue . . . death: most probably refers to the legal rescue of those unjustly condemned to death.
24, 16: The just man overcomes every misfortune which oppresses him. Seven times: i.e., an indefinite number; cf Mt 18, 21f; Lk 17, 4.
24, 21f: One owes obedience to God and to supreme civil authority (Mt 22, 21; Rom 13, 1ff; 1 Pt 2, 13f). The punishments for failure in either duty transcend the limits of private justice.
24, 23–34: This collection of sayings continues in the same vein as the preceding: it instructs in fairness (23–26) and preparation for the future (27); and warns against vengeance (28f) and slothfulness (30–34).
24, 26: He gives a kiss on the lips: shows himself a true friend.
24, 27: This verse is commonly interpreted as advocating careful and practical preparation for marriage.
24, 29: This verse indicates great progress from the principle on the law of Talion (see note on Ex 21, 23ff) toward the teaching found in Rom 12, 17ff. Cf also Prv 25, 21ff.
25, 1: The men of Hezekiah: literary men at the royal court

2 God has glory in what he conceals,
kings have glory in what they fathom.
3 As the heavens in height, and the earth in depth,
the heart of kings is unfathomable.

4 Remove the dross from silver,
and it comes forth perfectly purified;
5 Remove the wicked from the presence of the king,
and his throne is made firm through righteousness.

6 Claim no honor in the king's presence,*
nor occupy the place of great men;
7 For it is better that you be told, "Come up closer!"
than that you be humbled before the prince.[e]

8 What your eyes have seen
bring not forth hastily against an opponent;
For what will you do later on
when your neighbor puts you to shame?
9 Discuss your case with your neighbor,
but another man's secret do not disclose;
10 Lest, hearing it, he reproach you,
and your ill repute cease not.

11 Like golden apples in silver settings
are words spoken at the proper time.

12 Like a golden earring, or a necklace of fine gold,
is a wise reprover to an obedient ear.

13 Like the coolness of snow in the heat of the harvest
is a faithful messenger for the one who sends him.
[He refreshes the soul of his master.]

14 Like clouds and wind when no rain follows
is the man who boastfully promises what he never gives.

15 By patience is a ruler persuaded,[f]
and a soft tongue will break a bone.

16 If you find honey, eat only what you need,
lest you become glutted with it and vomit it up.

17 Let your foot be seldom in your neighbor's house,
lest he have more than enough of you, and hate you.

18 Like a club, or a sword, or a sharp arrow,
is the man who bears false witness against his neighbor.

19 Like an infected tooth or an unsteady foot
is [dependence on] a faithless man in time of trouble.

20 Like a moth in clothing, or a maggot in wood,
sorrow gnaws at the human heart.[g]

21 If your enemy be hungry, give him food to eat,*
if he be thirsty, give him to drink;[h]

22 For live coals you will heap on his head,
and the LORD will vindicate you.

23 The north wind brings rain,
and a backbiting tongue an angry countenance.

24 It is better to dwell in a corner of the housetop
than in a roomy house with a quarrelsome woman.[i]

25 Like cool water to one faint from thirst
is good news from a far country.

26 Like a troubled fountain or a polluted spring
is a just man who gives way before the wicked.

27 To eat too much honey is not good;
nor to seek honor after honor.*

28 Like an open city with no defenses
is the man with no check on his feelings.

## CHAPTER 26*

1 Like snow in summer, or rain in harvest,
honor for a fool is out of place.

2 Like the sparrow in its flitting, like the swallow in its flight,
a curse uncalled-for arrives nowhere.

3 The whip for the horse, the bridle for the ass,
and the rod for the back of fools.[j]

e Lk 14, 8ff.
f Prv 15, 1. 4.
g Sir 30, 24.
h Rom 12, 20.
i Prv 21, 9.
j Pv 19, 29; Sir 33, 25.

* of Hezekiah who are represented as transcribing the proverbs from other collections. Hezekiah was a reformer of national religious life (2 Chr 29, 25–30).

25, 6f: Compare the lesson on humility which was taught by Christ (Lk 14, 7–11).

25, 21f: Charity is invaluable in resolving enmities and restoring peace. Live coals: i.e., either remorse and embarrassment for the harm done, or increased punishment for refusing reconciliation. Cf Mt 5, 44; Rom 12, 20.

25, 27: Nor . . . honor after honor: the text is uncertain.

26, 1–28: Concrete images describe the vices of fools (1–12), of sluggards (13–16), of meddlers (17–19), of talebearers (20ff), and of flatterers (23–28).

4 Answer not the fool according to his folly,*
lest you too become like him.

5 Answer the fool according to his folly,
lest he become wise in his own eyes.

6 He cuts off his feet, he drinks down
violence,
who sends messages by a fool.

7 A proverb in the mouth of a fool*
hangs limp, like crippled legs.

8 Like one who entangles the stone in the
sling
is he who gives honor to a fool.

9 Like a thorn stick brandished by the hand of
a drunkard
is a proverb in the mouth of fools.

10 Like an archer wounding all who pass by
is he who hires a drunken fool.

11 As the dog returns to his vomit,
so the fool repeats his folly.[k]

12 You see a man wise in his own eyes?
There is more hope for a fool than for
him.

13 The sluggard says, "There is a lion in the
street,
a lion in the middle of the square!"[l]

14 The door turns on its hinges,
the sluggard, on his bed!

15 The sluggard loses his hand in the dish;
he is too weary to lift it to his mouth.[m]

16 The sluggard imagines himself wiser
than seven men who answer with good
sense.

17 Like the man who seizes a passing dog by
the ears
is he who meddles in a quarrel not his
own.

18 Like a crazed archer
scattering firebrands and deadly arrows

19 Is the man who deceives his neighbor,
and then says, "I was only joking."

20 For lack of wood, the fire dies out;
and when there is no talebearer, strife
subsides.

21 What a bellows is to live coals, what wood
is to fire,
such is a contentious man in enkindling
strife.[n]

22 The words of a talebearer are like dainty
morsels
that sink into one's inmost being.[o]

23 Like a glazed finish on earthenware
are smooth lips with a wicked heart.

24 With his lips an enemy pretends,
but in his inmost being he maintains
deceit;

25 When he speaks graciously, trust him not,[p]
for seven abominations* are in his heart.

26 A man may conceal hatred under
dissimulation,
but his malice will be revealed in the
assembly.

27 He who digs a pit falls into it;
and a stone comes back upon him who
rolls it.[q]

28 The lying tongue is its owner's enemy,
and the flattering mouth works ruin.

## CHAPTER 27

1 Boast not of tomorrow,
for you know not what any day may bring
forth.

2 Let another praise you—not your own
mouth;
someone else—not your own lips.

3 Stone is heavy, and sand a burden,
but a fool's provocation is heavier than
both.[r]

4 Anger is relentless, and wrath
overwhelming—
but before jealousy who can stand?

5 Better is an open rebuke
than a love that remains hidden.

6 Wounds from a friend may be accepted as
well meant,
but the greetings of an enemy one prays
against.

7 One who is full, tramples on virgin honey;

k 2 Pt 2, 22.
l Prv 22, 13.
m Prv 19, 24.
n Prv 15, 18; 29, 22.
o Prv 18, 8.
p Sir 12, 10; 27, 23.
q Eccl 10, 8; Sir 27, 25f.
r Sir 22, 14f.

*

26, 4f: There is no contradiction between these two proverbs. In any answer the wise man gives he must protect his own interest against the fool.

26, 7ff: The fool abuses whatever knowledge he possesses.

26, 25: Seven abominations: many evil intentions.

but to the man who is hungry, any bitter
thing is sweet.

8 Like a bird that is far from its nest
is a man who is far from his home.

9 Perfume and incense gladden the heart,
but by grief the soul is torn asunder.

10 Your own friend and your father's friend
forsake not;
but if ruin befalls you, enter not a
kinsman's house.
Better is a neighbor near at hand than a
brother far away.

11 If you are wise, my son, you will gladden
my heart,
and I will be able to rebut him who taunts
me.

12 The shrewd man perceives evil and hides;
simpletons continue on and suffer the
penalty.[s]

13 Take his garment who becomes surety for
another,[t]
and for the sake of a stranger, yield it
up!*

14 When one greets his neighbor with a loud
voice in the early morning,
a curse can be laid to his charge.*

15 For a persistent leak on a rainy day
the match is a quarrelsome woman.[u]

16 He who keeps her stores up a stormwind;
he cannot tell north from south.

17 As iron sharpens iron,
so man sharpens his fellow man.

18 He who tends a fig tree eats its fruit,
and he who is attentive to his master will
be enriched.

19 As one face differs from another,
so does one human heart from another.

20 The nether world and the abyss are never
satisfied;[v]
so too the eyes of men.

21 As the crucible tests silver and the furnace
gold,
so a man is tested by the praise he
receives.

22 Though you should pound the fool to bits
with the pestle, amid the grits in a mortar,
his folly would not go out of him.

23 Take good care of your flocks,*
give careful attention to your herds;

24 For wealth lasts not forever,
nor even a crown from age to age.

25 When the grass is taken away and the
aftergrowth appears,
and the mountain greens are gathered in,

26 The lambs will provide you with clothing,
and the goats will bring the price of a
field,

27 And there will be ample goat's milk to
supply you,
to supply your household,
and maintenance for your maidens.

## CHAPTER 28

1 The wicked man flees although no one
pursues him;
but the just man, like a lion, feels sure of
himself.

2 If a land is rebellious, its princes will be
many;
but with a prudent man it knows
security.*

3 A rich man who oppresses the poor
is like a devastating rain that leaves no
food.

4 Those who abandon the law* praise the
wicked man,
but those who keep the law war against
him.

5 Evil men understand nothing of justice,
but those who seek the LORD understand
all.

6 Better a poor man who walks in his integrity
than he who is crooked in his ways and
rich.[w]

7 He who keeps the law is a wise son,
but the gluttons' companion disgraces his
father.

s Prv 22, 3.
t Prv 20, 16.
u Prv 21, 9; 25, 24.
v Prv 30, 16; Eccl 4, 8.
w Prv 19, 1.

*

27, 13: See note on Prv 20, 16.

27, 14: The loud voice suggests hypocrisy in the greeting.

27, 23–27: The land of Palestine was very suitable for flocks and herds, which formed the principal source of wealth for their owners.

28, 2: The meaning of this poorly preserved verse seems to be that frequent changes of rulers often result from moral corruption and political disorder.

28, 4: The law: religious and moral teaching.

8 He who increases his wealth by interest and overcharge*
gathers it for him who is kind to the poor.

9 When one turns away his ear from hearing the law,[x]
even his prayer is an abomination.*

10 He who seduces the upright into an evil way
will himself fall into his own pit.
[And blameless men will gain prosperity.]

11 The rich man is wise in his own eyes,
but a poor man who is intelligent sees through him.

12 When the just are triumphant, there is great jubilation;
but when the wicked gain pre-eminence, people hide.

13 He who conceals his sins prospers not,
but he who confesses and forsakes them obtains mercy.

14 Happy the man who is always on his guard;
but he who hardens his heart will fall into evil.

15 Like a roaring lion or a ravenous bear
is a wicked ruler over a poor people.

16 The less prudent the prince, the more his deeds oppress.
He who hates ill-gotten gain prolongs his days.

17 Though a man burdened with human blood
were to flee to the grave, none should support him.

18 He who walks uprightly is safe,
but he whose ways are crooked falls into the pit.

19 He who cultivates his land will have plenty of food,
but from idle pursuits a man has his fill of poverty.[y]

20 The trustworthy man will be richly blessed;
he who is in haste to grow rich will not go unpunished.[z]

21 To show partiality is never good:[a]
for even a morsel of bread a man may do wrong.

22 The avaricious man is perturbed about his wealth,
and he knows not when want will come upon him.

23 He who rebukes a man gets more thanks in the end
than one with a flattering tongue.

24 He who defrauds father or mother and calls it no sin,[b]
is a partner of the brigand.

25 The greedy man stirs up disputes,
but he who trusts in the LORD will prosper.

26 He who trusts in himself is a fool,
but he who walks in wisdom is safe.

27 He who gives to the poor suffers no want,[c]
but he who ignores them gets many a curse.

28 When the wicked gain pre-eminence, other men hide;
but at their fall the just flourish.

## CHAPTER 29

1 The man who remains stiff-necked and hates rebuke
will be crushed suddenly beyond cure.

2 When the just prevail, the people rejoice;
but when the wicked rule, the people groan.[d]

3 He who loves wisdom makes his father glad,
but he who consorts with harlots
squanders his wealth.[e]

4 By justice a king gives stability to the land;
but he who imposes heavy taxes ruins it.

5 The man who flatters his neighbor
is spreading a net under his feet.

6 The wicked man steps into a snare,
but the just man runs on joyfully.

7 The just man has a care for the rights of the poor;
the wicked man has no such concern.

8 Arrogant men set the city ablaze,
but wise men calm the fury.[f]

x Prv 21, 27.
y Prv 12, 11.
z Prv 13, 11.
a Prv 24, 23.
b Mk 7, 11ff.
c Prv 19, 17; Sir 4, 3-8.
d Prv 11, 10.
e Prv 5, 10; 10, 1.
f Prv 11, 11.

*

28, 8: Interest and overcharge were strictly forbidden in the old law among Israelites because it was presumed that the borrower was in distress; cf Ex 22, 25; Lv 25, 35ff; Dt 23, 19; Ps 15, 5; Ez 18, 8. Civil and divine law will take the offender's wealth from him.

28, 9: Prayers offered in bad faith are displeasing to God.

9 If a wise man disputes with a fool,
he may rage or laugh but can have no peace.

10 Bloodthirsty men hate the honest man,
but the upright show concern for his life.

11 The fool gives vent to all his anger;
but by biding his time, the wise man calms it.[g]

12 If a ruler listens to lying words,
his servants all become wicked.

13 The poor and the oppressor* have a common bond:[h]
the LORD gives light to the eyes of both.

14 If a king is zealous for the rights of the poor,
his throne stands firm forever.

15 The rod of correction gives wisdom,
but a boy left to his whims disgraces his mother.[i]

16 When the wicked prevail, crime increases;
but their downfall the just will behold.

17 Correct your son, and he will bring you comfort,
and give delight to your soul.

18 Without prophecy the people become demoralized;
but happy is he who keeps the law.

19 By words no servant can be trained;[j]
for he understands what is said, but obeys not.

20 Do you see a man hasty in his words?[k]
More can be hoped for from a fool!

21 If a man pampers his servant from childhood,
he will turn out to be stubborn.

22 An ill-tempered man stirs up disputes,
and a hotheaded man is the cause of many sins.[l]

23 Man's pride causes his humiliation,
but he who is humble of spirit obtains honor.[m]

24 The accomplice of a thief is his own enemy:*
he hears himself put under a curse, yet discloses nothing.

25 The fear of man brings a snare,
but he who trusts in the LORD is safe.

26 Many curry favor with the ruler,
but the rights of each are from the LORD.

27 The evildoer is an abomination to the just,
and he who walks uprightly is an abomination to the wicked.

## *VI: The Words of Agur*

### CHAPTER 30

1 The words of Agur,* son of Jakeh the Massaite:

The pronouncement of mortal man: "I am not God;*
I am not God, that I should prevail.
2 Why, I am the most stupid of men,
and have not even human intelligence;
3 Neither have I learned wisdom,
nor have I the knowledge of the Holy One.
4 Who has gone up to heaven and come down again—
who has cupped the wind in his hands?
Who has bound up the waters in a cloak—
who has marked out all the ends of the earth?
What is his name, what is his son's name,
if you know it?"
5 Every word of God is tested;[n]
he is a shield to those who take refuge in him.
6 Add nothing to his words,[o]
lest he reprove you, and you be exposed as a deceiver.

## *VII: Numerical Proverbs*

7 Two things I ask of you,
deny them not to me before I die:
8 Put falsehood and lying far from me,
give me neither poverty nor riches;
[provide me only with the food I need;]
9 Lest, being full, I deny you,
saying, "Who is the Lord?"
Or, being in want, I steal,
and profane the name of my God.

g Prv 12, 16; 25, 28; Sir 21, 26.
h Prv 22, 2.
i Prv 13, 24; 22, 15; 23, 13f; Sir 22. 6; 30, 1.
j Sir 33, 25f.
k Eccl 5, 1.
l Prv 15, 18; 26, 21.
m Prv 11, 2; 16, 18; 18, 12; Jb 22, 29.
n Ps 12, 7.
o Dt 4, 2.

*

29, 13: God gives life to all classes of people; cf Prv 22, 2.

29, 24: Is his own enemy: because he not only incurs guilt as an accomplice but, by his silence, brings down on himself the curse invoked on the unknown guilty partner.

30, 1: Agur: an unknown person. Massaite: from Massa in northern Arabia, elsewhere referred to as an encampment of the Ishmaelites (Gn 25, 14). But the word may not be intended as a place name; it might signify "an oracle," "a prophecy."

30, 1ff: Agur wishes to stress man's insignificance when he is compared to God; cf Jb 38—39.

10 Slander not a servant to his master,
lest he curse you, and you have to pay the penalty.

11 There is a group of people that curses its father,*
and blesses not its mother.[p]
12 There is a group that is pure in its own eyes,
yet is not purged of its filth.
13 There is a group—how haughty their eyes!
how overbearing their glance!
14 There is a group whose incisors are swords,
whose teeth are knives,
Devouring the needy from the earth,
and the poor from among men.

15 The two daughters of the leech are, "Give, Give."*
Three things are never satisfied,
four never say, "Enough!"
16 The nether world, and the barren womb;[q]
the earth, that is never saturated with water,
and fire, that never says, "Enough!"
17 The eye that mocks a father,
or scorns an aged mother,
Will be plucked out by the ravens in the valley;
the young eagles will devour it.

18 Three things are too wonderful for me,*
yes, four I cannot understand:
19 The way of an eagle in the air,
the way of a serpent upon a rock,
The way of a ship on the high seas,
and the way of a man with a maiden.
20 Such is the way of an adulterous woman:
she eats, wipes her mouth,
and says, "I have done no wrong."*

21 Under three things the earth trembles,
yes, under four it cannot bear up:
22 Under a slave when he becomes king,
and a fool when he is glutted with food;[r]
23 Under an odious woman when she is wed,
and a maidservant when she displaces her mistress.

24 Four things are among the smallest on the earth,
and yet are exceedingly wise:
25 Ants—a species not strong,
yet they store up their food in the summer;
26 Rock-badgers*—a species not mighty,
yet they make their home in the crags;
27 Locusts—they have no king,
yet they migrate all in array;
28 Lizards—you can catch them with your hands,
yet they find their way into kings' palaces.

29 Three things are stately in their stride,
yes, four are stately in their carriage:
30 The lion, mightiest of beasts,
who retreats before nothing;
31 The strutting cock, and the he-goat,
and the king at the head of his people.

32 If you have foolishly been proud*
or presumptuous—put your hand on your mouth;
33 For the stirring of milk brings forth curds,
and the stirring of anger brings forth blood.

## *VIII: The Words of Lemuel*

## CHAPTER 31

1 The words of Lemuel, king of Massa. The advice which his mother gave him:

2 What, my son, my first-born!
what, O son of my womb;
what, O son of my vows!
3 Give not your vigor to women,
nor your strength to those who ruin kings.[s]
4 It is not for kings, O Lemuel,
not for kings to drink wine;
strong drink is not for princes![t]
5 Lest in drinking they forget what the law decrees,
and violate the rights of all who are in need.
6 Give strong drink to one who is perishing,
and wine to the sorely depressed;
7 When they drink, they will forget their misery,
and think no more of their burdens.
8 Open your mouth in behalf of the dumb,
and for the rights of the destitute;
9 Open your mouth, decree what is just,
defend the needy and the poor!

p Prv 20. 20.
q Prv 27, 20.
r Prv 19, 10; Eccl 10, 6f.
s Prv 5, 9.
t Prv 20, 1.

*

30, 11–14: Perverted people are here classified as unfilial (11), self-righteous (12), proud (13) and rapacious (14).

30, 15f: The two daughters ... "Give, Give": the text is obscure but the sense seems to be that the leech is insatiable in its desire for blood, just as are the nether world for victims, the barren womb for offspring, the parched earth for water, and fire for fuel (16).

30, 18f: The soaring flight of the eagle, the mysterious movement upon a rock of the serpent which has no feet, the path of the ship through the trackless deep, and the marvelous procreation of human life, excite great wonderment.

30, 20: This verse portrays the indifference of an adulterous woman who thinks there is no trace of her wicked act.

30, 26: Rock-badgers: cf note on Ps 104, 18.

30, 32f: The anger aroused by overweening pride threatens an awesome punishment.

## *IX: The Ideal Wife*

**10** When one finds a worthy wife,[u]
her value is far beyond pearls.
**11** Her husband, entrusting his heart to her,
has an unfailing prize.
**12** She brings him good, and not evil,*
all the days of her life.
**13** She obtains wool and flax
and makes cloth with skillful hands.
**14** Like merchant* ships,
she secures her provisions from afar.
**15** She rises while it is still night,
and distributes food to her household.
**16** She picks out a field to purchase;
out of her earnings she plants a vineyard.
**17** She is girt about with strength,
and sturdy are her arms.
**18** She enjoys the success of her dealings;
at night her lamp is undimmed.*
**19** She puts her hands to the distaff,
and her fingers ply the spindle.
**20** She reaches out her hands to the poor,
and extends her arms to the needy.
**21** She fears not the snow for her household;
all her charges are doubly clothed.
**22** She makes her own coverlets;
fine linen and purple are her clothing.
**23** Her husband is prominent at the city gates
as he sits with the elders of the land.
**24** She makes garments and sells them,
and stocks the merchants with belts.
**25** She is clothed with strength and dignity,
and she laughs at the days to come.*
**26** She opens her mouth in wisdom,
and on her tongue is kindly counsel.
**27** She watches the conduct of her household,
and eats not her food in idleness.
**28** Her children rise up and praise her;
her husband, too, extols her:
**29** ''Many are the women of proven worth,
but you have excelled them all.''
**30** Charm is deceptive and beauty fleeting;
the woman who fears the LORD is to be praised.*
**31** Give her a reward of her labors,
and let her works praise her at the city gates.

---

u 10-31: Sir 26, 1ff. 13-18.

---

31, 12: Good and not evil: i.e., prosperity, not adversity.

31, 14: Merchant: literally, "Canaanite" (cf v 24), probably because the merchant class had been composed chiefly of Canaanites.

31, 18: Her lamp is undimmed: indicates abundance of productive work and its accompanying prosperity; cf Prv 20, 20; Jb 18, 6.

31, 25: Laughs at the days to come: anticipates the future with gladness free from anxiety.

31, 30: The true charm of the ideal wife is her religious spirit, for she fears the Lord; cf note on Prv 1, 7.

# The Book of
# ECCLESIASTES

*The title* Ecclesiastes *given to this book is the Greek translation of the Hebrew name* Qoheleth *meaning, perhaps, "one who convokes an assembly." The book, however, does not consist of public addresses, but is a treatise, more or less logically developed, on the vanity of all things. Reflections in prose and aphorisms in verse are intermingled in Ecclesiastes, which contains, besides, an introduction and an epilogue.*

*The book is concerned with the purpose and value of human life. While admitting the existence of a divine plan, it considers such a plan to be hidden from man, who seeks happiness without ever finding it here below (3, 11; 8, 7. 17). Ecclesiastes applies his "Vanity of vanities" to everything "under the sun," even to that wisdom which seeks to find at last a semblance of good in the things of the world. Merit does not yield happiness for it is often tried by suffering. Riches and pleasures do not avail. Existence is monotonous, enjoyment fleeting and vain; darkness quickly follows. Life, then, is an enigma beyond human ability to solve.*

*While Ecclesiastes concedes that there is an advantage for man in the enjoyment of certain legitimate pleasures lest he lapse into pessimism and despair, he nevertheless considers this indulgence also vanity unless man returns due thanks to the Creator who has given him all. Under this aspect, earthly wisdom would rise to the higher level of true spiritual wisdom. This true wisdom is not found "under the sun" but is perceived only by the light of faith, inasmuch as it rests with God, who is the final Judge of the good and the bad, and whose reign endures forever. The Epilogue gives the clue to this thought (12, 13f).*

*The moral teaching of the book is imperfect, like the Old Testament itself (Heb 7, 19), yet it marks an advance in the development of the doctrine of divine retribution. While rejecting the older solution of earthly rewards and punishments, Ecclesiastes looks forward to a more lasting one. The clear answer to the problem was to come with the light of Christ's teaching concerning future life.*

*The author of the book was a teacher of popular wisdom (12, 9). Qoheleth was obviously only his literary name. Because he is called "David's son, king in Jerusalem," it was commonly thought that he was King Solomon. Such personation, however, was but a literary device to lend greater dignity and authority to the book—a circumstance which does not in any way impugn its inspired character. The Epilogue seems to have been written by an editor, probably a disciple of Qoheleth. The entire work differs considerably in language and style from earlier books of the Old Testament. It reflects a late period of Hebrew, and was probably written about three centuries before Christ.*

## CHAPTER 1

**1** The words of David's son, Qoheleth,*
king in Jerusalem:[a]

### Vanity of Toil without Profit

**2** Vanity of vanities,* says Qoheleth,
vanity of vanities! All things are vanity![b]
**3** What profit has man from all the labor[c]
which he toils at under the sun?*
**4** One generation passes and another comes,
but the world forever stays.
**5** The sun rises and the sun goes down;
then it presses on to the place where it rises.
**6** Blowing now toward the south, then toward the north,
the wind turns again and again, resuming its rounds.
**7** All rivers go to the sea,
yet never does the sea become full.
To the place where they go,
the rivers keep on going.

a Eccl 7, 27; 12, 8f.
b Eccl 12, 8.
c Eccl 2, 11. 22; 3, 9; 5, 15.

*

1, 1: Qoheleth: see Introduction.
1, 2: Vanity of vanities: a Hebrew superlative expressing the supreme degree of futility and emptiness.
1, 3: Under the sun: used throughout this book to signify "on the earth."

**8** All speech is labored;
there is nothing man can say.*
The eye is not satisfied with seeing
nor is the ear filled with hearing.[d]

**9** What has been, that will be; what has been
done, that will be done. Nothing is new under
the sun.[e] **10** Even the thing of which we say,
"See, this is new!" has already existed in the
ages that preceded us.[f] **11** There is no remembrance of the men of old;[g] nor of those to come
will there be any remembrance among those
who come after them.*

## I: *Qoheleth's Investigation of Life*

**Twofold Introduction.** **12** I, Qoheleth,
was king over Israel in Jerusalem, **13** and I
applied my mind to search and investigate in
wisdom all things that are done under the sun.[h]

A thankless task God has appointed
for men to be busied about.

**14** I have seen all things that are done under the
sun,[i] and behold, all is vanity and a chase after
wind.*

**15** What is crooked cannot be made straight,
and what is missing cannot be supplied.

**16** [j]Though I said to myself, "Behold, I
have become great and stored up wisdom beyond all who were before me in Jerusalem, and
my mind has broad experience of wisdom and
knowledge"; **17** yet when I applied my mind to
know wisdom and knowledge, madness and folly, I learned that this also is a chase after wind.[k]

**18** For in much wisdom there is much sorrow,
and he who stores up knowledge stores up
grief.

### CHAPTER 2

**Study of Pleasure-seeking.** **1** I said to
myself,* "Come, now, let me try you with
pleasure and the enjoyment of good things."[l]
But behold, this too was vanity. **2** Of laughter
I said: "Mad!" and of mirth: "What good does
this do?" **3** I thought of beguiling my senses
with wine, though my mind was concerned with
wisdom,* and of taking up folly, until I should
understand what is best for men to do under the
heavens during the limited days of their life.

**4** I undertook great works; I built myself
houses and planted vineyards; **5** I made gardens
and parks, and set out in them fruit trees of all
sorts. **6** And I constructed for myself reservoirs
to water a flourishing woodland. **7** I acquired
male and female slaves, and slaves were born in
my house. I also had growing herds of cattle and
flocks of sheep, more than all who had been
before me in Jerusalem. **8** I amassed for myself
silver and gold, and the wealth of kings and
provinces. I got for myself male and female
singers and all human luxuries. **9** I became
great, and I stored up more than all others before
me in Jerusalem; my wisdom, too, stayed with
me. **10** [m]Nothing that my eyes desired did I
deny them, nor did I deprive myself of any joy,
but my heart rejoiced in the fruit of all my toil.
This was my share for all my toil. **11** [n]But
when I turned to all the works that my hands had
wrought, and to the toil at which I had taken
such pains, behold! all was vanity and a chase
after wind, with nothing gained under the sun.
**12** For what will the man do who is to come
after the king? What men have already done!

**Study of Wisdom and Folly.** I went on to
the consideration of wisdom, madness and folly. **13** And I saw that wisdom has the advantage
over folly as much as light has the advantage
over darkness.

**14** The wise man has eyes in his head,
but the fool walks in darkness.[o]

Yet I knew that one lot befalls both of them.
**15** So I said to myself, if the fool's lot is to
befall me also, why then should I be wise?
Where is the profit for me? And I concluded in
my heart that this too is vanity. **16** [p]Neither of
the wise man nor of the fool will there be an
abiding remembrance, for in days to come both
will have been forgotten. How is it that the wise
man dies as well as the fool! **17** Therefore I
loathed life, since for me the work that is done
under the sun is evil; for all is vanity and a chase
after wind.

### Study of the Fruits of Toil

**To Others the Profits.** **18** And I detested
all the fruits of my labor under the sun, because
I must leave them to a man who is to come after
me. **19** And who knows whether he will be a
wise man or a fool? Yet he will have control
over all the fruits of my wise labor under the

d Eccl 8, 17.
e Eccl 3, 15; 6, 10.
f Eccl 3, 15.
g Eccl 2, 16.
h Eccl 8, 9.
i Eccl 2, 11. 17.
j Eccl 2, 9.
k Eccl 2, 3; 7, 25.
l Wis 2, 6.
m Eccl 3, 22; 5, 18.
n Eccl 1, 17; Sir 44, 9.
o 14f: Eccl 6, 8; 9, 2f.
p Eccl 1, 11; Wis 2, 4.

*

1, 8: All speech . . . man can say: or "All things are wearisome beyond man's power to tell."

1, 11: Men remember nothing long; God, however, never forgets.

1, 14: Chase after wind: futility, like an attempt to corral the winds. Cf Hos 12, 2. The ancient versions understood "affliction of spirit." These words are used to conclude sections of the discourse, as far as Eccl 6, 9.

2, 1-11: The author here assumes the role of Solomon.

2, 3: Though my mind . . . wisdom: while indulging in pleasure the author hopes to discover wherein man's true happiness consists.

sun. This also is vanity. **20** So my feelings
turned to despair of all the fruits of my labor
under the sun. **21** For there is a man who has
labored with wisdom and knowledge and skill,
and to another, who has not labored over it, he
must leave his property. This also is vanity and
a great misfortune. **22** [q]For what profit comes
to a man from all the toil and anxiety of heart
with which he has labored under the sun?
**23** All his days sorrow and grief are his occupation; even at night his mind is not at rest. This
also is vanity.

**24** [r]There is nothing better for man than to
eat and drink and provide himself with good
things by his labors. Even this, I realized, is
from the hand of God.* **25** For who can eat or
drink apart from him? **26** [s]For to whatever man
he sees fit he gives wisdom and knowledge and
joy; but to the sinner he gives the task of gathering possessions to be given to whatever man
God sees fit. This also is vanity and a chase after
wind.

## CHAPTER 3

### Man Cannot Hit on the Right Time To Act

**1** There is an appointed time for everything,
and a time for every affair under the
heavens.
**2** A time to be born, and a time to die;
a time to plant, and a time to uproot the
plant.
**3** A time to kill, and a time to heal;
a time to tear down, and a time to build.
**4** A time to weep, and a time to laugh;
a time to mourn, and a time to dance.
**5** A time to scatter stones, and a time to
gather them;
a time to embrace, and a time to be far
from embraces.
**6** A time to seek, and a time to lose;
a time to keep, and a time to cast away.
**7** A time to rend, and a time to sew;
a time to be silent, and a time to speak.
**8** A time to love, and a time to hate;
a time of war, and a time of peace.

**9** [t]What advantage has the worker from his
toil? **10** I have considered the task which God
has appointed for men to be busied about.
**11** [u]He has made everything appropriate to its
time, and has put the timeless into their hearts,
without men's ever discovering, from beginning to end, the work which God has done. **12** I
recognized that there is nothing better than to be
glad and to do well during life. **13** [v]For every
man, moreover, to eat and drink and enjoy the
fruit of all his labor is a gift of God. **14** I recognized that whatever God does will endure forever; there is no adding to it, or taking from it.
Thus has God done that he may be revered.
**15** [w]What now is has already been; what is to
be, already is; and God restores* what would
otherwise be displaced.

**The Problem of Retribution.** **16** [x]And
still under the sun in the judgment place I saw
wickedness, and in the seat of justice, iniquity.
**17** [y]And I said to myself, both the just and the
wicked God will judge, since there is a time for
every affair and on every work a judgment. **18** I
said to myself: As for the children of men, it is
God's way of testing them and of showing that
they are in themselves like beasts. **19** For the
lot of man and of beast is one lot; the one dies
as well as the other. Both have the same life-
breath, and man has no advantage over the
beast; but all is vanity. **20** [z]Both go to the same
place; both were made from the dust, and to the
dust they both return. **21** [a]Who knows if the
life-breath of the children of men goes upward
and the life-breath of beasts goes earthward?
**22** [b]And I saw that there is nothing better for
a man than to rejoice in his work; for this is his
lot. Who will let him see what is to come after
him?

## CHAPTER 4

**Vanity of Toil.** **1** Again I considered all the
oppressions that take place under the sun: the
tears of the victims with none to comfort them!
From the hand of their oppressors comes violence, and there is none to comfort them![c]
**2** And those now dead, I declared more fortunate in death than are the living to be still alive.[d]
**3** And better off than both is the yet unborn,
who has not seen the wicked work that is done
under the sun. **4** Then I saw that all toil and
skillful work is the rivalry of one man for another. This also is vanity and a chase after wind.

**5** "The fool folds his arms
and consumes his own flesh"*—
**6** Better is one handful with tranquility
than two with toil and a chase after wind!

---

q Eccl 1, 3.
r Eccl 3, 12f. 22; 5, 17f; 8, 15.
s Prv 13, 22.
t Eccl 1, 3.
u Eccl 8, 17; 11, 5; Gn 1, 31.
v Eccl 2, 24.
w Eccl 1, 9.
x Eccl 4, 1.
y Eccl 12, 14.
z Eccl 12, 7; Gn 2, 7; 3, 19; Ps 103, 14; Wis 2, 3; Sir 10, 9; 17, 1; 40, 11.
a Wis 2, 2.
b Eccl 8, 7; 10, 14.
c Eccl 5, 7.
d Eccl 7, 2.

*

2, 24: Unrestrained indulgence is not advocated here, but legitimate pleasure and the cheerfulness it begets.

3, 15: God restores: the meaning is probably that God allows no part of his creation to drop out of existence.

4, 5: Consumes his own flesh: refuses to work for the necessities of life and consequently suffers hunger and impairs his bodily health.

**Companions and Successors.** 7 Again
I found this vanity under the sun: **8** a solitary
man with no companion; with neither son nor
brother. Yet there is no end to all his toil, and
riches do not satisfy his greed. "For whom do
I toil and deprive myself of good things?" This
also is vanity and a worthless task. **9** Two are
better than one: they get a good wage for their
labor. **10** If the one falls, the other will lift up
his companion. Woe to the solitary man! For if
he should fall, he has no one to lift him up.
**11** So also, if two sleep together, they keep
each other warm. How can one alone keep
warm? **12** Where a lone man may be overcome,
two together can resist. A three-ply cord is not
easily broken.

**13** Better is a poor but wise youth than an old
but foolish king who no longer knows caution;
**14** for from a prison house* one comes forth to
rule, since even in his royalty he was poor at
birth. **15** Then I saw all those who are to live
and move about under the sun with the heir
apparent who will succeed to his place.*
**16** There is no end to all these people, to all
over whom he takes precedence; yet the later
generations will not applaud him. This also is
vanity and a chase after wind.

**Vanity of Many Words.** **17** [e]Guard your
step when you go to the house of God. Let your
approach be obedience, rather than the fools'
offering of sacrifice;* for they know not how to
keep from doing evil.

## CHAPTER 5

**1** Be not hasty in your utterance and let not
your heart be quick to make a promise in God's
presence. God is in heaven and you are on earth;
therefore let your words be few.

**2** For nightmares* come with many cares,
and a fool's utterance with many words.

**3** [f]When you make a vow to God, delay not
its fulfillment. For God has no pleasure in fools;
fulfill what you have vowed. **4** You had better
not make a vow than make it and not fulfill it.
**5** Let not your utterances make you guilty, and
say not before his representative, "It was a
mistake," lest God be angered by such words
and destroy the works of your hands.
**6** [g]Rather, fear God!

**Gain and Loss of Goods.** **7** [h]If you see
oppression of the poor, and violation of rights
and justice in the realm, do not be shocked by
the fact, for the high official has another higher
than he watching him and above these are others
higher still—. **8** Yet an advantage for a country
in every respect is a king for the arable land.*

**9** [i]The covetous man is never satisfied with
money, and the lover of wealth reaps no fruit
from it; so this too is vanity. **10** Where there are
great riches, there are also many to devour
them. Of what use are they to the owner except
to feast his eyes upon? **11** Sleep is sweet to the
laboring man, whether he eats little or much,
but the rich man's abundance allows him no
sleep.

**12** [j]This is a grievous evil which I have seen
under the sun: riches kept by their owner to his
hurt. **13** Should the riches be lost through some
misfortune, he may have a son when he is without means. **14** [k]As he came forth from his
mother's womb, so again shall he depart, naked
as he came, having nothing from his labor that
he can carry in his hand. **15** This too is a grievous evil, that he goes just as he came. What then
does it profit him to toil for wind? **16** All the
days of his life are passed in gloom and sorrow,
under great vexation, sickness and wrath.

**17** [l]Here is what I recognize as good: it is
well for a man to eat and drink and enjoy all the
fruits of his labor under the sun during the
limited days of the life which God gives him; for
this is his lot. **18** Any man to whom God gives
riches and property, and grants power to partake
of them, so that he receives his lot and finds joy
in the fruits of his toil, has a gift from God.
**19** For he will hardly dwell on the shortness of
his life, because God lets him busy himself with
the joy of his heart.*

## CHAPTER 6

**Limited Worth of Enjoyment.** **1** There is
another evil which I have seen under the sun,
and it weighs heavily upon man: **2** [m]there is the
man to whom God gives riches and property and
honor, so that he lacks none of all the things he
craves; yet God does not grant him power to
partake of them, but a stranger devours them.
This is vanity and a dire plague. **3** Should a man
have a hundred children and live many years, no
matter to what great age, still if he has not the

e 1 Sm 15, 22; Hos 6, 6.
f Nm 30, 3; Dt 23, 23; Ps 50, 14.
g Eccl 12, 13; Dt 10, 12.
h Eccl 3, 16; 4, 1.
i Prv 28, 22.
j Jb 20, 20.
k Jb 1, 21; 1 Tm 6, 7.
l 17f: Eccl 2, 24.
m Eccl 2, 18f.

*

4, 14: Prison house: probably his mother's womb, from which the king issues without possessions. Cf Eccl 5, 14.

4, 15: The king is no sooner dead than the people transfer their allegiance to his successor.

4, 17: The fools' . . . sacrifice: unacceptable to God because of their disobedience; cf 1 Sm 15, 22; Hos 6, 6.

5, 2: Nightmares: literally, "dreams."

5, 8: The wording of this verse has perhaps never been adequately explained.

5, 19: The meaning is that the joys of life, though temporary, keep a man from dwelling on the ills which afflict humanity.

6, 3: A large family, a long life, an honorable burial, all were highly esteemed by the Hebrews, and it was considered a great misfortune to be deprived of them.

full benefit of his goods, or if he is deprived of
burial, of this man I proclaim that the child born
dead is more fortunate than he.* 4 Though it
came in vain and goes into darkness and its
name is enveloped in darkness; 5 though it has
not seen or known the sun, yet the dead child is
at rest rather than such a man. 6 Should he live
twice a thousand years and not enjoy his goods,
do not both go to the same place?*

7 All man's toil is for his mouth,* yet his
desire is not fulfilled. 8 For what advantage has
the wise man over the fool, or what advantage
has the poor man in knowing how to conduct
himself in life? 9 "What the eyes see is better
than what the desires wander after."* This also
is vanity and a chase after wind.

## *II: Qoheleth's Conclusions*

10 Whatever is, was long ago given its
name, and the nature of man is known, and that
he cannot contend in judgment with one who is
stronger than he.* 11 For though there are
many sayings that multiply vanity, what profit
is there for a man? 12 [n]For who knows what is
good for a man in life, the limited days of his
vain life (which God has made like a shadow)?
Because—who is there to tell a man what will
come after him under the sun?

### A. Man Cannot Find Out What Is Good for Him To Do

### CHAPTER 7

### Critique of Sages on the Day of Adversity

1 A good name is better than good ointment,*
and the day of death than the day of
birth.[o]
2 It is better to go to the house of mourning
than to the house of feasting,
For that is the end of every man,
and the living should take it to heart.[p]
3 Sorrow is better than laughter,
because when the face is sad the heart
grows wiser.
4 The heart of the wise is in the house of
mourning,
but the heart of fools is in the house of
mirth.
5 It is better to hearken to the wise man's
rebuke
than to hearken to the song of fools;
6 For as the crackling of thorns under a pot,
so is the fool's laughter.

This also is vanity,
7 For oppression can make a fool of a wise
man,
and a bribe corrupts the heart.
8 Better is the end of speech than its
beginning;
better is the patient spirit than the lofty
spirit.
9 Do not in spirit become quickly
discontented,
for discontent lodges in the bosom of a
fool.

10 Do not say: How is it that former times were
better than these? For it is not in wisdom that
you ask about this.

11 Wisdom and an inheritance are good,
and an advantage to those that see the
sun.

12 For the protection of wisdom is as the protection of money; and the advantage of knowledge is that wisdom preserves the life of its
owner.

13 Consider the work of God. Who can make
straight what he has made crooked? 14 On a
good day enjoy good things, and on an evil day
consider: Both the one and the other God has
made, so that man cannot find fault with him in
anything.

**Critique of Sages on Justice and Wicked-
ness.** 15 I have seen all manner of things in
my vain days: a just man perishing in his justice,
and a wicked one surviving in his wickedness.
16 [q]"Be not just to excess, and be not over-
wise, lest you be ruined.* 17 Be not wicked to
excess, and be not foolish. Why should you die
before your time?"* 18 It is good to hold to this
rule, and not to let that one* go; but he who fears
God will win through at all events.

19 Wisdom is a better defense for the wise
man than would be ten princes in the city,
20 [r]yet there is no man on earth so just as to do

n Jb 8, 9; 14, 2; Ps 102, 12.
o Eccl 4, 2; Prv 22, 1; Sir 41, 13.
p Eccl 4, 2.
q 16f: Eccl 8, 12ff.
r Jb 25, 4; Prv 20, 9; 1 Kgs 8, 46; Rom 3, 23; Jas 3, 2; 1 Jn 1, 8.

*

6, 6: Same place: the grave.

6, 7: Mouth: appetite, and therefore, body.

6, 9: Better . . . wander after: the good that is present to us is better than that which is absent and, perhaps, unattainable.

6, 10: The one who is stronger than man is God.

7, 1: Ointment: applied to the child at birth; a good name remains even after death.

7, 16: St. Jerome explains the warning against excessive justice in reference to the self-righteous man who is so stern that he is never willing to forgive sin in others; cf vv 20ff.

7, 17: Untimely death was traditionally recognized as a divine punishment of the wicked; cf 1 Sm 2, 31–34; Jer 17, 11; Ps 55, 24; Prv 10, 27. This warning against presumptuous wickedness is not an endorsement of any lesser degree of misconduct.

7, 18: This rule . . . that one: the sayings cited in vv 16f. Others refer this and that to riches and wisdom (cf 7, 12), justice and wisdom, or justice and wickedness. This last supposition makes the author's thought hard to follow.

7, 20: This is to be understood in the sense of Rom 5, 12.

good and never sin.* **21** [s]Do not give heed to
every word that is spoken lest you hear your
servant speaking ill of you, **22** for you know in
your heart that you have many times spoken ill
of others.

**23** All these things I probed in wisdom. I
said, "I will acquire wisdom"; but it was beyond me. **24** What exists is far-reaching; it is
deep, very deep: who can find it out? **25** [t]I
turned my thoughts toward knowledge; I sought
and pursued wisdom and reason, and I recognized that wickedness is foolish and folly is
madness.

**Critique of Sages on Women.** **26** [u]"More
bitter than death I find the woman who is a
hunter's trap, whose heart is a snare and whose
hands are prison bonds. He who is pleasing to
God will escape her, but the sinner will be entrapped by her. **27** Behold, this have I found,
says Qoheleth, adding one thing to another that
I might discover the answer **28** which my soul
still seeks and has not found: One man out of a
thousand have I come upon, but a woman
among them all I have not found.* **29** Behold,
only this have I found out: God made mankind
straight, but men have had recourse to many
calculations.*

## CHAPTER 8

### Critique of Sages on the Wise Man and the King

**1** Who is like the wise man,
and who knows the explanation of things?
A man's wisdom illumines his face,
but an impudent look is resented.

**2** Observe the precept of the king, and in
view of your oath to God, **3** be not hasty to
withdraw from the king; do not join in with a
base plot, for he does whatever he pleases,
**4** because his word is sovereign, and who can
say to him, "What are you doing?"

**5** "He who keeps the commandment experiences no evil, and the wise man's heart knows
times and judgments; **6** for there is a time and
a judgment for everything."—Yet it is a great
affliction for man **7** [v]that he is ignorant of what
is to come; for who will make known to him
how it will be? **8** There is no man who is master
of the breath of life so as to retain it, and none
has mastery of the day of death. There is no
exemption from the struggle, nor are the wicked
saved by their wickedness. **9** [w]All these things
I considered and I applied my mind to every
work that is done under the sun, while one man
tyrannizes over another to his hurt.

**The Problem of Retribution.** **10** Meanwhile I saw wicked men approach and enter; and
as they left the sacred place, they were praised
in the city for what they had done. This also is
vanity.* **11** Because the sentence against evildoers is not promptly executed, therefore the
hearts of men are filled with the desire to commit evil— **12** because the sinner does evil a
hundred times and survives. Though indeed I
know that it shall be well with those who fear
God, for their reverence toward him; **13** and
that it shall not be well with the wicked man,
and he shall not prolong his shadowy* days, for
his lack of reverence toward God.

**14** This is a vanity which occurs on earth:
there are just men treated as though they had
done evil and wicked men treated as though they
had done justly. This, too, I say is vanity.
**15** [x]Therefore I commend mirth, because there
is nothing good for man under the sun except
eating and drinking and mirth: for this is the
accompaniment of his toil during the limited
days of the life which God gives him under the
sun.*

**16** [y]When I applied my heart to know wisdom and to observe what is done on earth, **17** [z]I
recognized that man is unable to find out all
God's work that is done under the sun, even
though neither by day nor by night do his eyes
find rest in sleep. However much man toils in
searching, he does not find it out; and even if the
wise man says that he knows, he is unable to
find it out.

## B. Man Does Not Know What Is To Come

## CHAPTER 9

**1** All this I have kept in mind and recognized:* the just, the wise, and their deeds are in
the hand of God. Love from hatred* man cannot
tell; both appear equally vain, **2** [a]in that there
is the same lot for all, for the just and the wicked, for the good and the bad, for the clean and

s 21f: 1 Kgs 8, 46.
t Eccl 1, 17.
u Prv 5, 4.
v Eccl 3, 22; 10, 14.
w Eccl 1, 13f.
x Eccl 2, 24; 9, 7.
y Eccl 1, 13; 3, 10.
z Eccl 3, 11.
a Eccl 2, 14.

* See note there.

7, 28: The author found sincerity rare among men, but among women still more rare.

7, 29: Calculations: the many vain attempts and schemes of men to attain happiness by their own efforts.

8, 10: The text is obscure. The Latin has "wicked men buried, who, while still alive, were in the holy place, and were praised in the city as if their works were just."

8, 13: Shadowy: perhaps an addition here; cf Eccl 6, 12.

8, 15: See notes on Eccl 2, 24; 5, 19.

9, 1–10: These statements are based on a very imperfect concept of life beyond the grave. With Christian revelation about the future life came the only satisfactory solution of the problem which so perplexed the author.

9, 1: Love from hatred: divine favor or disfavor.

the unclean, for him who offers sacrifice and
him who does not. As it is for the good man, so
it is for the sinner; as it is for him who swears
rashly, so it is for him who fears an oath.
**3** Among all the things that happen under the
sun, this is the worst, that things turn out the
same for all. Hence the minds of men are filled
with evil, and madness is in their hearts during
life; and afterward they go to the dead.

**4** Indeed, for any among the living there is
hope; a live dog is better off than a dead lion.
**5** [b]For the living know that they are to die, but
the dead no longer know anything. There is no
further recompense for them, because all memory of them is lost. **6** For them, love and hatred
and rivalry have long since perished. They will
never again have part in anything that is done
under the sun.

**7** [c]Go, eat your bread with joy and drink
your wine with a merry heart, because it is now
that God favors your works. **8** At all times let
your garments be white, and spare not the perfume for your head. **9** Enjoy life with the wife
whom you love, all the days of the fleeting life
that is granted you under the sun. This is your
lot in life, for the toil of your labors under the
sun. **10** Anything you can turn your hand to, do
with what power you have; for there will be no
work, nor reason, nor knowledge, nor wisdom
in the nether world where you are going . . .

**The Evil Time Not Known.** **11** Again I
saw under the sun that the race is not won by the
swift, nor the battle by the valiant, nor a livelihood by the wise, nor riches by the shrewd, nor
favor by the experts; for a time of calamity
comes to all alike. **12** Man no more knows his
own time* than fish taken in the fatal net, or
birds trapped in the snare; like these the children
of men are caught when the evil time falls suddenly upon them.

### The Uncertain Future and the Sages.

**13** On the other hand I saw this wise deed under
the sun, which I thought sublime. **14** Against a
small city with few men in it advanced a mighty
king, who surrounded it and threw up great
siegeworks about it. **15** But in the city lived a
man who, though poor, was wise, and he delivered it through his wisdom. Yet no one remembered this poor man. **16** [d]Though I had said,
"Wisdom is better than force," yet the wisdom
of the poor man is despised and his words go
unheeded.

**17** "The quiet words of the wise are better
heeded
than the shout of a ruler of fools"—!

**18** "A fly that dies can spoil the perfumer's
ointment,
and a single slip can ruin much that is
good."

## CHAPTER 10

**1** More weighty than wisdom or wealth is a
little folly!
**2** The wise man's understanding turns him to
his right;
the fool's understanding turns him to his
left.*

**3** When the fool walks through the street, in
his lack of understanding he calls everything
foolish.

**4** Should the anger of the ruler burst upon
you, forsake not your place; for mildness abates
great offenses.

**5** I have seen under the sun another evil, like
a mistake that proceeds from the ruler: **6** a fool
put in lofty position while the rich sit in lowly
places. **7** I have seen slaves on horseback,
while princes walked on the ground like slaves.

**8** He who digs a pit may fall into it,[e]
and he who breaks through a wall may be
bitten by a serpent.

**9** He who moves stones may be hurt by them,
and he who chops wood is in danger from
it.

**10** If the iron becomes dull, though at first he
made easy progress, he must increase his efforts; but the craftsman has the advantage of his
skill.

**11** If the serpent bites because it has not been
charmed,
then there is no advantage for the
charmer.

**12** Words from the wise man's mouth win
favor,
but the fool's lips consume him.[f]
**13** The beginning of his words is folly,
and the end of his talk is utter madness;
**14** yet the fool multiplies words.
Man knows not what is to come,
for who can tell him what is to come after
him?[g]
**15** When will the fool be weary of his labor,
he who knows not the way to the city?*

---

b Eccl 1, 11.
c Eccl 2, 1. 24; 8, 15; 11, 9.
d Prv 24, 5.
e 8f: Prv 26, 27; Sir 27, 29.
f Sir 21, 19.
g Eccl 5, 2; 8, 7.

---

*9, 12: His own time: the time of death or sudden disaster.
10, 2: It is doubtful whether the author is endorsing either direction; cf Prv 4, 25ff.
10, 15: He who . . . city: perhaps a proverbial expression for supreme stupidity.

### Man Does Not Know What Evil Will Come

16 Woe to you, O land, whose king was a
servant,
and whose princes dine in the morning!
17 Blessed are you, O land, whose king is of
noble birth,
and whose princes dine at the right time
(for vigor and not in drinking bouts).
18 When hands are lazy, the rafters sag;
when hands are slack, the house leaks.
19 Bread and oil call forth merriment
and wine makes the living glad,
but money answers for everything.
20 Even in your thoughts do not make light of
the king,
nor in the privacy of your bedroom revile
the rich,
Because the birds of the air may carry your
voice,
a winged creature may tell what you say.

## CHAPTER 11

1 Cast your bread upon the waters;*
after a long time you may find it again.
2 Make seven or eight portions;*
you know not what misfortune may come
upon the earth.

### Man Does Not Know What Good Will Come

3 When the clouds are full,
they pour out rain upon the earth.
Whether a tree falls to the south or to the
north,
wherever it falls, there shall it lie.
4 One who pays heed to the wind will not
sow,
and one who watches the clouds will
never reap.
5 Just as you know not how the breath of life
fashions the human frame in the mother's
womb,
So you know not the work of God
which he is accomplishing in the
universe.[h]
6 In the morning sow your seed,
and at evening let not your hand be idle:
For you know not which of the two will be
successful,
or whether both alike will turn out well.

**Poem on Youth and Old Age.** 7 Light is
sweet! and it is pleasant for the eyes to see the
sun. 8 However many years a man may live, let
him, as he enjoys them all, remember that the
days of darkness will be many. All that is to
come is vanity.

9 Rejoice, O young man, while you are
young,
and let your heart be glad in the days of
your youth.
Follow the ways of your heart,
the vision of your eyes;
Yet understand that as regards all this
God will bring you to judgment.
10 Ward off grief from your heart
and put away trouble from your presence,
though the dawn of youth is fleeting.*

## CHAPTER 12

1 Remember your Creator in the days of your
youth,
before the evil days come
And the years approach of which you will
say,
I have no pleasure in them;
2 Before the sun is darkened,
and the light, and the moon, and the
stars,
while the clouds return* after the rain;
3 When the guardians* of the house tremble,
and the strong men are bent,
And the grinders are idle because they are
few,
and they who look through the windows
grow blind;
4 When the doors* to the street are shut,
and the sound of the mill is low;
When one waits for the chirp of a bird,
but all the daughters of song are
suppressed;
5 And one fears heights,
and perils in the street;
When the almond tree blooms,*
and the locust grows sluggish
and the caper berry is without effect,
Because man goes to his lasting home,
and mourners go about the streets;
6 Before the silver cord is snapped
and the golden bowl* is broken,
And the pitcher is shattered at the spring,
and the broken pulley falls into the well,

---

h Eccl 8, 17.

---

11, 1: This may refer to a spirit of adventure in business or to generosity in almsgiving. Waters: of the ocean, which sometimes carry lost treasures to the shore.

11, 2: This verse refers either to almsgiving or to the wisdom of not putting all one's cargo into a single vessel.

11, 10: Dawn . . . fleeting: literally, "youth and the dawn [of life] are vanity."

12, 2: The sun . . . return: the cloudy and rainy Palestinian winter, a natural symbol of old age.

12, 3: Guardians: the arms; strong men: the legs; grinders; the teeth; they who . . . windows: the eyes.

12, 4: Doors: the tightly compressed lips; sound of the mill: perhaps the sound of mastication; daughters of song: the voice.

12, 5: The almond tree blooms: resembling the white hair of age. The locust . . . sluggish: an image of the stiffness in movement of the aged. The caper berry: a stimulant for appetite.

12, 6: The golden bowl suspended by the silver cord was a symbol of life; the snapping of the cord and the breaking of the bowl, a symbol of death. The pitcher . . . the broken pulley: another pair of metaphors for life and its ending.

7 And the dust returns to the earth as it once
was,
and the life breath returns to God who
gave it.[i]

8 Vanity of vanities, says Qoheleth,
all things are vanity![j]

**Epilogue.** 9 Besides being wise, Qoheleth
taught the people knowledge, and weighed,
scrutinized and arranged many proverbs.
10 Qoheleth sought to find pleasing sayings,
and to write down true sayings with precision.
11 The sayings of the wise are like goads; like
fixed spikes are the topics given by one collector.* 12 [k]As to more than these, my son, beware. Of the making of many books there is no
end, and in much study there is weariness for the
flesh.
13 [l]The last word, when all is heard: Fear
God and keep his commandments, for this is
man's all;* 14 [m]Because God will bring to
judgment every work, with all its hidden qualities, whether good or bad.

i Eccl 3, 20f; Jb 34, 15.
j Eccl 1, 2.
k Eccl 1, 18.
l Eccl 5, 6.
m Eccl 11, 9.

12, 11: Goads . . . one collector: the sayings were stimulants to thought and also spikes or centers around which to group correlated pronouncements of the wise.

12, 13: Man's all: St. Jerome explains: "Unto this is every man born, that, knowing his Maker, he may revere him in fear, honor, and the observance of his commandments."

# THE SONG OF SONGS

*The Song of Songs, meaning the greatest of songs (1, 1), contains in exquisite poetic form the sublime portrayal and praise of the mutual love of the Lord and his people. The Lord is the Lover and his people are the beloved. Describing this relationship in terms of human love, the author simply follows Israel's tradition. Isaiah (5, 1–7; 54, 4–8), Jeremiah (2, 2f. 32), and Ezekiel (16; 23) all characterize the covenant between the Lord and Israel as a marriage. Hosea the prophet sees the idolatry of Israel in the adultery of Gomer (1—3). He also represents the Lord speaking to Israel's heart (2, 16) and changing her into a new spiritual people, purified by the Babylonian captivity and betrothed anew to her divine Lover "in justice and uprightness, in love and mercy" (2, 21).*

*The author of the Song, using the same literary figure, paints a beautiful picture of the ideal Israel, the chosen people of the Old and New Testaments, whom the Lord led by degrees to an exalted spiritual union with himself in the bond of perfect love. When the Song is thus interpreted there is no reason for surprise at the tone of the poem, which employs in its descriptions the courtship and marriage customs of the author's time. Moreover, the poem is not an allegory in which each remark, e.g., in the dialogue of the lovers, has a higher meaning. It is a parable in which the true meaning of mutual love comes from the poem as a whole.*

*While the Song is thus commonly understood by most Catholic scholars, it is also possible to see in it an inspired portrayal of ideal human love. Here we would have from God a description of the sacredness and the depth of married union.*

*Although the poem is attributed to Solomon in the traditional title (1, 1), the language and style of the work, among other considerations, point to a time after the end of the Babylonian Exile (538 B.C.) as that in which an unknown poet composed this masterpiece. The structure of the Song is difficult to analyze; here it is regarded as a lyric dialogue, with dramatic movement and interest.*

*The use of marriage as a symbol, characteristic of the Song, is found extensively also in the New Testament (Mt 9, 15; 25, 1–13; Jn 3; 29; 2 Cor 11, 2; Eph 5, 23–32; Rv 19, 7ff; 21, 9ff). In Christian tradition, the Song has been interpreted in terms of the union between Christ and the Church and, particularly by St. Bernard, of the union between Christ and the individual soul. Throughout the liturgy, especially in the Little Office, there is a consistent application of the Song of Songs to the Blessed Virgin Mary.*

## *I: The Song of Songs by Solomon**

### CHAPTER 1

#### Love's Desires

**2** ***B*** Let him kiss me with kisses of his
mouth!*

More delightful is your love than wine![a]
**3** Your name spoken is a spreading
perfume—
that is why the maidens love you.
**4** Draw me!—
***D*** We will follow you eagerly!
***B*** Bring me, O king, to your chambers.

***D*** With you we rejoice and exult,
we extol your love; it is beyond wine:[b]
how rightly you are loved!

#### Love's Boast

**5** ***B*** I am as dark—but lovely,
O daughters of Jerusalem*—
As the tents of Kedar,
as the curtains of Salma.
**6** Do not stare at me because I am swarthy,*

a 2f: Song 4, 10. b Song 4, 10.

*

1, 1: This title is actually the first verse of chapter 1.

1, 2ff: The marginal letters indicate the speaker of the verses: B—Bride; D—Daughters of Jerusalem; G—Bridegroom. In vv 2–7 the bride and the daughters address the bridegroom who appears here as a king, but more often in the poem as a shepherd. King and shepherd are familiar figures of the Lord in the Sacred Scriptures. Cf Ps 23, 1; Is 40, 11; Jn 10, 1–16.

1, 5: Daughters of Jerusalem: the chorus whom the bride addresses and who ask her questions (Song 5, 9; 6, 1), thus developing action within the poem. Kedar: a Syrian desert region whose name suggests blackness; tents were often made of black goat hair. Curtains: tent coverings of Salma, a region close to Kedar.

1, 6: Swarthy: tanned by the sun from working in her broth-

because the sun has burned me.
My brothers have been angry with me;
they charged me with the care of the vineyards:
my own vineyard I have not cared for.

## Love's Inquiry

7 *B* Tell me, you whom my heart loves,*
where you pasture your flock,
where you give them rest at midday,
Lest I be found wandering
after the flocks of your companions.

8 *G* If you do not know,
O most beautiful among women,
Follow the tracks of the flock
and pasture the young ones
near the shepherds' camps.

## Love's Vision

9 *G* To the steeds of Pharaoh's chariots*
would I liken you, my beloved:
10 Your cheeks lovely in pendants,
your neck in jewels.
11 We will make pendants of gold for you,
and silver ornaments.

## Love's Union

12 *B* For the king's banquet
my nard* gives forth its fragrance.
13 My lover is for me a sachet of myrrh*
to rest in my bosom.
14 My lover is for me a cluster of henna*
from the vineyards of Engedi.

15 *G* Ah, you are beautiful, my beloved,[c]
ah, you are beautiful; your eyes are doves!*

16 *B* Ah, you are beautiful, my lover—
yes, you are lovely.
Our couch, too, is verdant;*
17 the beams of our house are cedars,
our rafters, cypresses.

# CHAPTER 2

1 I am a flower of Sharon,*
a lily of the valley.

2 *G* As a lily among thorns,
so is my beloved among women.
3 *B* As an apple tree among the trees of the woods,
so is my lover among men.
I delight to rest in his shadow,
and his fruit is sweet to my mouth.
4 He brings me into the banquet hall*
and his emblem over me is love.[d]
5 Strengthen me with raisin cakes,
refresh me with apples,
for I am faint with love.[e]
6 His left hand is under my head
and his right arm embraces me.[f]
7 I adjure you, daughters of Jerusalem,[g]
by the gazelles and hinds* of the field,
Do not arouse, do not stir up love
before its own time.

## A Tryst in the Spring

8 *B* Hark! my lover—here he comes*
springing across the mountains,
leaping across the hills.
9 My lover is like a gazelle
or a young stag.
Here he stands behind our wall,
gazing through the windows,
peering through the lattices.
10 My lover speaks; he says to me,
"Arise, my beloved, my beautiful one,
and come!
11 "For see, the winter is past,
the rains are over and gone.
12 The flowers appear on the earth,
the time of pruning the vines has come,
and the song of the dove is heard in our land.
13 The fig tree puts forth its figs,
and the vines, in bloom, give forth fragrance.
Arise, my beloved, my beautiful one,
and come!

14 "O my dove in the clefts of the rock,*

c Song 4, 1. 7.
d Song 1, 4.
e Song 5, 8.
f Song 8, 3.
g Song 3, 5; 8, 4.

* ers' vineyards. My own vineyard: the bride herself; cf Is 5, 1–7, where Israel is designated as the vineyard and the Lord is the Lover.

1, 7: Here and elsewhere in the Song (3, 1; 5, 8; 6, 1), the bride expresses her desire to be in the company of her lover. These verses point to a certain tension in the poem. Only at the end (Song 8, 5ff) does mutual possession of the lovers become final.

1, 9ff: The bridegroom compares the girl's beauty to the rich adornment of the royal chariot of Pharaoh.

1, 12: Nard: a precious perfume, a figure of the bride; cf Song 4, 14.

1, 13: Myrrh: produced from aromatic resin of balsam or roses.

1, 14: Henna: a plant which bears white scented flowers.

1, 15: Doves: suggesting innocence and charm.

1, 16f: Though the meeting place of the lovers is but a shepherd's hut of green branches, it becomes a palace with beams of cedar and rafters of cypress when adorned with their love.

2, 1: Flower of Sharon: probably the narcissus, which grows in the fertile Plain of Sharon lying between Mount Carmel and Jaffa on the Mediterranean coast.

2, 4ff: The banquet hall, the sweet things of the table, the embrace of the bride and bridegroom, express the delicacy of their affection and the intimacy of their love.

2, 7: By the gazelles and hinds: the swiftness of these animals and the luster and soft expression of their eyes are suggestive of love; cf Prv 5, 19.

2, 8ff: In this sudden change of scene, the bride pictures her lover hastening toward her dwelling until his voice is heard bidding her come to him.

2, 14: The bride is addressed as though she were a dove in a mountain fastness out of sight and reach.

in the secret recesses of the cliff,
Let me see you,
let me hear your voice,
For your voice is sweet,
and you are lovely."

15 *B* Catch us the foxes, the little foxes*
that damage the vineyards; for our
vineyards are in bloom!

16 My lover belongs to me and I to him;
he browses among the lilies.[h]
17 Until the day breathes cool* and the
shadows lengthen,
roam, my lover,
Like a gazelle or a young stag
upon the mountains of Bether.[i]

## CHAPTER 3

### Loss and Discovery

1 *B* On my bed at night I sought him*
whom my heart loves—
I sought him but I did not find him.[j]
2 I will rise then and go about the city;
in the streets and crossings I will seek
Him whom my heart loves.
I sought him but I did not find him.
3 The watchmen came upon me,
as they made their rounds of the city:
Have you seen him whom my heart loves?
4 I had hardly left them
when I found him whom my heart loves.
I took hold of him and would not let him go
till I should bring him to the home of my
mother,[k]
to the room of my parent.
5 I adjure you, daughters of Jerusalem,
by the gazelles and hinds of the field,
Do not arouse, do not stir up love
before its own time.[l]

### Regal State of the Bridegroom

6 *D* What is this coming up from the desert,*
like a column of smoke
Laden with myrrh, with frankincense,
and with the perfume of every exotic
dust?[m]
7 Ah, it is the litter of Solomon;
sixty valiant men surround it,
of the valiant men of Israel:
8 All of them expert with the sword,
skilled in battle,
Each with his sword at his side
against danger in the watches of the night.

9 King Solomon made himself a carriage
of wood from Lebanon.
10 He made its columns of silver,
its roof of gold,
Its seat of purple cloth,
its framework inlaid with ivory.
11 Daughters of Jerusalem, come forth
and look upon King Solomon
In the crown with which his mother has
crowned him
on the day of his marriage,
on the day of the joy of his heart.

## CHAPTER 4

### The Charms of the Beloved

1 *G* Ah, you are beautiful, my beloved,[n]
ah, you are beautiful!
Your eyes are doves[o]
behind your veil.
Your hair is like a flock of goats
streaming down the mountains of Gilead.
2 Your teeth* are like a flock of ewes to be
shorn,
which come up from the washing,
All of them big with twins,
none of them thin and barren.
3 Your lips are like a scarlet strand;
your mouth is lovely.
Your cheek is like a half-pomegranate*
behind your veil.

4 Your neck is like David's tower[p]
girt with battlements;
A thousand bucklers hang upon it,
all the shields of valiant men.*
5 Your breasts are like twin fawns,[q]
the young of a gazelle
that browse among the lilies.
6 Until the day breathes cool and the shadows
lengthen,[r]
I will go to the mountain of myrrh,
to the hill of incense.*
7 You are all-beautiful, my beloved,
and there is no blemish in you.*

h Song 6, 3; 7, 10.
i Song 4, 6; 8, 14.
j 1ff: Song 5, 2ff.
k Song 8, 2.
l Song 2, 7; 8, 4.
m Song 6, 10; 8, 5.
n Song 1, 15.
o 1ff: Song 6, 5ff.
p Song 7, 5.
q Song 7, 4.
r Song 2, 17.

*

2, 15: A snatch of song in answer to the request of v 14; cf Song 8, 13f. Foxes: all who threaten to disturb the security of love symbolized by the vineyard; cf v 16.

2, 17: Breathes cool: in the evening when the sun is going down. Cf Gn 3, 8. Bether: a very obscure word; some interpret it in the sense of ruggedness; others, of spices; still others, of sacrifice (Gn 15, 10).

3, 1ff: See the parallel in Song 5, 2–8.

3, 6ff: The lover is portrayed as King Solomon, escorted by sixty armed men, coming in royal procession to meet his bride.

4, 2: Teeth: praised for whiteness and regularity.

4, 3: Pomegranate: a fruit somewhat like an orange, with a firm skin and deep red color. The girl's cheek is compared, in roundness and tint, to a half-pomegranate.

4, 4: The ornaments about her neck are compared to the trophies on the city walls. Cf 1 Kgs 10, 10; 14, 26ff; Ez 27, 10.

4, 6: Mountain of myrrh . . . hill of incense: spoken figuratively of the bride; cf Song 8, 14.

4, 7: Cf St. Paul's description of the church in Eph 5, 27. This verse is also applied to Our Lady, especially in the liturgy of the feast of the Immaculate Conception.

8 Come from Lebanon, my bride,
come from Lebanon, come!
Descend from the top of Amana,
from the top of Senir and Hermon,*
From the haunts of lions,
from the leopards' mountains.
9 You have ravished my heart, my sister,* my
bride;[s]
you have ravished my heart with one
glance of your eyes,
with one bead of your necklace.
10 How beautiful is your love, my sister, my
bride,[t]
how much more delightful is your love
than wine,
and the fragrance of your ointments than
all spices!
11 Your lips drip honey,* my bride,
sweetmeats and milk are under your
tongue;
And the fragrance of your garments
is the fragrance of Lebanon.

## The Lover and His Garden

12 *G* You are an enclosed garden, my sister,
my bride,[u]
an enclosed garden, a fountain sealed.*
13 You are a park that puts forth pomegranates,
with all choice fruits;
14 Nard and saffron, calamus and cinnamon,
with all kinds of incense;
Myrrh and aloes,
with all the finest spices.*
15 You are a garden fountain, a well of water
flowing fresh from Lebanon.
16 Arise, north wind? Come, south wind!
blow upon my garden*
that its perfumes may spread abroad.
*B* Let my lover come to his garden
and eat its choice fruits.

## CHAPTER 5

1 *G* I have come to my garden, my sister, my
bride;[v]
I gather my myrrh and my spices,
I eat my honey and my sweetmeats,
I drink my wine and my milk.

*D* Eat, friends; drink!* Drink freely of love!

## A Fruitless Search

2 *B* I was sleeping, but my heart kept vigil;*
I heard my lover knocking:
"Open to me, my sister, my beloved,
my dove, my perfect one![w]
For my head is wet with dew,
my locks with the moisture of the night."
3 I have taken off my robe,*
am I then to put it on?
I have bathed my feet,
am I then to soil them?
4 My lover put his hand through the opening;
my heart trembled within me,
and I grew faint when he spoke.
5 I rose to open to my lover,
with my hands dripping myrrh:
With my fingers dripping choice myrrh
upon the fittings of the lock.
6 I opened to my lover—
but my lover had departed, gone.[x]
I sought him but I did not find him;
I called to him but he did not answer
me.*

7 The watchmen came upon me[y]
as they made their rounds of the city;
They struck me, and wounded me,
and took my mantle from me,
the guardians of the walls.*
8 I adjure you, daughters of Jerusalem,[z]
if you find my lover—
What shall you tell him?—
that I am faint with love.

## The Charms of the Lost Lover

9 *D* How does your lover differ from any
other,
O most beautiful among women?
How does your lover differ from any other,
that you adjure us so?

10 *B* My lover is radiant and ruddy;*
he stands out among thousands.
11 His head is pure gold;
his locks are palm fronds,
black as the raven.
12 His eyes are like doves
beside running waters,
His teeth would seem bathed in milk,

s Song 6, 5.
t Song 1, 2f.
u Song 6, 2. 11.
v Song 6, 2.
w 2ff: Song 3, 1f.
x Song 3, 1.
y Song 3, 3.
z Song 2, 5.

*

4, 8: Amana . . . Senir and Hermon: these rugged heights symbolize obstacles that would separate the lovers; cf Song 2, 14.

4, 9: Sister: a term of endearment; it forms part of the conventional language of love used in this canticle.

4, 11: Honey: sweet words. Cf Prv 5, 3.

4, 12: Enclosed garden . . . fountain sealed: reserved for the bridegroom alone. The bride's fidelity is implied. Cf Prv 5, 15–19.

4, 14: These plants are all known for their sweet scent.

4, 16: The last two lines of the verse are spoken by the girl, inviting her lover to herself, the garden.

5, 1: Eat, friends; drink!: the lovers are encouraged to enjoy the delights of their love, symbol of Christ's union with the church.

5, 2–8: A trial similar to that in Song 3, 1ff.

5, 3f: The bride's hesitation is due, not to levity, but to strong emotion.

5, 6: The disappearance of the lover seems to be a deliberate trial and test inflicted on the girl.

5, 7: The watchmen do not know the reason for the girl's appearance in the city streets; cf Song 3, 2ff.

5, 10f: In answer to the question of v 9, the girl sings her lover's praises (vv 10–16). Gold: indicates how precious the lover is. Palm fronds: his thick, luxuriant growth of hair.

and are set like jewels.
13 His cheeks are like beds of spice
with ripening aromatic herbs.
His lips are red blossoms;
they drip choice myrrh.

14 His arms are rods of gold
adorned with chrysolites.
His body is a work of ivory
covered with sapphires.
15 His legs are columns of marble
resting on golden bases.
His stature is like the trees on Lebanon,
imposing as the cedars.
16 His mouth is sweetness itself;
he is all delight.
Such is my lover, and such my friend,
O daughters of Jerusalem.

## CHAPTER 6

### Discovery

1 *D* Where has your lover gone,
O most beautiful among women?
Where has your lover gone
that we may seek him with you?*
2 *B* My lover has come down to his garden,*
to the beds of spice,
To browse in the garden[a]
and to gather lilies.
3 My lover belongs to me and I to him;
he browses among the lilies.[b]

### The Charms of the Beloved

4 *G* You are as beautiful as Tirzah, my
beloved,*
as lovely as Jerusalem,
as awe-inspiring as bannered troops.
5 Turn your eyes from me,[c]
for they torment me.
Your hair is like a flock of goats
streaming down from Gilead.
6 Your teeth are like a flock of ewes[d]
which come up from the washing,
All of them big with twins,
none of them thin and barren.
7 Your cheek is like a half-pomegranate
behind your veil.

8 There are sixty queens, eighty concubines,
and maidens without number—
9 One alone is my dove, my perfect one,
her mother's chosen,
the dear one of her parent.
The daughters saw her and declared her
fortunate,
the queens and concubines, and they sang
her praises;
10 *D* Who is this that comes forth like the
dawn,[e]
as beautiful as the moon, as resplendent
as the sun,
as awe-inspiring as bannered troops?

### Love's Meeting

11 *B* I came down to the nut garden[f]
to look at the fresh growth of the valley,
To see if the vines were in bloom,
if the pomegranates had blossomed.
12 Before I knew it, my heart had made me
the blessed one of my kinswomen.*

## CHAPTER 7

### The Beauty of the Bride

1 *D* Turn, turn, O Shulammite,*
turn, turn, that we may look at you!
*B* Why would you look at the Shulammite
as at the dance of the two companies?

2 *D* How beautiful are your feet in sandals,*
O prince's daughter!
Your rounded thighs are like jewels,
the handiwork of an artist.
3 Your navel is a round bowl
that should never lack for mixed wine.
Your body is a heap of wheat
encircled with lilies.
4 Your breasts are like twin fawns,
the young of a gazelle.[g]
5 Your neck is like tower of ivory.[h]
Your eyes are like the pools in Heshbon
by the gate of Bath-rabbim.
Your nose is like the tower on Lebanon
that looks toward Damascus.*
6 Your head rises like Carmel;

a Song 4, 12; 5, 1.
b Song 2, 16; 7, 11.
c Song 4, 9.
d 6f: Song 4, 1ff.
e Song 3, 6; 8, 5.
f Song 4, 12ff; 7, 13.
g Song 4, 5.
h Song 4, 4.

*

6, 1: The daughters of Jerusalem are won by this description of the lover and offer their aid in seeking him.

6, 2f: Determined to share her lover with no one, the girl refuses the aid offered by the daughters in seeking him. She implies that she had never really lost him, for he has come down to his garden.

6, 4–9: The lover again celebrates her beauty. Tirzah: probably meaning "pleasant"; it was the early capital of the northern kingdom of Israel (1 Kgs 16).

6, 12: The text is obscure in Hebrew and in the ancient versions. The Vulgate reads: "I did not know; my soul disturbed me because of the chariots of Aminadab."

7, 1: Shulammite: so called either because the girl is considered to be from Shulam in the plain of Esdraelon (cf 1 Kgs 1, 3) or because the name may mean "the peaceful one," and thus recall the name of Solomon. As at the dance of the two companies: the meaning is uncertain. The question in this verse could be construed as a refusal to dance; more probably, however, the girl accedes, as the following verses suggest.

7, 2–6: A flattering description of the girl's charms. Rounded . . . jewels: the meaning of these Hebrew words is not certain. Wine and wheat are symbolic of fertility; they are here associated with parts of the body which have a close relation to fruitfulness.

7, 5: The comparison emphasizes the stateliness and whiteness of the neck, and the limpidity of the eyes. Bath-rabbim: a proper name which occurs only here; there was a city of Rabbah northeast of Heshbon in Transjordan. Cf Jer 49, 3.

your hair is like draperies of purple;
a king is held captive in its tresses.

## Love's Desires

7 *G* How beautiful you are, how pleasing,
my love, my delight!
8 Your very figure is like a palm tree,*
your breasts are like clusters.
9 I said: I will climb the palm tree,
I will take hold of its branches.
Now let your breasts be like clusters of the vine
and the fragrance of your breath like apples,
10 And your mouth like an excellent wine—

## Love's Union

*B* that flows smoothly for my lover,
spreading over the lips and the teeth.*
11 I belong to my lover*
and for me he yearns.[i]
12 Come, my lover, let us go forth to the fields
and spend the night among the villages.
13 Let us go early to the vineyards, and see
if the vines are in bloom,
If the buds have opened,
if the pomegranates have blossomed;[j]
There will I give you my love.
14 The mandrakes* give forth fragrance,
and at our doors are all choice fruits;
Both fresh and mellowed fruits, my lover,
I have kept in store for you.

## CHAPTER 8

1 Oh, that you were my brother,
nursed at my mother's breasts!
If I met you out of doors, I would kiss you
and none would taunt me.
2 I would lead you, bring you in
to the home of my mother.[k]
There you would teach me to give you
spiced wine to drink, and pomegranate juice.

3 His left hand is under my head
and his right arm embraces me.[l]
4 I adjure you, daughters of Jerusalem,
by the gazelles and hinds of the field,
Do not arouse, do not stir up love,
before its own time.[m]

## Homecoming

5 *D* Who is this coming up from the desert,[n]
leaning upon her lover?*
*G* Under the apple tree I awakened you;
it was there that your mother conceived you,
it was there that your parent conceived.

## True Love

6 *B* Set me as a seal* on your heart,
as a seal on your arm;
For stern as death is love,
relentless as the nether world is devotion;
its flames are a blazing fire.
7 Deep waters cannot quench love,
nor floods sweep it away.
Were one to offer all he owns to purchase love,
he would be roundly mocked.

## Chastity and Its Welcome

8 "Our sister is little*
and she has no breasts as yet.
What shall we do for our sister
when her courtship begins?
9 If she is a wall,
we will build upon it a silver parapet;
If she is a door,
we will reinforce it with a cedar plank."

10 I am a wall,
and my breasts are like towers.
So now in his eyes I have become
one to be welcomed.

## The Bride and Her Dowry

11 *B* Solomon had a vineyard at Baalhamon;*
he gave over the vineyard to caretakers.
For its fruit one would have to pay
a thousand silver pieces.
12 My vineyard is at my own disposal;

i Song 2, 16; 6, 3.
j Song 6, 11.
k Song 3, 4.
l Song 2, 6.
m Song 2, 7; 3, 5.
n Song 3, 6; 6, 10.

*

7, 8f: Palm tree: a figure of stateliness. The bridegroom is eager to enjoy the possession of his bride.

7, 10: The bride delicately turns his compliment into an expression of the love and tenderness she feels for him.

7, 11–14: The girl's answer assures him of her affection and invites him to return with her to the rural delights which are associated with their love and which recall the meeting described in Song 6, 11f.

7, 14: Mandrakes: herbs believed to have power to arouse love and promote fertility; cf Gn 30, 14ff.

8, 5: The lovers are pictured walking homeward, enjoying the fulfillment of the desire which the girl expressed in vv 1f. The groom speaks of their first meeting.

8, 6f: Seal: this could be worn bound to the arm, as here, or suspended at the neck, or as a ring (Jer 22, 24). It was used for identification and signatures. Stern . . . relentless: in human experience, death and the nether world are inevitable, unrelenting; in the end they always triumph. Love, which is just as certain of its victory, matches its strength against the natural enemies of life; waters cannot extinguish it nor floods carry it away. It is more priceless than all riches.

8, 8ff: The bride affirms her chastity. In 8, 9 she quotes the course of action which her elder brothers had decided on. While she is yet immature, they will shelter her in view of eventual marriage. If she is virtuous, she will be honored; if she is unchaste, she will be kept under strict vigilance. In reply to this she proclaims her virtue and boasts of having found welcome from her lover.

8, 11f: These enigmatic verses have been variously interpreted. In v 11 the girl alludes to a vineyard of great value which is compared to her own self in v 12. Her enormous dowry, a thousand silver pieces, is in keeping with her intrinsic worth. She has been the generous lover, giving herself and a dowry to her lover, referred to as Solomon, and also smaller gifts to her brothers, the caretakers (cf vv 8ff).

the thousand pieces are for you, O
Solomon,
and two hundred for the caretakers of its
fruit.

## Life Together

13 *G* O garden-dweller,*
my friends are listening for your voice,
let me hear it!

14 *B* Be swift, my lover,
like a gazelle or a young stag
on the mountains of spices![o]

---

o Song 2, 9. 17; 4, 6.

---

* 8, 13f: As in Song 2, 14f, her lover asks for a word or a song and she replies in words similar to those found in Song 2, 17.

The Book of

# WISDOM

*The Book of Wisdom was written about a hundred years before the coming of Christ. Its author, whose name is not known to us, was a member of the Jewish community at Alexandria, in Egypt. He wrote in Greek, in a style patterned on that of Hebrew verse. At times he speaks in the person of Solomon, placing his teachings on the lips of the wise king of Hebrew tradition in order to emphasize their value. His profound knowledge of the earlier Old Testament writings is reflected in almost every line of the book, and marks him, like Ben Sira, as an outstanding representative of religious devotion and learning among the sages of postexilic Judaism.*

*The primary purpose of the sacred author was the edification of his co-religionists in a time when they had experienced suffering and oppression, in part at least at the hands of apostate fellow Jews. To convey his message he made use of the most popular religious themes of his time, namely the splendor and worth of divine wisdom (6, 22–11, 1), the glorious events of the Exodus (11, 2–16; 12, 23–27; 15, 18–19, 22), God's mercy (11, 17–12, 22), the folly of idolatry (13, 1–15, 17), and the manner in which God's justice is vindicated in rewarding or punishing the individual soul (1, 1–6, 21). The first ten chapters especially form a preparation for the fuller teachings of Christ and his church. Many passages from this section of the book, notably 3, 1–8, are used by the church in her liturgy.*

*The principal divisions of the Book of Wisdom are:*
*I. The Reward of Justice (1, 1—6, 21).*
*II. Praise of Wisdom by Solomon (6, 22—11, 1).*
*III. Special Providence of God during the Exodus (11, 2–16; 12, 23–27; 15, 18—19, 22) with digressions on God's mercy (11, 17—12, 22) and on the folly and shame of idolatry (13, 1—15, 17).*

## I: The Reward of Justice

### CHAPTER 1

#### Exhortation to Justice, the Key to Life

**1** Love justice,* you who judge the earth;[a]
think of the LORD in goodness,
and seek him in integrity of heart;[b]
**2** Because he is found by those who test him not,
and he manifests himself to those who do not disbelieve him.[c]
**3** For perverse counsels separate a man from God,
and his power, put to the proof, rebukes the foolhardy;[d]
**4** Because into a soul that plots evil wisdom enters not,
nor dwells she in a body under debt of sin.[e]
**5** For the holy spirit of discipline* flees deceit
and withdraws from senseless counsels;
and when injustice occurs it is rebuked.[f]
**6** For wisdom is a kindly spirit,
yet she acquits not the blasphemer of his guilty lips;
Because God is the witness of his inmost self[g]
and the sure observer of his heart
and the listener to his tongue.[h]
**7** For the spirit of the LORD fills the world,[i]
is all-embracing, and knows what man says.*
**8** Therefore no one who utters wicked things can go unnoticed,
nor will chastising condemnation pass him by.[j]
**9** For the devices of the wicked man shall be scrutinized,

a 1 Chr 29, 17; Ps 2, 10; Is 26, 9.
b 1f: Sir 1, 25.
c 1 Chr 28, 9.
d Is 59, 2.
e Sir 15, 7f; Rom 7, 14.
f Is 63, 10.
g Jer 17, 10.
h 6f: Jer 23, 24f.
i Wis 12, 1.
j Prv 19, 5.

*

1, 1: Justice: not merely the cardinal virtue of that name (cf Wis 8, 7), but the universal moral quality which is the application of Wisdom to moral conduct.

1, 5: Discipline: here and elsewhere, another name for Wisdom; injustice: the opposite of the virtue in Wis 1, 1.

1, 7: This verse is applied to the Holy Spirit in the liturgy at Pentecost.

and the sound of his words shall reach the
LORD,
for the chastisement of his transgressions;
10 Because a jealous ear hearkens to
everything,[k]
and discordant grumblings are no secret.
11 Therefore guard against profitless grumbling,
and from calumny* withhold your
tongues;
For a stealthy utterance does not go
unpunished,
and a lying mouth slays the soul.
12 Court not death by your erring way of life,
nor draw to yourselves destruction by the
works of your hands.
13 Because God did not make death,[l]
nor does he rejoice in the destruction of
the living.
14 For he fashioned all things that they might
have being;
and the creatures of the world are
wholesome,
And there is not a destructive drug among
them
nor any domain of the nether world on
earth,
15 For justice is undying.[m]

## The Wicked Reject Immortality and Justice Alike

16 It was the wicked who with hands and
words invited death,
considered it a friend, and pined for it,
and made a covenant with it,
Because they deserve to be in its
possession,[n]

## CHAPTER 2

1 they who said among themselves, thinking
not aright:
"Brief and troublous is our lifetime;[o]
neither is there any remedy for man's
dying,
nor is anyone known to have come back
from the nether world.
2 For haphazard were we born,
and hereafter we shall be as though we
had not been;
Because the breath in our nostrils is a smoke
and reason is a spark at the beating of our
hearts,
3 And when this is quenched, our body will
be ashes
and our spirit will be poured abroad like
unresisting air,[p]
4 Even our name will be forgotten in time,
and no one will recall our deeds.
So our life will pass away like the traces of
a cloud,
and will be dispersed like a mist
pursued by the sun's rays
and overpowered by its heat.
5 For our lifetime is the passing of a shadow;
and our dying cannot be deferred
because it is fixed with a seal; and no one
returns.[q]
6 Come, therefore, let us enjoy the good
things that are real,
and use the freshness of creation avidly.[r]
7 Let us have our fill of costly wine and
perfumes,
and let no springtime blossom pass us by;
8 let us crown ourselves with rosebuds ere
they wither.
9 Let no meadow be free from our
wantonness;*
everywhere let us leave tokens of our
rejoicing,
for this our portion is, and this our lot.[s]
10 Let us oppress the needy just man;
let us neither spare the widow
nor revere the old man for his hair grown
white with time.[t]
11 But let our strength be our norm of justice;
for weakness proves itself useless.
12 *Let us beset the just one, because he is
obnoxious to us;
he sets himself against our doings,
Reproaches us for transgressions of the law*
and charges us with violations of our
training.[u]
13 He professes to have knowledge of God
and styles himself a child of the LORD.[v]
14 To us he is the censure of our thoughts;
merely to see him is a hardship for us,[w]
15 Because his life is not like other men's,
and different are his ways.
16 He judges us debased;
he holds aloof from our paths as from
things impure.
He calls blest the destiny of the just
and boasts that God is his Father.[x]
17 Let us see whether his words be true;
let us find out what will happen to him.[y]
18 For if the just one be the son of God, he
will defend him
and deliver him from the hand of his
foes.[z]

k 10f: Nm 14, 27f.
l 13f: Ez 18, 32; 33, 11; 2 Pt 3, 9.
m Is 51, 6ff.
n Is 28, 15.
o Jb 14, 1; 7, 9.
p Jb 7, 9; Jas 4, 14.
q Ps 144, 4.
r Is 22, 13; 1 Cor 15, 32.
s Jer 13, 25.
t Ex 22, 22ff; Lv 19, 32.
u Hos 8, 1.
v Mt 27, 43; Jn 8, 55; 10, 36-39.
w Mt 9, 4.
x Jer 6, 30.
y Gn 37, 20.
z Ps 22, 9; Is 42, 1; Mt 27, 43; Jn 5, 18.

*

1, 11: Calumny: speech against God and his providence is meant.

2, 9: Let no meadow . . . wantonness: the extant Greek Mss have "Let none of us be without part in our wanton doings." Most Latin Mss have both forms of this line.

2, 12–20: Often applied to the Passion of our Lord; many have understood these verses as a direct prophecy. Cf Mt 27, 41–44.

2, 12: Law: the law of Moses; training has the same meaning.

19 With revilement and torture let us put him to the test
that we may have proof of his gentleness and try his patience.
20 Let us condemn him to a shameful death;
for according to his own words, God will take care of him."[a]
21 These were their thoughts, but they erred;
for their wickedness blinded them,[b]
22 And they knew not the hidden counsels of God;
neither did they count on a recompense of holiness
nor discern the innocent souls' reward.[c]
23 For God formed man to be imperishable;
the image of his own nature he made him.[d]
24 But by the envy of the devil, death entered the world,
and they who are in his possession experience it.[e]

## CHAPTER 3

## The Hidden Counsels of God

### A. On Suffering

1 But the souls of the just are in the hand of God,[f]
and no torment shall touch them.*
2 They seemed, in the view of the foolish, to be dead;
and their passing away was thought an affliction
3 and their going forth from us, utter destruction.
But they are in peace.[g]
4 For if before men, indeed, they be punished,
yet is their hope full of immortality;
5 Chastised a little, they shall be greatly blessed,
because God tried them
and found them worthy of himself.[h]
6 As gold in the furnace, he proved them,
and as sacrificial offerings* he took them to himself.[i]
7 In the time of their visitation* they shall shine,
and shall dart about as sparks through stubble;[j]
8 They shall judge nations and rule over peoples,
and the LORD shall be their King forever.[k]
9 Those who trust in him shall understand truth,
and the faithful shall abide with him in love:
Because grace and mercy are with his holy ones,[l]
and his care is with his elect.
10 But the wicked shall receive a punishment to match their thoughts,*
since they neglected justice and forsook the LORD.
11 For he who despises wisdom and instruction is doomed.[m]
Vain is their hope, fruitless are their labors,
and worthless are their works.[n]
12 Their wives are foolish and their children wicked;
accursed is their brood.[o]

### B. On Childlessness

13 Yes, blessed is she who, childless and undefiled,
knew not transgression of the marriage bed;
she shall bear fruit at the visitation of souls.*
14 So also the eunuch whose hand wrought no misdeed,
who held no wicked thoughts against the LORD—
For he shall be given fidelity's choice reward*
and a more gratifying heritage in the LORD's temple.[p]
15 For the fruit of noble struggles is a glorious one;
and unfailing is the root of understanding.[q]
16 But the children of adulterers will remain without issue,
and the progeny of an unlawful bed will disappear.[r]
17 For should they attain long life, they will be held in no esteem,
and dishonored will their old age be at last;
18 While should they die abruptly, they have no hope
nor comfort in the day of scrutiny;
19 for dire is the end of the wicked generation.[s]

a Jas 5, 6.
b Rom 1, 21.
c Ps 18, 24f; Prv 11, 18; Mt 11, 25.
d Gn 1, 26f; Is 54, 16 LXX.
e Gn 3, 1-24; Rom 5, 12.
f Jb 12, 10; 5, 19.
g Is 57, 2.
h Tb 12, 13; 2 Cor 4, 17; 1 Pt 1, 6f.
i Ps 51, 19; Prv 17, 3; Sir 2, 5; Is 48, 10.
j Dn 12, 3; Ob 18; Mal 3, 3; Mt 13, 43.
k Wis 8, 14; Prv 8, 16; Dn 7, 22; 1 Cor 6, 2; Rv 20, 4.
l Wis 3, 9; 4, 15; Jb 10, 12; Jn 15, 10.
m Prv 1, 7.
n 11f: Sir 41, 8.
o Dt 28, 18ff.
p Is 56, 2-5.
q Sir 1, 18.
r 2 Sm 12, 14.
s Ps 34, 22.

*

3, 1–8: Verses frequently applied to the martyrs.

3, 6: Offerings: the image is that of the holocaust, in which the victim is completely consumed by fire.

3, 7: Visitation: God's loving judgment of those who have been faithful to him; the same word is used in Wis 14, 11 for the punishment of the wicked at God's final judgment. Cf also Wis 3, 13.

3, 10: To match their thoughts: a fate as empty as that which they describe; cf Wis 2, 1–5.

3, 13: Visitation of souls: that is, the last judgment. Cf Wis 3, 7–9.

3, 14: Fidelity's choice reward: cf Is 56, 1–8. More gratifying: better than sons and daughters; cf Is 56, 5.

## CHAPTER 4

1 Better is childlessness with virtue;
for immortal is its memory:*
because both by God is it acknowledged,
and by men.[t]
2 When it is present men imitate it,
and they long for it when it is gone;
And forever it marches crowned in triumph,
victorious in unsullied deeds of valor.
3 But the numerous progeny of the wicked
shall be of no avail;
their spurious offshoots shall not strike
deep root
nor take firm hold.[u]
4 For even though their branches flourish for a
time,
they are unsteady and shall be rocked by
the wind
and, by the violence of the winds,
uprooted;[v]
5 Their twigs shall be broken off untimely,
and their fruit be useless, unripe for
eating,
and fit for nothing.
6 For children born of lawless unions
give evidence of the wickedness of their
parents, when they are examined.

### C. On Early Death

7 But the just man, though he die early, shall
be at rest.[w]
8 For the age that is honorable comes not with
the passing of time,[x]
nor can it be measured in terms of years.
9 Rather, understanding is the hoary crown for
men,
and an unsullied life, the attainment of old
age.
10 He who pleased God was loved;[y]
he who lived among sinners was
transported—*
11 Snatched away, lest wickedness pervert his
mind
or deceit beguile his soul;[z]
12 For the witchery of paltry things obscures
what is right
and the whirl of desire transforms the
innocent mind.[a]
13 Having become perfect in a short while, he
reached the fullness of a long career;
14 for his soul was pleasing to the LORD,
therefore he sped him out of the midst of
wickedness.[b]
But the people saw and did not understand,
nor did they take this into account.*
16 Yes, the just man dead condemns the sinful
who live,
and youth swiftly completed
condemns the many years of the wicked
man grown old.[c]
17 For they see the death of the wise man
and do not understand what the LORD
intended for him,
or why he made him secure.
18 They see, and hold him in contempt;
but the LORD laughs them to scorn.[d]
19 And they shall afterward become dishonored
corpses[e]
and an unceasing mockery among the
dead.
For he shall strike them down speechless
and prostrate[f]
and rock them to their foundations;
They shall be utterly laid waste
and shall be in grief
and their memory shall perish.

### The Final Judgment of the Wicked

20 Fearful shall they come, at the counting up*
of their sins,
and their lawless deeds shall convict them
to their face.

## CHAPTER 5

1 Then shall the just one with great assurance
confront[g]
his oppressors who set at nought his
labors.[h]
2 Seeing this, they shall be shaken with
dreadful fear,
and amazed at the unlooked-for salvation.
3 They shall say among themselves, rueful
and groaning through anguish of spirit:
"This is he whom once we held as a
laughingstock
and as a type for mockery, 4 fools that
we were!
His life we accounted madness,
and his death dishonored.
5 See how he is accounted among the sons of
God;
how his lot is with the saints![i]
6 We, then, have strayed from the way of
truth,[j]
and the light of justice did not shine for
us,
and the sun did not rise for us.[k]

t Sir 16, 1ff; Prv 3, 3f.
u Sir 23, 25.
v Sir 40, 15; Is 40, 24.
w Wis 3, 3.
x 8f: Jb 12, 12; 32, 9; Sir 25, 4ff.
y Gn 5, 24; Sir 44, 16; Heb 11, 5.
z Is 57, 1f.
a Wis 2, 21; Dn 13, 9.
b Gn 19, 22. 29; 2 Pt 2, 7.
c Mt 12, 41f.
d Ps 37, 13.
e Neh 1, 10 LXX; Ps 18, 8; Is 14, 19; Jer 23, 39f.
f 2 Mc 3, 29.
g 1f: 2 Thes 1, 6f.
h Col 2, 15.
i Acts 26, 18; Col 1, 12.
j Prv 4, 18f; Jn 12, 35.
k 6f. Is 59, 6-14.

*

4, 1: The Latin form of this line, "Oh, how fair is the chaste generation in its glory!" is a later adaptation, which is applied in the liturgy to the splendor of virginity.

4, 10f: There are allusions here to Enoch (Gn 5, 21–24), who was young by patriarchal standards, and to Lot (Gn 19, 10f; 2 Pt 2, 7f). Cf also is 57, 1f.

4, 15: The verse here omitted repeats the last two lines of Wis 3, 9.

4, 20: Counting up: the last judgment.

7 We had our fill of the ways of mischief and
of ruin;
we journeyed through impassable deserts,
but the way of the LORD we knew not.
8 What did our pride avail us?
What have wealth and its boastfulness
afforded us?[l]
9 All of them passed like a shadow
and like a fleeting rumor;[m]
10 Like a ship traversing the heaving water,
of which, when it has passed, no trace
can be found,
no path of its keel in the waves.
11 Or like a bird flying through the air;
no evidence of its course is to be found—
But the fluid air, lashed by the beat of
pinions,
and cleft by the rushing force
Of speeding wings, is traversed:
and afterward no mark of passage can be
found in it.
12 Or as, when an arrow has been shot at a
mark,
the parted air straightway flows together
again
so that none discerns the way it went
through—
13 Even so we, once born, abruptly came to
nought
and held no sign of virtue to display,
but were consumed in our wickedness."[n]
14 Yes, the hope of the wicked is like
thistledown borne on the wind,
and like fine, tempest-driven foam;
Like smoke scattered by the wind,
and like the passing memory of the nomad
camping for a single day.[o]
15 But the just live forever,
and in the LORD is their recompense,
and the thought of them is with the Most
High.[p]
16 Therefore shall they receive the splendid
crown,
the beauteous diadem, from the hand of
the LORD—
For he shall shelter them with his right
hand,
and protect them with his arm.[q]
17 He shall take his zeal for armor[r]
and he shall arm creation to requite the
enemy;
18 He shall don justice for a breastplate
and shall wear sure judgment for a
helmet;
19 He shall take invincible rectitude as a
shield[s]
20 and whet his sudden anger for a sword,
And the universe shall war with him against
the foolhardy.
21 Well-aimed shafts of lightnings shall go
forth
and from the clouds as from a well-drawn
bow shall leap to the mark;[t]
22 and as from his sling, wrathful hailstones
shall be hurled.
The water of the sea shall be enraged
against them
and the streams shall abruptly overflow;[u]
23 A mighty wind shall confront them
and a tempest winnow them out;
Thus lawlessness shall lay the whole earth
waste
and evildoing overturn the thrones of
potentates.[v]

# CHAPTER 6

## Exhortation to Seek Wisdom

1 Hear, therefore, kings, and understand;[w]
learn, you magistrates of the earth's
expanse!
2 Hearken, you who are in power over the
multitude
and lord it over throngs of peoples!
3 Because authority was given you by the
LORD
and sovereignty by the Most High,
who shall probe your works and scrutinize
your counsels![x]
4 Because, though you were ministers of his
kingdom, you judged not rightly,
and did not keep the law,*
nor walk according to the will of God,
5 Terribly and swiftly shall he come against
you,
because judgment is stern for the
exalted—
6 For the lowly may be pardoned out of
mercy[y]
but the mighty shall be mightily put to the
test.
7 For the Lord of all shows no partiality,
nor does he fear greatness,[z]
Because he himself made the great as well
as the small,
and he provides for all alike;
8 but for those in power a rigorous scrutiny
impends.
9 To you, therefore, O princes, are my words
addressed[a]
that you may learn wisdom and that you
may not sin.
10 For those who keep the holy precepts
hallowed shall be found holy,

l Ps 49, 7; Prv 10, 2.
m 9ff. 1 Chr 20, 15; Ps 144, 4; Jb 9, 25f LXX.
n Ez 33, 10.
o Jb 21, 18; Ps 1, 4; 37, 20; Is 17, 13.
p Is 62, 11; Ez 18, 9.
q Ex 33, 22; Is 62, 3; 2 Tm 4, 8; 1 Pt 5, 4.
r 17: Is 59, 16.
s 19f: Dt 32, 40ff.
t Hb 3, 9ff.
u Dt 11, 4.
v Wis 11, 20; Sir 10, 13f.
w 1f: Wis 1, 1; Sir 33, 19; Mi 3, 1. 9.
x 2 Chr 36, 23; Prv 8, 15f; Jn 19, 11; Rom 13, 1ff.
y 6ff: Lk 12, 48.
z Dt 1, 17; Prv 22, 2.
a 9ff: Dt 4, 10; Ps 2, 12; Sir 32, 14; 1 Jn 3, 7.

*

6, 4: Law; that of Moses; cf v 10; Wis 2, 12.
6, 10: Response: a suitable plea before the great Judge. Cf Prv 22, 21; Jb 31, 14; Hb 2, 1; Sir 8, 9.

and those learned in them will have ready
a response.*
11 Desire therefore my words;
long for them and you shall be instructed.
12 Resplendent and unfading is Wisdom,
and she is readily perceived by those who
love her,
and found by those who seek her.[b]
13 She hastens to make herself known in
anticipation of men's desire;[c]
14 he who watches for her at dawn shall not
be disappointed,
for he shall find her sitting by his gate.
15 For taking thought of her is the perfection of
prudence,
and he who for her sake keeps vigil shall
quickly be free from care;
16 Because she makes her own rounds, seeking
those worthy of her,
and graciously appears to them in the
ways,
and meets them with all solicitude.[d]
17 For the first step toward discipline is a very
earnest desire for her;[e]
then, care for discipline is love of her;
18 love means the keeping of her laws;
To observe her laws is the basis for
incorruptibility;
19 and incorruptibility makes one close to
God;
20 thus the desire for Wisdom leads up to a
kingdom.
21 If, then, you find pleasure in throne and
scepter, you princes of the peoples,
honor Wisdom, that you may reign as
kings forever.

## II: *Praise of Wisdom by Solomon*

### Introduction

22 Now what Wisdom is, and how she came to
be, I shall relate;
and I shall hide no secrets from you,
But from the very beginning I shall search
out
and bring to light knowledge of her,
nor shall I diverge from the truth.[f]
23 Neither shall I admit consuming jealousy to
my company,
because that can have no fellowship with
Wisdom.[g]
24 A great number of wise men is the safety of
the world,
and a prudent king, the stability of his
people;[h]
25 so take instruction from my words, to
your profit.

## CHAPTER 7

### Solomon Is Like All Other Men

1 I too am a mortal man, the same as all the
rest,[i]
and a descendant of the first man formed
of earth.*
And in my mother's womb I was molded
into flesh
2 in a ten-months' period*—body and
blood,
from the seed of man, and the pleasure
that accompanies marriage.
3 And I too, when born, inhaled the common
air,
and fell upon the kindred earth;
wailing, I uttered that first sound common
to all.
4 In swaddling clothes and with constant care
I was nurtured.
5 For no king has any different origin or birth,
6 but one is the entry into life for all; and in
one same way they leave it.[j]

### Solomon Prayed and Wisdom and Riches Came to Him

7 Therefore I prayed, and prudence was given
me;
I pleaded, and the spirit of Wisdom came
to me.[k]
8 I preferred her to scepter and throne,[l]
And deemed riches nothing in comparison
with her,
9 nor did I liken any priceless gem to her;
Because all gold, in view of her, is a little
sand,
and before her, silver is to be accounted
mire.
10 Beyond health and comeliness I loved her,
And I chose to have her rather than the
light,
because the splendor of her never yields
to sleep.[m]
11 Yet all good things together came to me in
her company,[n]
and countless riches at her hands;
12 And I rejoiced in them all, because Wisdom
is their leader,
though I had not known that she is the
mother of these.[o]

b Wis 7, 10; Prv 8, 17; Jer 29, 13.
c 13ff: Prv 8, 3. 17. 34.
d Prv 8, 20f; Sir 15, 1ff.
e 17-21: Ps 2, 10ff; Prv 4, 4-9; 7, 1-4; 8, 15f; Dn 7, 27; Jn 14, 15. 21; 1 Jn 5, 3.
f Tb 12, 7. 11; Mt 13, 11; Jn 15, 15.
g Wis 7, 13; Jas 3, 14f.
h Prv 24, 6; 29, 4; Sir 10, 1ff.
i 1f: Wis 10, 1; Gn 2, 7; Jb 10, 9-12; 33, 6; 1 Cor 15, 47ff.
j Jb 1, 21; 1 Tm 6, 7f.
k 1 Kgs 3, 5-15; Prv 2, 3-11.
l 8f: Wis 8, 5; 1 Kgs 10, 21; Prv 3, 14ff; 8, 10. 18f; Jb 28, 15-19.
m Prv 6, 23.
n Prv 8, 21.
o Prv 8, 14f.

*

7, 1: First man formed of earth: Adam. The author omits throughout the book the proper names of the characters in sacred history of whom he speaks; see especially chapter 10.

7, 2: In a ten-months' period: thus the ancients were accustomed to reckon the period of pregnancy.

## Solomon Prays for Help To Speak of Wisdom

13 Simply I learned about her, and
ungrudgingly do I share—
her riches I do not hide away;[p]
14 For to men she is an unfailing treasure;
those who gain this treasure win the
friendship of God,
to whom the gifts they have from
discipline* commend them.
15 Now God grant I speak suitably
and value these endowments at their
worth:
For he is the guide of Wisdom
and the director of the wise.
16 For both we and our words are in his hand,
as well as all prudence and knowledge of
crafts.[q]
17 For he gave me sound knowledge of existing
things,
that I might know the organization of the
universe and the force of its elements,
18 The beginning and the end and the midpoint
of times,
the changes in the sun's course and the
variations of the seasons.
19 Cycles of years, positions of the stars,
20 natures of animals, tempers of beasts,
Powers of the winds and thoughts of men,
uses of plants and virtues of roots—
21 Such things as are hidden I learned, and
such as are plain;
22 for Wisdom, the artificer of all, taught
me.[r]

## Nature and Incomparable Dignity of Wisdom

For in her is a spirit
intelligent, holy, unique,
Manifold, subtle, agile,
clear, unstained, certain,
Not baneful, loving the good, keen,[s]
unhampered, beneficient, **23** kindly,
Firm, secure, tranquil,
all-powerful, all-seeing,
And pervading all spirits,
though they be intelligent, pure and very
subtle.
24 For Wisdom is mobile beyond all motion,
and she penetrates and pervades all things
by reason of her purity.[t]
25 For she is an aura of the might of God
and a pure effusion of the glory of the
Almighty;
therefore nought that is sullied enters into
her.
26 For she is the refulgence of eternal light,
the spotless mirror of the power of God,
the image of his goodness.[u]
27 And she, who is one, can do all things,
and renews everything while herself
perduring;
And passing into holy souls from age to
age,
she produces friends of God and
prophets.[v]
28 For there is nought God loves, be it not one
who dwells with Wisdom.
29 For she is fairer than the sun[w]
and surpasses every constellation of the
stars.
Compared to light, she takes precedence;
30 for that, indeed, night supplants,
but wickedness prevails not over Wisdom.

## CHAPTER 8

1 Indeed, she reaches from end to end*
mightily
and governs all things well.[x]

## Solomon Sought Wisdom, the Source of Blessings

2 Her I loved and sought after from my youth;
I sought to take her for my bride
and was enamored of her beauty.[y]
3 She adds to nobility the splendor of
companionship with God;
even the LORD of all loved her.
4 For she is instructress in the understanding
of God,
the selector of his works.[z]
5 And if riches be a desirable possession in
life,
what is more rich than Wisdom, who
produces all things?[a]
6 And if prudence renders service,[b]
who in the world is a better craftsman
than she?
7 Or if one loves justice,
the fruits of her works are virtues;
For she teaches moderation and prudence,
justice and fortitude,*
and nothing in life is more useful for men
than these.
8 Or again, if one yearns for copious learning,
she knows the things of old, and infers
those yet to come.
She understands the turns of phrases and the
solutions of riddles;
signs and wonders she knows in advance
and the outcome of times and ages.[c]

p Wis 6, 23.
q Wis 3, 1.
r Wis 14, 2; Prv 8, 30.
s 22f: Heb 4, 12f; Jas 3, 17.
t Wis 8, 1.
u 2 Cor 4, 4; Col 1, 15; Heb 1, 3.
v Ex 33, 11; Jb 42, 2; Ps 104, 29; Jl 3, 1.
w 29f: Song 6, 3. 9.
x Wis 7, 24; 15, 1.
y 1 Kgs 3, 7ff; Ps 45, 12; Prv 5, 18; 8, 17.
z Prv 8, 27-31.
a Prv 8, 18f.
b 6f: Prv 8, 14f.
c Prv 1, 6; Sir 39, 1ff; 42, 19f; Dn 2, 21.

*

7, 14: Discipline: cf note on Wis 1, 5.

8, 1: End to end: from one end of the heavens to the other.

8, 7: Moderation . . . fortitude: what are now known as the cardinal virtues.

## Solomon Sought Wisdom as His Counselor and Comfort

9 So I determined to take her to live with me,
knowing that she would be my counselor while all was well,
and my comfort in care and grief.
10 For her sake I should have glory among the masses,[d]
and esteem from the elders, though I be but a youth.
11 I should become keen in judgment,
and should be a marvel before rulers.
12 They would abide my silence and attend my utterance;
and as I spoke on further,
they would place their hands upon their mouths.*
13 For her sake I should have immortality
and leave to those after me an everlasting memory.[e]
14 I should govern peoples, and nations would be my subjects—[f]
15 terrible princes, hearing of me, would be afraid;
in the assembly I should appear noble,
and in war courageous.
16 Within my dwelling, I should take my repose beside her;
For association with her involves no bitterness
and living with her no grief,
but rather joy and gladness.[g]

## Solomon Realizes That Wisdom Is a Gift of God

17 Thinking thus within myself,
and reflecting in my heart
That there is immortality in kinship with Wisdom,[h]
18 and good pleasure in her friendship,
and unfailing riches in the works of her hands,
And that in frequenting her society there is prudence,
and fair renown in sharing her discourses,
I went about seeking to take her for my own.
19 Now, I was a well-favored child,*
and I came by a noble nature;
20 or rather, being noble, I attained an unsullied body.
21 And knowing that I could not otherwise possess her* except God gave it—
and this, too, was prudence, to know whose is the gift—
I went to the LORD and besought him,[i]
and said with all my heart:

## CHAPTER 9

## Solomon's Prayer

1 God of my fathers, LORD of mercy,[j]
you who have made all things by your word[k]
2 And in your wisdom have established man
to rule the creatures produced by you,[l]
3 To govern the world in holiness and justice,
and to render judgment in integrity of heart:[m]
4 Give me Wisdom, the attendant at your throne,
and reject me not from among your children;[n]
5 For I am your servant, the son of your handmaid,
a man weak and short-lived
and lacking in comprehension of judgment and of laws.[o]
6 Indeed, though one be perfect among the sons of men,
if Wisdom, who comes from you, be not with him,
he shall be held in no esteem.[p]
7 You have chosen me king over your people
and magistrate for your sons and daughters.[q]
8 You have bid me build a temple on your holy mountain
and an altar in the city that is your dwelling place,
a copy of the holy tabernacle which you had established from of old.[r]
9 Now with you is Wisdom, who knows your works
and was present when you made the world;
Who understands what is pleasing in your eyes
and what is conformable with your commands.[s]
10 Send her forth from your holy heavens
and from your glorious throne dispatch her

d 10ff: 1 Kgs 3, 28; Jb 29, 8ff. 21f.
e Sir 15, 6; 41, 12f; Is 56, 5.
f Wis 3, 8; Ps 18, 48; 47, 4.
g Prv 29, 6; Sir 15, 6; Bar 3, 38.
h Prv 3, 18.
i 1 Kgs 3, 9; 4, 29; Prv 2, 6; Jas 1, 5.
j Ps 86, 15.
k 1f: Gn 1; Ps 33, 6; Prv 3, 19; Jer 10, 12; Jn 1, 3. 10.
l Ps 8, 7ff; Sir 17, 2ff.
m 1 Kgs 3, 6; 9 4f; Ps 9, 8f.
n 2 Chr 1, 10.
o 1 Kgs 3, 7; Ps 116, 16.
p Wis 3, 17; 1 Kgs 11, 4; 1 Cor 3, 18ff.
q 1 Chr 28, 5.
r Ex 25, 8f; 2 Sm 7, 13; 1 Chr 28, 5; 2 Chr 6, 1f; 7, 7; Tb 1, 4; Pss 15. 1; 48, 2f.
s Dt 6, 17f; Prv 8, 22-31; Jn 1, 1ff. 10.
t Wis 18, 15; Mt 5, 34; Jn 3, 17; 20, 21.

*

8, 12: Hands upon their mouths: an oft-mentioned sign of respect among the ancients for unanswerable wisdom; cf Jb 40, 4.

8, 19f: Here the sacred writer mentions first bodily, then spiritual, excellence. To make it plain that the latter is the governing factor in the harmonious development of the human person, he then reverses the order.

8, 21: Possess her: in the Latin, "be continent." Though this verse has often been cited in connection with the virtue of chastity, the original must certainly mean "be possessed of Wisdom."

That she may be with me and work with
me,
that I may know what is your pleasure,[t]
11 For she knows and understands all things,
and will guide me discreetly in my affairs
and safeguard me by her glory;[u]
12 Thus my deeds will be acceptable,
and I shall judge your people justly
and be worthy of my father's throne.[v]
13 For what man knows God's counsel,
or who can conceive what the LORD
intends?[w]
14 For the deliberations of mortals are timid,
and unsure are our plans.
15 For the corruptible body burdens the soul
and the earthen shelter weighs down the
mind that has many concerns.[x]
16 And scarce do we guess the things on earth,
and what is within our grasp we find with
difficulty;
but when things are in heaven, who can
search them out?[y]
17 Or who ever knew your counsel, except you
had given Wisdom
and sent your holy spirit from on high?[z]
18 And thus were the paths of those on earth
made straight,
and men learned what was your pleasure,
and were saved by Wisdom.[a]

## CHAPTER 10*

### Wisdom Preserves Her Followers

1 She preserved the first-formed father* of the
world[b]
when he alone had been created;[c]
And she raised him up from his fall,
2 and gave him power to rule all things.[d]
3 But when the unjust man* withdrew from
her in his anger,
he perished through his fratricidal wrath.[e]
4 When on his account the earth was flooded,
Wisdom again saved it,
piloting the just man* on frailest wood.[f]
5 She, when the nations were sunk in
universal wickedness,
knew the just man,* kept him blameless
before God,
and preserved him resolute against pity for
his child.[g]
6 She delivered the just man* from among the
wicked who were being destroyed,[h]
when he fled as fire descended upon
Pentapolis—
7 Where as a testimony to its wickedness,
there yet remain a smoking desert,
Plants bearing fruit that never ripens,
and the tomb of a disbelieving soul,* a
standing pillar of salt.[i]
8 For those who forsook Wisdom
first were bereft of knowledge of the
right,
And then they left mankind a memorial of
their folly—
so that they could not even be hidden in
their fall.
9 But Wisdom delivered from tribulations
those who served her.[j]
10 She, when the just man fled from his
brother's anger,[k]
guided him in direct ways,*
Showed him the kingdom of God
and gave him knowledge of holy things;
She prospered him in his labors
and made abundant the fruit of his works,
11 Stood by him against the greed of his
defrauders,
and enriched him;[l]
12 She preserved him from foes,
and secured him against ambush,
And she gave him the prize for his stern
struggle
that he might know that devotion to God*
is mightier than all else.[m]
13 She did not abandon the just man* when he
was sold,[n]
but delivered him from sin.[o]
14 She went down with him into the dungeon,
and did not desert him in his bonds,
Until she brought him the scepter of royalty
and authority over his oppressors,
Showed those who had defamed him false,
and gave him eternal glory.
15 The holy people and blameless race—it was
she
who delivered them from the nation that
oppressed them.[p]
16 She entered the soul of the LORD's servant,*
and withstood fearsome kings with signs
and portents;[q]

u Wis 8, 8.
v 1 Kgs 3, 6-9.
w Is 40, 13; Bar 3, 31.
x Jb 4, 19.
y Sir 1. 3; Jn 3, 12.
z Jn 14, 26.
a Wis 10, 9; Prv 28, 26.
b 1-16: Heb 11, 17-27.
c Wis 7, 1.
d Gn 1, 28.
e Gn 4, 1-16.
f Wis 14, 5f; Gn 6, 5-9.
g Gn 22, 7-10.
h Gn 18, 22-33; 19, 15-25; 2 Pt 2, 6f.
i Gn 19, 26; Lk 17, 32.
j Wis 16, 8.
k Gn 27, 43ff; 28, 12-15.
l Gn 30, 29f; 31, 5-12.
m Gn 32, 24-29; 1 Tm 4, 8.
n 13f: Gn 37-45.
o Gn 39, 7-10.
p Ex 3, 9; 14, 30; 19, 6.
q Wis 1, 4; 7, 27; Ex 4, 10; Ps 76, 13.

*

10, 1–21: This chapter prepares for the following section (11, 2—19, 22) on the history of Israel in the Exodus, by reviewing the dealings of Wisdom with the patriarchs. It has a parallel in Sir 44–50; cf also Wis 18, 9.

10, 1f: Adam.

10, 3: Cain.

10, 4: Noah.

10, 5: Abraham.

10, 6: Lot. Pentapolis: the five cities, including Sodom; cf Gn 14, 2.

10, 7: Disbelieving soul: Lot's wife; cf Gn 19, 26.

10, 10ff: Jacob.

10, 12: Devotion to God: in the Greek this signifies "piety" or "religion," and is the equivalent of the Hebrew "fear of the Lord"; cf Prv 1, 7.

10, 13f: Joseph.

10, 16: Moses.

17 she gave the holy ones the recompense of
their labors,[r]
Conducted them by a wondrous road,
and became a shelter for them by day
and a starry flame by night.
18 She took them across the Red Sea
and brought them through the deep
waters—
19 But their enemies she overwhelmed,
and cast them up* from the bottom of the
depths.
20 Therefore the just despoiled the wicked;
and they sang, O LORD, your holy name
and praised in unison your conquering
hand[s]—
21 Because Wisdom opened the mouths of the
dumb,
and gave ready speech to infants.[t]

## CHAPTER 11

1 She made their affairs prosper through the
holy prophet.[u]

# III: Special Providence of God During the Exodus

## Introduction

2 They journeyed through the uninhabited
desert,*
and in solitudes they pitched their tents;[v]
3 they withstood enemies and took
vengeance on their foes.[w]
4 When they thirsted, they called upon you,
and water was given them from the sheer
rock,
assuagement for their thirst from the hard
stone.
5 For by the things through which their foes
were punished
they in their need were benefited.[x]

## First Example: Water Punishes the Egyptians and Benefits the Israelites

6 Instead of a spring, when the perennial
river*
was troubled with impure blood[y]
7 as a rebuke to the decree for the slaying
of infants,
You gave them abundant water in an
unhoped-for way,
8 once you had shown by the thirst they
then had
how you punished their adversaries.
9 For when they had been tried, though only
mildly chastised,[z]
they recognized how the wicked,
condemned in anger, were being
tormented.
10 the latter you tested, admonishing them as
a father;
the former as a stern king you probed and
condemned.
11 Both those afar off and those close by were
afflicted:[a]
12 For a twofold grief took hold of them[b]
and a groaning at the remembrance of the
ones who had departed.
13 For when they heard that the cause of their
own torments
was a benefit to these others, they
recognized the LORD.
14 Him who of old had been cast out in
exposure they indeed mockingly
rejected;
but in the end of events, they marveled at
him,
since their thirst proved unlike that of the
just.[c]

## Second Example: Animals Punish the Egyptians and Benefit the Israelites

15 And in return for their senseless, wicked
thoughts,
which misled them into worshiping dumb*
serpents and worthless insects,
You sent upon them swarms of dumb
creatures for vengeance;[d]
16 that they might recognize that a man is
punished by the very things through
which he sins.[e]

## Digression on God's Mercy

17 For not without means was your almighty
hand,[f]
that had fashioned the universe from
formless matter,
to send upon them a drove of bears or
fierce lions,
18 Or new-created, wrathful, unknown beasts
to breathe forth fiery breath,
Or pour out roaring smoke,
or flash terrible sparks from their eyes.

---

r 17ff; Wis 14, 3; 19, 7; Ex 13, 21f; 14—15; Pss 77, 20f; 78, 13. 53; Is 4, 5f.
s Ex 12, 35f; 15, 1-21.
t Ex 4, 10-15; Ps 8, 3; Mt 11, 25.
u Dt 2, 7; Hos 12, 14.
v 2ff: Ex 17, 2-6; Nm 20, 1-13; Pss 63, 2; 107, 4-7; Jer 2, 6.
w Ex 17, 8-16; Nm 21, 1ff. 21-35; 31, 1-12; Ps 118, 10ff.
x Wis 16, 1f.
y 6ff: Wis 18, 5; Ex 1, 22; 7, 17-24.
z 9ff: Wis 3, 5; 16, 3f; Dt 8, 2-5; Ps 6, 2; Prv 3, 12; 2 Mc 6, 12-11.11
a Ps 6, 2.
b 12f: Wis 16, 8; Ex 14, 4. 18.
c Ex 2, 3.
d Wis 12, 23f; 15, 18—16, 1; Ex 7, 26ff.
e Wis 12, 23. 27; Ex 10, 16; Prv 1, 31f; 26, 27.
f 17ff: Wis 12, 8f; 16, 1. 5; Gn 1, 1f; Dt 32, 24; 2 Kgs 17, 25f; Hos 13, 4-8.

---

10, 19: Cast them up: their bodies, on the shore.

11, 2ff: Few verses in these later chapters can be fully understood without consulting the passages in the Mosaic books which are indicated in the cross references. The theme of this part of the book is expressed in Wis 11, 5, and is illustrated in the following chapters by five examples drawn from Exodus events.

11, 6ff: The perennial river: the Nile; the contrast is between the first plague of Egypt (Ex 7, 17–24) and the water drawn from the rock in Horeb (Ex 17, 5–7; Num 20, 8–11).

11, 15: Dumb: that is, irrational.

19 Not only could these attack and completely
destroy them;
even their frightful appearance itself could
slay.
20 Even without these, they could have been
killed at a single blast,
pursued by retribution
and winnowed out by your mighty spirit;
But you have disposed all things by measure
and number and weight.[g]
21 For with you great strength abides always;
who can resist the might of your arm?[h]
22 Indeed, before you the whole universe is as
a grain from a balance,*
or a drop of morning dew come down
upon the earth.[i]
23 But you have mercy on all, because you can
do all things;
and you overlook the sins of men that
they may repent.[j]
24 For you love all things that are
and loathe nothing that you have made;
for what you hated, you would not have
fashioned.[k]
25 And how could a thing remain, unless you
willed it;
or be preserved, had it not been called
forth by you?[l]
26 But you spare all things, because they
are yours, O LORD and lover of souls,[m]

## CHAPTER 12

1 for your imperishable spirit is in all things![n]
2 Therefore you rebuke offenders little by
little,
warn them, and remind them of the sins
they are committing,
that they may abandon their wickedness
and believe in you, O LORD!
3 For, truly, the ancient inhabitants of your
holy land,[o]
4 whom you hated for deeds most odious—
Works of witchcraft and impious sacrifices;
5 a cannibal feast of human flesh
and of blood, from the midst of . . . .*—
These merciless murderers of children,
6 and parents who took with their own
hands defenseless lives,[p]
You willed to destroy by the hands of our
fathers,
7 that the land that is dearest of all to you
might receive a worthy colony of God's
children.[q]
8 But even these, as they were men, you
spared,
and sent wasps as forerunners of your
army
that they might exterminate them by
degrees.[r]
9 Not that you were without power to have the
wicked vanquished in battle by the just,
or wiped out at once by terrible beasts or
by one decisive word;[s]
10 But condemning them bit by bit, you gave
them space for repentance.
You were not unaware that their race was
wicked
and their malice ingrained,[t]
And that their dispositions would never
change;
11 for they were a race accursed from the
beginning.
Neither out of fear for anyone
did you grant amnesty for their sins.[u]
12 For who can say to you, "What have you
done?"
or who can oppose your decree?
Or when peoples perish, who can challenge
you, their maker;
or who can come into your presence as
vindicator of unjust men?[v]
13 For neither is there any god besides you
who have the care of all,
that you need show you have not unjustly
condemned;[w]
14 Nor can any king or prince confront you on
behalf of those you have punished.[x]
15 But as you are just, you govern all things
justly;
you regard it as unworthy of your power
to punish one who has incurred no
blame.[y]
16 For your might is the source of justice;
your mastery over all things makes you
lenient to all.[z]
17 For you show your might when the
perfection of your power is
disbelieved;*
and in those who know you, you rebuke
temerity.[a]
18 But though you are master of might, you
judge with clemency,
and with much lenience you govern us;

g Jb 4, 9.
h Wis 12, 12; 2 Chr 20, 6.
i Hos 13, 3.
j Wis 12, 10; Dt 9, 27; Acts 17, 30; Rom 2, 4; 11, 32; 2 Pt 3, 9.
k Ps 145, 9.
l Is 41, 4.
m Wis 12, 16; Is 63, 9.
n Wis 1, 7.
o 3ff: Wis 14, 23; Dt 18, 9-12; Pss 5, 6; 106, 28. 34-39; Jer 19, 4f; Ez 16, 3. 20f. 36.
p Nm 33, 52.
q Dt 11, 12.
r Ex 23, 28ff; Dt 7, 17-24.
s Wis 11, 18; 18, 15; Nm 16, 21.
t Wis 11, 23; Ps 55, 20; Sir 16, 9.
u Gn 9, 25.
v 2 Sm 16, 10; Eccl 8, 4; Sir 46, 19; Is 45, 9; Dn 4, 32; Rom 9, 19ff.
w Wis 6, 7; Dt 3, 24; 32, 39; Is 44, 6. 8.
x Jer 49, 19; 50, 44.
y Gn 18, 23ff; Dt 32, 4.
z Wis 2, 11; 11, 26; Ps 103, 19.
a Wis 15, 2f; Ex 9, 16.

*

11, 22: Grain from a balance: a tiny particle used for weighing on sensitive scales.

12, 5: And of blood, from the midst of . . . : this line is obscure in the current Greek text and in all extant translations. Either one or two words would complete it. The horrible crimes here spoken of (cf Wis 14, 23) were not unheard of in the ancient pagan world.

12, 17: The brunt of God's anger and vindictive justice is borne by those who know him and yet defy his authority and might. Cf Wis 1, 2; 15, 2, but also Wis 12, 27; 18. 13.

for power, whenever you will, attends
you.
19 And you taught your people, by these
deeds,[b]
that those who are just must be kind;
And you gave your sons good ground for
hope
that you would permit repentance for their
sins.
20 For these were enemies of your servants,
doomed to death;
yet, while you punished them with such
solicitude and pleading,
granting time and opportunity to abandon
wickedness,
21 With what exactitude you judged your sons,
to whose fathers you gave the sworn
covenants of goodly promises![c]
22 Us, therefore, you chastise, and our enemies
with a thousand blows you punish,
that we may think earnestly of your
goodness when we judge,
and, when being judged, may look for
mercy.

## Second Example Resumed

23 Hence those unjust also, who lived a life of
folly,
you tormented through their own
abominations.[d]
24 For they went far astray in the paths of
error,
taking for gods the worthless and
disgusting among beasts,
deceived like senseless infants.[e]
25 Therefore as though upon unreasoning
children,
you sent your judgment on them as a
mockery;[f]
26 But they who took no heed of punishment
which was but child's play
were to experience a condemnation
worthy of God.
27 For in the things through which they
suffered distress,
since they were tortured by the very
things they deemed gods,
They saw and recognized the true God
whom before they had refused to know;
with this, their final condemnation came
upon them.[g]

## Digression on False Worship

# CHAPTER 13

### A. Nature Worship

1 For all men were by nature foolish who
were in ignorance of God,
and who from the good things seen did
not succeed in knowing him who is,*
and from studying the works did not
discern the artisan;[h]
2 But either fire, or wind, or the swift air,
or the circuit of the stars, or the mighty
water,
or the luminaries of heaven,* the
governors of the world, they considered
gods.[i]
3 Now if out of joy in their beauty they
thought them gods,
let them know how far more excellent is
the Lord than these;
for the original source of beauty fashioned
them.[j]
4 Or if they were struck by their might and
energy,
let them from these things realize how
much more powerful is he who made
them.[k]
5 For from the greatness and the beauty of
created things
their original author, by analogy, is seen.
6 But yet, for these the blame is less;*
For they indeed have gone astray perhaps,
though they seek God and wish to find
him.
7 For they search busily among his works,
but are distracted by what they see,
because the things seen are fair.
8 But again, not even these are pardonable.
9 For if they so far succeeded in knowledge
that they could speculate about the world,
how did they not more quickly find its
LORD?

### B. Idolatry

10 But doomed are they, and in dead things are
their hopes,
who termed gods things made by human
hands:
Gold and silver, the product of art, and
likenesses of beasts,
or useless stone, the work of an ancient
hand.[l]

## The Carpenter and Wooden Idols

11 A carpenter may saw out a suitable tree[m]
and skillfully scrape off all its bark,
And deftly plying his art,
produce something fit for daily use,[n]

b 19f: Wis 11, 23; Sir 17, 24.
c Wis 18, 22; Gn 50, 24; Dt 7, 6-14; Ps 105, 8ff.
d Wis 11, 16; 16, 1.
e Dt 11, 28; Jer 5, 28; Rom 1, 23.
f Jer 4, 22.
g Wis 16, 16; Ex 14, 4. 28.
h Acts 14, 17; Eph 4, 17ff.
i Gn 1, 14-19; Dt 4, 19; Jb 31, 26ff.
j Ps 8, 4.
k Jer 10, 2; Bar 6, 39.
l Wis 3, 11; 15, 5. 17; Dt 4, 25-28; 7, 25; 27, 15; Ps 115, 4; Hos 14, 4; Acts 17, 29.
m 11-19: Is 44, 9-20.
n Wis 15, 7; Bar 6, 58.

*

13, 1: Him who is: the Hebrew sacred name of God; cf Ex 3, 14.

13, 2: Luminaries of heaven: the Latin interprets, "sun and moon"; governors: cf Gn 1, 16.

13, 6: The blame is less: the greater blame is incurred by those mentioned in Wis 13, 10 and 15, 14ff.

12 and use up the refuse from his handiwork
in preparing his food, and have his fill;
13 Then the good-for-nothing refuse from these
remnants,
crooked wood grown full of knots,
he takes and carves to occupy his spare
time.[o]
This wood he models with listless skill,
and patterns it on the image of a man
14 or makes it resemble some worthless
beast.
When he has daubed it with red and
crimsoned its surface with red stain,
and daubed over every blemish in it,[p]
15 He makes a fitting shrine for it
and puts it on the wall, fastening it with a
nail.[q]
16 Thus lest it fall down he provides for it,
knowing that it cannot help itself;
for, truly, it is an image and needs help.[r]
17 But when he prays about his goods or
marriage or children,[s]
he is not ashamed to address the thing
without a soul.
And for vigor he invokes the powerless;
18 and for life he entreats the dead;
And for aid he beseeches the wholly
incompetent,
and about travel, something that cannot
even walk.
19 And for profit in business and success with
his hands
he asks facility of a thing with hands
completely inert.

## CHAPTER 14

1 Again, one preparing for a voyage and about
to traverse the wild waves
cries out to wood more unsound than the
boat that bears him.[t]
2 For the urge for profits devised this latter,
and Wisdom the artificer produced it.
3 But your providence, O Father! guides it,
for you have furnished even in the sea a
road,
and through the waves a steady path,[u]
4 Showing that you can save from any danger,
so that even one without skill may
embark.[v]
5 But you will that the products of your
Wisdom be not idle;
therefore men trust their lives even to
frailest wood,
and have been safe crossing the surge on
a raft.[w]
6 For of old, when the proud giants were
being destroyed,
the hope of the universe, who took refuge
on a raft,*
left to the world a future for his race,
under the guidance of your hand.[x]
7 For blest is the wood through which justice
comes about;*
8 but the handmade idol is accursed, and its
maker as well:
he for having produced it, and it, because
though corruptible, it was termed a
god.[y]
9 Equally odious to God are the evildoer and
his evil deed;
10 and the thing made shall be punished with
its contriver.
11 Therefore upon even the idols of the nations
shall a visitation come,
since they have become abominable amid
God's works,
Snares for the souls of men
and a trap for the feet of the senseless.[z]

### The Origin and Evils of Idolatry

12 For the source of wantonness is the devising
of idols;
and their invention was a corruption of
life.[a]
13 For in the beginning they were not,
nor shall they continue forever;[b]
14 for by the vanity of men they came into
the world,
and therefore a sudden end is devised for
them.
15 For a father, afflicted with untimely
mourning,
made an image of the child so quickly
taken from him,
And now honored as a god what was
formerly a dead man
and handed down to his subjects mysteries
and sacrifices.
16 Then, in time, the impious practice gained
strength and was observed as law,
and graven things were worshiped by
princely decrees.[c]
17 Men who lived so far away that they could
not honor him in his presence
copied the appearance of the distant king
And made a public image of him they
wished to honor,
out of zeal to flatter him when absent, as
though present.
18 And to promote this observance among those
to whom it was strange,
the artisan's ambition provided a stimulus.
19 For he, mayhap in his determination to
please the ruler,

o Dt 4, 16.
p Jer 10, 9.
q Is 40, 20; 41, 7; 44, 13.
r 1 Sm 5, 3ff; Bar 6, 57.
s 17ff: Wis 15, 15.
t Is 46, 7.
u Ps 107, 23-30; Is 43, 16.
v Wis 16, 8.
w Wis 10, 4.
x Gn 6, 4; 17, 1ff. 21f.
y Rom 1, 23.
z Wis 3, 7; 23, 33; Nm 33, 4; Jos 23, 13; Ps 115, 4; Jer 6, 15; 10, 15; 46, 25; Hos 9, 15.
a Rom 1, 23ff.
b Is 2, 18.
c Dn 3, 4ff; 1 Mc 1, 47-50.
d Is 44, 12f LXX.

* 14, 6: Noah.
14, 7: Often applied to the Cross of our Lord.

labored over the likeness to the best of his skill;[d]
20 And the masses, drawn by the charm of the workmanship,
soon thought he should be worshiped who shortly before was honored as a man.[e]
21 And this became a snare for mankind,
that men enslaved to either grief or tyranny
conferred the incommunicable Name on stocks and stones.
22 Then it was not enough for them to err in their knowledge of God;[f]
but even though they live in a great war of ignorance,
they call such evils peace.[g]
23 For while they celebrate either child-slaying sacrifices or clandestine mysteries,
or frenzied carousals in unheard-of rites,[h]
24 They no longer safeguard either lives or pure wedlock;
but each either waylays and kills his neighbor, or aggrieves him by adultery.
25 And all is confusion—blood and murder, theft and guile,[i]
corruption, faithlessness, turmoil, perjury,
26 Disturbance of good men, neglect of gratitude,
besmirching of souls, unnatural lust,
disorder in marriage, adultery and shamelessness.
27 For the worship of infamous idols
is the reason and source and extremity of all evil.[j]
28 For they either go mad with enjoyment, or prophesy lies,
or live lawlessly or lightly forswear themselves.[k]
29 For as their trust is in soulless idols,
they expect no harm when they have sworn falsely.
30 But on both counts shall justice overtake them:
because they thought ill of God and devoted themselves to idols,[l]
and because they deliberately swore false oaths, despising piety.*
31 For not the might of those that are sworn by
but the retribution of sinners
ever follows upon the transgression of the wicked.*

## CHAPTER 15

1 But you, our God, are good and true,
slow to anger, and governing all with mercy.[m]
2 For even if we sin, we are yours, and know your might;
but we will not sin, knowing that we belong to you.[n]
3 For to know you well is complete justice,
and to know your might is the root of immortality.[o]
4 For neither did the evil creation of men's fancy deceive us,
nor the fruitless labor of painters,[p]
A form smeared with varied colors,
5 the sight of which arouses yearning in the senseless man,
till he longs for the inanimate form of a dead image.
6 Lovers of evil things, and worthy of such hopes
are they who make them and long for them and worship them.[q]

### The Potter's Clay Idols

7 For truly the potter, laboriously working the soft earth,
molds for our service each several article:
Both the vessels that serve for clean purposes
and their opposites, all alike;
As to what shall be the use of each vessel of either class
the worker in clay is the judge.[r]
8 And with misspent toil he molds a meaningless god from the selfsame clay;
though he himself shortly before was made from the earth
And after a little, is to go whence he was taken,
when the life that was lent him is demanded back.[s]
9 But his concern is not that he is to die
nor that his span of life is brief;
Rather, he vies with goldsmiths and silversmiths
and emulates molders of bronze,
and takes pride in modeling counterfeits.[t]
10 Ashes his heart is! more worthless than earth is his hope,[u]
and more ignoble than clay his life;
11 Because he knew not the one who fashioned him,
and breathed into him a quickening soul,
and infused a vital spirit.[v]
12 Instead, he esteemed our life a plaything,
and our span of life a holiday for gain;
"For one must," says he, "make profit every way, be it even out of evil."[w]

---

e Wis 15, 4.
f 22-31: Jer 2, 20; 3, 1-25; Hos 4, 1f. 9-19; Rom 1, 26-31; Gal 5, 19ff; 1 Tm 1, 9f.
g Jer 6, 14; Ez 13, 10.
h Wis 12, 4f; 14, 15; Is 57, 5.
i 25f: Jer 7, 8f; 22, 17.
j Ex 23, 13.
k Jer 5, 31; 29, 26.
l Wis 1, 1. 8; 11, 20; Jer 5, 2. 7.
m Ex 34, 6f; Pss 86, 5. 15; 145, 8. 9. 14.
n Jb 10, 14f LXX.
o Wis 3, 15; Jn 17, 3.
p Wis 13, 14.
q Ps 115, 8.
r Wis 13, 11; Jer 18, 3f; Rom 9, 21; 2 Tm 2, 20f.
s Gn 3, 19; Eccl 12, 7.
t Bar 6, 46.
u Jb 13, 12 LXX.
v Gn 2, 7; Zec 12, 1.
w Jas 4, 13f.

*

14, 30: Piety: the sanctity of oaths.

14, 31: Perjury is a form of deceit which calls for punishment even though it be practiced in the name of a lifeless idol.

13 For this man more than any knows that he is sinning,
when out of earthen stuff he creates fragile vessels and idols alike.
14 But all quite senseless, and worse than childish in mind,
are the enemies of your people who enslaved them.[x]
15 For they esteemed all the idols of the nations, gods,
which have no use of the eyes for vision,
nor nostrils to snuff the air,
Nor ears to hear,
nor fingers on their hands for feeling;
even their feet are useless to walk with.[y]
16 For a man made them;[z]
one whose spirit has been lent him fashioned them.
For no man succeeds in fashioning a god like himself;
17 being mortal, he makes a dead thing with his lawless hands.
For he is better than the things he worships;
he at least lives, but never they.

## Second Example Resumed

18 And besides, they worship* the most loathsome beasts—[a]
for compared as to folly, these are worse than the rest,*
19 Nor for their looks are they good or desirable beasts,
but they have escaped both the approval of God and his blessing.[b]

## CHAPTER 16

1 Therefore they* were fittingly punished by similar creatures,
and were tormented by a swarm of insects.[c]
2 Instead of this punishment, you benefited your people
with a novel dish, the delight they craved,
by providing quail for their food;[d]
3 That those others, when they desired food,
since the creatures sent to plague them were so loathsome,
should be turned from even the craving of necessities,
While these, after a brief period of privation,
partook of a novel dish.[e]
4 For upon those oppressors, inexorable want had to come;
but these needed only be shown how their enemies were being tormented.[f]
5 For when the dire venom of beasts came upon them[g]
and they were dying from the bite of crooked serpents,
your anger endured not to the end.
6 But as a warning, for a short time they were terrorized,
though they had a sign* of salvation, to remind them of the precept of your law.
7 For he who turned toward it was saved,
not by what he saw,
but by you, the savior of all.
8 And by this also you convinced our foes
that you are he who delivers from all evil.[h]
9 For the bites of locusts and of flies slew them,
and no remedy was found to save their lives
because they deserved to be punished by such means;[i]
10 But not even the fangs of poisonous reptiles overcame your sons,
for your mercy brought the antidote to heal them.[j]
11 For as a reminder of your injunctions, they were stung,
and swiftly they were saved,
Lest they should fall into deep forgetfulness
and become unresponsive to your beneficence.[k]
12 For indeed, neither herb nor application cured them,
but your all-healing word, O LORD![l]
13 For you have dominion over life and death;[m]
you lead down to the gates of the nether world, and lead back.
14 Man, however, slays in his malice,
but when the spirit has come away, it does not return,
nor can he bring back the soul once it is confined.*
15 But your hand none can escape.

## Third Example: A Rain of Manna for Israel instead of the Plague of Storms

16 For the wicked who refused to know you

x Ex 1, 13.
y Wis 14, 11; Dt 4, 28; Pss 115, 4-7; 135, 15ff.
z 16f: Wis 13. 10.
a Wis 11, 15; 12, 24.
b Gn 1, 25; 3, 14.
c Wis 11, 15f; 12, 23. 27; Ex 7, 27; 8, 12. 17.
d Wis 11, 13; 19, 11f; Ex 16, 13; Nm 11, 31f; Ps 105, 40.
e Wis 11, 15; Ex 8, 10; 16, 3.
f Wis 11, 8f.
g 5f: Nm 21, 4-9; Dt 32, 24; Jer 8, 7 LXX.
h Gn 48, 16; 2 Mc 1, 24f.
i Ex 8, 16-28; 10, 4-19; Pss 78, 45f; 105, 31. 34; Rv 9, 1-11.
j Dt 32, 33.
k Ps 78, 11.
l Ex 15, 26.
m 13ff: Dt 32, 39; 1 Sm 2, 6; Tb 13, 2; Ps 78, 34. 39; Eccl 8, 8; Dn 5, 19; 2 Mc 6, 26; 7, 23.
n Wis 11, 21; 12, 27; Ex 5, 2; 9, 29-34.

*

15, 18ff: The author here returns to the main theme of chapters 11—19, which was interrupted by the digression 13, 1—15, 17.

15, 18: For . . . rest: this may mean that the creatures worshiped by the Egyptians (e.g., crocodiles, serpents, scarabs, etc.) were more patently lacking in intelligence than the general run of beasts; cf Wis 11, 15; 12, 24.

16, 1: They: the Egyptian idolaters.

16, 6: Sign: the brazen serpent; cf Nm 21, 9.

16, 14: Confined: in the nether world, in limbo.

were punished by the might of your arm,
Pursued by unwonted rains and hailstorms
and unremitting downpours,
and consumed by fire.[n]
17 For against all expectation, in water which
quenches anything,
the fire grew more active;
For the universe fights on behalf of the
just.[o]
18 For now the flame was tempered[p]
so that the beasts might not be burnt up
that were sent upon the wicked,
but that these might see and know they
were struck by the judgment of God;
19 And again, even in the water, fire blazed
beyond its strength
so as to consume the produce of the
wicked land.
20 Instead of this, you nourished your people
with food of angels
and furnished them bread from heaven,
ready to hand, untoiled-for,
endowed with all delights and conforming
to every taste.[q]
21 For this substance of yours revealed your
sweetness toward your children,
and serving the desire of him who
received it,
was blended to whatever flavor each one
wished.[r]
22 Yet snow and ice* withstood fire and were
not melted,
that they might know that their enemies'
fruits
Were consumed by a fire that blazed in the
hail
and flashed lightning in the rain.[s]
23 But this fire, again, that the just might be
nourished,
forgot even its proper strength;[t]
24 For your creation, serving you, its maker,
grows tense for punishment against the
wicked,
but is relaxed in benefit for those who
trust in you.[u]
25 Therefore at that very time, transformed in
all sorts of ways,
it was serving your all-nourishing bounty
according to what they needed and
desired;
26 That your sons whom you loved might
learn, O LORD,
that it is not the various kinds of fruits
that nourish man, but it is your word
that preserves those who believe you![v]
27 For what was not destroyed by fire,
when merely warmed by a momentary
sunbeam, melted;[w]
28 So that men might know that one must give
you thanks before the sunrise,
and turn to you at daybreak.[x]
29 For the hope of the ingrate melts like a
wintry frost
and runs off like useless water.[y]

## CHAPTER 17

### Fourth Example: Darkness Afflicts the Egyptians, While the Israelites Have Light

1 For great are your judgments, and hardly to
be described;
therefore the unruly souls were wrong.[z]
2 For when the lawless thought to enslave the
holy nation,
shackled with darkness, fettered by the
long night,
they lay confined beneath their own roofs
as exiles from the eternal providence.[a]
3 For they who supposed their secret sins were
hid[b]
under the dark veil of oblivion
Were scattered in fearful trembling,
terrified by apparitions.
4 For not even their inner chambers kept them
fearless,
for crashing sounds on all sides terrified
them,
and mute phantoms with somber looks
appeared.
5 No force, even of fire, was able to give
light,
nor did the flaming brilliance of the stars
succeed in lighting up that gloomy night.[c]
6 But only intermittent, fearful fires*
flashed through upon them;
And in their terror they thought beholding
these was worse
than the times when that sight was no
longer to be seen.[d]
7 And mockeries of the magic art were in
readiness,
and a jeering reproof of their vaunted
shrewdness.[e]
8 For they who undertook to banish fears and
terrors from the sick soul
themselves sickened with a ridiculous
fear.
9 For even though no monstrous thing
frightened them,
they shook at the passing of insects and
the hissing of reptiles,[f]
10 And perished trembling,

o Wis 10, 20; 19, 20; Ex 9, 23-28; 2 Mc 8, 36; 14, 34.
p 18f: Wis 19, 20f.
q Ex 16, 4; Nm 11, 8; Ps 78, 24f; Jn 6, 31.
r Ps 34, 9.
s Ex 9, 25-31; 10, 12; Ps 148, 8.
t Wis 19, 21.
u Wis 5, 17. 20; 19, 6; Sir 39, 25ff.
v Dt 8, 3; Mt 4, 4.
w Ex 16, 21.
x Pss 57, 9f; 92, 3.
y Wis 5, 14; 2 Sm 14, 14.
z Ex 6, 6 LXX.
a Wis 18, 4; Ex 1, 13f; 19, 6; 10, 21ff.
b 3f: Wis 1, 7f; 10, 8; 18, 17.
c Wis 10, 17; Jer 23, 24 LXX.
d Ex 9, 23f.
e Wis 12, 25f; Ex 7, 11f. 22; 8, 3; 9, 11; 10, 2.
f Wis 16, 1; Jer 26, 22 LXX.

*

16, 22: Snow and ice: the manna; cf Wis 16, 27; 19, 21.
17, 6: Fires: that is, lightnings.

reluctant to face even the air that they
could nowhere escape.
11 For wickedness, of its nature cowardly,
testifies in its own condemnation,
and because of a distressed conscience,
always magnifies misfortunes.[g]
12 For fear is nought but the surrender of the
helps that come from reason;
13 and the more one's expectation is of itself
uncertain,
the more one makes of not knowing the
cause that brings on torment.
14 So they, during that night, powerless though
it was,
that had come upon them from the
recesses of a powerless* nether world,
while all sleeping the same sleep,
15 Were partly smitten by fearsome apparitions
and partly stricken by their soul's
surrender;
for fear came upon them, sudden and
unexpected.[h]
16 Thus, then, whoever was there fell
into that unbarred prison and was kept
confined.[i]
17 For whether one was a farmer, or a
shepherd, or a worker at tasks in the
wasteland,
Taken unawares, he served out the
inescapable sentence;
18 for all were bound by the one bond of
darkness.[j]
And were it only the whistling wind,
or the melodious song of birds in the
spreading branches,
Or the steady sound of rushing water,
19 or the rude crash of overthrown rocks,
Or the unseen gallop of bounding animals,
or the roaring cry of the fiercest beasts,
Or an echo resounding from the hollow of
the hills,
these sounds, inspiring terror, paralyzed
them.
20 For the whole world shone with brilliant
light[k]
and continued its works without
interruption;
21 Over them alone was spread oppressive
night,
an image of the darkness that next should
come upon them;
yet they were to themselves more
burdensome than the darkness.

## CHAPTER 18

1 But your holy ones had very great light;
And those others, who heard their voices but
did not see their forms,
since now they themselves had suffered,
called them blest;
2 And because they who formerly had been
wronged did not harm them, they
thanked them,
and pleaded with them, for the sake of the
difference between them.*
3 Instead of this, you furnished the flaming
pillar
which was a guide on the unknown way,
and the mild sun for an honorable
migration.[l]
4 For those deserved to be deprived of light
and imprisoned by darkness,
who had kept your sons confined
through whom the imperishable light of
the law was to be given to the world.[m]

### Fifth Example: Death of the Egyptian First-born; the Israelites Are Spared

5 When they determined to put to death the
infants of the holy ones,
and when a single boy* had been cast
forth but saved,
As a reproof you carried off their multitude
of sons
and made them perish all at once in the
mighty water.[n]
6 That night was known beforehand to our
fathers,
that, with sure knowledge of the oaths in
which they put their faith, they might
have courage.[o]
7 Your people awaited
the salvation of the just and the
destruction of their foes.[p]
8 For when you punished our adversaries,
in this you glorified us whom you had
summoned.[q]
9 For in secret the holy children of the good
were offering sacrifice
and putting into effect with one accord the
divine institution,
That your holy ones should share alike the
same good things and dangers,[r]
having previously sung the praises of the
fathers.*
10 But the discordant cry of their enemies
responded,
and the piteous wail of mourning for
children was borne to them.[s]

g Wis 4, 6; 10, 7; Rom 2, 15.
h Ex 11, 9f.
i Wis 18, 4; Ex 10, 23.
j 18f: Lv 26, 36.
k 20f: Ex 10, 23; Is 9, 1; 60, 1ff; 2 Pt 2, 17.
l Ex 13, 21.
m Wis 17, 2; Ps 119, 105; Is 2, 3. 5.
n Wis 11, 7. 14; Ex 1, 16. 22; 2, 3. 6-10; 15, 10; Neh 9, 11.
o Wis 12, 21; Ex 6, 8; 13, 5.
p Ex 14, 13.
q Wis 19, 22; Ex 3, 18; Is 43, 3f.
r Ex 12, 21-28; Sir 44—50.
s Ex 12, 30; Jer 9, 17. 19.

*

17, 14: Powerless: the nether world, the home of darkness, has no power against God, nor even against such men as do not submit to it of themselves; cf Wis 1, 14ff.

18, 2: The difference between them: God's distinctive manner of treating the Israelites and the Egyptians according to their respective merits.

18, 5: Single boy: Moses.

18, 9: Praises of the fathers: cf Sir 44—50; Wis 10.

11 And the slave was smitten with the same
retribution as his master;
even the plebeian suffered the same as the
king.[t]
12 And all alike by a single death
had countless dead;
For the living were not even sufficient for
the burial,
since at a single instant their nobler
offspring were destroyed.[u]
13 For though they disbelieved at every turn on
account of sorceries,
at the destruction of the first-born they
acknowledged that the people* was
God's son.[v]
14 For when peaceful stillness compassed
everything
and the night in its swift course was half
spent,
15 Your all-powerful word from heaven's royal
throne
bounded, a fierce warrior, into the
doomed land,[w]
16 bearing the sharp sword of your
inexorable decree.
And as he alighted, he filled every place
with death;
he still reached to heaven, while he stood
upon the earth.[x]
17 Then, forthwith, visions in horrible dreams
perturbed them[y]
and unexpected fears assailed them;
18 And cast half-dead, one here, another there,
each was revealing the reason for his
dying.
19 For the dreams that disturbed them had
proclaimed this beforehand,
lest they perish unaware of why they
suffered ill.
20 But the trial of death touched at one time
even the just,
and in the desert a plague struck the
multitude;
Yet not for long did the anger last.[z]
21 For the blameless man* hastened to be their
champion,
bearing the weapon of his special office,
prayer and the propitiation of incense;
He withstood the wrath and put a stop to the
calamity,
showing that he was your servant.[a]
22 And he overcame the bitterness
not by bodily strength, not by force of
arms;
But by word he overcame the smiter,*
recalling the sworn covenants with their
fathers.[b]
23 For when corpses had already fallen one on
another in heaps,
he stood in the midst and checked the
anger,
and cut off the way to the living.[c]
24 For on his full-length robe was the whole
world,
and the glories of the fathers were carved
in four rows upon the stones,
and your grandeur* was on the crown
upon his head.[d]
25 To these names the destroyer yielded, and
these he feared;
for the mere trial of anger was enough.[e]

## CHAPTER 19

1 But the wicked, merciless wrath assailed
until the end.
For he* knew beforehand what they were
yet to do:[f]
2 That though they themselves had agreed to
the departure
and had anxiously sent them* on their
way,
they would regret it and pursue them.[g]
3 For while they* were still engaged in funeral
rites
and were mourning at the burials of the
dead,
They adopted another senseless plan;
and those whom they had sent away with
entreaty,
they pursued as fugitives.[h]
4 For a compulsion suited to this ending drew
them on,
and made them forgetful of what had
befallen them,
That they might fill out the torments of their
punishment,
5 and your people might experience a
glorious* journey
while those others met an extraordinary
death.
6 For all creation, in its several kinds, was
being made over anew,
serving its natural laws,
that your children might be preserved
unharmed.[i]
7 The cloud overshadowed their camp;

t Ex 11, 5; 12, 29.
u Nm 33, 4.
v Wis 17, 7; Ex 4, 22f; 12, 12. 29; 13, 2. 13. 15.
w Wis 9, 10; Ex 15, 3.
x 1 Chr 21, 16; Heb 4, 12; Rv 1, 16.
y 17ff: Wis 17, 3f.
z Wis 16, 5; Nm 17, 9-15.
a Wis 12, 21; Ex 32, 12f; Ps 20, 8.
b 12, 21; Ex 32, 12f.
c Nm 14, 29f.
d Ex 28, 15-21. 31-38; Sir 45, 8-12; 50, 11.
e 1 Chr 21, 15.
f Ex 14, 4.
g Ex 12, 33; 14, 5. 8.
h Wis 18, 10. 12; Ex 12, 30ff.
i Wis 5, 17; 16, 24.
j Ex 14, 21-29.

*

18, 13: People: the Hebrews.

18, 21: Blameless man: Aaron acting according to his office of high priest and intercessor.

18, 22: Smiter: the destroying angel; cf v 25.

18, 24: Glories . . . grandeur: the name of God and the names of the tribes were inscribed on the high priest's apparel.

19, 1: He: i.e., God.

19, 2: Them: the Hebrews.

19, 3: They: the Egyptians.

19, 5: Glorious: more precisely, "wondrous," but the word reflects glorified in Wis 18, 8 and 19, 22.

and out of what had before been water,
dry land was seen emerging:
Out of the Red Sea an unimpeded road,
and a grassy plain out of the mighty flood.[j]
8 Over this crossed the whole nation sheltered by your hand,
after they beheld stupendous wonders.
9 For they ranged about like horses,
and bounded about like lambs,
praising you, O Lord! their deliverer.[k]
10 For they were still mindful of what had happened in their sojourn:
how instead of the young of animals the land brought forth gnats,
and instead of fishes the river swarmed with countless frogs.[l]
11 And later they saw also a new kind of bird[m]
when, prompted by desire, they asked for pleasant foods;
12 For to appease them quail came to them from the sea.
13 And the punishments came upon the sinners
only after forewarnings from the violence of the thunderbolts.
For they justly suffered for their own misdeeds,
since indeed they treated their guests with the more grievous* hatred.[n]
14 For those others did not receive unfamiliar visitors,[o]
but these were enslaving beneficent guests.
15 And not that only; but what punishment was to be theirs*
since they received strangers unwillingly!
16 Yet these, after welcoming them with festivities,
oppressed with awful toils
those who now shared with them the same rights.[p]
17 And they were struck with blindness,
as those others had been at the portals of the just—
When, surrounded by yawning darkness,
each sought the entrance of his own gate.[q]
18 For the elements, in variable harmony among themselves,
like strings of the harp, produce new melody,
while the flow of music steadily persists.
And this can be perceived exactly from a review of what took place.

19 For land creatures were changed into water creatures,
and those that swam went over on to the land.
20 Fire in water maintained its own strength,[r]
and water forgot its quenching nature;
21 Flames, by contrast, neither consumed the flesh
of the perishable animals that went about in them,
nor melted the icelike, quick-melting kind of ambrosial food.
22 For every way, O LORD! you magnified and glorified your people;
unfailing, you stood by them in every time and circumstance.[s]

k Wis 10, 20; 16, 8; Ex 15, 1-18; Ps 114, 4-6.
l Ex 7, 27ff; 8, 12-15; Ps 105, 30f.
m 11f: Wis 16, 2; Ps 78, 18.
n 2 Mc 7, 18. 32.
o 14f: Gn 15, 13; Ex 2, 22.
p Gn 45, 17-20; 47, 4ff; Ex 1, 11.
q Wis 17, 2; Gn 19, 11.
r 20f: Wis 16, 17ff. 22f. 27.
s Wis 18, 8; Lv 26, 44; Ps 126, 3.

19, 13: More grievous: than that of the people of Sodom; cf Gn 19.

19, 15: Theirs: the people of Sodom.

# The Book of
# Sirach
## (Ecclesiasticus)

*The Book of Sirach derives its name from the author,* Jesus, son of Eleazar, son of Sirach *(50, 27). Its earliest title seems to have been "Wisdom of the Son of Sirach." The designation "Liber Ecclesiasticus," meaning "Church Book," appended to some Greek and Latin manuscripts was due to the extensive use which the church made of this book in presenting moral teaching to catechumens and to the faithful.*

*The author, a sage who lived in Jerusalem, was thoroughly imbued with love for the law, the priesthood, the temple, and divine worship. As a wise and experienced observer of life he addressed himself to his contemporaries with the motive of helping them to maintain religious faith and integrity through study of the holy books, and through tradition.*

*The book contains numerous maxims formulated with care, grouped by affinity, and dealing with a variety of subjects such as the individual, the family, and the community in their relations with one another and with God. It treats of friendship, education, poverty and wealth, the law, religious worship, and many other matters which reflect the religious and social customs of the time.*

*Written in Hebrew between 200 and 175 B.C., the text was translated into Greek sometime after 132 B.C. by the author's grandson, who also wrote a Foreword which contains information about the book, the author, and the translator himself. Until the close of the nineteenth century Sirach was known only in translations, of which this Greek rendering was the most important. From it the Latin version was made. Between 1896 and 1900, again in 1931, and several times since 1956, manuscripts were discovered containing in all about two thirds of the Hebrew text, which agrees substantially with the Greek. One such text, from Masada, is pre-Christian in date.*

*Though not included in the Hebrew Bible after the first century A.D., nor accepted by Protestants, the Book of Sirach has always been recognized by the Catholic Church as divinely inspired and canonical. The Foreword, though not inspired, is placed in the Bible because of its antiquity and importance.*

*The contents of Sirach are of a discursive nature not easily divided into separate parts. Chapters 1—43 deal largely with moral instruction; chapters 44, 1—50, 24 contain a eulogy of the heroes of Israel and some of the patriarchs. There are two appendices in which the author expresses his gratitude to God, and appeals to the unlearned to acquire true wisdom.*

*The church uses the Book of Sirach extensively in her liturgy.*

## FOREWORD

Many important truths have been handed down to us through the law, the prophets, and the later authors; and for these the instruction and wisdom of Israel merit praise. Now, those who are familiar with these truths must not only understand them themselves but, as lovers of wisdom, be able, in speech and in writing, to help others less familiar. Such a one was my grandfather, Jesus, who, having devoted himself for a long time to the diligent study of the law, the prophets, and the rest of the books[1] of our ancestors, and having developed a thorough familiarity with them, was moved to write something himself in the nature of instruction and wisdom, in order that those who love wisdom might, by acquainting themselves with what he too had written, make even greater progress in living in conformity with the divine law.

You therefore are now invited to read it in a spirit of attentive good will, with indulgence

*

[1] The law, the prophets and the rest of the books: the Sacred Scriptures of the Old Testament written before the time of Sirach, according to the threefold division of the present Hebrew Bible.

for any apparent failure on our part, despite earnest efforts, in the interpretation of particular passages. For words spoken originally in Hebrew are not as effective when they are translated into another language. That is true not only of this book but of the law itself, the prophets and the rest of the books, which differ no little when they are read in the original.

I arrived in Egypt in the thirty-eighth year of the reign of King Euergetes,[2] and while there, I found a reproduction of our valuable teaching.[3] I therefore considered myself in duty bound to devote some diligence and industry to the translation of this book. Many sleepless hours of close application have I devoted in the interval to finishing the book for publication, for the benefit of those living abroad who wish to acquire wisdom and are disposed to live their lives according to the standards of the law.

# THE WISDOM OF SIRACH

## CHAPTER 1

### Praise of Wisdom*

1 All wisdom* comes from the LORD
and with him it remains forever.[a]
2 The sand of the seashore, the drops of rain,
the days of eternity: who can number these?
3 Heaven's height, earth's breadth,
the depths of the abyss: who can explore these?
4 Before all things else wisdom was created;
and prudent understanding, from eternity.
5 To whom has wisdom's root been revealed?
Who knows her subtleties?[b]
6 There is but one, wise and truly awe-inspiring,
seated upon his throne:
7 It is the LORD; he created her,
has seen her and taken note of her.[c]
8 He has poured her forth upon all his works,
upon every living thing according to his bounty;
he has lavished her upon his friends.
9 Fear of the LORD* is glory and splendor,
gladness and a festive crown.*
10 Fear of the LORD warms the heart,
giving gladness and joy and length of days.
11 He who fears the LORD will have a happy end;
even on the day of his death he will be blessed.
12 The beginning of wisdom is fear of the LORD,
which is formed with the faithful in the womb.[d]
13 With devoted men was she created from of old,
and with their children her beneficence abides.
14 Fullness of wisdom is fear of the LORD;
she inebriates men with her fruits.[e]
15 Her entire house she fills with choice foods,
her granaries with her harvest.
16 Wisdom's garland is fear of the LORD,
with blossoms of peace and perfect health.[f]
17 Knowledge and full understanding she showers down;
she heightens the glory of those who possess her.
18 The root of wisdom is fear of the LORD;
her branches are length of days.
19 One cannot justify unjust anger;*
anger plunges a man to his downfall.
20 A patient man need stand firm but for a time,
and then contentment comes back to him.
21 For a while he holds back his words,
then the lips of many herald his wisdom.
22 Among wisdom's treasures is the paragon of prudence;
but fear of the LORD is an abomination to the sinner.
23 If you desire wisdom, keep the commandments,
and the LORD will bestow her upon you;
24 For fear of the LORD is wisdom and culture;
loyal humility is his delight.
25 Be not faithless to the fear of the LORD,*
nor approach it with duplicity of heart.
26 Play not the hypocrite before men;
over your lips keep watch.

a 1 Kgs 3, 9. Prv 1, 7; 9, 10.
b Bar 3, 15.
c Jb 28, 27.
d Jb 28, 28; Ps 111, 10;
e Eccl 12, 13.
f Sir 21, 11.

*

2 Thirty-eighth . . . Euergetes: 132 B.C. The reference is to Ptolemy VII, Physkon Euergetes II (170–163; 145, 117 B.C.)

3 Reproduction . . . teaching; may refer to the Septuagint (Greek) translation of Hebrew wisdom writings predating Sirach.

1, 1–8: The Lord is the source and preserver of wisdom (1); he created her from eternity, before all things else (4–7); all his works reflect wisdom (2f. 8).

1, 1: Wisdom: here the author speaks of true wisdom, namely God's external revelation of himself. Throughout the book he describes in great detail just what wisdom is; sometimes it is divine; sometimes it is a synonym for God's law; sometimes it is human. But the author makes clear that even human wisdom, properly understood, comes from God.

1, 9–18: Here are described the spiritual and temporal blessings that come during the lifetime of him who fears the Lord, i.e. practice true religion.

1, 9: Fear of the Lord: see note on Ps 111, 10.

1, 19–22: The disciple of wisdom shuns unjust anger which brings downfall. By patience and self-control he preserves calm, recovers contentment, and receives public praise. The sinner, on the contrary, despises the restraints which religion imposes.

1, 25–29: Infidelity to religion, or the use of it for any but the single purpose of serving God, is hypocrisy and self-exaltation, deserving of public disgrace.

27 Exalt not yourself lest you fall
and bring upon you dishonor;
28 For then the LORD will reveal your secrets
and publicly cast you down,
29 Because you approached the fear of the
LORD
with your heart full of guile.

## CHAPTER 2

## Duties toward God

1 My son, when you come to serve the
LORD,*
prepare yourself for trials.[g]
2 Be sincere of heart and steadfast,
undisturbed in time of adversity.
3 Cling to him, forsake him not;
thus will your future be great.
4 Accept whatever befalls you,
in crushing misfortune be patient;
5 For in fire gold is tested,
and worthy men in the crucible of
humiliation.[h]
6 Trust God and he will help you;
make straight your ways and hope in him.

7 You who fear the LORD, wait for his mercy,
turn not away lest you fall.
8 You who fear the LORD, trust him,
and your reward will not be lost.
9 You who fear the LORD, hope for good
things,
for lasting joy and mercy.
10 Study the generations long past and
understand;
has anyone hoped in the LORD and been
disappointed?
Has anyone persevered in his fear and been
forsaken?
has anyone called upon him and been
rebuffed?[i]
11 Compassionate and merciful is the LORD;
he forgives sins, he saves in time of
trouble.

12 Woe to craven hearts and drooping hands,*
to the sinner who treads a double path!
13 Woe to the faint of heart who trust not,
who therefore will have no shelter!
14 Woe to you who have lost hope!
what will you do at the visitation of the
LORD?
15 Those who fear the LORD disobey not his
words;
those who love him keep his ways.[j]
16 Those who fear the LORD seek to please
him,
those who love him are filled with his
law.
17 Those who fear the LORD prepare their
hearts
and humble themselves before him.
18 Let us fall into the hands of the LORD
and not into the hands of men,
For equal to his majesty
is the mercy that he shows.[k]

## CHAPTER 3

## Duties toward Parents*

1 Children, pay heed to a father's right;
do so that you may live.
2 For the LORD sets a father in honor over his
children;
a mother's authority he confirms over her
sons.
3 He who honors his father atones for sins;
4 he stores up riches who reveres his
mother.
5 He who honors his father is gladdened by
children,
and when he prays he is heard.
6 He who reveres his father will live a long
life;
he obeys the LORD who brings comfort to
his mother.

7 He who fears the LORD honors his father,
and serves his parents as rulers.
8 In word and deed honor your father
that his blessing may come upon you;[l]
9 For a father's blessing gives a family firm
roots,
but a mother's curse uproots the growing
plant.[m]
10 Glory not in your father's shame,
for his shame is no glory to you!
11 His father's honor is a man's glory;
disgrace for her children, a mother's
shame.
12 My son, take care of your father when he is
old;
grieve him not as long as he lives.[n]
13 Even if his mind fail, be considerate with
him;

g 2 Tm 3, 12.
h Prv 17, 3; Wis 3, 6; 1 Pt 1, 7.
i Pss 31, 2; 145, 18f.
j Jn 14, 23.
k Sir 18, 3.
l Ex 20, 12; Dt 5, 16; Mt 15, 4; Mk 7, 10; Eph 6, 2.
m Gn 27, 29; 49, 2-27.
n Prv 23, 22.

*

2, 1–11: Serving God is not without its trials (1); moreover, it must be done with sincerity, steadfastness and fidelity (2f). Misfortune and humiliation merely purify man and prove his worth (4f). Patience and unwavering trust in God are always rewarded with the benefits of God's mercy and of lasting joy (6–11).

2, 12–18: A warning to those who compromise their religion in time of affliction; they fail in courage and trust and therefore have no security (12ff). But those who fear the Lord through obedience, reverence, love and humility find his mercy equal to his majesty (15–18).

3, 1–16: Besides the virtues that must characterize our conduct toward God, special duties toward our neighbor are enjoined, such as honor and respect toward parents, with corresponding blessings (1–9). Even to old and infirm parents this respect is due (10–13); through it, the sins of children are pardoned (14f). Failure to render respect is blasphemy and merits a curse from God (16). Cf Ex 20, 12; Eph 6, 2f.

revile him not in the fullness of your strength.
14 For kindness to a father will not be forgotten,
it will serve as a sin offering—it will take lasting root.
15 In time of tribulation it will be recalled to your advantage,
like warmth upon frost it will melt away your sins.
16 A blasphemer is he who despises his father;
accursed of his Creator, he who angers his mother.[o]

## Humility*

17 My son, conduct your affairs with humility,
and you will be loved more than a giver of gifts.
18 Humble yourself the more, the greater you are,
and you will find favor with God.[p]
19 For great is the power of God;
by the humble he is glorified.*
20 What is too sublime for you, seek not,
into things beyond your strength search not.[q]
21 What is committed to you, attend to;
for what is hidden is not your concern.
22 With what is too much for you meddle not,
when shown things beyond human understanding.
23 Their own opinion has misled many,
and false reasoning unbalanced their judgment.
24 Where the pupil of the eye is missing, there is no light,
and where there is no knowledge, there is no wisdom.

25 A stubborn man will fare badly in the end,
and he who loves danger will perish in it.
26 A stubborn man will be burdened with sorrow;
a sinner will heap sin upon sin.
27 For the affliction of the proud man there is no cure;
he is the offshoot of an evil plant.[r]
28 The mind of a sage appreciates proverbs,
and an attentive ear is the wise man's joy.

## Alms for the Poor*

29 Water quenches a flaming fire,
and alms atone for sins.[s]
30 He who does a kindness is remembered afterward;
when he falls, he finds a support.

## CHAPTER 4

1 My son, rob not the poor man of his livelihood:
force not the eyes of the needy* to turn away.[t]
2 A hungry man grieve not,
a needy man anger not;
3 Do not exasperate the downtrodden;
delay not to give to the needy.
4 A beggar in distress do not reject;
avert not your face from the poor.
5 From the needy turn not your eyes,
give no man reason to curse you;
6 For if in the bitterness of his soul he curse you,
his Creator will hear his prayer.
7 Endear yourself to the assembly;
before a ruler bow your head.
8 Give a hearing to the poor man,
and return his greeting with courtesy;
9 Deliver the oppressed from the hand of the oppressor;
let not justice be repugnant to you.
10 To the fatherless be as a father,
and help their mother as a husband would;
Thus will you be like a son to the Most High,
and he will be more tender to you than a mother.

## The Rewards of Wisdom*

11 Wisdom instructs her children
and admonishes those who seek her.
12 He who loves her loves life;
those who seek her out win her favor.
13 He who holds her fast inherits glory;
wherever he dwells, the LORD bestows blessings.
14 Those who serve her serve the Holy One;
those who love her the LORD loves.[u]
15 He who obeys her judges nations;
he who hearkens to her dwells in her inmost chambers.
16 If one trusts her, he will possess her;
his descendants too will inherit her.
17 She walks with him as a stranger,
and at first she puts him to the test;

o Prv 19, 26; 30, 11. 14. 17.
p Mt 23, 12.
q Ps 131, 1.
r Dt 32, 32; Wis 12, 10.
s Dn 4, 27.
t Tb 4, 7-11.
u Wis 7, 28.

*

3, 17–27: Humility gives a true estimate of self (17ff). Through it a man performs duty, avoids what is beyond his understanding and strength (20ff). Pride, however, begets false greatness, misjudgment, stubbornness, sorrow, affliction and perdition (23–27).

3, 19: An alternate or additional line would read: "For though many have been great in the course of time, it is to the humble he reveals his secrets." Cf Mt 11, 25f; 1 Cor 1, 26–29.

3, 29—4, 10: Mercy and kindness toward those in misfortune atone for sin and endear a man to God and to his fellow men.

4, 1: Eyes of the needy: when they look for help; cf Sir 18, 17.

4, 11–19: The Hebrew text presents wisdom speaking in the first person, as in ch 24. The precious fruits of wisdom: life, favor, glory, blessings, God's love, are intended to arouse desire for her (11–14). Her disciples are like priests (14) and judges (15), even partners who possess her for themselves and their descendants (16). They enjoy happiness and penetrate her profound secrets after surviving her tests (17f). Those who fail her are abandoned to destruction (19).

Fear and dread she brings upon him
and tries him with her discipline;
With her precepts she puts him to the proof,
until his heart is fully with her.
18 Then she comes back to bring him happiness
and reveal her secrets to him.
19 But if he fails her, she will abandon him
and deliver him into the hands of
despoilers.

## Sincerity and Justice*

20 Use your time well; guard yourself from
evil,
and bring upon yourself no shame.
21 There is a sense of shame laden with guilt,
and a shame that merits honor and
respect.
22 Show no favoritism to your own discredit;
let no one intimidate you to your own
downfall.
23 Refrain not from speaking at the proper
time,
and hide not away your wisdom;
24 For it is through speech that wisdom
becomes known,
and knowledge through the tongue's
rejoinder.
25 Never gainsay the truth,
and struggle not against the rushing
stream.
26 Be not ashamed to acknowledge your guilt,
but of your ignorance rather be ashamed.
27 Do not abase yourself before an impious
man,
nor refuse to do so before rulers.
28 Even to the death fight for truth,
and the LORD your God will battle for
you.
29 Be not surly in your speech,
nor lazy and slack in your deeds.
30 Be not a lion at home,
nor sly and suspicious at work.
31 Let not your hand be open to receive
and clenched when it is time to give.

## CHAPTER 5

## Against Presumption*

1 Rely not on your wealth;
say not: "I have the power."[v]
2 Rely not on your strength
in following the desires of your heart.
3 Say not: "Who can prevail against me?"
for the LORD will exact the punishment.
4 Say not: "I have sinned, yet what has
befallen me?"
for the LORD bides his time.
5 Of forgiveness be not overconfident,
adding sin upon sin.
6 Say not: "Great is his mercy;
my many sins he will forgive."
7 For mercy and anger alike are with him;
upon the wicked alights his wrath.
8 Delay not your conversion to the LORD,
put it not off from day to day;
9 For suddenly his wrath flames forth;
at the time of vengeance, you will be
destroyed.
10 Rely not upon deceitful wealth,
for it will be no help on the day of
wrath.[w]

## Sincerity in Speech

11 Winnow not in every wind,
and start not off in every direction.*
12 Be consistent in your thoughts;
steadfast be your words.*
13 Be swift to hear,
but slow to answer.[x]
14 If you have the knowledge, answer your
neighbor;
if not, put your hand over your mouth.
15 Honor and dishonor through talking!
A man's tongue can be his downfall.
16 Be not called a detractor;
use not your tongue for calumny;
17 For shame has been created for the thief,
and the reproach of his neighbor for the
double-tongued.

## CHAPTER 6

1 Say nothing harmful, small or great;
be not a foe instead of a friend;
A bad name and disgrace will you acquire:
"That for the evil man with double
tongue!"*

2 Fall not into the grip of desire,[y]
lest, like fire, it consume your strength;
3 Your leaves it will eat, your fruits destroy,
and you will be left a dry tree,
4 For contumacious desire destroys its owner
and makes him the sport of his enemies.

v Lk 12, 19.
w Prv 10, 2; 11, 4. 28.
x Prv 29, 20; Jas 1, 19.
y 2-3: Sir 9, 8; 23, 17; Jb 31, 12; Is 56, 3.

*

4, 20–31: Besides the interior trials of discipline and precept, the disciple of wisdom is warned against external dangers to his sincerity and justice, namely evil, human respect (20f), compromise of liberty in speech and action (22–25), false shame, and ignorance (26). He must fight for the truth (28), and avoid cynicism and laziness (29), and inconsistency in his conduct (30).

5, 1–10: The vices of the rich are pride and independence (1f), presumption (3), false security (4–7), and impenitence (8), which cannot escape the divine wrath (9f). Cf Prv 18, 23; 19, 1; 28, 6.

5, 11: A proverbial expression condemning inconstancy and advocating sincerity and honesty.

5, 12—6, 1: Proper use of the tongue requires constancy in speech (5, 12), prudence (13f), reserve (15), charity (6, 1), as well as the avoidance of detraction, calumny (16) and double talk, which bring shame and disgrace (5, 17; 6, 1).

6, 1: "That . . . double tongue!": people will say this against the man whose deceitful tongue has brought him to disgrace.

## True Friendship*

5 A kind mouth multiplies friends,
and gracious lips prompt friendly greetings.
6 Let your acquaintances be many,
but one in a thousand your confidant.
7 When you gain a friend, first test him,[z]
and be not too ready to trust him.
8 For one sort of friend is a friend when it suits him,
but he will not be with you in time of distress.
9 Another is a friend who becomes an enemy,
and tells of the quarrel to your shame.
10 Another is a friend, a boon companion,
who will not be with you when sorrow comes.
11 When things go well, he is your other self,
and lords it over your servants;
12 But if you are brought low, he turns against you
and avoids meeting you.
13 Keep away from your enemies;
be on your guard with your friends.
14 A faithful friend is a sturdy shelter;
he who finds one finds a treasure.
15 A faithful friend is beyond price,
no sum can balance his worth.
16 A faithful friend is a life-saving remedy,
such as he who fears God finds;
17 For he who fears God behaves accordingly,
and his friend will be like himself.

## Blessings of Wisdom*

18 My son, from your youth embrace discipline;
thus will you find wisdom with graying hair.
19 As though plowing and sowing, draw close to her;
then await her bountiful crops.
20 For in cultivating her you will labor but little,
and soon you will eat of her fruits.
21 How irksome she is to the unruly!
The fool cannot abide her.
22 She will be like a burdensome stone to test him,
and he will not delay in casting her aside.
23 For discipline* is like her name,
she is not accessible to many.

24 Listen, my son, and heed my advice;
refuse not my counsel.
25 Put your feet into her fetters,
and your neck under her yoke.
26 Stoop your shoulders and carry her
and be not irked at her bonds.
27 With all your soul draw close to her;
with all your strength keep her ways.
28 Search her out, discover her; seek her and you will find her.
Then when you have her, do not let her go;
29 Thus will you afterward find rest in her,
and she will become your joy.
30 Her fetters will be your throne of majesty;
her bonds, your purple cord.
31 You will wear her as your robe of glory,[a]
bear her as your splendid crown.*

32 My son, if you wish, you can be taught;
if you apply yourself, you will be shrewd.
33 If you are willing to listen, you will learn;
if you give heed, you will be wise.
34 Frequent the company of the elders;
whoever is wise, stay close to him.
35 Be eager to hear every godly discourse;
let no wise saying escape you.[b]
36 If you see a man of prudence, seek him out;
let your feet wear away his doorstep!
37 Reflect on the precepts of the LORD,
let his commandments be your constant meditation;
Then he will enlighten your mind,
and the wisdom you desire he will grant.[c]

## CHAPTER 7

### Conduct in Public Life*

1 Do no evil, and evil will not overtake you;
2 avoid wickedness, and it will turn aside from you.
3 Sow not in the furrows of injustice,
lest you harvest it sevenfold.[d]
4 Seek not from the LORD authority,
nor from the king a place of honor.
5 Parade not your justice before the LORD,
and before the king flaunt not your wisdom.[e]
6 Seek not to become a judge
if you have not strength to root out crime,
Or you will show favor to the ruler
and mar your integrity.
7 Be guilty of no evil before the city's populace,
nor disgrace yourself before the assembly.

---

z 7ff: Sir 12, 8f; 37, 1-5; Prv 19, 4.
a Is 62, 3.
b Sir 8, 9.
c Ps 1, 2.
d Prv 22, 8.
e Jb 9, 2; Ps 143, 2; Prv 25, 6; 1 Cor 4, 4.

---

6, 5–17: True friends are discerned not by prosperity (11) but through the trials of adversity: distress, quarrels (9), sorrow (10) and misfortune (12). Such friends are rare and their value is beyond estimation, a gift from God (14–17).

6, 18–37: The various figures in each of the three strophes urge the search for wisdom through patients (19–23), docility (32–37), and perseverance in trials (25ff), promising rich rewards (28–31). Cf 4, 11–19.

6, 23: Discipline (musar, in the sense of wisdom) is a perfect homonym for musar, "removed, withdrawn"; thus the path of discipline is inaccessible to many.

6, 31: Some forms of the text speak also of the "yoke" of wisdom under the imagery of golden ornaments.

7, 1–17: In the conduct of social relations wisdom forbids evil and injustice (1ff), pride (5. 15ff), ambition and human respect (4, 6), public disorder (7), presumption and impatience toward God (9f), ridicule (11), mischief and deceit toward one's neighbor (8, 12f).

8 Do not plot to repeat a sin;
not even for one will you go unpunished.
9 Say not: "He will appreciate my many gifts;
the Most High will accept my offerings."[f]
10 Be not impatient in prayers,
and neglect not the giving of alms.
11 Laugh not at an embittered man;
be mindful of him who exalts and humbles.*
12 Plot no mischief against your brother,
nor against your friend and companion.
13 Delight not in telling lie after lie,
for it never results in good.
14 Thrust not yourself into the deliberations of princes,[g]
and repeat not the words of your prayer.*
15 Hate not laborious tasks,
nor farming, which was ordained by the Most High.[h]
16 Do not esteem yourself better than your fellows;
remember, his wrath will not delay.
17 More and more, humble your pride;
what awaits man is worms.[i]

## Duties of Family Life, Religion and Charity*

18 Barter not a friend for money,
nor a dear brother for the gold of Ophir.*
19 Dismiss not a sensible wife;
a gracious wife is more precious than corals.
20 Mistreat not a servant who faithfully serves,
nor a laborer who devotes himself to his task.[j]
21 Let a wise servant be dear to you as your own self;
refuse him not his freedom.*
22 If you have livestock, look after them;
if they are dependable, keep them.
23 If you have sons, chastise them;
bend their necks* from childhood.[k]
24 If you have daughters, keep them chaste,
and be not indulgent to them.[l]
25 Giving your daughter in marriage ends a great task;
but give her to a worthy man.[m]
26 If you have a wife, let her not seem odious to you;
but where there is ill-feeling, trust her not.
27 With your whole heart honor your father;
your mother's birthpangs forget not.[n]
28 Remember, of these parents you were born;
what can you give them for all they gave you?
29 With all your soul, fear God,
revere his priests.
30 With all your strength, love your Creator,
forsake not his ministers.
31 Honor God and respect the priest;
give him his portion as you have been commanded:[o]
First fruits and contributions,
due sacrifices and holy offerings.*
32 To the poor man also extend your hand,
that your blessing may be complete;
33 Be generous to all the living,
and withhold not your kindness from the dead.*
34 Avoid not those who weep,
but mourn with those who mourn;[p]
35 Neglect not to visit the sick—
for these things you will be loved.[q]
36 In whatever you do, remember your last days,
and you will never sin.

# CHAPTER 8

## Prudence in Dealing with Other Men*

1 Contend not with an influential man,
lest you fall into his power.
2 Quarrel not with a rich man,
lest he pay out the price of your downfall;
For gold has dazzled many,
and perverts the character of princes.[r]
3 Dispute not with a man of railing speech,
heap no wood upon his fire.[s]
4 Be not too familiar with an unruly man,
lest he speak ill of your forebears.

f Sir 34, 18; 35, 12.
g Sir 32, 7ff; Mt 6, 7.
h Gn 2, 15; 3, 17.
i Is 66, 24.
j Lv 19, 13; Dt 24, 14f; Jas 5, 4.
k Sir 30, 8-13; Prv 13, 24.
l Sir 42, 9ff.
m 1 Cor 7, 36ff.
n Ex 20, 12.
o Lv 7, 31; Nm 18, 18.
p Rom 12, 15.
q Mt 25, 36.
r Sir 31, 6; Dt 16, 19.
s Prv 26, 20.

*

7, 11: Him who exalts and humbles: God; cf 1 Sm 2, 7; Ps 75, 8; Lk 1, 52.

7, 14: Repeat not . . . prayer: brevity of speech in dealings with superiors and more especially with God is a sign of reverence and respect; cf Eccl 5, 1; Mt 6, 7.

7, 18–36: The duties of respect and appreciation, justice and kindness should characterize relations toward members of the household (18–28), and also toward God and his priests (29ff), the poor and afflicted, the living and the dead (32–36).

7, 18: Ophir was the port, at present unidentified, to which the ships of Solomon sailed and from which they brought back gold and silver; cf note on Ps 45, 10.

7, 21: After six years of service a Hebrew slave was entitled to freedom; cf Ex 21, 2; Dt 15, 12–15.

7, 23: Bend their necks: keep them from rebellious pride; so with the Greek. Cf Sir 30, 12. The present Hebrew text, which is probably not original here, reads: "Choose wives for them while they are young."

7, 31: First fruits . . . holy offerings: cf Ex 29, 27; Lv 7, 31–34; Nm 18, 8–20; Dt 18, 1–5.

7, 33: This seems to refer to the observances ordained toward the dead, that is, proper mourning and burial. Cf 2 Sm 21, 12ff; Tb 1, 20; 12, 12. When this verse is read in the light of later teaching, prayers for the souls of the deceased would also be recommended. Cf 2 Mc 12, 43ff.

8, 1–19: A prudent man will be circumspect, avoiding conflict with the powerful, the rich and insolent, the impious, the irascible, and with judges (1ff. 10ff. 14. 16). He will seek friendship not with the undisciplined (4. 12f) and the ruthless (15), nor with fools and strangers (17ff), but with the wise and the ancients of the people (8f).

5 Shame not a repentant sinner;[t]
remember, we all are guilty.*
6 Insult no man when he is old,
for some of us, too, will grow old.
7 Rejoice not when a man dies;
remember, we are all to die.
8 Spurn not the discourse of the wise,[u]
but acquaint yourself with their proverbs;
From them you will acquire the training
to serve in the presence of princes.
9 Reject not the tradition of old men
which they have learned from their fathers;
From it you will obtain the knowledge
how to answer in time of need.
10 Kindle not the coals of a sinner,
lest you be consumed in his flaming fire.
11 Let not the impious man intimidate you;
it will set him in ambush against you.*
12 Lend not to one more powerful than yourself;
and whatever you lend, count it as lost.[v]
13 Go not surety beyond your means;
think any pledge a debt you must pay.
14 Contend not at law with a judge,
for he will settle it according to his whim.
15 Travel not with a ruthless man,
lest he weigh you down with calamity;
For he will go his own way straight,
and through his folly you will perish with him.
16 Provoke no quarrel with a quick-tempered man
nor ride with him through the desert;
For bloodshed is nothing to him;
when there is no one to help you, he will destroy you.
17 Take no counsel with a fool,
for he can keep nothing to himself.
18 Before a stranger do nothing that should be kept secret,
for you know not what it will engender.[w]
19 Open your heart to no man,
and banish not your happiness.

## CHAPTER 9

### Advice Concerning Women*

1 Be not jealous of the wife of your bosom,
lest you teach her to do evil against you.*
2 Give no woman power over you
to trample upon your dignity.[x]
3 Be not intimate with a strange woman,
lest you fall into her snares.
4 With a singing girl be not familiar,
lest you be caught in her wiles.
5 Entertain no thoughts against a virgin,
lest you be enmeshed in damages for her.*
6 Give not yourself to harlots,
lest you surrender your inheritance.[y]
7 Gaze not about the lanes of the city
and wander not through its squares;
8 Avert your eyes from a comely woman;
gaze not upon the beauty of another's wife—
Through woman's beauty many perish,
for lust for it burns like fire.[z]
9 With a married woman dine not,
recline not at table to drink by her side,
Lest your heart be drawn to her
and you go down in blood to the grave.

### Choice of Friends*

10 Discard not an old friend,
for the new one cannot equal him.
A new friend is like new wine
which you drink with pleasure only when it has aged.
11 Envy not a sinner's fame,
for you know not what disaster awaits him.
12 Rejoice not at a proud man's success;
remember he will not reach death unpunished.
13 Keep far from the man who has power to kill,
and you will not be filled with the dread of death.
But if you approach him, offend him not,
lest he take away your life;
Know that you are stepping among snares
and walking over a net.
14 As best you can, take your neighbors' measure,
and associate with the wise.
15 With the learned be intimate;
let all your conversation be about the law of the LORD.
16 Have just men for your table companions;
in the fear of God be your glory.

### Concerning Rulers*

17 Skilled artisans are esteemed for their deftness;

t 1 Kgs 8, 46; 1 Jn 1, 8.
u 8f: Sir 6, 35.
v Sir 29, 4-7; Prv 17, 18.
w Prv 25, 9f.
x Sir 25, 21.
y Prv 5, 3-11; 6, 24; 29, 3.
z Sir 25, 20; 41, 21.

8, 5: We all are guilty: cf 1 Kgs 8, 46; 2 Chr 6, 36; Eccl 7, 20; Rom 3, 9f; 1 Jn 1, 8.

8, 11: To give in to the wicked in one instance becomes an occasion of sin for the future.

9, 1–9: Prudence and reserve in dealing with women are the best defense of morality. To preserve the liberty and dignity of his person and the integrity of his possessions, a man must avoid jealousy toward his own wife and familiarity toward all other women. Cf Sir 25, 12—26, 18.

9, 1: Unjust suspicions often engender hatred between husband and wife and may prompt a wife to commit those faults of which heretofore she had been innocent.

9, 5: Cf Ex 22, 15f; Dt 22, 28f; Jb 31, 1.

9, 10–16: In social relations, adherence to the law of the Lord should serve as a guide (15). Associate with true friends (10), with the just and the learned (14ff); avoid the company of the mighty and of sinners doomed to punishment (11ff). Cf Sir 8, 1–19.

9, 17—10, 5: Public office as conducted justly, or unjustly benefits or destroys the people, according to the axiom, "as

but the ruler of his people is the skilled sage.
18 Feared in the city is the man of railing speech,
and he who talks rashly is hated.

## CHAPTER 10

1 A wise magistrate lends stability to his people,
and the government of a prudent man is well ordered.[a]
2 As the people's judge, so are his ministers;[b]
as the head of a city, its inhabitants.
3 A wanton king destroys his people,
but a city grows through the wisdom of its princes.[c]
4 Sovereignty over the earth is in the hand of God,
who raises up on it the man of the hour;
5 Sovereignty over every man is in the hand of God,
who imparts his majesty to the ruler.

### The Sin of Pride*

6 No matter the wrong, do no violence to your neighbor,
and do not walk the path of arrogance.[d]
7 Odious to the LORD and to men is arrogance,
and the sin of oppression they both hate.
8 Dominion is transferred from one people to another
because of the violence of the arrogant.
9 Why are dust and ashes proud?*
even during life man's body decays;
10 A slight illness—the doctor jests,
a king today—tomorrow he is dead.
11 When a man dies, he inherits corruption;
worms and gnats and maggots.[e]
12 The beginning of pride is man's stubbornness
in withdrawing his heart from his Maker;
13 For pride is the reservoir of sin,
a source which runs over with vice;
Because of it God sends unheard-of afflictions
and brings men to utter ruin.[f]
14 The thrones of the arrogant God overturns
and establishes the lowly in their stead.
15 The roots of the proud God plucks up,
to plant the humble in their place:
16 He breaks down their stem to the level of the ground,
then digs their roots from the earth.
17 The traces of the proud God sweeps away
and effaces the memory of them from the earth.
18 Insolence is not allotted to a man,
nor stubborn anger to one born of woman.

### True Glory*

19 Whose offspring can be in honor? Those of men.
Which offspring are in honor? Those who fear God.
Whose offspring can be in disgrace? Those of men.
Which offspring are in disgrace? Those who transgress the commandments.
20 Among brethren their leader is in honor;
he who fears God is in honor among his people.
21 Be it tenant or wayfarer, alien or pauper,
his glory is the fear of the LORD.
22 It is not just to despise a man who is wise but poor,
nor proper to honor any sinner.[g]
23 The prince, the ruler, the judge are in honor;
but none is greater than he who fears God.
24 When free men serve a prudent slave,
the wise man does not complain.[h]
25 Flaunt not your wisdom in managing your affairs,
and boast not in your time of need.
26 Better the worker who has plenty of everything
than the boaster who is without bread.[i]
27 My son, with humility have self-esteem;
prize yourself as you deserve.
28 Who will acquit him who condemns himself?
who will honor him who discredits himself?
29 The poor man is honored for his wisdom
as the rich man is honored for his wealth;
30 Honored in poverty, how much more so in wealth!
Dishonored in wealth, in poverty how much the more!

## CHAPTER 11

1 The poor man's wisdom lifts his head high
and sets him among princes.
2 Praise not a man for his looks;
despise not a man for his appearance.
3 Least is the bee among winged things,

a Wis 6, 24.
b 2f: Prv 29, 12.
c Prv 29, 4. 8.
d Lv 19, 18.
e Jb 17, 14.
f Prv 18, 12.
g Jas 2, 1-4.
h Prv 17, 2.
i Prv 12, 9.

* the prince, so the people." Cf Is 24, 2. God, however, has sovereignty over both.

10, 6–18: Glory displayed through arrogance and pride is false and displeasing to God and men, because founded on dust and ashes (6–11). It is the denial of the glory due to God, and therefore the source of all sin (12f). Even the memory of the proud is destroyed and God transfers their power to the lowly (14–18).

10, 9f: The text is uncertain. Its general implication is that man deteriorates physically even while alive: a slight illness today may be followed by death tomorrow. The uncertainty of life leaves no room for pride.

10, 19—11, 6: Regardless of social barriers, genuine honor among men comes from fear of the Lord and a true estimate of self. The Lord exalts the lowly and oppressed; transgressors of the commandments merit dishonor and disgrace.

but she reaps the choicest of all harvests.
4 Mock not the worn cloak
and jibe at no man's bitter day:
For strange are the works of the LORD,
hidden from men his deeds.
5 The oppressed often rise to a throne,
and some that none would consider wear a crown.*
6 The exalted often fall into utter disgrace;
the honored are given into enemy hands.

## Moderation*

7 Before investigating, find no fault;
examine first, then criticize.
8 Before hearing, answer not,
and interrupt no one in the middle of his speech.[j]
9 Dispute not about what is not your concern;
in the strife of the arrogant take no part.
10 My son, why increase your cares,
since he who is avid for wealth will not be blameless?
Even if you run after it, you will never overtake it;
however you seek it, you will not find it.
11 One may toil and struggle and drive,
and fall short all the more.[k]
12 Another goes his way a weakling and a failure,
with little strength and great misery—
Yet the eyes of the LORD look favorably upon him;
he raises him free of the vile dust,
13 Lifts up his head and exalts him
to the amazement of the many.
14 Good and evil, life and death,[l]
poverty and riches, are from the LORD.*
15 Wisdom and understanding and knowledge of affairs,*
love and virtuous paths are from the LORD.
16 Error and darkness were formed with sinners from their birth,
and evil grows old with evildoers.
17 The LORD's gift remains with the just;
his favor brings continued success.
18 A man may become rich through a miser's life,
and this is his allotted reward:
19 When he says: "I have found rest,[m]
now I will feast on my possessions,"
He does not know how long it will be
till he dies and leaves them to others.*
20 My son, hold fast to your duty, busy yourself with it,
grow old while doing your task.
21 Admire not how sinners live,
but trust in the LORD and wait for his light;
For it is easy with the LORD
suddenly, in an instant, to make a poor man rich.
22 God's blessing is the lot of the just man,
and in due time his hopes bear fruit.
23 Say not: "What do I need?
What further pleasure can be mine?"
24 Say not: "I am independent.
What harm can come to me now?"
25 The day of prosperity makes one forget adversity;
the day of adversity makes one forget prosperity.[n]
26 For it is easy with the LORD on the day of death*
to repay man according to his deeds.
27 A moment's affliction brings forgetfulness of past delights;
when a man dies, his life is revealed.
28 Call no man happy before his death,
for by how he ends, a man is known.

## Care in Choosing Friends

29 Bring not every man into your house,
for many are the snares of the crafty one;
30 Though he seem like a bird confined in a cage,
yet like a spy he will pick out the weak spots.
31 The talebearer turns good into evil;
with a spark he sets many coals afire.
32 The evil man lies in wait for blood,
and plots against your choicest possessions.
33 Avoid a wicked man, for he breeds only evil,
lest you incur a lasting stain.
34 Lodge a stranger with you, and he will subvert your course,
and make a stranger of you to your own household.

## CHAPTER 12

1 If you do good, know for whom you are doing it,*
and your kindness will have its effect.
2 Do good to the just man and reward will be yours,

j Prv 18, 13.
k Ps 127, 2; Eccl 4, 8.
l Jb 1, 21; 2, 10.
m Eccl 4, 8; 6, 2; Lk 12, 19.
n Sir 18, 25.

*

11, 5: Cf 1 Sm 2, 8; Ps 105, 17–22; Lk 1, 52.

11, 7–25: Discretion regulates a man's conduct toward others and their affairs (7ff); as regards his own interests, a man should avoid solicitude for the passing external benefits of life and property (10–14. 18f. 21. 23ff), and cultivate the lasting inward gifts of wisdom and virtue (15. 17. 20. 22).

11, 14: Divine Providence ultimately governs the lives of men. Evil: misfortune and calamity sent by God either in punishment or as an incentive to repentance or to greater virtue.

11, 15f: Some ancient witnesses omit these two verses.

11, 19: Cf the parable of the rich man, Lk 12, 16–21.

11, 26ff: Sirach, writing before Christian revelation, did not go beyond the hour of death to find full divine retribution.

12, 1–7: The limitations to the practice of charity here reflected were removed by Christ, who requires that good be done even to enemies and to those who hate, persecute and calumniate us (Mt 5, 43–48).

if not from him, from the LORD.
3 No good comes to him who gives comfort to
the wicked,*
nor is it an act of mercy that he does.
4 Give to the good man, refuse the sinner;[o]
refresh the downtrodden, give nothing to
the proud man.
5 No arms for combat should you give him,
lest he use them against yourself;
6 With twofold evil you will meet
for every good deed you do for him.
7 The Most High himself hates sinners,
and upon the wicked he takes vengeance.

8 In our prosperity we cannot know our
friends;*
in adversity an enemy will not remain
concealed.[p]
9 When a man is successful even his enemy is
friendly;
in adversity even his friend disappears.[q]
10 Never trust your enemy,
for his wickedness is like corrosion in
bronze.
11 Even though he acts humbly and peaceably
toward you,
take care to be on your guard against him.
Rub him as one polishes a brazen mirror,*
and you will find that there is still
corrosion.
12 Let him not stand near you,
lest he oust you and take your place.
Let him not sit at your right hand,
lest he then demand your seat,
And in the end you appreciate my advice,
when you groan with regret, as I warned
you.
13 Who pities a snake charmer when he is
bitten,
or anyone who goes near a wild beast?
14 So is it with the companion of the proud
man,
who is involved in his sins:
15 While you stand firm, he makes no bold
move;
but if you slip, he cannot hold back.
16 With his lips an enemy speaks sweetly,
but in his heart he schemes to plunge you
into the abyss.
Though your enemy has tears in his eyes,
if given the chance, he will never have
enough of your blood.
17 If evil comes upon you, you will find him at
hand;
feigning to help, he will trip you up,
18 Then he will nod his head and clap his
hands
and hiss repeatedly, and show his true
face.

## CHAPTER 13

## Caution Regarding Associates*

1 He who touches pitch blackens his hand;
he who associates with an impious man
learns his ways.
2 Bear no burden too heavy for you;
go with no one greater or wealthier than
yourself.
How can the earthen pot go with the metal
cauldron?
When they knock together, the pot will be
smashed:
3 The rich man does wrong and boasts of it,
the poor man is wronged and begs
forgiveness.
4 As long as the rich man can use you he will
enslave you,
but when you are exhausted, he will
abandon you.
5 As long as you have anything he will speak
fair words to you,
and with smiles he will win your
confidence;
6 When he needs something from you he will
cajole you,
then without regret he will impoverish
you.
7 While it serves his purpose he will beguile
you,
then twice or three times he will terrify
you;
When later he sees you he will pass you by,
and shake his head over you.
8 Guard against being presumptuous;
be not as those who lack sense.
9 When invited by a man of influence, keep
your distance;
then he will urge you all the more.
10 Be not bold with him lest you be rebuffed,
but keep not too far away lest you be
forgotten.
11 Engage not freely in discussion with him,
trust not his many words;
For by prolonged talk he will test you,
and though smiling he will probe you.
12 Mercilessly he will make of you a
laughingstock,
and will not refrain from injury or chains.
13 Be on your guard and take care
never to accompany men of violence.

14 Every living thing loves its own kind,
every man a man like himself.
15 Every being is drawn to its own kind;
with his own kind every man associates.

o 4f: Gal 6, 10.
p Prv 17, 17.
q Prv 19, 4-7.

*

12, 3ff: The author advises against generosity to those who would abuse it.

12, 8–18: Through adversity friends are distinguished from enemies; to trust the latter or permit them intimacy is to invite disaster. Cf note on Sir 6, 5–17.

12, 11: Brazen mirror: see note on Ex 38, 8.

13, 1—14, 2: By means of various figures Sirach indicates the practical impossibility of genuine and sincere companionship between the poor and the proud rich. He lays down the principle of associating with equals (13, 15).

16 Is a wolf ever allied with a lamb?
So it is with the sinner and the just.[r]
17 Can there be peace between the hyena and the dog?
Or between the rich and the poor can there be peace?*
18 Lion's prey are the wild asses of the desert;
so too the poor are feeding grounds for the rich.
19 A proud man abhors lowliness;
so does the rich man abhor the poor.
20 When a rich man stumbles he is supported by a friend;
when a poor man trips he is pushed down by a friend.
21 Many are the supporters for a rich man when he speaks;
though what he says is odious, it wins approval.
When a poor man speaks they make sport of him;
he speaks wisely and no attention is paid him.
22 A rich man speaks and all are silent,
his wisdom they extol to the clouds.
A poor man speaks and they say: "Who is that?"
If he slips they cast him down.
23 Wealth is good when there is no sin;
but poverty is evil by the standards of the proud.
24 The heart of a man changes his countenance,
either for good or for evil.[s]
25 The sign of a good heart is a cheerful countenance;
withdrawn and perplexed is the laborious schemer.

## CHAPTER 14

1 Happy the man whose mouth brings him no grief,
who is not stung by remorse for sin.[t]
2 Happy the man whose conscience does not reproach him,
who has not lost hope.

### The Use of Wealth

3 Wealth ill becomes the mean man;*
and to the miser, of what use is gold?
4 What he denies himself he collects for others,
and in his possessions a stranger will revel.[u]
5 To whom will he be generous who is stingy with himself
and does not enjoy what is his own?
6 None is more stingy than he who is stingy with himself;
he punishes his own miserliness.
7 If ever he is generous, it is by mistake;
and in the end he displays his greed.
8 In the miser's opinion his share is too small;
9 he refuses his neighbor and brings ruin on himself.
10 The miser's eye is rapacious for bread,
but on his own table he sets it stale.
11 My son, use freely whatever you have
and enjoy it as best you can;[v]
12 Remember that death does not tarry,
nor have you been told the grave's appointed time.
13 Before you die, be good to your friend,
and give him a share in what you possess.[w]
14 Deprive not yourself of present good things,
let no choice portion escape you.
15 Will you not leave your riches to others,
and your earnings to be divided by lot?
16 Give, take, and treat yourself well,
for in the nether world there are no joys to seek.
17 All flesh grows old, like a garment;
the age-old law is: All must die.[x]
18 As with the leaves that grow on a vigorous tree:
one falls off and another sprouts—
So with the generations of flesh and blood:
one dies and another is born.[y]
19 All man's works will perish in decay,
and his handiwork will follow after him.

### The Search for Wisdom and Its Blessings*

20 Happy the man who meditates on wisdom,
and reflects on knowledge;[z]
21 Who ponders her ways in his heart,
and understands her paths;
22 Who pursues her like a scout,
and lies in wait at her entry way;
23 Who peeps through her windows,
and listens at her doors;
24 Who encamps near her house,
and fastens his tent pegs next to her walls;
25 Who pitches his tent beside her,
and lives as her welcome neighbor;
26 Who builds his nest in her leafage,
and lodges in her branches;

r 2 Cor 6, 14ff.
s Prv 15, 13.
t Sir 19, 15; 25, 8; Jas 3, 2.
u Eccl 6, 2.
v Prv 3, 9.
w Sir 4, 1; Tb 4, 7.
x Ps 103; 14ff; Is 40, 6; Jas 1, 10; 1 Pt 1, 24.
y Eccl 1, 4.
z Ps 1, 2.

13, 17: The hostility between the dogs which guard the flocks at night and the rapacious hyenas is proverbial in Palestine.

14, 3–16: The miser does no good even to himself (3–10); wealth should be wisely used during life, for it must be left behind at death (11–16). In the light of the gospel, generosity has a higher motivation and promise of reward than the Old Testament writer could propose. Cf Mt 6, 19ff; Lk 12, 32ff.

14, 20—15, 20: From his social teaching the sage now turns to consider individual responsibility. Happiness is to be found in the pursuit and possession of wisdom (14, 20—15, 5). Joy and honor are given, not to the sinner (7ff), but to him who fears God and observes his law (1–6. 10). The sinner is fully responsible for his conduct because God, who sees all things (18f), is not the author of wickedness (11ff. 20): he gives to every man the liberty to choose between good and evil (14–17).

27 Who takes shelter with her from the heat,
and dwells in her home.

## CHAPTER 15

1 He who fears the LORD will do this;
he who is practiced in the law will come to wisdom.
2 Motherlike she will meet him,
like a young bride she will embrace him,
3 Nourish him with the bread of understanding,
and give him the water of learning to drink.[a]
4 He will lean upon her and not fall,
he will trust in her and not be put to shame.
5 She will exalt him above his fellows;
in the assembly she will make him eloquent.
6 Joy and gladness he will find,
an everlasting name inherit.[b]
7 Worthless men will not attain to her,
haughty men will not behold her.
8 Far from the impious is she,
not to be spoken of by liars.
9 Unseemly is praise on a sinner's lips,
for it is not accorded to him by God.
10 But praise is offered by the wise man's tongue;
its rightful steward will proclaim it.

### Man's Free Will

11 Say not: "It was God's doing that I fell away";
for what he hates he does not do.
12 Say not: "It was he who set me astray";
for he has no need of wicked man.[c]
13 Abominable wickedness the LORD hates,
he does not let it befall those who fear him.
14 When God, in the beginning, created man,
he made him subject to his own free choice.[d]
15 If you choose you can keep the commandments;
it is loyalty to do his will.
16 There are set before you fire and water;
to whichever you choose, stretch forth your hand.
17 Before man are life and death,
whichever he chooses shall be given him.[e]
18 Immense is the wisdom of the LORD;
he is mighty in power, and all-seeing.
19 The eyes of God see all he has made;
he understands man's every deed.[f]
20 No man does he command to sin,
to none does he give strength for lies.

## CHAPTER 16

### God's Punishment of Sinners*

1 Desire not a brood of worthless children,
nor rejoice in wicked offspring.
2 Many though they be, exult not in them
if they have not the fear of the LORD.
3 Count not on their length of life,[g]
have no hope in their future.
For one can be better than a thousand;
rather die childless than have godless children!
4 Through one wise man can a city be peopled;
through a clan of rebels it becomes desolate.
5 Many such things has my eye seen,
even more than these has my ear heard.
6 Against a sinful band fire is enkindled,[h]
upon a godless people wrath flames out.*
7 He forgave not the leaders of old*
who rebelled long ago in their might;[i]
8 He spared not the neighbors of Lot[j]
whom he detested for their pride;*
9 Nor did he spare the doomed people*
who were uprooted because of their sin;
10 Nor the six hundred thousand foot soldiers[k]
who perished for the impiety of their hearts.*
11 And had there been but one stiffnecked man,
it were a wonder had he gone unpunished.
For mercy and anger alike are with him
who remits and forgives, though on the wicked alights his wrath.
12 Great as his mercy is his punishment;
he judges men, each according to his deeds.
13 A criminal does not escape with his plunder;
a just man's hope God does not leave unfulfilled.
14 Whoever does good has his reward,
which each receives according to his deeds.
15 Say not: "I am hidden from God;
in heaven who remembers me?
Among so many people I cannot be known;
what am I in the world of spirits?
16 Behold, the heavens, the heaven of heavens,

a Jn 4, 10; 6, 31ff.
b Sir 6, 29-32.
c Jas 1, 13.
d Gn 1, 27.
e Dt 30, 15.
f Pss 33, 18; 34, 16; Heb 4, 13.
g 3f: Wis 4, 1f.
h Sir 21, 9.
i Gn 6, 4; Wis 14, 6; Bar 3, 26ff.
j Gn 19, 24ff.
k Nm 14, 29.

*

16, 1–21: Sinful offspring are a great misfortune (1–4), for history and experience show how God punishes sin (5–10). He judges everyone according to his deeds (11ff); no one is hidden from him or escapes retribution at his hand (15–21).

16, 6: For Korah and his band (6a), see Nm 16, 35; Ps 106, 18; for the disgruntled Israelites (6b), Ps 78, 21f.

16, 7: The leaders of old: the "mighty men of old" who were destroyed by the flood: Gn 6, 4; Wis 14, 6; Bar 3, 26ff.

16, 8: The people of Sodom and Gomorrah: Gn 19, 24f; Ez 16, 49f.

16, 9: The Canaanites: Ex 23, 23f. 27–31; 33, 2; Dt 7, 1; Wis 12, 3.

16, 10: The Israelites who murmured against Moses: Nm 11, 20; 14, 12. 22ff.

the earth and the abyss tremble at his visitation;
17 The roots of the mountains, the earth's foundations,
at his mere glance, quiver and quake.
18 Of me, therefore, he will take no thought;
with my ways who will concern himself?
19 If I sin, no eye will see me;
if all in secret I am disloyal, who is to know?[l]
20 Who tells him of just deeds
and what could I expect for doing my duty?"
21 Such are the thoughts of senseless men,
which only the foolish knave will think.

## Divine Wisdom Seen in Creation*

22 Hearken to me, my son, take my advice,
apply your mind to my words,
23 While I propose measured wisdom,
and impart accurate knowledge.
24 When at the first God created his works
and, as he made them, assigned their tasks,[m]
25 He ordered for all time what they were to do
and their domains from generation to generation.
They were not to hunger, nor grow weary,
nor ever cease from their tasks.
26 Not one should ever crowd its neighbor,
nor should they ever disobey his word.
27 Then the LORD looked upon the earth,
and filled it with his blessings.[n]
28 Its surface he covered with all manner of life
which must return into it again.

## CHAPTER 17

1 The LORD from the earth created man,
and in his own image he made him.[o]
2 Limited days of life he gives him[p]
and makes him return to earth again.
3 He endows man with a strength of his own,
and with power over all things else on earth.
4 He puts the fear of him in all flesh,
and gives him rule over beasts and birds.
5 He forms men's tongues and eyes and ears,
and imparts to them an understanding heart.
6 With wisdom and knowledge he fills them;
good and evil he shows them.
7 He looks with favor upon their hearts,
and shows them his glorious works,
8 That they may describe the wonders of his deeds
and praise his holy name.
9 He has set before them knowledge,
a law of life as their inheritance;
10 An everlasting covenant* he has made with them,
his commandments he has revealed to them.
11 His majestic glory their eyes beheld,
his glorious voice their ears heard.
12 He says to them, "Avoid all evil";
each of them he gives precepts about his fellow men.
13 Their ways are ever known to him,
they cannot be hidden from his eyes.
14 Over every nation he places a ruler,*
but the LORD's own portion is Israel.[q]
15 All their actions are clear as the sun to him,
his eyes are ever upon their ways.
16 Their wickedness cannot be hidden from him;
all of their sins are before the LORD.
17 A man's goodness God cherishes like a signet ring,
a man's virtue, like the apple of his eye.
18 Later he will rise up and repay them,
and requite each one of them as they deserve.[r]

## Appeal for a Return to God*

19 But to the penitent he provides a way back,
he encourages those who are losing hope!
20 Return to the LORD and give up sin,
pray to him and make your offenses few.
21 Turn again to the Most High and away from sin,
hate intensely what he loathes;
22 Who in the nether world can glorify the Most High[s]
in place of the living who offer their praise?
23 No more can the dead give praise than those who have never lived;
they glorify the LORD who are alive and well.
24 How great the mercy of the LORD,
his forgiveness of those who return to him!

l Sir 23, 18.
m Gn 1, 4ff.
n Gn 1, 20ff.
o Gn 2, 7; 3. 19.
p 2ff: Gn 1, 26ff; Ps 8, 4-8.
q Ex 19, 5; Dt 4, 19f; 32, 8f; Dn 10, 13-21; 12, 1; Rom 13, 1.
r Jb 19, 25; Jl 3, 4.
s 22f: Pss 6, 6; 115, 17; Is 38, 18.

*

16, 22—17, 18: In harmony with Gn 1—2, the author describes God's wisdom in creating the universe and all things in it (22–28), endowing man with a moral nature, with wisdom and knowledge and freedom of will according to his own image (17, 1. 6), so that man may govern the earth (3f), praise God's name (8), obey his law (9–12), and render to him an account of his deeds (18). Cf Pss 19; 104.

17, 10: An everlasting covenant . . . his commandments: the various covenants which God entered into with mankind, e.g., Gn 2, 15ff; 17, 1–22, especially on Mount Sinai where the people saw God's glory and heard his voice (Ex 19, 16—24, 18).

17, 14: Ruler: this may refer to civil authority or to angels placed over nations as guardians; see note on Dt 32, 8, and the cross references above.

17, 19–27: Exhorting the sinner to return to God (19ff. 24ff), the author implies that the Lord will postpone death for a repentant sinner so that he may fulfill his destiny of praising God on earth (22f). In the light of Christian teaching, the gift of final penitence extends this divine purpose into life everlasting. See note on Ps 6, 6; cf also Ez 18, 23; 33, 11–16.

**25** The like cannot be found in men,
for not immortal is any son of man.
**26** Is anything brighter than the sun? Yet it can be eclipsed.
How obscure* then the thoughts of flesh and blood!
**27** God watches over the hosts of highest heaven,
while all men are dust and ashes.

## CHAPTER 18

### The Divine Power and Mercy*

**1** The Eternal is the judge of all things without exception;
the LORD alone is just.
**2** Whom has he made equal to describing his works,
and who can probe his mighty deeds?
**3** Who can measure his majestic power,
or exhaust the tale of his mercies?
**4** One cannot lessen, nor increase,
nor penetrate the wonders of the LORD.
**5** When a man ends he is only beginning,
and when he stops he is still bewildered.
**6** What is man, of what worth is he?
the good, the evil in him, what are these?
**7** The sum of a man's days is great
if it reaches a hundred years:[t]
**8** Like a drop of sea water, like a grain of sand,
so are these few years among the days of eternity.
**9** That is why the LORD is patient with men
and showers upon them his mercy.
**10** He sees and understands that their death is grievous,
and so he forgives them all the more.
**11** Man may be merciful to his fellow man,
but the LORD's mercy reaches all flesh,
**12** Reproving, admonishing, teaching,
as a shepherd guides his flock;[u]
**13** Merciful to those who accept his guidance,
who are diligent in his precepts.

### The Necessity of Prudence

**14** My son, to your charity add no reproach,*
nor spoil any gift by harsh words.
**15** Like dew that abates a burning wind,
so does a word improve a gift.
**16** Sometimes the word means more than the gift;
both are offered by a kindly man.
**17** Only a fool upbraids before giving;
a grudging gift wears out the expectant eyes.[v]
**18** Be informed before speaking;
before sickness prepare the cure.
**19** Before you are judged, seek merit for yourself,
and at the time of visitation you will have a ransom.*
**20** Before you have fallen, humble yourself;
when you have sinned, show repentance.
**21** Delay not to forsake sins,
neglect it not till you are in distress.
**22** Let nothing prevent the prompt payment of your vows;*
wait not to fulfill them when you are dying.[w]
**23** Before making a vow have the means to fulfill it;
be not one who tries the LORD.
**24** Think of wrath and the day of death,
the time of vengeance when he will hide his face.[x]
**25** Remember the time of hunger in the time of plenty,
poverty and want in the day of wealth.[y]
**26** Between morning and evening the weather changes;
before the LORD all things are fleeting.
**27** A wise man is circumspect in all things;
when sin is rife he keeps himself from wrongdoing.
**28** Any learned man should make wisdom known,*
and he who attains to her should declare her praise;
**29** Those trained in her words must show their wisdom,
dispensing sound proverbs like life-giving waters.

### Self-Control*

**30** Go not after your lusts,[z]
but keep your desires in check.
**31** If you satisfy your lustful appetites
they will make you the sport of your enemies.
**32** Have no joy in the pleasures of a moment

t Ps 90, 10. Eccl 5, 4.
u Jn 10, 11.
v Sir 20, 13.
w Nm 30, 3; Dt 23, 22; Ps 50, 14; Prv 20, 25;
x Sir 7, 16.
y Sir 11, 25.
z Rom 6, 12; 13, 14.

*

17, 26: Obscure: literally, evil; compare Gn 6, 5. Though moral fault is not excluded, the thought here is the inability to understand the merciful designs of God. Cf Wis 9, 14–18.

18, 1–13: Not only are God's justice and power beyond man's understanding (1–5), his mercy also is boundless and surpasses all human compassion (6–13).

18, 14–27: The practice of charity is an art which avoids every offense to the recipient (14–18). Prudence directs the changing circumstances of daily life toward the attainment of its reward at the time of visitation, i.e., the day of reckoning (19–27).

18, 19: Merit . . . ransom: almsgiving is often portrayed in the Bible as a means of approach to the forgiving mercy of God. Cf Sir 3, 29f; 29, 11f; Tb 12, 12f; Dn 4, 24; Lk 16, 9; Acts 10, 31.

18, 22f: The usual object of a vow in Old Testament times was the offering of a bloody sacrifice.

18, 28f: A general statement on the teaching of wisdom, serving either as a conclusion to the preceding section or as an introduction to the following one. The neighbors of the wise man are regarded as the field into which he channels the waters of wisdom to encourage growth. Cf Sir 24, 28–31.

18, 30—19, 4: Inordinate gratification of the senses makes a man unreasonable, the slave of passion, the sport of his enemies. In the end it destroys him physically and spiritually.

which bring on poverty redoubled;
33 Become not a glutton and a winebibber
with nothing in your purse.

## CHAPTER 19

1 He who does so grows no richer;
he who wastes the little he has will be stripped bare.
2 Wine and women make the mind giddy,
and the companion of harlots becomes reckless.[a]
4 He who lightly trusts in them has no sense,
and he who strays after them sins against his own life.
3 Rottenness and worms will possess him,
for contumacious desire destroys its owner.

### The Proper Use of Speech*

5 He who gloats over evil will meet with evil,
and he who repeats an evil report has no sense.
6 Never repeat gossip,
and you will not be reviled.[b]
7 Tell nothing to friend or foe;
if you have a fault, reveal it not,[c]
8 For he who hears it will hold it against you,
and in time become your enemy.
9 Let anything you hear die within you;
be assured it will not make you burst.
10 When a fool hears something, he is in labor,
like a woman giving birth to a child.
11 Like an arrow lodged in a man's thigh
is gossip in the breast of a fool.
12 Admonish your friend—he may not have done it;
and if he did, that he may not do it again.[d]
13 Admonish your neighbor—he may not have said it;
and if he did, that he may not say it again.
14 Admonish your friend—often it may be slander;
every story you must not believe.
15 Then, too, a man can slip and not mean it;
who has not sinned with his tongue?[e]
16 Admonish your neighbor before you break with him;
thus will you fulfill the law of the Most High.[f]

### How To Recognize True Wisdom*

17 All wisdom is fear of the LORD;
perfect wisdom is the fulfillment of the law.[g]
18 The knowledge of wickedness is not wisdom,
nor is there prudence in the counsel of sinners.
19 There is a shrewdness that is detestable,
while the simple man may be free from sin.
20 There are those with little understanding
who fear God,
and those of great intelligence who violate the law.
21 There is a shrewdness keen but dishonest,
which by duplicity wins a judgment.
22 There is the wicked man who is bowed in grief,
but is full of guile within;
23 He bows his head and feigns not to hear,
but when not observed, he will take advantage of you:
24 Even though his lack of strength keeps him from sinning,
when he finds the opportunity, he will do harm.
25 One can tell a man by his appearance;
a wise man is known as such when first met.
26 A man's attire, his hearty laughter and his gait,
proclaim him for what he is.

## CHAPTER 20

### Conduct of the Wise and the Foolish

1 An admonition can be inopportune,*
and a man may be wise to hold his peace.
2 It is much better to admonish than to lose one's temper,
for one who admits his fault will be kept from disgrace.
3 Like a eunuch lusting for intimacy with a maiden
is he who does right under compulsion.*
4 One man is silent and is thought wise,
another is talkative and is disliked.
5 One man is silent because he has nothing to say;
another is silent, biding his time.[h]
6 A wise man is silent till the right time comes,

a Prv 20, 1; 23, 20ff.
b Prv 25, 10.
c Sir 8, 18f.
d Lv 19, 17; Mt 18, 15; Lk 17, 3.
e Sir 14, 1; Jas 3, 2.
f Lv 19, 17.
g Sir 1, 1. 12. 14; Jb 28, 28; Ps 111, 10; Prv 1, 7; 9, 10.
h Sir 20, 1; Prv 10, 19; 17, 28.

*

19, 5–16: An excellent commentary on the eighth commandment of the Decalogue, forbidding intemperance in speech through calumny, rash judgment, and detraction (5f), and inculcating discreet silence in defense of self and of neighbor (7–11). Justice requires that an accused neighbor be given a hearing, and charity urges fraternal correction; both together fulfill the law of the Most High (12–16); cf Mt 7, 1f; 18, 15f.

19, 17–26: True and false wisdom as here described are synonymous with virtue and vice, with the fulfillment of the law and the violation of it.

20, 1–7: Wisdom indicates the proper times for speech and silence, that is, the occasions when the most benefit can be gained from them.

20, 3: The sense is that violence or force against a person can prevent an external act of sin or compel a good deed without eliminating the internal sin or desire of wrongdoing. Cf Sir 20, 20.

but a boasting fool ignores the proper
time.
7 He who talks too much is detested;
he who pretends to authority is hated.

8 Some misfortunes bring success;*
some things gained are a man's loss.
9 Some gifts do one no good,
and some must be paid back double.*
10 Humiliation can follow fame,
while from obscurity a man can lift up his
head.
11 A man may buy much for little,
but pay for it seven times over.
12 A wise man makes himself popular by a few
words,
but fools pour forth their blandishments in
vain.
13 A gift from a rogue will do you no good,
for in his eyes his one gift is equal to
seven.
14 He gives little and criticizes often,
and like a crier he shouts aloud.
He lends today, he asks it back tomorrow;
hateful indeed is such a man.
15 A fool has no friends,
nor thanks for his generosity;
16 Those who eat his bread have an evil
tongue.
How many times they laugh him to scorn!

17 A fall to the ground is less sudden than a
slip of the tongue;*
that is why the downfall of the wicked
comes so quickly.
18 Insipid food is the untimely tale;
the unruly are always ready to offer it.
19 A proverb when spoken by a fool is
unwelcome,
for he does not utter it at the proper time.
20 A man through want may be unable to sin,
yet in this tranquility he cannot rest.
21 One may lose his life through shame,
and perish through a fool's intimidation.
22 A man makes a promise to a friend out of
shame,
and has him for his enemy needlessly.
23 A lie is a foul blot in a man,
yet it is constantly on the lips of the
unruly.
24 Better a thief than an inveterate liar,
yet both will suffer disgrace;
25 A liar's way leads to dishonor,
his shame remains ever with him.
26 A wise man advances himself by his
words,*
a prudent man pleases the great.
27 He who works his land has abundant crops,
he who pleases the great is pardoned his
faults.
28 Favors and gifts blind the eyes;
like a muzzle over the mouth they silence
reproof.[i]
29 Hidden wisdom and unseen treasure—
of what value is either?
30 Better the man who hides his folly
than the one who hides his wisdom.

## CHAPTER 21

### Sin Must Be Avoided*

1 My son, if you have sinned, do so no more,
and for your past sins pray to be forgiven.
2 Flee from sin as from a serpent
that will bite you if you go near it;
Its teeth are lion's teeth,
destroying the souls of men.
3 Every offense is a two-edged sword;
when it cuts, there can be no healing.
4 Violence and arrogance wipe out wealth;
so too a proud man's home is destroyed.
5 Prayer from a poor man's lips is heard at
once,
and justice is quickly granted him.
6 He who hates correction walks the sinner's
path,
but he who fears the LORD repents in his
heart.
7 Widely known is the boastful speaker,
but the wise man knows his own faults.
8 He who builds his house with another's
money
is collecting stones for his funeral mound.
9 A band of criminals is like a bundle of tow;
they will end in a flaming fire.[j]
10 The path of sinners is smooth stones
that end in the depths of the nether
world,*

### The Wise and the Foolish Differ*

11 He who keeps the law controls his impulses;

i Ex 23, 8; Dt 16, 19. j Ps 21, 9.

*

20, 8–16: In a series of paradoxes the author indicates how much true and lasting values differ from apparent ones.

20, 9: And some . . . double: or perhaps, "but some are doubly precious."

20, 17–25: The ill-timed speech of the wicked, the unruly and a fool is repulsive (17ff); human respect exposes one to intimidation, rash promises and enmity (21f); lies bring dishonor and lasting disgrace (23ff).

20, 26–30: Unlike the fool who invites disaster through misuse of his tongue, the sage through prudent speech gains in honor and esteem among the great (26f). He must beware, however, of accepting bribes, lest he share in evil through silence when he should reprove (28ff).

21, 1–10: Under various figures the consequences of sin are described as destructive of wealth, and even of bodily life, and deserving of death and a place in the depths of the nether world (2ff. 6a. 8ff). Through prayer, forgiveness can be sought (1), and through fear of the Lord, repentance is achieved (1, 5. 6b).

21, 10: The path of sinners . . . nether world: eternal retribution is not yet proposed in this reference. It became clearly revealed through the teaching of Christ; cf Mt 7, 13f; 25, 41–46; Lk 16, 19–31.

21, 11–28: The mind of the wise man is a fountain of knowledge (13. 15); his will is trained to keep the law (11); his words are gracious, valued, carefully weighed, sincere (16f. 25f); his conduct is respectful, cultured and restrained (20. 22ff). The fool's mind is devoid of knowledge and impenetrable

he who is perfect in fear of the LORD has
wisdom.
12 He can never be taught who is not shrewd,
but one form of shrewdness is thoroughly
bitter.
13 A wise man's knowledge wells up in a
flood,
and his counsel, like a living spring;[k]
14 A fool's mind is like a broken jar—
no knowledge at all can it hold.
15 When an intelligent man hears words of
wisdom,
he approves them and adds to them;
The wanton hears them with scorn
and casts them behind his back.
16 A fool's chatter is like a load on a journey,
but there is charm to be found upon the
lips of the wise.
17 The views of a prudent man are sought in an
assembly,
and his words are considered with care.
18 Like a house in ruins is wisdom to a fool;
the stupid man knows it only as
inscrutable words.
19 Like fetters on the legs is learning to a fool,
like a manacle on his right hand.
20 A fool raises his voice in laughter,
but a prudent man at the most smiles
gently.[l]
21 Like a chain of gold is learning to a wise
man,
like a bracelet on his right arm.

22 The fool steps boldly into a house,
while the well-bred man remains
outside;[m]
23 A boor peeps through the doorway of a
house,
but a cultured man keeps his glance cast
down.
24 It is rude for one to listen at a door;
a cultured man would be overwhelmed by
the disgrace of it.
25 The lips of the impious talk of what is not
their concern,
but the words of the prudent are carefully
weighed.
26 Fools' thoughts are in their mouths,
wise men's words are in their hearts.
27 When a godless man curses his adversary,*
he really curses himself.
28 A slanderer besmirches himself,
and is hated by his neighbors.

## CHAPTER 22

### On Laziness and Foolishness

1 The sluggard is like a stone in the mud;*
everyone hisses at his disgrace.
2 The sluggard is like a lump of dung;
whoever touches him wipes his hands.
3 An unruly child is a disgrace to its father;
if it be a daughter, she brings him to
poverty.[n]
4 A thoughtful daughter becomes a treasure to
her husband,
a shameless one is her father's grief.
5 A hussy shames her father and her husband;
by both she is despised.
6 Like a song in time of mourning is
inopportune talk,*
but lashes and discipline are at all times
wisdom.
7 Teaching a fool is like gluing a broken pot,[o]
or like disturbing a man in the depths of
sleep;
8 He talks with a slumberer who talks with a
fool,
for when it is over, he will say, "What
was that?"
9 Weep over the dead man, for his light has
gone out;
weep over the fool, for sense has left
him.
10 Weep but a little over the dead man, for he
is at rest;
but worse than death is the life of a fool.
11 Seven days of mourning for the dead,
but for the wicked fool a whole lifetime.[p]

12 Speak but seldom with the stupid man,
be not the companion of a brute;
13 Beware of him lest you have trouble
and be spattered when he shakes himself;
Turn away from him and you will find rest
and not be wearied by his lack of sense.
14 What is heavier than lead,
and what is its name but "Fool"?
15 Sand and salt and an iron mass
are easier to bear than a stupid man.[q]

16 Masonry bonded with wooden beams*
is not loosened by an earthquake;

k Prv 13, 14; 16, 22.
l Eccl 7, 6.
m Prv 25, 17.
n Prv 17, 21; 19, 13.
o 7-11: Prv 23, 9.
p Gn 50, 10.
q Prv 27, 3.

*

to it (12. 14. 18f); his will rejects it (15); his talk is burdensome (16), his laughter unrestrained (20), his conversation shallow and meddlesome (25f); his conduct is bold and rude (22ff); his abuse of others redounds on himself (27f).

21, 27: Adversary: this can be understood in the sense that, if a man curses one who led him into sin, he implicitly curses himself for having yielded to the sin; or in the sense that the enemy is the man's own sinful nature; or even in the sense that the enemy is the devil, since the Hebrew word used here is satan. Cf 1 Chr 21, 1; Zec 3, 2; 2 Pt 2, 12f; Jude 9.

22, 1–15: To Sirach, a lazy person and an unruly child are a cause of shame and disgrace; everyone wishes to be rid of them (1–5). A wicked fool is as senseless as a man asleep or dead, but the grief he causes others lasts a lifetime (7–11). He is like a brute, troublesome and intolerable (12–15).

22, 6: Like a song . . . is . . . talk: some understand talk in the sense of a rebuke unheeded by the unruly as a joyful song is out of place among mourners. Corporal punishment, however, is always effective.

22, 16ff: A prudent mind firmly resolved is undisturbed by violent and conflicting thoughts, whereas a foolish person is tossed about by the winds of fear, like small stones whipped about by high winds.

Neither is a resolve constructed with careful deliberation
shaken in a moment of fear.
17 A resolve that is backed by prudent understanding
is like the polished surface of a smooth wall.
18 Small stones lying on an open height
will not remain when the wind blows;
Neither can a timid resolve based on foolish plans
withstand fear of any kind.

### The Preservation of Friendship*

19 One who jabs the eye brings tears:
he who pierces the heart bares its feelings.
20 He who throws stones at birds drives them away,
and he who insults a friend breaks up the friendship.
21 Should you draw a sword against a friend,
despair not, it can be undone.
22 Should you speak sharply to a friend,
fear not, you can be reconciled.
But a contemptuous insult, a confidence broken,
or a treacherous attack will drive away any friend.

23 Make fast friends with a man while he is poor;
thus will you enjoy his prosperity with him.
In time of trouble remain true to him,
so as to share in his inheritance when it comes.
24 Before flames burst forth an oven smokes;
so does abuse come before bloodshed.
25 From a friend in need of support
no one need hide in shame;
26 But from him who brings harm to his friend
all will stand aloof who hear of it.

### Prayer*

27 Who will set a guard over my mouth,
and upon my lips an effective seal,
That I may not fail through them,
that my tongue may not destroy me?[r]

## CHAPTER 23

1 LORD, Father and Master of my life,*
permit me not to fall by them!
2 Who will apply the lash to my thoughts,
to my mind the rod of discipline,
That my failings may not be spared,
nor the sins of my heart overlooked;
3 Lest my failings increase,
and my sins be multiplied;
Lest I succumb to my foes,
and my enemy rejoice over me?
4 LORD, Father and God of my life,
abandon me not into their control!
5 A brazen look allow me not;
ward off passion from my heart,
6 Let not the lustful cravings of the flesh
master me,
surrender me not to shameless desires.

### The Proper Use of the Tongue*

7 Give heed, my children, to the instruction
that I pronounce,
for he who keeps it will not be enslaved.
8 Through his lips is the sinner ensnared;
the railer and the arrogant man fall thereby.
9 Let not your mouth form the habit of swearing,
or becoming too familiar with the Holy Name.[s]
10 Just as a slave that is constantly under scrutiny*
will not be without welts,
So one who swears continually by the Holy Name
will not remain free from sin.
11 A man who often swears heaps up obligations;
the scourge will never be far from his house.
If he swears in error, he incurs guilt;
if he neglects his obligation, his sin is doubly great.[t]
If he swears without reason he cannot be found just,
and all his house will suffer affliction.
12 There are words which merit death;
may they never be heard among Jacob's heirs.
For all such words are foreign to the devout,
who do not wallow in sin.
13 Let not your mouth become used to coarse talk,
for in it lies sinful matter.
14 Keep your father and mother in mind

r Ps 141, 3.
s Ex 20, 7; Lv 19, 12; Dt 5, 11; Mt 5, 33ff.
t Lv 5, 4ff.
u Sir 7, 27; Ex 20, 12; Dt 5, 16.

*

22, 19–26: As disputes and violence weaken friendship, and disloyalty and abuse of confidence destroy it utterly (19–22. 24. 26), so kindness to a poor man in time of poverty and adversity builds up friendship and merits a share in his prosperity and inheritance (23. 25).

22, 27—23, 6: The sage implores the divine assistance to preserve him through stern discipline from sins of the tongue (22, 27; 23, 1); ignorance of mind and weakness of will (2f); and inclinations of the senses and the flesh, lest he fall into the hands of his enemies, or become a prey of shameful desires (3–6).

23, 1: Lord, Father and Master of my life: these words express the tender personal relationship between the author's soul and God, the need of his assistance, and the truth of his providence.

23, 7–15: A warning against sins of the tongue through misuse of the Holy Name, thoughtless swearing which involves obligation and incurs guilt (7–11), blasphemy (12), talk that is coarse and blundersome (13f), and the incorrigible habit of abusive language (15).

23, 10: As a slave . . . under scrutiny, so is he who calls on God to witness the truth of what he says.

when you sit among the mighty,
Lest in their presence you commit a blunder
and disgrace your upbringing,
By wishing you had never been born
or cursing the day of your birth.[u]
15 A man who has the habit of abusive language
will never mature in character as long as he lives.

## Sins of the Flesh*

16 Two types of men multiply sins,
a third* draws down wrath;
For burning passion is a blazing fire,
not to be quenched till it burns itself out:
A man given to sins of the flesh,
who never stops until the fire breaks forth;
17 The rake to whom all bread is sweet
and who is never through till he dies;[v]
18 And the man who dishonors his marriage bed
and says to himself, "Who can see me?
Darkness surrounds me, walls hide me;
no one sees me; why should I fear to sin?"[w]
Of the Most High he is not mindful,
19 fearing only the eyes of men;
He does not understand that the eyes of the LORD,
ten thousand times brighter than the sun,
Observe every step a man takes
and peer into hidden corners.
20 He who knows all things before they exist
still knows them all after they are made.
21 Such a man will be punished in the streets of the city;[x]
when he least expects it, he will be apprehended.*

22 So also with the woman who is unfaithful to her husband
and offers as heir her son by a stranger.
23 First, she has disobeyed the law of the Most High;
secondly, she has wronged her husband;
Thirdly, in her wanton adultery
she has borne children by another man.*
24 Such a woman will be dragged before the assembly,*
and her punishment will extend to her children;
25 Her children will not take root;
her branches will not bring forth fruit.
26 She will leave an accursed memory;
her disgrace will never be blotted out.
27 Thus all who dwell on the earth shall know,
and all who inhabit the world shall understand,
That nothing is better than the fear of the LORD,
nothing more salutary than to obey his commandments.[y]

## CHAPTER 24

### Praise of Wisdom

1 Wisdom sings her own praises,*
before her own people she proclaims her glory;
2 In the assembly of the Most High she opens her mouth,
in the presence of his hosts she declares her worth:
3 "From the mouth of the Most High I came forth,[z]
and mistlike covered the earth.
4 In the highest heavens did I dwell,
my throne on a pillar of cloud.
5 The vault of heaven I compassed alone,
through the deep abyss I wandered.
6 Over waves of the sea, over all the land,
over every people and nation I held sway.
7 Among all these I sought a resting place;
in whose inheritance should I abide?

8 "Then the Creator of all gave me his command,
and he who formed me chose the spot for my tent,
Saying, 'In Jacob make your dwelling,
in Israel your inheritance.'
9 Before all ages, in the beginning, he created me,
and through all ages I shall not cease to be.
10 In the holy tent I ministered before him,
and in Zion I fixed my abode.

v Prv 9, 17.
w Is 29, 15.
x 21f: Lv 20, 10; Dt 22, 21.
y Sir 1, 10-18. 24; Prv 3, 1f.
z 3ff: Sir 1, 1; Prv 2, 6; 8, 22-36; Wis 7, 24f.

*

23, 16–27: From sins of the tongue the author proceeds to treat of sins of the flesh and their dire consequences. The passion of lust tyrannizes over its victims and, like fire, consumes and utterly destroys them (16f. 22–26). The false security of the adulterer serves but to aggravate his inevitable fate (18–21). Only the fear of the Lord and observance of his commandments can assure moral safety (27).

23, 16: Two types . . . a third: three kinds of sins of impurity, with increasing degrees of gravity: solitary sins (16), fornication (17) and adultery (18–21).

23, 21: Cf Lv 20, 19; Dt 22, 22.

23, 23: The detailed evil of adultery includes disobedience to God's law (Ex 20, 14), injustice to a partner in marriage, and disgraceful offspring.

23, 24f: The judgment of the assembly determined the illegitimacy of children born of adultery or incest and excluded them from the "community of the Lord" (Dt 23, 3). Cf Wis 3, 16–19; 4, 3–6.

24, 1–27: In this chapter Wisdom speaks in the first person, describing her origin, her dwelling place in Israel, and the reward she gives her followers. As in Prv 8, Wisdom is described as a being who comes from God and is distinct from him. While we do not say with certainty that this description applies to a personal being, it does foreshadow the beautiful doctrine of the Word of God later developed in St. John's Gospel (Jn 1, 1–14). In the liturgy this chapter is applied to the Blessed Virgin because of her constant and intimate association with Christ, the Incarnate Wisdom.

11 Thus in the chosen city he has given me
rest,
in Jerusalem is my domain.
12 I have struck root among the glorious
people,
in the portion of the LORD, his heritage.

13 "Like a cedar on Lebanon I am raised aloft,
like a cypress on Mount Hermon,
14 Like a palm tree in Engedi,
like a rosebush in Jericho,
Like a fair olive tree in the field,
like a plane tree growing beside the water.
15 Like cinnamon, or fragrant balm, or
precious myrrh,
I give forth perfume;[a]
Like galbanum and onycha and sweet spices,
like the odor of incense in the holy
place.*
16 I spread out my branches like a terebinth,
my branches so bright and so graceful.
17 I bud forth delights like the vine,
my blossoms become fruit fair and rich.
18 Come to me, all you that yearn for me,
and be filled with my fruits;*
19 You will remember me as sweeter than
honey,
better to have than the honeycomb.
20 He who eats of me will hunger still,*
he who drinks of me will thirst for more;[b]
21 He who obeys me will not be put to shame,
he who serves me will never fail."

22 All this is true of the book of the Most
High's covenant,[c]
the law which Moses commanded us
as an inheritance for the community of
Jacob.*
23 It overflows, like the Pishon, with
wisdom—[d]
like the Tigris in the days of the new
fruits.
24 It runs over, like the Euphrates, with
understanding,
like the Jordan at harvest time.
25 It sparkles like the Nile with knowledge,
like the Gihon* at vintage time.
26 The first man never finished comprehending
wisdom,
nor will the last succeed in fathoming her.
27 For deeper than the sea are her thoughts;
her counsels, than the great abyss.

28 Now I, like a rivulet from her stream,*
channeling the waters into a garden,
29 Said to myself, "I will water my plants,
my flower bed I will drench";
And suddenly this rivulet of mine became a
river,
then this stream of mine, a sea.
30 Thus do I send my teachings forth shining
like the dawn,
to become known afar off.
31 Thus do I pour out instruction like prophecy
and bestow it on generations to come.

## CHAPTER 25

### Those Who Are Worthy of Praise*

1 With three things I am delighted,
for they are pleasing to the LORD and to
men:
Harmony among brethren, friendship among
neighbors,
and the mutual love of husband and wife.
2 Three kinds of men I hate;
their manner of life I loathe indeed:
A proud pauper, a rich dissembler,
and an old man lecherous in his dotage.

3 What you have not saved in your youth,
how will you acquire in your old age?
4 How becoming to the gray-haired is
judgment,
and a knowledge of counsel to those on in
years!
5 How becoming to the aged is wisdom,
understanding and prudence to the
venerable!
6 The crown of old men is wide experience;
their glory, the fear of the LORD.

7 There are nine who come to my mind as
blessed,
a tenth whom my tongue proclaims:
The man who finds joy in his children,
and he who lives to see his enemies'
downfall.
8 Happy is he who dwells with a sensible
wife,
and he who plows not like a donkey
yoked with an ox.*
Happy is he who sins not with his tongue,
and he who serves not his inferior.

---

a Ex 30, 22-25.
b Is 55, 1; Jn 6, 35.
c Ex 24, 7.
d 23ff: Gn 2, 11-14.

---

*

24, 15: These substances were associated with worship, being mentioned in Ex 30, 22f. 34 as the ingredients of the anointing oil and the sacred incense. Israel was a priestly nation.

24, 18: Compare the words of the Savior in Mt 11, 28ff.

24, 20: So pleasing is wisdom to man that, far from being satiated, he will always desire more.

24, 22: Here the author begins to speak once more, Wisdom having ended her discourse in the preceding verse. Wisdom and the law of Moses are now identified.

24, 25: Gihon: understood by some to have been a name for the Nile; cf Gn 2, 13.

24, 28–31: Spoken by the author. He had at first drawn a small portion of the water of wisdom for his own private benefit, but finding it so useful, he soon began to let others share in this boon by teaching them the lessons of wisdom.

25, 1–11: While praising brotherly love, love of neighbor, and conjugal love, the sage condemns their opposites in the arrogant pauper who despises his brother, the fraudulent rich man who cheats his neighbor, and the lecherous old man unfaithful to his wife (1f). This last, sensual from his youth, lacks the mature blessings of judgment and wisdom in old age (3–6), and the joy of a peaceful household, where honesty and dignity, friendship, wisdom and fear of God prevail (7–11).

25, 8: Like a donkey yoked with an ox: incompatibility between husband and wife.

9 Happy is he who finds a friend
and he who speaks to attentive ears.
10 He who finds wisdom is great indeed,
but not greater than he who fears the LORD.
11 Fear of the LORD surpasses all else,
its possessor is beyond compare.

### Wicked and Virtuous Women*

12 Worst of all wounds is that of the heart,
worst of all evils is that of a woman.
13 Worst of all sufferings is that from one's foes,
worst of all vengeance is that of one's enemies:
14 No poison worse than that of a serpent,
no venom greater than that of a woman.
15 With a dragon or a lion I would rather dwell
than live with an evil woman.
16 Wickedness changes a woman's looks,
and makes her sullen as a female bear.
17 When her husband sits among his neighbors,
a bitter sigh escapes him unawares.

18 There is scarce any evil like that in a woman;
may she fall to the lot of the sinner!
19 Like a sandy hill to aged feet
is a railing wife to a quiet man.
20 Stumble not through woman's beauty,
nor be greedy for her wealth;
21 The man is a slave, in disgrace and shame,
when a wife supports her husband.
22 Depressed mind, saddened face,
broken heart—this from an evil wife.
Feeble hands and quaking knees—
from a wife who brings no happiness to her husband.
23 In woman was sin's beginning,
and because of her we all die.*
24 Allow water no outlet,
and be not indulgent to an erring wife.
25 If she walks not by your side,
cut her away from you.

## CHAPTER 26

1 Happy the husband of a good wife,*
twice-lengthened are his days;[e]
2 A worthy* wife brings joy to her husband.
peaceful and full is his life.
3 A good wife is a generous gift
bestowed upon him who fears the LORD;[f]
4 Be he rich or poor, his heart is content,
and a smile is ever on his face.

5 There are three things at which my heart quakes,
a fourth before which I quail:
Though false charges in public, trial before all the people,
and lying testimony are harder to bear than death,
6 A jealous wife is heartache and mourning*
and a scourging tongue like the other three.
7 A bad wife is a chafing yoke;
he who marries her seizes a scorpion.
8 A drunken wife arouses great anger,
for she does not hide her shame.
9 By her eyelids and her haughty stare
an unchaste wife can be recognized.
10 Keep a strict watch over an unruly wife,
lest, finding an opportunity, she make use of it;[g]
11 Follow close if her eyes are bold,
and be not surprised if she betrays you:
12 As a thirsty traveler with eager mouth
drinks from any water that he finds,
So she settles down before every tent peg
and opens her quiver for every arrow.
13 A gracious wife delights her husband,
her thoughtfulness puts flesh on his bones;
14 A gift from the LORD is her governed speech,
and her firm virtue is of surpassing worth.
15 Choicest of blessings is a modest wife,
priceless her chaste person.
16 Like the sun rising in the LORD's heavens,
the beauty of a virtuous wife is the radiance of her home.
17 Like the light which shines above the holy lampstand,*
are her beauty of face and graceful figure.
18 Golden columns on silver bases
are her shapely limbs and steady feet.*

e Sir 25, 8; Prv 18, 22; 31, 10ff.
f Sir 36, 24.
g Sir 42, 11.

*

25, 12–25: Wickedness in a woman is most grievous, painful and bitter to her husband. Through it she becomes, vengeful, dangerous and intolerable, jealous, talkative, intemperate and unchaste. Even her very appearance is changed (12–17). The worst of all evils, a source of grief, a snare and a disgrace to her husband, she depresses his mind, saddens and breaks his heart, destroys his strength (18–22). She must not be indulged but made obedient or punished (24f).

25, 23: According to the account in Gn 3, to which Ben Sirach refers, sin, the cause of death, originated in woman: Eve, the first human being to sin, induced Adam to follow her example. But it is through Adam, as head of the race, that original sin and its punishment of spiritual death are presented by St. Paul (Rom 5) as having entered the world, to become the occasion for the redemptive work of Christ our Lord.

26, 1–4. 13–18: A good wife is as a gift from God, bringing joy and peace, happiness and contentment to her husband (1–4) through her thoughtfulness, reserve, modesty and chastity, beauty, grace and virtue (13–18).

26, 2: Worthy: gifted spiritually, mentally and physically. Cf Prv 31, 10.

26, 6–12: A repetition of the thought expressed in Sir 25, 12–25.

26, 17f: The holy lampstand and the golden columns stood in the holy place of the ancient Tabernacle (Ex 25, 31–40; 26, 32).

26, 18: Among the additions found here in some manuscripts are the following lines:
"My son, take care in the prime of life
not to surrender your strength to strangers;
Single out from the land a goodly field
and there with confidence sow the seed of your increase;
So shall you have your offspring around you,
and in confidence shall they grow up.

### Dangers to Integrity and Friendship

**19** These two bring grief to my heart,
and the third arouses my horror:
A wealthy man reduced to want;
illustrious men held in contempt;
And the man who passes from justice to sin,
for whom the LORD makes ready the sword.[h]
**20** A merchant can hardly remain upright,*
nor a shopkeeper free from sin;

## CHAPTER 27

**1** For the sake of profit many sin,
and the struggle for wealth blinds the eyes.[i]
**2** Like a peg driven between fitted stones,
between buying and selling sin is wedged in.
**3** Unless you earnestly hold fast to the fear of the LORD,
suddenly your house will be thrown down.
**4** When a sieve is shaken, the husks appear;
so do a man's faults when he speaks.
**5** As the test of what the potter molds is in the furnace,
so in his conversation is the test of a man.[j]
**6** The fruit of a tree shows the care it has had;
so too does a man's speech disclose the bent of his mind.[k]
**7** Praise no man before he speaks,
for it is then that men are tested.
**8** If you strive after justice you will attain it,
and put it on like a splendid robe.
**9** Birds nest with their own kind,
and fidelity comes to those who live by it.
**10** As a lion crouches in wait for prey,
so do sins for evildoers
**11** Ever wise are the discourses of the devout,
but the godless man, like the moon, is inconstant.
**12** Limit the time you spend among fools,
but frequent the company of thoughtful men.
**13** The conversation of the wicked is offensive,
their laughter is wanton guilt.
**14** Their oath-filled talk makes the hair stand on end,
their brawls make one stop one's ears.
**15** Wrangling among the haughty ends in bloodshed,
their cursing is painful to hear.[l]

**16** He who betrays a secret cannot be trusted,*
he will never find an intimate friend.[m]
**17** Cherish your friend, keep faith with him;
but if you betray his confidence, follow him not;
**18** For as an enemy might kill a man,
you have killed your neighbor's friendship.
**19** Like a bird released from the hand,
you have let your friend go and cannot recapture him;
**20** Follow him not, for he is far away,
he has fled like a gazelle from the trap.
**21** A wound can be bound up, and an insult forgiven,
but he who betrays secrets does hopeless damage.[n]

### Malice, Anger and Vengeance

**22** He who has shifty eyes plots mischief
and no one can ward him off;
**23** In your presence he uses honeyed talk,
and admires your every word,
But later he changes his tone
and twists your words to your ruin.[o]
**24** There is nothing that I hate so much,
and the LORD hates him as well.[p]
**25** As a stone falls back on him who throws it up,[q]
so a blow struck in treachery injures more than one.
**26** As he who digs a pit falls into it,
and he who lays a snare is caught in it,
**27** Whoever does harm will be involved in it
without knowing how it came upon him.

**28** Mockery and abuse will be the lot of the proud,
and vengeance lies in wait for them like a lion.
**29** The trap seizes those who rejoice in pitfalls,
and pain will consume them before they die;
**30** Wrath and anger are hateful things,
yet the sinner hugs them tight.

h Ez 18, 24ff.
i Sir 7, 18; 31, 6; Prv 30, 8f.
j 1 Pt 1, 7.
k Mt 7, 20.
l Sir 23, 9-15.
m Prv 11, 13; 20, 19.
n Sir 22, 20.
o Prv 26, 24ff.
p Prv 6, 13. 16.
q 25f: Ps 7, 16f; Prv 26, 27: Eccl 10, 8.

*

"Though a woman for hire be thought of as a trifle,
a married woman is a deadly snare for those who embrace her. [Cf Prv 6, 26.]
"A wife's complaint should be made in meekness,
and show itself in a slight flush;
But a loud-mouthed, scolding wife
is a trumpet signaling for battle:
Any human being who answers that challenge
will spend his life amid the turbulence of war."

26, 20—27, 15: From proper conduct in family life, the author proceeds to social morality, warning especially against injustice in commerce (26, 20—27, 3), and perversity of speech in business (4–7). The pursuit of justice in these matters is all the more meritorious as it is difficult (8ff). The discourses of the devout are marked with wisdom, but the conversations of the wicked, with offense, swearing, cursing, quarrels and even bloodshed (11–15).

27, 16—28, 11: Betrayal of confidence through indiscretion destroys friendship and does irreparable harm (16–21); cf Sir 22, 22. False friendship based on hypocrisy and deceit is hateful to God and man (22ff); it soon becomes a victim of its own treachery (25ff). The same fate awaits the malicious and vengeful (27, 28—28, 1). They can obtain mercy and forgiveness only by first forgiving their neighbor, being mindful of death and of the commandments of the Most High (28, 2–7). And they must avoid quarrels and strife (8–11).

## CHAPTER 28

1 The vengeful will suffer the LORD's
vengeance,
for he remembers their sins in detail.[r]
2 Forgive your neighbor's injustice;
then when you pray, your own sins will
be forgiven.[s]
3 Should a man nourish anger against his
fellows
and expect healing from the LORD?[t]
4 Should a man refuse mercy to his fellows,
yet seek pardon for his own sins?
5 If he who is but flesh cherishes wrath,
who will forgive his sins?
6 Remember your last days, set enmity aside;
remember death and decay, and cease
from sin![u]
7 Think of the commandments, hate not your
neighbor;
of the Most High's covenant, and
overlook faults.

8 Avoid strife and your sins will be fewer,
for a quarrelsome man kindles disputes,
9 Commits the sin of disrupting friendship
and sows discord among those at peace.[v]
10 The more wood, the greater the fire,[w]
the more underlying it, the fiercer the
fight;
The greater a man's strength, the sterner his
anger,
the greater his power, the greater his
wrath.
11 Pitch and resin make fires flare up,
and insistent quarrels provoke bloodshed.

### The Evil Tongue*

12 If you blow upon a spark, it quickens into
flame,
if you spit on it, it dies out;
yet both you do with your mouth!
13 Cursed be gossips and the double-tongued,
for they destroy the peace of many.[x]
14 A meddlesome tongue subverts many,
and makes them refugees among the
peoples;
It destroys walled cities,
and overthrows powerful dynasties.
15 A meddlesome tongue can drive virtuous
women from their homes
and rob them of the fruit of their toil;
16 Whoever heeds it has no rest,
nor can he dwell in peace.

17 A blow from a whip raises a welt,
but a blow from the tongue smashes
bones;
18 Many have fallen by the edge of the sword,
but not as many as by the tongue.[y]
19 Happy he who is sheltered from it,
and has not endured its wrath;
Who has not borne its yoke
nor been fettered with its chains;
20 For its yoke is a yoke of iron
and its chains are chains of bronze!
21 Dire is the death it inflicts,
besides which even the nether world is a
gain;
22 It will not take hold among the just
nor scorch them in its flame,
23 But those who forsake the LORD will fall
victims to it,
as it burns among them unquenchably!
It will hurl itself against them like a lion;
like a panther, it will tear them to pieces.
24 As you hedge round your vineyard with
thorns,
set barred doors over your mouth;[z]
25 As you seal up your silver and gold,
so balance and weigh your words.
26 Take care not to slip by your tongue
and fall victim to your foe waiting in
ambush.

## CHAPTER 29

### Loans, Alms and Surety*

1 He does a kindness who lends to his
neighbor,
and he fulfills the precepts who holds out
a helping hand.[a]
2 Lend to your neighbor in his hour of need,
and pay back your neighbor when a loan
falls due;[b]
3 Keep your promise, be honest with him,
and you will always come by what you
need.
4 Many a man who asks for a loan
adds to the burdens of those who help
him;
5 When he borrows, he kisses the lender's
hand
and speaks with respect of his creditor's
wealth;

r Dt 32, 35; Rom 12, 19.
s Mt 6, 14.
t Mt 18, 23ff.
u Sir 7, 36; 38, 20.
v Prv 15, 18.
w 10ff: Prv 26, 20f.
x Sir 5, 16f.
y Jas 3, 5ff.
z Sir 22, 27; Ps 141, 3.
a Dt 15, 8; Ps 112, 5; Prv 19, 17.
b Ex 22, 24ff; Lv 25, 36; Mt 5, 42.

* 28, 12–26: Further treatment of sins of the tongue and their havoc; cf Sir 5, 12—6, 1; 19, 5–16; 20, 17–25; 23, 7–15. Gossips and the double-tongue destroy domestic peace (12–16). The whip, the sword, chains, even the nether world, are not so cruel as the suffering inflicted by an evil tongue (17–21). Not the just but those who forsake the Lord are victims of their evil tongues (22f). Therefore, guard your mouth and tongue as you would guard treasure against an enemy (24ff).

29, 1–20: Some practical maxims concerning the use of wealth. Give to a poor man (8f), lend to a needy neighbor, but repay when a loan falls due lest the lender's burden be increased (1–5) and his kindness abused (6f); through charity build up defense against evil (10–13). Go surety for your neighbor according to your means, but take care (20) not to fall, for the shameless play false and bring their protectors and themselves to misfortune and ruin (14–19).

But when payment is due he disappoints him
and says he is helpless to meet the claim.
6 If the lender is able to recover barely half,
he considers this an achievement;
If not, he is cheated of his wealth
and acquires an enemy at no extra charge;
With curses and insults the borrower pays
him back,
with abuse instead of honor.
7 Many refuse to lend, not out of meanness,
but from fear of being cheated.

8 To a poor man, however, be generous;
keep him not waiting for your alms;
9 Because of the precept, help the needy,
and in their want, do not send them away
empty-handed.[c]

10 Spend your money for your brother and
friend,
and hide it not under a stone to perish;
11 Dispose of your treasure as the Most High
commands,
for that will profit you more than the
gold.[d]
12 Store up almsgiving in your treasure house,
and it will save you from every evil;
13 Better than a stout shield and a sturdy spear
it will fight for you against the foe.

14 A good man goes surety for his neighbor,
and only the shameless would play him
false;[e]
15 Forget not the kindness of your backer,
for he offers his very life for you.
16 The wicked turn a pledge on their behalf
into misfortune,
and the ingrate abandons his protector;
17 Going surety has ruined many prosperous
men
and tossed them about like waves of the
sea,[f]
18 Has exiled men of prominence
and sent them wandering through foreign
lands.
19 The sinner through surety comes to grief,
and he who undertakes too much falls into
lawsuits.
20 Go surety for your neighbor according to
your means,
but take care lest you fall thereby.

## Frugality and Its Rewards*

21 Life's prime needs are water, bread, and
clothing,
a house, too, for decent privacy.[g]
22 Better a poor man's fare under the shadow
of one's own roof
than sumptuous banquets among
strangers.[h]
23 Be it little or much, be content with what
you have,
and pay no heed to him who would
disparage your home;
24 A miserable life it is to go from house to
house,
for as a guest you dare not open your
mouth.
25 The visitor has no thanks for filling the
cups;
besides, you will hear these bitter words:
26 "Come here, stranger, set the table,
give me to eat the food you have!
27 Away, stranger, for one more worthy;
for my brother's visit I need the room!"
28 Painful things to a sensitive man
are abuse at home and insults from his
creditors.

## CHAPTER 30

### The Training of Children*

1 He who loves his son chastises him often,
that he may be his joy when he grows
up.[i]
2 He who disciplines his son will benefit from
him,
and boast of him among his intimates.
3 He who educates his son makes his enemy
jealous,
and shows his delight in him among his
friends.
4 At the father's death, he will seem not dead,
since he leaves after him one like himself,
5 Whom he looks upon through life with joy,
and even in death, without regret:
6 The avenger he leaves against his foes,
and the one to repay his friends with
kindness.

7 He who spoils his son will have wounds to
bandage,
and will quake inwardly at every outcry.
8 A colt untamed turns out stubborn;
a son left to himself grows up unruly.
9 Pamper your child and he will be a terror
for you,
indulge him and he will bring you grief.
10 Share not in his frivolity lest you share in
his sorrow,
when finally your teeth are clenched in
remorse.

c Sir 4, 1ff; Lv 19, 9f; 23, 22; Dt 15, 8.
d Sir 17, 17; Tb 4, 7ff.
e Sir 8, 13.
f Prv 6, 1f; 11, 15.
g Sir 39, 26.
h Sir 40, 29.
i Prv 13, 24; 23, 13; 29, 15; Heb 12, 7.

*

29, 21–28: The man who provides his own basic needs of food, clothing and dwelling, and is content with what he has, preserves his freedom and self-respect (21ff). But if he lives as a guest, even among the rich, he exposes himself to insult and abuse (24–28).

30, 1–13: Sound discipline and careful education of children correct frivolity and stubbornness, prevent remorse and humiliation, and bring to parents lasting joy and delight, prestige among friends, jealousy of enemies, perpetuation and vindication of themselves through their offspring (1–6). Lack of discipline and overindulgence of children bring sorrow and disappointment, terror and grief (7–13).

11 Give him not his own way in his youth,
and close not your eyes to his follies.
12 Bend him to the yoke when he is young,
thrash his sides while he is still small,
Lest he become stubborn, disobey you,
and leave you disconsolate.[j]
13 Discipline your son, make heavy his yoke,
lest his folly humiliate you.

### Health of Soul and Body*

14 Better a poor man strong and robust,
than a rich man with wasted frame.
15 More precious than gold is health and well-being,
contentment of spirit than coral.
16 No treasure greater than a healthy body;
no happiness, than a joyful heart!
17 Preferable is death to a bitter life,[k]
unending sleep to constant illness.*
18 Dainties set before one who cannot eat
are like the offerings placed before a tomb.[l]
19 What good is an offering to an idol
that can neither taste nor smell?
20 So it is with the afflicted man
who groans at the good things his eyes behold!

21 Do not give in to sadness,
torment not yourself with brooding;[m]
22 Gladness of heart is the very life of man,
cheerfulness prolongs his days.
23 Distract yourself, renew your courage,
drive resentment far away from you;
For worry has brought death to many,
nor is there aught to be gained from resentment.[n]
24 Envy and anger shorten one's life,
worry brings on premature old age.
25 One who is cheerful and gay while at table
benefits from his food.[o]

## CHAPTER 31

### The Proper Attitude toward Riches*

1 Keeping watch over riches wastes the flesh,
and the care of wealth drives away rest.
2 Concern for one's livelihood banishes slumber;
more than a serious illness it disturbs repose.*
3 The rich man labors to pile up wealth,
and his only rest is wanton pleasure;
4 The poor man toils for a meager subsistence,
and if ever he rests, he finds himself in want.
5 The lover of gold will not be free from sin,
for he who pursues wealth is led astray by it.
6 Many have been ensnared by gold,
though destruction lay before their eyes;[p]
7 It is a stumbling block to those who are avid for it,
a snare for every fool.
8 Happy the rich man found without fault,*
who turns not aside after gain![q]
9 Who is he, that we may praise him?
he, of all his kindred, has done wonders,
10 For he has been tested by gold and come off safe,
and this remains his glory;
He could have sinned but did not,
could have done evil but would not,
11 So that his possessions are secure,
and the assembly recounts his praises.[r]

### Table Etiquette*

12 If you are dining with a great man,
bring not a greedy gullet to his table,
Nor cry out, ''How much food there is here?''
13 Remember that gluttony is evil.
No creature is greedier than the eye:
therefore it weeps for any cause.[s]
14 Toward what he eyes, do not put out a hand;
nor reach when he does for the same dish.
15 Recognize that your neighbor feels as you do,
and keep in mind your own dislikes:
16 Behave at table like a favored guest,
and be not greedy, lest you be despised.
17 Be the first to stop, as befits good manners;
gorge not yourself, lest you give offense.[t]
18 If there are many with you at table,
be not the first to reach out your hand.

j Sir 7, 23.
k Sir 41, 2.
l Tb 4, 17.
m Sir 38, 20; Prv 12, 25; 15, 13; 17, 22.
n Sir 38, 18f.
o Prv 15, 15.
p Sir 8, 2.
q Sir 5, 1. 10.
r Prv 29, 14.
s Sir 37, 28ff; Prv 23, 1f.
t Sir 37, 29.

*

30, 14–25: Health of mind and body and joy of heart are judged more precious than wealth (14ff); bitterness, constant illness and affliction more difficult to bear than death (17–20). Sadness, resentment, anxiety, envy and anger shorten . . . life; they should be dispelled by cheerfulness and gladness of heart, which help to prolong one's days (21–25).

30, 17: Preferable is death . . . constant illness: the true value of human suffering was revealed through the passion and death of Christ. It serves as reparation for sin, and when united with Christ's suffering, as merit for eternal life.

31, 1–11: Solicitude for acquiring wealth and anxiety over preserving it disturb repose and easily lead to sin and ruin (1–7). Cf Mt 6, 25–34. A rich man who has not sinned or been seduced by wealth is worthy of praise (8–11).

31, 2: The Hebrew adds a verse that seems out of place here: "A faithful comrade drives away reproach, and the friend who keeps secrets is as dear as life."

31, 8ff: The church in her liturgy applies this passage to holy confessors of the Faith.

31, 12—32, 13: A man observing etiquette at table avoids greed and selfishness (31, 12f), is considerate of a neighbor's likes and dislikes and generous toward him (14f. 23f), observes proper manners (16ff), is moderate in eating and drinking (19–22. 25–30). A good host makes himself one with his guests, is solicitous for them (32, 1f), provides conversation and diversion (3–6), is modest in speech (7f. 10), is respectful of elders (9), polite in comportment and grateful to God for his favors (11ff).

19 Does not a little suffice for a well-bred
man?
When he lies down, it is without
discomfort.[u]
20 Distress and anguish and loss of sleep,
and restless tossing for the glutton!
Moderate eating ensures sound slumber
and a clear mind next day on rising.
21 If perforce you have eaten too much,
once you have emptied your stomach,*
you will have relief.
22 Listen to me, my son, and scorn me not;
later you will find my advice good.
In whatever you do, be moderate,
and no sickness will befall you.
23 On a man generous with food, blessings are
invoked,
and this testimony to his goodness is
lasting;[v]
24 He who is miserly with food is denounced
in public,
and this testimony to his stinginess is
lasting.
25 Let not wine-drinking be the proof of your
strength,
for wine has been the ruin of many.
26 As the furnace probes the work of the smith,
so does wine the hearts of the insolent.
27 Wine is very life to man
if taken in moderation.
Does he really live who lacks the wine
which was created for his joy?[w]
28 Joy of heart, good cheer and merriment
are wine drunk freely at the proper time.
29 Headache, bitterness and disgrace
is wine drunk amid anger and strife.
30 More and more wine is a snare for the fool;
it lessens his strength and multiplies his
wounds.
31 Rebuke not your neighbor when wine is
served,
nor put him to shame while he is merry;
Use no harsh words with him
and distress him not in the presence of
others.

## CHAPTER 32

1 If you are chosen to preside at dinner, be
not puffed up,
but with the guests be as one of
themselves;
Take care of them first before you sit down;
2 when you have fulfilled your duty, then
take your place,
To share in their joy
and win praise for your hospitality.
3 Being older, you may talk; that is only your
right,
but temper your wisdom, not to disturb
the singing.
4 When wine is present, do not pour out
discourse,
and flaunt not your wisdom at the wrong
time.
5 Like a seal of carnelian in a setting of gold
is a concert when wine is served.
6 Like a gold mounting with an emerald seal
is string music with delicious wine.
7 Young man, speak only when necessary,[x]
when they have asked you more than
once;
8 Be brief, but say much in those few words,
be like the wise man, taciturn.
9 When among your elders be not forward,
and with officials be not too insistent.
10 Like the lightning that flashes before a storm
is the esteem that shines on modesty.
11 When it is time to leave, tarry not;
be off for home! There take your ease,
12 And there enjoy doing as you wish,
but without sin or words of pride.
13 Above all, give praise to your Creator,
who showers his favors upon you.

## The Providence of God

14 He who would find God must accept
discipline;*
he who seeks him obtains his request.[y]
15 He who studies the law masters it,
but the hypocrite finds it a trap.[z]
16 His judgment is sound who fears the LORD;
out of obscurity he draws forth a clear
plan.[a]
17 The sinner turns aside reproof
and distorts the law to suit his purpose.[b]
18 The thoughtful man will not neglect
direction;
the proud and insolent man is deterred by
nothing.
19 Do nothing without counsel,
and then you need have no regrets.[c]
20 Go not on a way that is set with snares,
and let not the same thing trip you twice.
21 Be not too sure even of smooth roads,
22 be careful on all your paths.
23 Whatever you do, be on your guard,
for in this way you will keep the
commandments.
24 He who keeps the law preserves himself;
and he who trusts in the LORD shall not
be put to shame.

u Eccl 5, 11.
v Prv 22, 9.
w Ps 104, 15; 1 Tm 5, 23.
x 7ff: Sir 7, 14.
y Sir 4, 13.
z Sir 2, 16.
a Ps 37, 6.
b Sir 21, 6; Prv 12, 1.
c Sir 37, 16; Tb 4, 18.
d Ps 91, 10.

*

31, 21: Emptied your stomach: the practice of induced vomiting, well-known among pagan Romans, and less well-known among the Jews, seems to be referred to here.

32, 14—33, 4: God is shown to reveal himself through the discipline of his law, a clear and safe plan of life for the pious Jew of old. Direction and counsel are aids in following it (14ff. 18–24); 33, 1. 3f). Sinners and hypocrites, hating the law or distorting it, fail in wisdom and are devoid of security (32, 15. 17f; 33, 2).

## CHAPTER 33

**1** No evil can harm the man who fears the LORD;
through trials, again and again he is safe.[d]
**2** He who hates the law is without wisdom,
and is tossed about like a boat in a storm.
**3** The prudent man trusts in the word of the LORD,
and the law is dependable for him as a divine oracle.*
**4** Prepare your words and you will be listened to;
draw upon your training, and then give your answer.

**5** Like the wheel of a cart is the mind of a fool;*
his thoughts revolve in circles.
**6** A fickle friend is like the stallion
that neighs, no matter who the rider.
**7** Why is one day more important than another,
when it is the sun that lights up every day?
**8** It is due to the LORD's wisdom that they differ;
it is through him the seasons and feasts come and go.[e]
**9** Some he dignifies and sanctifies,
and others he lists as ordinary days.[f]
**10** So too, all men are of clay,
for from earth man was formed;[g]
**11** Yet with his great knowledge the LORD makes men unlike;
in different paths he has them walk.
**12** Some he blesses and makes great,
some he sanctifies and draws to himself.
Others he curses and brings low,
and expels them from their place.
**13** Like clay in the hands of a potter,
to be molded according to his pleasure,
So are men in the hands of their Creator,
to be assigned by him their function.[h]
**14** As evil contrasts with good, and death with life,
so are sinners in contrast with the just;[i]
**15** See now all the works of the Most High:
they come in pairs, the one the opposite of the other.

**16** Now I am the last to keep vigil,*
like a gleaner after the vintage;
**17** Since by the LORD's blessing I have made progress
till like a vintager I have filled my winepress,
**18** I would inform you that not for myself only have I toiled,
but for every seeker after wisdom.

### Property and Servants*

**19** Listen to me, O leaders of the multitude;
O rulers of the assembly, give ear![j]
**20** Let neither son nor wife, neither brother nor friend,
have power over you as long as you live.
**21** While breath of life is still in you,
let no man have dominion over you.
Give not to another your wealth,
lest then you have to plead with him;
**22** Far better that your children plead with you
than that you should look to their generosity.
**23** Keep control over all your affairs;
let no one tarnish your glory.
**24** When your few days reach their limit,
at the time of death distribute your inheritance.

**25** Fodder and whip and loads for an ass;
the yoke and harness and the rod of his master.
**26** Make a slave work and he will look for his rest;
let his hands be idle and he will seek to be free.[k]
**27** Food, correction and work for a slave;
and for a wicked slave, punishment in the stocks.
**28** Force him to work that he be not idle,
for idleness is an apt teacher of mischief.
**29** Put him to work, for that is what befits him;
if he becomes unruly, load him with chains.
**30** But never lord it over any human being,
and do nothing unjust.
**31** If you have but one slave, treat him like yourself,
for you have acquired him with your life's blood;[l]
**32** If you have but one slave, deal with him as a brother,
for you need him as you need your life:
**33** If you mistreat him and he runs away,
in what direction will you look for him?

e Gn 1, 14.
f Ex 20, 11.
g Gn 2, 7.
h Wis 15, 7; Jer 18, 1-6; Rom 9, 20f.
i Sir 42, 25.
j Wis 6, 1f.
k Prv 29, 19.
l Sir 7, 21.

* 33, 3: Oracle: as the answer given through the Urim and Thummim to the high priest is true, so the law proves itself true to him who obeys it. Cf Ex 28, 30; Nm 27, 21.

33, 5–15: Contrasts observable in the physical universe as well as in the moral order serve the purposes of divine wisdom (5–9). All creatures are like clay . . . in the hands of their Creator—the fool and the wise man, the sinner, and the just (10–15). This does not imply that man is created to be a sinner: God is not the author of wickedness. Cf Jas 1, 13f.

33, 16ff: Here the author refers to himself as the most recent of the writers who have endeavored to present true wisdom to their readers.

33, 19–33: Public officials should reject every influence that would restrict their freedom in the management of their affairs. They must make their own household subservient to them rather than be subservient to it (19–24). Slaves are to be given food and work and correction but never to be treated unjustly (25–29). Great care should be taken of good slaves (30–33).

## CHAPTER 34

### Trust in the Lord and Not in Dreams*

1 Empty and false are the hopes of the senseless,
and fools are borne aloft by dreams.
2 Like a man who catches at shadows or chases the wind,
is the one who believes in dreams.
3 What is seen in dreams is to reality
what the reflection of a face is to the face itself.
4 Can the unclean produce the clean?
can the liar ever speak the truth?[m]
5 Divination, omens and dreams all are unreal;
what you already expect, the mind depicts.
6 Unless it be a vision specially sent by the Most High,
fix not your heart on it;
7 For dreams have led many astray,
and those who believed in them have perished.
8 The law is fulfilled without fail,
and perfect wisdom is found in the mouth of the faithful man.
9 A man with training gains wide knowledge;
a man of experience speaks sense.
10 One never put to the proof knows little,
whereas with travel a man adds to his resourcefulness.
11 I have seen much in my travels,
learned more than ever I could say.
12 Often I was in danger of death,
but by these attainments I was saved.

13 Lively is the courage of those who fear the LORD,
for they put their hope in their savior;
14 He who fears the LORD is never alarmed,
never afraid; for the LORD is his hope.[n]
15 Happy the soul that fears the LORD!
In whom does he trust, and who is his support?
16 The eyes of the LORD are upon those who love him;
he is their mighty shield and strong support,
A shelter from the heat, a shade from the noonday sun,
a guard against stumbling, a help against falling.[o]
17 He buoys up the spirits, brings a sparkle to the eyes,
gives health and life and blessing.

### True Worship of God*

18 Tainted his gifts who offers in sacrifice ill-gotten goods!
Mock presents from the lawless win not God's favor.[p]
19 The Most High approves not the gifts of the godless,
nor for their many sacrifices does he forgive their sins.
20 Like the man who slays a son in his father's presence
is he who offers sacrifice from the possessions of the poor.
21 The bread of charity is life itself for the needy;[q]
he who withholds it is a man of blood.
22 He slays his neighbor who deprives him of his living;
he sheds blood who denies the laborer his wages.
23 If one man builds up and another tears down,
what do they gain but trouble?
24 If one man prays and another curses,
whose voice will the LORD hear?
25 If a man again touches a corpse after he has bathed,
what did he gain by the purification?[r]
26 So with a man who fasts for his sins,
but then goes and commits them again:
Who will hear his prayer,
and what has he gained by his mortification?

## CHAPTER 35*

1 To keep the law is a great oblation,[s]
and he who observes the commandments sacrifices a peace offering.
2 In works of charity one offers fine flour,*
and when he gives alms he presents his sacrifice of praise.
3 To refrain from evil pleases the LORD,
and to avoid injustice is an atonement.
4 Appear not before the LORD empty-handed,
for all that you offer is in fulfillment of the precepts.[t]

m Jb 14, 4.
n Pss 23, 4; 112, 7f; Prv 3, 23ff; 28, 1.
o Pss 33, 18; 34, 16.
p Sir 35, 11; Prv 21, 27.
q 21f: Lv 19, 13; Dt 24, 14f; Tb 4, 14.
r Nm 19, 11f; Prv 26, 11; 2 Pt 2, 22.
s 1ff: 1 Sm 15, 22; Ps 51, 18f; Is 1, 11-18; Hos 6, 6; Am 5, 21-24.
t Ex 23, 15; 34, 20; Dt 16, 16.

*

34, 1–17: Confidence placed in dreams, divinations and omens is false because these are devoid of reality (1–8). True confidence is founded on knowledge and experience (9–12), and above all on the fear of the Lord, with its accompanying blessings of divine assistance and protection (13–17).

34, 18–26: To be acts of true religion, sacrifice and penance must be accompanied by the proper moral dispositions. To offer to God goods taken from the poor (18–22), or to practice penance without interior reform, is a mockery, worthless in the sight of God (23–26). Cf Mt 15, 4–7; Mk 7, 9–13.

35, 1–24: Keeping the commandments of the law and avoiding injustice constitute sacrifice pleasing and acceptable to God (1ff). Offerings also should be made to him, cheerfully and generously; these he repays . . . sevenfold (4–10). Extortion from widows and orphans is injustice, which God quickly repays (11–18). Punishing the proud and the merciless and coming to the aid of the distressed, he requites all according to their deeds (19–24).

35, 2: Fine flour, together with oil and frankincense, was a prescribed offering to God; cf Lv 2, 1ff.

5 The just man's offering enriches the altar
and rises as a sweet odor before the Most High.
6 The just man's sacrifice is most pleasing,
nor will it ever be forgotten.
7 In generous spirit pay homage to the LORD,
be not sparing of freewill gifts.[u]
8 With each contribution show a cheerful countenance,
and pay your tithes in a spirit of joy.[v]
9 Give to the Most High as he has given to you,
generously, according to your means.

10 For the LORD is one who always repays,
and he will give back to you sevenfold.[w]
11 But offer no bribes, these he does not accept!
Trust not in sacrifice of the fruits of extortion,[x]
12 For he is a God of justice,
who knows no favorites.[y]
13 Though not unduly partial toward the weak,
yet he hears the cry of the oppressed.*
14 He is not deaf to the wail of the orphan,[z]
nor to the widow when she pours out her complaint;

15 Do not the tears that stream down her cheek
cry out against him that causes them to fall?
16 He who serves God willingly is heard;
his petition reaches the heavens.
17 The prayer of the lowly pierces the clouds;
it does not rest till it reaches its goal,
18 Nor will it withdraw till the Most High responds,
judges justly and affirms the right.

19 God indeed will not delay,
and like a warrior, will not be still[a]
20 Till he breaks the backs of the merciless
and wreaks vengeance upon the proud;
21 Till he destroys the haughty root and branch,
and smashes the scepter of the wicked;
22 Till he requites mankind according to its deeds,
and repays men according to their thoughts;
23 Till he defends the cause of his people,
and gladdens them by his mercy.
24 Welcome is his mercy in time of distress
as rain clouds in time of drought.

## CHAPTER 36

### A Prayer for God's People*

1 Come to our aid, O God of the universe,
and put all the nations in dread of you!
2 Raise your hand against the heathen,
that they may realize your power.
3 As you have used us to show them your holiness,
so now use them to show us your glory.
4 Thus they will know, as we know,
that there is no God but you.

5 Give new signs and work new wonders;
show forth the splendor of your right hand and arm;
6 Rouse your anger, pour out wrath,
humble the enemy, scatter the foe.[b]
7 Hasten the day, bring on the time;
9 crush the heads of the hostile rulers.
8 Let raging fire consume the fugitive,
and your people's oppressors meet destruction.
10 Gather all the tribes of Jacob,
that they may inherit the land as of old.
11 Show mercy to the people called by your name;
Israel, whom you named your firstborn.[c]
12 Take pity on your holy city,
Jerusalem, your dwelling place.[d]
13 Fill Zion with your majesty,
your temple with your glory.

14 Give evidence of your deeds of old;
fulfill the prophecies spoken in your name,
15 Reward those who have hoped in you,
and let your prophets be proved true.
16 Hear the prayer of your servants,
for you are ever gracious to your people;
17 Thus it will be known to the very ends of the earth
that you are the eternal God.

### Choice of Associates*

18 The throat can swallow any food,
yet some foods are more agreeable than others;
19 As the palate tests meat by its savor,
so does a keen mind insincere words.

u Sir 7, 31.
v 2 Cor 9, 7.
w Prv 19, 17.
x Sir 34, 18f; Prv 21, 27.
y Dt 10, 17; 2 Chr 19, 7; Jb 34, 19; Wis 6, 7; Acts 10, 34; Rom 2, 11; Gal 2, 6; 1 Pt 1, 17.
z 14f: Ex 22, 22.
a Is 42, 13ff: 2 Pt 3, 9.
b Ps 79, 6.
c Ex 4, 22.
d 2 Chr 6, 41; Ps 132, 8. 14; Is 2, 1ff; Mi 4, 1ff.

35, 13: Cf Lv 19, 15.

36, 1–17: Making an act of faith and hope in the supreme Lord of the universe, the author begs God to continue manifesting his holiness and mercy through Israel, his people (1ff. 10–13), and his power and justice through the punishment of the nations (2. 5–9), that all the earth may acknowledge him the eternal God (4. 14–17).

36, 18—37, 15: In the choice of wife, friend or associate, experience is a discerner of character (18–21). Beauty and kindly speech make a woman desirable as wife (22f). The good wife becomes her husband's richest treasure, his helpmate in establishing his household (24–27). A true friend fights for his comrade and shares his spoils with him (37, 5f); a false one deceives and abandons him in time of need (1–4). A true counselor and associate should be sought among those who keep the commandments, not among those who break them and seek their own advantage (7–12). In all things pray to God for light and follow conscience (13ff).

20 A deceitful character causes grief,
but an experienced man can turn the tables on him.
21 Though any man may be accepted as a husband,
yet one girl will be more suitable than another:
22 A woman's beauty makes her husband's face light up,
for it surpasses all else that charms the eye;[e]
23 And if, besides, her speech is kindly,
his lot is beyond that of mortal men.
24 A wife is her husband's richest treasure,
a helpmate, a steadying column.[f]
25 A vineyard with no hedge will be overrun;
a man with no wife becomes a homeless wanderer.
26 Who will trust an armed band
that shifts from city to city?
27 Or a man who has no nest,
but lodges where night overtakes him?[g]

## CHAPTER 37

1 Every friend declares his friendship,
but there are friends who are friends in name only.[h]
2 Is it not a sorrow unto death
when your bosom companion becomes your enemy?
3 "Alas, my companion! Why were you created
to blanket the earth with deceit?"
4 A false friend will share your joys,
but in time of trouble he stands afar off.
5 A true friend will fight with you against the foe,
against your enemies he will be your shieldbearer.
6 Forget not your comrade during the battle,
and neglect him not when you distribute your spoils.

7 Every counselor points out a way,
but some counsel ways of their own;
8 Be on the alert when one proffers advice,
find out first of all what he wants.
For he may be thinking of himself alone;
why should the profit fall to him?
9 He may tell you how good your way will be,
and then stand by to watch your misfortune.
10 Seek no advice from one who regards you with hostility;
from those who envy you, keep your intentions hidden.
11 Speak not to a woman about her rival,
nor to a coward about war,
to a merchant about business,
to a buyer about value,
to a miser about generosity,
to a cruel man about mercy,
to a lazy man about work,
to a seasonal laborer about the harvest,
to an idle slave about a great task:
pay no attention to any advice they give.
12 Instead, associate with a religious man,
who you are sure keeps the commandments;
Who is like-minded with yourself
and will feel for you if you fall.
13 Then, too, heed your own heart's counsel;
for what have you that you can depend on more?
14 A man's conscience can tell him his situation
better than seven watchmen in a lofty tower.
15 Most important of all, pray to God
to set your feet in the path of truth.

### Wisdom and Temperance

16 A word is the source of every deed;*
a thought, of every act.[i]
17 The root of all conduct is the mind;
four branches it shoots forth:
18 Good and evil, death and life,
their absolute mistress is the tongue.[j]
19 A man may be wise and benefit many,
yet be of no use to himself.
20 Though a man may be wise, if his words are rejected
he will be deprived of all enjoyment.
21 When a man is wise to his own advantage,
the fruits of his knowledge are seen in his own person;
22 When a man is wise to his people's advantage,
the fruits of his knowledge are enduring:[k]
23 Limited are the days of one man's life,
but the life of Israel is days without number.
24 One wise for himself has full enjoyment,
and all who see him praise him;
25 One wise for his people wins a heritage of glory,
and his name endures forever.[l]

26 My son, while you are well, govern your appetite*
so that you allow it not what is bad for you;
27 For not every food is good for everyone,
nor is everything suited to every taste.[m]

e Sir 26, 13ff.
f Gn 2, 18; Prv 18, 22.
g Prv 27, 8.
h Sir 6, 7ff.
i Sir 32, 19.
j Prv 18, 21.
k Sir 15, 1ff.
l Sir 39, 9; 44, 13f.
m 1 Cor 6, 12; 10, 23.

*

37, 16–25: Thoughts determine action. Wisdom is the source of good and life; folly, of evil and death (16ff). If the fruits of a man's wisdom benefit himself, he may be praised in his own lifetime; if they benefit his people, his praise endures after him, in their lives (19–25).

37, 26–30: Temperance and self-control should govern a man's appetite for food, which is intended not to destroy but to preserve life.

28 Be not drawn after every enjoyment,[n]
neither become a glutton for choice foods,
29 For sickness comes with overeating,
and gluttony brings on biliousness.
30 Through lack of self-control many have
died,
but the abstemious man prolongs his life.

## CHAPTER 38

### Sickness and Death

1 Hold the physician in honor, for he is
essential to you,*
and God it was who established his
profession.
2 From God the doctor has his wisdom,
and the king provides for his sustenance.
3 His knowledge makes the doctor
distinguished,
and gives him access to those in authority.
4 God makes the earth yield healing herbs
which the prudent man should not neglect;
5 Was not the water sweetened by a twig
that men might learn his power?[o]
6 He endows men with the knowledge
to glory in his mighty works,
7 Through which the doctor eases pain
and the druggist prepares his medicines;
8 Thus God's creative work continues without
cease
in its efficacy on the surface of the earth.

9 My son, when you are ill, delay not,
but pray to God, who will heal you:[p]
10 Flee wickedness; let your hands be just,
cleanse your heart of every sin;
11 Offer your sweet-smelling oblation and
petition,
a rich offering according to your means.[q]
12 Then give the doctor his place
lest he leave; for you need him too.
13 There are times that give him an advantage,
14 and he too beseeches God
That his diagnosis may be correct
and his treatment bring about a cure.
15 He who is a sinner toward his Maker
will be defiant toward the doctor.

16 My son, shed tears for one who is dead*
with wailing and bitter lament;
As is only proper, prepare the body,
absent not yourself from his burial:[r]
17 Weeping bitterly, mourning fully,
pay your tribute of sorrow, as he
deserves,
18 One or two days, to prevent gossip;
then compose yourself after your grief,
19 For grief can bring on an extremity
and heartache destroy one's health.[s]
20 Turn not your thoughts to him again;
cease to recall him; think rather of the
end.[t]
21 Recall him not, for there is no hope of his
return;
it will not help him, but will do you
harm.[u]
22 Remember that his fate will also be yours;
for him it was yesterday, for you today.[v]
23 With the departed dead, let memory fade;
rally your courage, once the soul has left.

### Vocations of the Craftsman and the Scribe*

24 The scribe's profession increases his
wisdom;
whoever is free from toil can become a
wise man.
25 How can he become learned who guides the
plow,
who thrills in wielding the goad like a
lance,
Who guides the ox and urges on the
bullock,
and whose every concern is for cattle?
26 His care is for plowing furrows,
and he keeps a watch on the beasts in the
stalls.

27 So with every engraver and designer
who, laboring night and day,
Fashions carved seals,
and whose concern is to vary the pattern.
His care is to produce a vivid impression,
and he keeps watch till he finishes his
design.

28 So with the smith standing near his anvil,
forging crude iron.
The heat from the fire sears his flesh,
yet he toils away in the furnace heat.
The clang of the hammer deafens his ears,

n 28f: Sir 31, 13. 16ff.
o Ex 15, 25.
p Is 38, 2f.
q Lv 2, 1ff.
r Sir 22, 9f.
s Prv 12, 25; 15, 13; 17, 22.
t Sir 7, 36; 18, 24; 30, 21.
u 2 Sm 12, 23; Wis 2, 1.
v Jas 4, 13ff.

38, 1–15: The profession of medicine comes from God, who makes the earth yield healing herbs and gives the physician knowledge of their virtue (1–8). In illness the sick man should cleanse his soul from sin and petition God for help through an offering of sacrifice; the physician, too, does well to invoke God that he may understand the illness and apply the proper remedy (9–14). The sinner, in contrast, defies both his Maker and the doctor (15).

38, 16–23: A period of mourning for the deceased and care for their burial is becoming (16ff). But grief should not be excessive, for it neither helps the dead, who cannot return, nor fails to harm the living. The mourner's own end will quickly follow, and the time to prepare for it is now (19–23).

38, 24—39, 11: More excellent than the useful service of craftsmen—farmer, engraver, smith, potter (25–34)—is the profession of the scribe (24), who studies and meditates on the law of the Most High, seeks him in prayer of thanksgiving, petition and repentance for sin (39, 1. 6f), explores the wisdom of the past and present, travels abroad to observe the conduct of many peoples, and attends rulers and great men. Through the spirit of understanding granted by God, he will show forth his wisdom to the glory of God's law, gaining renown for generations to come (2–5. 8–11).

His eyes are fixed on the tool he is shaping.
His care is to finish his work,
and he keeps watch till he perfects it in detail.

29 So with the potter sitting at his labor
revolving the wheel with his feet.
He is always concerned for his products,
and turns them out in quantity.
30 With his hands he molds the clay,
and with his feet softens it.
His care is for proper coloring,
and he keeps watch on the fire of his kiln.
31 All these men are skilled with their hands,
each one an expert at his own task;
32 Without them no city could be lived in,
and wherever they stay, they need not hunger.
33 They do not occupy the judge's bench,
nor are they prominent in the assembly;
They set forth no decisions or judgments,
nor are they found among the rulers;
34 Yet they maintain God's ancient handiwork,
and their concern is for exercise of their skill.

## CHAPTER 39

1 How different the man who devotes himself
to the study of the law of the Most High!
He explores the wisdom of the men of old
and occupies himself with the prophecies;
2 He treasures the discourses of famous men,
and goes to the heart of involved sayings;
3 He studies obscure parables,
and is busied with the hidden meanings of the sages.
4 He is in attendance on the great,
and has entrance to the ruler.
5 He travels among the peoples of foreign lands
to learn what is good and evil among men.
6 His care is to seek the LORD, his Maker,
to petition the Most High,
To open his lips in prayer,
to ask pardon for his sins.
Then, if it pleases the LORD Almighty,
he will be filled with the spirit of understanding;
He will pour forth his words of wisdom
and in prayer give thanks to the LORD,
7 Who will direct his knowledge and his counsel,
as he meditates upon his mysteries.
8 He will show the wisdom of what he has learned
and glory in the law of the LORD's covenant.
9 Many will praise his understanding;
his fame can never be effaced;
Unfading will be his memory,
through all generations his name will live;[w]
10 Peoples will speak of his wisdom,
and in assembly sing his praises.
11 While he lives he is one out of a thousand,
and when he dies his renown will not cease.

### Praise of God the Creator*

12 Once more I will set forth my theme
to shine like the moon in its fullness!
13 Listen, my faithful children: open up your petals,
like roses planted near running waters;
14 Send up the sweet odor of incense,
break forth in blossoms like the lily.
Send up the sweet odor of your hymn of praise;
bless the LORD for all he has done!
15 Proclaim the greatness of his name,
loudly sing his praises,
With music on the harp and all stringed instruments;
sing out with joy as you proclaim:

16 The works of God are all of them good;
in its own time every need is supplied.[x]
17 At his word the waters become still as in a flask;
he had but to speak and the reservoirs were made.[y]
18 He has but to command and his will is done;
nothing can limit his achievement.
19 The works of all mankind are present to him;
not a thing escapes his eye.[z]
20 His gaze spans all the ages;
to him there is nothing unexpected.
21 No cause then to say: "What is the purpose of this?"
Everything is chosen to satisfy a need.
22 His blessing overflows like the Nile;
like the Euphrates it enriches the surface of the earth.
23 Again, his wrath expels the nations
and turns fertile land into a salt marsh.[a]
24 For the virtuous his paths are level,
to the haughty they are steep;
25 Good things for the good he provided from the beginning,
but for the wicked good things and bad.
26 Chief of all needs for human life
are water and fire, iron and salt,

w Sir 37, 25; 44, 14.
x Gn 1, 31; Eccl 3, 11.
y Gn 1, 6-10; Ex 14, 21f; Jos 3, 16.
z Sir 15, 19; 42, 20.
a Jos 1, 2-6.
b Sir 29, 21.

*

39, 12–35: The sage invites his disciples to join him in joyfully proclaiming his favorite theme: The works of God are all of them good; in its own time every need is supplied (12–16. 32–35). He describes God's omniscience, supreme power and wisdom, whereby all created things, good in themselves, are ever present to him, obey him, and fulfill their intended purpose (17–21), bringing blessing to the virtuous, but evil and punishment to the wicked who misuse them (22–31). Cf similar hymns of praise, Sir 36, 1–17; 42, 15—43, 35.

The heart of the wheat, milk and honey,
the blood of the grape, and oil, and cloth;[b]
27 For the good all these are good,
but for the wicked they turn out evil.
28 There are storm winds created to punish,
which in their fury can dislodge mountains;
When destruction must be, they hurl all their force
and appease the anger of their Maker.
29 In his treasury also, kept for the proper time,
are fire and hail, famine, disease,
30 Ravenous beasts, scorpions, vipers,
and the avenging sword to exterminate the wicked;
31 In doing his bidding they rejoice,
in their assignments they disobey not his command.
32 So from the first I took my stand,
and wrote down as my theme:
33 The works of God are all of them good;
every need when it comes he fills.[c]
34 No cause then to say: "This is not as good as that";
for each shows its worth at the proper time.
35 So now with full joy of heart proclaim
and bless the name of the Holy One.

## CHAPTER 40

### Joys and Miseries of Life

1 A great anxiety has God allotted,*
and a heavy yoke, to the sons of men;[d]
From the day one leaves his mother's womb
to the day he returns to the mother of all the living,*
2 His thoughts, the fear in his heart,
and his troubled forebodings till the day he dies—
3 Whether he sits on a lofty throne
or grovels in dust and ashes,
4 Whether he bears a splendid crown
or is wrapped in the coarsest of cloaks—
5 Are of wrath and envy, trouble and dread,
terror of death, fury and strife.
Even when he lies on his bed to rest,
his cares at night disturb his sleep.
6 So short is his rest it seems like none,
till in his dreams he struggles as he did by day,
Terrified by what his mind's eye sees,
like a fugitive being pursued;
7 As he reaches safety, he wakes up
astonished that there was nothing to fear.
8 So it is with all flesh, with man and with beast,
but for sinners seven times more.
9 Plague and bloodshed, wrath and the sword,
plunder and ruin, famine and death:[e]
10 For the wicked, these were created evil,
and it is they who bring on destruction.
11 All that is of earth returns to earth,
and what is from above returns above.*
12 All that comes from bribes or injustice will be wiped out,
but loyalty remains for ages.
13 Wealth out of wickedness is like a wadi in spate:
like a mighty stream with lightning and thunder,
14 Which, in its rising, rolls along the stones,
but suddenly, once and for all, comes to an end.[f]
15 The offshoot of violence will not flourish,
for the root of the godless is on sheer rock;
16 Or they are like reeds on the riverbank,
withered before all other plants.
17 But goodness will never be cut off,
and justice endures forever.

Wealth or wages can make life sweet,*
but better than either is finding a treasure.
18 A child or a city will preserve one's name,
but better than either, attaining wisdom.[g]
19 Sheepfolds and orchards bring flourishing health;
but better than either, a devoted wife;
20 Wine and music delight the soul,
but better than either, conjugal love.[h]
21 The flute and the harp offer sweet melody,
but better than either, a voice that is true.
22 Charm and beauty delight the eye,
but better than either, the flowers of the field.[i]
23 A friend, a neighbor, are timely guides,
but better than either, a prudent wife.
24 A brother, a helper, for times of stress;
but better than either, charity that rescues.
25 Gold and silver make one's way secure,
but better than either, sound judgment.
26 Wealth and vigor build up confidence,
but better than either, fear of God.
Fear of the LORD leaves nothing wanting;

c Sir 39, 16; Gn 1, 31; Eccl 3, 11.
d Gn 3, 17; Jb 7, 1; 14, 1; Eccl 2, 23.
e Sir 39, 28ff.
f Sir 23, 25; Wis 4, 3ff.
g Prv 19, 14.
h Ps 104, 15.
i Mt 6, 28f.

*

40, 1–16: The former idyllic description of the universe is contrasted with the picture of the evils afflicting humanity. Every man, high or low, is burdened from birth to death with fears, anxieties and troubles, by day and often by night, the time appointed for rest (1–7). For sinners, the suffering is much greater (8ff). What they gained by violence and injustice is quickly destroyed; but justice endures forever (14ff).

40, 1: Mother of all the living: the earth from which man was taken. Cf Gn 2, 7; 3, 19f; Jb 1, 21; Ps 139, 15.

40, 11: All that is of earth . . . returns above: a reference to bodily mortality and to the divine origin of life from the Spirit of God. Cf Sir 41, 10; Gn 2, 7; 3, 19; Jb 34, 14f; Pss 104, 29f; 146, 4; Eccl 12, 7. The Greek and the Latin render the second half of the verse: "all waters shall return to the sea."

40, 17–27: Of the many treasures making life sweet, such as health, children, friends, music, vigor, the best are called true conjugal love, wisdom, and above all, fear of God; cf Sir 25, 6–11.

he who has it need seek no other support:
27 The fear of God is a paradise of blessings;
its canopy, all that is glorious.[j]

28 My son, live not the life of a beggar,*
better to die than to beg;
29 When one has to look to another's table,
his life is not really a life.
His neighbor's delicacies bring revulsion of spirit
to one who understands inward feelings:[k]
30 In the mouth of the shameless man begging is sweet,
but within him it burns like fire.

## CHAPTER 41

1 O death! how bitter the thought of you*
for the man at peace amid his possessions,
For the man unruffled and always successful,
who still can enjoy life's pleasures.
2 O death! how welcome your sentence
to the weak man of failing strength,
Tottering and always rebuffed,
with no more sight, with vanished hope.[l]
3 Fear not death's decree for you;
remember, it embraces those before you, and those after.[m]
4 Thus God has ordained for all flesh;
why then should you reject the will of the Most High?
Whether one has lived a thousand years, a hundred, or ten,
in the nether world he has no claim on life.

5 A reprobate line are the children of sinners,[n]
and witless offspring are in the homes of the wicked.
6 Their dominion is lost to sinners' children,
and reproach abides with their descendants.
7 Children curse their wicked father,
for they suffer disgrace through him.
8 Woe to you, O sinful men,
who forsake the law of the Most High.
9 If you have children, calamity will seize them;
you will beget them only for groaning.
When you stumble, there is lasting joy;
at death, you become a curse.
10 Whatever is of nought returns to nought,
so too the godless from void to void.[o]
11 Man's body is a fleeting thing,
but a virtuous name will never be annihilated.[p]
12 Have a care for your name, for it will stand by you
better than precious treasures in the thousands;[q]
13 The boon of life is for limited days,
but a good name, for days without number.

### True and False Shame*

14 My children, heed my instruction about shame;
judge of disgrace only according to my rules,
For it is not always well to be ashamed,
nor is it always the proper thing to blush:
15 Before father and mother be ashamed of immorality,
before master and mistress, of falsehood;
16 Before prince and ruler, of flattery;
before the public assembly, of crime;
17 Before friend and companion, of disloyalty,
and of breaking an oath or agreement.
18 Be ashamed of theft from the people where you settle,
and of stretching out your elbow when you dine;
19 Of refusing to give when asked,
of defrauding another of his appointed share,
20 Of failing to return a greeting,
and of rebuffing a friend;
21 Of gazing at a married woman,
and of entertaining thoughts about another's wife;[r]
Of trifling with a servant girl you have,
and of violating her couch;
22 Of using harsh words with friends,
and of following up your gifts with insults;[s]
23 Of repeating what you hear,
and of betraying secrets—[t]
24 These are the things you should rightly avoid as shameful
if you would be looked upon by everyone with favor.

## CHAPTER 42

1 But of these things be not ashamed,
lest you sin through human respect:[u]
2 Of the law of the Most High and his precepts,

j Is 4, 5.
k Sir 29, 24.
l Sir 30, 17.
m Sir 38, 20ff.
n 5ff: Sir 3, 9ff; Wis 3, 16-19.
o Sir 40, 11; Wis 4, 19.
p Prv 10, 7.
q Prv 22, 1; Eccl 7, 1.
r Sir 9, 8; Mt 5, 28.
s Sir 18, 14; 20, 13.
t Sir 27, 16.
u Prv 24, 23; Jas 2, 1.

*

40, 28ff: Among the Jews, beggary was considered degrading to human dignity; it was agreeable only to the shameless, who had lost their sense of honor. Cf Sir 29, 22f.

41, 1–13: Whether death seems bitter to one who enjoys peace, success and pleasure, or welcome to one who is weak and in despair, it comes to all and must be accepted as the will of God (1–4). As the human body passes away (11), so do those who have sinned through the body and their offspring alike, who, needy and accursed, pass on with their parents as if they had never been (5–10). Only the good name of the virtuous endures (11ff).

41, 14—42, 8: The author illustrates the subject of true and false shame with numerous and detailed examples of sin (14–24) and virtue (42, 1–8), following the norm of the commandments.

or of the sentence to be passed upon the sinful;
3 Of sharing the expenses of a business or a journey,
or of dividing an inheritance or property;
4 Of accuracy of scales and balances,
or of tested measures and weights;[v]
5 Of acquiring much or little,
or of bargaining in dealing with a merchant;
Of constant training of children,
or of beating the sides of a disloyal servant;[w]
6 Of a seal to keep an erring wife at home,
or of a lock placed where there are many hands;
7 Of numbering every deposit,
or of recording all that is given or received;
8 Of chastisement of the silly and the foolish,
or of the aged and infirm answering for wanton conduct.
Thus you will be truly cautious
and recognized by all men as discreet.

## A Father's Care for His Daughter*

9 A daughter is a treasure that keeps her father wakeful,
and worry over her drives away rest:[x]
Lest she pass her prime unmarried,
or when she is married, lest she be disliked;
10 While unmarried, lest she be seduced,
or, as a wife, lest she prove unfaithful;
Lest she conceive in her father's home,
or be sterile in that of her husband.
11 Keep a close watch on your daughter,
lest she make you the sport of your enemies,
A byword in the city, a reproach among the people,
an object of derision in public gatherings.
See that there is no lattice in her room,
no place that overlooks the approaches to the house.[y]
12 Let her not parade her charms before men,[z]
or spend her time with married women;
13 For just as moths come from garments,
so harm to women comes from women:
14 Better a man's harshness than a woman's indulgence,
and a frightened daughter than any disgrace.

## The Works of God in Nature*

15 Now will I recall God's works;
what I have seen, I will describe.
At God's word were his works brought into being;
they do his will as he has ordained for them.[a]
16 As the rising sun is clear to all,
so the glory of the LORD fills all his works;
17 Yet even God's holy ones must fail
in recounting the wonders of the LORD,
Though God has given these, his hosts, the strength
to stand firm before his glory.
18 He plumbs the depths and penetrates the heart;
their innermost being he understands.
The Most High possesses all knowledge,
and sees from of old the things that are to come:
19 He makes known the past and the future,
and reveals the deepest secrets.
20 No understanding does he lack;
no single thing escapes him.[b]
21 Perennial is his almighty wisdom;
he is from all eternity one and the same,
22 With nothing added, nothing taken away;
no need of a counselor for him![c]
23 How beautiful are all his works!
even to the spark and fleeting vision!
24 The universe lives and abides forever;
to meet each need, each creature is preserved.
25 All of them differ, one from another,
yet none of them has he made in vain,
For each in turn, as it comes, is good;
can one ever see enough of their splendor?[d]

## CHAPTER 43

1 The clear vault of the sky shines forth[e]
like heaven itself, a vision of glory.
2 The orb of the sun, resplendent at its rising:
what a wonderful work of the Most High!
3 At noon it seethes the surface of the earth,
and who can bear its fiery heat?
4 Like a blazing furnace of solid metal,
it sets the mountains aflame with its rays;
By its fiery darts the land is consumed;
the eyes are dazzled by its light.
5 Great indeed is the LORD who made it,
at whose orders it urges on its steeds.
6 The moon, too, that marks the changing times,
governing the seasons, their lasting sign,[f]

v Prv 11, 1.
w Sir 30, 1-13; 33, 25-33.
x Sir 7, 24f.
y Sir 26, 10.
z 12f: Sir 9, 1-9.
a Ps 77, 12f.
b Sir 39, 19; Wis 1, 6-10.
c Is 40, 13; Rom 11, 34.
d Sir 33, 15.
e 1ff: Ps 19, 2f.
f Lv 23, 5; Nm 28, 11-14; Ps 81, 4.

* 42, 9–14: The author considers a daughter to be a source of anxiety to her father, lest she fail to marry, or be seduced, or lest, marrying, she be disliked, prove unfaithful, or find herself sterile (9f). He is advised to keep a close watch on her at home, and on her companionship while abroad, lest he suffer on her account among the people (11–14).

42, 15—43, 35: These verses comprise a new section. In them the author contemplates God's power, beauty and goodness as manifested in the mighty work of creating and preserving the universe (42, 15ff. 23. 25; 43, 1–27), his omniscience (42, 18ff), his perfect wisdom (21f), his eternity (24). The conclusion is a fervent hymn of praise (43, 28–35). Cf Sir 16, 22—18, 13.

7 By which we know the feast days and fixed dates,
this light-giver which wanes in its course:
8 As its name says, each month it renews itself;
how wondrous in this change!
9 The beauty, the glory, of the heavens are the stars
that adorn with their sparkling the heights of God,[g]
10 At whose command they keep their place
and never relax in their vigils.
A weapon against the flood waters stored on high,
lighting up the firmament by its brilliance,
11 Behold the rainbow! Then bless its Maker,
for majestic indeed is its splendor;[h]
12 It spans the heavens with its glory,
this bow bent by the mighty hand of God.

13 His rebuke marks out the path for the lightning,
and speeds the arrows of his judgment to their goal.
14 At it the storehouse is opened,
and like vultures the clouds hurry forth.
15 In his majesty he gives the storm its power
and breaks off the hailstones.
16 The thunder of his voice makes the earth writhe;
before his might the mountains quake.
17 A word from him drives on the south wind,
the angry north wind, the hurricane and the storm.
18 He sprinkles the snow like fluttering birds;
it comes to settle like swarms of locusts.
19 Its shining whiteness blinds the eyes,
the mind is baffled by its steady fall.
20 He scatters frost like so much salt;
it shines like blossoms on the thornbush.
21 Cold northern blasts he sends
that turn the ponds to lumps of ice.
He freezes over every body of water,
and clothes each pool with a coat of mail.
22 When the mountain growth is scorched with heat,
and the flowering plains as though by flames,
23 The dripping clouds restore them all,
and the scattered dew enriches the parched land.
24 His is the plan that calms the deep,
and plants the islands in the sea.
25 Those who go down to the sea tell part of its story,
and when we hear them we are thunderstruck;[i]
26 In it are his creatures, stupendous, amazing,
all kinds of life, and the monsters of the deep.
27 For him each messenger succeeds,
and at his bidding accomplishes his will.[j]
28 More than this we need not add;
let the last word be, he is all in all!*
29 Let us praise him the more, since we cannot fathom him,
for greater is he than all his works;
30 Awful indeed is the LORD's majesty,
and wonderful is his power.
31 Lift up your voices to glorify the LORD,
though he is still beyond your power to praise;
32 Extol him with renewed strength,
and weary not, though you cannot reach the end:
33 For who can see him and describe him?
or who can praise him as he is?[k]
34 Beyond these, many things lie hid;
only a few of his works have we seen.
35 It is the LORD who has made all things,
and to those who fear him he gives wisdom.[l]

## CHAPTER 44

### Praise of Israel's Great Ancestors

1 Now will I praise those godly men,*
our ancestors, each in his own time:*
2 The abounding glory of the Most High's portion,
his own part, since the days of old.
Subduers of the land in kingly fashion,
men of renown for their might,[m]
3 Or counselors in their prudence,
or seers of all things in prophecy;[n]
4 Resolute princes of the folk,
and governors with their staves;
Authors skilled in composition,
and forgers of epigrams with their spikes;
5 Composers of melodious psalms,
or discoursers on lyric themes;
6 Stalwart men, solidly established
and at peace in their own estates—
7 All these were glorious in their time,
each illustrious in his day.
8 Some of them have left behind a name
and men recount their praiseworthy deeds;
9 But of others there is no memory,
for when they ceased, they ceased.
And they are as though they had not lived,

g Ps 8, 4.
h Gn 9, 13.
i Ps 104, 25-30.
j Ps 33, 6.
k Ps 106, 2.
l Jb 28, 28.
m Dt 32, 8f.
n Sir 39, 1.

*

43, 28: All in all: the perfections reflected in creation are found in a transcendent way in God, who alone is their source.

44, 1—50, 24: As in the previous section God's wisdom shone forth in the works of nature, so in these chapters it is also revealed through the history of God's people as seen in the lives of their patriarchs, prophets, priests and rulers. The example of these great men, whose virtues are here recalled, constitutes a high point of the author's teaching and illustrates his belief in the canonical Scriptures.

44, 1–15: The reader is here introduced to those men of Israel, later mentioned by name, who through various achievements and beneficial social activities have acquired great renown (1–8. 14f); and also to those who, though forgotten, endure through the fruit of their virtues and through their families because of God's covenant with them (9–13).

they and their children after them.
10 Yet these also were godly men
whose virtues have not been forgotten;
11 Their wealth remains in their families,
their heritage with their descendants;
12 Through God's covenant with them their
family endures,
their posterity for their sake.
13 And for all time their progeny will endure,
their glory will never be blotted out;
14 Their bodies are peacefully laid away,
but their name lives on and on.[o]
15 At gatherings their wisdom is retold,
and the assembly proclaims their praise.

### The Early Patriarchs

16 [ENOCH* walked with the LORD and was
taken up,[p]
that succeeding generations might learn by
his example.]
17 NOAH, found just and perfect,
renewed the race in the time of
devastation.[q]
Because of his worth there were survivors,
and with a sign to him the deluge ended;
18 A lasting agreement was made with him,
that never should all flesh be destroyed.
19 ABRAHAM, father of many peoples,
kept his glory without stain:[r]
20 He observed the precepts of the Most High,
and entered into an agreement with him;
In his own flesh he incised the ordinance,*
and when tested he was found loyal.[s]
21 For this reason, God promised him with an
oath
that in his descendants the nations would
be blessed,
That he would make him numerous as the
grains of dust,
and exalt his posterity like the stars;
That he would give them an inheritance
from sea to sea,
and from the River* to the ends of the
earth.
22 And for ISAAC he renewed the same promise
because of Abraham, his father.
The covenant with all his forebears was
confirmed,
and the blessing rested upon the head of
JACOB.[t]
23 God acknowledged him as the firstborn,
and gave him his inheritance.
He fixed the boundaries for his tribes,
and their division into twelve.

## CHAPTER 45

### Praise of Moses, Aaron and Phinehas

1 From him was to spring the man*
who won the favor of all:[u]
Dear to God and men,
MOSES, whose memory is held in
benediction.
2 God's honor[v] devolved upon him,*
and the Lord strengthened him with
fearful powers;[w]
3 God wrought swift miracles at his words
and sustained him in the king's presence.
He gave him the commandments for his
people,
and revealed to him his glory.[x]
4 For his trustworthiness and meekness
God selected him from all mankind;[y]
5 He permitted him to hear his voice,
and led him into the cloud,
Where, face to face,* he gave him the
commandments,
the law of life and understanding,
That he might teach his precepts to Jacob,
his judgments and decrees to Israel.

6 He raised up also, like Moses in holiness,*
his brother AARON, of the tribe of Levi.[z]
7 He made him perpetual in his office
when he bestowed on him the priesthood*
of his people;
He established him in honor

o Wis 3, 3.
p Sir 49, 14; Gn 5, 18-24; Heb 11, 5.
q Gn 6, 8—9, 29; Heb 11, 7.
r Gn 12, 1—25, 10; Gal 3, 6; Heb 11, 8-19.
s Gn 17, 10; 22, 1.
t Gn 26, 3. 5. 24; 27, 28f; 28, 14.
u Ex 2, 2; 11, 3; 33, 11; Nm 12, 7.
v Ex 7, 1—13, 22.
w 2-5: Ex 7—Dt 34.
x Ex 4, 17; 7, 1.
y Nm 12, 3. 7.
z 6ff: Ex 28f; Wis 18, 24.

*

44, 16: Enoch: because of his friendship with God and also by reason of his unusual disappearance from the earth, this prophet's renown was great among the chosen people, particularly in the two centuries just before the coming of Christ; cf Gn 5, 21–24; Heb 11, 5. The present verse is an expansion of the original text; cf Sir 49, 14.

44, 20: In his own flesh ... ordinance: the covenant of circumcision; cf Gn 17, 10–14. And when tested ... loyal: Abraham's willingness to sacrifice his son Isaac at the Lord's command; cf Gn 22, 9–12.

44, 21: The River: the Euphrates; cf Gn 2, 14.

45, 1–5: Moses manifested God's power through miracles (1ff), God's authority through the promulgation of the commandments and the law (5), and God's mercy through the intimacy granted him by the Lord for his own faithfulness and meekness (4f). The very personification of the old covenant, Moses was also a type of Christ, the Prophet and Legislator of the new; cf Dt 18, 15.

45, 2: God's honor devolved upon him: Moses was actually God's substitute in dealing with Pharaoh, hence God entrusted his own honor to Moses.

45, 5: Face to face: on God's intimacy with Moses, see Ex 33, 11; Nm 12, 8. St. Paul alluded to this in 1 Cor 13, 12.

45, 6–21: The author here expresses his reverence and esteem for the priesthood of the old covenant. He recalls God's choice of Aaron and his sons for this sublime office (6f), and describes in detail the beauty of the high priest's vestments (8–13). He relates the ordination of Aaron at the hands of Moses, his brother (15), and describes the priestly functions, of offering sacrifice to God (16), and of blessing (15), teaching, governing and judging the people (17); the inheritance of the high priest (20ff); the punishment of those families who were jealous of Aaron (18f); and the confirmation of the covenant of the priesthood with Aaron's descendants through Phinehas (23ff).

45, 7: The priesthood of Aaron was superseded by the priesthood of Christ; cf Heb 7, 18–28.

and crowned him with lofty majesty;
8 He clothed him with splendid apparel,
and adorned him with the glorious vestments:
Breeches and tunic and robe
with pomegranates around the hem,
9 And a rustle of bells round about,
through whose pleasing sound at each step
He would be heard within the sanctuary,
and the children of his race would be remembered;
10 The sacred vestments of gold, of violet,
and of crimson, wrought with embroidery;
The breastpiece for decision, the ephod and cincture
11 with scarlet yarn, the work of the weaver;
Precious stones with seal engravings
in golden settings, the work of the jeweler,
To commemorate in incised letters
each of the tribes of Israel;
12 On his turban the diadem of gold,
its plate wrought with the insignia of holiness,
Majestic, glorious, renowned for splendor,
a delight to the eyes, beauty supreme.
13 Before him, no one was adorned with these,
nor may they ever be worn by any
Except his sons and them alone,
generation after generation, for all time.
14 His cereal offering is wholly burnt
with the established sacrifice twice each day;
15 For Moses ordained him
and anointed him with the holy oil,
In a lasting covenant with him
and with his family, as permanent as the heavens,
That he should serve God in his priesthood
and bless his people in his name.
16 He chose him from all mankind
to offer holocausts and choice offerings,
To burn sacrifices of sweet odor for a memorial,
and to atone for the people of Israel.
17 He gave to him his laws,
and authority to prescribe and to judge:
To teach the precepts to his people,
and the ritual to the descendants of Israel.
18 Men of other families were inflamed against him,
were jealous of him in the desert,
The followers of Dathan and Abiram,
and the band of Korah in their defiance.[a]

19 But the LORD saw this and became angry,
he destroyed them in his burning wrath.
He brought down upon them a miracle,
and consumed them with his flaming fire.
20 Then he increased the glory of Aaron[b]
and bestowed upon him his inheritance:
The sacred offerings he allotted to him,
with the showbread as his portion;
21 The oblations of the LORD are his food,
a gift to him and his descendants.
22 But he holds no land among the people
nor shares with them their heritage;
For the LORD himself is his portion,
his inheritance in the midst of Israel.

23 PHINEHAS too, the son of Eleazar,
was the courageous third of his line
When, zealous for the God of all,
he met the crisis of his people[c]
And, at the prompting of his noble heart,
atoned for the children of Israel.
24 Therefore on him again God conferred the right,
in a covenant of friendship, to provide for the sanctuary,
So that he and his descendants
should possess the high priesthood forever.
25 For even his covenant with David,
the son of Jesse of the tribe of Judah,
Was an individual heritage through one son alone;
but the heritage of Aaron is for all his descendants.[d]

26 And now bless the LORD
who has crowned you with glory!
May he grant you wisdom of heart
to govern his people in justice,
Lest their welfare should ever be forgotten,
or your authority, throughout all time.

## CHAPTER 46

### Joshua, Caleb and the Judges

1 Valiant leader was JOSHUA, son of Nun*
assistant to Moses in the prophetic office,
Formed to be, as his name implies,
the great savior of God's chosen ones,
To punish the enemy
and to win the inheritance for Israel.[e]
2 What glory was his when he raised his arm,
to brandish his javelin against the city![f]
3 And who could withstand him
when he fought the battles of the LORD?*
4 Did he not by his power stop the sun,
so that one day became two?[g]
5 He called upon the Most High God
when his enemies beset him on all sides,
And God Most High gave answer to him
in hailstones of tremendous power,
6 Which he rained down upon the hostile army
till on the slope he destroyed the foe;
That all the doomed nations might know

a Nm 16, 1ff.
b 20f: Nm 18, 11-21; Dt 10, 9.
c Nm 25, 7-13; Ps 106, 30f; 1 Mc 2, 26. 54.
d 2 Sm 7, 12-16.
e Ex 17, 9; Nm 27, 18; Dt 34, 9; Jos 1, 1-4.
f Jos 8, 18.
g Jos 10, 13.

46, 1–6: Joshua: whose name means "the LORD is savior" (1), was the instrument through which God delivered his people in miraculous ways (2–6) by destroying their enemies, whose land he gave to the Israelites as an inheritance (1).
46, 3: The battles of the Lord: cf Jos 6—10.

that the LORD was watching over his
people's battles.
And because he was a devoted follower of
God
7 and in Moses' lifetime showed himself
loyal,
He and CALEB,* son of Jephunneh,
when they opposed the rebel assembly,
Averted God's anger from the people
and suppressed the wicked complaint—[h]
8 Because of this, they were the only two
spared
from the six hundred thousand infantry,
To lead the people into their inheritance,
the land flowing with milk and honey.[i]
9 And the strength he gave to Caleb
remained with him even in his old age
Till he won his way onto the summits of the
land;
his family too received an inheritance,[j]
10 That all the people of Jacob might know
how good it is to be a devoted follower of
the LORD.
11 The JUDGES,* too, each one of them,
whose hearts were not deceived,
Who did not abandon God:
may their memory be ever blessed,[k]
12 Their bones return to life from their resting
place,
and their names receive fresh luster in
their children!
13 Beloved of his people, dear to his Maker,
dedicated from his mother's womb,
Consecrated to the LORD as a prophet,
was SAMUEL, the judge and priest.
At God's word he established the kingdom
and anointed princes to rule the people.[l]
14 By the law of the LORD he judged the
nation,
when he visited the encampments of
Jacob.
15 As a trustworthy prophet he was sought out
and his words proved him true as a seer.
16 He, too, called upon God,
and offered him a suckling lamb;[m]
17 Then the LORD thundered forth from heaven,
and the tremendous roar of his voice was
heard.[n]
18 He brought low the rulers of the enemy
and destroyed all the lords of the
Philistines.
19 When Samuel approached the end of his
life,
he testified before the LORD and his
anointed prince,
"No bribe or secret gift have I taken from
any man!"
and no one dared gainsay him.[o]
20 Even when he lay buried, his guidance was
sought;
he made known to the king his fate,
And from the grave he raised his voice
as a prophet, to put an end to
wickedness.[p]

## CHAPTER 47

### Nathan, David and Solomon

1 After him came NATHAN*
who served in the presence of David.[q]
2 Like the choice fat of the sacred offerings,
so was DAVID in Israel.[r]
3 He made sport of lions as though they were
kids,
and of bears, like lambs of the flock.[s]
4 As a youth he slew the giant
and wiped out the people's disgrace,
When his hand let fly the slingstone
that crushed the pride of Goliath.[t]
5 Since he called upon the Most High God,
who gave strength to his right arm
To defeat the skilled warrior
and raise up the might of his people,
6 Therefore the women sang his praises
and ascribed to him tens of thousands.
When he assumed the royal crown, he
battled[u]
7 and subdued the enemy on every side.
He destroyed the hostile Philistines
and shattered their power till our own
day.[v]
8 With his every deed he offered thanks
to God Most High, in words of praise.
With his whole being he loved his Maker
and daily had his praises sung;
9 He added beauty to the feasts
and solemnized the seasons of each year
With string music before the altar,
providing sweet melody for the psalms[w]
10 So that when the Holy Name was praised,

h Nm 13, 30; 14, 6.
i Nm 14, 22-38.
j Jos 14, 6; 15, 13.
k Jgs 1, 1—16, 31.
l 1 Sm 1, 10ff; 8, 4ff; 10, 1; 16, 13.
m 1 Sm 7, 9.
n Sir 12, 18.
o 1 Sm 12, 3.
p 1 Sm 28, 14.
q 2 Sm 7, 2.
r 1 Sm 16, 11.
s 1 Sm 17, 35.
t 1 Sm 17, 49.
u 1 Sm 18, 7.
v 2 Sm 5, 6-25.
w 1 Chr 16, 4ff; 23, 2ff; 25, 1-7.

*

46, 7–10: Caleb, who with Joshua advised Moses and the people in the desert to conquer Canaan, despite the counsel of their companion scouts and the rebellion of the people, merited to lead the Israelites of the succeeding generation into the Promised Land. Caleb in his old age received as his inheritance a portion of land which he himself had previously conquered; cf Jos 15, 13f.

46, 11–20: Of the Judges praised and blessed for their fidelity to God in opposing idolatry, Samuel, a man of spotless integrity, was the greatest (11f. 19). He was judge of the entire nation, and was also a prophet and priest who through his sacrificial offering obtained victory over the Philistines. He established the kingdom, anointed kings (13–18), and even after his death foretold the king's fate and put an end to wickedness (20).

47, 1–11: David, a youthful and fearless warrior, the favorite of all Israel, by defeating Goliath, the boastful Philistine giant, removed the people's disgrace and greatly strengthened their power (1–7). With his whole being he loved and praised God, and his devotion to divine worship led him to develop liturgical cult. David fell into sin, but repenting, received pardon from God and the promise of an everlasting kingdom (8–11).

before daybreak the sanctuary would
resound.
11 The LORD forgave him his sins
and exalted his strength forever;
He conferred on him the rights of royalty
and established his throne in Israel.[x]

12 Because of his merits he had as his
successor*
a wise son, who lived in security:[y]
13 SOLOMON reigned during an era of peace,
for God made tranquil all his borders.
He built a house to the name of God,
and established a lasting sanctuary.[z]
14 How wise you were when you were young,
overflowing with instruction, like the Nile
in flood![a]
15 Your understanding covered the whole earth,
and, like a sea, filled it with knowledge.
16 Your fame reached distant coasts,
and their peoples came to hear you;
17 With song and story and riddle,
and with your answers, you astounded the
nations.
18 You were called by that glorious name
which was conferred upon Israel.*
Gold you gathered like so much iron,
you heaped up silver as though it were
lead;
19 But you abandoned yourself to women
and gave them dominion over your
body.[b]
20 You brought dishonor upon your reputation,
shame upon your marriage,
Wrath upon your descendants,
and groaning upon your domain;
21 Thus two governments came into being,
when in Ephraim kingship was usurped.[c]
22 But God does not withdraw his mercy,
nor permit even one of his promises to
fail.
He does not uproot the posterity of his
chosen one,
nor destroy the offspring of his friend.
So he gave to Jacob a remnant,
to David a root from his own family.[d]
23 Solomon finally slept with his fathers,
and left behind him one of his sons,
Expansive* in folly, limited in sense,
REHOBOAM, who by his policy made the
people rebel;
Until one arose who should not be
remembered,
the sinner who led Israel into sin,[e]
Who brought ruin to Ephraim
24 and caused them to be exiled from their
land.

## Elijah and Elisha

Their sinfulness grew more and more,
25 and they lent themselves to every evil,*
48, 1 Till like a fire there appeared the prophet
whose words were as a flaming furnace.[f]
2 Their staff of bread he shattered,
in his zeal he reduced them to straits;
3 By God's word he shut up the heavens
and three times brought down fire.[g]
4 How awesome are you, ELIJAH!
Whose glory is equal to yours?
5 You brought a dead man back to life
from the nether world, by the will of the
LORD.[h]
6 You sent kings down to destruction,
and nobles, from their beds of sickness.[i]
7 You heard threats at Sinai,
at Horeb avenging judgments.[j]
8 You anointed kings who should inflict
vengeance,
and a prophet as your successor.[k]
9 You were taken aloft in a whirlwind,
in a chariot with fiery horses.[l]
10 You are destined, it is written, in time to
come
to put an end to wrath before the day of
the LORD,
To turn back the hearts of fathers toward
their sons,
and to re-establish the tribes of Jacob.[m]
11 Blessed is he who shall have seen you
before he dies,
12 O Elijah, enveloped in the whirlwind![n]

x 2 Sm 12, 13; 7, 12-16.
y 1 Kgs 2, 12.
z 1 Kgs 5, 1. 5.
a 14-18: 1 Kgs 5, 9-14; 10, 14-28.
b 1 Kgs 11, 1ff.
c 1 Kgs 12, 1ff.
d 2 Sm 7, 15; Ps 89, 34ff.
e 1 Kgs 11, 43; 12, 13. 21; 13, 34; 2 Kgs 17, 6ff.
f 1 Kgs 17, 1.
g 1 Kgs 17, 1; 2 Kgs 1, 9-14.
h 1 Kgs 17, 22.
i 1 Kgs 21, 19; 2 Kgs 1, 17.
j 1 Kgs 19, 8ff.
k 1 Kgs 19, 15ff.
l 2 Kgs 2, 11.
m Mal 3, 23f; Mt 17, 10.
n 2 Kgs 2, 9; 3, 13.

*

47, 12–24: Solomon, son and successor of David, inherited peace through his father's conquests. He built the magnificent temple of Jerusalem (12f) and received from God the favor of unparalleled wisdom, through which he obtained great fame (14–17). Luxury and sensuality, however, brought disgrace upon him, and because of his oppressive burdens, he disposed the kingdom for division after his death (19–21. 23f). Nevertheless God did not withdraw his promise of establishing his throne in the descendants of David (22).

47, 18: Cf 2 Sm 12, 25, where Solomon is called Jedidiah, "beloved of the Lord." The same term is used of Israel in Jer 11, 15.

47, 23: Expansive: the name Rehoboam means "the people is expansive," that is, widespread. The sinner: Jeroboam; cf 1 Kgs 12, 2. 20. 26–32.

47, 25—48, 11: The prophetic ministry of Elijah amid widespread idolatry is here described as a judgment by fire (47, 25f). Through his preaching, miracles and vengeance against God's enemies within and without Israel, the prophet succeeded for a time in destroying idols and in restoring faith and the worship of the true God (48, 2–8). His miraculous departure from this life gave rise to the belief that he did not die but would return before the end of the world to put an end to wrath and restore the tribes of Israel (9ff). Cf Mt 17, 9–13.

48, 12–16: Elisha fearlessly continued the work of his predecessor by numerous miracles (12ff), but the obstinacy of the people eventually brought on the destruction of the kingdom of Israel and the dispersion of its subjects. Judah, however, survived under the rule of Davidic kings, both good and bad (15f).

Then ELISHA, filled with a twofold portion
of his spirit,*
wrought many marvels by his mere word.
During his lifetime he feared no one,
nor was any man able to intimidate his
will.
13 Nothing was beyond his power;[o]
beneath him flesh was brought back into
life.
14 In life he performed wonders,
and after death, marvelous deeds.
15 Despite all this the people did not repent,
nor did they give up their sins,
Until they were rooted out of their land
and scattered all over the earth.
But Judah remained, a tiny people,
with its rulers from the house of David.[p]
16 Some of these did what was right,
but others were extremely sinful.

### Hezekiah and Isaiah*

17 HEZEKIAH fortified his city
and had water brought into it;[q]
With iron tools he cut through the rock
and he built reservoirs for water.
18 During his reign Sennacherib led an
invasion,
and sent his adjutant;
He shook his fist at Zion
and blasphemed God in his pride.[r]
19 The people's hearts melted within them,
and they were in anguish like that of
childbirth.
20 But they called upon the Most High God
and lifted up their hands to him;
He heard the prayer they uttered,
and saved them through ISAIAH.[s]
21 God struck the camp of the Assyrians
and routed them with a plague.[t]
22 For Hezekiah did what was right
and held fast to the paths of David,
As ordered by the illustrious prophet
Isaiah, who saw the truth in visions.
23 In his lifetime he turned back the sun
and prolonged the life of the king.[u]
24 By his powerful spirit he looked into the
future[v]
and consoled the mourners of Zion;
25 He foretold what should be till the end of
time,
hidden things yet to be fulfilled.

## CHAPTER 49

### Josiah and the Prophets*

1 The name JOSIAH is like blended incense,
made lasting by a skilled perfumer.[w]
Precious is his memory, like honey to the
taste,
like music at a banquet.
2 For he grieved over our betrayals
and destroyed the abominable idols.
3 He turned to God with his whole heart,
and, though times were evil, he practiced
virtue.
4 Except for David, Hezekiah and Josiah,
they all were wicked;
They abandoned the law of the Most High,
these kings of Judah, right to the very
end.
5 So he gave over their power to others,
their glory to a foolish foreign nation
6 Who burned the holy city
and left its streets desolate,
As JEREMIAH had foretold;[x]
7 for they had treated him badly
who even in the womb had been made a
prophet,
To root out, pull down, and destroy,
and then to build and to plant.[y]
8 EZEKIEL beheld the vision
and described the different creatures of the
chariot;[z]
9 He also referred to JOB,
who always persevered in the right path.[a]
10 Then, too, the TWELVE PROPHETS—
may their bones return to life from their
resting place!—
Gave new strength to Jacob
and saved him by their faith and hope.

### The Heroes after the Exile

11 How can we fittingly praise ZERUBBABEL,*
who was like a signet ring on God's right
hand,[b]
12 And Jeshua, Jozadak's son?
In their time they built the house of God;
They erected the holy temple,
destined for everlasting glory.
13 Extolled be the memory of NEHEMIAH!
He rebuilt our ruined walls,
Restored our shattered defenses,
and set up gates and bars.[c]

o 13f: 2 Kgs 13, 21.
p 2 Kgs 15, 29; 18, 11.
q 2 Kgs 20, 20; 2 Chr 32, 3ff. 30.
r 2 Kgs 18, 13ff; Is 36, 1ff.
s 2 Kgs 19, 20.
t 2 Kgs 19, 35; Is 37, 36.
u 2 Kgs 20, 11; Is 38, 8.
v 24f: 2 Kgs 20, 17; Is 40, 1ff; 42, 9; 46, 10; 48, 6; 61, 2.
w 2 Kgs 22, 1; 2 Chr 34, 1.
x 2 Kgs 25, 9; 2 Chr 36, 19.
y Jer 1, 5, 10.
z Ez 1, 4ff.
a Ez 14, 14. 20.
b 11f: Ezr 3, 2; Hg 1, 12; Zec 3, 1.
c Neh 1, 1; 3, 1.

*

48, 17–25: The fidelity, trust and courage of King Hezekiah (17. 22), the zeal of the prophet Isaiah, and the prayer of the people (20) availed with God. The Assyrian oppressors were routed (18f. 21), the king's life was prolonged, and consolations were granted the people through Isaiah's prophecies concerning the future (23ff), especially the coming of the Messiah and the establishment of his kingdom; cf Is 7, 14; 9, 6f; 40—65.

49, 1–10: The author's praise of King Josiah (1–3), of the prophets Jeremiah and Ezekiel and likewise the minor prophets (7–10) derives from their spirit of fidelity to the Lord and his law amid the infidelity of kings and people (4ff. 10).

49, 11ff: Zerubbabel and Jeshua, in rebuilding the temple, and Nehemiah, the governor, in repairing the walls of the Holy City, also restored what these constructions signify, namely, religious worship and civil authority as prescribed in the law.

## The Earliest Patriarchs

14 Few on earth have been made the equal of
ENOCH,*
for he was taken up bodily.[d]
15 Was ever a man born like JOSEPH?
Even his dead body was provided for.[e]
16 Glorious, too, were SHEM and SETH and
ENOS;
but beyond that of any living being
was the splendor of ADAM.[f]

## CHAPTER 50

### Simon, Son of Jochanan

1 The greatest among his brethren, the glory
of his people,
was SIMON the priest, son of Jochanan,*
In whose time the house of God was
renovated,
in whose days the temple was reinforced.
2 In his time also the wall was built
with powerful turrets for the temple
precincts;
3 In his time the reservoir was dug,
the pool with a vastness like the sea's.
4 He protected his people against brigands
and strengthened his city against the
enemy.
5 How splendid he was as he appeared from
the tent,
as he came from within the veil!
6 Like a star shining among the clouds,
like the full moon at the holyday season;
7 Like the sun shining upon the temple,
like the rainbow appearing in the cloudy
sky;
8 Like the blossoms on the branches in
springtime,
like a lily on the banks of a stream;
Like the trees of Lebanon in summer,
9 like the fire of incense at the sacrifice;
Like a vessel of beaten gold,
studded with precious stones;
10 Like a luxuriant olive tree thick with fruit,
like a cypress standing against the clouds;
11 Vested in his magnificent robes,
and wearing his garments of splendor,[g]
As he ascended the glorious altar
and lent majesty to the court of the
sanctuary.

12 When he received the sundered victims from
the priests
while he stood before the sacrificial wood,
His brethren ringed him about like a
garland,
like a stand of cedars on Lebanon;
13 All the sons of Aaron in their dignity
clustered around him like poplars,
With the offerings to the LORD in their
hands,
in the presence of the whole assembly of
Israel.
14 Once he had completed the services at the
altar
with the arranging of the sacrifices for the
Most High,
15 And had stretched forth his hand for the
cup,[h]
to offer blood of the grape,
And poured it out at the foot of the altar,
a sweet-smelling odor to the Most High
God,
16 The sons of Aaron would sound a blast,
the priests, on their trumpets of beaten
metal;
A blast to resound mightily
as a reminder before the Most High.[i]
17 Then all the people with one accord
would quickly fall prostrate to the ground
In adoration before the Most High,
before the Holy One of Israel.

18 Then hymns would re-echo,
and over the throng sweet strains of praise
resound.
19 All the people of the land would shout for
joy,
praying to the Merciful One,
As the high priest completed the services at
the altar
by presenting to God the sacrifice due;
20 Then coming down he would raise his hands
over all the congregation of Israel.[j]
The blessing of the LORD would be upon his
lips,
the name of the LORD would be his glory.
21 Then again the people would lie prostrate
to receive from him the blessing of the
Most High.

22 And now, bless the God of all,*

d Sir 44, 16; Gn 5, 18-24.
e Gn 37—50; Ex 13, 19; Jos 24, 32.
f Gn 1, 27; 4, 25f.
g Sir 45, 8-12; Ex 28, 2-5; 39, 1-21.
h 15f: Nm 15, 5; 28, 7.
i Nm 10, 10.
j Nm 6, 23-26.

*

49, 14ff: The patriarchs here mentioned were glorious because of their spirit of religion, i.e., their profound reverence for God and obedience to him. The splendor of Adam, moreover, was due to his direct origin from God.

50, 1–21: The son of Jochanan here mentioned was Simon II, in whose time as high priest (219–196 B.C.) great works were accomplished for the benefit of public worship and welfare (1–4). The author, a contemporary of this high priest, describes in great detail and by numerous comparisons the impression of awful majesty received, the lofty joy aroused, at sight of the high priest fully vested entering the sanctuary, ascending the altar (6–11), and, in the presence of the whole assembly of Israel, encircled by assistant priests bearing offerings, sacrificing the burnt offering on the Day of Atonement, while the trumpets blast and the people bow down in adoration of the Most High (12–17). The hymnody, the joyful shouts of the multitude, and finally the high priest's blessing, in which he pronounces—once only in the year, on this occasion—the holy name of Yahweh, climax the description of this most solemn Jewish liturgical function (18–21).

50, 22ff: Praise and thanksgiving are given to God for his wondrous works, and a blessing is invoked on man that he

who has done wondrous things on earth;
Who fosters men's growth from their
mother's womb,
and fashions them according to his will!
23 May he grant you joy of heart
and may peace abide among you;
24 May his goodness toward us endure in Israel
as long as the heavens are above.

## Epilogue and Canticles

25 My whole being loathes two nations,*
the third is not even a people:*
26 Those who live in Seir* and Philistia,
and the degenerate folk who dwell in
Shechem.[k]

27 Wise instruction, appropriate proverbs,*
I have written in this book,
I, Jesus, son of Eleazar, son of Sirach,
as they gushed forth from my heart's
understanding.
28 Happy the man who meditates upon these
things,
wise the man who takes them to heart!
29 If he puts them into practice, he can cope
with anything,
for the fear of the LORD is his lamp.

## CHAPTER 51

1 I give you thanks, O God of my father;*
I praise you, O God my savior!
I will make known your name, refuge of my
life;[l]
2 you have been my helper against my
adversaries.
You have saved me from death,
and kept back my body from the pit,
From the clutches of the nether world you
have snatched my feet;[m]
3 you have delivered me, in your great
mercy,
From the scourge of a slanderous tongue,
and from lips that went over to falsehood;
From the snare of those who watched for
my downfall,
and from the power of those who sought
my life;[n]
From many a danger you have saved me,
4 from flames that hemmed me in on every
side;[o]
From the midst of unremitting fire,
5 From the deep belly of the nether world;
From deceiving lips and painters of lies,
6 from the arrows of dishonest tongues.
I was at the point of death,
my soul was nearing the depths of the
nether world;[p]
7 I turned every way, but there was no one to
help me,
I looked for one to sustain me, but could
find no one.[q]
8 But then I remembered the mercies of the
LORD,
his kindness through ages past;
For he saves those who take refuge in him,
and rescues them from every evil.
9 So I raised my voice from the very earth,
from the gates of the nether world, my
cry.
10 I called out: O Lord, you are my father,
you are my champion and my savior;
Do not abandon me in time of trouble,
in the midst of storms and dangers.[r]
11 I will ever praise your name
and be constant in my prayers to you.
Thereupon the LORD heard my voice,
he listened to my appeal;
12 He saved me from evil of every kind

k 2 Kgs 17, 24; Jn 4, 9.
l Ps 138, 1.
m Ps 91, 3.
n Pss 40, 5; 91, 3.
o Ps 66, 12.
p Pss 88, 4; 94, 17.
q Pss 22, 12; 142, 5.
r Ps 89, 27.

* may enjoy peace and gladness of heart and the abiding goodness of the Most High.

50, 25f: The author's abhorrence of the pagan Edomites (Idumeans), Philistines and Samaritans can be understood in the light of Old Testament thinking, which does not always distinguish between hatred of evildoers and hatred of the evil they do.

50, 25: Not even a people: the Samaritans.

50, 26: Seir: Mount Seir in the territory of the Edomites. Shechem: a city in Samaria.

50, 27ff: These verses contain the subscription of the author, Jesus, son of Eleazar, son of Sirach, to his long and beautiful treatise on wisdom as applying to all of human life, integrating it under the direction of the fear of the Lord.

51, 1–12: A canticle of praise and thanks to God for delivering the author from slander, dangers, destruction, death, the nether world, and evil of every kind.

51, 12: After this verse the Hebrew text gives the litany of praise contained below. It is similar to Ps 136. Though not found in any versions, and therefore of doubtful authenticity, the litany seems from internal evidence to go back to the time of Sirach:

Give thanks to the Lord, for he is good, for his mercy endures forever;
Give thanks to the God of glory, for his mercy endures forever;
Give thanks to the guardian of Israel, for his mercy endures forever;
Give thanks to the creator of the universe, for his mercy endures forever;
Give thanks to the redeemer of Israel, for his mercy endures forever;
Give thanks to him who gathers the dispersed of Israel, for his mercy endures forever;
Give thanks to him who builds his city and his sanctuary, for his mercy endures forever;
Give thanks to him who makes a horn to sprout forth, for the house of David, for his mercy endures forever;
Give thanks to him who has chosen for his priests the sons of Zadok, for his mercy endures forever;
Give thanks to the shield of Abraham, for his mercy endures forever;
Give thanks to the rock of Isaac, for his mercy endures forever;
Give thanks to the mighty one of Jacob, for his mercy endures forever;
Give thanks to him who has chosen Zion, for his mercy endures forever;
Give thanks to the king over kings of kings, for his mercy endures forever;
He has lifted up the horn of his people, be this his praise from

and preserved me in time of trouble.
For this reason I thank him and I praise him;
I bless the name of the LORD.*

13 *When I was young and innocent,*
I sought wisdom.[s]
14 She came to me in her beauty,
and until the end I will cultivate her.
15 As the blossoms yielded to ripening grapes,
the heart's joy,
My feet kept to the level path
because from earliest youth I was familiar
with her.
16 In the short time I paid heed,
I met with great instruction.
17 Since in this way I have profited,
I will give my teacher grateful praise.

18 I became resolutely devoted to her—
the good I persistently strove for.
19 I burned with desire for her,
never turning back.
I became preoccupied with her,
never weary of extolling her.
My hand opened her gate
and I came to know her secrets.
20 For her I purified my hands;
in cleanness I attained to her.
At first acquaintance with her, I gained
understanding
such that I will never forsake her.[t]
21 My whole being was stirred as I learned
about her;
therefore I have made her my prize
possession.
22 The LORD has granted me my lips as a
reward,
and my tongue will declare his praises.

23 Come aside to me, you untutored,
and take up lodging in the house of
instruction;[u]
24 How long will you be deprived of wisdom's
food,
how long will you endure such bitter
thirst?
25 I open my mouth and speak of her:
gain, at no cost, wisdom for yourselves.[v]
26 Submit your neck to her yoke,
that your mind may accept her teaching.
For she is close to those who seek her,
and the one who is in earnest finds her.[w]
27 See for yourselves! I have labored only a
little,
but have found much.
28 Acquire but a little instruction;
you will win silver and gold through her.
29 Let your spirits rejoice in the mercy of God,
and be not ashamed to give him praise.
30 Work at your tasks in due season,
and in his own time God will give you
your reward.[x]

s Sir 34, 11.
t Prv 4, 6.
u Prv 8, 5.
v Sir 6, 20.
w Sir 6, 25.
x Sir 2, 8; Jb 34, 11; Jn 9, 4.

* all his faithful ones,
From the children of Israel, the people close to him. Alleluia! (Cf Ps 148, 14.)

51, 13–30: An alphabetic canticle describing: a) the approach to wisdom through prayer, persistent study and instruction (13–17), purification from sin, enlightenment and ardent desire; b) the possession of wisdom (18–22). The author concludes with an urgent invitation to men to receive instruction in wisdom from him, and to live by it, because wisdom gives herself to those who seek her (23–26); and for their labor. God will reward them in the end (27–30). Cf Mt 11, 28; Eccl 12, 14.

In the Greek of 13f there is an expansion introducing Solomon as the speaker. This deviates from the original author's intent. It reads, "Publicly, in my prayer, facing the temple, I asked for her."

# THE PROPHETIC BOOKS

*The prophetic books bear the names of the four major and twelve minor prophets, besides Lamentations and Baruch. The terms "major" and "minor" refer merely to the length of the respective compositions and not to any distinction in the prophetic office. Jonah is a story of the mission of the prophet rather than a collection of prophecies. Lamentations and Daniel are listed among the hagiographa in the Hebrew Bible, not among the prophetic books. The former contains a series of elegies on the fate of Jerusalem; the latter is apocalyptic in character. Daniel, who lived far removed from Palestine, was not called by God to preach; yet the book is counted as prophecy. Baruch, though excluded from the Hebrew canon, is found in the Septuagint version, and the church has always acknowledged it to be sacred and inspired.*

*The prophetic books, together with the oral preaching of the prophets, were the result of the institution of prophetism, in which a succession of Israelites chosen by God and appointed by him to be prophets received communications from him and transmitted them to the people in his name (Dt 18, 15–20). The prophets were spokesmen of God, intermediaries between him and his people. The communications they received from God came through visions, dreams, and ecstasies and were transmitted to the people through sermons, writings, and symbolic actions.*

*The office of prophet was due to a direct call from God. It was not the result of heredity, just as it was not a permanent gift but a transient one, subject entirely to the divine will. The prophets preserved and developed revealed religion (1 Sm 12, 6–25), denounced idolatry (1 Kgs 14, 1–13), defended the moral law (2 Sm 12, 1–15), gave counsel in political matters (Is 31, 1ff), and often also in matters of private life (1 Sm 9, 6–9). At times miracles confirmed their preaching, and their predictions of the future intensified the expectation of the Messiah and of his kingdom.*

*The prophetic literature in this volume contains the substance of the prophets' authentic preaching, resumes, and genuine samples of such preaching. Some parts were recorded by the prophets themselves, some by persons other than the prophets who uttered them.*

*The prophecies express judgments of the people's moral conduct, on the basis of the Mosaic alliance between God and Israel. They teach sublime truths and lofty morals. They contain exhortations, threats, announcements of punishment, promises of deliverance, made with solemn authority and in highly imaginative language. In the affairs of men, their prime concern is the interests of God, especially in what pertains to the chosen people through whom the Messiah is to come; hence their denunciations of idolatry and of that externalism in worship which excludes the interior spirit of religion. They are concerned also with the universal nature of the moral law, with personal responsibility, with the person and office of the Messiah, and with the conduct of foreign nations.*

*In content, the literary genre of prophecy uses warning and threat besides exhortation and promise to declare in God's name events of the near and distant future (Is 8–9). In form, the divine source of prophetic declaration appears in: "The word (or oracle) of the Lord," or "Thus says the Lord," followed by the announcement of a coming event and its moral cause (Hos 4, 7–10). Divine exhortation and promise are introduced by such forms as: "Hear this word, O men of Israel, that the Lord pronounces over you" (Am 3, 1). Kindly and persuasive tones pervade the promises of reward and even the threats of punishment (Am 5, 14–15).*

*Disregard for exact chronological perspective in the prophecies is an additional characteristic. Predictions of the immediate and distant future are often interrelated, not on the basis of years separating the events but on the analogy of the pattern joining present with very distant, though similar, conditions and circumstances. This is prophetic compenetration, idealization in which persons and things of the more immediate present, in the prophet's day, fade into a wider and more perfect order of persons and things of the future; the former are figures and types of the latter. Thus, some details of what the Psalmist said of the kingdom of David and Solomon (Ps 72) went beyond what was fulfilled in these men, as St. Thomas points out, and found their realization only in the kingdom of Christ, St. Jerome*

***before him, and still earlier the apostles themselves—Peter (Acts 2, 14–36) and Paul (Gal 4, 21–31)—taught us that through anticipation in types we discover in Sacred Scripture the truth of things to come.***

***Thus the universal blessing for mankind, often promised by God through the mouths of his prophets in figures and types, was in time to become personalized and to confer its full benefit on us through the Word made flesh, who became for us the New Covenant through his life, death, and resurrection, as the prophets had foretold.***

# The Book of

# ISAIAH

*The greatest of the prophets appeared at a critical moment of Israel's history. The second half of the eighth century B.C. witnessed the collapse of the northern kingdom under the hammerlike blows of Assyria (722), while Jerusalem itself saw the army of Sennacherib drawn up before its walls (701). In the year that Uzziah, king of Judah, died (742), Isaiah received his call to the prophetic office in the Temple of Jerusalem. Close attention should be given to chapter 6, where this divine summons to be the ambassador of the Most High is circumstantially described.*

*The vision of the Lord enthroned in glory stamps an indelible character on Isaiah's ministry and provides the key to the understanding of his message. The majesty, holiness and glory of the Lord took possession of his spirit and, conversely, he gained a new awareness of human pettiness and sinfulness. The enormous abyss between God's sovereign holiness and man's sin overwhelmed the prophet. Only the purifying coal of the seraphim could cleanse his lips and prepare him for acceptance of the call: "Here I am, send me!"*

*The ministry of Isaiah may be divided into three periods, covering the reigns of Jotham (742–735), Ahaz (735–715), and Hezekiah (715–687). To the first period belong, for the most part, the early oracles (1—5) which exposed the moral breakdown of Judah and its capital, Jerusalem. With the accession of Ahaz, the prophet became adviser to the king, whose throne was threatened by the Syro-Ephraimite coalition. Rejecting the plea of Isaiah for faith and courage, the weak Ahaz turned to Assyria for help. From this period came the majority of messianic oracles found in the section of Immanuel prophecies (6—12).*

*Hezekiah succeeded his father and undertook a religious reform which Isaiah undoubtedly supported. But the old intrigues began again, and the king was soon won over to the pro-Egyptian party. Isaiah denounced this "covenant with death" and again summoned Judah to faith in Yahweh as her only hope. But it was too late; the revolt had already begun. Assyria acted quickly and her army, after ravaging Judah, laid siege to Jerusalem (701). "I shut up Hezekiah like a bird in his cage," boasts the famous inscription of Sennacherib. But Yahweh delivered the city, as Isaiah had promised: God is the Lord of history, and Assyria but an instrument in his hands.*

*Little is known about the last days of this great religious leader, whose oracles, of singular poetic beauty and power constantly reminded his wayward people of their destiny and the fidelity of Yahweh to his promises.*

*The complete Book of Isaiah is an anthology of poems composed chiefly by the great prophet, but also by disciples, some of whom came many years after Isaiah. In 1—39 most of the oracles come from Isaiah and faithfully reflect the situation in eighth-century Judah. To disciples deeply influenced by the prophet belong sections such as the Apocalypse of Isaiah (24—27), the oracles against Babylon (13—14), and probably the poems of 34—35.*

*Chapters 40—55, sometimes called the Deutero-Isaiah, are generally attributed to an anonymous poet who prophesied toward the end of the Babylonian exile. From this section come the great messianic oracles known as the songs of the Servant, whose mysterious destiny of suffering and glorification is fulfilled in the passion and glorification of Christ. Chapters 56—66 contain oracles from a later period and were composed by disciples who inherited the spirit and continued the work of the great prophet.*

*The principal divisions of the Book of Isaiah are the following:*

*A. The Book of Judgment:*

*I. Indictment of Israel and Judah (1, 1—5, 30).*

*II. Immanuel Prophecies (6, 1—12, 6).*

*III. Oracles against the Pagan Nations (13, 1—23, 18).*

*IV. Apocalypse of Isaiah (24, 1—27, 13).*

*V. The Lord Alone, Israel's and Judah's Salvation (28, 1—33, 24).*
*VI. The Lord, Zion's Avenger (34, 1—35, 10).*
*VII. Historical Appendix (36, 1—39, 8).*
*B. The Book of Consolation:*
*I. The Lord's Glory in Israel's Liberation (40, 1—48, 21).*
*II. Expiation of Sin, Spiritual Liberation of Israel (49, 1—55, 13).*
*III. Return of the First Captives (56, 1—66, 24).*

# A. THE BOOK OF JUDGMENT

## I: *Indictment of Israel and Judah*

### CHAPTER 1

**Israel's Sinfulness.** **1** The vision* which
Isaiah, son of Amoz, had concerning Judah and
Jerusalem in the days of Uzziah, Jotham, Ahaz
and Hezekiah, kings of Judah.

**2** Hear, O heavens, and listen, O earth,
for the LORD speaks:
Sons have I raised and reared,
but they have disowned me![a]
**3** An ox knows its owner,
and an ass, its master's manger;
But Israel* does not know,
my people has not understood.
**4** Ah! sinful nation, people laden with wickedness,
evil race, corrupt children!
They have forsaken the LORD,
spurned the Holy One of Israel,*
apostatized.[b]
**5** Where would you yet be struck,*
you that rebel again and again?
The whole head is sick,
the whole heart faint.
**6** From the sole of the foot to the head
there is no sound spot:
Wound and welt and gaping gash,
not drained, or bandaged,
or eased with salve.
**7** Your country is waste,
your cities burnt with fire;
Your land before your eyes
strangers devour
[a waste, like Sodom overthrown]—
**8** And daughter Zion* is left
like a hut in a vineyard,
Like a shed in a melon patch,
like a city blockaded.

**9** Unless the LORD of hosts*
had left us a scanty remnant,
We had become as Sodom,
we should be like Gomorrah.[c]
**10** Hear the word of the LORD,
princes of Sodom!
Listen to the instruction of our God,
people of Gomorrah!
**11** What care I for the number of your sacrifices?*
says the LORD.
I have had enough of whole-burnt rams
and fat of fatlings;
In the blood of calves, lambs and goats
I find no pleasure.[d]

**12** When you come in to visit me,
who asks these things of you?
**13** Trample my courts no more!
Bring no more worthless offerings;
your incense is loathsome to me.
New moon and sabbath, calling of assemblies,
octaves with wickedness:* these I cannot bear.[e]
**14** Your new moons and festivals I detest;
they weigh me down, I tire of the load.
**15** When you spread out your hands,*
I close my eyes to you;
Though you pray the more,
I will not listen.

a Dt 32, 1. 5f. Mi 6, 7.
b Is 5, 24; Dt 32, 15.
c Rom 9, 29.
d Ps 50, 8-13; Sir 34, 19;
e Prv 15, 8; Jer 6, 20.
f Prv 1, 28; Sir 34, 21-25.

*

1, 1: The title of the book: an editorial addition. Isaiah: meaning "the salvation of the Lord," or "The Lord is salvation." Amoz: not the minor prophet. Judah: The southern kingdom of the tribes of Judah and Benjamin. Uzziah: also called Azariah; cf 2 Kgs 15, 1; 2 Chr 26, 1.

1, 3: Israel, not the northern kingdom, as in Is 9, 11, exclusively, which Isaiah usually calls "Ephraim" from the tribe bordering on the southern kingdom, but the entire chosen people; cf Is 8, 14.

1, 4: Holy One of Israel: a title used frequently by Isaiah, rarely by other writers.

1, 5-8: Sufferings inflicted upon God's people for their sins.

1, 8: Daughter Zion: Jerusalem. Hut . . . shed: for the shelter of watchmen and laborers.

1, 9: Lord of hosts: God, who is the Creator and Ruler of the heavenly armies of the angels, stars, etc. Remnant: St. Paul uses this text in Rom 9, 29, where he speaks of God's saving mercy toward the Jews and Gentiles. Sodom . . . Gomorrah: cf Gn 19.

1, 11: The number of your sacrifices: however numerous, they are not acceptable without the right dispositions on the part of the worshipers.

1, 13: Octaves with wickedness: the solemnity of the feasts marred by evil deeds.

1, 15: Spread out your hands: in prayer.

Your hands are full of blood![f]
16 Wash yourselves clean!
Put away your misdeeds from before my eyes;
cease doing evil; 17 learn to do good.
Make justice your aim: redress the wronged,
hear the orphan's plea, defend the widow.[g]

18 Come now, let us set things right,
says the LORD:
Though your sins be like scarlet,
they may become white as snow;
Though they be crimson red,
they may become white as wool.[h]
19 If you are willing, and obey,
you shall eat the good things of the land;
20 But if you refuse and resist,
the sword shall consume you:
for the mouth of the LORD has spoken!

21 How has she turned adulteress,
the faithful city, so upright!*
Justice used to lodge within her,
but now, murderers.[i]
22 Your silver is turned to dross,
your wine is mixed with water.
23 Your princes are rebels
and comrades of thieves;
Each one of them loves a bribe
and looks for gifts.
The fatherless they defend not,
and the widow's plea does not reach them.[j]
24 Now, therefore, says the Lord,
the LORD of hosts, the Mighty One of Israel:
Ah! I will take vengeance on my foes
and fully repay my enemies![k]
25 I will turn my hand against you,
and refine your dross in the furnace,
removing all your alloy.
26 I will restore your judges as at first,
and your counselors as in the beginning;
After that you shall be called
city of justice, faithful city.[l]

27 Zion shall be redeemed by judgment,
and her repentant ones by justice.*
28 Rebels and sinners alike shall be crushed,
those who desert the LORD shall be consumed.
29 You shall be ashamed of the terebinths
which you prized,
and blush for the groves which you chose.*
30 You shall become like a tree with falling leaves,
like a garden that has no water.
31 The strong man shall turn to tow,
and his work shall become a spark;
Both shall burn together,
and there shall be none to quench the flames.

## CHAPTER 2

**Zion, the Messianic Capital.** 1 This is what Isaiah, son of Amoz, saw concerning Judah and Jerusalem.*

2 In days to come,*
The mountain of the LORD's house[m]
shall be established as the highest mountain
and raised above the hills.
All nations shall stream toward it;[n]
3 many peoples shall come and say:
"Come, let us climb the LORD's mountain,
to the house of the God of Jacob,
That he may instruct us in his ways,
and we may walk in his paths."[o]
For from Zion shall go forth instruction,
and the word of the LORD from Jerusalem.*
4 He shall judge between the nations,
and impose terms on many peoples.
They shall beat their swords into plowshares
and their spears into pruning hooks;
One nation shall not raise the sword against another,
nor shall they train for war again.[p]

5 O house of Jacob, come,
let us walk in the light of the LORD!

### The Lord's Judgment against Idols

6 You have abandoned your people,
the house of Jacob,
Because they are filled with fortunetellers
and soothsayers,* like the Philistines;
they covenant with strangers.[q]
7 Their land is full of silver and gold,

g Ex 23, 6; Dt 24, 17; Sir 4, 9f; Jer 22, 3; Ez 22, 7; Zec 7, 9f.
h Ps 51, 9.
i Jer 3, 8; Hos 2, 7.
j Ex 23, 8; Dt 16, 19.
k Dt 32, 41.
l Jer 33, 7ff; Zec 8, 3.
m 2ff: Mi 4, 1ff.
n Is 56, 7.
o Zec 8, 20-23.
p Is 9, 7; 11, 4; Ps 72, 3f; Zec 9, 10.
q Is 8, 19; 19, 3.

*

1, 21: A picture of Jerusalem, once so faithful to God. Apostasy from the covenant is often likened by the prophets to unfaithfulness to the marriage vow.

1, 27: This verse is the key to the whole Book of Isaiah. Zion's defiant persistence in sin has demanded a divine judgment, by which her survivors will be cleansed and will return to God in justice; cf Is 40, 2.

1, 29: Terebinths which you prized . . . groves which you chose: as popular shrines for idolatrous worship.

2, 1: An editorial addition introducing chapters 2–5.

2, 2–4: The messianic destiny which ensures Judah's later restoration. In the messianic kingdom the prophets generally see the Lord's house as the seat of authority and the source of clear and certain doctrine; also, its rule willingly accepted by all peoples, maintained by spiritual sanctions, and tending to universal peace. This passage is found substantially unchanged in Mi 4, 1–3; it probably, although not certainly, has Isaiah as its author.

2, 3: Zion . . . Jerusalem: types of the earthly center of the messianic kingdom.

2, 6: Fortunetellers and soothsayers: divination was strictly forbidden; cf Dt 18, 9–14.

and there is no end to their treasures;
Their land is full of horses,
and there is no end to their chariots.
8 Their land is full of idols;
they worship the works of their hands,
that which their fingers have made.[r]

9 But man is abased,
each one brought low.
[Do not pardon them!]
10 Get behind the rocks,
hide in the dust,
From the terror of the LORD
and the splendor of his majesty![s]
11 The haughty eyes of man will be lowered,
the arrogance of men will be abased,
and the LORD alone will be exalted, on that day.*
12 For the LORD of hosts will have his day
against all that is proud and arrogant,
all that is high, and it will be brought low;
13 Yes, against all the cedars of Lebanon*
and all the oaks of Bashan,
14 Against all the lofty mountains
and all the high hills,
15 Against every lofty tower
and every fortified wall,
16 Against all the ships of Tarshish*
and all stately vessels.
17 Human pride will be abased,
the arrogance of men brought low,
And the LORD alone will be exalted, on that day.

18 The idols will perish forever.

19 Men will go into caves in the rocks
and into holes in the earth,
From the terror of the LORD
and the splendor of his majesty,
when he arises to overawe the earth.

20 On that day men will throw to the moles and the bats the idols of silver and gold which they made for worship.

21 They go into caverns in the rocks
and into crevices in the cliffs,
From the terror of the LORD
and the splendor of his majesty,
when he arises to overawe the earth.

22 As for you, let man alone,
in whose nostrils is but a breath;
for what is he worth?

## CHAPTER 3

## Judgment of Judah and Jerusalem

1 The Lord, the LORD of hosts,*
shall take away from Jerusalem and from Judah
support and prop [all supplies of bread and water]:[t]
2 Hero and warrior,
judge and prophet, fortuneteller and elder,
3 The captain of fifty and the nobleman,
counselor, skilled magician, and expert charmer.
4 I will make striplings their princes;
the fickle shall govern them,
5 And the people shall oppress one another,
yes, every man his neighbor.
The child shall be bold toward the elder,
and the base toward the honorable.
6 When a man seizes his brother
in his father's house, saying,
"You have clothes! Be our ruler,
and take in hand this ruin!"—
7 Then shall he answer in that day:
"I will not undertake to cure this,
when in my own house there is no bread or clothing!
You shall not make me ruler of the people."

8 Jerusalem is crumbling, Judah is falling;
for their speech and their deeds are before the LORD,
a provocation in the sight of his majesty.
9 Their very look bears witness against them;
their sin like Sodom they vaunt,
They hide it not. Woe to them!
they deal out evil to themselves.
10 Happy the just, for it will be well with them,
the fruit of their works they will eat.
11 Woe to the wicked man! All goes ill,
with the work of his hands he will be repaid.
12 My people—a babe in arms will be their tyrant,
and women will rule them!
O my people, your leaders mislead,
they destroy the paths you should follow.

13 The LORD rises to accuse,
standing to try his people.
14 The Lord enters into judgment
with his people's elders and princes:
It is you who have devoured the vineyard;
the loot wrested from the poor is in your houses.
15 What do you mean by crushing my people,
and grinding down the poor when they look to you?

r Is 31, 1ff.
s 2 Thes 1, 9.
t Lv 26, 26; Ez 4, 16.
u Lv 25, 42. 55.

*

2, 11: That day: the day of the Lord, a day of retribution, often referred to, especially by the minor prophets, and described in terms of natural phenomena: earthquake, fire, storm.

2, 13: Lebanon: Mount Lebanon in Syria, famed for its cedars. Bashan: the wooded uplands east of the Jordan River.

2, 16: Tarshish: of note on Ps 48, 8.

3, 1–12: Anarchy will reign in Jerusalem and Judah. In the prevailing desperation, even the most unworthy and the least qualified will be sought as rulers.

says the Lord, the God of hosts.[u]
16 The LORD said:[v]
Because the daughters of Zion are haughty,
and walk with necks outstretched
Ogling and mincing as they go,
their anklets tinkling with every step,
17 The Lord shall cover the scalps of Zion's daughters with scabs,
and the LORD shall bare their heads.*

18 On that day the LORD will do away with the
finery of the anklets, sunbursts, and crescents;
19 the pendants, bracelets, and veils; 20 the
headdresses, bangles, cinctures, perfume
boxes, and amulets; 21 the signet rings, and the
nose rings;* 22 the court dresses, wraps,
cloaks, and purses; 23 the mirrors, linen tunics,
turbans, and shawls.

24 Instead of perfume there will be stench,
instead of the girdle, a rope,
And for the coiffure, baldness;
for the rich gown, a sackcloth skirt. Then, instead of beauty:
25 Your men will fall by the sword,
and your champions, in war;
26 Her gates will lament and mourn,
as the city sits desolate on the ground.

## CHAPTER 4

1 Seven women will take hold of one man*
on that day, saying:
"We will eat our own food
and wear our own clothing;
Only let your name be given us,
put an end to our disgrace!"

### The Messianic Branch

2 On that day,
The branch of the LORD* will be luster and glory,
and the fruit of the earth will be honor and splendor
for the survivors of Israel.[w]
3 He who remains in Zion
and he that is left in Jerusalem
Will be called holy:
every one marked down for life* in Jerusalem.[x]
4 When the Lord washes away
the filth of the daughters of Zion,
And purges Jerusalem's blood from her midst
with a blast of searing judgment,
5 Then will the LORD create,
over the whole site of Mount Zion
and over her place of assembly,
A smoking cloud by day
and a light of flaming fire by night.[y]
6 For over all, his glory will be shelter and protection:
shade from the parching heat of day,
refuge and cover from storm and rain.

## CHAPTER 5

### The Vineyard Song

1 Let me now sing of my friend,
my friend's song concerning his vineyard.
My friend had a vineyard*
on a fertile hillside;
2 He spaded it, cleared it of stones,
and planted the choicest vines;
Within it he built a watchtower,
and hewed out a wine press.
Then he looked for the crop of grapes,
but what it yielded was wild grapes.

3 Now, inhabitants of Jerusalem and men of Judah,
judge between me and my vineyard:
4 What more was there to do for my vineyard
that I had not done?
Why, when I looked for the crop of grapes,
did it bring forth wild grapes?
5 Now, I will let you know
what I mean to do to my vineyard:
Take away its hedge, give it to grazing,
break through its wall, let it be trampled!
6 Yes, I will make it a ruin:
it shall not be pruned or hoed,
but overgrown with thorns and briers;
I will command the clouds
not to send rain upon it.
7 The vineyard of the LORD of hosts is the house of Israel,
and the men of Judah are his cherished plant;
He looked for judgment, but see, bloodshed!
for justice, but hark, the outcry!*

### Doom of the Unjust

8 Woe to you who join house to house,*
who connect field with field,
Till no room remains, and you are left to dwell
alone in the midst of the land![z]

v 16ff: Is 32, 11f.
w Is 11, 1; Jer 23, 5; 33, 15.
x Is 6, 13; 10, 20; Ob 17.
y Ex 13, 21.
z Mi 2, 2.

3, 17: Bare their heads: a mark of social disgrace; cf Nm 5, 18.

3, 21: Nose rings: of gold, a feminine ornament in the East; cf note on Gn 24, 22.

4, 1: Seven women . . . one man: the disproportion of the sexes due to war leaves the female population almost without male partners. The women are eager to marry, not for support, but to avoid the disgrace of being childless.

4, 2: Branch of the Lord: divine blessings in general, which later culminated in the Messiah; cf Jer 23, 5; Zec 3, 8; 6, 12.

4, 3: Marked down for life: in God's list of his elect; cf Ex 32, 32.

5, 1: My friend had a vineyard: the Lord and his chosen people.

5, 7: Judgment . . . bloodshed . . . justice . . . outcry: in Hebrew, these adversative terms constitute a play on words.

5, 8–10: Land-grabbers who unjustly acquire property will be impoverished instead of enriched.

9 In my hearing the LORD of hosts has sworn:
Many houses shall be in ruins,
large ones and fine, with no one to live in
them.[a]
10 Ten acres* of vineyard
shall yield but one liquid measure,
And a homer of seed
shall yield but an ephah.
17 Lambs shall graze there at pasture,
and kids shall eat in the ruins of the rich.

11 Woe to those who demand strong drink
as soon as they rise in the morning,
And linger into the night
while wine inflames them!
12 With harp and lyre, timbrel and flute,
they feast on wine;
But what the LORD does, they regard not,
the work of his hands they see not.[b]
13 Therefore my people go into exile,
because they do not understand;
Their nobles die of hunger,
and their masses are parched with thirst.
14 Therefore the nether world* enlarges its
throat
and opens its maw without limit;
Down go their nobility and their masses,
their throngs and their revelry.[c]
15 Men shall be abased, each one brought low,
and the eyes of the haughty lowered,
16 But the LORD of hosts shall be exalted by
his judgment,
and God the Holy shall be shown holy by
his justice.

18 Woe to those who tug at guilt with cords of
perversity,
and at sin as if with cart ropes!
19 To those who say, "Let him make haste
and speed his work, that we may see it;
On with the plan of the Holy One of Israel!
let it come to pass, that we may know
it!"[d]
20 Woe to those who call evil good, and good
evil,
who change darkness into light, and light
into darkness,
who change bitter into sweet, and sweet
into bitter!
21 Woe to those who are wise in their own
sight,
and prudent in their own esteem![e]
22 Woe to the champions at drinking wine,
the valiant at mixing strong drink![f]
23 To those who acquit the guilty for bribes,
and deprive the just man of his rights![g]
24 Therefore, as the tongue of fire licks up
stubble,
as dry grass shrivels in the flame,
Even so their root shall become rotten
and their blossom scatter like dust;
For they have spurned the law of the LORD
of hosts,
and scorned the word of the Holy One of
Israel.
25 Therefore the wrath of the LORD blazes
against his people,
he raises his hand to strike them;
When the mountains quake,
their corpses shall be like refuse in the
streets.
For all this, his wrath is not turned back,
and his hand is still outstretched.

### Invasion*

26 He will give a signal to a far-off nation,
and whistle to them from the ends of the
earth;
speedily and promptly will they come.
27 None of them will stumble with weariness,
none will slumber and none will sleep.
None will have his waist belt loose,
nor the thong of his sandal broken.
28 Their arrows are sharp,
and all their bows are bent.
The hoofs of their horses seem like flint,
and their chariot wheels like the
hurricane.
29 Their roar is that of the lion,
like the lion's whelps they roar;
They growl and seize the prey,
they carry it off and none will rescue it.
30 [They will roar over it, on that day,
with a roaring like that of the sea.][h]

## II: *Immanuel Prophecies*

## CHAPTER 6

**Call of Isaiah.** 1 In the year king Uzziah
died,* I saw the Lord seated on a high and lofty
throne,[i] with the train of his garment filling the
temple.* 2 Seraphim were stationed above;
each of them had six wings: with two they veiled
their faces, with two they veiled their feet, and
with two they hovered aloft.[j]

a Is 6, 12.
b Am 6, 5f.
c Hb 2, 5.
d Jer 5, 12: 2 Pt 3, 4.
e Prv 3, 7; Rom 12, 16.
f Sir 31, 3.
g Ex 23, 8; Prv 17, 15.
h Is 8, 22.
i Jn 12, 41.
j Rv 4, 8.

*

5, 10: Ten acres: a field requiring ten days of plowing by a yoke of oxen. Liquid measure: in Hebrew, a "bath," i.e., about ten gallons. Homer: a dry measure of about ten bushels. Ephah: a dry measure of about one bushel.

5, 14: Nether world: cf note on Ps 6, 6.

5, 26–30: A description of the invading Assyrian army, God's instrument for punishing his people.

6, 1: In the year King Uzziah died: 742 B.C.

6, 1ff: Temple: the holy place, just in front of the holy of holies. Seraphim: literally "the burning ones," are celestial beings who surround the throne of God. Each has six wings. Reverence for the divine majesty causes them to veil their faces with two wings; modesty, to veil their extremities in similar fashion; alacrity in God's service, to extend two wings in preparation for flight. Holy, holy, holy: God's perfect interior holiness whose exterior manifestation is his glory. These words are found in the Roman liturgy just before the Canon of the Mass.

3 "Holy, holy, holy is the LORD of hosts!"
they cried one to the other. "All the earth is
filled with his glory!" 4 [k]At the sound of that
cry, the frame of the door shook and the house
was filled with smoke.*

5 Then I said, "Woe is me, I am doomed!*
For I am a man of unclean lips, living among a
people of unclean lips; yet my eyes have seen
the King, the LORD of hosts!"[l] 6 Then one of
the seraphim flew to me, holding an ember
which he had taken with tongs from the altar.

7 He touched my mouth with it. "See," he
said, "now that this has touched your lips,*
your wickedness is removed, your sin
purged."[m]

8 Then I heard the voice of the Lord saying,
"Whom shall I send? Who will go for us?"
"Here I am;" I said; "send me!" 9 And he
replied: Go and say to this people:*

Listen carefully, but you shall not
understand!
Look intently, but you shall know
nothing![n]
10 You are to make the heart of this people
sluggish,
to dull their ears and close their eyes;
Else their eyes will see, their ears hear,
their heart understand,
and they will turn and be healed.[o]

11 "How long, O Lord?" I asked. And he
replied:

Until the cities are desolate,
without inhabitants,
Houses, without a man,
and the earth is a desolate waste.
12 Until the LORD removes men far away,
and the land is abandoned more and
more.*
13 If there be still a tenth part in it,
then this in turn shall be laid waste;
As with a terebinth or an oak
whose trunk remains when its leaves have
fallen.
[Holy offspring is the trunk.][p]

## CHAPTER 7

**Birth of Immanuel.** 1 In the days of
Ahaz,* king of Judah, son of Jotham, son of
Uzziah, Rezin, king of Aram, and Pekah, king
of Israel, son of Remaliah, went up to attack
Jerusalem,[q] but they were not able to conquer
it. 2 When word came to the house of David
that Aram was encamped in Ephraim, the heart
of the king and the heart of the people trembled,
as the trees of the forest tremble in the wind.

3 [r]Then the LORD said to Isaiah: Go out to
meet Ahaz, you and your son Shear-jashub,* at
the end of the conduit of the upper pool, on the
highway of the fuller's field, 4 and say to him:
Take care you remain tranquil and do not fear;
let not your courage fail before these two stumps
of smoldering brands [the blazing anger of Rezin and the Arameans, and of the son of Remali-
ah], 5 because of the mischief that Aram
[Ephraim and the son of Remaliah] plots against
you, saying, 6 "Let us go up and tear Judah
asunder, make it our own by force, and appoint
the son of Tabeel* king there."

7 Thus says the LORD:
This shall not stand, it shall not be!
8 Damascus is the capital of Aram,
and Rezin the head of Damascus;
Samaria is the capital of Ephraim,
and Remaliah's son the head of Samaria.
9 But within sixty years and five,*
Ephraim shall be crushed, no longer a
nation.
Unless your faith is firm
you shall not be firm![s]

10 Again the LORD spoke to Ahaz: 11 Ask
for a sign from the LORD, your God; let it be
deep deep as the nether world, or high as the
sky!* 12 But Ahaz answered, "I will not ask!
I will not tempt the LORD!* 13 Then he said:
Listen, O house of David! Is it not enough for
you to weary men, must you also weary my
God!? 14 Therefore the Lord himself will give

k 1 Kgs 8, 10f; Rv 15, 8.
l Gn 32, 3; Ex 20, 19; 33, 20; Jgs 6, 22; 13, 22.
m Jer 1, 9; Dn 10, 16.
n Mt 13, 14f; Mk 4, 12; Lk 8, 10; Acts 28, 26f.
o Jer 5, 21; Jn 12, 40.
p Is 10, 22.
q 2 Kgs 16, 5; 2 Chr 28, 5-15.
r Is 36, 2; 2 Chr 32, 3.
s Is 8, 6ff.

*

6, 4: Smoke: reminiscent of the clouds which surrounded God at Mount Sinai; cf Ex 19, 16–19; Dt 4, 11f.

6, 5: Doomed: it was popularly believed that to see God would lead to one's death; cf Gn 32, 31; Ex 33, 20; Jgs 13, 22.

6, 7: Touched your lips: Isaiah is thus symbolically purified to be worthy of his vocation as God's prophet. In the Roman liturgy, the celebrant at Mass makes reference to this incident just before he reads the gospel.

6, 9f: The truth that the nation will remain impenitent is vividly foretold, as if its obstinacy would be caused, instead of merely occasioned, by the prophet's warning. Cf Mt 13, 13ff; Mk 4, 12; Lk 8, 10.

6, 12: Several limited deportations in the time of Isaiah would later culminate in the Babylonian Exile.

7, 1: Days of Ahaz: who ruled from 735 to 715 B.C. This attack against Jerusalem by the kings of Aram (Syria) and Israel was occasioned by Ahaz' refusal to enter with them into an anti-Assyrian alliance; cf 2 Kgs 16.

7, 3: Shear-jashub: this name means "a remnant will return."

7, 6: Son of Tabeel: an adherent of Jerusalem's enemies. His appointment would interrupt the lawful succession from David.

7, 9: Within sixty years and five: if the text is correct, its reference is unknown.

7, 11: Deep . . . sky: an extraordinary or miraculous sign that would prove God's firm will to save the royal house of David from its oppressors.

7, 12: Tempt the Lord: Ahaz expresses in this hypocritical way his preference for depending upon the might of Assyria rather than upon God.

7, 14: The sign proposed by Isaiah was concerned with the

you this sign:* the virgin shall be with child, and
bear a son, and shall name him Immanuel.
**15** He shall be living on curds and honey* by
the time he learns to reject the bad and choose
the good. **16** For before the child learns to reject the bad and choose the good, the land of
those two kings whom you dread shall be deserted.

**17** The LORD shall bring upon you and your
people and your father's house days worse than
any since Ephraim seceded from Judah. [This
means the king of Assyria.] **18** On that day

The LORD shall whistle
for the fly that is in the farthest streams of Egypt,
and for the bee in the land of Assyria.
**19** All of them shall come and settle
in the steep ravines and in the rocky clefts,
on all thornbushes and in all pastures.

**20** On that day the LORD shall shave with the
razor hired from across the River [with the king
of Assyria] the head, and the hair between the
legs. It shall also shave off the beard.*

**21** On that day a man shall keep a heifer or
a couple of sheep, **22** and from their abundant
yield of milk he shall live on curds; curds and
honey shall be the food of all who remain in the
land. **23** On that day every place where there
used to be a thousand vines, worth a thousand
pieces of silver, shall be turned to briers and
thorns. **24** Men shall go there with bow and
arrows; for all the country shall be briers and
thorns. **25** For fear of briers and thorns you
shall not go upon any mountainside which used
to be hoed with the mattock; they shall be grazing land for cattle and shall be trampled upon by
sheep.

## CHAPTER 8

**The Son of Isaiah.** **1** The LORD said to me:
Take a large cylinder-seal, and inscribe on it in
ordinary letters:* "Belonging to Maher-shalal-hash-baz." **2** And I took reliable witnesses,*
Uriah the priest, and Zechariah, son of Jebere-
chiah. **3** Then I went to the prophetess* and she
conceived and bore a son. The LORD said to me:
Name him Maher-shalal-hash-baz, **4** for before
the child knows how to call his father or mother
by name, the wealth of Damascus and the spoil
of Samaria shall be carried off by the king of
Assyria.

**5** Again the LORD spoke to me:

**6** Because this people* has rejected the waters of Shiloah that flow gently,[t]
And melts with fear before the loftiness of Rezin
and Remaliah's son,
**7** Therefore the LORD raises against them
the waters of the River, great and mighty
[the king of Assyria and all his power].
It shall rise above all its channels,
and overflow all its banks;
**8** It shall pass into Judah, and flood it all throughout:
up to the neck it shall reach;
It shall spread its wings
the full width of your land, Immanuel!
**9** Know, O peoples, and be appalled!
Give ear, all you distant lands!
Arm, but be crushed! Arm, but be crushed!
**10** Form a plan,* and it shall be thwarted;
make a resolve, and it shall not be carried out,
for "With us is God!"

**Disciples of Isaiah.** **11** For thus said the
LORD to me, taking hold of me and warning me
not to walk in the way of this people:[u]

**12** Call not alliance what this people calls alliance,
and fear not, nor stand in awe of what they fear.
**13** But with the LORD of hosts make your alliance—

t Jn 9, 7. 11. u Ez 3, 14.

*

preservation of Judah in the midst of distress (cf Is 7, 15. 17), but more especially with the fulfillment of God's earlier promise to David (2 Sm 7, 12–16) in the coming of Immanuel (meaning, "With us is God") as the ideal king (cf Is 9, 5–6; 11, 1–5). The church has always followed St. Matthew in seeing the transcendent fulfillment of this verse in Christ and his Virgin Mother. The prophet need not have known the full force latent in his own words; and some Catholic writers have sought a preliminary and partial fulfillment in the conception and birth of the future King Hezekiah, whose mother, at the time Isaiah spoke, would have been a young, unmarried woman (Hebrew, almah). The Holy Spirit was preparing, however, for another Nativity which alone could fulfill the divinely given terms of Immanuel's mission, and in which the perpetual virginity of the Mother of God was to fulfill also the words of this prophecy in the integral sense intended by the divine Wisdom.

7, 15: Curds and honey: the restricted diet of those who remain after devastation has changed the once fertile fields of Judah into grazing land; cf Is 7, 21–25.

7, 20: God will use the Assyrians from across the River (the Euphrates) as his instrument (razor) to inflict disgrace and suffering upon his people.

8, 1: Ordinary letters: easily read by all. Maher-shalal-hash-baz: a symbolic name to be given to another son of Isaiah (v 3); it means "quick spoils; speedy plunder," and describes what the Assyrians will do.

8, 2: Reliable witnesses: who would testify that Isaiah had indeed prophesied the future destruction. Uriah the priest: cf 2 Kgs 16, 10.

8, 3: The prophetess: wife of Isaiah.

8, 6ff: This people: Judah. Waters of Shiloah: the stream that flows into the pool of Shiloah in Jerusalem, its slow current symbolizing the silent, divine protection which Judah has rejected. God will therefore summon the mighty Assyrian army, symbolized by the River (Euphrates), to devastate Judah, which, however, will not be entirely destroyed, because it is the land of Immanuel.

8, 10: The plan of Israel's enemies will be thwarted because, as the name "Immanuel" signifies, With us is God.

for him be your fear and your awe.
14 Yet he shall be a snare, an obstacle and a
stumbling stone
to both the houses of Israel,
A trap and a snare
to those who dwell in Jerusalem;[v]
15 And many among them shall stumble and
fall,
broken, snared, and captured.

16 The record is to be folded and the sealed
instruction kept among my disciples.* 17 For I
will trust in the LORD, who is hiding his face
from the house of Jacob; yes, I will wait for
him. 18 Look at me and the children whom the
Lord has given me: we are signs* and portents
in Israel from the LORD of hosts who dwells on
Mount Zion. 19 [w]And when they say to you,
"Inquire of mediums and fortunetellers (who
chirp and mutter!*); should not a people inquire
of their gods, apply to the dead on behalf of the
living!"— 20 then this document will furnish
its instruction. That kind of thing they will surely say.*

**The Prince of Peace.** 23 First he degraded
the land of Zebulun and the land of Naphtali;*
but in the end he has glorified the seaward road,
the land west of the Jordan, the District of the
Gentiles.

Anguish has taken wing, dispelled is
darkness:
for there is no gloom where but now there
was distress.

## CHAPTER 9

1 The people who walked in darkness[x]
have seen a great light;
Upon those who dwelt in the land of gloom
a light has shone.
2 You have brought them abundant joy
and great rejoicing,
As they rejoice before you as at the harvest,
as men make merry when dividing spoils.
3 For the yoke that burdened them,
the pole on their shoulder,
And the rod of their taskmaster
you have smashed, as on the day of
Midian.
4 For every boot that tramped in battle,
every cloak rolled in blood,
will be burned as fuel for flames.[y]
5 For a child* is born to us, a son is given us;
upon his shoulder dominion rests.
They name him Wonder-Counselor,
God-Hero,
Father-Forever, Prince of Peace.[z]
6 His dominion is vast
and forever peaceful,
From David's throne, and over his kingdom,
which he confirms and sustains
By judgment and justice,
both now and forever.
The zeal of the LORD of hosts will do this![a]

## Fall of the Northern Kingdom

7 The Lord has sent word against Jacob,
it falls upon Israel;
8 And all the people know it,
Ephraim and those who dwell in Samaria,
those who say in arrogance and pride of
heart,
9 "Bricks have fallen,
but we will build with cut stone;
Sycamores are felled,
but we will replace them with cedars."
10 But the LORD raises up their foes against
them
and stirs up their enemies to action:
11 Aram* on the east and the Philistines on the
west
devour Israel with open mouth.
For all this, his wrath is not turned back,
and his hand is still outstretched!

12 The people do not turn to him who struck
them,
nor seek the LORD of hosts.
13 So the LORD severs from Israel head and
tail,
palm branch and reed in one day.
14 [The elder and the noble are the head,
the prophet who teaches falsehood is the
tail.]
15 The leaders of this people mislead them
and those to be led are engulfed.[b]
16 For this reason, the Lord does not spare
their young men,
and their orphans and widows he does not
pity;
They are wholly profaned and sinful,

v Rom 9, 33; 1 Pt 2, 8.
w Lv 19, 31; Dt 18, 10ff.
x 1f: Mt 4, 15f.
y Sir 39, 9.
z Ps 72, 7; Lk 2, 11. 14.
a Jer 23, 5; Lk 1, 32f.
b Is 28, 7; Jer 2, 8; 5, 31; 20, 6; 23, 13f; 29, 30ff; Ez 13, 1-7; 22, 28; Mi 3, 11.

8, 16: Kept among my disciples: for preservation and transmission.

8, 18: Signs: Isaiah and his sons had symbolic names.

8, 19: Chirp and mutter: a mocking reference to the sounds uttered by necromancers, as if the dead were speaking; all such practices were forbidden.

8, 21f: These verses have been transposed and placed within Is 14, 25, which affords the context in which they can be understood.

8, 23: Zebulun . . . Naphtali: northern Palestine, which was first to be attacked by the Assyrians; God, however, redeems it, as he redeems all his people. Seaward road; from Damascus, across southern Galilee to the Mediterranean Sea. District of the Gentiles: northern Galilee, inhabited by pagans; cf Jos 20, 7; Is 9, 1. Mt 4, 15f refers to this, since Jesus began his public mission in Galilee.

9, 5: A child: the Immanuel of Is 7, 14 and 8, 8; cf Is 11, 1. 2. 9. In Christian tradition and liturgy, this passage is used to refer to Christ. Upon his shoulder dominion rests: authority. Wonder-Counselor: remarkable for his wisdom and prudence. God-Hero: a warrior and a defender of his people, like God himself. Father-Forever: ever devoted to his people. Prince of Peace: his reign will be characterized by peace.

9, 11: Aram: the Syrian kingdom, with its capital at Damascus.

# The Farmer's Year

In Bible times, most people had some involvement with farming, every family having at least a small plot of land.

**Grain**

The main crops were wheat and barley. Following the autumn rains, the farmer plowed the soil and sowed the grain by hand. If there were winter rains, he could harvest the crop in April or May.

**Harvest**

The farmer would cut the grain with a sickle, leaving the sheaves in the field to dry. Next he threshed the grain on a threshing-floor. After this, the farmer winnowed the grain, throwing it in the air to separate the grain from the lighter chaff, which blew away. Finally, the grain was sieved and stored away in sacks or large jars.

**Fruit**

The Israelites also grew fruit such as grapes, figs and olives as well as melons, dates, pomegranates and nuts. Often they also cultivated vegetables such as beans, lentils, onions and cucumbers, and some herbs.

**Animals**

Sheep and goats were herded for their meat and their milk, and for their wool and hair, which could be utilised for making garments. Farmers would often use asses for load-bearing and oxen for pulling the plow.

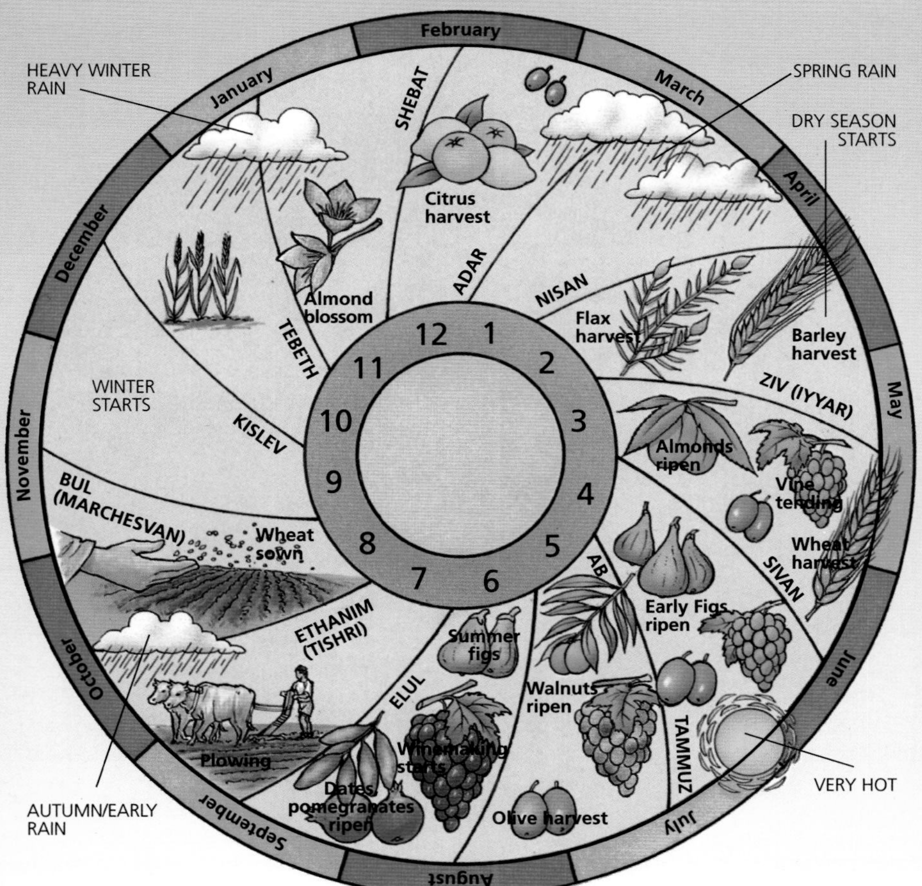

# Herod's Temple



Around 20 B.C., Herod the Great embarked on reconstructing the Temple in Jerusalem. First, the Temple Mount area on which the Temple stood was doubled in size in a huge earth-moving operation.

The new Temple was magnificent, constructed in white marble and decorated in gold. Its plan was similar to Solomon's Temple, with the Holy Place and the Holiest Place within, the latter only visited once a year, and only by the high priest.

Although anyone could enter the outer Court of the Gentiles, only Jewish people were allowed inside the inner courtyards. The Court of the Gentiles was a market-place where visitors bought and sold, and changed their money into special coins needed for offerings and for the temple tax (Mark 11:15-17).

***Below*: Photograph of the magnificent accurate scale model of Herod's Temple, built by a farmer in England.**

*By permission A. Garrard*

# The Synagogue

In Jesus' time, there was at least one synagogue in nearly every town and village (Luke 4:14-30). The Jews started having services in synagogues during the Exile when they had no access to the Temple. The synagogues developed their own form of service, parallel to that of the Temple.

There were synagogue services every Sabbath and on the Jewish festival days. The synagogue was also open for prayer three times a day.

In the main room of the synagogue stood a seven-branched lampstand, or *Menorah*, and a lamp of eternity. During worship there would be prayers, Scripture readings and praise.

The sacred rolls of the Law (the *Torah*) were kept in a special cupboard.

Sometimes in larger buildings there would be a courtyard with small rooms leading off it that were built onto the main structure.

**Women and Children**

Women and children were allowed only into the gallery of the synagogue.

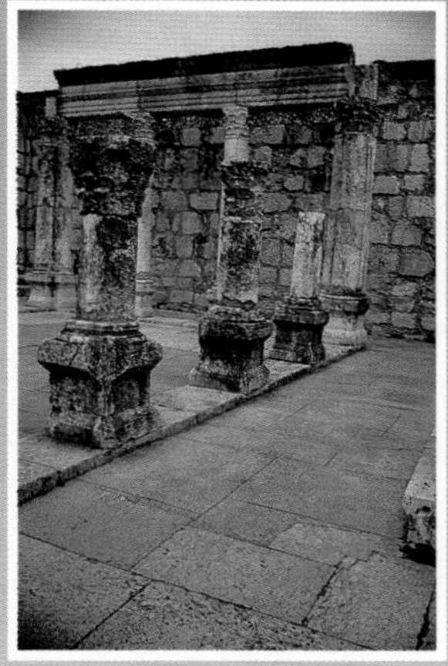

***Above*: The fourth-century Capernaum synagogue has been carefully excavated and partially reconstructed.**

***Below*: An artist's cutaway illustration of a synagogue from around the time of Jesus.**

**gallery for women and children**

**reading desk**

**men's area**

**cloister**

**entrance**

# Travel in Bible Times

In Jesus' time, most people traveled on foot. Those who could afford it traveled on horseback or in horse-drawn carriages. Palestine is a bare, hilly country, which is difficult for travel. Walkers could usually cover 16-20 Roman miles (15-18 miles/24-30 km) per day. Jesus traveled on foot around Galilee, and Paul walked long distances taking the gospel to new places.

Sometimes travelers were carried in chairs hung on poles and supported on slaves' shoulders. The rich also traveled in horse-drawn carriages, and merchants used heavy carts to transport grain and other goods. Asses and mules were also useful for carrying loads.

**By Jesus' time, the Romans were building large sailing vessels. When he was taken to Rome (Acts 27:1-44), Paul traveled in a grain-ship which carried 276 people. Such vessels had a single main sail and were difficult to handle in bad weather.**

***Below*: A passenger carriage from Roman times.**

***Above*: Wealthy people could be carried in a litter, supported on slaves' shoulders.**

***Above*: A goods cart drawn by two oxen.**

every mouth gives vent to folly.
For all this, his wrath is not turned back,
his hand is still outstretched!

17 For wickedness burns like fire,
devouring brier and thorn;
It kindles the forest thickets,
which go up in columns of smoke.
18 At the wrath of the LORD of hosts the land
quakes,
and the people are like fuel for fire;
No man spares his brother,
each devours the flesh of his neighbor.
19 Though they hack on the right, they are
hungry;
though they eat on the left, they are not
filled.
20 Manasseh devours Ephraim,* and Ephraim
Manasseh;
together they turn on Judah.
For all this, his wrath is not turned back.
his hand is still outstretched!

## CHAPTER 10

### Social Injustice

1 Woe to those who enact unjust statutes
and who write oppressive decrees,[c]
2 Depriving the needy of judgment
and robbing my people's poor of their
rights.
Making widows their plunder,
and orphans their prey![d]
3 What will you do on the day of punishment,
when ruin comes from afar?
To whom will you flee for help?
Where will you leave your wealth,
4 Lest it sink beneath the captive
or fall beneath the slain?
For all this, his wrath is not turned back,
his hand is still outstretched!

### Assyria the Unconscious Instrument of God

5 Woe to Assyria! My rod in anger,
my staff in wrath.
6 Against an impious nation* I send him.
and against a people under my wrath I
order him
To seize plunder, carry off loot,
and tread them down like the mud of the
streets.
7 But this is not what he intends,
nor does he have this in mind;
Rather, it is in his heart to destroy,
to make an end of nations not a few.
8 "Are not my commanders all kings?" he
says,
9 "Is not Calno like Carchemish,[e]
Or Hamath like Arpad,
or Samaria like Damascus?*
10 Just as my hand reached out to idolatrous
kingdoms
that had more images than Jerusalem and
Samaria,
11 Just as I treated Samaria and her idols,
shall I not do to Jerusalem and her graven
images?"[f]

12 *[But when the LORD has brought to an end
all his work on Mount Zion and in Jerusalem,

I will punish the utterance of the king of
Assyria's proud heart,
13 and the boastfulness of his haughty eyes.
For he says:]

"By my own power I have done it,
and by my wisdom, for I am shrewd.
I have moved the boundaries of peoples,
their treasures I have pillaged,
and, like a giant, I have put down the
enthroned.
14 My hand has seized like a nest
the riches of nations;
As one takes eggs left alone,
so I took in all the earth;
No one fluttered a wing,
or opened a mouth, or chirped!"

15 Will the axe boast against him who hews
with it?
Will the saw exalt itself above him who
wields it?
As if a rod could sway him who lifts it,
or a staff him who is not wood!
16 Therefore the Lord, the LORD of hosts,
will send among his fat ones* leanness,
And instead of his glory there will be
kindling
like the kindling of fire.
17 The Light of Israel will become a fire,
Israel's Holy One a flame,
That burns and consumes his briers
and his thorns in a single day.
18 His splendid forests and orchards
will be consumed, soul and body;
19 And the remnant of the trees in his forest
will be so few,
Like poles set up for signals,
that any boy can record them.
20 On that day
The remnant of Israel,
the survivors of the house of Jacob,
will no more lean upon him who struck
them;
But they will lean upon the LORD,
the Holy One of Israel, in truth

c Jer 8, 8.
d Is 1, 23.
e Is 36, 19; Am 6, 2.
f Is 36, 20.

*

9, 20: Manasseh . . . Ephraim: two of the leading tribes of the northern kingdom.

10, 6f: Impious nation: Israel. It was God's intention to use Assyria merely to punish, not to destroy, his people.

10, 9: Calno . . . Damascus: cities captured by the Assyrians.

10, 16: His fat ones: the strong men of the king of Assyria.

21 A remnant will return,* the remnant of
Jacob,
to the mighty God.
22 For though your people, O Israel,
were like the sand of the sea,
Only a remnant of them will return;
their destruction is decreed
as overwhelming justice demands.[g]

23 Yes, the destruction he has decreed, the
Lord the GOD of hosts, will carry out within the
whole land. 24 Therefore thus says the Lord,
the GOD of hosts: O my people, who dwell in
Zion, do not fear the Assyrian, though he strikes
you with a rod, and raises his staff against you.
25 For only a brief moment more, and my anger shall be over; but them I will destroy in
wrath. 26 Then the LORD of hosts will raise
against them a scourge such as struck Midian at
the rock of Oreb; and he will raise his staff over
the sea as he did against Egypt.[h] 27 On that
day,*

His burden shall be taken from your
shoulder,
and his yoke shattered from your neck.

## Sennacherib's Invasion

He has come up from the direction of
Rimmon,
28 he has reached Aiath, passed through
Migron,
at Michmash his supplies are stored.
29 They cross the ravine:
"We will spend the night at Geba."
Ramah is in terror,
Gibeah of Saul has fled.
30 Cry and shriek, O daughter of Gallim!
Hearken, Laishah! Answer her, Anathoth!
31 Madmenah is in flight,
the inhabitants of Gebim seek refuge.
32 Even today he will halt at Nob,*
he will shake his fist at the mount of
daughter Zion,
the hill of Jerusalem!
33 Behold, the Lord, the LORD of hosts,
lops off the boughs with terrible violence;
The tall of stature are felled,
and the lofty ones brought low;
34 The forest thickets are felled with the axe,
and Lebanon in its splendor falls.

## CHAPTER 11

### The Rule of Immanuel

1 But a shoot shall sprout from the stump of
Jesse,*
and from his roots a bud shall blossom.[i]
2 The spirit of the LORD shall rest upon him:[j]
a spirit of wisdom and of understanding,
A spirit of counsel and of strength,
a spirit of knowledge and of fear of the
LORD,*
3 and his delight shall be the fear of the
LORD.
Not by appearance shall he judge,
nor by hearsay shall he decide,
4 But he shall judge the poor with justice,
and decide aright for the land's afflicted.[k]
He shall strike the ruthless with the rod of
his mouth,
and with the breath of his lips he shall
slay the wicked.
5 Justice shall be the band around his waist,
and faithfulness a belt upon his hips.

6 Then the wolf shall be a guest of the lamb,*
and the leopard shall lie down with the
kid;
The calf and the young lion shall browse
together,
with a little child to guide them.[l]
7 The cow and the bear shall be neighbors,
together their young shall rest;
the lion shall eat hay like the ox.
8 The baby shall play by the cobra's den,
and the child lay his hand on the adder's
lair.
9 There shall be no harm or ruin on all my
holy mountain;
for the earth shall be filled with
knowledge of the LORD,
as water covers the sea.[m]

### Union of Ephraim and Judah

10 On that day,
The root of Jesse,
set up as a signal for the nations,
The Gentiles shall seek out,
for his dwelling shall be glorious.[n]
11 On that day,
The Lord shall again take it in hand[o]

g Rom 9, 27f.
h Jgs 7, 25.
i Lk 3, 32.
j Mt 3, 16; Mk 1, 10.
k Pss 72, 2. 4; 98, 9; 2 Thes 2, 8.
l Is 65, 25.
m Hb 2, 14.
n Is 49, 22; Rom 15, 12.
o Is 27, 13; Mi 7, 12; Zec 10, 10.

*

10, 21: A remnant will return: in Hebrew, shear-jashub, an allusion to the name of Isaiah's son, Shear-jashub; cf Is 7, 3.

10, 27–32: A poetic description of the progress of the Assyrian army, advancing from the north through Judah to the gates of Jerusalem.

10, 32ff: Just when the enemy is about to capture Jerusalem, God intervenes and destroys the hostile army.

11, 1: Jesse: David's father. Shoot . . . stump: after the Babylonian exile only a stump of the Davidic dynasty will remain; from it will arise the new shoot, the messianic King.

11, 2f: The source of the traditional names of the gifts of the Holy Spirit. The Septuagint and the Vulgate read "piety" for fear of the Lord in its first occurrence, thus listing seven gifts.

11, 6–9: This picture of the idyllic harmony of paradise is a dramatic symbol of the universal peace and justice of messianic times.

11, 11: Pathros . . . sea: where God's people lived in exile. Pathros: upper Egypt. Elam: east of Babylonia. Shinar: Babylonia. Hamath: on the Orontes River in Syria. Isles: or coastlands, in the Mediterranean.

to reclaim the remnant of his people
that is left from Assyria and Egypt,
Pathros, Ethiopia, and Elam,
Shinar, Hamath, and the isles of sea.*
12 He shall raise a signal to the nations
and gather the outcasts of Israel;
The dispersed of Judah he shall assemble
from the four corners of the earth.
13 The envy of Ephraim shall pass away,
and the rivalry of Judah be removed;
Ephraim shall not be jealous of Judah,
and Judah shall not be hostile to
Ephraim;[p]
14 But they shall swoop down on the foothills
of the Philistines to the west,
together they shall plunder the
Kedemites;*
Edom and Moab shall be their possessions,
and the Ammonites their subjects.
15 The LORD shall dry up the tongue of the Sea
of Egypt,*
and wave his hand over the Euphrates in
his fierce anger
And shatter it into seven streamlets,
so that it can be crossed in sandals.[q]
17 There shall be a highway for the remnant of
his people
that is left from Assyria,
As there was for Israel
when he came up from the land of Egypt.

## CHAPTER 12

### Song of Thanksgiving*

1 On that day, you will say:
I give you thanks O LORD;
though you have been angry with me,
your anger has abated, and you have
consoled me.
2 God indeed is my savior;
I am confident and unafraid.
My strength and my courage is the LORD,
and he has been my savior.[r]

3 With joy you will draw water
at the fountain of salvation, 4 and say on
that day:
Give thanks to the LORD, acclaim his name;
among the nations make known his deeds,
proclaim how exalted is his name.
5 Sing praise to the LORD for his glorious
achievement;
let this be known throughout all the
earth.[s]
6 Shout with exultation, O city of Zion,
for great in your midst
is the Holy One of Israel![t]

## III: *Oracles Against the Pagan Nations*

## CHAPTER 13

**Babylon.** 1 An oracle concerning Babylon;
a vision of Isaiah, son of Amoz.

2 Upon the bare mountains set up a signal;
cry out to them,*
Wave for them to enter
the gates of the volunteers.[u]

3 I have commanded my dedicated soldiers,*
I have summoned my warriors,
eager and bold to carry out my anger.
4 Listen! the rumble on the mountains:
that of an immense throng!
Listen! the noise of kingdoms, nations
assembled!
The LORD of hosts is mustering
an army for battle.[v]
5 They come from a far-off country,
and from the end of the heavens,
The LORD and the instruments of his wrath,
to destroy all the land.

6 Howl, for the day of the LORD* is near;
as destruction from the Almighty it
comes.[w]
7 Therefore all hands fall helpless,[x]
the bows of the young men fall from their
hands.
Every man's heart melts 8 in terror.
Pangs and sorrows take hold of them,
like a woman in labor they writhe;
They look aghast at each other,
their faces aflame.[y]
9 Lo, the day of the LORD comes,
cruel, with wrath and burning anger;
To lay waste the land
and destroy the sinners within it!
10 The stars and constellations of the heavens

p Ex 37, 16-17.
q Ex 14, 29.
r Ex 15, 2; Ps 118, 14.
s Ex 15, 1.
t Is 41, 14. 16; 54, 1; Zep 3, 14; Zec 2, 10.
u Is 5, 26.
v Jer 50, 9.
w Jer 46, 10; Jl 1, 15.
x Ez 7, 17.
y Is 21, 3; Ps 48, 7; Mi 4, 9.
z Is 24, 23.

*

11, 14: Kedemites: tribes in the Arabian Desert.

11, 15: Tongue . . . Egypt: the body of water between Egypt and Palestine.

12, 1–6: Israel's thanksgiving to the Lord, expressed in language like that of the Psalms.

13, 2: To them: the Medes (v 17) and Persians, who would destroy Babylon. Gates of the volunteers: the mustering places of Babylon's enemies for war against her.

13, 3: Dedicated soldiers: in the sense that they will wage a "holy war" and carry out God's plan.

13, 6ff: Day of the Lord: described often in prophetical writings, it generally signified the coming of the Lord in power and majesty to destroy his enemies and inaugurate his kingdom. Here it refers to the overthrow of Babylon. The figures used convey the idea of horror and destruction. Read vv 6–8 with vv 14–16.

send forth no light;
The sun is dark when it rises,
and the light of the moon does not shine.[z]
11 Thus I will punish the world for its evil
and the wicked for their guilt.
I will put an end to the pride of the arrogant,
the insolence of tyrants I will humble.[a]
12 I will make mortals more rare than pure gold,
men, than gold of Ophir.*
13 For this I will make the heavens tremble
and the earth shall be shaken from its place,
At the wrath of the LORD of hosts
on the day of his burning anger.

14 Like a hunted gazelle,
or a flock that no one gathers,
Every man shall turn to his kindred
and flee to his own land.[b]
15 Everyone who is caught shall be run through;
to a man, they shall fall by the sword.
16 Their infants shall be dashed to pieces in their sight;
their houses shall be plundered
and their wives ravished.[c]

17 I am stirring up against them the Medes,
who think nothing of silver
and take no delight in gold.[d]
18 The fruit of the womb they shall not spare,
nor shall they have eyes of pity for children.
19 And Babylon, the jewel of kingdoms,
the glory and pride of the Chaldeans,
Shall be overthrown by God
like Sodom and like Gomorrah.
20 She shall never be inhabited,
nor dwelt in, from age to age;
The Arab shall not pitch his tent there,
nor shepherds couch their flocks.[e]
21 But wildcats shall rest there
and owls shall fill the houses;
There ostriches shall dwell,
and satyrs* shall dance.[f]
22 Desert beasts shall howl in her castles,
and jackals in her luxurious palaces.
Her time is near at hand
and her days shall not be prolonged.

## CHAPTER 14

**The King of Babylon.** 1 When the LORD
has pity on Jacob and again chooses Israel and
settles them on their own soil, the aliens will
join them and be counted with the house of
Jacob.[g] 2 The house of Israel will take them
and bring them along to its place, and possess
them as male and female slaves on the Lord's
soil, making captives of its captors and ruling
over its oppressors.[h] 3 On the day the LORD
relieves you of sorrow and unrest and the hard
service in which you have been enslaved,[i]
4 you will take up this taunt-song* against the
king of Babylon:[j]

How the oppressor has reached his end!
how the turmoil is stilled!
5 The LORD has broken the rod of the wicked,
the staff of the tyrants
6 That struck the peoples in wrath
relentless blows;
That beat down the nations in anger,
with oppression unchecked.
7 The whole earth rests peacefully,
song breaks forth;
8 The very cypresses rejoice over you,
and the cedars of Lebanon:
"Now that you are laid to rest,
there will be none to cut us down."[k]

9 The nether world below is all astir
preparing for your coming;
It awakens the shades to greet you,
all the leaders of the earth;
It has the kings of all nations
rise from their thrones.
10 All of them speak out
and say to you,
"You too have become weak like us,
you are the same as we.
11 Down to the nether world your pomp is brought,
the music of your harps.
The couch beneath you is the maggot,
your covering, the worm."[l]

12 How have you fallen from the heavens,
O morning star,* son of the dawn!
How are you cut down to the ground,
you who mowed down the nations!
13 You said in your heart:[m]
"I will scale the heavens:
Above the stars of God
I will set up my throne;
I will take my seat on the Mount of Assembly,
in the recesses of the North.*
14 I will ascend above the tops of the clouds;
I will be like the Most High!"[n]

a Is 2, 17; Jer 50. 32.
b Jer 50, 16.
c Na 3, 10.
d Is 21, 2; Jer 51, 11. 28.
e Jer 51, 62.
f Is 34, 13f; 35, 7.
g Is 56, 3; 60, 4; Ps 102, 14; Jer 24, 6; Zec 1, 17.
h Is 66, 20.
i Jer 30, 10.
j Hb 2, 6.
k Ez 31, 16.
l Sir 10, 13.
m Jer 51, 53; Am 9, 2.
n Ez 28, 2.

*

13, 12: Ophir: cf note to Ps 45, 10.

13, 21: Satyrs: in the popular mind, demons of goatlike form dwelling in ruins, symbols of immorality; cf Lv 17, 7.

14, 4–21: This taunt-song, or satire, is one of the finest in the Bible.

14, 12: Morning star: the king of Babylon. The Vulgate has "Lucifer," a name applied by the church Fathers to Satan.

14, 13: Recesses of the North: see note on Ps 48, 3.

**15** Yet down to the nether world you go
to the recesses of the pit!
**16** When they see you they will stare,
pondering over you:
"Is this the man who made the earth
tremble,
and kingdoms quake!
**17** Who made the world a desert,
razed its cities,
and gave his captives no release?
**18** All the kings of the nations lie in glory,
each in his own tomb;
**19** But you are cast forth without burial,
loathsome and corrupt,
Cloathed as those slain at sword-point,
a trampled corpse.
Going down to the pavement of the pit,
**20** you will never be one with them in the
grave."
For you have ruined your land,
you have slain your people!

Let him not be named forever,
that scion of an evil race!
**21** Make ready to slaughter his sons
for the guilt of their fathers;
Lest they rise and possess the earth,
and fill the breadth of the world with
tyrants.

**22** I will rise up against them, says the LORD
of hosts, and cut off from Babylon name and
remnant, progeny and offspring, says the
LORD.[o] **23** I will make it a haunt of hoot owls
and a marshland; I will sweep it with the broom
of destruction, says the LORD of hosts.

## Assyria

**24** The LORD of hosts has sworn:
As I have resolved,
so shall it be;
As I have proposed,
so shall it stand:
**25** I will break the Assyrian in my land
and trample him on my mountains;
**8, 21** *He shall pass through it hard-pressed and
hungry,
and in his hunger he shall become
enraged,
and curse his king and his gods.
He shall look upward,
but there shall be strict darkness
without any dawn;
**8, 22** He shall gaze at the earth,
but there shall be distress and darkness,
with the light blacked out by its clouds.
**(25)** Then his yoke shall be removed from
them,
and his burden from their shoulder.
**26** This is the plan proposed for the whole
earth,
and this the hand outstretched over all
nations.
**27** The LORD of hosts has planned;
who can thwart him?
His hand is stretched out;
who can turn it back?

**Philistia.** **28** In the year that King Ahaz
died,* there came this oracle:

**29** Rejoice not, O Philistia, not a man of you,
that the rod* which smote you is broken;
For out of the serpent's root shall come an
adder,
its fruit shall be a flying saraph.
**30** In my pastures the poor shall eat,
and the needy lie down in safety;
But I will kill your root with famine
that shall slay even your remnant.
**31** Howl, O gate; cry out, O city!
Philistia, all of you melts away!
For there comes a smoke from the north.
without a straggler in the ranks.
**32** What will one answer the messengers of the
nation?
"The LORD has established Zion,
and in her the afflicted of his people find
refuge."[p]

## CHAPTER 15

## Moab

**1** Oracle on Moab:
Laid waste in a night,
Ar of Moab is destroyed;
Laid waste in a night,
Kir of Moab is destroyed.[q]
**2** Up goes daughter Dibon[r]
to the high places to weep;
Over Nebo and over Medeba
Moab wails.
Every head is shaved,
every beard sheared off.*
**3** In the streets they wear sackcloth, lamenting
and weeping;
On rooftops and in the squares everyone
wails.
**4** Heshbon and Elealeh cry out,
they are heard as far as Jahaz.
At this the loins of Moab tremble,
his soul quivers within him;[s]
**5** The heart of Moab cries out,
his fugitives reach Zoar
[Eglath-shelishiyah].
The ascent of Luhith
they climb weeping;
On the way to Horonaim[t]

o Jer 51, 62.
p Pss 87, 5; 102, 17f; Zep 3, 12.
q Is 16, 7.
r Jer 48, 38f.
s Jer 48, 34.
t Is 16, 9; Jer 48, 3.

*

8, 21f: He . . . clouds: the two verses have been transposed from chap. 8.

14, 28: The year that King Ahaz died: 715 B.C.

14, 29: Rod: an Assyrian oppressor whose identity is uncertain. Flying saraph: a poisonous serpent, distinguished by its speedy movement; cf note on Nm 21, 6.

15, 2: Every head . . . sheared off: traditional signs of grief.

they utter rending cries.

6 The waters of Nimrim
have become a waste;
The grass is withered,
new growth is gone,
nothing is green.
7 So now whatever they have acquired or
stored away
they carry across the Gorge of the
Poplars,
8 For the cry has gone round
the land of Moab;
As far as Eglaim the wailing, and to
Beer-elim,
the wail.
9 The waters of Dimon were filled with
blood,*
but I will bring still more upon Dimon:
Lion for those who are fleeing from Moab
and for those who remain in the land!

## CHAPTER 16

1 Send them forth, hugging the earth like
reptiles,
from Sela across the desert,
to the mount of daughter Zion.
2 Like flushed birds,
like startled nestlings,
Are the daughters of Moab
at the fords of the Arnon.*
3 Offer counsel, take their part:*
at high noon let your shadow be like the
night,
To hide the outcasts,
to conceal the fugitives.
4 Let the outcasts of Moab live with you,
be their shelter from the destroyer.
When the struggle is ended, the ruin
complete,
and they have done with trampling the
land,
5 A throne shall be set up in mercy,
and on it shall sit in fidelity
[in David's tent]
A judge upholding right
and prompt to do justice.[u]

6 We have heard of the pride of Moab,
how very proud he is,
With his haughty, arrogant insolence
that his empty words do not match.[v]

7 Therefore Moab wails for Moab,*
everywhere they wail;
For the raisin cakes* of Kir-hareseth
they sigh, stricken with grief.[w]
8 The terraced slopes of Heshbon languish,
the vines of Sibmah,
Whose clusters overpowered
the lords of nations,
While they reached as far as Jazer
and scattered over the desert,*
And whose branches spread forth
and extended over the sea.
9 Therefore I weep with Jazer
for the vines of Sibmah;
I water you with tears,
Heshbon and Elealeh;
For on your summer fruits and harvests
the battle cry has fallen.[x]
10 From the orchards are taken away
joy and gladness,
In the vineyards there is no singing,
no shout of joy;
In the wine presses no one treads grapes,
the vintage shout is stilled.[y]
11 Therefore for Moab
my breast moans like a lyre,
and my heart for Kir-hareseth.[z]
12 When Moab grows weary on the high
places,[a]
he shall enter his sanctuary to pray,
but it shall avail him nothing.*

13 *This is the word the LORD spoke against
Moab in times past. 14 But now the LORD has
spoken: In three years, like those of a hireling,
the glory of Moab shall be degraded despite all
its great multitude; there shall be a remnant,
very small and weak.

## CHAPTER 17

### Damascus

1 Oracle on Damascus:*
Lo, Damascus shall cease to be a city
and become a ruin;[b]
2 Her cities shall be forever abandoned,
given over to flocks to lie in undisturbed.
3 The fortress shall be lost to Ephraim*
and the kingdom to Damascus;
The remnant of Aram shall have the same
glory
as the Israelites,

u Is 32, 1.
v Jer 48, 29.
w Is 15, 3.
x Is 15, 5; Jer 48, 32.
y Is 24, 8.
z Is 15, 5; Jer 48, 36.
a Jer 48, 13.
b Jer 49, 23.

*

15, 9: There is in the Hebrew a play on words: Dimon and dam, the latter signifying "blood."

16, 2: The Amon: principal river of Moab.

16, 3–5: Directed to Jerusalem, which should receive the suffering Moabites with mercy, as befits the city of David's family, who were partly descended from Ruth the Moabite.

16, 7–14: Moab had been prosperous; now it has become a desert.

16, 7: Raisin cakes: masses of dried compressed grapes used as food (cf 2 Sm 6, 19; 1 Chr 16, 3; Ct 2, 5), and also in pagan cult (Hos 3, 1).

16, 8: Desert: to the east. Sea: the Dead Sea.

16, 12: In fain do the Moabites appeal to their god Chemosh.

16, 13f: A prose application of the preceding poetic oracle against Moab (15, 1—16, 12); cf Jer 4, 8. Like those of a hireling: who fulfills his period of service according to the shortest manner of reckoning; cf Is 21, 16.

17, 1: Damascus: capital of Syria, destroyed in 732 B.C.

17, 3: Ephraim: Israel, leagued with Syria against Assyria and Judah; destroyed in 721 B.C. Aram: Syria.

says the LORD of hosts.
4 On that day
The glory of Jacob shall fade,
and his full body grow thin,[c]
5 Like the reaper's mere armful of stalks
when he gathers the standing grain;
Or as when one gleans the ears
in the Valley of Rephaim.*
6 Only a scattering of grapes shall be left!
As when an olive tree has been beaten,
Two or three olives remain at the very top,
four or five on its fruitful branches,*
says the LORD, the God of Israel.[d]

7 On that day man shall look to his maker,
his eyes turned toward the Holy One of
Israel.[e]
8 He shall not look to the altars, his
handiwork,
nor shall he regard what he fingers have
made:
the sacred poles* or the incense stands.
9 On that day his strong cities shall be
like those abandoned by the Hivites and
Amorites
When faced with the children of Israel:
they shall be laid waste.[f]
10 For you have forgotten God, your savior,
and remembered not the Rock, your
strength.
Therefore, though you plant your pagan
plants*
and set your foreign vine slips,[g]
11 Though you make them grow the day you
plant them
and make your sprouts blossom on the
next morning.
The harvest shall disappear on the day of the
grievous blow,
the incurable blight.

12 Ah! the roaring of many peoples*
that roar like the roar of the seas!
The surging of nations
that surge like the surging of mighty
waves!
13 But God shall rebuke them,
and they shall flee far away;
Windswept, like chaff on the mountains,
like tumbleweed in a storm.
14 In the evening, they spread terror,
before morning, they are gone!
Such is the portion of those who despoil us,
the lot of those who plunder us.

## CHAPTER 18

### Ethiopia

1 Ah, land of buzzing insects,*
beyond the rivers of Ethiopia,*
2 Sending ambassadors by sea,
in papyrus boats on the waters!
Go, swift messengers,
to a nation tall and bronzed,
To a people dreaded near and far,
a nation strong and conquering,
whose land is washed by rivers.[h]
3 All you who inhabit the *world*,
who dwell on earth,
When the signal is raised on the mountain,
look!
When the trumpet blows, listen!
4 For thus says the LORD to me:
I will quietly look on from where I dwell,
Like the glowing heat of sunshine,
like a cloud of dew at harvest time.
5 Before the vintage, when the flowering is
ended,
and the blooms are succeeded by ripening
grapes,
Then comes the cutting of branches with
pruning hooks
and the discarding of the lopped-off
shoots.
6 They shall all be left to the mountain birds
of prey,
and to the beasts in the land;
The birds of prey shall summer on them
and on them all the beasts of the earth
shall winter.

7 Then will gifts be brought to the LORD of
hosts from a people tall and bronzed, from a
people dreaded near and far, a nation strong and
conquering, whose land is washed by rivers—to
Mount Zion where dwells the name of the LORD
of hosts.[i]

## CHAPTER 19

### Egypt

1 Oracle on Egypt:
See, the LORD is riding on a swift cloud
on his way to Egypt;
The idols of Egypt tremble before him,

c Is 10, 16.
d Is 24, 13.
e Mi 5, 12.
f Is 27, 10.
g Jer 2, 32; Hos 8, 14.
h Is 18, 7.
i Is 45, 14; Zep 3, 10; Mal 1, 11.

*

17, 5: Valley of Rephaim: a fertile plain to the southwest of Jerusalem; cf Jos 15, 8; 2 Sm 5, 18.

17, 6: Olives not easily picked by hand were knocked from the tree by means of a long stick; cf Is 24, 13.

17, 8: Sacred poles: see note on Ex 34, 13. Incense stands: small altars on which incense was burned in idolatrous worship; cf Is 27, 9; Lv 26, 30.

17, 10: Pagan plants: literally, "plants of delights," understood by some as planted in honor of the god of fertility.

17, 12f: Many peoples: the hordes that accompanied the invading Assyrians, whom God repels just as he vanquished the primeval waters of chaos; see notes on Jb 3, 8; 7, 12; Ps 89, 11.

18, 1: Land of buzzing insects: the region of the Upper Nile where these multiplied with great rapidity.

18, 1f: Papyrus boats: light and serviceable vessels made of bundles of papyrus stalks and sealed with pitch. Egypt, ruled by a dynasty from Ethiopia, had invited Judah to join a coalition against Assyria, but Isaiah bade the ambassadors return to their own people.

the hearts of the Egyptians melt within them.
2 I will rouse Egypt against Egypt:
brother will war against brother,
Neighbor against neighbor,
city against city, kingdom against kingdom.
3 The courage of the Egyptians ebbs away within them,
and I will bring to nought their counsel;
They shall consult idols and charmers,
ghosts and spirits.[j]
4 I will deliver Egypt
into the power of a cruel master,*
A harsh king who shall rule over them,
says the Lord, the LORD of hosts.[k]
5 The waters shall be drained from the sea,
the river shall shrivel and dry up;[l]
6 Its streams shall become foul,
and the canals of Egypt shall dwindle and dry up.
Reeds and rushes shall wither away,
7 and bulrushes on the bank of the Nile;
All the sown land along the Nile
shall dry up and blow away, and be no more.
8 The fishermen shall mourn and lament,
all who cast hook in the Nile;
Those who spread their nets in the water
shall pine away.
9 The linen-workers shall be disappointed,
the combers and weavers shall turn pale;[m]
10 The spinners shall be crushed,
all the hired laborers shall be despondent.
11 Utter fools are the princes of Zoan!*
the wisest of Pharaoh's advisers give stupid counsel.
How can you say to Pharaoh,
"I am a disciple of wise men, of ancient kings"?
12 Where then are your wise men?
Let them tell you and make known
What the LORD of hosts has planned
against Egypt.
13 The princes of Zoan have become fools,
the princes of Memphis have been deceived.
The chiefs of her tribes
have led Egypt astray.
14 The LORD has prepared among them
a spirit of dizziness,
And they have made Egypt stagger in
whatever she does,
as a drunkard staggers in his vomit.
15 Egypt shall have no work to do[n]
for head or tail, palm branch or reed.*

16 On that day the Egyptians shall be like
women, trembling with fear, because of the
LORD of hosts shaking his fist at them.[o] 17 And
the land of Judah shall be a terror to the Egyptians. Every time they remember Judah, they
shall stand in dread because of the plan which
the LORD of hosts has in mind for them.[p]
18 On that day there shall be five cities* in
the land of Egypt speaking the language of Canaan and swearing by the LORD of hosts; one
shall be called "City of the Sun."
19 On that day there shall be an altar to the
LORD in the land of Egypt, and a sacred pillar
to the LORD near the boundary. 20 It shall be a
sign and a witness to the LORD of hosts in the
land of Egypt, when they cry out to the LORD
against their oppressors, and he sends them a
savior to defend and deliver them. 21 The LORD
shall make himself known to Egypt, and the
Egyptians shall know the LORD in that day; they
shall offer sacrifices and oblations, and fulfill
the vows they make to the LORD.[q] 22 Although
the LORD shall smite Egypt severely, he shall
heal them; they shall turn to the LORD and he
shall be won over and heal them.
23 On that day there shall be a highway from
Egypt to Assyria; the Assyrians shall enter
Egypt, and the Egyptians enter Assyria, and
Egypt shall serve Assyria.
24 On that day Israel shall be a third party
with Egypt and Assyria, a blessing in the midst
of the land,[r] 25 when the LORD of hosts blesses
it: "Blessed be my people Egypt, and the work
of my hands Assyria, and my inheritance, Israel."

## CHAPTER 20

**Captivity of Egypt and Ethiopia.** 1 In
the year the general sent by Sargon, king of
Assyria, fought against Ashdod and captured it,
2 the LORD gave a warning through Isaiah,* the
son of Amoz: Go and take off the sackcloth from
your waist, and remove the sandals from your
feet. This he did, walking naked and barefoot.
3 Then the LORD said: Just as my servant Isaiah
has gone naked and barefoot for three years as
a sign and portent against Egypt and Ethiopia,
4 so shall the king of Assyria lead away captives from Egypt, and exiles from Ethiopia,
young and old, naked and barefoot, with buttocks uncovered [the shame of Egypt]. 5 They

j Is 44, 25.
k Ez 29, 19; 30, 10.
l Ez 30, 12; 32, 2.
m Ez 27, 7.
n Is 9, 14.
o Na 3, 13.
p Ex 14, 25.
q Zec 14, 16. 18.
r Gn 12, 2.
s Is 30, 3. 5.

*

19, 4: Cruel master: the king of Assyria.

19, 11. 13: Zoan: later known as Tanis, and Memphis (in Hebrew Noph) were the key cities of the Nile Delta.

19, 15: Head or tail, palm branch or reed: the leaders or the people; cf Is 9, 13f.

19, 18: Five cities: colonies of Jews living together and speaking their languages, Hebrew and Aramaic; cf Jer, chap. 43. City of the Sun: the meaning is uncertain, but the reference seems to be to the city known later as Heliopolis.

20, 2–6: The symbolic act of the prophet conveyed the idea that Assyria would lead captive the Egyptians and Ethiopians. The Judeans and their allies would then realize the folly of having trusted in them.

shall be dismayed and ashamed because of Ethiopia, their hope, and because of Egypt, their
boast.[s] 6 The inhabitants of this coastland shall
say on that day, "Look at our hope! We have
fled here for help and deliverance from the king
of Assyria; where can we flee now?"[t]

## CHAPTER 21

### Fall of Babylon

1 Oracle on the wastelands by the sea:*
Like whirlwinds sweeping in waves through
the Negeb,
there comes from the desert,
from the fearful land,
2 A cruel sight, revealed to me:
the traitor betrays,
the despoiler spoils.
"Go up, Elam; besiege, O Media;*
I will put an end to all groaning!"[u]
3 Therefore my loins are filled with anguish,
pangs have seized me like those of a
woman in labor;
I am to bewildered to hear,
too dismayed to look.[v]
4 My mind reels,
shuddering assails me;
My yearning for twilight
has turned into dread.
5 They set the table,
spread out the rugs;
they eat, they drink.*
Rise up, O princes,
oil the shield!

6 For thus says my Lord to me:
Go, station a watchman,
let him tell what he sees.
7 If he sees a chariot,
a pair of horses,
Someone riding an ass,
someone riding a camel,
Then let him pay heed,
very close heed.
8 Then the watchman cried,
"On the watchtower, O my Lord,
I stand constantly by day;
And I stay at my post
through all the watches of the night.[w]
9 Here he comes now:
a single chariot,
a pair of horses;
He calls out and says,
'Fallen, fallen is Babylon,
And all the images of her gods
are smashed to the ground.' "[x]

10 O my people who have been threshed,
beaten on my threshing floor!
What I have heard
from the LORD of hosts,
The God of Israel,
I have announced to you.[y]

### Edom

11 Oracle on Edom:
They call to me from Seir,*
"Watchman, how much longer the night?
Watchman, how much longer the night?"
12 The watchman replies,
"Morning has come, and again night.
If you will ask, ask; come back again."

### Arabia

13 Oracle on Arabia:*
In the thicket in the nomad country spend
the night,
O caravans of Dedanites.
14 Meet the thirsty, bring them water;
you who dwell in the land of Tema,
greet the fugitives with bread.
15 They flee from the sword,
from the whetted sword;
From the taut bow,
from the fury of battle.

16 For thus says the Lord to me: In another
year, like those of a hireling,* all the glory of
Kedar shall come to an end. 17 Few of Kedar's
stalwart archers shall remain, for the LORD, the
God of Israel, has spoken.

## CHAPTER 22

### Jerusalem

1 Oracle of the Valley of Vision:*
What is the matter with you now, that you
have gone up,
all of you, to the housetops,
2 O city full of noise and chaos,
O wanton town!
Your slain are not slain with the sword,
nor killed in battle.[z]

t Is 31, 3; 36. 6.
u Is 13, 17.
v Ps 38, 8.
w Hb 2, 1.
x Is 46, 1; Jer 50, 2: 51, 8; Rv 14, 8.
y Is 51, 23.
z Is 32. 13.

*

21, 1: Wastelands by the sea: Babylonia. Negeb: the desert south of Judah.

21, 2: Elam . . . Media: nations which, under the leadership of Cyrus, captured Babylon in 538 B.C. End to all groaning: those who were captives of Babylon shall be freed.

21, 5: Babylon is destroyed while its leaders are feasting; cf Dn 5. Oil the shield: shields were oiled and greased so as to divert blows more easily.

21, 11f: Seir: another name for Edom. The Edomites ask the prophet how much longer they must suffer (the night of suffering); he answers ambiguously: "Liberation (morning) and further suffering (night," but perhaps they will later receive a more encouraging answer (ask; come back again).

21, 13f: Arabia: that is, the nomad country. Dedanites: an Arab tribe associated with Edom and Tema, and living east of the Red Sea; cf Gn 10, 7; 25, 3; Jer 25, 23.

21, 16: Year . . . of a hireling: see note on Is 16, 14. Kedar: a nomad tribe in Arabia; cf Is 42, 11; 60, 7; Ps 120, 5.

22, 1–8: Valley of Vision: while the people live in revelry and disorder, the prophet foresees the impending doom of the city.

3 All your leaders fled away together,
fled afar off;
All who were in you were captured together,
captured without the use of a bow.[a]
4 At this I say: Turn away from me,
let me weep bitterly;
Do not try to comfort me
for the ruin of the daughter of my
people.[b]
5 It is a day of panic, rout and confusion,
from the Lord, the GOD of hosts, in the
Valley of Vision.
Walls crash;
they cry for help to the mountains.[c]
6 Elam* takes up the quivers,
Aram mounts the horses,
and Kir uncovers the shields.
7 Your choice valleys are filled with chariots,
and horses are posted at the gates,
8 and shelter over Judah is removed.*

On that day you looked to the weapons in the
House of the Forest; 9 you saw the the breaches
in the City of David were many; you collected
the water of the lower pool. 10 You numbered
the houses of Jerusalem, tearing some down to
strengthen the wall; 11 you made a reservoir
between the two walls for the water of the old
pool. But you did not look to the city's Maker,
nor did you consider him who built it long ago.

12 On that day the Lord,
the GOD of hosts, called on you
To weep and mourn,
to shave your head and put on sackcloth.[d]
13 But look! you feast and celebrate,
you slaughter oxen and butcher sheep,
You eat meat and drink wine:
"Eat and drink, for tomorrow we die!"[e]
14 This reaches the ears of the LORD of hosts—
You shall not be pardoned this wickedness
till you die,
says the Lord, the GOD of hosts.

## Shebna and Eliakim

15 Thus says the Lord, the GOD of hosts:
Up, go to that official,
Shebna,* master of the palace,
16 Who has hewn for himself a sepulcher on a
height
and carved his tomb in the rock:
"What are you doing here, and what people
have you here,
that here you have hewn for yourself a
tomb?"
17 The LORD shall hurl you down headlong,
mortal man!
He shall grip you firmly
18 And roll you up and toss you like a ball
into an open land
To perish there, you and the chariots you
glory in,
you disgrace to your master's house!
19 I will thrust you from your office
and pull you down from your station.
20 On that day I will summon my servant
Eliakin,* son of Hilkiah;[f]
21 I will clothe him with your robe,
and gird him with your sash,
and give over to him your authority.
He shall be a father to the inhabitants of
Jerusalem,
and to the house of Judah.
22 I will place the key* of the House of David
on his shoulder;
when he opens, no one shall shut,
when he shuts, no one shall open.[g]
23 I will fix him like a peg in a sure spot,
to be a place of honor for his family;
24 On him shall hang all the glory of his
family:*
descendants and offspring,
all the little dishes, from bowls to jugs.

25 On that day, says the LORD of hosts, the
peg fixed in a sure spot shall give way, break off
and fall, and the weight that hung on it shall be
done away with; for the LORD has spoken.

# CHAPTER 23

## Tyre and Sidon

1 Oracle on Tyre:
Wail, O ships of Tarshish,*
for your port is destroyed;
From the land of the Kittim*
the news reaches them.
2 Silence! you who dwell on the coast,
you merchants of Sidon,
Whose messengers crossed the sea
3 over the deep waters.
The grain of Shihor,* the harvest of the
Nile, was her revenue,
and she the merchant among nations.
4 Shame, O Sidon, fortress on the sea,
for the sea has spoken:*
"I have not been in labor, nor given birth,
nor raised young men,
nor reared virgins."

a 2 Kgs 25, 4.
b Jer 6, 26; 9, 1; 14, 17.
c Is 37, 3.
d Jl 2, 17.
e Is 56, 12; Wis 2, 6; 1 Cor 15, 32.
f 2 Kgs 18, 18. 37.
g Rv 3, 7.

*

22, 6: Elam, Aram, Kir: all allies of Assyria. Kir: perhaps the same people referred to in Am 1, 5.

22, 8–11: Defense measures, in which the inhabitants of Jerusalem placed their trust instead of relying on God. House of the Forest: an armory built by Solomon; its columns of wood suggested the trees of a forest; cf 1 Kgs 7, 2; 10, 17.

22, 15: Shebna: referred to as the scribe in Is 36, 3.

22, 20: Eliakim: also referred to in Is 36, 3; he is described as loyal to God.

22, 22: Key: symbol of authority; cf Mt 16, 19; Rv 3, 7.

22, 24f: If Eliakim should anger God, he and his family (compared here to dishes, bowls and jugs) will suffer disaster.

23, 1–4. 12ff: These verses refer to Sidon, vv 5–11 to Tyre.

23, 1: Kittim: Cyprus.

23, 3: Shihor: a synonym for the Nile.

23, 4: The sea brings to distant coasts the news that Sidon must disown her children; her people are dispersed.

5 When it is heard in Egypt
they shall be in anguish at the news of Tyre.
6 Pass over to Tarshish, wailing,
you who dwell on the coast!
7 Is this your wanton city,
whose origin is from of old,
Whose feet have taken her
to dwell in distant lands?
8 Who has planned such a thing
against Tyre, the bestower of crowns,
Whose merchants are princes,
whose traders are the earth's honored men?
9 The LORD of hosts has planned it, to
disgrace all pride of majesty,
to degrade all the earth's honored men.[h]
10 Cross to your own land,
O ship of Tarshish;
the harbor is no more.
11 His hand he stretches out over the sea,
he shakes kingdoms;
The LORD has ordered the destruction
of Canaan's strongholds.*
12 You shall exult no more, he says,
you who are now oppressed, virgin daughter Sidon.
Arise, pass over to the Kittim, even there
you shall find no rest.[i]

13 *[This people is the land of the Chaldeans, not Assyria.]

She whom the impious founded,
setting up towers for her,
Has had her castles destroyed,
and has been turned into a ruin.[j]
14 Lament, O ships of Tarshish,
for your haven is destroyed.

15 On that day, Tyre shall be forgotten for
seventy years. With the days of another king, at
the end of seventy years,* it shall be for Tyre
as in the song about the harlot:[k]

16 Take a harp, go about the city,
O forgotten harlot;
Pluck the strings skillfully, sing many songs,
that they may remember you.

17 At the end of the seventy years the LORD
shall visit Tyre. She shall return to her hire and
deal with all the world's kingdoms on the face
of the earth.[l] 18 But her merchandise and her
hire shall be sacred to the LORD. It shall not be
stored up or laid away, but from her merchandise those who dwell before the LORD shall eat
their fill and clothe themselves in choice attire.*

## *IV: Apocalypse of Isaiah**

## CHAPTER 24

### Devastation of the World: A Remnant Saved

1 Lo, the LORD empties the land and lays it waste;
he turns it upside down,
scattering its inhabitants:[m]
2 Layman and priest alike,
servant and master,
The maid as her mistress,
the buyer as the seller,
The lender as the borrower,
the creditor as the debtor.
3 The earth is utterly laid waste, utterly stripped,
for the LORD has decreed this thing.
4 The earth mourns and fades,
the world languishes and fades;
both heaven and earth languish.
5 The earth is polluted because of its inhabitants,
who have transgressed laws, violated statutes,
broken the ancient covenant.*
6 Therefore a curse devours the earth,
and its inhabitants pay for their guilt;
Therefore they who dwell on earth turn pale,
and a few men are left.
7 The wine mourns, the vine languishes,
all the merry-hearted groan.[n]
8 Stilled are the cheerful timbrels,
ended the shouts of the jubilant,
stilled is the cheerful harp.[o]
9 They cannot sing and drink wine;
strong drink is bitter to those who partake of it.
10 Broken down is the city of chaos,*
shut against entry, every house.[p]
11 In the streets they cry out for lack of wine;
all joy has disappeared
and cheer has left the land.[q]
12 In the city nothing remains but ruin;
its gates are battered and desolate.

h Ez 28, 7.
i Ez 28, 21f.
j Ez 26, 7.
k Jer 25, 11.
l Ez 27, 12.
m Is 13, 9; Hos 4, 9.
n Jl 1, 10.
o Jer 7, 34; Hos 2, 13.
p Is 25, 2.
q Jer 48, 33; Lam 5, 14f.

*

23, 11: Canaan's strongholds: the fortresses of Phoenicia.

23, 13: The gloss here identifies she whom the impious founded with the land of the Chaldeans.

23, 15: Seventy years: a conventional period of time indicating simply a long disaster; cf Jer 25, 11 and 29, 10.

23, 18: Describes the conversion of Tyre.

24, 1—27, 13: This section, probably composed at a later date, contains oracles on the day of the Lord, combined with hymns of thanksgiving and of supplication.

24, 5: Ancient covenant: God's commandments to all mankind.

24, 10: City of chaos: a symbol of godlessness as opposed to Jerusalem, the city of God.

13 Thus it is within the land,
and among the peoples,
As with an olive tree after it is beaten,
as with a gleaning when the vintage is done.[r]
14 These* lift up their voice in acclaim;
from the sea they proclaim the majesty of the LORD:
15 "For this, in the coastlands,
give glory to the LORD!
In the coastlands of the sea,
to the name of the LORD, the God of Israel!"[s]
16 From the end of the earth we hear songs:
"Splendor to the Just One!"
But I said, "I am wasted, wasted away.
Woe is me! The traitors betray:
with treachery have the traitors betrayed!
17 Terror, pit, and trap[t]
are upon you, inhabitant of the earth;
18 He who flees at the sound of terror
will fall into the pit;
He who climbs out of the pit
will be caught in the trap.
For the windows on high will be opened
and the foundations of the earth will shake.
19 The earth will burst asunder,
the earth will be shaken apart,
the earth will be convulsed.
20 The earth will reel like a drunkard,
and it will sway like a hut;
Its rebellion will weigh it down,
until it falls, never to rise again."[u]

21 On that day the LORD will punish
the host of the heavens* in the heavens,
and the kings of the earth on the earth.[v]
22 They will be gathered together
like prisoners into a pit;
They will be shut up in a dungeon,
and after many days they will be punished.
23 Then the moon will blush[w]
and the sun grow pale,
For the LORD of hosts will reign
on Mount Zion and in Jerusalem,
glorious in the sight of his elders.*

## CHAPTER 25

1 O LORD, you are my God,*
I will extol you and praise your name;
For you have fulfilled your wonderful plans of old,
faithful and true.[x]
2 For you have made the city a heap,
the fortified city a ruin;
The castle of the insolent is a city no more,
nor ever to be rebuilt.[y]
3 Therefore a strong people will honor you,
fierce nations will fear you.
4 For you are a refuge to the poor,
a refuge to the needy in distress;
Shelter from the rain,
shade from the heat.[z]
As with the cold rain,
5 as with the desert heat,
even so you quell the uproar of the wanton.
6 On this mountain* the LORD of hosts
will provide for all peoples
A feast of rich food and choice wines,
juicy, rich food and pure, choice wines.
7 On this mountain he will destroy
the veil that veils all peoples,
The web that is woven over all nations;[a]
8 he will destroy death forever.
The Lord GOD will wipe away
the tears from all faces;
The reproach of his people he will remove
from the whole earth; for the LORD has spoken.

9 On that day it will be said:
"Behold our God, to whom we looked to save us!
This is the LORD for whom we looked;
let us rejoice and be glad that he has saved us!"[b]
10 For the hand of the LORD will rest on this mountain,
but Moab* will be trodden down
as a straw is trodden down in the mire.[c]
11 He will stretch forth his hands in Moab;
as a swimmer extends his hands to swim;
He will bring low their pride
as his hands sweep over them.[d]
12 The high-walled fortress he will raze,
and strike it down level with the earth,
with the very dust.[e]

## CHAPTER 26

**The Divine Vindicator.** 1 On that day they will sing this song in the land of Judah:

"A strong city have we;
he sets up walls and ramparts to protect us.
2 Open up the gates
to let in a nation that is just,

r Is 17, 6; Mi 7, 1.
s Is 42. 10. 12; Zep 2, 11.
t 17f. Jer 48, 43f.
u Is 9, 14.
v Ps 76, 13.
w Is 13, 10; Jl 3, 3f; 4, 15.
x Ex 15, 2.
y Jer 9, 11.
z Is 14, 32; 32, 2; Na 1, 7.
a Is 60, 1. 3; 1 Cor 15, 53ff; Rv 7, 17; 21, 4.
b Is 30, 18f.
c Zep 2, 9f.
d Is 16, 6f. 14.
e Is 26, 5.
f Ps 118, 19f.

24, 14: These: the saved.

24, 21: Host of the heavens: the stars, which were regarded by the pagans as gods; cf Dt 4, 19; Jer 8, 2.

24, 23: His elders: the heavenly courtiers surrounding the throne of God.

25, 1–8: Victory in messianic times.

25, 6: This mountain: Zion, symbol of the heavenly Jerusalem.

25, 10: Moab: symbol of God's enemies.

one that keeps faith.[f]
3 A nation of firm purpose you keep in peace;
in peace, for its trust in you."[g]

4 Trust in the LORD forever!
For the LORD is an eternal Rock.[h]
5 He humbles those in high places,
and the lofty city he brings down;
He tumbles it to the ground,
levels it with the dust.[i]
6 It is trampled underfoot by the needy,
by the footsteps of the poor.
7 The way of the just is smooth;
the path of the just you make level.[j]
8 Yes, for your way and your judgments, O LORD,
we look to you;
Your name and your title
are the desire of our souls,
9 My soul yearns for you in the night,
yes, my spirit within me keeps vigil for you;
When your judgment dawns upon the earth,
the world's inhabitants learn justice.[k]
10 The wicked man, spared, does not learn justice;
in an upright land he acts perversely,
and sees not the majesty of the LORD.[l]
11 O LORD, your hand is uplifted,
but they behold it not;
Let them be shamed when they see your zeal for your people:
let the fire prepared for your enemies consume them.
12 O LORD, you mete out peace to us,
for it is you who have accomplished all we have done.[m]
13 O LORD, our God, other lords than you have ruled us;
it is from you only that we can call upon your name.

14 Dead they are, they have no life,
shades that cannot rise;
For you have punished and destroyed them,
and wiped out all memory of them.
15 You have increased the nation, O LORD,
increased the nation to your own glory,
and extended far all the borders of the land.[n]
16 O LORD, oppressed by your punishment,
we cried out in anguish under your chastising.[o]
17 As a woman about to give birth
writhes and cries out in her pains,
so were we in your presence, O LORD.[p]
18 We conceived and writhed in pain,
giving birth to wind;
Salvation we have not achieved for the earth,
the inhabitants of the world cannot bring it forth.
19 But your dead shall live, their corpses shall rise;
awake and sing, you who lie in the dust.[q]
For your dew is a dew of light,
and the land of shades gives birth.*

## Day of the Lord: Reward and Punishment

20 Go, my people, enter your chambers,
and close your doors behind you;
Hide yourselves for a brief moment,
until the wrath is past.
21 See, the LORD goes forth from his place,
to punish the wickedness of the earth's inhabitants;
The earth will reveal the blood upon her,
and no longer conceal her slain.[r]

## CHAPTER 27

1 On that day,
The LORD will punish with his sword
that is cruel, great, and strong,
Leviathan the fleeing serpent,
Leviathan the coiled serpent;
and he will slay the dragon* that is in the sea.[s]
2 On that day—
The pleasant vineyard, sing about it![t]
3 I, the LORD, am its keeper,
I water it every moment;
Lest anyone harm it,
night and day I guard it.[u]
4 I am not angry,
but if I were to find briers and thorns,
In battle I should march against them;
I should burn them all.[v]
8 Expunging and expelling, I should strive against them,
carrying them off with my cruel wind in time of storm.[w]
6 In days to come Jacob shall take root,
Israel shall sprout and blossom,
covering all the world with fruit.
7 Is he to be smitten as his smiter was smitten?
or slain as his slayer was slain?*
5 Or shall he cling to me for refuge?*
He must make peace with me;

g Is 32, 17f; 54, 13.
h Is 30, 29; Ps 62, 8.
i Is 25, 12; 32, 19.
j Ps 23, 3f; Prv 11, 3. 5.
k Ps 94, 15.
l Is 5, 12.
m Jer 29, 11.
n Is 54, 2f; Neh 9, 23.
o Hos 6, 1.
p Mi 4, 10.
q Ez 37, 5f; Dn 12. 2; Hos 6, 2.
r Mi 1, 3.
s Jb 40, 25-32; Ez 32, 2.
t Is 5, 1.
u Is 5, 2ff; Ps 121, 4f.
v Is 10, 17.
w Jer 18, 17.
x Is 37, 31; Rom 11, 12.

*

26, 19: This verse refers to the restoration of Israel in messianic times under the figure of the resurrection of the dead; cf Ez, chap. 37.

27, 1: Leviathan . . . dragon: symbols of the forces of evil which God vanquishes even as he overcame primeval chaos; cf notes on Jb 3, 8; 7, 12.

27, 7: God's people will not be treated as sternly as were their enemies.

27, 5. 9: Israel will make peace with God and destroy all signs of idolatrous worship.

peace shall he make with me![x]
9 This, then, shall be the expiation of Jacob's guilt,
this the whole fruit of the removal of his sin:
He shall pulverize all the stones of the altars
like pieces of chalk;
no sacred poles or incense altars shall stand.
10 For the fortified city* shall be desolate,
an abandoned pasture, a forsaken wilderness,
where calves shall browse and lie.[y]
Its boughs shall be destroyed,
11 its branches shall wither and be broken off,
and women shall come to build a fire with them.
This is not an understanding people;
therefore their maker shall not spare them,
nor shall he who formed them have mercy on them.[z]
12 On that day,
The LORD shall beat out the grain
between the Euphrates and the Wadi of Egypt,*
and you shall be gleaned one by one, O sons of Israel.
13 On that day,*
A great trumpet shall blow,
and the lost in the land of Assyria
and the outcasts in the land of Egypt
Shall come and worship the LORD
on the holy mountain, in Jerusalem.[a]

## *V: The Lord Alone, Israel's and Judah's Salvation*

## CHAPTER 28

### The Fate of Samaria

1 Woe to the majestic garland
of the drunkard Ephraim,*
To the fading blooms of his glorious beauty,
on the head of him who is stupefied with wine.[b]
2 Behold, the LORD has a strong one and a mighty,*
who, like a downpour of hail, a destructive storm,
Like a flood of water, great and overflowing,
levels to the ground with violence;[c]
3 With feet that will trample
the majestic garland of the drunkard Ephraim.
4 The fading blooms of his glorious beauty
on the head of the fertile valley
Will be like an early fig before summer:
when a man sees it,
he picks and swallows it at once.
5 On that day the LORD of hosts
will be a glorious crown
And a brilliant diadem
to the remnant of his people,
6 A spirit of justice
to him who sits in judgment,
And strength to those
who turn back the battle at the gate.

### Against Judah

7 But these also stagger from wine
and stumble from strong drink:
Priest and prophet stagger from strong drink,
overpowered by wine;
Led astray by strong drink,
staggering in their visions,
tottering when giving judgment.[d]
8 Yes, all the tables
are covered with filthy vomit,
with no place left clean.
9 "To whom would he impart knowledge?*
To whom would he convey the message?
To those just weaned from milk,
those taken from the breast? **10** For he says,
'Command on command, command on command,
rule on rule, rule on rule,
here a little, there a little!' "
11 Yes, with stammering lips and in a strange language*
he will speak to this people[e]
12 to whom he said:
This is the resting place,
give rest to the weary;
Here is repose—
but they would not listen.
13 So for them the word of the LORD shall be:
"Command on command, command on command,
Rule on rule, rule on rule,
here a little, there a little!"
So that when they walk, they stumble backward,

y Is 6, 11.
z Jer 4, 22.
a Hos 11, 11.
b Hos 7, 5; Am 6, 6.
c Is 30, 30.
d Is 56, 10. 12.
e Jer 5, 15; 1 Cor 14, 21; Dt 28, 49; Bar 4, 15.

*

27, 10f: The fortified city: symbol of the powers of evil; see note on Is 24, 10.

27, 12: The Euphrates and the Wadi of Egypt: the ideal borders of Israel; cf Gn 15, 18; 2 Kgs 24, 7.

27, 13: The triumph of God's people is described in eschatological language; they will gather in Jerusalem from Assyria and Egypt.

28, 1: Ephraim: the northern kingdom. Its capital, Samaria, was built upon a hill, suggestive of a majestic garland adorning the head of the drunken kingdom.

28, 2: A strong one and a mighty: Assyria.

28, 9f: The words of those who ridicule Isaiah. The Hebrew of v 10, by its very sound, conveys the idea of mocking imitation of what the prophet says, as though he spoke like a stammering child: SAU LASAU, SAU LASAU, CAU LACAU, CAU LACAU, ZE'ER SHAM, ZE'ER SHAM. But in v 13 God repeats these words in deadly earnest, putting them in the mouth of the victorious pagan army.

28, 11: God will answer the mockers and defend Isaiah. Strange language: spoken by the invading army.

broken, ensnared, and captured.

14 Therefore, hear the word of the LORD, you arrogant,
who rule this people in Jerusalem:
15 Because you say, "We have made a covenant with death,
and with the nether world* we have made a pact;
When the overwhelming scourge passes,
it will not reach us;
For we have made lies our refuge,
and in falsehood we have found a hiding place,"—[f]
16 Therefore, thus says the Lord GOD:
See, I am laying a stone in Zion,*
a stone that has been tested,
A precious cornerstone as a sure foundation;
he who puts his faith in it shall not be shaken.[g]
17 I will make of right a measuring line,
of justice a level.—
Hail shall sweep away the refuge of lies,
and waters shall flood the hiding place.
18 Your covenant with death shall be canceled
and your pact with the nether world shall not stand.
When the overwhelming scourge passes,
you shall be trampled down by it.
19 Whenever it passes, it shall take you;
morning after morning it shall pass,
By day and by night;
terror alone shall convey the message.
20 For the bed shall be too short to stretch out in,
and the cover too narrow to wrap in.
21 For the LORD shall rise up as on Mount Perazim,*
bestir himself as in the Valley of Gibeon,
To carry out his work, his singular work,
to perform his deed, his strange deed.[h]
22 Now, be arrogant no more
lest your bonds be tightened,
For I have heard from the Lord, the GOD of hosts,
the destruction decreed for the whole earth.[i]
23 Give ear and hear my voice,*
pay attention and listen to what I say:
24 Is the plowman forever plowing,
always loosening and harrowing his land for planting?
25 When he has leveled the surface,
does he not scatter gith and sow cumin,*
Put in wheat and barley,
with spelt as its border?
26 He has learned this rule,
instructed by his God.
27 Gith is not threshed with a sledge,
nor does a cartwheel roll over cumin.
But gith is beaten out with a staff,
and cumin crushed for food with a rod.
28 No, he does not thresh it unendingly,
nor does he crush it
with his noisy cartwheels and horses.
29 This too comes from the LORD of hosts;
wonderful is his counsel and great his wisdom.

## CHAPTER 29

### The Fall of Jerusalem

1 Woe to Ariel, Ariel,*
the city where David encamped!
Add year to year,
let the feasts come round.[j]
2 But I will bring distress upon Ariel,
with mourning and grief.
You shall be to me like Ariel,[k]
3 I will encamp like David against you;
I will encircle you with outposts
and set up siege works against you.[l]
4 Prostrate you shall speak from the earth,
and from the base dust your words shall come.
Your voice shall be like a ghost's from the earth,
and your words like chirping* from the dust.
5 The horde of your arrogant shall be like fine dust,
the horde of the tyrants like flying chaff.
Then suddenly, in an instant,[m]
6 you shall be visited by the LORD of hosts,
With thunder, earthquake, and great noise,
whirlwind, storm, and the flame of consuming fire.

f Wis 1, 16; Jer 5, 12.
g Ps 118, 22; Mt 21, 42; Acts 4, 11; Rom 9, 33; 1 Pt 2, 6.
h Jos 10, 10; 2 Sm 5, 20; 1 Chr 14, 11.
i Is 10, 23.
j 2 Sm 5, 9.
k Is 33, 7.
l 2 Kgs 25, 1; Ez 4, 2.
m Is 17, 13; Ps 18, 43; Jb 21, 18.

*

28, 15. 18: A covenant with death, and with the nether world: an alliance with foreign powers, such as Egypt and Babylon, to prevent death and destruction. Have made lies . . . a hiding place: this confidence in human aid proves to be false and deceitful, incapable of averting the dreaded disaster. Overwhelming scourge: the flood of the Assyrian invasion; cf Is 8, 7f.

28, 16: A stone in Zion: the true and sure foundation of salvation promised by God to the Davidic dynasty (cf Is 7, 13–16; 9, 1–6), which the Apostles saw fulfilled in Christ the universal Savior; cf 1 Pt 2, 6–8; Rom 9, 33; 10, 9ff. Cornerstone: the assurance of salvation rejected by Israel in the prophet's time, is reflected by the psalmist (Ps 118, 22) and fulfilled in the Person of Christ; cf Mt 21, 42; Lk 20, 17; Acts 4, 11; Rom 9. 33; 1 Pt 2, 7.

28, 21: Mount Perazim . . . Valley of Gibeon: where David defeated the Philistines; cf 2 Sm 5, 20. 25; 1 Chr 14, 11. 16.

28, 23–29: The practical variation of the farmer's work taught him by God reflects God's dealing with his people, wisely adapted to circumstances; he does not crush their weakness altogether; cf ch 29.

28, 25: Gith . . . cumin: herbs used in seasoning food. Spelt: a variety of wheat.

29, 1f: Ariel: variously interpreted to mean "lion of God" or "hearth (altar) of God," a poetic name for Jerusalem; or perhaps to be read as Uru-el, "foundation of God," an archaic name for the Jebusite city of Jerusalem; like that Ariel, against which David encamped, it will be besieged by God.

29, 4: Chirping: see note on Is 8, 19.

7 Then like a dream,*
a vision in the night,
Shall be the horde of all the nations
who war against Ariel
with all the earthworks of her besiegers.
8 As when a hungry man dreams he is eating
and awakens with an empty stomach,
Or when a thirsty man dreams he is drinking
and awakens faint and dry,
So shall the horde of all the nations be,
who make war against Zion.

## Blindness and Perversity

9 Be irresolute, stupefied;*
blind yourselves and stay blind!
Be drunk, but not from wine,
stagger, but not from strong drink![n]
10 For the LORD has poured out on you
a spirit of deep sleep.
He has shut your eyes [the prophets]
and covered your heads [the seers].[o]

11 For you the revelation of all this has become like the words of a sealed scroll. When it
is handed to one who can read, with the request,
"Read this," he replies, "I cannot; it is
sealed."[p] 12 When it is handed to one who
cannot read, with the request, "Read this," he
replies, "I cannot read."

13 The Lord said:
Since this people draws near with words
only
and honors me with their lips alone,
though their hearts are far from me,
And their reverence for me has become
routine observance of the precepts of
men,[q]
14 Therefore I will again deal with this people
in surprising and wondrous fashion:
The wisdom of its wise men shall perish
and the understanding of its prudent men
be hid.[r]
15 Woe to those who would hide their plans
too deep for the LORD!
Who work in the dark, saying,
"Who sees us, or who knows us?"[s]
16 Your perversity is as though the potter
were taken to be the clay:
As though what is made should say of its
maker,
"He made me not!"
Or the vessel should say of the potter,
"He does not understand."[t]

## Redemption*

17 But a very little while,
and Lebanon shall be changed into an
orchard,
and the orchard be regarded as a forest![u]
18 On that day the deaf shall hear
the words of a book;
And out of gloom and darkness,
the eyes of the blind shall see.[v]
19 The lowly will ever find joy in the LORD,
and the poor rejoice in the Holy One of
Israel.[w]
20 For the tyrant will be no more
and the arrogant will have gone;
All who are alert to do evil will be cut off,[x]
21 those whose mere word condemns a man,
Who ensnare his defender at the gate,
and leave the just man with an empty
claim.[y]
22 Therefore thus says the LORD,
the God of the house of Jacob,
who redeemed Abraham:*
Now Jacob shall have nothing to be ashamed
of,
nor shall his face grow pale.[z]
23 When his children see
the work of my hands in his midst,
They shall keep my name holy;
they shall reverence the Holy One of
Jacob,
and be in awe of the God of Israel.
24 Those who err in spirit shall acquire
understanding,
and those who find fault shall receive
instruction.

## CHAPTER 30

## Futile Alliance with Egypt

1 Woe to the rebellious children,
says the LORD,
Who carry out plans that are not mine,
who weave webs that are not inspired by
me,
adding sin upon sin.[a]
2 They go down to Egypt,
but my counsel they do not seek.
They find their strength in Pharaoh's
protection
and take refuge in Egypt's shadow;[b]
3 Pharaoh's protection shall be your shame,
and refuge in Egypt's shadow your
disgrace.[c]
4 When their princes are at Zoan
and their messengers reach Hanes,[d]

n Is 19, 14; 28, 7f.
o Is 6, 10; Rom 11, 8.
p Dn 12, 4.
q Ez 33, 31; Mt 15, 8f; Mk 7, 6f.
r Jer 49, 7; 1 Cor 1, 19.
s Is 30, 1; Ez 8, 12; Jn 3, 19f.
t Is 45, 9; Jer 18, 6; Rom 9, 20.
u Is 32, 15.
v Is 35, 5; 42, 6f.
w Is 61, 1.
x Is 28, 22.
y Am 5, 10. 12.
z Is 45, 17.
a Is 1, 4.
b Is 31, 1; 36, 6.
c Is 20, 5; Jer 2, 26f.
d Is 19, 11.

*

29, 7f: Just when the Assyrians think their capture of Jerusalem to be certain, the Lord will snatch victory from their hands and save his city.

29, 9–12: Jerusalem in her blindness refuses to believe God's revelation that she will be saved.

29, 17–24: The prophet presents God's plan of redemption in terms of unheard-of natural phenomena as if such changes in nature took place, e. g., the change of the cedars of Lebanon into an orchard (v 17).

29, 22: Who redeemed Abraham: by freeing him from the idolatry of his native land.

5 All shall be ashamed
of a people that gain them nothing,
Neither help nor benefit,
but only shame and reproach.[e]

6 [Oracle on the Beasts of the Negeb]

Through the distressed and troubled land
of the lioness and roaring lion,
of the viper and flying saraph,*
They carry their riches on the backs of asses
and their treasures on the humps of camels
To a people good for nothing,
7 to Egypt whose help is futile and vain.
Therefore I call her
"Rahab* quelled."
8 Now come, write it on a tablet they can keep,
inscribe it in a record;*
That it may be in future days
an eternal witness:[f]
9 This is a rebellious people,
deceitful children,
Children who refuse
to obey the law of the LORD.[g]
10 They say to the seers, "Have no visions" ;
to the prophets, "Do not descry for us
what is right;
speak flatteries to us, conjure up illusions.[h]
11 Out of the way! Out of our path!
Let us hear no more
of the Holy One of Israel."[i]
12 Therefore, thus says the Holy One of Israel:
Because you reject this word,
And put your trust in what is crooked and devious,
and depend on it,
13 This guilt of yours shall be
like a descending rift
Bulging out in a high wall
whose crash comes suddenly, in an instant.[j]
14 It crashes like a potter's jar
smashed beyond rescue,
And among it fragments cannot be found
a sherd to scoop fire from the hearth
or dip water from the cistern.[k]

15 For thus said the Lord GOD,
the Holy One of Israel:
By waiting and by calm you shall be saved,
in quiet and in trust your strength lies.
But this you did not wish.[l]
16 "No," you said,
"Upon horses we will flee."
—Very well, flee!
"Upon swift steeds we will ride."
—Not so swift as your pursuers.[m]
17 A thousand shall tremble at the threat of one;
if five threaten you, you shall flee,
Until you are left like a flagstaff on the mountaintop,
like a flag on the hill.
18 Yet the LORD is waiting to show you favor,
and he rises to pity you;
For the LORD is a God of justice:
blessed are all who wait for him![n]

19 O people of Zion, who dwell in Jerusalem,
no more will you weep;
He will be gracious to you when you cry out,
as soon as he hears he will answer you.[o]
20 The Lord will give you the bread you need
and the water for which you thirst.
No longer will your Teacher* hide himself,
but with your own eyes you shall see your Teacher,
21 While from behind, a voice shall sound in your ears:
"This is the way; walk in it,"
when you would turn to the right or to the left.[p]
22 And you shall consider unclean your
silver-plated idols
and your gold-covered images;
You shall throw them away like filthy rags
to which you say, "Begone!"[q]

## Zion's Future Prosperity

23 He will give rain for the seed
that you sow in the ground,
And the wheat that the soil produces
will be rich and abundant.
On that day your cattle will graze
in spacious meadows;[r]
24 The oxen and the asses that till the ground
will eat silage tossed to them
with shovel and pitchfork.
25 Upon every high mountain and lofty hill
there will be streams of running water.
On the day of the great slaughter,
when the towers fall,[s]
26 The light of the moon will be like that of the sun
and the light of the sun will be seven times greater
[like the light of seven days].

e 36, 6.
f Is 8, 1. 16; Jer 36, 2; Heb 2, 2.
g Is 1, 4; Jer 7, 28.
h Jer 5, 31.
i Jb 21, 14f.
j Ez 13, 14.
k Jer 19, 11.
l Is 7, 4; Mi 7, 7.
m Is 31, 3.
n Ps 34, 9; Jer 17, 7.
o Is 58, 9.
p Jer 31, 33f.
q Is 31, 7.
r Lv 26, 3. 5.
s Jl 4, 18.
t Jer 30, 17.

*

30, 6: Flying saraph: see note on Nm 21, 6.

30, 7: Rahab: Egypt, here as elsewhere (cf Ps 87, 4), is compared to the stormy, impetuous sea monster (cf Is 51, 9; Jb 26, 12; Ps 89, 11), which yet, when asked for aid by Judah, becomes silent, quelled.

30, 8: Isaiah will write down his condemnation of the people so that (vv 12–18) its fulfillment may afterward be admitted.

30, 20: Teacher: God, who in the past taught in a veiled manner through his prophets, will in future help them to understand his teaching clearly. This was eminently true when the Son of God became Man.

On the day the LORD binds up the wounds
of his people,
he will heal the bruises left by his blows.[t]

### Divine Judgment on Assyria*

27 See the name of the LORD coming from afar
in burning wrath, with lowering clouds!
His lips are filled with fury,
his tongue is like a consuming fire;
28 His breath, like a flood in a ravine
that reaches suddenly to the neck,
Will winnow the nations with a destructive
winnowing,
and with repeated winnowings will he
battle against them
[and a bridle on the jaws of the peoples to
send them astray].
30 The LORD will make his glorious voice
heard,
and let it be seen how his arm descends
In raging fury and flame of consuming fire,
in driving storm and hail.
31 When the LORD speaks, Assyria will be
shattered,
as he strikes with the rod;
32 While at every sweep of the rod
which the LORD will bring down on him
in punishment,
29 You will sing
as on a night when a feast is observed,
And be merry of heart,
as one marching along with a flute
Toward the mountain of the LORD,
toward the Rock of Israel,
accompanied by the timbrels and lyres.
33 For the pyre* has long been ready,
prepared for the king;
Broad and deep it is piled
with dry grass and wood in abundance,
And the breath of the LORD, like a stream of
sulphur,
will set it afire.

## CHAPTER 31

### Against the Egyptian Alliance

1 Woe to those who go down to Egypt for
help,
who depend upon horses;
Who put their trust in chariots because of
their number,
and in horsemen because of their
combined power,
But look not to the Holy One of Israel
nor seek the LORD![u]
2 Yet he too is wise and will bring disaster;
he will not turn from what he has
threatened to do.
He will rise up against the house of the
wicked
and against those who help evildoers.
3 The Egyptians are men, not God,
their horses are flesh, not spirit;
When the LORD stretches forth his hand,
the helper shall stumble, the one helped
shall fall,
and both of them shall perish together.[v]

4 Thus says the LORD to me:
As a lion or a lion cub
growling over its prey,
With a band of shepherds
assembled against it,
Is neither frightened by their shouts
nor disturbed by their noise,
So shall the LORD of hosts come down
to wage war upon the mountain and hill
of Zion.
5 Like hovering birds, so the LORD of hosts
shall shield Jerusalem,
To protect and deliver,
to spare and rescue it.[w]

6 Return, O children of Israel, to him whom
you have utterly deserted.[x] 7 On that day each
one of you shall spurn his sinful idols of silver
and gold, which he made with his hands.[y]

### Downfall of Assyria

8 Assyria shall fall by a sword not wielded by
man,
no mortal sword shall devour him;
He shall flee before the sword,
and his young men shall be impressed as
laborers.[z]
9 He shall rush past his crag* in panic,
and his princes shall flee in terror from
his standard,
Says the LORD who has a fire in Zion
and a furnace in Jerusalem.

## CHAPTER 32

### The Kingdom of Justice

1 See, a king will reign justly
and princes will rule rightly.[a]
2 Each of them will be a shelter from the
wind,
a retreat from the rain.
They will be like streams of water in a dry
country,
like the shade of a great rock in a parched
land.[b]
3 The eyes of those who see will not be
closed;
the ears of those who hear will be
attentive.

u Is 30, 2; 36, 6.
v Ps 146, 3ff.
w Ps 91, 4.
x Jer 3, 12.
y Is 30, 22.
z Is 37, 36.
a Is 16, 5; Ps 72, 2ff; Jer 23, 5.
b Is 4, 6; 25, 4.

30, 27–33: God's punishment of Assyria. The name of the Lord: God himself; cf Ps 20, 2.

30, 29–33: Pyre: on which the corpse of the king of Assyria is burned. This is the occasion of festal rejoicing for the Israelites, who are now free from his yoke.

31, 9: Crag: the king as the rallying point of the princes.

4 The flighty will become wise and capable,
and the stutterers will speak fluently and clearly.
5 No more will the fool be called noble,
nor the trickster be considered honorable.
6 For the fool speaks foolishly,
planning evil in his heart:
How to do wickedness,
to speak perversely against the LORD,
To let the hungry go empty
and the thirsty be without drink.[c]
7 And the trickster uses wicked trickery,
planning crimes:
How to ruin the poor with lies,
and the needy when they plead their case.
8 But the noble man plans noble things,
and by noble things he stands.

### The Women of Jerusalem

9 O complacent ladies, rise up and hear my voice,
overconfident women, give heed to my words.
10 In a little more than a year
you overconfident ones will be shaken;
The vintage will fail,
there will be no harvest.[d]
11 Tremble, you who are complacent!
Shudder, you who are overconfident!
Strip yourselves bare,
with only a loincloth to cover you.[e]
12 Beat your breasts
for the pleasant fields, the fruitful vine,
13 And the soil of my people,
overgrown with thorns and briers;
For all the joyful houses,
the wanton city.[f]
14 Yes, the castle* will be forsaken,
the noisy city deserted;[g]
19 Down it comes, as trees come down in the forest!
The city will be utterly laid low.
Hill and tower will become wasteland forever
for wild asses to frolic in, and flocks to pasture,
15 Until the spirit from on high*
is poured out on us.
Then will the desert become an orchard
and the orchard be regarded as a forest.[h]

16 Right will dwell in the desert
and justice abide in the orchard.
17 Justice will bring about peace;
right will produce calm and security.[i]
18 My people will live in peaceful country,
in secure dwellings and quiet resting places.[j]
20 Happy are you who sow beside every stream,
and let the ox and the ass go freely![k]

## CHAPTER 33

### Overthrow of Assyria

1 Woe, O destroyer never destroyed,
O traitor never betrayed!
When you finish destroying, you will be destroyed;
when wearied with betraying, you will be betrayed.
2 O LORD, have pity on us, for you we wait.
Be our strength every morning,
our salvation in time of trouble![l]
3 At the roaring sound, peoples flee;
when you rise in your majesty, nations are scattered.
4 Men gather spoil as caterpillars are gathered up;
they rush upon it like the onrush of locusts.[m]
5 The LORD is exalted, enthroned on high;
he fills Zion with right and justice.[n]
6 That which makes her seasons lasting,
the riches that save her, are wisdom and knowledge;
the fear of the LORD is her treasure.[o]

7 See, the men of Ariel cry out in the streets,
the messengers of Shalem* weep bitterly.
8 The highways are desolate,
travelers have quit the paths,
Covenants are broken, their terms are spurned;
yet no man gives it a thought.[p]
9 The country languishes in mourning,
Lebanon withers with shame;
Sharon* is like the steppe,
Bashan and Carmel are stripped bare.[q]
10 Now will I rise up, says the LORD,
now will I be exalted, now be lifted up.
11 You conceive dry grass, bring forth stubble;
my spirit shall consume you like fire.
12 The peoples shall be as in a limekiln,
like brushwood cut down for burning in the fire.[r]
13 Hear, you who are far off, what I have done;
you who are near, acknowledge my might.

c Prv 10, 32; Eccl 10, 12f.
d Zep 1, 13.
e Jer 4, 8.
f Is 7, 23; 34, 13.
g Is 27, 10.
h Is 35, 1; 44, 3.
i Is 54, 13f; Ps 72, 7; Jas 3, 18.
j Mi 4, 4.
k Is 30, 23.
l Is 25, 9.
m 2 Chr 20, 25.
n Is 1, 26.
o Prv 9, 10.
p Jgs 5, 6.
q Na 1, 4.
r Is 10, 17.

*

32, 14. 19: The castle: the citadel of Jerusalem. Hill and tower: the fortified hill, in Hebrew Ophel, with its stronghold called "the great projecting tower" in Neh 3, 27.

32, 15–18. 20: Extraordinary peace and prosperity will come to Israel under just rulers.

33, 7: Ariel . . . Shalem: Jerusalem; cf Is 29, 1; Gn 14, 18.

33, 9: Sharon: the fertile plain near the Mediterranean.

14 On Zion sinners are in dread,
trembling grips the impious:
"Who of us can live with the consuming fire?
who of us can live with the everlasting flames?"[s]
15 He who practices virtue and speaks honestly,
who spurns what is gained by oppression,
Brushing his hands free of contact with a bribe,
stopping his ears lest he hear of bloodshed,
closing his eyes lest he look on evil—[t]
16 He shall dwell on the heights,
his stronghold shall be the rocky fastness,
his food and drink in steady supply.

### Restoration of Zion

17 Your eyes will see a king* in his splendor,
they will look upon a vast land.
18 Your mind will dwell on the terror:
"Where is he who counted, where is he who weighed?
Where is he who counted the towers?"
19 To the people of alien tongue you will look no more,
the people of obscure speech,
stammering in a language not understood.
20 Look to Zion, the city of our festivals;
let your eyes see Jerusalem
as a quiet abode, a tent not to be struck,
Whose pegs will never be pulled up,
nor any of its ropes severed.
22 Indeed the LORD will be there with us, majestic;
yes, the LORD our judge, the LORD our lawgiver,
the LORD our king, he it is who will save us.
21 In a place of rivers and wide streams
on which no boat is rowed,
where no majestic ship* passes,
23 The rigging hangs slack;
it cannot hold the mast in place,
nor keep the sail spread out.
Then the blind will divide great spoils
and the lame will carry off the loot.
24 No one who dwells there will say, "I am sick";
the people who live there will be forgiven their guilt.

## *VI: The Lord, Zion's Avenger*

## CHAPTER 34

### Judgment upon Edom

1 Come near, O nations, and hear;
be attentive, O peoples!
Let the earth and what fills it listen,
the world and all it produces.[u]
2 The LORD is angry with all the nations
and is wrathful against all their host;
he has doomed them and given them over to slaughter.
3 Their slain shall be cast out,
their corpses shall send up a stench;
The mountains shall run with their blood,[v]
4 and all the hills shall rot;
The heavens shall be rolled up like a scroll,
and all their host shall wither away,
As the leaf wilts on the vine,
or as the fig withers on the tree.[w]

5 When my sword has drunk its fill in the heavens,
lo, it shall come down in judgment
upon Edom, a people I have doomed.[x]
6 The LORD has a sword filled with blood,[y]
greasy with fat,
With the blood of lambs and goats,
with the fat of rams' kidneys;
For the LORD has a sacrifice in Bozrah,
a great slaughter in the land of Edom.
7 Wild oxen shall be struck down with fatlings,
and bullocks with bulls;
Their land shall be soaked with blood,
and their earth greasy with fat.
8 For the LORD has a day of vengeance,
a year of requital by Zion's defender.[z]
9 Edom's streams shall be changed into pitch
and her earth into sulphur,
and her land shall become burning pitch;
10 Night and day it shall not be quenched,
its smoke shall rise forever.
From generation to generation she shall lie waste,
never again shall anyone pass through her.
11 But the desert owl and hoot owl shall possess her,
the screech owl and raven shall dwell in her.
The LORD will measure her with line and plummet
to be an empty waste
for satyrs* to dwell in.[a]

12 Her nobles shall be no more,
nor shall kings be proclaimed there;
all her princes are gone.[b]
13 Her castles shall be overgrown with thorns,
her fortresses with thistles and briers.
She shall become an abode for jackals and a haunt for ostriches.[c]
14 Wildcats shall meet with desert beasts,

s Na 1, 6.
t Pss 15, 2-6; 24, 4f.
u Dt 32, 1.
v Ez 32, 4. 6.
w Is 13, 10; Ez 32, 7f; 4, 15.
x Jer 46, 10.
y 6f: Jer 49, 12f.
z Is 13, 9; 63, 4.
a Is 14, 23; Zep 2, 14.
b Ob 18.
c Is 13, 21; Hos 9, 6.

*

33, 17: King: the messianic King, or God; cf v 22.

33, 21. 23: Boat . . . majestic ship: of a foreign oppressor.

34, 11: Satyrs: see note on Is 13, 21; cf Is 34, 14.

34, 14: Lilith: a female demon thought to roam about the desert.

satyrs shall call to one another;
There shall the lilith* repose,
and find for herself a place to rest.
15 There the hoot owl shall nest and lay eggs,
hatch them out and gather them in her shadow;
There shall the kites assemble,
none shall be missing its mate.

16 Look in the book of the LORD* and read:
No one of these shall be lacking,
For the mouth of the LORD has ordered it,
and his spirit shall gather them there.[d]
17 It is he who casts the lot for them,
and with his hand he marks off their shares of her;
They shall possess her forever,
and dwell there from generation to generation.

## CHAPTER 35

### Israel's Deliverance*

1 The desert and the parched land will exult;
the steppe will rejoice and bloom.[e]
2 They will bloom with abundant flowers,
and rejoice with joyful song.
The glory of Lebanon will be given to them,
the splendor of Carmel and Sharon;
They will see the glory of the LORD,
the splendor of our God.[f]
3 Strengthen the hands that are feeble,
make firm the knees that are weak,[g]
4 Say to those whose hearts are frightened:
Be strong, fear not!
Here is your God,
he comes with vindication;
With divine recompense
he comes to save you.[h]
5 Then will the eyes of the blind be opened,
the ears of the deaf be cleared;[i]
6 Then will the lame leap like a stag,
then the tongue of the dumb will sing.[j]

Streams will burst forth in the desert,
and rivers in the steppe.
7 The burning sands will become pools,
and the thirsty ground, springs of water;
The abode where jackals lurk
will be a marsh for the reed and papyrus.
8 A highway will be there,
called the holy way;
No one unclean may pass over it,
nor fools go astray on it.
9 No lion will be there,
nor beast of prey go up to be met upon it.
It is for those with a journey to make,
and on it the redeemed will walk.[k]
10 Those whom the LORD has ransomed will return
and enter Zion singing,
crowned with everlasting joy;
They will meet with joy and gladness,
sorrow and mourning will flee.[l]

## *VII: Historical Appendix*

## CHAPTER 36

**Invasion of Sennacherib.*** 1 In the fourteenth year of King Hezekiah, Sennacherib,
king of Assyria, went on an expedition against
all the fortified cities of Judah and captured
them.[m] 2 From Lachish the king of Assyria
sent his commander with a great army to King
Hezekiah in Jerusalem. When he stopped at the
conduit of the upper pool, on the highway of the
fuller's field, 3 there came out to him the master of the palace, Eliakim, son of Hilkiah, and
Shebna the scribe, and the herald Joah, son of
Asaph. 4 The commander said to them, "Tell
King Hezekiah: Thus says the great king, the
king of Assyria, 'On what do you base this
confidence of yours? 5 Do you think mere
words substitute for strategy and might in war?
On whom, then, do you rely, that you rebel
against me? 6 This Egypt, the staff on which
you rely, is in fact a broken reed which pierces
the hand of anyone who leans on it. That is what
Pharaoh, king of Egypt, is to all who rely on
him.[n] 7 But if you say to me: "We rely on the
LORD, our God," is not he the one whose high
places and altars Hezekiah removed,* commanding Judah and Jerusalem to worship before
this altar?'[o]
8 "Now, make a wager with my lord the
king of Assyria: 'I will give you two thousand
horses, if you can put riders on them.' 9 How
then can you repulse even one of the least servants of my lord? And yet you rely on Egypt for
chariots and horsemen! 10 'Was it without the
LORD's will that I have come up to destroy this
land? The LORD said to me, "Go up and destroy
that land!" '"[p]
11 Then Eliakim and Shebna and Joah said

d Jos 18, 10; Ps 78, 55.
e Is 55, 12f.
f Is 60, 13; Ps 96, 12.
g Jb 4, 3f; Heb 12, 12.
h Is 41, 10; Zec 8, 13.
i Is 29, 18; 32, 3.
j Is 41, 18; 43, 10. 19.
k Is 62, 10; Lv 26, 6.
l Is 51, 11.
m 2 Kgs 18, 13; 2 Chr 32, 1.
n Is 30, 2.
o 2 Kgs 18, 4.
p Is 10, 5f.

*

34, 16: Book of the Lord: God's list of all his creatures; cf Ps 69, 29, "the book of the living"; Ps 139, 16, "your book."

35, 1–10: Similar to the description of the return from the Exile, as found in chaps. 40–55.

36, 1—39, 8: Except for 38, 9–20, this historical appendix describing the siege, etc., is paralleled in 2 Kgs 18, 13—20, 19, which, however, has certain details proper to itself. The events are also recorded in substantially the same way in the cuneiform inscriptions of Sennacherib.

36, 7: The Assyrians pretend that Hezekiah's removal of the high places and altars (illegal sanctuaries) was taken by the Lord as an insult. They declare to Jerusalem's emissaries that the city therefore no longer has a right to the Lord's protection and that they are the ones who truly carry out his will (cf v 10).

36, 11: The Jewish emissaries ask that the conversation be carried on in Aramaic, not in Judean, for they fear the effect

to the commander, "Please speak to your servants in Aramaic; we understand it. Do not
speak to us in Judean within earshot of the people who are on the wall."*

**12** But the commander replied, "Was it to
you and your master that my lord sent me to
speak these words? Was it not rather to the men
sitting on the wall, who, with you, will have to
eat their own excrement and drink their own
urine?" **13** Then the commander stepped forward and cried out in a loud voice in Judean,
"Listen to the words of the great king, the king
of Assyria. **14** Thus says the king: 'Do not let
Hezekiah deceive you, since he cannot deliver
you. **15** Let not Hezekiah induce you to rely on
the LORD, saying, "The LORD will surely save
us; this city will not be handed over to the king
of Assyria." ' **16** Do not listen to Hezekiah, for
the king of Assyria says: 'Make peace with me
and surrender! Then each of you will eat of his
own vine and of his own fig tree, and drink the
water of his own cistern,[q] **17** until I come to
take you to a land like your own, a land of grain
and wine, of bread and vineyards. **18** Do not let
Hezekiah seduce you by saying, "The LORD
will save us." Has any of the gods of the nations
ever rescued his land from the hand of the king
of Assyria?[r] **19** Where are the gods of Hamath
and Arpad? Where are the gods of Sepharvaim?
Where are the gods of Samaria? Have they
saved Samaria from my hand?[s] **20** Which of all
the gods of these lands ever rescued his land
from my hand? Will the LORD then save Jerusalem from my hand?' " **21** But they remained
silent and did not answer him one word, for the
king had ordered them not to answer him.

**22** Then the master of the palace, Eliakim,
son of Hilkiah, Shebna the scribe, and the herald Joah, son of Asaph, came to Hezekiah with
their garments torn, and reported to him what
the commander had said.

## CHAPTER 37

**1** When King Hezekiah heard this, he tore
his garments, wrapped himself in sackcloth, and
went into the temple of the LORD. **2** He sent
Eliakim, the master of the palace, and Shebna
the scribe, and the elders of the priests, wrapped
in sackcloth, to tell the prophet Isaiah, son of
Amoz: **3** "Thus says Hezekiah: 'This is a day
of distress, of rebuke, and of disgrace. Children
are at the point of birth, but there is no strength
to bring them forth.* **4** Perhaps the LORD, your
God, will hear the words of the commander,
whom his master, the king of Assyria, sent to
taunt the living God, and will rebuke him for the
words which the LORD, your God, has heard.
Send up a prayer for the remnant that is here.' "

**5** When the servants of King Hezekiah had
come to Isaiah, **6** he said to them: "Tell this to
your master: 'Thus says the LORD: Do not be
frightened by the words you have heard, with
which the servants of the king of Assyria have
blasphemed me.[t] **7** I am about to put in him
such a spirit that, when he hears a certain report,
he will return to his own land, and there I will
cause him to fall by the sword.' "

**8** When the commander returned to Lachish
and heard that the king of Assyria had left there,
he found him besieging Libnah. **9** The king of
Assyria heard a report that Tirhakah,* king of
Ethiopia, had come out to fight against him.
Again he sent envoys to Hezekiah with this
message: "Thus shall you say to Hezekiah, king
of Judah: **10** 'Do not let your God on whom you
rely deceive you by saying that Jerusalem will
not be handed over to the king of Assyria.[u]
**11** You yourself have heard what the kings of
Assyria have done to all the countries: They
doomed them! Will you, then, be saved?
**12** Did the gods of the nations whom my fathers
destroyed save them? Gozen, Haran, Rezeph,
and the Edenites in Telassar? **13** Where is the
king of Hamath, the king of Arpad, or a king of
the cities of Sepharvaim, Hena or Ivvah?' "

**14** Hezekiah took the letter from the hand of
the messengers and read it; then he went up to
the temple of the LORD, and spreading it out
before him, **15** he prayed to the LORD: **16** "O
LORD of hosts, God of Israel, enthroned upon
the cherubim! You alone are God over all the
kingdoms of the earth. You have made the heavens and the earth.* **17** Incline your ear, O
LORD, and listen! Open your eyes, O LORD, and
see! Hear all the words of the letter that Sennacherib sent to taunt the living God. **18** Truly,
O LORD, the kings of Assyria have laid waste all
the nations and their lands, **19** and cast their
gods into the fire; they destroyed them because
they were not gods but the work of human
hands, wood and stone.[v] **20** Therefore, O
LORD, our God, save us from his hand, that all
the kingdoms of the earth may know that you,
O LORD, alone are God."

q 1 Kgs 4, 25; Zec 3, 10.
r Is 37, 11.
s Is 10, 9; 37, 13.
t Is 41, 10-14; 51, 7.
u Is 36, 14.
v Jer 16, 20.

* of the Assyrian claims upon the morale of the people.

37, 3: A proverbial expression. In the Bible the pangs of childbirth often typify extreme anguish; cf Is 13, 8; Jer 6, 24; Mi 4, 9f. In this instance there is reference to the desperate situation of Hezekiah from which he was scarcely able to free himself.

37, 9: Tirhakah: may have been general of the Egyptian army in 701 B.C.; later he became king, one of the Ethiopian dynasty of Egyptian kings (c. 690–664 B.C.). Many consider that this account in Isaiah combines features of two originally distinct sieges of Jerusalem by Sennacherib.

37, 16: In contrast to the empty boasting of the Assyrians, Hezekiah proclaims the Lord as God over all the kingdoms of the earth.

**Punishment of Sennacherib.** 21 Then
Isaiah, son of Amoz, sent this message to Hezekiah: Thus says the LORD, the God of Israel: In
answer to your prayer for help against Sennacherib, king of Assyria, 22 this is the word the
LORD has spoken concerning him:[w]

She despises you, laughs you to scorn,
 the virgin daughter Zion;
Behind you she wags her head,
 daughter Jerusalem.
23 Whom have you insulted and blasphemed,
 against whom have you raised your voice
And lifted up your eyes on high?
 Against the Holy One of Israel![x]
24 Through your servants you have insulted the
 LORD:
 You said, "With my many chariots
I climbed the mountain heights,
 the recesses of Lebanon;
I cut down its lofty cedars,
 its choice cypresses;
I reached the remotest heights,
 its forest park.
25 I dug wells and drank water in foreign
 lands;
 I dried up with the soles of my feet
 all the rivers of Egypt.

26 Have you not heard?
 Long ago I prepared it,
From days of old I planned it,
 now I have brought it to pass:
That you should reduce fortified cities
 into heaps of ruins,
27 While their inhabitants, shorn of power,
 are dismayed and ashamed,
Becoming like the plants of the field,
 like the green growth,
 like the scorched grass on the housetops.
28 I am aware whether you stand or sit;
 I know whether you come or go,
 and also your rage against me.
29 Because of your rage against me
 and your fury which has reached my ears,
I will put my hook in your nose
 and my bit in your mouth,
 and make you return the way you came.

30 This shall be a sign for you:*
 this year you shall eat the aftergrowth,
 next year, what grows of itself;
But in the third year, sow and reap,
 plant vineyards and eat their fruit!
31 The remaining survivors of the house of
 Judah
 shall again strike root below
 and bear fruit above.[y]
32 For out of Jerusalem shall come a remnant,
 and from Mount Zion, survivors.
 The zeal of the LORD of hosts shall do
 this.

33 Therefore, thus says the LORD concerning
the king of Assyria: He shall not reach this city,
nor shoot an arrow at it, nor come before it with
a shield, nor cast up siegeworks against it.
34 He shall return by the same way he came,
without entering the city, says the LORD.[z] 35 I
will shield and save this city for my own sake,
and for the sake of my servant David.[a]

36 The angel of the LORD went forth and
struck down one hundred and eighty-five thousand in the Assyrian camp.[b] Early the next
morning, there they were, all the corpses of the
dead.* 37 So Sennacherib, the king of Assyria,
broke camp and went back home to Nineveh.[c]

38 When he was worshiping in the temple of
his god Nisroch, his sons Adrammelech and
Sharezer slew him with the sword and fled into
the land of Ararat.* His son Esarhaddon reigned
in his stead.

## CHAPTER 38

### Sickness and Recovery of Hezekiah.*

1 In those days,* when Hezekiah was mortally
ill, the prophet Isaiah, son of Amoz, came and
said to him: "Thus says the LORD: Put your
house in order, for you are about to die; you
shall not recover."[d] 2 Then Hezekiah turned
his face to the wall and prayed to the LORD: 3 O
LORD, remember how faithfully and wholeheartedly I conducted myself in your presence,
doing what was pleasing to you!" And Hezekiah wept bitterly.[e]

4 Then the word of the LORD came to Isaiah:
5 "Go, tell Hezekiah:* Thus says the LORD, the
God of your father David: I have heard your
prayer and seen your tears. I will heal you: in
three days you shall go up to the LORD's temple;
I will add fifteen years to your life. 6 I will
rescue you and this city from the hand of the
king of Assyria; I will be a shield to this city."[f]

w 2 Kgs 19, 21.
x Is 1, 4.
y Is 27, 6.
z Is 37, 29.
a 1 Kgs 15, 4f.
b Is 10, 12; 17, 14.
c 2 Kgs 19, 35f.
d 2 Kgs 20, 1.
e 2 Kgs 18, 5f.
f Is 37, 35.

37, 30: You: Hezekiah. A sign: it is difficult to know the nature of this sign. Either it is merely a proverbial expression to signify that prosperity follows adversity, or it indicates that after two years the normal conditions of life will be resumed.

37, 36: The destruction of Sennacherib's army is also recorded by Herodotus, a Greek historian of the fifth century B.C. It was probably due to the bubonic plague, but the sacred author attributes it to its ultimate cause, God through his angel.

37, 38: The violent death of Sennacherib (681 B.C.) is also mentioned in non-biblical sources. It occurred twenty years after his invasion of Judea.

38, 1—39, 8: The events of this section—sickness and recovery of Hezekiah, embassy of Merodach-baladan—point forward to Babylon (cc 40–66). They occurred prior to the events of Is 36, 1—37, 38, which point back to Assyria (Is 1, 1—35, 10).

38, 1: In those days: a time prior to the siege of Jerusalem in 701 B.C.

38, 5: Since Hezekiah died in 687 B.C. this sickness of his seems to have been in 702 B.C., that is, fifteen years before.

21 Isaiah then ordered a poultice of figs to be
taken and applied to the boil, that he might
recover. 22 Then Hezekiah asked, "What is
the sign that I shall go up to the temple of the
LORD?"

7 [Isaiah answered:] "This will be the sign
for you from the LORD that he will do what he
has promised: 8 See, I will make the shadow
cast by the sun on the stairway to the terrace of
Ahaz* go back the ten steps it has advanced."
So the sun came back the ten steps it had advanced.[g]

### Hezekiah's Hymn of Thanksgiving.

9 The song of Hezekiah, king of Judah, after he
had been sick and had recovered from his illness:

10 Once I said,
"In the noontime of life* I must depart!
To the gates of the nether world I shall be consigned
for the rest of my years."[h]
11 I said, "I shall see the LORD* no more
in the land of the living.
No longer shall I behold my fellow men
among those who dwell in the world."
12 My dwelling, like a shepherd's tent,
is struck down and borne away from me;
You have folded up my life, like a weaver
who severs the last thread.*
Day and night you give me over to torment;[i]
13 I cry out until the dawn.
Like a lion he breaks all my bones;
[day and night you give me over to torment].
14 Like a swallow I utter shrill cries;
I moan like a dove.
My eyes grow weak, gazing heavenward:
O LORD, I am in straits; be my surety!

15 What am I to say or tell him?*
He has done it!
I shall go on through all my years
despite the bitterness of my soul.
16 Those live whom the LORD protects;
yours . . . the life of my spirit.*
You have given me health and life;
17 thus is my bitterness transformed into peace.
You have preserved my life
from the pit of destruction,
When you cast behind your back
all my sins.*
18 For it is not the nether world that gives you thanks,*
nor death that praises you;
Neither do those who go down into the pit
await your kindness.[j]
19 The living, the living give you thanks,
as I do today.
Fathers declare to their sons,
O God, your faithfulness.
20 The LORD is our savior;
we shall sing to stringed instruments
In the house of the LORD
all the days of our life.

## CHAPTER 39

### Embassy from Merodach-baladan.

1 At that time when Merodach-baladan,* son
of Baladan, king of Babylon, heard that Hezekiah
had recovered from his sickness, he sent
letters and gifts to him.[k] 2 Hezekiah was
pleased at this, and therefore showed the messengers
his treasury, the silver and gold, the
spices and fine oil, his whole armory, and everything
that was in his storerooms; there was
nothing in his house or in his whole realm that
he did not show them.[l]

3 Then Isaiah the prophet came to King Hezekiah
and asked him, "What did these men say
to you? Where did they come from?" Hezekiah
answered, "They came to me from a distant
land, from Babylon." 4 "What did they see in
your house?" he asked. Hezekiah replied,
"They saw everything in my house; there is
nothing in my storerooms that I did not show
them."

5 Then Isaiah said to Hezekiah, "Hear the
word of the LORD of hosts: 6 Behold, the days
shall come when all that is in your house, and

g 2 Kgs 20, 9. 11.
h Jb 17, 11; Ps 102, 25.
i Jb 7, 6.
j Pss 6, 6; 88, 11-13.
k 1-8: 2 Kgs 20, 12.
l 2 Chr 32, 25ff.
m 2 Kgs 24, 13; 25, 13ff.

*

38, 8: Stairway to the terrace of Ahaz: this interpretation is based on a reading of the Hebrew text revised according to the Dead Sea Scroll of Isaiah; cf 2 Kgs 23, 12. Many translate the phrase as "steps of Ahaz" and understand this as referring to a sundial.

38, 10: In the noontime of life: long before the end of a full span of life; cf Pss 55, 24; 102, 25.

38, 11: See the Lord: go to the temple and take part in its service.

38, 12: These two metaphors emphasize the suddenness and finality of death.

38, 15: What am I to say or tell him?: a rhetorical question, as if the poet were at a loss in giving fitting expression to his gratitude; cf Ps 116, 12. He has done it: accomplished the cure. Despite the bitterness: even though the one praying was previously so dejected.

38, 16: Yours . . . the life of my spirit: the current Hebrew text is corrupt. The revised Latin psalter renders it: "You have revived my soul."

38, 17: You cast behind your back all my sins: figurative language to express the divine forgiveness of sins, as if God no longer saw or cared about them. This expression is ordinarily used of men forgetting God; cf 1 Kgs 14, 9; Ez 23, 35; Ps 50, 17.

38, 18f: See note on Ps 6, 6.

39, 1: Merodach-baladan: twice king of Babylon, probably from 721 to 710 B.C., and again for nine months, in 704–703. This visit of his messengers, certainly before 701, was in reality a political one. Babylon hoped to lead an anti-Assyrian confederation composed of neighboring states.

39, 6: Because Judah preferred to follow a pro-Babylonian policy, instead of trusting in God, it would later be exiled to Babylon.

everything that your fathers have stored up until
this day, shall be carried off to Babylon;* nothing shall be left, says the LORD.[m] 7 Some of
your own bodily descendants shall be taken and
made servants in the palace of the king of Babylon."[n] 8 Hezekiah replied to Isaiah, "The
word of the LORD which you have spoken is
favorable."* For he thought, "There will be
peace and security in my lifetime."[o]

### B. The Book of Consolation

## I: *The Lord's Glory in Israel's Liberation*

## CHAPTER 40

### Promise of Salvation

1 Comfort, give comfort to my people,
says your God.
2 Speak tenderly to Jerusalem, and proclaim to her
that her service* is at an end,
her guilt is expiated;
Indeed, she has received from the hand of the LORD
double for all her sins.[p]

3 A voice cries out:*
In the desert prepare the way of the LORD!
Make straight in the wasteland a highway for our God![q]
4 Every valley shall be filled in,
every mountain and hill shall be made low;
The rugged land shall be made a plain,
the rough country, a broad valley.
5 Then the glory of the LORD shall be revealed,
and all mankind shall see it together;
for the mouth of the LORD has spoken.

6 A voice says, "Cry out!"
I answer, "What shall I cry out?"
"All mankind is grass,
and all their glory like the flower of the field.[r]
7 The grass withers, the flower wilts,
when the breath of the LORD blows upon it.
[So then, the people is the grass.]
8 Though the grass withers and the flower wilts,
the word of our God stands forever."

9 Go up onto a high mountain,
Zion, herald of glad tidings;
Cry out at the top of your voice,
Jerusalem, herald of good news!
Fear not to cry out
and say to the cities of Judah:
Here is your God!
10 Here comes with power
the Lord GOD,
who rules by his strong arm;
Here is his reward with him,
his recompense before him.
11 Like a shepherd he feeds his flock;
in his arms he gathers the lambs,
Carrying them in his bosom,
and leading the ewes with care.[s]

### Power of the Creator To Save His People

12 Who has cupped in his hand the waters of the sea,
and marked off the heavens with a span?*
Who has held in a measure the dust of the earth,
weighed the mountains in scales
and the hills in a balance?
13 Who has directed the spirit of the LORD,
or has instructed him as his counselor?[t]
14 Whom did he consult to gain knowledge?
Who taught him the path of judgment,
or showed him the way of understanding?

15 Behold, the nations count as a drop of the bucket,
as dust on the scales;
the coastlands weigh no more than powder.
16 Lebanon would not suffice for fuel,*
nor its animals be enough for holocausts.
17 Before him all the nations are as nought,
as nothing and void he accounts them.

18 To whom can you liken God?[u]
With what equal can you confront him?
19 An idol, cast by a craftsman,
which the smith plates with gold
and fits with silver chains?[v]
20 Mulberry wood, the choice portion
which a skilled craftsman picks out for himself,
Choosing timber that will not rot,

n 2 Chr 33, 11; Dn 1, 2f.
o 2 Chr 32, 26.
p Is 50, 21.
q Mt 3, 3; Jn 1, 23.
r Jb 8, 12; 14, 2; Ps 37, 2; Sir 14, 18; Jas 1, 10; 1 Pt 1, 24.
s Is 49, 9f; 63, 11; Ez 34, 23; 37, 24; Jn 10, 11.
t Wis 9, 13; Rom 11, 34; 1 Cor 2, 16; Jb 38, 1ff.
u 18f: Acts 17, 29.
v Ps 115, 4-7.
w Is 44, 13.

*

39, 8: Favorable: for the Exile would not occur in his lifetime.

40, 2: Service: servitude and exile.

40, 3–5: The figurative language here describes the actual return of the exiles from Babylon to Jerusalem. It is the Lord who leads them; their road is made easy for them. Mt 3, 3 and parallels see in these verses a prophecy of the Baptizer and Christ.

40, 12: Span: the distance between the extended little finger and the thumb. Measure: literally, "third"; here a small container.

40, 16: Lebanon . . . fuel: the famed cedars would not be enough to keep the fires of sacrifice burning.

to set up an idol that will not be
unsteady?[w]
41, 6 One man helps another,*
one says to the other, "Keep on!"
41, 7 The craftsman encourages the goldsmith,
the one who beats with the hammer, him
who strikes on the anvil;
He says the soldering is good,
and he fastens it with nails to steady it.

21 Do you not know? Have you not heard?
Was it not foretold you from the
beginning?
Have you not understood? Since the earth
was founded
22 He sits enthroned above the vault of the
earth,
and its inhabitants are like grasshoppers;
He stretches out the heavens like a veil,
spreads them out like a tent to dwell in.[x]
23 He brings princes to nought
and makes the rulers of the earth as
nothing.
24 Scarcely are they planted or sown,
scarcely is their stem rooted in the earth,
When he breathes upon them and they
wither,
and the stormwind carries them away like
straw.

25 To whom can you liken me as an equal?
says the Holy One.
26 Lift up your eyes on high
and see who has created* these:
He leads out their army and numbers them,
calling them all by name.
By his great might and the strength of his
power
not one of them is missing![y]
27 Why, O Jacob, do you say,*
and declare, O Israel,
"My way is hidden from the LORD,
and my right is disregarded by my God"?
28 Do you not know
or have you not heard?
The LORD is the eternal God,
creator of the ends of the earth.
He does not faint nor grow weary,
and his knowledge is beyond scrutiny.
29 He gives strength to the fainting;
for the weak he makes vigor abound.
30 Though young men faint and grow weary,
and youths stagger and fall,
31 They that hope in the LORD will renew their
strength,
they will soar as with eagles' wings;
They will run and not grow weary,
walk and not grow faint.

## CHAPTER 41

## The Liberator of Israel

1 Keep silence before me, O coastlands;*
you peoples, wait for my words!
Let them draw near and speak;
let us come together for judgment.

2 Who has stirred up from the East the
champion of justice,*
and summoned him to be his attendant?
To him he delivers the nations
and subdues the kings;
With his sword he reduces them to dust,
with his bow, to driven straw.
3 He pursues them, passing on without loss,
by a path his feet do not even tread.
4 Who has performed these deeds?
He who has called forth the generations
since the beginning.[z]

I, the LORD, am the first,
and with the last I will also be.
5 The coastlands see, and fear;
the ends of the earth tremble:
these things are near, they come to pass.
8 But you, Israel, my servant,[a]
Jacob, whom I have chosen,
offspring of Abraham my friend—
9 You whom I have taken from the ends of
the earth
and summoned from its far-off places,
You whom I have called my servant,
whom I have chosen and will not cast
off—
10 Fear not, I am with you;
be not dismayed; I am your God.
I will strengthen you, and help you,
and uphold you with my right hand of
justice.

11 Yes, all shall be put to shame and disgrace
who vent their anger against you;
Those shall perish and come to nought
who offer resistance.
12 You shall seek out, but shall not find,
those who strive against you;
They shall be as nothing at all
who do battle with you.

13 For I am the LORD, your God,
who grasp your right hand;
It is I who say to you, "Fear not,
I will help you."
14 Fear not, O worm Jacob,

x Ps 104, 2.
y Ps 147, 4f.
z Is 44, 7; 46, 10.
a 8f: Is 44, 1f. 21; 45, 4.

*

41, 6–7: These two verses have been transposed from chap. 41.

40, 26: Created: see note on Gn 1, 1. By name: for he is their Creator.

40, 27f: God's people, here called Jacob and Israel, must not give way to discouragement: their Lord is the eternal God.

41, 1–4: It is generally agreed that these verses describe the vocation and victory of Cyrus, whom the Lord used as his instrument to redeem Israel.

41, 2: Cyrus is the champion of justice and God's attendant.

41, 14: Redeemer: in Hebrew, goel, one who frees another

O maggot Israel;
I will help you, says the LORD;
your redeemer* is the Holy One of Israel.
15 I will make of you a threshing sledge,
sharp, new, and double-edged,
To thresh the mountains and crush them,
to make the hills like chaff.
16 When you winnow them, the wind shall carry them off
and the storm shall scatter them.
But you shall rejoice in the LORD,
and glory in the Holy One of Israel.
17 The afflicted and the needy seek water in vain,
their tongues are parched with thirst.
I, the LORD, will answer them;
I, the God of Israel, will not forsake them.
18 I will open up rivers on the bare heights,
and fountains in the broad valleys;
I will turn the desert into a marshland,
and the dry ground into springs of water.
19 I will plant in the desert the cedar,
acacia, myrtle, and olive;
I will set in the wasteland the cypress,
together with the plane tree and the pine,
20 That all may see and know,
observe and understand,
That the hand of the LORD has done this,
the Holy One of Israel has created it.

21 Present your case, says the LORD;*
bring forward your reasons, says the King of Jacob.
22 Let them come near and foretell to us
what it is that shall happen!
What are the things of long ago?
Tell us, that we may reflect on them
And know their outcome;
or declare to us the things to come!
23 Foretell the things that shall come afterward,
that we may know that you are gods!
Do something, good or evil,
that will put us in awe and in fear.
24 Why, you are nothing and your work is nought!
To choose you is an abomination.

25 I have stirred up one from the north, and he comes;
from the east I summon him* by name;
He shall trample the rulers down like red earth,
as the potter treads the clay.
26 Who announced this from the beginning,
that we might know;
beforehand, that we might say it is true?
Not one of you foretold it, not one spoke;
no one heard you say,
27 "The first news for Zion: they are coming now,"
or, "For Jerusalem I will pick out a bearer of the glad tidings."
28 When I look, there is not one,
no one of them to give counsel,
to make an answer when I question them.
29 Ah, all of them are nothing,
their works are nought,
their idols are empty wind!

## CHAPTER 42

### The Servant of the Lord

1 Here is my servant* whom I uphold,
my chosen one with whom I am pleased,
Upon whom I have put my spirit;
he shall bring forth justice to the nations,[b]
2 Not crying out, not shouting,
not making his voice heard in the street.
3 A bruised reed he shall not break,
and a smoldering wick he shall not quench,*
4 Until he establishes justice on the earth;
the coastlands* will wait for his teaching.

5 Thus says God, the LORD,
who created the heavens and stretched them out,
who spreads out the earth with its crops,
Who gives breath to its people
and spirit to those who walk on it:
6 I, the LORD, have called you for the victory of justice,
I have grasped you by the hand;
I formed you, and set you
as a covenant of the people,
a light for the nations,[c]
7 To open the eyes of the blind,
to bring out prisoners from confinement,
and from the dungeon, those who live in darkness.
8 I am the LORD, this is my name;
my glory I give to no other,
nor my praise to idols.
9 See, the earlier things have come to pass,
new ones I now foretell;
Before they spring into being,
I announce them to you.

### The Salvation of Israel despite Its Sins

10 Sing to the LORD a new song,
his praise from the end of the earth:
Let the sea and what fills it resound,

---

b Is 45, 6; 49, 6. c Is 45, 13.

---

from slavery and avenges his sufferings; cf Lv 25, 48: Dt 19. 6. 12.

41, 21–24: An indictment of idols.

41, 25: I summon him: Cyrus.

42, 1–4: Servant: there are three other "Servant-of-the-Lord" oracles, Is 49, 1–7; 50, 4–11; 52, 13—53, 12. Many identifications have been proposed, e.g., historical Israel, ideal Israel, an Old Testament historical character before or during the lifetime of the prophet, the prophet himself. The New Testament and Christian tradition, however, have seen a fulfillment of these prophecies in Jesus Christ.

42, 3: A reference to the mercy of Christ.

42, 4: Coastlands: the lands of the Mediterranean. In the Old Testament the word often refers to the pagan lands of the west.

the coastlands, and those who dwell in
them.
11 Let the steppe and its cities cry out,
the villages where Kedar* dwells;
Let the inhabitants of Sela exult,
and shout from the top of the mountains.
12 Let them give glory to the LORD,
and utter his praise in the coastlands.
13 The LORD goes forth like a hero,
like a warrior he stirs up his ardor;
He shouts out his battle cry,
against his enemies he shows his might:[d]
14 I have looked away, and kept silence,
I have said nothing, holding myself in;
But now, I cry out as a woman in labor,
gasping and panting.
15 I will lay waste mountains and hills,
all their herbage I will dry up;
I will turn the rivers into marshes,
and the marshes I will dry up.[e]
16 I will lead the blind on their journey;
by paths unknown I will guide them.
I will turn darkness into light before them,
and make crooked ways straight.
These things I do for them,
and I will not forsake them.[f]
17 They shall be turned back in utter shame
who trust in idols;
Who say to molten images,
"You are our gods."
18 You who are deaf, listen,*
you who are blind, look and see!
19 Who is blind but my servant,
or deaf like the messenger I send?
20 You see many things without taking note;
your ears are open, but without hearing.
21 Though it pleased the LORD in his justice
to make his law great and glorious,
22 This is a people* despoiled and plundered,
all of them trapped in holes,
hidden away in prisons.
They are taken as booty, with no one to
rescue them,
as spoil, with no one to demand their
return.
23 Who of you gives ear to this?
Who listens and pays heed for the time to
come?
24 Who was it that gave Jacob to be plundered,
Israel to the despoilers?*
Was it not the LORD, against whom we have
sinned?
In his ways they refused to walk,
his law they disobeyed.
25 So he poured out wrath upon them,
his anger, and the fury of battle;
It blazed round about them, yet they did not
realize,
it burned them, but they took it not to
heart.

## CHAPTER 43

### Promises of Redemption and Restoration

1 But now, thus says the LORD,
who created you, O Jacob, and formed
you, O Israel:
Fear not, for I have redeemed you;
I have called you by name: you are mine.
2 When you pass through the water, I will be
with you;
in the rivers you shall not drown.
When you walk through fire, you shall not
be burned;
the flames shall not consume you.
3 For I am the LORD, your God,
the Holy One of Israel, your savior.
I give Egypt as your ransom,
Ethiopia and Seba* in return for you.
4 Because you are precious in my eyes
and glorious, and because I love you.
I give men in return for you
and peoples in exchange for your life.[g]
5 Fear not, for I am with you;
from the east I will bring back your
descendants,
from the west I will gather you.
6 I will say to the north: Give them up!
and to the south: Hold not back!
Bring back my sons from afar,
and my daughters from the ends of the
earth:[h]
7 Everyone who is named as mine,
whom I created for my glory,
whom I formed and made.
8 Lead out the people who are blind though
they have eyes,
who are deaf though they have ears.

9 Let all the nations gather together,
let the peoples assemble!
Who among them could have revealed this,
or foretold to us the earlier things?*
Let them produce witnesses to prove
themselves right,
that one may hear and say, "It is true!"
10 You are my witnesses, says the LORD,
my servants whom I have chosen
To know and believe in me
and understand that it is I.

d Ex 14, 3.
e Ex 9, 25; 10, 15; 14, 21; Ps 105, 33ff.
f Ex 13, 21.
g Dt 4, 37; Hos 11, 1.
h Is 49, 22; Ez 16, 20.

*

42, 11: Kedar: cf footnote to Is 21, 16. Sela: Petra, the capital of Edom.

42, 18–20: Because of their unbelief, the Lord rebukes his people, whom he calls his servant, his messenger.

42, 22: A people: Israel in exile.

42, 24: Despoilers: the Assyrians and Babylonians.

43, 3f: Egypt . . . Ethiopia and Seba: countries which God permitted the Persians to conquer in return for having given Israel its freedom.

43, 9: Only God can know and predict future events; cf Is 41, 1–5. 21–29.

Before me no god was formed,
and after me there shall be none.

11 It is I, I the LORD;
there is no savior but me.
12 It is I who foretold, I who saved;
I made it known, not any strange god among you;
You are my witnesses, says the LORD.
I am God, 13 yes, from eternity I am He;
There is none who can deliver from my hand:
who can countermand what I do?[i]

14 Thus says the LORD, your redeemer,*
the Holy One of Israel:
For your sakes I send to Babylon;
I will lower all the bars,
and the Chaldeans shall cry out in lamentation.
15 I am the LORD, your Holy One,
the creator of Israel, your King.
16 Thus says the LORD,
who opens a way in the sea
and a path in the mighty waters,[j]
17 Who leads out chariots and horsemen,
a powerful army,
Till they lie prostrate together, never to rise,
snuffed out and quenched like a wick.[k]
18 Remember not the events of the past,
the things of long ago consider not;*
19 See, I am doing something new!
Now it springs forth, do you not perceive it?
In the desert I make a way,
in the wasteland, rivers.
20 Wild beasts honor me,
jackals and ostriches,
For I put water in the desert
and rivers in the wasteland
for my chosen people to drink,
21 The people whom I formed for myself,
that they might announce my praise.

22 Yet you did not call upon me, O Jacob,*
for you grew weary of me, O Israel.
23 You did not bring me sheep for your holocausts,
nor honor me with your sacrifices.
I did not exact from you the service of offerings,
nor weary you for frankincense.[l]
24 You did not buy me sweet cane* for money,
nor fill me with the fat of your sacrifices;
Instead, you burdened me with your sins,
and wearied me with your crimes.
25 It is I, I, who wipe out,
for my own sake, your offenses;
your sins I remember no more.
26 Would you have me remember, have us come to trial?
Speak up, prove your innocence!
27 Your first father* sinned;
your spokesmen rebelled against me
28 Till I repudiated the holy gates,
put Jacob under the ban,
and exposed Israel to scorn.

## CHAPTER 44

1 Hear then, O Jacob, my servant,
Israel, whom I have chosen.
2 Thus says the LORD who made you,
your help, who formed you from the womb:
Fear not, O Jacob, my servant,
the darling* whom I have chosen.
3 I will pour out water upon the thirsty ground,
and streams upon the dry land;
I will pour out my spirit upon your offspring,
and my blessing upon your descendants.
4 They shall spring up amid the verdure
like poplars beside the flowing waters.[m]
5 One shall say, "I am the LORD's,"
another shall be named after Jacob,
And this one shall write on his hand,* "The LORD's,"
and Israel shall be his surname.[n]

### The True God and False Gods

6 Thus says the LORD, Israel's King
and redeemer, the LORD of hosts:
I am the first and I am the last;
there is no God but me.[o]
7 Who is like me? Let him stand up and speak,
make it evident, and confront me with it.
Who of old announced future events?
Let them foretell to us the things to come.
8 Fear not, be not troubled:
did I not announce and foretell it long ago?
You are my witnesses! Is there a God
or any Rock* besides me?[p]
9 *Idol makers all amount to nothing, and

i Is 41, 4.
j Is 51, 10f; Ex 14, 21.
k Ex 15, 4.
l Jer 6, 20.
m Is 54, 1ff.
n Is 43, 7; 45, 14.
o Is 41, 44; 43, 15; 45, 21; 48, 3. 12; 51, 15; 54, 5.
p Is 43, 10. 12; Dt 32, 4.
q Is 48, 5. 7.

*

43, 14–17: The destruction of Babylon.

43, 18: No need to think solely of the past wonders of the exodus from Egypt; equally great is the exodus from Babylon.

43, 22–28: The reason for the liberation of the Israelites is not their fidelity but rather God's mercy.

43, 24: Sweet cane: a fragrant substance used in making incense and the sacred anointing oil; cf Ex 30, 23; Jer, 6, 20.

43, 27: First father: Adam or Jacob, or collectively "early ancestors." Spokesmen: leaders, priests, prophets.

44, 2: The darling: see note on Dt 32, 15; cf also Dt 33, 5. 26.

44, 5: Write on his hand: an allusion to the Babylonian custom of tatooing the owner's name on the hand of his slave; cf also Rv 13, 16.

44, 8: Rock: place of refuge; said of God in Dt 32, 4. 18; 1 Sm 2, 2; etc.

44, 9–20: Satire on the makers and worshipers of idols.

their precious works are of no avail, as they themselves give witness. To their shame, they neither see nor know anything; and they are more deaf than men are.[q] 10 Indeed, all the associates of anyone who forms a god, or casts an idol to no purpose, will be put to shame;
11 they will all assemble and stand forth, to be reduced to fear and shame.

12 The smith fashions an iron image, works it over the coals, shapes it with hammers, and forges it with his strong arm. He is hungry and weak, drinks no water and becomes exhausted.[r]

13 The carpenter stretches a line and marks with a stylus the outline of an idol. He shapes it with a plane and measures it off with a compass, making it like a man in appearance and
dignity, to occupy a shrine. 14 He cuts down cedars, takes a holm or an oak, and lays hold of other trees of the forest, which the Lord had
planted and the rain made grow 15 to serve man for fuel. With a part of their wood he warms himself, or makes a fire for baking bread; but with another part he makes a god which he
adores, an idol which he worships. 16 Half of it he burns in the fire, and on its embers he roasts his meat; he eats what he has roasted until he is full, and then warms himself and says, "Ah! I
am warm, I feel the fire." 17 Of what remains he makes a god, his idol, and prostrate before it in worship, he implores it, "Rescue me, for you are my god."

18 The idols have neither knowledge nor reason; their eyes are coated so that they cannot see, and their hearts so that they cannot under-
stand. 19 Yet he does not reflect, nor have the intelligence and sense to say, "Half of the wood I burned in the fire, and on its embers I baked bread and roasted meat which I ate. Shall I then make an abomination out of the rest, or worship
a block of wood?" 20 He is chasing ashes*—a thing that cannot save itself when the flame consumes it; yet he does not say, "Is not this thing in my right hand a fraud?"

21 Remember this, O Jacob,
you, O Israel, who are my servant!
I formed you to be a servant to me;
O Israel, by me you shall never be forgotten:
22 I have brushed away your offenses like a cloud,
your sins like a mist;
return to me, for I have redeemed you.

23 Raise a glad cry, you heavens: the LORD has done this;
shout, you depths of the earth.
Break forth, you mountains, into song,
you forest, with all your trees.
For the LORD has redeemed Jacob,
and shows his glory through Israel.

## Cyrus, Anointed of the Lord, Liberator of Israel

24 Thus says the LORD, your redeemer,
who formed you from the womb:
I am the LORD, who made all things,
who alone stretched out the heavens;
when I spread out the earth, who was with me?[s]
25 It is I who bring to nought the omens of liars,
who make fools of diviners;
I turn wise men back
and make their knowledge foolish.
26 It is I who confirm the words of my servants,
I carry out the plan announced by my messengers;
I say to Jerusalem: Be inhabited;
to the cities of Judah: Be rebuilt;
I will raise up their ruins.
27 It is I who said to the deep: Be dry;
I will dry up your wellsprings.[t]
28 I say of Cyrus:* My shepherd,
who fulfills my every wish;
He shall say of Jerusalem, "Let her be rebuilt,"
and of the temple, "Let its foundations be laid."[u]

## CHAPTER 45

1 Thus says the LORD to his anointed,* Cyrus,
whose right hand I grasp,
Subduing nations before him,
and making kings run in his service,
Opening doors before him
and leaving the gates unbarred:
2 I will go before you
and level the mountains;
Bronze doors* I will shatter,
and iron bars I will snap.[v]
3 I will give you treasures out of the darkness,
and riches that have been hidden away,
That you may know that I am the LORD,
the God of Israel, who calls you by your name.
4 For the sake of Jacob, my servant,
of Israel my chosen one,
I have called you by your name,

r Wis 13, 11ff.
s Is 40, 22; Jb 9, 8.
t Is 42, 15; 51, 10.
u Jer 3, 15; Ez 34, 23.
v Ps 107, 16.
w Is 40, 26.

44, 20: Chasing ashes: exerting efforts in vain; cf Hos 12, 2; Eccl 1, 14; 2, 11. 17.

44, 28: Cyrus: king of Persia (559–529 B.C.) and conqueror of Babylon (538 B.C.), who liberated the Jews, permitting them to return to their native land and to rebuild Jerusalem and the Temple.

45, 1: Anointed: in Hebrew, meshiah, from which the word "Messiah" is derived; from its Greek translation, Christos, we have the name "Christ." Applied to kings, "anointed" originally referred only to those of Israel, but it is here given to Cyrus because he is the agent of the Lord.

45, 2: Bronze doors: of Babylon.

giving you a title, though you knew me
not.[w]
5 I am the LORD and there is no other,
there is no God besides me.
It is I who arm you, though you know me
not,
6 so that toward the rising and the setting of
the sun
men may know that there is none besides
me.*

I am the LORD, there is no other;
7 I form the light, and create the darkness,
I make well-being and create woe;*
I, the LORD, do all these things.
8 Let justice descend, O heavens, like dew
from above,
like gentle rain let the skies drop it down.
Let the earth open and salvation bud forth;
let justice also spring up!*
I, the LORD, have created this.[x]
9 Woe to him who contends with his Maker;[y]
a potsherd among potsherds of the earth!*
Dare the clay say to its modeler, "What are
you doing?"
or, "What you are making has no
hands"?
10 Woe to him who asks a father, "What are
you begetting?"
or a woman, "What are you giving birth
to?"
11 Thus says the LORD,
the Holy One of Israel, his maker:
You question me about my children,
or prescribe the work of my hands for
me!
12 It was I who made the earth
and created mankind upon it;
It was my hands that stretched out the
heavens;
I gave the order to all their host.
13 It was I who stirred up one* for the triumph
of justice;
all his ways I make level.
He shall rebuild my city
and let my exiles go free
Without price or ransom,
says the LORD of hosts.
14 Thus says the LORD:
The earnings of Egypt, the gain of Ethiopia,
and the Sabeans,* tall of stature,
Shall come over to you and belong to you;
they shall follow you, coming in chains.
Before you they shall fall prostrate,
saying in prayer:
"With you only is God, and nowhere else;
the gods are nought.[z]
15 Truly with you God is hidden,*
the God of Israel, the savior![a]
16 Those are put to shame and disgrace
who vent their anger against him;
Those go in disgrace
who carve images.
17 Israel, you are saved by the LORD,
saved forever!
You shall never be put to shame or disgrace
in future ages."
18 For thus says the LORD,
The creator of the heavens,
who is God,
The designer and maker of the earth
who established it,
Not creating it to be a waste,*
but designing it to be lived in:
I am the LORD, and there is no other.
19 I have not spoken from hiding
nor from some dark place of the earth,
And I have not said to the descendants of
Jacob,
"Look for me in an empty waste."
I, the LORD, promise justice,
I foretell what is right.
20 Come and assemble, gather together,
you fugitives from among the gentiles!
They are without knowledge who bear
wooden idols*
and pray to gods that cannot save.
21 Come here and declare
in counsel together:
Who announced this from the beginning
and foretold it from of old?
Was it not I, the LORD,
besides whom there is no other God?
There is no just and saving God but me.
22 Turn to me and be safe,
all you ends of the earth,
for I am God; there is no other!
23 By myself I swear,
uttering my just decree
and my unalterable word:
To me every knee shall bend;
by me every tongue shall swear,[b]

x Pss 72, 6; 85, 11.
y Jer 18, 6; Rom 9, 20.
z Is 43, 3.
a Is 55, 8; Prv 25, 2.
b Rom 14, 11; Phil 2, 10.

*

45, 6: The Gentiles will come to know the true God; cf also vv 20–25.

45, 7: Create woe: God permits evil for the sake of a greater good.

45, 8: The Vulgate rendering gives a more precise Messianic sense to this verse, using "just one" and "savior" in place of justice and salvation. The Advent liturgy uses the Vulgate form, Rorate coeli desuper . . . , to express the world's longing for the coming of Christ.

45, 9: No one may challenge God's freedom of action, exemplified here by the selection of Cyrus as his anointed.

45, 13: One: Cyrus, called by God for the deliverance and restoration of Israel.

45, 14: Egypt . . . Ethiopia . . . Sabeans: the Egyptians and their allies who, when conquered by Cyrus, are seen as acknowledging the God of Israel to be the one true God; cf Is 43, 3.

45, 15: God is hidden: he dwells invisibly in the holy of holies.

45, 18: Waste: an allusion to the beginning of creation, when the earth was waste and void (Gn 1, 2), the same Hebrew word, tohu, being used in both passages. The further reference here is to Palestine, which God wishes again to be inhabited by the returning exiles.

45, 20: Who bear wooden idols: in their religious processions. The gods of the pagans have feet but cannot walk; cf Ps 115, 7; Bar 6, 25.

24 Saying, "Only in the LORD
are just deeds and power.
Before him in shame shall come
all who vent their anger against him.
25 In the LORD shall be the vindication and the glory
of all the descendants of Israel."

## CHAPTER 46

### The Gods of Babylon

1 Bel bows down, Nebo* stoops,
their idols are upon beasts and cattle;
They must be borne up on shoulders,
carried as burdens by the weary.
2 They stoop and bow down together;
unable to save those who bear them,
they too go into captivity.

3 Hear me, O house of Jacob,
all who remain of the house of Israel,
My burden since your birth,
whom I have carried from your infancy.[c]
4 Even to your old age I am the same,
even when your hair is gray I will bear you;
It is I who have done this, I who will continue,
and I who will carry you to safety.

5 Whom would you compare me with, as an equal,
or match me against, as though we were alike?
6 There are those who pour out gold from a purse
and weigh out silver on the scales;
Then they hire a goldsmith to make it into a god
before which they fall down in worship.
7 They lift it to their shoulders to carry;
when they set it in place again, it stays,
and does not move from the spot.
Although they cry out to it, it cannot answer;
it delivers no one from distress.

8 Remember this and be firm,
bear it well in mind, you rebels;
remember the former things, those long ago:
9 I am God, there is no other;
I am God, there is none like me.
10 At the beginning I foretell the outcome;
in advance, things not yet done.
I say that my plan shall stand,
I accomplish my every purpose.

11 I call from the east a bird of prey,*
from a distant land, one to carry out my plan.
Yes, I have spoken, I will accomplish it;
I have planned it, and I will do it.
12 Listen to me, you fainthearted,
you who seem far from the victory of justice:
13 I am bringing on my justice, it is not far off,
my salvation shall not tarry;
I will put salvation within Zion,
and give to Israel my glory.

## CHAPTER 47

### The Fall of Babylon*

1 Come down, sit in the dust,
O virgin daughter Babylon;
Sit on the ground, dethroned,
O daughter of the Chaldeans.
No longer shall you be called
dainty and delicate.
2 Take the millstone and grind flour,
remove your veil;
Strip off your train, bare your legs,
pass through the streams.
3 Your nakedness shall be uncovered
and your shame be seen;
I will take vengeance,
I will yield to no entreaty,
says our redeemer.
4 Whose name is the LORD of hosts,
the Holy One of Israel.

5 Go into darkness and sit in silence,
O daughter of the Chaldeans,
No longer shall you be called
sovereign mistress of kingdoms.
6 Angry at my people,
I profaned my inheritance,
And I gave them into your hand;
but you showed them no mercy,
And upon old men
you laid a very heavy yoke.
7 You said, "I shall remain always,
a sovereign mistress forever!"
But you did not lay these things to heart,
you disregarded their outcome.[d]
8 Now hear this, voluptuous one,
enthroned securely,
Saying to yourself,
"I, and no one else!
I shall never be a widow,
or suffer the loss of my children"—[e]
9 Both these things shall come to you
suddenly, in a single day:
Complete bereavement and widowhood
shall come upon you
For your many sorceries

c Is 44, 2.
d Is 14, 13f.
e Zep 2, 15; Rv 18, 7.

46, 1: Bel . . . Nebo: gods of Babylon; their complete helplessness is here contrasted with God's omnipotence.

46, 11: From the east a bird of prey: Cyrus; cf Is 41, 2–4.

47, 1–15: A taunt-song, mocking Babylon, once queen of the nations, now made a slave girl.

47, 9. 13. 15: Babylon was known for its sorcery and astrology.

and the great number of your spells;*
10 Because you felt secure in your wickedness,
and said, "No one sees me."
Your wisdom and your knowledge
led you astray,
And you said to yourself,
"I, and no one else!"
11 But upon you shall come evil
you will not know how to predict;
Disaster shall befall you
which you cannot allay.
Suddenly there shall come upon you
ruin which you will not expect.
12 Keep up, now, your spells
and your many sorceries;
Perhaps you can make them avail,
perhaps you can strike terror!
13 You wearied yourself with many
consultations,
at which you toiled from your youth;
Let the astrologers stand forth to save you,
the stargazers who forecast at each new
moon
what would happen to you.
14 Lo, they are like stubble,
fire consumes them;
They cannot save themselves
from the spreading flames.
This is no warming ember,
no fire to sit before.
15 Thus do your wizards serve you
with whom you have toiled from your
youth;
Each wanders his own way,
with none to save you.

## CHAPTER 48

### Exhortations to the Exiles

1 Hear this, O house of Jacob
called by the name Israel,
sprung from the stock of Judah,
You who swear by the name of the LORD
and invoke the God of Israel
without sincerity or justice,
2 Though you are named after the holy city
and rely on the God of Israel,
whose name is the LORD of hosts.
3 Things of the past I foretold long ago,
they went forth from my mouth, I let you
hear of them;
then suddenly I took action and they came
to be.
4 Because I know that you are stubborn
and that your neck is an iron sinew
and your forehead bronze,
5 I foretold them to you of old;
before they took place I let you hear of
them,
That you might not say, "My idol did them,
my statue, my molten image commanded
them."
6 Now that you have heard, look at all this;
must you not admit it?[f]
From now on I announce new things to you,
hidden events of which you knew not.
7 Now, not long ago, they are brought into
being,
and beforetime you did not hear of them,
so that you cannot claim to have known
them;
8 You neither heard nor knew,
they did not reach your ears beforehand.
Yes, I know you are utterly treacherous,
a rebel you were called from birth.[g]
9 For the sake of my name I restrain my
anger,
for the sake of my renown I hold it back
from you,
lest I should destroy you.
10 See, I have refined you like silver,
tested you in the furnace of affliction.[h]
11 For my sake, for my own sake, I do this;
why should I suffer profanation?
My glory I will not give to another.

12 Listen to me, Jacob,
Israel, whom I named!
I, it is I who am the first,
and also the last am I.[i]
13 Yes, my hand laid the foundations of the
earth;
my right hand spread out the heavens.
When I call them,
they stand forth at once.[j]

14 All of you assemble and listen:
Who among you foretold these things?
The LORD's friend* shall do his will
against Babylon and the progeny of
Chaldea.
15 I myself have spoken, I have called him,
I have brought him, and his way
succeeds!
16 Come near to me and hear this!
Not from the beginning did I speak it in
secret;
At the time it comes to pass, I am present:
"Now the Lord* GOD has sent me,
and his spirit."
17 Thus says the LORD, your redeemer,
the Holy One of Israel:
I, the LORD, your God,
teach you what is for your good,
and lead you on the way you should go.
18 If you would hearken to my commandments,
your prosperity would be like a river,
and your vindication like the waves of the
sea;
19 Your descendants would be like the sand,

f Is 42, 9.
g Is 43, 22ff.
h Is 1, 25; Jer 6, 29f; Zec 13, 9; Mal 3, 2.
i Is 41, 4; 44, 6; 48, 12; Rv 1, 8. 17.
j Is 40, 22. 26; 45, 12. 18.

48, 14: The Lord's friend: Cyrus, who carries out God's plans.

48, 16: "Now the Lord . . . spirit": said by Cyrus; cf v 14.

and those born of your stock like its grains,
Their name never cut off
or blotted out from my presence.
20 Go forth from Babylon, flee from Chaldea!
With shouts of joy proclaim this, make it known;
Publish it to the ends of the earth, and say,
"The LORD has redeemed his servant Jacob.
21 They did not thirst
when he led them through dry lands;
Water from the rock he set flowing for them;
he cleft the rock, and waters welled forth."[k]
22 [There is no peace for the wicked,
says the LORD.]

## II: *Expiation of Sin, Spiritual Liberation of Israel*

## CHAPTER 49

### The Servant of the Lord*

1 Hear me, O coastlands,
listen, O distant peoples.[l]
The LORD called me from birth,
from my mother's womb he gave me my name.*
2 He made of me a sharp-edged sword
and concealed me in the shadow of his arm.
He made me a polished arrow,
in his quiver he hid me.*
3 You are my servant, he said to me,
Israel,* through whom I show my glory.

4 Though I thought I had toiled in vain,
and for nothing, uselessly, spent my strength,
Yet my reward is with the LORD,
my recompense is with my God.[m]
5 For now the LORD has spoken
who formed me as his servant from the womb,
That Jacob may be brought back to him
and Israel gathered to him;
And I am made glorious in the sight of the LORD,
and my God is now my strength!
6 It is too little, he says, for you to be my servant,
to raise up the tribes of Jacob,
and restore the survivors of Israel;[n]
I will make you a light to the nations,
that my salvation may reach to the ends of the earth.*

7 Thus says the LORD,
the redeemer and the Holy One of Israel,
To the one despised, whom the nations abhor,
the slave of rulers:
When kings see you, they shall stand up,
and princes shall prostrate themselves
Because of the LORD who is faithful,
the Holy One of Israel who has chosen you.[o]

### The Liberation and Restoration of Zion

8 Thus says the LORD:
In a time of favor I answer you,
on the day of salvation I help you,
To restore the land
and allot the desolate heritages,[p]
9 Saying to the prisoners: Come out!
To those in darkness: Show yourselves!
Along the ways they shall find pasture,
on every bare height shall their pastures be.[q]
10 They shall not hunger or thirst,
nor shall the scorching wind or the sun strike them;
For he who pities them leads them
and guides them beside springs of water.[r]
11 I will cut a road through all my mountains,
and make my highways level.[s]
12 See, some shall come from afar,
others from the north and the west,
and some from the land of Syene.*

13 Sing out, O heavens, and rejoice, O earth,
break forth into song, you mountains.
For the LORD comforts his people
and shows mercy to his afflicted.

14 But Zion said, "The LORD has forsaken me;
my Lord has forgotten me."[t]
15 Can a mother forget her infant,
be without tenderness for the child of her womb?
Even should she forget,
I will never forget you.[u]
16 See, upon the palms of my hands I have written your name;*

k Ex 17, 6; Nm 20, 11.
l Is 41, 9; 43, 1; 44, 2. 24; 46, 3.
m Is 40, 27.
n Is 42, 1-6; 44, 5; 45, 14; Lk 2, 32; Acts 13, 46f.
o Is 49, 23; 55, 5.
p 2 Cor 6, 2.
q Is 42, 7. 18ff.
r Is 51, 14; Rv 7, 16.
s Is 40, 3f.
t Is 40, 27.
u Is 43, 4; 44, 21; 46, 3f.

*

49, 1-7: The second of the four "Servant-of-the-Lord" oracles.

49, 1: Gave me my name: designated me for a special office (cf Jer 1, 5), or perhaps, made me renowned (cf Ps 45, 18).

49, 2: The servant was made ready and fit for the preaching of God's word.

49, 3: Israel: the Servant is identified with the people of Israel as their ideal representative; however, since vv 5f seem to distinguish the Servant from Israel, some regard the word Israel here as a gloss.

49, 6: The Servant's vocation will be not only the restoration of Israel but the conversion of the world; cf Lk 2, 32.

49, 12: Syene: now called Aswan, at the first cataract of the Nile in southern Egypt.

49, 16: Upon the palms . . . name: for continual remem-

your walls are ever before me.
17 Your rebuilders make haste,
as those who tore you down and laid you waste
go forth from you;
18 Look about and see,
they are all gathering and coming to you.
As I live, says the LORD,
you shall be arrayed with them all as with adornments,
like a bride you shall fasten them on you.

19 Though you were waste and desolate,
a land of ruins,
Now you shall be too small for your inhabitants,
while those who swallowed you up will be far away.
20 The children whom you had lost
shall yet say to you,
"This place is too small for me,
make room for me to live in."
21 You shall ask yourself:
"Who has borne me these?
I was bereft and barren
[exiled and repudiated];
who has reared them?
I was left all alone;
where then do these come from?"[v]

22 Thus says the LORD GOD:
See, I will lift up my hand to the nations,
and raise my signal to the peoples;
They shall bring your sons in their arms,
and your daughters shall be carried on their shoulders.[w]
23 Kings shall be your foster fathers,
their princesses your nurses;
Bowing to the ground, they shall worship you
and lick the dust at your feet.
Then you shall know that I am the LORD,
and those who hope in me shall never be disappointed.

24 Thus says the LORD:
Can booty be taken from a warrior?
or captives be rescued from a tyrant?
25 Yes, captives can be taken from a warrior,
and booty be rescued from a tyrant;
Those who oppose you I will oppose,
and your sons I will save.
26 I will make your oppressors eat their own flesh,
and they shall be drunk with their own blood
as with the juice of the grape.
All mankind shall know
that I, the LORD, am your savior,
your redeemer, the mighty one of Jacob.[x]

## CHAPTER 50

## Salvation Only through the Lord's Servant

1 Thus says the LORD:
Where is the bill of divorce
with which I dismissed your mother?*
Or to which of my creditors
have I sold you?
It was for your sins that you were sold,
for your crimes that your mother was dismissed.[y]

2 Why was no one there when I came?
Why did no one answer when I called?*
Is my hand too short to ransom?
Have I not the strength to deliver?
Lo, with my rebuke I dry up the sea,
I turn rivers into a desert;
Their fish rot for lack of water,
and die of thirst.[z]
3 I clothe the heavens in mourning,
and make sackcloth their vesture.

4 The Lord GOD has given me*
a well-trained tongue,
That I might know how to speak to the weary
a word that will rouse them.
Morning after morning
he opens my ear that I may hear;
5 And I have not rebelled,
have not turned back.*
6 I gave my back to those who beat me,
my cheeks to those who plucked my beard;*
My face I did not shield
from buffets and spitting.[a]

7 The Lord GOD is my help,
therefore I am not disgraced;
I have set my face like flint,
knowing that I shall not be put to shame.[b]
8 He is near who upholds my right;
if anyone wishes to oppose me,
let us appear together.

---

v Is 54, 1ff.
w Is 5, 26; 13, 2.
x Is 19, 2; Ez 38, 21; Zec 14, 13.
y Dt 24, 1-4; Mt 19, 3; Mk 10, 2ff; Is 54, 6ff.
z Ex 7, 18; Ps 105, 29.
a 2 Sm 10, 4ff; Mt 26, 67; 27, 30.
b Ez 3, 9.

---

brance; cf Ex 13, 9. 16; Dt 6, 6–9.

50, 1: Responding to the people's complaint of utter abandonment by God, the prophet shows that their sins were responsible for their banishment. Since there was no bill of divorce, the bond between the Lord and his people still exists and he will ultimately save them.

50, 2: Israel's faith in God is weak; she does not answer his call, nor believe in his promises of deliverance.

50, 4–11: The third of the four "Servant-of-the-Lord" oracles; in vv 4–9 the Servant speaks; in vv 10f God reproves the people for not following the Servant.

50, 5: The Servant does not refuse the divine vocation.

50, 6: He willingly submits to insults and beatings. Plucked my beard: a grave insult.

Who disputes my right?
Let him confront me.
9 See, the Lord GOD is my help;
who will prove me wrong?
Lo, they will all wear out like cloth,
the moth will eat them up.[c]

10 Who among you fears the LORD,*
heeds his servant's voice,
And walks in darkness
without any light,
Trusting in the name of the LORD
and relying on his God?[d]
11 All of you kindle flames
and carry about you fiery darts;
Walk by the light of your own fire
and by the flares you have burnt!
This is your fate from my hand:
you shall lie down in a place of pain.

## CHAPTER 51

### Exhortation To Trust in the Lord

1 Listen to me, you who pursue justice,
who seek the LORD;
Look to the rock from which you were
hewn,
to the pit* from which you were
quarried;[e]
2 Look to Abraham, your father,
and to Sarah, who gave you birth;
When he was but one I called him,
I blessed him and made him many.[f]
3 Yes, the LORD shall comfort Zion
and have pity on all her ruins;
Her deserts he shall make like Eden,
her wasteland like the garden of the LORD;
Joy and gladness shall be found in her,
thanksgiving and the sound of song.

4 Be attentive to me, my people;*
my folk, give ear to me.
For law shall go forth from my presence,
and my judgment, as the light of the
peoples.[g]
5 I will make my justice come speedily;
my salvation shall go forth
[and my arm shall judge the nations];
In me shall the coastlands hope,
and my arm they shall await.

6 Raise your eyes to the heavens,
and look at the earth below;
Though the heavens grow thin like smoke,
the earth wears out like a garment
and its inhabitants die like flies,
My salvation shall remain forever
and my justice shall never be dismayed.*
7 Hear me, you who know justice,
you people who have my teaching at
heart:
Fear not the reproach of men,
be not dismayed at their revilings.
8 They shall be like a garment eaten by
moths,
like wool consumed by grubs;
But my justice shall remain forever
and my salvation, for all generations.[h]

9 Awake, awake, put on strength,
O arm of the LORD!
Awake as in the days of old,
in ages long ago!
Was it not you who crushed Rahab,*
you who pierced the dragon?[i]
10 Was it not you who dried up the sea,
the waters of the great deep,*
Who made the depths of the sea into a way
for the redeemed to pass over?
11 Those whom the LORD has ransomed will
return
and enter Zion singing,
crowned with everlasting joy;
They will meet with joy and gladness,
sorrow and mourning will flee.
12 I, it is I who comfort you.
Can you then fear mortal man,
who is human only, to be looked upon as
grass,
13 And forget the LORD, your maker,
who stretched out the heavens
and laid the foundations of the earth?
All the day you are in constant dread
of the fury of the oppressor;
But when he sets himself to destroy,
what is there of the oppressor's fury?

14 The oppressed shall soon be released;
they shall not die and go down into the
pit,
nor shall they want for bread.
15 For I am the LORD, your God,
who stirs up the sea so that its waves
roar;
the LORD of hosts by name.[j]
16 I have put my words into your mouth
and shielded you in the shadow of my
hand,
I, who stretched out the heavens,
who laid the foundations of the earth,
who say to Zion: You are my people.

c Is 51, 6-8; Ps 102, 27.
d Is 43, 1f; 44, 1f.
e Rom 9, 30f.
f Ez 33, 24; Gn 12, 2ff; 22, 17.
g Is 2, 3.
h Is 50, 9.
i Ex 15, 16; Jb 9, 13; 26, 12; Pss 74, 13; 89, 11.
j Jer 31, 35.

*

50, 10f: Instead of trusting in the Lord and his Servant, the people rely on their own devices, to their own destruction.

51, 1: Rock . . . pit: your glorious ancestry.

51, 4f: The conversion of the Gentiles.

51, 6: God's salvation and justice are eternal, in contrast to the impermanence of the heavens and the earth: cf Mt 24, 35.

51, 9: Rahab: see note on Is 30, 7. The dragon: see notes on Is 27, 1; Ps 74, 13.

51, 10: Great deep: another reference to the primeval chaos of Gn 1, 2.

## The Cup of the Lord

17 Awake, awake!
Arise, O Jerusalem,
You who drank at the LORD's hand
the cup of his wrath;
Who drained to the dregs
the bowl of staggering![k]
18 She has no one to guide her
of all the sons she bore;
She has no one to grasp her by the hand,
of all the sons she reared!—
19 Your misfortunes are double;
who is there to condole with you?
Desolation and destruction, famine and
sword!
Who is there to comfort you?
20 Your sons lie helpless
at every street corner
like antelopes in a net.
They are filled with the wrath of the LORD,
the rebuke of your God.

21 But now, hear this, O afflicted one,
drunk, but not with wine,[l]
22 Thus says the LORD, your Master,
your God, who defends his people:
See, I am taking from your hand
the cup of staggering;
The bowl of my wrath
you shall no longer drink.
23 I will put it into the hands of your
tormentors,
those who ordered you
to bow down, that they might walk over
you,
While you offered your back like the
ground,
like the street for them to walk on.

## CHAPTER 52

### Let Zion Rejoice

1 Awake, awake!
Put on your strength, O Zion;
Put on your glorious garments,
O Jerusalem, holy city.
No longer shall the uncircumcised
or the unclean enter you.
2 Shake off the dust,
ascend to the throne, Jerusalem;
Loose the bonds from your neck,
O captive daughter Zion!
3 For thus says the LORD:
You were sold for nothing,
and without money you shall be
redeemed.
4 Thus says the Lord GOD:
To Egypt in the beginning my people went
down,
to sojourn there;
Assyria, too, oppressed them for nought.
5 But now, what am I to do here?
says the LORD.
My people have been taken away without
redress;
their rulers make a boast of it, says the
LORD;
all the day my name is constantly reviled.
6 Therefore on that day my people shall know
my renown,
that it is I who have foretold it. Here I
am!
7 How beautiful upon the mountains*
are the feet of him who brings glad
tidings,
Announcing peace, bearing good news,
announcing salvation, and saying to Zion,
"Your God is King!"[m]
8 Hark! Your watchmen raise a cry,
together they shout for joy,
For they see directly, before their eyes,
the LORD restoring Zion.[n]
9 Break out together in song,
O ruins of Jerusalem!
For the LORD comforts his people,
he redeems Jerusalem.
10 The LORD has bared his holy arm
in the sight of all the nations;
All the ends of the earth will behold
the salvation of our God.

11 Depart, depart, come forth from there,
touch nothing unclean!
Out from there!* Purify yourselves,
you who carry the vessels of the LORD.
12 Yet not in fearful haste will you come out,
nor leave in headlong flight,
For the LORD comes before you,
and your rear guard is the God of Israel.[o]

### Suffering and Triumph of the Servant of the Lord*

13 See, my servant shall prosper,
he shall be raised high and greatly
exalted.
14 Even as many were amazed at him—
so marred was his look beyond that of
man,
and his appearance beyond that of
mortals—[p]
15 So shall he startle many nations,

k Jer 25, 15ff; Ez 23, 32ff.
l Is 29, 9.
m Is 40, 9; Rom 10, 15.
n 1 Is 62, 6.
o Ex 12, 11.
p Ps 69, 8.
q Mi 7, 16.

*

52, 7–10: God leads his people back from Babylon to Zion, from whose ruined walls watchmen . . . shout for joy; cf Rom 10, 15.

52, 11: From there: from Babylon. Vessels of the Lord: taken to Babylon by Nebuchadnezzar, now carried back by the exiled priests returning in procession to Zion; cf Ezr 1, 7.

52, 13—53, 12: The last of the four "Servant-of-the-Lord" oracles. An extraordinary description of the sinless Servant, who by his voluntary suffering atones for the sins of his people, and saves them from just punishment at the hands of God. Only in Jesus Christ is the prophecy perfectly fulfilled.

because of him kings shall stand
speechless;
For those who have not been told shall see,
those who have not heard shall ponder
it.[q]

## CHAPTER 53

1 Who would believe what we have heard?
To whom has the arm of the LORD been
revealed?[r]
2 He grew up like a sapling before him,[s]
like a shoot from the parched earth;
There was in him no stately bearing to make
us look at him,
nor appearance that would attract us to
him.*
3 He was spurned* and avoided by men,
a man of suffering, accustomed to
infirmity,
One of those from whom men hide their
faces,
spurned, and we held him in no esteem.[t]

4 Yet it was our infirmities that he bore,*
our sufferings that he endured,
While we thought of him as stricken,
as one smitten by God and afflicted.[u]
5 But he was pierced for our offenses,
crushed for our sins,
Upon him was the chastisement that makes
us whole,
by his stripes we were healed.[v]
6 We had all gone astray like sheep,
each following his own way;
But the LORD laid upon him
the guilt of us all.[w]
7 Though he was harshly treated, he submitted
and opened not his mouth;
Like a lamb led to the slaughter
or a sheep before the shearers,
he was silent and opened not his mouth.[x]
8 Oppressed and condemned, he was taken
away,
and who would have thought any more of
his destiny?
When he was cut off from the land of the
living,
and smitten for the sin of his people,
9 A grave was assigned him among the
wicked
and burial place with evildoers,
Though he had done no wrong
nor spoken any falsehood.[y]
10 [But the LORD was pleased*
to crush him in infirmity.]

If he gives his life as an offering for sin,
he shall see his descendants in a long life,
and the will of the LORD shall be
accomplished through him.
11 Because of his affliction
he shall see the light in fullness of days;
Through his suffering, my servant shall
justify many,
and their guilt he shall bear.
12 Therefore I will give him his portion among
the great,
and he shall divide the spoils with the
mighty,
Because he surrendered himself to death
and was counted among the wicked;
And he shall take away the sins of many,
and win pardon for their offenses.[z]

## CHAPTER 54

### The New Zion

1 Raise a glad cry, you barren one* who did
not bear,
break forth in jubilant song, you who
were not in labor,
For more numerous are the children of the
deserted wife
than the children of her who has a
husband,
says the LORD.[a]
2 Enlarge the space for your tent,
spread out your tent cloths unsparingly;
lengthen your ropes and make firm your
stakes.[b]
3 For you shall spread abroad to the right and
to the left;
your descendants shall dispossess the
nations
and shall people the desolate cities.
4 Fear not, you shall not be put to shame;
you need not blush, for you shall not be
disgraced.
The shame of your youth you shall forget,
the reproach of your widowhood no
longer remember.
5 For he who has become your husband is
your Maker;
his name is the LORD of hosts;
Your redeemer* is the Holy One of Israel,
called God of all the earth.
6 The LORD calls you back,

r Is 52, 10; Jn 12, 38; Rom 10, 16.
s Is 11, 1.
t Jb 19, 18; Ps 31, 11ff; Mk 9, 11.
u Jer 10, 19; Mt 8, 17.
v 1 Cor 15, 3; 1 Pt 2, 24.
w Lv 16, 21ff.
x Mt 26, 63; Acts 8, 32.
y 1 Pt 2, 22f; 1 Jn 3, 5.
z Mk 15, 28; Lk 22, 37.
a Gal 4, 27.
b Is 49, 20.
c Mal 2, 14f.

*

53, 2: Only God appreciated his Servant's true greatness.

53, 3: Because he suffered, he was regarded as a sinner and therefore as one to be spurned.

53, 4ff: He did indeed suffer but it was for the sins of mankind, and through his sufferings men are healed.

53, 10ff: Because he fulfilled the divine will by suffering for the sins of others, the Servant will be rewarded by the Lord. See the light: enjoy happiness. This line may originally have read, "he shall drink and eat to the full"—at the thanksgiving sacrifice at which he shall divide the spoils (v 12).

54, 1: Jerusalem, pictured as a wife who had been barren and deserted, now suddenly finds herself with innumerable children (the returning exiles); cf Gal 4, 27 for the application of this text to the church, the New Zion.

54, 5: Redeemer: cf note on Is 41, 14.

like a wife forsaken and grieved in spirit,
A wife married in youth and then cast off,
says your God.[c]
**7** For a brief moment I abandoned you,
but with great tenderness I will take you back.
**8** In an outburst of wrath, for a moment
I hid my face from you;
But with enduring love I take pity on you,
says the LORD, your redeemer.

**9** This is for me like the days of Noah,
when I swore that the waters of Noah
should never again deluge the earth;
So I have sworn not to be angry with you,
or to rebuke you.[d]
**10** Though the mountains leave their place
and the hills be shaken,
My love shall never leave you
nor my covenant of peace be shaken,
says the LORD, who has mercy on you.[e]

**11** O afflicted one, storm-battered and unconsoled,*
I lay your pavements in carnelians,
and your foundations in sapphires;[f]
**12** I will make your battlements of rubies,
your gates of carbuncles,
and all your walls of precious stones.
**13** All your sons shall be taught by the LORD,
and great shall be the peace of your children.
**14** In justice shall you be established,
far from the fear of oppression,
where destruction cannot come near you.
**15** Should there be any attack, it shall not be of my making;
whoever attacks you shall fall before you.
**16** Lo, I have created the craftsman
who blows on the burning coals
and forges weapons as his work;
It is I also who have created
the destroyer to work havoc.
**17** No weapon fashioned against you shall prevail;
every tongue you shall prove false
that launches an accusation against you.
This is the lot of the servants of the LORD,
their vindication from me, says the LORD.

## CHAPTER 55

### An Invitation to Grace

**1** All you who are thirsty,*
come to the water!
You who have no money,
come, receive grain and eat;
Come, without paying and without cost,
drink wine and milk![g]
**2** Why spend your money for what is not bread;
your wages for what fails to satisfy?
Heed me, and you shall eat well,
you shall delight in rich fare.
**3** Come to me heedfully,
listen, that you may have life.
I will renew with you the everlasting covenant,
the benefits assured to David.[h]
**4** As I made him a witness to the peoples,
a leader and commander of nations,
**5** So shall you summon a nation you knew not,
and nations that knew you not shall run to you,
Because of the LORD, your God,
the Holy One of Israel, who has glorified you.[i]

**6** Seek the LORD while he may be found,
call him while he is near.
**7** Let the scoundrel forsake his way,
and the wicked man his thoughts;
Let him turn to the LORD for mercy;
to our God, who is generous in forgiving.
**8** For my thoughts are not your thoughts,
nor are your ways my ways, says the LORD.
**9** As high as the heavens are above the earth,
so high are my ways above your ways
and my thoughts above your thoughts.
**10** For just as from the heavens
the rain and snow come down
And do not return there
till they have watered the earth,
making it fertile and fruitful,
Giving seed to him who sows
and bread to him who eats,
**11** So shall my word be
that goes forth from my mouth;
It shall not return to me void,
but shall do my will,
achieving the end for which I sent it.

**12** Yes, in joy you shall depart,
in peace you shall be brought back;
Mountains and hills shall break out in song before you,
and all the trees of the countryside shall clap their hands.
**13** In place of the thornbush, the cypress shall grow,
instead of nettles,* the myrtle.
This shall be to the LORD's renown,
an everlasting imperishable sign.

---

d Gn 9, 15.
e Pss 76, 5; 46, 3.
f Rv 21, 18-21.
g Jn 4, 10ff; 6, 35; 7, 37ff; Rv 21, 6; 22, 17.
h 2 Sm 7, 12-16.
i Acts 13, 34.

---

54, 11f: Cf Rv 21. Afflicted one: Jerusalem; camelians: reddish quartz, hard and durable; carbuncles: another precious stone of red color.

55, 1ff: God's salvation is freely extended to his people and to all nations; through him will the benefits assured to David be renewed; cf Is 12, 3; Jn 7, 37.

55, 13: Thornbush . . . nettles: suggestive of the desert and therefore symbolic of suffering and hardship; cypress, myrtle: suggestive of fertile land and therefore symbolic of joy and strength.

## *III: Return of the First Captives*

### CHAPTER 56

### The Lord's House Open to All*

1 Thus says the LORD:
Observe what is right, do what is just;
for my salvation is about to come,
my justice, about to be revealed.
2 Happy is the man who does this,
the son of man who holds to it;
Who keeps the sabbath free from
profanation,
and his hand from any evildoing.
3 Let not the foreigner say,
when he would join himself to the LORD,
"The LORD will surely exclude me from
his people";
Nor let the eunuch say,
"See, I am a dry tree."*
4 For thus says the LORD:
To the eunuchs who observe my sabbaths
and choose what pleases me
and hold fast to my covenant,[j]
5 I will give, in my house
and within my walls, a monument and a
name*
Better than sons and daughters;
an eternal, imperishable name will I give
them.

6 And the foreigners who join themselves to
the LORD,
ministering to him,
Loving the name of the LORD,
and becoming his servants—
All who keep the sabbath free from
profanation
and hold to my covenant,
7 Them I will bring to my holy mountain
and make joyful in my house of prayer;
Their holocausts and sacrifices
will be acceptable on my altar,
For my house shall be called
a house of prayer for all peoples.[k]
8 Thus says the Lord GOD,
who gathers the dispersed of Israel:
Others will I gather to him
besides those already gathered.

### Blind Leaders

9 *All you wild beasts* of the field,
come and eat,
all you beasts in the forest![l]
10 My watchmen are blind,
all of them unaware;
They are all dumb dogs,
they cannot bark;
Dreaming as they lie there,
loving their sleep.
11 They are relentless dogs,
they know not when they have enough.
These are the shepherds
who know no discretion;
Each of them goes his own way,
every one of them to his own gain:
12 "Come, I will fetch some wine;
let us carouse with strong drink,
And tomorrow will be like today,
or even greater."[m]

### CHAPTER 57

1 The just man perishes,
but no one takes it to heart;
Devout men are swept away,
with no one giving it a thought.
Though he is taken away from the presence
of evil,
the just man 2 enters into peace;
There is rest on his couch
for the sincere, straightforward man.

### Faithless People

3 But you, draw near,
you sons of a sorceress,
adulterous, wanton race!
4 Of whom do you make sport,
at whom do you open wide your mouth,
and put out your tongue?
Are you not rebellious children,
a worthless race;
5 You who are in heat among the terebinths,
under every green tree;
You who immolate children in the wadies,
behind the crevices in the cliffs?[n]

6 Among the smooth stones* of the wadi is
your portion,
these are your lot;
To these you poured out libations,
and brought offerings.
Should I decide not to punish these
things?

---

j Wis 3, 14f.
k 1 Kgs 8, 29f; Mt 21, 13.
l Ez 34, 5.
m Is 28, 7ff; Wis 2, 7.
n Jer 7, 31; 19, 5; Ez 20, 28. 31.

---

56, 1–8: Participation in the future messianic salvation is offered to all who believe in the Lord and keep his commandments, regardless of origin or social condition.

56, 3: Eunuchs had originally been excluded from the community of the Lord; cf Dt 23, 2; Wis 3, 14. Dry tree: unable to produce the fruit of offspring.

56, 5: A monument and a name: a memorial inscription to prevent oblivion for one who had no children; cf 2 Sm 18, 18; Neh 7, 15; 13, 14.

56, 9—57, 13: This section is apparently preexilic, written in the manner of the older prophets who condemned the pagan rites of Baal worship.

56, 9: Wild beasts: foreign nations, which are invited to come and ravage Israel.

57, 6: Smooth stones: the Hebrew word for this expression has the same consonants as the word for "portion"; instead of making the Lord their portion (cf Ps 16, 5), the people adored slabs of stone which they took from the streambeds in valleys and set up as idols; cf Jer 3, 9. Therefore, it is implied, they will be swept away as by a sudden torrent of waters carrying them down the rocky-bottomed gorge to destruction and death without burial.

7 Upon a high and lofty mountain
you made your bed,
and there you went up to offer sacrifice.[o]
8 Behind the door and the doorpost
you placed your indecent symbol.
Deserting me, you spread out
your high, wide bed;
And of those whose embraces you love
you carved the symbol and gazed upon it
9 While you approached the king* with
scented oil,
and multiplied your perfumes;
While you sent your ambassadors far away,
down even to the nether world.
10 Though worn out by your many misdeeds,
you never said, "It is hopeless";
New strength you found,
and so you did not weaken.

11 Of whom were you afraid? Whom did you
fear,
that you became false
And did not remember me
or give me any thought?
Was I to remain silent and unseeing,
so that you would not have me to fear?
12 I will expose your justice*
and your works;
13 They shall not help you when you cry out,
nor save you in your distress.
All these* the wind shall carry off,
the breeze shall bear away;
But he who takes refuge in me shall inherit
the land,
and possess my holy mountain.

## Comfort for the Afflicted

14 Build up, build up, prepare the way,
remove the stumbling blocks from my
people's path.[p]
15 For thus says he who is high and exalted,
living eternally, whose name is the Holy
One:
On high I dwell, and in holiness,
and with the crushed and dejected in
spirit,
To revive the spirits of the dejected,
to revive the hearts of the crushed.[q]
16 I will not accuse forever,
nor always be angry;
For their spirits would faint before me,
the souls that I have made.
17 Because of their wicked avarice I was angry,
and struck them, hiding myself in wrath,
as they went their own rebellious way.[r]
18 I saw their ways,
but I will heal them and lead them;
I will give full comfort
to them and to those who mourn for
them,
19 I, the Creator, who gave them life.

Peace, peace to the far and the near,
says the LORD; and I will heal them.

20 But the wicked are like the tossing sea
which cannot be calmed,
And its waters cast up mud and filth.
21 No peace for the wicked! says my God.[s]

## CHAPTER 58

### True Fasting

1 Cry out full-throated and unsparingly,
lift up your voice like a trumpet blast;
Tell my people their wickedness,
and the house of Jacob their sins.*
2 They seek me day after day,*
and desire to know my ways,
Like a nation that has done what is just
and not abandoned the law of their God;
They ask me to declare what is due them,
pleased to gain access to God.
3 "Why do we fast, and you do not see it?
afflict ourselves, and you take no note of
it?"

Lo, on your fast day you carry out your own
pursuits,
and drive all your laborers.
4 Yes, your fast ends in quarreling and
fighting,
striking with wicked claw.
Would that today you might fast
so as to make your voice heard on high!
5 Is this the manner of fasting I wish,
of keeping a day of penance:
That a man bow his head like a reed,
and lie in sackcloth and ashes?
Do you call this a fast,
a day acceptable to the LORD?[t]
6 This, rather, is the fasting that I wish:
releasing those bound unjustly,
untying the thongs of the yoke;
Setting free the oppressed,
breaking every yoke;
7 Sharing your bread with the hungry,
sheltering the oppressed and the homeless;
Clothing the naked when you see them,
and not turning your back on your own.[u]
8 Then your light shall break forth like the
dawn,
and your wound shall quickly be healed;
Your vindication shall go before you,
and the glory of the LORD shall be your
rear guard.
9 Then you shall call, and the LORD will
answer,

o Hos 4, 13; Jer 2, 20; Ez 6, 13.
p Is 40, 3f.
q Is 61, 2f.
r Is 56, 11.
s Is 48, 21.
t Zec 7, 5.
u Ez 18, 7. 16; Mt 25, 35.

*

57, 9: The king: the pagan god Moloch. Ambassadors: children sent to him through a sacrificial death.

57, 12: Justice: here used ironically.

57, 13: All these: the wicked mentioned in Is 57, 3–10.

58, 1: This command is directed to the prophet.

58, 2–14: Merely external worship does not avail with God; it must be joined to internal sincerity.

you shall cry for help, and he will say:
Here I am!
If you remove from your midst oppression,
false accusation and malicious speech;
10 If you bestow your bread on the hungry
and satisfy the afflicted;
Then light shall rise for you in the darkness,
and the gloom shall become for you like
midday;
11 Then the LORD will guide you always
and give you plenty even on the parched
land.
He will renew your strength,
and you shall be like a watered garden,
like a spring whose water never fails.[v]
12 The ancient ruins shall be rebuilt for your
sake,
and the foundations from ages past you
shall raise up;
''Repairer of the breach,'' they shall call
you,
''Restorer of ruined homesteads.''[w]

13 If you hold back your foot on the sabbath
from following your own pursuits on my
holy day;
If you call the sabbath a delight,
and the LORD's holy day honorable;
If you honor it by not following your ways,
seeking your own interests, or speaking
with malice—
14 Then you shall delight in the LORD,
and I will make you ride on the heights of
the earth;
I will nourish you with the heritage of
Jacob, your father,
for the mouth of the LORD has spoken.

## CHAPTER 59

### Sin and Confession

1 Lo, the hand of the LORD is not too short to
save,
nor his ear too dull to hear.[x]
2 Rather, it is your crimes
that separate you from your God,
It is your sins that make him hide his face
so that he will not hear you.
3 For your hands are stained with blood,
your fingers with guilt;
Your lips speak falsehood,
and your tongue utters deceit.[y]
4 No one brings suit justly,
no one pleads truthfully;
They trust in emptiness* and tell lies;
they conceive mischief and bring forth
malice.
5 They hatch adders' eggs,*
and weave spiders' webs:
Whoever eats their eggs will die,
if one of them is pressed, it will hatch as
a viper;[z]
6 Their webs cannot serve as clothing,
nor can they cover themselves with their
works.
Their works are evil works,
and deeds of violence come from their
hands.
7 Their feet run to evil,
and they are quick to shed innocent blood;
Their thoughts are destructive thoughts,
plunder and ruin are on their highways.[a]
8 The way of peace they know not,
and there is nothing that is right in their
paths;
Their ways they have made crooked,
whoever threads them knows no peace.

9 That is why right is far from us*
and justice does not reach us.
We look for light, and lo, darkness;
for brightness, but we walk in gloom!
10 Like blind men we grope along the wall,
like people without eyes we feel our way.
We stumble at midday as at dusk,
in Stygian darkness, like the dead.
11 We all growl like bears,
like doves we moan without ceasing.
We look for right, but it is not there;
for salvation, and it is far from us.[b]
12 For our offenses before you are many,
our sins bear witness against us.
Yes, our offenses are present to us,
and our crimes we know:
13 Transgressing, and denying the LORD,
turning back from following our God,
Threatening outrage, and apostasy,
uttering words of falsehood the heart has
conceived.
14 Right is repelled,
and justice stands far off;
For truth stumbles in the public square,
uprightness cannot enter.
15 Honesty is lacking,
and the man who turns from evil is
despoiled.

### The Redeemer in Zion

The LORD saw this, and was aggrieved
that right did not exist.
16 He saw that there was no one,
and was appalled that there was none to
intervene;
So his own arm brought about the victory,
and his justice lent him its support.
17 He put on justice as his breastplate,

v Is 51, 3; Ps 24.
w Is 61, 4.
x Is 50, 2; Nm 11, 23.
y Is 1, 15.
z Jb 20, 12-16.
a Rom 3, 15.
b Is 38, 14.
c Wis 5, 17ff; Eph 6, 14; 1 Thes 5, 8.

59, 4: Emptiness: things having no value.

59, 5f: A proverb signifying evil works—adders' eggs—and useless devices—spiders' webs; the former do positive harm to oneself and others, the latter serve no useful purpose.

59, 9-15: Spoken by the people through the mouth of the prophet.

salvation, as the helmet on his head;
He clothed himself with garments of
vengeance,
wrapped himself in a mantle of zeal.[c]
18 He repays his enemies their deserts,
and requites his foes with wrath.
19 Those in the west shall fear the name of the
LORD,
and those in the east, his glory;
For it shall come like a pent-up river
which the breath of the LORD drives on.
20 He shall come to Zion a redeemer
to those of Jacob who turn from sin, says
the LORD.[d]
21 This is the covenant with them
which I myself have made, says the
LORD:
My spirit which is upon you
and my words that I have put into your
mouth
Shall never leave your mouth,
nor the mouths of your children
Nor the mouths of your children's children
from now on and forever, says the LORD.

## CHAPTER 60

### Glory of the New Zion

1 Rise up in splendor! Your light has come,*
the glory of the Lord shines upon you.
2 See, darkness covers the earth,
and thick clouds cover the peoples;
But upon you the LORD shines,
and over you appears his glory.
3 Nations shall walk by your light,
and kings by your shining radiance.[e]
4 Raise your eyes and look about;
they all gather and come to you:
Your sons come from afar,
and your daughters in the arms of their
nurses.[f]

5 Then you shall be radiant at what you see,
your heart shall throb and overflow,
For the riches of the sea shall be emptied
out before you,
the wealth of nations shall be brought to
you.
6 Caravans of camels shall fill you,
dromedaries from Midian and Ephah;
All from Sheba shall come
bearing gold and frankincense,
and proclaiming the praises of the LORD.
7 All the flocks of Kedar shall be gathered for
you,
the rams of Nebaioth shall be your
sacrifices;
They will be acceptable offerings on my
altar,
and I will enhance the splendor of my
house.

8 What are these that fly along like clouds,
like doves* to their cotes?
9 All the vessels of the sea are assembled,
with the ships of Tarshish in the lead,
To bring your children from afar
with their silver and gold,
In the name of the LORD, your God,
the Holy One of Israel, who has glorified
you.

10 Foreigners shall rebuild your walls,
and their kings shall be your attendants;
Though I struck you in my wrath,
yet in my good will I have shown you
mercy.
11 Your gates shall stand open constantly;
day and night they shall not be closed
But shall admit to you the wealth of nations,
and their kings, in the vanguard.[g]
12 For the people or kingdom shall perish
that does not serve you;
those nations shall be utterly destroyed.
13 The glory of Lebanon* shall come to you:
the cypress, the plane and the pine,
To bring beauty to my sanctuary,
and glory to the place where I set my
feet.[h]
14 The children of your oppressors shall come,
bowing low before you;
All those who despised you
shall fall prostrate at your feet.
They shall call you "City of the LORD,"
"Zion of the Holy One of Israel."

15 Once you were forsaken,
hated and unvisited,
Now I will make you the pride of the ages,
a joy to generation after generation.[i]
16 You shall suck the milk of nations,
and be nursed at royal breasts;
You shall know that I, the LORD, am your
savior,
your redeemer, the mighty one of Jacob.
17 In place of bronze I will bring gold,
instead of iron, silver;
In place of wood, bronze,
instead of stones, iron;
I will appoint peace your governor,
and justice your ruler.
18 No longer shall violence be heard of in your
land,
or plunder and ruin within your
boundaries.
You shall call your walls "Salvation"
and your gates "Praise."

d Rom 11, 26f.
e Is 42. 6; 45, 14; 49, 6.
f Is 49, 18.
g Rv 21, 25.
h Is 35, 2.
i Ez 16.

60, 1–6: The Church makes use of these verses for the first reading of the Mass on the feast of Epiphany, for she sees in them symbols of her universality.

60, 8f: Like clouds, like doves: the white sails of the ships of Tarshish; cf note on Ps 48, 8.

60, 13: Glory of Lebanon: the cedars, together with the cypress, the plane and the pine, all precious, durable wood.

19 No longer shall the sun
be your light by day,
Nor the brightness of the moon
shine upon you at night;
The LORD shall be your light forever,
your God shall be your glory.[j]
20 No longer shall your sun go down,
or your moon withdraw,
For the LORD will be your light forever,
and the days of your mourning shall be at an end.
21 Your people shall all be just,
they shall always possess the land,
They, the bud of my planting,
my handiwork to show my glory.
22 The smallest shall become a thousand,
the youngest, a mighty nation;
I, the LORD, will swiftly accomplish these things
when their time comes.[k]

## CHAPTER 61

### The Mission to the Afflicted

1 The spirit of the Lord GOD is upon me,*
because the LORD has anointed me;
He has sent me to bring glad tidings to the lowly,
to heal the brokenhearted,
To proclaim liberty to the captives
and release to the prisoners,[l]
2 To announce a year of favor from the LORD
and a day of vindication by our God,
to comfort all who mourn;[m]
3 To place on those who mourn in Zion
a diadem instead of ashes,
To give them oil of gladness in place of mourning,
a glorious mantle instead of a listless spirit.
They will be called oaks of justice,
planted by the LORD to show his glory.

### The Reward of Israel

4 They shall rebuild the ancient ruins,
the former wastes they shall raise up
And restore the ruined cities,
desolate now for generations.[n]
5 Strangers shall stand ready to pasture your flocks,
foreigners shall be your farmers and vinedressers.
6 You yourselves shall be named priests of the LORD,
ministers of our God you shall be called.
You shall eat the wealth of the nations
and boast of riches from them.
7 Since their shame was double
and disgrace and spittle were their portion,
They shall have a double inheritance in their land,
everlasting joy shall be theirs.[o]
8 For I, the LORD, love what is right,
I hate robbery and injustice;
I will give them their recompense faithfully,
a lasting covenant I will make with them.[p]
9 Their descendants shall be renowned among the nations,
and their offspring among the peoples;
All who see them shall acknowledge them
as a race the LORD has blessed.
10 I rejoice heartily in the LORD,
in my God is the joy of my soul;
For he has clothed me with a robe of salvation,
and wrapped me in a mantle of justice,
Like a bridegroom adorned with a diadem,
like a bride bedecked with her jewels.
11 As the earth brings forth its plants,
and a garden makes its growth spring up,
So will the Lord GOD make justice and praise
spring up before all the nations.

## CHAPTER 62

### Jerusalem the Lord's Bride

1 For Zion's sake I will not be silent,
for Jerusalem's sake I will not be quiet,
Until her vindication shines forth like the dawn
and her victory like a burning torch.
2 Nations shall behold your vindication,
and all kings your glory;
You shall be called by a new name*
pronounced by the mouth of the LORD.[q]
3 You shall be a glorious crown in the hand of the LORD,
a royal diadem held by your God.
4 No more shall men call you "Forsaken,"
or your land "Desolate,"
But you shall be called "My Delight,"
and your land "Espoused."
For the LORD delights in you,
and makes your land his spouse.[r]
5 As a young man marries a virgin,
your Builder shall marry you;
And as a bridegroom rejoices in his bride
so shall your God rejoice in you.

j Rv 21, 23; 22, 5.
k Gn 12, 2; 17, 6.
l Is 42, 1; 48, 16; Lk 4, 18f.
m Mt 5, 5.
n Is 58, 12.
o Is 40, 2.
p Is 55, 3; 59, 21.
q Rv 2, 17; 3, 12.
r Is 49, 15f; 54, 1ff.

*

61, 1f: This was spoken by the prophet in regard to the restoration of Zion, but quoted by Christ as referring to his mission; cf Lk 4, 18f. Year of favor . . . day of vindication: the time of God's salvation.

62, 2: New name: figurative expression for a new state of happiness; cf Rv 2, 17; 3, 12.

## Restoration of Zion

6 Upon your walls, O Jerusalem,
I have stationed watchmen;
Never, by day or by night,
shall they be silent.
O you who are to remind the LORD,*
take no rest
7 And give no rest to him,
until he re-establishes Jerusalem
And makes of it
the pride of the earth.

8 The LORD has sworn by his right hand
and by his mighty arm:
No more will I give your grain
as food to your enemies;
Nor shall foreigners drink your wine,
for which you toiled.[s]
9 But you who harvest the grain shall eat it,
and you shall praise the LORD;
You who gather the grapes shall drink the
wine
in the courts of my sanctuary.[t]

10 Pass through, pass through the gates,
prepare the way for the people;[u]
Build up, build up the highway,
clear it of stones,
raise up a standard over the nations.*
11 See, the LORD proclaims
to the ends of the earth:
Say to daughter Zion,
your savior comes!
Here is his reward with him,
his recompense before him.[v]
12 They shall be called the holy people,
the redeemed of the LORD,
And you shall be called "Frequented,"
a city that is not forsaken.[w]

## CHAPTER 63

## Punishment of Edom*

1 Who is this that comes from Edom,
in crimsoned garments, from Bozrah—
This one arrayed in majesty,
marching in the greatness of his strength?
"It is I, I who announce vindication,
I who am mighty to save."
2 Why is your apparel red,
and your garments like those of the wine
presser?[x]

3 "The wine press I have trodden alone,
and of my people there was no one with
me.
I trod them in my anger,
and trampled them down in my wrath;
Their blood spurted on my garments;
all my apparel I stained.
4 For the day of vengeance was in my heart,
my year for redeeming was at hand.[y]
5 I looked about, but there was no one to
help,
I was appalled that there was no one to
lend support;
So my own arm brought about the victory
and my own wrath lent me its support.[z]
6 I trampled down the peoples in my anger,
I crushed them in my wrath,
and I let their blood run out upon the
ground."

## Prayer for the Return of God's Favor*

7 The favors of the LORD I will recall,
the glorious deeds of the LORD,
Because of all he has done for us;
for he is good to the house of Israel,
He has favored us according to his mercy
and his great kindness.[a]

8 He said: They are indeed my people,
children who are not disloyal;
So he became their savior
9 in their every affliction.
It was not a messenger or an angel,
but he himself who saved them.
Because of his love and pity
he redeemed them himself,
Lifting them and carrying them
all the days of old.[b]
10 But they rebelled, and grieved
his holy spirit;
So he turned on them like an enemy,
and fought against them.

11 Then they remembered the days of old
and Moses, his servant;
Where is he who brought up out of the sea
the shepherd of his flock?
Where is he who put his holy spirit
in their midst;
12 Whose glorious arm
was the guide at Moses' right;
Who divided the waters before them,
winning for himself eternal renown;
13 Who led them without stumbling through the
depths

s Is 52, 10.
t Dt 12, 17f; 14, 23.
u Is 58, 14.
v Is 40, 10.
w Is 62, 4.
x Rv 19, 13.
y Is 34, 8; 61, 2.
z Is 59, 16.
a Is 26, 15.
b Dt 4, 37f.

*

62, 6f: Remind the Lord . . . give no rest to him: figuratively, as though to make certain that the Lord will remember his pledge to Jerusalem. Cf Lk 11, 7f.

62, 10: The command is given to the workmen to begin the reconstruction of the city.

63, 1–6: In a dramatic dialogue between God and the prophet, the Lord is portrayed as the sole avenger of justice against his enemies.

63, 7—64, 11: A prayer probably composed toward the end of the exile, in which the prophet, after recalling God's blessings on Israel in its past history (63, 7–10), especially at the Exodus (11–14), begs the Lord to come once more to the aid of his people (63, 15—64, 3), who now humbly confess their sins (4–11).

like horses in the open country,
14 Like cattle going down into the plain,
the spirit of the LORD guiding them?
Thus you led your people,
bringing glory to your name.

15 Look down from heaven and regard us
from your holy and glorious palace!
Where is your zealous care and your might,
your surge of pity and your mercy?[c]
O Lord, hold not back,
16 for you are our father.
Were Abraham not to know us,
nor Israel to acknowledge us,
You, LORD, are our father,
our redeemer you are named forever.
17 Why do you let us wander, O Lord, from your ways,
and harden our hearts so that we fear you not?
Return for the sake of your servants,
the tribes of your heritage.
18 Why have the wicked invaded your holy place,
why have our enemies trampled your sanctuary?
19 Too long have we been like those you do not rule,
who do not bear your name.
Oh, that you would rend the heavens and come down,
with the mountains quaking before you,

## CHAPTER 64

1 As when brushwood is set ablaze,
or fire makes the water boil!
Thus your name would be made known to your enemies
and the nations would tremble before you,
2 While you wrought awesome deeds we could
not hope for,
3 such as they had not heard of from of old.
No ear has ever heard, no eye ever seen,
any God but you
doing such deeds for those who wait for him.[d]
4 Would that you might meet us doing right,
that we were mindful of you in our ways!
Behold, you are angry, and we are sinful;
5 all of us have become like unclean men,
all our good deeds are like polluted rags;
We have all withered like leaves,
and our guilt carries us away like the wind.
6 There is none who calls upon your name,
who rouses himself to cling to you;
For you have hidden your face from us
and have delivered us up to our guilt.
7 Yet, O LORD, you are our father;
we are the clay and you the potter:
we are all the work of your hands.
8 Be not so very angry, LORD,
keep not our guilt forever in mind;
look upon us, who are all your people.
9 Your holy cities have become a desert,
Zion is a desert, Jerusalem a waste.[e]
10 Our holy and glorious temple
in which our fathers praised you
Has been burned with fire;
all that was dear to us is laid waste.
11 Can you hold back, O LORD, after all this?
Can you remain silent, and afflict us so severely?

## CHAPTER 65

### Necessity of Punishment

1 I was ready to respond to those who asked me not,
to be found by those who sought me not.
I said: Here I am! Here I am!
To a nation that did not call upon my name.[f]
2 I have stretched out my hands all the day
to a rebellious people,
Who walk in evil paths
and follow their own thoughts,[g]
3 People who provoke me
continually, to my face,
Offering sacrifices in the groves
and burning incense on bricks,
4 Living among the graves
and spending the night in caverns,
Eating swine's flesh,
with carrion broth in their dishes,
5 Crying out, "Hold back,
do not touch me; I am too sacred for you!" *

These things enkindle my wrath,
a fire that burns all the day.
6 Lo, before me it stands written;
I will not be quiet until I have paid in full
7 Your crimes and the crimes of your fathers as well,
says the LORD.
Since they burned incense on the mountains,
and disgraced me on the hills,
I will at once pour out in full measure
their recompense into their laps.

### Fate of the Good and the Bad in Israel

8 Thus says the LORD:
When the juice is pressed from grapes,
men say, "Do not discard them,
for there is still good in them";
Thus will I do with my servants:
I will not discard them all;
9 From Jacob I will save offspring,

c Dt 26, 15; Bar 2, 16.
d 1 Cor 2, 9.
e Ps 79, 1.
f Rom 10, 20.
g Rom 10, 21.

* 65, 5: I am too sacred for you: the uncleanness of pork, obvious to a Semite, is what these people claim has made them sacred! The prophet ridicules them. Some translate: "I will render you sacred," and understand this as referring to the concept of sacredness as something contagious.

from Judah, those who are to inherit my mountains;
My chosen ones shall inherit the land,
my servants shall dwell there.
10 Sharon shall be a pasture for the flocks
and the valley of Achor a resting place for the cattle
of my people who have sought me.

11 But you who forsake the LORD,
forgetting my holy mountain,
You who spread a table for Fortune
and fill cups of blended wine for Destiny,*
12 You I will destine for the sword;
you shall all go down in slaughter.
Since I called and you did not answer,
I spoke and you did not listen,
But did what was evil in my sight
and preferred things which displease me,[h]
13 therefore thus says the Lord GOD:
Lo, my servants shall eat,
but you shall go hungry;
My servants shall drink,
but you shall be thirsty;
My servants shall rejoice,
but you shall be put to shame;
14 My servants shall shout
for joy of heart,
But you shall cry out for grief of heart
and howl for anguish of spirit.
15 The Lord GOD shall slay you,
and the name you leave
Shall be used by my chosen ones for cursing;
but my servants shall be called by another name
16 By which he will be blessed
on whom a blessing is invoked in the land;
He who takes an oath in the land
shall swear by the God of truth;
For the hardships of the past shall be forgotten,
and hidden from my eyes.

## The World Renewed

17 Lo, I am about to create new heavens
and a new earth;
The things of the past shall not be remembered
or come to mind.[i]
18 Instead, there shall always be rejoicing and happiness
in what I create;
For I create Jerusalem to be a joy
and its people to be a delight;
19 I will rejoice in Jerusalem
and exult in my people.
No longer shall the sound of weeping be heard there,
or the sound of crying;
20 No longer shall there be in it
an infant who lives but a few days,
or an old man who does not round out his full lifetime;
He dies a mere youth who reaches but a hundred years,
and he who fails of a hundred shall be thought accursed.

21 They shall live in the houses they build,
and eat the fruit of the vineyards they plant;
22 They shall not build houses for others to live in,
or plant for others to eat.
As the years of a tree, so the years of my people;
and my chosen ones shall long enjoy
the produce of their hands.
23 They shall not toil in vain,
nor beget children for sudden destruction;
For a race blessed by the LORD
are they and their offspring.
24 Before they call, I will answer;
while they are yet speaking, I will hearken to them.
25 The wolf and the lamb shall graze alike,
and the lion shall eat hay like the ox
[but the serpent's food shall be dust].[j]
None shall hurt or destroy
on all my holy mountain, says the LORD.*

## CHAPTER 66

## True and False Worship

1 Thus says the LORD:
The heavens are my throne,
the earth is my footstool.
What kind of house can you build for me;
what is to be my resting place?[k]
2 My hand made all these things
when all of them came to be, says the LORD.
This is the one whom I approve:
the lowly and afflicted man who trembles at my word.

3 Merely slaughtering an ox is like slaying a man;
sacrificing a lamb, like breaking a dog's neck;
Bringing a cereal offering, like offering swine's blood;
burning incense, like paying homage to an idol.
Since these have chosen their own ways
and taken pleasure in their own abominations,[l]

h Is 66, 4; Prv 1, 24; Jer 7, 13.
i Is 66, 22; Rv 21, 1.
j Is 11, 6-9.
k 2 Sm 7, 4ff; 1 Kgs 8, 27; Acts 7, 49; 17, 24.
l Lv 11, 7.

*

65, 11f: Destiny: the Hebrew also has a play on the words: Destiny and destine; meni and manithi.

65, 25: See note on Is 11, 6–9.

4 I in turn will choose ruthless treatment for them*
and bring upon them what they fear.

Because, when I called, no one answered,
when I spoke, no one listened;
Because they did what was evil in my sight,
and chose what gave me displeasure,[m]
5 Hear the word of the LORD,
you who tremble at his word:
Your brethren who, because of my name,
hate and reject you, say,
"Let the LORD show his glory
that we may see your joy";
but they shall be put to shame.
6 A sound of roaring from the city,
a sound from the temple,
The sound of the LORD
repaying his enemies their deserts![n]

## Mother Zion

7 Before she comes to labor,*
she gives birth;[o]
Before the pains come upon her,
she safely delivers a male child.
8 Who ever heard of such a thing,
or saw the like?
Can a country be brought forth in one day,
or a nation be born in a single moment?
Yet Zion is scarcely in labor
when she gives birth to her children.
9 Shall I bring a mother to the point of birth,
and yet not let her child be born? says the LORD;
Or shall I who allow her to conceive,
yet close her womb? says your God.

10 Rejoice with Jerusalem and be glad because of her,
all you who love her;
Exult, exult with her,
all you who were mourning over her!
11 Oh, that you may suck fully
of the milk of her comfort,
That you may nurse with delight
at her abundant breasts!
12 For thus says the LORD:
Lo, I will spread prosperity over her like a river,
and the wealth of the nations like
an overflowing torrent.
As nurslings, you shall be carried in her arms,
and fondled in her lap;
13 As a mother comforts her son,
so will I comfort you;
in Jerusalem you shall find your comfort.

14 When you see this, your heart shall rejoice,
and your bodies flourish like the grass;
The LORD's power shall be known to his servants,
but to his enemies, his wrath.

15 Lo, the LORD shall come in fire,
his chariots like the whirlwind,
To wreak his wrath with burning heat
and his punishment with fiery flames.
16 For the LORD shall judge all mankind
by fire and sword,
and many shall be slain by the LORD.

17 They who sanctify and purify themselves
to go to the groves, as followers of one who
stands within, they who eat swine's flesh, loathsome things and mice, shall all perish with their
deeds and their thoughts, says the LORD.[p]

**Gathering of the Nations.** 18 I come to
gather nations of every language; they shall
come and see my glory.* 19 I will set a sign
among them; from them I will send fugitives to
the nations: to Tarshish, Put and Lud, Mosoch,
Tubal and Javan, to the distant coastlands that
have never heard of my fame, or seen my glory;
and they shall proclaim my glory among the
nations. 20 They shall bring all your brethren
from all the nations as an offering to the LORD,
on horses and in chariots, in carts, upon mules
and dromedaries, to Jerusalem, my holy mountain, says the LORD, just as the Israelites bring
their offering to the house of the LORD in clean
vessels. 21 Some of these I will take as priests
and Levites, says the LORD.

## Lasting Reward and Punishment

22 As the new heavens and the new earth
which I will make
Shall endure before me, says the LORD,
so shall your race and your name endure.[q]
23 From one new moon to another,
and from one sabbath to another,
All mankind shall come to worship
before me, says the LORD.
24 They shall go out and see the corpses[r]
of the men who rebelled against me;
Their worm shall not die,
nor their fire be extinguished;
and they shall be abhorrent to all mankind.*

m Is 65, 12; Prv 1, 24; Jer 7, 13.
n Jl 4, 16; Am 1, 2.
o 7-9: Is 49, 18-21; 54, 1.
p Lv 11, 29.
q Is 65, 17; Rv 21, 1.
r Mk 9, 45.

*

66, 4f: Worship which is merely external is as evil as though it were idolatry.

66, 7–9: The absence of labor in Zion's childbearing is a symbol of the joyful begetting of the new people of God.

66, 18–21: God summons the neighboring nations to Zion and from among them will send some to far distant lands to proclaim his glory. All your brethren: Jews in exile.

66, 24: God's enemies lie dead outside the walls of the New Jerusalem; Just as in the past, corpses, filth and refuse lay in the Valley of Hinnom outside the city, where huge fires were constantly burning; cf Jos 15, 8; 2 Chr 28, 3; Mk 9, 45–48.

# The Book of

# JEREMIAH

*The Book of Jeremiah combines history, biography, and prophecy. It portrays a nation in crisis and introduces the reader to an extraordinary leader upon whom the Lord placed the heavy burden of the prophetic office. Jeremiah was born about 650 B.C. of a priestly family from the little village of Anathoth, near Jerusalem. While still very young he was called to his task in the thirteenth year of King Josiah (628), whose reform, begun with enthusiasm and hope, ended with his death on the battlefield of Megiddo (609) as he attempted to stop the northward march of the Egyptian Pharaoh Neco.*

*The prophet heartily supported the reform of the pious King Josiah, which began in 629 B.C. Nineveh, the capital of Assyria, fell in 612, preparing the way for the new colossus, Babylon, which was soon to put an end to Judean independence.*

*After the death of Josiah the old idolatry returned. Jeremiah opposed it with all his strength. Arrest, imprisonment, and public disgrace were his lot. Jeremiah saw in the nation's impenitence the sealing of its doom. Nebuchadnezzar captured Jerusalem and carried King Jehoiachin into exile (22, 24).*

*During the years 598–587, Jeremiah attempted to counsel Zedekiah in the face of bitter opposition. The false prophet Hananiah proclaimed that the yoke of Babylon was broken and a strong pro-Egyptian party in Jerusalem induced Zedekiah to revolt. Nebuchadnezzar took swift and terrible vengeance; Jerusalem was destroyed in 587 and its leading citizens sent into exile. About this time Jeremiah uttered the great oracle of the "New Covenant" (31, 31–34) sometimes called "The Gospel before the Gospel." This passage contains his most sublime teaching and is a landmark in Old Testament theology.*

*The prophet remained amidst the ruins of Jerusalem, but was later forced into Egyptian exile by a band of conspirators. There, according to an old tradition, he was murdered by his own countrymen. The influence of Jeremiah was greater after his death than before. The exiled community read and meditated the lessons of the prophet, and his influence can be seen in Ezekiel, certain of the psalms, and the second part of Isaiah. Shortly after the exile, the Book of Jeremiah as we have it today was published in a final edition.*

*It is divided as follows:*

*I. Oracles in the Days of Josiah (1, 1—6, 30).*
*II. Oracles Mostly in the Days of Jehoiakim (7, 1—20, 18).*
*III. Oracles in the Last Years of Jerusalem (21, 1—33, 26).*
*IV. Fall of Jerusalem (34, 1—45, 5).*
*V. Oracles against the Nations (46, 1—51, 64).*
*VI. Historical Appendix (52, 1—34).*

## *I: Oracles in the Days of Josiah*

### CHAPTER 1

**1** The words of Jeremiah, son of Hilkiah, of
a priestly family in Anathoth,* in the land of
Benjamin. **2** The word of the LORD first came
to him in the days of Josiah, son of Amon, king
of Judah, in the thirteenth year of his reign,[a]
**3** and continued through the reign of Jehoiakim, son of Josiah, king of Judah, and until the
downfall* and exile of Jerusalem in the fifth
month of the eleventh year of Zedekiah, son of
Josiah, king of Judah.[b]

#### Call of Jeremiah

**4** The word of the LORD came to me thus:

a Jer 25, 3. b Jer 25, 1.

*

1, 1: Anathoth: a village about three miles northeast of Jerusalem, where Solomon exiled Abiathar (1 Kgs 2, 26f); it is probable that Jeremiah belonged to the priestly family of Abiathar.

1, 3: Until the downfall: these words were originally prefixed as a title to a collection of Jeremiah's prophecies which lacked chapters 40–44. The new title in Jer 40, 1 and the oracles that follow clearly show that Jeremiah continued to prophesy after the destruction of Jerusalem in 587 B.C.

5 Before I formed you in the womb I knew
you,*
before you were born I dedicated you,
a prophet to the nations I appointed you.[c]
6 "Ah, LORD GOD!" I said,
"I know not how to speak; I am too
young."*

7 But the LORD answered me,

Say not, "I am too young."
To whomever I send you, you shall go;
whatever I command you, you shall
speak.
8 Have no fear before them,
because I am with you to deliver you,
says the LORD.

9 Then the LORD extended his hand and
touched my mouth, saying,

See, I place my words in your mouth![d]
10 This day I set you
over nations and over kingdoms,
To root up and to tear down,
to destroy and to demolish,
to build and to plant.

11 The word of the LORD came to me with
the question: What do you see, Jeremiah? "I see
a branch of the watching-tree,"* I replied.
12 Then the LORD said to me: Well have you
seen, for I am watching to fulfill my word.
13 [e]A second time the word of the LORD came
to me with the question: What do you see? "I
see a boiling cauldron," I replied, "that appears
from the north."*
14 And from the north, said the LORD to me,
evil will boil over upon all who dwell in the
land.[f]

15 Lo, I am summoning
all the kingdoms of the north, says the
LORD;
Each king shall come and set up his throne
at the gateways of Jerusalem,
Opposite her walls all around
and opposite all the cities of Judah.[g]
16 I will pronounce my sentence against them
for all their wickedness in forsaking me,
And in burning incense to strange gods
and adoring their own handiwork.[h]

17 But do you gird your loins;
stand up and tell them
all that I command you.
Be not crushed on their account,
as though I would leave you crushed
before them;
18 For it is I this day
who have made you a fortified city,
A pillar of iron, a wall of brass,
against the whole land:
Against Judah's kings and princes,
against its priests and people.[i]
19 They will fight against you, but not prevail
over you,
for I am with you to deliver you, says the
LORD.

## CHAPTER 2

**Infidelity of Israel.** 1 *This word of the
LORD came to me: 2 Go, cry out this message
for Jerusalem to hear!

I remember the devotion* of your youth,
how you loved me as a bride,
Following me in the desert,
in a land unsown.[j]
3 Sacred to the LORD was Israel,
the first fruits* of his harvest;
Should anyone presume to partake of them,
evil would befall him, says the LORD.[k]

4 Listen to the word of the LORD, O house of
Jacob!
All you clans of the house of Israel,
5 thus says the LORD:
What fault did your fathers find in me
that they withdrew from me,
Went after empty idols,
and became empty themselves?[l]
6 They did not ask, "Where is the LORD
who brought us up from the land of
Egypt,
Who led us through the desert,
through a land of wastes and gullies,

c Jer 49, 1; Gal 1, 15f.
d Is 6, 7.
e Ez 11, 3. 7; 24, 3.
f Jer 4, 6; 6, 1.
g Jer 6, 22.
h Is 2, 8.
i Jer 6, 27; 15, 20; Ex 3, 8.
j Dt 2, 7; 32, 9-12; Mi 6, 4.
k Jer 12, 14; Ex 4, 22; Dt 7, 6; 14, 2.
l Is 5, 4; Mi 6, 3.
m Ex 20, 2f; Dt 8, 14; Is 63, 11ff.

*

1, 5: Jeremiah was destined to the office of prophet before his birth; cf Is 49, 1. 5; Lk 1, 15; Gal 1, 15f. I knew you: I loved you and chose you. I dedicated you: I set you apart to be a prophet. Some Fathers and later theologians understand this to mean that Jeremiah was freed from original sin before his birth. The context does not justify this conclusion. The nations: the pagan neighbors of Judah, besides the great world powers—Assyria, Babylonia, Egypt—intimately associated with Judah's destiny.

1, 6: I am too young: Jeremiah's youth (he was less than thirty years old) must not be an obstacle to the responsibilities of the prophetic office; God will supply for his human defects (cf vv 7f).

1, 11: The watching-tree: the almond tree, which is the first to blossom in the springtime as though it had not slept. The Hebrew name contains a play on words with "I am watching."

1, 13: Boiling cauldron . . . the north: symbol of an invasion from the north; cf vv 14f.

2, 1—3, 5: These verses probably contain the earliest of Jeremiah's preachings. The covenant relationship, symbolized by the figure of a marriage, was frequently broken by Israel, seen here as an unfaithful wife unworthy of reconciliation with God (Jer 3, 1–5).

2, 2: Devotion: Israel's gratitude, fidelity, and love for God.

2, 3: First fruits: an offering to God which became his exclusive property, and could therefore not be put to profane use; cf Lv 22, 1.

Through a land of drought and darkness,
through a land which no one crosses,
where no man dwells?"[m]

7 When I brought you into the garden land
to eat its goodly fruits,
You entered and defiled my land,
you made my heritage loathsome.[n]
8 The priests asked not,
"Where is the LORD?"
Those who dealt with the law* knew me
not:
the shepherds rebelled against me.
The prophets prophesied by Baal,
and went after useless idols.[o]
9 Therefore will I yet accuse you, says the
LORD,
and even your children's children I will
accuse.[p]
10 Pass over to the coast of the Kittim* and
see,
send to Kedar and carefully inquire:
Where has the like of this been done?
11 Does any other nation change its gods?—
yet they are not gods at all!
But my people have changed their glory
for useless things.[q]
12 Be amazed at this, O heavens,
and shudder with sheer horror, says the
LORD.
13 Two evils have my people done:
they have forsaken me, the source of
living waters;
They have dug themselves cisterns,
broken cisterns, that hold no water.[r]

14 Is Israel a slave, a bondman by birth?*
Why then has he become booty?
15 Against him lions roar
full-throated cries.
They have made his land a waste;
his cities are charred ruins, without
inhabitant.[s]
16 Yes, the people of Memphis* and
Tahpanhes
shave the crown of your head.
17 Has not the forsaking of the LORD, your
God,
done this to you?[t]
18 And now, why go to Egypt,*
to drink the waters of the Nile?
Why go to Assyria,
to drink the waters of the Euphrates?
19 Your own wickedness chastises you,
your own infidelities punish you.
Know then, and see, how evil and bitter
is your forsaking the LORD, your God,
And showing no fear of me,
says the Lord, the GOD of hosts.[u]

20 Long ago you broke your yoke,[v]
you tore off your bonds.
"I will not serve," you said.
On every high hill, under every green tree,
you gave yourself to harlotry.*
21 I had planted you, a choice vine
of fully tested stock;
How could you turn out obnoxious to me,
a spurious vine?[w]
22 Though you scour it with soap,
and use much lye,
The stain of your guilt is still before me,
says the Lord GOD.[x]
23 How can you say, "I am not defiled,
I have not gone after the Baals"?
Consider your conduct in the Valley,*
recall what you have done:
A frenzied she-camel, coursing near and far,
24 breaking away toward the desert,
Snuffing the wind in her ardor—
who can restrain her lust?
No beasts need tire themselves seeking her;
in her month they will meet her.

25 Stop wearing out your shoes
and parching your throat!
But you say, "No use! no!
I love these strangers,
and after them I must go."[y]
26 As the thief is shamed when caught,
so shall the house of Israel be shamed:
They, their kings and their princes,
their priests and their prophets;[z]
27 They who say to a piece of wood, "You are
my father,"
and to a stone, "You gave me birth."
They turn to me their backs, not their faces;
yet, in their time of trouble they cry out,
"Rise up and save us!"
28 Where are the gods you made for
yourselves?
Let them rise up!

n Lv 18, 24f; Dt 8, 7-10; 32, 13f.
o Jer 8, 8ff; 23, 1. 13.
p Ex 20, 5.
q Jer 16, 20; Ps 106, 20.
r Jer 17, 13; Ps 36, 9; Is 1, 4.
s Jer 9, 11.
t Jer 4, 18; 30, 15.
u Prv 5, 22; Hos 5, 5.
v Jer 3, 6. 13; Jgs 10, 6.
w Ex 15, 17; Ps 80, 9; Is 5, 4.
x Jb 9, 30.
y Jer 18, 12.
z Jer 48, 27; Rom 6, 21.
a Jer 11, 13; Dt 32, 38; Jgs 10, 14.

*

2, 8: Those who dealt with the law: the priests. The shepherds: the kings and nobles.

2, 10: Kittim: a Phoenician colony in Cyprus. Kedar: a nomad tribe of the Syrian desert. These two names represent West and East.

2, 14: Bondman by birth: a perpetual slave, different from the debt-slave, who was to be freed after six years; cf Ex 21, 2.

2, 16: Memphis: the capital of Lower Egypt. Tahpanhes: a frontier city of Egypt, east of the Delta. Shave the crown of your head: the spoliation of Judah at the hands of the Egyptians.

2, 18: Egypt and Assyria were the protecting foreign powers favored by rival parties within Judah. The desire for such foreign alliances is a further desertion of the Lord, the source of living waters (v 13), in favor of the above-named powers, symbolized by the Nile and the Euphrates rivers.

2, 20: Harlotry: idolatry (because Israel is the bride of God).

2, 23: The Valley: of Ben-hinnom, south of Jerusalem, site of the infamous sanctuary of Topheth where children were sacrificed to Molech; cf Jer 7, 31.

Will they save you in your time of trouble?
For as numerous as your cities are your gods, O Judah!
And as many as the streets of Jerusalem are the altars you have set up for Baal.[a]

29 How dare you still plead with me?
You have all rebelled against me, says the LORD.
30 In vain I struck your children;
the correction they did not take.
Your sword devoured your prophets
like a ravening lion.[b]
31 You, of this generation,
take note of the word of the Lord:
Have I been a desert to Israel,
a land of darkness?
Why do my people say, "We have moved on,
we will come to you no more"?
32 Does a virgin forget her jewelry,
a bride her sash?
Yet my people have forgotten me
days without number.[c]

33 How well you pick your way
when seeking love!
You who, in your wickedness,
have gone by ways unclean!
34 You, on whose clothing there is
the life-blood of the innocent,
whom you found committing no burglary;
35 Yet withal you say, "I am innocent;
at least, his anger is turned away from me."
Behold, I will judge you
on that word of yours, "I have not sinned."
36 How very base you have become
in changing your course!
By Egypt will you be shamed,
as you were shamed by Assyria.[d]
37 From there also shall you go away
with hands upon your head;
For the LORD has rejected those in whom you trust,
with them you will have no success.[e]

## CHAPTER 3

1 If a man sends away his wife[f]
and, after leaving him,
she marries another man,
Does the first husband come back to her?
Would not the land be wholly defiled?
But you have sinned with many lovers,
and yet you would return to me! says the LORD.*
2 Lift your eyes to the heights, and see,
where have men not lain with you?
By the waysides you waited for them
like an Arab* in the desert.
You defiled the land
by your wicked harlotry.[g]
3 Therefore the showers were withheld,
the spring rain failed.
But because you have a harlot's brow,
you refused to blush.[h]

4 Even now do you not call me, "My father,
you who are the bridegroom of my youth"?
5 "Will he keep his wrath forever,
will he hold his grudge to the end?"
This is what you say; yet you do
all the evil you can.

**Judah and Israel.** 6 The LORD said to me
in the days of King Josiah: See now what rebellious Israel has done! She has gone up every
high mountain, and under every green tree she
has played the harlot.[i] 7 And I thought, after
she has done all this she will return to me. But
she did not return. Then, even though her traitor
sister Judah saw 8 that for all the adulteries
rebellious Israel had committed, I put her away
and gave her a bill of divorce, nevertheless her
traitor sister Judah was not frightened; she too
went off and played the harlot.[j] 9 Eager to sin,
she polluted the land, committing adultery with
stone and wood.[k] 10 With all this, the traitor
sister Judah did not return to me wholeheartedly, but insincerely, says the LORD.

**Restoration of Israel.** 11 Then the LORD
said to me: Rebel Israel is inwardly more just
than traitorous Judah.[l] 12 Go, proclaim these
words toward the north, and say:

Return, rebel Israel, says the LORD,
I will not remain angry with you;
For I am merciful, says the LORD,
I will not continue my wrath forever.[m]
13 Only know your guilt:
how you rebelled against the LORD, your God,
How you ran hither and yon to strangers
[under every green tree]
and would not listen to my voice, says the LORD.[n]
14 Return, rebellious children, says the LORD,*

b Jer 5, 3; Neh 9, 26.
c Jer 13, 25; Dt 32, 18.
d 2 Chr 28, 16-21.
e 2 Sm 13, 19.
f Dt 24, 1-4.
g Ex 16, 24f.
h Jer 6, 15; 8, 12.
i Jer 2, 20; Dt 12, 2.
j 2 Kgs 17, 6. 18-23; Ez 23, 11.
k Jer 2, 27.
l Ez 16, 51; 23, 11.
m Dt 4, 29ff.
n Jer 2, 20. 25; Lv 26, 40.
o Jer 23, 3; Is 10, 21f.

*

3, 1: Such remarriage of divorced spouses was forbidden by Dt 24, 1–4. Under this figure the prophet sees the presumption of Judah, the unfaithful spouse, who thinks she can return to the Lord after uniting herself to other gods.

3, 2: An Arab: a marauding nomad who lay in wait for caravans.

3, 14–18: A remnant of Israel (14) will reunite with Judah (18). The elementary cult of the Lord represented by the ark of the covenant will now be replaced by a more deeply spiritual

for I am your Master;
I will take you, one from a city, two from a clan,
and bring you to Zion.[o]
15 I will appoint over you shepherds after my own heart,
who will shepherd you wisely and prudently.[p]
16 When you multiply and become fruitful in the land,
says the LORD,
They will in those days no longer say,
"The ark of the covenant of the LORD!"
They will no longer think of it, or remember it,
or miss it, or make another.

17 At that time they will call Jerusalem the
LORD's throne; there all nations will be gathered
together to honor the name of the LORD at Jerusalem, and they will walk no longer in their
hardhearted wickedness.[q] 18 In those days the
house of Judah will join the house of Israel;
together they will come from the land of the
north to the land which I gave to your fathers as
a heritage.[r]

## Conditions for Forgiveness

19 I had thought:
How I should like to treat you as sons,
And give you a pleasant land,
a heritage most beautiful among the nations!
You would call me, "My Father," I thought,
and never cease following me.[s]
20 But like a woman faithless to her lover,
even so have you been faithless to me,
O house of Israel, says the LORD.[t]
21 A cry is heard on the heights!
the plaintive weeping of Israel's children,
Because they have perverted their ways
and forgotten the LORD, their God.
22 Return, rebellious children,
and I will cure you of your rebelling.
"Here we are, we now come to you
because you are the LORD, our God.[u]
23 Deceptive indeed are the hills,
the thronging mountains;
In the LORD, our God, alone
is the salvation of Israel.[v]
24 The shame-god* has devoured
our fathers' toil from our youth,
Their sheep and their cattle,
their sons and their daughters.
25 Let us lie down in our shame,
let our disgrace cover us,
for we have sinned against the LORD, our God,
From our youth to this day, we and our fathers also;
we listened not to the voice of the LORD, our God."[w]

## CHAPTER 4

1 If you wish to return, O Israel, says the LORD,
return to me.
If you put your detestable things out of my sight,
and do not stray,[x]
2 Then you can swear, "As the LORD lives,"*
in truth, in judgment, and in justice;
Then shall the nations use his name in blessing,
and glory in him.[y]

3 For to the men of Judah and to Jerusalem,
thus says the LORD:

Till your untilled ground,
sow not among thorns.[z]
4 For the sake of the LORD, be circumcised,*
remove the foreskins of your hearts,
O men of Judah and citizens of Jerusalem:
Lest my anger break out like fire,
and burn till none can quench it,
because of your evil deeds.[a]

## The Invasion from the North

5 Proclaim it in Judah,
make it heard in Jerusalem;
Blow the trumpet through the land,
summon the recruits!
Say, "Fall in, let us march
to the fortified cities."
6 Bear the standard to Zion,
seek refuge without delay!
Evil I bring from the north,
and great destruction.
7 Up comes the lion from his lair,
the destroyer of nations has set out,
has left his place,
To turn your land into desolation,
till your cities lie waste and empty.[b]
8 So gird yourselves with sackcloth,
mourn and wail:
"The blazing wrath of the LORD
is not turned away from us."[c]

p Ez 34, 23; Jn 21, 15.
q Is 2, 2.
r Jer 30, 3; 31, 8.
s Jer 31, 9. 20; Is 63, 16.
t Jer 5, 11.
u Hos 3, 5.
v Jer 14, 8.
w Jer 16, 11f; 22, 21.
x Jer 25, 5.
y Jer 12, 16; Dt 10, 20; Is 65, 16.
z Hos 10, 12; Mt 13, 7. 22.
a Jer 9, 24.
b Jer 2, 15; 5, 6.
c Jer 6, 26; Is 5, 25.

* and universal alliance, symbolized by his throne in the ideal Jerusalem around which all nations will be gathered together (17).

3, 24: Shame-god: literally, shame, a term commonly substituted for Baal, the Canaanite god with many local shrines.

4, 2: As the Lord lives: this oath, made sincerely, implies Israel's return to God and loyal adherence to him. Thus the ancient promises are fulfilled; cf Gn 12, 3; 18, 18; 22, 18; 26, 4; Ps 72, 17.

4, 4: The mere external rite of circumcision avails nothing unless accompanied by the removal of blindness and obstinacy of heart; cf Rm 2, 25. 29; 1 Cor 7, 19; Gal 5, 6; 6, 13. 15.

9 In that day, says the LORD,
The king will lose heart, and the princes;
the priests will be amazed,
and the prophets stunned.
10 "Alas! Lord GOD," they will say,
"You only deceived us*
When you said: Peace shall be yours;
for the sword touches our very soul."[d]
11 At that time it will be said
of this people and of Jerusalem,
"From the glaring heights through the desert
a wind comes toward the daughter of my people."
Not to winnow, not to cleanse,
12 does this wind from the heights come at my
bidding;
And I myself now pronounce
sentence upon them.[e]

13 See! like storm clouds he advances,
like a hurricane his chariots;
Swifter than eagles are his steeds:
"Woe to us! we are ruined."
14 Cleanse your heart of evil, O Jerusalem,
that you may be saved.
How long must your pernicious thoughts
lodge within you?
15 Listen! They proclaim it from Dan,
from Mount Ephraim they announce
destruction:
16 "Make this known to the nations,
announce it to Jerusalem:
The besiegers are coming from the distant
land,
shouting their war cry against the cities of
Judah."[f]
17 Like watchmen of the fields they surround
her,
for she has rebelled against me, says the
LORD.[g]
18 Your conduct, your misdeeds, have done
this to you;
how bitter is this disaster of yours,
how it reaches to your very heart![h]

19 My breast! my breast! how I suffer!*
The walls of my heart!
My heart beats wildly,
I cannot be still;
For I have heard the sound of the trumpet,
the alarm of war.
20 Ruin after ruin is reported;
the whole earth is laid waste.
In an instant my tents are ravaged;
in a flash, my shelters.[i]
21 How long must I see that signal,
hear that trumpet sound!

22 Fools my people are,
they know me not;
Senseless children they are,
having no understanding;
They are wise in evil,
but know not how to do good.[j]

23 I looked at the earth, and it was waste and
void;
at the heavens, and their light had gone
out![k]
24 I looked at the mountains, and they were
trembling,
and all the hills were crumbling!
25 I looked and behold, there was no man;
even the birds of the air had flown away!
26 I looked and behold, the garden land was a
desert,
with all its cities destroyed
before the LORD, before his blazing
wrath.[l]

27 For thus says the LORD:
Waste shall the whole land be;
I will [not] wholly destroy it.[m]
28 Because of this the earth shall mourn,
the heavens above shall darken;
I have spoken, I will not repent,
I have resolved, I will not turn back.[n]
29 At the shout of horseman and bowman
each city takes to flight;
They shrink into the thickets,
they scale the rocks:
All the cities are abandoned,
and no one dwells in them.
30 You now who are doomed, what do you
mean
by putting on purple,
bedecking yourself with gold,
Shading your eyes with cosmetics,
beautifying yourself in vain?
Your lovers spurn you,
they seek your life.
31 Yes, I hear the moaning, as of a woman in
travail,
like the anguish of a mother with her first
child—
The cry of daughter Zion gasping,
as she stretches forth her hands:
"Ah, woe is me! I sink exhausted
before the slayers!"[o]

## CHAPTER 5

## Universal Corruption

1 Roam the streets of Jerusalem,
look about and observe,
Search through her public places,
to find even one
Who lives uprightly
and seeks to be faithful,

d Jer 6, 14.
e Jer 1, 16.
f Jer 5, 15.
g Jer 6, 3.
h Jer 2, 17. 19.
i Jer 10, 20.
j Dt 32, 5f. 28.
k Is 24, 1. 3.
l Lv 26, 31.
m Jer 5, 18.
n Is 24, 4.
o Jer 6, 24.

*

4, 10: You only deceived us: the false prophets blame their deception on God; cf Jer 14, 13–16.

4, 19ff: Probably the prophet's own anguish at the coming destruction of Judah.

and I will pardon her!
2 Though they say, "As the LORD lives,"
they swear falsely.
3 O LORD, do your eyes not look for honesty?
You struck them, but they did not cringe;
you laid them low, but they refused correction;
They set their faces harder than stone,
and refused to return to you.[p]
4 It is only the lowly, I thought,
who are foolish;
For they know not the way of the LORD,
their duty to their God.[q]
5 I will go to the great ones
and speak with them;
For they know the way of the LORD,
their duty to their God.
But, one and all, they had broken the yoke,
torn off the harness.[r]
6 Therefore lions from the forest slay them,
wolves of the desert ravage them,
Leopards keep watch round their cities:
all who come out are torn to pieces
For their many crimes
and their numerous rebellions.

7 Why should I pardon you these things?
Your sons have forsaken me,
they swear by gods that are not.
I fed them, but they committed adultery;
to the harlot's house they throng.
8 Lustful stallions they are,
each neighs after another's wife.[s]
9 Shall I not punish them for these things?
says the LORD;
On a nation such as this shall I not take vengeance?
10 Climb to her terraces, and ravage them,
destroy them [not] wholly.
Tear away her tendrils,
they do not belong to the LORD.[t]
11 For they have openly rebelled against me,
both the house of Israel and the house of Judah,
says the LORD,[u]
12 They denied the LORD,*
saying, "Not he—
No evil shall befall us,
neither sword nor famine shall we see.[v]
13 The prophets have become wind,
and the word is not in them.
May their threats be carried out against themselves!"

14 Now, for this that you have said,
says the LORD, the God of hosts—
Behold, I make my words
in your mouth, a fire,
And this people is the wood
that it shall devour!—
15 Beware, I will bring against you
a nation from afar,
O house of Israel, says the LORD;
A long-lived nation, an ancient nation,
a people whose language you know not,
whose speech you cannot understand.[w]
16 Their quivers are like open graves;
all of them are warriors.
17 They will devour your harvest and your bread,
devour your sons and your daughters,
Devour your sheep and cattle,
devour your vines and fig trees;
They will beat flat with the sword
the fortified city in which you trust.[x]

18 Yet even in those days, says the LORD, I will
not wholly destroy you.[y] 19 And when they
ask, "Why has the LORD done all these things
to us?" say to them, "As you have forsaken me
to serve strange gods in your own land, so shall
you serve strangers in a land not your own."

20 Announce this to the house of Jacob,
proclaim it in Judah:
21 Pay attention to this,
foolish and senseless people
Who have eyes and see not,
who have ears and hear not.[z]
22 Should you not fear me, says the LORD,
should you not tremble before me?
I made the sandy shore the sea's limit,
which by eternal decree it may not overstep.
Toss though it may, it is to no avail;
though its billows roar, they cannot pass.[a]
23 But this people's heart is stubborn and rebellious;
they turn and go away,
24 And say not in their hearts,
"Let us fear the LORD, our God,
Who gives us rain
early and late,* in its time;
Who watches for us
over the appointed weeks of harvest."[b]
25 Your crimes have prevented these things,
your sins have turned back these blessings from you.[c]
26 For there are among my people criminals;
like fowlers they set traps,
but it is men they catch.[d]
27 Their houses are as full of treachery
as a bird-cage is of birds;
Therefore they grow powerful and rich,
28 fat and sleek.
They go their wicked way;

p Jer 2, 30.
q Jer 8, 7.
r Jer 6, 13.
s Jer 13, 27.
t Jer 2, 21.
u Jer 3, 20.
v Jer 14, 13; Is 28, 15.
w Dt 28, 49.
x Dt 28, 31.
y Jer 4, 27.
z Is 6, 9.
a Jb 38, 10f.
b Gn 8, 22; Dt 11, 14.
c Jer 2, 17. 19.
d Prv 1, 11.
e Jer 12, 1; Is 1, 23.

*

5, 12: They denied the Lord: the people act as though God does not exist and will not interfere.

5, 24: Rain early and late: autumn and spring rains respectively. Appointed weeks of harvest: the seven weeks between the Passover (Dt 16, 9f) and Pentecost, during which it ordinarily did not rain.

justice they do not defend
By advancing the claim of the fatherless
or judging the cause of the poor.[e]
29 Shall I not punish these things? says the LORD;
on a nation such as this shall I not take vengeance?
30 A shocking, horrible thing
has happened in the land:
31 The prophets prophesy falsely,
and the priests teach as they wish;
Yet my people will have it so;
what will you do when the end comes?[f]

## CHAPTER 6

### The Enemy at the Gates

1 Flee, sons of Benjamin,
out of Jerusalem!
Blow the trumpet in Tekoa,
raise a signal over Beth-haccherem;
For evil threatens from the north,
and mighty destruction.[g]
2 O lovely and delicate
daughter Zion, you are ruined!
3 Against her, shepherds come with their flocks;*
all around, they pitch their tents,
each one grazes his portion.[h]
4 "Prepare for war against her,
Up! let us rush upon her at midday!
Alas! the day is waning,
evening shadows lengthen;
5 Up! let us rush upon her by night,
destroy her palaces!"[i]

6 For thus says the LORD of hosts:
Hew down her trees,
throw up a siege mound against Jerusalem.
Woe to the city marked for punishment;
nought but oppression within her![j]
7 As the well gushes out its waters,
so she gushes out her wickedness.
Violence and destruction resound in her;
ever before me are wounds and blows.[k]
8 Be warned, O Jerusalem,
lest I be estranged from you;
Lest I turn you into a desert,
a land where no man dwells.

9 Thus says the LORD of hosts:
Glean, glean like a vine
the remnant of Israel;
Pass your hand, like a vintager,
repeatedly over the tendrils.
10 To whom shall I speak?
whom shall I warn, and be heard?
See! their ears are uncircumcised,
they cannot give heed;
See, the word of the LORD has become for them
an object of scorn, which they will not have.[l]
11 Therefore my wrath brims up within me,
I am weary of holding it in;
I will pour it out upon the child in the street,
upon the young men gathered together.
Yes, all will be taken, husband and wife,
graybeard with ancient.[m]
12 Their houses will fall to strangers,
their fields and their wives as well;
For I will stretch forth my hand
against those who dwell in this land, says the LORD.[n]
13 Small and great alike, all are greedy for gain;
prophet and priest, all practice fraud.[o]
14 They would repair, as though it were nought,*
the injury to my people:
"Peace, peace!" they say,
though there is no peace.[p]
15 They are odious; they have done abominable things,
yet they are not at all ashamed,
they know not how to blush.
Hence they shall be among those who fall;
in their time of punishment they shall go down,
says the LORD.[q]

16 Thus says the LORD:
Stand beside the earliest roads,
ask the pathways of old*
Which is the way to good, and walk it;
thus you will find rest for your souls.
But they said, "We will not walk it."[r]
17 When I raised up watchmen* for them:
"Hearken to the sound of the trumpet!"
they said, "We will not hearken."
18 Therefore hear, O nations,
and know, O earth,
what I will do with them:
19 See, I bring evil upon this people,
the fruit of their own schemes,
Because they heeded not my words,
because they despised my law.[s]
20 Of what use to me incense that comes from Sheba,
or sweet cane from far-off lands?

---

f Jer 14, 14; Mi 2, 11.
g Jer 1, 14f.
h Jer 4, 17.
i 2 Chr 36, 19.
j Jer 32, 24; Zep 3, 1-4.
k Is 57, 20.
l Jer 7, 26; 20, 8.
m Ez 9, 6.
n Jer 8, 10; Dt 28, 30ff.
o Jer 8, 10; 23, 11.
p Jer 8, 11.
q Jer 3, 3; 8, 12.
r Jer 7, 23f; 18, 15.
s Prv 1, 31.
t Is 1, 11; 43, 24.

---

*

6, 3: Shepherds . . . with their flocks: foreign invaders with their armies.

6, 14: As though it were nought: the false assurance of well-being given by priest and prophet cannot reduce the harm which universal materialism and corruption have done to the people.

6, 16: Earliest roads . . . pathways of old: history and the lessons to be learned from it.

6, 17: Watchmen: the prophets who, like Jeremiah, had upheld God's moral law.

Your holocausts find no favor with me,
your sacrifices please me not.[t]
21 Therefore, thus says the LORD:
See, I will place before this people
obstacles to bring them down;
Fathers and sons alike,
neighbors and friends shall perish.[u]

22 Thus says the LORD:
See, a people comes from the land of the
north,
a great nation, roused from the ends of
the earth.[v]
23 Bow and javelin they wield;
cruel and pitiless are they.
They sound like the roaring sea
as they ride forth on steeds,
Each in his place, for battle
against you, daughter Zion.
24 We hear the report of them;
helpless fall our hands,
Anguish takes hold of us,
throes like a mother's in childbirth.[w]
25 Go not forth into the field,
step not into the street,
Beware of the enemy's sword;
terror on every side!
26 O daughter of my people, gird on sackcloth,
roll in the ashes.
Mourn as for an only child
with bitter wailing,
For sudden upon us
comes the destroyer.[x]

27 A tester among my people I have appointed
you,
to search and test their way.[y]
28 Arch-rebels are they all,
dealers in slander,
all of them corrupt.
29 The bellows roars,
the lead is consumed by the fire;
In vain has the smelter refined,
the wicked are not drawn off.
30 "Silver rejected" they shall be called,
for the LORD has rejected them.

## *II: Oracles Mostly in the Days of Jehoiakim*

## CHAPTER 7

**The Temple Sermon.*** 1 The following
message came to Jeremiah from the LORD:
2 Stand at the gate of the house of the LORD,
and there proclaim this message: Hear the word
of the LORD, all you of Judah who enter these
gates to worship the LORD! 3 Thus says the
LORD of hosts, the God of Israel: Reform your
ways and your deeds, so that I may remain with
you in this place.[z] 4 Put not your trust in the
deceitful words: "This is the temple of the
LORD! The temple of the LORD! The temple of
the LORD!"[a] 5 Only if you thoroughly reform
your ways and your deeds; if each of you deals
justly with his neighbor; 6 if you no longer
oppress the resident alien,* the orphan, and the
widow; if you no longer shed innocent blood in
this place, or follow strange gods to your own
harm,[b] 7 will I remain with you in this place,
in the land which I gave your fathers long ago
and forever.[c]

8 But here you are, putting your trust in deceitful words to your own loss! 9 Are you to
steal and murder, commit adultery and perjury,
burn incense to Baal, go after strange gods that
you know not,[d] 10 and yet come to stand before me in this house which bears my name, and
say: "We are safe; we can commit all these
abominations again"?[e] 11 Has this house
which bears my name become in your eyes a den
of thieves? I too see what is being done, says the
LORD.[f] 12 You may go to Shiloh,* which I
made the dwelling place of my name in the
beginning. See what I did to it because of the
wickedness of my people Israel.[g] 13 And now,
because you have committed all these misdeeds,
says the LORD, because you did not listen,
though I spoke to you untiringly; because you
did not answer, though I called you, 14 I will
do to this house named after me, in which you
trust, and to this place which I gave to you and
your fathers, just as I did to Shiloh.[h] 15 I will
cast you away from me, as I cast away all your
brethren, all the offspring of Ephraim.[i]

**Abuses in Worship.** 16 You, now, do not
intercede for this people; raise not in their behalf
a pleading prayer![j] Do not urge me, for I will
not listen to you. 17 Do you not see what they
are doing in the cities of Judah, in the streets of
Jerusalem? 18 The children gather wood, their
fathers light the fire, and the women knead
dough to make cakes for the queen of heaven,*

u Is 8, 14f.
v Jer 1, 15; 5, 15.
w Jer 4, 31.
x Jer 25, 34; Am 8, 10.
y Jer 1, 18.
z Jer 18, 11; 26, 13.
a Mi 3, 11.
b Ex 22, 21-24.
c Dt 4, 40.
d Jer 44, 17.
e Jer 32, 34.
f Mt 21, 13.
g Jos 18, 1.
h Jer 26, 9.
i 1 Kgs 9, 7; 2 Kgs 17, 23.
j Jer 11, 14; 14, 11.
k Jer 44, 17.19.

7, 1–15: The temple of the Lord will not serve as a place of refuge for the Jews against their enemies if they fail to reform their evil ways.

7, 6: The resident alien: specially protected by law; cf Ex 20, 10; Nm 9, 14; 15, 14; Dt 5, 14; 28, 43.

7, 12: Shiloh: original place of worship from the time of Joshua to that of Samuel. The sanctuary was later rejected by God and destroyed by the Philistines; cf 1 Sm 1, 9; 4, 3f; Ps 78, 60. 68f.

7, 18: Queen of heaven: the Assyro-Babylonian Ishtar, goddess of fertility, whose worship was introduced under King Manasseh and was revived after Josiah's death. Cakes shaped like stars (Ishtar was identified with the planet Venus) were offered in her honor.

while libations are poured out to strange gods in
order to hurt me.[k] **19** Is it I whom they hurt,
says the LORD; is it not rather themselves, to
their own confusion?[l] **20** See now, says the
Lord GOD, my anger and my wrath will pour out
upon this place, upon man and beast, upon the
trees of the field and the fruits of the earth; it will
burn without being quenched.[m]

**21** Thus says the LORD of hosts, the God of
Israel: Heap your holocausts upon your sacrifices; eat up the flesh! **22** In speaking to your
fathers on the day I brought them out of the land
of Egypt, I gave them no command* concerning
holocaust or sacrifice. **23** This rather is what I
commanded them: Listen to my voice; then I
will be your God and you shall be my people.
Walk in all the ways that I command you, so
that you may prosper.[n]

**24** But they obeyed not, nor did they pay
heed. They walked in the hardness of their evil
hearts and turned their backs, not their faces, to
me.[o] **25** From the day that your fathers left the
land of Egypt even to this day, I have sent you
untiringly all my servants the prophets.[p] **26** Yet
they have not obeyed me nor paid heed; they
have stiffened their necks and done worse than
their fathers.[q] **27** When you speak all these
words to them, they will not listen to you either;
when you call to them, they will not answer
you. **28** Say to them: This is the nation which
does not listen to the voice of the LORD, its God,
or take correction. Faithfulness has disappeared; the word itself is banished from their
speech.

**29** Cut off your dedicated hair* and throw it
away!
on the heights intone an elegy;
For the LORD has rejected and cast off
the generation that draws down his
wrath.[r]

**30** The people of Judah have done what is
evil in my eyes, says the LORD. They have
defiled the house which bears my name by setting up in it their abominable idols.[s] **31** In the
Valley of Ben-hinnom they have built the high
place of Topheth to immolate in fire their sons
and their daughters, such a thing as I never
commanded or had in mind. **32** Therefore, beware! days will come, says the LORD, when
Topheth and the Valley of Ben-hinnom will no
longer be called such, but rather the Valley of
Slaughter. For lack of space, Topheth will be a
burial place.[t] **33** The corpses of this people will
be food for the birds of the sky and for the beasts
of the field, which no one will drive away.[u]
**34** In the cities of Judah and in the streets of
Jerusalem I will silence the cry of joy, the cry
of gladness, the voice of the bridegroom and the
voice of the bride; for the land will be turned to
rubble.[v]

## CHAPTER 8

**1** At that time, says the LORD, the bones of
the kings and princes of Judah, the bones of the
priests and the prophets, and the bones of the
citizens of Jerusalem will be emptied out of their
graves[w] **2** and spread out before the sun and the
moon and the whole army of heaven,* which
they loved and served, which they followed,
consulted, and worshiped. They will not be
gathered up for burial, but will lie like dung
upon the ground.[x] **3** Death will be preferred to
life by all the survivors of this wicked race who
remain in any of the places to which I banish
them, says the LORD of hosts.

### Israel's Conduct Incomprehensible

**4** Tell them: Thus says the LORD:
When someone falls, does he not rise again?
if he goes astray, does he not turn back?
**5** Why do these people rebel
with obstinate resistance?
Why do they cling to deceptive idols,
refuse to turn back?[y]
**6** I listen closely:
they speak what is not true;
No one repents of his wickedness,
saying "What have I done!"
Everyone keeps on running his course,
like a steed dashing into battle.[z]
**7** Even the stork in the air
knows its seasons;
Turtledove, swallow and thrush
observe their time of return,
But my people do not know
the ordinance of the LORD.[a]
**8** How can you say, "We are wise,[b]
we have the law of the LORD"?
Why, that has been changed into falsehood
by the lying pen of the scribes!*
**9** The wise are confounded,
dismayed and ensnared;

l Jb 35, 6.
m Jer 36, 29; 2 Kgs 22, 17.
n Jer 11, 4; Lv 26, 3. 12.
o Jer 17, 23.
p 2 Chr 36, 15f; Bar 1, 19.
q Jer 19, 15; 2 Chr 30, 8.
r Jer 9, 17-21.
s Jer 32, 34.
t Jer 19, 6; 32, 35.
u Jer 16, 4; 34, 20.
v Jer 16, 9.
w Bar 2, 24.
x Dt 4, 19.
y Jer 5, 3; 7, 24. 26.
z Jb 34, 31f.
a Is 1, 3.
b Mal 2, 8; Rom 2, 17-23.
c 1 Cor 3, 20.

*

7, 22: I gave them no command: right conduct rather than mere external cult was God's will concerning his people (v 23).

7, 29: Dedicated hair: the unshorn hair of the nazirite, regarded as sacred because of a vow, temporary or permanent, to abstain from cutting or shaving the hair, from contact with a corpse, and from all products of the vine; cf Nm 6, 4–8. The cutting of this hair was a sign of extreme mourning.

8, 2: Army of heaven: the stars, worshiped by the pagan nations and even by the inhabitants of Jerusalem during the reigns of Manasseh and Amon.

8, 8f: Lying pen of the scribes: because the interpretations and ordinances of the scribes ran counter to the word of the Lord.

Since they have rejected the word of the
LORD,
of what avail is their wisdom?[c]

## Shameless in Their Crimes

10 Therefore, I will give their wives to
strangers,
their fields to spoilers.
Small and great alike, all are greedy for
gain,
prophet and priest, all practice fraud.[d]
11 They would repair, as though it were
nought,
the injury to the daughter of my people:*
"Peace, peace!" they say,
though there is no peace.[e]
12 They are odious; they have done abominable
things,
yet they are not at all ashamed,
they know not how to blush.
Hence they shall be among those who fall;
in their time of punishment they shall go
down,
says the LORD.[f]

## Threats of Punishment

13 I will gather them all in, says the LORD:
no grapes on the vine,
No figs on the fig trees,
foliage withered!
14 Why do we remain here?
Let us form ranks and enter the walled
cities,
to perish there;
For the LORD has wrought our destruction,
he has given us poison to drink,
because we have sinned against the
LORD.[g]
15 We wait for peace to no avail;
for a time of healing, but terror comes
instead.[h]
16 From Dan is heard
the snorting of his steeds;
The neighing of his stallions
shakes the whole land.
They come devouring the land and all it
contains,
the city and those who dwell in it.
17 Yes, I will send against you
poisonous snakes,
Against which no charm will work
when they bite you, says the LORD.[i]

## The Prophet's Grief over the People's Suffering

18 My grief is incurable,
my heart within me is faint.
19 Listen! the cry of the daughter of my
people,
far and wide in the land!
Is the LORD no longer in Zion,
is her King no longer in her midst?
[Why do they provoke me with their idols,
with their foreign nonentities?][j]
20 "The harvest has passed, the summer is at
an end,
and yet we are not safe!"
21 I am broken by the ruin of the daughter of
my people.
I am disconsolate; horror has seized me.[k]
22 Is there no balm in Gilead,*
no physician there?
Why grows not new flesh
over the wound of the daughter of my
people?[l]
23 Oh, that my head were a spring of water,
my eyes a fountain of tears,
That I might weep day and night
over the slain of the daughter of my
people!

# CHAPTER 9

## The Corruption of the People

1 Would that I had in the desert
a travelers' lodge!
That I might leave my people
and depart from them.
They are all adulterers,
a faithless band.
2 They ready their tongues like a drawn bow;
with lying, and not with truth,
they hold forth in the land.
They go from evil to evil,
but me they know not, says the LORD.
3 Be on your guard, everyone against his
neighbor;
put no trust in any brother.
Every brother apes Jacob, the supplanter,*
every friend is guilty of slander.
4 Each one deceives the other,
no one speaks the truth.
They have accustomed their tongues to
lying,
and are perverse, and cannot repent.[m]
5 Violence upon violence,
deceit upon deceit:
They refuse to recognize me,
says the LORD.

6 Therefore, thus says the LORD of hosts:
I will smelt them and test them;
how else should I deal with their
wickedness?
7 A murderous arrow is his tongue,

d Jer 6, 13; Dt 28, 30.
e Jer 6, 14.
f Jer 6, 15.
g Jer 9, 14; 23, 15.
h Jer 14, 19.
i Dt 32, 24.
j Dt 32, 21; Mi 4, 9.
k Jer 14, 17.
l Jer 46, 11.
m Jer 12, 6.
n Pss 28, 3; 62, 4.

8, 11: Daughter of my people: the people itself personified as a woman.

8, 22: Gilead: noted for its healing balm but unable to heal the moral wound of the people.

9, 3: Jacob, the supplanter: in Hebrew, a play on words. Jacob, as his name indicates ("he supplants"), deprived his brother Esau of his birthright; cf Gn 25, 26. 33.

his mouth utters deceit;
He speaks cordially with his friends,
but in his heart he lays an ambush![n]
8 For these things, says the LORD,
shall I not punish them?
On a nation such as this
shall I not take vengeance?[o]

## Dirge over the Ravaged Land

9 Over the mountains, break out in cries of
lamentation,
over the pasture lands, intone a dirge:
They are scorched, and no man crosses
them,
unheard is the bleat of the flock;
Birds of the air as well as beasts,
all have fled, and are gone.[p]
10 I will turn Jerusalem into a heap of ruins,
a haunt of jackals;
The cities of Judah I will make into a waste,
where no one dwells.[q]

11 Who is so wise that he can understand
this? Let him to whom the mouth of the LORD
has spoken make it known:

Why is the land ravaged,
scorched like a wasteland untraversed?[r]

12 The LORD answered: Because they have
abandoned my law, which I set before them,
and have not followed it or listened to my voice,
13 but followed rather the hardness of their
hearts and the Baals, as their fathers had taught
them;[s] 14 therefore, thus says the LORD of
hosts, the God of Israel: See now, I will give
them wormwood to eat and poison to drink.[t]
15 I will scatter them among nations whom
neither they nor their fathers have known; I will
send the sword to pursue them until I have completely destroyed them.[u]

16 Thus says the LORD of hosts:
Attention! tell the wailing women to come,
summon the best of them;
17 Let them come quickly
and intone a dirge for us,
That our eyes may be wet with weeping,
our cheeks run with tears.[v]
18 The dirge is heard from Zion:
Ruined we are, and greatly ashamed;
We must leave the land,
give up our homes!
19 Hear, you women, the word of the LORD,
let your ears receive his message.
Teach your daughters this dirge,
and each other this lament.
20 Death has come up through our windows,
has entered our palaces;
It cuts down the children in the street,
young people in the squares.[w]
21 The corpses of the slain
lie like dung on a field,
Like sheaves behind the harvester,
with no one to gather them.

## True Glory

22 Thus says the LORD:
Let not the wise man glory in his wisdom,
nor the strong man glory in his strength,
nor the rich man glory in his riches;[x]
23 But rather, let him who glories, glory in
this,
that in his prudence he knows me,
Knows that I, the LORD, bring about
kindness,
justice and uprightness on the earth;
For with such am I pleased, says the LORD.

**Circumcision Worthless.** 24 See, days
are coming, says the LORD, when I will demand
an account of all those circumcised in their
flesh:[y] 25 Egypt and Judah, Edom and the Ammonites, Moab and the desert dwellers who
shave their temples.* For all these nations, like
the whole house of Israel, are uncircumcised in
heart.

## CHAPTER 10

**The Folly of Idolatry.** 1 Hear the word
which the LORD speaks to you, O house of
Israel. 2 Thus says the LORD:

Learn not the customs of the nations,
and have no fear of the signs of the
heavens,*
though the nations fear them.[z]
3 For the cult idols of the nations are nothing,
wood cut from the forest,
Wrought by craftsmen with the adze,[a]
4 adorned with silver and gold.
With nails and hammers they are fastened,
that they may not totter.[b]
5 Like a scarecrow in a cucumber field are
they,
they cannot speak;
They must be carried about,
for they cannot walk.
Fear them not, they can do no harm,
neither is it in their power to do good.[c]
6 No one is like you, O LORD,
great are you,
great and mighty is your name.[d]
7 Who would not fear you,
King of the nations,

o Jer 5, 9. 29.
p Jer 4, 25; 12, 4.
q Is 13, 22.
r Ps 107, 43; Hos 14, 10.
s Jer 7, 24; 19, 4f.
t Jer 23, 15.
u Lv 26, 33; Dt 28, 36. 64.
v Jer 14, 17.
w Jer 14, 16.
x Prv 21, 30.
y Jer 4, 4.
z Bar 6, 6.
a Wis 13, 11; Is 44, 9.
b Is 40, 19; 41, 7.
c Ps 115, 4-8; Bar 6, 15.
d Ps 86, 8ff.
e Jer 5, 22; Ps 47, 2. 8.

*

9, 25: Desert dwellers . . . temples: Arab tribesmen who cut off their hair and shaved their temples in honor of the pagan god of Dushara. This was forbidden the Israelites (Lv 19, 27).

10, 2: Signs of the heavens: phenomena in the sky superstitiously regarded by the pagans as dire omens.

for it is your due!
Among all the wisest of the nations,
and in all their domain,
there is none like you.[e]

8 One and all they are dumb and senseless,
these idols they teach about are wooden:
9 Silver strips brought from Tarshish,
and gold from Ophir,
The work of the craftsman
and the handiwork of the smelter,
Clothed with violet and purple—
all of them the work of artisans.

11 Thus shall you say of them: Let the gods
that did not make heaven and earth perish from
the earth, and from beneath these heavens![f]

10 The LORD is true God,
he is the living God, the eternal King,
Before whose anger the earth quakes,
whose wrath the nations cannot endure:[g]
12 He who made the earth by his power,
established the world by his wisdom,
and stretched out the heavens by his
skill.[h]
13 When he thunders, the waters in the heavens
roar,
and he brings up clouds from the end of
the earth;
He makes the lightning flash in the rain,
and releases stormwinds from their
chambers.
14 Every man is stupid, ignorant;
every artisan is put to shame by his idol:
He has molded a fraud,
without breath of life.[i]
15 Nothingness are they, a ridiculous work;
they will perish in their time of
punishment.
16 Not like these is the portion of Jacob:
he is the creator of all things;
Israel is his very own tribe,
LORD of hosts is his name.[j]

### Abandonment of Judah

17 Lift your bundle and leave the land,
O city living in a state of siege!
18 For thus says the LORD:
Behold, this time
I will sling away the inhabitants of the
land;
I will hem them in,
that they may be taken.
19 Woe is me! I am undone,
my wound is incurable;
Yet I had thought:
if I make light of my wound, I can bear
it.
20 My tent is ruined,
all its cords are severed.
My sons have left me, they are no more:
no one to pitch my tent,
no one to raise its curtains.[k]
21 Yes, the shepherds were stupid as cattle,
the LORD they sought not;
Therefore they had no success,
and all their flocks were scattered.[l]
22 Listen! a noise! it comes closer,
a great uproar from the northern land:
To turn the cities of Judah
into a desert haunt of jackals.

### Prayer of Jeremiah

23 You know, O LORD,
that man is not master of his way;
Man's course is not within his choice,
nor is it for him to direct his step.
24 Punish us, O LORD, but with equity,
not in anger, lest you have us dwindle
away.
25 Pour out your wrath on the nations that
know you not,
on the tribes that call not upon your
name;
For they have devoured Jacob utterly,
and laid waste his dwelling.[m]

## CHAPTER 11

**Plea for Fidelity to the Covenant.** 1 The
following message came to Jeremiah from the
LORD: 2 Speak to the men of Judah and to the
citizens of Jerusalem, 3 saying to them: Thus
says the LORD, the God of Israel: Cursed be the
man who does not observe the terms of this
covenant,[n] 4 which I enjoined upon your fathers the day I brought them up out of the land
of Egypt, that iron foundry, saying: Listen to
my voice and do all that I command you. Then
you shall be my people, and I will be your
God.[o] 5 Thus I will fulfill the oath which I
swore to your fathers, to give them a land flowing with milk and honey: the one you have
today. "Amen, LORD," I answered.
6 Then the LORD said to me: Proclaim all
these words in the cities of Judah and in the
streets of Jerusalem: Hear the words of this
covenant and obey them. 7 Urgently and constantly I warned your fathers to obey my voice,
from the day I brought them up out of the land
of Egypt even to this day. 8 But they did not
listen or give ear. Each one followed the hardness of his evil heart, till I brought upon them
all the threats of this covenant which they had
failed to observe as I commanded them.[p]
9 A conspiracy has been found, the LORD
said to me, among the men of Judah and the
citizens of Jerusalem. 10 They have returned to
the crimes of their forefathers who refused to

f Ps 96, 5.
g Ps 10, 16.
h Ps 104, 5.
i Rom 1, 22f.
j Jer 31, 35.
k Jer 4, 20.
l Jer 23, 1; Ez 34, 5f.
m Ps 79, 6f.
n Dt 27, 26.
o Dt 4, 20; 1 Kgs 8, 51.
p 2 Kgs 17, 14.
q Dt 31, 16; Ez 20, 21-30.

obey my words. They also have followed and
served strange gods; the covenant which I had
made with their fathers, the house of Israel and
the house of Judah have broken.[q] 11 Therefore, thus says the LORD: See, I bring upon them
misfortune which they cannot escape. Though
they cry out to me, I will not listen to them.[r]
12 Then the cities of Judah and the citizens of
Jerusalem will go and cry out to the gods to
which they have been offering incense. But
these gods will give them no help whatever
when misfortune strikes.[s]

13 For as numerous as your cities
are your gods, O Judah!
And as many as the streets of Jerusalem
are the altars for offering sacrifice to
Baal.[t]

14 Do not intercede on behalf of this people,
nor utter a plea for them. I will not listen when
they call to me at the time of their misfortune.[u]

### Sacrifices of No Avail

15 What right has my beloved in my house,
while she prepares her plots?
Can vows and sacred meat turn away
your misfortune from you?
Will you still be jubilant
16 when you hear the great invasion?
A spreading olive tree, goodly to behold,
the LORD has named you;
Now he sets fire to it,
its branches burn.

17 The LORD of hosts who planted you has
decreed misfortune for you because of the evil
done by the house of Israel and by the house of
Judah, who provoked me by sacrificing to
Baal.[v]

**The Plot against Jeremiah.** 18 I knew it
because the LORD informed me; at that time
you, O LORD, showed me their doings.

## CHAPTER 12

1 You would be in the right, O LORD,
if I should dispute with you;
even so, I must discuss the case with you.
Why does the way of the godless prosper,
why live all the treacherous in
contentment?[w]
2 You planted them; they have taken root,
they keep on growing and bearing fruit.
You are upon their lips,
but far from their inmost thoughts.[x]
3 You, O LORD, know me, you see me,
you have found that at heart I am with
you.[y]
Pick them out like sheep for the slaughter,
set them apart for the day of carnage.*
4 How long must the earth mourn,
the green of the whole countryside wither?
For the wickedness of those who dwell in it
beasts and birds disappear,
because they say, "God does not see our
ways."

5 If running against men has wearied you,
how will you race against horses?
And if in a land of peace you fall headlong,
what will you do in the thickets of the
Jordan?

6 For even your own brothers, the members of
your father's house, betray you; they have recruited a force against you. Do not believe
them, even if they are friendly to you in their
words.[z]

11, 19 *Yet I, like a trusting lamb led to
slaughter, had not realized that they were hatch-
ing plots against me: "Let us destroy the tree in
its vigor; let us cut him off from the land of the
living, so that his name will be spoken no
more."[a]

11, 20 But, you, O LORD of hosts, O just
Judge,
searcher of mind and heart,
Let me witness the vengeance you take on
them,
for to you I have entrusted my cause![b]

11, 21 Therefore, thus says the LORD concerning the men of Anathoth who seek your life,
saying, "Do not prophesy in the name of the
LORD; else you shall die by our hand."[c]
11, 22 Therefore, thus says the LORD of hosts:
I am going to punish them. The young men shall
die by the sword; their sons and daughters shall
die by famine.[d] 11, 23 None shall be spared
among them, for I will bring misfortune upon
the men of Anathoth, the year of their punishment.[e]

### The Lord's Complaint

7 I abandon my house,
cast off my heritage;
The beloved of my soul I deliver
into the hand of her foes.[f]
8 My heritage has turned on me
like a lion in the jungle;
Because she has roared against me,
I treat her as an enemy.[g]

---

r Jer 14, 12; Mi 3, 4.
s Dt 32, 37f.
t Jer 2, 28; Hos 10, 1.
u Jer 7, 16; 14, 11.
v Is 5, 2.
w Jb 21, 7; Mal 3, 15.
x Is 29, 13.
y Jer 17, 18; Jb 23, 10.
z Jer 9, 4.
a Jer 18, 18; 20, 10; Wis 2, 20.
b Jer 15, 15.
c Am 7, 13. 16.
d Jer 18, 21f.
e Jer 23, 12.
f Ps 78, 62; Lam 2, 1f.
g Ps 106, 40.

---

12, 3: Jeremiah does not seek private vengeance but the punishment of the wicked by the Lord; cf Jer 20, 12. Nevertheless, the prophet's reaction to persecution shows the difference between the spirit of the Old Testament and the New.

11, 19–23: These verses have been transposed from ch 11.

9 My heritage is a prey for hyenas,
is surrounded by vultures;
Come, gather together, all you beasts of the field,
come and eat![h]
10 Many shepherds have ravaged my vineyard,
have trodden my heritage underfoot;
The portion that delighted me they have turned
into a desert waste.[i]
11 They have made it a mournful waste,
desolate it lies before me,
Desolate, all the land,
because no one takes it to heart.
12 Upon every desert height
brigands have come up.
The LORD has a sword which consumes
the land, from end to end:
no peace for all mankind.[j]
13 They have sown wheat and reaped thorns,
they have tired themselves out to no purpose;
They recoil before their harvest,
the flaming anger of the LORD.

**Judah's Neighbors.** 14 Thus says the
LORD against all my evil neighbors* who plunder the heritage which I gave my people Israel
as their own: See, I will pluck them up from
their land; the house of Judah I will pluck up in
their midst.[k] 15 But after plucking them up, I
will pity them again and bring them back, each
to his heritage, each to his land.[l] 16 And if they
carefully learn my people's custom of swearing
by my name, "As the LORD lives," they who
formerly taught my people to swear by Baal
shall be built up in the midst of my people.[m]
17 But if they do not obey, I will uproot and
destroy that nation entirely, says the LORD.[n]

## CHAPTER 13

**Judah's Corruption.*** 1 The LORD said to
me: Go buy yourself a linen loincloth; wear it
on your loins, but do not put it in water. 2 I
bought the loincloth, as the LORD commanded,
and put it on. 3 A second time the word of the
LORD came to me thus: 4 Take the loincloth
which you bought and are wearing, and go now
to the Parath; there hide it in a cleft of the rock.
5 Obedient to the LORD's command, I went to
the Parath and buried the loincloth. 6 After a
long interval, he said to me: Go now to the
Parath and fetch the loincloth which I told you
to hide there. 7 Again I went to the Parath,
sought out and took the loincloth from the place
where I had hid it. But it was rotted, good for
nothing! 8 Then the message came to me from
the LORD: 9 Thus says the LORD: So also I will
allow the pride of Judah to rot, the great pride
of Jerusalem.[o] 10 This wicked people who refuse to obey my words, who walk in the stubbornness of their hearts, and follow strange
gods to serve and adore them, shall be like this
loincloth which is good for nothing.[p] 11 For, as
close as the loincloth clings to a man's loins, so
had I made the whole house of Israel and the
whole house of Judah cling to me, says the
LORD; to my people, my renown, my praise, my
beauty. But they did not listen.[q]

**The Broken Wineflask.** 12 Now speak to
them this word: Thus says the LORD, the God of
Israel: Every wineflask is meant to be filled with
wine. If they reply, "Do we not know that every
wineflask is meant to be filled with wine?"
13 say to them: Thus says the LORD: Beware!
I am filling with drunkenness all the inhabitants
of this land, the kings who succeed to David's
throne, the priests and prophets, and all the
citizens of Jerusalem.[r] 14 I will dash them
against each other, fathers and sons together,
says the LORD; I will show no compassion, I will
not spare or pity, but will destroy them.[s]

### A Last Warning

15 Give ear, listen humbly,
for the LORD speaks.
16 Give glory to the LORD, your God,
before it grows dark;
Before your feet stumble
on darkening mountains;
Before the light you look for turns to darkness,
changes into black clouds.[t]
17 If you do not listen to this in your pride,
I will weep in secret many tears;
My eyes will run with tears
for the LORD's flock, led away to exile.[u]

### Exile

18 Say to the king and to the queen mother:
come down from your throne;
From your heads fall
your magnificent crowns.[v]
19 The cities of the Negeb are besieged,
with no one to relieve them;
All Judah is banished
in universal exile.

h 2 Kgs 24, 2; Is 56, 9.
i Jer 6, 3; Is 63, 18.
j Is 42, 25; 57, 21.
k 2 Kgs 24, 2.
l Am 9, 14.
m Dt 6, 13.
n Is 60, 12.
o Prv 16, 18.
p Jer 2, 20; 7, 24; 16, 11.
q Ex 19, 5; Dt 26, 18f.
r Jer 25, 15-18; Is 51, 17.
s Jer 19, 10f.
t Prv 4, 18f; Is 5, 30; Am 8, 9.
u Jer 14, 17; Ps 119, 136.
v Jer 22, 26; 2 Kgs 24, 12. 15.

*

12, 14: My evil neighbors: nations surrounding Israel, the land belonging to the Lord; cf Is 8, 8.

13, 1-11: This is probably a vision of the prophet symbolizing the religious corruption of Judah at the hands of the Babylonians, represented here by the river Parath, the Euphrates; though a spring of the same name, northeast of Anathoth, may be directly meant.

### Jerusalem's Disgrace

20 Lift up your eyes and see
men coming from the north.
Where is the flock entrusted to you,
the sheep that were your glory?[w]
21 What will you say when they place as rulers over you
those whom you taught to be your lovers?
Will not pangs seize you
like those of a woman giving birth?[x]
22 If you ask in your heart
why these things befall you:
For your great guilt your skirts are stripped away
and you are violated.[y]
23 Can the Ethiopian change his skin?
the leopard his spots?
As easily would you be able to do good,
accustomed to evil as you are.[z]
24 I will scatter them like chaff that flies
when the desert wind blows.[a]
25 This is your lot, the portion measured out to you
from me, says the LORD.
Because you have forgotten me,
and trusted in the lying idol,[b]
26 I now will strip off your skirts from you,
so that your shame will appear.[c]
27 Your adulteries, your neighings,
your shameless prostitutions:
On the hills in the highlands
I see these horrible crimes of yours.
Woe to you, Jerusalem, how long will it yet be
before you become clean![d]

## CHAPTER 14

**The Great Drought.** 1 The word of the
LORD that came to Jeremiah concerning the
drought:[e]

2 Judah mourns,
her gates are lifeless;
Her people sink down in mourning:
from Jerusalem ascends a cry of anguish.[f]
3 The nobles send their servants for water,
but when they come to the cisterns
They find no water
and return with empty jars.[g]
Ashamed, despairing, they cover their heads
4 because of the stricken soil;
Because there is no rain in the land
the farmers are ashamed, they cover their heads.[h]
5 Even the hind in the field deserts her offspring
because there is no grass.
6 The wild asses stand on the bare heights,
gasping for breath like jackals;
Their eyes grow dim,
because there is no vegetation to be seen.
7 Even though our crimes bear witness against us,
take action, O LORD, for the honor of your name—
Even though our rebellions are many,
though we have sinned against you.[i]
8 O Hope of Israel, O LORD,
our savior in time of need!
Why should you be a stranger in this land,
like a traveler who has stopped but for a night?
9 Why are you like a man dumbfounded,
a champion who cannot save?
You are in our midst, O LORD,
your name we bear:
do not forsake us![j]

10 Thus says the LORD of this people:
They so love to wander
that they do not spare their feet.
The LORD has no pleasure in them;
now he remembers their guilt,
and will punish their sins.[k]

11 Then the LORD said to me: Do not intercede for this people.[l] 12 If they fast, I will not
listen to their supplication. If they offer holocausts or cereal offerings, I will not accept
them. Rather, I will destroy them with the
sword, famine, and pestilence.[m]
13 Ah! Lord GOD, I replied, it is the prophets
who say to them, "You shall not see the sword;
famine shall not befall you. Indeed, I will give
you lasting peace in this place."[n]
14 Lies these prophets utter in my name, the
LORD said to me. I did not send them; I gave
them no command nor did I speak to them.
Lying visions, foolish divination, dreams of
their own imagination, they prophesy to you.[o]
15 Therefore, thus says the LORD: Concerning
the prophets who prophesy in my name, though
I did not send them; who say, "Sword and
famine shall not befall this land": by the sword
and famine shall these prophets meet their end.[p]
16 The people to whom they prophesy shall be
cast out into the streets of Jerusalem by famine
and the sword. No one shall bury them, their
wives, their sons, or their daughters, for I will
pour out upon them their own wickedness.[q]
17 Speak to them this word:

Let my eyes stream with tears
day and night, without rest,
Over the great destruction which overwhelms
the virgin daughter of my people,
over her incurable wound.[r]

w Jer 6, 22f.
x 2 Kgs 16, 7.
y Is 47, 2f.
z Ps 55, 20.
a Pss 1, 4; 83, 14.
b Jb 20, 29.
c Ez 16, 32.
d Jer 2, 20.
e Lv 26, 19f.
f Is 3, 26.
g Am 4, 8.
h Dt 28, 23.
i Dn 9, 4-14.
j Is 59, 1f; 63, 19.
k Jer 2, 25.
l Jer 11, 14; Ex 32, 10.
m Jer 6, 20; Is 1, 11. 13.
n Jer 4, 10; 5, 12.
o Jer 5, 31; 23, 16.
p Jer 5, 12f.
q Jer 7, 33; 19, 7.
r Jer 9, 17.

18 If I walk out into the field,
look! those slain by the sword;
If I enter the city,
look! those consumed by hunger.
Even the prophet and the priest
forage in a land they know not.

19 Have you cast Judah off completely?
Is Zion loathsome to you?
Why have you struck us a blow
that cannot be healed?
We wait for peace, to no avail;
for a time of healing, but terror comes
instead.[s]
20 We recognize, O LORD, our wickedness,
the guilt of our fathers;
that we have sinned against you.[t]
21 For your name's sake spurn us not,
disgrace not the throne of your glory;
remember your covenant with us, and
break it not.[u]
22 Among the nations' idols is there any that
gives rain?
Or can the mere heavens send showers?
Is it not you alone, O LORD,
our God, to whom we look?
You alone have done all these things.[v]

## CHAPTER 15

1 The LORD said to me: Even if Moses and
Samuel stood before me, my heart would not
turn toward this people. Send them away from
me.[w] 2 If they ask you where they should go,
tell them, Thus says the LORD: Whoever is
marked for death, to death; whoever is marked
for the sword, to the sword; whoever is marked
for famine, to famine; whoever is marked for
captivity, to captivity.[x] 3 Four kinds of scourge
I have decreed against them, says the LORD: the
sword to slay them; dogs to drag them about; the
birds of the sky and the beasts of the earth to
devour and destroy them.[y] 4 And I will make
them an object of horror to all the kingdoms of
the earth because of what Manasseh, son of
Hezekiah, king of Judah, did in Jerusalem.[z]

### Scene of Tragedy

5 Who will pity you, Jerusalem,
who will console you?
Who will stop to ask
about your welfare?[a]
6 You have disowned me, says the LORD,
turned your back upon me;
And so I stretched out my hand to destroy
you,
I was weary of sparing you.[b]
7 I winnowed them with the fan
in every city gate.
I destroyed my people through bereavement;
they returned not from their evil ways.[c]
8 Their widows were more numerous before
me
than the sands of the sea.
I brought against the mother of youths
the spoiler at midday;
Suddenly I struck her
with anguish and terror.
9 The mother of seven swoons away,
gasping out her life;
Her sun sets in full day,
she is disgraced, despairing.
Their survivors I will give to the sword
before their enemies, says the LORD.[d]

### Jeremiah's Complaint

10 Woe to me, mother, that you gave me birth!
a man of strife and contention to all the
land!
I neither borrow nor lend,
yet all curse me.[e]
11 Tell me, LORD, have I not served you for
their good?
Have I not interceded with you
in the time of misfortune and anguish?[f]*
15 You know I have.
Remember me, LORD, visit me,
and avenge me on my persecutors.
Because of your long-suffering banish me
not;
know that for you I have borne insult.[g]
16 When I found your words, I devoured them;
they became my joy and the happiness of
my heart,
Because I bore your name,
O LORD, God of hosts.
17 I did not sit celebrating
in the circle of merrymakers;
Under the weight of your hand I sat alone
because you filled me with indignation.[h]
18 Why is my pain continuous,
my wound incurable, refusing to be
healed?
You have indeed become for me a
treacherous brook,*
whose waters do not abide![i]
19 Thus the LORD answered me:
If you repent, so that I restore you,
in my presence you shall stand;
If you bring forth the precious without the
vile,
you shall be my mouthpiece.
Then it shall be they who turn to you,
and you shall not turn to them;

s Jer 8, 15; 2 Chr 36, 16.
t Ps 106, 6; Dn 9, 5. 8.
u Jer 14, 7; Lv 26, 44; Ps 25, 11.
v Jer 5, 24; Zec 10, 1.
w Ps 99, 6; Ez 14, 14. 16.
x Jer 14, 12; Ez 5, 12.
y Ez 14, 21.
z Jer 24, 9; 2 Kgs 21, 11-16; 23, 26; 24, 3f.
a Is 51, 19.
b Am 7, 8.
c Is 41, 16.
d 1 Sm 2, 5.
e Jer 20, 14.
f Jer 39, 11-14.
g Jer 11, 20; 12, 3; Ps 69, 8.
h Ps 25, 4.
i Jer 14, 19; 30, 15.

*

15, 12ff: These verses are corruptions of the text and are therefore omitted.

15, 18: A treacherous brook: that dries up when its waters are needed. The prophet complains that he cannot rely on God with unfailing assurance of his assistance.

**20** And I will make you toward this people
a solid wall of brass.
Though they fight against you,
they shall not prevail,
For I am with you,
to deliver and rescue you, says the LORD.[j]
**21** I will free you from the hand of the wicked,
and rescue you from the grasp of the
violent.

## CHAPTER 16

**Jeremiah's Life a Warning.** **1** This message came to me from the LORD: **2** Do not marry any woman; you shall not have sons or
daughters in this place, **3** for thus says the LORD
concerning the sons and daughters who will be
born in this place, the mothers who will give
them birth, the fathers who will beget them in
this land: **4** Of deadly disease they shall die.
Unlamented and unburied they will lie like dung
on the ground. Sword and famine will make an
end of them, and their corpses will become food
for the birds of the sky and the beasts of the
field.[k]
**5** Go not into a house of mourning, the LORD
continued: go not there to lament or offer sympathy. For I have withdrawn my friendship from
this people, says the LORD, my kindness and my
pity.[l] **6** They shall die, the great and the lowly,
in this land, and shall go unburied and unlamented.* No one will gash himself or shave his
head for them.[m] **7** They will not break bread
with the bereaved to console them in their bereavement; they will not give them the cup of
consolation to drink over the death of father or
mother.[n]
**8** Enter not a house where people are celebrating, to sit with them eating and drinking.
**9** For thus says the LORD of hosts, the God of
Israel: Before your very eyes and during your
lifetime I will silence from this place the cry of
joy and the cry of gladness, the voice of the
bridegroom and the voice of the bride.[o]
**10** When you proclaim all these words to this
people and they ask you: "Why has the LORD
pronounced all these great evils against us?
What is our crime? What sin have we committed
against the LORD, our God?"[p] — **11** [q]you shall
answer them: It is because your fathers have
forsaken me, says the LORD, and followed
strange gods, which they served and worshiped;
but me they have forsaken, and my law they
have not observed. **12** And you have done
worse than your fathers. Here you are, every
one of you, walking in the hardness of his evil
heart instead of listening to me.[r] **13** I will cast
you out of this land into a land that neither you
nor your fathers have known; there you can
serve strange gods day and night, because I will
not grant you my mercy.

**Return from Exile.** **14** However, days will
surely come, says the LORD, when it will no
longer be said, "As the LORD lives, who
brought the Israelites out of Egypt";[s] **15** but
rather, "As the LORD lives, who brought the
Israelites out of the land of the north and out of
all the countries to which he had banished
them." I will bring them back to the land which
I gave their fathers.[t]

**Double Punishment.** **16** Look! I will send
many fishermen, says the LORD, to catch them.
After that, I will send many hunters to hunt them
out from every mountain and hill and from the
clefts of the rocks.[u] **17** For my eyes are upon
all their ways; they are not hidden from me, nor
does their guilt escape my view.[v] **18** I will at
once repay them double for their crime and their
sin of profaning my land with their detestable
corpses of idols, and filling my heritage with
their abominations.[w]

### Conversion of the Heathen

**19** O LORD, my strength, my fortress,
my refuge in the day of distress!
To you will the nations come
from the ends of the earth, and say,
"Mere frauds are the heritage of our fathers,
empty idols of no use."[x]
**20** Can man make for himself gods?
These are not gods.[y]
**21** Look, then: I will give them knowledge;
this time I will leave them in no doubt
Of my strength and my power:
they shall know that my name is LORD.[z]

## CHAPTER 17

### The Sin of Judah and Its Punishment

**1** The sin of Judah is written
with an iron stylus,
Engraved with a diamond point
upon the tablets of their hearts.[a]

[And the horns of their altars, **2** when their sons
remember their altars and their sacred poles,
beside the green trees, on the high hills, **3** the
peaks in the highland.]

Your wealth and all your treasures
I will give as spoil.
In recompense for all your sins
throughout your borders,

j Jer 1, 18; 6, 27.
k Jer 7, 33; 22, 18.
l Ez 24, 16f.
m Lv 19, 28; Dt 14, 1.
n Ez 24, 17.
o Jer 7, 34; 25, 10.
p Jer 2, 35; 5, 19; 13, 22.
q Jer 22, 9; Dt 29, 25.
r Jer 7, 24ff.
s Jer 23, 7f.
t Jer 24, 6.
u 2 Kgs 24, 2; Lam 4, 19.
v Jer 32, 19; Jb 34, 21.
w Is 40, 2.
x Jer 2, 11; Is 2, 2f.
y Jer 2, 11; Gal 4, 8.
z Am 5, 8.
a Jb 19, 24.

* 16, 6f: These verses refer to popular mourning practices, sometimes connected with pagan superstition; cf Dt 14, 1f.

4 You will relinquish your hold on your heritage
which I have given you.
I will enslave you to your enemies
in a land that you know not:
For a fire has been kindled by my wrath
that will burn forever.[b]

## True Wisdom

5 Thus says the LORD:
Cursed is the man who trusts in human beings,
who seeks his strength in flesh,
whose heart turns away from the LORD.[c]
6 He is like a barren bush in the desert
that enjoys no change of season,
But stands in a lava waste,
a salt and empty earth.
7 Blessed is the man who trusts in the LORD,
whose hope is the LORD.[d]
8 He is like a tree planted beside the waters
that stretches out its roots to the stream:
It fears not the heat when it comes,
its leaves stay green;
In the year of drought it shows no distress,
but still bears fruit.[e]
9 More tortuous than all else is the human heart,
beyond remedy; who can understand it?
10 I, the LORD, alone probe the mind
and test the heart,
To reward everyone according to his ways,
according to the merit of his deeds.[f]
11 A partridge that mothers a brood not her own
is the man who acquires wealth unjustly:
In midlife it will desert him;
in the end he is only a fool.[g]

## The Source of Life

12 A throne of glory, exalted from the beginning,
such is our holy place.[h]
13 O hope of Israel, O LORD!
all who forsake you shall be in disgrace;
The rebels in the land shall be put to shame;
they have forsaken the source of living waters [the LORD].[i]

## Prayer for Vengeance

14 Heal me, LORD, that I may be healed;
save me, that I may be saved,
for it is you whom I praise.
15 See how they say to me,
"Where is the word of the LORD?
Let it come to pass!"[j]
16 Yet I did not press you to send calamity;
the day without remedy I have not desired.
You know what passed my lips;
it is present before you.
17 Do not be my ruin,
you, my refuge in the day of misfortune.[k]
18 Let my persecutors, not me, be confounded;
let them, not me, be broken.
Bring upon them the day of misfortune,
crush them with repeated destruction.[l]

**Observance of the Sabbath.** 19 Thus
said the LORD to me: Go, stand at the Gate of
Benjamin,* where the kings of Judah enter and
leave, and at the other gates of Jerusalem.[m]
20 There say to them: Hear the word of the
LORD, you kings of Judah, and all Judah, and
all you citizens of Jerusalem who enter these
gates! 21 Thus says the LORD: As you love your
lives, take care not to carry burdens on the
sabbath day, to bring them in through the gates
of Jerusalem.[n] 22 Bring no burden from your
homes on the sabbath. Do no work whatever,
but keep holy the sabbath, as I commanded your
fathers,[o] 23 though they did not listen or give
ear, but stiffened their necks so as not to hear
or take correction.[p] 24 If you obey me wholeheartedly, says the LORD, and carry no burden
through the gates of this city on the sabbath,
keeping the sabbath holy and abstaining from all
work on it,[q] 25 then, through the gates of this
city, kings who sit upon the throne of David will
continue to enter, riding in their chariots or upon
their horses, along with their princes, and the
men of Judah, and the citizens of Jerusalem.
This city will remain inhabited forever.[r] 26 To
it people will come from the cities of Judah and
the neighborhood of Jerusalem, from the land of
Benjamin and from the foothills, from the hill
country and the Negeb, to bring holocausts and
sacrifices, cereal offerings and incense and
thank offerings to the house of the LORD.[s]
27 But if you do not obey me and keep holy the
sabbath, if you carry burdens and come through
the gates of Jerusalem on the sabbath, I will set
unquenchable fire to its gates, which will consume the palaces of Jerusalem.[t]

## CHAPTER 18

**The Potter's Vessel.*** 1 This word came
to Jeremiah from the LORD: 2 Rise up, be off
to the potter's house; there I will give you my

b Jer 5, 19; Dt 32, 22.
c Ps 146, 2f.
d Ps 1, 3.
e Is 58, 11.
f Jer 32, 19; 1 Sm 16, 7; Eccl 12, 14.
g Prv 13, 11; Lk 12, 20.
h Jer 14, 21.
i Jer 2, 13.
j Is 5, 19; 2 Pt 3, 4.
k Jer 16, 19.
l Jer 15, 15; 18, 20-23; Ps 35, 5f.
m Jer 7, 2.
n Neh 13, 15-19.
o Ex 20, 8; 23, 12.
p Jer 5, 3; 7, 24.
q Is 58, 14.
r Jer 22, 4.
s Jer 32, 44.
t Ez 22, 8.

*

17, 19: The Gate of Benjamin: probably the northern gate of the temple area and city wall of Jerusalem; cf Jer 20, 2; 37, 12; 38, 7.

18, 1-12: The lesson of the potter is not that God deals arbitrarily with his people, but that he is almighty to destroy or restore, accordingly as they disobey him or fulfill his plans.

message. 3 I went down to the potter's house
and there he was, working at the wheel.
4 Whenever the object of clay which he was
making turned out badly in his hand, he tried
again, making of the clay another object of
whatever sort he pleased.[u] 5 Then the word of
the Lord came to me: 6 Can I not do to you,
house of Israel, as this potter has done? says the
LORD. Indeed, like clay in the hand of the potter, so are you in my hand, house of Israel.[v]
7 [w]Sometimes I threaten to uproot and tear
down and destroy a nation or a kingdom. 8 But
if that nation which I have threatened turns from
its evil, I also repent of the evil which I threatened to do.[x] 9 Sometimes, again, I promise to
build up and plant a nation or a kingdom.
10 But if that nation does what is evil in my
eyes, refusing to obey my voice, I repent of the
good with which I promised to bless it.[y]

11 And now, tell this to the men of Judah and
the citizens of Jerusalem: Thus says the LORD:
Take care! I am fashioning evil against you and
making a plan. Return, each of you, from his
evil way; reform your ways and your deeds.[z]
12 But they will say, "No use! We will follow
our own devices; each one of us will behave
according to the stubbornness of his evil
heart!"[a]

### Judah's Apostasy Unnatural

13 Therefore thus says the LORD:
Ask among the nations—
who has ever heard the like?
Truly horrible things
has virgin Israel done![b]
14 Does the snow of Lebanon*
desert the rocky heights?
Do the gushing waters dry up
that flow fresh down the mountains?
15 Yet my people have forgotten me:
they burn incense to a thing that does not
exist.
They stumble out of their ways,
the paths of old,
To travel on bypaths,
not the beaten track.[c]
16 Their land shall be turned into a desert,
an object of lasting ridicule:
All passers-by will be amazed,
will shake their heads.[d]
17 Like the east wind, I will scatter them
before their enemies;
I will show them my back, not my face,
in their day of disaster.[e]

### Another Prayer for Vengeance.

18 "Come," they said, "let us contrive a plot
against Jeremiah. It will not mean the loss of
instruction from the priests, nor of counsel from
the wise, nor of messages from the prophets.
And so, let us destroy him by his own tongue;
let us carefully note his every word."[f]

19 Heed me, O LORD,
and listen to what my adversaries say.
20 Must good be repaid with evil
that they should dig a pit to take my life?
Remember that I stood before you
to speak in their behalf,
to turn away your wrath from them.[g]
21 So now, deliver their children to famine,[h]
do away with them by the sword.
Let their wives be made childless and
widows;
let their men die of pestilence,
their men be slain by the sword in battle.*
22 May cries be heard from their homes,
when suddenly you send plunderers
against them.
For they have dug a pit to capture me,
they have hid snares for my feet;
23 But you, O LORD, know
all their plans to slay me.
Forgive not their crime,
blot not out their sin in your sight!
Let them go down before you,
proceed against them in the time of your
anger.[i]

## CHAPTER 19

**Symbol of the Potter's Flask.** 1 Thus
said the LORD: Go, buy a potter's earthen flask.
Take along some of the elders of the people and
of the priests, 2 and go out toward the Valley
of Ben-hinnom, at the entrance of the Potsherd
Gate;* there proclaim the words which I will
speak to you: 3 Listen to the word of the LORD,
kings of Judah and citizens of Jerusalem: Thus
says the LORD of hosts, the God of Israel: I am
going to bring such evil upon this place that all
who hear of it will feel their ears tingle. 4 This
is because they have forsaken me and alienated
this place by burning in it incense to strange
gods which neither they nor their fathers knew;
and the kings of Judah have filled this place with
the blood of the innocent.[j] 5 They have built

u Rom 9, 20f.
v Wis 15, 7; Is 45, 9.
w Jer 1, 10.
x Jer 26, 3; Is 55, 7; Ez 18, 21. 27.
y Nm 14, 22f.
z Jer 7, 3; 25, 5; 35, 15.
a Jer 2, 25; 7, 24.
b Jer 2, 10f; 5, 30.
c Jer 2, 13. 32.
d Jer 19, 8; Lv 26, 32; 1 Kgs 9, 8.
e Prv 1, 24-31.
f Jer 11, 19; Ps 35, 15f.
g Ps 35, 12.
h Ps 109, 9f.
i Neh 4, 5; Pss 35, 4; 37, 32f.
j Jer 1, 16; 2 Kgs 21, 16; 24, 4.
k Jer 7, 31f; 32, 35.

*

18, 14: Lebanon: here apparently including Mount Hermon, whose snow-capped peak can be seen from parts of Palestine all year round. The prophet contrasts the certainties of nature with Israel's unnatural desertion of the Lord for idols (v 15).

18, 21: In the Old Testament a man's family was regarded as part of his personality, to be rewarded or punished along with him; cf Jos 7, 24ff.

19, 2: Potsherd Gate: in the south wall of Jerusalem, through which potsherds and other refuse were carried to the Valley of Ben-hinnom.

high places for Baal to immolate their sons in
fire as holocausts to Baal: such a thing as I
neither commanded nor spoke of, nor did it ever
enter my mind.[k] **6** Therefore, days will come,
says the LORD when this place will no longer be
called Topheth, or the Valley of Ben-hinnom,
but rather, the Valley of Slaughter.[l] **7** In this
place I will foil the plan of Judah and Jerusalem;
I will make them fall by the sword before their
enemies, by the hand of those that seek their
lives. Their corpses I will give as food to the
birds of the sky and the beasts of the field.[m] **8** I
will make this city an object of amazement and
derision. Because of all its wounds, every passer-by will be amazed and will catch his breath.
**9** I will have them eat the flesh of their sons and
daughters; they shall eat one another's flesh
during the strict siege by which their enemies
and those who seek their lives will confine
them.[n]

**10** And you shall break the flask in the sight
of the men who went with you, **11** and say to
them: Thus says the LORD of hosts: Thus will I
smash this people and this city, as one smashes
a clay pot so that it cannot be repaired. And
Topheth shall be a burial place, for lack of place
to bury elsewhere.[o] **12** Thus I will do to this
place and to its inhabitants, says the LORD; I will
make this city like Topheth.[p] **13** And the
houses of Jerusalem and the palaces of the kings
of Judah shall be defiled like the place of Topheth, all the houses upon whose roofs they
burnt incense to the whole host of heaven and
poured out libations to strange gods.[q]

**14** When Jeremiah returned from Topheth,
where the LORD had sent him to prophesy, he
stood in the court of the house of God and said
to all the people:[r] **15** Thus says the LORD of
hosts, the God of Israel: I will surely bring upon
this city all the evil with which I threatened it,
because they have stiffened their necks and have
not obeyed my words.[s]

## CHAPTER 20

**1** Jeremiah was heard prophesying these
things by the priest Pashhur,[t] son of Immer,
chief officer in the house of the LORD.* **2** So he
had the prophet scourged and placed in the
stocks at the upper Gate of Benjamin in the
house of the LORD.[u] **3** The next morning, after
Pashhur had released Jeremiah from the stocks,
the prophet said to him:[v] Instead of Pashhur, the
LORD will name you "Terror on every side."*
**4** For thus says the LORD: Indeed, I will deliver
you to terror, you and all your friends. Your
own eyes shall see them fall by the sword of
their enemies. All Judah I will deliver to the
king of Babylon,* who shall take them captive
to Babylon or slay them with the sword. **5** All
the wealth of this city, all it has toiled for and
holds dear, all the treasures of the kings of
Judah, I will give as plunder into the hands of
their foes, who shall seize it and carry it away
to Babylon.[w] **6** You, Pashhur, and all the members of your household shall go into exile. To
Babylon you shall go, you and all your friends;
there you shall die and be buried, because you
have prophesied lies to them.[x]

### Jeremiah's Interior Crisis

**7** You duped me,* O LORD, and I let myself
be duped;
you were too strong for me, and you
triumphed.
All the day I am an object of laughter;
everyone mocks me.
**8** Whenever I speak, I must cry out,
violence and outrage is my message;
The word of the LORD has brought me
derision and reproach all the day.
**9** I say to myself, I will not mention him,
I will speak in his name no more.
But then it becomes like fire burning in my
heart,
imprisoned in my bones;
I grow weary holding it in,
I cannot endure it.[y]
**10** Yes, I hear the whisperings of many:
"Terror on every side!
Denounce! let us denounce him!"
All those who were my friends
are on the watch for any misstep of mine.
"Perhaps he will be trapped; then we can
prevail,
and take our vengeance on him."[z]
**11** But the LORD is with me, like a mighty
champion:
my persecutors will stumble, they will not
triumph.
In their failure they will be put to utter
shame,
to lasting, unforgettable confusion.[a]
**12** O LORD of hosts, you who test the just,
who probe mind and heart,

l Jer 7, 32.
m Jer 7, 33.
n Lv 26, 29.
o Jer 7, 32.
p 2 Kgs 23, 10.
q Jer 32, 29.
r Jer 26, 2.
s Jer 7, 26; Prv 29, 1.
t Jer 21, 1.
u Jer 29, 26.
v Jer 6, 25.
w 2 Kgs 20, 17; 24, 12-16.
x Jer 14, 13f; 28, 15.
y Jer 6, 11; Jb 32, 18.
z Jb 19, 19; Ps 31, 13; Lk 20, 20.
a Jer 1, 8; 15, 20.
b Jer 11, 20.

*

20, 1: Chief officer in the house of the Lord: head of the temple police; cf Jer 29, 26. By entering the temple court (Jer 19, 14), Jeremiah had put himself under Pashhur's jurisdiction.

20, 3: Terror on every side: Pashhur will share the fate of doomed Jerusalem and will experience personally all that the people as a whole have had to endure.

20, 4: Babylon: mentioned here for the first time as the land of exile. The prophecy probably dates from after 605 B.C., when Nebuchadnezzar defeated Egypt and made the Chaldean empire dominant in Syria and Palestine.

20, 7: You duped me: to be understood in the light of Jeremiah's intimate dealings with God; cf Jer 15, 18.

Let me witness the vengeance you take on
them,
for to you I have entrusted my cause.[b]
13 Sing to the LORD,
praise the LORD,
For he has rescued the life of the poor
from the power of the wicked![c]

14 Cursed be the day*
on which I was born!
May the day my mother gave me birth
never be blessed![d]
15 Cursed be the man who brought the news
to my father, saying,
"A child, a son, has been born to you!"
filling
him with great joy.
16 Let that man be like the cities
which the LORD relentlessly overthrew;
Let him hear war cries in the morning,
battle alarms at noonday,[e]
17 because he did not dispatch me in the
womb!
Then my mother would have been my grave,
her womb confining me forever.[f]
18 Why did I come forth from the womb,
to see sorrow and pain,
to end my days in shame?[g]

## *III: Oracles in the Last Years of Jerusalem*

### CHAPTER 21

**Fate of Zedekiah and Jerusalem.** 1 The
message which came to Jeremiah from the LORD
when King Zedekiah* sent him Pashhur, son of
Malchiah, and the priest Zephaniah, son of Maaseiah, with this request: 2 Inquire for us of the
LORD, because Nebuchadnezzar, king of Babylon, is attacking us. Perhaps the LORD will deal
with us according to all his wonderful works, so
that he will withdraw from us. 3 But Jeremiah
answered them: This is what you shall report to
Zedekiah: 4 Thus says the LORD, the God of
Israel: I will turn back in your hands the weapons with which you intend to fight the king of
Babylon and the Chaldeans who besiege you
outside the walls. These weapons I will pile up
in the midst of this city,[h] 5 and I myself will
fight against you with outstretched hand and
mighty arm, in anger, and wrath, and great
rage![i] 6 I will strike the inhabitants of this city,
both man and beast; they shall die in a great
pestilence.[j] 7 After that, says the LORD, I will
hand over Zedekiah, king of Judah, and his
ministers and the people in this city who survive
pestilence, sword, and famine, into the hand of
Nebuchadnezzar, king of Babylon, into the
hands of their enemies and those who seek their
lives. He shall strike them with the edge of the
sword, without quarter, without pity or mercy.[k]
8 And to this people you shall say: Thus says
the LORD: See, I am giving you a choice between life and death.[l] 9 Whoever remains in
this city shall die by the sword or famine or
pestilence. But whoever leaves and surrenders
to the besieging Chaldeans shall live and have
his life as booty. 10 For I have turned against
this city, for its woe and not for its good, says
the LORD. It shall be given into the power of the
king of Babylon who shall burn it with fire.*

### Oracles regarding the Kings

11 To the royal house of Judah:*
Hear the word of the LORD, 12 O house of
David!
Thus says the LORD:
Each morning dispense justice,
rescue the oppressed from the hand of the
oppressor,
Lest my fury break out like fire
which burns without being quenched,
because of the evil of your deeds.[m]
13 Beware! I am against you, Valley-site,
Rock of the Plain,* says the LORD.
You who say, "Who will attack us,
who can penetrate our retreats?"
14 I will punish you, says the LORD,
as your deeds deserve!
I will kindle a fire in its forest*
that shall devour all its surroundings.[n]

---

c Pss 35, 9f; 109, 30f.
d Jer 15, 10; Jb 3, 1-10; 10, 18.
e Gn 19, 25; Is 13, 19.
f Jb 3, 10f; 10, 19.
g Jb 14, 1.
h Jer 37, 8ff.
i Is 63, 10; Lam 2, 4f.
j Jer 16, 4.
k Jer 24, 8ff; Dt 28, 49f.
l Jer 21, 9; Dt 30, 15. 19.
m Jer 4, 4; 22, 3; Zec 7, 9.
n 2 Kgs 25, 9; 2 Chr 36, 19.

---

*20, 14–18: Deception, sorrow and terror have brought the prophet close to the point of despair; nevertheless he has expressed his utmost confidence in the triumph of God's will (vv 11ff); cf Jb 3, 3–12.

21, 1: Zedekiah: brother of Jehoiakim, appointed king by Nebuchadnezzar after he had carried Jehoiachin away to captivity (2 Kgs 24, 17). Passhur: different from the one in Jer 20, 1ff but also one of Jeremiah's enemies; cf Jer 38, 1. 4.

21, 10: Jeremiah consistently pointed out the uselessness of resistance to Babylon, since the Lord had delivered Judah to Nebuchadnezzar (Jer 27, 6). Because of this the prophet was denounced and imprisoned as a traitor (Jer 37, 13f).

21, 11—23, 8: This section contains an editor's collection of Jeremiah's oracles against the kings of Judah. They are placed in the chronological order of the kings, and are prefaced by the oracles against the kings of Judah in general (Jer 21, 11—22, 9).

21, 13: Valley-site, Rock of the Plain: Mount Zion, surrounded by valleys, was regarded by the royal house as impregnable. Despite this natural fortification, God shows derisively that it is no more than a rock rising from the plain, undefendable against the attack of his fury.

21, 14: Its forest: probably the royal palace, built of cedar wood; cf Jer 22, 14; in 1 Kgs 7, 2 the armory of Solomon's palace is called "the house of the forest of Lebanon."

## CHAPTER 22

1 The LORD told me this: Go down to the
palace of the king of Judah and there deliver this
message: 2 You shall say: Listen to the word of
the LORD, king of Judah, who sit on the throne
of David, you, your ministers, and your people
that enter by these gates![o] 3 Thus says the
LORD: Do what is right and just. Rescue the
victim from the hand of his oppressor. Do not
wrong or oppress the resident alien, the orphan,
or the widow, and do not shed innocent blood
in this place.[p] 4 If you carry out these commands, kings who succeed to the throne of David will continue to enter the gates of this palace, riding in chariots or mounted on horses,
with their ministers, and their people. 5 But if
you do not obey these commands, I swear by
myself, says the LORD: this palace shall become
rubble. 6 For thus says the LORD concerning the
palace of the king of Judah:

Though you be to me like Gilead,
like the peak of Lebanon,*
I will turn you into a waste,
a city uninhabited.
7 Against you I will send destroyers,
each with his axe:
They shall cut down your choice cedars,
and cast them into the fire.[q]

8 Many people will pass by this city and ask
one another: "Why has the LORD done this to
so great a city?"[r] 9 And the answer will be
given: "Because they have deserted their covenant with the LORD, their God, by worshiping
and serving strange gods."[s]

### Jehoahaz

10 Weep not for him who is dead,*
mourn not for him!
Weep rather for him who is going away;
never again will he see
the land of his birth.[t]

11 Thus says the LORD concerning Shallum,* son of Josiah, king of Judah, who succeeded his father as king. He has left this place
never to return. 12 Rather, he shall die in the
place where they exiled him; this land he shall
not see again.

### Jehoiakim

13 Woe to him who builds his house on wrong,
his terraces on injustice;
Who works his neighbor without pay,*
and gives him no wages.[u]
14 Who says, "I will build myself a spacious
house,
with airy rooms,"
Who cuts out windows for it,
panels it with cedar,
and paints it with vermillion.
15 Must you prove your rank among kings*
by competing with them in cedar?
Did not your father eat and drink?
He did what was right and just,
and it went well with him.[v]
16 Because he dispensed justice to the weak
and the poor,
it went well with him.
Is this not true knowledge of me?
says the LORD.[w]
17 But your eyes and heart are set on nothing
except on your own gain,
On shedding innocent blood,
on practicing oppression and extortion.[x]

18 Therefore, thus says the LORD concerning
Jehoiakim, son of Josiah, king of Judah:

They shall not lament him,
"Alas! my brother"; "Alas! sister."*
They shall not lament him,
"Alas, Lord! alas, Majesty!"[y]
19 The burial of an ass* shall he be given,
dragged forth and cast out
beyond the gates of Jerusalem.[z]

### Jeconiah

20 Scale Lebanon and cry out,*
in Bashan lift up your voice;
Cry out from Abarim,

o Jer 17, 20.
p Jer 21, 12; Ex 22, 21-24; Dt 24, 17.
q Jer 21, 14.
r Dt 29, 24ff.
s Jer 19, 4; 40, 2f.
t 2 Chr 35, 23ff.
u Lv 19, 13; Dt 24, 14; Hb 2, 9. 12.
v 2 Kgs 23, 25.
w Prv 31, 9.
x Ez 22, 13. 27.
y Jer 16, 4ff; 1 Kgs 13, 30.
z Jer 36, 30.
a Jer 30, 14f; Dt 32, 49.

*

22, 6: Gilead . . . Lebanon: both were known for their trees; cf v 7.

22, 10: Him who is dead: Josiah. His successor, Jehoahaz, who is going away, was deported by Pharaoh Neco to Egypt, where he died (2 Kgs 23, 33f).

22, 11: Shallum: Jehoahaz is called this only here. Presumably it was his name at birth, while Jehoahaz was his royal name.

22, 13: Without pay: either by forced labor in public works, or in as much as workers were defrauded of their hire. Despite the impoverishment caused in Judah by the payment of foreign tribute, Jehoiakim embarked on a program of lavish building in Jerusalem (v 14). Social injustice is the cause of much of the prophetic condemnation of the kings (v 17).

22, 15f: Josiah, the reforming king, prospered materially without oppressing his people; he embodied all the ideals of kingship.

22, 18: "Alas! my brother"; "Alas! sister": customary cries of mourning.

22, 19: The burial of an ass: no burial at all, except to be cast outside the city as refuse. This prophecy regards the popular feeling toward Jehoiakim rather than the actual circumstances of his burial. According to 2 Kgs 24, 5 he was buried with his fathers in Jerusalem. However, his grave may have been profaned by Nebuchadnezzar.

22, 20–23: The prophet first apostrophizes Jerusalem, which is bidden to scale Lebanon, Bashan, and Abarim, i.e., the highest surrounding mountains to the north, northeast, and southeast, to gaze on the ruin of its lovers, i.e., the false leaders of Judah, called its shepherds (22); cf Jer 2, 8. The year is 597 B.C., after Nebuchadnezzar's deportation of Jehoiachin. Jerusalem still stands (23), apparently as secure as the heights of Lebanon, but destruction is to follow (cf v 6).

for all your lovers are crushed.[a]
21 I spoke to you when you were secure,
but you answered, "I will not listen."
This has been your way from your youth,
not to listen to my voice.
22 The wind shall shepherd all your shepherds,
your lovers shall go into exile.
Surely then you shall be ashamed and
confounded
because of all your wickedness.
23 You who dwell on Lebanon,
who nest in the cedars,
How you shall groan when pains come upon
you,
like the pangs of a woman in travail!

24 As I live, says the LORD, if you, Coniah,*
son of Jehoiakim, king of Judah, are a signet
ring on my right hand, I will snatch you from
it. 25 I will deliver you into the hands of those
who seek your life; the hands of those whom
you fear; the hands of Nebuchadnezzar, king of
Babylon, and the Chaldeans.[b] 26 I will cast
you out, you and the mother who bore you,*
into a different land from the one you were born
in; and there you shall die.[c] 27 Neither of them
shall come back to the land for which they
yearn.[d]

28 Is this man Coniah a vessel despised, to be
broken up,
an instrument that no one wants?
Why are he and his descendants cast out?
why thrown into a land they know not?
29 O land, land, land,
hear the word of the LORD—
30 Thus says the LORD:
[e]Write this man down as one childless,*
who will never thrive in his lifetime!
No descendant of his shall achieve
a seat on the throne of David
as ruler again over Judah.

## CHAPTER 23

**Messianic Reign.*** 1 [f]Woe to the shepherds who mislead and scatter the flock of my
pasture, says the LORD. 2 Therefore, thus says
the LORD, the God of Israel, against the shepherds who shepherd my people: You have scattered my sheep and driven them away. You
have not cared for them, but I will take care to
punish your evil deeds.[g] 3 I myself will gather
the remnant of my flock from all the lands to
which I have driven them and bring them back
to their meadow; there they shall increase and
multiply.[h] 4 I will appoint shepherds for them
who will shepherd them so that they need no
longer fear and tremble; and none shall be missing, says the LORD.[i]

5 Behold, the days are coming, says the
LORD,
when I will raise up a righteous shoot to
David;
As king he shall reign and govern wisely,
he shall do what is just and right in the
land.[j]
6 In his days Judah shall be saved,
Israel shall dwell in security.
This is the name they give him:
"The LORD our justice."[k]

7 [l]Therefore, the days will come, says the
LORD, when they shall no longer say, "As the
LORD lives, who brought the Israelites out of the
land of Egypt"; 8 but rather, "As the LORD
lives, who brought the descendants of the house
of Israel up from the land of the north"—and
from all the lands to which I banished them; they
shall again live on their own land.

### The False Prophets*

9 Concerning the prophets:
My heart within me is broken,
my bones all tremble;
I am like a man who is drunk,

b Jer 21, 7; 34, 20.
c 2 Kgs 24, 15.
d Jer 44, 14.
e Jer 36, 30; 1 Chr 3, 16f; Mt 1, 12.
f Jer 22, 22.
g Ez 34, 4ff; Zec 11, 16f.
h Jer 29, 14; 32, 37.
i Jer 3, 15; Ez 34, 11f.
j Jer 33, 14ff; Is 4, 2; 9, 5f; 11, 1-5.
k Dn 9, 24.
l 7f: Jer 16, 14f.

*

22, 24: Coniah: a shortened form of Jeconiah, the name which Jeremiah gives the king called elsewhere in the Bible Jehoiachin. A signet ring: the seal used by important men—in a sense, their most valuable possession—mounted in a ring worn constantly on the hand. The Lord says that even were Jehoiachin such a precious possession, he would reject him. The words in vv 24–30 date from the short three-month reign of Jehoiachin, before he was carried away by Nebuchadnezzar.

22, 26: You and the mother who bore you: the queen mother held a special position in the monarchy of Judah, and in the Books of Kings she is invariably mentioned by name along with the king (1 Kgs 15, 2; 2 Kgs 18, 2). Jehoiachin did indeed die in Babylon.

22, 30: Childless: Jehoiachin is so considered because none of his descendants will be king. From the Book of Ezekiel, who dates his oracles according to Jehoiachin's fictitious regnal years, it is evident that the people expected Jehoiachin to return. The above prophecy of Jeremiah was uttered to dispel this hope (Jer 28, 4). Of the seven sons born to Jehoiachin in exile, none became king. His grandson Zerubbabel presided for a time over the Jewish community after the return from exile, but not as king.

23, 1–8: With the false rulers who have governed his people the Lord contrasts himself, the good shepherd, who will in the times of restoration appoint worthy rulers (1–4). A messianic King will arise from the line of David who will rule over Judah and Israel with the justice of the Lord, fulfilling all the kingly ideals (5f). "The Lord our justice" is probably an ironic wordplay on the name of the weak King Zedekiah ("The Lord is justice"); the messianic King will be in reality what Zedekiah's name falsely proclaims him. The final verses, 7–8, were probably added during the exile.

23, 9–40: After the collection of oracles against the kings, the editor of the book placed this collection of oracles against the false prophets. With them are associated the priests, for both have betrayed their trust as instructors in the religion of the Lord; cf Jer 2, 8; 4, 9; 6, 13f.

overcome by wine,
Because of the LORD,
because of his holy words.
10 With adulterers the land is filled;
on their account the land mourns,
the pasture ranges are seared.[m]
Theirs is an evil course,
theirs is unjust power.
11 Both prophet and priest are godless!
In my very house I find their wickedness,
says the LORD.[n]
12 Hence their way shall become for them
slippery ground.
In the darkness they shall lose their footing,
and fall headlong;
Evil I will bring upon them:
the year of their punishment, says the
LORD.[o]
13 Among Samaria's prophets
I saw unseemly deeds:
They prophesied by Baal
and led my people Israel astray.[p]
14 But among Jerusalem's prophets
I saw deeds still more shocking:
Adultery, living in lies,
siding with the wicked,
so that no one turns from evil;
To me they are all like Sodom,
its citizens like Gomorrah.[q]

15 Therefore, thus says the LORD of hosts
against the prophets:

Behold, I will give them wormwood to eat,
and poison to drink;
For from Jerusalem's prophets
ungodliness has gone forth into the whole
land.[r]
16 Thus says the LORD of hosts:
Listen not to the words of your prophets,
who fill you with emptiness;
Visions of their own fancy they speak,
not from the mouth of the LORD.[s]
17 They say to those who despise the word of
the LORD,*
"Peace shall be yours";
And to everyone who walks in hardness of
heart,
"No evil shall overtake you."[t]
18 Now, who has stood in the council of the
LORD,
to see him and to hear his word?
Who has heeded his word, so as to
announce it?[u]
19 See, the storm of the LORD!
His wrath breaks forth
In a whirling storm
that bursts upon the heads of the wicked.[v]
20 The anger of the LORD shall not abate
until he has done and fulfilled
what he has determined in his heart.
When the time comes,
you shall fully understand.
21 I did not send these prophets,
yet they ran;
I did not speak to them,
yet they prophesied.[w]
22 Had they stood in my council,
and did they but proclaim to my people
my words,
They would have brought them back from
evil ways
and from their wicked deeds.
23 Am I a God near at hand only, says the
LORD,[x]
and not a God far off?*
24 Can a man hide in secret
without my seeing him? says the LORD.
Do I not fill
both heaven and earth? says the LORD.

25 I have heard the prophets who prophesy
lies in my name say, "I had a dream! I had a
dream!" 26 How long will this continue? Is my
name in the hearts of the prophets who prophesy
lies and their own deceitful fancies? 27 By their
dreams which they recount to each other, they
think to make my people forget my name, just
as their fathers forgot my name for Baal.[y]
28 Let the prophet who has a dream recount his
dream; let him who has my word speak my word
truthfully!

What has straw to do with the wheat?*
says the LORD.[z]
29 Is not my word like fire, says the LORD,
like a hammer shattering rocks?

30 Therefore I am against the prophets, says
the LORD, who steal my words from each other.[a] 31 Yes, I am against the prophets, says the
LORD, who borrow speeches to pronounce oracles. 32 Yes, I am against the prophets who
prophesy lying dreams, says the LORD, and who
lead my people astray by recounting their lies
and by their empty boasting. From me they have
no mission or command, and they do this people
no good at all, says the LORD.[b]
33 *And when this people, or a prophet or a

m Jer 4, 22; 5, 7f; 9, 2. 10.
n Jer 6, 13.
o Ps 35, 6.
p 1 Kgs 18, 19.
q Jer 29, 21ff; Is 1, 9f.
r Jer 8, 14; 9, 14.
s Jer 14, 14.
t Jer 5, 12; Ez 13, 10; Mi 3, 11; Zec 10, 2.
u Jb 15, 8; Is 40, 13; 1 Cor 2, 16.
v Jer 30, 23.
w Jer 29, 9.
x Jer 16, 17; Ps 139, 8.
y Jgs 3, 7; 8, 33.
z Nm 12, 6.
a Dt 18, 20.
b Jer 28, 15ff.

*

23, 17–20: Not only are the false prophets personally immoral, but they encourage immorality by prophesying good of those who do evil. The true prophet, on the other hand, sees the inevitable consequences of sin.

23, 23: Near at hand only . . . far off: God knows not merely the present but also the future.

23, 28f: Straw . . . wheat: such is the contrast between false and true prophecy. True prophecy is like fire (cf Jer 5, 14; 20, 9), producing violent results (v 29); Jeremiah's own life is a testimony of this.

23, 33–40: A wordplay on massa, which means both oracle (usually of woe) and burden. In 34ff it appears that the word massa itself is forbidden the people in the meaning of a divine oracle. Doubtless this was because of some association un-

priest asks you, "What is the burden of the
LORD?" you shall answer, "You are the burden, and I cast you off, says the LORD." **34** If
a prophet or a priest or anyone else mentions
"the burden of the LORD," I will punish that
man and his house. **35** Thus you shall ask,
when speaking to one another, "What answer
did the LORD give?" or, "What did the LORD
say?" **36** But the burden of the LORD you shall
mention no more. For each man his own word
becomes the burden so that you pervert the
words of the living God, the LORD of hosts, our
God. **37** Thus shall you ask the prophet, "What
answer did the LORD give?" or, "What did the
LORD say?" **38** But if you ask about "the burden of the LORD," then thus says the LORD:
Because you use this phrase, "the burden of the
LORD," though I forbade you to use it,
**39** therefore I will lift you on high and cast you
from my presence, you and the city which I gave
to you and your fathers. **40** And I will bring
upon you eternal reproach, eternal, unforgettable shame.[c]

## CHAPTER 24

**The Two Baskets of Figs.*** **1** The LORD
showed me two baskets of figs placed before the
temple of the LORD.[d] —This was after Nebuchadnezzar, king of Babylon, had exiled from
Jerusalem Jeconiah, son of Jehoiakim, king of
Judah, and the princes of Judah, the artisans and
the skilled workers, and brought them to Babylon.— **2** One basket contained excellent figs,
the early-ripening kind. But the other basket
contained very bad figs, so bad they could not
be eaten. **3** Then the LORD said to me: What do
you see, Jeremiah?[e] "Figs," I replied; "the
good ones are very good, but the bad ones very
bad, so bad they cannot be eaten." **4** Thereupon this word of the LORD came to me: **5** Thus
says the LORD, the God of Israel: Like these
good figs, even so will I regard with favor Judah's exiles whom I sent away from this place
into the land of the Chaldeans.[f] **6** I will look
after them for their good, and bring them back
to this land, to build them up, not to tear them
down; to plant them, not to pluck them out.[g] **7** I
will give them a heart with which to understand
that I am the LORD. They shall be my people and
I will be their God, for they shall return to me
with their whole heart.[h] **8** And like the figs that
are bad, so bad they cannot be eaten—yes, thus
says the LORD—even so will I treat Zedekiah,
king of Judah, and his princes, the remnant of
Jerusalem remaining in this land and those who
have settled in the land of Egypt.[i] **9** I will make
them an object of horror to all the kingdoms of
the earth, a reproach and a byword, a taunt and
a curse, in all the places to which I will drive
them.[j] **10** I will send upon them the sword,
famine, and pestilence, until they have disappeared from the land which I gave them and
their fathers.[k]

## CHAPTER 25

**Seventy Years of Exile.*** **1** The word that
came to Jeremiah concerning all the people of
Judah, in the fourth year of Jehoiakim, son of
Josiah, king of Judah (the first year of Nebuchadnezzar, king of Babylon).[l] **2** This word the
prophet Jeremiah spoke to all the people of Judah and all the citizens of Jerusalem: **3** Since
the thirteenth year of Josiah, son of Amon, king
of Judah, to this day—these three and twenty
years—the word of the LORD has come to me
and I spoke to you untiringly, but you would not
listen.[m] **4** Though you refused to listen or pay
heed, the LORD has sent you without fail all his
servants the prophets[n] **5** with this message:
Turn back, each of you, from your evil way and
from your evil deeds; then you shall remain in
the land which the LORD gave you and your
fathers, from of old and forever. **6** Do not follow strange gods to serve and adore them, lest
you provoke me with your handiwork, and I
bring evil upon you.[o] **7** But you would not
listen to me, says the LORD, and so you provoked me with your handiwork to your own
harm.[p] **8** Hence, thus says the LORD of hosts:
Since you would not listen to my words, **9** lo!
I will send for and fetch all the tribes of the
north, says the LORD (and I will send to Nebuchadnezzar, king of Babylon, my servant); I
will bring them against this land, against its
inhabitants, and against all these neighboring
nations. I will doom them, making them an
object of horror, of ridicule, of everlasting reproach.[q] **10** Among them I will bring to an end

c Jer 20, 11.
d Am 8, 1f.
e Jer 1, 11.
f Jer 29, 11; Lv 26, 44f.
g Jer 12, 15; Am 9, 15.
h Jer 30, 22; 31, 1; 32, 37; Bar 2, 31.
i Jer 29, 18.
j Jer 15, 4; Dt 28, 37.
k Jer 14, 12.
l Jer 36, 1.
m Jer 1, 2.
n 2 Chr 36, 15.
o Jer 7, 6f.
p Jer 7, 17ff.
q Jer 1, 15; 43, 10.

*

known to us. In Hos 2, 18 it is forbidden to call God "Baal" ("master"), because of the association of this title with the Canaanite god.

24, 1–10: Jeremiah, like Ezekiel, saw that no good could be expected from the people who had been left in Judah under Zedekiah or who had fled into Egypt; good was to be hoped for only from those who would pass through the purifying experience of the exile to form the new Israel.

25, 1–14: The fourth year of Jehoiakim: 605 B.C. Officially, the first year of Nebuchadnezzar began the following year; but as early as his victory over Egypt at Carchemish in 605, Nebuchadnezzar was the dominant power in the Near East, in whom Jeremiah now saw the fulfillment of his prophecy of the enemy to come from the north (cf Jer 1, 13; 6 22ff). In vv 11f occurs for the first time the prophecy of the seventy years' exile; cf Jer 29, 10. This Jeremiah intends as a round number, to signify that the present generation must die out.

the song of joy and the song of gladness, the
voice of the bridegroom and the voice of the
bride, the sound of the millstone and the light
of the lamp. **11** This whole land shall be a ruin
and a desert. Seventy years these nations shall
be enslaved to the king of Babylon:[r] **12** but
when the seventy years have elapsed, I will
punish the king of Babylon and the nation and
the land of the Chaldeans for their guilt, says the
LORD. Their land I will turn into everlasting
desert.[s] **13** Against that land I will fulfill all the
words I have spoken against it [all that is written
in this book, which Jeremiah prophesied against
all the nations]. **14** They also shall be enslaved
to great nations and mighty kings, and thus I
will repay them according to their own deeds
and according to their own handiwork.[t]

## The Cup of Judgment on the Nations.

**15** For thus said the LORD, the God of Israel,
to me:* Take this cup of foaming wine from my
hand, and have all the nations to whom I will
send you drink it.[u] **16** They shall drink, and be
convulsed, and go mad, because of the sword I
will send among them.[v] **17** I took the cup from
the hand of the LORD and gave drink to all the
nations to which the LORD sent me: **18** [Jerusa-
lem, the cities of Judah, her kings and her
princes, to make them a ruin and a desert, an
object of ridicule and cursing, as they are today;] **19** Pharaoh, king of Egypt, and his servants, his princes, all the people under him,
native **20** and foreign; all the kings of the land
of Uz;* all the kings of the land of the Philistines: Ashkelon, Gaza, Ekron, and the remnant
of Ashdod; **21** Edom, Moab, and the Ammonites; **22** all the kings of Tyre, of Sidon, and of
the shores beyond the sea;* **23** Dedan and
Tema and Buz,* all the desert dwellers who
shave their temples; **24** [all the kings of Arabia;] **25** all the kings of Zimri, of Elam, of the
Medes; **26** all the kings of the north, near and
far, one after the other; all the kingdoms upon
the face of the earth [and after them the king of
Sheshach* shall drink].

**27** Tell them: Thus says the LORD of hosts,
the God of Israel: Drink! become drunk and
vomit; fall, never to rise, before the sword that
I will send among you![w] **28** If they refuse to
take the cup from your hand and drink, say to
them: Thus says the LORD of hosts: You must
drink![x] **29** For since with this city, which is
called by my name, I begin to inflict evil, how
can you possibly be spared? You shall not be
spared! I will call down the sword upon all who
inhabit the earth, says the LORD of hosts.

**30** Prophesy against them all these things
and say to them:

The LORD roars from on high,
from his holy dwelling he raises his voice;
Mightily he roars over the range,
a shout like that of vintagers over
the grapes.[y]
**31** To all who inhabit the earth to its very ends
the uproar spreads;
For the LORD has an indictment against the
nations,
he is to pass judgment upon all mankind:
The godless shall be given to the sword,
says the LORD.
**32** Thus says the LORD of hosts:
Lo! calamity stalks
from nation to nation;
A great storm is unleashed
from the ends of the earth.

**33** On that day, those whom the LORD has slain
will be strewn from one end of the earth to the
other. None will mourn them, none will gather
them for burial; they shall lie like dung on the
field.[z]

**34** Howl, you shepherds, and wail!
roll in the dust, leaders of the flock!
The time for your slaughter has come;
like choice rams you shall fall.
**35** There is no flight for the shepherds,
no escape for the leaders of the flock.[a]
**36** Listen! Wailing from the shepherds,
howling by the leaders of the flock!
For the LORD lays waste their grazing place,
**37** desolate lie the peaceful pastures;
**38** The lion leaves his lair,
and their land is made desolate
By the sweeping sword,
by the burning wrath of the LORD.[b]

## CHAPTER 26

**Jeremiah Threatened with Death.** **1** In
the beginning of the reign* of Jehoiakim, son of
Josiah, king of Judah, this message came from
the LORD: **2** Thus says the LORD: Stand in the
court of the house of the LORD and speak to the
people of all the cities of Judah who come to

r Lv 26, 32-35.
s Is 13, 20ff.
t Jer 27, 7; 50, 9. 41f; 51, 6. 24.
u Rv 14, 10.
v Jer 51, 7.
w Ob 1, 16.
x Jer 49, 12.
y Jer 51, 14.
z Jer 8, 2; 16, 4. 6.
a Jer 32, 4.
b Jer 4, 7.
c Jer 7, 2.

*

25, 15ff: Jeremiah is a prophet to the nations (cf 1, 5) as well as to his own people. All the nations mentioned here appear again in the more extensive collection of Jeremiah's oracles against the nations in chapters 46–51.

25, 20: Uz: the homeland of Job, in Edomite or Arabian territory.

25, 22: The shores beyond the sea: Phoenician commercial colonies planted throughout the Mediterranean world.

25, 23: Dedan and Tema and Buz: North Arabian tribes.

25, 26: Sheshach: Babylon. The word is formed from babel by substituting letters of the Hebrew alphabet in inverse order.

26, 1: The beginning of the reign: a technical expression for the time between a king's accession to the throne and the beginning of his first official (calendar) year as king. Jehoiakim's first regnal year was 608 B.C.

worship in the house of the LORD; whatever I
command you, tell them, and omit nothing.[c]
**3** Perhaps they will listen and turn back, each
from his evil way, so that I may repent of the
evil I have planned to inflict upon them for their
evil deeds.[d] **4** Say to them: Thus says the
LORD: If you disobey me, not living according
to the law I placed before you **5** and not listening to the words of my servants the prophets,
whom I send you constantly though you do not
obey them,[e] **6** I will treat this house like Shiloh, and make this the city which all the nations
of the earth shall refer to when cursing another.[f]

**7** Now the priests, the prophets, and all the
people heard Jeremiah speak these words in the
house of the LORD. **8** When Jeremiah finished
speaking all that the LORD bade him speak to all
the people, the priests and prophets laid hold of
him, crying, "You must be put to death! **9** Why
do you prophesy in the name of the LORD: 'This
house shall be like Shiloh,' and 'This city shall
be desolate and deserted'?" And all the people
gathered about Jeremiah in the house of the
LORD.

**10** When the princes of Judah were informed
of these things, they came up from the king's
palace to the house of the LORD and held court
at the New Gate of the house of the LORD.
**11** The priests and prophets said to the princes
and to all the people, "This man deserves death;
he has prophesied against this city, as you have
heard with your own ears."[g] **12** Jeremiah gave
this answer to the princes and all the people: "It
was the LORD who sent me to prophesy against
this house and city all that you have heard.
**13** Now, therefore, reform your ways and your
deeds; listen to the voice of the LORD your God,
so that the LORD will repent of the evil with
which he threatens you.[h] **14** As for me, I am in
your hands; do with me what you think good and
right. **15** But mark well: if you put me to death,
it is innocent blood you bring on yourselves, on
this city and its citizens. For in truth it was the
LORD who sent me to you, to speak all these
things for you to hear."

**16** Thereupon the princes and all the people
said to the priests and the prophets, "This man
does not deserve death; it is in the name of the
LORD, our God, that he speaks to us." **17** At
this, some of elders of the land came forward
and said to all the people assembled, **18** "Micah of Moresheth* used to prophesy in the days
of Hezekiah, king of Judah, and he told all the
people of Judah: Thus says the LORD of hosts:

Zion shall become a plowed field,
  Jerusalem a heap of ruins,
  and the temple mount a forest ridge.[i]

**19** Did Hezekiah, king of Judah, and all Judah
condemn him to death? Did they not rather fear
the LORD and entreat the favor of the LORD, so
that he repented of the evil with which he had
threatened them? But we are on the point of
committing this great evil to our own undoing."[j]

**The Fate of Uriah.** **20** There was another
man who prophesied in the name of the LORD,
Uriah, son of Shemaiah, from Kiriath-jearim;
he prophesied the same things against this city
and land as Jeremiah did. **21** When King Jehoiakim and all his officers and princes were informed of his words, the king sought to kill him.
But Uriah heard of it and fled in fear to Egypt.
**22** Thereupon King Jehoiakim sent Elnathan,
son of Achbor, and others with him into Egypt
**23** to bring Uriah back to the king, who had him
slain by the sword and his corpse cast into the
common grave. **24** But Ahikam, son of Shaphan,* protected Jeremiah, so that he was not
handed over to the people to be put to death.

## CHAPTER 27

**Serve Babylon or Perish.*** **1** [In the beginning of the reign of Jehoiakim, son of Josiah,
king of Judah,] . . . this message came to Jeremiah from the LORD: **2** Thus said the LORD to
me: Make for yourself bands and yoke bars and
put them over your shoulders. **3** Send to the
kings of Edom, of Moab, of the Ammonites, of
Tyre, and of Sidon, through the ambassadors
who have come to Jerusalem to Zedekiah, king
of Judah, **4** and charge them thus: Tell your
masters: Thus says the LORD of hosts, the God
of Israel: **5** It was I who made the earth, and
man and beast on the face of the earth, by my
great power, with my outstretched arm; and I
can give them to whomever I think fit.[k] **6** Now
I have given all these lands into the hand of
Nebuchadnezzar, king of Babylon, my servant;
even the beasts of the field I have given him for

d Jer 18, 3.
e Jer 25, 4.
f Jer 7, 12. 14.
g Jer 38, 4.
h Jer 7, 3.
i Mi 1, 1; 3, 12.
j 2 Chr 32, 26.
k Jer 32, 17.
l Jer 25, 9; 43, 10; Ez 30, 21. 25.

*

26, 18: Micah of Moresheth: the prophet Micah, who appears among the canonical minor prophets (cf Mi 1, 1).

26, 24: Ahikam, son of Shaphan: one of Josiah's officials (2 Kgs 22, 12) and father of Gedaliah, Jeremiah's friend, who was governor of Judah after Zedekiah's deportation (cf Jer 39, 14; 40, 5ff).

27, 1—29, 32: A special collection of Jeremiah's prophecies dealing with false prophets. From stylistic peculiarities, quite evident in the Hebrew, it is plain that these three chapters once existed independently of the other prophecies of Jeremiah.

27, 1: [In the beginning of the reign of Jehoiakim . . . Judah]: this gloss cannot be correct because according to Jer 28, 1 the time is the fourth year of Zedekiah, 594 B.C., the occasion of an embassy of the neighboring states (v 3), doubtless for the purpose of laying plans against Nebuchadnezzar.

his use.[l] 7 All nations shall serve him and his
son and his grandson, until the time of his land,
too, shall come. Then it in turn shall serve great
nations and mighty kings.[m] 8 Meanwhile, if
any nation or kingdom will not serve Nebuchadnezzar, king of Babylon, or will not bend its
neck under the yoke of the king of Babylon, I
will punish that nation with sword, famine, and
pestilence, says the LORD, until I give them into
his hand.[n]

9 You, however, must not listen to your
prophets,* to your diviners and dreamers, to
your soothsayers and sorcerers, who say to you,
"You need not serve the king of Babylon."[o]
10 For they prophesy lies to you, in order to
drive you far from your land, to make me banish
you so that you will perish.[p] 11 The people that
submits its neck to the yoke of the king of
Babylon to serve him I will leave in peace on its
own land, says the LORD, to till it and dwell in
it.[q]

12 To Zedekiah, king of Judah, I spoke the
same words: Submit your necks to the yoke of
the king of Babylon; serve him and his people,
so that you may live.[r] 13 Why should you and
your people die by sword, famine, and pestilence, with which the LORD has threatened the
nation that will not serve the king of Babylon?[s]
14 Do not listen to the words of those prophets
who say, "You need not serve the king of Babylon," for they prophesy lies to you.[t] 15 I did
not send them, says the LORD, but they prophesy falsely in my name, with the result that I must
banish you, and you will perish, you and the
prophets who are prophesying to you.[u]

16 [v]To the priests and to all the people I
spoke as follows: Thus says the LORD: Do not
listen to the words of your prophets who prophesy to you: "The vessels of the house of the LORD
will be brought back from Babylon soon now,"
for they prophesy lies to you. 17 Do not listen
to them! Serve the king of Babylon that you may
live; else this city will become a heap of ruins.
18 If they were prophets, if the word of the
LORD were with them, they would intercede
with the LORD of hosts, that the vessels which
remain in the house of the LORD and in the
palace of the king of Judah and in Jerusalem
might not be taken to Babylon. 19 *For thus
says the LORD of hosts concerning the pillars,
the bronze sea, the stands, and the rest of the
vessels that remain in this city, 20 which Nebuchadnezzar, king of Babylon, did not take when
he exiled Jeconiah, son of Jehoiakim, king of
Judah, from Jerusalem to Babylon, along with
all the nobles of Judah and Jerusalem— 21 yes,
thus says the LORD of hosts, the God of Israel,
concerning the vessels that remain in the house
of the LORD, in the palace of the king of Judah,
and in Jerusalem:[w] 22 To Babylon they shall be
brought, and there they shall remain, until the
day I look for them, says the LORD; then I will
bring them back and restore them to this place.

## CHAPTER 28

**The Two Yokes.** 1 That same year, in [the
beginning of] the reign of Zedekiah, king of
Judah, in the fifth month of the fourth year, the
prophet Hananiah, son of Azzur, from Gibeon,
said to me in the house of the LORD in the
presence of the priests and all the people:
2 "Thus says the LORD of hosts, the God of
Israel: 'I will break the yoke of the king of
Babylon. 3 Within two years I will restore to
this place all the vessels of the temple of the
LORD which Nebuchadnezzar, king of Babylon,
took away from this place to Babylon. 4 And I
will bring back to this place Jeconiah, son of
Jehoiakim, king of Judah, and all the exiles of
Judah who went to Babylon,' says the LORD,
'for I will break the yoke of the king of Babylon.' "

5 The prophet Jeremiah answered the prophet Hananiah in the presence of the priests and all
the people assembled in house of the LORD,
6 and said: Amen! thus may the LORD do! May
he fulfill the things you have prophesied by
bringing the vessels of the house of the LORD
and all the exiles back from Babylon to this
place! 7 But now, listen to what I am about to
state in your hearing and the hearing of all the
people. 8 From of old, the prophets who were
before you and me prophesied war, woe, and
pestilence against many lands and mighty kingdoms. 9 But the prophet who prophesies peace
is recognized as truly sent by the LORD only
when his prophetic prediction is fulfilled.[x]

10 Thereupon the prophet Hananiah took the
yoke from the neck of the prophet Jeremiah,
broke it, 11 and said in the presence of all the
people: "Thus says the LORD: 'Even so, within
two years I will break the yoke of Nebuchadnezzar, king of Babylon, from off the neck of all
the nations.' " At that, the prophet Jeremiah
went away.

12 Some time after the prophet Hananiah had
broken the yoke from off the neck of the prophet
Jeremiah, the word of the LORD came to Jeremiah: 13 Go tell Hananiah this: Thus says the
LORD: By breaking a wooden yoke, you forge

m Jer 25, 11; 2 Chr 36, 20.
n Jer 25, 9; Bar 2, 22.
o Jer 29, 8.
p Jer 14, 13-16.
q Bar 2, 21.
r Jer 38, 17.
s Jer 24, 8ff.
t Jer 14, 14; 23, 21.
u Jer 20, 6.
v Jer 28, 3; 2 Chr 36, 7. 10. 18.
w 21f: 2 Kgs 25, 13-17; 2 Chr 36, 18. 22.
x Dt 18, 22.

*

27, 9: Your prophets: seers and diviners served the Gentile kings as the professional prophets served the kings of Judah.

27, 19–22: This prophecy was fulfilled after Zedekiah's disastrous defeat; cf 2 Kgs 25, 13ff.

an iron yoke! **14** For thus says the LORD of
hosts, the God of Israel: A yoke of iron I will
place on the necks of all these nations serving
Nebuchadnezzar, king of Babylon, and they
shall serve him; even the beasts of the field I
give him.[y]
**15** To the prophet Hananiah the prophet Jeremiah said: Hear this, Hananiah! The LORD has
not sent you, and you have raised false confidence in this people. **16** For this, says the
LORD, I will dispatch you from the face of the
earth; this very year you shall die, because you
have preached rebellion against the LORD.[z]
**17** That same year, in the seventh month, Hananiah the prophet died.

## CHAPTER 29

**Letter to the Exiles in Babylon.** **1** This
is the contents of the letter which the prophet
Jeremiah sent from Jerusalem to the remaining
elders among the exiles, to the priests, the
prophets, and all the people who were exiled by
Nebuchadnezzar from Jerusalem to Babylon.
**2** This was after King Jeconiah and the queen
mother, the courtiers, the princes of Judah and
Jerusalem, the artisans and the skilled workmen
had left Jerusalem.[a] **3** Delivered in Babylon by
Elasah,* son of Shaphan, and by Gemariah, son
of Hilkiah, whom Zedekiah, king of Judah, sent
to the king of Babylon, the letter read:
**4** Thus says the LORD of hosts, the God of
Israel, to all the exiles whom I exiled from
Jerusalem to Babylon: **5** Build houses to dwell
in; plant gardens, and eat their fruits. **6** Take
wives and beget sons and daughters; find wives
for your sons and give your daughters husbands,
so that they may bear sons and daughters. There
you must increase in number, not decrease.
**7** Promote the welfare of the city to which I
have exiled you; pray for it to the LORD, for
upon its welfare depends your own.[b]
**10** Thus says the LORD: Only after seventy
years have elapsed for Babylon will I visit you
and fulfill for you my promise to bring you back
to this place.[c] **11** For I know well the plans I
have in mind for you, says the LORD, plans for
your welfare, not for woe! plans to give you a
future full of hope. **12** When you call me, when
you go to pray to me, I will listen to you.[d]
**13** When you look for me, you will find me.
Yes, when you seek me with all your heart,
**14** you will find me with you, says the LORD,
and I will change your lot; I will gather you
together from all the nations and all the places
to which I have banished you, says the LORD,
and bring you back to the place from which I
have exiled you.[e]
**16** Thus says the LORD concerning the king
who sits on David's throne, and all the people
who remain in this city, your brethren who did
not go with you into exile; **17** thus says the
LORD of hosts: I am sending against them
sword, famine and pestilence. I will make them
like rotten figs, too bad to be eaten. **18** I will
pursue them with sword, famine, and pestilence, and make them an object of horror to all
the kingdoms of the earth, of malediction, astonishment, ridicule, and reproach to all the
nations among which I will banish them.[f]
**19** For they did not listen to my words, says the
LORD, though I kept sending them my servants
the prophets, only to have them go unheeded,
says the LORD.[g]
**20** You, now, listen to the word of the LORD,
all you exiles whom I sent away from Jerusalem
to Babylon. **15** As for your saying, "The LORD
has raised up for us prophets here in Babylon"— **8** thus says the LORD of hosts, the God
of Israel: Do not let yourselves be deceived by
the prophets and diviners who are among you;
do not listen to those among you who dream
dreams.[h] **9** For they prophesy lies to you in my
name; I did not send them, says the LORD.[i]
**21** This is what the LORD of hosts, the God of
Israel, has to say about those who prophesy lies
to you in my name, Ahab, son of Kolaiah, and
Zedekiah, son of Maaseiah: I am handing them
over to Nebuchadnezzar, king of Babylon, who
will slay them before your eyes.[j] **22** All the
exiles of Judah in Babylon will pattern a curse
after them: "May the LORD make you like Zedekiah and Ahab, whom the king of Babylon
roasted in the flames." **23** For they are criminals in Israel, committing adultery with their
neighbors' wives, and alleging in my name
things I did not command. I know, I am witness,
says the LORD.[k]

**The False Prophet Shemaiah.** **24** Say
this to Shemaiah, the Nehelamite: **25** Thus says
the LORD of hosts, the God of Israel: Because
you sent letters on your own authority to all the
people of Jerusalem, to all the priests and to
Zephaniah, the priest, son of Maaseiah, with
this message: **26** *"The LORD has appointed

y Jer 27, 6f; Dt 28, 48.
z Dt 13, 6.
a 2 Kgs 24, 15.
b 1 Tm 2, 1f.
c Jer 25, 11; 2 Chr 36, 21f; Ezr 1, 1; Dn 9, 2; Zec 1, 12; 7, 5.
d Jer 33, 3.
e Jer 23, 3. 8.
f Jer 15, 4; 24, 9; 34, 17f.
g Jer 25, 4.
h Jer 27, 9. 14.
i Jer 5, 31.
j Jer 14, 14.
k Jer 23, 14.

*

29, 3: Elasah: possibly the brother of Ahikam (cf Jer 26, 24). Gemariah; perhaps the son of the high priest Hilkiah; cf 2 Kgs 22, 4. Zedekiah had dispatched these men to Nebuchadnezzar for some other purpose, possibly the payment of tribute, but Jeremiah took advantage of their mission to send his letter by them.

29, 26–29: The words of Jeremiah to the false prophet Shemaiah are not fully preserved in the current Hebrew text, as is seen in the incomplete sentence of this translation (vv 25–28). In his letter to Zephaniah Shemaiah reminds him of his

you priest in place of the priest Jehoiada, so that
there may be police officers in the house of the
LORD, to take action against all madmen and
those who pose as prophets, by putting them
into the stocks or the pillory. **27** Why, then, do
you not rebuke Jeremiah of Anathoth who poses
as a prophet among you? **28** For he sent us in
Babylon this message: It will be a long time;
build houses to live in; plant gardens and eat
their fruits. . . .''

**29** When the priest Zephaniah read this letter
to the prophet, **30** the word of the LORD came
to Jeremiah: **31** Send the message to all the
exiles: Thus says the LORD concerning Shemaiah, the Nehelamite: Because Shemaiah prophesies to you without a mission from me, and
raises false confidence, **32** says the LORD, I will
therefore punish Shemaiah, the Nehelamite,
and his offspring. None of them shall survive
among this people to see the good I will do to
this people, says the LORD, because he preached
rebellion against the LORD.

## CHAPTER 30

**The Restoration.*** **1** The following message came to Jeremiah from the LORD: **2** Thus
says the LORD, the God of Israel: Write all the
words I have spoken to you in a book.[l] **3** For
behold, the days will come, says the LORD,
when I will change the lot of my people (of
Israel and Judah, says the LORD), and bring
them back to the land which I gave to their
fathers; they shall have it as their possession.[m]

**4** These are the words which the LORD spoke
to Israel and to Judah: **5** thus says the LORD:

A cry of dismay we hear;
  fear reigns, not peace.
**6** Inquire, and see:
  since when do men bear children?
Why, then, do I see all these men,
  with their hands on their loins
  like women in childbirth?
Why have all their faces turned deathly
  pale?[n]
**7** How mighty is that day—
  none like it!
At time of distress for Jacob,
  though he shall be saved from it.[o]

**8** On that day, says the LORD of hosts, ''I
will break his yoke from off your necks and snap
your bonds.'' Strangers shall no longer enslave
them;[p] **9** instead, they shall serve the LORD,
their God, and David, their king,* whom I will
raise up for them.[q]

**10** But you, my servant Jacob, fear not, says
  the LORD,
  be not dismayed, O Israel!
Behold, I will deliver you from the faroff
  land,
  your descendants, from their land of exile;
Jacob shall again find rest,
  shall be tranquil and undisturbed,[r]
**11** for I am with you, says the LORD, to
  deliver you.
I will make an end of all the nations
  among which I have scattered you;
  but of you I will not make an end.
I will chastise you as you deserve,
  I will not let you go unpunished.[s]

**12** For thus says the LORD:
Incurable is your wound,
  grievous your bruise;[t]
**13** There is none to plead your cause,
  no remedy for your running sore,
  no healing for you.
**14** All your lovers have forgotten you,
  they do not seek you.
I struck you as an enemy would strike,
  punished you cruelly;[u]
**15** Why cry out over your wound?
  your pain is without relief.
Because of your guilt,
  your numerous sins,
  I have done this to you.[v]
**16** Yet all who devour you shall be devoured,
  all your enemies shall go into exile.
All who plunder you shall be plundered,
  all who pillage you I will hand over to
  pillage.[w]
**17** For I will restore you to health;
  of your wounds I will heal you, says the
  LORD.
''The outcast'' they have called you,
  ''with no avenger.''[x]
**18** Thus says the LORD:
See! I will restore the tents of Jacob,
  his dwellings I will pity;
City shall be rebuilt upon hill,
  and palace restored as it was.[y]
**19** From them will resound songs of praise,

l Jer 36, 2; Hb 2, 2; Rv 1, 11.
m Jer 29, 14; 31, 8. 10. 23; 32, 37. 44; Ez 39, 25; Am 9, 14.
n Jer 6, 24; 50, 43.
o Am 5, 18; Zep 1, 14f.
p Is 14, 5f; Ez 34, 27.
q Ez 34, 23; 37, 24; Hos 3, 5; Lk 1, 69.
r Jer 46, 27; Is 43, 5.
s Jer 46, 28; Ez 11, 16f; Am 9, 8f.
t Jer 10, 19; 14, 17; 15, 18.
u Jer 22, 22; Lam 1, 19.
v Jer 15, 18.
w Jer 2, 3.
x Jer 33, 6.
y Jer 33, 7. 11; Ezr 6, 3-15; Ez 36, 10.
z Is 35, 10; 51, 11.

*

authority, as Pashhur's successor, to imprison Jeremiah. Zephaniah, however, merely reads the letter to Jeremiah but does not imprison him.

30, 1—31, 40: These two chapters do not belong chronologically to those that precede or follow. They contain mainly oracles of salvation which Jeremiah originally uttered on behalf of the conquered remnants of the northern kingdom; then, after Judah began to share Samaria's fate, the oracles were extended to include Judah. Their composition is to be placed early in Jeremiah's ministry, probably after the fall of Nineveh (612 B.C.), when Josiah assumed power over the North; cf 2 Kgs 23, 15ff.

30, 9: David, their king: the messianic King of the Davidic line, often called David by the prophets; cf Ez 34, 23f; 37, 24f; Hos 3, 5.

the laughter of happy men.
I will make them not few, but many;
they will not be tiny, for I will glorify them.[z]
20 His sons shall be as of old,
his assembly before me shall stand firm;
I will punish all his oppressors.[a]
21 His leader* shall be one of his own,
and his rulers shall come from his kin.
When I summon him, he shall approach me;
how else should one take the deadly risk
of approaching me? says the LORD.
22 You shall be my people,
and I will be your God.[b]

23 See, the storm of the LORD!
His wrath breaks forth
In a whirling storm
that bursts upon the heads of the wicked.[c]
24 The anger of the LORD will not abate
until he has done and fulfilled
what he has determined in his heart.
When the time comes,
you will fully understand.[d]

## CHAPTER 31

### Good News of the Return

1 At that time, says the LORD,
I will be the God of all the tribes of Israel,
and they shall be my people.[e]
2 Thus says the LORD:
The people that escaped the sword*
have found favor in the desert.
As Israel comes forward to be given his rest,
3 the LORD appears to him from afar:
With age-old love I have loved you;
so I have kept my mercy toward you.[f]
4 Again I will restore you, and you shall be rebuilt,
O virgin Israel;
Carrying your festive tambourines,
you shall go forth dancing with the merry-makers.
5 Again you shall plant vineyards
on the mountains of Samaria;
those who plant them shall enjoy the fruits.[g]
6 Yes, a day will come when the watchmen
will call out on Mount Ephraim:
"Rise up, let us go to Zion,
to the LORD, our God."[h]

### The Road of Return

7 For thus says the LORD:
Shout with joy for Jacob,
exult at the head of the nations;
proclaim your praise and say:
The LORD has delivered his people,
the remnant of Israel.[i]
8 Behold, I will bring them back
from the land of the north;
I will gather them from the ends of the world,
with the blind and the lame in their midst,
The mothers and those with child;
they shall return as an immense throng.[j]
9 They departed in tears,
but I will console them and guide them;
I will lead them to brooks of water,
on a level road, so that none shall stumble.
For I am a father to Israel,
Ephraim is my first-born.[k]
10 Hear the word of the LORD, O nations,
proclaim it on distant coasts, and say:
He who scattered Israel, now gathers them together,
he guards them as a shepherd his flock.
11 The LORD shall ransom Jacob,
he shall redeem him from the hand of his conqueror.[l]
12 Shouting, they shall mount the heights of Zion,
they shall come streaming to the LORD's blessings:
The grain, the wine, and the oil,
the sheep and the oxen;
They themselves shall be like watered gardens,
never again shall they languish.[m]
13 Then the virgins shall make merry and dance,
and young men and old as well.
I will turn their mourning into joy,
I will console and gladden them after their sorrows.
14 I will lavish choice portions upon the priests,
and my people shall be filled with my blessings,
says the LORD.

### End of Rachel's Mourning

15 Thus says the LORD:

a Is 49, 26.
b Jer 24, 7; 31, 1. 33; 32, 38; Lv 26, 12; Ez 11, 20; 36, 28.
c Jer 23, 19.
d Jer 23, 20.
e Jer 30, 22.
f Dt 7, 8; 10, 15; Is 43, 4; 63, 9; Hos 11, 1. 4.
g Is 65, 21; Am 9, 14.
h Is 2, 3; 27, 13; Mi 4, 2.
i Is 12, 6.
j Jer 3, 18; 23, 3. 8; Is 35, 5f.
k Ex 4, 22.
l Is 44, 23; 48, 20.
m Is 58, 11.
n Mt 2, 18.

*

30, 21: His leader: probably not the messianic King, but simply any one of the rulers of the restored Israel, who will no longer be foreigners, and with whom the Lord will be on terms of intimacy, as with the whole people. The deadly risk of approaching me: to approach God unsummoned brings death; cf Lv 16, 1f.

31, 2: The people that escaped the sword: the exiles who were not killed but deported; they have found favor in the desert, across which they were driven into captivity. The prophet alludes to the first desert wandering of Israel (Ex 16ff), in which the people found the Lord. His rest: the land of promise. The perfect fulfillment of this promised rest is found only in the New Testament (Heb., chapters 3 and 4).

31, 15: Ramah: a village about five miles north of Jerusa-

In Ramah* is heard the sound of moaning,
of bitter weeping!
Rachel mourns her children,
she refuses to be consoled
because her children are no more.[n]
16 Thus says the LORD:
Cease your cries of mourning,
wipe the tears from your eyes.
The sorrow you have shown shall have its
reward,
says the LORD,
they shall return from the enemy's land.
17 There is hope for your future, says the
LORD;
your sons shall return to their own
borders.[o]

18 I hear, I hear Ephraim pleading:
You chastised me, and I am chastened;
I was an untamed calf.
If you allow me, I will return,
for you are the LORD, my God.[p]
19 I turn in repentance;
I have come to myself, I strike my breast;
I blush with shame,
I bear the disgrace of my youth.[q]
20 Is Ephraim not my favored son,
the child in whom I delight?
Often as I threaten him,
I still remember him with favor;
My heart stirs for him,
I must show him mercy, says the LORD.[r]

### Summons To Return Home

21 Set up road markers,
put up guideposts;
Turn your attention to the highway,
the road by which you went.
Turn back, O virgin Israel,
turn back to these your cities.
22 How long will you continue to stray,
rebellious daughter?
The LORD has created a new thing upon the
earth:
the woman must encompass the man*
with devotion.

23 Thus says the LORD of hosts, the God of
Israel: When I change their lot in the land of
Judah and her cities, they shall again repeat this
greeting: "May the LORD bless you, holy mountain, abode of justice!"[s] 24 Judah and all her
cities, the farmers and those who lead the flock,
shall dwell there together. 25 For I will refresh
the weary soul; every soul that languishes I will
replenish. 26 Upon this I awoke and opened my
eyes; but my sleep was sweet to me.*
27 The days are coming, says the LORD,
when I will seed the house of Israel and the
house of Judah with the seed of man and the
seed of beast. 28 As I once watched over them
to uproot and pull down, to destroy, to ruin, and
to harm, so I will watch over them to build and
to plant, says the LORD.[t] 29 In those days they
shall no longer say,

"The fathers ate unripe grapes,[u]
and the children's teeth are set on
edge,"*

30 but through his own fault only shall anyone
die: the teeth of him who eats the unripe grapes
shall be set on edge.

**The New Covenant.*** 31 The days are
coming, says the LORD, when I will make a new
covenant with the house of Israel and the house
of Judah.[v] 32 It will not be like the covenant I
made with their fathers the day I took them by
the hand to lead them forth from the land of
Egypt; for they broke my covenant and I had to
show myself their master, says the LORD.[w]
33 But this is the covenant which I will make
with the house of Israel after those days, says
the LORD. I will place my law within them, and
write it upon their hearts; I will be their God,
and they shall be my people.[x] 34 No longer will

o Jer 29, 10-14.
p Lv 26, 40ff.
q Dt 30, 1ff.
r Hos 11, 8.
s Jer 30, 3; Ps 122, 8.
t Jer 1, 10; 18, 7.
u Dt 24, 16; Ez 18, 2.
v Jer 32, 40; Heb 9, 15.
w Ex 24, 7f; Dt 5, 2.
x Jer 32, 40; Ez 37, 26; Heb 10, 16.
y Is 54, 13.

* lem, where Rachel was buried (1 Sm 10, 2). Rachel: said to mourn for her children since she was the ancestress of Ephraim, the chief of the northern tribes. Mt 2, 18 applies this verse to the slaughter of the innocents by Herod.

31, 22: The woman must encompass the man: the words "with devotion," not in the Hebrew, are added for the sense. No fully satisfactory explanation has been given this text. Among the more probable are these: (a) Formerly the man (the Lord) encompassed the woman (Israel) with mercy and devotion; now in the spiritual religion of Israel which will follow on the restoration, this order will be reversed. (b) So secure will Israel be after the restoration that women will no longer need the natural protection of their husbands, but even weak women can protect men. (c) St. Jerome in his commentary on this verse understood it of Mary's virginal conception of Christ. "The Lord has created a new thing on earth; without seed of man, without carnal union and conception, 'a woman will encompass a man' within her womb—One who, though He will later appear to advance in wisdom and age through the stages of infancy and childhood, yet, while confined for the usual number of months in his mother's womb, will already be perfect man."

31, 26: I awoke . . . sweet to me: probably said by the prophet himself.

31, 29: "The fathers . . . on edge": a proverb used in Israel, expressing the idea that children suffer for the sins of their parents (cf Ez 18, 2). The Israel of the restoration will be characterized instead by personal responsibility and retribution for one's acts (v 30; cf vv 31–34).

31, 31–34: The new covenant to be made with Israel is a common theme of the prophets, beginning with Hosea. According to Jeremiah, the qualities of the new covenant that make it different from the old are: (a) It will not be broken, but will last forever; (b) Its law will be written in the heart, not merely on tablets of stone; (c) The knowledge of God will be so generally shown forth in the life of the people that it will no longer be necessary to put it into words of instruction. In the fullest sense, this prophecy was fulfilled only through the work of Jesus Christ; cf Lk 22, 20; 1 Cor 11, 25.

they have need to teach their friends and kinsmen how to know the LORD. All, from least to
greatest, shall know me, says the LORD, for I
will forgive their evildoing and remember their
sin no more.[y]

### Certainty of God's Promise

35 Thus says the LORD,
He who gives the sun to light the day,
moon and stars to light the night;
Who stirs up the sea till its waves roar,
whose name is LORD of hosts:[z]
36 If ever these natural laws give way
in spite of me, says the LORD,
Then shall the race of Israel cease
as a nation before me forever.[a]
37 Thus says the LORD:
If the heavens on high can be measured,
or the foundations below the earth be
sounded,
Then will I cast off the whole race of Israel
because of all they have done, says the
LORD.

**Rebuilding of Jerusalem.** 38 The days
are coming, says the LORD, when the city shall
be rebuilt as the LORD'S,[b] from the Tower of
Hananel to the Corner Gate.* 39 The measuring line shall be stretched from there straight to
the hill Gareb and then turn to Goah. 40 The
whole valley of corpses and ashes,* all the
slopes toward the Kidron Valley, as far as the
corner of the Horse Gate at the east, shall be
holy to the LORD. Never again shall the city be
rooted up or thrown down.

## CHAPTER 32

**Pledge of Restoration.*** 1 This message
came to Jeremiah from the LORD in the tenth
year of Zedekiah,* king of Judah, the eighteenth year of Nebuchadnezzar. 2 At that time
the army of the king of Babylon was besieging
Jerusalem, and the prophet Jeremiah was imprisoned in the quarters of the guard, at the
king's palace.[c] 3 Zedekiah, king of Judah, had
imprisoned him there, remonstrating: "How
dare you prophesy: Thus says the LORD: I am
handing over this city to the king of Babylon,
who will capture it.[d] 4 Neither shall Zedekiah,
king of Judah, escape the hands of the Chaldeans; rather shall he be handed over to the king
of Babylon. They shall meet and speak face to
face,[e] 5 and Zedekiah shall be taken to Babylon. There he shall remain, until I attend to
him, says the LORD; in fighting the Chaldeans,
you cannot win!"[f]
6 *This message came to me from the LORD,
said Jeremiah: 7 Hanamel, son of your uncle
Shallum, will come to you with the offer:[g]
"Buy for yourself my field in Anathoth, since
you, as nearest relative, have the first right of
purchase."* 8 Then, as the LORD foretold,
Hanamel, my uncle's son, came to me to the
quarters of the guard and said, "Please buy my
field in Anathoth, in the district of Benjamin; as
nearest relative, you have the first claim to possess it; make it yours." I knew this was what the
LORD meant, 9 so I bought the field in Anathoth
from my cousin Hanamel, paying him the money, seventeen silver shekels.
10 When I had written and sealed the deed,
called witnesses and weighed out the silver on
the scales, 11 I accepted the deed of purchase,
both the sealed copy, containing title and conditions, and the open one.* 12 This deed of purchase I gave to Baruch, son of Neriah, son of
Mahseiah, in the presence of my cousin Hanamel and of the witnesses who had signed the
deed, and before all the men of Judah who
happened to be in the quarters of the guard.[h]
13 In their presence I gave Baruch this
charge: 14 Thus says the LORD of hosts, the
God of Israel: Take these deeds, both the sealed
and the open deed of purchase, and put them in
an earthen jar,* so that they can be kept there
a long time. 15 For thus says the LORD of hosts,
the God of Israel: Houses and fields and vineyards shall again be bought in this land.
16 After giving the deed of purchase to Baruch, son of Neriah, I prayed thus to the LORD:

z Gn 1, 14-18.
a Jer 33, 20f.
b Neh 12, 38; Zec 14, 10f.
c Jer 33, 1; 37, 20; 38, 6; 39, 14.
d Jer 26, 9; 34, 2; 37, 6-10.
e Jer 34, 3; 38, 18. 23; 39, 4-7.
f Jer 39, 7; 52, 11.
g Lv 25, 24-34; Ru 4, 4.
h Jer 36, 4.

*

31, 38: From the Tower of Hananel to the Corner Gate: from the northeast to the northwest.

31, 40: Valley of corpses and ashes: the Valley of Benhinnom, which joins the Kidron at the southeast of ancient Jerusalem. The Horse Gate: in the eastern city wall, at the southeast corner of the temple area.

32, 1–44: This chapter recounts a prophecy "in action." At the Lord's command, Jeremiah fulfills his family duty to purchase the land of his cousin, carrying out all the legal forms, including records, to testify that Judah will be restored and that the life of the past will be resumed.

32, 1: The tenth year of Zedekiah: 588 B.C. The eighteenth year of Nebuchadnezzar: dating his reign from his victory at Carchemish; see note on Jer 25, 1–14.

32, 6–9: Jeremiah's imprisonment by the weak-willed Zedekiah was a technical custody that did not deprive him of all freedom of action. The siege maintained by the Chaldeans (v 2) was only now beginning (v 24), and could be bypassed by individual persons going to and fro between Jerusalem and nearby Anathoth.

32, 7: The first right of purchase: the obligation of the closest relative to redeem the property of one in economic distress, so that the ancestral land might remain within the family (Lv 25, 25–28); see note on Ru 2, 20.

32, 11: The sealed copy . . . and the open one: the legal deed of sale was written on a scroll, which was then rolled up and sealed; about it was rolled another scroll, left unsealed, containing a copy or a summary of the first.

32, 14: In an earthen jar: the first of the Dead Sea Scrolls were found in such a jar.

**17** Ah, Lord GOD, you have made heaven and earth by your great might, with your outstretched arm; nothing is impossible to you.[i] **18** You continue your kindness through a thousand generations; and you repay the fathers' guilt, even into the lap of their sons who follow them. O God, great and mighty, whose name is LORD of hosts,[j] **19** great in counsel, mighty in deed, whose eyes are open to all the ways of men, giving to each according to his ways, according to the fruit of his deeds:[k] **20** you have wrought signs and wonders in the land of Egypt and to this day, both in Israel and among all other men, until now you have gained renown.[l] **21** With strong hand and outstretched arm you brought your people Israel out of the land of Egypt amid signs and wonders and great terror. **22** This land you gave them, as you had promised their fathers under oath, a land flowing with milk and honey.[m] **23** They entered and took possession of it, but they did not listen to your voice; by your law they did not live, and what you commanded they failed to do. Hence you let all these evils befall them.[n] **24** See, the siegeworks have arrived at this city to breach it; the city will be handed over to the Chaldeans who are attacking it, amid sword, famine, and pestilence. What you threatened has happened, you see it yourself;[o] **25** and yet you tell me, O Lord GOD: Buy the field with money, call in witnesses. But the city has already been handed over to the Chaldeans!

**26** Then this word of the LORD came to Jeremiah: **27** I am the LORD, the God of all mankind! Is anything impossible to me? **28** This now is what the LORD says: I will hand over this city to the Chaldeans, for Nebuchadnezzar, king of Babylon, to take. **29** The Chaldeans who are attacking it shall enter this city and set fire to it, burning it and its houses, on the roofs of which incense was burned to Baal and libations were poured out to strange gods as a provocation to me.[p] **30** The Israelites and the Judeans from their youth have done only what is evil in my eyes; the Israelites did nothing but provoke me with the works of their hands, says the LORD.[q] **31** From the day it was built to this day, this city has excited my anger and wrath, **32** so that I must put it out of my sight for all the wickedness the Israelites and Judeans, with their kings and their princes, their priests and their prophets, the men of Judah and the citizens of Jerusalem, have done to provoke me.[r] **33** They turned their backs to me, not their faces; though I kept teaching them, they would not listen to my correction.[s] **34** They defiled the house named after me by the horrid idols they set up in it.[t] **35** They built high places to Baal in the Valley of Ben-hinnom, and immolated their sons and daughters to Molech,* bringing sin upon Judah; this I never commanded them, nor did it even enter my mind that they should practice such abominations.[u]

**36** Now, therefore, thus says the LORD, the God of Israel, concerning this city, which as you say is handed over to the king of Babylon amid sword, famine, and pestilence: **37** Behold, I will gather them together from all the lands to which in anger, wrath, and great rage I banish them; I will bring them back to this place and settle them here in safety.[v] **38** They shall be my people, and I will be their God.[w] **39** One heart and one way I will give them, that they may fear me always, to their own good and that of their children after them. **40** I will make with them an eternal covenant, never to cease doing good to them; into their hearts I will put the fear of me, that they may never depart from me.[x] **41** I will take delight in doing good to them: I will replant them firmly in this land, with all my heart and soul.[y]

**42** For thus says the LORD: Just as I brought upon this people all this great evil, so I will bring upon them all the good I promise them.[z] **43** Fields shall again be bought in this land, which you call a desert, without man or beast, handed over to the Chaldeans.[a] **44** Fields shall be bought with money, deeds written and sealed, and witnesses shall be used in the land of Benjamin, in the suburbs of Jerusalem, in the cities of Judah and of the hill country, in the cities of the foothills and of the Negeb, when I change their lot, says the LORD.[b]

## CHAPTER 33

**Restoration of Jerusalem.** **1** The word of the LORD came to Jeremiah a second time while he was still imprisoned in the quarters of the guard: **2** Thus says the LORD who made the earth and gave it form and firmness, whose name is LORD: **3** Call to me, and I will answer you; I will tell to you things great beyond reach of your knowledge.[c] **4** Thus says the LORD, the God of Israel, concerning the houses of this city and the palaces of Judah's kings, which are being destroyed in the face of siegeworks and

i 2 Kgs 19, 15; Jb 42, 2.
j Ex 20, 5f; Dt 5, 9.
k Jb 34, 21; Ps 33, 13ff.
l Ex 6, 6; Dt 4, 34; Ps 135, 9.
m Jer 11, 5; Gn 15, 18; 17, 8; 26, 3.
n Jer 7, 24ff; Dn 9, 10-14.
o Jer 21, 5; 33, 4.
p Jer 21, 10; 37, 8ff.
q Jer 3, 25; 44, 8.
r Jer 2, 26; Is 3, 8.
s Jer 7, 24.
t Jer 7, 30; 2 Kgs 21, 4f.
u Jer 7, 31; 19, 5; Ps 106, 37f.
v Jer 23, 3; 29, 14; Is 11, 12; Ez 11, 17.
w Jer 24, 7; 31, 33.
x Jer 31, 31ff.
y Dt 30, 9.
z Jer 33, 10-14; Zec 8, 13.
a Jer 33, 10.
b Jer 17, 26; 33, 7.
c Is 48, 6.
d Jer 32, 24.

*

32, 35: Molech: the god to whom human sacrifice was offered in the Valley of Ben-hinnom. Here, as in Jer 19, 5, he is given the name Baal; see note on Lv 18, 21.

the sword:[d] **5** men come to battle the Chaldeans, and these houses will be filled with the
corpses of those whom I slay in my anger and
wrath, when I hide my face from this city for all
their wickedness.[e]

**6** Behold, I will treat and assuage the city's
wounds; I will heal them, and reveal to them an
abundance of lasting peace.[f] **7** I will change the
lot of Judah and the lot of Israel, and rebuild
them as of old.[g] **8** I will cleanse them of all the
guilt they incurred by sinning against me; all
their offenses by which they sinned and rebelled
against me, I will forgive.[h] **9** Then Jerusalem
shall be my joy, my praise, my glory, before all
the nations of the earth, as they hear of all the
good I will do among them. They shall be in fear
and trembling over all the peaceful benefits I
will give her.

**10** Thus says the LORD: In this place of
which you say, "How desolate it is, without
man, without beast!" and in the cities of Judah,
in the streets of Jerusalem that are now deserted,
without man, without citizen, without beast,
there shall yet be heard[i] **11** the cry of joy, the
cry of gladness, the voice of the bridegroom, the
voice of the bride, the sound of those who bring
thank offerings to the house of the LORD, singing, "Give thanks to the LORD of hosts, for the
LORD is good; his mercy endures forever." For
I will restore this country as of old, says the
LORD.[j]

**12** Thus says the LORD of hosts: In this place,
now desolate, without man or beast, and in all
its cities there shall again be sheepfolds for the
shepherds to couch their flocks. **13** In the cities
of the hill country, of the foothills, and of the
Negeb, in the land of Benjamin and the suburbs
of Jerusalem, and in the cities of Judah, flocks
will again pass under the hands of the one who
counts them, says the LORD.

**14** *The days are coming, says the LORD,
when I will fulfill the promise I made to the
house of Israel and Judah. **15** In those days, in
that time, I will raise up for David a just shoot;
he shall do what is right and just in the land.[k]
**16** In those days Judah shall be safe and Jerusalem shall dwell secure; this is what they shall
call her: "The LORD our justice." **17** For thus
says the LORD: Never shall David lack a successor on the throne of the house of Israel,[l] **18** nor
shall priests of Levi ever be lacking, to offer
holocausts before me, to burn cereal offerings,
and to sacrifice victims.[m]

This word of the LORD also came to Jeremiah:
**19** Thus says the LORD: **20** If you can break my
covenant with day,[n] and my covenant with
night, so that day and night no longer alternate
in sequence, **21** then can my covenant with my
servant David also be broken, so that he will not
have a son to be king upon his throne, and my
covenant with the priests of Levi who minister
to me. **22** Like the host of heaven which cannot
be numbered, and the sands of the sea which
cannot be counted, I will multiply the descendants of my servant David and the Levites who
minister to me.

**23** This word of the LORD came to Jeremiah:
**24** Have you not noticed what these people are
saying: "The LORD has rejected the two tribes
which he had chosen"? They spurn my people
as if it were no longer a nation in their eyes.[o]
**25** [p]Thus says the LORD: When I have no covenant with day and night, and have given no
laws to heaven and earth, **26** then too will I
reject the descendants of Jacob and of my servant David, so as not to take from his descendants rulers for the race of Abraham, Isaac, and
Jacob. For I will change their lot and show them
mercy.

## IV: Fall of Jerusalem

### CHAPTER 34

**Fate of Zedekiah.** **1** This word came to
Jeremiah from the LORD while Nebuchadnezzar, king of Babylon, and his armies and the
earth's kingdoms subject to him, as well as the
other peoples, were all attacking Jerusalem and
all her cities:[q] **2** Thus says the LORD, the God
of Israel: Go to Zedekiah, king of Judah, and tell
him: Thus says the LORD: I am handing this city
over to the king of Babylon; he will destroy it
with fire.[r] **3** Neither shall you escape his hand;
rather you will be captured and fall into his
hands. You shall see the king of Babylon and
speak to him face to face. Then you shall be
taken to Babylon.[s]

**4** But if you obey the word of the LORD,
Zedekiah, king of Judah, then, says the LORD to
you, you shall not die by the sword. **5** You shall
die in peace, and they will lament you as their
lord, and burn spices for your burial as they did

e Jer 21, 4ff.
f Is 57, 18.
g Jer 30, 3; 32, 44.
h Ez 36, 25.
i Jer 32, 43.
j 1 Chr 16, 34; Ezr 3, 11; Ps 136, 1.
k Jer 23, 5; Ps 72, 1-4. 12ff; Is 11.1.
l 2 Sm 7, 16; 1 Kgs 2, 4; Ps 89, 4f. 29. 36f.
m Ez 44, 15f.
n 20f: Jer 31, 36f; Ps 89, 37f.
o Rom 11, 1f.
p 25f: Jer 31, 36f; 32, 44.
q Jer 52, 4; 2 Kgs 25, 1.
r Jer 21, 10; 32, 3. 28.
s Jer 32, 4; 52, 11.

* 33, 14–26: This is the longest continuous passage in the Book of Jeremiah that is lacking in the Greek. It appears to be the postexilic composition of an inspired writer who used parts of the prophecies of Jeremiah—often, however, in a sense different from the prophet's. The prediction of an eternal Davidic dynasty (14–17) to fulfill the prophecy of Nathan (2 Sm 7, 11–16), and of a perpetual priesthood and sacrifice (18), was not to be realized in the restoration of the Jewish nation. It finds its fulfillment only in Jesus of Nazareth, who combined with his messianic Davidic kingship an eternal priesthood; cf Heb 6, 20; 7, 24f.

for your fathers, the kings who preceded you
from the first; it is I who make this promise,
says the LORD.
6 The prophet Jeremiah told all these things
to Zedekiah, king of Judah, in Jerusalem,
7 while the armies of the king of Babylon were
attacking Jerusalem and the remaining cities of
Judah, Lachish, and Azekah,* since these alone
were left of the fortified cities of Judah.

**The Pact Broken.*** 8 This is the word that
came to Jeremiah from the LORD after King
Zedekiah had made an agreement with all the
people in Jerusalem to issue an edict of emancipation. 9 Everyone was to free his Hebrew
slaves, male and female, so that no one should
hold a man of Judah, his brother, in slavery.[t]
10 All the princes and the others who entered
the agreement consented to set free their male
and female servants, so that they should be
slaves no longer. But though they agreed and
freed them, 11 afterward they took back their
male and female slaves whom they had set free
and again forced them into service.
12 Then this word of the LORD came to Jeremiah: 13 Thus says the LORD, the God of Israel:
The day I brought your fathers out of the land
of Egypt, out of the place where they were
slaves, I made this covenant with them: 14 Every seventh year each of you shall set free his
Hebrew brother who has sold himself to you; six
years he shall serve you, but then you shall let
him go free. Your fathers, however, did not
heed me or obey me. 15 Today you indeed
repented and did what is right in my eyes by
proclaiming the emancipation of your brethren
and making an agreement before me in the
house that is named after me. 16 But then you
changed your mind and profaned my name by
taking back your male and female slaves to
whom you had given their freedom; you forced
them once more into slavery.[u] 17 Therefore,
thus says the LORD: You did not obey me by
proclaiming your neighbors and kinsmen free.
I now proclaim you free, says the LORD, for the
sword, famine, and pestilence. I will make you
an object of horror to all the kingdoms of the
earth. 18 *The men who violated my covenant
and did not observe the terms of the agreement
which they made before me, I will make like the
calf which they cut in two, between whose two
parts they passed. 19 The princes of Judah and
of Jerusalem, the courtiers, the priests, and the
common people, who passed between the parts
of the calf, 20 I will hand over, all of them, to
their enemies, to those who seek their lives:
their corpses shall be food for the birds of the
air and the beasts of the field.[v]
21 Zedekiah, too, king of Judah, and his
princes, I will hand over to their enemies, to
those who seek their lives, to the soldiers of the
king of Babylon who have at present withdrawn
from you.[w] 22 I will give the command, says
the LORD, and bring them back to this city. They
shall attack and capture it, and destroy it with
fire; the cities of Judah I will turn into a desert
where no man dwells.[x]

## CHAPTER 35

**The Faithful Rechabites.** 1 This word
came to Jeremiah from the LORD in the days of
Jehoiakim, son of Josiah, king of Judah: 2 Approach the Rechabites* and speak to them; bring
them into the house of the LORD, to one of the
rooms, and give them wine to drink. 3 So I
went and brought Jaazaniah, son of Jeremiah,
son of Habazzaniah, his brothers and all his
sons, the whole company of the Rechabites,
4 into the house of the LORD, to the room of the
sons of Hanan,* son of Igdaliah, the man of
God, next to the princes' room, above the room
of Maaseiah, son of Shallum, keeper of the
doorway. 5 I set before these Rechabite men
bowls full of wine and offered them cups to
drink the wine.
6 "We do not drink wine," they said to me:
"Jonadab,* Rechab's son, our father, forbade

t Ex 21, 2ff; Lv 25, 39. 46; Dt 15, 12-15.
u Lv 19, 12.
v Jer 7, 33; 16, 4; 19, 7.
w Jer 37, 5. 11.
x Jer 37, 8; 52, 7-13; 2 Chr 36, 17. 19.

34, 7: Lachish and Azekah: fortress towns to the southwest of Jerusalem which Nebuchadnezzar besieged to prevent help coming to Jerusalem from Egypt. Between 1935 and 1938, archaeologists found at Lachish several letters written on pottery fragments which date from 598 or 588 B.C., and which mention both Lachish and Azekah.

34, 8–22: While the Chaldean siege of Jerusalem was in progress, the citizens of Jerusalem made a covenant at Zedekiah's instigation to free their brother Judeans who were in slavery. Doubtless this was both to provide additional free defenders for the city and to offer reparation for past violations of the law, according to which Hebrew slaves were to serve no longer than six years (Dt 15, 12–15). But when the siege was temporarily lifted, probably because of the help promised by Pharaoh Hophra (cf Jer 37, 5), the inhabitants of Jerusalem broke the covenant and once more pressed their brethren into slavery (v 11).

34, 18f: As the Bible (Gn 15, 10–17) and also contemporary inscriptions make clear, agreements were sometimes ratified by walking between the divided pieces of animals while the contracting parties invoked on themselves a fate similar to that of the slaughtered beast if they should fail to keep their word. The agreement: that mentioned in vv 10. 15.

35, 2: The Rechabites: reactionaries who believed that the Lord could not be well served except by maintaining the original nomadic conditions of Israel's life. Without sharing their convictions, the prophet holds up their fidelity to their ideals as an example to put to shame his faithless countrymen. In the days of Jehoiakim: probably in 599 or 598 B.C.

35, 4: The sons of Hanan: probably the disciples of this man of God or prophet. Maaseiah: possibly the father of the priest Zephaniah (Jer 29, 25; 37, 3). Keeper of the doorway: a priestly function of responsibility; cf Jer 52, 24.

35, 6: Jonadab: a contemporary of King Jehu; cf 2 Kgs 10, 15ff.

us in these words: 'Neither you nor your children shall ever drink wine. 7 Build no house
and sow no seed; neither plant nor own a vineyard. You shall dwell in tents all your life, so
that you may live long on the earth where you
are wayfarers.' 8 Now we have heeded Jonadab, Rechab's son, our father, in all his prohibitions. All our lives we have not drunk wine,
neither we, nor our wives, nor our sons, nor our
daughters. 9 We build no houses to live in; we
own no vineyards or fields or crops, 10 and we
live in tents; we obediently do everything our
father Jonadab commanded us. 11 But when
Nebuchadnezzar, king of Babylon, invaded this
land, we decided to come into Jerusalem to
escape the army of the Chaldeans and the army
of Aram;* that is why we are now living in
Jerusalem."

12 Then this word of the LORD came to Jeremiah: 13 Thus says the LORD of hosts, the God
of Israel: Go, say to the men of Judah and to the
citizens of Jerusalem: Will you not take correction and obey my words? says the LORD.[y]
14 The advice of Jonadab, Rechab's son, by
which he forbade his children to drink wine, has
been followed: to this day they have not drunk
it; they obeyed their father's command. Me,
however, you have not obeyed, although I
spoke to you untiringly and insistently.[z] 15 I
kept sending you all my servants the prophets,
telling you to turn back, all of you, from your
evil way; to reform your conduct, and not follow strange gods or serve them, if you would
remain on the land which I gave you and your
fathers; but you did not heed me or obey me.[a]
16 Yes, the children of Jonadab, Rechab's son,
observed the command which their father laid
on them; but this people does not obey me!
17 Now, therefore, says the LORD God of
hosts, the God of Israel: I will bring upon Judah
and all the citizens of Jerusalem every evil that
I threatened; because when I spoke they did not
obey, when I called they did not answer.[b]

18 But to the company of the Rechabites Jeremiah said: Thus says the LORD of hosts, the
God of Israel: Since you have obeyed the command of Jonadab, your father, kept all his commands and done everything he commanded you,
19 thus therefore says the LORD of hosts, the
God of Israel: Never shall there fail to be a
descendant of Jonadab, Rechab's son, standing
in my service.

## CHAPTER 36

**Baruch Writes the Prophecies of Jeremi-
ah.** 1 In the fourth year of Jehoiakim, son of
Josiah, king of Judah, this word came to Jeremiah from the LORD: 2 Take a scroll and write on
it all the words I have spoken to you against
Israel, Judah, and all the nations, from the day
I first spoke to you, in the days of Josiah, until
today. 3 Perhaps, when the house of Judah
hears all the evil I have in mind to do to them,
they will turn back each from his evil way, so
that I may forgive their wickedness and their
sin.[c] 4 So Jeremiah called Baruch, son of Neriah, who wrote down on a scroll, as Jeremiah
dictated, all the words which the LORD had spoken to him.

9 In the ninth month, in the fifth year of
Jehoiakim, son of Josiah, king of Judah, a fast
to placate the LORD was proclaimed for all the
people of Jerusalem and all who came from
Judah's cities to Jerusalem. 5 Then Jeremiah
charged Baruch: I cannot go to the house of the
LORD: I am prevented* from doing so. 6 Do
you go on the fast day and read publicly in the
LORD's house the LORD's words from the scroll
you wrote at my dictation; read them also to all
the men of Judah who come up from their cities.
7 Perhaps they will lay their supplication before
the LORD and will all turn back from their evil
way; for great is the fury of anger with which
the LORD has threatened this people.[d]

8 Baruch, son of Neriah, did everything the
prophet Jeremiah commanded; from the book-
scroll he read the LORD's words in the LORD's
house. 10 It was in the room of Gemariah,* son
of the scribe Shaphan, in the upper court of the
LORD's house, at the entrance of the New Tem-
ple-Gate, that Baruch publicly read the words of
Jeremiah from his book.

11 Now Micaiah, son of Gemariah, son of
Shaphan, heard all the words of the LORD read
from the book. 12 So he went down to the
king's palace, into the scribe's chamber,*
where the princes were just then in session:
Elishama, the scribe, Delaiah, son of Shemaiah,
Elnathan, son of Achbor, Gemariah, son of
Shaphan, Zedekiah, son of Hananiah, and the
other princes. 13 To them Micaiah reported all
that he had heard Baruch read publicly from his
book. 14 Thereupon the princes sent Jehudi,
son of Nethaniah, son of Shelemiah, son of
Cushi, to Baruch with the order: "Come, and
bring with you the scroll you read publicly to the
people." Scroll in hand, Baruch, son of Neriah,

y Jer 32, 33.
z Jer 7, 13; 25, 3; 2 Chr 36, 15f.
a Jer 25, 4f. 7.
b Jer 11, 8f.
c Jer 26, 3; Is 55, 6f.
d 2 Kgs 22, 13.

*

35, 11: The army of Aram; Nebuchadnezzar enlisted the help of Judah's foreign neighbors in his assault on Jerusalem.

36, 5: I am prevented: probably because of his temple sermon (Jer 7, 1–15), or because of temporary ritual uncleanness.

36, 10: Gemariah: member of a family friendly to Jeremiah, which had rights to a room in the fortress of the temple gateway overlooking the court of the temple; from a window in this room Baruch read Jeremiah's prophetic sermon to the people.

36, 12: The scribe's chamber: the office of the royal secretary.

went to them. **15** "Sit down," they said to him,
"and read it to us." Baruch read it to them,
**16** and when they heard all its words, they were
frightened and said to one another, "We must
certainly tell the king all these things."
**17** Then they asked Baruch: "Tell us, please,
how you came to write down all these words."
**18** "Jeremiah dictated all these words to me,"
Baruch answered them, "and I wrote them
down with ink in the book." **19** At this the
princes said to Baruch, "Go into hiding, you
and Jeremiah; let no one know where you are."

**20** Leaving the scroll in safekeeping in the
room of Elishama the scribe, they entered the
room where the king was. When they told him
everything that had happened, **21** he sent Jehudi to fetch the scroll. Jehudi brought it from the
room of Elishama the scribe, and read it to the
king and to all the princes who were in attendance on the king. **22** Now the king was sitting
in his winter house, since it was the ninth
month, and fire was burning in a brazier before
him. **23** Each time Jehudi finished reading
three or four columns, the king would cut off the
piece with a scribe's knife* and cast it into the
fire in the brazier, until the entire roll was consumed in the fire. **24** Hearing all these words
did not frighten the king and his ministers or
cause them to rend their garments. **25** And
though Elnathan, Delaiah, and Gemariah urged
the king not to burn the scroll, he would not
listen to them, **26** but commanded Jerahmeel,
a royal prince, and Seraiah, son of Azriel, and
Shelemiah, son of Abdeel, to arrest Baruch, the
secretary, and the prophet Jeremiah. But the
LORD kept them concealed.

**27** This word of the LORD came to Jeremiah,
after the king burned the scroll with the text
Jeremiah had dictated to Baruch: **28** Take another scroll, and write on it everything that the
first scroll contained, which Jehoiakim, king of
Judah, burned up. **29** And against Jehoiakim,
king of Judah, say this: Thus says the LORD:
You burned that scroll, saying, "Why did you
write on it: Babylon's king shall surely come
and lay waste this land and empty it of man and
beast?" **30** The LORD now says of Jehoiakim,
king of Judah:[e] No descendant of his shall succeed to David's throne; his corpse shall be cast
out, exposed to the heat of day, to the cold of
night.* **31** I will punish him and his descendants and his ministers for their wickedness;
against them and the citizens of Jerusalem and
the men of Judah I will fulfill all the threats of
evil which went unheeded.

**32** Jeremiah took another scroll, and gave it
to his secretary, Baruch, son of Neriah; he wrote
on it at Jeremiah's dictation all the words contained in the book which Jehoiakim, king of
Judah, had burned in the fire, and many others
of the same kind in addition.

## CHAPTER 37

**Jeremiah in the Dungeon.** **1** Coniah, son
of Jehoiakim, was succeeded by King Zedekiah, son of Josiah; he was made king over the
land of Judah by Nebuchadnezzar, king of Babylon.[f] **2** Neither he, nor his ministers, nor the
people of the land would listen to the words of
the LORD spoken by Jeremiah the prophet.
**3** Yet King Zedekiah sent Jehucal, son of Shelemiah, and Zephaniah, son of Maaseiah the
priest, to the prophet Jeremiah with this request:
"Pray to the LORD, our God, for us."[g] **4** At
this time Jeremiah had not yet been put into
prison;* he still came and went freely among the
people. **5** Also, Pharaoh's army* had set out
from Egypt, and when the Chaldeans who were
besieging Jerusalem heard this report they
marched away from the city.[h]

**6** This word of the LORD then came to the
prophet Jeremiah: **7** Thus says the LORD, the
God of Israel: Give this answer to the king of
Judah who sent you to me to consult me: Pharaoh's army which has set out to help you will
return to its own land, Egypt.[i] **8** The Chaldeans
shall return to the fight against this city; they
shall capture it and destroy it with fire.[j]

**9** Thus says the LORD: Do not deceive yourselves with the thought that the Chaldeans will
leave you for good, because they shall not
leave! **10** Even if you were to defeat the whole
Chaldean army now attacking you, and only the
wounded remained, each in his tent, these
would rise up and destroy the city with fire.[k]

**11** When the Chaldean army lifted the siege
of Jerusalem at the threat of the army of Pharaoh,[l] **12** Jeremiah set out from Jerusalem for
the district of Benjamin, to take part with his
family in the division of an inheritance. **13** But
when he reached the Gate of Benjamin, he met
the captain of the guard, a man named Irijah,
son of Shelemiah, son of Hananiah; he seized
the prophet Jeremiah, saying, "You are deserting to the Chaldeans!" **14** "That is a lie!" Jeremiah answered, "I am not deserting to the Chal-

e Jer 22, 19.
f Jer 52, 1; 2 Kgs 24, 17; 2 Chr 36, 10.
g Jer 21, 1.
h Ez 17, 15; 29, 6f.
i Ez 17, 17.
j Jer 34, 22.
k Jer 21, 4.
l Zec 14, 10.

36, 23: A scribe's knife: used to sharpen the reeds which were employed as pens.

36, 30: Jehoiakim's son Jehoiachin was named king, but reigned only three months; he was known better for his thirty-seven-year exile in Babylon. His corpse shall be cast out: see note on Jer 22, 19.

37, 4: Put into prison: as described in Jer 32, 1ff. Chronologically, the present episode follows Jer 34, 1–7.

37, 5: Pharaoh's army: the force sent by Pharaoh Hophra which caused the Chaldeans momentarily to lift the siege of Jerusalem (cf Jer 34, 21).

deans.'' Without listening, Irijah kept Jeremiah
in custody and brought him to the princes.
**15** The princes were enraged, and had Jeremiah beaten and thrown into prison in the house
of Jonathan the scribe, which they were using
as a jail.[m] **16** And so Jeremiah entered the
vaulted dungeon, where he remained a long
time.
**17** Once King Zedekiah had him brought to
his palace and he asked him secretly whether
there was any message from the LORD. Yes!
Jeremiah answered: you shall be handed over to
the king of Babylon.[n] **18** Jeremiah then asked
King Zedekiah: In what have I wronged you, or
your ministers, or this people, that you should
put me in prison?[o] **19** And where are your own
prophets now, **20** who prophesied to you that
the king of Babylon would not attack you or this
land? Hear now, my lord king, and grant my
petition: do not send me back into the house of
Jonathan the scribe, or I shall die there.
**21** King Zedekiah ordered that Jeremiah be
confined in the quarters of the guard, and given
a loaf of bread each day from the bakers' shop
until all the bread in the city was eaten up. Thus
Jeremiah remained in the quarters of the guard.[p]

## CHAPTER 38

**Jeremiah in the Miry Cistern.** **1** Shephatiah, son of Mattan, Gedaliah, son of Pashhur,
Jucal, son of Shelemiah, and Pashhur, son of
Malchiah, heard Jeremiah speaking these words
to all the people:* **2** Thus says the LORD: He
who remains in this city shall die by sword, or
famine, or pestilence; but he who goes out to the
Chaldeans shall live; his life shall be spared him
as booty, and he shall live.[q] **3** Thus says the
LORD: This city shall certainly be handed over
to the army of the king of Babylon; he shall
capture it.
**4** ''This man ought to be put to death,'' the
princes said to the king; ''he demoralizes the
soldiers* who are left in this city, and all the
people, by speaking such things to them; he is
not interested in the welfare of our people, but
in their ruin.''[r] **5** King Zedekiah answered:
''He is in your power''; for the king could do
nothing with them. **6** And so they took Jeremiah and threw him into the cistern of Prince
Malchiah, which was in the quarters of the
guard, letting him down with ropes. There was
no water in the cistern, only mud, and Jeremiah
sank into the mud.[s]
**7** Now Ebed-melech, a Cushite,* a courtier
in the king's palace, heard that they had put
Jeremiah into the cistern. The king happened
just then to be at the Gate of Benjamin, **8** and
Ebed-melech went there from the palace and
said to him, **9** ''My lord king, these men have
been at fault in all they have done to the prophet
Jeremiah, casting him into the cistern. He will
die of famine on the spot, for there is no more
food in the city.''[t] **10** Then the king ordered
Ebed-melech the Cushite to take three men
along with him, and draw the prophet Jeremiah
out of the cistern before he should die.
**11** Ebed-melech took the men along with him,
and went first to the linen closet in the palace,
from which he took some old, tattered rags;
these he sent down to Jeremiah in the cistern,
with ropes. **12** Then he said to Jeremiah, ''Put
the old, tattered rags between your armpits and
the ropes.'' Jeremiah did so, **13** and they drew
him up with the ropes out of the cistern. But
Jeremiah remained in the quarters of the guard.
**14** Once King Zedekiah summoned the
prophet Jeremiah to come to him at the third
entrance to the house of the LORD. ''I have a
question to ask you,'' the king said to Jeremiah;
''hide nothing from me.''[u] Jeremiah answered
Zedekiah: **15** If I tell you anything, you will
have me killed, will you not? If I counsel you,
you will not listen to me![v] **16** But King Zedekiah swore to Jeremiah secretly: ''As the LORD
lives who gave us the breath of life, I will not
kill you; nor will I hand you over to these men
who seek your life.''
**17** Thereupon Jeremiah said to Zedekiah:
Thus says the LORD God of hosts, the God of
Israel: If you surrender to the princes of Babylon's king, you shall save your life; this city
shall not be destroyed with fire, and you and
your family shall live.[w] **18** But if you do not
surrender to the princes of Babylon's king, this
city shall fall into the hands of the Chaldeans,
who shall destroy it with fire, and you shall not
escape their hands.[x]
**19** King Zedekiah, however, said to Jeremiah, ''I am afraid of the men of Judah who have
deserted to the Chaldeans; I may be handed over
to them, and they will mistreat me.''[y] **20** You
will not be handed over, Jeremiah answered.
Please obey the voice of the LORD and do as I
tell you; then it shall go well with you, and your
life will be spared.[z] **21** But if you refuse to
surrender, this is what the LORD shows me:

m Jer 38, 6-13.
n Jer 21, 7; 32, 3; 34, 21.
o Jer 26, 19.
p Jer 32, 2; 38, 28.
q Jer 21, 9f; 39, 18; 45, 5.
r Jer 26, 11.
s Jer 37, 14f.
t Jer 52, 6.
u Jer 37, 16.
v Lk 22, 67f.
w Jer 27, 12f; 2 Kgs 24, 12.
x Jer 32, 4.
y 1 Sm 31, 4.
z 2 Chr 20, 20.

38, 1: Jeremiah enjoyed sufficient liberty in the quarters of the guard (Jer 37, 21) to speak to the people; cf Jer 32, 6–9. Gedaliah, son of Pashhur: the latter is possibly the Pashhur of Jer 20, 1. Pashhur, son of Malchiah; mentioned in Jer 21, 1.

38, 4: He demoralizes the soldiers: literally, "he weakens their hands." One of the Lachish ostraca (see note on Jer 34, 7) uses the same expression of the princes in Jerusalem.

38, 7: A Cushite: an Ethiopian. Ebed-melech evidently held a position of some authority at court.

22 All the women left in the house of Judah's
king shall be brought out to the princes of Babylon's king, and they shall taunt you thus:

"They betrayed you, outdid you,
your good friends!
Now that your feet are stuck in the mud,
they slink away."[a]

23 All your wives and sons shall be led forth
to the Chaldeans, and you shall not escape their
hands; you shall be handed over to the king of
Babylon, and this city shall be destroyed with
fire.[b]

24 Then Zedekiah said to Jeremiah, "Let no
one know about this conversation, or you shall
die. 25 If the princes hear I spoke to you, if they
come and ask you, 'Tell us what you said to the
king; do not hide it from us, or we will kill you,'
or, 'What did the king say to you?' 26 give
them this answer: 'I petitioned the king not to
send me back to Jonathan's house to die
there.'" 27 When all the princes came to Jeremiah, they questioned him, and he answered
them in the very words the king had commanded. They said no more to him, for nothing had
been heard of the earlier conversation. 28 Thus
Jeremiah stayed in the quarters of the guard till
the day Jerusalem was taken.[c]

## CHAPTER 39

**Jeremiah and Gedaliah.** When Jerusalem
was taken. . . . 1 In the tenth month of the ninth
year* of Zedekiah,[d] king of Judah, Nebuchadnezzar, king of Babylon, and all his army
marched against Jerusalem and besieged it.
2 On the ninth day of the fourth month, in the
eleventh year* of Zedekiah, a breach was made
in the city's defenses. 3 All the princes of the
king of Babylon came and occupied the middle
gate: Nergal-sharezer, of Simmagir, the chief
officer, Nebushazban, the high dignitary, and
all the other princes of the king of Babylon. . . .
4 When Zedekiah, king of Judah, saw them, he
and all his warriors fled by night, leaving the
city on the Royal Garden Road* through the
gate between the two walls. He went in the
direction of the Arabah,[e] 5 but the Chaldean
army pursued them, and overtook and captured
Zedekiah in the desert near Jericho. He was
brought to Riblah,* in the land of Hamath,
where Nebuchadnezzar, king of Babylon, pronounced sentence upon him.[f] 6 As Zedekiah
looked on, his sons were slain at Riblah by order
of the king of Babylon, who slew also all the
nobles of Judah.[g] 7 He then blinded Zedekiah
and bound him in chains to bring him to Babylon.[h]

8 The Chaldeans set fire to the king's palace
and the houses of the people, and demolished
the walls of Jerusalem.[i] 9 Nebuzaradan, chief
of the bodyguard, deported to Babylon the rest
of the people left in the city, those who had
deserted to him, and the rest of the workmen.[j]
10 But some of the poor who had no property
were left in the land of Judah by Nebuzaradan,
chief of the bodyguard, and were given at the
same time vineyards and farms.[k]

11 Concerning Jeremiah, Nebuchadnezzar,
king of Babylon, gave the following orders
through Nebuzaradan, chief of the bodyguard:
12 "Take him and look after him; let no harm
befall him, but treat him as he himself requests."[l] 13 Thereupon Nebuzaradan, chief of
the bodyguard, and Nebushazban, the high dignitary, and Nergal-sharezer, the chief officer,
and all the nobles of the king of Babylon,
14 had Jeremiah taken out of the quarters of the
guard, and entrusted to Gedaliah, son of Ahikam, son of Shaphan, to be brought home. And
so he remained among the people.[m]

**A Word of Comfort for Ebed-melech.**
15 While Jeremiah was still imprisoned in the
quarters of the guard, the word of the LORD
came to him: 16 Go, tell this to Ebed-melech
the Cushite: Thus says the LORD of hosts, the
God of Israel: Behold, I am now fulfilling the
words I spoke against this city, for evil and not
for good; and this before your very eyes.[n]
17 But on that day I will rescue you, says the
LORD; you shall not be handed over to the men
of whom you are afraid. 18 I will make certain
that you escape and do not fall by the sword.
Your life shall be spared as booty, because you
trusted in me, says the LORD.[o]

## CHAPTER 40

**Jeremiah Still in Judah.** 1 This word*
came to Jeremiah from the LORD, after Nebu-

a Jb 6, 15; 19, 13f. 19.
b Jer 41, 10.
c Jer 39, 14.
d 1f: Jer 52, 4-16; 2 Kgs 25, 1-12; Ez 24, 1.
e Jer 52, 7.
f Jer 32, 4f; 38, 18.
g Jer 34, 21.
h Jer 32, 4f; Ez 12, 13.
i Jer 21, 10; 34, 2; 52, 13.
j 2 Kgs 25, 11.
k 2 Kgs 25, 12. 22.
l Jer 40, 4.
m Jer 26, 24; 38, 28.
n Jer 21, 10; Dn 9, 12.
o Jer 45, 5; Pss 25, 3; 36, 40.
p Jer 39, 14.

39, 1: The tenth month of the ninth year: the month Tebet (mid-December to mid-January) of the year 589/8 B.C.

39, 2: The ninth day of the fourth month, in the eleventh year: in July of 587 B.C.

39, 4: The Royal Garden Road: along the southeast side of the city; the royal garden was in the Kidron Valley. The gate between the two walls: the southernmost city gate, at the end of the Tyropoean Valley. The Arabah: the Jordan Valley. Zedekiah was attempting to escape across the Jordan when he was captured near Jericho.

39, 5: Riblah: Nebuchadnezzar's headquarters in Syria, which had also been used by Pharaoh Neco (2 Kgs 23, 33).

40, 1: This word: actually, no further word of the Lord is recorded until Jer 42, 7ff. This is a title affixed to the following

zaradan, captain of the bodyguard, had released
him in Ramah, where he had found him a prisoner in chains, among the captives of Jerusalem
and Judah who were being exiled to Babylon.[p]
**2** When the captain of the bodyguard took
charge of Jeremiah, he said to him, "The LORD,
your God, foretold the ruin of this place. **3** Now
he has brought about in deed what he threatened; because you sinned against the LORD and
did not obey his voice, this fate has befallen
you. **4** And now, I am freeing you today from
the fetters that bind your hands; if it seems good
to you to come with me to Babylon, you may
come: I will look after you well. But if it does
not please you to come to Babylon, you need not
come. See, the whole land is before you; go
wherever you think good and proper";[q] **5** and
then, before he left—"or go to Gedaliah, son of
Ahikam, son of Shaphan, whom the king of
Babylon has appointed ruler over the cities of
Judah; stay with him among the people, or go
wherever you please." The captain of the bodyguard gave him food and gifts and let him go.[r]
**6** Jeremiah went to Gedaliah, son of Ahikam,
in Mizpah,* and stayed with him among the
people left in the land.[s]

**7** When the army leaders who were still in
the field with all their men heard that the king
of Babylon had given Gedaliah, son of Ahikam,
charge of the land, of men, women, and children, and of those poor who had not been led
captive to Babylon, **8** they came with their men
to Gedaliah in Mizpah: Ishmael, son of Nethaniah; Johanan, son of Kareah; Seraiah, son of
Tanhumeth; the sons of Ephai of Netophah; and
Jezaniah* of Bethmaacah. **9** Gedaliah, son of
Ahikam, son of Shaphan, adjured them and
their men not to be afraid to serve the Chaldeans: to stay in the land and submit to the king
of Babylon, for their own welfare,[t] **10** saying
that he himself would remain in Mizpah, as their
intermediary with the Chaldeans who should
come to them. They were to collect the wine,
the fruit, and the oil, to store them in jars, and
to settle in the cities they occupied. **11** When
the people of Judah in Moab, those among the
Ammonites, those in Edom, and those in all
other lands heard that the king of Babylon had
left a remnant in Judah, and had appointed over
them Gedaliah, son of Ahikam, son of Shaphan,
**12** they all returned to the land of Judah from
the places to which they had scattered. They
went to Gedaliah at Mizpah and had a rich harvest of wine and fruit.

**Assassination of Gedaliah.** **13** Now Johanan, son of Kareah, and all the leaders of the
armies in the field came to Gedaliah in Mizpah
**14** and asked him whether he did not know that
Baalis, the king of the Ammonites,* had sent
Ishmael, son of Nethaniah, to assassinate him.[u]
**15** But Gedaliah, son of Ahikam, would not
believe them. Then Johanan, son of Kareah,
said secretly to Gedaliah in Mizpah: "Let me go
and kill Ishmael, son of Nethaniah; no one will
know it. Why should he be allowed to kill you?
All the Jews who have now rallied to you will
be dispersed and the remnant of Judah will perish." **16** Nevertheless, Gedaliah, son of Ahikam, answered Johanan, son of Kareah, "You
shall do nothing of the kind; you have lied about
Ishmael."

## CHAPTER 41

**1** In the seventh month Ishmael, son of Nethaniah, son of Elishama, of royal descent, one of
the king's nobles, came with ten men to Gedaliah, son of Ahikam, at Mizpah.[v] And while they
were together at table in Mizpah, **2** Ishmael,
son of Nethaniah, and the ten who were with
him, rose up and attacked with swords Gedaliah, son of Ahikam, son of Shaphan, whom the
king of Babylon had made ruler over the land;
and they killed him. **3** Ishmael also slew all the
men of Judah of military age who were with
Gedaliah and the Chaldean soldiers who were
there.

**4** The second day after the murder of Gedaliah, before anyone knew of it, **5** eighty men
with beards shaved off, clothes in rags, and with
gashes on their bodies came from Shechem,
Shiloh, and Samaria, bringing food offerings
and incense for the house of the LORD. **6** Ishmael, son of Nethaniah, went out from Mizpah to
meet them, weeping as he went. **7** "Come to
Gedaliah, son of Ahikam," he said as he met
them. When they were once inside the city,
Ishmael, son of Nethaniah, and his men slew
them and threw them into the cistern. **8** But
there were ten among them who pleaded with
Ishmael: "Do not kill us; we have stores buried
in the field: wheat and barley, oil and honey."
And so he spared them and did not kill them, as
he had killed their companions. **9** The cistern
into which Ishmael threw all the corpses of the

q Jer 39, 12.
r Jer 39, 14; 2 Kgs 25, 22.
s Jer 39, 14.
t Jer 27, 12f; 2 Kgs 25, 24.
u Jer 41, 1ff. 10.
v Jer 40, 14ff; 2 Kgs 25, 25.
w 1 Kgs 15, 16; 2 Chr 16, 6.

*

chapters after they were attached to an earlier form of the book ending with chapter 39.

40, 6: Mizpah: some five miles northwest of Jerusalem, where Israel chose its first king (1 Sm 10, 17–24). Presumably Jerusalem had been damaged too much by the Chaldean conquest to remain a seat of government.

40, 8: Jezaniah: the seal ring of a high official of this name was discovered in 1932 at the site usually identified with Mizpah, Tell en-Nasbe.

40, 14: The Ammonites: they resented the survival of their ancient enemy, Judah. Ishmael: their willing tool, who doubtless aspired to rule over Judah himself, as he was of the house of David; cf Jer 41, 1.

men he had killed was the large one made by
King Asa to defend himself against Baasha,
king of Israel; this cistern Ishmael, son of Nethaniah, filled with the slain.[w]
**10** Ishmael, son of Nethaniah, led away the
remnant of the people left in Mizpah and the
princesses,* whom Nebuzaradan, captain of the
bodyguard, had confided to Gedaliah, son of
Ahikam. With these captives, Ishmael, son of
Nethaniah, set out to make his way to the Ammonites.

**Flight to Egypt.** **11** But when Johanan, son
of Kareah, and the other army leaders with him
heard of the crimes Ishmael, son of Nethaniah,
had committed, **12** they took all their men and
set out to attack Ishmael, son of Nethaniah.
They overtook him at the Great Waters in Gibeon.* **13** At the sight of Johanan, son of Kareah,
and the other army leaders, the people who were
Ishmael's captives rejoiced. **14** All of those
whom Ishmael had brought away from Mizpah
went over to Johanan, son of Kareah. **15** But
Ishmael, son of Nethaniah, escaped from Johanan and fled to the Ammonites with eight men.
**16** Then Johanan, son of Kareah, and all his
army leaders took charge of the remnant of the
people, both the soldiers and the women and
children with their guardians, whom Ishmael,
son of Nethaniah, had brought away from Mizpah after he killed Gedaliah, son of Ahikim.
From Gibeon, **17** they retreated to the lodging
place of Chimham near Bethlehem, where they
stopped, intending to flee into Egypt. **18** They
were afraid of the Chaldeans, because Ishmael,
son of Nethaniah, had slain Gedaliah, son of
Ahikam, whom the king of Babylon had made
ruler in the land of Judah.

## CHAPTER 42

**1** Then all the army leaders, Johanan, son of
Kareah, Azariah, son of Hoshaiah, and all the
people, high and low, approached the prophet
Jeremiah **2** and said, "Grant our petition; pray
for us to the LORD, your God, for all this remnant. We are now few who once were many, as
you well see. **3** Let the LORD, your God, show
us what way we should take and what we should
do." **4** Very well! the prophet Jeremiah answered them: I will pray to the LORD, your God,
as you desire; whatever the LORD answers you,
I will tell you; I will withhold nothing from
you.[x] **5** And they said to Jeremiah, "May the
LORD be our witness: we will truly and faithfully
follow all the instructions the LORD, your God,
will send us.[y] **6** Whether it is pleasant or difficult, we will obey the command of the LORD,
our God, to whom we are sending you, so that
it will go well with us for obeying the command
of the LORD, our God."[z]

**7** Ten days passed before the word of the
LORD came to Jeremiah. **8** Then he called Johanan, son of Kareah, his army leaders, and all the
people, high and low, **9** and said to them: Thus
says the LORD, the God of Israel, to whom you
sent me to offer your prayer: **10** If you remain
quietly in this land I will build you up, and not
tear you down; I will plant you, not uproot you;
for I regret the evil I have done you.[a] **11** Do not
fear the king of Babylon, before whom you are
now afraid; do not fear him, says the LORD, for
I am with you to save you, to rescue you from
his power.[b] **12** I will grant you mercy, so that
he will be sorry for you and let you return to
your land.[c] **13** But if you disobey the voice of
the LORD, your God, and decide not to remain
in this land, **14** saying, "No, we will go to
Egypt, where we will see no more of war, hear
the trumpet alarm no longer, nor hunger for
bread; there we will live";[d] **15** then listen to the
word of the LORD, remnant of Judah: Thus says
the LORD of hosts, the God of Israel: If you are
determined to go to Egypt, when you arrive
there to stay, **16** the sword you fear shall reach
you in the land of Egypt; the hunger you dread
shall cling to you no less in Egypt, and there you
shall die.[e] **17** All those men who determine to
go to Egypt to stay, shall die by the sword,
famine, and pestilence; not one shall survive or
escape the evil that I will bring upon them.[f]
**18** For thus says the LORD of hosts, the God of
Israel: Just as my furious anger was poured out
upon the citizens of Jerusalem, so shall my anger be poured out on you when you reach Egypt.
You shall become an example of malediction
and horror, a curse and a reproach, and you shall
never see this place again.[g]
**19** It is the LORD who has spoken to you,
remnant of Judah; do not go to Egypt! You can
never say that I did not warn you this day. **20** At
the cost of your lives you have deceived me,
sending me to the LORD, your God, saying,
"Pray for us to the LORD, our God; make known
to us all that the LORD, our God, shall say, and
we will do it." **21** Today I proclaim his message, but you obey the voice of the LORD, your
God, in nothing that he has commissioned me
to make known to you.[h] **22** Have no doubt of
this, you shall die by the sword, famine, and

x 1 Sm 3, 18.
y Jgs 11, 10.
z Jer 7, 23; Dt 5, 33; 6, 3.
a Jer 31, 28; 32, 41.
b Jer 30, 10f.
c Ps 106, 45f; Prv 16, 7.
d Dt 28, 68.
e Jer 44, 13f. 27.
f Jer 29, 17f; 44, 14. 28.
g Jer 44, 12.
h Zec 7, 11f.
i Jer 44, 12; Hos 9, 6.

*

41, 10: The princesses: of the royal house of Judah. They had not been deported to Babylon with the men of this house.

41, 12: Gibeon: today called El-Jib; it is northwest of Jerusalem. The most recent excavations have revealed the extensive dimensions of the city spring and well, called here the Great Waters; cf 2 Sm 2, 12ff.

pestilence in the place where you wish to go and settle.[i]

## CHAPTER 43

**1** When Jeremiah finished speaking to the people all these words of the LORD, their God, with which the LORD had sent him to them, **2** Azariah, son of Hoshaiah, Johanan, son of Kareah, and all the insolent men shouted to Jeremiah: "You lie; it was not the LORD, our God, who sent you to tell us not to go to Egypt to settle. **3** It is Baruch, son of Neriah, who stirs you up against us, to hand us over to the Chaldeans to be killed or exiled to Babylon."[j]

**4** Johanan, son of Kareah, and the rest of the leaders and the people did not obey the LORD's command to stay in the land of Judah.[k] **5** Instead, Johanan, son of Kareah, and all the army leaders took along the whole remnant of Judah that had been dispersed among the nations and had returned thence to dwell again in the land of Judah: **6** men, women, and children, the princesses and everyone whom Nebuzaradan, captain of the bodyguard, had entrusted to Gedaliah, son of Ahikam, son of Shaphan; also Jeremiah, the prophet, and Baruch, son of Neriah.[l] **7** Against the LORD's command they went to Egypt, and arrived at Tahpanhes. . . .[m]

**Jeremiah in Egypt.** **8** This word of the LORD came to Jeremiah in Tahpanhes: **9** Take with you large stones and sink them in mortar in the brickyard at the entrance to the royal building* in Tahpanhes, while the men of Judah look on, **10** and then say to them: Thus says the LORD of hosts, the God of Israel: I will send for my servant Nebuchadnezzar, king of Babylon, and bring him here. He will set his throne upon these stones which I, Jeremiah, have sunk, and stretch his canopy over them.[n] **11** He shall come and strike the land of Egypt: with death, whoever is marked for death; with exile, everyone destined for exile; with the sword, all who are intended for the sword.[o] **12** He shall set fire to the temples of Egypt's gods, and burn the gods or carry them off. As a shepherd delouses his cloak, he shall delouse the land of Egypt and depart victorious.[p] **13** He shall smash the obelisks of the temple of the sun in the land of Egypt and destroy with fire the temples of the Egyptian gods.

## CHAPTER 44

**1** This word came to Jeremiah for all the people of Judah who were living in Egypt, at Migdol, Tahpanhes, and Memphis, and in Upper Egypt: **2** *Thus says the LORD of hosts, the God of Israel: You have seen all the evil I brought on Jerusalem and the other cities of Judah. Today they are ruins and uninhabited,[q] **3** because of the evil they did to provoke me, going after strange gods, serving them and sacrificing to them, gods which neither they, nor you, nor your fathers knew.[r] **4** Though I kept sending to you all my servants the prophets, with the plea not to commit this horrible deed which I hate, **5** they would not listen or accept the warning to turn away from the evil of sacrificing to strange gods.[s] **6** Therefore the fury of my anger poured forth in flame over the cities of Judah and the streets of Jerusalem, so that they became the ruinous waste they are today.

**7** Now thus says the LORD God of hosts, the God of Israel: Why do you inflict so great an evil upon yourselves? Will you root out from Judah man and wife, child and nursling, and not leave yourselves even a remnant? **8** Will you go on provoking me by the works of your hands, by sacrificing to strange gods here in the land of Egypt where you have come to live? Will you be rooted out and become a curse and a disgrace among all the nations of the earth?[t] **9** Have you forgotten the evil deeds which your fathers, and the kings of Judah and their wives, and you yourselves and your wives have done in the land of Judah and the streets of Jerusalem?[u] **10** To this day they have not been crushed; they do not fear or follow the law and the statutes which I set before you and your fathers.[v]

**11** Hence, thus says the LORD of hosts, the God of Israel: I have determined evil against you; and I will uproot all Judah. **12** I will take away the remnant of Judah who insisted on coming to dwell in Egypt, so that they shall be wholly destroyed. In the land of Egypt they shall fall by the sword or be consumed by hunger. High and low, they shall die by the sword, or by hunger, and become an example of malediction, a horror, a curse and a reproach.[w] **13** Thus will I punish those who live in Egypt, just as I punished Jerusalem with sword, hunger, and pestilence. None of the remnant of Judah that have come to settle in the land of Egypt shall escape or survive.[x] **14** None shall return to the land of Judah, though they yearn to return and live there. Only scattered refugees shall return.

**15** From all the men who knew that their

---

j Jer 38, 4.
k Jer 41, 16.
l Jer 41, 10.
m Jer 42, 13f; 44, 1.
n Jer 27, 6; Ez 29, 19.
o Jer 46, 13; Ez 30, 10.
p Jer 46, 25; Ez 30, 13f.
q Jer 34, 22; Lv 26, 32f.
r Jer 11, 17; Dt 32, 17.
s Jer 7, 24. 26; 19, 4.
t Jer 25, 6f.
u 1 Kgs 11, 1. 8; Ezr 9, 7. 14.
v Jer 7, 24.
w Jer 42, 15. 18. 22.
x Jer 43, 11.

---

*

43, 9: The royal building: residence of the Egyptian governor.

44, 2–30: Chronologically, this is the last of Jeremiah's prophecies to his countrymen. The narrative leaves him an old man nearing seventy, rejected by his people. According to tradition, he was murdered in Egypt by fellow Judeans.

wives were burning incense to strange gods,
from all the women who were present in the
immense crowd, and from all the people who
lived in Lower and Upper Egypt, Jeremiah received this answer: **16** "We will not listen to
what you say in the name of the LORD.[y]
**17** Rather will we continue doing what we had
proposed; we will burn incense to the queen of
heaven and pour out libations to her, as we and
our fathers, our kings and princes have done in
the cities of Judah and the streets of Jerusalem.
Then we had enough food to eat and we were
well off; we suffered no misfortune.[z] **18** But
since we stopped burning incense to the queen
of heaven and pouring out libations to her, we
are in need of everything and are being destroyed by the sword and by hunger. **19** And
when we burned incense to the queen of heaven
and poured out libations to her, was it without
our husbands' consent that we baked for her
cakes in her image and poured out libations to
her?"[a]

**20** To all the people, men and women, who
gave him this answer, Jeremiah said: **21** Was it
not this that the LORD remembered and brought
to mind, that you burned incense in the cities of
Judah and the streets of Jerusalem: you, your
fathers, your kings and princes, and the people
generally?[b] **22** The LORD could no longer bear
your evil deeds, the horrible things which you
were doing; and so your land became a waste,
a desert, a thing accursed and without inhabitants, as it is today.[c] **23** Because you burned
incense and sinned against the LORD, not obeying the voice of the LORD, not living by his law,
his statutes, and his decrees, this evil has befall-
en you at the present day.[d]

**24** Jeremiah said further to all the people,
including the women: Hear the word of the
LORD, all you Judeans in the land of Egypt:
**25** Thus says the LORD of hosts, the God of
Israel: You and your wives have stated your
intentions, and kept them in fact: "We will
continue to fulfill the vows we have made to
burn incense to the queen of heaven and to pour
out libations to her." Very well! keep your
vows, carry out your resolutions! **26** But listen
then to the word of the LORD, all you people of
Judah who live in Egypt; I swear by my own
great name, says the LORD, in the whole land of
Egypt no man of Judah shall henceforth pronounce my name, saying, "As the Lord GOD
lives." **27** I am watching over them to do evil,
not good. All the men of Judah in Egypt shall
perish by the sword or famine until they are
utterly destroyed.[e] **28** Those who escape the
sword to return from the land of Egypt to the
land of Judah shall be few in number. The whole
remnant of Judah who came to settle in Egypt
shall know whose word stands, mine or theirs.[f]
**29** That you may know how surely my
threats of punishment for you shall be fulfilled,
this shall be a sign to you, says the LORD, that
I will punish you in this place. **30** Thus says the
LORD: See! I will hand over Pharaoh Hophra,*
king of Egypt, to his enemies, to those who seek
his life, just as I handed over Zedekiah, king of
Judah, to his enemy and mortal foe, Nebuchadnezzar, king of Babylon.[g]

## CHAPTER 45

**A Message to Baruch.*** **1** This is the message that the prophet Jeremiah gave to Baruch,
son of Neriah, when he wrote in a book the
prophecies that Jeremiah dictated in the fourth
year of Jehoiakim, son of Josiah, king of Judah:[h] **2** Thus says the LORD, God of Israel, to
you, Baruch, **3** because you said, "Alas! the
LORD adds grief to my pain;[i] I am weary from
groaning, and can find no rest": **4** say this to
him, says the LORD: What I have built, I am
tearing down; what I have planted, I am uproot-
ing: even the whole land.[j] **5** And do you seek
great things for yourself? Seek them not! I am
bringing evil on all mankind, says the LORD, but
your life I will leave you as booty, wherever you
may go.[k]

# *V: Oracles against the Nations**

## CHAPTER 46

**1** This is the word of the LORD that came to
the prophet Jeremiah against the nations.

**Against Egypt.** **2** Concerning Egypt.
Against the army of Pharaoh Neco, king of

y Jer 6, 16f.
z Jer 5, 3; 7, 18.
a Jer 7, 18.
b Jer 11, 13.
c Jer 15, 6.
d 2 Kgs 17, 15; Dn 9, 11f.
e Ez 7, 3-7.
f Dt 28, 62; Is 10, 22.
g Jer 39, 5ff; 46, 25f; Ez 29, 3f; 30, 21.
h Jer 36, 4. 18. 32.
i Lam 1, 3; 5, 5.
j Jer 18, 7; Is 5, 5f.
k Jer 25, 26-29.

*

44, 30: Hophra: killed by his own people. The ruler of Egypt at the time of its conquest by Nebuchadnezzar was Hophra's successor Amasis, who was also slain by his enemies.

45, 1–5: At the conclusion of his narrative, Baruch appends a prophecy given him personally by Jeremiah when he first wrote down Jeremiah's words (cf chap. 36). The future revealed by the prophet had depressed Baruch; this prophecy was to assure him of his personal safety, while repeating the Lord's determination to destroy Judah.

46—51: In these chapters most of Jeremiah's oracles against the foreign nations have been gathered together and placed at the end of his book; in the Greek text they appear with the other oracles against the nations, in chap. 25. In general, they are in chronological order: 46, 1—49, 33, from the fourth year of Jehoiakim; 49, 34–39, at the beginning of Zedekiah's reign; 50, 1—51, 64, from the fourth year of Zedekiah.

46, 2: Carchemish on the Euphrates: the western terminus of the Mesopotamian trade route, where Nebuchadnezzar defeated Neco in 605 B.C., thus gaining undisputed control of Syria and Palestine.

Egypt, which was defeated at Carchemish on the Euphrates* by Nebuchadnezzar, king of Babylon, in the fourth year of Jehoiakim, son of Josiah, king of Judah:

3 Prepare shield and buckler!
march to battle!
4 Harness the horses,
mount, charioteers
Fall in with your helmets;
polish your spears, put on your breastplates.
5 What do I see?
With broken ranks
They fall back;
their heroes are routed,
They flee headlong
without making a stand.
Terror on every side,
says the LORD![l]
6 The swift cannot flee,
nor the hero escape:
There in the north, on the Euphrates' bank,
they stumble and fall.

7 Who is this that surges forward like the Nile,
like rivers of billowing waters?
8 Egypt surges like the Nile,
like rivers of billowing waters.
"I will surge forward," he says, "and cover the earth,
destroying the city and its people.[m]
9 Forward, horses!
drive madly, chariots!
Set out, warriors,
Cush and Put, bearing your shields,
Men of Lud, stretching your bows!"
10 But this is the day of the Lord GOD of hosts,
a day of vengeance, vengeance on his foes!
The sword devours, is sated, drunk with their
blood:
for the Lord GOD of hosts holds a slaughter feast
in the northland, on the Euphrates.[n]

11 Go up to Gilead, and take balm,
O virgin daughter Egypt!
No use to multiply remedies;
for you there is no cure.[o]
12 The nations hear of your shame,
your cries fill the earth.
Warrior trips over warrior,
both fall together.[p]

13 [q]The message which the LORD gave to the
prophet Jeremiah concerning the advance of
Nebuchadnezzar, king of Babylon, to attack the
land of Egypt:*

14 Announce it in Egypt, publish it in Migdol,
proclaim it in Memphis and Tahpanhes!
Say: Take your stand, prepare yourselves,
the sword has already devoured your neighbors.[r]
15 Why has Apis* fled,
your mighty one failed to stand?
The LORD thrust him down;
16 he stumbled repeatedly, and fell.
They said one to another,
"Up! let us return to our own people,
To the land of our birth,
away from the destroying sword."[s]

17 Call Pharaoh, king of Egypt, by the name
"The noise that let its time go by."*
18 As I live, says the King
whose name is LORD of hosts,
Like Tabor among the mountains he shall come,
like Carmel* above the sea.
19 Pack your baggage exile,
capital city of daughter Egypt;
Memphis shall become a desert,
an empty ruin.
20 Egypt is a pretty heifer,
from the north a horsefly lights upon her.
21 The mercenaries in her ranks
are like fatted calves;
They too turn and flee together,
stand not their ground,
When the day of their ruin comes upon them,
the time of their punishment.
22 She sounds like a retreating reptile!
Yes, they come in force;
like woodchoppers, they attack her with axes.
23 They cut down her forest, says the LORD,
impenetrable though it be;
More numerous than locusts,
they cannot be counted.
24 Disgraced is daughter Egypt,
handed over to the people of the north.

25 The LORD of hosts, the God of Israel, has
said: See! I will punish Amon* of Thebes, and
Egypt, her gods and her kings, Pharaoh, and
those who trust in him.[t] 26 I will hand them

l Jer 6, 25; 49, 29.
m Ez 29, 3; 32, 2.
n Dt 32, 42; Is 13, 9; Ez 39, 17-20.
o Jer 8, 22; 51, 8; Ez 30, 21f.
p Ez 32, 9-12.
q Jer 43, 10f; 44, 30; Is 19, 1.
r Jer 44, 1.
s Lv 26, 37.
t Ez 30, 15f.
u Jer 44, 30; Ez 30, 4; 32, 11f.

*

46, 13: In 601 B.C. Nebuchadnezzar advanced against Egypt and even entered the country, but finally had to withdraw to Syria.

46, 15: Apis: the chief god of Memphis, venerated in the form of a black bull.

46, 17: "The noise . . . go by": in Hebrew there is wordplay here on the name Hophra, who still made a pretense of power though his career was at an end.

46, 18: Tabor . . . Carmel: outstanding mountains of Palestine, symbols of strength, to which Nebuchadnezzar is compared.

46, 25: Amon: the sun-god worshiped at Thebes, in Upper Egypt.

over to those who seek their lives, to Nebuchadnezzar, king of Babylon, and his ministers. But
later on Egypt shall be inhabited again, as in
times past, says the LORD.[u]

27 But you, my servant Jacob, fear not;
be not dismayed, O Israel.
Behold, I will deliver you from the faroff land,
your descendants, from their land of exile.
Jacob shall again find rest,
shall be tranquil and undisturbed.[v]
28 You, my servant Jacob, never fear, says the LORD,
for I am with you;
I will make an end of all the nations
to which I have driven you,
But of you I will not make an end:
I will chastise you as you deserve,
I will not let you go unpunished.[w]

## CHAPTER 47

**Against the Philistines.** 1 This is the
word that came from the LORD to the prophet
Jeremiah concerning the Philistines, before
Pharaoh attacked Gaza:[x] 2 Thus says the LORD:

*Behold: waters are rising from the north,
a torrent in flood;
It shall flood the land and all that is in it,
the cities and their people.
All the people of the land
set up a wailing cry.
3 They hear the stamping hooves of his steeds,
the rattling chariots, the rumbling wheels.
Fathers turn not to save their children;
their hands fall helpless
4 Because of the day which has come
to ruin all the Philistines,
And cut off from Tyre and Sidon*
the last of their allies.
Yes, the LORD is destroying the Philistines,
the remnant from the coasts of Caphtor.[y]
5 Gaza is shaved bald,[z]
Ashkelon is reduced to silence;
Ashdod, the remnant of their strength,
how long will you gash yourself?*
6 Alas, sword of the LORD!
how long till you find rest?
Return into your scabbard;
stop, be still!*
7 How can it find rest
when the LORD has commanded it?
Against Ashkelon and the seashore
he has appointed it.[a]

## CHAPTER 48

**Against Moab.*** 1 Concerning Moab, thus
says the LORD of hosts, the God of Israel:

Woe to Nebo, it is laid waste;
Kiriathaim is disgraced and captured,
Disgraced and overthrown is the stronghold:
2 Moab's glory is no more.
Evil they plan against Heshbon:
"Come, let us put an end to her as a people."
You, too, Madmen, shall be reduced to silence;
behind you stalks the sword.
3 Listen! a cry from Horonaim[b]
of ruin and great destruction!
4 Moab is crushed,
their outcry is heard in Zoar.
5 The ascent of Luhith
they climb weeping;
On the descent to Horonaim
the cry of destruction is heard.
6 "Flee, save your lives,
to survive like the wild ass in the desert!"
7 Because you trusted in your works and your treasures,
you also shall be captured.
Chemosh* shall go into exile,
his priests and princes with him.[c]
8 The destroyer comes upon every city,
not a city escapes;
Ruined is the valley,
wasted the plain, as the LORD has said.
9 Set up a memorial for Moab,
for it is an utter wasteland;
Its cities are turned into ruins
where no one dwells.
10 [Cursed be he who does the LORD's work remissly,
cursed he who holds back his sword from blood.]
11 Moab has been tranquil from his youth,
has rested upon his lees;
He was not poured from one flask to another,
he went not into exile.
Thus he kept his taste,
and his scent was not lost.[d]

12 Hence, the days shall come, says the
LORD, when I will send him coopers to turn him
over; they shall empty his flasks and break his

v Jer 30, 10; 43, 5.
w Jer 30, 11.
x Ez 25, 15f; Zep 2, 4.
y Jer 25, 22; Ez 25, 16f; Am 1, 8; 9, 7.
z Am 1, 7.
a Zep 2, 5f.
b 3ff: Is 15, 5.
c Nm 21, 29.
d Zep 1, 12.

*

47, 2–7: This prophecy was fulfilled in 605/4 B.C.

47, 4: Tyre and Sidon: Phoenician cities associated commercially with the Philistines, and enemies of Nebuchadnezzar; cf Jer 27, 1–4. Nebuchadnezzar carried out a thirteen-year siege of Tyre which was only partially successful. Caphtor: probably the island of Crete, the traditional place of origin of the Philistines; cf Am 9, 7.

47, 5: Of the ancient Philistine cities, neither Gath nor Ekron (Jer 25, 20) is mentioned in this period of waning independence of the seacoast.

47, 6: Words of the Philistines.

48, 1–47: Moab was one of the Israelites' bitterest enemies. According to Flavius Josephus, Moab and Ammon were conquered by Nebuchadnezzar in this twenty-third year, 582 B.C., five years after the destruction of Jerusalem.

48, 7: Chemosh: chief god of the Moabites.

jars. 13 Chemosh shall disappoint Moab, as
Israel was disappointed by Bethel in which they
trusted.[e]

14 How can you say, "We are heroes,
men valiant in war"?
15 The ravager of Moab and his cities
advances,
the flower of his youth goes down to be
slaughtered,
says the King, the LORD of hosts by
name.
16 Near at hand is Moab's ruin,
his disaster hastens apace.
17 Mourn for him, all you his neighbors,
all you who knew him well!
Say: How the strong staff is broken,
the glorious rod!
18 Come down from glory, sit on the ground,
you that dwell in Dibon;
Moab's ravager has come up against you,
he has ruined your strongholds.[f]
19 Stand by the wayside, watch closely,
you that dwell in Aroer;
Ask the man who flees, the woman who
tries to escape:
say to them, "What has happened?"[g]
20 Moab is disgraced, yes, destroyed,
howl and cry out;
Publish it at the Arnon,
Moab is ruined![h]

21 For judgment has come on the land of the
plateau: on Holon, Jahzah, and Mephaath,[i]
22 on Dibon, Nebo, and Beth-diblathaim,
23 on Kiriathaim, Beth-gamul, and Beth-
meon, 24 on Kerioth and on Bozrah: on all the
cities of Moab, far and near.

25 Moab's strength is broken,
his might is shattered, says the LORD.

26 Because he boasted against the LORD,
make Moab drunk so that he retches and vomits,
and he too becomes a laughingstock. 27 Is Israel a laughingstock to you? Was she caught
among thieves, that you shake your head whenever you speak of her?[j]

28 Leave the cities, dwell in the crags,
you that dwell in Moab.
Be like a dove that nests
out of reach on the edge of a chasm.
29 We have heard of the pride of Moab,[k]
pride beyond bounds:
His loftiness, his pride, his scorn,
his insolence of heart.
30 I know, says the LORD, his arrogance;
liar in boast, liar in deed.
31 And so I wail over Moab,
over all Moab I cry,
over the men of Kir-heres I moan.[l]
32 More than for Jazer I weep over you,
vineyard of Sibmah.
Your tendrils trailed down to the sea,
as far as Jazer they stretched.
Upon your harvest, upon your vintage,
the ravager has fallen.[m]
33 Joy and jubilation are at an end
in the fruit gardens of the land of Moab.
I drain the wine from the wine vats,
the treader treads no more,
the vintage shout is stilled.

34 The cry of Heshbon and Elealeh is heard
as far as Jahaz; they call from Zoar to Horonaim, and to Eglath-shelishiyah, for even the waters of Nimrim turn into a desert.[n] 35 I will
leave no one in Moab, says the LORD, to offer
a holocaust on the high place, or to burn incense
to his gods. 36 Hence the wail of flutes for
Moab is in my heart; for the men of Kir-heres
the wail of flutes is in my heart: the wealth they
acquired has perished.[o] 37 Every head has
been made bald, every beard shaved; every
hand is gashed, and the loins of all are clothed
in sackcloth.[p] 38 On every roof of Moab and in
all his squares there is mourning; I have shattered Moab like a pot that no one wants, says the
LORD. 39 How terror seizes Moab, and wailing! How he turns his back in shame! Moab has
become a laughingstock and a horror to all his
neighbors! 40 For thus says the LORD:

Behold, like an eagle he soars,
spreads his wings over Moab.[q]
41 Cities are taken,
strongholds seized:
On that day the hearts of Moab's heroes
are like the heart of a woman in travail.[r]
42 Moab shall be destroyed, no more a people,
because he boasted against the LORD.[s]
43 Terror, pit, and trap be upon you,
people of Moab, says the LORD.[t]
44 He who flees from the terror
falls into the pit;
He who climbs from the pit
is caught in the trap;
For I will bring these things upon Moab
in the year of their punishment, says the
LORD.
45 In Heshbon's shadow stop short
the exhausted refugees;
For fire breaks forth from Heshbon,
and a blaze from the house of Sihon:
It consumes the brow of Moab,
the skull of the noisemakers.[u]
46 Woe to you, O Moab,
you are ruined, O people of Chemosh!
Your sons are taken into exile,
your daughters into captivity.
47 But I will change the lot of Moab

e Is 16, 12.
f Nm 21, 30.
g Dt 2, 36.
h Is 16, 7.
i Is 15, 4.
j Zep 2, 8ff.
k 29f: Is 16, 6.
l Is 16, 7.
m Is 16, 8f.
n Is 15, 4f.
o Is 16, 11.
p Jer 47, 5; Is 15, 2f; Ez 7, 18.
q Jer 49, 22.
r Jer 6, 24; 30, 6.
s Zep 2, 9f.
t Is 24, 17f.
u Nm 21, 28f.
v Jer 49, 39.

in the days to come, says the LORD.[v]
Thus far the judgment of Moab.

## CHAPTER 49

**Against the Ammonites.** 1 Concerning the Ammonites, thus says the LORD:

Has Israel no sons?
has he no heir?
Why then has Milcom* disinherited Gad,
why have his people settled in Gad's cities?
2 But the days are coming, says the LORD,
when against Rabbah of the Ammonites*
I will sound the battle alarm;
She shall become a mound of ruins,
and her daughter cities shall be destroyed by fire.
Israel shall inherit those who disinherited her,
says the LORD.[w]
3 Howl, Heshbon, for the ravager approaches,
shriek, daughters of Rabbah!
Put on sackcloth and mourn,
run to and fro, gashing yourselves;
For Milcom goes into exile
along with his priests and captains.[x]
4 Why do you glory in your strength,
your ebbing strength, rebellious daughter?
You who trust in your treasures, saying,
"Who can come against me?"
5 I am bringing terror upon you,
says the Lord GOD of hosts,
from all round about you;
You shall be scattered, each man in headlong flight,
with no one to rally the fugitives.[y]
6 But afterward I will change the lot
of the Ammonites, says the LORD.

**Against Edom.*** 7 Concerning Edom, thus says the LORD of hosts:

Is there no more wisdom in Teman,*
has counsel perished from the prudent,
has their wisdom become corrupt?
8 Flee, retreat, hide in deep holes,
you who live in Dedan:
For I will bring destruction upon Esau*
when I come to punish him.[z]
9 If vintagers came upon you,
they would leave no gleanings;
If thieves by night,
they would destroy as they pleased.[a]
10 So I myself will strip Esau;
I will uncover his retreats so that he cannot hide.
He is ruined: sons, and brothers,
and neighbors, so that he is no more.[b]
11 Leave your orphans behind, I will keep them alive;
your widows, let them trust in me.[c]

12 For thus says the LORD: Even those not
sentenced to drink the cup must drink it! Shall
you then go unpunished? You shall not go unpunished; you shall surely drink it.[d] 13 By my
own self I have sworn, says the LORD: Bozrah*
shall become an object of horror and a disgrace,
a desolation and a curse; she and all her cities
shall become ruins forever.[e]

14 I have heard a report from the LORD,
a herald has been sent among the nations:
Gather together, move against her,
rise up for battle.
15 Small will I make you among the nations,
despised among men![f]
16 The terror you spread beguiled you,
and your presumption of heart;
You that live in rocky crags,
that hold the heights of the hill:
Though you build your nest high as the eagle,
from there I will drag you down, says the LORD.[g]

17 Edom shall become an object of horror.
Every passer-by shall be appalled and catch his
breath at all her wounds. 18 As when Sodom,
Gomorrah, and their neighbors were overthrown, says the LORD, not a man shall dwell
there: no one shall visit there.[h]

19 As when a lion comes up from the thicket of Jordan
to the permanent feeding grounds,
So I, in an instant, will drive men off;
and whom I choose I will establish there!
For who is like me? who can call me to account?
What shepherd can stand against me?[i]
20 Therefore, hear the counsel of the LORD,
which he has taken against Edom;
Hear the plans he has made
against those that live in Teman:
They shall be dragged away, even the smallest sheep,
their own pasture shall be aghast because

w Am 1, 14.
x Is 15, 2ff.
y Jer 48, 47.
z Ez 25, 13.
a Ob 5.
b Mal 1, 3.
c Dt 10, 18; Ps 68, 6.
d Jer 25, 15. 28; Lam 4, 21f.
e Is 34, 6; Ez 35, 3-9; Ob 16.
f Ob 2.
g Jer 48, 29f.
h Jer 50, 40; Dt 29, 23.
i Jer 12, 5; 25, 9; 50, 44f.

*

49, 1: Milcom: chief god of the Ammonites. The Transjordan tribe of Gad bordered on Ammon, and after the collapse of the northern kingdom the Ammonites occupied its territory.

49, 2: Rabbah of the Ammonites: or Rabbath-Ammon, capital of the Ammonite kingdom. The modern Amman is the capital of the kingdom of Jordan.

49, 7–22: Edom: this implacable enemy from ancient times profited from Judah's downfall; cf Ob 11f.

49, 7: Teman: a district of Edom, used here for the whole country; it was famous for its wise men; cf Jb 2, 11.

49, 8: Esau: Jacob's brother, the traditional ancestor of the Edomites; cf Gn 36.

49, 13: Bozrah: capital of Edom, southeast of the Dead Sea.

of them.
21 At the noise of their fall the earth quakes,
to the Red Sea the outcry is heard!
22 See! like an eagle he soars aloft,
and spreads his wings over Bozrah;
On that day the hearts of Edom's heroes
shall be
like the heart of a woman in travail.[j]

**Against Damascus.** Concerning Damascus:

23 Hamath and Arpad* are covered with
shame,
they have heard bad news;
Worried, they toss like the sea
which cannot rest.[k]
24 Damascus is weakened, she turns to flee,
panic has seized her.
Distress and pangs take hold of her,
like those of a woman in travail.
25 How can the city of glory be forsaken,
the town of delight!
26 But now her young men shall fall in her
streets,
and all her warriors shall be stilled.
On that day, says the LORD of hosts,
27 I will set fire to the wall of Damascus,
and it shall devour the palaces of
Benhadad.*

**Against Arabia.** 28 Of Kedar and the kingdoms of Hazor, defeated by Nebuchadnezzar,
king of Babylon, thus says the LORD:

Rise up, attack Kedar,
ravage the Easterners.[l]
29 Their tents and herds shall be taken away,
their tent curtains and all their goods;
Their camels they shall carry off for
themselves,
and shout from upon them, "Terror on
every side!"[m]
30 Flee! leave your homes, hide in deep holes,
you that live in Hazor, says the LORD;
For counsel has been taken against you,
a plan has been formed against you
[Nebuchadnezzar, king of Babylon].
31 Rise up! set out against a nation that is at
peace,
that lives secure, says the LORD,
That has no gates or bars,
and dwells alone.
32 Their camels shall be your booty,
their many herds your spoil;
I will scatter to the winds those who shave
their temples,
from all sides I will bring ruin upon them,
says the LORD.[n]
33 Hazor shall become a haunt of jackals,
a desert forever,
Where no man lives,
no human being stays.

**Against Elam.** 34 The following word of
the LORD against Elam* came to the prophet
Jeremiah at the beginning of the reign of Zedekiah, king of Judah: 35 Thus says the LORD of
hosts:

Behold, I will break the bow of Elam,
the mainstay of their might.
36 I will bring upon Elam the four winds
from the four ends of the heavens:
I will scatter them to all these winds, till
there is no nation
to which the outcasts of Elam shall not
come.
37 I will break Elam before their foes,
before those who seek their life;
I will bring evil upon them,
my burning wrath, says the LORD.
I will send the sword to pursue them
until I have completely made an end of
them;
38 My throne I will set up in Elam
and destroy from there king and princes,
says the LORD.
39 But in the days to come I will change
the lot of Elam, says the LORD.

## CHAPTER 50

### The First Prophecy against Babylon.

1 The word which the LORD spoke against Babylon,* against the land of the Chaldeans,
through the prophet Jeremiah:[o]

2 Announce and publish it among the nations;
publish it, hide it not, but say:
Babylon is taken, Bel* confounded,
Merodach shattered;
her images are put to shame, her idols
shattered.
3 A people from the north advances against
her
to turn her land into a desert,

j Jer 4, 13.
k Is 36, 19; 37, 13.
l Is 21, 16.
m Jer 4, 20.
n Jer 9, 25.
o Jer 51, 1; Is 13, 1-14; 21, 1-10.
p Jer 51, 48; Is 13, 17.

*

49, 23: Hamath and Arpad: independent Aramean states to the north of Damascus; the invasion is conceived as coming from the north. The situation is of the eighth century B.C. Cf Is 10, 9ff.

49, 27: The palaces of Ben-hadad: the royal palaces in Damascus where at least three kings bore this name; cf 1 Kgs 15, 18; 20.

49, 34: Elam: the ancient kingdom to the east of Babylonia.

50, 1—51, 58: A collection of miscellaneous prophecies against Babylon which now stands as the introduction to the story in Jer 51, 59–64. The Greek text of Jer 50, 1 omits through the prophet Jeremiah, and it is in fact likely that these oracles are not Jeremiah's, but were composed by other inspired writers after the fall of Jerusalem, who may have used some of Jeremiah's texts. Babylon fell to the Persians in 538 B.C.

50, 2: Bel: originally the name of the god of Nippur in Mesopotamia, then identified with Merodach (Marduk), chief god of Babylon.

So that no one shall live there,
because man and beast have fled away.[p]
4 In those days, at that time, says the LORD,
the men of Israel and of Judah shall come,
Weeping as they come, to seek the
LORD, their God;[q]
5 to their goal in Zion they shall ask the way.
"Come, let us join ourselves to the LORD
with covenant everlasting, never to be forgotten."[r]
6 Lost sheep were my people,
their shepherds misled them,
straggling on the mountains;
From mountain to hill they wandered, losing
the way to their fold.[s]
7 Whoever came upon them devoured them,
and their enemies said, "We incur no guilt,
Because they sinned against the LORD,
the hope of their fathers, their abode of justice."[t]

8 Flee from Babylon, leave the land of the Chaldeans,
be like the rams at the head of the flock.[u]
9 See, I am stirring up against Babylon
a band of great nations from the north;
from there they advance, and she shall be taken.
Their arrows are arrows of the skilled warrior;
none shall return without effect.[v]
10 Chaldea shall be their plunder,
and all her plunderers shall be enriched,
says the LORD.
11 Yes, rejoice and exult,
you that plunder my portion;
Frisk like calves on the green,
snort like stallions!
12 Your mother shall be sorely put to shame,
she that bore you shall be abashed;
See, the last of the nations,
a desert, dry and waste.[w]
13 Because of the LORD's wrath she shall be empty,
and become a total desert;
Everyone who passes by Babylon will be appalled
and catch his breath, at all her wounds.[x]
14 Take your posts encircling Babylon,
you who bend the bow;
Shoot at her, spare not your arrows,[y]
15 raise the war cry against her on all sides.
She surrenders, her bastions fall,
her walls are torn down:*
Vengeance of the LORD is this! Take revenge on her,
as she has done, do to her;
for she sinned against the LORD.[z]
16 Cut off from Babylon the sower
and him who wields the sickle in harvest time!
Before the destroying sword,
each of them turns to his own people,
everyone flees to his own land.[a]
17 A stray sheep was Israel
that lions pursued;
Formerly the king of Assyria devoured her,
now Nebuchadnezzar of Babylon gnaws her bones.[b]

18 Therefore, thus says the LORD of hosts,
the God of Israel:

I will punish the king of Babylon and his land,
as once I punished the king of Assyria;[c]
19 But I will bring back Israel to her fold,
to feed on Carmel and Bashan,
And on Mount Ephraim and Gilead,
till she has her fill.[d]

20 In those days, at that time, says the LORD:

They shall seek Israel's guilt, but it shall be no more,
and Judah's sins, but these shall no longer be found;
for I will forgive the remnant I preserve.[e]

21 Attack the land of Merathaim,*
and those who live in Pekod;
Slaughter and doom them, says the LORD,
do all I have commanded you.
22 Battle alarm in the land,
dire destruction!
23 How has the hammer of the whole earth
been broken and shattered!
What an object of horror
Babylon has become among the nations![f]
24 You ensnared yourself, and were caught,
O Babylon, before you knew it!
You were discovered and seized,
because you challenged the LORD.[g]
25 The LORD opens his armory
and brings forth the weapons of his wrath;
For the Lord GOD of hosts has work to do
in the land of the Chaldeans.[h]

26 Come upon her from every side,
open her granaries,
Pile up her goods in heaps and doom it,

q Jer 3, 18; Ps 126, 6.
r Jer 31, 31; 32, 40.
s Is 53, 6; I Pt 2, 25.
t Jer 31, 23.
u Jer 51, 6. 45; Is 48, 20.
v Jer 51, 27.
w Jer 51, 43; Is 13, 20ff.
x Jer 25, 12.
y Jer 51, 11; Is 21, 2.
z Jer 51, 11. 44, 58; Ps 137, 8.
a Is 13, 14.
b 2 Kgs 17, 24; 18, 14.
c Is 10, 12; 14, 24f.
d Jer 23, 3; Ez 34, 13f.
e Jer 31, 34; Is 43, 25; Mi 7, 19.
f Jer 51, 20; Is 14, 6.
g Jer 51, 57.
h Jer 51, 11; Is 13, 5.

* 50, 15: Her walls are torn down: the prophet is not predicting the details of Babylon's downfall, but describing such a downfall in conventional language. Actually, Babylon was surrendered peaceably, without destruction.

50, 21: Merathaim, "twice bitter," and Pekod, "punishment," are here symbolic terms for Babylonia, though probably they suggest also the names of regions in that country.

leave not a remnant.
27 Slay all her oxen,
let them go down to the slaughter;
Woe to them! their day has come,
the time of their punishment.
28 Listen! the fugitives, the escaped
from the land of Babylon:
They announce in Zion
the vengeance of the LORD, our God.[i]
29 Call up against Babylon archers,
all who bend the bow;
Encamp around her,
let no one escape.
Repay her for her deeds;
as she has done, do to her,
For she insulted the LORD,
the Holy One of Isreal.[j]
30 Therefore her young men shall fall in her streets,
all her warriors shall perish on that day;
says the LORD.[k]

31 I am against you, man of insolence,
says the Lord GOD of hosts;
For your day has come,
the time for me to punish you.
32 Insolence stumbles and falls;
there is no one to raise him up.
I will kindle in his cities a fire
that shall devour everything around him.
33 Thus says the LORD of hosts:
Oppressed are the men of Israel,
and with them the men of Judah;
All their captors hold them fast
and refuse to let them go.
34 Strong is their avenger,
whose name is LORD of hosts;
He will defend their cause with success,
and give rest to the earth,
but unrest to those who live in Babylon.[l]

35 A sword upon the Chaldeans, says the LORD,
upon Babylon's people, her princes and wise men!
36 A sword upon the soothsayers,
that they may become fools!
A sword upon her warriors,
that they may tremble;
37 A sword upon her motley throng,
that they may become women!
A sword upon her treasures,
that they may be plundered;[m]
38 A sword upon her waters,
that they may dry up!
For it is a land of idols,
and they shall be made frantic by fearful things.[n]
39 Hence, wildcats and desert beasts shall dwell there,
and ostriches shall occupy it;
Never again shall it be peopled, or lived in,
from age to age.[o]
40 As when God overturned Sodom
and Gomorrah, with their neighbors, says the LORD,
Not a man shall dwell there,
no human being shall tarry there.[p]
41 See! a people comes from the north,
a great nation, and mighty kings
roused from the ends of the earth.[q]
42 Bow and javelin they wield,
cruel and pitiless are they;
They sound like the roaring sea,
as they ride forth on steeds,
Each in his place for battle
against you, daughter Babylon.
43 The king of Babylon hears news of them,
and helpless fall his hands;
Anguish seizes him,
throes like a mother's in childbirth.[r]
44 As when a lion comes up from the Jordan's thicket
to the permanent feeding grounds,
So I, in one instant, will drive them off,
and whom I choose I will establish there;
For who is like me? who calls me to account?
what shepherd can stand against me?[s]
45 Therefore hear the counsel of the LORD
which he has taken against Babylon;
Hear the plans he has made
against the land of the Chaldeans:
They shall be dragged away, even the smallest sheep;
their own pasture shall be aghast because of them.[t]
46 At the cry "Babylon is captured!" the earth quakes;
the outcry is heard among the nations.[u]

## CHAPTER 51

### The Second Prophecy against Babylon

1 Thus says the LORD:
See! I rouse against Babylon,
and against those who live in Chaldea,
a destroying wind.
2 Against Babylon I will send winnowers
to winnow her and lay waste her land;
They shall besiege her from all sides
on the day of affliction.[v]
3 Let the bowman draw his bow,
and flaunt his coat of mail;
Spare not her young men,
doom her entire army.[w]
4 The slain shall fall in the land of Chaldea,
the transfixed, in her streets;[x]
5 For Israel and Judah are not widowed
of their God, the LORD of hosts,
And the Chaldean land is full of guilt

i Jer 51, 10f.
j Jer 51, 56.
k Jer 49, 26; 51, 4.
l Jer 51, 36.
m Jer 51, 30; Na 3, 13.
n Jer 51, 32. 36.
o Jer 51, 37; Is 13, 21f.
p Jer 51, 43.
q Jer 51, 27f.
r Is 13, 7.
s Jer 49, 19.
t Jer 51, 12. 29.
u Jer 51, 29.
v Jer 15, 7; Is 41, 16.
w Jer 50, 14. 29.
x Jer 50, 30.

to be punished by the Holy One of Israel.

6 Flee out of Babylon;
let each one save his life,
perish not for her guilt;
This is a time of vengeance for the LORD,
he pays her her due.[y]
7 Babylon was a golden cup in the hand of the LORD
which made the whole earth drunk;
The nations drank its wine,
with this they have become mad.[z]
8 Babylon suddenly falls and is crushed:
howl over her!
Bring balm for her wounds,
in case she can be healed.[a]
9 "We have tried to heal Babylon,
but she cannot be healed.
Leave her, let us go, each to his own land."
Her judgment reaches heaven,
it touches the clouds.[b]
10 The LORD has brought to light our just cause;
come, let us tell in Zion
what the LORD, our God, has done.[c]

11 Sharpen the arrows,
fill the quivers;
The LORD has stirred up the spirit of Media's kings;*
Babylon he is resolved to destroy.
Yes, it is the vengeance of the LORD,
vengeance for his temple.[d]
12 Against the walls of Babylon raise a signal,
make strong the watch;
Post sentries,
arrange ambushes!
For the LORD has planned and he will carry out
his threat against the inhabitants of Babylon.
13 You who dwell by mighty waters,
rich in treasure,
Your end has come,
the term at which you shall be cut off![e]
14 The LORD of hosts has sworn by himself:
I will fill you with men as numerous as locusts,
who shall raise over you the vintage shout!
15 He has sworn who made the earth by his power,
and established the world by his wisdom,
and stretched out the heavens by his skill.[f]
16 When he thunders, the waters in the heavens roar,
and he brings up clouds from the end of the earth;
He makes the lightning flash in the rain,
and releases stormwinds from their chambers.
17 Every man is stupid, ignorant;
every artisan is put to shame by his idol:
He molded a fraud,
without breath of life.
18 Nothingness are they, a ridiculous work,
that will perish in their time of punishment.
19 Not like these is the portion of Jacob,
he is the creator of all things;
Israel is his very own tribe,
LORD of hosts is his name.

20 You are my hammer,
my weapon for war;
With you I shatter nations,
with you I destroy kingdoms.
21 With you I shatter horse and rider,
with you I shatter chariot and driver.[g]
22 With you I shatter man and wife,
with you I shatter old and young,
with you I shatter youth and maiden.[h]
23 With you I shatter the shepherd and his flock,
with you I shatter the farmer and his team,
with you I shatter satraps and prefects.
24 Thus will I repay Babylon,
and all who live in Chaldea
All the evil they did to Zion,
as you shall see with your own eyes, says the LORD.[i]
25 Beware! I am against you,
destroying mountain,
destroyer of the entire earth, says the LORD;
I will stretch forth my hand against you,
roll you down over the cliffs,
and make you a burnt mountain:[j]
26 They will not take from you a cornerstone,
or a foundation stone;
Ruins forever shall you be,
say the LORD.[k]

27 Raise a signal on the earth,
blow the trumpet among the nations;
Dedicate peoples to war against her,
summon against her the kingdoms,
Ararat, Minni, and Ashkenaz;*
Appoint recruiting officers against her,
send up horses like bristling locusts.[l]
28 Dedicate peoples to war against her:
the king of Media,
Its governors and all its prefects,

y Jer 50, 8. 15. 29; Is 48, 20.
z Rv 14, 8; 17, 4.
a Rv 18, 9-18.
b Is 13, 14; Rv 18, 5.
c Jer 50, 28.
d 2 Kgs 17, 6; Is 13, 17.
e Na 2, 1.
f Jer 10, 12.
g Dn 7, 7. 19. 23.
h Is 13, 16. 18.
i Jer 25, 14; 50, 29; Ps 137, 8.
j Rv 8, 7; 18, 8f.
k Jer 25, 12; Ps 118, 22.
l Na 3, 17.

*

51, 11: Media's kings: the Medes dwelt with the Persians in the land now known as Iran. At the time these words were written the Medes were the dominant people of the two, but within a short time the Persians had gained the ascendancy.

51, 27: Ararat, Minni, and Ashkenaz: regions or people in what is now Armenia, subject at this time to Media.

every land in his domain.
29 The earth quakes and writhes,
the LORD's plan against Babylon is carried out,
Turning the land of Babylon
into a desert where no one lives.
30 Babylon's warriors have ceased to fight,
they remain in their strongholds;
Dried up is their strength,
they have become women.
Burned are their homes,
and broken their bars.
31 One runner meets another,
herald meets herald,
Telling the king of Babylon
that all his city is taken.[m]
32 The fords have been seized,
and the fortresses set on fire,
while warriors are in panic.

33 For thus says the LORD of hosts, the God of Israel:

Daughter Babylon is like a threshing floor
at the time it is trodden;
Yet a little while,
and the harvest time will come for her.[n]
34 He has consumed me,* routed me,
[Nebuchadnezzar, king of Babylon,]
he has left me as an empty vessel;
He has swallowed me like a dragon:
filled his belly with my delights, and cast me out.
35 My torn flesh be upon Babylon,
says the city on Zion;
My blood upon the people of Chaldea,
says Jerusalem.
36 But now, thus says the LORD:
Surely I will defend your cause,
I will avenge you;
I will dry up her sea,
and drain her fountain.
37 Babylon shall become a heap of ruins,
a haunt of jackals;
A place of horror and ridicule,
where no one lives.[o]
38 They all roar like lions,
growl like lion cubs.[p]
39 When they are parched, I will set a drink before them
to make them drunk, that they may be overcome
with perpetual sleep, never to awaken,
says the LORD.

40 I will bring them down like lambs to the slaughter,
like rams and goats.
41 How has she been seized, made captive,
the glory of the whole world!
What a horror has Babylon become among nations:[q]
42 against Babylon the sea rises,
she is overwhelmed by the roaring waves!
43 Her cities have become a desert,
parched and arid land
Where no man lives,
and no one passes through.
44 I will punish Bel in Babylon,
and make him disgorge what he swallowed;
peoples shall stream to him no more.
The wall of Babylon falls!
45 Leave her, my people, let each one save himself
from the burning wrath of the LORD.

46 Be not discouraged for fear of rumors
spread in the land; this year the rumor comes,
then violence in the land, tyrant against tyrant.[r]
47 But behold, the days are coming when I will
punish the idols of Babylon; her whole land
shall be put to shame, and all her slain shall lie
fallen within her. 48 Then heaven, and earth,
and everything in them shall shout over Babylon
with joy, when the destroyers come against her
from the north, says the LORD.[s] 49 Babylon,
too, must fall, O slain of Israel, as at the hands
of Babylon have fallen the slain of all the earth.

50 You who have escaped the sword,
go on, stand not still;
Remember the LORD from afar,
let Jerusalem come to your minds.
51 We are ashamed because we have heard taunts,
confusion covers our faces; strangers have entered
the holy places of the house of the LORD.[t]
52 But behold, the days are coming, says the LORD,
when I will punish her idols,
and in her whole land the wounded will groan.
53 Though Babylon scale the heavens,
and make her strong heights inaccessible,
destroyers from me shall reach her, says the LORD.[u]
54 Hear! loud cries from Babylon,
dire destruction from the land of the Chaldeans;
55 For the LORD lays Babylon waste,
stills her loud cry,
Though her waves were roaring like mighty waters,
and their clamor was heard afar.
56 For the destroyer comes upon her,
[Babylon,]
her heroes are captured, their bows broken;
The LORD is a God who requites,
he will surely repay.[v]

m 2 Chr 30, 6; Jb 1, 14-18.
n Rv 14, 15.
o Is 25, 2.
p Na 2, 11f.
q Is 13, 19.
r Mt 24, 6f.
s Rv 18, 20.
t Pss 44, 16f; 78, 1-4.
u Is 14, 13.
v Na 1, 2.

* 51, 34: Me, my: refers to Jerusalem.

**57** I will make her princes and her wise men drunk, her governors, her prefects, and her warriors, so that they sleep an eternal sleep, never to awaken, says the King, whose name is the LORD of hosts. **58** Thus says the LORD of hosts:

The walls of spacious Babylon shall be
leveled utterly;
her lofty gates shall be destroyed by fire.
The toil of the nations is for nothing;
for the flames the peoples weary
themselves.[w]

**The Prophecy Sent to Babylon.** **59** This was the errand given by the prophet Jeremiah to Seraiah,* son of Neriah, son of Mahseiah, when he went to Babylon for the king in the fourth year of the reign of Zedekiah; Seraiah was chief quartermaster. **60** Jeremiah had written all the misfortune that was to befall Babylon in a single book:* all these words that were written against Babylon. **61** And Jeremiah said to Seraiah: When you reach Babylon, see that you read aloud all these words,[x] **62** and then say: O LORD, you yourself threatened to destroy this place, so that neither man nor beast should dwell in it, since it would remain an everlasting desert. **63** When you have finished reading this book, tie a stone to it and throw it in the Euphrates,[y] **64** and say: Thus shall Babylon sink. Never shall she rise, because of the evil I am bringing upon her. [To "weary themselves" are the words of Jeremiah.]*

## *VI: Historical Appendix**

### CHAPTER 52

**Capture of Jerusalem.** **1** Zedakiah was twenty-one years old when he became king, and he reigned eleven years in Jerusalem.[z] His mother's name was Hamutal, daughter of Jeremiah of Libnah. **2** He did what was evil in the eyes of the LORD, just as Jehoiakim had done. **3** Indeed, what was done in Jerusalem and in Judah so angered the LORD that he cast them out from his presence.

Zedekiah rebelled against the king of Babylon. **4** [a]In the tenth month of the ninth year of his reign, on the tenth day of the month,* Nebuchadnezzar, king of Babylon, and his whole army advanced against Jerusalem, encamped around it, and built siege walls on every side. **5** The siege of the city continued until the eleventh year of King Zedekiah.

**6** On the ninth day of the fourth month, when famine had gripped the city and the people had no more bread, **7** the city walls were breached. Then all the soldiers took to flight and left the city by night through the gate between the two walls which was near the king's garden. With the Chaldeans surrounding the city, they went in the direction of the Arabah. **8** But the Chaldean army pursued the king and overtook Zedekiah in the desert near Jericho, while his whole army fled from him.

**9** The king, therefore, was arrested and brought to Riblah, in the land of Hamath, to the king of Babylon, who pronounced sentence on him. **10** As Zedekiah looked on, the king of Babylon slew his sons as well as all the princes of Judah at Riblah. **11** Then he blinded Zedekiah, bound him with fetters, and had him brought to Babylon and kept in prison until the day of his death.

**Destruction of Jerusalem.** **12** On the tenth day of the fifth month (this was in the nineteenth year* of Nebuchadnezzar, king of Babylon), Nebuzaradan, captain of the bodyguard, came to Jerusalem as the representative of the king of Babylon. **13** He burned the house of the LORD, the palace of the king, and all the houses of Jerusalem; every large building he destroyed with fire. **14** And the Chaldean troops who were with the captain of the guard tore down all the walls that surrounded Jerusalem.

**15** Then Nebuzaradan, captain of the guard, led into exile the rest of the people left in the city, and those who had deserted to the king of Babylon, and the rest of the artisans. **16** But some of the country's poor, Nebuzaradan, captain of the guard, left behind as vinedressers and farmers.

**17** The bronze pillars that belonged to the house of the LORD, and the wheeled carts and the bronze sea in the house of the LORD, the Chaldeans broke into pieces; they carried away all the bronze to Babylon. **18** They took also

w Hb 2, 13.
x Jer 50, 1-51.
y Rv 18, 21.
z 1-27: 2 Kgs 24, 18—25, 21.
a 4-16: Jer 39, 1-10.

51, 59: Seraiah: the brother of Baruch; cf Jer 32, 12. The king: Zedekiah. Perhaps Seraiah went to Babylon to explain away the presence of foreign ambassadors in Jerusalem that same year; cf Jer 27, 3.

51, 60: Jeremiah prophesied against Babylon, even as he foretold Judah's release from Babylon's power (Jer 3, 14–18; 32, 15; 33, 6–9. 12f); but his book against Babylon was thrown in the Euphrates (v 63). The preceding oracles were composed by later writers; see note on Jer 50, 1—51, 58.

51, 64: To "weary themselves" are the words of Jeremiah: an editorial remark concerning the end of v 58.

52, 1–34: This supplement to the Book of Jeremiah was taken by the final editor from 2 Kgs 24, 18—25, 30 and placed here in order to show the fulfillment of Jeremiah's prophecies. In part this repeats the history given in Jer 39—41; the history of Gedaliah in 2 Kgs 25, 22–26, however, has not been reproduced here.

52, 4: In the tenth month of the ninth year of his reign, on the tenth day of the month: January 15, 588 B.C. Cf Jer 39, 1.

52, 12: On the tenth day of the fifth month . . . nineteenth year: the tenth of Ab—July/August in 587 B.C.

the pots, the shovels, the snuffers, the bowls,
the pans, and all the bronze vessels used for
service. **19** The basins also, the fire holders, the
bowls, the pots, the lampstands, the pans, the
sacrificial bowls which were of gold or silver,
these too the captain of the guard carried off,
**20** as well as the two pillars, the one sea, and
the twelve oxen of bronze under the sea, and the
wheeled carts which King Solomon had made
for the house of the LORD. The bronze of all
these furnishings could not be weighed.

**21** Each of the pillars was eighteen cubits
high and twelve cubits in diameter; each was
four fingers thick, and hollow inside. **22** A
bronze capital five cubits high surmounted the
one pillar, and a network with pomegranates
encircled the capital, all of brass; and so for the
other pillar. The pomegranates . . . **23** there
were ninety-six pomegranates. There were a
hundred pomegranates, all around the network.

**24** The captain of the guard also took Seraiah, the high priest, Zephaniah, the second
priest, and the three keepers of the entry.
**25** And from the city he took one courtier, a
commander of soldiers, and seven men in the
personal service of the king who were present
in the city, and the scribe of the army commander who mustered the people of the land, and
sixty of the common people who were in the
city. **26** The captain of the guard, Nebuzaradan, arrested these and brought them to the king
of Babylon at Riblah, **27** who had them struck
down and put to death in Riblah, in the land of
Hamath.

Thus was Judah exiled from her land.
**28** *This is the number of the people whom
Nebuchadnezzar led away captive: in his seventh year, three thousand and twenty-three people of Judah; **29** in the eighteenth year of Nebuchadnezzar, eight hundred and thirty-two
persons from Jerusalem; **30** in the twenty-third
year of Nebuchadnezzar, Nebuzaradan, captain
of the guard, exiled seven hundred and forty-
five people of Judah: four thousand six hundred
persons in all.

**Favor Shown to Jehoiachin.*** **31** [b]In the
thirty-seventh year of the exile of Jehoiachin,
king of Judah, on the twenty-fifth day of the
twelth month, Evil-merodach, king of Babylon,
in the inaugural year of his reign, took up the
case of Jehoiahcin, king of Judah, and released
him from prison. **32** He spoke kindly to him
and gave him a throne higher than that of the
other kings* who were with him in Babylon.
**33** Jehoiachin took off his prison garb and ate
at the king's table as long as he lived. **34** The
allowance given him by the king of Babylon
was a perpetual allowance, in fixed daily
amounts, all the days of his life until the day of
his death.

b 31-34: 2 Kgs 25, 27-30.

*

52, 28–30: These verses are missing in the Greek text and have not been taken from 2 Kgs 25, but from some other source using a different system of chronology. Besides the deportations of 598 and 587 B.C., mention is made here of a final one that took place in the year 582/1, possibly as a sequel to the murder of Gedaliah; cf Jer 41, 2.

52, 31–34: In the year 561/0 B.C., Jehoiachin was released from prison by Nebuchadnezzar's successor Awel-Marduk (Evil-merodach), who reigned only two years. Babylonian records confirm the fact that Jehoiachin and his family were supported at public expense.

52, 32: The other kings: who had also been brought as captives to Babylon.

# The Book of
# LAMENTATIONS

*The sixth century B.C. was an age of crisis, a turning point in the history of Israel. With the destruction of the temple and the interruption of its ritual, the exile of the leaders and loss of national sovereignty, an era came to an end. Not long after the fall of Jerusalem (587) an eyewitness of the national humiliation composed these five laments. They combine confession of sin, grief over the suffering and humiliation of Zion, submission to merited chastisement, and strong faith in the constancy of Yahweh's love and power to restore. The union of poignant grief and unquenchable hope reflects the constant prophetic vision of the weakness of man and the strength of God's love; it also shows how Israel's faith in Yahweh could survive the shattering experience of national ruin.*

*As a literary work, the Book of Lamentations is carefully constructed according to a familiar structural device. The first four poems are acrostics in which the separate stanzas begin with successive letters of the Hebrew alphabet from the first to the last. Far from destroying the spontaneous pathos of the songs, this literary feature permits a symbolic and disciplined expression of the profound grief, the sinful responsibility, and the enduring hope of the suffering community. The figure of Israel as the bride of Yahweh, familiar from the prophets, appears here again; but now Zion is a desolate widow, the* Judaea Capta *of Titus' memorial coins, sustained only by the faith that God's chastisement will eventually give place to his infinite compassion.*

## CHAPTER 1

### Jerusalem Abandoned and Disgraced*

**1** How lonely she is now,
the once crowded city!
Widowed is she
who was mistress over nations;
The princess among the provinces
has been made a toiling slave.

**2** Bitterly she weeps at night,
tears upon her cheeks,
With not one to console her
of all her dear ones;
Her friends have all betrayed her
and become her enemies.[a]

**3** Judah has fled into exile
from oppression and cruel slavery;
Yet where she lives among the nations
she finds no place to rest:
All her persecutors come upon her
where she is narrowly confined.[b]

**4** The roads to Zion mourn
for lack of pilgrims going to her feasts;
All her gateways are deserted,
her priests groan,
Her virgins sigh;
she is in bitter grief.[c]

**5** Her foes are uppermost,
her enemies are at ease;
The LORD has punished her
for her many sins.
Her little ones have gone away,
captive before the foe.

**6** Gone from daughter Zion
is all her glory:
Her princes, like rams
that find no pasture,
Have gone off without strength
before their captors.

**7** Jerusalem is mindful of the days
of her wretched homelessness,
When her people fell into enemy hands,
and she had no one to help her;
When her foes gloated over her,
laughed at her ruin.

**8** Through the sin of which she is guilty,
Jerusalem is defiled;
All who esteemed her think her vile
now that they see her nakedness;
She herself groans
and turns away.[d]

a Jer 30, 14; Ez 16, 37.
b Dt 28, 65; Jer 45, 3.
c Jer 14, 2.
d Is 47, 2; Jer 13, 22. 26.

* 1, 1–22: In this poem the poet first describes Jerusalem's miserable state after the destruction wrought by the Chaldeans (vv 1–11a); in v 11b the city itself takes up the lament.

9 Her filth is on her skirt;
she gave no thought how she would end.
Astounding is her downfall,
with no one to console her.
Look, O LORD, upon her misery,
for the enemy has triumphed!

10 The foe stretched out his hand
to all her treasures;
She has seen those nations
enter her sanctuary
Whom you forbade to come
into your assembly.[e]

11 All her people groan,
searching for bread;
They give their treasures for food,
to retain the breath of life.
"Look, O LORD, and see
how worthless I have become![f]

12 "Come, all you who pass by the way,
look and see
Whether there is any suffering like my
suffering,
which has been dealt me
When the LORD afflicted me
on the day of his blazing wrath.

13 "From on high he sent fire
down into my very frame;
He spread a net for my feet,
and overthrew me.
He left me desolate,
in pain all the day.[g]

14 "He has kept watch over my sins;
by his hand they have been plaited:
They have settled about my neck,*
he has brought my strength to its knees;
The Lord has delivered me into their grip,
I am unable to rise.

15 "All the mighty ones in my midst
the Lord has cast away;
He summoned an army against me
to crush my young men;
The LORD has trodden in the wine press
virgin daughter Judah.[h]

16 "At this I weep,
my eyes run with tears:
Far from me are all who could console me,
any who might revive me;
My sons were reduced to silence
when the enemy prevailed."[i]

17 Zion stretched out her hands,
but there was no one to console her;
The LORD gave orders against Jacob
for his neighbors to be his foes;
Jerusalem has become in their midst
a thing unclean.[j]

18 "The LORD is just;
I had defied his command.
Listen, all you peoples,
and behold my suffering:
My maidens and my youths
have gone into captivity.[k]

19 "I cried out to my lovers,*
but they failed me.
My priests and my elders
perished in the city;
Where they sought food for themselves,
they found it not.[l]

20 "Look, O LORD, upon my distress:
all within me is in ferment,
My heart recoils within me
from my monstrous rebellion.
In the streets the sword bereaves,
at home death stalks.[m]

21 "Give heed to my groaning;
there is no one to console me.
All my enemies rejoice at my misfortune:
it is you who have wrought it.
Bring on the day you have proclaimed,
that they may be even as I.

22 "Let all their evil come before you;*
deal with them
As you have dealt with me
for all my sins;
My groans are many,
and I am sick at heart."[n]

## CHAPTER 2

### The Lord's Wrath against Zion

1 How the Lord in his wrath
has detested daughter Zion!
He has cast down from heaven to earth
the glory of Israel,*
Unmindful of his footstool
on the day of his wrath.

2 The Lord has consumed without pity
all the dwellings of Jacob;
He has torn down in his anger

e Jer 51, 51.
f Jer 52, 6.
g Ez 12, 13.
h Jer 8, 16.
i Jer 13, 17; 14, 17.
j Ps 74, 7.
k Dt 28, 41.
l Jer 30, 14.
m Lam 2, 11.
n Lam 3, 64.

*

1, 14: They have been plaited . . . my neck: the sins of the people have been bound together and laid as a yoke on their back; cf Mt 23, 4.

1, 19: My lovers: Zion's foreign allies, who failed to help her, as the prophets had warned.

1, 22: Zion fully acknowledges her guilt and the justness of divine punishment; nevertheless, she pleads that her enemies also be punished for their guilt.

2, 1: The glory of Israel: the temple. His footstool: the ark of the covenant (1 Chr 28, 2; Pss 99, 5; 132, 7); or again, the temple (Ez 43, 7).

the fortresses of daughter Judah;
He has brought to the ground in dishonor
her king and her princes.

3 He broke off, in fiery wrath,
the horn* that was Israel's whole strength;
He withheld the support of his right hand
when the enemy approached;
He blazed up in Jacob like a flaming fire
devouring all about it.[o]

4 Like an enemy he made taut his bow;
with his arrows in his right hand
He took his stand as a foe, and slew
all on whom the eye doted;
Over the tent of daughter Zion
he poured out his wrath like fire.[p]

5 The Lord has become an enemy,
he has consumed Israel:
Consumed all her castles
and destroyed her fortresses;
For daughter Judah he has multiplied
moaning and groaning.

6 He has demolished his shelter like a garden
booth,
he has destroyed his dwelling;
In Zion the LORD has made
feast and sabbath to be forgotten;
He has scorned in fierce wrath
both king and priest.[q]

7 The Lord has disowned his altar,
rejected his sanctuary;
The walls of her towers
he has handed over to the enemy,
Who shout in the house of the LORD
as on a feast day.[r]

8 The LORD marked for destruction
the wall of daughter Zion:
He stretched out the measuring line;*
his hand brought ruin, yet he did not
relent—
He brought grief on wall and rampart
till both succumbed.[s]

9 Sunk into the ground are her gates;
he has removed and broken her bars.
Her king and her princes are among the
pagans;
priestly instruction is wanting,
And her prophets have not received
any vision from the LORD.[t]

10 On the ground in silence sit
the old men of daughter Zion;
They strew dust* on their heads
and gird themselves with sackcloth;
The maidens of Jerusalem
bow their heads to the ground.[u]

11 Worn out from weeping are my eyes,
within me all is in ferment;
My gall is poured out on the ground*
because of the downfall of the daughter of
my people,
As child and infant faint away
in the open spaces of the town.[v]

12 They ask their mothers,
"Where is the cereal?"—in vain,
As they faint away like the wounded
in the streets of the city,
And breathe their last
in their mothers' arms.[w]

13 To what can I liken or compare you,
O daughter Jerusalem?
What example can I show you for your
comfort,
virgin daughter Zion?
For great as the sea is your downfall;
who can heal you?[x]

14 Your prophets had for you
false and specious visions;
They did not lay bare your guilt,
to avert your fate;
They beheld for you in vision
false and misleading portents.[y]

15 All who pass by
clap their hands at you;
They hiss and wag their heads
over daughter Jerusalem:
"Is this the all-beautiful city,
the joy of the whole earth?"[z]

16 All your enemies
open their mouths against you;
They hiss and gnash their teeth.
They say, "we have devoured her.
This at last is the day we hoped for;
we have lived to see it!"[a]

17 The LORD has done as he decreed:
he has fulfilled the threat
He set forth from days of old;
he has destroyed and had no pity,
Letting the enemy gloat over you
and exalting the horn of your foes.[b]

o Lam 1, 12.
p Jer 30, 14.
q Lam 1, 4; Is 1, 13; 5, 5.
r Ez 24, 21.
s Jer 52, 13.
t Dt 28, 36.
u Is 3, 26.
v Lam 3, 48.
w Lam 1, 11.
x Lam 1, 12.
y Is 58, 1; Jer 2, 8; 23, 16.
z Jer 18, 16.
a Lam 3, 46.
b Dt 28, 15.

2, 3: Horn: symbol of power and strength; cf Lam 2, 17; 1 Sm 2, 10; Lk 1, 69; etc.

2, 8: The measuring line: used not only in building, but in deciding what must be destroyed; cf Is 34, 11; 2 Kgs 21, 13.

2, 10: They strew dust: as a sign of penance; cf Jb 2, 12.

2, 11: My gall is poured out on the ground: I am afflicted with bitter sorrow; cf Jb 16, 13.

18 Cry out to the Lord;
moan, O daughter Zion!
Let your tears flow like a torrent
day and night;
Let there be no respite for you,
no repose for your eyes.

19 Rise up, shrill in the night,
at the beginning of every watch;
Pour out your heart like water
in the presence of the Lord;
Lift up your hands to him
for the lives of your little ones
[Who faint from hunger
at the corner of every street].

20 "Look, O LORD, and consider:
whom have you ever treated thus?
Must women eat their offspring,*
their well-formed children?
Are priest and prophet to be slain
in the sanctuary of the LORD?[c]

21 "Dead in the dust of the streets
lie young and old;
My maidens and young men
have fallen by the sword;
You have slain on the day of your wrath,
slaughtered without pity.[d]

22 "You summoned as for a feast day
terrors against me from all sides;
There was not, on the day of your wrath,
either fugitive or survivor;
Those whom I bore and reared
my enemy has utterly destroyed."[e]

## CHAPTER 3

### Sufferings of the Prophet and His People

1 I am a man who knows affliction*
from the rod of his anger,[f]
2 One whom he has led and forced to walk
in darkness, not in the light;
3 Against me alone he brings back his hand
again and again all the day.
4 He has worn away my flesh and my skin,
he has broken my bones;[g]
5 He has beset me round about
with poverty and weariness;
6 He has left me to dwell in the dark
like those long dead.[h]

7 He has hemmed me in with no escape
and weighed me down with chains;
8 Even when I cry out for help,
he stops my prayer;[i]
9 He has blocked my ways with fitted stones,
and turned my paths aside.

10 A lurking bear he has been to me,
a lion in ambush![j]
11 He deranged my ways, set me astray,
left me desolate.[k]
12 He bent his bow, and set me up
as the target for his arrow.[l]

13 He pierces my sides
with shafts from his quiver.[m]
14 I have become a laughingstock for all
nations,
their taunt all the day long;[n]
15 He has sated me with bitter food,
made me drink my fill of wormwood.[o]

16 He has broken my teeth with gravel,
pressed my face in the dust;
17 My soul is deprived of peace,
I have forgotten what happiness is;
18 I tell myself my future is lost,
all that I hoped for from the LORD.

19 The thought of my homeless poverty
is wormwood and gall;
20 Remembering it over and over
leaves my soul downcast within me.
21 But I will call this to mind,
as my reason to have hope:

22 The favors of the LORD are not exhausted,
his mercies are not spent;[p]
23 They are renewed each morning,
so great is his faithfulness.
24 My portion is the LORD, says my soul;
therefore will I hope in him.[q]

25 Good is the LORD to one who waits for him,
to the soul that seeks him;[r]
26 It is good to hope in silence
for the saving help of the LORD.
27 It is good for a man to bear
the yoke* from his youth.

28 Let him sit alone and in silence,
when it is laid upon him.
29 Let him put his mouth to the dust;*
there may yet be hope.[s]
30 Let him offer his cheek to be struck,
let him be filled with disgrace.[t]

31 For the Lord's rejection

c Lam 4, 10.
d Lam 3, 43; 2 Chr 36, 17; Jer 6, 11.
e Jer 42, 17.
f Jer 20, 18.
g Jb 30, 30; Is 38, 13.
h Ps 143, 3.
i Ps 22, 2.
j Jb 10, 16; Hos 13, 8.
k Lam 1, 13.
l Lam 2, 4; Jb 16, 12.
m Jb 6, 4; Ps 38, 3.
n Jb 30, 9; Ps 69, 13.
o Jer 9, 14; 23, 15.
p Neh 9, 31.
q Pss 16, 5; 73, 26.
r Ps 130, 6; Is 30, 18.
s Jb 42, 6.
t Is 50, 6; Mt 5, 39.
u Ps 103, 9.

*

2, 20: Must women eat their offspring: extreme famine in a besieged city sometimes led to this form of cannibalism; cf Lam 4, 10; 2 Kgs 6, 28f; Bar 2, 3; Ez 5, 10.

3, 1–21: The author identifies Zion's sufferings with his own.

3, 27: To bear the yoke: to do God's will; cf Jer 2, 20.

3, 29: Let him put his mouth to the dust: in humble submission; cf Ps 72, 9.

does not last forever;[u]
32 Though he punishes, he takes pity,
in the abundance of his mercies;[v]
33 He has no joy in afflicting
or grieving the sons of men.[w]

34 When anyone tramples underfoot
all the prisoners in the land,
35 When he distorts men's rights
in the very sight of the Most High,
36 When he presses a crooked claim,
the Lord does not look on unconcerned.

37 Who commands, so that it comes to pass,
except the Lord ordains it;
38 Except it proceeds from the mouth of the
Most High,
whether the thing be good or bad![x]
39 Why should any living man complain,
any mortal, in the face of his sins?[y]

40 Let us search and examine our ways
that we may return to the LORD![z]
41 Let us reach out our hearts
toward God in heaven!
42 We have sinned and rebelled;
you have not forgiven us.

43 You veiled yourself in wrath and pursued
us,
you slew us and took no pity;[a]
44 You wrapped yourself in a cloud
which prayer could not pierce.
45 You have made us offscourings and refuse
among the nations.[b]

46 All our enemies
have opened their mouths against us;
47 Terror and the pit have been our lot,
desolation and destruction;[c]
48 My eyes run with streams of water
over the downfall of the daughter of my
people.[d]

49 My eyes flow without ceasing,
there is no respite,
50 Till the LORD from heaven
looks down and sees.
51 My eyes torment my soul
at the sight of all the daughters of my
city.

52 Those who were my enemies without cause
hunted me down like a bird;
53 They struck me down alive in the pit,
and sealed me in with a stone.[e]
54 The waters flowed over my head,
and I said, "I am lost!"

55 I called upon your name, O LORD,[f]
from the bottom of the pit;
56 You heard me call, "Let not your ear
be deaf to my cry for help!"
57 You came to my aid when I called to you;
you said, "Have no fear!"

58 You defended me in mortal danger,
you redeemed my life.
59 You see, O LORD, how I am wronged;
do me justice![g]
60 You see all their vindictiveness,
all their plots against me.

61 You hear their insults, O LORD,
[all their plots against me],
62 The whispered murmurings of my foes,
against me all the day;
63 Whether they sit or stand,
see, I am their taunt song.

64 Requite them as they deserve, O LORD,
according to their deeds;
65 Give them hardness of heart,
as your curse upon them;[h]
66 Pursue them in wrath and destroy them
from under your heavens!

## CHAPTER 4

### Miseries of the Besieged City

1 How tarnished is the gold,
how changed the noble metal;
How the sacred stones lie strewn
at every street corner!

2 Zion's precious sons,
fine gold their counterpart,
Now worth no more than earthen jars
made by the hands of a potter![i]

3 Even the jackals bare their breasts
and suckle their young;
The daughter of my people has become as
cruel
as the ostrich* in the desert.[j]

4 The tongue of the suckling cleaves
to the roof of its mouth in thirst;
The babes cry for food,
but there is no one to give it to them.

5 Those accustomed to dainty food
perish in the streets;
Those brought up in purple
now cling to the ash heaps.[k]

v Is 54, 8f.
w Heb 12, 10f.
x Is 45, 7.
y Prv 19, 3.
z Jl 2, 12f.
a Lam 2, 21.
b 1 Cor 4, 13.
c Is 24, 17; Jer 48, 43.
d Ps 119, 136.
e Jer 37, 16; 38, 6-9.
f 55f: Ps 130, 1f.
g Ps 35, 23.
h Jer 11, 20; 2 Tm 4, 14.
i Jer 19, 11.
j Jb 39, 16.
k Dt 28, 56.

*

4, 3: Cruel as the ostrich: see note on Jb 39, 14ff. Jerusalem, in her distress, had abandoned her children.

6 The punishment of the daughter of my
people
is greater than the penalty of Sodom,
Which was overthrown in an instant
without the turning of a hand.[l]

7 Brighter than snow were her princes,
whiter than milk,
More ruddy than coral,
more precious than sapphire.

8 Now their appearance is blacker than soot,
they are unrecognized on the streets;
Their skin shrinks on their bones,
as dry as wood.[m]

9 Better for those who perish by the sword
than for those who die of hunger,
Who waste away, as though pierced
through,
lacking the fruits of the field!

10 The hands of compassionate women
boiled their own children,
To serve them as mourners' food
in the downfall of the daughter of my
people.[n]

11 The LORD has spent his anger,
poured out his blazing wrath;
He has kindled a fire in Zion
that has consumed her foundations.[o]

12 The kings of the earth did not believe,
nor any of the world's inhabitants,
That enemy or foe could enter
the gates of Jerusalem.

13 Because of the sins of her prophets*
and the crimes of her priests,
Who shed in her midst
the blood of the just!—[p]

14 They staggered blindly in the streets,
soiled with blood,
So that people could not touch
even their garments:[q]

15 "Away, you unclean!" they cried to them,
"Away, away, do not draw near!"
If they left and wandered among the nations,
nowhere could they remain.

16 The LORD himself has dispersed them,
he regards them no more;
He does not receive the priests with favor,
nor show kindness to the elders.

17 Our eyes ever wasted away,
looking in vain for aid;
From our watchtower we watched
for a nation* that could not save us.

18 Men dogged our steps
so that we could not walk in our streets;
Our end drew near, and came;
our time had expired.

19 Our pursuers were swifter
than eagles in the air,
They harassed us on the mountains
and waylaid us in the desert.[r]

20 The anointed one of the LORD, our breath of
life,*
was caught in their snares,
He in whose shadow we thought
we could live on among the nations.[s]

21 Though you rejoice and are glad, O daughter
Edom,
you who dwell in the land of Uz,*
To you also shall the cup be passed;
you shall become drunk and naked.[t]

22 Your chastisement is completed, O daughter
Zion,
he will not prolong your exile;
But your wickedness, O daughter Edom, he
will punish,
he will lay bare your sins.[u]

## CHAPTER 5

### The Prophet's Lament and Supplication

1 Remember, O LORD, what has befallen us,
look, and see our disgrace:
2 Our inherited lands have been turned over to
strangers,
our homes to foreigners.[v]
3 We have become orphans, fatherless;
widowed are our mothers.
4 The water we drink we must buy,
for our own wood we must pay.
5 On our necks is the yoke of those who drive
us;
we are worn out, but allowed no rest.

l Gn 19, 23-29; 2 Pt 2, 6; Jude 1, 7.
m Lam 3, 4.
n Lam 2, 20; Dt 28, 56f; 2 Kgs 6, 29.
o Jer 7, 20; Ez 5, 13.
p Jer 6, 13.
q Is 59, 10.
r Jer 4, 13; Hb 1, 8.
s Lam 2, 9; Ez 19, 4. 8.
t Lam 1, 21; Jer 25, 15.
u Is 40, 2.
v Ps 79, 1.

*

4, 13ff: The priests and the false prophets lulled the people into an illusory security (Jer 2, 8; 5, 31; 6, 13; etc.), condoning and entering into their crimes so that they themselves became unclean.

4, 17: A nation: Egypt, which failed to give effective aid against Babylon.

4, 20: Our breath of life: the king. This is a royal epithet borrowed from Egyptian usage, while the anointed one of the Lord is Israelite. After the disaster of 598 B.C. (2 Kgs 24, 1–17), Jerusalem could have hoped to live in peace amidst her neighbors; but they (vv 21f) as well as Babylon turned against her to ensure her total devastation in 587 B.C.

4, 21: Uz: see note on Jer 25, 20.

**6** To Egypt we submitted,
and to Assyria, to fill our need of bread.*
**7** Our fathers,* who sinned, are no more;
but we bear their guilt.
**8** Slaves rule over us;
there is no one to rescue us from their hands.*
**9** At the peril of our lives we bring in our sustenance,
in the face of the desert heat;[w]
**10** Our skin is shriveled up, as though by a furnace,
with the searing blasts of famine.[x]

**11** The wives in Zion were ravished by the enemy,
the maidens in the cities of Judah;[y]
**12** Princes were gibbeted by them,
elders shown no respect.[z]
**13** The youths carry the millstones,
boys stagger under their loads of wood;
**14** The old men have abandoned the gate,*
the young men their music.

**15** The joy of our hearts has ceased,
our dance has turned into mourning;[a]
**16** The garlands have fallen from our heads:
woe to us, for we have sinned!
**17** Over this our hearts are sick,
at this our eyes grow dim:
**18** That Mount Zion should be desolate,
with jackals roaming there!

**19** You, O LORD, are enthroned forever;
your throne stands from age to age.[b]
**20** Why, then, should you forget us,
abandon us so long a time?[c]
**21** Lead us back to you, O LORD, that we may be restored:
give us anew such days as we had of old.[d]
**22** For now you have indeed rejected us,
and in full measure turned your wrath against us.[e]

---

w Jer 6, 25.
x Lam 4, 8.
y Zec 14, 2.
z Lam 4, 16.
a Jer 16, 9; 25, 10; Am 8, 10.
b Pss 9, 8; 45, 7; 102, 13. 27.
c Pss 13, 1; 42, 10.
d Ps 80, 19f.
e Jer 14, 19.

---

*

5, 6: In its state of abjection, Judah was forced to depend on its traditional enemies to the west and the east for subsistence. Mesopotamia is here called by the name it had long borne, Assyria, though in these times the power of the Assyrians had been superseded by that of the Chaldeans.

5, 7: Our fathers: collective responsibility, for good and for evil, was recognized in the Old Testament; cf Jer 31, 29. But the present generation is also personally guilty of sin (v 16).

5, 8: Administrations imposed by foreign powers were notoriously corrupt and inept. The Hebrew word for "slave" is the same as that used for an official (servant of the ruler); the author doubtless intends the double meaning here.

5, 14: The gate: the place of assembly, where city decisions were made and judgment given by the elders and other notables; see note on Ru 4, 1.

# The Book of

# BARUCH

*The opening verses of this book ascribe it, or at least its first part, to Baruch, the well-known secretary of the prophet Jeremiah. It contains five very different compositions, the first and the last in prose, the others in poetic form. The prose sections were certainly composed in Hebrew, though the earliest known form of the book is in Greek.*

*An observance of the feast of Booths with a public prayer of penitence and petition (1, 15—3, 8), such as is supposed by the introduction (1, 1–14), would not have been possible during the lifetime of Baruch after the fall of Jerusalem; this indeed is suggested in the prayer itself (2, 26). The prayer is therefore to be understood as the pious reflection of a later Jewish writer upon the circumstances of the exiles in Babylon as he knew them from the Book of Jeremiah. He expresses in their name sentiments called for by the prophet, and ascribes the wording of these sentiments to the person most intimately acquainted with Jeremiah's teaching, namely, Baruch. The purpose of this literary device is to portray for his own and later generations the spirit of repentance which prompted God to bring the Exile to an end.*

*The lesson thus gained is followed by a hymn in praise of Wisdom (3, 9—4, 4), exalting the law of Moses as the unique gift of God to Israel, the observance of which is the way to life and peace. The ideal city of Jerusalem is then represented (4, 5–29) as the solicitous mother of all exiles, who is assured in the name of God that all her children will be restored to her (4, 30—5, 9).*

*The final chapter is really a separate work, with a title of its own (6, 1). It is patterned after the earlier letter of Jeremiah (Jer 29), in the spirit of the warnings against idolatry contained in Jer 10 and Is 44. Its earnestness is impressive, but in restating previous inspired teachings at a later day, it does so with no special literary grace.*

*Thus the principal divisions of the book are seen to be: I. Prayer of the Exiles (1, 1—3, 8). II. Praise of Wisdom in the Law of Moses (3, 9—4, 4). III. Jerusalem Bewails and Consoles Her Captive Children (4, 5–29). IV. Jerusalem Consoled: The Captivity about To End (4, 30—5, 9). V. The Letter of Jeremiah against Idolatry (6, 1–72).*

## I: Prayer of the Exiles

### CHAPTER 1

**Meeting in Babylon.** 1 Now these are the
words of the scroll which Baruch, son of Neriah, son of Mahseiah, son of Zedekiah, son of
Hasadiah, son of Hilkiah, wrote in Babylon,[a]
2 in the fifth year [on the seventh day of the
month,* at the time when the Chaldeans took
Jerusalem and burnt it with fire].[b] 3 [c]And Baruch read the words of this scroll for Jeconiah,
son of Jehoiakim, king of Judah, to hear it, as
well as all the people who came to the reading:[d]
4 the nobles, the kings' sons, the elders, and
the whole people, small and great alike—all
who lived in Babylon by the river Sud.*
5 They wept and fasted and prayed before the
LORD, 6 and collected such funds as each could
furnish.[e] 7 These they sent to Jerusalem, to
Jehoiakim, son of Hilkiah, son of Shallum, the
priest, and to the priests and the whole people
who were with him in Jerusalem. 8 [This was

a Jer 32, 12; 36, 4; 45, 1-5.
b 2 Kgs 25, 8ff.
c 2 Kgs 24, 8-17; Jer 22, 24-30; 51, 59-64.
d 3-4; 2 Kgs 23, 1-2.
e Dt 16, 17.

*

1, 2: In the fifth year on the seventh day of the month: Jerusalem fell on the seventh day of the fifth month; cf 2 Kgs 25, 8; Jer 52, 12. Either the text read originally "the fifth month," or it refers to the observance of an anniversary of the fall of Jerusalem in 587 B.C.

1, 4: The river Sud: one of the Babylonian canals, not otherwise identified. In ancient non-Biblical Hebrew fragments discovered in 1952, there is reference to a river "Sur" in a similar context.

1, 8f: He: possibly Baruch; less likely Jehoiakim . . . the priest (v 7), a member of the high-priestly family not mentioned elsewhere. The silver vessels here described are distinct from the vessels referred to in 2 Kgs 25, 14 and Ezr 1, 7ff. The author of this note may have thought of the fifth year (v 1) of Zedekiah, in view of Jer 28, 1; 29, 1ff. A "fifth year," again with

when he* received the vessels of the house of
the LORD that had been removed from the temple, to restore them to the land of Judah, on the
tenth of Sivan. These silver vessels Zedekiah,
son of Josiah, king of Judah, had had made
**9** after Nebuchadnezzar, king of Babylon, carried off Jeconiah, and the princes, and the
skilled workers, and the nobles, and the people
of the land from Jerusalem, as captives, and
brought them to Babylon.]

**10** Their message was: "We send you funds,
with which you are to procure holocausts, sin
offerings, and frankincense, and to prepare cereal offerings; offer these on the altar of the
LORD our God,[f] **11** and pray for the life of
Nebuchadnezzar, king of Babylon, and that of
Belshazzar, his son,* that their lifetimes may
equal the duration of the heavens above the
earth;[g] **12** and that the LORD may give us
strength, and light to our eyes, that we may live
under the protective shadow of Nebuchadnezzar, king of Babylon, and that of Belshazzar, his
son, and serve them long, finding favor in their
sight.

**Confession of Guilt.** **13** "Pray for us also
to the LORD, our God; for we have sinned
against the LORD, our God, and the wrath and
anger of the LORD have not yet been withdrawn
from us at the present day. **14** And read out
publicly this scroll which we send you, in the
house of the LORD, on the feast day and during
the days of assembly:[h]

**15** "Justice is with the LORD, our God; and
we today are flushed with shame, we men of
Judah and citizens of Jerusalem,[i] **16** that we,
with our kings and rulers and priests and prophets, and with our fathers, **17** have sinned in the
LORD's sight **18** and disobeyed him. We have
neither heeded the voice of the LORD, our God,
nor followed the precepts which the LORD set
before us. **19** From the time the LORD led our
fathers out of the land of Egypt until the present
day, we have been disobedient to the LORD, our
God, and only too ready to disregard his voice.
**20** And the evils and the curse which the LORD
enjoined upon Moses, his servant, at the time he
led our fathers forth from the land of Egypt to
give us the land flowing with milk and honey,
cling to us even today.[j] **21** For we did not heed
the voice of the LORD, our God, in all the words
of the prophets whom he sent us, **22** but each
one of us went off after the devices of our own
wicked hearts, served other gods, and did evil
in the sight of the LORD, our God.

## CHAPTER 2

**1** "And the LORD fulfilled the warning he
had uttered against us: against our judges, who
governed Israel, against our kings and princes,
and against the men of Israel and Judah. **2** He
brought down upon us evils so great that there
has not been done anywhere under heaven what
has been done in Jerusalem, as was written in
the law of Moses:[k] **3** that one after another of
us should eat* the flesh of his son or of his
daughter. **4** He has made us subject to all the
kingdoms round about us, a reproach and a
horror among all the nations round about to
which the LORD has scattered us.[l] **5** We are
brought low, not raised up, because we sinned
against the LORD, our God, not heeding his
voice.

**6** "Justice is with the LORD, our God; and
we, like our fathers, are flushed with shame
even today.[m] **7** All the evils of which the LORD
had warned us have come upon us; **8** and we did
not plead before the LORD, or turn, each from
the figments of his evil heart. **9** And the LORD
kept watch over the evils, and brought them
home to us; for the LORD is just in all the works
he commanded us to do,[n] **10** but we did not
heed his voice, or follow the precepts of the
LORD which he set before us.

**Prayer for Deliverance.** **11** "And now,
LORD, God of Israel, you who led your people
out of the land of Egypt with your mighty hand,
with signs and wonders and great might, and
with your upraised arm, so that you have made
for yourself a name till the present day:[o] **12** we
have sinned, been impious, and violated, O
LORD, our God, all your statutes.[p] **13** Let your
anger be withdrawn from us, for we are left few
in number among the nations to which you scattered us. **14** Hear, O LORD, our prayer of supplication, and deliver us for your own sake:
grant us favor in the presence of our captors,
**15** that the whole earth may know that you are
the LORD, our God, and that Israel and his descendants bear your name.[q] **16** O LORD, look
down from your holy dwelling and take thought
of us; turn, O LORD, your ear to hear us.[r]
**17** Look directly at us, and behold: it is not the
dead in the nether world, whose spirits have

f Jer 17, 26.
g Dt 11, 21; Jer 29, 7; Dn 5, 1-2; 1 Tm 2, 1f.
h Ex 23, 14ff; Lv 23, 35f; Hos 9, 5; Sir 50, 6.
i Bar 2, 6; 3, 8; Neh 9, 6-37; Ezr 9, 6-15; Dn 9, 4-19.
j Lv 26, 14-39; Dt 28, 15-68.
k 2f: 2 Kgs 6, 28f; Jer 19, 9; Lam 2, 20; 4, 10; Ez 5, 10.
l Jer 29, 18.
m Bar 1, 15.
n Jer 1, 12; 31, 28; 44, 27.
o Dt 6, 21-22.
p Ps 106, 6.
q Sir 36, 11; Jer 14, 9.
r Dt 26, 15.
s Ps 6, 6; Is 38, 18.

*

no month mentioned, is given in Ez 1, 2 for the inaugural vision of Ezekiel's prophetic career.

1, 11: Nebuchadnezzar . . . Belshazzar, his son: as in Dn 5, 1f. Later Jewish tradition seems to have simplified the history of the past by making the last Chaldean ruler of Babylon the son of the conqueror of Jerusalem.

2, 3: One after another of us should eat: see note on Lam 2, 20.

been taken from within them, who will give
glory and vindication to the LORD.[s] 18 He
whose soul is deeply grieved, who walks bowed
and feeble, with failing eyes and famished soul,
will declare your glory and justice, LORD![t]
19 "Not on the just deeds of our fathers and
our kings do we base our plea for mercy in your
sight, O LORD, our God. 20 You have brought
your wrath and anger down upon us, as you had
warned us through your servants the prophets:
21 'Thus says the LORD: Bend your shoulders
to the service of the king of Babylon, that you
may continue in the land I gave your fathers:[u]
22 for if you do not hear the LORD's voice so
as to serve the king of Babylon,

23 I will make to cease from the cities of Judah
and from the streets of Jerusalem
The sounds of joy and the sounds of
gladness,
the voice of the bridegroom
and the voice of the bride;
And all the land shall be deserted,
without inhabitants.'[v]

24 But we did not heed your voice, or serve the
king of Babylon, and you fulfilled the threats
you had made through your servants the prophets, to have the bones of our kings and the bones
of our fathers brought out from their burial
places.[w] 25 And indeed, they lie exposed* to
the heat of day and the frost of night. They died
in dire anguish, by hunger and the sword and
plague.[x] 26 And you reduced the house which
bears your name* to what it is today, for the
wickedness of the kingdom of Israel and the
kingdom of Judah.[y]

**God's Promises Recalled.** 27 "But with
us, O LORD, our God, you have dealt in all your
clemency and in all your great mercy. 28 This
was your warning through your servant Moses,
the day you ordered him to write down your law
in the presence of the Israelites: 29 If you do not
heed my voice, surely this great and numerous
throng will dwindle away among the nations to
which I will scatter them. 30 For I know they
will not heed me, because they are a stiff-
necked people. But in the land of their captivity
they shall have a change of heart;[z] 31 they shall
know that I, the LORD, am their God. I will give
them hearts, and heedful ears;[a] 32 and they
shall praise me in the land of their captivity, and
shall invoke my name.[b] 33 Then they shall turn
back from their stiff-necked stubbornness, and
from their evil deeds, because they shall remember the fate of their fathers who sinned
against the LORD.[c] 34 And I will bring them
back to the land which with my oath I promised
to their fathers, to Abraham, Isaac and Jacob;
and they shall rule it. I will make them increase;
they shall not then diminish. 35 And I will establish for them, as an eternal covenant, that I
will be their God, and they shall be my people;
and I will not again remove my people Israel
from the land I gave them.[d]

## CHAPTER 3

1 "LORD Almighty, God of Israel, afflicted
souls and dismayed spirits call to you. 2 Hear,
O LORD, for you are a God of mercy; and have
mercy on us, who have sinned against you:
3 for you are enthroned forever, while we are
perishing forever.[e] 4 LORD Almighty, God of
Israel, hear the prayer of Israel's few, the sons
of those who sinned against you; they did not
heed the voice of the LORD, their God, and the
evils cling to us. 5 Remember at this time not
the misdeeds of our fathers, but your own hand
and name: 6 for you are the LORD our God; and
you, O LORD, we praise! 7 For this, you put
into our hearts the fear of you: that we may call
upon your name, and praise you in our captivity, when we have removed from our hearts all
the wickedness of our fathers who sinned
against you.[f] 8 Behold us today in our captivity, where you scattered us, a reproach, a curse,
and a requital for all the misdeeds of our fathers,
who withdrew from the LORD, our God."

## *II: Praise of Wisdom in the Law of Moses*

9 Hear, O Israel, the commandments of life:
listen, and know prudence![g]
10 How is it, Israel,
that you are in the land of your foes,
grown old in a foreign land,
Defiled with the dead,
11 accounted with those destined for the
nether world?[h]
12 You have forsaken the fountain of wisdom![i]
13 Had you walked in the way of God,
you would have dwelt in enduring peace.[j]
14 Learn where prudence is,
where strength, where understanding;
That you may know also
where are length of days, and life,
where light of the eyes, and peace.[k]
15 Who has found the place of wisdom,[l]

t Zep 2, 3.
u Jer 27, 12.
v Jer 7, 34.
w Jer 8, 1f.
x Jer 7, 34; 14, 12; 31, 30.
y Jer 7, 10-15.
z Dt 30, 1f; 31, 27.
a Jer 24, 7; Ez 36, 26; Ps 40, 7.
b Tb 13, 7.
c 33ff: Dt 30, 1-10.
d Jer 31, 31; Lam 4, 22.
e Pss 29, 10; 102, 12f.
f Jer 31, 33.
g Prv 4, 20ff.
h Ps 88, 5.
i Jer 2, 13; Jn 4, 10. 14.
j Is 48, 18.
k Prv 3, 2; 8, 14.
l 15ff: Jb 28, 1-28.

*

2, 25: They lie exposed: probably an allusion to Jer 36, 30; see note on Jer 22, 19.

2, 26: The house which bears your name: the temple of Jerusalem. What it is today: during the exile it lay in ruins.

who has entered into her treasuries?
16 Where are the rulers of the nations,
they who lorded it over the wild beasts of the earth,[m]
17 and made sport of the birds of the heavens:
They who heaped up the silver
and the gold in which men trust;
of whose possessions there was no end?
18 They schemed anxiously for money,
but there is no trace of their work:
19 They have vanished down into the nether world,
and others have risen up in their stead.

20 Later generations have seen the light,
have dwelt in the land,
But the way to understanding they have not known,
21 they have not perceived her paths, or reached her;
their offspring were far from the way to her.
22 She has not been heard of in Canaan,*
nor seen in Teman.[n]
23 The sons of Hagar who seek knowledge on earth,
the merchants of Midian and Teman,
the phrasemakers seeking knowledge,
These have not known the way to wisdom,
nor have they her paths in mind.

24 O Israel, how vast is the house of God,*
how broad the scope of his dominion:
25 Vast and endless,
high and immeasurable!
26 In it were born the giants,
renowned at the first,
stalwarts, skilled in war.[o]
27 Not these did God choose,
nor did he give them the way of understanding;[p]
28 They perished for lack of prudence,
perished through their folly.[q]
29 Who has gone up to the heavens and taken her,
or brought her down from the clouds?[r]
30 Who has crossed the sea and found her,
bearing her away rather than choice gold?
31 None knows the way to her,
nor has any understood her paths.

32 Yet he who knows all things knows her;
he has probed her by his knowledge—
He who established the earth for all time,
and filled it with four-footed beasts;
33 He who dismisses the light, and it departs,
calls it, and it obeys him trembling;
34 Before whom the stars at their posts
shine and rejoice;
35 When he calls them, they answer, "Here we are!"
shining with joy for their Maker.[s]
36 Such is our God;
no other is to be compared to him:
37 He has traced out all the way of understanding,
and has given her to Jacob, his servant,
to Israel, his beloved son.[t]

38 Since then she has appeared on earth,
and moved among men.[u]

## CHAPTER 4

1 She is the book of the precepts of God,
the law that endures forever;
All who cling to her will live,
but those will die who forsake her.[v]
2 Turn, O Jacob, and receive her:
walk by her light toward splendor.[w]
3 Give not your glory to another,
your privileges to an alien race.
4 Blessed are we, O Israel;
for what pleases God is known to us![x]

### *III: Jerusalem Bewails and Consoles Her Captive Children*

5 Fear not, my people!
Remember, Israel,
6 You were sold to the nations
not for your destruction;
It was because you angered God
that you were handed over to your foes.[y]
7 For you provoked your Maker[z]
with sacrifices to demons, to no-gods;
8 You forsook the Eternal God who nourished you,
and you grieved Jerusalem who fostered you.
9 She indeed saw coming upon you
the anger of God; and she said:

"Hear, you neighbors of Zion!
God has brought great mourning upon me,
10 For I have seen the captivity
that the Eternal God has brought
upon my sons and daughters.
11 With joy I fostered them;
but with mourning and lament I let them go.
12 Let no one gloat over me, a widow,
bereft of many:

m Jer 27, 6.
n Jer 49, 7; Ez 28, 4-5; Zec 9, 2; Jb 2, 11.
o Gn 6, 4; Wis 14, 6.
p 1 Sm 16, 7-10.
q Sir 10, 8.
r Dt 30, 12f; Sir 24, 4; Rom 10, 6f.
s Jb 38, 7; Ps 147, 4; Is 40, 26.
t Ps 147, 19; Sir 24, 8-12.
u Wis 9, 18; Jn 1, 14.
v Dt 4, 6-8; Prv 8, 35f; Sir 24, 22.
w Prv 4, 13. 19.
x Dt 4, 32-37; 33, 29.
y Jgs 2, 14; Is 50, 1; 52, 3.
z 7-8: Dt 32, 13-18; 1 Cor 10, 20.
a Lam 1, 1. 2. 7.

*

3, 22f: Despite the renown for wisdom of the peoples of Canaan or Phoenicia (Ez 28, 3f), of Teman (Jer 49, 7), of the sons of Hagar or the Arabians, they did not possess true wisdom, which is found only in the law of God.

3, 24: The house of God: here, the created universe.

For the sins of my children I am left
desolate,
because they turned from the law of
God,[a]
13 and did not acknowledge his statutes;
In the ways of God's commandments they
did not walk,
nor did they tread the disciplined paths of
his justice.

14 "Let Zion's neighbors come,
to take note of the captivity of my sons
and daughters,
brought upon them by the Eternal God.
15 He has brought against them a nation from
afar,
a nation ruthless and of alien speech,
That has neither reverence for age
nor tenderness for childhood:[b]
16 They have led away this widow's cherished
sons,
have left me solitary, without daughters.
17 What can I do to help you?
18 He who has brought this evil upon you
must himself deliver you from your
enemies' hands.[c]
19 Farewell, my children, farewell:
I am left desolate.
20 I have taken off the garment of peace,
have put on sackcloth for my prayer of
supplication,
and while I live I will cry out to the
Eternal God.[d]

21 "Fear not, my children; call upon God,
who will deliver you from oppression at
enemy hands.[e]
22 I have trusted in the Eternal God for your
welfare,
and joy has come to me from the Holy
One
Because of the mercy that will swiftly reach
you
from your eternal savior.
23 With mourning and lament I sent you forth,
but God will give you back to me
with enduring gladness and joy.[f]
24 As Zion's neighbors lately saw you taken
captive,
so shall they soon see God's salvation
come to you,
with great glory and the splendor of the
Eternal God.[g]

25 "My children, bear patiently the anger[h]
that has come from God upon you;
Your enemies have persecuted you,
and you will soon see their destruction
and trample upon their necks.*
26 My pampered children have trodden rough
roads,
carried off by their enemies like sheep in
a raid.[i]
27 Fear not, my children; call out to God!
He who brought this upon you will
remember you.[j]
28 As your hearts have been disposed to stray
from God,
turn now ten times the more to seek him;
29 For he who has brought disaster upon you
will, in saving you, bring you back
enduring joy."[k]

## *IV: Jerusalem Consoled: The Captivity About to End*

30 Fear not, Jerusalem!
He who gave you your name is your
encouragement.[l]
31 Fearful are those who harmed you,
who rejoiced at your downfall;
32 Fearful are the cities where your children
were enslaved,
fearful the city that took your sons.[m]
33 As that city rejoiced at your collapse,[n]
and made merry at your downfall,
so shall she grieve over her own
desolation.
34 I will take from her the joyous throngs,
and her exultation shall be turned to
mourning:
35 For fire shall come upon her[o]
from the Eternal God, for a long time,
and demons shall dwell in her from that
time on.*

36 Look to the east, Jerusalem!
behold the joy that comes to you from
God.[p]
37 Here come your sons whom you once let
go,
gathered in from the east and from the
west
By the word of the Holy One,
rejoicing in the glory of God.

## CHAPTER 5

1 Jerusalem, take off your robe of mourning
and misery;
put on the splendor of glory from God
forever:[q]
2 Wrapped in the cloak of justice from God,
bear on your head the mitre

b Dt 28, 49f; Jer 5, 15; 6, 22f.
c Jer 32, 42.
d Jdt 9, 1; Est 4, 16.
e Jer 51, 5.
f Jer 31, 12f.
g Is 60, 1ff.
h Is 51, 23.
i Lam 2, 22.
j Is 40, 1.
k Is 35, 10.
l Ps 46, 5; Is 60, 14.
m Jer 51, 43.
n 33f: Is 13, 20ff; 47, 1-11; Jer 50, 13.
o Is 34, 9-14.
p Is 60, 4f.
q Is 52, 1.
r Ex 39, 30; Wis 18, 24; Is 61. 10; 62, 3.

*

4, 25: Trample upon their necks: love of enemies was not an Old Testament ideal. The Babylonians are considered here, however, to be God's enemies as well as Israel's.

4, 35: Deserts and desolate places were looked upon as the special habitations of demons; Tb 8, 3; Lk 11, 24.

that displays the glory of the eternal
name.[r]
3 For God will show all the earth your
splendor:
4 you will be named by God forever
the peace of justice, the glory of God's
worship.[s]

5 Up, Jerusalem! stand upon the heights;
look to the east and see your children
Gathered from the east and the west
at the word of the Holy One,
rejoicing that they are remembered by
God.
6 Led away on foot by their enemies they left
you:
but God will bring them back to you
borne aloft in glory as on royal thrones.[t]
7 For God has commanded
that every lofty mountain be made low,
And that the age-old depths and gorges
be filled to level ground,
that Israel may advance secure in the
glory of God.[u]
8 The forests and every fragrant kind of tree
have overshadowed Israel at God's
command;[v]
9 For God is leading Israel in joy
by the light of his glory,
with his mercy and justice for company.

## *V: The Letter of Jeremiah Against Idolatry*

## CHAPTER 6

1 A copy of the letter which Jeremiah sent to
those who were being led captive to Babylon by
the king of the Babylonians, to convey to them
what God had commanded him:[w]

For the sins you committed before God, you
are being led captive to Babylon by Nebuchadnezzar, king of the Babylonians. 2 When you
reach Babylon you will be there many years, a
period seven generations* long; after which I
will bring you back from there in peace. 3 And
now in Babylon you will see borne upon men's
shoulders gods of silver and gold and wood,
which cast fear upon the pagans.[x] 4 Take care
that you yourselves do not imitate their alien
example and stand in fear of them, 5 when you
see the crowd before them and behind worshiping them. Rather, say in your hearts, "You, O
LORD, are to be worshiped!"; 6 for my angel is
with you, and he is the custodian of your lives.[y]

7 Their tongues are smoothed by woodworkers; they are covered with gold and silver—but
they are a fraud, and cannot speak.[z] 8 People
bring gold, as to a maiden in love with ornament, 9 and furnish crowns for the heads of
their gods. Then sometimes the priests take the
silver and gold from their gods and spend it on
themselves, 10 or give part of it to the harlots
on the terrace.* They trick them out in garments
like men, these gods of silver and gold and
wood; 11 but though they are wrapped in purple
clothing, they are not safe from corrosion or
insects. 12 They wipe their faces clean of the
house dust which is thick upon them. 13 Each
has a scepter, like the human ruler of a district;
but none does away with those that offend
against it. 14 Each has in its right hand an axe
or dagger, but it cannot save itself from war or
pillage. Thus it is known they are not gods; do
not fear them.

15 As useless as one's broken tools 16 are
their gods, set up in their houses; their eyes are
full of dust from the feet of those who enter.
17 Their courtyards are walled in like those of
a man brought to execution for a crime against
the king; the priests reinforce their houses with
gates and bars and bolts, lest they be carried off
by robbers. 18 They light more lamps for them
than for themselves, yet not one of these can
they see. 19 They are like any beam in the
house; it is said their hearts are eaten away.
Though the insects out of the ground consume
them and their garments, they do not feel it.
20 Their faces are blackened by the smoke of
the house. 21 Bats and swallows alight on their
bodies and on their heads; and cats as well as
birds. 22 Know, therefore, that they are not
gods, and do not fear them.

23 Despite the gold that covers them for
adornment, unless someone wipes away the corrosion, they do not shine; nor did they feel
anything when they were molded. 24 They are
bought at any price, and there is no spirit in
them. 25 Having no feet, they are carried on
men's shoulders, displaying their shame to all;
and those who worship them are put to confusion[a] 26 because, if they fall to the ground, the
worshipers must raise them up. They neither
move of themselves if one sets them upright,
nor come upright if they fall; but one puts gifts
beside them as beside the dead. 27 *Their
priests resell their sacrifices for their own advantage. Even their wives cure parts of the
meat, but do not share it with the poor and the

s Is 1, 26; 32, 17; Jer 33, 16.
t Is 49, 22.
u Is 40, 3f.
v Is 41, 19.
w Jer 29, 1.
x Is 46, 7; Jer 10, 1-16.
y Ex 23, 20.
z Ps 135, 16.
a Wis 13, 16.
b Lv 12. 4; 15, 19f; Dt 14, 28f.

*

6, 2: Seven generations: possibly an indication of the date of this composition by an author writing for his contemporaries for whom the conditions of the exile were still realities. He has multiplied the seventy years of Jer 29, 10 by three or four.

6, 10: Harlots on the terrace: cult prostitutes, common in the idolatrous religions of the Gentiles.

6, 27–31: From the point of view of Jewish ritual law, the practices named here were grotesque and depraved; cf Lv 12, 2ff; 15, 19–23.

weak;[b] **28** the menstruous and women in
childbed handle their sacrifices. Knowing from
this that they are not gods, do not fear them.

**29** How can they be called gods? For women
bring the offerings to these gods of silver and
gold and wood; **30** and in their temples the
priests squat with torn tunic and with shaven
hair and beard, and with their heads uncovered.[c] **31** They shout and wail before their gods
as others do at a funeral banquet. **32** The priests
take some of their clothing and put it on their
wives and children. **33** *Whether they are treated well or ill by anyone, they cannot requite it;
they can neither set up a king nor remove him.[d]
**34** Similarly, they cannot give anyone riches or
coppers; if one fails to fulfill a vow to them,
they cannot exact it of him. **35** They neither
save a man from death, nor deliver the weak
from the strong.[e] **36** To no blind man do they
restore his sight, nor do they save any man in
an emergency. **37** They neither pity the widow
nor benefit the orphan. **38** These gilded and
silvered wooden statues are like stones from the
mountains; and their worshipers will be put to
shame. **39** How then can it be thought or
claimed that they are gods?

**40** Even the Chaldeans themselves have no
respect for them; for when they see a deaf mute,
incapable of speech, they bring forward Bel*
and ask the god to make noise, as though the
man could understand; **41** and they are themselves unable to reflect and abandon these gods,
for they have no sense. **42** *And their women,
girt with cords, sit by the roads, burning chaff
for incense;[f] **43** and whenever one of them is
drawn aside by some passerby who lies with
her, she mocks her neighbor who has not been
dignified as she has, and has not had her cord
broken. **44** All that takes place around these
gods is a fraud: how then can it be thought or
claimed that they are gods?

**45** They are produced by woodworkers and
goldsmiths, and they are nothing else than what
these craftsmen wish them to be. **46** Even those
who produce them are not long-lived; **47** how
then can what they have produced be gods?
They have left frauds and opprobrium to their
successors. **48** For when war or disaster comes
upon them, the priests deliberate among themselves where they can hide with them. **49** How
then can one not know that these are no-gods,
which do not save themselves either from war
or from disaster? **50** They are wooden, gilded
and silvered; they will later be known for
frauds. To all peoples and kings it will be clear
that they are not gods, but human handiwork;
and that God's work is not in them.

**51** Who does not know that they are not
gods? **52** They set no king over the land, nor do
they give men rain. **53** They neither vindicate
their own rights, nor do they recover what is
unjustly taken, for they are unable; **54** they are
like crows between heaven and earth. For when
fire breaks out in the temple of these wooden or
gilded or silvered gods, though the priests flee
and are safe, they themselves are burnt up in the
fire like beams. **55** They cannot resist a king,
or enemy forces. **56** How then can it be admitted or thought that they are gods?

They are safe from neither thieves nor bandits, these wooden and silvered and gilded gods;
**57** those who seize them strip off the gold and
the silver, and go away with the clothing that
was on them, and they cannot help themselves.
**58** How much better to be a king displaying his
valor, or a handy tool in a house, the joy of its
owner, than these false gods; or the door of a
house, that keeps safe those who are within,
rather than these false gods; or a wooden post
in a palace, rather than these false gods![g]
**59** The sun and moon and stars are bright, and
obedient in the service for which they are sent.
**60** Like wise the lightning, when it flashes, is
a goodly sight; and the same wind blows over
all the land. **61** The clouds, too, when commanded by God to proceed across the whole
world, fulfill the order; **62** and fire, sent from
on high to burn up the mountains and the forests, does what has been commanded. But these
false gods are not their equal, whether in beauty
or in power; **63** so that it is unthinkable, and
cannot be claimed, that they are gods. They can
neither execute judgment, nor benefit man.
**64** Know, therefore, that they are not gods, and
do not fear them.

**65** Kings they neither curse nor bless.
**66** They show the nations no signs in the heavens, nor are they brilliant like the sun, nor shining like the moon. **67** The beasts which can
help themselves by fleeing to shelter are better
than they are. **68** Thus in no way is it clear to
us that they are gods; so do not fear them.
**69** For like a scarecrow in a cucumber patch,
that is no protection, are their wooden, gilded,
silvered gods. **70** Just like a thornbush in a
garden on which perches every kind of bird, or
like a corpse hurled into darkness, are their
silvered and gilded wooden gods. **71** From the
rotting of the purple and the linen upon them,
it can be known that they are not gods; they
themselves will in the end be consumed, and be

---

c Lv 10, 6; 21, 5. 10.
d Dn 2, 21.
e Pss 68, 6; 146, 7ff.
f 42-43: Jer 3, 2.
g Wis 13, 10-15; 15, 7ff.

---

* 6, 33–39: All that the gods cannot do, the true God does; cf 1 Sm 2, 7; Dt 23, 22; Pss 68, 6; 146, 7–9; Is 35, 4f.

6, 40: Bel: cf note on Jer 50, 2.

6, 42f: This seems to refer to the obligation of Babylonian women to serve once in their lives as cult prostitutes. The unbroken cord was a sign that this duty had not yet been fulfilled. Chaff: burnt as an aphrodisiac or for use in erotic rites.

a disgrace in the land. **72** The better for the just
man who has no idols: he shall be far from
disgrace!

# The Book of
# EZEKIEL

*Ezekiel's complex character makes him one of the most interesting figures in Israelite prophecy. In many ways he resembles the more primitive type of prophet represented by Elijah and Elisha; yet he clearly depends on all his predecessors in prophecy, and his teaching is a development of theirs. His unique contribution to the history of prophetism lies in his manifest interest in the temple and the liturgy, an interest paralleled in no other prophet—not even Jeremiah who, like Ezekiel, was also a priest. Particularly because of this interest, Ezekiel's influence on postexilic religion was enormous, and not without reason has he been called "the father of Judaism." This has resulted in his prophecies reaching us with the evident marks of editing and addition by the postexilic circles that shared his intense interest. However, we may be sure that in this book we have throughout what is in substance the prophet's own work.*

*Ezekiel became a prophet in Babylon—the first prophet to receive the call to prophesy outside the Holy Land. As one of the exiles deported by Nebuchadnezzar in 597, his first task was to prepare his fellow countrymen in Babylon for the final destruction of Jerusalem, which they believed to be inviolable. Accordingly, the first part of his book consists of reproaches for Israel's past and present sins and the confident prediction of yet a further devastation of the land of promise and a more general exile. In 587, when Nebuchadnezzar destroyed Jerusalem, Ezekiel was vindicated before his unbelieving compatriots.*

*After this time, Ezekiel's message changes. From now on his prophecy is characterized by the promise of salvation in a new covenant, and he is anxious to lay down the conditions necessary to obtain it. Even as Jeremiah had believed, Ezekiel thought that the exiles were the hope of Israel's restoration, once God's allotted time for the exile had been accomplished. His final eight chapters are an utopian vision of the Israel of the future, rid of its past evils and re-established firmly under the rule of the Lord. The famous vision of the dry bones in chapter 37 expresses his firm belief in a forthcoming restoration, Israel rising to new life from the graveyard of Babylon. But Ezekiel's new covenant, like Jeremiah's, was to see its true fulfillment only in the New Testament.*

*Perhaps no other prophet has stressed the absolute majesty of God as Ezekiel does. This appears not only in the tremendous vision by the river Chebar with which his prophecy opens, but throughout the book. Ultimately, says Ezekiel, whatever God does to or for man is motivated by zeal for his own holy name. The new heart and the new spirit which must exist under the new covenant cannot be the work of man; they too must be the work of God. By such teachings he helped prepare for the New Testament doctrine of salvation through grace.*

*The Book of Ezekiel is divided as follows:*

*I. Call of the Prophet (1, 1—3, 27).*
*II. Before the Siege of Jerusalem (4, 1—24, 27).*
*III. Prophecies against Foreign Nations (25, 1—32, 32).*
*IV. Salvation for Israel (33, 1—39, 29).*
*V. The New Israel (40, 1—48, 35).*

## *I: Call of the Prophet*

### CHAPTER 1

**The Vision: God on the Cherubim.** **1** In
the thirtieth year,* on the fifth day of the fourth
month, while I was among the exiles by the river
Chebar, the heavens opened, and I saw divine
visions.[a] ——**2** On the fifth day of the month,
the fifth year,* that is, of King Jehoiachin's
exile, **3** the word of the LORD came to the priest
Ezekiel, the son of Buzi, in the land of the
Chaldeans by the river Chebar.—There the
hand of the LORD came upon me.

**4** As I looked, a stormwind came from the
North,* a huge cloud with flashing fire [envel-
oped in brightness], from the midst of which
[the midst of the fire] something gleamed like
electrum. **5** Within it were figures resembling
four living creatures* that looked like this: their
form was human, **6** but each had four faces and
four wings, **7** and their legs went straight down;
the soles of their feet were round. They sparkled
with a gleam like burnished bronze.

**10** *Their faces were like this:[b] each of the
four had the face of a man, but on the right side
was the face of a lion, and on the left side the
face of an ox, and finally each had the face of
an eagle. **9** Their faces [and their wings] looked
out on all their four sides; they did not turn when
they moved, but each went straight forward.
**12** [Each went straight forward; wherever the
spirit wished to go, there they went; they did not
turn when they moved.]

**8** Human hands were under their wings, and
the wings of one touched those of another.
**11** Each had two wings spread out above so that
they touched one another's, while the other two
wings of each covered his body. **13** In among
the living creatures something like burning
coals of fire could be seen; they seemed like
torches, moving to and fro among the living
creatures. The fire gleamed, and from it came
forth flashes of lightning.

**15** As I looked at the living creatures, I saw
wheels on the ground, one beside each of the
four living creatures. **16** The wheels had the
sparkling appearance of chrysolite, and all four
of them looked the same: they were constructed
as though one wheel were within another.
**17** They could move in any of the four directions they faced, without veering as they
moved. **18** [c]The four of them had rims, and I
saw that their rims were full of eyes all around.
**19** When the living creatures moved, the
wheels moved with them; and when the living
creatures were raised from the ground, the
wheels also were raised. **20** Wherever the spirit
wished to go, there the wheels went, and they
were raised together with the living creatures;
for the spirit of the living creatures was in the
wheels.

**22** *Over the heads of the living creatures,
something like a firmament could be seen,
seeming like glittering crystal, stretched straight
out above their heads. **23** Beneath the firmament their wings were stretched out, one toward
the other. [Each of them had two covering his
body.] **24** Then I heard the sound of their
wings, like the roaring of mighty waters, like
the voice of the Almighty. When they moved,
the sound of the tumult was like the din of an
army. [And when they stood still, they lowered
their wings.]

**26** Above the firmament over their heads
something like a throne could be seen, looking
like sapphire. Upon it was seated, up above, one
who had the appearance of a man.* **27** Upward
from what resembled his waist I saw what
gleamed like electrum; downward from what
resembled his waist I saw what looked like fire;
he was surrounded with splendor. **28** Like the
bow which appears in the clouds on a rainy day
was the splendor that surrounded him. Such was
the vision of the likeness of the glory of the
LORD.

### CHAPTER 2

**Eating of the Scroll.** When I had seen it,
I fell upon my face and heard a voice that said
to me: **1** Son of man,* stand up! I wish to speak
with you. **2** As he spoke to me, spirit* entered
into me and set me on my feet, and I heard the
one who was speaking **3** say to me: Son of man,
I am sending you to the Israelites, rebels who
have rebelled against me; they and their fathers

a Ez 3, 23; 10, 20; 43, 3. c Ez 10, 12; Rv 4, 6. 8.
b Rv 4, 6f.

*

1, 1: The thirtieth year, which corresponds to the fifth year of exile (v 2), has never been satisfactorily explained; possibly it refers to the prophet's age. The river Chebar: probably a canal near Nippur, southeast of Babylon, one of the sites on which the Jewish exiles were settled.

1, 2: The fifth day of the fourth month, the fifth year: July 31, 593 B.C.; cf v 1.

1, 4: The North: the abode of God; see notes on Jb 37, 22; Ps 48, 3. Electrum: an alloy of gold and silver, used here for some undetermined bright metal.

1, 5: Four living creatures: identified as cherubim in Ez 10, 20f.

1, 10–22: Note the changed order of the verses and the omission of the textually uncertain verses 14 and 21. Such changes also occur elsewhere in this book.

1, 22f. 26: This symbolic description of God's throne is similar to that in Ex 24, 9f.

1, 26: One who had the appearance of a man: God appearing in human form (v 28); cf Ex 33, 18–23.

2, 1: Son of man: a formal way of saying simply "man"; God's habitual way of addressing the prophet throughout this book. Probably the title is used to emphasize the separation of the divine and the human.

2, 2: Spirit: vital power, coming from God, which enables the prophet to hear the word of God; cf Ez 8, 3; 9, 24; 11, 1.

have revolted against me to this very day.
4 Hard of face and obstinate of heart are they
to whom I am sending you. But you shall say
to them: Thus says the Lord GOD! 5 And
whether they heed or resist—for they are a rebellious house—they shall know that a prophet
has been among them. 6 But as for you, son of
man, fear neither them nor their words when
they contradict you and reject you, and when
you sit on scorpions.* Neither fear their words
nor be dismayed at their looks, for they are a
rebellious house. 7 [But speak my words to
them, whether they heed or resist, for they are
rebellious.] 8 As for you, son of man, obey me
when I speak to you: be not rebellious like this
house of rebellion, but open your mouth and eat
what I shall give you.

9 [d]It was then I saw a hand stretched out to
me, in which was a written scroll 10 which he
unrolled before me. It was covered with writing
front and back, and written on it was: Lamentation and wailing and woe!

## CHAPTER 3

1 He said to me: Son of man, eat what is
before you; eat this scroll, then go, speak to the
house of Israel. 2 So I opened my mouth and
he gave me the scroll to eat. 3 [e]Son of man, he
then said to me, feed your belly and fill your
stomach with this scroll I am giving you. I ate
it, and it was as sweet as honey* in my mouth.
He said: 4 Son of man, go now to the house of
Israel, and speak my words to them.

5 Not to a people with difficult speech and
barbarous language am I sending you, 6 nor to
the many peoples [with difficult speech and barbarous language] whose words you cannot understand. If I were to send you to these, they
would listen to you; 7 but the house of Israel
will refuse to listen to you, since they will not
listen to me. For the whole house of Israel is
stubborn of brow and obstinate in heart. 8 But
I will make your face as hard as theirs, and your
brow as stubborn as theirs, 9 like diamond,
harder than flint. Fear them not, nor be dismayed at their looks, for they are a rebellious
house.

10 Son of man, he said to me, take into your
heart all my words that I speak to you; hear them
well. 11 Now go to the exiles, to your countrymen, and say to them: Thus says the Lord
GOD!—whether they heed or resist!

12 Then spirit lifted me up, and I heard behind me the noise of a loud rumbling as the
glory of the LORD* rose from its place: 13 the
noise made by the wings of the living creatures
striking one another, and by the wheels alongside them, a loud rumbling. 14 The spirit which
had lifted me up seized me, and I went off
spiritually stirred, while the hand of the LORD
rested heavily upon me. 15 Thus I came to the
exiles who lived at Tel-abib* by the river Chebar, and for seven days I sat among them dis-
traught.

**The Prophet as Watchman.*** 17 Thus the
word of the LORD came to me: Son of man, I
have appointed you a watchman for the house
of Israel.[f] When you hear a word from my
mouth, you shall warn them for me.

18 If I say to the wicked man, You shall
surely die; and you do not warn him or speak out
to dissuade him from his wicked conduct so that
he may live: that wicked man shall die for his
sin, but I will hold you responsible for his death.
19 If, on the other hand, you have warned the
wicked man, yet he has not turned away from
his evil nor from his wicked conduct, then he
shall die for his sin, but you shall save your life.

20 If a virtuous man turns away from virtue
and does wrong when I place a stumbling block
before him, he shall die. He shall die for his sin,
and his virtuous deeds shall not be remembered;
but I will hold you responsible for his death if
you did not warn him. 21 When, on the other
hand, you have warned a virtuous man not to
sin, and he has in fact not sinned, he shall surely
live because of the warning, and you shall save
your own life.

**Ezekiel's Dumbness.*** 22 The hand of the
Lord came upon me, and he said to me: Get up
and go out into the plain, where I will speak
with you. 23 [g]So I got up and went out into the
plain, and I saw that the glory of the LORD was
in that place, like the glory I had seen by the
river Chebar. I fell prone, 24 but then spirit
entered into me and set me on my feet, and he
spoke with me.

He said to me: Go shut yourself up in your
house. 25 [As for you, son of man, they will
put cords upon you and bind you with them, so
that you cannot go out among them.] 26 I will

d Rv 5, 1.
e Rv 10, 9f.
f Ez 33, 7.
g Ez 1, 3; 10, 15. 20. 22; 43, 3.

2, 6: When you sit on scorpions: the prophet must be prepared for the bitterest opposition.

3, 3: As sweet as honey: though the prophet must foretell terrible things the word of God is sweet to him who receives it.

3, 12: The glory of the Lord: the divine presence, manifested here in visible form.

3, 15: Tel-abib: one of the sites where the exiles were settled, probably near Nippur.

3, 17–21: This passage refers to one of the prophet's most characteristic qualities. It was placed here by an editor, though it properly belongs to a later stage in Ezekiel's ministry; cf chapter 33.

3, 22–27: This passage also belongs to a later period, with Ez 24, 25ff and 33, 21f, during the time of the final siege of Jerusalem, when Ezekiel's prophecies consisted mainly of symbolic actions rather than words.

3, 26: Dumb: unwilling to speak to the people in exile while

make your tongue stick to your palate so that
you will be dumb* and unable to rebuke them
for being a rebellious house. **27** Only when I
speak with you and open your mouth, shall you
say to them: Thus says the Lord GOD! Let him
heed who will, and let him resist who will, for
they are a rebellious house.

## *II: Before the Siege of Jerusalem*

## CHAPTER 4

### Acts Symbolic of Siege and Exile.

**3, 16** At the end of seven days . . . :* **1** As for
you, son of man, take a clay tablet; lay it in front
of you, and draw on it a city [Jerusalem].
**2** Raise a siege against it: build a tower, lay out
a ramp, pitch camps, and set up battering rams
all around. **3** Then take an iron griddle and set
it up as an iron wall between you and the city.
Fix your gaze on it: it shall be in the state of
siege, and you shall besiege it. This shall be a
sign for the house of Israel. **4** Then you shall lie
on your left side, while I place the sins of the
house of Israel upon you. As many days as you
lie thus, you shall bear their sins. **5** For the
years of their sins I allot you the same number
of days, three hundred and ninety,* during
which you will bear the sins of the house of
Israel. **6** When you finish this, you are to lie
down again, but on your right side, and bear the
sins of the house of Judah forty days; one day
for each year I have allotted you. **7** Fixing your
gaze on the siege of Jerusalem, with bared arm*
you shall prophesy against it. **8** See, I will bind
you with cords so that you cannot turn from one
side to the other until you have completed the
days of your siege.

**9** *Again, take wheat and barley, and beans
and lentils, and millet and spelt; put them in a
single vessel and make bread out of them. Eat
it for as many days as you lie upon your side,
three hundred and ninety. **10** The food you eat
shall be twenty shekels a day by weight; each
day the same. **11** And the water you drink shall
be the sixth of a hin by measure; each day the
same. **16** [h]Then he said to me: Son of man, I
am breaking the staff of bread* in Jerusalem.
They shall eat bread which they have weighed
out anxiously, and they shall drink water which
they have measured out fearfully, **17** so that,
owing to the scarcity of bread and water, everyone shall be filled with terror and waste away
because of his sins.

**12** For your food you must bake barley
loaves over human excrement in their sight, said
the LORD. **13** Thus the Israelites shall eat their
food unclean among the nations where I scatter
them.[i] **14** "Oh no, Lord GOD!" I protested.
"Never have I been made unclean, and from my
youth till now, never have I eaten carrion flesh
or that torn by wild beasts: never has any unclean meat entered my mouth." **15** Very well,
he replied, I allow you cow's dung in place of
human excrement; bake your bread on that.

## CHAPTER 5

**1** As for you, son of man, take a sharp sword
and use it like a barber's razor, passing it over
your head and beard. Then take a set of scales
and divide the hair you have cut. **2** Burn a third
in the fire, within the city,* when the days of
your siege are completed; place another third
around the city and strike it with the sword; the
final third strew in the wind, and pursue it with
the sword. **3** [But of the last take a small number and tie them in the hem of your garment.
**4** Then take some of these and throw them in
the midst of the fire and burn them.]

Say to the whole house of Israel: **5** Thus says
the Lord GOD: This is Jerusalem! In the midst
of the nations I placed her, surrounded by foreign countries. **6** But she rebelled against my
ordinances more wickedly than the nations, and
against my statutes more than the foreign countries surrounding her; she has spurned my ordinances and has not lived by my statutes.
**7** Therefore thus says the Lord GOD: Because
you have been more rebellious than the nations
surrounding you, not living by my statutes nor
fulfilling my ordinances, but acting according to
the ordinances of the surrounding nations;
**8** therefore thus says the Lord GOD: see, I am
coming at you!* I will inflict punishments in
your midst while the nations look on. **9** Because of all your abominations I will do with
you what I have never done before, the like of

---

h Ez 5, 16; 14, 13. i Hos 9, 4.

* Jerusalem was being besieged; cf Ez 24, 27.

3, 16: At the end of seven days . . . : the incomplete sentence probably contained some such words as "the word of the Lord came to me." For seven days, see v 15. (This verse has been transposed from ch 3.)

4, 5f: Three hundred and ninety days . . . forty days: symbolically representing the respective lengths of the periods of exile of northern Israelites and Judahites. Northern Israel had already fallen to Assyria in 722 B.C. The letters in the Hebrew phrase for the days of your siege (v 8), each of which has its own numerical value, add up to three hundred and ninety. Forty years represent one generation.

4, 7: Bared arm: a symbol of unrestrained power.

4, 9–17: This action represents the scarcity of food during the siege of Jerusalem, and the consequent need to eat whatever is at hand. Twenty shekels: about nine ounces. The sixth of a hin: about one quart.

4, 16: Breaking the staff of bread: reducing the supply of bread which sustains the life of man as the walking staff sustains the traveler on his journey; cf Ez 5, 16; 14, 13; Lv 26, 26; Ps 105, 16; Is 3, 1.

5, 2: The city: the one drawn on the tablet.

5, 8: I am coming at you: an expression borrowed from the language of warfare in which enemies attacked one another with the sword. You in vv 8–17 is Jerusalem.

which I will never do again. **10** This means that
fathers within you shall eat sons, and sons shall
eat fathers.* I will inflict punishments upon you
and scatter all that remain of your people in
every direction.

**11** Therefore, as I live, says the Lord GOD,
because you have defiled my sanctuary with all
your detestable abominations, I swear to cut you
down. I will not look upon you with pity nor
have mercy. **12** A third of your people shall die
of pestilence and perish of hunger within you;
another third shall fall by the sword all around
you; and a third I will scatter in every direction,
and I will pursue them with the sword.
**16** [j]When I loose against you the cruel, destructive arrows of hunger, I will break your
staff of bread; **17** I will send famine against
you, and wild beasts that shall rob you of your
children. Pestilence and bloodshed shall stalk
through you, and I will bring the sword upon
you. I, the LORD, have spoken!

**13** Thus shall my anger spend itself, and I
will wreak my fury upon them till I am appeased; they shall know that I, the LORD, have
spoken in my jealousy when I spend my fury
upon them. **14** I will make you a waste and a
reproach among the nations that surround you,
which every passer-by may see. **15** When I execute judgment upon you in anger and fury and
with furious chastisements, you shall be a reproach and an object of scorn, a terrible warning
to the nations that surround you. I, the LORD,
have spoken!

## CHAPTER 6

**Against the Mountains of Israel.** **1** Thus
the word of the LORD came to me: **2** Son of
man, turn toward the mountains of Israel, and
prophesy against them: **3** Mountains of Israel,
hear the word of the Lord GOD. Thus says the
Lord GOD [to the mountains and hills, the ravines and valleys]:[k] See, I am bringing a sword
against you, and I will destroy your high
places.* **4** Your altars shall be laid waste, your
incense stands shall be broken, and I will cast
down your slain ones before your idols; **5** I will
scatter their bones all around your altars.* **6** In
all your dwelling places cities shall be made
desolate and high places laid waste, so that your
altars will be made desolate and laid waste, your
idols broken and removed, and your incense
stands smashed to bits. **7** [The slain shall fall in
your midst, and you shall know that I am the
LORD. **8** I have warned you.]

When some of your people have escaped to
other nations from the sword, and have been
scattered over the foreign lands, **9** then those
who have escaped will remember me among the
nations to which they have been exiled, after I
have broken their adulterous hearts that turned
away from me [and their eyes which lusted after
idols]. They shall loathe themselves because of
their evil deeds, all their abominations.
**10** Then they shall know that it was not in vain
that I, the LORD, threatened to inflict this calamity upon them.

**11** Thus says the Lord GOD: Clap your
hands, stamp your feet,* and cry "Alas!" because of all the abominations of the house of
Israel, for which they shall fall by the sword, by
famine, and by pestilence. **12** He that is far off
shall die of pestilence, he that is near shall fall
by the sword, and he that is besieged shall perish
by famine; so will I spend my fury upon them.
**13** Then shall they know that I am the LORD,
when their slain shall lie amid their idols, all
about their altars, on every high hill and mountaintop, beneath every green tree and leafy
oak,* wherever they offered appeasing odors to
any of their gods. **14** I will stretch out my hand
against them, and wherever they live I will
make the land a desolate waste, from the desert
to Riblah;* thus shall they know that I am the
LORD.

## CHAPTER 7

**The End Has Come.** **1** Thus the word of
the LORD came to me: **2** Son of man, now say:
Thus says the Lord GOD to the land of Israel: An
end! The end has come upon the four corners of
the land! **3** Now the end is upon you; I will
unleash my anger against you and judge you
according to your conduct and lay upon you the
consequences of all your abominations. **4** I will
not look upon you with pity nor have mercy; I
will bring your conduct down upon you, and the
consequences of your abominations shall be in
your midst; then shall you know that I am the
LORD.

**5** Thus says the Lord GOD: Disaster upon
disaster! See it coming! **6** An end is coming,
the end is coming upon you! See it coming!
**7** The climax has come for you who dwell in the
land! The time has come, near is the day: a time
of consternation, not of rejoicing. **8** Soon now

---

j Ez 4, 16; 14, 13. k Ez 36, 1.

*

5, 10: Fathers . . . shall eat sons, and sons . . . fathers: see note on Lam 2, 20.

6, 3: High places: the sanctuaries on the mountaintops where illegal worship, whether of the Lord or of Canaanite deities, was performed.

6, 5: Scatter their bones . . . altars: dead men's bones defiled a place; cf 2 Kgs 23, 14.

6, 11: Clap your hands, stamp your feet: here evidently signs of mourning; in Ez 25, 6, signs of joy.

6, 13: Every green tree and leafy oak: sacred groves had a long history in Palestine as places of worship; cf Dt 12, 2; note on Gn 12, 6.

6, 14: From the desert to Riblah: the whole land, from the far south to the far north.

I will pour out my fury upon you and spend my
anger upon you; I will judge you according to
your conduct and lay upon you the consequences of all your abominations. **9** I will not
look upon you with pity nor have mercy; I will
deal with you according to your conduct, and
the consequences of your abominations shall be
in your midst; then shall you know that it is I,
the LORD, who strike.

**10** See, the day of the LORD! See, the end is
coming! Lawlessness is in full bloom, insolence
flourishes, **11** violence has risen to support
wickedness. It shall not be long in coming, nor
shall it delay. **12** *The time has come, the day
dawns. Let not the buyer rejoice nor the seller
mourn, for wrath shall be upon all the throng.
**13** The seller shall not regain what he sold as
long as he lives, for wrath shall be upon all the
throng. Because of his sins, no one shall preserve his life. **14** They shall sound the trumpet
and make everything ready, yet no one shall go
to war, for my wrath is upon all the throng.

**15** The sword is outside; pestilence and hunger are within. He that is in the country shall die
by the sword; pestilence and famine shall devour those in the city. **16** Even those who escape and flee to the mountains like the doves of
the valleys—I will put them all to death, each
one for his own sins. **17** All their hands shall be
limp, and all their knees shall run with water.
**18** [l]They shall put on sackcloth, and horror
shall cover them; shame shall be on all their
faces and baldness* on all their heads. **19** They
shall fling their silver into the streets, and their
gold shall be considered refuse.[m] Their silver
and gold cannot save them on the day of the
LORD's wrath. They shall not be allowed to
satisfy their craving or fill their bellies, for this
has been the occasion of their sin. **20** In the
beauty of their ornaments they put their pride:
they made of them their abominable images
[their idols]. For this reason I make them refuse.
**21** I will hand them over as booty to foreigners,
to be spoiled and defiled by the wicked of the
earth. **22** I will turn away my face from them,
and my treasure* shall be profaned: robbers
shall enter and profane it.

**23** They shall wreak slaughter, for the land
is filled with bloodshed and the city full of
violence. **24** I will bring in the worst of the
nations, who shall take possession of their
houses. I will put an end to their proud strength,
and their sanctuaries shall be profaned.
**25** When anguish comes they shall seek peace,
but there will be none. **26** There shall be disaster after disaster, rumor after rumor. Prophetic
vision shall fade; instruction shall be lacking to
the priest, and counsel to the elders, **27** while
the prince shall be enveloped in terror, and the
hands of the common people shall tremble. I
will deal with them according to their conduct,
and according to their judgments I will judge
them; thus they shall know that I am the LORD.

## CHAPTER 8

### Vision of Abominations in the Temple.

**3** Spirit lifted me up in the air and brought me
in divine visions to Jerusalem,[n] to the entrance
of the north gate, where stood the statue of
jealousy which stirs up jealousy.* **5** He* said to
me: Son of man, look toward the north! I looked
toward the north and saw northward of the gate
the altar of the statue of jealousy. **6** Son of man,
he asked me, do you see what they are doing?
Do you see the great abominations that the
house of Israel is practicing here, so that I must
depart from my sanctuary? But you shall see
still greater abominations!

**7** Then he brought me to the entrance of the
court, where I saw there was a hole in the wall.
**8** Son of man, he ordered, dig through the wall.
I dug through the wall and saw a door. **9** Enter,
he said to me, and see the abominable evils
which they are doing here. **10** I entered and saw
that all around upon the wall were pictured the
figures of all kinds of creeping things and loathsome beasts* [all the idols of the house of Isra-
el]. **11** Before these stood seventy of the elders
of the house of Israel, among whom stood Jaazaniah, son of Shaphan, each of them with his
censer in his hand, and the fragrance of the
incense was rising upward. **12** Then he said to
me: Do you see, son of man, what each of these
elders of the house of Israel is doing in his idol
room? They think: "The LORD cannot see us;
the LORD has forsaken the land." **13** He continued: You shall see still greater abominations
that they are practicing.

**14** Then he brought me to the entrance of the
north gate of the temple, and I saw sitting there

l Is 15, 2; Jer 48, 37. Zep 1, 18.
m Prv 11, 4; Sir 5, 10; n Dn 14, 6.

*

7, 12f: Mundane affairs will cease to have any meaning in view of the disaster that is to come.

7, 18: Baldness: shaving the head was a sign of mourning.

7, 22: My treasure: the temple of Jerusalem.

8, 3: The statue of jealousy which stirs up jealousy: the statue which provokes the Lord's jealousy for his honor. This was probably the statue of the goddess Asherah erected by the wicked King Manasseh (cf 2 Kgs 21, 7; 2 Chr 33, 7. 15). Though it had been removed by King Josiah (2 Kgs 23, 6), it had no doubt been set up again in the repaganizing of Jerusalem that followed on Josiah's death.

8, 5: He: an angel accompanies Ezekiel in these visions and represents the voice of the Lord; cf Ez 40, 3f.

8, 10: Creeping things and loathsome beasts: probably Egyptian deities, which were represented in animal form. During the last days of Jerusalem King Zedekiah was allied with Egypt, trusting in it for protection against the Chaldeans.

8, 14: Weeping for Tammuz: the withering of trees and plants in autumn was thought to be due to the descent of Tammuz, the Babylonian god of fertility, to the nether world of the dead; this descent was bewailed by the women.

the women who were weeping for Tammuz.*
15 Then he said to me: Do you see this, son of
man? You shall see other abominations, greater
than these!
16 Then he brought me into the inner court
of the LORD's house, and there at the door of the
LORD's temple, between the vestibule and the
altar, were about twenty-five men with their
backs to the LORD's temple and their faces toward the east; they were bowing down to the
sun.* 17 Do you see, son of man? he asked me.
Is it such a trivial matter for the house of Judah
to do the abominable things they have done
here—for they have filled the land with violence, and again and again they have provoked
me—that now they must also put the branch to
my nose?* 18 Therefore I in turn will act furiously: I will not look upon them with pity nor
will I show mercy.

## CHAPTER 9

**Slaughter of the Idolaters.** 1 Then he
cried loud for me to hear: Come, you scourges
of the city! 2 With that I saw six men coming
from the direction of the upper gate which faces
the north, each with a destroying weapon in his
hand. In their midst was a man dressed in linen,
with a writer's case at his waist. They entered
and stood beside the bronze altar. 3 Then he
called to the man dressed in linen with the writer's case at his waist, 4 [o]saying to him:* Pass
through the city [through Jerusalem] and mark
an X on the foreheads of those who moan and
groan over all the abominations that are practiced within it. 5 To the others I heard him say:
Pass through the city after him and strike! Do
not look on them with pity nor show any mercy!
6 Old men, youths and maidens, women and
children—wipe them out! But do not touch any
marked with the X; begin at my sanctuary. So
they began with the men [the elders] who were
in front of the temple. 7 Defile the temple, he
said to them, and fill the courts with the slain;
then go out and strike in the city.
8 As they began to strike, I was left alone.
I fell prone, crying out, "Alas, Lord GOD! Will
you destroy all that is left of Israel when you
pour out your fury on Jerusalem?" 9 He answered me: The sins of the house of Israel are
great beyond measure; the land is filled with
bloodshed, the city with lawlessness. They
think that the LORD has forsaken the land, that
he does not see them. 10 I, however, will not
look upon them with pity, nor show any mercy.
I will bring down their conduct upon their
heads.
11 Then I saw the man dressed in linen with
the writing case at his waist make his report: "I
have done as you ordered."
11, 24 *Spirit lifted me up and brought me
back to the exiles in Chaldea [in a vision, by
God's spirit]. Then the vision I had seen left me,
11, 25 and I told the exiles everything the
LORD had shown me.

## CHAPTER 10

**God's Glory Leaves Jerusalem.**
8, 1 *On the fifth day of the sixth month, in the
sixth year,* as I was sitting in my house, and the
elders of Judah sat before me, the hand of the
Lord GOD fell upon me there. 8, 2 I looked up
and saw a form that looked like a man. Downward from what seemed to be his waist, there
was fire; from his waist upward there seemed to
be a brightness like the sheen of electrum. He
stretched out what appeared to be a hand and
seized me by the hair of my head. . . .*
8, 4 I saw there the glory of the God of Israel, like the vision I had seen in the plain. The
cherubim were stationed to the right of the temple; 20 these were the living creatures I had
seen beneath the God of Israel by the river Chebar,[p] whom I now recognized to be cherubim.
21 Each had four faces and four wings; something like human hands were under their wings.
22 Their faces looked just like those I had seen
by the river Chebar; each one went straight forward. 14 [q]Each had four faces: the first face
was that of an ox, the second that of a man, the
third that of a lion, and the fourth that of an
eagle. 15 Such were the living creatures I had
seen by the river Chebar.
9 [r]I also saw four wheels beside them, one
wheel beside each cherub; the wheels appeared
to have the luster of chrysolite stone. 10 All
four of them seemed to be made the same, as
though there were a wheel within a wheel.

o Ex 12, 7; Rv 7, 3.
p Ez 1, 1. 3.
q Ez 1, 10.
r Ez 1, 15f.

*

8, 16: Bowing down to the sun: sun worship had been made an important part of Judahite idolatry by the impious kings; cf 2 Kgs 23, 11.

8, 17: Put the branch to my nose: the meaning is uncertain. Perhaps it refers to an Egyptian practice imported into Judah; the Egyptian sun god Re is pictured with a vine branch at his nose, signifying the transfer of creative power (divine breath) to living things. Such rites were abominable to the Lord.

9, 4: Ezekiel is pre-eminently the prophet of personal retribution; the innocent inhabitants of Jerusalem are to be spared when the idolatrous are punished. An X: literally, the Hebrew letter taw, which had the form of a cross.

9, 24f: These verses have been transposed from ch 11.

10, 1: In chapters 8, 1—11, 25 of the current Hebrew text, several visions involving the temple of Jerusalem were combined to form a single continuous vision. The redistribution of verses in this translation is an attempt to separate the original visions. (10, 1. 2. 4. have been transposed from ch 8)

10, 1: The fifth day of the sixth month, in the sixth year: September 17, 592 B.C.

10, 2: The dots suppose the omission of some words describing the prophet's being transported in his visions to the court of the temple.

**11** When they moved, they went in any one of
their four directions without veering as they
moved; for in whichever direction they were
faced, they went straight towards it without
veering as they moved. **12** [s]The rims of the four
wheels were full of eyes all around. **13** I heard
the wheels given the name "wheelwork."
**16** [t]When the cherubim moved, the wheels
went beside them; when the cherubim lifted
their wings to rise from the earth, even then the
wheels did not leave their sides. **17** When they
stood still, the wheels stood still; when they
rose, the wheels rose with them; for the living
creatures' spirit was in them.
**1** I looked and saw in the firmament above
the cherubim what appeared to be sapphire
stone; something like a throne could be seen
upon it. **2** He said to the man dressed in linen:
Go within the wheelwork under the cherubim;
fill both your hands with burning coals* from
among the cherubim, then scatter them over the
city. As I looked on, he entered.
The glory of the God of Israel had gone up
from the cherubim, upon which it had been, to
the threshold of the temple. **3** As the man entered, the cloud filled the inner court, **4** and the
glory of the LORD rose from over the cherubim
to the threshold of the temple; the temple was
filled with the cloud, and all the court was bright
with the glory of the LORD. **5** The noise of the
wings of the cherubim could be heard as far as
the outer court; it was like the voice of God the
Almighty when he speaks.
**6** When he had commanded the man dressed
in linen to take fire from within the wheelwork,
among the cherubim, the man entered and stood
by one of the wheels. **7** Thereupon its cherub
stretched out his hand toward the fire that was
among the cherubim. He took up some of it and
put it in the hands of the one dressed in linen,
who took it and came out. **8** [Something like
human hands could be seen under the wings of
the cherubim.]
**18** Then the glory of the LORD left the threshold of the temple and rested upon the cherubim.
**19** These lifted their wings, and I saw them rise
from the earth, the wheels rising along with
them. They stood at the entrance of the eastern
gate of the LORD's house, and the glory of the
God of Israel was up above them.
**11, 22** *Then the cherubim lifted their wings,
and the wheels went along with them, while up
above them was the glory of the God of Israel.
**11, 23** And the glory of the LORD rose from the
city and took a stand on the mountain which is
to the east of the city.

## CHAPTER 11

**Judgment of the Princes.** **1** Spirit lifted
me up and brought me to the east gate of the
temple. At the entrance of the gate I saw twenty-five men, among whom were Jaazaniah, son
of Azzur, and Pelatiah, son of Benaiah, princes
of the people. **2** The LORD said to me: Son of
man, these are the men who are planning evil
and giving wicked counsel in this city. **3** "Shall
we not," they say, "be building houses soon?
The city is the kettle, and we are the meat."*
**4** Therefore prophesy against them, son of
man, prophesy! **5** Then the spirit of the LORD
fell upon me, and he told me to say: Thus says
the LORD: This is the way you talk, house of
Israel, and what you are plotting I well know.
**6** You have slain many in this city and have
filled its streets with your slain. **7** Therefore
thus says the Lord GOD: Your slain whom you
have placed within it, they are the meat, and the
city is the kettle; but you I will take out of it.
**8** You fear the sword, but the sword I will bring
upon you, says the Lord GOD. **9** I will bring you
out of the city, and hand you over to foreigners,
and inflict punishments upon you. **10** By the
sword you shall fall; at the boundaries of Israel
I will judge you; thus you shall know that I am
the LORD. **11** The city shall not be a kettle for
you, nor shall you be the meat within it. At the
boundaries of Israel I will judge you, **12** and
you shall know that I am the LORD, by whose
statutes you have not lived, and whose ordinances you have not kept; rather, you have acted
according to the ordinances of the nations
around you.
**13** While I was prophesying, Pelatiah, the
son of Benaiah, died. I fell prone and cried out
in a loud voice: "Alas, Lord GOD! will you
utterly wipe out what remains of Israel?"

**Restoration of the Exiles.** **14** Thus the
word of the LORD came to me: **15** *Son of man,
it is about your kinsmen, your fellow exiles, and
the whole house of Israel that the inhabitants of
Jerusalem say, "They are far away from the
LORD; to us the land of Israel has been given as
our possession." **16** Therefore say: Thus says
the Lord GOD: Though I have removed them far
among the nations and scattered them over foreign countries—and was for a while their only

s Ez 1, 18. t Ez 1, 19.

*

10, 2: The burning coals within the wheelwork under God's throne, a sign of the divine presence (cf Ez 28, 14; Ps 18, 13), symbolize the judgment to be visited on the city.

10, 22f: These verses have been transposed from ch 11.

11, 3: These words reflect the false confidence of the inhabitants of Jerusalem in the face of the Chaldean invasion. Jerusalem, they think, is like an iron kettle protecting the meat within it from harm; but cf Ez 24, 3–6.

11, 15–21: Like Jeremiah (cf chapter 29), Ezekiel knows that no reform is to be expected from the men of Judah who remained in Palestine; but the exiles will be the ones to form the new Israel. The new, spiritual covenant will replace the former covenant; cf Jer 24, 7.

sanctuary in the countries to which they had gone— **17** I will gather you from the nations and assemble you from the countries over which you have been scattered, and I will restore to you the land of Israel. **18** They shall return to it and remove from it all its detestable abominations. **19** [u]I will give them a new heart and put a new spirit within them; I will remove the stony heart from their bodies, and replace it with a natural heart, **20** so that they will live according to my statutes, and observe and carry out my ordinances; thus they shall be my people and I will be their God. **21** But as for those whose hearts are devoted to their detestable abominations, I will bring down their conduct upon their heads, says the Lord GOD.

## CHAPTER 12

**Acts Symbolic of the Exile.** **1** Thus the word of the LORD came to me: **2** Son of man, you live in the midst of a rebellious house; they have eyes to see but do not see, and ears to hear but do not hear, for they are a rebellious house. **3** Now, son of man, during the day while they are looking on, prepare your baggage as though for exile, and again while they are looking on, migrate from where you live to another place; perhaps they will see that they are a rebellious house. **4** You shall bring out your baggage like an exile in the daytime while they are looking on; in the evening, again while they are looking on, you shall go out like one of those driven into exile; **5** while they look on, dig a hole in the wall* and pass through it; **6** while they look on, shoulder the burden and set out in the darkness; cover your face that you may not see the land, for I have made you a sign for the house of Israel.

**7** I did as I was told. During the day I brought out my baggage as though it were that of an exile, and at evening I dug a hole through the wall with my hand and, while they looked on, set out in the darkness, shouldering my burden.

**8** Then, in the morning, the word of the LORD came to me: **9** Son of man, did not the house of Israel, that rebellious house, ask you what you were doing? **10** Tell them: Thus says the Lord GOD: This oracle concerns Jerusalem and the whole house of Israel within it. **11** I am a sign for you: as I have done, so shall it be done to them; as captives they shall go into exile. **12** The prince who is among them shall shoulder his burden and set out in darkness, going through a hole that he has dug in the wall, and covering his face lest he be seen by anyone. **13** [v]But I will spread my net over him, and he shall be taken in my snare. I will bring him to Babylon, into the land of the Chaldeans—but he shall not see it*—and there he shall die. **14** All his retinue, his aides, and his troops I will scatter in every direction, and pursue them with the sword. **15** Then shall they know that I am the LORD, when I disperse them among the nations and scatter them over foreign lands. **16** Yet I will leave a few of them to escape the sword, famine and pestilence, so that they may tell of all their abominations among the nations to which they will come; thus they shall know that I am the LORD.

**17** Thus the word of the LORD came to me: **18** Son of man, eat your bread trembling, and drink your water shaking with anxiety. **19** Then say to the people of the land: Thus says the Lord GOD of the inhabitants of Jerusalem [to the land of Israel]: They shall eat their bread in anxiety and drink their water in horror, that their land may be emptied of the violence of all its inhabitants that now fills it. **20** Inhabited cities shall be in ruins, and the land shall be a waste; thus you shall know that I am the LORD.

**Prophecy Ridiculed.** **21** Thus the word of the LORD came to me: **22** Son of man, what is this proverb that you have in the land of Israel: "The days drag on, and no vision ever comes to anything"?* **23** Say to them therefore: Thus says the Lord GOD: I will put an end to this proverb; they shall never quote it again in Israel. Rather, say to them: The days are at hand, and also the fulfillment of every vision. **25** Whatever I speak is final, and it shall be done without further delay. In your days, rebellious house, whatever I speak I will bring about, says the Lord GOD.

**24** There shall no longer be any false visions or deceitful divinations within the house of Israel, because it is I, the LORD, who will speak.

**26** Thus the word of the LORD came to me: **27** Son of man, listen to the house of Israel saying, "The vision he sees is a long way off; he prophesies of the distant future!" **28** Say to them therefore: Thus says the Lord GOD: None of my words shall be delayed any longer; whatever I speak is final, and it shall be done, says the Lord GOD.

## CHAPTER 13

**Against the Prophets of Peace.** **1** Thus the word of the LORD came to me: **2** Son of man, prophesy against the prophets of Israel, prophesy! Say to those who prophesy their own

---

u Ez 36, 26; Jer 31, 33. v Ez 17, 20; 32, 3.

---

* 12, 5: Dig a hole in the wall: the exiles are to leave Jerusalem through the broken walls of the ruined city.

12, 13: But he shall not see it: Zedekiah was blinded by Nebuchadnezzar before being deported to Babylonia; cf 2 Kgs 25, 7.

12, 22. 27: These words used against Ezekiel because of the apparent failure of his prophecies; cf Jer 20, 7ff.

thought: Hear the word of the LORD: **5** You did not step into the breach, nor did you build a wall about the house of Israel that would stand firm against attack on the day of the LORD. **7** Was not the vision you saw false, and your divination lying? **8** Therefore thus says the Lord GOD: Because you have spoken falsehood and have seen lying visions, therefore see! I am coming at you, says the Lord GOD.

**10** For the very reason that they led my people astray, saying, "Peace!" when there was no peace, and that, as one built a wall, they would cover it with whitewash,* **11** say then to the whitewashers: I will bring down a flooding rain; hailstones shall fall, and a stormwind shall break out. **12** And when the wall has fallen, will you not be asked: Where is the whitewash you spread on?

**13** Therefore thus says the Lord GOD: In my fury I will let loose stormwinds; because of my anger there shall be a flooding rain, and hailstones shall fall with destructive wrath. **14** I will tear down the wall that you have whitewashed and level it to the ground, laying bare its foundations. When it falls, you shall be crushed beneath it; thus you shall know that I am the LORD. **15** When I have spent my fury on the wall and its whitewashers, I tell you there shall be no wall, nor shall there be whitewashers— **16** those prophets of Israel who prophesied to Jerusalem and saw for it visions of peace when there was no peace, says the Lord GOD.

### Against False Prophets in Chaldea.

**3** [w]Thus says the Lord GOD: Woe to those prophets who are fools, who follow their own spirit and have seen no vision. **4** Like foxes among ruins are your prophets, O Israel! **6** Their visions are false and their divination lying. They say, "Thus says the LORD!" though the LORD did not send them; then they wait for him to fulfill their word! **9** But I will stretch out my hand against the prophets who have false visions and who foretell lies. They shall not belong to the community of my people, nor be recorded in the register of the house of Israel, nor enter the land of Israel; thus you shall know that I am the LORD.

### Against False Prophetesses.

**17** Now, son of man, turn toward the daughters of your people who prophesy their own thoughts; against these, prophesy: Thus says the Lord GOD: **22** Because you have disheartened the upright man with lies when I did not wish him grieved, and have encouraged the wicked man not to turn from his evil conduct and save his life; **23** therefore you shall no longer see false visions and practice divination, but I will rescue my people from your power. Thus you shall know that I am the LORD.

### Against Sorceresses.

**18** Woe to those who sew bands for everyone's wrists and make veils* for every size of head so as to entrap their owners. Do you think to entrap the lives of my people, yet keep yourselves alive? **19** You dishonor me before my people with handfuls of barley and crumbs of bread,* killing those who should not die and keeping alive those who should not live, lying to my people who willingly hear lies. **20** Therefore thus says the Lord GOD: See! I am coming at those bands of yours in which you entrap men's lives: I will tear them from their arms and set free those you have caught. **21** I will tear off your veils and rescue my people from your power, so that they shall no longer be prey to your hands. Thus you shall know that I am the LORD.

## CHAPTER 14

### Prophecy Useless for Idolaters.

**1** When certain elders of Israel came and sat down before me, **2** the word of the LORD came to me: **3** Son of man, these men have the memory of their idols fresh in their hearts, and they keep the occasion of their sin before them. Why should I allow myself to be consulted by them? **4** Therefore speak with them, and say to them: Thus says the Lord GOD: If anyone of the house of Israel, holding the memory of his idols in his heart and keeping the occasion of his sin before him, has recourse to a prophet, I, the LORD, will be his answer in person because of his many idols. **5** Thus would I bring back to their senses the house of Israel, who have become estranged from me through all their idols.

**6** Therefore say to the house of Israel: Thus says the Lord GOD: Return and be converted from your idols; turn yourselves away from all your abominations. **7** For if anyone of the house of Israel or any alien resident in Israel is estranged from me, and holds the memory of his idols in his heart and keeps the occasion of his sin before him, yet asks a prophet to consult me for him, I, the LORD, will be his answer in person. **8** I will turn against that man, and make of him an example and a byword. I will cut him off from the midst of my people. Thus you shall know that I am the LORD.

---

w Ez 14, 9; 34, 2; Jer 23, 1.

---

13, 10: To the confidence which the people had in their defenses against the Chaldeans, the false prophets contributed the illusion of security by predictions of peace, like men who whitewash a wall rather than allow its defects to be seen.

13, 18: Sew bands . . . make veils: magical practices believed to give to the sorceresses power over those on whom they placed these objects.

13, 19: Handfuls of barley and crumbs of bread: used in divination and forecasting the future.

**9** [x]As for the prophet, if he is beguiled into speaking a word, I, the LORD, shall have beguiled that prophet;* I will stretch out my hand against him and root him out of my people Israel. **10** Each shall receive punishment for his sin, the inquirer and the prophet shall be punished alike, **11** so that the house of Israel may no longer stray from me and may no longer be defiled by all their sins. Thus they shall be my people, and I will be their God, says the Lord GOD.

**Personal Responsibility.*** **12** Thus the word of the LORD came to me: **13** [y]Son of man, when a land sins against me by breaking faith, I stretch out my hand against it and break its staff of bread, I let famine loose upon it and cut off from it both man and beast; **14** and even if these three men were in it, Noah, Daniel, and Job,* they could save only themselves by their virtue, says the Lord GOD. **15** If I were to cause wild beasts to prowl the land, depopulating it so that it became a waste, traversed by none because of the wild beasts, **16** and these three men were in it, as I live, says the Lord GOD, I swear they could save neither sons nor daughters; they alone would be saved, and the land would be a waste. **17** Or if I brought the sword upon this country, commanding the sword to pass through the land cutting off from it man and beast, **18** and these three men were in it, as I live, says the Lord GOD, they would be unable to save either sons or daughters; they alone would be saved. **19** Or if I were to send pestilence into this land, pouring out upon it my bloodthirsty fury, cutting off from it man and beast, **20** even if Noah, Daniel, and Job were in it, as I live, says the Lord GOD, I swear that they could save neither son nor daughter; they would save only themselves by their virtue.

**21** Thus says the Lord GOD: Even though I send Jerusalem my four cruel punishments, the sword, famine, wild beasts, and pestilence, to cut off from it man and beast, **22** still some survivors shall be left in it who will bring out sons and daughters; when they come out to you, you shall see their conduct and their actions and be consoled regarding the evil I have brought on Jerusalem [all that I have brought upon it]. **23** They shall console you when you see their conduct and actions, for you shall then know that it was not without reason that I did to it what I did, says the Lord GOD.

## CHAPTER 15

**Parable of the Vine.** **1** Thus the word of the LORD came to me: **2** Son of man, what makes the wood of the vine better than any other wood? That branch among the trees of the forest! **3** Can you use its wood to make anything worthwhile? Can you make even a peg from it, to hand on it any kind of vessel? **4** If you throw it on the fire as fuel and the fire devours both ends and even the middle is scorched, is it still good for anything? **5** Why, even when it was whole it was good for nothing; how much less, when the fire has devoured and scorched it, can it be used for anything! **6** Therefore, thus says the Lord GOD: Like the wood of the vine among the trees of the forest, which I have destined as fuel for the fire, do I make the inhabitants of Jerusalem. **7** I will set my face against them; they have escaped from the fire, but the fire shall devour them. Thus you shall know that I am the LORD, when I turn my face against them. **8** I will make the land a waste, because they have broken faith, says the Lord God.

## CHAPTER 16

**The Faithless Spouse.** **1** Thus the word of the LORD came to me: **2** Son of man, make known to Jerusalem her abominations. **3** Thus says the Lord GOD to Jerusalem: By origin and birth you are of the land of Canaan; your father was an Amorite and your mother a Hittite.* **4** As for your birth, the day you were born your navel cord was not cut; you were neither washed with water nor anointed, nor were you rubbed with salt, nor swathed in swaddling clothes. **5** No one looked on you with pity or compassion to do any of these things for you. Rather, you were thrown out on the ground as something loathsome, the day you were born.

**6** Then I passed by and saw you weltering in your blood. I said to you: Live in your blood **7** and grow like a plant in the field. You grew and developed, you came to the age of puberty; your breasts were formed, your hair had grown, but you were still stark naked. **8** Again I passed by you and saw that you were now old enough

---

x 1 Kgs 22, 23. y Ez 4, 16.

*

14, 9: I, the Lord, shall have beguiled that prophet: the ancient Israelites attributed to God every action, good or evil; cf 1 Sm 18, 10; 2 Sm 24, 1ff. We would say, rather, that God permitted this deceit.

14, 12–23: The doctrine of personal responsibility before God was not new (cf Ez 3, 16–21; 18; 33, 1–20); but it had not been emphasized by the prophets before the Exile, who mostly predicted national retribution and called for national repentance.

14, 14: Noah, Daniel, and Job: proverbially virtuous men. The Daniel named here may be the traditional just judge of the ancient past, celebrated in Canaanite literature, who is possibly reflected in Dn 13, but is not the hero of Dn 1–12.

16, 3f: By origin and birth . . . Canaan . . . Amorite . . . Hittite: the inhabitants of Jerusalem and Judah absorbed not only pre-Israelite racial strains, but also many elements of the country's pagan cult and customs.

16, 8: I spread the corner of my cloak over you to cover your nakedness: and also to signify the intention of marriage; cf Ru 3, 9.

for love. So I spread the corner of my cloak over
you to cover your nakedness;* I swore an oath
to you and entered into a covenant with you; you
became mine, says the Lord GOD. **9** Then I
bathed you with water, washed away your
blood, and anointed you with oil. **10** I clothed
you with an embroidered gown, put sandals of
fine leather on your feet; I gave you a fine linen
sash and silk robes to wear. **11** I adorned you
with jewelry: I put bracelets on your arms, a
necklace about your neck, **12** a ring in your
nose, pendants in your ears, and a glorious diadem upon your head. **13** Thus you were
adorned with gold and silver; your garments
were of fine linen, silk, and embroidered cloth.
Fine flour, honey, and oil were your food. You
were exceedingly beautiful, with the dignity of
a queen. **14** You were renowned among the
nations for your beauty, perfect as it was, because of my splendor which I had bestowed on
you, says the Lord God.

**15** But you were captivated by your own
beauty, you used your renown to make yourself
a harlot, and you lavished your harlotry on every passer-by, whose own you became.
**16** *You took some of your gowns and made
for yourself gaudy high places, where you
played the harlot. . . . **17** You took the splendid
gold and silver ornaments that I had given you
and made for yourself male images, with which
also you played the harlot. **18** You took your
embroidered gowns to cover them; my oil and
my incense you set before them; **19** the food
that I had given you, the fine flour, the oil, and
the honey with which I fed you, you set before
them as an appeasing odor, says the Lord GOD.
**20** [z]The sons and daughters you had borne me
you took and offered as sacrifices* to be devoured by them! Was it not enough that you had
become a harlot? **21** [a]You slaughtered and immolated my children to them, making them pass
through fire. **22** And through all your abominations and harlotries you remembered nothing of
when you were a girl, stark naked and weltering
in your blood.

**23** Then after all your evildoing—woe, woe
to you! says the Lord GOD— **24** you raised for
yourself a platform and a dais* in every public
place. **25** [b]At every street corner you built a
dais for yourself to use your beauty obscenely,
spreading your legs for every passer-by, playing
the harlot countless times. **26** You played the
harlot with the Egyptians, your lustful neighbors, so many times that I was provoked to
anger. **27** Therefore I stretched out my hand
against you, I diminished your allowance and
delivered you over to the will of your enemies,
the Philistines, who revolted at your lewd conduct. **28** You also played the harlot with the
Assyrians, because you were not satisfied; and
after playing the harlot with them, you were still
not satisfied. **29** Again and again you played
the harlot, now going to Chaldea, the land of the
traders; but despite this, you were still not satisfied.

**30** How wild your lust! says the Lord GOD,
that you did all these things, acting like a shameless prostitute, **31** building your platform at every street corner and erecting your dais in every
public place! Yet you were unlike a prostitute,
since you disdained payment. **32** The adulterous wife receives, instead of her husband, payment. **33** All harlots receive gifts. But you rather bestowed your gifts on all your lovers,
bribing them to come to you from all sides for
your harlotry. **34** Thus in your harlotry you
were different from all other women. No one
sought you out for prostitution. Since you gave
payment instead of receiving it, how different
you were!

**35** Therefore, harlot, hear the word of the
LORD! **36** Thus says the Lord GOD: Because
you poured out your lust and revealed your nakedness in your harlotry with your lovers and
abominable idols, and because you sacrificed
the life-blood of your children to them, **37** [c]I
will now gather together all your lovers whom
you tried to please, whether you loved them or
loved them not; I will gather them against you
from all sides and expose you naked for them to
see. **38** I will inflict on you the sentence of
adulteresses and murderesses; I will wreak fury
and jealousy upon you. **39** I will hand you over
to them to tear down your platform and demolish your dais; they shall strip you of your garments and take away your splendid ornaments,
leaving you stark naked. **40** They shall lead an
assembly against you to stone you and hack you
with their swords. **41** [d]They shall burn your
apartments with fire and inflict punishments on
you while many women look on. Thus I will put
an end to your harlotry, and you shall never
again give payment. **42** When I have wreaked
my fury upon you I will cease to be jealous of
you, I will be quiet and no longer vexed. **43** Because you did not remember what happened
when you were a girl, but enraged me with all
these things, therefore in return I am bringing

z Ez 20, 26. 31; 23, 37ff; Lv 18, 21; 20, 2; Dt 12, 31; 18, 10; 2 Kgs 21, 6; 23, 10; 24. 4; Jer 7, 31; 19, 5; 32, 34; Mi 6, 7.
a 2 Kgs 16, 3; 17, 17; 21, 6; 23, 10.
b Ez 23, 8; Is 57, 7; Jer 2, 20; 3, 2; 5, 7; 13, 27; Hos 2, 4; 4, 13.
c Ez 23, 10.
d 2 Kgs 25, 9.

*

16, 16: Fine robes were used to cover a couch for harlotry; cf Prv 7, 16f. In the allegory of this chapter the viewpoint often shifts from the figure (harlotry) to the reality (idolatry).

16, 20f: Human sacrifice was introduced under Judah's impious kings; cf 2 Kgs 16, 3; 17, 17; Jer 7, 31.

16, 24: A platform and a dais: associated with ritual prostitution, which the Israelites borrowed from Canaanite practice.

down your conduct upon your head, says the Lord GOD. For did you not add lewdness to the rest of your abominable deeds?

44 See, everyone who is fond of proverbs will say of you, 'Like mother, like daughter.'
45 Yes, you are the true daughter of the mother* who spurned her husband and children, and you are a true sister to those who spurned their husbands and children—your mother was a Hittite and your father an Amorite. 46 Your elder
sister was Samaria* with her daughters, living to the north of you; and your younger sister, living to the south of you, was Sodom with her daughters. 47 Yet not only in their ways did
you walk, and act as abominably as they did; in a very short time you became more corrupt in all your ways than they. 48 As I live, says the
Lord GOD, I swear that your sister Sodom, with her daughters, has not done as you and your daughters have done! 49 [e]And look at the guilt
of your sister Sodom: she and her daughters were proud, sated with food, complacent in their prosperity, and they gave no help to the poor and needy. 50 Rather, they became
haughty and committed abominable crimes in my presence; then, as you have seen, I removed them. 51 Samaria did not commit half your
sins! You have done more abominable things than they, and have even made your sisters appear just, with all the abominable deeds you have done. 52 You, then, bear your shame; you
are an argument in favor of your sisters! In view of your sinful deeds, more abominable than theirs, they appear just in comparison with you. Blush for shame, and bear the shame of having made your sisters appear just.

53 I will restore their fortunes, the fortune of
Sodom and her daughters and of Samaria and her daughters [and I will restore your fortune along with them], 54 that you may bear your
shame and be disgraced for all the comfort you brought them. 55 Yes, your sisters, Sodom and
her daughters, Samaria and her daughters, shall return to their former state [you and your daughters shall return to your former state]. 56 Was
not your sister Sodom kept in bad repute by you while you felt proud of yourself, 57 before your
wickedness became evident? Now you are like her, reproached by the Edomites and all your neighbors, despised on all sides by the Philistines. 58 The penalty of your lewdness and
your abominations—you must bear it all, says the LORD.

59 For thus speaks the Lord GOD: I will deal
with you according to what you have done, you who despised your oath, breaking a covenant.
60 Yet I will remember the covenant I made
with you when you were a girl, and I will set up an everlasting covenant with you. 61 Then you
shall remember your conduct and be ashamed when I take your sisters, those older and younger than you, and give them to you as daughters, even though I am not bound by my covenant with you. 62 For I will re-establish my covenant with you, that you may know that I am the LORD, 63 that you may remember and be cov-
ered with confusion, and that you may be utterly silenced for shame when I pardon you for all you have done, says the Lord GOD.

## CHAPTER 17

**The Eagles and the Vine.** 1 Thus the
word of the LORD came to me: 2 Son of man,
propose a riddle, and speak this proverb to the house of Israel: 3 Thus speaks the Lord GOD:

The great eagle, with great wings, with long
 pinions,
 with thick plumage, many-hued, came to
 Lebanon.
He took the crest of the cedar,
4 tearing off its topmost branch,
And brought it to a land of tradesmen, set it
 in a city of merchants.
5 Then he took some seed of the land,
 and planted it in a seedbed;
A shoot by plentiful waters,
 like a willow he placed it,
6 To sprout and grow up a vine,
 dense and low-lying,
Its branches turned toward him,
 its roots lying under him.
Thus it became a vine, produced branches
 and put forth shoots.
7 But there was another great eagle,
 great of wing, rich in plumage;
To him this vine bent its roots,
 sent out its branches,
That he might water it more freely
 than the bed where it was planted.
8 In a fertile field by plentiful waters it was
 planted,
 to grow branches, bear fruit,
 and become a majestic vine.

9 Say: Thus says the Lord GOD: Can it pros-
per? Will he not rather tear it out by the roots and strip off its fruit, so that all its green growth will wither when he pulls it up by the roots? [No need of a mighty arm or many people to do this.]
10 True, it is planted, but will it prosper? Will
it not rather wither, when touched by the east wind, in the bed where it grew?

11 *Thus the word of the LORD came to me:

e Gn 19, 24.

*

16, 45: True daughter of the mother: Jerusalem has followed in the footsteps of its heathen forebears; cf v 3.

16, 46: Your elder sister was Samaria: Samaria can be called an elder sister in view of the relatively greater importance of the northern kingdom, Israel, during most of Old Testament history. Also, the relatively insignificant Sodom of ancient history can be called your younger sister.

17, 11-21: These verses explain the foregoing allegory. In

**12** Son of man, say now to the rebellious house:
Do you not understand what this means? It is
this: The king of Babylon came to Jerusalem
and took away its king and princes with him to
Babylon. **13** Then he selected a man of the
royal line with whom he made a covenant, binding him under oath, while removing the nobles
of the land, **14** so that the kingdom would remain a modest one, without aspirations, and
would keep his covenant and obey him. **15** But
this man rebelled against him, sending envoys
to Egypt to obtain horses and a great army. Can
he prosper? Can he who does such things escape? Can he break a covenant and still go free?
**16** As I live, says the Lord GOD, in the home
of the king who set him up to rule, whose oath
he spurned, whose covenant with him he broke,
there in Babylon I swear he shall die! **17** When
ramps are cast up and siege towers are built for
the destruction of many lives, he shall not be
saved in the conflict by Pharaoh with a great
army and numerous troops. **18** He spurned his
oath, breaking his covenant. Though he gave
his hand in pledge, he did all these things. He
shall not escape!

**19** Therefore say: Thus says the Lord GOD:
As live, my oath which he spurned, my covenant which he broke, I swear to bring down
upon his head. **20** [f]I will spread my net over
him, and he shall be taken in my snare. I will
bring him to Babylon and enter into judgment
with him there over his breaking faith with me.
**21** All the crack troops among his forces shall
fall by the sword, and the survivors shall be
scattered in every direction. Thus you shall
know that I, the LORD, have spoken.

**22** *Therefore say: Thus says the Lord GOD:

I, too, will take from the crest of the cedar,
from its topmost branches tear off a tender
shoot,
And plant it on a high and lofty mountain;
**23** on the mountain heights of Israel I will
plant it.
It shall put forth branches and bear fruit,
and become a majestic cedar.
Birds of every kind shall dwell beneath it,
every winged thing in the shade of its
boughs.
**24** And all the trees of the field shall know
that I, the LORD,
Bring low the high tree,
lift high the lowly tree,
Wither up the green tree,
and make the withered tree bloom.

As I, the LORD, have spoken, so will I do.

## CHAPTER 18

**Personal Responsibility.** **1** Thus the
word of the LORD came to me: Son of man,
**2** what is the meaning of this proverb that you
recite in the land of Israel:

"Fathers have eaten green grapes,[g]
thus their children's teeth are on edge"?*

**3** As I live, says the Lord GOD: I swear that
there shall no longer be anyone among you who
will repeat this proverb in Israel. **4** For all lives
are mine; the life of the father is like the life of
the son, both are mine; only the one who sins
shall die.

**5** If a man is virtuous—if he does what is
right and just, **6** if he does not eat on the mountains,* nor raise his eyes to the idols of the
house of Israel; if he does not defile his neighbor's wife, nor have relations with a woman in
her menstrual period; **7** [h]if he oppresses no one,
gives back the pledge received for a debt, commits no robbery; if he gives food to the hungry
and clothes the naked; **8** if he does not lend at
interest nor exact usury; if he holds off from
evildoing, judges fairly between a man and his
opponent; **9** if he lives by my statutes and is
careful to observe my ordinances, that man is
virtuous—he shall surely live, says the Lord
GOD.

**10** But if he begets a son who is a thief, a
murderer, or who does any of these things
**11** (though the father does none of them), a son
who eats on the mountains, defiles the wife of
his neighbor, **12** oppresses the poor and needy,
commits robbery, does does not give back a
pledge, raises his eyes to idols, does abominable things, **13** lends at interest and exacts usury—this son certainly shall not live. Because he
practiced all these abominations, he shall surely
die; his death shall be his own fault.

**14** On the other hand, if a man begets a son
who, seeing all the sins his father commits, yet
fears and does not imitate him; **15** a son who
does not eat on the mountains, or raise his eyes
to the idols of the house of Israel, or defile his
neighbor's wife; **16** who does not oppress anyone, or exact a pledge, or commit robbery; who
gives his food to the hungry and clothes the
naked; **17** who holds off from evildoing, ac-

---

f Ez 12, 13; 32, 3.
g Jer 13, 29.
h Is 58, 7; Mt 25, 35.

---

*

597 B.C. Nebuchadnezzar removed King Jehoiachin and took him into exile; in his place he set Zedekiah, Jehoiachin's uncle, on the throne and received from him the oath of loyalty. But Zedekiah was beguiled into rebellion by Pharaoh Hophra of Egypt, and thereby merited punishment; cf 2 Kgs 24, 10—25, 7.

17, 22f: I, too, will take from the crest of the cedar . . . plant it: the Lord will restore Israel under a messianic King from the same Davidic dynasty.

18, 2: Fathers . . . on edge: a proverb by which the people claimed that they were being punished for their ancestors' sins rather than for their own; cf Jer 31, 29.

18, 6: Eat on the mountains: partake of ritual meals at the heathen high places.

cepts no interest or usury, but keeps my ordinances and lives by my statutes—this one shall
not die for the sins of his father, but shall surely
live. **18** Only the father, since he violated
rights, and robbed, and did what was not good
among his people, shall in truth die for his sins.
**19** You ask: "Why is not the son charged with
the guilt of his father?" Because the son has
done what is right and just, and has been careful
to observe all my statutes, he shall surely live.
**20** [i]Only the one who sins shall die. The son
shall not be charged with the guilt of his father,
nor shall the father be charged with the guilt of
his son. The virtuous man's virtue shall be his
own, as the wicked man's wickedness shall be
his own.
**21** But if the wicked man turns away from all
the sins he committed, if he keeps all my statutes and does what is right and just, he shall
surely live, he shall not die. **22** None of the
crimes he committed shall be remembered
against him; he shall live because of the virtue
he has practiced. **23** [j]Do I indeed derive any
pleasure from the death of the wicked? says the
Lord GOD. Do I not rather rejoice when he turns
from his evil way that he may live?
**24** And if the virtuous man turns from the
path of virtue to do evil, the same kind of abominable things that the wicked man does, can he
do this and still live? None of his virtuous deeds
shall be remembered, because he has broken
faith and committed sin; because of this, he
shall die. **25** [k]You say, "The LORD's way is not
fair!" Hear now, house of Israel: Is it my way
that is unfair, or rather, are not your ways unfair? **26** When a virtuous man turns away from
virtue to commit iniquity, and dies, it is because
of the iniquity he committed that he must die.
**27** But if a wicked man, turning from the wickedness he has committed, does what is right and
just, he shall preserve his life; **28** since he has
turned away from all the sins which he committed, he shall surely live, he shall not die.
**29** And yet the house of Israel says, "The
LORD's way is not fair!" Is it my way that is not
fair, house of Israel, or rather, is it not that your
ways are not fair?
**30** [l]Therefore I will judge you, house of Israel, each one according to his ways, says the
Lord GOD. Turn and be converted from all your
crimes, that they may be no cause of guilt for
you. **31** Cast away from you all the crimes you
have committed, and make for yourselves a new
heart and a new spirit. Why should you die, O
house of Israel? **32** [m]For I have no pleasure in
the death of anyone who dies, says the Lord
GOD. Return and live!

## CHAPTER 19

**1** As for you, son of man, raise a lamentation
over the prince of Israel:

### Allegory of the Lions*

**2** What a lioness was your mother,
a lion of lions!
Among young lions she couched
to rear her whelps.
**3** One whelp she raised up,
a young lion he became;
He learned to seize prey,
men he devoured.
**4** Then nations raised cries against him,
in their pit he was caught;
They took him away with hooks
to the land of Egypt.
**5** Then she saw that in vain she had waited,
her hope was destroyed.
She took another of her whelps,
him she made a young lion.
**6** He prowled among the lions,
a young lion he became;
He learned to seize prey,
men he devoured;
**7** He ravaged their strongholds,
their cities he wasted.
The land and all in it were appalled
at the noise of his roar.
**8** Nations laid out against him
snares all about him;
They spread their net to take him,
in their pit he was caught.
**9** They put him in a cage and took him away
to the king of Babylon,
So that his voice would not be heard
on the mountains of Israel.

### Allegory of the Vine Branch

**10** Your mother was like a vine*
planted by the water;
Fruitful and branchy was she
because of the abundant water.
**11** One strong branch she put out
as a royal scepter.
Stately was her height
amid the dense foliage;
Notably tall was she
with her many clusters.
**12** But she was torn up in fury
and flung to the ground;
The east wind withered her up,
her fruit was torn off;
Then her strong branch withered up,
fire devoured it.[n]
**13** So now she is planted in the desert,
in a land dry and parched,

i Dt 24, 16; 2 Kgs 14, 6; 2 Chr 25, 4.
j Ez 33, 11; 2 Pt 3, 9.
k Ez 33, 20.
l Mt 3, 2; Lk 3, 3.
m Ez 18, 23; 33, 11; 2 Pt 3, 9.
n Hos 13, 15.

*

19, 2–9: The meaning of this allegory is uncertain. Probably the two young lions are Jehoahaz and Zedekiah, sons of the same mother, who were deported to Egypt and Babylonia respectively. Cf 2 Kgs 23, 31–34; 24, 18ff.

19, 10–14: A vine: Judah. One strong branch: the Davidic king.

**14** For fire came out of the branch
and devoured her shoots;
She is now without a strong branch,
a ruler's scepter.

This is a lamentation and serves as a lamentation.

## CHAPTER 20

**Israel's History of Infidelity.** **1** In the seventh year, on the tenth day of the fifth month,*
some of the elders of Israel came to consult the
LORD and sat down before me. **2** Then the word
of the LORD came to me: **3** Son of man, speak
with the elders of Israel and say to them: Thus
says the Lord GOD: Have you come to consult
me? As I live! I swear I will not allow myself
to be consulted by you, says the Lord GOD.
**4** Will you judge them? Will you judge, son
of man? Make known to them the abominations
of their ancestors **5** in these words: Thus speaks
the Lord GOD: The day I chose Israel, I swore
to the decendants of the house of Jacob; in the
land of Egypt I revealed myself to them and
swore: I am the LORD, your God. **6** That day I
swore to bring them out of the land of Egypt to
the land I had scouted for them, a land flowing
with milk and honey, a jewel among all lands.
**7** Then I said to them: Throw away, each of
you, the detestable things that have held your
eyes; do not defile yourselves with the idols of
Egypt: I am the LORD, your God.
**8** But they rebelled against me and refused to
listen to me; none of them threw away the detestable things that had held their eyes, they did
not abandon the idols of Egypt. Then I thought
of pouring out my fury on them and spending
my anger on them there in the land of Egypt;
**9** but I acted for my name's sake, that it should
not be profaned in the sight of the nations among
whom they were, in whose presence I had made
myself known to them, revealing that I would
bring them out of the land of Egypt. **10** Therefore I led them out of the land of Egypt and
brought them into the desert. **11** [o]Then I gave
them my statutes and made known to them my
ordinances, which everyone must keep, to have
life through them. **12** [p]I also gave them my
sabbaths to be a sign between me and them, to
show that it was I, the LORD, who made them
holy.
**13** But the house of Israel rebelled against
me in the desert. They did not observe my statutes, and they despised my ordinances that
bring life to those who keep them. My sabbaths,
too, they desecrated grievously. Then I thought
of pouring out my fury on them in the desert to
put an end to them, **14** but I acted for my
name's sake, that it should not be profaned in
the sight of the nations in whose presence I had
brought them out. **15** Nevertheless I swore to
them in the desert not to bring them to the land
I had given them, a land flowing with milk and
honey, a jewel among all lands. **16** So much
were their hearts devoted to their idols, they had
not lived by my statutes, but despised my ordinances and desecrated my sabbaths. **17** But I
looked on them with pity, not wanting to destroy them, so I did not put an end to them in
the desert.
**18** Then I said to their children in the desert:
Do not observe the statutes of your parents or
keep their ordinances; do not defile yourselves
with their idols. **19** I am the LORD, your God:
observe my statutes and be careful to keep my
ordinances; **20** keep holy my sabbaths, as a sign
between me and you to show that I am the
LORD, your God. **21** But their children rebelled
against me: they did not observe my statutes or
keep my ordinances that bring life to those who
observe them, and my sabbaths they desecrated.
Then I thought of pouring out my fury on them,
of spending my anger on them in the desert;
**22** but I stayed my hand, acting for my name's
sake, lest it be profaned in the sight of the
nations in whose presence I brought them out.
**23** Nevertheless I swore to them in the desert
that I would disperse them among the nations
and scatter them over foreign lands; **24** for they
did not keep my ordinances, but despised my
statutes and desecrated my sabbaths with eyes
only for the idols of their fathers. **25** Therefore
I gave them statutes that were not good,* and
ordinances through which they could not live.
**26** I let them become defiled by their gifts, by
their immolation of every first-born, so as to
make them an object of horror.
**27** Therefore speak to the house of Israel,
son of man, and tell them: Thus says the Lord
GOD: In this way also your fathers blasphemed
me, breaking faith with me: **28** when I had
brought them to the land I had sworn to give
them, and they saw all its high hills and leafy
trees, there they offered their sacrifices [there
they brought their offensive offerings], there
they sent up appeasing odors, and there they
poured out their libations. **29** I asked them: To
what sort of high place do you betake yourselves?—and so they call it a high place even to
the present day. **30** Therefore say to the house
of Israel: Thus says the Lord GOD: Will you
defile yourselves like your fathers? Will you
lust after their detestable idols? **31** By offering

o Lv 18, 5; Rom 10, 5.
p Ex 20, 8; 31, 13; Dt 5, 12.

*

20, 1: The seventh year, on the tenth day of the fifth month: August 14, 591 B.C.

20, 25f: I gave them statutes that were not good: the Lord permitted them to adopt pagan practices, including the abominable sacrifice of their newborn infants, which could only merit their destruction. See note on Ez 14, 9.

your gifts, by making your children pass
through the fire, you defile yourselves with all
your idols even to this day. Shall I let myself be
consulted by you, house of Israel? As I live!
says the Lord GOD: I swear I will not let myself
be consulted by you.

**32** What you are thinking of shall never happen: "We shall be like the nations, like the
peoples of foreign lands, serving wood and
stone." **33** As I live, says the Lord GOD, with
a mighty hand and outstretched arm, with
poured-out wrath, I swear I will be king over
you! **34** With a mighty hand and outstretched
arm, with poured-out wrath, I will bring you out
from the nations and gather you from the countries over which you are scattered; **35** *then I
will lead you to the desert of the peoples, where
I will enter into judgment with you face to face.
**36** Just as I entered into judgment with your
fathers in the desert of the land of Egypt, so will
I enter into judgment with you, says the Lord
GOD. **37** I will count you with the staff and
bring back but a small number. **38** I will separate from you those who have rebelled and
transgressed against me; from the land where
they sojourned as aliens I will bring them out,
but they shall not return to the land of Israel.
Thus you shall know that I am the LORD.

**39** As for you, house of Israel, thus says the
Lord GOD: Come, each one of you, destroy you
idols! Then listen to me, and never again profane my holy name with your gifts and your
idols. **40** For on my holy mountain, on the
mountain height of Israel, says the Lord GOD,
there the whole house of Israel without exception shall worship me; there I will accept them,
and there I will claim your tributes and the first
fruits of your offerings, and all that you dedicate. **41** As a pleasing odor I will accept you,
when I have brought you from among the nations and gathered you out of the countries over
which you were scattered; and by means of you
I will manifest my holiness in the sight of the
nations. **42** Thus you shall know that I am the
LORD, when I bring you back to the land of
Israel, the land which I swore to give to your
fathers. **43** There you shall recall your conduct
and all the deeds by which you defiled yourselves; and you shall loathe yourselves because
of all the evil things you did. **44** And you shall
know that I am the LORD when I deal with you
thus, for my name's sake, and not according to
your evil conduct and corrupt actions, O house
of Israel, says the Lord GOD.

## CHAPTER 21

**The Sword of the Lord.** **1** Thus the word
of the LORD came to me: **2** *Son of man, look
southward, preach toward the south, and prophesy against the forest of the southern land.
**3** Hear the word of the LORD! you shall say to
the southern forest. Thus says the Lord GOD:
See! I am kindling a fire in you that shall devour
all trees, the green as well as the dry. The blazing flame shall not be quenched, but from south
to north every face shall be scorched by it.
**4** Everyone shall see that I, the LORD, have
kindled it, and it shall not be quenched.

**5** But I said, "Alas! Lord GOD, they say to
me, 'Is not this the one who is forever spinning
parables?' " **6** Then the word of the LORD came
to me: **7** Son of man, look toward Jerusalem,
preach against their sanctuary, and prophesy
against the land of Israel, **8** saying to the land
of Israel: Thus says the LORD: See! I am coming
at you; I will draw my sword from its sheath and
cut off from you the virtuous and the wicked.*
**9** Thus my sword shall leave its sheath against
everyone from south to north, **10** and everyone
shall know that I, the LORD, have drawn my
sword from its sheath, and it shall not be
sheathed again.

**Act Symbolic of the City's Fall.** **11** As
for you, son of man, groan! with shattered
strength groan bitterly while they look on.
**12** And when they ask you, "Why are you
groaning?" you shall say: Because of a report;*
when it comes every heart shall fail, every hand
shall fall helpless, every spirit shall be daunted,
and every knee shall run with water. See, it is
coming, it is here! says the Lord GOD.

**Song of the Sword.** **13** Thus the word of
the LORD came to me: **14** Son of man, prophesy! say: Thus says the LORD:

A sword, a sword has been sharpened,
a sword, a sword has been burnished:
**15** To work slaughter has it been sharpened,
to flash lightning has it been burnished.
Why should I now withdraw it?
You have spurned the rod and every
judgment!
**16** I have given it over to the burnisher
that he might hold it in his hand,
A sword sharpened and burnished
to be put in the hand of a slayer.
**17** Cry out and wail, son of man,
for it is destined for my people;
It is for all the princes of Israel,

*

20, 35–38: Exile in the pagan lands will serve the same purpose as the desert journey after the Exodus from Egypt: the rebellious will be eliminated, and only a remnant will survive.

21, 2ff: The southern kingdom, Judah, is likened to a forest about to be burned; cf Jer 21, 14.

21, 8: Cut off from you the virtuous and the wicked: a more complete devastation of Jerusalem than that described in Ez 9, 6.

21, 12: A report: the news of the fall of Jerusalem; cf Ez 33, 21f.

21, 17: Slap your thigh: a gesture signifying grief and dread.

victims of the sword with my people.

Therefore, slap your thigh,* **18** for the sword
has been tested; and why should it not be so?
says the Lord GOD, since you have spurned the
rod.

**19** As for you, son of man, prophesy,
brushing one hand against the other:
While the sword is doubled and tripled,
this sword of slaughter,
This great sword of slaughter
which threatens all around,
**20** That every heart may tremble;
for many will be the fallen.
At all their gates
I have appointed the sword for slaughter,
Fashioned to flash lightning,
burnished for slaughter.
**21** Cleave to the right! destroy!
to the left! wherever your edge is turned.

**22** Then I, too, shall brush one hand against the
other* and wreak my fury. I, the LORD, have
spoken.

## Nebuchadnezzar at the Crossroads.

**23** Thus the word of the LORD came to me:
**24** Son of man, make for yourself two roads
over which the sword of the king of Babylon can
come. Both roads shall lead out from the same
land. Then put a signpost at the head of each
road, **25** so that the sword can come to Rabbah
of the Ammonites or to Judah's capital, Jerusalem. **26** For at the fork where the two roads
divide stands the king of Babylon, divining;* he
has shaken the arrows, inquired of the teraphim,
inspected the liver. **27** In his right hand is the
divining arrow marked "Jerusalem,"* bidding
him to give the order for slaying, to raise his
voice in the battle cry, to post battering rams at
the gates, to cast up a ramp, to build a siege
tower. **28** In their eyes this is but a lying oracle;
yet they are bound by the oaths they have sworn,
and the arrow taken in hand marks their guilt.
**29** Therefore thus says the Lord GOD: Because you have drawn attention to your guilt,
with your crimes laid bare and your sinfulness
in all your wicked deeds revealed (because attention has been drawn to you), you shall be
taken in hand. **30** And as for you, depraved and
wicked prince of Israel, whose day is coming
when your life of crime will be ended, **31** thus
says the Lord GOD: Off with the turban and
away with the crown! Nothing shall be as it was!
Up with the low and down with the high!
**32** Twisted, twisted, twisted will I leave it; it
shall not be the same until he comes who has the
claim against the city; and to him I will hand it
over.

## Against the Ammonites*

**33** As for you,
son of man, prophesy: Thus says the Lord GOD
against the Ammonities and their insults: A
sword, a sword is drawn for slaughter, burnished to consume and to flash lightning,
**34** because you planned with false visions and
lying divinations to lay it on the necks of depraved and wicked men whose day has come
when their crimes are at an end. **35** Return it to
its sheath! In the place where you were created,
in the land of your origin, I will judge you. **36** I
will pour out my indignation upon you, breathing my fiery wrath upon you; I will hand you
over to ravaging men, artisans of destruction.
**37** You shall be fuel for the fire, your blood
shall flow throughout the land. You shall not be
remembered, for I, the LORD, have spoken.

# CHAPTER 22

## Crimes of Jerusalem.

**1** Thus the word of
the LORD came to me: **2** You, son of man,
would you judge, would you judge the bloody
city? Then make known all her abominations,
**3** and say: Thus says the Lord GOD: Woe to the
city which sheds blood within herself so that her
time has come, and which has made idols for her
own defilement. **4** By the blood which you shed
you have been made guilty, and with the idols
you made you have become defiled; you have
brought on your day, so that the end of your
years has come. Therefore I make you an object
of scorn to the nations and a laughingstock to all
foreign lands. **5** Those near you and those far
off shall deride you because of your foul reputation and your great perversity. **6** See! the
princes of Israel, family by family, are in you
only for bloodshed. **7** Within you, father and
mother are despised; in your midst, they extort
from the resident alien; within you, they oppress
orphans and widows. **8** What is holy to me you
have spurned, and my sabbaths you have desecrated. **9** There are those in you who slander to
cause bloodshed; within you are those who feast
on the mountains; in your midst are those who
do lewd things. **10** In you are those who uncover the nakedness of their fathers, and in you
those who coerce women in their menstrual pe-

*

21, 22: Brush one hand against the other: a gesture signifying the rejection of responsibility; cf Ez 22, 13; Nm 24, 10.

21, 26: Three forms of divination are mentioned: arrow divination, consisting in the use of differently marked arrows extracted or shaken from a case at random; the consultation of the teraphim or household idols; and liver divination, scrutiny of the configurations of the livers of newly slaughtered animals, a common form of divination in Mesopotamia.

21, 27f: An arrow marked "Jerusalem" is picked out, which marks the guilt of the city's inhabitants for having broken their oath of allegiance to Nebuchadnezzar.

21, 33–37: In the preceding section Nebuchadnezzar is represented as deciding whether to attack Jerusalem or Rabath-Ammon. As it happened, Jerusalem was chosen for attack; later, however, the Chaldeans also invaded Ammon. The present oracle against Ammon is inserted here, rather than in chapters 25–32, in order to complement the oracle against Jerusalem.

riod. 11 [q]There are those in you who do abominable things with the wives of their neighbors,
men who defile their daughters-in-law by incest, men who coerce their sisters, the daughters
of their own fathers. 12 There are those in you
who take bribes to shed blood. You exact interest and usury; you despoil your neighbors violently; and me you have forgotten, says the Lord
GOD.

13 See, I am brushing one hand against the
other because of the unjust profits you have
made and because of the blood shed in your
midst. 14 Can your heart remain firm, will your
hands be strong, in the days when I deal with
you? I, the LORD, have spoken, and I will act.
15 I will disperse you among the nations and
scatter you over foreign lands, so that I may
purge your uncleanness. 16 In you I will allow
myself to be profaned in the eyes of the nations;
thus you shall know that I am the LORD.

17 Thus the word of the LORD came to me:
18 Son of man, the house of Israel has become
dross for me. All of them are bronze and tin,
iron and lead [in the midst of a furnace]: dross
from silver have they become. 19 Therefore
thus says the Lord GOD: Because all of you have
become dross, therefore I must gather you together within Jerusalem. 20 Just as silver,
bronze, iron, lead, and tin are gathered into a
furnace and smelted in the roaring flames, so I
will gather you together in my furious wrath,
put you in, and smelt you. 21 When I have
assembled you, I will blast you with the fire of
my anger and smelt you with it. 22 You shall
be smelted by it just as silver is smelted in a
furnace. Thus you shall know that I, the Lord,
have poured out my fury on you.

23 Thus the word of the LORD came to me:
24 Son of man, say to her: You are a land
unrained on [that is, not rained on] at the time
of my fury. 25 Her princes are like roaring lions
that tear prey; they devour people, seizing their
wealth and precious things, and make widows
of many within her. 26 Her priests violate my
law and profane what is holy to me; they do not
distinguish between the sacred and the profane,
nor teach the difference between the unclean
and the clean; they pay no attention to my sabbaths, so that I have been profaned in their
midst. 27 [r]Her nobles within her are like
wolves that tear prey, shedding blood and destroying lives to get unjust gain. 28 Her prophets cover them with whitewash, pretending to
visions that are false and performing lying divinations, saying, "Thus says the Lord GOD,"
although the LORD has not spoken. 29 The people of the land practice extortion and commit
robbery; they afflict the poor and the needy, and
oppress the resident alien without justice.
30 Thus I have searched among them for someone who could build a wall or stand in the
breach before me to keep me from destroying
the land; but I found no one. 31 Therefore I
have poured out my fury upon them; with my
fiery wrath I have consumed them; I have
brought down their conduct upon their heads,
says the Lord GOD.

## CHAPTER 23

**The Two Sisters.** 1 Thus the word of the
LORD came to me: 2 Son of man, there were
two women, daughters of the same mother,
3 who even as young girls played the harlot in
Egypt. There the Egyptians caressed their bo-
soms and fondled their virginal breasts. 4 Oholah was the name of the elder, and the name of
her sister was Oholibah.* They became mine
and bore sons and daughters. [As for their
names: Samaria is Oholah, and Jerusalem is
Oholibah.] 5 Oholah became a harlot faithless
to me; she lusted after her lovers, the Assyrians,
warriors 6 dressed in purple, governors and officers, all of them attractive young men, knights
mounted on horses. 7 Thus she gave herself as
a harlot to them, to all the elite of the Assyrians,
and she defiled herself with all those for whom
she lusted [with all their idols]. 8 She did not
give up the harlotry which she had begun in
Egypt, when they had lain with her as a young
girl, fondling her virginal breasts and pouring
out their impurities on her. 9 Therefore I handed her over to her lovers, the Assyrians for
whom she had lusted. 10 [s]They exposed her
nakedness, her sons and daughters they took
away, and herself they slew with the sword.
Thus she became a byword for women, for they
punished her grievously.

11 Though her sister Oholibah saw all this,
her lust was more depraved than her sister's,
and she outdid her in harlotry. 12 She too lusted
after the Assyrians, governors and officers,
warriers impeccably clothed, knights mounted
on horses, all of them attractive young men.
13 I saw that she had defiled herself. Both had
gone down the same path, 14 yet she went further in her harlotry. When she saw men drawn
on the wall, the images of Chaldeans drawn
with vermillion, 15 with sashes girded about
their waists, flowing turbans on their heads, all
looking like chariot warriors, the portraits of
Babylonians, natives of Chaldea, 16 she lusted
for them; no sooner had she set eyes on them

q Jer 5, 7f. s Ez 16, 37.
r Mi 3, 11; Zep 3, 3.

* 23, 4: Oholah . . . Oholibah: symbolic names. The first, standing for Samaria, may be read to mean "her own tent"; the latter, standing for Jerusalem, means "My tent is in her." The references seem to be to the schismatic temple and cult of the Lord in Samaria, as opposed to their authentic counterpart in Jerusalem.

than she sent messengers to them in Chaldea.
**17** Then the Babylonians came to her, to the
love couch, and defiled her with their intercourse. As soon as she was defiled by them, she
became disgusted with them. **18** Her harlotry
was discovered and her shame was revealed,
and I became disgusted with her as I had become
disgusted with her sister. **19** But she played the
harlot all the more, recalling the days of her
girlhood, when she had been a harlot in the land
of Egypt. **20** She lusted for the lechers of
Egypt, whose members are like that of an ass,
and whose heat is like those of stallions.

**21** You yearned for the lewdness of your
girlhood, when the Egyptians fondled your
breasts, caressing your bosom. **22** Therefore,
Oholibah, thus says the Lord GOD: I will now
stir up your lovers against you, those with
whom you are disgusted, and I will bring them
against you from every side: **23** the men of
Babylon and all of Chaldea, Pekod, Shoa and
Koa,* along with all those of Assyria, attractive
young men, all of them governors and officers,
charioteers and warriors, all of them horsemen.
**24** They shall come against you from the north
with chariots and wagons and many peoples.
Shields, bucklers, and helmets they shall array
against you everywhere. **25** I will leave it to
them to judge, and they will judge you by their
own ordinances. I will let loose my jealousy
against you, so that they shall deal with you in
fury, cutting off your nose and ears; and what
is left of you shall fall by the sword. They shall
take away your sons and daughters, and what is
left of you shall be devoured by fire. **26** They
shall strip off your clothes and seize your splendid ornaments. **27** I will put an end to your
lewdness and to the harlotry you began in
Egypt; you shall no longer look toward it, nor
shall you remember Egypt again.

**28** For thus says the Lord GOD: I am now
handing you over to those whom you hate, to
those who fill you with disgust. **29** They shall
deal with you in hatred, seizing all that you have
worked for and leaving you stark naked, so that
your indecent nakedness is exposed. Your lewdness and harlotry **30** have brought these things
upon you, because you played the harlot with
the nations by defiling yourself with their idols.

**31** Because you followed in the path of your
sister, I will hand you her cup. **32** Thus says the
Lord GOD:

The cup of your sister you shall drink,
so wide and deep, which holds so much,
**33** Filled with destruction and grief,
a cup of dismay, the cup of your sister.

**34** You shall drain it dry, and gnaw at the very
sherds of the cup, and you shall tear out your
breasts; for I have spoken, says the Lord GOD.
**35** Therefore thus says the Lord GOD: Because
you have forgotten me and cast me behind your
back, it is for you to bear the penalty of your
lewdness and harlotry.

**36** Then the LORD said to me: Son of man,
would you judge Oholah and Oholibah? Then
make known to them their abominations.
**37** For they committed adultery, and blood is
on their hands. They committed adultery with
their idols; to feed them they immolated the
children they had borne me. **38** [This, too, they
did to me: they defiled my sanctuary and desecrated my sabbaths. **39** On the very day they
slew their children for their idols, they entered
my sanctuary to desecrate it. Thus they acted
within my house.] **40** Moreover, they sent for
men who had to come from afar,* to whom
messengers were sent. And so they came—and
for them you bathed yourself, painted your
eyes, and put on ornaments. **41** You sat on a
couch prepared for them, with a table spread
before it, on which you had set my incense and
oil. **42** Then was heard the shout of a carefree
mob in the city, and these were men brought in
from the desert, who put bracelets on the wom-
en's arms and splendid diadems on their heads.
**43** So I said: "Oh, this woman jaded with adulteries! Now they will commit whoredom with
her, and as for her. . . ." **44** And indeed they
did come to her as men come to a harlot. Thus
they came to Oholah and Oholibah, the lewd
women. **45** But just men shall punish them with
the sentence meted out to adulteresses and murderesses, for they have committed adultery, and
blood is on their hands.

**46** Thus says the Lord GOD: Summon an assembly against them, and deliver them over to
terror and plunder. **47** The assembly shall stone
them and hack them to pieces with their swords.
They shall slay their sons and daughters, and
burn their houses with fire. **48** Thus I will put
an end to lewdness in the land, and all the
women will be warned not to imitate your lewdness. **49** They shall inflict on you the penalty of
your lewdness, and you shall pay for your sins
of idolatry. Thus you shall know that I am the
LORD.

## CHAPTER 24

**Allegory of the Pot.** **1** On the tenth day of
the tenth month, in the ninth year,* the word of
the LORD came to me: **2** Son of man, write
down this date today, for this very day the king

23, 23: Pekod, Shoa and Koa: peoples living about the Tigris, part of "greater Babylonia."

23, 40: Men who had to come from afar: ambassadors from Assyria and Babylon. Alliances with these countries aided in the corruption of both Israel and Judah.

24, 1: The tenth day of the tenth month, in the ninth year: January 15, 588 B.C. The same date is given in Jer 52, 4.

of Babylon has invested Jerusalem. **3** Propose
this parable to the rebellious house: Thus says
the Lord GOD:

*Set up the pot, set it up,
then pour in some water.
**4** Put in it pieces of meat,
all good pieces: thigh and shoulder;
Fill it with the choicest joints
**5** taken from the pick of the flock.
Then pile the wood beneath it;
bring to a boil these pieces
and the joints that are in it.
**6** Take out its pieces, one by one,
without casting lots for it.

Therefore, thus says the Lord GOD: Woe to the
bloody city,[t] a pot containing rust, whose rust
has not been removed. **7** For the blood she shed
is in her midst; she poured it on the bare rock;
she did not pour it out on the earth, to be covered
with dust.* **8** To work up my wrath, to excite
my vengeance, she put her blood on the bare
rock, not to be covered. **9** Therefore, thus says
the Lord GOD:

I, too, will heap up a great bonfire,
**10** piling on wood and kindling the fire,
Till the meat has been cooked,
till the broth has boiled.

**11** Then I will set the pot empty on the coals till
its metal glows red hot, till the impurities in it
melt, and its rust disappears. **12** Yet not even
with fire will its great rust be removed. **13** Because you have sullied yourself with lewdness
when I would have purified you, and you refused to be purified of your uncleanness, therefore you shall not be purified until I wreak my
fury on you. **14** I, the LORD, have spoken; it is
coming, for I will bring it about without fail. I
will not have pity nor repent. By your conduct
and your deeds you shall be judged, says the
Lord GOD.

**Symbol of the Destruction of the Tem-
ple.** **15** Thus the word of the LORD came to
me: **16** Son of man, by a sudden blow I am
taking away from you the delight of your eyes,
but do not mourn or weep or shed any tears.
**17** Groan in silence, make no lament for the
dead, bind on your turban, put your sandals on
your feet, do not cover your beard, and do not
eat the customary bread.* **18** That evening my
wife died, and the next morning I did as I had
been commanded. **19** Then the people asked
me, "Will you not tell us what all these things
that you are doing mean for us?" I therefore
spoke to the people that morning, **20** saying to
them: Thus the word of the LORD came to me:
**21** Say to the house of Israel: Thus says the
Lord GOD: I will now desecrate my sanctuary,
the stronghold of your pride, the delight of your
eyes, the desire of your soul. The sons and
daughters you left behind shall fall by the
sword. **24** Ezekiel shall be a sign for you: all
that he did you shall do when it happens. Thus
you shall know that I am the LORD. **22** *You
shall do as I have done, not covering your
beards nor eating the customary bread. **23** Your
turbans shall remain on your heads, your sandals on your feet. You shall not mourn or weep,
but you shall rot away because of your sins and
groan one to another.

**End of Ezekiel's Dumbness.** **25** [u]As for
you, son of man, truly, on the day I take away
from them their bulwark, their glorious joy, the
delight of their eyes, the desire of their soul, and
the pride of their hearts, their sons and daughters, **26** that day the fugitive will come to you,
that you may hear it for yourself; **27** that day
your mouth shall be opened and you shall be
dumb no longer. Thus you shall be a sign to
them, and they shall know that I am the LORD.

## III: *Prophecies Against Foreign Nations*

## CHAPTER 25

**Against Ammon.** **1** Thus the word of the
LORD came to me: **2** Son of man, turn toward
the Ammonites and prophesy against them.
**3** [v]Say to the Ammonites: Hear the word of the
LORD! Thus says the Lord GOD: Because you
cried out your joy over the desecration of my
sanctuary, the devastation of the land of Israel,
and the exile of the house of Judah, **4** therefore
I will deliver you into the possession of the
Easterners.* They shall set up their encampments among you and pitch their tents; they
shall eat your fruits and drink your milk. **5** I
will make Rabbah a pasture for camels, and the
villages of the Ammonites a resting place for
flocks. Thus you shall know that I am the LORD.
**6** For thus says the Lord GOD: Because you
clapped your hands and stamped your feet, rejoicing most maliciously in your heart over the

t Na 3, 1; Hb 2, 12.
u 25ff: Ez 3, 22-27.
v Jer 40, 14; 41, 10: 49, 2; Am 1, 13ff: Zep 2, 8ff.

*

24, 3ff: This present comparison of the inhabitants of Jerusalem to meat boiled in a pot symbolizes their punishment rather than their supposed protection as in Ez 11, 3.

24, 7: Blood . . . to be covered with dust: since blood was sacred to God, it had to be covered with earth (Lv 17, 13); the blood of a murdered man that was left uncovered cried to heaven for vengeance; cf Jb 16, 18; Gn 4, 10.

24, 17: The customary bread: eaten as a mourning observance; cf Jer 16, 7. The other gestures here forbidden were also popular mourning customs.

24, 22f: The fall of the city will be so sudden and final that the exiles will have no time to go into mourning.

25, 4: The Easterners: nomadic tribes to the east of Ammon and Moab.

land of Israel, **7** therefore I will stretch out my
hand against you. I will make you plunder for
the nations, I will cut you off from the peoples,
and remove you from the lands. I will destroy
you, and thus you shall know that I am the
LORD.

**Against Moab.** **8** [w]Thus says the Lord
GOD: Because Moab said, "See! the house of
Judah is like all other nations," **9** therefore I
will clear the shoulder of Moab* totally of its
cities, the jewels of the land: Beth-jesimoth,
Baalmeon, and Kiriathaim. **10** I will hand her
over, along with the Ammonites, into the possession of the Easterners, that she may not be
remembered among the peoples. **11** Thus I will
execute judgment upon Moab, that they may
know that I am the LORD.

**Against Edom.** **12** [x]Thus says the Lord
GOD: Because Edom has taken vengeance on
the house of Judah and has made itself grievously guilty by taking vengeance on them,
**13** therefore thus says the Lord GOD: I will
stretch out my hand against Edom and cut off
from it man and beast. I will make it a waste
from Teman to Dedan; they shall fall by the
sword. **14** My vengeance upon Edom I will
entrust to my people Israel, who will deal with
Edom in accordance with my anger and my
fury; thus they shall know my vengeance, says
the Lord GOD.

**Against the Philistines.** **15** Thus says the
Lord GOD: Because the Philistines have acted
revengefully, and have taken vengeance with
destructive malice in their hearts, with an undying enmity, **16** therefore thus says the Lord
GOD: See! I am stretching out my hand against
the Philistines; I will cut off the Cherethites*
and wipe out the remnant on the seacoast. **17** I
will execute great acts of vengeance on them,
punishing them furiously. Thus they shall know
that I am the LORD, when I wreak my vengeance
on them.

## CHAPTER 26

**Against the City of Tyre.** **1** On the first
day of the . . . month in the eleventh year, the
word of the LORD came to me: **2** Son of man,
because of what Tyre said of Jerusalem:

"Aha! it is broken, the gateway to the
peoples;
now that it is ruined, its wealth reverts to
me!"
**3** therefore thus says the Lord GOD:
See! I am coming at you, Tyre;
I will churn up against you many nations,
even as the sea churns up its waves;[y]
**4** They shall destroy the walls of Tyre
and raze her towers.
I will scrape the ground from her
and leave her a bare rock;*
**5** She shall be a drying place for nets
in the midst of the sea.

I have spoken, says the Lord GOD: and she shall
be booty for the nations. **6** And her daughters*
on the mainland shall be slaughtered by the
sword; thus they shall know that I am the LORD.
**7** For thus says the Lord GOD: I am now
bringing up against Tyre from the north Nebuchadnezzar the king of Babylon, the king of
kings, with horses and chariots, with cavalry
and a great and mighty army.

**8** Your daughters on the mainland
he shall slay with the sword;
He shall place a siege tower against you,
cast up a ramp about you,
and raise his shields against you.
**9** He shall pound your walls with
battering-rams
and break down your towers with his
weapons.
**10** The surge of his horses shall cover you with
dust,
amid the noise of steeds, of wheels and of
chariots.
Your walls shall shake as he enters your
gates,
even as one enters a city that is breached.
**11** With the hoofs of his horses
he shall trample all your streets;
Your people he shall slay by the sword;
your mighty pillars he shall pull to the
ground.
**12** Your wealth shall be plundered,
your merchandise pillaged;
Your walls shall be torn down,
your precious houses demolished;
Your stones, your timber, and your clay
shall be cast into the sea.
**13** I will put an end to the noise of your songs,
and the sound of your lyres shall be heard
no more.
**14** I will make you a bare rock;
a drying place for nets shall you be.

Never shall you be rebuilt, for I have spoken,
says the Lord GOD.

---

w Sir 50, 26; Is 15, 1-9; 16, 1-14; Jer 48, 1-47; Am 2, 1ff; Zep 2, 8f.
x 12ff: Ez 35, 1ff; Is 34, 5; Jer 49, 7-22; Jl 4, 19; Am 1, 11f; Ob 1, 1-21.
y Is 26, 1-21: 47, 4; Jl 4, 4f; Zec 9, 2ff.

---

*

25, 9: The shoulder of Moab: the edge of the Moabite plateau.

25, 16: Cherethites: a people forming part of the Philistine nation; cf Zep 2, 5.

26, 4f: A bare rock: the Tyre of Ezekiel's time was situated on a rocky island just off the Phoenician coast; it was not until the time of Alexander the Great that it was connected by a causeway to the mainland.

26, 6: Her daughters: tributary towns and villages on the mainland.

**15** Thus says the Lord GOD to Tyre: At the
noise of your fall, at the groaning of the wounded, when the sword slays in your midst, shall
not the isles quake? **16** All the princes of the
sea* shall step down from their thrones, lay
aside their robes, and strip off their embroidered
garments. They shall be clothed in mourning
and, sitting on the ground, they shall tremble at
every moment and be horrified at you. **17** Then
they shall utter a lament over you:

How have you perished, gone from the seas,
city most prized!
Once she was mighty on the sea,
she and her dwellers,
Who spread terror into all
that dwelt by the sea.
**18** On this, the day of your fall,
the islands quake!

The isles in the sea are terrified at your passing.
**19** For thus says the Lord GOD: When I make
you a city desolate like cities that are no longer
inhabited, when I churn up the abyss against
you, and its mighty waters cover you, **20** then
I will thrust you down with those who descend
into the pit,* those of the bygone age; and I will
make you dwell in the nether lands, in the everlasting ruins, with those who go down to the pit,
so that you may never return to take your place
in the land of the living. **21** I will make you a
devastation, and you shall be no more; you shall
be sought, but never again found, says the Lord
GOD.

## CHAPTER 27

**The Ship Tyre.** **1** Thus the word of the
LORD came to me: **2** As for you, son of man,
utter a lament over Tyre, **3** and say to Tyre that
is situated at the approaches of the sea, that
brought the trade of the peoples to many a coastland: Thus says the Lord GOD:

Tyre, you said, "I am a ship,
perfect in beauty."
**4** In the midst of the sea your builders placed
you,
perfected your beauty.
**5** With cypress from Senir* they built for you
all of your decks;
Cedar from Lebanon they took
to make you a mast;
**6** From the highest oaks of Bashan*
they made your oars;
Your bridge they made of cypress wood
from the coasts of Kittim.
**7** Fine embroidered linen from Egypt
became your sail [to serve you as a
banner].
Purple and scarlet from the coasts of
Elishah*
covered your cabin.
**8** Citizens of Sidon* and Arvad
served as your oarsmen;
Skilled men of Zemer were in you
to be your mariners;
**9** The elders and experts of Gebal were in you
to caulk your seams.

Every ship and sailor on the sea came to you
to carry trade. **10** Persia and Lud and Put were
in your army as warriors; shield and helmet they
hung upon you, increasing your splendor.
**11** The men of Arvad were all about your walls,
and the Gamadites were in your towers; they
hung their bucklers all around on your walls,
and made perfect your beauty. **12** Tarshish
traded with you, so great was your wealth, exchanging silver, iron, tin, and lead for your
wares. **13** Javan, Tubal, and Meshech were
also traders with you, exchanging slaves and
articles of bronze for your goods. **14** From
Beth-togarmah horses, steeds, and mules were
exchanged for your wares. **15** The Rhodanites
trafficked with you; many coastlands traded
with you; ivory tusks and ebony wood they gave
you for payment. **16** Edom traded with you, so
many were your products, exchanging garnets,
purple, embroidered cloth, fine linen, coral, and
rubies for your wares. **17** Judah and the land of
Israel trafficked with you, exchanging Minnith
wheat, figs, honey, oil, and balm for your
goods. **18** Damascus traded with you, so great
was your wealth, exchanging Helbon wine and
Zahar wool. **19** Javan exchanged wrought iron,
cassia, and aromatic cane from Uzal for your
wares. **20** Dedan traded with you for riding
gear. **21** The trade of Arabia and of all the
sheikhs of Kedar belonged to you; they dealt in
lambs, rams, and goats. **22** The merchants of
Sheba and Raamah also traded with you, exchanging for your wares the very choicest
spices, all kinds of precious stones, and gold.
**23** Haran, Canneh, and Eden, the merchants of
Sheba, Asshur, and Chilmad **24** traded with
you, marketing with you rich garments, violet
mantles, embroidered cloth, varicolored car-
pets, and firmly woven cords. **25** Ships of Tarshish journeyed for you in your merchandising.

You were full and heavily laden
in the heart of the sea.
**26** Through the deep waters your oarsmen
brought you home,
But the east wind smashed you

*

26, 16: The princes of the sea: the rulers of the islands and coastal cities leagued commercially with Tyre.

26, 20: Those who descend into the pit: the dead, pictured as dwelling in a place or cave of darkness.

27, 5: Senir: another name for Mount Hermon; cf Dt 3, 9.

27, 6: Bashan: northern Transjordan, which, like Lebanon, was noted for its great forests. Kittim: probably Cyprus.

27, 7: Elishah: probably another term for Cyprus.

27, 8f: Sidon . . . Arvad . . . Zemer . . . Gebal: Phoenician cities in Tyre's orbit of influence; the last-named is the classical Byblos.

in the heart of the sea.
27 Your wealth, your goods, your wares,
your sailors, and your crew,

[the caulkers of your seams, those who traded
for your goods, all your warriors who were in
you, and all the great crowd within you]

Sank into the heart of the sea
on the day of your shipwreck.
28 Hearing the shouts of your mariners,
the shores begin to quake.
29 Down from their ships
come all who ply the oar;
The sailors, all the mariners of the sea,
stand on the shore,
30 Making their voice heard on your behalf,
shouting bitter cries,
Strewing dust on their heads,
rolling in the ashes.
31 For you they shave their heads
and put on sackcloth,
For you they weep in anguish,
with bitter lament.
32 In their mourning they utter a lament over
you;
thus they wail over you:
Who was ever destroyed like Tyre
in the midst of the sea?
33 With your goods which you drew from the
seas
you filled many peoples;
With your great wealth and merchandise
you enriched the kings of the earth.
34 Now you are wrecked in the sea,
in the watery depths;
Your wares and all your crew
have gone down with you.
35 All who dwell on the coastlands
are aghast over you,
Their kings are terrified,
their faces convulsed.
36 The traders among the peoples
now hiss at you;
You have become a horror,
and you shall be no more.

## CHAPTER 28

**The Prince of Tyre.** 1 Thus the word of the
LORD came to me: 2 Son of man, say to the
prince of Tyre: Thus says the Lord GOD:

Because you are haughty of heart,
you say, "A god am I!
I occupy a godly throne
in the heart of the sea!"—
And yet you are a man, and not a god,
however you may think yourself like a
god.
3 Oh yes, you are wiser than Daniel,*
there is no secret that is beyond you.
4 By your wisdom and your intelligence
you have made riches for yourself;
You have put gold and silver
into your treasuries.
5 By your great wisdom applied to your
trading
you have heaped up your riches;
your heart has grown haughty from your
riches—
6 therefore thus says the Lord GOD:
Because you have thought yourself
to have the mind of a god,
7 Therefore I will bring against you
foreigners, the most barbarous of nations.
They shall draw their swords
against your beauteous wisdom,
they shall run them through your splendid
apparel.
8 They shall thrust you down to the pit, there
to die
a bloodied corpse, in the heart of the sea.
9 Will you then say, "I am a god!"
when you face your murderers?
No, you are a man, not a god,
handed over to those who will slay you.
10 You shall die the death of the uncircumcised
at the hands of foreigners,
for I have spoken, says the Lord GOD.

11 Thus the word of the LORD came to me:
12 Son of man, utter a lament over the king of
Tyre, saying to him: Thus says the Lord GOD:

*You were stamped with the seal of
perfection,
of complete wisdom and perfect beauty.
13 In Eden, the garden of God, you were,
and every precious stone was your
covering

[carnelian, topaz, and beryl, chrysolite, onyx,
and jasper, sapphire, garnet, and emerald];

Of gold your pendants and jewels
were made, on the day you were created.
14 With the Cherub I placed you;
you were on the holy mountain of God,*
walking among the fiery stones.
15 Blameless you were in your conduct
from the day you were created,
Until evil was found in you,
16 the result of your far-flung trade;
violence was your business, and you
sinned.
Then I banned you from the mountain of
God;
the Cherub drove you from among the
fiery stones.
17 You became haughty of heart because of
your beauty;
for the sake of splendor you debased your
wisdom.

---

28, 3: Wiser than Daniel: see note on Ez 14, 14.

28, 12–19: This picture of Tyre and its fall recalls images of the earthly paradise portraying the creation of man in perfection and his fall (Gn, chapters 2–3).

28, 14: The holy mountain of God: the residence of God was sometimes designated as a mountain; cf Is 14, 13. The fiery stones: associated with the divine presence; cf Ez 1, 13; Ps 18, 13.

I cast you to the earth, so great was your
guilt;
I made you a spectacle in the sight of
kings.
18 Because of your guilt, your sinful trade,
I have profaned your sanctuaries,
And I have brought out fire from your midst
which will devour you.
I have reduced you to dust on the earth
in the sight of all who should see you.
19 Among the peoples, all who knew you
stand aghast at you;
You have become a horror,
you shall be no more.

**Against Sidon.** 20 [z]Thus the word of the
LORD came to me: Son of man, look toward
Sidon, 21 [a]and prophesy against it: 22 Thus
says the Lord GOD:[b] See! I am coming at you,
Sidon; I will be glorified in your midst. Then
they shall know that I am the LORD, when I
inflict punishments upon it and use it to manifest
my holiness.

23 Into it I will send pestilence,
and blood shall flow in its streets.
Within it shall fall those slain
by the sword that comes against it from
every side.

Thus they shall know that I am the LORD. 24 Sidon shall no longer be a tearing thorn for the
house of Israel, a brier that scratches them more
than all the others about them who despise them;
thus they shall know that I am the LORD.

25 Thus says the Lord GOD: When I gather
the house of Israel from the peoples among
whom they are scattered, then I will manifest
my holiness through them in the sight of the
nations. Then they shall live on their land which
I gave to my servant Jacob; 26 they shall live
on it in security, building houses and planting
vineyards. They shall dwell secure while I inflict punishments on all their neighbors who
despised them; thus they shall know that I, the
LORD, am their God.

## CHAPTER 29

**Egypt the Crocodile.** 1 On the twelfth day
of the tenth month in the tenth year,* the word
of the LORD came to me: 2 Son of man, set your
face against Pharaoh, king of Egypt, and prophesy against him and against all Egypt.* 3 Say
this to him: Thus says the Lord GOD:

See! I am coming at you, Pharaoh,
king of Egypt,
Great crouching monster
amidst your Niles:*
Who say, "The Niles are mine;
it is I who made them!"

4 I will put hooks in your jaws and make the
fish of your Niles stick to your scales, then draw
you up from the midst of your Niles along with
all the fish of your Niles sticking to your scales.

5 I will cast you into the desert,
you and all the fish of your Niles;
You shall fall upon the open field,
you shall not be taken up or buried;
To the beasts of the earth and the birds of
the air
I give you as food,
6 That all who dwell in Egypt may know
that I am the LORD.
Because you have been a reed staff
for the house of Israel:[c]
7 When they held you in hand, you splintered,
throwing every shoulder out of joint;
When they leaned on you, you broke,
bringing each one of them down
headlong;

8 therefore thus says the Lord GOD: See! I will
bring the sword against you, and cut off from
you both man and beast. 9 The land of Egypt
shall become a desolate waste; thus they shall
know that I am the LORD.

Because you said, "The Niles are mine; it is
I who made them," 10 therefore see! I am coming at you and against your Niles; I will make
the land of Egypt a waste and a desolation from
Migdol to Syene,* and even to the frontier of
Ethiopia. 11 No foot of man or beast shall pass
through it; they shall not pass through it, and it
will be uninhabited for forty years. 12 I will
make the land of Egypt the most desolate of
lands, and its cities shall be the most deserted
of cities for forty years; and I will scatter the
Egyptians among the nations and strew them
over foreign lands. 13 Yet thus says the Lord
GOD: At the end of forty years I will gather the
Egyptians from the peoples among whom they
are scattered, 14 and I will restore Egypt's fortune, bringing them back to the land of Pathros,
the land of their origin,* where it will be the
lowliest 15 of kingdoms, never more to set itself above the nations. I will make them few,
that they may not dominate the nations. 16 No
longer shall they be for the house of Israel to
trust in, but the living reminder of its guilt for

z Is 23, 1-18.
a Jer 47, 4.
b Jl 4, 4; Zec 9, 2ff.
c Is 36, 6.

29, 1: The twelfth day of the tenth month in the tenth year: January 7, 587 B.C. The siege of Jerusalem had begun a year earlier; cf Ez 24, 1.

29, 2: Egypt was allied with Judah against the Chaldeans.

29, 3: Niles: the many rivulets of the Nile as it branches out into the Delta.

29, 10: From Migdol to Syene: from the northern to the southern extremity of Egypt. Syene is the modern Assuan.

29, 14: Pathros, the land of their origin: upper Egypt, that is, southern Egypt, where the Egyptians were thought to have originated; Is 11, 11; Jer 44, 1. 15.

having turned to follow after them. Thus they
shall know that I am the LORD.

**The Wages of Nebuchadnezzar.** 17 On
the first day of the first month in the twenty-seventh year,* the word of the LORD came to me:
18 Son of man, Nebuchadnezzar, the king of
Babylon, has led his army in an exhausting
campaign against Tyre.* Their heads became
bald and their shoulders were galled; but neither
he nor his army received any wages from Tyre
for the campaign he led against it. 19 Therefore
thus says the Lord GOD:[d] I am now giving the
land of Egypt to Nebuchadnezzar, king of Babylon. He shall carry off its riches, plundering
and pillaging it for the wages of his soldiers,
who did it for me; 20 as payment for his toil I
have given him the land of Egypt, says the Lord
GOD.

21 On that day I will make a horn sprout for
the house of Israel, and I will cause you to speak
out in their midst; thus they shall know that I am
the LORD.

## CHAPTER 30

### The Day of the Lord against Egypt.

1 Thus the word of the LORD came to me:
2 Son of man, speak this prophecy: Thus says
the Lord GOD: Cry, Oh, the day! 3 for near is
the day, near is the day of the Lord; a day of
clouds, doomsday for the nations shall it be.
4 Then a sword shall come upon Egypt, and
anguish shall be in Ethiopia, when the slain fall
in Egypt, when her riches are seized and her
foundations are overthrown. 5 Ethiopia, Put,
Lud, all Arabia, Libya, and people of the allied
territory shall fall by the sword with them.
6 Those who support Egypt shall fall, and down
shall come her proud strength; from Migdol to
Syene they shall fall there by the sword, says the
Lord GOD. 7 She shall be the most devastated
of lands, and her cities shall be the most desolate
of all. 8 Then they shall know that I am the
LORD, when I set fire to Egypt and when all who
help her are broken. 9 On that day messengers
shall hasten forth at my command to terrify
unsuspecting Ethiopia; they shall be in anguish
on the day of Egypt, which is surely coming.

10 Thus says the Lord GOD: I will put an end
to the throngs of Egypt by the hand of Nebuchadnezzar, king of Babylon. 11 He and his
people with him, the most ruthless of nations,
shall be brought in to devastate the land. They
shall draw their swords against Egypt, and fill
the land with the slain. 12 I will turn the Niles
into dry land and sell the land over to the power
of the wicked. The land and everything in it I
will hand over to foreigners to devastate. I, the
LORD, have spoken.

13 [e]Thus says the Lord GOD: I will put an
end to the great ones of Memphis and the
princes of the land of Egypt, that they may be
no more. I will cast fear into the land of Egypt,
and devastate Pathros. 14 I will set fire to Zoan,
and inflict punishments on Thebes. 15 I will
pour out my wrath on Pelusium, Egypt's stronghold, and cut down the crowds in Memphis.
16 I will set fire to Egypt; Syene shall writhe in
anguish; Thebes shall be breached and its walls
shall be demolished. 17 The young men of On
and of Pibeseth shall fall by the sword, and the
cities themselves shall go into captivity. 18 In
Tehaphnehes the day shall be darkened when I
break the scepter of Egypt. Her haughty pride
shall cease from her, clouds shall cover her, and
her daughters shall go into captivity. 19 Thus
will I inflict punishments on Egypt, that they
may know that I am the LORD.

**Pharaoh's Broken Arm.** 20 On the seventh day of the first month in the eleventh year,*
the word of the LORD came to me: 21 *Son of
man, I have broken the arm of Pharaoh, the king
of Egypt, and see, it has not been bound up with
bandages and healing remedies that it may be
strong enough to hold the sword. 22 Therefore
thus says the Lord GOD: See! I am coming at
Pharaoh, the king of Egypt. I will break his
strong arm, so that the sword drops from his
hand. 23 I will scatter the Egyptians among the
nations and strew them over foreign lands.
24 But I will strengthen the arms of the king of
Babylon, and put my sword in his hand, which
he will bring against Egypt so as to plunder and
pillage it. 25 [I will make the arms of the king
of Babylon strong, but the arms of Pharaoh shall
drop.] Then they shall know that I am the LORD,
when I put my sword in the hand of the king of
Babylon for him to wield against the land of
Egypt. 26 [I will scatter the Egyptians among
the nations and strew them over foreign lands.]
Thus they shall know that I am the LORD.

---

d Jer 46, 2. e Zec 13, 2.

---

*

29, 17: The first day of the first month in the twenty-seventh year: April 26, 571 B.C. This is the latest date attached to any prophecy in Ezekiel.

29, 18f: The fulfillment of Ezekiel's prophecy against Tyre (chapters 26–28) was a thirteen-year siege of the city by Nebuchadnezzar (587–574 B.C.). Tyre seems to have been taken, but its resources were exhausted and the booty was small. Therefore Ezekiel now prophesies that Nebuchadnezzar will collect his wages as God's instrument in the punishment of Tyre, by plundering Egypt.

30, 20: The seventh day of the first month in the eleventh year: April 29, 587 B.C.

30, 21–26: This oracle was uttered during the siege of Jerusalem, which had now lasted more than a year (Ez 24, 1). Pharaoh Hophra went to the aid of Jerusalem, causing the Chaldeans to lift the siege temporarily; cf Jer 34, 21; 37, 6f. In the prophet's eyes, this was interfering with the divine punishment of Judah that was to be inflicted by the Chaldeans. The Egyptians were routed by the Chaldeans, and were able to offer no more help to Jerusalem; cf chapter 31.

## CHAPTER 31

**Allegory of the Cypress.** 1 On the first
day of the third month in the eleventh year,* the
word of the LORD came to me: 2 Son of man,
say to Pharaoh, the king of Egypt, and to his
hordes: What are you like in your greatness?

3 Behold, a cypress [cedar] in Lebanon,
beautiful of branch, lofty of stature,
amid the very clouds lifted its crest.
4 Waters made it grow, the abyss made it
flourish,
sending its rivers round where it was
planted,
turning its streams to all the trees of the
field.
5 Thus it grew taller than every other tree of
the field,
and longer of branch because of the
abundant water.
6 In its boughs nested all the birds of the air,
under its branches all beasts of the field
gave birth,
in its shade dwelt numerous peoples of
every race.
7 It became beautiful and stately in its spread
of foliage,
for its roots were turned toward abundant
water.
8 The cedars in the garden of God were not its
equal,
nor could the fir trees match its boughs,
Neither were the plane trees like it for
branches;
no tree in the garden of God matched its
beauty.
9 I made it beautiful, with much foliage,
the envy of all Eden's trees in the garden
of God.

10 Therefore thus says the Lord GOD: Because
it became lofty in stature, raising its crest among
the clouds, and because it became proud in heart
at its height, 11 I have handed it over to the
mightiest of the nations, which has dealt with it
in keeping with its wickedness. I humiliated it.
12 Foreigners, the most ruthless of the nations,
cut it down and left it on the mountains. Its
foliage was brought low in all the valleys, its
branches lay broken in all the ravines of the
land, and all the peoples of the land withdrew
from its shade, abandoning it.

13 On its fallen trunk rested all the birds of the
air,
and by its branches were all the beasts of
the field.

14 Thus no tree may grow lofty in stature or
raise its crest among the clouds; no tree fed by
water may stand by itself in its loftiness.

For all of them are destined for death,
for the land below,
For the company of mortals,
those who go down into the pit.

15 Thus says the Lord GOD: On the day he
went down to the nether world I made the abyss
close up over him; I stopped its streams so that
the deep waters were held back. I cast gloom
over Lebanon because of him, so that all the
trees in the land drooped on his account. 16 At
the crash of his fall I made the nations rock,
when I cast him down to the nether world with
those who go down into the pit. In the land
below, all Eden's trees were consoled, Lebanon's choice and best, all that were fed by water. 17 They too have come down with him to
the nether world, to those slain by the sword;
those who dwelt in his shade are dispersed
among the nations. 18 Which was your equal in
glory or size among the trees of Eden? Yet you
have been brought down with the trees of Eden
to the land below. You shall lie with the uncircumcised, with those slain by the sword. Such
are Pharaoh and all his hordes, says the Lord
GOD.

## CHAPTER 32

**Dirge over Pharaoh.** 1 On the first day of
the twelfth month in the twelfth year,* the word
of the LORD came to me: 2 Son of man, utter
a lament over Pharaoh, the king of Egypt, saying to him: Lion of the nations, you are destroyed.

You were like a monster in the sea,
spouting in your streams,
Stirring the water with your feet
and churning its streams.
3 Thus says the Lord GOD:
I will spread my net over you
[with a host of many nations],
and draw you up in my seine.[f]
4 I will leave you on the land;
on the open field I will cast you.
I will have all the birds of the air alight on
you,
and all the beasts of the earth eat their fill
of you.
5 I will leave your flesh on the mountains,
and fill the valleys with your carcass.
6 I will water the land with what flows from
you,
and the river beds shall be filled with
your blood.
7 When I snuff you out I will cover the
heavens,
and all their stars I will darken;

f Ez 12, 13; 17, 20.
g Is 13, 10; Jl 2, 10; 4, 15; Mt 24, 29.

*

31, 1: The first day of the third month in the eleventh year: June 21, 587 B.C.

32, 1: The first day of the twelfth month in the twelfth year: March 3, 585 B.C.

The sun I will cover with clouds,
and the moon shall not give its light.[g]
**8** All the shining lights in the heavens
I will darken on your account,
And I will spread darkness over your land,
say the Lord GOD.

**9** I will grieve the hearts of many peoples
when I lead you captive among the nations, to
lands which you do not know. **10** Many peoples
shall be appalled at you, and their kings shall
shudder over you in horror when they see me
brandish my sword, and on the day of your
downfall every one of them shall continuously
tremble for his own life. **11** For thus says the
Lord GOD: The sword of the king of Babylon
shall come upon you.

**12** I will cut down your horde with the blades
of warriors,
all of them the most ruthless of the
nations;
They shall lay waste the glory of Egypt,
and all her hordes shall be destroyed.
**13** I will have all of her animals perish
beside her abundant waters;
The foot of man shall stir them no longer,
nor shall the hoof of beast disturb them.
**14** Then will I make their waters clear,
and their streams flow like oil,
says the Lord GOD.

**15** When I turn Egypt into a waste, the land
shall be devastated of all that is in it; when I
strike all who live there, they shall know that I
am the LORD. **16** This is a dirge, and it shall be
sung: the daughters of the nations shall chant it;
over Egypt and all its hordes shall they chant it,
says the Lord GOD.

**Dirge over Egypt.** **17** On the fifteenth day
of the first month in the twelfth year, the word
of the LORD came to me: **18** Son of man, lament
over the throngs of Egypt, for the mighty nations have thrust them down to the bottom of the
earth, with those who go down into the pit.
**20** In the midst of those slain by the sword shall
they fall, and place shall be made with them for
all their hordes. Then from the midst of the
nether world, the mighty warriors shall speak to
Egypt: **19** "Whom do you excel in beauty?
**21** Come down, you and your allies, lie with
the uncircumcised, with those slain by the
sword."

**22** There is Assyria with all her company, all
of them slain, **23** whose graves have been made
in the recesses of the pit; her company is around
Egypt's grave, all of them slain, fallen by the
sword, who spread terror in the land of the
living. **24** There is Elam with all her throng
about Egypt's grave, all of them slain, fallen by
the sword: they have gone down uncircumcised
to the bottom of the earth, who spread their
terror in the land of the living, and they bear
their disgrace with those who go down into the
pit; **25** in the midst of the slain they are placed.
**26** There are Meshech and Tubal and all their
throng about her grave, all of them uncircumcised, slain by the sword, for they spread their
terror in the land of the living.

**27** They do not lie with the mighty men fall-
en of old,* who went down to the nether world
with their weapons of war, whose swords were
placed under their heads and whose shields were
laid over their bones, though the mighty men
caused terror in the land of the living. **28** But
in the midst of the uncircumcised shall you lie,
with those slain by the sword.

**29** There are Edom, her kings, and all her
princes, who despite their might have been
placed with those slain by the sword; with the
uncircumcised they lie, and with those who go
down into the pit. **30** There are all the princes
of the north and all the Sidonians, who have
gone down with the slain, because of the terror
their might inspired; they lie uncircumcised
with those slain by the sword and bear their
disgrace with those who go down to the pit.
**31** When Pharaoh sees these, he shall be comforted for all his hordes slain by the sword—
Pharaoh and all his army, says the Lord GOD.
**32** Since he spread his terror in the land of the
living, therefore is he laid to rest among the
uncircumcised, with those slain by the sword
—Pharaoh and all his hordes, says the Lord
GOD.

## *IV: Salvation for Israel*

## CHAPTER 33

**The Prophet a Watchman.** **1** Thus the
word of the LORD came to me: **2** Son of man,
speak thus to your countrymen: When I bring
the sword against a country, and the people of
this country select one of their number to be
their watchman, **3** and the watchman, seeing
the sword coming against the country, blows the
trumpet to warn the people, **4** anyone hearing
but not heeding the warning of the trumpet and
therefore slain by the sword that comes against
him, shall be responsible for his own death.
**5** He heard the trumpet blast yet refused to take
warning; he is responsible for his own death, for
had he taken warning he would have escaped
with his life. **6** But if the watchman sees the
sword coming and fails to blow the warning
trumpet, so that the sword comes and takes
anyone, I will hold the watchman responsible
for that person's death, even though that person
is taken because of his own sin.

*

32, 27: The mighty men fallen of old: the semilegendary heroes of the prehistoric past, who were thought to have once dominated the world; cf Is 14, 9.

**7** [h]You, son of man, I have appointed watchman for the house of Israel; when you hear me say anything, you shall warn them for me. **8** If I tell the wicked man that he shall surely die, and you do not speak out to dissuade the wicked man from his way, he [the wicked man] shall die for his guilt, but I will hold you responsible for his death. **9** But if you warn the wicked man, trying to turn him from his way, and he refuses to turn from his way, he shall die for his guilt, but you shall save yourself.

**Individual Retribution.** **10** As for you, son of man, speak to the house of Israel: You people say, "Our crimes and our sins weigh us down; we are rotting away because of them. How can we survive?" **11** [i]Answer them: As I live, says the Lord GOD, I swear I take no pleasure in the death of the wicked man, but rather in the wicked man's conversion, that he may live. Turn, turn from your evil ways! Why should you die, O house of Israel?

**12** As for you, son of man, tell your countrymen: The virtue which a man has practiced will not save him on the day that he sins; neither will the wickedness that a man has done bring about his downfall on the day that he turns from his wickedness [nor can the virtuous man, when he sins, remain alive]. **13** Though I say to the virtuous man that he shall surely live, if he then presumes on his virtue and does wrong, none of his virtuous deeds shall be remembered; because of the wrong he has done, he shall die. **14** And though I say to the wicked man that he shall surely die, if he turns away from his sin and does what is right and just, **15** giving back pledges, restoring stolen goods, living by the statutes that bring life, and doing no wrong, he shall surely live, he shall not die. **16** None of the sins he committed shall be held against him; he has done what is right and just, he shall surely live.

**17** Yet your countrymen say, "The way of the LORD is not fair!"; but it is their way that is not fair. **18** When a virtuous man turns away from what is right and does wrong, he shall die for it. **19** But when a wicked man turns away from wickedness and does what is right and just, because of this he shall live. **20** [j]And still you say, "The way of the LORD is not fair!"? I will judge every one of you according to his ways, O house of Israel.

**The Fugitive from Jerusalem.*** **21** On the fifth day of the tenth month, in the twelfth year of our exile, the fugitive came to me from Jerusalem and said, "The city is taken!" **22** The hand of the LORD had come upon me the evening before the fugitive arrived, and he opened my mouth when the fugitive reached me in the morning. My mouth was opened, and I was dumb no longer.

**The Survivors in Judah.*** **23** Thus the word of the Lord came to me: **24** Son of man, they who live in the ruins on the land of Israel reason thus: "Abraham, though but a single individual, received possession of the land; we, therefore, being many, have as permanent possession the land that has been given to us." **25** Give them this answer: Thus says the Lord GOD: You eat on the mountains, you raise your eyes to your idols, you shed blood—yet you would keep possession of the land? **26** You rely on your sword, you do abominable things, each one of you defiles his neighbor's wife—yet you would keep possession of the land? **27** Tell them this: Thus says the Lord GOD: As I live, those who are in the ruins I swear shall fall by the sword; those who are in the open field I have given to the wild beasts for food; and those who are in fastnesses and in caves shall die by the plague. **28** I will make the land a desolate waste, so that its proud strength will come to an end, and the mountains of Israel shall be so desolate that no one will cross them. **29** Thus they shall know that I am the LORD, when I make the land a desolate waste because of all the abominable things they have done.

**The Prophet's False Popularity.** **30** As for you, son of man, your countrymen are talking about you along the walls and in the doorways of houses. They say to one another, "Come and hear the latest word that comes from the LORD."* **31** My people come to you as people always do; they sit down before you and hear your words, but they will not obey them, for lies are on their lips and their desires are fixed on dishonest gain. **32** For them you are only a ballad singer, with a pleasant voice and a clever touch. They listen to your words, but they will not obey them. **33** But when it comes—and it is surely coming!—they shall know that there was a prophet among them.

h Ez 3, 17. j Ez 18, 25.
i Ez 18, 23-32.

*

33, 21f: January 8, 585 B.C. According to Jeremiah (39, 2), Jerusalem was taken in July, 587. Some MSS read "eleventh" for twelfth year (January, 586); even so, there was ample time between the fall of Jerusalem and the arrival of the fugitive from that city to journey to Babylon. However, this is the fugitive sent to fulfill the promise of Ez 24, 25. 27, the eyewitness who would release Ezekiel from his dumbness; cf Ez, 2, 26f.

33, 23–29: News brought by the fugitive furnished the occasion of this prophecy. Like Jeremiah, Ezekiel rejects the idea that the survivors in Judah have any claim to the land. The new Israel is to be formed from the exiles.

33, 30: The fulfillment of Ezekiel's prophecies about Jerusalem was responsible for this temporary enthusiasm among the unstable people.

## CHAPTER 34

**Parable of the Shepherds.** **1** Thus the word of the LORD came to me: **2** Son of man, prophesy against the shepherds of Israel,* in these words prophesy to them [to the shepherds]: Thus says the Lord GOD: Woe to the shepherds of Israel who have been pasturing themselves![k] Should not shepherds, rather, pasture sheep? **3** You have fed off their milk, worn their wool, and slaughtered the fatlings, but the sheep you have not pastured. **4** You did not strengthen the weak nor heal the sick nor bind up the injured. You did not bring back the strayed nor seek the lost, but you lorded it over them harshly and brutally. **5** So they were scattered for lack of a shepherd, and became food for all the wild beasts. My sheep were scattered **6** and wandered over all the mountains and high hills; my sheep were scattered over the whole earth, with no one to look after them or to search for them.

**7** Therefore, shepherds, hear the word of the LORD: **8** As I live, says the Lord GOD, because my sheep have been given over to pillage, and because my sheep have become food for every wild beast, for lack of a shepherd; because my shepherds did not look after my sheep, but pastured themselves and did not pasture my sheep; **9** because of this, shepherds, hear the word of the LORD: **10** Thus says the Lord GOD: I swear I am coming against these shepherds. I will claim my sheep from them and put a stop to their shepherding my sheep so that they may no longer pasture themselves. I will save my sheep, that they may no longer be food for their mouths.

**11** For thus says the Lord GOD: I myself will look after and tend my sheep. **12** As a shepherd tends his flock when he finds himself among his scattered sheep, so will I tend my sheep. I will rescue them from every place where they were scattered when it was cloudy and dark. **13** I will lead them out from among the peoples and gather them from the foreign lands; I will bring them back to their own country and pasture them upon the mountains of Israel [in the land's ravines and all its inhabited places]. **14** In good pastures will I pasture them, and on the mountain heights of Israel shall be their grazing ground. There they shall lie down on good grazing ground, and in rich pastures shall they be pastured on the mountains of Israel. **15** I myself will pasture my sheep; I myself will give them rest, says the Lord GOD. **16** The lost I will seek out, the strayed I will bring back, the injured I will bind up, the sick I will heal [but the sleek and the strong I will destroy], shepherding them rightly.

**Separation of the Sheep.** **17** As for you, my sheep, says the Lord GOD, I will judge between one sheep and another, between rams and goats. **18** Was it not enough for you to graze on the best pasture, that you had to trample the rest of your pastures with your feet? Was it not enough for you to drink the clearest water, that you had to foul the remainder with your feet? **19** Thus my sheep had to graze on what your feet had trampled and drink what your feet had fouled. **20** Therefore thus says the Lord GOD: Now will I judge between the fat and the lean sheep. **21** Because you push with side and shoulder, and butt all the weak sheep with your horns until you have driven them out, **22** I will save my sheep so that they may no longer be despoiled, and I will judge between one sheep and another. **23** [l]I will appoint one shepherd over them to pasture them, my servant David;* he shall pasture them and be their shepherd. **24** I, the Lord, will be their God, and my servant David shall be prince among them. I, the LORD, have spoken.

**25** I will make a covenant of peace with them, and rid the country of ravenous beasts, that they may dwell securely in the desert and sleep in the forests. **26** I will place them about my hill, sending rain in due season, rains that shall be a blessing to them. **27** The trees of the field shall bear their fruits, and the land its crops, and they shall dwell securely on their own soil. Thus they shall know that I am the LORD when I break the bonds of their yoke and free them from the power of those who enslaved them. **28** They shall no longer be despoiled by the nations or devoured by beasts of the earth, but shall dwell secure, with no one to frighten them. **29** I will prepare for them peaceful fields for planting; they shall no longer be carried off by famine in the land, or bear the reproaches of the nations. **30** Thus they shall know that I, the LORD, am their God, and they are my people, the house of Israel, says the Lord GOD. **31** [You, my sheep, you are the sheep of my pasture, and I am your God, says the Lord GOD.]

## CHAPTER 35

**Against Edom.*** **1** Thus the word of the LORD came to me:[m] **2** Son of man, set your face

---

k Ez 13, 3; Jer 23, 1.
l Is 40, 21; Hos 3, 5; Jn 10, 11. 14.
m 1ff: Ez 25, 12ff.

---

*

34, 2: The shepherds of Israel: the leaders of the people.

34, 23: One shepherd . . . my servant David: a messianic Davidic King who will rule over the restored Israel (vv 25–31) in the name of the Lord.

35, 1–15: After the fall of Jerusalem, Edom assisted the Chaldeans in devastating the land and subduing the population, and ended by occupying part of Judah's former territory. For this reason these oracles against Edom are found in the

against Mount Seir, and prophesy against it.
**3** Say to it: Thus says the Lord GOD: See! I am
coming at you, Mount Seir. I will stretch out my
hand against you and make you a desolate
waste. **4** Your cities I will turn into ruins, and
you shall be a waste; thus you shall know that
I am the LORD.

**5** Because you never let die your hatred for
the Israelites, whom you delivered over to the
power of the sword at the time of their trouble,
when their crimes came to an end, **6** therefore,
as I live, says the Lord GOD, you have been
guilty of blood, and blood, I swear, shall pursue
you. **7** I will make Mount Seir a desolate waste,
and cut off from it any traveler. **8** With the slain
I will fill your hills, your valleys, and all your
ravines [in them the slain shall fall by the
sword]: **9** desolate will I make you forever, and
leave your cities without inhabitants; thus you
shall know that I am the LORD.

**10** Because you said: The two nations and
the two lands* have become mine; we shall
possess them—although the LORD was there—
**11** therefore, as I live, says the Lord GOD, I will
deal with you according to your anger and your
envy which you have exercised [in your hatred]
against them. I will make myself known among
you when I judge you, **12** and you shall know
that I am the LORD.

I have heard all the contemptuous things you
have uttered against the mountains of Israel:
"They are desolate, they have been given us to
devour." **13** I have heard the insolent and wild
words you have spoken against me. **14** Thus
says the Lord GOD: Just as you rejoiced over my
land because it was desolate, so will I do to you.
**15** In keeping with your glee over the devastation of the inheritance of the house of Israel, so
will I treat you. A waste shall you be, Mount
Seir, you and the whole of Edom. Thus they
shall know that I am the LORD.

## CHAPTER 36

**Regeneration of the Land.** **1** As for you,
son of man, prophesy to the mountains of Israel:
Mountains of Israel,[n] hear the word of the
LORD! **2** Thus says the Lord GOD: Because the
enemy has said of you, "Ha! the everlasting
heights have become our possession" **3** [there-
fore prophesy in these words: Thus says the
Lord GOD:]; because you have been ridiculed
and despised on all sides for having become a
possession for the rest of the nations, and have
become a byword and a popular jeer; **4** therefore, mountains of Israel, hear the word of the
LORD: [Thus says the Lord GOD to the mountains and hills, the ravines and valleys, the desolate ruins and abandoned cities, which have
been given over to the pillage and mockery of
the remaining nations round about; **5** therefore
thus says the Lord GOD:] Truly, with burning
jealousy I speak against the rest of the nations
[and against all of Edom] who with wholehearted joy and utter contempt have considered my
land their possession to be delivered over to
plunder. **6** [Therefore, prophesy concerning the
land of Israel, and say to the mountains and
hills, the ravines and valleys: Thus says the
Lord GOD:] With jealous fury I speak, because
you have borne the reproach of the nations.
**7** Therefore do I solemnly swear that your
neighboring nations shall bear their own reproach.

**8** As for you, mountains of Israel, you shall
grow branches and bear fruit for my people
Israel, for they shall soon return. **9** See, I come
to you, it is to you that I turn; you will be tilled
and sown, **10** and I will settle crowds of men
upon you, the whole house of Israel; cities shall
be repeopled, and ruins rebuilt. **11** I will settle
crowds of men and beasts upon you, to multiply
and be fruitful. I will repeople you as in the past,
and be more generous to you than in the beginning; thus you shall know that I am the LORD.

**12** [My people Israel are the ones whom I
will have walk upon you; they shall take possession of you, and you shall be their heritage.
Never again shall you rob them of their children.]

**13** Thus says the Lord GOD: Because they
have said of you, "You are a land that devours
men,* and you rob your people of their children"; **14** therefore, never again shall you devour men or rob your people of their children,
says the Lord GOD. **15** No more will I permit
you to hear the reproach of nations, or bear
insults from peoples, or rob your people of their
children, says the Lord GOD.

**Regeneration of the People.** **16** Thus the
word of the LORD came to me: **17** Son of man,
when the house of Israel lived in their land, they
defiled it by their conduct and deeds. In my
sight their conduct was like the defilement of a
menstruous woman. **18** Therefore I poured out
my fury upon them [because of the blood which
they poured out on the ground, and because they
defiled it with idols]. **19** I scattered them
among the nations, dispersing them over foreign
lands; according to their conduct and deeds I
judged them. **20** [o]But when they came among
the nations [wherever they came], they served
to profane my holy name, because it was said
of them: "These are the people of the LORD, yet

n Ez 6, 3. o Is 52, 5; Rom 2, 24.

context of the city's fall.

35, 10: The two nations and the two lands: the superseded kingdoms of Israel and Judah and their territories.

36, 13: A land that devours men: destroys its own population, as could be seen in its disastrous political history.

they had to leave their land.'' **21** So I have
relented because of my holy name which the
house of Israel profaned among the nations
where they came. **22** Therefore say to the house
of Israel: Thus says the Lord GOD: Not for your
sakes do I act, house of Israel, but for the sake
of my holy name, which you profaned among
the nations to which you came. **23** I will prove
the holiness of my great name, profaned among
the nations, in whose midst you have profaned
it. Thus the nations shall know that I am the
LORD, says the Lord GOD, when in their sight
I prove my holiness through you. **24** For I will
take you away from among the nations, gather
you from all the foreign lands, and bring you
back to your own land. **25** [p]I will sprinkle clean
water upon you to cleanse you from all your
impurities, and from all your idols I will cleanse
you. **26** [q]I will give you a new heart and place
a new spirit within you, taking from your bodies
your stony hearts and giving you natural hearts.
**27** [r]I will put my spirit within you and make
you live by my statutes, careful to observe my
decrees. **28** You shall live in the land I gave
your fathers; you shall be my people, and I will
be your God. **29** I will save you from all your
impurities; I will order the grain to be abundant,
and I will not send famine against you. **30** I will
increase the fruit on your trees and the crops in
your fields; thus you shall no longer bear among
the nations the reproach of famine. **31** Then
you shall remember your evil conduct, and that
your deeds were not good; you shall loathe
yourselves for your sins and your abominations.
**32** Not for your sakes do I act, says the Lord
GOD—let this be known to you! Be ashamed
and abashed because of your conduct, O house
of Israel.

**33** Thus says the Lord GOD: When I purify
you from all your crimes, I will repeople the
cities, and the ruins shall be rebuilt; **34** the desolate land shall be tilled, which was formerly a
wasteland exposed to the gaze of every passer-by. **35** ''This desolate land has been made
into a garden of Eden,'' they shall say. ''The
cities that were in ruins, laid waste, and destroyed are now repeopled and fortified.''
**36** Thus the neighboring nations that remain
shall know that I, the LORD, have rebuilt what
was destroyed and replanted what was desolate.
I, the LORD, have promised, and I will do it.

**37** Thus says the Lord GOD: This also I will
be persuaded to do for the house of Israel: to
multiply them like sheep. **38** As with sacrificial
sheep, the sheep of Jerusalem on its feast days,
the cities which were in ruins shall be filled with
flocks of men; thus they shall know that I am the
LORD.

## CHAPTER 37

**Vision of the Dry Bones.*** **1** The hand of
the LORD came upon me, and he led me out in
the spirit of the LORD and set me in the center
of the plain, which was now filled with bones.
**2** He made me walk among them in every direction so that I saw how many they were on the
surface of the plain. How dry they were! **3** He
asked me: Son of man, can these bones come to
life? ''Lord GOD,'' I answered, ''you alone
know that.'' **4** Then he said to me: Prophesy
over these bones, and say to them: Dry bones,
hear the word of the LORD! **5** Thus says the
Lord GOD to these bones: See! I will bring spirit
into you, that you may come to life. **6** I will put
sinews upon you, make flesh grow over you,
cover you with skin, and put spirit in you so that
you may come to life and know that I am the
LORD. **7** I prophesied as I had been told, and
even as I was prophesying I heard a noise; it was
a rattling as the bones came together, bone joining bone. **8** I saw the sinews and the flesh come
upon them, and the skin cover them, but there
was no spirit in them. **9** Then he said to me:
Prophesy to the spirit, prophesy, son of man,
and say to the spirit: Thus says the Lord GOD:
From the four winds come, O spirit, and breathe
into these slain that they may come to life. **10** I
prophesied as he told me, and the spirit came
into them; they came alive and stood upright, a
vast army. **11** Then he said to me: Son of man,
these bones are the whole house of Israel. They
have been saying, ''Our bones are dried up, our
hope is lost, and we are cut off.'' **12** Therefore,
prophesy and say to them: Thus says the Lord
GOD: O my people, I will open your graves and
have you rise from them, and bring you back to
the land of Israel. **13** Then you shall know that
I am the LORD, when I open your graves and
have you rise from them, O my people! **14** I
will put my spirit in you that you may live, and
I will settle you upon your land; thus you shall
know that I am the LORD. I have promised, and
I will do it, says the LORD.

**The Two Sticks.** **15** *Thus the word of the
LORD came to me: **16** Now, son of man, take
a single stick, and write on it: Judah and those
Israelites who are associated with him. Then
take another stick and write on it: Joseph [the
stick of Ephraim] and all the house of Israel

p Ps 51, 4; Zec 13, 1; Hb 10, 22; Jn 3, 5.
q Jer 31, 33.
r Ez 37, 14; 39, 29; Is 42, 1; 44, 3; 59, 21; Hg 2, 5; Jl 3, 1f.

*

37, 1–14: This vision is a prediction of the restoration of Israel under the figure of a resurrection from the dead; it is not concerned with the doctrine of resurrection itself.

37, 15–22: The symbolic action of joining two sticks into one signifies the future union of Israel and Judah under one messianic King.

associated with him. **17** Then join the two
sticks together, so that they form one stick in
your hand. **18** When your countrymen ask you,
"Will you not tell us what you mean by all
this?", **19** answer them: Thus says the Lord
GOD: [I will take the stick of Joseph, which is
in the hand of Ephraim, and of the tribes of
Israel associated with him, and I will join to it
the stick of Judah, making them a single stick;
they shall be one in my hand. **20** The sticks on
which you write you shall hold up before them
to see. **21** Tell them: Thus speaks the Lord
GOD:] I will take the Israelites from among the
nations to which they have come, and gather
them from all sides to bring them back to their
land. **22** I will make them one nation upon the
land, in the mountains of Israel, and there shall
be one prince for them all. Never again shall
they be two nations, and never again shall they
be divided into two kingdoms.

**23** No longer shall they defile themselves
with their idols, their abominations, and all their
transgressions. I will deliver them from all their
sins of apostasy, and cleanse them so that they
may be my people and I may be their God.
**24** [s]My servant David shall be prince over
them, and there shall be one shepherd for them
all; they shall live by my statutes and carefully
observe my decrees. **25** They shall live on the
land which I gave to my servant Jacob, the land
where their fathers lived; they shall live on it
forever, they, and their children, and their children's children, with my servant David their
prince forever. **26** [t]I will make with them a
covenant of peace; it shall be an everlasting
covenant with them, and I will multiply them,
and put my sanctuary among them forever.
**27** My dwelling shall be with them; I will be
their God, and they shall be my people.
**28** Thus the nations shall know that it is I, the
LORD, who make Israel holy, when my sanctuary shall be set up among them forever.

## CHAPTER 38

**First Prophecy against Gog.** **1** Thus the
word of the LORD came to me:* **2** Son of man,
turn toward Gog* [the land of Magog], [u] the
chief prince of Meshech and Tubal, and prophesy against him: **3** Thus says the Lord GOD: See!
I am coming at you, Gog, chief prince of Meshech and Tubal. **4** I will lead you forth with all
your army, horses and riders all handsomely
outfitted, a great horde with bucklers and
shields, all of them carrying swords: **5** Persia,
Cush, and Put with them [all with shields and
helmets], **6** Gomer with all its troops, Beth-togarmah from the recesses of the north with all
its troops, many peoples with you. **7** Prepare
yourself, be ready, you and all your horde assembled about you, and be at my disposal.
**8** After many days you will be mustered [in the
last years you will come] against a nation which
has survived the sword, which has been assembled from many peoples [on the mountains of
Israel which were long a ruin], which has been
brought forth from among the peoples and all of
whom now dwell in security. **9** You shall come
up like a sudden storm, advancing like a cloud
to cover the earth, you and all your troops and
the many peoples with you.

**10** Thus says the Lord GOD: At that time
thoughts shall arise in your mind, and you shall
devise an evil scheme: **11** "I will go up against
a land of open villages and attack the peaceful
people who are living in security, all of them
living without walls, having neither bars nor
gates, **12** to plunder and pillage, turning my
hand against the ruins that were repeopled and
against a people gathered from the nations, a
people concerned with cattle and goods, who
dwell at the navel of the earth."* **13** Sheba and
Dedan, the merchants of Tarshish and all her
young lions shall ask you: "Is it for plunder that
you have come? Is it for pillage that you have
summoned your horde, to carry off silver and
gold, to take away cattle and goods, to seize
much plunder?"

**17** Thus says the Lord GOD: It is of you that
I spoke in ancient times through my servants,
the prophets of Israel, who prophesied in those
days that I would bring you against them.
**18** But on that day, the day when Gog invades
the land of Israel, says the Lord GOD, my fury
shall be aroused. In my anger **19** and in my
jealousy, in my fiery wrath, I swear: On that day
there shall be a great shaking upon the land of
Israel. **20** Before me shall tremble the fish of
the sea and the birds of the air, the beasts of the
field and all the reptiles that crawl upon the
ground, and all men who are on the land. Mountains shall be overturned, and cliffs shall tum-
ble, and every wall shall fall to the ground.
**21** Against him I will summon every terror,

s Ez 34, 23; Jer 23, 5; 33, 15.
t Ps 110, 4.
u Rv 20, 7f.

*

38, 1—39, 20: These three oracles against Gog may refer either to a specific foreign invasion in the future, or to the apocalyptic struggle between good and evil at the end of time. By some they are ascribed to a later author than Ezekiel, who lived after the exile and the return to Palestine.

38, 2: Gog: the name is almost certainly a symbolic one taken from that of Gyges, king of Lydia, whether or not the prophet has a specific person in mind. The gloss Magog may be an Akkadian expression, mat-Gog, "the land of Gog." Meshech and Tubal, as well as Gomer and Beth-togarmah (v 6), were countries around the Black Sea, the northernmost countries known to the Hebrews: the north (cf also v 15) was the traditional direction from which invasion was expected; cf Jer 1, 13ff.

38, 12: Who dwell at the navel of the earth: the people of Israel (cf v 18; also Ez 5, 5). Many ancient peoples spoke of their own homelands as "the navel," that is, the center of the earth.

says the Lord GOD, every man's sword against
his brother. I will hold judgment with him in
pestilence and bloodshed; **22** flooding rain and
hailstones, fire and brimstone, I will rain upon
him, upon his troops, and upon the many peoples with him. **23** I will prove my greatness and
holiness and make myself known in the sight of
many nations; thus they shall know that I am the
LORD.

### Second Prophecy against Gog.

**14** Therefore prophesy, son of man, and say to
Gog: Thus says the Lord GOD: When my people
Israel are dwelling in security, will you not
bestir yourself **15** and come from your home in
the recesses of the north, you and many peoples
with you, all mounted on horses, a great horde
and a mighty army? **16** You shall come up
against my people Israel like a cloud covering
the land. In the last days I will bring you against
my land, that the nations may know of me,
when in their sight I prove my holiness through
you, O Gog.

## CHAPTER 39

**Third Prophecy against Gog.** **1** Now,
son of man, prophesy against Gog in these
words: Thus says the Lord GOD: See! I am
coming at you, Gog, chief prince of Meshech
and Tubal. **2** I will turn you about, I will urge
you on, and I will make you come up from the
recesses of the north; I will lead you against the
mountains of Israel. **3** Then I will strike the
bow from your left hand, and make the arrows
drop from your right. **4** Upon the mountains of
Israel you shall fall, you and all your troops and
the peoples who are with you. To birds of prey
of every kind and to the wild beasts I am giving
you to be eaten. **5** On the open field you shall
fall, for I have decreed it, says the Lord GOD.

**6** I will send fire upon Magog and upon those
who live securely in the coastlands; thus they
shall know that I am the LORD. **7** I will make
my holy name known among my people Israel;
I will no longer allow my holy name to be
profaned. Thus the nations shall know that I am
the LORD, the Holy One in Israel. **8** Yes, it is
coming and shall be fulfilled, says the Lord
GOD. This is the day I have decreed.

**9** Then shall those who live in the cities of
Israel go out and burn weapons: [shields and
bucklers,] bows and arrows, clubs and lances;
for seven years they shall make fires with them.
**10** They shall not have to bring in wood from
the fields or cut it down in the forests, for they
shall make fires with the weapons. Thus they
shall plunder those who plundered them and
pillage those who pillaged them, says the Lord
GOD.

**11** On that day I will give Gog for his tomb
a well-known place in Israel, the Valley of Abarim* east of the sea [it is blocked to travelers].
Gog shall be buried there with all his horde, and
it shall be named "Valley of Hamon-gog."
**12** To purify the land, the house of Israel shall
need seven months to bury them. **13** All the
people of the land shall bury them and gain
renown for it, when I reveal my glory, says the
Lord GOD. **14** Men shall be permanently employed to pass through the land burying those
who lie unburied, so as to purify the land. For
seven months they shall keep searching.
**15** When they pass through, should they see a
human bone, let them put up a marker beside it,
until others have buried it in the Valley of Hamon-gog. **16** [Also the name of the city shall be
Hamonah.] Thus the land shall be purified.

**17** As for you, son of man, says the Lord
GOD, say to birds of every kind and to all the
wild beasts: Come together, from all sides gather for the slaughter I am about to provide for
you, a great slaughter on the mountains of Israel: you shall have flesh to eat and blood to drink.
**18** You shall eat the flesh of warriors and drink
the blood of the princes of the land [rams,
lambs, and goats, bullocks, fatlings of Bashan,
all of them]. **19** From the slaughter which I will
provide for you, you shall eat fat until you are
filled and drink blood until you are drunk.
**20** You shall be filled at my table with horses
and riders, with warriors and soldiers of every
kind, says the Lord GOD.

**Israel's Return.** **21** Thus I will display my
glory among the nations, and all the nations
shall see the judgment I have executed and the
hand I have laid upon them. **22** From that day
forward the house of Israel shall know that I am
the LORD, their God. **23** The nations shall know
that because of its sins the house of Israel went
into exile; for they transgressed against me, and
I hid my face from them and handed them over
to their foes, so that all of them fell by the
sword. **24** According to their uncleanness and
their transgressions I dealt with them, hiding my
face from them.

**25** Therefore, thus says the Lord GOD: Now
I will restore the fortunes of Jacob and have pity
on the whole house of Israel, and I will be
jealous for my holy name. **26** They shall forget
their disgrace and all the times they broke faith
with me, when they live in security on their land
with no one to frighten them. **27** When I bring
them back from among the peoples, I will gather
them from the lands of their enemies, and will
prove my holiness through them in the sight of

---

39, 11: The Valley of Abarim: in the Abarim mountains, east of the Jordan. Hamon-gog: means "the horde of Gog."

many nations. **28** [v]Thus they shall know that I, the LORD, am their God, since I who exiled them among the nations, will gather them back on their land, not leaving any of them behind. **29** No longer will I hide my face from them, for I have poured out my spirit upon the house of Israel, says the Lord GOD.

## *V: The New Israel**

### The New Temple

### CHAPTER 40

**The Man with a Measure.** **1** On the tenth day of the month beginning the twenty-fifth year of our exile, fourteen years after the city was taken, that very day the hand of the LORD came upon me and brought me **2** in divine visions to the land of Israel, where he set me down on a very high mountain. On it there seemed to be a city being built before me. **3** When he had brought me there, all at once I saw a man whose appearance was that of bronze; he was standing in the gate, holding a linen cord and a measuring rod. **4** The man said to me, "Son of man, look carefully and listen intently, and pay strict attention to all that I will show you, for you have been brought here so that I might show it to you. Tell the house of Israel all that you see." **5** [Then I saw an outer wall that completely surrounded the temple. The man was holding a measuring rod six cubits long, each cubit being a cubit and a handbreadth;* he measured the width and the height of the structure, each of which was found to be one rod.]

**The East Gate.*** **6** Then he went to the gate which faced the east, climbed its steps, and measured the gate's threshold, which was found to be a rod wide. **7** The cells were a rod long and a rod wide, and the pilasters between the cells measured five cubits. The threshold of the gate adjoining the vestibule of the gate toward the inside measured one rod. **8** He measured the vestibule of the gate, **9** which was eight cubits, and its pilasters, which were two cubits. The vestibule of the gate was toward the inside. **10** The cells of the east gate were three on either side, of equal size, and the pilasters on either side were also of equal size. **11** He measured the gate's entrance, which was ten cubits wide, while the width of the gate's passage itself was thirteen cubits. **12** The border before each of the cells on both sides was one cubit; the cells themselves were six cubits on either side, from opening to opening. **13** He measured the gate from the back wall of one cell to the back wall of the cell on the opposite side: the width was twenty-five cubits. **14** He measured the vestibule, which was twenty-five cubits. The pilasters adjoining the court on either side were six cubits. **15** The length of the gate from the front entrance to the front of the vestibule on the inside was fifty cubits. **16** Within the gateway on both sides there were splayed windows let into the cells [and into their pilasters]; likewise, within the vestibule on both sides there were windows. The pilasters were decorated with palms.

**The Outer Court.** **17** Then he brought me to the outer court,* where there were chambers and a pavement. The pavement was laid all around the court, and the chambers, which were on the pavement, were thirty in number. **18** The pavement lay alongside the gates, as wide as the gates were long; this was the lower pavement. **19** He measured the width of the court from the front of the lower gate to the front of the inner gate; it was one hundred cubits between them.

**The North Gate.** Then he proceeded north, **20** where, on the outer court, there was a gate facing north, whose length and width he measured. **21** Its cells, three on either side, its pilasters, and its vestibule had the same measurements as those of the first gate; it was fifty cubits long and twenty-five cubits wide. **22** Its windows, the windows of its vestibule, and its palm decorations were of the same proportions as those of the gate facing the east. Seven steps led up to it, and its vestibule was toward the inside. **23** The inner court had a gate opposite the north gate, just as at the east gate; he measured one hundred cubits from one gate to the other.

**The South Gate.** **24** Then he led me south, to where there was a southern gate, whose cells, pilasters, and vestibule he measured; they were the same size as the others. **25** The gate and its vestibule had windows on both sides, like the

v Ez 36, 23.

*

40, 1—48, 35: This lengthy vision of the new Israel is dated (Ez 40, 1) April 28, 573 B.C. It is largely concerned with the new temple and the prescriptions to govern it, but other details of the restored commonwealth are included, forming a kind of program for the future. The literary form of the vision has been aptly termed "utopian": it is plain that the prophet did not expect a literal fulfillment of much of what he described. The passage doubtless underwent successive additions, both from the prophet and from later inspired writers.

40, 5: A cubit and a handbreadth: the ordinary cubit consisted of six handbreadths; the great cubit, of seven. In measuring the temple, a rod six great cubits long was used. The ordinary cubit was about one and a half feet, or, more exactly, 17.5 inches; the large cubit, 20.4 inches.

40, 6–16: The east gate, leading into the outer court of the temple, is described more fully than the north and south gates, which, however, were of the same dimensions. On the west side of the outer court there was a large building instead of a gate (Ez 41, 12).

40, 17: The outer court: the court outside the temple area proper, which had its own inner court (vv 28–37).

other windows. It was fifty cubits long and twenty-five cubits wide. **26** It was ascended by seven steps; its vestibule was toward the inside; and it was decorated with palms here and there on its pilasters. **27** The inner court also had a southern gate; from gate to gate he measured one hundred cubits.

**Gates of the Inner Court.*** **28** Then he brought me to the inner court by the south gate, where he measured the south gate. Its dimensions were the same as the others; **29** its cells, its pilasters, and its vestibule were the same size as the others. The gate and its vestibule had windows on both sides; and it was fifty cubits long and twenty-five cubits wide. **31** But its vestibule was toward the outer court; palms were on its pilasters, and it had a stairway of eight steps. **32** Then he brought me to the gate facing the east, where he measured the gate, whose dimensions were found to be the same. **33** Its cells, its pilasters, and its vestibule were the same size as the others; the gate and its vestibule had windows on both sides; it was fifty cubits long and twenty-five cubits wide. **34** But its vestibule was toward the outer court; palms were on its pilasters here and there, and it had a stairway of eight steps. **35** Then he brought me to the north gate, where he measured the dimensions **36** of its cells, its pilasters, and its vestibule, and found them the same. The gate and its vestibule had windows on both sides; it was fifty cubits long and twenty-five cubits wide. **37** Its vestibule was toward the outer court; palms were on its pilasters here and there, and it had a stairway of eight steps.

**Side Rooms.** **38** There was a chamber opening off the vestibule of the gate, where the holocausts were rinsed. **39** In the vestibule of the gate there were two tables on either side, on which were slaughtered the sin offerings and guilt offerings. **40** Along the wall of the vestibule, but outside, near the entrance of the north gate, were two tables, and on the other side of the vestibule of the gate there were two tables. **41** There were four tables on either side of the gate [eight tables], on which the sacrifices were slaughtered. **42** There were four tables for holocausts, made of cut stone, one and a half cubits long, one and a half cubits wide, and one cubit high. **43** The ledges, a handbreadth wide, were set on the inside all around, and on them were laid the instruments with which the holocausts were slaughtered. On the tables themselves the flesh was laid. **44** He then led me to the inner court where there were two chambers, one beside the north gate, facing south, and the other beside the south gate, facing north. **45** He said to me, "This chamber which faces south is for the priests who have charge of the temple, **46** and the chamber which faces north is for the priests who have charge of the altar. These are the Zadokites,* the only Levites who may come near to minister to the LORD." **47** Then he measured the court, which was a hundred cubits long and a hundred cubits wide, a perfect square. The altar stood in front of the temple.

**The Temple Building.*** **48** Then he brought me into the vestibule of the temple and measured the pilasters on each side, which were five cubits. The width of the doorway was fourteen cubits, and the side walls on either side of the door measured three cubits. **49** *The vestibule was twenty cubits wide and twelve cubits deep; ten steps led up to it, and there were columns by the pilasters, one on either side.

## CHAPTER 41

**1** Then he brought me to the nave and measured the pilasters, which were six cubits thick on either side. **2** The width of the entrance was ten cubits, and the walls at either side of it measured five cubits each. He measured the length of the nave, which was found to be forty cubits, while its width was twenty.

**3** Then he went in beyond and measured the pilasters flanking that entrance, which were two cubits; the width of the entrance was six cubits, and the walls at either side of it extended seven cubits each. **4** He measured the space beyond the nave, twenty cubits long and twenty cubits wide, and said to me, "This is the holy of holies."*

**5** Then he measured the wall of the temple, which was six cubits thick; the side chambers, which extended all the way around the temple, had a width of four cubits. **6** There were thirty side chambers built one above the other in three stories, and there were offsets in the outside wall of the temple that enclosed the side chambers; these served as supports, so that there were no supports in the temple wall proper. **7** There was a broad circular passageway that led upward to the side chambers, for the temple was enclosed all the way around and all the way upward; therefore the temple had a broad way running upward so that one could pass from the lowest to the middle and the highest story.

*

40, 28–37: The gates leading into the inner court of the temple area correspond to the gates leading into the outer court, with the exception that their vestibules are on the outer rather than the inner side. (Verse 30, a dittography of v 29, is omitted.)

40, 46: The Zadokites: descendants of the priestly line of Zadok; cf 2 Sm 15, 24–29; 1 Kgs 1, 32ff; 2, 35.

40, 48—41, 15: The description of Ezekiel's visionary temple closely follows the description of the temple of Solomon (1 Kgs 6).

40, 49—41, 4: Vestibule . . . nave . . . holy of holies: the three divisions of the temple building in progressing order of sanctity. The last is called "the inner sanctuary" in 1 Kgs 6.

**8** About the temple was a raised pavement completely enclosing it—the foundations of the side
chambers—a full rod of six cubits in extent.
**9** The width of the outside wall which enclosed
the side chambers was five cubits. Between the
side chambers of the temple **10** and the chambers of the court was an open space twenty
cubits wide going all around the temple. **11** The
side chambers had entrances to the open space,
one entrance on the north and another on the
south. The width of the wall surrounding the
open space was five cubits. **12** The building*
fronting the free area on the west side was seventy cubits front to back; the wall of the building
was five cubits thick all around, and it measured
ninety cubits from side to side. **13** He measured
the temple, which was one hundred cubits long.
The free area, together with the building and its
walls, was a hundred cubits in length. **14** The
façade of the temple, along with the free area,
on the east side, was one hundred cubits wide.
**15** He measured the building which lay the
length of the free area and behind it, and together with its walls on both sides it was one hundred cubits.

**Interior of the Temple.** The inner nave and
the outer vestibule **16** were paneled with precious wood all around, covered from the ground
to the windows. There were splayed windows
with trellises about them [facing the threshold].
**17** As high as the lintel of the door, even into
the interior part of the temple as well as outside,
on every wall on every side in both the inner and
outer rooms were carved **18** the figures of cherubim and palmtrees: a palmtree between every
two cherubim. Each cherub had two faces: **19** a
man's face looking at a palmtree on one side,
and a lion's face looking at a palmtree on the
other; thus they were figured on every side
throughout the whole temple. **20** From the
ground to the lintel of the door the cherubim and
palmtrees were carved on the walls. **21** The
way into the nave was a square doorframe. In
front of the holy place was something that
looked like **22** a wooden altar,* three cubits in
height, two cubits long, and two cubits wide. It
had corners, and its base and sides were of
wood. He said to me, "This is the table which
is before the LORD." **23** The nave had a double
door, and also the holy place had **24** a double
door. Each door had two movable leaves; two
leaves were on one doorjamb and two on the
other. **25** Carved upon them [on the doors of
the nave] were cherubim and palmtrees, like
those carved on the walls. Before the vestibule
outside was a wooden lattice. **26** There were
splayed windows [and palmtrees] on both side
walls of the vestibule, and the side chambers of
the temple. . . .

## CHAPTER 42

**Other Structures.** **1** Then he led me north
to the outer court, bringing me to some chambers on the north that lay across the free area and
which were also across from the building.
**2** Their length was a hundred cubits on the
north side, and they were fifty cubits wide.
**3** Across the twenty cubits of the inner court
and the pavement of the outer court, there were
three parallel rows of them on different levels.
**4** In front of the chambers, to the inside, was
a walk ten cubits broad and a wall of one cubit;
but the entrances of the chambers were on the
north. **5** The outermost chambers were the lowest, for the system of levels set them at a level
lower than the closest chambers and those in
between;* **6** for they were in three rows and had
no foundations to conform with the foundations
of the courts, therefore they were on a lower
terrace of the ground than the closest and the
middle chambers. **7** On the far side there was
a wall running parallel to the chambers along the
outer court; its length before these chambers
was fifty cubits, **8** for the length of the chambers belonging to the outer court was fifty cubits, but along its entire length the wall measured one hundred cubits. **9** Below these
chambers there was the way in from the east, so
that one could enter from the outer court
**10** where the wall of the court began.

To the south along the side of the free area
and the building there were also chambers,
**11** before which was a passage. These looked
like the chambers to the north, just as long and
just as wide, with the same exits and plan and
entrances. **12** Below the chambers to the south
there was an entrance at the beginning of the
way which led to the back wall, by which one
could enter from the east. **13** He said to me,
"The north and south chambers which border
on the free area are the sanctuary chambers; here
the priests who draw near to the LORD shall eat
the most sacred meals, and here they shall keep
the most sacred offerings: cereal offerings, sin
offerings, and guilt offerings; for it is a holy
place.* **14** When the priests have once entered,
they shall not leave the holy place for the outer
court until they have left here the clothing in
which they ministered, for it is holy. They shall
put on other garments, and then approach the
place destined for the people."

*

41, 12: The building: the function of this structure lying behind the temple is never specified.

41, 22: A wooden altar: the altar of incense, standing in the nave at the entrance to the holy of holies.

42, 5f: The three rows of identical chambers, since they rested on different ground levels, necessarily had roofs on correspondingly different levels.

42, 13: The function of these chambers is explained again in Ez 46, 19f.

**Measuring the Outer Court.** **15** When he
had finished measuring the inner temple area,
he brought me out by way of the gate which
faces east and measured all the limits of the
court. **16** He measured the east side: five hundred cubits by his measuring rod. Then he
turned **17** and measured the north side: five
hundred cubits by the measuring rod. He turned
**18** to the south and measured five hundred cubits by the measuring rod. **19** Then he turned to
the west and measured five hundred cubits by
the measuring rod. **20** Thus he measured it in
the four directions, five hundred cubits long and
five hundred cubits wide. It was surrounded by
a wall, to separate the sacred from the profane.

## Restoration of the Temple

## CHAPTER 43

**The Return of the Lord.** **1** Then he led me
to the gate which faces the east, **2** and there I
saw the glory of the God of Israel coming from
the east. I heard a sound like the roaring of many
waters, and the earth shone with his glory.
**3** [w]The vision was like that which I had seen
when he came to destroy the city, and like that
which I had seen by the river Chebar. I fell
prone **4** as the glory of the LORD entered the
temple by way of the gate which faces the east,
**5** but spirit lifted me up and brought me to the
inner court. And I saw that the temple was filled
with the glory of the LORD. **6** Then I heard
someone speaking to me from the temple, while
the man stood beside me. **7** The voice said to
me: Son of man, this is where my throne shall
be, this is where I will set the soles of my feet;
here I will dwell among the Israelites forever.
Never again shall they and their kings profane
my holy name with their harlotries and with the
corpses of their kings [their high places].
**8** When they placed their threshold against my
threshold* and their doorpost next to mine, so
that only a wall was between us, they profaned
my holy name by their abominable deeds; therefore I consumed them in my wrath. **9** From now
on they shall put far from me their harlotry and
the corpses of their kings, and I will dwell in
their midst forever.

**The Law of the Temple.** **10** As for you,
son of man, describe the temple to the house of
Israel [that they may be ashamed of their sins],
both its measurements and its design; **11** [and
if they are ashamed of all that they have done,]
make known to them the form and design of the
temple, its exits and entrances, all its statutes
and laws; write these down for them to see, that
they may carefully observe all its laws and statutes. **12** This is the law of the temple: its whole
surrounding area on the mountain top shall be
most sacred.

**The Altar.** **13** These were the measurements
of the altar* in cubits of one cubit plus a handbreadth. Its base was one cubit high and one
cubit deep, with a rim around its edge of one
span. The height of the altar itself was as follows: **14** from its base at the bottom up to the
lower ledge it was two cubits high, and this
ledge was one cubit deep; from the lower to the
upper ledge it was four cubits high, and this
ledge also was one cubit deep; **15** the hearth of
the altar was four cubits high, and extending
from the top of the hearth were the four horns
of the altar. **16** The hearth was a square: twelve
cubits long and twelve cubits wide. **17** The upper ledge was also a square: fourteen cubits long
and fourteen cubits wide. The lower ledge, likewise a square, was sixteen cubits long and sixteen cubits wide, with a half-cubit rim surrounding it. And there was a base of one cubit all
around. The steps of the altar face the east.
**18** Then he said to me: Son of man, thus says
the Lord GOD: These are the statutes for the altar
when it is set up for the offering of holocausts
upon it and for the sprinkling of blood against
it. **19** Give a young bull as a sin offering to the
priests, the Levites who are of the line of Zadok,
who draw near me to minister to me, says the
Lord GOD. **20** Take some of its blood and put
it on the four horns of the altar, and on the four
corners of the ledge, and on the rim all around.
Thus you shall purify it and make atonement for
it. **21** Then take the bull of the sin offering,
which is to be burnt in a designated part of the
temple, outside the sanctuary. **22** On the second day present an unblemished he-goat as a sin
offering, to purify the altar as was done with the
bull. **23** When you have finished the purification, bring an unblemished young bull and an
unblemished ram from the flock, **24** and
present them before the LORD; the priests shall
strew salt on them and offer them to the LORD
as holocausts. **25** Daily for seven days you shall
offer a he-goat as a sin offering, and a young
bull and a ram from the flock, all unblemished,
shall be offered **26** for seven days. Thus atonement shall be made for the altar, and it shall be
purified and dedicated. **27** And when these
days are over, from the eighth day on, the

w Ez 1, 1.

*

43, 8: They placed their threshold against my threshold: the preexilic temple and the royal palace belonged to the same complex of buildings, and this physical proximity was reflected in the use made of the temple by kings like Ahaz and Manasseh, who treated it as their private chapel for pagan rites. In the new Israel the temple is free, even physically, from civil jurisdiction; cf Ez 45, 7f.

43, 13: The altar: of holocausts, standing in the inner court of the temple area; cf Ez 40, 47.

priests shall offer your holocausts and peace offerings on the altar. Then I will accept you, says the Lord GOD.

## CHAPTER 44

**The Closed Gate.** **1** Then he brought me back to the outer gate of the sanctuary, facing the east; but it was closed. **2** He said to me: This gate is to remain closed; it is not to be opened for anyone to enter by it; since the LORD, the God of Israel, has entered by it, it shall remain closed. **3** Only the prince may sit down in it to eat his meal in the presence of the LORD. He must enter by way of the vestibule of the gate, and leave by the same way.*

### The New Law

**Admission to the Temple.** **4** Then he brought me by way of the north gate to the façade of the temple, and when I looked I saw the glory of the LORD filling the LORD's temple, and I fell prone. **5** Then he said to me: Son of man, pay strict attention, look carefully, and listen intently to all that I will tell you about the statutes and laws of the LORD's temple; be attentive in regard to those who are to be admitted to the temple and all those who are to be excluded from the sanctuary. **6** Say to that rebellious house, the house of Israel: Thus says the Lord GOD: Enough of all these abominations of yours, O house of Israel! **7** You have admitted foreigners, uncircumcised both in heart and flesh, to my sanctuary to profane it when you offered me food, fat, and blood;* thus you have broken my covenant by all your abominations. **8** Instead of caring for the service of my temple, you have appointed such as these to serve me in my sanctuary in your stead. **9** Thus says the Lord GOD: No foreigners, uncircumcised in heart and in flesh, shall ever enter my sanctuary; none of the foreigners who live among the Israelites.

**Levites.*** **10** But as for the Levites who departed from me when Israel strayed from me to pursue their idols, they shall bear the consequences of their sin. **11** They shall serve in my sanctuary as gatekeepers and temple servants; they shall slaughter the holocausts and the sacrifices for the people, and they shall stand before the people to minister for them. **12** Because they used to minister for them before their idols, and became an occasion of sin to the house of Israel, therefore I have sworn an oath against them, says the Lord GOD: they shall bear the consequences of their sin. **13** They shall no longer draw near me to serve as my priests, nor shall they touch any of my sacred things, or the most sacred things. Thus they shall bear their disgrace because of all their abominable deeds. **14** But I will set them to the service of the temple, for all its work and for everything that is to be done in it.

**Priests.** **15** As for the levitical priests, however, the Zadokites who cared for my sanctuary when the Israelites strayed from me, they shall draw near me to minister to me, and they shall stand before me to offer me fat and blood, says the Lord GOD. **16** It is they who shall enter my sanctuary, they who shall approach my table to minister to me, and they who shall carry out my service. **17** Whenever they enter the gates of the inner court, they shall wear linen garments; they shall not put on anything woolen when they minister at the gates of the inner court or within the temple. **18** [x]They shall have linen turbans on their heads and linen drawers on their loins; they shall not gird themselves with anything that causes sweat. **19** [y]When they are to go out to the people in the outer court, they shall take off the garments in which they ministered and leave them in the chambers of the sanctuary, putting on other garments; thus they will not transmit holiness to the people* with their garments.

**20** [z]They shall not shave their heads nor let their hair hang loose, but they shall keep their hair carefully trimmed. **21** [a]No priest shall drink wine when he is to enter the inner court. **22** [b]They shall not take for their wives either widows or divorced women, but only virgins of the race of Israel; however, they may marry women who are the widows of priests. **23** They shall teach my people to distinguish between the sacred and the profane, and make known to them the difference between the clean and the unclean. **24** [c]In capital cases they shall stand as judges, judging them according to my decrees.

x Ex 28, 40. 42; 29, 9; 38, 28; Lv 6, 3.
y Ez 42, 13. 14.
z Lv 21, 5.
a Lv 10, 9.
b Lv 21, 7. 14.
c Dt 17, 9; 19, 17.

*

44, 3: The prince stands at the eastern gate of the inner court while his sacrifice is offered up (Ez 46, 2); he then goes to the vestibule of the outer court, there to partake of his sacrificial meal. The closed outer gate on the eastern side signifies that the Lord has entered the temple permanently, not to depart again.

44, 7ff: In the preexilic temple various menial services had been performed by foreigners; cf Jos 9, 22–27. In the new temple the Levites will perform these services (vv 10–14).

44, 10–14: Levites other than the Zadokite priesthood of Jerusalem had performed priestly functions at the various sanctuaries and high places in Israel and Judah, where the worship of the Lord had often been corrupted with pagan elements. The demotion of the Levites to menial service in the temple was enforced in the actual restoration after the exile, and explains why relatively few Levites were willing to return; cf 1 Ezr 8, 15ff.

44, 19: Thus they will not transmit holiness to the people: holiness was thought of as something physical, as though it were communicable, and therefore not to be brought in contact with unconsecrated persons.

They shall observe my laws and statutes on all my festivals, and keep my sabbaths holy.

**25** [d]They shall not make themselves unclean by coming near any dead person, unless it be their father, mother, son, daughter, brother, or maiden sister; for these they may make themselves unclean. **26** After a priest has been cleansed, he must wait an additional seven days, **27** and on the day he enters the inner court to minister in the sanctuary, he shall present his sin offering, says the Lord GOD. **28** [e]They shall have no inheritance, for I am their inheritance; you shall give them no property in Israel, for I am their property. **29** [f]They shall eat the cereal offering, the sin offering, and the guilt offering; whatever is under the ban* in Israel shall be theirs. **30** [g]All the choicest first fruits of every kind, and all the best of your offerings of every kind, shall belong to the priests; likewise the best of your dough you shall give to the priests to bring a blessing down upon your house. **31** [h]The priests shall not eat anything, whether flesh or fowl, that has died of itself or has been killed by wild beasts.

## CHAPTER 45

**The Sacred Tract.** **1** When you apportion the land into inheritances, you shall set apart a sacred tract of land for the LORD, twenty-five thousand cubits long and twenty thousand wide; its whole area shall be sacred. **2** Of this land a square plot, five hundred by five hundred cubits, surrounded by a free space of fifty cubits, shall be assigned to the sanctuary. **3** Also from this sector measure off a strip, twenty-five thousand cubits long and ten thousand wide, within which shall be the sanctuary, the holy of holies. **4** This shall be the sacred part of the land belonging to the priests, the ministers of the sanctuary, who draw near to minister to the LORD; it shall be a place for their homes and pasture land for their cattle. **5** Also there shall be a strip twenty-five thousand cubits long and ten thousand wide as property for the Levites, the ministers of the temple, that they may have cities to live in. **6** As property of the City you shall designate a strip five thousand cubits wide and twenty-five thousand long, parallel to the sacred tract; this shall belong to the whole house of Israel. **7** The prince shall have a section bordering on both sides of the combined sacred tract and City property, extending westward on the western side and eastward on the eastern side, corresponding in length to one of the tribal portions from the western boundary to the eastern boundary **8** of the land. This shall be his property in Israel, so that the princes of Israel will no longer oppress my people, but will leave the land to the house of Israel according to their tribes.

**Weights and Measures.*** **9** Thus says the Lord GOD: Enough, you princes of Israel! Put away violence and oppression, and do what is right and just! Stop evicting my people! says the Lord GOD. **10** [i]You shall have honest scales, an honest ephah, and an honest liquid measure. **11** The ephah and the liquid measure shall be of the same size: the liquid measure equal to a tenth of a homer, and the ephah equal to a tenth of a homer; by the homer they shall be determined. **12** [j]The shekel shall be twenty gerahs. Twenty shekels, twenty-five shekels, plus fifteen shekels shall be your mina.

**Offerings.** **13** These are the offerings you shall make: one sixth of an ephah from each homer of wheat, and one sixth of an ephah from each homer of barley. **14** The regulation for oil: for every measure of oil, a tenth of a measure, computed by the kor* of ten liquid measures [or a homer, for ten liquid measures make a homer]. **15** One sheep from the flock for every two hundred from the pasturage of Israel, for sacrifice—holocausts and peace offerings and atonement sacrifices, says the Lord GOD. **16** All the people of the land shall be bound to this offering [for the prince in Israel]. **17** It shall be the duty of the prince to provide the holocausts, cereal offerings, and libations on the feasts, new moons, and sabbaths, on all the festivals of the house of Israel. He shall offer the sin offerings, cereal offerings, holocausts, and peace offerings, to make atonement on behalf of the house of Israel.

**The Passover.** **18** Thus says the Lord GOD: On the first day of the first month you shall use an unblemished young bull as a sacrifice to purify the sanctuary. **19** Then the priest shall take some of the blood from the sin offering and put it on the doorposts of the temple, on

d Lv 21, 1ff. 11.
e Nm 18, 20; Dt 18, 1.
f Lv 2, 3. 10; 6, 9. 22; 7, 9; 10, 12; Nm 18, 9; 18, 14.
g Ex 34, 26; Dt 18, 4.
h Lv 22, 8.
i Lv 19, 35; Dt 25, 13-16; Hos 12, 8; Am 8, 5; Mi 6, 10f.
j Ex 30, 13; Lv 27, 25; Nm 3, 47; 18, 16.

*

44, 29: Under the ban: dedicated to the Lord, withdrawn from profane use.

45, 9–12: Besides the land monopoly fostered by royal greed and collusion with the wealthy (Mi 2, 2; Is 3, 12–15; 5, 8–10), one grave social evil of preexilic Israel was dishonesty in business; cf Hos 12, 8; Am 8, 5. Ephah: a dry measure; liquid measure: in Hebrew, a "bath," standardized according to the homer (a dry measure of about 10 bushels, or 80 gallons). In v 12 reference is made to the change in value of the mina: before the exile it was valued at 50 shekels, but afterward, in imitation of Babylonian practice, the 60-shekel mina was adopted. The shekel was a unit of weight slightly less than half an ounce. As a monetary unit, the value obviously differed greatly, depending on whether it was a gold or a silver shekel.

45, 14: Kor: both a liquid and a dry measure, corresponding to the homer.

the four corners of the ledge of the altar, and on
the doorposts of the gates of the inner court.
**20** You shall repeat this on the first day of the
seventh month for those who have sinned
through inadvertence or ignorance; thus you
shall make atonement for the temple. **21** [k]On
the fourteenth day of the first month you shall
observe the feast of the Passover; for seven days
unleavened bread is to be eaten. **22** On that day
the prince shall offer on his own behalf, and on
behalf of all the people of the land, a bull as a
sin offering. **23** On each of the seven days of
the feast he shall offer as a holocaust to the Lord
seven bulls and seven rams without blemish,
and as a sin offering he shall offer one male goat
each day. **24** As a cereal offering he shall offer
one ephah for each bull and one ephah for each
ram; and he shall offer one hin* of oil for each
ephah.

**The Feast of Booths.** **25** On the fifteenth
day of the seventh month, the feast day, and for
seven days, he shall perform the same rites,
making the same sin offerings, the same holocausts, the same cereal offerings and offerings
of oil.

## CHAPTER 46

**Sabbaths.** **1** Thus says the Lord GOD: The
gate toward the east of the inner court shall
remain closed throughout the six working days,
but on the sabbath and on the day of the new
moon it shall be open. **2** The prince shall enter
from outside by way of the vestibule of the gate
and remain standing at the doorpost of the gate;
then while the priests offer his holocausts and
peace offerings, he shall worship at the threshold of the gate and then leave; the gate shall not
be closed until evening. **3** The people of the
land shall worship before the LORD at the door
of this gate on the sabbaths and new moons.
**4** [l]The holocausts which the prince presents to
the LORD on the sabbath shall consist of six
unblemished lambs and an unblemished ram,
**5** together with a cereal offering of one ephah
for the ram, whatever he pleases for the lambs,
and a hin of oil for each ephah. **6** [m]On the day
of the new moon he shall provide an unblemished young bull, also six lambs and a ram
without blemish, **7** with a cereal offering of one
ephah for the bull and one for the ram, for the
lambs as much as he has at hand, and for each
ephah a hin of oil.

**Ritual Laws.** **8** The prince shall always enter and depart by the vestibule of the gate.
**9** [n]When the people of the land enter the presence of the LORD to worship on the festivals, if
they enter by the north gate they shall leave by
the south gate, and if they enter by the south
gate they shall leave by the north gate; no one
shall return by the gate through which he has
entered, but he shall leave by the opposite gate.
**10** The prince shall be in their midst when they
enter, and he shall also leave with them. **11** On
the feasts and festivals the cereal offering shall
be an ephah for a bull, an ephah for a ram, but
for the lambs as much as one pleases, and a hin
of oil with each ephah. **12** When the prince
makes a freewill offering to the LORD, whether
holocausts or peace offerings, the eastern gate
shall be opened for him, and he shall offer his
holocausts or his peace offerings as on the sabbath; then he shall leave, and the gate shall be
closed after his departure. **13** [o]He shall offer as
a daily holocaust to the LORD an unblemished
yearling lamb; this he shall offer every morning.
**14** With it every morning he shall provide as a
cereal offering one sixth of an ephah, with a
third of a hin of oil to moisten the fine flour.
This cereal offering to the LORD is mandatory
with the established holocaust. **15** [p]The lamb,
the cereal offering, and the oil are to be offered
every morning as an established holocaust.

**The Prince and the Land.** **16** Thus says
the Lord GOD: If the prince makes a gift of part
of his inheritance to any of his sons, it shall
belong to his sons; that property is theirs by
inheritance. **17** But if he makes a gift of part of
his inheritance to one of his servants, it shall
belong to the latter only until the year of release,* when it shall revert to the prince. Only
the inheritance given to his sons is permanent.
**18** The prince shall not seize any part of the
inheritance of the people by evicting them from
their property. He shall provide an inheritance
for his sons from his own property, so that none
of my people will be driven from their property.

**The Temple Kitchens.** **19** Then he
brought me by the entrance which is on the side
of the gate to the chambers [of the sanctuary,
reserved to the priests] which face the north.
There, at their west end, I saw a place, **20** concerning which he said to me, "Here the priests
cook the guilt offerings and the sin offerings,
and bake the cereal offerings, so that they do not
have to take them into the outer court at the risk
of transmitting holiness to the people."
**21** Then he led me into the outer court and had
me pass around the four corners of the court,
and I saw that in each corner there was another

k Ex 12, 6; Lv 23, 5; Nm 28, 16.
l Nm 28, 9f.
m Nm 28, 11-15.
n Ex 23, 17; 34, 23; Dt 16, 16.
o Ex 29, 38-42; Nm 28, 3-8.
p Ex 29, 42.

*

45, 24: Hin: a sixth part of the liquid measure called a bath.
46, 17: The year of release: the jubilee year; cf Lv 25, 23–55.

court: **22** in the four corners of the court, minor
courts, forty cubits long and thirty wide, all four
of them the same size. **23** A wall of stones
surrounded each of the four, and hearths were
built beneath the stones all the way around.
**24** He said to me, "These are the kitchens
where the temple ministers cook the sacrifices
of the people."

## CHAPTER 47

**The Wonderful Stream.*** **1** Then he
brought me back to the entrance of the temple,
and I saw water flowing out from beneath the
threshold of the temple toward the east, for the
façade of the temple was toward the east; the
water flowed down from the southern side of the
temple, south of the altar.[q] **2** He led me outside
by the north gate, and around to the outer gate
facing the east, where I saw water trickling from
the southern side. **3** Then when he had walked
off to the east with a measuring cord in his hand,
he measured off a thousand cubits and had me
wade through the water, which was ankle-deep.
**4** He measured off another thousand and once
more had me wade through the water, which
was now knee-deep. Again he measured off a
thousand and had me wade; the water was up to
my waist. **5** Once more he measured off a thousand, but there was now a river through which
I could not wade; for the water had risen so high
it had become a river that could not be crossed
except by swimming. **6** He asked me, "Have
you seen this, son of man?" Then he brought
me to the bank of the river, where he had me sit.
**7** Along the bank of the river I saw very many
trees on both sides. **8** He said to me, "This
water flows into the eastern district down upon
the Arabah, and empties into the sea, the salt
waters, which it makes fresh. **9** Wherever the
river flows, every sort of living creature that can
multiply shall live, and there shall be abundant
fish, for wherever this water comes the sea shall
be made fresh. **10** Fishermen shall be standing
along it from En-gedi to En-eglaim,* spreading
their nets there. Its kinds of fish shall be like
those of the Great Sea, very numerous. **11** Only
its marshes and swamps shall not be made fresh;
they shall be left for salt. **12** Along both banks
of the river, fruit trees of every kind shall grow;
their leaves shall not fade, nor their fruit fail.
Every month they shall bear fresh fruit, for they
shall be watered by the flow from the sanctuary.
Their fruit shall serve for food, and their leaves
for medicine."

### The New Israel

**Boundaries of the Land.*** **13** Thus says
the Lord GOD: These are the boundaries within
which you shall apportion the land among the
twelve tribes of Israel [Joseph having two por-
tions]. **14** All of you shall have a like portion
in this land which I swore to give to your fathers, that it might fall to you as your inheritance. **15** [r]This is the boundary of the land on
the north side: from the Great Sea in the direction of Hethlon, past Labo of Hamath, to Zedad,
**16** Berothah, and Sibraim, along the frontiers
of Hamath and Damascus, to Hazar-enon which
is on the border of the Hauran. **17** Thus the
border shall extend from the sea to Hazar-enon,
with the frontier of Hamath and Damascus to the
north. This is the northern boundary. **18** The
eastern boundary: between the Hauran—toward
Damascus—and Gilead on the one side, and the
land of Israel on the other side, the Jordan shall
form the boundary down to the eastern sea as far
as Tamar. This is the eastern boundary. **19** The
southern boundary: from Tamar to the waters of
Meribath-kadesh, thence to the Wadi of Egypt,
and on to the Great Sea. This is the southern
boundary. **20** The western boundary: the Great
Sea forms the boundary up to a point parallel to
Labo of Hamath. This is the western boundary.

**The Northern Portions.** **21** You shall distribute this land among yourselves according to
the tribes of Israel. **22** [s]You shall allot it as
inheritances for yourselves and for the aliens
resident in your midst who have bred children
among you. The latter shall be to you like native
Israelites; along with you they shall receive inheritances among the tribes of Israel. **23** In
whatever tribe the alien may be resident, there
you shall assign him his inheritance, says the
Lord God.

## CHAPTER 48

**1** This is the list* of the tribes.[t] Dan: at the
northern extremity, adjoining Hamath, all along
from the approaches to Hethlon through Labo of
Hamath to Hazar-enon, on the northerly border
with Damascus, with his possession reaching

q Sir 24, 28f; Jl 4, 18; Zec 13, 1; Rv 22, 1f.
r Nm 34, 7ff.
s Ex 12, 48; Lv 19, 34; 24, 22; Nm 9, 14; Jos 8, 33.
t Ez 47, 15ff.

*

47, 1–12: The wonderful and superabundant stream flowing from the temple, restoring to fertility traditionally arid ground, is symbolic of the return of the conditions of primeval paradise; cf Gn 2, 10–14. Water signifies great blessings, just as dryness signifies a curse; cf Ez 26, 5. 14.

47, 10: From En-gedi to En-eglaim: the former was about halfway down the western shore of the Dead Sea, the latter may have been at its northern extremity.

47, 13–20: These boundaries of the restored Israel correspond to those of the Davidic kingdom at its fullest extent, the so-called "ideal boundaries" of the promised land; cf Nm 34, 3–12.

48, 1–29: This distribution of the land among the tribes does not correspond to the geographical realities of Palestine. It is a description of the ideal order, like that in Ez 47, 1–12.

from the eastern to the western boundary.
**2** Asher: on the frontier of Dan, from the eastern to the western boundary. **3** Naphtali: on the
frontier of Asher, from the eastern to the western boundary. **4** Manasseh: on the frontier of
Naphtali, from the eastern to the western boundary. **5** Ephraim: on the frontier of Manasseh,
from the eastern to the western boundary.
**6** Reuben: on the frontier of Ephraim, from the
eastern to the western boundary. **7** Judah: on
the frontier of Reuben, from the eastern to the
western boundary.

**The Sacred Tract.** **8** On the frontier of
Judah, from the eastern to the western boundary
there shall be the tract which you shall set apart,
twenty-five thousand cubits from north to south,
and as wide as one of the tribal portions from the
eastern to the western boundary. In the center of
the tract shall be the sanctuary. **9** The tract that
you set aside for the LORD shall be twenty-five
thousand cubits across by twenty thousand north
and south. **10** In this sacred tract the priests
shall have twenty-five thousand cubits on the
north, ten thousand on the west, ten thousand on
the east, and twenty-five thousand on the south;
and the sanctuary of the LORD shall be in its
center. **11** The consecrated priests, the Zadokites, who fulfilled my service and did not stray
along with the Israelites as the Levites did,
**12** shall have within this tract of land their own
most sacred domain, next to the territory of the
Levites. **13** The Levites shall have a territory
corresponding to that of the priests, twenty-five
thousand cubits by ten thousand. The whole
tract shall be twenty-five thousand cubits across
and twenty thousand north and south. **14** They
may not sell or exchange or alienate this, the
best part of the land, for it is sacred to the LORD.
**15** The remaining five thousand cubits along
the twenty-five-thousand-cubit line are profane
land, assigned to the City for dwellings and
pasture; the City shall be at their center.
**16** These are the dimensions of the City: the
north side, forty-five hundred cubits; the south
side, forty-five hundred cubits; the east side,
forty-five hundred cubits; and the west side,
forty-five hundred cubits. **17** The pasture lands
of the City shall extend north two hundred and
fifty cubits, south two hundred and fifty cubits,
east two hundred and fifty cubits, and west two
hundred and fifty cubits. **18** There shall remain
an area along the sacred tract, ten thousand
cubits to the east and ten thousand to the west,
whose produce shall provide food for the workers of the City. **19** The workers in the City shall
be taken from all the tribes of Israel. **20** The
entire tract shall be twenty-five thousand by
twenty-five thousand cubits; as a perfect square
you shall set apart the sacred tract together with
the City property.

**21** The remainder shall belong to the prince:
the land on both sides of the sacred tract and the
City property, extending along the twenty-
five-thousand-cubit line eastward to the eastern
boundary, and westward along the twenty-
five-thousand-cubit line to the western boundary, a territory parallel with the tribal portions
for the prince. The sacred tract and the sanctuary of the temple shall be in the middle.
**22** Thus, except for the property of the Levites
and the City property, which lie in the midst of
the prince's property, the territory between the
portions of Judah and of Benjamin shall belong
to the prince.

**The Southern Portions.** **23** These are the
remaining tribes. Benjamin: from the eastern to
the western boundary. **24** Simeon: on the frontier of Benjamin, from the eastern to the western
boundary. **25** Issachar: on the frontier of Simeon, from the eastern to the western boundary.
**26** Zebulun: on the frontier of Issachar, from
the eastern to the western boundary. **27** Gad: on
the frontier of Zebulun, from the eastern to the
western boundary. **28** Along the frontier of Gad
shall be the southern boundary, which shall extend from Tamar to the waters of Meribath-kadesh, and from there to the Wadi of Egypt, and
on to the Great Sea. **29** Such is the land which
you shall apportion as inheritances among the
tribes of Israel, and these are their portions, says
the Lord GOD.

**The Gates of the City.** **30** These are the
exits of the City, the gates of which are named
after the tribes of Israel. On the north side,
measuring forty-five hundred cubits, **31** there
shall be three gates: the gate of Reuben, the gate
of Judah, and the gate of Levi. **32** On the east
side, measuring forty-five hundred cubits, there
shall be three gates: the gate of Joseph, the gate
of Benjamin, and the gate of Dan. **33** On the
south side, measuring forty-five hundred cubits,
there shall be three gates: the gate of Simeon,
the gate of Issachar, and the gate of Zebulun.
**34** On the west side, measuring forty-five hundred cubits, there shall be three gates: the gate
of Gad, the gate of Asher, and the gate of Naphtali. **35** The perimeter of the City is eighteen
thousand cubits. The name of the City shall
henceforth be "The LORD is here."

# The Book of DANIEL

*This Book takes its name, not from the author, who is actually unknown, but from its hero, a young Jew taken early to Babylon, where he lived at least until 538 B.C. Strictly speaking, the book does not belong to the prophetic writings but rather to a distinctive type of literature known as "apocalyptic," of which it is an early specimen. Apocalyptic writing enjoyed its greatest popularity from 200 B.C. to 100 A.D., a time of distress and persecution for Jews, and later, for Christians. Though subsequent in time to the prophetic, apocalyptic literature has its roots in the teaching of the prophets, who often pointed ahead to the day of the Lord, the consummation of history. For both prophet and apocalyptist Yahweh was the Lord of history, and he would ultimately vindicate his people.*

*This work was composed during the bitter persecution carried on by Antiochus IV Epiphanes (167–164) and was written to strengthen and comfort the Jewish people in their ordeal.*

*The Book contains stories originating in and transmitted by popular traditions which tell of the trials and triumphs of the wise Daniel and his three companions. The moral is that men of faith can resist temptation and conquer adversity. The characters are not purely legendary but rest on older historical tradition. What is more important than the question of historicity, and closer to the intention of the author, is the fact that a persecuted Jew of the second century B.C. would quickly see the application of these stories to his own plight.*

*There follows a series of visions promising deliverance and glory to the Jews in the days to come. The great nations of the ancient world have risen in vain against Yahweh; his kingdom shall overthrow existing powers and last forever. Under this apocalyptic imagery are contained some of the best elements of prophetic teaching: the insistence on right conduct, the divine control over events, the certainty that the kingdom of God will ultimately triumph. The arrival of the kingdom is a central theme of the synoptic gospels, and Jesus, in calling himself the "Son of Man," reminds us that he fulfills the destiny of this mysterious figure in the seventh chapter of Daniel.*

*The added episodes of Susanna, Bel, and the Dragon, found only in the Greek version, are edifying short stories with a didactic purpose.*

*These three sections constitute the divisions of the Book of Daniel:*

*I. Daniel and the Kings of Babylon (1, 1–6, 29).*
*II. Daniel's Visions (7, 1–12, 13).*
*III. Appendix (13, 1–14, 42).*

## I: Daniel and the Kings of Babylon

### CHAPTER 1

**The Food Test.** 1 In the third year of the
reign of Jehoiakim, king of Judah, King Nebuchadnezzar of Babylon came and laid siege to
Jerusalem.[a] 2 [b]The Lord handed over to him
Jehoiakim, king of Judah, and some of the vessels of the temple of God, which he carried off
to the land of Shinar,* and placed in the temple
treasury of his god.
3 The king told Ashpenaz, his chief chamberlain, to bring in some of the Israelites of
royal blood and of the nobility, 4 young men
without any defect, handsome, intelligent and
wise, quick to learn, and prudent in judgment,
such as could take their place in the king's palace; they were to be taught the language and
literature of the Chaldeans; 5 after three years'
training they were to enter the king's service.
The king allotted them a daily portion of food
and wine from the royal table. 6 Among these
were men of Judah: Daniel, Hananiah, Mishael,

a 2 Kgs 24, 1; 2 Chr 36, 6; Jer 25, 1.
b Dn 5, 2; Gn 10, 10; 2 Kgs 24, 2; 2 Chr 36, 7.

* 1, 2: Shinar: ancient name for Babylonia, a deliberate archaism in this text: cf Gn 10. 10; 11. 2.

and Azariah. **7** The chief chamberlain changed
their names: Daniel to Belteshazzar, Hananiah
to Shadrach, Mishael to Meshach, and Azariah
to Abednego.*

**8** But Daniel was resolved not to defile himself with the king's food or wine; so he begged
the chief chamberlain to spare him this defilement.* **9** Though God had given Daniel the
favor and sympathy of the chief chamberlain,
**10** he nevertheless said to Daniel, "I am afraid
of my lord the king; it is he who allotted your
food and drink. If he sees that you look wretched by comparison with the other young men of
your age, you will endanger my life with the
king." **11** Then Daniel said to the steward
whom the chief chamberlain had put in charge
of Daniel, Hananiah, Mishael, and Azariah,
**12** "Please test your servants for ten days. Give
us vegetables to eat and water to drink. **13** Then
see how we look in comparison with the other
young men who eat from the royal table, and
treat your servants according to what you see."
**14** He acceded to this request, and tested them
for ten days; **15** after ten days they looked
healthier and better fed than any of the young
men who ate from the royal table. **16** So the
steward continued to take away the food and
wine they were to receive, and gave them vegetables.

**17** To these four young men God gave
knowledge and proficiency in all literature and
science, and to Daniel the understanding of all
visions and dreams. **18** At the end of the time
the king had specified for their preparation, the
chief chamberlain brought them before Nebuchadnezzar. **19** When the king had spoken with
all of them, none was found equal to Daniel,
Hananiah, Mishael, and Azariah; and so they
entered the king's service. **20** In any question
of wisdom or prudence which the king put to
them, he found them ten times better than all the
magicians and enchanters in his kingdom.
**21** [c]Daniel remained there until the first year of
King Cyrus.*

## CHAPTER 2

**The King's Dream*** **1** In the second year of
his reign, King Nebuchadnezzar had a dream
which left his spirit no rest and robbed him of
his sleep. **2** So he ordered that the magicians,
enchanters, sorcerers, and Chaldeans* be summoned to interpret the dream for him. When
they came and presented themselves to the king,
**3** he said to them, "I had a dream which will
allow my spirit no rest until I know what it
means." **4** The Chaldeans answered the king
[Aramaic]:* "O king, live forever! Tell your
servants the dream and we will give its meaning." **5** The king answered the Chaldeans,
"This is what I have decided: unless you tell me
the dream and its meaning, you shall be cut to
pieces and your houses destroyed. **6** But if you
tell me the dream and its meaning, you shall
receive from me gifts and presents and great
honors. Now tell me the dream and its meaning."

**7** Again they answered, "Let the king tell his
servants the dream and we will give its meaning." **8** But the king replied: "I know for certain that you are bargaining for time, since you
know what I have decided. **9** If you do not tell
me the dream, there can be but one decree for
you. You have framed a false and deceitful
interpretation to present me with till the crisis is
past. Tell me the dream, therefore, that I may
be sure that you can also give its correct interpretation."

**10** The Chaldeans answered the king:
"There is not a man on earth who can do what
you ask, O king; never has any king, however
great and mighty, asked such a thing of any
magician, enchanter, or Chaldean. **11** What
you demand, O king, is too difficult; there is no
one who can tell it to the king except the gods
who do not dwell among men." **12** At this the
king became violently angry and ordered all the
wise men of Babylon to be put to death.
**13** When the decree was issued that the wise
men should be slain, Daniel and his companions
were also sought out.

**14** Then Daniel prudently took counsel with
Arioch, the captain of the king's guard, who had
set out to kill the wise men of Babylon: **15** "O
officer of the king," he asked, "what is the
reason for this harsh order from the king?"
When Arioch told him, **16** Daniel went and
asked for time from the king, that he might give
him the interpretation.

**17** Daniel went home and informed his companions Hananiah, Mishael, and Azariah,
**18** that they might implore the mercy of the
God of heaven in regard to this mystery, so that

---

c Dn 6, 28.

---

1, 7: The young men are given Babylonian names as a sign of their adoption by the king.

1, 8: This defilement: the bread, meat, and wine of the Gentiles, which were unclean (Hos 9, 3; Tb 1, 12; Jdt 10, 5; 12, 1f) because they might have been offered to idols or prepared over firewood taken from a sacred grove. Only raw vegetables and water were safe from this danger (v 12).

1, 21: The first year of King Cyrus: the year of this Persian king's conquest of Babylon, 539/8 B.C.

2, 1–49: The chronology of v 1 is in conflict with that of Dn 1, 5. 18, and in v 25 Daniel appears to be introduced to the king for the first time. It seems that the story of this chapter was originally entirely independent of chapter 1, and later retouched slightly to fit its present setting.

2, 2: Chaldeans: here probably astrologers, who were so associated with the Chaldeans in the Hebrew mind that in the later language they are sometimes simply called by the name of that people.

2, 4: Aramaic: from Dn 2, 4 to 7, 28 the text of Daniel is in Aramaic, not Hebrew, as indicated by this gloss.

Daniel and his companions might not perish
with the rest of the wise men of Babylon.
**19** During the night the mystery was revealed
to Daniel in a vision, and he blessed the God of
heaven:

**20** "Blessed be the name of God forever and
ever,
for wisdom and power are his.
**21** He causes the changes of the times and
seasons,
makes kings and unmakes them.
He gives wisdom to the wise
and knowledge to those who understand.
**22** He reveals deep and hidden things
and knows what is in the darkness,
for the light dwells with him.[d]
**23** To you, O God of my fathers,
I give thanks and praise,
because you have given me wisdom and
power.
Now you have shown me what we asked of
you,
you have made known to us the king's
dream."

**24** So Daniel went to Arioch, whom the king
had appointed to destroy the wise men of Babylon, and said to him, "Do not put the wise men
of Babylon to death. Bring me before the king,
and I will tell him the interpretation of the
dream." Arioch quickly brought Daniel to the
king and said, **25** "I have found a man among
the Judean captives who can give the interpretation to the king." **26** The king asked Daniel,
whose name was Belteshazzar, "Can you tell
me the dream that I had, and its meaning?"
**27** In the king's presence Daniel made this reply:

"The mystery about which the king has inquired, the wise men, enchanters, magicians,
and astrologers could not explain to the king.
**28** But there is a God in heaven who reveals
mysteries, and he has shown King Nebuchadnezzar what is to happen in days to come; this
was the dream you saw as you lay in bed. **29** To
you in your bed there came thoughts about what
should happen in the future, and he who reveals
mysteries showed you what is to be. **30** To me
also this mystery has been revealed; not that I
am wiser than any other living person, but in
order that its meaning may be made known to
the king, that you may understand the thoughts
in your own mind.

**31** "In your vision, O king, you saw a statue, very large and exceedingly bright, terrifying
in appearance as it stood before you. **32** The
head of the statue was pure gold, its chest and
arms were silver, its belly and thighs bronze,
**33** the legs iron, its feet partly iron and partly
tile.* **34** While you looked at the statue, a stone
which was hewn from a mountain without a
hand being put to it, struck its iron and tile feet,
breaking them in pieces. **35** The iron, tile,
bronze, silver, and gold all crumbled at once,
fine as the chaff on the threshing floor in summer, and the wind blew them away without
leaving a trace. But the stone that struck the
statue became a great mountain and filled the
whole earth.

**36** *"This was the dream; the interpretation
we shall also give in the king's presence.
**37** You, O king, are the king of kings; to you
the God of heaven has given dominion and
strength, power and glory; **38** men, wild
beasts, and birds of the air, wherever they may
dwell, he has handed over to you, making you
ruler over them all; you are the head of gold.
**39** Another kingdom shall take your place, inferior to yours, then a third kingdom, of bronze,
which shall rule over the whole earth. **40** There
shall be a fourth kingdom, strong as iron; it shall
break in pieces and subdue all these others, just
as iron breaks in pieces and crushes everything
else. **41** The feet and toes you saw, partly of
potter's tile and partly of iron, mean that it shall
be a divided kingdom, but yet have some of the
hardness of iron. As you saw the iron mixed
with clay tile, **42** and the toes partly iron and
partly tile, the kingdom shall be partly strong
and partly fragile. **43** The iron mixed with clay
tile means that they shall seal their alliances by
intermarriage, but they shall not stay united,
any more than iron mixes with clay. **44** [e]In the
lifetime of those kings the God of heaven will
set up a kingdom that shall never be destroyed
or delivered up to another people; rather, it shall
break in pieces all these kingdoms and put an
end to them, and it shall stand forever. **45** That
is the meaning of the stone you saw hewn from
the mountain without a hand being put to it,
which broke in pieces the tile, iron, bronze,
silver, and gold. The great God has revealed to
the king what shall be in the future; this is
exactly what you dreamed, and its meaning is
sure."

**46** Then King Nebuchadnezzar fell down
and worshiped Daniel and ordered sacrifice and
incense offered to him. **47** To Daniel the king

d Jn 1, 9; 8, 12; 1 Cor 4, 5; 1 Jn 1, 6. e Mt 21, 44; Lk 20, 18.

*

2, 33: Partly tile: terra cotta tile was much in use among the Babylonians for decoration and for actual construction.

2, 36–45: The four successive kingdoms in this apocalyptic perspective are the Babylonian (gold), the Median (silver), the Persian (bronze), and the Hellenistic (iron). The last, after Alexander's death, was divided among his generals (vv 41f). The two resulting kingdoms, which most affected the Jews, were the dynasty of the Ptolemies in Egypt and that of the Seleucids in Syria, who tried in vain, by war and through intermarriage, to restore the unity of Alexander's empire (v 43). The stone hewn from the mountain is the messianic kingdom awaited by the Jews (vv 44f). Our Lord made this image personal to himself; cf Lk 20, 17f.

said, "Truly your God is the God of gods and
Lord of kings and a revealer of mysteries; that
is why you were able to reveal this mystery."
**48** He advanced Daniel to a high post, gave him
many generous presents, made him ruler of the
whole province of Babylon and chief prefect
over all the wise men of Babylon. **49** At Daniel's request the king made Shadrach, Meshach,
and Abednego administrators of the province of
Babylon, while Daniel himself remained at the
king's court.

## CHAPTER 3

**The Fiery Furnace.** **1** King Nebuchadnezzar had a golden statue made, sixty cubits high
and six cubits wide, which he set up in the plain
of Dura* in the province of Babylon. **2** He then
ordered the satraps,* prefects, and governors,
the counselors, treasurers, judges, magistrates
and all the officials of the provinces to be summoned to the dedication of the statue which he
had set up. **3** The satraps, prefects, and governors, the counselors, treasurers, judges, and
magistrates and all the officials of the provinces, all these came together for the dedication
and stood before the statue which King Nebuchadnezzar had set up. **4** A herald cried out:
"Nations and peoples of every language, when
you hear the sound of the trumpet, flute, lyre,
harp, psaltery,* bagpipe, and all the other musical instruments, **5** you are ordered to fall down
and worship the golden statue which King Nebuchadnezzar has set up. **6** Whoever does not
fall down and worship shall be instantly cast
into a white-hot furnace."* **7** Therefore, as
soon as they heard the sound of the trumpet,
flute, lyre, harp, psaltery, bagpipe, and all the
other musical instruments, the nations and peoples of every language all fell down and worshiped the golden statue which King Nebuchadnezzar had set up.

**8** At that point, some of the Chaldeans came
and accused the Jews **9** to King Nebuchadnezzar: "O king, live forever! **10** O king, you issued a decree that everyone who heard the
sound of the trumpet, flute, lyre, harp, psaltery,
bagpipe, and all the other musical instruments
should fall down and worship the golden statue;
**11** whoever did not was to be cast into a
white-hot furnace. **12** There are certain Jews
whom you have made administrators of the
province of Babylon: Shadrach, Meshach,
Abednego; these men, O king, have paid no
attention to you; they will not serve your god or
worship the golden statue which you set up."

**13** Nebuchadnezzar flew into a rage and sent
for Shadrach, Meshach, and Abednego, who
were promptly brought before the king.
**14** King Nebuchadnezzar questioned them: "Is
it true, Shadrach, Meshach, and Abednego, that
you will not serve my god, or worship the gold-
en statue that I set up? **15** Be ready now to fall
down and worship the statue I had made, whenever you hear the sound of the trumpet, flute,
lyre, harp, psaltery, bagpipe, and all the other
musical instruments; otherwise, you shall be
instantly cast into the white-hot furnace; and
who is the God that can deliver you out of my
hands?" **16** Shadrach, Meshach, and Abednego answered King Nebuchadnezzar, "There is
no need for us to defend ourselves before you
in this matter. **17** If our God, whom we serve,
can save us* from the white-hot furnace and
from your hands, O king, may he save us!
**18** But even if he will not, know, O king, that
we will not serve your god or worship the gold-
en statue which you set up."

**19** Nebuchadnezzar's face became livid with
utter rage against Shadrach, Meshach, and
Abednego. He ordered the furnace to be heated
seven times more than usual **20** and had some
of the strongest men in his army bind Shadrach,
Meshach, and Abednego and cast them into the
white-hot furnace. **21** They were bound and
cast into the white-hot furnace with their coats,
hats, shoes and other garments, **22** for the
king's order was urgent. So huge a fire was
kindled in the furnace that the flames devoured
the men who threw Shadrach, Meshach, and
Abednego into it. **23** But these three fell,
bound, into the midst of the white-hot furnace.

**24** *They walked about in the flames, singing to God and blessing the Lord. **25** In the fire
Azariah stood up and prayed aloud:

**26** "Blessed are you, and praiseworthy,
O Lord, the God of our fathers,
and glorious forever is your name.
**27** For you are just in all you have done;
all your deeds are faultless, all your ways
right,
and all your judgments proper.
**28** You have executed proper judgments
in all that you have brought upon us
and upon Jerusalem, the holy city of our
fathers.
By a proper judgment you have done all this
because of our sins;

*

3, 1: Dura: several places in Babylonia bore this name. Probably the present reference is to one a few miles south of Babylon. Colossi of the type mentioned here were not uncommon in antiquity; a cubit was seventeen and a half inches.

3, 2: Satraps: the Persian major governors.

3, 4: Psaltery: a harplike instrument.

3, 6: Death by fire was not unknown as a punishment in Babylonia; cf Jer 29, 22.

3, 17: If our God . . . can save us: the youths do not question the efficacy of the divine power, but whether it will be exercised (v 18).

3, 24–90: These verses are inspired additions to the Aramaic text of Daniel, translated from the Greek form of the book. They were originally composed in Hebrew or Aramaic, which has not been preserved. The church has always regarded them as part of the canonical Scriptures.

29 For we have sinned and transgressed
by departing from you,
and we have done every kind of evil.
30 Your commandments we have not heeded or observed,
nor have we done as you ordered us for our good.
31 Therefore all you have brought upon us,
all you have done to us,
you have done by a proper judgment.
32 You have handed us over to our enemies,
lawless and hateful rebels;
to an unjust king, the worst in all the world.
33 Now we cannot open our mouths;
we, your servants, who revere you,
have become a shame and a reproach.
34 For your name's sake, do not deliver us up forever,
or make void your covenant.
35 Do not take away your mercy from us,
for the sake of Abraham, your beloved,
Isaac your servant, and Israel your holy one,
36 To whom you promised to multiply their offspring
like the stars of heaven,
or the sand on the shore of the sea.
37 For we are reduced, O Lord, beyond any other nation,
brought low everywhere in the world this day
because of our sins.
38 We have in our day no prince, prophet, or leader,
no holocaust, sacrifice, oblation, or incense,
no place to offer first fruits, to find favor with you.
39 But with contrite heart and humble spirit
let us be received;
40 As though it were holocausts of rams and bullocks,
or thousands of fat lambs,
So let our sacrifice be in your presence today
as we follow you unreservedly;
for those who trust in you cannot be put to shame.
41 And now we follow you with our whole heart,
we fear you and we pray to you.
42 Do not let us be put to shame,
but deal with us in your kindness and great mercy.
43 Deliver us by your wonders,
and bring glory to your name, O Lord:
44 Let all those be routed
who inflict evils on your servants;
Let them be shamed and powerless,
and their strength broken;
45 Let them know that you alone are the Lord God,
glorious over the whole world."

46 Now the king's men who had thrown them
in continued to stoke the furnace with brimstone, pitch, tow, and faggots. 47 The flames
rose forty-nine cubits above the furnace, 48 and
spread out, burning the Chaldeans nearby.
49 But the angel of the Lord went down into the
furnace with Azariah and his companions,
drove the fiery flames out of the furnace,
50 and made the inside of the furnace as though
a dew-laden breeze were blowing through it.
The fire in no way touched them or caused them
pain or harm. 51 Then these three in the furnace
with one voice sang, glorifying and blessing
God:

52 "Blessed are you, O Lord, the God of our fathers,
praiseworthy and exalted above all forever;
And blessed is your holy and glorious name,
praiseworthy and exalted above all for all ages.
53 Blessed are you in the temple of your holy glory,
praiseworthy and glorious above all forever.
54 Blessed are you on the throne of your kingdom,
praiseworthy and exalted above all forever.
55 Blessed are you who look into the depths
from your throne upon the cherubim,
praiseworthy and exalted above all forever.
56 Blessed are you in the firmament of heaven,
praiseworthy and glorious forever.
57 Bless the Lord, all you works of the Lord,
praise and exalt him above all forever.
58 Angels of the Lord, bless the Lord,
praise and exalt him above all forever.
59 You heavens, bless the Lord,
praise and exalt him above all forever.[f]
60 All you waters above the heavens, bless the Lord,
praise and exalt him above all forever.
61 All you hosts of the Lord, bless the Lord;
praise and exalt him above all forever.
62 Sun and moon, bless the Lord;
praise and exalt him above all forever.
63 Stars of heaven, bless the Lord;
praise and exalt him above all forever.
64 Every shower and dew, bless the Lord;
praise and exalt him above all forever.
65 All you winds, bless the Lord;
praise and exalt him above all forever.
66 Fire and heat, bless the Lord;
praise and exalt him above all forever.
67 [Cold and chill, bless the Lord;
praise and exalt him above all forever.
68 Dew and rain, bless the Lord;
praise and exalt him above all forever.]
69 Frost and chill, bless the Lord;

f 59f: Ps 148, 4.

praise and exalt him above all forever.
**70** Ice and snow, bless the Lord;
praise and exalt him above all forever.
**71** Nights and days, bless the Lord;
praise and exalt him above all forever.
**72** Light and darkness, bless the Lord;
praise and exalt him above all forever.
**73** Lightnings and clouds, bless the Lord;
praise and exalt him above all forever.
**74** Let the earth bless the Lord,
praise and exalt him above all forever.
**75** Mountains and hills, bless the Lord;
praise and exalt him above all forever.
**76** Everything growing from the earth, bless the Lord;
praise and exalt him above all forever.
**77** You springs, bless the Lord;
praise and exalt him above all forever.
**78** Seas and rivers, bless the Lord;
praise and exalt him above all forever.
**79** You dolphins and all water creatures, bless the Lord;
praise and exalt him above all forever.
**80** All you birds of the air, bless the Lord;
praise and exalt him above all forever.
**81** All you beasts, wild and tame, bless the Lord;
praise and exalt him above all forever.
**82** You sons of men, bless the Lord;
praise and exalt him above all forever.
**83** O Israel, bless the Lord;
praise and exalt him above all forever.
**84** Priests of the Lord, bless the Lord;
praise and exalt him above all forever.
**85** Servants of the Lord, bless the Lord;
praise and exalt him above all forever.
**86** Spirits and souls of the just, bless the Lord;
praise and exalt him above all forever.
**87** Holy men of humble heart, bless the Lord;
praise and exalt him above all forever.
**88** Hananiah, Azariah, Mishael, bless the Lord;
praise and exalt him above all forever.
For he has delivered us from the nether world,
and saved us from the power of death;
He has freed us from the raging flame
and delivered us from the fire.
**89** Give thanks to the Lord, for he is good,
for his mercy endures forever.
**90** Bless the God of gods, all you who fear the Lord;
praise him and give him thanks,
because his mercy endures forever."

Hearing them sing, and astonished at seeing
them alive, **91** King Nebuchadnezzar rose in
haste and asked his nobles, "Did we not cast
three men bound into the fire?" "Assuredly, O
king," they answered. **92** "But," he replied,
"I see four men unfettered and unhurt, walking
in the fire, and the fourth looks like a son of
God."* **93** Then Nebuchadnezzar came to the
opening of the white-hot furnace and called to
Shadrach, Meshach, and Abednego: "Servants
of the most high God, come out." Thereupon
Shadrach, Meshach, and Abednego came out of
the fire. **94** When the satraps, prefects, governors, and nobles of the king came together, they
saw that the fire had had no power over the
bodies of these men; not a hair of their heads had
been singed, nor were their garments altered;
there was not even a smell of fire about them.
**95** Nebuchadnezzar exclaimed, "Blessed be
the God of Shadrach, Meshach, and Abednego,
who sent his angel to deliver the servants that
trusted in him; they disobeyed the royal command and yielded their bodies rather than serve
or worship any god except their own God.
**96** Therefore I decree for nations and peoples of
every language that whoever blasphemes the
God of Shadrach, Meshach, and Abednego
shall be cut to pieces and his house destroyed.
For there is no other God who can rescue like
this." **97** Then the king promoted Shadrach,
Meshach, and Abednego in the province of
Babylon.

**Vision of the Great Tree.*** **98** King Nebuchadnezzar to the nations and peoples of every
language, wherever they dwell on earth: abundant peace! **99** It has seemed good to me to
publish the signs and wonders which the most
high God* has accomplished in my regard.

**100** How great are his signs, how mighty his wonders;
his kingdom is an everlasting kingdom,
and his dominion endures through all generations.[g]

## CHAPTER 4

**1** I, Nebuchadnezzar, was at home in my
palace, content and prosperous. **2** I had a terrifying dream as I lay in bed, and the images and
the visions of my mind frightened me. **3** So I
issued a decree that all the wise men of Babylon
should be brought before me to give the interpretation of the dream. **4** When the magicians,
enchanters, Chaldeans, and astrologers had
come in, I related the dream before them; but
none of them could tell me its meaning.
**5** [h]Finally there came before me Daniel, whose

g Dn 4, 31; 7, 14. h Gn 41, 38.

*

3, 92: A son of God: an angel; cf Jb 1, 6.

3, 98—4, 34: This section has the form of a letter written by Nebuchadnezzar to his subjects.

3, 99: The most high God: the Jews, especially in the diaspora, used this title to distinguish their God from those of the pagans. On the lips of a polytheist (so also in v 93) it was merely the title of another god. It was an ancient divine name used in Canaan; cf Gn 14, 18.

4, 5: After the name of my god: Belteshazzar, the Babylonian name given to Daniel at the king's orders (Dn 1, 7), is Balatsuussur, "protect his life." In the king's intention, this would be an abbreviation for Bel-balatsu-ussur. It would thus include an appeal to the god Bel, originally the name of the city god of Nippur, and later identified with Marduk, the chief god

name is Belteshazzar after the name of my
god,* and in whom is the spirit of the holy God.
I repeated the dream to him: **6** "Belteshazzar,
chief of the magicians, I know that the spirit of
the holy God is in you and no mystery is too
difficult for you; tell me the meaning of the
visions that I saw in my dream.

**7** "These were the visions I saw while in
bed: I saw a tree of great height at the center of
the world. **8** It was large and strong, with its top
touching the heavens, and it could be seen to the
ends of the earth. **9** Its leaves were beautiful
and its fruit abundant, providing food for all.
Under it the wild beasts found shade, in its
branches the birds of the air nested; all men ate
of it. **10** In the vision I saw while in bed, a holy
sentinel* came down from heaven, **11** and
cried out:

*" 'Cut down the tree and lop off its
branches,
strip off its leaves and scatter its fruit;
let the beasts flee its shade, and the birds
its branches.
**12** But leave in the earth its stump and roots,
fettered with iron and bronze, in the grass
of the field.
Let him be bathed with the dew of heaven;
his lot be to eat, among beasts, the grass
of the earth.
**13** Let his mind be changed from the human;
let him be given the sense of a beast,
till seven years pass over him.
**14** By decree of the sentinels is this decided,
by order of the holy ones, this sentence;
That all who live may know
that the Most High rules over the kingdom
of men:
He can give it to whom he will,
or set over it the lowliest of men.'[i]

**15** "This is the dream that I, King Nebuchadnezzar, had. Now, Belteshazzar, tell me its
meaning. Although none of the wise men in my
kingdom can tell me the meaning, you can,
because the spirit of the holy God is in you."

**16** Then Daniel, whose name was Beltesha̲z-
zar, was appalled for a while, terrified by his
thoughts. "Belteshazzar," the king said to him,
"let not the dream or its meaning terrify you."
**17** "My lord," Belteshazzar replied, "this
dream should be for your enemies, and its
meaning for your foes.* The large, strong tree
that you saw, with its top touching the heavens,
that could be seen by the whole earth, **18** which
had beautiful foliage and abundant fruit, providing food for all, under which the wild beasts
lived, and in whose branches the birds of the air
dwelt— **19** you are that tree, O king, large and
strong! Your majesty has become so great as to
touch the heavens, and your rule extends over
the whole earth. **20** As for the king's vision of
a holy sentinel that came down from heaven and
proclaimed: 'Cut down the tree and destroy it,
but leave in the earth its stump and roots, fettered with iron and bronze in the grass of the
field; let him be bathed with the dew of heaven,
and let his lot be among wild beasts till seven
years pass over him'— **21** this is its meaning,
O king; this is the sentence which the Most High
has passed upon my lord king: **22** [j]You shall be
cast out from among men and dwell with wild
beasts; you shall be given grass to eat like an ox
and be bathed with the dew of heaven;* seven
years shall pass over you, until you know that
the Most High rules over the kingdom of men
and gives it to whom he will. **23** The command
that the stump and roots of the tree are to be left
means that your kingdom shall be preserved for
you, once you have learned it is heaven that
rules. **24** [k]Therefore, O king, take my advice;
atone for your sins by good deeds, and for your
misdeeds by kindness to the poor; then your
prosperity will be long."*

**25** All this happened to King Nebuchadnezzar. **26** Twelve months later, as he was walking
on the roof of the royal palace in Babylon,
**27** the king said, "Babylon the great! Was it
not I, with my great strength, who built it as a
royal residence for my splendor and majesty?"*
**28** While these words were still on the king's
lips, a voice spoke from heaven, "It has been
decreed for you, King Nebuchadnezzar, that
your kingdom is taken from you! **29** You shall
be cast out from among men, and shall dwell
with wild beasts; you shall be given grass to eat
like an ox, and seven years shall pass over you,
until you learn that the Most High rules over the
kingdom of men and gives it to whom he will."
**30** *At once this was fulfilled. Nebuchadnezzar

i 1 Sm 2, 8; 16, 11; Is 62, 6.
j Dn 5, 21.
k Sir 3, 30; 4, 8.

* of Babylon. Daniel's use of the name would refer the prayer rather to the true God.

4, 10: A holy sentinel: an angel. This term is found in the Bible only in this chapter of Daniel, but it is common in later Jewish literature.

4, 11ff: As the tree is Nebuchadnezzar (v 19), the description passes from metaphor to the reality.

4, 17: "This dream . . . for your foes": Daniel speaks as a courtier.

4, 22: The description is of a form of insanity called lycanthropy, in which the patient acts like a wolf.

4, 24: A classic Scriptural text for the efficacy of good works.

4, 27: The words attributed to the king are similar to the boastings in the royal inscriptions by which the Mesopotamian kings testified to their mighty works.

4, 30ff: There is no certainty of any such thing happening to Nebuchadnezzar as is described here. Some scholars think that the Nebuchadnezzar of this chapter is actually Nabonidus, the father of Belshazzar, who was mysteriously absent from Babylon for a number of years. The Biblical author's chief interest was not in the historicity of this popular tale, but in the object lesson it contained for the proud "divine" kings of the Seleucid dynasty.

was cast out from among men, he ate grass like an ox, and his body was bathed with the dew of heaven, until his hair grew like the feathers of an eagle, and his nails like the claws of a bird.
**31** [l]When this period was over, I, Nebuchadnezzar, raised my eyes to heaven; my reason was restored to me, and I blessed the Most High, I praised and glorified him who lives forever:

His dominion is an everlasting dominion,
and his kingdom endures through all generations.
**32** All who live on the earth are counted as nothing;
he does as he pleases with the powers of heaven
as well as with those who live on the earth.
There is no one who can stay his hand or say
to him, "What have you done?"

**33** At the same time my reason returned to me, and for the glory of my kingdom, my majesty and my splendor returned to me. My nobles and lords sought me out; I was restored to my kingdom, and became much greater than before. **34** Therefore, I, Nebuchadnezzar, now praise and exalt and glorify the King of heaven, because all his works are right and his ways just; and those who walk in pride he is able to humble.

## CHAPTER 5

**The Writing on the Wall.** **1** King Belshazzar* gave a great banquet for a thousand of his
lords, with whom he drank. **2** Under the influ-
ence of the wine, he ordered the gold and silver vessels which Nebuchadnezzar, his father,* had taken from the temple in Jerusalem, to be brought in so that the king, his lords, his wives and his entertainers might drink from them.
**3** When the gold and silver vessels taken from the house of God in Jerusalem had been brought in, and while the king, his lords, his wives and his entertainers were drinking **4** wine from
them, they praised their gods of gold and silver, bronze and iron, wood and stone.
**5** Suddenly, opposite the lampstand, the fingers of a human hand appeared, writing on the plaster of the wall in the king's palace. When the king saw the wrist and hand that wrote,
**6** his face blanched; his thoughts terrified him, his hip joints shook, and his knees knocked.
**7** The king shouted for the enchanters, Chaldeans, and astrologers to be brought in. "Whoever reads this writing and tells me what it means," he said to the wise men of Babylon, "shall be clothed in purple, wear a golden collar about his neck, and be third in the government of the kingdom." **8** But though all the king's
wise men came in, none of them could either read the writing or tell the king what it meant.
**9** Then King Belshazzar was greatly terrified; his face went ashen, and his lords were thrown into confusion.
**10** When the queen heard of the discussion between the king and his lords, she entered the banquet hall and said, "O king, live forever! Be not troubled in mind, nor look so pale!
**11** There is a man in your kingdom in whom is the spirit of the holy God; during the lifetime of your father he was seen to have brilliant knowledge and god-like wisdom. In fact, King Nebuchadnezzar, your father, made him chief of the magicians, enchanters, Chaldeans, and astrologers, **12** because of the extraordinary
mind possessed by this Daniel, whom the king named Belteshazzar. He knew and understood how to interpret dreams, explain enigmas, and solve difficulties. Now therefore, summon Daniel to tell you what this means."
**13** Then Daniel was brought into the presence of the king. The king asked him, "Are you the Daniel, the Jewish exile, whom my father, the king, brought from Judah? **14** I have heard
that the spirit of God is in you, that you possess brilliant knowledge and extraordinary wisdom.
**15** Now, the wise men and enchanters were brought in to me to read this writing and tell me its meaning, but they could not say what the words meant. **16** But I have heard that you can
interpret dreams and solve difficulties; if you are able to read the writing and tell me what it means, you shall be clothed in purple, wear a gold collar about your neck, and be third in the government of the kingdom."
**17** Daniel answered the king: "You may keep your gifts, or give your presents to someone else; but the writing I will read for you, O king, and tell you what it means. **18** The Most
High God gave your father Nebuchadnezzar a great kingdom and glorious majesty. **19** Be-
cause he made him so great, the nations and peoples of every language dreaded and feared him. Whomever he wished, he killed or let live; whomever he wished, he exalted or humbled.
**20** But when his heart became proud and his spirit hardened by insolence, he was put down from his royal throne and deprived of his glory;
**21** [m]he was cast out from among men and was made insensate as a beast; he lived with wild

l Dn 3, 100; 7, 14. m Dn 4, 22.

* 5, 1: King Belshazzar: Belshazzar was actually the crown prince, but he had been given royal authority in Babylon by his father Nabonidus.

5, 2: Nebuchadnezzar, his father: several kings of Babylon intervened between Nebuchadnezzar and Belshazzar. Either the term father is used here in the broad sense of "remote predecessor," or the name Nebuchadnezzar is used for "Nabonidus."

asses, and ate grass like an ox; his body was
bathed with the dew of heaven, until he learned
that the Most High God rules over the kingdom
of men and appoints over it whom he will.
**22** You, his son, Belshazzar, have not humbled
your heart, though you knew all this; **23** you
have rebelled against the Lord of heaven. You
had the vessels of his temple brought before
you, so that you and your nobles, your wives
and your entertainers, might drink wine from
them; and you praised the gods of silver and
gold, bronze and iron, wood and stone, that
neither see nor hear nor have intelligence. But
the God in whose hand is your life breath and
the whole course of your life, you did not glorify. **24** By him were the wrist and hand sent, and
the writing set down.

**25** "This is the writing that was inscribed:
MENE, TEKEL, and PERES.* These words mean:
**26** *MENE, God has numbered your kingdom
and put an end to it; **27** TEKEL, you have been
weighed on the scales and found wanting;
**28** PERES, your kingdom has been divided and
given to the Medes and Persians."

**29** Then by order of Belshazzar they clothed
Daniel in purple, with a gold collar about his
neck, and proclaimed him third in the government of the kingdom. **30** The same night Belshazzar, the Chaldean king, was slain:

## CHAPTER 6

**1** And Darius the Mede* succeeded to the
kingdom at the age of sixty-two.

**In the Lions' Den.** **2** Darius decided to appoint over his entire kingdom one hundred and
twenty satraps, to safeguard his interests;
**3** these were accountable to three supervisors,
one of whom was Daniel. **4** Daniel outshone all
the supervisors and satraps because an extraordinary spirit was in him, and the king thought
of giving him authority over the entire kingdom.
**5** Therefore the supervisors and satraps tried to
find grounds for accusation against Daniel as
regards the administration. But they could accuse him of no wrongdoing; because he was
trustworthy, no fault of neglect or misconduct
was to be found in him. **6** Then these men said
to themselves, "We shall find no grounds for
accusation against this Daniel unless by way of
the law of his God." **7** So these supervisors and
satraps went thronging to the king and said to
him, "King Darius, live forever! **8** [n]All the
supervisors of the kingdom, the prefects, satraps, nobles, and governors are agreed that the
following prohibition ought to be put in force by
royal decree: no one is to address any petition
to god or man for thirty days, except to you, O
king; otherwise he shall be cast into a den of
lions. **9** Now, O king, issue the prohibition
over your signature, immutable and irrevocable* under Mede and Persian law." **10** So King
Darius signed the prohibition and made it law.

**11** Even after Daniel heard that this law had
been signed, he continued his custom of going
home to kneel in prayer and give thanks to his
God in the upper chamber three times a day,
with the windows open toward Jerusalem.
**12** So these men rushed in and found Daniel
praying and pleading before his God. **13** Then
they went to remind the king about the prohibition: "Did you not decree, O king, that no one
is to address a petition to god or man for thirty
days, except to you, O king; otherwise he shall
be cast into a den of lions?" The king answered
them, "The decree is absolute, irrevocable under the Mede and Persian law." **14** To this they
replied, "Daniel, the Jewish exile, has paid no
attention to you, O king, or to the decree you
issued; three times a day he offers his prayer."
**15** The king was deeply grieved at this news
and he made up his mind to save Daniel; he
worked till sunset to rescue him. **16** But these
men insisted. "Keep in mind, O king," they
said, "that under the Mede and Persian law
every royal prohibition or decree is irrevocable." **17** So the king ordered Daniel to be
brought and cast into the lions' den.* To Daniel
he said, "May your God, whom you serve so
constantly, save you." **18** To forestall any tam-
pering, the king sealed with his own ring and the
rings of the lords the stone that had been brought
to block the opening of the den.

**19** Then the king returned to his palace for
the night; he refused to eat and he dismissed the
entertainers. Since sleep was impossible for
him, **20** the king rose very early the next morning and hastened to the lions' den. **21** As he

n Est 1, 19.

*

5, 25: Mene, Tekel, and Peres: these seem to be the Aramaic names of weights and monetary values: the mina, the shekel (the sixtieth part of a mina), and the parsu (a half-mina).

5, 26ff: Daniel interprets these three terms by a play on the words: Mene, connected with the verb meaning to number; Tekel, with the verb meaning to weigh; Peres, with the verb meaning to divide. There is also a play on the last term with the word for Persians.

6, 1: Darius the Mede: unknown in profane history. The Median kingdom had already been conquered by Cyrus the Persian, and it was Cyrus who captured Babylon. Evidently the author of Daniel has deliberately adopted an apocalyptic view of history, derived from prophecy (cf Is 13, 17ff; Jer 51, 11. 28ff), according to which the Medes formed the second of four world kingdoms preceding the messianic times; see note on Dn 2, 36–45. The character of Darius the Mede has probably been modeled on that of the Persian king Darius the Great (552–486 B.C.), the second successor of Cyrus.

6, 9: Immutable and irrevocable: the passages in Est 1, 19 and 8, 8 also refer to the immutability of Medo-Persian laws. The historian Diodorus Siculus indicates that such a concept existed in the time of Darius III (335–331 B.C.), the last of the Persian kings. Cf vv 13. 16.

6, 17: The lions' den: a pit too deep to be easily scaled; its opening was blocked with a stone (v 18).

drew near, he cried out to Daniel sorrowfully,
"O Daniel, servant of the living God, has the
God whom you serve so constantly been able to
save you from the lions?" 22 [o]Daniel answered
the king: "O king, live forever! 23 My God has
sent his angel and closed the lion's mouths so
that they have not hurt me. For I have been
found innocent before him; neither to you have
I done any harm, O king!" 24 This gave the
king great joy. At his order Daniel was removed
from the den, unhurt because he trusted in his
God. 25 The king then ordered the men who
had accused Daniel, along with their children
and their wives, to be cast into the lions' den.
Before they reached the bottom of the den, the
lions overpowered them and crushed all their
bones.
26 Then King Darius wrote to the nations
and peoples of every language, wherever they
dwell on the earth: "All peace to you! 27 I
decree that throughout my royal domain the
God of Daniel is to be reverenced and feared:

"For he is the living God, enduring forever;
his kingdom shall not be destroyed, and
his dominion shall be without end.
28 He is a deliverer and savior,
working signs and wonders in heaven and
on earth,
and he delivered Daniel from the lions'
power."[p]

29 So Daniel fared well during the reign of
Darius and the reign of Cyrus the Persian.

## *II: Daniel's Visions*

## CHAPTER 7

**Vision of the Four Beasts.*** 1 In the first
year of King Belshazzar of Babylon, Daniel had
a dream as he lay in bed, and was terrified by
the visions of his mind. Then he wrote down the
dream; the account began: 2 In the vision I saw
during the night, suddenly the four winds of
heaven stirred up the great sea,* 3 from which
emerged four immense beasts, each different
from the others. 4 The first was like a lion, but
with eagle's wings.* While I watched, the
wings were plucked; it was raised from the
ground to stand on two feet like a man, and
given a human mind. 5 The second was like a
bear;* it was raised up on one side, and among
the teeth in its mouth were three tusks. It was
given the order, "Up, devour much flesh."
6 After this I looked and saw another beast, like
a leopard;* on its back were four wings like
those of a bird, and it had four heads. To this
beast dominion was given. 7 After this, in the
visions of the night I saw the fourth beast,*
different from all the others, terrifying, horrible, and of extraordinary strength; it had great
iron teeth with which it devoured and crushed,
and what was left it trampled with its feet. 8 I
was considering the ten horns it had, when suddenly another, a little horn, sprang out of their
midst, and three of the previous horns were torn
away to make room for it. This horn had eyes
like a man, and a mouth that spoke arrogantly.
9 *As I watched,

Thrones were set up
and the Ancient One took his throne.
His clothing was snow bright,
and the hair on his head as white as wool;
His throne was flames of fire,
with wheels of burning fire.
10 A surging stream of fire
flowed out from where he sat;
Thousands upon thousands were ministering
to him,
and myriads upon myriads attended him.[q]

The court was convened, and the books were
opened. 11 I watched, then, from the first of
the arrogant words which the horn spoke, until
the beast was slain and its body thrown into the
fire to be burnt up. 12 The other beasts, which
also lost their dominion, were granted a prolon-
gation of life for a time and a season. 13 As the
visions during the night continued, I saw

o 1 Mc 2, 60.
p Dn 1, 21.
q Rv 5, 11.

*

7, 1–27: The significance of this vision is the same as that of Nebuchadnezzar's dream in chapter 2; see note on Dn 2, 36–45. To the four succeeding world kingdoms, Babylonian, Median, Persian, and Greek, is opposed and messianic kingdom of the people of God. The imagery of this chapter has been used extensively in the Revelation of St. John, where it is applied to the Roman empire, the persecutor of the church.

7, 2: The great sea: the primordial ocean beneath the earth, according to primitive cosmology (Gn 7, 11; 49, 25). This was thought to contain various monsters (Is 27, 1; Jb 7, 12), and in particular mythological monsters symbolizing the chaos which God had vanquished in ancient times (Jb 9, 13; 26, 13; etc.).

7, 4: The representation of the Babylonian empire as a winged lion, a common motif in Babylonian art, symbolizes the bestial power hostile to God. The two wings that are plucked represent Nebuchadnezzar and Belshazzar. On two feet like a man . . . a human mind: contrasts with what is said in Dn 4, 13. 30.

7, 5: A bear: represents the Median empire, its three tusks symbolizing its destructive nature; hence, the command: "Up, devour much flesh."

7, 6: A leopard: used to symbolize the swiftness with which Cyrus the Persian established his kingdom. Four heads: corresponding to the four Persian kings of Dn 11, 2.

7, 7f: Alexander's empire was different from all the others in that it was Western rather than Oriental in inspiration. The ten horns represent the kings of the Seleucid dynasty, the only part of the Hellenistic empire that concerned the author. The little horn is Antiochus IV Epiphanes (175–163 B.C.), the worst of the Seleucid kings, who usurped the throne.

7, 9f: A vision of the heavenly throne of God (the Ancient One), who sits in judgment (symbolized by fire) over the nations. Some of the details of the vision, depicting the divine majesty and omnipotence, are to be found in Ez 1.

7, 13f: One like a son of man: in contrast to the wordly kingdoms opposed to God, which appear as beasts, the glori-

One like a son of man* coming,
on the clouds of heaven;
When he reached the Ancient One
and was presented before him,
14 He received dominion, glory, and kingship;
nations and peoples of every language
serve him.
His dominion is an everlasting dominion
that shall not be taken away,
his kingship shall not be destroyed.[r]

15 I, Daniel, found my spirit anguished
within its sheath of flesh, and I was terrified by
the visions of my mind. 16 I approached one of
those present and asked him what all this meant
in truth; in answer, he made known to me the
meaning of the things: 17 "These four great
beasts stand for four kingdoms which shall arise
on the earth. 18 But the holy ones of the Most
High shall receive the kingship, to possess it
forever and ever."

19 But I wished to make certain about the
fourth beast, so very terrible and different from
the others, devouring and crushing with its iron
teeth and bronze claws, and trampling with its
feet what was left; 20 about the ten horns on its
head, and the other one that sprang up, before
which three horns fell; about the horn with the
eyes and the mouth that spoke arrogantly, which
appeared greater than its fellows. 21 For, as I
watched, that horn made war against the holy
ones and was victorious 22 until the Ancient
One arrived; judgment was pronounced in favor
of the holy ones of the Most High, and the time
came when the holy ones possessed the kingdom. 23 He answered me thus:

"The fourth beast shall be a fourth kingdom
on earth,
different from all the others;
It shall devour the whole earth,
beat it down, and crush it.
24 The ten horns shall be ten kings
rising out of that kingdom;
another shall rise up after them,
Different from those before him,
who shall lay low three kings.
25 He shall speak against the Most High
and oppress the holy ones of the Most
High, thinking to change the feast days
and the law.*
They shall be handed over to him
for a year, two years, and a half-year.
26 But when the court is convened,
and his power is taken away
by final and absolute destruction,
27 Then the kingship and dominion and majesty
of all the kingdoms under the heavens
shall be given to the holy people of the
Most High,
Whose kingdom shall be everlasting:
all dominions shall serve and obey him."

28 The report concluded: I, Daniel, was
greatly terrified by my thoughts, and my face
blanched, but I kept the matter to myself.*

## CHAPTER 8

**Vision of the Ram and He-goat.*** 1 After
this first vision, I, Daniel, had another, in the
third year of the reign of King Belshazzar. 2 In
my vision I saw myself in the fortress of Susa*
in the province of Elam; I was beside the river
Ulai. 3 I looked up and saw standing by the
river a ram with two great horns, the one larger
and newer than the other. 4 I saw the ram but-
ting toward the west, north, and south. No beast
could withstand it or be rescued from its power;
it did what it pleased and became very powerful.

5 As I was reflecting, a he-goat with a prominent horn on its forehead suddenly came from
the west across the whole earth without touching the ground. 6 It approached the two-horned
ram I had seen standing by the river, and rushed
toward it with savage force. 7 I saw it attack the
ram with furious blows when they met, and
break both its horns. It threw the ram, which had
not the force to withstand it, to the ground, and
trampled upon it; and no one could rescue it
from its power.

8 The he-goat became very powerful, but at
the height of its power the great horn was shattered, and in its place came up four others,
facing the four winds of heaven. 9 Out of one
of them came a little horn* which kept growing
toward the south, the east, and the glorious
country. 10 Its power extended to the host of

r Dn 3, 100; 4, 31; Mi 4, 7; Lk 1, 32.

*

fied people of God that will form his kingdom on earth is represented in human form (v 18). Just as our Lord applied the figure of the stone hewn from the mountain to himself (Dn 2, 36–45), he also made the title, "Son of Man" his most characteristic way of referring to himself, as the One in whom and through whom the salvation of God's people came to be realized.

7, 25: The reference is to the persecutions of Antiochus IV and his attempt to force the Jews to give up their customs and to adopt Hellenistic ways (1 Mc 1, 33f). A year, two years, and a half-year: an indefinite, evil period of time. As seven is the Jewish "perfect" number, half of it signifies great imperfection. Actually, this corresponds fairly accurately to the duration of Antiochus' persecution.

7, 28: This verse ends the Aramaic part of the Book of Daniel.

8, 1–27: This vision repeats the major part of the preceding one, though in a more explicit fashion. As explained in vv 20ff, the two-horned ram represents the combined kingdom of the Medes and Persians, destroyed by Alexander's Hellenistic empire originating in the west. Once again the author is interested only in the Seleucid dynasty, which emerged from the dissolution of Alexander's empire after his death in 323 B.C.

8, 2: The fortress of Susa: the royal palace of the Persian kings in the ancient territory of Elam, east of Babylonia. The river Ulai: a canal along the northern side of Susa.

8, 9: The little horn, as in chapter 7, is Antiochus IV. The glorious country: Palestine.

8, 10ff: The host of heaven: ordinarily meaning the stars,

heaven,* so that it cast down to earth some of
the host and some of the stars and trampled on
them. **11** It boasted even against the prince of
the host, from whom it removed the daily sacrifice, and whose sanctuary it cast down, **12** as
well as the host, while sin replaced the daily
sacrifice. It cast truth to the ground, and was
succeeding in its undertaking.

**13** I heard a holy one speaking, and another
said to whichever one it was that spoke, "How
long shall the events of this vision last concerning the daily sacrifice, the desolating sin* which
is placed there, the sanctuary, and the trampled
host?" **14** He answered him, "For two thousand three hundred evenings and mornings; then
the sanctuary shall be purified."

**15** While I, Daniel, sought the meaning of
the vision I had seen, a manlike figure stood
before me, **16** and on the Ulai I heard a human
voice that cried out, "Gabriel,* explain the vision to this man." **17** When he came near
where I was standing, I fell prostrate in terror.
But he said to me, "Understand, son of man,
that the vision refers to the end time."* **18** As
he spoke to me, I fell forward in a faint; he
touched me and made me stand up. **19** "I will
show you," he said, "what is to happen later in
the period of wrath; for at the appointed time,
there will be an end.

**20** "The two-horned ram you saw represents
the kings of the Medes and Persians. **21** The
he-goat is the king of the Greeks, and the great
horn on its forehead is the first king. **22** The
four that rose in its place when it was broken are
four kingdoms that will issue from his nation,
but without his strength.

**23** "After their reign,
 when sinners have reached their measure,
There shall arise a king, impudent
 and skilled in intrigue.
**24** He shall be strong and powerful,
 bring about fearful ruin,
 and succeed in his undertaking.
He shall destroy powerful peoples;
**25** his cunning shall be against the holy ones,
 his treacherous conduct shall succeed.
He shall be proud of heart
 and destroy many by stealth.
But when he rises against the prince of
 princes,
 he shall be broken without a hand being
 raised.
**26** The vision of the evenings and the mornings
 is true, as spoken;
Do you, however, keep this vision
 undisclosed,
 because the days are to be many."

**27** I, Daniel, was weak and ill for some days;
then I arose and took care of the king's affairs.
But I was appalled at the vision, which I could
not understand.

## CHAPTER 9

**Gabriel and the Seventy Weeks.** **1** It
was the first year that Darius,* son of Ahasuerus, of the race of the Medes, reigned over the
kingdom of the Chaldeans; **2** [s]in the first year
of his reign I, Daniel, tried to understand in the
Scriptures the counting of the years of which the
LORD spoke to the prophet Jeremiah: that for the
ruins of Jerusalem seventy years* must be fulfilled.

**3** I turned to the Lord God, pleading in earnest prayer, with fasting, sackcloth, and ashes.
**4** [t]I prayed to the LORD, my God, and confessed, "Ah, Lord, great and awesome God,
you who keep your merciful covenant toward
those who love you and observe your commandments! **5** [u]We have sinned, been wicked and
done evil; we have rebelled and departed from
your commandments and your laws. **6** We have
not obeyed your servants the prophets, who
spoke in your name to our kings, our princes,
our fathers, and all the people of the land.
**7** Justice, O Lord, is on your side; we are
shamefaced even to this day: the men of Judah,
the residents of Jerusalem, and all Israel, near
and far, in all the countries to which you have
scattered them because of their treachery toward
you. **8** O LORD, we are shamefaced, like our
kings, our princes, and our fathers, for having
sinned against you. **9** But yours, O Lord, our
God, are compassion and forgiveness! Yet we
rebelled against you **10** and paid no heed to
your command, O LORD, our God, to live by the
law you gave us through your servants the
prophets. **11** [v]Because all Israel transgressed
your law and went astray, not heeding your
voice, the sworn malediction, recorded in the

s 2f: Jer 25, 11; 29, 10.
t Neh 1, 5.
u Bar 1, 17.
v Dt 27, 15.

*

here refers to the people of God; cf Dn 12, 3. The prince of the host: God himself, with whose holy religion Antiochus interfered (1 Mc 1, 45).

8, 13: The desolating sin: the Hebrew contains a wordplay (shomem) on the name Baal Shamem ("lord of the heavens," the Greek Zeus Olympios), referring to the statue with which Antiochus profaned the temple of Jerusalem (2 Mc 6, 2).

8, 16: The angel Gabriel is mentioned here for the first time in the Bible. There is wordplay in the preceding verse on geber—manlike figure.

8, 17: The end time: the day of the Lord, when God sits in judgment on his enemies (v 19).

9, 1: Darius: see the note on Dn 6, 1.

9, 2: Seventy years: the prophet Jeremiah (25, 11; 29, 10) prophesied a Babylonian captivity of seventy years, a round number signifying the complete passing away of the existing generation. Jeremiah's prophecy was fulfilled in the capture of Babylon by Cyrus and the subsequent return of the Jews to Palestine. However, the author of Daniel, living during the persecution of Antiochus, sees the conditions of the exile still existing; therefore in his mediation he extends Jeremiah's number to seventy weeks of years (v 24, i.e., seven times seventy years, to characterize the Jewish victory over the Seleucids as the ultimate fulfillment of the prophecy.

law of Moses, the servant of God, was poured
out over us for our sins. **12** You carried out the
threats you spoke against us and against those
who governed us, by bringing upon us in Jerusalem the greatest calamity that has ever occurred
under heaven. **13** As it is written* in the law of
Moses, this calamity came full upon us. As we
did not appease the LORD, our God, by turning
back from our wickedness and recognizing his
constancy, **14** so the LORD kept watch over the
calamity and brought it upon us. You, O LORD,
our God, are just in all that you have done, for
we did not listen to your voice.

**15** [w]"Now, O Lord, our God, who led your
people out of the land of Egypt with a strong
hand, and made a name for yourself even to this
day, we have sinned, we are guilty. **16** O Lord,
in keeping with all your just deeds, let your
anger and your wrath be turned away from your
city Jerusalem, your holy mountain. On account
of our sins and the crimes of our fathers, Jerusalem and your people have become the reproach
of all our neighbors. **17** Hear, therefore, O
God, the prayer and petition of your servant;
and for your own sake, O Lord, let your face
shine upon your desolate sanctuary. **18** [x]Give
ear, O my God, and listen; open your eyes and
see our ruins and the city which bears your
name. When we present our petition before you,
we rely not on our just deeds, but on your great
mercy. **19** O Lord, hear! O Lord, pardon! O
Lord, be attentive and act without delay, for
your own sake, O my God, because this city and
your people bear your name!"

**20** I was still occupied with my prayer, confessing my sin and the sin of my people Israel,
presenting my petition to the LORD, my God, on
behalf of his holy mountain— **21** [y]I was still
occupied with this prayer, when Gabriel, the
one whom I had seen before in vision, came to
me in rapid flight at the time of the evening
sacrifice.* **22** He instructed me in these words:
"Daniel, I have now come to give you understanding. **23** When you began your petition, an
answer was given which I have come to announce, because you are beloved. Therefore,
mark the answer and understand the vision.

**24** "Seventy weeks* are decreed
for your people and for your holy city:
Then transgression will stop and sin will end,
guilt will be expiated,
Everlasting justice will be introduced,
vision and prophecy ratified,
and a most holy will be anointed.
**25** Know and understand this:
From the utterance of the word
that Jerusalem was to be rebuilt*
Until one who is anointed and a leader,
there shall be seven weeks.
During sixty-two weeks
it shall be rebuilt,
With streets and trenches,
in time of affliction.

**26** After the sixty-two weeks
an anointed* shall be cut down
when he does not possess the city;
And the people of a leader who will come
shall destroy the sanctuary.
Then the end shall come like a torrent;
until the end there shall be war,
the desolation that is decreed.
**27** For one week* he shall make
a firm compact with the many;
Half the week
he shall abolish sacrifice and oblation;
On the temple wing shall be the horrible abomination
until the ruin that is decreed
is poured out upon the horror."[z]

w Bar 2, 11; Ex 14, 22.
x Jer 25, 29.
y Dn 8, 16.
z Mt 24, 15; 2 Mc 6, 2.

*

9, 13: As it is written: the first time that this formula of Scriptural citation is used in the Bible. The reference (v 11) is to the sanctions of Lv 26, 14ff; Dt 28, 15ff.

9, 21: At the time of the evening sacrifice: between three and four in the afternoon.

9, 24: Seventy weeks: i. e., of years. Just as Jeremiah's seventy years was an approximation (see note on v 2), the four hundred and ninety years here is not to be taken literally. Similarly, the distribution of the "weeks" in the following verses indicates only relative proportions of the total figure. A most holy: an expression used almost always of an object, the altar or the temple, but once (1 Chr 23, 13) of Aaron the high priest. The author sees the definitive establishment of the kingdom of God, realized in the reconsecration of the temple after Antiochus' desecration, or personified in the holy community (like the Son of Man of chapter 7). The Fathers of the church almost unanimously understood the reference to be to Christ, the final realization of the prophecy.

9, 25: From the utterance . . . to be rebuilt: from the time of Jeremiah's prophecy. One . . . anointed and a leader: either Cyrus, who was called the anointed of the Lord to end the exile (Is 45, 1), or the high priest Joshua, who presided over the rebuilding of the altar of sacrifice after the exile (Ezr 3, 2). Seven weeks: forty-nine years, an approximation of the time of the exile. During sixty-two weeks . . . rebuilt: a period of 434 years, roughly approximating the interval between the rebuilding of Jerusalem after the exile and the beginning of the Seleucid persecution.

9, 26: An anointed: doubtless the high priest Onias III, murdered in 171 B.C., from which the author dates the beginning of the persecution. Onias was in exile when he was killed. A leader: Antiochus IV.

9, 27: One week: the final phase of the period in view, the time of Antiochus' persecution; he is Antiochus himself. The many: the faithless Jews who allied themselves with the heathen; cf 1 Mc 1, 11ff. Half the week: three and a half years; see note on Dn 7, 25. The temple was desecrated by Antiochus from 167 to 165 B.C. The temple wing: probably the main portal. The horrible abomination: see note on Dn 8, 13. Perhaps an inscription was placed on the portal of the temple dedicating it to the Olympian Zeus. Our Lord referred to this passage in his own prediction of the destruction of Jerusalem (Mt 24, 15).

## CHAPTER 10

**Vision of the Hellenistic Wars.*** **1** In the
third year of Cyrus, king of Persia, a revelation
was given to Daniel, who had been named Belteshazzar. The revelation was certain: a great
war; he understood it from the vision. **2** In
those days, I, Daniel, mourned* three full
weeks. **3** I ate no savory food, I took no meat
or wine, and I did not anoint myself at all until
the end of the three weeks.

**4** On the twenty-fourth day of the first
month* I was on the bank of the great river, the
Tigris. **5** As I looked up, I saw a man* dressed
in linen with a belt of fine gold around his waist.
**6** His body was like chrysolite, his face shone
like lightning, his eyes were like fiery torches,
his arms and feet looked like burnished bronze,
and his voice sounded like the roar of a multitude. **7** I alone, Daniel, saw the vision; but
great fear seized the men who were with me;
they fled and hid themselves, although they did
not see the vision. **8** So I was left alone, seeing
this great vision. No strength remained in me;
I turned the color of death and was powerless.
**9** When I heard the sound of his voice, I fell
face forward in a faint.

**10** But then a hand touched me, raising me
to my hands and knees. **11** "Daniel, beloved,"
he said to me, "understand the words which I
am speaking to you; stand up, for my mission
now is to you." When he said this to me, I stood
up trembling. **12** "Fear not, Daniel," he continued; "from the first day you made up your
mind to acquire understanding and humble
yourself before God, your prayer was heard.
Because of it I started out, **13** but the prince of
the kingdom of Persia* stood in my way for
twenty-one days, until finally Michael, one of
the chief princes, came to help me. I left him
there with the prince of the kings of Persia,
**14** and came to make you understand what shall
happen to your people in the days to come; for
there is yet a vision concerning those days."

**15** While he was speaking thus to me, I fell
forward and kept silent. **16** Then something
like a man's hand touched my lips; I opened my
mouth and said to the one facing me, "My lord,
I was seized with pangs at the vision and I was
powerless. **17** How can my lord's servant speak
with you, my lord? For now no strength or even
breath is left in me." **18** The one who looked
like a man touched me again and strengthened
me, saying, **19** "Fear not, beloved, you are
safe; take courage and be strong." **20** When he
spoke to me, I grew strong and said, "Speak,
my lord, for you have strengthened me." "Do
you know," he asked, "why I have come to
you? Soon I must fight the prince of Persia
again. When I leave, the prince of Greece will
come; **21** [a]but I shall tell you what is written in
the truthful book. No one supports me against
all these except Michael, your prince,

## CHAPTER 11

**1** standing* as a reinforcement and a bulwark
for me. **2** Now I shall tell you the truth.

"Three kings of Persia* are yet to come; and
a fourth shall acquire the greatest riches of all.
Strengthened by his riches, he shall rouse all the
kingdom of Greece. **3** But a powerful king shall
appear and rule with great might, doing as he
pleases. **4** No sooner shall he appear than his
kingdom shall be broken and divided in the four
directions under heaven; but not among his descendants or in keeping with his mighty rule, for
his kingdom shall be torn to pieces and belong
to others than they.

**5** *"The king of the south shall grow strong,
but one of his princes shall grow stronger still
and govern a domain greater than his. **6** After
some years they shall become allies: the daughter of the king of the south shall come to the king
of the north in the interest of peace. But her bid
for power shall fail: and her line shall not be
recognized, and she shall be given up, together
with those who brought her, her son and her
husband. But later **7** a descendant of her line
shall succeed to his rank, and shall come against
the rampart and enter the stronghold of the king

---

a Rv 12, 7.

---

* 10, 1—12, 13: This final vision repeats some of the material contained in the others. It is concerned with history of the worldly kingdoms from the time of Cyrus to the defeat of the tyrant Antiochus.

10, 2: Mourned: perhaps the author intends to recall the interruption in the rebuilding of the temple, which occurred during this time (Ezr 4, 1–4).

10, 4: The first month: the month Nisan (mid-March to mid-April).

10, 5f: The heavenly person of the vision is probably the angel Gabriel, as in Dn 9, 21. Chrysolite: or topaz, a yellowish precious stone.

10, 13: The prince of the kingdom of Persia: the guardian angel of Persia. The later Judaism ascribed protecting angels to various groups of human society, often as little more than personifications. Michael: the angel who is the protector of God's people (v 21).

11, 1f: Standing . . . truth: these are the first two verses of ch 11.

11, 2–4: The three kings of Persia who follow Cyrus are uncertain, since there were more than three Persian kings between Cyrus and the dissolution of the kingdom. The fourth is doubtless Xerxes I (486–465 B.C.), the great campaigner against Greece. The powerful king is Alexander the Great, who ended the Persian empire by his victory at Issus in 333 B.C.

11, 5–45: These verses describe the dynastic histories of the Ptolemies in Egypt (the king of the south) and the Seleucids in Syria (the king of the north), the two divisions of the Hellenistic empire that were of interest to the author (v 6). In vv 10–20 is described the struggle between the two kingdoms for the control of Palestine, in which the Seleucids were eventually victorious. The reference in v 20 is to Seleucus IV, who sent Heliodorus to plunder the temple treasure in Jerusalem (2 Mc 3). Finally, vv 21–45 describe the career of Antiochus IV and his persecution, in details that have been seen above.

of the north, and conquer them. **8** Even their
gods, with their molten images and their precious vessels of silver and gold, he shall carry
away as booty into Egypt. For years he shall
have nothing to do with the king of the north.
**9** Then the latter shall invade the land of the
king of the south, and return to his own country.

**10** "But his sons shall prepare and assemble
a great armed host, which shall advance like a
flood, then withdraw. When it returns and
surges around the stronghold, **11** the king of the
south, provoked, shall go out to fight against the
king of the north, whose great host shall make
a stand but shall be given into his hand **12** and
be carried off. In the pride of his heart, he shall
lay low tens of thousands, but he shall not triumph. **13** For the king of the north shall raise
another army, greater than before; after some
years he shall attack with this large army and
great resources. **14** [b]In those times many shall
resist the king of the south, and outlaws of your
people shall rise up in fulfillment of vision, but
they shall fail. **15** When the king of the north
comes, he shall set up siegeworks and take the
fortified city by storm. The power of the south
shall not withstand him, and not even his picked
troops shall have the strength to resist. **16** He
shall attack him and do as he pleases, with no
one to withstand him. He shall stop in the glorious land, dealing destruction. **17** He shall set
himself to penetrate the entire strength of his
kingdom. He shall conclude an agreement with
him and give him a daughter in marriage in
order to destroy the kingdom, but this shall not
succeed in his favor. **18** He shall turn to the
coastland and take many, but a leader shall put
an end to his shameful conduct, so that he cannot renew it against him. **19** He shall turn to the
strongholds of his own land, but shall stumble
and fall, to be found no more. **20** In his stead
one shall arise who will send a tax collector
through the glorious kingdom, but he shall soon
be destroyed, though not in conflict or in battle.

**21** "There shall rise in his place a despicable
person, to whom the royal insignia shall not be
given. By stealth and fraud he shall seize the
kingdom. **22** Armed might shall be completely
overwhelmed by him and crushed, and even the
prince of the covenant. **23** After allying with
him, he shall treacherously rise to power with
a small party. **24** By stealth he shall enter prosperous provinces and do that which his fathers
or grandfathers never did; he shall distribute
spoil, booty, and riches among them and devise
plots against their strongholds; but only for a
time. **25** He shall call on his strength and clev-
erness to meet the king of the south with a great
army; the king of the south shall prepare for
battle with a very large and strong army, but he
shall not succeed because of the plots devised
against him. **26** Even his table companions
shall seek to destroy him, his army shall be
overwhelmed, and many shall fall slain. **27** The
two kings, resolved on evil, shall sit at table
together and exchange lies, but they shall have
no success, because the appointed end is not
yet.

**28** "He shall turn back toward his land with
great riches, his mind set against the holy covenant; he shall arrange matters and return to his
land. **29** At the time appointed he shall come
again to the south, but this time it shall not be
as before. **30** When ships of the Kittim* confront him, he shall lose heart and retreat. Then
he shall direct his rage and energy against the
holy covenant; those who forsake it he shall
once more single out. **31** Armed forces shall
move at his command and defile the sanctuary
stronghold, abolishing the daily sacrifice and
setting up the horrible abomination. **32** By his
deceit he shall make some who were disloyal to
the covenant apostatize; but those who remain
loyal to their God shall take strong action.
**33** The nation's wise men shall instruct the
many; though for a time they will become victims of the sword, of flames, exile, and plunder.
**34** When they fall, few people shall help them,
but many shall join them out of treachery.
**35** Of the wise men, some shall fall, so that the
rest may be tested, refined, and purified, until
the end time which is still appointed to come.

**36** *"The king shall do as he pleases, exalting himself and making himself greater than any
god; he shall utter dreadful blasphemies against
the God of gods. He shall prosper only till divine wrath is ready, for what is determined must
take place. **37** He shall have no regard for the
gods of his ancestors or for the one in whom
women delight; for no god shall he have regard,
because he shall make himself greater than all.
**38** Instead, he shall give glory to the god of
strongholds; a god unknown to his fathers he
shall glorify with gold, silver, precious stones,
and other treasures. **39** To defend the strongholds he shall station a people of a foreign god.
Whoever acknowledges him he shall provide
with abundant honor; he shall make them rule
over the many and distribute the land as a reward.

**40** "At the appointed time the king of the
south shall come to grips with him, but the king

---

b Is 19, 1.

---

11, 30: Kittim: originally this word meant Cypriots or other island dwellers. Here it means the Romans, who forced Antiochus to withdraw from Egypt during his second campaign there.

11, 36–39: Instead of venerating Apollo, one of the gods of his ancestors, Antiochus venerated, and even identified himself with, Zeus Olympios, whom the Romans equated with the god of their fortress in Rome, Jupiter Capitolinus, the god of strongholds.

of the north shall overwhelm him with chariots
and horsemen and a great fleet, passing through
the countries like a flood. **41** He shall enter the
glorious land and many shall fall, except Edom,
Moab, and the chief part of Ammon, which
shall escape from his power. **42** He shall extend
his power over the countries, and not even the
land of Egypt shall escape. **43** He shall control
the riches of gold and silver and all the treasures
of Egypt; Libya and Ethiopia shall be in his
train. **44** When news from the east and the
north terrifies him, he shall set out with great
fury to slay and to doom many. **45** He shall
pitch the tents of his royal pavilion between the
sea and the glorious holy mountain, but he shall
come to his end with none to help him.

## CHAPTER 12

**1** "At that time there shall arise
Michael, the great prince,
guardian of your people;[c]
It shall be a time unsurpassed in distress
since nations began until that time.
At that time your people shall escape,
everyone who is found written in the
book.*
**2** Many of those who sleep
in the dust of the earth shall awake;*
Some shall live forever,
others shall be an everlasting horror and
disgrace.[d]
**3** But the wise shall shine brightly
like the splendor of the firmament,
And those who lead the many to justice
shall be like the stars forever.[e]

**4** "As for you, Daniel, keep secret the message and seal the book until the end time; many
shall fall away and evil shall increase."
**5** I, Daniel, looked and saw two others, one
standing on either bank of the river. **6** One of
them said to the man clothed in linen, who was
upstream, "How long shall it be to the end of
these appalling things?" **7** [f]The man clothed in
linen, who was upstream, lifted his right and left
hands to heaven; and I heard him swear by him
who lives forever that it should be for a year,
two years, a half-year;* and that, when the power of the destroyer of the holy people was
brought to an end, all these things should end.
**8** I heard, but I did not understand; so I asked,
"My lord, what follows this?" **9** "Go, Daniel," he said, "because the words are to be kept
secret and sealed until the end time. **10** Many
shall be refined, purified, and tested, but the
wicked shall prove wicked; none of them shall
have understanding, but the wise shall have it.
**11** From the time that the daily sacrifice is abolished and the horrible abomination is set up,
there shall be one thousand two hundred and
ninety days. **12** Blessed is the man who has
patience and perseveres until the one thousand
three hundred and thirty-five days. **13** Go, take
your rest, you shall rise for your reward at the
end of days."

## *III: Appendix**

## CHAPTER 13

**Susanna's Virtue.** **1** In Babylon there
lived a man named Joakim, **2** who married a
very beautiful and God-fearing woman, Susanna, the daughter of Hilkiah; **3** her pious parents
had trained their daughter according to the law
of Moses. **4** Joakim was very rich; he had a
garden near his house, and the Jews had recourse to him often because he was the most
respected of them all.
**5** That year, two elders of the people were
appointed judges, of whom the Lord said,
"Wickedness has come out of Babylon: from
the elders who were to govern the people as
judges." **6** These men, to whom all brought
their cases, frequented the house of Joakim.
**7** When the people left at noon, Susanna used
to enter her husband's garden for a walk.
**8** When the old men saw her enter every day for
her walk, they began to lust for her. **9** They
suppressed their consciences; they would not
allow their eyes to look to heaven, and did not
keep in mind just judgments. **10** Though both
were enamored of her, they did not tell each
other their trouble, **11** for they were ashamed to
reveal their lustful desire to have her. **12** Day
by day they watched eagerly for her. **13** One
day they said to each other, "Let us be off for
home, it is time for lunch." So they went out
and parted; **14** but both turned back, and when
they met again, they asked each other the reason. They admitted their lust, and then they
agreed to look for an occasion when they could
meet her alone.
**15** One day, while they were waiting for the
right moment, she entered the garden as usual,
with two maids only. She decided to bathe, for
the weather was warm. **16** Nobody else was

c Rv 12, 7.
d Mt 25, 46; Jn 5, 29.
e Wis 3, 7.
f Rv 10, 5f.

*

12, 1: Written in the book: the book of God's predestination.
12, 2: The first Israelites who have fallen (Dn 11, 33ff) shall awake, that is, rise to live forever. A resurrection of the wicked as in later, Christian teaching (Jn 5, 28f) is implied here if the others are included in the many; but cf Is 66, 24.
12, 7: A year, two years, a half-year: see note on Dn 7, 25. The author's perspective is the end of Antiochus, and beyond, the final consummation of all things.
13, 1—14, 42: The short stories in these two chapters may have originally been about some other Daniel or Daniels than the hero of the main part of the book. They exist now only in Greek, but probably were first composed in Hebrew or Aramaic. They are excluded from the Jewish canon of Scripture, but the church as always included them among the inspired writings.

there except the two elders, who had hidden
themselves and were watching her. 17 "Bring
me oil and soap," she said to the maids, "and
shut the garden doors while I bathe." 18 They
did as she said; they shut the garden doors and
left by the side gate to fetch what she had ordered, unaware that the elders were hidden inside.

19 As soon as the maids had left, the two old
men got up and hurried to her. 20 "Look,"
they said, "the garden doors are shut, and no
one can see us; give in to our desire, and lie with
us. 21 If you refuse, we will testify against you
that you dismissed your maids because a young
man was here with you."

22 "I am completely trapped," Susanna
groaned. "If I yield, it will be my death; if I
refuse, I cannot escape your power. 23 Yet it is
better for me to fall into your power without
guilt than to sin before the Lord." 24 Then
Susanna shrieked, and the old men also shouted
at her, 25 as one of them ran to open the garden
doors. 26 When the people in the house heard
the cries from the garden, they rushed in by the
side gate to see what had happened to her.
27 At the accusations by the old men, the servants felt very much ashamed, for never had any
such thing been said about Susanna.

28 When the people came to her husband
Joakim the next day, the two wicked elders also
came, fully determined to put Susanna to death.
Before all the people they ordered: 29 "Send
for Susanna, the daughter of Hilkiah, the wife
of Joakim." When she was sent for, 30 she
came with her parents, children and all her relatives. 31 Susanna, very delicate and beautiful,
32 was veiled; but those wicked men ordered
her to uncover her face so as to sate themselves
with her beauty. 33 All her relatives and the
onlookers were weeping.

34 In the midst of the people the two elders
rose up and laid their hands on her head.
35 Through her tears she looked up to heaven,
for she trusted in the Lord wholeheartedly.
36 The elders made this accusation: "As we
were walking in the garden alone, this woman
entered with two girls and shut the doors of the
garden, dismissing the girls. 37 A young man,
who was hidden there, came and lay with her.
38 When we, in a corner of the garden, saw this
crime, we ran toward them. 39 We saw them
lying together, but the man we could not hold,
because he was stronger than we; he opened the
doors and ran off. 40 Then we seized this one
and asked who the young man was, 41 but she
refused to tell us. We testify to this." The assembly believed them, since they were elders
and judges of the people, and they condemned
her to death.

42 But Susanna cried aloud: "O eternal God,
you know what is hidden and are aware of all
things before they come to be: 43 you know
that they have testified falsely against me. Here
I am about to die, though I have done none of
the things with which these wicked men have
charged me."

44 The Lord heard her prayer. 45 As she
was being led to execution, God stirred up the
holy spirit of a young boy named Daniel,
46 and he cried aloud: "I will have no part in
the death of this woman." 47 All the people
turned and asked him, "What is this you are
saying?" 48 He stood in their midst and continued, "Are you such fools, O Israelites! To condemn a woman of Israel without examination
and without clear evidence? 49 Return to court,
for they have testified falsely against her."

50 Then all the people returned in haste. To
Daniel the elders said, "Come, sit with us and
inform us, since God has given you the prestige
of old age." 51 But he replied, "Separate these
two far from one another that I may examine
them."

52 After they were separated one from the
other, he called one of them and said: "How
you have grown evil with age! Now have your
past sins come to term: 53 [g]passing unjust sentences, condemning the innocent, and freeing
the guilty, although the Lord says, 'The innocent and the just you shall not put to death.'
54 Now, then, if you were a witness, tell me
under what tree you saw them together."
55 "Under a mastic tree,"* he answered.
"Your fine lie has cost you your head," said
Daniel; "for the angel of God shall receive the
sentence from him and split you in two."
56 Putting him to one side, he ordered the other
one to be brought. "Offspring of Canaan, not
of Judah," Daniel said to him, "beauty has
seduced you, lust has subverted your conscience. 57 This is how your acted with the
daughters of Israel, and in their fear they yielded
to you; but a daughter of Judah did not tolerate
your wickedness.* 58 Now then, tell me under
what tree you surprised them together."
59 "Under an oak," he said. "Your fine lie has
cost you also your head," said Daniel; "for the
angel of God waits with a sword to cut you in
two so as to make an end of you both."

60 The whole assembly cried aloud, blessing
God who saves those that hope in him.

g Ex 23, 7.

*

13, 55–59: The contrast between the mastic tree, which is small, and the majestic oak emphasizes the contradiction between the statements of the two elders. In the Greek text there is a play on words between the names of these two trees and the mortal punishment decreed by Daniel for the elders.

13, 57: Besides the evident moral intent of this story, it appears to have served the purpose of contrasting the northern and the southern kingdom, Israel and Judah, in favor of the latter.

**61** [h]They rose up against the two elders, for by their own words Daniel had convicted them of perjury. According to the law of Moses, they inflicted on them the penalty they had plotted to impose on their neighbor: **62** they put them to death. Thus was innocent blood spared that day.

**63** Hilkiah and his wife praised God for their daughter Susanna, as did Joakim her husband and all her relatives, because she was found innocent of any shameful deed. **64** And from that day onward Daniel was greatly esteemed by the people.

## CHAPTER 14

**Bel and the Dragon.** **1** After King Astyages* was laid with his fathers, Cyrus the Persian succeeded to his kingdom. **2** Daniel was the king's favorite and was held in higher esteem than any of the friends of the king.* **3** The Babylonians had an idol called Bel,* and every day they provided for it six barrels of fine flour, forty sheep, and six measures of wine. **4** The king worshiped it and went every day to adore it; but Daniel adored only his God. **5** When the king asked him, "Why do you not adore Bel?" Daniel replied, "Because I worship not idols made with hands, but only the living God who made heaven and earth and has dominion over all mankind." **6** Then the king continued, "You do not think Bel is a living god? Do you not see how much he eats and drinks every day?" **7** Daniel began to laugh. "Do not be deceived, O king," he said; "it is only clay inside and bronze outside; it has never taken any food or drink." **8** Enraged, the king called his priests and said to them, "Unless you tell me who it is that consumes these provisions, you shall die. **9** But if you can show that Bel consumes them, Daniel shall die for blaspheming Bel." Daniel said to the king, "Let it be as you say!" **10** There were seventy priests of Bel, besides their wives and children.

When the king went with Daniel into the temple of Bel, **11** the priests of Bel said, "See, we are going to leave. Do you, O king, set out the food and prepare the wine; then shut the door and seal it with your ring. **12** If you do not find that Bel has eaten it all when you return in the morning, we are to die; otherwise Daniel shall die for his lies against us." **13** They were not perturbed, because under the table they had made a secret entrance through which they always came in to consume the food. **14** After they departed the king set the food before Bel, while Daniel ordered his servants to bring some ashes, which they scattered through the whole temple; the king alone was present. Then they went outside, sealed the closed door with the king's ring, and departed. **15** The priests entered that night as usual, with their wives and children, and they ate and drank everything.

**16** Early the next morning, the king came with Daniel. **17** "Are the seals unbroken, Daniel?" he asked. And Daniel answered, "They are unbroken, O king." **18** As soon as he had opened the door, the king looked at the table and cried aloud, "Great you are, O Bel; there is no trickery in you." **19** But Daniel laughed and kept the king from entering. "Look at the floor," he said; "whose footprints are these?" **20** "I see the footprints of men, women, and children!" said the king. **21** The angry king arrested the priests, their wives, and their children. They showed him the secret door by which they used to enter to consume what was on the table. **22** He put them to death, and handed Bel over to Daniel, who destroyed it and its temple.

**23** There was a great dragon which the Babylonians worshiped. **24** "Look!" said the king to Daniel, "you cannot deny that this is a living god, so adore it." **25** But Daniel answered, "I adore the Lord, my God, for he is the living God. **26** Give me permission, O king, and I will kill this dragon without sword or club." "I give you permission," the king said. **27** Then Daniel took some pitch, fat, and hair; these he boiled together and made into cakes. He put them into the mouth of the dragon, and when the dragon ate them, he burst asunder. "This," he said, "is what you worshiped."

**28** When the Babylonians heard this, they were angry and turned against the king. "The king has become a Jew," they said; "he has destroyed Bel, killed the dragon, and put the priests to death." **29** They went to the king and demanded: "Hand Daniel over to us, or we will kill you and your family." **30** When he saw himself threatened with violence, the king was forced to hand Daniel over to them. **31** They threw Daniel into a lions' den, where he remained six days. **32** In the den were seven lions, and two carcasses and two sheep had been given to them daily. But now they were given nothing, so that they would devour Daniel.

**33** In Judea there was a prophet, Habakkuk; he mixed some bread in a bowl with the stew he had boiled, and was going to bring it to the reapers in the field, **34** when an angel of the Lord told him, "Take the lunch you have to Daniel in the lions' den at Babylon." **35** But

h 61f: Dt 19, 18. 19.

*

14, 1: King Astyages: the last of the Median kings, defeated by Cyrus in 550 B.C. This story preserves the fiction of a successive Median and Persian rule of Babylon.

14, 2: This verse in the Septuagint Greek text reads: "There was once a priest, Daniel by name, the son of Abal, a favorite of the king of Babylon." This may represent an earlier form of the story, before it was attached to the Book of Daniel.

14, 3: Bel: see the note on Dn 4, 5.

Habakkuk answered, "Babylon, sir, I have never seen, and I do not know the den!" **36** *i*The
angel of the Lord seized him by the crown of his
head and carried him by the hair; with the speed
of the wind, he set him down in Babylon above
the den. **37** "Daniel, Daniel," cried Habakkuk, "take the lunch God has sent you."
**38** "You have remembered me, O God," said
Daniel; "you have not forsaken those who love
you." **39** While Daniel began to eat, the angel
of the Lord at once brought Habakkuk back to
his own place.

**40** On the seventh day the king came to
mourn for Daniel. As he came to the den and
looked in, there was Daniel, sitting there!
**41** The king cried aloud, "You are great, O
Lord, the God of Daniel, and there is no other
besides you!" **42** Daniel he took out, but those
who had tried to destroy him he threw into the
den, and they were devoured in a moment before his eyes.

i Ez 8, 3.

# The Book of
# HOSEA

*Hosea belonged to the northern kingdom and began his prophetic career in the last years of Jeroboam II (786–746 B.C.). Some believe that he was a priest, others that he was a cult prophet; the prophecy, our only source of information concerning his life, gives us no certain answer in the matter. The collected oracles reveal a very sensitive, emotional man who could pass quickly from violent anger to the deepest tenderness. The prophecy pivots around his own unfortunate marriage to Gomer, a personal tragedy which profoundly influenced his teaching. In fact, his own prophetic vocation and message were immeasurably deepened by the painful experience he underwent in his married life.*

*Gomer, the adulteress, symbolized faithless Israel. And just as Hosea could not give up his wife forever even when she played the harlot, so Yahweh could not renounce Israel, who had been betrothed to him. God would chastise, but it would be the chastisement of the jealous lover, longing to bring back the beloved to the fresh and pure joy of their first love.*

*Israel's infidelity took the form of idolatry and ruthless oppression of the poor. No amount of mechanically offered sacrifices could atone for her serious sins. Chastisement alone remained; God would have to strip her of the rich ornaments bestowed by her false lovers and thus bring her back to the true lover. A humiliated Israel would again seek Yahweh. The eleventh chapter of Hosea is one of the summits of Old Testament theology; God's love for his people has never been expressed more tenderly. Hosea began the tradition of describing the relation between Yahweh and Israel in terms of marriage. This symbolism appears later on in the Old Testament; and, in the New, both St. John and St. Paul express in the same imagery the union between Christ and his church.*

*The Book of Hosea is divided as follows:*
*I. The Prophet's Marriage and Its Lesson (1, 1—3, 5).*
*II. Israel's Guilt and Punishment (4, 1—14, 10).*

## I: The Prophet's Marriage and Its Lesson*

### CHAPTER 1

**Marriage with an Unfaithful Wife.** 1 The
word of the LORD that came to Hosea, the son
of Beeri, in the days of Uzziah, Jotham, Ahaz,
Hezekiah, kings of Judah, and in the days of
Jeroboam, son of Joash, king of Israel. 2 In the
beginning of the LORD's speaking to Hosea, the
LORD said to Hosea:

Go, take a harlot wife* and harlot's
children,
for the land gives itself to harlotry,
turning away from the LORD.

3 So he went and took Gomer, the daughter of
Diblaim; and she conceived and bore him a son.
4 Then the LORD said to him:

Give him the name Jezreel,*
for in a little while
I will punish the house of Jehu
for the bloodshed at Jezreel
And bring to an end the kingdom
of the house of Israel;
5 On that day I will break the bow of Israel
in the valley of Jezreel.

* 1—3: This section is ordinarily thought to be biographical, the prophet's personal tragedy figuring as the relation of God to his people Israel. Hosea's marriage to a harlot wife represents Israel's infidelity to her Lord; hence the symbolic names of the children (Hos 1, 4–9). In Hos 2, 4–25 the Lord protests this infidelity and decrees its consequences, but promises restoration in return for amendment; his punishments are medicinal. In chapter 3 Hosea once more takes back his wife, but only conditionally, signifying God's long-suffering love for Israel and hope for her return.

1, 2: A harlot wife: this does not necessarily mean that Gomer was a harlot when Hosea married her; the verse describes the event in its final consequences.

1, 4: Jezreel: the strategic valley in northern Israel where Jehu brought the dynasty of Omri to an end through bloodshed (2 Kgs 9–10). Jeroboam II was the last king but one of the house of Jehu; the prophecy in this verse was fulfilled by the murder of his son, who reigned only six months (2 Kgs 15, 8–10).

6 When she conceived again and bore a daughter, the LORD said to him:

Give her the name Lo-ruhama;*
I no longer feel pity for the house of Israel:
rather, I abhor them utterly.
7 Yet for the house of Judah I feel pity;
I will save them by the LORD, their God;
But I will not save them by war,
by sword or bow, by horses or
horsemen.*

8 After she weaned Lo-ruhama, she conceived
and bore a son. 9 Then the LORD said:

Give him the name Lo-ammi,*
for you are not my people,
and I will not be your God.

## CHAPTER 2

### Israel's Punishment and Restoration

4 Protest against your mother, protest!*
for she is not my wife,
and I am not her husband.
Let her remove her harlotry from before her,
her adultery from between her breasts,
5 Or I will strip her naked,*
leaving her as on the day of her birth;
I will make her like the desert,
reduce her to an arid land,
and slay her with thirst.
6 I will have no pity on her children,
for they are the children of harlotry.
7 Yes, their mother has played the harlot;
she that conceived them has acted
shamefully.
"I will go after my lovers,"* she said,
"who give me my bread and my water,
my wool and my flax, my oil and my
drink."

10 Since she has not known
that it was I who gave her
the grain, the wine, and the oil,
And her abundance of silver,
and of gold, which they used for Baal,
11 Therefore I will take back my grain in its
time,
and my wine in its season;
I will snatch away my wool and my flax,
with which she covers her nakedness.
12 So now I will lay bare her shame
before the eyes of her lovers,
and no one can deliver her out of my
hand.
13 I will bring an end to all her joy,
her feasts, her new moons, her sabbaths,
and all her solemnities.
14 I will lay waste her vines and fig trees,
of which she said, "These are the hire
my lovers have given me";
I will turn them into rank growth
and wild beasts shall devour them.
15 I will punish her for the days of the Baals,*
for whom she burnt incense
While she decked herself out with her rings
and her jewels,
and, in going after her lovers,
forgot me, says the LORD.
8 Therefore, I will hedge in her way with
thorns*
and erect a wall against her,
so that she cannot find her paths.
9 If she runs after her lovers, she shall not
overtake them;
if she looks for them she shall not find
them.
Then she shall say,
"I will go back to my first husband,
for it was better with me then than now."

16 So I will allure her;*
I will lead her into the desert
and speak to her heart.
17 From there I will give her the vineyards she
had,
and the valley of Achor as a door of
hope.
She shall respond there as in the days of her
youth,
when she came up from the land of
Egypt.

18 On that day, says the LORD,

---

1, 6: Lo-ruhama: "she is not pitied." The "pity" that is here withheld from Israel is God's gratuitous love which inspires his beneficent acts.

1, 7: The terrible punishments announced by the prophets were so fully realized that later generations made a point of recalling the same prophets' messages of consolation also, even though it meant taking these from another context. Thus, an editor placed the words of Hos 2, 1ff after the repudiation of Israel in Hos 1, 9; here the more natural order has been restored. The present verse is another example of the same thing. In addition, it may be the work of a later hand, dating from a time when the prophecies of Hosea were circulated in the south, after the dissolution of the northern kingdom that he had prophesied. The second part of the verse emphasizes the power of the Lord, who needs no human agents to fulfill his will. It may refer to the deliverance of Jerusalem from the siege of Sennacherib (2 Kgs 19, 35ff).

1, 9: Lo-ammi: "not my people."

2, 4: The Lord speaks of Israel, still using the example of Hosea's wife.

2, 5: I will strip her naked: contemporary documents indicate that this was a conventional punishment for adultery.

2, 7: My lovers: the local fertility deities to whom, rather than to the Lord (v 10), the unfaithful Israelites attributed the produce of the land.

2, 15: The days of the Baals: ritual observances held in various local shrines in honor of Baal.

2, 8f: The crop failures, blight, etc., sent by the Lord (vv 11–14) have as their purpose to make Israel see the folly of her ways.

2, 16f: Israel's journey in the desert represents for Hosea the time of Israel's fidelity, before it was corrupted by the ways of Canaan; cf Jer 2, 2–7; Am 5, 25. Thus, he pictures a restoration in terms of a new entry into the promised land.

2, 18: My baal: the word means "lord, master." It was commonly used by women of their husbands, but it is to be shunned as a title for the Lord because of its association with the pagan god Baal. Probably it had been so used by many

She shall call me "My husband,"
and never again "My baal."*
19 Then will I remove from her mouth the
names of the Baals,
so that they shall no longer be invoked.
20 I will make a covenant for them on that day,
with the beasts of the field,
With the birds of the air,
and with the things that crawl on the
ground.
Bow and sword and war
I will destroy from the land,
and I will let them take their rest in
security.

21 I will espouse you to me forever:*
I will espouse you in right and in justice,
in love and in mercy;
22 I will espouse you in fidelity,
and you shall know the LORD.
23 On that day I will respond, says the LORD;
I will respond to the heavens,
and they shall respond to the earth;
24 The earth shall respond to the grain, and
wine, and oil,
and these shall respond to Jezreel.
25 I will sow him for myself in the land,
and I will have pity on Lo-ruhama.
I will say to Lo-ammi, "You are my
people,"
and he shall say, "My God!"[a]

## CHAPTER 3

### Triumph of Love

1 *Again the LORD said to me:
Give your love to a woman
beloved of a paramour, an adulteress;
Even as the LORD loves the people of Israel,
though they turn to other gods
and are fond of raisin cakes.*
2 So I bought her for fifteen pieces of silver and
a homer* and a lethech of barley. 3 Then I said
to her:

"Many days you shall wait for me;
you shall not play the harlot
Or belong to any man;
I in turn will wait for you."
4 For the people of Israel shall remain many
days
without king or prince,
Without sacrifice or sacred pillar,*
without ephod or household idols.
5 Then the people of Israel shall turn back
and seek the LORD, their God,
and David, their king;*
They shall come trembling to the LORD
and to his bounty, in the last days.[b]
2, 1 *The number of the Israelites
shall be like the sand of the sea,
which can be neither measured nor
counted.
Whereas they were called,
"Lo-ammi,"
They shall be called,
"Children of the living God."[c]
2 Then the people of Judah and of Israel
shall be gathered together;
They shall appoint for themselves one head
and come up from other lands,
for great shall be the day of Jezreel.
3 Say to your brothers, "Ammi,"
and to your sisters, "Ruhama."

## II: *Israel's Guilt and Punishment*

## CHAPTER 4

### Crimes of Israel

1 Hear the word of the LORD, O people of
Israel,
for the LORD has a grievance
against the inhabitants of the land:
There is no fidelity, no mercy,
no knowledge of God in the land.

a Rom 9, 25; 1 Pt 2, 10. c Rom 9, 26.
b Ez 34, 23.

* Israelites, who saw little if any difference between the worship of the Lord and the worship of Baal.

2, 21f: The Lord will once more espouse Israel; the qualities ascribed to the renewed people are the bridal gift (cf Gn 24, 53) with which he will endow it. In right and in justice: two terms dear to Hosea, used by him especially to condemn the popular social injustice and corruption of the legal processes. Here they mean right conduct in general. Love: one of the most characteristic words of Hosea's prophecy. It means a dutiful love, based on a social relation; here it refers to the covenant between God and his people. It is a love fulfilled by the performance of mutual obligations. Mercy: from the same root as the word translated pity in Hos 1, 6; cf v 25. And you shall know the Lord: another characteristic expression of Hosea; cf Hos 4, 1; 5, 4; 6, 3. 6. It means not an abstract but a practical knowledge, i.e., acknowledgment of his will, obedience to his law.

3, 1–5: Hosea is instructed to take Gomer back, redeeming her from her paramours. On condition of her amendment, she will be restored to her former position of wife. This in turn signifies God's enduring love for his people. He will put the people through a period of trial—the dissolution of the kingdom—in order that they may return to him wholeheartedly.

3, 1: Raisin cakes: offerings to the fertility goddess Ashera, the female counterpart of Baal; cf Jer 7, 18; 44, 19.

3, 2: Homer: about ten bushels. Lethech: a half-homer.

3, 4: Sacred pillar: the stone massebah, originally perhaps a phallic symbol, representing Baal. These were also used, with another signification, in Israelite worship; see notes on Gn 28, 18; Ex 34, 13. Ephod: an instrument used in consulting the deity; cf 1 Sm 23, 6–12; 30, 7; see notes on Ex 28, 6. 15–30. Household idols: images regarded as the tutelary deities of the household; cf Gn 31, 19; Jgs 17, 5; 18, 14. 17f.

3, 5: David, their king: the messianic King of the Davidic line who will restore the kingdom of God's people; cf Jer 23, 5; Ez 34, 23f. The last days: the messianic age.

2, 1–3: These verses (The number . . . Ruhama) (transposed from ch 2) continue the conditional promise of restoration made in Hos 3, 1–5, reversing the dire predictions of chapter 1; the symbolic names now become names of honor: Jezreel, "God sows"; Ammi, "my people"; Ruhama, "she is pitied."

2 False swearing, lying, murder, stealing and
adultery!
in their lawlessness, bloodshed follows
bloodshed.[d]
3 Therefore the land mourns,
and everything that dwells in it
languishes:
The beasts of the field,
the birds of the air,
and even the fish of the sea perish.

## Guilt of the Priests

4 But let no one protest, let no one complain;
with you is my grievance, O priests!*
5 You shall stumble in the day,
and the prophets shall stumble with you at
night;
I will destroy your mother.
6 My people perish for want of knowledge!
Since you have rejected knowledge,
I will reject you from my priesthood;
Since you have ignored the law of your
God,
I will also ignore your sons.
7 One and all they sin against me,
exchanging their glory for shame.
8 They feed on the sin of my people,
and are greedy for their guilt.
9 The priests shall fare no better than the
people:
I will punish them for their ways,
and repay them for their deeds.[e]
10 They shall eat but not be satisfied,
they shall play the harlot but not increase,
Because they have abandoned the LORD
11 to practice harlotry.
Old wine and new
deprive my people of understanding.
12 They consult their piece of wood,
and their wand* makes pronouncements
for them,
For the spirit of harlotry has led them astray;
they commit harlotry, forsaking their God.
13 On the mountaintops they offer sacrifice
and on the hills they burn incense,
Beneath oak and poplar and terebinth,
because of their pleasant shade.
That is why your daughters play the harlot,
and your daughters-in-law are
adulteresses.
14 Am I then to punish your daughters for their
harlotry,
your daughters-in-law for their adultery?
You yourselves consort with harlots,
and with prostitutes you offer sacrifice!*
So must a people without understanding
come to ruin.
15 Though you play the harlot, O Israel,
let not Judah become guilty!
Come not to Gilgal,*
nor up to Beth-aven,
to swear, "As the Lord lives!"
16 For Israel is as stubborn as a heifer;
will the LORD now give them broad
pastures
as though they were lambs?
17 Ephraim* is an associate of idols,
let him alone!
18 When their carousing is over,
they give themselves to harlotry;
in their arrogance they love shame.
19 The wind has bound them up in its pinions;*
they shall have only shame from their
altars.

# CHAPTER 5

## Guilt of the Leaders

1 Hear this, O priests,
Pay attention, O house of Israel,
O household of the king, give ear!
It is you who are called to judgment.[f]
For you have become a snare at Mizpah,*
and a net spread upon Tabor.
2 In their perversity they have sunk into
wickedness,
and I am rejected by them all.
3 I know Ephraim,
and Israel is not hidden from me;
Now Ephraim has played the harlot,
Israel is defiled.
4 Their deeds do not allow them
to return to their God;
For the spirit of harlotry is in them,
and they do not recognize the LORD.

5 The arrogance of Israel bears witness against
him;
Ephraim stumbles in his guilt,

d Ex 20, 13-17.
e Is 24, 2.
f Mi 3, 1.

*

4, 4ff: Hosea is particularly severe with the priests in the northern kingdom, who had led the way in the general apostasy from God's law. The prophets here associated with the priests (v 5) were doubtless cult prophets, who were often unworthy of their pretended calling; cf Jer 2, 8; 4, 9f; 6, 13f; 23, 9–40.

4, 12: Wood . . . wand: an idol used in divination.

4, 14: With prostitutes you offer sacrifice: the ritual prostitution practiced at the Canaanite shrines was introduced even into sanctuaries dedicated to the Lord. In comparison, the adultery that had become common in Israel was a far less reprehensible crime.

4, 15: Gilgal: not the Gilgal of the south (Jos 4, 19f), but a sanctuary north of Bethel where there was an association of cult prophets (2 Kgs 2, 1ff; 4, 38). Beth-aven: literally, "house of iniquity," Hosea's nickname for Bethel, or a scribal substitute for Bethel, "house of god," in this context. Bethel was one of the royal shrines of Israel, where there was a schismatic public worhsip of the Lord; cf 1 Kgs 12, 26–30.

4, 17: Ephraim: the heartland of the northern kingdom. During the latter part of Hosea's prophetic career, Ephraim was all that remained of Israel after the Assyrians had overrun Transjordan and Galilee.

4, 19: The Israelites shall be carried from their country as by a whirlwind. To this their idolatry has brought them.

5, 1: Mizpah: probably the Mizpah in Transjordan is meant; cf Jos 11, 8. Tabor: the mountain that dominates the valley of Jezreel.

and Judah stumbles with them.
6 With their flocks and their herds they shall go
to seek the LORD, but they shall not find him:
he has withdrawn himself from them.
7 They have been untrue to the LORD,
for they have begotten illegitimate children;
Now shall the new moon devour them
together with their fields.

### Political Upheavals*

8 Blow the horn in Gibeah,
the trumpet in Ramah!
Sound the alarm in Beth-aven:
"Look behind you, O Benjamin!"*
9 Ephraim shall become a waste
on the day of chastisement:
Against the tribes of Israel
I announce what is sure to be.
10 The princes of Judah have become
like those that move a boundary line;*
Upon them I will pour out
my wrath like water.[g]

11 Is Ephraim maltreated, his rights violated?
No, he has willingly gone after filth!*
12 I am like a moth for Ephraim,
like maggots* for the house of Judah.
13 When Ephraim saw his infirmity,
and Judah his sore,
Ephraim went to Assyria,
and Judah sent to the great king.*
But he cannot heal you
nor take away your sore.
14 For I am like a lion to Ephraim,
like a young lion to the house of Judah;
It is I who rend the prey and depart,
I carry it away and no one can save it from me.

### Insincere Conversion

15 I will go back to my place
until they pay for their guilt
and seek my presence.*

## CHAPTER 6

*In their affliction, they shall look for me:
1 "Come, let us return to the LORD,
For it is he who has rent, but he will heal us;
he has struck us, but he will bind our wounds.
2 He will revive us after two days;*
on the third day he will raise us up,
to live in his presence.[h]
3 Let us know, let us strive to know the LORD;
as certain as the dawn is his coming,
and his judgment shines forth like the light of day!
He will come to us like the rain,
like spring rain that waters the earth."
4 What can I do with you, Ephraim?
What can I do with you, Judah?
Your piety* is like a morning cloud,
like the dew that early passes away.
5 For this reason I smote them through the prophets,
I slew them by the words of my mouth;
6 For it is love that I desire, not sacrifice,
and knowledge of God rather than holocausts.[i]
7 But they, in their land, violated the covenant;
there they were untrue to me.
8 Gilead is a city of evildoers,
tracked with blood.
9 As brigands ambush a man,
a band of priests slay on the way to Shechem,
committing monstrous crime.
10 In the house of Israel I have seen a horrible thing:
there harlotry is found in Ephraim,
Israel is defiled.
11 For you also, O Judah,
a harvest* has been appointed.

## CHAPTER 7

1 When I would bring about the restoration of my people,
when I would heal Israel,
The guilt of Ephraim stands out,

g Dt 19, 14; 27, 17.
h 1 Cor 15, 4.
i 1 Sm 15, 22; Eccl 4, 17; Mt 9, 13; 12, 7.

*

5, 8–14: This passage refers to the Syro-Ephraimite war of 735–734 B.C., when a coalition of Arameans and Israelites attempted to dethrone the king of Judah. Judah repulsed the attempt with the aid of Assyria, and the latter devastated both Aram and Israel; cf 2 Kgs 16, 5–9. Hosea condemns both Israel and Judah for the war.

5, 8: A vision of invasion, from Gibeah and Ramah in northern Judah, into Israel.

5, 10: Like those that move a boundary line: comparison of the invaders to a classic case of social injustice; cf Dt 19, 14; 27, 17; Prv 23, 10f.

5, 11: Gone after filth: by allying himself with Aram.

5, 12: Moth . . . maggots: internal corruption will work the Lord's punishment on both Israel and Judah.

5, 13: Ephraim went . . . the great king: in 738 B.C. the Israelite king Manahem had to pay tribute to the Assyrian king Tiglath-pileser III, whose vassal he became (2 Kgs 15, 19f). Under the threat of the Syro-Ephraimite invasion King Ahaz of Judah also submitted himself and his country to Tiglath-pileser (2 Kgs 16, 7–9). "The great king" was the title used by the Assyrian kings.

5, 15: The Lord withdraws himself from Israel, hoping for its repentance.

6, 1: In . . . me: this is the last line of ch 5.

6, 2: After two days; on the third day: after a short lapse of time.

6, 4: Piety: the word is translated "love" in Hos 2, 21 and in v 6 below.

6, 11: Harvest: when the land will reap the consequences of its sins.

the wickedness of Samaria;
They practice falsehood,
thieves break in, bandits plunder abroad.
2 Yet they do not remind themselves
that I remember all their wickedness.
Even now their crimes surround them,
present to my sight.

### Failure of the Monarchy*

3 In their wickedness they regale the king,
the princes too, with their deceits.
4 They are all kindled to wrath
like a blazing oven,
Whose fire the baker desists from stirring
once the dough is kneaded until it has
risen.
5 On the day of our king,
the princes are overcome with the heat of
wine.
He extends his hand among dissemblers;
6 the plotters approach with hearts like
ovens.
All the night their anger sleeps;
in the morning it flares like a blazing fire.
7 They are all heated like ovens,
and consume their rulers.
All their kings have fallen;
none of them calls upon me.

### Foreign Alliances

8 Ephraim mingles with the nations,
Ephraim is a hearth cake unturned.*
9 Strangers have sapped his strength,
but he takes no notice of it;
Of gray hairs, too, there is a sprinkling,
but he takes no notice of it.
10 The arrogance of Israel bears witness against
him;
yet they do not return to the LORD, their
God,
nor seek him, for all that.
11 Ephraim is like a dove,
silly and senseless;
They call upon Egypt,
they go to Assyria.
12 Even as they go I will spread my net around
them,
like birds in the air I will bring them
down.
In an instant I will send them captive
from their land.

### Perversity of Israel

13 Woe to them, they have strayed from me!
Ruin to them, they have sinned against
me!
Though I wished to redeem them,
they spoke lies against me.
14 They have not cried to me from their hearts
when they wailed upon their beds;
For wheat and wine they lacerated
themselves,*
while they rebelled against me.
15 Though I trained and strengthened their
arms,
yet they devised evil against me.
16 They have again become useless,
like a treacherous bow.
Their princes shall fall by the sword
because of the insolence of their tongues;
thus they shall be mocked in the land of
Egypt.

## CHAPTER 8

1 A trumpet to your lips,
You who watch over the house of the
LORD!
Since they have violated my covenant,
and sinned against my law,
2 While to me they cry out,
"O God of Israel, we know you!"
3 The men of Israel have thrown away what is
good;
the enemy shall pursue them.
4 *They made kings, but not by my authority;
they established princes, but without my
approval.
With their silver and gold they made
idols for themselves, to their own
destruction.
5 Cast away your calf, O Samaria!
my wrath is kindled against them;
How long will they be unable to attain
innocence in Israel?
6 The work of an artisan,
no god at all,
Destined for the flames—
such is the calf of Samaria!

7 When they sow the wind,
they shall reap the whirlwind;
The stalk of grain that forms no ear
can yield no flour;
Even if it could,

---

7, 3–7: This passage refers to the dynastic upheavals of Israel's declining days. Between the death of Jeroboam II and the fall of Samaria to the Assyrians, a matter of some twenty-five years, there were four separate dynasties on the throne and as many murdered kings. The prophet compares the Israelite nobles who were inflamed with passion to an overheated oven that consumes what it is supposed to bake; thus the land consumes its kings. Regale: with wine (v 3). Like fire smoldering through the night and blazing up in the morning, the sleeping anger of plotters soon breaks out in open rebellion; the succession of night and morning suggests the short reigns of the various kings of this troubled period.

7, 8: A hearth cake unturned: burnt on one side, half baked on the other, and therefore useless. Israel's decline in power is ascribed to its disastrous meddling in the power politics of the neighboring nations.

7, 14: They lacerated themselves: a common oriental practice in prayers of earnest impetration (1 Kgs 18, 28); the practice was forbidden in Israelite religion (Lv 19, 28; Dt 14, 1).

8, 4–6: Israel's monarchy and separate sanctuary are here associated, as in 1 Kgs 12, 20–33; both were the result of rebellion against the divinely approved Davidic dynasty and the Jerusalem temple with the ark of the covenant. The calf image set up by Jeroboam I in the royal shrines prevented Israel from attaining innocence (vv 5f).

strangers would swallow it.
8 Israel is swallowed up;
he is now among the nations
a thing of no value.
9 They went up to Assyria—
a wild ass off on its own—
Ephraim bargained for lovers.
10 Even though they bargain with the nations,
I will now gather an army;
King and princes shall shortly
succumb under the burden.

11 When Ephraim made many altars to expiate sin,
his altars became occasions of sin.*
12 Though I write for him my many ordinances,
they are considered as a stranger's.
13 Though they offer sacrifice,
immolate flesh and eat it,
the LORD is not pleased with them.
He shall still remember their guilt
and punish their sins;
they shall return to Egypt.
14 Israel has forgotten his maker
and built palaces.
Judah, too, has fortified many cities;
but I will send fire upon his cities,
to devour their castles.[j]

## CHAPTER 9

### Exile without Worship

1 Rejoice not, O Israel,
exult not like the nations!
For you have been unfaithful to your God,
loving a harlot's hire
upon every threshing floor.*
2 Threshing floor and wine press shall not nourish them,
the new wine shall fail them.

3 They shall not dwell in the LORD's land;
Ephraim shall return to Egypt,
and in Assyria they shall eat unclean food.
4 They shall not pour libations of wine to the LORD,
or proffer their sacrifices before him.
Theirs will be like mourners' bread,*
that makes unclean all who eat of it;
Such food as they have shall be for themselves;
it cannot enter the house of the LORD.

5 What will you do on the festival day,
the day of the LORD's feast?*
6 When they go from the ruins,
Egypt shall gather them in, Memphis shall bury them.
Weeds shall overgrow their silver treasures,
and thorns invade their tents.

### The Prophet Ridiculed

7 They have come, the days of punishment!
they have come, the days of recompense!
Let Israel know it!
"The prophet is a fool,
the man of the spirit is mad!"
Because your iniquity is great,
great, too, is your hostility.
8 A prophet is Ephraim's watchman with God,
yet a fowler's snare is on all his ways,
hostility in the house of his God.
9 They have sunk to the depths of corruption,
as in the days of Gibeah;*
He shall remember their iniquity
and punish their sins.

### Crime of Baal-peor

10 Like grapes in the desert,
I found Israel;
Like the first fruits of the fig tree in its prime,
I considered your fathers.
When they came to Baal-peor*
and consecrated themselves to the Shame,
they became as abhorrent as the thing they loved.
11 The glory of Ephraim flies away like a bird:
no birth, no carrying in the womb, no conception.
Were they to bear children,
I would slay the darlings of their womb.
12 Even though they bring up their children,
I will make them childless, till not one is left.
Woe to them
when I turn away from them!
13 Ephraim, as I saw, was like Tyre,
planted in a beauteous spot;
But Ephraim shall bring out
his children to the slayer.
14 Give them, O LORD!

j Am 2, 5.

*

8, 11: The very multiplicity of sanctuaries throughout the land was a danger to the purity of worship. The local shrines were speedily assimilated to the cult places used by the Canaanites, and the Lord was identified with the god Baal worshiped there. Thus the Deuteronomic writers, influenced by prophetic ideas, ended by restricting sacrificial worship to the one temple in Jerusalem.

9, 1f: Upon every threshing floor: an allusion to harvest festivals in honor of Baal, to whom the Israelites had attributed the fertility of the land; cf Hos 2, 7.

9, 4: Mourners' bread: bread eaten at funeral rites; cf Dt 26, 13f. Contact with a corpse made a person ritually unclean, together with everything he touched. Such bread could not be offered to the Lord.

9, 5: The Lord's feast: doubtless the autumn feast of Booths, the most important of the Israelite public celebrations; cf Lv 23, 34.

9, 9: The days of Gibeah: a reference to the outrage committed at Gibeah in the days of the Judges (Jgs 19, 22–30).

9, 10: At Baal-peor (Nm 25, 1–5) the Israelites consecrated themselves to Baal, here called the Shame.

9, 14: An unfruitful womb: this appears to be a reversal of the ancient blessing of Joseph contained in Gn 49, 25f, in

give them what?
Give them an unfruitful womb,*
and dry breasts!

## Crime of Gilgal

15 All their wickedness is in Gilgal;*
yes, there they incurred my hatred.
Because of their wicked deeds
I will drive them out of my house.
I will love them no longer;
all their princes are rebels.[k]
16 Ephraim is stricken,
their root is dried up;
they shall bear no fruit.

17 My God will disown them
because they have not listened to him;
they shall be wanderers among the
nations.

# CHAPTER 10

## Punishment of Idolatry

1 Israel is a luxuriant vine
whose fruit matches its growth.
The more abundant his fruit,
the more altars he built;
The more productive his land,
the more sacred pillars* he set up.
2 Their heart is false,
now they pay for their guilt;
God shall break down their altars
and destroy their sacred pillars.
3 If they would say,
"We have no king"—
Since they do not fear the LORD,
what can the king do for them?
4 Nothing but make promises,
swear false oaths, and make alliances,
While justice grows wild
like wormwood* in a plowed field!
5 The inhabitants of Samaria fear
for the calf of Beth-aven;*
The people mourn for it
and its priests wail over it,
because the glory has departed from it.
6 It too shall be carried to Assyria,
as an offering to the great king.
Ephraim shall be taken into captivity,
Israel be shamed by his schemes.

7 The king of Samaria shall disappear,
like foam upon the waters.
8 The high places of Aven shall be destroyed,
the sin of Israel;
thorns and thistles shall overgrow their
altars.
Then they shall cry out to the mountains,
"Cover us!"
and to the hills, "Fall upon us!"[l]

9 Since the days of Gibeah
you have sinned, O Israel.
There they took their stand;
war was not to reach them in Gibeah.[m]
10 Against the wanton people I came
and I chastised them;[n]
I gathered troops against them
when I chastised them for their two
crimes.*

## Time To Seek the Lord

11 Ephraim was a trained heifer,
willing to thresh;
I myself laid a yoke
upon her fair neck;
Ephraim was to be harnessed, Judah was to
plow,
Jacob was to break his furrows:
12 "Sow for yourselves justice,
reap the fruit of piety;
Break up for yourselves a new field,
for it is time to seek the LORD,
till he come and rain down justice upon
you."[o]
13 But you have cultivated wickedness,
reaped perversity,
and eaten the fruit of falsehood.

Because you have trusted in your chariots,
and in your many warriors,
14 Turmoil shall break out among your tribes
and all your fortresses shall be ravaged
As Salman ravaged Beth-arbel* in time of
war,
smashing mothers and their children.[p]
15 So shall it be done to you, Bethel,
because of your utter wickedness:
At dawn the king of Israel
shall perish utterly.

k 1 Sm 8, 5.
l Is 2, 19; Lk 23, 30; Rv 6, 16.
m Jgs 20, 1.
n Jer 4, 3.
o Is 45, 8.
p Jgs 8, 10ff.

* which the increase, hence fruitfulness, promised to the patriarch is even signified by the name of his son Ephraim, on whose descendants the prophet now invokes the curse of extinction.

9, 15: Gilgal: see note on Hos 4, 15.

10, 1: Sacred pillars: see note on Hos 3, 4.

10, 4: Justice . . . like wormwood: the administration of justice, which should have been the mainstay of the people, has in corrupt hands become another instrument of oppression; cf Am 6, 13.

10, 5: The calf of Beth-aven: see notes on Hos 4, 15; 8, 4ff.

10, 10: Their two crimes: possibly the outrage described in Jgs 19 is conceived as a double crime, of adultery and murder. Or the prophet regards the proclamation of the monarchy (cf 1 Sm 10, 23f) as a crime.

10, 14: As Salman ravaged Beth-arbel: allusion to an invasion not otherwise mentioned in the Bible. Salman may have been the Moabite king of this name mentioned in an inscription of Tiglath-pileser III. There were several Beth-arbels in Palestine; this one was probably in Transjordan.

## CHAPTER 11

### When Israel Was a Child

1 When Israel was a child I loved him,
out of Egypt* I called my son.[q]
2 The more I called them,
the farther they went from me,
Sacrificing to the Baals
and burning incense to idols.
3 Yet it was I who taught Ephraim to walk,
who took them in my arms;
4 I drew them with human cords,
with bands of love;*
I fostered them like one
who raises an infant to his cheeks;
Yet, though I stooped to feed my child,
they did not know that I was their healer.

5 He shall return to the land of Egypt,
and Assyria shall be his king;
6 The sword shall begin with his cities
and end by consuming his solitudes.
Because they refused to repent,
their own counsels shall devour them.
7 His people are in suspense about returning to him;
and God, though in unison they cry out to him,
shall not raise them up.

### End of the Exile

8 How could I give you up, O Ephraim,
or deliver you up, O Israel?
How could I treat you as Admah,
or make you like Zeboiim?*
My heart is overwhelmed,
my pity is stirred.[r]
9 I will not give vent to my blazing anger,
I will not destroy Ephraim again;
For I am God and not man,
the Holy One present among you;
I will not let the flames consume you.

10 They shall follow the LORD,
who roars like a lion;
When he roars,
his sons shall come frightened from the west,
11 Out of Egypt they shall come trembling, like sparrows,
from the land of Assyria, like doves;
And I will resettle them in their homes,
says the LORD.

## CHAPTER 12

### Infidelity of Israel

1 Ephraim has surrounded me with lies,
the house of Israel, with deceit;
Judah is still rebellious against God,
against the Holy One, who is faithful.
2 Ephraim chases the wind,
ever pursuing the gale.
His lies and falsehoods are many:
he comes to terms with Assyria,
and carries oil to Egypt.*
3 *The LORD has a grievance against Israel:
he shall punish Jacob for his conduct,
for his deeds he shall repay him.
4 In the womb he supplanted his brother,
and as a man he contended with God;[s]
5 He contended with the angel and triumphed,
entreating him with tears.
At Bethel he met God
and there he spoke with him:
6 The LORD, the God of hosts,
the LORD is his name!
7 You shall return by the help of your God,
if you remain loyal and do right
and always hope in your God.

8 A merchant who holds a false balance,
who loves to defraud!
9 Though Ephraim says,
"How rich I have become;
I have made a fortune!"
All his gain shall not suffice him
for the guilt of his sin.
10 I am the LORD, your God,
since the land of Egypt;
I will again have you live in tents,
as in that appointed time.
11 I granted many visions
and spoke to the prophets,
through whom I set forth examples.
12 In Gilead is falsehood, they have come to nought,
in Gilgal they sacrifice to bullocks;
Their altars are like heaps of stones
in the furrows of the field.

13 When Jacob fled to the land of Aram,
he served for a wife;
for a wife Israel tended sheep.[t]
14 By a prophet* the LORD brought Israel out
of Egypt,

q Mt 2, 15.
r Gn 19, 24f.
s Gn 25, 26; 32, 25.
t Gn 28, 5; 29, 20.
u Ex 14, 21f.

*

11, 1: Out of Egypt: Hosea, like most of the prophets, dates the real beginning of Israel from the time of Moses and the Exodus. Mt 2, 15 applies this text to the return of the Christ Child from Egypt.

11, 4: I drew them . . . with bands of love: not forcing them like draft animals, but drawing them with kindness and affection.

11, 8: Admah . . . Zeboiim: cities destroyed with Sodom and Gomorrah (Dt 29, 22).

12, 2: He comes . . . Egypt: allusion to the commercial and military pacts with the great powers, consistently condemned by the prophets as derogatory of the Lord's claim on his people.

12, 3–7: Contemporary Israel and the Israel represented by its ancestor Jacob (Israel) are here alternated, a splendid example of the Hebrew concept of "corporate personality" or easy transition from the individual to the community of which he is part. Hosea recalls the history of Jacob as it now appears in Genesis, but with some differences of detail and order.

12, 14: A prophet: Moses.

and by a prophet they were protected.[u]
15 Ephraim has exasperated his lord;
therefore he shall cast his blood-guilt upon him
and repay him for his outrage.

## CHAPTER 13

### Furrows of the Field

1 Ephraim's word caused fear,
for he was exalted in Israel;
but he sinned through Baal and died.

### Punishment for Ingratitude

2 Now they continue to sin,
making for themselves molten images,
Silver idols according to their fancy,
all of them the work of artisans.
"To these," they say, "offer sacrifice."
Men kiss calves!
3 Therefore, they shall be like a morning cloud
or like the dew that early passes away,
Like chaff storm-driven from the threshing floor
or like smoke out of the window.

4 I am the LORD, your God,
since the land of Egypt;
You know no God besides me,
and there is no savior but me.[v]
5 I fed you in the desert,
in the torrid land.
6 They ate their fill;
when filled, they became proud of heart
and forgot me.

7 Therefore, I will be like a lion to them,
like a panther by the road I will keep watch.
8 I will attack them like a bear robbed of its young,
and tear their hearts from their breasts;
I will devour them on the spot like a lion,
as though a wild beast were to rend them.

9 Your destruction, O Israel!
who is there to help you?
10 Where now is your king,
that he may rescue you in all your cities?
And your rulers, of whom you said,
"Give me a king and princes"?[w]
11 I give you a king in my anger,
and I take him away in my wrath.*

12 The guilt of Israel is wrapped up,
his sin is stored away.

13 The birth pangs shall come for him,
but he shall be an unwise child;
For when it is time he shall not present himself
where children break forth.*

14 Shall I deliver them from the power of the nether world?*
shall I redeem them from death?[x]
Where are your plagues, O death!
where is your sting, O nether world!
My eyes are closed to compassion.

15 Though he be fruitful among his fellows,
an east wind shall come, a wind from the LORDS,
rising from the desert,
That shall dry up his spring,
and leave his fountain dry.
It shall loot his land
of every precious thing.[y]

## CHAPTER 14

1 Samaria shall expiate her guilt,
for she has rebelled against her God.
They shall fall by the sword,
their little ones shall be dashed to pieces,
their expectant mothers shall be ripped open.

### Sincere Conversion

2 Return, O Israel, to the LORD, your God;
you have collapsed through your guilt.
3 Take with you words,
and return to the LORD;
Say to him, "Forgive all iniquity,
and receive what is good, that we may render
as offerings the bullocks from our stalls.
4 Assyria will not save us,
nor shall we have horses to mount;
We shall say no more, 'Our god,'
to the work of our hands;
for in you the orphan finds compassion."

5 I will heal their defection,
I will love them freely;
for my wrath is turned away from them.
6
I will be like the dew of Israel:
he shall blossom like the lily;
He shall strike root like the Lebanon cedar,
7 and put forth his shoots.
His splendor shall be like the olive tree

v Is 43, 11.
w 1 Sm 8, 5.
x 1 Cor 15, 54.
y Ex 19, 12.

13, 11: I give you a king . . . in my wrath: the Lord punishes the people of the northern kingdom by giving them incompetent kings who are soon deposed.

13, 13: Israel's sin is such as to warrant its destruction (v 12), because it refused to do penance. It will therefore perish as surely as the unborn child which dies in its mother's body because it does not properly employ the only way to safety.

13, 14: Shall . . . nether world: a vigorous affirmation of the Lord's determination to destroy Israel. St. Paul cites these words in a different sense (1 Cor 15, 54f), that of the ultimate victory of life over death in the resurrection of the body on the last day, wrought through the merits of Christ's passion and resurrection.

and his fragrance like the Lebanon cedar.
8 Again they shall dwell in his shade and
raise grain;
They shall blossom like the vine,
and his fame shall be like the wine of
Lebanon.

9 Ephraim! What more has he to do with
idols?
I have humbled him, but I will prosper
him.
"I am like a verdant cypress tree"—
Because of me you bear fruit!

* * *

10 Let him who is wise understand these things;
let him who is prudent know them.
Straight are the paths of the LORD,
in them the just walk,
but sinners stumble in them.*

---

* 14, 10: A later addition in the style of the wisdom literature.

# The Book of

# JOEL

*This prophecy is rich in apocalyptic imagery and strongly eschatological in tone. It was composed about 400 B.C. Its prevailing theme is the day of the Lord.*

*A terrible invasion of locusts ravaged Judah. So frightful was the scourge that the prophet visualized it as a symbol of the coming day of the Lord. In the face of this threatening catastrophe, the prophet summoned the people to repent, to turn to the Lord with fasting and weeping. They were ordered to convoke a solemn assembly in which the priests would pray for deliverance. The Lord answered their prayer and promised to drive away the locusts and bless the land with peace and prosperity. To these material blessings would be added an outpouring of the spirit on all flesh. St. Peter, in his first discourse before the people at Pentecost (Acts 2, 16–21), sees in the coming of the Holy Spirit the fulfillment of this promise (1, 1—3, 5).*

*The concluding poem pictures the nations gathered in the Valley of Jehoshaphat, where the Lord is about to pass judgment. Israel's enemies are summoned to hear the solemn indictment; their evil deeds are at last requited. The tumultuous throng assembled in the valley of decision is made up of the enemies of God and they face inevitable destruction. The oracle changes abruptly from the terrifying image of judgment to a vision of Israel restored and forever secure from her enemies. God is both the vindicator of his people and the source of their blessing (4, 1–21).*

## CHAPTER 1

**The Land Invaded.** 1 The word of the LORD which came to Joel, the son of Pethuel.

2 Hear this, you elders!
Pay attention, all you who dwell in the land!
Has the like of this happened in your days,
or in the days of your fathers?
3 Tell it to your children,
and your children to their children,
and their children to the next generation.
4 What the cutter left,
the locust swarm has eaten;
What the locust swarm left,
the grasshopper has eaten;
And what the grasshopper left,
the devourer* has eaten.

5 Wake up, you drunkards, and weep;
wail, all you drinkers of wine,
Because the juice of the grape
will be withheld from your mouths.
6 For a people* has invaded my land,
mighty and without number;
His teeth are the teeth of a lion,
and his molars those of a lioness.
7 He has laid waste my vine,
and blighted my fig tree;
He has stripped it, sheared off its bark;
its branches are made white.
8 Lament like a virgin girt with sackcloth
for the spouse of her youth.
9 Abolished are offering and libation
from the house of the LORD;
In mourning are the priests,
the ministers of the LORD.
10 The field is ravaged,
the earth mourns,
Because the grain is ravaged,
the must has failed,
the oil languishes.

11 Be appalled, you husbandmen!
wail, you vinedressers!
Over the wheat and the barley,
because the harvest of the field has perished.
12 The vine has dried up,
the fig tree is withered;
The pomegranate, the date palm also, and the apple,
all the trees of the field are dried up;
Yes, joy has withered away
from among mankind.

### Call to Penance

13 Gird yourselves and weep, O priests!
wail, O ministers of the altar!
Come, spend the night in sackcloth,
O ministers of my God!

---

1, 4: Cutter . . . locust . . . grasshopper . . . devourer: these names refer to various species of locusts: they can only be approximate.

1, 6: A people: the locusts compared to an invading army.

The house of your God is deprived
of offering and libation.
14 Proclaim a fast,
call an assembly;
Gather the elders,
all who dwell in the land,
Into the house of the LORD, your God,
and cry to the LORD![a]

15 Alas, the day!
for near is the day of the LORD,
and it comes as ruin from the Almighty.
16 From before our very eyes
has not the food been cut off;
And from the house of our God,
joy and gladness?
17 The seed lies shriveled under its clods;
the stores are destroyed,
The barns are broken down,
for the grain has failed.
18 How the beasts groan!
The herds of cattle are bewildered!
Because they have no pasturage,
even the flocks of sheep have perished.

19 To you, O LORD, I cry!
for fire has devoured the pastures of the plain,
and flame has enkindled all the trees of the field.
20 Even the beasts of the field
cry out to you;
For the streams of water are dried up,
and fire has devoured the pastures of the plain.

## CHAPTER 2

### The Day of the Lord

1 Blow the trumpet in Zion,
sound the alarm on my holy mountain!
Let all who dwell in the land tremble,
for the day of the LORD is coming;
2 Yes, it is near, a day of darkness and of gloom,
a day of clouds and somberness!
Like dawn spreading over the mountains,
a people numerous and mighty!
Their like has not been from of old,
nor will it be after them,
even to the years of distant generations.
3 Before them a fire devours,
and after them a flame enkindles;
Like the garden of Eden is the land before them,
and after them a desert waste;
from them there is no escape.

4 Their appearance is that of horses;
like steeds they run.
5 As with the rumble of chariots
they leap on the mountaintops;
As with the crackling of a fiery flame
devouring stubble;
Like a mighty people
arrayed for battle.
6 Before them peoples are in torment,
every face blanches.

7 Like warriors they run,
like soldiers they scale the wall;
They advance, each in his own lane,
without swerving from their paths.
8 No one crowds another,
each advances in his own track;
Though they fall into the ditches,
they are not checked.

9 They assault the city,
they run upon the wall,
they climb into the houses;
In at the windows
they come like thieves.
10 Before them the earth trembles,
the heavens shake;
The sun and the moon are darkened,
and the stars withhold their brightness.[b]

11 The LORD raises his voice
at the head of his army;
For immense indeed is his camp,
yes, mighty, and it does his bidding.
For great is the day of the LORD,
and exceedingly terrible; who can bear it?[c]
12 Yet even now, says the LORD,
return to me with your whole heart,
with fasting, and weeping, and mourning;
13 Rend your hearts, not your garments,
and return to the LORD, your God.
For gracious and merciful is he,
slow to anger, rich in kindness,
and relenting in punishment.[d]
14 Perhaps he will again relent
and leave behind him a blessing,
Offerings and libations
for the LORD, your God.[e]
15 Blow the trumpet Zion!
proclaim a fast,
call an assembly;[f]
16 Gather the people,
notify the congregation;
Assemble the elders,
gather the children
and the infants at the breast;
Let the bridegroom quit his room,
and the bride her chamber.
17 Between the porch and the altar*

a Jl 2, 15.
b Jl 4, 15; Is 13, 10; Ez 32, 7f; Mt 24, 29; Mk 13, 24; Lk 21, 25f.
c Jer 30, 7; Am 5, 18; Zep 1, 15.
d Ps 86, 5; Jon 4, 2.
e Jon 3, 9.
f Jl 1, 14.

* 2, 17: The priests stood in the open space between the outdoor altar of holocausts and the temple building, facing the latter in order thereby to look toward God present in the holy of holies.

let the priests, the ministers of the LORD,
weep,
And say, "Spare, O LORD, your people,
and make not your heritage a reproach,
with the nations ruling over them!
Why should they say among the peoples,
'Where is their God?'"

**Blessings for God's People.** 18 Then
the LORD was stirred to concern for his land and
took pity on his people. 19 The LORD answered
and said to his people:

See, I will send you
grain, and wine, and oil,
and you shall be filled with them;
No more will I make you
a reproach among the nations.
20 No, the northerner* I will remove far from
you,
and drive him out into a land arid and
waste,
With his van toward the eastern sea,
and his rear toward the western sea;
And his foulness shall go up,
and his stench shall go up.

21 Fear not, O land!
exult and rejoice!
for the LORD has done great things.
22 Fear not, beasts of the field!
for the pastures of the plain are green;
The tree bears its fruit,
the fig tree and the vine give their yield.
23 And do you, O children of Zion, exult
and rejoice in the LORD, your God!
He has given you the teacher of justice:*
he has made the rain come down for you,
the early and the late rain as before.[g]
24 The threshing floors shall be full of grain
and the vats shall overflow with wine and
oil.
25 And I will repay you for the years
which the locust has eaten,
The grasshopper, the devourer, and the
cutter,
my great army which I sent among you.
26 You shall eat and be filled,
and shall praise the name of the LORD,
your God,
Because he has dealt wondrously with you;
my people shall nevermore be put to
shame.
27 And you shall know that I am in the midst
of Israel;
I am the LORD, your God, and there is no
other;
my people shall nevermore be put to
shame.

## CHAPTER 3

1 Then afterward I will pour out[h]
my spirit* upon all mankind.
Your sons and daughters shall prophesy,
your old men shall dream dreams,
your young men shall see visions;
2 Even upon the servants and the handmaids,
in those days, I will pour out my spirit.

3 And I will work wonders in the heavens and
on the earth,
blood, fire, and columns of smoke;
4 The sun will be turned to darkness,
and the moon to blood,
At the coming of the day of the LORD,
the great and terrible day.[i]
5 Then everyone shall be rescued
who calls on the name of the LORD;
For on Mount Zion there shall be a remnant,
as the LORD has said,
And in Jerusalem survivors
whom the LORD shall call.[j]

## CHAPTER 4

### Judgment upon the Nations

1 Yes, in those days, and at that time,
when I would restore the fortunes
of Judah and Jerusalem,
2 I will assemble all the nations
and bring them down to the Valley of
Jehoshaphat,*
And I will enter into judgment with them
there
on behalf of my people and my
inheritance, Israel;
Because they have scattered them among the
nations,
and divided my land.
3 Over my people they have cast lots;
they gave a boy for a harlot,
and sold a girl for the wine they drank.

4 Moreover, what are you to me, Tyre and
Sidon, and all the regions of Philistia? Would
you take vengeance upon me by some action?

g Hos 10, 12.
h 1-5: Is 44, 3; Acts 2, 17-21.
i Jl 2, 10.
j Rom 10, 13.

*

2, 20: The northerner: the locusts, that are compared to an invading army which in Palestine came from the north; cf Jer 1, 14f; 4, 6; Ez 26, 7; 38, 6. 15.

2, 23: The teacher of justice: the rain sent by God to show his fidelity to his promises, and to teach his people to be faithful to his commandments; cf Dt 11, 14. There is also a play on words here between the Hebrew word moreh (teacher) and the Hebrew word yoreh (the early rain). The expression likewise has a messianic connotation; cf Is 30, 20. The founder of the Essene sect of Qumran (second century B.C.) was known as "The Teacher of Justice."

3, 1f: I will pour out my spirit: in the Old Testament the spirit is the gift of God bestowed on those acting as his agents. The promise of the spirit is quoted by St. Peter in Acts 2, 17–21 as fulfilled in an eminent way by the gift of the Holy Spirit, the Third Person of the Blessed Trinity, bestowed on the Apostles.

4, 2: Valley of Jehosphaphat: a symbolic name of the place of final judgment (v 14). The name Jehoshaphat signifies "Yahweh judges." This place has been popularly identified with the Kidron Valley.

But if you do take action against me, swiftly,
speedily, I will return your deed upon your own
head. **5** You took my silver and my gold, and
brought my precious treasures into your temples! **6** You sold the people of Judah and Jerusalem to the Greeks, removing them far from
their own country! **7** See, I will rouse them
from the place into which you have sold them,
and I will return your deed upon your own head.
**8** I will sell your sons and your daughters to the
people of Judah, who shall sell them to the
Sabeans,* a nation far off. Indeed, the LORD has
spoken.

**9** Declare this among the nations:
proclaim a war,
rouse the warriors to arms!
Let all the soldiers
report and march!
**10** Beat your plowshares into swords,
and your pruning hooks into spears;
let the weak man say, "I am a warrior!"*

**11** Hasten and come, all you neighboring
peoples,
assemble there!
[Bring down, O Lord, your warriors!*]
**12** Let the nations bestir themselves and come
up
to the Valley of Jehoshaphat;
For there will I sit in judgment
upon all the neighboring nations.

**13** Apply the sickle,[k]
for the harvest is ripe;
Come and tread,
for the wine press is full;
The vats overflow,
for great is their malice.*
**14** Crowd upon crowd
in the valley of decision;
For near is the day of the LORD
in the valley of decision.
**15** Sun and moon are darkened,
and the stars withhold their brightness.[l]
**16** The LORD roars from Zion,
and from Jerusalem raises his voice;
The heavens and the earth quake,
but the LORD is a refuge to his people,
a stronghold to the men of Israel.[m]

## Salvation for God's Elect

**17** Then shall you know that I, the LORD, am
your God,
dwelling on Zion, my holy mountain;
Jerusalem shall be holy,
and strangers shall pass through her no
more.
**18** And then, on that day,[n]
the mountains shall drip new wine,
and the hills shall flow with milk;
And the channels of Judah
shall flow with water:
A fountain shall issue from the house of the
LORD,
to water the Valley of Shittim.*
**19** Egypt shall be a waste,
and Edom a desert waste,
Because of violence done to the people of
Judah,
because they shed innocent blood in their
land.
**20** But Judah shall abide forever,
and Jerusalem for all generations.
**21** I will avenge their blood,
and not leave it unpunished.
The LORD dwells in Zion.

---

k Rv 14, 15.
l Jl 2, 10; 3, 4.
m Jer 25, 30; Am 1, 2.
n Am 9, 13; Ez 47, 1-12; Zec 14, 8.

---

4, 8: Sabeans: a south Arabian people known for their commerce.

4, 10: This imagery is used in the reverse sense in Is 2, 4; Mi 4, 3. Here the warlike weapons are made in response to God's summons to armies which he selected to expel forever the unlawful invaders from the land of his chosen people.

4, 11: Warriors: the angels; cf Zec 14, 5.

4, 13: Because of their numerous crimes, the nations are ripe for punishment. The use of warlike weapons against them is likened to the onslaught on the fields and vines at harvest time.

4, 18: The Valley of Shittim, or "the ravine of the acacia trees": perhaps a part of the Kidron Valley southeast of Jerusalem; the prophetic picture of a stream of water flowing from a fountain in the temple of Jerusalem is to be found in Ez 47, 1. The Shittim east of the Jordan (see note on Nm 25, 1) is hardly referred to here.

# The Book of
# AMOS

*Amos was a shepherd of Tekoa in Judah, who exercised his ministry during the prosperous reign of Jeroboam II (786–746 B.C.). He prophesied in Israel at the great cult center of Bethel, from which he was finally expelled by the priest in charge of this royal sanctuary. The poetry of Amos, who denounces the hollow prosperity of the northern kingdom, is filled with imagery and language taken from his own pastoral background. The book is an anthology of his oracles and was compiled either by the prophet or by some of his disciples.*

*The prophecy begins with a sweeping indictment of Damascus, Philistia, Tyre, and Edom; but the forthright herdsman saves his climactic denunciation for Israel, whose injustice and idolatry are sins against the light granted to her. Israel could indeed expect the day of Yahweh, but it would be a day of darkness and not light. When Amos prophesied the overthrow of the sanctuary, the fall of the royal house, and the captivity of the people, it was more than Israelite officialdom could bear. The priest of Bethel drove Amos from the shrine—but not before hearing a terrible sentence pronounced upon himself.*

*Amos is a prophet of divine judgment, and the sovereignty of Yahweh in nature and history dominates his thought. But he was no innovator; his conservatism was in keeping with the whole prophetic tradition calling the people back to the high moral and religious demands of Yahweh's revelation. In common with the other prophets, Amos knew that divine punishment is never completely destructive; it is part of the hidden plan of God to bring salvation to men. The perversity of the human will may retard, but it cannot totally frustrate, this design of a loving God. The last oracle opens up a perspective of restoration under a Davidic king.*

*The Book of Amos may be divided as follows:*
*I. Judgment of the Nations (1, 1–2, 16).*
*II. Words and Woes for Israel (3, 1–6, 14).*
*III. Symbolic Visions: Threats and Promises (7, 1–9, 8b); Epilogue: Messianic Perspective (9, 8c–15).*

## *I: Judgment of the Nations*

### CHAPTER 1

**1** The words of Amos, a shepherd from Tekoa,[a] which he received in vision concerning Israel, in the days of Uzziah, king of Judah, and in the days of Jeroboam, son of Joash, king of Israel, two years before the earthquake:*

**2** The LORD will roar from Zion,
and from Jerusalem raise his voice:
The pastures of the shepherds will languish,
and the summit of Carmel wither.[b]

### Aram

**3** Thus says the LORD:
For three crimes of Damascus, and for four,*
I will not revoke my word;
Because they threshed Gilead
with sledges of iron,
**4** I will send fire* upon the house of Hazael,
to devour the castles of Ben-hadad.
**5** I will break the bar of Damascus;*

a Zec 14, 5. b Jer 25, 30; Jl 3, 16.

1, 1: The earthquake: which according to Hebrew tradition marked the crime of Uzziah when he attempted to offer incense in the temple (2 Chr 26, 16–21). Zechariah mentions it several centuries later (Zec 14, 5).

1, 3: For three crimes . . . four: crime after crime, an indefinite number; cf Am 1, 6. The series of judgments on the foreign nations shows that the Lord demands the observance of the moral order everywhere; Israel and Judah, despite their privileged position, are no exception. I will not revoke my word: God will not withdraw his threat of punishment against each of these nations. They threshed Gilead: the people of Aram under King Hazael had devastated Gilead; cf 2 Kgs 10, 32f.

1, 4: Fire: devastation caused by the Assyrians (Am 1, 7. 10. 12. 14; 2, 2. 5); cf 1 Sm 15, 18. Hazael and Ben-hadad: kings of the Arameans whose capital was Damascus (v 5); they fought against Israel (2 Kgs 13, 3), and had long occupied the region of Gilead (v 3) in Transjordan.

1, 5: Bar of Damascus: the beam securing the main gate of the city against invaders, symbol of its defenses. Valley of Aven ("vale of wickedness") and Beth-eden ("house of plea-

I will root out those who live in the
Valley of Aven,
And the sceptered ruler of Beth-eden;
the people of Aram shall be exiled to Kir,
says the LORD.

### Philistia

6 Thus says the LORD:
For three crimes of Gaza, and for four,
I will not revoke my word;
Because they took captive whole groups
to hand over to Edom,
7 I will send fire upon the wall of Gaza,
to devour her castles;
8 I will root out those who live in Ashdod,
and the sceptered ruler of Ashkelon;
I will turn my hand against Ekron,
and the last of the Philistines shall perish,
says the Lord God.

### Tyre

9 Thus says the LORD:
For three crimes of Tyre, and for four,
I will not revoke my word;
Because they delivered whole groups captive
to Edom,
and did not remember the pact of
brotherhood,*
10 I will send fire upon the wall of Tyre, to
devour her castles.

### Edom

11 Thus says the LORD:
For three crimes of Edom, and for four,
I will not revoke my word;
Because he pursued his brother* with the
sword,
choking up all pity;
Because he persisted in his anger
and kept his wrath to the end,
12 I will send fire upon Teman,
and it will devour the castles of Bozrah.*

### Ammon

13 Thus says the LORD:
For three crimes of the Ammonites, and for
four,
I will not revoke my word;
Because they ripped open expectant mothers
in Gilead,
while extending their territory,
14 I will kindle a fire upon the wall of
Rabbah,*
and it will devour her castles
Amid clamor on the day of battle
and stormwind in a time of tempest.
15 Their king shall go into captivity,
he and his princes with him, says the
LORD.

## CHAPTER 2

### Moab

1 Thus says the LORD:
For three crimes of Moab, and for four,
I will not revoke my word;
Because he burned to ashes
the bones of Edom's king,*
2 I will send fire upon Moab,
to devour the castles of Kerioth;
Moab shall meet death amid uproar
and shouts and trumpet blasts.
3 I will root out the judge from her midst,
and her princes I will slay with him, says
the LORD.

### Judah

4 Thus says the LORD:
For three crimes of Judah, and for four,
I will not revoke my word;
Because they spurned the law of the LORD,
and did not keep his statutes;
Because the lies* which their fathers
followed
have led them astray,
5 I will send fire upon Judah,
to devour the castles of Jerusalem.

### Israel

6 Thus says the LORD:
For three crimes of Israel, and for four,*
I will not revoke my word;
Because they sell the just man for silver,
and the poor man for a pair of sandals.*
7 They trample the heads of the weak
into the dust of the earth,
and force the lowly out of the way.
Son and father go to the same prostitute,
profaning my holy name.
8 Upon garments taken in pledge

---

sure"): Aramean territory from southwest to northeast.

1, 9: Pact of brotherhood: Hiram of Tyre had made a pact with Solomon and called him brother (1 Kgs 5, 12; 9, 13).

1, 11: Pursued his brother: the Edomites were descended from Esau, the brother of Jacob (Gn 25—27); nevertheless they constantly nourished enmity against Jacob's descendants, the Israelites.

1, 12: Teman and Bozrah: two of the chief cities of Edom; cf Jer 49, 20.

1, 14: Rabbah: now called Amman, the modern capital of the Hashemite Kingdom of Jordan.

2, 1: Here the prophet stresses the gravity of Moab's violation of the Semitic custom of providing honorable burial for the dead.

2, 4: The lies: false gods, who exist only in the minds of their worshipers. The crimes of Judah are infidelity and idolatry, in contrast to the sins for which the surrounding nations are judged.

2, 6–13: The detailed crimes of Israel are placed in strong contrast with the benefits with which the Lord favored his people.

2, 6: A pair of sandals: indicating how cheaply the rich regarded the poor.

2, 8: Upon garments . . . any altar: usurers kept the garments taken as pledges from the poor; but instead of restoring them to their owners before nightfall (Ex 22, 25; Dt 24, 12), they

they recline beside any altar;*
And the wine of those who have been fined
they drink in the house of their god.

9 Yet it was I who destroyed the Amorites
before them,
who were as tall as the cedars,
and as strong as the oak trees.
I destroyed their fruit above,
and their roots beneath.[c]
10 It was I who brought you up from the land
of Egypt,
and who led you through the desert for
forty years,
to occupy the land of the Amorites:[d]
11 I who raised up prophets among your sons,
and nazirites* among your young men.
Is this not so, O men of Israel?
says the LORD.
12 But you gave the nazirites wine to drink,
and commanded the prophets not to
prophesy.

13 Beware, I will crush you into the ground
as a wagon crushes when laden with
sheaves.
14 Flight shall perish from the swift,
and the strong man shall not retain his
strength;
The warrior shall not save his life,
15 nor the bowman stand his ground;
The swift of foot shall not escape,
nor the horseman save his life.
16 And the most stouthearted of warriors
shall flee naked on that day, says the
LORD.

## II: *Words and Woes for Israel*

### CHAPTER 3

**First Word.** 1 Hear this word, O men of
Israel, that the LORD pronounces over you, over
the whole family that I brought up from the land
of Egypt:

2 You alone have I favored,
more than all the families of the earth;
Therefore I will punish you
for all your crimes.*

3 Do two walk together
unless they have agreed?
4 Does a lion roar in the forest
when it has no prey?
Does a young lion cry out from its den
unless it has seized something?
5 Is a bird brought to earth by a snare
when there is no lure for it?
Does a snare spring up from the ground
without catching anything?
6 If the trumpet sounds in a city,
will the people not be frightened?
If evil befalls a city,
has not the LORD caused it?*
7 Indeed, the Lord GOD does nothing
without revealing his plan
to his servants, the prophets.

8 The lion roars—
who will not be afraid!
The Lord GOD speaks—
who will not prophesy!

9 Proclaim this in the castles of Ashdod,
in the castles of the land of Egypt:
"Gather about the mountain of Samaria,
and see the great disorders within her,
the oppression in her midst."*
10 For they know not how to do what is right,
says the LORD,
Storing up in their castles
what they have extorted and robbed.
11 Therefore, thus says the Lord GOD:
An enemy shall surround the land,
and strip you of your strength,
and pillage your castles.

12 Thus says the LORD:
As the shepherd snatches from the mouth of
the lion
a pair of legs or the tip of an ear of his
sheep,
So the Israelites who dwell in Samaria shall
escape
with the corner of a couch or a piece of a
cot.

13 Hear and bear witness against the house
of Jacob, says the Lord GOD, the God of hosts:

14 On the day when I punish Israel for his
crimes,
I will visit also the altars of Bethel:
The horns of the altar shall be broken off
and fall to the ground.
15 Then will I strike the winter house
and the summer house;
The ivory apartments* shall be ruined,
and their many rooms shall be no more,
says the LORD.

c Nm 21, 24; Dt 2, 24. d Ex 14, 21; Dt 8, 2. 14.

*

used them in idolatrous worship. Wine . . . their god: under the guise of a religious ceremony they drink the wine obtained through unjust fines.

2, 11: Nazirites: see note on Nm 6, 1ff.

3, 2: God's choice of Israel brought its own responsibility.

3, 6: The sufferings which sinful man experiences through the permissive will of God are presented here, as elsewhere in the Old Testament, simply as caused by the Lord.

3, 9: Israel's southern neighbors, beyond Judah, are invited by the prophetic orator to witness the moral disorders of God's people.

3, 15: Ivory apartments: rooms containing furniture inlaid in ivory, similar to the pieces discovered in the excavations at Samaria.

## CHAPTER 4

### Second Word

**1** Hear this word, women of the mountain of
Samaria,
you cows of Bashan,*
You who oppress the weak
and abuse the needy;
Who say to your lords,
"Bring drink for us!"
**2** The Lord GOD has sworn by his holiness:
Truly the days are coming upon you
When they shall drag you away with hooks,
the last of you with fishhooks;
**3** You shall go out through the breached walls
each by the most direct way,
And you shall be cast into the mire,
says the LORD.

**4** Come to Bethel and sin,
to Gilgal, and sin the more;*
Each morning bring your sacrifices,
every third day, your tithes;
**5** Burn leavened food as a thanksgiving
sacrifice,
proclaim publicly your freewill offerings,
For so you love to do, O men of Israel, says
the Lord GOD.

**6** Though I have made your teeth
clean of food in all your cities,
and have made bread scarce in all your
dwellings,
Yet you returned not to me,
says the LORD.

**7** Though I also withheld the rain from you
when the harvest was still three months
away;
I sent rain upon one city
but not upon another;
One field was watered by rain,
but another without rain dried up;
**8** Though two or three cities staggered to one
city
for water that did not quench their thirst;
Yet you returned not to me,
says the LORD.

**9** I struck you with blight and searing wind;
your many gardens and vineyards,
your fig trees and olive trees the locust
devoured;
Yet you returned not to me,
says the LORD.[e]

**10** I sent upon you a pestilence like that of
Egypt,*
and with the sword I slew your young
men;
Your horses I let be captured,
to your nostrils I brought the stench of
your camps;
Yet you returned not to me,
says the LORD.
**11** I brought upon you such upheaval
as when God overthrew Sodom and
Gomorrah:
you were like a brand plucked from the
fire;
Yet you returned not to me,
says the LORD.[f]

**12** So now I will deal with you in my own
way, O Israel!
and since I will deal thus with you,
prepare to meet your God, O Israel:
**13** Him who formed the mountains, and created
the wind,
and declares to man his thoughts;
Who made the dawn and the darkness,
and strides upon the heights of the earth:
The LORD, the God of hosts by name.

## CHAPTER 5

### Third Word

**1** Hear this word which I utter over you,
a lament, O house of Israel:
**2** She is fallen, to rise no more,
the virgin Israel;
She lies abandoned upon her land,
with no one to raise her up.

**3** For thus says the Lord GOD:
The city that marched out with a thousand
shall be left with a hundred,
Another that marched out with a hundred
shall be left with ten,
of the house of Israel.

**4** For thus says the LORD
to the house of Israel:
Seek me, that you may live,
**5** but do not seek Bethel;
Do not come to Gilgal,
and do not cross to Beer-sheba.
For Gilgal shall be led into exile,
and Bethel shall become nought.
**6** Seek the LORD, that you may live,

---

e Hg 2, 17. f Gn 19, 24.

---

4, 1: Bashan: the region east of the Sea of Galilee, famous for its rich pasture and fattened herds, to which Amos likens the indolent women of Samaria.

4, 4f: This invitation to the sanctuaries of the northern kingdom is ironical. Pilgrimages to the shrines of Bethel and Gilgal were the more displeasing to God because they were contrary to his will and ineffective toward improvement of morals.

4, 10: Pestilence like that of Egypt: plagues were well known in Egypt; cf Dt 7, 15; 28, 27. 60. Stench of your camps: caused by the unburied bodies.

5, 6: House of Joseph: the kingdom of Israel or northern kingdom, the chief tribes of which were descended from Ephraim and Manasseh, the sons of Joseph; cf Am 5, 15; 6, 6.

lest he come upon the house of Joseph*
like a fire
That shall consume, with none to quench it
for the house of Israel:
8 He who made the Pleiades and Orion,
who turns darkness into dawn,
and darkens day into night;
Who summons the waters of the sea,
and pours them out upon the surface of
the earth;[g]
9 Who flashes destruction upon the strong,
and brings ruin upon the fortress;
whose name is LORD.

## First Woe

7 Woe to those who turn judgment to
wormwood
and cast justice to the ground!
10 They hate him who reproves at the gate*
and abhor him who speaks the truth.
11 Therefore, because you have trampled upon
the weak
and exacted of them levies of grain,
Though you have built houses of hewn
stone,
you shall not live in them!
Though you have planted choice vineyards,
you shall not drink their wine![h]

12 Yes, I know how many are your crimes,
how grievous your sins:
Oppressing the just, accepting bribes,
repelling the needy at the gate!
13 Therefore the prudent man is silent at this
time,
for it is an evil time.
14 Seek good and not evil,
that you may live;
Then truly will the LORD, the God of hosts,
be with you as you claim!
15 Hate evil and love good,
and let justice prevail at the gate;
Then it may be that the LORD, the God of
hosts,
will have pity on the remnant of Joseph.[i]

16 Therefore, thus says the LORD,
the God of hosts, the Lord:
In every square there shall be lamentation,
and in every street they shall cry, Alas!
Alas!
They shall summon the farmers to wail
and professional mourners to lament,
17 And in every vineyard there shall be
lamentation
when I pass through your midst, says the
LORD.

## Second Woe

18 Woe to those who yearn for the day of the
LORD!*
What will this day of the LORD mean for
you?
Darkness and not light![j]
19 As if a man were to flee from a lion,
and a bear should meet him;
Or as if on entering his house
he were to rest his hand against the wall,
and a snake should bite him.
20 Will not the day of the LORD be darkness
and not light,
gloom without any brightness?

21 *I hate, I spurn your feasts,
I take no pleasure in your solemnities;[k]
22 Your cereal offerings I will not accept,
nor consider your stall-fed peace
offerings.
23 Away with your noisy songs!
I will not listen to the melodies of your
harps.
But if you would offer me holocausts,
24 then let justice surge like water,
and goodness like an unfailing stream.
25 Did you bring me sacrifices and offerings[l]
for forty years in the desert, O house of
Israel?*
26 You will carry away Sakkuth, your king,
and Kaiwan, your star god,*
the images that you have made for
yourselves;
27 For I will exile you beyond Damascus,
say I, the LORD, the God of hosts by
name.

g Am 9, 6.
h Zep 1, 13.
i Ps 97, 10; Rom 12, 9.
j Jer 30, 7; Jl 2, 11; Zep 1, 15.
k Is 1, 11; Jer 6, 20; Mal 1, 12.
l Acts 7, 42.

*

5, 10: At the gate: see note on Ps 127, 5.

5, 18: Day of the Lord: a technical expression which in earliest times referred to God's special intervention in human affairs. Through it his power and justice triumphed in his people. The present passage is the first instance in which it means a day of punishment of sinners. During the exile it assumed the meaning of a time when God would avenge Israel against her oppressors and bring about her restoration (Jer 50, 27; Ez 30, 3ff). Still later it came to mean the day of final judgment of the world when the good will be rewarded and the wicked punished (Mal 3, 19ff; Jl 2, 1ff; Zep 1, 14ff).

5, 21–27: The Lord condemns, not ritual worship in itself, but the cult whose exterior rites and solemnity have no relation to interior morality and justice. The Israelites falsely worshiped him as neighboring nations adored Baal or Chamos, deities which were thought to protect their respective peoples against their enemies in return for ritual observances, without any relation to right conduct.

5, 25: The meaning is not certain; according to some, the idea is that during the forty years' wandering in the desert the simple, rudimentary worship of God was accompanied by the practice of justice, in contrast to the elaborate ritual unaccompanied by works of justice in the prophet's time.

5, 26: Sakkuth . . . star god: although the text is uncertain, it seems quite probable that reference is made to the Assyrian deities, Sakkuth, god of war and light, and Kaiwan, the planet Saturn. The people will go into exile, from which these gods have been unable to save them.

## CHAPTER 6

### Third Woe

1 *Woe to the complacent in Zion,
To the overconfident on the mount of Samaria,*
Leaders of a nation favored from the first,
to whom the people of Israel have recourse![m]
2 Pass over to Calneh and see,
go from there to Hamath the great,
and down to Gath of the Philistines!
Are you better than these kingdoms,
or is your territory wider than theirs?
3 You would put off the evil day,
yet you hasten the reign of violence!

4 Lying upon beds of ivory,
stretched comfortably on their couches,
They eat lambs taken from the flock,
and calves from the stall!
5 Improvising to the music of the harp,
like David, they devise their own accompaniment.
6 They drink wine from bowls
and anoint themselves with the best oils;
yet they are not made ill by the collapse of Joseph!
7 Therefore, now they shall be the first to go into exile,
and their wanton revelry shall be done away with.

8 The Lord GOD has sworn by his very self,
say I, the LORD, the God of hosts:
I abhor the pride of Jacob,
I hate his castles,
and I give over the city with everything in it;[n]
9 Should there remain ten men
in a single house, these shall die.
10 Only a few shall be left
to carry the dead out of the houses;
If one says to a man inside a house,
"Is anyone with you?" and he answers,
"No one,"
Then he shall say, "Silence!"
for no one must mention the name of the LORD.
11 Indeed, the LORD has given the command
to shatter the great house to bits,
and reduce the small house to rubble.

12 Can horses run across a cliff?
or can one plow the sea with oxen?*
Yet you have turned judgment into gall,
and the fruit of justice into wormwood.
13 You rejoice in Lodebar,
and say, "Have we not, by our own strength,
seized for ourselves Karnaim?"*
14 Beware, I am raising up against you, O house of Israel,
say I, the LORD, the God of hosts,
A nation* that shall oppress you
from Labo of Hamath even to the Wadi Arabah.

## *III: Symbolic Visions: Threats and Promises*

## CHAPTER 7

**Vision of Locusts.** 1 This is what the Lord
GOD showed me: He was forming a locust
swarm when the late growth began to come up
(the late growth after the king's mowing*).
2 While they were eating all the grass in the
land, I said:

Forgive, O Lord GOD!
How can Jacob stand?
He is so small!

3 And the LORD repented of this. "It shall
not be," said the Lord GOD.

**Vision of Fire.** 4 Then the Lord GOD
showed me this: he called for a judgment by
fire.* It had devoured the great abyss, and was
consuming the land, 5 when I said:

Cease, O Lord GOD!
How can Jacob stand?
He is so small!

6 The LORD repented of this. "This also shall
not be," said the Lord GOD.

**Vision of the Plummet.** 7 Then the Lord
GOD showed me this: he was standing by a wall,
plummet in hand.* 8 The LORD asked me,
"What do you see, Amos?" And when I answered, "A plummet," the LORD said:

See, I will lay the plummet
in the midst of my people Israel;
I will forgive them no longer.

m Lk 6, 24. n Jer 51, 14.

6, 1–7: The luxury of the people in Samaria will be punished by exile. They failed to learn the lesson from Calneh, Hamath and Gath at the approach of the powerful and warlike Assyrians.

6, 1: The complacent in Zion . . . the overconfident . . . of Samaria: the proud and self-interested rulers of Judah and Israel.

6, 12: Can horses . . . oxen?: one cannot change the course of nature, as the Israelites attempted to do by their sins of injustice.

6, 13: Lodebar . . . Karnaim: in Transjordan; they had been captured by the Israelites. Perhaps it is in irony that reference is made to these two cities, for the root of the first suggests "nothing" and that of the second, "horns" or "strength."

6, 14: A nation: Assyria.

7, 1: The king's mowing: the first mowing, a portion of which was payable to the king as a tax.

7, 4: Fire: understood by many as a burning drought.

7, 7: Plummet in hand: signifying that God is about to withdraw his mercy from his people and that the nation is to be measured for destruction.

9 The high places of Isaac shall be laid waste,
and the sanctuaries of Israel made desolate;
I will attack the house of Jeroboam with the sword.

**Amos and Amaziah.** 10 Amaziah, the
priest of Bethel, sent word to Jeroboam, king of
Israel: "Amos has conspired against you here
within Israel; the country cannot endure all his
words. 11 For this is what Amos says:

Jeroboam shall die by the sword,
and Israel shall surely be exiled from its land."

12 To Amos, Amaziah said: "Off with you,
visionary, flee to the land of Judah! There earn
your bread by prophesying, 13 but never again
prophesy in Bethel; for it is the king's sanctuary
and a royal temple." 14 Amos answered Amaziah, "I was no prophet, nor have I belonged to
a company of prophets; I was a shepherd and a
dresser of sycamores.* 15 The LORD took me
from following the flock, and said to me, Go,
prophesy to my people Israel. 16 Now hear the
word of the LORD!"

You say: prophesy not against Israel,
preach not against the house of Isaac.
17 Now thus says the LORD:
Your wife shall be made a harlot in the city,
and your sons and daughters shall fall by the sword;
Your land shall be divided by measuring line,
and you yourself shall die in an unclean land;
Israel shall be exiled far from its land.

## CHAPTER 8

**Vision of the Fruit Basket.** 1 This is what
the Lord GOD showed me: a basket of ripe fruit.
2 "What do you see, Amos?" he asked. I answered, "A basket of ripe fruit." Then the
LORD said to me:

The time is ripe to have done with my people Israel;
I will forgive them no longer.
3 The temple songs shall become wailings on that day,
says the Lord GOD.
Many shall be the corpses,
strewn everywhere.—Silence!

### Against Greed

4 Hear this, you who trample upon the needy
and destroy the poor of the land!
5 "When will the new moon be over," you ask,
"that we may sell our grain,
and the sabbath, that we may display the wheat?
We will diminish the ephah,*
add to the shekel,
and fix our scales for cheating!
6 We will buy the lowly man for silver,
and the poor man for a pair of sandals;
even the refuse of the wheat we will sell!"
7 The LORD has sworn by the pride of Jacob:*
Never will I forget a thing they have done!
8 Shall not the land tremble because of this,
and all who dwell in it mourn,
While it rises up and tosses like the Nile,
and settles back like the river of Egypt?*

9 On that day, says the Lord GOD,
I will make the sun set at midday
and cover the earth with darkness in broad daylight.
10 I will turn your feasts into mourning
and all your songs into lamentations.
I will cover the loins of all with sackcloth
and make every head bald.
I will make them mourn as for an only son,
and bring their day to bitter end.[o]

11 Yes, days are coming, says the Lord GOD,
when I will send famine upon the land:
Not a famine of bread, or thirst for water,
but for hearing the word of the LORD.
12 Then shall they wander from sea to sea
and rove from the north to the east
In search of the word of the LORD,
but they shall not find it.

13 On that day, fair virgins and young men
shall faint from thirst;
14 Those who swear by the shameful idol of Samaria,
"By the life of your god, O Dan!"
"By the life of your love, O Beer-sheba!"
those shall fall, never to rise again.*

## CHAPTER 9

**Vision of the Altar.*** 1 I saw the Lord
standing beside the altar, and he said:

o Tb 2, 6; 1 Mc 1, 41.

7, 14f: Amos denies that he belonged to the class of professional prophets; his vocation is due to the personal intervention of the Lord.

8, 5: Ephah: a standard of measure; a little more than a bushel.

8, 7: The pride of Jacob: the sinful pride detested by God (Am 6, 8), in contrast to God himself, who is the true Pride of Jacob.

8, 8: The figure is based on the annual flooding of the river Nile.

8, 14: Dan and Beer-sheba, the extreme northern and southern limits of the country, where idolatrous worship was offered.

9, 1–8: There will be no escape from God's punishment, symbolized here by the destruction of a building, probably the schismatic temple at Bethel.

Strike the bases, so that the doorjambs totter
till you break them off on the heads of them all!
Those who are left I will slay with the sword;
not one shall flee,
no survivor shall escape.
2 Though they break through to the nether world,
even from there my hand shall bring them out;
Though they climb to the heavens,
I will bring them down;[p]
3 Though they hide on the summit of Carmel,
there too I will hunt them out and take them away;
Though they hide from my gaze
in the bottom of the sea,
I will command the serpent* there to bite them;
4 Though they are led into captivity by their enemies,
there will I command the sword to slay them.
I will fix my gaze upon them
for evil, and not for good,[q]
5 I, the Lord GOD of hosts.
I melt the earth with my touch,
so that all who dwell on it mourn,
While it all rises up like the Nile,
and settles back like the river of Egypt;
6 I have built heaven, my upper chamber,
and established my vault over the earth;
I summon the waters of the sea
and pour them out upon the surface of the earth,
I, the LORD by name.[r]

7 Are you not like the Ethiopians to me,
O men of Israel, says the LORD?
Did I not bring the Israelites from the land of Egypt
As I brought the Philistines from Caphtor
and the Arameans* from Kir?[s]
8 The eyes of the Lord GOD are on this sinful kingdom:
I will destroy it from off the face of the earth.

## Epilogue: Messianic Perspective

But I will not destroy the house of Jacob completely,
says the LORD.
9 For see, I have given the command
to sift the house of Israel among all the nations,
As one sifts with a sieve,
letting no pebble fall to the ground.
10 By the sword shall all sinners among my people die,
those who say, "Evil will not reach or overtake us."
11 *On that day I will raise up
the fallen hut of David;
I will wall up its breaches,
raise up its ruins,
and rebuild it as in the days of old,[t]
12 That they may conquer what is left of Edom
and all the nations that shall bear my name,
say I, the LORD, who will do this.
13 Yes, days are coming,
says the LORD,
When the plowman shall overtake the reaper,
and the vintager, him who sows the seed;
The juice of grapes shall drip down the mountains,
and all the hills shall run with it.[u]
14 I will bring about the restoration of my people Israel;
they shall rebuild and inhabit their ruined cities,
Plant vineyards and drink the wine,
set out gardens and eat the fruits.
15 I will plant them upon their own ground;
never again shall they be plucked
From the land I have given them,
say I, the LORD, your God.

p Ps 139, 8.
q Jer 44, 11.
r Am 5, 8.
s Dt 2, 23; Jer 47, 4.
t Acts 15, 16.
u Jl 3, 18.

9, 3: Serpent: the sea monster of familiar legend, subdued by God at the time of creation and lurking still in the ocean depths; cf Ps 89, 10f.

9, 7: The Ethiopians . . . the Philistines . . . the Arameans: by nature Israel is not different from any other nation. It was not because of any merit on Israel's part that God delivered them from Egypt. Caphtor: the island of Crete.

9, 11f: In Acts 15, 15ff St. James interprets this passage in a messianic sense. Fallen hut: the kingdom. The nations that shall bear my name: the Gentile peoples who shall be converted to the Lord, that is, conquered by him, and therefore shall bear his name.

# The Book of
# OBADIAH

*The twenty-one verses of this book contain the shortest and sternest prophecy in the Old Testament. Nothing is known of the author, although his oracle against Edom, a long-standing enemy of Israel, indicates a date of composition sometime in the fifth century B.C. During this period the Edomites had been forced to abandon their ancient home near the Gulf of Aqaba and had settled in southern Judah, where they appear among the adversaries of the Jews returning from exile.*

*The prophecy is a bitter cry for vengeance against Edom for its heinous crimes. The mountain of Esau will be occupied and ravaged by the enemy but Zion shall remain inviolate. Judah and Israel shall again form one nation; and that triumphant refrain of Israelite eschatology will be heard once more: "The Kingdom is the Lord's!" Many of the verses in this prophecy can be paralleled in Jer 49, 7-22, but it is difficult to determine the precise relationship between these similar passages.*

### Title and Theme

**1** The vision of Obadiah.
[Thus says the LORD God:]
Of Edom we have heard a message from the LORD,
and a herald has been sent among the nations:
"Up! let us go to war against him!"[a]

### Edom Shall Perish

**2** See, I make you small among the nations;[b]
you are held in dire contempt.
**3** The pride of your heart has deceived you:
you who dwell in the clefts of the rock,
whose abode is in the heights,
Who say in your heart,
"Who will bring me down to earth?"
**4** Though you go as high as the eagle,
and your nest be set among the stars,
From there will I bring you down,
says the LORD.
**5** If thieves came to you, if robbers by night,[c]
how could you be thus destroyed:
would they not steal merely till they had enough?
If vintagers came to you,
would they not leave some gleanings?*
**6** How they search Esau,
seek out his hiding places!
**7** To the border they drive you—
all your allies;
They deceive you, they overpower you—
those at peace with you;
Those who eat your bread
lay snares beneath you:
There is no understanding in him!*
**8** Shall I not, says the LORD, on that day
make the wise men* disappear from Edom,
and understanding from the mount of Esau?[d]
**9** Your warriors, O Teman,* shall be crushed,
till all on Mount Esau are destroyed.

### The Cause

**10** Because of violence to your brother Jacob,*
disgrace shall cover you
and you shall be destroyed forever.[e]
**11** On the day when you stood by,
on the day when aliens carried off his possessions,
And strangers entered his gates
and cast lots over Jerusalem,
you too were one of them.*
**12** Gaze not upon the day of your brother,
the day of his disaster;
Exult not over the children of Judah
on the day of their ruin;
Speak not haughtily
on the day of distress!

---

a Jer 49, 14.
b 2ff: Jer 49, 15f.
c Jer 49, 9.
d Is 29, 14; 1 Cor 1, 19.
e Gn 27, 41f.

---

5: Something of value may escape the robber, and the vintager always leaves something for the gleaners, but God's devastation of Edom will be complete.

7: There is no understanding in him: Edom's faithless allies assure one another that he does not have sense enough to be able to defend himself.

8: The wise men: Edom was proverbial for its wise men; cf Jer 49, 7.

9: Teman: one of the names used for the land southeast of Palestine, here synonymous with Edom. Esau: here used as the name of the land.

10: Your brother Jacob: Esau, also called Edom, and Jacob, the father of Judah, were the sons of Isaac (Gn 25, 24ff).

11: After the devastation of Judah, Edom occupied the southern part of its territory. Edomites also joined the invading Chaldean forces (13) and assisted them in capturing the people of Judah (14).

13 Enter not the gate of my people
on the day of their calamity;
Gaze not, you at least, upon his misfortune
on the day of his calamity;
Lay not hands upon his possessions
on the day of his calamity!
14 Stand not at the crossroads
to slay his refugees;
Betray not his fugitives
on the day of distress!

## Judgment upon the Nations

15 For near is the day of the LORD[f]
for all the nations!
As you have done, so shall it be done to
you,
your deed shall come back upon your own
head:
16 As you have drunk* upon my holy
mountain,
so shall all the nations drink continually.
Yes, they shall drink and swallow,
and shall become as though they had not
been.

## Judah Shall Be Restored

17 But on Mount Zion there shall be a portion
saved;*
the mountain shall be holy,
And the house of Jacob shall take possession
of those that dispossessed them.
18 The house of Jacob shall be a fire,
and the house of Joseph a flame;
The house of Esau shall be stubble,
and they shall set them ablaze and devour
them;
Then none shall survive of the house of
Esau,
for the LORD has spoken.
19 They shall occupy the Negeb, the mount of
Esau,
and the foothills of the Philistines;
And they shall occupy the lands of Ephraim
and the lands of Samaria,
and Benjamin shall occupy Gilead.
20 The captives of this host of the children of
Israel
shall occupy the Canaanite land as far as
Zarephath,*
And the captives of Jerusalem who are in
Sepharad
shall occupy the cities of the Negeb.
21 And saviors* shall ascent Mount Zion
to rule the mount of Esau,
and the kingship shall be the LORD's.

---

f 15f: Ps 137, 7ff.

---

16: As you have drunk: the Lord addresses the people of Judah. As the people of Jerusalem have drunk the cup of retribution, so shall the nations, and especially Edom (18), suffer punishment. This metaphorical use of drinking the cup of God's wrath is common in the Bible; cf Jb 21, 20; Is 19, 14; Jer 25, 15f.

17ff: The Israelites shall be restored and shall occupy the lands of those who oppressed them. The survivors of Judah shall be rejoined by the returned exiles from northern Israel.

20: Zarephath: a town in Phoenicia, north of Tyre; cf 1 Kgs 17, 10. Ezekiel's ideal boundaries of the new Israel (Ez 47, 13ff) extend farther north. Sepharad: probably Sardis in western Asia Minor. The later rabbis thought it to be Spain.

21: Saviors: the victorious Israelites who will rule over their enemies after the fashion of the ancient Judges; cf Jgs 3, 9. 15. 31; 10, 1.

# The Book of
# JONAH

*Written in the postexilic era, probably in the fifth century B.C., this book is a didactic story with an important theological message. It concerns a disobedient prophet who attempted to run away from his divine commission, was cast overboard and swallowed by a great fish, rescued in a marvelous manner, and sent on his way to Nineveh, the traditional enemy of Israel. To the surprise of Jonah, the wicked city listened to his message of doom and repented immediately. All, from king to lowliest subject, humbled themselves in sackcloth and ashes. Seeing their repentance, God did not carry out the punishment he had planned for them. Whereupon Jonah complained to God about the unexpected success of his mission; he was bitter because Yahweh, instead of destroying had led the people to repentance and then spared them.*

*From this partly humorous story, a very sublime lesson may be drawn. Jonah stands for a narrow and vindictive mentality, all too common among the Jews of that period. Because they were the chosen people, a good many of them cultivated an intolerant nationalism which limited the mercy of God to their nation. It was abhorrent to their way of thinking that nations as wicked as Assyria should escape his wrath.*

*The prophecy, which is both instructive and entertaining, strikes directly at this viewpoint. It is a parable of mercy, showing that God's threatened punishments are but the expression of a merciful will which moves all men to repent and seek forgiveness. The universality of the story contrasts sharply with the particularistic spirit of many in the postexilic community. The book has also prepared the way for the gospel with its message of redemption for all, both Jew and Gentile.*

## CHAPTER 1

**The First Mission.** **1** This is the word of
the LORD that came to Jonah,[a] son of Amittai:*
**2** "Set out for the great city of Nineveh, and
preach against it; their wickedness has come up
before me."[b] **3** But Jonah made ready to flee
to Tarshish* away from the LORD. He went
down to Joppa, found a ship going to Tarshish,
paid the fare, and went aboard to journey with
them to Tarshish, away from the LORD.
**4** The LORD, however, hurled a violent wind
upon the sea, and in the furious tempest that
arose the ship was on the point of breaking up.
**5** Then the mariners became frightened and
each one cried to his god. To lighten the ship for
themselves, they threw its cargo into the sea.
Meanwhile, Jonah had gone down into the hold
of the ship, and lay there fast asleep. **6** The
captain came to him and said, "What are you
doing asleep? Rise up, call upon your God!
Perhaps God will be mindful of us so that we
may not perish."
**7** Then they said to one another, "Come, let
us cast lots to find out on whose account we
have met with this misfortune." So they cast
lots, and thus singled out Jonah. **8** "Tell us,"
they said, "what is your business? Where do
you come from? What is your country, and to
what people do you belong?" **9** "I am a Hebrew," Jonah answered them; "I worship the
LORD, the God of heaven, who made the sea and
the dry land."
**10** Now the men were seized with great fear
and said to him, "How could you do such a
thing!"—They knew that he was fleeing from
the LORD, because he had told them.—
**11** "What shall we do with you," they asked,
"that the sea may quiet down for us?" For the
sea was growing more and more turbulent.
**12** Jonah said to them, "Pick me up and throw
me into the sea, that it may quiet down for you;
since I know it is because of me that this violent
storm has come upon you."
**13** Still the men rowed hard to regain the
land, but they could not, for the sea grew ever
more turbulent. **14** Then they cried to the LORD:

a 2 Kgs 14, 25. b Jon 3, 3; 4, 11.

*

1, 1: Jonah, son of Amittai: a prophet of this name lived at the time of Jeroboam II (786–746 B.C.).

1, 3: Tarshish: identified by many with Tartessus, an ancient Phoenician colony in southwest Spain; precise identification with any particular Phoenician center in the western Mediterranean is uncertain. To the Hebrews it stood for the far west.

1, 14: Since it has pleased the Lord to punish Jonah, the mariners ask that in ridding themselves of him they be not

"We beseech you, O LORD, let us not perish for taking this man's life; do not charge us with shedding innocent blood, for you, LORD, have done as you saw fit."* **15** Then they took Jonah and threw him into the sea, and the sea's raging abated. **16** Struck with great fear of the LORD, the men offered sacrifice and made vows to him.

## CHAPTER 2

**1** But the LORD sent a large fish, that swallowed Jonah; and he remained in the belly of the fish three days and three nights.[c] **2** From the belly of the fish Jonah said this prayer to the LORD, his God:

### Psalm of Thanksgiving

**3** Out of my distress I called to the LORD,
and he answered me;
From the midst of the nether world I cried
for help,
and you heard my voice.[d]
**4** For you cast me into the deep, into the heart
of the sea,
and the flood enveloped me;
All your breakers and your billows passed
over me.[e]
**5** Then I said, "I am banished from your
sight!
yet would I again look upon your holy
temple."[f]
**6** The waters swirled about me, threatening
my life;
the abyss enveloped me;
seaweed clung about my head.[g]
**7** Down I went to the roots of the mountains;
the bars of the nether world
were closing behind me forever,
But you brought up my life from the pit,
O LORD, my God.[h]
**8** When my soul fainted within me,
I remembered the LORD;
My prayer reached you
in your holy temple.[i]
**9** Those who worship vain idols
forsake their source of mercy.[j]
**10** But I, with resounding praise,
will sacrifice to you;
What I have vowed I will pay:
deliverance is from the LORD.[k]

**11** Then the LORD commanded the fish to spew Jonah upon the shore.

## CHAPTER 3

**Conversion of Nineveh.** **1** The word of the LORD came to Jonah a second time: **2** "Set out for the great city of Nineveh, and announce to it the message that I will tell you." **3** So Jonah made ready and went to Nineveh, according to the LORD's bidding. Now Nineveh was an enormously large city; it took three days to go through it. **4** Jonah began his journey through the city, and had gone but a single day's walk announcing, "Forty days more and Nineveh shall be destroyed,"* **5** when the people of Nineveh believed God; they proclaimed a fast and all of them, great and small, put on sackcloth.[l]

**6** When the news reached the king of Nineveh, he rose from his throne, laid aside his robe, covered himself with sackcloth, and sat in the ashes. **7** Then he had this proclaimed throughout Nineveh, by decree of the king and his nobles: "Neither man nor beast, neither cattle nor sheep, shall taste anything; they shall not eat, nor shall they drink water. **8** Man and beast shall be covered with sackcloth* and call loudly to God; every man shall turn from his evil way and from the violence he has in hand. **9** Who knows, God may relent and forgive, and withold his blazing wrath, so that we shall not perish."[m] **10** When God saw by their actions how they turned from their evil way, he repented of the evil that he had threatened to do to them; he did not carry it out.

## CHAPTER 4

**Jonah's Anger: God's Reproof.** **1** But this was greatly displeasing to Jonah, and he became angry.* **2** "I beseech you, LORD," he prayed, "is not this what I said while I was still in my own country? This is why I fled at first to Tarshish. I knew that you are a gracious and merciful God, slow to anger, rich in clemency, loathe to punish.[n] **3** And now, LORD, please take my life from me; for it is better for me to die than to live."[o] **4** But the LORD asked, "Have you reason to be angry?"

**5** Jonah then left the city for a place to the east of it, where he built himself a hut and waited under it in the shade, to see what would happen to the city. **6** And when the LORD God provided a gourd plant,* that grew up over Jonah's head, giving shade that relieved him of any discomfort, Jonah was very happy over the

c Mt 12, 40; 16, 4; Lk 11, 30; 1 Cor 15, 4.
d Pss 18, 7; 120, 1.
e Ps 42, 8.
f Ps 31, 23; Is 38, 11.
g Pss 18, 5; 69, 2.
h Pss 16, 10; 30, 4.
i Pss 5, 8; 18, 7; 88, 3.
j Ps 31, 7.
k Ps 50, 14.
l Mt 12, 41; Lk 11, 32.
m Jl 2, 14.
n Ps 86, 5; Jl 2, 13.
o 1 Kgs 19, 4.

* charged with the crime of murder.

3, 4: Shall be destroyed: the Hebrew expression reminds the reader of the "overthrowing" of the wicked cities, Sodom and Gomorrah, by a special act of God.

3, 8: Beast . . . sackcloth: the animals carried the signs of this repentance, as on occasions of joy they bore garlands.

4, 1: He became angry: because of his narrowly nationalistic vindictiveness, Jonah did not wish the Lord to forgive the Ninevites.

4, 6: Gourd plant: the Hebrew word, kikayon, means here a wide-leafed plant of the cucumber or castor-bean variety.

plant. 7 But the next morning at dawn God sent
a worm which attacked the plant, so that it
withered. 8 And when the sun arose, God sent
a burning east wind; and the sun beat upon
Jonah's head till he became faint. Then he asked
for death, saying, "I would be better off dead
than alive."

9 But God said to Jonah, "Have you reason
to be angry over the plant?" "I have reason to
be angry," Jonah answered, "angry enough to
die." 10 Then the LORD said, "You are concerned over the plant which cost you no labor
and which you did not raise; it came up in one
night and in one night it perished.* 11 And
should I not be concerned over Nineveh, the
great city, in which there are more than a hundred and twenty thousand persons who cannot
distinguish their right hand from their left, not
to mention the many cattle?"

---

* 4, 10f: Jonah is selfish in bemoaning his personal loss of a shady gourd plant without any concern over the threat of loss of life to the Ninevites through the destruction of their city. If God in his kindness provided the plant for his prophet without the latter's effort or merit, how much more is he disposed to show love and mercy toward all men, Jew and Gentile, when they repent of their sins and implore his pardon! God's providence is also shown here to extend even to animals.

# The Book of
# MICAH

*Micah was a contemporary of Isaiah. Of his personal life and call we know nothing except that he came from the obscure village of Moresheth in the foothills. His were the broad vistas of the Judean lowland and the distant sea on the western horizon. With burning eloquence he attacked the rich exploiters of the poor, fraudulent merchants, venal judges, corrupt priests and prophets. To the man of the countryside the vices of the nation seemed centered in its capitals, for both Samaria and Jerusalem are singled out for judgment. An interesting notice in Jer 26, 17f informs us that the reform of Hezekiah was influenced by the preaching of Micah.*

*The prophecy may be divided into three parts: I. The impending judgment of the Lord, followed by an exposition of its causes, Israel's sins. Censure of Judah's leaders for betrayal of their responsibility (1, 1—3, 12). II. The glory of the restored Zion. A prince of David's house will rule over a reunited Israel. (St. Matthew's Nativity narrative points to Christ's birth in Bethlehem as the fulfillment of this prophecy.) A remnant shall survive the chastisement of Judah and her adversaries shall be destroyed (4, 1—5, 14). III. The case against Israel, in which the Lord is portrayed as the plaintiff who has maintained fidelity to the covenant. The somber picture closes with a prayer for national restoration and a beautiful expression of trust in God's pardoning mercy (6, 1—7, 20).*

*It should be noted that each of these three divisions begins with reproach and the threat of punishment, and ends on a note of hope and promise.*

## *I: Punishment of Israel's Sins*

### CHAPTER 1

**Divine Judgment.** 1 The word of the LORD which came to Micah of Moresheth in the days of Jotham, Ahaz, and Hezekiah, kings of Judah: that is, the vision he received concerning Samaria and Jerusalem.

2 Hear, O peoples, all of you,
give heed, O earth, and all that fills you![a]
Let the LORD GOD be witness against you,
the LORD from his holy temple!*
3 For see, the LORD comes forth from his place,[b]
he descends and treads upon the heights of the earth.
4 The mountains melt under him
and the valleys split open,
Like wax before the fire,
like water poured down a slope.

5 For the crime of Jacob all this comes to pass,
and for the sins of the house of Israel.
What is the crime of Jacob? Is it not Samaria?
And what is the sin of the house of Judah?
Is it not Jerusalem?
6 I will make Samaria a stone heap in the field,
a place to plant for vineyards;
I will throw down into the valley her stones,
and lay bare her foundations.
7 All her idols shall be broken to pieces,[c]
all her wages shall be burned in the fire,
and all her statues I will destroy.
As the wages of a harlot they were gathered,
and to the wages of a harlot shall they return.*

8 For this reason I lament and wail,
I go barefoot and naked;
I utter lamentation like the jackals,
and mourning like the ostriches.[d]
9 There is no remedy for the blow she has been struck;
rather, it has come even to Judah,
It reaches to the gate of my people,
even to Jerusalem.
10 Publish it not in Gath,*

---

a Dt 32, 1; Is 1, 2.
b 3f: Is 26, 21; Na 1, 5; Hb 3, 10.
c Hos 9, 1.
d Jb 30, 29.
e 2 Sm 1, 20.

---

*

1, 2: His holy temple: God's heavenly temple; the prophet pictures a theophany (3f).

1, 7: The comparison of the unfaithful people with a prostitute, first found in Hosea, is frequent with the prophets; probably ritual prostitution is meant; cf Am 2, 7f; Hos 4, 14.

1, 10–15: The Judean cities here named were in the vicinity of Moresheth, the region with which Micah was most familiar. They were to experience divine chastisement. In the Hebrew, wordplays on the names of these cities abound. The text is partly obscure.

weep not at all;
In Beth-leaphrah
roll in the dust.[e]
11 Pass by,
you who dwell in Shaphir!
The inhabitants of Zaanan
come not forth from their city.
The lamentation of Beth-ezel
finds in you its grounds.
12 How can the inhabitants of Maroth
hope for good?
For evil has come down from the LORD
to the gate of Jerusalem.
13 Harness steeds to the chariots,
O inhabitants of Lachish;
Lachish, the beginning of sin
for daughter Zion,
Because there were in you
the crimes of Israel.
14 Therefore you shall give parting gifts
to Moresheth-gath;
Beth-achzib is a deception
to the kings of Israel.
15 Yet must I bring to you the conqueror,
O inhabitants of Mareshah;
Even to Adullam shall go
the glory of Israel.

16 Make yourself bald, pluck out your hair,
for the children whom you cherish;
Let your baldness be as the eagle's,
because they are exiled from you.*

## CHAPTER 2

### Social Evils

1 Woe to those who plan iniquity,
and work out evil on their couches;
In the morning light they accomplish it
when it lies within their power.
2 They covet fields, and seize them;
houses, and they take them;
They cheat an owner of his house,
a man of his inheritance.*
3 Therefore thus says the LORD:
Behold, I am planning against this race an
evil
from which you shall not withdraw your
necks;
Nor shall you walk with head high,
for it will be a time of evil.

4 On that day a satire shall be sung over you,
and there shall be a plaintive chant:
"Our ruin is complete,
our fields are portioned out among our
captors,
The fields of my people are measured out,
and no one can get them back!"
5 Thus you shall have no one
to mark out boundaries by lot*
in the assembly of the LORD.

6 "Preach not," they preach,
"let them not preach of these things!"*
The shame will not withdraw.
7 How can it be said, O house of Jacob,
"Is the LORD short of patience,
or are such his deeds?"
Do not my words promise good
to him who walks uprightly?

8 But of late my people has risen up as an
enemy:
you have stripped off the mantle covering
the tunic
Of those who go their way in confidence,
as though it were spoils of war.
9 The women of my people you drive out
from their pleasant houses;
From their children you take away
forever the honor I gave them.*
10 "Up! Be off,
this is no place to rest";
For any trifle you exact
a crippling pledge.*

11 If one, acting on impulse, should make the
futile claim:
"I pour you wine and strong drink as my
prophecy,"
then he would be the prophet of this
people.
12 I will gather you, O Jacob, each and every
one,*
I will assemble all the remnant of Israel;
I will group them like a flock in the fold,
like a herd in the midst of its corral;
they shall not be thrown into panic by
men.
13 With a leader to break the path
they shall burst open the gate and go out
through it;
Their king shall go through before them,
and the LORD at their head.

*

1, 16: Shaving the head was a sign of mourning; cf Is 3, 24; Am 8, 10.

2, 2: Land monopoly, also denounced by Isaiah, was a chronic vice in Judah. To protect the poor against it, a man's inheritance, his ancestral property, was supposed to be inviolate; cf 1 Kgs 21, 1–4; but the wealthy in their greed were enslaving men for their debts and depriving them of their land.

2, 5: To mark out boundaries by lot: an allusion to the initial distribution of the land of Palestine among the Israelites; cf Jos 13–21. The appropriate punishment of those greedy for land will be the loss of their land to their enemies (v 4), a loss that will be irrevocable.

2, 6f: The words in quotation marks are the protestations of the people against the prophet's predictions of doom.

2, 9: The honor I gave them: their dignity as free Israelites.

2, 10: A crippling pledge: Israelite law forbade exacting pledges for loans that would work hardship on the borrower (Ex 22, 25f; Dt 24, 6. 10–13. 17); but the law was habitually violated.

2, 12f: This messianic passage concerning the restoration after the Babylonian exile seems out of place here and is probably a later addition.

## CHAPTER 3

### Downfall of Present Leaders

1 And I said:
Hear, you leaders of Jacob,
rulers of the house of Israel!
Is it not your duty to know what is right,
2 you who hate what is good, and love evil?
You who tear their skin from them,
and their flesh from their bones![f]
3 They eat the flesh of my people,
and flay their skin from them,
and break their bones.
They chop them in pieces like flesh in a kettle,
and like meat in a caldron.
4 When they cry to the LORD,
he shall not answer them;
Rather shall he hide his face from them at that time,
because of the evil they have done.

5 Thus says the LORD regarding the prophets*
who lead my people astray;
Who, when their teeth have something to bite,
announce peace,
But when one fails to put something in their mouth,
proclaim war against him.[g]
6 Therefore you shall have night, not vision,
darkness, not divination;
The sun shall go down upon the prophets,
and the day shall be dark for them.[h]
7 Then shall the seers be put to shame,
and the diviners confounded;
They shall cover their lips, all of them,
because there is no answer from God.
8 But as for me, I am filled with power,
with the spirit of the LORD,
with authority and with might;
To declare to Jacob his crimes
and to Israel his sins.
9 Hear this, you leaders of the house of Jacob,
you rulers of the house of Israel!
You who abhor what is just,
and pervert all that is right;
10 Who build up Zion with bloodshed,
and Jerusalem with wickedness!
11 Her leaders render judgment for a bribe,
her priests give decisions for a salary,
her prophets divine for money,
While they rely on the LORD, saying,
"Is not the LORD in the midst of us?
No evil can come upon us!"[i]
12 Therefore, because of you,
Zion shall be plowed like a field,
and Jerusalem reduced to rubble,
And the mount of the temple
to a forest ridge.[j]

## *II: The New Israel*

## CHAPTER 4

### The People To Be Restored

1 In days to come*
the mount of the LORD's house
Shall be established higher than the mountains;
it shall rise high above the hills,
And peoples shall stream to it:[k]
2 Many nations shall come, and say,
"Come, let us climb the mount of the LORD,
to the house of the God of Jacob,
That he may instruct us in his ways,
that we may walk in his paths."
For from Zion shall go forth instruction,
and the word of the LORD from Jerusalem.
3 He shall judge between many peoples
and impose terms on strong and distant nations;
They shall beat their swords into plowshares,
and their spears into pruning hooks;
One nation shall not raise the sword against another,
nor shall they train for war again.
4 Every man shall sit under his own vine
or under his own fig tree, undisturbed;
for the mouth of the LORD of hosts has spoken.[l]
5 For all the peoples walk
each in the name of its god,
But we will walk in the name of the LORD,
our God, forever and ever.
6 On that day, says the LORD,
I will gather the lame,
And I will assemble the outcasts,
and those whom I have afflicted.
7 I will make of the lame a remnant,
and of those driven far off a strong nation;
And the LORD shall be king over them on Mount Zion,
from now on forever.[m]
8 And you, O Magdal-eder,*
hillock of daughter Zion!
Unto you shall it come:
the former dominion shall be restored,
the kingdom of daughter Jerusalem.

---

f Am 2, 7.
g Ez 13, 10.
h Jer 15, 9; Am 8, 9; Zec 13, 3.
i Ez 22, 27; Zep 3, 3.
j Jer 26, 18.
k 1ff: Is 2, 2ff.
l Hos 14, 8; Am 9, 14.
m Is 6, 13; Dn 7, 14; Zep 3, 19; Lk 1, 32.

---

3, 5–8: Almost all the prophetic books contain oracles against the false prophets. Here Micah accuses them of prophesying for venal motives and determining the prophecy by the price that is paid them; he contrasts his own disinterested preaching of the word of God.

4, 1ff: See note on Is 2, 2ff.

4, 8: Magdal-eder: "tower of the flock," an ancient place name (cf Gn 35, 21), here used symbolically of Jerusalem.

9 Now why do you cry out so?
Are you without a king?
Or has your counselor perished,
That you are seized with pains
like a woman in travail?
10 Writhe in pain, grow faint,
O daughter Zion,
like a woman in travail;
For now shall you go forth from the city
and dwell in the fields;
To Babylon shall you go,
there shall you be rescued.
There shall the LORD redeem you
from the hand of your enemies.*

11 How many nations are gathered against you!
They say, "Let her be profaned,
let our eyes see Zion's downfall!"
12 But they know not the thoughts of the LORD,
nor understand his counsel,
When he has gathered them
like sheaves on the threshing floor.
13 Arise and thresh, O daughter Zion;
your horn I will make iron
And your hoofs bronze,
that you may crush many peoples;
You shall devote their spoils to the LORD,
and their riches to the Lord of the whole earth.[n]

## Restoration through the Messiah

14 Now fence yourself in, Bat-gader!*
"They have laid siege against us!"
With the rod they strike on the cheek
the ruler of Israel.

## CHAPTER 5

1 But you, Bethlehem-Ephrathah,[o]
too small to be among the clans of Judah,
From you shall come forth for me
one who is to be ruler in Israel;
Whose origin is from of old,
from ancient times.*
2 (Therefore the Lord will give them up, until the time
when she who is to give birth* has borne,
And the rest of his brethren shall return
to the children of Israel.)[p]
3 He shall stand firm and shepherd his flock
by the strength of the LORD,
in the majestic name of the LORD, his God;
And they shall remain, for now his greatness
shall reach to the ends of the earth;
4 he shall be peace.

If Assyria invades our country*
and treads upon our land,
We shall raise against it seven shepherds,
eight men of royal rank;
5 And they shall tend the land of Assyria with the sword,
and the land of Nimrod* with the drawn sword;
And we shall be delivered from Assyria,
if it invades our land
and treads upon our borders.

6 The remnant of Jacob shall be
in the midst of many peoples,
Like dew coming from the LORD,
like raindrops on the grass,
Which wait for no man,
nor tarry for the sons of men.
7 And the remnant of Jacob shall be among the nations,
in the midst of many peoples,
Like a lion among beasts of the forest,
like a young lion among flocks of sheep;
When it passes through, it tramples
and tears, and there is none to deliver.
8 Your hand shall be lifted above your foes,
and all your enemies shall be destroyed.

9 On that day, says the LORD,*
I will destroy the horses from your midst
and ruin your chariots;
10 I will demolish the cities of your land
and tear down all your fortresses.
11 I will abolish the means of divination from your use,
and there shall no longer be soothsayers among you.
12 I will abolish your carved images
and the sacred pillars* from your midst;
And you shall no longer adore

n Is 41, 15; Hos 10, 11.
o Ru 1, 2; 1 Sm 17, 12; Mt 2, 6; Jn 7, 42.
p 2f: Is 7, 14; 11, 1f.
q Hos 3, 4; 10, 1f.

*

4, 10: For now . . . your enemies; probably a later addition to the text, when the prediction of exile had been fulfilled in the Babylonian captivity. The prophet sees the exile as the means whereby God will purify and restore his people.

4, 14: Bat-gader: "fenced-in maiden," another symbolic name for Jerusalem, then under siege from the Assyrians.

5, 1: In contrast to Bat-gader (Mi 4, 14), where the ruler of Israel, the reigning king, is in peril of his life from the Assyrians, is the tiny city and clan of Bethlehem-Ephrathah, from which comes the ancient Davidic dynasty (whose origin is from of old, from ancient times) with its messianic King, one who is to be ruler in Israel.

5, 2: She who is to give birth: the mother of the Messiah: cf Is 7, 14.

5, 4f: This passage, expressing confidence in Judah's ability to deliver itself from Assyria, is in contrast with the preceding messianic oracle, which ascribes deliverance to the Lord and his agent. Some believe that here the prophet is quoting the words of the defiant men of Judah, The shepherds and men of royal rank are one and the same: warriors capable of routing Assyria. The same kind of numerical progression is used by Amos (1, 3), and elsewhere in the Bible.

5, 5: Nimrod: the legendary ancestor of the Mesopotamians; cf Gn 10, 10ff.

5, 9–13: Part of the messianic restoration will consist in the removal of everything that has drawn Israel away from the Lord; this includes not only the objects of false worship, but also the armaments in which the idolators had trusted.

5, 12f: Sacred pillars . . . sacred poles: see note on Ex 34, 13.

the works of your hands.[q]
13 I will tear out the sacred poles from your
midst,
and destroy your cities.
14 I will wreak vengeance in anger and wrath
upon the nations that have not hearkened.

## III: Admonition

## CHAPTER 6

### Accusation and Answer

1 Hear, then, what the LORD says:
Arise, present your plea before the
mountains,
and let the hills hear your voice![r]
2 Hear, O mountains, the plea of the LORD,
pay attention, O foundations of the earth!
For the LORD has a plea against his people,
and he enters into trial with Israel.

3 O my people, what have I done to you,
or how have I wearied you? Answer me![s]
4 For I brought you up from the land of
Egypt,
from the place of slavery I released you;
And I sent before you Moses,
Aaron, and Miriam.[t]
5 My people, remember what Moab's King
Balak planned,
and how Balaam, the son of Beor,
answered him
. . . from Shittim to Gilgal,*
that you may know the just deeds of the
LORD.[u]
6 With what shall I come before the LORD,*
and bow before God most high?
Shall I come before him with holocausts,
with calves a year old?[v]
7 Will the LORD be pleased with thousands of
rams,
with myriad streams of oil?
Shall I give my first-born* for my crime,
the fruit of my body for the sin of my
soul?
8 You have been told, O man, what is good,
and what the LORD requires of you:
Only to do the right and to love goodness,
and to walk humbly with your God.[w]

9 Hark! the LORD cries to the city.*
[It is wisdom to fear your name!]
Hear, O tribe and city council,
12 You whose rich men are full of violence,
whose inhabitants speak falsehood
with deceitful tongues in their heads!
10 Am I to bear any longer criminal hoarding
and the meager ephah that is accursed?
11 Shall I acquit criminal balances,
bags of false weights?

13 Rather I will begin to strike you
with devastation because of your sins.
15 You shall sow, yet not reap,
tread out the olive, yet pour no oil,
and the grapes, yet drink no wine.[x]
14 You shall eat, without being satisfied,
food that will leave you empty;
What you acquire, you cannot save;
what you do save, I will deliver up to the
sword.[y]
16 You have kept the decrees of Omri,
and all the works of the house of Ahab,
and you have walked in their counsels;
Therefore I will deliver you up to ruin,
and your citizens to derision;
and you shall bear the reproach of the
nations.*

## CHAPTER 7

### Condemnation and Prayer

1 Alas! I am as when the fruit is gathered,
as when the vines have been gleaned;
There is no cluster to eat,
no early fig that I crave.
2 The faithful are gone from the earth,
among men the upright are no more!
They all lie in wait to shed blood,
each one ensnares the other.[z]
3 Their hands succeed at evil;
the prince makes demands,
The judge is had for a price,
the great man speaks as he pleases,[a]
4 The best of them is like a brier,
the most upright like a thorn hedge.
The day announced by your watchmen!
your punishment has come;
now is the time of your confusion.
5 Put no trust in a friend,*

r Is 6, 2; Ob 1.
s Jer 2, 5.
t Ex 15, 20.
u Nm 22, 23.
v 6f: Hos 6, 6; 8, 13; Am 5, 21.
w Dt 26, 16; Zec 7, 9; Mt 23, 23.
x Dt 28, 38; Am 5, 11; Hg 1, 6.
y Hos 4, 10.
z Is 1, 21; Hos 4, 2.
a Is 1, 23.
b Jer 9, 3.

6, 5: From Shittim to Gilgal: from the east to the west side of the Jordan; the events described in Jos 3—5 are meant. The text is defective; however, it is evident that this verse continues the remembrance of God's deeds of mercy to Israel, beginning with the Exodus (v 4) and extending to the conquest, deeds which have provoked so little response from his people.

6, 6ff: The people ask how they shall worship the Lord, proposing the various forms of sacrifice. The prophet replies that sacrifice avails nothing without the true spirit of religion. This is one of the best expressions of the prophetic teaching on religion, the preparation for such New Testament passages as Jas 1, 27.

6, 7: Shall I give my first-born: through Canaanite influence the abominable practice of human sacrifice had been introduced under impious kings (cf 2 Kgs 16, 3; 21, 6).

6, 9: The city: Jerusalem as the embodiment of the crimes of the entire land.

6, 16: Judah has followed the example of the northern kingdom epitomized in the semipaganism of Omri and his son Ahab (1 Kgs 16, 25–34), copying both the corrupted worship and the social injustice of their reigns.

7, 5f: Corresponding to the widespread civil corruption and

have no confidence in a companion;
Against her who lies in your bosom
guard the portals of your mouth.[b]
6 For the son dishonors his father,
the daughter rises up against her mother,
The daughter-in-law against her
mother-in-law,
and a man's enemies are those of his
household.[c]
7 But as for me, I will look to the LORD,
I will put my trust in God my savior;
my God will hear me![d]

8 Rejoice not over me, O my enemy!*
though I have fallen, I will arise;
though I sit in darkness, the LORD is my
light.
9 The wrath of the LORD I will endure
because I have sinned against him,
Until he takes up my cause,
and establishes my right.
He will bring me forth to the light;
I will see his justice.
10 When my enemy sees this,
shame shall cover her:
She who said to me,
"Where is the LORD, thy God?"
My eyes shall see her downfall;
now shall she be trampled underfoot,
like the mire in the streets.

11 It is the day for building your walls;*
on that day the boundary shall be taken
away.
12 It is the day; and they shall come to you
from Assyria and from Egypt,
From Tyre even to the River,
from sea to sea, and from mountain to
mountain;[e]
13 And the land shall be a waste
because of its citizens,
as a result of their deeds.

14 Shepherd your people with your staff,*
the flock of your inheritance,
That dwells apart in a woodland,
in the midst of Carmel.
Let them feed in Bashan and Gilead,
as in the days of old;
15 As in the days when you came from the
land of Egypt,
show us wonderful signs.

16 The nations shall behold and be put to
shame,
in spite of all their strength;
They shall put their hands over their mouths;
their ears shall become deaf.
17 They shall lick the dust like the serpent,
like reptiles on the ground;
They shall come quaking from their
fastnesses,
trembling in fear of you [the LORD, our
God].

18 Who is there like you, the God who
removes guilt
and pardons sin for the remnant of his
inheritance;
Who does not persist in anger forever,
but delights rather in clemency,[f]
19 And will again have compassion on us,
treading underfoot our guilt?
You will cast into the depths of the sea all
our sins;
20 You will show faithfulness to Jacob,
and grace to Abraham,
As you have sworn to our fathers
from days of old.[g]

---

c Mt 10, 35f.
d Is 8, 17.
e Zec 14, 16.
f Jer 10, 6; Acts 10, 43.
g Ps 105, 6; Is 41, 8; 63, 16.

---

* apostasy from religion is the breakdown of normal human and family relations.

7, 8ff: The unnamed enemy of Judah mentioned in these verses may be Assyria or one of the neighboring countries, such as Edom, which stood by to profit at Judah's downfall.

7, 11ff: This prophecy of restoration and repopulation of the promised land by the Jews now in exile appears to be from the period after the destruction of Jerusalem by the Chaldeans (587 B.C.).

7, 14–17: This prayer appears to be from the time after the return from exile (537 B.C.), when the people few in number, possessed only a fragment of their former land, and were surrounded by hostile nations.

# The Book of
# NAHUM

*Shortly before the fall of Nineveh in 612 B.C., Nahum uttered his prophecy against the hated city. To understand the prophet's exultant outburst of joy over the impending destruction it is necessary to recall the savage cruelty of Assyria, which had made it the scourge of the ancient Near East for almost three centuries. The royal inscriptions of Assyria afford the best commentary on the burning denunciation of "the bloody city." In the wake of their conquests, mounds of heads, impaled bodies, enslaved citizens, and avaricious looters testified to the ruthlessness of the Assyrians. Little wonder that Judah joined in the general outburst of joy over the destruction of Nineveh!*

*But Nahum is not a prophet of unrestrained revenge. God's moral government of the world is asserted. Yahweh is the avenger but he is also merciful, a citadel in the day of distress. Nineveh's doom was a judgment on the wicked city. Before many years passed, Jerusalem too was to learn the meaning of such a judgment.*

*The book is divided as follows: The Lord's Coming in Judgment (1, 2—2, 1.3). The Fall of Nineveh (2, 2—3, 19).*

## CHAPTER 1

**1** Oracle about Nineveh. The book of the vision of Nahum of Elkosh.

### The Lord's Coming in Judgment

**2** *A jealous and avenging God* is the LORD,
an avenger is the LORD, and angry;
The LORD brings vengeance on his adversaries,
and lays up wrath for his enemies;
**3** The LORD is slow to anger, yet great in power,
and the LORD never leaves the guilty unpunished.
In hurricane and tempest is his path,
and clouds are the dust at his feet;[a]
**4** He rebukes the sea and leaves it dry,
and all the rivers he dries up.[b]
Withered are Bashan and Carmel,
and the bloom of Lebanon fades;*
**5** The mountains quake before him,
and the hills dissolve;
The earth is laid waste before him,
the world and all who dwell in it.
**6** Before his wrath, who can stand firm,[c]
and who can face his blazing anger?
His fury is poured out like fire,
and the rocks are rent asunder before him.*
**7** The LORD is good,
a refuge on the day of distress;
He takes care of those who have recourse to him,
**8** when the flood rages;
He makes an end of his opponents,
and his enemies he pursues with darkness.
**9** What are you imputing to the LORD?*
It is he who will make an end!
The enemy shall not rise a second time;
**10** As when a tangle of thornbushes is set aflame,
like dry stubble, they shall be utterly consumed.
**12** For, says the LORD,
be they* ever so many and so vigorous,
still they shall be mown down and disappear.
Though I have humbled you,
I will humble you no more.
**13** Now will I break his yoke from off you,
and burst asunder your bonds.[d]
**11** From you he came
who devised evil against the LORD,
the scoundrel planner.*
**14** The LORD has commanded regarding you:*
no descendant shall come to bear your name;

---

a Ex 19, 16ff. b Is 33, 9; Hb 3, 6ff. c Zep 1, 15; 2, 3. d Is 9, 4; 10, 27.

---

*

1, 2–8: A poem written in the style of the alphabetic psalms; cf Pss 9A; 25; 111; 119. Here, however, most of the verses beginning with the letters of the second half of the alphabet are not preserved.

1, 2: A jealous . . . God: see note on Ex 20, 5.

1, 4: Bashan, Carmel and Lebanon were famous for their forests.

1, 6f: The coming of God in judgment has two aspects: to those who oppose him it will be unbearable; to those who have recourse to him it will bring strength and consolation.

1, 9: What are you imputing to the Lord?: the people of Judah are asked what they think God has in mind.

1, 12f: They: the enemies of Judah. You: Judah. His yoke: the dominion of the Assyrian king over Judah.

1, 11: From you . . . the scoundrel planner: addressed to Nineveh, the capital city of Sennacherib, king of Assyria, who besieged Jerusalem c. 700 B.C.

1, 14: You: the king of Assyria.

From your temple I will abolish
the carved and the molten image;
I will make your grave a mockery.

## CHAPTER 2

1 See, upon the mountains there advances
the bearer of good news, announcing
peace!
Celebrate your feasts, O Judah,
fulfill your vows!
For nevermore shall you be invaded
by the scoundrel; he is completely
destroyed.[e]
3 The LORD will restore the vine of Jacob,
the pride of Israel,
Though ravagers have ravaged them
and ruined the tendrils.

### The Fall of Nineveh

2 The hammer comes up against you;*
guard the rampart,
Keep watch on the road, gird your loins,
marshal all your strength!
4 The shields of his warriors are crimsoned,
the soldiers colored in scarlet;
Fiery steel are the chariots
on the day of his mustering.
The horses are frenzied;
5 the chariots dash madly through the streets
And wheel in the squares,
looking like firebrands,
flashing like lightning bolts.
6 His picked troops are called,
ranks break at their charge;
To the wall they rush,
the mantelet* is set up.
7 The river gates are opened,
the palace shudders,
8 Its mistress is led forth captive,
and her handmaids,* under guard,
Moaning like doves,
beating their breasts.
9 Nineveh is like a pool
whose waters escape;
"Stop! Stop!"
but none turns back.
10 "Plunder the silver, plunder the gold!"
There is no end to the treasure,
to their wealth in precious things of every
kind!

11 Emptiness, desolation, waste;
melting hearts and trembling knees,
Writhing in every frame,
every face blanched![f]
12 Where is the lions' cave,
the young lions' den,
Where the lion* went in and out,
and the cub, with no one to disturb them?
13 The lion snatched enough for his cubs,
and strangled for his lionesses;
He filled his dens with prey,
and his caves with plunder.
14 I come against you,
says the LORD of hosts;
I will consume in smoke your chariots,
and the sword shall devour your young
lions;
Your preying on the land I will bring to an
end,
the cry of your lionesses shall be heard no
more.

## CHAPTER 3

### Ruin Imminent and Inevitable

1 Woe to the bloody city, all lies,
full of plunder, whose looting never
stops![g]
2 The crack of the whip, the rumbling sounds
of wheels;
horses a-gallop, chariots bounding,
3 Cavalry charging,
The flame of the sword, the flash of the
spear,
the many slain, the heaping corpses,
the endless bodies to stumble upon!
4 For the many debaucheries of the harlot,
fair and charming, a mistress of
witchcraft,
Who enslaved nations with her harlotries,
and peoples by her witchcraft:[h]
5 I am come against you,[i]
and I will strip your skirt from you;
I will show your nakedness to the nations,
to the kingdoms your shame!*
6 I will cast filth upon you,
disgrace you and put you to shame;
7 Till everyone who sees you runs from you,
saying,
"Nineveh is destroyed; who can pity her?
Where can one find any to console her?"

8 Are you better than No-amon*
that was set among the streams,
Surrounded by waters,
with the flood for her rampart
and water her wall?[j]
9 Ethiopia was her strength, and Egypt,
and others without end;
Put and the Libyans were her auxiliaries.
10 Yet even she went captive into exile,

e Is 52, 7; Rom 10, 15.
f Jl 2, 6.
g Hb 2, 12.
h Mi 1, 7; Rv 17, 1f.
i Is 47, 3; Jer 13, 26; Hos 2, 12.
j Jer 46, 25.

*

2, 2: The hammer comes up against you: the enemy is about to crush Nineveh.

2, 6: Mantelet: a movable shelter protecting the besiegers.

2, 8: Mistress . . . and her handmaids: either the queen of Nineveh with the ladies of her court, or the statute of Ishtar, Nineveh's chief goddess, with her temple prostitutes.

2, 12: The lion: the king of Assyria.

3, 5f: The punishment of adulteresses.

3, 8: No-amon: No was the Egyptian name of the capital of Upper Egypt, called Thebes by the Greeks; its tutelary deity was Amon. This great city was destroyed by the Assyrians in 663 B.C.

even her little ones were dashed to pieces
at the corner of every street;
For her nobles they cast lots,
and all her great men were put into chains.
11 You, too, shall drink of this till you faint away;
you, too, shall seek a refuge from the foe.[k]
12 All your fortresses are but fig trees,
bearing early figs
That fall, when shaken,
into the hungry mouth.
13 See, the troops are women in your midst;
to your foes the gates of your land are open wide,
fire has consumed their bars.[l]
14 Draw water for the siege,*
strengthen your fortresses;
Go down into the mud and tread the clay,
take hold of the brick mold!
15 There the fire shall consume you,
the sword shall cut you down.
Multiply like the grasshoppers,
multiply like the locusts!
16 Make your couriers more numerous than the stars,
17 your garrisons as many as grasshoppers,
And your scribes as locust swarms
gathered on the rubble fences on a cold day!
Yet when the sun warms them,
the grasshoppers will spread their wings and fly,
and vanish, no one knows where.
18 Alas! how your shepherds slumber, O king of Assyria,
your nobles have gone to rest;
Your people are scattered upon the mountains,
with none to gather them.

19 There is no healing for your hurt,
your wound is mortal.
All who hear this news of you
clap their hands over you;
For who has not been overwhelmed,
steadily, by your malice?

k Mi 2, 11. l Jer 51, 30.

* 3, 14: An ironic exhortation to prepare the city for a futile defense. Go down . . . brick mold: make bricks for the city walls.

# The Book of

# HABAKKUK

*This prophecy dates from the years 605–597 B.C., or between the great Babylonian victory at Carchemish and Nebuchadnezzar's invasion of Judah which culminated in the capture of Jerusalem. The situation of Judah was desperate at this time, with political intrigue and idolatry widespread in the small kingdom. The first two chapters consist of a dialogue between the prophet and the Lord. For what may be the first time in Israelite literature, a man questions the ways of God, as Habukkuk calls him to account for his government of the world. To this question God replies that he has prepared a chastising rod, Babylon, which will be the avenging instrument in his hand. There is added the divine assurance that the just Israelite will not perish in the calamities about to be visited on the nation.*

*The third chapter is a magnificent religious lyric, filled with reminiscences of Israel's past and rich in literary borrowings from the poetry of ancient Canaan, though still expressing authentic Israelite faith. God appears in all his majestic splendor and executes vengeance on Judah's enemies. The prophecy ends with a joyous profession of confidence in the Lord, the Savior.*

## CHAPTER 1

1 The oracle which Habakkuk the prophet received in vision.

### The Prophet's Complaint and Its Answer

2 How long, O LORD? I cry for help*
but you do not listen!
I cry out to you, "Violence!"
but you do not intervene.
3 Why do you let me see ruin;
why must I look at misery?
Destruction and violence are before me;
there is strife, and clamorous discord.
4 This is why the law is benumbed,
and judgment is never rendered:
Because the wicked circumvent the just;
this is why judgment comes forth perverted.

5 Look over the nations and see,*
and be utterly amazed!
For a work is being done in your days
that you would not have believed, were it told.[a]
6 For see, I am raising up Chaldea,
that bitter and unruly people,
That marches the breadth of the land
to take dwellings not his own.
7 Terrible and dreadful is he,
from himself derive his law and his majesty.
8 Swifter than leopards are his horses,
and keener than wolves at evening.*
His horses prance,
his horsemen come from afar:
They fly like the eagle hastening to devour;
9 each comes for the rapine,
Their combined onset is that of a stormwind
that heaps up captives like sand.
10 He scoffs at kings,
and princes are his laughingstock;
He laughs at any fortress,
heaps up a ramp, and conquers it.
11 Then he veers like the wind* and is gone—
this culprit who makes his own strength his god!

12 Are you not from eternity, O LORD,*
my holy God, immortal?
O LORD, you have marked him for judgment,

a Acts 13, 41.

*

1, 2–4: Traditionally, these verses have been taken as the prophet's complaint against the internal evils of Judah; the language used is that employed by Amos, Isaiah, and Jeremiah to condemn the social abuses of their day. In vv 5ff the Lord answers this complaint by indicating the Chaldean empire as his instrument for punishing his people for these sins.

1, 5: Look over the nations and see: after Nebuchadnezzar's defeat of Egypt in 605 B.C., there could be little doubt that it was the Chaldean ambition to dominate the entire Near East.

1, 8: Wolves at evening: the wolf is apparently thought of as more rabid and vicious in the evening when setting out for prey (Jer 5, 6; Zep 3, 3).

1, 11: Veers like the wind: the conquests of the ancient Near East were mainly raiding expeditions to collect tribute. As far as administration of conquered territories was concerned, both the Assyrians and Chaldeans were usually content to install friendly rulers and then depart. This culprit: though the Chaldeans were used by God as the agents of his punishment, this did not diminish their own guilt as ruthless marauders.

1, 12—2, 1: It is generally thought that this complaint is directed against the Chaldeans and their terrible destruction. But it may well be a continuation of Hb 1, 2–4, against the wicked Judahites who have merited God's punishment.

1, 12: O Rock: an ancient title celebrating the Lord's power; cf Ps 18, 32.

O Rock,* you have readied him for
punishment!
13 Too pure are your eyes to look upon evil,
and the sight of misery you cannot
endure.
Why, then, do you gaze on the faithless in
silence
while the wicked man devours
one more just than himself?
14 You have made man like the fish of the sea,
like creeping things without a ruler.
15 He* brings them all up with his hook,
he hauls them away with his net,
He gathers them in his seine;
and so he rejoices and exults.
16 Therefore he sacrifices to his net,*
and burns incense to his seine;
For thanks to them his portion is generous,
and his repast sumptuous.
17 Shall he, then, keep on brandishing his
sword
to slay peoples without mercy?

## CHAPTER 2

1 I will stand at my guard post,
and station myself upon the rampart,
And keep watch to see what he will say to
me,
and what answer he will give to my
complaint.[b]

2 Then the LORD answered me and said:
Write down the vision
Clearly upon the tablets,
so that one can read it readily.
3 For the vision still has its time,
presses on to fulfillment, and will not
disappoint;
If it delays, wait for it,
it will surely come, it will not be late.
4 The rash man has no integrity;[c]
but the just man, because of his faith,
shall live.*
Wealth, too, is treacherous:
the proud, unstable man—
5 He who opens wide his throat like the nether
world,
and is insatiable as death,
Who gathers to himself all the nations,
and rallies to himself all the peoples—
6 Shall not all these take up a taunt against
him,
satire and epigrams about him, to say:

Woe to him who stores up what is not his:
how long can it last!
he loads himself down with debts.
7 Shall not your creditors rise suddenly?
Shall not they who make you tremble
awake?
You shall become their spoil!
8 Because you despoiled many peoples
all the rest of the nations shall despoil
you;
Because of men's blood shed,
and violence done to the land,
to the city and to all who dwell in it.

9 Woe to him who pursues evil gain for his
household,
setting his nest on high
to escape the reach of misfortune!
10 You have devised shame for your
household,
cutting off many peoples, forfeiting your
own life:
11 For the stone in the wall shall cry out,*
and the beam in the woodwork shall
answer it!

12 Woe to him who builds a city by bloodshed,
and establishes a town by wickedness![d]
13 Is not this from the LORD of hosts:
peoples toil for the flames,*
and nations grow weary for nought![e]
14 But the earth shall be filled
with the knowledge of the LORD's glory
as water covers the sea.[f]
15 Woe to you who give your neighbors
a flood of your wrath to drink,
and make them drunk, till their nakedness
is seen!
16 You are filled with shame instead of glory;
drink, you too, and stagger!
On you shall revert the cup from the LORD's
right hand,
and utter shame on your glory.
17 For the violence done to Lebanon* shall
cover you,

b Ps 85, 9.
c Rom 1, 17; Gal 3, 11; Heb 10, 38.
d Ez 24, 9; Na 3, 1.
e Jer 51, 58.
f Is 11, 9.

1, 15: The he of this and the following verses, to whom is attributed such extensive evil and the destruction of many peoples, may be the wicked of Judah embodied in King Jehoiakim, ally of the powerful Pharaoh Neco of Egypt; the devastation wrought by Jehoiakim and Neco together is condemned.

1, 16: He sacrifices to his net: in v 15 the wicked ruler in question is represented as catching men in a net. This verse alludes to some rite involving the sacrificial veneration of the weapons of war.

2, 4: The just man, because of his faith, shall live: the faith which here enables the virtuous man to survive the impending doom is both a confident belief in God's justice, and patience in awaiting its execution. St. Paul quotes these words (Rom 1, 17; Gal 3, 11; Heb 10, 38) to confirm his teaching that man receives justification and supernatural life through faith in Christ.

2, 11f: The palaces, built at the expense of gross injustice (vv 6–10), call down vengeance on their builders. This is typical prophetic language for the condemnation of social crimes within Israel and Judah.

2, 13: Peoples toil for the flames: they build only to have fire consume their work, when they build contrary to God's will.

2, 17: The violence done to Lebanon: the spoliation of the cedar forests of Lebanon, used in lavish building projects by the great conquerors; cf Is 14, 8; 37, 24. The destruction of the beasts: the killing-off of the wild animals through excessive hunting by the same conquerors; cf Bar 3, 16.

and the destruction of the beasts shall
terrify you;
Because of men's blood shed,
and violence done to the land,
to the city and to all who dwell in it.
19 Woe to him who says to wood, "Awake!"
to dumb stone, "Arise!"
Can such a thing give oracles?
See, it is overlaid with gold and silver,
but there is no life breath in it.
18 Of what avail is the carved image,*
that its maker should carve it?
Or the molten image and lying oracle,
that its very maker should trust in it,
and make dumb idols?
20 But the LORD is in his holy temple;
silence before him, all the earth![g]

## CHAPTER 3

### Canticle

1 *Prayer of Habakkuk, the prophet. To a plaintive tune.**

2 O LORD, I have heard your renown,
and feared, O LORD, your work.
In the course of the years revive it,*
in the course of the years make it known;
in your wrath remember compassion!

3 *God comes from Teman,*
the Holy One from Mount Paran.
Covered are the heavens with his glory,
and with his praise the earth is filled.
4 His splendor spreads like the light;
rays shine forth from beside him,
where his power is concealed.
5 Before him goes pestilence,
and the plague follows in his steps.
6 He pauses to survey the earth;
his look makes the nations tremble.
The eternal mountains are shattered,
the age-old hills bow low
along his ancient ways.
7 I see the tents of Cushan collapse;
trembling are the pavilions of the land of
Midian.
8 Is your anger against the streams, O LORD?
Is your wrath against the streams,
your rage against the sea,
That you drive the steeds
of your victorious chariot?
9 Bared and ready is your bow,
filled with arrows is your quiver.
Into streams you split the earth;
10 at sight of you the mountains tremble.
A torrent of rain descends;
the ocean gives forth its roar.
The sun forgets to rise,
11 the moon remains in its shelter,
At the light of your flying arrows,
at the gleam of your flashing spear.[h]

12 In wrath you bestride the earth,
in fury you trample the nations.
13 You come forth to save your people,
to save your anointed one.*
You crush the heads of the wicked,
you lay bare their bases at the neck.[i]
14 You pierce with your shafts the heads of
their princes
whose boast would be of devouring
the wretched in their lair.
15 You tread the sea with your steeds
amid the churning of the deep waters.

16 I hear, and my body trembles;
at the sound, my lips quiver.
Decay invades my bones,
my legs tremble beneath me.
I await the day of distress
that will come upon the people who attack
us.
17 For though the fig tree blossom not
nor fruit be on the vines,
Though the yield of the olive fail
and the terraces produce no nourishment,
Though the flocks disappear from the fold
and there be no herd in the stalls,
18 Yet will I rejoice in the LORD[j]
and exult in my saving God.
19 GOD, my Lord, is my strength;
he makes my feet swift as those of hinds
and enables me to go upon the heights.

*For the leader; with stringed instruments.*

---

g Ps 11, 4.
h Jos 10, 12.
i Is 51, 9ff.
j 18f: Ps 18, 32f; Mi 7, 7.

---

2, 18–20: Idolatrous worship is here shown to be folly by contrasting man-made idols with the majesty of the one true God.

3, 1: A later liturgical rubric. So also the end of v 19.

3, 2: In the course of the years revive it: renew today your wondrous deeds of the past.

3, 3–15: Cf the theophanies in Dt 33, 2f; Jgs 5, 4f; Pss 18, 8–16; 68, 8f; 77, 17–21; 97, 1–5; Na 1, 3–6, etc. Conventional language is employed to describe the appearance of the Lord, as in Ex 19, 16–19.

3, 3: Teman: a region in Edom. Mount Paran: in the territory of Edom, or the northern part of the Sinaitic peninsula. The Lord is represented as coming from Sinai, where he had appeared to Moses and given Israel the covenant and the law.

3, 13: Your anointed one: the theocratic king, the head of God's people.

# The Book of
# ZEPHANIAH

*The title of the prophecy informs us that the ministry of Zephaniah took place during the reign of Josiah (640–609 B.C.). The protest against the worship of false gods, and the condemnation of the pro-Assyrian court ministers who served as regents during Josiah's minority, allow us to place the work in the first decade of the reign. Accordingly, the prophecy of Zephaniah comes rightly before that of Jeremiah, who was probably influenced by it in both language and ideas.*

*The age of Zephaniah was a time of religious degradation, when the old idolatries reappeared and men worshiped sun, moon, and stars. Rites completely alien to the pure monotheism taught by Moses flourished in Jerusalem. To the corrupt city Zephaniah announced the impending judgment, the day of the Lord. The prophecy may be divided into three sections, corresponding to the three chapters of the book:*

*The Day of the Lord: A day of doom. The last few verses of this oracle give the classic description of the Day of the Lord as an overwhelming disaster. The Christian hymn* Dies Irae *is based on this passage (1, 2–18).*

*The Day of the Lord: A day of judgment of the nations, traditional enemies of God's people (2, 1–15).*

*Reproach and Promise for Jerusalem: Despite Judah's infidelities, the Lord in his mercy will spare a holy remnant, which will finally enjoy peace. The prophecy closes with a hymn of joy sung by the remnant restored to Zion (3, 1–20).*

## CHAPTER 1

**1** The word of the LORD which came to Zephaniah, the son of Cushi, the son of Gedaliah, the son of Amariah, the son of Hezekiah, in the days of Josiah, the son of Amon, king of Judah.

### The Day of the Lord: A Day of Doom

**2** I will completely sweep away all things
from the face of the earth, says the LORD.
**3** I will sweep away man and beast,
I will sweep away the birds of the sky,
and the fishes of the sea.
I will overthrow the wicked;
I will destroy mankind
from the face of the earth, says the LORD.[a]
**4** I will stretch out my hand against Judah,
and against all the inhabitants of Jerusalem;
I will destroy from this place the last vestige of Baal,
the very names of his priests,
**5** And those who adore the host of heaven* on the roofs,
with those who adore the LORD
but swear by Milcom;[b]
**6** And those who have fallen away from the LORD,
and those who do not seek the LORD.
**7** Silence in the presence of the Lord GOD!
for near is the day of the LORD,
Yes, the LORD has prepared a slaughter feast,
he has consecrated his guests.*
**8** On the day of the LORD's slaughter feast
I will punish the princes, and the king's sons,
and all that dress in foreign apparel.
**9** I will punish, on that day,
all who leap over the threshold,*
Who fill the house of their master
with violence and deceit.
**10** On that day, says the LORD,
A cry will be heard from the Fish Gate,
a wail from the New Quarter,*
loud crashing from the hills.
**11** Wail, O inhabitants of the Mortar!
for all the merchants will be destroyed,
all who weigh out silver, done away with.

a Hos 4, 3.    b Jer 8, 2; 19, 13.

*

1, 5: The host of heaven: the stars, the worship of which was introduced into Judah by the Assyrians. Milcom: the god of the Ammonites; cf 1 Kgs 11, 5. 7. 33; 2 Kgs 23, 13.

1, 7: He has consecrated his guests: God has prepared those whom he has invited to share as soldiers in the booty, or as beast and bird scavengers of carrion, on the day of slaughter. Cf Jer 46, 10; Ez 39, 17.

1, 9: Leap over the threshold: the reference is to a superstitious custom of the pagans, witnessed to at least in regard to the worship of Dagon (1 Sm 5, 5).

1, 10f: The New Quarter . . . the Mortar: sections of Jerusalem (cf 2 Kgs 22, 14).

12 At that time I will explore Jerusalem with lamps;
I will punish the men who thicken on their lees,*
Who say in their hearts,
"Neither good nor evil can the LORD do."
13 Their wealth shall be given to pillage
and their houses to devastation;
They will build houses, but shall not dwell in them,
plant vineyards, but not drink their wine.[c]
14 Near is the great day of the LORD,
near and very swiftly coming;
Hark, the day of the LORD!
bitter, then, the warrior's cry.
15 A day of wrath is that day,[d]
a day of anguish and distress,
A day of destruction and desolation,
a day of darkness and gloom,
A day of thick black clouds,
16 a day of trumpet blasts and battle alarm
Against fortified cities,
against battlements on high.[e]
17 I will hem men in
till they walk like the blind,
because they have sinned against the LORD;
And their blood shall be poured out like dust,
and their brains like dung.
18 Neither their silver nor their gold
shall be able to save them
on the day of the LORD's wrath,
When in the fire of his jealousy
all the earth shall be consumed.
For he shall make an end, yes, a sudden end,
of all who live on the earth.[f]

## CHAPTER 2

### The Day of the Lord: A Day of Judgment

1 Gather, gather yourselves together,
O nation without shame!*
2 Before you are driven away,
like chaff that passes on;
Before there comes upon you
the blazing anger of the LORD;
Before there comes upon you
the day of the LORD's anger.
3 Seek the LORD, all you humble of the earth,
who have observed his law;
Seek justice, seek humility;
perhaps you may be sheltered
on the day of the LORD's anger.
4 For Gaza shall be forsaken,
and Ashkelon shall be a waste,
Ashdod they shall drive out at midday,
and Ekron* shall be uprooted.[g]
5 Woe to you who dwell by the seacoast,
to the Cretan folk!*
The word of the LORD is against you,
I will humble you, land of the Philistines,
and leave you to perish without an inhabitant!
6 The coastland of the Cretans shall become
fields for shepherds, and folds for flocks.
7 The coast shall belong
to the remnant of the house of Judah;
by the sea they shall pasture.
In the houses of Ashkelon at evening
they shall couch their flocks,
For the LORD their God shall visit them,
and bring about their restoration.

8 I have heard the revilings uttered by Moab,
and the insults of the Ammonites,
When they reviled my people
and made boasts against their territory.
9 Therefore, as I live, says the LORD of hosts,
the God of Israel,
Moab shall become like Sodom,
the land of Ammon like Gomorrah:
A field of nettles and a salt pit
and a waste forever.
The remnant of my people shall plunder them,
the survivors of my nation dispossess them.
10 Such shall be the requital of their pride,
because they reviled and boasted against
the people of the LORD of hosts.
11 The LORD shall inspire them with fear
when he makes all the gods of earth to waste away;
Then, each from its own place,
all the coastlands of the nations shall adore him.

12 You too, O Cushites,*
shall be slain by the sword of the LORD.
13 He will stretch out his hand against the north,
to destroy Assyria;
He will make Nineveh a waste,
dry as the desert.
14 In her midst shall settle in droves
all the wild life of the hollows;
The screech owl and the desert owl
shall roost in her columns;
Their call shall resound from the window,

c Am 5, 11.
d Jer 30, 7; Jl 2, 11; Am 5, 18.
e Am 2, 2.
f Zep 3, 8; Ez 7, 19.
g Am 1, 6ff, Zec 9, 5.
h Is 34, 11.

*

1, 12: The men who thicken on their lees: those who are overconfident because, like bottles of wine in which the sediment has settled to the bottom, they have remained at peace and undisturbed for a long time.

2, 1: Nation without shame: Judah.

2, 4: Gaza . . . Ashkelon . . . Ashdod . . . Ekron: four of the five cities of the Philistine confederation. The fifth city, Gath, is not mentioned, perhaps because it was already destroyed.

2, 5: Cretan folk: the Philistines, who came from Crete; see note on Dt 2, 23.

2, 12: Cushites: the Egyptians, at this time under a Cushite or Ethiopian dynasty.

the raven's croak from the doorway.[h]
15 Is this the exultant city*
that dwelt secure;
That told herself,
"There is no other than I!"
How has she become a waste,
a lair for wild beasts?
Whoever passes by her
hisses, and shakes his fist!

## CHAPTER 3

### Reproach and Promise for Jerusalem

1 Woe to the city, rebellious and polluted,
to the tyrannical city!
2 She hears no voice,
accepts no correction;
In the LORD she has not trusted,
to her God she has not drawn near.[i]
3 Her princes in her midst
are roaring lions;
Her judges are wolves of the night
that have had no bones to gnaw by
morning.[j]
4 Her prophets are insolent,
treacherous men;
Her priests profane what is holy,
and do violence to the law.[k]
5 The LORD within her is just,
who does no wrong;
Morning after morning he renders judgment
unfailingly, at dawn.

6 I have destroyed nations,
their battlements are laid waste;
I have made their streets deserted,
with no one passing through;
Their cities are devastated,
with no man dwelling in them.[l]
7 I said, "Surely now you will fear me,
you will accept correction";
She should not fail to see
all I have visited upon her.
Yet all the more eagerly have they done
all their corrupt deeds.
8 Therefore, wait for me, says the LORD,
against the day when I arise as accuser;
For it is my decision to gather together the
nations,
to assemble the kingdoms,
In order to pour out upon them my wrath,
all my blazing anger;
For in the fire of my jealousy
shall all the earth be consumed.[m]
9 For then I will change and purify
the lips of the peoples,
That they all may call upon the name of the
LORD,
to serve him with one accord;
10 From beyond the rivers of Ethiopia
and as far as the recesses of the North,
they shall bring me offerings.

11 On that day
You need not be ashamed
of all your deeds,
your rebellious actions against me;
For then will I remove from your midst
the proud braggarts,
And you shall no longer exalt yourself
on my holy mountain.
12 But I will leave as a remnant in your midst
a people humble and lowly,
Who shall take refuge in the name of the
LORD:[n]
13 the remnant of Israel.
They shall do no wrong
and speak no lies;
Nor shall there be found in their mouths
a deceitful tongue;
They shall pasture and couch their flocks
with none to disturb them.[o]

14 Shout for joy, O daughter Zion!
sing joyfully, O Israel!
Be glad and exult with all your heart,
O daughter Jerusalem![p]
15 The LORD has removed the judgment against
you,
he has turned away your enemies;
The King of Israel, the LORD, is in your
midst,
you have no further misfortune to fear.
16 On that day, it shall be said to Jerusalem:
Fear not, O Zion, be not discouraged![q]
17 The LORD, your God, is in your midst,
a mighty savior;
He will rejoice over you with gladness,
and renew you in his love,
He will sing joyfully because of you,
18 as one sings at festivals.
I will remove disaster from among you,
so that none may recount your disgrace.
19 Yes, at that time I will deal
with all who oppress you:
I will save the lame,
and assemble the outcasts;
I will give them praise and renown
in all the earth, when I bring about their
restoration.[r]
20 At that time I will bring you home,
and at that time I will gather you;
For I will give you renown and praise,
among all the peoples of the earth,
When I bring about your restoration
before your very eyes, says the LORD.

i Jer 2, 30; 7, 28.
j Ez 22, 27; Mi 3, 11.
k Jer 23, 32.
l Jer 2, 15.
m Zep 1, 18.
n Hos 14, 4.
o Mi 4, 4.
p Zec 9, 9.
q Mt 14, 27.
r Mi 4, 6.

*

2, 15: The exultant city: Nineveh.

# The Book of

# HAGGAI

*Postexilic prophecy begins with Haggai, who received the word of the Lord in the second year of Darius (520 B.C.). The Jews who returned from the Exile in Babylonia had encountered formidable obstacles in their efforts to re-establish Jewish life in Judah. The Samaritans had succeeded in blocking the rebuilding of the temple; but after Darius acceded to the throne (522), permission was given to resume the work. At this critical moment, when defeatism and a certain lethargy had overtaken his repatriated countrymen, Haggai came forward with his exhortations to them to complete the great task. The first oracle, an appeal to the Jews, is contained in chapter 1. To this appeal Haggai added a short oracle of encouragement (2, 1–9) for the sake of those who gloomily contrasted the former magnificence of Solomon's temple with the second temple: the Lord would be present in this new abode, and its glory, enhanced by the offerings of the Gentiles, would surpass the ancient splendor.*

*The prophecy may be divided into five oracles:*

*The call to rebuild the temple. The economic distress so apparent in Judah is due to the Jews' neglect of the Lord while they provide for their own needs (1, 1–15).*

*The future glory of the new temple, surpassing that of the old (2, 1–9).*

*Unworthiness of a people, who may be the Samaritans, to offer sacrifice at the newly restored altar. This oracle is cast in the literary form of a* torah, *an instruction given the people by a priest (2, 10–14).*

*A promise of immediate blessings, which follows upon the undertaking (chapter 1) to rebuild the temple (2, 15–19).*

*A pledge to Zerubbabel, descendant of David, repository of the Messianic hopes (2, 20–23).*

## CHAPTER 1

**Exhortation To Rebuild the Temple of the Lord.** 1 On the first day of the sixth month
in the second year* of King Darius, the word of
the LORD came through the prophet Haggai to
the governor of Judah, Zerubbabel, son of Shealtiel, and to the high priest Joshua, son of
Jehozadak:[a]
2 Thus says the LORD of hosts: This people
says: "Not now has the time come to rebuild the
house of the LORD." 3 (Then this word of the
LORD came through Haggai, the prophet:) 4 Is
it time for you to dwell in your own paneled
houses,[b] while this house lies in ruins?*

5 Now thus says the LORD of hosts:
Consider your ways!
6 You have sown much, but have brought in
little;
you have eaten, but have not been
satisfied;
You have drunk, but have not been
exhilarated;
have clothed yourselves, but not been
warmed;
And he who earned wages
earned them for a bag with holes in it.[c]

7 Thus says the LORD of hosts:
Consider your ways!
8 Go up into the hill country;
bring timber, and build the house
That I may take pleasure in it
and receive my glory, says the LORD.
9 You expected much, but it came to little;
and what you brought home, I blew away.
For what cause? says the LORD of hosts.
Because my house lies in ruins,
while each of you hurries to his own
house.[d]
10 Therefore the heavens withheld from you
their dew,
and the earth her crops.[e]
11 And I called for a drought
upon the land and upon the mountains;
Upon the grain, and upon the wine, and
upon the oil,

---

a Ezr 4, 24; 5, 1; 6, 14.
b 2 Sm 7, 2.
c Dt 28, 38ff; Mi 6, 15.
d 2 Kgs 25, 9.
e Gn 27, 28; Am 4, 6-9.

---

*

1, 1: The sixth month in the second year: August/September in 520 B.C.

1, 4: The luxury of the homes of the wealthy with their paneled houses contrasts sadly with the ruined state of the Lord's house.

and upon all that the ground brings forth;
Upon men and upon beasts,
and upon all that is produced by hand.

12 Then Zerubbabel, son of Shealtiel, and
the high priest Joshua, son of Jehozadak, and all
the remnant of the people* listened to the voice
of the LORD, their God, and to the words of the
prophet Haggai, because the LORD, their God,
had sent him, and the people feared because of
the LORD. 13 And the LORD's messenger, Haggai, proclaimed to the people as the message of
the LORD: I am with you, says the LORD.

14 Then the LORD stirred up the spirit of the
governor of Judah, Zerubbabel, son of Shealtiel, and the spirit of the high priest Joshua, son
of Jehozadak, and the spirit of all the remnant
of the people, so that they came and set to work
on the house of the LORD of hosts, their God,
15 on the twenty-fourth day of the sixth month.

## CHAPTER 2

**Future Glory of the New Temple.** In the
second year of King Darius, 1 on the twenty-
first day of the seventh month, the word of the
LORD came through the prophet Haggai: 2 Tell
this to the governor of Judah, Zerubbabel, son
of Shealtiel, and to the high priest Joshua, son
of Jehozadak, and to the remnant of the people:

3 Who is left among you
that saw this house in its former glory?
And how do you see it now?
Does it not seem like nothing in your eyes?
4 But now take courage, Zerubbabel, says the LORD,
and take courage, Joshua, high priest, son of Jehozadak,
And take courage, all you people of the land,
says the LORD, and work!
For I am with you, says the LORD of hosts.[f]
5 This is the pact that I made with you
when you came out of Egypt,
And my spirit continues in your midst;
do not fear![g]

6 For thus says the LORD of hosts:*
One moment yet, a little while,
and I will shake the heavens and the earth,
the sea and the dry land.[h]
7 I will shake all the nations,
and the treasures of all the nations will come in,
And I will fill this house with glory,
says the LORD of hosts.[i]
8 Mine is the silver and mine the gold,
says the LORD of hosts.
9 Greater will be the future glory of this house
than the former, says the LORD of hosts;
And in this place I will give peace,
says the LORD of hosts![j]

### Offerings of the Unclean Rejected.

10 On the twenty-fourth day of the ninth
month, in the second year of King Darius, the
word of the LORD came to the prophet Haggai:
11 Thus says the LORD of hosts: Ask the priests
for a decision:[k] 12 If a man carries sanctified
flesh in the fold of his garment and the fold
touches bread, or pottage, or wine, or oil, or any
other food, do they become sanctified? "No,"
the priests answered.* 13 Then Haggai said: If
a person unclean from contact with a corpse
touches any of these, do they become unclean?
The priests answered, "They become unclean."[l] 14 Then Haggai continued:

So is this people, and so is this nation
in my sight, says the LORD:
And so are all the works of their hands;
and what they offer there is unclean.

### Promise of Immediate Blessings.*

15 But now, consider from this day forward.
Before there was a stone laid upon a stone in the
temple of the LORD, 16 how did you fare?

When one went to a heap of grain for twenty measures,
it would yield but ten;
When another went to the vat to draw fifty measures,
there would be but twenty.[m]
17 I struck you in all the works of your hands
with blight, searing wind, and hail,
yet you did not return to me, says the LORD.

18 [Consider from this day forward: from the
twenty-fourth day of the ninth month.* From
the day on which the temple of the LORD was
founded, consider!]

19 Indeed, the seed has not sprouted,

f Zec 8, 9.
g Ex 29, 45; Lv 26, 45.
h Heb 12, 26.
i Gn 49, 10; Is 60, 5. 9. 11; Mal 3, 1; Rv 21, 26.
j Is 2, 2ff; Zec 6, 13.
k Dt 17, 8-13; Zec 7, 3.
l Nm 19, 11. 13, 22.
m Is 5, 10.

*

1, 12: The remnant of the people: a technical term in Haggai and Zechariah for the returned exiles.

2, 6–9: From the later period of Ezekiel's preaching onward, the temple became, as here, one of the dominant messianic themes. Greater will be the future glory of this house than the former: because Christ will enter it.

2, 12ff: According to the ritual concepts of the Jews, uncleanness was more contagious than sacredness. Inasmuch as the people were unclean, their offerings became unclean (Nm 19, 22).

2, 15–19: This prophecy is intimately linked with chapter 1, and should be read with it.

2, 18: The ninth month: the ordinal ninth has been copied incorrectly from Hg 2, 10. This note clearly concerns the twenty-fourth day of the sixth month, on which the temple of the Lord was founded (Hg 1, 15).

nor have the vine, the fig, the
pomegranate
and the olive tree yet borne.
From this day, I will bless!

**Pledge to Zerubbabel.** 20 The message
of the LORD came a second time to Haggai on
the twenty-fourth day of the month:* 21 Tell
this to Zerubbabel, the governor of Judah:

I will shake the heavens and the earth;
22 I will overthrow the thrones of kingdoms,
destroy the power of the kingdoms of the
nations.
I will overthrow the chariots and their riders,
and the riders with their horses
shall go down by one another's sword.[n]
23 On that day, says the LORD of hosts,[o]
I will take you, Zerubbabel,
son of Shealtiel, my servant, says the
LORD,
And I will set you as a signet ring;
for I have chosen you, says the LORD of
hosts.*

n Ez 38, 21; Dn 2, 44; Zec 14, 13; Lk 1, 52.
o Song 8, 6; Sir 49, 11; Is 42, 1; 44, 1f.

2, 20: The month: probably again the sixth month, as in Hg 1, 15 and 2, 18; see note on the latter.

2, 23: This promise to Zerubbabel, reversing the punishment of his grandfather (Jer 22, 24), is a continuation of the messianic hope; cf Zec 6, 11f.

# The Book of ZECHARIAH

*Zechariah's initial prophecy is dated to 520 B.C., the same year as that in which Haggai received the prophetic call. The first eight chapters of the Book of Zechariah contain oracles which certainly belong to him while the last six (sometimes called ''Deutero-Zechariah'') represent the work of one or more unknown authors. In the prophecies proper to Zechariah eight symbolic visions are recorded, all meant to promote the work of rebuilding the temple and to encourage the returned exiles, especially their leaders, Joshua and Zerubbabel. In the final chapter of this first division Zechariah portrays the messianic future under the figure of a prosperous land to which the nations come in pilgrimage, eager to follow the God of Israel.*

*The second part of Zechariah is divided into two sections, each with its own introductory title. The first (9—11) consists of oracles whose historical background, date and authorship are extremely difficult to determine. With 9, 9 begins the messianic vision of the coming of the Prince of Peace. The verses describing the triumphant appearance of the humble king are taken up by the four Evangelists to describe the entry of Christ into Jerusalem on Palm Sunday. Chapter 12 is introduced by an oracle proclaiming the victory of God's people over the heathen. The prophecy closes by describing, in apocalyptic imagery, the final assault of the enemy on Jerusalem, after which the messianic age begins.*

## CHAPTER 1

**Necessity of Conversion.** **1** In the second year of Darius, in the eighth month,* the
word of the LORD came to the prophet Zechariah, son of Berechiah, son of Iddo:[a] **2** The LORD
was indeed angry with your fathers. . . . **3** and
say to them: Thus says the LORD of hosts: Return to me, says the LORD of hosts, and I will
return to you, says the LORD of hosts. **4** Be not
like your fathers whom the former prophets
warned: Thus says the LORD of hosts: Turn from
your evil ways and from your wicked deeds. But
they would not listen or pay attention to me,
says the LORD.[b] **5** Your fathers, where are
they? And the prophets, can they live forever?
**6** But my words and my decrees, which I entrusted to my servants the prophets, did not
these overtake your fathers? Then they repented
and admitted: ''The LORD of hosts has treated
us according to our ways and deeds, just as he
had determined he would.''[c]

**The Four Horsemen.** **7** In the second year
of Darius, on the twenty-fourth day of Shebat,
the eleventh month,* the word of the LORD
came to the prophet Zechariah, son of Berechiah, son of Iddo, in the following way: **8** I
had a vision during the night. There appeared
the driver of a red horse,* standing among myrtle trees in a shady place, and behind him were
red, sorrel, and white horses.[d] **9** Then I asked,
''What are these, my lord?''; and the angel who
spoke with me answered me, ''I will show you
what these are.'' **10** The man who was standing
among the myrtle trees spoke up and said,
''These are they whom the LORD has sent to
patrol the earth.''[e] **11** And they answered the
angel of the LORD who was standing among the
myrtle trees and said, ''We have patrolled the
earth; see, the whole earth is tranquil and at
rest!''

**12** [f]Then the angel of the Lord spoke out and
said, ''O LORD of hosts, how long will you be
without mercy for Jerusalem and the cities of
Judah that have felt your anger these seventy
years?''* **13** To the angel who spoke with me,
the LORD replied with comforting words.[g]

**14** And the angel who spoke with me said to
me, Proclaim: Thus says the LORD of hosts: I am
deeply moved for the sake of Jerusalem and

a Ezr 4, 24; 5, 1; 6, 14.
b Jer 25, 5; 35, 15; Mal 3, 7.
c Lam 2, 17; Lv 26, 14ff; Dt 28, 15.
d Rv 6, 4.
e Zec 6, 7.
f Zec 7, 5; Jer 25, 11; Dn 9, 2.
g Jer 29, 10.
h Zec 8, 2; Jl 2, 18.

1, 1: The second year ... eighth month: October/November, 520 B.C.

1, 7: The second year ... eleventh month: January/February, 519 B.C.

1, 8–11: The driver of a red horse: apparently distinct from the man, or angel of the Lord . . . standing among the myrtle trees, who spoke with the prophet. The four horsemen are sent by God to the four corners of the earth (Zec 2, 10), to see if the whole earth is at peace.

1, 12: These seventy years: see note on Jer 25, 1–14.

Zion,[h] **15** and I am exceedingly angry with the complacent nations;* whereas I was but a little angry, they added to the harm.[i] **16** Therefore, says the LORD: I will turn to Jerusalem in mercy; my house shall be built in it, says the LORD of hosts, and a measuring line* shall be stretched over Jerusalem.[j] **17** Proclaim further: Thus says the LORD of hosts: My cities shall again overflow with prosperity; the LORD will again comfort Zion, and again choose Jerusalem.[k]

## CHAPTER 2

**Four Horns and Four Blacksmiths.** **1** I raised my eyes and looked: there were four horns.* **2** Then I asked the angel who spoke with me what these were. He answered me, "These are the horns that scattered Judah and Israel and Jerusalem."

**3** Then the LORD showed me four blacksmiths. And I asked, "What are these coming to do?" **4** And he said, "Here are the horns that scattered Judah, so that no man raised his head any more; but these have come to terrify them: to cast down the horns of the nations that raised their horns to scatter the land of Judah."

**The New Jerusalem.** **5** Again I raised my eyes and looked: there was a man with a measuring line in his hand.[l] **6** "Where are you going?" I asked. "To measure Jerusalem," he answered; "to see how great is its width and how great its length."[m]

**7** Then the angel who spoke with me advanced, and another angel came out to meet him **8** and said to him, "Run, tell this to that young man:* People will live in Jerusalem as though in open country, because of the multitude of men and beasts in her midst.[n] **9** But I will be for her an encircling wall of fire, says the LORD, and I will be the glory in her midst."

**10** Up, up! Flee from the land of the north,* says the LORD; for I scatter you to the four winds of heaven, says the LORD. **11** Up, escape to Zion! you who dwell in daughter Babylon. **12** For thus said the LORD of hosts (after he had already sent me) concerning the nations that have plundered you: Whoever touches you touches the apple of my eye.[o] **13** See, I wave my hand over them; they become plunder for their slaves. Thus you shall know that the LORD of hosts has sent me.

**14** Sing and rejoice, O daughter Zion! See, I am coming to dwell among you, says the LORD.[p] **15** Many nations shall join themselves to the LORD on that day, and they shall be his people, and he will dwell among you, and you shall know that the LORD of hosts has sent me to you. **16** The LORD will possess Judah as his portion in the holy land, and he will again choose Jerusalem. **17** Silence, all mankind, in the presence of the LORD! for he stirs forth from his holy dwelling.

## CHAPTER 3

**Joshua the High Priest.** **1** Then he showed me Joshua the high priest standing before the angel of the LORD, while Satan stood at his right hand to accuse him.[q] **2** And the angel of the LORD said to Satan, "May the LORD rebuke you, Satan; may the LORD who has chosen Jerusalem rebuke you! Is not this man a brand snatched from the fire?"[r]

**3** Now Joshua was standing before the angel, clad in filthy garments.* **4** He spoke and said to those who were standing before him, "Take off his filthy garments, and clothe him in festal garments."[s] **5** He also said, "Put a clean miter on his head." And they put a clean miter on his head and clothed him with the garments. Then the angel of the LORD, standing, said, "See, I have taken away your guilt."

**6** The angel of the LORD then gave Joshua this assurance: **7** "Thus says the LORD of hosts: If you walk in my ways and heed my charge, you shall judge my house and keep my courts, and I will give you access among these standing here. **8** Listen, O Joshua, high priest! You and your associates who sit before you are men of good omen.* Yes, I will bring my servant the Shoot.[t] **9** Look at the stone that I have placed

i Is 47, 6; Ob 10-14.
j Zec 8, 3; Ezr 6, 14.
k Is 51, 3.
l Rv 11, 1.
m Dt 28, 64.
n Ez 36, 11.
o Dt 32, 10; Ps 17, 8.
p Ez 37, 26.
q Hg 1, 1; 1 Chr 21, 1.
r Rom 8, 33; Jude 9.
s Lk 15, 22.
t Is 4, 2; 11, 1; Jer 23, 5; 33, 15.
u Zec 4, 10.

*

1, 15: The complacent nations: the neighbors of Judah, especially Edom, which enjoyed their present prosperity and security at Judah's expense.

1, 16: Measuring line: not for devastation, as in Is 34, 11, but for reconstruction.

2, 1–4: Four horns: symbolic of the hostile forces which, from the four corners of the earth, invaded and devastated the land of Judah. Four blacksmiths: the powers used by God to destroy these enemies of his people.

2, 8: That young man: the angel or man with a measuring line of v 5.

2, 10: The land of the north: Babylonia (v 11).

3, 3: Filthy garments: symbolic of mourning for the dead, or of national catastrophe, and implying acknowledgment of guilt (v 5).

3, 8: Men of good omen: the restoration of the priesthood is a sign of the coming of the messianic times. My servant the Shoot: identified, in the earliest form of Zec 6, 11f as the prophet composed it, with Zerubbabel, direct descendant of King David and rebuilder of the temple; and, as such, a type of the Messiah; cf Jer 23, 5.

3, 9: One stone with seven facets: apparently the same as the select stone of Zec 4, 10, which seems to be a precious gem. The seven facets are explained in Zec 4, 10 as signifying the Lord's vigilance over the world. I will engrave its inscription: the same Hebrew verb for engrave is used in Ex 28, 9. 11 in regard to the inscriptions on the twelve precious stones of the priestly breastpiece.

before Joshua, one stone with seven facets.* I
will engrave its inscription, says the LORD of
hosts, and I will take away the guilt of the land
in one day.[u] **10** On that day, says the LORD of
hosts, you will invite one another under your
vines and fig trees."[v]

## CHAPTER 4

**4** Then I said to the angel who spoke with
me, "What are these things, my lord?" **5** And
the angel who spoke with me replied, "Do you
not know what these things are?" "No, my
lord," I answered. **6** Then he said to me, "This
is the LORD's message to Zerubbabel: Not by an
army, nor by might, but by my spirit, says the
LORD of hosts. **7** What are you, O great mountain?* Before Zerubbabel you are but a plain.
He shall bring out the capstone amid exclama-
tions of 'Hail, Hail' to it."[w]
**8** This word of the LORD then came to me:
**9** The hands of Zerubbabel have laid the foundations of this house,[x] and his hands shall finish
it; then you shall know that the LORD of hosts
has sent me to you. **10** [y]For even they who were
scornful on that day of small beginnings shall
rejoice to see the select stone in the hands of
Zerubbabel. These seven facets are the eyes of
the LORD that range over the whole earth.

**The Lampstand.** **1** Then the angel who
spoke with me returned and awakened me, like
a man awakened from his sleep. **2** "What do
you see?" he asked me. "I see a lampstand all
of gold, with a bowl at the top," I replied; "on
it are seven lamps with their tubes,[z] **3** and beside it are two olive trees, one on the right and
the other on the left."[a] **11** I then asked him,
"What are these two olive trees at each side of
the lampstand?" **12** And again I asked, "What
are the two olive tufts which freely pour out
fresh oil through the two golden channels?"
**13** "Do you not know what these are?" he said
to me. "No, my lord," I answered him. **14** He
said, "These are the two anointed* who stand
by the LORD of the whole earth."

## CHAPTER 5

**The Flying Scroll.*** **1** Then I raised my
eyes again and saw a scroll flying.[b] **2** "What
do you see?" he asked me. I answered, "I see
a scroll flying; it is twenty cubits long and ten
cubits wide." **3** Then he said to me: "This is
the curse which is to go forth over the whole
earth; in accordance with it shall every thief be
swept away, and in accordance with it shall
every perjurer be expelled from here. **4** I will
send it forth, says the LORD of hosts, and it shall
come into the house of the thief, or into the
house of him who perjures himself with my
name; it shall lodge within his house, consuming it, timber and stones."[c]

**The Flying Bushel.*** **5** Then the angel who
spoke with me came forward and said to me,
"Raise your eyes and see what this is that comes
forth." **6** "What is it?" I asked. And he answered, "This is a bushel container coming.
This is their guilt in all the land." **7** Then a
leaden cover was lifted, and there was a woman
sitting inside the bushel. **8** "This is Wickedness," he said; and he thrust her inside the
bushel, pushing the leaden cover into the opening. **9** Then I raised my eyes and saw two wom-
en coming forth with a wind ruffling their
wings, for they had wings like the wings of a
stork. As they lifted up the bushel into the air,
**10** I said to the angel who spoke with me,
"Where are they taking the bushel?" **11** He
replied, "To build a temple for it in the land of
Shinar; when the temple is ready, they will deposit it there in its place."[d]

## CHAPTER 6

**Four Chariots.*** **1** Again I raised my eyes
and saw four chariots coming out from between
two mountains; and the mountains were of
bronze. **2** The first chariot had red horses, the
second chariot black horses,[e] **3** the third chariot
white horses, and the fourth chariot spotted
horses—all of them strong horses. **4** I asked the
angel who spoke with me, "What are these, my

---

v 1 Kgs 4, 25.
w Ezr 3, 11f; Ps 118, 22.
x Ezr 6, 14ff.
y Zec 3, 9.
z Rv 1, 12.
a Rv 11, 4.
b Ez 2, 9.
c Lv 19, 12.
d Gn 11, 2ff.
e Zec 1, 8; Rv 6, 4.

---

4, 7: Great mountain: figure of the obstacles confronting Zerubbabel in building the temple. A plain: figure of the ease with which he will overcome these obstacles.

4, 1ff. 11–14: The two anointed: literally, "the two sons of oil," Joshua, the anointed high priest, and Zerubbabel, the anointed prince. Just as the two olive trees in this imagery supply the sacred seven-branched lampstand (Ex 25, 31–40) with oil (v 12), so these two men, in ministering to the community, stand by (serve) the Lord.

5, 1–4: The enormous scroll, thirty feet by fifteen (the dimensions in length and breadth of the portico of Solomon's temple, 1 Kgs 6, 3), contains a list of maledictions on sinners, similar to that in Dt 27, 15–26. The thief and the perjurer represent all sinners, who are expelled from the holy community.

5, 5–11: The woman sealed in the bushel container is a figure of the general corruption of the people of Judah. She is removed from the Holy Land and transported to Shinar, that is, Babylonia, where a dwelling is being prepared for her; that is a symbol of the reign of Wickedness in pagan lands, contrasted with the reign of holiness in the Lord's dwelling on Mount Zion.

6, 1–8: The four chariots represent the angelic hosts sent by the Lord to the four ends of the earth. The chariot with the black horses brings the spirit, i.e., anger of the Lord against the land of the north, Babylonia.

lord?" **5** The angel said to me in reply, "These are the four winds of the heavens, which are coming forth after being reviewed by the LORD of all the earth."[f] **6** The chariot with the black horses was turning toward the land of the north, the red and the white horses went after them, and the spotted ones went toward the land of the south. **7** As these strong horses emerged, eager to set about patrolling the earth, he said, "Go, patrol the earth!" Then, as they patrolled the earth, **8** he called out to me and said, "See, they that go forth to the land of the north will make my spirit rest in the land of the north."

**The Coronation.** **9** This word of the LORD then came to me: **10** Take from the returned captives Heldai, Tobijah, Jedaiah; and go the same day to the house of Josiah, son of Zephaniah (these had come from Babylon). **11** Silver and gold you shall take, and make a crown; place it on the head of [Joshua, son of Jehozadak, the high priest] Zerubbabel.* **12** And say to him: Thus says the LORD of hosts: Here is a man whose name is Shoot, and where he is he shall sprout, and he shall build the temple of the LORD.[g] **13** Yes, he shall build the temple of the LORD, and taking up the royal insignia, he shall sit as ruler upon his throne. The priest shall be at his right hand, and between the two of them there shall be friendly understanding.[h] **14** The crown itself shall be a memorial offering in the temple of the LORD in favor of Heldai, Tobijah, Jedaiah, and the son of Zephaniah. **15** And they who are from afar shall come and build the temple of the LORD, and you shall know that the LORD of hosts has sent me to you.[i] And if you heed carefully the voice of the LORD your God. . . .

## CHAPTER 7

**True Fasting.** **1** In the fourth year of Darius the king [the word of the LORD came to Zechariah], on the fourth day of Chislev, the ninth month,* **2** Bethelsarezer sent Regemmelech and his men to implore favor of the LORD **3** and to ask the priests of the house of the LORD of hosts, and the prophets, "Must I mourn and abstain in the fifth month as I have been doing these many years?"[j] **4** Thereupon this word of the LORD of hosts came to me: **5** Say to all the people of the land and to the priests: When you fasted and mourned in the fifth and in the seventh month these seventy years, was it really for me that you fasted?[k] **6** And when you were eating and drinking, was it not for yourselves that you ate, and for yourselves that you drank? **7** Were not these the words which the LORD spoke through the former prophets, when Jerusalem and the surrounding cities were inhabited and at peace, when the Negeb and the foothills were inhabited?[l] **8** [This word of the LORD came to Zechariah: **9** Thus says the LORD of hosts:] Render true judgment, and show kindness and compassion toward each other.[m] **10** Do not oppress the widow or the orphan, the alien or the poor; do not plot evil against one another in your hearts.[n] **11** But they refused to listen; they stubbornly turned their backs and stopped their ears so as not to hear.[o] **12** And they made their hearts diamondhard so as not to hear the teaching and the message that the LORD of hosts had sent by his spirit through the former prophets.[p] **13** Then the LORD of hosts in his great anger said that, as they had not listened when he called, so he would not listen when they called,[q] **14** but would scatter them with a whirlwind among all the nations that they did not know. Thus the land was left desolate after them with no one traveling to and fro; they made the pleasant land into a desert.[r]

## CHAPTER 8

**In the Days of the Messiah.** **1** This word of the LORD of hosts came: Thus says the LORD of hosts:

**2** I am intensely jealous for Zion,
stirred to jealous wrath for her.[s]
**3** Thus says the LORD:
I will return to Zion,
and I will dwell within Jerusalem;
Jerusalem shall be called the faithful city,
and the mountain of the LORD of hosts,
the holy mountain.[t]

**4** Thus says the LORD of hosts: Old men and old women, each with staff in hand because of old age, shall again sit in the streets of Jerusalem. **5** The city shall be filled with boys and girls playing in her streets. **6** Thus says the LORD of hosts: Even if this should seem impossible in the eyes of the remnant of this people, shall it in those days be impossible in my eyes also, says the LORD of hosts? **7** Thus says the

f Ps 104, 4.
g Zec 3, 8; Eph 2, 20; Heb 3, 3.
h Ps 110, 4; Heb 3, 1.
i Eph 2, 19f.
j Zec 8, 19.
k Is 58, 5; Rom 14, 6.
l Jer 17, 26.
m Is 58, 6.
n Ex 22, 21-24; Dt 24, 17; Is 1, 17; Jer 5, 28.
o Neh 9, 29; Hos 4, 16.
p Ez 11, 19; 36, 26; Neh 9, 29.
q Is 1, 15; Mi 3, 4.
r Dt 4, 27.
s Na 1, 2.
t Is 2, 2; Jer 31, 23.
u Is 11, 11; Jer 30, 18.

*

6, 11: Make a crown; place it on the head of [Joshua, son of Jehozadak, the high priest] Zerubbabel: according to the current Hebrew text, Joshua the high priest is to be crowned. However, since the crown is a sign of royalty, the original text must have had the name of Zerubbabel here, not that of Joshua. In Zec 3, 8 Joshua is a different man from the one called the Shoot, and in v 12 it is upon the Shoot that the crown is to be placed.

7, 1: The fourth year of Darius . . . the fourth day of Chislev, the ninth month: November, 518 B.C.

LORD of hosts: Lo, I will rescue my people from the land of the rising sun, and from the land of the setting sun.[u] **8** I will bring them back to dwell within Jerusalem. They shall be my people, and I will be their God, with faithfulness and justice.[v]

**9** Thus says the LORD of hosts: Let your hands be strong, you who in these days hear these words spoken by the prophets on the day when the foundation of the house of the LORD of hosts was laid for the building of the temple.[w] **10** For before those days there were no wages for men, or hire for beasts; those who came and went had no security from the enemy, for I set every man against his neighbor. **11** But now I will not deal with the remnant of this people as in former days, says the LORD of hosts, **12** for it is the seedtime of peace: the vine shall yield its fruit, the land shall bear its crops, and the heavens shall give their dew; all these things I will have the remnant of the people possess. **13** Just as you were a curse among the nations, O house of Judah and house of Israel, so will I save you that you may be a blessing; do not fear, but let your hands be strong.[x]

**14** Thus says the LORD of hosts: As I determined to harm you when your fathers provoked me to wrath, says the LORD of hosts, and I did not relent,[y] **15** so again in these days I have determined to favor Jerusalem and the house of Judah; do not fear! **16** These then are the things you should do: Speak the truth to one another; let there be honesty and peace in the judgments at your gates,[z] **17** and let none of you plot evil against another in his heart, nor love a false oath. For all these things I hate, says the LORD.[a]

**18** This word of the LORD of hosts came to me: **19** Thus says the LORD of hosts: The fast days of the fourth, the fifth, the seventh, and the tenth months shall become occasions of joy and gladness, cheerful festivals for the house of Judah; only love faithfulness and peace.* **20** Thus says the LORD of hosts: There shall yet come peoples, the inhabitants of many cities; **21** and the inhabitants of one city shall approach those of another, and say, "Come! let us go to implore the favor of the LORD"; and, "I too will go to seek the LORD."[b] **22** Many peoples and strong nations shall come to seek the LORD of hosts in Jerusalem and to implore the favor of the LORD.[c] **23** Thus says the LORD of hosts: In those days ten men of every nationality, speaking different tongues, shall take hold, yes, take hold of every Jew by the edge of his garment and say, "Let us go with you, for we have heard that God is with you."[d]

## CHAPTER 9

### Invasion by the Lord*

1 An oracle:

The word of the LORD is upon the land of Hadrach,
and Damascus is its resting place,
For the cities of Aram are the LORD's,
as are all the tribes of Israel,
2 Hamath also, on its border,
Tyre, too, and Sidon, however wise they be.[e]
3 Tyre built herself a stronghold,
and heaped up silver like dust,
and gold like the mire of the streets.
4 Lo, the LORD will strip her of her possessions,
and smite her power on the sea,
and she shall be devoured by fire.[f]
5 Ashkelon shall see it and be afraid;
Gaza also: she shall be in great anguish;
Ekron, too, for her hope shall come to nought.
The king shall disappear from Gaza,
and Ashkelon shall not be inhabited,
6 and the baseborn* shall occupy Ashdod.
I will destroy the pride of the Philistine[g]
7 and take from his mouth his bloody meat,
and his abominations from between his teeth:
He also shall become a remnant* for our God,
and shall be like a family in Judah,
and Ekron shall be like the Jebusites.
8 I will encamp by my house* as a guard
that none may pass to and fro;
No oppressor shall pass over them again,
for now I have regard for their affliction.

### Restoration under the Messiah

9 Rejoice heartily, O daughter Zion,[h]

v Jer 4, 2.
w Ezr 5, 1; Hg 2, 18.
x Is 19, 24; Jer 42, 18; Hg 2, 19; Zep 3, 20.
y Jer 31, 28.
z Zec 7, 9.
a Zec 7, 10.
b Is 2, 3.
c Is 60, 3.
d Is 66, 23.
e Jer 49, 23.
f Is 23, 1-18; Ez 26, 1—28, 26.
g Am 1, 8.
h Is 62, 11; Jer 23, 5; Mt 21, 5; Jn 12, 15.

*

8, 19: The fast day of the fourth month recalled the fall of Jerusalem in June. 587 B.C. (2 Kgs 25, 3f); that of the fifth month, the burning of the temple by Nebuzaradan in July of the same year (2 Kgs 25, 8f); that of the seventh month, the murder of Gedaliah in September of the same year (Jer 41, 1f); that of the tenth month, the beginning of the final siege of Jerusalem in January, 588 B.C. (2 Kgs 25, 1).

9, 1–8: Divine judgment is about to fall on the surrounding hostile peoples: Aram (Syria), including the cities of Hadrach and Damascus; Phoenicia, with its cities of Tyre and Sidon; Philistia, with its cities of Ashkelon, Gaza, Ekron, and Ashdod.

9, 6: The baseborn: people of mixed ancestry.

9, 7: Remnant: see note on Hg 1, 12. The Jebusites: the pre-Israelite inhabitants of Jerusalem, conquered by David and incorporated into Israel.

9, 8: My house: the Holy Land; cf Hos 8, 1; 9, 15; Jer 12, 7.

9, 9: The Messiah will come, not as a conquering warrior, but in lowliness and peace. Not like the last kings of Judah, who rode in chariots and on horses (Jer 17, 25; 22, 4), but like the princes of old (Gn 49, 11; Jgs 5, 10; 10, 4), the Messiah will ride on an ass. The Evangelists see a literal fulfillment of

shout for joy, O daughter Jerusalem!
See, your king shall come to you;
a just savior is he,
Meek, and riding on an ass,
on a colt, the foal of an ass.*
10 He shall banish the chariot from Ephraim,
and the horse from Jerusalem;
The warrior's bow shall be banished,
and he shall proclaim peace to the nations.
His dominion shall be from sea to sea,
and from the River* to the ends of the earth.[i]
11 As for you, for the blood of your covenant with me,*
I will bring forth your prisoners from the dungeon.[j]
12 In the return to the fortress
of the waiting prisoners,*
This very day, I will return you
double for your exile.[k]
13 For I will bend Judah as my bow,
I will arm myself with Ephraim;
I will arouse your sons, O Zion,
[against your sons, O Yavan,]
and I will use you as a warrior's sword.
14 The LORD shall appear over them,
and his arrow shall shoot forth as lightning;
The LORD God shall sound the trumpet,
and come in a storm from the south.
15 The LORD of hosts shall be a shield over them,
they shall overcome sling stones
and trample them underfoot;
They shall drink blood like wine,
till they are filled with it like libation bowls,
like the corners of the altar.
16 And the LORD, their God, shall save them
on that day,
his people, like a flock.
For they are the jewels in a crown
raised aloft over his land.[l]
17 For what wealth is theirs, and what beauty!
grain that makes the youths flourish,
and new wine, the maidens!

## CHAPTER 10

### The New Order of Things

1 Ask of the LORD rain in the spring season!
It is the LORD who makes the storm clouds,
And sends men the pouring rain;
for everyone, grassy fields.[m]
2 For the teraphim* speak nonsense,
the diviners have false visions:
Deceitful dreams they tell,
empty comfort they offer.
This is why they wander like sheep,
wretched: they have no shepherd.[n]
3 My wrath is kindled against the shepherds,
and I will punish the leaders;
For the LORD of hosts will visit his flock,
the house of Judah,
and make them his stately war horse.

4 From him shall come leader and chief,
from him warrior's bow and every officer.
5 They shall all be warriors,
trampling the mire of the streets in battle;
They shall wage war because the LORD is with them,
and shall put the horsemen to rout.
6 I will strengthen the house of Judah,
the house of Joseph I will save;
I will bring them back, because I have mercy on them,
they shall be as though I had never cast them off,
for I am the LORD, their God, and I will hear them.
7 Then Ephraim shall be valiant men,
and their hearts shall be cheered as by wine.
Their children shall see it and be glad,
their hearts shall rejoice in the LORD.

8 I will whistle for them to come together,
and when I redeem them
they will be as numerous as before.[o]
9 I sowed them among the nations,
yet in distant lands they remember me;
they shall rear their children and return.
10 I will bring them back from the land of Egypt,
and gather them from Assyria.
I will bring them into Gilead and into Lebanon,
but these shall not suffice them;[p]
11 I will cross over to Egypt
and smite the waves of the sea
and all the depths of the Nile shall be dried up.
The pride of Assyria shall be cast down,
and the scepter of Egypt taken away.[q]
12 I will strengthen them in the LORD,
and they shall walk in his name, says the LORD.[r]

i Hos 1, 7.
j Is 42, 7; Ez 24, 8.
k Is 61, 7.
l Is 62, 3.
m Dt 11, 14; Jer 14, 22.
n Jer 10, 8; Ez 34, 5.
o Ez 36, 37.
p Is 11, 11; 49, 20; Hos 11, 11.
q Is 11, 15; Ez 30, 13.
r Mi 4, 5.

* this prophecy in the Savior's triumphant entry into Jerusalem (Mt 21, 4f; Jn 12, 14f).

9, 10: The River: the Euphrates; see note on Ps 72, 8.

9, 11: The blood of your covenant with me: the covenant between the Lord and Israel sealed with sacrificial blood (Ex 24, 8).

9, 12: The waiting prisoners: the exiles awaiting the return to their country, where they will receive a double compensation for the double punishment they had suffered; cf Is 40, 2; 61, 7.

10, 2: Teraphim: household idols, used for divination; cf Gn 31, 19. 34f; Jgs 17, 5; 18, 17f. 20; Ez 21, 26; Hos 3, 4.

## CHAPTER 11

1 Open your doors, O Lebanon,
that the fire may devour your cedars!
2 Wail, you cypress trees,
for the cedars are fallen,
the mighty have been despoiled.
Wail, you oaks of Bashan,
for the impenetrable forest is cut down!
3 Hark! the wailing of the shepherds,
their glory has been ruined.
Hark! the roaring of the young lions,
the jungle of the Jordan is laid waste.

**Allegory of the Shepherds.*** 4 Thus said
the LORD, my God: Shepherd the flock to be
slaughtered. 5 For they who buy them slay
them with impunity; while those who sell them
say, "Blessed be the LORD, I have become
rich!" Even their own shepherds do not feel for
them.[s] 6 (Nor shall I spare the inhabitants of
the earth any more, says the LORD. Yes, I will
deliver each of them into the power of his neighbor, or into the power of his king; they shall
crush the earth, and I will not deliver it out of
their power.)
7 So I became the shepherd of the flock to be
slaughtered for the sheep merchants. I took two
staffs, one of which I called "Favor," and the
other, "Bonds," and I fed the flock.[t] 8 In a
single month I did away with the three shepherds. I wearied of them, and they behaved
badly toward me. 9 "I will not feed you," I
said. "What is to die, let it die; what is to perish,
let it perish, and let those that are left devour one
another's flesh."[u]
10 Then I took my staff "Favor" and
snapped it asunder, breaking off the covenant
which I had made with all peoples; 11 that day
it was broken off. The sheep merchants who
were watching me understood that this was the
word of the LORD. 12 I said to them, "If it
seems good to you, give me my wages; but if
not, let it go." And they counted out my wages,
thirty pieces of silver.[v] 13 But the LORD said to
me, "Throw it in the treasury, the handsome
price at which they valued me." So I took the
thirty pieces of silver and threw them into the
treasury in the house of the LORD.[w] 14 Then I
snapped asunder my other staff, "Bonds,"
breaking off the brotherhood between Judah and
Israel. 15 The LORD said to me: This time take
the gear of a foolish shepherd. 16 For I will
raise up a shepherd in the land who will take no
note of those that perish, nor seek the strays, nor
heal the injured, nor feed what survives—he
will eat the flesh of the fat ones and tear off their
hoofs![x]
17 Woe to my foolish shepherd
who forsakes the flock!
May the sword fall upon his arm
and upon his right eye;
Let his arm wither away entirely,
and his right eye be blind forever![y]

## CHAPTER 12

**Jerusalem God's Instrument.*** 1 An oracle: the word of the LORD concerning Israel.
Thus says the LORD, who spreads out the heavens, lays the foundations of the earth, and forms
the spirit of man within him:[z] 2 See, I will
make Jerusalem a bowl to stupefy all peoples
round about. [Judah will be besieged, even Jerusalem.][a] 3 On that day I will make Jerusalem
a weighty stone for all peoples. All who attempt
to lift it shall injure themselves badly, and all the
nations of the earth shall be gathered against
her.[b] 4 On that day, says the LORD, I will strike
every horse with fright, and its rider with madness. I will strike blind all the horses of the
peoples, but upon the house of Judah I will open
my eyes, 5 and the princes of Judah shall say
to themselves, "The inhabitants of Jerusalem
have their strength in the LORD of hosts, their
God." 6 On that day I will make the princes of
Judah like a brazier of fire in the woodland, and
like a burning torch among sheaves, and they
shall devour right and left all the surrounding
peoples; but Jerusalem shall still abide on its
own site.[c] 7 The LORD shall save the tents of
Judah first, that the glory of the house of David
and the glory of the inhabitants of Jerusalem
may not be exalted over Judah. 8 On that day,
the LORD will shield the inhabitants of Jerusalem, and the weakling among them shall be like
David on that day, and the house of David god-
like, like an angel of the Lord before them.[d]
9 On that day I will seek the destruction of all
nations that come against Jerusalem.

---

s Jer 50, 7.
t Hos 5, 6.
u Jer 15, 2.
v Ex 21, 32; Mt 26, 15.
w Mt 27, 9f.
x Ez 34, 2ff.
y Jn 10, 12.
z Is 42, 5.
a Is 51, 17; Jer 51, 7.
b Mt 21, 44.
c Ob 18.
d Ex 32, 34.

---

* 11, 4–17: In this allegory the prophet becomes the good shepherd of God's flock, which is being slaughtered; he is the defender of the people exploited by bad rulers. The three shepherds, rulers in general, are to destroy one another in a short time (a single month). The service of the good shepherd is contemptuously valued at thirty pieces of silver, the legal indemnity (Ex 21, 32) for a gored slave. The prophet is thus a type of Christ whose mission of salvation to his people was appraised by the Sanhedrists, the false shepherds, at the same base price (Mt 26, 14ff). In the case of the prophet as well as of Christ (Mt 27, 5), the money is thrown into the temple treasury, i.e., paid to God, showing thereby how shamefully his divine love and care are requited.

12, 1–9: Under the image of the deliverance of Judah and Jerusalem from invading enemies, the prophet foretells the ultimate victory of God's people in the messianic age.

**Messianic Jerusalem.** 10 I will pour out
on the house of David and on the inhabitants of
Jerusalem a spirit of grace and petition;[e] and
they shall look on him whom they have thrust
through, and they shall mourn for him as one
mourns for an only son, and they shall grieve
over him as one grieves over a firstborn.*
11 *On that day the mourning in Jerusalem
shall be as great as the mourning of Hadadrimmon in the plain of Megiddo.[f] 12 And the land
shall mourn, each family apart: the family of the
house of David, and their wives; the family of
the house of Nathan, and their wives; 13 the
family of the house of Levi, and their wives; the
family of Shemei, and their wives; 14 and all
the rest of the families, each family apart, and
the wives apart.

## CHAPTER 13

**The End of Falsehood.** 1 On that day
there shall be open to the house of David and to
the inhabitants of Jerusalem, a fountain to purify from sin* and uncleanness.[g] 2 On that day,
says the LORD of hosts, I will destroy the names
of the idols from the land, so that they shall be
mentioned no more; I will also take away the
prophets and the spirit of uncleanness from the
land.[h] 3 If a man still prophesies, his parents,
father and mother, shall say to him, "You shall
not live, because you have spoken a lie in the
name of the LORD." When he prophesies, his
parents, father and mother, shall thrust him
through.[i]
4 On that day, every prophet shall be
ashamed to prophesy his vision, neither shall he
assume the hairy mantle* to mislead, 5 but he
shall say, "I am no prophet, I am a tiller of the
soil, for I have owned land since my youth."[j]
6 And if anyone asks him, "What are these
wounds on your chest?"* he shall answer,
"With these I was wounded in the house of my
dear ones."

### The Song of the Sword

7 Awake, O sword, against my shepherd,
against the man who is my associate,
says the LORD of hosts.
Strike the shepherd
that the sheep may be dispersed,*
and I will turn my hand against the little
ones.[k]
8 In all the land, says the LORD,
two thirds of them shall be cut off and
perish,
and one third shall be left.
9 I will bring the one third through fire,
and I will refine them as silver is refined,
and I will test them as gold is tested.[l]
They shall call upon my name, and I will
hear them.
I will say, "They are my people,"
and they shall say, "The LORD is my
God."

## CHAPTER 14

**The Fight for Jerusalem.*** 1 Lo, a day
shall come for the LORD when the spoils shall
be divided in your midst. 2 And I will gather all
the nations against Jerusalem for battle: the city
shall be taken, houses plundered, women ravished; half of the city shall go into exile, but the
rest of the people shall not be removed from the
city. 3 Then the LORD shall go forth and fight
against those nations, fighting as on a day of
battle. 4 That day his feet shall rest upon the
Mount of Olives, which is opposite Jerusalem to
the east. The Mount of Olives shall be cleft in
two from east to west by a very deep valley, and
half of the mountain shall move to the north and
half of it to the south. 5 And the valley of the
LORD's mountain shall be filled up when the

e Jer 6, 26; Jn 19, 34; Rv 1, 7.
f 2 Chr 35, 22-25.
g Heb 9, 14; 1 Pt 1, 18f; Rv 1, 5.
h Mi 5, 12; 2 Pt 2, 1.
i Dt 18, 20; Mi 3, 5ff.
j Am 7, 14.
k Mt 26, 31.
l Jer 30, 22; Ps 66, 10.

*

12, 10: The divine blessings (a spirit of grace and petition) will be poured out on God's people through the intervention of an unnamed sufferer (him whom they have thrust through), similar to the Servant of the Lord in Is 52, 13—53, 12. In Jn 19, 37 the Evangelist sees in this passage a prophecy fulfilled in the piercing of Christ's side.

12, 11: The mourning for the pierced victim in Jerusalem is compared to a lamentation in the plain of Megiddo apparently over a certain personage called Hadadrimmon. The reference is no longer clear. Both Hadad and Rimmon were names of the Semitic storm god, often identified with the god Baal. Some see here a reference to the annual mourning by the pagans over the death of the fertility god. According to others, Hadadrimmon is the name of a place near Megiddo, and the reference would then be to the mourning over the death of King Josiah, who was killed in battle there; cf 2 Chr 35, 22–25.

13, 1: A fountain to purify from sin: in contrast to the lustral water used in ritual purification; cf Nm 19, 9. 13. 20; 31, 23. The Lord himself is the fountain of living water (Jer 2, 13); cf Is 12, 2ff.

13, 4: Hairy mantle: worn by prophets as a mark of their calling; cf 2 Kgs 1, 8; Mt 3, 4.

13, 6: Wounds on your chest: literally "wounds between your hands." The false prophets, like the prophet of Baal (1 Kgs 13, 28), apparently inflicted wounds on themselves; to defend himself against the accusation of being a false prophet, a man will deny having inflicted wounds on himself and say instead that he received them at home, "in the house of my dear ones." In the liturgy this text is applied to Christ in an accommodated sense.

13, 7: When the shepherd is killed, the sheep are scattered. In Mt 26, 31 the Evangelist quotes from this verse, in somewhat different form, the words, I will smite the shepherd, and the sheep of the flock will be scattered, as said by Christ shortly before his arrest in the Garden of Olives and the flight of the Apostles.

14, 1–21: An apocalyptic description of the day of the Lord, in which Jerusalem, the figure of God's elect, after much suffering (siege: vv 1ff; riot: v 13; plague: vv 12, 15), is rescued by the Lord (vv 4f) and given great blessings (vv 6–11. 14. 16–21).

valley of those two mountains reaches its edge;
it shall be filled up as it was filled up by the
earthquake in the days of King Uzziah of Judah.
Then the LORD, my God, shall come, and all his
holy ones with him.
6 On that day there shall no longer be cold
or frost. 7 There shall be one continuous day,
known to the LORD, not day and night, for in the
evening time there shall be light.[m]
8 On that day, living waters shall flow from
Jerusalem, half to the eastern sea, and half to the
western sea, and it shall be so in summer and in
winter.[n] 9 The LORD shall become king over
the whole earth; on that day the LORD shall be
the only one, and his name the only one.[o]
10 And from Geba to Rimmon in the Negeb,
all the land shall turn into a plain; but Jerusalem
shall remain exalted in its place. From the Gate
of Benjamin to the place of the First Gate, to the
Corner Gate; and from the Tower of Hananel to
the king's wine presses,[p] 11 they shall occupy
her. Never again shall she be doomed; Jerusalem shall abide in security.[q]
12 And this shall be the plague with which
the LORD shall strike all the nations that have
fought against Jerusalem: their flesh shall rot
while they stand upon their feet, and their eyes
shall rot in their sockets, and their tongues shall
rot in their mouths.
13 On that day there shall be among them a
great tumult from the LORD: every man shall
seize the hand of his neighbor, and the hand of
each shall be raised against that of his neighbor.
14 Judah also shall fight against Jerusalem. The
riches of all the surrounding nations shall be
gathered together, gold, silver, and garments, in
great abundance.
15 Similar to this plague shall be the plague
upon the horses, mules, camels, asses, and
upon all the beasts that are in those camps.
16 All who are left of all the nations that
came against Jerusalem shall come up year after
year to worship the King, the LORD of hosts, and
to celebrate the feast of Booths.[r] 17 If any of
the families of the earth does not come up to
Jerusalem to worship the King, the LORD of
hosts, no rain shall fall upon them. 18 And if
the family of Egypt does not come up, or enter,
upon them shall fall the plague which the LORD
will inflict upon all the nations that do not come
up to celebrate the feast of Booths. 19 This
shall be the punishment of Egypt, and the punishment of all the nations that do not come up
to celebrate the feast of Booths.
20 On that day there shall be upon the bells
of the horses, "Holy to the LORD." The pots in
the house of the LORD shall be as the libation
bowls before the altar. 21 And every pot in
Jerusalem and in Judah shall be holy to the LORD
of hosts; and all who come to sacrifice shall take
them and cook in them. On that day there shall
no longer be any merchant in the house of the
LORD of hosts.[s]

---

m Rv 21, 23.
n Zec 13, 1; Ez 47, 1-8; Jl 3, 18.
o Dt 6, 4; Eph 4, 5f; Rv 11, 15.
p Zec 12, 6; Neh 3, 6; 12, 38.
q Jer 31, 40; Rv 22, 3.
r Lv 23, 34. 43; Neh 8, 14; Is 60, 6. 9.
s Mt 21, 12; Jn 2, 13-16.

# The Book of
# MALACHI

*This work was composed by an anonymous writer shortly before Nehemiah's arrival in Jerusalem (455 B.C.). Because of the sharp reproaches he was leveling against the priests and rulers of the people, the author probably wished to conceal his identity. To do this he made a proper name out of the Hebrew expression for "My Messenger" (Malachi), which occurs in 1, 1 and 3, 1. The historical value of the prophecy is considerable in that it gives us a picture of life in the Jewish community returned from Babylon, between the period of Haggai and the reform measures of Ezra and Nehemiah. It is likely that the author's trenchant criticism of abuses and religious indifference in the community prepared the way for these necessary reforms.*

*The chosen people had made a sorry return for divine love. The priests, who should have been leaders, had dishonored God by their blemished sacrifices. In his first chapter, the writer foresees the time when all nations will offer a pure oblation (1, 11)—a prophecy whose fulfillment the church sees in the Sacrifice of the Mass. The author then turns from priests to people, denouncing their marriages with pagans and their callous repudiation of Israelite wives. Imbued with the rationalist and critical spirit of the times, many had wearied God with the question, "Where is the God of justice?" To this question the prophet replies that the day of the Lord is coming. But first the forerunner must come, who will prepare the soil for repentance and true worship. The gospel writers point to John the Baptizer as the forerunner ushering in the messianic age, the true day of the Lord. When the ground is prepared God will appear, measuring out rewards and punishments and purifying the nation in the furnace of judgment. He will create a new order in which the ultimate triumph of good is inevitable.*

## CHAPTER 1

1 An oracle. The word of the LORD to Israel through Malachi.

### Israel Preferred to Edom

2 I have loved you, says the LORD;
but you say, "How have you loved us?"[a]
3 Was not Esau Jacob's brother? says the LORD:*
yet I loved Jacob, but hated Esau;
I made his mountains a waste,
his heritage a desert for jackals.[b]
4 If Edom says, "We have been crushed
but we will rebuild the ruins,"
Thus says the LORD of hosts:
They indeed may build, but I will tear down,
And they shall be called the land of guilt,[c]
the people with whom the LORD is angry forever.
5 Your own eyes shall see it, and you will say,
"Great is the LORD, even beyond the land of Israel."[d]

### Sins of the Priests and Levites

6 A son honors his father,
and a servant fears his master;
If then I am a father,
where is the honor due to me?
And if I am a master, where is the reverence due to me?—
So says the LORD of hosts to you, O priests,
who despise his name.
But you ask, "How have we despised your name?"
7 By offering polluted food on my altar!
Then you ask, "How have we polluted it?"
By saying the table of the LORD may be slighted!
8 When you offer a blind animal for sacrifice,[e]
is this not evil?
When you offer the lame or the sick,
is it not evil?

a Dt 7, 6ff; Ez 16; Am 1, 11.
b Gn 25, 23; Rom 9, 13.
c Is 34, 5f; 63, 1-6; Jer 49, 7-22; Ob 21.
d Is 60.
e Lv 22, 19-25; Dt 15, 21.

1, 3ff: The thought passes from the person Esau to his descendants, Edom, and from the person Jacob to his descendants, Israel. Loved: preferred; hated: rejected; cf Gn 25, 21ff. St. Paul uses this passage as an example of God's freedom of choice in calling the Gentiles to the faith (Rom 9, 13).

1, 8: The offering in sacrifice of a lame, sick or blind animal was forbidden in the law (Lv 22, 17–25; Dt 17, 1).

Present it to your governor; see if he will
accept it,
or welcome you, says the LORD of hosts.*
9 So now if you implore God for mercy on
us,
when you have done the like
Will he welcome any of you?
says the LORD of hosts.

10 Oh, that one among you would shut the
temple gates*
to keep you from kindling fire on my altar
in vain!
I have no pleasure in you, says the LORD of
hosts;
neither will I accept any sacrifice from
your hands,
11 For from the rising of the sun, even to its
setting,
my name is great among the nations;
And everywhere they bring sacrifice to my
name,
and a pure offering;
For great is my name among the nations,
says the LORD of hosts.[f]
12 But you behave profanely toward me by
thinking
the LORD's table and its offering may be
polluted,
and its food slighted.
13 You also say, "What a burden!"
and you scorn it, says the LORD of hosts;
You bring in what you seize, or the lame, or
the sick;
yes, you bring it as a sacrifice.
Shall I accept it from your hands?
says the LORD.
14 Cursed is the deceiver, who has in his flock
a male,
but under his vow sacrifices to the LORD a
gelding;
For a great King am I, says the LORD of
hosts,
and my name will be feared among the
nations.

## CHAPTER 2

1 And now, O priests, this commandment is
for you:
If you do not listen,
2 And if you do not lay it to heart,
to give glory to my name, says the LORD
of hosts,
I will send a curse upon you
and of your blessing I will make a curse.
Yes, I have already cursed it,
because you do not lay it to heart.[g]
3 Lo, I will deprive you of the shoulder*
and I will strew dung in your faces,
The dung of your feasts,
and you will be carried off with it.
4 Then you will know that I sent you this
commandment
because I have a covenant with Levi,
says the LORD of hosts.[h]
5 My covenant with him was one of life and
peace;
fear I put in him, and he feared me,
and stood in awe of my name.[i]
6 True doctrine was in his mouth,
and no dishonesty was found upon his
lips;
He walked with me in integrity and
uprightness,
and turned many away from evil.[j]
7 For the lips of the priest are to keep
knowledge,
and instruction is to be sought from his
mouth,
because he is the messenger of the LORD
of hosts.[k]
8 But you have turned aside from the way,
and have caused many to falter by your
instruction;
You have made void the covenant of Levi,
says the LORD of hosts.
9 I, therefore, have made you contemptible
and base before all the people,
Since you do not keep my ways,
but show partiality in your decisions.

### Sins of the People

10 Have we not all the one Father?*
Has not the one God created us?
Why then do we break faith with each other,
violating the covenant of our fathers?[l]
11 Judah has broken faith; an abominable thing
has been done in Israel and in Jerusalem.
Judah has profaned the temple which the
LORD loves,
and has married an idolatrous woman.[m]
12 May the LORD cut off from the man who
does this

f Ps 113, 3; Is 59, 19.
g Lv 26, 14-45; Dt 28, 15-68.
h Nm 25, 12f.
i Nm 25, 12; Ez 37, 26ff.
j Dt 33, 8-11.
k Lv 10, 10f; Dt 17, 9f; Jer 18, 18; Hg 2, 12.
l Mt 23, 9; Jb 31, 15; Eph 4, 6.
m Ezr 9, 2; Neh 13, 25.

*

1, 10f: The imperfect sacrifices offered without sincerity by the people of Judah are displeasing to the Lord. He will rather be pleased with the offerings of the Gentile nations throughout the world (from the rising of the sun, even to its setting), which anticipate the pure offering to be sacrificed in messianic times, the universal Sacrifice of the Mass, as we are told by the Council of Trent.

2, 3: I will deprive you of the shoulder: this part of a sacrificial animal, allotted by the law (Dt 18, 3) to the priests, will be withheld from them.

2, 10–16: Intermarriage of Israelites with foreigners was forbidden according to Dt 7, 1–4. After the exile this law was strictly enforced (Ezr 9—10). Foreign marriages are here portrayed as a violation of the covenant (v 10), which made the sacrifices offered by the offenders unacceptable to God (v 13). They were all the more reprehensible when accompanied by the divorce of Israelite wives (vv 14ff). This gradual return to the primitive ideal of the indissolubility of marriage was fully realized in New Testament times through the teaching of Christ; cf Mt 19, 3–12.

both witness and advocate out of the tents
of Jacob,
and anyone to offer sacrifice to the LORD
of hosts!

13 This also you do: the altar of the LORD you
cover
with tears, weeping and groaning,
Because he no longer regards your sacrifice
nor accepts it favorably from your hand;
14 And you say, "Why is it?"—
Because the LORD is witness
between you and the wife of your youth,
With whom you have broken faith
though she is your companion, your
betrothed wife.[n]
15 Did he not make one being, with flesh and
spirit:
and what does that one require but godly
offspring?
You must then safeguard life that is your
own,
and not break faith with the wife of your
youth.[o]
16 For I hate divorce,
says the LORD, the God of Israel,
And covering one's garment with injustice,
says the LORD of hosts;
You must then safeguard life that is your
own,
and not break faith.

17 You have wearied the LORD with your
words,
yet you say, "How have we wearied
him?"
By your saying, "Every evildoer
is good in the sight of the LORD,
And he is pleased with him";
or else, "Where is the just God?"

## CHAPTER 3

### The Messenger of the Covenant

1 Lo, I am sending my messenger
to prepare the way before me;*
And suddenly there will come to the temple
the LORD whom you seek,
And the messenger of the covenant whom
you desire.
Yes, he is coming, says the LORD of hosts.[p]
2 But who will endure the day of his coming?
And who can stand when he appears?
For he is like the refiner's fire,
or like the fuller's lye.
3 He will sit refining and purifying [silver],
and he will purify the sons of Levi,
Refining them like gold or like silver
that they may offer due sacrifice to the
LORD.[q]
4 Then the sacrifice of Judah and Jerusalem
will please the LORD,
as in the days of old, as in years gone by.
5 I will draw near to you for judgment,
and I will be swift to bear witness
Against the sorcerers, adulterers, and
perjurers,
those who defraud the hired man of his
wages,
Against those who defraud widows and
orphans;
those who turn aside the stranger,
and those who do not fear me, says the
LORD of hosts.

6 Surely I, the LORD, do not change,*
nor do you cease to be sons of Jacob.
7 Since the days of your fathers you have
turned aside
from my statutes, and have not kept them.
Return to me, and I will return to you,
says the LORD of hosts.
Yet you say, "How must we return?"[r]
8 Dare a man rob God? Yet you are robbing
me!
And you say, "How do we rob you?"
In tithes and in offerings![s]
9 You are indeed accursed,
for you, the whole nation, rob me.
10 Bring the whole tithe
into the storehouse,*
That there may be food in my house,
and try me in this, says the LORD of
hosts:
Shall I not open for you the floodgates of
heaven,
to pour down blessing upon you without
measure?[t]
11 For your sake I will forbid the locust to
destroy your crops;
And the vine in the field will not be barren,
says the LORD of hosts.
12 Then all nations will call you blessed,
for you will be a delightful land,
says the LORD of hosts.

13 You have defied me in word, says the
LORD,
yet you ask, "What have we spoken
against you?"
14 You have said, "It is vain to serve God,
and what do we profit by keeping his
command,
And going about in penitential dress
in awe of the LORD of hosts?[u]

n Gn 31, 49f; Prv 5, 18ff.
o Gn 2, 7. 22ff.
p Is 40, 3; Mt 11, 10; Mk 1, 2; Lk 1, 17; 7, 27.
q Is 1, 25; Zec 13, 9.
r Zec 1, 3f; Acts 7, 51.
s Neh 13, 10-14.
t 2 Chr 31, 10f; Neh 10, 38; 13, 12; Prv 3, 9f.
u Jb 21, 14f; 22, 17; Ps 73, 11f.

*

3, 1: My messenger . . . before me: in v 23 this messenger is called Elijah. In Mt 11, 10 these words are quoted by Christ as referring to John the Baptizer, who prepared the way for the coming of the Savior; cf Mt 3, 1ff. 11f; 17, 11ff; Mk 1, 2–8; Lk 3, 2–18; Jn 1, 31–34.

3, 6f: God is faithful to his promises. He will not abandon the Israelites, who are still his people.

3, 10: Storehouse: the temple treasury.

**15** Rather must we call the proud blessed;
for indeed evildoers prosper,
and even tempt God with impunity."
**16** Then they who fear the LORD spoke with one another,
and the LORD listened attentively;
And a record book* was written before him
of those who fear the LORD and trust in his name.[v]
**17** And they shall be mine, says the LORD of hosts,
my own special possession, on the day I take action.
And I will have compassion on them,
as a man has compassion on his son who serves him.[w]
**18** Then you will again see the distinction
between the just and the wicked;
Between him who serves God,
and him who does not serve him.
**19** For lo, the day is coming, blazing like an oven,
when all the proud and all evildoers will be stubble,
And the day that is coming will set them on fire,
leaving them neither root nor branch,
says the LORD of hosts.[x]
**20** But for you who fear my name, there will arise
the sun of justice with its healing rays;
And you will gambol like calves out of the stall
**21** and tread down the wicked;[y]
They will become ashes under the soles of your feet,
on the day I take action, says the LORD of hosts.

**22** Remember the law of Moses my servant,
which I enjoined upon him on Horeb,
The statutes and ordinances
for all Israel.[z]
**23** Lo, I will send you
Elijah,* the prophet,
Before the day of the LORD comes,
the great and terrible day,
**24** To turn the hearts of the fathers to their children,
and the hearts of the children to their fathers,[a]
Lest I come and strike
the land with doom.
Lo, I will send you
Elijah, the prophet,
Before the day of the LORD comes,
the great and terrible day.*

v Rv 20, 12.
w Ex 19, 5; Dt 7, 6; Pss 103, 13; 135, 4.
x Is 13, 9; 34, 8; Jl 3, 3; Zep 1, 18; 2 Pt 3, 7.
y Lk 1, 78f.
z Ex 20; Lv 26; Dt 4, 1. 5f.
a Mt 11, 14; 17, 10; Mk 9, 10ff; Lk 1, 17.

*

3, 16: Record book: see note on Ex 32, 32.

3, 23: Elijah: described in 2 Kgs 2, 11 as taken heavenward in a fiery chariot. Here his return to earth seems to be foretold. Jewish tradition has interpreted this literally; Christ declares it to be fulfilled in the coming of John the Baptizer (Mt 17, 10–13).

3, 24: The words in fine print, a repetition of v 23a-d, have been added by the scribes so that the collection of the twelve minor prophets will not end with the threat of doom.

# THE NEW TESTAMENT

# Preface to
# THE NEW TESTAMENT
## First Edition

The New Testament translation has been approached with essentially the same fidelity to the thought and individual style of the biblical writers as was applied in the Old Testament. In some cases, however, the problem of marked literary peculiarities had to be met. What by any Western standard are the limited vocabularies and stylistic infelicities of the evangelists cannot be retained in the exact form in which they appear in the originals without displeasing the modern ear. A compromise is here attempted whereby some measure of the poverty of the evangelists' expression is kept and placed at the service of their message in its richness. Similarly, the syntactical shortcomings of Paul, his frequent lapses into anacoluthon, and the like, are rendered as they occur in his epistles rather than "smoothed out." Only thus, the translators suppose, will contemporary readers have some adequate idea of the kind of writing they have before them. When the prose of the original flows more smoothly, as in Luke, Acts, and Hebrews, it is reflected in the translation.

The Gospel according to John comprises a special case. Absolute fidelity to his technique of reiterated phrasing would result in an assault on the English ear, yet the softening of the vocal effect by substitution of other words and phrases would destroy the effectiveness of his poetry. Again, resort is had to compromise. This is not an easy matter when the very repetitiousness which the author deliberately employed is at the same time regarded by those who read and speak English to be a serious stylistic defect. Only those familiar with the Greek originals can know what a relentless tattoo Johannine poetry can produce. A similar observation could be made regarding other New Testament books as well. Matthew and Mark are given to identical phrasing twice and three times in the same sentence. As for the rhetorical overgrowth and mixed figures of speech in the letters of Peter, James, and Jude, the translator must resist a powerful compulsion to tidy them up if only to render these letters intelligibly.

Without seeking refuge in complaints against the inspired authors, however, the translators of THE NEW AMERICAN BIBLE here state that what they have attempted is a translation rather than a paraphrase. To be sure, all translation can be called paraphrase by definition. Any striving for complete fidelity will shortly end in infidelity. Nonetheless, it must be pointed out that the temptation to improve overladen sentences by the consolidation or elimination of multiplied adjectives, or the simplification of clumsy hendiadys, has been resisted here. For the most part, rhetorically ineffective words and phrases are retained in this translation in some form, even when it is clear that a Western contemporary writer would never have employed them.

The spelling of proper names in THE NEW AMERICAN BIBLE follows the customary forms found in most English Bibles since the Authorized Version.

Despite the arbitrary character of the divisions into numbered verses (a scheme which in its present form is only four centuries old), the translators have made a constant effort to keep within an English verse the whole verbal content of the Greek verse. At times the effort has not seemed worth the result since it often does violence to the original author's flow of expression, which preceded it by so many centuries. If this translation had been prepared for purposes of public reading only, the editors would have forgone the effort at an early stage. But since they never departed from the three fold objective of preparing a translation suitable for liturgical use, private reading, and the purposes of students, the last-named consideration prevailed. Those familiar with Greek should be able to discover how the translators of the New Testament have rendered any given original verse of scripture, if their exegetical or theological tasks require them to know this. At the same time, the fact should be set down here that the editors did not commit themselves in the synoptic gospels to rendering repeated words or phrases identically.

This leads to a final consideration: the Greek text used for the New Testament. Here, punctuation and verse division are at least as important as variant readings. In general, Nestle-Aland's *Novum Testamentum Graece* (25th edition, 1963) was followed. Additional help was derived from *The Greek New Testament* (Aland, Black, Metzger, Wikgren), produced for the use of translators by the United Bible Societies in 1966. However, the editors did not confine themselves strictly to these texts: at times, they inclined toward readings otherwise attested. The omission of alternative translations does not mean that the translators think them without merit, but only that in every case they had to make a choice.

Poorly attested readings do not occur in this translation. Doubtful readings of some merit appear within brackets; public readers may include such words or phrases, or omit them entirely without any damage to sense. Parentheses are used, as ordinarily in English, as a punctuation device. Material they enclose is in no sense textually doubtful. It is simply thought to be parenthetical in the intention of the biblical author, even though there is no such punctuation mark in Greek. The difficulty in dealing with quotation marks is well known. Since they do not appear in any form in the original text, wherever they occur here they constitute an editorial decision.

# Preface to
# THE NEW TESTAMENT
## Revised Edition

The New Testament of THE NEW AMERICAN BIBLE, a fresh translation from the Greek text, was first published in complete form in 1970, together with the Old Testament translation that had been completed the previous year. Portions of the New Testament had appeared earlier, in somewhat different form, in the provisional Mass lectionary of 1964 and in the *Lectionary for Mass* of 1970.

Since 1970 many different printings of the New Testament have been issued by a number of publishers, both separately and in complete bibles, and the text has become widely known both in the United States and in other English-speaking countries. Most American Catholics have been influenced by it because of its widespread use in the liturgy, and it has received a generally favorable reception from many other Christians as well. It has taken its place among the standard contemporary translations of the New Testament, respected for its fidelity to the original and its attempt to render this into current American English.

Although the scriptures themselves are timeless, translations and explanations of them quickly become dated in an era marked by rapid cultural change to a degree never previously experienced. The explosion of biblical studies that has taken place in our century and the changing nature of our language itself require periodic adjustment both in translations and in the accompanying explanatory materials. The experience of actual use of the New Testament of THE NEW AMERICAN BIBLE, especially in oral proclamation, has provided a basis for further improvement. Accordingly, it was decided in 1978 to proceed with a thorough revision of the New Testament to reflect advances in scholarship and to satisfy needs identified through pastoral experience.

For this purpose a steering committee was formed to plan, organize, and direct the work of revision, to engage collaborators, and to serve as an editorial board to coordinate the work of the various revisers and to determine the final form of the text and the explanatory materials. Guidelines were drawn up and collaborators selected in 1978 and early 1979, and November of 1980 was established as the deadline for manuscripts. From December 1980 through September 1986 the editorial board met a total of fifty times and carefully reviewed and revised all the material in order to insure accuracy and consistency of approach. The editors also worked together with the ad hoc bishops' committee that was appointed by the National Conference of Catholic Bishops in 1982 to oversee the revision.

The threefold purpose of the translation that was expressed in the preface to the first edition has been maintained in the revision: to provide a version suitable for liturgical proclamation, for private reading, and for purposes of study. Special attention has been given to the first of these purposes, since oral proclamation demands special qualities in a translation, and experience had provided insights and suggestions that could lead to improvement in this area. Efforts have also been made, however, to facilitate devotional reading by providing suitable notes and introductory materials, and to assist the student by achieving greater accuracy and consistency in the translation and supplying more abundant information in the introductions and notes.

The primary aim of the revision is to produce a version as accurate and faithful to the meaning of the Greek original as is possible for a translation. The editors have consequently moved in the direction of a formal-equivalence approach to translation, matching the vocabulary, structure, and even word order of the original as closely as possible in the receptor language. Some other contemporary biblical versions have adopted, in varying degrees, a dynamic-equivalence approach, which attempts to respect the individuality of each language by expressing the meaning of the original in a linguistic structure suited to English, even though this may be very different from the corresponding Greek structure. While this approach often results in fresh and brilliant renderings, it has the disadvantages of more or less radically abandoning traditional biblical and liturgical terminology and phraseology, of expanding the text to include what more properly belongs in notes, commentaries, or preaching, and of tending toward paraphrase. A more formal approach seems better suited to the specific purposes intended for this translation.

At the same time, the editors have wished to produce a version in English that reflects contemporary American usage and is readily understandable to ordinary educated people, but one that will be recognized as dignified speech, on the level of formal rather than colloquial usage. These aims are not in fact contradictory, for there are different levels of language in current use: the language of formal situations is not that of colloquial conversation, though people understand both and may pass from one to the other without adverting to the transition. The liturgy is a formal situation that requires a level of discourse more dignified, formal, and hieratic than the world of business, sport, or informal communication. People readily understand this more formal level even though they may not often use it; our passive vocabulary is much larger than our active vocabulary. Hence this revision, while avoiding archaisms, does not shrink from traditional biblical terms that are easily understood even though not in common use in everyday speech. The level of language consciously aimed at is one appropriate for liturgical proclamation; this may also permit the translation to serve the purposes of devotional reading and serious study.

A particular effort has been made to insure consistency of vocabulary. Always to translate a given Greek word by the same English equivalent would lead to ludicrous results and to infidelity to the meaning of the text. But in passages where a particular Greek term retains the same meaning, it has been rendered in the same way insofar as this has been feasible; this is particularly significant in the case of terms that have a specific theological meaning. The synoptic gospels have been carefully translated so as to reveal both the similarities and the differences of the Greek.

An especially sensitive problem today is the question of discrimination in language. In recent years there has been much discussion about allegations of anti-Jewish expressions in the New Testament and of language that discriminates against various minorities. Above all, however, the question of discrimination against women affects the largest number of people and arouses the greatest degree of interest and concern. At present there is little agreement about these problems or about the best way to deal with them. In all these areas the present translation attempts to display a sensitivity appropriate to the present state of the questions under discussion, which are not yet resolved and in regard to which it is impossible to please everyone, since intelligent and sincere participants in the debate hold mutually contradictory views.

The primary concern in this revision is fidelity to what the text says. When the meaning of the Greek is inclusive of both sexes, the translation seeks to reproduce such inclusivity insofar as this is possible in normal English usage, without resort to inelegant circumlocutions or neologisms that would offend against the dignity of the language. Although the generic sense of *man* is traditional in English, many today reject it; its use has therefore generally been avoided, though it is retained in cases where no fully satisfactory equivalent could be found. English does not possess a gender-inclusive third personal pronoun in the singular, and this translation continues to use the masculine resumptive pronoun after *everyone* or *anyone*, in the traditional way, where this cannot be avoided without infidelity to the meaning.

The translation of the Greek word *adelphos*, particularly in the plural form *adelphoi*, poses an especially delicate problem. While the term literally means *brothers* or other male blood relatives, even in profane Greek the plural can designate two persons, one of either sex, who were born of the same parents. It was adopted by the early Christians to designate, in a figurative sense, the members of the Christian community, who were conscious of a new familial relationship to one another by reason of their adoption as children of God. They are consequently addressed as *adelphoi*. This has traditionally been rendered into English by *brothers* or, more archaically, *brethren*. There has never been any doubt that this designation includes *all* the members of the Christian community, both male and female. Given the absence in English of a corresponding term that explicitly includes both sexes, this translation retains the usage of *brothers*, with the inclusive meaning that has been traditionally attached to it in this biblical context.

Since the New Testament is the product of a particular time and culture, the views expressed in it and the language in which they are expressed reflect a particular cultural conditioning, which sometimes makes them quite different from contemporary ideas and concerns. Discriminatory language should be eliminated insofar as possible whenever it is unfaithful to the meaning of the New Testament, but the text should not be altered in order to adjust it to contemporary concerns. This translation does not introduce any changes, expansions, additions to, or subtractions from the text of scripture. It further retains the traditional biblical ways of speaking about God and about Christ, including the use of masculine nouns and pronouns.

The Greek text followed in this translation is that of the third edition of *The Greek New Testament*, edited by Kurt Aland, Matthew Black, Carlo Martini, Bruce Metzger, and Allen Wikgren, and published by the United Bible Societies in 1975. The same text, with a different critical apparatus and variations in punctuation and typography, was published as the twenty-sixth edition of the Nestle-Aland *Novum Tesetamentum Graece* in 1979 by the Deutsche Bibelstiftung, Stuttgart. This edition has also been consulted. When variant readings occur, the translation, with few exceptions, follows the reading that was placed in the text of these Greek editions, though the occurrence of the principal variants is pointed out in the notes.

The editors of the Greek text placed square brackets around words or portions of words of which the authenticity is questionable because the evidence of textual witnesses is inconclusive. The same has been done in the translation insofar as it is possible to reproduce this convention in English. It should be possible to read the text either with or without the disputed words, but in English it is not always feasible to provide this alternative, and in some passages the bracketed words must be included to make sense. As in the first edition, parentheses do not indicate textual uncertainty, but are simply a punctuation device to indicate a passage that in the editors' judgment appears parenthetical to the thought of the author.

Citations from the Old Testament are placed within quotation marks; longer citations are set off as block quotations in a separate indented paragraph. The sources of such citations, as well as those of many more or less subtle allusions to the Old Testament, are identified in the biblical cross-reference section at the bottom of each page. Insofar as possible, the translation of such Old Testament citations agrees with that of THE NEW AMERICAN BIBLE Old Testament whenever the underlying Greek agrees with the Hebrew (or, in some cases, the Aramaic or Greek) text from which the Old Testament translation was made. But citations in the New Testament frequently follow the Septuagint or some other version, or were made from memory; hence, in many cases the translation in the New Testament passage will not agree with what appears in the Old Testament. Some of these cases are explained in the notes.

It is a further aim of the revised edition to supply explanatory materials more abundantly than in the first edition. In most cases the introductions and notes have been entirely rewritten and expanded, and the cross-references checked and revised. It is intended that these materials should reflect the present state of sound biblical scholarship and should be presented in such a form that they can be assimilated by the ordinary intelligent reader without specialized biblical training. While they have been written with the ordinary educated Christian in mind, not all technical vocabulary can be entirely dispensed with in approaching the Bible, any more than in any other field. It is the hope of the editors that these materials, even if they sometimes demand an effort, will help the reader to a fuller and more intelligent understanding of the New Testament and a fruitful appropriation of its meaning for personal spiritual growth.

THE NEW AMERICAN BIBLE is a Roman Catholic translation. This revision, however, like the first edition, has been accomplished with the collaboration of scholars from other Christian churches, both among the revisers and on the editorial board, in response to the encouragement of Vatican Council II (*Dei Verbum,* 22). The editorial board expresses gratitude to all who have collaborated in the revision: to all the revisers, consultants, and bishops who contributed to it, to reviewers of the first edition, and to those who voluntarily submitted suggestions. May this translation fulfill its threefold purpose, "so that the word of the Lord may speed forward and be glorified" (2 Thes 3, 1).

The Feast of St. Jerome
September 30, 1986

# THE GOSPELS

The collection of writings that constitutes the New Testament begins with four gospels. Next comes the Acts of the Apostles, followed by twenty-one letters that are attributed to Paul, James, Peter, John, and Jude. Finally, at the end of the early church's scriptures stands the Revelation to John. Virtually all Christians agree that these twenty-seven books constitute the "canon," a term that means "rule" and designates the list of writings that are regarded as authoritative for Christian faith and life.

It is the purpose of this Introduction to describe those features that are common to the four gospels. A similar treatment of the letters of the New Testament is provided in the two Introductions that appear before the Letter to the Romans and before the Letter of James, respectively. The Acts of the Apostles, a work that is both historical and theological, and Revelation, an apocalyptic work, have no counterparts in the New Testament; the special Introductions prefixed to these books treat of the literary characteristics proper to each of them.

While the New Testament contains four writings called "gospels," there is in reality only one gospel running through all of the Christian scriptures, the gospel of and about Jesus Christ. Our English word "gospel" translates the Greek term *euangelion,* meaning "good news." This noun was used in the plural by the Greek translators of the Old Testament to render the Hebrew term for "good news" (2 Sm 4, 10; possibly also 18, 20.25). But it is the corresponding verb *euangelizomai,* "to proclaim good news," that was especially significant in preparing for the New Testament idea of "gospel," since this term is used by Deutero-Isaiah for announcing the great victory of God that was to establish his universal kingship and inaugurate the new age (Is 40, 9; 52, 7; 61, 1).

Paul used the word *euangelion* to designate the message that he and the other apostles proclaimed, the "gospel of God" (Rom 1, 1; 15, 16; 2 Cor 11, 7; 1 Thes 2, 2.8.9). He often referred to it simply as "the gospel" (Rom 1, 16; 10, 16; 11, 28; etc.) or, because of its content and origin, as "the gospel of Christ" (Rom 15, 19; 1 Cor 9, 12; 1 Thes 3, 2; etc.). Because of its personal meaning for him and his own particular manner of telling the story about Jesus Christ and of explaining the significance of his cross and resurrection, Paul also referred to this message as "my gospel" (Rom 2, 16; cf Gal 1, 11; 2, 2) or "our gospel" (2 Cor 4, 3; 1 Thes 1, 5; 2 Thes 2, 14).

It was Mark, as far as we know, who first applied the term "gospel" to a book telling the story of Jesus; see Mk 1, 1 and the note there. This form of presenting Jesus' life, works, teachings, passion, and resurrection was developed further by the other evangelists; see the Introduction to each gospel. The first three of the canonical gospels, Matthew, Mark, and Luke, are so similar at many points when viewed together, particularly when arranged in parallel columns or lines, that they are called "synoptic" gospels, from the Greek word for such a general view. The fourth gospel, John, often differs significantly from the synoptics in outline and approach. This work never uses the word "gospel" or its corresponding verb; nevertheless, its message concerns the same Jesus, and the reader is urged to believe in him as the Messiah, "that through this belief you may have life in his name" (20, 31).

From the second century onward, the practice arose of designating each of these four books as a "gospel," understood as a title, and of adding a phrase with a name that identified the traditional author, e.g., "The Gospel according to Matthew." The arrangement of the canon that was adopted, with the four gospels grouped together at the beginning followed by Acts, provides a massive focus upon Jesus and allows Acts to serve as a framework for the letters of the New Testament. This order, however, conceals the fact that Luke's two volumes, a gospel and Acts, were intended by their author to go together. It further obscures the point that Paul's letters were written before any of our gospels, though the sayings and deeds of Jesus stand behind all the New Testament writings.

# THE GOSPEL ACCORDING TO

# MATTHEW

## INTRODUCTION

*The position of the Gospel according to Matthew as the first of the four gospels in the New Testament reflects both the view that it was the first to be written, a view that goes back to the late second century A.D., and the esteem in which it was held by the church; no other was so frequently quoted in the noncanonical literature of earliest Christianity. Although the majority of scholars now reject the opinion about the time of its composition, the high estimation of this work remains. The reason for that becomes clear upon study of the way in which Matthew presents his story of Jesus, the demands of Christian discipleship, and the breaking-in of the new and final age through the ministry but particularly through the death and resurrection of Jesus.*

*The gospel begins with a narrative prologue (1, 1—2, 23), the first part of which is a genealogy of Jesus starting with Abraham, the father of Israel (1, 1–17). Yet at the beginning of that genealogy Jesus is designated as "the son of David, the son of Abraham" (1, 1). The kingly ancestor who lived about a thousand years after Abraham is named first, for this is the genealogy of Jesus Christ, the Messiah, the royal anointed one (1, 16). In the first of the episodes of the infancy narrative that follow the genealogy, the mystery of Jesus' person is declared. He is conceived of a virgin by the power of the Spirit of God (1, 18–25). The first of the gospel's fulfillment citations, whose purpose it is to show that he was the one to whom the prophecies of Israel were pointing, occurs here (1, 23): he shall be named Emmanuel, for in him God is with us.*

*The announcement of the birth of this newborn king of the Jews greatly troubles not only King Herod but all Jerusalem (2, 1–3), yet the Gentile magi are overjoyed to find him and offer him their homage and their gifts (2, 10–11). Thus his ultimate rejection by the mass of his own people and his acceptance by the Gentile nations is foreshadowed. He must be taken to Egypt to escape the murderous plan of Herod. By his sojourn there and his subsequent return after the king's death he relives the Exodus experience of Israel. The words of the Lord spoken through the prophet Hosea, "Out of Egypt I called my son," are fulfilled in him (2, 15); if Israel was God's son, Jesus is so in a way far surpassing the dignity of that nation, as his marvelous birth and the unfolding of his story show (see 3, 17; 4, 1–11; 11, 27; 14, 33; 16, 16; 27, 54). Back in the land of Israel, he must be taken to Nazareth in Galilee because of the danger to his life in Judea, where Herod's son Archelaus is now ruling (2, 22–23). The sufferings of Jesus in the infancy narrative anticipate those of his passion, and if his life is spared in spite of the dangers, it is because his destiny is finally to give it on the cross as "a ransom for many" (20, 28). Thus the word of the angel will be fulfilled, ". . . he will save his people from their sins" (1, 21; cf 26, 28).*

*In 4, 12 Matthew begins his account of the ministry of Jesus, introducing it by the preparatory preaching of John the Baptist (3, 1–12), the baptism of Jesus that culminates in God's proclaiming him his "beloved Son" (3, 13–17), and the temptation in which he proves his true sonship by his victory over the devil's attempt to deflect him from the way of obedience to the Father (4, 1–11). The central message of Jesus' preaching is the coming of the kingdom of heaven and the need for repentance, a complete change of heart and conduct, on the part of those who are to receive this great gift of God (4, 17). Galilee is the setting for most of his ministry; he leaves there for Judea only in 19, 1, and his ministry in Jerusalem, the goal of his journey, is limited to a few days (21, 1—25, 46).*

*In this extensive material there are five great discourses of Jesus, each concluding with the formula "When Jesus finished these words" or one closely similar (7, 28; 11, 1; 13, 53; 19, 1; 26, 1). These are an important structure of the gospel. In every case the discourse is preceded by a narrative section, each narrative and discourse together constituting a "book" of the gospel. The discourses are, respectively, the "Sermon on the Mount" (5, 3—7, 27), the missionary discourse (10, 5–42), the parable discourse (13, 3–52), the "church order" discourse (18, 3–35), and the eschatological discourse (24, 4—25, 46). In large measure the material of these discourses came to Matthew from his tradition, but his work in modifying and adding to what he had received is abundantly evident. No other evangelist gives the teaching of Jesus with such elegance and order as he.*

*In the "Sermon on the Mount" the theme of righteousness is prominent, and even at this early stage of the ministry the note of opposition is struck between Jesus and the Pharisees, who are designated as "the hypocrites" (6, 2.5.16). The righteousness of his disciples must surpass that of the scribes and Pharisees; otherwise, in spite of their alleged following of Jesus, they will not enter into the kingdom of heaven (5, 20). Righteousness means doing the will of the heavenly Father (7, 21), and his will is proclaimed in a manner that is startling to all who have identified it with the law of Moses. The antitheses of the Sermon (5, 21–48) both accept (5, 21–30.43–48) and reject (5, 31–42) elements of that law, and in the former case the understanding of the law's demands is deepened and extended. The antitheses are the best commentary on the meaning of Jesus' claim that he has come not to abolish but to fulfill the law (5, 17). What is meant by fulfillment of the law is not the demand to keep it exactly as it stood before the coming of Jesus, but rather his bringing the law to be a lasting expression of the will of God, and in that fulfillment there is much that will pass away. Should this appear contradictory to his saying that "until heaven and earth pass away" not even the smallest part of the law will pass (5, 18), that time of fulfillment is not the dissolution of the universe but the coming of the new age, which will occur with Jesus' death and resurrection. While righteousness in the new age will continue to mean conduct that is in accordance with the law, it will be conduct in accordance with the law as expounded and interpreted by Jesus (cf 28, 20, ". . . all that I have commanded you").*

*Though Jesus speaks harshly about the Pharisees in the Sermon, his judgment is not solely a condemnation of them. The Pharisees are portrayed as a negative example for his disciples, and his condemnation of those who claim to belong to him while disobeying his word is no less severe (7, 21–23.26–27).*

*In 4, 23 a summary statement of Jesus' activity speaks not only of his teaching and proclaiming the gospel but of his "curing every disease and illness among the people"; this is repeated almost verbatim in 9, 35. The narrative section that follows the Sermon on the Mount (8, 1—9, 38) is composed principally of accounts of those merciful deeds of Jesus, but it is far from being simply a collection of stories about miraculous cures. The nature of the community that Jesus will establish is shown; it will always be under the protection of him whose power can deal with all dangers (8, 23–27), but it is only for those who are prepared to follow him at whatever cost (8, 16–22), not only believing Israelites but Gentiles who have come to faith in him (8, 10–12). The disciples begin to have some insight, however imperfect, into the mystery of Jesus' person. They wonder about him whom "the winds and the sea obey" (8, 27), and they witness his bold declaration of the forgiveness of the paralytic's sins (9, 2). That episode of the narrative moves on two levels. When the crowd sees the cure that testifies to the authority of Jesus, the Son of Man, to forgive sins (9, 6), they glorify God "who had given such authority to human beings" (9, 8). The forgiveness of sins is now not the prerogative of Jesus alone but of "human beings," that is, of the disciples who constitute the community of Jesus, the church. The ecclesial character of this narrative section could hardly be more plainly indicated.*

*The end of the section prepares for the discourse on the church's mission (10, 5–42). Jesus is moved to pity at the sight of the crowds who are like sheep without a shepherd (9, 36), and he sends out the twelve disciples to make the proclamation with which his own ministry began, "The kingdom of heaven is at hand" (10, 7; cf 4, 17), and to drive out demons and cure the sick as he has done (10, 1). Their mission is limited to Israel (10, 5–6) as Jesus' own was (15, 24), yet in v 16 that perspective broadens and the discourse begins to speak of the mission that the disciples will have after the resurrection and of the severe persecution that will attend it (10, 18). Again, the discourse moves on two levels: that of the time of Jesus and that of the time of the church.*

*The narrative section of the third book (11, 2—12, 50) deals with the growing opposition to Jesus. Hostility toward him has already been manifested (8, 10; 9, 3.10–13.34), but here it becomes more intense. The rejection of Jesus comes, as before, from Pharisees, who take "counsel against him to put him to death" (12, 14) and repeat their earlier accusation that he drives out demons because he is in league with demonic power (12, 22–24). But they are not alone in their rejection. Jesus complains of the lack of faith of "this generation" of Israelites (11, 16–19) and reproaches the towns "where most of his mighty deeds had been done" for not heeding his call to repentance (11, 20–24). This dark picture is relieved by Jesus' praise of the Father who has enabled "the childlike" to accept him (11, 25–27), but on the whole the story is one of opposition to his word and blindness to the meaning of his deeds. The whole section ends with his declaring that not even the most intimate blood relationship with him counts for anything; his only true relatives are those who do the will of his heavenly Father (12, 48–50).*

*The narrative of rejection leads up to the parable discourse (13, 3–52). The reason given for Jesus' speaking to the crowds in parables is that they have hardened themselves against his clear teaching, unlike the disciples to whom knowledge of "the mysteries of the kingdom has been granted" (13, 10–16). In 13, 36 he dismisses the crowds and continues the discourse to his disciples alone, who claim, at the end, to have understood all that he has said (13, 51). But, lest the impression be given that the church of Jesus is made up only of true disciples, the explanation of the parable of the weeds among the wheat (13, 37–43), as well as the parable of the net thrown into the sea "which collects fish of every kind" (13, 47–49), shows that it is composed of both the righteous and the wicked, and that separation between the two will be made only at the time of the final judgment.*

*In the narrative that constitutes the first part of the fourth book of the gospel (13, 54—17, 27), Jesus is shown preparing for the establishment of his church with its teaching authority that will supplant the blind guidance of the Pharisees (15, 13–14), whose teaching, curiously said to be that of the Sadducees also, is repudiated by Jesus as the norm for his disciples (16, 6.11–12). The church of Jesus will be built on Peter (16, 18), who will be given authority to bind and loose on earth, an authority whose exercise will be confirmed in heaven (16, 19). The metaphor of binding and loosing has a variety of meanings, among them that of giving authoritative teaching. This promise is made to Peter directly after he has confessed Jesus to be the Messiah, the Son of the living God (16, 16), a confession that he has made as the result of revelation given to him by the heavenly Father (16, 17); Matthew's ecclesiology is based on his high christology.*

*Directly after that confession Jesus begins to instruct his disciples about how he must go the way of suffering and death (16, 21). Peter, who has been praised for his confession, protests against this and receives from Jesus the sharpest of rebukes for attempting to deflect Jesus from his God-appointed destiny. The future rock upon whom the church will be built is still a man of "little faith" (see 14, 31). Both he and the other disciples must know not only that Jesus will have to suffer and die but that they too will have to follow him on the way of the cross if they are truly to be his disciples (16, 24–25).*

*The discourse following this narrative (18, 1–35) is often called the "church order" discourse, although that title is perhaps misleading since the emphasis is not on the structure of the church but on the care that the disciples must have for one another in respect to guarding each other's faith in Jesus (18, 6–7), to seeking out those who have wandered from the fold (18, 10–14), and to repeated forgiving of their fellow disciples who have offended them (18, 21–35). But there is also the obligation to correct the sinful fellow Christian and, should one refuse to be corrected, separation from the community is demanded (18, 15–18).*

*The narrative of the fifth book (19, 1—23, 39) begins with the departure of Jesus and his disciples from Galilee for Jerusalem. In the course of their journey Jesus for the third time predicts the passion that awaits him at Jerusalem and also his resurrection (20, 17–19). At his entrance into the city he is hailed as the Son of David by the crowds accompanying him (21, 9). He cleanses the temple (21, 12–17), and in the few days of his Jerusalem ministry he engages in a series of controversies with the Jewish religious leaders (21, 23–27; 22, 15–22.23–33.34–*

*40.41–46), meanwhile speaking parables against them (21, 28–32.33–46), against all those Israelites who have rejected God's invitation to the messianic banquet (22, 1–10), and against all, Jew and Gentile, who have accepted but have shown themselves unworthy of it (22, 11–14). Once again, the perspective of the evangelist includes not only the time of Jesus' ministry but that of the preaching of the gospel after his resurrection. The narrative culminates in Jesus' denunciation of the scribes and Pharisees, reflecting not only his own opposition to them but that of Matthew's church (23, 1–36), and in Jesus' lament over Jerusalem (23, 37–39).*

*In the discourse of the fifth book (24, 1—25, 46), the last of the great structural discourses of the gospel, Jesus predicts the destruction of the temple and his own final coming. The time of the latter is unknown (24, 36.44), and the disciples are exhorted in various parables to live in readiness for it, a readiness that entails faithful attention to the duties of the interim period (24, 45—25, 30). The coming of Jesus will bring with it the great judgment by which the everlasting destiny of all will be determined (25, 31–46).*

*The story of Jesus' passion and resurrection (26, 1—28, 20), the climax of the gospel, throws light on all that has preceded. In Mt "righteousness" means both the faithful response to the will of God demanded of all to whom that will is announced and also the saving activity of God for his people (see 3, 15; 5, 6; 6, 33). The passion supremely exemplifies both meanings of that central Matthean word. In Jesus' absolute faithfulness to the Father's will that he drink the cup of suffering (26, 39), the incomparable model for Christian obedience is given; in his death "for the forgiveness of sins" (26, 28), the saving power of God is manifested as never before.*

*Matthew's portrayal of Jesus in his passion combines both the majestic serenity of the obedient Son who goes his destined way in fulfillment of the scriptures (26, 52–54), confident of his ultimate vindication by God, and the depths of fear and abandonment that he feels in face of death (26, 38–39; 27, 46). These two aspects are expressed by an Old Testament theme that occurs often in the narrative, i.e., the portrait of the suffering Righteous One who complains to God in his misery, but is certain of eventual deliverance from his terrible ordeal.*

*The passion-resurrection of God's Son means nothing less than the turn of the ages, a new stage of history, the coming of the Son of Man in his kingdom (28, 18; cf 16, 28). That is the sense of the apocalyptic signs that accompany Jesus' death (27, 51–53) and resurrection (28, 2). Although the old age continues, as it will until the manifestation of Jesus' triumph at his parousia, the final age has now begun. This is known only to those who have seen the Risen One and to those, both Jews and Gentiles, who have believed in their announcement of Jesus' triumph and have themselves become his disciples (cf 28, 19). To them he is constantly, though invisibly, present (28, 20), verifying the name Emmanuel, "God is with us" (cf 1, 23).*

*The questions of authorship, sources, and the time of composition of this gospel have received many answers, none of which can claim more than a greater or less degree of probability. The one now favored by the majority of scholars is the following.*

*The ancient tradition that the author was the disciple and apostle of Jesus named Matthew (see 10, 3) is untenable because the gospel is based, in large part, on the Gospel according to Mark (almost all the verses of that gospel have been utilized in this), and it is hardly likely that a companion of Jesus would have followed so extensively an account that came from one who admittedly never had such an association rather than rely on his own memories. The attribution of the gospel to the disciple Matthew may have been due to his having been responsible for some of the traditions found in it, but that is far from certain.*

*The unknown author, whom we shall continue to call Matthew for the sake of convenience, drew not only upon the Gospel according to Mark but upon a large body of material (principally, sayings of Jesus) not found in Mk that corresponds, sometimes exactly, to material found also in the Gospel according to Luke. This material, called "Q" (probably from the first letter of the German word Quelle, meaning ("source"), represents traditions, written and oral, used by both Matthew and Luke. Mark and Q are sources common to the two other synoptic gospels;*

*hence the name the "Two-Source Theory" given to this explanation of the relation among the synoptics.*

*In addition to what Matthew drew from Mk and Q, his gospel contains material that is found only there. This is often designated "M," written or oral tradition that was available to the author. Since Mk was written shortly before or shortly after A.D. 70 (see Introduction to Mk), Mt was composed certainly after that date, which marks the fall of Jerusalem to the Romans at the time of the First Jewish Revolt (A.D. 66–70), and probably at least a decade later since Matthew's use of Mk presupposes a wide diffusion of that gospel. The post-A.D. 70 date is confirmed within the text by 22, 7, which refers to the destruction of Jerusalem.*

*As for the place where the gospel was composed, a plausible suggestion is that it was Antioch, the capital of the Roman province of Syria. That large and important city had a mixed population of Greek-speaking Gentiles and Jews. The tensions between Jewish and Gentile Christians there in the time of Paul (see Gal 2, 1–14) in respect to Christian obligation to observe Mosaic law are partially similar to tensions that can be seen between the two groups in Matthew's gospel. The church of Matthew, originally strongly Jewish Christian, had become one in which Gentile Christians were predominant. His gospel answers the question how obedience to the will of God is to be expressed by those who live after the "turn of the ages," the death and resurrection of Jesus.*

*The principal divisions of the Gospel according to Matthew are the following:*

*I. The Infancy Narrative (1, 1—2, 23)*
*II. The Proclamation of the Kingdom (3, 1—7, 29)*
*III. Ministry and Mission in Galilee (8, 1—11, 1)*
*IV. Opposition from Israel (11, 2—13, 53)*
*V. Jesus, the Kingdom, and the Church (13, 54—18, 35)*
*VI. Ministry in Judea and Jerusalem (19, 1—25, 46)*
*VII. The Passion and Resurrection (26, 1—28, 20)*

# I: THE INFANCY NARRATIVE

## CHAPTER 1

**The Genealogy of Jesus** 1 [a]*The book of the genealogy of Jesus Christ, the son of David, the son of Abraham.
2 [bc]Abraham became the father of Isaac,
Isaac the father of Jacob, Jacob the father of
Judah and his brothers. 3 [d]Judah became the
father of Perez and Zerah, whose mother was
Tamar. Perez became the father of Hezron,
Hezron the father of Ram, 4 [e]Ram the father of
Amminadab. Amminadab became the father of
Nahshon, Nahshon the father of Salmon,
5 [f]Salmon the father of Boaz, whose mother
was Rahab. Boaz became the father of Obed,
whose mother was Ruth. Obed became the father of Jesse, 6 [g]Jesse the father of David the
king.

David became the father of Solomon, whose mother had been the wife of Uriah.

a Gn 5, 1 / 1 Chr 17, 11 / Gn 22, 18.
b Lk 3, 23-38.
c Gn 21, 3; 25, 26; 29, 35; 1 Chr 2, 1.
d Gn 38, 29-30; Ru 4, 18; 1 Chr 2, 4-9.
e Ru 4, 19-20; 1 Chr 2, 10-11.
f Ru 4, 21-22; 1 Chr 2, 11-12.
g 2 Sm 12, 24; 1 Chr 2, 15; 3, 5.

*

1, 1—2, 23: The infancy narrative forms the prologue of the gospel. Consisting of a genealogy and five stories, it presents the coming of Jesus as the climax of Israel's history, and the events of his conception, birth, and early childhood as the fulfillment of Old Testament prophecy. The genealogy is probably traditional material that Matthew edited. In its first two sections (1, 2–11) it was drawn from Ru 4, 18–22 and 1 Chr 1–3. Except for Jechoniah, Shealtiel, and Zerubbabel, none of the names in the third section (1, 12–16) is found in any Old Testament genealogy. While the genealogy shows the continuity of God's providential plan from Abraham on, discontinuity is also present. The women Tamar (1, 3), Rahab and Ruth (1, 5), and the wife of Uriah, Bathsheba (1, 6), bore their sons through unions that were in varying degrees strange and unexpected. These "irregularities" culminate in the supreme "irregularity" of the Messiah's birth of a virgin mother; the age of fulfillment is inaugurated by a creative act of God.

Drawing upon both biblical tradition and Jewish stories, Matthew portrays Jesus as reliving the Exodus experience of Israel and the persecutions of Moses. His rejection by his own people and his passion are foreshadowed by the troubled reaction of "all Jerusalem" to the question of the magi who are seeking the "newborn king of the Jews" (2, 2–3), and by Herod's attempt to have him killed. The magi who do him homage prefigure the Gentiles who will accept the preaching of the gospel. The infancy narrative proclaims who Jesus is, the savior of his people from their sins (1, 21), Emmanuel in whom "God is with us" (1, 23), and the Son of God (2, 15).

1, 1: *The Son of David, the son of Abraham:* two links of the genealogical chain are singled out. Although the later, David is placed first in order to emphasize that Jesus is the royal Messiah. The mention of Abraham may be due not only to his being the father of the nation Israel but to Matthew's interest in the universal scope of Jesus' mission; cf Gn 22, 18, ". . . in your descendants all the nations of the earth shall find blessing."

7 [h]*Solomon became the father of Rehoboam,
Rehoboam the father of Abijah, Abijah the father of Asaph. 8 Asaph became the father of
Jehoshaphat, Jehoshaphat the father of Joram,
Joram the father of Uzziah. 9 Uzziah became
the father of Jotham, Jotham the father of Ahaz,
Ahaz the father of Hezekiah. 10 *Hezekiah became the father of Manasseh, Manasseh the
father of Amos, Amos the father of Josiah.
11 Josiah became the father of Jechoniah and
his brothers at the time of the Babylonian exile.

12 [i]After the Babylonian exile, Jechoniah
became the father of Shealtiel, Shealtiel the father of Zerubbabel, 13 Zerubbabel the father of
Abiud. Abiud became the father of Eliakim,
Eliakim the father of Azor, 14 Azor the father
of Zadok. Zadok became the father of Achim,
Achim the father of Eliud, 15 Eliud the father
of Eleazar. Eleazar became the father of Matthan, Matthan the father of Jacob, 16 Jacob the
father of Joseph, the husband of Mary. Of her
was born Jesus who is called the Messiah.

17 *Thus the total number of generations
from Abraham to David is fourteen generations;
from David to the Babylonian exile, fourteen
generations; from the Babylonian exile to the
Messiah, fourteen generations.

**The Birth of Jesus** 18 *Now this is how
the birth of Jesus Christ came about. When his
mother Mary was betrothed to Joseph, but before they lived together, she was found with
child through the holy Spirit. 19 *Joseph her
husband, since he was a righteous man, yet
unwilling to expose her to shame, decided to
divorce her quietly. 20 [j]*Such was his intention when, behold, the angel of the Lord appeared to him in a dream and said, "Joseph, son
of David, do not be afraid to take Mary your
wife into your home. For it is through the holy
Spirit that this child has been conceived in her.
21 *She will bear a son and you are to name
him Jesus, because he will save his people from
their sins." 22 All this took place to fulfill what
the Lord had said through the prophet:

23 [k]*"Behold, the virgin shall be with child
and bear a son,
and they shall name him Emmanuel,"

which means "God is with us." 24 When Joseph awoke, he did as the angel of the Lord had
commanded him and took his wife into his
home. 25 [l]*He had no relations with her until
she bore a son, and he named him Jesus.

h 2 Kgs 25, 1-21; 1 Chr 3, 10-15.
i 1 Chr 3, 16-19.
j 2, 13.19; Lk 1, 35.
k Is 7, 14 LXX.
l Lk 2, 7.

*

1, 7: The successor of Abijah was not Asaph but Asa (see 1 Chr 3, 10). Some textual witnesses read the latter name; however, *Asaph* is better attested. Matthew may have deliberately introduced the psalmist Asaph into the genealogy (and in v 10 the prophet Amos) in order to show that Jesus is the fulfillment not only of the promises made to David (see 2 Sm 7) but of all the Old Testament.

1, 10: *Amos:* some textual witnesses read *Amon,* who was the actual successor of Manasseh (see 1 Chr 3, 14).

1, 17: Matthew is concerned with fourteen generations, probably because fourteen is the numerical value of the Hebrew letters forming the name of David. In the second section of the genealogy (6b–11), three kings of Judah, Ahaziah, Joash, and Amaziah, have been omitted (see 1 Chr 3, 11–12), so that there are fourteen generations in that section. Yet the third (12–16) apparently has only thirteen. Since Matthew here emphasizes that each section has fourteen, it is unlikely that the thirteen of the last was due to his oversight. Some scholars suggest that *Jesus who is called the Messiah* (16b) doubles the final member of the chain: *Jesus,* born within the family of David, opens up the new age as *Messiah,* so that in fact there are fourteen generations in the third section. This is perhaps too subtle, and the hypothesis of a slip not on the part of Matthew but of a later scribe seems likely. On *Messiah,* see the note on Lk 2, 11.

1, 18–25: This first story of the infancy narrative spells out what is summarily indicated in v 16. The virginal conception of Jesus is the work of the Spirit of God. Joseph's decision to divorce Mary is overcome by the heavenly command that he take her into his home and accept the child as his own. The natural genealogical line is broken but the promises to David are fulfilled; through Joseph's adoption the child belongs to the family of David. Matthew sees the virginal conception as the fulfillment of Is 7, 14.

1, 18: *Betrothed to Joseph:* betrothal was the first part of the marriage, constituting a man and woman as husband and wife. Subsequent infidelity was considered adultery. The betrothal was followed some months later by the husband's taking his wife into his home, at which time normal married life began.

1, 19: *A righteous man:* as a devout observer of the Mosaic law, Joseph wished to break his union with someone whom he suspected of gross violation of the law. It is commonly said that the law required him to do so, but the texts usually given in support of that view, e.g., Dt 22, 20–21, do not clearly pertain to Joseph's situation. *Unwilling to expose her to shame:* the penalty for proved adultery was death by stoning; cf Dt 22, 21–23.

1, 20: *The angel of the Lord:* in the Old Testament a common designation of God in communication with a human being. *In a dream:* see 2, 13.19.22. These dreams may be meant to recall the dreams of Joseph, son of Jacob the patriarch (Gn 37, 5–11.19). A closer parallel is the dream of Amram, father of Moses, related by Josephus (*Antiquities* 2, 9, 3 **212, 215–16).

1, 21: *Jesus:* in first-century Judaism the Hebrew name Joshua (Greek *Iēsous*) meaning "Yahweh helps" was interpreted as "Yahweh saves."

1, 23: *God is with us:* God's promise of deliverance to Judah in Isaiah's time is seen by Matthew as fulfilled in the birth of Jesus, in whom God is with his people. The name Emmanuel is alluded to at the end of the gospel where the risen Jesus assures his disciples of his continued presence, ". . . I am with you always, until the end of the age" (28, 20).

1, 25: *Until she bore a son:* the evangelist is concerned to emphasize that Joseph was not responsible for the conception of Jesus. The Greek word translated "until" does not imply normal marital conduct after Jesus' birth, nor does it exclude it.

## CHAPTER 2

**The Visit of the Magi** 1 *When Jesus was
born in Bethlehem of Judea, in the days of King
Herod, behold, magi from the east arrived in
Jerusalem, 2 [m]*saying, "Where is the newborn king of the Jews? We saw his star at its
rising and have come to do him homage."
3 When King Herod heard this, he was greatly
troubled, and all Jerusalem with him. 4 *Assembling all the chief priests and the scribes of
the people, he inquired of them where the Messiah was to be born. 5 [n]They said to him, "In
Bethlehem of Judea, for thus it has been written
through the prophet:

6 'And you, Bethlehem, land of Judah,
are by no means least among the rulers of
Judah;
since from you shall come a ruler,
who is to shepherd my people Israel.' "

7 Then Herod called the magi secretly and ascertained from them the time of the star's appearance. 8 He sent them to Bethlehem and
said, "Go and search diligently for the child.
When you have found him, bring me word, that
I too may go and do him homage." 9 After
their audience with the king they set out. And
behold, the star that they had seen at its rising
preceded them, until it came and stopped over
the place where the child was. 10 They were
overjoyed at seeing the star, 11 [o]*and on entering the house they saw the child with Mary his
mother. They prostrated themselves and did him
homage. Then they opened their treasures and
offered him gifts of gold, frankincense, and
myrrh. 12 And having been warned in a dream
not to return to Herod, they departed for their
country by another way.

**The Flight to Egypt** 13 *When they had
departed, behold, the angel of the Lord appeared to Joseph in a dream and said, "Rise,
take the child and his mother, flee to Egypt, and
stay there until I tell you. Herod is going to
search for the child to destroy him." 14 Joseph
rose and took the child and his mother by night
and departed for Egypt. 15 [p]*He stayed there
until the death of Herod, that what the Lord had
said through the prophet might be fulfilled,
"Out of Egypt I called my son."

**The Massacre of the Infants** 16 When
Herod realized that he had been deceived by the
magi, he became furious. He ordered the massacre of all the boys in Bethlehem and its vicinity
two years old and under, in accordance with the
time he had ascertained from the magi. 17 Then
was fulfilled what had been said through Jeremiah the prophet:

18 [q]*"A voice was heard in Ramah,
sobbing and loud lamentation;
Rachel weeping for her children,
and she would not be consoled,
since they were no more."

**The Return from Egypt** 19 When Herod
had died, behold, the angel of the Lord appeared
in a dream to Joseph in Egypt 20 [r]*and said,
"Rise, take the child and his mother and go to
the land of Israel, for those who sought the
child's life are dead." 21 He rose, took the
child and his mother, and went to the land of
Israel. 22 *But when he heard that Archelaus

m Nm 24, 17.
n Mi 5, 1 / 2 Sm 5, 2.
o Ps 72, 10-11.15; Is 60, 6.
p Hos 11, 1.
q Jer 31, 15.
r Ex 4, 19.

*

2, 1–12: The future rejection of Jesus by Israel and his acceptance by the Gentiles are retrojected into this scene of the narrative.

2, 1: *In the days of King Herod:* Herod reigned from 37 to 4 B.C. *Magi:* originally a designation of the Persian priestly caste, the word became used of those who were regarded as having more than human knowledge. Matthew's magi are astrologers.

2, 2: *We saw his star:* it was a common ancient belief that a new star appeared at the time of a ruler's birth. Matthew also draws upon the Old Testament story of Balaam, who had prophesied that "A star shall advance from Jacob" (Nm 24, 17), though there the star means not an astral phenomenon but the king himself.

2, 4: Herod's consultation with the chief priests and scribes has some similarity to a Jewish legend about the child Moses in which the "sacred scribes" warn Pharaoh about the imminent birth of one who will deliver Israel from Egypt and the king makes plans to destroy him.

2, 11: Cf Ps 72, 10.15; Is 60, 6. These Old Testament texts led to the interpretation of the magi as kings.

2, 13–23: Biblical and nonbiblical traditions about Moses are here applied to the child Jesus, though the dominant Old Testament type is not Moses but Israel (see v 15).

2, 13: *Flee to Egypt:* Egypt was a traditional place of refuge for those fleeing from danger in Palestine (see 1 Kgs 11, 40; Jer 26, 21), but the main reason why the child is to be taken to Egypt is that he may relive the Exodus experience of Israel.

2, 15: The fulfillment citation is taken from Hos 11, 1. Israel, God's son, was called out of Egypt at the time of the Exodus; Jesus, the Son of God, will similarly be called out of that land in a new exodus. The father-son relationship between God and the nation is set in a higher key. Here the son is not a group adopted as "son of God," but the child who, as conceived by the holy Spirit, stands in unique relation to God. He is son of David and of Abraham, of Mary and of Joseph, but, above all, of God.

2, 18: Jer 31, 15 portrays Rachel, wife of the patriarch Jacob, weeping for her children taken into exile at the time of the Assyrian invasion of the northern kingdom (722–21 B.C.). Bethlehem was traditionally identified with Ephrath, the place near which Rachel was buried (see Gn 35, 19; 48, 7), and the mourning of Rachel is here applied to her lost children of a later age. *Ramah:* about six miles north of Jerusalem. The lamentation of Rachel is so great as to be heard at a far distance.

2, 20: *For those who sought the child's life are dead:* Moses, who had fled from Egypt because the Pharaoh sought to kill him (see Ex 2, 15), was told to return there, "for all the men who sought your life are dead" (Ex 4, 19).

2, 22: With the agreement of the emperor Augustus, Archelaus received half of his father's kingdom, including Judea, after Herod's death. He had the title "ethnarch" (i.e., "ruler of a nation") and reigned from 4 B.C. to A.D. 6.

was ruling over Judea in place of his father
Herod, he was afraid to go back there. And
because he had been warned in a dream, he
departed for the region of Galilee. **23** [s]*He
went and dwelt in a town called Nazareth, so
that what had been spoken through the prophets
might be fulfilled, "He shall be called a Nazorean."

## *II: THE PROCLAMATION OF THE KINGDOM*

## CHAPTER 3

### The Preaching of John the Baptist

**1** [t]*In those days John the Baptist appeared,
preaching in the desert of Judea **2** [u]*[and] saying, "Repent, for the kingdom of heaven is at
hand!" **3** [v]*It was of him that the prophet Isaiah had spoken when he said:

"A voice of one crying out in the desert,
'Prepare the way of the Lord,
make straight his paths.' "

**4** [w]*John wore clothing made of camel's hair
and had a leather belt around his waist. His food
was locusts and wild honey. **5** At that time
Jerusalem, all Judea, and the whole region
around the Jordan were going out to him **6** *and
were being baptized by him in the Jordan River
as they acknowledged their sins.

**7** [x]*When he saw many of the Pharisees and
Sadducees coming to his baptism, he said to
them, "You brood of vipers! Who warned you
to flee from the coming wrath? **8** Produce good
fruit as evidence of your repentance. **9** [y]And do
not presume to say to yourselves, 'We have
Abraham as our father.' For I tell you, God can
raise up children to Abraham from these stones.
**10** Even now the ax lies at the root of the trees.
Therefore every tree that does not bear good
fruit will be cut down and thrown into the fire.
**11** [z]*I am baptizing you with water, for repentance, but the one who is coming after me is
mightier than I.

I am not worthy to carry his sandals. He will
baptize you with the holy Spirit and fire.
**12** [a]*His winnowing fan is in his hand. He will
clear his threshing floor and gather his wheat
into his barn, but the chaff he will burn with
unquenchable fire."

s 13, 54; Mk 1, 9; Lk 2, 39; 4, 34; Jn 19, 19.
t Mk 1, 2-8; Lk 3, 2-17.
u 4, 17; 10, 7.
v Is 40, 3.
w 11, 7-8; 2 Kgs 1, 8; Zec 13, 4.
x 12, 34; 23, 33; Is 59, 5.
y Jn 8, 33.39; Rom 9, 7-8; Gal 4, 21-31.
z Jn 1, 26-27.33; Acts 1, 5.
a 13, 30; Is 41, 16; Jer 15, 7.

*

2, 23: *Nazareth . . . he shall be called a Nazorean:* the tradition of Jesus' residence in Nazareth was firmly established, and Matthew sees it as being in accordance with the foreannounced plan of God. The town of Nazareth is not mentioned in the Old Testament, and no such prophecy can be found there. The vague expression "through the prophets" may be due to Matthew's seeing a connection between Nazareth and certain texts in which there are words with a remote similarity to the name of that town. Some such Old Testament texts are Is 11, 1 where the Davidic king of the future is called "a bud" *(nēser)* that shall blossom from the roots of Jesse, and Jgs 13, 5.7 where Samson, the future deliverer of Israel from the Philistines, is called one who shall be consecrated (a *nāzîr*) to God.

3, 1–12: Here Matthew takes up the order of Jesus' ministry found in the gospel of Mark, beginning with the preparatory preaching of John the Baptist.

3, 1: Unlike Luke, Matthew says nothing of the Baptist's origins and does not make him a relative of Jesus. *The desert of Judea:* the barren region west of the Dead Sea extending up the Jordan valley.

3, 2: *Repent:* the Baptist calls for a change of heart and conduct, a turning of one's life from rebellion to obedience toward God. *The kingdom of heaven is at hand:* "heaven" (literally, "the heavens") is a substitute for the name "God" that was avoided by devout Jews of the time out of reverence. The expression "the kingdom of heaven" occurs only in the gospel of Matthew. It means the effective rule of God over his people. In its fullness it includes not only human obedience to God's word, but the triumph of God over physical evils, supremely over death. In the expectation found in Jewish apocalyptic, the kingdom was to be ushered in by a judgment in which sinners would be condemned and perish, an expectation shared by the Baptist. This was modified in Christian understanding where the kingdom was seen as being established in stages, culminating with the parousia of Jesus.

3, 3: See the note on Jn 1, 23.

3, 4: The clothing of John recalls the austere dress of the prophet Elijah (2 Kgs 1, 8). The expectation of the return of Elijah from heaven to prepare Israel for the final manifestation of God's kingdom was widespread, and according to Matthew this expectation was fulfilled in the Baptist's ministry (11, 14; 17, 11–13).

3, 6: Ritual washing was practiced by various groups in Palestine between 150 B.C. and A.D. 250. John's baptism may have been related to the purificatory washings of the Essenes at Qumran.

3, 7: *Pharisees and Sadducees:* the former were marked by devotion to the law, written and oral, and the scribes, experts in the law, belonged predominantly to this group. The Sadducees were the priestly aristocratic party, centered in Jerusalem. They accepted as scripture only the first five books of the Old Testament, followed only the letter of the law, rejected the oral legal traditions, and were opposed to teachings not found in the Pentateuch, such as the resurrection of the dead. Matthew links both of these groups together as enemies of Jesus (16, 1.6.11.12; cf Mk 8, 11–13.15). The threatening words that follow are addressed to them rather than to "the crowds" as in Lk 3, 7. *The coming wrath:* the judgment that will bring about the destruction of unrepentant sinners.

3, 11: *Baptize you with the holy Spirit and fire:* the water baptism of John will be followed by an "immersion" of the repentant in the cleansing power of the Spirit of God, and of the unrepentant in the destroying power of God's judgment. However, some see *the holy Spirit* and *fire* as synonymous, and the effect of this "baptism" as either purification or destruction. See the note on Lk 3, 16.

3, 12: The discrimination between the good and the bad is compared to the procedure by which a farmer separates wheat and chaff. The *winnowing fan* was a forklike shovel with which the threshed wheat was thrown into the air. The kernels fell to the ground; the light chaff, blown off by the wind, was gathered and burned up.

**The Baptism of Jesus** 13 [b]*Then Jesus
came from Galilee to John at the Jordan to be
baptized by him. 14 *John tried to prevent him,
saying, "I need to be baptized by you, and yet
you are coming to me?" 15 Jesus said to him
in reply, "Allow it now, for thus it is fitting for
us to fulfill all righteousness." Then he allowed
him. 16 [c]*After Jesus was baptized, he came
up from the water and behold, the heavens were
opened [for him], and he saw the Spirit of God
descending like a dove [and] coming upon him.
17 [d]*And a voice came from the heavens, saying, "This is my beloved Son, with whom I am
well pleased."

## CHAPTER 4

**The Temptation of Jesus** 1 [e]*Then Jesus
was led by the Spirit into the desert to be tempted by the devil. 2 [f]*He fasted for forty days and
forty nights, and afterwards he was hungry.
3 The tempter approached and said to him, "If
you are the Son of God, command that these
stones become loaves of bread." 4 [g]*He said
in reply, "It is written:

'One does not live by bread alone,
but by every word that comes forth
from the mouth of God.'"

5 *Then the devil took him to the holy city, and
made him stand on the parapet of the temple,
6 [h]and said to him, "If you are the Son of God,
throw yourself down. For it is written:

'He will command his angels concerning
you'
and "with their hands they will support
you,
lest you dash your foot against a stone.'"

7 [i]Jesus answered him, "Again it is written,
'You shall not put the Lord, your God, to the
test.'" 8 Then the devil took him up to a very
high mountain, and showed him all the kingdoms of the world in their magnificence,
9 *and he said to him, "All these I shall give
to you, if you will prostrate yourself and worship me." 10 [j]At this, Jesus said to him, "Get
away, Satan! It is written:

'The Lord, your God, shall you worship
and him alone shall you serve.'"

11 Then the devil left him and, behold, angels
came and ministered to him.

**The Beginning of the Galilean Ministry**
12 [k]*When he heard that John had been arrested, he withdrew to Galilee. 13 [l]He left Nazareth and went to live in Capernaum by the sea,
in the region of Zebulun and Naphtali, 14 that
what had been said through Isaiah the prophet
might be fulfilled:

15 [m]"Land of Zebulun and land of Naphtali,
the way to the sea, beyond the Jordan,
Galilee of the Gentiles,
16 [n]the people who sit in darkness
have seen a great light,
on those dwelling in a land overshadowed
by death
light has arisen."

b Mk 1, 9-11; Lk 3, 21-22; Jn 1, 31-34.
c Is 42, 1.
d 12, 18; 17, 5; Gn 22, 2; Ps 2, 7; Is 42, 1.
e Mk 1, 12-13; Lk 4, 1-13.
f Ex 24, 18; Dt 8, 2.
g Dt 8, 3.
h Ps 91, 11-12.
i Dt 6, 16.
j 16, 23; Dt 6, 13.
k Mk 1, 14-15; Lk 4, 14.31.
l Jn 2, 12.
m Is 8, 23 LXX; 9, 1.
n Lk 1, 79.

*

3, 13–17: The baptism of Jesus is the occasion on which he is equipped for his ministry by the holy Spirit and proclaimed to be the Son of God.

3, 14–15: This dialogue, peculiar to Matthew, reveals John's awareness of Jesus' superiority to him as the mightier one who is coming and who will baptize with the holy Spirit (11). His reluctance to admit Jesus among the sinners whom he is baptizing with water is overcome by Jesus' response. *To fulfill all righteousness:* in this gospel to *fulfill* usually refers to fulfillment of prophecy, and *righteousness* to moral conduct in conformity with God's will. Here, however, as in 5, 6 and 6, 33, *righteousness* seems to mean the saving activity of God. *To fulfill all righteousness* is to submit to the plan of God for the salvation of the human race. This involves Jesus' identification with sinners; hence the propriety of his accepting John's baptism.

3, 16: *The Spirit . . . coming upon him:* cf Is 42, 1.

3, 17: *This is my beloved Son:* the Marcan address to Jesus (Mk 1, 11) is changed into a proclamation. The Father's voice speaks in terms that reflect Is 42, 1, Ps 2, 7, and Gn 22, 2.

4, 1–11: Jesus, proclaimed Son of God at his baptism, is subjected to a triple temptation. Obedience to the Father is a characteristic of true sonship, and Jesus is tempted by the devil to rebel against God, overtly in the third case, more subtly in the first two. Each refusal of Jesus is expressed in language taken from the Book of Deuteronomy (Dt 8, 3; 6, 13.16). The testings of Jesus resemble those of Israel during the wandering in the desert and later in Canaan, and the victory of Jesus, the true Israel and the true Son, contrasts with the failure of the ancient and disobedient "son," the old Israel. In the temptation account Matthew is almost identical with Luke; both seem to have drawn upon the same source.

4, 2: *Forty days and forty nights:* the same time as that during which Moses remained on Sinai (Ex 24, 18). The time reference, however, seems primarily intended to recall the forty years during which Israel was tempted in the desert (Dt 8, 2).

4, 4: Cf Dt 8, 3. Jesus refuses to use his power for his own benefit and accepts whatever God wills.

4, 5–7: The devil supports his proposal by an appeal to the scriptures, Ps 91, 11a.12. Unlike Israel (Dt 6, 16), Jesus refuses to "test" God by demanding from him an extraordinary show of power.

4, 9: The worship of Satan to which Jesus is tempted is probably intended to recall Israel's worship of false gods. His refusal is expressed in the words of Dt 6, 13.

4, 12–17: Isaiah's prophecy of the light rising upon Zebulun and Naphtali (Is 8, 23—9, 1) is fulfilled in Jesus' residence at Capernaum. The territory of these two tribes was the first to be devastated (733–32 B.C.) at the time of the Assyrian invasion. In order to accommodate Jesus' move to Capernaum to the prophecy, Matthew speaks of that town as being "in the region of Zebulun and Naphtali" (13), whereas it was only in the territory of the latter, and he understands the sea of the prophecy, the Mediterranean, as the sea of Galilee.

**17** [o]*From that time on, Jesus began to preach
and say, "Repent, for the kingdom of heaven is
at hand."

**The Call of the First Disciples** 18 [p]*As
he was walking by the Sea of Galilee, he saw
two brothers, Simon who is called Peter, and his
brother Andrew, casting a net into the sea; they
were fishermen. **19** He said to them, "Come
after me, and I will make you fishers of men."
**20** *At once they left their nets and followed
him. **21** He walked along from there and saw
two other brothers, James, the son of Zebedee,
and his brother John. They were in a boat, with
their father Zebedee, mending their nets. He
called them, **22** and immediately they left their
boat and their father and followed him.

**Ministering to a Great Multitude**
**23** [q]*He went around all of Galilee, teaching in
their synagogues, proclaiming the gospel of the
kingdom, and curing every disease and illness
among the people. **24** *His fame spread to all
of Syria, and they brought to him all who were
sick with various diseases and racked with pain,
those who were possessed, lunatics, and para-
lytics, and he cured them. **25** [r]*And great
crowds from Galilee, the Decapolis, Jerusalem,
and Judea, and from beyond the Jordan followed him.

## CHAPTER 5

**The Sermon on the Mount** 1 *When he
saw the crowds, he went up the mountain, and
after he had sat down, his disciples came to him.
**2** He began to teach them, saying:

### The Beatitudes

**3** [s]*"Blessed are the poor in spirit,
for theirs is the kingdom of heaven.
**4** [t]*Blessed are they who mourn,
for they will be comforted.
**5** [u]*Blessed are the meek,
for they will inherit the land.
**6** *Blessed are they who hunger and thirst for
righteousness,
for they will be satisfied.
**7** [v]Blessed are the merciful,
for they will be shown mercy.
**8** [w]*Blessed are the clean of heart,
for they will see God.
**9** Blessed are the peacemakers,
for they will be called children of God.

o 3, 2.
p Mk 1, 16-20; Lk 5, 1-11.
q 9, 35; Mk 1, 39; Lk 4, 15.44.
r Mk 3, 7-8; Lk 6, 17-19.
s Lk 6, 20-23.
t Is 61, 2-3; Rv 21, 4.
u Gn 13, 15; Ps 37, 11.
v 18, 33; Jas 2, 13.
w Pss 24, 4-5; 73, 1.

*

4, 17: At the beginning of his preaching Jesus takes up the words of John the Baptist (3, 2) although with a different meaning; in his ministry the kingdom of heaven has already begun to be present (12, 28).

4, 18–22: The call of the first disciples promises them a share in Jesus' work and entails abandonment of family and former way of life. Three of the four, Simon, James, and John, are distinguished among the disciples by a closer relation with Jesus (17, 1; 26, 37).

4, 20: Here and in v 22, as in Mark (1, 16–20) and unlike the Lucan account (5, 1–11), the disciples' response is motivated only by Jesus' invitation, an element that emphasizes his mysterious power.

4, 23–25: This summary of Jesus' ministry concludes the narrative part of the first book of Matthew's gospel (chs 3–4). The activities of his ministry are teaching, proclaiming the gospel, and healing; cf 9, 35.

4, 23: *Their synagogues:* Matthew usually designates the Jewish synagogues as *their synagogue(s)* (9, 35; 10, 17; 12, 9; 13, 54) or, in address to Jews, *your synagogues* (23, 34), an indication that he wrote after the break between church and synagogue.

4, 24: *Syria:* the Roman province to which Palestine belonged.

4, 25: *The Decapolis:* a federation of Greek cities in Palestine, originally ten in number, all but one east of the Jordan.

5, 1—7, 29: The first of the five discourses that are a central part of the structure of this gospel. It is the discourse section of the first book and contains sayings of Jesus derived from Q and from M. The Lucan parallel is in that gospel's "Sermon on the Plain" (Lk 6, 20–49), although some of the sayings in Matthew's "Sermon on the Mount" have their parallels in other parts of Luke. The careful topical arrangement of the sermon is probably not due only to Matthew's editing; he seems to have had a structured discourse of Jesus as one of his sources. The form of that source may have been as follows: four beatitudes (5, 3–4.6.11–12), a section on the new righteousness with illustrations (5, 17.20–24.27–28.33–48), a section on good works (6, 1–6.16–18), and three warnings (7, 1–2.15–21.24–27).

5, 1–2: Unlike Luke's sermon, this is addressed not only to the disciples but to the crowds (see 7, 28).

5, 3–12: The form *Blessed are (is)* occurs frequently in the Old Testament in the Wisdom literature and in the psalms. Although modified by Matthew, the first, second, fourth, and ninth beatitudes have Lucan parallels (5, 3 // Lk 6, 20; 5, 4 // Lk 6, 21b; 5, 6 // Lk 6, 21a; 5, 11–12 // Lk 5, 22–23). The others were added by the evangelist and are probably his own composition. A few manuscripts, Western and Alexandrian, and many versions and patristic quotations give the second and third beatitudes in inverted order.

5, 3: *The poor in spirit:* in the Old Testament, the *poor (ănāwîm) are those who are without material possessions and whose confidence is in God (see Is 61, 1; Zep 2, 3; in the NAB the word is translated lowly and humble, respectively, in those texts). Matthew added in spirit in order either to indicate that only the devout poor were meant or to extend the beatitude to all, of whatever social rank, who recognized their complete dependence on God. The same phrase poor in spirit is found in the Qumran literature (1QM 14, 7).*

5, 4: Cf Is 61, 2, "(The Lord has sent me) . . . to comfort all who mourn." *They will be comforted:* here the passive is a "theological passive" equivalent to the active "God will comfort them"; so also in vv 6 and 7.

5, 5: Cf Ps 37, 11, ". . . the meek shall possess the land." In the psalm "the land" means the land of Palestine; here it means the kingdom.

5, 6: *For righteousness:* a Matthean addition. For the meaning of *righteousness* here, see the note on 3, 14–15.

5, 8: Cf Ps 24, 4. Only one "whose heart is clean" can take part in the temple worship. To be with God in the temple is described in Ps 42, 3 as "beholding his face," but here the promise to *the clean of heart* is that they will *see God* not in the temple but in the coming kingdom.

**10** [x]*Blessed are they who are persecuted for
the sake of righteousness,
for theirs is the kingdom of heaven.

**11** [y]Blessed are you when they insult you
and persecute you and utter every kind of
evil against you [falsely] because of me.
**12** [z]*Rejoice and be glad, for your reward will
be great in heaven. Thus they persecuted the
prophets who were before you.

## The Similes of Salt and Light

**13** [a]*"You are the salt of the earth. But if salt
loses its taste, with what can it be seasoned? It
is no longer good for anything but to be thrown
out and trampled underfoot. **14** [b]You are the
light of the world. A city set on a mountain
cannot be hidden. **15** [c]Nor do they light a lamp
and then put it under a bushel basket; it is set on
a lampstand, where it gives light to all in the
house. **16** [d]Just so, your light must shine before
others, that they may see your good deeds and
glorify your heavenly Father.

## Teaching about the Law

**17** *"Do not
think that I have come to abolish the law or the
prophets. I have come not to abolish but to
fulfill. **18** [e]Amen, I say to you, until heaven
and earth pass away, not the smallest letter or
the smallest part of a letter will pass from the
law, until all things have taken place.
**19** *Therefore, whoever breaks one of the least
of these commandments and teaches others to
do so will be called least in the kingdom of
heaven. But whoever obeys and teaches these
commandments will be called greatest in the
kingdom of heaven. **20** I tell you, unless your
righteousness surpasses that of the scribes and
Pharisees, you will not enter into the kingdom
of heaven.

## Teaching about Anger

**21** [f]*"You have
heard that it was said to your ancestors, 'You
shall not kill; and whoever kills will be liable to
judgment.' **22** [g]*But I say to you, whoever is
angry with his brother will be liable to judgment, and whoever says to his brother, 'Raqa,'
will be answerable to the Sanhedrin, and whoever says, 'You fool,' will be liable to fiery
Gehenna. **23** [h]Therefore, if you bring your gift
to the altar, and there recall that your brother has
anything against you, **24** leave your gift there
at the altar, go first and be reconciled with your
brother, and then come and offer your gift.
**25** [i]Settle with your opponent quickly while on
the way to court with him. Otherwise your op-

x 1 Pt 2, 20; 3, 14; 4, 14.
y 10, 22; Acts 5, 41.
z 2 Chr 36, 16; Heb 11, 32-38; Jas 5, 10.
a Mk 9, 50; Lk 14, 34-35.
b Jn 8, 12.
c Mk 4, 21; Lk 8, 16; 11, 33.
d Jn 3, 21.
e Lk 16, 17.
f Ex 20, 13; Dt 5, 17.
g Jas 1, 19-20.
h Mk 11, 25.
i 18, 34-35; Lk 12, 58-59.

*

5, 10: *Righteousness* here, as usually in Matthew, means conduct in conformity with God's will.

5, 12: *The prophets who were before you:* the disciples of Jesus stand in the line of the persecuted prophets of Israel. Some would see the expression as indicating also that Matthew considered all Christian disciples as prophets.

5, 13–16: By their deeds the disciples are to influence the world for good. They can no more escape notice than *a city set on a mountain.* If they fail in good works, they are as useless as flavorless salt or as a lamp whose light is concealed.

5, 13: The unusual supposition of salt losing its flavor has led some to suppose that the saying refers to the salt of the Dead Sea that, because chemically impure, could lose its taste.

5, 17–20: This statement of Jesus' position concerning the Mosaic law is composed of traditional material from Matthew's sermon documentation (see the note on 5, 1—7, 29), other Q material (cf 18 and Lk 16, 17), and the evangelist's own editorial touches. *To fulfill* the law appears at first to mean a literal enforcement of the law in the least detail: *until heaven and earth pass away* nothing of the law *will pass* (18). Yet the "passing away" of heaven and earth is not necessarily the end of the world understood, as in much apocalyptic literature, as the dissolution of the existing universe. The "turning of the ages" comes with the apocalyptic event of Jesus' death and resurrection, and those to whom this gospel is addressed are living in the new and final age, prophesied by Isaiah as the time of "new heavens and a new earth" (Is 65, 17; 66, 22). Meanwhile, during Jesus' ministry when the kingdom is already breaking in, his mission remains within the framework of the law, though with significant anticipation of the age to come, as the following antitheses (vv 21–48) show.

5, 19: Probably *these commandments* means those of the Mosaic law. But this is an interim ethic "until heaven and earth pass away."

5, 21–48: Six examples of the conduct demanded of the Christian disciple. Each deals with a commandment of the law, introduced by *You have heard that it was said to your ancestors* or an equivalent formula, followed by Jesus' teaching in respect to that commandment, *But I say to you;* thus their designation as "antitheses." Three of them accept the Mosaic law but extend or deepen it (21–22; 27–28; 43–44); three reject it as a standard of conduct for the disciples (31–32; 33–37; 38–39).

5, 21: Cf Ex 20, 13; Dt 5, 17. The second part of the verse is not an exact quotation from the Old Testament, but cf Ex 21, 12.

5, 22: Anger is the motive behind murder, as the insulting epithets are steps that may lead to it. They, as well as the deed, are all forbidden. *Raqa:* an Aramaic word *rêqa'* or *rêqâ* probably meaning "imbecile," "blockhead," a term of abuse. The ascending order of punishment, *judgment* (by a local council?), trial before *the Sanhedrin,* condemnation to *Gehenna,* points to a higher degree of seriousness in each of the offenses. *Sanhedrin:* the highest judicial body of Judaism. *Gehenna:* in Hebrew *gê-hinnōm,* "Valley of Hinnom," or *gê ben-hinnōm,* "Valley of the son of Hinnom," southwest of Jerusalem, the center of an idolatrous cult during the monarchy in which children were offered in sacrifice (see 2 Kgs 23, 10; Jer 7, 31). In Jos 18, 16 (Septuagint, Codex Vaticanus) the Hebrew is transliterated into Greek as *gaienna,* which appears in the New Testament as *geenna.* The concept of punishment of sinners by fire either after death or after the final judgment is found in Jewish apocalyptic literature (e.g., Enoch 90, 26) but the name *geenna* is first given to the place of punishment in the New Testament.

5, 22–26: Reconciliation with an offended brother is urged in the admonition of vv 23–24 and the parable of vv 25–26 (// Lk 12, 58–59). The severity of the judge in the parable is a warning of the fate of unrepentant sinners in the coming judgment by God.

ponent will hand you over to the judge, and the
judge will hand you over to the guard, and you
will be thrown into prison. **26** Amen, I say to
you, you will not be released until you have paid
the last penny.

### Teaching about Adultery

**27** j* "You
have heard that it was said, 'You shall not commit adultery.' **28** But I say to you, everyone
who looks at a woman with lust has already
committed adultery with her in his heart.
**29** k* If your right eye causes you to sin, tear it
out and throw it away. It is better for you to lose
one of your members than to have your whole
body thrown into Gehenna. **30** And if your
right hand causes you to sin, cut it off and throw
it away. It is better for you to lose one of your
members than to have your whole body go into
Gehenna.

### Teaching about Divorce

**31** l* "It was
also said, 'Whoever divorces his wife must give
her a bill of divorce.' **32** m But I say to you,
whoever divorces his wife (unless the marriage
is unlawful) causes her to commit adultery, and
whoever marries a divorced woman commits
adultery.

### Teaching about Oaths

**33** n* "Again you
have heard that it was said to your ancestors,
'Do not take a false oath, but make good to the
Lord all that you vow.' **34** o* But I say to you,
do not swear at all; not by heaven, for it is God's
throne; **35** nor by the earth, for it is his footstool; nor by Jerusalem, for it is the city of the
great King. **36** Do not swear by your head, for
you cannot make a single hair white or black.
**37** * Let your 'Yes' mean 'Yes,' and your 'No'
mean 'No.' Anything more is from the evil one.

### Teaching about Retaliation

**38** p* "You
have heard that it was said, 'An eye for an eye
and a tooth for a tooth.' **39** q But I say to you,
offer no resistance to one who is evil. When
someone strikes you on [your] right cheek, turn
the other one to him as well. **40** If anyone wants
to go to law with you over your tunic, hand him
your cloak as well. **41** r* Should anyone press
you into service for one mile, go with him for
two miles. **42** s Give to the one who asks of
you, and do not turn your back on one who
wants to borrow.

### Love of Enemies

**43** tu* "You have heard
that it was said, 'You shall love your neighbor
and hate your enemy.' **44** But I say to you, love
your enemies, and pray for those who persecute
you, **45** that you may be children of your heavenly Father, for he makes his sun rise on the bad
and the good, and causes rain to fall on the just
and the unjust. **46** * For if you love those who
love you, what recompense will you have? Do
not the tax collectors do the same? **47** * And if

j Ex 20, 14; Dt 5, 18.
k 18, 8-9; Mk 9, 43-47.
l 19, 3-9; Dt 24, 1.
m Lk 16, 18; 1 Cor 7, 10-11.
n Lv 19, 12; Nm 30, 3.
o Ps 48, 3; Sir 23, 9; Is 66, 1; Jas 5, 12.
p Ex 21, 24; Lv 24, 19-20.
q Lk 6, 29-30.
r Lam 3, 30.
s Dt 15, 7-8.
t Lk 6, 27.32-36.
u Lv 19, 18.

*

5, 27: See Ex 20, 14; Dt 5, 18.

5, 29–30: No sacrifice is too great to avoid total destruction in *Gehenna.*

5, 31–32: See Dt 24, 1–5. The Old Testament commandment that a bill of divorce be given to the woman assumes the legitimacy of divorce itself. It is this that Jesus denies. (*Unless the marriage is unlawful*): this "exceptive clause," as it is often called, occurs also in 19, 9, where the Greek is slightly different. There are other sayings of Jesus about divorce that prohibit it absolutely (see Mk 10, 11–12; Lk 16, 18; cf 1 Cor 7, 10.11b), and most scholars agree that they represent the stand of Jesus. Matthew's "exceptive clauses" are understood by some as a modification of the absolute prohibition. It seems, however, that the unlawfulness that Matthew gives as a reason why a marriage must be broken refers to a situation peculiar to his community: the violation of Mosaic law forbidding marriage between persons of certain blood and/or legal relationship (Lv 18, 6–18). Marriages of that sort were regarded as incest (*porneia*), but some rabbis allowed Gentile converts to Judaism who had contracted such marriages to remain in them. Matthew's "exceptive clause" is against such permissiveness for Gentile converts to Christianity; cf the similar prohibition of *porneia* in Acts 15, 20.29. In this interpretation, the clause constitutes no exception to the absolute prohibition of divorce when the marriage is lawful.

5, 33: This is not an exact quotation of any Old Testament text, but see Ex 20, 7, Dt 5, 11, and Lv 19, 12. The purpose of an oath was to guarantee truthfulness by one's calling on God as witness.

5, 34–36: The use of these oath formularies that avoid the divine name is in fact equivalent to swearing by it, for all the things sworn by are related to God.

5, 37: *Let your 'Yes' mean 'Yes,' and your 'No' mean 'No':* literally, "let your speech be 'Yes, yes,' 'No, no.' " Some have understood this as a milder form of oath, permitted by Jesus. In view of v 34, "Do not swear at all," that is unlikely. *From the evil one:* i.e., from the devil. Oath-taking presupposes a sinful weakness of the human race, namely, the tendency to lie. Jesus demands of his disciples a truthfulness that makes oaths unnecessary.

5, 38–42: See Lv 24, 20. The Old Testament commandment was meant to moderate vengeance; the punishment should not exceed the injury done. Jesus forbids even this proportionate retaliation. Of the five examples that follow, only the first deals directly with retaliation for evil; the others speak of liberality.

5, 41: Roman garrisons in Palestine had the right to requisition the property and services of the native population.

5, 43–48: See Lv 19, 18. There is no Old Testament commandment demanding hatred of one's enemy, but the "neighbor" of the love commandment was understood as one's fellow countryman. Both in the Old Testament (Ps 139, 19–22) and at Qumran (1QS 9, 21) hatred of evil persons is assumed to be right. Jesus extends the love commandment to the enemy and the persecutor. His disciples, as children of God, must imitate the example of their Father, who grants his gifts of sun and rain to both the good and the bad.

5, 46: *Tax collectors:* Jews who were engaged in the collection of indirect taxes such as tolls and customs. See the note on Mk 2, 14.

5, 47: Jesus' disciples must not be content with merely usual standards of conduct; see v 20 where the verb "surpass"

you greet your brothers only, what is unusual
about that? Do not the pagans do the same?
**48** *v**So be perfect, just as your heavenly Father is perfect.

## CHAPTER 6

**Teaching about Almsgiving** **1** *w**"[But]
take care not to perform righteous deeds in order
that people may see them; otherwise, you will
have no recompense from your heavenly Father.
**2** *x**When you give alms, do not blow a trumpet before you, as the hypocrites do in the synagogues and in the streets to win the praise of
others. Amen, I say to you, they have received
their reward. **3** But when you give alms, do not
let your left hand know what your right is doing,
**4** so that your almsgiving may be secret. And
your Father who sees in secret will repay you.

**5** "When you
pray, do not be like the hypocrites, who love to
stand and pray in the synagogues and on street
corners so that others may see them. Amen, I
say to you, they have received their reward.
**6** But when you pray, go to your inner room,
close the door, and pray to your Father in secret.
And your Father who sees in secret will repay
you. **7** *In praying, do not babble like the pagans, who think that they will be heard because
of their many words. **8** Do not be like them.
Your Father knows what you need before you
ask him.

**The Lord's Prayer** **9** *y**"This is how you
are to pray:

Our Father in heaven,
hallowed be your name,
**10** *z**your kingdom come,
your will be done,
on earth as in heaven.
**11** *a**Give us today our daily bread;
**12** *b**and forgive us our debts,
as we forgive our debtors;
**13** *c**and do not subject us to the final test,
but deliver us from the evil one.

**14** *d**If you forgive others their transgressions,
your heavenly Father will forgive you. **15** *e*But
if you do not forgive others, neither will your
Father forgive your transgressions.

**Teaching about Fasting** **16** *"When you
fast, do not look gloomy like the hypocrites.

v Lv 11, 44; 19, 2; Dt 18, 13; Jas 1, 4; 1 Pt 1, 16; 1 Jn 3, 3.
w 23, 5.
x Jn 12, 43.
y Lk 11, 2-4.
z 26, 42.
a Prv 30, 8-9.
b 18, 21-22; Sir 28, 2.
c Jn 17, 15; 2 Thes 3, 3.
d 18, 35; Sir 28, 1-5; Mk 11, 25.
e Jas 2, 13.

* (Greek *perisseuō*) is cognate with the *unusual* (*perisson*) of this verse.

5, 48: *Perfect:* in the gospels this word occurs only in Matthew, here and in 19, 21. The Lucan parallel (6, 36) demands that the disciples be *merciful.*

6, 1–18: The sermon continues with a warning against doing good in order to be seen and gives three examples, almsgiving (2–4), prayer (5, 15), and fasting (16–18). In each, the conduct of *the hypocrites* (2) is contrasted with that demanded of the disciples. The sayings about *reward* found here and elsewhere (5, 12.46; 10, 41–42) show that this is a genuine element of Christian moral exhortation. Possibly to underline the difference between the Christian idea of *reward* and that of *the hypocrites,* the evangelist uses two different Greek verbs to express the rewarding of the disciples and that of *the hypocrites;* in the latter case it is the verb *apechō,* a commercial term for giving a receipt for what has been paid in full (2.5.16).

6, 2: *The hypocrites:* the scribes and Pharisees, see 23, 13.15. 23.25.27.29. The designation reflects an attitude resulting not only from the controversies at the time of Jesus' ministry but from the opposition between Pharisaic Judaism and the church of Matthew. *They have received their reward:* they desire praise and have received what they were looking for.

6, 7–15: Matthew inserts into his basic traditional material an expansion of the material on prayer that includes the model prayer, the "Our Father." That prayer is found in Lk 11, 2–4 in a different context and in a different form.

6, 7: The example of what Christian prayer should be like contrasts it now not with the prayer of the hypocrites but with that of *the pagans.* Their babbling probably means their reciting a long list of divine names, hoping that one of them will force a response from the deity.

6, 9–13: Matthew's form of the "Our Father" follows the liturgical tradition of his church. Luke's less developed form also represents the liturgical tradition known to him, but it is probably closer than Matthew's to the original words of Jesus.

6, 9: *Our Father in heaven:* this invocation is found in many rabbinic prayers of the post-New Testament period. *Hallowed be your name:* though the "hallowing" of the divine name could be understood as reverence done to God by human praise and by obedience to his will, this is more probably a petition that God hallow his own name, i.e., that he manifest his glory by an act of power (cf Ez 36, 23), in this case, by the establishment of his kingdom in its fullness.

6, 10: *Your kingdom come:* this petition sets the tone of the prayer, and inclines the balance toward divine rather than human action in the petitions that immediately precede and follow it. *Your will be done, on earth as in heaven:* a petition that the divine purpose to establish the kingdom, a purpose present now *in heaven,* be executed *on earth.*

6, 11: *Give us today our daily bread:* the rare Greek word *epiousios,* here *daily,* occurs in the New Testament only here and in Lk 11, 3. A single occurrence of the word outside of these texts and of literature dependent on them has been claimed, but the claim is highly doubtful. The word may mean *daily* or "future" (other meanings have also been proposed). The latter would conform better to the eschatological tone of the whole prayer. So understood, the petition would be for a speedy coming of the kingdom (*today*), which is often portrayed in both the Old Testament and the New under the image of a feast (Is 25, 6; Mt 8, 11; 22, 1–10; Lk 13, 29; 14, 15–24).

6, 12: *Forgive us our debts:* the word *debts* is used metaphorically of sins, "debts" owed to God (see Lk 11, 4). The request is probably for forgiveness at the final judgment.

6, 13: Jewish apocalyptic writings speak of a period of severe trial before the end of the age, sometimes called the "messianic woes." This petition asks that the disciples be spared that *final test.*

6, 14–15: These verses reflect a set pattern called "Principles of Holy Law." Human action now will be met by a corresponding action of God at the final judgment.

6, 16: The only fast prescribed in the Mosaic law was that of the Day of Atonement (Lv 16, 31), but the practice of regular

They neglect their appearance, so that they may
appear to others to be fasting. Amen, I say to
you, they have received their reward. **17** But
when you fast, anoint your head and wash your
face, **18** so that you may not appear to be fasting, except to your Father who is hidden. And
your Father who sees what is hidden will repay
you.

**Treasure in Heaven** **19** *f**"Do not store
up for yourselves treasures on earth, where
moth and decay destroys, and thieves break in
and steal. **20** *g* But store up treasures in heaven,
where neither moth nor decay destroy, nor
thieves break in and steal. **21** For where your
treasure is, there also will your heart be.

**The Light of the Body** **22** *h**"The lamp of
the body is the eye. If your eye is sound, your
whole body will be filled with light; **23** but if
your eye is bad, your whole body will be in
darkness. And if the light in you is darkness,
how great will the darkness be.

**God and Money** **24** *i**"No one can serve
two masters. He will either hate one and love the
other, or be devoted to one and despise the
other. You cannot serve God and mammon.

**Dependence on God** **25** *j**"Therefore I
tell you, do not worry about your life, what you
will eat [or drink], or about your body, what you
will wear. Is not life more than food and the
body more than clothing? **26** *k* Look at the birds
in the sky; they do not sow or reap, they gather
nothing into barns, yet your heavenly Father
feeds them. Are not you more important than
they? **27** *Can any of you by worrying add a
single moment to your life-span? **28** Why are
you anxious about clothes? Learn from the way
the wild flowers grow. They do not work or
spin. **29** But I tell you that not even Solomon
in all his splendor was clothed like one of them.
**30** *If God so clothes the grass of the field,
which grows today and is thrown into the oven
tomorrow, will he not much more provide for
you, O you of little faith? **31** So do not worry
and say, 'What are we to eat?' or 'What are we
to drink?' or 'What are we to wear?' **32** All
these things the pagans seek. Your heavenly
Father knows that you need them all. **33** *But
seek first the kingdom [of God] and his righteousness, and all these things will be given you
besides. **34** Do not worry about tomorrow; tomorrow will take care of itself. Sufficient for a
day is its own evil.

## CHAPTER 7

**Judging Others** **1** *lm**"Stop judging, that
you may not be judged. **2** *n* For as you judge,
so will you be judged, and the measure with
which you measure will be measured out to you.
**3** Why do you notice the splinter in your brother's eye, but do not perceive the wooden beam
in your own eye? **4** How can you say to your
brother, 'Let me remove that splinter from your
eye,' while the wooden beam is in your eye?
**5** *You hypocrite, remove the wooden beam
from your eye first; then you will see clearly to
remove the splinter from your brother's eye.

**Pearls before Swine** **6** *o**"Do not give
what is holy to dogs, or throw your pearls before
swine, lest they trample them underfoot, and
turn and tear you to pieces.

**The Answer to Prayers** **7** *pq*"Ask and it
will be given to you; seek and you will find;

f Jas 5, 2-3.
g Lk 12, 33-34.
h Lk 11, 34-36.
i Lk 16, 13.
j Lk 12, 22-31.
k Pss 145, 15-16; 147, 9.
l Lk 6, 37-38.41-42.
m Rom 2, 1-2; 1 Cor 4, 5.
n Wis 12, 22; Mk 4, 24.
o Prv 23, 9.
p Mk 11, 24; Lk 11, 9-13.
q 18, 19.

*

fasting was common in later Judaism; cf *Didache* 9, 1.

6, 19–34: The remaining material of this chapter is taken almost entirely from Q. It deals principally with worldly possessions, and the controlling thought is summed up in v 24: the disciple can serve only one master and must choose between God and wealth (*mammon*). See further the note on Lk 16, 9.

6, 22–23: In this context the parable probably points to the need for the disciple to be enlightened by Jesus' teaching on the transitory nature of earthly riches.

6, 24: *Mammon:* an Aramaic word meaning wealth or property.

6, 25–34: Jesus does not deny the reality of human needs (32), but forbids making them the object of anxious care and, in effect, becoming their slave.

6, 27: *Life-span:* the Greek word can also mean "stature." If it is taken in that sense, the word here translated *moment* (literally, "cubit") must be translated literally as a unit not of time but of spatial measure. The cubit is about eighteen inches.

6, 30: *Of little faith:* except for the parallel in Lk 12, 28, the word translated *of little faith* is found in the New Testament only in Matthew. It is used by him of those who are disciples of Jesus but whose faith in him is not as deep as it should be (see Mt 8, 26; 14, 31; 16, 8 and the cognate noun in 17, 20).

6, 33: *Righteousness:* see the note on 3, 14–15.

7, 1–12: In v 1 Matthew returns to the basic traditional material of the sermon (Lk 6, 37–38.41–42). The governing thought is the correspondence between conduct toward one's fellows and God's conduct toward the one so acting.

7, 1: This is not a prohibition against recognizing the faults of others, which would be hardly compatible with vv 5 and 6, but against passing judgment in a spirit of arrogance, forgetful of one's own faults.

7, 5: *Hypocrite:* the designation previously given to the scribes and Pharisees is here given to the Christian disciple who is concerned with the faults of another and ignores his own more serious offenses.

7, 6: *Dogs* and *swine* were Jewish terms of contempt for Gentiles. This saying may originally have derived from a Jewish Christian community opposed to preaching the gospel (*what is holy, pearls*) to Gentiles. In the light of 28, 19 that can hardly be Matthew's meaning. He may have taken the saying as applying to a Christian dealing with an obstinately impenitent fellow Christian (18, 17).

knock and the door will be opened to you.
8 [r]For everyone who asks, receives; and the
one who seeks, finds; and to the one who
knocks, the door will be opened. 9 *Which one
of you would hand his son a stone when he asks
for a loaf of bread, 10 or a snake when he asks
for a fish? 11 [s]If you then, who are wicked,
know how to give good gifts to your children,
how much more will your heavenly Father give
good things to those who ask him.

### The Golden Rule
12 [t]*"Do to others
whatever you would have them do to you. This
is the law and the prophets.

### The Narrow Gate
13 [u]*"Enter through the
narrow gate; for the gate is wide and the road
broad that leads to destruction, and those who
enter through it are many. 14 How narrow the
gate and constricted the road that leads to life.
And those who find it are few.

### False Prophets
15 [v]*"Beware of false
prophets, who come to you in sheep's clothing,
but underneath are ravenous wolves. 16 [w]By
their fruits you will know them. Do people pick
grapes from thornbushes, or figs from thistles?
17 Just so, every good tree bears good fruit,
and a rotten tree bears bad fruit. 18 A good tree
cannot bear bad fruit, nor can a rotten tree bear
good fruit. 19 [x]Every tree that does not bear
good fruit will be cut down and thrown into the
fire. 20 So by their fruits you will know them.

### The True Disciple
21 [y]*"Not everyone
who says to me, 'Lord, Lord,' will enter the
kingdom of heaven, but only the one who does
the will of my Father in heaven. 22 [z a]Many
will say to me on that day, 'Lord, Lord, did we
not prophesy in your name? Did we not drive
out demons in your name? Did we not do mighty
deeds in your name?' 23 [b]*Then I will declare
to them solemnly, 'I never knew you. Depart
from me, you evildoers.'

### The Two Foundations
24 [c]*"Everyone
who listens to these words of mine and acts on
them will be like a wise man who built his house
on rock. 25 [d]The rain fell, the floods came, and
the winds blew and buffeted the house. But it
did not collapse; it had been set solidly on rock.
26 And everyone who listens to these words of
mine but does not act on them will be like a fool
who built his house on sand. 27 The rain fell,
the floods came, and the winds blew and buffeted the house. And it collapsed and was completely ruined."

28 *When Jesus finished these words, the
crowds were astonished at his teaching,
29 [e]*for he taught them as one having authority, and not as their scribes.

## *III: MINISTRY AND MISSION IN GALILEE*

## CHAPTER 8

### The Cleansing of a Leper
1 [f]*When
Jesus came down from the mountain, great

r Lk 18, 1-8; Jn 14, 13.
s 1 Jn 5, 14-15.
t Lk 6, 31.
u Lk 13, 24.
v 2 Pt 2, 1.
w 12, 33; Lk 6, 43-44.
x 3, 10.
y Is 29, 13; Lk 6, 46.
z Lk 13, 26-27.
a 25, 11-12.
b Pss 5, 5; 6, 9.
c Lk 6, 47-49.
d Prv 10, 25.
e Mk 1, 22; Lk 4, 32.
f Mk 1, 40-44; Lk 5, 12-14.

*

7, 9–10: There is a resemblance between a stone and a round loaf of bread and between a serpent and the scaleless fish called *barbut*.

7, 12: See Lk 6, 31. This saying, known since the eighteenth century as the "Golden Rule," is found in both positive and negative form in pagan and Jewish sources, both earlier and later than the gospel. *This is the law and the prophets* is an addition probably due to the evangelist.

7, 13–28: The final section of the discourse is composed of a series of antitheses, contrasting two kinds of life within the Christian community, that of those who obey the words of Jesus and that of those who do not. Most of the sayings are from Q and are found also in Luke.

7, 13–14: The metaphor of the "two ways" was common in pagan philosophy and in the Old Testament. In Christian literature it is found also in the *Didache* (1–6) and the *Epistle of Barnabas* (18–20).

7, 15–20: Christian disciples who claimed to speak in the name of God are called *prophets* (15) in 10, 41 and in 23, 34. They were presumably an important group within the church of Matthew. As in the case of the Old Testament prophets, there were both true and false ones, and for Matthew the difference could be recognized by the quality of their deeds, the *fruits* (16). The mention of *fruits* leads to the comparison with trees, some producing good fruit, others bad.

7, 21–23: The attack on the false prophets is continued, but is broadened to include those disciples who perform works of healing and exorcism in the name of Jesus (*Lord*) but live evil lives. Entrance into the kingdom is only for those who do the will of the Father. On the day of judgment (*on that day*) the morally corrupt prophets and miracle workers will be rejected by Jesus.

7, 23: *I never knew you:* cf 10, 33. *Depart from me, you evildoers:* cf Ps 6, 9.

7, 24–27: The conclusion of the discourse (cf Lk 6, 47–49). Here the relation is not between saying and doing as in vv 15–23 but between hearing and doing, and the words of Jesus are applied to every Christian (*everyone who listens*).

7, 28–29: *When Jesus finished these words:* this or a similar formula is used by Matthew to conclude each of the five great disccourses of Jesus (cf 11, 1; 13, 53; 19, 1; 26, 1).

7, 29: *Not as their scribes:* scribal instruction was a faithful handing down of the traditions of earlier teachers; Jesus' teaching is based on his own authority. *Their scribes:* for the implications of *their,* see the note on 4, 23.

8, 1—9, 38: This narrative section of the second book of the gospel is composed of nine miracle stories, most of which are found in Mark, although Matthew does not follow the Marcan order and abbreviates the stories radically. The stories are arranged in three groups of three, each group followed by a section composed principally of sayings of Jesus about discipleship. Verse 9, 35 is an almost verbatim repetition of 4, 23. Each speaks of Jesus' teaching, preaching, and healing. The teaching and preaching form the content of chs 5–7; the healing, that of chs 8–9. Some scholars speak of a portrayal of Jesus as "Messiah of the Word" in 5–7 and "Messiah of the

crowds followed him. **2** *And then a leper approached, did him homage, and said, "Lord, if
you wish, you can make me clean." **3** He
stretched out his hand, touched him, and said,
"I will do it. Be made clean." His leprosy was
cleansed immediately. **4** [g]*Then Jesus said to
him, "See that you tell no one, but go show
yourself to the priest, and offer the gift that
Moses prescribed; that will be proof for them."

## The Healing of a Centurion's Servant

**5** [h]*When he entered Capernaum, a centurion
approached him and appealed to him, **6** saying,
"Lord, my servant is lying at home paralyzed,
suffering dreadfully." **7** He said to him, "I will
come and cure him." **8** *The centurion said in
reply, "Lord, I am not worthy to have you enter
under my roof; only say the word and my servant will be healed. **9** For I too am a person
subject to authority, with soldiers subject to me.
And I say to one, 'Go,' and he goes; and to
another, 'Come here,' and he comes; and to my
slave, 'Do this,' and he does it." **10** *When
Jesus heard this, he was amazed and said to
those following him, "Amen, I say to you, in
no one in Israel have I found such faith. **11** [i]*I
say to you, many will come from the east and
the west, and will recline with Abraham, Isaac,
and Jacob at the banquet in the kingdom of
heaven, **12** but the children of the kingdom will
be driven out into the outer darkness, where
there will be wailing and grinding of teeth."
**13** And Jesus said to the centurion, "You may
go; as you have believed, let it be done for
you." And at that very hour [his] servant was
healed.

## The Cure of Peter's Mother-in-Law

**14** [j]*Jesus entered the house of Peter, and saw
his mother-in-law lying in bed with a fever.
**15** [k]He touched her hand, the fever left her, and
she rose and waited on him.

## Other Healings

**16** *When it was evening,
they brought him many who were possessed by
demons, and he drove out the spirits by a word
and cured all the sick, **17** [l]*to fulfill what had
been said by Isaiah the prophet:

"He took away our infirmities
  and bore our diseases."

## The Would-be Followers of Jesus

**18** [m]*When Jesus saw a crowd around him, he
gave orders to cross to the other side. **19** [n]*A
scribe approached and said to him, "Teacher, I
will follow you wherever you go." **20** *Jesus
answered him, "Foxes have dens and birds of
the sky have nests, but the Son of Man has
nowhere to rest his head." **21** Another of [his]
disciples said to him, "Lord, let me go first and
bury my father." **22** *But Jesus answered him,
"Follow me, and let the dead bury their dead."

g Lv 14, 2-32; Lk 17, 14.
h Lk 7, 1-10; Jn 4, 46-53.
i 13, 42.50; 22, 13; 24, 51; 25, 30; Lk 13, 28-29.
j Mk 1, 29-34; Lk 4, 38-41.
k 9, 25.
l Is 53, 4.
m Mk 4, 35.
n Lk 9, 57-60.

* Deed" in 8–9. That is accurate so far as it goes, but there is also a strong emphasis on discipleship in 8–9; these chapters have not only christological but ecclesiological import.

8, 2: *A leper:* see the note on Mk 1, 40.

8, 4: Cf Lv 14, 2–9. *That will be proof for them:* the Greek can also mean "that will be proof against them." It is not clear whether *them* refers to the priests or the people.

8, 5–13: This story comes from Q (see Lk 7, 1–10) and is also reflected in Jn 4, 46–54. The similarity between the Q story and the Johannine is due to a common oral tradition, not to a common literary source. As in the later story of the daughter of the Canaanite woman (15, 21–28) Jesus here breaks with his usual procedure of ministering only to Israelites and anticipates the mission to the Gentiles.

8, 5: *A centurion:* a military officer commanding a hundred men. He was probably in the service of Herod Antipas, tetrarch of Galilee; see the note on 14, 1.

8, 8–9: Acquainted by his position with the force of a command, the centurion expresses faith in the power of Jesus' mere word.

8, 10: *In no one in Israel:* there is good textual attestation (e.g., Codex Sinaiticus) for a reading identical with that of Lk 7, 9, "not even in Israel." But that seems to be due to a harmonization of Matthew with Luke.

8, 11–12: Matthew inserts into the story a Q saying (see Lk 13, 28–29) about the entrance of Gentiles into the kingdom and the exclusion of those Israelites who, though descended from the patriarchs and members of the chosen nation (*the children of the kingdom*), refused to believe in Jesus. *There will be wailing and grinding of teeth:* the first occurrence of a phrase used frequently in this gospel to describe final condemnation (13, 42.50; 22, 13; 24, 51; 25, 30). It is found elsewhere in the New Testament only in Lk 13, 28.

8, 14–15: Cf Mk 1, 29–31. Unlike Mark, Matthew has no implied request by others for the woman's cure. Jesus acts on his own initiative, and the cured woman rises and waits not on "them" (Mk 1, 31) but on *him.*

8, 16: *By a word:* a Matthean addition to Mk 1, 34; cf 8, 8.

8, 17: This fulfillment citation from Is 53, 4 follows the MT, not the LXX. The prophet speaks of the Servant of the Lord who suffers vicariously for the sins ("infirmities") of others; Matthew takes the *infirmities* as physical afflictions.

8, 18–22: This passage between the first and second series of miracles about following Jesus is taken from Q (see Lk 9, 57–62). The third of the three sayings found in the source is absent from Matthew.

8, 18: *The other side:* i.e., of the Sea of Galilee.

8, 19: *Teacher:* for Matthew, this designation of Jesus is true, for he has Jesus using it of himself (10, 24.25; 23, 8; 26, 18), yet when it is used of him by others they are either his opponents (9, 11; 12, 38; 17, 24; 22, 16.24.36) or, as here and in 19, 16, well-disposed persons who cannot see more deeply. Thus it reveals an inadequate recognition of who Jesus is.

8, 20: *Son of Man:* see the note on Mk 8, 31. This is the first occurrence in Mt of a term that appears in the New Testament only in sayings of Jesus, except for Acts 7, 56 and possibly 9, 6 (// Mk 2, 10; Lk 5, 24). In Mt it refers to Jesus in his ministry (seven times, as here), in his passion and resurrection (nine times, e.g., 17, 22), and in his glorious coming at the end of the age (thirteen times, e.g., 24, 30).

8, 22: *Let the dead bury their dead:* the demand of Jesus overrides what both the Jewish and the Hellenistic world regarded as a filial obligation of the highest importance. See the note on Lk 9, 60.

### The Calming of the Storm at Sea
23 [o]*He got into a boat and his disciples followed him. 24 *Suddenly a violent storm came
up on the sea, so that the boat was being
swamped by waves; but he was asleep.
25 [p]*They came and woke him, saying,
"Lord, save us! We are perishing!" 26 *He
said to them, "Why are you terrified, O you of
little faith?" Then he got up, rebuked the winds
and the sea, and there was great calm. 27 The
men were amazed and said, "What sort of man
is this, whom even the winds and the sea
obey?"

### The Healing of the Gadarene Demoniacs
28 [q]*When he came to the other side,
to the territory of the Gadarenes, two demoniacs
who were coming from the tombs met him.
They were so savage that no one could travel by
that road. 29 *They cried out, "What have you
to do with us, Son of God? Have you come here
to torment us before the appointed time?"
30 *Some distance away a herd of many swine
was feeding. 31 [r]The demons pleaded with
him, "If you drive us out, send us into the herd
of swine." 32 And he said to them, "Go
then!" They came out and entered the swine,
and the whole herd rushed down the steep bank
into the sea where they drowned. 33 The swineherds ran away, and when they came to the town
they reported everything, including what had
happened to the demoniacs. 34 Thereupon the
whole town came out to meet Jesus, and when
they saw him they begged him to leave their
district.

## CHAPTER 9

### The Healing of a Paralytic
1 [s]*He en-
tered a boat, made the crossing, and came into
his own town. 2 [t]And there people brought to
him a paralytic lying on a stretcher. When Jesus
saw their faith, he said to the paralytic, "Courage, child, your sins are forgiven." 3 *At that,
some of the scribes said to themselves, "This
man is blaspheming." 4 Jesus knew what they
were thinking, and said, "Why do you harbor
evil thoughts? 5 Which is easier, to say, 'Your
sins are forgiven,' or to say, 'Rise and walk'?
6 [u]*But that you may know that the Son of Man
has authority on earth to forgive sins"—he then
said to the paralytic, "Rise, pick up your
stretcher, and go home." 7 He rose and went
home. 8 *When the crowds saw this they were
struck with awe and glorified God who had
given such authority to human beings.

### The Call of Matthew
9 [v]*As Jesus passed
on from there, he saw a man named Matthew
sitting at the customs post. He said to him,
"Follow me." And he got up and followed him.

o Mk 4, 35-40; Lk 8, 22-25.
p Ps 107, 28-29.
q Mk 5, 1-17; Lk 8, 26-37.
r Lk 4, 34.41.
s Mk 2, 3-12; Lk 5, 18-26.
t Lk 7, 48.
u Jn 5, 27.
v Mk 2, 14-17; Lk 5, 27-32.

*

8, 23: *His disciples followed him:* the first miracle in the second group (8, 23—9, 8) is introduced by a verse that links it with the preceding sayings by the catchword "follow." In Mk the initiative in entering the boat is taken by the disciples (Mk 4, 35–41); here, Jesus enters first and the disciples follow.

8, 24: *Storm:* literally, "earthquake," a word commonly used in apocalyptic literature for the shaking of the old world when God brings in his kingdom. All the synoptics use it in depicting the events preceding the parousia of the Son of Man (24, 7; Mk 13, 8; Lk 21, 11). Matthew has introduced it here and in his account of the death and resurrection of Jesus (27, 51–54; 28, 2).

8, 25: The reverent plea of the disciples contrasts sharply with their reproach of Jesus in Mk 4, 38.

8, 26: *You of little faith:* see the note on 6, 30. *Great calm:* Jesus' calming the sea may be meant to recall the Old Testament theme of God's control over the chaotic waters (Pss 65, 8; 89, 10; 93, 3–4; 107, 29).

8, 28: *Gadarenes:* this is the reading of Codex Vaticanus, supported by other important textual witnesses. The original reading of Codex Sinaiticus was Gazarenes, later changed to Gergesenes, and a few versions have Gerasenes. Each of these readings points to a different territory connected, respectively, with the cities Gadara, Gergesa, and Gerasa (modern Jerash). There is the same confusion of readings in the parallel texts, Mk 5, 1 and Lk 8, 26; there the best reading seems to be "Gerasenes," whereas "Gadarenes" is probably the original reading in Mt. The town of Gadara was about five miles southeast of the Sea of Galilee, and Josephus (*Life* 9 *42) refers to it as possessing territory that lay on that sea. *Two demoniacs:* Mark (5, 1–20) has one.

8, 29: *What have you to do with us?:* see the note on Jn 2, 4. *Before the appointed time:* the notion that evil spirits were allowed by God to afflict human beings until the time of the final judgment is found in Enoch 16, 1 and Jubilees 10, 7–10.

8, 30: The tending of pigs, animals considered unclean by Mosaic law (Lv 11, 6–7), indicates that the population was Gentile.

9, 1: *His own town:* Capernaum; see 4, 13.

9, 3: *Scribes:* see the note on Mk 2, 6. Matthew omits the reason given in the Marcan story for the charge of blasphemy: "Who but God alone can forgive sins?" (Mk 2, 7).

9, 6: It is not clear whether "But that you may know . . . to forgive sins" is intended to be a continuation of the words of Jesus or a parenthetical comment of the evangelist to those who would hear or read this gospel. In any case, Matthew here follows the Marcan text.

9, 8: *Who had given such authority to human beings:* a significant difference from Mk 2, 12 ("They . . . glorified God saying, 'We have never seen anything like this.' "). Matthew's extension to *human beings* of the authority to forgive sins points to the belief that such authority was being claimed by Matthew's church.

9, 9–17: In this section the order is the same as that of Mk 2, 13–22.

9, 9: *A man named Matthew:* Mark names this tax collector Levi (2, 14). No such name appears in the four lists of the twelve who were the closest companions of Jesus (10, 2–4; Mk 3, 16–19; Lk 6, 14–16; Acts 1, 13 [eleven, because of the defection of Judas Iscariot]), whereas all four list a Matthew, designated in 10, 3 as "the tax collector." The evangelist may have changed the "Levi" of his source to *Matthew* so that this man, whose call is given special notice, like that of the first four disciples (4, 18–22), might be included among the twelve. Another reason for the change may be that the disciple Matthew was the source of traditions peculiar to the church for

**10** [w]*While he was at table in his house, many
tax collectors and sinners came and sat with
Jesus and his disciples. **11** *The Pharisees saw
this and said to his disciples, "Why does your
teacher eat with tax collectors and sinners?"
**12** *He heard this and said, "Those who are
well do not need a physician, but the sick do.
**13** [x]*Go and learn the meaning of the words,
'I desire mercy, not sacrifice.' I did not come
to call the righteous but sinners."

**The Question about Fasting** **14** [y]Then
the disciples of John approached him and said,
"Why do we and the Pharisees fast [much], but
your disciples do not fast?" **15** *Jesus answered them, "Can the wedding guests mourn
as long as the bridegroom is with them? The
days will come when the bridegroom is taken
away from them, and then they will fast.
**16** *No one patches an old cloak with a piece
of unshrunken cloth, for its fullness pulls away
from the cloak and the tear gets worse. **17** People do not put new wine into old wineskins.
Otherwise the skins burst, the wine spills out,
and the skins are ruined. Rather, they pour new
wine into fresh wineskins, and both are preserved."

**The Official's Daughter and the Woman with a Hemorrhage** **18** [z]*While he was
saying these things to them, an official came
forward, knelt down before him, and said, "My
daughter has just died. But come, lay your hand
on her, and she will live." **19** Jesus rose and
followed him, and so did his disciples. **20** *A
woman suffering hemorrhages for twelve years
came up behind him and touched the tassel on
his cloak. **21** [a]She said to herself, "If only I
can touch his cloak, I shall be cured." **22** Jesus
turned around and saw her, and said, "Courage,
daughter! Your faith has saved you." And from
that hour the woman was cured.

**23** When Jesus arrived at the official's house
and saw the flute players and the crowd who
were making a commotion, **24** *he said, "Go
away! The girl is not dead but sleeping." And
they ridiculed him. **25** When the crowd was put
out, he came and took her by the hand, and the
little girl arose. **26** And news of this spread
throughout all that land.

**The Healing of Two Blind Men**
**27** [b][c]*And as Jesus passed on from there, two
blind men followed [him], crying out, "Son of
David, have pity on us!" **28** When he entered
the house, the blind men approached him and
Jesus said to them, "Do you believe that I can
do this?" "Yes, Lord," they said to him.
**29** Then he touched their eyes and said, "Let
it be done for you according to your faith."
**30** And their eyes were opened. Jesus warned
them sternly, "See that no one knows about
this." **31** But they went out and spread word of
him through all that land.

**The Healing of a Mute Person** **32** [d]*As
they were going out, a demoniac who could not

w 11, 19; Lk 15, 1-2.
x 12, 7; Hos 6, 6.
y Mk 2, 18-22; Lk 5, 33-39.
z Mk 5, 22-43; Lk 8, 41-56.
a 14, 36; Nm 15, 37.
b 20, 29-34.
c 15, 22.
d 12, 22-24; Lk 11, 14-15.

* which the evangelist was writing.

9, 10: *His house:* it is not clear whether *his* refers to Jesus or Matthew. *Tax collectors:* see the note on 5, 46. Table association with such persons would cause ritual impurity.

9, 11: *Teacher:* see the note on 8, 19.

9, 12: See the note on Mk 2, 17.

9, 13: *Go and learn . . . not sacrifice:* Matthew adds the prophetic statement of Hos 6, 6 to the Marcan account (see also 12, 7). If mercy is superior to the temple sacrifices, how much more to the laws of ritual impurity.

9, 15: Fasting is a sign of mourning and would be as inappropriate at this time of joy, when Jesus is proclaiming the kingdom, as it would be at a marriage feast. Yet the saying looks forward to the time when Jesus will no longer be with the disciples visibly, the time of Matthew's church. *Then they will fast:* see *Didache* 8, 1.

9, 16–17: Each of these parables speaks of the unsuitability of attempting to combine the old and the new. Jesus' teaching is not a patching up of Judaism, nor can the gospel be contained within the limits of Mosaic law.

9, 18–34: In this third group of miracles, the first (18–26) is clearly dependent on Mark (Mk 5, 21–43). Though it tells of two miracles, the cure of the woman had already been included within the story of the raising of the official's daughter, so that the two were probably regarded as a single unit. The other miracles seem to have been derived from Mark and Q respectively, though there Matthew's own editing is much more evident.

9, 18: *Official:* literally, "ruler." Mark calls him "one of the synagogue officials" (Mk 5, 22). *My daughter has just died:* Matthew heightens the Marcan "my daughter is at the point of death" (Mk 5, 23).

9, 20: *Tassel:* possibly "fringe." The Mosaic law prescribed that tassels be worn on the corners of one's garment as a reminder to keep the commandments (see Nm 15, 37–39; Dt 22, 12).

9, 24: *Sleeping:* sleep is a biblical metaphor for death (see Ps 87, 6 LXX; Dn 12, 2; 1 Thes 5, 10). Jesus' statement is not a denial of the child's real death, but an assurance that she will be roused from her sleep of death.

9, 27–31: This story was probably composed by Matthew out of Mark's story of the healing of a blind man named Bartimaeus (Mk 10, 46–52). Mark places the event late in Jesus' ministry, just before his entrance into Jerusalem, and Matthew has followed his Marcan source at that point in his gospel also (see 20, 29–34). In each of the Matthean stories the single blind man of Mark becomes two. The reason why Matthew would have given a double version of the Marcan story and placed the earlier one here may be that he wished to add a story of Jesus' curing the blind at this point in order to prepare for Jesus' answer to the emissaries of the Baptist (11, 4–6) in which Jesus, recounting his works, begins with his giving sight to the blind.

9, 27: *Son of David:* this messianic title is connected once with the healing power of Jesus in Mark (10, 47–48) and Luke (18, 38–39) but more frequently in Matthew (see also 12, 23; 15, 22; 20, 30–31).

9, 32–34: The source of this story seems to be Q (see Lk 11, 14–15). As in the preceding healing of the blind, Matthew

speak was brought to him, **33** [e]and when the
demon was driven out the mute person spoke.
The crowds were amazed and said, "Nothing
like this has ever been seen in Israel." **34** [f]*But
the Pharisees said, "He drives out demons by
the prince of demons."

**The Compassion of Jesus** **35** [g]*Jesus
went around to all the towns and villages, teaching in their synagogues, proclaiming the gospel
of the kingdom, and curing every disease and
illness. **36** [h]*At the sight of the crowds, his
heart was moved with pity for them because
they were troubled and abandoned, like sheep
without a shepherd. **37** [i]*Then he said to his
disciples, "The harvest is abundant but the laborers are few; **38** so ask the master of the
harvest to send out laborers for his harvest."

## CHAPTER 10

**The Mission of the Twelve** **1** [j]*Then he
summoned his twelve disciples and gave them
authority over unclean spirits to drive them out
and to cure every disease and every illness.
**2** *The names of the twelve apostles are these:
first, Simon called Peter, and his brother Andrew; James, the son of Zebedee, and his brother John; **3** Philip and Bartholomew, Thomas
and Matthew the tax collector; James, the son
of Alphaeus, and Thaddeus; **4** Simon the Cananean, and Judas Iscariot who betrayed him.

**The Commissioning of the Twelve**
**5** [k]*Jesus sent out these twelve after instructing
them thus, "Do not go into pagan territory or
enter a Samaritan town. **6** [l]Go rather to the lost
sheep of the house of Israel. **7** [m]As you go,
make this proclamation: 'The kingdom of heav-
en is at hand.' **8** *Cure the sick, raise the dead,
cleanse lepers, drive out demons. Without cost
you have received; without cost you are to give.
**9** [n]Do not take gold or silver or copper for your
belts; **10** [o]no sack for the journey, or a second
tunic, or sandals, or walking stick. The laborer
deserves his keep. **11** [p]Whatever town or village you enter, look for a worthy person in it,
and stay there until you leave. **12** As you enter
a house, wish it peace. **13** *If the house is worthy, let your peace come upon it; if not, let your
peace return to you. **14** [q]*Whoever will not
receive you or listen to your words—go outside
that house or town and shake the dust from your
feet. **15** [r]Amen, I say to you, it will be more
tolerable for the land of Sodom and Gomorrah
on the day of judgment than for that town.

**Coming Persecutions** **16** [s]"Behold, I
am sending you like sheep in the midst of
wolves; so be shrewd as serpents and simple as
doves. **17** [tu]*But beware of people, for they

e Mk 2, 12; 7, 37.
f 10, 25; Mk 3, 22.
g 4, 23; Lk 8, 1.
h Nm 27, 17; 1 Kgs 22, 17; Jer 50, 6; Ez 34, 5; Mk 6, 34.
i Lk 10, 2; Jn 4, 35.
j Mk 3, 14-19; Lk 6, 13-16; Acts 1, 13.
k Mk 6, 7-13; Lk 9, 1-6.
l 15, 24.
m 3, 2; 4, 17.
n Mk 6, 8-9; Lk 9, 3; 10, 4.
o Lk 10, 7; 1 Cor 9, 14; 2 Tm 5, 18.
p Mk 6, 10-11; Lk 9, 4-5; 10, 5-12.
q Acts 13, 51; 18, 6.
r 11, 24; Gn 19, 1-29; Jude 7.
s Lk 10, 3.
t Mk 13, 9-13; Lk 21, 12-19.
u Acts 5, 40.

has two versions of this healing, the later in 12, 22–24 and the earlier here.

9, 34: This spiteful accusation foreshadows the growing opposition to Jesus in chs 11 and 12.

9, 35: See the notes on 4, 23–25 and 8, 1—9, 38.

9, 36: See Mk 6, 34; Nm 27, 17; 1 Kgs 22, 17.

9, 37–38: This Q saying (see Lk 10, 2) is only imperfectly related to this context. It presupposes that only God (*the master of the harvest*) can take the initiative in sending out preachers of the gospel, whereas in Matthew's setting it leads into ch 10, where Jesus does so.

10, 1—11, 1: After an introductory narrative (10, 1–4), the second of the discourses of the gospel. It deals with the mission now to be undertaken by the disciples (5–15), but the perspective broadens and includes the missionary activity of the church between the time of the resurrection and the parousia.

10, 1: *His twelve disciples:* although, unlike Mark (3, 13–14) and Luke (6, 12–16), Matthew has no story of Jesus' choosing the Twelve, he assumes that the group is known to the reader. The earliest New Testament text to speak of it is 1 Cor 15, 5. The number probably is meant to recall the twelve tribes of Israel and implies Jesus' authority to call all Israel into the kingdom. While Luke (6, 13) and probably Mark (4, 10.34) distinguish between the Twelve and a larger group also termed disciples, Matthew tends to identify the disciples and the Twelve. *Authority . . . every illness:* activities the same as those of Jesus; see 4, 23; 9, 35; 10, 8. The Twelve also share in his proclamation of the kingdom (10, 7). But although he teaches (4, 23; 7, 28; 9, 35), they do not. Their commission to teach comes only after Jesus' resurrection, after they have been fully instructed by him (28, 20).

10, 2–4: Here, for the only time in Matthew, the Twelve are designated *apostles.* The word "apostle" means "one who is sent," and therefore fits the situation here described. In the Pauline letters, the place where the term occurs most frequently in the New Testament, it means primarily one who has seen the risen Lord and has been commissioned to proclaim the resurrection. With slight variants in Luke and Acts, the names of those who belong to this group are the same in the four lists given in the New Testament (see the note on 9, 9). *Cananean:* this represents an Aramaic word meaning "zealot." The meaning of that designation is unclear (see the note on Lk 6, 15).

10, 5–6: Like Jesus (15, 24), the Twelve are sent only to Israel. This saying may reflect an original Jewish Christian refusal of the mission to the Gentiles, but for Matthew it expresses rather the limitation that Jesus himself observed during his ministry.

10, 8–11: The Twelve have received their own call and mission through God's gift, and the benefits they confer are likewise to be given freely. They are not to take with them money, provisions, or unnecessary clothing; their lodging and food will be provided by those who receive them.

10, 13: The greeting of peace is conceived of not merely as a salutation but as an effective word. If it finds no worthy recipient, it will return to the speaker.

10, 14: *Shake the dust from your feet:* this gesture indicates a complete disassociation from such unbelievers.

10, 17: The persecutions attendant upon the post-resurrection mission now begin to be spoken of. Here Matthew brings

will hand you over to courts and scourge you in
their synagogues, **18** and you will be led before
governors and kings for my sake as a witness
before them and the pagans. **19** [v]When they
hand you over, do not worry about how you are
to speak or what you are to say. You will be
given at that moment what you are to say.
**20** For it will not be you who speak but the
Spirit of your Father speaking through you.
**21** [w]*Brother will hand over brother to death,
and the father his child; children will rise up
against parents and have them put to death.
**22** *You will be hated by all because of my
name, but whoever endures to the end will be
saved. **23** *When they persecute you in one
town, flee to another. Amen, I say to you, you
will not finish the towns of Israel before the Son
of Man comes. **24** [x]No disciple is above his
teacher, no slave above his master. **25** *It is
enough for the disciple that he become like his
teacher, for the slave that he become like his
master. If they have called the master of the
house Beelzebul, how much more those of his
household!

## Courage under Persecution

**26** [y z]*"Therefore do not be afraid of them.
Nothing is concealed that will not be revealed,
nor secret that will not be known. **27** What I say
to you in the darkness, speak in the light; what
you hear whispered, proclaim on the housetops.
**28** [a]And do not be afraid of those who kill the
body but cannot kill the soul; rather, be afraid
of the one who can destroy both soul and body
in Gehenna. **29** Are not two sparrows sold for
a small coin? Yet not one of them falls to the
ground without your Father's knowledge.
**30** Even all the hairs of your head are counted.
**31** So do not be afraid; you are worth more than
many sparrows. **32** *Everyone who acknowledges me before others I will acknowledge before my heavenly Father. **33** [b]But whoever denies me before others, I will deny before my
heavenly Father.

## Jesus: A Cause of Division

**34** [c]"Do not
think that I have come to bring peace upon the
earth. I have come to bring not peace but the
sword. **35** For I have come to set

a man "against his father,
  a daughter against her mother,
and a daughter-in-law against her
    mother-in-law;
**36** and one's enemies will be those of his
    household.'

## The Conditions of Discipleship

**37** [d]"Whoever loves father or mother more
than me is not worthy of me, and whoever loves
son or daughter more than me is not worthy of
me; **38** *and whoever does not take up his cross
and follow after me is not worthy of me.
**39** [e]*Whoever finds his life will lose it, and
whoever loses his life for my sake will find it.

## Rewards

**40** [f]*"Whoever receives you receives me, and whoever receives me receives
the one who sent me. **41** *Whoever receives a
prophet because he is a prophet will receive a
prophet's reward, and whoever receives a righteous man because he is righteous will receive a
righteous man's reward. **42** [g]And whoever
gives only a cup of cold water to one of these
little ones to drink because he is a disciple—

v Ex 4, 11-12; Jer 1, 6-10; Lk 12, 11-12.
w 24, 9.13.
x Lk 6, 40; Jn 13, 16; 15, 20.
y Lk 12, 2-9.
z Mk 4, 22; Lk 8, 17; 1 Tm 5, 25.
a Jas 4, 12.
b Mk 8, 38; Lk 9, 26; 2 Tm 2, 12; Rv 3, 5.
c Lk 12, 51-53.
d 16, 24-25; Lk 14, 26-27.
e Mk 8, 35; Lk 9, 24; Jn 12, 25.
f Lk 10, 16; Jn 12, 44; 13, 20.
g 25, 40; Mk 9, 41.

* into the discourse sayings found in Mk 13, which deals with events preceding the parousia.

10, 21: See Mi 7, 6, which is cited in vv 35.36.

10, 22: *To the end:* the original meaning was probably "until the parousia." But it is not likely that Matthew expected no missionary disciples to suffer death before then, since he envisages the martyrdom of other Christians (21). For him, *the end* is probably that of the individual's life (see 28).

10, 23: *Before the Son of Man comes:* since the coming of the Son of Man at the end of the age had not taken place when this gospel was written, much less during the mission of the Twelve during Jesus' ministry, Matthew cannot have meant the coming to refer to the parousia. It is difficult to know what he understood it to be: perhaps the "proleptic parousia" of 28, 16–20, or the destruction of the temple in A.D. 70, viewed as a coming of Jesus in judgment on unbelieving Israel.

10, 25: *Beelzebul:* see 9, 34 for the charge linking Jesus with "the prince of demons," who is named *Beelzebul* in 12, 24. The meaning of the name is uncertain; possibly, "lord of the house."

10, 26: The *concealed* and *secret* coming of the kingdom is to be proclaimed by them, and no fear must be allowed to deter them from that proclamation.

10, 32–33: In the Q parallel (Lk 12, 8–9), the Son of Man will acknowledge those who have acknowledged Jesus, and those who deny him will be denied (by the Son of Man) before the angels of God at the judgment. Here Jesus and the Son of Man are identified, and the acknowledgment or denial will be before his heavenly Father.

10, 38: The first mention of the cross in Matthew, explicitly that of the disciple, but implicitly that of Jesus (*and follow after me*). Crucifixion was a form of capital punishment used by the Romans for offenders who were not Roman citizens.

10, 39: One who denies Jesus in order to save one's earthly life will be condemned to everlasting destruction; loss of earthly life for Jesus' sake will be rewarded by everlasting life in the kingdom.

10, 40–42: All who receive the disciples of Jesus receive him, and God who sent him, and will be rewarded accordingly.

10, 41: *A prophet:* one who speaks in the name of God; here, the Christian prophets who proclaim the gospel. *Righteous man:* since righteousness is demanded of all the disciples, it is difficult to take the *righteous man* of this verse and *one of these little ones* (42) as indicating different groups within the followers of Jesus. Probably all three designations are used here of Christian missionaries as such.

amen, I say to you, he will surely not lose his
reward."

## CHAPTER 11

**1** *When Jesus finished giving these commands to his twelve disciples, he went away
from that place to teach and to preach in their
towns.

# *IV: OPPOSITION FROM ISRAEL*

### The Messengers from John the Baptist

**2** [h]*When John heard in prison of the works of
the Messiah, he sent his disciples to him
**3** *with this question, "Are you the one who is
to come, or should we look for another?"
**4** Jesus said to them in reply, "Go and tell John
what you hear and see: **5** [i]*the blind regain
their sight, the lame walk, lepers are cleansed,
the deaf hear, the dead are raised, and the poor
have the good news proclaimed to them. **6** And
blessed is the one who takes no offense at me."

### Jesus' Testimony to John

**7** [j]*As they
were going off, Jesus began to speak to the
crowds about John, "What did you go out to the
desert to see? A reed swayed by the wind?
**8** Then what did you go out to see? Someone
dressed in fine clothing? Those who wear fine
clothing are in royal palaces. **9** *Then why did
you go out? To see a prophet? Yes, I tell you,
and more than a prophet. **10** [k]This is the one
about whom it is written:

'Behold, I am sending my messenger ahead
of you;
he will prepare your way before you.'

**11** *Amen, I say to you, among those born of
women there has been none greater than John
the Baptist; yet the least in the kingdom of heav-
en is greater than he. **12** [l]*From the days of
John the Baptist until now, the kingdom of
heaven suffers violence, and the violent are taking it by force. **13** *All the prophets and the law
prophesied up to the time of John. **14** [m]And if
you are willing to accept it, he is Elijah, the one
who is to come. **15** Whoever has ears ought to
hear.

**16** [n]*"To what shall I compare this generation? It is like children who sit in marketplaces
and call to one another, **17** 'We played the flute
for you, but you did not dance, we sang a dirge
but you did not mourn.' **18** [o]For John came
neither eating nor drinking, and they said, 'He
is possessed by a demon.' **19** [p]The Son of Man
came eating and drinking and they said, 'Look,
he is a glutton and a drunkard, a friend of tax
collectors and sinners.' But wisdom is vindicated by her works."

### Reproaches to Unrepentant Towns

**20** [q]Then he began to reproach the towns where
most of his mighty deeds had been done, since
they had not repented. **21** [r]*"Woe to you,

h Lk 7, 18-28.
i Is 26, 19; 29, 18-19; 35, 5-6; 61, 1.
j 3, 3.5.
k Ex 23, 20; Mal 3, 1; Mk 1, 2; Lk 1, 76.
l Lk 16, 16.
m 17, 10-13; Mal 3, 23; Lk 1, 17.
n Lk 7, 31-35.
o Lk 1, 15.
p 9, 10-11.
q Lk 10, 12-15.
r Jl 4, 4-7.

*

11, 1: The closing formula of the discourse refers back to the original addressees, the Twelve.

11, 2—12, 50: The narrative section of the third book deals with the growing opposition to Jesus. It is largely devoted to disputes and attacks relating to faith and discipleship and thus contains much sayings-material, drawn in large part from Q.

11, 2: *In prison:* see 4, 12; 14, 1–12. *The works of the Messiah:* the deeds of chs 8–9.

11, 3: The question probably expresses a doubt of the Baptist that Jesus is *the one who is to come* (cf Mal 3, 1) because his mission has not been one of fiery judgment as John had expected (3, 2).

11, 5–6: Jesus' response is taken from passages of Isaiah (26, 19; 29, 18–19; 35, 5–6; 61, 1) that picture the time of salvation as marked by deeds such as those that Jesus is doing. The beatitude is a warning to the Baptist not to disbelieve because his expectations have not been met.

11, 7–19: Jesus' rebuke of John is counterbalanced by a reminder of the greatness of the Baptist's function (7–15) that is followed by a complaint about those who have heeded neither John nor Jesus (16–19).

11, 9–10: In common Jewish belief there had been no prophecy in Israel since the last of the Old Testament prophets, Malachi. The coming of a new prophet was eagerly awaited, and Jesus agrees that John was such. Yet he was *more than a prophet,* for he was the precursor of the one who would bring in the new and final age. The Old Testament quotation is a combination of Mal 3, 1 and Ex 23, 20, with the significant change that the *before me* of Malachi becomes *before you.* The messenger now precedes not God, as in the original, but Jesus.

11, 11: John's preeminent greatness lies in his function of announcing the imminence of the kingdom (3, 1). But to be in the kingdom is so great a privilege that the least who has it is greater than the Baptist.

11, 12: The meaning of this difficult saying is probably that the opponents of Jesus are trying to prevent people from accepting the kingdom and to snatch it away from those who have received it.

11, 13: *All the prophets and the law:* Matthew inverts the usual order, "law and prophets," and says that both have *prophesied.* This emphasis on the prophetic character of the law points to its fulfillment in the teaching of Jesus and to the transitory nature of some of its commandments (see the note on 5, 17–20).

11, 16–19: See Lk 7, 31–35. The meaning of the parable (16–17) and its explanation (18–19b) is much disputed. A plausible view is that the *children* of the parable are two groups, one of which proposes different entertainments to the other that will not agree with either proposal. The first represents John, Jesus, and their disciples; the second those who reject John for his asceticism and Jesus for his table association with those despised by the religiously observant. Verse 19c (*her works*) forms an inclusion with v 2 ("the works of the Messiah"). The original form of the saying is better preserved in Lk 7, 35, ". . . wisdom is vindicated by all her children." There John and Jesus are the children of Wisdom; here the works of Jesus the Messiah are those of divine Wisdom, of which he is the embodiment. Some important textual witnesses, however, have essentially the same reading as in Luke.

11, 21: Tyre and Sidon were pagan cities denounced for

Chorazin! Woe to you, Bethsaida! For if the
mighty deeds done in your midst had been done
in Tyre and Sidon, they would long ago have
repented in sackcloth and ashes. **22** But I tell
you, it will be more tolerable for Tyre and Sidon
on the day of judgment than for you. **23** [s]*And
as for you, Capernaum:

'Will you be exalted to heaven?
You will go down to the netherworld.'

For if the mighty deeds done in your midst had
been done in Sodom, it would have remained
until this day. **24** [t]But I tell you, it will be more
tolerable for the land of Sodom on the day of
judgment than for you."

**The Praise of the Father** **25** [u]*At that
time Jesus said in reply, "I give praise to you,
Father, Lord of heaven and earth, for although
you have hidden these things from the wise and
the learned you have revealed them to the childlike. **26** Yes, Father, such has been your gracious will. **27** [v]All things have been handed
over to me by my Father. No one knows the Son
except the Father, and no one knows the Father
except the Son and anyone to whom the Son
wishes to reveal him.

## The Gentle Mastery of Christ

**28** *"Come to me, all you who labor and are
burdened, and I will give you rest. **29** [w]*Take
my yoke upon you and learn from me, for I am
meek and humble of heart; and you will find rest
for yourselves. **30** For my yoke is easy, and my
burden light."

## CHAPTER 12

**Picking Grain on the Sabbath** **1** [xy]*At
that time Jesus was going through a field of
grain on the sabbath. His disciples were hungry
and began to pick the heads of grain and eat
them. **2** When the Pharisees saw this, they said
to him, "See, your disciples are doing what is
unlawful to do on the sabbath." **3** [z]*He said to
them, "Have you not read what David did when
he and his companions were hungry, **4** [a]how he
went into the house of God and ate the bread of
offering, which neither he nor his companions
but only the priests could lawfully eat? **5** [b]*Or
have you not read in the law that on the sabbath
the priests serving in the temple violate the sabbath and are innocent? **6** I say to you, something greater than the temple is here. **7** [c]*If you
knew what this meant, 'I desire mercy, not sacrifice,' you would not have condemned these
innocent men. **8** [d]*For the Son of Man is Lord
of the sabbath."

## The Man with a Withered Hand

**9** [e]Moving on from there, he went into their
synagogue. **10** *And behold, there was a man
there who had a withered hand. They questioned him, "Is it lawful to cure on the sabbath?" so that they might accuse him. **11** *He
said to them, "Which one of you who has a

s Is 14, 13-15.
t 10, 15.
u Lk 10, 21-22.
v Jn 3, 35; 6, 46; 7, 28; 10, 15.
w Sir 51, 26; Jer 6, 16.
x Mk 2, 23-28; Lk 6, 1-5.
y Dt 23, 26.
z 1 Sm 21, 2-7.
a Lv 24, 5-9.
b Lv 24, 8; Nm 28, 9-10.
c Hos 6, 6.
d Jn 5, 16-17.
e Mk 3, 1-6; Lk 6, 6-11.

* their wickedness in the Old Testament; cf Jl 4, 4–7.

11, 23: Capernaum's pride and punishment are described in language taken from the taunt song against the king of Babylon (Is 14, 13–15).

11, 25–27: This Q saying, identical with Lk 10, 21–22 except for minor variations, introduces a joyous note into this section, so dominated by the theme of unbelief. While the *wise and the learned,* the scribes and Pharisees, have rejected Jesus' preaching and the significance of his mighty deeds, *the childlike* have accepted them. Acceptance depends upon the Father's revelation, but this is granted to those who are open to receive it and refused to the arrogant. Jesus can speak of all mysteries because he is *the Son* and there is perfect reciprocity of knowledge between him and the Father; what has been *handed over* to him is revealed only to those whom he wishes.

11, 28–29: These verses are peculiar to Matthew and are similar to Ben Sirach's invitation to learn wisdom and submit to her yoke (Sir 51, 23.26).

11, 28: *Who labor and are burdened:* burdened by the law as expounded by the scribes and Pharisees (23, 4).

11, 29: In place of the yoke of the law, complicated by scribal interpretation, Jesus invites the burdened to take the yoke of obedience to his word, under which they *will find rest;* cf Jer 6, 16.

12, 1–14: Matthew here returns to the Marcan order that he left in 9, 18. The two stories depend on Mk 2, 23–28 and 3, 1–6, respectively, and are the only places in either gospel that deal explicitly with Jesus' attitude toward sabbath observance.

12, 1–2: The picking of the heads of grain is here equated with reaping, which was forbidden on the sabbath (Ex 34, 21).

12, 3–4: See 1 Sm 21, 2–7. In the Marcan parallel (2, 25–26) the high priest is called Abiathar, although in 1 Sm this action is attributed to Ahimelech. The Old Testament story is not about a violation of the sabbath rest; its pertinence to this dispute is that a violation of the law was permissible because of David's men being without food.

12, 5–6: This and the following argument (7) are peculiar to Matthew. The temple service seems to be the changing of the showbread on the sabbath (Lv 24, 8) and the doubling on the sabbath of the usual daily holocausts (Nm 28, 9–10). The argument is that the law itself requires work that breaks the sabbath rest, because of the higher duty of temple service. If temple duties outweigh the sabbath law, how much more does the presence of Jesus, with his proclamation of the kingdom (*something greater than the temple*), justify the conduct of his disciples.

12, 7: See the note on 9, 13.

12, 8: The ultimate justification for the disciples' violation of the sabbath rest is that Jesus, the Son of Man, has supreme authority over the law.

12, 10: Rabbinic tradition later than the gospels allowed relief to be given to a sufferer on the sabbath if life was in danger. This may also have been the view of Jesus' Pharisaic contemporaries. But the case here is not about one in danger of death.

12, 11: Matthew omits the question posed by Jesus in Mk 3, 4 and substitutes one about rescuing a sheep on the sabbath, similar to that in Lk 14, 5.

sheep that falls into a pit on the sabbath will not
take hold of it and lift it out? **12** How much
more valuable a person is than a sheep. So it is
lawful to do good on the sabbath." **13** Then he
said to the man, "Stretch out your hand." He
stretched it out, and it was restored as sound as
the other. **14** [f]*But the Pharisees went out and
took counsel against him to put him to death.

**The Chosen Servant** **15** *When Jesus realized this, he withdrew from that place. Many
[people] followed him, and he cured them all,
**16** but he warned them not to make him known.
**17** This was to fulfill what had been spoken
through Isaiah the prophet:

**18** [g]"Behold, my servant whom I have chosen,
my beloved in whom I delight;
I shall place my spirit upon him,
and he will proclaim justice to the
Gentiles.
**19** *He will not contend or cry out,
nor will anyone hear his voice in the
streets.
**20** A bruised reed he will not break,
a smoldering wick he will not quench,
until he brings justice to victory.
**21** *And in his name the Gentiles will
hope."

**Jesus and Beelzebul** **22** [h]*Then they
brought to him a demoniac who was blind and
mute. He cured the mute person so that he could
speak and see. **23** [i]*All the crowd was astounded, and said, "Could this perhaps be the Son of
David?" **24** [j]*But when the Pharisees heard
this, they said, "This man drives out demons
only by the power of Beelzebul, the prince of
demons." **25** [k]*But he knew what they were
thinking and said to them, "Every kingdom
divided against itself will be laid waste, and no
town or house divided against itself will stand.
**26** And if Satan drives out Satan, he is divided
against himself; how, then, will his kingdom
stand? **27** *And if I drive out demons by Beelzebul, by whom do your own people drive them
out? Therefore they will be your judges.
**28** [l]*But if it is by the Spirit of God that I drive
out demons, then the kingdom of God has come
upon you. **29** *How can anyone enter a strong
man's house and steal his property, unless he
first ties up the strong man? Then he can plunder
his house. **30** [m]*Whoever is not with me is
against me, and whoever does not gather with
me scatters. **31** [n]*Therefore, I say to you, every sin and blasphemy will be forgiven people,
but blasphemy against the Spirit will not be
forgiven. **32** And whoever speaks a word
against the Son of Man will be forgiven; but
whoever speaks against the holy Spirit will not
be forgiven, either in this age or in the age to
come.

**A Tree and Its Fruits** **33** [o]*"Either declare the tree good and its fruit is good, or
declare the tree rotten and its fruit is rotten, for
a tree is known by its fruit. **34** [p]*You brood of

f Jn 5, 18.
g Is 42, 1-4.
h 9, 32-34; Lk 11, 14-15.
i 9, 27.
j 10, 25; Mk 3, 22.
k Mk 3, 23-27; Lk 11, 17-22.
l Lk 11, 20.
m Lk 11, 23.
n Mk 3, 28-30; Lk 12, 10.
o Lk 6, 43-45.
p 3, 7; 23, 33; 15, 11-12; Lk 3, 7.

*

12, 14: See Mk 3, 6. Here the plan to bring about Jesus' death is attributed to the Pharisees only. This is probably due to the situation of Matthew's church, when the sole opponents were the Pharisees.

12, 15–21: Matthew follows Mk 3, 7–12 but summarizes his source in two verses (15.16) that pick up the withdrawal, the healings, and the command for silence. To this he adds a fulfillment citation from the first Servant Song (Is 42, 1–4) that does not correspond exactly to either the Hebrew or the LXX of that passage. It is the longest Old Testament citation in this gospel, emphasizing the meekness of Jesus, the Servant of the Lord, and foretelling the extension of his mission to the Gentiles.

12, 15: Jesus' knowledge of the Pharisees' plot and his healing *all* are peculiar to Matthew.

12, 19: The servant's not contending is seen as fulfilled in Jesus' withdrawal from the disputes narrated in 1–14.

12, 21: Except for a minor detail, Matthew here follows the LXX, although the meaning of the Hebrew ("the coastlands will wait for his teaching") is similar.

12, 22–32: For the exorcism, see the note on 9, 32–34. The long discussion combines Marcan and Q material (Mk 3, 22–30; Lk 11, 19–20.23; 12, 10). Mk 3, 20–21 is omitted, with a consequent lessening of the sharpness of 12, 48.

12, 23: See the note on 9, 27.

12, 24: See the note on 10, 25.

12, 25–26: Jesus' first response to the Pharisees' charge is that if it were true, Satan would be destroying his own kingdom.

12, 27: Besides pointing out the absurdity of the charge, Jesus asks how the work of Jewish exorcists (*your own people*) is to be interpreted. Are they, too, to be charged with collusion with Beelzebul? For an example of Jewish exorcism see Josephus, Antiquities 8, 2, 5 **42–49.

12, 28: The Q parallel (Lk 11, 20) speaks of the "finger" rather than of the "spirit" of God. While the difference is probably due to Matthew's editing, he retains *the kingdom of God* rather than changing it to his usual "kingdom of heaven." *Has come upon you:* see 4, 17.

12, 29: A short parable illustrates what Jesus is doing. The *strong man* is Satan, whom Jesus has tied up and whose *house* he is plundering. Jewish expectation was that Satan would be chained up in the last days (Rv 20, 2); Jesus' exorcisms indicate that those days have begun.

12, 30: This saying, already attached to the preceding verses in Q (see Lk 11, 23), warns that there can be no neutrality where Jesus is concerned. Its pertinence in a context where Jesus is addressing not the neutral but the bitterly opposed is not clear. The accusation of scattering, however, does fit the situation. Jesus is the shepherd of God's people (2, 6), his mission is to the lost sheep of Israel (15, 24); the Pharisees, who oppose him, are guilty of scattering the sheep.

12, 31: *Blasphemy against the Spirit:* the sin of attributing to Satan (24) what is the work of the Spirit of God (28).

12, 33: *Declare:* literally, "make." The meaning of this verse is obscure. Possibly it is a challenge to the Pharisees either to declare Jesus and his exorcisms good or both of them bad. A tree is known by its fruit; if the fruit is good, so must the tree be. If the driving out of demons is good, so must its source be.

12, 34: The admission of Jesus' goodness cannot be made

vipers, how can you say good things when you
are evil? For from the fullness of the heart the
mouth speaks. **35** A good person brings forth
good out of a store of goodness, but an evil
person brings forth evil out of a store of evil.
**36** [q]*I tell you, on the day of judgment people
will render an account for every careless word
they speak. **37** By your words you will be acquitted, and by your words you will be condemned."

**The Demand for a Sign** **38** [r]*Then some
of the scribes and Pharisees said to him,
"Teacher, we wish to see a sign from you."
**39** *He said to them in reply, "An evil and
unfaithful generation seeks a sign, but no sign
will be given it except the sign of Jonah the
prophet. **40** *Just as Jonah was in the belly of
the whale three days and three nights, so will the
Son of Man be in the heart of the earth three
days and three nights. **41** *At the judgment, the
men of Nineveh will arise with this generation
and condemn it, because they repented at the
preaching of Jonah; and there is something
greater than Jonah here. **42** [s]At the judgment
the queen of the south will arise with this generation and condemn it, because she came from
the ends of the earth to hear the wisdom of
Solomon; and there is something greater than
Solomon here.

### The Return of the Unclean Spirit

**43** [t]*"When an unclean spirit goes out of a
person it roams through arid regions searching
for rest but finds none. **44** Then it says, 'I will
return to my home from which I came.' But
upon returning, it finds it empty, swept clean,
and put in order. **45** Then it goes and brings
back with itself seven other spirits more evil
than itself, and they move in and dwell there;
and the last condition of that person is worse
than the first. Thus it will be with this evil
generation."

**The True Family of Jesus** **46** [u]*While he
was still speaking to the crowds, his mother and
his brothers appeared outside, wishing to speak
with him. [ **47** *Someone told him, "Your
mother and your brothers are standing outside,
asking to speak with you."] **48** But he said in
reply to the one who told him, "Who is my
mother? Who are my brothers?" **49** And
stretching out his hand toward his disciples, he
said, "Here are my mother and my brothers.
**50** For whoever does the will of my heavenly
Father is my brother, and sister, and mother."

## CHAPTER 13

**The Parable of the Sower** **1** [v]*On that
day, Jesus went out of the house and sat down
by the sea. **2** Such large crowds gathered
around him that he got into a boat and sat down,
and the whole crowd stood along the shore.
**3** *And he spoke to them at length in parables,

q Jas 3, 1-2.
r 16, 1-4; Jon 2, 1; 3, 1-10; Mk 8, 11-12; Lk 11, 29-32.
s 1 Kgs 10, 1-10.
t Lk 11, 24-26.
u Mk 3, 31-35; Lk 8, 19-21.
v Mk 4, 1-12; Lk 8, 4-10.

*

by the Pharisees, for they are evil, and the words that proceed from their evil hearts cannot be good.

12, 36–37: If on the day of judgment people will be held accountable for even their *careless* words, the vicious accusations of the Pharisees will surely lead to their condemnation.

12, 38–42: This section is mainly from Q (see Lk 11, 29–32). Mk 8, 11–12, which Matthew has followed in 16, 1–4, has a similar demand for a sign. The scribes and Pharisees refuse to accept the exorcisms of Jesus as authentication of his claims and demand a sign that will end all possibility of doubt. Jesus' response is that no such sign will be given. Because his opponents are evil and see him as an agent of Satan, nothing will convince them.

12, 38: *Teacher:* see the note on 8, 19. In 16, 1 the request is for a sign "from heaven" (Mk 8, 11).

12, 39: *Unfaithful:* literally, "adulterous." The covenant between God and Israel was portrayed as a marriage bond, and unfaithfulness to the covenant as adultery; cf Hos 2, 4–15; Jer 3, 6–10.

12, 40: See Jon 2, 1. While in Q the sign was simply Jonah's preaching to the Ninevites (Lk 11, 30.32), Matthew here adds Jonah's sojourn *in the belly of the whale* for *three days and three nights,* a prefigurement of Jesus' sojourn in the abode of the dead and, implicitly, of his resurrection.

12, 41–42: The Ninevites who *repented* (see Jon 3, 1–10) *and the queen of the south* (i.e., of Sheba; see 1 Kgs 10, 1–13) were pagans who responded to lesser opportunities than have been offered to Israel in the ministry of Jesus, *something greater than Jonah* or *Solomon.* At the final judgment they will condemn the faithless *generation* that has rejected him.

12, 43–45: Another Q passage; cf 11, 24–26. Jesus' ministry has broken Satan's hold over Israel, but the refusal of *this evil generation* to accept him will lead to a worse situation than what preceded his coming.

12, 46–50: See Mk 3, 31–35. Matthew has omitted Mk 3, 20–21, which is taken up in Mk 3, 31 (see the note on 12, 22–32), yet the point of the story is the same in both gospels: natural kinship with Jesus counts for nothing; only one who *does the will* of *his heavenly Father* belongs to his true family.

12, 47: This verse is omitted in some important textual witnesses, including Codex Sinaiticus (original reading) and Codex Vaticanus.

13, 1–53: The discourse in parables is the third great discourse of Jesus in Mt and constitutes the second part of the third book of the gospel. Matthew follows the Marcan outline (Mk 4, 1–35) but has only two of Mark's parables, the five others being from Q and M. In addition to the seven parables, the discourse gives the reason why Jesus uses this type of speech (10–15), declares the blessedness of those who understand his teaching (16–17), explains the parable of the sower (18–23) and of the weeds (36–43), and ends with a concluding statement to the disciples (51–52).

13, 3: *In parables:* the word "parable" (Greek *parabolē*) is used in the LXX to translate the Hebrew *māshāl,* a designation covering a wide variety of literary forms such as axioms, proverbs, similitudes, and allegories. In the New Testament the same breadth of meaning of the word is found, but there it primarily designates stories that are illustrative comparisons between Christian truths and events of everyday life. Sometimes the event has a strange element that is quite different from usual experience (e.g., in v 33, the enormous amount of dough in the parable of the yeast); this is meant to sharpen the

saying: "A sower went out to sow. **4** And as he
sowed, some seed fell on the path, and birds
came and ate it up. **5** Some fell on rocky
ground, where it had little soil. It sprang up at
once because the soil was not deep, **6** and when
the sun rose it was scorched, and it withered for
lack of roots. **7** Some seed fell among thorns,
and the thorns grew up and choked it. **8** But
some seed fell on rich soil, and produced fruit,
a hundred or sixty or thirtyfold. **9** Whoever has
ears ought to hear."

### The Purpose of Parables

**10** The disci-
ples approached him and said, "Why do you
speak to them in parables?" **11** *He said to
them in reply, "Because knowledge of the mysteries of the kingdom of heaven has been granted to you, but to them it has not been granted.
**12** [w]*To anyone who has, more will be given
and he will grow rich; from anyone who has not,
even what he has will be taken away. **13** [x]*This
is why I speak to them in parables, because
'they look but do not see and hear but do not
listen or understand.' **14** [y]Isaiah's prophecy is
fulfilled in them, which says:

'You shall indeed hear but not understand,
you shall indeed look but never see.
**15** Gross is the heart of this people,
they will hardly hear with their ears,
they have closed their eyes,
lest they see with their eyes
and hear with their ears
and understand with their heart and be
converted,
and I heal them.'

### The Privilege of Discipleship

**16** [z]*"But
blessed are your eyes, because they see, and
your ears, because they hear. **17** Amen, I say
to you, many prophets and righteous people
longed to see what you see but did not see it, and
to hear what you hear but did not hear it.

### The Explanation of the Parable of the Sower

**18** [a]*"Hear then the parable of the
sower. **19** The seed sown on the path is the one
who hears the word of the kingdom without
understanding it, and the evil one comes and
steals away what was sown in his heart. **20** The
seed sown on rocky ground is the one who hears
the word and receives it at once with joy.
**21** But he has no root and lasts only for a time.
When some tribulation or persecution comes
because of the word, he immediately falls away.
**22** The seed sown among thorns is the one who
hears the word, but then worldly anxiety and the
lure of riches choke the word and it bears no
fruit. **23** But the seed sown on rich soil is the
one who hears the word and understands it, who
indeed bears fruit and yields a hundred or sixty
or thirtyfold."

### The Parable of the Weeds among the Wheat

**24** *He proposed another parable to

w 25, 29; Mk 4, 25; Lk 8, 18; 19, 26.
x Jn 9, 39.
y Is 6, 9-10; Jn 12, 40; Acts 28, 26-27; Rom 11, 8.
z Lk 10, 23-24; 1 Pt 1, 10-12.
a Mk 4, 13-20; Lk 8, 11-15.

*

curiosity of the hearer. If each detail of such a story is given a figurative meaning, the story is an allegory. Those who maintain a sharp distinction between parable and allegory insist that a parable has only one point of comparison, and that while parables were characteristic of Jesus' teaching, to see allegorical details in them is to introduce meanings that go beyond their original intention and even falsify it. However, to exclude any allegorical elements from a parable is an excessively rigid mode of interpretation, now abandoned by many scholars.

13, 3–8: Since in Palestine sowing often preceded plowing, much of the seed is scattered on ground that is unsuitable. Yet while much is wasted, the seed that falls on good ground bears fruit in extraordinarily large measure. The point of the parable is that, in spite of some failure because of opposition and indifference, the message of Jesus about the coming of the kingdom will have enormous success.

13, 11: Since a parable is figurative speech that demands reflection for understanding, only those who are prepared to explore its meaning can come to know it. To understand is a gift of God, granted to the disciples but not to the crowds. In Semitic fashion, both the disciples' understanding and the crowd's obtuseness are attributed to God. The question of human responsibility for the obtuseness is not dealt with, although it is asserted in v 13. *The mysteries:* as in Lk 8, 10; Mk 4, 11 has "the mystery." The word is used in Dn 2, 18.19.27 and in the Qumran literature (1QpHab 7, 8; 1QS 3, 23; 1QM 3, 9) to designate a divine plan or decree affecting the course of history that can be known only when revealed. *Knowledge of the mysteries of the kingdom of heaven* means recognition that the kingdom has become present in the ministry of Jesus.

13, 12: In the New Testament use of this axiom of practical "wisdom" (see 25, 29; Mk 4, 25; Lk 8, 18; 19, 26), the reference transcends the original level. God gives further understanding to one who accepts the revealed mystery; from the one who does not, he will take it away (note the "theological passive," *more will be given, what he has will be taken away*).

13, 13: *Because 'they look . . . or understand':* Matthew softens his Marcan source, which states that Jesus speaks in parables so that the crowds may not understand (Mk 4, 12), and makes such speaking a punishment given *because* they have not accepted his previous clear teaching. However, his citation of Is 6, 9–10 in v 14 supports the harsher Marcan view.

13, 16–17: Unlike the unbelieving crowds, the disciples have seen that which the *prophets* and the *righteous* of the Old Testament *longed to see* without having their longing fulfilled.

13, 18–23: See Mk 4, 14–20; Lk 8, 11–15. In this explanation of the parable the emphasis is on the various types of soil on which the seed falls, i.e., on the dispositions with which the preaching of Jesus is received. The second and third types particularly are explained in such a way as to support the view held by many scholars that the explanation derives not from Jesus but from early Christian reflection upon apostasy from the faith that was the consequence of persecution and worldliness respectively. Others, however, hold that the explanation may come basically from Jesus even though it was developed in the light of later Christian experience. The four types of persons envisaged are (1) those who never accept *the word of the kingdom* (19); (2) those who believe for a while but fall away because of *persecution* (20–21); (3) those who believe, but in whom *the word* is choked by *worldly anxiety* and the seduction of *riches* (22); (4) those who respond to *the word* and produce *fruit* abundantly (23).

13, 24–30: This parable is peculiar to Matthew. The comparison in v 24 does not mean that *the kingdom of heaven may*

them. "The kingdom of heaven may be likened
to a man who sowed good seed in his field.
**25** *While everyone was asleep his enemy
came and sowed weeds all through the wheat,
and then went off. **26** When the crop grew and
bore fruit, the weeds appeared as well. **27** The
slaves of the householder came to him and said,
'Master, did you not sow good seed in your
field? Where have the weeds come from?'
**28** He answered, 'An enemy has done this.' His
slaves said to him, 'Do you want us to go and
pull them up?' **29** He replied, 'No, if you pull
up the weeds you might uproot the wheat along
with them. **30** [b]*Let them grow together until
harvest; then at harvest time I will say to the
harvesters, "First collect the weeds and tie them
in bundles for burning; but gather the wheat into
my barn." ' "

### The Parable of the Mustard Seed

**31** [c]*He proposed another parable to them.
"The kingdom of heaven is like a mustard seed
that a person took and sowed in a field. **32** [d]*It
is the smallest of all the seeds, yet when full-
grown it is the largest of plants. It becomes a
large bush, and the 'birds of the sky come and
dwell in its branches.' "

### The Parable of the Yeast

**33** [e]*He spoke
to them another parable. "The kingdom of
heaven is like yeast that a woman took and
mixed with three measures of wheat flour until
the whole batch was leavened."

### The Use of Parables

**34** [f]*All these things
Jesus spoke to the crowds in parables. He spoke
to them only in parables, **35** [g]*to fulfill what
had been said through the prophet:

"I will open my mouth in parables,
I will announce what has lain hidden from
the foundation
[of the world]."

### The Explanation of the Parable of the Weeds

**36** *Then, dismissing the crowds,
he went into the house. His disciples approached him and said, "Explain to us the parable of the weeds in the field." **37** *He said in
reply, "He who sows good seed is the Son of
Man, **38** *the field is the world, the good seed
the children of the kingdom. The weeds are the
children of the evil one, **39** *and the enemy
who sows them is the devil. The harvest is the
end of the age, and the harvesters are angels.
**40** Just as weeds are collected and burned [up]
with fire, so will it be at the end of the age.
**41** *The Son of Man will send his angels, and
they will collect out of his kingdom all who
cause others to sin and all evildoers. **42** [h]They
will throw them into the fiery furnace, where
there will be wailing and grinding of teeth.
**43** [i]*Then the righteous will shine like the sun
in the kingdom of their Father. Whoever has
ears ought to hear.

### More Parables

**44** [j]*"The kingdom of
heaven is like a treasure buried in a field, which

b 3, 12.
c Mk 4, 30-32; Lk 13, 18-19.
d Ez 17, 23; 31, 6; Dn 4, 7-9.17-19.
e Lk 13, 20-21.
f Mk 4, 33-34.
g Ps 78, 2.
h 8, 12; Rv 21, 8.
i Dn 12, 3.
j Prv 2, 4; 4, 7.

*

*be likened* simply to the person in question but to the situation narrated in the whole story. The refusal of the *householder* to allow his *slaves* to separate *the wheat* from *the weeds* while they are still growing is a warning to the disciples not to attempt to anticipate the final judgment of God by a definitive exclusion of sinners from the kingdom. In its present stage it is composed of the good and the bad. The judgment of God alone will eliminate the sinful. Until then there must be patience and the preaching of repentance.

13, 25: *Weeds:* darnel, a poisonous weed that in its first stage of growth resembles wheat.

13, 30: *Harvest:* a common biblical metaphor for the time of God's judgment; cf Jer 51, 33; Jl 4, 13; Hos 6, 11.

13, 31–33: See Mk 4, 30–32; Lk 13, 18–21. The parables of the mustard seed and the yeast illustrate the same point: the amazing contrast between the small beginnings of the kingdom and its marvelous expansion.

13, 32: See Dn 4, 7–9.17–19, where the birds nesting in the tree represent the people of Nebuchadnezzar's kingdom. See also Ez 17, 23 and 31, 6.

13, 33: Except in this Q parable and in 16, 12, *yeast* (or "leaven") is, in New Testament usage, a symbol of corruption (see 16, 6.11–12; Mk 8, 15; Lk 12, 1; 1 Cor 5, 6–8; Gal 5, 9). *Three measures:* an enormous amount, enough to feed a hundred people. The exaggeration of this element of the parable points to the greatness of the kingdom's effect.

13, 34: *Only in parables:* see vv 10–15.

13, 35: *The prophet:* some textual witnesses read "Isaiah the prophet." The quotation is actually from Ps 78, 2; the first line corresponds to the LXX text of the psalm. The psalm's title ascribes it to Asaph, the founder of one of the guilds of temple musicians. He is called "the prophet" (NAB "the seer") in 2 Chr 29, 30, but it is doubtful that Matthew averted to that; for him, any Old Testament text that could be seen as fulfilled in Jesus was prophetic.

13, 36: *Dismissing the crowds:* the return of Jesus to the house marks a break with the crowds, who represent unbelieving Israel. From now on his attention is directed more and more to his disciples and to their instruction. The rest of the discourse is addressed to them alone.

13, 37–43: In the explanation of the parable of the weeds emphasis lies on the fearful end of the wicked, whereas the parable itself concentrates on patience with them until judgment time.

13, 38: *The field is the world:* this presupposes the resurrection of Jesus and the granting to him of "all power in heaven and on earth" (28, 18).

13, 39: *The end of the age:* this phrase is found only in Mt (13, 40.49; 24, 3; 28, 20).

13, 41: *His kingdom:* the *kingdom* of the *Son of Man* is distinguished from that of the Father (43); see 1 Cor 15, 24–25. The church is the place where Jesus' kingdom is manifested, but his royal authority embraces the entire world; see the note on 13, 38.

13, 43: See Dn 12, 3.

13, 44–50: The first two of the last three parables of the discourse have the same point. The *person* who *finds* a buried *treasure* and the *merchant* who finds a *pearl of great price* sell *all* that they have to acquire these finds; similarly, the one who

a person finds and hides again, and out of joy
goes and sells all that he has and buys that field.
**45** Again, the kingdom of heaven is like a merchant searching for fine pearls. **46** When he
finds a pearl of great price, he goes and sells all
that he has and buys it. **47** Again, the kingdom
of heaven is like a net thrown into the sea, which
collects fish of every kind. **48** When it is full
they haul it ashore and sit down to put what is
good into buckets. What is bad they throw
away. **49** Thus it will be at the end of the age.
The angels will go out and separate the wicked
from the righteous **50** and throw them into the
fiery furnace, where there will be wailing and
grinding of teeth.

**Treasures New and Old** 51 *"Do you
understand all these things?" They answered,
"Yes." **52** *And he replied, "Then every
scribe who has been instructed in the kingdom
of heaven is like the head of a household who
brings from his storeroom both the new and the
old." **53** When Jesus finished these parables,
he went away from there.

## V: JESUS, THE KINGDOM, AND THE CHURCH

**The Rejection at Nazareth** 54 [kl]*He
came to his native place and taught the people
in their synagogue. They were astonished and
said, "Where did this man get such wisdom and
mighty deeds? **55** [m]Is he not the carpenter's
son? Is not his mother named Mary and his
brothers James, Joseph, Simon, and Judas?
**56** Are not his sisters all with us? Where did
this man get all this?" **57** [n]And they took offense at him. But Jesus said to them, "A prophet is not without honor except in his native place
and in his own house." **58** And he did not work
many mighty deeds there because of their lack
of faith.

### CHAPTER 14

**Herod's Opinion of Jesus** 1 [opq]*At that
time Herod the tetrarch heard of the reputation
of Jesus **2** and said to his servants, "This man
is John the Baptist. He has been raised from the
dead; that is why mighty powers are at work in
him."

**The Death of John the Baptist** 3 [r]*Now
Herod had arrested John, bound [him], and put
him in prison on account of Herodias, the wife
of his brother Philip, **4** [s]for John had said to
him, "It is not lawful for you to have her."
**5** [t]Although he wanted to kill him, he feared
the people, for they regarded him as a prophet.
**6** But at a birthday celebration for Herod, the
daughter of Herodias performed a dance before
the guests and delighted Herod **7** so much that
he swore to give her whatever she might ask for.
**8** Prompted by her mother, she said, "Give me
here on a platter the head of John the Baptist."

k Mk 6, 1-6; Lk 4, 16-30.
l 2, 23; Jn 1, 46; 7, 15.
m 12, 46; 27, 56; Jn 6, 42.
n Jn 4, 44.
o Mk 6, 14-29.
p Lk 3, 1.
q Lk 9, 7-9.
r Lk 3, 19-20.
s Lv 18, 16; 20, 21.
t 21, 26.

* understands the supreme value of the kingdom gives up whatever he must to obtain it. The *joy* with which this is done is made explicit in the first parable, but it may be presumed in the second also. The concluding parable of the fishnet resembles the explanation of the parable of the weeds with its stress upon the final exclusion of evil persons from the kingdom.

13, 44: In the unsettled conditions of Palestine in Jesus' time, it was not unusual to guard valuables by burying them in the ground.

13, 51: Matthew typically speaks of the understanding of the disciples.

13, 52: Since Matthew tends to identify the disciples and the Twelve (see the note on 10, 1), this saying about the Christian *scribe* cannot be taken as applicable to all who accept the message of Jesus. While the Twelve are in many ways representative of all who believe in him, they are also distinguished from them in certain respects. The church of Matthew has leaders among whom are a group designated as "scribes" (23, 34). Like the scribes of Israel, they are teachers. It is the Twelve and these their later counterparts to whom this verse applies. The *scribe . . . instructed in the kingdom of heaven* knows both the teaching of Jesus (*the new*) and the law and prophets (*the old*) and provides in his own teaching *both the new and the old* as interpreted and fulfilled by *the new*. On the translation *head of a household* (for the same Greek word translated *householder* in v 27), see the note on 24, 45–51.

13, 54—17, 27: This section is the narrative part of the fourth book of the gospel.

13, 54–58: After the Sermon on the Mount the crowds are in admiring astonishment at Jesus' teaching (7, 28); here the astonishment is of those who take *offense at him*. Familiarity with his background and family leads them to regard him as pretentious. Matthew modifies his Marcan source (6, 1–6). Jesus is not the carpenter but *the carpenter's son* (55), "and among his own kin" is omitted (57), *he did not work many mighty deeds* in face of such unbelief (58) rather than the Marcan ". . . he was not able to perform any mighty deed there" (6, 5), and there is no mention of his amazement at his townspeople's lack of faith.

14, 1–12: The murder of the Baptist by Herod Antipas prefigures the death of Jesus (see 17, 12). The Marcan source (6, 14–29) is much reduced and in some points changed. In Mk Herod reveres John as a holy man and the desire to kill him is attributed to Herodias (6, 19.20), whereas here that desire is Herod's from the beginning (5).

14, 1: *Herod the tetrarch:* Herod Antipas, son of Herod the Great. When the latter died, his territory was divided among three of his surviving sons, Archelaus who received half of it (2, 23), Herod Antipas who became ruler of Galilee and Perea, and Philip who became ruler of northern Transjordan. Since he received a quarter of his father's domain, Antipas is accurately designated *tetrarch* ("ruler of a fourth [part]"), although in v 9 Matthew repeats the "king" of his Marcan source (6, 26).

14, 3: Herodias was not the wife of Herod's half-brother Philip but of another half-brother, Herod Boethus. The union was prohibited by Lv 18, 16; 20, 21. According to Josephus (*Antiquities* 18, 5, 2 **116–19), Herod imprisoned and then executed John because he feared that the Baptist's influence over the people might enable him to lead a rebellion.

**9** The king was distressed, but because of his
oaths and the guests who were present, he ordered that it be given, **10** and he had John beheaded in the prison. **11** His head was brought
in on a platter and given to the girl, who took
it to her mother. **12** His disciples came and took
away the corpse and buried him; and they went
and told Jesus.

## The Return of the Twelve and the Feeding of the Five Thousand

**13** [u]*When
Jesus heard of it, he withdrew in a boat to a
deserted place by himself. The crowds heard of
this and followed him on foot from their towns.
**14** When he disembarked and saw the vast
crowd, his heart was moved with pity for them,
and he cured their sick. **15** When it was evening, the disciples approached him and said,
"This is a deserted place and it is already late;
dismiss the crowds so that they can go to the
villages and buy food for themselves."
**16** [Jesus] said to them, "There is no need for
them to go away; give them some food yourselves." **17** But they said to him, "Five loaves
and two fish are all we have here." **18** Then he
said, "Bring them here to me," **19** *and he
ordered the crowds to sit down on the grass.
Taking the five loaves and the two fish, and
looking up to heaven, he said the blessing,
broke the loaves, and gave them to the disciples,
who in turn gave them to the crowds. **20** *They
all ate and were satisfied, and they picked up the
fragments left over—twelve wicker baskets
full. **21** Those who ate were about five thousand men, not counting women and children.

## The Walking on the Water

**22** [v]*Then he
made the disciples get into the boat and precede
him to the other side, while he dismissed the
crowds. **23** [w]After doing so, he went up on the
mountain by himself to pray. When it was evening he was there alone. **24** Meanwhile the
boat, already a few miles offshore, was being
tossed about by the waves, for the wind was
against it. **25** *During the fourth watch of the
night, he came toward them, walking on the
sea. **26** When the disciples saw him walking on
the sea they were terrified. "It is a ghost," they
said, and they cried out in fear. **27** *At once
[Jesus] spoke to them, "Take courage, it is I; do
not be afraid." **28** Peter said to him in reply,
"Lord, if it is you, command me to come to you
on the water." **29** He said, "Come." Peter got
out of the boat and began to walk on the water
toward Jesus. **30** [x]But when he saw how
[strong] the wind was he became frightened;
and, beginning to sink, he cried out, "Lord,
save me!" **31** *Immediately Jesus stretched out
his hand and caught him, and said to him, "O
you of little faith, why did you doubt?" **32** After they got into the boat, the wind died down.
**33** [y]*Those who were in the boat did him homage, saying, "Truly, you are the Son of God."

## The Healings at Gennesaret

**34** [z]After
making the crossing, they came to land at Gennesaret. **35** When the men of that place recognized him, they sent word to all the surrounding
country. People brought to him all those who
were sick **36** [a]and begged him that they might
touch only the tassel on his cloak, and as many
as touched it were healed.

# CHAPTER 15

## The Tradition of the Elders

**1** [b]*Then
Pharisees and scribes came to Jesus from Jeru-

u 15, 32-38; Mk 6, 32-44; Lk 9, 10-17; Jn 6, 1-13.
v Mk 6, 45-52; Jn 6, 16-21.
w Mk 1, 35; Lk 5, 16; 6, 12.
x 8, 25-26.
y 16, 16.
z Mk 6, 53-56.
a 9, 20-22.
b Mk 7, 1-23.

*

14, 13–21: The feeding of the five thousand is the only miracle of Jesus that is recounted in all four gospels. The principal reason for that may be that it was seen as anticipating the Eucharist and the final banquet in the kingdom (8, 11; 26, 29), but it looks not only forward but backward, to the feeding of Israel with manna in the desert at the time of the Exodus (Ex 16), a miracle that in some contemporary Jewish expectation would be repeated in the messianic age (2 Baruch 29, 8). It may also be meant to recall Elisha's feeding a hundred men with small provisions (2 Kgs 4, 42–44).

14, 19: The *taking,* saying the blessing, breaking, and giving to the disciples correspond to the actions of Jesus over the bread at the Last Supper (26, 26). Since they were usual at any Jewish meal, that correspondence does not necessarily indicate a eucharistic reference here. Matthew's silence about Jesus' dividing the fish among the people (Mk 6, 41) is perhaps more significant in that regard.

14, 20: *The fragments left over:* as in Elisha's miracle, food was *left over* after all had been fed. The word *fragments* (Greek *klasmata*) is used, in the singular, of the broken bread of the Eucharist in *Didache* 9, 3–4.

14, 22–33: The disciples, laboring against the turbulent sea, are saved by Jesus. For his power over the waters, see the note on 8, 26. Here that power is expressed also by his *walking on the sea* (25; cf Ps 77, 20; Jb 9, 8). Matthew has inserted into the Marcan story (Mk 6, 45–52) material that belongs to his special traditions on Peter (28–31).

14, 25: *The fourth watch of the night:* between 3 a.m. and 6 a.m. The Romans divided the twelve hours between 6 p.m. and 6 a.m. into four equal parts called "watches."

14, 27: *It is I:* see the note on Mk 6, 50.

14, 31: *You of little faith:* see the note on 6, 30. *Why did you doubt?:* the verb is peculiar to Matthew and occurs elsewhere only in 28, 17.

14, 33: This confession is in striking contrast to the Marcan parallel (6, 51) where the disciples are "completely astounded."

15, 1–20: This dispute begins with the question of the Pharisees and scribes why Jesus' disciples are breaking *the tradition of the elders* about washing one's hands before eating (2). Jesus' counterquestion accuses his opponents of breaking *the commandment of God for the sake of* their *tradition* (3) and illustrates this by their interpretation of the commandment of the Decalogue concerning parents (4–6). Denouncing them as hypocrites, he applies to them a derogatory prophecy of Isaiah (7–8). Then with a wider audience (*the crowd,* 10) he goes beyond the violation of tradition with which the dispute

salem and said, **2** [c]*"Why do your disciples
break the tradition of the elders? They do not
wash [their] hands when they eat a meal."
**3** *He said to them in reply, "And why do you
break the commandment of God for the sake of
your tradition? **4** [d]For God said, 'Honor your
father and your mother,' and 'Whoever curses
father or mother shall die.' **5** *But you say,
'Whoever says to father or mother, "Any support you might have had from me is dedicated
to God," **6** need not honor his father.' You
have nullified the word of God for the sake of
your tradition. **7** Hypocrites, well did Isaiah
prophesy about you when he said:

**8** [e]*'This people honors me with their lips,
but their hearts are far from me;
**9** [f]in vain do they worship me,
teaching as doctrines human precepts.' "

**10** [g]He summoned the crowd and said to them,
"Hear and understand. **11** It is not what enters
one's mouth that defiles that person; but what
comes out of the mouth is what defiles one."
**12** Then his disciples approached and said to
him, "Do you know that the Pharisees took
offense when they heard what you said?"
**13** *He said in reply, "Every plant that my
heavenly Father has not planted will be uprooted. **14** [h]Let them alone; they are blind guides
[of the blind]. If a blind person leads a blind
person, both will fall into a pit." **15** *Then
Peter said to him in reply, "Explain [this] parable to us." **16** He said to them, "Are even you
still without understanding? **17** Do you not realize that everything that enters the mouth
passes into the stomach and is expelled into the
latrine? **18** [i]But the things that come out of the
mouth come from the heart, and they defile.
**19** *For from the heart come evil thoughts,
murder, adultery, unchastity, theft, false witness, blasphemy. **20** These are what defile a
person, but to eat with unwashed hands does not
defile."

## The Canaanite Woman's Faith

**21** [j]*Then Jesus went from that place and withdrew to the region of Tyre and Sidon. **22** And
behold, a Canaanite woman of that district came
and called out, "Have pity on me, Lord, Son of
David! My daughter is tormented by a demon."
**23** But he did not say a word in answer to her.
His disciples came and asked him, "Send her
away, for she keeps calling out after us."
**24** *He said in reply, "I was sent only to the
lost sheep of the house of Israel." **25** [k]But the
woman came and did him homage, saying,
"Lord, help me." **26** *He said in reply, "It is
not right to take the food of the children and
throw it to the dogs." **27** She said, "Please,
Lord, for even the dogs eat the scraps that fall
from the table of their masters." **28** [l]*Then
Jesus said to her in reply, "O woman, great is
your faith! Let it be done for you as you wish."
And her daughter was healed from that hour.

## The Healing of Many People

**29** Moving
on from there Jesus walked by the Sea of Galilee, went up on the mountain, and sat down
there. **30** [m]Great crowds came to him, having
with them the lame, the blind, the deformed, the
mute, and many others. They placed them at his
feet, and he cured them. **31** The crowds were
amazed when they saw the mute speaking, the
deformed made whole, the lame walking, and
the blind able to see, and they glorified the God
of Israel.

c Lk 11, 38.
d Ex 20, 12; 21, 17; Lv 20, 9; Dt 5, 16; Prv 20, 20.
e Is 29, 13 LXX.
f Col 2, 23.
g Mk 7, 14.
h 23, 16.19.24; Lk 6, 39; Jn 9, 40.
i 12, 34.
j Mk 7, 24-30.
k 10, 6.
l 8, 10.
m Is 35, 5-6.

*

has started. The parable (11) is an attack on the Mosaic law concerning clean and unclean foods, similar to those antitheses that abrogate the law (5, 31–32.33–34.38–39). After a warning to his disciples not to follow the moral guidance of the Pharisees (13–14), he explains the *parable (15)* to them, saying that defilement comes not from what *enters the mouth* (17) but from the evil thoughts and deeds that rise from within, *from the heart* (18–20). The last verse returns to the starting point of the dispute (eating *with unwashed hands*). Because of Matthew's omission of Mk 7, 19b, some scholars think that Matthew has weakened the Marcan repudiation of the Mosaic food laws. But that half verse is ambiguous in the Greek, which may be the reason for its omission here.

15, 2: *The tradition of the elders:* see the note on Mk 7, 5. The purpose of the handwashing was to remove defilement caused by contact with what was ritually unclean.

15, 3–4: For the commandment see Ex 20, 12 (// Dt 5, 16); 21, 17. The honoring of one's parents had to do with supporting them in their needs.

15, 5: See the note on Mk 7, 11.

15, 8: The text of Is 29, 13 is quoted approximately according to the Septuagint.

15, 13–14: Jesus leads his disciples away from the teaching authority of the Pharisees.

15, 15: Matthew specifies *Peter* as the questioner, unlike Mk 7, 17. Given his tendency to present the disciples as more understanding than in his Marcan source, it is noteworthy that here he retains the Marcan rebuke, although in a slightly milder form. This may be due to his wish to correct the Jewish Christians within his church who still held to the food laws and thus separated themselves from Gentile Christians who did not observe them.

15, 19: The Marcan list of thirteen things that defile (7, 21–22) is here reduced to seven that partially cover the content of the Decalogue.

15, 21–28: See the note on 8, 5–13.

15, 24: See the note on 10, 5–6.

15, 26: *The children:* the people of Israel. *Dogs:* see the note on 7, 6.

15, 28: As in the case of the cure of the centurion's servant (8, 10), Matthew ascribes Jesus' granting the request to the woman's *great faith*, a point not made equally explicit in the Marcan parallel (7, 24–30).

### The Feeding of the Four Thousand

32 [n]*Jesus summoned his disciples and said,
"My heart is moved with pity for the crowd, for
they have been with me now for three days and
have nothing to eat. I do not want to send them
away hungry, for fear they may collapse on the
way." 33 The disciples said to him, "Where
could we ever get enough bread in this deserted
place to satisfy such a crowd?" 34 Jesus said to
them, "How many loaves do you have?" "Sev-
en," they replied, "and a few fish." 35 He
ordered the crowd to sit down on the ground.
36 *Then he took the seven loaves and the fish,
gave thanks, broke the loaves, and gave them to
the disciples, who in turn gave them to the
crowds. 37 [o]They all ate and were satisfied.
They picked up the fragments left over—seven
baskets full. 38 Those who ate were four thousand men, not counting women and children.
39 And when he had dismissed the crowds, he
got into the boat and came to the district of
Magadan.

## CHAPTER 16

### The Demand for a Sign

1 [p]*The Phari-
sees and Sadducees came and, to test him, asked
him to show them a sign from heaven. 2 *He
said to them in reply, "[In the evening you say,
'Tomorrow will be fair, for the sky is red';
3 [q]and, in the morning, 'Today will be stormy,
for the sky is red and threatening.' You know
how to judge the appearance of the sky, but you
cannot judge the signs of the times.] 4 [r]*An
evil and unfaithful generation seeks a sign, but
no sign will be given it except the sign of Jonah." Then he left them and went away.

### The Leaven of the Pharisees and Sadducees

5 [s]*In coming to the other side of the
sea, the disciples had forgotten to bring bread.
6 [t]*Jesus said to them, "Look out, and beware
of the leaven of the Pharisees and Sadducees."
7 *They concluded among themselves, saying,
"It is because we have brought no bread."
8 When Jesus became aware of this he said,
"You of little faith, why do you conclude
among yourselves that it is because you have no
bread? 9 [u]Do you not yet understand, and do
you not remember the five loaves for the five
thousand, and how many wicker baskets you
took up? 10 [v]Or the seven loaves for the four
thousand, and how many baskets you took up?
11 How do you not comprehend that I was not
speaking to you about bread? Beware of the
leaven of the Pharisees and Sadducees."
12 *Then they understood that he was not telling them to beware of the leaven of bread, but
of the teaching of the Pharisees and Sadducees.

### Peter's Confession about Jesus

13 [w]*When Jesus went into the region of Caes-

n Mk 8, 1-10.
o 16, 10.
p Mk 8, 11-21.
q Lk 12, 54-56.
r 12, 39; Jon 2, 1.
s Mk 8, 14-21.
t Lk 12, 1.
u 14, 17-21; Jn 6, 9.
v 15, 34-38.
w Mk 8, 27-29; Lk 9, 18-20.

*

15, 32–39: Most probably this story is a doublet of that of the feeding of the five thousand (14, 13–21). It differs from it notably only in that Jesus takes the initiative, not the disciples (32), and in the numbers: the crowd has been with Jesus *three days* (32), *seven loaves* are multiplied (36), *seven baskets* of *fragments* remain after the feeding (37), and *four thousand* men are fed (38).

15, 36: *Gave thanks:* see 14, 19, "said the blessing." There is no difference in meaning. The thanksgiving was a blessing of God for his benefits.

16, 1: *A sign from heaven:* see the note on 12, 38–42.

16, 2–3: The answer of Jesus in these verses is omitted in many important textual witnesses, and it is very uncertain that it is an original part of this gospel. It resembles Lk 12, 54–56 and may have been inserted from there. It rebukes the Pharisees and Sadducees who are able to read indications of coming weather but not the indications of the coming kingdom in the signs that Jesus does offer, his mighty deeds and teaching.

16, 4: See the notes on 12, 39.40.

16, 5–12: Jesus' warning his disciples against *the teaching of the Pharisees and Sadducees* comes immediately before his promise to confer on Peter the authority to bind and to loose on earth (19), an authority that will be confirmed in heaven. Such authority most probably has to do, at least in part, with teaching. The rejection of the teaching authority of the Pharisees (see also 12, 12–14) prepares for a new one derived from Jesus.

16, 6: *Leaven:* see the note on 13, 33. *Sadducees:* Matthew's Marcan source speaks rather of "the leaven of Herod" (8, 15).

16, 7–11: The disciples, men *of little faith,* misunderstand Jesus' metaphorical use of *leaven,* forgetting that, as the feeding of the crowds shows, he is not at a loss to provide them with bread.

16, 12: After his rebuke, the disciples understand that by *leaven* he meant the corrupting influence of the *teaching of the Pharisees and Sadducees.* The evangelist probably understands this *teaching* as common to both groups. Since at the time of Jesus' ministry the two differed widely on points of teaching, e.g., the resurrection of the dead, and at the time of the evangelist the Sadducee party was no longer a force in Judaism, the supposed common *teaching* fits neither period. The disciples' eventual understanding of Jesus' warning contrasts with their continuing obtuseness in the Marcan parallel (8, 14–21).

16, 13–20: The Marcan confession of Jesus as Messiah, made by Peter as spokesman for the other disciples (8, 27–29; cf also Lk 9, 18–20), is modified significantly here. The confession is of Jesus both as *Messiah* and as *Son of the living God* (16). Jesus' response, drawn principally from material peculiar to Matthew, attributes the confession to a divine revelation granted to Peter alone (17) and makes him the *rock* on which Jesus *will build* his *church* (18) and the disciple whose authority in the church *on earth* will be confirmed in *heaven,* i.e., by God (19).

16, 13: *Caesarea Philippi:* situated about twenty miles north of the Sea of Galilee in the territory ruled by Philip, a son of Herod the Great, tetrarch from 4 B.C. until his death in A.D. 34 (see the note on 14, 1). He rebuilt the town of Paneas, naming it *Caesarea* in honor of the emperor, and *Philippi* ("of Philip") to distinguish it from the seaport in Samaria that was also called Caesarea. *Who do people say that the Son of Man is?:* although the question differs from the Marcan parallel (8, 27: "Who . . . that I am?"), the meaning is the same, for Jesus

area Philippi he asked his disciples, "Who do
people say that the Son of Man is?" **14** [x]*They
replied, "Some say John the Baptist, others
Elijah, still others Jeremiah or one of the prophets." **15** He said to them, "But who do you say
that I am?" **16** [y]*Simon Peter said in reply,
"You are the Messiah, the Son of the living
God." **17** *Jesus said to him in reply, "Blessed
are you, Simon son of Jonah. For flesh and
blood has not revealed this to you, but my heavenly Father. **18** [z]*And so I say to you, you are
Peter, and upon this rock I will build my church,
and the gates of the netherworld shall not prevail
against it. **19** [a]*I will give you the keys to the
kingdom of heaven. Whatever you bind on earth
shall be bound in heaven; and whatever you
loose on earth shall be loosed in heaven."
**20** [b]*Then he strictly ordered his disciples to
tell no one that he was the Messiah.

## The First Prediction of the Passion

**21** [c][d]*From that time on, Jesus began to show
his disciples that he must go to Jerusalem and
suffer greatly from the elders, the chief priests,
and the scribes, and be killed and on the third
day be raised. **22** *Then Peter took him aside
and began to rebuke him, "God forbid, Lord!
No such thing shall ever happen to you."
**23** [e]He turned and said to Peter, "Get behind
me, Satan! You are an obstacle to me. You are
thinking not as God does, but as human beings
do."

x 14, 2.
y Jn 6, 69.
z Jn 1, 42.
a Is 22, 22; Rv 3, 7.
b Mk 8, 30; Lk 9, 21.
c Mk 8, 31–9, 1; Lk 9, 22-27.
d 17, 22-23; 20, 17-19.
e 4, 10.

* here refers to himself as the *Son of Man* (cf 15).

16, 14: *John the Baptist:* see 14, 2. *Elijah:* cf Mal 3, 23–24; Sir 48, 10; and see the note on 3, 4. *Jeremiah:* an addition of Matthew to the Marcan source.

16, 16: *The Son of the living God:* see 2, 15; 3, 17. The addition of this exalted title to the Marcan confession eliminates whatever ambiguity was attached to the title Messiah. This, among other things, supports the view proposed by many scholars that Matthew has here combined his source's confession with a post-resurrectional confession of faith in Jesus as *Son of the living God* that belonged to the appearance of the risen Jesus to Peter; cf 1 Cor 15, 5; Lk 24, 34.

16, 17: *Flesh and blood:* a Semitic expression for human beings, especially in their weakness. *Has not revealed this . . . but my heavenly Father:* that Peter's faith is spoken of as coming not through human means but through a revelation from God is similar to Paul's description of his recognition of who Jesus was; see Gal 1, 15–16, ". . . when he [God] . . . was pleased to reveal his Son to me. . . ."

16, 18: *You are Peter, and upon this rock I will build my church:* the Aramaic word *kēpā'* meaning *rock* and transliterated into Greek as *Kēphas* is the name by which Peter is called in the Pauline letters (1 Cor 1, 12; 3, 22; 9, 5; 15, 4; Gal 1, 18; 2, 9.11.14) except in Gal 2, 7–8 ("Peter"). It is translated as *Petros* ("Peter") in Jn 1, 42. The presumed original Aramaic of Jesus' statement would have been, in English, "You are the Rock (*Kēpā'*) and upon this rock (*kēpā'*) I will build my church." The Greek text probably means the same, for the difference in gender between the masculine noun *petros,* the disciple's new name, and the feminine noun *petra* (rock) may be due simply to the unsuitability of using a feminine noun as the proper name of a male. Although the two words were generally used with slightly different nuances, they were also used interchangeably with the same meaning, "rock." *Church:* this word (Greek *ekklēsia*) occurs in the gospels only here and in 18, 17 (twice). There are several possibilities for an Aramaic original. Jesus' *church* means the community that he *will* gather and that, like a building, will have Peter as its solid foundation. That function of Peter consists in his being witness to Jesus as *the Messiah, the Son of the living God. The gates of the netherworld shall not prevail against it:* the netherworld (Greek *Hadēs,* the abode of the dead) is conceived of as a walled city whose *gates* will not close in upon the church of Jesus, i.e., it will not be overcome by the power of death.

16, 19: *The keys to the kingdom of heaven:* the image of the *keys* is probably drawn from Is 22, 15–25, where Eliakim, who succeeds Shebnah as master of the palace, is given "the key of the house of David," which he authoritatively "opens" and "shuts" (22, 22). *Whatever you bind . . . loosed in heaven:* there are many instances in rabbinic literature of the binding-loosing imagery. Of the several meanings given there to the metaphor, two are of special importance here: the giving of authoritative teaching, and the lifting or imposing of the ban of excommunication. It is disputed whether the image of *the keys* and that of binding and loosing are different metaphors meaning the same thing. In any case, the promise of the keys is given to Peter alone. In 18, 18 all the disciples are given the power of binding and loosing, but the context of that verse suggests that there the power of excommunication alone is intended. That *the keys* are those to *the kingdom of heaven* and that Peter's exercise of authority in the church *on earth* will be confirmed *in heaven* show an intimate connection between, but not an identification of, the church and *the kingdom of heaven.*

16, 20: Cf Mk 8, 30. Matthew makes explicit that the prohibition has to do with speaking of Jesus as *the Messiah;* see the note on Mk 8, 27–30.

16, 21–23: This first prediction of the passion follows Mk 8, 31–33 in the main and serves as a corrective to an understanding of Jesus' messiahship as solely one of glory and triumph. By his addition of *from that time on* (21) Matthew has emphasized that Jesus' revelation of his coming suffering and death marks a new phase of the gospel. Neither this nor the two later passion predictions (17, 22–23; 20, 17–19) can be taken as sayings that, as they stand, go back to Jesus himself. However, it is probable that he foresaw that his mission would entail suffering and perhaps death, but was confident that he would ultimately be vindicated by God (see 26, 29).

16, 21: *He:* the Marcan parallel (8, 31) has "the Son of Man." Since Matthew has already designated Jesus by that title (13), its omission here is not significant. The Matthean prediction is equally about the sufferings of the Son of Man. *Must:* this necessity is part of the tradition of all the synoptics; cf Mk 8, 31; Lk 9, 21. *The elders, the chief priests, and the scribes:* see the note on Mk 8, 31. *On the third day:* so also Lk 9, 22, against the Marcan "after three days" (8, 31). Matthew's formulation is, in the Greek, almost identical with the pre-Pauline fragment of the kerygma in 1 Cor 15, 4, and also with Hos 6, 2, which many take to be the Old Testament background to the confession that Jesus was raised *on the third day.* Josephus uses "after three days" and "on the third day" interchangeably (*Antiquities* 7, 11, 6 **280–81; 8, 8, 1–2 **214, 218) and there is probably no difference in meaning between the two phrases.

16, 22–23: Peter's refusal to accept Jesus' predicted suffering and death is seen as a satanic attempt to deflect Jesus from his God-appointed course, and the disciple is addressed in terms that recall Jesus' dismissal of the devil in the temptation account (4, 10: "Get away, Satan!"). Peter's satanic purpose is emphasized by Matthew's addition to the Marcan source of the words *You are an obstacle to me.*

## The Conditions of Discipleship

24 [f]*Then Jesus said to his disciples, "Whoever wishes to come after me must deny himself,
take up his cross, and follow me. 25 [g]*For
whoever wishes to save his life will lose it, but
whoever loses his life for my sake will find it.
26 What profit would there be for one to gain
the whole world and forfeit his life? Or what can
one give in exchange for his life? 27 [h]*For the
Son of Man will come with his angels in his
Father's glory, and then he will repay everyone
according to his conduct. 28 *Amen, I say to
you, there are some standing here who will not
taste death until they see the Son of Man coming
in his kingdom."

# CHAPTER 17

## The Transfiguration of Jesus

1 [i]*After
six days Jesus took Peter, James, and John his
brother, and led them up a high mountain by
themselves. 2 [j]*And he was transfigured before them; his face shone like the sun and his
clothes became white as light. 3 *And behold,
Moses and Elijah appeared to them, conversing
with him. 4 *Then Peter said to Jesus in reply,
"Lord, it is good that we are here. If you wish,
I will make three tents here, one for you, one for
Moses, and one for Elijah." 5 [k]*While he was
still speaking, behold, a bright cloud cast a
shadow over them, then from the cloud came a
voice that said, "This is my beloved Son, with
whom I am well pleased; listen to him."
6 *When the disciples heard this, they fell prostrate and were very much afraid. 7 But Jesus
came and touched them, saying, "Rise, and do
not be afraid." 8 And when the disciples raised
their eyes, they saw no one else but Jesus alone.

## The Coming of Elijah

9 [l]*As they were
coming down from the mountain, Jesus charged
them, "Do not tell the vision to anyone until the
Son of Man has been raised from the dead."
10 [m]*Then the disciples asked him, "Why do
the scribes say that Elijah must come first?"
11 [n]*He said in reply, "Elijah will indeed
come and restore all things; 12 [o]but I tell you
that Elijah has already come, and they did not
recognize him but did to him whatever they
pleased. So also will the Son of Man suffer at
their hands." 13 *Then the disciples understood that he was speaking to them of John the
Baptist.

f Lk 14, 27.
g Lk 17, 33; Jn 12, 25.
h 25, 31-33; Jb 34, 11; Ps 62, 13; Jer 17, 10; 2 Thes 1, 7-8.
i Mk 9, 2-8; Lk 9, 28-36.
j 28, 3; Dn 7, 9; 10, 6; Rv 4, 4; 7, 9; 19, 14.
k 3, 17; Dt 18, 15; 2 Pt 1, 17.
l Mk 9, 9-13.
m Mal 3, 23-24.
n Lk 1, 17.
o 11, 14.

*

16, 24–28: A readiness to follow Jesus even to giving up one's life for him is the condition for true discipleship; this will be repaid by him at the final judgment.

16, 24: *Deny himself:* to deny someone is to disown him (see 10, 33; 26, 34–35) and to deny oneself is to disown oneself as the center of one's existence.

16, 25: See the notes on 10, 38.39.

16, 27: The parousia and final judgment are described in 25, 31 in terms almost identical with these.

16, 28: *Coming in his kingdom:* since the *kingdom* of *the Son of Man* has been described as "the world" and Jesus' sovereignty precedes his final coming in glory (13, 38.41), the *coming* in this verse is not the parousia as in the preceding but the manifestation of Jesus' rule after his resurrection; see the notes on 13, 38.41.

17, 1–8: The account of the transfiguration confirms that Jesus is the *Son* of God (5) and points to fulfillment of the prediction that he will come *in his Father's glory* at the end of the age (16, 27). It has been explained by some as a resurrection appearance retrojected into the time of Jesus' ministry, but that is not probable since the account lacks many of the usual elements of the resurrection-appearance narratives. It draws upon motifs from the Old Testament and noncanonical Jewish apocalyptic literature that express the presence of the heavenly and the divine, e.g., brilliant light, white garments, and the overshadowing cloud.

17, 1: These three disciples are also taken apart from the others by Jesus in Gethsemane (26, 37). *A high mountain:* this has been identified with Tabor or Hermon, but probably no specific mountain was intended by the evangelist or by his Marcan source (9, 2). Its meaning is theological rather than geographical, possibly recalling the revelation to Moses on Mount Sinai (Ex 24, 12–18) and to Elijah at the same place (1 Kgs 19, 8–18; Horeb Sinai).

17, 2: *His face shone like the sun:* this is a Matthean addition; cf Dn 10, 6. *His clothes became white as light:* cf Dn 7, 9, where the clothing of God appears "snow bright." For the *white* garments of other heavenly beings, see Rv 4, 4; 7, 9; 19, 14.

17, 3: See the note on Mk 9, 5.

17, 4: *Three tents:* the booths in which the Israelites lived during the feast of Tabernacles (cf Jn 7, 2) were meant to recall their ancestors' dwelling in booths during the journey from Egypt to the promised land (Lv 23, 39–42). The same Greek word, *skēnē,* here translated *tents,* is used in the LXX for the booths of that feast, and some scholars have suggested that there is an allusion here to that liturgical custom.

17, 5: *Cloud cast a shadow over them:* see the note on Mk 9, 7. *This is my beloved Son . . . listen to him:* cf 3, 17. The voice repeats the baptismal proclamation about Jesus, with the addition of the command *listen to him.* The latter is a reference to Dt 18, 15 in which the Israelites are commanded to *listen to* the prophet like Moses whom God will raise up for them. The command to *listen to* Jesus is general, but in this context it probably applies particularly to the preceding predictions of his passion and resurrection (16, 21) and of his coming (16, 27.28).

17, 6–7: A Matthean addition; cf Dn 10, 9–10.18–19.

17, 9–13: In response to the disciples' question about the expected return of Elijah, Jesus interprets the mission of the Baptist as the fulfillment of that expectation. But that was not suspected by those who opposed and finally killed him, and Jesus predicts a similar fate for himself.

17, 9: *The vision:* Matthew alone uses this word to describe the transfiguration. *Until the Son of Man has been raised from the dead:* only in the light of Jesus' resurrection can the meaning of his life and mission be truly understood; until then no testimony to *the vision* will lead people to faith.

17, 10: See the notes on 3, 4; 16, 14.

17, 11–12: The preceding question and this answer may reflect later controversy with Jews who objected to the Christian claims for Jesus that Elijah had not yet come.

17, 13: See 11, 14.

## The Healing of a Boy with a Demon

14 [p]*When they came to the crowd a man approached, knelt down before him, 15 *and
said, "Lord, have pity on my son, for he is a
lunatic and suffers severely; often he falls into
fire, and often into water. 16 I brought him to
your disciples, but they could not cure him."
17 [q]*Jesus said in reply, "O faithless and perverse generation, how long will I be with you?
How long will I endure you? Bring him here to
me." 18 *Jesus rebuked him and the demon
came out of him, and from that hour the boy was
cured. 19 Then the disciples approached Jesus
in private and said, "Why could we not drive
it out?" 20 [r]*He said to them, "Because of
your little faith. Amen, I say to you, if you have
faith the size of a mustard seed, you will say to
this mountain, 'Move from here to there,' and
it will move. Nothing will be impossible for
you." **[21*]**

## The Second Prediction of the Passion

22 [s]*As they were gathering in Galilee, Jesus
said to them, "The Son of Man is to be handed
over to men, 23 and they will kill him, and he
will be raised on the third day." And they were
overwhelmed with grief.

## Payment of the Temple Tax

24 [t]*When
they came to Capernaum, the collectors of the
temple tax approached Peter and said, "Doesn't
your teacher pay the temple tax?" 25 *"Yes,"
he said. When he came into the house, before
he had time to speak, Jesus asked him, "What
is your opinion, Simon? From whom do the
kings of the earth take tolls or census tax? From
their subjects or from foreigners?" 26 *When
he said, "From foreigners," Jesus said to him,
"Then the subjects are exempt. 27 *But that we
may not offend them, go to the sea, drop in a
hook, and take the first fish that comes up. Open
its mouth and you will find a coin worth twice
the temple tax. Give that to them for me and for
you."

p Mk 9, 14-29; Lk 9, 37-43.
q Dt 32, 5 LXX.
r 21, 21; Lk 17, 6; 1 Cor 13, 2.
s 16, 21; 20, 18-19.
t Ex 30, 11-16; Neh 10, 33.

*

17, 14–20: Matthew has greatly shortened the Marcan story (9, 14–29). Leaving aside several details of the boy's illness, he concentrates on the need for faith, not so much on the part of the boy's father (as does Mark, for Matthew omits Mk 9, 22b–24) but on that of his own disciples whose inability to drive out the demon is ascribed to their *little faith* (20).

17, 15: *A lunatic:* this description of the boy is peculiar to Matthew. The word occurs in the New Testament only here and in 4, 24 and means one affected or struck by the moon. The symptoms of the boy's illness point to epilepsy, and attacks of this were thought to be caused by phases of the moon.

17, 17: *Faithless and perverse:* so Matthew and Luke (9, 41) against Mark's *faithless* (9, 19). The Greek word here translated *perverse* is the same as that in Dt 32, 5 LXX, where Moses speaks to his people. There is a problem in knowing to whom the reproach is addressed. Since the Matthean Jesus normally chides his disciples for their *little faith* (as in 20), it would appear that the charge of lack of faith could not be made against them and that the reproach is addressed to unbelievers among the Jews. However in v 20b (*if you have faith the size of a mustard seed*), which is certainly addressed to the disciples, they appear to have not even the smallest faith; if they had, they would have been able to cure the boy. In the light of v 20b the reproach of v 17 could have applied to the disciples. There seems to be an inconsistency between the charge of *little faith* in v 20a and that of not even a little in v 20b.

17, 18: *The demon came out of him:* not until this verse does Matthew indicate that the boy's illness is a case of demoniacal possession.

17, 20: The entire verse is an addition of Matthew who (according to the better attested text) omits the reason given for the disciples' inability in Mk 9, 29. *Little faith:* see the note on 6, 30. *Faith the size of a mustard seed . . . and it will move:* a combination of a Q saying (cf Lk 17, 6) with a Marcan saying (cf Mk 11, 23).

17, 21: Some manuscripts add, "But this kind does not come out except by prayer and fasting"; this is a variant of the better reading of Mk 9, 29.

17, 22–23: The second passion prediction (cf 16, 21–23) is the least detailed of the three and may be the earliest. In the Marcan parallel the disciples do not understand (9, 32); here they understand and are *overwhelmed with grief* at the prospect of Jesus' death (23).

17, 24–27: Like 14, 28–31 and 16, 16b–19, this episode comes from Matthew's special material on Peter. Although the question of *the collectors* concerns Jesus' payment of *the temple tax,* it is put to *Peter.* It is he who receives instruction from Jesus about freedom from the obligation of payment and yet why it should be made. The means of doing so is provided miraculously. The pericope deals with a problem of Matthew's church, whether its members should pay the temple tax, and the answer is given through a word of Jesus conveyed to Peter. Some scholars see here an example of the teaching authority of Peter exercised in the name of Jesus (see 16, 19). The specific problem was a Jewish Christian one and may have arisen when the Matthean church was composed largely of that group.

17, 24: *The temple tax:* before the destruction of the Jerusalem temple in A.D. 70 every male Jew above nineteen years of age was obliged to make an annual contribution to its upkeep (cf Ex 30, 11–16; Neh 10, 33). After the destruction the Romans imposed upon Jews the obligation of paying that tax for the temple of Jupiter Capitolinus. There is disagreement about which period the story deals with.

17, 25: *From their subjects or from foreigners?:* the Greek word here translated *subjects* literally means "sons."

17, 26: *Then the subjects are exempt:* just as *subjects* are not bound by laws applying to *foreigners,* neither are Jesus and his disciples, who belong to the kingdom of heaven, bound by the duty of paying the temple tax imposed on those who are not of the kingdom. If the Greek is translated "sons," the freedom of Jesus, the Son of God, and of his disciples, children ("sons") of the kingdom (cf 13, 38), is even more clear.

17, 27: *That we may not offend them:* though they are *exempt* (26), Jesus and his disciples are to avoid giving offense; therefore the tax is to be paid. *A coin worth twice the temple tax:* literally, "a stater," a Greek coin worth two double drachmas. Two double drachmas were equal to the Jewish shekel and the tax was a half-shekel. *For me and for you:* not only Jesus but Peter pays the tax, and this example serves as a standard for the conduct of all the disciples.

## CHAPTER 18

### The Greatest in the Kingdom
1 [u]*At
that time the disciples approached Jesus and
said, "Who is the greatest in the kingdom of
heaven?" 2 He called a child over, placed it in
their midst, 3 [v]*and said, "Amen, I say to you,
unless you turn and become like children, you
will not enter the kingdom of heaven.
4 [w]Whoever humbles himself like this child is
the greatest in the kingdom of heaven. 5 *And
whoever receives one child such as this in my
name receives me.

### Temptations to Sin
6 [x]*"Whoever
causes one of these little ones who believe in me
to sin, it would be better for him to have a great
millstone hung around his neck and to be
drowned in the depths of the sea. 7 *Woe to the
world because of things that cause sin! Such
things must come, but woe to the one through
whom they come! 8 [y]*If your hand or foot
causes you to sin, cut it off and throw it away.
It is better for you to enter into life maimed or
crippled than with two hands or two feet to be
thrown into eternal fire. 9 And if your eye
causes you to sin, tear it out and throw it away.
It is better for you to enter into life with one eye
than with two eyes to be thrown into fiery
Gehenna.

### The Parable of the Lost Sheep
10 [z]*"See that you do not despise one of these
little ones, for I say to you that their angels in
heaven always look upon the face of my heavenly Father. [11[a]*] 12 What is your opinion? If
a man has a hundred sheep and one of them goes
astray, will he not leave the ninety-nine in the
hills and go in search of the stray? 13 And if he
finds it, amen, I say to you, he rejoices more
over it than over the ninety-nine that did not
stray. 14 In just the same way, it is not the will
of your heavenly Father that one of these little
ones be lost.

u Mk 9, 36-37; Lk 9, 46-48.
v 19, 14; Mk 10, 15; Lk 18, 17.
w 23, 12.
x Mk 9, 42; Lk 17, 1-2.
y 5, 29-30; Mk 9, 43-47.
z Ez 34, 1-3.16; Lk 15, 3-7.
a Lk 19, 10.

*

18, 1–35: This discourse of the fourth book of the gospel is often called the "church order" discourse, but it lacks most of the considerations usually connected with church order, such as various offices in the church and the duties of each, and deals principally with the relations that must obtain among the members of the church. Beginning with the warning that greatness in *the kingdom of heaven* is measured not by rank or power but by childlikeness (1–5), it deals with the care that the disciples must take not to cause the *little ones to sin* or to neglect them if they stray from the community (6–14), the correction of members who sin (15–18), the efficacy of the prayer of the disciples because of the presence of Jesus (19–20), and the forgiveness that must be repeatedly extended to sinful members who repent (21–35).

18, 1: The initiative is taken not by Jesus as in the Marcan parallel (9, 33–34) but by the disciples. *Kingdom of heaven:* this may mean *the kingdom* in its fullness, i.e., after the parousia and the final judgment. But what follows about causes of sin, church discipline, and forgiveness, all dealing with the present age, suggests that the question has to do with rank also in the church, where *the kingdom* is manifested here and now, although only partially and by anticipation; see the notes on 3, 2; 4, 17.

18, 3: *Become like children:* the child is held up as a model for the disciples not because of any supposed innocence of children but because of their complete dependence on, and trust in, their parents. So must the disciples be, in respect to God.

18, 5: Cf 10, 40.

18, 6: *One of these little ones:* the thought passes from the child of vv 2–4 to the disciples, *little ones* because of their becoming *like children.* It is difficult to know whether this is a designation of all who are disciples or of those who are insignificant in contrast to others, e.g., the leaders of the community. Since apart from this chapter the designation *little ones* occurs in Mt only in 10, 42 where it means disciples as such, that is its more likely meaning here. *Who believe in me:* since discipleship is impossible without at least some degree of faith, this further specification seems superfluous. However, it serves to indicate that the warning against causing a *little one* to sin is principally directed against whatever would lead such a one to a weakening or loss of faith. The Greek verb *skandalizein,* here translated *causes . . . to sin,* means literally "causes to stumble"; what the stumbling is depends on the context. It is used of falling away from faith in 13, 21. According to the better reading of Mk 9, 42, *in me* is a Matthean addition to the Marcan source. *It would be better . . . depths of the sea:* cf Mk 9, 42.

18, 7: This is a Q saying; cf Lk 17, 1. The inevitability of *things that cause sin* (literally, "scandals") does not take away the responsibility of *the one through whom they come.*

18, 8–9: These verses are a doublet of 5, 29–30. In that context they have to do with causes of sexual sin. As in the Marcan source from which they have been drawn (Mk 9, 42–48), they differ from the first warning about scandal, which deals with causing another person to sin, for they concern what *causes* oneself *to sin* and they do not seem to be related to another's loss of faith, as the first warning is. It is difficult to know how Matthew understood the logical connection between these verses and vv 6–7.

18, 10–14: The first and last verses are peculiar to Mt. The parable itself comes from Q; see Lk 15, 3–7. In Lk it serves as justification for Jesus' table-companionship with sinners; here, it is an exhortation for the disciples to seek out fellow disciples who have gone *astray.* Not only must no one cause a fellow disciple to sin, but those who have strayed must be sought out and, if possible, brought back to the community. The joy of the shepherd on finding the sheep, though not absent in Mt (13), is more emphasized in Lk. By his addition of vv 10 and 14, Matthew has drawn out explicitly the application of the parable to the care of the *little ones.*

18, 10: *Their angels in heaven . . . my heavenly Father:* for the Jewish belief in angels as guardians of nations and individuals, see Dn 10, 13.20–21; Tb 5, 4–7; 1QH 5, 20–22; as intercessors who present the prayers of human beings to God, see Tb 13, 12.15. The high worth of the *little ones* is indicated by their being represented before God by these heavenly beings.

18, 11: Some manuscripts add, "For the Son of Man has come to save what was lost"; cf 9, 13. This is practically identical with Lk 19, 10 and is probably a copyist's addition from that source.

## A Brother Who Sins

15 [b]*“If your broth-
er sins [against you], go and tell him his fault
between you and him alone. If he listens to you,
you have won over your brother. 16 [c]*If he
does not listen, take one or two others along
with you, so that ‘every fact may be established
on the testimony of two or three witnesses.’
17 [d]*If he refuses to listen to them, tell the
church. If he refuses to listen even to the church,
then treat him as you would a Gentile or a tax
collector. 18 [e]*Amen, I say to you, whatever
you bind on earth shall be bound in heaven, and
whatever you loose on earth shall be loosed in
heaven. 19 [f]*Again, [amen,] I say to you, if
two of you agree on earth about anything for
which they are to pray, it shall be granted to
them by my heavenly Father. 20 [g]*For where
two or three are gathered together in my name,
there am I in the midst of them.”

## The Parable of the Unforgiving Servant

21 [h]*Then Peter approaching asked him,
“Lord, if my brother sins against me, how often
must I forgive him? As many as seven times?”
22 *Jesus answered, “I say to you, not seven
times but seventy-seven times. 23 [i]That is why
the kingdom of heaven may be likened to a king
who decided to settle accounts with his servants. 24 *When he began the accounting, a
debtor was brought before him who owed him
a huge amount. 25 Since he had no way of
paying it back, his master ordered him to be
sold, along with his wife, his children, and all
his property, in payment of the debt. 26 *At
that, the servant fell down, did him homage,
and said, ‘Be patient with me, and I will pay you
back in full.’ 27 Moved with compassion the
master of that servant let him go and forgave
him the loan. 28 *When that servant had left,
he found one of his fellow servants who owed
him a much smaller amount. He seized him and
started to choke him, demanding, ‘Pay back
what you owe.’ 29 Falling to his knees, his

b Lv 19, 17; Sir 19, 13; Gal 6, 1.
c Dt 19, 15; Jn 8, 17; 1 Tm 5, 19.
d 1 Cor 5, 1-13.
e 16, 19; Jn 20, 23.
f 7, 7-8; Jn 15, 7.
g 1 Cor 5, 4.
h 6, 12; Lk 17, 4.
i 25, 19.

*

18, 15–20: Passing from the duty of Christian disciples toward those who have strayed from their number, the discourse now turns to how they are to deal with one who sins and yet remains within the community. First there is to be private correction (15); if this is unsuccessful, further correction before *two or three witnesses* (16); if this fails, the matter is to be brought before the assembled community (*the church*), and if the sinner refuses to attend to the correction of *the church,* he is to be expelled (17). The church's judgment will be ratified *in heaven,* i.e., by God (18). This three-step process of correction corresponds, though not exactly, to the procedure of the Qumran community; see 1QS 5, 25—6, 1; 6, 24—7, 25; CD 9, 2–8. The section ends with a saying about the favorable response of God to prayer, even to that of a very small number, for Jesus is in the midst of any gathering of his disciples, however small (19–20). Whether this prayer has anything to do with the preceding judgment is uncertain.

18, 15: *Your brother:* a fellow disciple; see 23, 8. The bracketed words, *against you,* are widely attested but they are not in the important codices Sinaiticus and Vaticanus or in some other textual witnesses. Their omission broadens the type of sin in question. *Won over:* literally, “gained.”

18, 16: Cf Dt 19, 15.

18, 17: *The church:* the second of the only two instances of this word in the gospels; see the note on 16, 18. Here it refers not to the entire *church* of Jesus, as in 16, 18, but to the local congregation. *Treat him . . . a Gentile or a tax collector:* just as the observant Jew avoided the company of Gentiles and tax collectors, so must the congregation of Christian disciples separate itself from the arrogantly sinful member who refuses to repent even when convicted of his sin by the whole *church.* Such a one is to be set outside the fellowship of the community. The harsh language about *Gentile* and *tax collector* probably reflects a stage of the Matthean *church* when it was principally composed of Jewish Christians. That time had long since passed, but the principle of exclusion for such a sinner remained. Paul makes a similar demand for excommunication in 1 Cor 5, 1–13.

18, 18: Except for the plural of the verbs *bind* and *loose,* this verse is practically identical with 16, 19b, and many scholars understand it as granting to all the disciples what was previously given to Peter alone. For a different view, based on the different contexts of the two verses, see the note on 16, 19.

18, 19–20: Some take these verses as applying to prayer on the occasion of the church's gathering to deal with the sinner of v 17. Unless an *a fortiori* argument is supposed, this seems unlikely. God's answer to the prayer of *two or three* envisages a different situation from one that involves the entire congregation. In addition, the object of this prayer is expressed in most general terms as *anything for which they are to pray.*

18, 20: *For where two or three . . . midst of them:* the presence of Jesus guarantees the efficacy of the prayer. This saying is similar to one attributed to a rabbi executed in A.D. 135 at the time of the second Jewish revolt: “. . . When two sit and there are between them the words of the Torah, the divine presence (Shekinah) rests upon them” (*Pirqê ’Abôt* 3, 3).

18, 21–35: The final section of the discourse deals with the forgiveness that the disciples are to give to their fellow disciples who sin against them. To the question of Peter how often forgiveness is to be granted (21), Jesus answers that it is to be given without limit (22) and illustrates this with the parable of the unmerciful servant (23–34), warning that his *heavenly Father* will give those who do not forgive the same treatment as that given to the unmerciful servant (35). Verses 21–22 correspond to Lk 17, 4; the parable and the final warning are peculiar to Mt. That the parable did not originally belong to this context is suggested by the fact that it really does not deal with repeated forgiveness, which is the point of Peter's question and Jesus' reply.

18, 22: *Seventy-seven times:* the Greek corresponds exactly to the LXX of Gn 4, 24. There is probably an allusion, by contrast, to the limitless vengeance of Lamech in the Gn text. In any case, what is demanded of the disciples is limitless forgiveness.

18, 24: *A huge amount:* literally, “ten thousand talents.” The talent was a unit of coinage of high but varying value depending on its metal (gold, silver, copper) and its place of origin. It is mentioned in the New Testament only here and in 25, 14–30.

18, 26: *Pay you back in full:* an empty promise, given the size of the debt.

18, 28: *A much smaller amount:* literally, “a hundred denarii.” A denarius was the normal daily wage of a laborer. The difference between the two debts is enormous and brings out the absurdity of the conduct of the Christian who has received the great forgiveness of God and yet refuses to forgive the relatively minor offenses done to him.

fellow servant begged him, 'Be patient with me,
and I will pay you back.' **30** But he refused.
Instead, he had him put in prison until he paid
back the debt. **31** Now when his fellow servants
saw what had happened, they were deeply disturbed, and went to their master and reported the
whole affair. **32** His master summoned him and
said to him, 'You wicked servant! I forgave you
your entire debt because you begged me to.
**33** [j]Should you not have had pity on your fellow servant, as I had pity on you?' **34** *Then in
anger his master handed him over to the tortur-
ers until he should pay back the whole debt.
**35** [k]*So will my heavenly Father do to you,
unless each of you forgives his brother from his
heart."

## *VI: MINISTRY IN JUDEA AND JERUSALEM*

## CHAPTER 19

**Marriage and Divorce** **1** *When Jesus finished these words, he left Galilee and went to
the district of Judea across the Jordan. **2** Great
crowds followed him, and he cured them there.
**3** [l]*Some Pharisees approached him, and tested him, saying, "Is it lawful for a man to divorce his wife for any cause whatever?"
**4** [m]*He said in reply, "Have you not read that
from the beginning the Creator 'made them
male and female' **5** [n]and said, 'For this reason
a man shall leave his father and mother and be
joined to his wife, and the two shall become one
flesh'? **6** So they are no longer two, but one
flesh. Therefore, what God has joined together,
no human being must separate." **7** [o]*They said
to him, "Then why did Moses command that
the man give the woman a bill of divorce and
dismiss [her]?" **8** He said to them, "Because of
the hardness of your hearts Moses allowed you
to divorce your wives, but from the beginning
it was not so. **9** [p]*I say to you, whoever divorces his wife (unless the marriage is unlawful)
and marries another commits adultery."
**10** [His] disciples said to him, "If that is the
case of a man with his wife, it is better not to
marry." **11** *He answered, "Not all can accept
[this] word, but only those to whom that is

j Sir 28, 4.
k 6, 15; Jas 2, 13.
l Mk 10, 2-12.
m Gn 1, 27.
n Gn 2, 24; 1 Cor 6, 16; Eph 5, 31.
o Dt 24, 1-4.
p 5, 32; Lk 16, 18; 1 Cor 7, 10-11.

*

18, 34: Since the debt is so great as to be unpayable, the punishment will be endless.

18, 35: The Father's forgiveness, already given, will be withdrawn at the final judgment for those who have not imitated his forgiveness by their own.

19, 1—23, 39: The narrative section of the fifth book of the gospel. The first part (19, 1—20, 34) has for its setting the journey of Jesus from Galilee to Jerusalem; the second (21, 1—23, 39) deals with Jesus' ministry in Jerusalem up to the final great discourse of the gospel (chs 24–25). Matthew follows the Marcan sequence of events, though adding material both special to this gospel and drawn from Q. The second part ends with the denunciation of the scribes and Pharisees (23, 1–36) followed by Jesus' lament over Jerusalem (37–39). This long and important speech raises a problem for the view that Mt is structured around five other discourses of Jesus (see Introduction) and that this one has no such function in the gospel. However, it is to be noted that this speech lacks the customary concluding formula that follows the five discourses (see the note on 7, 28), and that those discourses are all addressed either exclusively (chs 10, 18, 24–25) or primarily (chs 5–7, 13) to the disciples, whereas this is addressed primarily to the scribes and Pharisees (13–36). Consequently, it seems plausible to maintain that the evangelist did not intend to give it the structural importance of the five other discourses, and that, in spite of its being composed of sayings-material, it belongs to the narrative section of this book. In that regard, it is similar to the sayings-material of 11, 7–30. Some have proposed that Matthew wished to regard it as part of the final discourse of chs 24–25, but the intervening material (24, 1–4) and the change in matter and style of those chapters do not support that view.

19, 1–12: In giving Jesus' teaching on divorce (3–9), Matthew here follows his Marcan source (10, 2–12) as he does Q in 5, 31–32 (cf Lk 16, 18). Verses 10–12 are peculiar to Mt.

19, 1: *When Jesus finished these words:* see the note on 7, 28–29. *The district of Judea across the Jordan:* an inexact designation of the territory. Judea did not extend *across the Jordan;* the territory east of the river was Perea. The route to Jerusalem by way of Perea avoided passage through Samaria.

19, 3: *Tested him:* the verb is used of attempts of Jesus' opponents to embarrass him by challenging him to do something they think impossible (16, 1; Mk 8, 11; Lk 11, 16) or by having him say something that they can use against him (22, 18.35; Mk 10, 2; 12, 15). *For any cause whatever:* this is peculiar to Mt and has been interpreted by some as meaning that Jesus was being asked to take sides in the dispute between the schools of Hillel and Shammai on the reasons for divorce, the latter holding a stricter position than the former. It is unlikely, however, that to ask Jesus' opinion about the differing views of two Jewish schools, both highly respected, could be described as "testing" him, for the reason indicated above.

19, 4–6: Matthew recasts his Marcan source, omitting Jesus' question about Moses' command (Mk 10, 3) and having him recall at once two Genesis texts that show the will and purpose of *the Creator* in making human beings *male and female* (Gn 1, 27), namely, that *a man* may *be joined to his wife* in marriage in the intimacy of *one flesh* (Gn 2, 24). *What God has* thus *joined* must not be separated by any *human being.* (The NAB translation of the Hebrew *bāśār* of Gn 2, 24 as "body" rather than "flesh" obscures the reference of Mt to that text.)

19, 7: See Dt 24, 1–4.

19, 9: Moses' concession to human sinfulness (*the hardness of your hearts,* 8) is repudiated by Jesus, and the original will of the Creator is reaffirmed against that concession. (*Unless the marriage is unlawful*): see the note on 5, 31–32. There is some evidence suggesting that Jesus' absolute prohibition of divorce was paralleled in the Qumran community (see 11QTemple 57, 17–19; CD 4, 12b—5, 14). Matthew removes Mark's setting of this verse as spoken to the disciples alone "in the house" (Mk 10, 10) and also his extension of the divorce prohibition to the case of a woman's divorcing her husband (10, 12), probably because in Palestine, unlike the places where Roman and Greek law prevailed, the woman was not allowed to initiate the divorce.

19, 11: [*This*] *word:* probably the disciples' *it is better not to marry* (10). Jesus agrees but says that celibacy is not for all but only for those *to whom that is granted* by God.

granted. **12** *Some are incapable of marriage
because they were born so; some, because they
were made so by others; some, because they
have renounced marriage for the sake of the
kingdom of heaven. Whoever can accept this
ought to accept it."

**Blessing of the Children** **13** [q]*Then children were brought to him that he might lay his
hands on them and pray. The disciples rebuked
them, **14** [r]but Jesus said, "Let the children
come to me, and do not prevent them; for the
kingdom of heaven belongs to such as these."
**15** After he placed his hands on them, he went
away.

**The Rich Young Man** **16** [s]*Now someone
approached him and said, "Teacher, what good
must I do to gain eternal life?" **17** *He answered him, "Why do you ask me about the
good? There is only One who is good. If you
wish to enter into life, keep the commandments." **18** [t]*He asked him, "Which ones?"
And Jesus replied, " 'You shall not kill; you
shall not commit adultery; you shall not steal;
you shall not bear false witness; **19** honor your
father and your mother'; and 'you shall love
your neighbor as yourself.' " **20** *The young
man said to him, "All of these I have observed.
What do I still lack?" **21** [u]*Jesus said to him,
"If you wish to be perfect, go, sell what you
have and give to [the] poor, and you will have
treasure in heaven. Then come, follow me."
**22** When the young man heard this statement,
he went away sad, for he had many possessions.
**23** *Then Jesus said to his disciples, "Amen,
I say to you, it will be hard for one who is rich
to enter the kingdom of heaven. **24** [v]Again I
say to you, it is easier for a camel to pass
through the eye of a needle than for one who is
rich to enter the kingdom of God." **25** *When
the disciples heard this, they were greatly astonished and said, "Who then can be saved?"
**26** [w]Jesus looked at them and said, "For human beings this is impossible, but for God all
things are possible." **27** [x]Then Peter said to
him in reply, "We have given up everything
and followed you. What will there be for us?"
**28** [y]*Jesus said to them, "Amen, I say to you

q Mk 10, 13-16; Lk 18, 15-17.
r 18, 3; Acts 8, 36.
s Mk 10, 17-31; Lk 18, 18-30.
t Ex 20, 12-16; Dt 5, 16-20 / Lv 19, 18; Rom 13, 9.
u 5, 48; 6, 20.
v 7, 14.
w Gn 18, 14; Jb 42, 2; Lk 1, 37.
x 4, 20.22.
y 25, 31; Dn 7, 9.22; Lk 22, 30; Rv 3, 21; 20, 4.

*

19, 12: *Incapable of marriage:* literally, "eunuchs." Three classes are mentioned, eunuchs from birth, eunuchs by castration, and those who have voluntarily *renounced marriage* (literally, "have made themselves eunuchs") *for the sake of the kingdom,* i.e., to devote themselves entirely to its service. Some scholars take the last class to be those who have been divorced by their spouses and have refused to enter another marriage. But it is more likely that it is rather those who have chosen never to marry, since that suits better the optional nature of the decision: *whoever can . . . ought to accept it.*

19, 13–15: This account is understood by some as intended to justify the practice of infant baptism. That interpretation is based principally on the command not to *prevent* the children from coming, since that word sometimes has a baptismal connotation in the New Testament; see Acts 8, 36.

19, 16–30: Cf Mk 10, 17–31. This story does not set up a "two-tier" morality, that of those who seek (only) *eternal life* (16) and that of those who *wish to be perfect* (21). It speaks rather of the obstacle that riches constitute for the following of Jesus and of the impossibility, humanly speaking, for one who has *many possessions* (22) *to enter the kingdom* (24). Actual renunciation of riches is not demanded of all; Matthew counts the rich Joseph of Arimathea as a disciple of Jesus (27, 57). But only the poor in spirit (5, 3) can *enter the kingdom* and, as here, such poverty may entail the sacrifice of one's *possessions.* The Twelve, who *have given up everything* (27) to follow Jesus, will have as their reward a share in Jesus' (the Son of Man's) *judging the twelve tribes of Israel* (28), and all who have similarly sacrificed family or property for his sake *will inherit eternal life* (29).

19, 16: *Gain eternal life:* this is equivalent to "entering into life" (17) and "being saved" (25); the *life* is that of the new age after the final judgment (see 25, 46). It probably is also equivalent here to "entering the kingdom of heaven" (23) or "the kingdom of God" (24), but see the notes on 3, 2; 4, 17; 18, 1 for the wider reference of *the kingdom* in Mt.

19, 17: By Matthew's reformulation of the Marcan question and reply (Mk 10, 17–18) Jesus' repudiation of the term "good" for himself has been softened. Yet the Marcan assertion that "no one is good but God alone" stands, with only unimportant verbal modification.

19, 18–19: The first five commandments cited are from the Decalogue (see Ex 20, 12–16; Dt 5, 16–20). Matthew omits Mark's "you shall not defraud" (10, 19; see Dt 24, 14) and adds Lv 19, 18. This combination of commandments of the Decalogue with Lv 19, 18 is partially the same as Paul's enumeration of the demands of Christian morality in Rom 13, 9.

19, 20: *Young man:* in Mt alone of the synoptics the questioner is said to be a *young man;* thus the Marcan "from my youth" (10, 20) is omitted.

19, 21: *If you wish to be perfect: to be perfect is* demanded of all Christians; see 5, 48. In the case of this man, it involves selling his possessions and giving to the poor; only so can he *follow* Jesus.

19, 23–24: Riches are an obstacle to entering *the kingdom* that cannot be overcome by human power. The comparison with the impossibility of a camel's passing *through the eye of a needle* should not be mitigated by such suppositions as that *the eye of a needle* means a low or narrow gate. *The kingdom of God:* as in 12, 28; 21, 31.43, instead of Mt's usual *kingdom of heaven.*

19, 25–26: See the note on Mk 10, 23–27.

19, 28: This saying, directed to the Twelve, is from Q; see Lk 22, 29–30. *The new age:* the Greek word here translated "new age" occurs in the New Testament only here and in Ti 3, 5. Literally, it means "rebirth" or "regeneration," and is used in Ti of spiritual rebirth through baptism. Here it means the "rebirth" effected by the coming of the kingdom. Since that coming has various stages (see the notes on 3, 2; 4, 17), *the new age* could be taken as referring to the time after the resurrection when the Twelve will govern the true Israel, i.e., the church of Jesus. (For "judge" in the sense of "govern," cf Jgs 12, 8.9.11; 15, 20; 16, 31; Ps 2, 10). But since it is connected here with the time when *the Son of Man* will be *seated on his throne of glory,* language that Matthew uses in 25, 31 for the time of final judgment, it is more likely that what the Twelve are promised is that they will be joined with Jesus then in judging the people of Israel.

that you who have followed me, in the new age,
when the Son of Man is seated on his throne of
glory, will yourselves sit on twelve thrones,
judging the twelve tribes of Israel. **29** And everyone who has given up houses or brothers or
sisters or father or mother or children or lands
for the sake of my name will receive a hundred
times more, and will inherit eternal life.
**30** [z]*But many who are first will be last, and
the last will be first.

## CHAPTER 20

### The Workers in the Vineyard

**1** *"The
kingdom of heaven is like a landowner who
went out at dawn to hire laborers for his vineyard. **2** After agreeing with them for the usual
daily wage, he sent them into his vineyard.
**3** Going out about nine o'clock, he saw others
standing idle in the marketplace, **4** *and he said
to them, 'You too go into my vineyard, and I
will give you what is just.' **5** So they went off.
[And] he went out again around noon, and
around three o'clock, and did likewise. **6** Going out about five o'clock, he found others
standing around, and said to them, 'Why do you
stand here idle all day?' **7** They answered, 'Because no one has hired us.' He said to them,
'You too go into my vineyard.' **8** [a]*When it
was evening the owner of the vineyard said to
his foreman, 'Summon the laborers and give
them their pay, beginning with the last and ending with the first.' **9** When those who had started about five o'clock came, each received the
usual daily wage. **10** So when the first came,
they thought that they would receive more, but
each of them also got the usual wage. **11** And
on receiving it they grumbled against the landowner, **12** saying, 'These last ones worked
only one hour, and you have made them equal
to us, who bore the day's burden and the heat.'
**13** *He said to one of them in reply, 'My
friend, I am not cheating you. Did you not agree
with me for the usual daily wage? **14** *Take
what is yours and go. What if I wish to give this
last one the same as you? **15** [Or] am I not free
to do as I wish with my own money? Are you
envious because I am generous?' **16** *Thus, the
last will be first, and the first will be last."

### The Third Prediction of the Passion

**17** [b]*As Jesus was going up to Jerusalem, he
took the twelve [disciples] aside by themselves,
and said to them on the way, **18** "Behold, we
are going up to Jerusalem, and the Son of Man
will be handed over to the chief priests and the
scribes, and they will condemn him to death,
**19** and hand him over to the Gentiles to be
mocked and scourged and crucified, and he will
be raised on the third day."

### The Request of James and John

**20** [c]*Then the mother of the sons of Zebedee
approached him with her sons and did him homage, wishing to ask him for something. **21** He
said to her, "What do you wish?" She answered him, "Command that these two sons of
mine sit, one at your right and the other at your
left, in your kingdom." **22** *Jesus said in reply,
"You do not know what you are asking. Can
you drink the cup that I am going to drink?"
They said to him, "We can." **23** He replied,
"My cup you will indeed drink, but to sit at my
right and at my left [, this] is not mine to give
but is for those for whom it has been prepared

z 20, 16.
a Lv 19, 13; Dt 24, 15.
b 16, 21; 17, 22-23; Mk 10, 32-34; Lk 18, 31-33.
c Mk 10, 35-45.

*

19, 30: Different interpretations have been given to this saying, which comes from Mk 10, 31. In view of Matthew's associating it with the following parable (20, 1–15) and substantially repeating it (in reverse order) at the end of that parable (20, 16), it may be that his meaning is that all who respond to the call of Jesus, at whatever time (*first* or *last*), will be the same in respect to inheriting the benefits of the kingdom, which is the gift of God.

20, 1–16: This parable is peculiar to Mt. It is difficult to know whether the evangelist composed it or received it as part of his traditional material and, if the latter is the case, what its original reference was. In its present context its close association with 19, 30 suggests that its teaching is the equality of all the disciples in the reward of inheriting eternal life.

20, 4: *What is just:* although the wage is not stipulated as in the case of those first hired, it will be fair.

20, 8: *Beginning with the last . . . the first:* this element of the parable has no other purpose than to show how *the first* knew what *the last* were given (12).

20, 13: *I am not cheating you:* literally, "I am not treating you unjustly."

20, 14–15: The owner's conduct involves no violation of justice (4.13), and that all the workers receive the same wage is due only to his generosity to the latest arrivals; the resentment of the first comes from envy.

20, 16: See the note on 19, 30.

20, 17–19: Cf Mk 10, 32–34. This is the third and the most detailed of the passion predictions (16, 21–23; 17, 22–23). It speaks of Jesus' *being handed over to the Gentiles* (27, 2), his being *mocked* (27, 27–30), *scourged* (27, 26), and *crucified* (27, 31.35). In all but the last of these points Matthew agrees with his Marcan source, but whereas Mk speaks of Jesus' being killed (10, 34), Mt has the specific *to be . . . crucified.*

20, 20–28: Cf Mk 10, 35–45. The request of the sons of Zebedee, made through their mother, for the highest places of honor in the *kingdom,* and the indignation of *the* other *ten* disciples at this request, show that neither *the two brothers* nor the others have understood that what makes for greatness in the kingdom is not lordly power but humble service. Jesus gives the example, and his ministry of service will reach its highest point when he gives his life for the deliverance of the human race from sin.

20, 20–21: The reason for Matthew's making *the mother* the petitioner (cf Mk 10, 35) is not clear. Possibly he intends an allusion to Bathsheba's seeking the kingdom for Solomon; see 1 Kgs 1, 11–21. *Your kingdom:* see the note on 16, 28.

20, 22: *You do not know what you are asking:* the Greek verbs are plural and, with the rest of the verse, indicate that the answer is addressed not to the woman but to her sons. *Drink the cup:* see the note on Mk 10, 38–40. Matthew omits the Marcan "or be baptized with the baptism with which I am baptized" (10, 38).

by my Father." **24** [d]When the ten heard this,
they became indignant at the two brothers.
**25** But Jesus summoned them and said, "You
know that the rulers of the Gentiles lord it over
them, and the great ones make their authority
over them felt. **26** But it shall not be so among
you. Rather, whoever wishes to be great among
you shall be your servant; **27** [e] whoever wishes
to be first among you shall be your slave.
**28** [f]*Just so, the Son of Man did not come to
be served but to serve and to give his life as a
ransom for many."

**The Healing of Two Blind Men** **29** [g]*As
they left Jericho, a great crowd followed him.
**30** [h]*Two blind men were sitting by the roadside, and when they heard that Jesus was passing by, they cried out, "[Lord,] Son of David,
have pity on us!" **31** The crowd warned them
to be silent, but they called out all the more,
"Lord, Son of David, have pity on us!"
**32** Jesus stopped and called them and said,
"What do you want me to do for you?"
**33** They answered him, "Lord, let our eyes be
opened." **34** Moved with pity, Jesus touched
their eyes. Immediately they received their
sight, and followed him.

## CHAPTER 21

**The Entry into Jerusalem** **1** [i]*When they
drew near Jerusalem and came to Bethphage on
the Mount of Olives, Jesus sent two disciples,
**2** *saying to them, "Go into the village opposite you, and immediately you will find an ass
tethered, and a colt with her. Untie them and
bring them here to me. **3** And if anyone should
say anything to you, reply, 'The master has
need of them.' Then he will send them at once."
**4** *This happened so that what had been spoken
through the prophet might be fulfilled:

**5** [j]"Say to daughter Zion,
'Behold, your king comes to you,
meek and riding on an ass,
and on a colt, the foal of a beast of
burden.'"

**6** The disciples went and did as Jesus had ordered them. **7** *They brought the ass and the
colt and laid their cloaks over them, and he sat
upon them. **8** [k]*The very large crowd spread
their cloaks on the road, while others cut
branches from the trees and strewed them on the
road. **9** [l]*The crowds preceding him and those
following kept crying out and saying:

"Hosanna to the Son of David;

---

d Lk 22, 25-27.
e Mk 9, 35.
f 26, 28; Is 53, 12; Rom 5, 6; 1 Tm 2, 6.
g Mk 10, 46-52; Lk 18, 35-43.
h 9, 27.
i Mk 11, 1-11; Lk 19, 28-38; Jn 12, 12-15.
j Is 62, 11; Zec 9, 9.
k 2 Kgs 9, 13.
l Ps 118, 25-26.

*

20, 28: *Ransom:* this noun, which occurs in the New Testament only here and in the Marcan parallel (10, 45), does not necessarily express the idea of liberation by payment of some price. The cognate verb is used frequently in the LXX of God's liberating Israel from Egypt or from Babylonia after the Exile; see Ex 6, 6; 15, 13; Ps 77 (76 LXX), 16; Is 43, 1; 44, 22. The liberation brought by Jesus' death will be *for many;* cf Is 53, 12. *Many* does not mean that some are excluded, but is a Semitism designating the collectivity who benefit from the service of the one, and is equivalent to "all." While there are few verbal contacts between this saying and the fourth Servant Song (Is 52, 13—53, 12), the ideas of that passage are reflected here.

20, 29–34: The cure of the blind men is probably symbolic of what will happen to the disciples, now blind to the meaning of Jesus' passion and to the necessity of their sharing his suffering. As the men are given sight, so, after the resurrection, will the disciples come to see that to which they are now blind. Matthew has abbreviated his Marcan source (10, 46–52) and has made Mk's one man two. Such doubling is characteristic of this gospel; see 8, 28–34 (// Mk 5, 1–20) and the note on 9, 27–31.

20, 30: *[Lord]:* some important textual witnesses omit this, but that may be because copyists assimilated this verse to 9, 27. *Son of David:* see the note on 9, 27.

21, 1–11: Jesus' coming to Jerusalem is in accordance with the divine will that he must go there (cf 16, 21) to suffer, die, and be raised. He prepares for his entry into the city in such a way as to make it a fulfillment of the prophecy of Zec 9, 9 (2) that emphasizes the humility of the *king* who *comes* (5). That prophecy, absent from the Marcan parallel account (11, 1–11) although found also in the Johannine account of the entry (12, 15), is the center of the Matthean story. During the procession from Bethphage to Jerusalem, Jesus is acclaimed as the Davidic messianic king by the crowds who accompany him (9). On his arrival *the whole city was shaken,* and to the inquiry of the amazed populace about Jesus' identity the crowds with him reply that he is *the prophet, from Nazareth in Galilee* (10.11).

21, 1: *Bethphage:* a village that can no longer be certainly identified. Mk mentions it before Bethany (11, 1), which suggests that it lay to the east of the latter. *The Mount of Olives:* the hill east of Jerusalem that is spoken of in Zec 14, 4 as the place where the Lord will come to rescue Jerusalem from the enemy nations.

21, 2: *An ass tethered, and a colt with her:* instead of the one animal of Mk 11, 2, Mt has two, as demanded by his understanding of Zec 9, 9.

21, 4–5: *The prophet:* this fulfillment citation is actually composed of two distinct Old Testament texts, Is 62, 11 *(Say to daughter Zion)* and Zec 9, 9. The *ass* and the *colt* are the same animal in the prophecy, mentioned twice in different ways, the common Hebrew literary device of poetic parallelism. That Matthew takes them as two is one of the reasons why some scholars think that he was a Gentile rather than a Jewish Christian who would presumably not make that mistake (see Introduction).

21, 7: *Upon them:* upon the two animals; an awkward picture resulting from Matthew's misunderstanding of the prophecy.

21, 8: *Spread . . . on the road:* cf 2 Kgs 9, 13. There is a similarity between the cutting and strewing of the *branches* and the festivities of Tabernacles (Lv 23, 39–40); see also 2 Mc 10, 5–8 where the celebration of the rededication of the temple is compared to that of Tabernacles.

21, 9: *Hosanna:* the Hebrew means "(O LORD) grant salvation"; see Ps 118, 25, but that invocation had become an acclamation of jubilation and welcome. *Blessed is he . . . in the name of the Lord:* see Ps 118, 26 and the note on Jn 12, 13. *In the highest:* probably only an intensification of the acclamation, although *Hosanna in the highest* could be taken as a prayer, "May God save (him)."

blessed is he who comes in the name of
the Lord;
hosanna in the highest.''

**10** *And when he entered Jerusalem the whole
city was shaken and asked, ''Who is this?''
**11** *And the crowds replied, ''This is Jesus the
prophet, from Nazareth in Galilee.''

## The Cleansing of the Temple

**12** [m n]*Jesus entered the temple area and drove
out all those engaged in selling and buying
there. He overturned the tables of the money
changers and the seats of those who were selling
doves. **13** [o]*And he said to them, ''It is written:

'My house shall be a house of prayer,'
but you are making it a den of thieves.''

**14** [p]*The blind and the lame approached him in
the temple area, and he cured them. **15** *When
the chief priests and the scribes saw the wondrous things he was doing, and the children
crying out in the temple area, ''Hosanna to the
Son of David,'' they were indignant **16** [q]*and
said to him, ''Do you hear what they are saying?'' Jesus said to them, ''Yes; and have you
never read the text, 'Out of the mouths of infants
and nurslings you have brought forth praise'?''
**17** And leaving them, he went out of the city to
Bethany, and there he spent the night.

## The Cursing of the Fig Tree

**18** [r]*When
he was going back to the city in the morning, he
was hungry. **19** [s]Seeing a fig tree by the road,
he went over to it, but found nothing on it except
leaves. And he said to it, ''May no fruit ever
come from you again.'' And immediately the
fig tree withered. **20** When the disciples saw
this, they were amazed and said, ''How was it
that the fig tree withered immediately?''
**21** [t]*Jesus said to them in reply, ''Amen, I say
to you, if you have faith and do not waver, not
only will you do what has been done to the fig
tree, but even if you say to this mountain, 'Be
lifted up and thrown into the sea,' it will be
done. **22** [u]Whatever you ask for in prayer with
faith, you will receive.''

## The Authority of Jesus Questioned

**23** [v w]*When he had come into the temple area,
the chief priests and the elders of the people
approached him as he was teaching and said,
''By what authority are you doing these things?
And who gave you this authority?'' **24** *Jesus
said to them in reply, ''I shall ask you one
question, and if you answer it for me, then I
shall tell you by what authority I do these things.
**25** Where was John's baptism from? Was it of
heavenly or of human origin?'' They discussed
this among themselves and said, ''If we say 'Of
heavenly origin,'' he will say to us, ''Then why
did you not believe him?'' **26** [x]*But if we say,

m Mk 11, 15-19; Lk 19, 45-48; Jn 2, 14-22.
n Lv 5, 7.
o Is 56, 7; Jer 7, 11.
p 2 Sm 5, 8 LXX.
q Ps 8, 2 LXX; Wis 10, 21.
r Mk 11, 12-14.20-24.
s Jer 8, 13; Lk 13, 6-9.
t 17, 20; Lk 17, 6.
u 7, 7; 1 Jn 3, 22.
v Mk 11, 27-33; Lk 20, 1-8.
w Jn 2, 18.
x 14, 5.

*

21, 10: *Was shaken:* in the gospels this verb is peculiar to Mt where it is used also of the earthquake at the time of the crucifixion (27, 51) and of the terror of the guards of Jesus' tomb at the appearance of the angel (28, 4). For Matthew's use of the cognate noun, see the note on 8, 24.

21, 11: *The prophet:* see 16, 14 ("one of the prophets") and 21, 46.

21, 12–17: Matthew changes the order of Mk (11, 11.12.15) and places the cleansing of the temple on the same day as the entry into Jerusalem, immediately after it. The activities going on in *the temple area* were not secular but connected with the temple worship. Thus Jesus' attack on those so engaged and his charge that they were *making* God's *house of prayer a den of thieves* (12–13) constituted a claim to authority over the religious practices of Israel and were a challenge to the priestly authorities. Verses 14–17 are peculiar to Mt. Jesus' healings and his countenancing the children's cries of praise rouse the indignation of *the chief priests and the scribes* (15). These two groups appear in the infancy narrative (2, 4) and have been mentioned in the first and third passion predictions (16, 21; 20, 18). Now, as the passion approaches, they come on the scene again, exhibiting their hostility to Jesus.

21, 12: These activities were carried on in the court of the Gentiles, the outermost court of *the temple area.* Animals for sacrifice were sold; the *doves* were for those who could not afford a more expensive offering; see Lv 5, 7. *Tables of the money changers:* only the coinage of Tyre could be used for the purchases; other money had to be exchanged for that.

21, 13: *'My house . . . prayer':* cf Is 56, 7. Matthew omits the final words of the quotation, "for all peoples" ("all nations"), possibly because for him the worship of the God of Israel by all nations belongs to the time after the resurrection; see 28, 19. *A den of thieves:* the phrase is taken from Jer 7, 11.

21, 14: *The blind and the lame:* according to 2 Sm 5, 8 (LXX) *the blind and the lame* were forbidden to enter "the house of the Lord," the temple. These are the last of Jesus' healings in Mt.

21, 15: *The wondrous things:* the healings.

21, 16: *'Out of the mouths . . . praise':* cf Ps 8, 3 (LXX).

21, 18–22: In Mk the effect of Jesus' cursing the fig tree is not immediate; see 11, 14.20. By making it so, Matthew has heightened the miracle. Jesus' act seems arbitrary and ill-tempered, but it is a prophetic action similar to those of Old Testament prophets that vividly symbolize some part of their preaching; see, e.g., Ez 12, 1–20. It is a sign of the judgment that is to come upon the Israel that with all its apparent piety lacks the fruit of good deeds (3, 10) and will soon bear the punishment of its fruitlessness (43). Some scholars propose that this story is the development in tradition of a parable of Jesus about the destiny of a fruitless tree, such as Lk 13, 6–9. Jesus' answer to the question of the amazed disciples (20) makes the miracle an example of the power of prayer made with unwavering *faith* (21–22).

21, 21: See 17, 20.

21, 23–27: Cf Mk 11, 27–33. This is the first of five controversies between Jesus and the religious authorities of Judaism in 21, 23—22, 46, presented in the form of questions and answers.

21, 23: *These things:* probably his entry into the city, his cleansing of the temple, and his healings there.

21, 24: To reply by counterquestion was common in rabbinical debate.

21, 26: *We fear . . . as a prophet:* cf 14, 5.

"Of human origin," we fear the crowd, for they
all regard John as a prophet." **27** *So they said
to Jesus in reply, "We do not know." He himself said to them, "Neither shall I tell you by
what authority I do these things.

## The Parable of the Two Sons

**28** *"What is your opinion? A man had two
sons. He came to the first and said, 'Son, go out
and work in the vineyard today.' **29** He said in
reply, "I will not," but afterwards he changed
his mind and went. **30** The man came to the
other son and gave the same order. He said in
reply, "Yes, sir," but did not go. **31** *Which
of the two did his father's will?" They answered, "The first." Jesus said to them,
"Amen, I say to you, tax collectors and prostitutes are entering the kingdom of God before
you. **32** [y]*When John came to you in the way
of righteousness, you did not believe him; but
tax collectors and prostitutes did. Yet even
when you saw that, you did not later change
your minds and believe him.

## The Parable of the Tenants

**33** [z][a]*"Hear another parable. There was a
landowner who planted a vineyard, put a hedge
around it, dug a wine press in it, and built a
tower. Then he leased it to tenants and went on
a journey. **34** *When vintage time drew near,
he sent his servants to the tenants to obtain his
produce. **35** But the tenants seized the servants
and one they beat, another they killed, and a
third they stoned. **36** Again he sent other servants, more numerous than the first ones, but
they treated them in the same way. **37** Finally,
he sent his son to them, thinking, 'They will
respect my son.' **38** *But when the tenants saw
the son, they said to one another, 'This is the
heir. Come, let us kill him and acquire his inheritance.' **39** [b]*They seized him, threw him out
of the vineyard, and killed him. **40** What will
the owner of the vineyard do to those tenants
when he comes?" **41** *They answered him,
"He will put those wretched men to a wretched
death and lease his vineyard to other tenants
who will give him the produce at the proper
times." **42** [c]*Jesus said to them, "Did you
never read in the scriptures:

'The stone that the builders rejected

y Lk 7, 29-30.
z Mk 12, 1-12; Lk 20, 9-19.
a Is 5, 1-2.7.
b Heb 13, 12.
c Ps 118, 22-23; Is 28, 16; Acts 4, 11; 1 Pt 2, 7.

*

21, 27: Since through embarrassment on the one hand and fear on the other the religious authorities claim ignorance of the origin of John's baptism, they show themselves incapable of speaking with authority; hence Jesus refuses to discuss with them the grounds of his authority.

21, 28–32: The series of controversies is interrupted by three parables on the judgment of Israel (21, 28—22, 14) of which this, peculiar to Mt, is the first. The second (21, 33–46) comes from Mk (12, 1–12), and the third (22, 1–14) from Q; see Lk 14, 15–24. This interruption of the controversies is similar to that in Mk, although Mk has only one parable between the first and second controversy. As regards Mt's first parable, vv 28–30 if taken by themselves could point simply to the difference between saying and doing, a theme of much importance in this gospel (cf 7, 21; 12, 50); that may have been the parable's original reference. However, it is given a more specific application by the addition of vv 31–32. The two sons represent, respectively, the religious leaders and the religious outcasts who followed John's call to repentance. By the answer they give to Jesus' question (31) the leaders condemn themselves. There is much confusion in the textual tradition of the parable. Of the three different forms of the text given by important textual witnesses, one has the leaders answer that the son who agreed to go but did not was the one who did the father's will. Although some scholars accept that as the original reading, their arguments in favor of it seem unconvincing. The choice probably lies only between a reading that puts the son who agrees and then disobeys before the son who at first refuses and then obeys, and the reading followed in the present translation. The witnesses to the latter reading are slightly better than those that support the other.

21, 31: *Entering . . . before you:* this probably means "they enter; you do not."

21, 32: Cf Lk 7, 29–30. Although the thought is similar to that of the Lucan text, the formulation is so different that it is improbable that the saying comes from Q. *Came to you . . . way of righteousness:* several meanings are possible: that John himself was righteous, that he taught righteousness to others, or that he had an important place in God's plan of salvation. For the last, see the note on 3, 14–15.

21, 33–46: Cf Mk 12, 1–12. In this parable there is a close correspondence between most of the details of the story and the situation that it illustrates, the dealings of God with his people. Because of that heavy allegorizing, some scholars think that it does not in any way go back to Jesus, but represents the theology of the later church. That judgment applies to the Marcan parallel as well, although the allegorizing has gone farther in Mt. There are others who believe that while many of the allegorical elements are due to church sources, they have been added to a basic parable spoken by Jesus. This view is now supported by the Gospel of Thomas, 65, where a less allegorized and probably more primitive form of the parable is found.

21, 33: *Planted a vineyard . . . a tower:* cf Is 5, 1–2. The *vineyard* is defined in Is 5, 7 as "the house of Israel."

21, 34–35: *His servants:* Mt has two sendings of *servants* as against Mk's three sendings of a single servant (11, 2–5a) followed by a statement about the sending of "many others" (11, 2.5b). That these *servants* stand for the prophets sent by God to Israel is clearly implied but not made explicit here, but see 23, 37. *His produce:* cf Mk 12, 2, "some of the produce." The *produce* is the good works demanded by God, and his claim to them is total.

21, 38: *Acquire his inheritance:* if a Jewish proselyte died without heir, the tenants of his land would have final claim on it.

21, 39: *Threw him out . . . and killed him:* the change in the Marcan order where the son is killed and his corpse then thrown out (12, 8) was probably made because of the tradition that Jesus died outside the city of Jerusalem; see Jn 19, 17; Heb 13, 12.

21, 41: *They answered:* in Mk 12, 9 the question is answered by Jesus himself; here the leaders answer and so condemn themselves; cf v 31. Matthew adds that the new *tenants* to whom the vineyard will be transferred *will give* the owner *the produce at the proper times.*

21, 42: Cf Ps 118, 22–23. The psalm was used in the early church as a prophecy of Jesus' resurrection; see Acts 4, 11; 1 Pt 2, 7. If, as some think, the original parable ended at v 39, it was thought necessary to complete it by a reference to Jesus' vindication by God.

has become the cornerstone;
by the Lord has this been done,
and it is wonderful in our eyes'?

**43** *Therefore, I say to you, the kingdom of
God will be taken away from you and given to
a people that will produce its fruit. [**44** *The
one who falls on this stone will be dashed to
pieces; and it will crush anyone on whom it
falls.]" **45** *When the chief priests and the
Pharisees heard his parables, they knew that he
was speaking about them. **46** And although
they were attempting to arrest him, they feared
the crowds, for they regarded him as a prophet.

## CHAPTER 22

### The Parable of the Wedding Feast

**1** [d]*Jesus again in reply spoke to them in parables, saying, **2** *"The kingdom of heaven may
be likened to a king who gave a wedding feast
for his son. **3** *He dispatched his servants to
summon the invited guests to the feast, but they
refused to come. **4** A second time he sent other
servants, saying, 'Tell those invited: "Behold,
I have prepared my banquet, my calves and
fattened cattle are killed, and everything is
ready; come to the feast."' **5** Some ignored the
invitation and went away, one to his farm, another to his business. **6** [e]The rest laid hold of
his servants, mistreated them, and killed them.
**7** *The king was enraged and sent his troops,
destroyed those murderers, and burned their
city. **8** Then he said to his servants, 'The feast
is ready, but those who were invited were not
worthy to come. **9** Go out, therefore, into the
main roads and invite to the feast whomever you
find.' **10** *The servants went out into the streets
and gathered all they found, bad and good alike,
and the hall was filled with guests. **11** *But
when the king came in to meet the guests he saw
a man there not dressed in a wedding garment.
**12** He said to him, 'My friend, how is it that
you came in here without a wedding garment?'
But he was reduced to silence. **13** [f]*Then the
king said to his attendants, 'Bind his hands and
feet, and cast him into the darkness outside,
where there will be wailing and grinding of
teeth.' **14** Many are invited, but few are chosen."

### Paying Taxes to the Emperor

**15** [g]*Then the Pharisees went off and plotted
how they might entrap him in speech. **16** *They
sent their disciples to him, with the Herodians,
saying, "Teacher, we know that you are a truthful man and that you teach the way of God in
accordance with the truth. And you are not concerned with anyone's opinion, for you do not
regard a person's status. **17** *Tell us, then,
what is your opinion: Is it lawful to pay the
census tax to Caesar or not?" **18** Knowing their
malice, Jesus said, "Why are you testing me,
you hypocrites? **19** *Show me the coin that
pays the census tax." Then they handed him the
Roman coin. **20** He said to them, "Whose im-

d Lk 14, 15-24.
e 21, 35.
f 8, 12; 25, 30.
g Mk 12, 13-17; Lk 20, 20-26.

*

21, 43: Peculiar to Mt. *Kingdom of God:* see the note on 19, 23–24. Its presence here instead of Mt's usual "kingdom of heaven" may indicate that the saying came from Matthew's own traditional material. *A people that will produce its fruit:* believing Israelites and Gentiles, the church of Jesus.

21, 44: The majority of textual witnesses omit this verse. It is probably an early addition to Mt from Lk 20, 18 with which it is practically identical.

21, 45: *The Pharisees:* Matthew inserts into the group of Jewish leaders (23) those who represented the Judaism of his own time.

22, 1–14: This parable is from Q; see Lk 14, 15–24. It has been given many allegorical traits by Matthew, e.g., the burning of the *city* of the guests who refused the invitation (7), which corresponds to the destruction of Jerusalem by the Romans in A.D. 70. It has similarities with the preceding parable of the tenants: the sending of two groups of *servants* (3.4), the murder of the *servants* (6), the punishment of the *murderers* (7), and the entrance of a new group into a privileged situation of which the others had proved themselves unworthy (8–10). The parable ends with a section that is peculiar to Mt (11–14), which some take as a distinct parable. Mt presents the *kingdom* in its double aspect, already present and something that can be entered here and now (1–10), and something that will be possessed only by those present members who can stand the scrutiny of the final judgment (11–14). The parable is not only a statement of God's judgment on Israel but a warning to Matthew's church.

22, 2: *Wedding feast:* the Old Testament's portrayal of final salvation under the image of a banquet (Is 25, 6) is taken up also in 8, 11; cf Lk 13, 15.

22, 3–4: *Servants . . . other servants:* probably Christian missionaries in both instances; cf 23, 34.

22, 7: See the note on vv 1–14.

22, 10: *Bad and good alike:* cf 13, 47.

22, 11: *A wedding garment:* the repentance, change of heart and mind, that is the condition for entrance into the kingdom (3, 2; 4, 17) must be continued in a life of good deeds (7, 21–23).

22, 13: *Wailing and grinding of teeth:* the Christian who lacks the wedding garment of good deeds will suffer the same fate as those Jews who have rejected Jesus; see the note on 8, 11–12.

22, 15–22: The series of controversies between Jesus and the representatives of Judaism (see the note on 21, 23–27) is resumed. As in the first (21, 23–27), here and in the following disputes Matthew follows his Marcan source with few modifications.

22, 15: *The Pharisees:* while Matthew retains the Marcan union of Pharisees and Herodians in this account, he clearly emphasizes the Pharisees' part. They alone are mentioned here, and the Herodians are joined with them only in a prepositional phrase of v 16. *Entrap him in speech:* the question that they will pose is intended to force Jesus to take either a position contrary to that held by the majority of the people or one that will bring him into conflict with the Roman authorities.

22, 16: *Herodians:* see the note on Mk 3, 6. They would favor payment of the tax; the Pharisees did not.

22, 17: *Is it lawful:* the law to which they refer is the law of God.

22, 19: *They handed him the Roman coin:* their readiness in producing the money implies their use of it and their acceptance of the financial advantages of the Roman administration in Palestine.

age is this and whose inscription?" **21** [h]*They
replied, "Caesar's." At that he said to them,
"Then repay to Caesar what belongs to Caesar
and to God what belongs to God." **22** When
they heard this they were amazed, and leaving
him they went away.

## The Question about the Resurrection

**23** [i]*On that day Sadducees approached him,
saying that there is no resurrection. They put
this question to him, **24** [j]*saying, "Teacher,
Moses said, 'If a man dies without children, his
brother shall marry his wife and raise up descendants for his brother.' **25** Now there were
seven brothers among us. The first married and
died and, having no descendants, left his wife
to his brother. **26** The same happened with the
second and the third, through all seven. **27** Finally the woman died. **28** Now at the resurrection, of the seven, whose wife will she be? For
they all had been married to her." **29** *Jesus
said to them in reply, "You are misled because
you do not know the scriptures or the power of
God. **30** At the resurrection they neither marry
nor are given in marriage but are like the angels
in heaven. **31** *And concerning the resurrection
of the dead, have you not read what was said to
you by God, **32** [k]'I am the God of Abraham,
the God of Isaac, and the God of Jacob'? He is
not the God of the dead but of the living."
**33** When the crowds heard this, they were astonished at his teaching.

## The Greatest Commandment

**34** [l]*When the Pharisees heard that he had silenced the Sadducees, they gathered together,
**35** *and one of them [a scholar of the law]
tested him by asking, **36** *"Teacher, which
commandment in the law is the greatest?"
**37** [m]*He said to him, "You shall love the
Lord, your God, with all your heart, with all
your soul, and with all your mind. **38** This is
the greatest and the first commandment.
**39** [n]*The second is like it: You shall love your
neighbor as yourself. **40** [o]*The whole law and
the prophets depend on these two commandments."

h Rom 13, 7.
i Mk 12, 18-27; Lk 20, 27-40.
j Gn 38, 8; Dt 25, 5-6.
k Ex 3, 6.
l Mk 12, 28-34; Lk 10, 25-28.
m Dt 6, 5.
n Lv 19, 18; Jas 2, 8.
o Rom 13, 8-10; Gal 5, 14.

*

22, 21: *Caesar's:* the emperor Tiberius (A.D. 14–37). *Repay to Caesar what belongs to Caesar:* those who willingly use the coin that is Caesar's should *repay* him in kind. The answer avoids taking sides in the question of the lawfulness of the tax. *To God what belongs to God:* Jesus raises the debate to a new level. Those who have hypocritically asked about tax in respect to its relation to the law of God should be concerned rather with repaying *God* with the good deeds that are his due; cf 21, 41.43.

22, 23–33: Here Jesus' opponents are the *Sadducees,* members of the powerful priestly party of his time; see the note on 3, 7. Denying the resurrection of the dead, a teaching of relatively late origin in Judaism (cf Dn 12, 2), they appeal to a law of the Pentateuch (Dt 25, 5–10) and present a case based on it that would make resurrection from the dead ridiculous (24–28). Jesus chides them for knowing neither *the scriptures* nor *the power of God* (29). His argument in respect to God's *power* contradicts the notion, held even by many proponents as well as by opponents of the teaching, that the life of those raised from the dead would be essentially a continuation of the type of life they had had before death (30). His argument based on the scriptures (31–32) is of a sort that was accepted as valid among Jews of the time.

22, 23: *Saying that there is no resurrection:* in the Marcan parallel (12, 18) the Sadducees are correctly defined as those "who say there is no resurrection"; see also Lk 20, 27. Matthew's rewording of Mk can mean that these particular Sadducees deny the resurrection, which would imply that he was not aware that the denial was characteristic of the party. For some scholars this is an indication of his being a Gentile Christian; see the note on 21, 4–5.

22, 24: *'If a man dies . . . his brother':* this is known as the "law of the levirate," from the Latin *levir,* "brother-in-law." Its purpose was to continue the family line of the deceased *brother* (Dt 25, 6).

22, 29: The sexual relationships of this world will be transcended; the risen body will be the work of the creative *power of God.*

22, 31–32: Cf Ex 3, 6. In the Pentateuch, which the Sadducees accepted as normative for Jewish belief and practice, God speaks even now (*to you*) of himself as the God of the patriarchs who died centuries ago. He identifies himself in relation to them, and because of their relation to him, the living God, they too are alive. This might appear no argument for the resurrection, but simply for life after death as conceived in Wis 3, 1–3. But the general thought of early first-century Judaism was not influenced by that conception; for it human immortality was connected with the existence of the body.

22, 34–40: The Marcan parallel (12, 28–34) is an exchange between Jesus and a scribe who is impressed by the way in which Jesus has conducted himself in the previous controversy (12, 28), who compliments him for the answer he gives him (12, 32), and who is said by Jesus to be "not far from the kingdom of God" (12, 34). Matthew has sharpened that scene. The questioner, as the representative of other Pharisees, tests Jesus by his question (34–35), and both his reaction to Jesus' reply and Jesus' commendation of him are lacking.

22, 35: [*A scholar of the law*]: meaning "scribe." Although this reading is supported by the vast majority of textual witnesses, it is the only time that the Greek word so translated occurs in Mt. It is relatively frequent in Lk, and there is reason to think that it may have been added here by a copyist since it occurs in the Lucan parallel (10, 25–28). *Tested:* see the note on 19, 3.

22, 36: For the devout Jew all the commandments were to be kept with equal care, but there is evidence of preoccupation in Jewish sources with the question put to Jesus.

22, 37–38: Cf Dt 6, 5. Matthew omits the first part of Mk's fuller quotation (12, 29; Dt 6, 4–5), probably because he considered its monotheistic emphasis needless for his church. The love of God must engage the total person (*heart, soul, mind*).

22, 39: Jesus goes beyond the extent of the question put to him and joins *to the greatest and the first commandment* a *second,* that of *love* of *neighbor,* Lv 19, 18; see the note on 19, 18–19. This combination of the two commandments may already have been made in Judaism.

22, 40: The double commandment is the source from which *the whole law and the prophets* are derived.

## The Question about David's Son

**41** [p]*While the Pharisees were gathered together, Jesus questioned them, **42** *saying,
"What is your opinion about the Messiah?
Whose son is he?" They replied, "David's."
**43** He said to them, "How, then, does David,
inspired by the Spirit, call him 'lord,' saying:

**44** [q]'The Lord said to my lord,
"Sit at my right hand
until I place your enemies under your
feet" '?

**45** *If David calls him 'lord,' how can he be his
son?" **46** [r]No one was able to answer him a
word, nor from that day on did anyone dare to
ask him any more questions.

## CHAPTER 23

### Denunciation of the Scribes and Pharisees

**1** [s]*Then Jesus spoke to the crowds
and to his disciples, **2** *saying, "The scribes
and the Pharisees have taken their seat on the
chair of Moses. **3** Therefore, do and observe all
things whatsoever they tell you, but do not follow their example. For they preach but they do
not practice. **4** [t]*They tie up heavy burdens
[hard to carry] and lay them on people's shoulders, but they will not lift a finger to move them.
**5** [u]*All their works are performed to be seen.
They widen their phylacteries and lengthen their
tassels. **6** [v]*They love places of honor at banquets, seats of honor in synagogues, **7** greetings in marketplaces, and the salutation 'Rabbi.' **8** *As for you, do not be called 'Rabbi.'
You have but one teacher, and you are all brothers. **9** Call no one on earth your father; you
have but one Father in heaven. **10** Do not be

p Mk 12, 35-37; Lk 20, 41-44.
q Ps 110, 1; Acts 2, 35; Heb 1, 13.
r Lk 20, 40.
s Mk 12, 38-39; Lk 11, 37-52; 13, 34-35.
t Lk 11, 46.
u 6, 1-6; Ex 13, 9.16; Nm 15, 38-39; Dt 6, 8; 11, 18.
v Mk 12, 38-39; Lk 11, 43; 20, 46.

*

22, 41–46: Having answered the questions of his opponents in the preceding three controversies, Jesus now puts a question to them about the sonship of the Messiah. Their easy response (43a) is countered by his quoting a verse of Ps 110 that raises a problem for their response (43b–45). They are unable to solve it and *from that day on* their questioning of him is ended.

22, 41: *The Pharisees ... questioned them:* Mk is not specific about who are questioned (12, 35).

22, 42–44: *David's:* this view of the Pharisees was based on such Old Testament texts as Is 11, 1–9; Jer 23, 5; and Ez 34, 23; see also the extrabiblical Psalms of Solomon 17, 21. *How, then ... saying:* Jesus cites Ps 110, 1, accepting the Davidic authorship of the psalm, a common view of his time. The psalm was probably composed for the enthronement of a Davidic king of Judah. Matthew assumes that the Pharisees interpret it as referring to the Messiah, although there is no clear evidence that it was so interpreted in the Judaism of Jesus' time. It was widely used in the early church as referring to the exaltation of the risen Jesus. *My lord:* understood as the Messiah.

22, 45: Since Matthew presents Jesus both as Messiah (16, 16) and as Son of David (1, 1; see also the note on 9, 27), the question is not meant to imply Jesus' denial of Davidic sonship. It probably means that although he is the Son of David, he is someone greater, Son of Man and Son of God, and recognized as greater by David who calls him my *'lord.'*

23, 1–39: The final section of the narrative part of the fifth book of the gospel is a denunciation by Jesus of the scribes and the Pharisees (see the note on 3, 7). It depends in part on Mk and Q (cf Mk 12, 38–39; Lk 11, 37–52; 13, 34–35), but in the main it is peculiar to Mt. (For the reasons against considering this extensive body of sayings-material either as one of the structural discourses of this gospel or as part of the one that follows in chs 24–25, see the note on 19, 1—23, 39.) While the tradition of a deep opposition between Jesus and the Pharisees is well founded, this speech reflects an opposition that goes beyond that of Jesus' ministry and must be seen as expressing the bitter conflict between Pharisaic Judaism and the church of Matthew at the time when the gospel was composed. The complaint often made that the speech ignores the positive qualities of Pharisaism and of its better representatives is true, but the complaint overlooks the circumstances that gave rise to the invective. Nor is the speech purely anti-Pharisaic. The evangelist discerns in his church many of the same faults that he finds in its opponents and warns his fellow Christians to look to their own conduct and attitudes.

23, 2–3: *Have taken their seat ... Moses:* it is uncertain whether this is simply a metaphor for Mosaic teaching authority or refers to an actual *chair* on which the teacher sat. It has been proved that there was a seat so designated in synagogues of a later period than that of this gospel. *Do and observe ... they tell you:* since the Matthean Jesus abrogates Mosaic law (5, 31–42), warns his disciples against the teaching of the Pharisees (14, 1–12), and, in this speech, denounces the Pharisees as blind guides in respect to their teaching on oaths (16–22), this commandment *to observe all things whatsoever they* (the scribes and Pharisees) *tell you* cannot be taken as the evangelist's understanding of the proper standard of conduct for his church. The saying may reflect a period when the Matthean community was largely Jewish Christian and was still seeking to avoid a complete break with the synagogue. Matthew has incorporated this traditional material into the speech in accordance with his view of the course of salvation history, in which he portrays the time of Jesus' ministry as marked by the fidelity to the law, although with significant pointers to the new situation that would exist after his death and resurrection (see the note on 5, 17–20). The crowds and the disciples (1) are exhorted not to *follow* the *example* of the Jewish leaders, whose deeds do not conform to their teaching (3).

23, 4: *Tie up heavy burdens:* see the note on 11, 28.

23, 5: To the charge of preaching but not practicing (3), Jesus adds that of acting in order to earn praise. The disciples have already been warned against this same fault (see the note on 6, 1–18). *Phylacteries:* the Mosaic law required that during prayer small boxes containing parchments on which verses of scripture were written be worn on the left forearm and the forehead (see Ex 13, 9.16; Dt 6, 8; 11, 18). *Tassels:* see the note on 9, 20. The widening of *phylacteries* and the lengthening of *tassels* were for the purpose of making these evidences of piety more noticeable.

23, 6–7: Cf Mk 12, 38–39. *'Rabbi':* literally, "my great one," a title of respect for teachers and leaders.

23, 8–12: These verses, warning against the use of various titles, are addressed to the disciples alone. While only the title *'Rabbi'* has been said to be used in addressing the scribes and Pharisees (7), the implication is that *Father* and *'Master'* also were. The prohibition of these titles to the disciples suggests that their use was present in Matthew's church. The Matthean Jesus forbids not only the titles but the spirit of superiority and pride that is shown by their acceptance. *Whoever exalts ... will be exalted:* cf Lk 14, 11.

called 'Master'; you have but one master, the
Messiah. 11 [w] The greatest among you must be
your servant. 12 [x] Whoever exalts himself will
be humbled; but whoever humbles himself will
be exalted.

13 [y]* "Woe to you, scribes and Pharisees,
you hypocrites. You lock the kingdom of heaven before human beings. You do not enter yourselves, nor do you allow entrance to those trying
to enter. [14*]

15 * "Woe to you, scribes and Pharisees,
you hypocrites. You traverse sea and land to make one convert, and when that happens you make him a child of Gehenna twice as much as yourselves.

16 [z]* "Woe to you, blind guides, who say,
'If one swears by the temple, it means nothing, but if one swears by the gold of the temple, one
is obligated.' 17 Blind fools, which is greater, the gold, or the temple that made the gold sacred? 18 And you say, 'If one swears by the altar, it means nothing, but if one swears by the
gift on the altar, one is obligated.' 19 You blind ones, which is greater, the gift, or the altar that
makes the gift sacred? 20 [a] One who swears by the altar swears by it and all that is upon it;
21 one who swears by the temple swears by it
and by him who dwells in it; 22 one who swears by heaven swears by the throne of God and by him who is seated on it.

23 [b]* "Woe to you, scribes and Pharisees,
you hypocrites. You pay tithes of mint and dill and cummin, and have neglected the weightier things of the law: judgment and mercy and fidelity. [But] these you should have done, without neglecting the others. 24 [c]* Blind
guides, who strain out the gnat and swallow the camel!

25 [d]* "Woe to you, scribes and Pharisees,
you hypocrites. You cleanse the outside of cup and dish, but inside they are full of plunder and self-indulgence. 26 Blind Pharisee, cleanse
first the inside of the cup, so that the outside also may be clean.

27 * "Woe to you, scribes and Pharisees,
you hypocrites. You are like whitewashed tombs, which appear beautiful on the outside, but inside are full of dead men's bones and every kind of filth. 28 [e] Even so, on the outside
you appear righteous, but inside you are filled with hypocrisy and evildoing.

w 20, 26.
x Lk 14, 11; 18, 14.
y Lk 11, 52.
z 15, 14.
a 5, 34-35.
b Lv 27, 30; Dt 14, 22; Lk 11, 42.
c Lv 11, 41-45.
d Mk 7, 4; Lk 11, 39.
e Lk 16, 15; 18, 9.

*

23, 13–36: This series of seven "woes," directed against the *scribes and Pharisees* and addressed to them, is the heart of the speech. The phrase *woe to* occurs often in the prophetic and apocalyptic literature, expressing horror of a sin and punishment for those who commit it. *Hypocrites:* see the note on 6, 2. The hypocrisy of the *scribes and Pharisees* consists in the difference between their speech and action (3) and in demonstrations of piety that have no other purpose than to enhance their reputation as religious persons (5).

23, 13: *You lock the kingdom of heaven:* cf 16, 19 where Jesus tells Peter that he will give him the keys to *the kingdom of heaven.* The purpose of the authority expressed by that metaphor is to give entrance into the kingdom (the kingdom is closed only to those who reject the authority); here the charge is made that the authority of the *scribes and Pharisees* is exercised in such a way as to be an obstacle to entrance. Cf Lk 11, 52 where the accusation against the "scholars of the law" (Mt's *scribes*) is that they "have taken away the key of knowledge."

23, 14: Some manuscripts add a verse here or after v 12, "Woe to you, scribes and Pharisees, you hypocrites. You devour the houses of widows and, as a pretext, recite lengthy prayers. Because of this, you will receive a very severe condemnation." Cf Mk 12, 40; Lk 20, 47. This "woe" is almost identical with Mk 12, 40 and seems to be an interpolation derived from that text.

23, 15: In the first century A.D. until the First Jewish Revolt against Rome (A.D. 66–70), many Pharisees conducted a vigorous missionary campaign among Gentiles. *Convert:* literally, "proselyte," a Gentile who accepted Judaism fully by submitting to circumcision and all other requirements of Mosaic law. *Child of Gehenna:* worthy of everlasting punishment; for *Gehenna,* see the note on 5, 22. *Twice as much as yourselves:* possibly this refers simply to the zeal of the *convert,* surpassing that of the one who converted him.

23, 16–22: An attack on the casuistry that declared some oaths binding (*one is obligated*) and others not (*it means nothing*) and held the binding oath to be the one made by something of lesser value (*the gold; the gift on the altar*). Such teaching, which inverts the order of values, reveals the teachers to be *blind guides;* cf 15, 14. Since the Matthean Jesus forbids all oaths to his disciples (5, 33–37), this *woe* does not set up a standard for Christian moral conduct, but ridicules the Pharisees on their own terms.

23, 23: The Mosaic law ordered tithing of the produce of the land (Lv 27, 30; Dt 14, 22–23), and the scribal tradition is said here to have extended this law to even the smallest herbs. The practice is criticized not in itself but because it shows the Pharisees' preoccupation with matters of less importance while they neglect *the weightier things of the law.*

23, 24: Cf Lv 11, 41–45 that forbids the eating of any "swarming creature." The Pharisees' scrupulosity about minor matters and neglect of greater ones (23) is further brought out by this contrast between straining liquids that might contain a tiny "swarming creature" and yet swallowing *the camel.* The latter was one of the unclean animals forbidden by the law (Lv 11, 4), but it is hardly possible that the scribes and Pharisees are being denounced as guilty of so gross a violation of the food laws. To *swallow the camel* is only a hyperbolic way of speaking of their neglect of what is important.

23, 25–26: The ritual washing of utensils for dining (cf Mk 7, 4) is turned into a metaphor illustrating a concern for appearances while inner purity is ignored. The *scribes and Pharisees* are compared to cups carefully washed on the outside but filthy within. *Self-indulgence:* the Greek word here translated means lack of self-control, whether in drinking or in sexual conduct.

23, 27–28: The sixth *woe,* like the preceding one, deals with concern for externals and neglect of what is *inside.* Since contact with dead bodies, even when one was unaware of it, caused ritual impurity (Nm 19, 11–22), tombs were whitewashed so that no one would contract such impurity inadvertently.

**29** *"Woe to you, scribes and Pharisees,
you hypocrites. You build the tombs of the
prophets and adorn the memorials of the righteous, **30** [f]and you say, 'If we had lived in the
days of our ancestors, we would not have joined them in shedding the prophets' blood.'
**31** [g]Thus you bear witness against yourselves
that you are the children of those who murdered
the prophets; **32** now fill up what your ancestors measured out! **33** [h]You serpents, you
brood of vipers, how can you flee from the
judgment of Gehenna? **34** [i]*Therefore, behold,
I send to you prophets and wise men and scribes;
some of them you will kill and crucify, some of
them you will scourge in your synagogues and
pursue from town to town, **35** so that there may
come upon you all the righteous blood shed
upon earth, from the righteous blood of Abel to
the blood of Zechariah, the son of Barachiah,
whom you murdered between the sanctuary and
the altar. **36** Amen, I say to you, all these things
will come upon this generation.

## The Lament over Jerusalem

**37** [jk]*"Jerusalem, Jerusalem, you who kill the
prophets and stone those sent to you, how many
times I yearned to gather your children together,
as a hen gathers her young under her wings, but
you were unwilling! **38** [l]Behold, your house
will be abandoned, desolate. **39** [m]I tell you,
you will not see me again until you say,
'Blessed is he who comes in the name of the
Lord.'"

# CHAPTER 24

## The Destruction of the Temple Foretold

**1** [n]*Jesus left the temple area and was
going away, when his disciples approached him
to point out the temple buildings. **2** *He said to
them in reply, "You see all these things, do you
not? Amen, I say to you, there will not be left
here a stone upon another stone that will not be
thrown down."

## The Beginning of Calamities

**3** *As he
was sitting on the Mount of Olives, the disciples

f Lk 11, 47.
g Acts 7, 52.
h 3, 7; 12, 34.
i 5, 12; Gn 4, 8; 2 Chr 24, 20-22; Zec 1, 1; Lk 11, 49-51;Rv 18, 24.
j Lk 13, 34-35; 19, 41-44.
k 21, 35.
l Jer 12, 7.
m Ps 118, 26.
n Mk 13, 1-37; Lk 21, 5-36.

*

23, 29–36: The final *woe* is the most serious indictment of all. It portrays the *scribes and Pharisees* as standing in the same line as their *ancestors* who murdered *the prophets* and *the righteous.*

23, 29–32: In spite of honoring the slain dead by building their *tombs* and adorning their *memorials,* and claiming that they would not have joined in their ancestors' crimes if they *had lived in* their *days,* the *scribes and Pharisees* are true *children* of their ancestors and are defiantly ordered by Jesus to *fill up* what those *ancestors measured out.* This order reflects the Jewish notion that there was an allotted measure of suffering that had to be completed before God's final judgment would take place.

23, 34–36: There are important differences between the Matthean and the Lucan form of this Q material; cf Lk 11, 49–51. In Lk the one who sends the emissaries is the "wisdom of God." If, as many scholars think, that is the original wording of Q, Matthew, by making Jesus the sender, has presented him as the personified divine wisdom. In Lk, wisdom's emissaries are the Old Testament "prophets" and the Christian "apostles." Mt's *prophets and wise men and scribes* are probably Christian disciples alone; cf 10, 41 and see the note on 13, 52. *You will kill:* see 24, 9. *Scourge in your synagogues . . . town to town:* see 10, 17.23 and the note on 10, 17. *All the righteous blood shed upon the earth:* the slaying of the disciples is in continuity with all the shedding of *righteous blood* beginning with that of *Abel.* The persecution of Jesus' disciples by *this generation* involves the persecutors in the guilt of their murderous ancestors. *The blood of Zechariah:* see the note on Lk 11, 51. By identifying him as *the son of Barachiah* Matthew understands him to be Zechariah the Old Testament minor prophet; see Zec 1, 1.

23, 37–39: Cf Lk 13, 34–35. The denunciation of Pharisaic Judaism ends with this lament over *Jerusalem,* which has repeatedly rejected and murdered those whom God has *sent to* her. *How many times:* this may refer to various visits of Jesus to the city, an aspect of his ministry found in Jn but otherwise not in the synoptics. *As a hen . . . under her wings:* for imagery similar to this, see Pss 17, 8; 91, 4. *Your house . . . desolate:* probably an allusion to the destruction of the temple in A.D. 70. *You will not see me . . . in the name of the Lord:* Israel will not see Jesus again until he comes in glory for the final judgment. The acclamation has been interpreted in contrasting ways, as an indication that Israel will at last accept Jesus at that time, and as its troubled recognition of him as its dreaded judge who will pronounce its condemnation; in support of the latter view see 24, 30.

24, 1—25, 46: The discourse of the fifth book, the last of the five around which the gospel is structured. It is called the "eschatological" discourse since it deals with the coming of the new age (the *eschaton*) in its fullness, with events that will precede it, and with how the disciples are to conduct themselves while awaiting an event that is as certain as its exact time is unknown to all but the Father (24, 36). The discourse may be divided into two parts, 24, 1–44 and 24, 45—25, 46. In the first, Matthew follows his Marcan source (13, 1–37) closely. The second is drawn from Q and from the evangelist's own traditional material. Both parts show Matthew's editing of his sources by deletions, additions, and modifications. The vigilant waiting that is emphasized in the second part does not mean a cessation of ordinary activity and concentration only on what is to come, but a faithful accomplishment of duties at hand, with awareness that the end, for which the disciples must always be ready, will entail the great judgment by which the everlasting destiny of all will be determined.

24, 2: As in Mk, Jesus predicts the destruction of the temple. By omitting the Marcan story of the widow's contribution (12, 41–44) that immediately precedes the prediction in that gospel, Matthew has established a close connection between it and 23, 38, ". . . your house will be abandoned desolate."

24, 3: *The Mount of Olives:* see the note on 21, 1. *The disciples:* cf Mk 13, 3–4 where only Peter, James, John, and Andrew put the question that is answered by the discourse. In both gospels, however, the question is put *privately:* the ensuing discourse is only for those who are *disciples* of Jesus. *When will this happen . . . end of the age?:* Matthew distinguishes carefully between the destruction of the temple [*this*] and the *coming* of Jesus that will bring *the end of the age.* In Mk the two events are more closely connected, a fact that may be explained by Mark's believing that the one would immediately succeed the other. *Coming:* this translates the Greek

approached him privately and said, "Tell us,
when will this happen, and what sign will there
be of your coming, and of the end of the age?"
4 *Jesus said to them in reply, "See that no one
deceives you. 5 For many will come in my
name, saying, 'I am the Messiah,' and they will
deceive many. 6 [o]*You will hear of wars and
reports of wars; see that you are not alarmed, for
these things must happen, but it will not yet be
the end. 7 [p]Nation will rise against nation, and
kingdom against kingdom; there will be famines
and earthquakes from place to place. 8 *All
these are the beginning of the labor pains.
9 [q]*Then they will hand you over to persecution, and they will kill you. You will be hated
by all nations because of my name. 10 And
then many will be led into sin; they will betray
and hate one another. 11 Many false prophets
will arise and deceive many; 12 and because of
the increase of evildoing, the love of many will
grow cold. 13 [r]But the one who perseveres to
the end will be saved. 14 [s]*And this gospel of
the kingdom will be preached throughout the
world as a witness to all nations, and then the
end will come.

## The Great Tribulation

15 [t]*"When you
see the desolating abomination spoken of
through Daniel the prophet standing in the holy
place (let the reader understand), 16 *then
those in Judea must flee to the mountains,
17 [u]* person on the housetop must not go
down to get things out of his house, 18 a person
in the field must not return to get his cloak.
19 Woe to pregnant women and nursing mothers in those days. 20 *Pray that your flight not

o Dn 2, 28 LXX.
p Is 19, 2.
q 10, 17.
r 10, 22.
s 28, 19; Rom 10, 18.
t Dn 9, 27; 11, 31; 12, 11; Mk 13, 14.
u Lk 17, 31.

* word *parousia,* which is used in the gospels only here and in vv 27, 37, and 39. It designated the official visit of a ruler to a city or the manifestation of a saving deity, and it was used by Christians to refer to the final coming of Jesus in glory, a term first found in the New Testament with that meaning in 1 Thes 2, 19. *The end of the age:* see the note on 13, 39.

24, 4–14: This section of the discourse deals with calamities in the world (6–7) and in the church (9–12). The former *must happen* before *the end* comes (6), but they are only *the beginning of the labor pains* (8). (It may be noted that the Greek word translated *the end* in v 6 and in vv 13–14 is not the same as the phrase "the end of the age" in v 3, although the meaning is the same.) The latter are sufferings of the church, both from within and without, that will last until the *gospel* is *preached . . . to all nations. Then the end will come* and those who have endured the sufferings with fidelity *will be saved* (13–14).

24, 6–7: The disturbances mentioned here are a commonplace of apocalyptic language, as is the assurance that they *must happen* (see Dn 2, 28 LXX), for that is the plan of God. *Kingdom against kingdom:* see Is 19, 2.

24, 8: *The labor pains:* the tribulations leading up to the end of the age are compared to the pains of a woman about to give birth. There is much attestation for rabbinic use of the phrase "the woes (or birth pains) of the Messiah" after the New Testament period, but in at least one instance it is attributed to a rabbi who lived in the late first century A.D. In this Jewish usage it meant the distress of the time preceding the coming of the Messiah; here, the *labor pains* precede the coming of the Son of Man in glory.

24, 9–12: Matthew has used Mk 13, 9–12 in his missionary discourse (10, 17–21) and omits it here. Besides the sufferings, including death, and the hatred of *all nations* that the disciples will have to endure, there will be worse affliction within the church itself. This is described in vv 10–12, which are peculiar to Mt. *Will be led into sin:* literally, "will be scandalized," probably meaning that they will become apostates; see 13, 21 where "fall away" translates the same Greek word as here. *Betray:* in the Greek this is the same word as the *hand over* of v 9. The handing over to persecution and hatred from outside will have their counterpart within the church. *False prophets:* these are Christians; see the note on 7, 15–20. *Evildoing:* see 7, 23. Because of the apocalyptic nature of much of this discourse, the literal meaning of this description of the church should not be pressed too hard. However, there is reason to think that Mt's addition of these verses reflects in some measure the condition of his community.

24, 14: Except for the last part (*and then the end will come*), this verse substantially repeats Mk 13, 10. The Matthean addition raises a problem since what follows in vv 15–23 refers to the horrors of the First Jewish Revolt including the destruction of the temple, and Matthew, writing after that time, knew that the parousia of Jesus was still in the future. A solution may be that the evangelist saw the events of those verses as foreshadowing the cosmic disturbances that he associates with the parousia (29) so that the period in which the former took place could be understood as belonging to *the end.*

24, 15–28: Cf Mk 13, 14–23; Lk 17, 23–24.37. A further stage in the tribulations that will precede the coming of the Son of Man, and an answer to the question of v 3a, "when will this (the destruction of the temple) happen?"

24, 15: *The desolating abomination:* in 167 B.C. the Syrian king Antiochus IV Epiphanes desecrated the temple by setting up in it a statue of Zeus Olympios (see 1 Mc 1, 54). That event is referred to in Dn 12, 11 LXX as the "desolating abomination" (NAB "horrible abomination") and the same Greek term is used here; cf also Dn 9, 27; 11, 31. Although the desecration had taken place before Dn was written, it is presented there as a future event, and Matthew sees that "prophecy" fulfilled in the desecration of the temple by the Romans. *In the holy place:* the temple; more precise than Mk's *where he should not* (13, 14). *Let the reader understand:* this parenthetical remark, taken from Mk 13, 14, invites *the reader* to realize the meaning of Dn's "prophecy."

24, 16: The tradition that the Christians of Jerusalem fled from that city to Pella, a city of Transjordan, at the time of the First Jewish Revolt is found in Eusebius (*Ecclesiastical History,* 3, 5, 3), who attributes the flight to "a certain oracle given by revelation before the war." The tradition is not improbable but the Matthean command, derived from its Marcan source, is vague in respect to the place of flight (*to the mountains*), although some scholars see it as applicable to the flight to Pella.

24, 17–19: Haste is essential, and the journey will be particularly difficult for women who are burdened with unborn or infant children.

24, 20: *On the sabbath:* this addition to *in winter* (cf Mk 13, 18) has been understood as an indication that Mt was addressed to a church still observing the Mosaic law of sabbath rest and the scribal limitations upon the length of journeys that might lawfully be made on that day. That interpretation conflicts with Mt's view on sabbath observance (cf 12, 1–14). The meaning of the addition may be that those undertaking on the sabbath a journey such as the one here ordered would be offending the sensibilities of law-observant Jews and would incur their hostility.

be in winter or on the sabbath, **21** [v]*for at that
time there will be great tribulation, such as has
not been since the beginning of the world until
now, nor ever will be. **22** And if those days had
not been shortened, no one would be saved; but
for the sake of the elect they will be shortened.
**23** [w]If anyone says to you then, 'Look, here is
the Messiah!' or, 'There he is!' do not believe
it. **24** False messiahs and false prophets will
arise, and they will perform signs and wonders
so great as to deceive, if that were possible,
even the elect. **25** Behold, I have told it to you
beforehand. **26** *So if they say to you, 'He is
in the desert,' do not go out there; if they say,
'He is in the inner rooms,' do not believe it.
**27** [x]For just as lightning comes from the east
and is seen as far as the west, so will the coming
of the Son of Man be. **28** Wherever the corpse
is, there the vultures will gather.

## The Coming of the Son of Man

**29** [y]*"Immediately after the tribulation of
those days,

the sun will be darkened,
    and the moon will not give its light,
and the stars will fall from the sky,
    and the powers of the heavens will be shaken.

**30** [z]*And then the sign of the Son of Man will
appear in heaven, and all the tribes of the earth
will mourn, and they will see the Son of Man
coming upon the clouds of heaven with power
and great glory. **31** [a]*And he will send out his
angels with a trumpet blast, and they will gather
his elect from the four winds, from one end of
the heavens to the other.

## The Lesson of the Fig Tree

**32** *"Learn
a lesson from the fig tree. When its branch
becomes tender and sprouts leaves, you know
that summer is near. **33** In the same way, when
you see all these things, know that he is near,
at the gates. **34** *Amen, I say to you, this generation will not pass away until all these things
have taken place. **35** [b]Heaven and earth will
pass away, but my words will not pass away.

## The Unknown Day and Hour

**36** [c]*"But
of that day and hour no one knows, neither the
angels of heaven, nor the Son, but the Father
alone. **37** [d]*For as it was in the days of Noah,
so it will be at the coming of the Son of Man.
**38** In [those] days before the flood, they were
eating and drinking, marrying and giving in
marriage, up to the day that Noah entered the
ark. **39** They did not know until the flood came
and carried them all away. So will it be [also]
at the coming of the Son of Man. **40** [e]*Two
men will be out in the field; one will be taken,
and one will be left. **41** Two women will be
grinding at the mill; one will be taken, and one
will be left. **42** [f]*Therefore, stay awake! For
you do not know on which day your Lord will
come. **43** [g]Be sure of this: if the master of the
house had known the hour of night when the

v Dn 12, 1.
w Lk 17, 23.
x Lk 17, 24.37.
y Is 13, 10.13; Ez 32, 7; Am 8, 9.
z Dn 7, 13; Zec 12, 12-14; Rv 1, 7.
a Is 27, 13; 1 Cor 15, 52; 1 Thes 4, 16.
b Is 40, 8.
c Acts 1, 7.
d Gn 6, 5—7, 23; Lk 17, 26-27; 2 Pt 3, 6.
e Lk 17, 34-35.
f 25, 13; Lk 12, 39-40.
g 1 Thes 5, 2.

*

24, 21: For the unparalleled distress of that time, see Dn 12, 1.

24, 26–28: Claims that the Messiah is to be found in some distant or secret place must be ignored. *The coming of the Son of Man* will be as clear as *lightning* is to all and as *the corpse* of an animal is to *vultures;* cf Lk 17, 24.37. Here there is clear identification of *the Son of Man* and the Messiah; cf v 23.

24, 29: The answer to the question of v 3b, "What will be the sign of your coming?" *Immediately after . . . those days:* the shortening of time between the preceding *tribulation* and the parousia has been explained as Matthew's use of a supposed device of Old Testament prophecy whereby certainty that a predicted event will occur is expressed by depicting it as imminent. While it is questionable that that is an acceptable understanding of the Old Testament predictions, it may be applicable here, for Matthew knew that the parousia had not come *immediately after* the fall of Jerusalem, and it is unlikely that he is attributing a mistaken calculation of time to Jesus. *The sun . . . be shaken:* cf Is 13, 10.13.

24, 30: *The sign of the Son of Man:* perhaps this means *the sign* that is the glorious appearance *of the Son of Man;* cf 12, 39–40 where "the sign of Jonah" is Jonah's being in the "belly of the whale." *Tribes of the earth will mourn:* peculiar to Mt; cf Zec 12, 12–14. *Coming upon the clouds . . . glory:* cf Dn 7, 13, although there the "one like a son of man" comes to God to receive kingship; here *the Son of Man* comes from heaven for judgment.

24, 31: *Send out his angels:* cf 13, 41 where they are sent out to collect the wicked for punishment. *Trumpet blast:* cf Is 27, 13; 1 Thes 4, 16.

24, 32–35: Cf Mk 13, 28–31.

24, 34: The difficulty raised by this verse cannot be satisfactorily removed by the supposition that *this generation* means the Jewish people throughout the course of their history, much less the entire human race. Perhaps for Matthew it means the *generation* to which he and his community belonged.

24, 36–44: The statement of v 34 is now counterbalanced by one that declares that the exact time of the parousia is known only to *the Father* (36), and the disciples are warned to be always ready for it. This section is drawn from Mk and Q (cf Lk 17, 26–27.34–35; 12, 39–40).

24, 36: Many textual witnesses omit *nor the Son,* which follows Mk 13, 32. Since its omission can be explained by reluctance to attribute this ignorance to *the Son,* the reading that includes it is probably original.

24, 37–39: Cf Lk 17, 26–27. *In the days of Noah:* the Old Testament account of the flood lays no emphasis upon what is central for Matthew, i.e., the unexpected coming of the flood upon those who were unprepared for it.

24, 40–41: Cf Lk 17, 34–35. *Taken . . . left:* the former probably means *taken* into the kingdom; the latter, *left* for destruction. People in the same situation will be dealt with in opposite ways. In this context, the discrimination between them will be based on their readiness for the coming of the Son of Man.

24, 42–44: Cf Lk 12, 39–40. The theme of vigilance and readiness is continued with the bold comparison of the Son of Man to a thief who comes to break into a house.

thief was coming, he would have stayed awake
and not let his house be broken into. **44** So too,
you also must be prepared, for at an hour you
do not expect, the Son of Man will come.

### The Faithful or the Unfaithful Servant

**45** [h]*"Who, then, is the faithful and prudent
servant, whom the master has put in charge of
his household to distribute to them their food at
the proper time? **46** Blessed is that servant
whom his master on his arrival finds doing so.
**47** Amen, I say to you, he will put him in
charge of all his property. **48** *But if that wicked servant says to himself, 'My master is long
delayed,' **49** and begins to beat his fellow servants, and eat and drink with drunkards, **50** the
servant's master will come on an unexpected
day and at an unknown hour **51** [i]*and will punish him severely and assign him a place with the
hypocrites, where there will be wailing and
grinding of teeth.

## CHAPTER 25

### The Parable of the Ten Virgins

**1** *"Then the kingdom of heaven will be like
ten virgins who took their lamps and went out
to meet the bridegroom. **2** *Five of them were
foolish and five were wise. **3** The foolish ones,
when taking their lamps, brought no oil with
them, **4** but the wise brought flasks of oil with
their lamps. **5** Since the bridegroom was long
delayed, they all became drowsy and fell
asleep. **6** At midnight, there was a cry, 'Behold, the bridegroom! Come out to meet him!'
**7** Then all those virgins got up and trimmed
their lamps. **8** The foolish ones said to the wise,
'Give us some of your oil, for our lamps are
going out.' **9** But the wise ones replied, 'No,
for there may not be enough for us and you. Go
instead to the merchants and buy some for yourselves.' **10** While they went off to buy it, the
bridegroom came and those who were ready
went into the wedding feast with him. Then the
door was locked. **11** [j]*Afterwards the other virgins came and said, 'Lord, Lord, open the door
for us!' **12** But he said in reply, 'Amen, I say
to you, I do not know you.' **13** [k]*Therefore,
stay awake, for you know neither the day nor the
hour.

### The Parable of the Talents

**14** [l]*"It will
be as when a man who was going on a journey
called in his servants and entrusted his possessions to them. **15** *To one he gave five talents;
to another, two; to a third, one—to each according to his ability. Then he went away. Immediately **16** the one who received five talents went
and traded with them, and made another five.
**17** Likewise, the one who received two made
another two. **18** *But the man who received one
went off and dug a hole in the ground and buried
his master's money. **19** After a long time the
master of those servants came back and settled
accounts with them. **20** *The one who had received five talents came forward bringing the
additional five. He said, 'Master, you gave me
five talents. See, I have made five more.'
**21** [m]His master said to him, 'Well done, my
good and faithful servant. Since you were faithful in small matters, I will give you great responsibilities. Come, share your master's joy.'
**22** [Then] the one who had received two talents
also came forward and said, 'Master, you gave
me two talents. See, I have made two more.'
**23** His master said to him, 'Well done, my
good and faithful servant. Since you were faithful in small matters, I will give you great responsibilities. Come, share your master's joy.'

---

h Lk 12, 41-46.
i 13, 42; 25, 30.
j 7, 21.23; Lk 13, 25.27.
k 24, 42; Mk 13, 33.
l Lk 19, 12-27.
m Lk 16, 10.

---

*

24, 45–51: The second part of the discourse (see the note on 24, 1—25, 46) begins with this parable of *the faithful* or unfaithful *servant;* cf Lk 12, 41–46. It is addressed to the leaders of Matthew's church; *the servant has* been *put in charge* of his master's *household* (45) even though that *household* is composed of those who are his *fellow servants* (49).

24, 45: *To distribute . . . proper time:* readiness for the master's return means a vigilance that is accompanied by faithful performance of the duty assigned.

24, 48: *My master . . . delayed:* the note of delay is found also in the other parables of this section; cf 25, 5.19.

24, 51: *Punish him severely:* the Greek verb, found in the New Testament only here and in the Lucan parallel (12, 46), means, literally, "cut in two." *With the hypocrites:* see the note on 6, 2. Matthew classes the unfaithful Christian leader with the unbelieving leaders of Judaism. *Wailing and grinding of teeth:* see the note on 8, 11–12.

25, 1–13: Peculiar to Mt.

25, 1: *Then:* at the time of the parousia. *Kingdom . . . will be like:* see the note on 13, 24–30.

25, 2–4: *Foolish . . . wise:* cf the contrasted "wise man" and "fool" of 7, 24.26, where the two are distinguished by good deeds and lack of them, and such deeds may be signified by the *oil* of this parable.

25, 11–12: *Lord, Lord:* cf 7, 21. *I do not know you:* cf 7, 23, where the Greek verb is different but synonymous.

25, 13: *Stay awake:* some scholars see this command as an addition to the original parable of Matthew's traditional material, since in v 5 all the virgins, wise and foolish, fall asleep. But the wise virgins are adequately equipped for their task, and *stay awake* may mean no more than to be prepared; cf 24, 42.44.

25, 14–30: Cf Lk 19, 12–27.

25, 14: *It will be as when . . . journey:* literally, "For just as a man who was going on a journey." Although the comparison is not completed, the sense is clear; the kingdom of heaven is like the situation here described. Faithful use of one's gifts will lead to participation in the fullness of the kingdom, lazy inactivity to exclusion from it.

25, 15: *Talents:* see the note on 18, 24.

25, 18: *Buried his master's money:* see the note on 13, 44.

25, 20–23: Although the first two servants have received and doubled large sums, their faithful trading is regarded by the master as fidelity *in small matters* only, compared with the *great responsibilities* now to be given to them. The latter are unspecified. *Share your master's joy:* probably the joy of the banquet of the kingdom; cf 8, 11.

**24** Then the one who had received the one talent came forward and said, 'Master, I knew you
were a demanding person, harvesting where you
did not plant and gathering where you did not
scatter; **25** so out of fear I went off and buried
your talent in the ground. Here it is back.'
**26** *His master said to him in reply, 'You wicked, lazy servant! So you knew that I harvest
where I did not plant and gather where I did not
scatter? **27** Should you not then have put my
money in the bank so that I could have got it
back with interest on my return? **28** Now then!
Take the talent from him and give it to the one
with ten. **29** [n]*For to everyone who has, more
will be given and he will grow rich; but from the
one who has not, even what he has will be taken
away. **30** *And throw this useless servant into
the darkness outside, where there will be wailing and grinding of teeth.'

## The Judgment of the Nations

**31** [o]*"When the Son of Man comes in his glory, and all the angels with him, he will sit upon
his glorious throne, **32** [p]*and all the nations
will be assembled before him. And he will separate them one from another, as a shepherd separates the sheep from the goats. **33** He will place
the sheep on his right and the goats on his left.
**34** Then the king will say to those on his right,
'Come, you who are blessed by my Father.
Inherit the kingdom prepared for you from the
foundation of the world. **35** [q]For I was hungry
and you gave me food, I was thirsty and you
gave me drink, a stranger and you welcomed
me, **36** naked and you clothed me, ill and you
cared for me, in prison and you visited me.'
**37** *Then the righteous will answer him and
say, 'Lord, when did we see you hungry and
feed you, or thirsty and give you drink?
**38** When did we see you a stranger and welcome you, or naked and clothe you? **39** When
did we see you ill or in prison, and visit you?'
**40** [r]And the king will say to them in reply,
'Amen, I say to you, whatever you did for one
of these least brothers of mine, you did for me.'
**41** [s]*Then he will say to those on his left, 'Depart from me, you accursed, into the eternal fire
prepared for the devil and his angels. **42** [t]For
I was hungry and you gave me no food, I was
thirsty and you gave me no drink, **43** a stranger
and you gave me no welcome, naked and you
gave me no clothing, ill and in prison, and you
did not care for me.' **44** *Then they will answer
and say, 'Lord, when did we see you hungry or
thirsty or a stranger or naked or ill or in prison,
and not minister to your needs?' **45** He will
answer them, 'Amen, I say to you, what you did
not do for one of these least ones, you did not
do for me.' **46** [u]And these will go off to eternal
punishment, but the righteous to eternal life."

# *VII: THE PASSION AND RESURRECTION*

## CHAPTER 26

### The Conspiracy against Jesus

**1** *When Jesus finished all these words, he said

n 13, 12; Mk 4, 25; Lk 8, 18; 19, 26.
o 16, 27; Dt 33, 2 LXX.
p Ez 34, 17.
q Is 58, 7; Ez 18, 7.
r 10, 40.42.
s 7, 23; Lk 13, 27.
t Jb 22, 7; Jas 2, 15-16.
u Dn 12, 2.

*

25, 26–28: *Wicked, lazy servant:* this man's inactivity is not negligible but seriously culpable. As punishment, he loses the gift he had received, that is now given to the first servant, whose possessions are already great.

25, 29: See the note on 13, 12 where there is a similar application of this maxim.

25, 30: See the note on 8, 11–12.

25, 31–46: The conclusion of the discourse, which is peculiar to Mt, portrays the final judgment that will accompany the parousia. Although often called a "parable," it is not really such, for the only parabolic elements are the depiction of *the Son of Man* as *a shepherd* and of *the righteous* and the wicked as *sheep* and *goats* respectively (32–33). The criterion of judgment will be the deeds of mercy that have been done for the *least* of Jesus' *brothers* (40). A difficult and important question is the identification of these *least brothers.* Are they all people who have suffered hunger, thirst, etc. (35.36) or a particular group of such sufferers? Scholars are divided in their response and arguments can be made for either side. But leaving aside the problem of what the traditional material that Matthew edited may have meant, it seems that a stronger case can be made for the view that in the evangelist's sense the sufferers are Christians, probably Christian missionaries whose sufferings were brought upon them by their preaching of the gospel. The criterion of judgment for *all the nations* is their treatment of those who have borne to the world the message of Jesus, and this means ultimately their acceptance or rejection of Jesus himself; cf 10, 40, "Whoever receives you, receives me."

25, 31: See the note on 16, 27.

25, 32: *All the nations:* before the end the gospel will have been preached throughout the world (24, 14); thus the Gentiles will be judged on their response to it. But the phrase *all the nations* includes the Jews also, for at the judgment "the Son of Man . . . will repay everyone according to his conduct" (16, 27).

25, 37–40: *The righteous* will be astonished that in caring for the needs of the sufferers they were ministering to the *Lord* himself. *One of these least brothers of mine:* cf 10, 42.

25, 41: *Fire prepared . . . his angels:* cf 1 Enoch 10, 13 where it is said of the evil angels and Semyaza, their leader, "In those days they will lead them into the bottom of the fire—and in torment—in the prison (where) they will be locked up forever."

25, 44–45: The *accursed* (41) will be likewise astonished that their neglect of the sufferers was neglect of the *Lord* and will receive from him a similar answer.

26, 1—28, 20: The five books with alternating narrative and discourse (3, 1—25, 46) that give this gospel its distinctive structure lead up to the climactic events that are the center of Christian belief and the origin of the Christian church, the passion and resurrection of Jesus. In his passion narrative (chs 26–27) Matthew follows his Marcan source closely but with omissions (e.g., Mk 14, 51–52) and additions (e.g., 27, 3–10.19). Some of the additions indicate that he utilized traditions that he had received from elsewhere; others are due to his own theological insight (e.g., 26, 28, ". . . for the forgiveness of sins"; 27, 52). In his editing Matthew also altered Mk

to his disciples, 2 [v]"You know that in two
days' time it will be Passover, and the Son of
Man will be handed over to be crucified."
3 *Then the chief priests and the elders of the
people assembled in the palace of the high
priest, who was called Caiaphas, 4 [w]and they
consulted together to arrest Jesus by treachery
and put him to death. 5 *But they said, "Not
during the festival, that there may not be a riot
among the people."

**The Anointing at Bethany** 6 [x]*Now
when Jesus was in Bethany in the house of
Simon the leper, 7 a woman came up to him
with an alabaster jar of costly perfumed oil, and
poured it on his head while he was reclining at
table. 8 When the disciples saw this, they were
indignant and said, "Why this waste? 9 It could
have been sold for much, and the money given
to the poor." 10 Since Jesus knew this, he said
to them, "Why do you make trouble for the
woman? She has done a good thing for me.
11 [y]The poor you will always have with you;
but you will not always have me. 12 *In pouring this perfumed oil upon my body, she did it
to prepare me for burial. 13 Amen, I say to you,
wherever this gospel is proclaimed in the whole
world, what she has done will be spoken of, in
memory of her."

**The Betrayal by Judas** 14 [z]*Then one of
the Twelve, who was called Judas Iscariot, went
to the chief priests 15 [a]*and said, "What are
you willing to give me if I hand him over to
you?" They paid him thirty pieces of silver,
16 and from that time on he looked for an opportunity to hand him over.

**Preparations for the Passover**
17 [bc]*On the first day of the Feast of Unleavened Bread, the disciples approached Jesus and
said, "Where do you want us to prepare for you
to eat the Passover?" 18 *He said, "Go into
the city to a certain man and tell him, 'The
teacher says, "My appointed time draws near;
in your house I shall celebrate the Passover with
my disciples."'" 19 The disciples then did as
Jesus had ordered, and prepared the Passover.

**The Betrayer** 20 When it was evening, he
reclined at table with the Twelve. 21 *And
while they were eating, he said, "Amen, I say
to you, one of you will betray me." 22 Deeply
distressed at this, they began to say to him one
after another, "Surely it is not I, Lord?" 23 He
said in reply, "He who has dipped his hand into
the dish with me is the one who will betray me.
24 [d]*The Son of Man indeed goes, as it is
written of him, but woe to that man by whom
the Son of Man is betrayed. It would be better
for that man if he had never been born."
25 *Then Judas, his betrayer, said in reply,
"Surely it is not I, Rabbi?" He answered,
"You have said so."

**The Lord's Supper** 26 [ef]*While they
were eating, Jesus took bread, said the blessing,

v Mk 14, 1-2; Lk 22, 1-2.
w Jn 11, 47-53.
x Mk 14, 3-9; Jn 12, 1-8.
y Dt 15, 11.
z Mk 14, 10-11; Lk 22, 3-6.
a Zec 11, 12.
b Mk 14, 12-21; Lk 22, 7-23.
c Ex 12, 14-20.
d Is 53, 8-10.
e Mk 14, 22-26; Lk 22, 14-23; 1 Cor 11, 23-25.
f 1 Cor 10, 16.

* in some minor details. But there is no need to suppose that he knew any passion narrative other than Mark's.

26, 1–2: *When Jesus finished all these words:* see the note on 7, 28–29. *"You know . . . crucified":* Matthew turns Mk's statement of the time (14, 1) into Jesus' final prediction of his passion. *Passover:* see the note on Mk 14, 1.

26, 3: *Caiaphas* was high priest from A.D. 18 to 36.

26, 5: *Not during the festival:* the plan to delay Jesus' arrest and execution until after *the festival* was not carried out, for according to the synoptics he was arrested on the night of Nisan 14 and put to death the following day. No reason is given why the plan was changed.

26, 6–13: See the notes on Mk 14, 3–9 and Jn 12, 1–8.

26, 12: *To prepare me for burial:* cf Mk 14, 8. In accordance with the interpretation of this act as Jesus' *burial* anointing, Matthew, more consistent than Mark, changes the purpose of the visit of the women to Jesus' tomb; they do not go to anoint him (Mk 16, 1) but "to see the tomb" (28, 1).

26, 14: *Iscariot:* see the note on Lk 6, 16.

26, 15: The motive of avarice is introduced by Judas's question about the price for betrayal, which is absent in the Marcan source (14, 10–11). *Hand him over:* the same Greek verb is used to express the saving purpose of God by which Jesus is handed over to death (cf 17, 22; 20, 18; 26, 2) and the human malice that hands him over. *Thirty pieces of silver:* the price of the betrayal is found only in Mt. It is derived from Zec 11, 12 where it is the wages paid to the rejected shepherd, a cheap price (Zec 11, 13). That amount is also the compensation paid to one whose slave has been gored by an ox (Ex 21, 32).

26, 17: *The first day of the Feast of Unleavened Bread:* see the note on Mk 14, 1. Matthew omits Mk's "when they sacrificed the Passover lamb."

26, 18: By omitting much of Mk 14, 13–15, adding *My appointed time draws near,* and turning the question into a statement, *in your house I shall celebrate the Passover,* Matthew has given this passage a solemnity and majesty greater than that of his source.

26, 21: Given Matthew's interest in the fulfillment of the Old Testament, it is curious that he omits the Marcan designation of Jesus' betrayer as "one who is eating with me" (14, 18), since that is probably an allusion to Ps 41, 10. However, the shocking fact that the betrayer is one who shares table fellowship with Jesus is emphasized in v 23.

26, 24: *It would be better . . . born:* the enormity of the deed is such that it would be better not to exist than to do it.

26, 25: Peculiar to Mt. *You have said so:* cf 26, 64; 27, 11. This is a half-affirmative. Emphasis is laid on the pronoun and the answer implies that the statement would not have been made if the question had not been asked.

26, 26–29: See the note on Mk 14, 22–24. The Marcan-Matthean is one of the two major New Testament traditions of the words of Jesus when instituting the Eucharist. The other (and earlier) is the Pauline-Lucan (1 Cor 11, 23–25; Lk 22, 19–20). Each shows the influence of Christian liturgical usage, but the Marcan-Matthean is more developed in that regard than the Pauline-Lucan. The words over the bread and cup succeed each other without the intervening meal mentioned in

broke it, and giving it to his disciples said,
"Take and eat; this is my body." 27 *Then he
took a cup, gave thanks, and gave it to them,
saying, "Drink from it, all of you, 28 [g]for this
is my blood of the covenant, which will be shed
on behalf of many for the forgiveness of sins.
29 *I tell you, from now on I shall not drink this
fruit of the vine until the day when I drink it with
you new in the kingdom of my Father."
30 *Then, after singing a hymn, they went out
to the Mount of Olives.

### Peter's Denial Foretold

31 [h i]*Then
Jesus said to them, "This night all of you will
have your faith in me shaken, for it is written:

> 'I will strike the shepherd,
> and the sheep of the flock will be
> dispersed';

32 but after I have been raised up, I shall go
before you to Galilee." 33 Peter said to him in
reply, "Though all may have their faith in you
shaken, mine will never be." 34 [j k]*Jesus said
to him, "Amen, I say to you, this very night
before the cock crows, you will deny me three
times." 35 Peter said to him, "Even though I
should have to die with you, I will not deny
you." And all the disciples spoke likewise.

### The Agony in the Garden

36 [l m]*Then
Jesus came with them to a place called Gethsemane, and he said to his disciples, "Sit here
while I go over there and pray." 37 [n]*He took
along Peter and the two sons of Zebedee, and
began to feel sorrow and distress. 38 [o]*Then he
said to them, "My soul is sorrowful even to
death. Remain here and keep watch with me."
39 [p]*He advanced a little and fell prostrate in
prayer, saying, "My Father, if it is possible, let
this cup pass from me; yet, not as I will, but as
you will." 40 When he returned to his disciples
he found them asleep. He said to Peter, "So you
could not keep watch with me for one hour?
41 *Watch and pray that you may not undergo
the test. The spirit is willing, but the flesh is
weak." 42 [q]*Withdrawing a second time, he
prayed again, "My Father, if it is not possible
that this cup pass without my drinking it, your
will be done!" 43 Then he returned once more

g Ex 24, 8; Is 53, 12.
h Mk 14, 7-31.
i Zec 13, 7; Jn 16, 32.
j Lk 22, 33-34; Jn 13, 37-38.
k 26, 69-75.
l Mk 14, 32-42; Lk 22, 39-46.
m Jn 18, 1.
n Heb 5, 7.
o Ps 42, 6.12; Jon 4, 9.
p Jn 4, 34; 6, 38; Phil 2, 8.
q 6, 10; Heb 10, 9.

*

1 Cor 11, 25; Lk 22, 20; and there is parallelism between the consecratory words (*this is my body . . . this is my blood*). Matthew follows Mk closely but with some changes.

26, 26: See the note on 14, 19. *Said the blessing:* a prayer blessing God. *Take and eat:* literally, *Take, eat. Eat* is an addition to Mk's "take it" (literally, "take"; 14, 22). *This is my body:* the bread is identified with Jesus himself.

26, 27–28: *Gave thanks:* see the note on 15, 36. *Gave it to them . . . all of you:* cf Mk 14, 23–24. In the Marcan sequence the disciples drink and then Jesus says the interpretative words. Matthew has changed this into a command to *drink* followed by those words. *My blood:* see Lv 17, 11 for the concept that the *blood* is "the seat of life" and that when placed on the altar it "makes atonement." *Which will be shed:* the present participle, "being shed" or "going to be shed," is future in relation to the Last Supper. *On behalf of:* Greek *peri;* see the note on Mk 14, 24. *Many:* see the note on 20, 28. *For the forgiveness of sins:* a Matthean addition. The same phrase occurs in Mk 1, 4 in connection with John's baptism but Matthew avoids it there (3, 11). He places it here probably because he wishes to emphasize that it is the sacrificial death of Jesus that brings *forgiveness of sins.*

26, 29: Although his death will interrupt the table fellowship he has had with the disciples, Jesus confidently predicts his vindication by God and a new table fellowship with them at the banquet of the kingdom.

26, 30: See the note on Mk 14, 26.

26, 31: *Will have . . . shaken:* literally, "will be scandalized in me"; see the note on 24, 9–12. *I will strike . . . dispersed:* cf Zec 13, 7.

26, 34: *Before the cock crows:* see the note on 14, 25. The third watch of the night was called "cockcrow." *Deny me:* see the note on 16, 24.

26, 36–56: Cf Mk 14, 32–52. The account of Jesus in Gethsemane is divided between that of his agony (36–46) and that of his betrayal and arrest (47–56). Jesus' *sorrow and distress* (37) in face of death is unrelieved by the presence of his three disciples who, though urged to *watch with* him (38.41), fall asleep (40.43). He prays that *if . . . possible* his death may be avoided (39) but that his Father's will be done (39.42.44). Knowing then that his death must take place, he announces to his companions that *the hour* for his being *handed over* has come (45). Judas arrives with an armed band provided by the Sanhedrin and greets Jesus with a kiss, the prearranged sign for his identification (47–49). After his arrest, he rebukes a disciple who has attacked the *high priest's servant* with a *sword* (51–54), and chides those who have come out to seize him with *swords and clubs* as if he were a *robber* (55–56). In both rebukes Jesus declares that the treatment he is now receiving is the fulfillment of the scriptures (55.56). The subsequent flight of *all the disciples* is itself the fulfillment of his own prediction (cf 31). In this episode, Matthew follows Mk with a few alterations.

26, 36: *Gethsemane:* the Hebrew name means "oil press" and designates an olive orchard on the western slope of the Mount of Olives; see the note on 21, 1. The name appears only in Mt and Mk. The place is called a "garden" in Jn 18, 1.

26, 37: *Peter and the two sons of Zebedee:* cf 17, 1.

26, 38: Cf Ps 42, 6.12. In the Septuagint (Ps 41, 5.12) the same Greek word for *sorrowful* is used as here. *To death:* i.e., "enough to die"; cf Jon 4, 9.

26, 39: *My Father:* see the note on Mk 14, 36. Matthew omits the Aramaic *'abba'* and adds the qualifier *my. This cup:* see the note on Mk 10, 38–40.

26, 41: *Undergo the test:* see the note on 6, 13. In that verse "the final test" translates the same Greek word as is here translated *the test,* and these are the only instances of the use of that word in Mt. It is possible that the passion of Jesus is seen here as an anticipation of the great tribulation that will precede the parousia (see the notes on 24, 8; 24, 21) to which 6, 13 refers, and that just as Jesus prays to be delivered from death (39), so he exhorts the disciples to pray that they will not have to *undergo the* great *test* that his passion would be for them. Some scholars, however, understand *not undergo* (literally, "not enter") *the test* as meaning not that the disciples may be spared *the test* but that they may not yield to the temptation of falling away from Jesus because of his passion even though they will have to endure it.

26, 42: *Your will be done:* cf 6, 10.

and found them asleep, for they could not keep
their eyes open. **44** He left them and withdrew
again and prayed a third time, saying the same
thing again. **45** [r]Then he returned to his disciples and said to them, "Are you still sleeping
and taking your rest? Behold, the hour is at hand
when the Son of Man is to be handed over to
sinners. **46** Get up, let us go. Look, my betrayer is at hand."

## The Betrayal and Arrest of Jesus

**47** [s]While he was still speaking, Judas, one of
the Twelve, arrived, accompanied by a large
crowd, with swords and clubs, who had come
from the chief priests and the elders of the people. **48** His betrayer had arranged a sign with
them, saying, "The man I shall kiss is the one;
arrest him." **49** *Immediately he went over to
Jesus and said, "Hail, Rabbi!" and he kissed
him. **50** Jesus answered him, "Friend, do what
you have come for." Then stepping forward
they laid hands on Jesus and arrested him.
**51** And behold, one of those who accompanied
Jesus put his hand to his sword, drew it, and
struck the high priest's servant, cutting off his
ear. **52** Then Jesus said to him, "Put your
sword back into its sheath, for all who take the
sword will perish by the sword. **53** Do you
think that I cannot call upon my Father and he
will not provide me at this moment with more
than twelve legions of angels? **54** But then how
would the scriptures be fulfilled which say that
it must come to pass in this way?" **55** *At that
hour Jesus said to the crowds, "Have you come
out as against a robber, with swords and clubs
to seize me? Day after day I sat teaching in the
temple area, yet you did not arrest me. **56** [t]But
all this has come to pass that the writings of the
prophets may be fulfilled." Then all the disciples left him and fled.

## Jesus before the Sanhedrin

**57** [u]*Those
who had arrested Jesus led him away to Caiaphas the high priest, where the scribes and the
elders were assembled. **58** Peter was following
him at a distance as far as the high priest's
courtyard, and going inside he sat down with the
servants to see the outcome. **59** *The chief
priests and the entire Sanhedrin kept trying to
obtain false testimony against Jesus in order to
put him to death, **60** [v]*but they found none,
though many false witnesses came forward. Finally two came forward **61** who stated, "This
man said, 'I can destroy the temple of God and
within three days rebuild it.' " **62** The high
priest rose and addressed him, "Have you no
answer? What are these men testifying against
you?" **63** [w]*But Jesus was silent. Then the
high priest said to him, "I order you to tell us
under oath before the living God whether you
are the Messiah, the Son of God." **64** [x]*Jesus
said to him in reply, "You have said so. But I
tell you:

From now on you will see 'the Son of Man
seated at the right hand of the Power'
and 'coming on the clouds of heaven.' "

**65** *Then the high priest tore his robes and said,

r Jn 12, 23; 13, 1; 17, 1.
s Mk 14, 43-50; Lk 22, 47-53; Jn 18, 3-11.
t 26, 31.
u Mk 14, 53-65; Lk 22, 54-55.63-71; Jn 18, 12-14.19-24.
v Dt 19, 15; Jn 2, 19; Acts 6, 14.
w Is 53, 7.
x Ps 110, 1; Dn 7, 13.

*

26, 49: *Rabbi:* see the note on 23, 6–7. Jesus is so addressed twice in Mt (cf 25), both times by Judas. For the significance of the closely related address "teacher" in Mt, see the note on 8, 19.

26, 55: *Day after day . . . arrest me:* cf Mk 14, 49. This suggests that Jesus had taught for a relatively long period in Jerusalem, whereas 21, 1–11 puts his coming to the city for the first time only a few days before.

26, 57–68: Following Mk 14, 53–65, Matthew presents the nighttime appearance of Jesus before *the Sanhedrin* as a real trial. After *many false witnesses* bring charges against him that do not suffice for the death sentence (60), *two came forward* who charge him with claiming to be able to *destroy the temple . . . and within three days* to *rebuild it* (60–61). Jesus makes no answer even when challenged to do so by *the high priest,* who then orders him to declare *under oath . . . whether* he is *the Messiah, the Son of God* (62–63). Matthew changes Mk's clear affirmative response (14, 62) to the same one as that given to Judas (cf 25), but follows Mk almost verbatim in Jesus' predicting that his judges will see him (*the Son of Man*) *seated at the right hand of* God *and coming on the clouds of heaven* (64). *The high priest* then charges him with blasphemy (65), a charge with which the other members of *the Sanhedrin* agree by declaring that *he deserves to die* (66). They then attack him (67) and mockingly demand that he *prophesy* (68). This account contains elements that are contrary to the judicial procedures prescribed in the Mishnah, the Jewish code of law that dates in written form from ca. A.D. 200, e.g., trial on a feast day, a night session of the court, pronouncement of a verdict of condemnation at the same session at which testimony was received. Consequently, some scholars regard the account entirely as a creation of the early Christians without historical value. However, it is disputable whether the norms found in the Mishnah were in force at the time of Jesus. More to the point is the question whether the Matthean-Marcan night trial derives from a combination of two separate incidents, a nighttime preliminary investigation (cf Jn 18, 13.19–24) and a formal trial on the following morning (cf Lk 22, 66–71).

26, 57: *Caiaphas:* see the note on 26, 3.

26, 59: *Sanhedrin:* see the note on Lk 22, 66.

26, 60–61: *Two:* cf Dt 19, 15. *I can destroy . . . rebuild it:* there are significant differences from the Marcan parallel (14, 58). Matthew omits "made with hands" and "not made with hands" and changes Mk's "will destroy" and "will build another" to *can destroy* and (can) *rebuild.* The charge is probably based on Jesus' prediction of the temple's destruction; see the notes on 23, 37–39; 24, 2; and Jn 2, 19. A similar prediction by Jeremiah was considered as deserving death; cf Jer 7, 1–15; 26, 1–8.

26, 63: *Silent:* possibly an allusion to Is 53, 7. *I order you . . . living God:* peculiar to Mt; cf Mk 14, 61.

26, 64: *You have said so:* see the note on 26, 25. *From now on . . . heaven:* the Son of Man who is to be crucified (cf 20, 19) will be seen in glorious majesty (cf Ps 110, 1) and *coming on the clouds of heaven* (cf Dn 7, 13). *The Power:* see the note on Mk 14, 61–62.

26, 65: *Blasphemed:* the punishment for *blasphemy* was death by stoning (see Lv 24, 10–16). According to the Mish-

"He has blasphemed! What further need have
we of witnesses? You have now heard the blasphemy; **66** what is your opinion?" They said in
reply, "He deserves to die!" **67** [y]*Then they
spat in his face and struck him, while some
slapped him, **68** saying, "Prophesy for us,
Messiah: who is it that struck you?"

**Peter's Denial of Jesus** **69** [z]Now Peter
was sitting outside in the courtyard. One of the
maids came over to him and said, "You too
were with Jesus the Galilean." **70** *But he denied it in front of everyone, saying, "I do not
know what you are talking about!" **71** As he
went out to the gate, another girl saw him and
said to those who were there, "This man was
with Jesus the Nazorean." **72** Again he denied
it with an oath, "I do not know the man!"
**73** *A little later the bystanders came over and
said to Peter, "Surely you too are one of them;
even your speech gives you away." **74** At that
he began to curse and to swear, "I do not know
the man." And immediately a cock crowed.
**75** [a]Then Peter remembered the word that
Jesus had spoken: "Before the cock crows you
will deny me three times." He went out and
began to weep bitterly.

## CHAPTER 27

**Jesus before Pilate** **1** [b]*When it was
morning, all the chief priests and the elders of
the people took counsel against Jesus to put him
to death. **2** They bound him, led him away, and
handed him over to Pilate, the governor.

**The Death of Judas** **3** [c d]*Then Judas, his
betrayer, seeing that Jesus had been condemned, deeply regretted what he had done. He
returned the thirty pieces of silver to the chief
priests and elders, **4** saying, "I have sinned in
betraying innocent blood." They said, "What
is that to us? Look to it yourself." **5** *Flinging
the money into the temple, he departed and went
off and hanged himself. **6** The chief priests
gathered up the money, but said, "It is not
lawful to deposit this in the temple treasury, for
it is the price of blood." **7** After consultation,
they used it to buy the potter's field as a burial
place for foreigners. **8** That is why that field
even today is called the Field of Blood.
**9** *Then was fulfilled what had been said
through Jeremiah the prophet, "And they took
the thirty pieces of silver, the value of a man
with a price on his head, a price set by some of
the Israelites, **10** [e]and they paid it out for the
potter's field just as the Lord had commanded
me."

**Jesus Questioned by Pilate** **11** [f]*Now
Jesus stood before the governor, and he ques-

---

y Wis 2, 19; Is 50, 6.
z Mk 14, 66-72; Lk 22, 56-62; Jn 18, 17-18.25-27.
a 26, 34.
b Mk 15, 1; Lk 23, 1; Jn 18, 28.
c Acts 1, 18-19.
d 26, 15.
e Zec 11, 12-13.
f Mk 15, 2-5; Lk 23, 2-3; Jn 18, 29-38.

---

nah, to be guilty of *blasphemy* one had to pronounce "the Name itself," i.e. Yahweh; cf *Sanhedrin* 7, 4.5. Those who judge the gospel accounts of Jesus' trial by the later Mishnah standards point out that Jesus uses the surrogate "the Power," and hence no Jewish court would have regarded him as guilty of *blasphemy;* others hold that the Mishnah's narrow understanding of *blasphemy* was a later development.

26, 67–68: The physical abuse, apparently done to Jesus by the members of the Sanhedrin themselves, recalls the sufferings of the Isaian Servant of the Lord; cf Is 50, 6. The mocking challenge to *prophesy* is probably motivated by Jesus' prediction of his future glory (64).

26, 70: *Denied it in front of everyone:* see 10, 33. Peter's repentance (75) saves him from the fearful destiny of which Jesus speaks there.

26, 73: *Your speech . . . away:* Matthew explicates Mk's "you too are a Galilean" (14, 70).

27, 1–31: Cf Mk 15, 1–20. Matthew's account of the Roman trial before *Pilate* is introduced by a consultation of the Sanhedrin after which Jesus is *handed over to . . . the governor* (1–2). Matthew follows his Marcan source closely but adds some material that is peculiar to him, the death of *Judas* (3–10), possibly the name *Jesus* as the name of *Barabbas* also (16–17), the intervention of Pilate's *wife* (19), Pilate's washing *his hands* in token of his disclaiming responsibility for Jesus' death (24), and the assuming of that responsibility by *the whole people* (25).

27, 1–2: There is scholarly disagreement about the meaning of the Sanhedrin's taking *counsel* (*symboulion elabon;* cf 12, 14; 22, 15; 27, 7; 28, 12); see the note on Mk 15, 1. Some understand it as a discussion about the strategy for putting their death sentence against *Jesus* into effect since they lacked the right to do so themselves. Others see it as the occasion for their passing that sentence, holding that Matthew, unlike Mark (14, 64), does not consider that it had been passed in the night session (26, 66). Even in the latter interpretation, their handing *him over to Pilate* is best explained on the hypothesis that they did not have competence to put their sentence into effect, as is stated in Jn 18, 31.

27, 3: *The thirty pieces of silver:* see 26, 15.

27, 5–8: For another tradition about the death of Judas, cf Acts 1, 18–19. The two traditions agree only in the purchase of a field with *the money* paid to Judas for his betrayal of Jesus and the name given to the *field, the Field of Blood.* In Acts Judas himself buys the field and its name comes from his own blood shed in his fatal accident on it. *The potter's field:* this designation of the field is based on the fulfillment citation in v 10.

27, 9–10: Cf 26, 15. Matthew's attributing this text to Jeremiah is puzzling, for there is no such text in that book, and *the thirty pieces of silver* thrown by Judas "into the temple" (5) recall rather Zec 11, 12–13. It is usually said that the attribution of the text to Jeremiah is due to Matthew's combining the Zechariah text with texts from Jeremiah that speak of a *potter* (18, 2–3), the buying of a *field* (32, 6–9), or the breaking of a potter's flask at Topheth in the valley of Ben-Hinnom with the prediction that it will become a burial place (19, 1–13).

27, 11: *King of the Jews:* this title is used of Jesus only by pagans. The Matthean instances are, besides this verse, 2, 2; 27, 29.37. Matthew equates it with "Messiah"; cf 2, 2.4 and 27, 17.22 where he has changed "the king of the Jews" of his Marcan source (15, 9.12) to "(Jesus) called Messiah." The normal political connotation of both titles would be of concern to the Roman *governor. You say so:* see the note on 26, 25. An unqualified affirmative response is not made because Jesus' kingship is not what Pilate would understand it to be.

tioned him, "Are you the king of the Jews?" Jesus said, "You say so." **12** [g]*And when he was accused by the chief priests and elders, he made no answer. **13** Then Pilate said to him, "Do you not hear how many things they are testifying against you?" **14** But he did not answer him one word, so that the governor was greatly amazed.

**The Sentence of Death** **15** [h]*Now on the occasion of the feast the governor was accustomed to release to the crowd one prisoner whom they wished. **16** *And at that time they had a notorious prisoner called [Jesus] Barabbas. **17** So when they had assembled, Pilate said to them, "Which one do you want me to release to you, [Jesus] Barabbas, or Jesus called Messiah?" **18** *For he knew that it was out of envy that they had handed him over. **19** *While he was still seated on the bench, his wife sent him a message, "Have nothing to do with that righteous man. I suffered much in a dream today because of him." **20** [i]The chief priests and the elders persuaded the crowds to ask for Barabbas but to destroy Jesus. **21** The governor said to them in reply, "Which of the two do you want me to release to you?" They answered, "Barabbas!" **22** *Pilate said to them, "Then what shall I do with Jesus called Messiah?" They all said, "Let him be crucified!" **23** But he said, "Why? What evil has he done?" They only shouted the louder, "Let him be crucified!" **24** [j]*When Pilate saw that he was not succeeding at all, but that a riot was breaking out instead, he took water and washed his hands in the sight of the crowd, saying, "I am innocent of this man's blood. Look to it yourselves." **25** And the whole people said in reply, "His blood be upon us and upon our children." **26** *Then he released Barabbas to them, but after he had Jesus scourged, he handed him over to be crucified.

**Mockery by the Soldiers** **27** [k]*Then the soldiers of the governor took Jesus inside the praetorium and gathered the whole cohort around him. **28** *They stripped off his clothes and threw a scarlet military cloak about him. **29** [l]*Weaving a crown out of thorns, they placed it on his head, and a reed in his right hand. And kneeling before him, they mocked him, saying, "Hail, King of the Jews!" **30** [m]*They spat upon him and took the reed and kept striking him on the head. **31** And when they had mocked him, they stripped him of the cloak, dressed him in his own clothes, and led him off to crucify him.

g Is 53, 7.
h Mk 15, 6-15; Lk 23, 17-25; Jn 18, 39—19, 16.
i Acts 3, 14.
j Dt 21, 1-8.
k Mk 15, 16-20; Jn 19, 2-3.
l 27, 11.
m Is 50, 6.

*

27, 12–14: Cf 26, 62–63. As in the trial before the Sanhedrin, Jesus' silence may be meant to recall Is 53, 7. *Greatly amazed:* possibly an allusion to Is 52, 14–15.

27, 15–26: The choice that Pilate offers *the crowd* between *Barabbas* and *Jesus* is said to be in accordance with a custom of releasing at the Passover feast *one prisoner* chosen by *the crowd* (15). This custom is mentioned also in Mk 15, 6 and Jn 18, 39 but not in Lk; see the note on Lk 23, 17. Outside of the gospels there is no direct attestation of it, and scholars are divided in their judgment of the historical reliability of the claim that there was such a practice.

27, 16–17: [*Jesus*] *Barabbas:* it is possible that the double name is the original reading; *Jesus* was a common Jewish name; see the note on 1, 21. This reading is found in only a few textual witnesses, although its absence in the majority can be explained as an omission of *Jesus* made for reverential reasons. That name is bracketed because of its uncertain textual attestation. The Aramaic name *Barabbas* means "son of the father"; the irony of the choice offered between him and Jesus, the true son of the Father, would be evident to those addressees of Mt who knew that.

27, 18: Cf Mk 14, 10. This is an example of the tendency, found in varying degree in all the gospels, to present Pilate in a relatively favorable light and emphasize the hostility of the Jewish authorities and eventually of the people.

27, 19: Jesus' innocence is declared by a Gentile woman. *In a dream:* in Mt's infancy narrative, dreams are the means of divine communication; cf 1, 20; 2, 12.13.19.22.

27, 22: *Let him be crucified:* incited by the chief priests and elders (20), the crowds demand that Jesus be executed by crucifixion, a peculiarly horrible form of Roman capital punishment. The Marcan parallel, "Crucify him" (15, 3), addressed to Pilate, is changed by Matthew to the passive, probably to emphasize the responsibility of the crowds.

27, 24–25: Peculiar to Mt. *Took water . . . blood:* cf Dt 21, 1–8, the handwashing prescribed in the case of a murder when the killer is unknown. The elders of the city nearest to where the corpse is found must wash their hands, declaring, "Our hands did not shed this blood." *Look to it yourselves:* cf v 4. *The whole people:* Matthew sees in those who speak these words *the* entire *people* (Greek *laos*) of Israel. *His blood . . . and upon our children:* cf Jer 26, 15. The responsibility for Jesus' death is accepted by the nation that was God's special possession (Ex 19, 5), his own *people* (Hos 2, 25), and they thereby lose that high privilege; see 21, 43 and the note on that verse. The controversy between Matthew's church and Pharisaic Judaism about which was the true people of God is reflected here. As the Second Vatican Council has pointed out, guilt for Jesus' death is not attributable to all the Jews of his time or to any Jews of later times.

27, 26: *He had Jesus scourged:* the usual preliminary to crucifixion.

27, 27: *The praetorium:* the residence of the Roman *governor.* His usual place of residence was at Caesarea Maritima on the Mediterranean coast, but he went to Jerusalem during the great feasts, when the influx of pilgrims posed the danger of a nationalistic riot. It is disputed whether *the praetorium* in Jerusalem was the old palace of Herod in the west of the city or the fortress of Antonia northwest of the temple area. *The whole cohort:* normally six hundred soldiers.

27, 28: *Scarlet military cloak:* so Mt as against the royal purple of Mk 15, 17 and Jn 19, 2.

27, 29: *Crown out of thorns:* probably of long *thorns* that stood upright so that it resembled the "radiant" *crown,* a diadem with spikes worn by Hellenistic kings. The soldiers' purpose was mockery, not torture. *A reed:* peculiar to Mt; a mock scepter.

27, 30: *Spat upon him:* cf 26, 67 where there also is a possible allusion to Is 50, 6.

**The Way of the Cross** 32 [n]*As they were going out, they met a Cyrenian named Simon; this man they pressed into service to carry his cross.

**The Crucifixion** 33 [o]And when they came to a place called Golgotha (which means Place of the Skull), 34 [p]*they gave Jesus wine to drink mixed with gall. But when he had tasted it, he refused to drink. 35 [q]*After they had crucified him, they divided his garments by casting lots; 36 then they sat down and kept watch over him there. 37 *And they placed over his head the written charge against him: This is Jesus, the King of the Jews. 38 *Two revolutionaries were crucified with him, one on his right and the other on his left. 39 [r]*Those passing by reviled him, shaking their heads 40 [s]and saying, "You who would destroy the temple and rebuild it in three days, save yourself, if you are the Son of God, [and] come down from the cross!" 41 Likewise the chief priests with the scribes and elders mocked him and said, 42 *"He saved others; he cannot save himself. So he is the king of Israel! Let him come down from the cross now, and we will believe in him. 43 [t]*He trusted in God; let him deliver him now if he wants him. For he said, 'I am the Son of God.' " 44 The revolutionaries who were crucified with him also kept abusing him in the same way.

**The Death of Jesus** 45 [u][v]*From noon onward, darkness came over the whole land until three in the afternoon. 46 [w]*And about three o'clock Jesus cried out in a loud voice, "*Eli, Eli, lema sabachthani*?" which means, "My God, my God, why have you forsaken me?" 47 *Some of the bystanders who heard it said, "This one is calling for Elijah." 48 [x]Immediately one of them ran to get a sponge; he soaked it in wine, and putting it on a reed, gave it to him to drink. 49 But the rest said, "Wait, let us see if Elijah comes to save him." 50 *But Jesus cried out again in a loud voice, and gave up his spirit. 51 [y]*And behold, the veil of the sanctuary was torn in two from top to bottom. The earth quaked, rocks were

n Mk 15, 21; Lk 23, 26.
o Mk 15, 22-32; Lk 23, 32-38; Jn 19, 17-19.23-24.
p Ps 69, 21.
q Ps 22, 19.
r Ps 22, 8.
s 4, 3.6; 26, 61.
t Ps 22, 9; Wis 2, 12-20.
u Mk 15, 33-41; Lk 23, 44-49; Jn 19, 28-30.
v Am 8, 9.
w Ps 22, 2.
x Ps 69, 21.
y Ex 26, 31-36; Ps 68, 9; 77, 19.

*

27, 32: See the note on Mk 15, 21. *Cyrenian named Simon:* Cyrenaica was a Roman province on the north coast of Africa and Cyrene was its capital city. The city had a large population of Greek-speaking Jews. *Simon* may have been living in Palestine or have come there for the Passover as a pilgrim. *Pressed into service:* see the note on 5, 41.

27, 34: *Wine . . . mixed with gall:* cf Mk 15, 23 where the drink is "wine drugged with myrrh," a narcotic. Mt's text is probably an inexact allusion to Ps 69, 22. That psalm belongs to the class called the individual lament, in which a persecuted just man prays for deliverance in the midst of great suffering and also expresses confidence that his prayer will be heard. That theme of the suffering Just One is frequently applied to the sufferings of Jesus in the passion narratives.

27, 35: The clothing of an executed criminal went to his executioner(s), but the description of that procedure in the case of Jesus, found in all the gospels, is plainly inspired by Ps 22, 19. However, that psalm verse is quoted only in Jn 19, 24.

27, 37: The offense of a person condemned to death by crucifixion was written on a tablet that was displayed on his cross. The *charge* against *Jesus* was that he had claimed to be the *King of the Jews* (cf 11), i.e., the Messiah (cf 17.22).

27, 38: *Revolutionaries:* see the note on Jn 18, 40 where the same Greek word as that found here is used for Barabbas.

27, 39–40: *Reviled him . . . heads:* cf Ps 22, 8. *You who would destroy . . . three days:* cf 26, 61. *If you are the Son of God:* the same words as those of the devil in the temptation of Jesus; cf 4, 3.6.

27, 42: *King of Israel:* in their mocking of Jesus the members of the Sanhedrin call themselves and their people not "the Jews" but *Israel.*

27, 43: Peculiar to Mt. *He trusted in God . . . wants him:* cf Ps 22, 9. *He said . . . of God:* probably an allusion to Wis 2, 12–20 where the theme of the suffering just one appears.

27, 45: Cf Amos 8, 9 where on the day of the Lord "the sun will set at midday."

27, 46: *Eli, Eli, lema sabachthani?:* Jesus cries out in the words of Ps 22, 2a, a psalm of lament that is the Old Testament passage most frequently drawn upon in this narrative. In Mk the verse is cited entirely in Aramaic, which Matthew partially retains but changes the invocation of God to the Hebrew *Eli,* possibly because that is more easily related to the statement of the following verse about Jesus' calling for Elijah.

27, 47: *Elijah:* see the note on 3, 4. This prophet, taken up into heaven (2 Kgs 2, 11), was believed to come to the help of those in distress, but the evidences of that belief are all later than the gospels.

27, 50: *Gave up his spirit:* cf the Marcan parallel (15, 37), "breathed his last." Matthew's alteration expresses both Jesus' control over his destiny and his obedient giving up of his life to God.

27, 51–53: *Veil of the sanctuary . . . bottom:* cf Mk 15, 38; Lk 23, 45. Lk puts this event immediately before the death of Jesus. There were two veils in the Mosaic tabernacle on the model of which the temple was constructed, the outer one before the entrance of the Holy Place and the inner one before the Holy of Holies (see Ex 26, 31–36). Only the high priest could pass through the latter and that only on the Day of Atonement (see Lv 16, 1–18). Probably the *torn veil* of the gospels is the inner one. The meaning of the scene may be that now, because of Jesus' death, all people have access to the presence of God, or that the temple, its holiest part standing exposed, is now profaned and will soon be destroyed. *The earth quaked . . . appeared to many:* peculiar to Mt. The earthquake, the splitting of the *rocks,* and especially the resurrection of the dead *saints* indicate the coming of the final age. In the Old Testament the coming of God is frequently portrayed with the imagery of an earthquake (see Pss 68, 9; 77, 19), and Jesus speaks of the earthquakes that will accompany the "labor pains" that signify the beginning of the dissolution of the old world (24, 7–8). For the expectation of the resurrection of the dead at the coming of the new and final age, see Dn 12, 1–3. Matthew knows that the end of the old age has not yet come (28, 20), but the new age has broken in with the death (and resurrection; cf the earthquake in 28, 2) of Jesus; see the note on 16, 28. *After his resurrection:* this qualification seems to be due to Matthew's wish to assert the primacy of Jesus' *resurrection* even though he has placed the resurrection of the dead *saints* immediately after Jesus' death.

split, **52** [z]tombs were opened, and the bodies of
many saints who had fallen asleep were raised.
**53** And coming forth from their tombs after his
resurrection, they entered the holy city and appeared to many. **54** *The centurion and the men
with him who were keeping watch over Jesus
feared greatly when they saw the earthquake
and all that was happening, and they said, "Truly, this was the Son of God!" **55** *There were
many women there, looking on from a distance,
who had followed Jesus from Galilee, ministering to him. **56** [a]Among them were Mary Magdalene and Mary the mother of James and Joseph, and the mother of the sons of Zebedee.

**The Burial of Jesus** **57** [b c]*When it was
evening, there came a rich man from Arimathea
named Joseph, who was himself a disciple of
Jesus. **58** He went to Pilate and asked for the
body of Jesus; then Pilate ordered it to be handed over. **59** Taking the body, Joseph wrapped
it [in] clean linen **60** and laid it in his new tomb
that he had hewn in the rock. Then he rolled a
huge stone across the entrance to the tomb and
departed. **61** But Mary Magdalene and the other Mary remained sitting there, facing the tomb.

**The Guard at the Tomb** **62** *The next
day, the one following the day of preparation,
the chief priests and the Pharisees gathered before Pilate **63** [d]and said, "Sir, we remember
that this impostor while still alive said, 'After
three days I will be raised up.' **64** *Give orders, then, that the grave be secured until the
third day, lest his disciples come and steal him
and say to the people, "He has been raised from
the dead." This last imposture would be worse
than the first." **65** *Pilate said to them, "The
guard is yours; go secure it as best you can."
**66** So they went and secured the tomb by fixing
a seal to the stone and setting the guard.

## CHAPTER 28

**The Resurrection of Jesus** **1** [e]*After the
sabbath, as the first day of the week was dawning, Mary Magdalene and the other Mary came
to see the tomb. **2** [f]*And behold, there was a
great earthquake; for an angel of the Lord descended from heaven, approached, rolled back

z Dn 12, 1-3.
a 13, 55.
b Mk 15, 42-47; Lk 23, 50-56; Jn 19, 38-42.
c Is 53, 9.
d 12, 40; 16, 21; 17, 23; 20, 19.
e Mk 16, 1-8; Lk 24, 1-12; Jn 20, 1-10.
f 25, 51.

*

27, 54: Cf Mk 15, 39. The Christian confession of faith is made by Gentiles, not only *the centurion,* as in Mk, but the other soldiers *who were keeping watch over Jesus* (cf 36).

27, 55–56: *Looking on from a distance:* cf Ps 38, 12. *Mary Magdalene . . . Joseph:* these two women are mentioned again in v 61 and 28, 1 and are important as witnesses of the reality of the empty tomb. A *James* and *Joseph* are referred to in 13, 55 as brothers of Jesus.

27, 57–61: Cf Mk 15, 42–47. Matthew drops Mk's designation of *Joseph* of *Arimathea* as "a distinguished member of the council" (the Sanhedrin), and makes him *a rich man* and *a disciple of Jesus.* The former may be an allusion to Is 53, 9 (the Hebrew reading of that text is disputed and the one followed in the NAB OT has nothing about the rich, but they are mentioned in the LXX version). That the tomb was the *new tomb* of *a rich man* and that it was seen by the women are indications of an apologetic intent of Matthew; there could be no question about the identity of Jesus' burial place. *The other Mary:* the mother of James and Joseph (56).

27, 62–66: Peculiar to Mt. The story prepares for 28, 11–15 and the Jewish charge that the tomb was empty because the *disciples* had stolen the body of Jesus (28, 13.15).

27, 62: *The next day . . . preparation:* the sabbath. According to the synoptic chronology, in that year *the day of preparation* (for the sabbath) was the Passover; cf Mk 15, 42. *The Pharisees:* the principal opponents of Jesus during his ministry and, in Matthew's time, of the Christian church, join with *the chief priests* to guarantee against a possible attempt of Jesus' *disciples* to steal his body.

27, 64: *This last imposture . . . the first:* the claim that Jesus *has been raised from the dead* is clearly the *last imposture; the first* may be either his claim that he would *be raised up* (63) or his claim that he was the one with whose ministry the kingdom of God had come (see 12, 28).

27, 65: *The guard is yours:* literally, "have a guard" or "you have a guard." Either the imperative or the indicative could mean that Pilate granted the petitioners some Roman soldiers as guards, which is the sense of the present translation. However, if the verb is taken as an indicative it could also mean that Pilate told them to use their own Jewish guards.

28, 1–20: Except for vv 1–8, based on Mk 16, 1–8, the material of this final chapter is peculiar to Mt. Even where he follows Mk, Matthew has altered his source so greatly that a very different impression is given from that of the Marcan account. The two points that are common to the resurrection testimony of all the gospels are that the tomb of Jesus had been found empty and that the risen Jesus had appeared to certain persons, or, in the original form of Mk, that such an appearance was promised as soon to take place (see Mk 16, 7). On this central and all-important basis, Matthew has constructed an account that interprets the resurrection as the turning of the ages (2–4), shows the Jewish opposition to Jesus as continuing *to the present* in the claim that the resurrection is a deception perpetrated by the *disciples* who stole his body from the tomb (11–15), and marks a new stage in the mission of *the disciples* once limited to Israel (10, 5–6); now they are to *make disciples of all nations.* In this work they will be strengthened by the presence of the exalted Son of Man, who will be with them *until* the kingdom comes in fullness at *the end of the age* (16–20).

28, 1: *After the sabbath . . . dawning:* since the sabbath ended at sunset, this could mean in the early evening, for *dawning* can refer to the appearance of the evening star; cf Lk 23, 54. However, it is probable that Matthew means the morning dawn of the day after the sabbath, as in the similar though slightly different text of Mk, "when the sun had risen" (16, 2). *Mary Magdalene and the other Mary:* see the notes on 27, 55–56; 57–61. *To see the tomb:* cf Mk 16, 1–2 where the purpose of the women's visit is to anoint Jesus' body.

28, 2–4: Peculiar to Mt. *A great earthquake:* see the note on 27, 51–53. *Descended from heaven:* this trait is peculiar to Mt, although his interpretation of the "young man" of his Marcan source (16, 5) as an *angel* is probably true to Mk's intention; cf Lk 24, 23 where the "two men" of 24, 4 are said to be "angels." *Rolled back the stone . . . upon it:* not to allow the risen Jesus to leave the tomb but to make evident that the tomb is empty (see 6). Unlike the apocryphal Gospel of Peter (9, 35—11, 44), the New Testament does not describe the resurrection of Jesus, nor is there anyone who sees it. *His appearance was like lightning . . . snow:* see the note on 17, 2.

the stone, and sat upon it. **3** [g]His appearance
was like lightning and his clothing was white as
snow. **4** The guards were shaken with fear of
him and became like dead men. **5** Then the
angel said to the women in reply, "Do not be
afraid! I know that you are seeking Jesus the
crucified. **6** *He is not here, for he has been
raised just as he said. Come and see the place
where he lay. **7** [h]Then go quickly and tell his
disciples, 'He has been raised from the dead,
and he is going before you to Galilee; there you
will see him.' Behold, I have told you."
**8** *Then they went away quickly from the
tomb, fearful yet overjoyed, and ran to announce this to his disciples. **9** [i]*And behold,
Jesus met them on their way and greeted them.
They approached, embraced his feet, and did
him homage. **10** Then Jesus said to them, "Do
not be afraid. Go tell my brothers to go to Galilee, and there they will see me."

**The Report of the Guard** **11** *While they
were going, some of the guard went into the city
and told the chief priests all that had happened.
**12** They assembled with the elders and took
counsel; then they gave a large sum of money
to the soldiers, **13** telling them, "You are to
say, 'His disciples came by night and stole him
while we were asleep.' **14** And if this gets to the
ears of the governor, we will satisfy [him] and
keep you out of trouble." **15** The soldiers took
the money and did as they were instructed. And
this story has circulated among the Jews to the
present [day].

## The Commissioning of the Disciples

**16** [j]*The eleven disciples went to Galilee, to
the mountain to which Jesus had ordered them.
**17** *When they saw him, they worshiped, but
they doubted. **18** [k]*Then Jesus approached and
said to them, "All power in heaven and on earth
has been given to me. **19** [l]*Go, therefore, and
make disciples of all nations, baptizing them in
the name of the Father, and of the Son, and of
the holy Spirit, **20** [m]*teaching them to observe
all that I have commanded you. And behold, I
am with you always, until the end of the age."

g 17, 2.
h 26, 32.
i Jn 20, 17.
j Mk 16, 14-16; Lk 24, 36-49; Jn 20, 19-23.
k Dn 7, 14 LXX.
l Acts 1, 8.
m 1, 23; 13, 39; 24, 3.

*

28, 6–7: Cf Mk 16, 6–7. *Just as he said:* a Matthean addition referring to Jesus' predictions of his resurrection, e.g., 16, 21; 17, 23; 20, 19. *Tell his disciples:* like the angel of the Lord of the infancy narrative, the angel interprets a fact and gives a commandment about what is to be done; cf 1, 20–21. Matthew omits Mk's "and Peter" (16, 7); considering his interest in Peter, this omission is curious. Perhaps the reason is that the Marcan text may allude to a first appearance of Jesus to Peter alone (cf 1 Cor 15, 5; Lk 24, 34) which Matthew has already incorporated into his account of Peter's confession at Caesarea Philippi; see the note on 16, 16. *He is going . . . Galilee:* like Mk 16, 7, a reference to Jesus' prediction at the Last Supper (26, 32; Mk 14, 28). Matthew changes Mk's "as he told you" to a declaration of the angel.

28, 8: Contrast Mk 16, 8 where the women in their fear "said nothing to anyone."

28, 9–10: Although these verses are peculiar to Mt, there are similarities between them and Jn's account of the appearance of Jesus to Mary Magdalene (20, 17). In both there is a touching of Jesus' body, and a command of Jesus to bear a message to his disciples, designated as his *brothers.* Matthew may have drawn upon a tradition that appears in a different form in Jn. Jesus' words to the women are mainly a repetition of those of the angel (5a; 7b).

28, 11–15: This account indicates that the dispute between Christians and Jews about the empty tomb was not whether the tomb was empty but why.

28, 16–20: This climactic scene has been called a "proleptic parousia," for it gives a foretaste of the final glorious coming of the Son of Man (26, 64). Then his triumph will be manifest to all; now it is revealed only to *the disciples,* who are commissioned to announce it to *all nations* and bring them to belief in Jesus and obedience to his commandments.

28, 16: *The eleven:* the number recalls the tragic defection of Judas Iscariot. *To the mountain . . . ordered them:* since the message to *the disciples* was simply that they were to go to Galilee (10), some think that *the mountain* comes from a tradition of the message known to Matthew and alluded to here. For the significance of *the mountain,* see the note on 17, 1.

28, 17: *But they doubted:* the Greek can also be translated, "but some doubted." The verb occurs elsewhere in the New Testament only in 14, 31 where it is associated with Peter's being of "little faith." For the meaning of that designation, see the note on 6, 30.

28, 18: *All power . . . me:* the Greek word here translated *power* is the same as that found in the LXX translation of Dn 7, 13–14 where one "like a son of man" is given *power* and an everlasting kingdom by God. The risen Jesus here claims universal power, i.e., *in heaven and on earth.*

28, 19: *Therefore:* since universal power belongs to the risen Jesus (18), he gives the eleven a mission that is universal. They are to *make disciples of all nations.* While *all nations* is understood by some scholars as referring only *to all* Gentiles, it is probable that it included the Jews as well. *Baptizing them:* baptism is the means of entrance into the community of the risen one, the Church. *In the name of the Father . . . holy Spirit:* this is perhaps the clearest expression in the New Testament of trinitarian belief. It may have been the baptismal formula of Matthew's church, but primarily it designates the effect of baptism, the union of the one baptized with the Father, Son, and holy Spirit.

28, 20: *All that I have commanded you:* the moral teaching found in this gospel, preeminently that of the Sermon on the Mount (chs 5–7). The commandments of Jesus are the standard of Christian conduct, not the Mosaic law as such, even though some of the Mosaic commandments have now been invested with the authority of Jesus. *Behold, I am with you always:* the promise of Jesus' real though invisible presence echoes the name Emmanuel given to him in the infancy narrative; see the note on 1, 23. End of the age: see the notes on 13, 39 and 24, 3.

# THE GOSPEL ACCORDING TO

# MARK

## INTRODUCTION

*This shortest of all New Testament gospels is likely the first to have been written, yet it often tells of Jesus' ministry in more detail than either Matthew or Luke (for example, the miracle stories at 5, 1–20 or 9, 14–29). It recounts what Jesus did in a vivid style, where one incident follows directly upon another. In this almost breathless narrative, Mark stresses Jesus' message about the kingdom of God now breaking into human life as good news (1, 14–15) and Jesus himself as the gospel of God (1, 1; 8, 35; 10, 29). Jesus is the Son whom God has sent to rescue humanity by serving and by sacrificing his life (10, 45).*

*The opening verse about good news in Mark (1, 1) serves as a title for the entire book. The action begins with the appearance of John the Baptist, a messenger of God attested by scripture. But John points to a mightier one, Jesus, at whose baptism God speaks from heaven, declaring Jesus his Son. The Spirit descends upon Jesus, who eventually, it is promised, will baptize "with the holy Spirit." This presentation of who Jesus really is (1, 1–13) is rounded out with a brief reference to the temptation of Jesus and how Satan's attack fails. Jesus as Son of God will be victorious, a point to be remembered as one reads of Jesus' death and the enigmatic ending to Mark's Gospel.*

*The key verses at 1, 14–15, which are programmatic, summarize what Jesus proclaims as gospel: fulfillment, the nearness of the kingdom, and therefore the need for repentance and for faith. After the call of the first four disciples, all fishermen (1, 16–20), we see Jesus engaged in teaching (1, 21.22.27), preaching (1, 38.39), and healing (1, 29–31.34.40–45), and exorcising demons (1, 22–27.34.39). The content of Jesus' teaching is only rarely stated, and then chiefly in parables (ch 4) about the kingdom. His cures, especially on the sabbath (3, 1–5); his claim, like God, to forgive sins (2, 3–12); his table fellowship with tax collectors and sinners (2, 14–17); and the statement that his followers need not now fast but should rejoice while Jesus is present (2, 18–22), all stir up opposition that will lead to Jesus' death (3, 6).*

*In Mark, Jesus is portrayed as immensely popular with the people in Galilee during his ministry (2, 2; 3, 7; 4, 1). He appoints twelve disciples to help preach and drive out demons, just as he does (3, 13–19). He continues to work many miracles; the blocks 4, 35—6, 44 and 6, 45—7, 10 are cycles of stories about healings, miracles at the Sea of Galilee, and marvelous feedings of the crowds. Jesus' teaching in ch 7 exalts the word of God over "the tradition of the elders" and sees defilement as a matter of the heart, not of unclean foods. Yet opposition mounts. Scribes charge that Jesus is possessed by Beelzebul (3, 22). His relatives think him "out of his mind" (3, 21). Jesus' kinship is with those who do the will of God, in a new eschatological family, not even with mother, brothers, or sisters by blood ties (3, 31–35; cf 6, 1–6). But all too often his own disciples do not understand Jesus (4, 13.40; 6, 52; 8, 17–21). The fate of John the Baptist (6, 17–29) hints ominously at Jesus' own passion (9, 13; cf 8, 31).*

*A breakthrough seemingly comes with Peter's confession that Jesus is the Christ (Messiah; 8, 27–30). But Jesus himself emphasizes his passion (8, 31; 9, 31; 10, 33–34), not glory in the kingdom (10, 35–45). Momentarily he is glimpsed in his true identity when he is transfigured before three of the disciples (9, 2–8), but by and large Jesus is depicted in Mark as moving obediently along the way to his cross in Jerusalem. Occasionally there are miracles (9, 17–27; 10, 46–52; 11, 12–14.20–21, the only such account in Jerusalem), sometimes teachings (10, 2–11.23–31), but the greatest concern is with discipleship (8, 34—9, 1; 9, 33–50). For the disciples do not grasp the mystery being revealed (9, 32; 10, 32.38). One of them will betray him, Judas (14, 10–11.43–45); one will deny him, Peter (14, 27.31.54.66–72); all eleven men will desert Jesus (14, 27.50).*

*The passion account, with its condemnation of Jesus by the Sanhedrin (14, 53.55–65; 15, 1a) and sentencing by Pilate (15, 1b-15), is prefaced with the entry into Jerusalem (11, 1–11), ministry and controversies there (11, 15—12, 44), Jesus' Last Supper with the disciples (14, 1–26), and his arrest at Gethsemane (14, 32–52). A chapter of apocalyptic tone about the destruction of the temple (13, 1–2.14–23) and the coming of the Son of Man (13, 24–27), a discourse filled with promises (13, 11.31) and admonitions to be watchful (13, 2.23.37), is significant for Mark's Gospel, for it helps one see that God, in Jesus, will be victorious after the cross and at the end of history.*

*The Gospel of Mark ends in the most ancient manuscripts with an abrupt scene at Jesus' tomb, which the women find empty (16, 1–8). His own prophecy of 14, 28 is reiterated, that Jesus goes before the disciples into Galilee; "there you will see him." These words may imply resurrection appearances there, or Jesus' parousia there, or the start of Christian mission, or a return to the roots depicted in 1, 9.14–15 in Galilee. Other hands have attached additional endings after 16, 8; see the note on 16, 9–20.*

*The framework of Mark's Gospel is partly geographical: Galilee (1, 14—9, 49), through the area "across the Jordan" (10, 1) and through Jericho (10, 46–52), to Jerusalem (11, 1—16, 8). Only rarely does Jesus go into Gentile territory (5, 1–20; 7, 24–37), but those who acknowledge him there and the centurion who confesses Jesus at the cross (15, 39) presage the gospel's expansion into the world beyond Palestine.*

*Mark's Gospel is even more oriented to christology. Jesus is the Son of God (1, 11; 9, 7; 15, 39; cf 1, 1; 14, 61). He is the Messiah, the anointed king of Davidic descent (12, 35; 15, 32), the Greek for which, Christos, has, by the time Mark wrote, become in effect a proper name (1, 1; 9, 41). Jesus is also seen as Son of Man, a term used in Mark not simply as a substitute for "I" or for humanity in general (cf 2, 10.27–28; 14, 21) or with reference to a mighty figure who is to come (13, 26; 14, 62), but also in connection with Jesus' predestined, necessary path of suffering and vindication (8, 31; 10, 45).*

*The unfolding of Mark's story about Jesus is sometimes viewed by interpreters as centered around the term "mystery." The word is employed just once, at 4, 11, in the singular, and its content there is the kingdom, the open secret that God's reign is now breaking into human life with its reversal of human values. There is a related sense in which Jesus' real identity remained a secret during his lifetime, according to Mark, although demons and demoniacs knew it (1, 24; 3, 11; 5, 7); Jesus warned against telling of his mighty deeds and revealing his identity (1, 44; 3, 12; 5, 43; 7, 36; 8, 26.30), an injunction sometimes broken (1, 45; cf 5, 19–20). Further, Jesus teaches by parables, according to Mark, in such a way that those "outside" the kingdom do not understand, but only those to whom the mystery has been granted by God.*

*Mark thus shares with Paul, as well as with other parts of the New Testament, an emphasis on election (13, 20.22) and upon the gospel as Christ and his cross (cf 1 Cor 1, 23). Yet in Mark the person of Jesus is also depicted with an unaffected naturalness. He reacts to events with authentic human emotion: pity (1, 44), anger (3, 5), triumph (4, 40), sympathy (5, 36; 6, 34), surprise (6, 9), admiration (7, 29; 10, 21), sadness (14, 33–34), and indignation (14, 48–49).*

*Although the book is anonymous, apart from the ancient heading "According to Mark" in manuscripts, it has traditionally been assigned to John Mark, in whose mother's house (at Jerusalem) Christians assembled (Acts 12, 12). This Mark was a cousin of Barnabas (Col 4, 10) and accompanied Barnabas and Paul on a missionary journey (Acts 12, 25; 13, 3; 15, 36–39). He appears in Pauline letters (Phlm 24; 2 Tm 4, 11) and with Peter (1 Pt 5, 13). Papias (ca. A.D. 135) described Mark as Peter's "interpreter," a view found in other patristic writers. Petrine influence should not, however, be exaggerated. The evangelist has put together various oral and possibly written sources—miracle stories, parables, sayings, stories of controversies, and the passion—so as to speak of the crucified Messiah for Mark's own day.*

*Traditionally, the gospel is said to have been written shortly before A.D. 70 in Rome, at a time of impending persecution and when destruction loomed over Je-*

*rusalem. Its audience seems to have been Gentile, unfamiliar with Jewish customs (hence 7, 3–4.11). The book aimed to equip such Christians to stand faithful in the face of persecution (13, 9–13), while going on with the proclamation of the gospel begun in Galilee (13, 10; 14, 9). Modern research often proposes as the author an unknown Hellenistic Jewish Christian, possibly in Syria, and perhaps shortly after the year 70.*

*The principal divisions of the Gospel according to Mark are the following:*
*I. The Preparation for the Public Ministry of Jesus (1, 1–13)*
*II. The Mystery of Jesus (1, 14—8, 26)*
*III. The Mystery Begins to Be Revealed (8, 27—9, 32)*
*IV. The Full Revelation of the Mystery (9, 33—16, 8)*
*The Longer Ending (16, 9–20)*
*The Shorter Ending*
*The Freer Logion (in the note on 16, 9–20)*

# I: THE PREPARATION FOR THE PUBLIC MINISTRY OF JESUS

## CHAPTER 1

**1** *The beginning of the gospel of Jesus
Christ [the Son of God].

### The Preaching of John the Baptist

**2** [a][b]*As it is written in Isaiah the prophet:

"Behold, I am sending my messenger ahead
of you;
he will prepare your way.
**3** [c]A voice of one crying out in the desert:
'Prepare the way of the Lord,
make straight his paths.' "

**4** John [the] Baptist appeared in the desert proclaiming a baptism of repentance for the forgiveness of sins. **5** People of the whole Judean
countryside and all the inhabitants of Jerusalem
were going out to him and were being baptized
by him in the Jordan River as they acknowledged their sins. **6** *John was clothed in camel's hair, with a leather belt around his waist. He
fed on locusts and wild honey. **7** And this is
what he proclaimed: "One mightier than I is
coming after me. I am not worthy to stoop and
loosen the thongs of his sandals. **8** [d]*I have
baptized you with water; he will baptize you
with the holy Spirit."

### The Baptism of Jesus

**9** [e]It happened in
those days that Jesus came from Nazareth of
Galilee and was baptized in the Jordan by John.
**10** *On coming up out of the water he saw the
heavens being torn open and the Spirit, like a
dove, descending upon him. **11** [f]And a voice
came from the heavens, "You are my beloved
Son; with you I am well pleased."

### The Temptation of Jesus

**12** [g]*At once
the Spirit drove him out into the desert, **13** and
he remained in the desert for forty days, tempted

a Mt 3, 1-11; Lk 3, 2-16.
b Mal 3, 1.
c Is 40, 3; Jn 1, 23.
d Jn 1, 27; Acts 1, 5; 11, 16.
e Mt 3, 13-17; Lk 3, 21-23; Jn 1, 32-33.
f Ps 2, 7.
g Mt 4, 1-11; Lk 4, 1-13.

*

1, 1–13: The prologue of the Gospel according to Mark begins with the title (1) followed by three events preparatory to Jesus' preaching: (1) the appearance in the Judean wilderness of John, baptizer, preacher of repentance, and precursor of Jesus (2–8); (2) the baptism of Jesus, at which a voice from heaven acknowledges Jesus to be God's Son, and the holy Spirit descends on him (9–11); (3) the temptation of Jesus by Satan (12–13).

1, 1: *The gospel of Jesus Christ [the Son of God]:* the "good news" of salvation in and through Jesus, crucified and risen, acknowledged by the Christian community as Messiah (8, 29; 14, 61–62) and Son of God (11; 9, 7; 15, 39), although some important manuscripts here omit *the Son of God.*

1, 2–3: Although Mark attributes the prophecy to Isaiah, the text is a combination of Mal 3, 1; Is 40, 3; and Ex 23, 20; cf Mt 11, 10; Lk 7, 27. John's ministry is seen as God's prelude to the saving mission of his Son. *The way of the Lord:* this prophecy of Deutero-Isaiah concerning the end of the Babylonian exile is here applied to the coming of Jesus; John the Baptist is to prepare the way for him.

1, 6: *Clothed in camel's hair . . . waist:* the Baptist's garb recalls that of Elijah in 2 Kgs 1, 8. Jesus speaks of the Baptist as Elijah who has already come (9, 11–13; Mt 17, 10–12; cf Mal 3, 23–24; Lk 1, 17).

1, 8–9: Through the life-giving baptism with the holy Spirit (8), Jesus will create a new people of God. But first he identifies himself with the people of Israel in submitting to John's baptism of repentance and in bearing on their behalf the burden of God's decisive judgment (9; cf 4). As in the desert of Sinai, so here in the wilderness of Judea, Israel's sonship with God is to be renewed.

1, 10–11: *He saw the heavens . . . and the Spirit . . . upon him:* indicating divine intervention in fulfillment of promise. Here the descent of the Spirit on Jesus is meant, anointing him for his ministry; cf Is 11, 2; 42, 1; 61, 1; 63, 9. *A voice . . . with you I am well pleased:* God's acknowledgment of Jesus as his unique Son, the object of his love. His approval of Jesus is the assurance that Jesus will fulfill his messianic mission of salvation.

1, 12–13: The same Spirit who descended on Jesus in his baptism now drives him into the desert for forty days. The result is radical confrontation and temptation by Satan who attempts to frustrate the work of God. The presence of wild beasts may indicate the horror and danger of the desert regarded as the abode of demons or may reflect the paradise motif of harmony among all creatures; cf Is 11, 6–9. The

by Satan. He was among wild beasts, and the
angels ministered to him.

## II: THE MYSTERY OF JESUS

### The Beginning of the Galilean Ministry

14 [h]*After John had been arrested, Jesus came
to Galilee proclaiming the gospel of God:
15 [i]"This is the time of fulfillment. The kingdom of God is at hand. Repent, and believe in
the gospel."

**The Call of the First Disciples** 16 [j]*As
he passed by the Sea of Galilee, he saw Simon
and his brother Andrew casting their nets into
the sea; they were fishermen. 17 Jesus said to
them, "Come after me, and I will make you
fishers of men." 18 Then they left their nets
and followed him. 19 He walked along a little
farther and saw James, the son of Zebedee, and
his brother John. They too were in a boat mending their nets. 20 Then he called them. So they
left their father Zebedee in the boat along with
the hired men and followed him.

**The Cure of a Demoniac** 21 [k]*Then they
came to Capernaum, and on the sabbath he entered the synagogue and taught. 22 [l]The people
were astonished at his teaching, for he taught
them as one having authority and not as the
scribes. 23 *In their synagogue was a man with
an unclean spirit; 24 *he cried out, "What have
you to do with us, Jesus of Nazareth? Have you
come to destroy us? I know who you are—the
Holy One of God!" 25 Jesus rebuked him and
said, "Quiet! Come out of him!" 26 The unclean spirit convulsed him and with a loud cry
came out of him. 27 All were amazed and
asked one another, "What is this? A new teaching with authority. He commands even the unclean spirits and they obey him." 28 His fame
spread everywhere throughout the whole region
of Galilee.

### The Cure of Simon's Mother-in-Law

29 [m]On leaving the synagogue he entered the
house of Simon and Andrew with James and
John. 30 Simon's mother-in-law lay sick with
a fever. They immediately told him about her.
31 He approached, grasped her hand, and
helped her up. Then the fever left her and she
waited on them.

**Other Healings** 32 When it was evening,
after sunset, they brought to him all who were
ill or possessed by demons. 33 The whole town
was gathered at the door. 34 He cured many
who were sick with various diseases, and he
drove out many demons, not permitting them to
speak because they knew him.

**Jesus Leaves Capernaum** 35 [n]Rising
very early before dawn, he left and went off to
a deserted place, where he prayed. 36 Simon
and those who were with him pursued him
37 and on finding him said, "Everyone is looking for you." 38 He told them, "Let us go on
to the nearby villages that I may preach there
also. For this purpose have I come." 39 So he
went into their synagogues, preaching and driving out demons throughout the whole of Galilee.

**The Cleansing of a Leper** 40 [o]*A leper
came to him [and kneeling down] begged him
and said, "If you wish, you can make me

h Mt 4, 12-17; Lk 4, 14-15.
i Mt 3, 2.
j Mt 4, 18-22; Lk 5, 2-11.
k Lk 4, 31-37.
l Mt 7, 28-29.
m Mt 8, 14-16; Lk 4, 38-41.
n Lk 4, 42-44.
o Mt 8, 2-4; Lk 5, 12-14.

* presence of ministering angels to sustain Jesus recalls the angel who guided the Israelites in the desert in the first Exodus (14, 19; 23, 20) and the angel who supplied nourishment to Elijah in the wilderness (1 Kgs 19, 5–7). The combined forces of good and evil were present to Jesus in the desert. His sustained obedience brings forth the new Israel of God there where Israel's rebellion had brought death and alienation.

1, 14–15: *After John had been arrested:* in the plan of God, Jesus was not to proclaim the good news of salvation prior to the termination of the Baptist's active mission. *Galilee:* in the Marcan account, scene of the major part of Jesus' public ministry before his arrest and condemnation. *The gospel of God:* not only the good news from God but about God at work in Jesus Christ. *This is the time of fulfillment:* i.e., of God's promises. *The kingdom of God . . . repent:* see the note on Mt 3, 2.

1, 16–20: These verses narrate the call of the first disciples. See the notes on Mt 4, 18–22 and 4, 20.

1, 21–45: The account of a single day's ministry of Jesus on a sabbath in and outside the synagogue of Capernaum (21–31) combines teaching and miracles of exorcism and healing. Mention is not made of the content of the teaching but of the effect of astonishment and alarm on the people. Jesus' teaching with authority, making an absolute claim on the hearer, was in the best tradition of the ancient prophets, not of the scribes. The narrative continues with events that evening (32–34; see the notes on Mt 8, 14–17) and the next day (35–39). The cleansing in vv 40–45 stands as an isolated story.

1, 23: *An unclean spirit:* so called because of the spirit's resistance to the holiness of God. The spirit knows and fears the power of Jesus to destroy his influence; cf 32.34; 3, 11; 6, 13.

1, 24: *What have you to do with us?:* see the note on Jn 2, 4.

1, 24–25: *The Holy One of God:* not a confession but an attempt to ward off Jesus' power, reflecting the notion that use of the precise name of an opposing spirit would guarantee mastery over him. Jesus silenced the cry of the unclean spirit and drove him out of the man.

1, 40: *A leper:* for the various forms of skin disease, see Lv 13, 1–50 and the note on Lv 13, 2–4. There are only two instances in the Old Testament in which God is shown to have cured a leper (Nm 12, 10–15 and 2 Kgs 5, 1–14). The law of Moses provided for the ritual purification of a leper. In curing the leper, Jesus assumes that the priests will reinstate the cured man into the religious community. See also the note on Lk 5, 14.

clean." 41 [p]Moved with pity, he stretched out
his hand, touched him, and said to him, "I do
will it. Be made clean." 42 [q]The leprosy left
him immediately, and he was made clean.
43 Then, warning him sternly, he dismissed
him at once. 44 [r]Then he said to him, "See that
you tell no one anything, but go, show yourself
to the priest and offer for your cleansing what
Moses prescribed; that will be proof for them."
45 The man went away and began to publicize
the whole matter. He spread the report abroad
so that it was impossible for Jesus to enter a
town openly. He remained outside in deserted
places, and people kept coming to him from
everywhere.

## CHAPTER 2

### The Healing of a Paralytic
1 [s]*When
Jesus returned to Capernaum after some days, it
became known that he was at home. 2 Many
gathered together so that there was no longer
room for them, not even around the door, and
he preached the word to them. 3 They came
bringing to him a paralytic carried by four men.
4 Unable to get near Jesus because of the
crowd, they opened up the roof above him.
After they had broken through, they let down
the mat on which the paralytic was lying.
5 *When Jesus saw their faith, he said to the
paralytic, "Child, your sins are forgiven."
6 *Now some of the scribes were sitting there
asking themselves, 7 [t]*"Why does this man
speak that way? He is blaspheming. Who but
God alone can forgive sins?" 8 Jesus immediately knew in his mind what they were thinking
to themselves, so he said, "Why are you thinking such things in your hearts? 9 Which is easier, to say to the paralytic, 'Your sins are forgiv-
en,' or to say, 'Rise, pick up your mat and
walk'? 10 *But that you may know that the Son
of Man has authority to forgive sins on earth"—
11 he said to the paralytic, "I say to you, rise,
pick up your mat, and go home." 12 He rose,
picked up his mat at once, and went away in the
sight of everyone. They were all astounded and
glorified God, saying, "We have never seen
anything like this."

### The Call of Levi
13 [u]*Once again he went
out along the sea. All the crowd came to him
and he taught them. 14 [v]*As he passed by, he
saw Levi, son of Alphaeus, sitting at the customs post. He said to him, "Follow me." And
he got up and followed him. 15 *While he was
at table in his house, many tax collectors and
sinners sat with Jesus and his disciples; for there
were many who followed him. 16 *Some
scribes who were Pharisees saw that he was
eating with sinners and tax collectors and said
to his disciples, "Why does he eat with tax
collectors and sinners?" 17 *Jesus heard this
and said to them [that], "Those who are well do
not need a physician, but the sick do. I did not
come to call the righteous but sinners."

### The Question about Fasting
18 [w]*The
disciples of John and of the Pharisees were accustomed to fast. People came to him and objected, "Why do the disciples of John and the
disciples of the Pharisees fast, but your disciples
do not fast?" 19 *Jesus answered them, "Can

p 5, 30.
q Lk 17, 14.
r Lv 14, 2-32.
s Mt 9, 2-8; Lk 5, 18-26.
t Is 43, 25.
u 4, 1.
v Mt 9, 9-13; Lk 5, 27-32.
w Mt 9, 14-17; Lk 5, 33-39.

*

2, 1—3, 6: This section relates a series of conflicts between Jesus and the scribes and Pharisees in which the growing opposition of the latter leads to their plot to put Jesus to death (3, 6).

2, 1–2: *He was at home:* to the crowds that gathered in and outside the house Jesus *preached the word,* i.e., the gospel concerning the nearness of the kingdom and the necessity of repentance and faith (1, 14).

2, 5: It was the faith of the paralytic and those who carried him that moved Jesus to heal the sick man. Accounts of other miracles of Jesus reveal more and more his emphasis on faith as the requisite for exercising his healing powers (5, 34; 9, 23–24; 10, 52).

2, 6: *Scribes:* trained in oral interpretation of the written law; in Mark's gospel, adversaries of Jesus, with one exception (12, 28.34).

2, 7: *He is blaspheming:* an accusation made here and repeated during the trial of Jesus (14, 60–64).

2, 10: *But that you may know that the Son of Man . . . on earth:* although vv 8–9 are addressed to the scribes, the sudden interruption of thought and structure in v 10 seems not addressed to them nor to the paralytic. Moreover, the early public use of the designation "Son of Man" to unbelieving scribes is most unlikely. The most probable explanation is that Mark's insertion of v 10 is a commentary addressed to Christians for whom he recalls this miracle and who already accept in faith that Jesus is Messiah and Son of God.

2, 13: *He taught them:* see the note on 1, 21–45.

2, 14: *As he passed by:* see the note on 1, 16–20. *Levi, son of Alphaeus:* see the note on Mt 9, 9. *Customs post:* such tax collectors paid a fixed sum for the right to collect customs duties within their districts. Since whatever they could collect above this amount constituted their profit, the abuse of extortion was widespread among them. Hence, Jewish customs officials were regarded as sinners (16), outcasts of society, and disgraced along with their families. *He got up and followed him:* i.e., became a disciple of Jesus.

2, 15: *In his house:* cf v 1; Mt 9, 10. Lk 5, 29 clearly calls it Levi's house.

2, 16–17: This and the following conflict stories reflect a similar pattern: a statement of fact, a question of protest, and a reply by Jesus.

2, 17: *Do not need a physician:* this maxim of Jesus with its implied irony was uttered to silence his adversaries who objected that he ate with *tax collectors and sinners* (16). Because the scribes and Pharisees were self-righteous, they were not capable of responding to Jesus' call to repentance and faith in the gospel.

2, 18–22: This conflict over the question of fasting has the same pattern as vv 16–17; see the notes on Mt 9, 15 and 9, 16–17.

2, 19: *Can the wedding guests fast?:* the bridal metaphor expresses a new relationship of love between God and his people in the person and mission of Jesus to his disciples. It

the wedding guests fast while the bridegroom is
with them? As long as they have the bridegroom
with them they cannot fast. **20** But the days will
come when the bridegroom is taken away from
them, and then they will fast on that day. **21** No
one sews a piece of unshrunken cloth on an old
cloak. If he does, its fullness pulls away, the
new from the old, and the tear gets worse.
**22** Likewise, no one pours new wine into old
wineskins. Otherwise, the wine will burst the
skins, and both the wine and the skins are ruined. Rather, new wine is poured into fresh
wineskins."

**The Disciples and the Sabbath** **23** [x]*As
he was passing through a field of grain on the
sabbath, his disciples began to make a path
while picking the heads of grain. **24** [y]At this the
Pharisees said to him, "Look, why are they
doing what is unlawful on the sabbath?"
**25** *He said to them, "Have you never read
what David did when he was in need and he and
his companions were hungry? **26** [z]How he
went into the house of God when Abiathar was
high priest and ate the bread of offering that only
the priests could lawfully eat, and shared it with
his companions?" **27** [a]*Then he said to them,
"The sabbath was made for man, not man for
the sabbath. **28** *That is why the Son of Man
is lord even of the sabbath."

## CHAPTER 3

**A Man with a Withered Hand** **1** [b]*Again
he entered the synagogue. There was a man
there who had a withered hand. **2** They watched
him closely to see if he would cure him on the
sabbath so that they might accuse him. **3** He
said to the man with the withered hand, "Come
up here before us." **4** Then he said to them, "Is
it lawful to do good on the sabbath rather than
to do evil, to save life rather than to destroy it?"
But they remained silent. **5** [c]Looking around at
them with anger and grieved at their hardness of
heart, he said to the man, "Stretch out your
hand." He stretched it out and his hand was
restored. **6** *The Pharisees went out and immediately took counsel with the Herodians against
him to put him to death.

**The Mercy of Jesus** **7** [d]*Jesus withdrew
toward the sea with his disciples. A large number of people [followed] from Galilee and from
Judea. **8** Hearing what he was doing, a large
number of people came to him also from Jerusalem, from Idumea, from beyond the Jordan, and
from the neighborhood of Tyre and Sidon. **9** He
told his disciples to have a boat ready for him
because of the crowd, so that they would not
crush him. **10** [e]He had cured many and, as a
result, those who had diseases were pressing
upon him to touch him. **11** [f]*And whenever
unclean spirits saw him they would fall down
before him and shout, "You are the Son of
God." **12** He warned them sternly not to make
him known.

**The Mission of the Twelve** **13** [g]*He went
up the mountain and summoned those whom he
wanted and they came to him. **14** [h]*He ap-

x Mt 12, 1-8; Lk 6, 1-5.
y Dt 23, 25.
z 1 Sm 21, 2-7 / Lv 24, 5-9.
a 2 Mc 5, 19.
b Mt 12, 9-14; Lk 6, 6-11.
c Lk 14, 4.
d Mt 4, 23-25; 12, 15; Lk 6, 17-19.
e 5, 30.
f 1, 34; Lk 4, 41.
g Mt 10, 1-4; Lk 6, 12-16.
h 6, 7.

* is the inauguration of the new and joyful messianic time of fulfillment and the passing of the old. Any attempt at assimilating the Pharisaic practice of fasting, or of extending the preparatory discipline of John's disciples beyond the arrival of the bridegroom, would be as futile as sewing *a piece of unshrunken cloth on an old cloak* or pouring *new wine into old wineskins* with the resulting destruction of both cloth and wine (21–22). Fasting is rendered superfluous during the earthly ministry of Jesus; cf v 20.

2, 23–28: This conflict regarding the sabbath follows the same pattern as in vv 18–22.

2, 25–26: *Have you never read what David did?:* Jesus defends the action of his disciples on the basis of 1 Sm 21, 2–7 in which an exception is made to the regulation of Lv 24, 9 because of the extreme hunger of David and his men. According to 1 Sm, the priest who gave the bread to David was Ahimelech, father of Abiathar.

2, 27: *The sabbath was made for man:* a reaffirmation of the divine intent of the sabbath to benefit Israel as contrasted with the restrictive Pharisaic tradition added to the law.

2, 28: *The Son of Man is lord even of the sabbath:* Mark's comment on the theological meaning of the incident is to benefit his Christian readers; see the note on 2, 10.

3, 1–5: Here Jesus is again depicted in conflict with his adversaries over the question of sabbath-day observance. His opponents were already ill disposed toward him because they regarded Jesus as a violator of the sabbath. Jesus' question *Is it lawful to do good on the sabbath rather than to do evil?* places the matter in the broader theological context outside the casuistry of the scribes. The answer is obvious. Jesus heals the man with the withered hand in the sight of all and reduces his opponents to silence; cf Jn 5, 17–18.

3, 6: In reporting the plot of the Pharisees and Herodians to put Jesus to death after this series of conflicts in Galilee, Mark uses a pattern that recurs in his account of later controversies in Jerusalem (11, 17–18; 12, 13–17). The help of the Herodians, supporters of Herod Antipas, tetrarch of Galilee and Perea, is needed to take action against Jesus. Both series of conflicts point to their gravity and to the impending passion of Jesus.

3, 7–19: This overview of the Galilean ministry manifests the power of Jesus to draw people to himself through his teaching and deeds of power. The crowds of Jews from many regions surround Jesus (7–12). This phenomenon prepares the way for creating a new people of Israel. The choice and mission of the Twelve is the prelude (13–19).

3, 11–12: See the note on 1, 24–25.

3, 13: *He went up the mountain:* here and elsewhere the mountain is associated with solemn moments and acts in the mission and self-revelation of Jesus (6, 46; 9, 2–8; 13, 3). Jesus acts with authority as he *summoned those whom he wanted and they came to him.*

3, 14–15: *He appointed twelve [whom he also named apostles] that they might be with him:* literally "he made," i.e., instituted them as apostles to extend his messianic mission

pointed twelve [whom he also named apostles]
that they might be with him and he might send
them forth to preach 15 and to have authority to
drive out demons: 16 *[he appointed the
twelve:] Simon, whom he named Peter;
17 [i]James, son of Zebedee, and John the brother of James, whom he named Boanerges, that is,
sons of thunder; 18 Andrew, Philip, Bartholomew, Matthew, Thomas, James the son of
Alphaeus; Thaddeus, Simon the Cananean,
19 and Judas Iscariot who betrayed him.

**Blasphemy of the Scribes** 20 [j]*He came
home. Again [the] crowd gathered, making it
impossible for them even to eat. 21 [k]When his
relatives heard of this they set out to seize him,
for they said, "He is out of his mind."
22 [l]*The scribes who had come from Jerusalem
said, "He is possessed by Beelzebul," and "By
the prince of demons he drives out demons."

**Jesus and Beelzebul** 23 Summoning
them, he began to speak to them in parables,
"How can Satan drive out Satan? 24 If a kingdom is divided against itself, that kingdom cannot stand. 25 And if a house is divided against
itself, that house will not be able to stand.
26 And if Satan has risen up against himself
and is divided, he cannot stand; that is the end
of him. 27 But no one can enter a strong man's
house to plunder his property unless he first ties
up the strong man. Then he can plunder his
house. 28 [m]Amen, I say to you, all sins and all
blasphemies that people utter will be forgiven
them. 29 *But whoever blasphemes against the
holy Spirit will never have forgiveness, but is
guilty of an everlasting sin." 30 For they had
said, "He has an unclean spirit."

**Jesus and His Family** 31 [n]His mother
and his brothers arrived. Standing outside they
sent word to him and called him. 32 *A crowd
seated around him told him, "Your mother and
your brothers [and your sisters] are outside asking for you." 33 But he said to them in reply,
"Who are my mother and [my] brothers?"
34 And looking around at those seated in the
circle he said, "Here are my mother and my
brothers. 35 [For] whoever does the will of God
is my brother and sister and mother."

## CHAPTER 4

**The Parable of the Sower** 1 [o][p]*On another occasion he began to teach by the sea. A
very large crowd gathered around him so that he
got into a boat on the sea and sat down. And the
whole crowd was beside the sea on land. 2 And
he taught them at length in parables, and in the
course of his instruction he said to them,
3 *"Hear this! A sower went out to sow.
4 And as he sowed, some seed fell on the path,
and the birds came and ate it up. 5 Other seed
fell on rocky ground where it had little soil. It
sprang up at once because the soil was not deep.
6 And when the sun rose, it was scorched and
it withered for lack of roots. 7 Some seed fell
among thorns, and the thorns grew up and
choked it and it produced no grain. 8 And some
seed fell on rich soil and produced fruit. It came
up and grew and yielded thirty, sixty, and a
hundredfold." 9 He added, "Whoever has ears
to hear ought to hear."

**The Purpose of the Parables** 10 And
when he was alone, those present along with the
Twelve questioned him about the parables.
11 *He answered them, "The mystery of the

i Mt 16, 18; Jn 1, 42.
j 2, 2.
k Jn 10, 20.
l Mt 12, 24-32; Lk 11, 15-22; 12, 10.
m Lk 12, 10.
n Mt 12, 46-50; Lk 8, 19-21.
o Mt 13, 1-13; Lk 8, 4-10.
p 2, 13; Lk 5, 1.

* through them (6, 7–13). See the notes on Mt 10, 1 and 10, 2–4.

3, 16: *Simon, whom he named Peter:* Mark indicates that Simon's name was changed on this occasion. Peter is first in all lists of the apostles (Mt 10, 2; Lk 6, 14; Acts 1, 13; cf 1 Cor 15, 5–8).

3, 20–35: Within the narrative of the coming of Jesus' relatives (20–21) is inserted the account of the unbelieving scribes from Jerusalem who attributed Jesus' power over demons to Beelzebul (22–30); see the note on 5, 21–43. There were those even among the relatives of Jesus who disbelieved and regarded Jesus as *out of his mind* (21). Against this background, Jesus is informed of the arrival of his mother and brothers [and sisters] (32). He responds by showing that not family ties but doing God's will (35) is decisive in the kingdom; cf the note on Mt 12, 46–50.

3, 20: *He came home:* cf 2, 1–2 and see the note on 2, 15.

3, 22: *By Beelzebul:* see the note on Mt 10, 25. Two accusations are leveled against Jesus: (1) that *he is possessed* by an unclean spirit, and (2) *by the prince of demons he drives out demons.* Jesus answers the second charge by a parable (24–27) and responds to the first charge in vv 28–29.

3, 29: *Whoever blasphemes against the holy Spirit:* this sin is called *an everlasting sin* because it attributes to Satan, who is the power of evil, what is actually the work of the holy Spirit, namely, victory over the demons.

3, 32: *Your brothers:* see the note on 6, 3.

4, 1–34: *In parables* (2): see the note on Mt 13, 3. The use of parables is typical of Jesus' enigmatic method of teaching the crowds (2–9.12) as compared with the interpretation of the parables he gives to his disciples (10–25.33–34), to each group according to its capacity to understand (9–11). The key feature of the parable at hand is the sowing of the seed (3), representing the breakthrough of the kingdom of God into the world. The various types of soil refer to the diversity of response accorded the word of God (4–7). The climax of the parable is the harvest of thirty, sixty, and a hundredfold, indicating the consummation of the kingdom (8). Thus both the present and the future action of God, from the initiation to the fulfillment of the kingdom, is presented through this and other parables (26–29.30–32).

4, 1: *By the sea:* the shore of the Sea of Galilee or a boat near the shore (2, 13; 3, 7–8) is the place where Mark depicts Jesus teaching the crowds. By contrast the mountain is the scene of Jesus at prayer (6, 46) or in the process of forming his disciples (3, 13; 9, 2).

4, 3–8: See the note on Mt 13, 3–8.

4, 11–12: These verses are to be viewed against their

kingdom of God has been granted to you. But
to those outside everything comes in parables,
**12** [q]so that

> 'they may look and see but not perceive,
> and hear and listen but not understand,
> in order that they may not be converted
> and be forgiven.' "

**13** [r]*Jesus said to them, "Do you not understand this parable? Then how will you understand any of the parables? **14** The sower sows
the word. **15** These are the ones on the path
where the word is sown. As soon as they hear,
Satan comes at once and takes away the word
sown in them. **16** And these are the ones sown
on rocky ground who, when they hear the word,
receive it at once with joy. **17** But they have no
root; they last only for a time. Then when tribulation or persecution comes because of the
word, they quickly fall away. **18** Those sown
among thorns are another sort. They are the
people who hear the word, **19** but worldly anxiety, the lure of riches, and the craving for other
things intrude and choke the word, and it bears
no fruit. **20** But those sown on rich soil are the
ones who hear the word and accept it and bear
fruit thirty and sixty and a hundredfold."

**Parable of the Lamp** **21** [s][t]He said to
them, "Is a lamp brought in to be placed under
a bushel basket or under a bed, and not to be
placed on a lampstand? **22** [u]For there is nothing
hidden except to be made visible; nothing is
secret except to come to light. **23** Anyone who
has ears to hear ought to hear." **24** [v]He also
told them, "Take care what you hear. The measure with which you measure will be measured
out to you, and still more will be given to you.
**25** [w]To the one who has, more will be given;
from the one who has not, even what he has will
be taken away."

**Seed Grows of Itself** **26** [x]*He said, "This
is how it is with the kingdom of God; it is as if
a man were to scatter seed on the land **27** and
would sleep and rise night and day and the seed
would sprout and grow, he knows not how.
**28** Of its own accord the land yields fruit, first
the blade, then the ear, then the full grain in the
ear. **29** And when the grain is ripe, he wields
the sickle at once, for the harvest has come."

**The Mustard Seed** **30** [y]He said, "To what
shall we compare the kingdom of God, or what
parable can we use for it? **31** It is like a mustard
seed that, when it is sown in the ground, is the
smallest of all the seeds on the earth. **32** *But
once it is sown, it springs up and becomes the
largest of plants and puts forth large branches,
so that the birds of the sky can dwell in its
shade." **33** [z]With many such parables he spoke
the word to them as they were able to understand
it. **34** Without parables he did not speak to
them, but to his own disciples he explained
everything in private.

**The Calming of a Storm at Sea** **35** [a]*On
that day, as evening drew on, he said to them,
"Let us cross to the other side." **36** Leaving
the crowd, they took him with them in the boat
just as he was. And other boats were with him.
**37** A violent squall came up and waves were
breaking over the boat, so that it was already
filling up. **38** Jesus was in the stern, asleep on
a cushion. They woke him and said to him,
"Teacher, do you not care that we are perishing?" **39** *He woke up, rebuked the wind, and
said to the sea, "Quiet! Be still!" The wind
ceased and there was great calm. **40** Then he
asked them, "Why are you terrified? Do you
not yet have faith?" **41** [b]*They were filled with
great awe and said to one another, "Who then
is this whom even wind and sea obey?"

## CHAPTER 5

**The Healing of the Gerasene Demo-
niac** **1** [c]*They came to the other side of the

q Is 6, 9; Jn 12, 40; Acts 28, 26; Rom 11, 8.
r Mt 13, 18-23; Lk 8, 11-15.
s Lk 8, 16-18.
t Mt 5, 15; Lk 11, 33.
u Mt 10, 26; Lk 12, 2.
v Mt 7, 2; Lk 6, 38.
w Mt 13, 12; Lk 19, 26.
x Jas 5, 7.
y Mt 13, 31-32; Lk 13, 18-19.
z Mt 13, 34.
a Mt 8, 18.23-37; Lk 8, 22-25.
b 1, 27.
c Mt 8, 28-34; Lk 8, 26-39.

*

background in 3, 6.22 concerning the unbelief and opposition Jesus encountered in his ministry. It is against this background that the distinction in Jesus' method becomes clear of presenting the kingdom to the disbelieving crowd in one manner and to the disciples in another. To the former it is presented in parables and the truth remains hidden; for the latter the parable is interpreted and the mystery is partially revealed because of their faith; see the notes on Mt 13, 11 and 13, 13.

4, 13–20: See the note on Mt 13, 18–23.

4, 26–29: Only Mark records the parable of the seed's growth. Sower and harvester are the same. The emphasis is on the power of the seed to grow of itself without human intervention (27). Mysteriously it produces *blade* and *ear* and *full grain* (28). Thus the kingdom of God initiated by Jesus in proclaiming the word develops quietly yet powerfully until it is fully established by him at the final judgment (29); cf Rv 14, 15.

4, 32: The universality of the kingdom of God is indicated here; cf Ez 17, 23; 31, 6; Dn 4, 17–19.

4, 35—5, 43: After the chapter on parables, Mark narrates four miracle stories: 4, 35–41; 5, 1–20; and two joined together in 5, 21–43. See also the notes on Mt 8, 23–34 and 9, 8–26.

4, 39: *Quiet! Be still!:* as in the case of silencing a demon (1, 25), Jesus rebukes the wind and subdues the turbulence of the sea by a mere word; see the note on Mt 8, 26.

4, 41: Jesus is here depicted as exercising power over wind and sea. In the Christian community this event was seen as a sign of Jesus' saving presence amid persecutions that threatened its existence.

5, 1: *The territory of the Gerasenes:* the reference is to pagan territory; cf Is 65, 1. Another reading is "Gadarenes"; see the note on Mt 8, 28.

sea, to the territory of the Gerasenes. **2** *When
he got out of the boat, at once a man from the
tombs who had an unclean spirit met him.
**3** The man had been dwelling among the
tombs, and no one could restrain him any longer, even with a chain. **4** In fact, he had frequently been bound with shackles and chains,
but the chains had been pulled apart by him and
the shackles smashed, and no one was strong
enough to subdue him. **5** Night and day among
the tombs and on the hillsides he was always
crying out and bruising himself with stones.
**6** Catching sight of Jesus from a distance, he
ran up and prostrated himself before him,
**7** *crying out in a loud voice, "What have you
to do with me, Jesus, Son of the Most High
God? I adjure you by God, do not torment me!"
**8** (He had been saying to him, "Unclean spirit,
come out of the man!") **9** [d]*He asked him,
"What is your name?" He replied, "Legion is
my name. There are many of us." **10** And he
pleaded earnestly with him not to drive them
away from that territory.

**11** *Now a large herd of swine was feeding
there on the hillside. **12** And they pleaded with
him, "Send us into the swine. Let us enter
them." **13** And he let them, and the unclean
spirits came out and entered the swine. The herd
of about two thousand rushed down a steep bank
into the sea, where they were drowned. **14** The
swineherds ran away and reported the incident
in the town and throughout the countryside.
And people came out to see what had happened.
**15** As they approached Jesus, they caught sight
of the man who had been possessed by Legion,
sitting there clothed and in his right mind. And
they were seized with fear. **16** Those who witnessed the incident explained to them what had
happened to the possessed man and to the
swine. **17** Then they began to beg him to leave
their district. **18** As he was getting into the
boat, the man who had been possessed pleaded
to remain with him. **19** *But he would not permit him but told him instead, "Go home to your
family and announce to them all that the Lord
in his pity has done for you." **20** Then the man
went off and began to proclaim in the Decapolis
what Jesus had done for him; and all were
amazed.

### Jairus's Daughter and the Woman with a Hemorrhage

**21** [e]*When Jesus had crossed
again [in the boat] to the other side, a large
crowd gathered around him, and he stayed close
to the sea. **22** [f]One of the synagogue officials,
named Jairus, came forward. Seeing him he fell
at his feet **23** *and pleaded earnestly with him,
saying, "My daughter is at the point of death.
Please, come lay your hands on her that she may
get well and live." **24** He went off with him,
and a large crowd followed him and pressed
upon him.

**25** There was a woman afflicted with hemorrhages for twelve years. **26** She had suffered greatly at the hands of many doctors and
had spent all that she had. Yet she was not
helped but only grew worse. **27** She had heard
about Jesus and came up behind him in the
crowd and touched his cloak. **28** *She said, "If
I but touch his clothes, I shall be cured."
**29** Immediately her flow of blood dried up. She
felt in her body that she was healed of her affliction. **30** Jesus, aware at once that power had
gone out from him, turned around in the crowd
and asked, "Who has touched my clothes?"
**31** But his disciples said to him, "You see how
the crowd is pressing upon you, and yet you ask,
'Who touched me?' " **32** And he looked
around to see who had done it. **33** The woman,
realizing what had happened to her, approached
in fear and trembling. She fell down before
Jesus and told him the whole truth. **34** [g]He said
to her, "Daughter, your faith has saved you. Go
in peace and be cured of your affliction."

**35** *While he was still speaking, people from
the synagogue official's house arrived and said,
"Your daughter has died; why trouble the
teacher any longer?" **36** Disregarding the message that was reported, Jesus said to the synagogue official, "Do not be afraid; just have

d Mt 12, 45; Lk 8, 2; 11, 26.
e 2, 13.
f Mt 9, 18-26; Lk 8, 41-56.
g Lk 7, 30.

*

5, 2–6: The man was an outcast from society, dominated by unclean spirits (8.13), living among the tombs. The prostration before Jesus (6) indicates Jesus' power over evil spirits.

5, 7: *What have you to do with me?:* cf 1, 24 and see the note on Jn 2, 4.

5, 9: *Legion is my name:* the demons were numerous and the condition of the possessed man was extremely serious; cf Mt 12, 45.

5, 11: *Herd of swine:* see the note on Mt 8, 30.

5, 19: *Go home:* Jesus did not accept the man's request *to remain with him* as a disciple (18), yet invited him to announce to his own people what the Lord had done for him, i.e., proclaim the gospel message to his pagan family; cf 1, 14.39; 3, 14; 13, 10.

5, 21–43: The story of the raising to life of Jairus's daughter is divided into two parts: vv 21–24 and 35–43. Between these two separated parts the account of the cure of the hemorrhage victim (25–34) is interposed. This technique of intercalating or sandwiching one story within another occurs several times in Mk: 3, 19b–21 (22–30) 31–35; 6, 6b–13 (14–29) 30; 11, 12–14 (15–19) 20–25; 14, 53 (54) 55–65 (66–73).

5, 23: *Lay your hands on her:* this act for the purpose of healing is frequent in Mk (6, 5; 7, 32–35; 8, 23–25; 16, 18) and is also found in Mt 9, 18; Lk 4, 40; 13, 13; Acts 9, 17; 28, 8.

5, 28: Both in the case of Jairus and his daughter (23) and in the case of the hemorrhage victim, the inner conviction that physical contact (30) accompanied by faith in Jesus' saving power could effect a cure was rewarded.

5, 35: The faith of Jairus was put to a twofold test: (1) that his daughter might be cured and, now that she had died, (2) that she might be restored to life. His faith contrasts with the lack of faith of the crowd.

faith." **37** He did not allow anyone to accompany him inside except Peter, James, and John,
the brother of James. **38** When they arrived at
the house of the synagogue official, he caught
sight of a commotion, people weeping and wailing loudly. **39** [h]*So he went in and said to
them, "Why this commotion and weeping? The
child is not dead but asleep." **40** And they ridiculed him. Then he put them all out. He took
along the child's father and mother and those
who were with him and entered the room where
the child was. **41** *He took the child by the
hand and said to her, "*Talitha koum,*" which
means, "Little girl, I say to you, arise!"
**42** The girl, a child of twelve, arose immediately and walked around. [At that] they were utterly astounded. **43** He gave strict orders that no
one should know this and said that she should
be given something to eat.

## CHAPTER 6

### The Rejection at Nazareth

**1** [i]*He de-
parted from there and came to his native place,
accompanied by his disciples. **2** *When the
sabbath came he began to teach in the synagogue, and many who heard him were astonished. They said, "Where did this man get all
this? What kind of wisdom has been given him?
What mighty deeds are wrought by his hands!
**3** [j]*Is he not the carpenter, the son of Mary,
and the brother of James and Joses and Judas
and Simon? And are not his sisters here with
us?" And they took offense at him. **4** [k]*Jesus
said to them, "A prophet is not without honor
except in his native place and among his own
kin and in his own house." **5** *So he was not
able to perform any mighty deed there, apart
from curing a few sick people by laying his
hands on them. **6** He was amazed at their lack
of faith.

### The Mission of the Twelve

He went
around to the villages in the vicinity teaching.
**7** [l]*He summoned the Twelve and began to
send them out two by two and gave them authority over unclean spirits. **8** *He instructed them
to take nothing for the journey but a walking
stick—no food, no sack, no money in their
belts. **9** They were, however, to wear sandals
but not a second tunic. **10** *He said to them,
"Wherever you enter a house, stay there until
you leave from there. **11** Whatever place does
not welcome you or listen to you, leave there
and shake the dust off your feet in testimony
against them." **12** So they went off and
preached repentance. **13** [m]*They drove out
many demons, and they anointed with oil many
who were sick and cured them.

h Acts 9, 40.
i Mt 13, 54-58; Lk 4, 16-30.
j 15, 40; Mt 12, 46; Jn 6, 42.
k Jn 4, 44.
l Mt 10, 1.9-14; Lk 9, 15; 10, 4-11.
m Jas 5, 14.

*

5, 39: *Not dead but asleep:* the New Testament often refers to death as sleep (Mt 27, 52; Jn 11, 11; 1 Cor 15, 6; 1 Thes 4, 13–15); see the note on Mt 9, 24.

5, 41: *Arise:* the Greek verb *egeirein* is the verb generally used to express resurrection from death (6, 14.16; Mt 11, 5; Lk 7, 14) and Jesus' own resurrection (16, 6; Mt 28, 6; Lk 24, 6).

6, 1: *His native place:* the Greek word *patris* here refers to Nazareth (cf 1, 9; Lk 4, 16.23–24), though it can also mean native land.

6, 2–6: See the note on Mt 13, 54–58.

6, 3: *Is he not the carpenter?:* no other gospel calls Jesus a carpenter. Some witnesses have "the carpenter's son," as in Mt 13, 55. *Son of Mary:* contrary to Jewish custom, which calls a man the son of his father, this expression may reflect Mark's own faith that God is the Father of Jesus (1, 1.11; 8, 38; 13, 32; 14, 36). *The brother of James . . . Simon:* in Semitic usage, the terms 'brother,' 'sister' are applied not only to children of the same parents, but to nephews, nieces, cousins, half-brothers, and half-sisters; cf Gn 14, 16; 29, 15; Lv 10, 4. While one cannot suppose that the meaning of a Greek word should be sought in the first place from Semitic usage, the Septuagint often translates the Hebrew *'āḥ* by the Greek word *adelphos,* "brother," as in the cited passages, a fact that may argue for a similar breadth of meaning in some New Testament passages. For instance, there is no doubt that in v 17, "brother" is used of Philip, who was actually the half-brother of Herod Antipas. On the other hand, Mark may have understood the terms literally; see also Mt 3, 31–32; 12, 46; 13, 55–56; Lk 8, 19; Jn 7, 3.5. The question of meaning here would not have arisen but for the faith of the church in Mary's perpetual virginity.

6, 4: *A prophet is not without honor except . . . in his own house:* a saying that finds parallels in other literatures, especially Jewish and Greek, but without reference to a prophet. Comparing himself to previous Hebrew prophets whom the people rejected, Jesus intimates his own eventual rejection by the nation especially in view of the dishonor his own relatives had shown him (3, 21) and now his townspeople as well.

6, 5: *He was not able to perform any mighty deed there:* according to Mark, Jesus' power could not take effect because of a person's lack of faith.

6, 7–13: The preparation for the mission of the Twelve is seen in the call (1) of the first disciples to be fishers of men (1, 16–20), (2) then of the Twelve set apart to be with Jesus and to receive authority to preach and expel demons (3, 13–19). Now they are given the specific mission to exercise that authority in word and power as representatives of Jesus during the time of their formation.

6, 8–9: In Mk the use of a *walking stick* (8) and *sandals* (9) is permitted, but not in Mt 10, 10 nor in Lk 10, 4. Mark does not mention any prohibition to visit pagan territory and to enter Samaritan towns. These differences indicate a certain adaptation to conditions in and outside of Palestine and suggest in Mark's account a later activity in the church. For the rest, Jesus required of his apostles a total dependence on God for food and shelter; cf vv 35–44; 8, 1–9.

6, 10–11: Remaining in the same house as a guest (10) rather than moving to another offering greater comfort avoided any impression of seeking advantage for oneself and prevented dishonor to one's host. Shaking the dust off one's feet served as testimony against those who rejected the call to repentance.

6, 13: *Anointed with oil . . . cured them:* a common medicinal remedy, but seen here as a vehicle of divine power for healing.

## Herod's Opinion of Jesus
14 [no]*King
Herod heard about it, for his fame had become
widespread, and people were saying, "John the
Baptist has been raised from the dead; that is
why mighty powers are at work in him."
15 [p]Others were saying, "He is Elijah"; still
others, "He is a prophet like any of the prophets." 16 But when Herod learned of it, he said,
"It is John whom I beheaded. He has been
raised up."

## The Death of John the Baptist
17 [q]*Herod was the one who had John arrested
and bound in prison on account of Herodias, the
wife of his brother Philip, whom he had married. 18 [r]John had said to Herod, "It is not
lawful for you to have your brother's wife."
19 *Herodias harbored a grudge against him
and wanted to kill him but was unable to do so.
20 Herod feared John, knowing him to be a
righteous and holy man, and kept him in custody. When he heard him speak he was very much
perplexed, yet he liked to listen to him. 21 She
had an opportunity one day when Herod, on his
birthday, gave a banquet for his courtiers, his
military officers, and the leading men of Galilee. 22 Herodias's own daughter came in and
performed a dance that delighted Herod and his
guests. The king said to the girl, "Ask of me
whatever you wish and I will grant it to you."
23 [s]He even swore [many things] to her, "I
will grant you whatever you ask of me, even to
half of my kingdom." 24 She went out and said
to her mother, "What shall I ask for?" She
replied, "The head of John the Baptist."
25 The girl hurried back to the king's presence
and made her request, "I want you to give me
at once on a platter the head of John the Baptist." 26 The king was deeply distressed, but
because of his oaths and the guests he did not
wish to break his word to her. 27 [t]So he
promptly dispatched an executioner with orders
to bring back his head. He went off and beheaded him in the prison. 28 He brought in the head
on a platter and gave it to the girl. The girl in
turn gave it to her mother. 29 When his disciples heard about it, they came and took his body
and laid it in a tomb.

## The Return of the Twelve
30 [u]*The
apostles gathered together with Jesus and reported all they had done and taught. 31 [v]*He
said to them, "Come away by yourselves to a
deserted place and rest a while." People were
coming and going in great numbers, and they
had no opportunity even to eat. 32 [w]So they
went off in the boat by themselves to a deserted
place. 33 People saw them leaving and many
came to know about it. They hastened there on
foot from all the towns and arrived at the place
before them.

## The Feeding of the Five Thousand
34 When he disembarked and saw the vast
crowd, his heart was moved with pity for them,
for they were like sheep without a shepherd; and
he began to teach them many things. 35 *By
now it was already late and his disciples approached him and said, "This is a deserted
place and it is already very late. 36 Dismiss
them so that they can go to the surrounding
farms and villages and buy themselves something to eat." 37 He said to them in reply,
"Give them some food yourselves." But they
said to him, "Are we to buy two hundred days'
wages worth of food and give it to them to eat?"
38 He asked them, "How many loaves do you
have? Go and see." And when they had found
out they said, "Five loaves and two fish."
39 So he gave orders to have them sit down in
groups on the green grass. 40 *The people took
their places in rows by hundreds and by fifties.
41 *Then, taking the five loaves and the two

n Lk 9, 7-8.
o Mt 14, 1-12.
p Mt 16, 14.
q Lk 3, 19-20.
r Lv 18, 16.
s Est 5, 3.
t Lk 9, 9.
u Lk 9, 10.
v 3, 20; Mt 14, 13; Lk 9, 10.
w Mt 14, 13-21; Lk 9, 10-17; Jn 6, 1-13.

*

6, 14–16: The various opinions about Jesus anticipate the theme of his identity that reaches its climax in 8, 27–30.

6, 14: *King Herod:* see the note on Mt 14, 1.

6, 17–29: Similarities are to be noted between Mark's account of the imprisonment and death of John the Baptist in this pericope, and that of the passion of Jesus (15, 1–47). Herod and Pilate, each in turn, acknowledges the holiness of life of one over whom he unjustly exercises the power of condemnation and death (26–27; 15, 9–10.14–15). The hatred of Herodias toward John parallels that of the Jewish leaders toward Jesus. After the deaths of John and of Jesus, well-disposed persons request the bodies of the victims of Herod and of Pilate in turn to give them respectful burial (29; 15, 45–46).

6, 19: *Herodias:* see the note on Mt 14, 3.

6, 30: *Apostles:* here, and in some manuscripts at 3, 14, Mark calls apostles (i.e., those sent forth) the Twelve whom Jesus sends as his emissaries, empowering them to preach, to expel demons, and to cure the sick (13). Only after Pentecost is the title used in the technical sense.

6, 31–34: The withdrawal of Jesus with his disciples to a desert place to rest attracts a great number of people to follow them. Toward this people of the new exodus Jesus is moved with pity; he satisfies their spiritual hunger by teaching them many things, thus gradually showing himself the faithful shepherd of a new Israel; cf Nm 27, 17; Ez 34, 15.

6, 35–44: See the note on Mt 14, 13–21. Compare this section with 8, 1–9. The various accounts of the multiplication of loaves and fishes, two each in Mark and in Matthew and one each in Luke and in John, indicate the wide interest of the early church in their eucharistic gatherings; see, e.g., v 41; 8, 6; 14, 22; and recall also the sign of bread in Ex 16; Dt 8, 3–16; Pss 78, 24–25; 105, 40; Wis 16, 20–21.

6, 40: *The people . . . in rows by hundreds and by fifties:* reminiscent of the groupings of Israelites encamped in the desert (Ex 18, 21–25) and of the wilderness tradition of the prophets depicting the transformation of the wasteland into pastures where the true shepherd feeds his flock (Ez 34, 25–26) and makes his people beneficiaries of messianic grace.

6, 41: On the language of this verse as eucharistic (cf 14, 22), see the notes on Mt 14, 19.20. Jesus observed the Jewish

fish and looking up to heaven, he said the blessing, broke the loaves, and gave them to [his]
disciples to set before the people; he also divided the two fish among them all. **42** They all ate
and were satisfied. **43** And they picked up
twelve wicker baskets full of fragments and
what was left of the fish. **44** Those who ate [of
the loaves] were five thousand men.

**The Walking on the Water** **45** [x]*Then he
made his disciples get into the boat and precede
him to the other side toward Bethsaida, while he
dismissed the crowd. **46** *And when he had
taken leave of them, he went off to the mountain
to pray. **47** When it was evening, the boat was
far out on the sea and he was alone on shore.
**48** *Then he saw that they were tossed about
while rowing, for the wind was against them.
About the fourth watch of the night, he came
towards them walking on the sea. He meant to
pass by them. **49** But when they saw him walking on the sea, they thought it was a ghost and
cried out. **50** *They had all seen him and were
terrified. But at once he spoke with them,
"Take courage, it is I, do not be afraid!" **51** He
got into the boat with them and the wind died
down. They were [completely] astounded.
**52** [y]*They had not understood the incident of
the loaves. On the contrary, their hearts were
hardened.

**The Healings at Gennesaret** **53** [z]After
making the crossing, they came to land at Gennesaret and tied up there. **54** As they were leaving the boat, people immediately recognized
him. **55** They scurried about the surrounding
country and began to bring in the sick on mats
to wherever they heard he was. **56** [a]Whatever
villages or towns or countryside he entered,
they laid the sick in the marketplaces and
begged him that they might touch only the tassel
on his cloak; and as many as touched it were
healed.

## CHAPTER 7

**The Tradition of the Elders** **1** [b]*Now
when the Pharisees with some scribes who had
come from Jerusalem gathered around him,
**2** they observed that some of his disciples ate
their meals with unclean, that is, unwashed,
hands. **3** *(For the Pharisees and, in fact, all
Jews, do not eat without carefully washing their
hands, keeping the tradition of the elders.
**4** And on coming from the marketplace they do
not eat without purifying themselves. And there
are many other things that they have traditionally observed, the purification of cups and jugs
and kettles [and beds].) **5** *So the Pharisees and
scribes questioned him, "Why do your disciples
not follow the tradition of the elders but instead
eat a meal with unclean hands?" **6** [c]He responded, "Well did Isaiah prophesy about you
hypocrites, as it is written:

'This people honors me with their lips,
but their hearts are far from me;
**7** In vain do they worship me,
teaching as doctrines human precepts.'

**8** You disregard God's commandment but cling
to human tradition." **9** He went on to say,
"How well you have set aside the commandment of God in order to uphold your tradition!
**10** [d]For Moses said, 'Honor your father and
your mother,' and 'Whoever curses father or
mother shall die.' **11** *Yet you say, 'If a person
says to father or mother, "Any support you
might have had from me is qorban" ' (meaning,
dedicated to God), **12** you allow him to do
nothing more for his father or mother. **13** You
nullify the word of God in favor of your tradition that you have handed on. And you do many
such things." **14** [e]He summoned the crowd
again and said to them, "Hear me, all of you,

x Mt 14, 22-32; Jn 6, 15-21.
y 4, 13.
z Mt 14, 34-36.
a 5, 27-28; Acts 5, 15.
b Mt 15, 1-20.
c Is 29, 13.
d Ex 21, 17; Lv 20, 9; Dt 5, 16; Eph 6, 2.
e Mt 15, 10-20.

* table ritual of blessing God before partaking of food.

6, 45–52: See the note on Mt 14, 22–33.

6, 45: *To the other side toward Bethsaida:* a village at the northeastern shore of the Sea of Galilee.

6, 46: *He went off to the mountain to pray:* see 1, 35–38. In Jn 6, 15 Jesus withdrew to evade any involvement in the false messianic hopes of the multitude.

6, 48: *Walking on the sea:* see the notes on Mt 14, 22–33 and on Jn 6, 19.

6, 50: *It is I, do not be afraid!:* literally, "I am." This may reflect the divine revelatory formula of Ex 3, 14; Is 41, 4.10.14; 43, 1–3.10.13. Mark implies the hidden identity of Jesus as Son of God.

6, 52: *They had not understood . . . the loaves:* the revelatory character of this sign and that of the walking on the sea completely escaped the disciples. *Their hearts were hardened:* in 3, 5–6 hardness of heart was attributed to those who did not accept Jesus and plotted his death. Here the same disposition prevents the disciples from comprehending Jesus' self-revelation through signs; cf 8, 17.

7, 1–23: See the note on Mt 15, 1–20. Against the Pharisees' narrow, legalistic, and external practices of piety in matters of purification (2–5), external worship (6–7), and observance of commandments, Jesus sets in opposition the true moral intent of the divine law (8–13). But he goes beyond contrasting the law and Pharisaic interpretation of it. The parable of vv 14–15 in effect sets aside the law itself in respect to clean and unclean food. He thereby opens the way for unity between Jew and Gentile in the kingdom of God, intimated by Jesus' departure for pagan territory beyond Galilee. For similar contrast see 2, 1—3, 6; 3, 20–35; 6, 1–6.

7, 3: *Carefully washing their hands:* refers to ritual purification.

7, 5: *Tradition of the elders:* the body of detailed, unwritten, human laws regarded by the scribes and Pharisees to have the same binding force as that of the Mosaic law; cf Gal 1, 14.

7, 11: *Qorban:* a formula for a gift to God, dedicating the offering to the temple, so that the giver might continue to use it for himself but not give it to others, even needy parents.

# Palestine
## IN JESUS' TIME

Herod the Great, who was trusted by the Romans, was king at the time of Jesus' birth. However, when he died in 4 B.C., his cruel son Archelaus succeeded him in Judea. He was soon removed by the Romans. Herod's son, Herod Antipas, ruled Galilee and Perea; it was he who had John the Baptist executed (Mark 6:14-29). A third son of Herod, Philip, ruled Iturea and Trachonitis from Caesarea Philippi.

After the exile of Archelaus, Rome ruled Judea directly through officials called procurators, who lived at Caesarea, and only came to Jerusalem for special festivals. The Procurator Pontius Pilate was temporarily in Jerusalem when he sentenced Jesus to death (Luke 22:66-23:25).

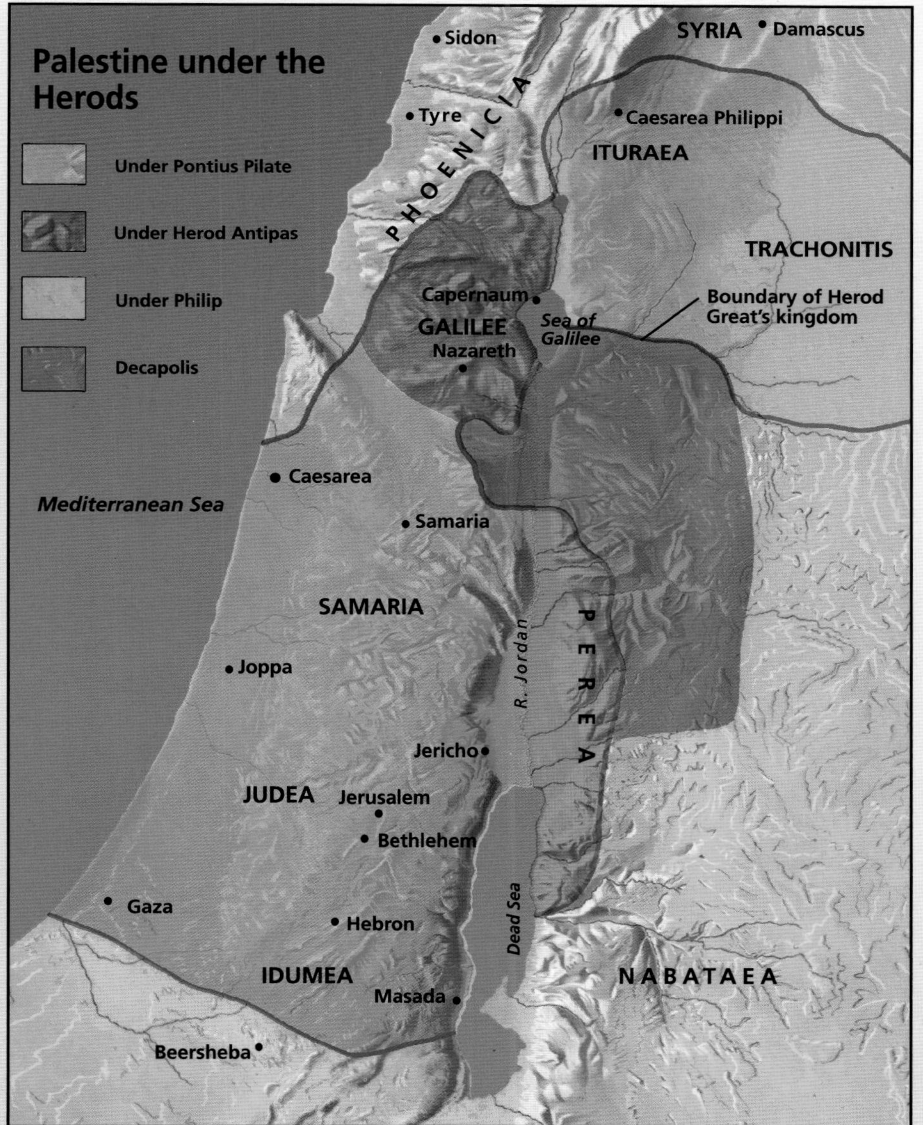

# Great Characters of the
## NEW TESTAMENT

**Andrew**
Peter's fisherman brother and one of the twelve apostles.
*Matthew 4:18, 10:2; John 1:35-44, 6:8-9, 12:20-22; Acts 1:12-14*

**Aquila**
A tent-maker and Jewish Christian friend of Paul; husband of Priscilla.
*Acts 18:1-3, 18-26*

**Barnabas**
Barnabas was a nickname for Joses, a Jewish Christian who was born in Cyprus, and who traveled extensively with Paul on his missionary work. His name means "son of encouragement."
*Acts 4:36-37, 9:27, 11:22-30, 13:1-15:39; 1 Corinthians 9:6; Galatians 2:1-13*

**Caiaphas**
The high priest in Jerusalem is said in the Bible to have found Jesus guilty of blasphemy and to have sent him to Pilate for sentencing.
*Matthew 26:3-5, 57-68; John 11:49-53*

**Cleopas**
One of the disciples who met the risen Christ on the Emmaus road.
*Luke 24:13-35*

**Cornelius**
A Roman centurion, stationed at Caesarea, who was converted to Christianity.
*Acts 10:1-48*

**Dorcas**
A disciple in Joppa, who did much good among the poor and widows. When she died, Peter restored her to life.
*Acts 9:36-42*

**Elizabeth**
Wife of the priest Zechariah and mother, in old age, of John the Baptist.
*Luke 1:5-66*

**Herod the Great**
Herod was king of Judea at the time of Jesus' birth. Trusted by the Romans, he undertook a huge building program in Judea. He ordered the killing of male children to eliminate any rival.
*Matthew 2:1-20; Luke 1:5*

**Herod the Tetrarch**
Son of Herod the Great, he imprisoned, and later beheaded, John the Baptist. Pilate sent Jesus to him for trial since Jesus came from Galilee, Herod's territory.
*Matthew 14:1-12; Luke 9:7-9, 13:31-32, 23:6-15*

**James**
Jesus' relative. After Pentecost he became the Bishop of the Jerusalem church and may be the writer of the letter of James. A martyr in 62 A.D.
*Matthew 13:55; Acts 15:13-21; Galatians 1:19, 2:9*

**James**
James was a fisherman like his brother John. Called by Jesus to follow him as one of the twelve apostles, he was present at Jesus' transfiguration. He was executed by Herod Agrippa in 44 A.D.
*Matthew 4:21-22; Mark 1:19-20; Luke 9:28-36; Acts 12:1-3*

**James**
Son of Alphaeus and one of the twelve apostles.
*Matthew 10:3*

**John**
James' brother and another fisherman, John was "the disciple whom Jesus loved." Jesus told him to look after Mary, his mother, when he was dying on the cross. John is believed to be the writer of John's Gospel, 1, 2 and 3 John and Revelation.
*Matthew 4:21-22, 10:2, 17:1-13; Mark 10:35-45; Luke 22:8; John; Acts 3:1-10, 4:1-31; 1,2,3 John, Revelation*

**John the Baptist**
John was sent to prepare the way for Jesus, the Messiah. He lived simply, and preached repentance and baptism. He was imprisoned and beheaded by Herod the Tetrarch.
*Matthew 3:1-15, 11:2-19, 14:1-12; Luke 1:5-17, 3:1-20, 7:18-35*

**Judas Iscariot**
Judas was one of the twelve apostles. His second name means "man from Kerioth," a town close to Hebron. Judas betrayed Jesus, and later hanged himself.
*Matthew 10:2-4, 26:47-49, 27:1-10; Mark 14:43-46; John 12:4-7, 13:26-30*

**Lazarus**
The brother of Mary and Martha, he lived in Bethany and was raised from the dead by Jesus.
*John 11:1-44*

**Lydia**
A business woman from Thyatira who traded in costly purple cloth, she was converted through the preaching of Paul
*Acts 16:12-15, 40*

**Martha**
The sister of Mary and Lazarus, Martha lived with her siblings in Bethany.
*Luke 10:38-42; John 11:1-44*

**Mary**
Mother of Jesus and wife of Joseph. Her song of faith, called the *Magnificat*, is found in Luke 1. When he was dying on the cross, Jesus told John to care for his mother.
*Matthew 1:16-25; Luke 1:26-56, 2:1-39; John 2:1-5, 19:25-27; Acts 1:14*

**Mary**
The sister of Martha, Mary anointed Jesus with oil just before his death.
*Luke 10:38-42; John 11:1-44, 12:1-8*

**Mary Magdalene**
She was from Magdala in Galilee: she was healed by Jesus. Later, she was the first to meet the risen Christ.
*Matthew 27:56,61, 28:1-10; Luke 8:1-3; John 20:1-18*

**Matthew**
Matthew, or Levi, was a tax-collector who was called by Jesus to become one of the twelve apostles. The Gospel of Matthew is attributed to him.
*Matthew 9:9-13, 10:3; Mark 2:13-17; Luke 5:27-32*

**Nicodemus**
A Pharisee and ruler of the Jews, Nicodemus came to talk to Jesus secretly by night and later assisted at his burial.
*John 3:1-36, 7:50-52, 19:38-42*

**Paul**
Paul was born in Tarsus and brought up as a strict Pharisee. Suddenly converted to Christ on the road to Damascus, he became the great missionary to the Gentiles. He undertook three major missionary journeys, founding and building up Christian communities wherever he went. He wrote letters to many new churches to encourage them in the faith. Paul is thought to have been executed by Nero in Rome about A.D. 67.
*Acts 7:1-28:31; Romans–Philemon*

**Peter (Simon Peter)**
Peter was a fisherman called by Jesus to become one of the twelve apostles. After the resurrection, Christ appeared specially to Peter, who became the leader of the young church. He was probably executed in Rome. 1 and 2 Peter are attributed to him.
*Matthew 4:18-20, 16:13-17:8, 26:31-35, 69-75; John 13:1-9,24,31-38; 21:1-22; Acts 1:13-5:42, 8:14-25, 9:32-12:18, 15:1-11; 1 and 2 Peter*

**Philip**
One of the twelve apostles, Philip came from Bethsaida in Galilee.
*Matthew 10:3; John 1:43-46, 6:7, 12:20-22*

**Pontius Pilate**
The Bible says that Pilate was the Roman procurator of Judea who sentenced Jesus to death, though he declared him to be innocent.
*Matthew 27:11-26; John 18:28-36*

**Priscilla**
Wife of Aquila; a faithful Jewish Christian and a friend of Paul.
*Acts 18:1-3,18-26*

**Silas**
Silas was a leader of the Jerusalem church and went with Paul on his second missionary journey.
*Acts 15:22-18:22*

**Stephen**
A Greek-speaking Jew and one of the seven men chosen to help the apostles in Jerusalem. Stephen became the first martyr in the church.
*Acts 6:1-8:2*

**Tabitha**
Also known as **Dorcas** (*see entry*).

**Thomas**
Thomas was one of the twelve apostles and was initially very sceptical when he heard that the risen Christ had appeared after the crucifixion.
*Matthew 10:3; Mark 3:18; John 11:16, 20:24-29, 21:2*

**Timothy**
Timothy was a young convert of Paul who accompanied the apostle on his second missionary journey. He later led the church in Ephesus. 1 and 2 Timothy are presented as being written to him by Paul.
*Acts 16:1-18:22; 1 and 2 Timothy*

**Titus**
A Gentile convert, sent as a missionary to Crete. A letter to him is attributed to Paul.
*2 Corinthians 2:13; Galatians 2:1-3; Titus*

**Zacchaeus**
A wealthy and dishonest tax-collector, Zacchaeus climbed a tree in Jericho to see Jesus. When Jesus invited himself to his home, Zacchaeus made full restitution.
*Luke 19:1-10*

# Jesus in Galilee

Jesus spent much of his ministry preaching and healing in Galilee. Although this Roman province was largely Jewish, many non-Jews also settled there. The Galileans, with a dialect of their own, were despised by many Jews from Jerusalem.

• In Jesus' time, many towns clustered around the **Sea of Galilee**. It was while sailing across the lake that Jesus calmed a sudden storm (Mark 4:35-41).

• Jesus came to live in **Capernaum** (Matthew 4:13) and cured a Roman officer's slave (Matthew 8:5-13), a leper (Matthew 8:2-4), Peter's mother-in-law (Matthew 8:14-15), a man with an evil spirit (Mark 1:21-26) and a paralysed man (Mark 2:1-12). Jesus preached in the Capernaum synagogue (Mark 1:21), called Matthew (Matthew 9:9), paid the Temple tax here (Matthew 17:24), and denounced the town for its lack of faith (Matthew 11:23).

• In **Chorazin**, Jesus performed miracles and later denounced the people for their lack of faith (Matthew 11:21)

• Jesus also visited **Bethsaida**, where he restored the sight of a blind man (Mark 8:22) and withdrew for a time of rest (Luke 9:10).

• At **Magdala**, Jesus was dining with Simon the Pharisee when Mary anointed him (Luke 7:36-8:2).

• **Tabgha** may be the place where the risen Christ met the disciples and ate with them (John 21:1-14).

• The **Mount of Beatitudes** is the hill where, by tradition, Jesus taught the Sermon on the Mount (Matthew 5:1-7:29).

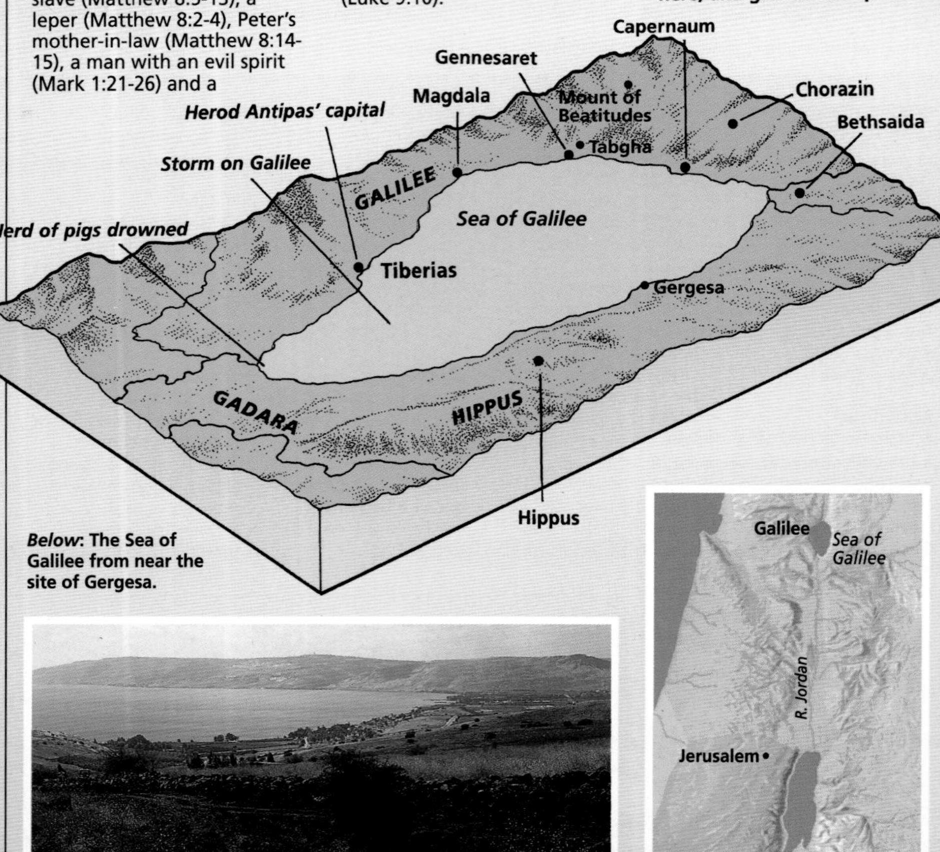


*Below*: The Sea of Galilee from near the site of Gergesa.

and understand. **15** Nothing that enters one
from outside can defile that person; but the
things that come out from within are what defile." **[16*]**

**17** [f]*When he got home away from the
crowd his disciples questioned him about the
parable. **18** He said to them, "Are even you
likewise without understanding? Do you not realize that everything that goes into a person
from outside cannot defile, **19** [g]*since it enters
not the heart but the stomach and passes out into
the latrine?" (Thus he declared all foods clean.)
**20** "But what comes out of a person, that is
what defiles. **21** [h]From within people, from
their hearts, come evil thoughts, unchastity,
theft, murder, **22** adultery, greed, malice, deceit, licentiousness, envy, blasphemy, arrogance, folly. **23** All these evils come from
within and they defile."

## The Syrophoenician Woman's Faith

**24** [i]*From that place he went off to the district
of Tyre. He entered a house and wanted no one
to know about it, but he could not escape notice.
**25** Soon a woman whose daughter had an unclean spirit heard about him. She came and fell
at his feet. **26** [j]The woman was a Greek, a
Syrophoenician by birth, and she begged him to
drive the demon out of her daughter. **27** *He
said to her, "Let the children be fed first. For
it is not right to take the food of the children and
throw it to the dogs." **28** She replied and said
to him, "Lord, even the dogs under the table eat
the children's scraps." **29** Then he said to her,
"For saying this, you may go. The demon has
gone out of your daughter." **30** When the
woman went home, she found the child lying in
bed and the demon gone.

## The Healing of a Deaf Man

**31** [k]Again he
left the district of Tyre and went by way of
Sidon to the Sea of Galilee, into the district of
the Decapolis. **32** And people brought to him a
deaf man who had a speech impediment and
begged him to lay his hand on him. **33** He took
him off by himself away from the crowd. He put
his finger into the man's ears and, spitting,
touched his tongue; **34** then he looked up to
heaven and groaned, and said to him, "Ephpha-
tha!" (that is, "Be opened!") **35** And [imme-
diately] the man's ears were opened, his speech
impediment was removed, and he spoke plainly. **36** *He ordered them not to tell anyone. But
the more he ordered them not to, the more they
proclaimed it. **37** [l]They were exceedingly astonished and they said, "He has done all things
well. He makes the deaf hear and [the] mute
speak."

# CHAPTER 8

## The Feeding of the Four Thousand

**1** [m]*In those days when there again was a great
crowd without anything to eat, he summoned
the disciples and said, **2** "My heart is moved
with pity for the crowd, because they have been
with me now for three days and have nothing to
eat. **3** If I send them away hungry to their
homes, they will collapse on the way, and some
of them have come a great distance." **4** His
disciples answered him, "Where can anyone
get enough bread to satisfy them here in this
deserted place?" **5** Still he asked them, "How
many loaves do you have?" "Seven," they
replied. **6** *He ordered the crowd to sit down on
the ground. Then, taking the seven loaves he
gave thanks, broke them, and gave them to his
disciples to distribute, and they distributed them
to the crowd. **7** They also had a few fish. He
said the blessing over them and ordered them

---

f 4, 10.13.
g Acts 10, 15.
h Jer 17, 9.
i Mt 15, 21-28.
j Mt 8, 29.
k Mt 15, 29-31.
l Mt 15, 31.
m 6, 34-44; Mt 15, 32-39.

---

7, 16: Verse 16, "Anyone who has ears to hear ought to hear," is omitted because it is lacking in some of the best Greek manuscripts and was probably transferred here by scribes from 4, (9).23.

7, 17: *Away from the crowd . . . the parable:* in this context of privacy the term *parable* refers to something hidden, about to be revealed to the disciples; cf 4, 10–11.34. Jesus sets the Mosaic food laws in the context of the kingdom of God where they are abrogated, and he declares moral defilement the only cause of uncleanness.

7, 19: *(Thus he declared all foods clean):* if this bold declaration goes back to Jesus, its force was not realized among Jewish Christians in the early church; cf Acts 10, 1—11, 18.

7, 24–37: The withdrawal of Jesus to the district of Tyre may have been for a respite (24), but he soon moved onward to Sidon and, by way of the Sea of Galilee, to the Decapolis. These districts provided a Gentile setting for the extension of his ministry of healing because the people there acknowledged his power (29.37). The actions attributed to Jesus (33–35) were also used by healers of the time.

7, 27–28: The figure of a household in which children at table are fed first and then their leftover food is given to the dogs under the table is used effectively to acknowledge the prior claim of the Jews to the ministry of Jesus; however, Jesus accedes to the Gentile woman's plea for the cure of her afflicted daughter because of her faith.

7, 36: *The more they proclaimed it:* the same verb *proclaim* attributed here to the crowd in relation to the miracles of Jesus is elsewhere used in Mark for the preaching of the gospel on the part of Jesus, of his disciples, and of the Christian community (1, 14; 13, 10; 14, 9). Implied in the action of the crowd is a recognition of the salvific mission of Jesus; see the note on Mt 11, 5–6.

8, 1–10: The two accounts of the multiplication of loaves and fishes (8, 1–10 and 6, 31–44) have eucharistic significance. Their similarity of structure and themes but dissimilarity of detail are considered by many to refer to a single event that, however, developed in two distinct traditions, one Jewish Christian and the other Gentile Christian, since Jesus in Mark's presentation (7, 24–37) has extended his saving mission to the Gentiles.

8, 6: See the note on 6, 41.

distributed also. **8** They ate and were satisfied.
They picked up the fragments left over—seven
baskets. **9** There were about four thousand people.
He dismissed them **10** and got into the boat
with his disciples and came to the region of
Dalmanutha.

**The Demand for a Sign** **11** [n,o]*The Pharisees came forward and began to argue with him,
seeking from him a sign from heaven to test
him. **12** He sighed from the depth of his spirit
and said, "Why does this generation seek a
sign? Amen, I say to you, no sign will be given
to this generation." **13** Then he left them, got
into the boat again, and went off to the other
shore.

**The Leaven of the Pharisees** **14** [p]They
had forgotten to bring bread, and they had only
one loaf with them in the boat. **15** *He enjoined
them, "Watch out, guard against the leaven of
the Pharisees and the leaven of Herod."
**16** They concluded among themselves that it
was because they had no bread. **17** [q]When he
became aware of this he said to them, "Why do
you conclude that it is because you have no
bread? Do you not yet understand or comprehend? Are your hearts hardened? **18** [r]Do you
have eyes and not see, ears and not hear? And
do you not remember, **19** when I broke the five
loaves for the five thousand, how many wicker
baskets full of fragments you picked up?" They
answered him, "Twelve." **20** "When I broke
the seven loaves for the four thousand, how
many full baskets of fragments did you pick
up?" They answered [him], "Seven." **21** He
said to them, "Do you still not understand?"

**The Blind Man of Bethsaida** **22** *When
they arrived at Bethsaida, they brought to him
a blind man and begged him to touch him.
**23** [s]He took the blind man by the hand and led
him outside the village. Putting spittle on his
eyes he laid his hands on him and asked, "Do
you see anything?" **24** Looking up he replied,
"I see people looking like trees and walking."
**25** Then he laid hands on his eyes a second time
and he saw clearly; his sight was restored and
he could see everything distinctly. **26** Then he
sent him home and said, "Do not even go into
the village."

## III: THE MYSTERY BEGINS TO BE REVEALED

**Peter's Confession about Jesus**
**27** [t]*Now Jesus and his disciples set out for the
villages of Caesarea Philippi. Along the way he
asked his disciples, "Who do people say that I
am?" **28** They said in reply, "John the Baptist,
others Elijah, still others one of the prophets."
**29** And he asked them, "But who do you say
that I am?" Peter said to him in reply, "You are
the Messiah." **30** Then he warned them not to
tell anyone about him.

**The First Prediction of the Passion**
**31** [u]*He began to teach them that the Son of
Man must suffer greatly and be rejected by the
elders, the chief priests, and the scribes, and be
killed, and rise after three days. **32** He spoke
this openly. Then Peter took him aside and began to rebuke him. **33** At this he turned around
and, looking at his disciples, rebuked Peter and
said, "Get behind me, Satan. You are thinking
not as God does, but as human beings do."

n Mt 12, 38-39; 16, 1-4.
o Lk 11, 16.
p Mt 16, 5-12; Lk 12, 1.
q 4, 13.
r Jer 5, 21; Ez 12, 2.
s 7, 33; Jn 9, 6.
t Mt 16, 13-20; Lk 9, 18-21.
u Mt 16, 21-27; Lk 9, 22-26.

*

8, 11–12: The objection of the Pharisees that Jesus' miracles are unsatisfactory for proving the arrival of God's kingdom is comparable to the request of the crowd for a sign in Jn 6, 30–31. Jesus' response shows that a sign originating in human demand will not be provided; cf Nm 14, 11.22.

8, 15: *The leaven of the Pharisees . . . of Herod:* the corruptive action of leaven (1 Cor 5, 6–8; Gal 5, 9) was an apt symbol of the evil dispositions both of the Pharisees (11–13; 7, 5–13) and of Herod (6, 14–29) toward Jesus. The disciples of Jesus are warned against sharing such rebellious attitudes toward Jesus; cf vv 17, 21.

8, 22–26: Jesus' actions and the gradual cure of the blind man probably have the same purpose as in the case of the deaf man (7, 31–37). Some commentators regard the cure as an intended symbol of the gradual enlightenment of the disciples concerning Jesus' messiahship.

8, 27–30: This episode is the turning point in Mark's account of Jesus in his public ministry. Popular opinions concur in regarding him as a prophet. The disciples by contrast believe him to be the Messiah. Jesus acknowledges this identification but prohibits them from making his messianic office known to avoid confusing it with ambiguous contemporary ideas on the nature of that office. See further the notes on Mt 16, 13–20.

8, 31: *Son of Man:* an enigmatic title. It is used in Dn 7, 13–14 as a symbol of "the saints of the Most High," the faithful Israelites who receive the everlasting kingdom from the Ancient One (God). They are represented by a human figure that contrasts with the various beasts who represent the previous kingdoms of the earth. In the Jewish apocryphal books of 1 Enoch and 4 Ezra the "Son of Man" is not, as in Dn, a group, but a unique figure of extraordinary spiritual endowments, who will be revealed as the one through whom the everlasting kingdom decreed by God will be established. It is possible though doubtful that this individualization of the Son of Man figure had been made in Jesus' time, and therefore his use of the title in that sense is questionable. Of itself, this expression means simply a human being, or, indefinitely, someone, and there are evidences of this use in pre-Christian times. Its use in the New Testament is probably due to Jesus' speaking of himself in that way, "a human being," and the later church's taking this in the sense of the Jewish apocrypha and applying it to him with that meaning. *Rejected by the elders, the chief priests, and the scribes:* the supreme council called the Sanhedrin was made up of seventy-one members of these three groups and presided over by the high priest. It exercised authority over the Jews in religious matters. See the note on Mt 8, 20.

### The Conditions of Discipleship

34 [v]*He summoned the crowd with his disciples and said to them, "Whoever wishes to come after me must deny himself, take up his cross, and follow me. 35 [w]*For whoever wishes to save his life will lose it, but whoever loses his life for my sake and that of the gospel will save it. 36 What profit is there for one to gain the whole world and forfeit his life? 37 What could one give in exchange for his life? 38 [x]Whoever is ashamed of me and of my words in this faithless and sinful generation, the Son of Man will be ashamed of when he comes in his Father's glory with the holy angels."

## CHAPTER 9

1 [y]*He also said to them, "Amen, I say to you, there are some standing here who will not taste death until they see that the kingdom of God has come in power."

### The Transfiguration of Jesus

2 [z]*After six days Jesus took Peter, James, and John and led them up a high mountain apart by themselves. And he was transfigured before them, 3 and his clothes became dazzling white, such as no fuller on earth could bleach them. 4 Then Elijah appeared to them along with Moses, and they were conversing with Jesus. 5 *Then Peter said to Jesus in reply, "Rabbi, it is good that we are here! Let us make three tents: one for you, one for Moses, and one for Elijah." 6 He hardly knew what to say, they were so terrified. 7 *Then a cloud came, casting a shadow over them; then from the cloud came a voice, "This is my beloved Son. Listen to him." 8 Suddenly, looking around, they no longer saw anyone but Jesus alone with them.

### The Coming of Elijah

9 [a]*As they were coming down from the mountain, he charged them not to relate what they had seen to anyone, except when the Son of Man had risen from the dead. 10 So they kept the matter to themselves, questioning what rising from the dead meant. 11 [b]Then they asked him, "Why do the scribes say that Elijah must come first?" 12 He told them, "Elijah will indeed come first and restore all things, yet how is it written regarding the Son of Man that he must suffer greatly and be treated with contempt? 13 [c]But I tell you that Elijah has come and they did to him whatever they pleased, as it is written of him."

### The Healing of a Boy with a Demon

14 [d]*When they came to the disciples, they saw a large crowd around them and scribes arguing with them. 15 Immediately on seeing him, the whole crowd was utterly amazed. They ran up to him and greeted him. 16 He asked them, "What are you arguing about with them?" 17 Someone from the crowd answered him, "Teacher, I have brought to you my son possessed by a mute spirit. 18 Wherever it seizes him, it throws him down; he foams at the mouth, grinds his teeth, and becomes rigid. I asked your disciples to drive it out, but they were unable to do so." 19 He said to them in reply, "O faithless generation, how long will I be with you? How long will I endure you? Bring him to me." 20 They brought the boy to him. And when he saw him, the spirit immediately threw the boy into convulsions. As he fell to the ground, he began to roll around and foam at the

---

v Mt 10, 38-39; 16, 24-27; Lk 14, 26-27.
w Jn 12, 25.
x Mt 10, 33; Lk 12, 8.
y Mt 16, 28; Lk 9, 27.
z Mt 17, 1-13; Lk 9, 28-36.
a 8, 31.
b Is 53, 3; Mal 3, 23.
c 1 Kgs 19, 2-10.
d Mt 17, 14-21; Lk 9, 37-43.

---

*

8, 34–35: This utterance of Jesus challenges all believers to authentic discipleship and total commitment to himself through self-renunciation and acceptance of the cross of suffering, even to the sacrifice of life itself. *Whoever wishes to save his life will lose it . . . will save it:* an expression of the ambivalence of life and its contrasting destiny. Life seen as mere self-centered earthly existence and lived in denial of Christ ends in destruction, but when lived in loyalty to Christ, despite earthly death, it arrives at fullness of life.

8, 35: *For my sake and that of the gospel:* Mark here, as at 10, 29, equates Jesus with the gospel.

9, 1: *There are some standing . . . come in power:* understood by some to refer to the establishment by God's power of his kingdom on earth in and through the church; more likely, as understood by others, a reference to the imminent parousia.

9, 2–8: Mk and Mt 17, 1 place the transfiguration of Jesus six days after the first prediction of his passion and death and his instruction to the disciples on the doctrine of the cross; Lk 9, 28 has "about eight days." Thus the transfiguration counterbalances the prediction of the passion by affording certain of the disciples insight into the divine glory that Jesus possessed. His glory will overcome his death and that of his disciples; cf 2 Cor 3, 18; 2 Pt 1, 16–19. The heavenly voice (7) prepares the disciples to understand that in the divine plan Jesus must die ignominiously before his messianic glory is made manifest; cf Lk 24, 25–27. See further the note on Mt 17, 1–8.

9, 5: Moses and Elijah represent respectively law and prophecy in the Old Testament and are linked to Mt. Sinai; cf Ex 19, 16—20, 17; 1 Kgs 19, 2.8–14. They now appear with Jesus as witnesses to the fulfillment of the law and the prophets taking place in the person of Jesus as he appears in glory.

9, 7: *A cloud came, casting a shadow over them:* even the disciples enter into the mystery of his glorification. In the Old Testament the cloud covered the meeting tent, indicating the Lord's presence in the midst of his people (Ex 40, 34–35) and came to rest upon the temple in Jerusalem at the time of its dedication (1 Kgs 8, 10).

9, 9–13: At the transfiguration of Jesus his disciples had seen Elijah. They were perplexed because, according to the rabbinical interpretation of Mal 3, 23–24, Elijah was to come first. Jesus' response shows that Elijah has come, in the person of John the Baptist, to prepare for the day of the Lord. Jesus *must suffer greatly and be treated with contempt* (12) like the Baptist (13); cf 6, 17–29.

9, 14–29: The disciples' failure to effect a cure seems to reflect unfavorably on Jesus (14–18.22). In response Jesus exposes their lack of trust in God (19) and scores their lack of prayer (29), i.e., of conscious reliance on God's power when acting in Jesus' name. For Mt, see the note on 17, 14–20. Luke 9, 37–43 centers attention on Jesus' sovereign power.

mouth. **21** Then he questioned his father,
"How long has this been happening to him?"
He replied, "Since childhood. **22** It has often
thrown him into fire and into water to kill him.
But if you can do anything, have compassion on
us and help us." **23** Jesus said to him, "'If you
can!' Everything is possible to one who has
faith." **24** Then the boy's father cried out, "I
do believe, help my unbelief!" **25** Jesus, on
seeing a crowd rapidly gathering, rebuked the
unclean spirit and said to it, "Mute and deaf
spirit, I command you: come out of him and
never enter him again!" **26** Shouting and
throwing the boy into convulsions, it came out.
He became like a corpse, which caused many to
say, "He is dead!" **27** But Jesus took him by
the hand, raised him, and he stood up. **28** When
he entered the house, his disciples asked him in
private, "Why could we not drive it out?"
**29** *He said to them, "This kind can only come
out through prayer."

### The Second Prediction of the Passion

**30** [e,f]They left from there and began a journey
through Galilee, but he did not wish anyone to
know about it. **31** He was teaching his disciples
and telling them, "The Son of Man is to be
handed over to men and they will kill him, and
three days after his death he will rise." **32** But
they did not understand the saying, and they
were afraid to question him.

## *IV: THE FULL REVELATION OF THE MYSTERY*

### The Greatest in the Kingdom

**33** [g]*They
came to Capernaum and, once inside the house,
he began to ask them, "What were you arguing
about on the way?" **34** But they remained silent. They had been discussing among themselves on the way who was the greatest.
**35** [h]Then he sat down, called the Twelve, and
said to them, "If anyone wishes to be first, he
shall be the last of all and the servant of all."
**36** Taking a child he placed it in their midst,
and putting his arms around it he said to them,
**37** [i]"Whoever receives one child such as this
in my name, receives me; and whoever receives
me, receives not me but the One who sent me."

### Another Exorcist

**38** [j]*John said to him,
"Teacher, we saw someone driving out demons
in your name, and we tried to prevent him because he does not follow us." **39** Jesus replied,
"Do not prevent him. There is no one who
performs a mighty deed in my name who can at
the same time speak ill of me. **40** [k]For whoever
is not against us is for us. **41** [l]Anyone who
gives you a cup of water to drink because you
belong to Christ, amen, I say to you, will surely
not lose his reward.

### Temptations to Sin

**42** [m]"Whoever
causes one of these little ones who believe [in
me] to sin, it would be better for him if a great
millstone were put around his neck and he were
thrown into the sea. **43** *If your hand causes
you to sin, cut it off. It is better for you to enter
into life maimed than with two hands to go into
Gehenna, into the unquenchable fire. **[44*]**
**45** And if your foot causes you to sin, cut it off.
It is better for you to enter into life crippled than
with two feet to be thrown into Gehenna. **[46*]**
**47** And if your eye causes you to sin, pluck it
out. Better for you to enter into the kingdom of
God with one eye than with two eyes to be
thrown into Gehenna, **48** [n]where 'their worm
does not die, and the fire is not quenched.'

### The Simile of Salt

**49** *"Everyone will be
salted with fire. **50** [o]Salt is good, but if salt
becomes insipid, with what will you restore its
flavor? Keep salt in yourselves and you will
have peace with one another."

## CHAPTER 10

### Marriage and Divorce

**1** He set out from
there and went into the district of Judea [and]
across the Jordan. Again crowds gathered
around him and, as was his custom, he again
taught them. **2** [p]*The Pharisees approached

e Jn 7, 1.
f 8, 31; Mt 17, 22-23; Lk 9, 43-45.
g Mt 18, 1-5; Lk 9, 46-48.
h Mt 20, 27.
i Mt 10, 40; 18, 5; Jn 13, 20.
j Nm 11, 28; Lk 9, 49-50; 1 Cor 12, 3.
k Mt 12, 30.
l Mt 10, 42; 1 Cor 3, 23.
m Mt 5, 29-30; 18, 6-9; Lk 17, 1-2.
n Is 66, 24.
o Lv 2, 13; Mt 5, 13; Lk 14, 34-35; Col 4, 6.
p Mt 19, 3-9.

*

9, 29: *This kind can only come out through prayer:* a variant reading adds "and through fasting."

9, 33–37: Mark probably intends this incident and the sayings that follow as commentary on the disciples' lack of understanding (32). Their role in Jesus' work is one of service, especially to the poor and lowly. Children were the symbol Jesus used for the *anawim,* the poor in spirit, the lowly in the Christian community.

9, 38–41: Jesus warns against jealousy and intolerance toward others, such as exorcists who do *not follow us.* The saying in v 40 is a broad principle of the divine tolerance. Even the smallest courtesies shown to those who teach in Jesus' name do not go unrewarded.

9, 43.45.47: *Gehenna:* see the note on Mt 5, 22.

9, 44.46: These verses, lacking in some important early manuscripts, are here omitted as scribal additions. They simply repeat v 48, itself a modified citation of Is 66, 24.

9, 49: *Everyone will be salted with fire:* so the better manuscripts. Some add "every sacrifice will be salted with salt." The purifying and preservative use of salt in food (Lv 2, 13) and the refinement effected through fire refer here to comparable effects in the spiritual life of the disciples of Jesus.

10, 2–9: In the dialogue between Jesus and the Pharisees on the subject of divorce, Jesus declares that the law of Moses permitted divorce (Dt 24, 1) only *because of the hardness of your hearts* (4–5). In citing Gn 1, 27 and 2, 24, Jesus proclaims permanence to be the divine intent from the beginning con-

and asked, "Is it lawful for a husband to divorce
his wife?" They were testing him. **3** He said to
them in reply, "What did Moses command
you?" **4** [q]They replied, "Moses permitted him
to write a bill of divorce and dismiss her."
**5** But Jesus told them, "Because of the hardness of your hearts he wrote you this commandment. **6** [r]But from the beginning of creation,
'God made them male and female. **7** [s]For this
reason a man shall leave his father and mother
[and be joined to his wife], **8** and the two shall
become one flesh.' So they are no longer two
but one flesh. **9** Therefore what God has joined
together, no human being must separate."
**10** In the house the disciples again questioned
him about this. **11** [t]He said to them, "Whoever
divorces his wife and marries another commits
adultery against her; **12** and if she divorces her
husband and marries another, she commits adultery."

## Blessing of the Children

**13** [u][v]And peo-
ple were bringing children to him that he might
touch them, but the disciples rebuked them.
**14** When Jesus saw this he became indignant
and said to them, "Let the children come to me;
do not prevent them, for the kingdom of God
belongs to such as these. **15** [w]*Amen, I say to
you, whoever does not accept the kingdom of
God like a child will not enter it." **16** Then he
embraced them and blessed them, placing his
hands on them.

## The Rich Man

**17** [x]As he was setting out on
a journey, a man ran up, knelt down before him,
and asked him, "Good teacher, what must I do
to inherit eternal life?" **18** *Jesus answered
him, "Why do you call me good? No one is
good but God alone. **19** [y]You know the commandments: 'You shall not kill; you shall not
commit adultery; you shall not steal; you shall
not bear false witness; you shall not defraud;
honor your father and your mother.'" **20** He
replied and said to him, "Teacher, all of these
I have observed from my youth." **21** Jesus,
looking at him, loved him and said to him,
"You are lacking in one thing. Go, sell what
you have, and give to [the] poor and you will
have treasure in heaven; then come, follow
me." **22** At that statement his face fell, and he
went away sad, for he had many possessions.
**23** [z]*Jesus looked around and said to his disciples, "How hard it is for those who have
wealth to enter the kingdom of God!" **24** The
disciples were amazed at his words. So Jesus
again said to them in reply, "Children, how
hard it is to enter the kingdom of God! **25** It is
easier for a camel to pass through [the] eye of
[a] needle than for one who is rich to enter the
kingdom of God." **26** They were exceedingly
astonished and said among themselves, "Then
who can be saved?" **27** Jesus looked at them
and said, "For human beings it is impossible,
but not for God. All things are possible for
God." **28** Peter began to say to him, "We have
given up everything and followed you."
**29** Jesus said, "Amen, I say to you, there is no
one who has given up house or brothers or sisters or mother or father or children or lands for
my sake and for the sake of the gospel **30** who
will not receive a hundred times more now in
this present age: houses and brothers and sisters
and mothers and children and lands, with persecutions, and eternal life in the age to come.
**31** [a]But many that are first will be last, and
[the] last will be first."

## The Third Prediction of the Passion

**32** [b]They were on the way, going up to Jerusalem, and Jesus went ahead of them. They were
amazed, and those who followed were afraid.
Taking the Twelve aside again he began to tell
them what was going to happen to him.
**33** "Behold, we are going up to Jerusalem, and
the Son of Man will be handed over to the chief
priests and the scribes, and they will condemn
him to death and hand him over to the Gentiles
**34** who will mock him, spit upon him, scourge
him, and put him to death, but after three days
he will rise."

## Ambition of James and John

**35** [c]Then
James and John, the sons of Zebedee, came to
him and said to him, "Teacher, we want you to
do for us whatever we ask of you." **36** He
replied, "What do you wish [me] to do for

q Dt 24, 1-4.
r Gn 1, 27.
s Gn 2, 24; 1 Cor 6, 16; Eph 5, 31.
t Mt 5, 32; Lk 16, 18; 1 Cor 7, 10-11.
u Mt 19, 13-15; Lk 18, 15-17.
v Lk 9, 47.
w Mt 18, 3.
x Mt 19, 16-30; Lk 18, 18-30.
y Ex 20, 12-16; Dt 5, 16-21.
z Prv 11, 28.
a Mt 19, 30; Lk 13, 30.
b 8, 31; Mt 20, 17-19; Lk 18, 31-33.
c Mt 20, 20-28.

*

cerning human marriage (6–8). He reaffirms this with the declaration that *what God has joined together, no human being must separate* (9). See further the notes on Mt 5, 31–32 and 19, 3–9.

10, 15: *Whoever does not accept the kingdom of God like a child:* i.e., in total dependence upon and obedience to the gospel; cf Mt 18, 3–4.

10, 18: *Why do you call me good?:* Jesus repudiates the term "good" for himself and directs it to God, the source of all goodness who alone can grant the gift of eternal life; cf Mt 19, 16–17.

10, 23–27: In the Old Testament wealth and material goods are considered a sign of God's favor (Jb 1, 10; Ps 128, 1–2; Is 3, 10). The words of Jesus in 23–25 provoke astonishment among the disciples because of their apparent contradiction of the Old Testament concept (24.26). Since wealth, power, and merit generate false security, Jesus rejects them utterly as a claim to enter the kingdom. Achievement of salvation is beyond human capability and depends solely on the goodness of God who offers it as a gift (27).

you?" **37** They answered him, "Grant that in your glory we may sit one at your right and the other at your left." **38** [d]*Jesus said to them, "You do not know what you are asking. Can you drink the cup that I drink or be baptized with the baptism with which I am baptized?" **39** They said to him, "We can." Jesus said to them, "The cup that I drink, you will drink, and with the baptism with which I am baptized, you will be baptized; **40** but to sit at my right or at my left is not mine to give but is for those for whom it has been prepared." **41** When the ten heard this, they became indignant at James and John. **42** [e]*Jesus summoned them and said to them, "You know that those who are recognized as rulers over the Gentiles lord it over them, and their great ones make their authority over them felt. **43** But it shall not be so among you. Rather, whoever wishes to be great among you will be your servant; **44** whoever wishes to be first among you will be the slave of all. **45** For the Son of Man did not come to be served but to serve and to give his life as a ransom for many."

**The Blind Bartimaeus** **46** [f]*They came to Jericho. And as he was leaving Jericho with his disciples and a sizable crowd, Bartimaeus, a blind man, the son of Timaeus, sat by the roadside begging. **47** On hearing that it was Jesus of Nazareth, he began to cry out and say, "Jesus, son of David, have pity on me." **48** And many rebuked him, telling him to be silent. But he kept calling out all the more, "Son of David, have pity on me." **49** Jesus stopped and said, "Call him." So they called the blind man, saying to him, "Take courage; get up, he is calling you." **50** He threw aside his cloak, sprang up, and came to Jesus. **51** Jesus said to him in reply, "What do you want me to do for you?" The blind man replied to him, "Master, I want to see." **52** Jesus told him, "Go your way; your faith has saved you." Immediately he received his sight and followed him on the way.

## CHAPTER 11

**The Entry into Jerusalem** **1** [g]*When they drew near to Jerusalem, to Bethphage and Bethany at the Mount of Olives, he sent two of his disciples **2** and said to them, "Go into the village opposite you, and immediately on entering it, you will find a colt tethered on which no one has ever sat. Untie it and bring it here. **3** If anyone should say to you, 'Why are you doing this?' reply, 'The Master has need of it and will send it back here at once.'" **4** So they went off and found a colt tethered at a gate outside on the street, and they untied it. **5** Some of the bystanders said to them, "What are you doing, untying the colt?" **6** They answered them just as Jesus had told them to, and they permitted them to do it. **7** So they brought the colt to Jesus and put their cloaks over it. And he sat on it. **8** Many people spread their cloaks on the road, and others spread leafy branches that they had cut from the fields. **9** [h]Those preceding him as well as those following kept crying out:

"Hosanna!
Blessed is he who comes in the name of the Lord!
**10** Blessed is the kingdom of our father David that is to come!
Hosanna in the highest!"

**11** [i]He entered Jerusalem and went into the temple area. He looked around at everything and, since it was already late, went out to Bethany with the Twelve.

**Jesus Curses a Fig Tree** **12** [j]*The next day as they were leaving Bethany he was hungry. **13** Seeing from a distance a fig tree in leaf, he went over to see if he could find anything on it. When he reached it he found nothing but leaves; it was not the time for figs. **14** And he

d Lk 12, 50.
e Lk 22, 25-27.
f Mt 20, 29-34; Lk 18, 35-43.
g Mt 21, 1-9; Lk 19, 29-38; Jn 12, 12-15.
h 2 Sm 7, 16; Ps 118, 26.
i Mt 21, 10.17.
j Mt 21, 18-20; Lk 13, 6-9.

*

10, 38–40: *Can you drink the cup . . . I am baptized?:* the metaphor of drinking the cup is used in the Old Testament to refer to acceptance of the destiny assigned by God; see the note on Ps 11, 6. In Jesus' case, this involves divine judgment on sin that Jesus the innocent one is to expiate on behalf of the guilty (14, 24; Is 53, 5). His baptism is to be his crucifixion and death for the salvation of the human race; cf Lk 12, 50. The request of James and John for a share in the glory (35–37) must of necessity involve a share in Jesus' sufferings, the endurance of tribulation and suffering for the gospel (39). The authority of assigning places of honor in the kingdom is reserved to God (40).

10, 42–45: Whatever authority is to be exercised by the disciples must, like that of Jesus, be rendered as service to others (45) rather than for personal aggrandizement (42–44). The service of Jesus is his passion and death for the sins of the human race (45); cf 14, 24; Is 53, 11–12; Mt 26, 28; Lk 22, 19–20.

10, 46–52: See the notes on Mt 9, 27–31 and 20, 29–34.

11, 1–11: In Mark's account Jesus takes the initiative in ordering the preparation for his entry into Jerusalem (1–6) even as he later orders the preparation of his last Passover Supper (14, 12–16). In vv 9–10 the greeting Jesus receives stops short of proclaiming him Messiah. He is greeted rather as the prophet of the coming messianic kingdom. Contrast Mt 21, 9.

11, 12–14: Jesus' search for fruit on the fig tree recalls the prophets' earlier use of this image to designate Israel; cf Jer 8, 13; 29, 17; Jl 1, 7; Hos 9, 10.16. Cursing the fig tree is a parable in action representing Jesus' judgment (20) on barren Israel and the fate of Jerusalem for failing to receive his teaching; cf Is 34, 4; Hos 2, 14; Lk 13, 6–9.

said to it in reply, "May no one ever eat of your
fruit again!" And his disciples heard it.

**Cleansing of the Temple** **15** [k]*They
came to Jerusalem, and on entering the temple
area he began to drive out those selling and
buying there. He overturned the tables of the
money changers and the seats of those who were
selling doves. **16** He did not permit anyone to
carry anything through the temple area.
**17** [l]Then he taught them saying, "Is it not written:

> 'My house shall be called a house of prayer
> for all peoples'?
> But you have made it a den of thieves."

**18** The chief priests and the scribes came to
hear of it and were seeking a way to put him
to death, yet they feared him because the
whole crowd was astonished at his teaching.
**19** [m]When evening came, they went out of the
city.

**The Withered Fig Tree** **20** [n]Early in the
morning, as they were walking along, they saw
the fig tree withered to its roots. **21** Peter remembered and said to him, "Rabbi, look! The
fig tree that you cursed has withered." **22** Jesus
said to them in reply, "Have faith in God.
**23** [o]Amen, I say to you, whoever says to this
mountain, 'Be lifted up and thrown into the
sea,' and does not doubt in his heart but believes
that what he says will happen, it shall be done
for him. **24** [p]Therefore I tell you, all that you
ask for in prayer, believe that you will receive
it and it shall be yours. **25** [q]When you stand to
pray, forgive anyone against whom you have a
grievance, so that your heavenly Father may in
turn forgive you your transgressions. **[26*]**"

**The Authority of Jesus Questioned**
**27** [r]*They returned once more to Jerusalem.
As he was walking in the temple area, the chief
priests, the scribes, and the elders approached
him **28** and said to him, "By what authority are
you doing these things? Or who gave you this
authority to do them?" **29** Jesus said to them,
"I shall ask you one question. Answer me, and
I will tell you by what authority I do these
things. **30** Was John's baptism of heavenly or
of human origin? Answer me." **31** They discussed this among themselves and said, "If we
say, 'Of heavenly origin,' he will say, '[Then]
why did you not believe him?' **32** But shall we
say, 'Of human origin'?"—they feared the
crowd, for they all thought John really was a
prophet. **33** So they said to Jesus in reply, "We
do not know." Then Jesus said to them, "Neither shall I tell you by what authority I do these
things."

## CHAPTER 12

**Parable of the Tenants** **1** [s t]*He began to
speak to them in parables. "A man planted a
vineyard, put a hedge around it, dug a wine
press, and built a tower. Then he leased it to
tenant farmers and left on a journey. **2** At the
proper time he sent a servant to the tenants to
obtain from them some of the produce of the
vineyard. **3** But they seized him, beat him, and
sent him away empty-handed. **4** Again he sent
them another servant. And that one they beat
over the head and treated shamefully. **5** He sent
yet another whom they killed. So, too, many
others; some they beat, others they killed. **6** He
had one other to send, a beloved son. He sent
him to them last of all, thinking, 'They will
respect my son.' **7** But those tenants said to one
another, 'This is the heir. Come, let us kill him,
and the inheritance will be ours.' **8** So they
seized him and killed him, and threw him out of
the vineyard. **9** What [then] will the owner of
the vineyard do? He will come, put the tenants
to death, and give the vineyard to others.
**10** [u]Have you not read this scripture passage:

> 'The stone that the builders rejected
> has become the cornerstone;
> **11** by the Lord has this been done,
> and it is wonderful in our eyes'?"

**12** They were seeking to arrest him, but they
feared the crowd, for they realized that he had
addressed the parable to them. So they left him
and went away.

k Mt 21, 12-13; Lk 19, 45-46; Jn 2, 14-16.
l Is 56, 7; Jer 7, 11.
m Lk 21, 37.
n Mt 21, 20-22.
o Mt 17, 20-21; Lk 17, 6.
p Mt 7, 7; Jn 11, 22; 14, 13.
q Mt 6, 14; 18, 35.
r Mt 21, 23-27; Lk 20, 1-8.
s Mt 21, 33-46; Lk 20, 9-19.
t Is 5, 1-7; Jer 2, 21.
u Ps 118, 22-23; Is 28, 16.

*

11, 15–19: See the note on Mt 21, 12–17.

11, 26: This verse, which reads, "But if you do not forgive, neither will your heavenly Father forgive your transgressions," is omitted in the best manuscripts. It was probably added by copyists under the influence of Mt 6, 15.

11, 27–33: The mounting hostility toward Jesus came from the chief priests, the scribes, and the elders (27); the Herodians and the Pharisees (12, 13); and the Sadducees (12, 18). By their rejection of God's messengers, John the Baptist and Jesus, they incurred the divine judgment implied in vv 27–33 and confirmed in the parable of the vineyard tenants (12, 1–12).

12, 1–12: The vineyard denotes Israel (Is 5, 1–7). The tenant farmers are the religious leaders of Israel. God is the owner of the vineyard. His servants are his messengers, the prophets. The beloved son is Jesus (1, 11; 9, 7; Mt 3, 17; 17, 5; Lk 3, 22; 9, 35). The punishment of the tenants refers to the religious leaders, and the transfer of the vineyard to others refers to the people of the new Israel.

## Paying Taxes to the Emperor

13 [v][w]*They sent some Pharisees and Herodians to him to ensnare him in his speech.
14 They came and said to him, "Teacher, we
know that you are a truthful man and that you
are not concerned with anyone's opinion. You
do not regard a person's status but teach the way
of God in accordance with the truth. Is it lawful
to pay the census tax to Caesar or not? Should
we pay or should we not pay?" 15 Knowing
their hypocrisy he said to them, "Why are you
testing me? Bring me a denarius to look at."
16 They brought one to him and he said to
them, "Whose image and inscription is this?"
They replied to him, "Caesar's." 17 [x]So Jesus
said to them, "Repay to Caesar what belongs to
Caesar and to God what belongs to God." They
were utterly amazed at him.

## The Question about the Resurrection

18 *Some Sadducees, who say there is no resurrection, came to him and put this question to
him, 19 [y]saying, "Teacher, Moses wrote for
us, 'If someone's brother dies, leaving a wife
but no child, his brother must take the wife and
raise up descendants for his brother.' 20 Now
there were seven brothers. The first married a
woman and died, leaving no descendants.
21 So the second married her and died, leaving
no descendants, and the third likewise. 22 And
the seven left no descendants. Last of all the
woman also died. 23 At the resurrection [when
they arise] whose wife will she be? For all seven
had been married to her." 24 Jesus said to
them, "Are you not misled because you do not
know the scriptures or the power of God?
25 When they rise from the dead, they neither
marry nor are given in marriage, but they are
like the angels in heaven. 26 [z]As for the dead
being raised, have you not read in the Book of
Moses, in the passage about the bush, how God
told him, 'I am the God of Abraham, [the] God
of Isaac, and [the] God of Jacob'? 27 He is not
God of the dead but of the living. You are
greatly misled."

## The Greatest Commandment

28 [a]*One
of the scribes, when he came forward and heard
them disputing and saw how well he had answered them, asked him, "Which is the first of
all the commandments?" 29 Jesus replied,
"The first is this: 'Hear, O Israel! The Lord our
God is Lord alone! 30 [b]You shall love the Lord
your God with all your heart, with all your soul,
with all your mind, and with all your strength.'
31 [c]The second is this: 'You shall love your
neighbor as yourself.' There is no other commandment greater than these." 32 The scribe
said to him, "Well said, teacher. You are right
in saying, 'He is One and there is no other than
he.' 33 [d]And 'to love him with all your heart,
with all your understanding, with all your
strength, and to love your neighbor as yourself'
is worth more than all burnt offerings and sacrifices." 34 [e]And when Jesus saw that [he] answered with understanding, he said to him,
"You are not far from the kingdom of God."
And no one dared to ask him any more questions.

## The Question about David's Son

35 [f]*As Jesus was teaching in the temple area
he said, "How do the scribes claim that the
Messiah is the son of David? 36 [g]David himself, inspired by the holy Spirit, said:

'The Lord said to my lord,
"Sit at my right hand
until I place your enemies under
your feet." '

37 David himself calls him 'lord'; so how is he
his son?" [The] great crowd heard this with
delight.

## Denunciation of the Scribes

38 [h]*In the
course of his teaching he said, "Beware of the
scribes, who like to go around in long robes and
accept greetings in the marketplaces, 39 seats
of honor in synagogues, and places of honor at
banquets. 40 They devour the houses of widows and, as a pretext, recite lengthy prayers.
They will receive a very severe condemnation."

## The Poor Widow's Contribution

41 [i]*He sat down opposite the treasury and
observed how the crowd put money into the
treasury. Many rich people put in large sums.
42 A poor widow also came and put in two
small coins worth a few cents. 43 Calling his
disciples to himself, he said to them, "Amen,
I say to you, this poor widow put in more than

v Mt 22, 15-33; Lk 20, 20-39.
w 3, 6.
x Rom 13, 7.
y Dt 25, 5.
z Ex 3, 6.
a Mt 22, 34-40; Lk 10, 25-28.
b Dt 6, 4-5.
c Lv 19, 18; Rom 13, 9; Gal 5, 14; Jas 2, 8.
d Dt 6, 4; Ps 40, 7-9.
e Mt 22, 46; Lk 20, 40.
f Mt 22, 41-45; Lk 20, 41-44.
g Ps 110, 1.
h Mt 23, 1-7; Lk 11, 43; 20, 45-47.
i Lk 21, 1-4.

*

12, 13–34: In the ensuing conflicts (cf also 2, 1—3, 6) Jesus vanquishes his adversaries by his responses to their questions and reduces them to silence (34).

12, 13–17: See the note on Mt 22, 15–22.

12, 18–27: See the note on Mt 22, 23–33.

12, 28–34: See the note on Mt 22, 34–40.

12, 35–37: Jesus questions the claim of the scribes about the Davidic descent of the Messiah, not to deny it (Mt 1, 1; Acts 2, 20.34; Rom 1, 3; 2 Tm 2, 8) but to imply that he is more than this. His superiority derives from his transcendent origin, to which David himself attested when he spoke of the Messiah with the name "Lord" (Ps 110, 1). See also the note on Mt 22, 41–46.

12, 38–40: See the notes on 7, 1–23 and Mt 23, 1–39.

12, 41–44: See the note on Lk 21, 1–4.

all the other contributors to the treasury. 44 For
they have all contributed from their surplus
wealth, but she, from her poverty, has contributed all she had, her whole livelihood."

## CHAPTER 13

**The Destruction of the Temple Fore-
told** 1 [j]*As he was making his way out of
the temple area one of his disciples said to him,
"Look, teacher, what stones and what buildings!" 2 Jesus said to him, "Do you see these
great buildings? There will not be one stone left
upon another that will not be thrown down."

**The Signs of the End** 3 [k]*As he was sitting on the Mount of Olives opposite the temple
area, Peter, James, John, and Andrew asked
him privately, 4 "Tell us, when will this happen, and what sign will there be when all these
things are about to come to an end?" 5 [l]Jesus
began to say to them, "See that no one deceives
you. 6 Many will come in my name saying, 'I
am he,' and they will deceive many. 7 When
you hear of wars and reports of wars do not be
alarmed; such things must happen, but it will
not yet be the end. 8 Nation will rise against
nation and kingdom against kingdom. There
will be earthquakes from place to place and
there will be famines. These are the beginnings
of the labor pains.

**The Coming Persecution** 9 [m]"Watch
out for yourselves. They will hand you over to
the courts. You will be beaten in synagogues.
You will be arraigned before governors and
kings because of me, as a witness before them.
10 *But the gospel must first be preached to all
nations. 11 [n]When they lead you away and
hand you over, do not worry beforehand about
what you are to say. But say whatever will be
given to you at that hour. For it will not be you
who are speaking but the holy Spirit. 12 Brother will hand over brother to death, and the father
his child; children will rise up against parents
and have them put to death. 13 You will be
hated by all because of my name. But the one
who perseveres to the end will be saved.

**The Great Tribulation** 14 [op]*"When you
see the desolating abomination standing where
he should not (let the reader understand), then
those in Judea must flee to the mountains,
15 [q][and] a person on a housetop must not go
down or enter to get anything out of his house,
16 and a person in a field must not return to get
his cloak. 17 Woe to pregnant women and nursing mothers in those days. 18 Pray that this
does not happen in winter. 19 [r]For those times
will have tribulation such as has not been since
the beginning of God's creation until now, nor
ever will be. 20 If the Lord had not shortened
those days, no one would be saved; but for the
sake of the elect whom he chose, he did shorten
the days. 21 If anyone says to you then, 'Look,
here is the Messiah! Look, there he is!' do not
believe it. 22 False messiahs and false prophets
will arise and will perform signs and wonders in
order to mislead, if that were possible, the elect.
23 Be watchful! I have told it all to you beforehand.

**The Coming of the Son of Man**
24 [st]"But in those days after that tribulation

the sun will be darkened,
    and the moon will not give its light,
25 and the stars will be falling from the sky,
    and the powers in the heavens will be
        shaken.

26 [u]*And then they will see 'the Son of Man
coming in the clouds' with great power and
glory, 27 and then he will send out the angels
and gather [his] elect from the four winds, from
the end of the earth to the end of the sky.

---

j Mt 24, 1-2; Lk 21, 5-6.
k Mt 24, 3-8; Lk 21, 7-11.
l Eph 5, 6; 2 Thes 2, 3.
m Mt 24, 9-14; Lk 21, 12-19.
n Mt 10, 19-22; Lk 12, 11-12.
o Mt 24, 15-22; Lk 21, 20-24.
p Dn 9, 27; Mt 24, 15.
q Lk 17, 31.
r Dn 12, 1.
s Mt 24, 29-31; Lk 21, 25-27.
t Is 13, 10; Ez 32, 7; Jl 2, 10.
u 14, 62; Dn 7, 13-14.

---

*

13, 1–2: The reconstructed temple with its precincts, begun under Herod the Great ca. 20 B.C., was completed only some seven years before it was destroyed by fire in A.D. 70 at the hands of the Romans; cf Jer 26, 18; Mt 24, 1–2. For the dating of the reconstruction of the temple, see further the note on Jn 2, 20.

13, 3–37: Jesus' prediction of the destruction of the temple (2) provoked questions that the four named disciples put to him in private regarding the time and the sign when all *these things are about to come to an end* (3–4). The response to their questions was Jesus' eschatological discourse prior to his imminent death. It contained instruction and consolation exhorting the disciples and the church to faith and obedience through the trials that would confront them (5–13). The sign is the presence of *the desolating abomination* (14; see Dn 9, 27), i.e., of the Roman power profaning the temple. Flight from Jerusalem is urged rather than defense of the city through misguided messianic hope (14–23). Intervention will occur only after destruction (24–27), which will happen before the end of the first Christian generation (28–31). No one but the Father knows the precise time, or that of the parousia (32); hence the necessity of constant vigilance (33–37). Luke sets the parousia at a later date, after "the time of the Gentiles" (Lk 21, 24). See also the notes on Mt 24, 1—25, 46.

13, 10: *The gospel . . . to all nations:* the period of the Christian mission.

13, 14: The participle *standing* is masculine, in contrast to the neuter at Mt 24, 15.

13, 26: *Son of Man . . . with great power and glory:* Jesus cites this text from Dn 7, 13 in his response to the high priest, *Are you the Messiah?* (14, 61). In Ex 34, 5; Lv 16, 2; and Nm 11, 25 the clouds indicate the presence of the divinity. Thus in his role of Son of Man, Jesus is a heavenly being who will come in power and glory.

**The Lesson of the Fig Tree** 28 [v]"Learn
a lesson from the fig tree. When its branch
becomes tender and sprouts leaves, you know
that summer is near. 29 In the same way, when
you see these things happening, know that he is
near, at the gates. 30 Amen, I say to you, this
generation will not pass away until all these
things have taken place. 31 Heaven and earth
will pass away, but my words will not pass
away.

**Need for Watchfulness** 32 "But of that
day or hour, no one knows, neither the angels
in heaven, nor the Son, but only the Father.
33 [w]Be watchful! Be alert! You do not know
when the time will come. 34 [x]It is like a man
traveling abroad. He leaves home and places his
servants in charge, each with his work, and
orders the gatekeeper to be on the watch.
35 Watch, therefore; you do not know when the
lord of the house is coming, whether in the
evening, or at midnight, or at cockcrow, or in
the morning. 36 May he not come suddenly and
find you sleeping. 37 What I say to you, I say
to all: 'Watch!' "

## CHAPTER 14

**The Conspiracy against Jesus** 1 [y]*The
Passover and the Feast of Unleavened Bread
were to take place in two days' time. So the
chief priests and the scribes were seeking a way
to arrest him by treachery and put him to death.
2 They said, "Not during the festival, for fear
that there may be a riot among the people."

**The Anointing at Bethany** 3 [z]*When he
was in Bethany reclining at table in the house of
Simon the leper, a woman came with an alabaster jar of perfumed oil, costly genuine spike-
nard. She broke the alabaster jar and poured it
on his head. 4 There were some who were indignant. "Why has there been this waste of
perfumed oil? 5 It could have been sold for
more than three hundred days' wages and the
money given to the poor." They were infuriated
with her. 6 Jesus said, "Let her alone. Why do
you make trouble for her? She has done a good
thing for me. 7 The poor you will always have
with you, and whenever you wish you can do
good to them, but you will not always have me.
8 She has done what she could. She has anticipated anointing my body for burial. 9 Amen, I
say to you, wherever the gospel is proclaimed
to the whole world, what she has done will be
told in memory of her."

**The Betrayal by Judas** 10 [a]Then Judas
Iscariot, one of the Twelve, went off to the chief
priests to hand him over to them. 11 When they
heard him they were pleased and promised to
pay him money. Then he looked for an opportunity to hand him over.

**Preparations for the Passover** 12 [b]*On
the first day of the Feast of Unleavened Bread,
when they sacrificed the Passover lamb, his
disciples said to him, "Where do you want us
to go and prepare for you to eat the Passover?"
13 *He sent two of his disciples and said to
them, "Go into the city and a man will meet
you, carrying a jar of water. Follow him.
14 Wherever he enters, say to the master of the
house, 'The Teacher says, "Where is my guest
room where I may eat the Passover with my
disciples?" ' 15 Then he will show you a large
upper room furnished and ready. Make the
preparations for us there." 16 The disciples
then went off, entered the city, and found it just
as he had told them; and they prepared the Passover.

**The Betrayer** 17 [c]When it was evening, he
came with the Twelve. 18 *And as they re-

v Mt 24, 32-36; Lk 21, 29-33.
w Mt 24, 42; 25, 13-15.
x Mt 25, 14-30; Lk 19, 12-27.
y Mt 26, 2-5; Lk 22, 1-2; Jn 11, 45-53.
z Mt 26, 6-13; Jn 12, 1-8.
a Mt 26, 14-16; Lk 22, 3-6.
b Mt 26, 17-19; Lk 22, 7-13.
c Mt 26, 20-24; Lk 22, 21-23; Jn 13, 21-26.

*

14, 1—16, 8: In the movement of Mark's gospel the cross is depicted as Jesus' way to glory in accordance with the divine will. Thus the passion narrative is seen as the climax of Jesus' ministry.

14, 1: *The Passover and the Feast of Unleavened Bread:* the connection between the two festivals is reflected in Ex 12, 3–20; 34, 18; Lv 23, 4–8; Nm 9, 2–14; 28, 16–17; Dt 16, 1–8. The Passover commemorated the redemption from slavery and the departure of the Israelites from Egypt by night. It began at sundown after the Passover lamb was sacrificed in the temple in the afternoon of the fourteenth day of the month of Nisan. With the Passover Supper on the same evening was associated the eating of unleavened bread. The latter was continued through Nisan 21, a reminder of the affliction of the Israelites and of the haste surrounding their departure. Praise and thanks to God for his goodness in the past were combined at this dual festival with the hope of future salvation. *The chief priests . . . to death:* the intent to put Jesus to death was plotted for a long time but delayed for fear of the crowd (3, 6; 11, 18; 12, 12).

14, 3–9: At Bethany on the Mount of Olives, a few miles from Jerusalem, *in the house of Simon the leper,* Jesus defends a woman's loving action of anointing his head with perfumed oil in view of his impending death and burial as a criminal, in which case his body would not be anointed. See further the note on Jn 12, 7. He assures the woman of the remembrance of her deed in the worldwide preaching of the good news.

14, 12: *The first day of the Feast of Unleavened Bread . . . the Passover lamb:* a less precise designation of the day for sacrificing the Passover lamb as evidenced by some rabbinical literature. For a more exact designation, see the note on 14, 1. It was actually Nisan 14.

14, 13: *A man . . . carrying a jar of water:* perhaps a prearranged signal, for only women ordinarily carried water in jars. The Greek word used here, however, implies simply a person and not necessarily a male.

14, 18: *One of you will betray me, one who is eating with*

clined at table and were eating, Jesus said,
"Amen, I say to you, one of you will betray me,
one who is eating with me." **19** They began to
be distressed and to say to him, one by one,
"Surely it is not I?" **20** He said to them, "One
of the Twelve, the one who dips with me into
the dish. **21** *For the Son of Man indeed goes,
as it is written of him, but woe to that man by
whom the Son of Man is betrayed. It would be
better for that man if he had never been born."

**The Lord's Supper** **22** [d]*While they were
eating, he took bread, said the blessing, broke
it, and gave it to them, and said, "Take it; this
is my body." **23** Then he took a cup, gave
thanks, and gave it to them, and they all drank
from it. **24** *He said to them, "This is my blood
of the covenant, which will be shed for many.
**25** Amen, I say to you, I shall not drink again
the fruit of the vine until the day when I drink
it new in the kingdom of God." **26** [e]*Then,
after singing a hymn, they went out to the
Mount of Olives.

**Peter's Denial Foretold** **27** [f]*Then Jesus
said to them, "All of you will have your faith
shaken, for it is written:

'I will strike the shepherd,
and the sheep will be dispersed.'

**28** But after I have been raised up, I shall go
before you to Galilee." **29** Peter said to him,
"Even though all should have their faith shak-
en, mine will not be." **30** Then Jesus said to
him, "Amen, I say to you, this very night before the cock crows twice you will deny me
three times." **31** But he vehemently replied,
"Even though I should have to die with you, I
will not deny you." And they all spoke similarly.

**The Agony in the Garden** **32** [g][h]*Then
they came to a place named Gethsemane, and he
said to his disciples, "Sit here while I pray."
**33** He took with him Peter, James, and John,
and began to be troubled and distressed.
**34** Then he said to them, "My soul is sorrowful
even to death. Remain here and keep watch."
**35** He advanced a little and fell to the ground
and prayed that if it were possible the hour
might pass by him; **36** *he said, "Abba, Father, all things are possible to you. Take this cup
away from me, but not what I will but what you
will." **37** When he returned he found them
asleep. He said to Peter, "Simon, are you
asleep? Could you not keep watch for one hour?
**38** [i]*Watch and pray that you may not undergo
the test. The spirit is willing but the flesh is
weak." **39** Withdrawing again, he prayed, saying the same thing. **40** Then he returned once
more and found them asleep, for they could not
keep their eyes open and did not know what to
answer him. **41** He returned a third time and
said to them, "Are you still sleeping and taking
your rest? It is enough. The hour has come.
Behold, the Son of Man is to be handed over to
sinners. **42** Get up, let us go. See, my betrayer
is at hand."

## The Betrayal and Arrest of Jesus

**43** [j]Then, while he was still speaking, Judas,
one of the Twelve, arrived, accompanied by a
crowd with swords and clubs who had come
from the chief priests, the scribes, and the elders. **44** His betrayer had arranged a signal with
them, saying, "The man I shall kiss is the one;
arrest him and lead him away securely." **45** He
came and immediately went over to him and
said, "Rabbi." And he kissed him. **46** At this

d Mt 26, 26-30; Lk 22, 19-20; 1 Cor 11, 23-25.
e Mt 26, 30-35; Lk 22, 34.39; Jn 13, 36-38.
f Zec 13, 7; Jn 16, 32.
g Mt 26, 36-46; Lk 22, 40-46.
h Jn 18, 1.
i Rom 7, 5.
j Mt 26, 47-56; Lk 22, 47-53; Jn 18, 3-11.

*

*me:* contrasts the intimacy of table fellowship at the Passover meal with the treachery of the traitor; cf Ps 41, 10.

14, 21: *The Son of Man indeed goes, as it is written of him:* a reference to Ps 41, 10 cited by Jesus concerning Judas at the Last Supper; cf Jn 13, 18–19.

14, 22–24: The actions and words of Jesus express within the framework of the Passover meal and the transition to a new covenant the sacrifice of himself through the offering of his body and blood in anticipation of his passion and death. His *blood of the covenant* both alludes to the ancient rite of Ex 24, 4–8 and indicates the new community that the sacrifice of Jesus will bring into being (Mt 26, 26–28; Lk 22, 19–20; 1 Cor 11, 23–25).

14, 24: *Which will be shed:* see the note on Mt 26, 27–28. *For many:* the Greek preposition *hyper* is a different one from that at Mt 26, 28 but the same as that found at Lk 22, 19.20 and 1 Cor 11, 24. The sense of both words is vicarious, and it is difficult in Hellenistic Greek to distinguish between them. For *many* in the sense of "all," see the note on Mt 20, 28.

14, 26: *After singing a hymn:* Pss 114–118, thanksgiving songs concluding the Passover meal.

14, 27–31: Jesus predicted that the Twelve would waver in their faith, even abandon him, despite their protestations to the contrary. Yet he reassured them that after his resurrection he would regather them in Galilee (16, 7; cf Mt 26, 32; 28, 7.10.16; Jn 21), where he first summoned them to be his followers as he began to preach the good news (1, 14–20).

14, 32–34: The disciples who had witnessed the raising to life of the daughter of Jairus (5, 37) and the transfiguration of their Master (9, 2) were now invited to witness his degradation and agony and to watch and pray with him.

14, 36: *Abba, Father:* an Aramaic term, here also translated by Mark, Jesus' special way of addressing God with filial intimacy. The word *'abbā'* seems not to have been used in earlier or contemporaneous Jewish sources to address God without some qualifier. Cf Rom 8, 15; Gal 4, 6 for other occurrences of the Aramaic word in the Greek New Testament. *Not what I will but what you will:* note the complete obedient surrender of the human will of Jesus to the divine will of the Father; cf Jn 4, 34; 8, 29; Rom 5, 19; Phil 2, 8; Heb 5, 8.

14, 38: *The spirit is willing but the flesh is weak:* the spirit is drawn to what is good yet found in conflict with the flesh, inclined to sin; cf Ps 51, 7.12. Everyone is faced with this struggle, the full force of which Jesus accepted on our behalf and, through his bitter passion and death, achieved the victory.

they laid hands on him and arrested him.
**47** One of the bystanders drew his sword,
struck the high priest's servant, and cut off his
ear. **48** Jesus said to them in reply, "Have you
come out as against a robber, with swords and
clubs, to seize me? **49** Day after day I was with
you teaching in the temple area, yet you did not
arrest me; but that the scriptures may be fulfilled." **50** And they all left him and fled.
**51** Now a young man followed him wearing
nothing but a linen cloth about his body. They
seized him, **52** but he left the cloth behind and
ran off naked.

**Jesus before the Sanhedrin** **53** [k]*They
led Jesus away to the high priest, and all the
chief priests and the elders and the scribes came
together. **54** Peter followed him at a distance
into the high priest's courtyard and was seated
with the guards, warming himself at the fire.
**55** The chief priests and the entire Sanhedrin
kept trying to obtain testimony against Jesus in
order to put him to death, but they found none.
**56** Many gave false witness against him, but
their testimony did not agree. **57** *Some took
the stand and testified falsely against him, alleging, **58** [l]"We heard him say, 'I will destroy this
temple made with hands and within three days
I will build another not made with hands.' "
**59** Even so their testimony did not agree.
**60** The high priest rose before the assembly and
questioned Jesus, saying, "Have you no answer? What are these men testifying against
you?" **61** *But he was silent and answered
nothing. Again the high priest asked him and
said to him, "Are you the Messiah, the son of
the Blessed One?" **62** [m]Then Jesus answered,
"I am;

and 'you will see the Son of Man
seated at the right hand of the Power
and coming with the clouds of heaven.' "

**63** At that the high priest tore his garments and
said, "What further need have we of witnesses?
**64** You have heard the blasphemy. What do
you think?" They all condemned him as deserving to die. **65** [n]Some began to spit on him.
They blindfolded him and struck him and said
to him, "Prophesy!" And the guards greeted
him with blows.

**Peter's Denial of Jesus** **66** [o]While Peter
was below in the courtyard, one of the high
priest's maids came along. **67** Seeing Peter
warming himself, she looked intently at him and
said, "You too were with the Nazarene,
Jesus." **68** *But he denied it saying, "I neither
know nor understand what you are talking
about." So he went out into the outer court.
[Then the cock crowed.] **69** The maid saw him
and began again to say to the bystanders, "This
man is one of them." **70** Once again he denied
it. A little later the bystanders said to Peter once
more, "Surely you are one of them; for you too
are a Galilean." **71** He began to curse and to
swear, "I do not know this man about whom
you are talking." **72** [p]And immediately a cock
crowed a second time. Then Peter remembered
the word that Jesus had said to him, "Before the
cock crows twice you will deny me three
times." He broke down and wept.

## CHAPTER 15

**Jesus before Pilate** **1** [q r]*As soon as
morning came, the chief priests with the elders
and the scribes, that is, the whole Sanhedrin,
held a council. They bound Jesus, led him
away, and handed him over to Pilate. **2** *Pilate
questioned him, "Are you the king of the
Jews?" He said to him in reply, "You say so."
**3** The chief priests accused him of many things.
**4** Again Pilate questioned him, "Have you no
answer? See how many things they accuse you
of." **5** Jesus gave him no further answer, so
that Pilate was amazed.

k Mt 26, 57-68; Lk 22, 54-55.63-65.67-71; Jn 18, 12-13.
l 15, 29; 2 Cor 5, 1.
m 13, 26; Ps 110, 1; Dn 7, 13; Mt 24, 30.
n Lk 22, 63-65.
o Mt 26, 69-75; Lk 22, 56-62; Jn 18, 16-18.25-27.
p Jn 13, 38.
q Mt 27, 1-2.11-14; Lk 23, 1-3.
r Jn 18, 28.

*

14, 53: *They led Jesus away . . . came together:* Mark presents a formal assembly of the whole Sanhedrin (chief priests, elders, and scribes) at night, leading to the condemnation of Jesus (64), in contrast to Lk 22, 66.71, where Jesus is condemned in a daytime meeting of the council; see also Jn 18, 13.19–24.

14, 57–58: See the notes on Mt 26, 60–61 and Jn 2, 19.

14, 61–62: *The Blessed One:* a surrogate for the divine name, which Jews did not pronounce. *I am:* indicates Jesus' acknowledgment that he is the Messiah and Son of God; cf 1, 1. Contrast Mt 26, 64 and Lk 22, 67–70, in which Jesus leaves his interrogators to answer their own question. *You will see the Son of Man . . . with the clouds of heaven:* an allusion to Dn 7, 13 and Ps 110, 1, portending the enthronement of Jesus as judge in the transcendent glory of God's kingdom. *The Power:* another surrogate for the name of God.

14, 68: [*Then the cock crowed*]: found in most manuscripts, perhaps in view of vv 30 and 72, but omitted in others.

15, 1: *Held a council:* the verb here, *poieō*, can mean either "convene a council" or "take counsel." This reading is preferred to a variant "reached a decision" (cf 3, 6), which 14, 64 describes as having happened at the night trial; see the note on Mt 27, 1–2. *Handed him over to Pilate:* lacking authority to execute their sentence of condemnation (14, 64), the Sanhedrin had recourse to Pilate to have Jesus tried and put to death (15); cf Jn 18, 31.

15, 2: *The king of the Jews:* in the accounts of the evangelists a certain irony surrounds the use of this title as an accusation against Jesus (see the note on 15, 26). While Pilate uses this term (2.9.12), he is aware of the evil motivation of the chief priests who handed Jesus over for trial and condemnation (10; Lk 23, 14–16.20; Mt 27, 18.24; Jn 18, 38; 19, 4.6.12).

**The Sentence of Death** **6** [s]*Now on the occasion of the feast he used to release to them one prisoner whom they requested. **7** *A man called Barabbas was then in prison along with the rebels who had committed murder in a rebellion. **8** The crowd came forward and began to ask him to do for them as he was accustomed. **9** Pilate answered, "Do you want me to release to you the king of the Jews?" **10** For he knew that it was out of envy that the chief priests had handed him over. **11** But the chief priests stirred up the crowd to have him release Barabbas for them instead. **12** Pilate again said to them in reply, "Then what [do you want] me to do with [the man you call] the king of the Jews?" **13** *They shouted again, "Crucify him." **14** Pilate said to them, "Why? What evil has he done?" They only shouted the louder, "Crucify him." **15** *So Pilate, wishing to satisfy the crowd, released Barabbas to them and, after he had Jesus scourged, handed him over to be crucified.

**Mockery by the Soldiers** **16** [t]*The soldiers led him away inside the palace, that is, the praetorium, and assembled the whole cohort. **17** They clothed him in purple and, weaving a crown of thorns, placed it on him. **18** They began to salute him with, "Hail, King of the Jews!" **19** and kept striking his head with a reed and spitting upon him. They knelt before him in homage. **20** And when they had mocked him, they stripped him of the purple cloak, dressed him in his own clothes, and led him out to crucify him.

**The Way of the Cross** **21** [u]*They pressed into service a passer-by, Simon, a Cyrenian, who was coming in from the country, the father of Alexander and Rufus, to carry his cross.

**The Crucifixion** **22** [v]They brought him to the place of Golgotha (which is translated Place of the Skull). **23** They gave him wine drugged with myrrh, but he did not take it. **24** [w]*Then they crucified him and divided his garments by casting lots for them to see what each should take. **25** *It was nine o'clock in the morning when they crucified him. **26** *The inscription of the charge against him read, "The King of the Jews." **27** [x]With him they crucified two revolutionaries, one on his right and one on his left. **[28*]** **29** [y]*Those passing by reviled him, shaking their heads and saying, "Aha! You who would destroy the temple and rebuild it in three days, **30** save yourself by coming down from the cross." **31** Likewise the chief priests, with the scribes, mocked him among themselves and said, "He saved others; he cannot save himself. **32** [z]Let the Messiah, the King of Israel, come down now from the cross that we may see and believe." Those who were crucified with him also kept abusing him.

**The Death of Jesus** **33** At noon darkness came over the whole land until three in the afternoon. **34** [a]*And at three o'clock Jesus cried out in a loud voice, "*Eloi, Eloi, lema sabachthani?*" which is translated, "My God, my God, why have you forsaken me?" **35** *Some of the bystanders who heard it said, "Look, he is calling Elijah." **36** One of them ran, soaked a sponge with wine, put it on a reed, and gave it to him to drink, saying, "Wait, let us see if Elijah comes to take him down." **37** Jesus gave a loud cry and breathed his last. **38** *The veil of the sanctuary was torn in two from top to bottom. **39** [b]*When the centurion who stood facing him saw how he breathed his last he said, "Truly this man was the Son of God!" **40** [c]*There were also women looking on from a distance. Among them were Mary Magdalene, Mary the mother of the younger

s Mt 27, 15-26; Lk 23, 17-25; Jn 18, 39-40.
t Mt 27, 27-31; Jn 19, 2-3.
u Mt 27, 32; Lk 23, 26.
v Mt 27, 33-51; Lk 23, 32-46; Jn 19, 17-30.
w Ps 22, 18.
x Lk 23, 33
y Jn 2, 19.
z Lk 23, 39.
a Ps 22, 2.
b Mt 27, 54-56; Lk 23, 47-49.
c 6, 3; Lk 8, 2-3.

*

15, 6–15: See the note on Mt 27, 15–26.

15, 7: *Barabbas:* see the note on Mt 27, 16–17.

15, 13: *Crucify him:* see the note on Mt 27, 22.

15, 15: See the note on Mt 27, 26.

15, 16: *Praetorium:* see the note on Mt 27, 27.

15, 21: *They pressed into service . . . Simon, a Cyrenian:* a condemned person was constrained to bear his own instrument of torture, at least the crossbeam. The precise naming of Simon and his sons is probably due to their being known among early Christian believers to whom Mark addressed his gospel. See also the notes on Mt 27, 32 and Lk 23, 26–32.

15, 24: See the notes on Mt 27, 35 and Jn 19, 23–25a.

15, 25: *It was nine o'clock in the morning:* literally, "the third hour," thus between 9 a.m. and 12 noon. Cf vv 33.34.42 for Mark's chronological sequence, which may reflect liturgical or catechetical considerations rather than the precise historical sequence of events; contrast the different chronologies in the other gospels, especially Jn 19, 14.

15, 26: *The inscription . . . the King of the Jews:* the political reason for the death penalty falsely charged by the enemies of Jesus. See further the notes on Mt 27, 37 and Jn 19, 19.

15, 28: This verse, "And the scripture was fulfilled that says, 'And he was counted among the wicked,'" is omitted in the earliest and best manuscripts. It contains a citation from Is 53, 12, and was probably introduced from Lk 22, 37.

15, 29: See the note on Mt 27, 39–40.

15, 34: An Aramaic rendering of Ps 22, 2. See also the note on Mt 27, 46.

15, 35: *Elijah:* a verbal link with *Eloi* (34). See the note on 9, 9–13; cf Mal 3, 23–24. See also the note on Mt 27, 47.

15, 38: See the note on Mt 27, 51–53.

15, 39: The closing portion of Mark's gospel returns to the theme of its beginning in the Gentile centurion's climactic declaration of belief that Jesus *was the Son of God.* It indicates the fulfillment of the good news announced in the prologue (1, 1) and may be regarded as the firstfruit of the passion and death of Jesus.

15, 40–41: See the note on Mt 27, 55–56.

James and of Joses, and Salome. **41** These
women had followed him when he was in Galilee and ministered to him. There were also
many other women who had come up with him
to Jerusalem.

**The Burial of Jesus** **42** [d]When it was already evening, since it was the day of preparation, the day before the sabbath, **43** *Joseph of
Arimathea, a distinguished member of the council, who was himself awaiting the kingdom of
God, came and courageously went to Pilate and
asked for the body of Jesus. **44** Pilate was
amazed that he was already dead. He summoned the centurion and asked him if Jesus had
already died. **45** And when he learned of it
from the centurion, he gave the body to Joseph.
**46** Having bought a linen cloth, he took him
down, wrapped him in the linen cloth and laid
him in a tomb that had been hewn out of the
rock. Then he rolled a stone against the entrance
to the tomb. **47** Mary Magdalene and Mary the
mother of Joses watched where he was laid.

## CHAPTER 16

**The Resurrection of Jesus** **1** [e f]*When
the sabbath was over, Mary Magdalene, Mary,
the mother of James, and Salome bought spices
so that they might go and anoint him. **2** Very
early when the sun had risen, on the first day of
the week, they came to the tomb. **3** They were
saying to one another, "Who will roll back the
stone for us from the entrance to the tomb?"
**4** When they looked up, they saw that the stone
had been rolled back; it was very large. **5** [g]On
entering the tomb they saw a young man sitting
on the right side, clothed in a white robe, and
they were utterly amazed. **6** He said to them,
"Do not be amazed! You seek Jesus of Nazareth, the crucified. He has been raised; he is not
here. Behold, the place where they laid him.
**7** [h]But go and tell his disciples and Peter, 'He
is going before you to Galilee; there you will see
him, as he told you.' " **8** Then they went out
and fled from the tomb, seized with trembling
and bewilderment. They said nothing to anyone, for they were afraid.

## THE LONGER ENDING

**The Appearance to Mary Magdalene**
[**9** [i]*When he had risen, early on the first day
of the week, he appeared first to Mary Magdalene, out of whom he had driven seven demons.
**10** [j]She went and told his companions who
were mourning and weeping. **11** When they
heard that he was alive and had been seen by
her, they did not believe.

**The Appearance to Two Disciples**
**12** [k]After this he appeared in another form to
two of them walking along on their way to the
country. **13** They returned and told the others;
but they did not believe them either.

**The Commissioning of the Eleven**
**14** [l][But] later, as the eleven were at table, he
appeared to them and rebuked them for their
unbelief and hardness of heart because they had
not believed those who saw him after he had
been raised. **15** [m]He said to them, "Go into the
whole world and proclaim the gospel to every
creature. **16** Whoever believes and is baptized
will be saved; whoever does not believe will be
condemned. **17** These signs will accompany
those who believe: in my name they will drive
out demons, they will speak new languages.

d Mt 27, 57-61; Lk 23, 50-56; Jn 19, 38-42.
e Mt 28, 1-8; Lk 24, 1-10; Jn 20, 1-10.
f Mt 28, 1; Lk 23, 56.
g Jn 20, 12.
h 14, 28.
i Mt 28, 1-10; Jn 20, 11-18.
j Lk 24, 10-11; Jn 20, 18.
k Lk 24, 13-35.
l Lk 24, 36-49; 1 Cor 15, 5.
m 13, 10; Mt 28, 18-20; Lk 24, 47; Jn 20, 21.

*

15, 43: *Joseph of Arimathea:* see the note on Mt 27, 57–61.

16, 1–8: The purpose of this narrative is to show that the tomb is empty and that Jesus *has been raised* (6) and *is going before you to Galilee* (7) in fulfillment of 14, 28. The women find the tomb empty, and an angel stationed there announces to them what has happened. They are told to proclaim the news to Peter and the disciples in order to prepare them for a reunion with him. Mark's composition of the gospel ends at v 8 with the women telling no one, because they were afraid. This abrupt termination causes some to believe that the original ending of this gospel may have been lost. See the following note.

16, 9–20: This passage, termed the Longer Ending to the Marcan gospel by comparison with a much briefer conclusion found in some less important manuscripts, has traditionally been accepted as a canonical part of the gospel and was defined as such by the Council of Trent. Early citations of it by the Fathers indicate that it was composed by the second century, although vocabulary and style indicate that it was written by someone other than Mark. It is a general resume of the material concerning the appearances of the risen Jesus, reflecting, in particular, traditions found in Luke (24) and John (20).

The Shorter Ending: Found after v 8 before the Longer Ending in four seventh-to-ninth-century Greek manuscripts as well as in one Old Latin version, where it appears alone without the Longer Ending.

The Freer Logion: Found after v 14 in a fourth-fifth century manuscript preserved in the Freer Gallery of Art, Washington, DC, this ending was known to Jerome in the fourth century. It reads: "And they excused themselves, saying, 'This age of lawlessness and unbelief is under Satan, who does not allow the truth and power of God to prevail over the unclean things dominated by the spirits [*or,* does not allow the unclean things dominated by the spirits to grasp the truth and power of God]. Therefore reveal your righteousness now.' They spoke to Christ. And Christ responded to them, 'The limit of the years of Satan's power is completed, but other terrible things draw near. And for those who sinned I was handed over to death, that they might return to the truth and no longer sin, in order that they might inherit the spiritual and incorruptible heavenly glory of righteousness. But . . . .' "

**18** [n]They will pick up serpents [with their
hands], and if they drink any deadly thing, it
will not harm them. They will lay hands on the
sick, and they will recover."

**The Ascension of Jesus** 19 [o]So then the
Lord Jesus, after he spoke to them, was taken
up into heaven and took his seat at the right hand
of God. 20 [p]But they went forth and preached
everywhere, while the Lord worked with them
and confirmed the word through accompanying
signs.]

## THE SHORTER ENDING

[And they reported all the instructions briefly to Peter's companions. Afterwards Jesus himself, through them, sent forth from east to west the sacred and imperishable proclamation of eternal salvation. Amen.]

n Mt 10, 1; Lk 10, 19; Acts 28, 3-6.
o Lk 24, 50-53.
p 1 Tm 3, 16.

# THE GOSPEL ACCORDING TO

# LUKE

*The Gospel according to Luke is the first part of a two-volume work that continues the biblical history of God's dealings with humanity found in the Old Testament, showing how God's promises to Israel have been fulfilled in Jesus and how the salvation promised to Israel and accomplished by Jesus has been extended to the Gentiles. The stated purpose of the two volumes is to provide Theophilus and others like him with certainty—assurance—about earlier instruction they have received (1, 4). To accomplish his purpose, Luke shows that the preaching and teaching of the representatives of the early church are grounded in the preaching and teaching of Jesus, who during his historical ministry (Acts 1, 21–22) prepared his specially chosen followers and commissioned them to be witnesses to his resurrection and to all else that he did (Acts 10, 37–42). This continuity between the historical ministry of Jesus and the ministry of the apostles is Luke's way of guaranteeing the fidelity of the church's teaching to the teaching of Jesus.*

*Luke's story of Jesus and the church is dominated by a historical perspective. This history is first of all salvation history. God's divine plan for human salvation was accomplished during the period of Jesus, who through the events of his life (22, 22) fulfilled the Old Testament prophecies (4, 21; 18, 31; 22, 37; 24, 26–27.44), and this salvation is now extended to all humanity in the period of the church (Acts 4, 12). This salvation history, moreover, is a part of human history. Luke relates the story of Jesus and the church to events in contemporary Palestinian (1, 5; 3, 1–2; Acts 4, 6) and Roman (2, 1–2; 3, 1; Acts 11, 28; 18, 2.12) history, for, as Paul says in Acts 26, 26, "this was not done in a corner." Finally, Luke relates the story of Jesus and the church to contemporaneous church history. Luke is concerned with presenting Christianity as a legitimate form of worship in the Roman world, a religion that is capable of meeting the spiritual needs of a world empire like that of Rome. To this end, Luke depicts the Roman governor Pilate declaring Jesus innocent of any wrongdoing three times (Acts 23, 29; 25, 25; 26, 31–32). At the same time Luke argues in Acts that Christianity is the logical development and proper fulfillment of Judaism and is therefore deserving of the same toleration and freedom traditionally accorded Judaism by Rome (Acts 13, 16–41; 23, 6–9; 24, 10–21; 26, 2–23).*

*The prominence given to the period of the church in the story has important consequences for Luke's interpretation of the teachings of Jesus. By presenting the time of the church as a distinct phase of salvation history, Luke accordingly shifts the early Christian emphasis away from the expectation of an imminent parousia to the day-to-day concerns of the Christian community in the world. He does this in the gospel by regularly emphasizing the words "each day" (9, 23; cf Mk 8, 34; 11, 3; 16, 19; 19, 47) in the sayings of Jesus. Although Luke still believes the parousia to be a reality that will come unexpectedly (12, 38.45–46), he is more concerned with presenting the words and deeds of Jesus as guides for the conduct of Christian disciples in the interim period between the ascension and the parousia and with presenting Jesus himself as the model of Christian life and piety.*

*Throughout the gospel, Luke calls upon the Christian disciple to identify with the master Jesus, who is caring and tender toward the poor and lowly, the outcast, the sinner, and the afflicted, toward all those who recognize their dependence on God (4, 18; 6, 20–23; 7, 36–50; 14, 12–14; 15, 1–32; 16, 19–31; 18, 9–14; 19, 1–10; 21, 1–4), but who is severe toward the proud and self-righteous, and particularly toward those who place their material wealth before the service of God and his people (6, 24–26; 12, 13–21; 16, 13–15.19–31; 18, 9–14.15–25; cf 1, 50–53). No gospel writer is more concerned than Luke with the mercy and compassion of Jesus (7, 41–43; 10, 29–37; 13, 6–9; 15, 11–32). No gospel writer is more concerned with the role of the Spirit in the life of Jesus and the Christian disciple (1, 35.41; 2, 25–27; 4, 1.14.18; 10, 21; 11, 13; 24, 49), with the importance of prayer (3, 21; 5, 16; 6, 12; 9, 28; 11, 1–13; 18, 1–8), or with Jesus' concern for women (7, 11–17.36–50; 8, 2–3; 10, 38–42). While Jesus calls all humanity to repent (5, 32; 10, 13; 11, 32; 13, 1–5; 15, 7–10; 16, 30; 17, 3–4; 24, 47), he is particularly demanding of those who would be his disciples. Of them he demands absolute and total detachment from family and material possessions (9, 57–62; 12, 32–34; 14, 25–35). To all who respond in faith and repentance to the word Jesus preaches, he brings salvation (2, 30–32; 3, 6; 7, 50; 8, 48.50; 17, 19; 19, 9) and peace (2, 14; 7, 50; 8, 48; 19, 38.42) and life (10, 25–28; 18, 26–30).*

*Early Christian tradition, from the late second century on, identifies the author of this gospel and of the Acts of the Apostles as Luke, a Syrian from Antioch, who is mentioned in the New Testament in Col 4, 14, Phlm 24, and 2 Tm 4, 11. The prologue of the gospel makes it clear that Luke is not part of the first generation of Christian disciples but is himself dependent upon the traditions he received from those who were eyewitnesses and ministers of the word (1, 2). His two-volume work marks him as someone who was highly literate both in the Old Testament traditions according to the Greek versions and in Hellenistic Greek writings.*

*Among the likely sources for the composition of this gospel (1, 3) were the Gospel of Mark, a written collection of sayings of Jesus known also to the author of the Gospel of Matthew (Q; see Introduction to Matthew), and other special traditions that were used by Luke alone among the gospel writers. Some hold that Luke used Mark only as a complementary source for rounding out the material he took from other traditions. Because of its dependence on the Gospel of Mark and because details in Luke's Gospel (13, 35a; 19, 43–44; 21, 20; 23, 28–31) imply that the author was acquainted with the destruction of the city of Jerusalem by the Romans in A.D. 70, the Gospel of Luke is dated by most scholars after that date; many propose A.D. 80–90 as the time of composition.*

*Luke's consistent substitution of Greek names for the Aramaic or Hebrew names occurring in his sources (e.g., 23, 33 // Mk 15, 22; 18, 41 // Mk 10, 51), his omission from the gospel of specifically Jewish Christian concerns found in his sources (e.g., Mk 7, 1–23), his interest in Gentile Christians (2, 30–32; 3, 6.38; 4, 16–30; 13, 28–30; 14, 15–24; 17, 11–19; 24, 47–48), and his incomplete knowledge of Palestinian geography, customs, and practices are among the characteristics of this gospel that suggest that Luke was a non-Palestinian writing to a non-Palestinian audience that was largely made up of Gentile Christians.*

*The principal divisions of the Gospel according to Luke are the following:*

*I. The Prologue (1, 1–4)*
*II. The Infancy Narrative (1, 5—2, 52)*
*III. The Preparation for the Public Ministry (3, 1—4, 13)*
*IV. The Ministry in Galilee (4, 14—9, 50)*
*V. The Journey to Jerusalem: Luke's Travel Narrative (9, 51—19, 27)*
*VI. The Teaching Ministry in Jerusalem (19, 28—21, 38)*
*VII. The Passion Narrative (22, 1—23, 56)*
*VIII. The Resurrection Narrative (24, 1–53)*

# *I: THE PROLOGUE*

## CHAPTER 1

**1** [a]*Since many have undertaken to compile
a narrative of the events that have been fulfilled
among us, **2** [b]just as those who were eyewitnesses from the beginning and ministers of the
word have handed them down to us, **3** I too
have decided, after investigating everything accurately anew, to write it down in an orderly
sequence for you, most excellent Theophilus,

a Acts 1, 1; 1 Cor 15, 3. 1, 21-22.
b 24, 48; Jn 15, 27; Acts

*

1, 1–4: The Gospel according to Luke is the only one of the synoptic gospels to begin with a literary prologue. Making use of a formal, literary construction and vocabulary, the author writes the prologue in imitation of Hellenistic Greek writers and, in so doing, relates his story about Jesus to contemporaneous Greek and Roman literature. Luke is not only interested in the words and deeds of Jesus, but also in the larger context of the birth, ministry, death, and resurrection of Jesus as the fulfillment of the promises of God in the Old Testament. As a second- or third-generation Christian, Luke acknowledges his debt to earlier *eyewitnesses* and *ministers of the word,* but claims that his contribution to this developing tradition is a complete and accurate account, told in an orderly manner, and intended to provide *Theophilus* ("friend of God," literally) and other readers with certainty about earlier teachings they have received.

**4** so that you may realize the certainty of the
teachings you have received.

## *II: THE INFANCY NARRATIVE*

### Announcement of the Birth of John

**5** [c]*In the days of Herod, King of Judea, there
was a priest named Zechariah of the priestly
division of Abijah; his wife was from the daughters of Aaron, and her name was Elizabeth.
**6** Both were righteous in the eyes of God, observing all the commandments and ordinances
of the Lord blamelessly. **7** [d]*But they had no
child, because Elizabeth was barren and both
were advanced in years. **8** Once when he was
serving as priest in his division's turn before
God, **9** [e]according to the practice of the priestly
service, he was chosen by lot to enter the sanctuary of the Lord to burn incense. **10** Then, when
the whole assembly of the people was praying
outside at the hour of the incense offering,
**11** the angel of the Lord appeared to him,
standing at the right of the altar of incense.
**12** Zechariah was troubled by what he saw, and
fear came upon him. **13** [f]*But the angel said to
him, "Do not be afraid, Zechariah, because
your prayer has been heard. Your wife Elizabeth will bear you a son, and you shall name
him John. **14** And you will have joy and gladness, and many will rejoice at his birth,
**15** [g]*for he will be great in the sight of [the]
Lord. He will drink neither wine nor strong
drink. He will be filled with the holy Spirit even
from his mother's womb, **16** and he will turn
many of the children of Israel to the Lord their
God. **17** [h]*He will go before him in the spirit
and power of Elijah to turn the hearts of fathers
toward children and the disobedient to the understanding of the righteous, to prepare a people
fit for the Lord." **18** Then Zechariah said to the
angel, "How shall I know this? For I am an old
man, and my wife is advanced in years."
**19** [i]*And the angel said to him in reply, "I am
Gabriel, who stand before God. I was sent to
speak to you and to announce to you this good
news. **20** [j]*But now you will be speechless and
unable to talk until the day these things take
place, because you did not believe my words,
which will be fulfilled at their proper time."

**21** Meanwhile the people were waiting for
Zechariah and were amazed that he stayed so
long in the sanctuary. **22** But when he came
out, he was unable to speak to them, and they
realized that he had seen a vision in the sanctuary. He was gesturing to them but remained

---

c 1 Chr 24, 10.
d Gn 18, 11; Jgs 13, 2-5; 1 Sm 1, 5-6.
e Ex 30, 7.
f 1, 57.60.63; Mt 1, 20-21.
g 7, 33; Nm 6, 1-21; Jgs 13, 4; 1 Sm 1, 11 LXX.
h Sir 48, 10; Mal 3, 1; 3, 23-24; Mt 11, 14; 17, 11-13.
i Dn 8, 16; 9, 21.
j 1, 45.

---

*

1, 5—2, 52: Like the Gospel according to Matthew, this gospel opens with an infancy narrative, a collection of stories about the birth and childhood of Jesus. The narrative uses early Christian traditions about the birth of Jesus, traditions about the birth and circumcision of John the Baptist, and canticles such as the Magnificat (1, 46–55) and Benedictus (1, 67–79), composed of phrases drawn from the Greek Old Testament. It is largely, however, the composition of Luke who writes in imitation of Old Testament birth stories, combining historical and legendary details, literary ornamentation and interpretation of scripture, to answer in advance the question, "Who is Jesus Christ?" The focus of the narrative, therefore, is primarily christological. In this section Luke announces many of the themes that will become prominent in the rest of the gospel: the centrality of Jerusalem and the temple, the journey motif, the universality of salvation, joy and peace, concern for the lowly, the importance of women, the presentation of Jesus as savior, Spirit-guided revelation and prophecy, and the fulfillment of Old Testament promises. The account presents parallel scenes (diptychs) of angelic announcements of the birth of John the Baptist and of Jesus, and of the birth, circumcision, and presentation of John and Jesus. In this parallelism, the ascendency of Jesus over John is stressed: John is prophet of the Most High (1, 76); Jesus is Son of the Most High (1, 32). John is great in the sight of the Lord (1, 15); Jesus will be Great (a LXX attribute, used absolutely, of God) (1, 32). John will go before the Lord (1, 16–17); Jesus will be Lord (1, 43; 2, 11).

1, 5: *In the days of Herod, King of Judea:* Luke relates the story of salvation history to events in contemporary world history. Here and in 3, 1–2, he connects his narrative with events in Palestinian history; in 2, 1–2 and 3, 1, he casts the Jesus story in the light of events of Roman history. Herod the Great, the son of the Idumean Antipater, was declared "King of Judea" by the Roman Senate in 40 B.C., but became the undisputed ruler of Palestine only in 37 B.C. He continued as king until his death in 4 B.C. *Priestly division of Abijah:* a reference to the eighth of the twenty-four divisions of priests who, for a week at a time, twice a year, served in the Jerusalem temple.

1, 7: *They had no child:* though childlessness was looked upon in contemporaneous Judaism as a curse or punishment for sin, it is intended here to present Elizabeth in a situation similar to that of some of the great mothers of important Old Testament figures: Sarah (Gn 15, 3; 16, 1); Rebekah (Gn 25, 21); Rachel (Gn 29, 31; 30, 1); the mother of Samson and wife of Manoah (Jgs 13, 2–3); Hannah (1 Sm 1, 2).

1, 13: *Do not be afraid:* a stereotyped Old Testament phrase spoken to reassure the recipient of a heavenly vision (Gn 15, 1; Jos 1, 9; Dn 10, 12.19 and elsewhere in 1, 30; 2, 10). *You shall name him John:* the name means "Yahweh has shown favor," an indication of John's role in salvation history.

1, 15: *He will drink neither wine nor strong drink:* like Samson (Jgs 13, 4–5) and Samuel (1 Sm 1, 11 LXX and 4QSam[a]), John is to be consecrated by Nazirite vow and set apart for the Lord's service.

1, 17: *He will go before him in the spirit and power of Elijah:* John is to be the messenger sent before Yahweh, as described in Mal 3, 1–2. He is cast, moreover, in the role of the Old Testament fiery reformer, the prophet Elijah, who according to Mal 3, 23 (4, 5) is sent before "the great and terrible day of the Lord comes."

1, 19: *I am Gabriel:* "the angel of the Lord" is identified as Gabriel, the angel who in Dn 9, 20–25 announces the seventy weeks of years and the coming of an anointed one, a prince. By alluding to Old Testament themes in vv 17 and 19, such as the coming of the day of the Lord and the dawning of the messianic era, Luke is presenting his interpretation of the significance of the births of John and Jesus.

1, 20: *You will be speechless and unable to talk:* Zechariah's becoming mute is the sign given in response to his question in v 18. When Mary asks a similar question in 1, 34, unlike Zechariah who was punished for his doubt, she, in spite of her doubt, is praised and reassured (35–37).

mute. **23** Then, when his days of ministry were
completed, he went home. **24** After this time
his wife Elizabeth conceived, and she went into
seclusion for five months, saying, **25** [k]"So has
the Lord done for me at a time when he has seen
fit to take away my disgrace before others."

## Announcement of the Birth of Jesus

**26** *In the sixth month, the angel Gabriel was
sent from God to a town of Galilee called Nazareth, **27** [l]to a virgin betrothed to a man named
Joseph, of the house of David, and the virgin's
name was Mary. **28** [m]And coming to her, he
said, "Hail, favored one! The Lord is with
you." **29** But she was greatly troubled at what
was said and pondered what sort of greeting this
might be. **30** Then the angel said to her, "Do
not be afraid, Mary, for you have found favor
with God. **31** [n]Behold, you will conceive in
your womb and bear a son, and you shall name
him Jesus. **32** [o]*He will be great and will be
called Son of the Most High, and the Lord God
will give him the throne of David his father,
**33** [p]and he will rule over the house of Jacob
forever, and of his kingdom there will be no
end." **34** *But Mary said to the angel, "How
can this be, since I have no relations with a
man?" **35** [q]And the angel said to her in reply,
"The holy Spirit will come upon you, and the
power of the Most High will overshadow you.
Therefore the child to be born will be called
holy, the Son of God. **36** *And behold, Elizabeth, your relative, has also conceived a son in
her old age, and this is the sixth month for her
who was called barren; **37** [r]for nothing will be
impossible for God." **38** Mary said, "Behold,
I am the handmaid of the Lord. May it be done
to me according to your word." Then the angel
departed from her.

## Mary Visits Elizabeth

**39** During those
days Mary set out and traveled to the hill country in haste to a town of Judah, **40** where she
entered the house of Zechariah and greeted Elizabeth. **41** [s]When Elizabeth heard Mary's greeting, the infant leaped in her womb, and Elizabeth, filled with the holy Spirit, **42** [t]cried out
in a loud voice and said, "Most blessed are you
among women, and blessed is the fruit of your
womb. **43** *And how does this happen to me,
that the mother of my Lord should come to me?
**44** For at the moment the sound of your greeting reached my ears, the infant in my womb
leaped for joy. **45** [u]*Blessed are you who believed that what was spoken to you by the Lord
would be fulfilled."

## The Canticle of Mary

**46** [v w]*And Mary
said:

"My soul proclaims the greatness of the
Lord;
**47** [x]my spirit rejoices in God my savior.
**48** [y]For he has looked upon his handmaid's
lowliness;
behold, from now on will all ages call me
blessed.
**49** [z]The Mighty One has done great things for
me,
and holy is his name.
**50** [a]His mercy is from age to age
to those who fear him.

k Gn 30, 23.
l 2, 5; Mt 1, 16.18.
m Jgs 6, 12; Ru 2, 4; Jdt 13, 18.
n Gn 16, 11; Jgs 13, 3; Is 7, 14; Mt 1, 21-23.
o 2 Sm 7, 12.13.16; Is 9, 7.
p Dn 2, 44; 7, 14; Mi 4, 7; Mt 28, 18.
q Mt 1, 20.
r Gn 18, 14; Jer 32, 27; Mt 19, 26.
s 1, 15; Gn 25, 22 LXX.
t 11, 27-28; Jgs 5, 24; Jdt 13, 18; Dt 28, 4.
u 1, 20.
v 1 Sm 2, 1-10.
w Ps 35, 9; Is 61, 10; Hb 3, 18.
x Ti 3, 4; Jude 25.
y 11, 27; 1 Sm 1, 11; 2 Sm 16, 12; 2 Kgs 14, 26; Ps 113, 7.
z Dt 10, 21; Pss 71, 19; 111, 9; 126, 2-3.
a Pss 89, 2; 103, 13.17.

*

1, 26–38: The announcement to Mary of the birth of Jesus is parallel to the announcement to Zechariah of the birth of John. In both the angel Gabriel appears to the parent who is troubled by the vision (11–12.26–29) and then told by the angel not to fear (13.30). After the announcement is made (14–17.31–33) the parent objects (18.34) and a sign is given to confirm the announcement (20.36). The particular focus of the announcement of the birth of Jesus is on his identity as Son of David (32–33) and Son of God (32.35).

1, 32: *Son of the Most High:* cf 1, 76 where John is described as "prophet of the Most High." "Most High" is a title for God commonly used by Luke (35.76; 6, 35; 8, 28; Acts 7, 48; 16, 17).

1, 34: Mary's questioning response is a denial of sexual relations and is used by Luke to lead to the angel's declaration about the Spirit's role in the conception of this child (35). According to Luke, the virginal conception of Jesus takes place through the holy Spirit, the power of God, and therefore Jesus has a unique relationship to Yahweh: he is Son of God.

1, 36–37: The sign given to Mary in confirmation of the angel's announcement to her is the pregnancy of her aged relative Elizabeth. If a woman past the childbearing age could become pregnant, why, the angel implies, should there be doubt about Mary's pregnancy, for *nothing will be impossible for God.*

1, 43: Even before his birth, Jesus is identified in Lk as the Lord.

1, 45: *Blessed are you who believed:* Luke portrays Mary as a believer whose faith stands in contrast to the disbelief of Zechariah (20). Mary's role as believer in the infancy narrative should be seen in connection with the explicit mention of her presence among "those who believed" after the resurrection at the beginning of the Acts of the Apostles (14).

1, 46–55: Although Mary is praised for being the mother of the Lord and because of her belief, she reacts as the servant in a psalm of praise, the Magnificat. Because there is no specific connection of the canticle to the context of Mary's pregnancy and her visit to Elizabeth, the Magnificat (with the possible exception of v 48) may have been a Jewish Christian hymn that Luke found appropriate at this point in his story. Even if not composed by Luke, it fits in well with themes found elsewhere in Lk: joy and exultation in the Lord; the lowly being singled out for God's favor; the reversal of human fortunes; the fulfillment of Old Testament promises. The loose connection between the hymn and the context is further seen in the fact that a few Old Latin manuscripts identify the speaker of the hymn as Elizabeth, even though the overwhelming textual evidence makes Mary the speaker.

**51** [b]He has shown might with his arm,
dispersed the arrogant of mind and heart.
**52** [c]He has thrown down the rulers from their thrones
but lifted up the lowly.
**53** [d]The hungry he has filled with good things;
the rich he has sent away empty.
**54** [e]He has helped Israel his servant,
remembering his mercy,
**55** [f]according to his promise to our fathers,
to Abraham and to his descendants forever.''

**56** Mary remained with her about three months
and then returned to her home.

**The Birth of John** **57** *When the time arrived for Elizabeth to have her child she gave
birth to a son. **58** [g]Her neighbors and relatives
heard that the Lord had shown his great mercy
toward her, and they rejoiced with her.
**59** [h]*When they came on the eighth day to
circumcise the child, they were going to call
him Zechariah after his father, **60** [i]but his
mother said in reply, "No. He will be called
John." **61** But they answered her, "There is no
one among your relatives who has this name."
**62** So they made signs, asking his father what
he wished him to be called. **63** He asked for a
tablet and wrote, "John is his name," and all
were amazed. **64** [j]Immediately his mouth was
opened, his tongue freed, and he spoke blessing
God. **65** Then fear came upon all their neighbors, and all these matters were discussed
throughout the hill country of Judea. **66** All
who heard these things took them to heart, saying, "What, then, will this child be?" For surely the hand of the Lord was with him.

**The Canticle of Zechariah** **67** Then
Zechariah his father, filled with the holy Spirit,
prophesied, saying:

**68** [k]*"Blessed be the Lord, the God of Israel,
for he has visited and brought redemption to his people.
**69** [l]*He has raised up a horn for our salvation
within the house of David his servant,
**70** even as he promised through the mouth of his holy
prophets from of old:
**71** [m]salvation from our enemies and from the hand
of all who hate us,
**72** [n o]to show mercy to our fathers
and to be mindful of his holy covenant
**73** [p]and of the oath he swore to Abraham our father,
and to grant us that,
**74** rescued from the hand of enemies,
without fear we might worship him
**75** [q]in holiness and righteousness
before him all our days.
**76** [r]*And you, child, will be called prophet of the Most High,
for you will go before the Lord to prepare his ways,
**77** to give his people knowledge of salvation
through the forgiveness of their sins,
**78** [s t]*because of the tender mercy of our God
by which the daybreak from on high will visit us
**79** to shine on those who sit in darkness and death's shadow,
to guide our feet into the path of peace."
**80** [u]The child grew and became strong in spirit,

b Pss 89, 10; 118, 15; Jer 32, 17 (39, 17 LXX).
c 1 Sm 2, 7; 2 Sm 22, 28; Jb 5, 11; 12, 19; Ps 147, 6; Sir 10, 14;Jas 4, 6; 1 Pt 5, 5.
d 1 Sm 2, 5; Ps 107, 9.
e Ps 98, 3; Is 41, 8-9.
f Gn 13, 15; 17, 7; 18, 18; 22, 17-18; Mi 7, 20.
g 1, 14.
h 2, 21; Gn 17, 10.12; Lv 12, 3.
i 1, 13.
j 1, 20.
k 7, 16; Pss 41, 13; 72, 18; 106, 48; 111, 9.
l Ps 18, 3.
m Ps 106, 10.
n Ps 106, 45-46.
o Gn 17, 7; Lv 26, 42; Ps 105, 8-9; Mi 7, 20.
p Gn 22, 16-17.
q Ti 2, 12.
r Is 40, 3; Mal 3, 1; Mt 3, 3; 11, 10.
s Mal 3, 20.
t Is 60, 1-2.
u 2, 40; Mt 3, 1.

*

1, 57–66: The birth and circumcision of John above all emphasize John's incorporation into the people of Israel by the sign of the covenant (Gn 17, 1–12). The narrative of John's circumcision also prepares the way for the subsequent description of the circumcision of Jesus in 2, 21. At the beginning of his two-volume work Luke shows those who play crucial roles in the inauguration of Christianity to be wholly a part of the people of Israel. At the end of the Acts of the Apostles (21, 20; 22, 3; 23, 6–9; 24, 14–16; 26, 2–8.22–23) he will argue that Christianity is the direct descendant of Pharisaic Judaism.

1, 59: The practice of Palestinian Judaism at this time was to name the child at birth; moreover, though naming a male child after the father is not completely unknown, the usual practice was to name the child after the grandfather (see 61). The naming of the child John and Zechariah's recovery from his loss of speech should be understood as fulfilling the angel's announcement to Zechariah in 1, 13 and 20.

1, 68–79: Like the canticle of Mary (46–55) the canticle of Zechariah is only loosely connected with its context. Apart from vv 76–77, the hymn in speaking of *a horn for our salvation* (69) and *the daybreak from on high* (78) applies more closely to Jesus and his work than to John. Again like Mary's canticle, it is largely composed of phrases taken from the Greek Old Testament and may have been a Jewish Christian hymn of praise that Luke adapted to fit the present context by inserting vv 76–77 to give Zechariah's reply to the question asked in v 66.

1, 69: *A horn for our salvation:* the horn is a common Old Testament figure for strength (Pss 18, 3; 75, 5–6; 89, 18; 112, 9; 148, 14). This description is applied to God in Ps 18, 3 and is here transferred to Jesus. The connection of the phrase with *the house of David* gives the title messianic overtones and may indicate an allusion to a phrase in Hannah's song of praise (1 Sm 2, 10), "the horn of his anointed."

1, 76: *You will go before the Lord:* here *the Lord* is most likely a reference to Jesus (contrast 15–17 where Yahweh is meant) and John is presented as the precursor of Jesus.

1, 78: *The daybreak from on high:* three times in the LXX (Jer 23, 5; Zec 3, 8; 6, 12), the Greek word used here for *daybreak* translates the Hebrew word for "scion, branch," an Old Testament messianic title.

and he was in the desert until the day of his
manifestation to Israel.

## CHAPTER 2

**The Birth of Jesus** 1 *In those days a
decree went out from Caesar Augustus that the
whole world should be enrolled. 2 This was the
first enrollment, when Quirinius was governor
of Syria. 3 So all went to be enrolled, each to
his own town. 4 [v]And Joseph too went up from
Galilee from the town of Nazareth to Judea, to
the city of David that is called Bethlehem, because he was of the house and family of David,
5 [w]to be enrolled with Mary, his betrothed,
who was with child. 6 While they were there,
the time came for her to have her child, 7 [x]*and
she gave birth to her firstborn son. She wrapped
him in swaddling clothes and laid him in a manger, because there was no room for them in the
inn.
8 *Now there were shepherds in that region
living in the fields and keeping the night watch
over their flock. 9 [y]The angel of the Lord appeared to them and the glory of the Lord shone
around them, and they were struck with great
fear. 10 The angel said to them, "Do not be
afraid; for behold, I proclaim to you good news
of great joy that will be for all the people.
11 [z]*For today in the city of David a savior has
been born for you who is Messiah and Lord.
12 And this will be a sign for you: you will find
an infant wrapped in swaddling clothes and lying in a manger." 13 And suddenly there was
a multitude of the heavenly host with the angel,
praising God and saying:
14 [a]*"Glory to God in the highest
and on earth peace to those on whom his
favor rests."

**The Visit of the Shepherds** 15 When the
angels went away from them to heaven, the
shepherds said to one another, "Let us go, then,
to Bethlehem to see this thing that has taken
place, which the Lord has made known to us."
16 So they went in haste and found Mary and
Joseph, and the infant lying in the manger.
17 When they saw this, they made known the
message that had been told them about this

v Mi 5, 2; Mt 2, 6.
w 1, 27; Mt 1, 18.
x Mt 1, 25.
y 1, 11.26.
z Mt 1, 21; 16, 16; Jn 4, 42; Acts 2, 36; 5, 31; Phil 2, 11.
a 19, 38.

*

2, 1–2: Although universal registrations of Roman citizens are attested in 28 B.C., 8 B.C., and A.D. 14 and enrollments in individual provinces of those who are not Roman citizens are also attested, such a universal census of the Roman world under Caesar Augustus is unknown outside the New Testament. Moreover, there are notorious historical problems connected with Luke's dating the census *when Quirinius was governor of Syria,* and the various attempts to resolve the difficulties have proved unsuccessful. P. Sulpicius Quirinius became legate of the province of Syria in A.D. 6–7 when Judea was annexed to the province of Syria. At that time, a provincial census of Judea was taken up. If Quirinius had been legate of Syria previously, it would have to have been before 10 B.C. because the various legates of Syria from 10 B.C. to 4 B.C. (the death of Herod) are known, and such a dating for an earlier census under Quirinius would create additional problems for dating the beginning of Jesus' ministry (3, 1.23). A previous legateship after 4 B.C. (and before A.D. 6) would not fit with the dating of Jesus' birth in the days of Herod (1, 5; Mt 2, 1). Luke may simply be combining Jesus' birth in Bethlehem with his vague recollection of a census under Quirinius (see also Acts 5, 37) to underline the significance of this birth for the whole Roman world: through this child born in Bethlehem peace and salvation come to the empire.

2, 1: *Caesar Augustus:* the reign of the Roman emperor Caesar Augustus is usually dated from 27 B.C. to his death in A.D. 14. According to Greek inscriptions, Augustus was regarded in the Roman Empire as "savior" and "god," and he was credited with establishing a time of peace, the *pax Augusta,* throughout the Roman world during his long reign. It is not by chance that Luke relates the birth of Jesus to the time of Caesar Augustus: the real savior (11) and peace-bearer (14; see also 19, 38) is the child born in Bethlehem. The great emperor is simply God's agent (like the Persian king Cyrus in Is 44, 28—45, 1) who provides the occasion for God's purposes to be accomplished. *The whole world:* that is, the whole Roman world: Rome, Italy, and the Roman provinces.

2, 7: *Firstborn son:* the description of Jesus as *firstborn son* does not necessarily mean that Mary had other sons. It is a legal description indicating that Jesus possessed the rights and privileges of the firstborn son (Gn 27; Ex 13, 2; Nm 3, 12–13; 18, 15–16; Dt 21, 15–17). See the notes on Mt 1, 25 and Mk 6, 3. *Wrapped him in swaddling clothes:* there may be an allusion here to the birth of another descendant of David, his son Solomon, who though a great king was wrapped in swaddling clothes like any other infant (Wis 7, 4–6). *Laid him in a manger:* a feeding trough for animals. A possible allusion to Is 1, 3 LXX.

2, 8–20: The annoucement of Jesus' birth to the shepherds is in keeping with Luke's theme that the lowly are singled out as the recipients of God's favors and blessings (see also 1, 48.52).

2, 11: The basic message of the infancy narrative is contained in the angel's announcement: this child is *savior, Messiah,* and *Lord.* Luke is the only synoptic gospel writer to use the title *savior* for Jesus (11; Acts 5, 31; 13, 23; see also 1, 69; 19, 9; Acts 4, 12). As savior, Jesus is looked upon by Luke as the one who rescues humanity from sin and delivers humanity from the condition of alienation from God. The title *christos,* "Christ," is the Greek equivalent of the Hebrew *māšîaḥ,* "Messiah," "anointed one." Among certain groups in first-century Palestinian Judaism, the title was applied to an expected royal leader from the line of David who would restore the kingdom to Israel (see Acts 1, 6). The political overtones of the title are played down in Lk and instead the Messiah of the Lord (26) or the Lord's anointed is the one who now brings salvation to all humanity, Jew and Gentile (29–32). *Lord* is the most frequently used title for Jesus in Lk and Acts. In the New Testament it is also applied to Yahweh, as it is in the Old Testament. When used of Jesus it points to his transcendence and dominion over humanity.

2, 14: *On earth peace to those on whom his favor rests:* the peace that results from the Christ event is for those whom God has favored with his grace. This reading is found in the oldest representatives of the Western and Alexandrian text traditions and is the preferred one; the Byzantine text tradition, on the other hand, reads: "on earth peace, good will toward men." The peace of which Luke's gospel speaks (14; 7, 50; 8, 48; 10, 5–6; 19, 38.42; 24, 36) is more than the absence of war of the *pax Augusta;* it also includes the security and well-being characteristic of peace in the Old Testament.

child. 18 All who heard it were amazed by what
had been told them by the shepherds. 19 And
Mary kept all these things, reflecting on them in
her heart. 20 Then the shepherds returned,
glorifying and praising God for all they had
heard and seen, just as it had been told to
them.

### The Circumcision and Naming of Jesus

21 [b]*When eight days were completed for his circumcision, he was named Jesus,
the name given him by the angel before he was
conceived in the womb.

### The Presentation in the Temple

22 [c]*When the days were completed for their
purification according to the law of Moses, they
took him up to Jerusalem to present him to the
Lord, 23 [d]just as it is written in the law of the
Lord, "Every male that opens the womb shall
be consecrated to the Lord," 24 and to offer the
sacrifice of "a pair of turtledoves or two young
pigeons," in accordance with the dictate in the
law of the Lord.

25 *Now there was a man in Jerusalem
whose name was Simeon. This man was righteous and devout, awaiting the consolation of
Israel, and the holy Spirit was upon him. 26 It
had been revealed to him by the holy Spirit that
he should not see death before he had seen the
Messiah of the Lord. 27 He came in the Spirit
into the temple; and when the parents brought
in the child Jesus to perform the custom of the
law in regard to him, 28 he took him into his
arms and blessed God, saying:

29 "Now, Master, you may let your servant go
in peace, according to your word,
30 [e]for my eyes have seen your salvation,
31 which you prepared in sight of all the
peoples,
32 [f]a light for revelation to the Gentiles,
and glory for your people Israel."

33 The child's father and mother were amazed
at what was said about him; 34 [g]and Simeon
blessed them and said to Mary his mother, "Behold, this child is destined for the fall and rise
of many in Israel, and to be a sign that will be
contradicted 35 *(and you yourself a sword
will pierce) so that the thoughts of many hearts
may be revealed." 36 There was also a prophetess, Anna, the daughter of Phanuel, of the
tribe of Asher. She was advanced in years, having lived seven years with her husband after her
marriage, 37 and then as a widow until she was
eighty-four. She never left the temple, but worshiped night and day with fasting and prayer.
38 [h]And coming forward at that very time, she
gave thanks to God and spoke about the child to
all who were awaiting the redemption of Jerusalem.

### The Return to Nazareth

39 [i]When they
had fulfilled all the prescriptions of the law of
the Lord, they returned to Galilee, to their own
town of Nazareth. 40 [j]The child grew and became strong, filled with wisdom; and the favor
of God was upon him.

### The Boy Jesus in the Temple

41 [k]*Each
year his parents went to Jerusalem for the feast
of Passover, 42 and when he was twelve years
old, they went up according to festival custom.
43 After they had completed its days, as they
were returning, the boy Jesus remained behind

b 1, 31; Gn 17, 12; Mt 1, 21.
c Lv 12, 2-8.
d Ex 13, 2.12.
e 3, 6; Is 40, 5 LXX; 52, 10.
f Is 42, 6; 46, 13; 49, 6; Acts 13, 47; 26, 23.
g 12, 51; Is 8, 14; Jn 9, 39; Rom 9, 33; 1 Cor 1, 23; 1 Pt 2, 7-8.
h Is 52, 9.
i Mt 2, 23.
j 1, 80; 2, 52.
k Ex 12, 24-27; 23, 15; Dt 16, 1-8.

*

2, 21: Just as John before him had been incorporated into the people of Israel through his circumcision, so too this child (see the note on 1, 57–66).

2, 22–40: The presentation of Jesus in the temple depicts the parents of Jesus as devout Jews, faithful observers of the law of the Lord (23.24.39), i.e., the law of Moses. In this respect, they are described in a fashion similar to the parents of John (1, 6) and Simeon (25) and Anna (36–37).

2, 22: *Their purification:* syntactically, *their* must refer to Mary and Joseph, even though the Mosaic law never mentions the purification of the husband. Recognizing the problem, some Western scribes have altered the text to read "his purification," understanding the presentation of Jesus in the temple as a form of purification; the Vulgate version has a Latin form that could be either "his" or "her." According to the Mosaic law (Lv 12, 2–8), the woman who gives birth to a boy is unable for forty days to touch anything sacred or to enter the temple area by reason of her legal impurity. At the end of this period she is required to offer a year-old lamb as a burnt offering and a turtledove or young pigeon as an expiation of sin. The woman who could not afford a lamb offered instead two turtledoves or two young pigeons, as Mary does here. *They took him up to Jerusalem to present him to the Lord:* as the firstborn son (7) Jesus was consecrated to the Lord as the law required (Ex 13, 2.12), but there was no requirement that this be done at the temple. The concept of a presentation at the temple is probably derived from 1 Sm 1, 24–28, where Hannah offers the child Samuel for sanctuary services. The law further stipulated (Nm 3, 47–48) that the firstborn son should be redeemed by the parents through their payment of five shekels to a member of a priestly family. About this legal requirement Luke is silent.

2, 25: *Awaiting the consolation of Israel:* Simeon here and later Anna who speak about the child to all who were awaiting the redemption of Jerusalem represent the hopes and expectations of faithful and devout Jews who at this time were looking forward to the restoration of God's rule in Israel. The birth of Jesus brings these hopes to fulfillment.

2, 35: (And you yourself a sword will pierce): Mary herself will not be untouched by the various reactions to the role of Jesus (34). Her blessedness as mother of the Lord will be challenged by her son who describes true blessedness as "hearing the word of God and observing it" (11, 27–28 and 8, 20–21).

2, 41–52: This story's concern with an incident from Jesus' youth is unique in the canonical gospel tradition. It presents Jesus in the role of the faithful Jewish boy, raised in the traditions of Israel, and fulfilling all that the law requires. With this episode, the infancy narrative ends just as it began, in the setting of the Jerusalem temple.

in Jerusalem, but his parents did not know it.
**44** Thinking that he was in the caravan, they
journeyed for a day and looked for him among
their relatives and acquaintances, **45** but not
finding him, they returned to Jerusalem to look
for him. **46** After three days they found him in
the temple, sitting in the midst of the teachers,
listening to them and asking them questions,
**47** and all who heard him were astounded at his
understanding and his answers. **48** When his
parents saw him, they were astonished, and his
mother said to him, "Son, why have you done
this to us? Your father and I have been looking
for you with great anxiety." **49** *And he said
to them, "Why were you looking for me? Did
you not know that I must be in my Father's
house?" **50** But they did not understand what
he said to them. **51** [l]He went down with them
and came to Nazareth, and was obedient to
them; and his mother kept all these things in her
heart. **52** [m]And Jesus advanced [in] wisdom
and age and favor before God and man.

## *III: THE PREPARATION FOR THE PUBLIC MINISTRY*

## CHAPTER 3

### The Preaching of John the Baptist

**1** [n]*In the fifteenth year of the reign of Tiberius
Caesar, when Pontius Pilate was governor of
Judea, and Herod was tetrarch of Galilee, and
his brother Philip tetrarch of the region of Itura-
ea and Trachonitis, and Lysanias was tetrarch of
Abilene, **2** [o]*during the high priesthood of Annas and Caiaphas, the word of God came to John
the son of Zechariah in the desert. **3** [p]*He went
throughout [the] whole region of the Jordan,
proclaiming a baptism of repentance for the forgiveness of sins, **4** [qr]*as it is written in the
book of the words of the prophet Isaiah:

"A voice of one crying out in the desert:
'Prepare the way of the Lord,
make straight his paths.
**5** Every valley shall be filled
and every mountain and hill shall be made low.
The winding roads shall be made straight,
and the rough ways made smooth,
**6** [s]and all flesh shall see the salvation of God.' "

**7** [t]He said to the crowds who came out to be
baptized by him, "You brood of vipers! Who
warned you to flee from the coming wrath?
**8** [u]Produce good fruits as evidence of your repentance; and do not begin to say to yourselves,
'We have Abraham as our father,' for I tell
you, God can raise up children to Abraham from
these stones. **9** [v]Even now the ax lies at the root
of the trees. Therefore every tree that does not

l 2, 19.
m 1, 80; 2, 40; 1 Sm 2, 26.
n Mt 3, 1-12; Mk 1, 1-8; Jn 1, 19-28.
o 1, 80.
p Acts 13, 24; 19, 4.
q Is 40, 3-5.
r Jn 1, 23.
s 2, 30-31.
t Mt 12, 34.
u Jn 8, 39.
v Mt 7, 19; Jn 15, 6.

*

2, 49: *I must be in my Father's house:* this phrase can also be translated, "I must be about my Father's work." In either translation, Jesus refers to God as his Father. His divine sonship, and his obedience to his heavenly Father's will, take precedence over his ties to his family.

3, 1–20: Although Luke is indebted in this section to his sources, the Gospel of Mark and a collection of sayings of John the Baptist, he has clearly marked this introduction to the ministry of Jesus with his own individual style. Just as the gospel began with a long periodic sentence (1, 1–4), so too this section (1–2). He casts the call of John the Baptist in the form of an Old Testament prophetic call (2) and extends the quotation from Isaiah found in Mk 1, 3 (Is 40, 3) by the addition of Is 40, 4–5 in vv 5–6. In doing so, he presents his theme of the universality of salvation, which he has announced earlier in the words of Simeon (2, 30–32). Moreover, in describing the expectation of the people (15), Luke is characterizing the time of John's preaching in the same way as he had earlier described the situation of other devout Israelites in the infancy narrative (2, 25–26.37–38). In vv 7–18 Luke presents the preaching of John the Baptist who urges the crowds to reform in view of *the coming wrath* (7.9: eschatological preaching), and who offers the crowds certain standards for reforming social conduct (10–14: ethical preaching), and who announces to the crowds the coming of *one mightier than* he (15–18: messianic preaching).

3, 1: *Tiberius Caesar:* Tiberius succeeded Augustus as emperor in A.D. 14 and reigned until A.D. 37. The fifteenth year of his reign, depending on the method of calculating his first regnal year, would have fallen between A.D. 27 and 29. *Pontius Pilate:* prefect of Judea from A.D. 26 to 36. The Jewish historian Josephus describes him as a greedy and ruthless prefect who had little regard for the local Jewish population and their religious practices (see 13, 1). *Herod:* i.e., Herod Antipas, the son of Herod the Great. He ruled over Galilee and Perea from 4 B.C. to A.D. 39. His official title *tetrarch* means literally, "ruler of a quarter," but came to designate any subordinate prince. *Philip:* also a son of Herod the Great, tetrarch of the territory to the north and east of the Sea of Galilee from 4 B.C. to A.D. 34. Only two small areas of this territory are mentioned by Luke. *Lysanias:* nothing is known about this Lysanias who is said here to have been tetrarch of Abilene, a territory northwest of Damascus.

3, 2: *During the high priesthood of Annas and Caiaphas:* after situating the call of John the Baptist in terms of the civil rulers of the period, Luke now mentions the religious leadership of Palestine (see the note on 1, 5). Annas had been high priest A.D. 6–15. After being deposed by the Romans in A.D. 15 he was succeeded by various members of his family and eventually by his son-in-law, Caiaphas, who was high priest A.D. 18–36. Luke refers to Annas as high priest at this time (but see Jn 18, 13.19), possibly because of the continuing influence of Annas or because the title continued to be used for the ex-high priest. *The word of God came to John:* Luke is alone among the New Testament writers in associating the preaching of John with a call from God. Luke is thereby identifying John with the prophets whose ministries began with similar calls. In 7, 26 John will be described as "more than a prophet"; he is also the precursor of Jesus (7, 27), a transitional figure inaugurating the period of the fulfillment of prophecy and promise.

3, 3: See the note on Mt 3, 2.

3, 4: The Essenes from Qumran used the same passage to explain why their community was in the desert studying and observing the law and the prophets (1QS 8, 12–15).

produce good fruit will be cut down and thrown
into the fire."
**10** And the crowds asked him, "What then
should we do?" **11** He said to them in reply,
"Whoever has two cloaks should share with the
person who has none. And whoever has food
should do likewise." **12** [w]Even tax collectors
came to be baptized and they said to him,
"Teacher, what should we do?" **13** He answered them, "Stop collecting more than what
is prescribed." **14** Soldiers also asked him,
"And what is it that we should do?" He told
them, "Do not practice extortion, do not falsely
accuse anyone, and be satisfied with your
wages."
**15** [x]Now the people were filled with expectation, and all were asking in their hearts whether John might be the Messiah. **16** [y]*John answered them all, saying, "I am baptizing you
with water, but one mightier than I is coming.
I am not worthy to loosen the thongs of his
sandals. He will baptize you with the holy Spirit
and fire. **17** [z]*His winnowing fan is in his hand
to clear his threshing floor and to gather the
wheat into his barn, but the chaff he will burn
with unquenchable fire." **18** Exhorting them in
many other ways, he preached good news to the
people. **19** [a]*Now Herod the tetrarch, who had
been censured by him because of Herodias, his
brother's wife, and because of all the evil deeds
Herod had committed, **20** added still another to
these by [also] putting John in prison.

**The Baptism of Jesus** **21** [b]*After all the
people had been baptized and Jesus also had
been baptized and was praying, heaven was
opened **22** [c]*and the holy Spirit descended
upon him in bodily form like a dove. And a
voice came from heaven, "You are my beloved
Son; with you I am well pleased."

**The Genealogy of Jesus** **23** [de]*When
Jesus began his ministry he was about thirty
years of age. He was the son, as was thought,
of Joseph, the son of Heli, **24** the son of Matthat, the son of Levi, the son of Melchi, the son
of Jannai, the son of Joseph, **25** the son of
Mattathias, the son of Amos, the son of Nahum,
the son of Esli, the son of Naggai, **26** the son
of Maath, the son of Mattathias, the son of
Semein, the son of Josech, the son of Joda,
**27** [f]the son of Joanan, the son of Rhesa, the son
of Zerubbabel, the son of Shealtiel, the son of
Neri, **28** the son of Melchi, the son of Addi, the
son of Cosam, the son of Elmadam, the son of
Er, **29** the son of Joshua, the son of Eliezer, the
son of Jorim, the son of Matthat, the son of
Levi, **30** the son of Simeon, the son of Judah,
the son of Joseph, the son of Jonam, the son of
Eliakim, **31** [ghi]*the son of Melea, the son of
Menna, the son of Mattatha, the son of Nathan,
the son of David, **32** the son of Jesse, the son
of Obed, the son of Boaz, the son of Sala, the
son of Nahshon, **33** [j]the son of Amminadab,
the son of Admin, the son of Arni, the son of
Hezron, the son of Perez, the son of Judah,
**34** [kl]the son of Jacob, the son of Isaac, the son
of Abraham, the son of Terah, the son of Nahor,
**35** the son of Serug, the son of Reu, the son of
Peleg, the son of Eber, the son of Shelah,

w 7, 29.
x Acts 13, 25.
y 7, 19-20; Jn 1, 27; Acts 1, 5; 11, 16.
z Mt 3, 12.
a Mt 14, 3-4; Mk 6, 17-18.
b Mt 3, 13-17; Mk 1, 9-11.
c 9, 35; Ps 2, 7; Is 42, 1; Mt 12, 18; 17, 5; Mk 9, 7; Jn 1, 32; 2 Pt 1, 17.
d Mt 1, 1-17.
e 4, 22; Jn 6, 42.
f 1 Chr 3, 17; Ez 3, 2.
g 2 Sm 5, 14.
h 1 Sm 16, 1.18.
i Ru 4, 17-22; 1 Chr 2, 1-15.
j Gn 29, 35; 38, 29.
k Gn 21, 3; 25, 26; 1 Chr 1, 34; 28, 34.
l Gn 11, 10-26; 1 Chr 1, 24-27.

*

3, 16: *He will baptize you with the holy Spirit and fire:* in contrast to John's baptism with water, Jesus is said to baptize with the holy Spirit and with fire. From the point of view of the early Christian community, the Spirit and fire must have been understood in the light of the fire symbolism of the pouring out of the Spirit at Pentecost (Acts 2, 1–4); but as part of John's preaching, the Spirit and fire should be related to their purifying and refining characteristics (Ez 36, 25–27; Mal 3, 2–3). See the note on Mt 3, 11.

3, 17: *Winnowing fan:* see the note on Mt 3, 12.

3, 19–20: Luke separates the ministry of John the Baptist from that of Jesus by reporting the imprisonment of John before the baptism of Jesus (21–22). Luke uses this literary device to serve his understanding of the periods of salvation history. With John the Baptist, the time of promise, the period of Israel, comes to an end; with the baptism of Jesus and the descent of the Spirit upon him, the time of fulfillment, the period of Jesus, begins. In his second volume, the Acts of the Apostles, Luke will introduce the third epoch in salvation history, the period of the church.

3, 21–22: This episode in Luke focuses on the heavenly message identifying Jesus as *Son* and, through the allusion to Is 42, 1, as Servant of Yahweh. The relationship of Jesus to the Father has already been announced in the infancy narrative (1, 32.35; 2, 49); it occurs here at the beginning of Jesus' Galilean ministry and will reappear in 9, 35 before another major section of Luke's gospel, the travel narrative (9, 51—19, 27). Elsewhere in Luke's writings (4, 18; Acts 10, 38), this incident will be interpreted as a type of anointing of Jesus.

3, 21: *Was praying:* Luke regularly presents Jesus at prayer at important points in his ministry: here at his baptism; at the choice of the Twelve (6, 12); before Peter's confession (9, 18); at the transfiguration (9, 28); when he teaches his disciples to pray (11, 1); at the Last Supper (22, 32); on the Mount of Olives (22, 41); on the cross (23, 46).

3, 22: *You are my beloved Son; with you I am well pleased:* this is the best attested reading in the Greek manuscripts. The Western reading, "You are my Son, this day I have begotten you," is derived from Ps 2, 7.

3, 23–38: Whereas Mt 1, 2 begins the genealogy of Jesus with Abraham to emphasize Jesus' bonds with the people of Israel, Luke's universalism leads him to trace the descent of Jesus beyond Israel to Adam and beyond that to God (38) to stress again Jesus' divine sonship.

3, 31: *The son of Nathan, the son of David:* in keeping with Jesus' prophetic role in Lk and Acts (e.g., 7, 16.39; 9, 8; 13, 33; 24, 19; Acts 3, 22–23; 7, 37) Luke traces Jesus' Davidic ancestry through the prophet Nathan (see 2 Sm 7, 2) rather than through King Solomon, as Mt 1, 6–7.

36 [m]the son of Cainan, the son of Arphaxad,
the son of Shem, the son of Noah, the son of
Lamech, 37 the son of Methuselah, the son of
Enoch, the son of Jared, the son of Mahalaleel,
the son of Cainan, 38 the son of Enos, the son
of Seth, the son of Adam, the son of God.

## CHAPTER 4

**The Temptation of Jesus** 1 [n]*Filled with
the holy Spirit, Jesus returned from the Jordan
and was led by the Spirit into the desert 2 [o]*for
forty days, to be tempted by the devil. He ate
nothing during those days, and when they were
over he was hungry. 3 The devil said to him,
"If you are the Son of God, command this stone
to become bread." 4 [p]Jesus answered him, "It
is written, 'One does not live by bread alone.' "
5 Then he took him up and showed him all the
kingdoms of the world in a single instant.
6 [q]The devil said to him, "I shall give to you
all this power and their glory; for it has been
handed over to me, and I may give it to whomever I wish. 7 All this will be yours, if you
worship me." 8 [r]Jesus said to him in reply, "It
is written:

'You shall worship the Lord, your God,
and him alone shall you serve.' "

9 *Then he led him to Jerusalem, made him
stand on the parapet of the temple, and said to
him, "If you are the Son of God, throw yourself
down from here, 10 [s]for it is written:

'He will command his angels concerning
you,
to guard you,'

11 [t]and:

'With their hands they will support you,
lest you dash your foot against a stone.' "

12 [u]Jesus said to him in reply, "It also says,
'You shall not put the Lord, your God, to the
test.' " 13 [v]*When the devil had finished every
temptation, he departed from him for a time.

## IV: THE MINISTRY IN GALILEE

### The Beginning of the Galilean Ministry

14 [wx]*Jesus returned to Galilee in the power of
the Spirit, and news of him spread throughout
the whole region. 15 He taught in their synagogues and was praised by all.

**The Rejection at Nazareth** 16 [y]*He came
to Nazareth, where he had grown up, and went
according to his custom into the synagogue on
the sabbath day. He stood up to read 17 and was
handed a scroll of the prophet Isaiah. He unrolled the scroll and found the passage where it
was written:

18 [z]*"The Spirit of the Lord is upon me,
because he has anointed me
to bring glad tidings to the poor.
He has sent me to proclaim liberty to
captives
and recovery of sight to the blind,
to let the oppressed go free,
19 and to proclaim a year acceptable to the
Lord."

20 Rolling up the scroll, he handed it back to
the attendant and sat down, and the eyes of all
in the synagogue looked intently at him.
21 *He said to them, "Today this scripture pas-

m Gn 4, 25—5, 32; 1 Chr 1, 1-4.
n Mt 4, 1-11; Mk 1, 12-13.
o Heb 4, 15.
p Dt 8, 3.
q Jer 27, 5; Mt 28, 18.
r Dt 6, 13.
s Ps 91, 11.
t Ps 91, 12.
u Dt 6, 16; 1 Cor 10, 9.
v 22, 3; Jn 13, 2.27; Heb 4, 15.
w Mt 4, 12-17; Mk 1, 14-15.
x 5, 15; Mt 3, 16.
y Mt 13, 53-58; Mk 6, 1-6.
z Is 61, 1-2; 58, 6.

*

4, 1–13: See the note on Mt 4, 1–11.

4, 1: *Filled with the holy Spirit:* as a result of the descent of the Spirit upon him at his baptism (3, 21–22), Jesus is now equipped to overcome the devil. Just as the Spirit is prominent at this early stage of Jesus' ministry (1.14.18), so too it will be at the beginning of the period of the church in Acts (Acts 1, 4; 2, 4.17).

4, 2: *For forty days:* the mention of forty days recalls the forty years of the wilderness wanderings of the Israelites during the Exodus (Dt 8, 2).

4, 9: *To Jerusalem:* the Lucan order of the temptations concludes on the parapet of the temple in Jerusalem, the city of destiny in Luke-Acts. It is in Jerusalem that Jesus will ultimately face his destiny (9, 51; 13, 33).

4, 13: *For a time:* the devil's opportune time will occur before the passion and death of Jesus (Lk 22, 3.31–32.53).

4, 14: *News of him spread:* a Lucan theme; see v 37; 5, 15; 7, 17.

4, 16–30: Luke has transposed to the beginning of Jesus' ministry an incident from his Marcan source, which situated it near the end of the Galilean ministry (Mk 6, 1–6a). In doing so, Luke turns the initial admiration (22) and subsequent rejection of Jesus (28–29) into a foreshadowing of the whole future ministry of Jesus. Moreover, the rejection of Jesus in his own hometown hints at the greater rejection of him by Israel (Acts 13, 46).

4, 16: *According to his custom:* Jesus' practice of regularly attending synagogue is carried on by the early Christians' practice of meeting in the temple (Acts 2, 46; 3, 1; 5, 12).

4, 18: *The Spirit of the Lord is upon me, because he has anointed me:* see the note on 3, 21–22. As this incident develops, Jesus is portrayed as a prophet whose ministry is compared to that of the prophets Elijah and Elisha. Prophetic anointings are known in first-century Palestinian Judaism from the Qumran literature that speaks of prophets as God's anointed ones. *To bring glad tidings to the poor:* more than any other gospel writer Luke is concerned with Jesus' attitude toward the economically and socially poor (see 6, 20.24; 12, 16–21; 14, 12–14; 16, 19–26; 19, 8). At times, the poor in Luke's gospel are associated with the downtrodden, the oppressed and afflicted, the forgotten and the neglected (18; 6, 20–22; 7, 22; 14, 12–14), and it is they who accept Jesus' message of salvation.

4, 21: *Today this scripture passage is fulfilled in your hearing:* this sermon inaugurates the time of fulfillment of Old Testament prophecy. Luke presents the ministry of Jesus as fulfilling Old Testament hopes and expectations (7, 22); for Luke, even Jesus' suffering, death, and resurrection are done in

sage is fulfilled in your hearing.” 22 [a]And all
spoke highly of him and were amazed at the
gracious words that came from his mouth. They
also asked, “Isn't this the son of Joseph?”
23 *He said to them, “Surely you will quote
me this proverb, ‘Physician, cure yourself,’ and
say, ‘Do here in your native place the things that
we heard were done in Capernaum.’” 24 And
he said, “Amen, I say to you, no prophet is
accepted in his own native place. 25 [b]*Indeed,
I tell you, there were many widows in Israel in
the days of Elijah when the sky was closed for
three and a half years and a severe famine spread
over the entire land. 26 [c]*It was to none of
these that Elijah was sent, but only to a widow
in Zarephath in the land of Sidon. 27 [d]Again,
there were many lepers in Israel during the time
of Elisha the prophet; yet not one of them was
cleansed, but only Naaman the Syrian.”
28 When the people in the synagogue heard
this, they were all filled with fury. 29 They rose
up, drove him out of the town, and led him to
the brow of the hill on which their town had
been built, to hurl him down headlong. 30 But
he passed through the midst of them and went
away.

### The Cure of a Demoniac

31 [e,f]*Jesus
then went down to Capernaum, a town of Galilee. He taught them on the sabbath, 32 [g]and
they were astonished at his teaching because he
spoke with authority. 33 [h]In the synagogue
there was a man with the spirit of an unclean
demon, and he cried out in a loud voice,
34 [i]*“Ha! What have you to do with us, Jesus
of Nazareth? Have you come to destroy us? I
know who you are—the Holy One of God!”
35 Jesus rebuked him and said, “Be quiet!
Come out of him!” Then the demon threw the
man down in front of them and came out of him
without doing him any harm. 36 They were all
amazed and said to one another, “What is there
about his word? For with authority and power
he commands the unclean spirits, and they come
out.” 37 And news of him spread everywhere
in the surrounding region.

### The Cure of Simon's Mother-in-Law

38 [j]*After he left the synagogue, he entered the
house of Simon. Simon's mother-in-law was
afflicted with a severe fever, and they interceded with him about her. 39 He stood over her,
rebuked the fever, and it left her. She got up
immediately and waited on them.

### Other Healings

40 [k]At sunset, all who had
people sick with various diseases brought them
to him. He laid his hands on each of them and
cured them. 41 [l]*And demons also came out
from many, shouting, “You are the Son of
God.” But he rebuked them and did not allow
them to speak because they knew that he was the
Messiah.

### Jesus Leaves Capernaum

42 [m]*At day-
break, Jesus left and went to a deserted place.
The crowds went looking for him, and when
they came to him, they tried to prevent him from
leaving them. 43 [n]But he said to them, “To the
other towns also I must proclaim the good news
of the kingdom of God, because for this purpose
I have been sent.” 44 *And he was preaching
in the synagogues of Judea.

---

a 3, 23; Jn 6, 42.
b 1 Kgs 17, 1-7; 18, 1; Jas 5, 17.
c 1 Kgs 17, 9.
d 2 Kgs 5, 1-14.
e Mk 1, 21-28.
f Mt 4, 13; Jn 2, 12.
g Mt 7, 28-29.
h 8, 28; Mt 8, 29; Mk 1, 23-24; 5, 7.
i 4, 41; Jn 6, 69.
j Mt 8, 14-15; Mk 1, 29-31.
k Mt 8, 16; Mk 1, 32-34.
l 4, 34; Mt 8, 29; Mk 3, 11-12.
m Mk 1, 35-39.
n 8, 1; Mk 1, 14-15.

---

* fulfillment of the scriptures (24, 25–27.44–46; Acts 3, 18).

4, 23: *The things that we heard were done in Capernaum:* Luke's source for this incident reveals an awareness of an earlier ministry of Jesus in Capernaum that Luke has not yet made use of because of his transposition of this Nazareth episode to the beginning of Jesus' Galilean ministry. It is possible that by use of the future tense *you* will quote me. . . , Jesus is being portrayed as a prophet.

4, 25–26: The references to Elijah and Elisha serve several purposes in this episode: they emphasize Luke's portrait of Jesus as a prophet like Elijah and Elisha; they help to explain why the initial admiration of the people turns to rejection; and they provide the scriptural justification for the future Christian mission to the Gentiles.

4, 26: *A widow in Zarephath in the land of Sidon:* like Naaman the Syrian in v 27, a non-Israelite becomes the object of the prophet's ministry.

4, 31–44: The next several incidents in Jesus' ministry take place in Capernaum and are based on Luke's source, Mk 1, 21–39. To the previous portrait of Jesus as prophet (16–30) they now add a presentation of him as teacher (31–32), exorcist (32–37.41), healer (38–40), and proclaimer of God's kingdom (43).

4, 34: *What have you to do with us?:* see the note on Jn 2, 4. *Have you come to destroy us?:* the question reflects the current belief that before the day of the Lord control over humanity would be wrested from the evil spirits, evil destroyed, and God's authority over humanity reestablished. The synoptic gospel tradition presents Jesus carrying out this task.

4, 38: *The house of Simon:* because of Luke's arrangement of material, the reader has not yet been introduced to Simon (cf Mk 1, 16–18.29–31). Situated as it is before the call of Simon (5, 1–11), it helps the reader to understand Simon's eagerness to do what Jesus says (5, 5) and to follow him (5, 11).

4, 41: *They knew that he was the Messiah:* that is, the Christ (see the note on 2, 11).

4, 42: *They tried to prevent him from leaving them:* the reaction of these strangers in Capernaum is presented in contrast to the reactions of those in his hometown who rejected him (28–30).

4, 44: *In the synagogues of Judea:* instead of *Judea,* which is the best reading of the manuscript tradition, the Byzantine text tradition and other manuscripts read “Galilee,” a reading that harmonizes Lk with Mt 4, 23 and Mk 1, 39. Up to this point Luke has spoken only of a ministry of Jesus in Galilee. Luke may be using *Judea* to refer to the land of Israel, the territory of the Jews, and not to a specific portion of it.

## CHAPTER 5

### The Call of Simon the Fisherman
**1** [o,p]*While the crowd was pressing in on Jesus
and listening to the word of God, he was standing by the Lake of Gennesaret. **2** He saw two
boats there alongside the lake; the fishermen
had disembarked and were washing their nets.
**3** Getting into one of the boats, the one belonging to Simon, he asked him to put out a short
distance from the shore. Then he sat down and
taught the crowds from the boat. **4** [q]After he
had finished speaking, he said to Simon, "Put
out into deep water and lower your nets for a
catch." **5** Simon said in reply, "Master, we
have worked hard all night and have caught
nothing, but at your command I will lower the
nets." **6** When they had done this, they caught
a great number of fish and their nets were tearing. **7** They signaled to their partners in the
other boat to come to help them. They came and
filled both boats so that they were in danger of
sinking. **8** When Simon Peter saw this, he fell
at the knees of Jesus and said, "Depart from
me, Lord, for I am a sinful man." **9** For astonishment at the catch of fish they had made seized
him and all those with him, **10** [r]and likewise
James and John, the sons of Zebedee, who were
partners of Simon. Jesus said to Simon, "Do
not be afraid; from now on you will be catching
men." **11** [s]*When they brought their boats to
the shore, they left[t] everything and followed
him.

### The Cleansing of a Leper
**12** [t]*Now
there was a man full of leprosy in one of the
towns where he was; and when he saw Jesus, he
fell prostrate, pleaded with him, and said,
"Lord, if you wish, you can make me clean."
**13** Jesus stretched out his hand, touched him,
and said, "I do will it. Be made clean." And
the leprosy left him immediately. **14** [u]*Then he
ordered him not to tell anyone, but "Go, show
yourself to the priest and offer for your cleansing what Moses prescribed; that will be proof
for them." **15** The report about him spread all
the more, and great crowds assembled to listen
to him and to be cured of their ailments, **16** [v]but
he would withdraw to deserted places to pray.

### The Healing of a Paralytic
**17** [w]*One day
as Jesus was teaching, Pharisees and teachers of
the law were sitting there who had come from
every village of Galilee and Judea and Jerusalem, and the power of the Lord was with him for
healing. **18** And some men brought on a
stretcher a man who was paralyzed; they were
trying to bring him in and set [him] in his presence. **19** *But not finding a way to bring him
in because of the crowd, they went up on the
roof and lowered him on the stretcher through
the tiles into the middle in front of Jesus.
**20** *When he saw their faith, he said, "As for
you, your sins are forgiven." **21** [x]*Then the
scribes and Pharisees began to ask themselves,
"Who is this who speaks blasphemies? Who but
God alone can forgive sins?" **22** [y]Jesus knew
their thoughts and said to them in reply, "What
are you thinking in your hearts? **23** Which is
easier, to say, 'Your sins are forgiven,' or to

o Mt 4, 18-22; Mk 1, 16-20.
p Mt 13, 1-2; Mk 2, 13; 3, 9-10; 4, 1-2.
q Jn 21, 1-11.
r Jer 16, 16.
s Mt 19, 27.
t Mt 8, 2-4; Mk 1, 40-45.
u 8, 56; Lv 14, 2-32; Mk 7, 36.
v Mk 1, 35.
w Mt 9, 1-8; Mk 2, 1-12.
x 7, 49; Is 43, 25.
y 6, 8; 9, 47.

*

5, 1–11: This incident has been transposed from his source, Mk 1, 16–20, which places it immediately after Jesus makes his appearance in Galilee. By this transposition Luke uses this example of Simon's acceptance of Jesus to counter the earlier rejection of him by his hometown people, and since several incidents dealing with Jesus' power and authority have already been narrated, Luke creates a plausible context for the acceptance of Jesus by Simon and his partners. Many commentators have noted the similarity between the wondrous catch of fish reported here (4–9) and the post-resurrectional appearance of Jesus in Jn 21, 1–11. There are traces in Luke's story that the post-resurrectional context is the original one: in v 8 Simon addresses Jesus as *Lord* (a post-resurrectional title for Jesus—see 24, 34; Acts 2, 36—that has been read back into the historical ministry of Jesus) and recognizes himself as a sinner (an appropriate recognition for one who has denied knowing Jesus—22, 54–62). As used by Luke, the incident looks forward to Peter's leadership in Luke-Acts (6, 14; 9, 20; 22, 31–32; 24, 34; Acts 1, 15; 2, 14–40; 10, 11–18; 15, 7–12) and symbolizes the future success of Peter as fisherman (Acts 2, 41).

5, 11: *They left everything:* in Mk 1, 16–20 and Mt 4, 18–22 the fishermen who follow Jesus leave their nets and their father; in Luke, they leave *everything* (see also 28; 12, 33; 14, 33; 18, 22), an indication of Luke's theme of complete detachment from material possessions.

5, 12: *Full of leprosy:* see the note on Mk 1, 40.

5, 14: *Show yourself to the priest . . . what Moses prescribed:* this is a reference to Lv 14, 2–9 that gives detailed instructions for the purification of one who had been a victim of leprosy and thereby excluded from contact with others (see Lv 13, 45–46.49; Nm 5, 2–3). *That will be proof for them:* see the note on Mt 8, 4.

5, 17—6, 11: From his Marcan source, Luke now introduces a series of controversies with Pharisees: controversy over Jesus' power to forgive sins (17–26); controversy over his eating and drinking with tax collectors and sinners (27–32); controversy over not fasting (33–36); and finally two episodes narrating controversies over observance of the sabbath (1–11).

5, 17: *Pharisees:* see the note on Mt 3, 7.

5, 19: *Through the tiles:* Luke has adapted the story found in Mk to his non-Palestinian audience by changing "opened up the roof" (Mk 2, 4, a reference to Palestinian straw and clay roofs) to *through the tiles,* a detail that reflects the Hellenistic Greco-Roman house with tiled roof.

5, 20: *As for you, your sins are forgiven:* literally, "O man, your sins are forgiven you." The connection between the forgiveness of sins and the cure of the paralytic reflects the belief of first-century Palestine (based on the Old Testament: Ex 20, 5; Dt 5, 9) that sickness and infirmity are the result of sin, one's own or that of one's ancestors (see also 13, 2; Jn 5, 14; 9, 2).

5, 21: *The scribes:* see the note on Mk 2, 6.

say, 'Rise and walk'? **24** [z]*But that you may know that the Son of Man has authority on earth to forgive sins"—he said to the man who was paralyzed, "I say to you, rise, pick up your stretcher, and go home." **25** He stood up immediately before them, picked up what he had been lying on, and went home, glorifying God. **26** Then astonishment seized them all and they glorified God, and, struck with awe, they said, "We have seen incredible things today."

**The Call of Levi** **27** [a]After this he went out and saw a tax collector named Levi sitting at the customs post. He said to him, "Follow me." **28** *And leaving everything behind, he got up and followed him. **29** [b]Then Levi gave a great banquet for him in his house, and a large crowd of tax collectors and others were at table with them. **30** The Pharisees and their scribes complained to his disciples, saying, "Why do you eat and drink with tax collectors and sinners?" **31** Jesus said to them in reply, "Those who are healthy do not need a physician, but the sick do. **32** I have not come to call the righteous to repentance but sinners."

**The Question about Fasting** **33** [c]And they said to him, "The disciples of John fast often and offer prayers, and the disciples of the Pharisees do the same; but yours eat and drink." **34** *Jesus answered them, "Can you make the wedding guests fast while the bridegroom is with them? **35** But the days will come, and when the bridegroom is taken away from them, then they will fast in those days." **36** *And he also told them a parable. "No one tears a piece from a new cloak to patch an old one. Otherwise, he will tear the new and the piece from it will not match the old cloak. **37** Likewise, no one pours new wine into old wineskins. Otherwise, the new wine will burst the skins, and it will be spilled, and the skins will be ruined. **38** Rather, new wine must be poured into fresh wineskins. **39** *[And] no one who has been drinking old wine desires new, for he says, 'The old is good.'"

## CHAPTER 6

**Debates about the Sabbath** **1** [de]*While he was going through a field of grain on a sabbath, his disciples were picking the heads of grain, rubbing them in their hands, and eating them. **2** Some Pharisees said, "Why are you doing what is unlawful on the sabbath?" **3** [f]Jesus said to them in reply, "Have you not read what David did when he and those [who were] with him were hungry? **4** [g]*[How] he went into the house of God, took the bread of offering, which only the priests could lawfully eat, ate of it, and shared it with his companions." **5** Then he said to them, "The Son of Man is lord of the sabbath."

**6** [h]On another sabbath he went into the synagogue and taught, and there was a man there whose right hand was withered. **7** [i]The scribes and the Pharisees watched him closely to see if he would cure on the sabbath so that they might discover a reason to accuse him. **8** [j]But he realized their intentions and said to the man with the withered hand, "Come up and stand before us." And he rose and stood there. **9** Then Jesus said to them, "I ask you, is it lawful to do good on the sabbath rather than to do evil, to save life rather than to destroy it?" **10** Looking around at them all, he then said to him, "Stretch out your hand." He did so and his hand was restored. **11** But they became enraged and discussed together what they might do to Jesus.

**The Mission of the Twelve** **12** [k]*In those days he departed to the mountain to pray, and he spent the night in prayer to God. **13** *When

z Jn 5, 8-9.27.
a Mt 9, 9-13; Mk 2, 13-17.
b 15, 1-2.
c Mt 9, 14-17; Mk 2, 18-22.
d Mt 12, 1-8; Mk 2, 23-28.
e Dt 23, 26.
f 1 Sm 21, 1-6.
g Lv 24, 5-9.
h Mt 12, 9-14; Mk 3, 1-6.
i 14, 1.
j 5, 22; 9, 47.
k Mt 10, 1-4; Mk 3, 13-19.

*

5, 24: See the notes on Mt 9, 6 and Mk 2, 10.

5, 28: *Leaving everything behind:* see the note on 5, 11.

5, 34–35: See the notes on Mt 9, 15 and Mk 2, 19.

5, 34: *Wedding guests:* literally, "sons of the bridal chamber."

5, 36–39: See the notes on Mt 9, 16–17 and Mk 2, 19.

5, 39: *The old is good:* this saying is meant to be ironic and offers an explanation for the rejection by some of the new wine that Jesus offers: satisfaction with old forms will prevent one from sampling the new.

6, 1–11: The two episodes recounted here deal with gathering grain and healing, both of which were forbidden on the sabbath. In his defense of his disciples' conduct and his own charitable deed, Jesus argues that satisfying human needs such as hunger and performing works of mercy take precedence even over the sacred sabbath rest. See also the notes on Mt 12, 1–14 and Mk 2, 25–26.

6, 4: *The bread of offering:* see the note on Mt 12, 5–6.

6, 12–16: See the notes on Mt 10, 1—11, 1 and Mk 3, 14–15.

6, 12: *Spent the night in prayer:* see the note on 3, 21.

6, 13: *He chose Twelve:* the identification of this group as the *Twelve* is a part of early Christian tradition (see 1 Cor 15, 5), and in Mt and Lk, the Twelve are associated with the twelve tribes of Israel (22, 29–30; Mt 19, 28). After the fall of Judas from his position among the Twelve, the need is felt on the part of the early community to reconstitute this group before the Christian mission begins at Pentecost (Acts 1, 15–26). From Luke's perspective, they are an important group who because of their association with Jesus from the time of his baptism to his ascension (Acts 1, 21–22) provide the continuity between the historical Jesus and the church of Luke's day and who as the original eyewitnesses guarantee the fidelity of the church's beliefs and practices to the teachings of Jesus (1, 1–4). *Whom he also named apostles:* only Luke among the gospel writers attributes to Jesus the bestowal of the name *apostles* upon the Twelve. See the note on Mt 10, 2–4. "Apostle" becomes a technical term in early Christianity for a missionary sent out to

day came, he called his disciples to himself, and
from them he chose Twelve, whom he also
named apostles: **14** [l]*Simon, whom he named
Peter, and his brother Andrew, James, John,
Philip, Bartholomew, **15** *Matthew, Thomas,
James the son of Alphaeus, Simon who was
called a Zealot, **16** *and Judas the son of
James, and Judas Iscariot, who became a traitor.

## Ministering to a Great Multitude

**17** [m]*And he came down with them and stood
on a stretch of level ground. A great crowd of
his disciples and a large number of the people
from all Judea and Jerusalem and the coastal
region of Tyre and Sidon **18** came to hear him
and to be healed of their diseases; and even
those who were tormented by unclean spirits
were cured. **19** Everyone in the crowd sought
to touch him because power came forth from
him and healed them all.

## Sermon on the Plain

**20** [n]*And raising his
eyes toward his disciples he said:

"Blessed are you who are poor,
for the kingdom of God is yours.
**21** [o]Blessed are you who are now hungry,
for you will be satisfied.
Blessed are you who are now weeping,
for you will laugh.
**22** [p]Blessed are you when people hate you,
and when they exclude and insult you,
and denounce your name as evil
on account of the Son of Man.
**23** [q]Rejoice and leap for joy on that day!
Behold, your reward
will be great in heaven. For their
ancestors treated the prophets
in the same way.
**24** [r]But woe to you who are rich,
for you have received your consolation.
**25** [s]But woe to you who are filled now,
for you will be hungry.
Woe to you who laugh now,
for you will grieve and weep.
**26** [t]Woe to you when all speak well of you,
for their ancestors treated the false
prophets in this way.

## Love of Enemies

**27** [uv]*"But to you who
hear I say, love your enemies, do good to those
who hate you, **28** [w]bless those who curse you,
pray for those who mistreat you. **29** To the
person who strikes you on one cheek, offer the
other one as well, and from the person who
takes your cloak, do not withhold even your
tunic. **30** Give to everyone who asks of you,
and from the one who takes what is yours do not
demand it back. **31** [x]Do to others as you would
have them do to you. **32** For if you love those
who love you, what credit is that to you? Even
sinners love those who love them. **33** And if
you do good to those who do good to you, what
credit is that to you? Even sinners do the same.
**34** [y]If you lend money to those from whom you
expect repayment, what credit [is] that to you?
Even sinners lend to sinners, and get back the
same amount. **35** [z]But rather, love your enemies and do good to them, and lend expecting

---

l Acts 1, 13.
m Mt 4, 23-25; Mk 3, 7-10.
n Mt 5, 1-12.
o Ps 126, 5-6; Is 61, 3; Jer 31, 25; Rv 7, 16-17.
p Jn 15, 19; 16, 2; 1 Pt 4, 14.
q 11, 47-48; 2 Chr 36, 16; Mt 23, 30-31.
r Jas 5, 1.
s Is 65, 13-14.
t Jas 4, 4.
u Mt 5, 38-48.
v Prv 25, 21; Rom 12, 20-21.
w Rom 12, 14; 1 Pt 3, 9.
x Mt 7, 12.
y Dt 15, 7-8.
z Lv 25, 35-36.

---

* preach the word of God. Although Luke seems to want to restrict the title to the Twelve (only in Acts 4, 4.14 are Paul and Barnabas termed apostles), other places in the New Testament show an awareness that the term was more widely applied (1 Cor 15, 5–7; Gal 1, 19; 1 Cor 1, 1; 9, 1; Rom 16, 7).

6, 14: *Simon, whom he named Peter:* see the note on Mk 3, 16.

6, 15: *Simon who was called a Zealot:* the Zealots were the instigators of the First Revolt of Palestinian Jews against Rome in A.D. 66–70. Because the existence of the Zealots as a distinct group during the lifetime of Jesus is the subject of debate, the meaning of the identification of Simon as a Zealot is unclear.

6, 16: *Judas Iscariot:* the name *Iscariot* may mean "man from Kerioth."

6, 17: *The coastal region of Tyre and Sidon:* not only Jews from Judea and Jerusalem, but even Gentiles from outside Palestine come to hear Jesus (see 2, 31–32; 3, 6; 4, 24–27).

6, 20–49: Luke's "Sermon on the Plain" is the counterpart to Mt's "Sermon on the Mount" (Mt 5, 1—7, 27). It is addressed to the disciples of Jesus, and, like the sermon in Mt, it begins with beatitudes (20–22) and ends with the parable of the two houses (46–49). Almost all the words of Jesus reported by Lk are found in Mt's version, but because Mt includes sayings that were related to specifically Jewish Christian problems (e.g., Mt 5, 17–20; 6, 1–8.16–18) that Luke did not find appropriate for his predominantly Gentile Christian audience, the "Sermon on the Mount" is considerably longer. Lk's sermon may be outlined as follows: an introduction consisting of blessings and woes (20–26); the love of one's enemies (27–36); the demands of loving one's neighbor (37–42); good deeds as proof of one's goodness (43–45); a parable illustrating the result of listening to and acting on the words of Jesus (46–49). At the core of the sermon is Jesus' teaching on the love of one's enemies (27–36) that has as its source of motivation God's graciousness and compassion for all humanity (35–36) and Jesus' teaching on the love of one's neighbor (37–42) that is characterized by forgiveness and generosity.

6, 20–26: The introductory portion of the sermon consists of blessings and woes that address the real economic and social conditions of humanity (the poor—the rich; the hungry—the satisfied; those grieving—those laughing; the outcast—the socially acceptable). By contrast, Matthew emphasizes the religious and spiritual values of disciples in the kingdom inaugurated by Jesus ("poor in spirit," 5, 5; "hunger and thirst for righteousness" 5, 6). In the sermon, *blessed* extols the fortunate condition of persons who are favored with the blessings of God; the woes, addressed as they are to the disciples of Jesus, threaten God's profound displeasure on those so blinded by their present fortunate situation that they do not recognize and appreciate the real values of God's kingdom. In all the blessings and woes, the present condition of the persons addressed will be reversed in the future.

6, 27–36: See the notes on Mt 5, 43–48 and 5, 48.

nothing back; then your reward will be great and
you will be children of the Most High, for he
himself is kind to the ungrateful and the wicked.
36 Be merciful, just as [also] your Father is
merciful.

**Judging Others** 37 [ab]*"Stop judging and
you will not be judged. Stop condemning and
you will not be condemned. Forgive and you
will be forgiven. 38 [c]Give and gifts will be
given to you; a good measure, packed together,
shaken down, and overflowing, will be poured
into your lap. For the measure with which you
measure will in return be measured out to you."
39 [d]And he told them a parable, "Can a blind
person guide a blind person? Will not both fall
into a pit? 40 [e]No disciple is superior to the
teacher; but when fully trained, every disciple
will be like his teacher. 41 Why do you notice
the splinter in your brother's eye, but do not
perceive the wooden beam in your own?
42 How can you say to your brother, 'Brother,
let me remove that splinter in your eye,' when
you do not even notice the wooden beam in your
own eye? You hypocrite! Remove the wooden
beam from your eye first; then you will see
clearly to remove the splinter in your brother's
eye.

**A Tree Known by Its Fruit** 43 [f]*"A good
tree does not bear rotten fruit, nor does a rotten
tree bear good fruit. 44 For every tree is known
by its own fruit. For people do not pick figs
from thornbushes, nor do they gather grapes
from brambles. 45 A good person out of the
store of goodness in his heart produces good,
but an evil person out of a store of evil produces
evil; for from the fullness of the heart the mouth
speaks.

**The Two Foundations** 46 [g]"Why do you
call me, 'Lord, Lord,' but not do what I command? 47 [h]*I will show you what someone is
like who comes to me, listens to my words, and
acts on them. 48 That one is like a person building a house, who dug deeply and laid the foundation on rock; when the flood came, the river
burst against that house but could not shake it
because it had been well built. 49 But the one
who listens and does not act is like a person who
built a house on the ground without a foundation. When the river burst against it, it collapsed
at once and was completely destroyed."

## CHAPTER 7

### The Healing of a Centurion's Slave

1 [i]*When he had finished all his words to the
people, he entered Capernaum. 2 *A centurion
there had a slave who was ill and about to die,
and he was valuable to him. 3 When he heard
about Jesus, he sent elders of the Jews to him,
asking him to come and save the life of his
slave. 4 They approached Jesus and strongly
urged him to come, saying, "He deserves to
have you do this for him, 5 for he loves our
nation and he built the synagogue for us."
6 *And Jesus went with them, but when he was
only a short distance from the house, the centurion sent friends to tell him, "Lord, do not
trouble yourself, for I am not worthy to have
you enter under my roof. 7 Therefore, I did not
consider myself worthy to come to you; but say
the word and let my servant be healed. 8 For I
too am a person subject to authority, with soldiers subject to me. And I say to one, 'Go,' and
he goes; and to another, 'Come here,' and he
comes; and to my slave, 'Do this,' and he does
it." 9 When Jesus heard this he was amazed at
him and, turning, said to the crowd following
him, "I tell you, not even in Israel have I found
such faith." 10 When the messengers returned
to the house, they found the slave in good
health.

**Raising of the Widow's Son** 11 [j]*Soon
afterward he journeyed to a city called Nain,
and his disciples and a large crowd accompa-

a Mt 7, 1-5.
b Mt 6, 14; Jas 2, 13.
c Mk 4, 24.
d Mt 15, 14; 23, 16-17.24.
e Mt 10, 24-25; Jn 13, 16; 15, 20.
f Mt 7, 16-20; 12, 33.35.
g Mt 7, 21; Rom 2, 13; Jas 1, 22.
h Mt 7, 24-27.
i Mt 8, 5-13; Jn 4, 43-54
j 4, 25-26; 1 Kgs 17, 17-24.

*

6, 37–42: See the notes on Mt 7, 1–12; 7, 1; 7, 5.

6, 43–46: See the notes on Mt 7, 15–20 and 12, 33.

6, 47–49: See the note on Mt 7, 24–27.

7, 1—8, 3: The episodes in this section present a series of reactions to the Galilean ministry of Jesus and reflect some of Luke's particular interests: the faith of a Gentile (1–10); the prophet Jesus' concern for a widowed mother (11–17); the ministry of Jesus directed to the afflicted and unfortunate of Is 61, 1 (18–23); the relation between John and Jesus and their role in God's plan for salvation (24–35); a forgiven sinner's manifestation of love (36–50); the association of women with the ministry of Jesus (8, 1–3).

7, 1–10: This story about the faith of the centurion, a Gentile who cherishes the Jewish nation (5), prepares for the story in Acts of the conversion by Peter of the Roman centurion Cornelius who is similarly described as one who is generous to the Jewish nation (Acts 10, 2). See also Acts 10, 34–35 in the speech of Peter: "God shows no partiality . . . the person who fears him and acts righteously is acceptable to him." See also the notes on Mt 8, 5–13 and Jn 4, 43–54.

7, 2: *A centurion:* see the note on Mt 8, 5.

7, 6: *I am not worthy to have you enter under my roof:* to enter the house of a Gentile was considered unclean for a Jew; cf Acts 10, 28.

7, 11–17: In the previous incident Jesus power was displayed for a Gentile whose servant was dying; in this episode it is displayed toward a widowed mother whose only son has already died. Jesus' power over death prepares for his reply to John's disciples in v 22: "the dead are raised." This resuscitation in alluding to the prophet Elijah's resurrection of the only son of a widow of Zarephath (1 Kgs 7, 8–24) leads to the reaction of the crowd: "A great prophet has arisen in our midst" (16).

nied him. **12** [k]As he drew near to the gate of the
city, a man who had died was being carried out,
the only son of his mother, and she was a widow. A large crowd from the city was with her.
**13** When the Lord saw her, he was moved with
pity for her and said to her, "Do not weep."
**14** He stepped forward and touched the coffin;
at this the bearers halted, and he said, "Young
man, I tell you, arise!" **15** [l]The dead man sat
up and began to speak, and Jesus gave him to
his mother. **16** [m]Fear seized them all, and they
glorified God, exclaiming, "A great prophet
has arisen in our midst," and "God has visited
his people." **17** This report about him spread
through the whole of Judea and in all the surrounding region.

## The Messengers from John the Baptist

**18** [n]*The disciples of John told him about all
these things. John summoned two of his disciples **19** [o]and sent them to the Lord to ask, "Are
you the one who is to come, or should we look
for another?" **20** When the men came to him,
they said, "John the Baptist has sent us to you
to ask, 'Are you the one who is to come, or
should we look for another?' " **21** At that time
he cured many of their diseases, sufferings, and
evil spirits; he also granted sight to many who
were blind. **22** [p]And he said to them in reply,
"Go and tell John what you have seen and
heard: the blind regain their sight, the lame
walk, lepers are cleansed, the deaf hear, the
dead are raised, the poor have the good news
proclaimed to them. **23** *And blessed is the one
who takes no offense at me."

## Jesus' Testimony to John

**24** [q]*When
the messengers of John had left, Jesus began to
speak to the crowds about John. "What did you
go out to the desert to see—a reed swayed by
the wind? **25** Then what did you go out to see?
Someone dressed in fine garments? Those who
dress luxuriously and live sumptuously are
found in royal palaces. **26** [r]Then what did you
go out to see? A prophet? Yes, I tell you, and
more than a prophet. **27** [s]This is the one about
whom scripture says:

'Behold, I am sending my messenger ahead
of you,
he will prepare your way before you.'

**28** I tell you, among those born of women, no
one is greater than John; yet the least in the
kingdom of God is greater than he." **29** [t](All
the people who listened, including the tax collectors, and who were baptized with the baptism
of John, acknowledged the righteousness of
God; **30** but the Pharisees and scholars of the
law, who were not baptized by him, rejected the
plan of God for themselves.)
**31** [u]*"Then to what shall I compare the people of this generation? What are they like?
**32** They are like children who sit in the marketplace and call to one another,

'We played the flute for you, but you did
not dance.
We sang a dirge, but you did not weep.'

**33** For John the Baptist came neither eating
food nor drinking wine, and you said, 'He is
possessed by a demon.' **34** [v]The Son of Man
came eating and drinking and you said, 'Look,
he is a glutton and a drunkard, a friend of tax
collectors and sinners.' **35** But wisdom is vindicated by all her children."

## The Pardon of the Sinful Woman

**36** [w]*A Pharisee invited him to dine with him,
and he entered the Pharisee's house and reclined
at table. **37** [x][y]Now there was a sinful woman in
the city who learned that he was at table in the
house of the Pharisee. Bringing an alabaster
flask of ointment, **38** she stood behind him at
his feet weeping and began to bathe his feet with

k 8, 42; 1 Kgs 17, 17.
l 1 Kgs 17, 23; 2 Kgs 4, 36.
m 1, 68; 19, 44.
n Mt 11, 2-6.
o Mal 3, 1; Rv 1, 4.8; 4, 8.
p 4, 18; Is 35, 5-6; 61, 1.
q Mt 11, 7-15.
r 1, 76.
s Mal 3, 1 / Is 40, 3.
t 3, 7.12; Mt 21, 32.
u Mt 11, 16-19.
v 15, 2.
w 11, 37; 14, 1.
x Mt 26, 7; Mk 14, 3.
y Jn 12, 3.

*

7, 18–23: In answer to John's question, *Are you the one who is to come?*—a probable reference to the return of the fiery prophet of reform, Elijah, "before the day of the Lord comes, the great and terrible day" (Mal 3, 23)—Jesus responds that his role is rather to bring the blessings spoken of in Is 61, 1 to the oppressed and neglected of society (22; cf 4, 18).

7, 23: *Blessed is the one who takes no offense at me:* this beatitude is pronounced on the person who recognizes Jesus' true identity in spite of previous expectations of what "the one who is to come" would be like.

7, 24–30: In his testimony to John, Jesus reveals his understanding of the relationship between them: John is the precursor of Jesus (27); John is the messenger spoken of in Mal 3, 1 who in Mal 3, 23 is identified as Elijah. Taken with the previous episode, it can be seen that Jesus identifies John as precisely the person John envisioned Jesus to be: the Elijah who prepares the way for the coming of the day of the Lord.

7, 31–35: See the note on Mt 11, 16–19.

7, 36–50: In this story of the pardoning of the sinful woman Luke presents two different reactions to the ministry of Jesus. A Pharisee, suspecting Jesus to be a prophet, invites Jesus to a festive banquet in his house, but the Pharisee's self-righteousness leads to little forgiveness by God and consequently little love shown toward Jesus. The sinful woman, on the other hand, manifests a faith in God (50) that has led her to seek forgiveness for her sins, and because so much was forgiven, she now overwhelms Jesus with her display of love; cf the similar contrast in attitudes in 18, 9–14. The whole episode is a powerful lesson on the relation between forgiveness and love.

7, 36: *Reclined at table:* the normal posture of guests at a banquet. Other oriental banquet customs alluded to in this story include the reception by the host with a kiss (45), washing the feet of the guests (44), and the anointing of the guests' heads (46).

her tears. Then she wiped them with her hair,
kissed them, and anointed them with the ointment. **39** When the Pharisee who had invited
him saw this he said to himself, "If this man
were a prophet, he would know who and what
sort of woman this is who is touching him, that
she is a sinner." **40** Jesus said to him in reply,
"Simon, I have something to say to you."
"Tell me, teacher," he said. **41** *"Two people
were in debt to a certain creditor; one owed five
hundred days' wages and the other owed fifty.
**42** Since they were unable to repay the debt, he
forgave it for both. Which of them will love him
more?" **43** Simon said in reply, "The one, I
suppose, whose larger debt was forgiven." He
said to him, "You have judged rightly."
**44** Then he turned to the woman and said to
Simon, "Do you see this woman? When I entered your house, you did not give me water for
my feet, but she has bathed them with her tears
and wiped them with her hair. **45** You did not
give me a kiss, but she has not ceased kissing
my feet since the time I entered. **46** You did not
anoint my head with oil, but she anointed my
feet with ointment. **47** *So I tell you, her many
sins have been forgiven; hence, she has shown
great love. But the one to whom little is forgiv-
en, loves little." **48** [z]He said to her, "Your sins
are forgiven." **49** [a]The others at table said to
themselves, "Who is this who even forgives
sins?" **50** But he said to the woman, "Your
faith has saved you; go in peace."

## CHAPTER 8

### Galilean Women Follow Jesus

**1** [b]*Afterward he journeyed from one town and
village to another, preaching and proclaiming
the good news of the kingdom of God. Accompanying him were the Twelve **2** [c]and some
women who had been cured of evil spirits and
infirmities, Mary, called Magdalene, from
whom seven demons had gone out, **3** Joanna,
the wife of Herod's steward Chuza, Susanna,
and many others who provided for them out of
their resources.

### The Parable of the Sower

**4** [d]*When a
large crowd gathered, with people from one
town after another journeying to him, he spoke
in a parable. **5** "A sower went out to sow his
seed. And as he sowed, some seed fell on the
path and was trampled, and the birds of the sky
ate it up. **6** Some seed fell on rocky ground, and
when it grew, it withered for lack of moisture.
**7** Some seed fell among thorns, and the thorns
grew with it and choked it. **8** [e]And some seed
fell on good soil, and when it grew, it produced
fruit a hundredfold." After saying this, he
called out, "Whoever has ears to hear ought to
hear."

### The Purpose of the Parables

**9** [f]Then his
disciples asked him what the meaning of this
parable might be. **10** [g]He answered, "Knowledge of the mysteries of the kingdom of God has
been granted to you; but to the rest, they are
made known through parables so that 'they may
look but not see, and hear but not understand.'

### The Parable of the Sower Explained

**11** [h][i]*"This is the meaning of the parable. The
seed is the word of God. **12** Those on the path
are the ones who have heard, but the devil
comes and takes away the word from their
hearts that they may not believe and be saved.
**13** Those on rocky ground are the ones who,
when they hear, receive the word with joy, but
they have no root; they believe only for a time
and fall away in time of trial. **14** As for the seed
that fell among thorns, they are the ones who
have heard, but as they go along, they are
choked by the anxieties and riches and pleasures
of life, and they fail to produce mature fruit.
**15** But as for the seed that fell on rich soil, they
are the ones who, when they have heard the
word, embrace it with a generous and good
heart, and bear fruit through perseverance.

z 5, 20; Mt 9, 20; Mk 2, 5.
a 5, 21.
b 4, 43.
c 23, 49; 24, 10; Mt 27, 55-56; Mk 15, 40-41; Jn 19, 5.
d Mt 13, 1-9; Mk 4, 1-9.
e 14, 35; Mt 11, 15; 13, 43; Mk 4, 23.
f Mt 13, 10-13; Mk 4, 10-12.
g Is 6, 9.
h Mt 13, 18-23; Mk 4, 13-20.
i 1 Pt 1, 23.

*

7, 41: *Days' wages:* one denarius is the normal daily wage of a laborer.

7, 47: *Her many sins have been forgiven; hence, she has shown great love:* literally, "her many sins have been forgiven, seeing that she has loved much." That the woman's sins have been forgiven is attested by the great love she shows toward Jesus. Her love is the consequence of her forgiveness. This is also the meaning demanded by the parable in vv 41–43.

8, 1–3: Luke presents Jesus as an itinerant preacher traveling in the company of the Twelve and of the Galilean women who are sustaining them out of their means. These Galilean women will later accompany Jesus on his journey to Jerusalem and become witnesses to his death (23, 49) and resurrection (24, 9–11, where Mary Magdalene and Joanna are specifically mentioned; cf also Acts 1, 14). The association of women with the ministry of Jesus is most unusual in the light of the attitude of first-century Palestinian Judaism toward women. The more common attitude is expressed in Jn 4, 27, and early rabbinic documents caution against speaking with women in public.

8, 4–21: The focus in this section is on how one should hear the word of God and act on it. It includes the parable of the sower and its explanation (4–15), a collection of sayings on how one should act on the word that is heard (16–18), and the identification of the mother and brothers of Jesus as the ones who hear the word and act on it (19–21). See also the notes on Mt 13, 1–53 and Mk 4, 1–34.

8, 4–8: See the note on Mt 13, 3–8.

8, 11–15: On the interpretation of the parable of the sower, see the note on Mt 13, 18–23.

**The Parable of the Lamp** **16** [j][k]*"No one who lights a lamp conceals it with a vessel or sets it under a bed; rather, he places it on a lampstand so that those who enter may see the light. **17** [l]For there is nothing hidden that will not become visible, and nothing secret that will not be known and come to light. **18** [m]Take care, then, how you hear. To anyone who has, more will be given, and from the one who has not, even what he seems to have will be taken away."

**Jesus and His Family** **19** [n]*Then his mother and his brothers came to him but were unable to join him because of the crowd. **20** [o]He was told, "Your mother and your brothers are standing outside and they wish to see you." **21** *He said to them in reply, "My mother and my brothers are those who hear the word of God and act on it."

**The Calming of a Storm at Sea** **22** [p]*One day he got into a boat with his disciples and said to them, "Let us cross to the other side of the lake." So they set sail, **23** and while they were sailing he fell asleep. A squall blew over the lake, and they were taking in water and were in danger. **24** They came and woke him saying, "Master, master, we are perishing!" He awakened, rebuked the wind and the waves, and they subsided and there was a calm. **25** Then he asked them, "Where is your faith?" But they were filled with awe and amazed and said to one another, "Who then is this, who commands even the winds and the sea, and they obey him?"

**The Healing of the Gerasene Demoniac** **26** [q]*Then they sailed to the territory of the Gerasenes, which is opposite Galilee. **27** When he came ashore a man from the town who was possessed by demons met him. For a long time he had not worn clothes; he did not live in a house, but lived among the tombs. **28** [r]When he saw Jesus, he cried out and fell down before him; in a loud voice he shouted, "What have you to do with me, Jesus, son of the Most High God? I beg you, do not torment me!" **29** For he had ordered the unclean spirit to come out of the man. (It had taken hold of him many times, and he used to be bound with chains and shackles as a restraint, but he would break his bonds and be driven by the demon into deserted places.) **30** *Then Jesus asked him, "What is your name?" He replied, "Legion," because many demons had entered him. **31** *And they pleaded with him not to order them to depart to the abyss.

**32** A herd of many swine was feeding there on the hillside, and they pleaded with him to allow them to enter those swine; and he let them. **33** The demons came out of the man and entered the swine, and the herd rushed down the steep bank into the lake and was drowned. **34** When the swineherds saw what had happened, they ran away and reported the incident in the town and throughout the countryside. **35** *People came out to see what had happened and, when they approached Jesus, they discovered the man from whom the demons had come out sitting at his feet. He was clothed and in his right mind, and they were seized with fear. **36** Those who witnessed it told them how the possessed man had been saved. **37** The entire population of the region of the Gerasenes asked Jesus to leave them because they were seized with great fear. So he got into a boat and returned. **38** The man from whom the demons had come out begged to remain with him, but he sent him away, saying, **39** "Return home and recount what God has done for you." The man went off and proclaimed throughout the whole town what Jesus had done for him.

j Mk 4, 21-25.
k 11, 33; Mt 5, 15.
l 12, 2; Mt 10, 26.
m 19, 26; Mt 13, 12; 25, 29.
n Mt 12, 46-50; Mk 3, 31-35.
o 11, 27-28.
p Mt 8, 18.23-27; Mk 4, 35-41.
q Mt 8, 28-34; Mk 5, 1-20.
r 4, 33-35; Mt 8, 29; Mk 1, 23-24.

*

8, 16–18: These sayings continue the theme of responding to the word of God. Those who hear the word must become a light to others (16); even the mysteries of the kingdom that have been made known to the disciples (9–10) must come to light (17); a generous and persevering response to the word of God leads to a still more perfect response to the word.

8, 19: *His brothers:* see the note on Mk 6, 3.

8, 21: The family of Jesus is not constituted by physical relationship with him but by obedience to the word of God. In this, Luke agrees with the Marcan parallel (3, 31–35), although by omitting Mk 3, 33 and especially Mk 3, 20–21 Luke has softened the Marcan picture of Jesus' natural family. Probably he did this because Mary has already been presented in 1, 38 as the obedient handmaid of the Lord who fulfills the requirement for belonging to the eschatological family of Jesus; cf also 11, 27–28.

8, 22–56: This section records four miracles of Jesus that manifest his power and authority: (1) the calming of a storm on the lake (22–25); (2) the exorcism of a demoniac (26–39); (3) the cure of a hemorrhaging woman (40–48); (4) the raising of Jairus's daughter to life (49–56). They parallel the same sequence of stories at Mk 4, 35—5, 43.

8, 26: *Gerasenes:* other manuscripts read Gadarenes or Gergesenes. See also the note on Mt 8, 28. *Opposite Galilee:* probably Gentile territory (note the presence in the area of pigs—unclean animals to Jews) and an indication that the person who receives salvation (36) is a Gentile.

8, 30: *What is your name?:* the question reflects the popular belief that knowledge of the spirit's name brought control over the spirit. *Legion:* to Jesus' question the demon replies with a Latin word transliterated into Greek. The Roman legion at this period consisted of 5,000 to 6,000 foot soldiers; hence the name implies a very large number of demons.

8, 31: *Abyss:* the place of the dead (Rom 10, 7) or the prison of Satan (Rv 20, 3) or the subterranean "watery deep" that symbolizes the chaos before the order imposed by creation (Gn 1, 2).

8, 35: *Sitting at his feet:* the former demoniac takes the position of a disciple before the master (10, 39; Acts 22, 3).

**Jairus's Daughter and the Woman with a
Hemorrhage** 40 [s]*When Jesus returned,
the crowd welcomed him, for they were all
waiting for him. 41 And a man named Jairus,
an official of the synagogue, came forward. He
fell at the feet of Jesus and begged him to come
to his house, 42 *because he had an only
daughter, about twelve years old, and she was
dying. As he went, the crowds almost crushed
him. 43 *And a woman afflicted with hemorrhages for twelve years, who [had spent her whole
livelihood on doctors and] was unable to be
cured by anyone, 44 came up behind him and
touched the tassel on his cloak. Immediately her
bleeding stopped. 45 Jesus then asked, "Who
touched me?" While all were denying it, Peter
said, "Master, the crowds are pushing and
pressing in upon you." 46 [t]But Jesus said,
"Someone has touched me; for I know that
power has gone out from me." 47 When the
woman realized that she had not escaped notice,
she came forward trembling. Falling down before him, she explained in the presence of all the
people why she had touched him and how she
had been healed immediately. 48 [u]He said to
her, "Daughter, your faith has saved you; go in
peace."

49 While he was still speaking, someone
from the synagogue official's house arrived and
said, "Your daughter is dead; do not trouble the
teacher any longer." 50 On hearing this, Jesus
answered him, "Do not be afraid; just have faith
and she will be saved." 51 When he arrived at
the house he allowed no one to enter with him
except Peter and John and James, and the
child's father and mother. 52 [v]*All were weeping and mourning for her, when he said, "Do
not weep any longer, for she is not dead, but
sleeping." 53 And they ridiculed him, because
they knew that she was dead. 54 But he took
her by the hand and called to her, "Child,
arise!" 55 Her breath returned and she immediately arose. He then directed that she should be
given something to eat. 56 Her parents were
astounded, and he instructed them to tell no one
what had happened.

## CHAPTER 9

**The Mission of the Twelve** 1 [w]*He summoned the Twelve and gave them power and
authority over all demons and to cure diseases,
2 and he sent them to proclaim the kingdom of
God and to heal [the sick]. 3 *He said to them,
"Take nothing for the journey, neither walking
stick, nor sack, nor food, nor money, and let no
one take a second tunic. 4 [x]Whatever house
you enter, stay there and leave from there.
5 [y]*And as for those who do not welcome you,
when you leave that town, shake the dust from
your feet in testimony against them." 6 Then
they set out and went from village to village
proclaiming the good news and curing diseases
everywhere.

**Herod's Opinion of Jesus** 7 [z a]*Herod
the tetrarch heard about all that was happening,
and he was greatly perplexed because some
were saying, "John has been raised from the
dead"; 8 others were saying, "Elijah has appeared"; still others, "One of the ancient
prophets has arisen." 9 [b]*But Herod said,
"John I beheaded. Who then is this about whom
I hear such things?" And he kept trying to see
him.

**The Return of the Twelve and the Feed-
ing of the Five Thousand** 10 [c]When the
apostles returned, they explained to him what
they had done. He took them and withdrew in
private to a town called Bethsaida. 11 The

s Mt 9, 18-26; Mk 5, 21-43.
t 6, 19.
u 7, 50; 17, 19; 18, 42.
v 7, 13.
w Mt 10, 1.5-15; Mk 6, 7-13.
x 10, 5-7.
y 10, 10-11; Acts 13, 51.
z Mt 14, 1-12; Mk 6, 14-29.
a 9, 19; Mt 16, 14; Mk 8, 28.
b 23, 8.
c Mt 14, 13-21; Mk 6, 30-44; Jn 6, 1-14.

8, 40–56: Two interwoven miracle stories, one a healing and the other a resuscitation, present Jesus as master over sickness and death. In the Lucan account, faith in Jesus is responsible for the cure (48) and for the raising to life (50).

8, 42: *An only daughter:* cf the son of the widow of Nain whom Luke describes as an "only" son (7, 12; see also 9, 38).

8, 43: *Afflicted with hemorrhages for twelve years:* according to the Mosaic law (Lv 15, 25–30) this condition would render the woman unclean and unfit for contact with other people.

8, 52: *Sleeping:* her death is a temporary condition; cf Jn 11, 11–14.

9, 1–6: Armed with the power and authority that Jesus himself has been displaying in the previous episodes, the Twelve are now sent out to continue the work that Jesus has been performing throughout his Galilean ministry: (1) proclaiming the kingdom (4, 43; 8, 1); (2) exorcising demons (4, 33–37.41; 8, 26–39) and (3) healing the sick (4, 38–40; 5, 12–16.17–26; 6, 6–10; 7, 1–10.17.22; 8, 40–56).

9, 3: *Take nothing for the journey:* the absolute detachment required of the disciple (14, 33) leads to complete reliance on God (12, 22–31).

9, 5: *Shake the dust from your feet:* see the note on Mt 10, 14.

9, 7–56: This section in which Luke gathers together incidents that focus on the identity of Jesus is introduced by a question that Herod is made to ask in this gospel: "Who then is this about whom I hear such things?" (9). In subsequent episodes, Luke reveals to the reader various answers to Herod's question: Jesus is one in whom God's power is present and who provides for the needs of God's people (10–17); Peter declares Jesus to be "the Messiah of God" (18–21); Jesus says he is the suffering Son of Man (22.43–45); Jesus is the Master to be followed, even to death (23–27); Jesus is God's Son, his Chosen One (28–36).

9, 7: *Herod the tetrarch:* see the note on 3, 1.

9, 9: *And he kept trying to see him:* this indication of Herod's interest in Jesus prepares for 13, 31–33 and for 23, 8–12 where Herod's curiosity about Jesus' power to perform miracles remains unsatisfied.

crowds, meanwhile, learned of this and followed him. He received them and spoke to them
about the kingdom of God, and he healed those
who needed to be cured. **12** As the day was
drawing to a close, the Twelve approached him
and said, "Dismiss the crowd so that they can
go to the surrounding villages and farms and
find lodging and provisions; for we are in a
deserted place here." **13** [d]He said to them,
"Give them some food yourselves." They replied, "Five loaves and two fish are all we have,
unless we ourselves go and buy food for all
these people." **14** Now the men there numbered about five thousand. Then he said to his
disciples, "Have them sit down in groups of
[about] fifty." **15** They did so and made them
all sit down. **16** [e]*Then taking the five loaves
and the two fish, and looking up to heaven, he
said the blessing over them, broke them, and
gave them to the disciples to set before the
crowd. **17** They all ate and were satisfied. And
when the leftover fragments were picked up,
they filled twelve wicker baskets.

## Peter's Confession about Jesus

**18** [f]*Once when Jesus was praying in solitude,
and the disciples were with him, he asked them,
"Who do the crowds say that I am?" **19** [g]They
said in reply, "John the Baptist; others, Elijah;
still others, 'One of the ancient prophets has
arisen.'" **20** *Then he said to them, "But who
do you say that I am?" Peter said in reply, "The
Messiah of God." **21** He rebuked them and
directed them not to tell this to anyone.

## The First Prediction of the Passion

**22** [h]He said, "The Son of Man must suffer
greatly and be rejected by the elders, the chief
priests, and the scribes, and be killed and on the
third day be raised."

## The Conditions of Discipleship

**23** [i][j]*Then he said to all, "If anyone wishes to
come after me, he must deny himself and take
up his cross daily and follow me. **24** [k]For whoever wishes to save his life will lose it, but
whoever loses his life for my sake will save it.
**25** What profit is there for one to gain the whole
world yet lose or forfeit himself? **26** [l]Whoever
is ashamed of me and of my words, the Son of
Man will be ashamed of when he comes in his
glory and in the glory of the Father and of the
holy angels. **27** Truly I say to you, there are
some standing here who will not taste death
until they see the kingdom of God."

## The Transfiguration of Jesus

**28** [m]*About eight days after he said this, he
took Peter, John, and James and went up the
mountain to pray. **29** While he was praying his
face changed in appearance and his clothing
became dazzling white. **30** *And behold, two
men were conversing with him, Moses and Elijah, **31** [n]*who appeared in glory and spoke of
his exodus that he was going to accomplish in
Jerusalem. **32** [o]*Peter and his companions had
been overcome by sleep, but becoming fully
awake, they saw his glory and the two men
standing with him. **33** *As they were about to
part from him, Peter said to Jesus, "Master, it
is good that we are here; let us make three tents,
one for you, one for Moses, and one for Elijah." But he did not know what he was saying.
**34** *While he was still speaking, a cloud came

---

d 2 Kgs 4, 42-44.
e 22, 19; 24, 30-31; Acts 2, 42; 20, 11; 27, 35.
f Mt 16, 13-20; Mk 8, 27-30.
g 9, 7-8.
h 24, 7.26; Mt 16, 21; 20, 18-19; Mk 8, 31; 10, 33-34.
i Mt 16, 24-28; Mk 8, 34—9, 1.
j 14, 27; Mt 10, 38.
k 17, 33; Mt 10, 39; Jn 12, 25.
l 12, 9; Mt 10, 33; 2 Tm 2, 12.
m Mt 17, 1-8; Mk 9, 2-8.
n 9, 22; 13, 33.
o Jn 1, 14; 2 Pt 1, 16.

---

9, 16: *Then taking . . . :* the actions of Jesus recall the institution of the Eucharist in 22, 19; see also the note on Mt 14, 19.

9, 18–22: This incident is based on Mk 8, 27–33, but Luke has eliminated Peter's refusal to accept Jesus as suffering Son of Man (Mk 8, 32) and the rebuke of Peter by Jesus (Mk 8, 33). Elsewhere in the gospel, Luke softens the harsh portrait of Peter and the other apostles found in his Marcan source (cf 22, 39–46, which similarly lacks a rebuke of Peter that occurs in the source, Mk 14, 37–38).

9, 18: *When Jesus was praying in solitude:* see the note on 3, 21.

9, 20: *The Messiah of God:* on the meaning of this title in first-century Palestinian Judaism, see the notes on 2, 11 and on Mt 16, 13–20 and Mk 8, 27–30.

9, 23: *Daily:* this is a Lucan addition to a saying of Jesus, removing the saying from a context that envisioned the imminent suffering and death of the disciple of Jesus (as does the saying in Mk 8, 34–35) to one that focuses on the demands of daily Christian existence.

9, 28–36: Situated shortly after the first announcement of the passion, death, and resurrection, this scene of Jesus' transfiguration provides the heavenly confirmation to Jesus' declaration that his suffering will end in glory (32); see also the notes on Mt 17, 1–8 and Mk 9, 2–8.

9, 28: *Up the mountain to pray:* the "mountain" is the regular place of prayer in Lk (see 6, 12; 22, 39–41).

9, 30: *Moses and Elijah:* the two figures represent the Old Testament law and the prophets. At the end of this episode, the heavenly voice will identify Jesus as the one to be listened to now (35). See also the note on Mk 9, 5.

9, 31: *His exodus that he was going to accomplish in Jerusalem:* Luke identifies the subject of the conversation as the *exodus* of Jesus, a reference to the death, resurrection, and ascension of Jesus that will take place in Jerusalem, the city of destiny (see 9, 51). The mention of exodus, however, also calls to mind the Israelite Exodus from Egypt to the promised land.

9, 32: *They saw his glory:* the *glory* that is proper to God is here attributed to Jesus (see 24, 26).

9, 33: *Let us make three tents:* in a possible allusion to the feast of Tabernacles, Peter may be likening his joy on the occasion of the transfiguration to the joyful celebration of this harvest festival.

9, 34: *Over them:* it is not clear whether *them* refers to Jesus, Moses, and Elijah, or to the disciples. For the cloud casting its shadow, see the note on Mk 9, 7.

and cast a shadow over them, and they became
frightened when they entered the cloud.
**35** [p]*Then from the cloud came a voice that
said, "This is my chosen Son; listen to him."
**36** *After the voice had spoken, Jesus was
found alone. They fell silent and did not at that
time tell anyone what they had seen.

### The Healing of a Boy with a Demon

**37** [q]*On the next day, when they came down
from the mountain, a large crowd met him.
**38** There was a man in the crowd who cried out,
"Teacher, I beg you, look at my son; he is my
only child. **39** For a spirit seizes him and he
suddenly screams and it convulses him until he
foams at the mouth; it releases him only with
difficulty, wearing him out. **40** I begged your
disciples to cast it out but they could not."
**41** Jesus said in reply, "O faithless and perverse generation, how long will I be with you
and endure you? Bring your son here." **42** As
he was coming forward, the demon threw him
to the ground in a convulsion; but Jesus rebuked
the unclean spirit, healed the boy, and returned
him to his father. **43** [r]And all were astonished
by the majesty of God.

### The Second Prediction of the Passion

While they were all amazed at his everv deed,
he said to his disciples, **44** "Pay attention to
what I am telling you. The Son of Man is to be
handed over to men." **45** But they did not understand this saying; its meaning was hidden
from them so that they should not understand it,
and they were afraid to ask him about this saying.

### The Greatest in the Kingdom

**46** [st]*An
argument arose among the disciples about
which of them was the greatest. **47** Jesus realized the intention of their hearts and took a child
and placed it by his side **48** [u]and said to them,
"Whoever receives this child in my name receives me, and whoever receives me receives
the one who sent me. For the one who is least
among all of you is the one who is the greatest."

### Another Exorcist

**49** [v]Then John said in
reply, "Master, we saw someone casting out
demons in your name and we tried to prevent
him because he does not follow in our company." **50** Jesus said to him, "Do not prevent
him, for whoever is not against you is for you."

## *V: THE JOURNEY TO JERUSALEM: LUKE'S TRAVEL NARRATIVE*

### Departure for Jerusalem; Samaritan Inhospitality

**51** [w]*When the days for his be-
ing taken up were fulfilled, he resolutely determined to journey to Jerusalem, **52** [x]*and he
sent messengers ahead of him. On the way they
entered a Samaritan village to prepare for his
reception there, **53** but they would not welcome
him because the destination of his journey was
Jerusalem. **54** [y]When the disciples James and
John saw this they asked, "Lord, do you want
us to call down fire from heaven to consume
them?" **55** Jesus turned and rebuked them,
**56** and they journeyed to another village.

---

p 3, 22; Dt 18, 15; Ps 2, 7; Is 42, 1; Mt 3, 17; 12, 18; Mk 1, 11;2 Pt 1, 17-18.
q Mt 17, 14-18; Mk 9, 14-27.
r 18, 32-34; Mt 17, 22-23; Mk 9, 30-32.
s Mt 18, 1-5; Mk 9, 33-37.
t 22, 24.
u 10, 16; Mt 10, 40; Jn 13, 20.
v Mk 9, 38-40.
w 9, 53; 13, 22.33; 17, 11; 18, 31; 19, 28; 24; 51; Acts 1, 2.9-11.22.
x Mal 3, 1.
y 2 Kgs 1, 10.12.

---

9, 35: Like the heavenly voice that identified Jesus at his baptism prior to his undertaking the Galilean ministry (3, 22), so too here before the journey to the city of destiny is begun (51) the heavenly voice again identifies Jesus as Son. *Listen to him:* the two representatives of Israel of old depart (33) and Jesus is left alone (36) as the teacher whose words must be heeded (see also Acts 3, 22).

9, 36: *At that time:* i.e., before the resurrection.

9, 37–43a: See the note on Mk 9, 14–29.

9, 46–50: These two incidents focus on attitudes that are opposed to Christian discipleship: rivalry and intolerance of outsiders.

9, 51—18, 14: The Galilean ministry of Jesus finishes with the previous episode and a new section of Luke's gospel begins, the journey to Jerusalem. This journey is based on Mk 10, 1–52, but Luke uses his Marcan source only in 18, 15—19, 27. Before that point he has inserted into his gospel a distinctive collection of sayings of Jesus and stories about him that he has drawn from Q, a collection of sayings of Jesus used also by Matthew, and from his own special traditions. All of the material collected in this section is loosely organized within the framework of a journey of Jesus to Jerusalem, the city of destiny, where his exodus (suffering, death, resurrection, ascension) is to take place (9, 31), where salvation is accomplished, and from where the proclamation of God's saving word is to go forth (24, 47; Acts 1, 8). Much of the material in the Lucan travel narrative is teaching for the disciples. During the course of this journey Jesus is preparing his chosen Galilean witnesses for the role they will play after his exodus (9, 31): they are to be his witnesses to the people (Acts 10, 39; 13, 31) and thereby provide certainty to the readers of Luke's gospel that the teachings they have received are rooted in the teachings of Jesus (1, 1–4).

9, 51–55: Just as the Galilean ministry began with a rejection of Jesus in his hometown, so too the travel narrative begins with the rejection of him by Samaritans. In this episode Jesus disassociates himself from the attitude expressed by his disciples that those who reject him are to be punished severely. The story alludes to 2 Kgs 1, 10.12, where the prophet Elijah takes the course of action Jesus rejects, and Jesus thereby rejects the identification of himself with Elijah.

9, 51: *Days for his being taken up:* like the reference to his exodus in v 31, this is probably a reference to all the events (suffering, death, resurrection, ascension) of his last days in Jerusalem. He resolutely determined: literally, "he set his face."

9, 52: *Samaritan:* Samaria was the territory between Judea and Galilee west of the Jordan river. For ethnic and religious reasons, the Samaritans and the Jews were bitterly opposed to one another (see Jn 4, 9).

## The Would-be Followers of Jesus

**57** [z]*As they were proceeding on their journey
someone said to him, "I will follow you wherever you go." **58** Jesus answered him, "Foxes
have dens and birds of the sky have nests, but
the Son of Man has nowhere to rest his head."
**59** And to another he said, "Follow me." But
he replied, "[Lord,] let me go first and bury my
father." **60** *But he answered him, "Let the
dead bury their dead. But you, go and proclaim
the kingdom of God." **61** [a]And another said,
"I will follow you, Lord, but first let me say
farewell to my family at home." **62** [To him]
Jesus said, "No one who sets a hand to the plow
and looks to what was left behind is fit for the
kingdom of God."

# CHAPTER 10

## The Mission of the Seventy-two

**1** [b]*After this the Lord appointed seventy
[-two] others whom he sent ahead of him in
pairs to every town and place he intended to
visit. **2** [c]He said to them, "The harvest is abundant but the laborers are few; so ask the master
of the harvest to send out laborers for his harvest. **3** [d]Go on your way; behold, I am sending
you like lambs among wolves. **4** [ef]*Carry no
money bag, no sack, no sandals; and greet no
one along the way. **5** *Into whatever house you
enter, first say, 'Peace to this household.'
**6** *If a peaceful person lives there, your peace
will rest on him; but if not, it will return to you.
**7** [g]Stay in the same house and eat and drink
what is offered to you, for the laborer deserves
his payment. Do not move about from one
house to another. **8** [h]Whatever town you enter
and they welcome you, eat what is set before
you, **9** [i]cure the sick in it and say to them, 'The
kingdom of God is at hand for you.'
**10** [j]Whatever town you enter and they do not
receive you, go out into the streets and say,
**11** [k]'The dust of your town that clings to our
feet, even that we shake off against you.' Yet
know this: the kingdom of God is at hand. **12** I
tell you, it will be more tolerable for Sodom on
that day than for that town.

## Reproaches to Unrepentant Towns

**13** [mn]*"Woe to you, Chorazin! Woe to you,
Bethsaida! For if the mighty deeds done in your
midst had been done in Tyre and Sidon, they
would long ago have repented, sitting in sackcloth and ashes. **14** But it will be more tolerable
for Tyre and Sidon at the judgment than for you.
**15** [o]*And as for you, Capernaum, 'Will you be
exalted to heaven? You will go down to the
netherworld.'" **16** [p]Whoever listens to you
listens to me. Whoever rejects you rejects me.
And whoever rejects me rejects the one who
sent me."

## Return of the Seventy-two

**17** The sev-
enty[-two] returned rejoicing, and said, "Lord,
even the demons are subject to us because of
your name." **18** [q]*Jesus said, "I have observed Satan fall like lightning from the sky.
**19** [r]Behold, I have given you the power 'to
tread upon serpents' and scorpions and upon the
full force of the enemy and nothing will harm
you. **20** [s]Nevertheless, do not rejoice because
the spirits are subject to you, but rejoice because
your names are written in heaven."

---

z Mt 8, 19-22.
a 1 Kgs 19, 20.
b Mk 6, 7.
c Mt 9, 37-38; Jn 4, 35.
d Mt 10, 16.
e 9, 3; 2 Kgs 4, 29.
f Mt 10, 7-14.
g 9, 4; Mt 10, 10; 1 Cor 9, 6-14; 1 Tm 5, 18.
h 1 Cor 10, 27.
i Mt 3, 2; 4, 17; Mk 1, 15.
j 9, 5.
k Acts 13, 51; 18, 6.
l Mt 10, 15; 11, 24.
m Mt 11, 20-24.
n Is 23; Ez 26-28; Jl 3, 4-8; Am 1, 1-10; Zec 9, 2-4.
o Is 14, 13-15.
p Mt 10, 40; Jn 5, 23; 13, 20; 15, 23.
q Is 14, 12; Jn 12, 31; Rv 12, 7-12.
r Ps 19, 13; Mk 16, 18.
s Ex 32, 32; Dn 12, 1; Mt 7, 22; Phil 4, 3; Heb 12, 23; Rv 3, 5; 21, 27.

*

9, 57–62: In these sayings Jesus speaks of the severity and the unconditional nature of Christian discipleship. Even family ties and filial obligations, such as burying one's parents, cannot distract one no matter how briefly from proclaiming the kingdom of God. The first two sayings are paralleled in Mt 8, 19–22; see also the notes there.

9, 60: *Let the dead bury their dead:* i.e., let the spiritually dead (those who do not follow) bury their physically dead. See also the note on Mt 8, 22.

10, 1–12: Only the Gospel of Luke contains two episodes in which Jesus sends out his followers on a mission: the first (9, 1–6) is based on the mission in Mk 6, 6b–13 and recounts the sending out of the Twelve; here in vv 1–12 a similar report based on Q becomes the sending out of seventy-two in this gospel. The episode continues the theme of Jesus preparing witnesses to himself and his ministry. These witnesses include not only the Twelve but also the seventy-two who may represent the Christian mission in Luke's own day. Note that the instructions given to the Twelve and to the seventy-two are similar and that what is said to the seventy-two in v 4 is directed to the Twelve in 22, 35.

10, 1: *Seventy[-two]:* important representatives of the Alexandrian and Caesarean text types read "seventy," while other important Alexandrian texts and Western readings have "seventy-two."

10, 4: *Carry no money bag . . . greet no one along the way:* because of the urgency of the mission and the singlemindedness required of missionaries, attachment to material possessions should be avoided and even customary greetings should not distract from the fulfillment of the task.

10, 5: *First say, 'Peace to this household':* see the notes on 2, 14 and Mt 10, 13.

10, 6: *A peaceful person:* literally, "a son of peace."

10, 13–16: The call to repentance that is a part of the proclamation of the kingdom brings with it a severe judgment for those who hear it and reject it.

10, 15: *The netherworld:* the underworld, the place of the dead (Acts 2, 27.31), here contrasted with heaven; see also the note on Mt 11, 23.

10, 18: *I have observed Satan fall like lightning:* the effect of the mission of the seventy-two is characterized by the Lucan Jesus as a symbolic fall of Satan. As the kingdom of God is gradually being established, evil in all its forms is being defeated; the dominion of Satan over humanity is at an end.

## Praise of the Father

21 [t,u]*At that very
moment he rejoiced [in] the holy Spirit and said,
"I give you praise, Father, Lord of heaven and
earth, for although you have hidden these things
from the wise and the learned you have revealed
them to the childlike. Yes, Father, such has
been your gracious will. 22 [v]All things have
been handed over to me by my Father. No one
knows who the Son is except the Father, and
who the Father is except the Son and anyone to
whom the Son wishes to reveal him."

## The Privileges of Discipleship

23 [w]Turning to the disciples in private he said,
"Blessed are the eyes that see what you see.
24 For I say to you, many prophets and kings
desired to see what you see, but did not see it,
and to hear what you hear, but did not hear it."

## The Greatest Commandment

25 [x,y]*There was a scholar of the law who stood
up to test him and said, "Teacher, what must I
do to inherit eternal life?" 26 Jesus said to him,
"What is written in the law? How do you read
it?" 27 [z]He said in reply, "You shall love the
Lord, your God, with all your heart, with all
your being, with all your strength, and with all
your mind, and your neighbor as yourself."
28 [a]He replied to him, "You have answered
correctly; do this and you will live."

## The Parable of the Good Samaritan

29 But because he wished to justify himself, he
said to Jesus, "And who is my neighbor?"
30 Jesus replied, "A man fell victim to robbers
as he went down from Jerusalem to Jericho.
They stripped and beat him and went off leaving
him half-dead. 31 *A priest happened to be
going down that road, but when he saw him, he
passed by on the opposite side. 32 Likewise a
Levite came to the place, and when he saw him,
he passed by on the opposite side. 33 But a
Samaritan traveler who came upon him was
moved with compassion at the sight. 34 He
approached the victim, poured oil and wine over
his wounds and bandaged them. Then he lifted
him up on his own animal, took him to an inn
and cared for him. 35 The next day he took out
two silver coins and gave them to the innkeeper
with the instruction, 'Take care of him. If you
spend more than what I have given you, I shall
repay you on my way back.' 36 Which of these
three, in your opinion, was neighbor to the robbers' victim?" 37 He answered, "The one who
treated him with mercy." Jesus said to him,
"Go and do likewise."

## Martha and Mary

38 [b]*As they continued
their journey he entered a village where a woman whose name was Martha welcomed him.
39 *She had a sister named Mary [who] sat
beside the Lord at his feet listening to him
speak. 40 Martha, burdened with much serving, came to him and said, "Lord, do you not
care that my sister has left me by myself to do
the serving? Tell her to help me." 41 The Lord
said to her in reply, "Martha, Martha, you are
anxious and worried about many things.
42 *There is need of only one thing. Mary has
chosen the better part and it will not be taken
from her."

# CHAPTER 11

## The Lord's Prayer

1 [c]*He was praying in
a certain place, and when he had finished, one
of his disciples said to him, "Lord, teach us to

t Mt 11, 25-27.
u 1 Cor 1, 26-28.
v Jn 3, 35; 10, 15.
w Mt 13, 16-17.
x Mt 22, 34-40; Mk 12, 28-34.
y 18, 18; Mt 19, 16; Mk 10, 17.
z Lv 19, 18; Dt 6, 5; 10, 12; Jos 22, 5; Mt 19, 19; 22, 37-39; Rom 13, 9; Gal 5, 14; Jas 2, 8.
a Lv 18, 5; Prv 19, 16; Rom 10, 5; Gal 3, 12.
b Jn 11, 1; 12, 2-3.
c Mt 6, 9-15.

*

10, 21: *Revealed them to the childlike:* a restatement of the theme announced in 8, 10: the mysteries of the kingdom are revealed to the disciples. See also the note on Mt 11, 25–27.

10, 25–37: In response to a question from a Jewish legal expert about inheriting eternal life, Jesus illustrates the superiority of love over legalism through the story of the good Samaritan. The law of love proclaimed in the "Sermon on the Plain" (6, 27–36) is exemplified by one whom the legal expert would have considered ritually impure (see Jn 4, 9). Moreover, the identity of the "neighbor" requested by the legal expert (29) turns out to be a Samaritan, the enemy of the Jew (see the note on 9, 52).

10, 25: *Scholar of the law:* an expert in the Mosaic law, and probably a member of the group elsewhere identified as the scribes (5, 21).

10, 31–32: *Priest . . . Levite:* those religious representatives of Judaism who would have been expected to be models of "neighbor" to the victim pass him by.

10, 38–42: The story of Martha and Mary further illustrates the importance of hearing the words of the teacher and the concern with women in Lk.

10, 39: *Sat beside the Lord at his feet:* it is remarkable for first-century Palestinian Judaism that a woman would assume the posture of a disciple at the master's feet (see also 8, 35; Acts 22, 3), and it reveals a characteristic attitude of Jesus toward women in this gospel (see 8, 2–3).

10, 42: *There is need of only one thing:* some ancient versions read, "there is need of few things"; another important, although probably inferior, reading found in some manuscripts is, "there is need of few things, or of one."

11, 1–13: Luke presents three episodes concerned with prayer. The first (1–4) recounts Jesus teaching his disciples the Christian communal prayer, the "Our Father"; the second (5–8), the importance of persistence in prayer; the third (9–13), the effectiveness of prayer.

11, 1–4: The Matthean form of the "Our Father" occurs in the "Sermon on the Mount" (Mt 6, 9–15); the shorter Lucan version is presented while Jesus is at prayer (see the note on 3, 21) and his disciples ask him to teach them to pray just as John taught his disciples to pray. In answer to their question, Jesus presents them with an example of a Christian communal prayer that stresses the fatherhood of God and acknowledges him as the one to whom the Christian disciple owes daily sustenance (3), forgiveness (4), and deliverance from the final trial (4). See also the notes on Mt 6, 9–13.

pray just as John taught his disciples." 2 *He
said to them, "When you pray, say:

Father, hallowed be your name,
your kingdom come.
3 *Give us each day our daily bread
4 and forgive us our sins
for we ourselves forgive everyone in debt
to us,
and do not subject us to the final test."

**Further Teachings on Prayer** 5 [d]And he
said to them, "Suppose one of you has a friend
to whom he goes at midnight and says, 'Friend,
lend me three loaves of bread, 6 for a friend of
mine has arrived at my house from a journey and
I have nothing to offer him,' 7 and he says in
reply from within, 'Do not bother me; the door
has already been locked and my children and I
are already in bed. I cannot get up to give you
anything.' 8 I tell you, if he does not get up to
give him the loaves because of their friendship,
he will get up to give him whatever he needs
because of his persistence.

**The Answer to Prayer** 9 [ef]"And I tell
you, ask and you will receive; seek and you will
find; knock and the door will be opened to you.
10 For everyone who asks, receives; and the
one who seeks, finds; and to the one who
knocks, the door will be opened. 11 What father among you would hand his son a snake
when he asks for a fish? 12 Or hand him a
scorpion when he asks for an egg? 13 *If you
then, who are wicked, know how to give good
gifts to your children, how much more will the
Father in heaven give the holy Spirit to those
who ask him?"

**Jesus and Beelzebul** 14 [g]He was driving
out a demon [that was] mute, and when the
demon had gone out, the mute person spoke and
the crowds were amazed. 15 [h]Some of them
said, "By the power of Beelzebul, the prince of
demons, he drives out demons." 16 [i]Others, to
test him, asked him for a sign from heaven.
17 But he knew their thoughts and said to them,
"Every kingdom divided against itself will be
laid waste and house will fall against house.
18 And if Satan is divided against himself, how
will his kingdom stand? For you say that it is by
Beelzebul that I drive out demons. 19 *If I,
then, drive out demons by Beelzebul, by whom
do your own people drive them out? Therefore
they will be your judges. 20 [j]But if it is by the
finger of God that [I] drive out demons, then the
kingdom of God has come upon you. 21 When
a strong man fully armed guards his palace, his
possessions are safe. 22 *But when one stronger than he attacks and overcomes him, he takes
away the armor on which he relied and distributes the spoils. 23 [k]Whoever is not with me is
against me, and whoever does not gather with
me scatters.

**The Return of the Unclean Spirit**
24 [l]"When an unclean spirit goes out of someone, it roams through arid regions searching for
rest but, finding none, it says, 'I shall return to
my home from which I came.' 25 But upon
returning, it finds it swept clean and put in
order. 26 [m]Then it goes and brings back seven
other spirits more wicked than itself who move
in and dwell there, and the last condition of that
person is worse than the first."

**True Blessedness** 27 [n]*While he was
speaking, a woman from the crowd called out
and said to him, "Blessed is the womb that
carried you and the breasts at which you
nursed." 28 He replied, "Rather, blessed are
those who hear the word of God and observe
it."

**The Demand for a Sign** 29 [op]*While still
more people gathered in the crowd, he said to
them, "This generation is an evil generation; it
seeks a sign, but no sign will be given it, except
the sign of Jonah. 30 Just as Jonah became a
sign to the Ninevites, so will the Son of Man be
to this generation. 31 [q]At the judgment the
queen of the south will rise with the men of this
generation and she will condemn them, because

d 18, 1-5.
e Mt 7, 7-11.
f Mt 21, 22; Mk 11, 24; Jn 14, 13; 15, 7; 1 Jn 5, 14-15.
g Mt 12, 22-30; Mk 3, 20-27.
h Mt 9, 34.
i Mt 12, 38; 16, 1; Mk 8, 11; 1 Cor 1, 22.
j Ex 8, 19.
k 9, 50; Mk 9, 40.
l Mt 12, 43-45.
m Jn 5, 14.
n 1, 28.42.48.
o Mt 12, 38-42; Mk 8, 12.
p Mt 16, 1.4; Jn 6, 30; 1 Cor 1, 22.
q 1 Kgs 10, 1-10; 2 Chr 9, 1-12.

*

11, 2: *Your kingdom come:* in place of this petition, some early church Fathers record: "May your holy Spirit come upon us and cleanse us," a petition that may reflect the use of the "Our Father" in a baptismal liturgy.

11, 3–4: *Daily bread:* see the note on Mt 6, 11. *The final test:* see the note on Mt 6, 13.

11, 13: *The holy Spirit:* this is a Lucan editorial alteration of a traditional saying of Jesus (see Mt 7, 11). Luke presents the gift of the holy Spirit as the response of the Father to the prayer of the Christian disciple.

11, 19: *Your own people:* the Greek reads "your sons." Other Jewish exorcists (see Acts 19, 13–20), who recognize that the power of God is active in the exorcism, would themselves convict the accusers of Jesus. See also the note on Mt 12, 27.

11, 22: *One stronger:* i.e., Jesus. Cf 3, 16 where John the Baptist identifies Jesus as "more powerful than I."

11, 27–28: The beatitude in v 28 should not be interpreted as a rebuke of the mother of Jesus; see the note on 8, 21. Rather, it emphasizes (like 2, 35) that attentiveness to God's word is more important than biological relationship to Jesus.

11, 29–32: The "sign of Jonah" in Lk is the preaching of the need for repentance by a prophet who comes from afar. Cf Mt 12, 38–42 (and see the notes there) where the "sign of Jonah" is interpreted by Jesus as his death and resurrection.

she came from the ends of the earth to hear the
wisdom of Solomon, and there is something
greater than Solomon here. 32 [r]At the judgment the men of Nineveh will arise with this
generation and condemn it, because at the
preaching of Jonah they repented, and there is
something greater than Jonah here.

**The Simile of Light** 33 [s]"No one who
lights a lamp hides it away or places it [under
a bushel basket], but on a lampstand so that
those who enter might see the light. 34 [t]The
lamp of the body is your eye. When your eye is
sound, then your whole body is filled with light,
but when it is bad, then your body is in darkness. 35 Take care, then, that the light in you
not become darkness. 36 If your whole body is
full of light, and no part of it is in darkness, then
it will be as full of light as a lamp illuminating
you with its brightness."

**Denunciation of the Pharisees and Scholars of the Law** 37 [uv]*After he had
spoken, a Pharisee invited him to dine at his
home. He entered and reclined at table to eat.
38 [w]The Pharisee was amazed to see that he did
not observe the prescribed washing before the
meal. 39 [x]The Lord said to him, "Oh you Pharisees! Although you cleanse the outside of the
cup and the dish, inside you are filled with
plunder and evil. 40 You fools! Did not the
maker of the outside also make the inside?
41 But as to what is within, give alms, and
behold, everything will be clean for you.
42 [y]Woe to you Pharisees! You pay tithes of
mint and of rue and of every garden herb, but
you pay no attention to judgment and to love for
God. These you should have done, without
overlooking the others. 43 [z]Woe to you Pharisees! You love the seat of honor in synagogues
and greetings in marketplaces. 44 [a]*Woe to
you! You are like unseen graves over which
people unknowingly walk."

45 [b]*Then one of the scholars of the law said
to him in reply, "Teacher, by saying this you
are insulting us too." 46 And he said, "Woe
also to you scholars of the law! You impose on
people burdens hard to carry, but you yourselves do not lift one finger to touch them.
47 [c]Woe to you! You build the memorials of
the prophets whom your ancestors killed.
48 Consequently, you bear witness and give
consent to the deeds of your ancestors, for they
killed them and you do the building.
49 [d]*Therefore, the wisdom of God said, 'I
will send to them prophets and apostles; some
of them they will kill and persecute' 50 in order
that this generation might be charged with the
blood of all the prophets shed since the foundation of the world, 51 [e]*from the blood of Abel
to the blood of Zechariah who died between the
altar and the temple building. Yes, I tell you,
this generation will be charged with their blood!
52 [f]Woe to you, scholars of the law! You have
taken away the key of knowledge. You yourselves did not enter and you stopped those trying
to enter." 53 [g]When he left, the scribes and
Pharisees began to act with hostility toward him
and to interrogate him about many things,
54 [h]for they were plotting to catch him at something he might say.

## CHAPTER 12

### The Leaven of the Pharisees

1 [i]*Meanwhile, so many people were crowd-
ing together that they were trampling one another underfoot. He began to speak, first to his
disciples, "Beware of the leaven—that is, the
hypocrisy—of the Pharisees.

### Courage under Persecution

2 [jk]*"There is nothing concealed that will not
be revealed, nor secret that will not be known.
3 Therefore whatever you have said in the darkness will be heard in the light, and what you
have whispered behind closed doors will be proclaimed on the housetops. 4 I tell you, my
friends, do not be afraid of those who kill the

r Jon 3, 8.10.
s 8, 16; Mt 5, 15; Mk 4, 21.
t Mt 6, 22-23.
u 20, 45-47; Mt 23, 1-36; Mk 12, 38-40.
v 7, 36; 14, 1.
w Mt 15, 2; Mk 7, 2-5.
x Mt 23, 25-26.
y Lv 27, 30; Mt 23, 23.
z 20, 46; Mt 23, 6; Mk 12, 38-39.
a Mt 23, 27.
b Mt 23, 4.
c Mt 23, 29-32.
d Mt 23, 34-36.
e Gn 4, 8; 2 Chr 24, 20-22.
f Mt 23, 13.
g 6, 11; Mt 22, 15-22.
h 20, 20.
i Mt 16, 6; Mk 8, 15.
j Mt 10, 26-33.
k 8, 17; Mk 4, 22.

*

11, 37–54: This denunciation of the Pharisees (39–44) and the scholars of the law (45–52) is set by Luke in the context of Jesus' dining at the home of a Pharisee. Controversies with or reprimands of Pharisees are regularly set by Luke within the context of Jesus' eating with Pharisees (see 5, 29–39; 7, 36–50; 14, 1–24). A different compilation of similar sayings is found in Mt 23 (see also the notes there).

11, 44: *Unseen graves:* contact with the dead or with human bones or graves (see Nm 19, 16) brought ritual impurity. Jesus presents the Pharisees as those who insidiously lead others astray through their seeming attention to the law.

11, 45: *Scholars of the law:* see the note on 10, 25.

11, 49: *I will send to them prophets and apostles:* Jesus connects the mission of the church (apostles) with the mission of the Old Testament prophets who often suffered the rebuke of their contemporaries.

11, 51: *From the blood of Abel to the blood of Zechariah:* the murder of Abel is the first murder recounted in the Old Testament (Gn 4, 8). The Zechariah mentioned here may be the Zechariah whose murder is recounted in 2 Chr 24, 20–22, the last murder presented in the Hebrew canon of the Old Testament.

12, 1: See the notes on Mk 8, 15 and Mt 16, 5–12.

12, 2–9: Luke presents a collection of sayings of Jesus exhorting his followers to acknowledge him and his mission fearlessly and assuring them of God's protection even in times of persecution. They are paralleled in Mt 10, 26–33.

body but after that can do no more. **5** *I shall
show you whom to fear. Be afraid of the one
who after killing has the power to cast into
Gehenna; yes, I tell you, be afraid of that one.
**6** *Are not five sparrows sold for two small
coins? Yet not one of them has escaped the
notice of God. **7** [l]Even the hairs of your head
have all been counted. Do not be afraid. You are
worth more than many sparrows. **8** I tell you,
everyone who acknowledges me before others
the Son of Man will acknowledge before the
angels of God. **9** [m]But whoever denies me before others will be denied before the angels of
God.

## Sayings about the holy Spirit

**10** [n]*"Everyone who speaks a word against the
Son of Man will be forgiven, but the one who
blasphemes against the holy Spirit will not be
forgiven. **11** [o]When they take you before synagogues and before rulers and authorities, do not
worry about how or what your defense will be
or about what you are to say. **12** For the holy
Spirit will teach you at that moment what you
should say."

## Saying against Greed

**13** *Someone in
the crowd said to him, "Teacher, tell my brother to share the inheritance with me." **14** [p]He
replied to him, "Friend, who appointed me as
your judge and arbitrator?" **15** [q]Then he said to
the crowd, "Take care to guard against all
greed, for though one may be rich, one's life
does not consist of possessions."

## Parable of the Rich Fool

**16** Then he told
them a parable. "There was a rich man whose
land produced a bountiful harvest. **17** He asked
himself, 'What shall I do, for I do not have
space to store my harvest?' **18** And he said,
"This is what I shall do: I shall tear down my
barns and build larger ones. There I shall store
all my grain and other goods **19** [r s]and I shall
say to myself, "Now as for you, you have so
many good things stored up for many years,
rest, eat, drink, be merry!" ' **20** But God said
to him, 'You fool, this night your life will be
demanded of you; and the things you have prepared, to whom will they belong?' **21** *Thus
will it be for the one who stores up treasure for
himself but is not rich in what matters to God."

## Dependence on God

**22** [t]He said to [his]
disciples, "Therefore I tell you, do not worry
about your life and what you will eat, or about
your body and what you will wear. **23** For life
is more than food and the body more than clothing. **24** [u]Notice the ravens: they do not sow or
reap; they have neither storehouse nor barn, yet
God feeds them. How much more important are
you than birds! **25** Can any of you by worrying
add a moment to your life-span? **26** If even the
smallest things are beyond your control, why
are you anxious about the rest? **27** [v]Notice how
the flowers grow. They do not toil or spin. But
I tell you, not even Solomon in all his splendor
was dressed like one of them. **28** If God so
clothes the grass in the field that grows today
and is thrown into the oven tomorrow, will he
not much more provide for you, O you of little
faith? **29** As for you, do not seek what you are
to eat and what you are to drink, and do not
worry anymore. **30** All the nations of the world
seek for these things, and your Father knows
that you need them. **31** Instead, seek his kingdom, and these other things will be given you
besides. **32** [w]Do not be afraid any longer, little
flock, for your Father is pleased to give you the
kingdom. **33** [x]Sell your belongings and give
alms. Provide money bags for yourselves that
do not wear out, an inexhaustible treasure in
heaven that no thief can reach nor moth destroy.
**34** For where your treasure is, there also will
your heart be.

## Vigilant and Faithful Servants

**35** [y]*"Gird your loins and light your lamps
**36** [z]and be like servants who await their master's return from a wedding, ready to open immediately when he comes and knocks.
**37** Blessed are those servants whom the master
finds vigilant on his arrival. Amen, I say to you,
he will gird himself, have them recline at table,
and proceed to wait on them. **38** And should he
come in the second or third watch and find them

l 12, 24; 21, 18; Acts 27, 34.
m 9, 26; Mk 8, 38; 2 Tm 2, 12.
n Mt 12, 31-32; Mk 3, 28-29.
o 21, 12-15; Mt 10, 17-20; Mk 13, 11.
p Ex 2, 14; Acts 7, 27.
q 1 Tm 6, 9-10.
r Mt 6, 19-21; 1 Tm 6, 17.
s Sir 11, 19.
t Mt 6, 25-34.
u 12, 7.
v 1 Kgs 10, 4-7; 2 Chr 9, 3-6.
w 22, 29; Rv 1, 6.
x 18, 22; Mt 6, 20-21; Mk 10, 21.
y Mt 24, 45-51.
z Mt 25, 1-13; Mk 13, 35-37.

*

12, 5: *Gehenna:* see the note on Mt 5, 22.

12, 6: *Two small coins:* the Roman copper coin, the assarion (Latin *as*), was worth about one-sixteenth of a denarius (see the note on 7, 41).

12, 10–12: The sayings about the holy Spirit are set in the context of fearlessness in the face of persecution (2–9; cf Mt 12, 31–32). The holy Spirit will be presented in Luke's second volume, the Acts of the Apostles, as the power responsible for the guidance of the Christian mission and the source of courage in the face of persecution.

12, 13–34: Luke has joined together sayings contrasting those whose focus and trust in life is on material possessions, symbolized here by the rich fool of the parable (16–21), with those who recognize their complete dependence on God (21), those whose radical detachment from material possessions symbolizes their heavenly treasure (33–34).

12, 21: *Rich in what matters to God:* literally, "rich for God."

12, 35–48: This collection of sayings relates to Luke's understanding of the end time and the return of Jesus. Luke emphasizes for his readers the importance of being faithful to the instructions of Jesus in the period before the parousia.

prepared in this way, blessed are those servants.
39 [a] Be sure of this: if the master of the house
had known the hour when the thief was coming,
he would not have let his house be broken into.
40 You also must be prepared, for at an hour
you do not expect, the Son of Man will come."
41 Then Peter said, "Lord, is this parable
meant for us or for everyone?" 42 And the
Lord replied, "Who, then, is the faithful and
prudent steward whom the master will put in
charge of his servants to distribute [the] food
allowance at the proper time? 43 Blessed is that
servant whom his master on arrival finds doing
so. 44 Truly, I say to you, he will put him in
charge of all his property. 45 *But if that servant says to himself, 'My master is delayed in
coming,' and begins to beat the menservants
and the maidservants, to eat and drink and get
drunk, 46 then that servant's master will come
on an unexpected day and at an unknown hour
and will punish him severely and assign him a
place with the unfaithful. 47 [b] That servant who
knew his master's will but did not make preparations nor act in accord with his will shall be
beaten severely; 48 and the servant who was
ignorant of his master's will but acted in a way
deserving of a severe beating shall be beaten
only lightly. Much will be required of the person entrusted with much, and still more will be
demanded of the person entrusted with more.

**Jesus: A Cause of Division** 49 *"I have
come to set the earth on fire, and how I wish it
were already blazing! 50 [c]*There is a baptism
with which I must be baptized, and how great
is my anguish until it is accomplished! 51 [d][e] Do
you think that I have come to establish peace on
the earth? No, I tell you, but rather division.
52 From now on a household of five will be
divided, three against two and two against three;
53 [f] a father will be divided against his son and
a son against his father, a mother against her
daughter and a daughter against her mother, a
mother-in-law against her daughter-in-law and
a daughter-in-law against her mother-in-law."

**Signs of the Times** 54 [g] He also said to the
crowds, "When you see [a] cloud rising in the
west you say immediately that it is going to
rain—and so it does; 55 and when you notice
that the wind is blowing from the south you say
that it is going to be hot—and so it is. 56 You
hypocrites! You know how to interpret the appearance of the earth and the sky; why do you
not know how to interpret the present time?

**Settlement with an Opponent**
57 [h] "Why do you not judge for yourselves
what is right? 58 If you are to go with your
opponent before a magistrate, make an effort to
settle the matter on the way; otherwise your
opponent will turn you over to the judge, and the
judge hand you over to the constable, and the
constable throw you into prison. 59 *I say to
you, you will not be released until you have paid
the last penny."

## CHAPTER 13

**A Call to Repentance** 1 *At that time
some people who were present there told him
about the Galileans whose blood Pilate had mingled with the blood of their sacrifices. 2 [i] He
said to them in reply, "Do you think that because these Galileans suffered in this way they
were greater sinners than all other Galileans?
3 [j] By no means! But I tell you, if you do not
repent, you will all perish as they did! 4 *Or
those eighteen people who were killed when the
tower at Siloam fell on them—do you think they
were more guilty than everyone else who lived
in Jerusalem? 5 By no means! But I tell you, if
you do not repent, you will all perish as they
did!"

**The Parable of the Barren Fig Tree**
6 [k]*And he told them this parable: "There once

---

a Mt 24, 43-44; 1 Thes 5, 2.
b Jas 4, 17.
c Mk 10, 38-39.
d Mt 10, 34-35.
e 2, 14.
f Mi 7, 6.
g Mt 16, 2-3.
h Mt 5, 25-26.
i Jn 9, 2.
j Jn 8, 24.
k Jer 8, 13; Hb 3, 17; Mt 21, 19; Mk 11, 13.

---

*

12, 45: *My master is delayed in coming:* this statement indicates that early Christian expectations for the imminent return of Jesus had undergone some modification. Luke cautions his readers against counting on such a delay and acting irresponsibly. Cf the similar warning in Mt 24, 48.

12, 49–53: Jesus' proclamation of the kingdom is a refining and purifying fire. His message that meets with acceptance or rejection will be a source of conflict and dissension even within families.

12, 50: *Baptism:* i.e., his death.

12, 59: *The last penny:* Greek, *lepton,* a very small amount. Mt 5, 26 has for "the last penny" the Greek word *kodrantēs* (Latin *quadrans,* "farthing").

13, 1–5: The death of the Galileans at the hands of Pilate (1) and the accidental death of those on whom the tower fell (4) are presented by the Lucan Jesus as timely reminders of the need for all to repent, for the victims of these tragedies should not be considered outstanding sinners who were singled out for punishment.

13, 1: The slaughter of the Galileans by Pilate is unknown outside Lk; but from what is known about Pilate from the Jewish historian Josephus, such a slaughter would be in keeping with the character of Pilate. Josephus reports that Pilate had disrupted a religious gathering of the Samaritans on Mt. Gerizim with a slaughter of the participants (*Antiquities* 18, 4, 1 **86–87), and that on another occasion Pilate had killed many Jews who had opposed him when he appropriated money from the temple treasury to build an aqueduct in Jerusalem (*Jewish War* 2, 9, 4 **175–77; *Antiquities* 18, 3, 2 **60–62).

13, 4: Like the incident mentioned in v 1, nothing of this accident in Jerusalem is known outside Lk and the New Testament.

13, 6–9: Following on the call to repentance in vv 1–5, the parable of the barren fig tree presents a story about the contin-

was a person who had a fig tree planted in his
orchard, and when he came in search of fruit on
it but found none, **7** he said to the gardener,
'For three years now I have come in search of
fruit on this fig tree but have found none. [So]
cut it down. Why should it exhaust the soil?'
**8** He said to him in reply, "Sir, leave it for this
year also, and I shall cultivate the ground
around it and fertilize it; **9** it may bear fruit in
the future. If not you can cut it down.' "

**Cure of a Crippled Woman on the Sabbath** **10** *He was teaching in a synagogue on
the sabbath. **11** And a woman was there who
for eighteen years had been crippled by a spirit;
she was bent over, completely incapable of
standing erect. **12** When Jesus saw her, he
called to her and said, "Woman, you are set free
of your infirmity." **13** He laid his hands on her,
and she at once stood up straight and glorified
God. **14** [l]But the leader of the synagogue, indignant that Jesus had cured on the sabbath, said
to the crowd in reply, "There are six days when
work should be done. Come on those days to be
cured, not on the sabbath day." **15** [m]*The Lord
said to him in reply, "Hypocrites! Does not
each one of you on the sabbath untie his ox or
his ass from the manger and lead it out for
watering? **16** [n]*This daughter of Abraham,
whom Satan has bound for eighteen years now,
ought she not to have been set free on the sabbath day from this bondage?" **17** When he said
this, all his adversaries were humiliated; and the
whole crowd rejoiced at all the splendid deeds
done by him.

**The Parable of the Mustard Seed**
**18** [o]*Then he said, "What is the kingdom of
God like? To what can I compare it? **19** [p]It is
like a mustard seed that a person took and planted in the garden. When it was fully grown, it
became a large bush and 'the birds of the sky
dwelt in its branches.' "

**The Parable of the Yeast** **20** [q] Again he
said, "To what shall I compare the kingdom of
God? **21** It is like yeast that a woman took and
mixed [in] with three measures of wheat flour
until the whole batch of dough was leavened."

**The Narrow Door; Salvation and Rejection** **22** *He passed through towns and villages, teaching as he went and making his way
to Jerusalem. **23** Someone asked him, "Lord,
will only a few people be saved?" He answered
them, **24** [rs]"Strive to enter through the narrow
gate, for many, I tell you, will attempt to enter
but will not be strong enough. **25** [t]After the
master of the house has arisen and locked the
door, then will you stand outside knocking and
saying, 'Lord, open the door for us.' He will say
to you in reply, 'I do not know where you are
from.' **26** And you will say, 'We ate and drank
in your company and you taught in our streets.'
**27** [u]Then he will say to you, 'I do not know
where [you] are from. Depart from me, all you
evildoers!' **28** [v]And there will be wailing and
grinding of teeth when you see Abraham, Isaac,
and Jacob and all the prophets in the kingdom
of God and you yourselves cast out. **29** [w]And
people will come from the east and the west and
from the north and the south and will recline at
table in the kingdom of God. **30** [x]For behold,
some are last who will be first, and some are
first who will be last."

**Herod's Desire to Kill Jesus** **31** At that
time some Pharisees came to him and said, "Go
away, leave this area because Herod wants to
kill you." **32** *He replied, "Go and tell that

l 6, 7; 14, 3; Ex 20, 8-11; Dt 5, 12-15; Mt 12, 10; Mk 3, 2-4; Jn 5, 16; 7, 23; 9, 14.16.
m 14, 5; Dt 22, 4; Mt 12, 11.
n 19, 9.
o Mt 13, 31-32; Mk 4, 30-32.
p Ez 17, 23-24; 31, 6.
q Mt 13, 33.
r Mt 7, 13-14.21-23.
s Mk 10, 25.
t Mt 25, 10-12.
u Ps 6, 9; Mt 7, 23; 25, 41.
v Mt 8, 11-12.
w Ps 107, 2-3.
x Mt 19, 20; 20, 16; Mk 10, 31.

*

uing patience of God with those who have not yet given evidence of their repentance (see 3, 8). The parable may also be alluding to the delay of the end time, when punishment will be meted out, and the importance of preparing for the end of the age because the delay will not be permanent (8–9).

13, 10–17: The cure of the crippled woman on the sabbath and the controversy that results furnishes a parallel to an incident that will be reported by Lk in 14, 1–6, the cure of the man with dropsy on the sabbath. A characteristic of Luke's style is the juxtaposition of an incident that reveals Jesus' concern for a man with an incident that reveals his concern for a woman; cf, e.g., 7, 11–17 and 8, 49–56.

13, 15–16: If the law as interpreted by Jewish tradition allowed for the untying of bound animals on the sabbath, how much more should this woman who has been bound by Satan's power be freed on the sabbath from her affliction.

13, 16: *Whom Satan has bound:* affliction and infirmity are taken as evidence of Satan's hold on humanity. The healing ministry of Jesus reveals the gradual wresting from Satan of control over humanity and the establishment of God's kingdom.

13, 18–21: Two parables are used to illustrate the future proportions of the kingdom of God that will result from its deceptively small beginning in the preaching and healing ministry of Jesus. They are paralleled in Mt 13, 31–33 and Mk 4, 30–32.

13, 22–30: These sayings of Jesus follow in Lk upon the parables of the kingdom (18–21) and stress that great effort is required for entrance into the kingdom (24) and that there is an urgency to accept the present opportunity to enter because the narrow door will not remain open indefinitely (25). Lying behind the sayings is the rejection of Jesus and his message by his Jewish contemporaries (26) whose places at table in the kingdom will be taken by Gentiles from the four corners of the world (29). Those called last (the Gentiles) will precede those to whom the invitation to enter was first extended (the Jews). See also 14, 15–24.

13, 32: Nothing, not even Herod's desire to kill Jesus, stands in the way of Jesus' role in fulfilling God's will and in establishing the kingdom through his exorcisms and healings.

fox, 'Behold, I cast out demons and I perform
healings today and tomorrow, and on the third
day I accomplish my purpose. **33** [y]*Yet I must
continue on my way today, tomorrow, and the
following day, for it is impossible that a prophet
should die outside of Jerusalem.'

### The Lament over Jerusalem

**34** [z]"Jerusalem, Jerusalem, you who kill the
prophets and stone those sent to you, how many
times I yearned to gather your children together
as a hen gathers her brood under her wings, but
you were unwilling! **35** [a]Behold, your house
will be abandoned. [But] I tell you, you will not
see me until [the time comes when] you say,
'Blessed is he who comes in the name of the
Lord.' "

## CHAPTER 14

### Healing of the Man with Dropsy on the Sabbath

**1** [b][c]*On a sabbath he went to dine
at the home of one of the leading Pharisees, and
the people there were observing him carefully.
**2** *In front of him there was a man suffering
from dropsy. **3** [d]Jesus spoke to the scholars of
the law and Pharisees in reply, asking, "Is it
lawful to cure on the sabbath or not?" **4** But
they kept silent; so he took the man and, after
he had healed him, dismissed him. **5** [e]*Then he
said to them, "Who among you, if your son or
ox falls into a cistern, would not immediately
pull him out on the sabbath day?" **6** [f]But they
were unable to answer his question.

### Conduct of Invited Guests and Hosts

**7** [g]*He told a parable to those who had been
invited, noticing how they were choosing the
places of honor at the table. **8** [h]"When you are
invited by someone to a wedding banquet, do
not recline at table in the place of honor. A more
distinguished guest than you may have been
invited by him, **9** and the host who invited both
of you may approach you and say, 'Give your
place to this man," and then you would proceed
with embarrassment to take the lowest place.
**10** Rather, when you are invited, go and take
the lowest place so that when the host comes to
you he may say, 'My friend, move up to a
higher position.' Then you will enjoy the esteem of your companions at the table. **11** [i]For
everyone who exalts himself will be humbled,
but the one who humbles himself will be exalted." **12** [j]Then he said to the host who invited
him, "When you hold a lunch or a dinner, do
not invite your friends or your brothers or your
relatives or your wealthy neighbors, in case they
may invite you back and you have repayment.
**13** Rather, when you hold a banquet, invite the
poor, the crippled, the lame, the blind;
**14** [k]blessed indeed will you be because of their
inability to repay you. For you will be repaid at
the resurrection of the righteous."

### The Parable of the Great Feast

**15** *One
of his fellow guests on hearing this said to him,
"Blessed is the one who will dine in the kingdom of God." **16** [l]He replied to him, "A man
gave a great dinner to which he invited many.
**17** When the time for the dinner came, he dispatched his servant to say to those invited,
'Come, everything is now ready.' **18** But one
by one, they all began to excuse themselves.
The first said to him, 'I have purchased a field
and must go to examine it; I ask you, consider
me excused.' **19** And another said, 'I have purchased five yoke of oxen and am on my way to
evaluate them; I ask you, consider me excused.'
**20** And another said, 'I have just married a
woman, and therefore I cannot come.' **21** The
servant went and reported this to his master.
Then the master of the house in a rage commanded his servant, 'Go out quickly into the
streets and alleys of the town and bring in here
the poor and the crippled, the blind and the
lame.' **22** The servant reported, 'Sir, your orders have been carried out and still there is
room.' **23** The master then ordered the servant,
'Go out to the highways and hedgerows and
make people come in that my home may be
filled. **24** For, I tell you, none of those men
who were invited will taste my dinner.' "

---

y 2, 38; Jn 6, 30; 8, 20.
z 19, 41-44; Mt 23, 37-39.
a 19, 38; 1 Kgs 9, 7-8; Ps 118, 26; Jer 7, 4-7.13-15; 12, 7: 22, 5.
b 6, 6-11; 13, 10-17.
c 11, 37.
d 6, 9; Mk 3, 4.
e 13, 15; Dt 22, 4; Mt 12, 11.
f Mt 22, 46.
g 11, 43; Mt 23, 6; Mk 12, 38-39.
h Prv 25, 6-7.
i 18, 14.
j 6, 32-35.
k Jn 5, 29.
l Mt 22, 2-10.

---

*

13, 33: *It is impossible that a prophet should die outside of Jerusalem:* Jerusalem is the city of destiny and the goal of the journey of the prophet Jesus. Only when he reaches the holy city will his work be accomplished.

14, 1–6: See the note on 13, 10–17.

14, 2: *Dropsy:* an abnormal swelling of the body because of the retention and accumulation of fluid.

14, 5: *Your son or ox:* this is the reading of many of the oldest and most important New Testament manuscripts. Because of the strange collocation of *son* and *ox,* some copyists have altered it to "your ass or ox," on the model of the saying in 13, 15.

14, 7–14: The banquet scene found only in Luke provides the opportunity for these teachings of Jesus on humility and presents a setting to display Luke's interest in Jesus' attitude toward the rich and the poor (see the notes on 4, 18; 6, 20–26; 12, 13–34).

14, 15–24: The parable of the great dinner is a further illustration of the rejection by Israel, God's chosen people, of Jesus' invitation to share in the banquet in the kingdom and the extension of the invitation to other Jews whose identification as the poor, crippled, blind, and lame (21) classifies them among those who recognize their need for salvation, and to Gentiles (23). A similar parable is found in Mt 22, 1–10.

### Sayings on Discipleship
25 *Great
crowds were traveling with him, and he turned
and addressed them, 26 [mn]*"If anyone comes
to me without hating his father and mother,
wife and children, brothers and sisters, and
even his own life, he cannot be my disciple.
27 [o]Whoever does not carry his own cross and
come after me cannot be my disciple. 28 Which
of you wishing to construct a tower does not first
sit down and calculate the cost to see if there is
enough for its completion? 29 Otherwise, after
laying the foundation and finding himself unable to finish the work the onlookers should
laugh at him 30 and say, 'This one began to
build but did not have the resources to finish.'
31 Or what king marching into battle would not
first sit down and decide whether with ten thousand troops he can successfully oppose another
king advancing upon him with twenty thousand
troops? 32 But if not, while he is still far away,
he will send a delegation to ask for peace terms.
33 [p]In the same way, everyone of you who
does not renounce all his possessions cannot be
my disciple.

### The Simile of Salt
34 [q]*"Salt is good, but
if salt itself loses its taste, with what can its
flavor be restored? 35 [r]It is fit neither for the
soil nor for the manure pile; it is thrown out.
Whoever has ears to hear ought to hear."

## CHAPTER 15

### The Parable of the Lost Sheep
1 [s]*The
tax collectors and sinners were all drawing near
to listen to him, 2 [t]but the Pharisees and scribes
began to complain, saying, "This man wel-
comes sinners and eats with them." 3 So to
them he addressed this parable. 4 [uvw]"What
man among you having a hundred sheep and
losing one of them would not leave the ninety-nine in the desert and go after the lost one
until he finds it? 5 And when he does find it,
he sets it on his shoulders with great joy 6 and,
upon his arrival home, he calls together his
friends and neighbors and says to them, 'Rejoice with me because I have found my lost
sheep.' 7 [x]I tell you, in just the same way there
will be more joy in heaven over one sinner who
repents than over ninety-nine righteous people
who have no need of repentance.

### The Parable of the Lost Coin
8 *"Or
what woman having ten coins and losing one
would not light a lamp and sweep the house,
searching carefully until she finds it? 9 And
when she does find it, she calls together her
friends and neighbors and says to them, 'Rejoice with me because I have found the coin that
I lost.' 10 In just the same way, I tell you, there
will be rejoicing among the angels of God over
one sinner who repents."

### The Parable of the Lost Son
11 Then he
said, "A man had two sons, 12 and the younger
son said to his father, 'Father, give me the share
of your estate that should come to me.' So the
father divided the property between them.
13 [y]After a few days, the younger son collected
all his belongings and set off to a distant country
where he squandered his inheritance on a life of
dissipation. 14 When he had freely spent everything, a severe famine struck that country, and
he found himself in dire need. 15 So he hired
himself out to one of the local citizens who sent
him to his farm to tend the swine. 16 And he
longed to eat his fill of the pods on which the
swine fed, but nobody gave him any. 17 Coming to his senses he thought, 'How many of my
father's hired workers have more than enough
food to eat, but here am I, dying from hunger.
18 I shall get up and go to my father and I shall
say to him, "Father, I have sinned against heav-
en and against you. 19 I no longer deserve to
be called your son; treat me as you would treat
one of your hired workers."' 20 So he got up
and went back to his father. While he was still
a long way off, his father caught sight of him,
and was filled with compassion. He ran to his
son, embraced him and kissed him. 21 His son
said to him, 'Father, I have sinned against heav-
en and against you; I no longer deserve to be
called your son.' 22 But his father ordered his

m Mt 10, 37-38.
n 9, 57-62; 18, 29; Jn 12, 25.
o 9, 23; Mt 16, 24; Mk 8, 34.
p 5, 11.
q Mt 5, 13; Mk 9, 50.
r 8, 8; Mt 11, 15; 13, 9; Mk 4, 9.23.
s Mt 9, 10-13.
t 5, 30; 19, 7.
u Mt 18, 12-14.
v 19, 10.
w Ez 34, 11-12.16.
x Ez 18, 23.
y Prv 29, 3.

*

14, 25–33: This collection of sayings, most of which are peculiar to Lk, focuses on the total dedication necessary for the disciple of Jesus. No attachment to family (26) or possessions (33) can stand in the way of the total commitment demanded of the disciple. Also, acceptance of the call to be a disciple demands readiness to accept persecution and suffering (27) and a realistic assessment of the hardships and costs (28–32).

14, 26: *Hating his father . . . :* cf the similar saying in Mt 10, 37. The disciple's family must take second place to the absolute dedication involved in following Jesus (see also 9, 59–62).

14, 34–35: The simile of salt follows the sayings of Jesus that demanded of the disciple total dedication and detachment from family and possessions and illustrates the condition of one who does not display this total commitment. The halfhearted disciple is like salt that cannot serve its intended purpose. See the simile of salt in Mt 5, 13 and the note there.

15, 1–32: To the parable of the lost sheep (1–7) that Luke shares with Matthew (Mt 18, 12–14), Luke adds two parables (the lost coin, 8–10; the prodigal son, 11–32) from his own special tradition to illustrate Jesus' particular concern for the lost and God's love for the repentant sinner.

15, 8: *Ten coins:* literally, "ten drachmas." A drachma was a Greek silver coin.

servants, 'Quickly bring the finest robe and put
it on him; put a ring on his finger and sandals
on his feet. **23** Take the fattened calf and
slaughter it. Then let us celebrate with a feast,
**24** because this son of mine was dead, and has
come to life again; he was lost, and has been
found.' Then the celebration began. **25** Now
the older son had been out in the field and, on
his way back, as he neared the house, he heard
the sound of music and dancing. **26** He called
one of the servants and asked what this might
mean. **27** The servant said to him, 'Your brother has returned and your father has slaughtered
the fattened calf because he has him back safe
and sound.' **28** He became angry, and when he
refused to enter the house, his father came out
and pleaded with him. **29** He said to his father
in reply, 'Look, all these years I served you and
not once did I disobey your orders; yet you
never gave me even a young goat to feast on
with my friends. **30** But when your son returns
who swallowed up your property with prostitutes, for him you slaughter the fattened calf.'
**31** He said to him, 'My son, you are here with
me always; everything I have is yours. **32** But
now we must celebrate and rejoice, because
your brother was dead and has come to life
again; he was lost and has been found.' "

## CHAPTER 16

### The Parable of the Dishonest Steward

**1** *Then he also said to his disciples, "A rich
man had a steward who was reported to him for
squandering his property. **2** He summoned him
and said, 'What is this I hear about you? Prepare
a full account of your stewardship, because you
can no longer be my steward.' **3** The steward
said to himself, 'What shall I do, now that my
master is taking the position of steward away
from me? I am not strong enough to dig and I
am ashamed to beg. **4** I know what I shall do
so that, when I am removed from the stewardship, they may welcome me into their homes.'
**5** He called in his master's debtors one by one.
To the first he said, 'How much do you owe my
master?' **6** *He replied, 'One hundred measures of olive oil.' He said to him, 'Here is your
promissory note. Sit down and quickly write
one for fifty.' **7** *Then to another he said, 'And
you, how much do you owe?' He replied, 'One
hundred kors of wheat.' He said to him, 'Here
is your promissory note; write one for eighty.'
**8** [z]*And the master commended that dishonest
steward for acting prudently.

### Application of the Parable

"For the chil-
dren of this world are more prudent in dealing
with their own generation than are the children
of light. **9** [a]*I tell you, make friends for yourselves with dishonest wealth, so that when it
fails, you will be welcomed into eternal dwellings. **10** [b]*The person who is trustworthy in
very small matters is also trustworthy in great
ones; and the person who is dishonest in very
small matters is also dishonest in great ones.
**11** If, therefore, you are not trustworthy with
dishonest wealth, who will trust you with true
wealth? **12** If you are not trustworthy with what
belongs to another, who will give you what is
yours? **13** [c]*No servant can serve two masters.
He will either hate one and love the other, or be
devoted to one and despise the other. You cannot serve God and mammon."

### A Saying against the Pharisees

**14** *The Pharisees, who loved money, heard all
these things and sneered at him. **15** [d]And he

---

z Eph 5, 8; 1 Thes 5, 5.
a 12, 33.
b 19, 17; Mt 25, 20-23.
c Mt 6, 24.
d 18, 9-14.

---

*

16, 1–8a: The parable of the dishonest steward has to be understood in the light of the Palestinian custom of agents acting on behalf of their masters and the usurious practices common to such agents. The dishonesty of the steward consisted in the squandering of his master's property (1) and not in any subsequent graft. The master commends the dishonest steward who has forgone his own usurious commission on the business transaction by having the debtors write new notes that reflected only the real amount owed the master (i.e., minus the steward's profit). The dishonest steward acts in this way in order to ingratiate himself with the debtors because he knows he is being dismissed from his position (3). The parable, then, teaches the prudent use of one's material goods in light of an imminent crisis.

16, 6: *One hundred measures:* literally, "one hundred baths." A bath is a Hebrew unit of liquid measurement equivalent to eight or nine gallons.

16, 7: *One hundred kors:* a *kor* is a Hebrew unit of dry measure for grain or wheat equivalent to ten or twelve bushels.

16, 8b–13: Several originally independent sayings of Jesus are gathered here by Luke to form the concluding application of the parable by the dishonest steward.

16, 8b–9: The first conclusion recommends the prudent use of one's wealth (in the light of the coming of the end of the age) after the manner of the children of this world, represented in the parable by the dishonest steward.

16, 9: *Dishonest wealth:* literally, "mammon of iniquity." Mammon is the Greek transliteration of a Hebrew or Aramaic word that is usually explained as meaning "that in which one trusts." The characterization of this wealth as *dishonest* expresses a tendency of wealth to lead one to dishonesty. *Eternal dwellings:* or, "eternal tents," i.e., heaven.

16, 10–12: The second conclusion recommends constant fidelity to those in positions of responsibility.

16, 13: The third conclusion is a general statement about the incompatibility of serving God and being a slave to riches. To be dependent upon wealth is opposed to the teachings of Jesus who counseled complete dependence on the Father as one of the characteristics of the Christian disciple (12, 22–39). *God and mammon:* see the note on 16, 9. Mammon is used here as if it were itself a god.

16, 14–18: The two parables about the use of riches in ch 16 are separated by several isolated sayings of Jesus on the hypocrisy of the Pharisees (14–15), on the law (16–17), and on divorce (18).

16, 14–15: The Pharisees are here presented as examples of those who are slaves to wealth (see 16, 13) and, consequently, they are unable to serve God.

said to them, "You justify yourselves in the
sight of others, but God knows your hearts; for
what is of human esteem is an abomination in
the sight of God.

**Sayings about the Law** 16 [e]*"The law
and the prophets lasted until John; but from then
on the kingdom of God is proclaimed, and everyone who enters does so with violence. 17 [f]It
is easier for heaven and earth to pass away than
for the smallest part of a letter of the law to
become invalid.

**Sayings about Divorce** 18 [g]"Everyone
who divorces his wife and marries another commits adultery, and the one who marries a woman
divorced from her husband commits adultery.

**The Parable of the Rich Man and Laza-
rus** 19 *"There was a rich man who dressed
in purple garments and fine linen and dined
sumptuously each day. 20 And lying at his door
was a poor man named Lazarus, covered with
sores, 21 [h]who would gladly have eaten his fill
of the scraps that fell from the rich man's table.
Dogs even used to come and lick his sores.
22 When the poor man died, he was carried
away by angels to the bosom of Abraham. The
rich man also died and was buried, 23 *and
from the netherworld, where he was in torment,
he raised his eyes and saw Abraham far off and
Lazarus at his side. 24 And he cried out, 'Father Abraham, have pity on me. Send Lazarus
to dip the tip of his finger in water and cool my
tongue, for I am suffering torment in these
flames.' 25 [i]Abraham replied, 'My child, remember that you received what was good during your lifetime while Lazarus likewise received what was bad; but now he is comforted
here, whereas you are tormented. 26 Moreover, between us and you a great chasm is established to prevent anyone from crossing who
might wish to go from our side to yours or from
your side to ours.' 27 He said, 'Then I beg you,
father, send him to my father's house, 28 for I
have five brothers, so that he may warn them,
lest they too come to this place of torment.'
29 But Abraham replied, 'They have Moses
and the prophets. Let them listen to them.'
30 *He said, 'Oh no, father Abraham, but if
someone from the dead goes to them, they will
repent.' 31 [j]Then Abraham said, 'If they will
not listen to Moses and the prophets, neither
will they be persuaded if someone should rise
from the dead.'"

## CHAPTER 17

**Temptations to Sin** 1 [k]He said to his disciples, "Things that cause sin will inevitably
occur, but woe to the person through whom they
occur. 2 It would be better for him if a millstone
were put around his neck and he be thrown into
the sea than for him to cause one of these little
ones to sin. 3 [l]*Be on your guard! If your
brother sins, rebuke him; and if he repents,
forgive him. 4 [m]And if he wrongs you seven
times in one day and returns to you seven times
saying, 'I am sorry,' you should forgive him."

**Saying of Faith** 5 And the apostles said to
the Lord, "Increase our faith." 6 [n]The Lord
replied, "If you have faith the size of a mustard
seed, you would say to [this] mulberry tree, 'Be
uprooted and planted in the sea,' and it would
obey you.

**Attitude of a Servant** 7 *"Who among
you would say to your servant who has just
come in from plowing or tending sheep in the
field, 'Come here immediately and take your
place at table'? 8 Would he not rather say to
him, 'Prepare something for me to eat. Put on
your apron and wait on me while I eat and drink.
You may eat and drink when I am finished'?
9 Is he grateful to that servant because he did
what was commanded? 10 So should it be with
you. When you have done all you have been
commanded, say, 'We are unprofitable servants; we have done what we were obliged to
do.'"

e Mt 11, 12-13.
f Mt 5, 18.
g Mt 5, 32; 19, 9; Mk 10, 11-12; 1 Cor 7, 10-11.
h Mt 15, 27; Mk 7, 28.
i 6, 24-25.
j Jn 5, 46-47; 11, 44-48.
k Mt 18, 6-7.
l Mt 18, 15.
m Mt 6, 14; 18, 21-22.35; Mk 11, 25.
n Mt 17, 20; 21, 21; Mk 11, 23.

*

16, 16: John the Baptist is presented in Luke's gospel as a transitional figure between the period of Israel, the time of promise, and the period of Jesus, the time of fulfillment. With John, the fulfillment of the Old Testament promises has begun.

16, 19–31: The parable of the rich man and Lazarus again illustrates Luke's concern with Jesus' attitude toward the rich and the poor. The reversal of the fates of the rich man and Lazarus (22–23) illustrates the teachings of Jesus in Luke's "Sermon on the Plain" (6, 20–21.24–25).

16, 19: The oldest Greek manuscript of Lk dating from ca. A.D. 175–225 records the name of the rich man as an abbreviated form of "Nineveh," but there is very little textual support in other manuscripts for this reading. "Dives" of popular tradition is the Latin Vulgate's translation for "rich man."

16, 23: *The netherworld:* see the note on 10, 15.

16, 30–31: A foreshadowing in Luke's gospel of the rejection of the call to repentance even after Jesus' resurrection.

17, 3a: *Be on your guard:* the translation takes v 3a as the conclusion to the saying on scandal in vv 1–2. It is not impossible that it should be taken as the beginning of the saying on forgiveness in vv 3b–4.

17, 7–10: These sayings of Jesus, peculiar to Luke, which continue his response to the apostles' request to increase their faith (5–6), remind them that Christian disciples can make no claim on God's graciousness; in fulfilling the exacting demands of discipleship, they are only doing their duty.

**The Cleansing of Ten Lepers** 11 [o]*As
he continued his journey to Jerusalem, he traveled through Samaria and Galilee. 12 As he
was entering a village, ten lepers met [him].
They stood at a distance from him 13 [p]and
raised their voice, saying, "Jesus, Master!
Have pity on us!" 14 [q]*And when he saw
them, he said, "Go show yourselves to the
priests." As they were going they were
cleansed. 15 And one of them, realizing he had
been healed, returned, glorifying God in a loud
voice; 16 and he fell at the feet of Jesus and
thanked him. He was a Samaritan. 17 Jesus
said in reply, "Ten were cleansed, were they
not? Where are the other nine? 18 Has none but
this foreigner returned to give thanks to God?"
19 [r]Then he said to him, "Stand up and go;
your faith has saved you."

**The Coming of the Kingdom of God**
20 [s]*Asked by the Pharisees when the kingdom
of God would come, he said in reply, "The
coming of the kingdom of God cannot be observed, 21 [t]*and no one will announce, 'Look,
here it is,' or, 'There it is.' For behold, the
kingdom of God is among you."

**The Day of the Son of Man** 22 Then he
said to his disciples, "The days will come when
you will long to see one of the days of the Son
of Man, but you will not see it. 23 [u]There will
be those who will say to you, 'Look, there he
is,' [or] 'Look, here he is.' Do not go off, do
not run in pursuit. 24 [v]For just as lightning
flashes and lights up the sky from one side to the
other, so will the Son of Man be [in his day].
25 [w]But first he must suffer greatly and be rejected by this generation. 26 [x]As it was in the
days of Noah, so it will be in the days of the Son
of Man; 27 they were eating and drinking, marrying and giving in marriage up to the day that
Noah entered the ark, and the flood came and
destroyed them all. 28 [y]Similarly, as it was in
the days of Lot: they were eating, drinking,
buying, selling, planting, building; 29 on the
day when Lot left Sodom, fire and brimstone
rained from the sky to destroy them all. 30 So
it will be on the day the Son of Man is revealed.
31 [z][a]On that day, a person who is on the
housetop and whose belongings are in the house
must not go down to get them, and likewise a
person in the field must not return to what was
left behind. 32 Remember the wife of Lot.
33 [b]Whoever seeks to preserve his life will lose
it, but whoever loses it will save it. 34 I tell
you, on that night there will be two people in
one bed; one will be taken, the other left.
35 [c]And there will be two women grinding
meal together; one will be taken, the other left.
[36*] 37 [d]They said to him in reply, "Where,
Lord?" He said to them, "Where the body is,
there also the vultures will gather."

## CHAPTER 18

**The Parable of the Persistent Widow**
1 [e]*Then he told them a parable about the necessity for them to pray always without becoming weary. He said, 2 "There was a judge in a
certain town who neither feared God nor respected any human being. 3 And a widow in
that town used to come to him and say, 'Render
a just decision for me against my adversary.'
4 For a long time the judge was unwilling, but
eventually he thought, 'While it is true that I
neither fear God nor respect any human being,

---

o 9, 51-53; 13, 22.33; 18, 31; 19, 28; Jn 4, 4.
p 18, 38; Mt 9, 27; 15, 22.
q 5, 14; Lv 14, 2-32; Mt 8, 4; Mk 1, 44.
r 7, 50; 18, 42.
s Jn 3, 3.
t 17, 23; Mt 24, 23; Mk 13, 21.
u 17, 21; Mt 24, 23.26; Mk 13, 21.
v Mt 24, 27.
w 9, 22; 18, 32-33; Mt 16, 21; 17, 22-23; 20, 18-19; Mk 8, 31; 9, 31; 10, 33-34.
x Gn 6-8; Mt 24, 37-39.
y Gn 18, 20-21; 19, 1-29.
z Mt 24, 17-18; Mk 13, 15-16.
a Gn 19, 17.26.
b 9, 24; Mt 10, 39; 16, 25; Mk 8, 35; Jn 12, 25.
c Mt 24, 40-41.
d Jb 39, 30; Mt 24, 28.
e Rom 12, 12; Col 4, 2; 1 Thes 5, 17.

*

17, 11–19: This incident recounting the thankfulness of the cleansed Samaritan leper is narrated only in Luke's gospel and provides an instance of Jesus holding up a non-Jew (18) as an example to his Jewish contemporaries (cf 10, 33 where a similar purpose is achieved in the story of the good Samaritan). Moreover, it is the faith in Jesus manifested by the foreigner that has brought him salvation (19; cf the similar relationship between faith and salvation in 7, 50; 8, 48.50).

17, 11: *Through Samaria and Galilee:* or, "between Samaria and Galilee."

17, 14: See the note on 5, 14.

17, 20–37: To the question of the Pharisees about the time of the coming of God's kingdom, Jesus replies that the kingdom is *among you* (20–21). The emphasis has thus been shifted from an imminent observable coming of the kingdom to something that is already present in Jesus' preaching and healing ministry. Luke has also appended further traditional sayings of Jesus about the unpredictable suddenness of the day of the Son of Man, and assures his readers that in spite of the delay of that day (12, 45), it will bring judgment unexpectedly on those who do not continue to be vigilant.

17, 21: *Among you:* the Greek preposition translated as *among* can also be translated as "within." In the light of other statements in Luke's gospel about the presence of the kingdom (see 10, 9.11; 11, 20) "among" is to be preferred.

17, 36: The inclusion of v 36, "There will be two men in the field; one will be taken, the other left behind," in some Western manuscripts appears to be a scribal assimilation to Mt 24, 40.

18, 1–14: The particularly Lucan material in the travel narrative concludes with two parables on prayer. The first (1–8) teaches the disciples the need of persistent prayer so that they not fall victims to apostasy (8). The second (9–14) condemns the self-righteous, critical attitude of the Pharisee and teaches that the fundamental attitude of the Christian disciple must be the recognition of sinfulness and complete dependence on God's graciousness. The second parable recalls the story of the pardoning of the sinful woman (7, 36–50) where a similar contrast is presented between the critical attitude of the Pharisee Simon and the love shown by the pardoned sinner.

**5** [f]*because this widow keeps bothering me I
shall deliver a just decision for her lest she
finally come and strike me.' " **6** The Lord said,
"Pay attention to what the dishonest judge says.
**7** Will not God then secure the rights of his
chosen ones who call out to him day and night?
Will he be slow to answer them? **8** I tell you,
he will see to it that justice is done for them
speedily. But when the Son of Man comes, will
he find faith on earth?"

**The Parable of the Pharisee and the Tax**
**Collector** **9** [g]He then addressed this parable
to those who were convinced of their own righteousness and despised everyone else. **10** "Two
people went up to the temple area to pray; one
was a Pharisee and the other was a tax collector.
**11** The Pharisee took up his position and spoke
this prayer to himself, 'O God, I thank you that
I am not like the rest of humanity—greedy,
dishonest, adulterous—or even like this tax collector. **12** [h]I fast twice a week, and I pay tithes
on my whole income.' **13** [i]But the tax collector
stood off at a distance and would not even raise
his eyes to heaven but beat his breast and
prayed, 'O God, be merciful to me a sinner.'
**14** [j]I tell you, the latter went home justified,
not the former; for everyone who exalts himself
will be humbled, and the one who humbles
himself will be exalted."

**Saying on Children and the Kingdom**
**15** [k]*People were bringing even infants to him
that he might touch them, and when the disciples saw this, they rebuked them. **16** Jesus,
however, called the children to himself and
said, "Let the children come to me and do not
prevent them; for the kingdom of God belongs
to such as these. **17** [l]Amen, I say to you, whoever does not accept the kingdom of God like a
child will not enter it."

**The Rich Official** **18** [mn]An official asked
him this question, "Good teacher, what must I
do to inherit eternal life?" **19** Jesus answered
him, "Why do you call me good? No one is
good but God alone. **20** [o]You know the commandments, 'You shall not commit adultery;
you shall not kill; you shall not steal; you shall
not bear false witness; honor your father and
your mother.' " **21** And he replied, "All of
these I have observed from my youth."
**22** [p]*When Jesus heard this he said to him,
"There is still one thing left for you: sell all that
you have and distribute it to the poor, and you
will have a treasure in heaven. Then come,
follow me." **23** But when he heard this he became quite sad, for he was very rich.

**On Riches and Renunciation** **24** Jesus
looked at him [now sad] and said, "How hard
it is for those who have wealth to enter the
kingdom of God! **25** For it is easier for a camel
to pass through the eye of a needle than for a rich
person to enter the kingdom of God." **26** Those
who heard this said, "Then who can be saved?"
**27** [q]And he said, "What is impossible for human beings is possible for God." **28** Then Peter
said, "We have given up our possessions and
followed you." **29** [r]He said to them, "Amen,
I say to you, there is no one who has given up
house or wife or brothers or parents or children
for the sake of the kingdom of God **30** who will
not receive [back] an overabundant return in this
present age and eternal life in the age to come."

**The Third Prediction of the Passion**
**31** [s]*Then he took the Twelve aside and said to
them, "Behold, we are going up to Jerusalem
and everything written by the prophets about the
Son of Man will be fulfilled. **32** [t]He will be
handed over to the Gentiles and he will be
mocked and insulted and spat upon; **33** and after they have scourged him they will kill him,

f 11, 8.
g 16, 5; Mt 23, 25-28.
h Mt 23, 23.
i Ps 51, 3.
j 14, 11; Mt 23, 12.
k Mt 19, 13-15; Mk 10, 13-16.
l Mt 18, 3.
m Mt 19, 16-30; Mk 10, 17-31.
n 10, 25.
o Ex 20, 12-16; Dt 5, 16-20.
p 12, 33; Sir 29, 11; Mt 6, 20.
q Mk 14, 36.
r 14, 26.
s 24, 25-27.44; Mt 20, 17-19; Mk 10, 32-34; Acts 3, 18.
t 9, 22.44.

*

18, 5: *Strike me:* the Greek verb translated as strike means "to strike under the eye" and suggests the extreme situation to which the persistence of the widow might lead. It may, however, be used here in the much weaker sense of "to wear one out."

18, 15—19, 27: Luke here includes much of the material about the journey to Jerusalem found in his Marcan source (10, 1–52) and adds to it the story of Zacchaeus (19, 1–10) from his own particular tradition and the parable of the gold coins (minas) (19, 11–27) from Q, the source common to Lk and Mt.

18, 15–17: The sayings on children furnish a contrast to the attitude of the Pharisee in the preceding episode (9–14) and that of the wealthy official in the following one (18–23) who think that they can lay claim to God's favor by their own merit. The attitude of the disciple should be marked by the receptivity and trustful dependence characteristic of the child.

18, 22: Detachment from material possessions results in the total dependence on God demanded of one who would inherit eternal life. *Sell all that you have:* the original saying (cf Mk 10, 21) has characteristically been made more demanding by Luke's addition of "all."

18, 31–33: The details included in this third announcement of Jesus' suffering and death suggest that the literary formulation of the announcement has been directed by the knowledge of the historical passion and death of Jesus.

18, 31: *Everything written by the prophets . . . will be fulfilled:* this is a Lucan addition to the words of Jesus found in the Marcan source (Mk 10, 32–34). Luke understands the events of Jesus' last days in Jerusalem to be the fulfillment of Old Testament prophecy, but, as is usually the case in Luke-Acts, the author does not specify which Old Testament prophets he has in mind; cf 24, 25.27.44; Acts 3, 8; 13, 27; 26, 22–23.

but on the third day he will rise." **34** [u]But they
understood nothing of this; the word remained
hidden from them and they failed to comprehend what he said.

## The Healing of the Blind Beggar

**35** [v]Now as he approached Jericho a blind man
was sitting by the roadside begging, **36** and
hearing a crowd going by, he inquired what was
happening. **37** They told him, "Jesus of Nazareth is passing by." **38** [w]*He shouted, "Jesus,
Son of David, have pity on me!" **39** The people
walking in front rebuked him, telling him to be
silent, but he kept calling out all the more, "Son
of David, have pity on me!" **40** Then Jesus
stopped and ordered that he be brought to him;
and when he came near, Jesus asked him,
**41** [x]"What do you want me to do for you?" He
replied, "Lord, please let me see." **42** [y]Jesus
told him, "Have sight; your faith has saved
you." **43** He immediately received his sight
and followed him, giving glory to God. When
they saw this, all the people gave praise to God.

## CHAPTER 19

### Zacchaeus the Tax Collector

**1** *He
came to Jericho and intended to pass through the
town. **2** Now a man there named Zacchaeus,
who was a chief tax collector and also a wealthy
man, **3** was seeking to see who Jesus was; but
he could not see him because of the crowd, for
he was short in stature. **4** So he ran ahead and
climbed a sycamore tree in order to see Jesus,
who was about to pass that way. **5** When he
reached the place, Jesus looked up and said to
him, "Zacchaeus, come down quickly, for today I must stay at your house." **6** And he came
down quickly and received him with joy.
**7** [z]When they all saw this, they began to grumble, saying, "He has gone to stay at the house
of a sinner." **8** [a]But Zacchaeus stood there and
said to the Lord, "Behold, half of my possessions, Lord, I shall give to the poor, and if I
have extorted anything from anyone I shall repay it four times over." **9** [b]*And Jesus said to
him, "Today salvation has come to this house
because this man too is a descendant of Abraham. **10** [c]* For the Son of Man has come to seek
and to save what was lost."

### The Parable of the Ten Gold Coins

**11** [d]*While they were listening to him speak,
he proceeded to tell a parable because he was
near Jerusalem and they thought that the kingdom of God would appear there immediately.
**12** [e]So he said, "A nobleman went off to a
distant country to obtain the kingship for himself and then to return. **13** * He called ten of his
servants and gave them ten gold coins and told
them, 'Engage in trade with these until I return.'
**14** His fellow citizens, however, despised him
and sent a delegation after him to announce,
'We do not want this man to be our king.'
**15** But when he returned after obtaining the
kingship, he had the servants called, to whom
he had given the money, to learn what they had
gained by trading. **16** The first came forward
and said, 'Sir, your gold coin has earned ten
additional ones.' **17** [f]He replied, 'Well done,
good servant! You have been faithful in this
very small matter; take charge of ten cities.'
**18** Then the second came and reported, 'Your
gold coin, sir, has earned five more.' **19** And
to this servant too he said, 'You, take charge of
five cities.' **20** Then the other servant came and
said, 'Sir, here is your gold coin; I kept it stored

u Mk 9, 32.
v Mt 20, 29-34; Mk 10, 46-52.
w 17, 13; Mt 9, 27; 15, 22.
x Mk 10, 36.
y 7, 50; 17, 19.
z 5, 30; 15, 2.
a Ex 21, 37; Nm 5, 6-7; 2 Sm 12, 6.
b 13, 16; Mt 21, 31.
c 15, 4-10; Ez 34, 16.
d Mt 25, 14-30.
e Mk 13, 34.
f 16, 10.

*

18, 38: *Son of David:* the blind beggar identifies Jesus with a title that is related to Jesus' role as Messiah (see the note on 2, 11). Through this Son of David, salvation comes to the blind man. Note the connection between salvation and house of David mentioned earlier in Zechariah's canticle (1, 69). See also the note on Mt 9, 27.

19, 1–10: The story of the tax collector Zacchaeus is unique to this gospel. While a rich man (2), Zacchaeus provides a contrast to the rich man of 18, 18–23 who cannot detach himself from his material possessions to become a follower of Jesus. Zacchaeus, according to Luke, exemplifies the proper attitude toward wealth: he promises to give half of his possessions to the poor (8) and consequently is the recipient of salvation (9–10).

19, 9: *A descendant of Abraham:* literally, "a son of Abraham." The tax collector Zacchaeus, whose repentance is attested by his determination to amend his former ways, shows himself to be a true descendant of Abraham, the true heir to the promises of God in the Old Testament. Underlying Luke's depiction of Zacchaeus as a descendant of Abraham, the father of the Jews (1, 73; 16, 22–31), is his recognition of the central place occupied by Israel in the plan of salvation.

19, 10: This verse sums up for Luke his depiction of the role of Jesus as savior in this gospel.

19, 11–27: In this parable Luke has combined two originally distinct parables: (1) a parable about the conduct of faithful and productive servants (13.15b–26) and (2) a parable about a rejected king (12.14–15a.27). The story about the conduct of servants occurs in another form in Mt 25, 14–20. The story about the rejected king may have originated with a contemporary historical event. After the death of Herod the Great, his son Archelaus traveled to Rome to receive the title of king. A delegation of Jews appeared in Rome before Caesar Augustus to oppose the request of Archelaus. Although not given the title of king, Archelaus was made ruler over Judea and Samaria. As the story is used by Luke, however, it furnishes a correction to the expectation of the imminent end of the age and of the establishment of the kingdom in Jerusalem (11). Jesus is not on his way to Jerusalem to receive the kingly power; for that, he must go away and only after returning from the distant country (a reference to the parousia) will reward and judgment take place.

19, 13: *Ten gold coins:* literally, "ten minas." A mina was a monetary unit that in ancient Greece was the equivalent of one hundred drachmas.

away in a handkerchief, **21** for I was afraid of
you, because you are a demanding person; you
take up what you did not lay down and you
harvest what you did not plant.' **22** He said to
him, 'With your own words I shall condemn
you, you wicked servant. You knew I was a
demanding person, taking up what I did not lay
down and harvesting what I did not plant;
**23** why did you not put my money in a bank?
Then on my return I would have collected it with
interest.' **24** And to those standing by he said,
'Take the gold coin from him and give it to the
servant who has ten.' **25** But they said to him,
'Sir, he has ten gold coins.' **26** [g]'I tell you, to
everyone who has, more will be given, but from
the one who has not, even what he has will be
taken away. **27** Now as for those enemies of
mine who did not want me as their king, bring
them here and slay them before me.' "

## *VI: THE TEACHING MINISTRY IN JERUSALEM*

### The Entry into Jerusalem
**28** [h]*After he
had said this, he proceeded on his journey up to
Jerusalem. **29** [i]As he drew near to Bethphage
and Bethany at the place called the Mount of
Olives, he sent two of his disciples. **30** [j]He
said, "Go into the village opposite you, and as
you enter it you will find a colt tethered on
which no one has ever sat. Untie it and bring it
here. **31** And if anyone should ask you, 'Why
are you untying it?' you will answer, 'The Master has need of it.' " **32** [k]So those who had
been sent went off and found everything just as
he had told them. **33** And as they were untying
the colt, its owners said to them, "Why are you
untying this colt?" **34** They answered, "The
Master has need of it." **35** [l]So they brought it
to Jesus, threw their cloaks over the colt, and
helped Jesus to mount. **36** As he rode along, the
people were spreading their cloaks on the road;
**37** and now as he was approaching the slope of
the Mount of Olives, the whole multitude of his
disciples began to praise God aloud with joy for
all the mighty deeds they had seen. **38** [m]*They
proclaimed:

"Blessed is the king who comes
in the name of the Lord.
Peace in heaven
and glory in the highest."

**39** *Some of the Pharisees in the crowd said to
him, "Teacher, rebuke your disciples." **40** He
said in reply, "I tell you, if they keep silent, the
stones will cry out!"

### The Lament for Jerusalem
**41** [no]*As he
drew near, he saw the city and wept over it,
**42** [p]saying, "If this day you only knew what
makes for peace—but now it is hidden from
your eyes. **43** [q]*For the days are coming upon
you when your enemies will raise a palisade
against you; they will encircle you and hem you
in on all sides. **44** [r]They will smash you to the
ground and your children within you, and they
will not leave one stone upon another within you
because you did not recognize the time of your
visitation."

### The Cleansing of the Temple
**45** [st]*Then Jesus entered the temple area and
proceeded to drive out those who were selling
things, **46** [u]saying to them, "It is written, 'My
house shall be a house of prayer, but you have
made it a den of thieves.' " **47** [vw]And every
day he was teaching in the temple area. The
chief priests, the scribes, and the leaders of the
people, meanwhile, were seeking to put him to
death, **48** but they could find no way to accom-

g 8, 18; Mt 13, 12; Mk 4, 25.
h Mt 21, 1-11; Mk 11, 1-11; Jn 12, 12-19.
i Zec 14, 4.
j Nm 19, 2; Dt 21, 3, 1 Sm 6, 7; Zec 9, 9.
k 22, 13.
l 2 Kgs 9, 13.
m 2, 14; Ps 118, 26.
n 13, 34-35.
o 2 Kgs 8, 11-12; Jer 14, 17; 15, 5.
p 8, 10; Is 6, 9-10; Mt 13, 14; Mk 4, 12; Acts 28, 26-27; Rom 11, 8.10.
q Is 29, 3.
r 1, 68; 21, 6; Ps 137, 9; Mt 24, 2; Mk 13, 2.
s Mt 21, 12-13; Mk 11, 15-17; Jn 2, 13-17.
t 3, 1 / Hos 9, 15.
u Is 56, 7; Jer 7, 11.
v 20, 19; 22, 2; Mt 21, 46; Mk 11, 18; 12, 12; 14, 1-2; Jn 5, 18; 7, 30.
w 21, 37; 22, 53; Jn 18, 20.

*

19, 28—21, 38: With the royal entry of Jesus into Jerusalem, a new section of Luke's gospel begins, the ministry of Jesus in Jerusalem before his death and resurrection. Luke suggests that this was a lengthy ministry in Jerusalem (19, 47; 20, 1; 21, 37–38; 22, 53) and it is characterized by Jesus' daily teaching in the temple (21, 37–38). For the story of the entry of Jesus into Jerusalem, see also Mt 21, 1–11; Mk 11, 1–10; Jn 12, 12–19 and the notes there.

19, 38: *Blessed is the king who comes in the name of the Lord:* only in Lk is Jesus explicitly given the title *king* when he enters Jerusalem in triumph. Luke has inserted this title into the words of Ps 118, 26 that heralded the arrival of the pilgrims coming to the holy city and to the temple. Jesus is thereby acclaimed as *king* (see 1, 32) and as the one *who comes* (see Mal 3, 1; Lk 7, 19). *Peace in heaven . . . :* the acclamation of the disciples of Jesus in Lk echoes the announcement of the angels at the birth of Jesus (2, 14). The peace Jesus brings is associated with the salvation to be accomplished here in Jerusalem.

19, 39: *Rebuke your disciples:* this command, found only in Lk, was given so that the Roman authorities would not interpret the acclamation of Jesus as king as an uprising against them; cf 23, 2–3.

19, 41–44: The lament for Jerusalem is found only in Lk. By not accepting Jesus (the one who mediates peace), Jerusalem will not find peace but will become the victim of devastation.

19, 43–44: Luke may be describing the actual disaster that befell Jerusalem in A.D. 70 when it was destroyed by the Romans during the First Revolt.

19, 45–46: Immediately upon entering the holy city, Jesus in a display of his authority enters the temple (see Mal 3, 1–3) and lays claim to it after cleansing it that it might become a proper place for his teaching ministry in Jerusalem (19, 47; 20, 1; 21, 37; 22, 53). See Mt 21, 12–17; Mk 11, 15–19; Jn 2, 13–17 and the notes there.

plish their purpose because all the people were
hanging on his words.

## CHAPTER 20

### The Authority of Jesus Questioned

1 [x]*One day as he was teaching the people in
the temple area and proclaiming the good news,
the chief priests and scribes, together with the
elders, approached him 2 [y]and said to him,
"Tell us, by what authority are you doing these
things? Or who is the one who gave you this
authority?" 3 He said to them in reply, "I shall
ask you a question. Tell me, 4 [z]was John's
baptism of heavenly or of human origin?"
5 [a]They discussed this among themselves, and
said, "If we say, 'Of heavenly origin,' he will
say, 'Why did you not believe him?' 6 But if
we say, 'Of human origin,' then all the people
will stone us, for they are convinced that John
was a prophet." 7 So they answered that they
did not know from where it came. 8 Then Jesus
said to them, "Neither shall I tell you by what
authority I do these things."

### The Parable of the Tenant Farmers

9 [bc]*Then he proceeded to tell the people this
parable. "[A] man planted a vineyard, leased it
to tenant farmers, and then went on a journey for
a long time. 10 [d]At harvest time he sent a servant to the tenant farmers to receive some of the
produce of the vineyard. But they beat the servant and sent him away empty-handed. 11 So
he proceeded to send another servant, but him
also they beat and insulted and sent away empty-handed. 12 Then he proceeded to send a
third, but this one too they wounded and threw
out. 13 [e]The owner of the vineyard said, 'What
shall I do? I shall send my beloved son; maybe
they will respect him.' 14 But when the tenant
farmers saw him they said to one another, 'This
is the heir. Let us kill him that the inheritance
may become ours.' 15 *So they threw him out
of the vineyard and killed him. What will the
owner of the vineyard do to them? 16 He will
come and put those tenant farmers to death and
turn over the vineyard to others." When the
people heard this, they exclaimed, "Let it not
be so!" 17 [f]But he looked at them and asked,
"What then does this scripture passage mean:

'The stone which the builders rejected
has become the cornerstone'?

18 Everyone who falls on that stone will be
dashed to pieces; and it will crush anyone on
whom it falls." 19 [g]The scribes and chief
priests sought to lay their hands on him at that
very hour, but they feared the people, for they
knew that he had addressed this parable to them.

### Paying Taxes to the Emperor

20 [hi]*They watched him closely and sent
agents pretending to be righteous who were to
trap him in speech, in order to hand him over to
the authority and power of the governor.
21 [j]They posed this question to him, "Teacher,
we know that what you say and teach is correct,
and you show no partiality, but teach the way
of God in accordance with the truth. 22 *Is it
lawful for us to pay tribute to Caesar or not?"
23 Recognizing their craftiness he said to them,
24 *"Show me a denarius; whose image and
name does it bear?" They replied, "Caesar's."
25 [k]So he said to them, "Then repay to Caesar
what belongs to Caesar and to God what belongs
to God." 26 They were unable to trap him by
something he might say before the people, and
so amazed were they at his reply that they fell
silent.

### The Question about the Resurrection

27 [lm]*Some Sadducees, those who deny that
there is a resurrection, came forward and put
this question to him, 28 [n]*saying, "Teacher,

x Mt 21, 23-27; Mk 11, 27-33.
y Acts 4, 7.
z 3, 3.16.
a Mt 21, 32.
b Mt 21, 33-46; Mk 12, 1-12.
c Is 5, 1-7.
d 2 Chr 36, 15-16.
e 3, 22.
f Ps 118, 22; Is 28, 16.
g 19, 47-48; 22, 2; Mt 21, 46; Mk 11, 18; 12, 12; 14, 1-2; Jn 5, 18; 7, 30.
h Mt 22, 15-22; Mk 12, 13-17.
i 11, 54.
j Jn 3, 2.
k Rom 13, 6-7.
l Mt 22, 23-33; Mk 12, 18-27.
m Acts 23, 8.
n Gn 38, 8; Dt 25, 5.

*

20, 1–47: The Jerusalem religious leaders or their representatives, in an attempt to incriminate Jesus with the Romans and to discredit him with the people, pose a number of questions to him (about his authority, 2; about payment of taxes, 22; about the resurrection, 28–33).

20, 9–19: This parable about an absentee landlord and a tenant farmers' revolt reflects the social and economic conditions of rural Palestine in the first century. The synoptic gospel writers use the parable to describe how the rejection of the landlord's son becomes the occasion for the vineyard to be taken away from those to whom it was entrusted (the religious leadership of Judaism that rejects the teaching and preaching of Jesus; 19).

20, 15: *They threw him out of the vineyard and killed him:* cf Mk 12, 8. Luke has altered his Marcan source and reports that the murder of the son takes place outside the vineyard to reflect the tradition of Jesus' death outside the walls of the city of Jerusalem (see Heb 13, 12).

20, 20: *The governor:* i.e., Pontius Pilate, the Roman administrator responsible for the collection of taxes and maintenance of order in Palestine.

20, 22: Through their question the agents of the Jerusalem religious leadership hope to force Jesus to take sides on one of the sensitive political issues of first-century Palestine. The issue of nonpayment of taxes to Rome becomes one of the focal points of the First Jewish Revolt (A.D. 66–70) that resulted in the Roman destruction of Jerusalem and the temple. See also the note on Mt 22, 15–22.

20, 24: *Denarius:* a Roman silver coin (see the note on 7, 41).

20, 27: *Sadducees:* see the note on Mt 3, 7.

20, 28–33: The Saddducees' question, based on the law of

Moses wrote for us, 'If someone's brother dies
leaving a wife but no child, his brother must
take the wife and raise up descendants for his
brother.' **29** Now there were seven brothers;
the first married a woman but died childless.
**30** Then the second **31** and the third married
her, and likewise all the seven died childless.
**32** Finally the woman also died. **33** Now at the
resurrection whose wife will that woman be?
For all seven had been married to her."
**34** Jesus said to them, "The children of this age
marry and remarry; **35** but those who are
deemed worthy to attain to the coming age and
to the resurrection of the dead neither marry nor
are given in marriage. **36** *They can no longer
die, for they are like angels; and they are the
children of God because they are the ones who
will rise. **37** [o]That the dead will rise even Moses made known in the passage about the bush,
when he called 'Lord' the God of Abraham, the
God of Isaac, and the God of Jacob; **38** [p]and he
is not God of the dead, but of the living, for to
him all are alive." **39** Some of the scribes said
in reply, "Teacher, you have answered well."
**40** [q]And they no longer dared to ask him anything.

### The Question about David's Son

**41** [r]*Then he said to them, "How do they
claim that the Messiah is the Son of David?
**42** [s]For David himself in the Book of Psalms
says:

'The Lord said to my lord,
"Sit at my right hand
**43** till I make your enemies your
footstool."'

**44** Now if David calls him 'lord,' how can he
be his son?"

### Denunciation of the Scribes

**45** [t]Then,
within the hearing of all the people, he said to
[his] disciples, **46** [u]"Be on guard against the
scribes, who like to go around in long robes and
love greetings in marketplaces, seats of honor in
synagogues, and places of honor at banquets.
**47** They devour the houses of widows and, as
a pretext, recite lengthy prayers. They will receive a very severe condemnation."

## CHAPTER 21

### The Poor Widow's Contribution

**1** [v]*When he looked up he saw some wealthy
people putting their offerings into the treasury
**2** and he noticed a poor widow putting in two
small coins. **3** He said, "I tell you truly, this
poor widow put in more than all the rest; **4** for
those others have all made offerings from their
surplus wealth, but she, from her poverty, has
offered her whole livelihood."

### The Destruction of the Temple Foretold

**5** [w]*While some people were speaking
about how the temple was adorned with costly
stones and votive offerings, he said, **6** [x]"All
that you see here—the days will come when
there will not be left a stone upon another stone
that will not be thrown down."

### The Signs of the End

**7** [y]Then they asked
him, "Teacher, when will this happen? And
what sign will there be when all these things are
about to happen?" **8** [z]*He answered, "See that
you not be deceived, for many will come in my
name, saying, 'I am he,' and 'The time has
come.' Do not follow them! **9** When you hear
of wars and insurrections, do not be terrified; for
such things must happen first, but it will not
immediately be the end." **10** [a]Then he said to

---

o Ex 3, 2.6.15-16.
p Rom 14, 8-9.
q Mt 22, 46; Mk 12, 34.
r Mt 22, 41-45; Mk 12, 35-37.
s Ps 110, 1.
t 11, 37-54; Mt 23, 1-36; Mk 12, 38-40.
u 14, 7-11.
v Mk 12, 41-44.
w Mt 24, 1-2; Mk 13, 1-2.
x 19, 44.
y Mt 24, 3-14; Mk 13, 3-13.
z 17, 23; Mk 13, 5.6.21; 1 Jn 2, 18.
a 2 Chr 15, 6; Is 19, 2.

*

levirate marriage recorded in Dt 25, 5–10, ridicules the idea of the resurrection. Jesus rejects their naive understanding of the resurrection (35–36) and then argues on behalf of the resurrection of the dead on the basis of the written law (37–38) that the Sadducees accept. See also the notes on Mt 22, 23–33.

20, 36: *Because they are the ones who will rise:* literally, "being sons of the resurrection."

20, 41–44: After successfully answering the three questions of his opponents, Jesus now asks them a question. Their inability to respond implies that they have forfeited their position and authority as the religious leaders of the people because they do not understand the scriptures. This series of controversies between the religious leadership of Jerusalem and Jesus reveals Jesus as the authoritative teacher whose words are to be listened to (see 9, 35). See also the notes on Mt 22, 41–46.

21, 1–4: The widow is another example of the poor ones in this gospel whose detachment from material possessions and dependence on God leads to their blessedness (6, 20). Her simple offering provides a striking contrast to the pride and pretentiousness of the scribes denounced in the preceding section (20, 45–47). The story is taken from Mk 12, 41–44.

21, 5–36: Jesus' eschatological discourse in Lk is inspired by Mk 13, but Luke has made some significant alterations to the words of Jesus found there. Luke maintains, though in a modified form, the belief in the early expectation of the end of the age (see 27.28. 31.32.36), but, by focusing attention throughout the gospel on the importance of the day-to-day following of Jesus and by reinterpreting the meaning of some of the signs of the end from Mk 13, he has come to terms with what seemed to the early Christian community to be a delay of the parousia. Mark, for example, described the desecration of the Jerusalem temple by the Romans (Mk 13, 14) as the apocalyptic symbol (see Dn 9, 27; 12, 11) accompanying the end of the age and the coming of the Son of Man. Luke (21, 20–24), however, removes the apocalyptic setting and separates the historical destruction of Jerusalem from the signs of the coming of the Son of Man by a period that he refers to as "the times of the Gentiles" (21, 24). See also the notes on Mt 24, 1–36 and Mk 13, 1–37.

21, 8: *The time has come:* in Lk, the proclamation of the imminent end of the age has itself become a false teaching.

them, "Nation will rise against nation, and
kingdom against kingdom. 11 There will be
powerful earthquakes, famines, and plagues
from place to place; and awesome sights and
mighty signs will come from the sky.

### The Coming Persecution

12 [bc]*"Before all this happens, however, they
will seize and persecute you, they will hand you
over to the synagogues and to prisons, and they
will have you led before kings and governors
because of my name. 13 It will lead to your
giving testimony. 14 Remember, you are not to
prepare your defense beforehand, 15 [d]*for I
myself shall give you a wisdom in speaking that
all your adversaries will be powerless to resist
or refute. 16 [ef]You will even be handed over by
parents, brothers, relatives, and friends, and
they will put some of you to death. 17 You will
be hated by all because of my name, 18 [g]but
not a hair on your head will be destroyed.
19 [h]By your perseverance you will secure your
lives.

**The Great Tribulation** 20 [ij]*"When you
see Jerusalem surrounded by armies, know that
its desolation is at hand. 21 [k]Then those in
Judea must flee to the mountains. Let those
within the city escape from it, and let those in
the countryside not enter the city, 22 for these
days are the time of punishment when all the
scriptures are fulfilled. 23 [l]Woe to pregnant
women and nursing mothers in those days, for
a terrible calamity will come upon the earth and
a wrathful judgment upon this people.
24 [m]*They will fall by the edge of the sword
and be taken as captives to all the Gentiles; and
Jerusalem will be trampled underfoot by the
Gentiles until the times of the Gentiles are fulfilled.

### The Coming of the Son of Man

25 [no]"There will be signs in the sun, the
moon, and the stars, and on earth nations will
be in dismay, perplexed by the roaring of the sea
and the waves. 26 [p]*People will die of fright in
anticipation of what is coming upon the world,
for the powers of the heavens will be shaken.
27 [q]And then they will see the Son of Man
coming in a cloud with power and great glory.
28 [r]But when these signs begin to happen,
stand erect and raise your heads because your
redemption is at hand."

**The Lesson of the Fig Tree** 29 [s]He
taught them a lesson. "Consider the fig tree and
all the other trees. 30 When their buds burst
open, you see for yourselves and know that
summer is now near; 31 in the same way, when
you see these things happening, know that the
kingdom of God is near. 32 [t]Amen, I say to
you, this generation will not pass away until all
these things have taken place. 33 [u]Heaven and
earth will pass away, but my words will not pass
away.

**Exhortation to be Vigilant** 34 [v]"Beware
that your hearts do not become drowsy from
carousing and drunkenness and the anxieties of
daily life, and that day catch you by surprise
35 like a trap. For that day will assault everyone who lives on the face of the earth. 36 [w]Be
vigilant at all times and pray that you have the
strength to escape the tribulations that are imminent and to stand before the Son of Man."

**Ministry in Jerusalem** 37 [x]During the
day, Jesus was teaching in the temple area, but
at night he would leave and stay at the place
called the Mount of Olives. 38 And all the people would get up early each morning to listen to
him in the temple area.

## *VII: THE PASSION NARRATIVE*

## CHAPTER 22

### The Conspiracy against Jesus

1 [y]*Now the feast of Unleavened Bread, called

b 12, 11-12; Mt 10, 17-20; Mk 13, 9-11.
c Jn 16, 2; Acts 25, 24.
d Acts 6, 10.
e Mt 10, 21-22.
f 12, 52-53.
g 12, 7; 1 Sm 14, 45; Mt 10, 30; Acts 27, 34.
h 8, 15.
i Mt 24, 15-21; Mk 13, 14-19.
j 19, 41-44.
k 17, 31.
l 1 Cor 7, 26.
m Tb 14, 5; Ps 79, 1; Is 63, 18; Jer 21, 7; Rom 11, 25; Rv 11, 2.
n Mt 24, 29-31; Mk 13, 24-27.
o Wis 5, 22; Is 13, 10; Ez 32, 7; Jl 2, 10; 3, 3-4; 4, 15; Rv 6, 12-14.
p Hg 2, 6.21.
q Dn 7, 13-14; Mt 26, 64; Rv 1, 7.
r 2, 38.
s Mt 24, 32-35; Mk 13, 28-31.
t 9, 27; Mt 16, 28.
u 16, 17.
v 12, 45-46; Mt 24, 48-50; 1 Thes 5, 3.6-7.
w Mk 13, 33.
x 19, 47; 22, 39.
y Mt 26, 1-5; Mk 14, 1-2; Jn 11, 47-53.

*

21, 12: *Before all this happens . . . :* to Luke and his community, some of the signs of the end just described (10–11) still lie in the future. Now in dealing with the persecution of the disciples (12–19) and the destruction of Jerusalem (20–24) Luke is pointing to eschatological signs that have already been fulfilled.

21, 15: *A wisdom in speaking:* literally, "a mouth and wisdom."

21, 20–24: The actual destruction of Jerusalem by Rome in A.D. 70 upon which Luke and his community look back provides the assurance that, just as Jesus' prediction of Jerusalem's destruction was fulfilled, so too will be his announcement of their final redemption (27–28).

21, 24: *The times of the Gentiles:* a period of indeterminate length separating the destruction of Jerusalem from the cosmic signs accompanying the coming of the Son of Man.

21, 26: *The powers of the heavens:* the heavenly bodies mentioned in v 25 and thought of as cosmic armies.

22, 1—23, 56a: The passion narrative. Luke is still dependent upon Mk for the composition of the passion narrative but has incorporated much of his own special tradition into the narrative. Among the distinctive sections in Lk are: (1) the

the Passover, was drawing near, **2** [z]and the
chief priests and the scribes were seeking a way
to put him to death, for they were afraid of the
people. **3** [a][b]*Then Satan entered into Judas,
the one surnamed Iscariot, who was counted
among the Twelve, **4** and he went to the chief
priests and temple guards to discuss a plan for
handing him over to them. **5** They were pleased
and agreed to pay him money. **6** He accepted
their offer and sought a favorable opportunity to
hand him over to them in the absence of a
crowd.

## Preparations for the Passover

**7** [c][d]When the day of the feast of Unleavened
Bread arrived, the day for sacrificing the Passover lamb, **8** he sent out Peter and John, instructing them, "Go and make preparations for
us to eat the Passover." **9** They asked him,
"Where do you want us to make the preparations?" **10** *And he answered them, "When
you go into the city, a man will meet* you carrying a jar of water. Follow him into the house that
he enters **11** and say to the master of the house,
'The teacher says to you, "Where is the guest
room where I may eat the Passover with my
disciples?"' **12** He will show you a large upper
room that is furnished. Make the preparations
there." **13** [e]Then they went off and found everything exactly as he had told them, and there
they prepared the Passover.

## The Last Supper

**14** [f]When the hour
came, he took his place at table with the apostles. **15** *He said to them, "I have eagerly desired to eat this Passover with you before I
suffer, **16** [g]for, I tell you, I shall not eat it
[again] until there is fulfillment in the kingdom
of God." **17** *Then he took a cup, gave thanks,
and said, "Take this and share it among yourselves; **18** for I tell you [that] from this time on
I shall not drink of the fruit of the vine until the
kingdom of God comes." **19** [h]*Then he took
the bread, said the blessing, broke it, and gave
it to them, saying, "This is my body, which will
be given for you; do this in memory of me."
**20** [i]And likewise the cup after they had eaten,
saying, "This cup is the new covenant in my
blood, which will be shed for you.

## The Betrayal Foretold

**21** [j]"And yet be-
hold, the hand of the one who is to betray me
is with me on the table; **22** for the Son of Man
indeed goes as it has been determined; but woe
to that man by whom he is betrayed." **23** And
they began to debate among themselves who
among them would do such a deed.

## The Role of the Disciples

**24** [k]*Then an
argument broke out among them about which of
them should be regarded as the greatest.
**25** [l]*He said to them, "The kings of the Gentiles lord it over them and those in authority over
them are addressed as 'Benefactors'; **26** [m]but
among you it shall not be so. Rather, let the
greatest among you be as the youngest, and the
leader as the servant. **27** For who is greater: the
one seated at table or the one who serves? Is it
not the one seated at table? I am among you as
the one who serves. **28** It is you who have stood
by me in my trials; **29** [n]and I confer a kingdom
on you, just as my Father has conferred one on
me, **30** [o]that you may eat and drink at my table

z 19, 47-48; 20, 19; Mt 21, 46; Mk 12, 12; Jn 5, 18; 7, 30.
a Mt 26, 14-16; Mk 14, 10-11; Jn 13, 2.27.
b Acts 1, 17.
c Mt 26, 17-19; Mk 14, 12-16.
d Ex 12, 6.14-20.
e 19, 32.
f Mt 26, 20.26-30; Mk 14, 17.22-26; 1 Cor 11, 23-25.
g 13, 29.
h 24, 30; Acts 27, 35.
i Ex 24, 8; Jer 31, 31; 32, 40; Zec 9, 11.
j Ps 41, 10; Mt 26, 21-25; Mk 14, 18-21; Jn 13, 21-30.
k 9, 46; Mt 18, 1; Mk 9, 34.
l Mt 20, 25-27; Mk 10, 42-44; Jn 13, 3-16.
m Mt 23, 11; Mk 9, 35.
n 12, 32.
o Mt 19, 28.

*

tradition of the institution of the Eucharist (22, 15–20); (2) Jesus' farewell discourse (22, 21–38); (3) the mistreatment and interrogation of Jesus (22, 63–71); (4) Jesus before Herod and his second appearance before Pilate (23, 6–16); (5) words addressed to the women followers on the way to the crucifixion (23, 27–32); (6) words to the penitent thief (23, 39–41); (7) the death of Jesus (23, 46.47b–49). Luke stresses the innocence of Jesus (23, 4.14–15.22) who is the victim of the powers of evil (22, 3.31.53) and who goes to his death in fulfillment of his Father's will (22, 42.46). Throughout the narrative Luke emphasizes the mercy, compassion, and healing power of Jesus (22, 51; 23, 43) who does not go to death lonely and deserted, but is accompanied by others who follow him on the way of the cross (23, 26–31.49).

22, 1: *Feast of Unleavened Bread, called the Passover:* see the note on Mk 14, 1.

22, 3: *Satan entered into Judas:* see the note on 4, 13.

22, 10: *A man will meet you carrying a jar of water:* see the note on Mk 14, 13.

22, 15: *This Passover:* Luke clearly identifies this last supper of Jesus with the apostles as a Passover meal that commemorated the deliverance of the Israelites from slavery in Egypt. Jesus reinterprets the significance of the Passover by setting it in the context of the kingdom of God (16). The "deliverance" associated with the Passover finds its new meaning in the blood that will be shed (20).

22, 17: Because of a textual problem in vv 19 and 20, some commentators interpret this cup as the eucharistic cup.

22, 19c–20: *Which will be given . . . do this in memory of me:* these words are omitted in some important Western text manuscripts and a few Syriac manuscripts. Other ancient text types, including the oldest papyrus manuscript of Lk dating from the late second or early third century, contain the longer reading presented here. The Lucan account of the words of institution of the Eucharist bears a close resemblance to the words of institution in the Pauline tradition (see 1 Cor 11, 23–26). See also the notes on Mt 26, 26–29; 26, 27–28; and Mk 14, 22–24.

22, 24–38: The Gospel of Luke presents a brief farewell discourse of Jesus; compare the lengthy farewell discourses and prayer in Jn, chs 13–17.

22, 25: *'Benefactors':* this word occurs as a title of rulers in the Hellenistic world.

in my kingdom; and you will sit on thrones
judging the twelve tribes of Israel.

**Peter's Denial Foretold** 31 [pq]*“Simon,
Simon, behold Satan has demanded to sift all of
you like wheat, 32 but I have prayed that your
own faith may not fail; and once you have
turned back, you must strengthen your brothers.” 33 [r]He said to him, “Lord, I am prepared
to go to prison and to die with you.” 34 [s]But
he replied, “I tell you, Peter, before the cock
crows this day, you will deny three times that
you know me.”

**Instructions for the Time of Crisis**
35 [t]He said to them, “When I sent you forth
without a money bag or a sack or sandals, were
you in need of anything?” “No, nothing,” they
replied. 36 [u]*He said to them, “But now one
who has a money bag should take it, and likewise a sack, and one who does not have a sword
should sell his cloak and buy one. 37 [v]For I tell
you that this scripture must be fulfilled in me,
namely, ‘He was counted among the wicked’;
and indeed what is written about me is coming
to fulfillment.” 38 *Then they said, “Lord,
look, there are two swords here.” But he replied, “It is enough!”

**The Agony in the Garden** 39 [w]Then going out he went, as was his custom, to the
Mount of Olives, and the disciples followed
him. 40 [x]When he arrived at the place he said
to them, “Pray that you may not undergo the
test.” 41 [y]After withdrawing about a stone's
throw from them and kneeling, he prayed,
42 [z]saying, “Father, if you are willing, take
this cup away from me; still, not my will but
yours be done.” [ 43 *And to strengthen him
an angel from heaven appeared to him. 44 He
was in such agony and he prayed so fervently
that his sweat became like drops of blood falling
on the ground.] 45 When he rose from prayer
and returned to his disciples, he found them
sleeping from grief. 46 [a]He said to them,
“Why are you sleeping? Get up and pray that
you may not undergo the test.”

**The Betrayal and Arrest of Jesus**
47 [b]While he was still speaking, a crowd approached and in front was one of the Twelve, a
man named Judas. He went up to Jesus to kiss
him. 48 Jesus said to him, “Judas, are you
betraying the Son of Man with a kiss?” 49 [c]His
disciples realized what was about to happen,
and they asked, “Lord, shall we strike with a
sword?” 50 [d]And one of them struck the high
priest's servant and cut off his right ear.
51 *But Jesus said in reply, “Stop, no more of
this!” Then he touched the servant's ear and
healed him. 52 [e]And Jesus said to the chief
priests and temple guards and elders who had
come for him, “Have you come out as against
a robber, with swords and clubs? 53 [f]Day after
day I was with you in the temple area, and you
did not seize me; but this is your hour, the time
for the power of darkness.”

**Peter's Denial of Jesus** 54 [gh]After arresting him they led him away and took him into
the house of the high priest; Peter was following
at a distance. 55 They lit a fire in the middle of
the courtyard and sat around it, and Peter sat
down with them. 56 When a maid saw him
seated in the light, she looked intently at him
and said, “This man too was with him.”
57 But he denied it saying, “Woman, I do not
know him.” 58 A short while later someone
else saw him and said, “You too are one of
them”; but Peter answered, “My friend, I am
not.” 59 About an hour later, still another insisted, “Assuredly, this man too was with him,
for he also is a Galilean.” 60 But Peter said,
“My friend, I do not know what you are talking
about.” Just as he was saying this, the cock
crowed, 61 [i]*and the Lord turned and looked at
Peter; and Peter remembered the word of the
Lord, how he had said to him, “Before the cock
crows today, you will deny me three times.”

p Mt 26, 33-35; Mk 14, 29-31; Jn 13, 37-38.
q Jb 1, 6-12; Am 9, 9.
r 22, 54.
s 22, 54-62.
t 9, 3; 10, 4; Mt 10, 9-10; Mk 6, 7-9.
u 22, 49.
v Is 53, 12.
w Mt 26, 30.36-46; Mk 14, 26.32-42; Jn 18, 1-2.
x 22, 46.
y Heb 5, 7-8.
z Mt 6, 10.
a 22, 40.
b Mt 26, 47-56; Mk 14, 43-50; Jn 18, 3-4.
c 22, 36.
d Jn 18, 26.
e 22, 37.
f 19, 47; 21, 37; Jn 7, 30; 8, 20; Col 1, 13.
g Mt 26, 57-58.69-75; Mk 14, 53-54.66-72; Jn 18, 12-18.25-27.
h 22, 33.
i 22, 34.

*

22, 31: All of you: literally, “you.” The translation reflects the meaning of the Greek text that uses a second person plural pronoun here.

22, 31–32: Jesus' prayer for Simon's faith and the commission to strengthen his brothers anticipates the post-resurrectional prominence of Peter in the first half of Acts, where he appears as the spokesman for the Christian community and the one who begins the mission to the Gentiles (Acts 10–11).

22, 36: In contrast to the ministry of the Twelve and of the seventy-two during the period of Jesus (9, 3; 10, 4), in the future period of the church the missionaries must be prepared for the opposition they will face in a world hostile to their preaching.

22, 38: *It is enough!:* the farewell discourse ends abruptly with these words of Jesus spoken to the disciples when they take literally what was intended as figurative language about being prepared to face the world's hostility.

22, 43–44: These verses, though very ancient, were probably not part of the original text of Lk. They are absent from the oldest papyrus manuscripts of Lk and from manuscripts of wide geographical distribution.

22, 51: *And healed him:* only Luke recounts this healing of the injured servant.

22, 61: Only Luke recounts that *the Lord turned and looked at Peter.* This look of Jesus leads to Peter's weeping bitterly over his denial (62).

**62** He went out and began to weep bitterly.
**63** [j]The men who held Jesus in custody were
ridiculing and beating him. **64** They blindfolded him and questioned him, saying, "Prophesy!
Who is it that struck you?" **65** And they reviled
him in saying many other things against him.

### Jesus before the Sanhedrin

**66** [k][l]*When day came the council of elders of
the people met, both chief priests and scribes,
and they brought him before their Sanhedrin.
**67** [m]They said, "If you are the Messiah, tell
us," but he replied to them, "If I tell you, you
will not believe, **68** and if I question, you will
not respond. **69** [n]But from this time on the Son
of Man will be seated at the right hand of the
power of God." **70** They all asked, "Are you
then the Son of God?" He replied to them,
"You say that I am." **71** Then they said,
"What further need have we for testimony? We
have heard it from his own mouth."

## CHAPTER 23

### Jesus before Pilate

**1** [o]*Then the whole
assembly of them arose and brought him before
Pilate. **2** [p]They brought charges against him,
saying, "We found this man misleading our
people; he opposes the payment of taxes to Caesar and maintains that he is the Messiah, a
king." **3** [q]Pilate asked him, "Are you the king
of the Jews?" He said to him in reply, "You say
so." **4** [r]Pilate then addressed the chief priests
and the crowds, "I find this man not guilty."
**5** But they were adamant and said, "He is inciting the people with his teaching throughout all
Judea, from Galilee where he began even to
here."

### Jesus before Herod

**6** *On hearing this
Pilate asked if the man was a Galilean; **7** [s]and
upon learning that he was under Herod's jurisdiction, he sent him to Herod who was in Jerusalem at that time. **8** [t]Herod was very glad to see
Jesus; he had been wanting to see him for a long
time, for he had heard about him and had been
hoping to see him perform some sign. **9** [u]He
questioned him at length, but he gave him no
answer. **10** [v]The chief priests and scribes,
meanwhile, stood by accusing him harshly.
**11** [w][Even] Herod and his soldiers treated him
contemptuously and mocked him, and after
clothing him in resplendent garb, he sent him
back to Pilate. **12** Herod and Pilate became
friends that very day, even though they had been
enemies formerly. **13** Pilate then summoned
the chief priests, the rulers, and the people
**14** [x]and said to them, "You brought this man
to me and accused him of inciting the people to
revolt. I have conducted my investigation in
your presence and have not found this man
guilty of the charges you have brought against
him, **15** nor did Herod, for he sent him back to
us. So no capital crime has been committed by
him. **16** [y]Therefore I shall have him flogged
and then release him." **[17*]**

### The Sentence of Death

**18** [z]But all to-
gether they shouted out, "Away with this man!
Release Barabbas to us." **19** (Now Barabbas
had been imprisoned for a rebellion that had
taken place in the city and for murder.)
**20** Again Pilate addressed them, still wishing to
release Jesus, **21** but they continued their
shouting, "Crucify him! Crucify him!" **22** Pilate addressed them a third time, "What evil has
this man done? I found him guilty of no capital
crime. Therefore I shall have him flogged and
then release him." **23** With loud shouts, however, they persisted in calling for his crucifixion, and their voices prevailed. **24** The verdict
of Pilate was that their demand should be granted. **25** So he released the man who had been
imprisoned for rebellion and murder, for whom

---

j Mt 26, 67-68; Mk 14, 65.
k Mt 26, 59-66; Mk 14, 55-64.
l Mt 27, 1; Mk 15, 1.
m Jn 3, 12; 8, 45; 10, 24.
n Ps 110, 1; Dn 7, 13-14; Acts 7, 56.
o Mt 27, 1-2.11-14; Mk 15, 1-5; Jn 18, 28-38.
p 20, 22-25; Acts 17, 7; 24, 5.
q 22, 70; 1 Tm 6, 13.
r 23, 14.22.41; Mt 27, 24; Jn 19, 4.6; Acts 13, 28.
s 3, 1; 9, 7.
t 9, 9; Acts 4, 27-28.
u Mk 15, 5.
v Mt 27, 12; Mk 15, 3.
w Mt 27, 28-30; Mk 15, 17-19; Jn 19, 2-3.
x 23, 4.22.41.
y 23, 22; Jn 19, 12-14.
z Mt 27, 20-26; Mk 15, 6-7.11-15; Jn 18, 38b-40; 19, 14-16;Acts 3, 13-14.

---

*

22, 66–71: Luke recounts one daytime trial of Jesus (66–71) and hints at some type of preliminary nighttime investigation (54–65). Mark (and Matthew who follows Mk) has transferred incidents of this day into the nighttime interrogation with the result that there appear to be two Sanhedrin trials of Jesus in Mk (and Mt); see the note on Mk 14, 53.

22, 66: *Sanhedrin:* the word is a Hebraized form of a Greek word meaning a "council," and refers to the elders, chief priests, and scribes who met under the high priest's leadership to decide religious and legal questions that did not pertain to Rome's interests. Jewish sources are not clear on the competence of the Sanhedrin to sentence and to execute during this period.

23, 1–5.13–25: Twice Jesus is brought before Pilate in Luke's account, and each time Pilate explicitly declares Jesus innocent of any wrongdoing (4.14.22). This stress on the innocence of Jesus before the Roman authorities is also characteristic of John's gospel (Jn 18, 38; 19, 4.6). Luke presents the Jerusalem Jewish leaders as the ones who force the hand of the Roman authorities (1–2.5.10.13. 18.21.23–25).

23, 6–12: The appearance of Jesus before Herod is found only in this gospel. Herod has been an important figure in Lk (9, 7–9; 13, 31–33) and has been presented as someone who has been curious about Jesus for a long time. His curiosity goes unrewarded. It is faith in Jesus, not curiosity, that is rewarded (7, 50; 8, 48.50; 17, 19).

23, 17: This verse, "He was obliged to release one prisoner for them at the festival," is not part of the original text of Lk. It is an explanatory gloss from Mk 15, 6 (also Mt 27, 15) and is not found in many early and important Greek manuscripts. On its historical background, see the notes on Mt 27, 15–26.

they asked, and he handed Jesus over to them
to deal with as they wished.

**The Way of the Cross** **26** [a]*As they led
him away they took hold of a certain Simon, a
Cyrenian, who was coming in from the country;
and after laying the cross on him, they made him
carry it behind Jesus. **27** A large crowd of people followed Jesus, including many women who
mourned and lamented him. **28** [b]Jesus turned
to them and said, "Daughters of Jerusalem, do
not weep for me; weep instead for yourselves
and for your children, **29** for indeed, the days
are coming when people will say, 'Blessed are
the barren, the wombs that never bore and the
breasts that never nursed.' **30** [c]At that time
people will say to the mountains, 'Fall upon us!'
and to the hills, 'Cover us!' **31** for if these
things are done when the wood is green what
will happen when it is dry?" **32** Now two others, both criminals, were led away with him to
be executed.

**The Crucifixion** **33** [de]When they came to
the place called the Skull, they crucified him
and the criminals there, one on his right, the
other on his left. **34** [f]*[Then Jesus said, "Father, forgive them, they know not what they
do."] They divided his garments by casting
lots. **35** [gh]The people stood by and watched;
the rulers, meanwhile, sneered at him and said,
"He saved others, let him save himself if he is
the chosen one, the Messiah of God."
**36** [i]Even the soldiers jeered at him. As they
approached to offer him wine **37** they called
out, "If you are King of the Jews, save yourself." **38** Above him there was an inscription
that read, "This is the King of the Jews."
**39** *Now one of the criminals hanging there
reviled Jesus, saying, "Are you not the Messiah? Save yourself and us." **40** The other, however, rebuking him, said in reply, "Have you no
fear of God, for you are subject to the same
condemnation? **41** [j]And indeed, we have been
condemned justly, for the sentence we received
corresponds to our crimes, but this man has
done nothing criminal." **42** [k]Then he said,
"Jesus, remember me when you come into your
kingdom." **43** [l]He replied to him, "Amen, I
say to you, today you will be with me in Paradise."

**The Death of Jesus** **44** [mn]*It was now
about noon and darkness came over the whole
land until three in the afternoon **45** [o]because of
an eclipse of the sun. Then the veil of the temple
was torn down the middle. **46** [p]Jesus cried out
in a loud voice, "Father, into your hands I
commend my spirit"; and when he had said this
he breathed his last. **47** *The centurion who
witnessed what had happened glorified God and
said, "This man was innocent beyond doubt."
**48** [q]When all the people who had gathered for
this spectacle saw what had happened, they returned home beating their breasts; **49** [r]but all
his acquaintances stood at a distance, including
the women who had followed him from Galilee
and saw these events.

**The Burial of Jesus** **50** [s]Now there was a
virtuous and righteous man named Joseph who,
though he was a member of the council,
**51** [t]had not consented to their plan of action.
He came from the Jewish town of Arimathea
and was awaiting the kingdom of God. **52** He
went to Pilate and asked for the body of Jesus.
**53** [u]After he had taken the body down, he
wrapped it in a linen cloth and laid him in a
rock-hewn tomb in which no one had yet been
buried. **54** It was the day of preparation, and
the sabbath was about to begin. **55** [v]The wom-
en who had come from Galilee with him followed behind, and when they had seen the tomb
and the way in which his body was laid in it,
**56** [w]they returned and prepared spices and perfumed oils. Then they rested on the sabbath
according to the commandment.

a Mt 27, 32.38; Mk 15, 21.27; Jn 19, 17.
b 19, 41-44; 21, 23-24.
c Hos 10, 8; Rv 6, 16.
d Mt 27, 33-44; Mk 15, 22-32; Jn 19, 17-24.
e 22, 37; Is 53, 12.
f Nm 15, 27-31; Ps 22, 19; Mt 5, 44; Acts 7, 60.
g Ps 22, 8-9.
h 4, 23.
i Ps 69, 22; Mt 27, 48; Mk 15, 36.
j 23, 4.14.22.
k 9, 27; 23, 2.3.38.
l 2 Cor 12, 3; Rv 2, 7.
m Mt 27, 45-56; Mk 15, 33-41; Jn 19, 25-30.
n Am 8, 9.
o Ex 26, 31-33; 36, 35.
p Ps 31, 6; Acts 7, 59.
q 18, 13; Zec 12, 10.
r 8, 1-3; 23, 55-56; 24, 10; Ps 38, 12.
s Mt 27, 57-61; Mk 15, 42-47; Jn 19, 38-42; Acts 13, 29.
t 2, 25.38.
u 19, 30; Acts 13, 29.
v 8, 2; 23, 49; 24, 10.
w Ex 12, 16; 20, 10; Dt 5, 14.

*

23, 26–32: An important Lucan theme throughout the gospel has been the need for the Christian disciple to follow in the footsteps of Jesus. Here this theme comes to the fore with the story of Simon of Cyrene who takes up the cross and follows Jesus (see 9, 23; 14, 27) and with the large crowd who likewise follow Jesus on the way of the cross. See also the note on Mk 15, 21.

23, 34a: [*Then Jesus said, "Father, forgive them, they know not what they do."*]: this portion of v 34 does not occur in the oldest papyrus manuscript of Lk and in other early Greek manuscripts and ancient versions of wide geographical distribution.

23, 39–43: This episode is recounted only in this gospel. The penitent sinner receives salvation through the crucified Jesus. Jesus' words to the penitent thief reveal Luke's understanding that the destiny of the Christian is "to be with Jesus."

23, 44: *Noon . . . three in the afternoon:* literally, the sixth and ninth hours. See the note on Mk 15, 25.

23, 47: *This man was innocent:* or, "This man was righteous."

## VIII: THE RESURRECTION NARRATIVE

## CHAPTER 24

**The Resurrection of Jesus** **1** [x]*But at
daybreak on the first day of the week they took
the spices they had prepared and went to the
tomb. **2** They found the stone rolled away from
the tomb; **3** but when they entered, they did not
find the body of the Lord Jesus. **4** [y]While they
were puzzling over this, behold, two men in
dazzling garments appeared to them. **5** [z]They
were terrified and bowed their faces to the
ground. They said to them, "Why do you seek
the living one among the dead? **6** *He is not
here, but he has been raised. Remember what he
said to you while he was still in Galilee, **7** [a]that
the Son of Man must be handed over to sinners
and be crucified, and rise on the third day."
**8** [b]And they remembered his words. **9** [c]*Then
they returned from the tomb and announced all
these things to the eleven and to all the others.
**10** [d]The women were Mary Magdalene, Joanna, and Mary the mother of James; the others
who accompanied them also told this to the
apostles, **11** but their story seemed like nonsense and they did not believe them. **12** [e]*But
Peter got up and ran to the tomb, bent down, and
saw the burial cloths alone; then he went home
amazed at what had happened.

**The Appearance on the Road to Emma-
us** **13** [f]*Now that very day two of them were
going to a village seven miles from Jerusalem
called Emmaus, **14** and they were conversing
about all the things that had occurred. **15** And
it happened that while they were conversing and
debating, Jesus himself drew near and walked
with them, **16** [g]*but their eyes were prevented
from recognizing him. **17** He asked them,
"What are you discussing as you walk along?"
They stopped, looking downcast. **18** One of
them, named Cleopas, said to him in reply,
"Are you the only visitor to Jerusalem who does
not know of the things that have taken place
there in these days?" **19** [h]And he replied to
them, "What sort of things?" They said to him,
"The things that happened to Jesus the Nazarene, who was a prophet mighty in deed and
word before God and all the people, **20** how our
chief priests and rulers both handed him over to
a sentence of death and crucified him. **21** [i]But
we were hoping that he would be the one to
redeem Israel; and besides all this, it is now the
third day since this took place. **22** [j]Some wom-
en from our group, however, have astounded
us: they were at the tomb early in the morning
**23** and did not find his body; they came back
and reported that they had indeed seen a vision
of angels who announced that he was alive.
**24** [k]Then some of those with us went to the
tomb and found things just as the women had
described, but him they did not see." **25** [l]And
he said to them, "Oh, how foolish you are! How
slow of heart to believe all that the prophets
spoke! **26** *Was it not necessary that the Messiah should suffer these things and enter into his
glory?" **27** [m]Then beginning with Moses and
all the prophets, he interpreted to them what
referred to him in all the scriptures. **28** As they
approached the village to which they were going, he gave the impression that he was going

---

x Mt 28, 1-8; Mk 16, 1-8; Jn 20, 1-17.
y 2 Mc 3, 26; Acts 1, 10.
z Acts 2, 9.
a 9, 22.44; 17, 25; 18, 32-33; Mt 16, 21; 17, 22-23; Mk 9, 31; Acts 17, 3.
b Jn 2, 22.
c Mk 16, 10-11; Jn 20, 18.
d 8, 2-3; Mk 16, 9.
e Jn 20, 3-7.
f Mk 16, 12-13.
g Jn 20, 14; 21, 4.
h Mt 2, 23; 21, 11; Acts 2, 22.
i 1, 54.68; 2, 38.
j 24, 1-11; Mt 28, 1-8; Mk 16, 1-8.
k Jn 20, 3-10.
l 9, 22; 18, 31; 24, 44; Acts 3, 24; 17, 3.
m 24, 44; Dt 18, 25; Ps 22, 1-18; Is 53; 1 Pt 1, 10-11.

*

24, 1–53: The resurrection narrative in Lk consists of five sections: (1) the women at the empty tomb (23, 56b—24, 12); (2) the appearance to the two disciples on the way to Emmaus (24, 13–35); (3) the appearance to the disciples in Jerusalem (24, 36–43); (4) Jesus' final instructions (24, 44–49); (5) the ascension (24, 50–53). In Lk, all the resurrection appearances take place in and around Jerusalem; moreover, they are all recounted as having taken place on Easter Sunday. A consistent theme throughout the narrative is that the suffering, death, and resurrection of Jesus were accomplished in fulfillment of Old Testament promises and of Jewish hopes (19a.21.26–27.44.46). In his second volume, Acts, Luke will argue that Christianity is the fulfillment of the hopes of Pharisaic Judaism and its logical development (see Acts 24, 10–21).

24, 6a: *He is not here, but he has been raised:* this part of the verse is omitted in important representatives of the Western text tradition, but its presence in other text types and the slight difference in wording from Mt 28, 6 and Mk 16, 6 argue for its retention.

24, 9: The women in this gospel do not flee from the tomb and tell no one, as in Mk 16, 8, but return and tell the disciples about their experience. The initial reaction to the testimony of the women is disbelief (11).

24, 12: This verse is missing from the Western textual tradition but is found in the best and oldest manuscripts of other text types.

24, 13–35: This episode focuses on the interpretation of scripture by the risen Jesus and the recognition of him in the breaking of the bread. The references to the quotations of scripture and explanation of it (25–27), the kerygmatic proclamation (34), and the liturgical gesture (30) suggest that the episode is primarily catechetical and liturgical rather than apologetic.

24, 13: *Seven miles:* literally, "sixty stades." A stade was 607 feet. Some manuscripts read "160 stades" or more than eighteen miles. The exact location of Emmaus is disputed.

24, 16: A consistent feature of the resurrection stories is that the risen Jesus was different and initially unrecognizable (37; Mk 16, 12; Jn 20, 14; 21, 4).

24, 26: *That the Messiah should suffer . . . :* Luke is the only New Testament writer to speak explicitly of a suffering Messiah (26.46; Acts 3, 18; 17, 3; 26, 23). The idea of a suffering Messiah is not found in the Old Testament or in other Jewish literature prior to the New Testament period, although the idea is hinted at in Mk 8, 31–33. See the notes on Mt 26, 63 and 26, 67–68.

on farther. 29 But they urged him, "Stay with
us, for it is nearly evening and the day is almost
over." So he went in to stay with them. 30 And
it happened that, while he was with them at
table, he took bread, said the blessing, broke it,
and gave it to them. 31 With that their eyes
were opened and they recognized him, but he
vanished from their sight. 32 Then they said to
each other, "Were not our hearts burning [with-
in us] while he spoke to us on the way and
opened the scriptures to us?" 33 So they set out
at once and returned to Jerusalem where they
found gathered together the eleven and those
with them 34 [n]who were saying, "The Lord
has truly been raised and has appeared to Simon!" 35 Then the two recounted what had
taken place on the way and how he was made
known to them in the breaking of the bread.

**The Appearance to the Disciples in Jeru-
salem** 36 [op]*While they were still speaking
about this, he stood in their midst and said to
them, "Peace be with you." 37 [q]But they were
startled and terrified and thought that they were
seeing a ghost. 38 Then he said to them, "Why
are you troubled? And why do questions arise
in your hearts? 39 *Look at my hands and my
feet, that it is I myself. Touch me and see,
because a ghost does not have flesh and bones
as you can see I have." 40 [r]And as he said this,
he showed them his hands and his feet.
41 While they were still incredulous for joy and
were amazed, he asked them, "Have you anything here to eat?" 42 [s]They gave him a piece
of baked fish; 43 he took it and ate it in front
of them.

44 [t]He said to them, "These are my words
that I spoke to you while I was still with you,
that everything written about me in the law of
Moses and in the prophets and psalms must be
fulfilled." 45 [u]Then he opened their minds to
understand the scriptures. 46 [v]*And he said to
them, "Thus it is written that the Messiah
would suffer and rise from the dead on the third
day 47 [w]and that repentance, for the forgiveness of sins, would be preached in his name to
all the nations, beginning from Jerusalem.
48 [x]You are witnesses of these things.
49 [y]*And [behold] I am sending the promise of
my Father upon you; but stay in the city until
you are clothed with power from on high."

**The Ascension** 50 [z]*Then he led them
[out] as far as Bethany, raised his hands, and
blessed them. 51 As he blessed them he parted
from them and was taken up to heaven.
52 [a]They did him homage and then returned to
Jerusalem with great joy, 53 *and they were
continually in the temple praising God.

---

n 1 Cor 15, 4-5.
o Mk 16, 14-19; Jn 20, 19-20.
p 1 Cor 15, 5.
q Mt 14, 26.
r Jn 21, 5.9-10.13.
s Acts 10, 41.
t 18, 31; 24, 27; Mt 16, 21; Jn 5, 39.46.
u Jn 20, 9.
v 9, 22; Is 53; Hos 6, 2.
w Mt 3, 2; 28, 19-20; Mk 16, 15-16; Acts 10, 41.
x Acts 1, 8.
y Jn 14, 26; Acts 1, 4; 2, 3-4.
z Mk 16, 19; Acts 1, 9-11.
a Acts 1, 12.

---

24, 36–43.44–49: The Gospel of Luke, like each of the other gospels (Mt 28, 16–20; Mk 16, 14–15; Jn 20, 19–23), focuses on an important appearance of Jesus to the Twelve in which they are commissioned for their future ministry. As in vv 6 and 12, so in vv 36 and 40 there are omissions in the Western text.

24, 39–42: The apologetic purpose of this story is evident in the concern with the physical details and the report that Jesus ate food.

24, 46: See the note on 24, 26.

24, 49: *The promise of my Father:* i.e., the gift of the holy Spirit.

24, 50–53: Luke brings his story about the time of Jesus to a close with the report of the ascension. He will also begin the story of the time of the church with a recounting of the ascension. In the gospel, Luke recounts the ascension of Jesus on Easter Sunday night, thereby closely associating it with the resurrection. In Acts (1, 3.9–11; 13, 31) he historicizes the ascension by speaking of a forty-day period between the resurrection and the ascension. The Western text omits some phrases in vv 51 and 52, perhaps to avoid any chronological conflict with Acts 1 about the time of the ascension.

24, 53: The Gospel of Luke ends as it began (1, 9), in the Jerusalem temple.

# THE GOSPEL ACCORDING TO

# JOHN

*The Gospel according to John is quite different in character from the three synoptic gospels. It is highly literary and symbolic. It does not follow the same order or reproduce the same stories as the synoptic gospels. To a much greater degree, it is the product of a developed theological reflection and grows out of a different circle and tradition. It was probably written in 90's of the first century.*

*The Gospel of John begins with a magnificent prologue, which states many of the major themes and motifs of the gospel, much as an overture does for a musical work. The prologue proclaims Jesus as the preexistent and incarnate Word of God who has revealed the Father to us. The rest of the first chapter forms the introduction to the gospel proper and consists of the Baptist's testimony about Jesus (there is no baptism of Jesus in this gospel—John simply points him out as the Lamb of God), followed by stories of the call of the first disciples, in which various titles predicated of Jesus in the early church are presented.*

*The gospel narrative contains a series of "signs"—the gospel's word for the wondrous deeds of Jesus. The author is primarily interested in the significance of these deeds, and so interprets them for the reader by various reflections, narratives, and discourses. The first sign is the transformation of water into wine at Cana (2, 1–11); this represents the replacement of the Jewish ceremonial washings and symbolizes the entire creative and transforming work of Jesus. The second sign, the cure of the royal official's son (4, 46–54) simply by the word of Jesus at a distance, signifies the power of Jesus' life-giving word. The same theme is further developed by other signs, probably for a total of seven. The third sign, the cure of the paralytic at the pool with five porticoes in ch 5, continues the theme of water offering newness of life. In the preceding chapter, to the woman at the well in Samaria Jesus had offered living water springing up to eternal life, a symbol of the revelation that Jesus brings; here Jesus' life-giving word replaces the water of the pool that failed to bring life. Chapter 6 contains two signs, the multiplication of loaves and the walking on the waters of the Sea of Galilee. These signs are connected much as the manna and the crossing of the Red Sea are in the Passover narrative and symbolize a new exodus. The multiplication of the loaves is interpreted for the reader by the discourse that follows, where the bread of life is used first as a figure for the revelation of God in Jesus and then for the Eucharist. After a series of dialogues reflecting Jesus' debates with the Jewish authorities at the Feast of Tabernacles in chs 7 and 8, the sixth sign is presented in ch 9, the sign of the young man born blind. This is a narrative illustration of the theme of conflict in the preceding two chapters; it proclaims the triumph of light over darkness, as Jesus is presented as the Light of the world. This is interpreted by a narrative of controversy between the Pharisees and the young man who had been given his sight by Jesus, ending with a discussion of spiritual blindness and spelling out the symbolic meaning of the cure. And finally, the seventh sign, the raising of Lazarus in ch 11, is the climax of signs. Lazarus is presented as a token of the real life that Jesus, the Resurrection and the Life, who will now ironically be put to death because of his gift of life to Lazarus, will give to all who believe in him once he has been raised from the dead.*

*After the account of the seven signs, the "hour" of Jesus arrives, and the author passes from sign to reality, as he moves into the discourses in the upper room that interpret the meaning of the passion, death, and resurrection narratives that follow. The whole gospel of John is a progressive revelation of the glory of God's only Son, who comes to reveal the Father and then returns in glory to the Father. The author's purpose is clearly expressed in what must have been the original ending of the gospel at the end of ch 20: "Now Jesus did many other signs in the presence of [his] disciples that are not written in this book. But these are written that you may [come to] believe that Jesus is the Messiah, the Son of God, and that through this belief you may have life in his name."*

*Critical analysis makes it difficult to accept the idea that the gospel as it now stands was written by one person. Chapter 21 seems to have been added after the gospel was completed; it exhibits a Greek style somewhat different from that of the rest of the work. The prologue (1, 1–18) apparently contains an independent hymn, subsequently adapted to serve as a preface to the gospel. Within the gospel itself there are also some inconsistencies, e.g., there are two endings of Jesus' discourse in the upper room (14, 31; 18, 1). To solve these problems, scholars have proposed various rearrangements that would produce a smoother order. However, most have come to the conclusion that the inconsistencies were probably produced by subsequent editing in which homogeneous materials were added to a shorter original.*

*Other difficulties for any theory of eyewitness authorship of the gospel in its present form are presented by its highly developed theology and by certain elements of its literary style. For instance, some of the wondrous deeds of Jesus have been worked into highly effective dramatic scenes (ch 9); there has been a careful attempt to have these followed by discourses that explain them (chs 5 and 6); and the sayings of Jesus have been woven into long discourses of a quasi-poetic form resembling the speeches of personified Wisdom in the Old Testament.*

*The gospel contains many details about Jesus not found in the synoptic gospels, e.g., that Jesus engaged in a baptizing ministry (3, 22) before he changed to one of preaching and signs; that Jesus' public ministry lasted for several years (see the note on 2, 13); that he traveled to Jerusalem for various festivals and met serious opposition long before his death (2, 14–25; chs 5 and 7–8); and that he was put to death on the day before Passover (18, 28). These events are not always in chronological order because of the development and editing that took place. However, the accuracy of much of the detail of the fourth gospel constitutes a strong argument that the Johannine tradition rests upon the testimony of an eyewitness. Although tradition identified this person as John, the son of Zebedee, most modern scholars find that the evidence does not support this.*

*The fourth gospel is not simply history; the narrative has been organized and adapted to serve the evangelist's theological purposes as well. Among them are the opposition to the synagogue of the day and to John the Baptist's followers, who tried to exalt their master at Jesus' expense, the desire to show that Jesus was the Messiah, and the desire to convince Christians that their religious belief and practice must be rooted in Jesus. Such theological purposes have impelled the evangelist to emphasize motifs that were not so clear in the synoptic account of Jesus' ministry, e.g., the explicit emphasis on his divinity.*

*The polemic between synagogue and church produced bitter and harsh invective, especially regarding the hostility toward Jesus of the authorities—Pharisees and Sadducees—who are combined and referred to frequently as "the Jews" (see the note on 1, 19). These opponents are even described in 8, 44 as springing from their father the devil, whose conduct they imitate in opposing God by rejecting Jesus, whom God has sent. On the other hand, the author of this gospel seems to take pains to show that women are not inferior to men in the Christian community: the woman at the well in Samaria (ch 4) is presented as a prototype of a missionary (4, 4–42), and the first witness of the resurrection is a woman (20, 11–18).*

*The final editing of the gospel and arrangement in its present form probably dates from between A.D. 90 and 100. Traditionally, Ephesus has been favored as the place of composition, though many support a location in Syria, perhaps the city of Antioch, while some have suggested other places, including Alexandria.*

*The principal divisions of the Gospel according to John are the following:*

*I. Prologue (1, 1–18)*
*II. The Book of Signs (1, 19—12, 50)*
*III. The Book of Glory (13, 1—20, 31)*
*IV. Epilogue: The Resurrection Appearance in Galilee (21, 1–25)*

# I: PROLOGUE

## CHAPTER 1

1 [a]*In the beginning was the Word,
and the Word was with God,
and the Word was God.
2 He was in the beginning with God.
3 [b]*All things came to be through him,
and without him nothing came to be.
What came to be 4 [c]through him was life,
and this life was the light of the human
race;
5 [d]*the light shines in the darkness,
and the darkness has not overcome it.

6 [e]*A man named John was sent from God.
7 [f]*He came for testimony, to testify to the
light, so that all might believe through him.
8 [g]He was not the light, but came to testify to
the light. 9 [h]The true light, which enlightens
everyone, was coming into the world.

10 He was in the world,
and the world came to be through him,
but the world did not know him.
11 *He came to what was his own,
but his own people did not accept him.

12 [i]But to those who did accept him he gave
power to become children of God, to those who
believe in his name, 13 [j]*who were born not by
natural generation nor by human choice nor by
a man's decision but of God.

14 [k]*And the Word became flesh
and made his dwelling among us,
and we saw his glory,
the glory as of the Father's only Son,
full of grace and truth.

15 [l]*John testified to him and cried out, saying, "This was he of whom I said, 'The one
who is coming after me ranks ahead of me because he existed before me.'" 16 *From his
fullness we have all received, grace in place of
grace, 17 [m]because while the law was given
through Moses, grace and truth came through
Jesus Christ. 18 [n]*No one has ever seen God.

a 10, 30; Gn 1, 1-5; Jb 28, 12-27; Prv 8, 22-25; Wis 9, 1-2;1 Jn 1, 1-2; Col 1, 1.15; Rv 3, 14; 19, 13.
b Ps 33, 9; Wis 9, 1; Sir 42, 15; 1 Cor 8, 6; Col 1, 16; Heb 1, 2; Rv 3, 14.
c 5, 26; 8, 12; 1 Jn 1, 2.
d 3, 19; 8, 12; 9, 5; 12, 35.46; Wis 7, 29-30; 1 Thes 5, 4; 1 Jn 2, 8.
e Mt 3, 1; Mk 1, 4; Lk 3, 2-3.
f 1, 19-34; 5, 33.
g 5, 35.
h 3, 19; 8, 12; 9, 39; 12, 46.
i 3, 11-12; 5, 43-44; 12, 46-50; Gal 3, 26; 4, 6-7; Eph 1, 5;1 Jn 3, 2.
j 3, 5-6.
k Ex 16, 10; 24, 17; 25, 8-9; 33, 22; 34, 6; Sir 24, 4.8; Is 60, 1; Ez 43, 7; Jl 4, 17; Hb 2, 14; 1 Jn 1, 2; 4, 2; 2 Jn 7.
l 1, 30; 3, 27-30.
m 7, 19; Ex 31, 18; 34, 28.
n 5, 37; 6, 46; Ex 33, 20; Jgs 13, 21-22; 1 Tm 6, 16; 1 Jn 4, 12.

*

1, 1–18: The prologue states the main themes of the gospel: life, light, truth, the world, testimony, and the preexistence of Jesus Christ, the incarnate *Logos,* who reveals God the Father. In origin, it was probably an early Christian hymn. Its closest parallel is in other christological hymns, Col 1, 15–20 and Phil 2, 6–11. Its core (1–5.10–11.14) is poetic in structure, with short phrases linked by "staircase parallelism," in which the last word of one phrase becomes the first word of the next. Prose inserts (at least 6–8 and 15) deal with John the Baptist.

1, 1: *In the beginning:* also the first words of the Old Testament (Gn 1, 1). *Was:* this verb is used three times with different meanings in this verse: existence, relationship, and predication. *The Word* (Greek *logos*): this term combines God's dynamic, creative word (Genesis), personified preexistent Wisdom as the instrument of God's creative activity (Proverbs), and the ultimate intelligibility of reality (Hellenistic philosophy). *With God:* the Greek preposition here connotes communication with another. *Was God:* lack of a definite article with "God" in Greek signifies predication rather than identification.

1, 3: *What came to be:* while the oldest manuscripts have no punctuation here, the corrector of Bodmer Papyrus $P^{75}$, some manuscripts, and the Ante-Nicene Fathers take this phrase with what follows, as staircase parallelism. Connection with v 3 reflects fourth-century anti-Arianism.

1, 5: The ethical dualism of light and darkness is paralleled in intertestamental literature and in the Dead Sea Scrolls. *Overcome:* "comprehend" is another possible translation, but cf 12, 35; Wis 7, 29–30.

1, 6: John was *sent* just as Jesus was "sent" (4, 34) in divine mission. Other references to John the Baptist in this gospel emphasize the differences between them and John's subordinate role.

1, 7: *Testimony:* the testimony theme of Jn is introduced, which portrays Jesus as if on trial throughout his ministry. All testify to Jesus: John the Baptist, the Samaritan woman, scripture, his works, the crowds, the Spirit, and his disciples.

1, 11: *What was his own . . . his own people:* first a neuter, literally, "his own property = possession" (probably-Israel), then a masculine, "his own people" (the Israelites).

1, 13: Believers in Jesus become children of God not through any of the three natural causes mentioned but through God who is the immediate cause of the new spiritual life. *Were born:* the Greek verb can mean "begotten" (by a male) or "born" (from a female or of parents). The variant "he who was begotten," asserting Jesus' virginal conception, is weakly attested in Old Latin and Syriac versions.

1, 14: *Flesh:* the whole person, used probably against docetic tendencies (cf 1 Jn 4, 2; 2 Jn 7). *Made his dwelling.* literally, "pitched his tent/tabernacle." Cf the tabernacle or tent of meeting that was the place of God's presence among his people (Ex 25, 8–9). The incarnate Word is the new mode of God's presence among his people. The Greek verb has the same consonants as the Aramaic word for God's presence (Shekinah). *Glory:* God's visible manifestation of majesty in power, which once filled the tabernacle (Ex 40, 34) and the temple (1 Kgs 8, 10–11.27), is now centered in Jesus. *Only Son:* Greek, *monogenēs,* but see the note on 1, 18. *Grace and truth:* these words may represent two Old Testament terms describing Yahweh in covenant relationship with Israel (cf Ex 34, 6), thus God's "love" and "fidelity." The Word shares Yahweh's covenant qualities.

1, 15: This verse, interrupting vv 14 and 16, seems drawn from v 30.

1, 16: *Grace in place of grace:* replacement of the Old Covenant with the New (cf 17). Other possible translations are "grace upon grace" (accumulation) and "grace for grace" (correspondence).

1, 18: *The only Son, God:* while the vast majority of later textual witnesses have another reading, "the Son, the only one" or "the only Son," the translation above follows the best and earliest manuscripts, *monogenēs theos,* but takes the first term to mean not just "Only One" but to include a filial relationship with the Father, as at Lk 9, 38 ("only child") or Heb 11, 17 ("only son") and as translated at Jn 1, 14. The Logos is thus

The only Son, God, who is at the Father's side,
has revealed him.

# *II: THE BOOK OF SIGNS*

## John the Baptist's Testimony to Himself

**19** *And this is the testimony of John.
When the Jews from Jerusalem sent priests and
Levites [to him] to ask him, "Who are you?"
**20** [o]*he admitted and did not deny it, but admitted, "I am not the Messiah." **21** [p]*So they
asked him, "What are you then? Are you Elijah?" And he said, "I am not." "Are you the
Prophet?" He answered, "No." **22** So they
said to him, "Who are you, so we can give an
answer to those who sent us? What do you have
to say for yourself?" **23** [q]*He said:

"I am 'the voice of one crying out in the
desert,
"Make straight the way of the Lord," '

as Isaiah the prophet said." **24** *Some Pharisees were also sent. **25** [r]They asked him,
"Why then do you baptize if you are not the
Messiah or Elijah or the Prophet?" **26** [s]*John
answered them, "I baptize with water; but there
is one among you whom you do not recognize,
**27** the one who is coming after me, whose sandal strap I am not worthy to untie." **28** *This
happened in Bethany across the Jordan, where
John was baptizing.

## John the Baptist's Testimony to Jesus

**29** [t]*The next day he saw Jesus coming toward
him and said, "Behold, the Lamb of God, who
takes away the sin of the world. **30** [u]*He is the
one of whom I said, 'A man is coming after me
who ranks ahead of me because he existed before me.' **31** *I did not know him, but the reason why I came baptizing with water was that
he might be made known to Israel." **32** [v]*John
testified further, saying, "I saw the Spirit come
down like a dove from the sky and remain upon
him. **33** [w]I did not know him, but the one who
sent me to baptize with water told me, 'On
whomever you see the Spirit come down and
remain, he is the one who will baptize with the
holy Spirit.' **34** [x]*Now I have seen and testified
that he is the Son of God."

o 3, 28; Lk 3, 15; Acts 13, 25.
p Dt 18, 15.18; 2 Kgs 2, 11; Sir 48, 10; Mal 3, 1.23; Mt 11, 14; 17, 11-13; Mk 9, 13; Acts 3, 22.
q Is 40, 3; Mt 3, 3; Mk 1, 2; Lk 3, 4.
r Ez 36, 25; Zec 13, 1; Mt 16, 14.
s Mt 3, 11; Mk 1, 7-8; Lk 3, 16; Acts 13, 25.
t 1, 36; Ex 12; Is 53, 7; Rv 5-7; 17, 14.
u 1, 15; Mt 3, 11; Mk 1, 7; Lk 3, 16.
v Sg 5, 2; Is 11, 2; Hos 11, 11; Mt 3, 16; Mk 1, 10; Lk 3, 21-22.
w Is 42, 1; Mt 3, 11; Mk 1, 8; Lk 3, 16.
x Is 42, 1; Mt 3, 17; Mk 1, 11; Lk 9, 35.
y Mt 4, 18-22; Mk 1, 16-20; Lk 5, 1-11.

## The First Disciples

**35** [y]The next day John
was there again with two of his disciples,
**36** *and as he watched Jesus walk by, he said,
"Behold, the Lamb of God." **37** *The two dis-

* "only Son" and God but not Father/God.

1, 19–51: The testimony of John the Baptist about the Messiah and Jesus' self-revelation to the first disciples. This section constitutes the introduction to the gospel proper and is connected with the prose inserts in the prologue. It develops the major theme of testimony in four scenes: John's negative testimony about himself; his positive testimony about Jesus; the revelation of Jesus to Andrew and Peter; the revelation of Jesus to Philip and Nathanael.

1, 19: *The Jews:* throughout most of the gospel, the "Jews" does not refer to the Jewish people as such but to the hostile authorities, both Pharisees and Sadducees, particularly in Jerusalem, who refuse to believe in Jesus. The usage reflects the atmosphere, at the end of the first century, of polemics between church and synagogue, or possibly it refers to Jews as representative of a hostile world (10–11).

1, 20: *Messiah:* the anointed agent of Yahweh, usually considered to be of Davidic descent. See further the note on 1, 41.

1, 21: *Elijah:* the Baptist did not claim to be Elijah returned to earth (cf Mal 3, 23; Mt 11, 14). *The Prophet:* probably the prophet like Moses (Dt 18, 15; cf Acts 3, 22).

1, 23: This is a repunctuation and reinterpretation (as in the synoptic gospels and Septuagint) of the Hebrew text of Is 40, 3, which reads, "A voice cries out: In the desert prepare the way of the LORD."

1, 24: *Some Pharisees:* other translations, such as "Now they had been sent from the Pharisees," misunderstand the grammatical construction. This is a different group from that in v 19; the priests and Levites would have been Sadducees, not Pharisees.

1, 26: *I baptize with water:* the synoptics add "but he will baptize you with the holy Spirit" (Mk 1, 8) or ". . . holy Spirit and fire" (Mt 3, 11; Lk 3, 16). John's emphasis is on purification and preparation for a better baptism.

1, 28: *Bethany across the Jordan:* site unknown. Another reading is "Bethabara."

1, 29: *The Lamb of God:* the background for this title may be the victorious apocalyptic lamb who would destroy evil in the world (Rv 5–7; 17, 14); the paschal lamb, whose blood saved Israel (Ex 12); and/or the suffering servant led like a lamb to the slaughter as a sin-offering (Is 53, 7.10).

1, 30: *He existed before me:* possibly as Elijah (to come, 27); for the evangelist and his audience, Jesus' preexistence would be implied (see the note on 1, 1).

1, 31: *I did not know him:* this gospel shows no knowledge of the tradition (Lk 1) about the kinship of Jesus and John the Baptist. *The reason why I came baptizing with water:* in this gospel, John's baptism is not connected with forgiveness of sins; its purpose is revelatory, that Jesus may be made known to Israel.

1, 32: *Like a dove:* a symbol of the new creation (Gn 8, 8) or the community of Israel (Hos 11, 11). *Remain:* the first use of a favorite verb in Jn, emphasizing the permanency of the relationship between Father and Son (as here) and between the Son and the Christian. Jesus is the permanent bearer of the Spirit.

1, 34: *The Son of God:* this reading is supported by good Greek manuscripts, including the Chester Beatty and Bodmer Papyri and the Vatican Codex, but is suspect because it harmonizes this passage with the synoptic version: "This is my beloved Son" (Mt 3, 17; Mk 1, 11; Lk 3, 22). The poorly attested alternate reading, "God's chosen One," is probably a reference to the Servant of Yahweh (Is 42, 1).

1, 36: John the Baptist's testimony makes his disciples' following of Jesus plausible.

1, 37: *The two disciples:* Andrew (40) and, traditionally, John, son of Zebedee (see the note on 13, 23).

ciples heard what he said and followed Jesus.
**38** Jesus turned and saw them following him
and said to them, "What are you looking for?"
They said to him, "Rabbi" (which translated
means Teacher), "where are you staying?"
**39** *He said to them, "Come, and you will
see." So they went and saw where he was staying, and they stayed with him that day. It was
about four in the afternoon. **40** Andrew, the
brother of Simon Peter, was one of the two who
heard John and followed Jesus. **41** [z]*He first
found his own brother Simon and told him,
"We have found the Messiah" (which is translated Anointed). **42** [a]*Then he brought him to
Jesus. Jesus looked at him and said, "You are
Simon the son of John; you will be called Cephas" (which is translated Peter).

**43** *The next day he decided to go to Galilee,
and he found Philip. And Jesus said to him,
"Follow me." **44** Now Philip was from Bethsaida, the town of Andrew and Peter.
**45** [b]Philip found Nathanael and told him, "We
have found the one about whom Moses wrote in
the law, and also the prophets, Jesus, son of
Joseph, from Nazareth." **46** But Nathanael
said to him, "Can anything good come from
Nazareth?" Philip said to him, "Come and
see." **47** *Jesus saw Nathanael coming toward
him and said of him, "Here is a true Israelite.
There is no duplicity in him." **48** [c]*Nathanael
said to him, "How do you know me?" Jesus
answered and said to him, "Before Philip called
you, I saw you under the fig tree."
**49** [d]*Nathanael answered him, "Rabbi, you
are the Son of God; you are the King of Israel."
**50** *Jesus answered and said to him, "Do you
believe because I told you that I saw you under
the fig tree? You will see greater things than
this." **51** [e]*And he said to him, "Amen,
amen, I say to you, you will see the sky opened
and the angels of God ascending and descending
on the Son of Man."

## CHAPTER 2

### The Wedding at Cana

**1** [f]*On the third
day there was a wedding in Cana in Galilee, and
the mother of Jesus was there. **2** Jesus and his
disciples were also invited to the wedding.
**3** When the wine ran short, the mother of Jesus
said to him, "They have no wine." **4** [g]*[And]
Jesus said to her, "Woman, how does your
concern affect me? My hour has not yet come."
**5** [h]His mother said to the servers, "Do whatever he tells you." **6** [i]*Now there were six stone
water jars there for Jewish ceremonial washings, each holding twenty to thirty gallons.
**7** Jesus told them, "Fill the jars with water."
So they filled them to the brim. **8** *Then he told
them, "Draw some out now and take it to the
headwaiter." So they took it. **9** And when the

---

z 4, 25.
a Mt 16, 18; Mk 3, 16.
b 21, 2.
c Mi 4, 4; Zec 3, 10.
d 12, 13; Ex 4, 22; Dt 14, 1; 2 Sm 7, 14; Jb 1, 6; 2, 1; 38, 7; Pss 2, 7; 29, 1; 89, 27; Wis 2, 18; Sir 4, 10; Dn 3, 25;Hos 11, 1; Mt 14, 33; 16, 16; Mk 13, 32.
e Gn 28, 10-17; Dn 7, 13.
f 4, 46; Jgs 14, 12; Tb 11, 8.
g 7, 30; 8, 20; 12, 23; 13, 1; Jgs 11, 12; 1 Kgs 17, 18;2 Kgs 3, 13; 2 Chr 35, 21; Hos 14, 9; Mk 1, 24; 5, 7; 7, 30; 8, 20; 12, 23; 13, 1.
h Gn 41, 55.
i 3, 25; Lv 11, 33; Am 9, 13-14; Mt 15, 2; 23, 25-26; Mk 7, 2-4; Lk 11, 38.

---

1, 39: *Four in the afternoon:* literally, the tenth hour, from sunrise, in the Roman calculation of time. Some suggest that the next day, beginning at sunset, was the sabbath; they would have stayed with Jesus to avoid travel on it.

1, 41: *Messiah:* the Hebrew word *mašîah,* "anointed one" (see the note on Lk 2, 11), appears in Greek as the transliterated *messias* only here and in 4, 25. Elsewhere the Greek translation *christos* is used.

1, 42: *Simon, the son of John:* in Mt 16, 17, Simon is called *Bariōna,* "son of Jonah," a different tradition for the name of Simon's father. *Cephas:* in Aramaic = the Rock; cf Mt 16, 18. Neither the Greek equivalent *Petros* nor, with one isolated exception, *Cephas* is attested as a personal name before Christian times.

1, 43: *He:* grammatically, could be Peter, but logically is probably Jesus.

1, 47: *A true Israelite. There is no duplicity in him:* Jacob was the first to bear the name "Israel" (Gn 32, 29), but Jacob was a man of duplicity (Gn 27, 35–36).

1, 48: *Under the fig tree:* a symbol of messianic peace (cf Mi 4, 4; Zec 3, 10).

1, 49: *Son of God:* this title is used in the Old Testament, among other ways, as a title of adoption for the Davidic king (2 Sm 7, 14; Pss 2, 7; 89, 27), and thus here, with *King of Israel,* in a messianic sense. For the evangelist, Son of God also points to Jesus' divinity (cf 20, 28).

1, 50: Possibly a statement: "You [singular] believe because I saw you under the fig tree."

1, 51: The double "Amen" is characteristic of John. *You* is plural in Greek. The allusion is to Jacob's ladder (Gn 28, 12).

2, 1—6, 71: Signs revealing Jesus as the Messiah to all Israel. "Sign" (*sēmeion*) is John's symbolic term for Jesus' wondrous deeds (see Introduction). The Old Testament background lies in the Exodus story (cf Dt 11, 3; 29, 2). John is interested primarily in what the *sēmeia* signify: God's intervention in human history in a new way through Jesus.

2, 1–11: The first sign. This story of replacement of Jewish ceremonial washings (6) presents the initial revelation about Jesus at the outset of his ministry. He manifests his glory; the disciples believe. There is no synoptic parallel.

2, 1: *Cana:* unknown from the Old Testament. *The mother of Jesus:* she is never named in John.

2, 4: This verse may seek to show that Jesus did not work miracles to help his family and friends, as in the apocryphal gospels. *Woman:* a normal, polite form of address, but unattested in reference to one's mother. Cf also 19, 26. *How does your concern affect me?:* literally, "What is this to me and to you?"—a Hebrew expression of either hostility (Jgs 11, 12; 2 Chr 35, 21; 1 Kgs 17, 18) or denial of common interest (Hos 14, 9; 2 Kgs 3, 13). Cf Mk 1, 24; 5, 7, used by demons to Jesus. *My hour has not yet come:* the translation as a question ("Has not my hour now come?"), while preferable grammatically and supported by Greek Fathers, seems unlikely from a comparison with 7, 6.30. The "hour" is that of Jesus' passion, death, resurrection, and ascension (13, 1).

2, 6: *Twenty to thirty gallons:* literally, "two or three measures"; the Attic liquid measure contained 39.39 liters. The vast quantity recalls prophecies of abundance in the last days; cf Am 9, 13–14; Hos 14, 7; Jer 31, 12.

2, 8: *Headwaiter:* used of the official who managed a ban-

headwaiter tasted the water that had become
wine, without knowing where it came from (although the servers who had drawn the water
knew), the headwaiter called the bridegroom
10 and said to him, "Everyone serves good
wine first, and then when people have drunk
freely, an inferior one; but you have kept the
good wine until now." 11 [j]*Jesus did this as
the beginning of his signs in Cana in Galilee and
so revealed his glory, and his disciples began to
believe in him.
12 *After this, he and his mother, [his]
brothers, and his disciples went down to Capernaum and stayed there only a few days.

**Cleansing of the Temple** 13 [k]*Since the
Passover of the Jews was near, Jesus went up to
Jerusalem. 14 [l]*He found in the temple area
those who sold oxen, sheep, and doves, as well
as the money-changers seated there. 15 He
made a whip out of cords and drove them all out
of the temple area, with the sheep and oxen, and
spilled the coins of the money-changers and
overturned their tables, 16 [m]and to those who
sold doves he said, "Take these out of here, and
stop making my Father's house a marketplace."
17 [n]*His disciples recalled the words of scripture, "Zeal for your house will consume me."
18 [o]At this the Jews answered and said to him,
"What sign can you show us for doing this?"
19 [p]*Jesus answered and said to them, "Destroy this temple and in three days I will raise
it up." 20 *The Jews said, "This temple has
been under construction for forty-six years, and
you will raise it up in three days?" 21 But he
was speaking about the temple of his body.
22 [q]Therefore, when he was raised from the
dead, his disciples remembered that he had said
this, and they came to believe the scripture and
the word Jesus had spoken.
23 [r]While he was in Jerusalem for the feast
of Passover, many began to believe in his name
when they saw the signs he was doing. 24 But
Jesus would not trust himself to them because
he knew them all, 25 [s]and did not need anyone
to testify about human nature. He himself understood it well.

## CHAPTER 3

**Nicodemus** 1 [t]*Now there was a Pharisee
named Nicodemus, a ruler of the Jews. 2 [u]He
came to Jesus at night and said to him, "Rabbi,
we know that you are a teacher who has come
from God, for no one can do these signs that you
are doing unless God is with him." 3 *Jesus
answered and said to him, "Amen, amen, I say
to you, no one can see the kingdom of God
without being born from above."
4 [v]Nicodemus said to him, "How can a person
once grown old be born again? Surely he cannot
reenter his mother's womb and be born again,
can he?" 5 [w]Jesus answered, "Amen, amen, I
say to you, no one can enter the kingdom of God
without being born of water and Spirit.

j 4, 54.
k Mt 21, 12-13; Mk 11, 15-17; Lk 19, 45-46.
l Ex 30, 11-16; Lv 5, 7.
m Zec 14, 21.
n Ps 69, 9.
o 6, 30.
p Mt 24, 2; 26, 61; 27, 40; Mk 13, 2; 14, 58; 15, 29; Lk 21, 6; Acts 6, 14.
q 5, 39; 12, 16; 14, 26; 20, 9; Mt 12, 6; Lk 24, 6-8; Rv 21, 22.
r 4, 45.
s 1 Kgs 8, 39; Pss 33, 15; 94, 11; Sir 42, 18; Jer 17, 10; 20, 12.
t 7, 50-51; 19, 39.
u 9, 4.16.33; 10, 21; 11, 10; 13, 30; Mt 22, 16; Mk 12, 14; Lk 20, 21.
v 1, 13.
w 1, 32; 7, 39; 19, 30.34-35; Is 32, 15; 44, 3; Ez 36, 25-27; Jl 3, 1-2.

*

quet, but there is no evidence of such a functionary in Palestine. Perhaps here a friend of the family acted as master of ceremonies; cf Sir 32, 1.

2, 11: *The beginning of his signs:* the first of seven (see Introduction).

2, 12—3, 21: The next three episodes take place in Jerusalem. Only the first is paralleled in the synoptic gospels.

2, 12: This transitional verse may be a harmonization with the synoptic tradition in Lk 4, 31 and Mt 4, 13. There are many textual variants. John depicts no extended ministry in Capernaum as do the synoptics.

2, 13–22: This episode indicates the post-resurrectional replacement of the temple by the person of Jesus.

2, 13: *Passover:* this is the first Passover mentioned in John; a second is mentioned in 6, 4, a third in 13, 1. Taken literally, they point to a ministry of at least two years.

2, 14–22: The other gospels place the cleansing of the temple in the last days of Jesus' life (Mt, on the day Jesus entered Jerusalem; Mk, on the next day). The order of events in the gospel narratives is often determined by theological motives rather than by chronological data.

2, 14: *Oxen, sheep, and doves:* intended for sacrifice. The doves were the offerings of the poor (Lv 5, 7). *Money-changers:* for a temple tax paid by every male Jew more than nineteen years of age, with a half-shekel coin (Ex 30, 11–16), in Tyrian currency. See the note on Mt 17, 24.

2, 17: Ps 69, 10, changed to future tense to apply to Jesus.

2, 19: This saying about the destruction of the temple occurs in various forms (Mt 24, 2; 27, 40; Mk 13, 2; 15, 29; Lk 21, 6; cf Acts 6, 14). Mt 26, 61 has: "I *can* destroy the temple of God . . ."; see the note there. In Mk 14, 58, there is a metaphorical contrast with a new temple: "I will destroy this temple *made with hands* and within three days I will build another *not made with hands.*" Here it is symbolic of Jesus' resurrection and the resulting community (see 21 and Rv 21, 2). *In three days:* an Old Testament expression for a short, indefinite period of time; cf Hos 6, 2.

2, 20: *Forty-six years:* based on references in Josephus (*Jewish Wars* 1, 21, 1 #401; *Antiquities* 15, 11, 1 ¶380), possibly the spring of A.D. 28. Cf the note on Lk 3, 1.

3, 1–21: Jesus instructs Nicodemus on the necessity of a new birth from above. This scene in Jerusalem at Passover exemplifies the faith engendered by signs (2, 23). It continues the self-manifestation of Jesus in Jerusalem begun in ch 2. This is the first of the Johannine discourses, shifting from dialogue to monologue (11–15) to reflection of the evangelist (16–21). The shift from singular through v 10 to plural in v 11 may reflect the early church's controversy with the Jews.

3, 1: *A ruler of the Jews:* most likely a member of the Jewish council, the Sanhedrin; see the note on Mk 8, 31.

3, 3: *Born:* see the note on 1, 13. *From above:* the Greek adverb *anōthen* means both "from above" and "again." Jesus means "from above" (see 31), but Nicodemus misunderstands it as "again." This misunderstanding serves as a springboard for further instruction.

**6** [x]What is born of flesh is flesh and what is
born of spirit is spirit. **7** Do not be amazed that
I told you, 'You must be born from above.'
**8** [y]*The wind blows where it wills, and you can
hear the sound it makes, but you do not know
where it comes from or where it goes; so it is
with everyone who is born of the Spirit."
**9** Nicodemus answered and said to him, "How
can this happen?" **10** Jesus answered and said
to him, "You are the teacher of Israel and you
do not understand this? **11** [z]Amen, amen, I say
to you, we speak of what we know and we
testify to what we have seen, but you people do
not accept our testimony. **12** [a]If I tell you about
earthly things and you do not believe, how will
you believe if I tell you about heavenly things?
**13** [b]No one has gone up to heaven except the
one who has come down from heaven, the Son
of Man. **14** [c]*And just as Moses lifted up the
serpent in the desert, so must the Son of Man be
lifted up, **15** *so that everyone who believes in
him may have eternal life."

**16** [d]*For God so loved the world that he
gave his only Son, so that everyone who believes in him might not perish but might have
eternal life. **17** [e]*For God did not send his Son
into the world to condemn the world, but that
the world might be saved through him.
**18** [f]Whoever believes in him will not be condemned, but whoever does not believe has already been condemned, because he has not believed in the name of the only Son of God.
**19** [g]*And this is the verdict, that the light came
into the world, but people preferred darkness to
light, because their works were evil. **20** [h]For
everyone who does wicked things hates the light
and does not come toward the light, so that his
works might not be exposed. **21** [i]But whoever
lives the truth comes to the light, so that his
works may be clearly seen as done in God.

## Final Witness of the Baptist

**22** [j]*After
this, Jesus and his disciples went into the region
of Judea, where he spent some time with them
baptizing. **23** *John was also baptizing in Aenon near Salim, because there was an abundance of water there, and people came to be
baptized, **24** [k]*for John had not yet been imprisoned. **25** *Now a dispute arose between the
disciples of John and a Jew about ceremonial
washings. **26** [l]So they came to John and said to
him, "Rabbi, the one who was with you across
the Jordan, to whom you testified, here he is
baptizing and everyone is coming to him."
**27** [m]John answered and said, "No one can receive anything except what has been given him
from heaven. **28** [n]You yourselves can testify
that I said [that] I am not the Messiah, but that
I was sent before him. **29** [o]*The one who has
the bride is the bridegroom; the best man, who
stands and listens for him, rejoices greatly at the
bridegroom's voice. So this joy of mine has
been made complete. **30** [p]He must increase; I
must decrease."

## The One from Heaven

**31** [q]*The one who
comes from above is above all. The one who is
of the earth is earthly and speaks of earthly
things. But the one who comes from heaven [is
above all]. **32** [r]He testifies to what he has seen
and heard, but no one accepts his testimony.
**33** [s]Whoever does accept his testimony certi-
fies that God is trustworthy. **34** *For the one
whom God sent speaks the words of God. He

x 6, 63; 1 Cor 15, 44-50.
y Eccl 11, 4-5; Acts 2, 2-4.
z 3, 32.34; 8, 14; Mt 11, 27.
a 6, 62-65; Wis 9, 16-17; 1 Cor 15, 40; 2 Cor 5, 1; Phil 2, 10; 3, 19-20.
b 1, 18; 6, 62; Dn 7, 13; Rom 10, 6; Eph 4, 9.
c 8, 28; 12, 32.34; Nm 21, 4-9; Wis 16, 5-7.
d 1 Jn 4, 9.
e 5, 22.30; 8, 15-18; 12, 47.
f 5, 24; Mk 16, 16.
g 1, 5.9-11; 8, 12; 9, 5.
h Jb 24, 13-17.
i Gn 47, 29 LXX; Jos 2, 14 LXX; 2 Sm 2, 6 LXX; 15, 20 LXX; Tb 4, 6 LXX; 13, 6; Is 26, 10 LXX; Mt 5, 14-16.
j 4, 1-2.
k Mt 4, 12; 14, 3; Mk 1, 14; 6, 17; Lk 3, 20.
l 1, 26.32-34.36.
m 19, 11; 1 Cor 4, 7; 2 Cor 3, 5; Heb 5, 4.
n 1, 20-23; Lk 3, 15.
o 15, 11; 17, 13; Mt 9, 15.
p 2 Sm 3, 1.
q 8, 23.
r 3, 11.
s 8, 26; 12, 44-50; 1 Jn 5, 10.

*

3, 8: *Wind:* the Greek word *pneuma* (as well as the Hebrew rûah) means both "wind" and "spirit." In the play on the double meaning, "wind" is primary.

3, 14: *Lifted up:* in Nm 21, 9, Moses simply "mounted" a serpent upon a pole. John here substitutes a verb implying glorification. Jesus, exalted to glory at his cross and resurrection, represents healing for all.

3, 15: *Eternal life:* used here for the first time in John, this term stresses quality of life rather than duration.

3, 16: *Gave:* as a gift in the incarnation, and also "over to death" in the crucifixion; cf Rom 8, 32.

3, 17–19: *Condemn:* the Greek root means both judgment and condemnation. Jesus' purpose is to save, but his coming provokes judgment; some condemn themselves by turning from the light.

3, 19: Judgment is not only future but is partially realized here and now.

3, 22–26: Jesus' ministry in Judea is only loosely connected with 2, 13—3, 21; cf 1, 19–36. Perhaps John the Baptist's further testimony was transposed here to give meaning to "water" in v 5. Jesus is depicted as baptizing (22); contrast 4, 2.

3, 23: *Aenon near Salim:* site uncertain, either in the upper Jordan valley or in Samaria.

3, 24: A remark probably intended to avoid objections based on a chronology like that of the synoptics (Mt 4, 12; Mk 1, 14).

3, 25: *A Jew:* some think Jesus is meant. Many manuscripts read "Jews."

3, 29: *The best man:* literally, "the friend of the groom," the *shoshben* of Jewish tradition, who arranged the wedding. Competition between him and the groom would be unthinkable.

3, 31–36: It is uncertain whether these are words by the Baptist, Jesus, or the evangelist. They are reflections on the two preceding scenes.

3, 34: *His gift:* of God or to Jesus, perhaps both. This verse echoes vv 5 and 8.

does not ration his gift of the Spirit. **35** [t]The
Father loves the Son and has given everything
over to him. **36** [u]Whoever believes in the Son
has eternal life, but whoever disobeys the Son
will not see life, but the wrath of God remains
upon him.

## CHAPTER 4

**1** *Now when Jesus learned that the Pharisees had heard that Jesus was making and baptizing more disciples than John **2** *(although
Jesus himself was not baptizing, just his disciples), **3** he left Judea and returned to Galilee.

### The Samaritan Woman

**4** *He had to pass
through Samaria. **5** [v]*So he came to a town of
Samaria called Sychar, near the plot of land that
Jacob had given to his son Joseph. **6** Jacob's
well was there. Jesus, tired from his journey, sat
down there at the well. It was about noon.

**7** A woman of Samaria came to draw water.
Jesus said to her, "Give me a drink." **8** His
disciples had gone into the town to buy food.
**9** [w]*The Samaritan woman said to him, "How
can you, a Jew, ask me, a Samaritan woman, for
a drink?" (For Jews use nothing in common
with Samaritans.) **10** [x]*Jesus answered and
said to her, "If you knew the gift of God and
who is saying to you, 'Give me a drink,' you
would have asked him and he would have given
you living water." **11** *[The woman] said to
him, "Sir, you do not even have a bucket and
the cistern is deep; where then can you get this
living water? **12** [y]Are you greater than our father Jacob, who gave us this cistern and drank
from it himself with his children and his
flocks?" **13** Jesus answered and said to her,
"Everyone who drinks this water will be thirsty
again; **14** [z]but whoever drinks the water I shall
give will never thirst; the water I shall give will
become in him a spring of water welling up to
eternal life." **15** The woman said to him, "Sir,
give me this water, so that I may not be thirsty
or have to keep coming here to draw water."

**16** Jesus said to her, "Go call your husband
and come back." **17** The woman answered and
said to him, "I do not have a husband." Jesus
answered her, "You are right in saying, 'I do
not have a husband.' **18** [a]For you have had
five husbands, and the one you have now is not
your husband. What you have said is true."
**19** [b]The woman said to him, "Sir, I can see
that you are a prophet. **20** [c]*Our ancestors worshiped on this mountain; but you people say that
the place to worship is in Jerusalem." **21** Jesus
said to her, "Believe me, woman, the hour is
coming when you will worship the Father neither on this mountain nor in Jerusalem.
**22** [d]You people worship what you do not understand; we worship what we understand, because salvation is from the Jews. **23** *But the
hour is coming, and is now here, when true
worshipers will worship the Father in Spirit and
truth; and indeed the Father seeks such people
to worship him. **24** [e]God is Spirit, and those
who worship him must worship in Spirit and
truth." **25** [f]*The woman said to him, "I know
that the Messiah is coming, the one called the
Anointed; when he comes, he will tell us everything." **26** [g]*Jesus said to her, "I am he, the
one who is speaking with you."

**27** *At that moment his disciples returned,
and were amazed that he was talking with a
woman, but still no one said, "What are you
looking for?" or "Why are you talking with
her?" **28** The woman left her water jar and
went into the town and said to the people,
**29** "Come see a man who told me everything
I have done. Could he possibly be the Messi-

---

t 13, 3; Mt 11, 27; 28, 18; Lk 10, 22.
u 3, 16; 1 Jn 5, 13.
v Gn 33, 18-19; 48, 22; Jos 24, 32.
w Sir 50, 25-26; Mt 10, 5.
x Sir 24, 20-21; Is 55, 1; Jer 2, 13.
y 8, 53; Mt 12, 41.
z 6, 35.58; 7, 37-39; Is 44, 3; 49, 10; Jl 4, 18; Rv 7, 16; 21, 6.
a 2 Kgs 17, 24-34.
b 9, 17; Hos 1, 3.
c Dt 11, 29; 27, 4; Jos 8, 33; Ps 122, 1-5.
d 2 Kgs 17, 27; Ps 76, 2-3.
e 2 Cor 3, 17.
f 1, 41.
g 9, 37.

---

4, 1–42: Jesus in Samaria. The self-revelation of Jesus continues with his second discourse, on his mission to "half-Jews." It continues the theme of replacement, here with regard to cult (21). Water (7–15) serves as a symbol (as at Cana and in the Nicodemus episode).

4, 2: An editorial refinement of 3, 22, perhaps directed against followers of John the Baptist who claimed that Jesus imitated him.

4, 4: *He had to:* a theological necessity; geographically, Jews often bypassed Samaria by taking a route across the Jordan.

4, 5: *Sychar:* Jerome identifies this with Shechem, a reading found in Syriac manuscripts.

4, 9: Samaritan women were regarded by Jews as ritually impure, and therefore Jews were forbidden to drink from any vessel they had handled.

4, 10: *Living water:* the water of life, i.e., the revelation that Jesus brings; the woman thinks of "flowing water," so much more desirable than stagnant cistern water. On John's device of such misunderstanding, cf the note on 3, 3.

4, 11: *Sir:* the Greek *kyrios* means "master" or "lord," as a respectful mode of address for a human being or a deity; cf 4, 19. It is also the word used in the Septuagint for the Hebrew *'ădônai*, substituted for the tetragrammaton YHWH.

4, 20: *This mountain:* Gerizim, on which a temple was erected in the fourth century B.C. by Samaritans to rival Mt. Zion in Jerusalem; cf Dt 27, 4 (Mt. Ebal = the Jews' term for Gerizim).

4, 23: *In Spirit and truth:* not a reference to an interior worship within one's own spirit. The Spirit is the spirit given by God that reveals truth and enables one to worship God appropriately (14, 16–17). Cf "born of water and Spirit" (3, 5).

4, 25: The expectations of the Samaritans are expressed here in Jewish terminology. They did not expect a messianic king of the house of David but a prophet like Moses (Dt 18, 15).

4, 26: *I am he:* it could also be translated "I am," an Old Testament self-designation of Yahweh (Is 43, 3, etc.); cf 6, 20; 8, 24.28.58; 13, 19; 18, 5.6.8. See the note on Mk 6, 50.

4, 27: *Talking with a woman:* a religious and social restriction that Jesus is pictured treating as unimportant.

ah?" 30 They went out of the town and came to him. 31 Meanwhile, the disciples urged him, "Rabbi, eat." 32 But he said to them, "I have food to eat of which you do not know." 33 So the disciples said to one another, "Could someone have brought him something to eat?" 34 [h]Jesus said to them, "My food is to do the will of the one who sent me and to finish his work. 35 [i]*Do you not say, 'In four months the harvest will be here'? I tell you, look up and see the fields ripe for the harvest. 36 [j]*The reaper is already receiving his payment and gathering crops for eternal life, so that the sower and reaper can rejoice together. 37 [k]For here the saying is verified that 'One sows and another reaps.' 38 I sent you to reap what you have not worked for; others have done the work, and you are sharing the fruits of their work."

39 *Many of the Samaritans of that town began to believe in him because of the word of the woman who testified, "He told me everything I have done." 40 When the Samaritans came to him, they invited him to stay with them; and he stayed there two days. 41 Many more began to believe in him because of his word, 42 [l]and they said to the woman, "We no longer believe because of your word; for we have heard for ourselves, and we know that this is truly the savior of the world."

**Return to Galilee** 43 *After the two days, he left there for Galilee. 44 [m]*For Jesus himself testified that a prophet has no honor in his native place. 45 When he came into Galilee, the Galileans welcomed him, since they had seen all he had done in Jerusalem at the feast; for they themselves had gone to the feast.

**Second Sign at Cana** 46 [n]*Then he returned to Cana in Galilee, where he had made the water wine. Now there was a royal official whose son was ill in Capernaum. 47 When he heard that Jesus had arrived in Galilee from Judea, he went to him and asked him to come down and heal his son, who was near death. 48 [o]Jesus said to him, "Unless you people see signs and wonders, you will not believe." 49 The royal official said to him, "Sir, come down before my child dies." 50 [p]Jesus said to him, "You may go; your son will live." The man believed what Jesus said to him and left. 51 While he was on his way back, his slaves met him and told him that his boy would live. 52 He asked them when he began to recover. They told him, "The fever left him yesterday, about one in the afternoon." 53 The father realized that just at that time Jesus had said to him, "Your son will live," and he and his whole household came to believe. 54 [q][Now] this was the second sign Jesus did when he came to Galilee from Judea.

## CHAPTER 5

**Cure on a Sabbath** 1 [r]*After this, there was a feast of the Jews, and Jesus went up to Jerusalem. 2 [s]*Now there is in Jerusalem at the Sheep [Gate] a pool called in Hebrew Bethesda, with five porticoes. 3 *In these lay a large number of ill, blind, lame, and crippled. [4*] 5 One man was there who had been ill for thirty-eight

h 5, 30.36; 6, 38; 9, 4; 17, 4.
i Mt 9, 37-38; Lk 10, 2; Rv 14, 15.
j Ps 126, 5-6; Am 9, 13-14.
k Dt 20, 6; 28, 30; Jb 31, 8; Mi 6, 15.
l 1 Jn 4, 14.
m Mt 13, 57; Mk 6, 4; Lk 4, 24.
n 2, 1-11; Mt 8, 5-13; 15, 21-28; Mk 7, 24-30; Lk 7, 1-10.
o 2, 18.23; Wis 8, 8; Mt 12, 38; 1 Cor 1, 22.
p 1 Kgs 17, 23.
q 2, 11.
r 6, 4.
s Neh 3, 1.32; 12, 39.

*

4, 35: *'In four months . . .'*: probably a proverb; cf Mt 9, 37–38.

4, 36: *Already:* this word may go with the preceding verse rather than with 36.

4, 39: The woman is presented as a missionary, described in virtually the same words as the disciples are in Jesus' prayer (17, 20).

4, 43–54: Jesus' arrival in Cana in Galilee; the second sign. This section introduces another theme, that of the life-giving word of Jesus. It is explicitly linked to the first sign (2, 11). The royal official believes (50). The natural life given his son is a sign of eternal life.

4, 44: Probably a reminiscence of a tradition as in Mk 6, 4. Cf Gospel of Thomas 31: "No prophet is acceptable in his village, no physician heals those who know him."

4, 46–54: The story of the cure of the royal official's son may be a third version of the cure of the centurion's son (Mt 8, 5–13) or servant (Lk 7, 1–10). Cf also Mt 15, 21–28 // Mk 7, 24–30.

5, 1–47: The self-revelation of Jesus continues in Jerusalem at a feast. The third sign (cf 2, 11; 4, 54) is performed, the cure of a paralytic by Jesus' life-giving word. The water of the pool fails to bring life; Jesus' word does.

5, 1: The reference in vv 45–46 to Moses suggests that the feast was Pentecost. The connection of that feast with the giving of the law to Moses on Sinai, attested in later Judaism, may already have been made in the first century. The feast could also be Passover (cf 6, 4). John stresses that the day was a sabbath (9).

5, 2: There is no noun with *Sheep.* "Gate" is supplied on the grounds that there must have been a gate in the NE wall of the temple area where animals for sacrifice were brought in; cf Neh 3, 1.32; 12, 39. *Hebrew:* more precisely, Aramaic. *Bethesda:* preferred to variants "Be(th)zatha" and "Bethsaida"; *bêt-'ešdatayin* is given as the name of a double pool northeast of the temple area in the Qumran Copper Roll. *Five porticoes:* a pool excavated in Jerusalem actually has five porticoes.

5, 3: The Caesarean and Western recensions, followed by the Vulgate, add "waiting for the movement of the water." Apparently an intermittent spring in the pool bubbled up occasionally (see 7). This turbulence was believed to cure.

5, 4: Toward the end of the second century in the West and among the fourth-century Greek Fathers, an additional verse was known: "For [from time to time] an angel of the Lord used to come down into the pool; and the water was stirred up, so the first one to get in [after the stirring of the water] was healed of whatever disease afflicted him." The angel was a popular explanation of the turbulence and the healing powers attributed to it. This verse is missing from all early Greek manuscripts and the earliest versions, including the original Vulgate. Its vocabulary is markedly non-Johannine.

years. **6** When Jesus saw him lying there and
knew that he had been ill for a long time, he said
to him, "Do you want to be well?" **7** The sick
man answered him, "Sir, I have no one to put
me into the pool when the water is stirred up;
while I am on my way, someone else gets down
there before me." **8** [t]Jesus said to him, "Rise,
take up your mat, and walk." **9** [u]Immediately
the man became well, took up his mat, and
walked.

Now that day was a sabbath. **10** [v]So the Jews
said to the man who was cured, "It is the sabbath, and it is not lawful for you to carry your
mat." **11** He answered them, "The man who
made me well told me, 'Take up your mat and
walk.' " **12** They asked him, "Who is the man
who told you, 'Take it up and walk'?" **13** [w]The
man who was healed did not know who it was,
for Jesus had slipped away, since there was a
crowd there. **14** [x]*After this Jesus found him in
the temple area and said to him, "Look, you are
well; do not sin any more, so that nothing worse
may happen to you." **15** The man went and
told the Jews that Jesus was the one who had
made him well. **16** [y]Therefore, the Jews began
to persecute Jesus because he did this on a sabbath. **17** [z]*But Jesus answered them, "My Father is at work until now, so I am at work."
**18** [a]For this reason the Jews tried all the more
to kill him, because he not only broke the sabbath but he also called God his own father,
making himself equal to God.

## The Work of the Son

**19** [b]*Jesus an-
swered and said to them, "Amen, amen, I say
to you, a son cannot do anything on his own, but
only what he sees his father doing; for what he
does, his son will do also. **20** [c]For the Father
loves his Son and shows him everything that he
himself does, and he will show him greater
works than these, so that you may be amazed.
**21** [d]*For just as the Father raises the dead and
gives life, so also does the Son give life to
whomever he wishes. **22** [e]*Nor does the Father
judge anyone, but he has given all judgment to
his Son, **23** so that all may honor the Son just
as they honor the Father. Whoever does not
honor the Son does not honor the Father who
sent him. **24** [f]Amen, amen, I say to you, whoever hears my word and believes in the one who
sent me has eternal life and will not come to
condemnation, but has passed from death to
life. **25** [g]Amen, amen, I say to you, the hour
is coming and is now here when the dead will
hear the voice of the Son of God, and those who
hear will live. **26** [h]For just as the Father has life
in himself, so also he gave to his Son the possession of life in himself. **27** [i]And he gave him
power to exercise judgment, because he is the
Son of Man. **28** [j]*Do not be amazed at this,
because the hour is coming in which all who are
in the tombs will hear his voice **29** [k]and will
come out, those who have done good deeds to
the resurrection of life, but those who have done
wicked deeds to the resurrection of condemnation.

**30** [l]"I cannot do anything on my own; I
judge as I hear, and my judgment is just, because I do not seek my own will but the will of
the one who sent me.

## Witnesses to Jesus

**31** [m]"If I testify on
my own behalf, my testimony cannot be verified. **32** *But there is another who testifies on
my behalf, and I know that the testimony he
gives on my behalf is true. **33** [n]You sent emissaries to John, and he testified to the truth.
**34** [o]I do not accept testimony from a human
being, but I say this so that you may be saved.
**35** [p]*He was a burning and shining lamp, and

t Mt 9, 6; Mk 2, 11; Lk 5, 24; Acts 3, 6.
u Mk 2, 12; Lk 5, 25 / 9, 14.
v Ex 20, 8; Jer 17, 21-27; Mk 3, 2; Lk 13, 10; 14, 1.
w Mt 8, 18; 13, 36; Mk 4, 36; 7, 17.
x 8, 11; 9, 2; Ez 18, 20.
y 7, 23; Mt 12, 8.
z Ex 20, 11.
a 7, 1.25; 8, 37.40; 10, 33.36; 14, 28; Gn 3, 5-6; Wis 2, 16; Mt 26, 4; 2 Thes 2, 4.
b 3, 34; 8, 26; 12, 49; 9, 4; 10, 30.
c 3, 35.
d 11, 25; Dt 32, 39; 1 Sm 2, 6; 2 Kgs 5, 7; Tb 13, 2; Wis 16, 13;Is 26, 19; Dn 7, 10.13; 12, 2; Rom 4, 17; 2 Cor 1, 9.
e Acts 10, 42; 17, 31.
f 3, 18; 8, 51; 1 Jn 3, 14.
g 5, 28; 8, 51; 11, 25-26; Eph 2, 1; 5, 14; Rv 3, 1.
h 1, 4; 1 Jn 5, 11.
i 5, 22; Dn 7, 13.22; Mt 25, 31; Lk 21, 36.
j 11, 43.
k Dn 12, 2; Mt 16, 27; 25, 46; Acts 24, 15; 2 Cor 5, 10.
l 6, 38.
m 8, 13-14.18.
n 1, 19-27; Mt 11, 10-11.
o 1 Jn 5, 9.
p 1, 8; Ps 132, 17; Sir 48, 1.

*

5, 14: While the cure of the paralytic in Mk 2, 1–12 is associated with the forgiveness of sins, Jesus never drew a one-to-one connection between sin and suffering (cf 9, 3; Lk 12, 1–5), as did Ez 18, 20.

5, 17: Sabbath observance (10) was based on God's resting on the seventh day (cf Gn 2, 2–3; Ex 20, 11). Philo and some rabbis insisted that God's providence remains active on the sabbath, keeping all things in existence, giving life in birth and taking it away in death. Other rabbis taught that God rested from creating, but not from judging (= ruling, governing). Jesus here claims the same authority to work as the Father, and, in the discourse that follows, the same divine prerogatives: power over life and death (21.24–26) and judgment (22.27).

5, 19: This proverb or parable is taken from apprenticeship in a trade: the activity of a son is modeled on that of his father. Jesus' dependence on the Father is justification for doing what the Father does.

5, 21: *Gives life:* in the Old Testament, a divine prerogative (Dt 32, 39; 1 Sm 2, 6; 2 Kgs 5, 7; Tob 13, 2; Is 26, 19; Dan 12, 2).

5, 22: *Judgment:* another divine prerogative, often expressed as acquittal or condemnation (Dt 32, 36; Ps 43, 1).

5, 28–29: While vv 19–27 present realized eschatology, vv 28–29 are future eschatology; cf Dn 12, 2.

5, 32: *Another:* likely the Father, who in four different ways gives testimony to Jesus, as indicated in the verse groupings 33–34, 36, 37–38, 39–40.

5, 35: *Lamp:* cf Ps 132, 17: "I will place a lamp for my Anointed (= David)," and possibly the description of Elijah in

for a while you were content to rejoice in his
light. 36 [q]But I have testimony greater than
John's. The works that the Father gave me to
accomplish, these works that I perform testify
on my behalf that the Father has sent me.
37 [r]Moreover, the Father who sent me has testified on my behalf. But you have never heard
his voice nor seen his form, 38 [s]and you do not
have his word remaining in you, because you do
not believe in the one whom he has sent.
39 [t]*You search the scriptures, because you
think you have eternal life through them; even
they testify on my behalf. 40 But you do not
want to come to me to have life.

**Unbelief of Jesus' Hearers** 41 *"I do
not accept human praise; 42 [u]moreover, I know
that you do not have the love of God in you.
43 [v]I came in the name of my Father, but you
do not accept me; yet if another comes in his
own name, you will accept him. 44 [w]How can
you believe, when you accept praise from one
another and do not seek the praise that comes
from the only God? 45 [x]Do not think that I will
accuse you before the Father: the one who will
accuse you is Moses, in whom you have placed
your hope. 46 [y]For if you had believed Moses,
you would have believed me, because he wrote
about me. 47 But if you do not believe his
writings, how will you believe my words?"

## CHAPTER 6

**Multiplication of the Loaves** 1 [z]*After
this, Jesus went across the Sea of Galilee [of
Tiberias]. 2 A large crowd followed him, because they saw the signs he was performing on
the sick. 3 Jesus went up on the mountain, and
there he sat down with his disciples. 4 [a]The
Jewish feast of Passover was near. 5 [b]*When
Jesus raised his eyes and saw that a large crowd
was coming to him, he said to Philip, "Where
can we buy enough food for them to eat?"
6 *He said this to test him, because he himself
knew what he was going to do. 7 [c]*Philip answered him, "Two hundred days' wages worth
of food would not be enough for each of them
to have a little [bit]." 8 One of his disciples,
Andrew, the brother of Simon Peter, said to
him, 9 [d]*"There is a boy here who has five
barley loaves and two fish; but what good are
these for so many?" 10 [e]*Jesus said, "Have
the people recline." Now there was a great deal
of grass in that place. So the men reclined, about
five thousand in number. 11 [f]Then Jesus took
the loaves, gave thanks, and distributed them to
those who were reclining, and also as much of
the fish as they wanted. 12 When they had had
their fill, he said to his disciples, "Gather the
fragments left over, so that nothing will be wasted." 13 *So they collected them, and filled
twelve wicker baskets with fragments from the
five barley loaves that had been more than they
could eat. 14 [g]*When the people saw the sign
he had done, they said, "This is truly the Prophet, the one who is to come into the world."
15 [h]Since Jesus knew that they were going to
come and carry him off to make him king, he
withdrew again to the mountain alone.

**Walking on the Water** 16 [i]*When it was
evening, his disciples went down to the sea,
17 embarked in a boat, and went across the sea
to Capernaum. It had already grown dark, and
Jesus had not yet come to them. 18 The sea was
stirred up because a strong wind was blowing.

q 10, 25.
r 8, 18; Dt 4, 12.15; 1 Jn 5, 9.
s 1 Jn 2, 14.
t 12, 16; 19, 28; 20, 9; Lk 24, 27.44; 1 Pt 1, 10.
u 1 Jn 2, 15.
v Mt 24, 5.24.
w 12, 43.
x Dt 31, 26.
y 5, 39; Dt 18, 15; Lk 16, 31; 24, 44.
z Mt 14, 13-21; Mk 6, 32-44; Lk 9, 10-17.
a 2, 13; 11, 55.
b Nm 11, 13.
c Mt 20, 2.
d 2 Kgs 4, 42-44.
e Mt 14, 21; Mk 6, 44.
f 21, 13.
g Dt 18, 15.18; Mal 3, 1.23; Acts 3, 22.
h 18, 36.
i Mt 14, 22-27; Mk 6, 45-52.

*

Sir 48, 1. But only *for a while,* indicating the temporary and subordinate nature of John's mission.

5, 39: *You search:* this may be an imperative: "Search the scriptures, because you think that you have eternal life through them."

5, 41: *Praise:* the same Greek word means "praise" or "honor" (from others) and "glory" (from God). There is a play on this in v 44.

6, 1–15: This story of the multiplication of the loaves is the fourth sign (cf the note on 5, 1–47). It is the only miracle story found in all four gospels (occurring twice in Mk and Mt). See the notes on Mt 14, 13–21 and 15, 32–39. John differs on the roles of Philip and Andrew, the proximity of Passover (4), and the allusion to Elisha (see 9). The story here symbolizes the food that is really available through Jesus. It connotes a new exodus and has eucharistic overtones.

6, 1: *[Of Tiberias]:* the awkward apposition represents a later name of the Sea of Galilee. It was probably originally a marginal gloss.

6, 5: Jesus takes the initiative (in the synoptics, the disciples do), possibly pictured as (cf 14) the new Moses (cf Nm 11, 13).

6, 6: Probably the evangelist's comment; in this gospel Jesus is never portrayed as ignorant of anything.

6, 7: *Days' wages:* literally, "denarii"; a Roman denarius is a day's wage in Mt 20, 2.

6, 9: *Barley loaves:* the food of the poor. There seems an allusion to the story of Elisha multiplying the barley bread in 2 Kgs 4, 42–44.

6, 10: *Grass:* implies springtime, and therefore Passover. *Five thousand:* so Mk 6, 39.44 and parallels.

6, 13: *Baskets:* the word describes the typically Palestinian wicker basket, as in Mk 6, 43 and parallels.

6, 14: *The Prophet:* probably the prophet like Moses (see the note on 1, 21). *The one who is to come into the world:* probably Elijah; cf Mal 3, 1.23.

6, 16–21: The fifth sign is a nature miracle, portraying Jesus sharing Yahweh's power. Cf the parallel stories following the multiplication of the loaves in Mk 6, 45–52 and Mt 14, 22–33.

19 [j]*When they had rowed about three or four
miles, they saw Jesus walking on the sea and
coming near the boat, and they began to be
afraid. 20 *But he said to them, "It is I. Do not
be afraid." 21 They wanted to take him into the
boat, but the boat immediately arrived at the
shore to which they were heading.

**The Bread of Life Discourse** 22 *The
next day, the crowd that remained across the sea
saw that there had been only one boat there, and
that Jesus had not gone along with his disciples
in the boat, but only his disciples had left.
23 *Other boats came from Tiberias near the
place where they had eaten the bread when the
Lord gave thanks. 24 When the crowd saw that
neither Jesus nor his disciples were there, they
themselves got into boats and came to Capernaum looking for Jesus. 25 And when they found
him across the sea they said to him, "Rabbi,
when did you get here?" 26 Jesus answered
them and said, "Amen, amen, I say to you, you
are looking for me not because you saw signs
but because you ate the loaves and were filled.
27 [k]*Do not work for food that perishes but for
the food that endures for eternal life, which the
Son of Man will give you. For on him the Father, God, has set his seal." 28 So they said to
him, "What can we do to accomplish the works
of God?" 29 Jesus answered and said to them,
"This is the work of God, that you believe in
the one he sent." 30 [l]So they said to him,
"What sign can you do, that we may see and
believe in you? What can you do? 31 [m]*Our
ancestors ate manna in the desert, as it is written:

'He gave them bread from heaven to eat.'"

32 [n]So Jesus said to them, "Amen, amen, I say
to you, it was not Moses who gave the bread
from heaven; my Father gives you the true bread
from heaven. 33 For the bread of God is that
which comes down from heaven and gives life
to the world."

34 [o]So they said to him, "Sir, give us this
bread always." 35 [p]*Jesus said to them, "I am
the bread of life; whoever comes to me will
never hunger, and whoever believes in me will
never thirst. 36 [q]But I told you that although
you have seen [me], you do not believe. 37 Everything that the Father gives me will come to
me, and I will not reject anyone who comes to
me, 38 [r]because I came down from heaven not
to do my own will but the will of the one who
sent me. 39 [s]And this is the will of the one who
sent me, that I should not lose anything of what
he gave me, but that I should raise it [on] the last
day. 40 [t]For this is the will of my Father, that
everyone who sees the Son and believes in him
may have eternal life, and I shall raise him [on]
the last day."

41 The Jews murmured about him because
he said, "I am the bread that came down from
heaven," 42 [u]and they said, "Is this not Jesus,
the son of Joseph? Do we not know his father
and mother? Then how can he say, 'I have come
down from heaven'?" 43 [v]*Jesus answered
and said to them, "Stop murmuring among
yourselves. 44 No one can come to me unless
the Father who sent me draw him, and I will
raise him on the last day. 45 [w]It is written in the
prophets:

'They shall all be taught by God.'

Everyone who listens to my Father and learns
from him comes to me. 46 [x]Not that anyone has
seen the Father except the one who is from God;
he has seen the Father. 47 Amen, amen, I say
to you, whoever believes has eternal life. 48 I
am the bread of life. 49 [y]Your ancestors ate the
manna in the desert, but they died; 50 this is the
bread that comes down from heaven so that one
may eat it and not die. 51 [z]I am the living bread
that came down from heaven; whoever eats this
bread will live forever; and the bread that I will
give is my flesh for the life of the world."

52 The Jews quarreled among themselves,
saying, "How can this man give us [his] flesh
to eat?" 53 Jesus said to them, "Amen, amen,
I say to you, unless you eat the flesh of the Son
of Man and drink his blood, you do not have life

j Jb 9, 8; Pss 29, 3-4; 77, 20; Is 43, 16.
k 6, 50.51.54.58.
l Mt 16, 1-4; Lk 11, 29-30.
m Ex 16, 4-5; Nm 11, 7-9; Ps 78, 24.
n Mt 6, 11.
o 4, 15.
p Is 55, 1-3; Am 8, 11-13.
q 20, 29.
r 4, 34; Mt 26, 39; Heb 10, 9.
s 10, 28-29; 17, 12; 18, 9.
t 1 Jn 2, 25.
u Mt 13, 54-57; Mk 6, 1-4; Lk 4, 22.
v Ex 16, 2.7.8; Lk 4, 22.
w Is 54, 13; Jer 31, 33-34.
x 1, 18; 7, 29; Ex 33, 20.
y 1 Cor 10, 3.5.
z Mt 26, 26-27; Lk 22, 19.

*

6, 19: *Walking on the sea:* although the Greek (cf 16) could mean "on the seashore" or "by the sea" (cf 21, 1), the parallels, especially Mt 14, 25, make clear that Jesus walked upon the water. John may allude to Job 9, 8: God "treads upon the crests of the sea."

6, 20: *It is I:* literally, "I am." See also the notes on 4, 26 and Mk 6, 50.

6, 22–71: Discourse on the bread of life; replacement of the manna. Verses 22–34 serve as an introduction, vv 35–59 constitute the discourse proper, vv 60–71 portray the reaction of the disciples and Peter's confession.

6, 23: Possibly a later interpolation, to explain how the crowd got to Capernaum.

6, 27: *The food that endures for eternal life:* cf 4, 14, on water "springing up to eternal life."

6, 31: *Bread from heaven:* cf Ex 16, 4.15.32–34 and the notes there; Ps 78, 24. The manna, thought to have been hidden by Jeremiah (2 Mc 2, 5–8), was expected to reappear miraculously at Passover, in the last days.

6, 35–59: Up to v 50, "bread of life" is a figure for God's revelation in Jesus; in vv 51–58, the eucharistic theme comes to the fore. There may thus be a break between vv 50 and 51.

6, 43: *Murmuring:* the word may reflect the Greek of Ex 16, 2.7.8.

within you. **54** *Whoever eats my flesh and
drinks my blood has eternal life, and I will raise
him on the last day. **55** For my flesh is true
food, and my blood is true drink. **56** Whoever
eats my flesh and drinks my blood remains in
me and I in him. **57** [a]Just as the living Father
sent me and I have life because of the Father,
so also the one who feeds on me will have life
because of me. **58** This is the bread that came
down from heaven. Unlike your ancestors who
ate and still died, whoever eats this bread will
live forever." **59** These things he said while
teaching in the synagogue in Capernaum.

**The Words of Eternal Life** **60** *Then
many of his disciples who were listening said,
"This saying is hard; who can accept it?"
**61** Since Jesus knew that his disciples were
murmuring about this, he said to them, "Does
this shock you? **62** *What if you were to see the
Son of Man ascending to where he was before?
**63** *It is the spirit that gives life, while the flesh
is of no avail. The words I have spoken to you
are spirit and life. **64** [b]But there are some of
you who do not believe." Jesus knew from the
beginning the ones who would not believe and
the one who would betray him. **65** And he said,
"For this reason I have told you that no one can
come to me unless it is granted him by my
Father."

**66** As a result of this, many [of] his disciples
returned to their former way of life and no longer accompanied him. **67** Jesus then said to the
Twelve, "Do you also want to leave?" **68** Simon Peter answered him, "Master, to whom
shall we go? You have the words of eternal life.
**69** [c]We have come to believe and are convinced that you are the Holy One of God."
**70** Jesus answered them, "Did I not choose you
twelve? Yet is not one of you a devil?" **71** [d]He
was referring to Judas, son of Simon the Iscariot; it was he who would betray him, one of the
Twelve.

## CHAPTER 7

**The Feast of Tabernacles** **1** [e]After this,
Jesus moved about within Galilee; but he did not
wish to travel in Judea, because the Jews were
trying to kill him. **2** [f]But the Jewish feast of
Tabernacles was near. **3** *So his brothers said
to him, "Leave here and go to Judea, so that
your disciples also may see the works you are
doing. **4** [g]No one works in secret if he wants to
be known publicly. If you do these things,
manifest yourself to the world." **5** For his
brothers did not believe in him. **6** *So Jesus
said to them, "My time is not yet here, but the
time is always right for you. **7** [h]The world cannot hate you, but it hates me, because I testify
to it that its works are evil. **8** *You go up to the
feast. I am not going up to this feast, because
my time has not yet been fulfilled." **9** After he
had said this, he stayed on in Galilee.

**10** But when his brothers had gone up to the
feast, he himself also went up, not openly but
[as it were] in secret. **11** The Jews were looking
for him at the feast and saying, "Where is he?"
**12** And there was considerable murmuring
about him in the crowds. Some said, "He is a
good man," [while] others said, "No; on the
contrary, he misleads the crowd." **13** [i]Still, no
one spoke openly about him because they were
afraid of the Jews.

**The First Dialogue** **14** *When the feast
was already half over, Jesus went up into the

a 5, 26.
b 13, 11.
c 11, 27; Mt 16, 16; Mk 1, 24; Lk 4, 34.
d 12, 4; 13, 2.27.
e 5, 18; 8, 37.40.
f Ex 23, 16; Lv 23, 34; Nm 29, 12; Dt 16, 13-16; Zec 14, 16-19.
g 14, 22.
h 15, 18.
i 9, 22; 19, 38; 20, 19.

*

6, 54–58: *Eats:* the verb used in these verses is not the classical Greek verb used of human eating, but that of animal eating: "munch," "gnaw." This may be part of John's emphasis on the reality of the flesh and blood of Jesus (cf 55), but the same verb eventually became the ordinary verb in Greek meaning "eat."

6, 60–71: These verses refer more to themes of vv 35–50 than to those of 51–58 and seem to be addressed to members of the Johannine community who found it difficult to accept the high christology reflected in the bread of life discourse.

6, 62: This unfinished conditional sentence is obscure. Probably there is a reference to vv 49–51. Jesus claims to be *the bread that comes down from heaven* (50); this claim provokes incredulity (60); and so Jesus is pictured as asking what his disciples will say when he goes up to heaven.

6, 63: *Spirit . . . flesh:* probably not a reference to the eucharistic body of Jesus but to the supernatural and the natural, as in 3, 6. *Spirit and life:* all Jesus said about the bread of life is the revelation of the Spirit.

7—8: These chapters contain events about the feast of Tabernacles (Sukkoth, Ingathering: Ex 23, 16; Tents, Booths: Dt 16, 13–16), with its symbols of booths (originally built to shelter harvesters), rain (water from Siloam poured on the temple altar), and lights (illumination of the four torches in the Court of the Women). They continue the theme of the replacement of feasts (Passover, 2, 13; 6, 4; Hanukkah, 10, 22; Pentecost, 5, 1), here accomplished by Jesus as the Living Water. These chapters comprise seven miscellaneous controversies and dialogues. There is a literary inclusion with Jesus in hiding in 7, 4.10 and 8, 59. There are frequent references to attempts on his life: 7, 1.13.19.25.30.32.44; 8, 37.40.59.

7, 3: *Brothers:* these relatives (cf 2, 12 and see the note on Mk 6, 3) are never portrayed as disciples until after the resurrection (Acts 1, 14). Mt 13, 55 and Mk 6, 3 give the names of four of them. Jesus has already performed works/signs in Judea; cf 2, 23; 3, 2; 4, 45; 5, 8.

7, 6: *Time:* the Greek word means "opportune time," here a synonym for Jesus' "hour" (see the note on 2, 4), his death and resurrection. In the wordplay, any time is suitable for Jesus' brothers, because they are not dependent on God's will.

7, 8: *I am not going up:* an early attested reading "not yet" seems a correction, since Jesus in the story does go up to the feast. "Go up," in a play on words, refers not only to going up to Jerusalem but also to exaltation at the cross, resurrection, and ascension; cf 3, 14; 6, 62; 20, 17.

7, 14–31: Jesus teaches in the temple; debate with the

temple area and began to teach. **15** [j]*The Jews
were amazed and said, "How does he know
scripture without having studied?" **16** Jesus
answered them and said, "My teaching is not
my own but is from the one who sent me.
**17** [k]*Whoever chooses to do his will shall
know whether my teaching is from God or
whether I speak on my own. **18** Whoever
speaks on his own seeks his own glory, but
whoever seeks the glory of the one who sent him
is truthful, and there is no wrong in him.
**19** [l]Did not Moses give you the law? Yet none
of you keeps the law. Why are you trying to kill
me?" **20** [m]*The crowd answered, "You are
possessed! Who is trying to kill you?"
**21** [n]*Jesus answered and said to them, "I performed one work and all of you are amazed
**22** [o]because of it. Moses gave you circumcision—not that it came from Moses but rather
from the patriarchs—and you circumcise a man
on the sabbath. **23** [p]If a man can receive circumcision on a sabbath so that the law of Moses
may not be broken, are you angry with me
because I made a whole person well on a sabbath? **24** [q]Stop judging by appearances, but
judge justly."

**25** So some of the inhabitants of Jerusalem
said, "Is he not the one they are trying to kill?
**26** *And look, he is speaking openly and they
say nothing to him. Could the authorities have
realized that he is the Messiah? **27** [r]But we
know where he is from. When the Messiah
comes, no one will know where he is from."
**28** [s]So Jesus cried out in the temple area as he
was teaching and said, "You know me and also
know where I am from. Yet I did not come on
my own, but the one who sent me, whom you
do not know, is true. **29** [t]I know him, because
I am from him, and he sent me." **30** [u]So they
tried to arrest him, but no one laid a hand upon
him, because his hour had not yet come.
**31** [v]But many of the crowd began to believe in
him, and said, "When the Messiah comes, will
he perform more signs that this man has done?"

## Officers Sent to Arrest Jesus

**32** *The
Pharisees heard the crowd murmuring about
him to this effect, and the chief priests and the
Pharisees sent guards to arrest him. **33** [w]So
Jesus said, "I will be with you only a little while
longer, and then I will go to the one who sent
me. **34** [x]You will look for me but not find [me],
and where I am you cannot come." **35** *So the
Jews said to one another, "Where is he going
that we will not find him? Surely he is not going
to the dispersion among the Greeks to teach the
Greeks, is he? **36** What is the meaning of his
saying, 'You will look for me and not find [me],
and where I am you cannot come'?"

## Rivers of Living Water

**37** [y]*On the last
and greatest day of the feast, Jesus stood up and
exclaimed, "Let anyone who thirsts come to me
and drink. **38** [z]*Whoever believes in me, as
scripture says:

'Rivers of living water will flow from
within him.' "

**39** [a]*He said this in reference to the Spirit that
those who came to believe in him were to receive. There was, of course, no Spirit yet, because Jesus had not yet been glorified.

## Discussion about the Origins of the Messiah

**40** [b]*Some in the crowd who heard
these words said, "This is truly the Prophet."
**41** Others said, "This is the Messiah." But
others said, "The Messiah will not come from
Galilee, will he? **42** [c]Does not scripture say
that the Messiah will be of David's family and

j Lk 2, 47.
k 6, 29.
l Acts 7, 53.
m 8, 48-49; 10, 20.
n 5, 1-9.
o Gn 17, 10; Lv 12, 3.
p 5, 2-9.16; Mt 12, 11-12; Lk 14, 5.
q 8, 15; Lv 19, 15; Is 11, 3-4.
r Heb 7, 3.
s 8, 19.
t 6, 46; 8, 55.
u 7, 44; 8, 20; Lk 4, 29-30.
v 2, 11; 10, 42; 11, 45.
w 13, 33; 16, 16.
x 8, 21; 12, 36; 13, 33.36; 16, 5; Dt 4, 29; Prv 1, 28; Is 55, 6; Hos 5, 6.
y Rv 21, 6.
z 4, 10.14; 19, 34; Is 12, 3; Ez 47, 1.
a 16, 7.
b Dt 18, 15.18.
c 2 Sm 7, 12-14; Pss 89, 3-4; 132, 11; Mi 5, 1; Mt 2, 5-6.

*

Jews.

7, 15: *Without having studied:* literally, "How does he know letters without having learned?" Children were taught to read and write by means of the scriptures. But here more than Jesus' literacy is being discussed; the people are wondering how he can teach like a rabbi. Rabbis were trained by other rabbis and traditionally quoted their teachers.

7, 17: *To do his will:* presumably a reference back to the "work" of 6, 29: belief in the one whom God has sent.

7, 20: *You are possessed:* literally, "You have a demon." The insane were thought to be possessed by a demoniacal spirit.

7, 21: *One work:* the cure of the paralytic (5, 1–9) because of the reference to the sabbath (22; 5, 9–10).

7, 26: *The authorities:* the members of the Sanhedrin (same term as 3, 1).

7, 32–36: Jesus announces his approaching departure (cf also 8, 21; 12, 36; 13, 33) and complete control over his destiny.

7, 35: *Dispersion:* or "diaspora": Jews living outside Palestine. *Greeks:* probably refers to the Gentiles in the Mediterranean area; cf 12, 20.

7, 37–39: Promise of living water through the Spirit.

7, 38: *Living water:* not an exact quotation from any Old Testament passage; in the gospel context the gift of the Spirit is meant; cf 3, 5. *From within him:* either Jesus or the believer; if Jesus, it continues the Jesus-Moses motif (water from the rock, Ex 17, 6; Nm 20, 11) as well as Jesus as the new temple (cf Ez 47, 1). Grammatically, it goes better with the believer.

7, 39: *No Spirit yet:* Codex Vaticanus and early Latin, Syriac, and Coptic versions add "given." In this gospel, the sending of the Spirit cannot take place until Jesus' glorification through his death, resurrection, and ascension; cf 20, 22.

7, 40–53: Discussion of the Davidic lineage of the Messiah.

come from Bethlehem, the village where David
lived?" 43 So a division occurred in the crowd
because of him. 44 Some of them even wanted
to arrest him, but no one laid hands on him.
45 So the guards went to the chief priests and
Pharisees, who asked them, "Why did you not
bring him?" 46 The guards answered, "Never
before has anyone spoken like this one." 47 So
the Pharisees answered them, "Have you also
been deceived? 48 [d]Have any of the authorities
or the Pharisees believed in him? 49 But this
crowd, which does not know the law, is accursed." 50 [e]Nicodemus, one of their members who had come to him earlier, said to them,
51 [f]"Does our law condemn a person before it
first hears him and finds out what he is doing?"
52 They answered and said to him, "You are
not from Galilee also, are you? Look and see
that no prophet arises from Galilee."

### A Woman Caught in Adultery

[53 *Then
each went to his own house,

## CHAPTER 8

1 [g]*while Jesus went to the Mount of Olives.
2 But early in the morning he arrived again in
the temple area, and all the people started coming to him, and he sat down and taught them.
3 Then the scribes and the Pharisees brought a
woman who had been caught in adultery and
made her stand in the middle. 4 They said to
him, "Teacher, this woman was caught in the
very act of committing adultery. 5 [h]*Now in
the law, Moses commanded us to stone such
women. So what do you say?" 6 *They said
this to test him, so that they could have some
charge to bring against him. Jesus bent down
and began to write on the ground with his finger.
7 [i]*But when they continued asking him, he
straightened up and said to them, "Let the one
among you who is without sin be the first to
throw a stone at her." 8 Again he bent down
and wrote on the ground. 9 And in response,
they went away one by one, beginning with the
elders. So he was left alone with the woman
before him. 10 [j]Then Jesus straightened up and
said to her, "Woman, where are they? Has no
one condemned you?" 11 [k]She replied, "No
one, sir." Then Jesus said, "Neither do I condemn you. Go, [and] from now on do not sin
any more."]

### The Light of the World

12 [l]*Jesus spoke
to them again, saying, "I am the light of the
world. Whoever follows me will not walk in
darkness, but will have the light of life." 13 So
the Pharisees said to him, "You testify on your
own behalf, so your testimony cannot be verified." 14 [m]*Jesus answered and said to them,
"Even if I do testify on my own behalf, my
testimony can be verified, because I know
where I came from and where I am going. But
you do not know where I come from or where
I am going. 15 [n]*You judge by appearances,
but I do not judge anyone. 16 [o]And even if I
should judge, my judgment is valid, because I
am not alone, but it is I and the Father who sent
me. 17 [p]*Even in your law it is written that the
testimony of two men can be verified. 18 [q]I
testify on my behalf and so does the Father who
sent me." 19 [r]So they said to him, "Where is
your father?" Jesus answered, "You know neither me nor my Father. If you knew me, you
would know my Father also." 20 [s]He spoke
these words while teaching in the treasury in the
temple area. But no one arrested him, because
his hour had not yet come.

### Jesus, the Father's Ambassador

21 [t]*He said to them again, "I am going away

d 12, 42.
e 3, 1; 19, 39.
f Dt 1, 16-17.
g Lk 21, 37-38.
h Lv 20, 10; Dt 22, 22-29.
i Dt 17, 7.
j Ez 33, 11.
k 5, 14.
l 1, 4-5.9; 12, 46; Ex 13, 22; Is 42, 6; Zec 14, 8.
m 5, 31.
n 12, 47; 1 Sm 16, 7.
o 5, 30.
p Dt 17, 6; 19, 15; Nm 35, 30.
q 5, 23.37.
r 7, 28; 14, 7; 15, 21.
s 7, 30.
t 7, 34; 13, 33.

*

7, 53—8, 11: The story of the woman caught in adultery is a later insertion here, missing from all early Greek manuscripts. A Western text-type insertion, attested mainly in Old Latin translations, it is found in different places in different manuscripts: here, or after 7, 36, or at the end of this gospel, or after Lk 21, 38, or at the end of that gospel. There are many non-Johannine features in the language, and there are also many doubtful readings within the passage. The style and motifs are similar to those of Luke, and it fits better with the general situation at the end of Lk 21, but it was probably inserted here because of the allusion to Jer 17, 13 (cf the note on 8, 6) and the statement, "I do not judge anyone," in 8, 15. The Catholic Church accepts this passage as canonical scripture.

8, 1: *Mount of Olives:* not mentioned elsewhere in the gospel tradition outside of passion week.

8, 5: Lv 20, 10 and Dt 22, 22 mention only death, but Dt 22, 23–24 prescribes stoning for a betrothed virgin.

8, 6: Cf Jer 17, 13 (RSV): "Those who turn away from thee shall be written in the earth, for they have forsaken the LORD, the fountain of living water"; cf 7, 38.

8, 7: The first stones were to be thrown by the witnesses (Dt 17, 7).

8, 12–20: Jesus the light of the world. Jesus replaces the four torches of the illumination of the temple as the light of joy.

8, 14: *My testimony can be verified:* this seems to contradict 5, 31, but the emphasis here is on Jesus' origin from the Father and his divine destiny. *Where I am going:* indicates Jesus' passion and glorification.

8, 15: *By appearances:* literally, "according to the flesh." *I do not judge anyone:* superficial contradiction of 5, 22.27.30; here the emphasis is that the judgment is not by material standards.

8, 17: *Your law:* a reflection of later controversy between church and synagogue.

8, 21–30: He whose ambassador I am is with me. Jesus' origin is from God; he can reveal God.

8, 21: *You will die in your sin:* i.e., of disbelief; cf v 24. *Where I am going you cannot come:* except through faith in Jesus' passion-resurrection.

and you will look for me, but you will die in
your sin. Where I am going you cannot come."
**22** *So the Jews said, "He is not going to kill
himself, is he, because he said, 'Where I am
going you cannot come'?" **23** [u]He said to
them, "You belong to what is below, I belong
to what is above. You belong to this world, but
I do not belong to this world. **24** [v]*That is why
I told you that you will die in your sins. For if
you do not believe that I AM, you will die in
your sins." **25** [w]*So they said to him, "Who
are you?" Jesus said to them, "What I told you
from the beginning. **26** [x]I have much to say
about you in condemnation. But the one who
sent me is true, and what I heard from him I tell
the world." **27** They did not realize that he was
speaking to them of the Father. **28** [y]So Jesus
said [to them], "When you lift up the Son of
Man, then you will realize that I AM, and that
I do nothing on my own, but I say only what the
Father taught me. **29** The one who sent me is
with me. He has not left me alone, because I
always do what is pleasing to him." **30** Because he spoke this way, many came to believe
in him.

**Jesus and Abraham** **31** *Jesus then said
to those Jews who believed in him, "If you
remain in my word, you will truly be my disciples, **32** [z]and you will know the truth, and the
truth will set you free." **33** [a]*They answered
him, "We are descendants of Abraham and
have never been enslaved to anyone. How can
you say, 'You will become free'?" **34** [b]Jesus
answered them, "Amen, amen, I say to you,
everyone who commits sin is a slave of sin.
**35** [c]*A slave does not remain in a household
forever, but a son always remains. **36** So if a
son frees you, then you will truly be free. **37** I
know that you are descendants of Abraham. But
you are trying to kill me, because my word has
no room among you. **38** *I tell you what I have
seen in the Father's presence; then do what you
have heard from the Father."

**39** [d]*They answered and said to him, "Our
father is Abraham." Jesus said to them, "If you
were Abraham's children, you would be doing
the works of Abraham. **40** But now you are
trying to kill me, a man who has told you the
truth that I heard from God; Abraham did not do
this. **41** [e]You are doing the works of your father!" [So] they said to him, "We are not illegitimate. We have one Father, God." **42** [f]Jesus
said to them, "If God were your Father, you
would love me, for I came from God and am
here; I did not come on my own, but he sent me.
**43** Why do you not understand what I am saying? Because you cannot bear to hear my word.
**44** [g]You belong to your father the devil and you
willingly carry out your father's desires. He was
a murderer from the beginning and does not
stand in truth, because there is no truth in him.
When he tells a lie, he speaks in character,
because he is a liar and the father of lies. **45** But
because I speak the truth, you do not believe
me. **46** [h]Can any of you charge me with sin? If
I am telling the truth, why do you not believe
me? **47** [i]Whoever belongs to God hears the
words of God; for this reason you do not listen,
because you do not belong to God."

**48** *The Jews answered and said to him,
"Are we not right in saying that you are a
Samaritan and are possessed?" **49** Jesus answered, "I am not possessed; I honor my Father, but you dishonor me. **50** [j]I do not seek my
own glory; there is one who seeks it and he is
the one who judges. **51** [k]Amen, amen, I say to
you, whoever keeps my word will never see
death." **52** [So] the Jews said to him, "Now
we are sure that you are possessed. Abraham
died, as did the prophets, yet you say, 'Whoever
keeps my word will never taste death.'
**53** [l]*Are you greater than our father Abraham,
who died? Or the prophets, who died? Who do

u 3, 31; 17, 14; 18, 36.
v Ex 3, 14; Dt 32, 39; Is 43, 10.
w 10, 24.
x 12, 44-50.
y 3, 14; 12, 32.34.
z Is 42, 7; Gal 4, 31.
a Mt 3, 9.
b Rom 6, 16-17.
c Gn 21, 10; Gal 4, 30; Heb 3, 5-6.
d Gn 26, 5; Rom 4, 11-17; Jas 2, 21-23.
e Mal 2, 10.
f 1 Jn 5, 1.
g Gn 3, 4; Wis 1, 13; 2, 24; Acts 13, 10; 1 Jn 3, 8-15.
h Heb 4, 15; 1 Pt 2, 22; 1 Jn 3, 5.
i 10, 26; 1 Jn 4, 6.
j 7, 18.
k 5, 24-29; 6, 40.47; 11, 25-26.
l 4, 12.

*

8, 22: The Jews suspect that he is referring to his death. Johannine irony is apparent here; Jesus' death will not be self-inflicted but destined by God.

8, 24.28: *I AM:* an expression that late Jewish tradition understood as Yahweh's own self-designation (Is 43, 10); see the note on 4, 26. Jesus is here placed on a par with Yahweh.

8, 25: *What I told you from the beginning:* this verse seems textually corrupt, with several other possible translations: "(I am) what I say to you"; "Why do I speak to you at all?" The earliest attested reading (Bodmer Papyrus $P^{66}$) has (in a second hand), "I told you at the beginning what I am also telling you (now)." The answer here (cf Prv 8, 22) seems to hinge on a misunderstanding of v 24 "*that* I AM" as "*what* I am."

8, 31–59: Jesus' origin ("before Abraham") and destiny are developed; the truth will free them from sin (34) and death (51).

8, 31: *Those Jews who believed in him:* a rough editorial suture, since in v 37 they are described as trying to kill Jesus.

8, 33: *Have never been enslaved to anyone:* since, historically, the Jews were enslaved almost continuously, this verse is probably Johannine irony, about slavery to sin.

8, 35: *A slave . . . a son:* an allusion to Ishmael and Isaac (Gn 16 and 21), or to the release of a slave after six years (Ex 21, 2; Dt 15, 12).

8, 38: *The Father:* i.e., God. It is also possible, however, to understand the second part of the verse as a sarcastic reference to descent of the Jews from the devil (44), "You do what you have heard from [your] father."

8, 39: *The works of Abraham:* Abraham believed; cf Rom 4, 11–17; Jas 2, 21–23.

8, 48: *Samaritan:* therefore interested in magical powers; cf Acts 7, 14–24.

8, 53: *Are you greater than our father Abraham?:* cf 4, 12.

you make yourself out to be?" **54** Jesus answered, "If I glorify myself, my glory is worth
nothing; but it is my Father who glorifies me,
of whom you say, 'He is our God.' **55** [m]You
do not know him, but I know him. And if I
should say that I do not know him, I would be
like you a liar. But I do know him and I keep
his word. **56** [n]*Abraham your father rejoiced to
see my day; he saw it and was glad. **57** *So the
Jews said to him, "You are not yet fifty years
old and you have seen Abraham?" **58** [o]*Jesus
said to them, "Amen, amen, I say to you, before Abraham came to be, I AM." **59** [p]So they
picked up stones to throw at him; but Jesus hid
and went out of the temple area.

## CHAPTER 9

**The Man Born Blind** **1** [q]*As he passed by
he saw a man blind from birth. **2** [r]*His disciples asked him, "Rabbi, who sinned, this man
or his parents, that he was born blind?"
**3** [s]Jesus answered, "Neither he nor his parents
sinned; it is so that the works of God might be
made visible through him. **4** [t]We have to do the
works of the one who sent me while it is day.
Night is coming when no one can work.
**5** [u]While I am in the world, I am the light of
the world." **6** [v]When he had said this, he spat
on the ground and made clay with the saliva,
and smeared the clay on his eyes, **7** [w]*and said
to him, "Go wash in the Pool of Siloam"
(which means Sent). So he went and washed,
and came back able to see.

**8** His neighbors and those who had seen him
earlier as a beggar said, "Isn't this the one who
used to sit and beg?" **9** Some said, "It is," but
others said, "No, he just looks like him." He
said, "I am." **10** So they said to him, "[So]
how were your eyes opened?" **11** He replied,
"The man called Jesus made clay and anointed
my eyes and told me, 'Go to Siloam and wash.'
So I went there and washed and was able to
see." **12** And they said to him, "Where is he?"
He said, "I don't know."

**13** They brought the one who was once blind
to the Pharisees. **14** [x]*Now Jesus had made
clay and opened his eyes on a sabbath. **15** So
then the Pharisees also asked him how he was
able to see. He said to them, "He put clay on
my eyes, and I washed, and now I can see."
**16** [y]So some of the Pharisees said, "This man
is not from God, because he does not keep the
sabbath." [But] others said, "How can a sinful
man do such signs?" And there was a division
among them. **17** [z]So they said to the blind man
again, "What do you have to say about him,
since he opened your eyes?" He said, "He is a
prophet."

**18** Now the Jews did not believe that he had
been blind and gained his sight until they summoned the parents of the one who had gained his
sight. **19** They asked them, "Is this your son,
who you say was born blind? How does he now
see?" **20** His parents answered and said, "We
know that this is our son and that he was born
blind. **21** We do not know how he sees now,
nor do we know who opened his eyes. Ask him,
he is of age; he can speak for himself."
**22** [a]*His parents said this because they were
afraid of the Jews, for the Jews had already
agreed that if anyone acknowledged him as the
Messiah, he would be expelled from the synagogue. **23** [b]For this reason his parents said,
"He is of age; question him."

**24** [c]*So a second time they called the man
who had been blind and said to him, "Give God
the praise! We know that this man is a sinner."
**25** He replied, "If he is a sinner, I do not know.
One thing I do know is that I was blind and now
I see." **26** So they said to him, "What did he
do to you? How did he open your eyes?" **27** He
answered them, "I told you already and you did
not listen. Why do you want to hear it again? Do

m 7, 28-29.
n Gn 17, 17; Mt 13, 17; Lk 17, 22.
o 1, 30; 17, 5.
p 10, 31.39; 11, 8; Lk 4, 29-30.
q Is 42, 7.
r Ex 20, 5; Ez 18, 20; Lk 13, 2.
s 5, 14; 11, 4.
t 11, 9-10; 12, 35-36.
u 8, 12.
v 5, 11; Mk 7, 33; 8, 23.
w 2 Kgs 5, 10-14.
x 5, 9.
y 3, 2; Mt 12, 10-11; Lk 13, 10-11; 14, 1-4.
z 4, 19.
a 7, 13; 12, 42; 16, 2; 19, 38.
b 12, 42.
c Jos 7, 19; 1 Sm 6, 5 LXX.

*

8, 56: *He saw it:* this seems a reference to the birth of Isaac (Gn 17, 7; 21, 6), the beginning of the fulfillment of promises about Abraham's seed.

8, 57: The evidence of the third-century Bodmer Papyrus $P^{75}$ and the first hand of Codex Sinaiticus indicates that the text originally read: "How can Abraham have seen you?"

8, 58: *Came to be, I AM:* the Greek word used for "came to be" is the one used of all creation in the prologue, while the word used for "am" is the one reserved for the Logos.

9, 1—10, 21: Sabbath healing of the man born blind. This fifth sign is introduced to illustrate the saying, "I am the light of the world" (8, 12; 9, 5). The narrative of conflict about Jesus contrasts Jesus (light) with the Jews (blindness, 39–41). The theme of water is reintroduced in the reference to the pool of Siloam. Ironically, Jesus is being judged by the Jews, yet the Jews are judged by the Light of the world; cf 3, 19–21.

9, 2: See the note on 5, 14, and Ex 20, 5, that parents' sins were visited upon their children. Jesus denies such a cause and emphasizes the purpose: the infirmity was providential.

9, 7: *Go wash:* perhaps a test of faith; cf 2 Kgs 5, 10–14. The water tunnel Siloam (= Sent) is used as a symbol of Jesus, sent by his Father.

9, 14: In using spittle, kneading clay, and healing, Jesus had broken the sabbath rules laid down by Jewish tradition.

9, 22: This comment of the evangelist (in terms used again in 12, 42 and 16, 2) envisages a situation after Jesus' ministry. Rejection/excommunication from the synagogue of Jews who confessed Jesus as Messiah seems to have begun ca. A.D. 85, when the curse against the *mînîm* or heretics was introduced into the "Eighteen Benedictions."

9, 24: *Give God the praise!:* an Old Testament formula of adjuration to tell the truth; cf Jos 7, 19; 1 Sm 6, 5 LXX. Cf 5, 41.

you want to become his disciples, too?"
28 They ridiculed him and said, "You are that
man's disciple; we are disciples of Moses!
29 [d]We know that God spoke to Moses, but we
do not know where this one is from." 30 The
man answered and said to them, "This is what
is so amazing, that you do not know where he
is from, yet he opened my eyes. 31 [e]We know
that God does not listen to sinners, but if one is
devout and does his will, he listens to him.
32 *It is unheard of that anyone ever opened the
eyes of a person born blind. 33 [f]If this man
were not from God, he would not be able to do
anything." 34 They answered and said to him,
"You were born totally in sin, and are you
trying to teach us?" Then they threw him out.
35 When Jesus heard that they had thrown
him out, he found him and said, "Do you believe in the Son of Man?" 36 He answered and
said, "Who is he, sir, that I may believe in
him?" 37 [g]Jesus said to him, "You have seen
him and the one speaking with you is he."
38 He said, "I do believe, Lord," and he worshiped him. 39 [h]*Then Jesus said, "I came into
this world for judgment, so that those who do
not see might see, and those who do see might
become blind."
40 [i]Some of the Pharisees who were with
him heard this and said to him, "Surely we are
not also blind, are we?" 41 [j]Jesus said to them,
"If you were blind, you would have no sin; but
now you are saying, 'We see,' so your sin remains.

## CHAPTER 10

**The Good Shepherd** 1 [k]*"Amen, amen,
I say to you, whoever does not enter a sheepfold
through the gate but climbs over elsewhere is a
thief and a robber. 2 But whoever enters
through the gate is the shepherd of the sheep.
3 The gatekeeper opens it for him, and the
sheep hear his voice, as he calls his own sheep
by name and leads them out. 4 [l]*When he has
driven out all his own, he walks ahead of them,
and the sheep follow him, because they recognize his voice. 5 But they will not follow a
stranger; they will run away from him, because
they do not recognize the voice of strangers."
6 *Although Jesus used this figure of speech,
they did not realize what he was trying to tell
them.
7 *So Jesus said again, "Amen, amen, I say
to you, I am the gate for the sheep. 8 *All who
came [before me] are thieves and robbers, but
the sheep did not listen to them. 9 I am the gate.
Whoever enters through me will be saved, and
will come in and go out and find pasture. 10 A
thief comes only to steal and slaughter and destroy; I came so that they might have life and
have it more abundantly. 11 [m]I am the good
shepherd. A good shepherd lays down his life
for the sheep. 12 [n]A hired man, who is not a
shepherd and whose sheep are not his own, sees
a wolf coming and leaves the sheep and runs
away, and the wolf catches and scatters them.
13 This is because he works for pay and has no
concern for the sheep. 14 I am the good shepherd, and I know mine and mine know me,
15 [o]just as the Father knows me and I know the
Father; and I will lay down my life for the
sheep. 16 [p]*I have other sheep that do not belong to this fold. These also I must lead, and
they will hear my voice, and there will be one
flock, one shepherd. 17 [q]This is why the Father
loves me, because I lay down my life in order
to take it up again. 18 [r]*No one takes it from
me, but I lay it down on my own. I have power
to lay it down, and power to take it up again.
This command I have received from my Father."
19 [s]Again there was a division among the
Jews because of these words. 20 [t]Many of
them said, "He is possessed and out of his

d Ex 33, 11.
e 10, 21; Pss 34, 16; 66, 18; Prv 15, 29; Is 1, 15.
f 3, 2.
g 4, 26; Dn 7, 13.
h Mt 13, 33-35.
i Mt 15, 14; 23, 26; Rom 2, 19.
j 15, 22.
k Gn 48, 15; 49, 24; Pss 23, 1-4; 80, 2; Jer 23, 1-4; Ez 34, 1-31; Mi 7, 14.
l Mi 2, 12-13.
m Ps 23, 1-4; Is 40, 11; 49, 9-10; Heb 13, 20; Rv 7, 17.
n Zec 11, 17.
o 15, 13; 1 Jn 3, 16.
p 11, 52; Is 56, 8; Jer 23, 3; Ez 34, 23; 37, 24; Mi 2, 12.
q Heb 10, 10.
r 19, 11.
s 7, 43; 9, 16.
t 7, 20; 8, 48.

*

9, 32: *A person born blind:* the only Old Testament cure from blindness is found in Tobit (cf Tb 7, 7; 11, 7–13; 14, 1–2), but Tobit was not born blind.

9, 39–41: These verses spell out the symbolic meaning of the cure; the Pharisees are not the innocent blind, willing to accept the testimony of others.

10, 1–21: The good shepherd discourse continues the theme of attack on the Pharisees that ends ch 9. The figure is allegorical: the hired hands are the Pharisees who excommunicated the cured blind man. It serves as a commentary on ch 9. For the shepherd motif, used of Yahweh in the Old Testament, cf Ex 34; Gn 48, 15; 49, 24; Mi 7, 14; Pss 23, 1–4; 80, 1.

10, 1: *Sheepfold:* a low stone wall open to the sky.

10, 4: *Recognize his voice:* the Pharisees do not recognize Jesus, but the people of God, symbolized by the blind man, do.

10, 6: *Figure of speech:* John uses a different word for illustrative speech than the "parable" of the synoptics, but the idea is similar.

10, 7–10: In vv 7–8, the figure is of a gate for the shepherd to come to the sheep; in vv 9–10, the figure is of a gate for the sheep to *come in and go out.*

10, 8: [*Before me*]: these words are omitted in many good early manuscripts and versions.

10, 16: *Other sheep:* the Gentiles, possibly a reference to "God's dispersed children" of 11, 52 destined to be gathered into one, or "apostolic Christians" at odds with the community of the beloved disciple.

10, 18: *Power to take it up again:* contrast the role of the Father as the efficient cause of the resurrection in Acts 2, 24; 4, 10; etc.; Rom 1, 4; 4, 24. Yet even here is added: *This command I have received from my Father.*

mind; why listen to him?" 21 [u]Others said,
"These are not the words of one possessed;
surely a demon cannot open the eyes of the
blind, can he?"

**Feast of the Dedication** 22 [v]*The feast of
the Dedication was then taking place in Jerusalem. It was winter. 23 *And Jesus walked
about in the temple area on the Portico of Solomon. 24 [w]*So the Jews gathered around him
and said to him, "How long are you going to
keep us in suspense? If you are the Messiah, tell
us plainly." 25 [x]*Jesus answered them, "I told
you and you do not believe. The works I do in
my Father's name testify to me. 26 [y]But you do
not believe, because you are not among my
sheep. 27 My sheep hear my voice; I know
them, and they follow me. 28 [z]I give them
eternal life, and they shall never perish. No one
can take them out of my hand. 29 [a]*My Father,
who has given them to me, is greater than all,
and no one can take them out of the Father's
hand. 30 [b]*The Father and I are one."

31 [c]The Jews again picked up rocks to stone
him. 32 Jesus answered them, "I have shown
you many good works from my Father. For
which of these are you trying to stone me?"
33 [d]The Jews answered him, "We are not stoning you for a good work but for blasphemy.
You, a man, are making yourself God."
34 [e]*Jesus answered them, "Is it not written in
your law, 'I said, "You are gods" '? 35 If it
calls them gods to whom the word of God came,
and scripture cannot be set aside, 36 [f]*can you
say that the one whom the Father has consecrated and sent into the world blasphemes because
I said, 'I am the Son of God'? 37 If I do not
perform my Father's works, do not believe me;
38 [g]but if I perform them, even if you do not
believe me, believe the works, so that you may
realize [and understand] that the Father is in me
and I am in the Father." 39 [Then] they tried
again to arrest him; but he escaped from their
power.

40 [h]He went back across the Jordan to the
place where John first baptized, and there he
remained. 41 *Many came to him and said,
"John performed no sign, but everything John
said about this man was true." 42 [i]And many
there began to believe in him.

## CHAPTER 11

**The Raising of Lazarus** 1 [j]*Now a man
was ill, Lazarus from Bethany, the village of
Mary and her sister Martha. 2 Mary was the
one who had anointed the Lord with perfumed
oil and dried his feet with her hair; it was her
brother Lazarus who was ill. 3 So the sisters
sent word to him, saying, "Master, the one you
love is ill." 4 [k]*When Jesus heard this he said,
"This illness is not to end in death, but is for
the glory of God, that the Son of God may be
glorified through it." 5 Now Jesus loved Martha and her sister and Lazarus. 6 So when he
heard that he was ill, he remained for two days
in the place where he was. 7 Then after this he
said to his disciples, "Let us go back to Judea."
8 [l]The disciples said to him, "Rabbi, the Jews
were just trying to stone you, and you want to

u 3, 2.
v 1 Mc 4, 54.59.
w Lk 22, 67.
x 8, 25 / 5, 36; 10, 38.
y 8, 45.47.
z Dt 32, 39.
a Wis 3, 1; Is 43, 13.
b 1, 1; 12, 45; 14, 9; 17, 21.
c 8, 59.
d 5, 18; 19, 7; Lv 24, 16.
e Ps 82, 6.
f 5, 18.
g 14, 10-11.20.
h 1, 28.
i 2, 23; 7, 31; 8, 30.
j 12, 1-8; Lk 10, 38-42; 16, 19-31.
k 9, 3.24.
l 8, 59; 10, 31.

*

10, 22: *Feast of the Dedication:* an eight-day festival of lights (Hebrew, Hanukkah) held in December, three months after the feast of Tabernacles (7, 2), to celebrate the Maccabees' rededication of the altar and reconsecration of the temple in 164 B.C., after their desecration by Antiochus IV Epiphanes (Dn 8, 13; 9, 27; cf 1 Mc 4, 36–59; 2 Mc 1, 18—2, 19; 10, 1–8).

10, 23: *Portico of Solomon:* on the east side of the temple area, offering protection against the cold winds from the desert.

10, 24: *Keep us in suspense:* literally, "How long will you take away our life?" Cf 11, 48–50. *If you are the Messiah, tell us plainly:* cf Lk 22, 67. This is the climax of Jesus' encounters with the Jewish authorities. There has never yet been an open confession before them.

10, 25: *I told you:* probably at 8, 25, which was an evasive answer.

10, 29: The textual evidence for the first clause is very divided; it may also be translated: "As for the Father, what he has given me is greater than all," or "My Father is greater than all, in what he has given me."

10, 30: This is justification for v 29; it asserts unity of power and reveals that the words and deeds of Jesus are the words and deeds of God.

10, 34: This is a reference to the judges of Israel who, since they exercised the divine prerogative to judge (Dt 1, 17), were called "gods"; cf Ex 21, 6, besides Ps 82, 6, from which the quotation comes.

10, 36: *Consecrated:* this may be a reference to the rededicated altar at the Hanukkah feast; see the note on 10, 22.

10, 41: *Performed no sign:* this is to stress the inferior role of John the Baptist. The Transjordan topography recalls the great witness of John the Baptist to Jesus, as opposed to the hostility of the authorities in Jerusalem.

11, 1–44: The raising of Lazarus, the longest continuous narrative in John outside of the Passion account, is the climax of the signs. It leads directly to the decision of the Sanhedrin to kill Jesus. The theme of life predominates. Lazarus is a token of the real life that Jesus dead and raised will give to all who believe in him. Johannine irony is found in the fact that Jesus' gift of life leads to his own death. The story is not found in the synoptics, but cf Mk 5, 21 and parallels; Lk 7, 11–17. There are also parallels between this story and Luke's parable of the rich man and poor Lazarus (Lk 16, 19–31). In both a man named Lazarus dies; in Luke, there is a request that he return to convince his contemporaries of the need for faith and repentance, while in John, Lazarus does return and some believe but others do not.

11, 4: *Not to end in death:* this is misunderstood by the disciples as referring to physical death, but it is meant as spiritual death.

go back there?" **9** [mn]Jesus answered, "Are there not twelve hours in a day? If one walks during the day, he does not stumble, because he sees the light of this world. **10** *But if one walks at night, he stumbles, because the light is not in him." **11** He said this, and then told them, "Our friend Lazarus is asleep, but I am going to awaken him." **12** So the disciples said to him, "Master, if he is asleep, he will be saved." **13** [o]But Jesus was talking about his death, while they thought that he meant ordinary sleep. **14** So then Jesus said to them clearly, "Lazarus has died. **15** And I am glad for you that I was not there, that you may believe. Let us go to him." **16** [p]*So Thomas, called Didymus, said to his fellow disciples, "Let us also go to die with him."

**17** When Jesus arrived, he found that Lazarus had already been in the tomb for four days. **18** *Now Bethany was near Jerusalem, only about two miles away. **19** [q]And many of the Jews had come to Martha and Mary to comfort them about their brother. **20** When Martha heard that Jesus was coming, she went to meet him; but Mary sat at home. **21** [r]Martha said to Jesus, "Lord, if you had been here, my brother would not have died. **22** [But] even now I know that whatever you ask of God, God will give you." **23** Jesus said to her, "Your brother will rise." **24** [s]Martha said to him, "I know he will rise, in the resurrection on the last day." **25** [t]Jesus told her, "I am the resurrection and the life; whoever believes in me, even if he dies, will live, **26** and everyone who lives and believes in me will never die. Do you believe this?" **27** [u]*She said to him, "Yes, Lord. I have come to believe that you are the Messiah, the Son of God, the one who is coming into the world."

**28** When she had said this, she went and called her sister Mary secretly, saying, "The teacher is here and is asking for you." **29** As soon as she heard this, she rose quickly and went to him. **30** For Jesus had not yet come into the village, but was still where Martha had met him. **31** So when the Jews who were with her in the house comforting her saw Mary get up quickly and go out, they followed her, presuming that she was going to the tomb to weep there. **32** When Mary came to where Jesus was and saw him, she fell at his feet and said to him, "Lord, if you had been here, my brother would not have died." **33** *When Jesus saw her weeping and the Jews who had come with her weeping, he became perturbed and deeply troubled, **34** and said, "Where have you laid him?" They said to him, "Sir, come and see." **35** [v]And Jesus wept. **36** So the Jews said, "See how he loved him." **37** But some of them said, "Could not the one who opened the eyes of the blind man have done something so that this man would not have died?"

**38** So Jesus, perturbed again, came to the tomb. It was a cave, and a stone lay across it. **39** Jesus said, "Take away the stone." Martha, the dead man's sister, said to him, "Lord, by now there will be a stench; he has been dead for four days." **40** Jesus said to her, "Did I not tell you that if you believe you will see the glory of God?" **41** *So they took away the stone. And Jesus raised his eyes and said, "Father, I thank you for hearing me. **42** [w]I know that you always hear me; but because of the crowd here I have said this, that they may believe that you sent me." **43** *And when he had said this, he cried out in a loud voice, "Lazarus, come out!" **44** The dead man came out, tied hand and foot with burial bands, and his face was wrapped in a cloth. So Jesus said to them, "Untie him and let him go."

**Session of the Sanhedrin** **45** [x]Now many of the Jews who had come to Mary and seen what he had done began to believe in him. **46** But some of them went to the Pharisees and told them what Jesus had done. **47** [y]So the chief priests and the Pharisees convened the Sanhedrin and said, "What are we going to do? This man is performing many signs. **48** *If we leave him alone, all will believe in him, and the Romans will come and take away both our land and our nation." **49** [z]*But one of them, Caiaphas,

m 8, 12; 9, 4.
n 12, 35; 1 Jn 2, 10.
o Mt 9, 24.
p 14, 5.22.
q 12, 9.17-18.
r 11, 32.
s 5, 29; 6, 39-40.44.54; 12, 48; Is 2, 2; Mi 4, 1; Acts 23, 8;24, 15.
t 5, 24; 8, 51; 14, 6; Dn 12, 2.
u 1, 9; 6, 69.
v Lk 19, 41.
w 12, 30.
x Lk 16, 31.
y 12, 19; Mt 26, 3-5; Lk 22, 2; Acts 4, 16.
z 18, 13-14.

*

11, 10: *The light is not in him:* the ancients apparently did not grasp clearly the entry of light *through* the eye; they seem to have thought of it as being *in* the eye; cf Lk 11, 34; Mt 6, 23.

11, 16: *Called Didymus: Didymus* is the Greek word for twin. Thomas is derived from the Aramaic word for twin; in an ancient Syriac version and in the Gospel of Thomas (80, 11–12) his given name, Judas, is supplied.

11, 18: *About two miles:* literally, "about fifteen stades"; a stade was 607 feet.

11, 27: The titles here are a summary of titles given to Jesus earlier in the gospel.

11, 33: *Became perturbed:* a startling phrase in Greek, literally, "He snorted in spirit," perhaps in anger at the presence of evil (death).

11, 41: *Father:* in Aramaic, *"abba."* See the note on Mk 14, 36.

11, 43: *Cried out in a loud voice:* a dramatization of 5, 28: "the hour is coming when all who are in the tombs will hear his voice."

11, 48: *The Romans will come:* Johannine irony; this is precisely what happened after Jesus' death.

11, 49: *That year:* emphasizes the conjunction of the office and the year. Actually, Caiaphas was high priest A.D. 18–36. The Jews attributed a gift of prophecy, sometimes uncon-

who was high priest that year, said to them,
"You know nothing, **50** nor do you consider
that it is better for you that one man should die
instead of the people, so that the whole nation
may not perish." **51** He did not say this on his
own, but since he was high priest for that year,
he prophesied that Jesus was going to die for the
nation, **52** *and not only for the nation, but also
to gather into one the dispersed children of God.
**53** [a]So from that day on they planned to kill
him.

**54** *So Jesus no longer walked about in public among the Jews, but he left for the region
near the desert, to a town called Ephraim, and
there he remained with his disciples.

**The Last Passover** **55** [b]*Now the Passover of the Jews was near, and many went up
from the country to Jerusalem before Passover
to purify themselves. **56** They looked for Jesus
and said to one another as they were in the
temple area, "What do you think? That he will
not come to the feast?" **57** For the chief priests
and the Pharisees had given orders that if anyone knew where he was, he should inform them,
so that they might arrest him.

## CHAPTER 12

**The Anointing at Bethany** **1** [c][d]*Six days
before Passover Jesus came to Bethany, where
Lazarus was, whom Jesus had raised from the
dead. **2** [e]They gave a dinner for him there, and
Martha served, while Lazarus was one of those
reclining at table with him. **3** [f]*Mary took a
liter of costly perfumed oil made from genuine
aromatic nard and anointed the feet of Jesus and
dried them with her hair; the house was filled
with the fragrance of the oil. **4** Then Judas the
Iscariot, one [of] his disciples, and the one who
would betray him, said, **5** *"Why was this oil
not sold for three hundred days' wages and giv-
en to the poor?" **6** [g]He said this not because he
cared about the poor but because he was a thief
and held the money bag and used to steal the
contributions. **7** *So Jesus said, "Leave her
alone. Let her keep this for the day of my burial.
**8** [h]You always have the poor with you, but you
do not always have me."

**9** [i][The] large crowd of the Jews found out
that he was there and came, not only because of
Jesus, but also to see Lazarus, whom he had
raised from the dead. **10** And the chief priests
plotted to kill Lazarus too, **11** [j]because many of
the Jews were turning away and believing in
Jesus because of him.

**The Entry into Jerusalem** **12** [k]*On the
next day, when the great crowd that had come
to the feast heard that Jesus was coming to
Jerusalem, **13** [l]*they took palm branches and
went out to meet him, and cried out:

"Hosanna!
Blessed is he who comes in the name of the
Lord,
[even] the king of Israel."

**14** Jesus found an ass and sat upon it, as is
written:

**15** [m]*"Fear no more, O daughter Zion;
see, your king comes, seated upon an
ass's colt."

**16** [n]*His disciples did not understand this at
first, but when Jesus had been glorified they
remembered that these things were written
about him and that they had done this for him.
**17** *So the crowd that was with him when he

a 5, 18; 7, 1; Mt 12, 14.
b 2, 13; 5, 1; 6, 4; 18, 28; Ex 19, 10-11.15; Nm 9, 6-14; 19, 12; Dt 16, 6; 2 Chr 30, 1-3.15-18.
c Mt 26, 6-13; Mk 14, 3-9.
d 11, 1.
e Lk 10, 38-42.
f 11, 2.
g 13, 29.
h Dt 15, 11.
i 11, 19.
j 11, 45.
k Mt 21, 1-16; Mk 11, 1-10; Lk 19, 28-40.
l 1, 49; Lv 23, 40; 1 Mc 13, 51; 2 Mc 10, 7; Rv 7, 9.
m Is 40, 9; Zec 9, 9.
n 2, 22.

*

scious, to the high priest.

11, 52: *Dispersed children of God:* perhaps the "other sheep" of 10, 16.

11, 54: Ephraim is usually located about twelve miles northeast of Jerusalem, where the mountains descend into the Jordan valley.

11, 55: *Purify:* prescriptions for purity were based on Ex 19, 10–11.15; Nm 9, 6–14; 2 Chr 30, 1–3.15–18.

12, 1–8: This is probably the same scene of anointing found in Mk 14, 3–9 (see the note there) and Mt 26, 6–13. The anointing by a penitent woman in Lk 7, 36–38 is different. Details from these various episodes have become interchanged.

12, 3: *The feet of Jesus:* so Mk 14, 3; but in Mt 26, 6, Mary anoints Jesus' head as a sign of regal, messianic anointing.

12, 5: *Days' wages:* literally, "denarii." A denarius is a day's wage in Mt 20, 2; see the note on 6, 7.

12, 7: Jesus' response reflects the rabbinical discussion of what was the greatest act of mercy, almsgiving or burying the dead. Those who favored proper burial of the dead thought it an essential condition for sharing in the resurrection.

12, 12–19: In Jn, the entry into Jerusalem follows the anointing whereas in the synoptics it precedes. In John, the crowd, not the disciples, are responsible for the triumphal procession.

12, 13: *Palm branches:* used to welcome great conquerors; cf 1 Mc 13, 51; 2 Mc 10, 7. They may be related to the *lûlab*, the twig bundles used at the feast of Tabernacles. *Hosanna:* see Ps 118, 25–26. The Hebrew word means: "(O Lord), grant salvation." *He who comes in the name of the Lord:* referred in Ps 118, 26 to a pilgrim entering the temple gates, but here a title for Jesus (see the notes on Mt 11, 3 and Jn 6, 14; 11, 27). *The king of Israel:* perhaps from Zep 3, 14–15, in connection with the next quotation from Zec 9, 9.

12, 15: *Daughter Zion:* Jerusalem. *Ass's colt:* symbol of peace, as opposed to the war-horse.

12, 16: *They had done this:* the antecedent of *they* is ambiguous.

12, 17–18: There seem to be two different crowds in these verses. There are some good witnesses to the text that have another reading for v 17: "Then the crowd that was with him

called Lazarus from the tomb and raised him
from death continued to testify. 18 This was
[also] why the crowd went to meet him, because
they heard that he had done this sign. 19 [o]*So
the Pharisees said to one another, "You see that
you are gaining nothing. Look, the whole world
has gone after him."

**The Coming of Jesus' Hour** 20 [p]*Now
there were some Greeks among those who had
come up to worship at the feast. 21 [q]*They
came to Philip, who was from Bethsaida in
Galilee, and asked him, "Sir, we would like to
see Jesus." 22 [r]Philip went and told Andrew;
then Andrew and Philip went and told Jesus.
23 [s]*Jesus answered them, "The hour has
come for the Son of Man to be glorified.
24 [t]*Amen, amen, I say to you, unless a grain
of wheat falls to the ground and dies, it remains
just a grain of wheat; but if it dies, it produces
much fruit. 25 [u]*Whoever loves his life loses
it, and whoever hates his life in this world will
preserve it for eternal life. 26 [v]Whoever serves
me must follow me, and where I am, there also
will my servant be. The Father will honor whoever serves me.

27 [w]*"I am troubled now. Yet what should
I say? 'Father, save me from this hour'? But it
was for this purpose that I came to this hour.
28 [x]Father, glorify your name." Then a voice
came from heaven, "I have glorified it and will
glorify it again." 29 [y]The crowd there heard it
and said it was thunder; but others said, "An
angel has spoken to him." 30 [z]Jesus answered
and said, "This voice did not come for my sake
but for yours. 31 [a]*Now is the time of judgment on this world; now the ruler of this world
will be driven out. 32 [b]And when I am lifted up
from the earth, I will draw everyone to myself."
33 He said this indicating the kind of death he
would die. 34 [c]*So the crowd answered him,
"We have heard from the law that the Messiah
remains forever. Then how can you say that the
Son of Man must be lifted up? Who is this Son
of Man?" 35 [d]Jesus said to them, "The light
will be among you only a little while. Walk
while you have the light, so that darkness may
not overcome you. Whoever walks in the dark
does not know where he is going. 36 [e]While
you have the light, believe in the light, so that
you may become children of the light."

**Unbelief and Belief among the Jews**
After he had said this, Jesus left and hid from
them. 37 [f]*Although he had performed so
many signs in their presence they did not believe
in him, 38 [g]*in order that the word which Isaiah the prophet spoke might be fulfilled:

"Lord, who has believed our preaching,
to whom has the might of the Lord been
revealed?"

39 For this reason they could not believe, because again Isaiah said:

40 [h]"He blinded their eyes
and hardened their heart,
so that they might not see with their eyes
and understand with their heart and be
converted,
and I would heal them."

41 [i]*Isaiah said this because he saw his glory
and spoke about him. 42 [j]Nevertheless, many,

o 11, 47-48.
p Acts 10, 2.
q 1, 44.
r 1, 40.
s 2, 4.
t Is 53, 10-12; 1 Cor 15, 36.
u Mt 10, 39; 16, 25; Mk 8, 35; Lk 9, 24; 17, 33.
v 14, 3; 17, 24; Mt 16, 24; Mk 8, 34; Lk 9, 23.
w 6, 38; 18, 11; Mt 26, 38-39; Mk 14, 34-36; Lk 22, 42; Heb 5, 7-8.
x 2, 11; 17, 5; Dn 4, 31.34.
y Ex 9, 28; 2 Sm 22, 14; Jb 37, 4; Ps 29, 3; Lk 22, 43; Acts 23, 9.
z 11, 42.
a 16, 11; Lk 10, 18; Rv 12, 9.
b 3, 14; 8, 28; Is 52, 13.
c Pss 89, 5; 110, 4; Is 9, 7; Dn 7, 13-14; Rv 20, 1-6.
d 9, 4; 11, 10; Jb 5, 14.
e Eph 5, 8.
f Dt 29, 2-4; Mk 4, 11-12; Rom 9-11.
g Is 53, 1; Rom 10, 16.
h Is 6, 9-10; Mt 13, 13-15; Mk 4, 12.
i 5, 39; Is 6, 1.4.
j 9, 22.

*

began to testify that he had called Lazarus out of the tomb and raised him from the dead."

12, 19: *The whole world:* the sense is that everyone is following Jesus, but John has an ironic play on *world;* he alludes to the universality of salvation (3, 17; 4, 42).

12, 20–36: This announcement of glorification by death is an illustration of "the whole world" (19) going after him.

12, 20: *Greeks:* not used here in a nationalistic sense. These are probably Gentile proselytes to Judaism; cf 7, 35.

12, 21–22: *Philip . . . Andrew:* the approach is made through disciples who have distinctly Greek names, suggesting that access to Jesus was mediated to the Greek world through his disciples. Philip and Andrew were from Bethsaida (1, 44); Galileans were mostly bilingual. *See:* here seems to mean "have an interview with."

12, 23: Jesus' response suggests that only after the crucifixion could the gospel encompass both Jew and Gentile.

12, 24: This verse implies that through his death Jesus will be accessible to all. *It remains just a grain of wheat:* this saying is found in the synoptic triple and double traditions (Mk 8, 35 // Mt 16, 25 // Lk 9, 24; Mt 10, 39 // Lk 17, 33). John adds the phrases (25) *in this world* and *for eternal life.*

12, 25: *His life:* the Greek word *psychē* refers to a person's natural life. It does not mean "soul," for Hebrew anthropology did not postulate body/soul dualism in the way that is familiar to us.

12, 27: *I am troubled:* perhaps an allusion to the Gethsemane agony scene of the synoptics.

12, 31: *Ruler of this world:* Satan.

12, 34: There is no passage in the Old Testament that states precisely that *the Messiah remains forever.* Perhaps the closest is Ps 89, 37.

12, 37–50: These verses, on unbelief of the Jews, provide an epilogue to the Book of Signs.

12, 38–41: John gives a historical explanation of the disbelief of the Jewish people, not a psychological one. The Old Testament had to be fulfilled; the disbelief that met Isaiah's message was a foreshadowing of the disbelief that Jesus encountered. In v 42 and also in 3, 20, we see that there is no negation of freedom.

12, 41: *His glory:* Isaiah saw the glory of Yahweh enthroned in the heavenly temple, but in John the antecedent of *his* is Jesus.

even among the authorities, believed in him, but
because of the Pharisees they did not acknowledge it openly in order not to be expelled from
the synagogue. **43** [k]For they preferred human
praise to the glory of God.

**Recapitulation** **44** [l]Jesus cried out and
said, "Whoever believes in me believes not
only in me but also in the one who sent me,
**45** [m]and whoever sees me sees the one who
sent me. **46** [n]I came into the world as light, so
that everyone who believes in me might not
remain in darkness. **47** [o]And if anyone hears
my words and does not observe them, I do not
condemn him, for I did not come to condemn
the world but to save the world. **48** [p]Whoever
rejects me and does not accept my words has
something to judge him: the word that I spoke,
it will condemn him on the last day,
**49** [q]because I did not speak on my own, but the
Father who sent me commanded me what to say
and speak. **50** And I know that his commandment is eternal life. So what I say, I say as the
Father told me."

## *III: THE BOOK OF GLORY*

### CHAPTER 13

### The Washing of the Disciples' Feet

**1** [r]*Before the feast of Passover, Jesus knew
that his hour had come to pass from this world
to the Father. He loved his own in the world and
he loved them to the end. **2** [s]*The devil had
already induced Judas, son of Simon the Iscariot, to hand him over. So, during supper,
**3** [t]fully aware that the Father had put everything into his power and that he had come from
God and was returning to God, **4** he rose from
supper and took off his outer garments. He took
a towel and tied it around his waist. **5** [u]*Then
he poured water into a basin and began to wash
the disciples' feet and dry them with the towel
around his waist. **6** He came to Simon Peter,
who said to him, "Master, are you going to
wash my feet?" **7** Jesus answered and said to
him, "What I am doing, you do not understand
now, but you will understand later." **8** [v]Peter
said to him, "You will never wash my feet."
Jesus answered him, "Unless I wash you, you
will have no inheritance with me." **9** Simon
Peter said to him, "Master, then not only my
feet, but my hands and head as well."
**10** [w]*Jesus said to him, "Whoever has bathed
has no need except to have his feet washed, for
he is clean all over; so you are clean, but not
all." **11** [x]For he knew who would betray him;
for this reason, he said, "Not all of you are
clean."

**12** So when he had washed their feet [and]
put his garments back on and reclined at table
again, he said to them, "Do you realize what I
have done for you? **13** [y]You call me 'teacher'
and 'master,' and rightly so, for indeed I am.
**14** If I, therefore, the master and teacher, have
washed your feet, you ought to wash one another's feet. **15** [z]I have given you a model to follow, so that as I have done for you, you should
also do. **16** [a]*Amen, amen, I say to you, no
slave is greater than his master nor any messenger greater than the one who sent him. **17** If you
understand this, blessed are you if you do it.
**18** [b]I am not speaking of all of you. I know
those whom I have chosen. But so that the scripture might be fulfilled, 'The one who ate my
food has raised his heel against me.' **19** From
now on I am telling you before it happens, so
that when it happens you may believe that I AM.
**20** [c]Amen, amen, I say to you, whoever receives the one I send receives me, and whoever
receives me receives the one who sent me."

### Announcement of Judas's Betrayal

**21** [d]When he had said this, Jesus was deeply
troubled and testified, "Amen, amen, I say to
you, one of you will betray me." **22** The disciples looked at one another, at a loss as to whom

k 5, 44.
l 13, 20; 14, 1.
m 14, 7-9.
n 1, 9; 8, 12.
o 3, 17.
p Lk 10, 16; Heb 4, 12.
q 14, 10.31; Dt 18, 18-19.
r 2, 4; 7, 30; 8, 20; Mt 26, 17.45; Mk 14, 12.41; Lk 22, 7.
s 6, 71; 17, 12; Mt 26, 20-21; Mk 14, 17-18; Lk 22, 3.
t 3, 35.
u 1 Sm 25, 41.
v 2 Sm 20, 1.
w 15, 3.
x 6, 70.
y Mt 23, 8.10.
z Lk 22, 27; 1 Pt 2, 21.
a 15, 20; Mt 10, 24; Lk 6, 40.
b Ps 41, 10.
c Mt 10, 40; Mk 9, 37; Lk 9, 48.
d Mt 26, 21-25; Mk 14, 18-21; Lk 22, 21-23.

*

13, 1—19, 42: The Book of Glory. There is a major break here; the word "sign" is used again only in 20, 30. In this phase of Jesus' return to the Father, the discourses (chs 13–17) precede the traditional narrative of the passion (chs 18–20) to interpret them for the Christian reader. This is the only extended example of esoteric teaching of disciples in John.

13, 1–20: Washing of the disciples' feet. This episode occurs in John at the place of the narration of the institution of the Eucharist in the synoptics. It may be a dramatization of Lk 22, 27: "I am your servant." It is presented as a "model" ("pattern") of the crucifixion. It symbolizes cleansing from sin by sacrificial death.

13, 1: *Before the feast of Passover:* this would be Thursday evening, before the day of preparation; in the synoptics, the Last Supper is a Passover meal taking place, in John's chronology, on Friday evening. *To the end:* or, "completely."

13, 2: *Induced:* literally, "The devil put into the heart that Judas should hand him over."

13, 5: The act of washing another's feet was one that could not be required of the lowliest Jewish slave. It is an allusion to the humiliating death of the crucifixion.

13, 10: *Bathed:* many have suggested that this passage is a symbolic reference to baptism. The Greek root involved is used in baptismal contexts in 1 Cor 6, 11; Eph 5, 26; Ti 3, 5; Heb 10, 22.

13, 16: *Messenger:* the Greek has *apostolos,* the only occurrence of the term in John. It is not used in the technical sense here.

he meant. 23 [e]*One of his disciples, the one
whom Jesus loved, was reclining at Jesus' side.
24 So Simon Peter nodded to him to find out
whom he meant. 25 [f]He leaned back against
Jesus' chest and said to him, "Master, who is
it?" 26 *Jesus answered, "It is the one to
whom I hand the morsel after I have dipped it."
So he dipped the morsel and [took it and] handed it to Judas, son of Simon the Iscariot.
27 [g]After he took the morsel, Satan entered
him. So Jesus said to him, "What you are going
to do, do quickly." 28 [Now] none of those
reclining at table realized why he said this to
him. 29 [h]Some thought that since Judas kept
the money bag, Jesus had told him, "Buy what
we need for the feast," or to give something to
the poor. 30 So he took the morsel and left at
once. And it was night.

**The New Commandment** 31 *When he
had left, Jesus said, "Now is the Son of Man
glorified, and God is glorified in him. 32 [i][If
God is glorified in him,] God will also glorify
him in himself, and he will glorify him at once.
33 [j]My children, I will be with you only a little
while longer. You will look for me, and as I told
the Jews, 'Where I go you cannot come,' so
now I say it to you. 34 [k]*I give you a new
commandment: love one another. As I have
loved you, so you also should love one another.
35 This is how all will know that you are my
disciples, if you have love for one another."

**Peter's Denial Predicted** 36 [l]Simon Peter said to him, "Master, where are you going?" Jesus answered [him], "Where I am going, you cannot follow me now, though you will
follow later." 37 Peter said to him, "Master,
why can't I follow you now? I will lay down my
life for you." 38 [m]Jesus answered, "Will you
lay down your life for me? Amen, amen, I say
to you, the cock will not crow before you deny
me three times."

## CHAPTER 14

**Last Supper Discourses** 1 *"Do not let
your hearts be troubled. You have faith in God;
have faith also in me. 2 In my Father's house
there are many dwelling places. If there were
not, would I have told you that I am going to
prepare a place for you? 3 [n]*And if I go and
prepare a place for you, I will come back again
and take you to myself, so that where I am you
also may be. 4 *Where [I] am going you know
the way." 5 Thomas said to him, "Master, we
do not know where you are going; how can we
know the way?" 6 [o]*Jesus said to him, "I am
the way and the truth and the life. No one comes
to the Father except through me. 7 [p]*If you
know me, then you will also know my Father.
From now on you do know him and have seen
him." 8 [q]*Philip said to him, "Master, show
us the Father, and that will be enough for us."
9 [r]Jesus said to him, "Have I been with you for
so long a time and you still do not know me,
Philip? Whoever has seen me has seen the Father. How can you say, 'Show us the Father'?
10 [s]Do you not believe that I am in the Father
and the Father is in me? The words that I speak
to you I do not speak on my own. The Father
who dwells in me is doing his works.
11 [t]Believe me that I am in the Father and the
Father is in me, or else, believe because of the
works themselves. 12 [u]Amen, amen, I say to
you, whoever believes in me will do the works
that I do, and will do greater ones than these,
because I am going to the Father. 13 [v]And

e 19, 26; 20, 2; 21, 7.20; Mt 10, 37.
f 21, 20.
g 13, 2; Lk 22, 3.
h 12, 5-6.
i 17, 1-5.
j 7, 33; 8, 21.
k 15, 12-13.17; Lv 19, 18; 1 Thes 4, 9; 1 Jn 2, 7-10; 3, 23; 2 Jn 5.
l Mk 14, 27; Lk 22, 23.
m 18, 27; Mt 26, 33-35; Mk 14, 29-31; Lk 22, 33-34.
n 12, 26; 17, 24; 1 Jn 2, 28.
o 8, 31-47.
p 8, 19; 12, 45.
q Ex 24, 9-10; 33, 18.
r 1, 18; 10, 30; 12, 45; 2 Cor 4, 4; Col 1, 15; Heb 1, 3.
s 1, 1; 10, 37-38; 12, 49.
t 10, 38.
u 1, 50; 5, 20.
v 15, 7.16; 16, 23-24; Mt 7, 7-11.

*

13, 23: *The one whom Jesus loved:* also mentioned in 19, 26; 20, 2; 21, 7. A disciple, called "another disciple" or "the other disciple," is mentioned in 18, 15 and 20, 2; in the latter reference he is identified with the disciple whom Jesus loved. There is also an unnamed disciple in 1, 35–40; see the note on 1, 37.

13, 26: *Morsel:* probably the bitter herb dipped in salt water.

13, 31—17, 26: Two farewell discourses and a prayer. These seem to be Johannine compositions, including sayings of Jesus at the Last Supper and on other occasions, modeled on similar farewell discourses in Greek literature and the Old Testament (of Moses, Joshua, David).

13, 31–38: Introduction: departure and return. Terms of coming and going predominate. These verses form an introduction to the last discourse of Jesus, which extends through chs 14 to 17. In it John has collected Jesus' words to *his own* (13, 1). There are indications that several speeches have been fused together, e.g., in 14, 31 and 17, 1.

13, 34: *I give you a new commandment:* this puts Jesus on a par with Yahweh. The commandment itself is not new; cf Lv 19, 18 and the note there.

14, 1–31: Jesus' departure and return. This section is a dialogue marked off by a literary inclusion in vv 1 and 27: "Do not let your hearts be troubled."

14, 1: *You have faith:* could also be imperative: "Have faith."

14, 3: *Come back again:* a rare Johannine reference to the parousia; cf 1 Jn 2, 28.

14, 4: *The way:* here, of Jesus himself; also a designation of Christianity in Acts 9, 2; 19, 9.23; 22, 4; 24, 14.22.

14, 6: *The truth:* in John, the divinely revealed reality of the Father manifested in the person and works of Jesus. The possession of truth confers knowledge and liberation from sin (8, 32).

14, 7: An alternative reading, "If you knew me, then you would have known my Father also," would be a rebuke, as in 8, 19.

14, 8: *Show us the Father:* Philip is pictured asking for a theophany like Ex 24, 9–10; 33, 18.

whatever you ask in my name, I will do, so that
the Father may be glorified in the Son. **14** If
you ask anything of me in my name, I will do
it.

### The Advocate

**15** [w]"If you love me, you
will keep my commandments. **16** [x]*And I will
ask the Father, and he will give you another
Advocate to be with you always, **17** [y]*the Spirit of truth, which the world cannot accept, because it neither sees nor knows it. But you know
it, because it remains with you, and will be in
you. **18** *I will not leave you orphans; I will
come to you. **19** [z]In a little while the world will
no longer see me, but you will see me, because
I live and you will live. **20** [a]On that day you
will realize that I am in my Father and you are
in me and I in you. **21** [b]Whoever has my commandments and observes them is the one who
loves me. And whoever loves me will be loved
by my Father, and I will love him and reveal
myself to him." **22** [c]*Judas, not the Iscariot,
said to him, "Master, [then] what happened that
you will reveal yourself to us and not to the
world?" **23** [d]Jesus answered and said to him,
"Whoever loves me will keep my word, and my
Father will love him, and we will come to him
and make our dwelling with him. **24** Whoever
does not love me does not keep my words; yet
the word you hear is not mine but that of the
Father who sent me.

**25** "I have told you this while I am with you.
**26** [e]The Advocate, the holy Spirit that the Father will send in my name—he will teach you
everything and remind you of all that [I] told
you. **27** [f]*Peace I leave with you; my peace I
give to you. Not as the world gives do I give it
to you. Do not let your hearts be troubled or
afraid. **28** [g]*You heard me tell you, 'I am going away and I will come back to you.' If you
loved me, you would rejoice that I am going to
the Father; for the Father is greater than I.
**29** [h]And now I have told you this before it
happens, so that when it happens you may believe. **30** *I will no longer speak much with
you, for the ruler of the world is coming. He has
no power over me, **31** [i]but the world must
know that I love the Father and that I do just as
the Father has commanded me. Get up, let us
go.

## CHAPTER 15

### The Vine and the Branches

**1** [j]*"I am
the true vine, and my Father is the vine grower.
**2** *He takes away every branch in me that does
not bear fruit, and everyone that does he prunes
so that it bears more fruit. **3** [k]You are already
pruned because of the word that I spoke to you.
**4** Remain in me, as I remain in you. Just as a
branch cannot bear fruit on its own unless it
remains on the vine, so neither can you unless
you remain in me. **5** I am the vine, you are the
branches. Whoever remains in me and I in him
will bear much fruit, because without me you
can do nothing. **6** [l]*Anyone who does not remain in me will be thrown out like a branch and
wither; people will gather them and throw them
into a fire and they will be burned. **7** [m]If you
remain in me and my words remain in you, ask
for whatever you want and it will be done for
you. **8** [n]By this is my Father glorified, that you
bear much fruit and become my disciples.
**9** [o]As the Father loves me, so I also love you.

---

w 15, 10; Dt 6, 4-9; Ps 119; Wis 6, 18; 1 Jn 5, 3; 2 Jn 6.
x 15, 26; Lk 24, 49; 1 Jn 2, 1.
y 16, 13; Mt 28, 20; 2 Jn 1-2.
z 16, 16.
a 10, 38; 17, 21; Is 2, 17; 4, 2-3.
b 16, 27; 1 Jn 2, 5; 3, 24.
c 7, 4; Acts 10, 40-41.
d Rv 3, 20.
e 15, 26; 16, 7.13-14; Ps 51, 13; Is 63, 10.
f 16, 33; Eph 2, 14-18.
g 8, 40.
h 13, 19; 16, 4.
i 6, 38.
j Ps 80, 9-17; Is 5, 1-7; Jer 2, 21; Ez 15, 2; 17, 5-10; 19, 10.
k 13, 10.
l Ez 15, 6-7; 19, 10-14.
m 14, 13; Mt 7, 7; Mk 11, 24; 1 Jn 5, 14.
n Mt 5, 16.
o 17, 23.

*

14, 16: *Another Advocate:* Jesus is the first advocate (paraclete); see 1 Jn 2, 1, where Jesus is an advocate in the sense of intercessor in heaven. The Greek term derives from legal terminology for an advocate or defense attorney, and can mean spokesman, mediator, intercessor, comforter, consoler, although no one of these terms encompasses the meaning in John. The Paraclete in John is a teacher, a witness to Jesus, and a prosecutor of the world, who represents the continued presence on earth of the Jesus who has returned to the Father.

14, 17: *The Spirit of truth:* this term is also used at Qumran, where it is a moral force put into a person by God, as opposed to the spirit of perversity. It is more personal in John; it will teach the realities of the new order (26), and testify to the truth (6). While it has been customary to use masculine personal pronouns in English for the Advocate, the Greek word for "spirit" is neuter, and the Greek text and manuscript variants fluctuate between masculine and neuter pronouns.

14, 18: *I will come to you:* indwelling, not parousia.

14, 22: *Judas, not the Iscariot:* probably not the brother of Jesus in Mk 6, 3 // Mt 13, 55 or the apostle named Jude in Lk 6, 16, but Thomas (see the note on 11, 16), although other readings have "Judas the Cananean."

14, 27: *Peace:* the traditional Hebrew salutation *šalôm;* but Jesus' "Shalom" is a gift of salvation, connoting the bounty of messianic blessing.

14, 28: *The Father is greater than I:* because he *sent, gave,* etc., and Jesus is "a man who has told you the truth that I heard from God" (8, 40).

14, 30: *The ruler of the world:* Satan; cf 12, 31; 16, 11.

15, 1—16, 4: Discourse on the union of Jesus with his disciples. His words become a monologue and go beyond the immediate crisis of the departure of Jesus.

15, 1-17: Like 10, 1-5, this passage resembles a parable. Israel is spoken of as a vineyard at Is 5, 1-7; Mt 21, 33-46 and as a vine at Ps 80, 9-17; Jer 2, 21; Ez 15, 2; 17, 5-10; 19, 10; Hos 10, 1. The identification of the vine as the Son of Man in Ps 80, 16, and Wisdom's description of herself as a vine in Sir 24, 17, are further background for portrayal of Jesus by this figure. There may be secondary eucharistic symbolism here; cf Mk 14, 25, "the fruit of the vine."

15, 2: *Takes away . . . prunes:* in Greek there is a play on two related verbs.

15, 6: Branches were cut off and dried on the wall of the vineyard for later use as fuel.

Remain in my love. **10** *p* If you keep my commandments, you will remain in my love, just as
I have kept my Father's commandments and
remain in his love.

**11** *q* "I have told you this so that my joy
might be in you and your joy might be complete.
**12** *r* This is my commandment: love one another as I love you. **13** *s** No one has greater love
than this, to lay down one's life for one's
friends. **14** You are my friends if you do what
I command you. **15** *t** I no longer call you
slaves, because a slave does not know what his
master is doing. I have called you friends, because I have told you everything I have heard
from my Father. **16** *u* It was not you who chose
me, but I who chose you and appointed you to
go and bear fruit that will remain, so that whatever you ask the Father in my name he may give
you. **17** *v* This I command you: love one another.

**The World's Hatred** **18** *w** "If the world
hates you, realize that it hated me first. **19** *x* If
you belonged to the world, the world would
love its own; but because you do not belong to
the world, and I have chosen you out of the
world, the world hates you. **20** *y** Remember
the word I spoke to you, 'No slave is greater
than his master.' If they persecuted me, they
will also persecute you. If they kept my word,
they will also keep yours. **21** *z** And they will
do all these things to you on account of my
name, because they do not know the one who
sent me. **22** *a** If I had not come and spoken to
them, they would have no sin; but as it is they
have no excuse for their sin. **23** *b* Whoever
hates me also hates my Father. **24** *c* If I had not
done works among them that no one else ever
did, they would not have sin; but as it is, they
have seen and hated both me and my Father.
**25** *d** But in order that the word written in their
law might be fulfilled, 'They hated me without
cause.'

**26** *e** "When the Advocate comes whom I
will send you from the Father, the Spirit of truth
that proceeds from the Father, he will testify to
me. **27** *f* And you also testify, because you have
been with me from the beginning.

## CHAPTER 16

**1** "I have told you this so that you may not
fall away. **2** *g** They will expel you from the
synagogues; in fact, the hour is coming when
everyone who kills you will think he is offering
worship to God. **3** *h* They will do this because
they have not known either the Father or me.
**4** *i** I have told you this so that when their hour
comes you may remember that I told you.

**Jesus' Departure; Coming of the Advo-
cate** "I did not tell you this from the beginning, because I was with you. **5** *j** But now I am
going to the one who sent me, and not one of
you asks me, 'Where are you going?' **6** But
because I told you this, grief has filled your
hearts. **7** *k* But I tell you the truth, it is better for
you that I go. For if I do not go, the Advocate
will not come to you. But if I go, I will send him
to you. **8** * And when he comes he will convict

p 8, 29; 14, 15.
q 16, 22; 17, 13.
r 13, 34.
s Rom 5, 6-8; 1 Jn 3, 16.
t Dt 34, 5; Jos 24, 29; 2 Chr 20, 7; Ps 89, 21; Is 41, 8;Rom 8, 15; Gal 4, 7; Jas 2, 23.
u 14, 13; Dt 7, 6.
v 13, 34; 1 Jn 3, 23; 4, 21.
w 7, 7; 14, 17; Mt 10, 22; 24, 9; Mk 13, 13; Lk 6, 22; 1 Jn 3, 13.
x 17, 14-16; 1 Jn 4, 5.
y 13, 16; Mt 10, 24.
z 8, 19; 16, 3.
a 8, 21.24; 9, 41.
b 5, 23; Lk 10, 16; 1 Jn 2, 23.
c 3, 2; 9, 32; Dt 4, 32-33.
d Ps 35, 19; 69, 4.
e 14, 16.26; Mt 10, 19-20.
f Lk 1, 2; Acts 1, 8.
g 9, 22; 12, 42; Mt 10, 17; Lk 21, 12; Acts 26, 11.
h 15, 21.
i 13, 19; 14, 29.
j 7, 33; 13, 36; 14, 5.
k 7, 39; 14, 16-17.26; 15, 26.

*

15, 13: *For one's friends:* or: "those whom one loves." In 9–13a, the words for love are related to the Greek *agapaō*. In 13b–15, the words for love are related to the Greek *phileō*. For John, the two roots seem synonymous and mean "to love"; cf also 21, 15–17. The word *philos* is used here.

15, 15: *Slaves . . . friends:* in the Old Testament, Moses (Dt 34, 5), Joshua (Jos 24, 29), and David (Ps 89, 21) were called "servants" or "slaves of Yahweh"; only Abraham (Is 41, 8; 2 Chr 20, 7; cf Jas 2, 23) was called a "friend of God."

15, 18—16, 4: The hostile reaction of the world. There are synoptic parallels, predicting persecution, especially at Mt 10, 17–25; 24, 9–10.

15, 20: *The word I spoke to you:* a reference to 13, 16.

15, 21: *On account of my name:* the idea of persecution for Jesus' name is frequent in the New Testament (Mt 10, 22; 24, 9; Acts 9, 14). For John, association with Jesus' name implies union with Jesus.

15, 22.24: Jesus' words (*spoken*) and deeds (*works*) are the great motives of credibility. *They have seen and hated:* probably means that they have seen his works and still have hated; but the Greek can be read: "have seen both me and my Father and still have hated both me and my Father." *Works . . . that no one else ever did:* so Yahweh in Dt 4, 32–33.

15, 25: *In their law:* law is here used as a larger concept than the Pentateuch, for the reference is to Ps 35, 19 or 69, 5. See the notes on 10, 34; 12, 34. *Their* law reflects the argument of the church with the synagogue.

15, 26: *Whom I will send:* in 14, 16.26, the Paraclete is to be sent by the Father, at the request of Jesus. Here the Spirit comes from both Jesus and the Father in mission; there is no reference here to the eternal procession of the Spirit.

16, 2: *Hour:* of persecution, not Jesus' "hour" (see the note on 2, 4).

16, 4b–33: A duplicate of 14, 1–31 on departure and return.

16, 5: *Not one of you asks me:* the difficulty of reconciling this with Simon Peter's question in 13, 36 and Thomas' words in 14, 5 strengthens the supposition that the last discourse has been made up of several collections of Johannine material.

16, 8–11: These verses illustrate the forensic character of the Paraclete's role: in the forum of the disciples' conscience he prosecutes the world. He leads believers to see (a) that the basic sin was and is refusal to believe in Jesus; (b) that, although Jesus was found guilty and apparently died in disgrace, in reality righteousness has triumphed, for Jesus has returned to his Father; (c) finally, that it is *the ruler of this world*, Satan, who has been condemned through Jesus' death (12, 32).

the world in regard to sin and righteousness and
condemnation: **9** [l] sin, because they do not believe in me; **10** righteousness, because I am
going to the Father and you will no longer see
me; **11** [m] condemnation, because the ruler of
this world has been condemned.

**12** "I have much more to tell you, but you
cannot bear it now. **13** [n]*But when he comes,
the Spirit of truth, he will guide you to all truth.
He will not speak on his own, but he will speak
what he hears, and will declare to you the things
that are coming. **14** He will glorify me, because
he will take from what is mine and declare it to
you. **15** Everything that the Father has is mine;
for this reason I told you that he will take from
what is mine and declare it to you.

**16** [o] "A little while and you will no longer
see me, and again a little while later and you
will see me." **17** So some of his disciples said
to one another, "What does this mean that he
is saying to us, 'A little while and you will not
see me, and again a little while and you will see
me,' and 'Because I am going to the Father'?"
**18** So they said, "What is this 'little while' [of
which he speaks]? We do not know what he
means." **19** Jesus knew that they wanted to ask
him, so he said to them, "Are you discussing
with one another what I said, 'A little while and
you will not see me, and again a little while and
you will see me'? **20** [p] Amen, amen, I say to
you, you will weep and mourn, while the world
rejoices; you will grieve, but your grief will
become joy. **21** [q] When a woman is in labor,
she is in anguish because her hour has arrived;
but when she has given birth to a child, she no
longer remembers the pain because of her joy
that a child has been born into the world.
**22** [r] So you also are now in anguish. But I will
see you again, and your hearts will rejoice, and
no one will take your joy away from you.
**23** [s] On that day you will not question me about
anything. Amen, amen, I say to you, whatever
you ask the Father in my name he will give you.
**24** Until now you have not asked anything in
my name; ask and you will receive, so that your
joy may be complete.

**25** [t]*"I have told you this in figures of
speech. The hour is coming when I will no
longer speak to you in figures but I will tell you
clearly about the Father. **26** [u] On that day you
will ask in my name, and I do not tell you that
I will ask the Father for you. **27** For the Father
himself loves you, because you have loved me
and have come to believe that I came from God.
**28** [v] I came from the Father and have come into
the world. Now I am leaving the world and
going back to the Father." **29** His disciples
said, "Now you are talking plainly, and not in
any figure of speech. **30** *Now we realize that
you know everything and that you do not need
to have anyone question you. Because of this we
believe that you came from God." **31** Jesus
answered them, "Do you believe now?
**32** [w]*Behold, the hour is coming and has arrived when each of you will be scattered to his
own home and you will leave me alone. But I
am not alone, because the Father is with me.
**33** [x] I have told you this so that you might have
peace in me. In the world you will have trouble,
but take courage, I have conquered the world."

## CHAPTER 17

**The Prayer of Jesus** **1** [y]*When Jesus had
said this, he raised his eyes to heaven and said,
"Father, the hour has come. Give glory to your
son, so that your son may glorify you, **2** [z]*just
as you gave him authority over all people, so
that he may give eternal life to all you gave him.
**3** [a]*Now this is eternal life, that they should
know you, the only true God, and the one whom
you sent, Jesus Christ. **4** I glorified you on
earth by accomplishing the work that you gave
me to do. **5** [b] Now glorify me, Father, with you,

l 8, 21-24; 15, 22.
m 12, 31.
n 14, 17.26; 15, 26; Pss 25, 5; 143, 10; 1 Jn 2, 27; Rv 7, 17.
o 7, 33; 14, 19.
p Ps 126, 6.
q Is 26, 17-18; Jer 31, 13; Mic 4, 9.
r 14, 19; 15, 11; 20, 20.
s 14, 13.
t Mt 13, 34-35.
u 14, 13.
v 1, 1.
w 8, 29; Zec 13, 7; Mt 26, 31; Mk 14, 27.
x 14, 27.
y 13, 31.
z 3, 35; Mt 28, 18.
a 1, 17; Wis 14, 7; 15, 3; 1 Jn 5, 20.
b 1, 1.2; 12, 28; Phil 2, 6.9-11.

*

16, 13: *Declare to you the things that are coming:* not a reference to new predictions about the future, but interpretation of what has already occurred or been said.

16, 25: See the note on 10, 6. Here, possibly a reference to 15, 1–16 or 16, 21.

16, 30: The reference is seemingly to the fact that Jesus could anticipate their question in v 19. The disciples naively think they have the full understanding that is the climax of "the hour" of Jesus' death, resurrection, and ascension (25), but the only part of the hour that is at hand for them is their share in the passion (32).

16, 32: *You will be scattered:* cf Mk 14, 27 and Mt 26, 31, where both cite Zec 13, 7 about the sheep being dispersed.

17, 1–26: Climax of the last discourse(s). Since the sixteenth century, this chapter has been called the "high priestly prayer" of Jesus. He speaks as intercessor, with words addressed directly to the Father and not to the disciples, who supposedly only overhear. Yet the prayer is one of petition, for immediate (6–19) and future (20–21) disciples. Many phrases reminiscent of the Lord's Prayer occur. Although still in the world (13), Jesus looks on his earthly ministry as a thing of the past (4.12). Whereas Jesus has up to this time stated that the disciples could follow him (13, 33.36), now he wishes them to be with him in union with the Father (12–14).

17, 1: The action of looking up to heaven and the address *Father* are typical of Jesus at prayer; cf 11, 41 and Lk 11, 2.

17, 2: Another possible interpretation is to treat the first line of the verse as parenthetical and the second as an appositive to the clause that ends v 1: *so that your son may glorify you (just as . . . all people), so that he may give eternal life. . . .*

17, 3: This verse was clearly added in the editing of the gospel as a reflection on the preceding verse; Jesus nowhere else refers to himself as Jesus Christ.

with the glory that I had with you before the
world began.
**6** *"I revealed your name to those whom you
gave me out of the world. They belonged to
you, and you gave them to me, and they have
kept your word. **7** Now they know that everything you gave me is from you, **8** because the
words you gave to me I have given to them, and
they accepted them and truly understood that I
came from you, and they have believed that you
sent me. **9** [c]I pray for them. I do not pray for
the world but for the ones you have given me,
because they are yours, **10** [d]and everything of
mine is yours and everything of yours is mine,
and I have been glorified in them. **11** And now
I will no longer be in the world, but they are in
the world, while I am coming to you. Holy
Father, keep them in your name that you have
given me, so that they may be one just as we are.
**12** [e]When I was with them I protected them in
your name that you gave me, and I guarded
them, and none of them was lost except the son
of destruction, in order that the scripture might
be fulfilled. **13** [f]But now I am coming to you.
I speak this in the world so that they may share
my joy completely. **14** [g]I gave them your word,
and the world hated them, because they do not
belong to the world any more than I belong to
the world. **15** [h]*I do not ask that you take them
out of the world but that you keep them from the
evil one. **16** They do not belong to the world
any more than I belong to the world.
**17** [i]Consecrate them in the truth. Your word is
truth. **18** [j]As you sent me into the world, so I
sent them into the world. **19** And I consecrate
myself for them, so that they also may be consecrated in truth.
**20** "I pray not only for them, but also for
those who will believe in me through their
word, **21** [k]so that they may all be one, as you,
Father, are in me and I in you, that they also
may be in us, that the world may believe that
you sent me. **22** And I have given them the
glory you gave me, so that they may be one, as
we are one, **23** I in them and you in me, that
they may be brought to perfection as one, that
the world may know that you sent me, and that
you loved them even as you loved me.
**24** [l]*Father, they are your gift to me. I wish
that where I am they also may be with me, that
they may see my glory that you gave me, because you loved me before the foundation of the
world. **25** [m]Righteous Father, the world also
does not know you, but I know you, and they
know that you sent me. **26** *I made known to
them your name and I will make it known, that
the love with which you loved me may be in
them and I in them."

## CHAPTER 18

### Jesus Arrested

**1** [n]*When he had said
this, Jesus went out with his disciples across the
Kidron valley to where there was a garden, into
which he and his disciples entered. **2** Judas his
betrayer also knew the place, because Jesus had
often met there with his disciples. **3** [o]*So Judas
got a band of soldiers and guards from the chief
priests and the Pharisees and went there with
lanterns, torches, and weapons. **4** Jesus, knowing everything that was going to happen to him,
went out and said to them, "Whom are you
looking for?" **5** *They answered him, "Jesus
the Nazorean." He said to them, "I AM."
Judas his betrayer was also with them. **6** When
he said to them, "I AM," they turned away and
fell to the ground. **7** So he again asked them,
"Whom are you looking for?" They said,
"Jesus the Nazorean." **8** Jesus answered, "I
told you that I AM. So if you are looking for me,
let these men go." **9** [p]*This was to fulfill what
he had said, "I have not lost any of those you
gave me." **10** *Then Simon Peter, who had a
sword, drew it, struck the high priest's slave,
and cut off his right ear. The slave's name was

c 17, 20.
d 16, 15; 2 Thes 1, 10.12.
e 13, 18; 18, 9; Ps 41, 10; Mt 26, 24; Acts 1, 16.
f 15, 11.
g 15, 19.
h Mt 6, 13; 2 Thes 3, 3; 1 Jn 5, 18.
i 1 Pt 1, 22
j 20, 21-22.
k 10, 30; 14, 10-11.20.
l 14, 3; 1 Thes 4, 17.
m 1, 10.
n 2 Sm 15, 23; Mt 26, 30.36; Mk 14, 26.32; Lk 22, 39.
o Mt 26, 47-51; Mk 14, 43-44; Lk 22, 47.
p 6, 39; 10, 28; 17, 12.

*

17, 6: *I revealed your name:* perhaps the name *I AM;* cf 8, 24. 28.58; 13, 19.

17, 15: Note the resemblance to the petition of the Lord's Prayer, "deliver us from the evil one." Both probably refer to the devil rather than to abstract evil.

17, 24: *Where I am:* Jesus prays for the believers ultimately to join him in heaven. Then they will not see his glory as in a mirror but clearly (2 Cor 3, 18; 1 Jn 3, 2).

17, 26: *I will make it known:* through the Advocate.

18, 1–14: John does not mention the agony in the garden and the kiss of Judas, nor does he identify the place as Gethsemane or the Mount of Olives.

18, 1: *Jesus went out:* see 14, 31, where it seems he is leaving the supper room. *Kidron valley:* literally, "the winter-flowing Kidron"; this wadi has water only during the winter rains.

18, 3: *Band of soldiers:* seems to refer to Roman troops, either the full cohort of 600 men (1/10 of a legion), or more likely the maniple of 200 under their tribune (12). In this case, John is hinting at Roman collusion in the action against Jesus before he was brought to Pilate. The lanterns and torches may be symbolic of the hour of darkness.

18, 5: *Nazorean:* the form found in Mt 26, 71 (see the note on Mt 2, 23) is here used, not *Nazarene* of Mark. *I AM:* or "I am he," but probably intended by the evangelist as an expression of divinity (cf their appropriate response in 6); see the note on 8, 24. John sets the confusion of the arresting party against the background of Jesus' divine majesty.

18, 9: The citation may refer to 6, 39; 10, 28; or 17, 12.

18, 10: Only John gives the names of the two antagonists; both John and Luke mention the right ear.

Malchus. 11 [q]*Jesus said to Peter, "Put your
sword into its scabbard. Shall I not drink the cup
that the Father gave me?"

12 [r]So the band of soldiers, the tribune, and
the Jewish guards seized Jesus, bound him,
13 [s]*and brought him to Annas first. He was
the father-in-law of Caiaphas, who was high
priest that year. 14 [t]It was Caiaphas who had
counseled the Jews that it was better that one
man should die rather than the people.

**Peter's First Denial** 15 [u]*Simon Peter and
another disciple followed Jesus. Now the other
disciple was known to the high priest, and he
entered the courtyard of the high priest with
Jesus. 16 But Peter stood at the gate outside. So
the other disciple, the acquaintance of the high
priest, went out and spoke to the gatekeeper and
brought Peter in. 17 Then the maid who was the
gatekeeper said to Peter, "You are not one of
this man's disciples, are you?" He said, "I am
not." 18 Now the slaves and the guards were
standing around a charcoal fire that they had
made, because it was cold, and were warming
themselves. Peter was also standing there keeping warm.

**The Inquiry before Annas** 19 [v]The high
priest questioned Jesus about his disciples and
about his doctrine. 20 [w]*Jesus answered him,
"I have spoken publicly to the world. I have
always taught in a synagogue or in the temple
area where all the Jews gather, and in secret I
have said nothing. 21 Why ask me? Ask those
who heard me what I said to them. They know
what I said." 22 [x]When he had said this, one
of the temple guards standing there struck Jesus
and said, "Is this the way you answer the high
priest?" 23 Jesus answered him, "If I have
spoken wrongly, testify to the wrong; but if I
have spoken rightly, why do you strike me?"
24 [y]*Then Annas sent him bound to Caiaphas
the high priest.

**Peter Denies Jesus Again** 25 [z]Now Simon Peter was standing there keeping warm.
And they said to him, "You are not one of his
disciples, are you?" He denied it and said, "I
am not." 26 One of the slaves of the high
priest, a relative of the one whose ear Peter had
cut off, said, "Didn't I see you in the garden
with him?" 27 *Again Peter denied it. And
immediately the cock crowed.

**The Trial before Pilate** 28 [a]*Then they
brought Jesus from Caiaphas to the praetorium.
It was morning. And they themselves did not
enter the praetorium, in order not to be defiled
so that they could eat the Passover. 29 So Pilate
came out to them and said, "What charge do
you bring [against] this man?" 30 They answered and said to him, "If he were not a criminal, we would not have handed him over to
you." 31 *At this, Pilate said to them, "Take
him yourselves, and judge him according to
your law." The Jews answered him, "We do
not have the right to execute anyone," 32 [b]*in
order that the word of Jesus might be fulfilled
that he said indicating the kind of death he
would die. 33 So Pilate went back into the praetorium and summoned Jesus and said to him,
"Are you the King of the Jews?" 34 Jesus
answered, "Do you say this on your own or
have others told you about me?" 35 [c]Pilate
answered, "I am not a Jew, am I? Your own
nation and the chief priests handed you over to
me. What have you done?" 36 [d]Jesus answered, "My kingdom does not belong to this
world. If my kingdom did belong to this world,
my attendants [would] be fighting to keep me
from being handed over to the Jews. But as it
is, my kingdom is not here." 37 [e]*So Pilate
said to him, "Then you are a king?" Jesus
answered, "You say I am a king. For this I was

q Mt 20, 22; 26, 39; Mk 10, 38; Lk 22, 42.
r Mt 26, 57-58; Mk 14, 53-54; Lk 22, 54-55.
s Lk 3, 2.
t 11, 49-50.
u Mt 26, 58.69-70; Mk 14, 54.66-68; Lk 22, 54-57.
v Mt 26, 59-66; Mk 14, 55-64; Lk 22, 66-71.
w 6, 59; 7, 14.26; Is 48, 16; Mt 26, 55; Mk 4, 23; Lk 19, 47; 22, 53.
x Acts 23, 2.
y Mt 26, 57.
z Mt 26, 71-75; Mk 14, 69-72; Lk 22, 58-62.
a Mt 27, 1-2.11-25; Mk 15, 1-5; Lk 23, 1-5.
b 3, 14; 8, 28; 12, 32-33.
c 1, 11.
d 1, 10; 8, 23.
e 8, 47; 1 Tm 6, 13.

*

18, 11: The theme of the cup is found in the synoptic account of the agony (Mk 14, 36 and parallels).

18, 13: *Annas:* only John mentions an inquiry before Annas; cf 16.19–24; see the note on Lk 3, 2. It is unlikely that this nighttime interrogation before Annas is the same as the trial before Caiaphas placed by Matthew and Mark at night and by Luke in the morning.

18, 15–16: *Another disciple . . . the other disciple:* see the note on 13, 23.

18, 20: *I have always taught . . . in the temple area:* cf Mk 14, 49 for a similar statement.

18, 24: *Caiaphas:* see Mt 26, 3.57; Lk 3, 2; and the notes there. John may leave room here for the trial before Caiaphas described in the synoptic gospels.

18, 27: Cockcrow was the third Roman division of the night, lasting from midnight to 3 a.m.

18, 28: *Praetorium:* see the note on Mt 27, 27. *Morning:* literally, "the early hour," or fourth Roman division of the night, 3 to 6 a.m. *The Passover:* the synoptic gospels give the impression that the Thursday night supper was the Passover meal (Mk 14, 12); for John that meal is still to be eaten Friday night.

18, 31: *We do not have the right to execute anyone:* only John gives this reason for their bringing Jesus to Pilate. Jewish sources are not clear on the competence of the Sanhedrin at this period to sentence and to execute for political crimes.

18, 32: The Jewish punishment for blasphemy was stoning (Lv 24, 16). In coming to the Romans to ensure that Jesus would be crucified, the Jewish authorities fulfilled his prophecy that he would be *exalted* (3, 14; 12, 32–33). There is some historical evidence, however, for Jews crucifying Jews.

18, 37: *You say I am a king:* see Mt 26, 64 for a similar response to the high priest. It is at best a reluctant affirmative.

born and for this I came into the world, to testify
to the truth. Everyone who belongs to the truth
listens to my voice." 38 [f]Pilate said to him,
"What is truth?"

When he had said this, he again went out to
the Jews and said to them, "I find no guilt in
him. 39 *But you have a custom that I release
one prisoner to you at Passover. Do you want
me to release to you the King of the Jews?"
40 *They cried out again, "Not this one but
Barabbas!" Now Barabbas was a revolutionary.

## CHAPTER 19

1 [g]*Then Pilate took Jesus and had him
scourged. 2 And the soldiers wove a crown out
of thorns and placed it on his head, and clothed
him in a purple cloak, 3 and they came to him
and said, "Hail, King of the Jews!" And they
struck him repeatedly. 4 [h]Once more Pilate
went out and said to them, "Look, I am bringing him out to you, so that you may know that
I find no guilt in him." 5 [i]So Jesus came out,
wearing the crown of thorns and the purple
cloak. And he said to them, "Behold, the
man!" 6 [j]When the chief priests and the guards
saw him they cried out, "Crucify him, crucify
him!" Pilate said to them, "Take him yourselves and crucify him. I find no guilt in him."
7 [k]*The Jews answered, "We have a law, and
according to that law he ought to die, because
he made himself the Son of God." 8 Now when
Pilate heard this statement, he became even
more afraid, 9 [l]and went back into the praetorium and said to Jesus, "Where are you from?"
Jesus did not answer him. 10 So Pilate said to
him, "Do you not speak to me? Do you not
know that I have power to release you and I have
power to crucify you?" 11 [m]Jesus answered
[him], "You would have no power over me if
it had not been given to you from above. For this
reason the one who handed me over to you has
the greater sin." 12 [n]*Consequently, Pilate
tried to release him; but the Jews cried out, "If
you release him, you are not a Friend of Caesar.
Everyone who makes himself a king opposes
Caesar."

13 *When Pilate heard these words he
brought Jesus out and seated him on the judge's
bench in the place called Stone Pavement, in
Hebrew, Gabbatha. 14 *It was preparation day
for Passover, and it was about noon. And he
said to the Jews, "Behold, your king!"
15 They cried out, "Take him away, take him
away! Crucify him!" Pilate said to them,
"Shall I crucify your king?" The chief priests
answered, "We have no king but Caesar."
16 *Then he handed him over to them to be
crucified.

**The Crucifixion of Jesus** So they took
Jesus, 17 [o]*and carrying the cross himself he
went out to what is called the Place of the Skull,
in Hebrew, Golgotha. 18 There they crucified
him, and with him two others, one on either
side, with Jesus in the middle. 19 *Pilate also
had an inscription written and put on the cross.
It read, "Jesus the Nazorean, the King of the
Jews." 20 Now many of the Jews read this
inscription, because the place where Jesus was
crucified was near the city; and it was written in
Hebrew, Latin, and Greek. 21 [p]So the chief
priests of the Jews said to Pilate, "Do not write
'The King of the Jews,' but that he said, 'I am
the King of the Jews.'" 22 Pilate answered,
"What I have written, I have written."

f Mt 27, 15-26; Mk 15, 6-15; Lk 23, 18-25; Acts 3, 14.
g Mt 27, 27-31; Mk 15, 16-20; Lk 23, 13-25.
h 18, 38.
i Is 52, 14.
j 18, 31; 19, 15.
k 10, 33-36; Lv 24, 16.
l 7, 28.
m 3, 27; 10, 18; Rom 13, 1.
n Acts 17, 7.
o Mt 27, 32-37; Mk 15, 21-26; Lk 23, 26-35.
p 18, 33; Lk 19, 14.

*

18, 39: See the note on Mt 27, 15.

18, 40: *Barabbas:* see the note on Mt 27, 16–17. *Revolutionary:* a guerrilla warrior fighting for nationalistic aims, though the term can also denote a robber. See the note on Mt 27, 38.

19, 1: Luke places the mockery of Jesus at the midpoint in the trial when Jesus was sent to Herod. Mark and Matthew place the scourging and mockery at the end of the trial after the sentence of death. Scourging was an integral part of the crucifixion penalty.

19, 7: *Made himself the Son of God:* this question was not raised in John's account of the Jewish interrogations of Jesus as it was in the synoptic account. Nevertheless, see 5, 18; 8, 53; 10, 36.

19, 12: *Friend of Caesar:* a Roman honorific title bestowed upon high-ranking officials for merit.

19, 13: *Seated him:* others translate "(Pilate) sat down." In John's thought, Jesus is the real judge of the world, and John may here be portraying him seated on the judgment bench. *Stone Pavement:* in Greek *lithostrotos;* under the fortress Antonia, one of the conjectured locations of the praetorium, a massive stone pavement has been excavated. *Gabbatha* (Aramaic rather than Hebrew) probably means "ridge, elevation."

19, 14: *Noon:* Mk 15, 25 has Jesus crucified "at the third hour," which means either 9 a.m. or the period from 9 to 12. Noon, the time when, according to John, Jesus was sentenced to death, was the hour at which the priests began to slaughter Passover lambs in the temple; see Jn 1, 29.

19, 16: *He handed him over to them to be crucified:* in context this would seem to mean "handed him over to the chief priests." Lk 23, 25 has a similar ambiguity. There is a polemic tendency in the gospels to place the guilt of the crucifixion on the Jewish authorities and to exonerate the Romans from blame. But John later mentions the Roman soldiers (23), and it was to these soldiers that Pilate handed Jesus over.

19, 17: *Carrying the cross himself:* a different picture from that of the synoptics, especially Lk 23, 26, where Simon of Cyrene is made to carry the cross, walking behind Jesus. In John's theology, Jesus remained in complete control and master of his destiny (cf 10, 18). *Place of the Skull:* the Latin word for skull is *Calvaria;* hence "Calvary." *Golgotha* is actually an Aramaic rather than a Hebrew word.

19, 19: The inscription differs with slightly different words in each of the four gospels. John's form is fullest and gives the equivalent of the Latin *INRI—Iesus Nazarenus Rex Iudaeorum.* = Only John mentions its polyglot character (20) and Pilate's role in keeping the title unchanged (21–22).

**23** [q][r]*When the soldiers had crucified Jesus,
they took his clothes and divided them into four
shares, a share for each soldier. They also took
his tunic, but the tunic was seamless, woven in
one piece from the top down. **24** So they said
to one another, "Let's not tear it, but cast lots
for it to see whose it will be," in order that the
passage of scripture might be fulfilled [that
says]:

"They divided my garments among them,
and for my vesture they cast lots."

This is what the soldiers did. **25** [s]*Standing by
the cross of Jesus were his mother and his mother's sister, Mary the wife of Clopas, and Mary
of Magdala. **26** [t]*When Jesus saw his mother
and the disciple there whom he loved, he said
to his mother, "Woman, behold, your son."
**27** Then he said to the disciple, "Behold, your
mother." And from that hour the disciple took
her into his home.

**28** [u][v]*After this, aware that everything was
now finished, in order that the scripture might
be fulfilled, Jesus said, "I thirst." **29** *There
was a vessel filled with common wine. So they
put a sponge soaked in wine on a sprig of hyssop
and put it up to his mouth. **30** [w]*When Jesus
had taken the wine, he said, "It is finished."
And bowing his head, he handed over the spirit.

## The Blood and Water

**31** [x]Now since it
was preparation day, in order that the bodies
might not remain on the cross on the sabbath,
for the sabbath day of that week was a solemn
one, the Jews asked Pilate that their legs be
broken and they be taken down. **32** So the soldiers came and broke the legs of the first and
then of the other one who was crucified with
Jesus. **33** But when they came to Jesus and saw
that he was already dead, they did not break his
legs, **34** [y]*but one soldier thrust his lance into
his side, and immediately blood and water
flowed out. **35** [z]*An eyewitness has testified,
and his testimony is true; he knows that he is
speaking the truth, so that you also may [come
to] believe. **36** [a]For this happened so that the
scripture passage might be fulfilled:

"Not a bone of it will be broken."

**37** [b]And again another passage says:

"They will look upon him whom they
have pierced."

## The Burial of Jesus

**38** [c]*After this, Jo-
seph of Arimathea, secretly a disciple of Jesus
for fear of the Jews, asked Pilate if he could
remove the body of Jesus. And Pilate permitted
it. So he came and took his body.
**39** [d]Nicodemus, the one who had first come to
him at night, also came bringing a mixture of
myrrh and aloes weighing about one hundred
pounds. **40** They took the body of Jesus and
bound it with burial cloths along with the spices,
according to the Jewish burial custom. **41** Now
in the place where he had been crucified there
was a garden, and in the garden a new tomb, in
which no one had yet been buried. **42** So they
laid Jesus there because of the Jewish preparation day; for the tomb was close by.

---

q Mt 27, 38-44; Mk 15, 27-32; Lk 23, 36-43.
r Ps 22, 19; Mt 27, 35; Mk 15, 24; Lk 23, 34.
s Mt 27, 55; Mk 15, 40-41; Lk 8, 2; 23, 49.
t 13, 23.
u Mt 27, 45-56; Mk 15, 33-41; Lk 23, 44-49.
v Pss 22, 16; 69, 22.
w 4, 34; 10, 18; 17, 4; Lk 23, 46.
x Ex 12, 16; Dt 21, 23.
y Nm 20, 11; 1 Jn 5, 6.
z 7, 37-39; 21, 24.
a Ex 12, 46; Nm 9, 12; Ps 34, 21.
b Nm 21, 9; Zec 12, 10; Rv 1, 7.
c Mt 27, 57-60; Mk 15, 42-46; Lk 34, 50-54.
d 3, 1-2; 7, 50; Ps 45, 9.

*

19, 23–25a: While all four gospels describe the soldiers casting lots to divide Jesus' garments (see the note on Mt 27, 35), only John quotes the underlying passage from Ps 22, 19, and only John sees each line of the poetic parallelism literally carried out in two separate actions (23a; 23b–24).

19, 25: It is not clear whether four women are meant, or three (i.e., *Mary the wife of Cl[e]opas* [cf Lk 24, 18] is in apposition with *his mother's sister*) or two (his mother and his mother's sister, i.e., Mary of Cl[e]opas and Mary of Magdala). Only John mentions the mother of Jesus here. The synoptics have a group of women looking on from a distance at the cross (Mk 15, 40).

19, 26–27: This scene has been interpreted literally, of Jesus' concern for his mother; and symbolically, e.g., in the light of the Cana story in ch 2 (the presence of the mother of Jesus, the address *woman,* and the mention of the *hour*) and of the upper room in ch 13 (the presence of the beloved disciple; the *hour*). Now that the hour has come (28), Mary (a symbol of the church?) is given a role as the mother of Christians (personified by the beloved disciple); or, as a representative of those seeking salvation, she is supported by the disciple who interprets Jesus' revelation; or Jewish and Gentile Christianity (or Israel and the Christian community) are reconciled.

19, 28: *The scripture . . . fulfilled:* either in the scene of vv 25–27, or in the *I thirst* of v 28. If the latter, Pss 22, 16 and 69, 22 deserve consideration.

19, 29: *Wine:* John does not mention the drugged wine, a narcotic that Jesus refused as the crucifixion began (Mk 15, 23), but only this final gesture of kindness at the end (Mk 15, 36). *Hyssop,* a small plant, is scarcely suitable for carrying a sponge (Mark mentions a reed) and may be a symbolic reference to the hyssop used to daub the blood of the paschal lamb on the doorpost of the Hebrews (Ex 12, 22).

19, 30: *Handed over the spirit:* there is a double nuance of dying (giving up the last breath or spirit) and that of passing on the holy Spirit; see 7, 39, which connects the giving of the Spirit with Jesus' glorious return to the Father, and 20, 22, where the author portrays the conferral of the Spirit.

19, 34–35: John probably emphasizes these verses to show the reality of Jesus' death, against the docetic heretics. In the blood and water there may also be a symbolic reference to the Eucharist and baptism.

19, 35: *He knows:* it is not certain from the Greek that this *he* is the *eyewitness* of the first part of the sentence. *May [come to] believe:* see the note on 20, 31.

19, 38–42: In the first three gospels there is no anointing on Friday. In Mt and Lk, the women come to the tomb on Sunday morning precisely to anoint Jesus.

## CHAPTER 20

### The Empty Tomb
**1** [ef]*On the first day of
the week, Mary of Magdala came to the tomb
early in the morning, while it was still dark, and
saw the stone removed from the tomb. **2** *So
she ran and went to Simon Peter and to the other
disciple whom Jesus loved, and told them,
"They have taken the Lord from the tomb, and
we don't know where they put him." **3** *So
Peter and the other disciple went out and came
to the tomb. **4** They both ran, but the other
disciple ran faster than Peter and arrived at the
tomb first; **5** he bent down and saw the burial
cloths there, but did not go in. **6** [g]*When Simon Peter arrived after him, he went into the
tomb and saw the burial cloths there, **7** [h]and the
cloth that had covered his head, not with the
burial cloths but rolled up in a separate place.
**8** Then the other disciple also went in, the one
who had arrived at the tomb first, and he saw
and believed. **9** [i]*For they did not yet understand the scripture that he had to rise from the
dead. **10** Then the disciples returned home.

### The Appearance to Mary of Magdala
**11** [j]*But Mary stayed outside the tomb weeping. And as she wept, she bent over into the
tomb **12** and saw two angels in white sitting
there, one at the head and one at the feet where
the body of Jesus had been. **13** And they said
to her, "Woman, why are you weeping?" She
said to them, "They have taken my Lord, and
I don't know where they laid him." **14** [k]When
she had said this, she turned around and saw
Jesus there, but did not know it was Jesus.
**15** [l]Jesus said to her, "Woman, why are you
weeping? Whom are you looking for?" She
thought it was the gardener and said to him,
"Sir, if you carried him away, tell me where
you laid him, and I will take him." **16** *Jesus
said to her, "Mary!" She turned and said to him
in Hebrew, "Rabbouni," which means Teach-
er. **17** [m]*Jesus said to her, "Stop holding on to
me, for I have not yet ascended to the Father.
But go to my brothers and tell them, 'I am going
to my Father and your Father, to my God and
your God.' " **18** Mary of Magdala went and
announced to the disciples, "I have seen the
Lord," and what he told her.

### Appearance to the Disciples
**19** [n]*On
the evening of that first day of the week, when
the doors were locked, where the disciples
were, for fear of the Jews, Jesus came and stood
in their midst and said to them, "Peace be with
you." **20** [o]*When he had said this, he showed
them his hands and his side. The disciples rejoiced when they saw the Lord. **21** [p]*[Jesus]
said to them again, "Peace be with you. As the

e Mt 28, 1-10; Mk 16, 1-11; Lk 24, 1-12.
f 19, 25.
g Lk 24, 12.
h 11, 44; 19, 40.
i Acts 2, 26-27; 1 Cor 15, 4.
j Mk 16, 9-11.
k 21, 4; Mk 16, 12; Lk 24, 16; 1 Cor 15, 43-44.
l Mt 28, 9-10.
m Acts 1, 9.
n Mt 28, 16-20; Mk 16, 14-18; Lk 24, 36-44.
o 14, 27.
p 17, 18; Mt 28, 19; Mk 16, 15; Lk 24, 47-48.

*

20, 1–31: The risen Jesus reveals his glory and confers the Spirit. This story fulfills the basic need for testimony to the resurrection. What we have here is not a record but a series of single stories.

20, 1–10: The story of the empty tomb is found in both the Matthean and the Lucan traditions; John's version seems to be a fusion of the two.

20, 1: *Still dark:* according to Mark the sun had risen, Matthew describes it as "dawning," and Luke refers to early dawn. Mary sees the stone removed, not the empty tomb.

20, 2: Mary runs away, not directed by an angel/young man as in the synoptic accounts. The plural "we" in the second part of her statement might reflect a tradition of more women going to the tomb.

20, 3–10: The basic narrative is told of Peter alone in Lk 24, 12, a verse missing in important manuscripts and which may be borrowed from tradition similar to John. Cf also Lk 24, 24.

20, 6–8: Some special feature about the state of the burial cloths caused the beloved disciple to believe. Perhaps the details emphasized that the grave had not been robbed.

20, 9: Probably a general reference to the scriptures is intended, as in Lk 24, 26 and 1 Cor 15, 4. Some individual Old Testament passages suggested are Ps 16, 10; Hos 6, 2; Jon 2, 1.2.11.

20, 11–18: This appearance to Mary is found only in Jn, but cf Mt 28, 8–10 and Mk 16, 9–11.

20, 16: *Rabbouni:* Hebrew or Aramaic for "my master."

20, 17: *Stop holding on to me:* see Mt 28, 9, where the women take hold of his feet. *I have not yet ascended:* for John and many of the New Testament writers, the ascension in the theological sense of going to the Father to be glorified took place with the resurrection as one action. This scene in John dramatizes such an understanding, for by Easter night Jesus is glorified and can give the Spirit. Therefore his ascension takes place immediately after he has talked to Mary. In such a view, the ascension after forty days described in Acts 1, 1–11 would be simply a termination of earthly appearances or, perhaps better, an introduction to the conferral of the Spirit upon the early church, modeled on Elisha's being able to have a (double) share in the spirit of Elijah if he saw him being taken up (same verb as ascending) into heaven (2 Kgs 2, 9–12). *To my Father and your Father, to my God and your God:* this echoes Ru 1, 16: "Your people shall be my people, and your God my God." The Father of Jesus will now become the Father of the disciples because, once ascended, Jesus can give them the Spirit that comes from the Father and they can be reborn as God's children (3, 5). That is why he calls them *my brothers.*

20, 19–29: The appearances to the disciples, without or with Thomas (cf 11, 16; 14, 5), have rough parallels in the other gospels only for vv 19–23; cf Lk 24, 36–39; Mk 16, 14–18.

20, 19: *The disciples:* by implication from v 24, this means ten of the Twelve, presumably in Jerusalem. *Peace be with you:* although this could be an ordinary greeting, John intends here to echo 14, 27. The theme of rejoicing in v 20 echoes 16, 22.

20, 20: *Hands and . . . side:* Lk 24, 39–40 mentions "hands and feet," based on Ps 22, 17.

20, 21: By means of this sending, the Eleven were made apostles, that is, "those sent" (cf 17, 18), though John does not use the noun in reference to them (see the note on 13, 16). A solemn mission or "sending" is also the subject of the post-resurrection appearances to the Eleven in Mt 28, 19; Lk 24, 47; Mk 16, 15.

Father has sent me, so I send you." **22** [q]*And when he had said this, he breathed on them and said to them, "Receive the holy Spirit. **23** [r]*Whose sins you forgive are forgiven them, and whose sins you retain are retained."

**Thomas** **24** Thomas, called Didymus, one of the Twelve, was not with them when Jesus came. **25** [s]So the other disciples said to him, "We have seen the Lord." But he said to them, "Unless I see the mark of the nails in his hands and put my finger into the nailmarks and put my hand into his side, I will not believe." **26** [t]Now a week later his disciples were again inside and Thomas was with them. Jesus came, although the doors were locked, and stood in their midst and said, "Peace be with you." **27** Then he said to Thomas, "Put your finger here and see my hands, and bring your hand and put it into my side, and do not be unbelieving, but believe." **28** [u]*Thomas answered and said to him, "My Lord and my God!" **29** [v]*Jesus said to him, "Have you come to believe because you have seen me? Blessed are those who have not seen and have believed."

**Conclusion** **30** [w]*Now Jesus did many other signs in the presence of [his] disciples that are not written in this book. **31** [x]But these are written that you may [come to] believe that Jesus is the Messiah, the Son of God, and that through this belief you may have life in his name.

## *IV: EPILOGUE*

## *THE RESURRECTION APPEARANCE IN GALILEE*

### CHAPTER 21

**The Appearance to the Seven Disciples** **1** [y]*After this, Jesus revealed himself again to his disciples at the Sea of Tiberias. He revealed himself in this way. **2** *Together were Simon Peter, Thomas called Didymus, Nathanael from Cana in Galilee, Zebedee's sons, and two others of his disciples. **3** [z]*Simon Peter said to them, "I am going fishing." They said to him, "We also will come with you." So they went out and got into the boat, but that night they caught nothing. **4** [a]When it was already dawn, Jesus was standing on the shore; but the disciples did not realize that it was Jesus. **5** [b]Jesus said to them, "Children, have you caught anything to eat?" They answered him, "No." **6** So he said to them, "Cast the net over the right side of the boat and you will find something." So they cast it, and were not able to pull it in because of the number of fish. **7** So the disciple whom Jesus loved said to Peter, "It is the Lord." When Simon Peter heard that it was the Lord, he tucked in his garment, for he was lightly clad, and jumped into the sea. **8** The other disciples came in the boat, for they were not far from shore, only about a hundred yards, dragging the net with the fish. **9** [c]*When they climbed out on shore, they saw a charcoal fire with fish on it and bread. **10** Jesus said to them, "Bring some of the fish you just caught." **11** [d]*So Simon Peter went over and dragged the net ashore full of one hundred fifty-three large fish. Even though there were so many, the

q Gn 2, 7; Ez 37, 9; 1 Cor 15, 45.
r Mt 16, 19; 18, 18.
s 1 Jn 1, 1.
t 21, 14.
u 1, 1.
v 4, 48; Lk 1, 45; 1 Pt 1, 8.
w 21, 25.
x 3, 14.15; 1 Jn 5, 13.
y Mt 26, 32; 28, 7.
z Mt 4, 18; Lk 5, 4-10.
a 20, 14; Mt 28, 17; Lk 24, 16.
b Lk 24, 41.
c Lk 24, 41-43.
d 2 Chr 2, 16.

*

20, 22: This action recalls Gn 2, 7, where God breathed on the first man and gave him life; just as Adam's life came from God, so now the disciples' new spiritual life comes from Jesus. Cf also the revivification of the dry bones in Ez 37. This is the author's version of Pentecost. Cf also the note on 19, 30.

20, 23: The Council of Trent defined that this power to forgive sins is exercised in the sacrament of penance. See Mt 16, 19 and 18, 18.

20, 28: *My Lord and my God:* this forms a literary inclusion with the first verse of the gospel: "and the Word was God."

20, 29: This verse is a beatitude on future generations; faith, not sight, matters.

20, 30–31: These verses are clearly a conclusion to the gospel and express its purpose. While many manuscripts read *come to believe,* possibly implying a missionary purpose for John's gospel, a small number of quite early ones read "continue to believe," suggesting that the audience consists of Christians whose faith is to be deepened by the book; cf 19, 35.

21, 1–23: There are many non-Johannine peculiarities in this chapter, some suggesting Lucan Greek style; yet this passage is closer to John than 7, 53—8, 11. There are many Johannine features as well. Its closest parallels in the synoptic gospels are found in Lk 5, 1–11 and Mt 14, 28–31. Perhaps the tradition was ultimately derived from John but preserved by some disciple other than the writer of the rest of the gospel. The appearances narrated seem to be independent of those in ch 20. Even if a later addition, the chapter was added before publication of the gospel, for it appears in all manuscripts.

21, 2: *Zebedee's sons:* the only reference to James and John in this gospel (but see the note on 1, 37). Perhaps the phrase was originally a gloss to identify, among the five, *the two others of his disciples.* The anonymity of the latter phrase is more Johannine (1, 35). The total of seven may suggest the community of the disciples in its fullness.

21, 3–6: This may be a variant of Luke's account of the catch of fish; see the note on Lk 5, 1–11.

21, 9.12–13: It is strange that Jesus already has fish since none have yet been brought ashore. This meal may have had eucharistic significance for early Christians since v 13 recalls Jn 6, 11, which uses the vocabulary of Jesus' action at the Last Supper; but see also the note on Mt 14, 19.

21, 11: The exact number 153 is probably meant to have a symbolic meaning in relation to the apostles' universal mission; Jerome claims that Greek zoologists catalogued 153 species of fish. Or 153 is the sum of the numbers from 1 to 17. Others invoke Ez 47, 10.

net was not torn. **12** *Jesus said to them,
"Come, have breakfast." And none of the disciples dared to ask him, "Who are you?" because they realized it was the Lord. **13** [e]Jesus
came over and took the bread and gave it to
them, and in like manner the fish. **14** [f]*This
was now the third time Jesus was revealed to his
disciples after being raised from the dead.

**Jesus and Peter** **15** *When they had finished breakfast, Jesus said to Simon Peter, "Simon, son of John, do you love me more than
these?" He said to him, "Yes, Lord, you know
that I love you." He said to him, "Feed my
lambs." **16** He then said to him a second time,
"Simon, son of John, do you love me?" He said
to him, "Yes, Lord, you know that I love you."
He said to him, "Tend my sheep." **17** [g]He said
to him the third time, "Simon, son of John, do
you love me?" Peter was distressed that he had
said to him a third time, "Do you love me?"
and he said to him, "Lord, you know everything; you know that I love you." [Jesus] said
to him, "Feed my sheep. **18** [h]*Amen, amen, I
say to you, when you were younger, you used
to dress yourself and go where you wanted; but
when you grow old, you will stretch out your
hands, and someone else will dress you and lead
you where you do not want to go." **19** [i]He said
this signifying by what kind of death he would
glorify God. And when he had said this, he said
to him, "Follow me."

**The Beloved Disciple** **20** [j]Peter turned
and saw the disciple following whom Jesus
loved, the one who had also reclined upon his
chest during the supper and had said, "Master,
who is the one who will betray you?" **21** When
Peter saw him, he said to Jesus, "Lord, what
about him?" **22** [k]*Jesus said to him, "What if
I want him to remain until I come? What concern is it of yours? You follow me." **23** *So the
word spread among the brothers that that disciple would not die. But Jesus had not told him
that he would not die, just "What if I want him
to remain until I come? [What concern is it of
yours?]"

**Conclusion** **24** [l]*It is this disciple who testifies to these things and has written them, and
we know that his testimony is true. **25** [m]There
are also many other things that Jesus did, but if
these were to be described individually, I do not
think the whole world would contain the books
that would be written.

e Lk 24, 42.
f 20, 19.26.
g 13, 37-38; 18, 15-18.25-27; Mt 26, 69-75; Mk 14, 66-72; Lk 22, 55-62.
h Acts 21, 11.14; 2 Pt 1, 14.
i 13, 36.
j 13, 25.
k Mt 16, 28.
l 19, 35.
m 20, 30.

*

21, 12: *None . . . dared to ask him:* is Jesus' appearance strange to them? Cf Lk 24, 16; Mk 16, 12; Jn 20, 14. The disciples do, however, recognize Jesus *before* the breaking of the bread (opposed to Lk 24, 35).

21, 14: This verse connects chs 20 and 21; cf 20, 19.26.

21, 15–23: This section constitutes Peter's rehabilitation and emphasizes his role in the church.

21, 15–17: In these three verses there is a remarkable variety of synonyms: two different Greek verbs for *love* (see the note on 15, 13); two verbs for *feed/tend;* two nouns for *sheep;* two verbs for *know.* But apparently there is no difference of meaning. The threefold confession of Peter is meant to counteract his earlier threefold denial (18, 17.25.27). The First Vatican Council cited these verses in defining that Jesus after his resurrection gave Peter the jurisdiction of supreme shepherd and ruler over the whole flock.

21, 15: *More than these:* probably "more than these disciples do" rather than "more than you love them" or "more than you love these things [fishing, etc.]."

21, 18: Originally probably a proverb about old age, now used as a figurative reference to the crucifixion of Peter.

21, 22: *Until I come:* a reference to the parousia.

21, 23: This whole scene takes on more significance if the disciple is already dead. The death of the apostolic generation caused problems in the church because of a belief that Jesus was to have returned first. Loss of faith sometimes resulted; cf 2 Pt 3, 4.

21, 24: *Who . . . has written them:* this does not necessarily mean he wrote them with his own hand. The same expression is used in 19, 22 of Pilate, who certainly would not have written the inscription himself. *We know:* i.e., the Christian community; cf 1, 14.16.

# THE ACTS OF THE

# APOSTLES

*The Acts of the Apostles, the second volume of Luke's two-volume work, continues Luke's presentation of biblical history, describing how the salvation promised to Israel in the Old Testament and accomplished by Jesus has now under the guidance of the holy Spirit been extended to the Gentiles. This was accomplished through the divinely chosen representatives (10, 41) whom Jesus prepared during his historical ministry (1, 21–22) and commissioned after his resurrection as witnesses to all that he taught (1, 8; 10, 37–43; Lk 24, 48). Luke's preoccupation with the Christian community as the Spirit-guided bearer of the word of salvation rules out of his book detailed histories of the activity of most of the preachers. Only the main lines of the roles of Peter and Paul serve Luke's interest.*

*Peter was the leading member of the Twelve (1, 13.15), a miracle worker like Jesus in the gospel (3, 1–10; 5, 1–11.15; 9, 32–35.36–42), the object of divine care (5, 17–21; 12, 6–11), and the spokesman for the Christian community (2, 14–36; 3, 12–26; 4, 8–12; 5, 29–32; 10, 34–43; 15, 7–11), who, according to Luke, was largely responsible for the growth of the community in the early days (2, 4; 4, 4). Paul eventually joined the community at Antioch (11, 25–26), which subsequently commissioned him and Barnabas to undertake the spread of the gospel to Asia Minor. This missionary venture generally failed to win the Jews of the diaspora to the gospel but enjoyed success among the Gentiles (13, 14—14, 27).*

*Paul's refusal to impose the Mosaic law upon his Gentile converts provoked very strong objection among the Jewish Christians of Jerusalem (15, 1), but both Peter and James supported his position (15, 6–21). Paul's second and third missionary journeys (16, 36—21, 16) resulted in the same pattern of failure among the Jews generally but of some success among the Gentiles. Paul, like Peter, is presented as a miracle worker (14, 8–18; 19, 12; 20, 7–12; 28, 7–10) and the object of divine care (16, 25–31).*

*In Acts, Luke has provided a broad survey of the church's development from the resurrection of Jesus to Paul's first Roman imprisonment, the point at which the book ends. In telling this story, Luke describes the emergence of Christianity from its origins in Judaism to its position as a religion of worldwide status and appeal. Originally a Jewish Christian community in Jerusalem, the church was placed in circumstances impelling it to include within its membership people of other cultures: the Samaritans (8, 4–25), at first an occasional Gentile (8, 26–30; 10, 1–48), and finally the Gentiles on principle (11, 20–21). Fear on the part of the Jewish people that Christianity, particularly as preached to the Gentiles, threatened their own cultural heritage caused them to be suspicious of Paul's gospel (13, 42–45; 15, 1–5; 28, 17–24). The inability of Christian missionaries to allay this apprehension inevitably created a situation in which the gospel was preached more and more to the Gentiles. Toward the end of Paul's career, the Christian communities, with the exception of those in Palestine itself (9, 31), were mainly of Gentile membership. In tracing the emergence of Christianity from Judaism, Luke is insistent upon the prominence of Israel in the divine plan of salvation (see the note on 1, 26; see also 2, 5–6; 3, 13–15; 10, 36; 13, 16–41; 24, 14–15) and that the extension of salvation to the Gentiles has been a part of the divine plan from the beginning (see 15, 13–18; 26, 22–23).*

*In the development of the church from a Jewish Christian origin in Jerusalem, with its roots in Jewish religious tradition, to a series of Christian communities among the Gentiles of the Roman empire, Luke perceives the action of God in history laying open the heart of all humanity to the divine message of salvation. His approach to the history of the church is motivated by his theological interests. His history of the apostolic church is the story of a Spirit-guided community and a Spirit-guided spread of the Word of God (1, 8). The travels of Peter and Paul are in reality the travels of the Word of God as it spreads from Jerusalem, the city of destiny for Jesus, to Rome, the capital of the civilized world of Luke's day. Nonetheless, the historical data he utilizes are of value for the understanding of the church's early life and development and as general background to the Pauline epistles. In the interpretation of Acts, care must be exercised to determine Luke's theological aims and interests and to evaluate his historical data without either exaggerating their literal accuracy or underestimating their factual worth.*

*Finally, an apologetic concern is evident throughout Acts. By stressing the continuity between Judaism and Christianity (13, 16–41; 23, 6–9; 24, 10–21; 26, 2–23), Luke argues that Christianity is deserving of the same toleration accorded Judaism by Rome. Part of Paul's defense before Roman authorities is to show that Christianity is not a disturber of the peace of the Roman Empire (24, 5.12–13; 25, 7–8). Moreover, when he stands before Roman authorities, he is declared innocent of any crime against the empire (18, 13–15; 23, 29; 25, 25–27; 26, 31–32). Luke tells his story with the hope that Christianity will be treated as fairly.*

*Concerning the date of Acts, see the Introduction to the Gospel according to Luke.*

*The principal divisions of the Acts of the Apostles are the following:*

*I. The Preparation for the Christian Mission (1, 1—2, 13)*
*II. The Mission in Jerusalem (2, 14—8, 3)*
*III. The Mission in Judea and Samaria (8, 4—9, 43)*
*IV. The Inauguration of the Gentile Mission (10, 1—15, 35)*
*V. The Mission of Paul to the Ends of the Earth (15, 36—28, 31)*

# I: THE PREPARATION FOR THE CHRISTIAN MISSION

## CHAPTER 1

**The Promise of the Spirit** 1 [a]*In the first
book, Theophilus, I dealt with all that Jesus did
and taught 2 [b]until the day he was taken up,
after giving instructions through the holy Spirit
to the apostles whom he had chosen. 3 [c]*He
presented himself alive to them by many proofs
after he had suffered, appearing to them during
forty days and speaking about the kingdom of
God. 4 [d]*While meeting with them, he enjoined them not to depart from Jerusalem, but
to wait for "the promise of the Father about
which you have heard me speak; 5 [e]for John
baptized with water, but in a few days you will
be baptized with the holy Spirit."

**The Ascension of Jesus** 6 *When they
had gathered together they asked him, "Lord,
are you at this time going to restore the kingdom
to Israel?" 7 [f]*He answered them, "It is not
for you to know the times or seasons that the
Father has established by his own authority.
8 [g]*But you will receive power when the holy
Spirit comes upon you, and you will be my
witnesses in Jerusalem, throughout Judea and

a Lk 1, 1-4.
b Mt 28, 19-20; Lk 24, 44-49; Jn 20, 22; 1 Tm 3, 16.
c 10, 41; 13, 31.
d Jn 14, 16.17.26.
e 11, 16; Mt 3, 11; Mk 1, 8; Lk 3, 16; Jn 1, 26; Eph 1, 13.
f Mt 24, 36; 1 Thes 5, 1-2.
g 2, 1-13; 10, 39; Is 43, 10; Mt 28, 19; Lk 24, 47-48.

*

1, 1–26: This introductory material (1–2) connects Acts with the Gospel of Luke, shows that the apostles were instructed by the risen Jesus (3–5), points out that the parousia or second coming in glory of Jesus will occur as certainly as his ascension occurred (6–11), and lists the members of the Twelve, stressing their role as a body of divinely mandated witnesses to his life, teaching, and resurrection (12–26).

1, 3: *Appearing to them during forty days:* Luke considered especially sacred the interval in which the appearances and instructions of the risen Jesus occurred and expressed it therefore in terms of the sacred number forty (cf Dt 8, 2). In his gospel, however, Luke connects the ascension of Jesus with the resurrection by describing the ascension on Easter Sunday evening (Lk 24, 50–53). What should probably be understood as one event (resurrection, glorification, ascension, sending of the Spirit—the paschal mystery) has been historicized by Luke when he writes of a visible ascension of Jesus after forty days and the descent of the Spirit at Pentecost. For Luke, the ascension marks the end of the appearances of Jesus except for the extraordinary appearance to Paul. With regard to Luke's understanding of salvation history, the ascension also marks the end of the time of Jesus (Lk 24, 50–53) and signals the beginning of the time of the church.

1, 4: *The promise of the Father:* the holy Spirit, as is clear from the next verse. This gift of the Spirit was first promised in Jesus' final instructions to his chosen witnesses in Luke's gospel (Lk 24, 49) and formed part of the continuing instructions of the risen Jesus on the kingdom of God, of which Luke speaks in v 3.

1, 6: The question of the disciples implies that in believing Jesus to be the Christ (see the note on Lk 2, 11) they had expected him to be a political leader who would restore self-rule to Israel during his historical ministry. When this had not taken place, they ask if it is to take place at this time, the period of the church.

1, 7: This verse echoes the tradition that the precise time of the parousia is not revealed to human beings; cf Mk 13, 32; I Thes 5, 1–3.

1, 8: Just as Jerusalem was the city of destiny in the Gospel of Luke (the place where salvation was accomplished), so here at the beginning of Acts, Jerusalem occupies a central position. It is the starting point for the mission of the Christian disciples to "the ends of the earth," the place where the apostles were situated and the doctrinal focal point in the early days of the community (15, 2.6). *The ends of the earth:* for Luke, this means Rome.

Samaria, and to the ends of the earth."
9 [h]When he had said this, as they were looking
on, he was lifted up, and a cloud took him from
their sight. 10 [i]While they were looking intently at the sky as he was going, suddenly two men
dressed in white garments stood beside them.
11 [j]They said, "Men of Galilee, why are you
standing there looking at the sky? This Jesus
who has been taken up from you into heaven
will return in the same way as you have seen
him going into heaven." 12 [k]Then they returned to Jerusalem from the mount called Oli-
vet, which is near Jerusalem, a sabbath day's
journey away.

### The First Community in Jerusalem

13 When they entered the city they went to the
upper room where they were staying, Peter and
John and James and Andrew, Philip and Thomas, Bartholomew and Matthew, James son of
Alphaeus, Simon the Zealot, and Judas son of
James. 14 [l]All these devoted themselves with
one accord to prayer, together with some wom-
en, and Mary the mother of Jesus, and his brothers.

### The Choice of Judas's Successor

15 During those days Peter stood up in the
midst of the brothers (there was a group of about
one hundred and twenty persons in the one
place). He said, 16 [m]"My brothers, the scripture had to be fulfilled which the holy Spirit
spoke beforehand through the mouth of David,
concerning Judas, who was the guide for those
who arrested Jesus. 17 He was numbered
among us and was allotted a share in this ministry. 18 [n]*He bought a parcel of land with the
wages of his iniquity, and falling headlong, he
burst open in the middle, and all his insides
spilled out. 19 This became known to everyone
who lived in Jerusalem, so that the parcel of
land was called in their language 'Akeldama,'
that is, Field of Blood. 20 [o]For it is written in
the Book of Psalms:

'Let his encampment become desolate,
and may no one dwell in it.'

And:

'May another take his office.'

21 Therefore, it is necessary that one of the
men who accompanied us the whole time the
Lord Jesus came and went among us,
22 [p]beginning from the baptism of John until
the day on which he was taken up from us,
become with us a witness to his resurrection."
23 So they proposed two, Joseph called Barsabbas, who was also known as Justus, and
Matthias. 24 Then they prayed, "You, Lord,
who know the hearts of all, show which one of
these two you have chosen 25 to take the place
in this apostolic ministry from which Judas
turned away to go to his own place."
26 [q]*Then they gave lots to them, and the lot
fell upon Matthias, and he was counted with the
eleven apostles.

## CHAPTER 2

### The Coming of the Spirit

1 [r]*When the
time for Pentecost was fulfilled, they were all in
one place together. 2 [s]*And suddenly there
came from the sky a noise like a strong driving
wind, and it filled the entire house in which they
were. 3 [t]*Then there appeared to them tongues
as of fire, which parted and came to rest on each
one of them. 4 [u]*And they were all filled with
the holy Spirit and began to speak in different
tongues, as the Spirit enabled them to proclaim.
5 Now there were devout Jews from every
nation under heaven staying in Jerusalem. 6 At
this sound, they gathered in a large crowd, but
they were confused because each one heard
them speaking in his own language. 7 [v]They
were astounded, and in amazement they asked,
"Are not all these people who are speaking
Galileans? 8 Then how does each of us hear

h 2 Kgs 2, 11; Mk 16, 19; Lk 24, 51.
i Jn 20, 17.
j Lk 24, 51; Eph 4, 8-10; 1 Pt 3, 22; Rv 1, 7.
k Lk 6, 14-16.
l Lk 23, 49.
m Ps 41, 10; Lk 22, 47.
n Mt 27, 3-10.
o Pss 69, 26; 109, 8; Jn 17, 12.
p 1, 8-9; 10, 39.
q Prv 16, 33.
r Lv 23, 15-21; Dt 16, 9-11.
s Jn 3, 8.
t Lk 3, 16.
u 1, 5; 4, 31; 8, 15.17; 10, 44; 11, 15-16; 15, 8; 19, 6; Ps 104, 30; Jn 20, 33.
v 1, 11.

*

1, 18: Luke records a popular tradition about the death of Judas that differs from the one in Mt 27, 5, according to which Judas hanged himself. Here, although the text is not certain, Judas is depicted as purchasing a piece of property with the betrayal money and being killed on it in a fall.

1, 26: The need to replace Judas was probably dictated by the symbolism of the number twelve, recalling the twelve tribes of Israel. This symbolism also indicates that for Luke (see Lk 22, 30) the Christian church is a reconstituted Israel.

2, 1–41: Luke's pentecostal narrative consists of an introduction (1–13), a speech ascribed to Peter declaring the resurrection of Jesus and its messianic significance (14–36), and a favorable response from the audience (37–41). It is likely that the narrative telescopes events that took place over a period of time and on a less dramatic scale. The Twelve were not originally in a position to proclaim publicly the messianic office of Jesus without incurring immediate reprisal from those religious authorities in Jerusalem who had brought about Jesus' death precisely to stem the rising tide in his favor.

2, 2: *There came from the sky a noise like a strong driving wind:* wind and spirit are associated in Jn 3, 8. The sound of a great rush of wind would herald a new action of God in the history of salvation.

2, 3: *Tongues as of fire:* see Ex 19, 18 where fire symbolizes the presence of God to initiate the covenant on Sinai. Here the holy Spirit acts upon the apostles, preparing them to proclaim the new covenant with its unique gift of the Spirit (38).

2, 4: *To speak in different tongues:* ecstatic prayer in praise of God, interpreted in vv 6 and 11 as speaking in foreign languages, symbolizing the worldwide mission of the church.

them in his own native language? **9** We are
Parthians, Medes, and Elamites, inhabitants of
Mesopotamia, Judea and Cappadocia, Pontus
and Asia, **10** Phrygia and Pamphylia, Egypt
and the districts of Libya near Cyrene, as well
as travelers from Rome, **11** [w]both Jews and
converts to Judaism, Cretans and Arabs, yet we
hear them speaking in our own tongues of the
mighty acts of God." **12** They were all astounded and bewildered, and said to one another, "What does this mean?" **13** [x]But others
said, scoffing, "They have had too much new
wine."

## *II: THE MISSION IN JERUSALEM*

**Peter's Speech at Pentecost** **14** *Then
Peter stood up with the Eleven, raised his voice,
and proclaimed to them, "You who are Jews,
indeed all of you staying in Jerusalem. Let this
be known to you, and listen to my words.
**15** These people are not drunk, as you suppose,
for it is only nine o'clock in the morning.
**16** No, this is what was spoken through the
prophet Joel:

**17** [y]'It will come to pass in the last days,' God
says,
'that I will pour out a portion of my spirit
upon all flesh.
Your sons and your daughters shall
prophesy,
your young men shall see visions,
your old men shall dream dreams.
**18** Indeed, upon my servants and my
handmaids
I will pour out a portion of my spirit in
those days,
and they shall prophesy.
**19** And I will work wonders in the heavens
above
and signs on the earth below:
blood, fire, and a cloud of smoke.
**20** The sun shall be turned to darkness,
and the moon to blood,
before the coming of the great and
splendid day of the Lord,
**21** [z]and it shall be that everyone shall be saved
who calls on
the name of the Lord.'

**22** [a]You who are Israelites, hear these words.
Jesus the Nazorean was a man commended to
you by God with mighty deeds, wonders, and
signs, which God worked through him in your
midst, as you yourselves know. **23** [b]This man,
delivered up by the set plan and foreknowledge
of God, you killed, using lawless men to crucify
him. **24** [c]But God raised him up, releasing him
from the throes of death, because it was impossible for him to be held by it. **25** [d]For David
says of him:

'I saw the Lord ever before me,
with him at my right hand I shall not be
disturbed.
**26** Therefore my heart has been glad and my
tongue has exulted;
my flesh, too, will dwell in hope,
**27** [e]because you will not abandon my soul to
the nether world,
nor will you suffer your holy one to see
corruption.
**28** You have made known to me the paths of
life;
you will fill me with joy in your
presence.'

**29** My brothers, one can confidently say to you
about the patriarch David that he died and was
buried, and his tomb is in our midst to this day.
**30** [f]But since he was a prophet and knew that
God had sworn an oath to him that he would set
one of his descendants upon his throne, **31** [g]he
foresaw and spoke of the resurrection of the
Messiah, that neither was he abandoned to the
netherworld nor did his flesh see corruption.
**32** God raised this Jesus; of this we are all
witnesses. **33** [h]*Exalted at the right hand of
God, he received the promise of the holy Spirit
from the Father and poured it forth, as you
[both] see and hear. **34** [i]For David did not go
up into heaven, but he himself said:

'The Lord said to my Lord,
"Sit at my right hand
**35** until I make your enemies your
footstool."'

**36** [j]Therefore let the whole house of Israel
know for certain that God has made him both
Lord and Messiah, this Jesus whom you crucified."

**37** [k]Now when they heard this, they were cut
to the heart, and they asked Peter and the other
apostles, "What are we to do, my brothers?"
**38** [l]*Peter [said] to them, "Repent and be bap-

w 10, 46.
x 1 Cor 14, 23.
y Is 2, 2; 44, 3; Jl 3, 1-5.
z Rom 10, 13.
a 10, 38; Lk 24, 19.
b 1 Thes 2, 15.
c 13, 34.
d Ps 16, 8-11.
e 13, 35.
f 2 Sm 7, 12; Ps 132, 11.
g 13, 35; Ps 16, 10.
h 1, 4-5.
i Ps 110, 1.
j 9, 22; Rom 10, 9; Phil 2, 11.
k Lk 3, 10.
l 3, 19; 16, 31; Lk 3, 3.

*

2, 14–36: The first of six discourses in Acts (along with 3, 12–26; 4, 8–12; 5, 29–32; 10, 34–43; 13, 16–41) dealing with the resurrection of Jesus and its messianic import. Five of these are attributed to Peter, the final one to Paul. Modern scholars term these discourses in Acts the "kerygma," the Greek word for proclamation (cf I Cor 15, 11).

2, 33: *At the right hand of God:* or "by the right hand of God."

2, 38: *Repent and be baptized:* repentance is a positive concept, a change of mind and heart toward God reflected in the actual goodness of one's life. It is in accord with the apostolic teaching derived from Jesus (42) and ultimately recorded in the four gospels. Luke presents baptism in Acts as the expected response to the apostolic preaching about Jesus and associates it with the conferring of the Spirit (1, 5; 10, 44–48;

tized, every one of you, in the name of Jesus
Christ for the forgiveness of your sins; and you
will receive the gift of the holy Spirit. **39** [m]For
the promise is made to you and to your children
and to all those far off, whomever the Lord our
God will call.'' **40** [n]He testified with many
other arguments, and was exhorting them,
''Save yourselves from this corrupt generation.'' **41** [o]Those who accepted his message
were baptized, and about three thousand persons were added that day.

## Communal Life

**42** [pq]*They devoted
themselves to the teaching of the apostles and to
the communal life, to the breaking of the bread
and to the prayers. **43** [r]Awe came upon everyone, and many wonders and signs were done
through the apostles. **44** [s]All who believed
were together and had all things in common;
**45** they would sell their property and possessions and divide them among all according to
each one's need. **46** Every day they devoted
themselves to meeting together in the temple
area and to breaking bread in their homes. They
ate their meals with exultation and sincerity of
heart, **47** praising God and enjoying favor with
all the people. And every day the Lord added to
their number those who were being saved.

# CHAPTER 3

## Cure of a Crippled Beggar

**1** *Now Peter
and John were going up to the temple area for
the three o'clock hour of prayer. **2** [t]And a man
crippled from birth was carried and placed at the
gate of the temple called ''the Beautiful Gate''
every day to beg for alms from the people who
entered the temple. **3** When he saw Peter and
John about to go into the temple, he asked for
alms. **4** But Peter looked intently at him, as did
John, and said, ''Look at us.'' **5** He paid attention to them, expecting to receive something
from them. **6** [u]*Peter said, ''I have neither silver nor gold, but what I do have I give you: in
the name of Jesus Christ the Nazorean, [rise
and] walk.'' **7** Then Peter took him by the right
hand and raised him up, and immediately his
feet and ankles grew strong. **8** [v]He leaped up,
stood, and walked around, and went into the
temple with them, walking and jumping and
praising God. **9** When all the people saw him
walking and praising God, **10** they recognized
him as the one who used to sit begging at the
Beautiful Gate of the temple, and they were
filled with amazement and astonishment at what
had happened to him.

## Peter's Speech

**11** [w]As he clung to Peter
and John, all the people hurried in amazement
toward them in the portico called ''Solomon's
Portico.'' **12** [x]When Peter saw this, he addressed the people, ''You Israelites, why are
you amazed at this, and why do you look so
intently at us as if we had made him walk by our
own power or piety? **13** [y]*The God of Abraham, [the God] of Isaac, and [the God] of Jacob,
the God of our ancestors, has glorified his servant Jesus whom you handed over and denied
in Pilate's presence, when he had decided to
release him. **14** [z]*You denied the Holy and
Righteous One and asked that a murderer be

---

m Is 57, 19; Jl 3, 5; Eph 2, 17.
n Dt 32, 5; Ps 78, 8; Lk 9, 41; Phil 2, 15.
o 2, 47; 4, 4; 5, 14; 6, 7; 11, 21.24; 21, 20.
p 4, 32-35.
q 1, 14; 6, 4.
r 5, 12-16.
s 4, 32.34-35.
t 14, 8-10.
u 4, 10.
v Is 35, 6; Lk 7, 22.
w 5, 12; Jn 10, 23.
x 14, 15.
y Ex 3, 6.15; Is 52, 13; Lk 23, 14-25.
z Mt 27, 20-21; Mk 15, 11; Lk 23, 18; Jn 18, 40.

---

*

11, 16).

2, 42–47: The first of three summary passages (along with 4, 32–37 and 5, 12–16) that outline, somewhat idyllically, the chief characteristics of the Jerusalem community: adherence to the teachings of the Twelve and the centering of its religious life in the eucharistic liturgy (42); a system of distribution of goods that led wealthier Christians to sell their possessions when the needs of the community's poor required it (44 and the note on 4, 32–37); and continued attendance at the temple, since in this initial stage there was little or no thought of any dividing line between Christianity and Judaism (46).

3, 1—4, 31: This section presents a series of related events: the dramatic cure of a lame beggar (3, 1–10) produces a large audience for the kerygmatic discourse of Peter (3, 11–26). The Sadducees, taking exception to the doctrine of resurrection, have Peter, John, and apparently the beggar as well, arrested (4, 1–4) and brought to trial before the Sanhedrin. The issue concerns the authority by which Peter and John publicly teach religious doctrine in the temple (4, 5–7). Peter replies with a brief summary of the kerygma, implying that his authority is prophetic (4, 8–12). The court warns the apostles to abandon their practice of invoking prophetic authority in the name of Jesus (4, 13–18). When Peter and John reply that the prophetic role cannot be abandoned to satisfy human objections, the court nevertheless releases them, afraid to do otherwise since the beggar, lame from birth and over forty years old, is a well-known figure in Jerusalem and the facts of his cure are common property (4, 19–22). The narrative concludes with a prayer of the Christian community imploring divine aid against threats of persecution (4, 23–31).

3, 1: *For the three o'clock hour of prayer:* literally, "at the ninth hour of prayer." With the day beginning at 6 a.m., the ninth hour would be 3 p.m.

3, 6–10: The miracle has a dramatic cast; it symbolizes the saving power of Christ and leads the beggar to enter the temple, where he hears Peter's proclamation of salvation through Jesus.

3, 13: *Has glorified:* through the resurrection and ascension of Jesus, God reversed the judgment against him on the occasion of his trial. *Servant:* the Greek word can also be rendered as "son" or even "child" here and also in 3, 26; 4, 25 (applied to David); 4, 27; and 4, 30. Scholars are of the opinion, however, that the original concept reflected in the words identified Jesus with the suffering Servant of the Lord of Is 52, 13—53, 12.

3, 14: *The Holy and Righteous One:* so designating Jesus emphasizes his special relationship to the Father (see Lk 1, 35; 4, 34) and emphasizes his sinlessness and religious dignity that are placed in sharp contrast with the guilt of those who rejected him in favor of Barabbas.

released to you. **15** [a]*The author of life you put
to death, but God raised him from the dead; of
this we are witnesses. **16** And by faith in his
name, this man, whom you see and know, his
name has made strong, and the faith that comes
through it has given him this perfect health, in
the presence of all of you. **17** [b]*Now I know,
brothers, that you acted out of ignorance, just as
your leaders did; **18** [c]*but God has thus
brought to fulfillment what he had announced
beforehand through the mouth of all the prophets, that his Messiah would suffer. **19** [d]Repent,
therefore, and be converted, that your sins may
be wiped away, **20** *and that the Lord may
grant you times of refreshment and send you the
Messiah already appointed for you, Jesus,
**21** *whom heaven must receive until the times
of universal restoration of which God spoke
through the mouth of his holy prophets from of
old. **22** [e]*For Moses said:

'A prophet like me will the Lord, your God,
raise up for you
from among your own kinsmen;
to him you shall listen in all that he may say
to you.
**23** [f]Everyone who does not listen to that
prophet
will be cut off from the people.'

**24** Moreover, all the prophets who spoke, from
Samuel and those afterwards, also announced
these days. **25** [g]You are the children of the
prophets and of the covenant that God made
with your ancestors when he said to Abraham,
'In your offspring all the families of the earth
shall be blessed.' **26** [h]For you first, God raised
up his servant and sent him to bless you by
turning each of you from your evil ways."

## CHAPTER 4

**1** *While they were still speaking to the
people, the priests, the captain of the temple
guard, and the Sadducees confronted them,
**2** [i]disturbed that they were teaching the people
and proclaiming in Jesus the resurrection of the
dead. **3** They laid hands on them and put them
in custody until the next day, since it was already evening. **4** But many of those who heard
the word came to believe and [the] number of
men grew to [about] five thousand.

**Before the Sanhedrin** **5** On the next day,
their leaders, elders, and scribes were assembled in Jerusalem, **6** with Annas the high priest,
Caiaphas, John, Alexander, and all who were of
the high-priestly class. **7** They brought them
into their presence and questioned them, "By
what power or by what name have you done
this?" **8** [j]Then Peter, filled with the holy Spirit, answered them, "Leaders of the people and
elders: **9** If we are being examined today about
a good deed done to a cripple, namely, by what
means he was saved, **10** then all of you and all
the people of Israel should know that it was in
the name of Jesus Christ the Nazorean whom
you crucified, whom God raised from the dead;
in his name this man stands before you healed.
**11** [k]*He is 'the stone rejected by you, the builders, which has become the cornerstone.'
**12** [l]*There is no salvation through anyone else,

a 4, 10; 5, 31 / 1, 8; 2, 32.
b 13, 27; Lk 23, 34; 1 Cor 2, 8; 1 Tm 1, 13.
c Lk 18, 31.
d 2, 38.
e 7, 37; Dt 18, 15.18.
f Lv 23, 29; Dt 18, 19.
g Gn 12, 3; 18, 18; 22, 18; Sir 44, 19-21; Gal 3, 8-9.
h 13, 46; Rom 1, 16.
i 23, 6-8; 24, 21.
j Mt 10, 20.
k Ps 118, 22; Is 28, 16; Mt 21, 42; Mk 12, 10; Lk 20, 17; Rom 9, 33; 1 Pt 2, 7.
l Mt 1, 21; 1 Cor 3, 11.

*

3, 15: *The author of life:* other possible translations of the Greek title are "leader of life" or "pioneer of life." The title clearly points to Jesus as the source and originator of salvation.

3, 17: *Ignorance:* a Lucan motif, explaining away the actions not only of the people but also of their leaders in crucifying Jesus. On this basis the presbyters in Acts could continue to appeal to the Jews in Jerusalem to believe in Jesus, even while affirming their involvement in his death because they were unaware of his messianic dignity. See also 13, 27 and Lk 23, 34.

3, 18: *Through the mouth of all the prophets:* Christian prophetic insight into the Old Testament saw the crucifixion and death of Jesus as the main import of messianic prophecy. The Jews themselves did not anticipate a suffering Messiah; they usually understood the Servant Song in Is 52, 13—53, 12 to signify their own suffering as a people. In his typical fashion (cf Lk 18, 31; 24, 25.27.44), Luke does not specify the particular Old Testament prophecies that were fulfilled by Jesus. See also the note on Lk 24, 26.

3, 20: *The Lord . . . and send you the Messiah already appointed for you, Jesus:* an allusion to the parousia or second coming of Christ, judged to be imminent in the apostolic age. This reference to its nearness is the only explicit one in Acts. Some scholars believe that this verse preserves a very early christology, in which the title "Messiah" (Greek "Christ") is applied to him as of his parousia, his second coming (contrast 2, 36). This view of a future messiahship of Jesus is not found elsewhere in the New Testament.

3, 21: *The times of universal restoration:* like "the times of refreshment" (20), an apocalyptic designation of the messianic age, fitting in with the christology of v 20 that associates the messiahship of Jesus with his future coming.

3, 22: A loose citation of Dt 18, 15, which teaches that the Israelites are to learn the will of Yahweh from no one but their prophets. At the time of Jesus, some Jews expected a unique prophet to come in fulfillment of this text. Early Christianity applied this tradition and text to Jesus and used them especially in defense of the divergence of Christian teaching from traditional Judaism.

4, 1: *The priests, the captain of the temple guard, and the Sadducees:* the priests performed the temple liturgy; the temple guard was composed of Levites, whose captain ranked next after the high priest. The Sadducees, a party within Judaism at this time, rejected those doctrines, including bodily resurrection, which they believed alien to the ancient Mosaic religion. The Sadducees were drawn from priestly families and from the lay aristocracy.

4, 11: Early Christianity applied this citation from Ps 118, 22 to Jesus; cf Mk 12, 10; 1 Pt 2, 7.

4, 12: In the Roman world of Luke's day, salvation was often attributed to the emperor who was hailed as "savior" and

nor is there any other name under heaven given
to the human race by which we are to be
saved."

13 Observing the boldness of Peter and John
and perceiving them to be uneducated, ordinary
men, they were amazed, and they recognized
them as the companions of Jesus. 14 Then
when they saw the man who had been cured
standing there with them, they could say nothing in reply. 15 So they ordered them to leave
the Sanhedrin, and conferred with one another,
saying, 16 "What are we to do with these men?
Everyone living in Jerusalem knows that a remarkable sign was done through them, and we
cannot deny it. 17 [m]But so that it may not be
spread any further among the people, let us give
them a stern warning never again to speak to
anyone in this name."

18 So they called them back and ordered
them not to speak or teach at all in the name of
Jesus. 19 [n]Peter and John, however, said to
them in reply, "Whether it is right in the sight
of God for us to obey you rather than God, you
be the judges. 20 It is impossible for us not to
speak about what we have seen and heard."
21 After threatening them further, they released them, finding no way to punish them, on
account of the people who were all praising God
for what had happened. 22 For the man on
whom this sign of healing had been done was
over forty years old.

## Prayer of the Community

23 After their
release they went back to their own people and
reported what the chief priests and elders had
told them. 24 And when they heard it, they
raised their voices to God with one accord and
said, "Sovereign Lord, maker of heaven and
earth and the sea and all that is in them, 25 [o]you
said by the holy Spirit through the mouth of our
father David, your servant:

'Why did the Gentiles rage
and the peoples entertain folly?
26 The kings of the earth took their stand
and the princes gathered together
against the Lord and against his
anointed.'

27 [p]*Indeed they gathered in this city against
your holy servant Jesus whom you anointed,
Herod and Pontius Pilate, together with the
Gentiles and the peoples of Israel, 28 to do
what your hand and [your] will had long ago
planned to take place. 29 And now, Lord, take
note of their threats, and enable your servants to
speak your word with all boldness, 30 as you
stretch forth [your] hand to heal, and signs and
wonders are done through the name of your holy
servant Jesus." 31 [q]*As they prayed, the place
where they were gathered shook, and they were
all filled with the holy Spirit and continued to
speak the word of God with boldness.

## Life in the Christian Community

32 *The community of believers was of one
heart and mind, and no one claimed that any of
his possessions was his own, but they had everything in common. 33 With great power the
apostles bore witness to the resurrection of the
Lord Jesus, and great favor was accorded them
all. 34 [r]There was no needy person among
them, for those who owned property or houses
would sell them, bring the proceeds of the sale,
35 and put them at the feet of the apostles, and
they were distributed to each according to need.

36 [s]Thus Joseph, also named by the apostles
Barnabas (which is translated "son of encouragement"), a Levite, a Cypriot by birth,
37 sold a piece of property that he owned, then
brought the money and put it at the feet of the
apostles.

# CHAPTER 5

## Ananias and Sapphira

1 *A man named
Ananias, however, with his wife Sapphira, sold
a piece of property. 2 He retained for himself,
with his wife's knowledge, some of the purchase price, took the remainder, and put it at the
feet of the apostles. 3 [t]But Peter said, "Ananias, why has Satan filled your heart so that you
lied to the holy Spirit and retained part of the

m 5, 28.
n 5, 29-32.
o Ps 2, 1-2.
p Lk 23, 12-13.
q 2, 4.
r 2, 44-45.
s 9, 27; 11, 22.30; 12, 25; 13, 15; 1 Cor 9, 6; Gal 2, 1.9.13;Col 4, 10.
t Lk 22, 3; Jn 13, 2.

*

"god." Luke, in the words of Peter, denies that deliverance comes through anyone other than Jesus.

4, 27: *Herod:* Herod Antipas, ruler of Galilee and Perea from 4 B.C. to A.D. 39, who executed John the Baptist and before whom Jesus was arraigned; cf Lk 23, 6–12.

4, 31: *The place . . . shook:* the earthquake is used as a sign of the divine presence in Ex 19, 18; Is 6, 4. Here the shaking of the building symbolizes God's favorable response to the prayer. Luke may have had as an additional reason for using the symbol in this sense the fact that it was familiar in the Hellenistic world. Ovid and Virgil also employ it.

4, 32–37: This is the second summary characterizing the Jerusalem community (see the note on 2, 42–47). It emphasizes the system of the distribution of goods and introduces Barnabas, who appears later in Acts as the friend and companion of Paul, and who, as noted here (37), endeared himself to the community by a donation of money through the sale of property. This sharing of material possessions continues a practice that Luke describes during the historical ministry of Jesus (Lk 8, 3) and is in accord with the sayings of Jesus in Luke's gospel (Lk 12, 33; 16, 9.11.13).

5, 1–11: The sin of Ananias and Sapphira did not consist in the withholding of part of the money but in their deception of the community. Their deaths are ascribed to a lie to the holy Spirit (3.9), i.e., they accepted the honor accorded them by the community for their generosity, but in reality they were not deserving of it.

price of the land? **4** While it remained unsold,
did it not remain yours? And when it was sold,
was it not still under your control? Why did you
contrive this deed? You have lied not to human
beings, but to God." **5** When Ananias heard
these words, he fell down and breathed his last,
and great fear came upon all who heard of it.
**6** The young men came and wrapped him up,
then carried him out and buried him.

**7** After an interval of about three hours, his
wife came in, unaware of what had happened.
**8** Peter said to her, "Tell me, did you sell the
land for this amount?" She answered, "Yes,
for that amount." **9** Then Peter said to her,
"Why did you agree to test the Spirit of the
Lord? Listen, the footsteps of those who have
buried your husband are at the door, and they
will carry you out." **10** At once, she fell down
at his feet and breathed her last. When the young
men entered they found her dead, so they carried her out and buried her beside her husband.
**11** [u]And great fear came upon the whole church
and upon all who heard of these things.

## Signs and Wonders of the Apostles

**12** [v]*Many signs and wonders were done
among the people at the hands of the apostles.
They were all together in Solomon's portico.
**13** None of the others dared to join them, but
the people esteemed them. **14** Yet more than
ever, believers in the Lord, great numbers of
men and women, were added to them.
**15** [w]Thus they even carried the sick out into the
streets and laid them on cots and mats so that
when Peter came by, at least his shadow might
fall on one or another of them. **16** A large number of people from the towns in the vicinity of
Jerusalem also gathered, bringing the sick and
those disturbed by unclean spirits, and they
were all cured.

## Trial before the Sanhedrin

**17** [x]*Then
the high priest rose up and all his companions,
that is, the party of the Sadducees, and, filled
with jealousy, **18** laid hands upon the apostles
and put them in the public jail. **19** [y]But during
the night, the angel of the Lord opened the doors
of the prison, led them out, and said, **20** "Go
and take your place in the temple area, and tell
the people everything about this life."
**21** When they heard this, they went to the temple early in the morning and taught. When the
high priest and his companions arrived, they
convened the Sanhedrin, the full senate of the
Israelites, and sent to the jail to have them
brought in. **22** But the court officers who went
did not find them in the prison, so they came
back and reported, **23** "We found the jail securely locked and the guards stationed outside
the doors, but when we opened them, we found
no one inside." **24** When they heard this report, the captain of the temple guard and the
chief priests were at a loss about them, as to
what this would come to. **25** Then someone
came in and reported to them, "The men whom
you put in prison are in the temple area and are
teaching the people." **26** [z]Then the captain and
the court officers went and brought them in, but
without force, because they were afraid of being
stoned by the people.

**27** When they had brought them in and made
them stand before the Sanhedrin, the high priest
questioned them, **28** [a]"We gave you strict orders [did we not?] to stop teaching in that
name[.] Yet you have filled Jerusalem with your
teaching and want to bring this man's blood
upon us." **29** [b]But Peter and the apostles said
in reply, "We must obey God rather than men.
**30** [c]*The God of our ancestors raised Jesus,
though you had him killed by hanging him on
a tree. **31** [d]*God exalted him at his right hand
as leader and savior to grant Israel repentance
and forgiveness of sins. **32** [e]We are witnesses
of these things, as is the holy Spirit that God has
given to those who obey him."

**33** When they heard this, they became infuriated and wanted to put them to death.
**34** [f]*But a Pharisee in the Sanhedrin named
Gamaliel, a teacher of the law, respected by all
the people, stood up, ordered the men to be put
outside for a short time, **35** and said to them,
"Fellow Israelites, be careful what you are

u 2, 43; 5, 5; 19, 17.
v 2, 43; 6, 8; 14, 3; 15, 12.
w 19, 11-12; Mk 6, 56.
x 4, 1-3.6.
y 12, 7-10; 16, 25-26.
z Lk 20, 19.
a Mt 27, 25.
b 4, 19.
c 2, 23-24.
d 2, 38.
e Lk 24, 48; Jn 15, 26.
f 22, 3.

*

5, 12–16: This, the third summary portraying the Jerusalem community, underscores the Twelve as its bulwark, especially because of their charismatic power to heal the sick; cf 2, 42–47; 4, 32–37.

5, 17–42: A second action against the community is taken by the Sanhedrin in the arrest and trial of the Twelve; cf 4, 1–3. The motive is the jealousy of the religious authorities over the popularity of the apostles (17) who are now charged with the defiance of the Sanhedrin's previous order to them to abandon their prophetic role (28; cf 4, 18). In this crisis the apostles are favored by a miraculous release from prison (18–24). (For similar incidents involving Peter and Paul, see 12, 6–11; 16, 25–29.) The real significance of such an event, however, would be manifest only to people of faith, not to unbelievers; since the Sanhedrin already judged the Twelve to be inauthentic prophets, it could disregard reports of their miracles. When the Twelve immediately resumed public teaching, the Sanhedrin determined to invoke upon them the penalty of death (33) prescribed in Dt 13, 6–10. Gamaliel's advice against this course finally prevailed, but it did not save the Twelve from the punishment of scourging (40) in a last endeavor to shake their conviction of their prophetic mission.

5, 30: *Hanging him on a tree:* that is, crucifying him (cf also Gal 3, 13).

5, 31: *At his right hand:* see the note on 2, 33.

5, 34: *Gamaliel:* in 22, 3, Paul identifies himself as a disciple of this Rabbi Gamaliel I who flourished in Jerusalem between A.D. 25 and 50.

about to do to these men. **36** *Some time ago,
Theudas appeared, claiming to be someone important, and about four hundred men joined
him, but he was killed, and all those who were
loyal to him were disbanded and came to nothing. **37** After him came Judas the Galilean at
the time of the census. He also drew people after
him, but he too perished and all who were loyal
to him were scattered. **38** So now I tell you,
have nothing to do with these men, and let them
go. For if this endeavor or this activity is of
human origin, it will destroy itself. **39** But if it
comes from God, you will not be able to destroy
them; you may even find yourselves fighting
against God.'' They were persuaded by him.
**40** [g]After recalling the apostles, they had them
flogged, ordered them to stop speaking in the
name of Jesus, and dismissed them. **41** [h]So
they left the presence of the Sanhedrin, rejoicing that they had been found worthy to suffer
dishonor for the sake of the name. **42** [i]And all
day long, both at the temple and in their homes,
they did not stop teaching and proclaiming the
Messiah, Jesus.

## CHAPTER 6

**The Need for Assistants** **1** [j]*At that
time, as the number of disciples continued to
grow, the Hellenists complained against the Hebrews because their widows were being neglected in the daily distribution. **2** *So the Twelve
called together the community of the disciples
and said, ''It is not right for us to neglect the
word of God to serve at table. **3** Brothers, select
from among you seven reputable men, filled
with the Spirit and wisdom, whom we shall
appoint to this task, **4** whereas we shall devote
ourselves to prayer and to the ministry of the
word.'' **5** The proposal was acceptable to the
whole community, so they chose Stephen, a
man filled with faith and the holy Spirit, also
Philip, Prochorus, Nicanor, Timon, Parmenas,
and Nicholas of Antioch, a convert to Judaism.
**6** [k]*They presented these men to the apostles
who prayed and laid hands on them. **7** [l]The
word of God continued to spread, and the number of the disciples in Jerusalem increased greatly; even a large group of priests were becoming
obedient to the faith.

**Accusation against Stephen** **8** *Now
Stephen, filled with grace and power, was
working great wonders and signs among the
people. **9** Certain members of the so-called
Synagogue of Freedmen, Cyrenians, and Alex-
andrians, and people from Cilicia and Asia,
came forward and debated with Stephen,
**10** [m]but they could not withstand the wisdom
and the spirit with which he spoke. **11** [n]Then
they instigated some men to say, ''We have
heard him speaking blasphemous words against
Moses and God.'' **12** They stirred up the people, the elders, and the scribes, accosted him,
seized him, and brought him before the Sanhedrin. **13** *They presented false witnesses who
testified, ''This man never stops saying things

g Mt 10, 17; Acts 4, 17-18.
h Mt 5, 10-11; 1 Pt 4, 13.
i 2, 46; 5, 20-21.25; 8, 35; 17, 3; 18, 5.28; 19, 4-5.
j 2, 45; 4, 34-35.
k 1, 24; 13, 3; 14, 23.
l 9, 31; 12, 24; 16, 5; 19, 20; 28, 30-31.
m Lk 21, 15.
n Mt 26, 59-61; Mk 14, 55-58; Acts 21, 21.

*

5, 36–37: Gamaliel offers examples of unsuccessful contemporary movements to argue that if God is not the origin of this movement preached by the apostles it will perish by itself. The movement initiated by Theudas actually occurred when C. Cuspius Fadus was governor, A.D. 44–46. Luke's placing of Judas the Galilean after Theudas and at the time of the census (see the note on Lk 2, 1–2) is an indication of the vagueness of his knowledge of these events.

6, 1–7: *The Hellenists . . . the Hebrews:* the Hellenists were not necessarily Jews from the diaspora, but were more probably Palestinian Jews who spoke only Greek. The Hebrews were Palestinian Jews who spoke Hebrew or Aramaic and who may also have spoken Greek. Both groups belong to the Jerusalem Jewish Christian community. The conflict between them leads to a restructuring of the community that will better serve the community's needs. The real purpose of the whole episode, however, is to introduce Stephen as a prominent figure in the community whose long speech and martyrdom will be recounted in ch 7.

6, 2–4: The essential function of the Twelve is the ''service of the word,'' including development of the kerygma by formulation of the teachings of Jesus.

6, 2: *To serve at table:* some commentators think that it is not the serving of food that is described here but rather the keeping of the accounts that recorded the distribution of food to the needy members of the community. In any case, after Stephen and the others are chosen, they are never presented carrying out the task for which they were appointed (2–3). Rather, two of their number, Stephen and Philip, are presented as preachers of the Christian message. They, the Hellenist counterpart of the Twelve, are active in the ministry of the word.

6, 6: *They . . . laid hands on them:* the customary Jewish way of designating persons for a task and invoking upon them the divine blessing and power to perform it.

6, 8—8, 1: The summary (6, 7) on the progress of the Jerusalem community, illustrated by the conversion of the priests, is followed by a lengthy narrative regarding Stephen. Stephen's defense is not a response to the charges made against him but takes the form of a discourse that reviews the fortunes of God's word to Israel and leads to a prophetic declaration: a plea for the hearing of that word as announced by Christ and now possessed by the Christian community.

The charges that Stephen depreciated the importance of the temple and the Mosaic law and elevated Jesus to a stature above Moses (6, 13–14) were in fact true. Before the Sanhedrin, no defense against them was possible. With Stephen, who thus perceived the fuller implications of the teachings of Jesus, the differences between Judaism and Christianity began to appear. Luke's account of Stephen's martyrdom and its aftermath shows how the major impetus behind the Christian movement passed from Jerusalem, where the temple and law prevailed, to Antioch in Syria, where these influences were less pressing.

6, 13: *False witnesses:* here, and in his account of Stephen's execution (7, 54–60), Luke parallels the martyrdom of Stephen with the death of Jesus.

against [this] holy place and the law. 14 [o]For
we have heard him claim that this Jesus the
Nazorean will destroy this place and change the
customs that Moses handed down to us."
15 All those who sat in the Sanhedrin looked
intently at him and saw that his face was like the
face of an angel.

## CHAPTER 7

**Stephen's Discourses** 1 Then the high
priest asked, "Is this so?" 2 [p]*And he replied,
"My brothers and fathers, listen. The God of
glory appeared to our father Abraham while he
was in Mesopotamia, before he had settled in
Haran, 3 [q]and said to him, 'Go forth from your
land and [from] your kinsfolk to the land that I
will show you.' 4 [r]So he went forth from the
land of the Chaldeans and settled in Haran. And
from there, after his father died, he made him
migrate to this land where you now dwell.
5 [s]Yet he gave him no inheritance in it, not
even a foot's length, but he did promise to give
it to him and his descendants as a possession,
even though he was childless. 6 [t]And God
spoke thus, 'His descendants shall be aliens in
a land not their own, where they shall be enslaved and oppressed for four hundred years;
7 [u]but I will bring judgment on the nation they
serve,' God said, 'and after that they will come
out and worship me in this place.' 8 [v]Then he
gave him the covenant of circumcision, and so
he became the father of Isaac, and circumcised
him on the eighth day, as Isaac did Jacob, and
Jacob the twelve patriarchs.

9 [w]"And the patriarchs, jealous of Joseph,
sold him into slavery in Egypt; but God was
with him 10 [x]and rescued him from all his afflictions. He granted him favor and wisdom
before Pharaoh, the king of Egypt, who put him
in charge of Egypt and [of] his entire household. 11 [y]Then a famine and great affliction
struck all Egypt and Canaan, and our ancestors
could find no food; 12 [z]but when Jacob heard
that there was grain in Egypt, he sent our ancestors there a first time. 13 [a]The second time,
Joseph made himself known to his brothers, and
Joseph's family became known to Pharaoh.
14 [b]Then Joseph sent for his father Jacob, inviting him and his whole clan, seventy-five persons; 15 [c]and Jacob went down to Egypt. And
he and our ancestors died 16 [d]and were brought
back to Shechem and placed in the tomb that
Abraham had purchased for a sum of money
from the sons of Hamor at Shechem.

17 [e]"When the time drew near for the fulfillment of the promise that God pledged to Abraham, the people had increased and become very
numerous in Egypt, 18 [f]until another king who
knew nothing of Joseph came to power [in
Egypt]. 19 He dealt shrewdly with our people
and oppressed [our] ancestors by forcing them
to expose their infants, that they might not survive. 20 [g]At this time Moses was born, and he
was extremely beautiful. For three months he
was nursed in his father's house; 21 [h]but when
he was exposed, Pharaoh's daughter adopted
him and brought him up as her own son.
22 Moses was educated [in] all the wisdom of
the Egyptians and was powerful in his words
and deeds.

23 [i]"When he was forty years old, he decided to visit his kinsfolk, the Israelites. 24 When
he saw one of them treated unjustly, he defended and avenged the oppressed man by striking
down the Egyptian. 25 He assumed [his] kinsfolk would understand that God was offering
them deliverance through him, but they did not
understand. 26 [j]The next day he appeared to
them as they were fighting and tried to reconcile
them peacefully, saying, 'Men, you are brothers. Why are you harming one another?'
27 Then the one who was harming his neighbor
pushed him aside, saying, 'Who appointed you
ruler and judge over us? 28 Are you thinking of
killing me as you killed the Egyptian yesterday?' 29 [k]Moses fled when he heard this and
settled as an alien in the land of Midian, where
he became the father of two sons.

30 [l]"Forty years later, an angel appeared to
him in the desert near Mount Sinai in the flame
of a burning bush. 31 When Moses saw it, he
was amazed at the sight, and as he drew near to
look at it, the voice of the Lord came, 32 'I am
the God of your fathers, the God of Abraham,

---

o Mt 26, 59-61; 27, 40; Jn 2, 19.
p Gn 11, 31; 12, 1; Ps 29, 3.
q Gn 12, 1.
r Gn 12, 5; 15, 7.
s Gn 12, 7; 13, 15; 15, 2; 16, 1; Dt 2, 5.
t Gn 15, 13-14.
u Ex 3, 12.
v Gn 17, 10-14; 21, 2-4.
w Gn 37, 11.28; 39, 2.3.21.23.
x Gn 41, 37-43; Ps 105, 21; Wis 10, 13-14.
y Gn 41, 54-57; 42, 5.
z Gn 42, 1-2.
a Gn 45, 3-4.16.
b Gn 45, 9-11.18-19; 46, 27; Ex 1, 5 LXX; Dt 10, 22.
c Gn 46, 5-6; 49, 33.
d Gn 23, 3-20; 33, 19; 49, 29-30; 50, 13; Jos 24, 32.
e Ex 1, 7.
f Ex 1, 8.
g Ex 2, 2; Heb 11, 23.
h Ex 2, 3-10.
i Ex 2, 11-12.
j Ex 2, 13-14.
k Ex 2, 15.21-22; 18, 3-4.
l Ex 3, 2-3.

*

7, 2–53: Stephen's speech represents Luke's description of Christianity's break from its Jewish matrix. Two motifs become prominent in the speech: (1) Israel's reaction to God's chosen leaders in the past reveals that the people have consistently rejected them; and (2) Israel has misunderstood God's choice of the Jerusalem temple as the place where he is to be worshiped.

7, 2: *God . . . appeared to our father Abraham . . . in Mesopotamia:* the first of a number of minor discrepancies between the data of the Old Testament and the data of Stephen's discourse. According to Gn 12, 1, God first spoke to Abraham in Haran. The main discrepancies are these: in v 16 it is said that Jacob was buried in Shechem, whereas Gn 50, 13 says he was buried at Hebron; in the same verse it is said that the tomb was purchased by Abraham, but in Gn 33, 19 and Jos 24, 32 the purchase is attributed to Jacob himself.

of Isaac, and of Jacob.' Then Moses, trembling,
did not dare to look at it. **33** But the Lord said
to him, 'Remove the sandals from your feet, for
the place where you stand is holy ground. **34** I
have witnessed the affliction of my people in
Egypt and have heard their groaning, and I have
come down to rescue them. Come now, I will
send you to Egypt.' **35** [m]This Moses, whom
they had rejected with the words, 'Who appointed you ruler and judge?' God sent as [both] ruler
and deliverer, through the angel who appeared
to him in the bush. **36** [n]This man led them out,
performing wonders and signs in the land of
Egypt, at the Red Sea, and in the desert for forty
years. **37** [o]It was this Moses who said to the
Israelites, 'God will raise up for you, from
among your own kinsfolk, a prophet like me.'
**38** [p]It was he who, in the assembly in the
desert, was with the angel who spoke to him on
Mount Sinai and with our ancestors, and he
received living utterances to hand on to us.

**39** [q]"Our ancestors were unwilling to obey
him; instead, they pushed him aside and in their
hearts turned back to Egypt, **40** [r]saying to Aaron, 'Make us gods who will be our leaders. As
for that Moses who led us out of the land of
Egypt, we do not know what has happened to
him.' **41** [s]So they made a calf in those days,
offered sacrifice to the idol, and reveled in the
works of their hands. **42** [tu]Then God turned
and handed them over to worship the host of
heaven, as it is written in the book of the prophets:

'Did you bring me sacrifices and offerings
for forty years in the desert, O house of
Israel?
**43** No, you took up the tent of Moloch
and the star of [your] god Rephan,
the images that you made to worship.
So I shall take you into exile beyond
Babylon.'

**44** [v]"Our ancestors had the tent of testimony in
the desert just as the One who spoke to Moses
directed him to make it according to the pattern
he had seen. **45** [w]Our ancestors who inherited
it brought it with Joshua when they dispossessed
the nations that God drove out from before our
ancestors, up to the time of David, **46** [x]who
found favor in the sight of God and asked that
he might find a dwelling place for the house of
Jacob. **47** [y]But Solomon built a house for him.
**48** [z]Yet the Most High does not dwell in houses
made by human hands. As the prophet says:

**49** [a]'The heavens are my throne,
the earth is my footstool.
What kind of house can you build for me?
says the Lord,
or what is to be my resting place?
**50** Did not my hand make all these things?'

**Conclusion** **51** "You stiff-necked people,
uncircumcised in heart and ears, you always
oppose the holy Spirit; you are just like your
ancestors. **52** [b]Which of the prophets did your
ancestors not persecute? They put to death those
who foretold the coming of the righteous one,
whose betrayers and murderers you have now
become. **53** [c]You received the law as transmitted by angels, but you did not observe it."

**Stephen's Martyrdom** **54** When they
heard this, they were infuriated, and they
ground their teeth at him. **55** [d]*But he, filled
with the holy Spirit, looked up intently to heav-
en and saw the glory of God and Jesus standing
at the right hand of God, **56** and he said, "Behold, I see the heavens opened and the Son of
Man standing at the right hand of God."
**57** *But they cried out in a loud voice, covered
their ears, and rushed upon him together.
**58** [e]They threw him out of the city, and began
to stone him. The witnesses laid down their
cloaks at the feet of a young man named Saul.
**59** [f]*As they were stoning Stephen, he called
out, "Lord Jesus, receive my spirit." **60** [g]Then
he fell to his knees and cried out in a loud voice,
"Lord, do not hold this sin against them"; and
when he said this, he fell asleep.

## CHAPTER 8

**1** [h]*Now Saul was consenting to his execution.

m Ex 2, 14.
n Ex 7, 3.10; 14, 21; Nm 14, 33.
o Dt 18, 15; Acts 3, 22.
p Ex 19, 3; 20, 1-17; Dt 5, 4-22; 6, 4-25.
q Nm 14, 3.
r Ex 32, 1.23.
s Ex 32, 4-6.
t Am 5, 25-27.
u Jer 7, 18; 8, 2; 19, 13.
v Ex 25, 9.40.
w Jos 3, 14-17; 18, 1; 2 Sm 7, 5-7.
x 2 Sm 7, 1-2; 1 Kgs 8, 17; Ps 132, 1-5.
y 1 Kgs 6, 1; 1 Chr 17, 12.
z 17, 24.
a Is 66, 1-2.
b 2 Chr 36, 16; Mt 23, 31.34.
c Gal 3, 19; Heb 2, 2.
d Mt 26, 64; Mk 14, 62; Lk 22, 69; Acts 2, 34.
e 22, 20.
f Ps 31, 6; Lk 23, 46.
g Mt 27, 46.50; Mk 15, 34; Lk 23, 46.
h 22, 20.

*

7, 55: *He . . . saw . . . Jesus standing at the right hand of God:* Stephen affirms to the Sanhedrin that the prophecy Jesus made before them has been fulfilled (Mk 14, 62).

7, 57: *Covered their ears:* Stephen's declaration, like that of Jesus, is a scandal to the court, which regards it as blasphemy.

7, 59: Compare Lk 23, [34].46.

8, 1–40: Some idea of the severity of the persecution that now breaks out against the Jerusalem community can be gathered from 22, 4 and 26, 9–11. Luke, however, concentrates on the fortunes of the word of God among people, indicating how the dispersal of the Jewish community resulted in the conversion of the Samaritans (4–17.25). His narrative is further expanded to include the account of Philip's acceptance of an Ethiopian (26–39).

8, 1: *All were scattered . . . except the apostles:* this observation leads some modern scholars to conclude that the persecution was limited to the Hellenist Christians and that the Hebrew Christians were not molested, perhaps because their attitude toward the law and temple was still more in line with

**Persecution of the Church** On that day,
there broke out a severe persecution of the
church in Jerusalem, and all were scattered
throughout the countryside of Judea and Samaria, except the apostles. **2** Devout men buried
Stephen and made a loud lament over him.
**3** [i]*Saul, meanwhile, was trying to destroy the
church; entering house after house and dragging
out men and women, he handed them over for
imprisonment.

## *III: THE MISSION IN JUDEA AND SAMARIA*

**Philip in Samaria** **4** [j]Now those who had
been scattered went about preaching the word.
**5** [k]Thus Philip went down to [the] city of Samaria and proclaimed the Messiah to them.
**6** With one accord, the crowds paid attention to
what was said by Philip when they heard it and
saw the signs he was doing. **7** [l]For unclean
spirits, crying out in a loud voice, came out of
many possessed people, and many paralyzed
and crippled people were cured. **8** There was
great joy in that city.

**Simon the Magician** **9** *A man named Simon used to practice magic in the city and astounded the people of Samaria, claiming to be
someone great. **10** All of them, from the least
to the greatest, paid attention to him, saying,
"This man is the 'Power of God' that is called
'Great.'" **11** They paid attention to him because he had astounded them by his magic for
a long time, **12** [m]but once they began to believe
Philip as he preached the good news about the
kingdom of God and the name of Jesus Christ,
men and women alike were baptized. **13** Even
Simon himself believed and, after being baptized, became devoted to Philip; and when he
saw the signs and mighty deeds that were occurring, he was astounded.

**14** Now when the apostles in Jerusalem
heard that Samaria had accepted the word of
God, they sent them Peter and John, **15** who
went down and prayed for them, that they might
receive the holy Spirit, **16** *for it had not yet
fallen upon any of them; they had only been
baptized in the name of the Lord Jesus.
**17** [n]Then they laid hands on them and they
received the holy Spirit.

**18** *When Simon saw that the Spirit was
conferred by the laying on of the apostles'
hands, he offered them money **19** and said,
"Give me this power too, so that anyone upon
whom I lay my hands may receive the holy
Spirit." **20** But Peter said to him, "May your
money perish with you, because you thought
that you could buy the gift of God with money.
**21** You have no share or lot in this matter, for
your heart is not upright before God. **22** Repent
of this wickedness of yours and pray to the Lord
that, if possible, your intention may be forgiv-
en. **23** For I see that you are filled with bitter
gall and are in the bonds of iniquity." **24** Simon said in reply, "Pray for me to the Lord,
that nothing of what you have said may come
upon me." **25** So when they had testified and
proclaimed the word of the Lord, they returned
to Jerusalem and preached the good news to
many Samaritan villages.

**Philip and the Ethiopian** **26** *Then the
angel of the Lord spoke to Philip, "Get up and
head south on the road that goes down from
Jerusalem to Gaza, the desert route." **27** [o]*So
he got up and set out. Now there was an Ethiopian eunuch, a court official of the Candace, that
is, the queen of the Ethiopians, in charge of her
entire treasury, who had come to Jerusalem to

i 9, 1.13; 22, 4; 26, 9-11; 1 Cor 5, 9; Gal 1, 13.
j 11, 19.
k 6, 5; 21, 8-9.
l Mk 16, 17.
m 1, 3; 19, 8; 28, 23.31.
n 2, 4; 4, 31; 10, 44-47; 15, 8-9; 19, 2.6.
o Is 56, 3-5.

* that of their fellow Jews (see the charge leveled against the Hellenist Stephen in 6, 13–14). Whatever the facts, it appears that the Twelve took no public stand regarding Stephen's position, choosing, instead, to await the development of events.

8, 3: *Saul . . . was trying to destroy the church:* like Stephen, Saul was able to perceive that the Christian movement contained the seeds of doctrinal divergence from Judaism. A pupil of Gamaliel, according to 22, 3, and totally dedicated to the law as the way of salvation (Gal 1, 13–14), Saul accepted the task of crushing the Christian movement, at least insofar as it detracted from the importance of the temple and the law. His vehement opposition to Christianity reveals how difficult it was for a Jew of his time to accept a messianism that differed so greatly from the general expectation.

8, 9–13.18–24: Sorcerers were well known in the ancient world. Probably the incident involving Simon and his altercation with Peter is introduced to show that the miraculous charisms possessed by members of the Christian community (6–7) were not to be confused with the magic of sorcerers.

8, 16: Here and in 10, 44–48 and 19, 1–6, Luke distinguishes between baptism in the name of the Lord Jesus and the reception of the Spirit. In each case, the Spirit is conferred through members of the Twelve (Peter and John) or their representative (Paul). This may be Luke's way of describing the role of the church in the bestowal of the Spirit. Elsewhere in Acts, baptism and the Spirit are more closely related (1, 5; 11, 16).

8, 18–20: Simon attempts to buy the gift of God (20) with money. Peter's cursing of Simon's attempt so to use his money expresses a typically Lucan attitude toward material wealth (cf Lk 6, 24; 12, 16–21; 16, 13).

8, 26–40: In the account of the conversion of the Ethiopian eunuch, Luke adduces additional evidence to show that the spread of Christianity outside the confines of Judaism itself was in accord with the plan of God. He does not make clear whether the Ethiopian was originally a convert to Judaism or, as is more probable, a "God-fearer" (10, 1), i.e., one who accepted Jewish monotheism and ethic and attended the synagogue but did not consider himself bound by other regulations such as circumcision and observance of the dietary laws. The story of his conversion to Christianity is given a strong supernatural cast by the introduction of an angel (26), instruction from the holy Spirit (29), and the strange removal of Philip from the scene (39).

worship, **28** and was returning home. Seated in
his chariot, he was reading the prophet Isaiah.
**29** The Spirit said to Philip, "Go and join up
with that chariot." **30** *Philip ran up and heard
him reading Isaiah the prophet and said, "Do
you understand what you are reading?" **31** [p]He
replied, "How can I, unless someone instructs
me?" So he invited Philip to get in and sit with
him. **32** [q]This was the scripture passage he was
reading:

"Like a sheep he was led to the slaughter,
and as a lamb before its shearer is silent,
so he opened not his mouth.
**33** In [his] humiliation justice was denied him.
Who will tell of his posterity?
For his life is taken from the earth."

**34** Then the eunuch said to Philip in reply, "I
beg you, about whom is the prophet saying
this? About himself, or about someone else?"
**35** Then Philip opened his mouth and, beginning with this scripture passage, he proclaimed
Jesus to him. **36** [r]As they traveled along the
road they came to some water, and the eunuch
said, "Look, there is water. What is to prevent
my being baptized?"
**[37*] 38** Then he ordered the chariot to stop,
and Philip and the eunuch both went down into
the water, and he baptized him. **39** [s]When they
came out of the water, the Spirit of the Lord
snatched Philip away, and the eunuch saw him
no more, but continued on his way rejoicing.
**40** [t]Philip came to Azotus, and went about proclaiming the good news to all the towns until he
reached Caesarea.

## CHAPTER 9

### Saul's Conversion

**1** [u][v]*Now Saul, still
breathing murderous threats against the disciples of the Lord, went to the high priest **2** *and
asked him for letters to the synagogues in Damascus, that, if he should find any men or wom-
en who belonged to the Way, he might bring
them back to Jerusalem in chains. **3** [w]On his
journey, as he was nearing Damascus, a light
from the sky suddenly flashed around him.
**4** [x]He fell to the ground and heard a voice
saying to him, "Saul, Saul, why are you persecuting me?" **5** [y]He said, "Who are you, sir?"
The reply came, "I am Jesus, whom you are
persecuting. **6** [z]Now get up and go into the city
and you will be told what you must do."
**7** [a]The men who were traveling with him stood
speechless, for they heard the voice but could
see no one. **8** [b]*Saul got up from the ground,
but when he opened his eyes he could see nothing; so they led him by the hand and brought
him to Damascus. **9** For three days he was unable to see, and he neither ate nor drank.

### Saul's Baptism

**10** [c]There was a disciple
in Damascus named Ananias, and the Lord said
to him in a vision, "Ananias." He answered,
"Here I am, Lord." **11** [d]The Lord said to him,
"Get up and go to the street called Straight and
ask at the house of Judas for a man from Tarsus
named Saul. He is there praying, **12** and [in a
vision] he has seen a man named Ananias come
in and lay [his] hands on him, that he may regain
his sight." **13** [e]*But Ananias replied, "Lord,
I have heard from many sources about this man,
what evil things he has done to your holy ones
in Jerusalem. **14** [f]And here he has authority
from the chief priests to imprison all who call
upon your name." **15** [g]But the Lord said to
him, "Go, for this man is a chosen instrument
of mine to carry my name before Gentiles,
kings, and Israelites, **16** and I will show him
what he will have to suffer for my name."
**17** So Ananias went and entered the house; laying his hands on him, he said, "Saul, my broth-

p Jn 16, 13.
q Is 53, 7-8 LXX.
r 10, 47.
s 1 Kgs 18, 12.
t 21, 8.
u 8, 3; 9, 13; 22, 4; 1 Cor 15, 9; Gal 1, 13-14.
v 9, 14; 26, 10.
w 1 Cor 9, 1; 15, 8; Gal 1, 16.
x 22, 6; 26, 14.
y 22, 8; 26, 15; Mt 25, 40.
z 22, 10; 26, 16.
a 22, 9; 26, 13-14.
b 22, 11.
c 22, 12-16.
d 21, 39.
e 8, 3; 9, 1.
f 9, 1-2; 26, 10; 1 Cor 1, 2; 2 Tm 2, 22.
g 22, 15; 26, 1; 27, 24.

*

8, 27: *The Candace:* Candace is not a proper name here but the title of a Nubian queen.

8, 30–34: Philip is brought alongside the carriage at the very moment when the Ethiopian is pondering the meaning of Is 53, 7–8, a passage that Christianity, from its earliest origins, has applied to Jesus; cf the note on 3, 13.

8, 37: The oldest and best manuscripts of Acts omit this verse, which is a Western text reading: "And Philip said, 'If you believe with all your heart, you may.' And he said in reply, 'I believe that Jesus Christ is the Son of God.'"

9, 1–19: This is the first of three accounts of Paul's conversion (with 22, 3–16 and 26, 2–18) with some differences of detail owing to Luke's use of different sources. Paul's experience was not visionary but was precipitated by the appearance of Jesus, as he insists in 1 Cor 15, 8. The words of Jesus, "Saul, Saul, why are you persecuting me?" related by Luke with no variation in all three accounts, exerted a profound and lasting influence on the thought of Paul. Under the influence of this experience he gradually developed his understanding of justification by faith (see the letters to the Galatians and Romans) and of the identification of the Christian community with Jesus Christ (see 1 Cor 12, 27). That Luke would narrate this conversion three times is testimony to the importance he attaches to it. This first account occurs when the word is first spread to the Gentiles. At this point, the conversion of the hero of the Gentile mission is recounted. The emphasis in the account is on Paul as a divinely chosen instrument (15).

9, 2: *The Way:* a name used by the early Christian community for itself (18, 26; 19, 9.23; 22, 4; 24, 14.22). The Essene community at Qumran used the same designation to describe its mode of life.

9, 8: *He could see nothing:* a temporary blindness (18) symbolizing the religious blindness of Saul as persecutor (cf 26, 18).

9, 13: *Your holy ones:* literally, "your saints."

er, the Lord has sent me, Jesus who appeared to
you on the way by which you came, that you
may regain your sight and be filled with the holy
Spirit.'' **18** Immediately things like scales fell
from his eyes and he regained his sight. He got
up and was baptized, **19** *and when he had
eaten, he recovered his strength.

**Saul Preaches in Damascus** He stayed
some days with the disciples in Damascus,
**20** *and he began at once to proclaim Jesus in
the synagogues, that he is the Son of God.
**21** All who heard him were astounded and said,
"Is not this the man who in Jerusalem ravaged
those who call upon this name, and came here
expressly to take them back in chains to the
chief priests?'' **22** But Saul grew all the stronger and confounded [the] Jews who lived in
Damascus, proving that this is the Messiah.

**Saul Visits Jerusalem** **23** After a long
time had passed, the Jews conspired to kill him,
**24** [h]but their plot became known to Saul. Now
they were keeping watch on the gates day and
night so as to kill him, **25** but his disciples took
him one night and let him down through an
opening in the wall, lowering him in a basket.

**26** [i]*When he arrived in Jerusalem he tried
to join the disciples, but they were all afraid of
him, not believing that he was a disciple.
**27** Then Barnabas took charge of him and
brought him to the apostles, and he reported to
them how on the way he had seen the Lord and
that he had spoken to him, and how in Damascus he had spoken out boldly in the name of
Jesus. **28** He moved about freely with them in
Jerusalem, and spoke out boldly in the name of
the Lord. **29** *He also spoke and debated with
the Hellenists, but they tried to kill him.
**30** [j]And when the brothers learned of this, they
took him down to Caesarea and sent him on his
way to Tarsus.

**The Church at Peace** **31** *The church
throughout all Judea, Galilee, and Samaria was
at peace. It was being built up and walked in the
fear of the Lord, and with the consolation of the
holy Spirit it grew in numbers.

**Peter Heals Aeneas at Lydda** **32** As Peter was passing through every region, he went
down to the holy ones living in Lydda.
**33** There he found a man named Aeneas, who
had been confined to bed for eight years, for he
was paralyzed. **34** Peter said to him, "Aeneas,
Jesus Christ heals you. Get up and make your
bed.'' He got up at once. **35** And all the inhabitants of Lydda and Sharon saw him, and they
turned to the Lord.

**Peter Restores Tabitha to Life** **36** *Now
in Joppa there was a disciple named Tabitha
(which translated means Dorcas). She was completely occupied with good deeds and almsgiving. **37** Now during those days she fell sick and
died, so after washing her, they laid [her] out in
a room upstairs. **38** Since Lydda was near Joppa, the disciples, hearing that Peter was there,
sent two men to him with the request, "Please
come to us without delay.'' **39** So Peter got up
and went with them. When he arrived, they took
him to the room upstairs where all the widows
came to him weeping and showing him the tunics and cloaks that Dorcas had made while she
was with them. **40** [k]Peter sent them all out and
knelt down and prayed. Then he turned to her
body and said, "Tabitha, rise up.'' She opened
her eyes, saw Peter, and sat up. **41** He gave her
his hand and raised her up, and when he had
called the holy ones and the widows, he presented her alive. **42** This became known all over
Joppa, and many came to believe in the Lord.
**43** [l]*And he stayed a long time in Joppa with
Simon, a tanner.

## IV: THE INAUGURATION OF THE GENTILE MISSION

### CHAPTER 10

**The Vision of Cornelius** **1** [m]*Now in
Caesarea there was a man named Cornelius, a

h 2 Cor 11, 32-33.
i Gal 1, 18.
j 11, 25.
k Mk 5, 40-41.
l 10, 6.
m 10, 30-33.

*

9, 19–30: This is a brief resume of Paul's initial experience as an apostolic preacher. At first he found himself in the position of being regarded as an apostate by the Jews and suspect by the Christian community of Jerusalem. His acceptance by the latter was finally brought about through his friendship with Barnabas (27).

9, 20: *Son of God:* the title "Son of God" occurs in Acts only here, but cf the citation of Ps 2, 7 in Paul's speech at Antioch in Pisidia (13, 33).

9, 26: This visit of Paul to Jerusalem is mentioned by Paul in Gal 1, 18.

9, 29: *Hellenists:* see the note on 6, 1–7.

9, 31–43: In the context of the period of peace enjoyed by the community through the cessation of Paul's activities against it, Luke introduces two traditions concerning the miraculous power exercised by Peter as he was making a tour of places where the Christian message had already been preached. The towns of Lydda, Sharon, and Joppa were populated by both Jews and Gentiles and their Christian communities may well have been mixed.

9, 36: *Tabitha* (*Dorcas*), respectively the Aramaic and Greek words for "gazelle," exemplifies the right attitude toward material possessions expressed by Jesus in the Lucan Gospel (Lk 6, 30; 11, 41; 12, 33; 18, 22; 19, 8).

9, 43: The fact that Peter lodged with a tanner would have been significant to both the Gentile and Jewish Christians, for Judaism considered the tanning occupation unclean.

10, 1–48: The narrative centers on the conversion of Cornelius, a Gentile and a "God-fearer" (see the note on 8,

centurion of the Cohort called the Italica,
**2** *devout and God-fearing along with his
whole household, who used to give alms generously to the Jewish people and pray to God
constantly. **3** *One afternoon about three
o'clock, he saw plainly in a vision an angel of
God come in to him and say to him, "Cornelius." **4** He looked intently at him and, seized
with fear, said, "What is it, sir?" He said to
him, "Your prayers and almsgiving have ascended as a memorial offering before God.
**5** Now send some men to Joppa and summon
one Simon who is called Peter. **6** [n]He is staying
with another Simon, a tanner, who has a house
by the sea." **7** *When the angel who spoke to
him had left, he called two of his servants and
a devout soldier from his staff, **8** explained everything to them, and sent them to Joppa.

**The Vision of Peter** **9** *The next day,
while they were on their way and nearing the
city, Peter went up to the roof terrace to pray at
about noontime. **10** He was hungry and wished
to eat, and while they were making preparations
he fell into a trance. **11** [o]He saw heaven opened
and something resembling a large sheet coming
down, lowered to the ground by its four corners.
**12** In it were all the earth's four-legged animals
and reptiles and the birds of the sky. **13** A voice
said to him, "Get up, Peter. Slaughter and eat."
**14** [p]But Peter said, "Certainly not, sir. For
never have I eaten anything profane and unclean." **15** [q]The voice spoke to him again, a
second time, "What God has made clean, you
are not to call profane." **16** This happened
three times, and then the object was taken up
into the sky.

**17** *While Peter was in doubt about the meaning of the vision he had seen, the men sent by
Cornelius asked for Simon's house and arrived
at the entrance. **18** They called out inquiring
whether Simon, who is called Peter, was staying there. **19** [r]As Peter was pondering the vision, the Spirit said [to him], "There are three
men here looking for you. **20** So get up, go
downstairs, and accompany them without hesitation, because I have sent them." **21** Then
Peter went down to the men and said, "I am the
one you are looking for. What is the reason for
your being here?" **22** [s]They answered, "Cornelius, a centurion, an upright and God-fearing
man, respected by the whole Jewish nation, was
directed by a holy angel to summon you to his
house and to hear what you have to say." **23** So
he invited them in and showed them hospitality.

The next day he got up and went with them,
and some of the brothers from Joppa went with
him. **24** *On the following day he entered
Caesarea. Cornelius was expecting them and
had called together his relatives and close
friends. **25** [t]When Peter entered, Cornelius met
him and, falling at his feet, paid him homage.
**26** Peter, however, raised him up, saying,
"Get up. I myself am also a human being."
**27** While he conversed with him, he went in
and found many people gathered together
**28** [u]*and said to them, "You know that it is
unlawful for a Jewish man to associate with, or
visit, a Gentile, but God has shown me that I
should not call any person profane or unclean.
**29** And that is why I came without objection
when sent for. May I ask, then, why you summoned me?"

**30** *Cornelius replied, "Four days ago at
this hour, three o'clock in the afternoon, I was
at prayer in my house when suddenly a man in
dazzling robes stood before me and said,
**31** 'Cornelius, your prayer has been heard and
your almsgiving remembered before God.
**32** Send therefore to Joppa and summon Simon, who is called Peter. He is a guest in the
house of Simon, a tanner, by the sea.' **33** So I

n 9, 43.
o 11, 5-12.
p Lv 11, 1-47; Ez 4, 14.
q Mk 7, 15-19; Gal 2, 12.
r 13, 2.
s Lk 7, 4-5.
t 14, 13-15; Rv 19, 10.
u Gal 2, 11-16.

*

26–40). Luke considers the event of great importance, as is evident from his long treatment of it. The incident is again related in 11, 1–18 where Peter is forced to justify his actions before the Jerusalem community and alluded to in 15, 7–11 where at the Jerusalem "Council" Peter supports Paul's missionary activity among the Gentiles. The narrative divides itself into a series of distinct episodes, concluding with Peter's presentation of the Christian kerygma (34–43) and a pentecostal experience undergone by Cornelius' household preceding their reception of baptism (44–48).

10, 1: *The Cohort called the Italica:* this battalion was an auxiliary unit of archers formed originally in Italy but transferred to Syria shortly before A.D. 69.

10, 2: *Used to give alms generously:* like Tabitha (9, 36), Cornelius exemplifies the proper attitude toward wealth (see the note on 9, 36).

10, 3: *About three o'clock:* literally, "about the ninth hour." See the note on 3, 1.

10, 7: *A devout soldier:* by using this adjective, Luke probably intends to classify him as a "God-fearer" (see the note on 8, 26–40).

10, 9–16: The vision is intended to prepare Peter to share the food of Cornelius' household without qualms of conscience (48). The necessity of such instructions to Peter reveals that at first not even the apostles fully grasped the implications of Jesus' teaching on the law. In Acts, the initial insight belongs to Stephen.

10, 9: *At about noontime:* literally, "about the sixth hour."

10, 17–23: The arrival of the Gentile emissaries with their account of the angelic apparition illuminates Peter's vision: he is to be prepared to admit Gentiles, who were considered unclean like the animals of his vision, into the Christian community.

10, 24–27: So impressed is Cornelius with the apparition that he invites close personal friends to join him in his meeting with Peter. But his understanding of the person he is about to meet is not devoid of superstition, suggested by his falling down before him. For a similar experience of Paul and Barnabas, see 14, 11–18.

10, 28: Peter now fully understands the meaning of his vision; see the note on l0, l7–23.

10, 30: *Four days ago:* literally, "from the fourth day up to this hour."

sent for you immediately, and you were kind enough to come. Now therefore we are all here in the presence of God to listen to all that you have been commanded by the Lord."

**Peter's Speech** **34** [v]*Then Peter proceeded to speak and said, "In truth, I see that God shows no partiality. **35** Rather, in every nation whoever fears him and acts uprightly is acceptable to him. **36** [w]*You know the word [that] he sent to the Israelites as he proclaimed peace through Jesus Christ, who is Lord of all, **37** [x]what has happened all over Judea, beginning in Galilee after the baptism that John preached, **38** [y]*how God anointed Jesus of Nazareth with the holy Spirit and power. He went about doing good and healing all those oppressed by the devil, for God was with him. **39** *We are witnesses of all that he did both in the country of the Jews and [in] Jerusalem. They put him to death by hanging him on a tree. **40** This man God raised [on] the third day and granted that he be visible, **41** [z]not to all the people, but to us, the witnesses chosen by God in advance, who ate and drank with him after he rose from the dead. **42** [a]*He commissioned us to preach to the people and testify that he is the one appointed by God as judge of the living and the dead. **43** To him all the prophets bear witness, that everyone who believes in him will receive forgiveness of sins through his name."

**The Baptism of Cornelius** **44** [b]*While Peter was still speaking these things, the holy Spirit fell upon all who were listening to the word. **45** The circumcised believers who had accompanied Peter were astounded that the gift of the holy Spirit should have been poured out on the Gentiles also, **46** for they could hear them speaking in tongues and glorifying God. Then Peter responded, **47** [c]"Can anyone withhold the water for baptizing these people, who have received the holy Spirit even as we have?" **48** He ordered them to be baptized in the name of Jesus Christ. **49** Then they invited him to stay for a few days.

## CHAPTER 11

### The Baptism of the Gentiles Explained

**1** *Now the apostles and the brothers who were in Judea heard that the Gentiles too had accepted the word of God. **2** So when Peter went up to Jerusalem the circumcised believers confronted him, **3** *saying, "You entered the house of uncircumcised people and ate with them." **4** Peter began and explained it to them step by step, saying, **5** [d]"I was at prayer in the city of Joppa when in a trance I had a vision, something resembling a large sheet coming down, lowered from the sky by its four corners, and it came to me. **6** Looking intently into it, I observed and saw the four-legged animals of the earth, the wild beasts, the reptiles, and the birds of the sky. **7** I also heard a voice say to me, 'Get up, Peter. Slaughter and eat.' **8** But I said, 'Certainly not, sir, because nothing profane or unclean has ever entered my mouth.' **9** But a second time a voice from heaven answered, 'What God has made clean, you are not to call profane.' **10** This happened three times, and then everything was drawn up again into the sky. **11** Just then three men appeared at the house

v Dt 17, 2; 2 Chr 19, 7; Jb 34, 19; Wis 6, 7; Rom 2, 11; Gal 2, 6; Eph 6, 9; 1 Pt 1, 17.
w Is 52, 7; Na 2, 1.
x Mt 4, 12; Mk 1, 14; Lk 4, 14.
y Is 61, 1; Lk 4, 18.
z Lk 24, 41-43.
a 1, 8; 3, 15; 17, 31; Lk 24, 48; Rom 14, 9; 2 Tm 4, 1.
b 11, 15; 15, 8.
c 8, 36.
d 10, 11-20.

*

10, 34–43: Peter's speech to the household of Cornelius typifies early Christian preaching to Gentiles.

10, 34–35: The revelation of God's choice of Israel to be the people of God did not mean he withheld the divine favor from other people.

10, 36–43: These words are more directed to Luke's Christian readers than to the household of Cornelius, as indicated by the opening words, "You know." They trace the continuity between the preaching and teaching of Jesus of Nazareth and the proclamation of Jesus by the early community. The emphasis on this divinely ordained continuity (41) is meant to assure Luke's readers of the fidelity of Christian tradition to the words and deeds of Jesus.

10, 36: *To the Israelites:* Luke, in the words of Peter, speaks of the prominent position occupied by Israel in the history of salvation.

10, 38: *Jesus of Nazareth:* God's revelation of his plan for the destiny of humanity through Israel culminated in Jesus of Nazareth. Consequently, the ministry of Jesus is an integral part of God's revelation. This viewpoint explains why the early Christian communities were interested in conserving the historical substance of the ministry of Jesus, a tradition leading to the production of the four gospels.

10, 39: *We are witnesses:* the apostolic testimony was not restricted to the resurrection of Jesus but also included his historical ministry. This witness, however, was theological in character; the Twelve, divinely mandated as prophets, were empowered to interpret his sayings and deeds in the light of his redemptive death and resurrection. The meaning of these words and deeds was to be made clear to the developing Christian community as the bearer of the word of salvation (cf 1, 21–26). *Hanging him on a tree:* see the note on 5, 30.

10, 42: *As judge of the living and the dead:* the apostolic preaching to the Jews appealed to their messianic hope, while the preaching to Gentiles stressed the coming divine judgment; cf 1 Thes 1, 10.

10, 44: Just as the Jewish Christians received the gift of the Spirit, so too do the Gentiles.

11, 1–18: The Jewish Christians of Jerusalem were scandalized to learn of Peter's sojourn in the house of the Gentile Cornelius. Nonetheless, they had to accept the divine directions given to both Peter and Cornelius. They concluded that the setting aside of the legal barriers between Jew and Gentile was an exceptional ordinance of God to indicate that the apostolic kerygma was also to be directed to the Gentiles. Only in ch 15 at the "Council" in Jerusalem does the evangelization of the Gentiles become the official position of the church leadership in Jerusalem.

11, 3: *You entered . . . :* alternatively, this could be punctuated as a question.

where we were, who had been sent to me from
Caesarea. **12** *The Spirit told me to accompany
them without discriminating. These six brothers
also went with me, and we entered the man's
house. **13** [e]He related to us how he had seen
[the] angel standing in his house, saying, 'Send
someone to Joppa and summon Simon, who is
called Peter, **14** who will speak words to you by
which you and all your household will be
saved.' **15** [f]As I began to speak, the holy Spirit
fell upon them as it had upon us at the beginning, **16** [g]and I remembered the word of the
Lord, how he had said, 'John baptized with
water but you will be baptized with the holy
Spirit.' **17** [h]If then God gave them the same gift
he gave to us when we came to believe in the
Lord Jesus Christ, who was I to be able to hinder
God?'' **18** When they heard this, they stopped
objecting and glorified God, saying, ''God has
then granted life-giving repentance to the Gentiles too.''

## The Church at Antioch

**19** [i]*Now those
who had been scattered by the persecution that
arose because of Stephen went as far as Phoenicia, Cyprus, and Antioch, preaching the word
to no one but Jews. **20** There were some Cypriots and Cyrenians among them, however, who
came to Antioch and began to speak to the
Greeks as well, proclaiming the Lord Jesus.
**21** The hand of the Lord was with them and a
great number who believed turned to the Lord.
**22** The news about them reached the ears of the
church in Jerusalem, and they sent Barnabas [to
go] to Antioch. **23** When he arrived and saw the
grace of God, he rejoiced and encouraged them
all to remain faithful to the Lord in firmness of
heart, **24** for he was a good man, filled with the
holy Spirit and faith. And a large number of
people was added to the Lord. **25** Then he went
to Tarsus to look for Saul, **26** *and when he had
found him he brought him to Antioch. For a
whole year they met with the church and taught
a large number of people, and it was in Antioch
that the disciples were first called Christians.

## The Prediction of Agabus

**27** *At that
time some prophets came down from Jerusalem
to Antioch, **28** [j]and one of them named Agabus
stood up and predicted by the Spirit that there
would be a severe famine all over the world, and
it happened under Claudius. **29** [k]So the disciples determined that, according to ability, each
should send relief to the brothers who lived in
Judea. **30** *This they did, sending it to the presbyters in care of Barnabas and Saul.

## CHAPTER 12

## Herod's Persecution of the Christians

**1** *About that time King Herod laid hands upon
some members of the church to harm them.
**2** *He had James, the brother of John, killed by
the sword, **3** *and when he saw that this was
pleasing to the Jews he proceeded to arrest Peter
also. (It was [the] feast of Unleavened Bread.)
**4** He had him taken into custody and put in
prison under the guard of four squads of four
soldiers each. He intended to bring him before
the people after Passover. **5** [l]Peter thus was
being kept in prison, but prayer by the church
was fervently being made to God on his behalf.
**6** On the very night before Herod was to
bring him to trial, Peter, secured by double
chains, was sleeping between two soldiers,
while outside the door guards kept watch on the
prison. **7** Suddenly the angel of the Lord stood
by him and a light shone in the cell. He tapped
Peter on the side and awakened him, saying,
''Get up quickly.'' The chains fell from his
wrists. **8** The angel said to him, ''Put on your
belt and your sandals.'' He did so. Then he said
to him, ''Put on your cloak and follow me.''
**9** So he followed him out, not realizing that
what was happening through the angel was real;
he thought he was seeing a vision. **10** They

e 10, 3-5.22.30-32.
f 10, 44.
g 1, 5; 19, 4; Lk 3, 16.
h 15, 8-9.
i 8, 1-4.
j 21, 10.
k 12, 25.
l Jas 5, 16.

*

11, 12: *These six brothers:* companions from the Christian community of Joppa (see 10, 23).

11, 19–26: The Jewish Christian antipathy to the mixed community was reflected by the early missionaries generally. The few among them who entertained a different view succeeded in introducing Gentiles into the community at Antioch (in Syria). When the disconcerted Jerusalem community sent Barnabas to investigate, he was so favorably impressed by what he observed that he persuaded his friend Saul to participate in the Antioch mission.

11, 26: *Christians:* "Christians" is first applied to the members of the community at Antioch because the Gentile members of the community enable it to stand out clearly from Judaism.

11, 27–30: It is not clear whether the prophets from Jerusalem came to Antioch to request help in view of the coming famine or whether they received this insight during their visit there. The former supposition seems more likely. Suetonius and Tacitus speak of famines during the reign of Claudius (A.D. 41–54), while the Jewish historian Josephus mentions a famine in Judea in A.D. 46–48. Luke is interested, rather, in showing the charity of the Antiochene community toward the Jewish Christians of Jerusalem despite their differences on mixed communities.

11, 30: *Presbyters:* this is the same Greek word that elsewhere is translated "elders," primarily in reference to the Jewish community.

12, 1–19: Herod Agrippa ruled Judea A.D. 41–44. While Luke does not assign a motive for his execution of James and his intended execution of Peter, the broad background lies in Herod's support of Pharisaic Judaism. The Jewish Christians had lost the popularity they had had in Jerusalem (2, 47), perhaps because of suspicions against them traceable to the teaching of Stephen.

12, 2: *James, the brother of John:* this James, the son of Zebedee, was beheaded by Herod Agrippa ca. A.D. 44.

12, 3.4: *Feast of Unleavened Bread . . . Passover:* see the note on Lk 22, l.

passed the first guard, then the second, and
came to the iron gate leading out to the city,
which opened for them by itself. They emerged
and made their way down an alley, and suddenly the angel left him. **11** Then Peter recovered
his senses and said, "Now I know for certain
that [the] Lord sent his angel and rescued me
from the hand of Herod and from all that the
Jewish people had been expecting."
**12** [m]When he realized this, he went to the
house of Mary, the mother of John who is called
Mark, where there were many people gathered
in prayer. **13** When he knocked on the gateway
door, a maid named Rhoda came to answer it.
**14** She was so overjoyed when she recognized
Peter's voice that, instead of opening the gate,
she ran in and announced that Peter was standing at the gate. **15** They told her, "You are out
of your mind," but she insisted that it was so.
But they kept saying, "It is his angel." **16** But
Peter continued to knock, and when they
opened it, they saw him and were astounded.
**17** *He motioned to them with his hand to be
quiet and explained [to them] how the Lord had
led him out of the prison, and said, "Report this
to James and the brothers." Then he left and
went to another place. **18** [n]At daybreak there
was no small commotion among the soldiers
over what had become of Peter. **19** Herod, after
instituting a search but not finding him, ordered
the guards tried and executed. Then he left Judea to spend some time in Caesarea.

## Herod's Death

**20** *He had long been very
angry with the people of Tyre and Sidon, who
now came to him in a body. After winning over
Blastus, the king's chamberlain, they sued for
peace because their country was supplied with
food from the king's territory. **21** On an appointed day, Herod, attired in royal robes, [and]
seated on the rostrum, addressed them publicly.
**22** The assembled crowd cried out, "This is the
voice of a god, not of a man." **23** At once the
angel of the Lord struck him down because he
did not ascribe the honor to God, and he was
eaten by worms and breathed his last. **24** [o]But
the word of God continued to spread and grow.

## Mission of Barnabas and Saul

**25** [p]*After Barnabas and Saul completed their
relief mission, they returned to Jerusalem, taking with them John, who is called Mark.

## CHAPTER 13

**1** *Now there were in the church at Antioch
prophets and teachers: Barnabas, Symeon who
was called Niger, Lucius of Cyrene, Manaen
who was a close friend of Herod the tetrarch,
and Saul. **2** While they were worshiping the
Lord and fasting, the holy Spirit said, "Set apart
for me Barnabas and Saul for the work to which
I have called them." **3** Then, completing their
fasting and prayer, they laid hands on them and
sent them off.

## First Mission Begins in Cyprus

**4** *So
they, sent forth by the holy Spirit, went down
to Seleucia and from there sailed to Cyprus.
**5** *When they arrived in Salamis, they proclaimed the word of God in the Jewish synagogues. They had John also as their assistant.
**6** *When they had traveled through the whole
island as far as Paphos, they met a magician
named Bar-Jesus who was a Jewish false prophet. **7** He was with the proconsul Sergius Paulus,
a man of intelligence, who had summoned Barnabas and Saul and wanted to hear the word of
God. **8** But Elymas the magician (for that is
what his name means) opposed them in an attempt to turn the proconsul away from the faith.
**9** *But Saul, also known as Paul, filled with the

m 12, 25; 15, 37.
n 5, 22-24.
o 6, 7.
p 11, 29-30.

*

12, 17: *To James:* this James is not the son of Zebedee mentioned in v 2, but is James, the "brother of the Lord" (Gal 1, 19), who in chs 15 and 21 is presented as leader of the Jerusalem Christian community. *He left and went to another place:* the conjecture that Peter left for Rome at this time has nothing to recommend it. His chief responsibility was still the leadership of the Jewish Christian community in Palestine (see Gal 2, 7). The concept of the great missionary effort of the church was yet to come (see 13, 1–3).

12, 20–23: Josephus gives a similar account of Herod's death that occurred in A.D. 44. Early Christian tradition considered the manner of it to be a divine punishment upon his evil life. See 2 Kgs 19, 35 for the figure of the angel of the Lord in such a context.

12, 25: *They returned to Jerusalem:* many manuscripts read "from Jerusalem," since 11, 30 implies that Paul and Barnabas are already in Jerusalem. This present verse could refer to a return visit or subsequent relief mission.

13, 1–3: The impulse for the first missionary effort in Asia Minor is ascribed to the prophets of the Antiochene community, under the inspiration of the holy Spirit. Just as the Jerusalem community had earlier been the center of missionary activity, so too Antioch becomes the center from which the missionaries Barnabas and Saul are sent out.

13, 4—14, 27: The key event in Luke's account of the first missionary journey is the experience of Paul and Barnabas at Pisidian Antioch (13, 14–52). The Christian kerygma proclaimed by Paul in the synagogue was favorably received. Some Jews and "God-fearers" (see the note on 8, 26–40) became interested and invited the missionaries to speak again on the following sabbath (13, 42). By that time, however, the appearance of a large number of Gentiles from the city had so disconcerted the Jews that they became hostile toward the apostles (13, 44–50). This hostility of theirs appears in all three accounts of Paul's missionary journeys in Acts, the Jews of Iconium (14, 1–2) and Beroea (17, 11) being notable exceptions.

13, 5: *John:* that is, John Mark (see 12, 12.25).

13, 6: *A magician named Bar-Jesus who was a Jewish false prophet:* that is, he posed as a prophet. Again Luke takes the opportunity to dissociate Christianity from the magical acts of the time (7–11); see also 8, 18–24.

13, 9: *Saul, also known as Paul:* there is no reason to believe that his name was changed from Saul to Paul upon his conversion. The use of a double name, one Semitic (Saul), the other Greco-Roman (Paul), is well attested (cf 1, 23, Joseph

holy Spirit, looked intently at him
10 and said,
"You son of the devil, you enemy of all that is
right, full of every sort of deceit and fraud. Will
you not stop twisting the straight paths of [the]
Lord?
11 Even now the hand of the Lord is
upon you. You will be blind, and unable to see
the sun for a time." Immediately a dark mist fell
upon him, and he went about seeking people to
lead him by the hand.
12 When the proconsul
saw what had happened, he came to believe, for
he was astonished by the teaching about the
Lord.

### Paul's Arrival at Antioch in Pisidia

13 [q]From Paphos, Paul and his companions set
sail and arrived at Perga in Pamphylia. But John
left them and returned to Jerusalem.
14 They
continued on from Perga and reached Antioch in
Pisidia. On the sabbath they entered [into] the
synagogue and took their seats.
15 After the
reading of the law and the prophets, the synagogue officials sent word to them, "My brothers, if one of you has a word of exhortation for
the people, please speak."

### Paul's Address in the Synagogue

16 *So Paul got up, motioned with his hand,
and said, "Fellow Israelites and you others who
are God-fearing, listen.
17 [r]The God of this
people Israel chose our ancestors and exalted
the people during their sojourn in the land of
Egypt. With uplifted arms he led them out of it
18 [s]*and for about forty years he put up with
them in the desert.
19 [t]When he had destroyed
seven nations in the land of Canaan, he gave
them their land as an inheritance
20 [u]*at the
end of about four hundred and fifty years. After
these things he provided judges up to Samuel
[the] prophet.
21 [v]Then they asked for a king.
God gave them Saul, son of Kish, a man from
the tribe of Benjamin, for forty years.
22 [w]Then he removed him and raised up David
as their king; of him he testified, 'I have found
David, son of Jesse, a man after my own heart;
he will carry out my every wish.'
23 [x]From this
man's descendants God, according to his promise, has brought to Israel a savior, Jesus.
24 [y]John heralded his coming by proclaiming a
baptism of repentance to all the people of Israel;
25 [z]and as John was completing his course, he
would say, 'What do you suppose that I am? I
am not he. Behold, one is coming after me; I am
not worthy to unfasten the sandals of his feet.'

26 "My brothers, children of the family of
Abraham, and those others among you who are
God-fearing, to us this word of salvation has
been sent.
27 The inhabitants of Jerusalem and
their leaders failed to recognize him, and by
condemning him they fulfilled the oracles of the
prophets that are read sabbath after sabbath.
28 [a]For even though they found no grounds for
a death sentence, they asked Pilate to have him
put to death,
29 [b]and when they had accom-
plished all that was written about him, they took
him down from the tree and placed him in a
tomb.
30 [c]But God raised him from the dead,
31 [d]*and for many days he appeared to those
who had come up with him from Galilee to
Jerusalem. These are [now] his witnesses before
the people.
32 We ourselves are proclaiming
this good news to you that what God promised
our ancestors
33 [e]he has brought to fulfillment
for us, [their] children, by raising up Jesus, as
it is written in the second psalm, 'You are my
son; this day I have begotten you.'
34 [f]And that
he raised him from the dead never to return to
corruption he declared in this way, 'I shall give
you the benefits assured to David.'
35 [g]That is
why he also says in another psalm, 'You will not
suffer your holy one to see corruption.'
36 [h]Now David, after he had served the will of
God in his lifetime, fell asleep, was gathered to
his ancestors, and did see corruption.
37 But
the one whom God raised up did not see corruption.
38 *You must know, my brothers, that

---

q 15, 38.
r Ex 6, 1.6; 12, 51.
s Ex 16, 1.35; Nm 14, 34.
t Dt 7, 1; Jos 14, 1-2.
u Jgs 2, 16; 1 Sm 3, 20.
v 1 Sm 8, 5.19; 9, 16; 10, 1.20-21.24; 11, 15.
w 1 Sm 13, 14; 16, 12-13; Ps 89, 20-21.
x Is 11, 1.
y Mt 3, 1-2; Mk 1, 4-5; Lk 3, 2-3.
z Mt 3, 11; Mk 1, 7; Lk 3, 16; Jn 1, 20.27.
a Mt 27, 20.22-23; Mk 15, 13-14; Lk 23, 4.14-15.21-23; Jn 19, 4-6.15.
b Mt 27, 59-60; Mk 15, 46; Lk 23, 53; Jn 19, 38.41-42.
c 2, 24.32; 3, 15; 4, 10; 17, 31.
d 1, 3.8; 10, 39.41; Mt 28, 8-10.16-20; Mk 16, 9.12-20; Lk 24, 13-53; Jn 20, 11-29; 21, 1-23.
e Ps 2, 7.
f Is 55, 3.
g Ps 16, 10.
h 2, 29; 1 Kgs 2, 10.

---

* Justus; 12, 12.25, John Mark).

13, 16–41: This is the first of several speeches of Paul to Jews proclaiming that the Christian church is the logical development of Pharisaic Judaism (see also 24, 10–21; 26, 2–23).

13, 16: *Who are God-fearing:* see the note on 8, 26–40.

13, 18: *Put up with:* some manuscripts read "sustained."

13, 20: *At the end of about four hundred and fifty years:* the manuscript tradition makes it uncertain whether the mention of four hundred and fifty years refers to the sojourn in Egypt before the Exodus, the wilderness period and the time of the conquest (see Ex 12, 40–41), as the translation here suggests, or to the time between the conquest and the time of Samuel, the period of the judges, if the text is read, "After these things, for about four hundred and fifty years, he provided judges."

13, 31: The theme of the Galilean witnesses is a major one in the Gospel of Luke and in Acts and is used to signify the continuity between the teachings of Jesus and the teachings of the church and to guarantee the fidelity of the church's teachings to the words of Jesus.

13, 38–39: *Justified:* the verb is the same as that used in Paul's letters to speak of the experience of justification and, as in Paul, is here connected with the term "to have faith" ("every believer"). But this seems the only passage about Paul in Acts where justification is mentioned. In Lucan fashion it is paralleled with "forgiveness of sins" (a theme at 2, 38; 3, 19; 5, 31; 10, 43) based on Jesus' resurrection (37) rather than his cross, and is put negatively (38). Therefore, some would translate, "in regard to everything from which you could not be acquitted . . . every believer is acquitted."

through him forgiveness of sins is being proclaimed to you, [and] in regard to everything
from which you could not be justified under the
law of Moses, **39** [i]in him every believer is justified. **40** Be careful, then, that what was said in
the prophets not come about:

**41** [j]'Look on, you scoffers,
be amazed and disappear.
For I am doing a work in your days,
a work that you will never believe even
if someone
tells you.' "

**42** As they were leaving, they invited them to
speak on these subjects the following sabbath.
**43** After the congregation had dispersed, many
Jews and worshipers who were converts to Judaism followed Paul and Barnabas, who spoke
to them and urged them to remain faithful to the
grace of God.

**Address to the Gentiles** **44** On the following sabbath almost the whole city gathered
to hear the word of the Lord. **45** When the Jews
saw the crowds, they were filled with jealousy
and with violent abuse contradicted what Paul
said. **46** [k]*Both Paul and Barnabas spoke out
boldly and said, "It was necessary that the word
of God be spoken to you first, but since you
reject it and condemn yourselves as unworthy of
eternal life, we now turn to the Gentiles.
**47** [l]For so theLord has commanded us, 'I have
made you a light to the Gentiles, that you may
be an instrument of salvation to the ends of the
earth.' "

**48** The Gentiles were delighted when they
heard this and glorified the word of the Lord.
All who were destined for eternal life came to
believe, **49** and the word of the Lord continued
to spread through the whole region. **50** The
Jews, however, incited the women of prominence who were worshipers and the leading men
of the city, stirred up a persecution against Paul
and Barnabas, and expelled them from their
territory. **51** [m]*So they shook the dust from
their feet in protest against them and went to
Iconium. **52** The disciples were filled with joy
and the holy Spirit.

## CHAPTER 14

**Paul and Barnabas at Iconium** **1** In Iconium they entered the Jewish synagogue together and spoke in such a way that a great number
of both Jews and Greeks came to believe, **2** although the disbelieving Jews stirred up and poisoned the minds of the Gentiles against the
brothers. **3** [n]So they stayed for a considerable
period, speaking out boldly for the Lord, who
confirmed the word about his grace by granting
signs and wonders to occur through their hands.
**4** The people of the city were divided: some
were with the Jews; others, with the apostles.
**5** [o]When there was an attempt by both the Gentiles and the Jews, together with their leaders,
to attack and stone them, **6** they realized it and
fled to the Lycaonian cities of Lystra and Derbe
and to the surrounding countryside, **7** where
they continued to proclaim the good news.

**Paul and Barnabas at Lystra** **8** *At Lystra there was a crippled man, lame from birth,
who had never walked. **9** He listened to Paul
speaking, who looked intently at him, saw that
he had the faith to be healed, **10** and called out
in a loud voice, "Stand up straight on your
feet." He jumped up and began to walk about.
**11** [p]When the crowds saw what Paul had done,
they cried out in Lycaonian, "The gods have
come down to us in human form." **12** *They
called Barnabas "Zeus" and Paul "Hermes,"
because he was the chief speaker. **13** And the
priest of Zeus, whose temple was at the entrance
to the city, brought oxen and garlands to the
gates, for he together with the people intended
to offer sacrifice.

**14** *The apostles Barnabas and Paul tore
their garments when they heard this and rushed
out into the crowd, shouting, **15** [q]*"Men, why
are you doing this? We are of the same nature
as you, human beings. We proclaim to you good
news that you should turn from these idols to the
living God, 'who made heaven and earth and
sea and all that is in them.' **16** [r]In past generations he allowed all Gentiles to go their own

i Rom 3, 20.
j Hb 1, 5.
k 3, 26; Rom 1, 16.
l Is 49, 6.
m Mt 10, 14; Mk 6, 11; Lk 9, 5; 10, 11.
n Mk 16, 17-20.
o 2 Tm 3, 11.
p 28, 6.
q 3, 12; 10, 26; Ex 20, 11; Ps 146, 6.
r 17, 30.

*

13, 46: The refusal to believe frustrates God's plan for his chosen people; however, no adverse judgment is made here concerning their ultimate destiny. Again, Luke, in the words of Paul, speaks of the priority of Israel in the plan for salvation (see 10, 36).

13, 51: See the note on Lk 9, 5.

14, 8–18: In an effort to convince his hearers that the divine power works through his word, Paul cures the cripple. However, the pagan tradition of the occasional appearance of gods among human beings leads the people astray in interpreting the miracle. The incident reveals the cultural difficulties with which the church had to cope. Note the similarity of the miracle worked here by Paul to the one performed by Peter in 3, 2–10.

14, 12: *Zeus . . . Hermes:* in Greek religion, Zeus was the chief of the Olympian gods, the "father of gods and men"; Hermes was a son of Zeus and was usually identified as the herald and messenger of the gods.

14, 14: *Tore their garments:* a gesture of protest.

14, 15–17: This is the first speech of Paul to Gentiles recorded by Luke in Acts (cf 17, 22–31). Rather than showing how Christianity is the logical outgrowth of Judaism, as he does in speeches before Jews, Luke says that God excuses past Gentile ignorance and then presents a natural theology arguing for the recognition of God's existence and presence through his activity in natural phenomena.

ways; 17 [s]yet, in bestowing his goodness, he
did not leave himself without witness, for he
gave you rains from heaven and fruitful seasons, and filled you with nourishment and gladness for your hearts." 18 Even with these
words, they scarcely restrained the crowds from
offering sacrifice to them.

19 [t]However, some Jews from Antioch and
Iconium arrived and won over the crowds. They
stoned Paul and dragged him out of the city,
supposing that he was dead. 20 But when the
disciples gathered around him, he got up and
entered the city. On the following day he left
with Barnabas for Derbe.

**End of the First Mission** 21 After they
had proclaimed the good news to that city and
made a considerable number of disciples, they
returned to Lystra and to Iconium and to Antioch. 22 [u]They strengthened the spirits of the
disciples and exhorted them to persevere in the
faith, saying, "It is necessary for us to undergo
many hardships to enter the kingdom of God."
23 *They appointed presbyters for them in each
church and, with prayer and fasting, commended them to the Lord in whom they had put their
faith. 24 Then they traveled through Pisidia and
reached Pamphylia. 25 After proclaiming the
word at Perga they went down to Attalia.
26 [v]From there they sailed to Antioch, where
they had been commended to the grace of God
for the work they had now accomplished.
27 And when they arrived, they called the
church together and reported what God had
done with them and how he had opened the door
of faith to the Gentiles. 28 Then they spent no
little time with the disciples.

## CHAPTER 15

**Council of Jerusalem** 1 [w x]*Some who
had come down from Judea were instructing the
brothers, "Unless you are circumcised according to the Mosaic practice, you cannot be
saved." 2 Because there arose no little dissension and debate by Paul and Barnabas with
them, it was decided that Paul, Barnabas, and
some of the others should go up to Jerusalem to
the apostles and presbyters about this question.
3 They were sent on their journey by the
church, and passed through Phoenicia and Samaria telling of the conversion of the Gentiles,
and brought great joy to all the brothers.
4 When they arrived in Jerusalem, they were
welcomed by the church, as well as by the apostles and the presbyters, and they reported what
God had done with them. 5 But some from the
party of the Pharisees who had become believers stood up and said, "It is necessary to circumcise them and direct them to observe the
Mosaic law."

6 *The apostles and the presbyters met together to see about this matter. 7 [y]*After much
debate had taken place, Peter got up and said to
them, "My brothers, you are well aware that
from early days God made his choice among
you that through my mouth the Gentiles would
hear the word of the gospel and believe. 8 [z]And
God, who knows the heart, bore witness by
granting them the holy Spirit just as he did us.
9 [a]He made no distinction between us and
them, for by faith he purified their hearts.
10 [b]Why, then, are you now putting God to the
test by placing on the shoulders of the disciples
a yoke that neither our ancestors nor we have
been able to bear? 11 [c]*On the contrary, we
believe that we are saved through the grace of
the Lord Jesus, in the same way as they."
12 The whole assembly fell silent, and they
listened while Paul and Barnabas described the
signs and wonders God had worked among the
Gentiles through them.

**James on Dietary Law** 13 *After they had
fallen silent, James responded, "My brothers,

---

s Wis 13, 1.
t 2 Cor 11, 25; 2 Tm 3, 11.
u 1 Thes 3, 3.
v 13, 1-3.
w Gal 2, 1-9.
x Lv 12, 3; Gal 5, 2.
y 10, 27-43.
z 10, 44-48.
a 10, 34-35.
b Mt 23, 4; Gal 5, 1.
c Gal 2, 16; 3, 11; Eph 2, 5-8.

---

*

14, 23: *They appointed presbyters:* the communities are given their own religious leaders by the traveling missionaries. The structure in these churches is patterned on the model of the Jerusalem community (11, 30; 15, 2.5.22; 21, 18).

15, 1–35: The Jerusalem "Council" marks the official rejection of the rigid view that Gentile converts were obliged to observe the Mosaic law completely. From here to the end of Acts, Paul and the Gentile mission become the focus of Luke's writing.

15, 1–5: When some of the converted Pharisees of Jerusalem discover the results of the first missionary journey of Paul, they urge that the Gentiles be taught to follow the Mosaic law. Recognizing the authority of the Jerusalem church, Paul and Barnabas go there to settle the question of whether Gentiles can embrace a form of Christianity that does not include this obligation.

15, 6–12: The gathering is possibly the same as that recalled by Paul in Gal 2, 1–10. Note that in v 2 it is only the apostles and presbyters, a small group, with whom Paul and Barnabas are to meet. Here Luke gives the meeting a public character because he wishes to emphasize its doctrinal significance (see 22).

15, 7–11: Paul's refusal to impose the Mosaic law on the Gentile Christians is supported by Peter on the ground that within his own experience God bestowed the holy Spirit upon Cornelius and his household without preconditions concerning the adoption of the Mosaic law (see 10, 44–47).

15, 11: In support of Paul, Peter formulates the fundamental meaning of the gospel: that all are invited to be saved through faith in the power of Christ.

15, 13–35: Some scholars think that this apostolic decree suggested by James, the immediate leader of the Jerusalem community, derives from another historical occasion than the meeting in question. This seems to be the case if the meeting is the same as the one related in Gal 2, 1–10. According to that account, nothing was imposed upon Gentile Christians in re-

listen to me. **14** *Symeon has described how
God first concerned himself with acquiring from
among the Gentiles a people for his name.
**15** The words of the prophets agree with this,
as is written:

**16** [d]'After this I shall return
and rebuild the fallen hut of David;
from its ruins I shall rebuild it
and raise it up again,
**17** so that the rest of humanity may seek out
the Lord,
even all the Gentiles on whom my name
is invoked.
Thus says the Lord who accomplishes these
things,
**18** known from of old.'

**19** [e]It is my judgment, therefore, that we ought
to stop troubling the Gentiles who turn to God,
**20** [f]but tell them by letter to avoid pollution
from idols, unlawful marriage, the meat of
strangled animals, and blood. **21** For Moses,
for generations now, has had those who proclaim him in every town, as he has been read in
the synagogues every sabbath."

**Letter of the Apostles** **22** Then the apostles and presbyters, in agreement with the whole
church, decided to choose representatives and to
send them to Antioch with Paul and Barnabas.
The ones chosen were Judas, who was called
Barsabbas, and Silas, leaders among the brothers. **23** This is the letter delivered by them:
"The apostles and the presbyters, your brothers, to the brothers in Antioch, Syria, and Cilicia of Gentile origin: greetings. **24** Since we
have heard that some of our number [who went
out] without any mandate from us have upset
you with their teachings and disturbed your
peace of mind, **25** we have with one accord
decided to choose representatives and to send
them to you along with our beloved Barnabas
and Paul, **26** who have dedicated their lives to
the name of our Lord Jesus Christ. **27** So we are
sending Judas and Silas who will also convey
this same message by word of mouth: **28** [g]'It is
the decision of the holy Spirit and of us not to
place on you any burden beyond these necessities, **29** [h]namely, to abstain from meat sacrificed to idols, from blood, from meats of strangled animals, and from unlawful marriage. If
you keep free of these, you will be doing what
is right. Farewell.' "

**Delegates at Antioch** **30** And so they
were sent on their journey. Upon their arrival in
Antioch they called the assembly together and
delivered the letter. **31** When the people read it,
they were delighted with the exhortation.
**32** Judas and Silas, who were themselves
prophets, exhorted and strengthened the brothers with many words. **33** After they had spent
some time there, they were sent off with greetings of peace from the brothers to those who had
commissioned them. **[34*]** **35** But Paul and
Barnabas remained in Antioch, teaching and
proclaiming with many others the word of the
Lord.

## *V: THE MISSION OF PAUL TO THE ENDS OF THE EARTH*

**Paul and Barnabas Separate** **36** *After
some time, Paul said to Barnabas, "Come, let
us make a return visit to see how the brothers are
getting on in all the cities where we proclaimed
the word of the Lord." **37** Barnabas wanted to
take with them also John, who was called Mark,
**38** [i]but Paul insisted that they should not take
with them someone who had deserted them at
Pamphylia and who had not continued with
them in their work. **39** So sharp was their disagreement that they separated. Barnabas took
Mark and sailed to Cyprus. **40** But Paul chose
Silas and departed after being commended by
the brothers to the grace of the Lord. **41** He
traveled through Syria and Cilicia bringing
strength to the churches.

d Am 9, 11-12.
e 15, 28-29; 21, 25.
f Gn 9, 4; Lv 3, 17; 17, 10-14.
g 15, 19-20.
h Gn 9, 4; Lv 3, 17; 17, 10-14.
i 13, 13.

*

spect to Mosaic law; whereas the decree instructs Gentile Christians of mixed communities to abstain from meats sacrificed to idols and from blood-meats, and to avoid marriage within forbidden degrees of consanguinity and affinity (Lv 18), all of which practices were especially abhorrent to Jews. Luke seems to have telescoped two originally independent incidents here: the first a Jerusalem "Council" that dealt with the question of circumcision, and the second a Jerusalem decree dealing mainly with Gentile observance of dietary laws (see 21, 25 where Paul seems to be learning of the decree for the first time).

15, 14: *Symeon:* elsewhere in Acts he is called either Peter or Simon. The presence of the name Symeon here suggests that, in the source Luke is using for this part of the Jerusalem "Council" incident, the name may have originally referred to someone other than Peter (see 13, 1 where the Antiochene Symeon Niger is mentioned). As the text now stands, however, it is undoubtedly a reference to Simon Peter (7).

15, 34: Some manuscripts add, in various wordings, "But Silas decided to remain there."

15, 36—18, 22: This continuous narrative recounts Paul's second missionary journey. On the internal evidence of the Lucan account, it lasted about three years. Paul first visited the communities he had established on his first journey (16, 1–5), then pushed on into Macedonia, where he established communities at Philippi, Thessalonica, and Beroea (16, 7—17, 5). To escape the hostility of the Jews of Thessalonica, he left for Greece and while resident in Athens attempted, without success, to establish an effective Christian community there. From Athens he proceeded to Corinth and, after a stay of a year and a half, returned to Antioch by way of Ephesus and Jerusalem (17, 16—18, 22). Luke does not concern himself with the structure or statistics of the communities but aims to show the general progress of the gospel in the Gentile world as well as its continued failure to take root in the Jewish community.

## CHAPTER 16

**Paul in Lycaonia: Timothy** **1** [j]He reached [also] Derbe and Lystra where there was a disciple named Timothy, the son of a Jewish woman who was a believer, but his father was a Greek. **2** [k]The brothers in Lystra and Iconium spoke highly of him, **3** *and Paul wanted him to come along with him. On account of the Jews of that region, Paul had him circumcised, for they all knew that his father was a Greek. **4** As they traveled from city to city, they handed on to the people for observance the decisions reached by the apostles and presbyters in Jerusalem. **5** Day after day the churches grew stronger in faith and increased in number.

**Through Asia Minor** **6** They traveled through the Phrygian and Galatian territory because they had been prevented by the holy Spirit from preaching the message in the province of Asia. **7** *When they came to Mysia, they tried to go on into Bithynia, but the Spirit of Jesus did not allow them, **8** so they crossed through Mysia and came down to Troas. **9** During [the] night Paul had a vision. A Macedonian stood before him and implored him with these words, "Come over to Macedonia and help us." **10** *When he had seen the vision, we sought passage to Macedonia at once, concluding that God had called us to proclaim the good news to them.

**Into Europe** **11** *We set sail from Troas, making a straight run for Samothrace, and on the next day to Neapolis, **12** and from there to Philippi, a leading city in that district of Macedonia and a Roman colony. We spent some time in that city. **13** On the sabbath we went outside the city gate along the river where we thought there would be a place of prayer. We sat and spoke with the women who had gathered there. **14** *One of them, a woman named Lydia, a dealer in purple cloth, from the city of Thyatira, a worshiper of God, listened, and the Lord opened her heart to pay attention to what Paul was saying. **15** After she and her household had been baptized, she offered us an invitation, "If you consider me a believer in the Lord, come and stay at my home," and she prevailed on us.

**Imprisonment at Philippi** **16** *As we were going to the place of prayer, we met a slave girl with an oracular spirit, who used to bring a large profit to her owners through her fortune-telling. **17** She began to follow Paul and us, shouting, "These people are slaves of the Most High God, who proclaim to you a way of salvation." **18** She did this for many days. Paul became annoyed, turned, and said to the spirit, "I command you in the name of Jesus Christ to come out of her." Then it came out at that moment.

**19** When her owners saw that their hope of profit was gone, they seized Paul and Silas and dragged them to the public square before the local authorities. **20** *They brought them before the magistrates and said, "These people are Jews and are disturbing our city **21** and are advocating customs that are not lawful for us Romans to adopt or practice." **22** [l]The crowd joined in the attack on them, and the magistrates had them stripped and ordered them to be beaten with rods. **23** After inflicting many blows on them, they threw them into prison and instructed the jailer to guard them securely. **24** When he received these instructions, he put them in the innermost cell and secured their feet to a stake.

**Deliverance from Prison** **25** About midnight, while Paul and Silas were praying and singing hymns to God as the prisoners listened, **26** there was suddenly such a severe earthquake that the foundations of the jail shook; all the doors flew open, and the chains of all were pulled loose. **27** When the jailer woke up and saw the prison doors wide open, he drew [his] sword and was about to kill himself, thinking that the prisoners had escaped. **28** But Paul shouted out in a loud voice, "Do no harm to yourself; we are all here." **29** He asked for a

---

j 1 Tm 1, 2; 2 Tm 1, 5.
k Phil 2, 20.
l 2 Cor 11, 25; Phil 1, 30; 1 Thes 2, 2.

---

*

16, 3: *Paul had him circumcised:* he did this in order that Timothy might be able to associate with the Jews and so perform a ministry among them. Paul did not object to the Jewish Christians' adherence to the law. But he insisted that the law could not be imposed on the Gentiles. Paul himself lived in accordance with the law, or as exempt from the law, according to particular circumstances (see 1 Cor 9, 19–23).

16, 7: *The Spirit of Jesus:* this is an unusual formulation in Luke's writings. The parallelism with v 6 indicates its meaning, the holy Spirit.

16, 10–17: This is the first of the so-called "we-sections" in Acts, where Luke writes as one of Paul's companions. The other passages are 20, 5–15; 21, 1–18; 27, 1—28, 16. Scholars debate whether Luke may not have used the first person plural simply as a literary device to lend color to the narrative. The realism of the narrative, however, lends weight to the argument that the "we" includes Luke or another companion of Paul whose data Luke used as a source.

16, 11–40: The church at Philippi became a flourishing community to which Paul addressed one of his letters (see Introduction to the Letter to the Philippians).

16, 14: *A worshiper of God:* a "God-fearer." See the note on 8, 26–40.

16, 16: *With an oracular spirit:* literally, "with a Python spirit." The Python was the serpent or dragon that guarded the Delphic oracle. It later came to designate a "spirit that pronounced oracles" and also a ventriloquist who, it was thought, had such a spirit in the belly.

16, 20: *Magistrates:* in Greek, *strategoi,* the popular designation of the *duoviri,* the highest officials of the Roman colony of Philippi.

light and rushed in and, trembling with fear, he
fell down before Paul and Silas. **30** Then he
brought them out and said, "Sirs, what must I
do to be saved?" **31** And they said, "Believe
in the Lord Jesus and you and your household
will be saved." **32** So they spoke the word of
the Lord to him and to everyone in his house.
**33** He took them in at that hour of the night and
bathed their wounds; then he and all his family
were baptized at once. **34** He brought them up
into his house and provided a meal and with his
household rejoiced at having come to faith in
God.

**35** *But when it was day, the magistrates
sent the lictors with the order, "Release those
men." **36** The jailer reported the[se] words to
Paul, "The magistrates have sent orders that
you be released. Now, then, come out and go
in peace." **37** [m]*But Paul said to them, "They
have beaten us publicly, even though we are
Roman citizens and have not been tried, and
have thrown us into prison. And now, are they
going to release us secretly? By no means. Let
them come themselves and lead us out."
**38** [n]The lictors reported these words to the
magistrates, and they became alarmed when
they heard that they were Roman citizens.
**39** So they came and placated them, and led
them out and asked that they leave the city.
**40** When they had come out of the prison, they
went to Lydia's house where they saw and encouraged the brothers, and then they left.

## CHAPTER 17

**Paul in Thessalonica** **1** [o]When they took
the road through Amphipolis and Apollonia,
they reached Thessalonica, where there was a
synagogue of the Jews. **2** Following his usual
custom, Paul joined them, and for three sabbaths he entered into discussions with them
from the scriptures, **3** [p]expounding and demon-
strating that the Messiah had to suffer and rise
from the dead, and that "This is the Messiah,
Jesus, whom I proclaim to you." **4** Some of
them were convinced and joined Paul and Silas;
so, too, a great number of Greeks who were
worshipers, and not a few of the prominent
women. **5** [q]But the Jews became jealous and
recruited some worthless men loitering in the
public square, formed a mob, and set the city in
turmoil. They marched on the house of Jason,
intending to bring them before the people's assembly. **6** *When they could not find them,
they dragged Jason and some of the brothers
before the city magistrates, shouting, "These
people who have been creating a disturbance all
over the world have now come here, **7** [r]*and
Jason has welcomed them. They all act in opposition to the decrees of Caesar and claim instead
that there is another king, Jesus." **8** They
stirred up the crowd and the city magistrates
who, upon hearing these charges, **9** took a surety payment from Jason and the others before
releasing them.

**Paul in Beroea** **10** The brothers immediately sent Paul and Silas to Beroea during the
night. Upon arrival they went to the synagogue
of the Jews. **11** [s]These Jews were more fair-
minded than those in Thessalonica, for they
received the word with all willingness and examined the scriptures daily to determine whether these things were so. **12** Many of them became believers, as did not a few of the
influential Greek women and men. **13** But
when the Jews of Thessalonica learned that the
word of God had now been proclaimed by Paul
in Beroea also, they came there too to cause a
commotion and stir up the crowds. **14** [t]So the
brothers at once sent Paul on his way to the
seacoast, while Silas and Timothy remained behind. **15** After Paul's escorts had taken him to
Athens, they came away with instructions for
Silas and Timothy to join him as soon as possible.

**Paul in Athens** **16** *While Paul was waiting for them in Athens, he grew exasperated at
the sight of the city full of idols. **17** So he
debated in the synagogue with the Jews and with
the worshipers, and daily in the public square
with whoever happened to be there. **18** *Even

m 22, 25.
n 22, 29.
o 1 Thes 2, 1-2.
p 3, 18; Lk 24, 25-26.46.
q Rom 16, 21.
r Lk 23, 2; Jn 19, 12-15.
s Jn 5, 39.
t 1 Thes 3, 1-2.

*

16, 35: *The lictors:* the equivalent of police officers, among whose duties were the apprehension and punishment of criminals.

16, 37: Paul's Roman citizenship granted him special privileges in regard to criminal process. Roman law forbade under severe penalty the beating of Roman citizens (see also 22, 25).

17, 6–7: The accusations against Paul and his companions echo the charges brought against Jesus in Lk 23, 2.

17, 7: *There is another king, Jesus:* a distortion into a political sense of the apostolic proclamation of Jesus and the kingdom of God (see 8, 12).

17, 16–21: Paul's presence in Athens sets the stage for the great discourse before a Gentile audience in vv 22–31. Although Athens was a politically insignificant city at this period, it still lived on the glories of its past and represented the center of Greek culture. The setting describes the conflict between Christian preaching and Hellenistic philosophy.

17, 18: *Epicurean and Stoic philosophers:* for the followers of Epicurus (342–271 B.C.), the goal of life was happiness attained through sober reasoning and the searching out of motives for all choice and avoidance. The Stoics were followers of Zeno, a younger contemporary of Alexander the Great. Zeno and his followers believed in a type of pantheism that held that the spark of divinity was present in all reality and that, in order to be free, each person must live "according to nature." *This scavenger:* literally, "seed-picker," as of a bird that picks up grain. The word is later used of scrap collectors and of people who take other people's ideas and propagate them

some of the Epicurean and Stoic philosophers
engaged him in discussion. Some asked, "What
is this scavenger trying to say?" Others said,
"He sounds like a promoter of foreign deities,"
because he was preaching about 'Jesus' and
'Resurrection.' **19** [u]*They took him and led
him to the Areopagus and said, "May we learn
what this new teaching is that you speak of?
**20** For you bring some strange notions to our
ears; we should like to know what these things
mean." **21** Now all the Athenians as well as the
foreigners residing there used their time for
nothing else but telling or hearing something
new.

### Paul's Speech at the Areopagus

**22** *Then Paul stood up at the Areopagus and
said:
"You Athenians, I see that in every respect
you are very religious. **23** *For as I walked
around looking carefully at your shrines, I even
discovered an altar inscribed, 'To an Unknown
God.' What therefore you unknowingly worship, I proclaim to you. **24** [v]The God who
made the world and all that is in it, the Lord of
heaven and earth, does not dwell in sanctuaries
made by human hands, **25** nor is he served by
human hands because he needs anything. Rather
it is he who gives to everyone life and breath and
everything. **26** *He made from one the whole
human race to dwell on the entire surface of the
earth, and he fixed the ordered seasons and the
boundaries of their regions, **27** [w]so that people
might seek God, even perhaps grope for him
and find him, though indeed he is not far from
any one of us. **28** *For 'In him we live and
move and have our being,' as even some of your
poets have said, 'For we too are his offspring.'
**29** [x]Since therefore we are the offspring of
God, we ought not to think that the divinity is
like an image fashioned from gold, silver, or
stone by human art and imagination. **30** God
has overlooked the times of ignorance, but now
he demands that all people everywhere repent
**31** [y]because he has established a day on which
he will 'judge the world with justice' through a
man he has appointed, and he has provided
confirmation for all by raising him from the
dead."
**32** When they heard about resurrection of the
dead, some began to scoff, but others said, "We
should like to hear you on this some other
time." **33** And so Paul left them. **34** But some
did join him, and became believers. Among
them were Dionysius, a member of the Court of
the Areopagus, a woman named Damaris, and
others with them.

## CHAPTER 18

### Paul in Corinth

**1** After this he left Athens
and went to Corinth. **2** [z]*There he met a Jew
named Aquila, a native of Pontus, who had
recently come from Italy with his wife Priscilla
because Claudius had ordered all the Jews to
leave Rome. He went to visit them **3** and, because he practiced the same trade, stayed with
them and worked, for they were tentmakers by
trade. **4** Every sabbath, he entered into discussions in the synagogue, attempting to convince
both Jews and Greeks.
**5** When Silas and Timothy came down from
Macedonia, Paul began to occupy himself totally with preaching the word, testifying to the

u 1 Cor 1, 22.
v 7, 48-50; Gn 1, 1; 1 Kgs 8, 27; Is 42, 5.
w Jer 23, 23; Wis 13, 6; Rom 1, 19.
x 19, 26; Is 40, 18-20; 44, 10-17; Rom 1, 22-23.
y 10, 42.
z Rom 16, 3.

* as if they were their own. *Promoter of foreign deities:* according to Xenophon, Socrates was accused of promoting new deities. The accusation against Paul echoes the charge against Socrates. *'Jesus' and 'Resurrection':* the Athenians are presented as misunderstanding Paul from the outset; they think he is preaching about Jesus and a goddess named *Anastasis*, i.e., Resurrection.

17, 19: *To the Areopagus:* the "Areopagus" refers either to the Hill of Ares west of the Acropolis or to the Council of Athens, which at one time met on the hill but which at this time assembled in the Royal Colonnade (*Stoa Basileios*).

17, 22–31: In Paul's appearance at the Areopagus he preaches his climactic speech to Gentiles in the cultural center of the ancient world. The speech is more theological than christological. Paul's discourse appeals to the Greek world's belief in divinity as responsible for the origin and existence of the universe. It contests the common belief in a multiplicity of gods supposedly exerting their powers through their images. It acknowledges that the attempt to find God is a constant human endeavor. It declares, further, that God is the judge of the human race, that the time of the judgment has been determined, and that it will be executed through a man whom God raised from the dead. The speech reflects sympathy with pagan religiosity, handles the subject of idol worship gently, and appeals for a new examination of divinity, not from the standpoint of creation but from the standpoint of judgment.

17, 23: *'To an Unknown God':* ancient authors such as Pausanias, Philostratus, and Tertullian speak of Athenian altars with no specific dedication as altars of "unknown gods" or "nameless altars."

17, 26: *From one:* many manuscripts read "from one blood." *Fixed . . . seasons:* or "fixed limits to the epochs."

17, 28: *'In him we live and move and have our being':* some scholars understand this saying to be based on an earlier saying of Epimenides of Knossos (6th century B.C.). *'For we too are his offspring':* here Paul is quoting Aratus of Soli, a third-century B.C. poet from Cilicia.

18, 2: *Aquila . . . Priscilla:* both may already have been Christians at the time of their arrival in Corinth (see 26). According to 1 Cor 16, 19, their home became a meeting place for Christians. *Claudius:* the Emperor Claudius expelled the Jews from Rome ca. A.D. 40. The Roman historian Suetonius gives as reason for the expulsion disturbances among the Jews "at the instigation of Chrestos," probably meaning disputes about the messiahship of Jesus.

Jews that the Messiah was Jesus. **6** [a]*When
they opposed him and reviled him, he shook out
his garments and said to them, "Your blood be
on your heads! I am clear of responsibility.
From now on I will go to the Gentiles." **7** [b]*So
he left there and went to a house belonging to
a man named Titus Justus, a worshiper of God;
his house was next to a synagogue.
**8** [c]*Crispus, the synagogue official, came to
believe in the Lord along with his entire household, and many of the Corinthians who heard
believed and were baptized. **9** [d]One night in a
vision the Lord said to Paul, "Do not be afraid.
Go on speaking, and do not be silent, **10** for I
am with you. No one will attack and harm you,
for I have many people in this city." **11** He
settled there for a year and a half and taught the
word of God among them.

### Accusations before Gallio

**12** *But
when Gallio was proconsul of Achaia, the Jews
rose up together against Paul and brought him
to the tribunal, **13** *saying, "This man is induc-
ing people to worship God contrary to the law."
**14** When Paul was about to reply, Gallio spoke
to the Jews, "If it were a matter of some crime
or malicious fraud, I should with reason hear the
complaint of you Jews; **15** but since it is a question of arguments over doctrine and titles and
your own law, see to it yourselves. I do not wish
to be a judge of such matters." **16** And he
drove them away from the tribunal. **17** They all
seized Sosthenes, the synagogue official, and
beat him in full view of the tribunal. But none
of this was of concern to Gallio.

### Return to Syrian Antioch

**18** [e]*Paul re-
mained for quite some time, and after saying
farewell to the brothers he sailed for Syria, together with Priscilla and Aquila. At Cenchreae
he had his hair cut because he had taken a vow.
**19** When they reached Ephesus, he left them
there, while he entered the synagogue and held
discussions with the Jews. **20** Although they
asked him to stay for a longer time, he did not
consent, **21** but as he said farewell he promised, "I shall come back to you again, God
willing." Then he set sail from Ephesus.
**22** *Upon landing at Caesarea, he went up and
greeted the church and then went down to Antioch. **23** *After staying there some time, he left
and traveled in orderly sequence through the
Galatian country and Phrygia, bringing strength
to all the disciples.

### Apollos

**24** [f]*A Jew named Apollos, a native of Alexandria, an eloquent speaker, arrived
in Ephesus. He was an authority on the scriptures. **25** He had been instructed in the Way of
the Lord and, with ardent spirit, spoke and
taught accurately about Jesus, although he knew
only the baptism of John. **26** *He began to
speak boldly in the synagogue; but when Priscilla and Aquila heard him, they took him aside
and explained to him the Way [of God] more
accurately. **27** And when he wanted to cross to
Achaia, the brothers encouraged him and wrote
to the disciples there to welcome him. After his
arrival he gave great assistance to those who had
come to believe through grace. **28** He vigorously refuted the Jews in public, establishing from
the scriptures that the Messiah is Jesus.

## CHAPTER 19

### Paul in Ephesus

**1** *While Apollos was in
Corinth, Paul traveled through the interior of the
country and came [down] to Ephesus where he
found some disciples. **2** He said to them, "Did
you receive the holy Spirit when you became
believers?" They answered him, "We have
never even heard that there is a holy Spirit."
**3** He said, "How were you baptized?" They
replied, "With the baptism of John." **4** [g]Paul
then said, "John baptized with a baptism of
repentance, telling the people to believe in the
one who was to come after him, that is, in

---

a 13, 51; Mt 10, 14; 27, 24-25; Mk 6, 11; Lk 9, 5; 10, 10-11.
b 13, 46-47; 28, 28.
c 1 Cor 1, 14.
d Jer 1, 8.
e 21, 24; Nm 6, 18.
f 1 Cor 1, 12.
g 1, 5; 11, 16; 13, 24-25; Mt 3, 11; Mk 1, 8; Lk 3, 16.

---

*

18, 6: *Shook out his garments:* a gesture indicating Paul's repudiation of his mission to the Jews there; cf 28, 17–31.

18, 7: *A worshiper of God:* see the note on 8, 26–40.

18, 8: *Crispus:* in 1 Cor 1, 14, Paul mentions that Crispus was one of the few he himself baptized at Corinth.

18, 12: *When Gallio was proconsul of Achaia:* Gallio's proconsulship in Achaia is dated to A.D. 51–52 from an inscription discovered at Delphi. This has become an important date in establishing a chronology of the life and missionary work of Paul.

18, 13: *Contrary to the law:* Gallio (15) understands this to be a problem of Jewish, not Roman, law.

18, 18: *He had his hair cut because he had taken a vow:* a reference to a Nazirite vow (see Nm 6, 1–21, especially, 6, 18) taken by Paul (see also 21, 23–27).

18, 22: *He went up and greeted the church:* "going up" suggests a visit to the church in Jerusalem.

18, 23—21, 16: Luke's account of Paul's third missionary journey devotes itself mainly to his work at Ephesus (19, 1—20, 1). There is a certain restiveness on Paul's part and a growing conviction that the Spirit bids him return to Jerusalem and prepare to go to Rome (19, 21).

18, 24–25: Apollos appears as a preacher who knows the teaching of Jesus in the context of John's baptism of repentance. Aquila and Priscilla instruct him more fully. He is referred to in 1 Cor 1, 12; 3, 5–6.22.

18, 26: *The Way [of God]:* for the Way, see the note on 9, 2. Other manuscripts here read "the Way of the Lord," "the word of the Lord," or simply "the Way."

19, 1–6: Upon his arrival in Ephesus, Paul discovers other people at the same religious stage as Apollos, though they seem to have considered themselves followers of Christ, not of the Baptist. On the relation between baptism and the reception of the Spirit, see the note on 8, 16.

Jesus." **5** When they heard this, they were baptized in the name of the Lord Jesus. **6** [h]And
when Paul laid [his] hands on them, the holy
Spirit came upon them, and they spoke in
tongues and prophesied. **7** Altogether there
were about twelve men.

**8** He entered the synagogue, and for three
months debated boldly with persuasive arguments about the kingdom of God. **9** But when
some in their obstinacy and disbelief disparaged
the Way before the assembly, he withdrew and
took his disciples with him and began to hold
daily discussions in the lecture hall of Tyrannus.
**10** This continued for two years with the result
that all the inhabitants of the province of Asia
heard the word of the Lord, Jews and Greeks
alike. **11** So extraordinary were the mighty
deeds God accomplished at the hands of Paul
**12** [i]that when face cloths or aprons that touched
his skin were applied to the sick, their diseases
left them and the evil spirits came out of them.

**The Jewish Exorcists** **13** Then some itinerant Jewish exorcists tried to invoke the name
of the Lord Jesus over those with evil spirits,
saying, "I adjure you by the Jesus whom Paul
preaches." **14** When the seven sons of Sceva,
a Jewish high priest, tried to do this, **15** the evil
spirit said to them in reply, "Jesus I recognize,
Paul I know, but who are you?" **16** The person
with the evil spirit then sprang at them and
subdued them all. He so overpowered them that
they fled naked and wounded from that house.
**17** When this became known to all the Jews and
Greeks who lived in Ephesus, fear fell upon
them all, and the name of the Lord Jesus was
held in great esteem. **18** Many of those who had
become believers came forward and openly acknowledged their former practices. **19** Moreover, a large number of those who had practiced
magic collected their books and burned them in
public. They calculated their value and found it
to be fifty thousand silver pieces. **20** Thus did
the word of the Lord continue to spread with
influence and power.

**Paul's Plans** **21** [j]When this was conclud-
ed, Paul made up his mind to travel through
Macedonia and Achaia, and then to go on to
Jerusalem, saying, "After I have been there, I
must visit Rome also." **22** Then he sent to
Macedonia two of his assistants, Timothy and
Erastus, while he himself stayed for a while in
the province of Asia.

**The Riot of the Silversmiths** **23** About
that time a serious disturbance broke out concerning the Way. **24** *There was a silversmith
named Demetrius who made miniature silver
shrines of Artemis and provided no little work
for the craftsmen. **25** He called a meeting of
these and other workers in related crafts and
said, "Men, you know well that our prosperity
derives from this work. **26** [k]As you can now
see and hear, not only in Ephesus but throughout most of the province of Asia this Paul has
persuaded and misled a great number of people
by saying that gods made by hands are not gods
at all. **27** The danger grows, not only that our
business will be discredited, but also that the
temple of the great goddess Artemis will be of
no account, and that she whom the whole province of Asia and all the world worship will be
stripped of her magnificence."

**28** When they heard this, they were filled
with fury and began to shout, "Great is Artemis
of the Ephesians!" **29** [l]The city was filled with
confusion, and the people rushed with one accord into the theater, seizing Gaius and Aristarchus, the Macedonians, Paul's traveling companions. **30** Paul wanted to go before the
crowd, but the disciples would not let him,
**31** *and even some of the Asiarchs who were
friends of his sent word to him advising him not
to venture into the theater. **32** Meanwhile,
some were shouting one thing, others something
else; the assembly was in chaos, and most of the
people had no idea why they had come together.
**33** Some of the crowd prompted Alexander, as
the Jews pushed him forward, and Alexander
signaled with his hand that he wished to explain
something to the gathering. **34** But when they
recognized that he was a Jew, they all shouted
in unison, for about two hours, "Great is Artemis of the Ephesians!" **35** *Finally the town
clerk restrained the crowd and said, "You
Ephesians, what person is there who does not
know that the city of the Ephesians is the guardian of the temple of the great Artemis and of her
image that fell from the sky? **36** Since these
things are undeniable, you must calm yourselves and not do anything rash. **37** The men
you brought here are not temple robbers, nor

h 8, 15-17; 10, 44.46. 22-32.
i 5, 15-16; Lk 8, 44-47. k 17, 29.
j 23, 11; Rom 1, 13; 15, l Col 4, 10.

*

19, 24: *Miniature silver shrines of Artemis:* the temple of Artemis at Ephesus was one of the seven wonders of the ancient world. Artemis, originally the Olympian virgin hunter, moon goddess, and goddess of wild nature, was worshiped at Ephesus as an Asian mother goddess and goddess of fertility. She was one of the most widely worshiped female deities in the Hellenistic world (see 18, 27).

19, 31: *Asiarchs:* the precise status and role of the Asiarchs is disputed. They appear to have been people of wealth and influence who promoted the Roman imperial cult and who may also have been political representatives in a league of cities in the Roman province of Asia.

19, 35: *Guardian of the temple:* this title was accorded by Rome to cities that provided a temple for the imperial cult. Inscriptional evidence indicates that Ephesus was acknowledged as the temple keeper of Artemis and of the imperial cult. *That fell from the sky:* many scholars think that this refers to a meteorite that was worshiped as an image of the goddess.

have they insulted our goddess. 38 If Demetrius and his fellow craftsmen have a complaint
against anyone, courts are in session, and there
are proconsuls. Let them bring charges against
one another. 39 If you have anything further to
investigate, let the matter be settled in the lawful
assembly, 40 *for, as it is, we are in danger of
being charged with rioting because of today's
conduct. There is no cause for it. We shall [not]
be able to give a reason for this demonstration."
With these words he dismissed the assembly.

## CHAPTER 20

### Journey to Macedonia and Greece

1 [m]When the disturbance was over, Paul had
the disciples summoned and, after encouraging
them, he bade them farewell and set out on his
journey to Macedonia. 2 As he traveled
throughout those regions, he provided many
words of encouragement for them. Then he arrived in Greece, 3 where he stayed for three
months. But when a plot was made against him
by the Jews as he was about to set sail for Syria,
he decided to return by way of Macedonia.

**Return to Troas** 4 [n]Sopater, the son of
Pyrrhus, from Beroea, accompanied him, as did
Aristarchus and Secundus from Thessalonica,
Gaius from Derbe, Timothy, and Tychicus and
Trophimus from Asia 5 [o]*who went on ahead
and waited for us at Troas. 6 *We sailed from
Philippi after the feast of Unleavened Bread,
and rejoined them five days later in Troas,
where we spent a week.

**Eutychus Restored to Life** 7 *On the
first day of the week when we gathered to break
bread, Paul spoke to them because he was going
to leave on the next day, and he kept on speaking until midnight. 8 There were many lamps in
the upstairs room where we were gathered,
9 and a young man named Eutychus who was
sitting on the window sill was sinking into a
deep sleep as Paul talked on and on. Once overcome by sleep, he fell down from the third story
and when he was picked up, he was dead.
10 [p]*Paul went down, threw himself upon him,
and said as he embraced him, "Don't be
alarmed; there is life in him." 11 Then he returned upstairs, broke the bread, and ate; after
a long conversation that lasted until daybreak,
he departed. 12 And they took the boy away
alive and were immeasurably comforted.

**Journey to Miletus** 13 We went ahead to
the ship and set sail for Assos where we were
to take Paul on board, as he had arranged, since
he was going overland. 14 When he met us in
Assos, we took him aboard and went on to
Mitylene. 15 We sailed away from there on the
next day and reached a point off Chios, and a
day later we reached Samos, and on the following day we arrived at Miletus. 16 *Paul had
decided to sail past Ephesus in order not to lose
time in the province of Asia, for he was hurrying
to be in Jerusalem, if at all possible, for the day
of Pentecost.

### Paul's Farewell Speech at Miletus

17 From Miletus he had the presbyters of the
church at Ephesus summoned. 18 When they
came to him, he addressed them, "You know
how I lived among you the whole time from the
day I first came to the province of Asia. 19 I
served the Lord with all humility and with the
tears and trials that came to me because of the
plots of the Jews, 20 and I did not at all shrink
from telling you what was for your benefit, or
from teaching you in public or in your homes.
21 I earnestly bore witness for both Jews and
Greeks to repentance before God and to faith in
our Lord Jesus. 22 But now, compelled by the
Spirit, I am going to Jerusalem. What will happen to me there I do not know, 23 [q]except that
in one city after another the holy Spirit has been
warning me that imprisonment and hardships
await me. 24 [r]Yet I consider life of no importance to me, if only I may finish my course and
the ministry that I received from the Lord Jesus,
to bear witness to the gospel of God's grace.

25 "But now I know that none of you to
whom I preached the kingdom during my travels will ever see my face again. 26 And so I
solemnly declare to you this day that I am not
responsible for the blood of any of you, 27 for

m 1 Cor 16, 1.
n Rom 16, 21.
o 21, 29; 2 Tm 4, 20.
p 1 Kgs 17, 17-24; 2 Kgs 4, 30-37; Mt 9, 24; Mk 5, 39; Lk 8, 52.
q 9, 16.
r 2 Tm 4, 7.

*

19, 40: Some manuscripts omit the negative in [*not*] *be able*, making the meaning, "There is no cause for which we shall be able to give a reason for this demonstration."

20, 5: The second "we-section" of Acts begins here. See the note on 16, 10–17.

20, 6: *Feast of Unleavened Bread:* see the note on Lk 22, 1.

20, 7: *The first day of the week:* the day after the sabbath and the first day of the Jewish week, apparently chosen originally by the Jerusalem community for the celebration of the liturgy of the Eucharist in order to relate it to the resurrection of Christ.

20, 10: The action of Paul in throwing himself upon the dead boy recalls that of Elijah in 1 Kgs 17, 21 where the son of the widow of Zarephath is revived and that of Elisha in 2 Kgs 4, 34 where the Shunamite woman's son is restored to life.

20, 16–35: Apparently aware of difficulties at Ephesus and neighboring areas, Paul calls the presbyters together at Miletus, about thirty miles from Ephesus. He reminds them of his dedication to the gospel (18–21), speaks of what he is about to suffer for the gospel (22–27), and admonishes them to guard the community against false prophets, sure to arise upon his departure (28–31). He concludes by citing a saying of Jesus (35) not recorded in the gospel tradition. Luke presents this farewell to the Ephesian presbyters as Paul's last will and testament.

I did not shrink from proclaiming to you the
entire plan of God. **28** [s]*Keep watch over yourselves and over the whole flock of which the
holy Spirit has appointed you overseers, in
which you tend the church of God that he acquired with his own blood. **29** [t]I know that after
my departure savage wolves will come among
you, and they will not spare the flock. **30** [u]And
from your own group, men will come forward
perverting the truth to draw the disciples away
after them. **31** [v]So be vigilant and remember
that for three years, night and day, I unceasingly
admonished each of you with tears. **32** And
now I commend you to God and to that gracious
word of his that can build you up and give you
the inheritance among all who are consecrated.
**33** I have never wanted anyone's silver or gold
or clothing. **34** [w]You know well that these very
hands have served my needs and my companions. **35** [x]In every way I have shown you that
by hard work of that sort we must help the weak,
and keep in mind the words of the Lord Jesus
who himself said, 'It is more blessed to give
than to receive.'"

**36** When he had finished speaking he knelt
down and prayed with them all. **37** They were
all weeping loudly as they threw their arms
around Paul and kissed him, **38** for they were
deeply distressed that he had said that they
would never see his face again. Then they escorted him to the ship.

## CHAPTER 21

**Arrival at Tyre** 1 *When we had taken
leave of them we set sail, made a straight run for
Cos, and on the next day for Rhodes, and from
there to Patara. **2** Finding a ship crossing to
Phoenicia, we went on board and put out to sea.
**3** We caught sight of Cyprus but passed by it on
our left and sailed on toward Syria and put in at
Tyre where the ship was to unload cargo.
**4** There we sought out the disciples and stayed
for a week. They kept telling Paul through the
Spirit not to embark for Jerusalem. **5** At the end
of our stay we left and resumed our journey. All
of them, women and children included, escorted
us out of the city, and after kneeling on the
beach to pray, **6** we bade farewell to one another. Then we boarded the ship, and they returned
home.

**Arrival at Ptolemais and Caesarea**
**7** We continued the voyage and came from
Tyre to Ptolemais, where we greeted the brothers and stayed a day with them. **8** [y]*On the next
day we resumed the trip and came to Caesarea,
where we went to the house of Philip the evangelist, who was one of the Seven, and stayed
with him. **9** He had four virgin daughters gifted
with prophecy. **10** *We had been there several
days when a prophet named Agabus came down
from Judea. **11** [z]*He came up to us, took Paul's
belt, bound his own feet and hands with it, and
said, "Thus says the holy Spirit: This is the way
the Jews will bind the owner of this belt in
Jerusalem, and they will hand him over to the
Gentiles." **12** When we heard this, we and the
local residents begged him not to go up to Jerusalem. **13** [a]Then Paul replied, "What are you
doing, weeping and breaking my heart? I am
prepared not only to be bound but even to die
in Jerusalem for the name of the Lord Jesus."
**14** [b]*Since he would not be dissuaded we let
the matter rest, saying, "The Lord's will be
done."

**Paul and James in Jerusalem** 15 After
these days we made preparations for our journey, then went up to Jerusalem. **16** Some of the
disciples from Caesarea came along to lead us
to the house of Mnason, a Cypriot, a disciple of
long standing, with whom we were to stay.
**17** *When we reached Jerusalem the brothers
welcomed us warmly. **18** The next day, Paul
accompanied us on a visit to James, and all the
presbyters were present. **19** He greeted them,
then proceeded to tell them in detail what God
had accomplished among the Gentiles through
his ministry. **20** They praised God when they
heard it but said to him, "Brother, you see how
many thousands of believers there are from
among the Jews, and they are all zealous observers of the law. **21** They have been informed
that you are teaching all the Jews who live
among the Gentiles to abandon Moses and that

s Jn 21, 15-17; 1 Pt 5, 2.
t Jn 10, 12.
u Mt 7, 15; 2 Pt 2, 1-3; 1 Jn 2, 18-19.
v 1 Thes 2, 11.
w 1 Cor 4, 12; 1 Thes 2, 9; 2 Thes 3, 8.
x Sir 4, 31.
y 6, 5; 8, 5-6.
z 11, 28; 20, 23.
a 19, 15-16.
b Mt 6, 10; 26, 39; Mk 14, 36; Lk 22, 42.

*

20, 28: *Overseers:* see the note on Phil 1, 1. *The church of God:* because the clause "that he acquired with his own blood" following "the church of God" suggests that "his own blood" refers to God's blood, some early copyists changed "the church of God" to "the church of the Lord." Some prefer the translation "acquired with the blood of his own," i.e., Christ.

21, 1–18: The third "we-section" of Acts (see the note on 16, 10–17).

21, 8: *One of the Seven:* see the note on 6, 2–4.

21, 10: *Agabus:* mentioned in 11, 28 as the prophet who predicted the famine that occurred when Claudius was emperor.

21, 11: The symbolic act of Agabus recalls those of Old Testament prophets. Compare Is 20, 2; Ez 4, 1; Jer 13, l.

21, 14: The Christian disciples' attitude reflects that of Jesus (see Lk 22, 42).

21, 17–26: The leaders of the Jewish Christians of Jerusalem inform Paul that the Jews there believe he has encouraged the Jews of the diaspora to abandon the Mosaic law. According to Acts, Paul had no objection to the retention of the law by the Jewish Christians of Jerusalem and left the Jews of the diaspora who accepted Christianity free to follow the same practice.

you are telling them not to circumcise their children or to observe their customary practices.
**22** What is to be done? They will surely hear
that you have arrived. **23** [c]*So do what we tell
you. We have four men who have taken a vow.
**24** *Take these men and purify yourself with
them, and pay their expenses that they may have
their heads shaved. In this way everyone will
know that there is nothing to the reports they
have been given about you but that you yourself
live in observance of the law. **25** [d]*As for the
Gentiles who have come to believe, we sent
them our decision that they abstain from meat
sacrificed to idols, from blood, from the meat
of strangled animals, and from unlawful marriage." **26** [e]So Paul took the men, and on the
next day after purifying himself together with
them entered the temple to give notice of the day
when the purification would be completed and
the offering made for each of them.

**Paul's Arrest** **27** When the seven days
were nearly completed, the Jews from the province of Asia noticed him in the temple, stirred
up the whole crowd, and laid hands on him,
**28** [f]*shouting, "Fellow Israelites, help us.
This is the man who is teaching everyone everywhere against the people and the law and this
place, and what is more, he has even brought
Greeks into the temple and defiled this sacred
place." **29** For they had previously seen Trophimus the Ephesian in the city with him and
supposed that Paul had brought him into the
temple. **30** The whole city was in turmoil with
people rushing together. They seized Paul and
dragged him out of the temple, and immediately
the gates were closed. **31** *While they were
trying to kill him, a report reached the cohort
commander that all Jerusalem was rioting.
**32** He immediately took soldiers and centurions and charged down on them. When they saw
the commander and the soldiers they stopped
beating Paul. **33** The cohort commander came
forward, arrested him, and ordered him to be
secured with two chains; he tried to find out who
he might be and what he had done. **34** Some in
the mob shouted one thing, others something
else; so, since he was unable to ascertain the
truth because of the uproar, he ordered Paul to
be brought into the compound. **35** When he
reached the steps, he was carried by the soldiers
because of the violence of the mob, **36** [g]*for a
crowd of people followed and shouted, "Away
with him!"

**37** Just as Paul was about to be taken into the
compound, he said to the cohort commander,
"May I say something to you?" He replied,
"Do you speak Greek? **38** [h]*So then you are
not the Egyptian who started a revolt some time
ago and led the four thousand assassins into the
desert?" **39** Paul answered, "I am a Jew, of
Tarsus in Cilicia, a citizen of no mean city; I
request you to permit me to speak to the people." **40** *When he had given his permission,
Paul stood on the steps and motioned with his
hand to the people; and when all was quiet he
addressed them in Hebrew.

## CHAPTER 22

**Paul's Defense before the Jerusalem
Jews** **1** *"My brothers and fathers, listen to
what I am about to say to you in my defense."
**2** When they heard him addressing them in Hebrew they became all the more quiet. And he
continued, **3** [i]"I am a Jew, born in Tarsus in
Cilicia, but brought up in this city. At the feet
of Gamaliel I was educated strictly in our ances-

c 18, 18; Nm 6, 1-21.
d 15, 19-20.28-29.
e 1 Cor 9, 20.
f Rom 15, 31.
g 22, 22; Lk 23, 18; Jn 19, 15.
h 5, 36-37.
i 5, 34; 26, 4-5; 2 Cor 11, 22; Gal 1, 13-14; Phil 3, 5-6.

*

21, 23–26: The leaders of the community suggest that Paul, on behalf of four members of the Jerusalem community, make the customary payment for the sacrifices offered at the termination of the Nazirite vow (see Nm 6, 1–24) in order to impress favorably the Jewish Christians in Jerusalem with his high regard for the Mosaic law. Since Paul himself had once made this vow (18, 18), his respect for the law would be on public record.

21, 24: *Pay their expenses:* according to Nm 6, 14–15 the Nazirite had to present a yearling lamb for a holocaust, a yearling ewe lamb for a sin offering, and a ram for a peace offering, along with food and drink offerings, upon completion of the period of the vow.

21, 25: Paul is informed about the apostolic decree, seemingly for the first time (see the note on 15, 13–35). The allusion to the decree was probably introduced here by Luke to remind his readers that the Gentile Christians themselves were asked to respect certain Jewish practices deriving from the law.

21, 28: The charges against Paul by the diaspora Jews are identical to the charges brought against Stephen by diaspora Jews in 6, 13. *Brought Greeks into the temple:* non-Jews were forbidden, under penalty of death, to go beyond the Court of the Gentiles. Inscriptions in Greek and Latin on a stone ballustrade marked off the prohibited area.

21, 31: *Cohort commander:* literally, "the leader of a thousand in a cohort." At this period the Roman cohort commander usually led six hundred soldiers, a tenth of a legion; but the number in a cohort varied.

21, 36: *Away with him:* at the trial of Jesus before Pilate in Lk 23, 18, the people similarly shout, "Away with this man."

21, 38: *The Egyptian:* according to the Jewish historian Josephus, an Egyptian gathered a large crowd on the Mount of Olives to witness the destruction of the walls of Jerusalem that would fall at the Egyptian "prophet's" word. The commotion was put down by the Roman authorities and the Egyptian escaped, but only after thousands had been killed. *Four thousand assassins:* literally, *sicarii.* According to Josephus, these were political nationalists who removed their opponents by assassination with a short dagger, called in Latin a sica.

21, 40: *In Hebrew:* meaning, perhaps, in Aramaic, which at this time was the Semitic tongue in common use.

22, 1–21: Paul's first defense speech is presented to the Jerusalem crowds. Luke here presents Paul as a devout Jew (3) and zealous persecutor of the Christian community (4–5), and then recounts the conversion of Paul for the second time in Acts (see the note on 9, 1–19).

tral law and was zealous for God, just as all of you are today. **4** [j]I persecuted this Way to death, binding both men and women and delivering them to prison. **5** Even the high priest and the whole council of elders can testify on my behalf. For from them I even received letters to the brothers and set out for Damascus to bring back to Jerusalem in chains for punishment those there as well.

**6** [k]"On that journey as I drew near to Damascus, about noon a great light from the sky suddenly shone around me. **7** [l]I fell to the ground and heard a voice saying to me, 'Saul, Saul, why are you persecuting me?' **8** [m]I replied, 'Who are you, sir?' And he said to me, 'I am Jesus the Nazorean whom you are persecuting.' **9** [n]My companions saw the light but did not hear the voice of the one who spoke to me. **10** [o]I asked, 'What shall I do, sir?' The Lord answered me, 'Get up and go into Damascus, and there you will be told about everything appointed for you to do.' **11** [p]Since I could see nothing because of the brightness of that light, I was led by hand by my companions and entered Damascus.

**12** [q]"A certain Ananias, a devout observer of the law, and highly spoken of by all the Jews who lived there, **13** came to me and stood there and said, 'Saul, my brother, regain your sight.' And at that very moment I regained my sight and saw him. **14** Then he said, 'The God of our ancestors designated you to know his will, to see the Righteous One, and to hear the sound of his voice; **15** *for you will be his witness before all to what you have seen and heard. **16** Now, why delay? Get up and have yourself baptized and your sins washed away, calling upon his name.'

**17** "After I had returned to Jerusalem and while I was praying in the temple, I fell into a trance **18** and saw the Lord saying to me, 'Hurry, leave Jerusalem at once, because they will not accept your testimony about me.' **19** [r]But I replied, 'Lord, they themselves know that from synagogue to synagogue I used to imprison and beat those who believed in you. **20** [s]And when the blood of your witness Stephen was being shed, I myself stood by giving my approval and keeping guard over the cloaks of his murderers.' **21** [t]*Then he said to me, 'Go, I shall send you far away to the Gentiles.' "

**Paul Imprisoned** **22** [u]*They listened to him until he said this, but then they raised their voices and shouted, "Take such a one as this away from the earth. It is not right that he should live." **23** And as they were yelling and throwing off their cloaks and flinging dust into the air, **24** the cohort commander ordered him to be brought into the compound and gave instruction that he be interrogated under the lash to determine the reason why they were making such an outcry against him. **25** [v]*But when they had stretched him out for the whips, Paul said to the centurion on duty, "Is it lawful for you to scourge a man who is a Roman citizen and has not been tried?" **26** When the centurion heard this, he went to the cohort commander and reported it, saying, "What are you going to do? This man is a Roman citizen." **27** Then the commander came and said to him, "Tell me, are you a Roman citizen?" "Yes," he answered. **28** The commander replied, "I acquired this citizenship for a large sum of money." Paul said, "But I was born one." **29** At once those who were going to interrogate him backed away from him, and the commander became alarmed when he realized that he was a Roman citizen and that he had had him bound.

**Paul before the Sanhedrin** **30** The next day, wishing to determine the truth about why he was being accused by the Jews, he freed him and ordered the chief priests and the whole Sanhedrin to convene. Then he brought Paul down and made him stand before them.

## CHAPTER 23

**1** [w]Paul looked intently at the Sanhedrin and said, "My brothers, I have conducted myself with a perfectly clear conscience before God to this day." **2** *The high priest Ananias ordered his attendants to strike his mouth. **3** [x]*Then Paul said to him, "God will strike you, you whitewashed wall. Do you indeed sit in judgment upon me according to the law and yet in violation of the law order me to be struck?"

j 8, 3; 9, 1-2; 22, 19; 26, 9-11; Phil 3, 6.
k 9, 3; 26, 13; 1 Cor 15, 8.
l 9, 4; 26, 14.
m 9, 5; 26, 15; Mt 25, 40.
n 9, 7; 26, 13-14.
o 9, 6; 26, 16.
p 9, 8.
q 9, 10-19.
r 8, 3; 9, 1-2; 22, 4-5; 26, 9-11.
s 7, 58; 8, 1.
t 9, 15; Gal 2, 7-9.
u 21, 36; Lk 23, 18; Jn 19, 15.
v 16, 37.
w 24, 16.
x Ez 13, 10-15; Mt 23, 27.

*

22, 15: *His witness:* like the Galilean followers during the historical ministry of Jesus, Paul too, through his experience of the risen Christ, is to be a witness to the resurrection (compare 1, 8; 10, 39–41; Lk 24, 48).

22, 21: Paul endeavors to explain that his position on the law has not been identical with that of his audience because it has been his prophetic mission to preach to the Gentiles to whom the law was not addressed and who had no faith in it as a way of salvation.

22, 22: Paul's suggestion that his prophetic mission to the Gentiles did not involve his imposing the law on them provokes the same opposition as occurred in Pisidian Antioch (13, 45).

22, 25: *Is it lawful for you to scourge a man who is a Roman citizen and has not been tried?:* see the note on 16, 37.

23, 2: *The high priest Ananias:* Ananias, son of Nedebaeus, was high priest from A.D. 47 to 59.

23, 3: *God will strike you:* Josephus reports that Ananias was later assassinated in A.D. 66 at the beginning of the First Revolt.

**4** The attendants said, "Would you revile
God's high priest?" **5** [y]*Paul answered,
"Brothers, I did not realize he was the high
priest. For it is written, 'You shall not curse a
ruler of your people.'"
**6** [z]Paul was aware that some were Sadducees
and some Pharisees, so he called out before the
Sanhedrin, "My brothers, I am a Pharisee, the
son of Pharisees; [I] am on trial for hope in the
resurrection of the dead." **7** When he said this,
a dispute broke out between the Pharisees and
Sadducees, and the group became divided.
**8** [a]For the Sadducees say that there is no resurrection or angels or spirits, while the Pharisees
acknowledge all three. **9** A great uproar occurred, and some scribes belonging to the Pharisee party stood up and sharply argued, "We
find nothing wrong with this man. Suppose a
spirit or an angel has spoken to him?" **10** The
dispute was so serious that the commander,
afraid that Paul would be torn to pieces by them,
ordered his troops to go down and rescue him
from their midst and take him into the compound. **11** [b]*The following night the Lord
stood by him and said, "Take courage. For just
as you have borne witness to my cause in Jerusalem, so you must also bear witness in Rome."

**Transfer to Caesarea** **12** When day
came, the Jews made a plot and bound themselves by oath not to eat or drink until they had
killed Paul. **13** There were more than forty who
formed this conspiracy. **14** They went to the
chief priests and elders and said, "We have
bound ourselves by a solemn oath to taste nothing until we have killed Paul. **15** You, together
with the Sanhedrin, must now make an official
request to the commander to have him bring him
down to you, as though you meant to investigate
his case more thoroughly. We on our part are
prepared to kill him before he arrives." **16** The
son of Paul's sister, however, heard about the
ambush; so he went and entered the compound
and reported it to Paul. **17** *Paul then called one
of the centurions and requested, "Take this
young man to the commander; he has something
to report to him." **18** So he took him and
brought him to the commander and explained,
"The prisoner Paul called me and asked that I
bring this young man to you; he has something
to say to you." **19** The commander took him by
the hand, drew him aside, and asked him privately, "What is it you have to report to me?"
**20** He replied, "The Jews have conspired to
ask you to bring Paul down to the Sanhedrin
tomorrow, as though they meant to inquire
about him more thoroughly, **21** but do not believe them. More than forty of them are lying in
wait for him; they have bound themselves by
oath not to eat or drink until they have killed
him. They are now ready and only wait for your
consent." **22** As the commander dismissed the
young man he directed him, "Tell no one that
you gave me this information."
**23** *Then he summoned two of the centurions and said, "Get two hundred soldiers ready
to go to Caesarea by nine o'clock tonight, along
with seventy horsemen and two hundred auxiliaries. **24** Provide mounts for Paul to ride and
give him safe conduct to Felix the governor."
**25** Then he wrote a letter with this content:
**26** *"Claudius Lysias to his excellency the
governor Felix, greetings. **27** [c]This man,
seized by the Jews and about to be murdered by
them, I rescued after intervening with my troops
when I learned that he was a Roman citizen.
**28** I wanted to learn the reason for their accusations against him so I brought him down to their
Sanhedrin. **29** [d]I discovered that he was accused in matters of controversial questions of
their law and not of any charge deserving death
or imprisonment. **30** Since it was brought to my
attention that there will be a plot against the
man, I am sending him to you at once, and have
also notified his accusers to state [their case]
against him before you."
**31** So the soldiers, according to their orders,
took Paul and escorted him by night to Antipa-
tris. **32** The next day they returned to the compound, leaving the horsemen to complete the
journey with him. **33** When they arrived in
Caesarea they delivered the letter to the governor and presented Paul to him. **34** When he had
read it and asked to what province he belonged,
and learned that he was from Cilicia, **35** he

y Ex 22, 27.
z 24, 15.21; 26, 5; Phil 3, 5.
a Mt 22, 23; Lk 20, 27.
b 19, 21.
c 21, 30-34; 22, 27.
d 18, 14-15; 25, 18-19.

*

23, 5: Luke portrays Paul as a model of one who is obedient to the Mosaic law. Paul, because of his reverence for the law (Ex 22, 27), withdraws his accusation of hypocrisy, "white-washed wall" (cf Mt 23, 27), when he is told Ananias is the high priest.

23, 11: The occurrence of the vision of Christ consoling Paul and assuring him that he will be his witness in Rome prepares the reader for the final section of Acts: the journey of Paul and the word he preaches to Rome under the protection of the Romans.

23, 17: *Centurions:* a centurion was a military officer in charge of one hundred soldiers.

23, 23: *By nine o'clock tonight:* literally, "by the third hour of the night." The night hours began at 6 p.m. *Two hundred auxiliaries:* the meaning of the Greek is not certain. It seems to refer to spearmen from the local police force and not from the cohort of soldiers, which would have numbered only 500–1000 men.

23, 26-30: The letter emphasizes the fact that Paul is a Roman citizen and asserts the lack of evidence that he is guilty of a crime against the empire. The tone of the letter implies that the commander became initially involved in Paul's case because of his Roman citizenship, but this is not an exact description of what really happened (see 21, 31–33; 22, 25–29).

23, 26: M. Antonius Felix was procurator of Judea from A.D. 52 to 60. His procuratorship was marked by cruelty toward and oppression of his Jewish subjects.

said, "I shall hear your case when your accusers
arrive." Then he ordered that he be held in
custody in Herod's praetorium.

## CHAPTER 24

**Trial before Felix** 1 Five days later the
high priest Ananias came down with some elders and an advocate, a certain Tertullus, and
they presented formal charges against Paul to
the governor. 2 When he was called, Tertullus
began to accuse him, saying, "Since we have
attained much peace through you, and reforms
have been accomplished in this nation through
your provident care, 3 we acknowledge this in
every way and everywhere, most excellent Felix, with all gratitude. 4 But in order not to
detain you further, I ask you to give us a brief
hearing with your customary graciousness.
5 [e]*We found this man to be a pest; he creates
dissension among Jews all over the world and
is a ringleader of the sect of the Nazoreans.
6 [f]He even tried to desecrate our temple, but we
arrested him. [7*] 8 If you examine him you
will be able to learn from him for yourself about
everything of which we are accusing him."
9 The Jews also joined in the attack and asserted that these things were so.

10 *Then the governor motioned to him to
speak and Paul replied, "I know that you have
been a judge over this nation for many years and
so I am pleased to make my defense before you.
11 As you can verify, not more than twelve
days have passed since I went up to Jerusalem
to worship. 12 Neither in the temple, nor in the
synagogues, nor anywhere in the city did they
find me arguing with anyone or instigating a riot
among the people. 13 Nor can they prove to
you the accusations they are now making
against me. 14 [g]But this I do admit to you, that
according to the Way, which they call a sect, I
worship the God of our ancestors and I believe
everything that is in accordance with the law
and written in the prophets. 15 [h]I have the same
hope in God as they themselves have that there
will be a resurrection of the righteous and the
unrighteous. 16 [i]Because of this, I always
strive to keep my conscience clear before God
and man. 17 [j]After many years, I came to bring
alms for my nation and offerings. 18 [k]While I
was so engaged, they found me, after my purification, in the temple without a crowd or disturbance. 19 But some Jews from the province of
Asia, who should be here before you to make
whatever accusation they might have against
me— 20 or let these men themselves state what
crime they discovered when I stood before the
Sanhedrin, 21 [l]unless it was my one outcry as
I stood among them, that 'I am on trial before
you today for the resurrection of the dead.' "

22 Then Felix, who was accurately informed
about the Way, postponed the trial, saying,
"When Lysias the commander comes down, I
shall decide your case." 23 He gave orders to
the centurion that he should be kept in custody
but have some liberty, and that he should not
prevent any of his friends from caring for his
needs.

**Captivity in Caesarea** 24 *Several days
later Felix came with his wife Drusilla, who was
Jewish. He had Paul summoned and listened to
him speak about faith in Christ Jesus. 25 But as
he spoke about righteousness and self-restraint
and the coming judgment, Felix became frightened and said, "You may go for now; when I
find an opportunity I shall summon you again."
26 At the same time he hoped that a bribe
would be offered him by Paul, and so he sent for
him very often and conversed with him.

27 *Two years passed and Felix was succeeded by Porcius Festus. Wishing to ingratiate
himself with the Jews, Felix left Paul in prison.

## CHAPTER 25

**Appeal to Caesar** 1 Three days after his
arrival in the province, Festus went up from
Caesarea to Jerusalem 2 *where the chief
priests and Jewish leaders presented him their
formal charges against Paul. They asked him
3 as a favor to have him sent to Jerusalem, for
they were plotting to kill him along the way.
4 Festus replied that Paul was being held in
custody in Caesarea and that he himself would
be returning there shortly. 5 He said, "Let your
authorities come down with me, and if this man
has done something improper, let them accuse
him."

e 24, 14; Lk 23, 2.
f 21, 28.
g 24, 5.
h Dn 12, 2; Jn 5, 28-29.
i 23, 1.
j Rom 15, 25-26; Gal 2, 10.
k 21, 26-30.
l 23, 6; 24, 15.

*

24, 5: *Nazoreans:* that is, followers of Jesus of Nazareth.

24, 7: The Western text has added here a verse (really 6b–8a) that is not found in the best Greek manuscripts. It reads, "and would have judged him according to our own law, but the cohort commander Lysias came and violently took him out of our hands and ordered his accusers to come before you."

24, 10–21: Whereas the advocate Tertullus referred to Paul's activities on his missionary journeys, the apostle narrowed the charges down to the riot connected with the incident in the temple (see 21, 27–30; 24, 17–20). In his defense, Paul stresses the continuity between Christianity and Judaism.

24, 24–25: The way of Christian discipleship greatly disquiets Felix, who has entered into an adulterous marriage with Drusilla, daughter of Herod Agrippa I. This marriage provides the background for the topics Paul speaks about and about which Felix does not want to hear.

24, 27: Very little is known of Porcius Festus who was a procurator of Judea from A.D. 60 to 62.

25, 2: Even after two years the animosity toward Paul in Jerusalem had not subsided (see 24, 27).

6 After spending no more than eight or ten
days with them, he went down to Caesarea, and
on the following day took his seat on the tribunal
and ordered that Paul be brought in. 7 When he
appeared, the Jews who had come down from
Jerusalem surrounded him and brought many
serious charges against him, which they were
unable to prove. 8 In defending himself Paul
said, "I have committed no crime either against
the Jewish law or against the temple or against
Caesar." 9 *Then Festus, wishing to ingratiate
himself with the Jews, said to Paul in reply,
"Are you willing to go up to Jerusalem and
there stand trial before me on these charges?"
10 Paul answered, "I am standing before the
tribunal of Caesar; this is where I should be
tried. I have committed no crime against the
Jews, as you very well know. 11 If I have committed a crime or done anything deserving
death, I do not seek to escape the death penalty;
but if there is no substance to the charges they
are bringing against me, then no one has the
right to hand me over to them. I appeal to Caesar." 12 Then Festus, after conferring with his
council, replied, "You have appealed to Caesar. To Caesar you will go."

**Paul before King Agrippa** 13 *When a
few days had passed, King Agrippa and Bernice
arrived in Caesarea on a visit to Festus.
14 [m]Since they spent several days there, Festus
referred Paul's case to the king, saying, "There
is a man here left in custody by Felix. 15 When
I was in Jerusalem the chief priests and the
elders of the Jews brought charges against him
and demanded his condemnation. 16 I answered them that it was not Roman practice to
hand over an accused person before he has faced
his accusers and had the opportunity to defend
himself against their charge. 17 So when [they]
came together here, I made no delay; the next
day I took my seat on the tribunal and ordered
the man to be brought in. 18 [n]His accusers
stood around him, but did not charge him with
any of the crimes I suspected. 19 Instead they
had some issues with him about their own religion and about a certain Jesus who had died but
who Paul claimed was alive. 20 Since I was at
a loss how to investigate this controversy, I
asked if he were willing to go to Jerusalem and
there stand trial on these charges. 21 And when
Paul appealed that he be held in custody for the
Emperor's decision, I ordered him held until I
could send him to Caesar." 22 Agrippa said to
Festus, "I too should like to hear this man." He
replied, "Tomorrow you will hear him."

23 The next day Agrippa and Bernice came
with great ceremony and entered the audience
hall in the company of cohort commanders and
the prominent men of the city and, by command
of Festus, Paul was brought in. 24 And Festus
said, "King Agrippa and all you here present
with us, look at this man about whom the whole
Jewish populace petitioned me here and in Jerusalem, clamoring that he should live no longer.
25 I found, however, that he had done nothing
deserving death, and so when he appealed to the
Emperor, I decided to send him. 26 But I have
nothing definite to write about him to our sovereign; therefore I have brought him before all of
you, and particularly before you, King Agrippa,
so that I may have something to write as a result
of this investigation. 27 For it seems senseless
to me to send up a prisoner without indicating
the charges against him."

## CHAPTER 26

**King Agrippa Hears Paul** 1 Then Agrippa said to Paul, "You may now speak on your
own behalf." So Paul stretched out his hand and
began his defense. 2 *"I count myself fortunate, King Agrippa, that I am to defend myself
before you today against all the charges made
against me by the Jews, 3 especially since you
are an expert in all the Jewish customs and
controversies. And therefore I beg you to listen
patiently. 4 *My manner of living from my
youth, a life spent from the beginning among
my people and in Jerusalem, all [the] Jews
know. 5 [o]They have known about me from the
start, if they are willing to testify, that I have
lived my life as a Pharisee, the strictest party of
our religion. 6 [p]But now I am standing trial
because of my hope in the promise made by God
to our ancestors. 7 Our twelve tribes hope to
attain to that promise as they fervently worship
God day and night; and on account of this hope
I am accused by Jews, O king. 8 Why is it
thought unbelievable among you that God raises
the dead? 9 [q]I myself once thought that I had

m 24, 27.
n 18, 14-15; 23, 29.
o Phil 3, 5-6; Gal 1, 13-14; 2 Cor 11, 22.
p 23, 6; 24, 15.21; 28, 20.
q 8, 3; 9, 1-2; 22, 19; Phil 3, 6.

*

25, 9–12: Paul refuses to acknowledge that the Sanhedrin in Jerusalem has any jurisdiction over him now (11). Paul uses his right as a Roman citizen to appeal his case to the jurisdiction of the Emperor (Nero, ca. A.D. 60) (12). This move broke the deadlock between Roman protective custody of Paul and the plan of his enemies to kill him (3).

25, 13: *King Agrippa and Bernice:* brother and sister, children of Herod Agrippa I whose activities against the Jerusalem community are mentioned in 12, 1–19. Agrippa II was a petty ruler over small areas in northern Palestine and some villages in Perea. His influence on the Jewish population of Palestine was insignificant.

26, 2–23: Paul's final defense speech in Acts is now made before a king (see 9, 15). In the speech Paul presents himself as a zealous Pharisee and Christianity as the logical development of Pharisaic Judaism. The story of his conversion is recounted for the third time in Acts in this speech (see the note on 9, 1–19).

26, 4: *Among my people:* that is, among the Jews.

to do many things against the name of Jesus the
Nazorean, **10** [r]and I did so in Jerusalem. I imprisoned many of the holy ones with the authorization I received from the chief priests, and
when they were to be put to death I cast my vote
against them. **11** Many times, in synagogue after synagogue, I punished them in an attempt to
force them to blaspheme; I was so enraged
against them that I pursued them even to foreign
cities.

**12** "On one such occasion I was traveling to
Damascus with the authorization and commission of the chief priests. **13** [s t]At midday, along
the way, O king, I saw a light from the sky,
brighter than the sun, shining around me and my
traveling companions. **14** [u]*We all fell to the
ground and I heard a voice saying to me in
Hebrew, 'Saul, Saul, why are you persecuting
me? It is hard for you to kick against the goad.'
**15** [v]And I said, 'Who are you, sir?' And the
Lord replied, 'I am Jesus whom you are persecuting. **16** [w]*Get up now, and stand on your
feet. I have appeared to you for this purpose, to
appoint you as a servant and witness of what you
have seen [of me] and what you will be shown.
**17** [x]I shall deliver you from this people and
from the Gentiles to whom I send you, **18** [y]*to
open their eyes that they may turn from darkness
to light and from the power of Satan to God, so
that they may obtain forgiveness of sins and an
inheritance among those who have been consecrated by faith in me.'

**19** "And so, King Agrippa, I was not disobedient to the heavenly vision. **20** On the contrary, first to those in Damascus and in Jerusalem and throughout the whole country of Judea,
and then to the Gentiles, I preached the need to
repent and turn to God, and to do works giving
evidence of repentance. **21** [z]That is why the
Jews seized me [when I was] in the temple and
tried to kill me. **22** [a]*But I have enjoyed God's
help to this very day, and so I stand here testifying to small and great alike, saying nothing
different from what the prophets and Moses
foretold, **23** [b]*that the Messiah must suffer and
that, as the first to rise from the dead, he would
proclaim light both to our people and to the
Gentiles."

**Reactions to Paul's Speech** **24** While
Paul was so speaking in his defense, Festus said
in a loud voice, "You are mad, Paul; much
learning is driving you mad." **25** But Paul replied, "I am not mad, most excellent Festus; I
am speaking words of truth and reason.
**26** *The king knows about these matters and to
him I speak boldly, for I cannot believe that
[any] of this has escaped his notice; this was not
done in a corner. **27** *King Agrippa, do you
believe the prophets? I know you believe."
**28** Then Agrippa said to Paul, "You will soon
persuade me to play the Christian." **29** Paul
replied, "I would pray to God that sooner or
later not only you but all who listen to me today
might become as I am except for these chains."

**30** Then the king rose, and with him the governor and Bernice and the others who sat with
them. **31** *And after they had withdrawn they
said to one another, "This man is doing nothing
[at all] that deserves death or imprisonment."
**32** [c]And Agrippa said to Festus, "This man
could have been set free if he had not appealed
to Caesar."

## CHAPTER 27

**Departure for Rome** **1** *When it was decided that we should sail to Italy, they handed

r 9, 14.
s 9, 7.
t 9, 3; 22, 6.
u 9, 4; 22, 7.
v 9, 5; 22, 8; Mt 25, 40.
w 9, 6; 22, 10; Ez 2, 1.
x Jer 1, 7.
y Is 42, 7.16; 61, 1 LXX; Col 1, 13.
z 21, 31.
a 3, 18; Lk 24, 26-27.44-47.
b Is 42, 6; 49, 6; Lk 2, 32; 1 Cor 15, 20-23.
c 25, 11-12.

*

26, 14: *In Hebrew:* see the note on 21, 40. *It is hard for you to kick against the goad:* this proverb is commonly found in Greek literature and in this context signifies the senselessness and ineffectiveness of any opposition to the divine influence in his life.

26, 16: The words of Jesus directed to Paul here reflect the dialogues between Christ and Ananias (9, 15) and between Ananias and Paul (22, 14–15) in the two previous accounts of Paul's conversion.

26, 18: *To open their eyes:* though no mention is made of Paul's blindness in this account (cf 9, 8–9.12.18; 22, 11–13), the task he is commissioned to perform is the removal of other people's spiritual blindness.

26, 22: *Saying nothing different from what the prophets and Moses foretold:* see the note on Lk 18, 31.

26, 23: *That the Messiah must suffer:* see the note on Lk 24, 26.

26, 26: *Not done in a corner:* for Luke, this Greek proverb expresses his belief that he is presenting a story about Jesus and the church that is already well known. As such, the entire history of Christianity is public knowledge and incontestable. Luke presents his story in this way to provide "certainty" to his readers about the instructions they have received (Lk 1, 4).

26, 27–28: If the Christian missionaries proclaim nothing different from what the Old Testament prophets had proclaimed (22–23), then the logical outcome for the believing Jew, according to Luke, is to become a Christian.

26, 31–32: In recording the episode of Paul's appearance before Agrippa, Luke wishes to show that, when Paul's case was judged impartially, no grounds for legal action against him were found (see 23, 29; 25, 25).

27, 1—28, 16: Here Luke has written a stirring account of adventure on the high seas, incidental to his main purpose of showing how well Paul got along with his captors and how his prophetic influence saved the lives of all on board. The recital also establishes the existence of Christian communities in Puteoli and Rome. This account of the voyage and shipwreck also constitutes the final "we-section" in Acts (see the note on 16, 10–17).

27, 1: *Cohort Augusta:* the presence of a Cohort Augusta in Syria during the first century A.D. is attested in inscriptions. Whatever the historical background to this information given by Luke may be, the name Augusta serves to increase the prominence and prestige of the prisoner Paul whose custodi-

Paul and some other prisoners over to a centurion named Julius of the Cohort Augusta. **2** [d]We
went on board a ship from Adramyttium bound
for ports in the province of Asia and set sail.
Aristarchus, a Macedonian from Thessalonica,
was with us. **3** On the following day we put in
at Sidon where Julius was kind enough to allow
Paul to visit his friends who took care of him.
**4** From there we put out to sea and sailed
around the sheltered side of Cyprus because of
the headwinds, **5** and crossing the open sea off
the coast of Cilicia and Pamphylia we came to
Myra in Lycia.

**Storm and Shipwreck** **6** There the centurion found an Alexandrian ship that was sailing
to Italy and put us on board. **7** For many days
we made little headway, arriving at Cnidus only
with difficulty, and because the wind would not
permit us to continue our course we sailed for
the sheltered side of Crete off Salmone. **8** We
sailed past it with difficulty and reached a place
called Fair Havens, near which was the city of
Lasea.

**9** [e]*Much time had now passed and sailing
had become hazardous because the time of the
fast had already gone by, so Paul warned them,
**10** "Men, I can see that this voyage will result
in severe damage and heavy loss not only to the
cargo and the ship, but also to our lives."
**11** The centurion, however, paid more attention to the pilot and to the owner of the ship than
to what Paul said. **12** Since the harbor was
unfavorably situated for spending the winter,
the majority planned to put out to sea from there
in the hope of reaching Phoenix, a port in Crete
facing west-northwest, there to spend the winter.

**13** A south wind blew gently, and thinking
they had attained their objective, they weighed
anchor and sailed along close to the coast of
Crete. **14** Before long an offshore wind of hurricane force called a "Northeaster" struck.
**15** Since the ship was caught up in it and could
not head into the wind we gave way and let
ourselves be driven. **16** We passed along the
sheltered side of an island named Cauda and
managed only with difficulty to get the dinghy
under control. **17** They hoisted it aboard, then
used cables to undergird the ship. Because of
their fear that they would run aground on the
shoal of Syrtis, they lowered the drift anchor
and were carried along in this way. **18** We were
being pounded by the storm so violently that the
next day they jettisoned some cargo, **19** and on
the third day with their own hands they threw
even the ship's tackle overboard. **20** Neither
the sun nor the stars were visible for many days,
and no small storm raged. Finally, all hope of
our surviving was taken away.

**21** When many would no longer eat, Paul
stood among them and said, "Men, you should
have taken my advice and not have set sail from
Crete and you would have avoided this disastrous loss. **22** I urge you now to keep up your
courage; not one of you will be lost, only the
ship. **23** For last night an angel of the God to
whom [I] belong and whom I serve stood by me
**24** [f]and said, 'Do not be afraid, Paul. You are
destined to stand before Caesar; and behold, for
your sake, God has granted safety to all who are
sailing with you.' **25** Therefore, keep up your
courage, men; I trust in God that it will turn out
as I have been told. **26** We are destined to run
aground on some island."

**27** On the fourteenth night, as we were still
being driven about on the Adriatic Sea, toward
midnight the sailors began to suspect that they
were nearing land. **28** They took soundings and
found twenty fathoms; a little farther on, they
again took soundings and found fifteen fathoms.
**29** Fearing that we would run aground on a
rocky coast, they dropped four anchors from the
stern and prayed for day to come. **30** The sailors then tried to abandon ship; they lowered the
dinghy to the sea on the pretext of going to lay
out anchors from the bow. **31** But Paul said to
the centurion and the soldiers, "Unless these
men stay with the ship, you cannot be saved."
**32** So the soldiers cut the ropes of the dinghy
and set it adrift.

**33** Until the day began to dawn, Paul kept
urging all to take some food. He said, "Today
is the fourteenth day that you have been waiting,
going hungry and eating nothing. **34** I urge
you, therefore, to take some food; it will help
you survive. Not a hair of the head of anyone
of you will be lost." **35** [g]*When he said this,
he took bread, gave thanks to God in front of
them all, broke it, and began to eat. **36** They
were all encouraged, and took some food themselves. **37** In all, there were two hundred seventy-six of us on the ship. **38** After they had eaten
enough, they lightened the ship by throwing the
wheat into the sea.

**39** When day came they did not recognize
the land, but made out a bay with a beach. They
planned to run the ship ashore on it, if they
could. **40** So they cast off the anchors and abandoned them to the sea, and at the same time they
unfastened the lines of the rudders, and hoisting
the foresail into the wind, they made for the
beach. **41** But they struck a sandbar and ran the

d 19, 29; 20, 4.
e Lv 16, 29-31.
f 23, 11.
g Mt 15, 36; Mk 6, 41; 8, 6; Lk 22, 19; 1 Cor 11, 23-24.

ans bear so important a Roman name.

27, 9: *The time of the fast:* the fast kept on the occasion of the Day of Atonement (Lv 16, 29–31), which occurred in late September or early October.

27, 35: *He took bread . . . :* the words recall the traditional language of the celebration of the Eucharist (see Lk 22, 19).

ship aground. The bow was wedged in and
could not be moved, but the stern began to break
up under the pounding [of the waves]. **42** The
soldiers planned to kill the prisoners so that
none might swim away and escape, **43** but the
centurion wanted to save Paul and so kept them
from carrying out their plan. He ordered those
who could swim to jump overboard first and get
to the shore, **44** and then the rest, some on
planks, others on debris from the ship. In this
way, all reached shore safely.

## CHAPTER 28

**Winter in Malta** 1 Once we had reached
safety we learned that the island was called
Malta. **2** The natives showed us extraordinary
hospitality; they lit a fire and welcomed all of
us because it had begun to rain and was cold.
**3** Paul had gathered a bundle of brushwood and
was putting it on the fire when a viper, escaping
from the heat, fastened on his hand. **4** *When
the natives saw the snake hanging from his
hand, they said to one another, "This man must
certainly be a murderer; though he escaped the
sea, Justice has not let him remain alive."
**5** But he shook the snake off into the fire and
suffered no harm. **6** [h]They were expecting him
to swell up or suddenly to fall down dead but,
after waiting a long time and seeing nothing
unusual happen to him, they changed their
minds and began to say that he was a god. **7** In
the vicinity of that place were lands belonging
to a man named Publius, the chief of the island.
He welcomed us and received us cordially as his
guests for three days. **8** It so happened that the
father of Publius was sick with a fever and
dysentery. Paul visited him and, after praying,
laid his hands on him and healed him. **9** After
this had taken place, the rest of the sick on the
island came to Paul and were cured. **10** They
paid us great honor and when we eventually set
sail they brought us the provisions we needed.

**Arrival in Rome** 11 *Three months later
we set sail on a ship that had wintered at the
island. It was an Alexandrian ship with the Dioscuri as its figurehead. **12** We put in at Syra-
cuse and stayed there three days, **13** and from
there we sailed round the coast and arrived at
Rhegium. After a day, a south wind came up
and in two days we reached Puteoli. **14** There
we found some brothers and were urged to stay
with them for seven days. And thus we came to
Rome. **15** The brothers from there heard about
us and came as far as the Forum of Appius and
Three Taverns to meet us. On seeing them, Paul
gave thanks to God and took courage.
**16** *When he entered Rome, Paul was allowed
to live by himself, with the soldier who was
guarding him.

**Testimony to Jews in Rome** 17 [i]*Three
days later he called together the leaders of the
Jews. When they had gathered he said to them,
"My brothers, although I had done nothing
against our people or our ancestral customs, I
was handed over to the Romans as a prisoner
from Jerusalem. **18** [j]After trying my case the
Romans wanted to release me, because they
found nothing against me deserving the death
penalty. **19** [k]But when the Jews objected, I was
obliged to appeal to Caesar, even though I had
no accusation to make against my own nation.
**20** [l]*This is the reason, then, I have requested
to see you and to speak with you, for it is on
account of the hope of Israel that I wear these
chains." **21** They answered him, "We have
received no letters from Judea about you, nor
has any of the brothers arrived with a damaging
report or rumor about you. **22** [m]But we should
like to hear you present your views, for we
know that this sect is denounced everywhere."

**23** So they arranged a day with him and came
to his lodgings in great numbers. From early
morning until evening, he expounded his position to them, bearing witness to the kingdom of
God and trying to convince them about Jesus
from the law of Moses and the prophets.
**24** Some were convinced by what he had said,
while others did not believe. **25** *Without
reaching any agreement among themselves they
began to leave; then Paul made one final statement. "Well did the holy Spirit speak to your
ancestors through the prophet Isaiah, saying:
**26** [n]'Go to this people and say:

---

h 14, 11.
i 24, 12-13; 25, 8.
j 23, 29; 25, 25; 26, 31-32.
k 25, 11.
l 23, 6; 24, 15.21; 26, 6-8.
m 24, 5.14.
n Is 6, 9-10; Mt 13, 14-15; Mk 4, 12; Lk 8, 10; Jn 12, 40;Rom 11, 8.

*

28, 4: *Justice:* in Greek mythology, the pursuing goddess of vengeance and justice.

28, 11: *Dioscuri:* that is, the Twin Brothers, Castor and Pollux, the sons of Zeus and the patrons of the sailors.

28, 16: With Paul's arrival in Rome, the programmatic spread of the word of the Lord to "the ends of the earth" (1, 8) is accomplished. In Rome, Paul is placed under house arrest, and under this mild form of custody he is allowed to proclaim the word in the capital of the civilized world of his day.

28, 17–22: Paul's first act in Rome is to learn from the leaders of the Jewish community whether the Jews of Jerusalem plan to pursue their case against him before the Roman jurisdiction. He is informed that no such plan is afoot, but that the Jews of Rome have heard the Christian teaching denounced. Paul's offer to explain it to them is readily accepted.

28, 20: *The hope of Israel:* in the words of Paul (23, 6), Luke has identified this hope as hope in the resurrection of the dead.

28, 25–28: Paul's final words in Acts reflect a major concern of Luke's writings: how the salvation promised in the Old Testament, accomplished by Jesus, and offered first to Israel (13, 26), has now been offered to and accepted by the Gentiles. Quoting Is 6, 9–10, Paul presents the scriptural support for his indictment of his fellow Jews who refuse to accept the message he proclaims. Their rejection leads to its proclamation among the Gentiles.

You shall indeed hear but not understand.
You shall indeed look but never see.
27 Gross is the heart of this people;
they will not hear with their ears;
they have closed their eyes,
so they may not see with their eyes
and hear with their ears
and understand with their heart and be converted,
and I heal them.'
28 [o]Let it be known to you that this salvation
of God has been sent to the Gentiles; they will
listen." **[29*]**
30 *He remained for two full years in his
lodgings. He received all who came to him,
31 and with complete assurance and without
hindrance he proclaimed the kingdom of God
and taught about the Lord Jesus Christ.

o 13, 46; 18, 6; Ps 67, 2; Is 40, 5 LXX; Lk 3, 6.

*

28, 29: The Western text has added here a verse that is not found in the best Greek manuscripts: "And when he had said this, the Jews left, seriously arguing among themselves."

28, 30–31: Although the ending of Acts may seem to be abrupt, Luke has now completed his story with the establishment of Paul and the proclamation of Christianity in Rome. Paul's confident and unhindered proclamation of the gospel in Rome forms the climax to the story whose outline was provided in 1, 8: "You will be my witnesses in Jerusalem . . . and to the ends of the earth."

# NEW TESTAMENT LETTERS

*In the New Testament canon, between the Acts of the Apostles and Revelation, there are twenty-one documents that take the form of letters or epistles. Most of these are actual letters, but some are more like treatises in the guise of a letter. In a few cases even some of the more obvious elements of the letter form are absent; see the Introductions to Hebrews and to 1 John.*

*The virtually standard form found in these documents, though with some variation, is dependent upon the conventions of letter writing common in the ancient world, but these were modified to suit the purposes of Christian writers. The New Testament letters usually begin with a greeting including an identification of the sender or senders and of the recipients. Next comes a prayer, usually in the form of a thanksgiving. The body of the letter provides an exposition of Christian teaching, usually provoked by concrete circumstances, and generally also draws conclusions regarding ethical behavior. There often follows a discussion of practical matters, such as the writer's travel plans, and the letter concludes with further advice and a formula of farewell.*

*Fourteen of the twenty-one letters have been traditionally attributed to Paul. One of these, the Letter to the Hebrews, does not itself claim to be the work of Paul; when it was accepted into the canon after much discussion, it was attached at the very end of the Pauline corpus. The other thirteen identify Paul as their author, but most scholars believe that some of them were actually written by his disciples; see the Introductions to Ephesians, Colossians, 2 Thessalonians, and 1 Timothy.*

*Four of the letters in the Pauline corpus (Ephesians, Philippians, Colossians, and Philemon) are called the "Captivity Epistles" because in each of them the author speaks of being in prison at the time of writing. Three others (1–2 Timothy and Titus) are known as the "Pastoral Epistles" because, addressed to individuals rather than communities, they give advice to disciples about caring for the flock. The letters of the Pauline corpus are arranged in roughly descending order of length from Romans to Philemon, with Hebrews added at the end.*

*The other seven letters of the New Testament that follow the Pauline corpus are collectively referred to as the "Catholic Epistles." This term, which means "universal," refers to the fact that most of them are directed not to a single Christian community, as are most of the Pauline letters, but to a wider audience; see the Introduction to the catholic letters. Three of them (1–2–3 John) are closely related to the fourth gospel and thus belong to the Johannine corpus. The catholic letters, like those of the Pauline corpus, are also arranged in roughly descending order of length, but the three Johannine letters are kept together and Jude is placed at the end.*

*The genuine letters of Paul are earlier in date than any of our written gospels. The dates of the other New Testament letters are more difficult to determine, but for the most part they belong to the second and third Christian generations rather than to the first.*

# THE LETTER TO THE

# ROMANS

## INTRODUCTION

*Of all the letters of Paul, that to the Christians at Rome has long held pride of place. It is the longest and most systematic unfolding of the apostle's thought, expounding the gospel of God's righteousness that saves all who believe (1, 16–17); it reflects a universal outlook, with special implications for Israel's relation to the church (chs 9–11). Yet, like all Paul's letters, Romans too arose out of a specific situation, when the apostle wrote from Greece, likely Corinth, between A.D. 56 and 58 (cf Acts 20, 2–3).*

*Paul at that time was about to leave for Jerusalem with a collection of funds for the impoverished Jewish Christian believers there, taken up from his predominantly Gentile congregations (15, 25–27). He planned then to travel on to Rome and to enlist support there for a mission to Spain (15, 24.28). Such a journey had long been on his mind (1, 9–13; 15, 23). Now, with much missionary preaching successfully accomplished in the East (15, 19), he sought new opportunities in the West (15, 20–21), in order to complete the divine plan of evangelization in the Roman world. Yet he recognized that the visit to Jerusalem would be hazardous (15, 30–32), and we know from Acts that Paul was arrested there and came to Rome only in chains, as a prisoner (Acts 21–28, especially 21, 30–33 and 28, 14.30–31).*

*The existence of a Christian community in Rome antedates Paul's letter there. When it arose, likely within the sizable Jewish population at Rome, and how, we do not know. The Roman historian Suetonius mentions an edict of the Emperor Claudius about A.D. 49 ordering the expulsion of Jews from Rome in connection with a certain "Chrestus," probably involving a dispute in the Jewish community over Jesus as the Messiah ("Christus"). According to Acts 18, 2, Aquila and Priscilla (or Prisca, as in Rom 16, 3) were among those driven out; from them, in Corinth, Paul may have learned about conditions in the church at Rome.*

*Opinions vary as to whether Jewish or Gentile Christians predominated in the house churches (cf 16, 5) in the capital city of the empire at the time Paul wrote. Perhaps already by then Gentile Christians were in the majority. Paul speaks in Romans of both Jews and Gentiles (3, 9.29; see the note on 1, 14). The letter also refers to those "weak in faith" (14, 1) and those "who are strong" (15, 1); this terminology may reflect not so much differences between believers of Jewish and of Gentile background, respectively, as an ascetic tendency in some converts (14, 2) combined with Jewish laws about clean and unclean foods (14, 14.20). The issues were similar to problems that Paul had faced in Corinth (1 Cor 8). If Romans 16 is part of the letter to Rome (see the note on 16, 1–23), then Paul had considerable information about conditions in Rome through all these people there whom he knew, and our letter does not just reflect a generalized picture of an earlier situation in Corinth.*

*In any case, Paul writes to introduce himself and his message to the Christians at Rome, seeking to enlist their support for the proposed mission to Spain. He therefore employs formulations likely familiar to the Christians at Rome; see the note on the confessional material at 1, 3–4 and compare 3, 25–26 and 4, 25. He cites the Old Testament frequently (1, 17; 3, 10–18; ch 4; 9, 7.12–13.15.17.25–29.33; 10, 5–13.15–21; 15, 9–12). The gospel Paul presents is meant to be a familiar one to those in Rome, even though they heard it first from other preachers.*

*As the outline below shows, this gospel of Paul (see 16, 25) finds its center in salvation and justification through faith in Christ (1, 16–17). While God's wrath is revealed against all sin and wickedness of Gentile and Jew alike (1, 18—3, 20), God's power to save by divine righteous or justifying action in Christ is also revealed (1, 16–17; 3, 21—5, 21). The consequences and implications for those who believe are set forth (6, 1—8, 39), as are results for those in Israel (chs 9–11) who, to Paul's great sorrow (9, 1–5), disbelieve. The apostle's hope is that, just as rejection of the gospel by some in Israel has led to a ministry of salvation for non-Jews, so one day, in God's mercy, "all Israel" will be saved (11, 11–15.25–29.30– 32). The fuller ethical response of believers is also drawn out, both with reference to life in Christ's body (ch 12) and with regard to the world (13, 1–7), on the basis of the eschatological situation (13, 11–14) and conditions in the community (14, 1—15, 13).*

*Others have viewed Romans more in the light of Paul's earlier, quite polemical Letter to the Galatians and so see the theme as the relationship between Judaism and Christianity, a topic judged to be much in the minds of the Roman Christians. Each of these religious faiths claimed to be the way of salvation based upon a covenant between God and a people chosen and made the beneficiary of divine gifts. But Christianity regarded itself as the prophetic development and fulfillment of the faith of the Old Testament, declaring that the preparatory Mosaic covenant must now give way to the new and more perfect covenant in Jesus Christ. Paul himself had been the implacable advocate of freedom of Gentiles from the laws of the Mosaic covenant and, especially in Galatia, had refused to allow attempts to impose them on Gentile converts to the gospel. He had witnessed the personal hostilities that developed between the adherents of the two faiths and had written his strongly worded letter to the Galatians against those Jewish Christians who were seeking to persuade Gentile Christians to adopt the religious practices of Judaism. For him, the purity of the religious understanding of Jesus as the source of salvation would be seriously impaired if Gentile Christians were obligated to amalgamate the two religious faiths.*

*Still others find the theme of Israel and the church as expressed in Romans 9–11 to be the heart of Romans. Then the implication of Paul's exposition of justification by faith rather than by means of law is that the divine plan of salvation works itself out on a broad theological plane to include the whole of humanity, despite the differences in the content of the given religious system to which a human culture is heir. Romans presents a plan of salvation stretching from Adam through Abraham and Moses to Christ (chs 4 and 5) and on to the future revelation at Christ's parousia (8, 18–25). Its outlook is universal.*

*Paul's Letter to the Romans is a powerful exposition of the doctrine of the supremacy of Christ and of faith in Christ as the source of salvation. It is an implicit plea to the Christians at Rome, and to all Christians, to hold fast to that faith. They are to resist any pressure put on them to accept a doctrine of salvation through works of the law (see the note on 10, 4). At the same time they are not to exaggerate Christian freedom as an abdication of responsibility for others (12, 1–2) or as a repudiation of God's law and will (see the notes on 3, 9–26; 3, 31; 7, 7–12.13–25).*

*The principal divisions of the Letter to the Romans are the following:*

*I. Address (1, 1–15)*
*II. Humanity Lost without the Gospel (1, 16—3, 20)*
*III. Justification through Faith in Christ (3, 21—5, 21)*
*IV. Justification and the Christian Life (6, 1—8, 39)*
*V. Jews and Gentiles in God's Plan (9, 1—11, 36)*
*VI. The Duties of Christians (12, 1—15, 13)*
*VII. Conclusion (15, 14—16, 27)*

## *I: ADDRESS*

### CHAPTER 1

**Greeting** **1** [a]*Paul, a slave of Christ Jesus,
called to be an apostle and set apart for the
gospel of God, **2** [b]which he promised previously through his prophets in the holy scriptures,
**3** [c]*the gospel about his Son, descended from
David according to the flesh, **4** [d]but established
as Son of God in power according to the spirit
of holiness through resurrection from the dead,
Jesus Christ our Lord. **5** [e]*Through him we
have received the grace of apostleship, to bring
about the obedience of faith, for the sake of his
name, among all the Gentiles, **6** [f]among whom
are you also, who are called to belong to Jesus
Christ; **7** [g]*to all the beloved of God in Rome,
called to be holy. Grace to you and peace from
God our Father and the Lord Jesus Christ.

**Thanksgiving** **8** [h]*First, I give thanks to
my God through Jesus Christ for all of you,
because your faith is heralded throughout the
world. **9** [i]God is my witness, whom I serve
with my spirit in proclaiming the gospel of his
Son, that I remember you constantly,
**10** [j]*always asking in my prayers that somehow by God's will I may at last find my way
clear to come to you. **11** [k]For I long to see you,
that I may share with you some spiritual gift so
that you may be strengthened, **12** that is, that
you and I may be mutually encouraged by one
another's faith, yours and mine. **13** [l]*I do not
want you to be unaware, brothers, that I often
planned to come to you, though I was prevented
until now, that I might harvest some fruit among
you, too, as among the rest of the Gentiles.
**14** *To Greeks and non-Greeks alike, to the
wise and the ignorant, I am under obligation;
**15** [m]that is why I am eager to preach the gospel
also to you in Rome.

a Gal 1, 10; Phil 1, 1; Jas 1, 1 / Acts 9, 15; 13, 2; 1 Cor 1, 1; Gal 1, 15; Ti 1, 1.
b 16, 25-26; Ti 1, 2.
c 9, 5; 2 Sm 7, 12; Mt 1, 1; Mk 12, 35; Jn 7, 42; Acts 13, 22-23;2 Tm 2, 8; Rv 22, 16.
d 10, 9; Acts 13, 33; Phil 3, 10.
e 15, 15; Gal 2, 7.9 / 15, 18; Acts 9, 15; 26, 16-18; Gal 1, 16; 2, 7.9.
f 1 Cor 1, 9.
g Nm 6, 25-26; 1 Cor 1, 2-3; 2 Cor 1, 1-2.
h 16, 19; 1 Thes 1, 8.
i 2 Cor 1, 23; Eph 1, 16; Phil 1, 8; 1 Thes 1, 2; 2, 5.10;2 Tm 1, 3.
j 15, 23.32; Acts 18, 21; 1 Cor 4, 19; 1 Thes 2, 17.
k 1 Thes 2, 17; 3, 10.
l 15, 22; Jn 15, 16; Acts 19, 21.
m Acts 28, 30-31.

*

1, 1–7: In Paul's letters the greeting or *praescriptio* follows a standard form, though with variations. It is based upon the common Greco-Roman epistolary practice, but with the addition of Semitic and specifically Christian elements. The three basic components are: name of sender; name of addressee; greeting. In identifying himself, Paul often adds phrases to describe his apostolic mission; this element is more developed in Rom than in any other letter. Elsewhere he associates co-workers with himself in the greeting: Sosthenes (1 Cor), Timothy (2 Cor; Phil; Phlm), Silvanus (1–2 Thes). The standard secular greeting was the infinitive *chairein,* "greetings." Paul uses instead the similar-sounding *charis,* "grace," together with the Semitic greeting *šālôm* (Greek *eirēnē*), "peace." These gifts, foreshadowed in God's dealings with Israel (see Nm 6, 24–26), have been poured out abundantly in Christ, and Paul wishes them to his readers. In Rom the Pauline *praescriptio* is expanded and expressed in a formal tone; it emphasizes Paul's office as apostle to the Gentiles. Verses 3–4 stress the gospel or kerygma, v 2 the fulfillment of God's promise, and vv 1 and 5 Paul's office. On his call, see Gal 1, 15–16; 1 Cor 9, 1; 15, 8–10; Acts 9, 1–22; 22, 3–16; 26, 4–18.

1, 1: *Slave of Christ Jesus:* Paul applies the term slave to himself in order to express his undivided allegiance to the Lord of the church, the Master of all, including slaves and masters. "No one can serve (i.e., be a slave to) two masters," said Jesus (Mt 6, 24). It is this aspect of the slave-master relationship rather than its degrading implications that Paul emphasizes when he discusses Christian commitment.

1, 3–4: Paul here cites an early confession that proclaims Jesus' sonship as messianic descendant of David (cf Mt 22, 42; 2 Tm 2, 8; Rv 22, 16) and as Son of God by the resurrection. As "life-giving spirit" (1 Cor 15, 45), Jesus Christ is able to communicate the Spirit to those who believe in him.

1, 5: Paul recalls his apostolic office, implying that the Romans know something of his history. *The obedience of faith:* as Paul will show at length in chs 6–8 and 12–15, faith in God's justifying action in Jesus Christ relates one to God's gift of the new life that is made possible through the death and resurrection of Jesus Christ and the activity of the holy Spirit (see especially 8, 1–11).

1, 7: *Called to be holy:* Paul often refers to Christians as "the holy ones" or "the saints." The Israelite community was called a "holy assembly" because they had been separated for the worship and service of the Lord (see Lv 11, 44; 23, 1–44). The Christian community regarded its members as sanctified by baptism (6, 22; 15, 16; 1 Cor 6, 11; Eph 5, 26–27). Christians are called to holiness (1 Cor 1, 2; 1 Thes 4, 7), that is, they are called to make their lives conform to the gift they have already received.

1, 8: In Greco-Roman letters, the greeting was customarily followed by a prayer. The Pauline letters usually include this element (except Gal and Ti), expressed in Christian thanksgiving formulas and usually stating the principal theme of the letter. In 2 Cor the thanksgiving becomes a blessing, and in Eph it is preceded by a lengthy blessing. Sometimes the thanksgiving is blended into the body of the letter, especially in 1 Thes. In Rom it is stated briefly.

1, 10–12: Paul lays the groundwork for his more detailed statement in 15, 22–24 about his projected visit to Rome.

1, 13: *Brothers* is idiomatic for all Paul's "kin in Christ," all those who believe in the gospel; it includes women as well as men (cf 4, 3).

1, 14: *Greeks and non-Greeks:* literally, "Greeks and barbarians." As a result of Alexander's conquests, Greek became the standard international language of the Mediterranean world. *Greeks* in Paul's statement therefore means people who know Greek or who have been influenced by Greek culture. *Non-Greeks* were people whose cultures remained substantially unaffected by Greek influences. Greeks called such people "barbarians" (cf Acts 28, 2), meaning people whose speech was foreign. Roman citizens would scarcely classify themselves as such, and Nero, who was reigning when Paul wrote this letter, prided himself on his admiration for Greek culture. *Under obligation:* Paul will expand on the theme of obligation in 13, 8; 15, 1.27.

## *II: HUMANITY LOST WITHOUT THE GOSPEL*

**God's Power for Salvation** 16 [n]*For I
am not ashamed of the gospel. It is the power
of God for the salvation of everyone who believes: for Jew first, and then Greek. 17 [o]*For
in it is revealed the righteousness of God from
faith to faith; as it is written, "The one who is
righteous by faith will live."

**Punishment of Idolators** 18 [p]*The wrath
of God is indeed being revealed from heaven
against every impiety and wickedness of those
who suppress the truth by their wickedness.
19 [q]For what can be known about God is evident to them, because God made it evident to
them. 20 [r]Ever since the creation of the world,
his invisible attributes of eternal power and
divinity have been able to be understood and
perceived in what he has made. As a result, they
have no excuse; 21 [s]for although they knew
God they did not accord him glory as God or
give him thanks. Instead, they became vain in
their reasoning, and their senseless minds were
darkened. 22 [t]While claiming to be wise, they
became fools 23 [u]and exchanged the glory of
the immortal God for the likeness of an image
of mortal man or of birds or of four-legged
animals or of snakes.

24 [v]*Therefore, God handed them over to
impurity through the lusts of their hearts for the
mutual degradation of their bodies. 25 [w]They
exchanged the truth of God for a lie and revered
and worshiped the creature rather than the creator, who is blessed forever. Amen. 26 Therefore, God handed them over to degrading passions. Their females exchanged natural
relations for unnatural, 27 [x]and the males likewise gave up natural relations with females and
burned with lust for one another. Males did
shameful things with males and thus received in
their own persons the due penalty for their perversity. 28 And since they did not see fit to
acknowledge God, God handed them over to
their undiscerning mind to do what is improper.
29 [y]They are filled with every form of wickedness, evil, greed, and malice; full of envy, murder, rivalry, treachery, and spite. They are gossips 30 and scandalmongers and they hate God.
They are insolent, haughty, boastful, ingenious
in their wickedness, and rebellious toward their
parents. 31 They are senseless, faithless, heart-
less, ruthless. 32 [z]Although they know the just
decree of God that all who practice such things
deserve death, they not only do them but give
approval to those who practice them.

---

n Ps 119, 46; 1 Cor 1, 18.24 / 2, 9; Acts 3, 26; 13, 46.
o 3, 21-22; Hb 2, 4; Gal 3, 11; Heb 10, 38.
p 2, 5.8-9; Is 66, 15; Eph 5, 6; Col 3, 6.
q Wis 13-19; Acts 14, 15-17; 17, 23-29.
r Jb 12, 7-9; Pss 8, 4; 19, 2; Sir 17, 7-9; Is 40, 26; Acts 14, 17;17, 25-28.
s Eph 4, 17-18.
t Wis 13, 1-9; Is 5, 21; Jer 10, 14; Acts 17, 29-30;1 Cor 1, 19-21.
u Dt 4, 15-19; Ps 106, 20; Wis 11, 15; 12, 24; 13, 10-19;Jer 2, 11.
v Wis 12, 25; 14, 22-31; Acts 7, 41-42; Eph 4, 19.
w 9, 5; Jer 13, 25-27.
x Lv 18, 22; 20, 13; Wis 14, 26; 1 Cor 6, 9; 1 Tm 1, 10.
y 13, 13; Mt 15, 19; Mk 7, 21-22; Gal 5, 19-21; 2 Tm 3, 2-4.
z Acts 8, 1; 2 Thes 2, 12.

---

*

1, 16–17: The principal theme of the letter is salvation through faith. *I am not ashamed of the gospel:* Paul is not ashamed to proclaim the gospel, despite the criticism that Jews and Gentiles leveled against the proclamation of the crucified savior; cf 1 Cor 1, 23–24. Paul affirms, however, that it is precisely through the crucifixion and resurrection of Jesus that God's saving will and power become manifest. *Jew first* (cf 2, 9–10) means that Jews especially, in view of the example of Abraham (ch 4), ought to be the leaders in the response of faith.

1, 17: *In it is revealed the righteousness of God from faith to faith:* the gospel centers in Jesus Christ, in whom God's saving presence and righteousness in history have been made known. Faith is affirmation of the basic purpose and meaning of the Old Testament as proclamation of divine promise (2; 4, 13) and exposure of the inability of humanity to effect its salvation even through covenant law. Faith is the gift of the holy Spirit and denotes acceptance of salvation as God's righteousness, that is, God's gift of a renewed relationship in forgiveness and power for a new life. Faith is response to God's total claim on people and their destiny. *The one who is righteous by faith will live:* see the note on Hb 2, 4.

1, 18—3, 20: Paul aims to show that all humanity is in a desperate plight and requires God's special intervention if it is to be saved.

1, 18–32: In this passage Paul uses themes and rhetoric common in Jewish-Hellenistic mission proclamation (cf Wis 13, 1—14, 31) to indict especially the non-Jewish world. The close association of idolatry and immorality is basic, but the generalization needs in all fairness to be balanced against the fact that non-Jewish Christian society on many levels displayed moral attitudes and performance whose quality would challenge much of contemporary Christian culture. Romans themselves expressed abhorrence over devotion accorded to animals in Egypt. Paul's main point is that the wrath of God does not await the end of the world but goes into action at each present moment in humanity's history when misdirected piety serves as a facade for self-interest.

1, 18: *The wrath of God:* God's reaction to human sinfulness, an Old Testament phrase that expresses the irreconcilable opposition between God and evil (see Is 9, 11.16.18.20; 10, 4; 30, 27). It is not contrary to God's universal love for his creatures, but condemns Israel's turning aside from the covenant obligations. Hosea depicts Yahweh as suffering intensely at the thought of having to punish Israel (Hos 11, 8–9). God's wrath was to be poured forth especially on the "Day of Yahweh" and thus took on an eschatological connotation (see Zep 1, 15).

1, 24: In order to expose the depth of humanity's rebellion against the Creator, *God handed them over to impurity through the lusts of their hearts.* Instead of curbing people's evil interests, God abandoned them to self-indulgence, thereby removing the facade of apparent conformity to the divine will. Subsequently Paul will show that the Mosaic law produces the same effect; cf 5, 20; 7, 13–24. The divine judgment expressed here is related to the theme of hardness of heart described in 9, 17–18.

## CHAPTER 2

**God's Just Judgment** 1 [a]*Therefore,
you are without excuse, every one of you who
passes judgment. For by the standard by which
you judge another you condemn yourself, since
you, the judge, do the very same things. 2 We
know that the judgment of God on those who do
such things is true. 3 [b]Do you suppose, then,
you who judge those who engage in such things
and yet do them yourself, that you will escape
the judgment of God? 4 [c]Or do you hold his
priceless kindness, forbearance, and patience in
low esteem, unaware that the kindness of God
would lead you to repentance? 5 [d]By your stubbornness and impenitent heart, you are storing
up wrath for yourself for the day of wrath and
revelation of the just judgment of God,
6 [e]*who will repay everyone according to his
works: 7 eternal life to those who seek glory,
honor, and immortality through perseverance in
good works, 8 [f]but wrath and fury to those who
selfishly disobey the truth and obey wickedness.
9 Yes, affliction and distress will come upon
every human being who does evil, Jew first and
then Greek. 10 [g]But there will be glory, honor,
and peace for everyone who does good, Jew
first and then Greek. 11 [h]*There is no partiality
with God.

**Judgment by the Interior Law** 12 [i]*All
who sin outside the law will also perish without
reference to it, and all who sin under the law
will be judged in accordance with it. 13 [j]For it
is not those who hear the law who are just in the
sight of God; rather, those who observe the law
will be justified. 14 [k]For when the Gentiles
who do not have the law by nature observe the
prescriptions of the law, they are a law for themselves even though they do not have the law.
15 *They show that the demands of the law are
written in their hearts, while their conscience
also bears witness and their conflicting thoughts
accuse or even defend them 16 [l]on the day
when, according to my gospel, God will judge
people's hidden works through Christ Jesus.

**Judgment by the Mosaic Law**
17 [m]*Now if you call yourself a Jew and rely
on the law and boast of God 18 [n]and know his
will and are able to discern what is important
since you are instructed from the law, 19 [o]and
if you are confident that you are a guide for the
blind and a light for those in darkness, 20 [p]that
you are a trainer of the foolish and teacher of the
simple, because in the law you have the formulation of knowledge and truth— 21 [q]then you
who teach another, are you failing to teach yourself? You who preach against stealing, do you
steal? 22 You who forbid adultery, do you
commit adultery? You who detest idols, do you
rob temples? 23 You who boast of the law, do
you dishonor God by breaking the law?
24 [r]*For, as it is written, "Because of you the
name of God is reviled among the Gentiles."
25 [s][t]Circumcision, to be sure, has value if
you observe the law; but if you break the law,
your circumcision has become uncircumcision.
26 [u]Again, if an uncircumcised man keeps the
precepts of the law, will he not be considered
circumcised? 27 Indeed, those who are physically uncircumcised but carry out the law will
pass judgment on you, with your written law
and circumcision, who break the law. 28 [v]One
is not a Jew outwardly. True circumcision is not

a Mt 7, 1-2.
b Wis 16, 15-16.
c 3, 25-26; 9, 22; Wis 11, 23; 15, 1; 2 Pt 3, 9.15.
d Ex 33, 3; Acts 7, 51; Rv 6, 17; 11, 18.
e Ps 62, 12; Prv 24, 12; Sir 16, 14; Mt 16, 27; Jn 5, 29;2 Cor 5, 10.
f 2 Thes 1, 8.
g 1, 16; 3, 9.
h Dt 10, 17; 2 Chr 19, 7; Sir 35, 12-13; Acts 10, 34; Gal 2, 6;Eph 6, 9; Col 3, 25; 1 Pt 1, 17.
i 3, 19.
j Mt 7, 21; Lk 6, 46-49; 8, 21; Jas 1, 22-25; 1 Jn 3, 7.
k Acts 10, 35.
l Acts 10, 42; 17, 31.
m Is 48, 1-2; Mi 3, 11; Phil 3, 4-6.
n Phil 1, 10.
o Mt 15, 14; Lk 6, 39.
p 2 Tm 3, 15.
q Ps 50, 16-21; Mt 23, 3-4.
r Is 52, 5; Ez 36, 20; 2 Pt 2, 2.
s Jer 4, 4; 9, 24-25.
t 1 Cor 7, 19; Gal 5, 3.
u Gal 5, 6.
v Jn 7, 24; 8, 15.39.

*

2, 1—3, 20: After his general indictment of the Gentile, Paul shows that in spite of special revelation Jews enjoy no advantage in moral status before God (3, 1–8). With the entire human race now declared guilty before God (3, 9–20), Paul will then be able to display the solution for the total problem: salvation through God's redemptive work that is revealed in Christ Jesus for all who believe (3, 21–31).

2, 1–11: As a first step in his demonstration that Jews enjoy no real moral supremacy over Gentiles, Paul explains that the final judgment will be a review of performance, not of privilege. From this perspective Gentiles stand on an equal footing with Jews, and Jews cannot condemn the sins of Gentiles without condemning themselves.

2, 6: *Will repay everyone according to his works:* Paul reproduces the Septuagint text of Ps 62, 12 and Prv 24, 12.

2, 11: *No partiality with God:* this sentence is not at variance with the statements in vv 9–10. Since Jews are the first to go under indictment, it is only fair that they be given first consideration in the distribution of blessings. Basic, of course, is the understanding that God accepts no bribes (Dt 10, 17).

2, 12–16: Jews cannot reasonably demand from Gentiles the standard of conduct inculcated in the Old Testament since God did not address its revelation to them. Rather, God made it possible for Gentiles to know instinctively the difference between right and wrong. But, as Paul explained in 1, 18–32, humanity misread the evidence of God's existence, power, and divinity, and "while claiming to be wise, they became fools" (1, 22).

2, 15: Paul expands on the thought of Jer 31, 33; Wis 17, 11.

2, 17–29: Mere possession of laws is no evidence of virtue. By eliminating circumcision as an elitist moral sign, Paul clears away the last obstacle to his presentation of justification through faith without claims based on the receipt of circumcision and its attendant legal obligations.

2, 24: According to Is 52, 5 the suffering of Israel prompts her enemies to revile God. Paul uses the passage in support of his point that the present immorality of Israelites is the cause of such defamation.

outward, in the flesh. **29** [w]Rather, one is a Jew
inwardly, and circumcision is of the heart, in the
spirit, not the letter; his praise is not from human
beings but from God.

## CHAPTER 3

**Answers to Objections** **1** *What advantage is there then in being a Jew? Or what is the
value of circumcision? **2** [x]Much, in every respect. [For] in the first place, they were entrusted with the utterances of God. **3** [y]What if some
were unfaithful? Will their infidelity nullify the
fidelity of God? **4** [z]*Of course not! God must
be true, though every human being is a liar, as
it is written:

"That you may be justified in your words,
and conquer when you are judged."

**5** [a]But if our wickedness provides proof of
God's righteousness, what can we say? Is God
unjust, humanly speaking, to inflict his wrath?
**6** Of course not! For how else is God to judge
the world? **7** But if God's truth redounds to his
glory through my falsehood, why am I still being condemned as a sinner? **8** [b]And why not
say—as we are accused and as some claim we
say—that we should do evil that good may come
of it? Their penalty is what they deserve.

**Universal Bondage to Sin** **9** [c]*Well,
then, are we better off? Not entirely, for we
have already brought the charge against Jews
and Greeks alike that they are all under the
domination of sin, **10** [d]as it is written:

"There is no one just, not one,
**11** there is no one who understands,
there is no one who seeks God.
**12** All have gone astray; all alike are worthless;
there is not one who does good,
[there is not] even one.
**13** [e]Their throats are open graves;
they deceive with their tongues;
the venom of asps is on their lips;
**14** [f]their mouths are full of bitter cursing.
**15** [g]Their feet are quick to shed blood;
**16** ruin and misery are in their ways,
**17** and the way of peace they know not.
**18** [h]There is no fear of God before their
eyes."

**19** [i]*Now we know that what the law says is
addressed to those under the law, so that every
mouth may be silenced and the whole world
stand accountable to God, **20** [j]*since no human
being will be justified in his sight by observing
the law; for through the law comes consciousness of sin.

## *III: JUSTIFICATION THROUGH FAITH IN CHRIST*

**Justification apart from the Law**
**21** [k]*But now the righteousness of God has
been manifested apart from the law, though testified to by the law and the prophets, **22** [l]the
righteousness of God through faith in Jesus
Christ for all who believe. For there is no distinction; **23** [m]all have sinned and are deprived
of the glory of God. **24** [n]They are justified
freely by his grace through the redemption in

w Dt 30, 6; Jer 4, 4; 9, 25; Col 2, 11 / 1 Cor 4, 5; 2 Cor 10, 18.
x 9, 4; Dt 4, 7-8; Pss 103, 7; 147, 19-20.
y 9, 6; 11, 1.29; Ps 89, 30-37; 2 Tm 2, 13.
z Ps 116, 11 / Ps 51, 6.
a 9, 14; Jb 34, 12-17.
b 6, 1.
c 1, 18—2, 25; 3, 23; Sir 8, 5.
d Pss 14, 1-3; 53, 2-4; Eccl 7, 20.
e Pss 5, 10; 140, 4.
f Ps 10, 7.
g Prv 1, 16; Is 59, 7-8.
h Ps 36, 2.
i 7, 7.
j Ps 143, 2; Gal 2, 16 / 7, 7.
k Is 51, 6-8; Acts 10, 43.
l 1, 17; Gal 2, 16; Phil 3, 9.
m 3, 9; 5, 12.
n Eph 2, 8; Ti 3, 7 / 5, 1-2; Eph 1, 7.

*

3, 1–4: In keeping with the popular style of diatribe, Paul responds to the objection that his teaching on the sinfulness of all humanity detracts from the religious prerogatives of Israel. He stresses that Jews have remained the vehicle of God's revelation despite their sins, though this depends on the fidelity of God.

3, 4: *Though every human being is a liar:* these words reproduce the Greek text of Ps 116, 11. The rest of the verse is from Ps 51, 6.

3, 9–20: *Well, then, are we better off?:* this phrase can also be translated "Are we at a disadvantage?" but the latter version does not substantially change the overall meaning of the passage. Having explained that Israel's privileged status is guaranteed by God's fidelity, Paul now demonstrates the infidelity of the Jews by a catena of citations from scripture, possibly derived from an existing collection of *testimonia.* These texts show that all human beings share the common burden of sin. They are linked together by mention of organs of the body: throat, tongue, lips, mouth, feet, eyes.

3, 19: *The law:* Paul here uses the term in its broadest sense to mean all of the scriptures; none of the preceding texts is from the Torah or Pentateuch.

3, 20: *No human being will be justified in his sight:* these words are freely cited from Ps 143, 2. In place of the psalmist's "no living person," Paul substitutes "no human being" (literally "no flesh," a Hebraism), and he adds "by observing the law."

3, 21–31: These verses provide a clear statement of Paul's "gospel," i.e., the principle of justification by faith in Christ. God has found a means of rescuing humanity from its desperate plight: Paul's general term for this divine initiative is the righteousness of God (21). Divine mercy declares the guilty innocent and makes them so. God does this not as a result of the law but apart from it (21), and not because of any merit in human beings but through forgiveness of their sins (24), in virtue of the redemption wrought in Christ Jesus for all who believe (22.24–25). God has manifested his righteousness in the coming of Jesus Christ, whose saving activity inaugurates a new era in human history.

3, 21: *But now:* Paul adopts a common phrase used by Greek authors to describe movement from disaster to prosperity. The expressions indicate that vv 21–26 are the consolatory answer to vv 9–20.

Christ Jesus, **25** [o]*whom God set forth as an
expiation, through faith, by his blood, to prove
his righteousness because of the forgiveness of
sins previously committed, **26** through the forbearance of God—to prove his righteousness in
the present time, that he might be righteous and
justify the one who has faith in Jesus.

**27** [p]*What occasion is there then for boasting? It is ruled out. On what principle, that of
works? No, rather on the principle of faith.
**28** [q]For we consider that a person is justified by
faith apart from works of the law. **29** [r]Does
God belong to Jews alone? Does he not belong
to Gentiles, too? Yes, also to Gentiles, **30** [s]for
God is one and will justify the circumcised on
the basis of faith and the uncircumcised through
faith. **31** [t]*Are we then annulling the law by
this faith? Of course not! On the contrary, we
are supporting the law.

## CHAPTER 4

### Abraham Justified by Faith

**1** [u]*What
then can we say that Abraham found, our ancestor according to the flesh? **2** *Indeed, if Abraham was justified on the basis of his works, he
has reason to boast; but this was not so in the
sight of God. **3** [v]*For what does the scripture
say? "Abraham believed God, and it was credited to him as righteousness." **4** [w]A worker's
wage is credited not as a gift, but as something
due. **5** But when one does not work, yet believes in the one who justifies the ungodly, his
faith is credited as righteousness. **6** So also David declares the blessedness of the person to
whom God credits righteousness apart from
works:

**7** [x]"Blessed are they whose iniquities are
forgiven
and whose sins are covered.
**8** Blessed is the man whose sin the Lord does
not record."

**9** [y]*Does this blessedness apply only to the
circumcised, or to the uncircumcised as well?
Now we assert that "faith was credited to Abraham as righteousness." **10** Under what circumstances was it credited? Was he circumcised or
not? He was not circumcised, but uncircumcised. **11** [z]And he received the sign of circumcision as a seal on the righteousness received
through faith while he was uncircumcised. Thus
he was to be the father of all the uncircumcised
who believe, so that to them [also] righteousness might be credited, **12** as well as the father
of the circumcised who not only are circumcised, but also follow the path of faith that our
father Abraham walked while still uncircumcised.

### Inheritance through Faith

**13** [a]It was not
through the law that the promise was made to
Abraham and his descendants that he would
inherit the world, but through the righteousness
that comes from faith. **14** [b]For if those who
adhere to the law are the heirs, faith is null and
the promise is void. **15** [c]*For the law produces
wrath; but where there is no law, neither is there

o Lv 16, 12-15; Acts 17, 31; 1 Jn 4, 10.
p 8, 2; 1 Cor 1, 29-31.
q 5, 1; Gal 2, 16.
r 10, 12.
s Dt 6, 4; Gal 3, 20; Jas 2, 19 / 4, 11-12.
t 8, 4; Mt 5, 17.
u Gal 3, 6-9.
v Gn 15, 6; Gal 3, 6; Jas 2, 14.20-24.
w 11, 6.
x Ps 32, 1-2.
y 4, 3.
z Gn 17, 10-11; Gal 3, 6-8.
a Gn 12, 7; 18, 18; 22, 17-18; Sir 44, 21; Gal 3, 16-18.29.
b Gal 3, 18.
c 3, 20; 5, 13; 7, 8; Gal 3, 19.

*

3, 25: *Expiation:* this rendering is preferable to "propitiation," which suggests hostility on the part of God toward sinners. As Paul will be at pains to point out (5, 8–10), it is humanity that is hostile to God.

3, 27–31: People cannot boast of their own holiness, since it is God's free gift (27), both to the Jew who practices circumcision out of faith and to the Gentile who accepts faith without the Old Testament religious culture symbolized by circumcision (29–30).

3, 27: *Principle of faith:* literally, "law of faith." Paul is fond of wordplay involving the term "law"; cf 7, 21.23; 8, 2. Since "law" in Greek may also connote "custom" or "principle," his readers and hearers would have sensed no contradiction in the use of the term after the negative statement concerning law in v 20.

3, 31: *We are supporting the law:* giving priority to God's intentions. God is the ultimate source of law, and the essence of law is fairness. On the basis of the Mosaic covenant, God's justice is in question if those who sinned against the law are permitted to go free (see 23–26). In order to rescue all humanity rather than condemn it, God thinks of an alternative: the law or "principle" of faith (27). What can be more fair than to admit everyone into the divine presence on the basis of forgiveness grasped by faith? Indeed, this principle of faith antedates the Mosaic law, as Paul will demonstrate in ch 4, and does not therefore mark a change in divine policy.

4, 1–25: This is an expanded treatment of the significance of Abraham's faith, which Paul discusses in Gal 3, 6–18; see the notes there.

4, 2–5: Verse 2 corresponds to v 4, and v 3 to v 5. The Greek term here rendered *credited* means "made an entry." The context determines whether it is credit or debit. Verse 8 speaks of "recording sin" as a debit. Paul's repeated use of accountants' terminology in this and other passages can be traced both to the Old Testament texts he quotes and to his business activity as a tentmaker. The commercial term in Gn 15, 6, "credited it to him," reminds Paul in vv 7–8 of Ps 32, 2, in which the same term is used and applied to forgiveness of sins. Thus Paul is able to argue that Abraham's faith involved receipt of forgiveness of sins and that all believers benefit as he did through faith.

4, 3: Jas 2, 24 appears to conflict with Paul's statement. However, James combats the error of extremists who used the doctrine of justification through faith as a screen for moral self-determination. Paul discusses the subject of holiness in greater detail than does James and beginning with ch 6 shows how justification through faith introduces one to the gift of a new life in Christ through the power of the holy Spirit.

4, 9: *Blessedness:* evidence of divine favor.

4, 15: Law has the negative function of bringing the deep-seated rebellion against God to the surface in specific sins; see the note on 1, 18–32.

violation. **16** [d]For this reason, it depends on faith, so that it may be a gift, and the promise may be guaranteed to all his descendants, not to those who only adhere to the law but to those who follow the faith of Abraham, who is the father of all of us, **17** [e]as it is written, "I have made you father of many nations." He is our father in the sight of God, in whom he believed, who gives life to the dead and calls into being what does not exist. **18** [f]He believed, hoping against hope, that he would become "the father of many nations," according to what was said, "Thus shall your descendants be." **19** [g]He did not weaken in faith when he considered his own body as [already] dead (for he was almost a hundred years old) and the dead womb of Sarah. **20** *He did not doubt God's promise in unbelief; rather, he was empowered by faith and gave glory to God **21** [h]and was fully convinced that what he had promised he was also able to do. **22** [i]That is why "it was credited to him as righteousness." **23** But it was not for him alone that it was written that "it was credited to him"; **24** [j]it was also for us, to whom it will be credited, who believe in the one who raised Jesus our Lord from the dead, **25** [k]who was handed over for our transgressions and was raised for our justification.

## CHAPTER 5

**Faith, Hope, and Love** 1 [l]*Therefore, since we have been justified by faith, we have peace with God through our Lord Jesus Christ, **2** [m]through whom we have gained access [by faith] to this grace in which we stand, and we boast in hope of the glory of God. **3** Not only that, but we even boast of our afflictions, knowing that affliction produces endurance, **4** [n]and endurance, proven character, and proven character, hope, **5** [o]and hope does not disappoint, because the love of God has been poured out into our hearts through the holy Spirit that has been given to us. **6** For Christ, while we were still helpless, yet died at the appointed time for the ungodly. **7** *Indeed, only with difficulty does one die for a just person, though perhaps for a good person one might even find courage to die. **8** [p]But God proves his love for us in that while we were still sinners Christ died for us. **9** [q]How much more then, since we are now justified by his blood, will we be saved through him from the wrath. **10** [r]Indeed, if, while we were enemies, we were reconciled to God through the death of his Son, how much more, once reconciled, will we be saved by his life. **11** Not only that, but we also boast of God through our Lord Jesus Christ, through whom we have now received reconciliation.

**Humanity's Sin through Adam**

**12** [s]*Therefore, just as through one person sin entered the world, and through sin, death, and thus death came to all, inasmuch as all sinned— **13** [t]for up to the time of the law, sin was in the world, though sin is not accounted when there is no law. **14** [u]But death reigned from Adam to Moses, even over those who did not sin after the pattern of the trespass of Adam, who is the type of the one who was to come.

---

d Sir 44, 19; Gal 3, 7-9.
e Gn 17, 5; Heb 11, 19 / Is 48, 13.
f Gn 15, 5.
g Gn 17, 17; Heb 11, 11.
h Gn 18, 14; Lk 1, 37.
i Gn 15, 6.
j 10, 9; 1 Pt 1, 21.
k Is 53, 4-5.12; 1 Cor 15, 17; 1 Pt 1, 3 / 8, 11.
l 3, 24-28; Gal 2, 16.
m Eph 2, 18; 3, 12.
n 2 Cor 12, 9-10; Jas 1, 2-4; 1 Pt 1, 5-7; 4, 12-14.
o 8, 14-16; Pss 22, 5-6; 25, 20.
p Jn 3, 16; 1 Jn 4, 10.19.
q 1, 18; 1 Thes 1, 10.
r 8, 7-8; 2 Cor 5, 18; Col 1, 21-22.
s Gn 2, 17; 3, 1-19; Wis 2, 24 / 3, 19.23.
t 4, 15.
u 1 Cor 15, 21.

*

4, 20: *He did not doubt God's promise in unbelief:* any doubts Abraham might have had were resolved in commitment to God's promise. Heb 11, 8–12 emphasizes the faith of Abraham and Sarah.

5, 1–11: Popular piety frequently construed reverses and troubles as punishment for sin; cf Jn 9, 2. Paul therefore assures believers that God's justifying action in Jesus Christ is a declaration of peace. The crucifixion of Jesus Christ displays God's initiative in certifying humanity for unimpeded access into the divine presence. Reconciliation is God's gift of pardon to the entire human race. Through faith one benefits personally from this pardon or, in Paul's term, is justified. The ultimate aim of God is to liberate believers from the pre-Christian self as described in chs 1–3. Since this liberation will first find completion in the believer's resurrection, salvation is described as future in 5, 10. Because this fullness of salvation belongs to the future it is called the Christian hope. Paul's Greek term for hope does not, however, suggest a note of uncertainty, to the effect: "I wonder whether God really means it." Rather, God's promise in the gospel fills believers with expectation and anticipation for the climactic gift of unalloyed commitment in the holy Spirit to the performance of the will of God. The persecutions that attend Christian commitment are to teach believers patience and to strengthen this hope, which will not disappoint them because the holy Spirit dwells in their hearts and imbues them with God's love (5).

5, 1: *We have peace:* a number of manuscripts, versions, and church Fathers read "Let us have peace"; cf 14, 19.

5, 7: In the world of Paul's time the *good person* is especially one who is magnanimous to others.

5, 12–21: Paul reflects on the sin of Adam (Gn 3, 1–13) in the light of the redemptive mystery of Christ. Sin, as used in the singular by Paul, refers to the dreadful power that has gripped humanity, which is now in revolt against the Creator and engaged in the exaltation of its own desires and interests. But no one has a right to say, "Adam made me do it," for all are culpable (12): Gentiles under the demands of the law written in their hearts (2, 14–15), and Jews under the Mosaic covenant. Through the Old Testament law, the sinfulness of humanity that was operative from the beginning (13) found further stimulation, with the result that sins were generated in even greater abundance. According to vv 15–21, God's act in Christ is in total contrast to the disastrous effects of the virus of sin that invaded humanity through Adam's crime.

5, 12: *Inasmuch as all sinned:* others translate "because all sinned," and understand v 13 as a parenthetical remark. Unlike Wis 2, 24, Paul does not ascribe the entry of death to the devil.

**Grace and Life through Christ** 15 But
the gift is not like the transgression. For if by
that one person's transgression the many died,
how much more did the grace of God and the
gracious gift of the one person Jesus Christ
overflow for the many. 16 And the gift is not
like the result of the one person's sinning. For
after one sin there was the judgment that
brought condemnation; but the gift, after many
transgressions, brought acquittal. 17 For if, by
the transgression of one person, death came to
reign through that one, how much more will
those who receive the abundance of grace and
of the gift of justification come to reign in life
through the one person Jesus Christ. 18 [v]In
conclusion, just as through one transgression
condemnation came upon all, so through one
righteous act acquittal and life came to all.
19 [w]For just as through the disobedience of one
person the many were made sinners, so through
the obedience of one the many will be made
righteous. 20 [x]*The law entered in so that
transgression might increase but, where sin increased, grace overflowed all the more, 21 [y]so
that, as sin reigned in death, grace also might
reign through justification for eternal life
through Jesus Christ our Lord.

## *IV: JUSTIFICATION AND THE CHRISTIAN LIFE*

## CHAPTER 6

### Freedom from Sin; Life in God

1 [z]*What then shall we say? Shall we persist in
sin that grace may abound? Of course not!
2 [a]How can we who died to sin yet live in it?
3 [b]Or are you unaware that we who were baptized into Christ Jesus were baptized into his
death? 4 [c]We were indeed buried with him
through baptism into death, so that, just as
Christ was raised from the dead by the glory of
the Father, we too might live in newness of life.
5 [d]For if we have grown into union with him
through a death like his, we shall also be united
with him in the resurrection. 6 [e]We know that
our old self was crucified with him, so that our
sinful body might be done away with, that we
might no longer be in slavery to sin. 7 For a
dead person has been absolved from sin. 8 [f]If,
then, we have died with Christ, we believe that
we shall also live with him. 9 [g]We know that
Christ, raised from the dead, dies no more;
death no longer has power over him. 10 [h]As to
his death, he died to sin once and for all; as to
his life, he lives for God. 11 [i]Consequently,
you too must think of yourselves as [being] dead
to sin and living for God in Christ Jesus.
12 [j]*Therefore, sin must not reign over your
mortal bodies so that you obey their desires.
13 [k]And do not present the parts of your bodies
to sin as weapons for wickedness, but present
yourselves to God as raised from the dead to life
and the parts of your bodies to God as weapons
for righteousness. 14 [l]For sin is not to have any
power over you, since you are not under the law
but under grace.
15 [m]What then? Shall we sin because we are
not under the law but under grace? Of course
not! 16 [n o]Do you not know that if you present
yourselves to someone as obedient slaves, you
are slaves of the one you obey, either of sin,
which leads to death, or of obedience, which
leads to righteousness? 17 *But thanks be to
God that, although you were once slaves of sin,
you have become obedient from the heart to the
pattern of teaching to which you were entrusted.
18 Freed from sin, you have become slaves of
righteousness. 19 I am speaking in human
terms because of the weakness of your nature.
For just as you presented the parts of your bodies as slaves to impurity and to lawlessness for

v 1 Cor 15, 21-22.
w Is 53, 11; Phil 2, 8-9.
x 4, 15; 7, 7-8; Gal 3, 19.
y 6, 23.
z 3, 5-8.
a 1 Pt 4, 1.
b Gal 3, 27.
c Col 2, 12; 1 Pt 3, 21-22.
d Phil 3, 10-11; 2 Tm 2, 11.
e Gal 5, 24; 6, 14; Eph 4, 22-23.
f 1 Thes 4, 17.
g Acts 13, 34; 1 Cor 15, 26; 2 Tm 1, 10; Rv 1, 18.
h Heb 9, 26-28; 1 Pt 3, 18.
i 2 Cor 5, 15; 1 Pt 2, 24.
j Gn 4, 7.
k 12, 1; Eph 2, 5; 5, 14 / Col 3, 5.
l Gal 5, 18; 1 Jn 3, 6.
m 5, 17.21.
n Jn 8, 31-34; 2 Pt 2, 19.
o Jn 8, 32-36.

*

5, 20: *The law entered in:* sin had made its entrance (12); now the law comes in alongside sin. See the notes on 1, 18–32; 5, 12–21. *Where sin increased, grace overflowed all the more:* Paul declares that grace outmatches the productivity of sin.

6, 1–11: To defend the gospel against the charge that it promotes moral laxity (cf 3, 5–8), Paul expresses himself in the typical style of spirited diatribe. God's display of generosity or grace is not evoked by sin but, as stated in 5, 8, is the expression of God's love, and this love pledges eternal life to all believers (5, 21). Paul views the present conduct of the believers from the perspective of God's completed salvation when the body is resurrected and directed totally by the holy Spirit. Through baptism believers share the death of Christ and thereby escape from the grip of sin. Through the resurrection of Christ the power to live anew becomes reality for them, but the fullness of participation in Christ's resurrection still lies in the future. But life that is lived in dedication to God now is part and parcel of that future. Hence anyone who sincerely claims to be interested in that future will scarcely be able to say, "Let us sin so that grace may prosper" (cf 1).

6, 12–19: Christians have been released from the grip of sin, but sin endeavors to reclaim its victims. The antidote is constant remembrance that divine grace has claimed them and identifies them as people who are alive only for God's interests.

6, 17: In contrast to humanity, which was handed over to self-indulgence (1, 24–32), believers are *entrusted* ("handed over") to God's *pattern of teaching,* that is, the new life God aims to develop in Christians through the productivity of the holy Spirit. Throughout this passage Paul uses the slave-master model in order to emphasize the fact that one cannot give allegiance to both God and sin.

lawlessness, so now present them as slaves to
righteousness for sanctification. **20** [p]*For
when you were slaves of sin, you were free from
righteousness. **21** [q]But what profit did you get
then from the things of which you are now
ashamed? For the end of those things is death.
**22** [r]*But now that you have been freed from sin
and have become slaves of God, the benefit that
you have leads to sanctification, and its end is
eternal life. **23** [s]For the wages of sin is death,
but the gift of God is eternal life in Christ Jesus
our Lord.

## CHAPTER 7

**Freedom from the Law** **1** *Are you unaware, brothers (for I am speaking to people
who know the law), that the law has jurisdiction
over one as long as one lives? **2** [t]Thus a married
woman is bound by law to her living husband;
but if her husband dies, she is released from the
law in respect to her husband. **3** Consequently,
while her husband is alive she will be called an
adulteress if she consorts with another man. But
if her husband dies she is free from that law, and
she is not an adulteress if she consorts with
another man.
**4** In the same way, my brothers, you also
were put to death to the law through the body
of Christ, so that you might belong to another,
to the one who was raised from the dead in order
that we might bear fruit for God. **5** [u]For when
we were in the flesh, our sinful passions, awakened by the law, worked in our members to bear
fruit for death. **6** [v]But now we are released
from the law, dead to what held us captive, so
that we may serve in the newness of the spirit
and not under the obsolete letter.

**Acquaintance with Sin through the
Law** **7** [w]*What then can we say? That the
law is sin? Of course not! Yet I did not know
sin except through the law, and I did not know
what it is to covet except that the law said,
"You shall not covet." **8** [x]But sin, finding an
opportunity in the commandment, produced in
me every kind of covetousness. Apart from the
law sin is dead. **9** I once lived outside the law,
but when the commandment came, sin became
alive; **10** [y]then I died, and the commandment
that was for life turned out to be death for me.
**11** [z]For sin, seizing an opportunity in the commandment, deceived me and through it put me
to death. **12** [a]So then the law is holy, and the
commandment is holy and righteous and good.

**Sin and Death** **13** [b]*Did the good, then,
become death for me? Of course not! Sin, in
order that it might be shown to be sin, worked
death in me through the good, so that sin might
become sinful beyond measure through the
commandment. **14** [c]We know that the law is
spiritual; but I am carnal, sold into slavery to
sin. **15** What I do, I do not understand. For I do
not do what I want, but I do what I hate.
**16** Now if I do what I do not want, I concur that
the law is good. **17** So now it is no longer I who
do it, but sin that dwells in me. **18** [d]For I know
that good does not dwell in me, that is, in my
flesh. The willing is ready at hand, but doing the
good is not. **19** For I do not do the good I want,
but I do the evil I do not want. **20** Now if [I]
do what I do not want, it is no longer I who do
it, but sin that dwells in me. **21** So, then, I
discover the principle that when I want to do
right, evil is at hand. **22** For I take delight in the
law of God, in my inner self, **23** [e]*but I see in
my members another principle at war with the
law of my mind, taking me captive to the law
of sin that dwells in my members. **24** Miserable
one that I am! Who will deliver me from this
mortal body? **25** [f]Thanks be to God through

p Jn 8, 34.
q 8, 6.13; Prv 12, 28; Ez 16, 61.63.
r 1 Pt 1, 9.
s Gn 2, 17; Gal 6, 7-9; Jas 1, 15.
t 1 Cor 7, 39.
u 6, 21; 8, 6.13.
v 8, 2; 2 Cor 3, 6.
w 3, 20; Ex 20, 17; Dt 5, 21.
x 5, 13.20; 1 Cor 15, 56 / 4, 15.
y Lv 18, 5.
z Gn 3, 13; Heb 3, 13.
a 1 Tm 1, 8.
b 4, 15; 5, 20.
c 8, 7-8; Ps 51, 7.
d Gn 6, 5; 8, 21; Phil 2, 13.
e Gal 5, 17; 1 Pt 2, 11.
f 1 Cor 15, 57.

*

6, 20: *You were free from righteousness:* expressed ironically, for such freedom is really tyranny. The commercial metaphors in vv 21–23 add up only one way: sin is a bad bargain.

6, 22: *Sanctification:* or holiness.

7, 1–6: Paul reflects on the fact that Christians have a different understanding of the law because of their faith in Christ. Law binds the living, not the dead, as exemplified in marriage, which binds in life but is dissolved through death. Similarly, Christians who through baptism have died with Christ to sin (cf 6, 2–4) are freed from the law that occasioned transgressions, which in turn were productive of death. Now that Christians are joined to Christ, the power of Christ's resurrection makes it possible for them to bear the fruit of newness of life for God.

7, 7–25: In this passage Paul uses the first person singular in the style of diatribe for the sake of argument. He aims to depict the disastrous consequences when a Christian reintroduces the law as a means to attain the objective of holiness pronounced in 6, 22.

7, 7–12: The apostle defends himself against the charge of identifying the law with sin. Sin does not exist in law but in human beings, whose sinful inclinations are not overcome by the proclamation of law.

7, 13–25: Far from improving the sinner, law encourages sin to expose itself in transgressions or violations of specific commandments (see 1, 24; 5, 20). Thus persons who do not experience the justifying grace of God, and Christians who revert to dependence on law as the criterion for their relationship with God, will recognize a rift between their reasoned desire for the goodness of the law and their actual performance that is contrary to the law. Unable to free themselves from the slavery of sin and the power of death, they can only be rescued from defeat in the conflict by the power of God's grace working through Jesus Christ.

7, 23: As in 3, 27, Paul plays on the term *law,* which in Greek can connote custom, system, or *principle.*

Jesus Christ our Lord. Therefore, I myself, with
my mind, serve the law of God but, with my
flesh, the law of sin.

## CHAPTER 8

### The Flesh and the Spirit

1 *Hence, now
there is no condemnation for those who are in
Christ Jesus. 2 [g]For the law of the spirit of life
in Christ Jesus has freed you from the law of sin
and death. 3 [h]For what the law, weakened by
the flesh, was powerless to do, this God has
done: by sending his own Son in the likeness of
sinful flesh and for the sake of sin, he condemned sin in the flesh, 4 [i]so that the righteous
decree of the law might be fulfilled in us, who
live not according to the flesh but according to
the spirit. 5 For those who live according to the
flesh are concerned with the things of the flesh,
but those who live according to the spirit with
the things of the spirit. 6 [j]The concern of the
flesh is death, but the concern of the spirit is life
and peace. 7 [k]For the concern of the flesh is
hostility toward God; it does not submit to the
law of God, nor can it; 8 [l]and those who are in
the flesh cannot please God. 9 [m]But you are not
in the flesh; on the contrary, you are in the
spirit, if only the Spirit of God dwells in you.
Whoever does not have the Spirit of Christ does
not belong to him. 10 [n]But if Christ is in you,
although the body is dead because of sin, the
spirit is alive because of righteousness. 11 If
the Spirit of the one who raised Jesus from the
dead dwells in you, the one who raised Christ
from the dead will give life to your mortal bodies also, through his Spirit that dwells in you.
12 Consequently, brothers, we are not debtors
to the flesh, to live according to the flesh.
13 [o]For if you live according to the flesh, you
will die, but if by the spirit you put to death the
deeds of the body, you will live.

### Children of God through Adoption

14 [p]*For those who are led by the Spirit of God
are children of God. 15 [q]*For you did not receive a spirit of slavery to fall back into fear, but
you received a spirit of adoption, through which
we cry, "*Abba*, Father!" 16 [r]The Spirit itself
bears witness with our spirit that we are children
of God, 17 [s]and if children, then heirs, heirs of
God and joint heirs with Christ, if only we suffer
with him so that we may also be glorified with
him.

### Destiny of Glory

18 [t]*I consider that the
sufferings of this present time are as nothing
compared with the glory to be revealed for us.
19 For creation awaits with eager expectation
the revelation of the children of God; 20 [u]for
creation was made subject to futility, not of its
own accord but because of the one who subjected it, in hope 21 [v]that creation itself would be
set free from slavery to corruption and share in
the glorious freedom of the children of God.
22 [w]We know that all creation is groaning in
labor pains even until now; 23 [x]and not only
that, but we ourselves, who have the firstfruits
of the Spirit, we also groan within ourselves as
we wait for adoption, the redemption of our
bodies. 24 [y]For in hope we were saved. Now
hope that sees for itself is not hope. For who
hopes for what one sees? 25 But if we hope for
what we do not see, we wait with endurance.
26 In the same way, the Spirit too comes to
the aid of our weakness; for we do not know
how to pray as we ought, but the Spirit itself
intercedes with inexpressible groanings.
27 [z]And the one who searches hearts knows
what is the intention of the Spirit, because it
intercedes for the holy ones according to God's
will.

g 7, 23-24; 2 Cor 3, 17.
h Acts 13, 38; 15, 10 / Jn 3, 16-17; 2 Cor 5, 21; Gal 3, 13; 4, 4;Phil 2, 7; Col 1, 22; Heb 2, 17; 4, 15; 1 Jn 4, 9.
i Gal 5, 16-25.
j 6, 21; 7, 5; 8, 13; Gal 6, 8.
k 5, 10; Jas 4, 4.
l 1 Jn 2, 16.
m 1 Cor 3, 16.
n Gal 2, 20; 1 Pt 4, 6.
o Gal 5, 24; 6, 8; Eph 4, 22-24.
p Gal 5, 18.
q Mk 14, 36; Gal 4, 5-6; 2 Tm 1, 7.
r Jn 1, 12; Gal 3, 26-29.
s Gal 4, 7; 1 Pt 4, 13; 5, 1.
t 2 Cor 4, 17.
u Gn 3, 17-19.
v 2 Pt 3, 12-13; Rv 21, 1.
w 2 Cor 5, 2-5.
x 2 Cor 1, 22; Gal 5, 5.
y 2 Cor 5, 7; Heb 11, 1.
z Ps 139, 1; 1 Cor 4, 5.

*

8, 1–13: After his warning in ch 7 against the wrong route to fulfillment of the objective of holiness expressed in 6, 22, Paul points his addressees to the correct way. Through the redemptive work of Christ, Christians have been liberated from the terrible forces of sin and death. Holiness was impossible so long as the *flesh* (or our "old self"), that is, self-interested hostility toward God (7), frustrated the divine objectives expressed in the law. What is worse, sin used the law to break forth into all manner of lawlessness (8). All this is now changed. At the cross God broke the power of sin and pronounced sentence on it (3). Christians still retain the flesh, but it is alien to their new being, which is life in the spirit, namely the new self, governed by the holy Spirit. Under the direction of the holy Spirit Christians are able to fulfill the divine will that formerly found expression in the law (4). The same Spirit who enlivens Christians for holiness will also resurrect their bodies at the last day (11). Christian life is therefore the experience of a constant challenge to put to death the evil deeds of the body through life of the spirit (13).

8, 14–17: Christians, by reason of the Spirit's presence within them, enjoy not only new life but also a new relationship to God, that of adopted children and heirs through Christ, whose sufferings and glory they share.

8, 15: *Abba:* see the note on Mk 14, 36.

8, 18–27: The glory that believers are destined to share with Christ far exceeds the sufferings of the present life. Paul considers the destiny of the created world to be linked with the future that belongs to the believers. As it shares in the penalty of corruption brought about by sin, so also will it share in the benefits of redemption and future glory that comprise the ultimate liberation of God's people (19–22). After patient endurance in steadfast expectation, the full harvest of the Spirit's presence will be realized. On earth believers enjoy the firstfruits, i.e., the Spirit, as a guarantee of the total liberation of their bodies from the influence of the rebellious old self (23).

## God's Indomitable Love in Christ

28 [a]*We know that all things work for good for
those who love God, who are called according
to his purpose. 29 [b]*For those he foreknew he
also predestined to be conformed to the image
of his Son, so that he might be the firstborn
among many brothers. 30 [c]And those he predestined he also called; and those he called he
also justified; and those he justified he also glorified.
31 [d]*What then shall we say to this? If God
is for us, who can be against us? 32 [e]He who
did not spare his own Son but handed him over
for us all, how will he not also give us everything else along with him? 33 [f]Who will bring
a charge against God's chosen ones? It is God
who acquits us. 34 [g]Who will condemn? It is
Christ [Jesus] who died, rather, was raised, who
also is at the right hand of God, who indeed
intercedes for us. 35 What will separate us from
the love of Christ? Will anguish, or distress, or
persecution, or famine, or nakedness, or peril,
or the sword? 36 [h]As it is written:

"For your sake we are being slain all the
day;
we are looked upon as sheep to be
slaughtered."

37 [i]No, in all these things we conquer over-
whelmingly through him who loved us.
38 [j]*For I am convinced that neither death, nor
life, nor angels, nor principalities, nor present
things, nor future things, nor powers, 39 *nor
height, nor depth, nor any other creature will be
able to separate us from the love of God in
Christ Jesus our Lord.

# *V: JEWS AND GENTILES IN GOD'S PLAN*

## CHAPTER 9

**Paul's Love for Israel** 1 [k]*I speak the
truth in Christ, I do not lie; my conscience joins
with the holy Spirit in bearing me witness 2 that
I have great sorrow and constant anguish in my
heart. 3 [l]For I could wish that I myself were
accursed and separated from Christ for the sake
of my brothers, my kin according to the flesh.
4 [m]They are Israelites; theirs the adoption, the
glory, the covenants, the giving of the law, the
worship, and the promises; 5 [n]*theirs the patriarchs, and from them, according to the flesh, is
the Messiah. God who is over all be blessed
forever. Amen.

**God's Free Choice** 6 [o]But it is not that the
word of God has failed. For not all who are of
Israel are Israel, 7 [p]nor are they all children of
Abraham because they are his descendants; but
"It is through Isaac that descendants shall bear
your name." 8 [q]This means that it is not the
children of the flesh who are the children of
God, but the children of the promise are counted

a Eph 1, 4-14; 3, 11.
b Eph 1, 5; 1 Pt 1, 2.
c Is 45, 25; 2 Thes 2, 13-14.
d Ps 118, 6; Heb 13, 6.
e Jn 3, 16.
f Is 50, 8.
g Ps 110, 1; Heb 7, 25; 1 Jn 2, 1.
h Ps 44, 23; 1 Cor 4, 9; 15, 30; 2 Cor 4, 11; 2 Tm 3, 12.
i 1 Jn 5, 4.
j 1 Cor 3, 22; Eph 1, 21; 1 Pt 3, 22.
k 2 Cor 11, 31; 1 Tm 2, 7.
l Ex 32, 32.
m 3, 2; Ex 4, 22; Dt 7, 6; 14, 1-2.
n Mt 1, 1-16; Lk 3, 23-38 / 1, 25; Ps 41, 14.
o Nm 23, 19 / Mt 3, 9.
p Gn 21, 12; Gal 3, 29.
q Gal 4, 23.28.

*

8, 28–30: These verses outline the Christian vocation as it was designed by God: *to be conformed to the image of his Son,* who is to *be the firstborn among many brothers* (29). God's redemptive action on behalf of the believers has been in process before the beginning of the world. Those whom God chooses are *those he foreknew* (29) or elected. Those who are *called* (30) are *predestined* or predetermined. These expressions do not mean that God is arbitrary. Rather, Paul uses them to emphasize the thought and care that God has taken for the Christian's salvation.

8, 28: *We know that all things work for good for those who love God:* a few ancient authorities have God as the subject of the verb, and some translators render: "We know that God makes everything work for good for those who love God . . . ."

8, 29: *Image:* while man and woman were originally created in God's image (Gn 1, 26–27), it is through baptism into Christ, the image of God (2 Cor 4, 4; Col 1, 15), that we are renewed according to the image of the Creator (Col 3, 10).

8, 31–39: The all-conquering power of God's love has overcome every obstacle to Christians' salvation and every threat to separate them from God. That power manifested itself fully when God's own Son was delivered up to death for their salvation. Through him Christians can overcome all their afflictions and trials.

8, 38: *Present things* and *future things* may refer to astrological data. Paul appears to be saying that the gospel liberates believers from dependence on astrologers.

8, 39: *Height, depth* may refer to positions in the zodiac, positions of heavenly bodies relative to the horizon. In astrological documents the term for "height" means "exaltation" or the position of greatest influence exerted by a planet. Since hostile spirits were associated with the planets and stars, Paul includes *powers* (38) in his list of malevolent forces.

9, 1—11, 36: Israel's unbelief and its rejection of Jesus as savior astonished and puzzled Christians. It constituted a serious problem for them in view of God's specific preparation of Israel for the advent of the Messiah. Paul addresses himself here to the essential question of how the divine plan could be frustrated by Israel's unbelief. At the same time, he discourages both complacency and anxiety on the part of Gentiles. To those who might boast of their superior advantage over Jews, he warns that their enjoyment of the blessings assigned to Israel can be terminated. To those who might anxiously ask, "How can we be sure that Israel's fate will not be ours?" he replies that only unbelief can deprive one of salvation.

9, 1–5: The apostle speaks in strong terms of the depth of his grief over the unbelief of his own people. He would willingly undergo a curse himself for the sake of their coming to the knowledge of Christ (3; cf Lv 27, 28–29). His love for them derives from God's continuing choice of them and from the spiritual benefits that God bestows on them and through them on all of humanity (4–5).

9, 5: Some editors punctuate this verse differently and prefer the translation, "Of whom is Christ according to the flesh, who is God over all." However, Paul's point is that *God who is over all* aimed to use Israel, which had been entrusted with every privilege, in outreach to the entire world through the Messiah.

as descendants. **9** [r]For this is the wording of the
promise, "About this time I shall return and
Sarah will have a son." **10** [s]*And not only that,
but also when Rebecca had conceived children
by one husband, our father Isaac— **11** before
they had yet been born or had done anything,
good or bad, in order that God's elective plan
might continue, **12** [t]not by works but by his
call—she was told, "The older shall serve the
younger." **13** [u]*As it is written:

"I loved Jacob
but hated Esau."

**14** [v]*What then are we to say? Is there injustice
on the part of God? Of course not! **15** [w]For he
says to Moses:

"I will show mercy to whom I will,
I will take pity on whom I will."

**16** [x]So it depends not upon a person's will or
exertion, but upon God, who shows mercy.
**17** [y]For the scripture says to Pharaoh, "This is
why I have raised you up, to show my power
through you that my name may be proclaimed
throughout the earth." **18** [z]*Consequently, he
has mercy upon whom he wills, and he hardens
whom he wills.

**19** [a]*You will say to me then, "Why [then]
does he still find fault? For who can oppose his
will?" **20** [b]But who indeed are you, a human
being, to talk back to God? Will what is made
say to its maker, "Why have you created me
so?" **21** Or does not the potter have a right over
the clay, to make out of the same lump one
vessel for a noble purpose and another for an
ignoble one? **22** [c]What if God, wishing to show
his wrath and make known his power, has endured with much patience the vessels of wrath
made for destruction? **23** This was to make
known the riches of his glory to the vessels of
mercy, which he has prepared previously for
glory, **24** namely, us whom he has called, not
only from the Jews but also from the Gentiles.

## Witness of the Prophets

**25** [d]*As indeed
he says in Hosea:

"Those who were not my people I will call
'my people,'
and her who was not beloved I will call
'beloved.'
**26** [e]And in the very place where it was said to
them, 'You are not my people,'
there they shall be called children of the
living God."

**27** [f]And Isaiah cries out concerning Israel,
"Though the number of the Israelites were like
the sand of the sea, only a remnant will be
saved; **28** for decisively and quickly will the
Lord execute sentence upon the earth."
**29** [g]And as Isaiah predicted:

"Unless the Lord of hosts had left us
descendants,
we would have become like Sodom
and have been made like Gomorrah."

## Righteousness Based on Faith

**30** [h]*What then shall we say? That Gen-

r Gn 18, 10.14.
s Gn 25, 21.
t 11, 5-6 / Gn 25, 23-24.
u Mal 1, 3.
v Dt 32, 4.
w Ex 33, 19.
x Eph 2, 8; Ti 3, 5.
y Ex 9, 16.
z 11, 30-32; Ex 4, 21; 7, 3.
a 3, 7; Wis 12, 12.
b Wis 15, 7; Is 29, 16; 45, 9; Jer 18, 6.
c 2, 4; Wis 12, 20-21; Jer 50, 25.
d Hos 2, 25.
e Hos 2, 1.
f Is 10, 22-23; Hos 2, 1 / 11, 5 / Is 28, 22.
g Is 1, 9; Mt 10, 15.
h 10, 4.20.

*

9, 10: *Children by one husband, our father Isaac:* Abraham had two children, Ishmael and Isaac, by two wives, Hagar and Sarah, respectively. In that instance Isaac, although born later than Ishmael, became the bearer of the messianic promise. In the case of twins born to Rebecca, God's elective procedure is seen even more dramatically, and again the younger, contrary to Semitic custom, is given the preference.

9, 13: The literal rendering, *"Jacob I loved, but Esau I hated,"* suggests an attitude of divine hostility that is not implied in Paul's statement. In Semitic usage "hate" means to love less; cf Lk 14, 26 with Mt 10, 37. Israel's unbelief reflects the mystery of the divine election that is always operative within it. Mere natural descent from Abraham does not ensure the full possession of the divine gifts; it is God's sovereign prerogative to bestow this fullness upon, or to withhold it from, whomsoever he wishes; cf Mt 3, 9; Jn 8, 39. The choice of Jacob over Esau is a case in point.

9, 14–18: The principle of divine election does not invite Christians to theoretical inquiry concerning the nonelected, nor does this principle mean that God is unfair in his dealings with humanity. The instruction concerning divine election is a part of the gospel and reveals that the gift of faith is the enactment of God's mercy (16). God raised up Moses to display that mercy, and Pharaoh to display divine severity in punishing those who obstinately oppose their Creator.

9, 18: The basic biblical principle is: those who will not see or hear *shall* not see or hear. On the other hand, the same God who thus makes stubborn or hardens the heart can reconstruct it through the work of the holy Spirit.

9, 19–29: The apostle responds to the objection that if God rules over faith through the principle of divine election, God cannot then accuse unbelievers of sin (19). For Paul, this objection is in the last analysis a manifestation of human insolence, and his "answer" is less an explanation of God's ways than the rejection of an argument that places humanity on a level with God. At the same time, Paul shows that God is far less arbitrary than appearances suggest, for God endures *with much patience* (22) a person like the Pharaoh of the Exodus.

9, 25: *Beloved:* in Semitic discourse means "preferred" or "favorite" (cf 13). See Hos 2, 1, which is transposed after Hos 3, 5 in the NAB.

9, 30–33: In the conversion of the Gentiles and, by contrast, of relatively few Jews, the Old Testament prophecies are seen to be fulfilled; cf 25–29. Israel feared that the doctrine of justification through faith would jeopardize the validity of the Mosaic law, and so they never reached their goal of righteousness that they had sought to attain through meticulous observance of the law (31). Since Gentiles, including especially Greeks and Romans, had a great regard for righteousness, Paul's statement concerning Gentiles in v 30 is to be understood from a Jewish perspective: quite evidently they had not been interested in "God's" righteousness, for it had not been revealed to them; but now in response to the proclamation of the gospel they respond in faith.

tiles, who did not pursue righteousness, have
achieved it, that is, righteousness that comes
from faith; 31 [i]but that Israel, who pursued the
law of righteousness, did not attain to that law?
32 [j]*Why not? Because they did it not by faith,
but as if it could be done by works. They stumbled over the stone that causes stumbling,
33 [k]as it is written:

"Behold, I am laying a stone in Zion
that will make people stumble
and a rock that will make them fall,
and whoever believes in him shall not be put
to shame."

## CHAPTER 10

1 [l]*Brothers, my heart's desire and prayer to
God on their behalf is for salvation. 2 [m]I testify
with regard to them that they have zeal for God,
but it is not discerning. 3 [n]For, in their una-
wareness of the righteousness that comes from
God and their attempt to establish their own
[righteousness], they did not submit to the righteousness of God. 4 [o]*For Christ is the end of
the law for the justification of everyone who has
faith.

5 [p]*Moses writes about the righteousness
that comes from [the] law, "The one who does
these things will live by them." 6 [q]But the
righteousness that comes from faith says, "Do
not say in your heart, 'Who will go up into
heaven?' (that is, to bring Christ down) 7 [r]*or
'Who will go down into the abyss?' (that is,
to bring Christ up from the dead)." 8 [s]But what
does it say?

"The word is near you,
in your mouth and in your heart"

(that is, the word of faith that we preach),
9 [t]*for, if you confess with your mouth that
Jesus is Lord and believe in your heart that God
raised him from the dead, you will be saved.
10 For one believes with the heart and so is
justified, and one confesses with the mouth and
so is saved. 11 [u]For the scripture says, "No
one who believes in him will be put to shame."
12 [v]For there is no distinction between Jew and
Greek; the same Lord is Lord of all, enriching
all who call upon him. 13 [w]For "everyone who
calls on the name of the Lord will be saved."

14 [x]*But how can they call on him in whom
they have not believed? And how can they believe in him of whom they have not heard? And
how can they hear without someone to preach?
15 [y]*And how can people preach unless they
are sent? As it is written, "How beautiful are the
feet of those who bring [the] good news!"
16 [z]But not everyone has heeded the good
news; for Isaiah says, "Lord, who has believed
what was heard from us?" 17 [a]Thus faith
comes from what is heard, and what is heard
comes through the word of Christ. 18 [b]But I
ask, did they not hear? Certainly they did; for

"Their voice has gone forth to all the earth,
and their words to the ends of the
world."

19 [c]But I ask, did not Israel understand? First
Moses says:

"I will make you jealous of those who are
not a nation;
with a senseless nation I will make you
angry."

20 [d]Then Isaiah speaks boldly and says:

"I was found [by] those who were not
seeking me;
I revealed myself to those who were not
asking for me."

21 But regarding Israel he says, "All day long

---

i 10, 3.
j Is 8, 14.
k Is 28, 16; 1 Pt 2, 6-8.
l 9, 1.3.
m Acts 22, 3.
n 9, 31-32; Phil 3, 9.
o Acts 13, 38-39; 2 Cor 3, 14; Heb 8, 13.
p Lv 18, 5; Gal 3, 12.
q Dt 9, 4; 30, 12.
r Dt 30, 13; 1 Pt 3, 19.
s Dt 30, 14.
t 1 Cor 12, 3.
u 9, 33; Is 28, 16.
v 1, 16; 3, 22.29; Acts 10, 34; 15, 9.11; Gal 3, 28; Eph 2, 14.
w Jl 3, 5; Acts 2, 21.
x Acts 8, 31.
y Is 52, 7; Na 2, 1; Eph 6, 15.
z Is 53, 1; Jn 12, 38.
a Jn 17, 20.
b Ps 19, 5; Mt 24, 14.
c 11, 11.14; Dt 32, 21.
d 9, 30; Is 65, 1-2.

---

*

9, 32: Paul discusses Israel as a whole from the perspective of contemporary Jewish rejection of Jesus as Messiah. The Old Testament and much of Jewish noncanonical literature in fact reflect a fervent faith in divine mercy.

10, 1–13: Despite Israel's lack of faith in God's act in Christ, Paul does not abandon hope for her salvation (1). However, Israel must recognize that the Messiah's arrival in the person of Jesus Christ means the termination of the Mosaic law as the criterion for understanding oneself in a valid relationship to God. Faith in God's saving action in Jesus Christ takes precedence over any such legal claim (6).

10, 4: The Mosaic legislation has been superseded by God's action in Jesus Christ. Others understand *end* here in the sense that Christ is the goal of the law, i.e., the true meaning of the Mosaic law, which cannot be correctly understood apart from him. Still others believe that both meanings are intended.

10, 5–6: The subject of the verb *says* (6) is *righteousness* personified. Both of the statements in vv 5 and 6 derive from Moses, but Paul wishes to contrast the language of law and the language of faith.

10, 7: Here Paul blends Dt 30, 13 and Ps 107, 26.

10, 9–11: To confess Jesus as Lord was frequently quite hazardous in the first century (cf Mt 10, 18; 1 Thes 2, 2; 1 Pt 2, 18–21; 3, 14). For a Jew it could mean disruption of normal familial and other social relationships, including great economic sacrifice. In the face of penalties imposed by the secular world, Christians are assured that *no one who believes in* Jesus *will be put to shame* (11).

10, 14–21: The gospel has been sufficiently proclaimed to Israel, and Israel has adequately understood God's plan for the messianic age, which would see the gospel brought to the uttermost parts of the earth. As often in the past, Israel has not accepted the prophetic message; cf Acts 7, 51–53.

10, 15: *How beautiful are the feet of those who bring [the] good news:* in Semitic fashion, the parts of the body that bring the messenger with welcome news are praised; cf Lk 11, 27.

I stretched out my hands to a disobedient and
contentious people.''

## CHAPTER 11

### The Remnant of Israel

1 [ef]*I ask, then,
has God rejected his people? Of course not! For
I too am an Israelite, a descendant of Abraham,
of the tribe of Benjamin. 2 God has not rejected
his people whom he foreknew. Do you not
know what the scripture says about Elijah, how
he pleads with God against Israel? 3 [g]''Lord,
they have killed your prophets, they have torn
down your altars, and I alone am left, and they
are seeking my life.'' 4 [h]But what is God's
response to him? ''I have left for myself seven
thousand men who have not knelt to Baal.''
5 [i]So also at the present time there is a remnant,
chosen by grace. 6 [j]But if by grace, it is no
longer because of works; otherwise grace would
no longer be grace. 7 [k]What then? What Israel
was seeking it did not attain, but the elect attained it; the rest were hardened, 8 [l]as it is
written:

''God gave them a spirit of deep sleep,
eyes that should not see
and ears that should not hear,
down to this very day.''

9 [m]And David says:

''Let their table become a snare and a trap,
a stumbling block and a retribution for
them;
10 let their eyes grow dim so that they may not
see,
and keep their backs bent forever.''

### The Gentiles' Salvation

11 [n]*Hence I
ask, did they stumble so as to fall? Of course
not! But through their transgression salvation
has come to the Gentiles, so as to make them
jealous. 12 Now if their transgression is enrichment for the world, and if their diminished number is enrichment for the Gentiles, how much
more their full number.

13 [o]Now I am speaking to you Gentiles. Inasmuch then as I am the apostle to the Gentiles,
I glory in my ministry 14 in order to make my
race jealous and thus save some of them. 15 For
if their rejection is the reconciliation of the
world, what will their acceptance be but life
from the dead? 16 [p]*If the firstfruits are holy,
so is the whole batch of dough; and if the root
is holy, so are the branches.

17 [q]But if some of the branches were broken
off, and you, a wild olive shoot, were grafted
in their place and have come to share in the rich
root of the olive tree, 18 [r]do not boast against
the branches. If you do boast, consider that you
do not support the root; the root supports you.
19 Indeed you will say, ''Branches were broken off so that I might be grafted in.'' 20 [s]That
is so. They were broken off because of unbelief,
but you are there because of faith. So do not
become haughty, but stand in awe. 21 [t]For if
God did not spare the natural branches, [per-
haps] he will not spare you either. 22 [u]See,
then, the kindness and severity of God: severity
toward those who fell, but God's kindness to
you, provided you remain in his kindness; otherwise you too will be cut off. 23 [v]And they
also, if they do not remain in unbelief, will be
grafted in, for God is able to graft them in again.
24 For if you were cut from what is by nature
a wild olive tree, and grafted, contrary to nature, into a cultivated one, how much more will
they who belong to it by nature be grafted back
into their own olive tree.

### God's Irrevocable Call

25 [w]*I do not
want you to be unaware of this mystery, brothers, so that you will not become wise [in] your
own estimation: a hardening has come upon
Israel in part, until the full number of the Gentiles comes in, 26 [xy]and thus all Israel will be
saved, as it is written:

e 2 Cor 11, 22; Phil 3, 5.
f 1 Sm 12, 22; Ps 94, 14.
g 1 Kgs 19, 10.14.
h 1 Kgs 19, 18.
i 9, 27.
j 4, 4; Gal 3, 18.
k 9, 31.
l Dt 29, 3; Is 29, 10; Mt 13, 13-15; Acts 28, 26-27.
m Pss 69, 23-24; 35, 8.
n Acts 13, 46; 18, 6; 28, 28 / 10, 19; Dt 32, 21.
o 1, 5.
p Nm 15, 17-21; Ez 44, 30; Neh 10, 36-38.
q Eph 2, 11-19.
r 1 Cor 1, 31.
s 12, 16.
t 1 Cor 10, 12.
u Jn 15, 2.4; Heb 3, 14.
v 2 Cor 3, 16.
w Prv 3, 7 / 12, 16; Mk 13, 10; Lk 21, 24; Jn 10, 16.
x Mt 23, 39.
y Ps 14, 7; Is 59, 20-21.

*

11, 1–10: Although Israel has been unfaithful to the prophetic message of the gospel (10, 14–21), God remains faithful to Israel. Proof of the divine fidelity lies in the existence of Jewish Christians like Paul himself. The unbelieving Jews, says Paul, have been blinded by the Christian teaching concerning the Messiah.

11, 11–15: The unbelief of the Jews has paved the way for the preaching of the gospel to the Gentiles and for their easier acceptance of it outside the context of Jewish culture. Through his mission to the Gentiles Paul also hopes to fill his fellow Jews with jealousy. Hence he hastens to fill the entire Mediterranean world with the gospel. Once all the Gentile nations have heard the gospel, Israel as a whole is expected to embrace it. This will be tantamount to resurrection of the dead, that is, the reappearance of Jesus Christ with all the believers at the end of time.

11, 16–24: Israel remains holy in the eyes of God and stands as a witness to the faith described in the Old Testament because of *the firstfruits* (or the first piece baked) (16), that is, the converted remnant, and *the root* that *is holy,* that is, the patriarchs (16). The Jews' failure to believe in Christ is a warning to Gentile Christians to be on guard against any semblance of anti-Jewish arrogance, that is, failure to recognize their total dependence on divine grace.

11, 25–29: In God's design, Israel's unbelief is being used to grant the light of faith to the Gentiles. Meanwhile, Israel remains dear to God (cf 9, 13), still the object of special providence, the mystery of which will one day be revealed.

"The deliverer will come out of Zion,
he will turn away godlessness from Jacob;
**27** [z]and this is my covenant with them
when I take away their sins."

**28** [a]In respect to the gospel, they are enemies
on your account; but in respect to election, they
are beloved because of the patriarchs. **29** [b]For
the gifts and the call of God are irrevocable.

**Triumph of God's Mercy** **30** *Just as you
once disobeyed God but have now received
mercy because of their disobedience, **31** so
they have now disobeyed in order that, by virtue
of the mercy shown to you, they too may [now]
receive mercy. **32** [c]For God delivered all to
disobedience, that he might have mercy upon
all.

**33** [d]*Oh, the depth of the riches and wisdom
and knowledge of God! How inscrutable are his
judgments and how unsearchable his ways!

**34** [e]*"For who has known the mind of the
Lord
or who has been his counselor?"
**35** [f]*"Or who has given him anything
that he may be repaid?"

**36** [g]For from him and through him and for him
are all things. To him be glory forever. Amen.

## *VI: THE DUTIES OF CHRISTIANS*

## CHAPTER 12

**Sacrifice of Body and Mind** **1** [h]*I urge
you therefore, brothers, by the mercies of God,
to offer your bodies as a living sacrifice, holy
and pleasing to God, your spiritual worship.
**2** [i]Do not conform yourself to this age but be
transformed by the renewal of your mind, that
you may discern what is the will of God, what
is good and pleasing and perfect.

**Many Parts in One Body** **3** [j]For by the
grace given to me I tell everyone among you not
to think of himself more highly than one ought
to think, but to think soberly, each according to
the measure of faith that God has apportioned.
**4** [k]For as in one body we have many parts, and
all the parts do not have the same function,
**5** *so we, though many, are one body in Christ
and individually parts of one another. **6** [l]*Since
we have gifts that differ according to the grace
given to us, let us exercise them: if prophecy,
in proportion to the faith; **7** if ministry, in ministering; if one is a teacher, in teaching; **8** *if
one exhorts, in exhortation; if one contributes,
in generosity; if one is over others, with diligence; if one does acts of mercy, with cheerfulness.

**Mutual Love** **9** [m]Let love be sincere; hate
what is evil, hold on to what is good; **10** [n]love
one another with mutual affection; anticipate
one another in showing honor. **11** [o]Do not

z Is 27, 9; Jer 31, 33-34.
a 15, 8; 1 Thes 2, 15-16.
b 9, 6; Nm 23, 19; Is 54, 10.
c Gal 3, 22; 1 Tm 2, 4.
d Jb 11, 7-8; Ps 139, 6.17-18; Wis 17, 1; Is 55, 8-9.
e Jb 15, 8; Wis 9, 13; Is 40, 13; Jer 23, 18; 1 Cor 2, 11-16.
f Jb 41, 3; Is 40, 14.
g 1 Cor 8, 6; Col 1, 16-17.
h 2 Cor 1, 3 / 6, 13; 1 Pt 2, 5.
i Eph 4, 17.22-23; 1 Pt 1, 14 / Eph 5, 10.17; Phil 1, 10.
j 15, 15 / Phil 2, 3 / 1 Cor 12, 11; Eph 4, 7.
k 1 Cor 12, 12.27; Eph 4, 25.
l 1 Cor 12, 4-11.28-31; Eph 4, 7-12; 1 Pt 4, 10-11 / 2 Cor 9, 7.
m 2 Cor 6, 6; 1 Tm 1, 5; 1 Pt 1, 22 / Am 5, 15.
n Jn 13, 34; 1 Thes 4, 9; 1 Pt 2, 17; 2 Pt 1, 7 / Phil 2, 3.
o Acts 18, 25.

*

11, 30–32: Israel, together with the Gentiles who have been handed over to all manner of vices (ch 1), has been *delivered . . . to disobedience.* The conclusion of v 32 repeats the thought of 5, 20, "Where sin increased, grace overflowed all the more."

11, 33–36: This final reflection celebrates the wisdom of God's plan of salvation. As Paul has indicated throughout these chapters, both Jew and Gentile, despite the religious recalcitrance of each, have received the gift of faith. The methods used by God in making this outreach to the world stagger human comprehension but are at the same time a dazzling invitation to abiding faith.

11, 34: The citation is from the Greek text of Is 40, 13. Paul does not explicitly mention Isaiah in this verse, nor Job in v 35.

11, 35: Paul quotes from an old Greek version of Jb 41, 3a, which differs from the Hebrew text (Jb 41, 11a).

12, 1—13, 14: Since Christ marks the termination of the Mosaic law as the primary source of guidance for God's people (10, 4), the apostle explains how Christians can function, in the light of the gift of justification through faith, in their relation to one another and the state.

12, 1–8: The Mosaic code included elaborate directions on sacrifices and other cultic observances. The gospel, however, invites believers to present their *bodies as a living sacrifice* (1). Instead of being limited by specific legal maxims, Christians are liberated for the exercise of good judgment as they are confronted with the many and varied decisions required in the course of daily life. To assist them, God distributes a variety of gifts to the fellowship of believers, including those of prophecy, teaching, and exhortation (6–8). Prophets assist the community to understand the will of God as it applies to the present situation (6). Teachers help people to understand themselves and their responsibilities in relation to others (7). One who *exhorts* offers encouragement to the community to exercise their faith in the performance of all that is pleasing to God (8). Indeed, this very section, beginning with v 1, is a specimen of Paul's own style of exhortation.

12, 5: *One body in Christ:* on the church as the body of Christ, see 1 Cor 12, 12–27.

12, 6: Everyone has some gift that can be used for the benefit of the community. When the instruction on justification through faith is correctly grasped, the possesser of a gift will understand that it is not an instrument of self-aggrandizement. Possession of a gift is not an index to quality of faith. Rather, the gift is a challenge to faithful use.

12, 8: *Over others:* usually taken to mean "rule over" but possibly "serve as a patron." Wealthier members in Greco-Roman communities were frequently asked to assist in public service projects. In view of the references to contributing *in generosity* and to *acts of mercy,* Paul may have in mind people like Phoebe (16, 1–2), who is called a *benefactor* (or "patron") because of the services she rendered to many Christians, including Paul.

grow slack in zeal, be fervent in spirit, serve the
Lord. **12** [p]Rejoice in hope, endure in affliction,
persevere in prayer. **13** [q]Contribute to the
needs of the holy ones, exercise hospitality.
**14** [r s]*Bless those who persecute [you], bless
and do not curse them. **15** [t]Rejoice with those
who rejoice, weep with those who weep.
**16** [u]Have the same regard for one another; do
not be haughty but associate with the lowly; do
not be wise in your own estimation. **17** [v]Do not
repay anyone evil for evil; be concerned for
what is noble in the sight of all. **18** [w]If possible,
on your part, live at peace with all.
**19** [x]Beloved, do not look for revenge but leave
room for the wrath; for it is written, "Vengeance is mine, I will repay, says the Lord."
**20** [y]Rather, "if your enemy is hungry, feed
him; if he is thirsty, give him something to
drink; for by so doing you will heap burning
coals upon his head." **21** Do not be conquered
by evil but conquer evil with good.

## CHAPTER 13

### Obedience to Authority

**1** [z]*Let every
person be subordinate to the higher authorities,
for there is no authority except from God, and
those that exist have been established by God.
**2** Therefore, whoever resists authority opposes
what God has appointed, and those who oppose
it will bring judgment upon themselves. **3** [a]For
rulers are not a cause of fear to good conduct,
but to evil. Do you wish to have no fear of
authority? Then do what is good and you will
receive approval from it, **4** [b]for it is a servant
of God for your good. But if you do evil, be
afraid, for it does not bear the sword without
purpose; it is the servant of God to inflict wrath
on the evildoer. **5** [c]Therefore, it is necessary to
be subject not only because of the wrath but also
because of conscience. **6** This is why you also
pay taxes, for the authorities are ministers of
God, devoting themselves to this very thing.
**7** [d]Pay to all their dues, taxes to whom taxes are
due, toll to whom toll is due, respect to whom
respect is due, honor to whom honor is due.

### Love Fulfills the Law

**8** [e]*Owe nothing to
anyone, except to love one another; for the one
who loves another has fulfilled the law. **9** [f]The
commandments, "You shall not commit adultery; you shall not kill; you shall not steal; you
shall not covet," and whatever other commandment there may be, are summed up in this saying, [namely] "You shall love your neighbor as
yourself." **10** [g]Love does no evil to the neighbor; hence, love is the fulfillment of the law.

### Awareness of the End of Time

**11** [h]*And do this because you know the time;
it is the hour now for you to awake from sleep.
For our salvation is nearer now than when we
first believed; **12** [i]the night is advanced, the
day is at hand. Let us then throw off the works
of darkness [and] put on the armor of light;
**13** [j]*let us conduct ourselves properly as in the
day, not in orgies and drunkenness, not in promiscuity and licentiousness, not in rivalry and
jealousy. **14** [k]But put on the Lord Jesus Christ,
and make no provision for the desires of the
flesh.

p 5, 2-3; Col 4, 2; 1 Thes 5, 17.
q Heb 13, 2; 1 Pt 4, 9.
r Mt 5, 38-48; 1 Cor 4, 12; 1 Pt 3, 9.
s Lk 6, 27-28.
t Ps 35, 13; Sir 7, 34; 1 Cor 12, 26.
u 15, 5; Phil 2, 2-3 / 11, 20; Prv 3, 7; Is 5, 21.
v Prv 3, 4; 1 Thes 5, 15; 1 Pt 3, 9.
w Heb 12, 14.
x Lv 19, 18; Dt 32, 35.41; Mt 5, 39; 1 Cor 6, 6-7; Heb 10, 30.
y Prv 25, 21-22; Mt 5, 44.
z Prv 8, 15-16; Wis 6, 3; Jn 19, 11; 1 Pt 2, 13-17; Ti 3, 1.
a 1 Pt 2, 13-14; 3, 13.
b 12, 19.
c 1 Pt 2, 19.
d Mt 22, 21; Mk 12, 17; Lk 20, 25.
e Jn 13, 34; Gal 5, 14.
f Ex 20, 13-17 / Lv 19, 18; Dt 5, 17-21; Mt 5, 43-44; 19, 18-19;22, 39; Mk 12, 31; Lk 10, 27; Gal 5, 14; Jas 2, 8.
g Mt 22, 40; 1 Cor 13, 4-7.
h Eph 5, 8-16; 1 Thes 5, 5-7.
i Jn 8, 12; 1 Thes 5, 4-8; 1 Jn 2, 8 / 2 Cor 6, 7; 10, 4;Eph 5, 11; 6, 13-17.
j Lk 21, 34; Eph 5, 18.
k Gal 3, 27; 5, 16; Eph 4, 24; 6, 11.

*

12, 14–21: Since God has justified the believers, it is not necessary for them to take justice into their own hands by taking vengeance. God will ultimately deal justly with all, including those who inflict injury on the believers. This question of personal rights as a matter of justice prepares the way for more detailed consideration of the state as adjudicator.

13, 1–7: Paul must come to grips with the problem raised by a message that declares people free from the law. How are they to relate to Roman authority? The problem was exacerbated by the fact that imperial protocol was interwoven with devotion to various deities. Paul builds on the traditional instruction exhibited in Wis 6, 1–3, according to which kings and magistrates rule by consent of God. From this perspective, then, believers who render obedience to the governing authorities are obeying the one who is highest in command. At the same time, it is recognized that Caesar has the responsibility to make just ordinances and to commend uprightness; cf Wis 6, 4–21. That Caesar is not entitled to obedience when such obedience would nullify God's prior claim to the believers' moral decision becomes clear in the light of the following verses.

13, 8–10: When love directs the Christian's moral decisions, the interest of law in basic concerns, such as familial relationships, sanctity of life, and security of property, is safeguarded (9). Indeed, says Paul, the same applies to any *other commandment* (9), whether one in the Mosaic code or one drawn up by local magistrates under imperial authority. Love anticipates the purpose of public legislation, namely, to secure the best interests of the citizenry. Since Caesar's obligation is to punish the wrongdoer (4), the Christian who acts in love is free from all legitimate indictment.

13, 11–14: These verses provide the motivation for the love that is encouraged in vv 8–10.

13, 13: *Let us conduct ourselves properly as in the day:* the behavior described in 1, 29–30 is now to be reversed. Secular moralists were fond of making references to people who could not wait for nightfall to do their carousing. Paul says that Christians claim to be people of the new day that will dawn with the return of Christ. Instead of planning for nighttime behavior they should be concentrating on conduct that is consonant with avowed interest in the Lord's return.

## CHAPTER 14

### To Live and Die for Christ
1 [lm]*Welcome anyone who is weak in faith,
but not for disputes over opinions. 2 [n]One person believes that one may eat anything, while
the weak person eats only vegetables. 3 [o]The
one who eats must not despise the one who
abstains, and the one who abstains must not pass
judgment on the one who eats; for God has
welcomed him. 4 [p]Who are you to pass judgment on someone else's servant? Before his
own master he stands or falls. And he will be
upheld, for the Lord is able to make him stand.
5 [q]*[For] one person considers one day more
important than another, while another person
considers all days alike. Let everyone be fully
persuaded in his own mind. 6 Whoever observes the day, observes it for the Lord. Also
whoever eats, eats for the Lord, since he gives
thanks to God; while whoever abstains, abstains
for the Lord and gives thanks to God. 7 None
of us lives for oneself, and no one dies for
oneself. 8 [r]*For if we live, we live for the
Lord, and if we die, we die for the Lord; so then,
whether we live or die, we are the Lord's.
9 [s]For this is why Christ died and came to life,
that he might be Lord of both the dead and the
living. 10 [t]Why then do you judge your brother? Or you, why do you look down on your
brother? For we shall all stand before the judgment seat of God; 11 [u]for it is written:

"As I live, says the Lord, every knee shall
bend before me,
and every tongue shall give praise to
God."

12 [v]So [then] each of us shall give an account
of himself [to God].

### Consideration for the Weak Conscience
13 [w]Then let us no longer judge
one another, but rather resolve never to put a
stumbling block or hindrance in the way of a
brother. 14 [x]I know and am convinced in the
Lord Jesus that nothing is unclean in itself; still,
it is unclean for someone who thinks it unclean.
15 [y]If your brother is being hurt by what you
eat, your conduct is no longer in accord with
love. Do not because of your food destroy him
for whom Christ died. 16 [z]So do not let your
good be reviled. 17 [a]For the kingdom of God
is not a matter of food and drink, but of righteousness, peace, and joy in the holy Spirit;
18 whoever serves Christ in this way is pleasing
to God and approved by others. 19 [b]*Let us
then pursue what leads to peace and to building
up one another. 20 [c]For the sake of food, do not
destroy the work of God. Everything is indeed
clean, but it is wrong for anyone to become a
stumbling block by eating; 21 it is good not to
eat meat or drink wine or do anything that
causes your brother to stumble. 22 Keep the
faith [that] you have to yourself in the presence
of God; blessed is the one who does not condemn himself for what he approves. 23 [d]*But
whoever has doubts is condemned if he eats,
because this is not from faith; for whatever is not
from faith is sin.

## CHAPTER 15

### Patience and Self-Denial
1 [e]We who are
strong ought to put up with the failings of the
weak and not to please ourselves; 2 [f]let each of
us please our neighbor for the good, for building
up. 3 [g]*For Christ did not please himself; but,
as it is written, "The insults of those who insult
you fall upon me." 4 [h]For whatever was written previously was written for our instruction,
that by endurance and by the encouragement of

l 1 Cor 8, 1-13.
m 15, 1.7; 1 Cor 9, 22.
n Gn 1, 29; 9, 3; 1 Cor 8, 1-13; 10, 14-33.
o Col 2, 16.
p 2, 1; Mt 7, 11; Jas 4, 11-12.
q Gal 4, 10.
r Lk 20, 38; 2 Cor 5, 15; Gal 2, 20; 1 Thes 5, 10.
s Acts 10, 42.
t Acts 17, 31; 2 Cor 5, 10.
u Is 49, 18 / Is 45, 23; Phil 2, 10-11.
v Gal 6, 5.
w 1 Cor 8, 9.13.
x Mk 7, 5.20; Acts 10, 15; 1 Cor 10, 25-27; 1 Tm 4, 4.
y 1 Cor 8, 11-13.
z 2, 24; Ti 2, 5.
a 1 Cor 8, 8.
b 12, 18 / 15, 2.
c 1 Cor 8, 11-13; 10, 28-29; Ti 1, 15.
d Ti 1, 15; Jas 4, 17.
e 14, 1-2.
f 14, 1.19; 1 Cor 9, 19; 10, 24.33.
g Ps 69, 10.
h 4, 23-24; 1 Mc 12, 9; 1 Cor 10, 11; 2 Tm 3, 16.

*

14, 1—15, 6: Since Christ spells termination of the law, which included observance of specific days and festivals as well as dietary instruction, the jettisoning of long-practiced customs was traumatic for many Christians brought up under the Mosaic code. Although Paul acknowledges that in principle no food is a source of moral contamination (14), he recommends that the consciences of Christians who are scrupulous in this regard be respected by other Christians (21). On the other hand, those who have scruples are not to sit in judgment on those who know that the gospel has liberated them from such ordinances (10). See 1 Cor 8 and 10.

14, 5: Since the problem to be overcome was humanity's perverted mind or judgment (1, 28), Paul indicates that the *mind* of the Christian is now able to function with appropriate discrimination (cf 12, 2).

14, 8: *The Lord:* Jesus, our Master. The same Greek word, *kyrios,* was applied to both rulers and holders of slaves. Throughout the Letter to the Romans Paul emphasizes God's total claim on the believer; see the note on 1, 1.

14, 19: Some manuscripts, versions, and church Fathers read, "We then pursue . . ."; cf 5, 1.

14, 23: *Whatever is not from faith is sin:* Paul does not mean that all the actions of unbelievers are sinful. He addresses himself to the question of intracommunity living. *Sin* in the singular is the dreadful power described in 5, 12–14.

15, 3: Liberation from the law of Moses does not make the scriptures of the old covenant irrelevant. Much consolation and motivation for Christian living can be derived from the Old Testament, as in the citation from Ps 69, 10. Because this psalm is quoted several times in the New Testament, it has been called indirectly messianic.

the scriptures we might have hope. 5 [i]*May the
God of endurance and encouragement grant you
to think in harmony with one another, in keeping with Christ Jesus, 6 that with one accord
you may with one voice glorify the God and
Father of our Lord Jesus Christ.

**God's Fidelity and Mercy** 7 [j]*Welcome
one another, then, as Christ welcomed you, for
the glory of God. 8 [k]For I say that Christ became a minister of the circumcised to show
God's truthfulness, to confirm the promises to
the patriarchs, 9 [l]but so that the Gentiles might
glorify God for his mercy. As it is written:

"Therefore, I will praise you among the
Gentiles
and sing praises to your name."

10 [m]*And again it says:

"Rejoice, O Gentiles, with his people."

11 [n]And again:

"Praise the Lord, all you Gentiles,
and let all the peoples praise him."

12 [o]And again Isaiah says:

"The root of Jesse shall come,
raised up to rule the Gentiles;
in him shall the Gentiles hope."

13 [p]May the God of hope fill you with all joy
and peace in believing, so that you may abound
in hope by the power of the holy Spirit.

## *VII: CONCLUSION*

**Apostle to the Gentiles** 14 *I myself am
convinced about you, my brothers, that you
yourselves are full of goodness, filled with all
knowledge, and able to admonish one another.
15 [q]But I have written to you rather boldly in
some respects to remind you, because of the
grace given me by God 16 [r]to be a minister of
Christ Jesus to the Gentiles in performing the
priestly service of the gospel of God, so that the
offering up of the Gentiles may be acceptable,
sanctified by the holy Spirit. 17 In Christ Jesus,
then, I have reason to boast in what pertains to
God. 18 [s]For I will not dare to speak of anything except what Christ has accomplished
through me to lead the Gentiles to obedience by
word and deed, 19 *by the power of signs and
wonders, by the power of the Spirit [of God],
so that from Jerusalem all the way around to
Illyricum I have finished preaching the gospel
of Christ. 20 [t]*Thus I aspire to proclaim the
gospel not where Christ has already been
named, so that I do not build on another's foundation, 21 [u]*but as it is written:

"Those who have never been told of him
shall see,
and those who have never heard of him
shall understand."

**Paul's Plans; Need for Prayers** 22 That
is why I have so often been prevented from
coming to you. 23 [v]But now, since I no longer
have any opportunity in these regions and since
I have desired to come to you for many years,
24 [w]I hope to see you in passing as I go to Spain
and to be sent on my way there by you, after I
have enjoyed being with you for a time.
25 [x]*Now, however, I am going to Jerusalem
to minister to the holy ones. 26 [y]*For Macedonia and Achaia have decided to make some

i 12, 16; Phil 2, 2; 4, 2.
j 14, 1.
k Mt 15, 24 / Mi 7, 20; Acts 3, 25.
l 11, 30 / 2 Sm 22, 50; Ps 18, 50.
m Dt 32, 43.
n Ps 117, 1.
o Is 11, 10; Rv 5, 5; 22, 16.
p 5, 1-2.
q 1, 5; 12, 3.
r 11, 13; Phil 2, 17.
s Acts 15, 12; 2 Cor 12, 12.
t 2 Cor 10, 13-18.
u Is 52, 15.
v 1, 10-13; Acts 19, 21-22.
w 1 Cor 16, 6.
x Acts 19, 21; 20, 22.
y 1 Cor 16, 1; 2 Cor 8, 1-4; 9, 2.12.

*

15, 5: *Think in harmony:* a Greco-Roman ideal. Not rigid uniformity of thought and expression but thoughtful consideration of other people's views finds expression here.

15, 7–13: True oneness of mind is found in pondering the ultimate mission of the church: to bring it about that God's name be glorified throughout the world and that Jesus Christ be universally recognized as God's gift to all humanity. Paul here prepares his addressees for the climactic appeal he is about to make.

15, 10: Paul's citation of Dt 32, 43 follows the Greek version.

15, 14–33: Paul sees himself as apostle and benefactor in the priestly service of the gospel and so sketches plans for a mission in Spain, supported by those in Rome.

15, 14: *Full of goodness:* the opposite of what humanity was filled with according to 1, 29–30.

15, 19: *Illyricum:* Roman province northwest of Greece on the eastern shore of the Adriatic.

15, 20: *I aspire:* Paul uses terminology customarily applied to philanthropists. Unlike some philanthropists of his time, Paul does not engage in cheap competition for public acclaim. This explanation of his missionary policy is to assure the Christians in Rome that he is also not planning to remain in that city and build on other people's foundations (cf 2 Cor 10, 12–18). However, he does solicit their help in sending him on his way to Spain, which was considered the limit of the western world. Thus Paul's addressees realize that evangelization may be understood in the broader sense of mission or, as in Rom 1, 15, of instruction within the Christian community that derives from the gospel.

15, 21: The citation from Is 52, 15 concerns the Servant of the Lord. According to Isaiah, the Servant is first of all Israel, which was to bring the knowledge of Yahweh to the nations. In chs 9–11 Paul showed how Israel failed in this mission. Therefore, he himself undertakes almost singlehandedly Israel's responsibility as the Servant and moves as quickly as possible with the gospel through the Roman empire.

15, 25–27: Paul may have viewed the contribution he was gathering from Gentile Christians for the poor in Jerusalem (cf 2 Cor 8 and 9) as a fulfillment of the vision of Is 60, 5–6. In confidence that the messianic fulfillment was taking place, Paul stresses in chs 14–16 the importance of harmonious relationships between Jews and Gentiles.

15, 26: *Achaia:* the Roman province of southern Greece.

contribution for the poor among the holy ones
in Jerusalem; 27 [z]they decided to do it, and in
fact they are indebted to them, for if the Gentiles
have come to share in their spiritual blessings,
they ought also to serve them in material blessings. 28 So when I have completed this and
safely handed over this contribution to them, I
shall set out by way of you to Spain; 29 and I
know that in coming to you I shall come in the
fullness of Christ's blessing.

30 [a]I urge you, [brothers,] by our Lord Jesus
Christ and by the love of the Spirit, to join me
in the struggle by your prayers to God on my
behalf, 31 that I may be delivered from the
disobedient in Judea, and that my ministry for
Jerusalem may be acceptable to the holy ones,
32 so that I may come to you with joy by the
will of God and be refreshed together with you.
33 [b]The God of peace be with all of you.
Amen.

## CHAPTER 16

### Phoebe Commended

1 [c]*I commend to
you Phoebe our sister, who is [also] a minister
of the church at Cenchreae, 2 that you may
receive her in the Lord in a manner worthy of
the holy ones, and help her in whatever she may
need from you, for she has been a benefactor to
many and to me as well.

### Paul's Greetings

3 [d]*Greet Prisca and
Aquila, my co-workers in Christ Jesus, 4 who
risked their necks for my life, to whom not only
I am grateful but also all the churches of the
Gentiles; 5 [e]*greet also the church at their
house. Greet my beloved Epaenetus, who was
the firstfruits in Asia for Christ. 6 Greet Mary,
who has worked hard for you. 7 *Greet Andronicus and Junia, my relatives and my fellow
prisoners; they are prominent among the apostles and they were in Christ before me. 8 Greet
Ampliatus, my beloved in the Lord. 9 Greet
Urbanus, our co-worker in Christ, and my beloved Stachys. 10 Greet Apelles, who is approved in Christ. Greet those who belong to the
family of Aristobulus. 11 Greet my relative He-
rodion. Greet those in the Lord who belong to
the family of Narcissus. 12 Greet those workers
in the Lord, Tryphaena and Tryphosa. Greet the
beloved Persis, who has worked hard in the
Lord. 13 [f]*Greet Rufus, chosen in the Lord,
and his mother and mine. 14 Greet Asyncritus,
Phlegon, Hermes, Patrobas, Hermas, and the
brothers who are with them. 15 Greet Philolo-
gus, Julia, Nereus and his sister, and Olympas,
and all the holy ones who are with them.
16 [g]Greet one another with a holy kiss. All the
churches of Christ greet you.

### Against Factions

17 [h]*I urge you, broth-
ers, to watch out for those who create dissensions and obstacles, in opposition to the teaching that you learned; avoid them. 18 [i]For such
people do not serve our Lord Christ but their
own appetites, and by fair and flattering speech
they deceive the hearts of the innocent. 19 [j]For
while your obedience is known to all, so that I
rejoice over you, I want you to be wise as to
what is good, and simple as to what is evil;
20 [k]*then the God of peace will quickly crush
Satan under your feet. The grace of our Lord
Jesus be with you.

### Greetings from Corinth

21 [l]Timothy,
my co-worker, greets you; so do Lucius and
Jason and Sosipater, my relatives. 22 I, Terti-
us, the writer of this letter, greet you in the
Lord. 23 [m]*Gaius, who is host to me and to the

z 9, 4 / 1 Cor 9, 11.
a 2 Cor 1, 11; Phil 1, 27; Col 4, 3; 2 Thes 3, 1.
b 16, 20; 2 Cor 13, 11; Phil 4, 9; 1 Thes 5, 23; 2 Thes 3, 16;Heb 13, 20.
c Acts 18, 18.
d Acts 18, 2.18-26; 1 Cor 16, 19; 2 Tm 4, 19.
e 1 Cor 16, 19; Col 4, 15; Phlm 2 / 1 Cor 16, 15.
f Mk 15, 21.
g 1 Cor 16, 20; 2 Cor 13, 12; 1 Thes 5, 26; 1 Pt 5, 14.
h Mt 7, 15; Ti 3, 10.
i Phil 3, 18-19 / Col 2, 4; 2 Pt 2, 3.
j 1, 8; Mt 10, 16; 1 Cor 14, 20.
k 15, 33; Gn 3, 15; Lk 10, 19 / 1 Cor 16, 23; 1 Thes 5, 28;2 Thes 3, 18.
l Acts 16, 1-2; 19, 22; 20, 4; 1 Cor 4, 17; 16, 10; Phil 2, 19-22;Heb 13, 23.
m Acts 19, 29; 1 Cor 1, 14 / 2 Tm 4, 20.

*

16, 1–23: Some authorities regard these verses as a later addition to the letter, but in general the evidence favors the view that they were included in the original. Paul endeavors through the long list of greetings (3–16; 21–23) to establish strong personal contact with congregations that he has not personally encountered before. The combination of Jewish and Gentile names dramatically attests the unity in the gospel that transcends previous barriers of nationality, religious ceremony, or racial status.

16, 1: *Minister:* in Greek, *diakonos;* see the note on Phil 1, 1.

16, 3: *Prisca and Aquila:* presumably the couple mentioned at Acts 18, 2; 1 Cor 16, 19; 2 Tm 4, 19.

16, 5: *The church at their house:* i.e., that meets there. Such local assemblies (cf 1 Cor 16, 19; Col 4, 15; Phlm 2) might consist of only one or two dozen Christians each. It is understandable, therefore, that such smaller groups might experience difficulty in relating to one another on certain issues. *Firstfruits:* cf 8, 23; 11, 16; 1 Cor 16, 15.

16, 7: The name Junia is a woman's name. One ancient Greek manuscript and a number of ancient versions read the name "Julia." Most editors have interpreted it as a man's name, Junias.

16, 13: This Rufus cannot be identified to any degree of certainty with the Rufus of Mk 15, 21.

16, 17–18: Paul displays genuine concern for the congregations in Rome by warning them against self-seeking teachers. It would be a great loss, he intimates, if their obedience, which is known to all (cf 1, 8), would be diluted.

16, 20: This verse contains the only mention of Satan in Romans.

16, 23: This Erastus is not necessarily to be identified with the Erastus of Acts 19, 22 or of 2 Tm 4, 20.

16, 24 Some manuscripts add, similarly to v 20, "The grace of our Lord Jesus Christ be with you all. Amen."

whole church, greets you. Erastus, the city treasurer, and our brother Quartus greet you. [24*]

**Doxology** [25 [n]*Now to him who can
strengthen you, according to my gospel and the
proclamation of Jesus Christ, according to the
revelation of the mystery kept secret for long
ages 26 [o]but now manifested through the prophetic writings and, according to the command
of the eternal God, made known to all nations
to bring about the obedience of faith, 27 [p]to the
only wise God, through Jesus Christ be glory
forever and ever. Amen.]

n 1 Cor 2, 7; Eph 1, 9; 3, 3-9; Col 1, 26.
o 2 Tm 1, 10 / 1, 5; Eph 3, 4-5.9; 1 Pt 1, 20.
p 11, 36; Gal 1, 5; Eph 3, 20-21; Phil 4, 20; 1 Tm 1, 17; 2 Tm 4, 18; Heb 13, 21; 1 Pt 4, 11; 2 Pt 3, 18; Jude 25, Rev 1, 6.

*

16, 25–27: This doxology is assigned variously to the end of chs 14, 15, and 16 in the manuscript tradition. Some manuscripts omit it entirely. Whether written by Paul or not, it forms an admirable conclusion to the letter at this point.

16, 25: Paul's gospel reveals *the mystery kept secret for long ages:* justification and salvation through faith, with all the implications for Jews and Gentiles that Paul has developed in the letter.

# THE FIRST LETTER TO THE
# CORINTHIANS

## INTRODUCTION

*Paul's first letter to the church of Corinth provides us with a fuller insight into the life of an early Christian community of the first generation than any other book of the New Testament. Through it we can glimpse both the strengths and the weaknesses of this small group in a great city of the ancient world, men and women who had accepted the good news of Christ and were now trying to realize in their lives the implications of their baptism. Paul, who had founded the community and continued to look after it as a father, responds both to questions addressed to him and to situations of which he had been informed. In doing so, he reveals much about himself, his teaching, and the way in which he conducted his work of apostleship. Some things are puzzling because we have the correspondence only in one direction. For the person studying this letter, it seems to raise as many questions as it answers, but without it our knowledge of church life in the middle of the first century would be much poorer.*

*Paul established a Christian community in Corinth about the year 51, on his second missionary journey. The city, a commercial crossroads, was a melting pot full of devotees of various pagan cults and marked by a measure of moral depravity not unusual in a great seaport. The Acts of the Apostles suggests that moderate success attended Paul's efforts among the Jews in Corinth at first, but that they soon turned against him (Acts 18, 1–8). More fruitful was his year and a half spent among the Gentiles (Acts 18, 11), which won to the faith many of the city's poor and underprivileged (1, 26). After his departure the eloquent Apollos, an Alexandrian Jewish Christian, rendered great service to the community, expounding "from the scriptures that the Messiah is Jesus" (Acts 18, 24–28).*

*While Paul was in Ephesus on his third journey (16, 8; Acts 19, 1–20), he received disquieting news about Corinth. The community there was displaying open factionalism, as certain members were identifying themselves exclusively with individual Christian leaders and interpreting Christian teaching as a superior wisdom for the initiated few (1, 10—4, 21). The community lacked the decisiveness to take appropriate action against one of its members who was living publicly in an incestuous union (5, 1–13). Other members engaged in legal conflicts in pagan courts of law (6, 1–11); still others may have participated in religious prostitution (6, 12–20) or temple sacrifices (10, 14–22).*

*The community's ills were reflected in its liturgy. In the celebration of the Eucharist certain members discriminated against others, drank too freely at the agape, or fellowship meal, and denied Christian social courtesies to the poor among the membership (11, 17–22). Charisms such as ecstatic prayer, attributed freely to the impulse of the holy Spirit, were more highly prized than works of charity (13, 1–2.8), and were used at times in a disorderly way (14, 1–40). Women appeared at the assembly without the customary head-covering (11, 3–16), and perhaps were quarreling over their right to address the assembly (14, 34–35).*

*Still other problems with which Paul had to deal concerned matters of conscience discussed among the faithful members of the community: the eating of meat that had been sacrificed to idols (8, 1–13), the use of sex in marriage (7, 1–7), and the attitude to be taken by the unmarried toward marriage in view of the possible proximity of Christ's second coming (7, 25–40). There was also a doctrinal matter that called for Paul's attention, for some members of the community, despite their belief in the resurrection of Christ, were denying the possibility of general bodily resurrection.*

*To treat this wide spectrum of questions, Paul wrote this letter from Ephesus about the year 56. The majority of the Corinthian Christians may well have been quite faithful. Paul writes on their behalf to guard against the threats posed to the community by the views and conduct of various minorities. He writes with confidence in the authority of his apostolic mission, and he presumes that the Corinthians, despite their deficiencies, will recognize and accept it. On the other hand, he does not hesitate to exercise his authority as his judgment dictates in each situation, even going so far as to promise a direct confrontation with recalcitrants, should the abuses he scores remain uncorrected (4, 18–21).*

*The letter illustrates well the mind and character of Paul. Although he is impelled to insist on his office as founder of the community, he recognizes that he is only one servant of God among many and generously acknowledges the labors of Apollos (3, 5–8). He provides us in this letter with many valuable examples of his method of theological reflection and exposition. He always treats the questions at issue on the level of the purity of Christian teaching and conduct. Certain passages of the letter are of the greatest importance for the understanding of early Christian teaching on the Eucharist (10, 14–22; 11, 17–34) and on the resurrection of the body (15, 1–58).*

*Paul's authorship of 1 Corinthians, apart from a few verses that some regard as later interpolations, has never been seriously questioned. Some scholars have proposed, however, that the letter as we have it contains portions of more than one original Pauline letter. We know that Paul wrote at least two other letters to Corinth (see 5, 9; 2 Cor 2, 3–4) in addition to the two that we now have; this theory holds that the additional letters are actually contained within the two canonical ones. Most commentators, however, find 1 Corinthians quite understandable as a single coherent work.*

*The principal divisions of the First Letter to the Corinthians are the following:*

*I. Address (1, 1–9)*
*II. Disorders in the Corinthian Community (1, 10—6, 20)*
*A. Divisions in the Church (1, 10—4, 21)*
*B. Moral Disorders (5, 1—6, 20)*
*III. Answers to the Corinthians' Questions (7, 1—11, 1)*
*A. Marriage and Virginity (7, 1–40)*
*B. Offerings to Idols (8, 1—11, 1)*
*IV. Problems in Liturgical Assemblies (11, 2—14, 40)*
*A. Women's Headdresses (11, 3–16)*
*B. The Lord's Supper (11, 17–34)*
*C. Spiritual Gifts (12, 1—14, 40)*
*V. The Resurrection (15, 1–58)*
*A. The Resurrection of Christ (15, 1–11)*
*B. The Resurrection of the Dead (15, 12–34)*
*C. The Manner of the Resurrection (15, 35–58)*
*VI. Conclusion (16, 1–24)*

# *I: ADDRESS*

## CHAPTER 1

**Greeting** **1** [a]*Paul, called to be an apostle of Christ Jesus by the will of God, and Sosthenes our brother, **2** [b]to the church of God that is in Corinth, to you who have been sanctified in Christ Jesus, called to be holy, with all those everywhere who call upon the name of our Lord Jesus Christ, their Lord and ours. **3** Grace to you and peace from God our Father and the Lord Jesus Christ.

**Thanksgiving** **4** I give thanks to my God always on your account for the grace of God bestowed on you in Christ Jesus, **5** that in him you were enriched in every way, with all discourse and all knowledge, **6** *as the testimony to Christ was confirmed among you, **7** [c]so that

a Rom 1, 1. b Acts 18, 1-11. c Ti 2, 13.

*

1, 1-9: Paul follows the conventional form for the opening of a Hellenistic letter (cf Rom 1, 1–7), but expands the opening with details carefully chosen to remind the readers of their situation and to suggest some of the issues the letter will discuss.

1, 1: *Called . . . by the will of God:* Paul's mission and the church's existence are grounded in God's initiative. God's call, grace, and fidelity are central ideas in this introduction, emphasized by repetition and wordplays in the Greek.

1, 6: *The testimony:* this defines the purpose of Paul's mission (see also 15, 15 and the note on 2, 1). The forms of his testimony include oral preaching and instruction, his letters, and the life he leads as an apostle.

you are not lacking in any spiritual gift as you wait for the revelation of our Lord Jesus Christ.
**8** [d]He will keep you firm to the end, irreproachable on the day of our Lord Jesus [Christ].
**9** [e]God is faithful, and by him you were called to fellowship with his Son, Jesus Christ our Lord.

## *II: DISORDERS IN THE CORINTHIAN COMMUNITY*

## A. Divisions in the Church

**Groups and Slogans** **10** [f]*I urge you, brothers, in the name of our Lord Jesus Christ, that all of you agree in what you say, and that there be no divisions among you, but that you be united in the same mind and in the same purpose.
**11** For it has been reported to me about you, my brothers, by Chloe's people, that there are rivalries among you.
**12** [g]*I mean that each of you is saying, "I belong to Paul," or "I belong to Apollos," or "I belong to Cephas," or "I belong to Christ."
**13** *Is Christ divided? Was Paul crucified for you? Or were you baptized in the name of Paul?
**14** [h]I give thanks [to God] that I baptized none of you except Crispus and Gaius,
**15** so that no one can say you were baptized in my name.
**16** [i](I baptized the household of Stephanas also; beyond that I do not know whether I baptized anyone else.)
**17** [j]*For Christ did not send me to baptize but to preach the gospel, and not with the wisdom of human eloquence, so that the cross of Christ might not be emptied of its meaning.

**Paradox of the Cross** **18** [k]The message of the cross is foolishness to those who are perishing, but to us who are being saved it is the power of God.
**19** [l]For it is written:

"I will destroy the wisdom of the wise,
and the learning of the learned I will set aside."

**20** [m]Where is the wise one? Where is the scribe? Where is the debater of this age? Has not God made the wisdom of the world foolish?
**21** *For since in the wisdom of God the world did not come to know God through wisdom, it was the will of God through the foolishness of the proclamation to save those who have faith.
**22** [n]For Jews demand signs and Greeks look for wisdom,
**23** [o]but we proclaim Christ crucified, a stumbling block to Jews and foolishness to Gentiles,
**24** but to those who are called, Jews and Greeks alike, Christ the power of God and the wisdom of God.
**25** For the foolishness of God is wiser than human wisdom, and the weakness of God is stronger than human strength.

**The Corinthians and Paul** **26** *Consider your own calling, brothers. Not many of you were wise by human standards, not many were powerful, not many were of noble birth.
**27** [p]Rather, God chose the foolish of the world to shame the wise, and God chose the weak of

d Phil 1, 6.
e 1 Jn 1, 3.
f Phil 2, 2.
g 3, 4.22; 16, 12; Acts 18, 24-28.
h Acts 18, 8 / Rom 16, 23.
i 16, 15-17.
j 2, 1.4.
k 2, 14 / Rom 1, 16.
l Is 29, 14.
m Is 19, 12.
n Mt 12, 38; 16, 1 / Acts 17, 18-21.
o 2, 2; Gal 3, 1 / Gal 5, 11.
p Jas 2, 5.

*

1, 10—4, 21: The first problem Paul addresses is that of divisions within the community. Although we are unable to reconstruct the situation in Corinth completely, Paul clearly traces the divisions back to a false self-image on the part of the Corinthians, coupled with a false understanding of the apostles who preached to them (cf 4, 6.9; 9, 1–5) and of the Christian message itself. In these chapters he attempts to deal with those underlying factors and to bring the Corinthians back to a more correct perspective.

1, 12: *I belong to:* the activities of Paul and Apollos in Corinth are described in Acts 18. *Cephas* (i.e., "the Rock," a name by which Paul designates Peter also in 3, 22; 9, 5; 15, 5 and in Gal 1, 18; 2, 9.11.14) may well have passed through Corinth; he could have baptized some members of the community either there or elsewhere. The reference to *Christ* may be intended ironically here.

1, 13–17: The reference to baptism and the contrast with preaching the gospel in v 17a suggest that some Corinthians were paying special allegiance to the individuals who initiated them into the community.

1, 17b–18: The basic theme of chs 1–4 is announced. Adherence to individual leaders has something to do with differences in rhetorical ability and also with certain presuppositions regarding wisdom, eloquence, and effectiveness (power), which Paul judges to be in conflict with the gospel and the cross.

1, 17b: *Not with the wisdom of human eloquence:* both of the nouns employed here involve several levels of meaning, on which Paul deliberately plays as his thought unfolds. *Wisdom* (*sophia*) may be philosophical and speculative, but in biblical usage the term primarily denotes practical knowledge such as is demonstrated in the choice and effective application of means to achieve an end. The same term can designate the arts of building (cf 3, 10) or of persuasive speaking (cf 2, 4) or effectiveness in achieving salvation. *Eloquence* (*logos*): this translation emphasizes one possible meaning of the term *logos* (cf the references to rhetorical style and persuasiveness in 2, 1.4). But the term itself may denote an internal reasoning process, plan, or intention, as well as an external word, speech, or message. So by his expression *ouk en sophia logou* in the context of gospel preaching, Paul may intend to exclude both human ways of reasoning or thinking about things and human rhetorical technique. *Human:* this adjective does not stand in the Greek text but is supplied from the context. Paul will begin immediately to distinguish between *sophia* and *logos* from their divine counterparts and play them off against each other.

1, 21–25: True wisdom and power are to be found paradoxically where one would least expect them, in the place of their apparent negation. To human eyes the crucified Christ symbolizes impotence and absurdity.

1, 26—2, 5: The pattern of God's wisdom and power is exemplified in their own experience, if they interpret it rightly (1, 26–31), and can also be read in their experience of Paul as he first appeared among them preaching the gospel (2, 1–5).

the world to shame the strong, **28** and God chose the lowly and despised of the world, those who count for nothing, to reduce to nothing those who are something, **29** [q]*so that no human being might boast before God. **30** [r]It is due to him that you are in Christ Jesus, who became for us wisdom from God, as well as righteousness, sanctification, and redemption, **31** [s]so that, as it is written, "Whoever boasts, should boast in the Lord."

## CHAPTER 2

**1** [t]*When I came to you, brothers, proclaiming the mystery of God, I did not come with sublimity of words or of wisdom. **2** [u]For I resolved to know nothing while I was with you except Jesus Christ, and him crucified. **3** *I came to you in weakness and fear and much trembling, **4** [v]*and my message and my proclamation were not with persuasive [words of] wisdom, but with a demonstration of spirit and power, **5** [w]so that your faith might rest not on human wisdom but on the power of God.

**The True Wisdom** **6** *Yet we do speak a wisdom to those who are mature, but not a wisdom of this age, nor of the rulers of this age who are passing away. **7** *Rather we speak God's wisdom, mysterious, hidden, which God predetermined before the ages for our glory, **8** *and which none of the rulers of this age knew, for if they had known it, they would not have crucified the Lord of glory. **9** [x]But as it is written:

"What eye has not seen, and ear has not heard,
and what has not entered the human heart,
what God has prepared for those who love him,"

**10** [y]this God has revealed to us through the Spirit.

For the Spirit scrutinizes everything, even the depths of God. **11** Among human beings, who knows what pertains to a person except the spirit of the person that is within? Similarly, no one knows what pertains to God except the Spirit of God. **12** We have not received the spirit of the world but the Spirit that is from God, so that we may understand the things freely given us by God. **13** *And we speak about them not with words taught by human wisdom, but with words taught by the Spirit, describing spiritual realities in spiritual terms.

**14** *Now the natural person does not accept what pertains to the Spirit of God, for to him it is foolishness, and he cannot understand it, because it is judged spiritually. **15** *The spiritual person, however, can judge everything but is not subject to judgment by anyone.

**16** [z]For "who has known the mind of the Lord, so as to counsel him?" But we have the mind of Christ.

q Eph 2, 9.
r Rom 4, 17 / 6, 11; Rom 3, 24-26; 2 Cor 5, 21 / Eph 1, 7;Col 1, 14; 1 Thes 5, 23.
s Jer 9, 23; 2 Cor 10, 17.
t 1, 17.
u 1, 23; Gal 6, 14.
v 4, 20; Rom 15, 19; 1 Thes 1, 5.
w 2 Cor 4, 7.
x Is 64, 3.
y Mt 11, 25; 13, 11; 16, 17.
z Wis 9, 13; Is 40, 13; Rom 11, 34.

*

1, 29–31: "Boasting (about oneself)" is a Pauline expression for the radical sin, the claim to autonomy on the part of a creature, the illusion that we live and are saved by our own resources. "Boasting in the Lord" (31), on the other hand, is the acknowledgment that we live only from God and for God.

2, 1: *The mystery of God:* God's secret, known only to himself, is his plan for the salvation of his people; it is clear from 1, 18–25; 2, 2.8–10 that this secret involves Jesus and the cross. In place of *mystery,* other good manuscripts read "testimony" (cf 1, 6).

2, 3: The *weakness* of the crucified Jesus is reflected in Paul's own bearing (cf 2 Cor 10–13). *Fear and much trembling:* reverential fear based on a sense of God's transcendence permeates Paul's existence and preaching. Compare his advice to the Philippians to work out their salvation with "fear and trembling" (Phil 2, 12), because God is at work in them just as his exalting power was paradoxically at work in the emptying, humiliation, and obedience of Jesus to death on the cross (Phil 2, 6–11).

2, 4: Among many manuscript readings here the best is either "not with the persuasion of wisdom" or "not with persuasive words of wisdom," which differ only by a nuance. Whichever reading is accepted, the inefficacy of human wisdom for salvation is contrasted with the power of the cross.

2, 6—3, 4: Paul now asserts paradoxically what he has previously been denying. To the Greeks who "are looking for wisdom" (1, 22), he does indeed bring a wisdom, but of a higher order and an entirely different quality, the only wisdom really worthy of the name. The Corinthians would be able to grasp Paul's preaching as wisdom and enter into a wisdom-conversation with him if they were more open to the Spirit and receptive to the new insight and language that the Spirit teaches.

2, 7–10a: *God's wisdom:* his plan for our salvation. This was his own eternal secret that no one else could fathom, but in this new age of salvation he has graciously revealed it to us. For the pattern of God's secret, hidden to others and now revealed to the Church, cf also Rom 11, 25–36; 16, 25–27; Eph 1, 3–10; 3, 3–11; Col 1, 25–28.

2, 8: *The rulers of this age:* this suggests not only the political leaders of the Jews and Romans under whom Jesus was crucified (cf Acts 4, 25–28) but also the cosmic powers behind them (cf Eph 1, 20–23; 3, 10). *They would not have crucified the Lord of glory:* they became the unwitting executors of God's plan, which will paradoxically bring about their own conquest and submission (15, 24–28).

2, 13: *In spiritual terms:* the Spirit teaches spiritual people a new mode of perception (12) and an appropriate language by which they can share their self-understanding, their knowledge about what God has done in them. The final phrase in v 13 can also be translated "describing spiritual realities to spiritual people," in which case it prepares for vv 14–16.

2, 14: *The natural person:* see the note on 3, 1.

2, 15: *The spiritual person . . . is not subject to judgment:* since spiritual persons have been given knowledge of what pertains to God (11–12), they share in God's own capacity to judge. One to whom the mind of the Lord (and of Christ) is revealed (16) can be said to share in some sense in God's exemption from counseling and criticism.

## CHAPTER 3

**1** *My brothers, I could not talk to you as
spiritual people, but as fleshly people, as infants
in Christ. **2** [a]I fed you milk, not solid food,
because you were unable to take it. Indeed, you
are still not able, even now, **3** [b]*for you are still
of the flesh. While there is jealousy and rivalry
among you, are you not of the flesh, and behaving in an ordinary human way? **4** [c]Whenever
someone says, "I belong to Paul," and another,
"I belong to Apollos," are you not merely human?

**The Role of God's Ministers** **5** *What is
Apollos, after all, and what is Paul? Ministers
through whom you became believers, just as the
Lord assigned each one. **6** [d]I planted, Apollos
watered, but God caused the growth. **7** Therefore neither the one who plants nor the one who
waters is anything, but only God, who causes
the growth. **8** The one who plants and the one
who waters are equal, and each will receive
wages in proportion to his labor. **9** [e]For we are
God's co-workers; you are God's field, God's
building.

**10** *According to the grace of God given to
me, like a wise master builder I laid a foundation, and another is building upon it. But each
one must be careful how he builds upon it,
**11** for no one can lay a foundation other than
the one that is there, namely, Jesus Christ. **12** If
anyone builds on this foundation with gold, silver, precious stones, wood, hay, or straw,
**13** [f]*the work of each will come to light, for the
Day will disclose it. It will be revealed with fire,
and the fire [itself] will test the quality of each
one's work. **14** If the work stands that someone
built upon the foundation, that person will receive a wage. **15** *But if someone's work is
burned up, that one will suffer loss; the person
will be saved, but only as through fire. **16** [g]Do
you not know that you are the temple of God,
and that the Spirit of God dwells in you? **17** *If
anyone destroys God's temple, God will destroy
that person; for the temple of God, which you
are, is holy.

**18** [h]Let no one deceive himself. If anyone
among you considers himself wise in this age,
let him become a fool, so as to become wise.
**19** [i]For the wisdom of this world is foolishness
in the eyes of God, for it is written:

"He catches the wise in their own ruses,"

**20** [j]and again:

"The Lord knows the thoughts of the wise,
that they are vain."

**21** [k]*So let no one boast about human beings,
for everything belongs to you, **22** Paul or Apollos or Cephas, or the world or life or death, or

---

a Heb 5, 12-14.
b Jas 3, 13-16.
c 1, 12.
d Acts 18, 1-11.24-28.
e Eph 2, 20-22; 1 Pt 2, 5.
f Mt 3, 11-12; 2 Thes 1, 7-10.
g 6, 19; 2 Cor 6, 16; Eph 2, 20-22.
h 8, 2; Is 5, 21; Gal 6, 3.
i 1, 20 / Jb 5, 13.
j Ps 94, 11.
k 4, 6 / Rom 8, 32.

---

*

3, 1–4: The Corinthians desire a sort of wisdom dialogue or colloquy with Paul; they are looking for solid, adult food, and he appears to disappoint their expectations. Paul counters: if such a dialogue has not yet taken place, the reason is that they are still at an immature stage of development (cf 2, 6).

3, 1: *Spiritual people . . . fleshly people:* Paul employs two clusters of concepts and terms to distinguish what later theology will call the "natural" and the "supernatural." (1) The natural person (2, 14) is one whose existence, perceptions, and behavior are determined by purely natural principles, the *psychē* (2, 14) and the *sarx* (flesh, a biblical term that connotes creatureliness, 1.3). Such persons are only infants (1); they remain on a purely human level (*anthrōpoi*, 4). (2) On the other hand, they are called to be animated by a higher principle, the *pneuma*, God's spirit. They are to become spiritual (*pneumatikoi*, 1) and mature (2, 6) in their perceptions and behavior (cf Gal 5, 16–26). The culmination of existence in the Spirit is described in 15, 44–49.

3, 3–4: Jealousy, rivalry, and divisions in the community are symptoms of their arrested development; they reveal the immaturity both of their self-understanding (4) and of the judgments about their apostles (21).

3, 5—4, 5: The Corinthians tend to evaluate their leaders by the criteria of human wisdom and to exaggerate their importance. Paul views the role of the apostles in the light of his theology of spiritual gifts (cf chs 12–14, where the charism of the apostle heads the lists). The essential aspects of all spiritual gifts (12, 4–6 presents them as gifts of grace, as services, and as modes of activity) are exemplified by the apostolate, which is a gift of grace (3, 10) through which God works (3, 9) and a form of service (3, 5) for the common good (elsewhere expressed by the verb "build up," suggested here by the image of the building, 3, 9). The apostles serve the church, but their accountability is to God and to Christ (4, 1–5).

3, 5: *Ministers:* for other expressions of Paul's understanding of himself as minister or steward to the church, cf 4, 1; 9, 17.19–27; 2 Cor 3, 6–9; 4, 1; 5, 18; 6, 3–4; and 11, 23 (the climax of Paul's defense).

3, 10–11: There are diverse functions in the service of the community, but each individual's task is serious, and each will stand accountable for the quality of his contribution.

3, 13: *The Day:* the great day of Yahweh, the day of judgment, which can be a time of either gloom or joy. *Fire* both destroys and purifies.

3, 15: *Will be saved:* although Paul can envision very harsh divine punishment (cf 17), he appears optimistic about the success of divine corrective means both here and elsewhere (cf 5, 5; 11, 32 [discipline]). The text of v 15 has sometimes been used to support the notion of purgatory, though it does not envisage this.

3, 17: *Holy:* i.e., "belonging to God." The cultic sanctity of the community is a fundamental theological reality to which Paul frequently alludes (cf 1, 2.30; 6, 11; 7, 14).

3, 21–23: These verses pick up the line of thought of 1, 10–13. If the Corinthians were genuinely wise (18–20), their perceptions would be reversed, and they would see everything in the world and all those with whom they exist in the church in their true relations with one another. Paul assigns all the persons involved in the theological universe a position on a scale: God, Christ, church members, church leaders. Read from top to bottom, the scale expresses ownership; read from bottom to top, the obligation to serve. This picture should be complemented by similar statements such as those in 8, 6 and 15, 20–28.

the present or the future: all belong to you,
**23** and you to Christ, and Christ to God.

## CHAPTER 4

**1** [l]Thus should one regard us: as servants of
Christ and stewards of the mysteries of God.
**2** Now it is of course required of stewards that
they be found trustworthy. **3** It does not concern me in the least that I be judged by you or
any human tribunal; I do not even pass judgment
on myself; **4** [m]I am not conscious of anything
against me, but I do not thereby stand acquitted;
the one who judges me is the Lord. **5** Therefore
do not make any judgment before the appointed
time, until the Lord comes, for he will bring to
light what is hidden in darkness and will manifest the motives of our hearts, and then everyone
will receive praise from God.

**Paul's Life as Pattern** **6** *I have applied
these things to myself and Apollos for your
benefit, brothers, so that you may learn from us
not to go beyond what is written, so that none
of you will be inflated with pride in favor of one
person over against another. **7** Who confers
distinction upon you? What do you possess that
you have not received? But if you have received
it, why are you boasting as if you did not receive
it? **8** *You are already satisfied; you have already grown rich; you have become kings without us! Indeed, I wish that you had become
kings, so that we also might become kings with
you.
**9** [n]*For as I see it, God has exhibited us
apostles as the last of all, like people sentenced
to death, since we have become a spectacle to
the world, to angels and human beings alike.
**10** [o]We are fools on Christ's account, but you
are wise in Christ; we are weak, but you are
strong; you are held in honor, but we in disre-
pute. **11** [p]To this very hour we go hungry and
thirsty, we are poorly clad and roughly treated,
we wander about homeless **12** [q]and we toil,
working with our own hands. When ridiculed,
we bless; when persecuted, we endure;
**13** when slandered, we respond gently. We
have become like the world's rubbish, the scum
of all, to this very moment.
**14** *I am writing you this not to shame you,
but to admonish you as my beloved children.
**15** [r]Even if you should have countless guides
to Christ, yet you do not have many fathers, for
I became your father in Christ Jesus through the
gospel. **16** [s]Therefore, I urge you, be imitators
of me. **17** [t]For this reason I am sending you
Timothy, who is my beloved and faithful son in
the Lord; he will remind you of my ways in
Christ [Jesus], just as I teach them everywhere
in every church.
**18** *Some have become inflated with pride,
as if I were not coming to you. **19** But I will
come to you soon, if the Lord is willing, and I
shall ascertain not the talk of these inflated people but their power. **20** [u]For the kingdom of
God is not a matter of talk but of power.

l Ti 1, 7; 1 Pt 4, 10.
m 2 Cor 1, 12 / Rom 2, 16; 2 Cor 5, 10.
n 15, 31; Rom 8, 36; 2 Cor 4, 8-12; 11, 23 / Heb 10, 33.
o 1, 18; 3, 18; 2 Cor 11, 19 / 2, 3; 2 Cor 13, 9.
p Rom 8, 35; 2 Cor 11, 23-27.
q Acts 9, 6-14; 18, 3; 20, 34; 1 Thes 2, 9 / 1 Pt 3, 9.
r Gal 4, 19; Phlm 10.
s 11, 1; Phil 3, 17; 4, 9; 1 Thes 1, 6; 2 Thes 3, 7.9.
t 16, 10; Acts 19, 22.
u 2, 4; 1 Thes 1, 5.

*

4, 6–21: This is an emotionally charged peroration to the discussion about divisions. It contains several exhortations and statements of Paul's purpose in writing (cf 6.14–17.21) that counterbalance the initial exhortation at 1, 10.

4, 6: *That you may learn from us not to go beyond what is written:* the words "to go" are not in the Greek, but have here been added as the minimum necessary to elicit sense from this difficult passage. It probably means that the Corinthians should avoid the false wisdom of vain speculation, contenting themselves with Paul's proclamation of the cross, which is the fulfillment of God's promises in the Old Testament (what is written). *Inflated with pride:* literally, "puffed up," i.e., arrogant, filled with a sense of self-importance. The term is particularly Pauline, found in the New Testament only in 1 Cor 4, 6.18–19; 5, 2; 8, 1; 13, 4; Col 2, 18 (cf the related noun at 2 Cor 12, 20). It sometimes occurs in conjunction with the theme of "boasting," as in vv 6–7 here.

4, 8: *Satisfied . . . rich . . . kings:* these three statements could also be punctuated as questions continuing the series begun in v 7. In any case these expressions reflect a tendency at Corinth toward an overrealized eschatology, a form of self-deception that draws Paul's irony. The underlying attitude has implications for the Corinthians' thinking about other issues, notably morality and the resurrection, that Paul will address later in the letter.

4, 9–13: A rhetorically effective catalogue of the circumstances of apostolic existence, in the course of which Paul ironically contrasts his own sufferings with the Corinthians' illusion that they have passed beyond the folly of the passion and have already reached the condition of glory. His language echoes that of the beatitudes and woes, which assert a future reversal of present conditions. Their present sufferings ("to this very hour," 11) place the apostles in the class of those to whom the beatitudes promise future relief (Mt 5, 3–11; Lk 6, 20–23); whereas the Corinthians' image of themselves as "already" filled, rich, ruling (8), as wise, strong, and honored (10) places them paradoxically in the position of those whom the woes threaten with future undoing (Lk 6, 24–26). They have lost sight of the fact that the reversal is predicted for the future.

4, 14–17: *My beloved children:* the close of the argument is dominated by the tender metaphor of the father who not only gives his children life but also educates them. Once he has begotten them through his preaching, Paul continues to present the gospel to them existentially, by his life as well as by his word, and they are to learn, as children do, by imitating their parents (16). The reference to the *rod* in v 21 belongs to the same image-complex. So does the image of the *ways* in v 17: the ways that Paul teaches everywhere, "his ways in Christ Jesus," mean a behavior pattern quite different from the human ways along which the Corinthians are walking (3, 3).

4, 18–21: Verse 20 picks up the contrast between a certain kind of talk (*logos*) and true power (*dynamis*) from 1, 17–18 and 2, 4–5. The kingdom, which many of them imagine to be fully present in their lives (8), will be rather unexpectedly disclosed in the strength of Paul's encounter with them, if they make a powerful intervention on his part necessary. Compare the similar ending to an argument in 2 Cor 13, 1–4.10.

**21** [v]Which do you prefer? Shall I come to you
with a rod, or with love and a gentle spirit?

## B. Moral Disorders

### CHAPTER 5

**A Case of Incest** **1** [w]*It is widely reported
that there is immorality among you, and immorality of a kind not found even among pagans
—a man living with his father's wife. **2** *And
you are inflated with pride. Should you not
rather have been sorrowful? The one who did
this deed should be expelled from your midst.
**3** [x]I, for my part, although absent in body but
present in spirit, have already, as if present,
pronounced judgment on the one who has committed this deed, **4** in the name of [our] Lord
Jesus: when you have gathered together and I
am with you in spirit with the power of the Lord
Jesus, **5** [y]*you are to deliver this man to Satan
for the destruction of his flesh, so that his spirit
may be saved on the day of the Lord.
**6** [z]*Your boasting is not appropriate. Do you
not know that a little yeast leavens all the
dough? **7** [a]*Clear out the old yeast, so that you
may become a fresh batch of dough, inasmuch
as you are unleavened. For our paschal lamb,
Christ, has been sacrificed. **8** [b]Therefore let us
celebrate the feast, not with the old yeast, the
yeast of malice and wickedness, but with the
unleavened bread of sincerity and truth.
**9** *I wrote you in my letter not to associate
with immoral people, **10** [c]not at all referring to
the immoral of this world, or the greedy and
robbers or idolaters; for you would then have to
leave the world. **11** [d]But I now write to you not
to associate with anyone named a brother, if he
is immoral, greedy, an idolater, a slanderer, a
drunkard, or a robber, not even to eat with such
a person. **12** For why should I be judging outsiders? Is it not your business to judge those
within? **13** [e]God will judge those outside.
"Purge the evil person from your midst."

### CHAPTER 6

**Lawsuits before Unbelievers** **1** *How
can any one of you with a case against another
dare to bring it to the unjust for judgment instead
of to the holy ones? **2** [f]*Do you not know that
the holy ones will judge the world? If the world
is to be judged by you, are you unqualified for
the lowest law courts? **3** Do you not know that
we will judge angels? Then why not everyday
matters? **4** If, therefore, you have courts for
everyday matters, do you seat as judges people
of no standing in the church? **5** I say this to
shame you. Can it be that there is not one among
you wise enough to be able to settle a case
between brothers? **6** But rather brother goes to
court against brother, and that before unbelievers?
**7** [g]Now indeed [then] it is, in any case, a
failure on your part that you have lawsuits
against one another. Why not rather put up with
injustice? Why not rather let yourselves be
cheated? **8** Instead, you inflict injustice and

v 2 Cor 1, 23; 10, 2.
w Lv 18, 7-8; 20, 11; Dt 27, 20.
x Col 2, 5.
y 1 Tm 1, 20.
z Gal 5, 9.
a Ex 12, 1-13; Dt 16, 1-2; 1 Pt 1, 19.
b Ex 12, 15-20; 13, 7; Dt 16, 3.
c 10, 27; Jn 17, 15.
d Mt 18, 17; 2 Thes 3, 6.14; 2 Jn 10.
e Dt 13, 6; 17, 7; 22, 24.
f Wis 3, 8; Mt 19, 28; Rv 20, 4.
g Mt 5, 38-42; Rom 12, 17-21; 1 Thes 5, 15.

*

5, 1—6, 20: Paul now takes up a number of other matters that require regulation. These have come to his attention by hearsay (5, 1), probably in reports brought by "Chloe's people" (1, 11).

5, 1–13: Paul first deals with the incestuous union of a man with his stepmother (1–8) and then attempts to clarify general admonitions he has given about associating with fellow Christians guilty of immorality (9–13). Each of these three brief paragraphs expresses the same idea: the need of separation between the holy and the unholy.

5, 2: *Inflated with pride:* this remark and the reference to *boasting* in v 6 suggest that they are proud of themselves despite the infection in their midst, tolerating and possibly even approving the situation. The attitude expressed in 6, 2.13 may be influencing their thinking in this case.

5, 5: *Deliver this man to Satan:* once the sinner is expelled from the church, the sphere of Jesus' lordship and victory over sin, he will be in the region outside over which Satan is still master. *For the destruction of his flesh:* the purpose of the penalty is medicinal: through affliction, sin's grip over him may be destroyed and the path to repentance and reunion laid open. With Paul's instructions for an excommunication ceremony here, contrast his recommendations for the reconciliation of a sinner in 2 Cor 2, 5–11.

5, 6: *A little yeast:* yeast, which induces fermentation, is a natural symbol for a source of corruption that becomes all-pervasive. The expression is proverbial.

5, 7–8: In the Jewish calendar, Passover was followed immediately by the festival of Unleavened Bread. In preparation for this feast all traces of old bread were removed from the house, and during the festival only unleavened bread was eaten. The sequence of these two feasts provides Paul with an image of Christian existence: Christ's death (the true Passover celebration) is followed by the life of the Christian community, marked by newness, purity, and integrity (a perpetual feast of unleavened bread). Paul may have been writing around Passover time (cf 16, 5); this is a little Easter homily, the earliest in Christian literature.

5, 9–13: Paul here corrects a misunderstanding of his earlier directives against associating with immoral fellow Christians. He concedes the impossibility of avoiding contact with sinners in society at large but urges the Corinthians to maintain the inner purity of their own community.

6, 1–11: Christians at Corinth are suing one another before pagan judges in Roman courts. A barrage of rhetorical questions (1–9) betrays Paul's indignation over this practice, which he sees as an infringement upon the holiness of the Christian community.

6, 2–3: The principle to which Paul appeals is an eschatological prerogative promised to Christians: they are to share with Christ the judgment of the world (cf Dn 7, 22.27). Hence they ought to be able to settle minor disputes within the community.

cheat, and this to brothers. **9** [h]*Do you not
know that the unjust will not inherit the kingdom of God? Do not be deceived; neither for-
nicators nor idolaters nor adulterers nor boy
prostitutes nor sodomites **10** nor thieves nor the
greedy nor drunkards nor slanderers nor robbers
will inherit the kingdom of God. **11** [i]That is
what some of you used to be; but now you have
had yourselves washed, you were sanctified,
you were justified in the name of the Lord Jesus
Christ and in the Spirit of our God.

**Sexual Immorality** **12** [j]*"Everything is
lawful for me," but not everything is beneficial.
"Everything is lawful for me," but I will not let
myself be dominated by anything. **13** "Food
for the stomach and the stomach for food," but
God will do away with both the one and the
other. The body, however, is not for immorality, but for the Lord, and the Lord is for the body;
**14** [k]God raised the Lord and will also raise us
by his power.

**15** [l]*Do you not know that your bodies are
members of Christ? Shall I then take Christ's
members and make them the members of a prostitute? Of course not! **16** [m][Or] do you not
know that anyone who joins himself to a prostitute becomes one body with her? For "the
two," it says, "will become one flesh."
**17** [n]But whoever is joined to the Lord becomes
one spirit with him. **18** *Avoid immorality. Every other sin a person commits is outside the
body, but the immoral person sins against his
own body. **19** [o]*Do you not know that your
body is a temple of the holy Spirit within you,
whom you have from God, and that you are not
your own? **20** [p]For you have been purchased at
a price. Therefore glorify God in your body.

## *III: ANSWERS TO THE CORINTHIANS' QUESTIONS*

## A. Marriage and Virginity

### CHAPTER 7

**Advice to the Married** **1** *Now in regard
to the matters about which you wrote: "It is a

h 15, 50; Gal 5, 19-21; Eph 5, 5.
i Ti 3, 3-7.
j 10, 23.
k Rom 8, 11; 2 Cor 4, 14.
l 12, 27; Rom 6, 12-13; 12, 5; Eph 5, 30.
m Gn 2, 24; Mt 19, 5; Mk 10, 8; Eph 5, 31.
n Rom 8, 9-10; 2 Cor 3, 17.
o 3, 16-17; Rom 5, 5.
p 3, 23; 7, 23; Acts 20, 28 / Rom 12, 1; Phil 1, 20.

*

6, 9–10: A catalogue of typical vices that exclude from the kingdom of God and that should be excluded from God's church. Such lists (cf 5, 10) reflect the common moral sensibility of the New Testament period.

6, 9: The Greek word translated as *boy prostitutes* may refer to catamites, i.e., boys or young men who were kept for purposes of prostitution, a practice not uncommon in the Greco-Roman world. In Greek mythology this was the function of Ganymede, the "cupbearer of the gods," whose Latin name was Catamitus. The term translated *sodomites* would then refer to adult males who indulged in homosexual practices with such boys. See similar condemnations of such practices in Rom 1, 26–27; 1 Tm 1, 10.

6, 12–20: Paul now turns to the opinion of some Corinthians that sexuality is a morally indifferent area (12–13). This leads him to explain the mutual relation between the Lord Jesus and our bodies (13b) in a densely packed paragraph that contains elements of a profound theology of sexuality (15–20).

6, 12–13: *Everything is lawful for me:* the Corinthians may have derived this slogan from Paul's preaching about Christian freedom, but they mean something different by it: they consider sexual satisfaction a matter as indifferent as food, and they attribute no lasting significance to bodily functions (13a). Paul begins to deal with the slogan by two qualifications, which suggest principles for judging sexual activity. *Not everything is beneficial:* cf 10, 23, and the whole argument of chs 8–10 on the finality of freedom and moral activity. *Not let myself be dominated:* certain apparently free actions may involve in fact a secret servitude in conflict with the lordship of Jesus.

6, 15b–16: *A prostitute:* the reference may be specifically to religious prostitution, an accepted part of pagan culture at Corinth and elsewhere; but the prostitute also serves as a symbol for any sexual relationship that conflicts with Christ's claim over us individually. *The two . . . will become one flesh:* the text of Gn 2, 24 is applied positively to human marriage in Mt and Mk, and in Eph 5, 29–32: love of husband and wife reflect the love of Christ for his church. The application of the text to union with a prostitute is jarring, for such a union is a parody, an antitype of marriage, which does conflict with Christ's claim over us. This explains the horror expressed in 15b.

6, 18: *Against his own body:* expresses the intimacy and depth of sexual disorder, which violates the very orientation of our bodies.

6, 19–20: Paul's vision becomes trinitarian. *A temple:* sacred by reason of God's gift, his indwelling Spirit. *Not your own:* but "for the Lord," who acquires ownership by the act of redemption. *Glorify God in your body:* the argument concludes with a positive imperative to supplement the negative "avoid immorality" of v 18. Far from being a terrain that is morally indifferent, the area of sexuality is one in which our relationship with God (and his Christ and his Spirit) is very intimately expressed: he is either highly glorified or deeply offended.

7, 1–40: Paul now begins to answer questions addressed to him by the Corinthians (7, 1—11, 1). The first of these concerns marriage. This chapter contains advice both to the married (1–16) and to the unmarried (25–38) or widowed (39–40); these two parts are separated by vv 17–24, which enunciate a principle applicable to both.

7, 1–16: It seems that some Christians in Corinth were advocating asceticism in sexual matters. The pattern *it is a good thing . . . , but* occurs twice (1–2.8–9; cf 26), suggesting that in this matter as in others the Corinthians have seized upon a genuine value but are exaggerating or distorting it in some way. Once again Paul calls them to a more correct perspective and a better sense of their own limitations. The phrase *it is a good thing* (1) may have been the slogan of the ascetic party at Corinth.

7, 1–7: References to Paul's own behavior (7–8) suggest that his celibate way of life and his preaching to the unmarried (cf 25–35) have given some the impression that asceticism within marriage, i.e., suspension of normal sexual relations, would be a laudable ideal. Paul points to their experience of widespread immorality to caution them against overestimating their own strength (2); as individuals they may not have the particular gift that makes such asceticism feasible (7) and hence are to abide by the principle to be explained in vv 17–24.

good thing for a man not to touch a woman,"
**2** but because of cases of immorality every man
should have his own wife, and every woman her
own husband. **3** The husband should fulfill his
duty toward his wife, and likewise the wife
toward her husband. **4** A wife does not have
authority over her own body, but rather her
husband, and similarly a husband does not have
authority over his own body, but rather his wife.
**5** Do not deprive each other, except perhaps by
mutual consent for a time, to be free for prayer,
but then return to one another, so that Satan may
not tempt you through your lack of self-control.
**6** *This I say by way of concession, however,
not as a command. **7** [q]*Indeed, I wish everyone
to be as I am, but each has a particular gift from
God, one of one kind and one of another.

**8** [r]*Now to the unmarried and to widows, I
say: It is a good thing for them to remain as they
are, as I do, **9** but if they cannot exercise
self-control they should marry, for it is better to
marry than to be on fire. **10** [s]*To the married,
however, I give this instruction (not I, but the
Lord): A wife should not separate from her husband **11** —and if she does separate she must
either remain single or become reconciled to her
husband—and a husband should not divorce his
wife.

**12** *To the rest, I say (not the Lord): If any
brother has a wife who is an unbeliever, and she
is willing to go on living with him, he should not
divorce her; **13** and if any woman has a husband who is an unbeliever, and he is willing to
go on living with her, she should not divorce her
husband. **14** [t]For the unbelieving husband is
made holy through his wife, and the unbelieving
wife is made holy through the brother. Otherwise your children would be unclean, whereas
in fact they are holy.

**15** *If the unbeliever separates, however, let
him separate. The brother or sister is not bound
in such cases; God has called you to peace.
**16** For how do you know, wife, whether you
will save your husband; or how do you know,
husband, whether you will save your wife?

## The Life That the Lord Has Assigned

**17** *Only, everyone should live as the Lord has
assigned, just as God called each one. I give this
order in all the churches. **18** [u]Was someone
called after he had been circumcised? He should
not try to undo his circumcision. Was an uncircumcised person called? He should not be circumcised. **19** [v]Circumcision means nothing,
and uncircumcision means nothing; what matters is keeping God's commandments. **20** Everyone should remain in the state in which he
was called.

**21** Were you a slave when you were called?
Do not be concerned, but, rather, even if you
can gain your freedom, make the most of it.
**22** [w]For the slave called in the Lord is a freed
person in the Lord, just as the free person who
has been called is a slave of Christ. **23** [x]You
have been purchased at a price. Do not become
slaves to human beings. **24** Brothers, everyone
should continue before God in the state in which
he was called.

## Advice to Virgins and Widows

**25** *Now
in regard to virgins, I have no commandment
from the Lord, but I give my opinion as one who
by the Lord's mercy is trustworthy. **26** [y]So this
is what I think best because of the present distress: that it is a good thing for a person to
remain as he is. **27** Are you bound to a wife?
Do not seek a separation. Are you free of a
wife? Then do not look for a wife. **28** If you
marry, however, you do not sin, nor does an
unmarried woman sin if she marries; but such
people will experience affliction in their earthly
life, and I would like to spare you that.

**29** [z]*I tell you, brothers, the time is running
out. From now on, let those having wives act as
not having them, **30** those weeping as not

q Mt 19, 11-12.
r 1 Tm 5, 11-16 / 9, 5;
s Mt 5, 32; 19, 9.
t Rom 11, 16.
u 1 Mc 1, 15 / Acts 15, 1-2.
v Rom 2, 25.29; Gal 5, 6; 6, 15.
w Eph 6, 5-9; Col 3, 11; Phlm 16.
x 6, 20.
y 8.
z Rom 13, 11.

*

7, 6: *By way of concession:* this refers most likely to the concession mentioned in v 5a: temporary interruption of relations for a legitimate purpose.

7, 7: *A particular gift from God:* use of the term *charisma* suggests that marriage and celibacy may be viewed in the light of Paul's theology of spiritual gifts (chs 12–14).

7, 8: Paul was obviously unmarried when he wrote this verse. Some interpreters believe that he had previously been married and widowed; there is no clear evidence either for or against this view, which was expressed already at the end of the second century by Clement of Alexandria.

7, 10–11: *(Not I, but the Lord):* Paul reminds the married of Jesus' principle of nonseparation (Mk 10, 9). This is one of his rare specific references to the teaching of Jesus.

7, 12–14: *To the rest:* marriages in which only one partner is a baptized Christian. Jesus' prohibition against divorce is not addressed to them, but Paul extends the principle of nonseparation to such unions, provided they are marked by peacefulness and shared sanctification.

7, 15–16: *If the unbeliever separates:* the basis of the "Pauline privilege" in Catholic marriage legislation.

7, 17–24: On the ground that distinct human conditions are less significant than the whole new existence opened up by God's call, Paul urges them to be less concerned with changing their states of life than with answering God's call where it finds them. The principle applies both to the married state (1–16) and to the unmarried (25–38).

7, 25–28: Paul is careful to explain that the principle of v 17 does not bind under sin but that present earthly conditions make it advantageous for the unmarried to remain as they are (28). These remarks must be complemented by the statement about "particular gifts" from v 7.

7, 29–31: *The world . . . is passing away:* Paul advises Christians to go about the ordinary activities of life in a manner different from those who are totally immersed in them and unaware of their transitoriness.

weeping, those rejoicing as not rejoicing, those
buying as not owning, **31** those using the world
as not using it fully. For the world in its present
form is passing away.
**32** I should like you to be free of anxieties.
An unmarried man is anxious about the things
of the Lord, how he may please the Lord.
**33** [a]But a married man is anxious about the
things of the world, how he may please his wife,
**34** [b]and he is divided. An unmarried woman or
a virgin is anxious about the things of the Lord,
so that she may be holy in both body and spirit.
A married woman, on the other hand, is anxious
about the things of the world, how she may
please her husband. **35** [c]I am telling you this
for your own benefit, not to impose a restraint
upon you, but for the sake of propriety and
adherence to the Lord without distraction.
**36** *If anyone thinks he is behaving improp-
erly toward his virgin, and if a critical moment
has come and so it has to be, let him do as he
wishes. He is committing no sin; let them get
married. **37** The one who stands firm in his
resolve, however, who is not under compulsion
but has power over his own will, and has made
up his mind to keep his virgin, will be doing
well. **38** So then, the one who marries his virgin does well; the one who does not marry her
will do better.
**39** [d]*A wife is bound to her husband as long
as he lives. But if her husband dies, she is free
to be married to whomever she wishes, provided that it be in the Lord. **40** [e]She is more
blessed, though, in my opinion, if she remains
as she is, and I think that I too have the Spirit
of God.

## B. Offerings to Idols

## CHAPTER 8

**Knowledge Insufficient** **1** [f]*Now in regard to meat sacrificed to idols: we realize that
"all of us have knowledge"; knowledge inflates
with pride, but love builds up. **2** If anyone supposes he knows something, he does not yet
know as he ought to know. **3** [g]But if one loves
God, one is known by him.
**4** [h]So about the eating of meat sacrificed to
idols: we know that "there is no idol in the
world," and that "there is no God but one."
**5** Indeed, even though there are so-called gods
in heaven and on earth (there are, to be sure,
many "gods" and many "lords"), **6** [i]*yet for
us there is

one God, the Father,
from whom all things are and for whom
we exist,
and one Lord, Jesus Christ,
through whom all things are and through
whom we exist.

**Practical Rules** **7** [j]But not all have this
knowledge. There are some who have been so
used to idolatry up until now that, when they eat
meat sacrificed to idols, their conscience, which
is weak, is defiled.
**8** [k]*Now food will not bring us closer to

a Lk 14, 20.
b 1 Tm 5, 5.
c Lk 10, 39-42.
d Rom 7, 2.
e 25.
f Rom 15, 14 / 13, 1-13; Rom 14, 15.19.
g Rom 8, 29; Gal 4, 9;
h 10, 19; Dt 6, 4.
i Mal 2, 10 / Rom 11, 36; Eph 4, 5-6 / 1, 2-3 / Jn 1, 3; Col 1, 16.
j 10, 28; Rom 14, 23 / Rom 14, 1; 15, 1.
k Rom 14, 17.

*

7, 36–38: The passage is difficult to interpret, because it is unclear whether Paul is thinking of a father and his unmarried daughter (or slave), or of a couple engaged in a betrothal or spiritual marriage. The general principles already enunciated apply: there is no question of sin, even if they should marry, but staying as they are is "better" (for the reasons mentioned in 28–35). Once again the *charisma* of v 7, which applies also to the unmarried (8–9), is to be presupposed.

7, 36: *A critical moment has come:* either because the woman will soon be beyond marriageable age, or because their passions are becoming uncontrollable (cf 9).

7, 39–40: Application of the principles to the case of widows. If they do choose to remarry, they ought to prefer Christian husbands.

8, 1—11, 1: The Corinthians' second question concerns meat that has been sacrificed to idols; in this area they were exhibiting a disordered sense of liberation that Paul here tries to rectify. These chapters contain a sustained and unified argument that illustrates Paul's method of theological reflection on a moral dilemma. Although the problem with which he is dealing is dated, the guidelines for moral decisions that he offers are of lasting validity.

Essentially Paul urges them to take a communitarian rather than an individualistic view of their Christian freedom. Many decisions that they consider pertinent only to their private relationship with God have, in fact, social consequences. Nor can moral decisions be determined by merely theoretical considerations; they must be based on concrete circumstances, specifically on the value and needs of other individuals and on mutual responsibility within the community. Paul here introduces the theme of "building up" (*oikodomē*), i.e., of contributing by individual action to the welfare and growth of the community. This theme will be further developed in ch 14; see the note on 14, 3b–5. Several years later Paul would again deal with the problem of meat sacrificed to idols in Rom 14, 1—15, 6.

8, 1a: *Meat sacrificed to idols:* much of the food consumed in the city could have passed through pagan religious ceremonies before finding its way into markets and homes. *"All of us have knowledge":* a slogan, similar to 6, 12, which reveals the self-image of the Corinthians. Verse 4 will specify the content of this knowledge.

8, 6: This verse rephrases the monotheistic confession of v 4 in such a way as to contrast it with polytheism (5) and to express our relationship with the one God in concrete, i.e., in personal and Christian terms. *And for whom we exist:* since the Greek contains no verb here and the action intended must be inferred from the preposition *eis,* another translation is equally possible: "toward whom we return." *Through whom all things:* the earliest reference in the New Testament to Jesus' role in creation.

8, 8–9: Although the food in itself is morally neutral, extrinsic circumstances may make the eating of it harmful. *A stumbling block:* the image is that of tripping or causing someone to fall (cf 13; 9, 12; 10, 12.32; 2 Cor 6, 3; Rom 14, 13.20–21). This is a basic moral imperative for Paul, a counterpart to the positive imperative to "build one another up"; compare the

God. We are no worse off if we do not eat, nor
are we better off if we do. **9** [l]But make sure that
this liberty of yours in no way becomes a stumbling block to the weak. **10** If someone sees
you, with your knowledge, reclining at table in
the temple of an idol, may not his conscience
too, weak as it is, be "built up" to eat the meat
sacrificed to idols? **11** [m]Thus through your
knowledge, the weak person is brought to destruction, the brother for whom Christ died.
**12** When you sin in this way against your brothers and wound their consciences, weak as they
are, you are sinning against Christ.
**13** [n]*Therefore if food causes my brother to
sin, I will never eat meat again, so that I may
not cause my brother to sin.

## CHAPTER 9

**Paul's Rights as an Apostle** **1** [o]*Am I
not free? Am I not an apostle? Have I not seen
Jesus our Lord? Are you not my work in the
Lord? **2** Although I may not be an apostle for
others, certainly I am for you, for you are the
seal of my apostleship in the Lord.

**3** *My defense against those who would pass
judgment on me is this. **4** *Do we not have the
right to eat and drink? **5** Do we not have the
right to take along a Christian wife, as do the
rest of the apostles, and the brothers of the Lord,
and Cephas? **6** [p]Or is it only myself and Barnabas who do not have the right not to work?
**7** [q]Who ever serves as a soldier at his own
expense? Who plants a vineyard without eating
its produce? Or who shepherds a flock without
using some of the milk from the flock? **8** Am
I saying this on human authority, or does not the
law also speak of these things? **9** [r]It is written
in the law of Moses, "You shall not muzzle an
ox while it is treading out the grain." Is God
concerned about oxen, **10** [s]or is he not really
speaking for our sake? It was written for our
sake, because the plowman should plow in
hope, and the thresher in hope of receiving a
share. **11** [t]If we have sown spiritual seed for
you, is it a great thing that we reap a material
harvest from you? **12** [u]*If others share this
rightful claim on you, do not we still more?

**Reason for Not Using His Rights** Yet we
have not used this right. On the contrary, we
endure everything, so as not to place an obstacle
to the gospel of Christ. **13** [v]*Do you not know
that those who perform the temple services eat
[what] belongs to the temple, and those who
minister at the altar share in the sacrificial offerings? **14** [w]In the same way, the Lord ordered
that those who preach the gospel should live by
the gospel.

**15** [x]*I have not used any of these rights,
however, nor do I write this that it be done so
in my case. I would rather die. Certainly no one
is going to nullify my boast. **16** [y]If I preach the
gospel, this is no reason for me to boast, for an
obligation has been imposed on me, and woe to
me if I do not preach it! **17** [z]If I do so willingly,
I have a recompense, but if unwillingly, then I
have been entrusted with a stewardship.

---

l Rom 14, 13.20-21.
m Rom 14, 15.20.
n Mt 18, 6; Rom 14, 20-21.
o 19 / 2 Cor 12, 12 / 15, 8-9; Acts 9, 17; 26, 16.
p Acts 4, 36-37; 13, 1-2; Gal 2, 1.9.13; Col 4, 10.
q 2 Tm 2, 3-4.
r Dt 25, 4; 1 Tm 5, 18.
s 2 Tm 2, 6.
t Rom 15, 27.
u 2 Cor 11, 7-12; 12, 13-18; 2 Thes 3, 6-12.
v Nm 18, 8.31; Dt 18, 1-5.
w Mt 10, 10; Lk 10, 7-8.
x 2 Cor 11, 9-10.
y Acts 26, 14-18.
z 4, 1; Gal 2, 7.

---

* expression "giving offense" as opposed to "pleasing" in 10, 32–33.

8, 13: His own course is clear: he will avoid any action that might harm another Christian. This statement prepares for the paradigmatic development in ch 9.

9, 1–27: This chapter is an emotionally charged expansion of Paul's appeal to his own example in 8, 13; its purpose is to reinforce the exhortation of 8, 9. The two opening questions introduce the themes of Paul's freedom and his apostleship (1), themes that the chapter will develop in reverse order, vv 1–18 treating the question of his apostleship and the rights that flow from it, and vv 19–27 exploring dialectically the nature of Paul's freedom. The language is highly rhetorical, abounding in questions, wordplays, paradoxes, images, and appeals to authority and experience. The argument is unified by repetitions; its articulations are highlighted by inclusions and transitional verses.

9, 3: *My defense against those who would pass judgment on me:* the reference to a defense (*apologia*) is surprising, and suggests that Paul is incorporating some material here that he has previously used in another context. The defense will touch on two points: the fact of Paul's rights as an apostle (4–12a and 13–14) and his nonuse of those rights (12b and 15–18).

9, 4–12a: Apparently some believe that Paul is not equal to the other apostles and therefore does not enjoy equal privileges. His defense on this point (here and in 13–14) reinforces the assertion of his apostolic character in v 2. It consists of a series of analogies from natural equity (7) and religious custom (13) designed to establish his equal right to support from the churches (4–6.11–12a); these analogies are confirmed by the authority of the law (8–10) and of Jesus himself (14).

9, 12b: It appears, too, that suspicion or misunderstanding has been created by Paul's practice of not living from his preaching. The first reason he asserts in defense of this practice is an entirely apostolic one; it anticipates the developments to follow in vv 19–22. He will give a second reason in vv 15–18.

9, 13–14: The position of these verses produces an interlocking of the two points of Paul's defense. These arguments by analogy (13) and from authority (14) belong with those of vv 7–10 and ground the first point. But Paul defers them until he has had a chance to mention "the gospel of Christ" (12b), after which it is more appropriate to mention Jesus' injunction to his preachers and to argue by analogy from the sacred temple service to his own liturgical service, the preaching of the gospel (cf Rom 1, 9; 15, 16).

9, 15–18: Paul now assigns a more personal motive to his nonuse of his right to support. His preaching is not a service spontaneously undertaken on his part but a stewardship imposed by a sort of divine compulsion. Yet to merit any reward he must bring some spontaneous quality to his service, and this he does by freely renouncing his right to support. The material here is quite similar to that contained in Paul's "defense" at 2 Cor 11, 5–12; 12, 11–18.

**18** [a]What then is my recompense? That, when
I preach, I offer the gospel free of charge so as
not to make full use of my right in the gospel.

## All Things to All

**19** [b]*Although I am free
in regard to all, I have made myself a slave to
all so as to win over as many as possible. **20** To
the Jews I became like a Jew to win over Jews;
to those under the law I became like one under
the law—though I myself am not under the
law—to win over those under the law. **21** To
those outside the law I became like one outside
the law—though I am not outside God's law but
within the law of Christ—to win over those
outside the law. **22** [c]To the weak I became
weak, to win over the weak. I have become all
things to all, to save at least some. **23** All this
I do for the sake of the gospel, so that I too may
have a share in it.

**24** [d]*Do you not know that the runners in the
stadium all run in the race, but only one wins the
prize? Run so as to win. **25** [e]Every athlete exercises discipline in every way. They do it to win
a perishable crown, but we an imperishable one.
**26** Thus I do not run aimlessly; I do not fight
as if I were shadowboxing. **27** *No, I drive my
body and train it, for fear that, after having
preached to others, I myself should be disqualified.

## CHAPTER 10

## Warning against Overconfidence

**1** [f]*I
do not want you to be unaware, brothers, that
our ancestors were all under the cloud and all
passed through the sea, **2** [g]and all of them were
baptized into Moses in the cloud and in the sea.
**3** All ate the same spiritual food, **4** [h]*and all
drank the same spiritual drink, for they drank
from a spiritual rock that followed them, and the
rock was the Christ. **5** [i]Yet God was not
pleased with most of them, for they were struck
down in the desert.

**6** [j]*These things happened as examples for
us, so that we might not desire evil things, as
they did. **7** [k]And do not become idolaters, as
some of them did, as it is written, "The people
sat down to eat and drink, and rose up to revel."
**8** [l]Let us not indulge in immorality as some of
them did, and twenty-three thousand fell within
a single day. **9** [m]*Let us not test Christ as some
of them did, and suffered death by serpents.
**10** [n]Do not grumble as some of them did, and
suffered death by the destroyer. **11** *These
things happened to them as an example, and
they have been written down as a warning to us,
upon whom the end of the ages has come.
**12** *Therefore whoever thinks he is standing
secure should take care not to fall. **13** [o]No trial
has come to you but what is human. God is
faithful and will not let you be tried beyond your
strength; but with the trial he will also provide
a way out, so that you may be able to bear it.

## Warning against Idolatry

**14** [p]*Therefore, my beloved, avoid idolatry.
**15** I am speaking as to sensible people; judge
for yourselves what I am saying. **16** [q]The cup

a 2 Cor 11, 7-12.
b Mt 20, 26-27.
c 10, 33; Rom 15, 1; 2 Cor 11, 29.
d Heb 12, 1.
e 2 Tm 2, 5 / 2 Tm 4, 7-8; Jas 1, 12; 1 Pt 5, 4.
f Ex 13, 21-22; 14, 19-20 / Ex 14, 21-22.26-30.
g Rom 6, 3; Gal 3, 27 / Ex 16, 4-35.
h Ex 17, 1-7; Nm 20, 7-11; Dt 8, 15.
i Nm 14, 28-38; Jude 5.
j Nm 11, 4.34.
k Ex 32, 6.
l Nm 25, 1-9.
m Nm 21, 5-9.
n Nm 14, 2-37; 16, 1-35.
o Mt 6, 13; Jas 1, 13-14 / 1, 9.
p 1 Jn 5, 21.
q Mt 26, 26-29; Acts 2, 42.

*

9, 19–23: In a rhetorically balanced series of statements Paul expands and generalizes the picture of his behavior and explores the paradox of apostolic freedom. It is not essentially freedom *from* restraint but freedom *for* service—a possibility of constructive activity.

9, 24–27: A series of miniparables from sports, appealing to readers familiar with Greek gymnasia and the nearby Isthmian games.

9, 27: *For fear that . . . I myself should be disqualified:* a final paradoxical turn to the argument: what appears at first a free, spontaneous renunciation of rights (12–18) seems subsequently to be required for fulfillment of Paul's stewardship (to preach effectively he must reach his hearers wherever they are, 19–22), and finally is seen to be necessary for his own salvation (23–27). Mention of the possibility of disqualification provides a transition to ch 10.

10, 1–5: Paul embarks unexpectedly upon a panoramic survey of the events of the Exodus period. The privileges of Israel in the wilderness are described in terms that apply strictly only to the realities of the new covenant ("baptism," "spiritual food and drink"); interpreted in this way they point forward to the Christian experience (1–4). But those privileges did not guarantee God's permanent pleasure (5).

10, 4: *A spiritual rock that followed them:* the Torah speaks only about a rock from which water issued, but rabbinic legend amplified this into a spring that followed the Israelites throughout their migration. Paul uses this legend as a literary type: he makes the rock itself accompany the Israelites, and he gives it a spiritual sense. *The rock was the Christ:* in the Old Testament, Yahweh is the Rock of his people (cf Dt 32, Moses' song to Yahweh the Rock). Paul now applies this image to the Christ, the source of the living water, the true Rock that accompanied Israel, guiding their experiences in the desert.

10, 6–13: This section explicitates the typological value of these Old Testament events: the desert experiences of the Israelites are examples, meant as warnings, to deter us from similar sins (idolatry, immorality, etc.) and from a similar fate.

10, 9: *Christ:* to avoid Paul's concept of Christ present in the wilderness events, some manuscripts read "the Lord."

10, 11: *Upon whom the end of the ages has come:* it is our period in time toward which past ages have been moving and in which they arrive at their goal.

10, 12–13: *Take care not to fall:* the point of the whole comparison with Israel is to caution against overconfidence, a sense of complete security (12). This warning is immediately balanced by a reassurance, based, however, on God (13).

10, 14–22: The warning against idolatry from v 7 is now repeated (14) and explained in terms of the effect of sacrifices: all sacrifices, Christian (16–17), Jewish (18), or pagan (20), establish communion. But communion with Christ is exclusive, incompatible with any other such communion (21). Compare the line of reasoning at 6, 15.

of blessing that we bless, is it not a participation
in the blood of Christ? The bread that we break,
is it not a participation in the body of Christ?
17 [r]Because the loaf of bread is one, we,
though many, are one body, for we all partake
of the one loaf.

18 [s]Look at Israel according to the flesh; are
not those who eat the sacrifices participants in
the altar? 19 So what am I saying? That meat
sacrificed to idols is anything? Or that an idol
is anything? 20 [t]*No, I mean that what they
sacrifice, [they sacrifice] to demons, not to
God, and I do not want you to become participants with demons. 21 [u]You cannot drink the
cup of the Lord and also the cup of demons. You
cannot partake of the table of the Lord and of the
table of demons. 22 [v]Or are we provoking the
Lord to jealous anger? Are we stronger than he?

### Seek the Good of Others

23 [w]*"Everything is lawful," but not everything is beneficial. "Everything is lawful," but
not everything builds up. 24 [x]No one should
seek his own advantage, but that of his neighbor. 25 *Eat anything sold in the market, without raising questions on grounds of conscience,
26 [y]for "the earth and its fullness are the
Lord's." 27 If an unbeliever invites you and
you want to go, eat whatever is placed before
you, without raising questions on grounds of
conscience. 28 But if someone says to you,
"This was offered in sacrifice," do not eat it on
account of the one who called attention to it and
on account of conscience; 29 I mean not your
own conscience, but the other's. For why
should my freedom be determined by someone
else's conscience? 30 [z]If I partake thankfully,
why am I reviled for that over which I give
thanks?

31 So whether you eat or drink, or whatever
you do, do everything for the glory of God.
32 *Avoid giving offense, whether to Jews or
Greeks or the church of God, 33 [a]just as I try
to please everyone in every way, not seeking my
own benefit but that of the many, that they may
be saved.

## CHAPTER 11

1 [b]Be imitators of me, as I am of Christ.

# *IV: PROBLEMS IN LITURGICAL ASSEMBLIES*

2 [c]*I praise you because you remember me
in everything and hold fast to the traditions, just
as I handed them on to you.

## A. Women's Headdresses

**Man and Woman** 3 [d]*But I want you to
know that Christ is the head of every man, and

r Rom 12, 5; Eph 4, 4.
s Lv 7, 6.
t Dt 32, 17.
u 2 Cor 6, 14-18.
v Dt 32, 21 / Eccl 6, 10.
w 6, 12.
x Rom 15, 2; Phil 2, 4.21.
y Pss 24, 1; 50, 12.
z Rom 14, 6; 1 Tm 4, 3-4.
a 9, 22; Rom 15, 2.
b 4, 16; Phil 3, 17.
c 15, 3; 2 Thes 2, 15.
d Eph 5, 23.

*

10, 20: *To demons:* although Jews denied divinity to pagan gods, they often believed that there was some nondivine reality behind the idols, such as the dead, or angels, or demons. The explanation Paul offers in v 20 is drawn from Dt 32, 7: the power behind the idols, with which the pagans commune, consists of demonic powers hostile to God.

10, 23—11, 1: By way of peroration Paul returns to the opening situation (ch 8) and draws conclusions based on the intervening considerations (chs 9–10).

10, 23–24: He repeats in the context of this new problem the slogans of liberty from 6, 12, with similar qualifications. Liberty is not merely an individual perfection, nor an end in itself, but is to be used for the common good. The language of v 24 recalls the descriptions of Jesus' self-emptying in Phil 2.

10, 25–30: A summary of specific situations in which the eating of meat sacrificed to idols could present problems of conscience. Three cases are considered. In the first (the marketplace, 25–26) and the second (at table, 27), there is no need to be concerned with whether food has passed through a pagan sacrifice or not, for the principle of 8, 4–6 still stands, and the whole creation belongs to the one God. But in the third case (28), the situation changes if someone present explicitly raises the question of the sacrificial origin of the food; eating in such circumstances may be subject to various interpretations, some of which could be harmful to individuals. Paul is at pains to insist that the enlightened Christian conscience need not change its judgment about the neutrality, even the goodness, of the food in itself (29–30); yet the total situation is altered to the extent that others are potentially endangered, and this calls for a different response, for the sake of others.

10, 32—11, 1: In summary, the general rule of mutually responsible use of their Christian freedom is enjoined first negatively (32), then positively, as exemplified in Paul (33), and finally grounded in Christ, the pattern for Paul's behavior and theirs (11, 1; cf Rom 15, 1–3).

11, 2—14, 40: This section of the letter is devoted to regulation of conduct at the liturgy. The problems Paul handles have to do with the dress of women in the assembly (11, 3–16), improprieties in the celebration of community meals (11, 17–34), and the use of charisms or spiritual gifts (12, 1—14, 40). The statement in 11, 2 introduces all of these discussions, but applies more appropriately to the second (cf the mention of praise in 11, 17 and of tradition in 11, 23).

11, 3–16: Women have been participating in worship at Corinth without the head-covering normal in Greek society of the period. Paul's stated goal is to bring them back into conformity with contemporary practice and propriety. In his desire to convince, he reaches for arguments from a variety of sources, though he has space to develop them only sketchily and is perhaps aware that they differ greatly in persuasiveness.

11, 3: *A husband the head of his wife:* the specific problem suggests to Paul the model of the head as a device for clarifying relations within a hierarchical structure. The model is similar to that developed later in greater detail and nuance in Eph 5, 21–33. It is a hybrid model, for it grafts onto a strictly theological scale of existence (cf 3, 21–23) the hierarchy of sociosexual relations prevalent in the ancient world: men, dominant, reflect the active function of Christ in relation to his church; women, submissive, reflect the passive role of the church with

a husband the head of his wife, and God the
head of Christ. **4** *Any man who prays or
prophesies with his head covered brings shame
upon his head. **5** But any woman who prays or
prophesies with her head unveiled brings shame
upon her head, for it is one and the same thing
as if she had had her head shaved. **6** For if a
woman does not have her head veiled, she may
as well have her hair cut off. But if it is shameful
for a woman to have her hair cut off or her head
shaved, then she should wear a veil.

**7** [e]*A man, on the other hand, should not
cover his head, because he is the image and
glory of God, but woman is the glory of man.
**8** [f]For man did not come from woman, but
woman from man; **9** [g]nor was man created for
woman, but woman for man; **10** *for this reason a woman should have a sign of authority on
her head, because of the angels. **11** [h]*Woman
is not independent of man or man of woman in
the Lord. **12** [i]For just as woman came from
man, so man is born of woman; but all things
are from God.

**13** *Judge for yourselves: is it proper for a
woman to pray to God with her head unveiled?
**14** Does not nature itself teach you that if a man
wears his hair long it is a disgrace to him,
**15** whereas if a woman has long hair it is her
glory, because long hair has been given [her] for
a covering? **16** But if anyone is inclined to be
argumentative, we do not have such a custom,
nor do the churches of God.

## B. The Lord's Supper

**An Abuse at Corinth** **17** *In giving this
instruction, I do not praise the fact that your
meetings are doing more harm than good.
**18** [j]First of all, I hear that when you meet as a
church there are divisions among you, and to a
degree I believe it; **19** *there have to be factions
among you in order that [also] those who are
approved among you may become known.
**20** When you meet in one place, then, it is not
to eat the Lord's supper, **21** for in eating, each
one goes ahead with his own supper, and one
goes hungry while another gets drunk. **22** [k]Do
you not have houses in which you can eat and
drink? Or do you show contempt for the church
of God and make those who have nothing feel
ashamed? What can I say to you? Shall I praise
you? In this matter I do not praise you.

**Tradition of the Institution** **23** [l]*For I received from the Lord what I also handed on to
you, that the Lord Jesus, on the night he was
handed over, took bread, **24** and after he had
given thanks, broke it and said, "This is my
body that is for you. Do this in remembrance of
me." **25** [m]In the same way also the cup, after
supper, saying, "This cup is the new covenant
in my blood. Do this, as often as you drink it,
in remembrance of me." **26** For as often as you
eat this bread and drink the cup, you proclaim
the death of the Lord until he comes.

**27** *Therefore whoever eats the bread or

e Gn 1, 26-27; 5, 1.
f Gn 2, 21-23.
g Gn 2, 18.
h Gal 3, 27-28.
i 8, 6; Rom 11, 36.
j 1, 10-12; Gal 5, 20.
k Jas 2, 1-7.
l 2; 15, 3 / 10, 16-17; Mt 26, 26-29; Mk 14, 22-25; Lk 22, 14-20.
m Ex 24, 8; 2 Cor 3, 6; Heb 8, 6-13.

*

respect to its savior. This gives us the functional scale: God, Christ, man, woman.

11, 4–6: From man's direct relation to Christ, Paul infers that his head should not be covered. But woman, related not directly to Christ on the scale but to her husband, requires a covering as a sign of that relationship. *Shameful . . . to have her hair cut off:* certain less honored classes in society, such as lesbians and prostitutes, are thought to have worn their hair close-cropped.

11, 7–9: The hierarchy of v 3 is now expressed in other metaphors: the image (*eikōn*) and the reflected glory (*doxa*). Paul is alluding basically to the text of Gn 1, 27, in which mankind as a whole, the male-female couple, is created in God's image and given the command to multiply and together dominate the lower creation. But Gn 1, 24 is interpreted here in the light of the second creation narrative in Gn 2, in which each of the sexes is created separately (first the man and then the woman *from* man and *for* him, to be his helpmate, Gn 2, 20–23), and under the influence of the story of the fall, as a result of which the husband rules over the woman (Gn 3, 16). This interpretation splits the single image of God into two, at different degrees of closeness.

11, 10: *A sign of authority:* "authority" (*exousia*) may possibly be due to mistranslation of an Aramaic word for "veil"; in any case, the connection with v 9 indicates that the covering is a sign of woman's subordination. *Because of the angels:* a surprising additional reason, which the context does not clarify. Presumably the reference is to cosmic powers who might inflict harm on women or whose function is to watch over women or the cult.

11, 11–12: These parenthetical remarks relativize the argument from Gn 2–3. *In the Lord:* in the Christian economy the relation between the sexes is characterized by a mutual dependence, which is not further specified. And even in the natural order conditions have changed: the mode of origin described in Gn 2 has been reversed (12a). But the ultimately significant fact is the origin that all things have in common (12b).

11, 13–16: The argument for conformity to common church practice is summed up and pressed home. Verses 14–15 contain a final appeal to the sense of propriety that contemporary Greek society would consider "natural" (cf 5–6).

11, 17–34: Paul turns to another abuse connected with the liturgy, and a more serious one, for it involves neglect of basic Christian tradition concerning the meaning of the Lord's Supper. Paul recalls that tradition for them and reminds them of its implications.

11, 19: *That . . . those who are approved among you may become known:* Paul situates their divisions within the context of the eschatological separation of the authentic from the inauthentic and the final revelation of the difference. The notion of authenticity-testing recurs in the injunction to self-examination in view of present and future judgment (28–32).

11, 23–25: This is the earliest written account of the institution of the Lord's Supper in the New Testament. The narrative emphasizes Jesus' action of self-giving (expressed in the words over the bread and the cup) and his double command to repeat his own action.

11, 27: It follows that the only proper way to celebrate the Eucharist is one that corresponds to Jesus' intention, which fits with the meaning of his command to reproduce his action in

drinks the cup of the Lord unworthily will have to answer for the body and blood of the Lord. **28** *A person should examine himself, and so eat the bread and drink the cup. **29** *For anyone who eats and drinks without discerning the body, eats and drinks judgment on himself. **30** That is why many among you are ill and infirm, and a considerable number are dying. **31** If we discerned ourselves, we would not be under judgment; **32** [n]but since we are judged by [the] Lord, we are being disciplined so that we may not be condemned along with the world.

**33** Therefore, my brothers, when you come together to eat, wait for one another. **34** If anyone is hungry, he should eat at home, so that your meetings may not result in judgment. The other matters I shall set in order when I come.

## C. Spiritual Gifts

## CHAPTER 12

**Unity and Variety** **1** *Now in regard to spiritual gifts, brothers, I do not want you to be unaware. **2** [o]*You know how, when you were pagans, you were constantly attracted and led away to mute idols. **3** [p]Therefore I tell you that nobody speaking by the spirit of God says, "Jesus be accursed." And no one can say, "Jesus is Lord," except by the holy Spirit.

**4** [q]*There are different kinds of spiritual gifts but the same Spirit; **5** there are different forms of service but the same Lord; **6** there are different workings but the same God who produces all of them in everyone. **7** To each individual the manifestation of the Spirit is given for some benefit. **8** [r]To one is given through the Spirit the expression of wisdom; to another the expression of knowledge according to the same Spirit; **9** to another faith by the same Spirit; to another gifts of healing by the one Spirit; **10** [s]to another mighty deeds; to another prophecy; to another discernment of spirits; to another varieties of tongues; to another interpretation of tongues. **11** [t]But one and the same Spirit produces all of these, distributing them individually to each person as he wishes.

**One Body, Many Parts** **12** [u]*As a body is one though it has many parts, and all the parts of the body, though many, are one body, so also Christ. **13** [v]For in one Spirit we were all baptized into one body, whether Jews or Greeks, slaves or free persons, and we were all given to drink of one Spirit.

**14** Now the body is not a single part, but many. **15** If a foot should say, "Because I am not a hand I do not belong to the body," it does not for this reason belong any less to the body. **16** Or if an ear should say, "Because I am not an eye I do not belong to the body," it does not for this reason belong any less to the body. **17** If the whole body were an eye, where would the hearing be? If the whole body were hearing, where would the sense of smell be? **18** But as it is, God placed the parts, each one of them, in the body as he intended. **19** If they were all one part, where would the body be? **20** But as it is, there are many parts, yet one body. **21** The eye cannot say to the hand, "I do not need you," nor again the head to the feet, "I do not need you." **22** Indeed, the parts of the body that

n Dt 8, 5; Heb 12, 5-11.
o Eph 2, 11-18.
p Rom 10, 9; 1 Jn 4, 2-3.
q Rom 12, 6; Eph 4, 7.11.
r 2, 6-13.
s 14, 5.26.39; Acts 2, 4.
t 7, 7; Eph 4, 7.
u 10, 17; Rom 12, 4-5; Eph 2, 16; Col 3, 15.
v Gal 3, 28; Eph 2, 13-18; Col 3, 11 / Jn 7, 37-39.

*

the proper spirit. If the Corinthians eat and drink unworthily, i.e., without having grasped and internalized the meaning of his death for them, *they will have to answer for the body and blood,* i.e., will be guilty of a sin against the Lord himself (cf 8, 12).

11, 28: *Examine himself:* the Greek word is similar to that for "approved" in v 19, which means "having been tested and found true." The self-testing required for proper eating involves *discerning the body* (29), which, from the context, must mean understanding the sense of Jesus' death (26), perceiving the imperative to unity that follows from the fact that Jesus gives himself to all and requires us to repeat his sacrifice in the same spirit (18–25).

11, 29–32: *Judgment:* there is a series of wordplays in these verses that would be awkward to translate literally into English; it includes all the references to judgment (*krima,* 29.34; *krinō,* 31.32), discernment (*diakrinō,* 29.31), and condemnation (*katakrinō,* 32). The judgment is concretely described as the illness, infirmity, and death that have visited the community. These are signs that the power of Jesus' death is not yet completely recognized and experienced. Yet even the judgment incurred is an expression of God's concern; it is a medicinal measure meant to rescue us from condemnation with God's enemies.

12, 1—14, 40: Ecstatic and charismatic activity were common in early Christian experience, as they were in other ancient religions. But the Corinthians seem to have developed a disproportionate esteem for certain phenomena, especially tongues, to the detriment of order in the liturgy. Paul's response to this development provides us with the fullest exposition we have of his theology of the charisms.

12, 2–3: There is an experience of the Spirit and an understanding of ecstatic phenomena that are specifically Christian and that differ, despite apparent similarities, from those of the pagans. It is necessary to discern which spirit is leading one; ecstatic phenomena must be judged by their effect (2). Verse 3 illustrates this by an example: power to confess Jesus as Lord can come only from the Spirit, and it is inconceivable that the Spirit would move anyone to curse the Lord.

12, 4–6: There are some features common to all charisms, despite their diversity: all are *gifts* (*charismata*), grace from outside ourselves; all are *forms of service* (*diakoniai*), an expression of their purpose and effect; and all are *workings (energēmata),* in which God is at work. Paul associates each of these aspects with what later theology will call one of the persons of the Trinity, an early example of "appropriation."

12, 12–26: The image of *a body* is introduced to explain Christ's relationship with believers (12). Verse 13 applies this model to the church: by baptism all, despite diversity of ethnic or social origins, are integrated into one organism. Verses 14–26 then develop the need for diversity of function among the parts of a body without threat to its unity.

seem to be weaker are all the more necessary,
23 and those parts of the body that we consider
less honorable we surround with greater honor,
and our less presentable parts are treated with
greater propriety, 24 whereas our more presentable parts do not need this. But God has so
constructed the body as to give greater honor to
a part that is without it, 25 so that there may be
no division in the body, but that the parts may
have the same concern for one another. 26 If
[one] part suffers, all the parts suffer with it; if
one part is honored, all the parts share its joy.

**Application to Christ** 27 [w]*Now you are
Christ's body, and individually parts of it.
28 [x]*Some people God has designated in the
church to be, first, apostles; second, prophets;
third, teachers; then, mighty deeds; then gifts of
healing, assistance, administration, and varieties of tongues. 29 Are all apostles? Are all
prophets? Are all teachers? Do all work mighty
deeds? 30 Do all have gifts of healing? Do all
speak in tongues? Do all interpret? 31 Strive
eagerly for the greatest spiritual gifts.

**The Way of Love** But I shall show you a
still more excellent way.

## CHAPTER 13

1 [y]*If I speak in human and angelic tongues,
but do not have love, I am a resounding gong
or a clashing cymbal. 2 [z]And if I have the gift
of prophecy, and comprehend all mysteries and
all knowledge; if I have all faith so as to move
mountains, but do not have love, I am nothing.
3 [a]If I give away everything I own, and if I
hand my body over so that I may boast, but do
not have love, I gain nothing.
4 [b]*Love is patient, love is kind. It is not
jealous, [love] is not pompous, it is not inflated,
5 [c]it is not rude, it does not seek its own interests, it is not quick-tempered, it does not brood
over injury, 6 it does not rejoice over wrongdoing but rejoices with the truth. 7 [d]It bears all
things, believes all things, hopes all things, endures all things.
8 *Love never fails. If there are prophecies,
they will be brought to nothing; if tongues, they
will cease; if knowledge, it will be brought to
nothing. 9 For we know partially and we prophesy partially, 10 but when the perfect comes,
the partial will pass away. 11 When I was a
child, I used to talk as a child, think as a child,
reason as a child; when I became a man, I put
aside childish things. 12 [e]At present we see
indistinctly, as in a mirror, but then face to face.
At present I know partially; then I shall know
fully as I am fully known. 13 [f]*So faith, hope,
love remain, these three; but the greatest of
these is love.

## CHAPTER 14

### Prophecy Greater than Tongues

1 [g]*Pursue love, but strive eagerly for the spiritual gifts, above all that you may prophesy.
2 *For one who speaks in a tongue does not

w Rom 12, 5-8; Eph 1, 23; 4, 12; 5, 30; Col 1, 18.24.
x Eph 2, 20; 3, 5; 4, 11.
y 8, 1; 16, 14; Rom 12, 9-10; 13, 8-10.
z 4, 1; 14, 2 / 1, 5; 8, 1-3; 12, 8 / Mt 17, 20; 21, 21; Col 2, 3.
a Mt 6, 2.
b Eph 4, 2 / 4, 6.18; 5, 2; 8, 1.
c 10, 24.33; Phil 2, 4.21; 1 Thes 5, 15.
d Prv 10, 12; 1 Pt 4, 8.
e 2 Cor 5, 7; Heb 11, 1 / 2 Tm 2, 19; 1 Jn 3, 2.
f Col 1, 4; 1 Thes 1, 3; 5, 8.
g 5.12.39.

12, 27–30: Paul now applies the image again to the church as a whole and its members (27). The lists in vv 28–30 spell out the parallelism by specifying the diversity of functions found in the church (cf Rom 12, 6–8; Eph 4, 11).

12, 28: *First, apostles:* apostleship was not mentioned in vv 8–10, nor is it at issue in these chapters, but Paul gives it pride of place in his listing. It is not just one gift among others but a prior and fuller gift that includes the others. They are all demonstrated in Paul's apostolate, but he may have developed his theology of charisms by reflecting first of all on his own grace of apostleship (cf 3, 5—4, 14; 9, 1–27; 2 Cor 2, 14—6, 13; 10, 1—13, 30, esp. 11, 23 and 12, 12).

13, 1–13: This chapter involves a shift of perspective and a new point. All or part of the material may once have been an independent piece in the style of Hellenistic eulogies of virtues, but it is now integrated, by editing, into the context of chs 12–14 (cf the reference to tongues and prophecy) and into the letter as a whole (cf the references to knowledge and to behavior). The function of ch 13 within the discussion of spiritual gifts is to relativize all the charisms by contrasting them with the more basic, pervasive, and enduring value that gives them their purpose and their effectiveness. The rhetoric of this chapter is striking.

13, 1–3: An inventory of gifts, arranged in careful gradation: neither tongues (on the lowest rung), nor prophecy, knowledge, or faith, nor even self-sacrifice has value unless informed by love.

13, 4–7: This paragraph is developed by personification and enumeration, defining love by what it does or does not do. The Greek contains fifteen verbs; it is natural to translate many of them by adjectives in English.

13, 8–13: The final paragraph announces its topic, *Love never fails* (8), then develops the permanence of love in contrast to the charisms (9–12), and finally asserts love's superiority even over the other "theological virtues" (13).

13, 13: In speaking of love, Paul is led by spontaneous association to mention faith and hope as well. They are already a well-known triad (cf 1 Thes 1, 3), three interrelated (cf 7) features of Christian life, more fundamental than any particular charism. *The greatest . . . is love:* love is operative even within the other members of the triad (7), so that it has a certain primacy among them. Or, if the perspective is temporal, love will remain (cf "never fails," 8) even when faith has yielded to sight and hope to possession.

14, 1–5: Verse 1b returns to the thought of 12, 31a and reveals Paul's primary concern. The series of contrasts in vv 2–5 discloses the problem at Corinth: a disproportionate interest in tongues, with a corresponding failure to appreciate the worth of prophecy. Paul attempts to clarify the relative values of those gifts by indicating the kind of communication achieved in each and the kind of effect each produces.

14, 2–3a: They involve two kinds of communication: tongues, private speech toward God in inarticulate terms that need interpretation to be intelligible to others (see 27–28); prophecy, communication with others in the community.

speak to human beings but to God, for no one
listens; he utters mysteries in spirit. **3** [h]*On the
other hand, one who prophesies does speak to
human beings, for their building up, encouragement, and solace. **4** Whoever speaks in a
tongue builds himself up, but whoever prophesies builds up the church. **5** Now I should like
all of you to speak in tongues, but even more to
prophesy. One who prophesies is greater than
one who speaks in tongues, unless he interprets,
so that the church may be built up.

**6** *Now, brothers, if I should come to you
speaking in tongues, what good will I do you if
I do not speak to you by way of revelation, or
knowledge, or prophecy, or instruction?
**7** Likewise, if inanimate things that produce
sound, such as flute or harp, do not give out the
tones distinctly, how will what is being played
on flute or harp be recognized? **8** And if the
bugle gives an indistinct sound, who will get
ready for battle? **9** Similarly, if you, because of
speaking in tongues, do not utter intelligible
speech, how will anyone know what is being
said? For you will be talking to the air. **10** It
happens that there are many different languages
in the world, and none is meaningless; **11** but
if I do not know the meaning of a language, I
shall be a foreigner to one who speaks it, and
one who speaks it a foreigner to me. **12** So with
yourselves: since you strive eagerly for spirits,
seek to have an abundance of them for building
up the church.

## Need for Interpretation

**13** *Therefore
one who speaks in a tongue should pray to be
able to interpret. **14** *[For] if I pray in a tongue,
my spirit is at prayer but my mind is unproductive. **15** [i]So what is to be done? I will pray with
the spirit, but I will also pray with the mind. I
will sing praise with the spirit, but I will also
sing praise with the mind. **16** Otherwise, if you
pronounce a blessing [with] the spirit, how shall
one who holds the place of the uninstructed say
the "Amen" to your thanksgiving, since he
does not know what you are saying? **17** For you
may be giving thanks very well, but the other is
not built up. **18** I give thanks to God that I speak
in tongues more than any of you, **19** but in the
church I would rather speak five words with my
mind, so as to instruct others also, than ten
thousand words in a tongue.

## Functions of These Gifts

**20** [j]*Brothers,
stop being childish in your thinking. In respect
to evil be like infants, but in your thinking be
mature. **21** [k]It is written in the law:

"By people speaking strange tongues
 and by the lips of foreigners
I will speak to this people,
 and even so they will not listen to me,
says the Lord." **22** Thus, tongues are a sign not
for those who believe but for unbelievers,
whereas prophecy is not for unbelievers but for
those who believe.

**23** [l]*So if the whole church meets in one
place and everyone speaks in tongues, and then
uninstructed people or unbelievers should come
in, will they not say that you are out of your
minds? **24** But if everyone is prophesying, and
an unbeliever or uninstructed person should

h 4-5.12.17.26; 3, 9; 8, 1.10; 10, 23.
i Eph 5, 19; Col 3, 16.
j Mt 10, 16; Rom 16, 19; Eph 4, 14.
k Is 28, 11-12; Dt 28, 49.
l Acts 2, 6.13.

14, 3b–5: They produce two kinds of effect. One who speaks in tongues *builds himself up;* it is a matter of individual experience and personal perfection, which inevitably recalls Paul's previous remarks about being inflated, seeking one's own good, pleasing oneself. But a prophet *builds up the church:* the theme of "building up" or "edifying" others, the main theme of the letter, comes to clearest expression in this chapter (3.4.5.12.17). It has been anticipated at 8, 1 and 10, 23, and by the related concept of "the beneficial" in 6, 12; 10, 23; 12, 7; etc.

14, 6–12: Sound, in order to be useful, must be intelligible. This principle is illustrated by a series of analogies from music (7–8) and from ordinary human speech (10–11); it is applied to the case at hand in v 9 and v 12.

14, 13–19: The charism of interpretation lifts tongues to the level of intelligibility, enabling them to produce the same effect as prophecy (cf 5.26–28).

14, 14–15: *My spirit:* Paul emphasizes the exclusively ecstatic, nonrational quality of tongues. The tongues at Pentecost are also described as an ecstatic experience (Acts 2, 4.12–13), though Luke superimposes further interpretations of his own. *My mind:* the ecstatic element, dominant in earliest Old Testament prophecy as depicted in 1 Sam 10, 5–13; 19, 20–24, seems entirely absent from Paul's notion of prophecy and completely relegated to tongues. He emphasizes the role of reason when he specifies instruction as a function of prophecy (6.19.31). But he does not exclude intuition and emotion; cf references to encouragement and consolation (3.31) and the scene describing the ideal exercise of prophecy (24–25).

14, 20–22: The Corinthians pride themselves on tongues as a sign of God's favor, a means of direct communication with him (2.28). To challenge them to a more mature appraisal, Paul draws from scripture a less flattering explanation of what speaking in tongues may signify. Isaiah threatened the people that if they failed to listen to their prophets, the Lord would speak to them (in punishment) through the lips of Assyrian conquerors (Is 28, 11–12). Paul compresses Isaiah's text and makes God address his people directly. Equating tongues with foreign languages (cf 10–11), Paul concludes from Isaiah that *tongues are a sign not for those who believe,* i.e., not a mark of God's pleasure for those who listen to him but a mark of his displeasure with those in the community who are faithless, who have not heeded the message that he has sent through the prophets.

14, 23–25: Paul projects the possible missionary effect of two hypothetical liturgical experiences, one consisting wholly of tongues, the other entirely of prophecy. *Uninstructed (idiotai): the term may simply mean people who do not speak or understand tongues, as in v 16, where it seems to designate Christians. But coupled with the term "unbelievers" it may be another way of designating those who have not been initiated into the community of faith; some believe it denotes a special class of non-Christians who are close to the community, such as catechumens. Unbelievers (apistoi): he has shifted from the inner-community perspective of v 22; the term here designates non-Christians (cf 6, 6; 7, 15; 10, 27).*

come in, he will be convinced by everyone and
judged by everyone, **25** [m]and the secrets of his
heart will be disclosed, and so he will fall down
and worship God, declaring, "God is really in
your midst."

**Rules of Order** **26** [n]*So what is to be done,
brothers? When you assemble, one has a psalm,
another an instruction, a revelation, a tongue, or
an interpretation. Everything should be done for
building up. **27** If anyone speaks in a tongue,
let it be two or at most three, and each in turn,
and one should interpret. **28** But if there is no
interpreter, the person should keep silent in the
church and speak to himself and to God.

**29** Two or three prophets should speak, and
the others discern. **30** But if a revelation is giv-
en to another person sitting there, the first one
should be silent. **31** For you can all prophesy
one by one, so that all may learn and all be
encouraged. **32** Indeed, the spirits of prophets
are under the prophets' control, **33** *since he is
not the God of disorder but of peace.

As in all the churches of the holy ones,
**34** [o]women should keep silent in the churches,
for they are not allowed to speak, but should be
subordinate, as even the law says. **35** But if
they want to learn anything, they should ask
their husbands at home. For it is improper for
a woman to speak in the church. **36** Did the
word of God go forth from you? Or has it come
to you alone?

**37** If anyone thinks that he is a prophet or a
spiritual person, he should recognize that what
I am writing to you is a commandment of the
Lord. **38** If anyone does not acknowledge this,
he is not acknowledged. **39** So, [my] brothers,
strive eagerly to prophesy, and do not forbid
speaking in tongues, **40** but everything must be
done properly and in order.

# *V: THE RESURRECTION*

## A. The Resurrection of Christ

### CHAPTER 15

**The Gospel Teaching** **1** *Now I am reminding you, brothers, of the gospel I preached
to you, which you indeed received and in which
you also stand. **2** Through it you are also being
saved, if you hold fast to the word I preached
to you, unless you believed in vain. **3** [p]*For I
handed on to you as of first importance what I
also received: that Christ died for our sins in
accordance with the scriptures; **4** [q]that he was
buried; that he was raised on the third day in
accordance with the scriptures; **5** [r]that he appeared to Cephas, then to the Twelve. **6** After
that, he appeared to more than five hundred
brothers at once, most of whom are still living,
though some have fallen asleep. **7** After that he
appeared to James, then to all the apostles.
**8** [s]Last of all, as to one born abnormally, he
appeared to me. **9** [t]*For I am the least of the
apostles, not fit to be called an apostle, because

m 4, 5 / Is 45, 14; Zec 8, 23.
n Eph 4, 12.
o 1 Tm 2, 11-15; 1 Pt 3, 1.
p 11, 23 / 1 Pt 2, 24; 3, 18 / Is 53, 4-12.
q Acts 2, 23-24 / Ps 16, 8-11; Hos 6, 1-2; Jon 2, 1.
r Mk 16, 14; Mt 28, 16-17; Lk 24, 36; Jn 20, 19.
s 9, 1; Acts 9, 3-6; Gal 1, 16.
t Acts 8, 3; 9, 1-2; Gal 1, 23; Eph 3, 8; 1 Tm 1, 15.

*

14, 26–33a: Paul concludes with specific directives regarding exercise of the gifts in their assemblies. Verse 26 enunciates the basic criterion in the use of any gift: it must contribute to "building up."

14, 33b–36: Verse 33b may belong with what precedes, so that the new paragraph would begin only with v 34. Verses 34–35 change the subject. These two verses have the theme of submission in common with ch 11, despite differences in vocabulary, and a concern with what is or is not becoming; but it is difficult to harmonize the injunction to silence here with ch 11, which appears to take it for granted that women do pray and prophesy aloud in the assembly (cf 11, 5.13). Hence the verses are often considered an interpolation, reflecting the discipline of later churches; such an interpolation would have to have antedated our manuscripts, all of which contain them, though some transpose them to the very end of the chapter.

15, 1–58: Some consider this chapter an earlier Pauline composition inserted into the present letter. The problem that Paul treats is clear to a degree: some of the Corinthians are denying the resurrection of the dead (12), apparently because of their inability to imagine how any kind of bodily existence could be possible after death (35). It is plausibly supposed that their attitude stems from Greek anthropology, which looks with contempt upon matter and would be content with the survival of the soul, and perhaps also from an overrealized eschatology of gnostic coloration, such as that reflected in 2 Tm 2, 18, which considers the resurrection a purely spiritual experience already achieved in baptism and in the forgiveness of sins. Paul, on the other hand, will affirm both the essential corporeity of the resurrection and its futurity.

His response moves through three steps: a recall of the basic kerygma about Jesus' resurrection (1–11), an assertion of the logical inconsistencies involved in denial of the resurrection (12–34), and an attempt to perceive theologically what the properties of the resurrected body must be (35–58).

15, 1–11: Paul recalls the tradition (3–7), which he can presuppose as common ground and which provides a starting point for his argument. This is the fundamental content of all Christian preaching and belief (1–2.11).

15, 3–7: The language by which Paul expresses the essence of the "gospel" (1) is not his own but is drawn from older credal formulas. This credo highlights Jesus' death for our sins (confirmed by his burial) and Jesus' resurrection (confirmed by his appearances) and presents both of them as fulfillment of prophecy. *In accordance with the scriptures:* conformity of Jesus' passion with the scriptures is asserted in Mt 16, 1; Lk 24, 25–27.32.44–46. Application of some Old Testament texts (Pss 2, 7; 16, 8–11) to his resurrection is illustrated by Acts 2, 27–31; 13, 29–39; and Is 52, 13—53, 12 and Hos 6, 2 may also have been envisaged.

15, 9–11: A persecutor may have appeared disqualified (*ouk . . . hikanos*) from apostleship, but in fact God's grace has qualified him. Cf the remarks in 2 Cor about his qualifications (2, 16; 3, 5) and his greater labors (11, 23). These verses are parenthetical, but a nerve has been touched (the references to his abnormal birth and his activity as a persecutor may echo taunts from Paul's opponents), and he is instinctively moved to self-defense.

I persecuted the church of God. **10** But by the
grace of God I am what I am, and his grace to
me has not been ineffective. Indeed, I have
toiled harder than all of them; not I, however,
but the grace of God [that is] with me.
**11** Therefore, whether it be I or they, so we
preach and so you believed.

## B. The Resurrection of the Dead

**Results of Denial** **12** *But if Christ is
preached as raised from the dead, how can some
among you say there is no resurrection of the
dead? **13** [u]If there is no resurrection of the
dead, then neither has Christ been raised.
**14** And if Christ has not been raised, then empty [too] is our preaching; empty, too, your faith.
**15** [v]Then we are also false witnesses to God,
because we testified against God that he raised
Christ, whom he did not raise if in fact the dead
are not raised. **16** For if the dead are not raised,
neither has Christ been raised, **17** *and if Christ
has not been raised, your faith is vain; you are
still in your sins. **18** Then those who have fallen
asleep in Christ have perished. **19** If for this life
only we have hoped in Christ, we are the most
pitiable people of all.

**Christ the Firstfruits** **20** [w]*But now
Christ has been raised from the dead, the firstfruits of those who have fallen asleep. **21** *For
since death came through a human being, the
resurrection of the dead came also through a
human being. **22** [x]For just as in Adam all die,
so too in Christ shall all be brought to life,
**23** [y]but each one in proper order: Christ the
firstfruits; then, at his coming, those who belong to Christ; **24** [z]*then comes the end, when
he hands over the kingdom to his God and Father, when he has destroyed every sovereignty
and every authority and power. **25** [a]For he
must reign until he has put all his enemies under
his feet. **26** [b]*The last enemy to be destroyed
is death, **27** [c]*for "he subjected everything under his feet." But when it says that everything
has been subjected, it is clear that it excludes the
One who subjected everything to him.
**28** [d]When everything is subjected to him, then
the Son himself will [also] be subjected to the
One who subjected everything to him, so that
God may be all in all.

**Practical Arguments** **29** *Otherwise,
what will people accomplish by having themselves baptized for the dead? If the dead are not
raised at all, then why are they having themselves baptized for them?

**30** [e]*Moreover, why are we endangering
ourselves all the time? **31** [f]Every day I face
death; I swear it by the pride in you [brothers]
that I have in Christ Jesus our Lord. **32** [g]If at
Ephesus I fought with beasts, so to speak, what

u 1 Thes 4, 14.
v Acts 5, 32.
w Rom 8, 11; Col 1, 18; 1 Thes 4, 14.
x Gn 3, 17-19; Rom 5, 12-19.
y 1 Thes 4, 15-17.
z Eph 1, 22.
a Ps 110, 1.
b Rom 6, 9; 2 Tm 1, 10; Rv 20, 14; 21, 4.
c Ps 8, 7; Eph 1, 22; Phil 3, 21.
d Eph 4, 6; Col 3, 11.
e 2 Cor 4, 8-12; 11, 23-27.
f Ps 44, 23; Rom 8, 36.
g 4, 9; 2 Cor 4, 10-11 / Wis 2, 5-7; Is 22, 13.

*

15, 12–19: Denial of the resurrection (12) involves logical inconsistencies. The basic one, stated twice (13.16), is that if there is no such thing as (bodily) resurrection, then it has not taken place even in Christ's case.

15, 17–18: The consequences for the Corinthians are grave: both forgiveness of sins and salvation are an illusion, despite their strong convictions about both. Unless Christ is risen, their faith does not save.

15, 20–28: After a triumphant assertion of the reality of Christ's resurrection (20a), Paul explains its positive implications and consequences. As a soteriological event of both human (20–23) and cosmic (24–28) dimensions, Jesus' resurrection logically and necessarily involves ours as well.

15, 20: *The firstfruits:* the portion of the harvest offered in thanksgiving to God implies the consecration of the entire harvest to come. Christ's resurrection is not an end in itself; its finality lies in the whole harvest, ourselves.

15, 21–22: Our human existence, both natural and supernatural, is corporate, involves solidarity. *In Adam . . . in Christ:* the Hebrew word ʾādām in Genesis is both a common noun for mankind and a proper noun for the first man. Paul here presents Adam as at least a literary type of Christ; the parallelism and contrast between them will be developed further in vv 45–49 and in Rom 5, 12–21.

15, 24–28: Paul's perspective expands to cosmic dimensions, as he describes the climax of history, *the end.* His viewpoint is still christological, as in vv 20–23. Verses 24 and 28 describe Christ's final relations to his enemies and his Father in language that is both royal and military; vv 25–28 insert a proof from scripture (Pss 110, 1; 8, 7) into this description. But the viewpoint is also theological, for God is the ultimate agent and end, and likewise soteriological, for we are the beneficiaries of all the action.

15, 26: *The last enemy . . . is death:* a parenthesis that specifies the final fulfillment of the two Old Testament texts just referred to, Ps 110, 1 and Ps 8, 7. Death is not just one cosmic power among many, but the ultimate effect of sin in the universe (cf 56; Rom 5, 12). Christ defeats death where it prevails, in our bodies. The destruction of the last enemy is concretely the "coming to life" (22) of "those who belong to Christ" (23).

15, 27b–28: *The one who subjected everything to him:* the Father is the ultimate agent in the drama, and the final end of the process, to whom the Son and everything else is ordered (24.28). *That God may be all in all:* his reign is a dynamic exercise of creative power, an outpouring of life and energy through the universe, with no further resistance. This is the supremely positive meaning of "subjection": that God may fully be God.

15, 29–34: Paul concludes his treatment of logical inconsistencies with a listing of miscellaneous Christian practices that would be meaningless if the resurrection were not a fact.

15, 29: *Baptized for the dead:* this practice is not further explained here, nor is it necessarily mentioned with approval, but Paul cites it as something in their experience that attests in one more way to belief in the resurrection.

15, 30–34: A life of sacrifice, such as Paul describes in 4, 9–13 and 2 Cor, would be pointless without the prospect of resurrection; a life of pleasure, such as that expressed in the Epicurean slogan of v 32, would be far more consistent. *I fought with beasts:* since Paul does not elsewhere mention a combat with beasts at Ephesus, he may be speaking figuratively about struggles with adversaries.

benefit was it to me? If the dead are not raised:

> "Let us eat and drink,
> for tomorrow we die."

**33** Do not be led astray:

> "Bad company corrupts good morals."

**34** [h]Become sober as you ought and stop sinning. For some have no knowledge of God; I say
this to your shame.

## C. The Manner of the Resurrection

**35** *But someone may say, "How are the
dead raised? With what kind of body will they
come back?"

**The Resurrection Body** **36** [i]*You fool!
What you sow is not brought to life unless it
dies. **37** And what you sow is not the body that
is to be but a bare kernel of wheat, perhaps, or
of some other kind; **38** [j]but God gives it a body
as he chooses, and to each of the seeds its own
body. **39** *Not all flesh is the same, but there
is one kind for human beings, another kind of
flesh for animals, another kind of flesh for
birds, and another for fish. **40** There are both
heavenly bodies and earthly bodies, but the
brightness of the heavenly is one kind and that
of the earthly another. **41** The brightness of the
sun is one kind, the brightness of the moon
another, and the brightness of the stars another.
For star differs from star in brightness.
**42** *So also is the resurrection of the dead. It
is sown corruptible; it is raised incorruptible.
**43** [k]It is sown dishonorable; it is raised glorious. It is sown weak; it is raised powerful. **44** It
is sown a natural body; it is raised a spiritual
body. If there is a natural body, there is also a
spiritual one.
**45** [l]*So, too, it is written, "The first man,
Adam, became a living being," the last Adam
a life-giving spirit. **46** But the spiritual was not
first; rather the natural and then the spiritual.
**47** The first man was from the earth, earthly;
the second man, from heaven. **48** As was the
earthly one, so also are the earthly, and as is the
heavenly one, so also are the heavenly.
**49** [m]*Just as we have borne the image of the
earthly one, we shall also bear the image of the
heavenly one.

**The Resurrection Event** **50** [n]*This I declare, brothers: flesh and blood cannot inherit
the kingdom of God, nor does corruption inherit
incorruption. **51** [o]*Behold, I tell you a mystery. We shall not all fall asleep, but we will all
be changed, **52** [p]in an instant, in the blink of an
eye, at the last trumpet. For the trumpet will
sound, the dead will be raised incorruptible, and
we shall be changed. **53** [q]For this which is
corruptible must clothe itself with incorruptibil-

h Mt 22, 29; Mk 12, 24.
i Jn 12, 24.
j Gn 1, 11.
k Phil 3, 20-21; Col 3, 4.
l Gn 2, 7 / Jn 5, 21-29; 2 Cor 3, 6.17.
m Gn 5, 3 / Rom 8, 29; Phil 3, 21.
n Jn 3, 3-6.
o 1 Thes 4, 14-17.
p Jl 2, 1; Zec 9, 14; Mt 24, 31; Rv 11, 15-18.
q 2 Cor 5, 2-4.

*

15, 35–58: Paul imagines two objections that the Corinthians could raise: one concerning the manner of the resurrection (*how?*), the other pertaining to the qualities of the risen body (*what kind?*). These questions probably lie behind their denial of the resurrection (12), and seem to reflect the presumption that no kind of body other than the one we now possess would be possible. Paul deals with these objections in inverse order, in vv 36–49 and vv 50–58. His argument is fundamentally theological and its appeal is to the understanding.

15, 35–49: Paul approaches the question of the nature of the risen body (*what kind of body?*) by means of two analogies: the seed (36–44) and the first man, Adam (45–49).

15, 36–38: The analogy of the seed: there is a change of attributes from seed to plant; the old life-form must be lost for the new to emerge. By speaking about the seed as a *body* that dies and comes to life, Paul keeps the point of the analogy before the reader's mind.

15, 39–41: The expression "its own body" (38) leads to a development on the marvelous diversity evident in bodily life.

15, 42–44: The principles of qualitative difference before and after death (36–38) and of diversity on different levels of creation (39–41) are now applied to the human body. Before: a body animated by a lower, natural life-principle (*psyche*) and endowed with the properties of natural existence (corruptibility, lack of glory, weakness). After: a body animated by a higher life-principle (*pneuma;* cf 45) and endowed with other qualities (incorruptibility, glory, power, spirituality), which are properties of God himself.

15, 45: The analogy of *the first man, Adam,* is introduced by a citation from Gn 2, 7. Paul alters the text slightly, adding the adjective *first,* and translating the Hebrew ʾādām twice, so as to give it its value both as a common noun (*man*) and as a proper name (*Adam*). Verse 45b then specifies similarities and differences between the two Adams. *The last Adam,* Christ (cf 21–22) has become *a . . . spirit* (*pneuma*), a life-principle transcendent with respect to the natural soul (*psyche*) of the first Adam (on the terminology here, cf the note on 3, 1). Further, he is not just alive, but *life-giving,* a source of life for others.

15, 49: *We shall also bear the image:* although it has less manuscript support, this reading better fits the context's emphasis on futurity and the transforming action of God; on future transformation as conformity to the image of the Son, cf Rom 8, 29; Phil 3, 21. The majority reading, "let us bear the image," suggests that the image of the heavenly man is already present and exhorts us to conform to it.

15, 50–57: These verses, an answer to the first question of v 35, explain theologically how the change of properties from one image to another will take place: God has the power to transform, and he will exercise it.

15, 50–53: *Flesh and blood . . . corruption:* living persons and the corpses of the dead, respectively. In both cases, the gulf between creatures and God is too wide to be bridged unless God himself transforms us.

15, 51–52: *A mystery:* the last moment in God's plan is disclosed; cf the notes on 2, 1.7–10a. The final trumpet and the awakening of the dead are stock details of the apocalyptic scenario. *We shall not all fall asleep:* Paul expected that some of his contemporaries might still be alive at Christ's return; after the death of Paul and his whole generation, copyists altered this statement in various ways. *We will all be changed:* the statement extends to all Christians, for Paul is not directly speaking about anyone else. Whether they have died before the end or happen still to be alive, all must be transformed.

ity, and this which is mortal must clothe itself
with immortality. **54** [r]*And when this which is
corruptible clothes itself with incorruptibility
and this which is mortal clothes itself with immortality, then the word that is written shall
come about:

"Death is swallowed up in victory.
**55** [s]Where, O death, is your victory?
Where, O death, is your sting?"

**56** [t]*The sting of death is sin, and the power of
sin is the law. **57** [u]But thanks be to God who
gives us the victory through our Lord Jesus
Christ.
**58** Therefore, my beloved brothers, be firm,
steadfast, always fully devoted to the work of
the Lord, knowing that in the Lord your labor
is not in vain.

# *VI: CONCLUSION*

## CHAPTER 16

**The Collection** **1** [v]*Now in regard to the
collection for the holy ones, you also should do
as I ordered the churches of Galatia. **2** On the
first day of the week each of you should set
aside and save whatever one can afford, so that
collections will not be going on when I come.
**3** And when I arrive, I shall send with letters of
recommendation those whom you have approved to take your gracious gift to Jerusalem.
**4** *If it seems fitting that I should go also, they
will go with me.

**Paul's Travel Plans** **5** [w]*I shall come to
you after I pass through Macedonia (for I am
going to pass through Macedonia), **6** and perhaps I shall stay or even spend the winter with
you, so that you may send me on my way wherever I may go. **7** [x]For I do not wish to see you
now just in passing, but I hope to spend some
time with you, if the Lord permits. **8** [y]*I shall
stay in Ephesus until Pentecost, **9** [z]because a
door has opened for me wide and productive for
work, but there are many opponents.
**10** [a]If Timothy comes, see that he is without
fear in your company, for he is doing the work
of the Lord just as I am. **11** Therefore no one
should disdain him. Rather, send him on his
way in peace that he may come to me, for I am
expecting him with the brothers. **12** [b]Now in
regard to our brother Apollos, I urged him
strongly to go to you with the brothers, but it
was not at all his will that he go now. He will
go when he has an opportunity.

**Exhortation and Greetings** **13** Be on
your guard, stand firm in the faith, be courageous, be strong. **14** Your every act should be
done with love.
**15** [c]I urge you, brothers—you know that the
household of Stephanas is the firstfruits of
Achaia and that they have devoted themselves
to the service of the holy ones— **16** be subordinate to such people and to everyone who works
and toils with them. **17** I rejoice in the arrival
of Stephanas, Fortunatus, and Achaicus, because they made up for your absence, **18** [d]for
they refreshed my spirit as well as yours. So
give recognition to such people.
**19** [e]*The churches of Asia send you greetings. Aquila and Prisca together with the church
at their house send you many greetings in the
Lord. **20** [f]All the brothers greet you. Greet one
another with a holy kiss.
**21** [g]I, Paul, write you this greeting in my
own hand. **22** [h]*If anyone does not love the

r Is 25, 8; 2 Cor 5, 4; 2 Tm 1, 10; Heb 2, 14-15.
s Hos 13, 14.
t Rom 4, 15; 7, 7.13.
u Jn 16, 33; 1 Jn 5, 4.
v Acts 24, 17; Rom 15, 25-32; 2 Cor 8-9; Gal 2, 10.
w Acts 19, 21; Rom 15, 26; 2 Cor 1, 15-16.
x Acts 18, 21.
y 15, 32; Acts 18, 19; 19, 1-10.
z Acts 14, 27; 2 Cor 2, 12.
a 4, 17; Acts 16, 1; 19, 22; Phil 2, 19-23.
b 1, 12; 3, 4-6.22; Acts 18, 24-28.
c 1, 16.
d 1 Thes 5, 12-13.
e Acts 18, 2.18.26; Rom 16, 3-5.
f Rom 16, 16; 2 Cor 13, 12; 1 Thes 5, 26; 1 Pt 5, 14.
g Gal 6, 11; Col 4, 18; 2 Thes 3, 17.
h 12, 3; Rom 9, 3; Gal 1, 8-9; Rv 22, 20.

*

15, 54–55: *Death is swallowed up in victory:* scripture itself predicts death's overthrow. *O death:* in his prophetic vision Paul may be making Hosea's words his own, or imagining this cry of triumph on the lips of the risen church.

15, 56: *The sting of death is sin:* an explanation of Hosea's metaphor. Death, scorpion-like, is equipped with a sting, sin, by which it injects its poison. Christ defeats sin, the cause of death (Gn 3, 19; Rom 5, 12).

16, 1–4: This paragraph contains our earliest evidence for a project that became a major undertaking of Paul's ministry. The collection for the church at Jerusalem was a symbol in his mind for the unity of Jewish and Gentile Christianity. Cf Gal 2, 10; Rom 15, 25–29; 2 Cor 8–9 and the notes to this last passage.

16, 1: *In regard to the collection:* it has already begun in Galatia and Macedonia (cf 2 Cor 8), and presumably he has already instructed the Corinthians about its purpose.

16, 4: *That I should go also:* presumably Paul delivered the collection on his final visit to Jerusalem; cf Rom 15, 25–32; Acts 24, 14.

16, 5–12: The travel plans outlined here may not have materialized precisely as Paul intended; cf 2 Cor 1, 8—2, 13; 7, 4–16.

16, 8: *In Ephesus until Pentecost:* this tells us the place from which he wrote the letter and suggests he may have composed it about Easter time (cf 5, 7–8).

16, 19–24: These paragraphs conform to the normal epistolary conclusion, but their language is overlaid with liturgical coloration as well. The *greetings* of the Asian churches are probably to be read, along with the letter, in the liturgy at Corinth, and the union of the church is to be expressed by *a holy kiss* (19–20). Paul adds to this his own greeting (21) and blessings (23–24).

16, 22: *Accursed:* literally, "anathema." This expression (cf 12, 3) is a formula for exclusion from the community; it may imply here a call to self-examination before celebration of the Eucharist, in preparation for the Lord's coming and judgment

Lord, let him be accursed. *Marana tha.*
**23** [i]The grace of the Lord Jesus be with you.
**24** My love to all of you in Christ Jesus.

i Rom 16, 20.

* (cf 11, 17–34). *Marana tha:* an Aramaic expression, probably used in the early Christian liturgy. As understood here ("O Lord, come!"), it is a prayer for the early return of Christ. If the Aramaic words are divided differently (*Maran atha,* "Our Lord has come"), it becomes a credal declaration. The former interpretation is supported by what appears to be a Greek equivalent of this acclamation in Rv 22, 20: "Amen. Come, Lord Jesus!"

# THE SECOND LETTER TO THE

# CORINTHIANS

## INTRODUCTION

*The Second Letter to the Corinthians is the most personal of all of Paul's extant writings, and it reveals much about his character. In it he deals with one or more crises that have arisen in the Corinthian church. The confrontation with these problems caused him to reflect deeply on his relationship with the community and to speak about it frankly. One moment he is venting his feelings of frustration and uncertainty, the next he is pouring out his relief and affection. The importance of the issues at stake between them calls forth from him an enormous effort of personal persuasion, as well as doctrinal considerations that are of great value for us. Paul's ability to produce profound theological foundations for what may at first sight appear to be rather commonplace circumstances is perhaps nowhere better exemplified than in Second Corinthians. The emotional tone of the letter, its lack of order, and our ignorance of some of its background do not make it easy to follow, but it amply repays the effort required of the reader.*

*Second Corinthians is rich and varied in content. The interpretation of Exodus in chapter 3, for instance, offers a striking example of early apologetic use of the Old Testament. Paul's discussion of the collection in chs 8–9 contains a theology of sharing of possessions, of community of goods among Christian churches, which is both balanced and sensitive. Furthermore, the closing chapters provide an illustration of early Christian invective and polemic, because the conflict with intruders forces Paul to assert his authority. But in those same chapters Paul articulates the vision and sense of values that animate his own apostolate, revealing his faith that Jesus' passion and resurrection are the pattern for all Christian life and expressing a spirituality of ministry unsurpassed in the New Testament.*

*The letter is remarkable for its rhetoric. Paul falls naturally into the style and argumentation of contemporary philosophic preachers, employing with ease the stock devices of the "diatribe." By a barrage of questions, by challenges both serious and ironic, by paradox heaped upon paradox, even by insults hurled at his opponents, he strives to awaken in his hearers a true sense of values and an appropriate response. All his argument centers on the destiny of Jesus, in which a paradoxical reversal of values is revealed. But Paul appeals to his own personal experience as well. In passages of great rhetorical power (4, 7–15; 6, 3–10; 11, 21–29; 12, 5–10; 13, 3–4) he enumerates the circumstances of his ministry and the tribulations he has had to endure for Jesus and the gospel, in the hope of illustrating the pattern of Jesus' existence in his own and of drawing the Corinthians into a reappraisal of the values they cherish. Similar passages in the same style in his other letters (cf especially Rom 8, 31–39; 1 Cor 1, 26–31; 4, 6–21; 9, 1–27; 13, 1–13; Phil 4, 10–19) confirm Paul's familiarity with contemporary rhetoric and demonstrate how effectively it served to express his vision of Christian life and ministry.*

*Second Corinthians was occasioned by events and problems that developed after Paul's first letter reached Corinth. We have no information about these circumstances except what is contained in the letter itself, which of course supposes that they are known to the readers. Consequently the reconstruction of the letter's background is an uncertain enterprise about which there is not complete agreement.*

*The letter deals principally with these three topics: (1) a crisis between Paul and the Corinthians, occasioned at least partially by changes in his travel plans (1, 12—2, 13), and the successful resolution of that crisis (7, 5–16); (2) further directives and encouragement in regard to the collection for the church in Jerusalem (8, 1—9, 15); (3) the definition and defense of Paul's ministry as an apostle.*

*Paul's reflections on this matter are occasioned by visitors from other churches who passed through Corinth, missionaries who differed from Paul in a variety of ways, both in theory and in practice. Those differences led to comparisons. Either the visitors themselves or some of the local church members appear to have sown confusion among the Corinthians with regard to Paul's authority or his style, or both. Paul deals at length with aspects of this situation in 2, 14—7, 4 and again in 10, 1—13, 10, though the manner of treatment and the thrust of the argument differ in each of these sections.*

*Scholars have noticed a lack of continuity in this document. For example, the long section of 2, 14—7, 4 seems abruptly spliced into the narrative of a crisis and its resolution. Identical or similar topics, moreover, seem to be treated several times during the letter (compare 2, 14—7, 4 with 10, 1—13, 10, and 8, 1–24 with 9, 1–15). Many judge, therefore, that this letter as it stands incorporates several briefer letters sent to Corinth over a certain span of time. If this is so, then Paul himself or, more likely, some other editor clearly took care to gather those letters together and impose some literary unity upon the collection, thus producing the document that has come down to us as the Second Letter to the Corinthians. Others continue to regard it as a single letter, attributing its inconsistencies to changes of perspective in Paul that may have been occasioned by the arrival of fresh news from Corinth during its composition. The letter, or at least some sections of it, appears to have been composed in Macedonia (2, 12–13; 7, 5–6; 8, 1–4; 9, 2–4). It is generally dated about the autumn of A.D. 57; if it is a compilation, of course, the various parts may have been separated by intervals of at least some months.*

*The principal divisions of the Second Letter to the Corinthians are the following:*

- *I. Address (1, 1–11)*
- *II. The Crisis between Paul and the Corinthians (1, 12—7, 16)*
  - *A. Past Relationships (1, 12—2, 13)*
  - *B. Paul's Ministry (2, 14—7, 4)*
  - *C. Resolution of the Crisis (7, 5–16)*
- *III. The Collection for Jerusalem (8, 1—9, 15)*
- *IV. Paul's Defense of His Ministry (10, 1—13, 10)*
- *V. Conclusion (13, 11–13)*

# I: ADDRESS

## CHAPTER 1

**Greeting** 1 [a]*Paul, an apostle of Christ
Jesus by the will of God, and Timothy our
brother, to the church of God that is in Corinth,
with all the holy ones throughout Achaia:
2 grace to you and peace from God our Father
and the Lord Jesus Christ.

**Thanksgiving** 3 [b]*Blessed be the God and
Father of our Lord Jesus Christ, the Father of
compassion and God of all encouragement,
4 [c]who encourages us in our every affliction,
so that we may be able to encourage those who
are in any affliction with the encouragement
with which we ourselves are encouraged by
God. 5 *For as Christ's sufferings overflow to
us, so through Christ does our encouragement
also overflow. 6 If we are afflicted, it is for
your encouragement and salvation; if we are
encouraged, it is for your encouragement,
which enables you to endure the same sufferings
that we suffer. 7 *Our hope for you is firm, for
we know that as you share in the sufferings, you
also share in the encouragement.
8 [d]*We do not want you to be unaware,

a Eph 1, 1; Col 1, 1 / 1, 19; Acts 16 / Rom 1, 7; 1 Cor 1, 2.
b 1 Cor 15, 24; Eph 1, 3; 1 Pt 1, 3 / Rom 15, 5.
c 7, 6-7.13; 1 Thes 3, 6-8; 2 Thes 2, 16.
d Acts 20, 18-19; 1 Cor 15, 32.

*

1, 1–11: The opening follows the usual Pauline form, except that the thanksgiving takes the form of a doxology or glorification of God (3). This introduces a meditation on the experience of suffering and encouragement shared by Paul and the Corinthians (4–7), drawn, at least in part, from Paul's reflections on a recent affliction (8–10). The section ends with a modified and delayed allusion to thanksgiving (11).

1, 3: *God of all encouragement:* Paul expands a standard Jewish blessing so as to state the theme of the paragraph. The theme of "encouragement" or "consolation" (*paraklēsis*) occurs ten times in this opening, against a background formed by multiple references to "affliction" and "suffering."

1, 5: *Through Christ:* the Father of compassion is the Father of our Lord Jesus (3); Paul's sufferings and encouragement (or "consolation") are experienced in union with Christ. Cf Lk 2, 25: the "consolation of Israel" is Jesus himself.

1, 7: *You also share in the encouragement:* the eschatological reversal of affliction and encouragement that Christians expect (cf Mt 5, 4; Lk 6, 24) permits some present experience of reversal in the Corinthians' case, as in Paul's.

1, 8: *Asia:* a Roman province in western Asia Minor, the

brothers, of the affliction that came to us in the
province of Asia; we were utterly weighed
down beyond our strength, so that we despaired
even of life. **9** [e]*Indeed, we had accepted within ourselves the sentence of death, that we might
trust not in ourselves but in God who raises the
dead. **10** [f]He rescued us from such great danger
of death, and he will continue to rescue us; in
him we have put our hope [that] he will also
rescue us again, **11** [g]as you help us with prayer,
so that thanks may be given by many on our
behalf for the gift granted us through the prayers
of many.

## *II: THE CRISIS BETWEEN PAUL AND THE CORINTHIANS*

## A. Past Relationships

### Paul's Sincerity and Constancy

**12** *For our boast is this, the testimony of our
conscience that we have conducted ourselves in
the world, and especially toward you, with the
simplicity and sincerity of God, [and] not by
human wisdom but by the grace of God. **13** For
we write you nothing but what you can read and
understand, and I hope that you will understand
completely, **14** [h]as you have come to understand us partially, that we are your boast as you
also are ours, on the day of [our] Lord Jesus.
**15** *With this confidence I formerly intended
to come to you so that you might receive a
double favor, **16** [i]namely, to go by way of you
to Macedonia, and then to come to you again on
my return from Macedonia, and have you send
me on my way to Judea. **17** [j]*So when I intended this, did I act lightly? Or do I make my plans
according to human considerations, so that with
me it is "yes, yes" and "no, no"? **18** *As God
is faithful, our word to you is not "yes" and
"no." **19** [k]For the Son of God, Jesus Christ,
who was proclaimed to you by us, Silvanus and
Timothy and me, was not "yes" and "no," but
"yes" has been in him. **20** [l]For however many
are the promises of God, their Yes is in him;
therefore, the Amen from us also goes through
him to God for glory. **21** [m]*But the one who
gives us security with you in Christ and who
anointed us is God; **22** [n]he has also put his seal
upon us and given the Spirit in our hearts as a
first installment.

**Paul's Change of Plan** **23** [o]*But I call
upon God as witness, on my life, that it is to
spare you that I have not yet gone to Corinth.
**24** Not that we lord it over your faith; rather, we

e 4, 7-11; Rom 4, 17.
f 2 Tm 4, 18.
g 4, 15; 9, 12.
h Phil 2, 16; 1 Thes 2, 19-20.
i 1 Cor 16, 5-9; Acts 19, 21.
j Mt 5, 37; Jas 5, 12.
k Acts 16, 1-3; 1 Thes 1, 1; 2 Thes 1, 1.
l 1 Cor 14, 16; Rv 3, 14.
m 1 Jn 2, 20.27.
n Eph 1, 13-14; 4, 30 / 5, 5; Rom 5, 5; 8, 16.23.
o 13, 2.

* capital of which was Ephesus.

1, 9–10: *The sentence of death:* it is unclear whether Paul is alluding to a physical illness or to an external threat to life. The result of the situation was to produce an attitude of faith in God alone. *God who raises the dead:* rescue is the constant pattern of God's activity; his final act of encouragement is the resurrection.

1, 12—2, 13: The autobiographical remarks about the crisis in Asia Minor lead into consideration of a crisis that has arisen between Paul and the Corinthians. Paul will return to this question, after a long digression, in 7, 5–16. Both of these sections deal with travel plans Paul had made, changes in the plans, alternative measures adopted, a breach that opened between him and the community, and finally a reconciliation between them.

1, 12–14: Since Paul's own conduct will be under discussion here, he prefaces the section with a statement about his habitual behavior and attitude toward the community. He protests his openness, single-mindedness, and conformity to God's grace; he hopes that his relationship with them will be marked by mutual understanding and pride, which will constantly increase until it reaches its climax at the judgment. Two references to boasting frame this paragraph (12.14), the first appearances of a theme that will be important in the letter, especially in chs 10–13; the term is used in a positive sense here (cf the note on 1 Cor 1, 29–31).

1, 15: *I formerly intended to come:* this plan reads like a revision of the one mentioned in 1 Cor 16, 5. Not until 1, 23—2, 1 will Paul tell us something his original readers already knew, that he has canceled one or the other of these projected visits.

1, 17: *Did I act lightly?:* the subsequent change of plans casts suspicion on the original intention, creating the impression that Paul is vacillating and inconsistent or that *human considerations* keep dictating shifts in his goals and projects (cf the counterclaim of 12). *"Yes, yes" and "no, no":* stating something and denying it in the same or the next breath; being of two minds at once, or from one moment to the next.

1, 18–22: *As God is faithful:* unable to deny the change in plans, Paul nonetheless asserts the firmness of the original plan and claims a profound constancy in his life and work. He grounds his defense in God himself, who is firm and reliable; this quality can also be predicated in various ways of those who are associated with him. Christ, Paul, and the Corinthians all participate in analogous ways in the constancy of God. A number of the terms here, which appear related only conceptually in Greek or English, would be variations of the same root, *'mn,* in a Semitic language, and thus naturally associated in a Semitic mind, such as Paul's. These include the words *yes* (17–20), *faithful* (18), *Amen* (20), *gives us security* (21), *faith, stand firm* (24).

1, 21–22: The commercial terms *gives us security, seal, first installment* are here used analogously to refer to the process of initiation into the Christian life, perhaps specifically to baptism. The passage is clearly trinitarian. The Spirit is the *first installment* or "down payment" of the full messianic benefits that God guarantees to Christians. Cf Eph 1, 13–14.

1, 23–24: *I have not yet gone to Corinth:* some suppose that Paul received word of some affair in Corinth, which he decided to regulate by letter even before the first of his projected visits (cf 16). Others conjecture that he did pay the first visit, was offended there (cf 2, 5), returned to Ephesus, and sent a letter (2, 3–9) in place of the second visit. The expressions *to spare you* (23) and *work together for your joy* (24) introduce the major themes of the next two paragraphs, which are remarkable for insistent repetition of key words and ideas. These form two clusters of terms in the English translation: (1) cheer, rejoice, encourage, joy; (2) pain, affliction, anguish. These clusters reappear when Paul resumes treatment of this subject in 7, 5–16.

work together for your joy, for you stand firm
in the faith.

## CHAPTER 2

**1** For I decided not to come to you again in
painful circumstances. **2** For if I inflict pain
upon you, then who is there to cheer me except
the one pained by me? **3** *And I wrote as I did
so that when I came I might not be pained by
those in whom I should have rejoiced, confident
about all of you that my joy is that of all of you.
**4** For out of much affliction and anguish of
heart I wrote to you with many tears, not that
you might be pained but that you might know
the abundant love I have for you.

**The Offender** **5** *If anyone has caused
pain, he has caused it not to me, but in some
measure (not to exaggerate) to all of you.
**6** This punishment by the majority is enough
for such a person, **7** [p]so that on the contrary you
should forgive and encourage him instead, or
else the person may be overwhelmed by excessive pain. **8** Therefore, I urge you to reaffirm
your love for him. **9** [q]For this is why I wrote,
to know your proven character, whether you
were obedient in everything. **10** Whomever
you forgive anything, so do I. For indeed what
I have forgiven, if I have forgiven anything, has
been for you in the presence of Christ, **11** [r]so
that we might not be taken advantage of by
Satan, for we are not unaware of his purposes.

**Paul's Anxiety** **12** [s]*When I went to Troas
for the gospel of Christ, although a door was
opened for me in the Lord, **13** [t]*I had no relief
in my spirit because I did not find my brother
Titus. So I took leave of them and went on to
Macedonia.

## B. Paul's Ministry

**Ministers of a New Covenant** **14** *But
thanks be to God, who always leads us in triumph in Christ and manifests through us the
odor of the knowledge of him in every place.
**15** [u]For we are the aroma of Christ for God
among those who are being saved and among
those who are perishing, **16** *to the latter an
odor of death that leads to death, to the former
an odor of life that leads to life. Who is qualified

p Col 3, 13. q 7, 15. r Eph 4, 27. s Acts 16, 8. t 7, 6; 1 Tm 1, 3. u 4, 3; 1 Cor 1, 18.

*

2, 3–4: *I wrote as I did:* we learn for the first time about the sending of a letter in place of the proposed visit. Paul mentions the letter in passing, but emphasizes his motivation in sending it: to avoid being saddened by them (cf 1), and to help them realize the depth of his love. Another motive will be added in 7, 12: to bring to light their own concern for him. *With many tears:* it has been suggested that we may have all or part of this "tearful letter" somewhere in the Corinthian correspondence, either in 1 Cor 5 (the case of the incestuous man), or in 1 Cor as a whole, or in 2 Cor 10–13. None of these hypotheses is entirely convincing. See the note on 13, 1.

2, 5–11: The nature of the *pain* (5) is unclear, though some believe an individual at Corinth rejected Paul's authority, thereby scandalizing many in the community. In any case, action has been taken, and Paul judges the measures adequate to right the situation (6). The follow-up directives he now gives are entirely positive: forgive, encourage, love. *Overwhelmed* (7): a vivid metaphor (literally "swallowed") that Paul employs positively at 5, 4 and in 1 Cor 15, 54 (7). It is often used to describe satanic activity (cf 1 Pt 5, 8); note the reference to Satan here in v 11.

2, 12–13: *I had no relief:* Paul does not explain the reason for his anxiety until he resumes the thread of his narrative at 7, 5: he was waiting to hear how the Corinthians would respond to his letter. Since 7, 5–16 describes their response in entirely positive terms, we never learn in detail why he found it necessary to defend and justify his change of plans, as in 1, 15–24. Was this portion of the letter written before the arrival of Titus with his good news (7, 6–7)?

2, 13: *Macedonia:* a Roman province in northern Greece.

2, 14—7, 4: This section constitutes a digression within the narrative of the crisis and its resolution (1, 12—2, 13 and 7, 5–16). The main component (2, 14—6, 10) treats the nature of Paul's ministry and his qualifications for it; this material bears some similarity to the defense of his ministry in chs 10–13, but it may well come from a period close to the crisis. This is followed by a supplementary block of material quite different in character and tone (6, 14—7, 1). These materials may have been brought together into their present position during final editing of the letter; appeals to the Corinthians link them to one another (6, 11–13) and lead back to the interrupted narrative (7, 2–4).

2, 14—6, 10: The question of Paul's adequacy (16; cf 3, 5) and his credentials (3, 1–2) has been raised. Paul responds by an extended treatment of the nature of his ministry. It is a ministry of glory (3, 7—4, 6), of life (4, 7—5, 10), of reconciliation (5, 11—6, 10).

2, 14–16a: The initial statement plunges us abruptly into another train of thought. Paul describes his personal existence and his function as a preacher in two powerful images (14) that constitute a prelude to the development to follow.

2, 14a: *Leads us in triumph in Christ:* this metaphor of a festive parade in honor of a conquering military hero can suggest either a positive sharing in Christ's triumph or an experience of defeat, being led in captivity and submission (cf 4, 8–11; 1 Cor 4, 9). Paul is probably aware of the ambiguity, as he is in the case of the next metaphor.

2, 14b–16a: *The odor of the knowledge of him:* incense was commonly used in triumphal processions. The metaphor suggests the gradual diffusion of the knowledge of God through the apostolic preaching. *The aroma of Christ:* the image shifts from the fragrance Paul diffuses to the aroma that he is. Paul is probably thinking of the "sweet odor" of the sacrifices in the Old Testament (e.g., Gn 8, 21; Ex 29, 18) and perhaps of the metaphor of wisdom as a sweet odor (Sir 24, 15). *Death . . . life:* the aroma of Christ that comes to them through Paul is perceived differently by various classes of people. To some his preaching and his life (cf 1 Cor 1, 17—2, 6) are perceived as *death,* and the effect is death for them; others perceive him, despite appearances, as *life,* and the effect is life for them. This fragrance thus produces a separation and a judgment (cf the function of the "light" in John's gospel).

2, 16b–17: *Qualified:* Paul may be echoing either the self-satisfied claims of other preachers or their charges about Paul's deficiencies. No one is really qualified, but the apostle contrasts himself with those who dilute or falsify the preaching for personal advantage and insists on his totally good conscience: his ministry is from God, and he has exercised it with fidelity and integrity (cf 3, 5–6).

for this? **17** [v]For we are not like the many who
trade on the word of God; but as out of sincerity,
indeed as from God and in the presence of God,
we speak in Christ.

## CHAPTER 3

**1** [w]*Are we beginning to commend ourselves again? Or do we need, as some do, letters
of recommendation to you or from you? **2** *You
are our letter, written on our hearts, known and
read by all, **3** [x]*shown to be a letter of Christ
administered by us, written not in ink but by the
Spirit of the living God, not on tablets of stone
but on tablets that are hearts of flesh.

**4** *Such confidence we have through Christ
toward God. **5** [y]Not that of ourselves we are
qualified to take credit for anything as coming
from us; rather, our qualification comes from
God, **6** [z]*who has indeed qualified us as ministers of a new covenant, not of letter but of spirit;
for the letter brings death, but the Spirit gives
life.

### Contrast with the Old Covenant

**7** [a]*Now if the ministry of death, carved in
letters on stone, was so glorious that the Israelites could not look intently at the face of Moses
because of its glory that was going to fade,
**8** *how much more will the ministry of the
Spirit be glorious? **9** For if the ministry of condemnation was glorious, the ministry of righteousness will abound much more in glory.
**10** Indeed, what was endowed with glory has
come to have no glory in this respect because of
the glory that surpasses it. **11** For if what was
going to fade was glorious, how much more will
what endures be glorious.

**12** *Therefore, since we have such hope, we
act very boldly **13** *and not like Moses, who
put a veil over his face so that the Israelites
could not look intently at the cessation of what
was fading. **14** *Rather, their thoughts were

v 4, 2; 1 Cor 5, 8.
w Acts 18, 27; Rom 16, 1; 1 Cor 16, 3.
x Ex 24, 12; 31, 18; 32, 15-19 / Jer 31, 33; Ez 11, 19; 36, 26-27.
y Jn 3, 27.
z Eph 3, 7 / Jer 31, 31-34.
a Ex 34, 29-35.

*

3, 1: Paul seems to allude to certain preachers who pride themselves on their written credentials. Presumably they reproach him for not possessing similar credentials and compel him to spell out his own qualifications (4, 2; 5, 12; 6, 4). The Corinthians themselves should have performed this function for Paul (5, 12; cf 12, 11). Since he is forced to find something that can recommend him, he points to them: their very existence constitutes his *letter* of recommendation (1–2). Others who engage in self-commendation will also be mentioned in 10, 12–18.

3, 2–3: Mention of "letters of recommendation" generates a series of metaphors in which Paul plays on the word "letter": (1) the community is Paul's letter of recommendation (2a); (2) they are a letter engraved on his affections for all to see and read (2b); (3) they are a letter from Christ that Paul merely delivers (3a); (4) they are a letter written by the Spirit on the tablets of human hearts (3b). One image dissolves into another.

3, 3b: This verse contrasts Paul's letter with those *written . . . in ink* (like the credentials of other preachers) and those *written . . . on tablets of stone* (like the law of Moses). These contrasts suggest that the other preachers may have claimed special relationship with Moses. If they were Judaizers zealous for the Mosaic law, that would explain the detailed contrast between the old and the new covenants (6; 4, 7—6, 10). If they were charismatics who claimed Moses as their model, that would explain the extended treatment of Moses himself and his glory (3, 7—4, 6). *Hearts of flesh:* cf Ezekiel's contrast between the heart of flesh that the Spirit gives and the heart of stone that it replaces (Ez 36, 26); the context is covenant renewal and purification that makes observance of the law possible.

3, 4–6: These verses resume 2, 1—3, 3. Paul's confidence (4) is grounded in his sense of God-given mission (2, 17), the specifics of which are described in vv 1–3. Verses 5–6 return to the question of his qualifications (2, 16), attributing them entirely to God. Verse 6 further spells out the situation described in v 3b and "names" it: Paul is living within *a new covenant,* characterized by the Spirit, which *gives life.* The usage of a *new covenant* is derived from Jer 31, 31–33, a passage that also speaks of writing on the heart; cf 2.

3, 6b: This verse serves as a topic sentence for 3, 7—6, 10. For the contrast between *letter* and *spirit,* cf Rom 2, 29; 7, 5–6.

3, 7—4, 6: Paul now develops the contrast enunciated in 3, 6b in terms of the relative glory of the two covenants, insisting on the greater glory of the new. His polemic seems directed against individuals who appeal to the glorious Moses and fail to perceive any comparable glory either in Paul's life as an apostle or in the gospel he preaches. He asserts in response that Christians have a glory of their own that far surpasses that of Moses.

3, 7: The *ministry of death:* from his very first words, Paul describes the Mosaic covenant and ministry from the viewpoint of their limitations. They lead to *death* rather than life (6–7; cf 4, 7—5, 10), to *condemnation* rather than reconciliation (9; cf 5, 11—6, 10). *Was so glorious:* the basic text to which Paul alludes is Ex 34, 29–35, to which his opponents have undoubtedly laid claim. *Going to fade:* Paul concedes the glory of Moses' covenant and ministry, but grants them only temporary significance.

3, 8–11: *How much more:* the argument "from the less to the greater" is repeated three times (8.9.11). Verse 10 expresses another point of view: the difference in glory is so great that only the new covenant and ministry can properly be called "glorious" at all.

3, 12: *Such hope:* the glory is not yet an object of experience, but that does not lessen Paul's confidence. *Boldly:* the term parrēsia expresses outspoken declaration of Christian conviction (cf 4, 1–2). Paul has nothing to hide and no reason for timidity.

3, 13–14a: *Not like Moses:* in Exodus Moses veiled his face to protect the Israelites from God's reflected glory. Without impugning Moses' sincerity, Paul attributes another effect to the veil. Since it lies between God's glory and the Israelites, it explains how they could fail to notice the glory disappearing. *Their thoughts were rendered dull:* the problem lay with their understanding. This will be expressed in vv 14b–16 by a shift in the place of the veil: it is no longer over Moses' face but over their perception.

3, 14b–16: The parallelism in these verses makes it necessary to interpret corresponding parts in relation to one another. *To this present day:* this signals the shift of Paul's attention to his contemporaries; his argument is typological, as in 1 Cor 10. The Israelites of Moses' time typify the Jews of Paul's time, and perhaps also Christians of Jewish origin or mentality who may not recognize the temporary character of Moses' glory. *When they read the old covenant:* the lasting dullness prevents proper appraisal of Moses' person and covenant. When his writings are read in the synagogue, a veil still impedes their

rendered dull, for to this present day the same
veil remains unlifted when they read the old
covenant, because through Christ it is taken
away. **15** [b]To this day, in fact, whenever Moses is read, a veil lies over their hearts, **16** [c]but
whenever a person turns to the Lord the veil is
removed. **17** *Now the Lord is the Spirit, and
where the Spirit of the Lord is, there is freedom.
**18** [d]*All of us, gazing with unveiled face on
the glory of the Lord, are being transformed into
the same image from glory to glory, as from the
Lord who is the Spirit.

## CHAPTER 4

**Integrity in the Ministry** **1** *Therefore,
since we have this ministry through the mercy
shown us, we are not discouraged. **2** [e]Rather,
we have renounced shameful, hidden things; not
acting deceitfully or falsifying the word of God,
but by the open declaration of the truth we commend ourselves to everyone's conscience in the
sight of God. **3** [f]*And even though our gospel
is veiled, it is veiled for those who are perishing,
**4** [g]in whose case the god of this age has blinded
the minds of the unbelievers, so that they may
not see the light of the gospel of the glory of
Christ, who is the image of God. **5** *For we do
not preach ourselves but Jesus Christ as Lord,
and ourselves as your slaves for the sake of
Jesus. **6** [h]*For God who said, "Let light shine
out of darkness," has shone in our hearts to
bring to light the knowledge of the glory of God
on the face of [Jesus] Christ.

**The Paradox of the Ministry** **7** *But we
hold this treasure in earthen vessels, that the
surpassing power may be of God and not from
us. **8** [i]*We are afflicted in every way, but not
constrained; perplexed, but not driven to despair; **9** persecuted, but not abandoned; struck
down, but not destroyed; **10** [j]*always carrying
about in the body the dying of Jesus, so that the
life of Jesus may also be manifested in our body.
**11** [k]For we who live are constantly being given
up to death for the sake of Jesus, so that the life
of Jesus may be manifested in our mortal flesh.
**12** *So death is at work in us, but life in you.
**13** [l]*Since, then, we have the same spirit of

b Rom 11, 7-10.
c Ex 34, 34.
d Rom 8, 29-30; 12, 2; Gal 4, 19; Phil 3, 10.20-21 / 4, 4-6;1 Cor 15, 49; Col 1, 15; 3, 9-11; 1 Jn 3, 2.
e 2, 17; 1 Thes 2, 4-7.
f 2, 15-16; 2 Thes 2, 10.
g Jn 12, 31-36 / 1 Tm 1, 11.
h Gn 1, 3; Is 9, 1; Acts 26, 13-23; Gal 1, 15-16 / Jn 8, 12;Heb 1, 3.
i 6, 4-10; 1 Cor 4, 9-13.
j Col 1, 24.
k Rom 8, 36; 1 Cor 15, 31.
l Ps 116, 10.

* understanding. *Through Christ:* i.e., in the new covenant. *Whenever a person turns to the Lord:* Moses in Exodus appeared before God without the veil and gazed on his face unprotected. Paul applies that passage to converts to Christianity: when they turn to the Lord fully and authentically, the impediment to their understanding is removed.

3, 17: *The Lord is the Spirit:* the "Lord" to whom the Christian turns (16) is the Spirit of whom Paul has been speaking, the life-giving Spirit of the living God (6.8), the inaugurator of the new covenant and ministry, who is also the Spirit of Christ. *The Spirit of the Lord:* the Lord here is the living God (3), but there may also be an allusion to Christ as Lord (14.16). *Freedom:* i.e., from the ministry of death (7) and the covenant that condemned (9).

3, 18: Another application of the veil image. *All of us . . . with unveiled face:* Christians (Israelites from whom the veil has been removed) are like Moses, standing in God's presence, beholding and reflecting his glory. *Gazing:* the verb may also be translated "contemplating as in a mirror"; 4, 6 would suggest that the mirror is Christ himself. *Are being transformed:* elsewhere Paul speaks of transformation, conformity to Jesus, God's image, as a reality of the end time, and even v 12 speaks of the glory as an object of hope. But the life-giving Spirit, the distinctive gift of the new covenant, is already present in the community (cf 1, 22, the "first installment"), and the process of transformation has already begun. *Into the same image:* into the image of God, which is Christ (4, 4).

4, 1–2: A ministry of this sort generates confidence and forthrightness; cf 1, 12–14; 2, 17.

4, 3–4: *Though our gospel is veiled:* the final application of the image. Paul has been reproached either for obscurity in his preaching or for his manner of presenting the gospel. But he confidently asserts that there is no veil over his gospel. If some fail to perceive its light, that is because of unbelief. The veil lies over their eyes (3, 14), a blindness induced by Satan, and a sign that they are headed for destruction (cf 2, 15).

4, 5: *We do not preach ourselves:* the light seen in his gospel is the glory of Christ (4). Far from preaching himself, the preacher should be a transparent medium through whom Jesus is perceived (cf 10–11). *Your slaves:* Paul draws attention away from individuals as such and toward their role in relation to God, Christ, and the community; cf 1 Cor 3, 5; 4, 1.

4, 6: Autobiographical allusion to the episode at Damascus clarifies the origin and nature of Paul's service; cf Acts 9, 1–19; 22, 3–16; 26, 2–18. *"Let light shine out of darkness":* Paul seems to be thinking of Gn 1, 3 and presenting his apostolic ministry as a new creation. There may also be an allusion to Is 9, 1, suggesting his prophetic calling as servant of the Lord and light to the nations; cf Is 42, 6.16; 49, 6; 60, 1–2, and the use of light imagery in Acts 26, 13–23. *To bring to light the knowledge:* Paul's role in the process of revelation, expressed at the beginning under the image of the odor and aroma (2, 14–15), is restated now, at the end of this first moment of the development, in the imagery of light and glory (3–6).

4, 7—5, 10: Paul now confronts the difficulty that his present existence does not appear glorious at all; it is marked instead by suffering and death. He deals with this by developing the topic already announced in 3, 3.6, asserting his faith in the presence and ultimate triumph of life, in his own and every Christian existence, despite the experience of death.

4, 7: *This treasure:* the glory that he preaches and into which they are being transformed. *In earthen vessels:* the instruments God uses are human and fragile; some imagine small terracotta lamps in which light is carried.

4, 8–9: A catalogue of his apostolic trials and afflictions. Yet in these the negative never completely prevails; there is always some experience of rescue, of salvation.

4, 10–11: Both the negative and the positive sides of the experience are grounded christologically. The logic is similar to that of 1, 3–11. His sufferings are connected with Christ's, and his deliverance is a sign that he is to share in Jesus' resurrection.

4, 12–15: His experience does not terminate in himself, but in others (12.15; cf 1, 4–5). Ultimately, everything is ordered even beyond the community, toward God (15; cf 1, 11).

4, 13–14: Like the Psalmist, Paul clearly proclaims his faith, affirming life within himself despite death (10–11) and the

faith, according to what is written, "I believed,
therefore I spoke," we too believe and therefore
speak, **14** [m]knowing that the one who raised the
Lord Jesus will raise us also with Jesus and
place us with you in his presence.
**15** [n]Everything indeed is for you, so that the
grace bestowed in abundance on more and more
people may cause the thanksgiving to overflow
for the glory of God.
**16** [o]*Therefore, we are not discouraged;
rather, although our outer self is wasting away,
our inner self is being renewed day by day.
**17** [p]For this momentary light affliction is producing for us an eternal weight of glory beyond
all comparison, **18** [q]as we look not to what is
seen but to what is unseen; for what is seen is
transitory, but what is unseen is eternal.

## CHAPTER 5

**Our Future Destiny** **1** [r]*For we know that
if our earthly dwelling, a tent, should be destroyed, we have a building from God, a dwelling not made with hands, eternal in heaven.
**2** [s]*For in this tent we groan, longing to be
further clothed with our heavenly habitation
**3** *if indeed, when we have taken it off, we
shall not be found naked. **4** [t]*For while we are
in this tent we groan and are weighed down,
because we do not wish to be unclothed but to
be further clothed, so that what is mortal may
be swallowed up by life. **5** [u]*Now the one who
has prepared us for this very thing is God, who
has given us the Spirit as a first installment.
**6** *So we are always courageous, although
we know that while we are at home in the body
we are away from the Lord, **7** for we walk by
faith, not by sight. **8** [v]Yet we are courageous,
and we would rather leave the body and go
home to the Lord. **9** Therefore, we aspire to
please him, whether we are at home or away.
**10** [w]*For we must all appear before the judgment seat of Christ, so that each one may receive recompense, according to what he did in
the body, whether good or evil.

**The Ministry of Reconciliation**
**11** [x]*Therefore, since we know the fear of the

m Rom 4, 24-25; 8, 11; 1 Cor 6, 14; 1 Thes 4, 14.
n 1, 11.
o 4, 1.1.
p Mt 5, 11-12; Rom 8, 18.
q Rom 8, 24-25; Heb 11, 1.
r Is 38, 12 / Col 3, 1-4 / Mk 14, 58; Col 2, 11; Heb 9, 11.24.
s Rom 8, 23 / 1 Cor 15, 51-54.
t Is 25, 8; 1 Cor 15, 54.
u 1, 22.
v Phil 1, 21-23.
w Mt 16, 27; 25, 31-46; Rom 2, 16; 14, 10-11.
x 1, 12-14.

* life-giving effect of his experience upon the church (12.14–15). *And place us with you in his presence:* Paul imagines God presenting him and them to Jesus at the parousia and the judgment; cf 11, 2; Rom 14, 10.

4, 16–18: In a series of contrasts Paul explains the extent of his faith in life. Life is not only already present and revealing itself (8–11.16) but will outlast his experience of affliction and dying: it is eternal (17–18).

4, 16: *Not discouraged:* i.e., despite the experience of death. Paul is still speaking of himself personally, but he assumes his faith and attitude will be shared by all Christians. *Our outer self:* the individual subject of ordinary perception and observation, in contrast to the interior and hidden self, which undergoes renewal. *Is being renewed day by day:* this suggests a process that has already begun; cf 3, 18. The renewal already taking place even in Paul's dying is a share in the life of Jesus, but this is recognized only by faith (13.18; 5, 7).

5, 1: *Our earthly dwelling:* the same contrast is restated in the imagery of a dwelling. The language recalls Jesus' saying about the destruction of the temple and the construction of another building *not made with hands* (Mk 14, 58), a prediction later applied to Jesus' own body (Jn 2, 20).

5, 2–5: Verses 2–3 and 4 are largely parallel in structure. *We groan, longing:* see the note on 5, 5. *Clothed with our heavenly habitation:* Paul mixes his metaphors, adding the image of the garment to that of the building. *Further clothed:* the verb means strictly "to put one garment on over another." Paul may desire to put the resurrection body on over his mortal body, without dying; vv 2 and 4 permit this meaning but do not impose it. Or perhaps he imagines the resurrection body as a garment put on over the Christ-garment first received in baptism (Gal 3, 27) and preserved by moral behavior (Rom 13, 12–14; Col 3, 12; cf Mt 22, 11–13). Some support for this interpretation may be found in the context; cf the references to baptism (5), to judgment according to works (10), and to present renewal (4, 16), an idea elsewhere combined with the image of "putting on" a new nature (Eph 4, 22–24; Col 3, 1–5.9–10).

5, 3: *When we have taken it off:* the majority of witnesses read "when we have put it on," i.e., when we have been clothed (in the resurrection body), then we shall not be without a body (naked). This seems mere tautology, though some understand it to mean: whether we are "found" (by God at the judgment) clothed or naked depends upon whether we have preserved or lost our original investiture in Christ (cf the previous note). In this case to "put it on" does not refer to the resurrection body, but to keeping intact the Christ-garment of baptism. The translation follows the western reading (Codex Bezae, Tertullian), the sense of which is clear: to "take it off" is to shed our mortal body in death, after which we shall be clothed in the resurrection body and hence not "naked" (cf 1 Cor 15, 51–53).

5, 4: *We do not wish to be unclothed:* a clear allusion to physical death (4, 16; 5, 1). Unlike the Greeks, who found dissolution of the body desirable (cf Socrates), Paul has a Jewish horror of it. He seems to be thinking of the "intermediate period," an interval between death and resurrection. *Swallowed up by life:* cf 1 Cor 15, 54.

5, 5: God has created us for resurrected bodily life and already prepares us for it by the gift of the Spirit in baptism. *The Spirit as a first installment:* the striking parallel to 5, 1–5 in Rom 8, 17–30 describes Christians who have received the "firstfruits" (cf "first installment" here) of the Spirit as "groaning" (cf 2.4 here) for the resurrection, the complete redemption of their bodies. In place of clothing and building, Rom 8 uses other images for the resurrection: adoption and conformity to the image of the Son.

5, 6–9: Tension between present and future is expressed by another spatial image, the metaphor of the country and its citizens. At present we are like citizens in exile or far away from home. The Lord is the distant homeland, believed in but unseen (7).

5, 10: *We must all appear:* the verb is ambiguous: we are scheduled to "appear" for judgment, at which we will be "revealed" as we are (cf 11; 2, 14; 4, 10–11).

5, 11–15: This paragraph is transitional. Paul sums up much that has gone before. Still playing on the term "appearance," he reasserts his transparency before God and the Co-

Lord, we try to persuade others; but we are
clearly apparent to God, and I hope we are also
apparent to your consciousness. **12** [y]We are not
commending ourselves to you again but giving
you an opportunity to boast of us, so that you
may have something to say to those who boast
of external appearance rather than of the heart.
**13** *For if we are out of our minds, it is for God;
if we are rational, it is for you. **14** [z]*For the
love of Christ impels us, once we have come to
the conviction that one died for all; therefore, all
have died. **15** [a]He indeed died for all, so that
those who live might no longer live for themselves but for him who for their sake died and
was raised.

**16** *Consequently, from now on we regard
no one according to the flesh; even if we once
knew Christ according to the flesh, yet now we
know him so no longer. **17** [b]So whoever is in
Christ is a new creation: the old things have
passed away; behold, new things have come.
**18** *And all this is from God, who has reconciled us to himself through Christ and given us
the ministry of reconciliation, **19** [c]namely,
God was reconciling the world to himself in
Christ, not counting their trespasses against
them and entrusting to us the message of reconciliation. **20** [d]So we are ambassadors for
Christ, as if God were appealing through us. We
implore you on behalf of Christ, be reconciled
to God. **21** [e]*For our sake he made him to be
sin who did not know sin, so that we might
become the righteousness of God in him.

## CHAPTER 6

### The Experience of the Ministry

**1** [f]*Working together, then, we appeal to you
not to receive the grace of God in vain. **2** [g]*For
he says:

"In an acceptable time I heard you,
and on the day of salvation I helped
you."

Behold, now is a very acceptable time; behold,
now is the day of salvation. **3** [h]*We cause no
one to stumble in anything, in order that no fault
may be found with our ministry; **4** [i]*on the
contrary, in everything we commend ourselves
as ministers of God, through much endurance,
in afflictions, hardships, constraints,
**5** [j]beatings, imprisonments, riots, labors,

---

y 3, 1 / 1, 14; Phil 1, 26.
z Rom 6, 1-6.
a Rom 4, 25; 6, 4-11; 14, 9; Col 3, 3-4.
b Gal 6, 15; Eph 2, 15 / Is 43, 18-21; Rv 21, 5.
c Rom 5, 10-11; Col 1, 20.
d Eph 6, 20; Phlm 9.
e Is 53, 6-9; Gal 3, 13 / Rom 3, 24-26; 1 Cor 1, 30; 1 Pt 2, 24;1 Jn 3, 5-8.
f 1 Cor 3, 9; 1 Thes 3, 2.
g Is 49, 8.
h 1 Cor 9, 12; 10, 32 / 8, 20-21.
i 4, 8-11; 11, 23-27; 1 Cor 4, 9-13.
j Acts 16, 23.

---

*

rinthians, in contrast to the self-commendation, boasting, and preoccupation with externals that characterize some others (cf 1, 12–14; 2, 14; 3, 1; 3, 7—4, 6). Verse 14 recalls 3, 7—4, 6, and sums up 4, 7—5, 10.

5, 13: *Out of our minds:* this verse confirms that a concern for ecstasy and charismatic experience may lie behind the discussion about "glory" in 3, 7—4, 6. Paul also enjoys such experiences but, unlike others, does not make a public display of them or consider them ends in themselves. *Rational:* the Greek virtue *sōphrosynē,* to which Paul alludes, implies reasonableness, moderation, good judgment, self-control.

5, 14–15: These verses echo 4, 14 and resume the treatment of "life despite death" from 4, 7—5, 10.

5, 16–17: *Consequently:* the death of Christ described in vv 14–15 produces a whole new order (17) and a new mode of perception (16). *According to the flesh:* the natural mode of perception, characterized as "fleshly," is replaced by a mode of perception proper to the Spirit. Elsewhere Paul contrasts what Christ looks like according to the old criteria (weakness, powerlessness, folly, death) and according to the new (wisdom, power, life); cf vv 15.21; 1 Cor 1, 17—3, 3. Similarly, he describes the paradoxical nature of Christian existence, e.g., in 4, 10–11.14. *A new creation:* rabbis used this expression to describe the effect of the entrance of a proselyte or convert into Judaism or of the remission of sins on the Day of Atonement. The new order created *in Christ* is the new covenant (3, 6).

5, 18–21: Paul attempts to explain the meaning of God's action by a variety of different categories; his attention keeps moving rapidly back and forth from God's act to his own ministry as well. *Who has reconciled us to himself:* i.e., he has brought all into oneness. *Not counting their trespasses:* the reconciliation is described as an act of justification (cf "righteousness," 21); this contrasts with the covenant that condemned (3, 8). *The ministry of reconciliation:* Paul's role in the wider picture is described: entrusted with the message of reconciliation (19), he is Christ's ambassador, through whom God appeals (20a). In v 20b Paul acts in the capacity just described.

5, 21: This is a statement of God's purpose, expressed paradoxically in terms of sharing and exchange of attributes. As Christ became our righteousness (1 Cor 1, 30), we become God's righteousness (cf vv 14–15).

6, 1–10: This paragraph is a single long sentence in the Greek, interrupted by the parenthesis of v 2. The one main verb is "we appeal." In this paragraph Paul both exercises his ministry of reconciliation (cf 5, 20) and describes how his ministry is exercised: the "message of reconciliation" (5, 19) is lived existentially in his apostolic experience.

6, 1: *Not to receive . . . in vain:* i.e., conform to the gift of justification and new creation. The context indicates how this can be done concretely: become God's righteousness (5, 21), not live for oneself (5, 15), be reconciled with Paul (6, 11–13; 7, 2–3).

6, 2: *In an acceptable time:* Paul cites the Septuagint text of Is 49, 8; the Hebrew reads "in a time of favor"; it is parallel to "on the day of salvation." Now: God is bestowing favor and salvation at this very moment, as Paul is addressing his letter to them.

6, 3: *Cause no one to stumble:* the language echoes that of 1 Cor 8–10, as does the expression "no longer live for themselves" in 5, 15. *That no fault may be found:* i.e., at the eschatological judgment (cf 1 Cor 4, 2–5).

6, 4a: This is the central assertion, the topic statement for the catalogue that follows. *We commend ourselves:* Paul's self-commendation is ironical (with an eye on the charges mentioned in 3, 1–3) and paradoxical (pointing mostly to experiences that would not normally be considered points of pride but are perceived as such by faith). Cf also the self-commendation in 11, 23–29. *As ministers of God:* the same Greek word, *diakonos,* means "minister" and "servant"; cf 11, 23, the central assertion in a similar context, and 1 Cor 3, 5.

6, 4b–5: *Through much endurance:* this phrase functions as a subtitle; it is followed by an enumeration of nine specific types of trials endured.

vigils, fasts; 6 [k]*by purity, knowledge, patience, kindness, in a holy spirit, in unfeigned
love, 7 [l]in truthful speech, in the power of God;
with weapons of righteousness at the right and
at the left; 8 *through glory and dishonor, insult
and praise. We are treated as deceivers and yet
are truthful; 9 [m]as unrecognized and yet acknowledged; as dying and behold we live; as
chastised and yet not put to death; 10 [n]as sorrowful yet always rejoicing; as poor yet enriching many; as having nothing and yet possessing
all things.

11 *We have spoken frankly to you, Corinthians; our heart is open wide. 12 [o]You are not
constrained by us; you are constrained by your
own affections. 13 [p]As recompense in kind (I
speak as to my children), be open yourselves.

**Call to Holiness** 14 *Do not be yoked with
those who are different, with unbelievers. For
what partnership do righteousness and lawlessness have? Or what fellowship does light have
with darkness? 15 What accord has Christ with
Beliar? Or what has a believer in common with
an unbeliever? 16 [q]*What agreement has the
temple of God with idols? For we are the temple
of the living God; as God said:

"I will live with them and move among
them,
and I will be their God
and they shall be my people.
17 [r]Therefore, come forth from them
and be separate," says the Lord,
"and touch nothing unclean;
then I will receive you
18 [s]and I will be a father to you,
and you shall be sons and daughters to
me,
says the Lord Almighty."

## CHAPTER 7

1 Since we have these promises, beloved, let
us cleanse ourselves from every defilement of
flesh and spirit, making holiness perfect in the
fear of God.

2 *Make room for us; we have not wronged
anyone, or ruined anyone, or taken advantage of
anyone. 3 [t]I do not say this in condemnation,
for I have already said that you are in our hearts,
that we may die together and live together. 4 I
have great confidence in you, I have great pride
in you; I am filled with encouragement, I am
overflowing with joy all the more because of all
our affliction.

## C. Resolution of the Crisis

**Paul's Joy in Macedonia** 5 [u]*For even
when we came into Macedonia, our flesh had no
rest, but we were afflicted in every way—external conflicts, internal fears. 6 [v]But God, who

---

k Gal 5, 22-23.
l 10, 4; Rom 13, 12; Eph 6, 11-17.
m 4, 10-11; Rom 8, 36.
n Rom 8, 32; 1 Cor 3, 21.
o 7, 3.
p Gal 4, 19.
q 1 Cor 10, 20-21 / 1 Cor 3, 16-17; 6, 19 / Ex 25, 8; 29, 45;Lv 26, 12; Jer 31, 1; 32, 38; Ez 37, 27.
r Is 52, 11; Ez 20, 34.41; Rv 18, 4; 21, 27.
s 2 Sm 7, 14; Ps 2, 7; Is 43, 6; Jer 31, 9; Rv 21, 7 / Rv 4, 8;11, 17; 15, 3; 21, 22.
t 6, 11-13.
u 2, 13.
v 7, 13-14; 1 Thes 3, 6-8.

---

*

6, 6–7a: A list of virtuous qualities in two groups of four, the second fuller than the first.

6, 8b–10: A series of seven rhetorically effective antitheses, contrasting negative external impressions with positive inner reality. Paul perceives his existence as a reflection of Jesus' own and affirms an inner reversal that escapes outward observation. The final two members illustrate two distinct kinds of paradox or apparent contradiction that are characteristic of apostolic experience.

6, 11–13: Paul's tone becomes quieter, but his appeal for acceptance and affection is emotionally charged. References to the heart and their mutual relations bring the development begun in 2, 14—3, 3 to an effective conclusion.

6, 14—7, 1: Language and thought shift noticeably here. Suddenly we are in a different atmosphere, dealing with a quite different problem. Both the vocabulary and the thought, with their contrast between good and evil, are more characteristic of Qumran documents or the Book of Revelation than they are of Paul. Hence, critics suspect that this section was inserted by another hand.

6, 14–16a: The opening injunction to separate from unbelievers is reinforced by five rhetorical questions to make the point that Christianity is not compatible with paganism. Their opposition is emphasized also by the accumulation of five distinct designations for each group. These verses are a powerful statement of God's holiness and the exclusiveness of his claims.

6, 16c–18: This is a chain of scriptural citations carefully woven together. God's covenant relation to his people and his presence among them (16) is seen as conditioned on cultic separation from the profane and cultically impure (17); that relation is translated into the personal language of the parent-child relationship, an extension to the community of the language of 2 Sm 7, 14 (18). Some remarkable parallels to this chain are found in the final chapters of Revelation. God's presence among his people (21, 22) is expressed there, too, by applying 2 Sm 7, 14 to the community (21, 7). There is a call to separation (18, 4) and exclusion of the unclean from the community and its liturgy (21, 27). The title "Lord Almighty" (*Pantokratōr*) occurs in the New Testament only here in 18 and nine times in Rv.

7, 2–4: These verses continue the thought of 6, 11–13, before the interruption of 6, 14—7, 1. Verse 4 serves as a transition to the next section: the four themes it introduces (confidence; pride or "boasting"; encouragement; joy in affliction) are developed in vv 5–16. All have appeared previously in the letter.

7, 5–16: This section functions as a peroration or formal summing up of the whole first part of the letter, chs 1–7. It deals with the restoration of right relations between Paul and the Corinthians, and it is marked by fullness and intensity of emotion.

7, 5–7: Paul picks up the thread of the narrative interrupted at 2, 13 (5) and describes the resolution of the tense situation there depicted (6–7). Finally Titus arrives and his coming puts an end to Paul's restlessness (2, 13; 7, 5), casts out his fears, and reverses his mood. The theme of encouragement and affliction is reintroduced (cf 1, 3–11); here, too, encouragement is traced back to God and is described as contagious (6). The language of joy and sorrow also reappears in v 7 (cf 1, 23—2, 1 and the note on 1, 23–24).

7, 5: *Macedonia:* see the note on 2, 13.

encourages the downcast, encouraged us by the
arrival of Titus, 7 and not only by his arrival but
also by the encouragement with which he was
encouraged in regard to you, as he told us of
your yearning, your lament, your zeal for me,
so that I rejoiced even more. **8** [w]*For even if I
saddened you by my letter, I do not regret it; and
if I did regret it ([for] I see that that letter saddened you, if only for a while), **9** I rejoice now,
not because you were saddened, but because
you were saddened into repentance; for you
were saddened in a godly way, so that you did
not suffer loss in anything because of us. **10** For
godly sorrow produces a salutary repentance
without regret, but worldly sorrow produces
death. **11** For behold what earnestness this godly sorrow has produced for you, as well as readiness for a defense, and indignation, and fear,
and yearning, and zeal, and punishment. In every way you have shown yourselves to be innocent in the matter. **12** [x]So then even though I
wrote to you, it was not on account of the one
who did the wrong, or on account of the one
who suffered the wrong, but in order that your
concern for us might be made plain to you in the
sight of God. **13** *For this reason we are encouraged.

And besides our encouragement, we rejoice
even more because of the joy of Titus, since his
spirit has been refreshed by all of you. **14** For
if I have boasted to him about you, I was not put
to shame. No, just as everything we said to you
was true, so our boasting before Titus proved to
be the truth. **15** [y]And his heart goes out to you
all the more, as he remembers the obedience of
all of you, when you received him with fear and
trembling. **16** I rejoice, because I have confidence in you in every respect.

## *III: THE COLLECTION FOR JERUSALEM*

### CHAPTER 8

**Generosity in Giving** **1** [z]*We want you to
know, brothers, of the grace of God that has
been given to the churches of Macedonia,
**2** *for in a severe test of affliction, the abundance of their joy and their profound poverty
overflowed in a wealth of generosity on their
part. **3** *For according to their means, I can
testify, and beyond their means, spontaneously,
**4** [a]they begged us insistently for the favor of
taking part in the service to the holy ones,
**5** *and this, not as we expected, but they gave
themselves first to the Lord and to us through

w 2, 2-4; Heb 12, 11.
x 2, 3.9; 7, 8.
y 2, 9.
z 11, 9; Rom 15, 26.
a Acts 24, 17; Rom 15, 31.

*

7, 8–12: Paul looks back on the episode from the viewpoint of its ending. The goal of their common activity, promotion of their joy (1, 24), has been achieved, despite and because of the sorrow they felt. That sorrow was God-given. Its salutary effects are enumerated fully and impressively in vv 10–11; not the least important of these is that it has revealed to them the attachment they have to Paul.

7, 13–16: Paul summarizes the effect of the experience on Titus: encouragement, joy, love, relief. Finally, he describes its effects on himself: encouragement, joy, confidence, pride or "boasting" (i.e., the satisfaction resulting from a boast that proves well-founded; cf 4; 1, 12.14).

8, 1—9, 15: Paul turns to a new topic, the collection for the church in Jerusalem. There is an early precedent for this project in the agreement mentioned in Gal 2, 6–10. According to Acts, the church at Antioch had sent Saul and Barnabas to Jerusalem with relief (Acts 11, 27–30). Subsequently Paul organized a project of relief for Jerusalem among his own churches. Our earliest evidence for it comes in 1 Cor 16, 1–4, after it had already begun (see the notes there); by the time Paul wrote Rom 15, 25–28 the collection was completed and ready for delivery. Chapters 8 and 9 contain what appear to be two letters on the subject. In them Paul gives us his fullest exposition of the meaning he sees in the enterprise, presenting it as an act of Christian charity and as an expression of the unity of the church, both present and eschatological. These chapters are especially rich in the recurrence of key words, on which Paul plays; it is usually impossible to do justice to these wordplays in the translation.

8, 1–24: This is a letter of recommendation for Titus and two unnamed companions, written from Macedonia probably at least a year later than 1 Cor 16. The recommendation proper is prefaced by remarks about the ideals of sharing and equality within the Christian community (1–15). Phil 4, 10–20 shows that Paul has reflected on his personal experience of need and relief in his relations with the community at Philippi; he now develops his reflections on the larger scale of relations between his Gentile churches and the mother church in Jerusalem.

8, 1–5: The example of the Macedonians, a model of what ought to be happening at Corinth, provides Paul with the occasion for expounding his theology of "giving."

8, 1: *The grace of God:* the fundamental theme is expressed by the Greek noun *charis,* which will be variously translated throughout these chapters as "grace" (8, 1; 9, 8.14), "favor" (8, 4), "gracious act" (8, 6.7.9) or "gracious work" (8, 19), to be compared to "gracious gift" (1 Cor 16, 3). The related term, *eucharistia,* "thanksgiving," also occurs at 9, 11.12. The wordplay is not superficial; various mutations of the same root signal inner connection between aspects of a single reality, and Paul consciously exploits the similarities in vocabulary to highlight that connection.

8, 2: Three more terms are now introduced. *Test (dokimē):* the same root is translated as "to test" (8) and "evidence" (9, 13); it means to be tried and found genuine. *Abundance:* variations on the same root lie behind "overflow" (8, 2; 9, 12), "excel" (8, 7), "surplus" (8, 14), "superfluous" (9, 1), "make abundant" and "have an abundance" (9, 8). These expressions of fullness contrast with references to need (8, 14; 9, 12). *Generosity:* the word *haplotēs* has nuances of both simplicity and sincerity; here and in 9, 11.13 it designates the singleness of purpose that manifests itself in generous giving.

8, 3–4: Paul emphasizes the spontaneity of the Macedonians and the nature of their action. *They begged us insistently:* the same root is translated as "urge," "appeal," "encourage" (8, 6.17; 9, 5). *Taking part:* the same word is translated "contribution" in 9, 13 and a related term as "partner" in 8, 23. *Service (diakonia):* this word occurs also in 9, 1.13 as "service"; in 9, 12 it is translated "administration," and in 8, 19.20 the corresponding verb is rendered "administer."

8, 5: *They gave themselves . . . to the Lord and to us:* on its deepest level their attitude is one of self-giving.

the will of God, **6** [b]*so that we urged Titus that,
as he had already begun, he should also complete for you this gracious act also. **7** [c]*Now as
you excel in every respect, in faith, discourse,
knowledge, all earnestness, and in the love we
have for you, may you excel in this gracious act
also.

**8** I say this not by way of command, but to
test the genuineness of your love by your concern for others. **9** [d]*For you know the gracious
act of our Lord Jesus Christ, that for your sake
he became poor although he was rich, so that by
his poverty you might become rich. **10** [e]And I
am giving counsel in this matter, for it is appropriate for you who began not only to act but to
act willingly last year: **11** *complete it now, so
that your eager willingness may be matched by
your completion of it out of what you have.
**12** *For if the eagerness is there, it is acceptable
according to what one has, not according to
what one does not have; **13** not that others
should have relief while you are burdened, but
that as a matter of equality **14** your surplus at
the present time should supply their needs, so
that their surplus may also supply your needs,
that there may be equality. **15** [f]As it is written:

"Whoever had much did not have more,
and whoever had little did not have less."

**Titus and His Collaborators** **16** *But
thanks be to God who put the same concern for
you into the heart of Titus, **17** for he not only
welcomed our appeal but, since he is very concerned, he has gone to you of his own accord.
**18** [g]*With him we have sent the brother who is
praised in all the churches for his preaching of
the gospel. **19** [h]And not only that, but he has
also been appointed our traveling companion by
the churches in this gracious work administered
by us for the glory of the Lord [himself] and for
the expression of our eagerness. **20** *This we
desire to avoid, that anyone blame us about this
lavish gift administered by us, **21** [i]for we are
concerned for what is honorable not only in the
sight of the Lord but also in the sight of others.
**22** And with them we have sent our brother
whom we often tested in many ways and found
earnest, but who is now much more earnest
because of his great confidence in you. **23** As
for Titus, he is my partner and co-worker for
you; as for our brothers, they are apostles of the
churches, the glory of Christ. **24** *So give proof
before the churches of your love and of our
boasting about you to them.

## CHAPTER 9

**God's Indescribable Gift** **1** *Now about
the service to the holy ones, it is superfluous for
me to write to you, **2** [j]*for I know your eagerness, about which I boast of you to the Macedonians, that Achaia has been ready since last
year; and your zeal has stirred up most of them.
**3** *Nonetheless, I sent the brothers so that our
boast about you might not prove empty in this
case, so that you might be ready, as I said, **4** for
fear that if any Macedonians come with me and
find you not ready we might be put to shame (to

---

b 2, 13; 7, 6-7.13-14; 8, 16.23; 12, 18.
c 1 Cor 1, 5.
d 6, 10; Phil 2, 6-8.
e 9, 2; 1 Cor 16, 1-4.
f Ex 16, 18.
g 12, 18.
h 1 Cor 16, 3-4.
i Rom 12, 17.
j 8, 10; Rom 15, 26.

*

8, 6: *Titus:* 1 Cor 16 seemed to leave the organization up to the Corinthians, but apparently Paul has sent Titus to initiate the collection as well; 8, 16–17 will describe Titus' attitude as one of shared concern and cooperation.

8, 7: The charitable service Paul is promoting is seen briefly and in passing within the perspective of Paul's theology of the charisms. *Earnestness (spoudē):* this or related terms occur also in v 22 ("earnest") and 8, 8.16.17 ("concern").

8, 9: The dialectic of Jesus' experience, expressed earlier in terms of life and death (5, 15), sin and righteousness (5, 21), is now rephrased in terms of poverty and wealth. Many scholars think this is a reference to Jesus' preexistence with God (his "wealth") and to his incarnation and death (his "poverty"), and they point to the similarity between this verse and Phil 2, 6–8. Others interpret the wealth and poverty as succeeding phases of Jesus' earthly existence, e.g., his sense of intimacy with God and then the desolation and the feeling of abandonment by God in his death (cf Mk 15, 34).

8, 11: *Eager:* the word *prothymia* also occurs in 8, 12.19; 9, 2.

8, 12–15: Paul introduces the principle of *equality* into the discussion. The goal is not impoverishment but sharing of resources; balance is achieved at least over the course of time. In v 15 Paul grounds his argument unexpectedly in the experience of Israel gathering manna in the desert: equality was achieved, independently of personal exertion, by God, who gave with an even hand according to need. Paul touches briefly here on the theme of "living from God."

8, 16–24: In recommending Titus and his companions, Paul stresses their personal and apostolic qualities, their good dispositions toward the Corinthians, and their authority as messengers of the churches and representatives of Christ.

8, 18: *The brother:* we do not know the identity of this co-worker of Paul, nor of the third companion mentioned below in v 22.

8, 20–22: *That anyone blame us:* 12, 16–18 suggests that misunderstandings may indeed have arisen concerning Paul's management of the collection through the messengers mentioned here, but those same verses seem to imply that the Corinthians by and large would recognize the honesty of Paul's conduct in this area as in others (cf 6, 3).

8, 24: As Paul began by holding up the Macedonians as examples to be imitated, he closes by exhorting the Corinthians to show their love (by accepting the envoys and by cooperating as the Macedonians do), thus justifying the pride Paul demonstrates because of them before other churches.

9, 1–15: Quite possibly this was originally an independent letter, though it deals with the same subject and continues many of the same themes. In that case, it may have been written a few weeks later than ch 8, while the delegation there mentioned was still on its way.

9, 2: *Achaia:* see the note on Rom 15, 26.

9, 3: *I sent the brothers:* the Greek aorist tense here could be epistolary, referring to the present; in that case Paul would be sending them now, and ch 9 would merely conclude the letter of recommendation begun in ch 8. But the aorist may also refer to a sending that is past as Paul writes; then ch 9, with its apparently fresh beginning, is a follow-up message entrusted to another carrier.

say nothing of you) in this conviction. **5** So I
thought it necessary to encourage the brothers to
go on ahead to you and arrange in advance for
your promised gift, so that in this way it might
be ready as a bountiful gift and not as an exac-
tion.

**6** [k]Consider this: whoever sows sparingly
will also reap sparingly, and whoever sows
bountifully will also reap bountifully. **7** [l]Each
must do as already determined, without sadness
or compulsion, for God loves a cheerful giver.
**8** *Moreover, God is able to make every grace
abundant for you, so that in all things, always
having all you need, you may have an abundance for every good work. **9** [m]As it is written:

> "He scatters abroad, he gives to the poor;
> his righteousness endures forever."

**10** [n]The one who supplies seed to the sower
and bread for food will supply and multiply your
seed and increase the harvest of your righteousness.

**11** *You are being enriched in every way for
all generosity, which through us produces
thanksgiving to God, **12** for the administration
of this public service is not only supplying the
needs of the holy ones but is also overflowing
in many acts of thanksgiving to God.
**13** [o]Through the evidence of this service, you
are glorifying God for your obedient confession
of the gospel of Christ and the generosity of
your contribution to them and to all others,
**14** while in prayer on your behalf they long for
you, because of the surpassing grace of God
upon you. **15** [p]Thanks be to God for his indescribable gift!

## IV: PAUL'S DEFENSE OF HIS MINISTRY

### CHAPTER 10

**Accusation of Weakness** **1** *Now I myself, Paul, urge you through the gentleness and
clemency of Christ, I who am humble when face
to face with you, but brave toward you when
absent, **2** [q]*I beg you that, when present, I may
not have to be brave with that confidence with
which I intend to act boldly against some who
consider us as acting according to the flesh.
**3** *For, although we are in the flesh, we do not
battle according to the flesh, **4** [r]for the weapons
of our battle are not of flesh but are enormously
powerful, capable of destroying fortresses. We
destroy arguments **5** and every pretension raising itself against the knowledge of God, and
take every thought captive in obedience to
Christ, **6** [s]and we are ready to punish every
disobedience, once your obedience is complete.

---

k Prv 11, 24-25.
l Prv 22, 8 LXX.
m Ps 112, 9.
n Is 55, 10.
o 8, 4; Rom 15, 31.
p Rom 5, 15-16.
q 13, 2.10; 1 Cor 4, 21.
r 6, 7; 13, 2-3; 1 Cor 1, 25; Eph 6, 10-14.
s 2, 9.

---

*

9, 8–10: The behavior to which he exhorts them is grounded in God's own pattern of behavior. God is capable of overwhelming generosity, as scripture itself attests (9), so that they need not fear being short. He will provide in abundance, both supplying their natural needs and increasing their righteousness. Paul challenges them to godlike generosity and reminds them of the fundamental motive for encouragement: God himself cannot be outdone.

9, 11–15: Paul's vision broadens to take in all the interested parties in one dynamic picture. His language becomes liturgically colored and conveys a sense of fullness. With a final play on the words *charis* and *eucharistia* (see the note on 8, 1), he describes a circle that closes on itself: the movement of grace overflowing from God to them and handed on from them through Paul to others is completed by the prayer of praise and thanksgiving raised on their behalf to God.

10, 1—13, 10: These final chapters have their own unity of structure and theme and could well have formed the body of a separate letter. They constitute an *apologia* on Paul's part, i.e., a legal defense of his behavior and his ministry; the writing is emotionally charged and highly rhetorical. In the central section (11, 16—12, 10), the *apologia* takes the form of a boast. This section is prepared for by a prologue (11, 1–15) and followed by an epilogue (12, 11–18), which are similar in content and structure. These sections, in turn, are framed by an introduction (10, 1–18) and a conclusion (12, 19—13, 10), both of which assert Paul's apostolic authority and confidence and define the purpose of the letter. The structure that results from this disposition of the material is chiastic, i.e., the first element corresponds to the last, the second to the second last, etc., following the pattern *a b c b' a'*.

10, 1–18: Paul asserts his apostolic authority and expresses the confidence this generates in him. He writes in response to certain opinions that have arisen in the community and certain charges raised against him and in preparation for a forthcoming visit in which he intends to set things in order. This section gives us an initial glimpse of the situation in Corinth that Paul must address; much of its thematic material will be taken up again in the finale (12, 19—13, 10).

10, 1–2: A strong opening plunges us straight into the conflict. Contrasts dominate here: presence versus absence, gentleness-clemency-humility versus boldness-confidence-bravery. *Through the gentleness and clemency of Christ:* the figure of the gentle Christ, presented in a significant position before any specifics of the situation are suggested, forms a striking contrast to the picture of the bold and militant Paul (2–6); this tension is finally resolved in 13, 3–4. *Absent . . . present:* this same contrast, with a restatement of the purpose of the letter, recurs in 13, 10, which forms an inclusion with 10, 1–2.

10, 2b–4a: *Flesh:* the Greek word *sarx* can express both the physical life of the body without any pejorative overtones (as in "we are in the flesh," 3) and also our natural life insofar as it is marked by limitation and weakness (as in the other expressions) in contrast to the higher life and power conferred by the Spirit; cf the note on 1 Cor 3, 1. The wordplay is intended to express the paradoxical situation of a life already taken over by the Spirit but not yet seen as such except by faith. Lack of empirical evidence of the Spirit permits misunderstanding and misjudgment, but Paul resolutely denies that his behavior and effectiveness are as limited as some suppose.

10, 3b–6: Paul is involved in combat. The strong military language and imagery are both an assertion of his confidence in the divine power at his disposal and a declaration of war against those who underestimate his resources. The threat is echoed in 13, 2–3.

7 [t]*Look at what confronts you. Whoever is
confident of belonging to Christ should consider
that as he belongs to Christ, so do we. 8 [u]And
even if I should boast a little too much of our
authority, which the Lord gave for building you
up and not for tearing you down, I shall not be
put to shame. 9 *May I not seem as one fright-
ening you through letters. 10 [v]For someone
will say, "His letters are severe and forceful,
but his bodily presence is weak, and his speech
contemptible." 11 [w]Such a person must understand that what we are in word through letters
when absent, that we also are in action when
present.

12 [x]*Not that we dare to class or compare
ourselves with some of those who recommend
themselves. But when they measure themselves
by one another and compare themselves with
one another, they are without understanding.
13 *But we will not boast beyond measure but
will keep to the limits God has apportioned us,
namely, to reach even to you. 14 For we are not
overreaching ourselves, as though we did not
reach you; we indeed first came to you with the
gospel of Christ. 15 We are not boasting beyond measure, in other people's labors; yet our
hope is that, as your faith increases, our influence among you may be greatly enlarged, within our proper limits, 16 [y]so that we may preach
the gospel even beyond you, not boasting of
work already done in another's sphere.
17 [z]*"Whoever boasts, should boast in the
Lord." 18 [a]*For it is not the one who recommends himself who is approved, but the one
whom the Lord recommends.

## CHAPTER 11

**Preaching without Charge** 1 [b]*If only
you would put up with a little foolishness from
me! Please put up with me. 2 [c]*For I am jealous of you with the jealousy of God, since I
betrothed you to one husband to present you as
a chaste virgin to Christ. 3 [d]*But I am afraid
that, as the serpent deceived Eve by his cunning, your thoughts may be corrupted from a
sincere [and pure] commitment to Christ.
4 [e]*For if someone comes and preaches another Jesus than the one we preached, or if you
receive a different spirit from the one you received or a different gospel from the one you
accepted, you put up with it well enough.
5 [f]*For I think that I am not in any way inferior

t 1 Cor 1, 12.
u 13, 10.
v 1 Cor 2, 3.
w 13, 1-2.
x 3, 1-2; 4, 2; 5, 12; 6, 4; 10, 18; 12, 11.
y Rom 15, 20-21.
z Jer 9, 22-23; 1 Cor 1, 31.
a 13, 3-9.
b 11, 21; 12, 11.
c Hos 2, 21-22; Eph 5, 26-27.
d Gn 3, 1-6.
e Gal 1, 6-9.
f 12, 11.

*

10, 7–8: *Belonging to Christ . . . so do we:* these phrases already announce the pattern of Paul's boast in 11, 21b–29, especially 11, 22–23. *For building you up and not for tearing you down:* Paul draws on the language by which Jeremiah described the purpose of the prophetic power the Lord gave to him (Jer 1, 9–10; 12, 16–17; 24, 6). Though Paul's power may have destructive effects on others (2–6), its intended effect on the community is entirely constructive (cf 13, 10). *I shall not be put to shame:* his assertions will not be refuted; they will be revealed as true at the judgment.

10, 9–10: Paul cites the complaints of some who find him lacking in personal forcefulness and holds out the threat of a personal *parousia* (both "return" and "presence") that will be forceful, indeed will be a demonstration of Christ's own power (cf 13, 2–4).

10, 12–18: Paul now qualifies his claim to boldness, indicating its limits. He distinguishes his own behavior from that of others, revealing those "others" as they appear to him: as self-recommending, immoderately boastful, encroaching on territory not assigned to them, and claiming credit not due to them.

10, 13: *Will keep to the limits:* the notion of proper limits is expressed here by two terms with overlapping meanings, *metron* and *kanōn,* which are played off against several expressions denoting overreaching or expansion beyond a legitimate sphere.

10, 17: *Boast in the Lord:* there is a legitimate boasting, in contrast to the immoderate boasting to which vv 13 and 15 allude. God's work through Paul in the community is the object of his boast (13–16; 1, 12–14) and constitutes his recommendation (3, 1–3). Cf the notes on 1, 12–14 and 1 Cor 1, 29–31.

10, 18: *Approved:* to be approved is to come successfully through the process of testing for authenticity (cf 13, 3–7 and the note on 8, 2). *Whom the Lord recommends:* self-commendation is a premature and unwarranted anticipation of the final judgment, which the Lord alone will pass (cf 1 Cor 4, 3–5). Paul alludes to this judgment throughout chs 10–13, frequently in final or transitional positions; cf 11, 15; 12, 19a; 13, 3–7.

11, 1–15: Although these verses continue to reveal information about Paul's opponents and the differences he perceives between them and himself, 11, 1 signals a turn in Paul's thought. This section constitutes a prologue to the boasting that he will undertake in 11, 16—12, 10, and it bears remarkable similarities to the section that follows the central boast, 12, 11–18.

11, 1: *Put up with a little foolishness from me:* this verse indicates more clearly than the general statement of intent in 10, 13 the nature of the project Paul is about to undertake. He alludes ironically to the Corinthians' toleration for others. *Foolishness:* Paul qualifies his project as folly from beginning to end; see the note on 11, 16—12, 10.

11, 2: Paul gives us a sudden glimpse of the theological values that are at stake. *The jealousy of God:* the perspective is that of the covenant, described in imagery of love and marriage, as in the prophets; cf 1 Cor 10, 22. *I betrothed you:* Paul, like a father (cf 12, 14), betroths the community to Christ as his bride (cf Eph 5, 21–33) and will present her to him at his second coming. Cf Mt 25, 1–13 and the nuptial imagery in Rv 21.

11, 3: *As the serpent deceived Eve:* before Christ can return for the community Paul fears a repetition of the primal drama of seduction. Corruption of minds is satanic activity (see 2, 11; 4, 4). Satanic imagery recurs in 11, 13–15.20; 12, 7b.16–17; see the notes on these passages.

11, 4: *Preaches another Jesus:* the danger is specified, and Paul's opponents are identified with the cunning serpent. The battle for minds has to do with the understanding of Jesus, the Spirit, the gospel; the Corinthians have flirted with another understanding than the one that Paul handed on to them as traditional and normative.

11, 5: *These "superapostles":* this term, employed again in 12, 11b, designates the opponents of whom Paul has spoken in ch 10 and again in 11, 4. They appear to be intruders at

to these "superapostles." **6** [g]*Even if I am
untrained in speaking, I am not so in knowledge; in every way we have made this plain to
you in all things.

**7** [h]*Did I make a mistake when I humbled
myself so that you might be exalted, because I
preached the gospel of God to you without
charge? **8** I plundered other churches by accepting from them in order to minister to you.
**9** [i]And when I was with you and in need, I did
not burden anyone, for the brothers who came
from Macedonia supplied my needs. So I refrained and will refrain from burdening you in
any way. **10** [j]By the truth of Christ in me, this
boast of mine shall not be silenced in the regions
of Achaia. **11** [k]*And why? Because I do not
love you? God knows I do!

**12** And what I do I will continue to do, in
order to end this pretext of those who seek a
pretext for being regarded as we are in the mission of which they boast. **13** *For such people
are false apostles, deceitful workers, who masquerade as apostles of Christ. **14** And no wonder, for even Satan masquerades as an angel of
light. **15** So it is not strange that his ministers
also masquerade as ministers of righteousness.
Their end will correspond to their deeds.

**Paul's Boast: His Labors** **16** *I repeat,
no one should consider me foolish; but if you
do, accept me as a fool, so that I too may boast
a little. **17** What I am saying I am not saying
according to the Lord but as in foolishness, in
this boastful state. **18** Since many boast according to the flesh, I too will boast. **19** For you
gladly put up with fools, since you are wise
yourselves. **20** *For you put up with it if someone enslaves you, or devours you, or gets the
better of you, or puts on airs, or slaps you in the
face. **21** *To my shame I say that we were too
weak!

But what anyone dares to boast of (I am
speaking in foolishness) I also dare. **22** [l]*Are
they Hebrews? So am I. Are they Israelites? So
am I. Are they descendants of Abraham? So am
I. **23** [m]*Are they ministers of Christ? (I am

g 1 Cor 1, 5.17; 2, 1-5.
h 12, 13-18; Acts 18, 3; 1 Cor 9, 6-18.
i Phil 4, 15.18.
j 1 Cor 9, 15.
k 12, 15.
l Acts 22, 3 / Rom 11, 1; Phil 3, 5-6.
m 6, 5; Acts 16, 22-24; 1 Cor 15, 31-32.

* Corinth. Their preaching is marked at least by a different emphasis and style, and they do not hesitate to accept support from the community. Perhaps these itinerants appeal to the authority of church leaders in Jerusalem and even carry letters of recommendation from them. But it is not those distant leaders whom Paul is attacking here. The intruders are "superapostles" not in the sense of the "pillars" at Jerusalem (Gal 2), but in their own estimation. They consider themselves superior to Paul as apostles and ministers of Christ, and they are obviously enjoying some success among the Corinthians. Paul rejects their claim to be apostles in any superlative sense (*hyperlian*), judging them bluntly as "false apostles," ministers of Satan masquerading as apostles of Christ (13–15). On the contrary, he himself will claim to be a superminister of Christ (*hyper egō*, 23).

11, 6: Apparently found deficient in both rhetorical ability (cf 10, 10) and knowledge (cf 10, 5), Paul concedes the former charge but not the latter. *In every way:* in all their contacts with him revelation has been taking place. Paul, through whom God reveals the knowledge of himself (2, 14), and in whom the death and life of Jesus are revealed (4, 10–11; cf 6, 4), also demonstrates his own role as the bearer of true knowledge. Cf 1 Cor 1, 18—2, 16.

11, 7–10: Abruptly Paul passes to another reason for complaints: his practice of preaching without remuneration (cf 1 Cor 9, 3–18). He deftly defends his practice by situating it from the start within the pattern of Christ's own self-humiliation (cf 10, 1) and reduces objections to absurdity by rhetorical questions (cf 12, 13).

11, 11–12: Paul rejects lack of affection as his motive (possibly imputed to him by his opponents) and states his real motive, a desire to emphasize the disparity between himself and the others (cf 19–21). The topic of his gratuitous service will be taken up once more in 12, 13–18. 1 Cor 9, 15–18 gives a different but complementary explanation of his motivation.

11, 13–15: Paul picks up again the imagery of v 3 and applies it to the opponents: they are false apostles of Christ, really serving another master. *Deceitful . . . masquerade:* deception and simulation, like cunning (3), are marks of the satanic. *Angel of light:* recalls the contrast between light and darkness, Christ and Beliar at 6, 14–15. *Ministers of righteousness:* recalls the earlier contrast between the ministry of condemnation and that of righteousness (3, 9). *Their end:* the section closes with another allusion to the judgment, when all participants in the final conflict will be revealed or unmasked and dealt with as they deserve.

11, 16—12, 10: Paul now accepts the challenge of his opponents and indulges in boasting similar to theirs, but with differences that he has already signaled in 10, 12–18 and that become clearer as he proceeds. He defines the nature of his project and unmistakably labels it as folly at the beginning and the end (11, 16–23; 12, 11). Yet his boast does not spring from ignorance (11, 21; 12, 6) nor is it concerned merely with human distinctions (11, 18). Paul boasts "in moderation" (10, 13.15) and "in the Lord" (10, 17).

11, 16–29: The first part of Paul's boast focuses on labors and afflictions, in which authentic service of Christ consists.

11, 16–21: These verses recapitulate remarks already made about the foolishness of boasting and the excessive toleration of the Corinthians. They form a prelude to the boast proper.

11, 20: Paul describes the activities of the "others" in terms that fill out the picture drawn in vv 3–4.13–15. Much of the vocabulary suggests fleshly or even satanic activity. *Enslaves:* cf Gal 2, 4. *Devours:* cf 1 Pt 5, 8. *Gets the better:* the verb *lambanō* means "to take," but is used in a variety of senses; here it may imply financial advantage, as in the English colloquialism "to take someone." It is similarly used at 12, 16 and is there connected with cunning and deceit. *Puts on airs:* the same verb is rendered "raise oneself" (10, 5) and "be too elated" (12, 7).

11, 21: Paul ironically concedes the charge of personal weakness from 10, 1–18 but will refute the other charge there mentioned, that of lack of boldness, accepting the challenge to demonstrate it by his boast.

11, 22: The opponents apparently pride themselves on their "Jewishness." Paul, too, can claim to be a Jew by race, religion, and promise. *Descendants of Abraham:* elsewhere Paul distinguishes authentic from inauthentic heirs of Abraham and the promise (Rom 4, 13–18; 9, 7–13; 11, 1; Gal 3, 9.27–29; cf Jn 8, 33–47). Here he grants his opponents this title in order to concentrate on the principal claim that follows.

11, 23a: *Ministers of Christ . . . I am still more:* the central point of the boast (cf the note on 11, 5). *Like an insane person:*

talking like an insane person.) I am still more,
with far greater labors, far more imprisonments,
far worse beatings, and numerous brushes with
death. **24** [n]Five times at the hands of the Jews
I received forty lashes minus one. **25** [o]Three
times I was beaten with rods, once I was stoned,
three times I was shipwrecked, I passed a night
and a day on the deep; **26** on frequent journeys,
in dangers from rivers, dangers from robbers,
dangers from my own race, dangers from Gentiles, dangers in the city, dangers in the wilderness, dangers at sea, dangers among false brothers; **27** [p]in toil and hardship, through many
sleepless nights, through hunger and thirst,
through frequent fastings, through cold and exposure. **28** And apart from these things, there
is the daily pressure upon me of my anxiety for
all the churches. **29** [q]Who is weak, and I am
not weak? Who is led to sin, and I am not
indignant?

**Paul's Boast: His Weakness** **30** *If I
must boast, I will boast of the things that show
my weakness. **31** *The God and Father of the
Lord Jesus knows, he who is blessed forever,
that I do not lie. **32** At Damascus, the governor
under King Aretas guarded the city of Damascus, in order to seize me, **33** [r]but I was lowered
in a basket through a window in the wall and
escaped his hands.

## CHAPTER 12

**1** *I must boast; not that it is profitable, but
I will go on to visions and revelations of the
Lord. **2** I know someone in Christ who, fourteen years ago (whether in the body or out of the
body I do not know, God knows), was caught
up to the third heaven. **3** And I know that this
person (whether in the body or out of the body
I do not know, God knows) **4** [s]was caught up
into Paradise and heard ineffable things, which
no one may utter. **5** *About this person I will
boast, but about myself I will not boast, except
about my weaknesses. **6** Although if I should
wish to boast, I would not be foolish, for I
would be telling the truth. But I refrain, so that
no one may think more of me than what he sees
in me or hears from me **7** [t]*because of the
abundance of the revelations. Therefore, that I
might not become too elated, a thorn in the flesh
was given to me, an angel of Satan, to beat me,
to keep me from being too elated. **8** [u]*Three
times I begged the Lord about this, that it might
leave me, **9** [v]*but he said to me, "My grace is
sufficient for you, for power is made perfect in
weakness." I will rather boast most gladly of
my weaknesses, in order that the power of
Christ may dwell with me. **10** [w]*Therefore, I
*

n Dt 25, 2-3.
o Acts 14, 19; 27, 43-44.
p 1 Cor 4, 11.
q 1 Cor 9, 22.
r Acts 9, 23-25.
s Lk 23, 43; Rv 2, 7.
t Nm 33, 55; Jos 23, 13; Ez 28, 24.
u Mt 26, 39-44.
v 4, 7.
w 6, 4-5; Rom 5, 3 / Phil 4, 13.

the climax of his folly.

11, 23b–29: Service of the humiliated and crucified Christ is demonstrated by trials endured for him. This rhetorically impressive catalogue enumerates many of the labors and perils Paul encountered on his missionary journeys.

11, 30—12, 10: The second part of Paul's boast, marked by a change of style and a shift in focus. After recalling the project in which he is engaged, he states a new topic: his weaknesses as matter for boasting. Everything in this section, even the discussion of privileges and distinctions, will be integrated into this perspective.

11, 31–32: The episode at Damascus is symbolic. It aptly illustrates Paul's weakness but ends in deliverance (cf 4, 7–11).

12, 1–4: *In the body or out of the body:* he seemed no longer confined to bodily conditions, but he does not claim to understand the mechanics of the experience. *Caught up:* i.e., in ecstasy. *The third heaven . . . Paradise:* ancient cosmologies depicted a multitiered universe. Jewish intertestamental literature contains much speculation about the number of heavens. Seven is the number usually mentioned, but the Testament of Levi (2, 7–10; 3, 1–4) speaks of three; God himself dwelt in the third of these. Without giving us any clear picture of the cosmos, Paul indicates a mental journey to a nonearthly space, set apart by God, in which secrets were revealed to him. *Ineffable things:* i.e., privileged knowledge, which it was not possible or permitted to divulge.

12, 5–7: *This person:* the indirect way of referring to himself has the effect of emphasizing the distance between that experience and his everyday life, just as the indirect *someone in Christ* (2) and all the passive verbs emphasize his passivity and receptivity in the experience. The revelations were not a personal achievement, nor were they meant to draw attention to any quality of his own.

12, 7b: *That I might not become too elated:* God assures that there is a negative component to his experience, so that he cannot lose proper perspective; cf 1, 9; 4, 7–11. *A thorn in the flesh:* variously interpreted as a sickness or physical disability, a temptation, or a handicap connected with his apostolic activity. But since Hebrew "thorn in the flesh," like English "thorn in my side," refers to persons (cf Nm 33, 55; Ez 28, 24), Paul may be referring to some especially persistent and obnoxious opponent. The language of vv 7–8 permits this interpretation. If this is correct, the frequent appearance of singular pronouns in depicting the opposition may not be merely a stylistic variation; the singular may be provoked and accompanied by the image of one individual in whom criticism of Paul's preaching, way of life, and apostolic consciousness is concentrated, and who embodies all the qualities Paul attributes to the group. *An angel of Satan:* a personal messenger from Satan; cf the satanic language already applied to the opponents in 11, 3.13–15.20.

12, 8: *Three times:* his prayer was insistent, like that of Jesus in Gethsemane, a sign of how intolerable he felt the thorn to be.

12, 9: *But he said to me:* Paul's petition is denied; release and healing are withheld for a higher purpose. The Greek perfect tense indicates that Jesus' earlier response still holds at the time of writing. *My grace is sufficient for you:* this is not a statement about the sufficiency of grace in general. Jesus speaks directly to Paul's situation. *Is made perfect:* i.e., is given most fully and manifests itself fully.

12, 9b–10a: Paul draws the conclusion from the autobiographical anecdote and integrates it into the subject of this part of the boast. *Weaknesses:* the apostolic hardships he must endure, including active personal hostility, as specified in a final catalogue (10a). *That the power of Christ may dwell with me:* Paul pinpoints the ground for the paradoxical strategy he has adopted in his self-defense.

12, 10b: *When I am weak, then I am strong:* Paul recog-

am content with weaknesses, insults, hardships,
persecutions, and constraints, for the sake of
Christ; for when I am weak, then I am strong.

### Selfless Concern for the Church

11 [x]*I
have been foolish. You compelled me, for I
ought to have been commended by you. For I
am in no way inferior to these "superapostles,"
even though I am nothing.
12 [y]*The signs of an
apostle were performed among you with all endurance, signs and wonders, and mighty deeds.
13 [z]*In what way were you less privileged than
the rest of the churches, except that on my part
I did not burden you? Forgive me this wrong!
14 Now I am ready to come to you this third
time. And I will not be a burden, for I want not
what is yours, but you. Children ought not to
save for their parents, but parents for their children.
15 I will most gladly spend and be utterly
spent for your sakes. If I love you more, am I
to be loved less?
16 [a]But granted that I myself
did not burden you, yet I was crafty and got the
better of you by deceit.
17 Did I take advantage
of you through any of those I sent to you?
18 [b]I
urged Titus to go and sent the brother with him.
Did Titus take advantage of you? Did we not
walk in the same spirit? And in the same steps?

### Final Warnings and Appeals

19 *Have
you been thinking all along that we are defending ourselves before you? In the sight of God we
are speaking in Christ, and all for building you
up, beloved.
20 [c]*For I fear that when I come
I may find you not such as I wish, and that you
may find me not as you wish; that there may be
rivalry, jealousy, fury, selfishness, slander,
gossip, conceit, and disorder.
21 *I fear that
when I come again my God may humiliate me
before you, and I may have to mourn over many
of those who sinned earlier and have not repented of the impurity, immorality, and licentiousness they practiced.

## CHAPTER 13

1 [d]*This third time I am coming to you. "On
the testimony of two or three witnesses a fact
shall be established."
2 *I warned those who

x 11, 5.
y Rom 15, 19; 1 Thes 1, 5.
z 11, 9-12.
a 11, 3.13.
b 2, 13; 8, 16.23.
c 1 Cor 1, 11; 3, 3.
d Dt 19, 15; Mt 18, 16; Jn 8, 17; Heb 10, 28.

* nizes a twofold pattern in the resolution of the weakness-power (and death-life) dialectic, each of which looks to Jesus as the model and is experienced in him. The first is personal, involving a reversal in oneself (Jesus, 13, 4a; Paul, 1, 9–10; 4, 10–11; 6, 9). The second is apostolic, involving an effect on others (Jesus, 5, 14–15; Paul, 1, 6; 4, 12; 13, 9). The specific kind of "effectiveness in ministry" that Paul promises to demonstrate on his arrival (13, 4b; cf 10, 1–11) involves elements of both; this, too, will be modeled on Jesus' experience and a participation in that experience (9; 13, 3b).

12, 11–18: This brief section forms an epilogue or concluding observation to Paul's boast, corresponding to the prologue in 11, 1–15. A four-step sequence of ideas is common to these two sections: Paul qualifies his boast as folly (11, 1; 12, 11a), asserts his noninferiority to the "superapostles" (11, 5; 12, 11b), exemplifies this by allusion to charismatic endowments (11, 6; 12, 12), and finally denies that he has been a financial burden to the community (11, 7–12; 12, 13–18).

12, 12: Despite weakness and affliction (suggested by the mention *of endurance*), his ministry has been accompanied by demonstrations of power (cf 1 Cor 2, 3–4). *Signs of an apostle:* visible proof of belonging to Christ and of mediating Christ's power, which the opponents require as touchstones of apostleship (11; cf 13, 3).

12, 13–18: Paul insists on his intention to continue refusing support from the community (cf 11, 8–12). In defending his practice and his motivation, he once more protests his love (cf 11, 11) and rejects the suggestion of secret self-enrichment. He has recourse here again to language applied to his opponents earlier: "cunning" (11, 3), "deceit" (11, 13), "got the better of you" (see the note on 11, 20), "take advantage" (2, 11).

12, 19—13, 10: This concludes the development begun in ch 10. In the chiastic arrangement of the material (see the note on 10, 1—13, 10), this final part corresponds to the opening; there are important similarities of content between the two sections as well.

12, 19: This verse looks back at the previous chapters and calls them by their proper name, a defense, an *apologia* (cf 1 Cor 9, 3). Yet Paul insists on an important distinction: he has indeed been speaking for their benefit, but the ultimate judgment to which he submits is God's (cf 1 Cor 4, 3–5). This verse also leads into the final section, announcing two of its themes: judgment and building up.

12, 20: *I fear that . . . :* earlier Paul expressed fear that the Corinthians were being victimized, exploited, seduced from right thinking by his opponents (11, 3–4.19–21). Here he alludes unexpectedly to moral disorders among the Corinthians themselves. The catalogue suggests the effects of factions that have grown up around rival apostles.

12, 21: *Again:* one can also translate, "I fear that when I come my God may again humiliate me." Paul's allusion to the humiliation and mourning that may await him recall the mood he described in 2, 1–4, but there is no reference here to any individual such as there is in 2, 5–11. The crisis of ch 2 has happily been resolved by integration of the offender and repentance (7, 4–16), whereas 12, 21 is preoccupied with still unrepentant sinners. The sexual sins recall 1 Cor 5–7.

13, 1: *This third time I am coming:* designation of the forthcoming visit as the "third" (cf 12, 14) may indicate that, in addition to his founding sojourn in Corinth, Paul had already made the first of two visits mentioned as planned in 1, 15, and the next visit will be the long-postponed second of these. If so, the materials in 1, 12—2, 13 plus 7, 4–16 and chs 10–13 may date from the same period of time, presumably of some duration, between Paul's second and third visit, though it is not clear that they are addressing the same crisis. The chronology is too unsure and the relations between sections of 2 Cor too unclear to yield any certainty. The hypothesis that chs 10–13 are themselves the "tearful letter" mentioned at 2, 3–4 creates more problems than it solves.

13, 2: *I warned those who sinned earlier:* mention of unrepentant sinners (12, 21 and here) and of an oral admonition given them on an earlier visit complicates the picture at the very end of Paul's development. It provides, in fact, a second explanation for the show of power that has been threatened from the beginning (10, 1–6), but a different reason for it, quite unsuspected until now. It is not clear whether Paul is merely alluding to a dimension of the situation that he has not previously had occasion to mention, or whether some other community crisis, not directly connected with that behind chs 10–13, has influenced the final editing. *I will not be lenient:* contrast Paul's hesitation and reluctance to inflict pain in 1, 23

# Jerusalem
## JESUS' LAST DAYS

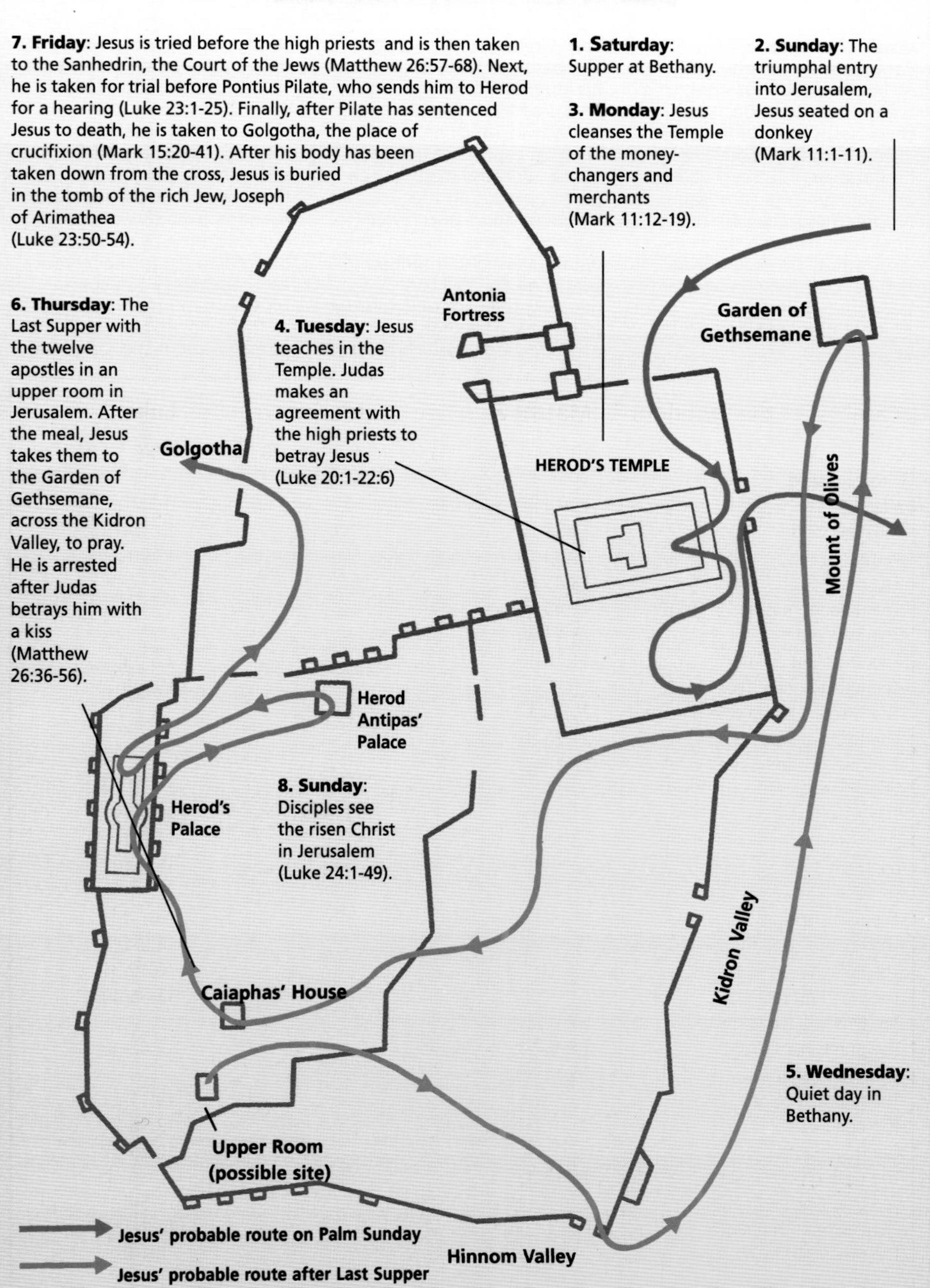

**7. Friday**: Jesus is tried before the high priests and is then taken to the Sanhedrin, the Court of the Jews (Matthew 26:57-68). Next, he is taken for trial before Pontius Pilate, who sends him to Herod for a hearing (Luke 23:1-25). Finally, after Pilate has sentenced Jesus to death, he is taken to Golgotha, the place of crucifixion (Mark 15:20-41). After his body has been taken down from the cross, Jesus is buried in the tomb of the rich Jew, Joseph of Arimathea (Luke 23:50-54).
**1. Saturday**: Supper at Bethany.
**2. Sunday**: The triumphal entry into Jerusalem, Jesus seated on a donkey (Mark 11:1-11).
**3. Monday**: Jesus cleanses the Temple of the money-changers and merchants (Mark 11:12-19).
**6. Thursday**: The Last Supper with the twelve apostles in an upper room in Jerusalem. After the meal, Jesus takes them to the Garden of Gethsemane, across the Kidron Valley, to pray. He is arrested after Judas betrays him with a kiss (Matthew 26:36-56).
Antonia Fortress
**4. Tuesday**: Jesus teaches in the Temple. Judas makes an agreement with the high priests to betray Jesus (Luke 20:1-22:6)
Garden of Gethsemane
Golgotha
HEROD'S TEMPLE
Mount of Olives
Herod Antipas' Palace
Herod's Palace
**8. Sunday**: Disciples see the risen Christ in Jerusalem (Luke 24:1-49).
Kidron Valley
Caiaphas' House
**5. Wednesday**: Quiet day in Bethany.
Upper Room (possible site)
Jesus' probable route on Palm Sunday
Jesus' probable route after Last Supper
Hinnom Valley

# Parables of Jesus
## EASY FINDER

**What Is a Parable?**
Parables make up about 35% of Jesus' recorded sayings, so it is important to understand them. Jesus repeatedly uses illustrations from daily life in his parables, but the parables are not merely illustrations in his preaching; they *are* the preaching. Though the illustrations are drawn from familiar objects and events, they often include exaggeration and unexpected behavior.

**The Kingdom**
The parables focus on God and his kingdom, and in doing so, reveal what kind of God he is, the way in which he works and what he expects of human beings. Because many of the parables focus on the kingdom, some also reveal aspects of Jesus' mission. The parables are also intended to challenge and call to a decision; they are told in order to bring the listener to concede a point which he or she has not regarded as relevant to himself or herself.

Yet we also read in Mark 4:10-12 that Jesus taught in parables to conceal his message. Some are far from self-evident, and teaching in this way helped conceal Jesus' message from those hostile to him. Teaching by parable also offered an aid to the memory and could serve to bypass resistance in Jesus' listeners.

The following are Jesus' parables about the Kingdom.

| Parables of the Kingdom | Matthew | Mark | Luke |
|---|---|---|---|
| The sower | 13:3-9, 18-23 | 4:3-9, 13-20 | 8:5-8, 11-15 |
| Growing seed | | 4:26-29 | |
| Weeds | 13:24-30, 36-43 | | |
| Mustard seed | 13:31-32 | 4:30-32 | 13:18-19 |
| Yeast | 13:33 | | 13:20-21 |
| The pearl | 13:45-46 | | |
| The hidden treasure | 13:44 | | |
| The fishing net | 13:47-50 | | |
| The unwilling children | 11:16-19 | | 7:31-35 |
| The unfruitful fig tree | | | 13:6-9 |
| The workers in the vineyard | 20:1-16 | | |
| The two brothers | 21:28-32 | | |
| The royal wedding feast | 22:1-14 | | |
| The great dinner | | | 14:16-24 |
| The wicked workers | 21:33-46 | 12:1-12 | 20:9-19 |
| Lost sheep | 18:12-14 | | 15:3-7 |
| Lost coin | | | 15:8-10 |
| Lost son | | | 15:11-32 |
| The two creditors | | | 7:41-47 |
| The Pharisee and the tax-collector | | | 18:9-14 |
| The rich man and Lazarus | | | 16:19-31 |
| The watchful servants | | | 12:35-40 |
| Ten girls at a wedding | 25:1-13 | | |
| The unreliable servant | 24:45-51 | | 12:42-46 |
| The five talents | 25:14-30 | | |
| The ten gold coins | | | 19:11-27 |
| The rich fool | | | 12:16-21 |
| Good Samaritan | | | 10:25-37 |
| The unforgiving servant | 18:23-35 | | |
| The troublesome friend | | | 11:5-8 |
| The dishonest manager | | | 16:1-13 |
| The unjust judge | | | 18:1-8 |

# Miracles of Jesus
## EASY FINDER

Three things are needed to make a true miracle: the event must be visible, the event must go beyond the powers of nature and the event must be the sign of a divine message.

Jesus did many miracles or signs. They show his power, his love for people and his desire to help.

Jesus' miracles explained his mission, revealed his divinity, proved him to be the Messiah and began the world's renewal.

**Miracles in John**
John's Gospel records seven miracles, apart from the death and resurrection of Jesus. John chose particular miracles to help his readers see Jesus as the Son of God and to show the need to trust in him.

| **Healings** | **Matthew** | **Mark** | **Luke** | **John** |
|---|---|---|---|---|
| Son of government official | | | | 4:46-54 |
| Sick man at a pool | | | | 5:1-18 |
| Man in synagogue | | 1:21-28 | 4:31-37 | |
| Man with skin disease | 8:1-4 | 1:40-45 | 5:12-14 | |
| Roman officer's servant | 8:5-13 | | 7:1-10 | |
| Dead son of a widow | | | 7:11-15 | |
| Peter's mother-in-law | 8:14-15 | 1:29-31 | 4:38-39 | |
| An uncontrollable man | | 5:1-20 | 8:26-39 | |
| Paralysed man | 9:1-8 | 2:1-12 | 5:17-26 | |
| Woman with severe bleeding | 9:20-22 | 5:25-34 | 8:43-48 | |
| Dead girl | 9:18-26 | 5:21-43 | 8:40-56 | |
| Dumb man | 9:32-34 | | | |
| Man with a paralysed hand | 12:9-14 | 3:1-6 | 6:6-11 | |
| Blind and dumb man | 12:22-23 | | 11:14 | |
| Canaanite woman's daughter | 15:21-28 | 7:24-30 | | |
| Deaf and dumb man | | 7:31-37 | | |
| Blind man at Bethsaida | | 8:22-26 | | |
| Boy with epilepsy | 17:14-20 | 9:14-29 | 9:37-43 | |
| Blind Bartimaeus | | 10:46-52 | 18:35-43 | |
| Woman with a bad back | | | 13:10-17 | |
| Sick man | | | 14:1-6 | |
| Man born blind | | | | 9:1-41 |
| Dead friend named Lazarus | | | | 11:1-44 |
| Slave's ear | | | 22:49-51 | |
| Crowd in Capernaum | 8:16-17 | 1:32-34 | 4:40-41 | |
| Two blind men | 9:27-31 | | | |
| Crowd by Lake Galilee | | 3:7-12 | | |
| Crowd on the hillsides by Galilee | 15:29-31 | | | |
| Ten men with leprosy | | | 17:11-19 | |
| **Control over Laws of Nature** | | | | |
| Water changed into wine | | | | 2:1-11 |
| Catch of fish | | | 5:1-11 | |
| Jesus calms a storm | 8:23-27 | 4:35-41 | 8:22-25 | |
| 5,000 men are fed, besides others | 14:13-21 | 6:30-44 | 9:10-17 | 6:1-15 |
| Jesus walks on the water | 14:22-33 | 6:45-52 | | 6:16-21 |
| 4,000 men are fed, besides others | 15:32-39 | 8:1-10 | | |
| A fish and the payment of taxes | 17:24-27 | | | |
| Fig tree withers away | 21:18-22 | 11:12-14, 20-24 | | |
| Another catch of fish | | | | 21:1-11 |
| Christ conquers death | 28:1-10 | 16:1-11 | 24:1-12 | 20:1-18 |

# Jesus' Resurrection
## APPEARANCES

The Gospels do not describe the resurrection itself; but they recount the meetings of many different people with the risen Christ. Many reliable witnesses claimed to have seen Jesus alive after his death (1 Corinthians 15:3-8).

*Right*: **The Garden Tomb, Jerusalem, is probably similar to the tomb in which Jesus was buried.**

**Mary Magdalene** (John 20:11-18).

**Simon Peter** (Luke 24:34).

**Two people on the way to Emmaus** (Luke 24:13-33).

**The disciples** – apart from Thomas (John 20:19-23).

**The disciples** – including **Thomas** (John 20:24-29).

**Mary Magdalene** and **"the other Mary"** (Matthew 28:1-10).

**The apostles** in Galilee (Matthew 28:16-17).

**Seven disciples** by the Sea of Tiberias (John 21:1-14).

**More than five hundred of his followers** (1 Corinthians 15:6).

**James** (1 Corinthians 15:7).

**His disciples** (Acts 1:4-9).

**Paul** (Acts 9:1-9).

sinned earlier and all the others, and I warn them
now while absent, as I did when present on my
second visit, that if I come again I will not be
lenient, **3** *since you are looking for proof of
Christ speaking in me. He is not weak toward
you but powerful in you. **4** For indeed he was
crucified out of weakness, but he lives by the
power of God. So also we are weak in him, but
toward you we shall live with him by the power
of God.

**5** *Examine yourselves to see whether you
are living in faith. Test yourselves. Do you not
realize that Jesus Christ is in you?—unless, of
course, you fail the test. **6** I hope you will discover that we have not failed. **7** But we pray to
God that you may not do evil, not that we may
appear to have passed the test but that you may
do what is right, even though we may seem to
have failed. **8** For we cannot do anything
against the truth, but only for the truth. **9** For
we rejoice when we are weak but you are strong.
What we pray for is your improvement.

**10** [e]*I am writing this while I am away, so
that when I come I may not have to be severe
in virtue of the authority that the Lord has given
me to build up and not to tear down.

## V: CONCLUSION

**11** *Finally, brothers, rejoice. Mend your
ways, encourage one another, agree with one
another, live in peace, and the God of love and
peace will be with you. **12** [f]Greet one another
with a holy kiss. All the holy ones greet you.

**13** [g]The grace of the Lord Jesus Christ and
the love of God and the fellowship of the holy
Spirit be with all of you.

---

e 10, 8.
f Rom 16, 16; 1 Cor 16, 20 / Phil 4, 22; 1 Thes 5, 26; 1 Pt 5, 14.
g Rom 16, 20; 1 Cor 16, 23.

---

* and 2, 1–4. The next visit will bring the showdown.

13, 3–4: Paul now gives another motive for severity when he comes, the charge of weakness leveled against him as an apostle. The motive echoes more closely the opening section (10, 1–18) and the intervening development (especially 11, 30—12, 10). *Proof of Christ speaking in me:* the threat of 10, 1–2 is reworded to recall Paul's conformity with the pattern of Christ, his insertion into the interplay of death and life, weakness and power (cf the note on 12, 10b).

13, 5–9: Paul turns the challenge mentioned in v 3 on them: they are to put themselves to the test to demonstrate whether Christ is in them. These verses involve a complicated series of plays on the theme of *dokimē* (testing, proof, passing and failing a test). Behind this stands the familiar distinction between present human judgment and final divine judgment. This is the final appearance of the theme (cf 10, 18; 11, 15; 12, 19).

13, 10: *Authority . . . to build up and not to tear down:* Paul restates the purpose of his letter in language that echoes 10, 2.8, emphasizing the positive purpose of his authority in their regard. This verse forms an inclusion with the topic sentence of the section (12, 19), as well as with the opening of this entire portion of the letter (10, 1–2).

13, 11–13: These verses may have originally concluded chs 10–13, but they have nothing specifically to do with the material of that section. It is also possible to consider them a conclusion to the whole of 2 Cor in its present edited form. The exhortations are general, including a final appeal for peace in the community. The letter ends calmly, after its many storms, with the prospect of ecclesial unity and divine blessing. The final verse is one of the clearest trinitarian passages in the New Testament.

# THE LETTER TO THE
# GALATIANS

## INTRODUCTION

*The Galatians to whom the letter is addressed were Paul's converts, most likely among the descendants of Celts who had invaded western and central Asia Minor in the third century B.C. and had settled in the territory around Ancyra (modern Ankara, Turkey). Paul had passed through this area on his second missionary journey (Acts 16, 6) and again on his third (Acts 18, 23). It is less likely that the recipients of this letter were Paul's churches in the southern regions of Pisidia, Lycaonia, and Pamphylia where he had preached earlier in the Hellenized cities of Perge, Iconium, Pisidian Antioch, Lystra, and Derbe (Acts 13, 13—14, 27); this area was part of the Roman province of Galatia, and some scholars think that South Galatia was the destination of this letter.*

*If it is addressed to the Galatians in the north, the letter was probably written around A.D. 54 or 55, most likely from Ephesus after Paul's arrival there for a stay of several years on his third missionary journey (Acts 19; 20, 31). On the South Galatian theory, the date would be earlier, perhaps A.D. 48–50. Involved is the question of how one relates the events of 2, 1–10 to the "Council of Jerusalem" described in Acts 15 (see the notes on each passage).*

*In any case, the new Christians whom Paul is addressing were converts from paganism (4, 8–9) who were now being enticed by other missionaries to add the observances of the Jewish law, including the rite of circumcision, to the cross of Christ as a means of salvation. For, since Paul's visit, some other interpretation of Christianity had been brought to these neophytes, probably by converts from Judaism (the name "Judaizers" is sometimes applied to them); it has specifically been suggested that they were Jewish Christians who had come from the austere Essene sect.*

*These interlopers insisted on the necessity of following certain precepts of the Mosaic law along with faith in Christ. They were undermining Paul's authority also, asserting that he had not been trained by Jesus himself, that his gospel did not agree with that of the original and true apostles in Jerusalem, that he had kept from his converts in Galatia the necessity of accepting circumcision and other key obligations of the Jewish law, in order more easily to win them to Christ, and that his gospel was thus not the full and authentic one held by "those of repute" in Jerusalem (2, 2). Some scholars also see in chapters 5 and 6 another set of opponents against whom Paul writes, people who in their emphasis on the Spirit set aside all norms for conduct and became libertines in practice.*

*When Paul learned of the situation, he wrote this defense of his apostolic authority and of the correct understanding of the faith. He set forth the unique importance of Christ and his redemptive sacrifice on the cross, the freedom that Christians enjoy from the old burdens of the law, the total sufficiency of Christ and of faith in Christ as the way to God and to eternal life, and the beauty of the new life of the Spirit. Galatians is thus a summary of basic Pauline theology. Its themes were more fully and less polemically developed in the Letter to the Romans.*

*Autobiographically, the letter gives us Paul's own accounts of how he came to faith (1, 15–24), the agreement in "the truth of the gospel" (2, 5.14) that he shared with the Jewish Christian leaders in Jerusalem, James, Kephas, and John (2, 1–10), and the rebuke he had to deliver to Kephas in Antioch for inconsistency, contrary to the gospel, on the issue of table fellowship in the racially mixed church of Jewish and Gentile Christians in Antioch (2, 11–14; cf 15–21). At the conclusion of the letter (6, 11–18), Paul wrote in his own hand (cf 2 Thes 3, 17–18) a vivid summary of the message to the Galatians.*

*In his vigorous emphasis on the absolute preeminence of Christ and his cross as God's way to salvation and holiness, Paul stresses Christian freedom and the ineffectiveness of the Mosaic law for gaining divine favor and blessings (3, 19–29). The pious Jew saw in the law a way established by God to win divine approval by a life of meticulous observance of ritual, social, and moral regulations. But Paul's profound insight into the higher designs of God in Christ led him to understand and welcome the priority of promise and faith (shown in the experience of Abraham, 3, 6–18) and the supernatural gifts of the Spirit (3, 2–5; 5, 16—6, 10). His enthusiasm for this new vision of the life of grace in Christ and of the uniquely salvific role of Christ's redemptive death on the cross shines through this whole letter.*

*The principal divisions of the Letter to the Galatians are the following:*

*I. Address (1, 1–5)*
*II. Loyalty to the Gospel (1, 6–10)*
*III. Paul's Defense of His Gospel and His Authority (1, 11—2, 21)*
*IV. Faith and Liberty (3, 1—4, 31)*
*V. Exhortation to Christian Living (5, 1—6, 10)*
*VI. Conclusion (6, 11–18)*

## I: ADDRESS

### CHAPTER 1

**Greeting** 1 [a][b]*Paul, an apostle not from
human beings nor through a human being but
through Jesus Christ and God the Father who
raised him from the dead, 2 *and all the brothers who are with me, to the churches of Galatia:
3 grace to you and peace from God our Father
and the Lord Jesus Christ, 4 [c]*who gave himself for our sins that he might rescue us from the
present evil age in accord with the will of our
God and Father, 5 [d]to whom be glory forever
and ever. Amen.

## II: LOYALTY TO THE GOSPEL

6 [e]*I am amazed that you are so quickly
forsaking the one who called you by [the] grace
[of Christ] for a different gospel 7 (not that
there is another). But there are some who are
disturbing you and wish to pervert the gospel of
Christ. 8 [f]*But even if we or an angel from
heaven should preach [to you] a gospel other
than the one that we preached to you, let that
one be accursed! 9 As we have said before, and
now I say again, if anyone preaches to you a
gospel other than the one that you received, let
that one be accursed!

10 [g]*Am I now currying favor with human
beings or God? Or am I seeking to please people? If I were still trying to please people, I
would not be a slave of Christ.

## III: PAUL'S DEFENSE OF HIS GOSPEL AND HIS AUTHORITY

**His Call by Christ** 11 [h]*Now I want you
to know, brothers, that the gospel preached by

a Rom 1, 1-7; 1 Cor 1, 1-3.
b 1, 11-12.
c 2, 20; Eph 5, 2; 1 Tm 2, 6 / 1 Jn 5, 19 / Rom 12, 2; Eph 5, 16; Heb 10, 10.
d Rom 16, 27; 2 Tm 4, 18.
e 5, 8.10; Acts 15, 1.24; 2 Cor 11, 4.
f 1 Cor 16, 22 / 5, 3.21; 2 Cor 13, 2.
g 2 Cor 5, 11 / 1 Thes 2, 4.
h 1 Cor 15, 1 / 1, 1; Eph 3, 3.

*

1, 1–5: See the note on Rom 1, 1–7, concerning the greeting.

1, 1: *Apostle:* because of attacks on his authority in Galatia, Paul defends his apostleship. He is not an apostle commissioned by a congregation (Phil 2, 25; 2 Cor 8, 23) or even by prophets (1 Tm 1, 18 and 4, 14) but *through Jesus Christ and God the Father.*

1, 2: *All the brothers:* fellow believers in Christ, male and female; cf 3, 27–28. Paul usually mentions the co-sender(s) at the start of a letter, but the use of all is unique, adding weight to the letter. *Galatia:* central Turkey more likely than the Roman province of Galatia; see Introduction.

1, 4: The greeting in v 3 is expanded by a christological formula that stresses deliverance through the Lord Jesus from a world dominated by Satan; cf 2 Cor 4, 4; Eph 2, 2; 6, 12.

1, 6–10: In place of the usual thanksgiving (see the note on Rom 1, 8), Paul, with little to be thankful for in the Galatian situation, expresses amazement at the way his converts are deserting the gospel of Christ for a perverted message. He reasserts the one gospel he has preached (7–9) and begins to defend himself (10).

1, 6: *The one who called you:* God or Christ, though in actuality Paul was the divine instrument to call the Galatians.

1, 8: *Accursed:* in Greek, *anathema;* cf Rom 9, 3; 1 Cor 12, 3; 16, 22.

1, 10: This charge by Paul's opponents, that he sought to conciliate people with flattery and to curry favor with God, might refer to his mission practices (cf 1 Cor 9, 19–23) but the word *still* suggests it refers to his pre-Christian days (cf 14; Phil 3, 6). The self-description *slave of Christ* is one Paul often uses in a greeting (Rom 1, 1).

1, 11—2, 21: Paul's presentation on behalf of his message and of his apostleship reflects rhetorical forms of his day: he first narrates the facts about certain past events (1, 12—2, 14) and then states his contention regarding justification by faith as the gospel message (2, 15–21). Further arguments follow from both experience and scripture in chs 3 and 4, before he draws out the ethical consequences (5, 1—6, 10). The specific facts that he takes up here to show that his gospel is not a human invention (1, 11) but *came through a revelation of*

me is not of human origin. **12** *For I did not receive it from a human being, nor was I taught it, but it came through a revelation of Jesus Christ.

**13** [i]*For you heard of my former way of life in Judaism, how I persecuted the church of God beyond measure and tried to destroy it, **14** [j]and progressed in Judaism beyond many of my contemporaries among my race, since I was even more a zealot for my ancestral traditions. **15** [k]But when [God], who from my mother's womb had set me apart and called me through his grace, was pleased **16** [l]*to reveal his Son to me, so that I might proclaim him to the Gentiles, I did not immediately consult flesh and blood, **17** *nor did I go up to Jerusalem to those who were apostles before me; rather, I went into Arabia and then returned to Damascus.

**18** [m]*Then after three years I went up to Jerusalem to confer with Cephas and remained with him for fifteen days. **19** [n]*But I did not see any other of the apostles, only James the brother of the Lord. **20** [o](As to what I am writing to you, behold, before God, I am not lying.) **21** [p]Then I went into the regions of Syria and Cilicia. **22** And I was unknown personally to the churches of Judea that are in Christ; **23** [q]they only kept hearing that "the one who once was persecuting us is now preaching the faith he once tried to destroy." **24** So they glorified God because of me.

## CHAPTER 2

### The Council of Jerusalem

**1** [r]*Then after fourteen years I again went up to Jerusalem with Barnabas, taking Titus along also. **2** [s]*I went up in accord with a revelation, and I presented to them the gospel that I preach to the Gentiles—but privately to those of repute—so that I might not be running, or have run, in vain. **3** [t]*Moreover, not even Titus, who was with me, although he was a Greek, was compelled to be circumcised, **4** [u]*but because of the false brothers secretly brought in, who slipped in to spy on our freedom that we have in Christ Jesus,

i Acts 8, 1-3; 9, 1-2; 1 Cor 15, 9.
j Acts 26, 4-5.
k Is 49, 1; Jer 1, 4.
l 1, 11-12; Rom 1, 5; 1 Cor 15, 10; Acts 9, 3-9 / 2, 2.7 /Mt 16, 17.
m Acts 9, 26-30 / Jn 1, 42.
n 2, 9; Mt 13, 55; Acts 12, 17.
o Rom 9, 1; 2 Cor 11, 31.
p Acts 9, 30.
q 1, 13.
r Acts 15, 2.
s 1, 11-12.16 / 1, 16 / Phil 2, 16.
t 2 Cor 2, 13; 7, 6-7; 8, 16-17; 12, 18; Ti 1, 4 / 2, 14; 6, 12.
u 5, 1; Acts 15, 1.24.

*

*Jesus Christ* (1, 12) deal with his own calling as a Christian missionary (1, 13–17), his initial relations with the apostles in Jerusalem (1, 18–24), a later journey to Jerusalem (2, 1–10), and an incident in Antioch involving Cephas and persons from James (2, 11–14). The content of Paul's revealed gospel is then set forth in the heart of the letter (2, 15–21).

1, 12: Although Paul received his gospel *through a revelation* from Christ, this did not exclude his use of early Christian confessional formulations. See the note on 1, 4.

1, 13–17: Along with Phil 3, 4–11, which also moves from autobiography to its climax in a discussion on justification by faith (cf Gal 2, 15–21), this passage is Paul's chief account of the change from his *former way of life* (13) to service as a Christian missionary (16); cf Acts 9, 1–22; 22, 4–16; 26, 9–18. Paul himself does not use the term "conversion" but stresses revelation (12.16). In v 15 his language echoes the Old Testament prophetic call of Jeremiah. Unlike the account in Acts (cf 22, 4–16), the calling of Paul here includes the mission to proclaim Christ *to the Gentiles* (16).

1, 16: *Flesh and blood:* human authorities (cf Mt 16, 17; 1 Cor 15, 50). Paul's apostleship comes from God (1).

1, 17: *Arabia:* probably the region of the Nabataean Arabs, east and south of Damascus.

1, 18–24: Paul's first journey to Jerusalem as a Christian, according to Galatians (cf Acts 9, 23–31 and the note on Acts 12, 25). He is quite explicit about contacts there, testifying under oath (20). On returning to *Syria* (perhaps specifically Damascus, cf v 17) *and Cilicia* (including his home town Tarsus, cf Acts 9, 30; 22, 3), Paul most likely engaged in missionary work. He underscores the fact that Christians in Judea knew of him only by reputation.

1, 18: *After three years:* two years and more, since Paul's call. To *confer with* Cephas may mean simply "pay a visit" or more specifically "get information from" him about Jesus, over a two-week period. *Cephas:* Aramaic name of Simon (Peter); cf Mt 16, 16–18 and the notes there.

1, 19: *James the brother of the Lord:* not one of the twelve, but a brother of Jesus (see the note on Mk 6, 3). He played an important role in the Jerusalem church (see the note on Gal 2, 9), the leadership of which he took over from Peter (Acts 12, 17). Paul may have regarded James as an apostle.

2, 1–10: Paul's second journey to Jerusalem, according to Galatians, involved a private meeting with *those of repute* (2). At issue was a Gentile, Titus, and the question of circumcision, which *false brothers* (4) evidently demanded for him. Paul insists that the gospel he preaches (2; cf 1, 9.11) remained intact with no addition by those of repute (6); that *Titus* was not *compelled* to accept circumcision (3); and that he and the reputed *pillars* in Jerusalem agreed on how each would advance the missionary task (7–10). Usually, 1–10 is equated with the "Council of Jerusalem," as it is called, described in Acts 15. See the notes on Acts 15, 6–12 and 15, 13–35, the latter concerning the "decree" that Paul does not mention.

2, 1: *After fourteen years:* thirteen or more years, probably reckoned from the return to Syria and Cilicia (1, 21), though possibly from Paul's calling as a Christian (1, 15). *Barnabas:* cf 9.13; 1 Cor 9, 6. A Jewish Christian missionary, with whom Paul worked (Acts 4, 36–37; 11, 22.25.30; 12, 25; 13, 1–3; 15, 2). *Titus:* a missionary companion of Paul (2 Cor 2, 13; 7, 6.13–15; 8, 6.16.23; 12, 18), non-Jewish (Gal 2, 3), never mentioned in Acts.

2, 2: *A revelation:* cf 1, 1.12. Paul emphasizes it was God's will, not Jerusalem authority, that led to the journey. Acts 15, 2 states that the church in Antioch appointed Paul and Barnabas for the task. *Those of repute:* leaders of the Jerusalem church; the term, while positive, may be slightly ironic (cf 6.9). *Run, in vain:* while Paul presents a positive picture in what follows, his missionary work in Galatia would have been to no purpose if his opponents were correct that circumcision is needed for complete faith in Christ.

2, 3: *Not even* a Gentile Christian like Titus was compelled to receive the rite of circumcision. The Greek text could be interpreted that he voluntarily accepted circumcision, but this is unlikely in the overall argument.

2, 4: *False brothers:* Jewish Christians who took the position that Gentile Christians must first become Jews through circumcision and observance of the Mosaic law in order to become Christians; cf Acts 15, 1.

that they might enslave us— **5** [v]*to them we
did not submit even for a moment, so that the
truth of the gospel might remain intact for you.
**6** [w]But from those who were reputed to be important (what they once were makes no difference to me; God shows no partiality)—those of
repute made me add nothing. **7** [x]*On the contrary, when they saw that I had been entrusted
with the gospel to the uncircumcised, just as
Peter to the circumcised, **8** for the one who
worked in Peter for an apostolate to the circumcised worked also in me for the Gentiles,
**9** [y]*and when they recognized the grace bestowed upon me, James and Cephas and John,
who were reputed to be pillars, gave me and
Barnabas their right hands in partnership, that
we should go to the Gentiles and they to the
circumcised. **10** [z]*Only, we were to be mindful
of the poor, which is the very thing I was eager
to do.

## Peter's Inconsistency at Antioch

**11** [a]*And when Cephas came to Antioch, I
opposed him to his face because he clearly was
wrong. **12** [b]*For, until some people came from
James, he used to eat with the Gentiles; but
when they came, he began to draw back and
separated himself, because he was afraid of the
circumcised. **13** [c]*And the rest of the Jews
[also] acted hypocritically along with him, with
the result that even Barnabas was carried away
by their hypocrisy. **14** [d]*But when I saw that
they were not on the right road in line with the
truth of the gospel, I said to Cephas in front of
all, "If you, though a Jew, are living like a
Gentile and not like a Jew, how can you compel
the Gentiles to live like Jews?"

## Faith and Works

**15** *We, who are Jews
by nature and not sinners from among the Gentiles, **16** [e]*[yet] who know that a person is not
justified by works of the law but through faith
in Jesus Christ, even we have believed in Christ
Jesus that we may be justified by faith in Christ
and not by works of the law, because by works
of the law no one will be justified. **17** *But if,
in seeking to be justified in Christ, we ourselves
are found to be sinners, is Christ then a minister
of sin? Of course not! **18** *But if I am building
up again those things that I tore down, then I
show myself to be a transgressor. **19** [f]*For
through the law I died to the law, that I might

v 2, 14; 4, 16.
w Dt 10, 17; Rom 2, 11.
x 1, 15-16; Acts 9, 15; 15, 12; 22, 21; Rom 1, 5.
y Rom 15, 15 / 1, 18-19; Jn 1, 42; Acts 12, 17 / 2, 1.
z Acts 11, 29-30; Rom 15, 25-28; 1 Cor 16, 1-4; 2 Cor 8, 9.
a 1, 18 / Acts 11, 19-30; 15, 1-2.
b Acts 10, 15.28; 11, 3.
c 2, 1.9.
d 2, 5 / 1, 18; 2, 9 / 2, 3.
e 3, 2.11; Ps 143, 1-2; Rom 3, 20.28; 4, 5; 11, 6; Eph 2, 8-9;Phil 3, 9.
f 6, 14; Rom 6, 6.8.10; 7, 6.

2, 5: *The truth of the gospel:* the true gospel, in contrast to the false one of the opponents (1, 6–9); the gospel of grace, used as a norm (14).

2, 7–9: Some think that actual "minutes" of the meeting are here quoted. Paul's apostleship to the Gentiles (1, 16) is recognized alongside that of Peter to the Jews. Moreover, the right to proclaim the gospel without requiring circumcision and the Jewish law is sealed by a handshake. That Paul and colleagues *should go to the Gentiles* did not exclude his preaching to the Jews as well (Rom 1, 13–16) or Cephas to Gentile areas.

2, 9: *James and Cephas and John:* see the notes on 1, 18 and 19; on Peter and John as leaders in the Jerusalem church, cf Acts 3, 1 and 8, 14. The order here, with James first, may reflect his prominence in Jerusalem after Peter (Cephas) departed (Acts 12, 17).

2, 10: *The poor:* Jerusalem Christians or a group within the church there (cf Rom 15, 26). The collection for them was extremely important in Paul's thought and labor (cf Rom 15, 25–28; 1 Cor 16, 1–4; 2 Cor 8 and 9).

2, 11–14: The decision reached in Jerusalem (3–7) recognized the freedom of Gentile Christians from the Jewish law. But the problem of table fellowship between Jewish Christians, who possibly still kept kosher food regulations, and Gentile believers was not yet settled. When Cephas first came to the racially mixed community of Jewish and Gentile Christians in Antioch (12), he ate with non-Jews. Pressure from persons arriving later from Jerusalem caused him and Barnabas to draw back. Paul therefore publicly rebuked Peter's inconsistency toward the gospel (14). Some think that what Paul said on that occasion extends through v 16 or v 21.

2, 11: *Clearly was wrong:* literally, "stood condemned," by himself and also by Paul. His action in breaking table fellowship was especially grievous if the eating involved the meal at the Lord's supper (cf 1 Cor 11, 17–25).

2, 12: *Some people came from James:* strict Jewish Christians (cf Acts 15, 1.5; 21, 20–21), either sent by James (1, 19; 2, 9) or claiming to be from the leader of the Jerusalem church. *The circumcised:* presumably Jewish Christians, not Jews.

2, 13: *The Jews:* Jewish Christians, like Barnabas. *Hypocrisy:* literally, "pretense," "play-acting"; moral insincerity.

2, 14: *Compel the Gentiles to live like Jews:* that is, conform to Jewish practices, such as circumcision (3–5) or regulations about food (12).

2, 15–21: Following on the series of incidents cited above, Paul's argument, whether spoken to Cephas at Antioch or only now articulated, is pertinent to the Galatian situation, where believers were having themselves circumcised (6, 12–13) and obeying other aspects of Jewish law (4, 9–10; 5, 1–4). He insists that salvation is by faith in Christ, not by works of the law. His teaching on the gospel concerns justification by faith (16) in relation to sin (17), law (19), life in Christ (19–20), and grace (21).

2, 16: *No one will be justified:* Ps 143, 2 is reflected.

2, 17: *A minister of sin:* literally, "a servant of sin" (cf Rom 15, 8), an agent of sin, one who promotes it. This is possibly a claim by opponents that justification on the basis of faith in Christ makes Christ an abettor of sin when Christians *are found to be sinners.* Paul denies the conclusion (cf Rom 6, 1–4).

2, 18: To return to observance of the law as the means to salvation would entangle one not only in inevitable transgressions of it but also in the admission that it was wrong to have abandoned the law in the first place.

2, 19: *Through the law I died to the law:* this is variously explained: the law revealed sin (Rom 7, 7–9) and led to death and then to belief in Christ; or, the law itself brought the insight that law cannot justify (16; Ps 143, 2); or, the "law of Christ" (6, 2) led to abandoning the Mosaic law; or, the law put Christ to death (cf 3, 13) and so provided a way to our salvation, through baptism into Christ, through which we die (*crucified with Christ;* see Rom 6, 6). Cf also 3, 19–25 on the role of the law in reference to salvation.

live for God. I have been crucified with Christ;
20 [g]yet I live, no longer I, but Christ lives in
me; insofar as I now live in the flesh, I live by
faith in the Son of God who has loved me and
given himself up for me. 21 [h]I do not nullify
the grace of God; for if justification comes
through the law, then Christ died for nothing.

## IV: FAITH AND LIBERTY

### CHAPTER 3

**Justification by Faith** 1 [i]*O stupid Galatians! Who has bewitched you, before whose
eyes Jesus Christ was publicly portrayed as crucified? 2 [j]*I want to learn only this from you:
did you receive the Spirit from works of the law,
or from faith in what you heard? 3 [k]*Are you
so stupid? After beginning with the Spirit, are
you now ending with the flesh? 4 *Did you
experience so many things in vain?—if indeed
it was in vain. 5 [l]Does, then, the one who
supplies the Spirit to you and works mighty
deeds among you do so from works of the law
or from faith in what you heard? 6 [m]*Thus
Abraham "believed God, and it was credited to
him as righteousness."

7 [n]*Realize then that it is those who
have faith who are children of Abraham.
8 [o]Scripture, which saw in advance that God
would justify the Gentiles by faith, foretold the
good news to Abraham, saying, "Through
you shall all the nations be blessed."
9 [p]Consequently, those who have faith are
blessed along with Abraham who had faith.
10 [q]*For all who depend on works of the law
are under a curse; for it is written, "Cursed be
everyone who does not persevere in doing all
the things written in the book of the law."
11 [r]And that no one is justified before God by
the law is clear, for "the one who is righteous
by faith will live." 12 [s]But the law does not
depend on faith; rather, "the one who does
these things will live by them." 13 [t]Christ ransomed us from the curse of the law by becoming
a curse for us, for it is written, "Cursed be
everyone who hangs on a tree," 14 [u]that the
blessing of Abraham might be extended to the
Gentiles through Christ Jesus, so that we might
receive the promise of the Spirit through faith.

**The Law Did Not Nullify the Promise**
15 [v]*Brothers, in human terms I say that no one
can annul or amend even a human will once
ratified. 16 [w]*Now the promises were made to
Abraham and to his descendant. It does not say,
"And to descendants," as referring to many,
but as referring to one, "And to your descendant," who is Christ. 17 [x]*This is what I mean:
the law, which came four hundred and thirty
years afterward, does not annul a covenant pre-

g 1, 4; Rom 8, 10-11; Col 3, 3-4.
h 5, 2.
i 5, 7; 1 Cor 1, 23.
j 2, 16 / 3, 14; Rom 10, 17.
k 5, 16-18.
l 2, 16.
m Gn 15, 6; Rom 4, 3; Jas 2, 23.
n 3, 29; Rom 4, 11-12 / Sir 44, 19-21.
o Gn 12, 3; 18, 17-19; Acts 3, 25.
p Rom 4, 16.
q Dt 27, 26; Jas 2, 10.
r 2, 16; Hb 2, 4; Rom 1, 17.
s Lv 18, 5; Rom 10, 5.
t Dt 21, 23; Rom 8, 3; 2 Cor 5, 21.
u 3, 2-3.5; Is 44, 3; Jl 3, 1-2; Acts 2, 33.
v Rom 3, 5 / Heb 9, 16-17.
w Gn 12, 7; 13, 15; 17, 8; 22, 17; 24, 7; Mt 1, 1.
x Ex 12, 40.

3, 1–14: Paul's contention that justification comes not through the law or the works of the law but by faith in Christ and in his death (2, 16.21) is supported by appeals to Christian experience (1–5) and to scripture (6–14). The gift of God's Spirit to the Galatians came from the gospel received in faith, not from doing what the law enjoins. The story of Abraham shows that faith in God brings *righteousness* (6; Gn 15, 6). The promise to Abraham (8; Gn 12, 3) extends to the Gentiles (14).

3, 1: *Stupid:* not just senseless, for they were in danger of deserting their salvation.

3, 2: *Faith in what you heard:* Paul's message received with faith. The Greek can also mean "the proclamation of the faith" or "a hearing that comes from faith."

3, 3: On the contrast of *Spirit* and *flesh,* cf Rom 8, 1–11. Having received the Spirit, they need not be circumcised now.

3, 4: *Experience so many things:* probably the *mighty deeds* of v 5 but possibly the experience of sufferings.

3, 6: *Abraham . . . righteousness:* see Gn 15, 6; Rom 4, 3. The Galatians like Abraham heard with faith and experienced justification. This first argument forms the basis for the further scriptural evidence that follows.

3, 7–9: *Faith* is what matters, for *Abraham* and the *children of Abraham,* in contrast to the claims of the opponents that circumcision and observance of the law are needed to bring the promised blessing of Gn 12, 3; cf Gn 18, 18; Sir 44, 21; Acts 3, 25.

3, 10–14: Those *who depend* not on promise and faith but *on works of the law are under a curse* because they do *not persevere in doing all the things written in the book of the law* (10; Dt 27, 26) in order to gain life (12; Lv 18, 5; cf Rom 10, 5). But scripture teaches that *no one is justified before God by the law* (11; Hb 2, 4, adapted from the Greek version of Habakkuk; cf Rom 1, 17; Heb 10, 38). Salvation, then, depends on faith in Christ who died on the cross (13), taking upon himself a curse found in Dt 21, 23 (about executed criminals hanged in public view), to free us from *the curse of the law* (13). That the Gentile Galatians have received the promised Spirit (14) by faith and in no other way returns the argument to the experience cited in vv 1–5.

3, 15–18: A third argument to support Paul's position that salvation is not through the law but by promise (1–14) comes from legal practice and scriptural history. A legal agreement or *human will,* duly *ratified,* is unalterable (15). God's *covenant* with *Abraham* and its repeated promises (Gn 12, 2–3.7; 13, 15; 17, 7–8; 22, 16–18; 24, 7) is not superseded by *the law,* which came much later, in the time of Moses. *The inheritance* (of the Spirit and the blessings) is by promise, not by law (18). Paul's argument hinges on the fact that the same Greek word, *diathēkē,* can be rendered as *will* or testament (15) and as *covenant* (17).

3, 16: Descendant: literally, "and to his seed." The Hebrew, as in Gn 12, 7; 15, 18; 22, 17–18, is a collective singular, traditionally rendered as a plural, *descendants,* but taken by Paul in its literal number to refer to *Christ* as descendant of Abraham.

3, 17: *Four hundred and thirty years afterward:* follows Ex 12, 40 in the Greek (Septuagint) version, in contrast to Gn 15, 13 and Acts 7, 6, for chronology.

viously ratified by God, so as to cancel the
promise. 18 [y]*For if the inheritance comes
from the law, it is no longer from a promise; but
God bestowed it on Abraham through a promise.

19 [z]*Why, then, the law? It was added for
transgressions, until the descendant came to
whom the promise had been made; it was promulgated by angels at the hand of a mediator.
20 [a]Now there is no mediator when only one
party is involved, and God is one. 21 [b]Is the
law then opposed to the promises [of God]? Of
course not! For if a law had been given that
could bring life, then righteousness would in
reality come from the law. 22 [c]But scripture
confined all things under the power of sin, that
through faith in Jesus Christ the promise might
be given to those who believe.

**What Faith Has Brought Us** 23 [d]*Before
faith came, we were held in custody under law,
confined for the faith that was to be revealed.
24 [e]*Consequently, the law was our disciplinarian for Christ, that we might be justified
by faith. 25 [f]But now that faith has come, we
are no longer under a disciplinarian. 26 [g]*For
through faith you are all children of God in
Christ Jesus. 27 [h]*For all of you who were
baptized into Christ have clothed yourselves
with Christ. 28 [i]There is neither Jew nor
Greek, there is neither slave nor free person,
there is not male and female; for you are all one
in Christ Jesus. 29 [j]And if you belong to
Christ, then you are Abraham's descendant,
heirs according to the promise.

## CHAPTER 4

**God's Free Children in Christ** 1 *I mean
that as long as the heir is not of age, he is no
different from a slave, although he is the owner
of everything, 2 but he is under the supervision
of guardians and administrators until the date set
by his father. 3 [k]*In the same way we also,
when we were not of age, were enslaved to the
elemental powers of the world. 4 [l]But when the
fullness of time had come, God sent his Son,
born of a woman, born under the law, 5 [m]to
ransom those under the law, so that we might
receive adoption. 6 [n]*As proof that you are
children, God sent the spirit of his Son into our
hearts, crying out, "Abba, Father!" 7 [o]So you
are no longer a slave but a child, and if a child
then also an heir, through God.

**Do Not Throw This Freedom Away**
8 [p]*At a time when you did not know God, you
became slaves to things that by nature are not
gods; 9 [q]but now that you have come to know
God, or rather to be known by God, how can
you turn back again to the weak and destitute

y Rom 4, 16; 11, 6.
z Rom 4, 15; 5, 20; 7, 7.13 / Acts 7, 38.53.
a Dt 6, 4.
b Rom 7, 7.10; 8, 2-4.
c Rom 3, 9-20.23; 11, 32.
d 4, 3-5; 5, 18.
e 2, 16.
f Rom 10, 4.
g 4, 5-7; Jn 1, 12; Rom 8, 14-17.
h Rom 6, 3; 13, 14; Eph 4, 24.
i Rom 10, 12; 1 Cor 12, 13; Col 3, 11.
j 3, 7.14.16.18; Rom 4, 16-17; 9, 7 / 4, 1.7; Rom 4, 13-14; 8, 17;Heb 6, 12; Jas 2, 5.
k 3, 23 / 4, 9; Col 2, 20.
l Mk 1, 15.
m 3, 13.26.
n 3, 26; Rom 8, 15.
o 3, 29; Rom 8, 16-17.
p 1 Cor 12, 2.
q 4, 3; Col 2, 20.

3, 18: This refutes the opponents' contention that the promises of God are fulfilled only as a reward for human observance of the law.

3, 19–22: A digression: if the Mosaic law, then, does not save or *bring life,* why was it given? Elsewhere, Paul says the law served to show what sin is (Rom 3, 20; 7, 7–8). Here the further implication is that the law in effect served to produce transgressions. Moreover, it was received at second hand *by angels,* through a *mediator,* not directly from God (19). The law does not, however, oppose God's purposes, for it carries out its function (22), so that *righteousness* comes by *faith* and *promise,* not by human works of the law.

3, 19: *The descendant:* Christ (16). *By angels:* Dt 33, 2–4 stressed their presence as enhancing the importance of the law; Paul uses their role to diminish its significance (cf Acts 7, 38.53). *A mediator:* Moses. But in a covenant of promise, where all depends on the one God, no mediator is needed (20).

3, 23–29: Paul adds a further argument in support of righteousness or justification by faith and through God's promise rather than by works of the law (2, 16; 3, 22): as *children of God, baptized into Christ,* the Galatians are all *Abraham's descendant* and *heirs* of *the promise* to Abraham (8.14.16–18.29). The teaching in 23–25, that since *faith* (Christianity) *has come, we are no longer under* the law, could be taken with the previous paragraph on the role of the Mosaic law, but it also fits here as a contrast between the situation *before faith* (23) and the results after faith has come (25–29).

3, 24–25: *Disciplinarian:* the Greek *paidagōgos* referred to a slave who escorted a child to school but did not teach or tutor; hence, a guardian or monitor. Applying this to the law fits the role of the law described in vv 19–25.

3, 26: *Children of God:* literally "sons," in contrast to the young child under the disciplinarian in vv 24–25. The term includes males and females (28). *Clothed yourselves with Christ:* literally, "have put on Christ"; cf Rom 13, 14; Eph 4, 24; Col 3, 10. Baptismal imagery, traceable to the Old Testament (Jb 29, 14; Is 59, 17) but also found in pagan mystery cults.

3, 27–28: Likely a formula used at baptism that expresses racial, social-economic, and sexual equality in Christ (cf Col 3, 11).

3, 27: *Clothed yourselves with Christ:* literally, "have put on Christ"; cf Rom 13, 14; Eph 4, 24; Col 3, 10. Baptismal imagery, traceable to the Old Testament (Jb 29, 14; Is 59, 17) but also found in pagan mystery cults.

4, 1–7: What Paul has argued in 3, 26–29 is now elaborated in terms of the Christian as *the heir* (1.7; cf 3, 18.29) freed from control by others. Again, as in 3, 2–5, the proof that Christians are children of God is the gift of the Spirit of Christ relating them intimately to God.

4, 1.3: *Not of age:* an infant or minor.

4, 3: *The elemental powers of the world:* while the term can refer to the "elements" like earth, air, fire, and water or to elementary forms of religion, the sense here is more likely that of celestial beings that were thought in pagan circles to control the world; cf 8; Col 2, 8.20.

4, 6: *Children:* see the note on 3, 26; here in contrast to the infant or young person *not of age* (1.3). *Abba:* cf Mk 14, 36 and the note; Rom 8, 15.

4, 8–11: On the basis of the arguments advanced from 3,

elemental powers? Do you want to be slaves to
them all over again? **10** [r]*You are observing
days, months, seasons, and years. **11** *I am
afraid on your account that perhaps I have labored for you in vain.

**Appeal to Former Loyalty** **12** [s]*I implore
you, brothers, be as I am, because I have also
become as you are. You did me no wrong;
**13** *you know that it was because of a physical
illness that I originally preached the gospel to
you, **14** and you did not show disdain or contempt because of the trial caused you by my
physical condition, but rather you received me
as an angel of God, as Christ Jesus. **15** *Where
now is that blessedness of yours? Indeed, I can
testify to you that, if it had been possible, you
would have torn out your eyes and given them
to me. **16** So now have I become your enemy
by telling you the truth? **17** [t]*They show interest in you, but not in a good way; they want to
isolate you, so that you may show interest in
them. **18** Now it is good to be shown interest
for good reason at all times, and not only when
I am with you. **19** [u]My children, for whom I am
again in labor until Christ be formed in you!
**20** I would like to be with you now and to
change my tone, for I am perplexed because of
you.

## An Allegory on Christian Freedom

**21** *Tell me, you who want to be under the law,
do you not listen to the law? **22** [v]For it is written that Abraham had two sons, one by the slave
woman and the other by the freeborn woman.
**23** [w]The son of the slave woman was born naturally, the son of the freeborn through a promise.
**24** [x]Now this is an allegory. These women represent two covenants. One was from Mount
Sinai, bearing children for slavery; this is Hagar. **25** *Hagar represents Sinai, a mountain in
Arabia; it corresponds to the present Jerusalem,
for she is in slavery along with her children.
**26** [y]But the Jerusalem above is freeborn, and
she is our mother. **27** [z]*For it is written:

"Rejoice, you barren one who bore no
children;
break forth and shout, you who were not
in labor;
for more numerous are the children of the
deserted one
than of her who has a husband."

**28** [a]Now you, brothers, like Isaac, are children
of the promise. **29** But just as then the child of
the flesh persecuted the child of the spirit, it is
the same now. **30** [b]But what does the scripture
say?

"Drive out the slave woman and her son!
For the son of the slave woman shall not
share the inheritance with the son"
of the freeborn. **31** [c]Therefore, brothers, we
are children not of the slave woman but of the
freeborn woman.

r Col 2, 16-20.
s 1 Cor 11, 1.
t 1, 7; 6, 12; Acts 20, 30.
u 1 Cor 4, 14-15; 2 Cor 6, 13; 1 Thes 2, 7-8.
v Gn 16, 15; 21, 2-3.
w Gn 17, 16; Rom 4, 19-20; 9, 7-9.
x 3, 17 / Ex 19, 20 / Gn 16, 1.
y Heb 12, 22; Rv 21, 2.
z Is 54, 1.
a Rom 9, 8.
b Gn 21, 10.
c 3, 29; Jn 8, 35.

*

1 through 4, 7, Paul now launches his appeal to the Galatians with the question, *how can you turn back* to the slavery of the law (9)? The question is posed with reference to bondage to the *elemental powers* (see the note on 4, 3) because the Galatians had originally been converted to Christianity from paganism, not Judaism (8). The use of the direct question is like 3, 3–5.

4, 8: *Things that by nature are not gods:* or "gods that by nature do not exist."

4, 10: This is likely a reference to ritual observances from the Old Testament, promoted by opponents: sabbaths or Yom Kippur, new moon, Passover or Pentecost, sabbatical years.

4, 11: Cf 2, 2. If the Galatians become *slaves . . . all over again* to the law (9), Paul will have worked in vain among them.

4, 12–20: A strongly personal section. Paul appeals to past ties between the Galatians and himself. He speaks sharply of the opponents (17–18) and pastorally to the Galatians (19–20).

4, 12: *Because I have also become as you are:* a terse phrase in Greek, meaning "Be as I, Paul, am," i.e., living by faith, independent of the law, for, in spite of my background in Judaism (1, 13), I have become as you Galatians are now, a brother in Christ.

4, 13: *Physical illness:* because its nature is not described, some assume an eye disease (15); others, epilepsy; some relate it to 2 Cor 12, 7–9. *Originally:* this may also be translated "formerly" or "on the first (of two) visit(s)"; cf Acts 16, 6; 18, 23.

4, 15: *That blessedness of yours:* possibly a reference to the Galatians' initial happy reception of Paul (14) and of his gospel (1, 6; 3, 1–4) and their felicitation at such blessedness, but the phrase could also refer ironically to earlier praise by Paul of the Galatians, no longer possible when they turn from the gospel to the claims of the opponents (17–18; 1, 7). If the word is a more literal reference to a beatitude, Gal 3, 26–28 may be in view.

4, 17: *Isolate you:* that is, from the blessings of the gospel and/or from Paul.

4, 21–31: Paul supports his appeal for the gospel (9; 1, 6–9; 2, 16; 3, 2) by a further argument from scripture (cf 3, 6–18). It involves the relationship of *Abraham* (3, 6–16) to his wife, Sarah, the *freeborn woman,* and to Hagar, *the slave woman,* and the contrast between the sons born to each, *Isaac,* child of promise, and Ishmael, son of Hagar (Gn 16 and 21). Only through Isaac is the promise of God preserved. This *allegory* (24), with its equation of the Sinai covenant and Mosaic law with slavery and of the promise of God with freedom, Paul uses only in light of previous arguments. His quotation of Gn 21, 10 at v 30 suggests on a scriptural basis that the Galatians should expel those who are troubling them (1, 7).

4, 25: *Hagar represents Sinai . . . :* some manuscripts have what seems a geographical note, "For Sinai is a mountain in Arabia."

4, 27: Is 54, 1 in the Septuagint translation is applied to Sarah as the *barren one* (in Gn 15) who ultimately becomes the mother not only of Isaac but now of numerous children, i.e., of all those who believe, the *children of the promise* (28).

## V: EXHORTATION TO CHRISTIAN LIVING

### CHAPTER 5

**The Importance of Faith** **1** [d]*For freedom Christ set us free; so stand firm and do not submit again to the yoke of slavery.

**2** [e]It is I, Paul, who am telling you that if you have yourselves circumcised, Christ will be of no benefit to you. **3** [f]*Once again I declare to every man who has himself circumcised that he is bound to observe the entire law. **4** You are separated from Christ, you who are trying to be justified by law; you have fallen from grace. **5** [g]For through the Spirit, by faith, we await the hope of righteousness. **6** [h]*For in Christ Jesus, neither circumcision nor uncircumcision counts for anything, but only faith working through love.

**Be Not Misled** **7** *You were running well; who hindered you from following [the] truth? **8** [i]*That enticement does not come from the one who called you. **9** [j]A little yeast leavens the whole batch of dough. **10** [k]I am confident of you in the Lord that you will not take a different view, and that the one who is troubling you will bear the condemnation, whoever he may be. **11** [l]*As for me, brothers, if I am still preaching circumcision, why am I still being persecuted? In that case, the stumbling block of the cross has been abolished. **12** *Would that those who are upsetting you might also castrate themselves!

**Freedom for Service** **13** [m]*For you were called for freedom, brothers. But do not use this freedom as an opportunity for the flesh; rather, serve one another through love. **14** [n]*For the whole law is fulfilled in one statement, namely, "You shall love your neighbor as yourself." **15** But if you go on biting and devouring one another, beware that you are not consumed by one another.

**16** [o]*I say, then: live by the Spirit and you will certainly not gratify the desire of the flesh. **17** [p]For the flesh has desires against the Spirit, and the Spirit against the flesh; these are opposed to each other, so that you may not do what you want. **18** [q]But if you are guided by the Spirit, you are not under the law. **19** [r]*Now the works of the flesh are obvious: immorality, impurity, licentiousness, **20** [s]idolatry, sorcery, hatreds, rivalry, jealousy, outbursts of fury, acts of selfishness, dissensions, factions, **21** *occasions of envy, drinking bouts, orgies, and the like. I warn you, as I warned you before, that those who do such things will not inherit the kingdom of God. **22** [t]In contrast, the fruit of the Spirit is love, joy, peace, patience, kindness, generosity, faithfulness, **23** [u]gentleness, self-control. Against such there is no law. **24** [v]Now those who belong to Christ [Jesus] have crucified their flesh with its passions and desires. **25** [w]If we live in the Spirit, let us also follow the Spirit. **26** [x]Let us not be conceited, provoking one another, envious of one another.

---

d 2, 4; 4, 5.9; Jn 8, 32.36.
e 2, 21; Acts 15, 1-29.
f 3, 10; Rom 2, 25; Jas 2, 10.
g Rom 8, 23.25.
h 3, 28; 6, 15; 1 Cor 7, 19.
i 1, 6.
j 1 Cor 5, 6.
k 1, 7.
l 6, 12.14; 1 Cor 1, 23.
m 5, 1 / Rom 6, 18; 1 Cor 8, 9; 1 Pt 2, 16.
n Lv 19, 18; Mt 22, 39; Rom 13, 8-10.
o 5, 24-25; Rom 8, 5.
p Rom 7, 15.23; 8, 6.
q Rom 6, 14; 8, 14.
r Rom 1, 29-31; 1 Cor 6, 9-10; Col 3, 5-6.8.
s Rv 22, 15.
t Eph 5, 9 / 1 Cor 13, 4-7; 2 Cor 6, 6; 1 Tm 4, 12; 2 Pt 1, 6.
u 1 Tm 1, 9.
v 2, 19; Rom 6, 6; 8, 13.
w 5, 16.
x Phil 2, 3.

*

5, 1–6: Paul begins the exhortations, continuing through 6, 10, with an appeal to the Galatians to side with freedom instead of slavery (1). He reiterates his message of justification or righteousness by faith instead of law and circumcision (2–5); cf 2, 16; 3, 3. Faith, not circumcision, is what counts (6).

5, 1: *Freedom:* Paul stresses as the conclusion from the allegory in 4, 21–31 this result of Christ's work for us. It is a principle previously mentioned (2, 4), the responsible use of which v 13 will emphasize.

5, 3: Cf 3, 10–12. Just as those who seek to live by the law must carry out all its contents, so those who have faith and live by promise must stand firm in their freedom (1.13).

5, 6: Cf Rom 2, 25–26; 1 Cor 7, 19; Gal 6, 15. The Greek for *faith working through love* or "faith expressing itself through love" can also be rendered as "faith energized by (God's) love."

5, 7–12: Paul addresses the Galatians directly: with questions (7.11), a proverb (9), a statement (8), and biting sarcasm (12), seeking to persuade the Galatians to break with those trying to add law and circumcision to Christ as a basis for salvation.

5, 7: *Running well:* as in an athletic contest; cf 2, 2; 1 Cor 9, 24–26; Phil 2, 16; 3, 14.

5, 8: *The one who called you:* see the note on 1, 6.

5, 11: *Preaching circumcision:* this could refer to Paul's pre-Christian period (possibly as a missionary for Judaism); more probably it arose as a charge from opponents, based perhaps on the story in Acts 16, 1–3 that Paul had circumcised Timothy "on account of the Jews." Unlike the Gentile Titus in Gal 2, 3, Timothy was the son of a Jewish mother. *The stumbling block of the cross:* cf 1 Cor 1, 23.

5, 12: A sarcastic half-wish that their knife would go beyond mere circumcision; cf Phil 3, 2 and the note there.

5, 13–26: In light of another reminder of the freedom of the gospel (13; cf 1), Paul elaborates on what believers are called to do and be: they fulfill the law by love of neighbor (14–15), walking in the Spirit (16–26), as is illustrated by concrete *fruit of the Spirit* in their lives.

5, 13: *Serve . . . through love:* cf v 6.

5, 14: Lv 19, 18, emphasized by Jesus (Mt 22, 39; Lk 10, 27); cf Rom 13, 8–10.

5, 16–25: *Spirit . . . flesh:* cf 3, 3 and the note on Rom 8, 1–13.

5, 19–23: Such lists of vices and virtues (cf Rom 1, 29–31; 1 Cor 6, 9–10) were common in the ancient world. Paul contrasts *works of the flesh* (19) with *fruit* (not "works") *of the Spirit* (22). Not law, but the Spirit, leads to such traits.

5, 21: *Occasions of envy:* after the Greek word *phthonoi,* "envies," some manuscripts add a similar sounding one, *phonoi,* "murders."

## CHAPTER 6

### Life in the Community of Christ

1 [y]*Brothers, even if a person is caught in some
transgression, you who are spiritual should correct that one in a gentle spirit, looking to yourself, so that you also may not be tempted.
2 [z]*Bear one another's burdens, and so you
will fulfill the law of Christ. 3 [a]For if anyone
thinks he is something when he is nothing, he
is deluding himself. 4 *Each one must examine
his own work, and then he will have reason to
boast with regard to himself alone, and not with
regard to someone else; 5 [b]for each will bear
his own load.

6 [c]*One who is being instructed in the word
should share all good things with his instructor.
7 Make no mistake: God is not mocked, for a
person will reap only what he sows, 8 [d]because
the one who sows for his flesh will reap corruption from the flesh, but the one who sows for the
spirit will reap eternal life from the spirit.
9 [e]Let us not grow tired of doing good, for in
due time we shall reap our harvest, if we do not
give up. 10 [f]*So then, while we have the opportunity, let us do good to all, but especially
to those who belong to the family of the faith.

## *VI: CONCLUSION*

**Final Appeal** 11 [g]*See with what large letters I am writing to you in my own hand!
12 [h]*It is those who want to make a good appearance in the flesh who are trying to compel
you to have yourselves circumcised, only that
they may not be persecuted for the cross of
Christ. 13 *Not even those having themselves
circumcised observe the law themselves; they
only want you to be circumcised so that they
may boast of your flesh. 14 [i]*But may I never
boast except in the cross of our Lord Jesus
Christ, through which the world has been crucified to me, and I to the world. 15 [j]*For neither
does circumcision mean anything, nor does uncircumcision, but only a new creation.
16 [k]*Peace and mercy be to all who follow this
rule and to the Israel of God.

17 [l]*From now on, let no one make troubles
for me; for I bear the marks of Jesus on my
body.

18 [m]The grace of our Lord Jesus Christ be
with your spirit, brothers. Amen.

y Mt 18, 15; Jas 5, 19 / 1 Cor 10, 12-13.
z Col 3, 13 / 1 Cor 9, 21.
a 1 Cor 3, 18; 8, 2; 2 Cor 12, 11.
b Rom 14, 12.
c 1 Cor 9, 14.
d Prv 11, 18; Rom 8, 6.13.
e 2 Thes 3, 13; Heb 12, 1-3.
f 1 Thes 5, 15.
g 1 Cor 16, 21.
h 5, 2.11.
i 2, 20; 1 Cor 2, 2.
j 5, 6; 1 Cor 7, 19 / 2 Cor 5, 17.
k Pss 125, 5; 128, 6.
l 2 Cor 4, 10.
m Phil 4, 23; 2 Tm 4, 22; Phlm 25.

*

6, 1–10: The ethical exhortations begun at 5, 1 continue with a variety of admonitions to the community (*brothers:* see the note on 1, 2). Nearly every sentence contains a separate item of practical advice; the faith and freedom of the gospel underlie each maxim. Tensions and temptation within communal life have previously been addressed in 5, 15.26, and v 1 continues with a case in which *a person is caught in some transgression* such as those in 5, 19–21; cf 2, 17.

6, 2: *The law of Christ:* cf Rom 8, 2; 1 Cor 9, 21; Gal 5, 14. The principle of love for others is meant. *To bear one another's burdens* is to "serve one another through love" (5, 13).

6, 4–5: Self-examination is the cure for self-deception. Compare what you are with what you were before, and give the glory to God; cf Rom 6, 19–22. *Load:* used elsewhere of a soldier's pack. Correcting one's own conduct avoids burdening others with it.

6, 6: Implies oral instruction in the faith by catechists; these are to be remunerated for their service; cf Rom 15, 27.

6, 10: *The family of the faith:* the Christian household or church. Doing good has a universal object (*to all*), but the local community makes specific the reality of those to be served.

6, 11–18: A postscript in Paul's own hand, as was his practice (see 1 Cor 16, 21; 2 Thes 3, 17). Paul summarizes his appeal against his opponents (12–13), then returns to his message of glorying in the cross, not in circumcision, as the means of salvation (14–15; cf 5, 11). A benediction follows at v 16. In the polemical spirit that the attack on his apostleship called forth (1, 11—2, 21), Paul reasserts his missionary credentials (17) before giving a final benediction (18).

6, 11: *Large letters:* in contrast to the finer hand of the scribe who wrote the letter up to this point. The larger Greek letters make Paul's message even more emphatic. Some find a hint of poor eyesight on Paul's part. See the note on 4, 13.

6, 12–15: The Jewish Christian opponents wished *not to be persecuted,* possibly by Jews. But since Judaism seems to have had a privileged status as a religion in the Roman empire, circumcised Christians might, if taken as Jews, thereby avoid persecution from the Romans. In any case, Paul instead stresses conformity with *the cross of our Lord Jesus Christ;* cf 2, 19–21; 5, 11.

6, 13: *Those having themselves circumcised:* other manuscripts read, "those who have had themselves circumcised."

6, 14: *Through which:* or "through whom."

6, 15: *New creation:* or "new creature"; cf 2 Cor 5, 17.

6, 16: *This rule:* the principle in vv 14 and 15. *The Israel of God:* while the church may be meant (the phrase can be translated "to all who follow this rule, even the Israel of God"; cf 10; 1 Cor 10, 18), the reference may also be to God's ancient people, Israel; cf Pss 125, 5; 128, 6.

6, 17: *The marks of Jesus:* slaves were often branded by marks (*stigmata*) burned into their flesh to show to whom they belonged; so also were devotees of pagan gods. Paul implies that instead of outdated circumcision, his body bears the scars of his apostolic labors (2 Cor 11, 22–31), such as floggings (Acts 16, 22; 2 Cor 11, 25) and stonings (Acts 14, 19), that mark him as belonging to the Christ who suffered (cf Rom 6, 3; 2 Cor 4, 10; Col 1, 24) and will protect his own.

# THE LETTER TO THE

# EPHESIANS

## INTRODUCTION

*Ephesians is the great Pauline letter about the church. It deals, however, not so much with a congregation in the city of Ephesus in Asia Minor as with the worldwide church, the head of which is Christ (4, 15), the purpose of which is to be the instrument for making God's plan of salvation known throughout the universe (3, 9–10). Yet this ecclesiology is anchored in God's saving love, shown in Jesus Christ (2, 4–10), and the whole of redemption is rooted in the plan and accomplishment of the triune God (1, 3–14). The language is often that of doxology (1, 3–14) and prayer (cf 1, 15–23; 3, 14–19), indeed of liturgy and hymns (3, 20–21; 5, 14).*

*The majestic chapters of Ephesians emphasize the unity in the church of Christ that has come about for both Jews and Gentiles within God's household (1, 15—2, 22, especially 2, 11–22) and indeed the "seven unities" of church, Spirit, hope; one Lord, faith, and baptism; and the one God (4, 4–6). Yet the concern is not with the church for its own sake but rather as the means for mission in the world (3, 1—4, 24). The gifts Christ gives its members are to lead to growth and renewal (4, 7–24). Ethical admonition is not lacking either; all aspects of human life and relationships are illumined by the light of Christ (4, 25—6, 20).*

*The letter is seemingly addressed by Paul to Christians in Ephesus (1, 1), a place where the apostle labored for well over two years (Acts 19, 10). Yet there is a curiously impersonal tone to the writing for a community with which Paul was so intimately acquainted (cf 3, 2 and 4, 21). There are no personal greetings (cf 6, 23). More significantly, important early manuscripts omit the words "in Ephesus" (see the note on 1, 1). Many therefore regard the letter as an encyclical or "circular letter" sent to a number of churches in Asia Minor, the addressees to be designated in each place by its bearer, Tychicus (6, 21–22). Others think that Ephesians is the letter referred to in Colossians 4, 16 as "to the Laodiceans."*

*Paul, who is designated as the sole author at 1, 1, is described in almost unparalleled terms with regard to the significant role he has in God's plan for bringing the Gentiles to faith in Christ (3, 1–12). Yet at the time of writing he is clearly in prison (3, 1; 4, 1; 6, 20), suffering afflictions (3, 13). Traditionally this "Captivity Epistle" has, along with Colossians, Philippians, and Philemon, been dated to an imprisonment in Rome, likely in A.D. 61–63. Others appeal to an earlier imprisonment, perhaps in Caesarea (Acts 23, 27—27, 2). Since the early nineteenth century, however, much of critical scholarship has considered the letter's style and use of words (especially when compared with Colossians), its concept of the church, and other points of doctrine put forward by the writer as grounds for serious doubt about authorship by Paul. The letter may then be the work of a secretary writing at the apostle's direction or of a later disciple who sought to develop Paul's ideas for a new situation around A.D. 80–100.*

*The principal divisions of the Letter to the Ephesians are the following:*

*I. Address (1, 1–14)*
*II. Unity of the Church in Christ (1, 15—2, 22)*
*III. World Mission of the Church (3, 1—4, 24)*
*IV. Daily Conduct, an Expression of Unity (4, 25—6, 20)*
*V. Conclusion (6, 21–24)*

## *I: ADDRESS*

### CHAPTER 1

**Greeting** 1 [a]*Paul, an apostle of Christ
Jesus by the will of God, to the holy ones who
are [in Ephesus] faithful in Christ Jesus:
2 [b]grace to you and peace from God our Father
and the Lord Jesus Christ.

**The Father's Plan of Salvation**
3 [c]*Blessed be the God and Father of our Lord
Jesus Christ, who has blessed us in Christ with
every spiritual blessing in the heavens, 4 [d]as he
chose us in him, before the foundation of the
world, to be holy and without blemish before
him. In love 5 [e]he destined us for adoption to
himself through Jesus Christ, in accord with the
favor of his will, 6 [f]for the praise of the glory
of his grace that he granted us in the beloved.

**Fulfillment through Christ** 7 [g]In him we
have redemption by his blood, the forgiveness
of transgressions, in accord with the riches of
his grace 8 [h]that he lavished upon us. In all
wisdom and insight, 9 [i]*he has made known to
us the mystery of his will in accord with his
favor that he set forth in him 10 [j]as a plan for
the fullness of times, to sum up all things in
Christ, in heaven and on earth.

**Inheritance through the Spirit** 11 [k]In
him we were also chosen, destined in accord
with the purpose of the One who accomplishes
all things according to the intention of his will,
12 *so that we might exist for the praise of his
glory, we who first hoped in Christ. 13 [l]*In
him you also, who have heard the word of truth,
the gospel of your salvation, and have believed
in him, were sealed with the promised holy
Spirit, 14 [m]*which is the first installment of our
inheritance toward redemption as God's possession, to the praise of his glory.

## *II: UNITY OF THE CHURCH IN CHRIST*

**The Church as Christ's Body**
15 [n]*Therefore, I, too, hearing of your faith in
the Lord Jesus and of your love for all the holy
ones, 16 [o]do not cease giving thanks for you,
remembering you in my prayers, 17 [p]that the
God of our Lord Jesus Christ, the Father of
glory, may give you a spirit of wisdom and
revelation resulting in knowledge of him.
18 [q]May the eyes of [your] hearts be enlight-

a Rom 1, 7; 1 Cor 1, 1-2; Col 1, 1.
b Col 1, 2.
c 2, 6; 2 Cor 1, 3.
d 5, 27; Jn 15, 16; 17, 24; Rom 8, 29; 2 Thes 2, 13.
e Jn 1, 12; 1 Jn 3, 1.
f Mt 3, 17; Col 1, 13.
g 2, 7-13; Rom 3, 24; Col 1, 14.20.
h Col 1, 9.
i 3, 3.9; Rom 16, 25.
j Gal 4, 4; Col 1, 16.20.
k Is 46, 10; Rom 8, 28; Col 1, 12; Rv 4, 11.
l 4, 30; Acts 2, 33; Col 1, 5-6.
m 2 Cor 1, 22; 5, 5.
n Col 1, 3-4; Phlm 4-5.
o Col 1, 3.9.
p 3, 14.16; Col 1, 9-10; 1 Jn 5, 20.
q 4, 4; Col 1, 12.27.

*

1, 1–2: For the epistolary form used at the beginning of letters, see the note on Rom 1, 1–7. Twenty-two of the thirty Greek words in vv 1–2 also occur in Col 1, 1–2.

1, 1: *[In Ephesus]:* the phrase is lacking in important early witnesses such as P46 (3rd cent.), and Sinaiticus and Vaticanus (4th cent.), appearing in the latter two as a fifth-century addition. Basil and Origen mention its absence from manuscripts. See Introduction. Without the phrase, the Greek can be rendered, as in Col 1, 2, "to the holy ones and faithful brothers in Christ."

1, 3–14: While a Pauline letter usually continues after the greeting with a prayer of thanksgiving, as in 15–23 below, Ephesians first inserts a blessing of God for the blessings Christians have experienced, as in 2 Cor 1, 3–4 and 1 Pt 1, 3–12. The blessing here, akin to a Jewish *berakah,* is rich in images almost certainly drawn from hymns and liturgy. Many ideas here are also found in Col 1, 3–23. Certain phrases are frequently repeated, such as *in Christ* (3.10.12) or *in him* (4.7.9.11.13) or *in the Beloved* (6) and *(for) the praise of (his) glory* (6.12.14). Some terms like *chose* (4) and *destined* (5) reflect Old Testament theology (Dt 7, 7; 9, 4–6; 23, 5) or Pauline themes (*redemption,* 7.14; *grace,* 6.7) or specific emphases in Col (*forgiveness,* Col 1, 14).

A triadic structure is discernible in vv 3–14: *God* the *Father* (3–6.8.11), *Christ* (3.5.7–10.12), and the *Spirit* (13–14). The spiritual blessings Christians have received through Christ (3) are gratefully enumerated: the call to holiness (4; cf Col 1, 22); the gift of divine *adoption* establishing a unique spiritual relationship with God the Father through Christ (5; cf Gal 4, 5); liberation from sin through Christ's sacrificial death (7); revelation of God's plan of salvation in Christ (9; cf 3, 3–4; Rom 16, 25); the gift of election and faith in Christ bestowed upon Jewish Christians (see the note on 12, *we who first hoped in Christ*); and finally, the same gift granted to Gentiles (13, *you also*). In the Christ-centered faith and existence of the Christian communities the apostle sees the predetermined *plan* of God to bring all creation under the final rule of Christ (4–5.9–10) being *made known* (9) and carried through, to God's glory (6.12.14).

1, 3: *In the heavens:* literally, "in the heavenlies" or "in the heavenly places," a term in Eph for the divine realm.

1, 9: *Mystery:* as in Rom 16, 25; Col 1, 26.27 and elsewhere, a secret of God now revealed in the *plan* to save and *sum up all things in Christ* (10); cf 3, 3–6.

1, 12: *We who first hoped:* probably Jewish Christians (contrast 13, *you,* the Gentiles); possibly the people of Israel, "we who already enjoyed the hope of Christ," or perhaps present hope in contrast to future redemption (cf 14).

1, 13: *Sealed:* by God, in baptism; cf 4, 30; 2 Cor 1, 22.

1, 14: *First installment:* down payment by God on full salvation, as at 2 Cor 1, 22.

1, 15–23: See the note on Rom 1, 8 for the thanksgiving form in a letter. Much of the content parallels thoughts in Col 1, 3–20. The prayer moves from God and Christ (17.20–21) to the Ephesians (17–19) and the church (22–23). Paul asks that the blessing imparted by God the Father (3) to the Ephesians will be strengthened in them through the message of the gospel (13.17–19). Those blessings are seen in the context of God's *might* in establishing the sovereignty of Christ over all other creatures (19–21) and in appointing him *head* of the church (22–23). For the allusion to angelic spirits in v 21, see Rom 8, 38 and Col 1, 16. Here, as in 1 Cor 15, 24–25 and Col 2, 15, every such *principality* and *power* is made subject to Christ.

1, 15: *Your faith . . . your love:* some manuscripts omit the latter phrase, but cf Col 1, 4.

ened, that you may know what is the hope that
belongs to his call, what are the riches of glory
in his inheritance among the holy ones, **19** [r]and
what is the surpassing greatness of his power for
us who believe, in accord with the exercise of
his great might, **20** [s]which he worked in Christ,
raising him from the dead and seating him at his
right hand in the heavens, **21** [t]far above every
principality, authority, power, and dominion,
and every name that is named not only in this
age but also in the one to come. **22** [u]And he put
all things beneath his feet and gave him as head
over all things to the church, **23** [v]*which is his
body, the fullness of the one who fills all things
in every way.

## CHAPTER 2

### Generosity of God's Plan

**1** [w]*You were
dead in your transgressions and sins **2** [x]*in
which you once lived following the age of this
world, following the ruler of the power of the
air, the spirit that is now at work in the disobedient. **3** [y]All of us once lived among them in the
desires of our flesh, following the wishes of the
flesh and the impulses, and we were by nature
children of wrath, like the rest. **4** But God, who
is rich in mercy, because of the great love he had
for us, **5** [z]*even when we were dead in our
transgressions, brought us to life with Christ (by
grace you have been saved), **6** [a]raised us up
with him, and seated us with him in the heavens
in Christ Jesus, **7** [b]that in the ages to come he
might show the immeasurable riches of his
grace in his kindness to us in Christ Jesus.
**8** [c]For by grace you have been saved through
faith, and this is not from you; it is the gift of
God; **9** [d]it is not from works, so no one may
boast. **10** [e]For we are his handiwork, created in
Christ Jesus for the good works that God has
prepared in advance, that we should live in
them.

### One in Christ

**11** *Therefore, remember
that at one time you, Gentiles in the flesh, called
the uncircumcision by those called the circumcision, which is done in the flesh by human hands,
**12** [f]*were at that time without Christ, alienated
from the community of Israel and strangers to
the covenants of promise, without hope and
without God in the world. **13** [g]But now in
Christ Jesus you who once were far off have
become near by the blood of Christ.
**14** [h]*For he is our peace, he who made both

r 2 Cor 13, 4; Col 1, 11; 2, 12.
s Ps 110, 1; Heb 1, 3.
t Phil 2, 9; Col 1, 16; 1 Pt 3, 22.
u 4, 15; Ps 8, 7; Mt 28, 18; Col 1, 18.
v 4, 10.12; Rom 12, 5; 1 Cor 12, 27; Col 1, 19.
w Col 1, 21; 2, 13.
x 6, 12; Jn 12, 31; Col 1, 13.
y Col 3, 6-7.
z Rom 5, 8; 6, 13; Col 2, 13.
a Rom 8, 10-11; Phil 3, 20; Col 2, 12.
b 1, 7.
c Rom 3, 24; Gal 2, 16.
d 1 Cor 1, 29.
e 4, 24; Ti 2, 14.
f Rom 9, 4; Col 1, 21.27
g 2, 17; Is 57, 19; Col 1, 20.
h Gal 3, 28.

*

1, 23: *His body:* the church (22); cf the note on Col 1, 18. Only in Eph and Col is Christ the *head* of the *body,* in contrast to the view in 1 Cor 12 and Rom 12, 4–8 where Christ is equated with the entire body or community. *Fullness:* see the note on Col 1, 19. Some take *the one who fills* as God, others as Christ (cf 4, 10). If in Christ "dwells the fullness of the deity bodily" (Col 2, 9), then, as God "fills" Christ, Christ in turn fills the church and the believer (3, 19; 5, 18). But the difficult phrases here may also allow the church to be viewed as the "complement" of Christ who is "being filled" as God's plan for the universe is carried out through the church (cf 3, 9–10).

2, 1–22: The gospel of *salvation* (1, 13) that God *worked in Christ* (1, 20) is reiterated in terms of what God's *great love* (4), expressed in Christ, means for us. The passage sometimes addresses *you,* Gentiles (1–2.8.11–13.19.22), but other times speaks of *all of us* who believe (3–7.10.14.18). In urging people to *remember* their grim past when they were *dead* in sins (1–3.11–12) and what they are *now in Christ* (4–10.13), the author sees both Jew and Gentile reconciled with God, now *one new person,* a new humanity, *one body, the household of God, a temple* and *dwelling place* of God's Spirit (15–16.19–22). The presentation falls into two parts, the second stressing more the meaning for the church.

2, 1–10: The recipients of Paul's letter have experienced, in their redemption from *transgressions and sins,* the effect of Christ's supremacy over the power of the devil (1–2; cf 6, 11–12), who rules not from the netherworld but from the *air* between God in heaven and human beings on earth. Both Jew and Gentile have experienced, through Christ, God's free gift of salvation that already marks them for a future heavenly destiny (3–7). The language *dead, raised us up,* and *seated us . . . in the heavens* closely parallels Jesus' own passion and Easter experience. The terms in vv 8–9 describe salvation in the way Paul elsewhere speaks of justification: *by grace, through faith, the gift of God, not from works;* cf Gal 2, 16–21; Rom 3, 24–28. Christians are a newly created people in Christ, fashioned by God for a life of goodness (10).

2, 1–7: These verses comprise one long sentence in Greek, the main verb coming in v 5, God *brought us to life,* the object you/us *dead in . . . transgressions* being repeated in 1 and 5; cf Col 2, 13.

2, 2: *Age of this world:* or "aeon," a term found in gnostic thought, possibly synonymous with the *rulers of this world,* but also reflecting the Jewish idea of "two ages," this present evil age and "the age to come"; cf 1 Cor 3, 19; 5, 10; 7, 31; Gal 1, 4; Ti 2, 12. *The disobedient:* literally, "the sons of disobedience," a Semitism as at Is 30, 9.

2, 5: Our relation through baptism *with Christ,* the risen Lord, is depicted in terms of realized eschatology, as already exaltation, though v 7 brings in the future aspect too.

2, 11–22: The Gentiles lacked Israel's messianic expectation, lacked the various *covenants* God made with *Israel,* lacked *hope* of salvation and knowledge of the true *God* (11–12); but through Christ all these religious barriers between Jew and Gentile have been transcended (13–14) by the abolition of the Mosaic covenant-law (15) for the sake of uniting Jew and Gentile into a single religious community (15–16), imbued with the same holy *Spirit* and worshiping the same *Father* (18). The Gentiles are now included in God's *household* (19) as it arises upon the *foundation* of *apostles* assisted by those endowed with the prophetic gift (3, 5), the preachers of Christ (20; cf 1 Cor 12, 28). With Christ as the *capstone* (20; cf Is 28, 16; Mt 21, 42), they are being built into the holy *temple* of God's people where the divine presence dwells (21–22).

2, 12: *The community of Israel:* or "commonwealth"; cf 4, 18. *The covenants:* cf Rom 9, 4: with Abraham, with Moses, with David.

2, 14–16: The elaborate imagery here combines pictures of Christ as *our peace* (Is 9, 5), his crucifixion, the ending of

one and broke down the dividing wall of enmity, through his flesh, 15 [i]*abolishing the law
with its commandments and legal claims, that
he might create in himself one new person in
place of the two, thus establishing peace,
16 [j]and might reconcile both with God, in one
body, through the cross, putting that enmity to
death by it. 17 [k]He came and preached peace
to you who were far off and peace to those who
were near, 18 [l]for through him we both have
access in one Spirit to the Father.
19 [m]So then you are no longer strangers and
sojourners, but you are fellow citizens with the
holy ones and members of the household of
God, 20 [n]*built upon the foundation of the
apostles and prophets, with Christ Jesus himself
as the capstone. 21 [o]Through him the whole
structure is held together and grows into a temple sacred in the Lord; 22 [p]in him you also are
being built together into a dwelling place of God
in the Spirit.

# *III: WORLD MISSION OF THE CHURCH*

## CHAPTER 3

### Commission to Preach God's Plan

1 [q]*Because of this, I, Paul, a prisoner of
Christ [Jesus] for you Gentiles— 2 [r]*if, as I
suppose, you have heard of the stewardship of
God's grace that was given to me for your benefit, 3 [s]*[namely, that] the mystery was made
known to me by revelation, as I have written
briefly earlier. 4 When you read this you can
understand my insight into the mystery of
Christ, 5 [t]which was not made known to human beings in other generations as it has now
been revealed to his holy apostles and prophets
by the Spirit, 6 [u]that the Gentiles are coheirs,
members of the same body, and copartners in
the promise in Christ Jesus through the gospel.
7 [v]Of this I became a minister by the gift of
God's grace that was granted me in accord with
the exercise of his power. 8 [w]To me, the very
least of all the holy ones, this grace was given,
to preach to the Gentiles the inscrutable riches
of Christ, 9 [x]*and to bring to light [for all] what
is the plan of the mystery hidden from ages past
in God who created all things, 10 [y]*so that the
manifold wisdom of God might now be made
known through the church to the principalities
and authorities in the heavens. 11 This was according to the eternal purpose that he accomplished in Christ Jesus our Lord, 12 [z]in whom
we have boldness of speech and confidence of
access through faith in him. 13 [a]So I ask you
not to lose heart over my afflictions for you; this
is your glory.

**Prayer for the Readers** 14 *For this reason I kneel before the Father, 15 from whom
every family in heaven and on earth is named,
16 [b]that he may grant you in accord with the
riches of his glory to be strengthened with power through his Spirit in the inner self, 17 [c]and

i 2 Cor 5, 17; Col 2, 14.
j Col 1, 20.22.
k Is 57, 19; Zec 9, 10.
l 3, 12.
m Heb 12, 22-23.
n Is 28, 16; Rv 21, 14.
o 1 Cor 3, 16; Col 2, 19.
p 1 Pt 2, 5.
q Phil 1, 7.13; Col 1, 24-29; 4, 18; Phlm 1, 9; 2 Tm 2, 9.
r Col 1, 25.
s 1, 9-10; Col 1, 26.
t Col 1, 26.
u 2, 13.18-19.
v Rom 15, 15; Col 1, 25.29.
w 1 Cor 15, 8-10; Gal 1, 16; 2, 7-9.
x Rom 16, 25; Col 1, 26-27.
y 1 Pt 1, 12.
z Rom 5, 1-2; Heb 4, 16.
a Col 1, 22.24; 2 Tm 2, 10.
b 6, 10; Rom 7, 22; 2 Cor 4, 16; Col 1, 11.
c Jn 14, 23; Col 1, 23; 2, 7.

*

the Mosaic law (cf Col 2, 14), reconciliation (2 Cor 5, 18–21), and the destruction of *the dividing wall* such as kept people from God in the temple or a barrier in the heavens.

2, 15: *One new person:* a corporate body, the Christian community, made up of Jews and Gentiles, replacing ancient divisions; cf Rom 1, 16.

2, 20: *Capstone:* the Greek can also mean cornerstone or keystone.

3, 1–13: Paul reflects on his mission to the Gentiles. He alludes to his call and appointment to the apostolic office (2–3) and how his *insight* through revelation, as well as that of the other apostles and charismatic prophets in the church (4–5), has deepened understanding of God's plan of salvation in Christ. Paul is the special herald (7) of a new *promise* to the *Gentiles* (6): that the divine plan includes them in the spiritual benefits promised to Israel. Not only is this unique apostolic role his; Paul also has been given the task of explaining to all the divine *plan* of salvation (8–9), once *hidden.* Through *the church,* God's plan to save through Christ is becoming manifest to angelic beings (10; cf 1, 21), in accord with God's *purpose* (11). The fulfillment of the plan in Christ gives the whole church more *confidence* through *faith* in God (12). The readers of this letter are also thereby encouraged to greater confidence despite Paul's imprisonment (13).

3, 1: A *prisoner of Christ:* see Introduction. Paul abruptly departs from his train of thought at the end of v 1, leaving an incomplete sentence.

3, 2: *Stewardship:* the Greek is the same term employed at 1, 10 for the *plan* that God administers (Col 1, 25) and in which Paul plays a key role.

3, 3–4: *The mystery:* God's resolve to deliver Gentiles along with Israel through Christ; cf the notes on 1, 10; 3, 9.

3, 9: *[For all]:* while some think this phrase was added so as to yield the sense "to enlighten all about the plan . . . ," it is more likely that some manuscripts and Fathers omitted it accidentally or to avoid the idea that *all* conflicted with Paul's assignment to preach to *the Gentiles* (8) specifically.

3, 10: *Principalities and authorities:* see the note on 1, 15–23 regarding v 21.

3, 14–21: The apostle prays that those he is addressing may, like the rest of the church, deepen their understanding of God's plan of salvation in Christ. It is a plan that affects the whole universe (15) *with the breadth and length and height and depth* of God's love in Christ (18) or possibly the universe in all its dimensions. The apostle prays that they may perceive the redemptive love of Christ for them and be completely immersed in the fullness of God (19). The prayer concludes with a doxology to God (20–21).

3, 14–15: *Every family:* in the Greek there is wordplay on the word for *the Father (patria, patēr).* The phrase could also mean "God's whole family" (cf 2, 21).

that Christ may dwell in your hearts through
faith; that you, rooted and grounded in love,
18 [d]may have strength to comprehend with all
the holy ones what is the breadth and length and
height and depth, 19 [e]and to know the love of
Christ that surpasses knowledge, so that you
may be filled with all the fullness of God.

20 [f]Now to him who is able to accomplish
far more than all we ask or imagine, by the
power at work within us, 21 to him be glory in
the church and in Christ Jesus to all generations,
forever and ever. Amen.

## CHAPTER 4

**Unity in the Body** 1 [g]*I, then, a prisoner
for the Lord, urge you to live in a manner worthy of the call you have received, 2 [h]with all
humility and gentleness, with patience, bearing
with one another through love, 3 [i]striving to
preserve the unity of the spirit through the bond
of peace: 4 [j]*one body and one Spirit, as you
were also called to the one hope of your call;
5 [k]one Lord, one faith, one baptism; 6 [l]one
God and Father of all, who is over all and
through all and in all.

**Diversity of Gifts** 7 [m]But grace was given
to each of us according to the measure of
Christ's gift. 8 [n]*Therefore, it says:

"He ascended on high and took prisoners
captive;
he gave gifts to men."

9 What does "he ascended" mean except that
he also descended into the lower [regions] of the
earth? 10 The one who descended is also the
one who ascended far above all the heavens,
that he might fill all things.

11 [o]*And he gave some as apostles, others
as prophets, others as evangelists, others as pastors and teachers, 12 *to equip the holy ones for
the work of ministry, for building up the body
of Christ, 13 [p]*until we all attain to the unity
of faith and knowledge of the Son of God, to
mature manhood, to the extent of the full stature
of Christ, 14 [q]so that we may no longer be
infants, tossed by waves and swept along by
every wind of teaching arising from human
trickery, from their cunning in the interests of
deceitful scheming. 15 [r]*Rather, living the
truth in love, we should grow in every way into
him who is the head, Christ, 16 [s]from whom
the whole body, joined and held together by
every supporting ligament, with the proper
functioning of each part, brings about the
body's growth and builds itself up in love.

**Renewal in Christ** 17 [t]*So I declare and
testify in the Lord that you must no longer live
as the Gentiles do, in the futility of their minds;
18 [u]darkened in understanding, alienated from
the life of God because of their ignorance, because of their hardness of heart, 19 [v]they have
become callous and have handed themselves
over to licentiousness for the practice of every
kind of impurity to excess. 20 That is not how
you learned Christ, 21 assuming that you have
heard of him and were taught in him, as truth is

---

d Col 2, 2.
e Col 2, 3.9.
f Rom 16, 25-27; Col 1, 29.
g 3, 1; Col 1, 10.
h Col 3, 12-13.
i Col 3, 14-15.
j Rom 12, 5; 1 Cor 10, 17; 12, 12-13.
k 1 Cor 8, 6.
l 1 Cor 12, 6.
m Rom 12, 3.6; 1 Cor 12, 28.
n Ps 68, 19; Col 2, 15.
o 1 Cor 12, 28.
p Col 1, 28.
q 1 Cor 14, 20; Col 2, 4.8; Heb 13, 9; Jas 1, 6.
r 1 Cor 11, 3; Col 1, 18; 2, 19.
s Col 2, 19.
t Rom 1, 21.
u Col 1, 21; 1 Pt 1, 14.
v Col 3, 5.

---

*

4, 1–16: A general plea for unity in the church. Christians have been fashioned through the *Spirit* into a single harmonious religious community (*one body*, 4.12; cf 16), belonging to a single *Lord* (in contrast to the many gods of the pagan world), and by one way of salvation through *faith*, brought out especially by the significance of *baptism* (1–6; cf Rom 6, 1–11). But Christian unity is more than adherence to a common belief. It is manifested in the exalted Christ's gifts to individuals to serve so as to make the community more Christlike (11–16). This teaching on Christ as the source of the gifts is introduced in v 8 by a citation of Ps 68, 18, which depicts Yahweh triumphantly leading Israel to salvation in Jerusalem. It is here understood of Christ, ascending *above all the heavens*, the *head* of the church; through his redemptive death, resurrection, and ascension he has become the source of the church's spiritual gifts. The "descent" of Christ (9–10) refers more probably to the incarnation (cf Phil 2, 6–8) than to Christ's presence after his death in the world of the dead (cf 1 Pt 3, 19).

4, 4–6: The "seven unities" (church, *Spirit, hope; Lord, faith* in Christ [1, 13], *baptism; one God*) reflect the triune structure of later creeds in reverse.

4, 8–10: While the emphasis is on an ascension and gift-giving by Christ, there is also a reference in taking *prisoners captive* to the aeons and powers mentioned at 1, 21; 2, 2; 3, 10; and 6, 12.

4, 11: Concerning this list of ministers, cf 1 Cor 12, 28 and Rom 12, 6–8. *Evangelists:* missionary preachers (cf Acts 21, 8 and 2 Tm 4, 5), not those who wrote gospels. *Pastors and teachers:* a single group in the Greek, shepherding congregations.

4, 12: The ministerial leaders in v 11 are to equip the whole people of God for their *work of ministry*.

4, 13: *Mature manhood:* literally, "a perfect man" (cf Col 1, 28), possibly the "one new person" of 2, 15, though there *anthrōpos* suggests humanity, while here *anēr* is the term for male. This personage becomes visible in the church's growing to its fullness in the unity of those who believe in Christ.

4, 15–16: *The head, Christ:* cf Col 1, 18 and contrast 1 Cor 12, 12–27 and Rom 12, 4–5 where Christ is identified with the whole body, including the head. The imagery may derive from ancient views in medicine, the *head* coordinating and caring for the body, each *ligament* (perhaps the ministers of v 11) supporting the whole. But as at 2, 19–22, where the temple is depicted as a growing organism, there may also be the idea here of growing toward the capstone, Christ.

4, 17–24: Paul begins to indicate how the new life in Christ contrasts with the Gentiles' old way of existence. Literally, *the old self* (22) and *the new self* (24) are "the old man" and "the new man" (*anthrōpos*, person), as at 2, 15; cf the note on 4, 13.

in Jesus, 22 [w]that you should put away the old
self of your former way of life, corrupted
through deceitful desires, 23 [x]and be renewed
in the spirit of your minds, 24 [y]*and put on the
new self, created in God's way in righteousness
and holiness of truth.

## IV: DAILY CONDUCT, AN EXPRESSION OF UNITY

**Rules for the New Life** 25 [z]*Therefore,
putting away falsehood, speak the truth, each
one to his neighbor, for we are members one of
another. 26 [a]*Be angry but do not sin; do not
let the sun set on your anger, 27 [b]and do not
leave room for the devil. 28 [c]*The thief must
no longer steal, but rather labor, doing honest
work with his [own] hands, so that he may have
something to share with one in need. 29 [d]No
foul language should come out of your mouths,
but only such as is good for needed edification,
that it may impart grace to those who hear.
30 *And do not grieve the holy Spirit of God,
with which you were sealed for the day of redemption. 31 [e]All bitterness, fury, anger,
shouting, and reviling must be removed from
you, along with all malice. 32 [f][And] be kind
to one another, compassionate, forgiving one
another as God has forgiven you in Christ.

## CHAPTER 5

1 [g]*So be imitators of God, as beloved children, 2 [h]and live in love, as Christ loved us and
handed himself over for us as a sacrificial offering to God for a fragrant aroma. 3 [i]Immorality
or any impurity or greed must not even be mentioned among you, as is fitting among holy
ones, 4 [j]no obscenity or silly or suggestive
talk, which is out of place, but instead, thanksgiving. 5 [k]Be sure of this, that no immoral or
impure or greedy person, that is, an idolater, has
any inheritance in the kingdom of Christ and of
God.

**Duty to Live in the Light** 6 [l]*Let no one
deceive you with empty arguments, for because
of these things the wrath of God is coming upon
the disobedient. 7 So do not be associated with
them. 8 [m]For you were once darkness, but now
you are light in the Lord. Live as children of
light, 9 [n]for light produces every kind of goodness and righteousness and truth. 10 [o]Try to
learn what is pleasing to the Lord. 11 [p]Take no
part in the fruitless works of darkness; rather
expose them, 12 for it is shameful even to mention the things done by them in secret; 13 [q]but
everything exposed by the light becomes visible, 14 [r]*for everything that becomes visible is
light. Therefore, it says:

"Awake, O sleeper,
and arise from the dead,
and Christ will give you light."

15 [s]*Watch carefully then how you live, not as
foolish persons but as wise, 16 making the most
of the opportunity, because the days are evil.
17 Therefore, do not continue in ignorance, but
try to understand what is the will of the Lord.
18 [t]And do not get drunk on wine, in which lies
debauchery, but be filled with the Spirit,
19 [u]addressing one another [in] psalms and
hymns and spiritual songs, singing and playing
to the Lord in your hearts, 20 [v]giving thanks
always and for everything in the name of our
Lord Jesus Christ to God the Father.

**Wives and Husbands** 21 [w]*Be subordinate to one another out of reverence for Christ.

w Rom 8, 13; Gal 6, 8; Col 3, 9.
x Rom 12, 2.
y Gn 1, 26-27; Col 3, 10.
z Zec 8, 16.
a Ps 4, 5 LXX; Mt 5, 22.
b 2 Cor 2, 11.
c 1 Thes 4, 11.
d 5, 4; Col 3, 16; 4, 6.
e Col 3, 8.
f Mt 6, 14; Col 3, 12-13.
g Mt 5, 45.48.
h Ex 29, 18; Ps 40, 7; Gal 2, 20; 1 Jn 3, 16.
i Gal 5, 19; Col 3, 5.
j 4, 29; Col 3, 8.
k 1 Cor 6, 9-10; Gal 5, 21; Col 3, 5.
l Rom 1, 18; Col 2, 4.8.
m 2, 11-13; Jn 12, 36; Col 1, 12-13.
n Gal 5, 22.
o Rom 12, 2.
p Rom 13, 12.
q Jn 3, 20-21.
r Is 26, 19; 60, 1.
s Col 4, 5.
t Prv 23, 31 LXX; Lk 21, 34.
u Ps 33, 2-3; Col 3, 16.
v Col 3, 17.
w 1 Pt 5, 5.

*

4, 24: *Put on:* in baptism. See the note on Gal 3, 27.

4, 25—6, 20: For similar exhortations to a morally good life in response to God's gift of faith, see the notes on Rom 12, 1—13, 14 and Gal 5, 13–26.

4, 26: If angry, seek reconciliation that day, not giving the devil (6, 11) opportunity to lead into sin.

4, 28: *Honest work:* literally, "the good." *His [own] hands:* some manuscripts have the full phrase as in 1 Cor 4, 12.

4, 30: See the note on 1, 13.

5, 1: *Imitators of God:* in forgiving (4, 32) and in loving (as exhibited in how *Christ loved us*).

5, 6: See the note on 2, 2.

5, 14: An early Christian hymn, possibly from a baptismal liturgy. For the content compare 2, 5–6; 3, 9 and Is 60, 1.

5, 15–16.19–20: The wording is similar to Col 4, 5 and 3, 16–17.

5, 21—6, 9: Cf the notes on Col 3, 18—4, 1 and 1 Pt 2, 18—3, 7 for a similar listing of household duties where the inferior is admonished first (*wives,* 5, 22; *children,* 6, 1; *slaves,* 6, 5), then the superior (*husbands,* 5, 25; *fathers,* 6, 4; *masters,* 6, 9). Paul varies this pattern by an emphasis on mutuality (see 5, 20); use of Old Testament material about *father and mother* in 6, 2; the judgment to come for slave-owners (*you have a Master in heaven,* 6, 9); and above all the initial principle of subordination *to one another* under *Christ,* thus effectively undermining exclusive claims to domination by one party. Into the section on *wives* and *husbands* an elaborate teaching on *Christ* and *the church* has been woven (5, 22–33).

5, 21–33: The apostle exhorts married Christians to a strong mutual love. Holding with Gn 2, 24 that marriage is a divine institution (31), Paul sees Christian marriage as taking on a new meaning symbolic of the intimate relationship of love between Christ and the church. The wife should serve her husband in the same spirit as that of the church's service to Christ (22.24), and the husband should care for his wife with the devotion of Christ to the church (25–30). Paul gives to the Genesis passage its highest meaning in the light of the union

22 [x]Wives should be subordinate to their husbands as to the Lord. 23 [y]For the husband is
head of his wife just as Christ is head of the
church, he himself the savior of the body.
24 As the church is subordinate to Christ, so
wives should be subordinate to their husbands in
everything. 25 [z]Husbands, love your wives,
even as Christ loved the church and handed
himself over for her 26 [a]to sanctify her, cleansing her by the bath of water with the word,
27 [b]that he might present to himself the church
in splendor, without spot or wrinkle or any such
thing, that she might be holy and without blemish. 28 So [also] husbands should love their
wives as their own bodies. He who loves his
wife loves himself. 29 For no one hates his own
flesh but rather nourishes and cherishes it, even
as Christ does the church, 30 [c]because we are
members of his body.

31 [d]"For this reason a man shall leave [his]
father and [his] mother
and be joined to his wife,
and the two shall become one flesh."

32 [e]This is a great mystery, but I speak in
reference to Christ and the church. 33 In any
case, each one of you should love his wife as
himself, and the wife should respect her husband.

## CHAPTER 6

**Children and Parents** 1 [f]Children, obey
your parents [in the Lord], for this is right.
2 [g]"Honor your father and mother." This is
the first commandment with a promise, 3 "that
it may go well with you and that you may have
a long life on earth." 4 [h]Fathers, do not provoke your children to anger, but bring them up
with the training and instruction of the Lord.

**Slaves and Masters** 5 [i]Slaves, be obedient to your human masters with fear and trembling, in sincerity of heart, as to Christ, 6 [j]not
only when being watched, as currying favor,
but as slaves of Christ, doing the will of God
from the heart, 7 willingly serving the Lord and
not human beings, 8 knowing that each will be
requited from the Lord for whatever good he
does, whether he is slave or free. 9 [k]Masters,
act in the same way towards them, and stop
bullying, knowing that both they and you have
a Master in heaven and that with him there is no
partiality.

**Battle against Evil** 10 *Finally, draw your
strength from the Lord and from his mighty
power. 11 [l]Put on the armor of God so that you
may be able to stand firm against the tactics of
the devil. 12 [m]For our struggle is not with flesh
and blood but with the principalities, with the
powers, with the world rulers of this present
darkness, with the evil spirits in the heavens.
13 [n]Therefore, put on the armor of God, that
you may be able to resist on the evil day and,
having done everything, to hold your ground.
14 [o]So stand fast with your loins girded in
truth, clothed with righteousness as a breastplate, 15 [p]and your feet shod in readiness for
the gospel of peace. 16 [q]In all circumstances,
hold faith as a shield, to quench all [the] flaming
arrows of the evil one. 17 [r]And take the helmet
of salvation and the sword of the Spirit, which
is the word of God.

**Constant Prayer** 18 [s]With all prayer and
supplication, pray at every opportunity in the
Spirit. To that end, be watchful with all perseverance and supplication for all the holy ones
19 [t]and also for me, that speech may be given
me to open my mouth, to make known with
boldness the mystery of the gospel 20 [u]for
which I am an ambassador in chains, so that I
may have the courage to speak as I must.

## V: CONCLUSION

**A Final Message** 21 [v]*So that you also
may have news of me and of what I am doing,
Tychicus, my beloved brother and trustworthy
minister in the Lord, will tell you everything.
22 [w]I am sending him to you for this very purpose, so that you may know about us and that
he may encourage your hearts.

x Col 3, 18—4, 1; 1 Pt 3, 1-7.
y 1 Cor 11, 3; Col 1, 18.
z Col 3, 19; 1 Tm 2, 6.
a Rom 6, 4; Ti 3, 5-7.
b 2 Cor 11, 2; Col 1, 22.
c Rom 12, 5; 1 Cor 6, 15.
d Gn 2, 24; Mt 19, 5; Mk 10, 7-8.
e Rv 19, 7.
f Prv 6, 20; Sir 3, 1-6; Col 3, 20.
g Ex 20, 12; Dt 5, 16.
h Col 3, 21-22.
i Col 3, 22-25; 1 Tm 6, 1-2; Ti 2, 9-10.
j 1 Pt 2, 18.
k Col 4, 1.
l Rom 13, 12; 2 Cor 6, 7; 10, 4; Jas 4, 7.
m 1, 21; 2, 2; Col 1, 13.
n Rom 13, 12.
o Wis 5, 17-20; Is 11, 5; Lk 12, 35; 1 Thes 5, 8.
p Is 52, 7.
q 1 Pt 5, 9.
r Is 59, 17; 1 Thes 5, 8.
s Mt 26, 41; Col 4, 2-3.
t Acts 4, 29; Col 4, 3; 2 Thes 3, 1.
u 2 Cor 5, 20; Col 4, 4.
v Acts 20, 4; Col 4, 7; 2 Tm 4, 12.
w Col 4, 8.

*

of Christ and the church, of which Christlike loyalty and devotion in Christian marriage are a clear reflection (31–33).

6, 10–20: A general exhortation to courage and prayer. Drawing upon the imagery and ideas of Is 11, 5; 59, 16–17; and Wis 5, 17–23, Paul describes the Christian in terms of the dress and equipment of Roman soldiers. He observes, however, that the Christian's readiness for combat is not directed against human beings but against the spiritual powers of evil (10–17; cf 1, 21; 2, 2; 3, 10). Unique importance is placed upon prayer (18–20).

6, 21–24: *Tychicus:* the bearer of the letter; see the note on Col 4, 7. Verses 21–22 parallel Col 4, 7–8, often word for word. If Ephesians is addressed to several Christian communities (see Introduction), it is understandable that no greetings to individual members of these communities should have been included in it.

**23** Peace be to the brothers, and love with
faith, from God the Father and the Lord Jesus
Christ. **24** [x]Grace be with all who love our Lord
Jesus Christ in immortality.

x 1 Pt 1, 8.

# THE LETTER TO THE

# PHILIPPIANS

## INTRODUCTION

*Philippi, in northeastern Greece, was a city of some importance in the Roman province of Macedonia. Lying on the great road from the Adriatic coast to Byzantium, the Via Egnatia, and in the midst of rich agricultural plains near the gold deposits of Mt. Pangaeus, it was in Paul's day a Roman town (Acts 16, 21), with a Greek-Macedonian population and a small group of Jews (see Acts 16, 13). Originally founded in the sixth century B.C. as Krenides by the Thracians, the town was taken over after 360 B.C. by Philip II of Macedon, the father of Alexander the Great, and was renamed for himself, "Philip's City." The area became Roman in the second century B.C. On the plains near Philippi in October 42 B.C., Antony and Octavian decisively defeated the forces of Brutus and Cassius, the slayers of Julius Caesar. Octavian (Augustus) later made Philippi a Roman colony and settled many veterans of the Roman armies there.*

*Paul, according to Acts (16, 9–40), established at Philippi the first Christian community in Europe. He came to Philippi, via its harbor town of Neapolis (modern Kavalla), on his second missionary journey, probably in A.D. 49 or 50, accompanied by Silas and Timothy (Acts 15, 40; 16, 3; cf Phil 1, 1) and Luke, if he is to be included in the "we" references of Acts 16, 10–17. The Acts account tells of the conversion of a business woman, Lydia; the exorcism of a slave girl; and, after an earthquake, while Paul and Silas were imprisoned in Philippi, the faith and baptism of a jailer and his family. None of these persons, however, is directly mentioned in Philippians (cf the notes on 4, 2 and 4, 3). Acts 16 concludes its account by describing how Paul (and Silas), asked by the magistrates to leave Philippi, went on to Thessalonica (Acts 17, 1–10), where several times his loyal Philippians continued to support him with financial aid (Phil 4, 16). Later, Paul may have passed through Philippi on his way from Ephesus to Greece (Acts 20, 1–2), and he definitely stopped there on his fateful trip to Jerusalem (Acts 20, 6).*

*Paul's letter to the Christians at Philippi was written while he was in a prison somewhere (1, 7.13.14.17), indeed in danger of death (1, 20–23). Although under guard for preaching Christ, Paul rejoices at the continuing progress of the gospel (1, 12–26) and expresses gratitude for the Philippians' renewed concern and help in an expression of thanks most clearly found at 4, 10–20. Much of the letter is devoted to instruction about unity and humility within the Christian community at Philippi (1, 27—2, 18) and exhortations to growth, joy, and peace in their life together (4, 1–9). The letter seems to be drawing to a close at the end of what we number as ch 2, as Paul reports the plans of his helper Timothy and of Epaphroditus (whom the Philippians had sent to aid Paul) to come to Philippi (2, 19—3, 1), and even Paul's own expectation that he will go free and come to Philippi (1, 25–26; 2, 24). Yet quite abruptly at 3, 2, Paul erupts into warnings against false teachers who threaten to impose on the Philippians the burdens of the Mosaic law, including circumcision. The section that follows, 3, 2–21, is a vigorous attack on these Judaizers (cf Gal 2, 11—3, 29) or Jewish Christian teachers (cf 2 Cor 11, 12–23), giving us insights into Paul's own life story (3, 4–6) and into the doctrine of justification, the Christian life, and ultimate hope (3, 7–21).*

*The location of Paul's imprisonment when he wrote to the Philippians, and thus the date of the letter, are uncertain. The traditional view has been that it stems from Paul's confinement in Rome, between A.D. 59 and 63 (cf Acts 28, 14–31). One modern view suggests the period when he was imprisoned at Caesarea, on the coast of Palestine, A.D. 57 or 58 (Acts 23, 23—26, 32); another suggests Corinth (cf 2 Cor 11, 9). Much recent scholarship favors Ephesus, around A.D. 55, a situation referred to in 2 Cor 1, 8 concerning "the affliction that came to us" in Asia Minor (cf also 1 Cor 15, 32). The reference at 1, 13 to the "praetorium" (cf also 4, 22) can be understood to mean the imperial guard or government house at Ephesus (or Caesarea), or the praetorian camp in Rome. Involved in a decision are the several journeys back and forth between Philippi and wherever Paul is imprisoned, mentioned in the letter (2, 25–28; 4, 14); this factor causes many to prefer Ephesus because of its proximity to Philippi. The Ephesian hypothesis dates the composition of Philippians to the mid-50s when most of Paul's major letters were written.*

*There is also a likelihood, according to some scholars, that the letter as we have it is a composite from parts of three letters by Paul to the Philippians. Seemingly 4, 10–20 is a brief note of appreciation for help sent through Epaphroditus. The long section from 1, 3 to 3, 1 is then another letter, with news of Paul's imprisonment and reports on Timothy and Epaphroditus (who has fallen ill while with Paul), along with exhortations to the Philippians about Christian conduct; and 3, 2–21 a third communication warning about threats to Philippian Christianity. The other verses in ch 4 and 1, 1–2, are variously assigned by critics to these three underlying letters, which an editor presumably put together to produce a picture of Paul writing earnestly from prison (chs 1–2), facing opponents of the faith (ch 3), and with serene joy advising and thanking his Philippians (ch 4). If all four chapters were originally a unity, then one must assume that a break occurred between the writing of 3, 1 and 3, 2, possibly involving the receipt of bad news from Philippi, and that Paul had some reasons for delaying his words of thanks for the aid brought by Epaphroditus till the end of his letter.*

*This beautiful letter is rich in insights into Paul's theology and his apostolic love and concern for the gospel and his converts. In Philippians, Paul reveals his human sensitivity and tenderness, his enthusiasm for Christ as the key to life and death (1, 21), and his deep feeling for those in Christ who dwell in Philippi. With them he shares his hopes and convictions, his anxieties and fears, revealing the total confidence in Christ that constitutes faith (3, 8–10). The letter incorporates a hymn about the salvation that God has brought about through Christ (2, 6–11), applied by Paul to the relations of Christians with one another (2, 1–5). Philippians has been termed "the letter of joy" (4, 4.10). It is the rejoicing of faith, based on true understanding of Christ's unique role in the salvation of all who profess his lordship (2, 11; 3, 8–12.14.20–21).*

*The principal divisions of the Letter to the Philippians are the following:*

*I. Address (1, 1–11)*
*II. Progress of the Gospel (1, 12–26)*
*III. Instructions for the Community (1, 27—2, 18)*
*IV. Travel Plans of Paul and His Assistants (2, 19—3, 1)*
*V. Polemic: Righteousness and the Goal in Christ (3, 2–21)*
*VI. Instructions for the Community (4, 1–9)*
*VII. Gratitude for the Philippians' Generosity (4, 10–20)*
*VIII. Farewell (4, 21–23)*

# *I: ADDRESS*

## CHAPTER 1

**Greeting** 1 [a]*Paul and Timothy, slaves of
Christ Jesus, to all the holy ones in Christ Jesus

a Rom 1, 1; 2 Cor 1, 1; 1 Thes 1, 1; Phlm 1 / 1 Tm 3, 1-13.

*

1, 1–2: See the note on Rom 1, 1–7, concerning the greeting.

1, 1: *Slaves:* Paul usually refers to himself at the start of a letter as an apostle. Here he substitutes a term suggesting the unconditional obligation of himself and Timothy to the service of Christ, probably because, in view of the good relationship with the Philippians, he wishes to stress his status as a co-servant rather than emphasize his apostolic authority. Reference to Timothy is a courtesy: Paul alone writes the letter, as the singular verb throughout shows (3–26), and the reference (2, 19–24) to Timothy in the third person. *Overseers:* the Greek term *episkopos* literally means "one who oversees" or "one who supervises," but since the second century it has come to designate the "bishop," the official who heads a local church. In New Testament times this office had not yet developed into the form that it later assumed, though it seems to be well on the way to such development in the Pastorals; see 1 Tm 3, 2 and Ti 1, 7, where it is translated *bishop.* At Philippi, however (and at Ephesus, according to Acts 20, 28), there was more than one *episkopos,* and the precise function of these officials is uncertain. In order to distinguish this office from the later stages into which it developed, the term is here translated as *overseers. Ministers:* the Greek term *diakonoi* is used frequently in the New Testament to designate "servants," "attendants," or "ministers." Paul refers to himself and to other apostles as "ministers of God" (2 Cor 6, 4) or "ministers of

who are in Philippi, with the overseers and ministers: 2 [b]*grace to you and peace from God our
Father and the Lord Jesus Christ.

**Thanksgiving** 3 [c]*I give thanks to my God
at every remembrance of you, 4 praying always
with joy in my every prayer for all of you,
5 because of your partnership for the gospel
from the first day until now. 6 [d]*I am confident
of this, that the one who began a good work in
you will continue to complete it until the day of
Christ Jesus. 7 It is right that I should think this
way about all of you, because I hold you in my
heart, you who are all partners with me in grace,
both in my imprisonment and in the defense and
confirmation of the gospel. 8 [e]For God is my
witness, how I long for all of you with the
affection of Christ Jesus. 9 [f]And this is my
prayer: that your love may increase ever more
and more in knowledge and every kind of perception, 10 [g]to discern what is of value, so that
you may be pure and blameless for the day of
Christ, 11 [h]filled with the fruit of righteousness
that comes through Jesus Christ for the glory
and praise of God.

## *II: PROGRESS OF THE GOSPEL*

12 [i]*I want you to know, brothers, that my
situation has turned out rather to advance the
gospel, 13 [j]*so that my imprisonment has become well known in Christ throughout the
whole praetorium and to all the rest, 14 *and so
that the majority of the brothers, having taken
encouragement in the Lord from my imprisonment, dare more than ever to proclaim the word
fearlessly.

15 Of course, some preach Christ from envy
and rivalry, others from good will. 16 The latter act out of love, aware that I am here for the
defense of the gospel; 17 the former proclaim
Christ out of selfish ambition, not from pure
motives, thinking that they will cause me trouble in my imprisonment. 18 [k]*What difference
does it make, as long as in every way, whether
in pretense or in truth, Christ is being proclaimed? And in that I rejoice.

Indeed I shall continue to rejoice, 19 [l]*for I
know that this will result in deliverance for me
through your prayers and support from the Spirit
of Jesus Christ. 20 [m]My eager expectation and
hope is that I shall not be put to shame in any
way, but that with all boldness, now as always,
Christ will be magnified in my body, whether
by life or by death. 21 [n]For to me life is Christ,
and death is gain. 22 [o]If I go on living in the
flesh, that means fruitful labor for me. And I do
not know which I shall choose. 23 [p]I am caught
between the two. I long to depart this life and
be with Christ, [for] that is far better. 24 Yet
that I remain [in] the flesh is more necessary for
your benefit. 25 And this I know with confidence, that I shall remain and continue in the
service of all of you for your progress and joy
in the faith, 26 so that your boasting in Christ
Jesus may abound on account of me when I
come to you again.

---

b Rom 1, 7; Gal 1, 3; Phlm 3.
c Rom 1, 8; 1 Cor 1, 4; 1 Thes 1, 2.
d 2, 13 / 1, 10; 2, 16; 1 Cor 1, 8.
e Rom 1, 9; 2 Cor 1, 23; 1 Thes 2, 5.
f Eph 3, 14-19; Col 1, 9-10; Phlm 6.
g Rom 2, 18; 12, 2 / 1, 6.
h Jn 15, 8.
i Eph 3, 1; 6, 20; 2 Tm 2, 9; Phlm 9.
j 4, 22.
k 4, 10.
l Jb 13, 16 / 2 Cor 1, 11.
m 1 Cor 6, 20; 1 Pt 4, 16.
n Gal 2, 20.
o Rom 1, 13.
p 2 Cor 5, 8.

---

Christ" (2 Cor 11, 23). In the Pastorals (1 Tm 3, 8.12) the *diakonos* has become an established official in the local church; hence the term is there translated as *deacon.* The *diakonoi* at Philippi seem to represent an earlier stage of development of the office; we are uncertain about their precise functions. Hence the term is here translated as *ministers.* See Rom 16, 1, where Phoebe is described as a *diakonos (minister)* of the church of Cenchreae.

1, 2: The gifts come *from* Christ the Lord, not simply through him from the Father; compare the christology in 2, 6–11.

1, 3–11: As in Rom 1, 8–15 and all the Pauline letters except Galatians, a thanksgiving follows, including a direct prayer for the Philippians (9–11); see the note on Rom 1, 8. On their *partnership for the gospel* (5), cf 29–30; 4, 10–20. Their devotion to the faith and to Paul made them his pride and joy (4, 1). The characteristics thus manifested are evidence of the community's continuing preparation for the Lord's parousia (6.10). Paul's especially warm relationship with the Philippians is suggested here (7.8) as elsewhere in the letter. The eschatology serves to underscore a concern for ethical growth (9–11), which appears throughout the letter.

1, 6: *The day of Christ Jesus:* the parousia or triumphant return of Christ, when those loyal to him will be with him and share in his eternal glory; cf 10; 2, 16; 3, 20–21; 1 Thes 4, 17; 5, 10; 2 Thes 1, 10; 1 Cor 1, 8.

1, 12–26: The body of the letter begins with an account of Paul's present *situation,* i.e., his *imprisonment* (12–13; see Introduction), and then goes on with advice for the Philippians (1, 27–2, 18). The *advance* of *the gospel* (12) and the *progress* of the Philippians *in the faith* (25) frame what is said.

1, 13: *Praetorium:* either the praetorian guard in the city where Paul was imprisoned or the governor's official residence in a Roman province (cf Mk 15, 16; Acts 23, 35). See Introduction on possible sites.

1, 14–18: Although Paul is imprisoned, Christians there nonetheless go on preaching Christ. But they do so with varied motives, *some* with personal hostility toward Paul, others out of personal ambition.

1, 18: *Rejoice:* a major theme in the letter; see Introduction.

1, 19–25: Paul earnestly debates his prospects of martyrdom or continued missionary labor. While he may *long to depart this life* and thus *be with Christ* (23), his overall and final expectation is that he will be delivered from this imprisonment and *continue in the service* of the Philippians and of others (19.25; 2, 24). In either case, Christ is central (20.21); if to live means Christ for Paul, death means to be united with Christ in a deeper sense.

1, 19: *Result in deliverance for me:* an echo of Jb 13, 16, hoping that God will turn suffering to ultimate good and deliverance from evil.

## *III: INSTRUCTIONS FOR THE COMMUNITY*

**Steadfastness in Faith** 27 [q]*Only, conduct yourselves in a way worthy of the gospel
of Christ, so that, whether I come and see you
or am absent, I may hear news of you, that you
are standing firm in one spirit, with one mind
struggling together for the faith of the gospel,
28 not intimidated in any way by your opponents. This is proof to them of destruction, but
of your salvation. And this is God's doing.
29 [r]For to you has been granted, for the sake
of Christ, not only to believe in him but also to
suffer for him. 30 [s]*Yours is the same struggle
as you saw in me and now hear about me.

## CHAPTER 2

**Plea for Unity and Humility** 1 *If there is
any encouragement in Christ, any solace in
love, any participation in the Spirit, any compassion and mercy, 2 [t]complete my joy by being of the same mind, with the same love, united
in heart, thinking one thing. 3 [u]Do nothing out
of selfishness or out of vainglory; rather, humbly regard others as more important than yourselves, 4 [v]each looking out not for his own
interests, but [also] everyone for those of others.
5 *Have among yourselves the same attitude
that is also yours in Christ Jesus,

6 [w]*Who, though he was in the form of God,
did not regard equality with God
something to be grasped.
7 [x]*Rather, he emptied himself,
taking the form of a slave,
coming in human likeness;
and found human in appearance,
8 [y]*he humbled himself,
becoming obedient to death,
even death on a cross.
9 [z]*Because of this, God greatly exalted him
and bestowed on him the name
that is above every name,
10 [a]*that at the name of Jesus
every knee should bend,
of those in heaven and on earth and under
the earth,
11 [b]*and every tongue confess that
Jesus Christ is Lord,
to the glory of God the Father.

*

1, 27–30: Ethical admonition begins at this early point in the letter, emphasizing steadfastness and congregational unity in the face of possible suffering. The *opponents* (28) are those in Philippi, probably pagans, who oppose the gospel cause. *This is proof . . .* (28) may refer to the whole outlook and conduct of the Philippians, turning out for their salvation but to the judgment of the opponents (cf 2 Cor 2, 15–16), or possibly the sentence refers to the opinion of the opponents, who hold that the obstinacy of the Christians points to the destruction of such people as defy Roman authority (though in reality, Paul holds, such faithfulness leads to salvation).

1, 30: A reference to Paul's earlier imprisonment in Philippi (Acts 16, 19–24; 1 Thes 2, 2) and to his present confinement.

2, 1–11: The admonition to likemindedness and unity (2–5) is based on the believers' threefold experience with Christ, God's love, and the Spirit. The appeal to humility (3) and to obedience (12) is rooted in christology, specifically in a statement about Christ Jesus (6–11) and his humbling of self and obedience to the point of death (8).

2, 5: *Have . . . the same attitude that is also yours in Christ Jesus:* or, "that also Christ Jesus had." While it is often held that Christ here functions as a model for moral imitation, it is not the historical Jesus but the entire Christ event that vv 6–11 depict. Therefore, the appeal is to have in relations among yourselves that same relationship you have in Jesus Christ, i.e., serving one another as you serve Christ (4).

2, 6–11: Perhaps an early Christian hymn quoted here by Paul. The short rhythmic lines fall into two parts, vv 6–8 where the subject of every verb is Christ, and vv 9–11 where the subject is God. The general pattern is thus of Christ's humiliation and then exaltation. More precise analyses propose a division into six three-line stanzas (6; 7abc; 7d–8; 9; 10; 11) or into three stanzas (6–7ab; 7cd–8; 9–11). Phrases such as *even death on a cross* (8c) are considered by some to be additions (by Paul) to the hymn, as are vv 10c and 11c.

2, 6: Either a reference to Christ's preexistence and those aspects of divinity that he was willing to give up in order to serve in human form, or to what the man Jesus refused to grasp at to attain divinity. Many see an allusion to the Genesis story: unlike Adam, Jesus, *though . . . in the form of God* (Gn 1, 26–27), did not reach out for *equality with God,* in contrast with the first Adam in Gn 3, 5–6.

2, 7: *Taking the form of a slave, coming in human likeness:* or ". . . taking the form of a slave. // Coming in human likeness, and found human in appearance." While it is common to take vv 6 and 7 as dealing with Christ's preexistence and v 8 with his incarnate life, so that lines 7b and c are parallel, it is also possible to interpret so as to exclude any reference to preexistence (see the note on 2, 6) and to take vv 6–8 as presenting two parallel stanzas about Jesus' human state (6–7b; 7cd–8); in the latter alternative, *coming in human likeness* begins the second stanza and parallels 6a to some extent.

2, 8: There may be reflected here language about the servant of the Lord, Is 52, 13—53, 12, especially 53, 12.

2, 9: *The name:* "Lord" (11), revealing the true nature of the one who is named.

2, 10–11: *Every knee should bend . . . every tongue confess:* into this language of Is 45, 23 there has been inserted a reference to the three levels in the universe, according to ancient thought, *heaven, earth, under the earth.*

2, 11: *Jesus Christ is Lord:* a common early Christian acclamation; cf 1 Cor 12, 3; Rom 10, 9. But doxology to God the Father is not overlooked here (11c) in the final version of the hymn.

---

q Eph 4, 1; Col 1, 10; 1 Thes 2, 12 / 4, 3.
r Mt 5, 10; 10, 38; Mk 8, 34; Acts 5, 41.
s 1, 13; Acts 16, 22-24.
t Rom 15, 5; 1 Cor 1, 10.
u Rom 12, 3.10; Gal 5, 26.
v 1 Cor 10, 24.33; 13, 5.
w Jn 1, 1-2; 17, 5; Col 2, 9; Heb 1, 3.
x Is 53, 3.11; Jn 1, 14; Rom 8, 3; 2 Cor 8, 9; Gal 4, 4; Heb 2, 14.17.
y Mt 26, 39; Jn 10, 17; Heb 5, 8; 12, 2.
z Acts 2, 33; Mt 23, 12; Eph 1, 20-21; Heb 1, 3-4.
a Is 45, 23; Jn 5, 23; Rom 14, 11; Rv 5, 13.
b Acts 2, 36; Rom 10, 9; 1 Cor 12, 3.

### Obedience and Service in the World
12 [c]*So then, my beloved, obedient as you
have always been, not only when I am present
but all the more now when I am absent, work
out your salvation with fear and trembling.
13 [d]For God is the one who, for his good purpose, works in you both to desire and to work.
14 [e]Do everything without grumbling or questioning, 15 [f]*that you may be blameless and
innocent, children of God without blemish in
the midst of a crooked and perverse generation,
among whom you shine like lights in the world,
16 [g]as you hold on to the word of life, so that
my boast for the day of Christ may be that I did
not run in vain or labor in vain. 17 [h]*But, even
if I am poured out as a libation upon the sacrificial service of your faith, I rejoice and share my
joy with all of you. 18 [i]In the same way you
also should rejoice and share your joy with me.

## *IV: TRAVEL PLANS OF PAUL AND HIS ASSISTANTS*

**Timothy and Paul** 19 [j]*I hope, in the Lord
Jesus, to send Timothy to you soon, so that I too
may be heartened by hearing news of you.
20 For I have no one comparable to him for
genuine interest in whatever concerns you.
21 [k]For they all seek their own interests, not
those of Jesus Christ. 22 But you know his
worth, how as a child with a father he served
along with me in the cause of the gospel. 23 He
it is, then, whom I hope to send as soon as I see
how things go with me, 24 *but I am confident
in the Lord that I myself will also come soon.

**Epaphroditus** 25 [l]*With regard to Epaphroditus, my brother and co-worker and fellow
soldier, your messenger and minister in my
need, I consider it necessary to send him to you.
26 For he has been longing for all of you and
was distressed because you heard that he was ill.
27 He was indeed ill, close to death; but God
had mercy on him, not just on him but also on
me, so that I might not have sorrow upon sorrow. 28 I send him therefore with the greater
eagerness, so that, on seeing him, you may
rejoice again, and I may have less anxiety.
29 [m]Welcome him then in the Lord with all joy
and hold such people in esteem, 30 because for
the sake of the work of Christ he came close to
death, risking his life to make up for those services to me that you could not perform.

## CHAPTER 3

**Concluding Admonitions** 1 [n]*Finally,
my brothers, rejoice in the Lord. Writing the
same things to you is no burden for me but is
a safeguard for you.

## *V: POLEMIC: RIGHTEOUSNESS AND THE GOAL IN CHRIST*

**Against Legalistic Teachers**
2 [o]*Beware of the dogs! Beware of the evil-

c Ps 2, 11; 1 Cor 2, 3; 2 Cor 7, 15.
d 1, 6; 1 Cor 12, 6; 15, 10; 2 Cor 3, 5.
e 1 Cor 10, 10; 1 Pt 4, 9.
f 1 Thes 3, 13 / Dt 32, 5; Mt 10, 16; Acts 2, 40 / Dn 12, 3;Mt 5, 14.16; Eph 5, 8.
g 1 Thes 2, 19 / Is 49, 4; 65, 23; Gal 2, 2.
h Rom 15, 16; 2 Tm 4, 6.
i 3, 1; 4, 4.
j Acts 16, 1-3; 17, 14-15; 1 Cor 4, 17; 16, 10.
k 1 Cor 13, 5; 2 Tm 4, 10.
l 4, 10-11.15-16.18.
m 1 Cor 16, 18.
n 2, 18; 4, 4.
o Ps 22, 17.21; Rv 22, 15 / 2 Cor 11, 13 / Gal 5, 6.12.

*

2, 12–18: Paul goes on to draw out further ethical implications for daily life (14–18) from the salvation God works in Christ.

2, 12: *Fear and trembling:* a common Old Testament expression indicating awe and seriousness in the service of God (cf Ex 15, 16; Jdt 2, 28; Ps 2, 11; Is 19, 16).

2, 15–16: *Generation . . . as you hold on to . . . :* or ". . . generation. Among them shine like lights in the world because you hold the word of life . . . ."

2, 17: *Libation:* in ancient religious ritual, the pouring out on the ground of a liquid offering as a sacrifice. Paul means that he may be facing death.

2, 19—3, 1: The plans of Paul and his assistants for future travel are regularly a part of a Pauline letter near its conclusion; cf Rom 15, 22–29; 1 Cor 16, 5–12.

2, 19: *Timothy:* already known to the Philippians (Acts 16, 1–15; cf 1 Cor 4, 17; 16, 10).

2, 24: *I myself will also come soon:* cf 1, 19–25 for the significance of this statement.

2, 25: *Epaphroditus:* sent by the Philippians as their *messenger* (literally, "apostle") to aid Paul in his imprisonment, he had fallen seriously ill; Paul commends him as he sends him back to Philippi.

3, 1: *Finally . . . rejoice:* the adverb often signals the close of a letter; cf 4, 8; 2 Cor 13, 11. While the verb could also be translated "good-bye" or "farewell," although it is never so used in Greek epistolography, the theme of joy has been frequent in the letter (1, 18; 2, 2.18); note also 4, 4 and the addition of "always" there as evidence for the meaning "rejoice." To write *the same things* may refer to what Paul has previously taught in Philippi or to what he has just written or to what follows.

3, 2–21: An abrupt change in content and tone, either because Paul at this point responds to disturbing news he has just heard about a threat to the faith of the Philippians in the form of false teachers, or because part of another Pauline letter was inserted here; see Introduction. The chapter describes these teachers in strong terms as *dogs.* The persons meant are evidently different from the rival preachers of 1, 14–18 and the opponents of 1, 28. Since vv 2–4 emphasize Jewish terms like *circumcision* (2–3.5), some relate them to the "Judaizers" of the Letter to the Galatians. Other phrases make them appear more like the false teachers of 2 Cor 11, 12–15, the *evil-workers.* The latter part of the chapter depicts the *many* who are *enemies* of Christ's cross in terms that may sound more Gentile or even "gnostic" than Jewish (18–19). Accordingly, some see two groups of false teachers in ch 3, others one group characterized by a claim of having attained "perfect maturity" (12–15).

3, 2–11: Paul sets forth the Christian claim, especially using personal, autobiographical terms that are appropriate to the situation. He presents his own experience in coming to know Christ Jesus in terms of *righteousness* or justification (cf Rom 1, 16–17; 3, 21—5, 11; Gal 2, 5–11), contrasting *the righteousness from God* through faith and that of one's own *based on the law* as two exclusive ways of pleasing God.

workers! Beware of the mutilation! **3** [p]*For we are the circumcision, we who worship through the Spirit of God, who boast in Christ Jesus and do not put our confidence in flesh, **4** [q]although I myself have grounds for confidence even in the flesh.

**Paul's Autobiography** If anyone else thinks he can be confident in flesh, all the more can I. **5** [r]*Circumcised on the eighth day, of the race of Israel, of the tribe of Benjamin, a Hebrew of Hebrew parentage, in observance of the law a Pharisee, **6** [s]in zeal I persecuted the church, in righteousness based on the law I was blameless.

**Righteousness from God** **7** [t]*[But] whatever gains I had, these I have come to consider a loss because of Christ. **8** More than that, I even consider everything as a loss because of the supreme good of knowing Christ Jesus my Lord. For his sake I have accepted the loss of all things and I consider them so much rubbish, that I may gain Christ **9** [u]and be found in him, not having any righteousness of my own based on the law but that which comes through faith in Christ, the righteousness from God, depending on faith **10** [v]to know him and the power of his resurrection and [the] sharing of his sufferings by being conformed to his death, **11** [w]if somehow I may attain the resurrection from the dead.

**Forward in Christ** **12** [x]*It is not that I have already taken hold of it or have already attained perfect maturity, but I continue my pursuit in hope that I may possess it, since I have indeed been taken possession of by Christ [Jesus]. **13** Brothers, I for my part do not consider myself to have taken possession. Just one thing: forgetting what lies behind but straining forward to what lies ahead, **14** [y]I continue my pursuit toward the goal, the prize of God's upward calling, in Christ Jesus. **15** Let us, then, who are "perfectly mature" adopt this attitude. And if you have a different attitude, this too God will reveal to you. **16** *Only, with regard to what we have attained, continue on the same course.

**Wrong Conduct and Our Goal** **17** [z]*Join with others in being imitators of me, brothers, and observe those who thus conduct themselves according to the model you have in us. **18** [a]For many, as I have often told you and now tell you even in tears, conduct themselves as enemies of the cross of Christ. **19** [b]Their end is destruction. Their God is their stomach; their glory is in their "shame." Their minds are occupied with earthly things. **20** [c]*But our citizenship is in heaven, and from it we also await a savior, the Lord Jesus Christ. **21** [d]He will change our lowly body to conform with his glorified body by the power that enables him also to bring all things into subjection to himself.

## *VI: INSTRUCTIONS FOR THE COMMUNITY*

## CHAPTER 4

**Live in Concord** **1** [e]*Therefore, my brothers, whom I love and long for, my joy and crown, in this way stand firm in the Lord, beloved.

**2** *I urge Euodia and I urge Syntyche to

p Rom 2, 28-29; Col 2, 11.
q 2 Cor 11, 18.21-23.
r Lk 1, 59; 2, 21 / Acts 22, 3; 23, 6; 26, 5.
s Acts 8, 3; 22, 4; 26, 9-11.
t Mt 13, 44.46; Lk 14, 33.
u Rom 3, 21-22.
v Rom 6, 3-5; 8, 17; Gal 6, 17.
w Jn 11, 23-26; Acts 4, 2; Rv 20, 5-6.
x 1 Tm 6, 12.19.
y 1 Cor 9, 24-25; 2 Tm 4, 7.
z 1 Cor 4, 16; 11, 1; 1 Thes 1, 7; 1 Pt 5, 3.
a 1 Cor 1, 17.23; Gal 6, 12.
b Rom 8, 5-6; 16, 18.
c Eph 2, 6.19; Col 3, 1-3; Heb 12, 22.
d Rom 8, 23.29; 1 Cor 15, 42-57; 2 Cor 3, 18; 5, 1-5 /1 Cor 15, 27-28.
e 1 Thes 2, 19-20.

*

3, 2: *Beware of the mutilation:* literally, "incision," an ironic wordplay on "circumcision"; cf Gal 5, 12. There may be an association with the self-inflicted mutilations of the prophets of Baal (1 Kgs 18, 28) and of devotees of Cybele who slashed themselves in religious frenzy.

3, 3: *We are the circumcision:* the true people of God, seed and offspring of Abraham (Gal 3, 7.29; 6, 15). *Spirit of God:* some manuscripts read "worship God by the Spirit."

3, 5: *Circumcised on the eighth day:* as the law required (Gn 17, 12; Lv 12, 3).

3, 7: *Loss:* his knowledge of Christ led Paul to reassess the ways of truly pleasing and serving God. His reevaluation indicates the profound and lasting effect of his experience of the meaning of Christ on the way to Damascus some twenty years before (Gal 1, 15–16; Acts 9, 1–22).

3, 12–16: To be *taken possession of by Christ* does not mean that one has already arrived at perfect spiritual maturity. Paul and the Philippians instead press on, trusting in God.

3, 12: *Attained perfect maturity:* possibly an echo of the concept in the mystery religions of being an initiate, admitted to divine secrets.

3, 16: Some manuscripts add, probably to explain Paul's cryptic phrase, "thinking alike."

3, 17–21: Paul and those who live a life centered in Christ, envisaging both his suffering and resurrection, provide a model that is the opposite of opponents who reject Christ's cross (cf 1 Cor 1, 23).

3, 17: *Being imitators of me:* not arrogance, but humble simplicity, since all his converts know that Paul is wholly dedicated to imitating Christ (1 Cor 11, 1; cf also Phil 4, 9; 1 Thes 1, 6; 2 Thes 3, 7.9; 1 Cor 4, 6).

3, 20: *Citizenship:* Christians constitute a colony of heaven, as Philippi was a *colonia* of Rome (Acts 16, 12). The hope Paul expresses involves the final coming of Christ, not a status already attained, such as the opponents claim.

4, 1–9: This series of ethical admonitions rests especially on the view of Christ and his coming (cf 5) in 3, 20–21. Paul's instructions touch on unity within the congregation, joy, prayer, and the Christian outlook on life.

4, 2: *Euodia . . . Syntyche:* two otherwise unknown women in the Philippian congregation; on the advice to them, cf 2, 2–4.

come to a mutual understanding in the Lord.
**3** [f]*Yes, and I ask you also, my true yokemate,
to help them, for they have struggled at my side
in promoting the gospel, along with Clement
and my other co-workers, whose names are in
the book of life.

**Joy and Peace** **4** [g]*Rejoice in the Lord
always. I shall say it again: rejoice! **5** [h]*Your
kindness should be known to all. The Lord is
near. **6** [i]Have no anxiety at all, but in everything, by prayer and petition, with thanksgiving, make your requests known to God.
**7** [j]Then the peace of God that surpasses all
understanding will guard your hearts and minds
in Christ Jesus.
**8** [k]*Finally, brothers, whatever is true,
whatever is honorable, whatever is just, whatever is pure, whatever is lovely, whatever is
gracious, if there is any excellence and if there
is anything worthy of praise, think about these
things. **9** [l]*Keep on doing what you have
learned and received and heard and seen in me.
Then the God of peace will be with you.

## *VII: GRATITUDE FOR THE PHILIPPIANS' GENEROSITY*

**10** [m]*I rejoice greatly in the Lord that now
at last you revived your concern for me. You
were, of course, concerned about me but lacked
an opportunity. **11** [n]Not that I say this because
of need, for I have learned, in whatever situation I find myself, to be self-sufficient. **12** I
know indeed how to live in humble circumstances; I know also how to live with abundance. In every circumstance and in all things
I have learned the secret of being well fed and
of going hungry, of living in abundance and of
being in need. **13** [o]I have the strength for everything through him who empowers me.
**14** Still, it was kind of you to share in my
distress.
**15** *You Philippians indeed know that at the
beginning of the gospel, when I left Macedonia,
not a single church shared with me in an account
of giving and receiving, except you alone.
**16** For even when I was at Thessalonica you
sent me something for my needs, not only once
but more than once. **17** It is not that I am eager
for the gift; rather, I am eager for the profit that
accrues to your account. **18** [p]*I have received
full payment and I abound. I am very well supplied because of what I received from you
through Epaphroditus, "a fragrant aroma," an
acceptable sacrifice, pleasing to God. **19** [q]My
God will fully supply whatever you need, in
accord with his glorious riches in Christ Jesus.
**20** [r]To our God and Father, glory for ever and
ever. Amen.

## *VIII: FAREWELL*

**21** *Give my greetings to every holy one in
Christ Jesus. The brothers who are with me send
you their greetings; **22** [s]*all the holy ones send
you their greetings, especially those of Caesar's
household. **23** The grace of the Lord Jesus
Christ be with your spirit.

f Ex 32, 32-33; Ps 69, 29; Dn 12, 1; Lk 10, 20; Rv 3, 5; 13, 8;17, 8; 20, 12.15; 21, 27.
g 2, 18; 3, 1.
h Ti 3, 2 / Ps 145, 18; Heb 10, 37; Jas 5, 8-9.
i Mt 6, 25-34; 1 Pt 5, 7 / Col 4, 2.
j Jn 14, 27; Col 3, 15.
k Rom 12, 17.
l 1 Thes 4, 1 / Rom 15, 33; 16, 20; 1 Cor 14, 33; 1 Thes 5, 23.
m 1, 18; 2, 25; 1 Cor 9, 11; 2 Cor 11, 9.
n 1 Cor 4, 11; 2 Cor 6, 10; 11, 27 / 2 Cor 12, 9-10.
o Col 1, 29; 2 Tm 4, 17.
p Gn 8, 21; Ex 29, 18; Eph 5, 2; Heb 13, 16.
q 1 Thes 3, 11.13.
r Rom 16, 27; Eph 5, 20.
s 1, 13.

*

4, 3: *Yokemate:* or "comrade," although the Greek *syzygos* could also be a proper name. *Clement:* otherwise unknown, although later writers sought to identify him with Clement, bishop of Rome (Eusebius, *Ecclesiastical History* 3.15.1).

4, 4: *Rejoice:* see the note on 3, 1.

4, 5: *Kindness:* considerateness, forbearance, fairness. *The Lord is near:* most likely a reference to Christ's parousia (1, 6.10; 3, 20–21; 1 Cor 16, 22), although some sense an echo of Ps 119, 151 and the perpetual presence of the Lord.

4, 8: The language employs terms from Roman Stoic thought.

4, 9: Cf the note on 3, 17.

4, 10-20: Paul, more directly than anywhere else in the letter (cf 1, 3–5), here thanks the Philippians for their gift of money sent through Epaphroditus (2, 25). Paul's own policy was *to be self-sufficient* as a missionary, supporting himself by his own labor (1 Thes 2, 5–9; 1 Cor 9, 15–18; cf Acts 18, 2–3). In spite of this reliance on self and on God to provide (11–13), Paul accepted gifts from the Philippians *not only once but more than once* (16) when he was in Thessalonica (Acts 17, 1–9), as he does now, in prison (*my distress,* 14). While commercial terms appear in the passage, like *an account of giving and receiving* (15) and *received full payment* (18), Paul is most concerned about the spiritual growth of the Philippians (10.17.19); he emphasizes that God will care for their needs, through Christ.

4, 15: *The beginning of the gospel:* it was at Philippi that Paul first preached Christ in Europe, going on from there to Thessalonica and Beroea (Acts 16, 9—17, 14).

4, 18: *Aroma . . . sacrifice:* Old Testament cultic language (cf Gn 8, 21; Ex 29, 18.25.41; Lv 1, 9.13; Ez 20, 41) applied to the Philippians' gift; cf Eph 5, 2; 2 Cor 2, 14–16.

4, 21-23: On the usual greetings at the conclusion of a letter, see the note on 1 Cor 16, 19–24. Inclusion of greetings from *all the holy ones* in the place from which Paul writes would involve even the Christians of 1, 14–18 who had their differences with Paul.

4, 22: *Those of Caesar's household:* minor officials or even slaves and freedmen, found in Ephesus or Rome, among other places.

# THE LETTER TO THE
# COLOSSIANS

## INTRODUCTION

*This letter is addressed to a congregation at Colossae in the Lycus Valley in Asia Minor, east of Ephesus. At the time of writing, Paul had not visited there, the letter says (1, 4; 2, 1). The community had apparently been established by Epaphras of Colossae (1, 7; 4, 12; Phlm 23). Problems, however, had arisen, brought on by teachers who emphasized Christ's relation to the universe (cosmos). Their teachings stressed angels (2, 18; "principalities and powers," 2, 15), which were connected with astral powers and cultic practices (see the note on 2, 16) and rules about food and drink and ascetical disciplines (2, 16.18). These teachings, Paul insists, detract from the person and work of Christ for salvation as set forth magnificently in a hymnic passage at 1, 15–20 and reiterated throughout the letter. Such teachings are but "shadows"; Christ is "reality" (2, 17).*

*For help in dealing with these problems that the new teachers posed at Colossae, Epaphras sought out Paul, who was then imprisoned (4, 10.18) at a place that the letter does not mention. Paul, without entering into debate over the existence of angelic spirits or their function, simply affirms that Christ possesses the sum total of redemptive power (1, 19) and that the spiritual renewal of the human person occurs through contact in baptism with the person of Christ, who died and rose again (2, 9–14). It is unnecessary for the Christian to be concerned about placating spirits (2, 15) or avoiding imagined defilement through ascetical practices in regard to food and drink (2, 20–23). True Christian asceticism consists in the conquering of personal sins (3, 5–10) and the practice of love of neighbor in accordance with the standard set by Christ (3, 12–16).*

*Paul commends the community as a whole (1, 3–8); this seems to indicate that, though the Colossians have been under pressure to adopt the false doctrines, they have not yet succumbed. The apostle expresses his prayerful concern for them (1, 9–14). His preaching has cost him persecution, suffering, and imprisonment, but he regards these as reflective of the sufferings of Christ, a required discipline for the sake of the gospel (see the note on 1, 24; cf 1, 29; 2, 1). His instructions to the Christian family and to slaves and masters require a new spirit of reflection and action. Love, obedience, and service are to be rendered "in the Lord" (3, 18—4, 1).*

*Colossians follows the outline of a typical Pauline letter. It is distinguished by the poetic lines in 1, 15–20 concerning who Christ is and what Christ means in creation and redemption. This hymn may be compared with similar passages in Philippians 2, 6–11; 1 Timothy 3, 16; and John 1, 1–18. It was apparently familiar liturgical material to the author, the audience, and the false teachers. In 1, 21—2, 7, however, Paul interprets the relation between the body of Christ, which he insists is the church (1, 18), and the world or cosmos to be one not simply of Christ's preexistence and rule but one of missionary advance into the world by the spreading of the word (1, 25.28). In this labor of the missionary body of Christ, Paul as a minister plays a prime part in bringing Christ and the gospel as hope to the Gentiles (1, 23.25.27). To "every creature under heaven" the word is to be proclaimed, so that everyone receives Christ, is established in faith, and walks in Christ (1, 28; 2, 6.7).*

*Paul wrote the Letter to the Colossians while in prison, but his several imprisonments leave the specific place and date of composition uncertain. On this point the same problem exists as with Ephesians and Philippians (see the Introductions to these letters). Traditionally the house arrest at Rome, in which Paul enjoyed a certain restricted freedom in preaching (see Acts 28, 16–28), or a second Roman imprisonment has been claimed as the setting. Others suggest a still earlier imprisonment at Caesarea (see Acts 23, 12—27, 1) or in Ephesus (see Acts 19). Still others regard the letter as the work of some pupil or follower of Paul, writing in his name. In any case, the contents are often closely paralleled by thoughts in Ephesians.*

*The principal divisions of the Letter to the Colossians are the following:*

*I. Address (1, 1–14)*
*II. The Preeminence of Christ (1, 15—2, 3)*
*III. Warnings against False Teachers (2, 4–23)*
*IV. The Ideal Christian Life in the World (3, 1—4, 6)*
*V. Conclusion (4, 7–18)*

## I: ADDRESS

### CHAPTER 1

**Greeting** **1** [a]*Paul, an apostle of Christ
Jesus by the will of God, and Timothy our
brother, **2** to the holy ones and faithful brothers
in Christ in Colossae: grace to you and peace
from God our Father.

**Thanksgiving** **3** [b]*We always give thanks
to God, the Father of our Lord Jesus Christ,
when we pray for you, **4** for we have heard of
your faith in Christ Jesus and the love that you
have for all the holy ones **5** [c]because of the
hope reserved for you in heaven. Of this you
have already heard through the word of truth,
the gospel, **6** that has come to you. Just as in
the whole world it is bearing fruit and growing,
so also among you, from the day you heard it
and came to know the grace of God in truth,
**7** [d]*as you learned it from Epaphras our beloved fellow slave, who is a trustworthy minister of Christ on your behalf **8** and who also told
us of your love in the Spirit.

**Prayer for Continued Progress**
**9** [e]*Therefore, from the day we heard this, we
do not cease praying for you and asking that you
may be filled with the knowledge of his will
through all spiritual wisdom and understanding
**10** to live in a manner worthy of the Lord, so
as to be fully pleasing, in every good work
bearing fruit and growing in the knowledge of
God, **11** strengthened with every power, in accord with his glorious might, for all endurance
and patience, with joy **12** [f]*giving thanks to the
Father, who has made you fit to share in the
inheritance of the holy ones in light. **13** He
delivered us from the power of darkness and
transferred us to the kingdom of his beloved
Son, **14** [g]in whom we have redemption, the
forgiveness of sins.

## II: THE PREEMINENCE OF CHRIST

### His Person and Work

**15** [h]*He is the image of the invisible God,

a Eph 1, 1.
b Eph 1, 15-16; Phlm 4-5.
c Eph 1, 13.18; 1 Pt 1, 4.
d Phlm 23.
e Eph 1, 15-17; 5, 17; Phil 1, 9.
f 3, 17; Jn 8, 12; Acts 26, 18; 1 Tm 6, 16; 1 Pt 2, 9.
g Eph 1, 7.
h Ps 89, 28; Jn 1, 3.18; 2 Cor 4, 4.

*

1, 1–2: For the epistolary form used by Paul at the beginning of his letters, see the note on Rom 1, 1–7. On *holy ones* or "God's people," see the note on Rom 1, 7. Awareness of their calling helps this group to be *faithful brothers* and sisters *in Christ,* i.e., dedicated to the tasks implied in their calling.

1, 3–8: On thanksgiving at the start of a letter, see the note on Rom 1, 8. The apostle, recalling his own prayers for them and the good report about them he has received (3–4), congratulates the Colossians upon their acceptance of Christ and their faithful efforts to live the gospel (3, 6–8). To encourage them he mentions the success of the gospel elsewhere (6) and assures them that his knowledge of their community is accurate, since he has been in personal contact with Epaphras (7–8), who likely had evangelized Colossae and other cities in the Lycus Valley of Asia Minor (cf 4, 12.13; Phlm 23). On *faith, love,* and *hope* (4.5.8), see the note on 1 Cor 13, 13; cf 1 Thes 1, 3; 5, 8.

1, 7: *Epaphras:* now with Paul but a Colossian, founder of the church there.

1, 9–14: Moved by Epaphras' account, the apostle has prayed and continues to pray fervently for the Colossians that, in their response to the gospel, they *may be filled with the knowledge of* God's *will* (9; cf 3, 10). Paul expects a mutual interaction between their life according to the gospel and this knowledge (10), yielding results (*fruit;* 10; cf 6) *in every good work:* growth, strength, *endurance, patience, with joy* (11), and the further giving of thanks (12).

1, 12–14: A summary about *redemption* by *the Father* precedes the statement in vv 15–20 about the *beloved Son* who is God's love in person (13). Christians share *the inheritance . . . in light* with *the holy ones,* here probably the angels (12). The imagery reflects the Exodus (*delivered . . . transferred*) and Jesus' theme of the *kingdom. Redemption* is explained as *forgiveness of sins* (cf Acts 2, 38; Rom 3, 24–25; Eph 1, 7).

1, 15–20: As the poetic arrangement indicates, these lines are probably an early Christian hymn, known to the Colossians and taken up into the letter from liturgical use (cf Phil 2, 6–11; 1 Tm 3, 16). They present Christ as the mediator of creation (15–18a) and of redemption (18b–20). There is a parallelism between *firstborn of all creation* (15) and firstborn from the dead (18). While many of the phrases were at home in Greek philosophical use and even in gnosticism, the basic ideas also

the firstborn of all creation.
16 [i]*For in him were created all things in
heaven and on earth,
the visible and the invisible,
whether thrones or dominions or
principalities or powers;
all things were created through him and
for him.
17 He is before all things,
and in him all things hold together.
18 [j]*He is the head of the body, the church.
He is the beginning, the firstborn from the
dead,
that in all things he himself might be
preeminent.
19 *For in him all the fullness was pleased to
dwell,
20 [k]*and through him to reconcile all things for
him,
making peace by the blood of his cross
[through him], whether those on earth or
those in heaven.

21 [l]*And you who once were alienated and
hostile in mind because of evil deeds 22 he has
now reconciled in his fleshly body through his
death, to present you holy, without blemish,
and irreproachable before him, 23 provided
that you persevere in the faith, firmly grounded,
stable, and not shifting from the hope of the
gospel that you heard, which has been preached
to every creature under heaven, of which I,
Paul, am a minister.

**Christ in Us** 24 *Now I rejoice in my sufferings for your sake, and in my flesh I am
filling up what is lacking in the afflictions of
Christ on behalf of his body, which is the
church, 25 of which I am a minister in accordance with God's stewardship given to me to
bring to completion for you the word of God,
26 [m]the mystery hidden from ages and from
generations past. But now it has been manifested to his holy ones, 27 [n]to whom God chose
to make known the riches of the glory of this
mystery among the Gentiles; it is Christ in you,
the hope for glory. 28 [o]It is he whom we proclaim, admonishing everyone and teaching everyone with all wisdom, that we may present
everyone perfect in Christ. 29 [p]For this I labor
and struggle, in accord with the exercise of his
power working within me.

## CHAPTER 2

1 *For I want you to know how great a struggle I am having for you and for those in Laodicea and all who have not seen me face to face,
2 [q]that their hearts may be encouraged as they
are brought together in love, to have all the
richness of fully assured understanding, for the

i 1 Cor 8, 6; Eph 1, 10.21.
j 1 Cor 11, 3; 12, 12.27; 15, 20; Eph 1, 22-23; Rv 1, 5.
k 2 Cor 5, 18-19; Eph 1, 10.
l Eph 2, 14-16.
m Rom 16, 25-26; 1 Cor 2, 7; Eph 3, 3.9.
n 3, 4; Rom 8, 10.
o Eph 4, 13.
p 2, 1; 4, 12; Phil 4, 13.
q 1, 26-27; Eph 3, 18-19.

* reflect Old Testament themes about Wisdom found in Prv 8, 22–31; Wis 7, 22—8, 1; and Sir 1, 4. See also the notes on what is possibly a hymn in Jn 1, 1–18.

1, 15: *Image:* cf Gn 1, 27. Whereas the man and the woman were originally created in the image and likeness of God (see also Gn 1, 26), Christ as image (2 Cor 4, 4) of *the invisible God* (Jn 1, 18) now shares this new nature in baptism with those redeemed (cf 3, 10–11).

1, 16–17: Christ (though not mentioned by name) is preeminent and supreme as God's agent in the creation of *all things* (cf Jn 1, 3), as prior to *all things* (17; cf Heb 1, 3).

1, 18: *Church:* such a reference seemingly belongs under "redemption" in the following lines, not under the "creation" section of the hymn. Stoic thought sometimes referred to the world as "the body of Zeus." Pauline usage is to speak of the church as the body of Christ (1 Cor 12, 12–27; Rom 12, 4–5). Some think that the author of Colossians has inserted the reference to the church here so as to define "head of the body" in Paul's customary way. See v 24. *Preeminent:* when Christ was raised by God as *firstborn from the dead* (cf Acts 26, 23; Rv 1, 5), he was placed over the community, the church, that he had brought into being, but he is also indicated as crown of the whole new creation, over *all things.* His further role is to *reconcile all things* (20) for God or possibly "to himself."

1, 19: *Fullness:* in gnostic usage this term referred to a spiritual world of beings above, between God and the world; many later interpreters take it to refer to *the fullness of the deity* (2, 9); the reference could also be to the fullness of grace (cf Jn 1, 16).

1, 20: *The blood of his cross:* the most specific reference in the hymn to redemption through Christ's death, a central theme in Paul; cf 2, 14–15; 1 Cor 1, 17.18.23. *[Through him]:* the phrase, lacking in some manuscripts, seems superfluous but parallels the reference to reconciliation through Christ earlier in the verse.

1, 21–23: Paul, in applying this hymn to the Colossians, reminds them that they have experienced the reconciling effect of Christ's death. He sees the effects of the cross in the redemption of human beings, not of cosmic powers such as those referred to in vv 16 and 20 (*all things*). Paul also urges adherence to Christ in faith and begins to point to his own role as minister (23), sufferer (24), and proclaimer (27–28) of this gospel.

1, 24—2, 3: As the community at Colossae was not personally known to Paul (see Introduction), he here invests his teaching with greater authority by presenting a brief sketch of his apostolic ministry and sufferings as they reflect those of Christ on behalf of the church (24). The preaching of God's word (25) carries out the divine plan (*the mystery,* 26) to make Christ known to the Gentiles (27). It teaches the God-given wisdom about Christ (28), whose power works mightily in the apostle (29). Even in those communities that do not know him personally (2, 1), he can increase the perception of God in Christ, unite the faithful more firmly in love, and so bring encouragement to them (2). He hopes that his apostolic authority will make the Colossians perceive more readily the defects in the teaching of others who have sought to delude them, the next concern in the letter.

1, 24: *What is lacking:* although variously interpreted, this phrase does not imply that Christ's atoning death on the cross was defective. It may refer to the apocalyptic concept of a quota of "messianic woes" to be endured before the end comes; cf Mk 13, 8.19–20.24 and the note on Mt 23, 29–32. Others suggest that Paul's mystical unity with Christ allowed him to call his own *sufferings the afflictions of Christ.*

2, 1: *Laodicea:* chief city in Phrygia, northwest of Colossae; cf 4, 13.16; Rv 3, 14–22.

knowledge of the mystery of God, Christ, **3** [r]in
whom are hidden all the treasures of wisdom
and knowledge.

## III: WARNINGS AGAINST FALSE TEACHERS

**A General Admonition** **4** [s]*I say this so
that no one may deceive you by specious arguments. **5** [t]For even if I am absent in the flesh,
yet I am with you in spirit, rejoicing as I observe
your good order and the firmness of your faith
in Christ. **6** So, as you received Christ Jesus the
Lord, walk in him, **7** [u]rooted in him and built
upon him and established in the faith as you
were taught, abounding in thanksgiving.
**8** [v]*See to it that no one captivate you with an
empty, seductive philosophy according to human tradition, according to the elemental powers of the world and not according to Christ.

**Sovereign Role of Christ** **9** [w]*For in him
dwells the whole fullness of the deity bodily,
**10** and you share in this fullness in him, who
is the head of every principality and power.
**11** [x]*In him you were also circumcised with a
circumcision not administered by hand, by
stripping off the carnal body, with the circumcision of Christ. **12** [y]You were buried with him
in baptism, in which you were also raised with
him through faith in the power of God, who
raised him from the dead. **13** [z]And even when
you were dead [in] transgressions and the uncircumcision of your flesh, he brought you to life
along with him, having forgiven us all our transgressions; **14** [a]*obliterating the bond against
us, with its legal claims, which was opposed to
us, he also removed it from our midst, nailing
it to the cross; **15** [b]*despoiling the principalities and the powers, he made a public spectacle
of them, leading them away in triumph by it.

**Practices Contrary to Faith** **16** [c]*Let no
one, then, pass judgment on you in matters of
food and drink or with regard to a festival or
new moon or sabbath. **17** [d]These are shadows
of things to come; the reality belongs to Christ.
**18** [e]*Let no one disqualify you, delighting in
self-abasement and worship of angels, taking
his stand on visions, inflated without reason by
his fleshly mind, **19** [f]and not holding closely to
the head, from whom the whole body, supported and held together by its ligaments and bonds,
achieves the growth that comes from God.

**20** If you died with Christ to the elemental
powers of the world, why do you submit to
regulations as if you were still living in the
world? **21** "Do not handle! Do not taste! Do
not touch!" **22** [g]These are all things destined to
perish with use; they accord with human precepts and teachings. **23** While they have a semblance of wisdom in rigor of devotion and
self-abasement [and] severity to the body, they
are of no value against gratification of the flesh.

---

r Prv 2, 4-5; Is 45, 3; Rom 11, 33; 1 Cor 1, 30.
s Eph 4, 14.
t 1 Cor 5, 3; Phil 1, 27.
u Eph 2, 20-22; 3, 17.
v Gal 4, 3; Eph 5, 6.
w 1, 19; Eph 3, 19.
x 1, 22; Jer 4, 4; Rom 2, 25-29; Phil 3, 3.
y Rom 6, 3-4.
z Eph 2, 1.5.
a Eph 2, 14-15.
b 1, 16.20; 2 Cor 2, 14; Eph 1, 21.
c Rom 14, 3-4; 1 Tm 4, 3.
d Heb 8, 5; 10, 1.
e 2, 23; Mt 24, 4.
f Eph 2, 21-22; 4, 16.
g Is 29, 13.

---

2, 4–23: In face of the threat posed by false teachers (4), the Colossians are admonished to adhere to the gospel as it was first preached to them (6), steeping themselves in it with grateful hearts (7). They must reject religious teachings originating in any source except the gospel (8) because in Christ alone will they have access to God, *the deity* (9). So fully has Christ enlightened them that they need no other source of religious knowledge or virtue (10). They do not require *circumcision* (11), for *in baptism* their whole being has been affected by Christ (12) through forgiveness of sin and resurrection to a new life (13; cf 3, 1 and Rom 6, 1–11).

On the cross Christ canceled the record of the debt that stood against us with all its claims (14), i.e., he eliminated the law (cf Eph 2, 15) that human beings could not observe—and that could not save them. He forgave sins against the law (14) and exposed as false and misleading (15) all other powers (cf 1, 16) that purport to offer salvation. Therefore, the Colossians are not to accept judgments from such teachers on *food and drink* or to keep certain religious festivals or engage in certain cultic practices (16), for the Colossians would thereby risk severing themselves from Christ (19). If, when they accepted the gospel, they believed in Christ as their savior, they must be convinced that their salvation cannot be achieved by appeasing ruling spirits through dietary practices or through a wisdom gained simply by means of harsh asceticism (20–23).

2, 8: *Elemental powers of the world:* see the note on Gal 4, 3.

2, 9: *Fullness of the deity:* the divine nature, not just attributes; see the note on 1, 19.

2, 11: A description of baptism (12) in symbolic terms of the Old Testament rite for entry into the community. The false teachers may have demanded physical circumcision of the Colossians.

2, 14: The elaborate metaphor here about how God canceled the legal claims against us through Christ's cross depicts not Christ being nailed to the cross by men but *the bond . . . with its legal claims* being nailed to the cross by God.

2, 15: The picture derives from the *public spectacle* and *triumph* of a Roman emperor's victory parade, where captives marched in subjection. *The principalities and the powers* are here conquered, not reconciled (cf 1, 16.20). An alternate rendering for *by it* (the cross) is "by him" (Christ).

2, 16: *Festival or new moon or sabbath:* yearly, monthly, and weekly observances determined by religious powers associated with a calendar set by the heavenly bodies, sun, moon, and stars (cf 8).

2, 18: Ascetic practices encouraged by the false teachers included subjection of self humbly to their rules, worship of angels, and cultivation of visions, though exact details are unclear.

# IV: THE IDEAL CHRISTIAN LIFE IN THE WORLD

## CHAPTER 3

**Mystical Death and Resurrection** 1 [h]*If then you were raised with Christ, seek what is above, where Christ is seated at the right hand of God. 2 Think of what is above, not of what is on earth. 3 [i]For you have died, and your life is hidden with Christ in God. 4 When Christ your life appears, then you too will appear with him in glory.

**Renunciation of Vice** 5 [j]*Put to death, then, the parts of you that are earthly: immorality, impurity, passion, evil desire, and the greed that is idolatry. 6 [k]*Because of these the wrath of God is coming [upon the disobedient]. 7 By these you too once conducted yourselves, when you lived in that way. 8 [l]*But now you must put them all away: anger, fury, malice, slander, and obscene language out of your mouths. 9 [m]Stop lying to one another, since you have taken off the old self with its practices 10 [n]*and have put on the new self, which is being renewed, for knowledge, in the image of its creator. 11 [o]*Here there is not Greek and Jew, circumcision and uncircumcision, barbarian, Scythian, slave, free; but Christ is all and in all.

12 [p]Put on then, as God's chosen ones, holy and beloved, heartfelt compassion, kindness, humility, gentleness, and patience, 13 [q]bearing with one another and forgiving one another, if one has a grievance against another; as the Lord has forgiven you, so must you also do. 14 [r]And over all these put on love, that is, the bond of perfection. 15 [s]And let the peace of Christ control your hearts, the peace into which you were also called in one body. And be thankful. 16 [t]Let the word of Christ dwell in you richly, as in all wisdom you teach and admonish one another, singing psalms, hymns, and spiritual songs with gratitude in your hearts to God. 17 [u]And whatever you do, in word or in deed, do everything in the name of the Lord Jesus, giving thanks to God the Father through him.

**The Christian Family** 18 [v]*Wives, be subordinate to your husbands, as is proper in the Lord. 19 Husbands, love your wives, and avoid any bitterness toward them. 20 [w]Children, obey your parents in everything, for this is pleasing to the Lord. 21 [x]Fathers, do not provoke your children, so they may not become discouraged.

**Slaves and Masters** 22 [y]*Slaves, obey your human masters in everything, not only when being watched, as currying favor, but in simplicity of heart, fearing the Lord. 23 Whatever you do, do from the heart, as for the Lord and not for others, 24 knowing that you will receive from the Lord the due payment of the inheritance; be slaves of the Lord Christ. 25 [z]For the wrongdoer will receive recompense for the wrong he committed, and there is no partiality.

## CHAPTER 4

1 Masters, treat your slaves justly and fairly, realizing that you too have a Master in heaven.

**Prayer and Apostolic Spirit**

2 [a]Persevere in prayer, being watchful in it with thanksgiving; 3 [b]at the same time, pray for us, too, that God may open a door to us for the word, to speak of the mystery of Christ, for

h 2, 12; Ps 110, 1; Phil 3, 20; Eph 2, 6.
i Rom 6, 2-5.
j Mt 15, 19; Rom 1, 29-30; Gal 5, 19-21; Eph 5, 3.5.
k Rom 1, 18.
l Eph 4, 22.25.31.
m Rom 6, 4.6; Eph 4, 22-25; Heb 12, 1; 1 Pt 2, 1; 4, 2.
n Gn 1, 26-27.
o 1 Cor 12, 13; Gal 3, 27-28.
p Eph 4, 1-2.32; 1 Thes 5, 15.
q Mt 6, 14; 18, 21-35; Eph 4, 32.
r Rom 13, 8-10.
s Rom 12, 5; 1 Cor 12, 12; Eph 2, 16; 4, 3-4; Phil 4, 7.
t Eph 5, 19-20.
u 1 Cor 10, 31.
v Eph 5, 22; Ti 2, 5; 1 Pt 3, 1.
w Eph 6, 1.
x Eph 6, 4.
y Eph 6, 5; 1 Tm 6, 1; Ti 2, 9-10; 1 Pt 2, 18.
z Rom 2, 11.
a Lk 18, 1; Rom 12, 12; Eph 6, 18-20; 1 Thes 5, 17.
b Rom 15, 30; 1 Cor 16, 9; Eph 6, 19; 2 Thes 3, 1.

*

3, 1–4: By retaining the message of the gospel that the risen, living Christ is the source of their salvation, the Colossians will be free from false religious evaluations of the things of the world (1–2). They have died to these; but one day *when Christ . . . appears,* they will live with Christ in the presence of God (3–4).

3, 5–17: In lieu of false asceticism and superstitious festivals, the apostle reminds the Colossians of the moral life that is to characterize their response to God through Christ. He urges their participation in the liturgical hymns and prayers that center upon God's plan of salvation in Christ (16).

3, 5.8: The two lists of five vices each are similar to enumerations at Rom 1, 29–31 and Gal 5, 19–21.

3, 6: *The wrath of God:* see the note on Rom 1, 18. Many manuscripts add, as at Eph 5, 6, "upon the disobedient."

3, 8–10: *Put . . . away; have taken off; have put on:* the terms may reflect baptismal practice, taking off garments and putting on new ones after being united with Christ, here translated into ethical terms.

3, 10: *Image:* see the note on 1, 15.

3, 11: *Scythian:* a barbarous people from north of the Black Sea.

3, 18—4, 6: After general recommendations that connect family life and the social condition of slavery with the service of Christ (3, 18—4, 1), Paul requests prayers for himself, especially in view of his imprisonment (2–3), and recommends friendly relations and meaningful discussions of Christian teaching with *outsiders,* i.e., non-Christians (5–6). See the note on Eph 5, 21—6, 9.

3, 22–25: *Slaves:* within this table of duties in family and societal relations, involving wives and husbands, children and parents (18–21), such as also appears in Eph 5, 22—6, 9, slaves here receive special attention because of the case of Onesimus the slave returning to his master (4, 9; Phlm 10–12).

which I am in prison, **4** that I may make it clear,
as I must speak. **5** [c]Conduct yourselves wisely
toward outsiders, making the most of the opportunity. **6** Let your speech always be gracious,
seasoned with salt, so that you know how you
should respond to each one.

## V: CONCLUSION

**Tychicus and Onesimus** 7 [d]*Tychicus,
my beloved brother, trustworthy minister, and
fellow slave in the Lord, will tell you all the
news of me. **8** I am sending him to you for this
very purpose, so that you may know about us
and that he may encourage your hearts,
**9** [e]together with Onesimus, a trustworthy and
beloved brother, who is one of you. They will
tell you about everything here.

**From Paul's Co-Workers**
**10** [f]*Aristarchus, my fellow prisoner, sends
you greetings, as does Mark the cousin of Barnabas (concerning whom you have received instructions; if he comes to you, receive him),
**11** *and Jesus, who is called Justus, who are of
the circumcision; these alone are my co-workers
for the kingdom of God, and they have been a
comfort to me. **12** [g]*Epaphras sends you greetings; he is one of you, a slave of Christ [Jesus],
always striving for you in his prayers so that you
may be perfect and fully assured in all the will
of God. **13** *For I can testify that he works very
hard for you and for those in Laodicea and those
in Hierapolis. **14** [h]*Luke the beloved physician
sends greetings, as does Demas.

**A Message for the Laodiceans**
**15** *Give greetings to the brothers in Laodicea
and to Nympha and to the church in her house.
**16** *And when this letter is read before you,
have it read also in the church of the Laodiceans, and you yourselves read the one from Laodicea. **17** [i]*And tell Archippus, "See that you
fulfill the ministry that you received in the
Lord."

**18** [j]*The greeting is in my own hand, Paul's.
Remember my chains. Grace be with you.

---

c Eph 5, 15-16.
d Acts 20, 4; Eph 6, 21-22; Phil 1, 12.
e Phlm 10-11.
f Acts 19, 29; 20, 4; 27, 2 / Acts 12, 12.25; 13, 13; 15, 37.40;2 Tm 4, 11; Phlm 24; 1 Pt 5, 13.
g 1, 7; Rom 15, 30.
h Phlm 24; 2 Tm 4, 10-11.
i Phlm 2.
j 1 Cor 16, 21; Gal 6, 11; Eph 3, 1; 2 Thes 3, 17.

---

4, 7–18: Paul concludes with greetings and information concerning various Christians known to the Colossians.

4, 7: *Tychicus:* Acts 20, 4 mentions his role in the collection for Jerusalem; Eph 6, 21 repeats what is said here; see also 2 Tm 4, 12; Ti 3, 12.

4, 10: *Aristarchus:* a Thessalonian who was with Paul at Ephesus and Caesarea and on the voyage to Rome (Acts 19, 29; 20, 4; 27, 2). *Mark:* also referred to at Phlm 24 and 2 Tm 4, 11 and, as "John Mark," in Acts (12, 12.25; 13, 13; 15, 37–40). See also 1 Pt 5, 13 and the note there. Traditionally the author of the second gospel.

4, 11: *Jesus:* a then common Jewish name, the Greek form of Joshua.

4, 12: *Epaphras:* see the notes on 1, 3–8 and 1, 7.

4, 13: *Laodicea:* see the note on 2, 1. *Hierapolis:* a city northeast of Laodicea and northwest of Colossae.

4, 14: *Luke:* only here described as a medical doctor; cf Phlm 24 and 2 Tm 4, 11. Traditionally the author of the third gospel. *Demas:* cf Phlm 24; he later deserted Paul (2 Tm 4, 10).

4, 15: *Nympha and . . . her house:* some manuscripts read a masculine for the house-church leader, "Nymphas and . . . his house."

4, 16: *The one from Laodicea:* either a letter by Paul that has been lost or the Letter to the Ephesians (cf the note on Eph 1, 1, *in Ephesus*).

4, 17: *Fulfill the ministry:* usually taken to mean that *Archippus,* the son of Philemon and Apphia (Phlm 1–2), is "pastor" at Colossae. An alternate interpretation is that Archippus, not Philemon, is the owner of the slave Onesimus and that Paul is asking Archippus to complete the service he has received in the Lord by sending Onesimus back to minister to Paul in his captivity (cf Phlm 20).

4, 18: *My own hand:* a postscript in Paul's own hand was his custom; cf Gal 6, 11–18 and 2 Thes 3, 17–18.

# THE FIRST LETTER TO THE
# THESSALONIANS

## INTRODUCTION

*When Paul parted from Barnabas (Acts 15, 36–41) at the beginning of what is called his second missionary journey, he chose Silvanus (Silas) as his traveling companion. Soon afterwards he took Timothy along with him (Acts 16, 1–3). Paul was now clearly at the head of his own missionary band. About A.D. 50, he arrived in Greece for the first time. In making converts in Philippi and, soon afterwards, in Thessalonica, he was beset by persecution from Jews and Gentiles alike. Moving on to Beroea, he was again harassed by enemies from Thessalonica and hurriedly left for Athens (Acts 16, 11—17, 15). Silvanus and Timothy remained behind for a while. Paul soon sent Timothy back to Thessalonica to strengthen that community in its trials (3, 1–5). Timothy and Silvanus finally returned to Paul when he reached Corinth (Acts 18, 1–18), probably in the early summer of A.D. 51. Timothy's return with a report on conditions at Thessalonica served as the occasion for Paul's first letter (3, 6–8).*

*The letter begins with a brief address (1, 1) and concludes with a greeting (5, 26–28). The body of the letter consists of two major parts. The first (1, 2—3, 13) is a set of three sections of thanksgiving connected by two* apologiae *(defenses) dealing, respectively, with the missionaries' previous conduct and their current concerns. Paul's thankful optimism regarding the Thessalonians' spiritual welfare is tempered by his insistence on their recognition of the selfless love shown by the missionaries. In an age of itinerant peddlers of new religions, Paul found it necessary to emphasize not only the content of his gospel but also his manner of presenting it, for both attested to God's grace as freely bestowed and powerfully effected.*

*The second part of the letter (4, 1—5, 25) is specifically hortatory or parenetic. The superabundant love for which Paul has just prayed (3, 12–13) is to be shown practically by living out the norms of conduct that he has communicated to them. Specific "imperatives" of Christian life, principles for acting morally, stem from the "indicative" of one's relationship to God through Christ by the sending of the holy Spirit. Thus, moral conduct is the practical, personal expression of one's Christian faith, love, and hope.*

*The principal divisions of the First Letter to the Thessalonians are the following:*

*I. Address (1, 1–10)*
*II. Previous Relations with the Thessalonians (2, 1—3, 13)*
*III. Specific Exhortations (4, 1—5, 25)*
*IV. Final Greeting (5, 26–28)*

### *I: ADDRESS*

#### CHAPTER 1

**Greeting** 1 [a]*Paul, Silvanus, and Timothy
to the church of the Thessalonians in God the
Father and the Lord Jesus Christ: grace to you
and peace.

**Thanksgiving for Their Faith** 2 [b]We
give thanks to God always for all of you, remembering you in our prayers, unceasingly
3 *calling to mind your work of faith and labor

a Acts 15, 40; 16, 1-3.19; 17, 14-15; 2 Thes 1, 1-2.
b 2 Thes 1, 3.

1, 1: On the address, see the note on Rom 1, 1–7.

1, 3: *Faith . . . love . . . hope:* this, along with 5, 8, is the earliest mention in Christian literature of the three "theological virtues" (see 1 Cor 13, 13). The order here stresses eschatological hope, in line with the letter's emphasis on the Lord's second, triumphal coming, or parousia (10; 2, 12.19; 3, 13; 4, 13—5, 11; 5, 23).

of love and endurance in hope of our Lord Jesus Christ, before our God and Father, **4** [c]knowing, brothers loved by God, how you were chosen. **5** [d]For our gospel did not come to you in word alone, but also in power and in the holy Spirit and [with] much conviction. You know what sort of people we were [among] you for your sake. **6** *And you became imitators of us and of the Lord, receiving the word in great affliction, with joy from the holy Spirit, **7** [e]so that you became a model for all the believers in Macedonia and in Achaia. **8** [f]For from you the word of the Lord has sounded forth not only in Macedonia and [in] Achaia, but in every place your faith in God has gone forth, so that we have no need to say anything. **9** [g]For they themselves openly declare about us what sort of reception we had among you, and how you turned to God from idols to serve the living and true God **10** [h]and to await his Son from heaven, whom he raised from [the] dead, Jesus, who delivers us from the coming wrath.

## *II: PREVIOUS RELATIONS WITH THE THESSALONIANS*

### CHAPTER 2

**Paul's Ministry Among Them** **1** For you yourselves know, brothers, that our reception among you was not without effect. **2** [i]Rather, after we had suffered and been insolently treated, as you know, in Philippi, we drew courage through our God to speak to you the gospel of God with much struggle. **3** Our exhortation was not from delusion or impure motives, nor did it work through deception. **4** [j]*But as we were judged worthy by God to be entrusted with the gospel, that is how we speak, not as trying to please human beings, but rather God, who judges our hearts. **5** Nor, indeed, did we ever appear with flattering speech, as you know, or with a pretext for greed—God is witness— **6** [k]nor did we seek praise from human beings, either from you or from others, **7** *although we were able to impose our weight as apostles of Christ. Rather, we were gentle among you, as a nursing mother cares for her children. **8** With such affection for you, we were determined to share with you not only the gospel of God, but our very selves as well, so dearly beloved had you become to us. **9** [l]You recall, brothers, our toil and drudgery. Working night and day in order not to burden any of you, we proclaimed to you the gospel of God. **10** You are witnesses, and so is God, how devoutly and justly and blamelessly we behaved toward you believers. **11** [m]As you know, we treated each one of you as a father treats his children, **12** [n]exhorting and encouraging you and insisting that you conduct yourselves as worthy of the God who calls you into his kingdom and glory.

**Further Thanksgiving** **13** And for this reason we too give thanks to God unceasingly, that, in receiving the word of God from hearing us, you received not a human word but, as it truly is, the word of God, which is now at work in you who believe. **14** *For you, brothers, have become imitators of the churches of God that are in Judea in Christ Jesus. For you suffer the same things from your compatriots as they did from the Jews, **15** [o]*who killed both the Lord Jesus and the prophets and persecuted us; they do not please God, and are opposed to everyone, **16** [p]trying to prevent us from speaking to the Gentiles that they may be saved, thus constantly filling up the measure of their sins. But the wrath of God has finally begun to come upon them.

**Paul's Recent Travel Plans** **17** [q]Brothers, when we were bereft of you for a short time, in person, not in heart, we were all the more eager in our great desire to see you in person. **18** [r]We decided to go to you—I, Paul, not only once but more than once—yet Satan thwarted us. **19** [s]For what is our hope or joy or

---

c 2 Thes 2, 13.
d Acts 13, 52; 17, 1-9.
e 2 Thes 1, 4; 1 Cor 4, 16; 11, 1 / 2, 14; Phil 3, 17.
f Rom 1, 8.
g Acts 14, 15; Gal 4, 8 / 4, 5.
h Rom 2, 1-16; 5, 9; 13, 4 / 5, 9.
i Acts 16, 19—17, 10.
j Gal 1, 10.
k Jn 5, 41.44; 1 Cor 10, 31; 2 Cor 4, 17.
l Acts 20, 34; 1 Cor 4, 12; 9, 3-18; 2 Thes 3, 7-9.
m Acts 20, 31.
n 1 Pt 5, 10 / 4, 7; 2 Thes 2, 14.
o Acts 2, 23; 7, 52.
p Gn 15, 16; 2 Mc 6, 14 / Rom 1, 18; 2, 5-6.
q 3, 10; Rom 1, 10-11.
r Rom 15, 22.
s 2 Cor 1, 14; Phil 2, 16; 4, 1.

*

1, 6: *Imitators:* the Pauline theme of "imitation" (see 2, 14; 1 Cor 4, 16; 11, 1; 2 Thes 3, 9) is rooted in Paul's view of solidarity in Christ through sharing in Jesus' cross and in the Spirit of the risen Lord.

2, 4: *Judged worthy:* Paul regards "worthiness" not as grounded in one's own talent or moral self-righteousness but in God's discernment of genuinely selfless attitudes and actions (see 2 Cor 10, 17–18).

2, 7: *Gentle:* many excellent manuscripts read "infants" (*nēpioi*), but "gentle" (*ēpioi*) better suits the context here.

2, 14: Luke's picture of the persecutions at Philippi (by Gentiles) and in Thessalonica and Beroea (by Jews) seems to be considerably schematized (Acts 16, 11–40; 17, 1–15). Paul pictures the Thessalonian community as composed of converts from paganism (1, 9) and speaks here of persecution by their (pagan) compatriots rather than by Jews.

2, 15–16: Paul is speaking of historical opposition on the part of Palestinian Jews in particular and does so only some twenty years after Jesus' crucifixion. Even so, he quickly proceeds to depict the persecutors typologically, in apocalyptic terms. His remarks give no grounds for anti-Semitism to those willing to understand him, especially in view of Paul's pride in his own ethnic and religious background (Rom 9, 1–5; 10, 1; 11, 1–3; Phil 3, 4–6). Sinful conduct (16) is itself an anticipation of the ultimate wrath or judgment of God (Rom 1, 18—2, 5), whether or not it is perceived as such.

crown to boast of in the presence of our Lord
Jesus at his coming if not you yourselves?
**20** For you are our glory and joy.

## CHAPTER 3

**1** [t]That is why, when we could bear it no
longer, we decided to remain alone in Athens
**2** [u]and sent Timothy, our brother and co-worker for God in the gospel of Christ, to strengthen
and encourage you in your faith, **3** *so that no
one be disturbed in these afflictions. For you
yourselves know that we are destined for this.
**4** [v]For even when we were among you, we used
to warn you in advance that we would undergo
affliction, just as has happened, as you know.
**5** For this reason, when I too could bear it no
longer, I sent to learn about your faith, for fear
that somehow the tempter had put you to the test
and our toil might come to nothing.
**6** But just now Timothy has returned to us
from you, bringing us the good news of your
faith and love, and that you always think kindly
of us and long to see us as we long to see you.
**7** Because of this, we have been reassured
about you, brothers, in our every distress and
affliction, through your faith. **8** For we now
live, if you stand firm in the Lord.

### Concluding Thanksgiving and Prayer

**9** *What thanksgiving, then, can we render to
God for you, for all the joy we feel on your
account before our God? **10** Night and day we
pray beyond measure to see you in person and
to remedy the deficiencies of your faith.
**11** Now may God himself, our Father, and our
Lord Jesus direct our way to you, **12** [w]and may
the Lord make you increase and abound in love
for one another and for all, just as we have for
you, **13** [x]so as to strengthen your hearts, to be
blameless in holiness before our God and Father
at the coming of our Lord Jesus with all his holy
ones. [Amen.]

# *III: SPECIFIC EXHORTATIONS*

## CHAPTER 4

**General Exhortations** **1** Finally, brothers, we earnestly ask and exhort you in the Lord
Jesus that, as you received from us how you
should conduct yourselves to please God—and
as you are conducting yourselves—you do so
even more. **2** *For you know what instructions
we gave you through the Lord Jesus.

**Holiness in Sexual Conduct** **3** *This is
the will of God, your holiness: that you refrain
from immorality, **4** that each of you know how
to acquire a wife for himself in holiness and
honor, **5** [y]not in lustful passion as do the Gentiles who do not know God; **6** not to take advantage of or exploit a brother in this matter, for the
Lord is an avenger in all these things, as we told
you before and solemnly affirmed. **7** For God
did not call us to impurity but to holiness.
**8** [z]Therefore, whoever disregards this, disregards not a human being but God, who [also]
gives his holy Spirit to you.

**Mutual Charity** **9** [a]On the subject of mutual charity you have no need for anyone to write
you, for you yourselves have been taught by
God to love one another. **10** [b]Indeed, you do
this for all the brothers throughout Macedonia.
Nevertheless we urge you, brothers, to progress
even more, **11** and to aspire to live a tranquil
life, to mind your own affairs, and to work with
your [own] hands, as we instructed you, **12** that
you may conduct yourselves properly toward
outsiders and not depend on anyone.

**Hope for the Christian Dead** **13** We do
not want you to be unaware, brothers, about
those who have fallen asleep, so that you may
not grieve like the rest, who have no hope.
**14** [c]For if we believe that Jesus died and rose,
so too will God, through Jesus, bring with him
those who have fallen asleep. **15** [d]*Indeed, we

---

t Acts 17, 14.
u Acts 16, l-2; 1 Cor 3, 5-9.
v Acts 14, 22; 2 Thes 2, 5-7; 2 Tm 3, 12.
w 4, 9-10; 2 Thes 1, 3.
x 5, 23; 1 Cor 1, 8.
y Ps 79, 6; Jer 10, 25; 2 Thes 1, 8; 1 Pt 3, 7.
z Lk 10, 16.
a Jn 6, 45; 13, 34; 1 Jn 2, 20-21.27; 4, 7.
b 2 Thes 3, 6-12.
c 1 Cor 15, 3-4.12.20.
d 1 Cor 15, 51; Rv 14, 13; 20, 4-6.

---

3, 3: *We are destined:* the Greek phraseology and the context suggest Paul's concern to alert his readers to difficulties he knew they would necessarily face and to enable them to see their present experience in the light of what he warned them would happen in the future. This line of thought is followed in 2 Thes 2, 1–15.

3, 9–10: The tension between Paul's optimism concerning the Thessalonians' faith and his worries about their perseverance remains unresolved. Perhaps this is accounted for not only by the continuing harassment but also by the shortness of his own stay in Thessalonica (even if that were over twice as long as the conventional three weeks that Luke assigns to it, Acts 17, 2).

4, 2: *Instructions:* these include specific guidelines on the basis of the Lord's authority, not necessarily sayings Jesus actually uttered. More profoundly, as v 8 implies, the instructions are practical principles that Paul worked out in accordance with his understanding of the role of the Spirit.

4, 3–8: Many think that this passage deals with a variety of moral regulations (fornication, adultery, sharp business practices). It can be more specifically interpreted as bringing general norms to bear on a specific problem, namely, marriage within degrees of consanguinity (as between uncle and niece) forbidden in Jewish law but allowed according to a Greek heiress law, which would insure retention of an inheritance within the family and perhaps thereby occasion divorce. In that case, "immorality" (3) should be rendered as "unlawful marriage" and "this matter" (6) as "a lawsuit." The phrase in v 4, "acquire a wife for himself," has often been interpreted to mean "control one's body."

4, 15: *Coming of the Lord:* Paul here assumes that the

tell you this, on the word of the Lord, that we
who are alive, who are left until the coming of
the Lord, will surely not precede those who
have fallen asleep. **16** [e]For the Lord himself,
with a word of command, with the voice of an
archangel and with the trumpet of God, will
come down from heaven, and the dead in Christ
will rise first. **17** *Then we who are alive, who
are left, will be caught up together with them in
the clouds to meet the Lord in the air. Thus we
shall always be with the Lord. **18** Therefore,
console one another with these words.

## CHAPTER 5

**Vigilance** **1** [f]Concerning times and seasons, brothers, you have no need for anything
to be written to you. **2** [g]For you yourselves
know very well that the day of the Lord will
come like a thief at night. **3** When people are
saying, "Peace and security," then sudden disaster comes upon them, like labor pains upon
a pregnant woman, and they will not escape.
**4** [h]But you, brothers, are not in darkness, for
that day to overtake you like a thief. **5** *For all
of you are children of the light and children of
the day. We are not of the night or of darkness.
**6** [i]Therefore, let us not sleep as the rest do, but
let us stay alert and sober. **7** Those who sleep
go to sleep at night, and those who are drunk get
drunk at night. **8** [j]But since we are of the day,
let us be sober, putting on the breastplate of faith
and love and the helmet that is hope for salvation. **9** For God did not destine us for wrath, but
to gain salvation through our Lord Jesus Christ,
**10** *who died for us, so that whether we are
awake or asleep we may live together with him.
**11** [k]Therefore, encourage one another and
build one another up, as indeed you do.

**Church Order** **12** We ask you, brothers, to
respect those who are laboring among you and
who are over you in the Lord and who admonish
you, **13** and to show esteem for them with special love on account of their work. Be at peace
among yourselves.
**14** We urge you, brothers, admonish the
idle, cheer the fainthearted, support the weak,
be patient with all. **15** [l]See that no one returns
evil for evil; rather, always seek what is good
[both] for each other and for all. **16** Rejoice
always. **17** Pray without ceasing. **18** [m]In all
circumstances give thanks, for this is the will of
God for you in Christ Jesus. **19** *Do not quench
the Spirit. **20** Do not despise prophetic utterances. **21** Test everything; retain what is good.
**22** Refrain from every kind of evil.

**Concluding Prayer** **23** [n]*May the God of
peace himself make you perfectly holy and may
you entirely, spirit, soul, and body, be preserved blameless for the coming of our Lord
Jesus Christ. **24** The one who calls you is faithful, and he will also accomplish it. **25** Brothers,
pray for us [too].

## *IV: FINAL GREETING*

**26** *Greet all the brothers with a holy kiss.
**27** I adjure you by the Lord that this letter be
read to all the brothers. **28** The grace of our
Lord Jesus Christ be with you.

---

e Mt 24, 31; 1 Cor 15, 23.52.
f Mt 24, 36-45.
g 2 Pt 3, 10.
h Eph 5, 8-9.
i Mt 24, 42; Rom 13, 12-13; 1 Pt 5, 8.
j Is 59, 17; Rom 13, 11-14; Eph 6, 11.14-17.
k Rom 15, 2; 1 Cor 8, 1; 14, 12.26; Eph 4, 29.
l Prv 20, 22; Mt 5, 38-42; Rom 12, 17.
m Eph 5, 20.
n 2 Thes 3, 16.

---

second coming, or parousia, will occur within his own lifetime but insists that the time or season is unknown (5, 1–2). Nevertheless, the most important aspect of the parousia for him was the fulfillment of union with Christ. His pastoral exhortation focuses first on hope for the departed faithful, then (5, 1–3) on the need of preparedness for those who have to achieve their goal.

4, 17: *Will be caught up together:* literally, snatched up, carried off; cf 2 Cor 12, 2; Rv 12, 5. From the Latin verb here used, *rapiemur,* has come the idea of "the rapture," when believers will be transported away from the woes of the world; this construction combines this verse with Mt 24, 40–41 (see the note there) // Lk 17, 34–35 and passages from Rv in a scheme of millennial dispensationalism.

5, 5: *Children of the light:* that is, belonging to the daylight of God's personal revelation and expected to achieve it (an analogous development of imagery that appears in Jn 12, 36).

5, 10: Characteristically, Paul plays on words suggesting ultimate and anticipated death and life. Union with the crucified and risen Lord at his parousia is anticipated in some measure in contrasted states of our temporal life. The essential element he urges is our indestructible personal union in Christ's own life (see Rom 5, 1–10).

5, 19–21: Paul's buoyant encouragement of charismatic freedom sometimes occasioned excesses that he or others had to remedy (see 1 Cor 14; 2 Thes 2, 1–15; 2 Pt 3, 1–16).

5, 23: Another possible translation is, "May the God of peace himself make you perfectly holy and sanctify your spirit fully, and may both soul and body be preserved blameless for the coming of our Lord Jesus Christ." In either case, Paul is not offering an anthropological or philosophical analysis of human nature. Rather, he looks to the wholeness of what may be called the supernatural and natural aspects of a person's service of God.

5, 26: *Kiss:* the holy embrace (see Rom 16, 16; 1 Cor 16, 20; 2 Cor 13, 12; 1 Pt 5, 14) was a greeting of respect and affection, perhaps given during a liturgy at which Paul's letter would have been read.

# THE SECOND LETTER TO THE

# THESSALONIANS

## INTRODUCTION

*This letter is addressed to the same church as the letter that precedes it in the canon and contains many expressions parallel to those in the First Letter to the Thessalonians, indeed verbatim with them. Yet other aspects of the contents of the Second Letter to the Thessalonians suggest a more impersonal tone and changed circumstances in the situation at Thessalonica.*

*The letter begins with an address (1, 1–2) that expands only slightly on that of 1 Thes 1, 1. It ends with a greeting insisting on its Pauline authority in the face of false claims made in Paul's name (see the note on 2, 2). The body of the letter falls into three short parts, of which the second is notoriously difficult (ch 2).*

*The opening thanksgiving and prayer (1, 3–12) speak of the Thessalonians' increasing faith and love in the face of outside persecution. God's eventual judgment against persecutors and his salvation for the faithful are already evidenced by the very fact of persecution. The second part (2, 1–17), the heart of the letter, deals with a problem threatening the faith of the community. A message involving a prophetic oracle and apparently a forged letter, possibly presented at a liturgical gathering (cf 2, 2 and 1 Cor 14, 26–33), to the effect that the day of the Lord and all that it means have already come, has upset the life of the Thessalonian church.*

*The writer counters their preoccupation with the date of the parousia (or coming again of the Lord Jesus from heaven, 2, 1) by recalling Paul's teaching concerning what must happen first and by going on to describe what will happen at the Lord's coming (2, 8); he indicates the twofold process by which the "activity of Satan" and God's actions (2, 9–11) are working out, namely, a growing division between believers and those who succumb to false prophecy and "the lie." He concludes by insisting on Pauline traditions and by praying for divine strength (2, 13–17). The closing part of the letter (3, 1–16) deals in particular with the apostle's directives and model style of life and with correction of disorderly elements within the community.*

*Traditional opinion holds that this letter was written shortly after 1 Thessalonians. Occasionally it has been argued that 2 Thessalonians was written first or that the two letters are addressed to different segments within the church at Thessalonica (2 Thessalonians being directed to the Jewish Christians there) or even that 2 Thessalonians was originally written to some other nearby place where Paul carried out mission work, such as Philippi or Beroea. Increasingly in recent times, however, the opinion has been advanced that 2 Thessalonians is a pseudepigraph, that is, a letter written authoritatively in Paul's name, to maintain apostolic traditions in a later period, perhaps during the last two decades of the first century.*

*In any case, the presumed audience of Second Thessalonians and certain features of its style and content require that it be read and studied in a Pauline context, particularly that provided by 1 Thessalonians. At the same time, and especially if the letter is regarded as not by Paul himself, its apocalyptic presentation of preconditions for the parousia (2, 1–12) may profit from and require recourse to a wider biblical basis for interpretation, namely Old Testament books such as Daniel and Isaiah and especially, in the New Testament, the synoptic apocalyptic discourse (Mk 13; Mt 24–25; Lk 21, 5–36) and the Book of Revelation.*

*The principal divisions of the Second Letter to the Thessalonians are the following:*

*I. Address (1, 1–12)*

*II. Warning against Deception Concerning the Parousia (2, 1–17)*
*III. Concluding Exhortations (3, 1–16)*
*IV. Final Greetings (3, 17–18)*

## *I: ADDRESS*

### CHAPTER 1

**Greeting** 1 [a]*Paul, Silvanus, and Timothy
to the church of the Thessalonians in God our
Father and the Lord Jesus Christ: 2 grace to you
and peace from God [our] Father and the Lord
Jesus Christ.

**Thanksgiving** 3 [b]*We ought to thank God
always for you, brothers, as is fitting, because
your faith flourishes ever more, and the love of
every one of you for one another grows ever
greater. 4 Accordingly, we ourselves boast of
you in the churches of God regarding your endurance and faith in all your persecutions and
the afflictions you endure.
5 [c]This is evidence of the just judgment of
God, so that you may be considered worthy of
the kingdom of God for which you are suffering. 6 For it is surely just on God's part to repay
with afflictions those who are afflicting you,
7 and to grant rest along with us to you who are
undergoing afflictions, at the revelation of the
Lord Jesus from heaven with his mighty angels,
8 [d]in blazing fire, inflicting punishment on
those who do not acknowledge God and on
those who do not obey the gospel of our Lord
Jesus. 9 [e]These will pay the penalty of eternal
ruin, separated from the presence of the Lord
and from the glory of his power, 10 [f]*when he
comes to be glorified among his holy ones and
to be marveled at on that day among all who
have believed, for our testimony to you was
believed.

**Prayer** 11 [g]To this end, we always pray for
you, that our God may make you worthy of his
calling and powerfully bring to fulfillment every
good purpose and every effort of faith,
12 [h]*that the name of our Lord Jesus may be
glorified in you, and you in him, in accord with
the grace of our God and Lord Jesus Christ.

## *II: WARNING AGAINST DECEPTION CONCERNING THE PAROUSIA*

### CHAPTER 2

**Christ and the Lawless One** 1 [i]*We ask
you, brothers, with regard to the coming of our
Lord Jesus Christ and our assembling with him,
2 [j]*not to be shaken out of your minds sudden-

a 1 Thes 1, 1.
b 1 Cor 1, 4; 1 Thes 1, 2; 3, 12.
c Phil 1, 28; 1 Thes 2, 12.
d Ps 79, 5-6; Is 66, 15; Jer 10, 25.
e Is 2, 10.19.21.
f Ps 89, 8; Dn 7, 18-22.27; 1 Thes 3, 13.
g 1 Thes 1, 2-3.
h Is 66, 5.
i 1 Thes 4, 13-17.
j Mt 24, 6; 1 Cor 14, 26.32-33; 1 Thes 5, 1-2.

*

1, 1–2: On the address, see the note on Rom 1, 1–7 and cf 1 Thes 1, 1.

1, 3–12: On the thanksgiving, see the note on Rom 1, 8 and cf 1 Thes 1, 2–10. Paul's gratitude to God for the faith and love of the Thessalonians (3) and his Christian pride in their faithful endurance (4–5) contrast with the condemnation announced for those who afflict them, a judgment to be carried out at the parousia (6–10), which is described in vivid language drawn from Old Testament apocalyptic. A prayer for the fulfillment of God's purpose in the Thessalonians (11–12) completes the section, as is customary in a Pauline letter (cf 1 Thes 1, 2–3).

1, 10: *Among his holy ones:* in the Old Testament, this term can refer to an angelic throng (cf also Jude 14), but here, in parallel with *among all who have believed,* it can refer to the triumphant people of God.

1, 12: *The grace of our God and Lord Jesus Christ:* the Greek can also be translated, "the grace of our God and of the Lord Jesus Christ."

2, 1–17: The Thessalonians have been *shaken* by a message purporting to come from Paul himself that *the day of the Lord* is already present. He warns against this deception in eschatology by citing a scenario of events that must first occur (3–12) before the end will come. The overall point Paul makes is the need to reject such lies as Satan sends; he also reaffirms the Thessalonians in their calling (13–14). They are to uphold what Paul himself has taught (15). There is a concluding prayer for their strengthening (16–17). As in 1, 8–10, the Old Testament provides a good deal of coloring; cf especially Is 14, 13–14; 66, 15.18–21; Ez 28, 2–9; Dn 11, 36–37. The contents of 2, 3b–8 may come from a previously existing apocalypse. The details have been variously interpreted.

An alternative to the possibilities noted below understands that an oracular utterance, supposedly coming from a prophetic spirit (2–3a), has so disrupted the community's thinking that its effects may be compared to those of the mania connected with the worship of the Greek god Dionysus. On this view, the writer seems to allude in vv 6–8 to Dionysiac "seizure," although, of course, ironically, somewhat as Paul alludes to witchcraft ("an evil eye") in Gal 3, 1 in speaking of the threat to faith posed by those disturbing the Galatians (Gal 1, 6–7; 5, 10b). On this view of 2 Thes 2, the Greek participles *katechon* (rendered above as *what is restraining*) and *katechōn* (*the one who restrains*) are to be translated "the seizing power" in v 6 and "the seizer" in v 7. They then allude to a pseudocharismatic force or spirit of Dionysiac character that has suddenly taken hold of the Thessalonian community (see 2). The addressees *know* (6) this force or spirit because of the problem it is causing. This pseudocharismatic force or spirit is a kind of anticipation and advance proof of the ultimate, climactic figure (*the lawless one* or the rebel, 3), of which the community has been warned (see the note on 1 Thes 3, 3). It is, however, only the beginning of the end that the latter's manifestation entails; the end is not yet. For in the course of *the mystery of lawlessness* (7), false prophetism, after it ceases in the Thessalonian community, will be manifested in the world at large (8–12), where it will also be eliminated in turn by the Lord Jesus.

2, 2: *"Spirit":* a Spirit-inspired utterance or ecstatic revela-

ly, or to be alarmed either by a "spirit," or by
an oral statement, or by a letter allegedly from
us to the effect that the day of the Lord is at
hand. **3** *Let no one deceive you in any way.
For unless the apostasy comes first and the lawless one is revealed, the one doomed to perdition, **4** [k]*who opposes and exalts himself above
every so-called god and object of worship, so as
to seat himself in the temple of God, claiming
that he is a god— **5** do you not recall that while
I was still with you I told you these things?
**6** *And now you know what is restraining, that
he may be revealed in his time. **7** [l]*For the
mystery of lawlessness is already at work. But
the one who restrains is to do so only for the
present, until he is removed from the scene.
**8** [m]And then the lawless one will be revealed,
whom the Lord [Jesus] will kill with the breath
of his mouth and render powerless by the manifestation of his coming, **9** [n]the one whose coming springs from the power of Satan in every
mighty deed and in signs and wonders that lie,
**10** and in every wicked deceit for those who are
perishing because they have not accepted the
love of truth so that they may be saved.
**11** Therefore, God is sending them a deceiving
power so that they may believe the lie, **12** that
all who have not believed the truth but have
approved wrongdoing may be condemned.

**13** [o]*But we ought to give thanks to God for
you always, brothers loved by the Lord, because God chose you as the firstfruits for salvation through sanctification by the Spirit and belief in truth. **14** [p]To this end he has [also] called
you through our gospel to possess the glory of
our Lord Jesus Christ. **15** *Therefore, brothers,
stand firm and hold fast to the traditions that you
were taught, either by an oral statement or by a
letter of ours.

**16** May our Lord Jesus Christ himself and
God our Father, who has loved us and given us
everlasting encouragement and good hope
through his grace, **17** encourage your hearts
and strengthen them in every good deed and
word.

## *III: CONCLUDING EXHORTATIONS*

## CHAPTER 3

**Request for Prayers** **1** [q]*Finally, brothers, pray for us, so that the word of the Lord
may speed forward and be glorified, as it did
among you, **2** and that we may be delivered
from perverse and wicked people, for not all

k Dn 11, 36-37; Ez 28, 2.
l Mt 13, 36-43; Acts 20, 29; Gal 5, 10; 2 Pt 2, 1; Rv 22, 11.
m Is 11, 4; Rv 19, 15.
n Mt 24, 24; Rv 13, 13.
o 1 Thes 2, 13; 5, 9.
p Rom 5, 1-10; 8, 29-30; 1 Thes 4, 7; 5, 9.
q Eph 6, 19; Col 4, 3.

*

tion. *An oral statement:* literally, a "word" or pronouncement, not necessarily of ecstatic origin. *A letter allegedly sent by us:* possibly a forged letter, so that Paul calls attention in 3, 17 to his practice of concluding a genuine letter with a summary note or greeting in his own hand, as at Gal 6, 11–18 and elsewhere.

2, 3b–5: This incomplete sentence (anacoluthon, 4) recalls what the Thessalonians had already been taught, an apocalyptic scenario depicting, in terms borrowed especially from Dn 11, 36–37 and related verses, human self-assertiveness against God in *the temple of God* itself. *The lawless one* represents the climax of such activity in this account.

2, 4: *Seat himself in the temple of God:* a reflection of the language in Dn 7, 23–25; 8, 9–12; 9, 27; 11, 36–37; and 12, 11 about the attempt of Antiochus IV Epiphanes to set up a statue of Zeus in the Jerusalem temple and possibly of the Roman emperor Caligula to do a similar thing (Mk 13, 14). Here the imagery suggests an attempt to install someone in the place of God, *claiming that he is a god* (cf Ez 28, 2). Usually, it is the Jerusalem temple that is assumed to be meant; on the alternative view sketched above (see the note on 2, 1–17), *the temple* refers to the Christian community.

2, 6–7: *What is restraining . . . the one who restrains:* neuter and masculine, respectively, of a force and person holding back the lawless one. The Thessalonians know what is meant (6), but the terms, seemingly found only in this passage and in writings dependent on it, have been variously interpreted. Traditionally, v 6 has been applied to the Roman empire and v 7 to the Roman emperor (in Paul's day, Nero) as bulwarks holding back chaos (cf Rom 13, 1–7). A second interpretation suggests that cosmic or angelic powers are binding Satan (9) and so restraining him; some relate this to an anti-Christ figure (1 Jn 2, 18) or to Michael the archangel (Rv 12, 7–9; 20, 1–3). A more recent view suggests that it is the preaching of the Christian gospel that restrains the end, for in God's plan the end cannot come until the gospel is preached to all nations (Mk 13, 10); in that case, Paul as missionary preacher par excellence is "the one who restrains," whose removal (death) will bring the end (7). On the alternative view (see the note on 2, 1–17), the phrases should be referred to that which and to him who seizes (a prophet) in ecstasy so as to have him speak pseudo-oracles.

2, 7–12: *The lawless one* and *the one who restrains* are involved in an activity or process, *the mystery of lawlessness,* behind which *Satan* stands (9). The action of the *Lord [Jesus]* in overcoming the lawless one is described in Old Testament language (*with the breath of his mouth;* cf Is 11, 4; Jb 4, 9; Rv 19, 15). His *coming* is literally the Lord's "parousia." The biblical concept of the "holy war," eschatologically conceived, may underlie the imagery.

2, 13: *As the firstfruits:* there is also strong manuscript evidence for the reading, "God chose you from the beginning," thus providing a focus on God's activity from beginning to end; *firstfruits* is a Pauline term, however; cf Rom 8, 23; 11, 16; 16, 5, among other references.

2, 15: Reference to *an oral statement* and *a letter* (2) and the content here, including a formula of conclusion (cf 1 Cor 16, 13; Gal 5, 1), suggest that vv 1–15 or even 1–17 are to be taken as a literary unit, notwithstanding the incidental thanksgiving formula in v 13.

3, 1–18: The final chapter urges the Thessalonians to pray for Paul and his colleagues (1–2) and reiterates confidence in the Thessalonians (3–5), while admonishing them about a specific problem in their community that has grown out of the intense eschatological speculation, namely, not to work but to become instead disorderly busybodies (6–15). A benediction (16) and postscript in Paul's own hand round out the letter. On vv 17–18, cf the note on 2, 2.

have faith. 3 [r]But the Lord is faithful; he will
strengthen you and guard you from the evil one.
4 [s]We are confident of you in the Lord that
what we instruct you, you [both] are doing and
will continue to do. 5 May the Lord direct your
hearts to the love of God and to the endurance
of Christ.

**Neglect of Work** 6 *We instruct you,
brothers, in the name of [our] Lord Jesus Christ,
to shun any brother who conducts himself in a
disorderly way and not according to the tradition they received from us. 7 For you know
how one must imitate us. For we did not act in
a disorderly way among you, 8 [t]nor did we eat
food received free from anyone. On the contrary, in toil and drudgery, night and day we
worked, so as not to burden any of you. 9 [u]Not
that we do not have the right. Rather, we wanted
to present ourselves as a model for you, so that
you might imitate us. 10 [v]In fact, when we
were with you, we instructed you that if anyone
was unwilling to work, neither should that one
eat. 11 [w]We hear that some are conducting
themselves among you in a disorderly way, by
not keeping busy but minding the business of
others. 12 Such people we instruct and urge in
the Lord Jesus Christ to work quietly and to eat
their own food. 13 But you, brothers, do not be
remiss in doing good. 14 If anyone does not
obey our word as expressed in this letter, take
note of this person not to associate with him,
that he may be put to shame. 15 [x]Do not regard
him as an enemy but admonish him as a brother.
16 [y]May the Lord of peace himself give you
peace at all times and in every way. The Lord
be with all of you.

## *IV: FINAL GREETINGS*

17 [z]This greeting is in my own hand, Paul's.
This is the sign in every letter; this is how I
write. 18 The grace of our Lord Jesus Christ be
with all of you.

r 1 Thes 5, 24 / 1 Cor 16, 13 / Mt 6, 13.
s 2 Cor 7, 16; 1 Thes 4, 1-2.
t 1 Thes 2, 9.
u Mt 10, 10; Phil 3, 17.
v 1 Thes 4, 11.
w 1 Thes 5, 14.
x 2 Cor 2, 7; Gal 6, 1.
y Jn 14, 27; Rom 15, 33.
z 1 Cor 16, 21; Gal 6, 11.

* 3, 6: Some members of the community, probably because they regarded the parousia as imminent or the new age of the Lord to be already here (2, 2), had apparently ceased to work for a living. The disciplinary problem they posed could be rooted in distorted thinking about Paul's own teaching (cf 1 Thes 2, 16; 3, 3–4; 5, 4–5) or, more likely, in a forged letter (2, 2) and the type of teaching dealt with in 2, 1–15. The apostle's own moral teaching, reflected in his selfless labors for others, was rooted in a deep doctrinal concern for the gospel message (cf 1 Thes 2, 3–10).

# THE FIRST LETTER TO

# TIMOTHY

## INTRODUCTION

*The three letters, First and Second Timothy and Titus, form a distinct group within the Pauline corpus. In the collection of letters by the Apostle to the Gentiles, they differ from the others in form and contents. All three suggest they were written late in Paul's career. The opponents are not "Judaizers" as in Galatians but false teachers stressing "knowledge" (gnōsis; see the note on 1 Tm 6, 20–21). Attention is given especially to correct doctrine and church organization. Jesus' second coming recedes into the background compared to references in Paul's earlier letters (though not Colossians and Ephesians). The three letters are addressed not to congregations but to those who shepherd congregations (Latin, pastores). These letters were first named "Pastoral Epistles" in the eighteenth century because they all are concerned with the work of a pastor in caring for the community or communities under his charge.*

*The first of the Pastorals, 1 Timothy, is presented as having been written from Macedonia. Timothy, whom Paul converted, was of mixed Jewish and Gentile parentage (Acts 16, 1–3). He was the apostle's companion on both the second and the third missionary journeys (Acts 16, 3; 19, 22) and was often sent by him on special missions (Acts 19, 22; 1 Cor 4, 17; 1 Thes 3, 2). In 1 Timothy (1, 3), he is described as the administrator of the entire Ephesian community.*

*The letter instructs Timothy on his duty to restrain false and useless teaching (1, 3–11; 4, 1–5; 6, 3–16) and proposes principles pertaining to his relationship with the older members of the community (5, 1–2) and with the presbyters (5, 17–22). It gives rules for aid to widows (5, 3–8) and their selection for charitable ministrations (5, 9–16) and also deals with liturgical celebrations (2, 1–15), selections for the offices of bishop and deacon (3, 1–13), relation of slaves with their masters (6, 1–2), and obligations of the wealthier members of the community (6, 17–19). This letter also reminds Timothy of the prophetic character of his office (1, 12–20) and encourages him in his exercise of it (4, 6–16). The central passage of the letter (3, 14–16) expresses the principal motive that should guide the conduct of Timothy—preservation of the purity of the church's doctrine against false teaching. On this same note the letter concludes (6, 20–21).*

*From the late second century to the nineteenth, Pauline authorship of the three Pastoral Epistles went unchallenged. Since then, the attribution of these letters to Paul has been questioned. Most scholars are convinced that Paul could not have been responsible for the vocabulary and style, the concept of church organization, or the theological expressions found in these letters. A second group believes, on the basis of statistical evidence, that the vocabulary and style are Pauline, even if at first sight the contrary seems to be the case. They state that the concept of church organization in the letters is not as advanced as the questioners of Pauline authorship hold since the notion of hierarchical order in a religious community existed in Israel before the time of Christ, as evidenced in the Dead Sea Scrolls. Finally, this group sees affinities between the theological thought of the Pastorals and that of the unquestionably genuine letters of Paul. Other scholars, while conceding a degree of validity to the positions mentioned above, suggest that the apostle made use of a secretary who was responsible for the composition of the letters. A fourth group of scholars believes that these letters are the work of a compiler, that they are based on traditions about Paul in his later years, and that they include, in varying amounts, actual fragments of genuine Pauline correspondence.*

*If Paul is considered the more immediate author, the Pastorals are to be dated between the end of his first Roman imprisonment (Acts 28, 16) and his execution under Nero (A.D. 63–67); if they are regarded as only more remotely Pauline, their date may be as late as the early second century. In spite of these problems of authorship and dating, the Pastorals are illustrative of early Christian life and remain an important element of canonical scripture.*

*The principal divisions of the First Letter to Timothy are the following:*

*I. Address (1, 1–2)*
*II. Sound Teaching (1, 3–20)*
*III. Problems of Discipline (2, 1—4, 16)*
*IV. Duties toward Others (5, 1—6, 2a)*
*V. False Teaching and True Wealth (6, 2b-19)*
*VI. Final Recommendation and Warning (6, 20–21)*

## *I: ADDRESS*

### CHAPTER 1

**Greeting** **1** [a]*Paul, an apostle of Christ
Jesus by command of God our savior and of
Christ Jesus our hope, **2** [b]to Timothy, my true
child in faith: grace, mercy, and peace from
God the Father and Christ Jesus our Lord.

## *II: SOUND TEACHING*

**Warning against False Doctrine** **3** [c]*I
repeat the request I made of you when I was on
my way to Macedonia, that you stay in Ephesus
to instruct certain people not to teach false doctrines **4** [d]*or to concern themselves with myths
and endless genealogies, which promote speculations rather than the plan of God that is to be
received by faith. **5** [e]The aim of this instruction
is love from a pure heart, a good conscience,
and a sincere faith. **6** [f]Some people have deviated from these and turned to meaningless
talk, **7** wanting to be teachers of the law, but
without understanding either what they are saying or what they assert with such assurance.
**8** [g]*We know that the law is good, provided
that one uses it as law, **9** with the understanding
that law is meant not for a righteous person but
for the lawless and unruly, the godless and sinful, the unholy and profane, those who kill their
fathers or mothers, murderers, **10** [h]*the unchaste, sodomites, kidnapers, liars, perjurers,
and whatever else is opposed to sound teaching,
**11** [i]according to the glorious gospel of the
blessed God, with which I have been entrusted.

**Gratitude for God's Mercy** **12** [j]*I am
grateful to him who has strengthened me, Christ
Jesus our Lord, because he considered me trustworthy in appointing me to the ministry. **13** [k]I
was once a blasphemer and a persecutor and an
arrogant man, but I have been mercifully treated
because I acted out of ignorance in my unbelief.
**14** [l]Indeed, the grace of our Lord has been
abundant, along with the faith and love that are
in Christ Jesus. **15** [m]*This saying is trustworthy and deserves full acceptance: Christ Jesus
came into the world to save sinners. Of these I
am the foremost. **16** But for that reason I was
mercifully treated, so that in me, as the foremost, Christ Jesus might display all his patience
as an example for those who would come to
believe in him for everlasting life. **17** [n]*To the

a 2, 3; Lk 1, 47; Ti 1, 3; 2, 10 / Col 1, 27.
b 2 Tm 1, 2; Ti 1, 4.
c Acts 20, 1.
d 4, 7; Ti 1, 14; 3, 9; 2 Pt 1, 16.
e Rom 13, 10.
f 6, 4.20; Ti 1, 10.
g Rom 7, 12.16.
h 4, 6; 6, 3; 2 Tm 4, 3; Ti 1, 9; 2, 1.
i Ti 1, 3.
j Phil 4, 13 / Acts 9, 15; Gal 1, 15-16.
k Acts 8, 3; 9, 1-2; 1 Cor 15, 9; Gal 1, 13.
l Rom 5, 20; 2 Tm 1, 13.
m Lk 15, 2; 19, 10.
n Rom 16, 27.

*

1, 1–2: For the Pauline use of the conventional epistolary form, see the note on Rom 1, 1–7.

1, 3–7: Here Timothy's initial task *in Ephesus* (cf Acts 20, 17–35) is outlined: to suppress the idle religious speculations, probably about Old Testament figures (3–4, but see the note on 6, 20–21), which do not contribute to the development of love within the community (5) but rather encourage similar useless conjectures (6–7).

1, 4: The *plan of God that is to be received by faith:* the Greek may also possibly mean "God's trustworthy plan" or "the training in faith that God requires."

1, 8–11: Those responsible for the speculations that are to be suppressed by Timothy do not present the Old Testament from the Christian viewpoint. The Christian values the Old Testament not as a system of law but as the first stage in God's revelation of his saving plan, which is brought to fulfillment in the good news of salvation through faith in Jesus Christ.

1, 10: *Sodomites:* see 1 Cor 6, 9 and the note there.

1, 12–17: Present gratitude for the Christian apostleship leads Paul to recall an earlier time when he had been a fierce persecutor of the Christian communities (cf Acts 26, 9–11) until his conversion by intervention of divine mercy through the appearance of Jesus. This and his subsequent apostolic experience testify to the saving purpose of Jesus' incarnation. The fact of his former ignorance of the truth has not kept the apostle from regarding himself as having been the worst of sinners (15). Yet he was chosen to be an apostle, that God might manifest his firm will to save sinful humanity through Jesus Christ (16). The recounting of so great a mystery leads to a spontaneous outpouring of adoration (17).

1, 15: *This saying is trustworthy:* this phrase regularly introduces in the Pastorals a basic truth of early Christian faith; cf 3, 1; 4, 9; 2 Tm 2, 11; Ti 3, 8.

1, 17: *King of ages:* through Semitic influence, the Greek expression could mean "everlasting king"; it could also mean "king of the universe."

king of ages, incorruptible, invisible, the only
God, honor and glory forever and ever. Amen.

**Responsibility of Timothy** 18 [o]*I entrust
this charge to you, Timothy, my child, in accordance with the prophetic words once spoken
about you. Through them may you fight a good
fight 19 [p]by having faith and a good conscience. Some, by rejecting conscience, have
made a shipwreck of their faith, 20 [q]*among
them Hymenaeus and Alexander, whom I have
handed over to Satan to be taught not to blaspheme.

## *III: PROBLEMS OF DISCIPLINE*

### CHAPTER 2

**Prayer and Conduct** 1 [r]*First of all, then,
I ask that supplications, prayers, petitions, and
thanksgivings be offered for everyone, 2 for
kings and for all in authority, that we may lead
a quiet and tranquil life in all devotion and
dignity. 3 [s]This is good and pleasing to God
our savior, 4 [t]who wills everyone to be saved
and to come to knowledge of the truth.

5 [u]For there is one God.
There is also one mediator between
God and
the human race,
Christ Jesus, himself human,
6 [v]*who gave himself as ransom for all.

This was the testimony at the proper time.
7 [w]For this I was appointed preacher and apostle (I am speaking the truth, I am not lying),
teacher of the Gentiles in faith and truth.

8 *It is my wish, then, that in every place the
men should pray, lifting up holy hands, without
anger or argument. 9 [x]Similarly, [too,] women
should adorn themselves with proper conduct,
with modesty and self-control, not with braided
hairstyles and gold ornaments, or pearls, or expensive clothes, 10 [y]but rather, as befits wom-
en who profess reverence for God, with good
deeds. 11 [z]A woman must receive instruction
silently and under complete control. 12 *I do
not permit a woman to teach or to have authority
over a man. She must be quiet. 13 [a]For Adam
was formed first, then Eve. 14 [b]Further, Adam
was not deceived, but the woman was deceived
and transgressed. 15 [c]But she will be saved
through motherhood, provided women persevere in faith and love and holiness, with self-
control.

### CHAPTER 3

**Qualifications of Various Ministers**
1 [d]*This saying is trustworthy: whoever as-
pires to the office of bishop desires a noble task.

---

o 4, 14 / 6, 12; 2 Tm 4, 7; Jude 3.
p 3, 9.
q 2 Tm 2, 17; 4, 14 / 1 Cor 5, 5.
r Eph 6, 18; Phil 4, 6.
s 1, 1; 4, 10.
t 2 Tm 3, 7; 2 Pt 3, 9.
u 1 Cor 8, 6; Heb 8, 6; 9, 15; 12, 24 / Rom 5, 15.
v Mk 10, 45; Gal 1, 4; 2, 20; Eph 5, 25; Ti 2, 14.
w Acts 9, 15; 1 Cor 9, 1; Gal 2, 7-8.
x 1 Pt 3, 3-5.
y 5, 10; 1 Pt 3, 1.
z 1 Cor 14, 34-35.
a Gn 1, 27; 2, 7.22; 1 Cor 11, 8-9.
b Gn 3, 6.13; 2 Cor 11, 3.
c 5, 14.
d Ti 1, 6-9.

---

1, 18–20: Timothy is to be mindful of his calling, which is here compared to the way Barnabas and Saul were designated by Christ as prophets for missionary service; cf Acts 13, 1–3. Such is probably the sense of the allusion to the prophetic words (18). His task is not to yield, whether in doctrine or in conduct, to erroneous opinions, taking warning from what has already happened at Ephesus in the case of Hymenaeus and Alexander (19–20).

1, 18: *The prophetic words once spoken about you:* the Greek may also be translated, "the prophecies that led (me) to you." It probably refers to testimonies given by charismatic figures in the Christian communities. *Fight a good fight:* this translation preserves the play on words in Greek. The Greek terms imply a lengthy engagement in battle and might well be translated "wage a good campaign."

1, 20: *Hymenaeus:* mentioned in 2 Tm 2, 17 as saying that the resurrection has already taken place (in baptism). *Alexander:* probably the Alexander mentioned in 2 Tm 4, 14 as the coppersmith who "did me a great deal of harm." *Whom I have handed over to Satan:* the same terms are used in the condemnation of the incestuous man in 1 Cor 5, 5.

2, 1–7: This marked insistence that the liturgical prayer of the community concern itself with the needs of all, whether Christian or not, and especially of those in authority, may imply that a disposition existed at Ephesus to refuse prayer for pagans. In actuality, such prayer aids the community to achieve peaceful relationships with non-Christians (2) and contributes to salvation, since it derives its value from the presence within the community of Christ, who is the one and only savior of all (3–6). The vital apostolic mission to the Gentiles (7) reflects Christ's purpose of universal salvation.

Verse 5 contains what may well have been a very primitive creed. Some interpreters have called it a Christian version of the Jewish *shema:* "Hear, O Israel, the LORD is our God, the LORD alone . . ." (Dt 6, 4–5). The assertion in v 7, "I am speaking the truth, I am not lying," reminds one of similar affirmations in Rom 9, 1; 2 Cor 11, 31; and Gal 1, 20.

2, 6: *The testimony:* to make sense of this overly concise phrase, many manuscripts supply "to which" (or "to whom"); two others add "was given." The translation has supplied "this was."

2, 8–15: The prayer of the community should be unmarred by internal dissension (8); cf Mt 5, 21–26; 6, 14; Mk 11, 25. At the liturgical assembly the dress of women should be appropriate to the occasion (9); their chief adornment is to be reputation for good works (10). Women are not to take part in the charismatic activity of the assembly (11–12; cf 1 Cor 14, 34) or exercise authority; their conduct there should reflect the role of man's helpmate (13; cf Gn 2, 18) and not the later relationship of Eve to Adam (14; cf Gn 3, 6–7). As long as women perform their role as wives and mothers in faith and love, their salvation is assured (15).

2, 12: *A man:* this could also mean "her husband."

3, 1–7: The passage begins by commending those who aspire to the office of bishop (*episkopos;* see the note on Phil 1, 1) within the community, but this first sentence (1) may also imply a warning about the great responsibilities involved. The writer proceeds to list the qualifications required: personal stability and graciousness; talent for teaching (2); moderation in habits and temperament (3); managerial ability (4); and experience in Christian living (5–6). Moreover, the candidate's

**2** Therefore, a bishop must be irreproachable,
married only once, temperate, self-controlled,
decent, hospitable, able to teach, **3** [e]not a
drunkard, not aggressive, but gentle, not contentious, not a lover of money. **4** He must manage his own household well, keeping his children under control with perfect dignity; **5** for if
a man does not know how to manage his own
household, how can he take care of the church
of God? **6** *He should not be a recent convert,
so that he may not become conceited and thus
incur the devil's punishment. **7** [f]He must also
have a good reputation among outsiders, so that
he may not fall into disgrace, the devil's trap.
**8** *Similarly, deacons must be dignified, not
deceitful, not addicted to drink, not greedy for
sordid gain, **9** holding fast to the mystery of the
faith with a clear conscience. **10** Moreover,
they should be tested first; then, if there is nothing against them, let them serve as deacons.
**11** [g]*Women, similarly, should be dignified,
not slanderers, but temperate and faithful in
everything. **12** Deacons may be married only
once and must manage their children and their
households well. **13** Thus those who serve well
as deacons gain good standing and much confidence in their faith in Christ Jesus.

**The Mystery of Our Religion** **14** *I am
writing you about these matters, although I hope
to visit you soon. **15** [h]But if I should be delayed, you should know how to behave in the
household of God, which is the church of the
living God, the pillar and foundation of truth.
**16** [i]*Undeniably great is the mystery of devotion,

Who was manifested in the flesh,
vindicated in the spirit,
seen by angels,
proclaimed to the Gentiles,
believed in throughout the world,
taken up in glory.

## CHAPTER 4

**False Asceticism** **1** [j]*Now the Spirit explicitly says that in the last times some will turn
away from the faith by paying attention to deceitful spirits and demonic instructions
**2** through the hypocrisy of liars with branded
consciences. **3** [k]They forbid marriage and require abstinence from foods that God created to
be received with thanksgiving by those who
believe and know the truth. **4** [l]For everything
created by God is good, and nothing is to be
rejected when received with thanksgiving,
**5** *for it is made holy by the invocation of God
in prayer.

**Counsel to Timothy** **6** *If you will give
these instructions to the brothers, you will be a
good minister of Christ Jesus, nourished on the
words of the faith and of the sound teaching you

e Heb 13, 5.
f 2 Cor 8, 21; 2 Tm 2, 26.
g Ti 2, 3.
h Eph 2, 19-22.
i Jn 1, 14; Rom 1, 3-4.
j 2 Tm 3, 1; 4, 3; 2 Pt 3, 3; Jude 18.
k Gn 9, 3; Rom 14, 6; 1 Cor 10, 30-31.
l Gn 1, 31; Acts 10, 15.

* previous life should provide no grounds for the charge that he did not previously practice what he now preaches. No list of qualifications for presbyters appears in 1 Tm. The presbyter-bishops here and in Ti (see the note on Ti 1, 5–9) lack certain functions reserved here for Paul and Timothy.

3, 1: *This saying is trustworthy:* the saying introduced is so unlike others after this phrase that some later Western manuscripts read, "This saying is popular." It is understood by some interpreters as concluding the preceding section (2, 8–15). *Bishop:* literally, "overseer"; see the note on Phil 1, 1.

3, 6: *The devil's punishment:* this phrase could mean the punishment once incurred by the devil (objective genitive) or a punishment brought about by the devil (subjective genitive).

3, 8–13: Deacons, besides possessing the virtue of moderation (8), are to be outstanding for their faith (9) and well respected within the community (10). Women in the same role, although some interpreters take them to mean wives of deacons, must be dignified, temperate, dedicated, and not given to malicious talebearing (11). Deacons must have shown stability in marriage and have a good record with their families (12), for such experience prepares them well for the exercise of their ministry on behalf of the community (13). See further the note on Phil 1, 1.

3, 11: *Women:* this seems to refer to women deacons but may possibly mean wives of deacons. The former is preferred because the word is used absolutely; if deacons' wives were meant, a possessive "their" would be expected. Moreover, they are also introduced by the word "similarly," as in v 8; this parallel suggests that they too exercised ecclesiastical functions.

3, 14–16: In case there is some delay in the visit to Timothy at Ephesus planned for the near future, the present letter is being sent on ahead to arm and enlighten him in his task of preserving sound Christian conduct in the Ephesian church. The care he must exercise over this community is required by the profound nature of Christianity. It centers in Christ, appearing in human flesh, vindicated by the holy Spirit; the mystery of his person was revealed to the angels, announced to the Gentiles, and accepted by them in faith. He himself was taken up (through his resurrection and ascension) to the divine glory (16). This passage apparently includes part of a liturgical hymn used among the Christian communities in and around Ephesus. It consists of three couplets in typical Hebrew balance: flesh-spirit (contrast), seen-proclaimed (complementary), world-glory (contrast).

3, 16: *Who:* the reference is to Christ, who is himself "the mystery of our devotion." Some predominantly Western manuscripts read "which," harmonizing the gender of the pronoun with that of the Greek word for mystery; many later (eighth/ninth century on), predominantly Byzantine manuscripts read "God," possibly for theological reasons.

4, 1–5: Doctrinal deviations from the true Christian message within the church have been prophesied, though the origin of the prophecy is not specified (1–2); cf Acts 20, 29–30. The letter warns against a false asceticism that prohibits marriage and regards certain foods as forbidden, though they are part of God's good creation (3).

4, 5: *The invocation of God in prayer:* literally, "the word of God and petition." The use of "word of God" without an article in Greek suggests that it refers to the name of God being invoked in blessing rather than to the "word of God" proclaimed to the community.

4, 6–10: Timothy is urged to be faithful, both in his teaching and in his own life, as he looks only to God for salvation.

have followed. **7** [m]Avoid profane and silly
myths. Train yourself for devotion, **8** [n]for,
while physical training is of limited value, devotion is valuable in every respect, since it holds
a promise of life both for the present and for the
future. **9** [o]This saying is trustworthy and deserves full acceptance. **10** [p]*For this we toil
and struggle, because we have set our hope on
the living God, who is the savior of all, especially of those who believe.
**11** *Command and teach these things.
**12** [q]*Let no one have contempt for your youth,
but set an example for those who believe, in
speech, conduct, love, faith, and purity.
**13** *Until I arrive, attend to the reading, exhortation, and teaching. **14** [r]*Do not neglect the
gift you have, which was conferred on you
through the prophetic word with the imposition
of hands of the presbyterate. **15** Be diligent in
these matters, be absorbed in them, so that your
progress may be evident to everyone. **16** Attend to yourself and to your teaching; persevere
in both tasks, for by doing so you will save both
yourself and those who listen to you.

## *IV: DUTIES TOWARD OTHERS*

### CHAPTER 5

**1** [s]*Do not rebuke an older man, but appeal
to him as a father. Treat younger men as brothers, **2** older women as mothers, and younger
women as sisters with complete purity.

**Rules for Widows** **3** Honor widows who
are truly widows. **4** But if a widow has children
or grandchildren, let these first learn to perform
their religious duty to their own family and to
make recompense to their parents, for this is
pleasing to God. **5** [t]The real widow, who is all
alone, has set her hope on God and continues in
supplications and prayers night and day. **6** But
the one who is self-indulgent is dead while she
lives. **7** Command this, so that they may be
irreproachable. **8** And whoever does not provide for relatives and especially family members has denied the faith and is worse than an
unbeliever.
**9** Let a widow be enrolled if she is not less
than sixty years old, married only once,
**10** [u]with a reputation for good works, namely,
that she has raised children, practiced hospitality, washed the feet of the holy ones, helped
those in distress, involved herself in every good
work. **11** But exclude younger widows, for
when their sensuality estranges them from
Christ, they want to marry **12** and will incur
condemnation for breaking their first pledge.
**13** [v]And furthermore, they learn to be idlers,
going about from house to house, and not only
idlers but gossips and busybodies as well, talking about things that ought not to be mentioned.
**14** [w]So I would like younger widows to marry,
have children, and manage a home, so as to give
the adversary no pretext for maligning us.
**15** For some have already turned away to follow Satan. **16** *If any woman believer has widowed relatives, she must assist them; the church
is not to be burdened, so that it will be able to
help those who are truly widows.

**Rules for Presbyters** **17** [x]*Presbyters
who preside well deserve double honor, espe-

m 1, 4; 2 Tm 2, 16; Ti 1, 14.
n 6, 6.
o 1, 15; 2 Tm 2, 11; Ti 3, 8.
p 2, 4; Ti 2, 11.
q 1 Cor 16, 11; Ti 2, 15 / Phil 3, 17.
r 5, 22; Acts 6, 6; 8, 17; 2 Tm 1, 6.
s Lv 19, 32; Ti 2, 2.
t Jer 49, 11; Lk 2, 37; 18, 7.
u Jn 13, 14; Heb 13, 2.
v 2 Thes 3, 11.
w 1 Cor 7, 9.
x 1 Cor 16, 18; Phil 2, 29.

*

4, 10: *Struggle:* other manuscripts and patristic witnesses read "suffer reproach."

4, 11–16: Timothy is urged to preach and teach with confidence, relying on the gifts and the mission that God has bestowed on him.

4, 12: *Youth:* some commentators find this reference a sign of pseudepigraphy. Timothy had joined Paul as a missionary already in A.D. 49, some fifteen years before the earliest supposed date of composition.

4, 13: *Reading:* the Greek word refers to private or public reading. Here, it probably designates the public reading of scripture in the Christian assembly.

4, 14: *Prophetic word:* this may mean the utterance of a Christian prophet designating the candidate or a prayer of blessing accompanying the rite. *Imposition of hands:* this gesture was used in the Old Testament to signify the transmission of authority from Moses to Joshua (Nm 27, 18–23; Dt 34, 9). The early Christian community used it as a symbol of installation into an office: the Seven (Acts 6, 6) and Paul and Barnabas (Acts 13, 3). *Of the presbyterate:* this would mean that each member of the college of presbyters imposed hands and appears to contradict 2 Tm 1, 6, in which Paul says that he imposed hands on Timothy. This latter text, however, does not exclude participation by others in the rite. Some prefer to translate "for the presbyterate," and thus understand it to designate the office into which Timothy was installed rather than the agents who installed him.

5, 1–16: After a few words of general advice based on common sense (1–2), the letter takes up, in its several aspects, the subject of widows. The first responsibility for their care belongs to the family circle, not to the Christian community as such (3–4.16). The widow left without the aid of relatives may benefit the community by her prayer, and the community should consider her material sustenance its responsibility (5–8). Widows who wish to work directly for the Christian community should not be accepted unless they are well beyond the probability of marriage, i.e., sixty years of age, married only once, and with a reputation for good works (9–10). Younger widows are apt to be troublesome and should be encouraged to remarry (11–15).

5, 16: *Woman believer:* some early Latin manuscripts and Fathers have a masculine here, while most later manuscripts and patristic quotations conflate the two readings, perhaps to avoid unfair restriction to women.

5, 17–25: The function of presbyters is not exactly the same as that of the *episkopos,* "bishop" (3, 1); in fact, the relation of the two at the time of this letter is obscure (but cf the note on Ti 1, 5–9). The Pastorals seem to reflect a transitional stage that developed in many regions of the church into

cially those who toil in preaching and teaching.
**18** [y]For the scripture says, "You shall not muzzle an ox when it is threshing," and, "A worker
deserves his pay." **19** [z]Do not accept an accusation against a presbyter unless it is supported
by two or three witnesses. **20** [a]Reprimand publicly those who do sin, so that the rest also will
be afraid. **21** I charge you before God and
Christ Jesus and the elect angels to keep these
rules without prejudice, doing nothing out of
favoritism. **22** [b]Do not lay hands too readily on
anyone, and do not share in another's sins. Keep
yourself pure. **23** Stop drinking only water, but
have a little wine for the sake of your stomach
and your frequent illnesses.

**24** Some people's sins are public, preceding
them to judgment; but other people are followed
by their sins. **25** Similarly, good works are also
public; and even those that are not cannot remain hidden.

## CHAPTER 6

**Rules for Slaves** **1** [c]*Those who are under
the yoke of slavery must regard their masters as
worthy of full respect, so that the name of God
and our teaching may not suffer abuse.
**2** [d]*Those whose masters are believers must
not take advantage of them because they are
brothers but must give better service because
those who will profit from their work are believers and are beloved.

## *V: FALSE TEACHING AND TRUE WEALTH*

**Teach and urge these things.**
**3** [e]Whoever teaches something different and
does not agree with the sound words of our Lord
Jesus Christ and the religious teaching **4** is conceited, understanding nothing, and has a morbid
disposition for arguments and verbal disputes.
From these come envy, rivalry, insults, evil
suspicions, **5** [f]and mutual friction among people with corrupted minds, who are deprived of
the truth, supposing religion to be a means of
gain. **6** [g]*Indeed, religion with contentment is
a great gain. **7** [h]For we brought nothing into the
world, just as we shall not be able to take anything out of it. **8** [i]If we have food and clothing,
we shall be content with that. **9** [j]Those who
want to be rich are falling into temptation and
into a trap and into many foolish and harmful
desires, which plunge them into ruin and destruction. **10** For the love of money is the root
of all evils, and some people in their desire for
it have strayed from the faith and have pierced
themselves with many pains.

**Exhortations to Timothy** **11** [k]*But you,
man of God, avoid all this. Instead, pursue
righteousness, devotion, faith, love, patience,
and gentleness. **12** [l]Compete well for the faith.
Lay hold of eternal life, to which you were
called when you made the noble confession in
the presence of many witnesses. **13** [m]I charge
[you] before God, who gives life to all things,
and before Christ Jesus, who gave testimony
under Pontius Pilate for the noble confession,
**14** to keep the commandment without stain or
reproach until the appearance of our Lord Jesus
Christ **15** [n]that the blessed and only ruler will
make manifest at the proper time, the King of
kings and Lord of lords, **16** [o]who alone has
immortality, who dwells in unapproachable
light, and whom no human being has seen or can
see. To him be honor and eternal power. Amen.

y Dt 25, 4; 1 Cor 9, 8 / Mt 10, 10; Lk 10, 7.
z Dt 17, 6; 19, 15; Mt 18, 16; 2 Cor 13, 1.
a Gal 2, 14; Eph 5, 11; 2 Tm 4, 2; Ti 1, 9.13.
b 4, 14; 2 Tm 1, 6.
c Eph 6, 5; Ti 2, 9-10.
d Phlm 16.
e Gal 1, 6-9; 2 Tm 1, 13; Ti 1, 1.
f 2 Tm 3, 8; 4, 4; Ti 1, 14.
g 4, 8; Phil 4, 11-12; Heb 13, 5.
h Jb 1, 21; Eccl 5, 14.
i Prv 30, 8.
j Prv 23, 4; 28, 22.
k 2 Tm 2, 22.
l 1 Cor 9, 26; 2 Tm 4, 7.
m Jn 18, 36-37; 19, 11.
n 2 Mc 13, 4; Rv 17, 14.
o Ex 33, 20; Ps 104, 2.

* the monarchical episcopate of the second and third centuries. The presbyters possess the responsibility of preaching and teaching, for which functions they are supported by the community (17–18). The realization that their position subjects them to adverse criticism is implied in the direction to Timothy (19–20) to make sure of the truth of any accusation against them before public reproof is given. He must be as objective as possible in weighing charges against presbyters (21), learning from his experience to take care in selecting them (22). Some scholars take v 22 as a reference not to ordination of presbyters but to reconciliation of public sinners. The letter now sounds an informal note of personal concern in its advice to Timothy not to be so ascetic that he even avoids wine (23). Judgment concerning the fitness of candidates to serve as presbyters is easy with persons of open conduct, more difficult and prolonged with those of greater reserve (24–25).

6, 1–2: Compare the tables for household duties, such as that of Col 3, 18—4, 1. Domestic relationships derive new meaning from the Christian faith.

6, 1: *Our teaching:* this refers to the teaching of the Christian community.

6, 2b–10: Timothy is exhorted to maintain steadfastly the position outlined in this letter, not allowing himself to be pressured into any other course. He must realize that false teachers can be discerned by their pride, envy, quarrelsomeness, and greed for material gain. Verse 6 is rather obscure and is interpreted, and therefore translated, variously. The suggestion seems to be that the important gain that religion brings is spiritual, but that there is material gain, too, up to the point of what is needed for physical sustenance (cf 17–19).

6, 6: *Contentment:* the word *autarkeia* is a technical Greek philosophical term for the virtue of independence from material goods (Aristotle, Cynics, Stoics).

6, 11–16: Timothy's position demands total dedication to God and faultless witness to Christ (11–14) operating from an awareness, through faith, of the coming revelation in Jesus of the invisible God (15–16).

6, 11: *Man of God:* a title applied to Moses and the prophets (Dt 33, 1; 1 Sm 2, 27; 1 Kgs 12, 22; 13, 1; etc.).

**Right Use of Wealth** 17 [p]*Tell the rich in
the present age not to be proud and not to rely
on so uncertain a thing as wealth but rather on
God, who richly provides us with all things for
our enjoyment. 18 Tell them to do good, to be
rich in good works, to be generous, ready to
share, 19 [q]thus accumulating as treasure a good
foundation for the future, so as to win the life
that is true life.

## *VI: FINAL RECOMMENDATION AND WARNING*

20 [r]*O Timothy, guard what has been entrusted to you. Avoid profane babbling and the
absurdities of so-called knowledge. 21 [s]By
professing it, some people have deviated from
the faith.

Grace be with all of you.

p Ps 62, 11; Lk 12, 20.
q Mt 6, 20.
r 2 Tm 1, 14 / 4, 7.
s 1, 6; 2 Tm 2, 18.

*

6, 17–19: Timothy is directed to instruct the rich, advising them to make good use of their wealth by aiding the poor.

6, 20–21: A final solemn warning against the heretical teachers, with what seems to be a specific reference to gnosticism, the great rival and enemy of the church for two centuries and more (the Greek word for "knowledge" is *gnōsis*). If gnosticism is being referred to here, it is probable that the warnings against "speculations" and "myths and genealogies" (cf especially 1, 4; Ti 3, 9) involve allusions to that same kind of heresy. Characteristic of the various gnostic systems of speculation was an elaborate mythology of innumerable superhuman intermediaries, on a descending scale ("genealogies"), between God and the world. Thus would be explained the emphasis upon Christ's being the one mediator (as in 2, 5). Although fully developed gnosticism belonged to the second and later centuries, there are signs that incipient forms of it belonged to Paul's own period.

# THE SECOND LETTER TO

# TIMOTHY

## INTRODUCTION

*The authorship and date of this letter, as one of the Pastoral Epistles, are discussed in the Introduction to the First Letter to Timothy.*

*The tone here is more personal than in First Timothy, for this letter addresses Timothy in vivid terms (1, 6–14; 2, 1–13) and depicts Paul's courage and hope in the face of discouragements late in the course of his apostolic ministry (1, 15–18; 3, 10–17; 4, 9–18). Indeed, the letter takes on the character of a final exhortation and testament from Paul to the younger Timothy (4, 1–8). Paul is portrayed as a prisoner (1, 8.16; 2, 9) in Rome (1, 17), and there is a hint that Timothy may be in Ephesus (2, 17). The letter reveals that, with rare exceptions, Christians have not rallied to Paul's support (1, 15–18) and takes a pessimistic view of the outcome of his case (4, 6). It describes Paul as fully aware of what impends, looking to God, not to human beings, for his deliverance (4, 3–8.18). It recalls his mission days with Timothy (1, 3–5; cf Acts 16, 1–4). It points to his preaching of the gospel as the reason for his imprisonment and offers Timothy, as a motive for steadfastness, his own example of firmness in faith despite adverse circumstances (1, 6–14). The letter suggests that Timothy should prepare others to replace himself as Paul has prepared Timothy to replace him (2, 1–2). Paul urges him not to desist out of fear from preserving and spreading the Christian message (2, 3–7). It presents the resurrection of Jesus and his messianic role as the heart of the gospel for which Paul has been ready to lay down his life (2, 8–9) and thus not only to express his own conviction fully but to support the conviction of others (2, 10–13).*

*This letter, like the preceding one, urges Timothy to protect the community from the inevitable impact of false teaching (2, 14—3, 9), without fear of the personal attacks that may result (3, 10–13). It recommends that he rely on the power of the scriptures, on proclamation of the word, and on sound doctrine (3, 14—4, 2), without being troubled by those who do not accept him (4, 3–5). The letter poignantly observes in passing that Paul has need of his reading materials and his cloak (4, 13) and, what will be best of all, a visit from Timothy.*

*On the theory of authorship by Paul himself, Second Timothy appears to be the last of the three Pastoral Epistles. The many scholars who argue that the Pastorals are products of the Pauline school often incline toward Second Timothy as the earliest of the three and the one most likely to have actual fragments of material from Paul himself.*

*The principal divisions of the Second Letter to Timothy are the following:*

*I. Address (1, 1–5)*
*II. Exhortations to Timothy (1, 6—2, 13)*
*III. Instructions Concerning False Teaching (2, 14—4, 8)*
*IV. Personal Requests and Final Greetings (4, 9–22)*

## *I: ADDRESS*

### CHAPTER 1

**Greeting** **1** [a]*Paul, an apostle of Christ
Jesus by the will of God for the promise of life
in Christ Jesus, **2** to Timothy, my dear child:
grace, mercy, and peace from God the Father
and Christ Jesus our Lord.

**Thanksgiving** **3** [b]*I am grateful to God,
whom I worship with a clear conscience as my
ancestors did, as I remember you constantly in
my prayers, night and day. **4** *I yearn to see
you again, recalling your tears, so that I may be
filled with joy, **5** [c]as I recall your sincere faith
that first lived in your grandmother Lois and in
your mother Eunice and that I am confident
lives also in you.

## *II: EXHORTATIONS TO TIMOTHY*

**The Gifts Timothy Has Received**
**6** [d]*For this reason, I remind you to stir into
flame the gift of God that you have through the
imposition of my hands. **7** [e]For God did not
give us a spirit of cowardice but rather of power
and love and self-control. **8** [f]*So do not be
ashamed of your testimony to our Lord, nor of
me, a prisoner for his sake; but bear your share
of hardship for the gospel with the strength that
comes from God.
**9** [g]*He saved us and called us to a holy life,
not according to our works but according to his
own design and the grace bestowed on us in
Christ Jesus before time began, **10** [h]but now
made manifest through the appearance of our
savior Christ Jesus, who destroyed death and
brought life and immortality to light through the
gospel, **11** [i]*for which I was appointed preacher and apostle and teacher. **12** [j]*On this account I am suffering these things; but I am not
ashamed, for I know him in whom I have believed and am confident that he is able to guard
what has been entrusted to me until that day.
**13** [k]Take as your norm the sound words that
you heard from me, in the faith and love that are
in Christ Jesus. **14** [l]Guard this rich trust with
the help of the holy Spirit that dwells within us.

**Paul's Suffering** **15** [m]*You know that everyone in Asia deserted me, including Phygelus
and Hermogenes. **16** [n]*May the Lord grant
mercy to the family of Onesiphorus because he
often gave me new heart and was not ashamed
of my chains. **17** But when he came to Rome,
he promptly searched for me and found me.
**18** [o]*May the Lord grant him to find mercy
from the Lord on that day. And you know very
well the services he rendered in Ephesus.

### CHAPTER 2

**Timothy's Conduct** **1** *So you, my child,
be strong in the grace that is in Christ Jesus.

a 1 Tm 4, 8.
b 1 Tm 3, 9 / Phil 3, 5.
c 1 Tm 1, 5 / Acts 16, 1.
d 1 Tm 4, 14; 5, 22 / Acts 6, 6; 8, 17.
e Rom 5, 5; 8, 15; 1 Cor 2, 4.
f 2, 3.15; Rom 1, 16.
g Eph 2, 8-9; Ti 3, 5 / Eph 1, 4; Ti 1, 2.
h Rom 16, 26; 1 Pt 1, 20 / 1 Tm 6, 14 / Phil 3, 20; Ti 1, 4; 2, 13; 2 Pt 1, 11 / 1 Cor 15, 54-55; Heb 2, 14 / 1 Cor 15, 53-54.
i 1 Tm 2, 7.
j 1 Pt 4, 16 / 1 Tm 1, 10-11.
k 1 Tm 1, 14.
l 1 Tm 6, 20 / Rom 8, 11.
m 4, 16.
n 4, 19.
o Jude 21.

*

1, 1–2: For the formula of address and greeting, see the note on Rom 1, 1–7.

1, 1: *The promise of life in Christ Jesus:* that God grants through union with Christ in faith and love; cf Col 3, 4; 1 Tm 4, 8.

1, 3: *As my ancestors did:* this emphasizes the continuity of Judaism and Christianity; for a similar view, see Rom 9, 3–5; Phil 3, 4–6.

1, 4–5: Purportedly written from prison in Rome (8.17; 4, 6–8) shortly before the writer's death, the letter recalls the earlier sorrowful parting from Timothy, commending him for his faith and expressing the longing to see him again.

1, 6: The *gift of God:* the grace resulting from the conferral of an ecclesiastical office. *The imposition of my hands:* see the note on 1 Tm 4, 14.

1, 8: *Do not be ashamed of your testimony to our Lord:* i.e., of preaching and suffering for the sake of the gospel.

1, 9–10: Redemption from sin and the call to holiness of life are not won by personal deeds but are freely and graciously bestowed according to God's eternal plan; cf Eph 1, 4.

1, 11: *Teacher:* the overwhelming majority of manuscripts and Fathers read "teacher of the nations," undoubtedly a harmonization with 1 Tm 2, 7.

1, 12: *He is able to guard . . . until that day:* the intervening words can also be translated "what I have entrusted to him" (i.e., the fruit of his ministry) as well as "what has been entrusted to me" (i.e., the faith). The same difficult term occurs in v 14, where it is modified by the adjective "rich" and used without a possessive.

1, 15: Keen disappointment is expressed, here and later (4, 16), that the Christians of the province of Asia, especially Phygelus and Hermogenes, should have abandoned the writer and done nothing to defend his case in court.

1, 16–18: *The family of Onesiphorus because he . . . of my chains:* Onesiphorus seems to have died before this letter was written. His family is mentioned twice (here and in 4, 19), though it was Onesiphorus himself who was helpful to Paul in prison and rendered much service to the community of Ephesus. Because the apostle complains of abandonment by all in Asia during his second imprisonment and trial, the assistance of Onesiphorus seems to have been given to Paul during his first Roman imprisonment (A.D. 61–63).

1, 18: *Lord . . . Lord:* the first "Lord" here seems to refer to Christ, the second "Lord" to the Father.

2, 1–7: This passage manifests a characteristic deep concern for safeguarding the faith and faithfully transmitting it through trustworthy people (1–2; cf 1, 14; 1 Tm 6, 20; Ti 1, 9). Comparisons to the soldier's detachment, the athlete's sportsmanship, and the farmer's arduous work as the price of recompense (4–6) emphasize the need of singleness of purpose in preaching the word, even at the cost of hardship, for the sake of Christ (3).

**2** And what you heard from me through many
witnesses entrust to faithful people who will
have the ability to teach others as well. **3** [p]Bear
your share of hardship along with me like a good
soldier of Christ Jesus. **4** [q]To satisfy the one
who recruited him, a soldier does not become
entangled in the business affairs of life.
**5** [r]Similarly, an athlete cannot receive the win-
ner's crown except by competing according to
the rules. **6** [s]The hardworking farmer ought to
have the first share of the crop. **7** [t]Reflect on
what I am saying, for the Lord will give you
understanding in everything.

**8** [u]*Remember Jesus Christ, raised from the
dead, a descendant of David: such is my gospel,
**9** [v]for which I am suffering, even to the point
of chains, like a criminal. But the word of God
is not chained. **10** [w]Therefore, I bear with everything for the sake of those who are chosen,
so that they too may obtain the salvation that is
in Christ Jesus, together with eternal glory.
**11** [x]This saying is trustworthy:

If we have died with him
 we shall also live with him;
**12** [y]if we persevere
 we shall also reign with him.
But if we deny him
 he will deny us.
**13** [z]If we are unfaithful
 he remains faithful,
 for he cannot deny himself.

## III: INSTRUCTIONS CONCERNING FALSE TEACHING

### Warning against Useless Disputes

**14** [a]*Remind people of these things and charge
them before God to stop disputing about words.
This serves no useful purpose since it harms
those who listen. **15** [b]Be eager to present yourself as acceptable to God, a workman who
causes no disgrace, imparting the word of truth
without deviation. **16** [c]Avoid profane, idle
talk, for such people will become more and
more godless, **17** [d]and their teaching will
spread like gangrene. Among them are Hymenaeus and Philetus, **18** [e]who have deviated
from the truth by saying that [the] resurrection
has already taken place and are upsetting the
faith of some. **19** [f]Nevertheless, God's solid
foundation stands, bearing this inscription,
"The Lord knows those who are his"; and,
"Let everyone who calls upon the name of the
Lord avoid evil."

**20** In a large household there are vessels not
only of gold and silver but also of wood and
clay, some for lofty and others for humble use.
**21** [g]If anyone cleanses himself of these things,
he will be a vessel for lofty use, dedicated,
beneficial to the master of the house, ready for
every good work. **22** [h]*So turn from youthful
desires and pursue righteousness, faith, love,
and peace, along with those who call on the
Lord with purity of heart. **23** [i]Avoid foolish
and ignorant debates, for you know that they
breed quarrels. **24** [j]A slave of the Lord should
not quarrel, but should be gentle with everyone,
able to teach, tolerant, **25** [k]correcting opponents with kindness. It may be that God will
grant them repentance that leads to knowledge
of the truth, **26** [l]*and that they may return to
their senses out of the devil's snare, where they
are entrapped by him, for his will.

## CHAPTER 3

**The Dangers of the Last Days** **1** [m]*But
understand this: there will be terrifying times in

p 1, 8; 4, 5; Phlm 2.
q 1 Cor 9, 6.
r 1 Cor 9, 25.
s 1 Cor 9, 7-10.
t Prv 2, 6.
u Rom 1, 3; 1 Cor 15, 4.20 / Rom 2, 16; Gal 1, 11; 2, 2.
v Phil 1, 12-14.
w Col 1, 24; 1 Tm 1, 15.
x Rom 6, 8.
y Mt 10, 22.33; Lk 12, 9.
z Nm 23, 19; Rom 3, 3-4; 1 Cor 10, 13; Ti 1, 2.
a 1 Tm 6, 4.
b 1, 8; 2 Cor 6, 7; Eph 1, 13; Col 1, 5.
c 1 Tm 4, 7.
d 1 Tm 1, 20.
e 2 Thes 2, 2.
f Is 28, 16; 1 Cor 3, 10-15 / Nm 16, 5; Jn 10, 14.
g 3, 17.
h Gal 5, 22; 1 Tm 6, 11 / Rom 10, 13; 1 Cor 1, 2.
i 1 Tm 1, 4; 4, 7; 6, 4; Ti 3, 9.
j 1 Tm 3, 2-3.
k 3, 7; 1 Tm 2, 4.
l 1 Tm 3, 7.
m 1 Tm 4, 1; 2 Pt 3, 3; Jude 18.

*

2, 8–13: The section begins with a sloganlike summary of Paul's gospel about Christ (8) and concludes with what may be part of an early Christian hymn (11b–12a; most exegetes include the rest of v 12 and all of v 13 as part of the quotation). The poetic lines suggest that through baptism Christians die spiritually with Christ and hope to live with him and reign with him forever, but the Christian life includes endurance, witness, and even suffering, as the final judgment will show and as Paul's own case makes clear; while he is imprisoned for preaching the gospel (9), his sufferings are helpful to the elect for obtaining the salvation and glory available in Christ (10), who will be true to those who are faithful and will disown those who deny him (12–13).

2, 14–19: For those who dispute about mere words (cf 23–24) and indulge in irreligious talk to the detriment of their listeners (16–19), see the notes on 1 Tm 1, 3–7; 6, 20–21. Hymenaeus and Philetus (17), while accepting the Christian's mystical death and resurrection in Christ through baptism, claimed that baptized Christians are already risen with Christ in this life and thus that there is no future bodily resurrection or eternal glory to come. The first quotation in v 19 is from Nm 16, 5; the other quotation is from some unidentified Jewish or Christian writing.

2, 14: *Before God:* many ancient manuscripts read "before the Lord."

2, 22: *Those who call on the Lord:* those who believe in Christ and worship him as Lord, i.e., Christians (Acts 9, 14–16.20–21; Rom 10, 12–13; cf 19, literally, "Everyone who names the name of the Lord").

2, 26: Some interpreters would render this passage, "Thus they may come to their senses and, forced to do his (i.e., God's) will, may escape the devil's trap." This interpretation of the Greek is possible, but the one accepted in the text seems more likely.

3, 1–9: The moral depravity and false teaching that will be rampant in the last days are already at work (1–5). The frivo-

the last days. **2** [n]People will be self-centered
and lovers of money, proud, haughty, abusive,
disobedient to their parents, ungrateful, irreligious, **3** callous, implacable, slanderous, licentious, brutal, hating what is good, **4** traitors,
reckless, conceited, lovers of pleasure rather
than lovers of God, **5** [o]as they make a pretense
of religion but deny its power. Reject them.
**6** [p]For some of these slip into homes and make
captives of women weighed down by sins, led
by various desires, **7** [q]always trying to learn but
never able to reach a knowledge of the truth.
**8** [r]Just as Jannes and Jambres opposed Moses,
so they also oppose the truth—people of depraved mind, unqualified in the faith. **9** But
they will not make further progress, for their
foolishness will be plain to all, as it was with
those two.

**Paul's Example and Teaching** **10** *You
have followed my teaching, way of life, purpose, faith, patience, love, endurance,
**11** [s]persecutions, and sufferings, such as happened to me in Antioch, Iconium, and Lystra,
persecutions that I endured. Yet from all these
things the Lord delivered me. **12** [t]In fact, all
who want to live religiously in Christ Jesus will
be persecuted. **13** But wicked people and char-
latans will go from bad to worse, deceivers and
deceived. **14** [u]But you, remain faithful to what
you have learned and believed, because you
know from whom you learned it, **15** [v]and that
from infancy you have known [the] sacred
scriptures, which are capable of giving you wisdom for salvation through faith in Christ Jesus.
**16** [w]*All scripture is inspired by God and is
useful for teaching, for refutation, for correction, and for training in righteousness, **17** [x]so
that one who belongs to God may be competent,
equipped for every good work.

## CHAPTER 4

**Solemn Charge** **1** [y]*I charge you in the
presence of God and of Christ Jesus, who will
judge the living and the dead, and by his appearing and his kingly power: **2** [z]proclaim the word;
be persistent whether it is convenient or incon-
venient; convince, reprimand, encourage
through all patience and teaching. **3** [a]*For the
time will come when people will not tolerate
sound doctrine but, following their own desires
and insatiable curiosity, will accumulate teachers **4** [b]and will stop listening to the truth and
will be diverted to myths. **5** But you, be
self-possessed in all circumstances; put up with
hardship; perform the work of an evangelist;
fulfill your ministry.

**Reward for Fidelity** **6** [c]*For I am already
being poured out like a libation, and the time of
my departure is at hand. **7** [d]*I have competed
well; I have finished the race; I have kept the
faith. **8** [e]*From now on the crown of righteousness awaits me, which the Lord, the just judge,
will award to me on that day, and not only to
me, but to all who have longed for his appearance.

---

n Rom 1, 29-31.
o Rom 2, 20-22; Ti 1, 16.
p Ti 1, 11.
q 2, 25.
r Ex 7, 11.22; 1 Tm 6, 5.
s Acts 13, 50; 14, 5.19 / Ps 34, 20.
t Jn 15, 20; Acts 14, 22.
u 2, 2.
v Jn 5, 39.
w Rom 15, 4; 2 Pt 1, 19-21.
x 2, 21.
y 1 Tm 5, 21; 6, 14 / Acts 10, 42; Rom 14, 9-10; 1 Pt 4, 5.
z Acts 20, 20.31; 1 Tm 5, 20.
a 1 Tm 4, 1.
b 1 Tm 1, 4; 4, 7; Ti 1, 14.
c Phil 2, 17.
d 1 Tm 1, 18; 6, 12; Jude 3 / Acts 20, 24; 1 Cor 9, 24; Heb 12, 1.
e 2, 5; Wis 5, 16; 1 Cor 9, 25; Phil 3, 14; Jas 1, 12; 1 Pt 5, 4;Rv 2, 10.

---

* lous and superficial, too, devoid of the true spirit of religion, will be easy victims of those who pervert them by falsifying the truth (6–8), just as Jannes and Jambres, Pharaoh's magicians of Egypt (Ex 7, 11–12.22), discredited the truth in Moses' time. Exodus does not name the magicians, but the two names are widely found in much later Jewish, Christian, and even pagan writings. Their origins are legendary.

3, 10–17: Paul's example for Timothy includes persecution, a frequent emphasis in the Pastorals. Timothy is to be steadfast to what he has been taught and to scripture. The scriptures are the source of wisdom, i.e., of belief in and loving fulfillment of God's word revealed in Christ, through whom salvation is given.

3, 16: *All scripture is inspired by God:* this could possibly also be translated, "All scripture inspired by God is useful for . . . ." In this classic reference to inspiration, God is its principal author, with the writer as the human collaborator. Thus the scriptures are the word of God in human language. See also 2 Pt 1, 20–21.

3, 16–17: *Useful for teaching . . . every good work:* because as God's word the scriptures share his divine authority. It is exercised through those who are ministers of the word.

4, 1–5: The gravity of the obligation incumbent on Timothy to preach the word can be gauged from the solemn adjuration: in the presence of God, and of Christ coming as universal judge, and by his appearance and his kingly power (1). Patience, courage, constancy, and endurance are required despite the opposition, hostility, indifference, and defection of many to whom the truth has been preached (2–5).

4, 3: *Insatiable curiosity:* literally, "with itching ears."

4, 6: The apostle recognizes his death through martyrdom to be imminent. He regards it as an act of worship in which his blood will be poured out in sacrifice; cf Ex 29, 38–40; Phil 2, 17.

4, 7: At the close of his life Paul could testify to the accomplishment of what Christ himself foretold concerning him at the time of his conversion, "I will show him what he will have to suffer for my name" (Acts 9, 16).

4, 8: When the world is judged at the parousia, all who have eagerly looked for the Lord's appearing and have sought to live according to his teachings will be rewarded. The crown is a reference to the laurel wreath placed on the heads of victorious athletes and conquerors in war; cf 2, 5; 1 Cor 9, 25.

## IV: PERSONAL REQUESTS AND FINAL GREETINGS

**Paul's Loneliness** 9 *Try to join me soon,
10 [f]*for Demas, enamored of the present
world, deserted me and went to Thessalonica,
Crescens to Galatia, and Titus to Dalmatia.
11 [g]Luke is the only one with me. Get Mark
and bring him with you, for he is helpful to me
in the ministry. 12 [h]I have sent Tychicus to
Ephesus. 13 [i]When you come, bring the cloak
I left with Carpus in Troas, the papyrus rolls,
and especially the parchments.
14 [j]*Alexander the coppersmith did me a
great deal of harm; the Lord will repay him
according to his deeds. 15 You too be on guard
against him, for he has strongly resisted our
preaching.
16 [k]At my first defense no one appeared on
my behalf, but everyone deserted me. May it
not be held against them! 17 [l]But the Lord
stood by me and gave me strength, so that
through me the proclamation might be completed and all the Gentiles might hear it. And I was
rescued from the lion's mouth. 18 [m]The Lord
will rescue me from every evil threat and will
bring me safe to his heavenly kingdom. To him
be glory forever and ever. Amen.

**Final Greeting** 19 [n]*Greet Prisca and Aquila and the family of Onesiphorus.
20 [o]*Erastus remained in Corinth, while I left
Trophimus sick at Miletus. 21 *Try to get here
before winter. Eubulus, Pudens, Linus, Claudia, and all the brothers send greetings.
22 [p]The Lord be with your spirit. Grace be
with all of you.

f Col 4, 14; Phlm 24 / 2 Cor 2, 13; 7, 6-7; 8, 23; Gal 2, 3;Ti 1, 4.
g Col 4, 14; Phlm 24 / Col 4, 10; Phlm 24.
h Acts 20, 4; Eph 6, 21; Col 4, 7.
i Acts 16, 8; 20, 6.
j 1 Tm 1, 20 / 2 Sm 3, 39; Pss 28, 4; 62, 12; Prv 24, 12; Rom 2, 6.
k 1, 15.
l Acts 23, 11; 27, 23; Phil 4, 13 / 1 Mc 2, 60; Ps 22, 22;Dn 6, 23.
m 2 Cor 1, 10 / Rom 16, 27.
n Acts 18, 2; Rom 16, 3; 1 Cor 16, 19 / 1, 16.
o Acts 19, 22; Rom 16, 24 / Acts 20, 4; 21, 29.
p Gal 6, 18; Phil 4, 23; Col 4, 18; 1 Tm 6, 21; Ti 3, 15.

*

4, 9–13: Demas either abandoned the work of the ministry for worldly affairs or, perhaps, gave up the faith itself (10). Luke (11) may have accompanied Paul on parts of his second and third missionary journeys (Acts 16, 10–12; 20, 5–7). Notice the presence of the first personal pronoun "we" in these Acts passages, suggesting to some that Luke (or at least some traveling companion of Paul's) was the author of Acts. Mark, once rejected by Paul (Acts 13, 13; 15, 39), is now to render him a great service (11); cf Col 4, 10; Phlm 24. For Tychicus, see Eph 6, 21; cf also Acts 20, 4; Col 4, 7.

4, 10: *Galatia:* some manuscripts read "Gaul" or "Gallia."

4, 14–18: *Alexander:* an opponent of Paul's preaching (14–15), perhaps the one who is mentioned in 1 Tm 1, 20. Despite Paul's abandonment by his friends in the province of Asia (cf 1, 15–16), the divine assistance brought this first trial to a successful issue, even to the point of making the gospel message known to those who participated in or witnessed the trial (16–17).

4, 19: *Prisca and Aquila:* they assisted Paul in his ministry in Corinth (Acts 18, 2–3) and Ephesus (Acts 18, 19.26; 1 Cor 16, 19). They risked death to save his life, and all the Gentile communities are indebted to them (Rom 16, 3–5).

4, 20: *Erastus:* he was the treasurer of the city of Corinth (Rom 16, 24); cf also Acts 19, 22. *Trophimus:* from the province of Asia, he accompanied Paul from Greece to Troas (Acts 20, 4–5).

4, 21: *Linus:* Western tradition sometimes identified this Linus with the supposed successor of Peter as bishop of Rome, and Claudia as the mother of Linus (*Apostolic Constitutions,* fourth century).

# THE LETTER TO

# TITUS

## INTRODUCTION

*The third of the Pastoral Epistles in the New Testament is addressed to a different co-worker of Paul than are First and Second Timothy. The situation is different, too, for Titus is addressed as the person in charge of developing the church on the large Mediterranean island of Crete (1, 5), a place Paul had never, according to the New Testament, visited. The tone is closer to that of First Timothy as three topics of church life and structure are discussed: presbyter-bishops (see the note on 1, 5–9), groups with which one must work in the church (2, 1–10), and admonitions for conduct based on the grace and love of God that appeared in Jesus Christ (2, 11—3, 10). The warmer personal tone of Second Timothy is replaced by emphasis on church office and on living in the society of the day, in which deceivers and heretics abound (1, 10–16; 3, 9–10).*

*The Pauline assistant who is addressed, Titus, was a Gentile Christian, but we are nowhere informed of his place of birth or residence. He went from Antioch with Paul and Barnabas to Jerusalem (Gal 2, 1; cf Acts 15, 2). According to 2 Corinthians (2, 13; 7, 6.13–14), he was with Paul on his third missionary journey; his name, however, does not appear in Acts. Besides being the bearer of Paul's severe letter to the Corinthians (2 Cor 7, 6–8), he had the responsibility of taking up the collection in Corinth for the Christian community of Jerusalem (2 Cor 8, 6.16–19.23). In the present letter (1, 5), he is mentioned as the administrator of the Christian community in Crete, charged with the task of organizing it through the appointment of presbyters and bishops (1, 5–9; here the two terms refer to the same personages).*

*The letter instructs Titus about the character of the assistants he is to choose in view of the pastoral difficulties peculiar to Crete (1, 5–16). It suggests the special individual and social virtues that the various age groups and classes in the Christian community should be encouraged to acquire (2, 1–10). The motivation for transformation of their lives comes from christology, especially the redemptive sacrifice of Christ and his future coming, as applied through baptism and justification (2, 11–14; 3, 4–8). The community is to serve as a leaven for Christianizing the social world about it (3, 1–3). Good works are to be the evidence of their faith in God (3, 8); those who engage in religious controversy are, after suitable warning, to be ignored (3, 9–11).*

*The authorship and date of the Letter to Titus are discussed in the Introduction to 1 Timothy. Those who assume authorship by Paul himself usually place Titus after 1 Timothy and before 2 Timothy. Others see it as closely related to 1 Timothy, in a growing emphasis on church structure and opposition to heresy, later than the letters of Paul himself and 2 Timothy. It has also been suggested that, if the three Pastorals once circulated as a literary unit, Titus was meant to be read ahead of 1 and 2 Timothy.*

*The principal divisions of the Letter to Titus are the following:*

*I. Address (1, 1–4)*
*II. Pastoral Charge (1, 5–16)*
*III. Teaching the Christian Life (2, 1—3, 15)*

## I: ADDRESS

### CHAPTER 1

**Greeting** 1 [a]*Paul, a slave of God and
apostle of Jesus Christ for the sake of the faith
of God's chosen ones and the recognition of
religious truth, 2 [b]in the hope of eternal life that
God, who does not lie, promised before time
began, 3 [c]who indeed at the proper time revealed his word in the proclamation with which
I was entrusted by the command of God our
savior, 4 [d]to Titus, my true child in our common faith: grace and peace from God the Father
and Christ Jesus our savior.

## II: PASTORAL CHARGE

**Titus in Crete** 5 *For this reason I left you
in Crete so that you might set right what remains
to be done and appoint presbyters in every town,
as I directed you, 6 [e]on condition that a man be
blameless, married only once, with believing
children who are not accused of licentiousness
or rebellious. 7 For a bishop as God's steward
must be blameless, not arrogant, not irritable,
not a drunkard, not aggressive, not greedy for
sordid gain, 8 but hospitable, a lover of goodness, temperate, just, holy, and self-controlled,
9 [f]holding fast to the true message as taught so
that he will be able both to exhort with sound
doctrine and to refute opponents. 10 *For there
are also many rebels, idle talkers and deceivers,
especially the Jewish Christians. 11 It is imperative to silence them, as they are upsetting
whole families by teaching for sordid gain what
they should not. 12 *One of them, a prophet of
their own, once said, "Cretans have always
been liars, vicious beasts, and lazy gluttons."
13 [g]That testimony is true. Therefore, admonish them sharply, so that they may be sound in
the faith, 14 [h]instead of paying attention to
Jewish myths and regulations of people who
have repudiated the truth. 15 [i]To the clean all
things are clean, but to those who are defiled
and unbelieving nothing is clean; in fact, both
their minds and their consciences are tainted.
16 They claim to know God, but by their deeds
they deny him. They are vile and disobedient
and unqualified for any good deed.

## III: TEACHING THE CHRISTIAN LIFE

### CHAPTER 2

**Christian Behavior** 1 [j]*As for yourself,
you must say what is consistent with sound
doctrine, namely, 2 that older men should be
temperate, dignified, self-controlled, sound in
faith, love, and endurance. 3 Similarly, older
women should be reverent in their behavior, not
slanderers, not addicted to drink, teaching what
is good, 4 so that they may train younger wom-
en to love their husbands and children, 5 [k]to be
self-controlled, chaste, good homemakers, under the control of their husbands, so that the
word of God may not be discredited.
6 Urge the younger men, similarly, to control themselves, 7 showing yourself as a model
of good deeds in every respect, with integrity in
your teaching, dignity, 8 and sound speech that
cannot be criticized, so that the opponent will be
put to shame without anything bad to say about
us.
9 [l]Slaves are to be under the control of their
masters in all respects, giving them satisfaction,
not talking back to them 10 [m]or stealing from
them, but exhibiting complete good faith, so as
to adorn the doctrine of God our savior in every
way.

---

a 1 Tm 2, 4; 4, 3; 2 Tm 2, 25; 3, 7; Heb 10, 26.
b 3, 7; 2 Tm 1, 1; 1 Jn 2, 25.
c 2, 10; 3, 4; Ps 24, 5; 1 Tm 1, 1; 2, 3; 4, 10; Jude 25.
d 2, 13; 3, 6; Phil 3, 20; 2 Tm 1, 10; 2 Pt 1, 1.11; 2, 20; 3, 2.18.
e 1 Tm 3, 2-7; 2 Tm 2, 24-26.
f 1, 13; 2, 1-2.8; 1 Tm 1, 10; 6, 3; 2 Tm 1, 13; 4, 3.
g 1, 9.
h 3, 9; 1 Tm 1, 4; 4, 7; 2 Tm 4, 4; 2 Pt 1, 16.
i Mk 7, 18-23; Acts 10, 15; Rom 14, 14-23.
j 1, 9.13; 2, 8; 1 Tm 1, 10; 6, 3; 2 Tm 1, 13; 4, 3.
k 1 Cor 11, 3; 14, 34; Eph 5, 22-24; Col 3, 18; 1 Tm 2, 11-15;1 Pt 3, 1-6.
l 1 Cor 7, 21-22; Eph 6, 5-8; Col 3, 22-25; 1 Tm 6, 1-2;1 Pt 2, 18.
m 1, 3; 3, 4; Ps 24, 5; 1 Tm 1, 1; 2, 3; 4, 10; Jude 25.

*

1, 1–4: On the epistolary form, see the note on Rom 1, 1–7. The apostolate is the divinely appointed mission to lead others to the true faith and through it to eternal salvation (1–3).

1, 5–9: This instruction on the selection and appointment of presbyters, substantially identical with that in 1 Tm 3, 1–7 on a bishop (see the note there), was aimed at strengthening the authority of Titus by apostolic mandate; cf 2, 15. In vv 5.7 and Acts 20, 17.28, the terms *episkopos* and *presbyteros* ("bishop" and "presbyter") refer to the same persons. Deacons are not mentioned in Titus. See also the note on Phil 1, 1.

1, 10–16: This adverse criticism of the defects within the community is directed especially against certain Jewish Christians, who busy themselves with useless speculations over persons mentioned in the Old Testament, insist on the observance of Jewish ritual purity regulations, and thus upset whole families by teaching things they have no right to teach; cf 3, 9; 1 Tm 1, 3–10.

1, 10: *Jewish Christians:* literally, "those of the circumcision."

1, 12: *Cretans . . . gluttons:* quoted from Epimenides, a Cretan poet of the sixth century B.C.

2, 1–10: One of Titus' main tasks in Crete is to become acquainted with the character of the Cretans and thereby learn to cope with its deficiencies (see 1, 12). The counsel is not only for Titus himself but for various classes of people with whom he must deal: older men and women (2–4), younger women and men (4–7), and slaves (9–10); cf Eph 6, 1–9; Col 3, 18—4, 1.

**Transformation of Life** 11 [n]*For the
grace of God has appeared, saving all 12 and
training us to reject godless ways and worldly
desires and to live temperately, justly, and devoutly in this age, 13 [o]*as we await the blessed
hope, the appearance of the glory of the great
God and of our savior Jesus Christ, 14 [p]who
gave himself for us to deliver us from all lawlessness and to cleanse for himself a people as
his own, eager to do what is good.
15 [q]Say these things. Exhort and correct
with all authority. Let no one look down on you.

## CHAPTER 3

1 [r]*Remind them to be under the control of
magistrates and authorities, to be obedient, to
be open to every good enterprise. 2 They are to
slander no one, to be peaceable, considerate,
exercising all graciousness toward everyone.
3 [s]For we ourselves were once foolish, disobedient, deluded, slaves to various desires and
pleasures, living in malice and envy, hateful
ourselves and hating one another.

4 [t]But when the kindness and generous love
of God our savior appeared,
5 [u]not because of any righteous deeds we had
done
but because of his mercy,
he saved us through the bath of rebirth
and renewal by the holy Spirit,
6 [v]whom he richly poured out on us
through Jesus Christ our savior,
7 [w]so that we might be justified by his grace
and become heirs in hope of eternal life.

8 [x]*This saying is trustworthy.

**Advice to Titus** I want you to insist on these
points, that those who have believed in God be
careful to devote themselves to good works;
these are excellent and beneficial to others.
9 [y]*Avoid foolish arguments, genealogies, rivalries, and quarrels about the law, for they are
useless and futile. 10 [z]After a first and second
warning, break off contact with a heretic, 11 realizing that such a person is perverted and sinful
and stands self-condemned.

**Directives, Greetings, and Blessing**
12 [a]*When I send Artemas to you, or Tychicus, try to join me at Nicopolis, where I have
decided to spend the winter. 13 [b]Send Zenas
the lawyer and Apollos on their journey soon,
and see to it that they have everything they need.
14 [c]But let our people, too, learn to devote
themselves to good works to supply urgent
needs, so that they may not be unproductive.
15 [d]All who are with me send you greetings.
Greet those who love us in the faith.
Grace be with all of you.

---

n 1 Tm 2, 4; 4, 10.
o 1 Cor 1, 7; Phil 3, 20; 1 Thes 1, 10 / 2 Tm 1, 10 / 1, 4; 3, 6;2 Pt 1, 1.11; 2, 20; 3, 2.18.
p Gal 1, 4; 2, 20; Eph 5, 2.25; 1 Tm 2, 6; 1 Pt 1, 18-19 /Ps 130, 8.
q 1 Tm 4, 12.
r Rom 13, 1-7; 1 Tm 2, 1-2; 1 Pt 2, 13-14.
s 1 Cor 6, 9-11; Eph 2, 1-3; 5, 8; Col 3, 5-7; 1 Pt 4, 3.
t 1, 3; 2, 10; Ps 24, 5; 1 Tm 1, 1; 2, 3; 4, 10; Jude 25.
u Dt 9, 5; Eph 2, 4-5.8-9; 2 Tm 1, 9.
v 1, 4; 2, 13; Phil 3, 20; 2 Tm 1, 10; 2 Pt 1, 1.11; 2, 20; 3, 2.18.
w 1, 2; 2 Tm 1, 1; 1 Jn 2, 25.
x 1 Tm 1, 15; 3, 1; 4, 9; 2 Tm 2, 11.
y 1 Tm 1, 4; 4, 7; 2 Tm 2, 23.
z Mt 18, 15-18; Rom 16, 17; 1 Cor 5, 11; 2 Thes 3, 6.14-15.
a Acts 20, 4; Eph 6, 21; Col 4, 7; 2 Tm 4, 12.
b Acts 18, 24-26; 1 Cor 1, 12; 3, 4-6.22; 4, 6; 16, 12.
c 2, 14; 3, 8; Heb 10, 24; 1 Pt 3, 13.
d Heb 13, 25.

---

2, 11–15: Underlying the admonitions for moral improvement in 1–10 as the moving force is the constant appeal to God's revelation of salvation in Christ, with its demand for transformation of life.

2, 13: *The blessed hope, the appearance:* literally, "the blessed hope and appearance," but the use of a single article in Greek strongly suggests an epexegetical, i.e., explanatory sense. *Of the great God and of our savior Jesus Christ:* another possible translation is "of our great God and savior Jesus Christ."

3, 1–8: The list of Christian duties continues from 2, 9–10, undergirded again as in 2, 11–13 by appeal to what God in Christ has done (4–7; cf 2, 11–14). The spiritual renewal of the Cretans, signified in God's merciful gift of baptism (4–7), should be reflected in their improved attitude toward civil authority and in their Christian relationship with all (1–3).

3, 1: *Magistrates and authorities:* some interpreters understand these terms as referring to the principalities and powers of the heavenly hierarchy. *To be open to every good enterprise:* this implies being good citizens. It could also be translated "ready to do every sort of good work" (as Christians); cf 14.

3, 8–11: In matters of good conduct and religious doctrine, Titus is to stand firm.

3, 9: See the note on 1 Tm 6, 20–21.

3, 12–15: *Artemas* or *Tychicus* (2 Tm 4, 12) is to replace Titus, who will join Paul in his winter sojourn at Nicopolis in Epirus, on the western coast of Greece.

# THE LETTER TO
# PHILEMON

## INTRODUCTION

*This short letter addressed to three specific individuals was written by Paul during an imprisonment, perhaps in Rome between A.D. 61 and 63 (see the Introduction to Colossians for other possible sites). It concerns Onesimus, a slave from Colossae (Col 4, 9), who had run away from his master, perhaps guilty of theft in the process (18). Onesimus was converted to Christ by Paul (10). Paul sends him back to his master (12) with this letter asking that he be welcomed willingly by his old master (8–10.14.17) not just as a slave but as a brother in Christ (16). Paul uses very strong arguments (especially 19) in his touching appeal on behalf of Onesimus. It is unlikely that Paul is subtly hinting that he would like to retain Onesimus as his own slave, lent to Paul by his master. Rather, he suggests he would like to have Onesimus work with him for the gospel (13.20–21). There is, however, little evidence connecting this Onesimus with a bishop of Ephesus of the same name mentioned by Ignatius of Antioch (ca. A.D. 110).*

*Paul's letter deals with an accepted institution of antiquity, human slavery. But Paul breathes into this letter the spirit of Christ and of equality within the Christian community. He does not attack slavery directly, for this is something the Christian communities of the first century were in no position to do, and the expectation that Christ would soon come again militated against social reforms. Yet Paul, by presenting Onesimus as "brother, beloved . . . to me, but even more so to you" (16), voiced an idea revolutionary in that day and destined to break down worldly barriers of division "in the Lord."*

**Address and Greeting** 1 [a]*Paul, a prisoner for Christ Jesus, and Timothy our brother,
to Philemon, our beloved and our co-worker,
2 [b]*to Apphia our sister, to Archippus our fellow soldier, and to the church at your house.
3 [c]*Grace to you and peace from God our Father and the Lord Jesus Christ.

**Thanksgiving** 4 [d]*I give thanks to my God always, remembering you in my prayers, 5 *as
I hear of the love and the faith you have in the
Lord Jesus and for all the holy ones, 6 [e]*so that
your partnership in the faith may become effective in recognizing every good there is in us that leads to Christ.

**Plea for Onesimus** 7 [f]*For I have experienced much joy and encouragement from your love, because the hearts of the holy ones have
been refreshed by you, brother. 8 *Therefore,
although I have the full right in Christ to order

a 9; Eph 3, 1; 4, 1; Phil 1, 7.13.
b Col 4, 17.
c Rom 1, 7; Gal 1, 3; Phil 1, 2.
d Rom 1, 8-9; Eph 1, 15-16.
e Phil 1, 9; Col 1, 9.
f 2 Cor 7, 4.

---

1: *Prisoner:* as often elsewhere (cf Rom, 1 Cor, Gal especially), the second word in Greek enunciates the theme and sets the tone of the letter. Here it is the prisoner appealing rather than the apostle commanding.

2: *Apphia our sister:* sister is here used (like brother) to indicate a fellow Christian. *The church at your house: your* here is singular. It more likely refers to Philemon than to the last one named, Archippus; Philemon is then the owner of the slave Onesimus (10). An alternate view is that the actual master of the slave is Archippus and that the one to whom the letter is addressed, Philemon, is the most prominent Christian there; see the note on Col 4, 17.

3: *Grace . . . and peace:* for this greeting, which may be a combination of Greek and Aramaic epistolary formulae, see the note on Rom 1, 1–7.

4: *In my prayers:* literally, "at the time of my prayers."

5: *Holy ones:* a common term for members of the Christian community (so also 7).

6: *In us:* some good ancient manuscripts have in you (plural). *That leads to Christ: leads to* translates the Greek preposition *eis,* indicating direction or purpose.

7: *Encouragement:* the Greek word *paraklēsis* is cognate with the verb translated "urge" in vv 9.10, and serves as an introduction to Paul's plea. *Hearts:* literally, "bowels," expressing in Semitic fashion the seat of the emotions, one's "inmost self." The same Greek word is used in v 12 and again in v 20, where it forms a literary inclusion marking off the body of the letter.

8: *Full right:* often translated "boldness," the Greek word *parrēsia* connotes the full franchise of speech, as the right of

you to do what is proper, **9** [g]*I rather urge you
out of love, being as I am, Paul, an old man, and
now also a prisoner for Christ Jesus. **10** [h]I urge
you on behalf of my child Onesimus, whose
father I have become in my imprisonment,
**11** *who was once useless to you but is now
useful to [both] you and me. **12** I am sending
him, that is, my own heart, back to you. **13** [i]*I
should have liked to retain him for myself, so
that he might serve me on your behalf in my
imprisonment for the gospel, **14** [j]but I did not
want to do anything without your consent, so
that the good you do might not be forced but
voluntary. **15** *Perhaps this is why he was away
from you for a while, that you might have him
back forever, **16** [k]*no longer as a slave but
more than a slave, a brother, beloved especially
to me, but even more so to you, as a man and
in the Lord. **17** So if you regard me as a partner,
welcome him as you would me. **18** *And if he
has done you any injustice or owes you anything, charge it to me. **19** [l]I, Paul, write this in
my own hand: I will pay. May I not tell you that
you owe me your very self. **20** Yes, brother,
may I profit from you in the Lord. Refresh my
heart in Christ.

**21** With trust in your compliance I write to
you, knowing that you will do even more than
I say. **22** [m]At the same time prepare a guest
room for me, for I hope to be granted to you
through your prayers.

**Final Greetings** **23** [n]*Epaphras, my fellow prisoner in Christ Jesus, greets you, **24** [o]as
well as Mark, Aristarchus, Demas, and Luke,
my co-workers. **25** The grace of the Lord Jesus
Christ be with your spirit.

g 1; Eph 3, 1; 4, 1; Phil 1, 7.13.
h 1 Cor 4, 14-15; Gal 4, 19; Col 4, 9.
i Phil 2, 30.
j 2 Cor 9, 7; 1 Pt 5, 2.
k 1 Tm 6, 2.
l Gal 6, 11; 2 Thes 3, 17.
m Heb 13, 19.
n Col 1, 7; 4, 12-13.
o Acts 12, 12.15; 13, 13; 15, 37-39; 19, 29; 20, 4; 27, 2; Col 4, 10.14; 2 Tm 4, 10-13.

*

a citizen to speak before the body politic, claimed by the Athenians as their privilege (Euripides).

9: *Old man:* some editors conjecture that Paul here used a similar Greek word meaning "ambassador" (cf Eph 6, 20). This conjecture heightens the contrast with "prisoner" but is totally without manuscript support.

11: *Useless . . . useful:* here Paul plays on the name Onesimus, which means "useful" or "beneficial." The verb translated "profit" in v 20 is cognate.

13: *Serve:* the Greek *diakoneō* could connote a ministry.

15: *Was away from:* literally, "was separated from," but the same verb means simply "left" in Acts 18, 1. It is a euphemism for his running away.

16: *As a man:* literally, "in the flesh." With this and the following phrase, Paul describes the natural and spiritual orders.

18–19: *Charge it to me . . . I will pay:* technical legal and commercial terms in account keeping and acknowledgment of indebtedness.

23–24: *Epaphras:* a Colossian who founded the church there (Col 1, 7) and perhaps also in Laodicea and Hierapolis (Col 2, 1; 4, 12–13). *Aristarchus:* a native of Thessalonica and fellow worker of Paul (Acts 19, 29; 20, 4; 27, 2). For Mark, Demas, and Luke, see 2 Tm 4, 9–13 and the note there.

# THE LETTER TO THE
# HEBREWS

## INTRODUCTION

*As early as the second century, this treatise, which is of great rhetorical power and force in its admonition to faithful pilgrimage under Christ's leadership, bore the title "To the Hebrews." It was assumed to be directed to Jewish Christians. Usually Hebrews was attached in Greek manuscripts to the collection of letters by Paul. Although no author is mentioned (for there is no address), a reference to Timothy (13, 23) suggested connections to the circle of Paul and his assistants. Yet the exact audience, the author, and even whether Hebrews is a letter have long been disputed.*

*The author saw the addressees in danger of apostasy from their Christian faith. This danger was due not to any persecution from outsiders but to a weariness with the demands of Christian life and a growing indifference to their calling (2, 1; 4, 14; 6, 1–12; 10, 23–32). The author's main theme, the priesthood and sacrifice of Jesus (chs 3–10), is not developed for its own sake but as a means of restoring their lost fervor and strengthening them in their faith. Another important theme of the letter is that of the pilgrimage of the people of God to the heavenly Jerusalem (11, 10; 12, 1–3.18–29; 13, 14). This theme is intimately connected with that of Jesus' ministry in the heavenly sanctuary (9, 11—10, 22).*

*The author calls this work a "message of encouragement" (13, 22), a designation that is given to a synagogue sermon in Acts 13, 15. Hebrews is probably therefore a written homily, to which the author gave an epistolary ending (13, 22–25).*

*The author begins with a reminder of the preexistence, incarnation, and exaltation of Jesus (1, 3) that proclaimed him the climax of God's word to humanity (1, 1–3). He dwells upon the dignity of the person of Christ, superior to the angels (1, 4—2, 2). Christ is God's final word of salvation communicated (in association with accredited witnesses to his teaching: cf 2, 3–4) not merely by word but through his suffering in the humanity common to him and to all others (2, 5–16). This enactment of salvation went beyond the pattern known to Moses, faithful prophet of God's word though he was, for Jesus as high priest expiated sin and was faithful to God with the faithfulness of God's own Son (2, 17—3, 6).*

*Just as the infidelity of the people thwarted Moses' efforts to save them, so the infidelity of any Christian may thwart God's plan in Christ (3, 6—4, 13). Christians are to reflect that it is their humanity that Jesus took upon himself, with all its defects save sinfulness, and that he bore the burden of it until death out of obedience to God. God declared this work of his Son to be the cause of salvation for all (4, 14—5, 10). Although Christians recognize this fundamental teaching, they may grow weary of it and of its implications, and therefore require other reflections to stimulate their faith (5, 11—6, 20).*

*Therefore, the author presents to the readers for their reflection the everlasting priesthood of Christ (7, 1–28), a priesthood that fulfills the promise of the Old Testament (8, 1–13). It also provides the meaning God ultimately intended in the sacrifices of the Old Testament (9, 1–28): these pointed to the unique sacrifice of Christ, which alone obtains forgiveness of sins (10, 1–18). The trial of faith experienced by the readers should resolve itself through their consideration of Christ's ministry in the heavenly sanctuary and his perpetual intercession there on their behalf (7, 25; 8, 1–13). They should also be strengthened by the assurance of his foreordained parousia, and by the fruits of faith that they have already enjoyed (10, 19–39).*

*It is in the nature of faith to recognize the reality of what is not yet seen and is the object of hope, and the saints of the Old Testament give striking example of that faith (11, 1–40). The perseverance to which the author exhorts the readers is shown forth in the early life of Jesus. Despite the afflictions of his ministry and the supreme trial of his suffering and death, he remained confident of the triumph that God would bring him (12, 1–3). The difficulties of human life have meaning when they are accepted as God's discipline (12, 4–13), and if Christians persevere in fidelity to the word in which they have believed, they are assured of possessing forever the unshakable kingdom of God (12, 14–29).*

*The letter concludes with specific moral commandments (13, 1–17), in the course of which the author recalls again his central theme of the sacrifice of Jesus and the courage needed to associate oneself with it in faith (13, 9–16).*

*As early as the end of the second century, the church of Alexandria in Egypt accepted Hebrews as a letter of Paul, and that became the view commonly held in the East. Pauline authorship was contested in the West into the fourth century, but then accepted. In the sixteenth century, doubts about that position were again raised, and the modern consensus is that the letter was not written by Paul. There is, however, no widespread agreement on any of the other suggested authors, e.g., Barnabas, Apollos, or Prisc(ill)a and Aquila. The document itself has no statement about its author.*

*Among the reasons why Pauline authorship has been abandoned are the great difference of vocabulary and style between Hebrews and Paul's letters, the alternation of doctrinal teaching with moral exhortation, the different manner of citing the Old Testament, and the resemblance between the thought of Hebrews and that of Alexandrian Judaism. The Greek of the letter is in many ways the best in the New Testament.*

*Since the letter of Clement of Rome to the Corinthians, written about A.D. 96, most probably cites Hebrews, the upper limit for the date of composition is reasonably certain. While the letter's references in the present tense to the Old Testament sacrificial worship do not necessarily show that temple worship was still going on, many older commentators and a growing number of recent ones favor the view that it was and that the author wrote before the destruction of the temple of Jerusalem in A.D. 70. In that case, the argument of the letter is more easily explained as directed toward Jewish Christians rather than those of Gentile origin, and the persecutions they have suffered in the past (cf 10, 32–34) may have been connected with the disturbances that preceded the expulsion of the Jews from Rome in A.D. 49 under the emperor Claudius. These were probably caused by disputes between Jews who accepted Jesus as the Messiah and those who did not.*

*The principal divisions of the Letter to the Hebrews are the following:*

*I. Introduction (1, 1–4)*
*II. The Son Higher than the Angels (1, 5—2, 18)*
*III. Jesus, Faithful and Compassionate High Priest (3, 1—5, 10)*
*IV. Jesus' Eternal Priesthood and Eternal Sacrifice (5, 11—10, 39)*
*V. Examples, Discipline, Disobedience (11, 1—12, 29)*
*VI. Final Exhortation, Blessing, Greetings (13, 1–25)*

# I: INTRODUCTION

## CHAPTER 1

**1** *In times past, God spoke in partial and
various ways to our ancestors through the

* 1, 1–4: The letter opens with an introduction consisting of a reflection on the climax of God's revelation to the human race in his Son. The divine communication was initiated and maintained during Old Testament times in fragmentary and varied ways through *the prophets* (1), including Abraham, Moses, and all through whom God spoke. But now *in these last days* (2), the final age, God's revelation of his saving purpose is achieved *through a son,* i.e., one who is Son, whose role is redeemer and mediator of creation. He was made *heir of all things* through his death and exaltation to glory, yet he existed before he appeared as man; through him God *created the universe.* Verses 3–4, which may be based upon a liturgical hymn, assimilate the Son to the personified Wisdom of the Old Testament as *refulgence of* God's *glory* and *imprint of his being* (3; cf Wis 7, 26). These same terms are used of the Logos in Philo. The author now turns from the cosmological role of the preexistent Son to the redemptive work of Jesus: he brought about purification from sins and has been exalted to the right hand of God (see Ps 110, 1). The once-humiliated and crucified Jesus has been declared God's Son, and this name shows his superiority to the angels. The reason for the author's insistence on that superiority is, among other things, that in some Jewish traditions angels were mediators of the old covenant (see Acts 7, 53; Gal 3, 19). Finally, Jesus' superiority to the angels emphasizes the superiority of the new covenant to the old because of the heavenly priesthood of Jesus.

prophets; 2 [a]in these last days, he spoke to us
through a son, whom he made heir of all things
and through whom he created the universe,

3 [b]who is the refulgence of his glory,
the very imprint of his being,
and who sustains all things by his mighty
word.
When he had accomplished purification from
sins,
he took his seat at the right hand of the
Majesty on high,
4 [c]as far superior to the angels
as the name he has inherited is more
excellent than theirs.

## *II: THE SON HIGHER THAN THE ANGELS*

**Messianic Enthronement** 5 [d]*For to
which of the angels did God ever say:

"You are my son; this day I have begotten
you"?

Or again:

"I will be a father to him, and he shall be a
son to me"?

6 [e]*And again, when he leads the first born
into the world, he says:

"Let all the angels of God worship him."

7 [f]Of the angels he says:

"He makes his angels winds
and his ministers a fiery flame";

8 [g]*but of the Son:

"Your throne, O God, stands forever and
ever;
and a righteous scepter is the scepter of
your kingdom.
9 You loved justice and hated wickedness;
therefore God, your God, anointed you
with the oil of gladness above your
companions";

10 [h]and:

"At the beginning, O Lord, you established
the earth,
and the heavens are the works of your
hands.
11 They will perish, but you remain;
and they will all grow old like a garment.
12 You will roll them up like a cloak,
and like a garment they will be changed.
But you are the same, and your years will
have no end."

13 [i]But to which of the angels has he ever said:

"Sit at my right hand
until I make your enemies your
footstool"?

14 [j]Are they not all ministering spirits sent to
serve, for the sake of those who are to inherit
salvation?

## CHAPTER 2

**Exhortation to Faithfulness** 1 *Therefore, we must attend all the more to what we
have heard, so that we may not be carried away.
2 [k]For if the word announced through angels
proved firm, and every transgression and disobedience received its just recompense, 3 [l]how
shall we escape if we ignore so great a salvation? Announced originally through the Lord, it
was confirmed for us by those who had heard.
4 [m]God added his testimony by signs, wonders, various acts of power, and distribution of
the gifts of the holy Spirit according to his will.

**Exaltation through Abasement** 5 *For
it was not to angels that he subjected the world

a Is 2, 2; Jer 23, 20; Ez 38, 16; Dn 10, 14 / Jn 3, 17; Rom 8, 3;Gal 4, 4 / Prv 8, 30; Wis 7, 22; Jn 1, 3; 1 Cor 8, 6; Col 1, 16.
b Wis 7, 26; 2 Cor 4, 4; Col 1, 15 / 8, 1; 10, 12; 12, 2; Mk 16, 19; Acts 2, 33; 7, 55-56; Rom 8, 34; Eph 1, 20;Col 3, 1; 1 Pt 3, 22.
c Eph 1, 21; Phil 2, 9-11.
d Ps 2, 7 / 2 Sm 7, 14.
e Dt 32, 43 LXX; Ps 97, 7.
f Ps 104, 4 LXX.
g Ps 45, 7-8.
h Ps 102, 26-28.
i Ps 110, 1.
j Ps 91, 11; Dn 7, 10.
k Acts 7, 38.53; Gal 3, 19.
l 10, 29; 12, 25.
m Mk 16, 20; Acts 14, 3; 19, 11.

*

1, 5–14: Jesus' superiority to the angels is now demonstrated by a series of seven Old Testament texts. Some scholars see in the stages of Jesus' exaltation an order corresponding to that of enthronement ceremonies in the ancient Near East, especially in Egypt, namely, elevation to divine status (5–6); presentation to the angels and proclamation of everlasting lordship (7–12); enthronement and conferral of royal power (13). The citations from the Psalms in vv 5 and 13 were traditionally used of Jesus' messianic sonship (cf Acts 13, 33) through his resurrection and exaltation (cf Acts 2, 33–35); those in vv 8 and 10–12 are concerned with his divine kingship and his creative function. The central quotation in v 7 serves to contrast the angels with the Son. The author quotes it according to the Septuagint translation, which is quite different in meaning from that of the Hebrew ("You make the winds your messengers, and flaming fire your ministers"). The angels are only *sent to serve . . . those who are to inherit salvation* (14).

1, 6: *And again, when he leads:* the Greek could also be translated "And when he again leads" in reference to the parousia.

1, 8–12: *O God:* the application of the name "God" to the Son derives from the preexistence mentioned in vv 2–3; the psalmist had already used it of the Hebrew king in the court style of the original. See the note on Ps 45, 7. It is also important for the author's christology that in vv 10–12 an Old Testament passage addressed to God is redirected to Jesus.

2, 1–4: The author now makes a transition into exhortation, using an a fortiori argument (as at 7, 21–22; 9, 13–14; 10, 28–29; 12, 25). The *word announced through angels* (2), the Mosaic law, is contrasted with the more powerful word that Christians have received (3–4). Christ's supremacy strengthens Christians against being *carried away* from their faith.

2, 5–18: The humanity and the suffering of Jesus do not constitute a valid reason for relinquishing the Christian faith. Ps 8 (6–7) is also applied to Jesus in 1 Cor 15, 27; Eph 1, 22; and probably 1 Pt 3, 22. This christological interpretation,

to come, of which we are speaking. 6 [n]Instead,
someone has testified somewhere:

> "What is man that you are mindful of him,
> or the son of man that you care for him?
> 7 You made him for a little while lower than
> the angels;
> you crowned him with glory and honor,
> 8 [o]subjecting all things under his feet."

In "subjecting" all things [to him], he left nothing not "subject to him." Yet at present we do
not see "all things subject to him," 9 [p]but we
do see Jesus "crowned with glory and honor"
because he suffered death, he who "for a little
while" was made "lower than the angels," that
by the grace of God he might taste death for
everyone.
10 [q]For it was fitting that he, for whom and
through whom all things exist, in bringing many
children to glory, should make the leader to
their salvation perfect through suffering. 11 He
who consecrates and those who are being consecrated all have one origin. Therefore, he is not
ashamed to call them "brothers," 12 [r]saying:

> "I will proclaim your name to my brothers,
> in the midst of the assembly I will praise
> you";

13 [s]and again:

> "I will put my trust in him";

and again:

> "Behold, I and the children God has given
> me."

14 [t]Now since the children share in blood and
flesh, he likewise shared in them, that through
death he might destroy the one who has the
power of death, that is, the devil, 15 and free
those who through fear of death had been subject to slavery all their life. 16 Surely he did not
help angels but rather the descendants of Abraham; 17 [u]therefore, he had to become like his
brothers in every way, that he might be a merciful and faithful high priest before God to expiate
the sins of the people. 18 Because he himself
was tested through what he suffered, he is able
to help those who are being tested.

## *III: JESUS, FAITHFUL AND COMPASSIONATE HIGH PRIEST*

## CHAPTER 3

**Jesus, Superior to Moses** 1 *Therefore,
holy "brothers," sharing in a heavenly calling,
reflect on Jesus, the apostle and high priest of
our confession, 2 [v]who was faithful to the one
who appointed him, just as Moses was "faithful
in [all] his house." 3 [w]But he is worthy of more
"glory" than Moses, as the founder of a house

n Ps 8, 5-7.
o Mt 28, 18; 1 Cor 15, 25-28; Eph 1, 20-23; Phil 3, 21; 1 Pt 3, 22.
p Phil 2, 6-11.
q 12, 2; Is 53, 4 / Rom 11, 36; 1 Cor 8, 6.
r Ps 22, 23.
s Is 8, 17.18.
t Is 25, 8; Hos 13, 14; Jn 12, 31; Rom 6, 9; 1 Cor 15, 54-55;2 Tm 1, 10; Rv 12, 10.
u 4, 15; 5, 1-3.
v Nm 12, 7.
w 2 Cor 3, 7-8.

therefore, probably reflects a common early Christian tradition, which may have originated in the expression *the son of man* (6). The psalm contrasts God's greatness with man's relative insignificance but also stresses the superiority of man to the rest of creation, of which he is lord. Heb applies this christologically: Jesus lived a truly human existence, *lower than the angels,* in the days of his earthly life, particularly in his suffering and death; now, *crowned with glory and honor,* he is raised above all creation. The author considers all things as already *subject to him* because of his exaltation (8–9), though *we do not see* this yet. The reference to Jesus as *leader* (10) sounds the first note of an important leitmotif in Heb: the journey of the people of God to the sabbath rest (4, 9), the heavenly sanctuary, following Jesus, their "forerunner" (6, 20). It was fitting that God should make him *perfect through suffering,* consecrated by obedient suffering. Because he is perfected as high priest, Jesus is then able to consecrate his people (11); access to God is made possible by each of these two consecrations. If Jesus is able to help human beings, it is because he has become one of us; we are his "brothers." The author then cites three Old Testament texts as proofs of this unity between ourselves and the Son. Psalm 22, 23 is inter preted so as to make Jesus the singer of this lament, which ends with joyful praise of the Lord in the assembly of "brothers." The other two texts are from Is 8, 17.18. The first of these seems intended to display in Jesus an example of the trust in God that his followers should emulate. The second curiously calls these followers "children"; probably this is to be understood to mean children of Adam, but the point is our solidarity with Jesus. By sharing human nature, including the ban of death, Jesus broke the power of the devil over death (14); the author shares the view of Hellenistic Judaism that death was not intended by God and that it had been introduced into the world by the devil. The *fear of death* (15) is a religious fear based on the false conception that death marks the end of a person's relations with God (cf Ps 115, 17–18; Is 38, 18). Jesus deliberately allied himself with the *descendants of Abraham* (16) in order to be a *merciful and faithful high priest.* This is the first appearance of the central theme of Heb, Jesus the great high priest expiating the *sins of the people* (17), as one who experienced the same tests as they (18).

3, 1–6: The author now takes up the two qualities of Jesus mentioned in 2, 17, but in inverse order: faithfulness (3, 1—4, 13) and mercy (4, 14—5, 10). Christians are called *holy "brothers"* because of their common relation to him (2, 11), the *apostle,* a designation for Jesus used only here in the New Testament (cf Jn 13, 16; 17, 3), meaning one sent as God's final word to us (1, 2). He is compared with Moses probably because he is seen as mediator of the new covenant (9, 15) just as Moses was of the old (9, 19–22, including his sacrifice). But when the author of Heb speaks of Jesus' sacrifice, he does not consider Moses as the Old Testament antitype, but rather the high priest on the Day of Atonement (9, 6–15). Moses' faithfulness *"in [all] his house"* refers back to Nm 12, 7, on which this section is a midrashic commentary. In vv 3–6, the author does not indicate that he thinks of either Moses or Christ as the founder of the household. *His house* (2.5.6) means God's house, not that of Moses or Christ; in the case of Christ, compare v 6 with 10, 21. The *house* of v 6 is the Christian community; the author suggests its continuity with Israel by speaking not of two houses but of only one. Verse 6 brings out the reason why Jesus is superior to Moses: the latter was the faithful *servant* laboring *in* the house founded by God, but Jesus is God's *son,* placed *over* the house.

has more "honor" than the house itself. 4 Every house is founded by someone, but the
founder of all is God. 5 Moses was "faithful in
all his house" as a "servant" to testify to what
would be spoken, 6 [x]*but Christ was faithful as
a son placed over his house. We are his house,
if [only] we hold fast to our confidence and
pride in our hope.

## Israel's Infidelity a Warning

7 [y]*Therefore, as the holy Spirit says:

"Oh, that today you would hear his voice,
8 'Harden not your hearts as at the rebellion
in the day of testing in the desert,
9 [z]where your ancestors tested and tried me
and saw my works 10 for forty years.
Because of this I was provoked with that
generation
and I said, "They have always been of
erring heart,
and they do not know my ways."
11 As I swore in my wrath,
"They shall not enter into my
rest." ' "

12 Take care, brothers, that none of you may
have an evil and unfaithful heart, so as to forsake the living God. 13 Encourage yourselves
daily while it is still "today," so that none of
you may grow hardened by the deceit of sin.
14 [a]We have become partners of Christ if only
we hold the beginning of the reality firm until
the end, 15 [b]for it is said:

"Oh, that today you would hear his voice:
"Harden not your hearts as at the
rebellion.' "

16 [c]Who were those who rebelled when they
heard? Was it not all those who came out of
Egypt under Moses? 17 [d]With whom was he
"provoked for forty years"? Was it not those
who had sinned, whose corpses fell in the
desert? 18 [e]And to whom did he "swear that
they should not enter into his rest," if not to
those who were disobedient? 19 And we see
that they could not enter for lack of faith.

## CHAPTER 4

**The Sabbath Rest** 1 Therefore, let us be
on our guard while the promise of entering into
his rest remains, that none of you seem to have
failed. 2 For in fact we have received the good
news just as they did. But the word that they
heard did not profit them, for they were not
united in faith with those who listened. 3 [f]For
we who believed enter into [that] rest, just as he
has said:

"As I swore in my wrath,
"They shall not enter into my rest,' "
and yet his works were accomplished at the
foundation of the world. 4 [g]For he has spoken
somewhere about the seventh day in this manner, "And God rested on the seventh day from
all his works"; 5 [h]and again, in the previously
mentioned place, "They shall not enter into my
rest." 6 Therefore, since it remains that some
will enter into it, and those who formerly received the good news did not enter because of
disobedience, 7 [i]he once more set a day, "today," when long afterwards he spoke through
David, as already quoted:

"Oh, that today you would hear his voice:
"Harden not your hearts.' "

8 [j]Now if Joshua had given them rest, he would
not have spoken afterwards of another day.
9 Therefore, a sabbath rest still remains for the
people of God. 10 And whoever enters into
God's rest, rests from his own works as God did
from his. 11 Therefore, let us strive to enter
into that rest, so that no one may fall after the
same example of disobedience.
12 [k]Indeed, the word of God is living and
effective, sharper than any two-edged sword,
penetrating even between soul and spirit, joints

x 10, 21; Eph 2, 19; 1 Tm 3, 15; 1 Pt 4, 17.
y Ps 95, 7-11.
z Ex 17, 7; Nm 20, 2-5.
a Rom 8, 17.
b Ps 95, 7-8.
c Nm 14, 1-38; Dt 1, 19-40.
d Nm 14, 29.
e Nm 14, 22-23; Dt 1, 35.
f 3, 11; Ps 95, 11.
g Gn 2, 2.
h Ps 95, 11.
i 3, 7-8.15; Ps 95, 7-8.
j Dt 31, 7; Jos 22, 4.
k Wis 18, 15-16; Is 49, 2; Eph 6, 17; Rv 1, 16; 2, 12.

*

3, 6: The majority of manuscripts add "firm to the end," but these words are not found in the three earliest and best witnesses and are probably an interpolation derived from v 14.

3, 7—4, 13: The author appeals for steadfastness of faith in Jesus, basing his warning on the experience of Israel during the Exodus. In the Old Testament the Exodus had been invoked as a symbol of the return of Israel from the Babylonian exile (Is 42, 9; 43, 16–21; 51, 9–11). In the New Testament the redemption was similarly understood as a new exodus, both in the experience of Jesus himself (Lk 9, 31) and in that of his followers (1 Cor 10, 1–4). The author cites Ps 95, 7–11, a salutary example of hardness of heart, as a warning against the danger of growing weary and giving up the journey. To call God *living* (12) means that he reveals himself in his works (cf Jos 3, 10; Jer 10, 10). The *rest* (11) into which Israel was to enter was only a foreshadowing of that rest to which Christians are called. They are to remember the example of Israel's revolt in the desert that cost a whole generation the loss of the promised land (15–19; cf Nm 14, 20–29). In 4, 1–11, the symbol of *rest* is seen in deeper dimension: because the promise to the ancient Hebrews foreshadowed that given to Christians, it is *good news;* and because the promised land was the place of rest that God provided for his people, it was a share in his own rest, which he enjoyed after he had finished his creative work (3–4; cf Gn 2, 2). The author attempts to read this meaning of God's rest into Ps 95, 7–11 (6–9). The Greek form of the name of Joshua, who led Israel into the promised land, is Jesus (8). The author plays upon the name but stresses the superiority of Jesus, who leads his followers into heavenly rest. Verses 12 and 13 are meant as a continuation of the warning, for the word of God brings judgment as well as salvation. Some would capitalize *the word of God* and see it as a personal title of Jesus, comparable to that of Jn 1, 1–18.

and marrow, and able to discern reflections and thoughts of the heart. **13** [l]No creature is concealed from him, but everything is naked and exposed to the eyes of him to whom we must render an account.

## Jesus, Compassionate High Priest

**14** [m]*Therefore, since we have a great high priest who has passed through the heavens, Jesus, the Son of God, let us hold fast to our confession. **15** [n]For we do not have a high priest who is unable to sympathize with our weaknesses, but one who has similarly been tested in every way, yet without sin. **16** [o]So let us confidently approach the throne of grace to receive mercy and to find grace for timely help.

## CHAPTER 5

**1** *Every high priest is taken from among men and made their representative before God, to offer gifts and sacrifices for sins. **2** *He is able to deal patiently with the ignorant and erring, for he himself is beset by weakness **3** [p]and so, for this reason, must make sin offerings for himself as well as for the people. **4** [q]No one takes this honor upon himself but only when called by God, just as Aaron was. **5** [r]In the same way, it was not Christ who glorified himself in becoming high priest, but rather the one who said to him:

"You are my son;
this day I have begotten you";

**6** [s]*just as he says in another place:

"You are a priest forever
according to the order of Melchizedek."

**7** [t]*In the days when he was in the flesh, he offered prayers and supplications with loud cries and tears to the one who was able to save him from death, and he was heard because of his reverence. **8** [u]*Son though he was, he learned obedience from what he suffered; **9** [v]and when he was made perfect, he became the source of eternal salvation for all who obey him, **10** [w]declared by God high priest according to the order of Melchizedek.

## *IV: JESUS' ETERNAL PRIESTHOOD AND ETERNAL SACRIFICE*

### Exhortation to Spiritual Renewal

**11** *About this we have much to say, and it is difficult to explain, for you have become sluggish in hearing. **12** [x]Although you should be teachers by this time, you need to have someone teach you again the basic elements of the utterances of God. You need milk, [and] not solid food. **13** Everyone who lives on milk lacks experience of the word of righteousness, for he is

---

l Jb 34, 21-22; Pss 90, 8; 139, 2-4.
m 9, 11.24.
n 2, 17-18; 5, 2.
o 8, 1; 10, 19.22.35; 12, 2; Eph 3, 12.
p Lv 9, 7; 16, 15-17.30.34.
q Ex 28, 1.
r Ps 2, 7.
s Ps 110, 4.
t Mt 26, 38-44; Mk 14, 34-40; Lk 22, 41-46; Jn 12, 27.
u Rom 5, 19; Phil 2, 8.
v 7, 24-25.28.
w 6, 20; Ps 110, 4.
x 1 Cor 3, 1-3.

*

4, 14–16: These verses, which return to the theme first sounded in 2, 16—3, 1, serve as an introduction to the section that follows. The author here alone calls Jesus *a great high priest* (14), a designation used by Philo for the Logos; perhaps he does so in order to emphasize Jesus' superiority over the Jewish high priest. He has *been tested in every way, yet without sin* (15); this indicates an acquaintance with the tradition of Jesus' temptations, not only at the beginning (as in Mk 1, 13) but throughout his public life (cf Lk 22, 28). Although the reign of the exalted Jesus is a theme that occurs elsewhere in Heb, and Jesus' throne is mentioned in 1, 8, *the throne of grace* (16) refers to the throne of God. The similarity of v 16 to 10, 19–22 indicates that the author is thinking of our confident access to God, made possible by the priestly work of Jesus.

5, 1–10: The true humanity of Jesus (see the note on 2, 5–18) makes him a more rather than a less effective high priest to the Christian community. In Old Testament tradition, the high priest was identified with the people, guilty of personal sin just as they were (1–3). Even so, the office was of divine appointment (4), as was also the case with the sinless Christ (5). For v 6, see the note on Ps 110, 4. Although Jesus was Son of God, he was destined as a human being to learn obedience by accepting the suffering he had to endure (8). Because of his perfection through this experience of human suffering, he is the cause of salvation for all (9), a *high priest according to the order of Melchizedek* (10; cf 6 and 7, 3).

5, 1: *To offer gifts and sacrifices for sins:* the author is thinking principally of the Day of Atonement rite, as is clear from 9, 7. This ritual was celebrated to atone for "all the sins of the Israelites" (Lv 16, 34).

5, 2: *Deal patiently:* the Greek word *metriopathein* occurs only here in the Bible; this term was used by the Stoics to designate the golden mean between excess and defect of passion. Here it means rather the ability to sympathize.

5, 6–8: The author of Heb is the only New Testament writer to cite v 4 of Ps 110, here and in 7, 17.21, to show that Jesus has been called by God to his role as priest. Verses 7–8 deal with his ability to sympathize with sinners, because of his own experience of the trials and weakness of human nature, especially fear of death. In his present exalted state, weakness is foreign to him, but he understands what we suffer because of his previous earthly experience.

5, 7: *He offered prayers . . . to the one who was able to save him from death:* at Gethsemane (cf Mk 14, 35), though some see a broader reference (see the note on Jn 12, 27).

5, 8: *Son though he was:* two different though not incompatible views of Jesus' sonship coexist in Heb, one associating it with his exaltation, the other with his preexistence. The former view is the older one (cf Rom 1, 4).

5, 11—6, 20: The central section of Heb (5, 11—10, 39) opens with a reprimand and an appeal. Those to whom the author directs his teaching about Jesus' priesthood, which is *difficult to explain*, have become *sluggish in hearing* and forgetful of even *the basic elements* (5, 12). But rather than treating of basic teachings, the author apparently believes that the challenge of more advanced ones may shake them out of their inertia (*therefore*, 6, 1). The six examples of *basic teaching* in 6, 1–3 are probably derived from a traditional catechetical list. No effort is made to address apostates, for their very hostility to the Christian message cuts them off completely from Christ (6, 4–8). This harsh statement seems to rule out repentance after apostasy, but perhaps the author deliberately uses hyperbole in order to stress the seriousness of abandon-

a child. 14 But solid food is for the mature, for
those whose faculties are trained by practice to
discern good and evil.

## CHAPTER 6

1 [y]Therefore, let us leave behind the basic
teaching about Christ and advance to maturity,
without laying the foundation all over again:
repentance from dead works and faith in God,
2 [z]*instruction about baptisms and laying on of
hands, resurrection of the dead and eternal judgment. 3 And we shall do this, if only God permits. 4 [a]*For it is impossible in the case of
those who have once been enlightened and tasted the heavenly gift and shared in the holy Spirit
5 *and tasted the good word of God and the
powers of the age to come, 6 [b]*and then have
fallen away, to bring them to repentance again,
since they are recrucifying the Son of God for
themselves and holding him up to contempt.
7 [c]Ground that has absorbed the rain falling
upon it repeatedly and brings forth crops useful
to those for whom it is cultivated receives a
blessing from God. 8 [d]But if it produces thorns
and thistles, it is rejected; it will soon be cursed
and finally burned.

9 But we are sure in your regard, beloved, of
better things related to salvation, even though
we speak in this way. 10 For God is not unjust
so as to overlook your work and the love you
have demonstrated for his name by having
served and continuing to serve the holy ones.
11 [e]We earnestly desire each of you to demonstrate the same eagerness for the fulfillment of
hope until the end, 12 [f]*so that you may not
become sluggish, but imitators of those who,
through faith and patience, are inheriting the
promises.

### God's Promise Immutable

13 [g]*When
God made the promise to Abraham, since he
had no one greater by whom to swear, "he
swore by himself," 14 [h]and said, "I will indeed bless you and multiply" you. 15 [i]*And
so, after patient waiting, he obtained the promise. 16 Human beings swear by someone greater than themselves; for them an oath serves as
a guarantee and puts an end to all argument.
17 [j]So when God wanted to give the heirs of his
promise an even clearer demonstration of the
immutability of his purpose, he intervened with
an oath, 18 [k]*so that by two immutable things,
in which it was impossible for God to lie, we
who have taken refuge might be strongly encouraged to hold fast to the hope that lies before
us. 19 [l]*This we have as an anchor of the soul,
sure and firm, which reaches into the interior
behind the veil, 20 [m]where Jesus has entered on
our behalf as forerunner, becoming high priest
forever according to the order of Melchizedek.

## CHAPTER 7

### Melchizedek, a Type of Christ

1 [n]*This
"Melchizedek, king of Salem and priest of God

---

y 9, 14.
z 9, 10; Mk 7, 4 / Acts 6, 6; 8, 17; 13, 3; 19, 6; 1 Tm 4, 14; 5, 22; 2 Tm 1, 6.
a 10, 26.32; Ps 34, 6; 2 Cor 4, 6.
b 2 Pt 2, 21.
c Gn 1, 11-12; Dt 11, 11.
d Gn 3, 17-18; Mt 7, 16; 13, 7; Mk 4, 7; Lk 8, 7.
e 3, 14.
f 5, 11; Gal 3, 14; Eph 1, 13-14.
g Gn 22, 16.
h Gn 22, 17.
i 12; Rom 4, 20.
j 12.
k Nm 23, 19; 1 Sm 15, 29; Jn 8, 17; 2 Tm 2, 13.
l 10, 20; Ex 26, 31-33; Lv 16, 2.
m 5, 10; Ps 110, 4.
n Gn 14, 17-20.

---

* ing Christ. With 6, 9 a milder tone is introduced, and the criticism of the community (6, 1–3.9) is now balanced by an expression of confidence that its members are living truly Christian lives, and that God will justly reward their efforts (10). The author is concerned especially about their persevering (11–12), citing in this regard the achievement of Abraham, who relied on God's promise and on God's oath (13–18; cf Gn 22, 16), and proposes to them as a firm anchor of Christian hope the high priesthood of Christ, who is now living with God (19–20).

6, 2: *Instruction about baptisms:* not simply about Christian baptism but about the difference between it and similar Jewish rites, such as proselyte baptism, John's baptism, and the washings of the Qumran sectaries. *Laying on of hands:* in Acts 8, 17; 19, 6 this rite effects the infusion of the holy Spirit; in Acts 6, 6; 13, 3; 1 Tm 4, 14; 5, 22; 2 Tm 1, 6 it is a means of conferring some ministry or mission in the early Christian community.

6, 4: *Enlightened and tasted the heavenly gift:* this may refer to baptism and the Eucharist, respectively, but more probably means the neophytes' enlightenment by faith and their experience of salvation.

6, 5: *Tasted the good word of God and the powers of the age to come:* the proclamation of the *word of God* was accompanied by signs of the Spirit's power (1 Thes 1, 5; 1 Cor 2, 4).

6, 6: *They are recrucifying the Son of God for themselves:* a colorful description of the malice of apostasy, which is portrayed as again crucifying and deriding the Son of God.

6, 12: *Imitators of those . . . inheriting the promises:* the author urges the addressees to imitate the faith of the holy people of the Old Testament, who now possess the promised goods of which they lived in hope. This theme will be treated fully in ch 11.

6, 13: *He swore by himself:* God's promise to Abraham, which he confirmed by an oath ("I swear by myself," Gen 22, 16) was the basis for the hope of all Abraham's descendants.

6, 15: *He obtained the promise:* this probably refers not to Abraham's temporary possession of the land but to the eschatological blessings that Abraham and the other patriarchs have now come to possess.

6, 18: *Two immutable things:* the promise and the oath, both made by God.

6, 19: *Anchor . . . into the interior behind the veil:* a mixed metaphor. The Holy of Holies, beyond the veil that separates it from the Holy Place (Ex 26, 31–33), is seen as the earthly counterpart of the heavenly abode of God. This theme will be developed in ch 9.

7, 1–3: Recalling the meeting between Melchizedek and Abraham described in Gn 14, 17–20, the author enhances the significance of this priest by providing the popular etymological meaning of his name and that of the city over which he ruled (2). Since Genesis gives no information on the parentage or the death of Melchizedek, he is seen here as a type of Christ, representing a priesthood that is unique and eternal (3).

7, 1: The author here assumes that Melchizedek was a priest of the God of Israel (cf Gn 14, 22 and the note there).

Most High," "met Abraham as he returned from his defeat of the kings" and "blessed him." **2** *And Abraham apportioned to him "a tenth of everything." His name first means righteous king, and he was also "king of Salem," that is, king of peace. **3** [o]*Without father, mother, or ancestry, without beginning of days or end of life, thus made to resemble the Son of God, he remains a priest forever.

**4** [p]*See how great he is to whom the patriarch "Abraham [indeed] gave a tenth" of his spoils. **5** [q]The descendants of Levi who receive the office of priesthood have a commandment according to the law to exact tithes from the people, that is, from their brothers, although they also have come from the loins of Abraham. **6** But he who was not of their ancestry received tithes from Abraham and blessed him who had received the promises. **7** *Unquestionably, a lesser person is blessed by a greater. **8** In the one case, mortal men receive tithes; in the other, a man of whom it is testified that he lives on. **9** *One might even say that Levi himself, who receives tithes, was tithed through Abraham, **10** for he was still in his father's loins when Melchizedek met him.

**11** [r]*If, then, perfection came through the levitical priesthood, on the basis of which the people received the law, what need would there still have been for another priest to arise according to the order of Melchizedek, and not reckoned according to the order of Aaron? **12** When there is a change of priesthood, there is necessarily a change of law as well. **13** *Now he of whom these things are said belonged to a different tribe, of which no member ever officiated at the altar. **14** [s]*It is clear that our Lord arose from Judah, and in regard to that tribe Moses said nothing about priests. **15** *It is even more obvious if another priest is raised up after the likeness of Melchizedek, **16** *who has become so, not by a law expressed in a commandment concerning physical descent but by the power of a life that cannot be destroyed. **17** [t]For it is testified:

"You are a priest forever
according to the order of Melchizedek."

**18** [u]On the one hand, a former commandment is annulled because of its weakness and uselessness, **19** *for the law brought nothing to perfection; on the other hand, a better hope is introduced, through which we draw near to God. **20** *And to the degree that this happened not

---

o 4, 14; 6, 6; 10, 29.
p Gn 14, 20.
q Nm 18, 21 / Gn 35, 11.
r 5, 6; Ps 110, 4.
s Gn 49, 10; Is 11, 1; Mt 1, 1-2.16.20; 2, 6; Lk 1, 27; 2, 4; Rom 1, 3; Rv 5, 5.
t 5, 6; Ps 110, 4.
u 10, 1.

---

*

7, 2: In Gn 14, the Hebrew text does not state explicitly who gave tithes to whom. The author of Heb supplies Abraham as the subject, according to a contemporary interpretation of the passage. This supports the argument of the midrash and makes it possible to see in Melchizedek a type of Jesus. The messianic blessings of righteousness and peace are foreshadowed in the names "Melchizedek" and "Salem."

7, 3: *Without father, mother, or ancestry, without beginning of days or end of life:* this is perhaps a quotation from a hymn about Melchizedek. The rabbis maintained that anything not mentioned in the Torah does not exist. Consequently, since the Old Testament nowhere mentions Melchizedek's ancestry, birth, or death, the conclusion can be drawn that he *remains . . . forever.*

7, 4–10: The tithe that Abraham gave to Melchizedek (4), a practice later followed by the levitical priesthood (5), was a gift (6) acknowledging a certain superiority in Melchizedek, the foreign priest (7). This is further indicated by the fact that the institution of the levitical priesthood was sustained by hereditary succession in the tribe of Levi, whereas the absence of any mention of Melchizedek's death in Gn implies that his personal priesthood is permanent (8). The levitical priesthood itself, through Abraham, its ancestor, paid tithes to Melchizedek, thus acknowledging the superiority of his priesthood over its own (9–10).

7, 7: *A lesser person is blessed by a greater:* though this sounds like a principle, there are some examples in the Old Testament that do not support it (cf 2 Sm 14, 22; Jb 31, 20). The author may intend it as a statement of a liturgical rule.

7, 9: *Levi:* for the author this name designates not only the son of Jacob mentioned in Genesis but the priestly tribe that was thought to be descended from him.

7, 11–14: The levitical priesthood was not typified by the priesthood of Melchizedek, for Ps 110, 4 speaks of a priesthood of a new order, the order of Melchizedek, to arise in messianic times (11). Since the levitical priesthood served the Mosaic law, a new priesthood (12) would not come into being without a change in the law itself. Thus Jesus was not associated with the Old Testament priesthood, for he was a descendant of the tribe of Judah, which had never exercised the priesthood (13–14).

7, 13: *He of whom these things are said:* Jesus, the priest "according to the order of Melchizedek." According to the author's interpretation, Ps 110 spoke prophetically of Jesus.

7, 14: *Judah:* the author accepts the early Christian tradition that Jesus was descended from the family of David (cf Mt 1, 1–2.16.20; Lk 1, 27; 2, 4; Rom 1, 3). The Qumran community expected two Messiahs, one descended from Aaron and one from David; Heb shows no awareness of this view or at least does not accept it. Our author's view is not attested in contemporaneous Judaism.

7, 15–19: Jesus does not exercise a priesthood through family lineage but through his immortal existence (15–16), fulfilling Ps 110, 4 (17; cf 3). Thus he abolishes forever both the levitical priesthood and the law it serves, because neither could effectively sanctify people (18) by leading them into direct communication with God (19).

7, 16: *A life that cannot be destroyed:* the life to which Jesus has attained by virtue of his resurrection; it is his exaltation rather than his divine nature that makes him priest. The Old Testament speaks of the Aaronic priesthood as eternal (see Ex 40, 15); our author does not explicitly consider this possible objection to his argument but implicitly refutes it in vv 23–24.

7, 19: *A better hope:* this hope depends upon the sacrifice of the Son of God; through it we "approach the throne of grace" (4, 16); cf 6, 19.20.

7, 20–25: As was the case with the promise to Abraham (6, 13), though not with the levitical priesthood, the eternal priesthood of the order of Melchizedek was confirmed by God's oath (20–21); cf Ps 110, 4. Thus Jesus becomes the guarantee of a permanent covenant (22) that does not require a succession of priests as did the levitical priesthood (23) because his high priesthood is eternal and unchangeable (24). Consequently, Jesus is able to save all who draw near to God through him since he is their ever-living intercessor (25).

without the taking of an oath—for others became priests without an oath, **21** [v]but he with
an oath, through the one who said to him:

> "The Lord has sworn, and he will not
> repent:
> 'You are a priest forever' "—

**22** [w]*to that same degree has Jesus [also] become the guarantee of an [even] better covenant. **23** Those priests were many because
they were prevented by death from remaining in
office, **24** [x]but he, because he remains forever,
has a priesthood that does not pass away.
**25** [y]*Therefore, he is always able to save those
who approach God through him, since he lives
forever to make intercession for them.
**26** [z]*It was fitting that we should have such
a high priest: holy, innocent, undefiled, separated from sinners, higher than the heavens.
**27** [a]*He has no need, as did the high priests,
to offer sacrifice day after day, first for his own
sins and then for those of the people; he did that
once for all when he offered himself. **28** [b]For
the law appoints men subject to weakness to be
high priests, but the word of the oath, which was
taken after the law, appoints a son, who has
been made perfect forever.

## CHAPTER 8

**Heavenly Priesthood of Jesus** **1** [c]*The
main point of what has been said is this: we have
such a high priest, who has taken his seat at the
right hand of the throne of the Majesty in heav-
en, **2** [d]*a minister of the sanctuary and of the
true tabernacle that the Lord, not man, set up.
**3** [e]Now every high priest is appointed to offer
gifts and sacrifices; thus the necessity for this
one also to have something to offer. **4** [f]If then
he were on earth, he would not be a priest, since
there are those who offer gifts according to the
law. **5** [g]They worship in a copy and shadow of
the heavenly sanctuary, as Moses was warned
when he was about to erect the tabernacle. For
he says, "See that you make everything according to the pattern shown you on the mountain."
**6** [h]Now he has obtained so much more excellent a ministry as he is mediator of a better
covenant, enacted on better promises.

**Old and New Covenants** **7** *For if that
first covenant had been faultless, no place
would have been sought for a second one.
**8** [i]*But he finds fault with them and says:

> "Behold, the days are coming, says the
> Lord,
> when I will conclude a new covenant with
> the house of
> Israel and the house of Judah.
> **9** It will not be like the covenant I made with
> their fathers

v Ps 110, 4.
w 8, 6-10; 9, 15-20; 10, 29; 12, 24; 13, 20.
x 5, 6; 13, 8.
y Rom 8, 34; 1 Jn 2, 1; Rv 1, 18.
z 4, 14.15.
a 5, 3; 9, 12.25-28; 10, 11-14; Ex 29, 38-39; Lv 16, 6.11.15-17;Nm 28, 3-4; Is 53, 10; Rom 6, 10.
b 5, 1.2.9.
c 1, 3; 4, 14; 7, 26-28.
d 9, 11; Ex 33, 7; Nm 24, 6 LXX.
e 5, 1.
f 7, 13.
g 9, 23; Ex 25, 40; Acts 7, 44; Col 2, 17.
h 7, 22; 9, 15.
i Jer 31, 31-34.

*

7, 20: *An oath:* God's oath in Ps 110, 4.

7, 22: *An [even] better covenant:* better than the Mosaic covenant because it will be eternal, like the priesthood of Jesus upon which it is based. Verse 12 argued that a change of priesthood involves a change of law; since "law" and "covenant" are used correlatively, a new covenant is likewise instituted.

7, 25: *To make intercession:* the intercession of the exalted Jesus, not the sequel to his completed sacrifice but its eternal presence in heaven; cf Rom 8, 34.

7, 26–28: Jesus is precisely the high priest whom the human race requires, holy and sinless, installed far above humanity (26); one having no need to offer sacrifice daily for sins but making a single offering of himself (27) once for all. The law could only appoint high priests with human limitations, but the fulfillment of God's oath regarding the priesthood of Melchizedek (Ps 110, 4) makes the Son of God the perfect priest forever (28).

7, 26: This verse with its list of attributes is reminiscent of v 3 and is perhaps a hymnic counterpart to it, contrasting the exalted Jesus with Melchizedek.

7, 27: Such daily sacrifice is nowhere mentioned in the Mosaic law; only on the Day of Atonement is it prescribed that the high priest must *offer sacrifice . . . for his own sins and then for those of the people* (Lv 16, 11–19). *Once for all:* this translates the Greek words *ephapax/hapax* that occur eleven times in Heb.

8, 1–6: The Christian community has in Jesus the kind of high priest described in 7, 26–28. In virtue of his ascension Jesus has taken his place at God's right hand in accordance with Ps 110, 1 (1), where he presides over the heavenly sanctuary established by God himself (2). Like every high priest, he has his offering to make (3; cf 9, 12.14), but it differs from that of the levitical priesthood in which he had no share (4) and which was in any case but a shadowy reflection of the true offering in the heavenly sanctuary (5). But Jesus' ministry in the heavenly sanctuary is that of mediator of a superior covenant that accomplishes what it signifies (6).

8, 2: *The sanctuary:* the Greek term could also mean "holy things" but bears the meaning "sanctuary" elsewhere in Heb (9, 8.12.24.25; 10, 19; 13, 11). *The true tabernacle:* the heavenly tabernacle *that the Lord . . . set up* is contrasted with the earthly tabernacle that Moses set up in the desert. *True* means "real" in contradistinction to a mere "copy and shadow" (5); compare the Johannine usage (e.g., Jn 1, 9; 6, 32; 15, 1). The idea that the earthly sanctuary is a reflection of a heavenly model may be based upon Ex 25, 9, but probably also derives from the Platonic concept of a real world of which our observable world is merely a shadow.

8, 7–13: Since the first covenant was deficient in accomplishing what it signified, it had to be replaced (7), as Jeremiah (31, 31–34) had prophesied (8–12). Even in the time of Jeremiah, the first covenant was antiquated (13). In 7, 22–24, the superiority of the new covenant was seen in the permanence of its priesthood; here the superiority is based on better promises, made explicit in the citation of Jer 31 (LXX: 38), 31–34, namely, in the immediacy of the people's knowledge of God (11) and in the forgiveness of sin (12).

8, 8–12: In citing Jer the author follows the Septuagint; some apparent departures from it may be the result of a different Septuagintal text rather than changes deliberately introduced.

the day I took them by the hand to lead
them forth from the land of Egypt;
for they did not stand by my covenant
and I ignored them, says the Lord.
10 [j]But this is the covenant I will establish with
the house of Israel
after those days, says the Lord:
I will put my laws in their minds
and I will write them upon their hearts.
I will be their God,
and they shall be my people.
11 And they shall not teach, each one his
fellow citizen
and kinsman, saying, "Know the Lord,"
for all shall know me,
from least to greatest.
12 For I will forgive their evildoing
and remember their sins no more."

13 [k]*When he speaks of a "new" covenant, he
declares the first one obsolete. And what has
become obsolete and has grown old is close to
disappearing.

## CHAPTER 9

### The Worship of the First Covenant

1 *Now [even] the first covenant had regulations for worship and an earthly sanctuary.
2 [l]*For a tabernacle was constructed, the outer
one, in which were the lampstand, the table, and
the bread of offering; this is called the Holy
Place. 3 [m]*Behind the second veil was the tabernacle called the Holy of Holies, 4 [n]*in which
were the gold altar of incense and the ark of the
covenant entirely covered with gold. In it were
the gold jar containing the manna, the staff of
Aaron that had sprouted, and the tablets of the
covenant. 5 [o]*Above it were the cherubim of
glory overshadowing the place of expiation.
Now is not the time to speak of these in detail.
6 [p]*With these arrangements for worship,
the priests, in performing their service, go into
the outer tabernacle repeatedly, 7 [q]*but the
high priest alone goes into the inner one once a
year, not without blood that he offers for himself and for the sins of the people. 8 In this way
the holy Spirit shows that the way into the sanctuary had not yet been revealed while the outer
tabernacle still had its place. 9 *This is a symbol of the present time, in which gifts and sacrifices are offered that cannot perfect the worshiper in conscience 10 [r]but only in matters of food
and drink and various ritual washings: regulations concerning the flesh, imposed until the
time of the new order.

**Sacrifice of Jesus** 11 [s]*But when Christ
came as high priest of the good things that have
come to be, passing through the greater and
more perfect tabernacle not made by hands, that
is, not belonging to this creation, 12 [t]he entered once for all into the sanctuary, not with the
blood of goats and calves but with his own
blood, thus obtaining eternal redemption.

---

j 10, 16-17.
k Rom 10, 4.
l Ex 25, 23-30.
m Ex 26, 31-34.
n Ex 16, 32-34; 25, 10.16.21; 30, 1-10; Lv 16, 12-13;Nm 17, 2-7.16-26.
o Ex 25, 16-22; 26, 34; Lv 16, 14-15.
p Ex 27, 21; 30, 7; Lv 24, 8.
q Ex 30, 10; Lv 16, 1-14.
r 13, 9; Lv 11; 14, 8; Nm 19, 11-21; Col 2, 16.
s 4, 14; 10, 1.20.
t 7, 27; Mt 26, 28.

---

8, 13: *Close to disappearing:* from the prophet's perspective, not that of the author of Heb.

9, 1–10: The regulations for worship under the old covenant permitted all the priests to enter the Holy Place (2, 6), but only the high priest to enter the Holy of Holies and then only once a year (3–5.7). The description of the sanctuary and its furnishings is taken essentially from Ex 25–26. This exclusion of the people from the Holy of Holies signified that they were not allowed to stand in God's presence (8) because their offerings and sacrifices, which were merely symbols of their need of spiritual renewal (10), could not obtain forgiveness of sins (9).

9, 2: *The outer one:* the author speaks of the *outer tabernacle* (6) and *the inner one* (7) rather than of one Mosaic tabernacle divided into two parts or sections.

9, 3: *The second veil:* what is meant is the veil that divided the Holy Place from the Holy of Holies. It is here called *the second,* because there was another veil at the entrance to the Holy Place, or "outer tabernacle" (Ex 26, 36).

9, 4: *The gold altar of incense:* Ex 30, 6 locates this altar in the Holy Place, i.e., the first tabernacle, rather than in the Holy of Holies. Neither is there any Old Testament support for the assertion that the jar of manna and the staff of Aaron were in the ark of the covenant. For the tablets of the covenant, see Ex 25, 16.

9, 5: *The place of expiation:* the gold "mercy seat" (Greek *hilastērion,* as in Rom 3, 25), where the blood of the sacrificial animals was sprinkled on the Day of Atonement (Lv 16, 14–15). This rite achieved "expiation" or atonement for the sins of the preceding year.

9, 6: *In performing their service:* the priestly services that had to be performed regularly in the Holy Place or *outer tabernacle* included burning incense on the incense altar twice each day (Ex 30, 7), replacing the loaves on the table of the bread of offering once each week (Lv 24, 8), and constantly caring for the lamps on the lampstand (Ex 27, 21).

9, 7: *Not without blood:* blood was essential to Old Testament sacrifice because it was believed that life was located in the blood. Hence blood was especially sacred, and its outpouring functioned as a meaningful symbol of cleansing from sin and reconciliation with God. Unlike Heb, the Old Testament never says that the blood is "offered." The author is perhaps retrojecting into his description of Mosaic ritual a concept that belongs to the New Testament antitype, as Paul does when he speaks of the Israelites' passage through the sea as a "baptism" (1 Cor 10, 2).

9, 9: *The present time:* this expression is equivalent to the "present age," used in contradistinction to the "age to come."

9, 11–14: Christ, the high priest of the spiritual blessings foreshadowed in the Old Testament sanctuary, has actually entered the true sanctuary of heaven that is not of human making (11). His place there is permanent, and his offering is his own blood that won eternal redemption (12). If the sacrifice of animals could bestow legal purification (13), how much more effective is the blood of the sinless, divine Christ who spontaneously offered himself to purge the human race of sin and render it fit for the service of God (14).

9, 11: *The good things that have come to be:* the majority of later manuscripts here read "the good things to come"; cf 10, 1.

**13** [u]*For if the blood of goats and bulls and the
sprinkling of a heifer's ashes can sanctify those
who are defiled so that their flesh is cleansed,
**14** [v]*how much more will the blood of Christ,
who through the eternal spirit offered himself
unblemished to God, cleanse our consciences
from dead works to worship the living God.

**15** [w]*For this reason he is mediator of a new
covenant: since a death has taken place for deliverance from transgressions under the first
covenant, those who are called may receive the
promised eternal inheritance. **16** *Now where
there is a will, the death of the testator must be
established. **17** For a will takes effect only at
death; it has no force while the testator is alive.
**18** Thus not even the first covenant was inaugurated without blood. **19** [x]*When every commandment had been proclaimed by Moses to all
the people according to the law, he took the
blood of calves [and goats], together with water
and crimson wool and hyssop, and sprinkled
both the book itself and all the people,
**20** [y]saying, "This is 'the blood of the covenant
which God has enjoined upon you.' " **21** [z]*In
the same way, he sprinkled also the tabernacle
and all the vessels of worship with blood.
**22** [a]*According to the law almost everything is
purified by blood, and without the shedding of
blood there is no forgiveness.

**23** [b]*Therefore, it was necessary for the copies of the heavenly things to be purified by these
rites, but the heavenly things themselves by
better sacrifices than these. **24** [c]For Christ did
not enter into a sanctuary made by hands, a copy
of the true one, but heaven itself, that he might
now appear before God on our behalf. **25** Not
that he might offer himself repeatedly, as the
high priest enters each year into the sanctuary
with blood that is not his own; **26** [d]*if that were
so, he would have had to suffer repeatedly from
the foundation of the world. But now once for
all he has appeared at the end of the ages to take
away sin by his sacrifice. **27** [e]Just as it is appointed that human beings die once, and after
this the judgment, **28** [f]*so also Christ, offered
once to take away the sins of many, will appear

u 10, 4; Lv 16, 6-16; Nm, 19, 9.14-21.
v 10, 10; Rom 5, 9; 1 Tm 3, 9; Ti 2, 14; 1 Pt 1, 18-19; 1 Jn 1, 7; Rv 1, 5.
w 1 Tm 2, 5.
x 12-13.
y Ex 24, 3-8; Mt 26, 28; Mk 14, 24.
z Ex 40, 9; Lv 8, 15.19.
a Lv 17, 11.
b Jb 15, 15.
c 7, 25; Rom 8, 34; 1 Jn 2, 1-2.
d 7, 27; Jn 1, 29; Gal 4, 4.
e Gn 3, 19.
f 10, 10; Is 53, 12.

*

9, 13: *A heifer's ashes:* ashes from a red heifer that had been burned were mixed with water and used for the cleansing of those who had become ritually defiled by touching a corpse; see Nm 19, 9.14–21.

9, 14: *Through the eternal spirit:* this expression does not refer either to the holy Spirit or to the divine nature of Jesus but to the life of the risen Christ, "a life that cannot be destroyed" (7, 16).

9, 15–22: Jesus' role as *mediator of the new covenant* is based upon his sacrificial *death* (cf 8, 6). His death has effected *deliverance from transgressions,* i.e., deliverance from sins committed under the old covenant, which the Mosaic sacrifices were incapable of effacing. Until this happened, the *eternal inheritance* promised by God could not be obtained (15). This effect of his work follows the human pattern by which a last will and testament becomes effective only with the death of the testator (16–17). The Mosaic covenant was also associated with death, for Moses made use of blood to seal the pact between God and the people (18–21). In Old Testament tradition, guilt could normally not be remitted without the use of blood (22; cf Lv 17, 11).

9, 16–17: *A will . . . death of the testator:* the same Greek word *diathēkē,* meaning "covenant" in vv 15 and 18, is used here with the meaning *will.* The new covenant, unlike the old, is at the same time a will that requires the *death of the testator.* Jesus as eternal Son is the one who established the new covenant together with his Father, author of both covenants; at the same time he is the testator whose death puts his *will* into effect.

9, 19–20: A number of details here are different from the description of this covenant rite in Ex 24, 5–8. Exodus mentions only calves ("young bulls," NAB), not goats (but this addition in Heb is of doubtful authenticity), says nothing of the use of *water and crimson wool and hyssop* (these features probably came from a different rite; cf Lv 14, 3–7; Nm 19, 6–18), and describes Moses as splashing blood on the altar, whereas Heb says he sprinkled it on the book (but both book and altar are meant to symbolize the agreement of God). The words of Moses are also slightly different from those in Exodus and are closer to the words of Jesus at the Last Supper in Mk 14, 24 // Mt 26, 28.

9, 21: According to Ex, the tabernacle did not yet exist at the time of the covenant rite. Moreover, nothing is said of sprinkling it with blood at its subsequent dedication (Ex 40, 9–11).

9, 22: *Without the shedding of blood there is no forgiveness:* in fact, ancient Israel did envisage other means of obtaining forgiveness; the Old Testament mentions contrition of heart (Ps 51, 19), fasting (Jl 2, 12), and almsgiving (Sir 3, 29). The author is limiting his horizon to the sacrificial cult, which did always involve the shedding of blood for its expiatory and unitive value.

9, 23–28: Since the blood of animals became a cleansing symbol among Old Testament prefigurements, it was necessary that the realities foreshadowed be brought into being by a shedding of blood that was infinitely more effective by reason of its worth (23). Christ did not simply prefigure the heavenly realities (24) by performing an annual sacrifice with a blood not his own (25); he offered the single sacrifice of himself as the final annulment of sin (26). Just as death is the unrepeatable act that ends a person's life, so Christ's offering of himself for all is the unrepeatable sacrifice that has once for all achieved redemption (27–28).

9, 26: *At the end of the ages:* the use of expressions such as this shows that the author of Heb, despite his interest in the Platonic concept of an eternal world above superior to temporal reality here below, nevertheless still clings to the Jewish Christian eschatology with its sequence of "the present age" and "the age to come."

9, 28: *To take away the sins of many:* the reference is to Is 53, 12. Since the Greek verb *anapherō* can mean both "to take away" and "to bear," the author no doubt intended to play upon both senses: Jesus took away sin by bearing it himself. See the similar wordplay in Jn 1, 29. *Many* is used in the Semitic meaning of "all" in the inclusive sense, as in Mk 14, 24. *To those who eagerly await him:* Jesus will appear *a second time* at the parousia, as the high priest reappeared on the Day of Atonement, emerging from the Holy of Holies, which he had entered *to take away sin.* This dramatic scene is described in Sir 50, 5–11.

a second time, not to take away sin but to bring
salvation to those who eagerly await him.

## CHAPTER 10

### One Sacrifice instead of Many

1 [g]*Since the law has only a shadow of the
good things to come, and not the very image of
them, it can never make perfect those who come
to worship by the same sacrifices that they offer
continually each year. 2 Otherwise, would not
the sacrifices have ceased to be offered, since
the worshipers, once cleansed, would no longer
have had any consciousness of sins? 3 [h]But in
those sacrifices there is only a yearly remembrance of sins, 4 [i]for it is impossible that the
blood of bulls and goats take away sins. 5 [j]*For
this reason, when he came into the world, he
said:

"Sacrifice and offering you did not desire,
but a body you prepared for me;
6 holocausts and sin offerings you took no
delight in.
7 Then I said, "As is written of me in the
scroll,
Behold, I come to do your will, O
God.' "

8 [k]*First he says, "Sacrifices and offerings,
holocausts and sin offerings, you neither desired
nor delighted in." These are offered according
to the law. 9 [l]Then he says, "Behold, I come
to do your will." He takes away the first to
establish the second. 10 [m]By this "will," we
have been consecrated through the offering of
the body of Jesus Christ once for all.

11 [n]*Every priest stands daily at his ministry, offering frequently those same sacrifices
that can never take away sins. 12 [o]But this one
offered one sacrifice for sins, and took his seat
forever at the right hand of God; 13 *now he
waits until his enemies are made his footstool.
14 [p]For by one offering he has made perfect
forever those who are being consecrated.
15 *The holy Spirit also testifies to us, for after
saying:

16 [q]"This is the covenant I will establish with
them after those days, says the Lord:
'I will put my laws in their hearts,
and I will write them upon their minds,' "
17 [r]*he also says:

"Their sins and their evildoing
I will remember no more."

18 Where there is forgiveness of these, there is
no longer offering for sin.

**Recalling the Past** 19 [s]*Therefore, brothers, since through the blood of Jesus we have
confidence of entrance into the sanctuary

---

g 8, 5; Col 2, 17.
h Lv 16, 21; Nm 5, 15 LXX.
i Is 1, 11; Mi 6, 6-8.
j Ps 40, 7-9.
k 5-6; Ps 40, 7.
l 7; Ps 40, 8; Mt 26, 39; Mk 14, 36; Lk 22, 42; Jn 6, 38.
m 9, 12.14.
n 7, 27; Dt 10, 8; 18, 7.
o Ps 110, 1.
p 9, 28.
q 8, 10; Jer 31, 33.
r 8, 12; Jer 31, 34.
s 3, 6; 4, 16; 6, 19-20; Eph 1, 7; 3, 12.

---

10, 1–10: Christian faith now realizes that the Old Testament sacrifices did not effect the spiritual benefits to come but only prefigured them (1). For if the sacrifices had actually effected the forgiveness of sin, there would have been no reason for their constant repetition (2). They were rather a continual reminder of the people's sins (3). It is not reasonable to suppose that human sins could be removed by the blood of animal sacrifices (4). Christ, therefore, is here shown to understand his mission in terms of Ps 40, 6–8, cited according to the Septuagint (5–7). Jesus acknowledged that the Old Testament sacrifices did not remit the sins of the people and so, perceiving the will of God, offered his own body for this purpose (8–10).

10, 1: *A shadow of the good things to come:* the term *shadow* was used in 8, 5 to signify the earthly counterpart of the Platonic heavenly reality. But here it means a prefiguration of what is to come in Christ, as it is used in the Pauline literature; cf Col 2, 17.

10, 5–7: A passage from Ps 40, 7–9a is placed in the mouth of the Son at his incarnation. As usual, the author follows the Septuagint text. There is a notable difference in v 5 ( Ps 40, 7b), where the Masoretic text reads "ears you have dug for me" ("ears open to obedience you gave me," NAB), but most Septuagint manuscripts have "a body you prepared for me," a reading obviously more suited to the interpretation of Heb.

10, 8: *Sacrifices and offerings, holocausts and sin offerings:* these four terms taken from the preceding passage of Ps 40 (with the first two changed to plural forms) are probably intended as equivalents to the four principal types of Old Testament sacrifices: peace offerings (Lv 3, here called *sacrifices*); cereal offerings (Lv 2, here called *offerings*); *holocausts* (Lv 1); and *sin offerings* (Lv 4–5). This last category includes the guilt offerings of Lv 5, 14–26.

10, 11–18: Whereas the levitical priesthood offered daily sacrifices that were ineffectual in remitting sin (11), Jesus offered a single sacrifice that won him a permanent place at God's right hand. There he has only to await the final outcome of his work (12–13; cf Ps 110, 1). Thus he has brought into being in his own person the new covenant prophesied by Jeremiah (31, 33–34) that has rendered meaningless all other offerings for sin (14–18).

10, 13: *Until his enemies are made his footstool:* Ps 110, 1 is again used; the reference here is to the period of time between the enthronement of Jesus and his second coming. The identity of the *enemies* is not specified; cf 1 Cor 15, 25–27.

10, 15–17: The testimony of the scriptures is now invoked to support what has just preceded. The passage cited is a portion of the new covenant prophecy of Jer 31, 31–34, which the author previously used in 8, 8–12.

10, 17: *He also says:* these words are not in the Greek text, which has only *kai*, "also," but the expression *after saying* in v 15 seems to require such a phrase to divide the Jeremiah text into two sayings. Others understand "the Lord says" of v 16 (here rendered *says the Lord*) as outside the quotation and consider v 16b as part of the second saying. Two ancient versions and a number of minuscules introduce the words "then he said" or a similar expression at the beginning of v 17.

10, 19–39: Practical consequences from these reflections on the priesthood and the sacrifice of Christ should make it clear that Christians may now have direct and confident access to God through the person of Jesus (19–20), who rules God's house as high priest (21). They should approach God with sincerity and faith, in the knowledge that through baptism their sins have been remitted (22), reminding themselves of

**20** [t]*by the new and living way he opened for
us through the veil, that is, his flesh, **21** [u]*and
since we have "a great priest over the house of
God," **22** [v]*let us approach with a sincere
heart and in absolute trust, with our hearts sprinkled clean from an evil conscience and our bodies washed in pure water. **23** [w]Let us hold un-
waveringly to our confession that gives us hope,
for he who made the promise is trustworthy.
**24** We must consider how to rouse one another
to love and good works. **25** [x]*We should not
stay away from our assembly, as is the custom
of some, but encourage one another, and this all
the more as you see the day drawing near.

**26** [y]*If we sin deliberately after receiving
knowledge of the truth, there no longer remains
sacrifice for sins **27** [z]but a fearful prospect of
judgment and a flaming fire that is going to
consume the adversaries. **28** [a]*Anyone who rejects the law of Moses is put to death without
pity on the testimony of two or three witnesses.
**29** [b]Do you not think that a much worse punishment is due the one who has contempt for the
Son of God, considers unclean the covenant-
blood by which he was consecrated, and insults
the spirit of grace? **30** [c]We know the one who
said:

"Vengeance is mine; I will repay,"

and again:

"The Lord will judge his people."

**31** [d]It is a fearful thing to fall into the hands of
the living God.

**32** [e]*Remember the days past when, after
you had been enlightened, you endured a great
contest of suffering. **33** [f]At times you were
publicly exposed to abuse and affliction; at other times you associated yourselves with those so
treated. **34** [g]You even joined in the sufferings
of those in prison and joyfully accepted the
confiscation of your property, knowing that you
had a better and lasting possession.
**35** [h]Therefore, do not throw away your confidence; it will have great recompense. **36** [i]You
need endurance to do the will of God and receive what he has promised.

**37** [j]*"For, after just a brief moment,
he who is to come shall come;
he shall not delay.
**38** [k]But my just one shall live by faith,
and if he draws back I take no pleasure in
him."

**39** We are not among those who draw back and
perish, but among those who have faith and will
possess life.

---

t Jn 14, 6 / 6, 19-20; 9, 8.11-12; Mt 27, 51; Mk 15, 38;Lk 23, 45.
u 3, 6.
v 9, 13-14; Ez 36, 25; 1 Cor 6, 11; Ti 3, 5; 1 Pt 3, 21.
w 3, 1.6; 4, 14; 1 Cor 10, 13.
x Rom 13, 12; 1 Cor 3, 13.
y 3, 12; 6, 4-8.
z 31; 9, 27; Is 26, 11 LXX; Zep 1, 18.
a Dt 17, 6.
b 6, 6.
c Dt 32, 35.36; Rom 12, 19.
d 27; Mt 10, 28; Lk 12, 4-5.
e 6, 4.
f 1 Cor 4, 9.
g 13, 3; Mt 6, 19-20; Lk 12, 33-34.
h 4, 16.
i Lk 21, 19.
j Is 26, 20; Hb 2, 3.
k Hb 2, 4; Rom 1, 17; Gal 3, 11.

---

* the hope they expressed in Christ at that event (23). They are to encourage one another to Christian love and activity (24). not refusing, no matter what the reason, to participate in the community's assembly, especially in view of the parousia (25; cf 1 Thes 4, 13–18). If refusal to participate in the assembly indicates rejection of Christ, no sacrifice exists to obtain forgiveness for so great a sin (26); only the dreadful judgment of God remains (27). For if violation of the Mosaic law could be punished by death, how much worse will be the punishment of those who have turned their backs on Christ by despising his sacrifice and disregarding the gifts of the holy Spirit (28–29). Judgment belongs to the Lord, and he enacts it by his living presence (30–31). There was a time when the spirit of their community caused them to welcome and share their sufferings (32–34). To revitalize that spirit is to share in the courage of the Old Testament prophets (cf Is 26, 20; Hb 2, 3–4), the kind of courage that must distinguish the faith of the Christian (35–39).

10, 20: *Through the veil, that is, his flesh:* the term *flesh* is used pejoratively. As the temple veil kept people from entering the Holy of Holies (it was rent at Christ's death, Mk 15, 38), so the flesh of Jesus constituted an obstacle to approaching God.

10, 21: *The house of God:* this refers back to 3, 6, "we are his house."

10, 22: *With our hearts sprinkled clean from an evil conscience:* as in 9, 13 (see the note there), the sprinkling motif refers to the Mosaic rite of cleansing from ritual impurity. This could produce only an external purification, whereas sprinkling with the blood of Christ (9, 14) cleanses the *conscience. Washed in pure water:* baptism is elsewhere referred to as a washing; cf 1 Cor 6, 11; Eph 5, 26.

10, 25: *Our assembly:* the liturgical *assembly* of the Christian community, probably for the celebration of the Eucharist. *The day:* this designation for the parousia also occurs in the Pauline letters, e.g., Rom 2, 16; 1 Cor 3, 13; 1 Thes 5, 2.

10, 26: *If we sin deliberately:* verse 29 indicates that the author is here thinking of apostasy; cf 3, 12; 6, 4–8.

10, 28: *Rejects the law of Moses:* evidently not any sin against the law, but idolatry. Dt 17, 2–7 prescribed capital punishment for idolaters who were convicted on the testimony of two or three witnesses.

10, 32: *After you had been enlightened:* "enlightenment" is an ancient metaphor for baptism (cf Eph 5, 14; Jn 9, 11), but see 6, 4 and the note there.

10, 37–38: In support of his argument, the author uses Hb 2, 3–4 in a wording almost identical with the text of the Codex Alexandrinus of the Septuagint but with the first and second lines of v 4 inverted. He introduces it with a few words from Is 26, 20: *after just a brief moment.* Note the Pauline usage of Hb 2, 4 in Rom 1, 17; Gal 3, 11.

# V: EXAMPLES, DISCIPLINE, DISOBEDIENCE

## CHAPTER 11

**Faith of the Ancients** **1** [l]*Faith is the realization of what is hoped for and evidence of
things not seen. **2** Because of it the ancients
were well attested. **3** [m]*By faith we understand
that the universe was ordered by the word of
God, so that what is visible came into being
through the invisible. **4** [n]*By faith Abel offered
to God a sacrifice greater than Cain's. Through
this he was attested to be righteous, God bearing
witness to his gifts, and through this, though
dead, he still speaks. **5** [o]By faith Enoch was
taken up so that he should not see death, and
"he was found no more because God had taken
him." Before he was taken up, he was attested
to have pleased God. **6** [p]*But without faith it is
impossible to please him, for anyone who approaches God must believe that he exists and
that he rewards those who seek him. **7** [q]By
faith Noah, warned about what was not yet
seen, with reverence built an ark for the salvation of his household. Through this he condemned the world and inherited the righteousness that comes through faith.

**8** [r]By faith Abraham obeyed when he was
called to go out to a place that he was to receive
as an inheritance; he went out, not knowing
where he was to go. **9** [s]By faith he sojourned
in the promised land as in a foreign country,
dwelling in tents with Isaac and Jacob, heirs of
the same promise; **10** [t]for he was looking forward to the city with foundations, whose architect and maker is God. **11** [u]By faith he received
power to generate, even though he was past the
normal age—and Sarah herself was sterile—for
he thought that the one who had made the promise was trustworthy. **12** [v]So it was that there
came forth from one man, himself as good as
dead, descendants as numerous as the stars in
the sky and as countless as the sands on the
seashore.

**13** [w]All these died in faith. They did not
receive what had been promised but saw it and
greeted it from afar and acknowledged themselves to be strangers and aliens on earth, **14** for
those who speak thus show that they are seeking
a homeland. **15** If they had been thinking of the
land from which they had come, they would
have had opportunity to return. **16** [x]But now
they desire a better homeland, a heavenly one.
Therefore, God is not ashamed to be called their
God, for he has prepared a city for them.

**17** [y]By faith Abraham, when put to the test,
offered up Isaac, and he who had received the
promises was ready to offer his only son, **18** [z]of
whom it was said, "Through Isaac descendants
shall bear your name." **19** [a]*He reasoned that
God was able to raise even from the dead, and

---

l 1, 3; 3, 14; Rom 8, 24; 2 Cor 4, 18.
m Gn 1, 3; Ps 33, 6; Wis 9, 1; Jn 1, 3.
n 12, 24; Gn 4, 4.10.
o Gn 5, 24; Sir 44, 16.
p Wis 4, 10.
q Gn 6, 8-22; Sir 44, 17-18; Mt 24, 37-39; Lk 17, 26-27;1 Pt 3, 20; 2, Pt 2, 5.
r Gn 12, 1-4; 15, 7-21; Sir 44, 19-22; Acts 7, 2-8; Rom 4, 16-22.
s Gn 12, 8; 13, 12; 23, 4; 26, 3; 35, 27.
t 12, 22; 13, 14; Rv 21, 10-22.
u Gn 17, 19; 21, 2; Rom 4, 19-21 / 1 Cor 10, 13.
v Gn 15, 5; 22, 17; 32, 13; Ex 32, 13; Dt 10, 22; Dn 3, 36 LXX.
w Gn 23, 4; Ps 39, 13.
x 13, 14; Ex 3, 6.
y Gn 22, 1-10; Sir 44, 20; 1 Mc 2, 52; Jas 2, 21.
z Gn 21, 12 LXX; Rom 9, 7.
a Rom 4, 16-22.

---

*

11, 1–40: This chapter draws upon the people and events of the Old Testament to paint an inspiring portrait of religious faith, firm and unyielding in the face of any obstacles that confront it. These pages rank among the most eloquent and lofty to be found in the Bible. They expand the theme announced in 6, 12, to which the author now returns (10, 39). The material of this chapter is developed chronologically. Verses 3–7 draw upon the first nine chapters of Gn; vv 8–22, upon the period of the patriarchs; vv 23–31, upon the time of Moses; vv 32–38, upon the history of the judges, the prophets, and the Maccabean martyrs. The author gives the most extensive description of faith provided in the New Testament, though his interest does not lie in a technical, theological definition. In view of the needs of his audience he describes what authentic faith does, not what it is in itself. Through faith God guarantees the blessings to be hoped for from him, providing evidence in the gift of faith that what he promises will eventually come to pass (1). Because they accepted in faith God's guarantee of the future, the biblical personages discussed in vv 3–38 were themselves commended by God (2). Christians have even greater reason to remain firm in faith since they, unlike the Old Testament men and women of faith, have perceived the beginning of God's fulfillment of his messianic promises (39–40).

11, 1: *Faith is the realization . . . evidence:* the author is not attempting a precise definition. There is dispute about the meaning of the Greek words *hypostasis* and *elenchos,* here translated *realization* and *evidence,* respectively. *Hypostasis* usually means "substance," "being" (as translated in 1, 3), or "reality" (as translated in 3, 14); here it connotes something more subjective, and so *realization* has been chosen rather than "assurance" (RSV). *Elenchos,* usually "proof," is used here in an objective sense and so translated *evidence* rather than the transferred sense of "(inner) conviction" (RSV).

11, 3: *By faith . . . God:* this verse does not speak of the faith of the Old Testament men and women but is in the first person plural. Hence it seems out of place in the sequence of thought.

11, 4: The "Praise of the Ancestors" in Sir 44, 1—50, 21 gives a similar list of heroes. The Cain and Abel narrative in Gn 4, 1–16 does not mention Abel's faith. It says, however, that God "looked with favor on Abel and his offering" (Gn 4, 4); in view of v 6 the author probably understood God's favor to have been activated by Abel's faith. *Though dead, he still speaks:* possibly because his blood "cries out to me from the soil" (Gn 4, 10), but more probably a way of saying that the repeated story of Abel provides ongoing witness to faith.

11, 6: One must believe not only that God exists but that he is concerned about human conduct; the Old Testament defines folly as the denial of this truth; cf Ps 52, 2.

11, 19: *As a symbol:* Isaac's "return from death" is seen as a *symbol* of Christ's resurrection. Others understand the words *en parabolē* to mean "in figure," i.e., the word *dead* is used figuratively of Isaac, since he did not really die. But in the one other place that *parabolē* occurs in Heb, it means symbol (9, 9).

he received Isaac back as a symbol. 20 [b]*By
faith regarding things still to come Isaac blessed
Jacob and Esau. 21 [c]By faith Jacob, when dying, blessed each of the sons of Joseph and
"bowed in worship, leaning on the top of his
staff." 22 [d]By faith Joseph, near the end of his
life, spoke of the Exodus of the Israelites and
gave instructions about his bones.

23 [e]By faith Moses was hidden by his parents for three months after his birth, because
they saw that he was a beautiful child, and they
were not afraid of the king's edict. 24 [f]*By
faith Moses, when he had grown up, refused to
be known as the son of Pharaoh's daughter;
25 he chose to be ill-treated along with the people of God rather than enjoy the fleeting pleasure of sin. 26 He considered the reproach of
the Anointed greater wealth than the treasures of
Egypt, for he was looking to the recompense.
27 [g]By faith he left Egypt, not fearing the
king's fury, for he persevered as if seeing the
one who is invisible. 28 [h]By faith he kept the
Passover and sprinkled the blood, that the Destroyer of the firstborn might not touch them.
29 [i]By faith they crossed the Red Sea as if it
were dry land, but when the Egyptians attempted it they were drowned. 30 [j]By faith the
walls of Jericho fell after being encircled for
seven days. 31 [k]By faith Rahab the harlot did
not perish with the disobedient, for she had
received the spies in peace.

32 [l]What more shall I say? I have not time
to tell of Gideon, Barak, Samson, Jephthah, of
David and Samuel and the prophets, 33 [m]who
by faith conquered kingdoms, did what was
righteous, obtained the promises; they closed
the mouths of lions, 34 [n]put out raging fires,
escaped the devouring sword; out of weakness
they were made powerful, became strong in
battle, and turned back foreign invaders.
35 [o]Women received back their dead through
resurrection. Some were tortured and would not
accept deliverance, in order to obtain a better
resurrection. 36 [p]Others endured mockery,
scourging, even chains and imprisonment.
37 [q]They were stoned, sawed in two, put to
death at sword's point; they went about in skins
of sheep or goats, needy, afflicted, tormented.
38 [r]The world was not worthy of them. They
wandered about in deserts and on mountains, in
caves and in crevices in the earth.

39 Yet all these, though approved because of
their faith, did not receive what had been promised. 40 *God had foreseen something better
for us, so that without us they should not be
made perfect.

## CHAPTER 12

**God our Father** 1 *Therefore, since we are
surrounded by so great a cloud of witnesses, let
us rid ourselves of every burden and sin that
clings to us and persevere in running the race
that lies before us 2 [s]while keeping our eyes
fixed on Jesus, the leader and perfecter of faith.
For the sake of the joy that lay before him he
endured the cross, despising its shame, and has
taken his seat at the right of the throne of God.
3 Consider how he endured such opposition
from sinners, in order that you may not grow
weary and lose heart. 4 In your struggle against
sin you have not yet resisted to the point of
shedding blood. 5 [t]You have also forgotten the
exhortation addressed to you as sons:

"My son, do not disdain the discipline of
the Lord
or lose heart when reproved by him;
6 for whom the Lord loves, he disciplines;
he scourges every son he acknowledges."

7 [u]Endure your trials as "discipline"; God
treats you as sons. For what "son" is there
whom his father does not discipline? 8 If you
are without discipline, in which all have shared,
you are not sons but bastards. 9 [v]Besides this,
we have had our earthly fathers to discipline us,

---

b Gn 27, 27-40.
c Gn 27, 38-40; 47, 31 LXX; 48, 15-16.
d Gn 50, 24-25.
e Ex 2, 2; Acts 7, 20.
f Ex 2, 10-15; Acts 7, 23-29.
g Ex 2, 15; Acts 7, 29.
h Ex 12, 21-23; Wis 18, 25; 1 Cor 10, 10.
i Ex 14, 22-28.
j Jos 6, 12-21.
k Jos 2, 1-21; 6, 22-25; Jas 2, 25.
l Jgs 4, 6—22; 6, 11—8, 32; 11, 1-12, 7.
m Dn 6, 23.
n Dn 3, 22-25.49-50.
o 1 Kgs 17, 17-24; 2 Kgs 4, 18-37; 2 Mc 6, 18—7, 42.
p 2 Chr 36, 16; Jer 20, 2; 37, 15.
q 2 Chr 24, 21.
r 1 Mc 2, 28-30.
s 2, 10; Ps 110, 1; Phil 2, 6-8.
t Prv 3, 11-12 / Dt 8, 5; 1 Cor 11, 32.
u Prv 13, 24; Sir 30, 1.
v Nm 16, 22; 27, 16 LXX.

---

11, 20–22: Each of these three patriarchs, Isaac, Jacob, and Joseph, had faith in the future fulfillment of God's promise and renewed this faith when near death.

11, 24–27: The reason given for Moses' departure from Egypt differs from the account in Ex 2, 11–15. The author also gives a christological interpretation of his decision to share the trials of his people.

11, 40: *So that without us they should not be made perfect:* the heroes of the Old Testament obtained their recompense only after the saving work of Christ had been accomplished. Thus they already enjoy what Christians who are still struggling do not yet possess in its fullness.

12, 1–13: Christian life is to be inspired not only by the Old Testament men and women of faith (1) but above all by Jesus. As the architect of Christian faith, he had himself to endure the cross before receiving the glory of his triumph (2). Reflection on his sufferings should give his followers courage to continue the struggle, if necessary even to the shedding of blood (3–4). Christians should regard their own sufferings as the affectionate correction of the Lord, who loves them as a father loves his children.

12, 1: *That clings to us:* the meaning is uncertain, since the Greek word *euperistatos,* translated *cling,* occurs only here. The papyrus P46 and one minuscule read *euperispastos,* "easily distracting," which also makes good sense.

and we respected them. Should we not [then]
submit all the more to the Father of spirits and
live? **10** They disciplined us for a short time as
seemed right to them, but he does so for our
benefit, in order that we may share his holiness.
**11** [w]At the time, all discipline seems a cause
not for joy but for pain, yet later it brings the
peaceful fruit of righteousness to those who are
trained by it.

**12** [x]So strengthen your drooping hands and
your weak knees. **13** [y]Make straight paths for
your feet, that what is lame may not be dislocat-
ed but healed.

**Penalties of Disobedience** **14** [z]Strive for
peace with everyone, and for that holiness without which no one will see the Lord. **15** [a]*See
to it that no one be deprived of the grace of God,
that no bitter root spring up and cause trouble,
through which many may become defiled,
**16** [b]that no one be an immoral or profane person like Esau, who sold his birthright for a
single meal. **17** [c]For you know that later, when
he wanted to inherit his father's blessing, he was
rejected because he found no opportunity to
change his mind, even though he sought the
blessing with tears.

**18** [d]*You have not approached that which
could be touched and a blazing fire and gloomy
darkness and storm **19** [e]and a trumpet blast and
a voice speaking words such that those who
heard begged that no message be further addressed to them, **20** [f]for they could not bear to
hear the command: "If even an animal touches
the mountain, it shall be stoned." **21** [g]Indeed,
so fearful was the spectacle that Moses said, "I
am terrified and trembling." **22** [h]No, you have
approached Mount Zion and the city of the living God, the heavenly Jerusalem, and countless
angels in festal gathering, **23** [i]*and the assembly of the firstborn enrolled in heaven, and God
the judge of all, and the spirits of the just made
perfect, **24** [j]*and Jesus, the mediator of a new
covenant, and the sprinkled blood that speaks
more eloquently than that of Abel.

**25** [k]See that you do not reject the one who
speaks. For if they did not escape when they
refused the one who warned them on earth, how
much more in our case if we turn away from the
one who warns from heaven. **26** [l]His voice
shook the earth at that time, but now he has
promised, "I will once more shake not only
earth but heaven." **27** [m]That phrase, "once
more," points to [the] removal of shaken, created things, so that what is unshaken may remain.
**28** [n]Therefore, we who are receiving the unshakable kingdom should have gratitude, with
which we should offer worship pleasing to God
in reverence and awe. **29** [o]For our God is a
consuming fire.

## *VI: FINAL EXHORTATION, BLESSING, GREETINGS*

## CHAPTER 13

**1** *Let mutual love continue. **2** [p]Do not neglect hospitality, for through it some have unknowingly entertained angels. **3** [q]Be mindful
of prisoners as if sharing their imprisonment,
and of the ill-treated as of yourselves, for you

w 2 Cor 4, 17; Phil 1, 11; Jas 3, 18.
x Is 35, 3; Sir 25, 23; Jb 4, 3-4.
y Prv 4, 26 LXX.
z Rom 12, 18; 14, 19.
a Dt 29, 18 (17 LXX).
b Gn 25, 33.
c Gn 27, 34-38.
d Ex 19, 12-14; Dt 4, 11; 5, 22-23.
e Ex 19, 16.19; 20, 18-19.
f Ex 19, 12-13.
g Dt 9, 19.
h Gal 4, 26; Rv 21, 2.
i Lk 10, 20; Rv 5, 11.
j 7, 22; 8, 6; 9, 15 / 11, 4; Gn 4, 10.
k Ex 20, 19.
l Ex 19, 18; Jgs 5, 4-5; Ps 68, 9; Hg 2, 6.
m Is 66, 22; Mt 24, 35; Mk 13, 31; Lk 21, 33.
n Dn 7, 14.18 / Rom 1, 9.
o Dt 4, 24; Is 33, 14.
p Gn 18, 3; 19, 2-3; Jgs 6, 11-22; Tb 5, 4.
q Mt 25, 36.

*

12, 15–17: Esau serves as an example in two ways: his *profane* attitude illustrates the danger of apostasy, and his inability to secure a blessing afterward illustrates the impossibility of repenting after falling away (see 6, 4–6).

12, 18–29: As a final appeal for adherence to Christian teaching, the two covenants, of Moses and of Christ, are compared. The Mosaic covenant, the author argues, is shown to have originated in fear of God and threats of divine punishment (18–21). The covenant in Christ gives us direct access to God (22), makes us members of the Christian community, God's children, a sanctified people (23), who have Jesus as mediator to speak for us (24). Not to heed the voice of the risen Christ is a graver sin than the rejection of the word of Moses (25–26). Though Christians fall away, God's kingdom in Christ will remain and his justice will punish those guilty of deserting it (28–29).

12, 18–24: This remarkably beautiful passage contrasts two great assemblies of people: that of the Israelites gathered at Mount Sinai for the sealing of the old covenant and the promulgation of the Mosaic law, and that of the followers of Jesus gathered at *Mount Zion, the heavenly Jerusalem,* the assembly of the *new covenant.* This latter scene, marked by the presence of *countless angels* and of *Jesus* with his redeeming *blood,* is reminiscent of the celestial liturgies of the Book of Revelation.

12, 23: *The assembly of the firstborn enrolled in heaven:* this expression may refer to the angels of v 22, or to the heroes of the Old Testament (see ch 11), or to the entire assembly of the new covenant.

12, 24: *Speaks more eloquently:* the blood of Abel, the first human blood to be shed, is contrasted with that of Jesus. Abel's blood cried out from the earth for vengeance, but the blood of Jesus has opened the way for everyone, providing cleansing and access to God (10, 19).

13, 1–16: After recommendations on social and moral matters (1–6), the letter turns to doctrinal issues. The fact that the original leaders are dead should not cause the recipients of this letter to lose their faith (7), for Christ still lives and he remains always the same (8). They must not rely for their personal sanctification on regulations concerning foods (9), nor should they entertain the notion that Judaism and Christianity can be intermingled (10; cf the notes on Gal 2, 11–14 and 2, 15–21). As Jesus died separated from his own people, so must the Christian community remain apart from the religious doctrines of Judaism (11–14). Christ must be the heart and center of the community (15–16).

also are in the body. **4** [r]Let marriage be honored among all and the marriage bed be kept
undefiled, for God will judge the immoral and
adulterers. **5** [s]Let your life be free from love of
money but be content with what you have, for
he has said, "I will never forsake you or abandon you." **6** [t]Thus we may say with confidence:

> "The Lord is my helper,
> [and] I will not be afraid.
> What can anyone do to me?"

**7** Remember your leaders who spoke the word
of God to you. Consider the outcome of their
way of life and imitate their faith. **8** [u]Jesus
Christ is the same yesterday, today, and forever.
**9** [v]*Do not be carried away by all kinds of
strange teaching. It is good to have our hearts
strengthened by grace and not by foods, which
do not benefit those who live by them. **10** *We
have an altar from which those who serve the
tabernacle have no right to eat. **11** [w]The bodies
of the animals whose blood the high priest
brings into the sanctuary as a sin offering are
burned outside the camp. **12** [x]Therefore, Jesus
also suffered outside the gate, to consecrate the
people by his own blood. **13** Let us then go to
him outside the camp, bearing the reproach that
he bore. **14** [y]For here we have no lasting city,
but we seek the one that is to come.
**15** [z]Through him [then] let us continually offer
God a sacrifice of praise, that is, the fruit of lips
that confess his name. **16** [a]Do not neglect to do
good and to share what you have; God is pleased
by sacrifices of that kind.
**17** *Obey your leaders and defer to them, for
they keep watch over you and will have to give
an account, that they may fulfill their task with
joy and not with sorrow, for that would be of no
advantage to you.
**18** Pray for us, for we are confident that we
have a clear conscience, wishing to act rightly
in every respect. **19** I especially ask for your
prayers that I may be restored to you very soon.
**20** [b]*May the God of peace, who brought up
from the dead the great shepherd of the sheep by
the blood of the eternal covenant, Jesus our
Lord, **21** furnish you with all that is good, that
you may do his will. May he carry out in you
what is pleasing to him through Jesus Christ, to
whom be glory forever [and ever]. Amen.
**22** Brothers, I ask you to bear with this message of encouragement, for I have written to you
rather briefly. **23** [c]I must let you know that our
brother Timothy has been set free. If he comes
soon, I shall see you together with him.
**24** Greetings to all your leaders and to all the
holy ones. Those from Italy send you greetings.
**25** [d]Grace be with all of you.

---

r 1 Cor 5, 13; Eph 5, 5.
s Dt 31, 6.8; Jos 1, 5.
t Pss 27, 1-3; 118, 6.
u 1, 12; 7, 24; Rv 1, 17.
v Rom 14, 17; 1 Cor 8, 8; Eph 4, 14; Col 2, 16.
w Ex 29, 14; Lv 16, 27.
x Mt 21, 39; Mk 12, 8; Lk 20, 15; Jn 19, 17.
y 11, 10.14.
z Hos 14, 3.
a Phil 4, 18.
b Is 63, 11; Zec 9, 11; Jn 10, 11; Acts 2, 24; Rom 15, 33.
c Acts 16, 1.
d Ti 3, 15.

---

13, 9: *Strange teaching:* this doctrine about *foods* probably refers to the Jewish food laws; in view of v 10, however, the author may be thinking of the Mosaic sacrificial banquets.

13, 10: *We have an altar:* this does not refer to the Eucharist, which is never clearly mentioned in Heb, but to the sacrifice of Christ.

13, 17–25: Recommending obedience to the leaders of the community, the author asks for prayers (17–19). The letter concludes with a blessing (20–21), a final request for the acceptance of its message (22), information regarding Timothy (23), and general greetings (24–25).

13, 20–21: These verses constitute one of the most beautiful blessings in the New Testament. The resurrection of Jesus is presupposed throughout Heb, since it is included in the author's frequently expressed idea of his exaltation, but this is the only place where it is explicitly mentioned.

# THE CATHOLIC LETTERS

*In addition to the thirteen letters attributed to Paul and the Letter to the Hebrews, the New Testament contains seven other letters. Three of these are attributed to John, two to Peter, and one each to James and Jude, all personages of the apostolic age. The term "catholic letter" first appears, with reference only to 1 John, in the writings of Apollonius of Ephesus, a second-century apologist, known only from a citation in Eusebius' Ecclesiastical History. Eusebius himself (A.D. 260–340) used the term to refer to all seven letters.*

*The reason for the term "catholic," which means "universal," was the perception that these letters, unlike those of Paul, which were directed to a particular local church, were apparently addressed more generally to the universal church. This designation is not entirely accurate, however. On the one hand, Hebrews has no specifically identified addressees, and originally this was probably true of Ephesians as well. On the other hand, 3 John is addressed to a named individual, 2 John to a specific, though unnamed, community, and 1 Peter to a number of churches that are specified as being located in Asia Minor.*

*While all seven of these writings begin with an epistolary formula, several of them do not appear to be real letters in the modern sense of the term. In the ancient world it was not unusual to cast an exhortation in the form of a letter for literary effect, a phenomenon comparable to the "open letter" that is sometimes used today.*

*With the exception of 1 Peter and 1 John, the ancient church showed reluctance to include the catholic letters in the New Testament canon. The reason for this was widespread doubt whether they had actually been written by the apostolic figures to whom they are attributed. The early Christians saw the New Testament as the depository of apostolic faith; therefore, they wished to include only the testimony of apostles. Today we distinguish more clearly between the authorship of a work and its canonicity: even though written by other, later witnesses than those whose names they bear, these writings nevertheless testify to the apostolic faith and constitute canonical scripture. By the late fourth or early fifth centuries, most objections had been overcome in both the Greek and Latin churches (though not in the Syriac), and all seven of the catholic letters have since been acknowledged as canonical.*

# THE LETTER OF

# JAMES

## INTRODUCTION

*The person to whom this letter is ascribed can scarcely be one of the two members of the Twelve who bore the name James (see Mt 10, 2–3; Mk 3, 17–18; Lk 6, 14–15), for he is not identified as an apostle but only as "slave of God and of the Lord Jesus Christ" (1, 1). This designation most probably refers to the third New Testament personage named James, a relative of Jesus who is usually called "brother of the Lord" (see Mt 13, 55; Mk 6, 3). He was the leader of the Jewish Christian community in Jerusalem whom Paul acknowledged as one of the "pillars" (Gal 2, 9). In Acts he appears as the authorized spokesman for the Jewish Christian position in the early Church (Acts 12, 17; 15, 13–21). According to the Jewish historian Josephus (*Antiquities *20, 9, 1 ¶¶200–203), he was stoned to death by the Jews under the high priest Ananus II in A.D. 62.*

*The letter is addressed to "the twelve tribes in the dispersion." In Old Testament terminology the term "twelve tribes" designates the people of Israel; the "dispersion" or "diaspora" refers to the non-Palestinian Jews who had settled throughout the Greco-Roman world (see Jn 7, 35). Since in Christian thought the church is the new Israel, the address probably designates the Jewish Christian churches located in Palestine, Syria, and elsewhere. Or perhaps the letter is meant more generally for all Christian communities, and the "dispersion" has the symbolic meaning of exile from our true home, as it has in the address of 1 Peter (1, 1). The letter is so markedly Jewish in character that some scholars have regarded it as a Jewish document subsequently "baptized" by a few Christian insertions, but such an origin is scarcely tenable in view of the numerous contacts discernible between the Letter of James and other New Testament literature.*

*From the viewpoint of its literary form, James is a letter only in the most conventional sense; it has none of the characteristic features of a real letter except the address. It belongs rather to the genre of *parenesis* or exhortation and is concerned almost exclusively with ethical conduct. It therefore falls within the tradition of Jewish wisdom literature, such as can be found in the Old Testament (Proverbs, Sirach) and in the extracanonical Jewish literature *(Testaments of the Twelve Patriarchs, *the* Books of Enoch, *the* Manual of Discipline *found at Qumran). More specifically, it consists of sequences of didactic proverbs, comparable to Tob 4, 5–19, to many passages in Sirach, and to sequences of sayings in the synoptic gospels. Numerous passages in James treat of subjects that also appear in the synoptic sayings of Jesus, especially in Matthew's Sermon on the Mount, but the correspondences are too general to establish any literary dependence. James represents a type of early Christianity that emphasized sound teaching and responsible moral behavior. Ethical norms are derived not primarily from christology, as in Paul, but from a concept of salvation that involves conversion, baptism, forgiveness of sin, and expectation of judgment (1, 17; 4, 12).*

*Paradoxically, this very Jewish work is written in an excellent Greek style, which ranks among the best in the New Testament and appears to be the work of a trained Hellenistic writer. Those who continue to regard James of Jerusalem as its author are therefore obliged to suppose that a secretary must have put the letter into its present literary form. This assumption is not implausible in the light of ancient practice. Some regard the letter as one of the earliest writings in the New Testament and feel that its content accurately reflects what we would expect of the leader of Jewish Christianity. Moreover, they argue that the type of Jewish Christianity reflected in the letter cannot be situated historically after the fall of Jerusalem in A.D. 70.*

*Others, however, believe it more likely that James is a pseudonymous work of a later period. In addition to its Greek style, they observe further that (a) the prestige that the writer is assumed to enjoy points to the later legendary reputation of James; (b) the discussion of the importance of good works seems to presuppose a debate subsequent to that in Paul's own day; (c) the author does not rely upon prescriptions of the Mosaic law, as we would expect from the historical James; (d) the letter contains no allusions to James's own history and to his relationship with Jesus or to the early Christian community of Jerusalem. For these reasons, many recent interpreters assign James to the period A.D. 90–100.*

*The principal divisions of the Letter of James are the following:*

*I. Address (1, 1)*
*II. The Value of Trials and Temptation (1, 2–18)*
*III. Exhortations and Warnings (1, 19—5, 12)*
*IV. The Power of Prayer (5, 13–20)*

## *I: ADDRESS*

### CHAPTER 1

**1** [a]*James, a slave of God and of the Lord
Jesus Christ, to the twelve tribes in the dispersion, greetings.

## *II: THE VALUE OF TRIALS AND TEMPTATION*

**Perseverance in Trial** **2** [b]*Consider it all
joy, my brothers, when you encounter various
trials, **3** *for you know that the testing of your
faith produces perseverance. **4** And let perseverance be perfect, so that you may be perfect
and complete, lacking in nothing. **5** [c]*But if
any of you lacks wisdom, he should ask God
who gives to all generously and ungrudgingly,
and he will be given it. **6** [d]But he should ask in
faith, not doubting, for the one who doubts is
like a wave of the sea that is driven and tossed
about by the wind. **7** For that person must not
suppose that he will receive anything from the
Lord, **8** since he is a man of two minds, unstable in all his ways.

**9** [e]*The brother in lowly circumstances
should take pride in his high standing, **10** [f]and
the rich one in his lowliness, for he will pass
away "like the flower of the field." **11** For the
sun comes up with its scorching heat and dries
up the grass, its flower droops, and the beauty
of its appearance vanishes. So will the rich person fade away in the midst of his pursuits.

**Temptation** **12** [g]*Blessed is the man who
perseveres in temptation, for when he has been
proved he will receive the crown of life that he
promised to those who love him. **13** [h]*No one
experiencing temptation should say, "I am being tempted by God"; for God is not subject to
temptation to evil, and he himself tempts no
one. **14** Rather, each person is tempted when he
is lured and enticed by his own desire. **15** Then
desire conceives and brings forth sin, and when
sin reaches maturity it gives birth to death.

**16** *Do not be deceived, my beloved brothers: **17** *all good giving and every perfect gift

a Jn 7, 35; 1 Pt 1, 1.
b Rom 5, 3-5; 1 Pt 1, 6; 4, 13-16.
c Prv 2, 2-6; Wis 9, 4.9-12.
d Mt 7, 7; Mk 11, 24.
e 2, 5.
f Is 40, 6-7.
g 1 Cor 9, 25; 2 Tm 4, 8; 1 Pt 5, 4; Rv 2, 10.
h Sir 15, 11-20; 1 Cor 10, 13.

*

1, 1: *James, a slave of God and of the Lord Jesus Christ:* a declaration of the writer's authority for instructing the Christian communities; cf Rom 1, 1. Regarding the identity of the author, see Introduction. *Dispersion:* see Introduction.

1, 2: *Consider it all joy . . . various trials:* a frequent teaching of the New Testament derived from the words and sufferings of Jesus (Mt 5, 10–12; Jn 10, 11; Acts 5, 41).

1, 3–8: The sequence of testing, perseverance, and being perfect and complete indicates the manner of attaining spiritual maturity and full preparedness for the coming of Christ (5, 7–12; cf 1 Pt 1, 6–7; Rom 5, 3–5). These steps require wisdom (5).

1, 5: *Wisdom:* a gift that God readily grants to all who ask in faith and that sustains the Christian in times of trial. It is a kind of knowledge or understanding not accessible to the unbeliever or those who doubt, which gives the recipient an understanding of the real importance of events. In this way a Christian can deal with adversity with great calm and hope (cf 1 Cor 2, 6–12).

1, 9–11: Throughout his letter (see 2, 5; 4, 10.13–16; 5, 1–6), the author reaffirms the teaching of Jesus that worldly prosperity is not necessarily a sign of God's favor but can even be a hindrance to proper humility before God (cf Lk 6, 20–25; 12, 16–21; 16, 19–31).

1, 12: *Temptation:* the Greek word used here is the same one used for "trials" in v 2. *The crown of life:* in ancient Palestine, crowns or wreaths of flowers were worn at festive occasions as signs of joy and honor. In the Hellenistic world, wreaths were given as a reward to great statesmen, soldiers, athletes. *Life:* here means eternal life. *He promised:* some manuscripts read "God" or "the Lord," while the best witnesses do not specify the subject of "promised."

1, 13–15: It is contrary to what we know of God for God to be the author of human temptation (13). In the commission of a sinful act, one is first beguiled by passion (14), then consent is given, which in turn causes the sinful act. When sin permeates the entire person, it incurs the ultimate penalty of death (15).

1, 16–18: The author here stresses that God is the source of all good and of good alone, and the evil of temptation does not come from him.

1, 17: *All good giving and every perfect gift* may be a proverb written in hexameter. *Father of lights:* God is here called the Father of the heavenly luminaries, i.e., the stars, sun, and moon that he created (Gn 1, 14–18). Unlike orbs

is from above, coming down from the Father of
lights, with whom there is no alteration or shadow caused by change. **18** [i]*He willed to give
us birth by the word of truth that we may be a
kind of firstfruits of his creatures.

## *III: EXHORTATIONS AND WARNINGS*

**Doers of the Word** **19** [j]*Know this, my
dear brothers: everyone should be quick to hear,
slow to speak, slow to wrath, **20** [k]for the wrath
of a man does not accomplish the righteousness
of God. **21** [l]Therefore, put away all filth and
evil excess and humbly welcome the word that
has been planted in you and is able to save your
souls.

**22** [m]Be doers of the word and not hearers
only, deluding yourselves. **23** For if anyone is
a hearer of the word and not a doer, he is like
a man who looks at his own face in a mirror.
**24** He sees himself, then goes off and promptly
forgets what he looked like. **25** [n]*But the one
who peers into the perfect law of freedom and
perseveres, and is not a hearer who forgets but
a doer who acts, such a one shall be blessed in
what he does.

**26** [o]*If anyone thinks he is religious and
does not bridle his tongue but deceives his heart,
his religion is vain. **27** [p]*Religion that is pure
and undefiled before God and the Father is this:
to care for orphans and widows in their affliction and to keep oneself unstained by the world.

## CHAPTER 2

**Sin of Partiality** **1** *My brothers, show no
partiality as you adhere to the faith in our glorious Lord Jesus Christ. **2** For if a man with gold
rings on his fingers and in fine clothes comes
into your assembly, and a poor person in shabby
clothes also comes in, **3** and you pay attention
to the one wearing the fine clothes and say, "Sit
here, please," while you say to the poor one,
"Stand there," or "Sit at my feet," **4** *have
you not made distinctions among yourselves
and become judges with evil designs?

**5** [q]*Listen, my beloved brothers. Did not
God choose those who are poor in the world to
be rich in faith and heirs of the kingdom that he
promised to those who love him? **6** But you
dishonored the poor person. Are not the rich
oppressing you? And do they themselves not
haul you off to court? **7** [r]Is it not they who
blaspheme the noble name that was invoked
over you? **8** [s]*However, if you fulfill the royal
law according to the scripture, "You shall love
your neighbor as yourself," you are doing well.
**9** [t]But if you show partiality, you commit sin,
and are convicted by the law as transgressors.
**10** [u]For whoever keeps the whole law, but falls
short in one particular, has become guilty in
respect to all of it. **11** [v]For he who said, "You
shall not commit adultery," also said, "You
shall not kill." Even if you do not commit adultery but kill, you have become a transgressor of
the law. **12** [w]*So speak and so act as people
who will be judged by the law of freedom.
**13** [x]For the judgment is merciless to one who
has not shown mercy; mercy triumphs over
judgment.

---

i Jn 1, 12-13; 1 Pt 1, 23.
j Prv 14, 17; Sir 5, 11.
k Eph 4, 26.
l Col 3, 8.
m Mt 7, 26; Rom 2, 13.
n 2, 12; Ps 19, 8; Rom 8, 2.
o 3, 2; Ps 34, 14.
p Ex 22, 21.
q 1 Cor 1, 26-28; Rv 2, 9.
r 1 Pt 4, 4.
s Lv 19, 18; Mt 22, 39; Rom 13, 9.
t Dt 1, 17.
u Gal 3, 10.
v Ex 20, 13-14; Dt 5, 17-18.
w 1, 25; Rom 8, 2.
x Mt 5, 7; 6, 14-15; 18, 32-33.

---

*

moving from nadir to zenith, he never changes or diminishes in brightness.

1, 18: Acceptance of the gospel message, *the word of truth,* constitutes new birth (Jn 3, 5–6) and makes the recipient the *firstfruits* (i.e., the cultic offering of the earliest grains, symbolizing the beginning of an abundant harvest) of a new creation; cf 1 Cor 15, 20; Rom 8, 23.

1, 19–25: *To be quick to hear* the gospel is to accept it readily and to act in conformity with it, removing from one's soul whatever is opposed to it, so that it may take root and effect salvation (19–21). To listen to the gospel message but not practice it is failure to improve oneself (22–24). Only conformity of life to the perfect law of true freedom brings happiness (25).

1, 25: *Peers into the perfect law:* the image of a person doing this is paralleled to that of hearing God's word. The *perfect law* applies the Old Testament description of the Mosaic law to the gospel of Jesus Christ that brings freedom.

1, 26–27: A practical application of v 22 is now made.

1, 26: For control of the tongue, see the note on 3, 1–12.

1, 27: In the Old Testament, orphans and widows are classical examples of the defenseless and oppressed.

2, 1–13: In the Christian community there must be no discrimination or favoritism based on status or wealth (2–4; cf Mt 5, 3; 11, 5; 23, 6; 1 Cor 1, 27–29). Divine favor rather consists in God's election and promises (5). The rich who oppress the poor blaspheme the name of Christ (6–7). By violating one law of love of neighbor, they offend against the whole law (8–11). On the other hand, conscious awareness of the final judgment helps the faithful to fulfill the whole law (12).

2, 4: When Christians show favoritism to the rich they are guilty of the worst kind of prejudice and discrimination. The author says that such Christians set themselves up as judges who judge not by divine law but by the basest, self-serving motives.

2, 5: The poor, "God's poor" of the Old Testament, were seen by Jesus as particularly open to God for belief in and reliance on him alone (Lk 6, 20). God's law cannot tolerate their oppression in any way (9).

2, 8: *Royal:* literally, "kingly"; because the Mosaic law came from God, the universal king. There may be an allusion to Jesus' uses of this commandment in his preaching of the kingdom of God (Mt 22, 39; Mk 12, 31; Lk 10, 27).

2, 12–13: The law upon which the last judgment will be based is the law of freedom. As Jesus taught, mercy (which participates in God's own loving mercy) includes forgiveness of those who wrong us (see Mt 6, 12.14–15).

**Faith and Works** 14 [y]*What good is it, my
brothers, if someone says he has faith but does
not have works? Can that faith save him? 15 If
a brother or sister has nothing to wear and has
no food for the day, 16 [z]and one of you says to
them, "Go in peace, keep warm, and eat well,"
but you do not give them the necessities of the
body, what good is it? 17 So also faith of itself,
if it does not have works, is dead.

18 Indeed someone might say, "You have
faith and I have works." Demonstrate your faith
to me without works, and I will demonstrate my
faith to you from my works. 19 You believe
that God is one. You do well. Even the demons
believe that and tremble. 20 Do you want
proof, you ignoramus, that faith without works
is useless? 21 [a]Was not Abraham our father
justified by works when he offered his son Isaac
upon the altar? 22 You see that faith was active
along with his works, and faith was completed
by the works. 23 [b]Thus the scripture was fulfilled that says, "Abraham believed God, and it
was credited to him as righteousness," and he
was called "the friend of God." 24 See how a
person is justified by works and not by faith
alone. 25 [c]And in the same way, was not Rahab the harlot also justified by works when she
welcomed the messengers and sent them out by
a different route? 26 For just as a body without
a spirit is dead, so also faith without works is
dead.

## CHAPTER 3

**Power of the Tongue** 1 *Not many of you
should become teachers, my brothers, for you
realize that we will be judged more strictly,
2 [d]for we all fall short in many respects. If
anyone does not fall short in speech, he is a
perfect man, able to bridle his whole body also.
3 If we put bits into the mouths of horses to
make them obey us, we also guide their whole
bodies. 4 It is the same with ships: even though
they are so large and driven by fierce winds,
they are steered by a very small rudder wherever
the pilot's inclination wishes. 5 In the same
way the tongue is a small member and yet has
great pretensions.

Consider how small a fire can set a huge
forest ablaze. 6 The tongue is also a fire. It
exists among our members as a world of malice,
defiling the whole body and setting the entire
course of our lives on fire, itself set on fire by
Gehenna. 7 For every kind of beast and bird, of
reptile and sea creature, can be tamed and has
been tamed by the human species, 8 [e]but no
human being can tame the tongue. It is a restless
evil, full of deadly poison. 9 With it we bless
the Lord and Father, and with it we curse human
beings who are made in the likeness of God.
10 From the same mouth come blessing and
cursing. This need not be so, my brothers.
11 Does a spring gush forth from the same
opening both pure and brackish water? 12 [f]Can
a fig tree, my brothers, produce olives, or a
grapevine figs? Neither can salt water yield
fresh.

**True Wisdom** 13 [g]*Who among you is
wise and understanding? Let him show his
works by a good life in the humility that comes
from wisdom. 14 But if you have bitter jealousy and selfish ambition in your hearts, do not
boast and be false to the truth. 15 Wisdom of
this kind does not come down from above but
is earthly, unspiritual, demonic. 16 For where
jealousy and selfish ambition exist, there is disorder and every foul practice. 17 [h]But the wisdom from above is first of all pure, then peaceable, gentle, compliant, full of mercy and good
fruits, without inconstancy or insincerity.
18 [i]And the fruit of righteousness is sown in
peace for those who cultivate peace.

## CHAPTER 4

**Causes of Division** 1 [j]*Where do the
wars and where do the conflicts among you

y Mt 25, 31-46; Gal 5, 6.
z 1 Jn 3, 17.
a Gn 22, 9-12; Heb 11, 17.
b Gn 15, 6; Rom 4, 3; Gal 3, 6 / 2 Chr 20, 7; Is 41, 8.
c Jos 2, 1-21.
d 1, 26; Prv 13, 3; Sir 28, 12-26.
e Ps 140, 4.
f Mt 7, 16-17.
g Eph 4, 1-2.
h 1, 17; Wis 7, 22-23.
i Mt 5, 9.
j Rom 7, 23; 1 Pt 2, 11.

*

2, 14–26: The theme of these verses is the relationship of faith and works (deeds). It has been argued that the teaching here contradicts that of Paul (see especially Rom 4, 5–6). The problem can only be understood if the different viewpoints of the two authors are seen. Paul argues against those who claim to participate in God's salvation because of their good deeds as well as because they have committed themselves to trust in God through Jesus Christ (Paul's concept of faith). Paul certainly understands, however, the implications of true faith for a life of love and generosity (see Gal 5, 6.13–15). The author of James is well aware that proper conduct can only come about with an authentic commitment to God in faith (18.26). Many think he was seeking to correct a misunderstanding of Paul's view.

3, 1–12: The use and abuse of the important role of teaching in the church (1) are here related to the good and bad use of the tongue (9–12), the instrument through which teaching was chiefly conveyed (see Sir 5, 11—6, 1; 28, 12–26).

3, 13–18: This discussion of true wisdom is related to the previous reflection on the role of the teacher as one who is in control of his speech. The qualities of the wise man endowed from above are detailed (17–18; cf Gal 5, 22–23), in contrast to the qualities of earthbound wisdom (14–16; cf 2 Cor 12, 20).

4, 1–12: The concern here is with the origin of conflicts in the Christian community. These are occasioned by love *of the world,* which *means enmity with God* (4). Further, the conflicts are bound up with failure to pray properly (cf Mt 7, 7–11; Jn 14, 13; 15, 7; 16, 23), that is, not asking God at all or using God's kindness only for one's pleasure (2–3). In contrast, the proper dispositions are submission to God, repentance, humility, and resistance to evil (7–10).

4, 1: *Passions:* the Greek word here (literally, "pleasures")

come from? Is it not from your passions that
make war within your members? 2 You covet
but do not possess. You kill and envy but you
cannot obtain; you fight and wage war. You do
not possess because you do not ask. 3 You ask
but do not receive, because you ask wrongly, to
spend it on your passions. 4 [k]*Adulterers! Do
you not know that to be a lover of the world
means enmity with God? Therefore, whoever
wants to be a lover of the world makes himself
an enemy of God. 5 *Or do you suppose that
the scripture speaks without meaning when it
says, "The spirit that he has made to dwell in
us tends toward jealousy"? 6 [l]*But he bestows
a greater grace; therefore, it says:

"God resists the proud,
but gives grace to the humble."

7 [m]So submit yourselves to God. Resist the
devil, and he will flee from you. 8 [n]Draw near
to God, and he will draw near to you. Cleanse
your hands, you sinners, and purify your hearts,
you of two minds. 9 Begin to lament, to mourn,
to weep. Let your laughter be turned into
mourning and your joy into dejection.
10 [o]Humble yourselves before the Lord and he
will exalt you.

11 *Do not speak evil of one another, brothers. Whoever speaks evil of a brother or judges
his brother speaks evil of the law and judges the
law. If you judge the law, you are not a doer of
the law but a judge. 12 [p]There is one lawgiver
and judge who is able to save or to destroy. Who
then are you to judge your neighbor?

## Warning against Presumption

13 *Come now, you who say, "Today or tomorrow we shall go into such and such a town,
spend a year there doing business, and make a
profit"—14 [q]*you have no idea what your life
will be like tomorrow. You are a puff of smoke
that appears briefly and then disappears.
15 *Instead you should say, "If the Lord wills
it, we shall live to do this or that." 16 But now
you are boasting in your arrogance. All such
boasting is evil. 17 [r]*So for one who knows the
right thing to do and does not do it, it is a sin.

## CHAPTER 5

### Warning to the Rich

1 [s]*Come now, you
rich, weep and wail over your impending miser-
ies. 2 [t]Your wealth has rotted away, your
clothes have become moth-eaten, 3 [u]your gold
and silver have corroded, and that corrosion will
be a testimony against you; it will devour your
flesh like a fire. You have stored up treasure for
the last days. 4 [v]Behold, the wages you withheld from the workers who harvested your fields
are crying aloud, and the cries of the harvesters
have reached the ears of the Lord of hosts.
5 [w]You have lived on earth in luxury and pleasure; you have fattened your hearts for the day
of slaughter. 6 [x]*You have condemned; you
have murdered the righteous one; he offers you
no resistance.

### Patience and Oaths

7 *Be patient, there-
fore, brothers, until the coming of the Lord. See

k Mt 6, 24; Lk 16, 13; Rom 8, 7; 1 Jn 2, 15-16.
l Jb 22, 29; Prv 3, 34; Mt 23, 12; 1 Pt 5, 5.
m 1 Pt 5, 8-9.
n Zec 1, 3; Mal 3, 7.
o Jb 5, 11; Mt 23, 12; Lk 14, 11; 18, 14; 1 Pt 5, 6.
p Mt 7, 1; Rom 2, 1; 14, 4.
q Prv 27, 1 / Ps 39, 6-7.
r Lk 12, 47.
s Lk 6, 24.
t Mt 6, 19.
u Ps 21, 10; Prv 11, 4; Jdt 16, 17.
v Lv 19, 13; Dt 24, 14-15; Mal 3, 5.
w Jer 12, 3; Lk 16, 19-25.
x Wis 2, 10-20.

* does not indicate that pleasure is evil. Rather, as the text points out (2–3), it is the manner in which one deals with needs and desires that determines good or bad. The motivation for any action can be wrong, especially if one does not pray properly but seeks only selfish enjoyment (3).

4, 4: *Adulterers:* a common biblical image for the covenant between God and his people is the marriage bond. In this image, breaking the covenant with God is likened to the unfaithfulness of adultery.

4, 5: The meaning of this saying is difficult because the author of Jas cites, probably from memory, a passage that is not in any extant manuscript of the Bible. Other translations of the text with a completely different meaning are possible: "The Spirit that he (God) made to dwell in us yearns (for us) jealously," or, "He (God) yearns jealously for the spirit that he has made to dwell in us." If this last translation is correct, the author perhaps had in mind an apocryphal religious text that echoes the idea that God is zealous for his creatures; cf Ex 20, 5; Dt 4, 24; Zec 8, 2.

4, 6: The point of this whole argument is that God wants the happiness of all, but that selfishness and pride can make that impossible. We must work with him in humility (10).

4, 11: Slander of a fellow Christian does not break just one commandment but makes mockery of the authority of law in general and therefore of God.

4, 13–17: The uncertainty of life (14), its complete dependence on God, and the necessity of submitting to God's will (15) all help one know and do what is right (17). To disregard this is to live in pride and arrogance (16); failure to do what is right is a sin (17).

4, 14: Some important Greek manuscripts here have, "You who have no idea what tomorrow will bring. Why, what is your life?"

4, 15: *If the Lord wills it:* often in piety referred to as the *"conditio Jacobaea,"* the condition James says we should employ to qualify all our plans.

4, 17: *It is a sin:* those who live arrogantly, forgetting the contingency of life and our dependence on God (13–16), are guilty of sin.

5, 1–6: Continuing with the theme of the transitory character of life on earth, the author points out the impending ruin of the godless. He denounces the unjust rich, whose victims cry to heaven for judgment on their exploiters (4–6). The decay and corrosion of the costly garments and metals, which symbolize wealth, prove them worthless and portend the destruction of their possessors (2–3).

5, 6: The author does not have in mind any specific crime in his readers' communities but rather echoes the Old Testament theme of the harsh oppression of the righteous poor (see Prv 1, 11; Wis 2, 10.12.20).

5, 7–11: Those oppressed by the unjust rich are reminded of the need for patience, both in bearing the sufferings of

how the farmer waits for the precious fruit of the
earth, being patient with it until it receives the
early and the late rains. **8** [y]You too must be
patient. Make your hearts firm, because the
coming of the Lord is at hand. **9** Do not complain, brothers, about one another, that you may
not be judged. Behold, the Judge is standing
before the gates. **10** Take as an example of
hardship and patience, brothers, the prophets
who spoke in the name of the Lord. **11** [z]Indeed
we call blessed those who have persevered. You
have heard of the perseverance of Job, and you
have seen the purpose of the Lord, because "the
Lord is compassionate and merciful."

**12** [a]*But above all, my brothers, do not
swear, either by heaven or by earth or with any
other oath, but let your "Yes" mean "Yes"
and your "No" mean "No," that you may not
incur condemnation.

## *IV: THE POWER OF PRAYER*

### Anointing of the Sick

**13** Is anyone
among you suffering? He should pray. Is anyone in good spirits? He should sing praise.
**14** [b]*Is anyone among you sick? He should
summon the presbyters of the church, and they
should pray over him and anoint [him] with oil
in the name of the Lord, **15** *and the prayer of
faith will save the sick person, and the Lord will
raise him up. If he has committed any sins, he
will be forgiven.

### Confession and Intercession

**16** There-
fore, confess your sins to one another and pray
for one another, that you may be healed. The
fervent prayer of a righteous person is very powerful. **17** [c]Elijah was a human being like us; yet
he prayed earnestly that it might not rain, and
for three years and six months it did not rain
upon the land. **18** [d]Then he prayed again, and
the sky gave rain and the earth produced its
fruit.

### Conversion of Sinners

**19** [e]My brothers,
if anyone among you should stray from the truth
and someone bring him back, **20** [f]*he should
know that whoever brings back a sinner from
the error of his way will save his soul from death
and will cover a multitude of sins.

y Lk 21, 19; Heb 10, 36 / Heb 10, 25; 1 Pt 4, 7.
z Ex 34, 6; Ps 103, 8.
a Mt 5, 34-37.
b Mk 6, 13.
c 1 Kgs 17, 1; Lk 4, 25.
d 1 Kgs 18, 45.
e Mt 18, 15; Gal 6, 1.
f Prv 10, 12; 1 Pt 4, 8.

*

human life (9) and in their expectation of the coming of the Lord. It is then that they will receive their reward (7–8.10–11; cf Heb 10, 25; 1 Jn 2, 18).

5, 7: *The early and the late rains:* an expression related to the agricultural season in ancient Palestine (see Dt 11, 14; Jer 5, 24; Jl 2, 23).

5, 12: This is the threat of condemnation for the abuse of swearing oaths (cf Mt 5, 33–37). *By heaven or by earth:* these words were substitutes for the original form of an oath, to circumvent its binding force and to avoid pronouncing the holy name of God (see Ex 22, 10).

5, 14: In case of sickness a Christian should ask for the presbyters of the church, i.e., those who have authority in the church (cf Acts 15, 2.22–23; 1 Tm 5, 17; Ti 1, 5). They are to pray over the person and anoint with oil; oil was used for medicinal purposes in the ancient world (see Is 1, 6; Lk 10, 34). In Mk 6, 13, the Twelve anoint the sick with oil on their missionary journey. *In the name of the Lord:* by the power of Jesus Christ.

5, 15: The results of the prayer and anointing are physical health and forgiveness of sins. The Roman Catholic Church (Council of Trent, Session 14) declared that this anointing of the sick is a sacrament "instituted by Christ and promulgated by blessed James the apostle."

5, 20: When a Christian is instrumental in the conversion of a sinner, the result is forgiveness of sins and a reinstatement of the sinner to the life of grace.

# THE FIRST LETTER OF
# PETER

## INTRODUCTION

*This letter begins with an address by Peter to Christian communities located in five provinces of Asia Minor (1, 1), including areas evangelized by Paul (Acts 16, 6–7; 18, 23). Christians there are encouraged to remain faithful to their standards of belief and conduct in spite of threats of persecution. Numerous allusions in the letter suggest that the churches addressed were largely of Gentile composition (1, 14.18; 2, 9–10; 4, 3–4), though considerable use is made of the Old Testament (1, 24; 2, 6–7.9–10.22; 3, 10–12).*

*The contents following the address both inspire and admonish these "chosen sojourners" (1, 1) who, in seeking to live as God's people, feel an alienation from their previous religious roots and the society around them. Appeal is made to Christ's resurrection and the future hope it provides (1, 3–5) and to the experience of baptism as new birth (1, 3.23–25; 3, 21). The suffering and death of Christ serve as both source of salvation and example (1, 19; 2, 21–25; 3, 18). What Christians are in Christ, as a people who have received mercy and are to proclaim and live according to God's call (2, 9–10), is repeatedly spelled out for all sorts of situations in society (2, 11–17), work (even as slaves, 2, 18–20), the home (3, 1–7), and general conduct (3, 8–12; 4, 1–11). But over all hangs the possibility of suffering as a Christian (3, 13–17). In 4, 12–19 persecution is described as already occurring, so that some have supposed the letter was addressed both to places where such a "trial by fire" was already present and to places where it might break out.*

*The letter constantly mingles moral exhortation* (paraklēsis) *with its catechetical summaries of mercies in Christ. Encouragement to fidelity in spite of suffering is based upon a vision of the meaning of Christian existence. The emphasis on baptism and allusions to various features of the baptismal liturgy suggest that the author has incorporated into his exposition numerous homiletic, credal, hymnic, and sacramental elements of the baptismal rite that had become traditional at an early date.*

*From Irenaeus in the late second century until modern times, Christian tradition regarded Peter the apostle as author of this document. Since he was martyred at Rome during the persecution of Nero between A.D. 64 and 67, it was supposed that the letter was written from Rome shortly before his death. This is supported by its reference to "Babylon" (5, 13), a code name for Rome in the early church.*

*Some modern scholars, however, on the basis of a number of features that they consider incompatible with Petrine authenticity, regard the letter as the work of a later Christian writer. Such features include the cultivated Greek in which it is written, difficult to attribute to a Galilean fisherman, together with its use of the Greek Septuagint translation when citing the Old Testament; the similarity in both thought and expression to the Pauline literature; and the allusions to widespread persecution of Christians, which did not occur until at least the reign of Domitian (A.D. 81–96). In this view the letter would date from the end of the first century or even the beginning of the second, when there is evidence for persecution of Christians in Asia Minor (the letter of Pliny the Younger to Trajan, A.D. 111–12).*

*Other scholars believe, however, that these objections can be met by appeal to use of a secretary, Silvanus, mentioned in 5, 12. Such secretaries often gave literary expression to the author's thoughts in their own style and language. The persecutions may refer to local harassment rather than to systematic repression by the state. Hence there is nothing in the document incompatible with Petrine authorship in the 60s.*

*Still other scholars take a middle position. The many literary contacts with the Pauline literature, James, and 1 John suggest a common fund of traditional formulations rather than direct dependence upon Paul. Such liturgical and catechetical traditions must have been very ancient and in some cases of Palestinian origin.*

*Yet it is unlikely that Peter addressed a letter to the Gentile churches of Asia Minor while Paul was still alive. This suggests a period after the death of the two apostles, perhaps A.D. 70–90. The author would be a disciple of Peter in Rome, representing a Petrine group that served as a bridge between the Palestinian origins of Christianity and its flowering in the Gentile world. The problem addressed would not be official persecution but the difficulty of living the Christian life in a hostile, secular environment that espoused different values and subjected the Christian minority to ridicule and oppression.*

*The principal divisions of the First Letter of Peter are the following:*

*I. Address (1, 1–2)*
*II. The Gift and Call of God in Baptism (1, 3—2, 10)*
*III. The Christian in a Hostile World (2, 11—4, 11)*
*IV. Advice to the Persecuted (4, 12—5, 11)*
*V. Conclusion (5, 12–14)*

## I: ADDRESS

### CHAPTER 1

**Greeting** **1** [a]*Peter, an apostle of Jesus
Christ, to the chosen sojourners of the disper-
sion in Pontus, Galatia, Cappadocia, Asia, and
Bithynia, **2** [b]in the foreknowledge of God the
Father, through sanctification by the Spirit, for
obedience and sprinkling with the blood of
Jesus Christ: may grace and peace be yours in
abundance.

## II: THE GIFT AND CALL OF GOD IN BAPTISM

**Blessing** **3** [c]*Blessed be the God and Father of our Lord Jesus Christ, who in his great
mercy gave us a new birth to a living hope
through the resurrection of Jesus Christ from the
dead, **4** [d]to an inheritance that is imperishable,
undefiled, and unfading, kept in heaven for you
**5** who by the power of God are safeguarded
through faith, to a salvation that is ready to be
revealed in the final time. **6** [e]*In this you rejoice, although now for a little while you may
have to suffer through various trials, **7** [f]so that
the genuineness of your faith, more precious
than gold that is perishable even though tested
by fire, may prove to be for praise, glory, and
honor at the revelation of Jesus Christ.
**8** [g]Although you have not seen him you love
him; even though you do not see him now yet
believe in him, you rejoice with an indescribable and glorious joy, **9** as you attain the goal
of [your] faith, the salvation of your souls.
**10** *Concerning this salvation, prophets who
prophesied about the grace that was to be yours
searched and investigated it, **11** [h]investigating
the time and circumstances that the Spirit of
Christ within them indicated when it testified in
advance to the sufferings destined for Christ and
the glories to follow them. **12** It was revealed
to them that they were serving not themselves
but you with regard to the things that have now
been announced to you by those who preached
the good news to you [through] the holy Spirit
sent from heaven, things into which angels
longed to look.

a Jas 1, 1.
b Rom 8, 29.
c Ti 3, 5.
d Mt 6, 19-20.
e Jas 1, 2-3.
f 1 Cor 3, 13.
g 2 Cor 5, 6-7.
h Is 52, 13—53, 12; Dn 9, 24.

*

1, 1–2: The introductory formula names *Peter* as the writer (but see Introduction). In his comments to the presbyters (5, 1), the author calls himself a "fellow presbyter." He addresses himself to the Gentile converts of Asia Minor. Their privileged status as a *chosen* and sanctified people makes them worthy of God's *grace* and *peace.* In contrast is their actual existence as aliens and *sojourners,* scattered among pagans, far from their true country.

1, 1: *Dispersion:* literally, diaspora; see Jas 1, 1 and Introduction to that letter. *Pontus . . . Bithynia:* five provinces in Asia Minor, listed in clockwise order from the north, perhaps in the sequence in which a messenger might deliver the letter.

1, 3–5: A prayer of praise and thanksgiving to God who bestows the gift of new life and hope in baptism (*new birth,* 3) *through the resurrection of Jesus Christ from the dead.* The new birth is a sign of an *imperishable inheritance* (4), of *salvation* that is still in the future (*to be revealed in the final time,* 5).

1, 6–9: As the glory of Christ's resurrection was preceded by his sufferings and death, the new life of faith that it bestows is to be subjected to many *trials* (6) while achieving its goal: the glory of the fullness of *salvation* (9) at the coming of Christ (7).

1, 10–12: The *Spirit of Christ* (11) is here shown to have been present in the prophets, moving them to search, investigate, and prophesy about the *grace* of *salvation* that was to come (10), and in the apostles impelling them to preach the fulfillment of salvation in the message of Christ's sufferings and glory (12).

**Obedience** 13 *Therefore, gird up the
loins of your mind, live soberly, and set your
hopes completely on the grace to be brought to
you at the revelation of Jesus Christ. 14 *Like
obedient children, do not act in compliance with
the desires of your former ignorance 15 [i]but, as
he who called you is holy, be holy yourselves
in every aspect of your conduct, 16 [j]for it is
written, "Be holy because I [am] holy."

**Reverence** 17 [k]Now if you invoke as Father him who judges impartially according to
each one's works, conduct yourselves with reverence during the time of your sojourning,
18 [l]realizing that you were ransomed from your
futile conduct, handed on by your ancestors, not
with perishable things like silver or gold
19 [m]*but with the precious blood of Christ as
of a spotless unblemished lamb. 20 He was
known before the foundation of the world but
revealed in the final time for you, 21 who
through him believe in God who raised him
from the dead and gave him glory, so that your
faith and hope are in God.

**Mutual Love** 22 [n]*Since you have purified
yourselves by obedience to the truth for sincere
mutual love, love one another intensely from a
[pure] heart. 23 [o]*You have been born anew,
not from perishable but from imperishable seed,
through the living and abiding word of God,
24 [p]for:

> "All flesh is like grass,
> and all its glory like the flower of the
> field;
> the grass withers,
> and the flower wilts;

25 but the word of the Lord remains forever."

This is the word that has been proclaimed to
you.

## CHAPTER 2

**God's House and People** 1 [q]*Rid yourselves of all malice and all deceit, insincerity,
envy, and all slander; 2 like newborn infants,
long for pure spiritual milk so that through it you
may grow into salvation, 3 [r]*for you have tasted that the Lord is good. 4 [s]*Come to him, a
living stone, rejected by human beings but chosen and precious in the sight of God, 5 [t]*and,
like living stones, let yourselves be built into a
spiritual house to be a holy priesthood to offer
spiritual sacrifices acceptable to God through
Jesus Christ. 6 [u]For it says in scripture:

> "Behold, I am laying a stone in Zion,
> a cornerstone, chosen and precious,
> and whoever believes in it shall not be put
> to shame."

7 [v]Therefore, its value is for you who have
faith, but for those without faith:

> "The stone which the builders rejected
> has become the cornerstone,"

8 [w]and

> "A stone that will make people stumble,
> and a rock that will make them fall."

They stumble by disobeying the word, as is their
destiny.
9 [x]*But you are "a chosen race, a royal
priesthood, a holy nation, a people of his own,

i Mt 5, 48; 1 Jn 3, 3.
j Lv 11, 44; 19, 2.
k 2, 11.
l Is 52, 3; 1 Cor 6, 20.
m Ex 12, 5; Jn 1, 29; Heb 9, 14.
n Rom 12, 10.
o 1 Jn 3, 9.
p Is 40, 6-8.
q Jas 1, 21.
r Ps 34, 9.
s Ps 118, 22; Mt 21, 42; Acts 4, 11.
t Eph 2, 21-22.
u Is 28, 16.
v Ps 118, 22; Mt 21, 42; Lk 20, 17; Acts 4, 11.
w Is 8, 14; Rom 9, 33.
x Ex 19, 6; Is 61, 6; Rv 1, 6; 20, 6.

*

1, 13–25: These verses are concerned with the call of God's people to holiness and to mutual love by reason of their redemption through the blood of Christ (18–21).

1, 13: *Gird up the loins of your mind:* a figure reminiscent of the rite of Passover when the Israelites were in flight from their oppressors (Ex 12, 11), and also suggesting the vigilance of the Christian people in expectation of the parousia of Christ (Lk 12, 35).

1, 14–16: The *ignorance* here referred to (14) was their former lack of knowledge of God, leading inevitably to godless conduct. Holiness (15–16), on the contrary, is the result of their call to the knowledge and love of God.

1, 19: Christians have received the redemption prophesied by Isaiah (52, 3), through the blood (Jewish symbol of life) of the spotless lamb (Is 53, 7.10; Jn 1, 29; Rom 3, 24–25; cf 1 Cor 6, 20).

1, 22–25: The new birth of Christians (23) derives from Christ, the *imperishable seed* or sowing that produces a new and lasting existence in those who accept the gospel (24–25), with the consequent duty of loving *one another* (22).

1, 23: *The living and abiding word of God:* or, "the word of the living and abiding God."

2, 1–3: Growth toward salvation is seen here as two steps: first, stripping away all that is contrary to the new life in Christ; second, the nourishment *(pure spiritual milk)* that the newly baptized have received.

2, 3: *Tasted that the Lord is good:* cf Ps 34, 9.

2, 4–8: Christ is the cornerstone (cf Is 28, 16) that is the foundation of the spiritual edifice of the Christian community (5). To unbelievers, Christ is an obstacle and a stumbling block on which they are destined to fall (8); cf Rom 11, 11.

2, 5: *Let yourselves be built:* the form of the Greek word could also be indicative passive, "you are being built" (cf 9).

2, 9–10: The prerogatives of ancient Israel mentioned here are now more fully and fittingly applied to the Christian people: "a chosen race" (cf Is 43, 20–21) indicates their divine election (Eph 1, 4–6); "a royal priesthood" (cf Ex 19, 6) to serve and worship God in Christ, thus continuing the priestly functions of his life, passion, and resurrection; "a holy nation" (Ex 19, 6) reserved for God, a people he claims for his own (cf Mal 3, 17) in virtue of their baptism into his death and resurrection. This transcends all natural and national divisions and unites the people into one community to glorify the one who led them from the darkness of paganism to the light of faith in Christ. From being "no people" deprived of all mercy, they have become the very people of God, the chosen recipients of his mercy (cf Hos 1, 9; 2, 25).

so that you may announce the praises" of him who called you out of darkness into his wonderful light.

10 [y]Once you were "no people"
but now you are God's people;
you "had not received mercy"
but now you have received mercy.

## III: THE CHRISTIAN IN A HOSTILE WORLD

**Christian Examples** 11 [z]*Beloved, I urge
you as aliens and sojourners to keep away from
worldly desires that wage war against the soul.
12 Maintain good conduct among the Gentiles, so that if they speak of you as evildoers, they may observe your good works and glorify God on the day of visitation.

**Christian Citizens** 13 [a]*Be subject to every human institution for the Lord's sake, whether it be to the king as supreme
14 or to
governors as sent by him for the punishment of evildoers and the approval of those who do
good.
15 For it is the will of God that by doing good you may silence the ignorance of foolish
people.
16 [b]Be free, yet without using freedom as a pretext for evil, but as slaves of God.
17 [c]Give honor to all, love the community, fear God, honor the king.

**Christian Slaves** 18 [d]*Slaves, be subject to your masters with all reverence, not only to those who are good and equitable but also to
those who are perverse.
19 For whenever anyone bears the pain of unjust suffering because of consciousness of God, that is a grace.
20 But
what credit is there if you are patient when beaten for doing wrong? But if you are patient when you suffer for doing what is good, this is
a grace before God.
21 [e]*For to this you have
been called, because Christ also suffered for you, leaving you an example that you should follow in his footsteps.

22 [f]*"He committed no sin,
and no deceit was found in his mouth."

23 [g]When he was insulted, he returned no insult; when he suffered, he did not threaten; instead, he handed himself over to the one who
judges justly.
24 [h]He himself bore our sins in
his body upon the cross, so that, free from sin, we might live for righteousness. By his wounds
you have been healed.
25 [i]*For you had gone
astray like sheep, but you have now returned to the shepherd and guardian of your souls.

## CHAPTER 3

**Christian Spouses** 1 *Likewise, you
wives should be subordinate to your husbands so that, even if some disobey the word, they may be won over without a word by their wives'
conduct
2 [j]when they observe your reverent
and chaste behavior.
3 [k]Your adornment
should not be an external one: braiding the hair, wearing gold jewelry, or dressing in fine
clothes,
4 but rather the hidden character of the
heart, expressed in the imperishable beauty of a gentle and calm disposition, which is precious

y Hos 1, 9; 2, 25 / Hos 1, 6.
z Gal 5, 24.
a Rom 13, 1-7.
b Gal 5, 13.
c Prv 24, 21; Mt 22, 21.
d Eph 6, 5.
e Mt 16, 24.
f Is 53, 9.
g Mt 5, 39.
h Is 53, 4.12 / Is 53, 5.
i Is 53, 6.
j 1 Cor 7, 12-16; Eph 5, 22-24; Col 3, 18; 1 Tm 2, 9-15.
k 1 Tm 2, 9-10.

*

2, 11—3, 12: After explaining the doctrinal basis for the Christian community, the author makes practical applications in terms of the virtues that should prevail in all the social relationships of the members of the community: good example to Gentile neighbors (2, 11–12); respect for human authority (2, 13–17); obedience, patience, and endurance of hardship in domestic relations (2, 18–25); Christian behavior of husbands and wives (3, 1–7); mutual charity (3, 8–12).

2, 11: *Aliens and sojourners:* no longer signifying absence from one's native land (Gn 23, 4), this image denotes rather their estrangement from the world during their earthly pilgrimage (see also 1, 1.17).

2, 13–17: True Christian freedom is the result of being servants of God (16; see the note on 2, 18–23). It includes reverence for God, esteem for every individual, and committed love for fellow Christians (17). Although persecution may threaten, subjection to human government is urged (13.17) and concern for the impact of Christians' conduct on those who are not Christians (12.15).

2, 18–21: Most of the labor in the commercial cities of first-century Asia Minor was performed by a working class of slaves. The sense of freedom contained in the gospel undoubtedly caused great tension among Christian slaves: witness the special advice given concerning them here and in 1 Cor 7, 21–24; Eph 6, 5–8; Col 3, 22–25; Phlm. The point made here does not have so much to do with the institution of slavery, which the author does not challenge, but with the nonviolent reaction (20) of slaves to unjust treatment. Their patient suffering is compared to that of Jesus (21), which won righteousness for all humanity.

2, 21: *Suffered:* some ancient manuscripts and versions read "died" (cf 3, 18).

2, 22–25: After the quotation of Is 53, 9b, the passage describes Jesus' passion with phrases concerning the Suffering Servant from Is 53, 4–12, perhaps as employed in an early Christian confession of faith; cf 1, 18–21 and 3, 18–22.

2, 25: *The shepherd and guardian of your souls:* the familiar shepherd and flock figures express the care, vigilance, and love of God for his people in the Old Testament (Ps 23; Is 40, 11; Jer 23, 4–5; Ez 34, 11–16) and of Jesus for all humanity in the New Testament (Mt 18, 10–14; Lk 15, 4–7; Jn 10, 1–16; Heb 13, 20).

3, 1–6: The typical marital virtues of women of the ancient world, obedience, reverence, and chastity (1–2), are outlined here by the author, who gives them an entirely new motivation: Christian wives are to be virtuous so that they may be instrumental in the conversion of their husbands. In imitation of *holy women* in the past (5) they are to cultivate the interior life (4) instead of excessive concern with their appearance (3).

in the sight of God. **5** For this is also how the
holy women who hoped in God once used to
adorn themselves and were subordinate to their
husbands; **6** thus Sarah obeyed Abraham, calling him "lord." You are her children when you
do what is good and fear no intimidation.

**7** [l]*Likewise, you husbands should live with
your wives in understanding, showing honor to
the weaker female sex, since we are joint heirs
of the gift of life, so that your prayers may not
be hindered.

### Christian Conduct

**8** *Finally, all of you,
be of one mind, sympathetic, loving toward one
another, compassionate, humble. **9** [m]Do not
return evil for evil, or insult for insult; but, on
the contrary, a blessing, because to this you
were called, that you might inherit a blessing.
**10** [n]For:

"Whoever would love life
  and see good days
must keep the tongue from evil
  and the lips from speaking deceit,
**11** must turn from evil and do good,
  seek peace and follow after it.
**12** For the eyes of the Lord are on the righteous
  and his ears turned to their prayer,
but the face of the Lord is against
  evildoers."

### Christian Suffering

**13** *Now who is go-
ing to harm you if you are enthusiastic for what
is good? **14** But even if you should suffer because of righteousness, blessed are you. Do not
be afraid or terrified with fear of them, **15** [o]but
sanctify Christ as Lord in your hearts. Always
be ready to give an explanation to anyone who
asks you for a reason for your hope, **16** but do
it with gentleness and reverence, keeping your
conscience clear, so that, when you are ma-
ligned, those who defame your good conduct in
Christ may themselves be put to shame. **17** For
it is better to suffer for doing good, if that be the
will of God, than for doing evil.

**18** [p]*For Christ also suffered for sins once,
the righteous for the sake of the unrighteous,
that he might lead you to God. Put to death in
the flesh, he was brought to life in the spirit.
**19** *In it he also went to preach to the spirits in
prison, **20** [q]who had once been disobedient
while God patiently waited in the days of Noah
during the building of the ark, in which a few
persons, eight in all, were saved through water.
**21** [r]*This prefigured baptism, which saves you
now. It is not a removal of dirt from the body
but an appeal to God for a clear conscience,
through the resurrection of Jesus Christ,
**22** [s]who has gone into heaven and is at the right
hand of God, with angels, authorities, and powers subject to him.

## CHAPTER 4

### Christian Restraint

**1** *Therefore, since
Christ suffered in the flesh, arm yourselves also
with the same attitude (for whoever suffers in
the flesh has broken with sin), **2** so as not to
spend what remains of one's life in the flesh on
human desires, but on the will of God. **3** [t]For
the time that has passed is sufficient for doing
what the Gentiles like to do: living in debauchery, evil desires, drunkenness, orgies, carousing, and wanton idolatry. **4** They are surprised
that you do not plunge into the same swamp of
profligacy, and they vilify you; **5** [u]but they will
give an account to him who stands ready to
judge the living and the dead. **6** *For this is why

l Eph 5, 25-33; Col 3, 19.
m Mt 5, 44; Lk 6, 28; Rom 12, 14.
n Ps 34, 13-17.
o Is 8, 12.
p 1 Cor 15, 45.
q Gn 7, 7.17; 2 Pt 2, 5.
r Eph 5, 26; Heb 10, 22.
s Eph 1, 20-21.
t Eph 2, 2-3; 4, 17-19; Col 3, 7; Ti 3, 3.
u Acts 10, 42; 2 Tm 4, 1.

*

3, 7: Husbands who do not respect their wives will have as little success in prayer as those who, according to Paul, have no love: their prayers will be "a resounding gong or a clashing cymbal" (1 Cor 13, 1). Consideration for others is shown as a prerequisite for effective prayer also in Mt 5, 23–24; 1 Cor 11, 20–22; Jas 4, 3. After all, whatever the social position of women in the world and in the family, they are equal recipients of the gift of God's salvation. Paul is very clear on this point, too (see 1 Cor 11, 11–12; Gal 3, 28).

3, 8–12: For the proper ordering of Christian life in its various aspects as described in 2, 11—3, 9, there is promised the blessing expressed in Ps 34, 13–17. In the Old Testament this refers to longevity and prosperity; here, it also refers to eternal life.

3, 13–22: This exposition, centering on v 17, runs as follows: by his suffering and death Christ the righteous one saved the unrighteous (18); by his resurrection he received new life in the spirit, which he communicates to believers through the baptismal bath that cleanses their consciences from sin. As Noah's family was saved *through water,* so Christians are saved through the waters of baptism (19–22). Hence they need not share the fear of sinners; they should rather rejoice in suffering because of their hope in Christ. Thus their innocence disappoints their accusers (13–16; cf Mt 10, 28; Rom 8, 35–39).

3, 18: *Suffered:* very many ancient manuscripts and versions read "died." *Put to death in the flesh:* affirms that Jesus truly died as a human being. *Brought to life in the spirit:* that is, in the new and transformed existence freed from the limitations and weaknesses of natural human life (cf 1 Cor 15, 45).

3, 19: *The spirits in prison:* it is not clear just who these spirits are. They may be the spirits of the sinners who died in the flood, or angelic powers, hostile to God, who have been overcome by Christ (cf 22; Gn 6, 4; Enoch 6–36, especially 21, 6; 2 Enoch 7, 1–5).

3, 21: *Appeal to God:* this could also be translated "pledge," that is, a promise on the part of Christians to live with a good conscience before God, or a pledge from God of forgiveness and therefore a good conscience for us.

4, 1–6: Willingness to suffer with Christ equips the Christian with the power to conquer sin (1). Christ is here portrayed as the judge to whom those guilty of pagan vices must render an account (5; cf Jn 5, 22–27; Acts 10, 42; 2 Tm 4, 1).

4, 6: *The dead:* these may be the sinners of the flood generation who are possibly referred to in 3, 19. But many scholars think that there is no connection between these two verses, and that *the dead* here are Christians who have died

the gospel was preached even to the dead that,
though condemned in the flesh in human estimation, they might live in the spirit in the estimation of God.

**Christian Charity** 7 *The end of all things
is at hand. Therefore, be serious and sober for
prayers. 8 [v]*Above all, let your love for one
another be intense, because love covers a multitude of sins. 9 [w]Be hospitable to one another
without complaining. 10 [x]As each one has received a gift, use it to serve one another as good
stewards of God's varied grace. 11 [y]*Whoever
preaches, let it be with the words of God; whoever serves, let it be with the strength that God
supplies, so that in all things God may be glorified through Jesus Christ, to whom belong glory
and dominion forever and ever. Amen.

## *IV: ADVICE TO THE PERSECUTED*

**Trial of Persecution** 12 [z]*Beloved, do not
be surprised that a trial by fire is occurring
among you, as if something strange were happening to you. 13 [a]But rejoice to the extent that
you share in the sufferings of Christ, so that
when his glory is revealed you may also rejoice
exultantly. 14 [b]If you are insulted for the name
of Christ, blessed are you, for the Spirit of glory
and of God rests upon you. 15 But let no one
among you be made to suffer as a murderer, a
thief, an evildoer, or as an intriguer. 16 But
whoever is made to suffer as a Christian should
not be ashamed but glorify God because of the
name. 17 [c]For it is time for the judgment to
begin with the household of God; if it begins
with us, how will it end for those who fail to
obey the gospel of God?

18 [d]"And if the righteous one is barely saved,
where will the godless and the sinner
appear?"

19 As a result, those who suffer in accord with
God's will hand their souls over to a faithful
creator as they do good.

## CHAPTER 5

**Advice to Presbyters** 1 *So I exhort the
presbyters among you, as a fellow presbyter and
witness to the sufferings of Christ and one who
has a share in the glory to be revealed. 2 [e]Tend
the flock of God in your midst, [overseeing] not
by constraint but willingly, as God would have
it, not for shameful profit but eagerly. 3 Do not
lord it over those assigned to you, but be examples to the flock. 4 [f]*And when the chief Shepherd is revealed, you will receive the unfading
crown of glory.

**Advice to the Community** 5 [g]*Likewise,
you younger members, be subject to the presbyters. And all of you, clothe yourselves with
humility in your dealings with one another, for:

"God opposes the proud
but bestows favor on the humble."

6 [h]So humble yourselves under the mighty
hand of God, that he may exalt you in due time.
7 [i]Cast all your worries upon him because he
cares for you.

8 [j]Be sober and vigilant. Your opponent the
devil is prowling around like a roaring lion looking for [someone] to devour. 9 Resist him,
steadfast in faith, knowing that your fellow believers throughout the world undergo the same
sufferings. 10 [k]The God of all grace who called
you to his eternal glory through Christ [Jesus]
will himself restore, confirm, strengthen, and

v Prv 10, 12; Jas 5, 20.
w Heb 13, 2.
x Rom 12, 6-8; 1 Cor 12, 4-11.
y 1 Cor 10, 31.
z 1, 6-7; 3, 14.17.
a Rom 5, 3-5; 8, 17; 2 Tm 2, 12.
b Acts 5, 41 / Is 11, 2.
c Lk 23, 31; 2 Thes 1, 8.
d Prv 11, 31 LXX.
e Acts 20, 28; Ti 1, 7.
f Wis 5, 15-16; 1 Cor 9, 25; 2 Tm 4, 8; Jas 1, 12.
g Prv 3, 34.
h Jb 22, 29; Jas 4, 10.
i Ps 55, 23; Mt 6, 25-33; Lk 12, 22-31; Phil 4, 6.
j 1 Thes 5, 6.
k Rom 8, 18; 2 Cor 4, 17.

*

since hearing the preaching of the gospel.

4, 7–11: The inner life of the eschatological community is outlined as *the end* (the parousia of Christ) and the judgment draws near in terms of seriousness, sobriety, prayer, and love expressed through hospitality and the use of one's gifts for the glory of God and of Christ.

4, 8: *Love covers a multitude of sins:* a maxim based on Prv 10, 12; see also Ps 32, 1; Jas 5, 20.

4, 11: Some scholars feel that this doxology concludes the part of the homily addressed specifically to the newly baptized, begun in 1, 3; others that it concludes a baptismal liturgy. Such doxologies do occur within a New Testament letter, e.g., Rom 9, 5. Some propose that v 11 was an alternate ending, with 4, 12—5, 14 being read in places where persecution was more pressing. But such doxologies usually do not occur at the end of letters (the only examples are 2 Pt 3, 18, Jude 25, and Rom 16, 27, the last probably a liturgical insertion).

4, 12–19: The suffering to which the author has already frequently referred is presented in more severe terms. This has led some scholars to see these verses as referring to an actual persecution. Others see the heightening of the language as only a rhetorical device used at the end of the letter to emphasize the suffering motif.

5, 1–4: In imitation of Christ, the chief shepherd, those entrusted with a pastoral office are to tend the flock by their care and example.

5, 1: *Presbyters:* the officially appointed leaders and teachers of the Christian community (cf 1 Tm 5, 17–18; Ti 1, 5–8; Jas 5, 14).

5, 4: See the note on 2, 25.

5, 5–11: The community is to be subject to the presbyters and to show humility toward one another and trust in God's love and care (5–7). With sobriety, alertness, and steadfast faith they must resist the evil one; their sufferings are shared with Christians everywhere (8–9). They will be strengthened and called to eternal glory (10–11).

5, 5: *Younger members:* this may be a designation for office-holders of lesser rank.

establish you after you have suffered a little.
**11** To him be dominion forever. Amen.

## V: CONCLUSION

**12** *I write you this briefly through Silvanus,
whom I consider a faithful brother, exhorting
you and testifying that this is the true grace of
God. Remain firm in it. **13** *The chosen one at
Babylon sends you greeting, as does Mark, my
son. **14** [l]Greet one another with a loving kiss.
Peace to all of you who are in Christ.

---

l Rom 16, 16; 1 Cor 16, 20; 2 Cor 13, 12.

---

5, 12: *Silvanus:* the companion of Paul (see 2 Cor 1, 19; 1 Thes 1, 1; 2 Thes 1, 1). Jews and Jewish Christians, like Paul, often had a Hebrew name (Saoul, Silas) and a Greek or Latin name (Paul, Silvanus). On Silvanus's possible role as amanuensis, see Introduction.

5, 13: *The chosen one:* feminine, referring to the Christian community *(ekklēsia)* at *Babylon,* the code name for Rome in Rv 14, 8; 17, 5; 18, 2. *Mark, my son:* traditionally a prominent disciple of Peter and co-worker at the church in Rome, perhaps the John Mark referred to in Acts 12, 12.25; 13, 5.13; and in 15, 37–39, a companion of Barnabas. Perhaps this is the same Mark mentioned as Barnabas's cousin in Col 4, 10, a co-worker with Paul in Phlm 24 (see also 2 Tm 4, 11).

# THE SECOND LETTER OF

# PETER

## INTRODUCTION

*This letter can be appreciated both for its positive teachings and for its earnest warnings. It seeks to strengthen readers in faith (1, 1), hope for the future (3, 1–10), knowledge (1, 2.6.8), love (1, 7), and other virtues (1, 5–6). This aim is carried out especially by warning against false teachers, the condemnation of whom occupies the long central section of the letter (2, 1–22). A particular crisis is the claim by "scoffers" that there will be no second coming of Jesus, a doctrine that the author vigorously affirms (3, 1–10). The concept of God's "promises" is particularly precious in the theology of 2 Peter (1, 4; 3, 4.9.13). Closing comments at 3, 17–18 well sum up the twin concerns: that you not "be led into" error and "fall" but instead "grow in grace" and "knowledge" of Jesus Christ.*

*Second Peter is clearly structured in its presentation of these points. It reminds its readers of the divine authenticity of Christ's teaching (1, 3–4), continues with reflections on Christian conduct (1, 5–15), then returns to the exalted dignity of Jesus by incorporating into the text the apostolic witness to his transfiguration (1, 16–18). It takes up the question of the interpretation of scripture by pointing out that it is possible to misunderstand the sacred writings (1, 19–21) and that divine punishment will overtake false teachers (2, 1–22). It proclaims that the parousia is the teaching of the Lord and of the apostles and is therefore an eventual certainty (3, 1–13). At the same time, it warns that the meaning of Paul's writings on this question should not be distorted (3, 14–18).*

*In both content and style this letter is very different from 1 Peter, which immediately precedes it in the canon. The opening verse attributes it to "Symeon Peter, a slave and apostle of Jesus Christ." Moreover, the author in 3, 1 calls his work a "second letter," referring probably to 1 Peter as his first, and in 1, 18 counts himself among those present at the transfiguration of Jesus.*

*Nevertheless, acceptance of 2 Peter into the New Testament canon met with great resistance in the early church. The oldest certain reference to it comes from Origen in the early third century. While he himself accepted both Petrine letters as canonical, he testifies that others rejected 2 Peter. As late as the fifth century some local churches still excluded it from the canon, but eventually it was universally adopted. The principal reason for the long delay was the persistent doubt that the letter stemmed from the apostle Peter.*

*Among modern scholars there is wide agreement that 2 Peter is a pseudonymous work, i.e., one written by a later author who attributed it to Peter according to a literary convention popular at the time. It gives the impression of being more remote in time from the apostolic period than 1 Peter; indeed, many think it is the latest work in the New Testament and assign it to the first or even the second quarter of the second century.*

*The principal reasons for this view are the following. The author refers to the apostles and "our ancestors" as belonging to a previous generation, now dead (3, 2–4). A collection of Paul's letters exists and appears to be well known, but disputes have arisen about the interpretation of them (3, 14–16). The passage about false teachers (2, 1–18) contains a number of literary contacts with Jude 4–16, and it is generally agreed that 2 Peter depends upon Jude, not vice versa. Finally, the principal problem exercising the author is the false teaching of "scoffers" who have concluded from the delay of the parousia that the Lord is not going to return. This could scarcely have been an issue during the lifetime of Simon Peter.*

*The Christians to whom the letter is addressed are not identified, though it may be the intent of 3, 1 to identify them with the churches of Asia Minor to which*

*1 Peter was sent. Except for the epistolary greeting in 1, 1–2, 2 Peter does not have the features of a genuine letter at all, but is rather a general exhortation cast in the form of a letter. The author must have been a Jewish Christian of the dispersion for, while his Jewish heritage is evident in various features of his thought and style, he writes in the rather stilted literary Greek of the Hellenistic period. He appeals to tradition against the twin threat of doctrinal error and moral laxity, which appear to reflect an early stage of what later developed into full-blown gnosticism. Thus he forms a link between the apostolic period and the church of subsequent ages.*

*The principal divisions of the Second Letter of Peter are the following:*

*I. Address (1, 1–2)*
*II. Exhortation to Christian Virtue (1, 3–21)*
*III. Condemnation of the False Teachers (2, 1–22)*
*IV. The Delay of the Second Coming (3, 1–16)*
*V. Final Exhortation and Doxology (3, 17–18)*

# I: ADDRESS

## CHAPTER 1

**Greeting** 1 *Symeon Peter, a slave and
apostle of Jesus Christ, to those who have received a faith of equal value to ours through the
righteousness of our God and savior Jesus
Christ: 2 *may grace and peace be yours in
abundance through knowledge of God and of
Jesus our Lord.

# II: EXHORTATION TO CHRISTIAN VIRTUE

**The Power of God's Promise** 3 [a]*His
divine power has bestowed on us everything
that makes for life and devotion, through the
knowledge of him who called us by his own
glory and power. 4 [b]Through these, he has bestowed on us the precious and very great promises, so that through them you may come to
share in the divine nature, after escaping from
the corruption that is in the world because of evil
desire. 5 [c]*For this very reason, make every
effort to supplement your faith with virtue, virtue with knowledge, 6 knowledge with self-
control, self-control with endurance, endurance
with devotion, 7 devotion with mutual affection, mutual affection with love. 8 If these are
yours and increase in abundance, they will keep
you from being idle or unfruitful in the knowledge of our Lord Jesus Christ. 9 [d]Anyone who
lacks them is blind and shortsighted, forgetful
of the cleansing of his past sins. 10 *Therefore,
brothers, be all the more eager to make your call
and election firm, for, in doing so, you will
never stumble. 11 For, in this way, entry into
the eternal kingdom of our Lord and savior
Jesus Christ will be richly provided for you.

**Apostolic Witness** 12 *Therefore, I will
always remind you of these things, even though
you already know them and are established in
the truth you have. 13 *I think it right, as long
as I am in this "tent," to stir you up by a
reminder, 14 [e]since I know that I will soon
have to put it aside, as indeed our Lord Jesus
Christ has shown me. 15 I shall also make ev-

a 2 Cor 4, 6; 1 Pt 2, 9.
b 2 Cor 7, 1; 1 Jn 2, 15.
c Gal 5, 22-23.
d 1 Jn 2, 9.11.
e Is 38, 12; Jn 21, 18-19.

*

1, 1: *Symeon Peter:* on the authorship of 2 Peter, see Introduction; on the spelling here of the Hebrew name *Šim'ôn,* cf Acts 15, 14. The greeting is especially similar to those in 1 Peter and Jude. The words translated *our God and savior Jesus Christ* could also be rendered "our God and the savior Jesus Christ"; cf 11; 2, 20; 3, 2.18.

1, 2: *Knowledge:* a key term in the letter (3.8; 2, 20; 3, 18), perhaps used as a Christian emphasis against gnostic claims.

1, 3–4: Christian life in its fullness is a gift of divine power effecting a knowledge of Christ and the bestowal of divine promises (3, 4.9). *To share in the divine nature,* escaping from a corrupt world, is a thought found elsewhere in the Bible but expressed only here in such Hellenistic terms, since it is said to be accomplished through knowledge (3); cf 2; 2, 20; but see also Jn 15, 4; 17, 22–23; Rom 8, 14–17; Heb 3, 14; 1 Jn 1, 3; 3, 2.

1, 3: *By his own glory and power:* the most ancient papyrus and the best codex read "through glory and power."

1, 5–9: Note the climactic gradation of qualities (5–7), beginning with faith and leading to the fullness of Christian life, which is love; cf Rom 5, 3–4; Gal 5, 6.22 for a similar series of "virtues," though the program and sense here are different than in Paul. The fruit of these is knowledge of Christ (8) referred to in v 3; their absence is spiritual blindness (9).

1, 10–11: Perseverance in the Christian vocation is the best preventative against losing it and the safest provision for attaining its goal, the kingdom. *Kingdom of . . . Christ,* instead of "God," is unusual; cf Col 1, 13 and Mt 13, 41, as well as the *righteousness of . . . Christ* (1).

1, 12–19: The purpose in writing is to call to mind the apostle's witness to the truth, even as he faces the end of his life (12–15), his eyewitness testimony to Christ (16–18), and the true prophetic message (19) through the Spirit in scripture (20–21), in contrast to what false teachers are setting forth (ch 2).

1, 13: *Tent:* a biblical image for transitory human life (Is 38, 12), here combined with a verb that suggests not folding or packing up a tent but its being discarded in death (cf 2 Cor 5, 1–4).

ery effort to enable you always to remember
these things after my departure.
**16** [f]*We did not follow cleverly devised
myths when we made known to you the power
and coming of our Lord Jesus Christ, but we had
been eyewitnesses of his majesty. **17** [g]*For he
received honor and glory from God the Father
when that unique declaration came to him from
the majestic glory, "This is my Son, my beloved, with whom I am well pleased." **18** *We
ourselves heard this voice come from heaven
while we were with him on the holy mountain.
**19** [h]Moreover, we possess the prophetic message that is altogether reliable. You will do well
to be attentive to it, as to a lamp shining in a dark
place, until day dawns and the morning star
rises in your hearts. **20** *Know this first of all,
that there is no prophecy of scripture that is a
matter of personal interpretation, **21** for no
prophecy ever came through human will; but
rather human beings moved by the holy Spirit
spoke under the influence of God.

## *III: CONDEMNATION OF THE FALSE TEACHERS*

### CHAPTER 2

**False Teachers** **1** [i]*There were also false
prophets among the people, just as there will be
false teachers among you, who will introduce
destructive heresies and even deny the Master
who ransomed them, bringing swift destruction
on themselves. **2** [j]Many will follow their licentious ways, and because of them the way of truth
will be reviled. **3** [k]In their greed they will exploit you with fabrications, but from of old their
condemnation has not been idle and their destruction does not sleep.

**Lessons from the Past** **4** [l]*For if God did
not spare the angels when they sinned, but condemned them to the chains of Tartarus and
handed them over to be kept for judgment;
**5** [m]*and if he did not spare the ancient world,
even though he preserved Noah, a herald of
righteousness, together with seven others, when
he brought a flood upon the godless world;
**6** [n]and if he condemned the cities of Sodom and
Gommorah [to destruction], reducing them to
ashes, making them an example for the godless
[people] of what is coming; **7** and if he rescued
Lot, a righteous man oppressed by the licentious
conduct of unprincipled people **8** (for day after
day that righteous man living among them was
tormented in his righteous soul at the lawless
deeds that he saw and heard), **9** [o]then the Lord
knows how to rescue the devout from trial and
to keep the unrighteous under punishment for
the day of judgment, **10** [p]*and especially those
who follow the flesh with its depraved desire
and show contempt for lordship.

f Lk 9, 28-36; Jn 1, 14.
g Ps 2, 7; Mt 17, 4-6.
h Lk 1, 78-79; Rv 2, 28.
i Mt 24, 11.24; 1 Tm 4, 1; Jude 4.
j Is 52, 5.
k Rom 16, 18.
l Jude 6.
m Gn 8, 15-19; Heb 11, 7.
n Gn 19, 24-25; Jude 7.
o 1 Cor 10, 13; Rv 3, 10.
p Jude 8.

*

1, 16: *Coming:* in Greek *parousia,* used at 3, 4.12 of the second coming of Christ. The word was used in the extrabiblical writings for the visitation of someone in authority; in Greek cult and Hellenistic Judaism it was used for the manifestation of the divine presence. What the apostles *made known* has been interpreted to refer to Jesus' transfiguration (17) or to his entire first coming or to his future coming in power (ch 3).

1, 17: The author assures the readers of the reliability of the apostolic message (including Jesus' power, glory, and coming; cf the note on 1, 16) by appeal to the transfiguration of Jesus in glory (cf Mt 17, 1–8 and parallels) and by appeal to the prophetic message (19; perhaps Nm 24, 17). Here, as elsewhere, the New Testament insists on continued reminders as necessary to preserve the historical facts about Jesus and the truths of the faith; cf 3, 1–2; 1 Cor 11, 2; 15, 1–3. *My Son, my beloved:* or, "my beloved Son."

1, 18: *We:* at Jesus' transfiguration, referring to Peter, James, and John (Mt 17, 1).

1, 20–21: Often cited, along with 2 Tm 3, 16, on the "inspiration" of scripture or against private interpretation, these verses in context are directed against the false teachers of ch 2 and clever tales (16). The prophetic word in scripture comes admittedly through *human beings* (21), but *moved by the holy Spirit,* not from their own interpretation, and is a matter of what the author and Spirit intended, not the *personal interpretation* of false teachers. Instead of *under the influence of God,* some manuscripts read "holy ones of God."

2, 1–3: The pattern of *false prophets* among the Old Testament people of God will recur through *false teachers* in the church. Such destructive opinions of heretical sects bring loss of faith in Christ, contempt for the way of salvation (cf 21), and immorality.

2, 4–6: The false teachers will be punished just as surely and as severely as were the fallen *angels* (4; cf Jude 6; Gn 6, 1–4), the sinners of Noah's day (5; Gn 7, 21–23), and the inhabitants of the cities of the Plain (6; Jude 7; Gn 19, 25). Whereas there are three examples in Jude 5–7 (Exodus and wilderness; rebellious angels; Sodom and Gomorrah), 2 Peter omitted the first of these, has inserted a new illustration about Noah (5) between Jude's second and third examples, and listed the resulting three examples in their Old Testament order (Gn 6; 7; 19).

2, 4: *Chains of Tartarus:* cf Jude 6; other manuscripts in 2 Peter read "pits of Tartarus." *Tartarus:* a term borrowed from Greek mythology to indicate the infernal regions.

2, 5–10a: Although God did not spare the sinful, he kept and saved the righteous, such as *Noah* (5) and *Lot* (7), and he *knows how to rescue the devout* (9), who are contrasted with the false teachers of the author's day. On Noah, cf Gn 5, 32—9, 29, especially 7, 1. On Lot, cf Gn 13 and 19.

2, 10b–22: Some take 10b and 11 with the preceding paragraph. Others begin the new paragraph with 10a, supplying from v 9 *The Lord knows how . . . to keep . . . under punishment,* with reference to God and probably specifically Christ (1). The conduct of the false teachers is described and condemned in language similar to that of Jude 8–16. This arrogance knows no bounds; animal-like, they are due to be caught and destroyed. They seduce even those who have knowledge of Christ (20).

2, 10b: *Glorious beings:* literally, "glories"; cf Jude 8. While some think that illustrious personages are meant or even political officials behind whom (fallen) angels stand, it is more likely that the reference is to glorious angelic beings (cf Jude 9).

**False Teachers Denounced** Bold and arrogant, they are not afraid to revile glorious
beings, **11** [q]*whereas angels, despite their superior strength and power, do not bring a reviling judgment against them from the Lord.
**12** [r]But these people, like irrational animals
born by nature for capture and destruction, revile things that they do not understand, and in
their destruction they will also be destroyed,
**13** [s]*suffering wrong as payment for wrongdoing. Thinking daytime revelry a delight, they
are stains and defilements as they revel in their
deceits while carousing with you. **14** Their eyes
are full of adultery and insatiable for sin. They
seduce unstable people, and their hearts are
trained in greed. Accursed children!
**15** [t]*Abandoning the straight road, they have
gone astray, following the road of Balaam, the
son of Bosor, who loved payment for wrongdoing, **16** [u]but he received a rebuke for his own
crime: a mute beast spoke with a human voice
and restrained the prophet's madness.
**17** [v]These people are waterless springs and
mists driven by a gale; for them the gloom of
darkness has been reserved. **18** [w]*For, talking
empty bombast, they seduce with licentious desires of the flesh those who have barely escaped
from people who live in error. **19** [x]They promise them freedom, though they themselves are
slaves of corruption, for a person is a slave of
whatever overcomes him. **20** [y]For if they, having escaped the defilements of the world
through the knowledge of [our] Lord and savior
Jesus Christ, again become entangled and overcome by them, their last condition is worse than
their first. **21** [z]*For it would have been better
for them not to have known the way of righteousness than after knowing it to turn back from
the holy commandment handed down to them.
**22** [a]*What is expressed in the true proverb has
happened to them, "The dog returns to its own
vomit," and "A bathed sow returns to wallow-
ing in the mire."

## *IV: THE DELAY OF THE SECOND COMING*

### CHAPTER 3

**Denial of the Parousia** **1** *This is now,
beloved, the second letter I am writing to you;
through them by way of reminder I am trying to
stir up your sincere disposition, **2** [b]to recall the
words previously spoken by the holy prophets
and the commandment of the Lord and savior
through your apostles. **3** [c]*Know this first of
all, that in the last days scoffers will come [to]
scoff, living according to their own desires
**4** [d]*and saying, "Where is the promise of his
coming? From the time when our ancestors fell
asleep, everything has remained as it was from
the beginning of creation." **5** [e]*They deliberately ignore the fact that the heavens existed of
old and earth was formed out of water and
through water by the word of God; **6** [f]*through
these the world that then existed was destroyed,
deluged with water. **7** [g]The present heavens
and earth have been reserved by the same word
for fire, kept for the day of judgment and of
destruction of the godless.
**8** [h]*But do not ignore this one fact, beloved,

q Jude 9.
r Ps 49, 13-15; Jude 10.
s Jude 12.
t Nm 31, 16; Jude 11.
u Nm 22, 28-33.
v Jude 12-13.
w Jude 16.
x Jn 8, 34; Rom 6, 16-17.
y Mt 12, 45.
z Ez 3, 20.
a Prv 26, 11.
b Jude 17.
c 1 Tm 4, 1; 2 Tm 3, 1; Jude 18.
d Is 5, 19.
e Gn 1, 2.6.8; Ps 24, 2.
f Gn 7, 21.
g Is 51, 6; Mt 3, 12.
h Ps 90, 4.

*

2, 11: *From the Lord:* some manuscripts read "before the Lord"; cf Jude 9.

2, 13: *Suffering wrong:* some manuscripts read "receiving a reward." *In their deceits:* some manuscripts read "in their love feasts" (Jude 12).

2, 15: *Balaam, the son of Bosor:* in Nm 22, 5, Balaam is said to be the son of Beor, and it is this name that turns up in a few ancient Greek manuscripts by way of "correction" of the text. Balaam is not portrayed in such a bad light in Nm 22. His evil reputation and his *madness* (16), and possibly his surname Bosor, may have come from a Jewish tradition about him in the first/second century, of which we no longer have any knowledge.

2, 18: *Barely escaped:* some manuscripts read "really escaped."

2, 21: *Commandment handed down:* cf 3, 2 and Jude 3.

2, 22: The second proverb is of unknown origin, while the first appears in Prv 26, 11.

3, 1–4: The false teachers not only flout Christian morality (cf Jude 8–19); they also deny the second coming of Christ and the judgment (4; cf 7). They seek to justify their licentiousness by arguing that the promised return of Christ has not been realized and the world is the same, no better than it was before (3–4). The author wishes to strengthen the faithful against such errors by reminding them in this *second letter* of the instruction in 1 Pt and of the teaching of the *prophets* and of Christ, conveyed through the *apostles* (1–2; cf Jude 17); cf 1 Pt 1, 10–12.16–21, especially 16–21; Eph 2, 20.

3, 3: *Scoffers:* cf Jude 18, where, however, only the passions of the scoffers are mentioned, not a denial on their part of Jesus' parousia.

3, 4–7: The false teachers tried to justify their immorality by pointing out that the promised *coming* (*parousia*) of the Lord has not yet occurred, even though early Christians expected it in their day. They thus insinuate that God is not guiding the world's history anymore, since nothing has changed and the first generation of Christians, *our ancestors* (4) has all died by this time. The author replies that, just as God destroyed the earth by water in the flood (5–6, cf 2, 5), so he will destroy it along with the false teachers on judgment day (7). *The word of God,* which called the world into being (Gn 1; Ps 33, 6) and *destroyed* it by the waters of a flood, will destroy it again by fire on *the day of judgment* (5–7).

3, 5: *Formed out of water and through water:* Gn 1, 2.6–8 is reflected as well as Greek views that water was the basic element from which all is derived.

3, 6: *Destroyed, deluged with water:* cf 2, 5; Gn 7, 11—8, 2.

3, 8–10: The scoffers' objection (4) is refuted also by showing that *delay* of the Lord's second coming is not a failure to

that with the Lord one day is like a thousand
years and a thousand years like one day. **9** [i]The
Lord does not delay his promise, as some regard
"delay," but he is patient with you, not wishing
that any should perish but that all should come
to repentance. **10** [j]*But the day of the Lord will
come like a thief, and then the heavens will pass
away with a mighty roar and the elements will
be dissolved by fire, and the earth and everything done on it will be found out.

## Exhortation to Preparedness

**11** [k]*Since everything is to be dissolved in this
way, what sort of persons ought [you] to be,
conducting yourselves in holiness and devotion,
**12** [l]*waiting for and hastening the coming of
the day of God, because of which the heavens
will be dissolved in flames and the elements
melted by fire. **13** [m]*But according to his
promise we await new heavens and a new earth
in which righteousness dwells.

**14** Therefore, beloved, since you await these
things, be eager to be found without spot or
blemish before him, at peace. **15** [n]And consider the patience of our Lord as salvation, as our
beloved brother Paul, according to the wisdom
given to him, also wrote to you, **16** *speaking
of these things as he does in all his letters. In
them there are some things hard to understand
that the ignorant and unstable distort to their
own destruction, just as they do the other scriptures.

## *V: FINAL EXHORTATION AND DOXOLOGY*

**17** [o]*Therefore, beloved, since you are forewarned, be on your guard not to be led into the
error of the unprincipled and to fall from your
own stability. **18** [p]But grow in grace and in the
knowledge of our Lord and savior Jesus Christ.
To him be glory now and to the day of eternity.
[Amen.]

i Ez 18, 23; 1 Tm 2, 4.
j Is 66, 15-16; Mt 24, 29.
k Acts 3, 19-21.
l Is 34, 4; Heb 10, 27.
m Is 65, 17; 66, 22; Rom 8, 21; Rv 21, 1.27.
n Rom 8, 19; Jude 24.
o Mk 13, 5; Heb 2, 1.
p Rom 16, 27.

* fulfill his word but rather a sign of his patience: God is giving time for repentance before the final judgment (cf Wis 11, 23–26; Ez 18, 23; 33, 11).

3, 8: Cf Ps 90, 4.

3, 10: *Like a thief:* Mt 24, 43; 1 Thes 5, 2; Rv 3, 3. *Will be found out:* cf 1 Cor 3, 13–15. Some few versions read, as the sense may demand, "will not be found out"; many manuscripts read "will be burned up"; there are further variants in other manuscripts, versions, and Fathers. Total destruction is assumed (11).

3, 11–16: The second coming of Christ and the judgment of the world are the doctrinal bases for the moral exhortation to readiness through vigilance and a virtuous life; cf Mt 24, 42.50–51; Lk 12, 40; 1 Thes 5, 1–11; Jude 20–21.

3, 12: *Flames . . . fire:* although this is the only New Testament passage about a final conflagration, the idea was common in apocalyptic and Greco-Roman thought. *Hastening:* eschatology is here used to motivate ethics (11), as elsewhere in the New Testament. Jewish sources and Acts 3, 19–20 assume that proper ethical conduct can help bring the promised day of the Lord; cf 9. Some render the phrase, however, "desiring it earnestly."

3, 13: *New heavens and a new earth:* cf Is 65, 17; 66, 22. The divine promises will be fulfilled after the day of judgment will have passed. The universe will be transformed by the reign of God's *righteousness* or justice; cf Is 65, 17–18; Acts 3, 21; Rom 8, 18–25; Rv 21, 1.

3, 16: *These things:* the teachings of this letter find parallels in Paul, e.g., God's will to save (Rom 2, 4; 9, 22–23; 1 Cor 1, 7–8), the coming of Christ (1 Thes 4, 16–17; 1 Cor 15, 23–52), and preparedness for the judgment (Col 1, 22–23; Eph 1, 4–14; 4, 30; 5, 5–14). *Other scriptures:* used to guide the faith and life of the Christian community. The letters of Paul are thus here placed on the same level as books of the Old Testament. Possibly other New Testament writings could also be included.

3, 17–18: To avoid the dangers *of error* and loss of *stability,* Christians are *forewarned* to be *on guard* and to *grow in grace and knowledge* (1, 2) of Christ. The doxology (18) recalls 1 Pt 4, 11. Some manuscripts add *Amen.*

# THE FIRST LETTER OF
# JOHN

## INTRODUCTION

*Early Christian tradition identified this work as a letter of John the apostle. Because of its resemblance to the fourth gospel in style, vocabulary, and ideas, it is generally agreed that both works are the product of the same school of Johannine Christianity. The terminology and the presence or absence of certain theological ideas in 1 John suggest that it was written after the gospel; it may have been composed as a short treatise on ideas that were developed more fully in the fourth gospel. To others, the evidence suggests that 1 John was written after the fourth gospel as part of a debate on the proper interpretation of that gospel. Whatever its relation to the gospel, 1 John may be dated toward the end of the first century. Unlike 2 and 3 John, it lacks in form the salutation and epistolary conclusion of a letter. These features, its prologue, and its emphasis on doctrinal teaching make it more akin to a theological treatise than to most other New Testament letters.*

*The purpose of the letter is to combat certain false ideas, especially about Jesus, and to deepen the spiritual and social awareness of the Christian community (3, 17). Some former members (2, 19) of the community refused to acknowledge Jesus as the Christ (2, 22) and denied that he was a true man (4, 2). The specific heresy described in this letter cannot be identified exactly, but it is a form of docetism or gnosticism; the former doctrine denied the humanity of Christ to insure that his divinity was untainted, and the latter viewed the appearance of Christ as a mere stepping-stone to higher knowledge of God. These theological errors are rejected by an appeal to the reality and continuity of the apostolic witness to Jesus. The author affirms that authentic Christian love, ethics, and faith take place only within the historical revelation and sacrifice of Jesus Christ. The fullness of Christian life as fellowship with the Father must be based on true belief and result in charitable living; knowledge of God and love for one another are inseparable, and error in one area inevitably affects the other. Although the author recognizes that Christian doctrine presents intangible mysteries of faith about Christ, he insists that the concrete Christian life brings to light the deeper realities of the gospel.*

*The structure and language of the letter are straightforward yet repetitious. The author sets forth the striking contrasts between light and darkness, Christians and the world, and truth and error to illustrate the threats and responsibilities of Christian life. The result is not one of theological argument but one of intense religious conviction expressed in simple truths. The letter is of particular value for its declaration of the humanity and divinity of Christ as an apostolic teaching and for its development of the intrinsic connection between Christian moral conduct and Christian doctrine.*

*The principal divisions of the First Letter of John are the following:*

*I. Prologue (1, 1–4)*
*II. God as Light (1, 5—3, 10)*
*III. Love for One Another (3, 11—5, 12)*
*IV. Epilogue (5, 13–21)*

## *I: PROLOGUE*

### CHAPTER 1

### The Word of Life

1 [a]*What was from the beginning,
what we have heard,
what we have seen with our eyes,
what we looked upon
and touched with our hands
concerns the Word of life—
2 [b]for the life was made visible;
we have seen it and testify to it
and proclaim to you the eternal life
that was with the Father and was made
visible to us—
3 [c]what we have seen and heard
we proclaim now to you,
so that you too may have fellowship with
us;
for our fellowship is with the Father
and with his Son, Jesus Christ.
4 [d]We are writing this so that our joy may be
complete.

## *II: GOD AS LIGHT*

**God is Light** 5 *Now this is the message
that we have heard from him and proclaim to
you: God is light, and in him there is no darkness at all. 6 [e]If we say, "We have fellowship
with him," while we continue to walk in darkness, we lie and do not act in truth. 7 [f]But if we
walk in the light as he is in the light, then we
have fellowship with one another, and the blood
of his Son Jesus cleanses us from all sin. 8 [g]*If
we say, "We are without sin," we deceive
ourselves, and the truth is not in us. 9 [h]If we
acknowledge our sins, he is faithful and just and
will forgive our sins and cleanse us from every
wrongdoing. 10 [i]If we say, "We have not
sinned," we make him a liar, and his word is
not in us.

### CHAPTER 2

**Christ and His Commandments** 1 [j]*My
children, I am writing this to you so that you
may not commit sin. But if anyone does sin, we
have an Advocate with the Father, Jesus Christ
the righteous one. 2 [k]He is expiation for our
sins, and not for our sins only but for those of
the whole world. 3 [l]*The way we may be sure
that we know him is to keep his commandments. 4 [m]Whoever says, "I know him," but
does not keep his commandments is a liar, and
the truth is not in him. 5 [n]But whoever keeps
his word, the love of God is truly perfected in
him. This is the way we may know that we are
in union with him: 6 whoever claims to abide
in him ought to live [just] as he lived.

**The New Commandment** 7 [o]*Beloved, I
am writing no new commandment to you but an
old commandment that you had from the beginning. The old commandment is the word that
you have heard. 8 [p]*And yet I do write a new
commandment to you, which holds true in him
and among you, for the darkness is passing
away, and the true light is already shining.
9 [q]Whoever says he is in the light, yet hates his
brother, is still in the darkness. 10 [r]Whoever
loves his brother remains in the light, and there
is nothing in him to cause a fall. 11 Whoever
hates his brother is in darkness; he walks in
darkness and does not know where he is going
because the darkness has blinded his eyes.

---

a 2, 13; Jn 1, 1.14; 20, 20.25.27.
b Jn 15, 27; 17, 5.
c Jn 17, 21; Acts 4, 20.
d Jn 15, 11; 2 Jn 12.
e Jn 12, 35.
f Mt 26, 28; Rom 3, 24-25; Heb 9, 14; 1 Pt 1, 19; Rv 1, 5.
g 2 Chr 6, 36; Prv 20, 9.
h Prv 28, 13; Jas 5, 16.
i 5, 10.
j Jn 14, 16; Heb 7, 25.
k 4, 10.
l Jn 14, 15; 15, 10.
m 4, 20.
n Jn 14, 23.
o 3, 11; Dt 6, 5; Mt 22, 37-40.
p Jn 13, 34 / Jn 1, 5; Rom 13, 12.
q Jn 8, 12.
r Eccl 2, 14; Jn 11, 10.

---

1, 1–4: There is a striking parallel to the prologue of the gospel of John (Jn 1, 1–18), but the emphasis here is not on the preexistent Word but rather on the apostles' witness to the incarnation of life by their experience of the historical Jesus. He is *the Word of life* (1; cf Jn 1, 4), *the eternal life that was with the Father and was made visible* (2; cf Jn 1, 14), and was *heard, seen, looked upon,* and *touched* by the apostles. The purpose of their teaching is to share that *life,* called *fellowship . . . with the Father and with his Son, Jesus Christ,* with those who receive their witness (3; Jn 1, 14.16).

1, 5–7: *Light* is to be understood here as truth and goodness; *darkness* here is error and depravity (cf Jn 3, 19–21; 17, 17; Eph 5, 8). To *walk* in light or darkness is to live according to truth or error, not merely intellectual but moral as well. Fellowship with God and with one another consists in a life according to the truth as found in God and in Christ.

1, 8–10: Denial of the condition of sin is self-deception and even contradictory of divine revelation; there is also the continual possibility of sin's recurrence. Forgiveness and deliverance from sin through Christ are assured through acknowledgment of them and repentance.

2, 1: *Children:* like the term "beloved," this is an expression of pastoral love (cf Jn 13, 33; 21, 5; 1 Cor 4, 14). *Advocate:* for the use of the term, see Jn 14, 16. Forgiveness of sin is assured through Christ's intercession and expiation or "offering"; the death of Christ effected the removal of sin.

2, 3–6: *The way we may be sure:* to those who claim, "I have known Christ and therefore I know him," our author insists on not mere intellectual knowledge but obedience to God's commandments in a life conformed to the example of Christ; this confirms our knowledge of him and is *the love of God . . . perfected.* Disparity between moral life and the commandments proves improper belief.

2, 7–11: The author expresses the continuity and freshness of mutual charity in Christian experience. Through Christ the commandment of love has become the *light* defeating the *darkness* of evil in a new age. All hatred as darkness is incompatible with the light and Christian life. Note also the characteristic Johannine polemic in which a positive assertion is emphasized by the negative statement of its opposite.

2, 8: *Which holds true in him and among you:* literally, "a thing that holds true in him and in you."

**Members of the Community** 12 [s]*I am
writing to you, children, because your sins have
been forgiven for his name's sake.
13 [t]I am writing to you, fathers, because you
know him who is from the beginning.
I am writing to you, young men, because you
have conquered the evil one.
14 I write to you, children, because you
know the Father.
I write to you, fathers, because you know him
who is from the beginning.
I write to you, young men, because you are
strong and the word of God remains in you, and
you have conquered the evil one.
15 [u]*Do not love the world or the things of
the world. If anyone loves the world, the love
of the Father is not in him. 16 *For all that is
in the world, sensual lust, enticement for the
eyes, and a pretentious life, is not from the
Father but is from the world. 17 [v]Yet the world
and its enticement are passing away. But whoever does the will of God remains forever.

**Antichrists** 18 [w]*Children, it is the last
hour; and just as you heard that the antichrist
was coming, so now many antichrists have appeared. Thus we know this is the last hour.
19 *They went out from us, but they were not
really of our number; if they had been, they
would have remained with us. Their desertion
shows that none of them was of our number.
20 [x]*But you have the anointing that comes
from the holy one, and you all have knowledge.
21 [y]I write to you not because you do not know
the truth but because you do, and because every
lie is alien to the truth. 22 [z]*Who is the liar?
Whoever denies that Jesus is the Christ. Whoever denies the Father and the Son, this is the
antichrist. 23 [a]No one who denies the Son has
the Father, but whoever confesses the Son has
the Father as well.

**Life from God's Anointing** 24 [b]*Let
what you heard from the beginning remain in
you. If what you heard from the beginning remains in you, then you will remain in the Son
and in the Father. 25 [c]And this is the promise
that he made us: eternal life. 26 I write you
these things about those who would deceive
you. 27 As for you, the anointing that you received from him remains in you, so that you do
not need anyone to teach you. But his anointing
teaches you about everything and is true and not
false; just as it taught you, remain in him.

**Children of God** 28 *And now, children,
remain in him, so that when he appears we may
have confidence and not be put to shame by him
at his coming. 29 If you consider that he is
righteous, you also know that everyone who
acts in righteousness is begotten by him.

## CHAPTER 3

1 [d]*See what love the Father has bestowed
on us that we may be called the children of God.
Yet so we are. The reason the world does not
know us is that it did not know him.
2 [e]*Beloved, we are God's children now; what
we shall be has not yet been revealed. We do
know that when it is revealed we shall be like
him, for we shall see him as he is. 3 [f]Everyone
who has this hope based on him makes himself
pure, as he is pure.

---

s 1 Cor 6, 11.
t 1, 1; Jn 1, 1.
u Rom 8, 7-8; Jas 4, 4; 2 Pt 1; 4.
v Is 40, 8; Mt 7, 21; 1 Cor 7, 31; 1 Pt 4, 2.
w 1 Tim 4, 1.
x Jn 14, 26.
y 3, 19; 2 Pt 1, 12.
z 2 Thes 2, 4.
a Jn 14, 7-9.
b Jn 14, 23.
c Jn 5, 24; 10, 28; 17, 2.
d Jn 1, 12; Eph 1, 5 / Jn 15, 21; 17, 25.
e Phil 3, 21.
f 2, 6.

*

2, 12–17: The Christian community that has experienced the grace of God through forgiveness of sin and knowledge of Christ is armed against the evil one.

2, 12: *For his name's sake:* because of Christ our sins are forgiven.

2, 15: *The world:* all that is hostile toward God and alienated from him. Love of the *world* and love of God are thus mutually exclusive; cf Jas 4, 4.

2, 16: *Sensual lust:* literally, "the lust of the flesh," inordinate desire for physical gratification. *Enticement for the eyes:* literally, "the lust of the eyes," avarice or covetousness; the eyes are regarded as the windows of the soul. *Pretentious life:* literally, "pride of life," arrogance or ostentation in one's earthly style of life that reflects a willful independence from God and others.

2, 18: *It is the last hour:* literally, "a last hour," the period between the death and resurrection of Christ and his second coming. *The antichrist:* opponent or adversary of Christ; the term appears only in 1–2 John, but "pseudochrists" (translated "false messiahs") in Mt 24, 24 and Mk 13, 22, and Paul's "lawless one" in 2 Thes 2, 3, are similar figures. *Many antichrists:* Mt, Mk, and Rv seem to indicate a collectivity of persons, here related to the false teachers.

2, 19: *Not really of our number:* the apostate teachers only proved their lack of faith by leaving the community.

2, 20: *The anointing that comes from the holy one:* this anointing is in the Old Testament sense of receiving the Spirit of God. The *Holy One* probably refers to Christ. True knowledge is the gift of the Spirit (cf Is 11, 2), and the function of the Spirit is to lead Christians to the truth (Jn 14, 17.26; 16, 13).

2, 22–23: Certain gnostics denied that the earthly Jesus was the Christ; to deny knowledge of the Son is to deny the Father, since only through the Son has God been fully revealed (Jn 1, 18; 14, 8–9).

2, 24: Continuity with the apostolic witness as proclaimed in the prologue is the safeguard of right belief.

2, 28–29: Our confidence at his judgment is based on the daily assurance of salvation. Our actions reflect our true relation to him.

3, 1–3: The greatest sign of God's love is the gift of his Son (Jn 3, 16) that has made Christians true children of God. This relationship is a present reality and also part of the life to come; true knowledge of God will ultimately be gained, and Christians prepare themselves now by virtuous lives in imitation of the Son.

3, 2: *When it is revealed:* or "when he is revealed" (the subject of the verb could be Christ).

**Avoiding Sin** 4 *Everyone who commits
sin commits lawlessness, for sin is lawlessness.
5 [g]You know that he was revealed to take away
sins, and in him there is no sin. 6 No one who
remains in him sins; no one who sins has seen
him or known him. 7 Children, let no one deceive you. The person who acts in righteousness
is righteous, just as he is righteous.
8 [h]Whoever sins belongs to the devil, because
the devil has sinned from the beginning. Indeed,
the Son of God was revealed to destroy the
works of the devil. 9 *No one who is begotten
by God commits sin, because God's seed remains in him; he cannot sin because he is begotten by God. 10 In this way, the children of God
and the children of the devil are made plain; no
one who fails to act in righteousness belongs to
God, nor anyone who does not love his brother.

## III: LOVE FOR ONE ANOTHER

11 [i]*For this is the message you have heard
from the beginning: we should love one another, 12 [j]unlike Cain who belonged to the evil
one and slaughtered his brother. Why did he
slaughter him? Because his own works were
evil, and those of his brother righteous. 13 [k]Do
not be amazed, [then,] brothers, if the world
hates you. 14 [l]We know that we have passed
from death to life because we love our brothers.
Whoever does not love remains in death.
15 [m]Everyone who hates his brother is a murderer, and you know that no murderer has eternal life remaining in him. 16 [n]The way we
came to know love was that he laid down his life
for us; so we ought to lay down our lives for our
brothers. 17 [o]If someone who has worldly
means sees a brother in need and refuses him
compassion, how can the love of God remain in
him? 18 [p]Children, let us love not in word or
speech but in deed and truth.

**Confidence before God** 19 *[Now] this
is how we shall know that we belong to the truth
and reassure our hearts before him 20 in whatever our hearts condemn, for God is greater than
our hearts and knows everything. 21 Beloved,
if [our] hearts do not condemn us, we have
confidence in God 22 [q]and receive from him
whatever we ask, because we keep his commandments and do what pleases him. 23 [r]And
his commandment is this: we should believe in
the name of his Son, Jesus Christ, and love one
another just as he commanded us. 24 [s]Those
who keep his commandments remain in him,
and he in them, and the way we know that he
remains in us is from the Spirit that he gave us.

## CHAPTER 4

**Testing the Spirits** 1 [t]*Beloved, do not
trust every spirit but test the spirits to see whether they belong to God, because many false
prophets have gone out into the world. 2 [u]This
is how you can know the Spirit of God: every
spirit that acknowledges Jesus Christ come in
the flesh belongs to God, 3 [v]*and every spirit
that does not acknowledge Jesus does not belong to God. This is the spirit of the antichrist
that, as you heard, is to come, but in fact is
already in the world. 4 You belong to God,
children, and you have conquered them, for the
one who is in you is greater than the one who
is in the world. 5 [w]They belong to the world;
accordingly, their teaching belongs to the
world, and the world listens to them. 6 [x]We
belong to God, and anyone who knows God

---

- g Is 53, 9; Jn 1, 29; 8, 46; 1 Pt 2, 22.
- h Jn 8, 44; 12, 31-32.
- i 2, 7; Jn 13, 34; 15, 12.17.
- j Gn 4, 8; Jude 11.
- k Mt 24, 9; Jn 15, 18; 17, 14.
- l Lv 19, 17; Jn 5, 24.
- m Jn 8, 44.
- n Mt 20, 28; Jn 10, 11; 15, 13.
- o Dt 15, 7.11; Jas 2, 15-16.
- p Jas 1, 22.
- q 5, 15; Mt 7, 7-11; 21, 22; Jn 14, 13-14.
- r Jn 13, 34; 15, 17.
- s 4, 13; Jn 14, 21-23.
- t 2, 18; Mt 24, 24.
- u 1 Cor 12, 3; 1 Thes 5, 21.
- v 1, 22.
- w Jn 15, 19.
- x Jn 8, 47; 10, 16.

---

3, 4: *Lawlessness:* a reference to the activity of the antichrist, so it is expressed as hostility toward God and a rejection of Christ. The author goes on to contrast the states of sin and righteousness. Christians do not escape sin but realize that when they sin they cease to have fellowship with God. Virtue and sin distinguish the children of God from the children of the devil.

3, 9: A habitual sinner is a child of the devil, while a child of God, who by definition is in fellowship with God, cannot sin. *Seed:* Christ or the Spirit who shares the nature of God with the Christian.

3, 11–18: Love, even to the point of self-sacrifice, is the point of the commandment. The story of Cain and Abel (12–15; Gn 4, 1–16) presents the rivalry of two brothers, in a contrast of evil and righteousness, where envy led to murder. For Christians, proof of deliverance is love toward others, after the example of Christ. This includes concrete acts of charity, out of our material abundance.

3, 19–24: Living a life of faith in Jesus and of Christian love assures us of abiding in God no matter what our feelings may at times tell us. Our obedience gives us confidence in prayer and trust in God's judgment. This obedience includes our belief in Christ and love for one another.

3, 19b–20: This difficult passage may also be translated "we shall be at peace before him in whatever our hearts condemn, for . . ." or "and before God we shall convince our hearts, if our hearts condemn us, that God is greater than our hearts."

4, 1–6: Deception is possible in spiritual phenomena and may be tested by its relation to Christian doctrine (cf 1 Cor 12, 3): those who fail to acknowledge Jesus Christ in the flesh are false prophets and belong to the antichrist. Even though these false prophets are well received in the world, the Christian who belongs to God has a greater power in the truth.

4, 3: *Does not acknowledge Jesus:* some ancient manuscripts add "Christ" and/or "to have come in the flesh" (cf 2), and others read "every spirit that annuls (or severs) Jesus."

listens to us, while anyone who does not belong
to God refuses to hear us. This is how we know
the spirit of truth and the spirit of deceit.

**God's Love and Christian Life** **7** *Beloved, let us love one another, because love is
of God; everyone who loves is begotten by God
and knows God. **8** Whoever is without love
does not know God, for God is love. **9** [y]In this
way the love of God was revealed to us: God
sent his only Son into the world so that we might
have life through him. **10** [z]In this is love: not
that we have loved God, but that he loved us and
sent his Son as expiation for our sins. **11** Beloved, if God so loved us, we also must love one
another. **12** [a]No one has ever seen God. Yet,
if we love one another, God remains in us, and
his love is brought to perfection in us.
**13** *This is how we know that we remain in
him and he in us, that he has given us of his
Spirit. **14** Moreover, we have seen and testify
that the Father sent his Son as savior of the
world. **15** Whoever acknowledges that Jesus is
the Son of God, God remains in him and he in
God. **16** We have come to know and to believe
in the love God has for us.
God is love, and whoever remains in love
remains in God and God in him. **17** [b]In this is
love brought to perfection among us, that we
have confidence on the day of judgment because
as he is, so are we in this world. **18** There is no
fear in love, but perfect love drives out fear
because fear has to do with punishment, and so
one who fears is not yet perfect in love. **19** We
love because he first loved us. **20** [c]*If anyone
says, "I love God," but hates his brother, he is
a liar; for whoever does not love a brother whom
he has seen cannot love God whom he has not
seen. **21** [d]This is the commandment we have
from him: whoever loves God must also love his
brother.

## CHAPTER 5

**Faith is Victory over the World**
**1** [e]*Everyone who believes that Jesus is the
Christ is begotten by God, and everyone who
loves the father loves [also] the one begotten by
him. **2** In this way we know that we love the
children of God when we love God and obey his
commandments. **3** [f]For the love of God is this,
that we keep his commandments. And his commandments are not burdensome, **4** [g]for whoever is begotten by God conquers the world. And
the victory that conquers the world is our faith.
**5** [h]Who [indeed] is the victor over the world
but the one who believes that Jesus is the Son
of God?
**6** [i]*This is the one who came through water
and blood, Jesus Christ, not by water alone, but
by water and blood. The Spirit is the one that
testifies, and the Spirit is truth. **7** So there are
three that testify, **8** [j]the Spirit, the water, and
the blood, and the three are of one accord. **9** [k]If
we accept human testimony, the testimony of
God is surely greater. Now the testimony of
God is this, that he has testified on behalf of his
Son. **10** [l]Whoever believes in the Son of God
has this testimony within himself. Whoever
does not believe God has made him a liar by not
believing the testimony God has given about his
Son. **11** [m]And this is the testimony: God gave
us eternal life, and this life is in his Son.
**12** Whoever possesses the Son has life; whoever does not possess the Son of God does not
have life.

## IV: EPILOGUE

**Prayer for Sinners** **13** [n]*I write these
things to you so that you may know that you

y Jn 3, 16.
z Rom 5, 8.
a Jn 1, 18; 1 Tm 6, 16.
b 2, 28.
c 2, 4.
d Jn 13, 34; 14, 15.21; 15, 17.
e Jn 8, 42; 1 Pt 1, 23.
f Jn 14, 15.
g Jn 16, 33.
h 1 Cor 15, 57.
i Jn 15, 26; 19, 34.
j Jn 5, 32.36; 15, 26.
k Jn 5, 32.37.
l 3, 33.
m 1, 2; Jn 1, 4; 5, 21.26; 17, 3.
n Jn 1, 12; 20, 31.

*

4, 7–12: Love as we share in it testifies to the nature of God and to his presence in our lives. One who loves shows that one is a child of God and knows God, for God's very being is love; one without love is without God. The revelation of the nature of God's love is found in the free gift of his Son to us, so that we may share life with God and be delivered from our sins. The love we have for one another must be of the same sort: authentic, merciful; this unique Christian love is our proof that we know God and can "see" the invisible God.

4, 13–21: The testimony of the Spirit and that of faith join the testimony of love to confirm our knowledge of God. Our love is grounded in the confession of Jesus as the Son of God and the example of God's love for us. Christian life is founded on the knowledge of God as love and on his continuing presence that relieves us from fear of judgment (16–18). What Christ is gives us confidence, even as we live and love in this world. Yet Christian love is not abstract but lived in the concrete manner of love for one another.

4, 20: *Cannot love God:* some ancient manuscripts read "how can he love . . . ?"

5, 1–5: Children of God are identified not only by their love for others (4, 7–9) and for God (5, 1–2) but by their belief in the divine sonship of Jesus Christ. Faith, the acceptance of Jesus in his true character and the obedience in love to God's commands (3), is the source of the Christian's power in the world and conquers the world of evil (4–5), even as Christ overcame the world (Jn 16, 33).

5, 6–12: *Water and blood* (6) refers to Christ's baptism (Mt 3, 16–17) and to the shedding of his blood on the cross (Jn 19, 34). *The Spirit* was present at the baptism (Mt 3, 16; Mk 1, 10; Lk 3, 22; Jn 1, 32.34). *The testimony* to Christ as the Son of God is confirmed by divine witness (7–9), greater by far than the two legally required human witnesses (Dt 17, 6). To deny this is to deny God's truth; cf Jn 8, 17–18. The gist of the divine witness or *testimony* is that *eternal life* (11–12) is given in Christ and nowhere else. To *possess the Son* is not acceptance of a doctrine but of a person who lives now and provides life.

5, 13–21: As children of God we have confidence in prayer

have eternal life, you who believe in the name
of the Son of God. **14** [o]And we have this confidence in him, that if we ask anything according
to his will, he hears us. **15** And if we know that
he hears us in regard to whatever we ask, we
know that what we have asked him for is ours.
**16** [p]If anyone sees his brother sinning, if the sin
is not deadly, he should pray to God and he will
give him life. This is only for those whose sin
is not deadly. There is such a thing as deadly
sin, about which I do not say that you should
pray. **17** All wrongdoing is sin, but there is sin
that is not deadly.

**18** We know that no one begotten by God
sins; but the one begotten by God he protects,
and the evil one cannot touch him. **19** We know
that we belong to God, and the whole world is
under the power of the evil one. **20** [q]We also
know that the Son of God has come and has
given us discernment to know the one who is
true. And we are in the one who is true, in his
Son Jesus Christ. He is the true God and eternal
life. **21** Children, be on your guard against
idols.

o 3, 21-22; Mt 7, 7; Jn 14, 13-14.
p Mt 12, 31.
q Jer 24, 7; Jn 17, 3; Eph 1, 17.

* because of our intimate relationship with him (14–15). In love, we pray (16–17) for those who are in *sin*, but not in *deadly sin* (literally, "sin unto death"), probably referring to apostasy or activities brought on under the antichrist; cf Mk 3, 29; Heb 6, 4–6; 10, 26–31. Even in the latter case, however, prayer, while not enjoined, is not forbidden. The letter concludes with a summary of the themes of the letter (18–20). There is a sharp antithesis between the children of God and those belonging to the world and to the evil one. The Son reveals the God of truth; Christians dwell in the true God, *in his Son,* and have eternal life. The final verse (21) voices a perennial warning about *idols,* any type of rival to God.

# THE SECOND LETTER OF
# JOHN

## INTRODUCTION

*Written in response to similar problems, the Second and Third Letters of John are of the same length, perhaps determined by the practical consideration of the writing space on one piece of papyrus. In each letter the writer calls himself "the Presbyter," and their common authorship is further evidenced by internal similarities in style and wording, especially in the introductions and conclusions. The literary considerations that link 2 and 3 John also link them with the First Letter and the Gospel of John. The concern with "truth," christology, mutual love, the new commandment, antichrist, and the integrity of witness to the earthly Jesus mark these works as products of the Johannine school. The identity of the Presbyter is problematic. The use of the title implies more than age, and refers to his position of leadership in the early church. The absence of a proper name indicates that he was well known and acknowledged in authority by the communities to which he writes. Although traditionally attributed to John the apostle, these letters were probably written by a disciple or scribe of an apostle. The traditional place and date of composition, Ephesus at the end of the first century, are plausible for both letters.*

*The Second Letter is addressed to "the chosen Lady" and "to her children." This literary image of a particular Christian community reflects the specific destination and purpose of the letter. Unlike 1 John, this brief letter is not a theological treatise but a reply to problems within the church. The Johannine themes of love and truth are used to support practical advice on Christian living. The Presbyter encourages community members to show their Christianity by adhering to the great commandment of mutual love and to the historical truth about Jesus. The false teaching present among them is a spiritualizing christology that may tempt some members to discount teachings about the incarnation and death of Jesus the Christ; cf 1 Jn 4, 2. For their protection the Presbyter forbids hospitality toward unknown or "progressive" Christians to prevent their infiltration of the community. The Second Letter preserves the Johannine concerns of doctrinal purity and active love in the form of pastoral advice to a threatened community.*

**1** [a]*The Presbyter to the chosen Lady and to
her children whom I love in truth—and not only
I but also all who know the truth— **2** because
of the truth that dwells in us and will be with us
forever. **3** *Grace, mercy, and peace will be
with us from God the Father and from Jesus
Christ the Father's Son in truth and love.

**4** [b]*I rejoiced greatly to find some of your
children walking in the truth just as we were
commanded by the Father. **5** [c]But now, Lady,
I ask you, not as though I were writing a new

a Jn 8, 32; 3 Jn 1.
b 3 Jn 3.
c Jn 13, 34; 15, 12; 1 Jn 4, 7.

*

1: *The chosen Lady:* literally "elected"; this could also be translated "Kyria (a woman's name) chosen (by God)" or "the lady Electa" or "Electa Kyria." The adjective "chosen" is applied to all Christians at the beginning of other New Testament letters (1 Pt 1, 1; Ti 1, 1). The description is of a specific community with "children" who are its members. *The truth:* the affirmation of Jesus in the flesh and in contrast to false teaching (7).

3: *Grace, mercy, and peace:* like 1 and 2 Tm this letter adds *mercy* to the terms used frequently in a salutation to describe Christian blessing; it appears only here in the Johannine writings. The author also puts the blessing in relation to *truth* and *love,* the watchwords of the Johannine teaching. *The Father's Son:* the title that affirms the close relationship of Christ to God; similar variations of this title occur elsewhere (Jn 1, 14; 3, 35), but the precise wording is not found elsewhere in the New Testament.

4: *Some of your children:* this refers to those whom the Presbyter has recently encountered, but it may also indicate the presence of false doctrine in the community: the Presbyter encourages those who have remained faithful. *Walking in the truth:* an expression used in the Johannine writings to describe a way of living in which the Christian faith is visibly expressed; cf 1 Jn 1, 6–7; 2, 6.11, 3 Jn 3.

commandment but the one we have had from the
beginning: let us love one another. **6** [d]*For this
is love, that we walk according to his commandments; this is the commandment, as you heard
from the beginning, in which you should walk.
**7** [e]*Many deceivers have gone out into the
world, those who do not acknowledge Jesus
Christ as coming in the flesh; such is the deceitful one and the antichrist. **8** *Look to yourselves that you do not lose what we worked for
but may receive a full recompense. **9** [f]*Anyone
who is so ''progressive'' as not to remain in the
teaching of the Christ does not have God; whoever remains in the teaching has the Father and
the Son. **10** [g]*If anyone comes to you and does
not bring this doctrine, do not receive him in
your house or even greet him; **11** for whoever
greets him shares in his evil works.

**12** [h]*Although I have much to write to you,
I do not intend to use paper and ink. Instead, I
hope to visit you and to speak face to face so that
our joy may be complete. **13** *The children of
your chosen sister send you greetings.

d Jn 13, 34; 14, 15; 1 Jn 5, 3.
e 1 Jn 2, 22; 4, 2.
f Jn 8, 31; 1 Jn 2, 23; 4, 15.
g Rom 16, 17; 2 Thes 3, 6.
h Jn 15, 11; 1 Jn 1, 4; 3 Jn 13.

*

6: *His commandments:* cf 1 Jn 3, 23; 2, 7–8; 4, 21; obedience to the commandment of faith and love includes all others.

7: *The antichrist:* see 1 Jn 2, 18–19.22; 4, 3.

8: *You* (plural): it is not certain whether this means the Christians addressed or includes the Presbyter, since some of the ancient Greek manuscripts and Greek Fathers have "we."

9: *Anyone who is so "progressive":* literally, "Anyone who goes ahead." Some gnostic groups held the doctrine of the Christ come in the flesh to be a first step in belief, which the more advanced and spiritual believer surpassed and abandoned in his knowledge of the spiritual Christ. The author affirms that fellowship with God may be gained only by holding to the complete doctrine of Jesus Christ (1 Jn 2, 22–23; 4, 2; 5, 5–6).

10–11: At this time false teachers were considered so dangerous and divisive as to be shunned completely. From this description they seem to be wandering preachers. We see here a natural suspicion of early Christians concerning such itinerants and can envisage the problems faced by missionaries such as those mentioned in 3 Jn 10.

12: *Our joy:* a number of other Greek manuscripts read "your joy."

13: *Chosen sister:* the community of which the Presbyter is now a part greets you (singular), the community of the Lady addressed.

# THE THIRD LETTER OF
# JOHN

## INTRODUCTION

*The Third Letter of John preserves a brief glimpse into the problems of missionary activity and local autonomy in the early church. In contrast to the other two letters of John, this work was addressed to a specific individual, Gaius. This letter is less theological in content and purpose. The author's goal was to secure hospitality and material support for his missionaries, and the Presbyter is writing to another member of the church who has welcomed missionaries in the past. The Presbyter commends Gaius for his hospitality and encourages his future help. He indicates he may come to challenge the policy of Diotrephes that is based on evil gossip.*

*The problems of the Presbyter in this short letter provide us with valuable evidence of the flexible and personal nature of authority in the early church. The Presbyter writes to Gaius, whom perhaps he had converted or instructed, on the basis of their personal links. The brothers have also confirmed him as a loyal Christian in action and belief. Gaius accepted the missionaries from the Presbyter and presumably will accept Demetrius on the Presbyter's recommendation. In contrast, Diotrephes refuses to receive either letters or friends of the Presbyter. Although he is portrayed as ambitious and hostile, he perhaps exemplifies the cautious and sectarian nature of early Christianity; for its own protection the local community mistrusted missionaries as false teachers. Most interestingly, Diotrephes seems comfortable in ignoring the requests of the Presbyter. The Presbyter seems to acknowledge that only a personal confrontation with Diotrephes will remedy the situation (10). The division, however, may also rest on doctrinal disagreement in which Gaius and the other "friends" accept the teaching of the Presbyter, and Diotrephes does not; the missionaries are not received for suspicion of theological error. Diotrephes has thus been viewed by some as an overly ambitious local upstart trying to thwart the advance of orthodox Christianity, by others as an orthodox church official suspicious of the teachings of the Presbyter and those in the Johannine school who think as he does, or by still others as a local leader anxious to keep the debates in the Johannine community out of his own congregation.*

*This brief letter and the situation that it mirrors show us how little we know about some details of early development in the church: schools of opinion existed around which questions of faith and life were discussed, and personal ties as well as doctrine and authority played a role in what happened amid divisions and unity.*

**1** [a]*The Presbyter to the beloved Gaius
whom I love in truth.
**2** Beloved, I hope you are prospering in every respect and are in good health, just as your
soul is prospering. **3** [b]*I rejoiced greatly when
some of the brothers came and testified to how
truly you walk in the truth. **4** [c]Nothing gives
me greater joy than to hear that my children are
walking in the truth.
**5** [d]*Beloved, you are faithful in all you do
for the brothers, especially for strangers;

a 2 Jn 1.
b 5; Gal 6, 10; 2 Jn 4.
c 1 Thes 2, 11-12; 1 Tm 1, 2; 2 Tm 1, 2; 1 Jn 2, 1; 2 Jn 4.
d Rom 12, 13; Gal 6, 10; Heb 13, 2.

*

1: *Beloved Gaius:* a frequent form of address for fellow Christians in New Testament epistolary literature.

3: *The brothers:* in this letter, the term may refer to Christians who have been missionaries and received hospitality from Gaius (5–6). *Walk in the truth:* the common Johannine term to describe Christian living; this description presents Gaius as following the teachings of the Presbyter in contrast to Diotrephes.

5: *You are faithful in all you do:* Gaius's aid to the mission-

**6** [e]*they have testified to your love before the
church. Please help them in a way worthy of
God to continue their journey. **7** *For they have
set out for the sake of the Name and are accepting nothing from the pagans. **8** Therefore, we
ought to support such persons, so that we may
be co-workers in the truth.
**9** *I wrote to the church, but Diotrephes,
who loves to dominate, does not acknowledge
us. **10** *Therefore, if I come, I will draw attention to what he is doing, spreading evil nonsense
about us. And not content with that, he will not
receive the brothers, hindering those who wish
to do so and expelling them from the church.
**11** [f]*Beloved, do not imitate evil but imitate
good. Whoever does what is good is of God;
whoever does what is evil has never seen God.
**12** [g]*Demetrius receives a good report from
all, even from the truth itself. We give our
testimonial as well, and you know our testimony is true.
**13** [h]I have much to write to you, but I do not
wish to write with pen and ink. **14** Instead, I
hope to see you soon, when we can talk face to
face.

**15** [i]*Peace be with you. The friends greet you;
greet the friends there each by name.

e Acts 15, 3; Col 1, 10; 1 Thes 2, 12.
f 1 Jn 2, 29; 3, 6.10.
g Jn 19, 35; 21, 24; 1 Tm 3, 7.
h 2 Jn 12.
i Jn 20, 19.21.26; Eph 6, 23; 1 Pt 5, 14.

*

aries is a manifestation of his true Christian faith.

6: *Help them . . . to continue their journey:* the Presbyter asks Gaius not only to continue to welcome the missionaries to his community but also to equip them for further travels.

7: *The Name:* of Jesus Christ (cf Acts 5, 41; 1 Jn 2, 12; 3, 23; 5, 13). *Accepting nothing:* not expecting support from the pagans to whom they preach the gospel, so that they will not be considered as beggars; they required support from other Christians; cf Paul's complaints to the Corinthians (1 Cor 9, 3–12).

9: *Who loves to dominate:* the Presbyter does not deny Diotrephes' place as leader but indicates that his ambition may have caused him to disregard his letter and his influence.

10: *If I come:* the Presbyter may visit the community to challenge the actions of Diotrephes toward himself and the missionaries. *Will not receive the brothers:* Diotrephes may have been critical of the teachings of the Presbyter and sought to maintain doctrinal purity; cf 1 Jn 2, 19 and 2 Jn 10–11.

11: *Do not imitate evil:* Gaius should not be influenced by the behavior of Diotrephes.

12: *Demetrius:* because of the fear of false teachers, Demetrius, perhaps the bearer of the letter, is provided with a recommendation from the Presbyter; cf 2 Cor 3, 1; Rom 16, 1. *Even from the truth itself:* this refers probably to the manner of Demetrius's life that testifies to his true belief; cf Gaius above (v 3).

15: *Friends:* although a Johannine term for Christians (Jn 15, 15), the word here may refer to those in the community loyal to the Presbyter and to Gaius.

# THE LETTER OF

# JUDE

## INTRODUCTION

*This letter is by its address attributed to "Jude, a slave of Jesus Christ and brother of James" (1). Since he is not identified as an apostle, this designation can hardly be meant to refer to the Jude or Judas who is listed as one of the Twelve (Lk 6, 16; Acts 1, 13; cf Jn 14, 22). The person intended is almost certainly the other Jude, named in the gospels among the relatives of Jesus (Mt 13, 55; Mk 6, 3), and the James who is listed there as his brother is the one to whom the Letter of James is attributed (see the Introduction to James). Nothing else is known of this Jude, and the apparent need to identify him by reference to his better-known brother indicates that he was a rather obscure personage in the early church.*

*The letter is addressed in the most general terms to "those who are called, beloved in God the Father and kept safe for Jesus Christ" (1), hence apparently to all Christians. But since its purpose is to warn the addressees against false teachers, the author must have had in mind one or more specific Christian communities located in the unidentified region where the errors in question constituted a danger. While the letter contains some Semitic features, there is nothing to identify the addressees specifically as Jewish Christians; indeed, the errors envisaged seem to reflect an early form of gnosticism, opposed to law, that points rather to the cultural context of the Gentile world. Like James and 2 Peter, the Letter of Jude manifests none of the typical features of the letter form except the address.*

*There is so much similarity between Jude and 2 Peter, especially Jude 4–16 and 2 Peter 2, 1–18, that there must be a literary relationship between them. Since there is no evidence for the view that both authors borrowed from the same source, it is usually supposed that one of them borrowed from the other. Most scholars believe that Jude is the earlier of the two, principally because he quotes two apocryphal Jewish works, the* Assumption of Moses *(9) and the* Book of Enoch *(14–15) as part of his structured argument, whereas 2 Peter omits both references. Since there was controversy in the early church about the propriety of citing non-canonical literature that included legendary material, it is more probable that a later writer would omit such references than that he would add them.*

*Many interpreters today consider Jude a pseudonymous work dating from the end of the first century or even later. In support of this view they adduce the following arguments: (a) the apostles are referred to as belonging to an age that has receded into the past (17–18); (b) faith is understood as a body of doctrine handed down by a process of tradition (3); (c) the author's competent Greek style shows that he must have had a Hellenistic cultural formation; (d) the gnostic character of the errors envisaged fits better into the early second century than into a period several decades earlier. While impressive, these arguments are not entirely compelling and do not completely rule out the possibility of composition around the year A.D. 80, when the historical Jude may still have been alive.*

*This little letter is an urgent note by an author who intended to write more fully about salvation to an unknown group of readers, but who was forced by dangers from false teachers worming their way into the community (3–4) to dash off a warning against them (5–16) and to deliver some pressing Christian admonitions (17–23). The letter is justly famous for its majestic closing doxology (24–25).*

**Address and Greeting** 1 [a]*Jude, a slave
of Jesus Christ and brother of James, to those
who are called, beloved in God the Father and
kept safe for Jesus Christ: 2 [b]may mercy,
peace, and love be yours in abundance.

**Occasion for Writing** 3 [c]*Beloved, although I was making every effort to write to you
about our common salvation, I now feel a need
to write to encourage you to contend for the faith
that was once for all handed down to the holy
ones. 4 [d]For there have been some intruders,
who long ago were designated for this condemnation, godless persons, who pervert the grace
of our God into licentiousness and who deny our
only Master and Lord, Jesus Christ.

**The False Teachers** 5 [e]*I wish to remind
you, although you know all things, that [the]
Lord who once saved a people from the land of
Egypt later destroyed those who did not believe.
6 [f]*The angels too, who did not keep to their
own domain but deserted their proper dwelling,
he has kept in eternal chains, in gloom, for the
judgment of the great day. 7 [g]*Likewise, Sodom, Gomorrah, and the surrounding towns,
which, in the same manner as they, indulged in
sexual promiscuity and practiced unnatural
vice, serve as an example by undergoing a punishment of eternal fire.

8 *Similarly, these dreamers nevertheless
also defile the flesh, scorn lordship, and revile
glorious beings. 9 [h]*Yet the archangel Michael, when he argued with the devil in a dispute
over the body of Moses, did not venture to
pronounce a reviling judgment upon him but
said, "May the Lord rebuke you!" 10 [i]But
these people revile what they do not understand
and are destroyed by what they know by nature
like irrational animals. 11 [j]*Woe to them!
They followed the way of Cain, abandoned
themselves to Balaam's error for the sake of
gain, and perished in the rebellion of Korah.
12 [k]*These are blemishes on your love feasts,
as they carouse fearlessly and look after themselves. They are waterless clouds blown about
by winds, fruitless trees in late autumn, twice
dead and uprooted. 13 They are like wild waves
of the sea, foaming up their shameless deeds,
wandering stars for whom the gloom of darkness has been reserved forever.

14 [l]*Enoch, of the seventh generation from
Adam, prophesied also about them when he
said, "Behold, the Lord has come with his
countless holy ones 15 to execute judgment on
all and to convict everyone for all the godless
deeds that they committed and for all the harsh
words godless sinners have uttered against
him." 16 [m]These people are complainers, disgruntled ones who live by their desires; their
mouths utter bombast as they fawn over people
to gain advantage.

---

a Mt 13, 55; Mk 6, 3; Acts 12, 17; Rom 1, 7.
b Gal 6, 16; 1 Tm 1, 2; 2 Pt 1, 2.
c 17.20; 1 Tm 6, 12.
d Gal 2, 4; 2 Tm 3, 6; 2 Pt 2, 1.
e Nm 14, 35; 1 Cor 10, 5; Heb 3, 16.17.
f 2 Pt 2, 4.9.
g Dt 29, 22-24; Mt 25, 41; 2 Thes 1, 8-9; 2 Pt 2, 6; 3, 7.
h Dn 10, 21; 12, 1.
i 2 Pt 2, 12.
j Gn 4, 8-16; 1 Jn 3, 12 / Nm 31, 15-16; 2 Pt 2, 15; Rv 2, 14 / Nm 16, 19-35.
k 2 Pt 2, 13.17.
l Mt 16, 27; Heb 12, 22-23.
m 18; 1 Cor 10, 10; 2 Pt 2, 10.18.

---

*

1: *Jude . . . brother of James:* for the identity of the author of this letter, see Introduction. *To those who are called:* the vocation to the Christian faith is God's free gift to those whom he loves and whom he safely protects in Christ until the Lord's second coming.

3–4: *Our common salvation:* the teachings of the Christian faith derived from the apostolic preaching and to be kept by the Christian community.

5: For this first example of divine punishment on those who had been saved but did not then keep faith, see Nm 14, 28–29 and the note there. Some manuscripts have the word "once" (*hapax* as at 3) after "you know"; some commentators have suggested that it means "knowing one thing" or "you know all things once for all." Instead of "[the] Lord" manuscripts vary, having "Jesus," "God," or no subject stated.

6: This second example draws on Gn 6, 1–4 as elaborated in the apocryphal Book of Enoch (cf 14): heavenly beings came to earth and had sexual intercourse with women. God punished them by casting them out of heaven into darkness and bondage.

7: *Practiced unnatural vice:* literally, "went after alien flesh." This example derives from Gn 19, 1–25, especially 4–11, when the townsmen of Sodom violated both hospitality and morality by demanding that Lot's two visitors (really messengers of Yahweh) be handed over to them so that they could abuse them sexually. *Unnatural vice:* this refers to the desire for intimacies by human beings with angels (the reverse of the example in 6). Sodom (whence "sodomy") and Gomorrah became proverbial as object lessons for God's punishment on sin (Is 1, 9; Jer 50, 40; Am 4, 11; Mt 10, 15; 2 Pt 2, 6).

8: *Dreamers:* the writer returns to the false teachers of v 4, applying charges from the three examples in vv 5, 6, 7. This may apply to claims they make for revelations they have received by night (to the author, hallucinations). *Defile the flesh:* this may mean bodily pollutions from the erotic dreams of sexual license (7). *Lordship . . . glorious beings:* these may reflect the Lord (5; Jesus, 4) whom they spurn and the angels (6; cf the note on 2 Pt 2, 10, here, as there, literally, "glories").

9: *The archangel Michael . . . judgment:* a reference to an incident in the apocryphal Assumption of Moses. Dt 34, 6 had said of Moses, literally in Greek, "they buried him" or "he (God?) buried him" (taken to mean "he was buried"). The later account tells how Michael, who was sent to bury him, was challenged by the devil's interest in the body. Our author draws out the point that if an archangel refrained from reviling even the devil, how wrong it is for mere human beings to revile glorious beings (angels).

11: *Cain . . . Balaam . . . Korah:* examples of rebellious men and of the punishment their conduct incurred; cf Gn 4, 8–16; Nm 16, 1–35; 31, 16. See the note on 2 Pt 2, 15.

12: *Blemishes on your love feasts:* or "hidden rocks" or "submerged reefs" (cf 13). The opponents engaged in scandalous conduct in connection with community gatherings called *love feasts* (agape meals), which were associated with eucharistic celebrations at certain stages of early Christian practice; cf 1 Cor 11, 18–34 and the note on 2 Pt 2, 13.

14–15: Cited from the apocryphal Book of Enoch 1, 9.

**Exhortations** 17 [n]But you, beloved, remember the words spoken beforehand by the
apostles of our Lord Jesus Christ, 18 [o]*for they
told you, "In [the] last time there will be scoffers who will live according to their own godless
desires." 19 [p]These are the ones who cause
divisions; they live on the natural plane, devoid
of the Spirit. 20 [q]But you, beloved, build yourselves up in your most holy faith; pray in the
holy Spirit. 21 [r]Keep yourselves in the love of
God and wait for the mercy of our Lord Jesus
Christ that leads to eternal life. 22 *On those
who waver, have mercy; 23 *save others by
snatching them out of the fire; on others have
mercy with fear, abhorring even the outer garment stained by the flesh.

**Doxology** 24 [s]*To the one who is able to
keep you from stumbling and to present you
unblemished and exultant, in the presence of his
glory, 25 [t]to the only God, our savior, through
Jesus Christ our Lord be glory, majesty, power,
and authority from ages past, now, and for ages
to come. Amen.

n Heb 2, 3; 2 Pt 3, 2.
o 1 Tm 4, 1; 2 Tm 3, 1-5; 2 Pt 3, 3.
p 1 Cor 2, 14; Jas 3, 15.
q 2; Eph 6, 18; Col 2, 7.
r Ti 2, 13.
s 2 Cor 4, 14; 1 Pt 4, 13.
t Rom 11, 36; 1 Tm 1, 17.

*

18: This is the substance of much early Christian preaching rather than a direct quotation of any of the various New Testament passages on this theme (see Mk 13, 22; Acts 20, 30; 1 Tm 4, 1–3; 2 Pt 3, 3).

22: *Have mercy:* some manuscripts read "convince," "confute," or reprove." Others have "even though you waver" or "doubt" instead of *who waver.*

23: *With fear:* some manuscripts connect the phrase "with fear" with the imperative "save" or with the participle "snatching." Other manuscripts omit the phrase "on others have mercy," so that only two groups are envisioned. Rescue of those led astray and caution in the endeavor are both enjoined. *Outer garment stained by the flesh:* the imagery may come from Zec 3, 3–5, just as that of *snatching . . . out of the fire* comes from Zec 3, 2; the very garments of the godless are to be abhorred because of their contagion.

24–25: With this liturgical statement about the power of God to keep the faithful from stumbling, and praise to him through Jesus Christ, the letter reaches its conclusion by returning to the themes with which it began (1–2).

# THE REVELATION TO
# JOHN

## INTRODUCTION

*The Apocalypse, or Revelation to John, the last book of the Bible, is one of the most difficult to understand because it abounds in unfamiliar and extravagant symbolism, which at best appears unusual to the modern reader. Symbolic language, however, is one of the chief characteristics of apocalyptic literature, of which this book is an outstanding example. Such literature enjoyed wide popularity in both Jewish and Christian circles from ca. 200 B.C. to A.D. 200.*

*This book contains an account of visions in symbolic and allegorical language borrowed extensively from the Old Testament, especially Ezekiel, Zechariah, and Daniel. Whether or not these visions were real experiences of the author or simply literary conventions employed by him is an open question.*

*This much, however, is certain: symbolic descriptions are not to be taken as literal descriptions, nor is the symbolism meant to be pictured realistically. One would find it difficult and repulsive to visualize a lamb with seven horns and seven eyes; yet Jesus Christ is described in precisely such words (5, 6). The author used these images to suggest Christ's universal (seven) power (horns) and knowledge (eyes). A significant feature of apocalyptic writing is the use of symbolic colors, metals, garments (1, 13–16; 3, 18; 4, 4; 6, 1–8; 17, 4; 19, 8), and numbers (*four *signifies the world,* six *imperfection,* seven *totality of perfection,* twelve *Israel's tribes or the apostles,* one thousand *immensity). Finally the vindictive language in the book (6, 9–10; 18, 1—19, 4) is also to be understood symbolically and not literally. The cries for vengeance on the lips of Christian martyrs that sound so harsh are in fact literary devices the author employed to evoke in the reader and hearer a feeling of horror for apostasy and rebellion that will be severely punished by God.*

*The lurid descriptions of the punishment of Jezebel (2, 22) and of the destruction of the great harlot, Babylon (16, 9—19, 2), are likewise literary devices. The metaphor of Babylon as harlot would be wrongly construed if interpreted literally. On the other hand, the stylized figure of the woman clothed with the sun (12, 1–6), depicting the New Israel, may seem to be a negative stereotype. It is necessary to look beyond the literal meaning to see that these images mean to convey a sense of God's wrath at sin in the former case and trust in God's providential care over the church in the latter.*

*The Book of Revelation cannot be adequately understood except against the historical background that occasioned its writing. Like Daniel and other apocalypses, it was composed as resistance literature to meet a crisis. The book itself suggests that the crisis was ruthless persecution of the early church by the Roman authorities; the harlot Babylon symbolizes pagan Rome, the city on seven hills (17, 9). The book is, then, an exhortation and admonition to Christians of the first century to stand firm in the faith and to avoid compromise with paganism, despite the threat of adversity and martyrdom; they are to await patiently the fulfillment of God's mighty promises. The triumph of God in the world of men and women remains a mystery, to be accepted in faith and longed for in hope. It is a triumph that unfolded in the history of Jesus of Nazareth and continues to unfold in the history of the individual Christian who follows the way of the cross, even, if necessary, to a martyr's death.*

*Though the perspective is eschatological—ultimate salvation and victory are said to take place at the end of the present age when Christ will come in glory at the parousia—the book presents the decisive struggle of Christ and his followers against Satan and his cohorts as already over. Christ's overwhelming defeat of the kingdom of Satan ushered in the everlasting reign of God (11, 15; 12, 10).*

*Even the forces of evil unwittingly carry out the divine plan (17, 17), for God is the sovereign Lord of history.*

*The Book of Revelation had its origin in a time of crisis, but it remains valid and meaningful for Christians of all time. In the face of apparently insuperable evil, either from within or from without, all Christians are called to trust in Jesus' promise, "Behold, I am with you always, until the end of the age" (Mt 28, 20). Those who remain steadfast in their faith and confidence in the risen Lord need have no fear. Suffering, persecution, even death by martyrdom, though remaining impenetrable mysteries of evil, do not comprise an absurd dead end. No matter what adversity or sacrifice Christians may endure, they will in the end triumph over Satan and his forces because of their fidelity to Christ the victor. This is the enduring message of the book; it is a message of hope and consolation and challenge for all who dare to believe.*

*The author of the book calls himself John (1, 1.4.9; 22, 8), who because of his Christian faith has been exiled to the rocky island of Patmos, a Roman penal colony. Although he never claims to be John the apostle, whose name is attached to the fourth gospel, he was so identified by several of the early church Fathers, including Justin, Irenaeus, Clement of Alexandria, Tertullian, Cyprian, and Hippolytus. This identification, however, was denied by other Fathers, including Denis of Alexandria, Eusebius of Caesarea, Cyril of Jerusalem, Gregory Nazianzen, and John Chrysostom. Indeed, vocabulary, grammar, and style make it doubtful that the book could have been put into its present form by the same person(s) responsible for the fourth gospel. Nevertheless, there are definite linguistic and theological affinities between the two books. The tone of the letters to the seven churches (1, 4—3, 22) is indicative of the great authority the author enjoyed over the Christian communities in Asia. It is possible, therefore, that he was a disciple of John the apostle, who is traditionally associated with that part of the world. The date of the book in its present form is probably near the end of the reign of Domitian (A.D. 81–96), a fierce persecutor of the Christians.*

*The principal divisions of the Book of Revelation are the following:*

*I. Prologue (1, 1–3)*
*II. Letters to the Churches of Asia (1, 4—3, 22)*
*III. God and the Lamb in Heaven (4, 1—5, 14)*
*IV. The Seven Seals, Trumpets, and Plagues, with Interludes (6, 1—16, 21)*
*V. The Punishment of Babylon and the Destruction of Pagan Nations (17, 1—20, 15)*
*VI. The New Creation (21, 1—22, 5)*
*VII. Epilogue (22, 6–21)*

## *I: PROLOGUE*

### CHAPTER 1

**1** [a]*The revelation of Jesus Christ, which God gave to him, to show his servants what must happen soon. He made it known by sending his angel to his servant John, **2** who gives witness to the word of God and to the testimony of Jesus Christ by reporting what he saw. **3** [b]*Blessed is the one who reads aloud and blessed are those who listen to this prophetic message and heed what is written in it, for the appointed time is near.

## *II: LETTERS TO THE CHURCHES OF ASIA*

**Greeting** **4** [c]*John, to the seven churches in Asia: grace to you and peace from him who is and who was and who is to come, and from the

a 22, 6-8.20; Dn 2, 28 / 19, 10.
b 22, 7 / Lk 11, 28.
c 8; 4, 8; 11, 17; 16, 5; Ex 3, 14.

*

1, 1–3: This prologue describes the source, contents, and audience of the book and forms an inclusion with the epilogue (22, 6–21), with its similar themes and expressions.

1, 3: *Blessed is the one:* this is the first of seven beatitudes in this book; the others are in 14, 13; 16, 15; 19, 9; 20, 6; 22, 7.14. *This prophetic message:* literally, "the words of the prophecy"; so 22, 7.10.18.19 by inclusion. *The appointed time:* when Jesus will return in glory; cf 1, 7; 3, 11; 22, 7.10.12.20.

1, 4–8: Although Revelation begins and ends (22, 21) with Christian epistolary formulae, there is nothing between chs 4 and 22 resembling a letter. The author here employs the standard word order for greetings in Greek letter writing: "N. to N., greetings . . ."; see the note on Rom 1, 1.

1, 4: *Seven churches in Asia:* Asia refers to the Roman province of that name in western Asia Minor (modern Turkey); these representative churches are mentioned by name in v 11, and each is the recipient of a message (2, 1—3, 22). *Seven* is the biblical number suggesting fullness and completeness; thus the seer is writing for the whole church.

seven spirits before his throne, **5** [d]*and from
Jesus Christ, the faithful witness, the firstborn
of the dead and ruler of the kings of the earth.
To him who loves us and has freed us from our
sins by his blood, **6** [e]who has made us into a
kingdom, priests for his God and Father, to him
be glory and power forever [and ever]. Amen.

**7** [f]Behold, he is coming amid the clouds,
and every eye will see him,
even those who pierced him.
All the peoples of the earth will lament him.
Yes. Amen.

**8** [g]*"I am the Alpha and the Omega," says the
Lord God, "the one who is and who was and
who is to come, the almighty."

**The First Vision** **9** *I, John, your brother,
who share with you the distress, the kingdom,
and the endurance we have in Jesus, found myself on the island called Patmos because I proclaimed God's word and gave testimony to
Jesus. **10** *I was caught up in spirit on the
Lord's day and heard behind me a voice as loud
as a trumpet, **11** *which said, "Write on a
scroll what you see and send it to the seven
churches: to Ephesus, Smyrna, Pergamum,
Thyatira, Sardis, Philadelphia, and Laodicea."
**12** *Then I turned to see whose voice it was that
spoke to me, and when I turned, I saw seven
gold lampstands **13** [h]*and in the midst of the
lampstands one like a son of man, wearing an
ankle-length robe, with a gold sash around his
chest. **14** *The hair of his head was as white as
white wool or as snow, and his eyes were like
a fiery flame. **15** *His feet were like polished
brass refined in a furnace, and his voice was like
the sound of rushing water. **16** [i]*In his right
hand he held seven stars. A sharp two-edged
sword came out of his mouth, and his face shone
like the sun at its brightest.

**17** [j]*When I caught sight of him, I fell down
at his feet as though dead. He touched me with
his right hand and said, "Do not be afraid. I am
the first and the last, **18** *the one who lives.
Once I was dead, but now I am alive forever and
ever. I hold the keys to death and the netherworld. **19** *Write down, therefore, what you
have seen, and what is happening, and what will
happen afterwards. **20** *This is the secret meaning of the seven stars you saw in my right hand,
and of the seven gold lampstands: the seven
stars are the angels of the seven churches, and
the seven lampstands are the seven churches.

## CHAPTER 2

**To Ephesus** **1** *"To the angel of the
church in Ephesus, write this:
" 'The one who holds the seven stars in his
right hand and walks in the midst of the seven

---

d 3, 14; 1 Cor 15, 20; Col 1, 18 / Heb 9, 14; 1 Pt 1, 19;1 Jn 1, 7.
e Ex 19, 6; 1 Pt 2, 9.
f Dn 7, 13 / Zec 12, 10; Mt 24, 30; Jn 19, 37.
g 17; 21, 6; 22, 13; Is 41, 4; 44, 6; 48, 12.
h Dn 7, 13; 10, 5.
i Heb 4, 12.
j Dn 8, 18 / 1, 8.

---

*

1, 5: *Freed us:* the majority of Greek manuscripts and several early versions read "washed us"; but "freed us" is supported by the best manuscripts and fits well with Old Testament imagery, e.g., Is 40, 2.

1, 8: *The Alpha and the Omega:* the first and last letters of the Greek alphabet. In 22, 13 the same words occur together with the expressions "the First and the Last, the Beginning and the End"; cf 17; 2, 8; 21, 6; Is 41, 4; 44, 6.

1, 9–20: In this first vision, the seer is commanded to write what he sees to the seven churches (9–11). He sees Christ in glory, whom he depicts in stock apocalyptic imagery (12–16), and hears him describe himself in terms meant to encourage Christians by emphasizing his victory over death (17–20).

1, 9: *Island called Patmos:* one of the Sporades islands in the Aegean Sea, some fifty miles south of Ephesus, used by the Romans as a penal colony. *Because I proclaimed God's word:* literally, "on account of God's word."

1, 10: *The Lord's day:* Sunday. *As loud as a trumpet:* the imagery is derived from the theophany at Sinai (Ex 19, 16.19; cf Heb 12, 19 and the trumpet in other eschatological settings in Is 27, 13; Jl 2, 1; Mt 24, 31; 1 Cor 15, 52; 1 Thes 4, 16).

1, 11: *Scroll:* a papyrus roll.

1, 12–16: A symbolic description of Christ in glory. The metaphorical language is not to be understood literally; cf Introduction.

1, 13: *Son of man:* see the note on Mk 8, 31. *Ankle-length robe:* Christ is priest; cf Ex 28, 4; 29, 5; Wis 18, 24; Zec 3, 4. *Gold sash:* Christ is king; cf Ex 28, 4; 1 Mc 10, 89; 11, 58; Dn 10, 5.

1, 14: *Hair . . . as white as white wool or as snow:* Christ is eternal, clothed with the dignity that belonged to the "Ancient of Days"; cf 18; Dn 7, 9. *His eyes were like a fiery flame:* Christ is portrayed as all-knowing; cf 2, 23; Ps 7, 10; Jer 17, 10; and similar expressions in 2, 18; 19, 12; cf Dn 10, 6.

1, 15: *His feet . . . furnace:* Christ is depicted as unchangeable; cf Ez 1, 27; Dn 10, 6. The Greek word translated "refined" is unconnected grammatically with any other word in the sentence. *His voice . . . water:* Christ speaks with divine authority; cf Ez 1, 24.

1, 16: *Seven stars:* in the pagan world, Mithras and the Caesars were represented with seven stars in their right hand, symbolizing their universal dominion. *A sharp two-edged sword:* this refers to the word of God (cf Eph 6, 17; Heb 4, 12) that will destroy unrepentant sinners; cf 2, 16; 19, 15; Wis 18, 15; Is 11, 4; 49, 2. *His face . . . brightest:* this symbolizes the divine majesty of Christ; cf 10, 1; 21, 23; Jgs 5, 31; Is 60, 19; Mt 17, 2.

1, 17: It was an Old Testament belief that for sinful human beings to see God was to die; cf Ex 19, 21; 33, 20; Jgs 6, 22–23; Is 6, 5.

1, 18: *Netherworld:* Greek Hades, Hebrew Sheol, the abode of the dead; cf 20, 13–14; Nm 16, 33.

1, 19: *What you have seen, and what is happening, and what will happen afterwards:* the three parts of the Book of Revelation, the vision (10–20), the situation in the seven churches (chs 2–3), and the events of chs 6–22.

1, 20: *Secret meaning:* literally, "mystery." *Angels:* these are the presiding spirits of the seven churches. Angels were thought to be in charge of the physical world (cf 7, 1; 14, 18; 16, 5) and of nations (Dn 10, 13; 12, 1), communities (the seven churches), and individuals (Mt 18, 10; Acts 12, 15). Some have seen in the "angel" of each of the seven churches its pastor or a personification of the spirit of the congregation.

2, 1—3, 22: Each of the seven letters follows the same pattern: address; description of the exalted Christ; blame and/or praise for the church addressed; threat and/or admoni-

gold lampstands says this: **2** *"I know your
works, your labor, and your endurance, and that
you cannot tolerate the wicked; you have tested
those who call themselves apostles but are not,
and discovered that they are impostors.
**3** Moreover, you have endurance and have suffered for my name, and you have not grown
weary. **4** Yet I hold this against you: you have
lost the love you had at first. **5** Realize how far
you have fallen. Repent, and do the works you
did at first. Otherwise, I will come to you and
remove your lampstand from its place, unless
you repent. **6** *But you have this in your favor:
you hate the works of the Nicolaitans, which I
also hate.

**7** [k]*" ' "Whoever has ears ought to hear
what the Spirit says to the churches. To the
victor I will give the right to eat from the tree
of life that is in the garden of God." ' "

**To Smyrna** **8** *"To the angel of the church
in Smyrna, write this:

" 'The first and the last, who once died but
came to life, says this: **9** [l]*"I know your tribulation and poverty, but you are rich. I know the
slander of those who claim to be Jews and are
not, but rather are members of the assembly of
Satan. **10** Do not be afraid of anything that you
are going to suffer. Indeed, the devil will throw
some of you into prison, that you may be tested,
and you will face an ordeal for ten days. Remain
faithful until death, and I will give you the
crown of life.

**11** [m]*" ' "Whoever has ears ought to hear
what the Spirit says to the churches. The victor
shall not be harmed by the second death." '

**To Pergamum** **12** *"To the angel of the
church in Pergamum, write this:

" 'The one with the sharp two-edged sword
says this: **13** *"I know that you live where
Satan's throne is, and yet you hold fast to my
name and have not denied your faith in me, not
even in the days of Antipas, my faithful witness,
who was martyred among you, where Satan
lives. **14** [n]*Yet I have a few things against you.
You have some people there who hold to the
teaching of Balaam, who instructed Balak to put
a stumbling block before the Israelites: to eat
food sacrificed to idols and to play the harlot.
**15** Likewise, you also have some people who
hold to the teaching of [the] Nicolaitans.
**16** Therefore, repent. Otherwise, I will come to
you quickly and wage war against them with the
sword of my mouth.

**17** [o]* ' "Whoever has ears ought to hear
what the Spirit says to the churches. To the

k 11.17.29; 3, 6.13.22; 13, 9; Mt 11, 15.
l Jas 2, 5.
m 20, 6.14; 21, 8.
n Nm 22-24; 25, 1-3; 31, 16; 2 Pt 2, 15; Jude 11.
o Is 62, 2; 65, 15.

* tion; final exhortation and promise to all Christians.

2, 1–7: The letter to Ephesus praises the members of the church there for their works and virtues, including discerning false teachers (2–3), but admonishes them to repent and return to their former devotion (4–5). It concludes with a reference to the Nicolaitans (see the note on 6) and a promise that the victor will have access to eternal life (7).

2, 1: *Ephesus:* this great ancient city had a population of ca. 250,000; it was the capital of the Roman province of Asia and the commercial, cultural, and religious center of Asia. The other six churches were located in the same province, situated roughly in a circle; they were selected for geographical reasons rather than for the size of their Christian communities. *Walks in the midst of the seven gold lampstands:* this signifies that Christ is always present in the church; see the note on 1, 4.

2, 2: *Who call themselves . . . impostors:* this refers to unauthorized and perverse missionaries; cf Acts 20, 29–30.

2, 6: *Nicolaitans:* these are perhaps the impostors of v 2; see the note on vv 14–15. There is little evidence for connecting this group with Nicolaus, the proselyte from Antioch, mentioned in Acts 6, 5.

2, 7: *Victor:* referring to any Christian individual who holds fast to the faith and does God's will in the face of persecution. *The tree of life that is in the garden of God:* this is a reference to the tree in the primeval paradise (Gn 2, 9); cf 22, 2.14.19. The decree excluding humanity from the tree of life has been revoked by Christ.

2, 8–11: The letter to Smyrna encourages the Christians in this important commercial center by telling them that although they are impoverished, they are nevertheless rich, and calls those Jews who are slandering them members of the assembly of Satan (9). There is no admonition; rather, the Christians are told that they will suffer much, even death, but the time of tribulation will be short compared to their eternal reward (10), and they will thus escape final damnation (11).

2, 8: *Smyrna:* modern Izmir, ca. thirty miles north of Ephesus, and the chief city of Lydia, with a temple to the goddess Roma. It was renowned for its loyalty to Rome, and it also had a large Jewish community very hostile toward Christians.

2, 9–10: The church in Smyrna was materially poor but spiritually rich. Accusations made by Jewish brethren there occasioned the persecution of Christians; cf Acts 14, 2.19; 17, 5.13.

2, 11: *The second death:* this refers to the eternal death, when sinners will receive their final punishment; cf 20, 6.14–15; 21, 8.

2, 12–17: The letter to Pergamum praises the members of the church for persevering in their faith in Christ even in the midst of a pagan setting and in face of persecution and martyrdom (13). But it admonishes them about members who advocate an unprincipled morality (14; cf 2 Pt 2, 15; Jude 11) and others who follow the teaching of the Nicolaitans (15; see the note there). It urges them to repent (16) and promises them the hidden manna and Christ's amulet (17).

2, 12: *Pergamum:* modern Bergama, ca. forty-five miles northeast of Smyrna, a center for various kinds of pagan worship. It also had an outstanding library (the word *parchment* is derived from its name).

2, 13: *Satan's throne:* the reference is to emperor worship and other pagan practices that flourished in Pergamum, perhaps specifically to the white marble altar erected and dedicated to Zeus by Eumenes II (197–160 B.C.).

2, 14–15: Like Balaam, the biblical prototype of the religious compromiser (cf Nm 25, 1–3; 31, 16; 2 Pt 2, 15; Jude 11), the Nicolaitans in Pergamum and Ephesus (6) accommodated their Christian faith to paganism. They abused the principle of liberty enunciated by Paul (1 Cor 9, 19–23).

2, 17: *The hidden manna:* this is the food of life; cf Ps 78, 24–25. *White amulet:* literally, "white stone," on which was written a magical name, whose power could be tapped by one who knew the secret name. It is used here as a symbol of victory and joy; cf 3, 4–5. *New name:* this is a reference to the

victor I shall give some of the hidden manna; I
shall also give a white amulet upon which is
inscribed a new name, which no one knows
except the one who receives it.'"

**To Thyatira** 18 *"To the angel of the
church in Thyatira, write this:
"'The Son of God, whose eyes are like a
fiery flame and whose feet are like polished
brass, says this: 19 "I know your works, your
love, faith, service, and endurance, and that
your last works are greater than the first.
20 *Yet I hold this against you, that you tolerate the woman Jezebel, who calls herself a
prophetess, who teaches and misleads my servants to play the harlot and to eat food sacrificed
to idols. 21 I have given her time to repent, but
she refuses to repent of her harlotry. 22 So I
will cast her on a sickbed and plunge those who
commit adultery with her into intense suffering
unless they repent of her works. 23 [p]*I will
also put her children to death. Thus shall all the
churches come to know that I am the searcher
of hearts and minds and that I will give each of
you what your works deserve. 24 *But I say to
the rest of you in Thyatira, who do not uphold
this teaching and know nothing of the so-called
deep secrets of Satan: on you I will place no
further burden, 25 except that you must hold
fast to what you have until I come.

26 [q]*" ' "To the victor, who keeps to my
ways until the end,
I will give authority over the nations.
27 He will rule them with an iron rod.
Like clay vessels will they be smashed,
28 just as I received authority from my Father.
And to him I will give the morning star.
29 " ' "Whoever has ears ought to hear
what the Spirit says to the churches." '

## CHAPTER 3

**To Sardis** 1 *"To the angel of the church
in Sardis, write this:
"'The one who has the seven spirits of God
and the seven stars says this: "I know your
works, that you have the reputation of being
alive, but you are dead. 2 Be watchful and
strengthen what is left, which is going to die, for
I have not found your works complete in the
sight of my God. 3 [r]Remember then how you
accepted and heard; keep it, and repent. If you
are not watchful, I will come like a thief, and
you will never know at what hour I will come
upon you. 4 [s]However, you have a few people
in Sardis who have not soiled their garments;
they will walk with me dressed in white, because they are worthy.
5 [t]*" ' "The victor will thus be dressed in
white, and I will never erase his name from the
book of life but will acknowledge his name in
the presence of my Father and of his angels.
6 " ' "Whoever has ears ought to hear what
the Spirit says to the churches." ' "

**To Philadelphia** 7 [u]*"To the angel of the
church in Philadelphia, write this:

p 1 Sm 16, 7; Jer 11, 20; 17, 10.
q 12, 5; Ps 2, 8-9.
r Mt 24, 42-44; Mk 13, 33; 1 Thes 5, 2; 2 Pt 3, 10.
s 7, 13-14.
t Ps 69, 29; Dn 12, 1 / Mt 10, 32.
u Is 22, 22; Mt 16, 19.

*

Christian's rebirth in Christ; cf 3, 12; 19, 12; Is 62, 2; 65, 15.

2, 18–29: The letter to Thyatira praises the progress in virtue of this small Christian community (19) but admonishes them for tolerating a false prophet who leads them astray (20). Her fate is sealed, but there is hope of repentance for her followers (21–22). Otherwise, they too shall die (23). They are warned against Satanic power or knowledge (24–25). Those who remain faithful will share in the messianic reign, having authority over nations (26–27), and will in fact possess Christ himself (28).

2, 18: *Thyatira:* modern Akhisar, ca. forty miles southeast of Pergamum, a frontier town famous for its workers' guilds (cf Acts 16, 14), membership in which may have involved festal meals in pagan temples.

2, 20: The scheming and treacherous Jezebel of old (cf 1 Kgs 19, 1–2; 21, 1–14; 2 Kgs 9, 22.30–34) introduced pagan customs into the religion of Israel; this new Jezebel was doing the same to Christianity.

2, 23: *Children:* spiritual descendants.

2, 24: *The so-called deep secrets of Satan:* literally, "the deep things of Satan," a scathing reference to the perverse teaching of the Nicolaitans (15).

2, 26–28: The Christian who perseveres in faith will share in Christ's messianic authority (cf Ps 2, 8–9) and resurrection victory over death, symbolized by the morning star; cf 22, 16.

2, 26: *Who keeps to my ways:* literally, "who keeps my works."

3, 1–6: The letter to Sardis does not praise the community but admonishes its members to watchfulness, mutual support, and repentance (2–3). The few who have remained pure and faithful will share Christ's victory and will be inscribed in the book of life (4–5).

3, 1: *Sardis:* this city, located ca. thirty miles southeast of Thyatira, was once the capital of Lydia, known for its wealth at the time of Croesus (6th century B.C.). Its citadel, reputed to be unassailable, was captured by surprise, first by Cyrus and later by Antiochus. The church is therefore warned to be on guard.

3, 5: *In white:* white is a sign of victory and joy as well as resurrection; see the note on 2, 17. *The book of life:* the roll in which the names of the redeemed are kept; cf 13, 8; 17, 8; 20, 12.15; 21, 27; Phil 4, 3; Dn 12, 1. They will be acknowledged by Christ in heaven; cf Mt 10, 32.

3, 7–13: The letter to Philadelphia praises the Christians there for remaining faithful even with their limited strength (8). Members of the assembly of Satan are again singled out (9; see 2, 9 above). There is no admonition; rather, the letter promises that they will be kept safe at the great trial (10–11) and that the victors will become pillars of the heavenly temple, upon which three names will be inscribed: God, Jerusalem, and Christ (12).

3, 7: *Philadelphia:* modern Alasehir, ca. thirty miles southeast of Sardis, founded by Attalus II Philadelphus of Pergamum to be an "open door" (8) for Greek culture; it was destroyed by an earthquake in A.D. 17. Rebuilt by money from the Emperor Tiberius, the city was renamed Neo-Caesarea; this may explain the allusions to "name" in v 12. *Key of David:* to the heavenly city of David (cf Is 22, 22), "the new Jerusalem" (12), over which Christ has supreme authority.

" 'The holy one, the true,
who holds the key of David,
who opens and no one shall close,
who closes and no one shall open,
says this:

8 *" ' "I know your works (behold, I have
left an open door before you, which no one can
close). You have limited strength, and yet you
have kept my word and have not denied my
name. 9 [v]Behold, I will make those of the assembly of Satan who claim to be Jews and are
not, but are lying, behold I will make them
come and fall prostrate at your feet, and they
will realize that I love you. 10 *Because you
have kept my message of endurance, I will keep
you safe in the time of trial that is going to come
to the whole world to test the inhabitants of the
earth. 11 [w]I am coming quickly. Hold fast to
what you have, so that no one may take your
crown.

12 [x]*" ' "The victor I will make into a pillar
in the temple of my God, and he will never leave
it again. On him I will inscribe the name of my
God and the name of the city of my God, the
new Jerusalem, which comes down out of heav-
en from my God, as well as my new name.

13 " ' "Whoever has ears ought to hear
what the Spirit says to the churches." '

**To Laodicea** 14 [y]*"To the angel of the
church in Laodicea, write this:

" 'The Amen, the faithful and true witness,
the source of God's creation, says this: 15 *"I
know your works; I know that you are neither
cold nor hot. I wish you were either cold or hot.
16 *So, because you are lukewarm, neither hot
nor cold, I will spit you out of my mouth.
17 [z]*For you say, 'I am rich and affluent and
have no need of anything," and yet do not
realize that you are wretched, pitiable, poor,
blind, and naked. 18 *I advise you to buy from
me gold refined by fire so that you may be rich,
and white garments to put on so that your
shameful nakedness may not be exposed, and
buy ointment to smear on your eyes so that you
may see. 19 [a]Those whom I love, I reprove and
chastise. Be earnest, therefore, and repent.

20 *" ' "Behold, I stand at the door and
knock. If anyone hears my voice and opens the
door, [then] I will enter his house and dine with
him, and he with me. 21 [b]I will give the victor
the right to sit with me on my throne, as I myself
first won the victory and sit with my Father on
his throne.

22 " ' "Whoever has ears ought to hear
what the Spirit says to the churches." ' "

## *III: GOD AND THE LAMB IN HEAVEN*

## CHAPTER 4

**Vision of Heavenly Worship** 1 *After
this I had a vision of an open door to heaven,
and I heard the trumpetlike voice that had spoken to me before, saying, "Come up here and

v 2, 9 / Is 45, 14; 60, 14.
w 2, 25; 22, 7.20.
x 21, 2-3; Ez 48, 35 / 19, 13.
y 1, 5.
z Prv 13, 7; Lk 12, 21.
a Prv 3, 11-12; 1 Cor 11, 32; Heb 12, 5-11.
b Lk 22, 28-30; Mt 19, 28.

*

3, 8: *An open door:* opportunities for sharing and proclaiming the faith; cf Acts 14, 27; 1 Cor 16, 9; 2 Cor 2, 12.

3, 10: *My message of endurance:* this does not refer to a saying of Jesus about patience but to the example of Christ's patient endurance. *The inhabitants of the earth:* literally, "those who live on the earth." This expression, which also occurs in 6, 10; 8, 13; 11, 10; 13, 8.12.14; 17, 2.8, always refers to the pagan world.

3, 12: *Pillar:* this may be an allusion to the rebuilding of the city; see the note on v 7. *New Jerusalem:* it is described in 21, 10—22, 5.

3, 14–22: The letter to Laodicea reprimands the community for being lukewarm (15–16), but no particular faults are singled out. Their material prosperity is contrasted with their spiritual poverty, the violet tunics that were the source of their wealth with the white robe of baptism, and their famous eye ointment with true spiritual perception (17–18). But Christ's chastisement is inspired by love and a desire to be allowed to share the messianic banquet with his followers in the heavenly kingdom (19–21).

3, 14: *Laodicea:* ca. forty miles southeast of Philadelphia and ca. eighty miles east of Ephesus, a wealthy industrial and commercial center, with a renowned medical school. It exported fine woolen garments and was famous for its eye salves. It was so wealthy that it was proudly rebuilt without outside aid after the devastating earthquake of A.D. 60/61. *The Amen:* this is a divine title (cf Hebrew text of Is 65, 16) applied to Christ; cf 2 Cor 1, 20. *Source of God's creation:* literally, "the beginning of God's creation," a concept found also in Jn 1, 3; Col 1, 16–17, Heb 1, 2; cf Prv 8, 22–31; Wis 9, 1–2.

3, 15–16: Halfhearted commitment to the faith is nauseating to Christ; cf Rom 12, 11.

3, 16: *Spit:* literally, "vomit." The image is that of a beverage that should be either hot or cold. Perhaps there is an allusion to the hot springs of Hierapolis across the Lycus river from Laodicea, which would have been lukewarm by the time they reached Laodicea.

3, 17: Economic prosperity occasioned spiritual bankruptcy.

3, 18: *Gold . . . fire:* God's grace. *White garments:* symbol of an upright life; the city was noted for its violet/purple cloth. *Ointment . . . eyes:* to remove spiritual blindness; one of the city's exports was eye ointment (see the note on 3, 14).

3, 20: Christ invites all to the messianic banquet in heaven; cf Is 25, 6; Lk 14, 15; 22, 30.

4, 1–11: The seer now describes a vision of the heavenly court in worship of God enthroned. He reverently avoids naming or describing God but pictures twenty-four elders in priestly and regal attire (4) and God's throne and its surroundings made of precious gems and other symbols that traditionally express the majesty of God (5–6). Universal creation is represented by the four living creatures (6–7). Along with the twenty-four elders, they praise God unceasingly in humble adoration (8–11).

4, 1: The ancients viewed heaven as a solid vault, entered by way of actual doors.

I will show you what must happen afterwards."
2 [c]*At once I was caught up in spirit. A throne
was there in heaven, and on the throne sat 3 one
whose appearance sparkled like jasper and carnelian. Around the throne was a halo as brilliant
as an emerald. 4 [d]*Surrounding the throne I
saw twenty-four other thrones on which twenty-four elders sat, dressed in white garments and
with gold crowns on their heads. 5 *From the
throne came flashes of lightning, rumblings,
and peals of thunder. Seven flaming torches
burned in front of the throne, which are the
seven spirits of God. 6 [e]*In front of the throne
was something that resembled a sea of glass like
crystal.

In the center and around the throne, there
were four living creatures covered with eyes in
front and in back. 7 *The first creature resembled a lion, the second was like a calf, the third
had a face like that of a human being, and the
fourth looked like an eagle in flight. 8 [f]*The
four living creatures, each of them with six
wings, were covered with eyes inside and out.
Day and night they do not stop exclaiming:

"Holy, holy, holy is the Lord God
almighty,
who was, and who is, and who is to
come."

9 Whenever the living creatures give glory
and honor and thanks to the one who sits on the
throne, who lives forever and ever,

10 the twenty-four elders fall down before
the one who sits on the throne and worship him,
who lives forever and ever. They throw down
their crowns before the throne, exclaiming:

11 [g]"Worthy are you, Lord our God,
to receive glory and honor and power,
for you created all things;
because of your will they came to be and
were created."

## CHAPTER 5

**The Scroll and the Lamb** 1 [h]*I saw a
scroll in the right hand of the one who sat on the
throne. It had writing on both sides and was
sealed with seven seals. 2 Then I saw a mighty
angel who proclaimed in a loud voice, "Who is
worthy to open the scroll and break its seals?"
3 But no one in heaven or on earth or under the
earth was able to open the scroll or to examine
it. 4 I shed many tears because no one was
found worthy to open the scroll or to examine
it. 5 [i]*One of the elders said to me, "Do not
weep. The lion of the tribe of Judah, the root of
David, has triumphed, enabling him to open the
scroll with its seven seals."
6 [j]*Then I saw standing in the midst of the
throne and the four living creatures and the elders, a Lamb that seemed to have been slain. He
had seven horns and seven eyes; these are the
[seven] spirits of God sent out into the whole
world. 7 He came and received the scroll from
the right hand of the one who sat on the throne.
8 When he took it, the four living creatures and
the twenty-four elders fell down before the
Lamb. Each of the elders held a harp and gold
bowls filled with incense, which are the prayers
of the holy ones. 9 They sang a new hymn:

"Worthy are you to receive the scroll
and to break open its seals,
for you were slain and with your blood
you purchased for God
those from every tribe and tongue, people
and nation.

---

c Is 6, 1 / Ez 1, 26-28.
d Is 24, 23.
e Ex 24, 10.
f Is 6, 2-3 / 1, 4.8; 11, 17; 16, 5.
g Rom 4, 17; 16, 27.
h Is 29, 11.
i Is 11, 1.10; Rom 15, 12.
j Jn 1, 29.

---

4, 2–8: Much of the imagery here is taken from Ez 1 and 10.

4, 4: *Twenty-four elders:* these represent the twelve tribes of Israel and the twelve apostles; cf 21, 12–14.

4, 5: *Flashes of lightning, rumblings, and peals of thunder:* as in other descriptions of God's appearance or activity; cf 8, 5; 11, 19; 16, 18; Ex 19, 16; Ez 1, 4.13. *The seven spirits of God:* the seven "angels of the presence" as in 8, 2 and Tb 12, 15.

4, 6: *A sea of glass like crystal:* an image adapted from Ez 1, 22–26. *Four living creatures:* these are symbols taken from Ez 1, 5–21; they are identified as cherubim in Ez 10, 20. *Covered with eyes:* these suggest God's knowledge and concern.

4, 7: *Lion . . . calf . . . human being . . . eagle:* these symbolize, respectively, what is noblest, strongest, wisest, and swiftest in creation. *Calf:* traditionally translated "ox," the Greek word refers to a heifer or young bull. Since the second century, these four creatures have been used as symbols of the evangelists Mark, Luke, Matthew, and John, respectively.

4, 8: *Six wings:* like the seraphim of Is 6, 2.

5, 1–14: The seer now describes a papyrus roll in God's right hand (1) with seven seals indicating the importance of the message. A mighty angel asks who is worthy to open the scroll, i.e., who can accomplish God's salvific plan (2). There is despair at first when no one in creation can do it (3–4). But the seer is comforted by an elder who tells him that Christ, called the lion of the tribe of Judah, has won the right to open it (5). Christ then appears as a Lamb, coming to receive the scroll from God (6–7), for which he is acclaimed as at a coronation (8–10). This is followed by a doxology of the angels (11–12) and then finally by the heavenly church united with all of creation (13–14).

5, 1: *A scroll:* a papyrus roll possibly containing a list of afflictions for sinners (cf Ez 2, 9–10) or God's plan for the world. *Sealed with seven seals:* it is totally hidden from all but God. Only the Lamb (7–9) has the right to carry out the divine plan.

5, 5: *The lion of the tribe of Judah, the root of David:* these are the messianic titles applied to Christ to symbolize his victory; cf 22, 16; Gn 49, 9; Is 11, 1.10; Mt 1, 1.

5, 6: Christ is the Paschal Lamb without blemish, whose blood saved the new Israel from sin and death; cf Ex 12; Is 53, 7; Jn 1, 29.36; Acts 8, 32; 1 Pt 1, 18–19. This is the main title for Christ in Rv, used twenty-eight times. *Seven horns and seven eyes:* Christ has the fullness (see the note on 1, 4) of power (horns) and knowledge (eyes); cf Zec 4, 10. *[Seven] spirits:* as in 1, 4; 3, 1; and 4, 5.

**10** [k]You made them a kingdom and priests for
our God,
and they will reign on earth."

**11** [l]*I looked again and heard the voices of
many angels who surrounded the throne and the
living creatures and the elders. They were
countless in number, **12** and they cried out in a
loud voice:

"Worthy is the Lamb that was slain
to receive power and riches, wisdom and
strength,
honor and glory and blessing."

**13** Then I heard every creature in heaven and
on earth and under the earth and in the sea,
everything in the universe, cry out:

"To the one who sits on the throne and to
the Lamb
be blessing and honor, glory and might,
forever and ever."

**14** The four living creatures answered,
"Amen," and the elders fell down and worshiped.

## *IV: THE SEVEN SEALS, TRUMPETS, AND PLAGUES, WITH INTERLUDES*

## CHAPTER 6

**The First Six Seals** **1** *Then I watched
while the Lamb broke open the first of the seven
seals, and I heard one of the four living creatures
cry out in a voice like thunder, "Come forward." **2** [m]*I looked, and there was a white
horse, and its rider had a bow. He was given a
crown, and he rode forth victorious to further
his victories.
**3** When he broke open the second seal, I
heard the second living creature cry out, "Come
forward." **4** [n]*Another horse came out, a red
one. Its rider was given power to take peace
away from the earth, so that people would
slaughter one another. And he was given a huge
sword.
**5** *When he broke open the third seal, I
heard the third living creature cry out, "Come
forward." I looked, and there was a black
horse, and its rider held a scale in his hand.
**6** [o]*I heard what seemed to be a voice in the
midst of the four living creatures. It said, "A
ration of wheat costs a day's pay, and three
rations of barley cost a day's pay. But do not
damage the olive oil or the wine."
**7** When he broke open the fourth seal, I
heard the voice of the fourth living creature cry
out, "Come forward." **8** [p]*I looked, and there
was a pale green horse. Its rider was named
Death, and Hades accompanied him. They were
given authority over a quarter of the earth, to kill
with sword, famine, and plague, and by means
of the beasts of the earth.
**9** *When he broke open the fifth seal, I saw
underneath the altar the souls of those who had
been slaughtered because of the witness they
bore to the word of God. **10** *They cried out in
a loud voice, "How long will it be, holy and
true master, before you sit in judgment and
avenge our blood on the inhabitants of the
earth?" **11** Each of them was given a white
robe, and they were told to be patient a little
while longer until the number was filled of their

---

k 1, 6; Ex 19, 6; Is 61, 6.
l Dn 7, 10; Jude 14-15.
m Zec 1, 8-10; 6, 1-3.
n Ez 21, 14-16.
o Lv 26, 26; Ez 4, 16-17.
p Ez 14, 21.

---

*

5, 11: *Countless:* literally, "100,000,000 plus 1,000,000," used by the author to express infinity.

6, 1—16, 21: A series of seven disasters now begins as each seal is broken (6, 1—8, 1), followed by a similar series as seven trumpets sound (8, 2—11, 19) and as seven angels pour bowls on the earth causing plagues (15, 1—16, 21). These gloomy sequences are interrupted by longer or shorter scenes suggesting the triumph of God and his witnesses (e.g., chs 7, 10, 11, 12, 13, 14).

6, 1–17: This chapter provides a symbolic description of the contents of the sealed scroll. The breaking of the first four seals reveals four riders. The first rider (of a white horse) is a conquering power (1–2), the second (red horse) a symbol of bloody war (3–4), the third (black horse) a symbol of famine (5–6), the fourth (pale green horse) a symbol of Death himself, accompanied by Hades (the netherworld) as his page (7–8). Verse 8b summarizes the role of all four riders. The breaking of the fifth seal reveals Christian martyrs in an attitude of sacrifice as blood poured out at the foot of an altar begging God for vindication, which will come only when their quota is filled; but they are given a white robe symbolic of victory (9–11). The breaking of the sixth seal reveals typical apocalyptic signs in the sky and the sheer terror of all people at the imminent divine judgment (12–17).

6, 1–8: The imagery is adapted from Zec 1, 8–10; 6, 1–8.

6, 2: *White horse . . . bow:* this may perhaps allude specifically to the Parthians on the eastern border of the Roman empire. Expert in the use of the bow, they constantly harassed the Romans and won a major victory in A.D. 62; see the note on 9, 13–21. But the Old Testament imagery typifies the history of oppression of God's people at all times.

6, 4: *Huge sword:* this is a symbol of war and violence; cf Ez 21, 14–17.

6, 5: *Black horse:* this is a symbol of famine, the usual accompaniment of war in antiquity; cf Lv 26, 26; Ez 4, 16–17. The *scale* is a symbol of shortage of food with a corresponding rise in price.

6, 6: *A day's pay:* literally, "a denarius," a Roman silver coin that constitutes a day's wage in Mt 20, 2. Because of the famine, food was rationed and sold at an exorbitant price. A liter of flour was considered a day's ration in the Greek historians Herodotus and Diogenes Laertius. *Barley:* food of the poor (Jn 6, 9.13; cf 2 Kgs 7, 1.16.18); it was also used to feed animals; cf 1 Kgs 5, 8. *Do not damage:* the olive and the vine are to be used more sparingly in time of famine.

6, 8: *Pale green:* symbol of death and decay; cf Ez 14, 21.

6, 9: *The altar:* this altar corresponds to the altar of holocausts in the temple in Jerusalem; see also 11, 1. *Because of the witness . . . word of God:* literally, "because of the word of God and the witness they had borne."

6, 10: *Holy and true master:* Old Testament usage as well as the context indicates that this is addressed to God rather than to Christ.

fellow servants and brothers who were going to
be killed as they had been.
12 [q]*Then I watched while he broke open
the sixth seal, and there was a great earthquake;
the sun turned as black as dark sackcloth and the
whole moon became like blood. **13** *The stars
in the sky fell to the earth like unripe figs shaken
loose from the tree in a strong wind. **14** [r]*Then
the sky was divided like a torn scroll curling up,
and every mountain and island was moved from
its place. **15** *The kings of the earth, the nobles, the military officers, the rich, the powerful, and every slave and free person hid themselves in caves and among mountain crags.
**16** [s]They cried out to the mountains and the
rocks, "Fall on us and hide us from the face of
the one who sits on the throne and from the
wrath of the Lamb, **17** *because the great day
of their wrath has come and who can withstand
it?"

## CHAPTER 7

**The 144,000 Sealed** 1 [t]*After this I saw
four angels standing at the four corners of the
earth, holding back the four winds of the earth
so that no wind could blow on land or sea or
against any tree. **2** *Then I saw another angel
come up from the East, holding the seal of the
living God. He cried out in a loud voice to the
four angels who were given power to damage
the land and the sea, **3** [u]"Do not damage the
land or the sea or the trees until we put the seal
on the foreheads of the servants of our God."
**4** [v]*I heard the number of those who had been
marked with the seal, one hundred and forty-
four thousand marked from every tribe of the
Israelites: **5** *twelve thousand were marked
from the tribe of Judah, twelve thousand from
the tribe of Reuben, twelve thousand from the
tribe of Gad, **6** twelve thousand from the tribe
of Asher, twelve thousand from the tribe of
Naphtali, twelve thousand from the tribe of Manasseh, **7** twelve thousand from the tribe of
Simeon, twelve thousand from the tribe of Levi,
twelve thousand from the tribe of Issachar,
**8** twelve thousand from the tribe of Zebulun,
twelve thousand from the tribe of Joseph, and
twelve thousand were marked from the tribe of
Benjamin.

**Triumph of the Elect** 9 *After this I had
a vision of a great multitude, which no one
could count, from every nation, race, people,
and tongue. They stood before the throne and
before the Lamb, wearing white robes and holding palm branches in their hands. **10** *They
cried out in a loud voice:

"Salvation comes from our God, who is
seated on the throne,
and from the Lamb."

**11** All the angels stood around the throne and
around the elders and the four living creatures.
They prostrated themselves before the throne,
worshiped God, **12** and exclaimed:

"Amen. Blessing and glory, wisdom and
thanksgiving,
honor, power, and might
be to our God forever and ever. Amen."

**13** Then one of the elders spoke up and said to
me, "Who are these wearing white robes, and
where did they come from?" **14** [w]*I said to
him, "My lord, you are the one who knows."
He said to me, "These are the ones who have
survived the time of great distress; they have

q Jl 3, 4; Mt 24, 29.
r Is 34, 4 / 16, 20.
s Is 2, 19; Hos 10, 8; Lk 23, 30.
t Jer 49, 36; Zec 6, 5.
u Ex 12, 7-14; Ez 9, 4; 2 Cor 1, 22; Eph 1, 13; 4, 30.
v 14, 1.
w Mt 24, 21.

*

6, 12–14: Symbolic rather than literal description of the cosmic upheavals attending the day of the Lord when the martyrs' prayer for vindication (10) would be answered; cf Am 8, 8–9; Is 34, 4; 50, 3; Jl 2, 10; 3, 3–4; Mt 24, 4–36; Mk 13, 5–37; Lk 21, 8–36.

6, 12: *Dark sackcloth:* for mourning, sackcloth was made from the skin of a black goat.

6, 13: *Unripe figs:* literally, "summer (or winter) fruit."

6, 14: *Was divided:* literally, "was split," like a broken papyrus roll torn in two, each half then curling up to form a roll on either side.

6, 15: *Nobles:* literally, "courtiers," "grandees." *Military officers:* literally, "commanders of 1,000 men," used in Josephus and other Greek authors as the equivalent of the Roman *tribunus militum.* The listing of various ranks of society represents the universality of terror at the impending doom.

6, 17: *Their:* this reading is attested in the best manuscripts, but the vast majority read "his" in reference to the wrath of the Lamb in the preceding verse.

7, 1–17: An interlude of two visions precedes the breaking of the seventh seal, just as two more will separate the sixth and seventh trumpets (ch 10). In the first vision (1–8), the elect receive the seal of the living God as protection against the coming cataclysm; cf 14, 1; Ez 9, 4–6; 2 Cor 1, 22; Eph 1, 13; 4, 30. The second vision (9–17) portrays the faithful Christians before God's throne to encourage those on earth to persevere to the end, even to death.

7, 1: *The four corners of the earth:* the earth is seen as a table or rectangular surface.

7, 2: *East:* literally, "rising of the sun." The east was considered the source of light and the place of paradise (Gn 2, 8). *Seal:* whatever was marked by the impression of one's signet ring belonged to that person and was under his protection.

7, 4–9: *One hundred and forty-four thousand:* the square of twelve (the number of Israel's tribes) multiplied by a thousand, symbolic of the new Israel (cf 14, 1–5; Gal 6, 16; Jas 1, 1) that embraces people *from every nation, race, people, and tongue* (9).

7, 5–8: Judah is placed first because of Christ; cf "the Lion of the tribe of Judah" (5, 5). Dan is omitted because of a later tradition that the antichrist would arise from it.

7, 9: *White robes . . . palm branches:* symbols of joy and victory; see the note on 3, 5.

7, 10: *Salvation comes from:* literally, "(let) salvation (be ascribed) to." A similar hymn of praise is found at the fall of the dragon (12, 10) and of Babylon (19, 1).

7, 14: *Time of great distress:* fierce persecution by the Romans; cf Introduction.

washed their robes and made them white in the blood of the Lamb.

15 "For this reason they stand before God's throne
and worship him day and night in his temple.
The one who sits on the throne will shelter them.
16 [x]They will not hunger or thirst anymore,
nor will the sun or any heat strike them.
17 [y]*For the Lamb who is in the center of the throne will shepherd them
and lead them to springs of life-giving water,
and God will wipe away every tear from their eyes."

## CHAPTER 8

**The Seven Trumpets** 1 [z]*When he broke
open the seventh seal, there was silence in heav-
en for about half an hour. 2 [a]And I saw that the
seven angels who stood before God were given
seven trumpets.

**The Gold Censer** 3 [b]*Another angel came
and stood at the altar, holding a gold censer. He
was given a great quantity of incense to offer,
along with the prayers of all the holy ones, on
the gold altar that was before the throne.
4 The smoke of the incense along with the
prayers of the holy ones went up before God
from the hand of the angel. 5 [c]Then the angel
took the censer, filled it with burning coals from
the altar, and hurled it down to the earth. There
were peals of thunder, rumblings, flashes of
lightning, and an earthquake.

**The First Four Trumpets** 6 [d]The seven
angels who were holding the seven trumpets
prepared to blow them.
7 *When the first one blew his trumpet, there
came hail and fire mixed with blood, which was
hurled down to the earth. A third of the land was
burned up, along with a third of the trees and all
green grass.
8 [e]*When the second angel blew his trumpet, something like a large burning mountain
was hurled into the sea. A third of the sea turned
to blood, 9 *a third of the creatures living in the
sea died, and a third of the ships were wrecked.
10 [f]When the third angel blew his trumpet,
a large star burning like a torch fell from the
sky. It fell on a third of the rivers and on the
springs of water. 11 [g]*The star was called
"Wormwood," and a third of all the water
turned to wormwood. Many people died from
this water, because it was made bitter.
12 [h]When the fourth angel blew his trumpet,
a third of the sun, a third of the moon, and a
third of the stars were struck, so that a third of
them became dark. The day lost its light for a
third of the time, as did the night.
13 *Then I looked again and heard an eagle
flying high overhead cry out in a loud voice,
"Woe! Woe! Woe to the inhabitants of the earth
from the rest of the trumpet blasts that the three
angels are about to blow!"

## CHAPTER 9

**The Fifth Trumpet** 1 [i]*Then the fifth angel
blew his trumpet, and I saw a star that had fallen
from the sky to the earth. It was given the key
for the passage to the abyss. 2 [j]It opened the
passage to the abyss, and smoke came up out of
the passage like smoke from a huge furnace.
The sun and the air were darkened by the smoke

x Is 49, 10.
y 21, 4; Is 25, 8.
z Hb 2, 20; Zep 1, 7; Zec 2, 17.
a 4, 5; Tb 12, 15.
b Ps 141, 2; Tb 12, 12.
c Ez 10, 2; Ps 11, 6 / 4, 5; 11, 19; 16, 18.
d 16, 1-21.
e Ex 7, 20.
f Is 14, 12.
g Jer 9, 14.
h Ex 10, 21-23.
i 20, 1.
j Gn 19, 28.

*

7, 17: *Life-giving water:* literally, "the water of life," God's grace, which flows from Christ; cf 21, 6; 22, 1.17; Jn 4, 10.14.

8, 1–13: The breaking of the seventh seal produces at first silence and then seven symbolic disasters, each announced by a trumpet blast, of which the first four form a unit as did the first four seals. A minor liturgy (3–5) is enclosed by a vision of seven angels (2.6). Then follow the first four trumpet blasts, each heralding catastrophes modeled on the plagues of Egypt affecting the traditional prophetic third (cf Ez 5, 12) of the earth, sea, fresh water, and stars (7–12). Finally, there is a vision of an eagle warning of the last three trumpet blasts (13).

8, 1: *Silence in heaven:* as in Zep 1, 7, a prelude to the eschatological woes that are to follow; cf Introduction.

8, 3: *Altar:* there seems to be only one altar in the heavenly temple, corresponding to the altar of holocausts in 6, 9, and here to the altar of incense in Jerusalem; cf also 9, 13; 11, 1; 14, 18; 16, 7.

8, 7: This woe resembles the seventh plague of Egypt (Ex 9, 23–24); cf Jl 3, 3.

8, 8–11: The background of these two woes is the first plague of Egypt (Ex 7, 20–21).

8, 9: *Creatures living in the sea:* literally, "creatures in the sea that had souls."

8, 11: *Wormwood:* an extremely bitter and malignant plant symbolizing the punishment God inflicts on the ungodly; cf Jer 9, 12–14; 23, 15.

8, 13: *Woe! Woe! Woe:* each of the three woes pronounced by the angel represents a separate disaster; cf 9, 12; 11, 14. The final woe, released by the seventh trumpet blast, includes the plagues of ch 16.

9, 1–12: The fifth trumpet heralds a woe containing elements from the eighth and ninth plagues of Egypt (Ex 10, 12–15.21–23) but specifically reminiscent of the invasion of locusts in Jl 1, 4—2, 10.

9, 1: *A star:* late Judaism represented fallen powers as stars (Is 14, 12–15; Lk 10, 18; Jude 13), but a comparison with 1, 20 and 20, 1 suggests that here it means an angel. *The passage to the abyss:* referring to Sheol, the netherworld, where Satan and the fallen angels are kept for a thousand years, to be cast afterwards into the pool of fire; cf 20, 7–10. The abyss was conceived of as a vast subterranean cavern full of fire. Its only link with the earth was a kind of passage or mine shaft, which was kept locked.

from the passage. **3** [k]*Locusts came out of the smoke onto the land, and they were given the same power as scorpions of the earth. **4** They were told not to harm the grass of the earth or any plant or any tree, but only those people who did not have the seal of God on their foreheads. **5** *They were not allowed to kill them but only to torment them for five months; the torment they inflicted was like that of a scorpion when it stings a person. **6** [l]During that time these people will seek death but will not find it, and they will long to die but death will escape them.

**7** [m]*The appearance of the locusts was like that of horses ready for battle. On their heads they wore what looked like crowns of gold; their faces were like human faces, **8** [n]and they had hair like women's hair. Their teeth were like lions' teeth, **9** and they had chests like iron breastplates. The sound of their wings was like the sound of many horse-drawn chariots racing into battle. **10** They had tails like scorpions, with stingers; with their tails they had power to harm people for five months. **11** *They had as their king the angel of the abyss, whose name in Hebrew is Abaddon and in Greek Apollyon.

**12** The first woe has passed, but there are two more to come.

**The Sixth Trumpet** **13** [o]*Then the sixth angel blew his trumpet, and I heard a voice coming from the [four] horns of the gold altar before God, **14** *telling the sixth angel who held the trumpet, "Release the four angels who are bound at the banks of the great river Euphrates." **15** So the four angels were released, who were prepared for this hour, day, month, and year to kill a third of the human race. **16** The number of cavalry troops was two hundred million; I heard their number. **17** [p]*Now in my vision this is how I saw the horses and their riders. They wore red, blue, and yellow breastplates, and the horses' heads were like heads of lions, and out of their mouths came fire, smoke, and sulfur. **18** By these three plagues of fire, smoke, and sulfur that came out of their mouths a third of the human race was killed. **19** For the power of the horses is in their mouths and in their tails; for their tails are like snakes, with heads that inflict harm.

**20** [q]*The rest of the human race, who were not killed by these plagues, did not repent of the works of their hands, to give up the worship of demons and idols made from gold, silver, bronze, stone, and wood, which cannot see or hear or walk. **21** Nor did they repent of their murders, their magic potions, their unchastity, or their robberies.

## CHAPTER 10

### The Angel with the Small Scroll

**1** *Then I saw another mighty angel come down from heaven wrapped in a cloud, with a halo around his head; his face was like the sun and his feet were like pillars of fire. **2** *In his hand he held a small scroll that had been opened. He placed his right foot on the sea and his left foot on the land, **3** [r]and then he cried out in a loud voice as a lion roars. When he cried out, the seven thunders raised their voices, too. **4** When the seven thunders had spoken, I was about to write it down; but I heard a voice from heaven say, "Seal up what the seven thunders have spoken, but do not write it down." **5** Then the angel I saw standing on the sea and on the land raised his right hand to heaven **6** [s]*and swore by the one who lives forever and ever, who created heaven and earth and sea and all that is in them, "There shall be no more delay.

k Ex 10, 12-15; Wis 16, 9.
l Jb 3, 21.
m Jl 2, 4.
n Jl 1, 6.
o Ex 30, 1-3.
p Jb 41, 10-13.
q Ps 135, 15-17; Is 17, 8; Dn 5, 4.
r Ps 29, 3-9; Jer 25, 30; Am 3, 8.
s Dt 32, 40; Dn 12, 7 / Ez 12, 28.

*

9, 3: *Scorpions:* their poisonous sting was proverbial; Ez 2, 6; Lk 11, 12.

9, 5: *For five months:* more or less corresponding to the life-span of locusts.

9, 7–10: Eight characteristics are listed to show the eschatological and diabolical nature of these locusts.

9, 11: *Abaddon:* Hebrew (more precisely, Aramaic) for destruction or ruin. *Apollyon:* Greek for the "Destroyer."

9, 13–21: The sixth trumpet heralds a woe representing another diabolical attack symbolized by an invasion by the Parthians living east of the Euphrates; see the note on 6, 2. At the appointed time (15), the frightful horses act as God's agents of judgment. The imaginative details are not to be taken literally; see Introduction and the note on 6, 12–14.

9, 13: *[Four]:* many Greek manuscripts and versions omit the word. The horns were situated at the four corners of the altar (Ex 27, 2; 30, 2–3); see the note on 8, 3.

9, 14–15: *The four angels:* they are symbolic of the destructive activity that will be extended throughout the universe.

9, 17: *Blue:* literally, "hyacinth-colored." *Yellow:* literally, "sulfurous."

9, 20: *The works of their hands:* i.e., the gods their hands had made.

10, 1—11, 14: An interlude in two scenes (10, 1–11 and 11, 1–14) precedes the sounding of the seventh trumpet; cf 7, 1–17. The first vision describes an angel astride sea and land like a colossus, with a small scroll open, the contents of which indicate that the end is imminent (ch 10). The second vision is of the measuring of the temple and of two witnesses, whose martyrdom means that the kingdom of God is about to be inaugurated.

10, 1–4: *The seven thunders:* God's voice announcing judgment and doom; cf Ps 29, 3–9, where thunder, as the voice of Yahweh, is praised seven times.

10, 2: *He placed . . . on the land:* this symbolizes the universality of the angel's message, as does the figure of the small scroll open to be read.

10, 6: *Heaven and earth and sea:* the three parts of the universe. *No more delay:* cf Dn 12, 7; Hb 2, 3.

**7** [t]*At the time when you hear the seventh angel blow his trumpet, the mysterious plan of
God shall be fulfilled, as he promised to his
servants the prophets."
**8** Then the voice that I had heard from heav-
en spoke to me again and said, "Go, take the
scroll that lies open in the hand of the angel who
is standing on the sea and on the land." **9** *So
I went up to the angel and told him to give me
the small scroll. He said to me, "Take and
swallow it. It will turn your stomach sour, but
in your mouth it will taste as sweet as honey."
**10** [u]I took the small scroll from the angel's
hand and swallowed it. In my mouth it was like
sweet honey, but when I had eaten it, my stomach turned sour. **11** *Then someone said to me,
"You must prophesy again about many peoples, nations, tongues, and kings."

## CHAPTER 11

**The Two Witnesses** **1** [v]*Then I was given
a measuring rod like a staff and I was told,
"Come and measure the temple of God and the
altar, and count those who are worshiping in it.
**2** *But exclude the outer court of the temple; do
not measure it, for it has been handed over to the
Gentiles, who will trample the holy city for
forty-two months. **3** *I will commission my
two witnesses to prophesy for those twelve hundred and sixty days, wearing sackcloth."
**4** [w]*These are the two olive trees and the two
lampstands that stand before the Lord of the
earth. **5** *If anyone wants to harm them, fire
comes out of their mouths and devours their
enemies. In this way, anyone wanting to harm
them is sure to be slain. **6** [x]They have the power
to close up the sky so that no rain can fall during
the time of their prophesying. They also have
power to turn water into blood and to afflict the
earth with any plague as often as they wish.
**7** [y]*When they have finished their testimony, the beast that comes up from the abyss will
wage war against them and conquer them and
kill them. **8** *Their corpses will lie in the main
street of the great city, which has the symbolic
names "Sodom" and "Egypt," where indeed
their Lord was crucified. **9** *Those from every
people, tribe, tongue, and nation will gaze on
their corpses for three and a half days, and they
will not allow their corpses to be buried. **10** The
inhabitants of the earth will gloat over them and
be glad and exchange gifts because these two
prophets tormented the inhabitants of the earth.
**11** [z]But after the three and a half days, a breath
of life from God entered them. When they stood
on their feet, great fear fell on those who saw
them. **12** [a]Then they heard a loud voice from
heaven say to them, "Come up here." So they
went up to heaven in a cloud as their enemies
looked on. **13** *At that moment there was a
great earthquake, and a tenth of the city fell in
ruins. Seven thousand people were killed during
the earthquake; the rest were terrified and gave
glory to the God of heaven.
**14** The second woe has passed, but the third
is coming soon.

**The Seventh Trumpet** **15** *Then the seventh angel blew his trumpet. There were loud
voices in heaven, saying, "The kingdom of the

t Am 3, 7.
u Ez 3, 1-3.
v Ez 40, 3-5 / Zec 2, 5-9.
w Zec 4, 3.14.
x Ex 7, 17.
y Dn 7, 21.
z Ez 37, 5.10.
a 2 Kgs 2, 11.

*

10, 7: *The mysterious plan of God:* literally, "the mystery of God," the end of the present age when the forces of evil will be put down (17, 1—19, 4.11–21; 20, 7–10; cf 2 Thes 2, 6–12; Rom 16, 25–26), and the establishment of the reign of God when all creation will be made new (21, 1—22, 5).

10, 9–10: The small scroll was sweet because it predicted the final victory of God's people; it was sour because it also announced their sufferings. Cf Ez 3, 1–3.

10, 11: This further prophecy is contained in chs 12–22.

11, 1: The temple and altar symbolize the new Israel; see the note on 7, 4–9. The worshipers represent Christians. The measuring of the temple (cf Ez 40, 3—42, 20; 47, 1–12; Zec 2, 5–6) suggests that God will preserve the faithful remnant (cf Is 4, 2–3) who remain true to Christ (14, 1–5).

11, 2: *The outer court:* the Court of the Gentiles. *Trample . . . forty-two months:* the duration of the vicious persecution of the Jews by Antiochus IV Epiphanes (Dn 7, 25; 12, 7); this persecution of three and a half years (half of seven, counted as 1260 days in 3; 12, 6) became the prototype of periods of trial for God's people; cf Lk 4, 25; Jas 5, 17. The reference here is to the persecution by the Romans; cf Introduction.

11, 3: The two witnesses, wearing sackcloth symbolizing lamentation and repentance, cannot readily be identified. Do they represent Moses and Elijah, or the Law and the Prophets, or Peter and Paul? Most probably they refer to the universal church, especially the Christian martyrs, fulfilling the office of witness (two because of Dt 19, 15; cf Mk 6, 7; Jn 8, 17).

11, 4: *The two olive trees and the two lampstands:* the martyrs who stand in the presence of the Lord; the imagery is taken from Zec 4, 1–3.11–14, where the olive trees refer to Zerubbabel and Joshua.

11, 5–6: These details are derived from stories of Moses, who turned *water into blood* (Ex 7, 17–20), and of Elijah, who called down fire from heaven (1 Kgs 18, 36–40; 2 Kgs 1, 10) and closed up the sky for three years (1 Kgs 17, 1; cf 18, 1).

11, 7: *The beast . . . from the abyss:* the Roman emperor Nero, who symbolizes the forces of evil, or the antichrist (13, 1.8; 17, 8); cf Dn 7, 2–8.11–12.19–22 and Introduction.

11, 8: *The great city:* this expression is used constantly in Rv for Babylon, i.e., Rome; cf 14, 8; 16, 19; 17, 18; 18, 2.10.21. *"Sodom" and "Egypt":* symbols of immorality (cf Is 1, 10) and oppression of God's people (cf Ex 1, 11–14). *Where indeed their Lord was crucified:* not the geographical but the symbolic Jerusalem that rejects God and his witnesses, i.e., Rome, called Babylon in chs 16–18; see the note on 17, 9 and Introduction.

11, 9–12: Over the martyrdom (7) of the two witnesses, now called prophets, the ungodly rejoice *for three and a half days,* a symbolic period of time; see the note on v 2. Afterwards they go in triumph to heaven, as did Elijah (2 Kgs 2, 11).

11, 13: *Seven thousand people:* a symbolic sum to represent all social classes (seven) and large numbers (thousands); cf Introduction.

11, 15–19: The seventh trumpet proclaims the coming of God's reign after the victory over diabolical powers; see the note on 10, 7.

world now belongs to our Lord and to his
Anointed, and he will reign forever and ever."
**16** The twenty-four elders who sat on their
thrones before God prostrated themselves and
worshiped God **17** and said:

"We give thanks to you, Lord God
almighty,
who are and who were.
For you have assumed your great power
and have established your reign.
**18** [b]The nations raged,
but your wrath has come,
and the time for the dead to be judged,
and to recompense your servants, the
prophets,
and the holy ones and those who fear
your name,
the small and the great alike,
and to destroy those who destroy the earth."

**19** Then God's temple in heaven was opened,
and the ark of his covenant could be seen in the
temple. There were flashes of lightning, rumblings, and peals of thunder, an earthquake, and
a violent hailstorm.

## CHAPTER 12

**The Woman and the Dragon** **1** [c]*A great
sign appeared in the sky, a woman clothed with
the sun, with the moon under her feet, and on
her head a crown of twelve stars. **2** *She was
with child and wailed aloud in pain as she labored to give birth. **3** [d]*Then another sign appeared in the sky; it was a huge red dragon, with
seven heads and ten horns, and on its heads were
seven diadems. **4** [e]Its tail swept away a third of
the stars in the sky and hurled them down to the
earth. Then the dragon stood before the woman
about to give birth, to devour her child when she
gave birth. **5** [f]*She gave birth to a son, a male
child, destined to rule all the nations with an
iron rod. Her child was caught up to God and
his throne. **6** *The woman herself fled into the
desert where she had a place prepared by God,
that there she might be taken care of for twelve
hundred and sixty days.

**7** *Then war broke out in heaven; Michael
and his angels battled against the dragon. The
dragon and its angels fought back, **8** but they
did not prevail and there was no longer any
place for them in heaven. **9** [g]*The huge dragon, the ancient serpent, who is called the Devil
and Satan, who deceived the whole world, was
thrown down to earth, and its angels were
thrown down with it.

**10** *Then I heard a loud voice in heaven say:
"Now have salvation and power come,
and the kingdom of our God
and the authority of his Anointed.
For the accuser of our brothers is cast out,
who accuses them before our God day and
night.
**11** They conquered him by the blood of the
Lamb
and by the word of their testimony;
love for life did not deter them from
death.
**12** Therefore, rejoice, you heavens,
and you who dwell in them.
But woe to you, earth and sea,
for the Devil has come down to you in
great fury,
for he knows he has but a short time."

**13** [h]When the dragon saw that it had been
thrown down to the earth, it pursued the woman

b Ps 2, 1.5 / Am 3, 7.
c Gn 37, 9.
d Dn 7, 7.
e Dn 8, 10.
f Is 66, 7 / Ps 2, 9.
g Gn 3, 1-4 / Lk 10, 18.
h Gn 3, 15.

*

12, 1—14, 20: This central section of Rv portrays the power of evil, represented by a dragon, in opposition to God and his people. First, the dragon pursues the woman about to give birth, but her son is saved and "caught up to God and his throne" (12, 5). Then Michael and his angels cast the dragon and his angels out of heaven (12, 7–9). After this, the dragon tries to attack the boy indirectly by attacking members of his church (12, 13–18). A beast, symbolizing the Roman empire, then becomes the dragon's agent, mortally wounded but restored to life and worshiped by all the world (13, 1–10). A second beast arises from the land, symbolizing the antichrist, which leads people astray by its prodigies to idolize the first beast (13, 11–18). This is followed by a vision of the Lamb and his faithful ones, and the proclamation of imminent judgment upon the world in terms of the wine of God's wrath (14, 1–20).

12, 1–6: The woman adorned with the sun, the moon, and the stars (images taken from Gn 37, 9–10) symbolizes God's people in the Old and the New Testament. The Israel of old gave birth to the Messiah (5) and then became the new Israel, the church, which suffers persecution by the dragon (6.13–17); cf Is 50, 1; 66, 7; Jer 50, 12. This corresponds to a widespread myth throughout the ancient world that a goddess pregnant with a savior was pursued by a horrible monster; by miraculous intervention, she bore a son who then killed the monster.

12, 2: Because of Eve's sin, the woman gives birth in distress and pain (Gn 3, 16; cf Is 66, 7–14).

12, 3: *Huge red dragon:* the Devil or Satan (cf 9; 20, 2), symbol of the forces of evil, a mythical monster known also as Leviathan (Ps 74, 13–14) or Rahab (Jb 26, 12–13; Ps 89, 11). *Seven diadems:* these are symbolic of the fullness of the dragon's sovereignty over the kingdoms of this world; cf Christ with many diadems (19, 12).

12, 5: *Rule . . . iron rod:* fulfilled in 19, 15; cf Ps 2, 9. *Was caught up to God:* reference to Christ's ascension.

12, 6: God protects the persecuted church in the desert, the traditional Old Testament place of refuge for the afflicted, according to the typology of the Exodus; see the note on 11, 2.

12, 7–12: Michael, mentioned only here in Rv, wins a victory over the dragon. A hymn of praise follows.

12, 7: *Michael:* the archangel, guardian and champion of Israel; cf Dn 10, 13.21; 12, 1; Jude 9. In Hebrew, the name Michael means "Who can compare with God?"; cf 13, 4.

12, 9: *The ancient serpent:* who seduced Eve (Gn 3, 1–6), mother of the human race; cf 20, 2; Eph 6, 11–12. *Was thrown down:* allusion to the expulsion of Satan from heaven; cf Lk 10, 18.

12, 10: *The accuser:* the meaning of the Hebrew word "Satan," found in v 9; Jb 1—2; Zec 3, 1; 1 Chr 21, 1; he continues to accuse Christ's disciples.

who had given birth to the male child. **14** [i]*But
the woman was given the two wings of the great
eagle, so that she could fly to her place in the
desert, where, far from the serpent, she was
taken care of for a year, two years, and a
half-year. **15** *The serpent, however, spewed a
torrent of water out of his mouth after the woman to sweep her away with the current. **16** But
the earth helped the woman and opened its
mouth and swallowed the flood that the dragon
spewed out of its mouth. **17** [j]*Then the dragon
became angry with the woman and went off to
wage war against the rest of her offspring, those
who keep God's commandments and bear witness to Jesus. **18** *It took its position on the
sand of the sea.

## CHAPTER 13

**The First Beast** **1** [k]*Then I saw a beast
come out of the sea with ten horns and seven
heads; on its horns were ten diadems, and on its
heads blasphemous name[s]. **2** [l]*The beast I
saw was like a leopard, but it had feet like a
bear's, and its mouth was like the mouth of a
lion. To it the dragon gave its own power and
throne, along with great authority. **3** *I saw that
one of its heads seemed to have been mortally
wounded, but this mortal wound was healed.
Fascinated, the whole world followed after the
beast. **4** *They worshiped the dragon because it
gave its authority to the beast; they also worshiped the beast and said, "Who can compare
with the beast or who can fight against it?"

**5** [m]*The beast was given a mouth uttering
proud boasts and blasphemies, and it was given
authority to act for forty-two months. **6** It
opened its mouth to utter blasphemies against
God, blaspheming his name and his dwelling
and those who dwell in heaven. **7** [n]It was also
allowed to wage war against the holy ones and
conquer them, and it was granted authority over
every tribe, people, tongue, and nation. **8** [o]All
the inhabitants of the earth will worship it, all
whose names were not written from the foundation of the world in the book of life, which
belongs to the Lamb who was slain.

**9** [p]Whoever has ears ought to hear these
words.
**10** [q]Anyone destined for captivity goes into
captivity.
Anyone destined to be slain by the sword
shall be slain by the sword.

Such is the faithful endurance of the holy ones.

**The Second Beast** **11** *Then I saw another beast come up out of the earth; it had two
horns like a lamb's but spoke like a dragon.
**12** It wielded all the authority of the first beast
in its sight and made the earth and its inhabitants
worship the first beast, whose mortal wound
had been healed. **13** [r]It performed great signs,
even making fire come down from heaven to
earth in the sight of everyone. **14** It deceived
the inhabitants of the earth with the signs it was
allowed to perform in the sight of the first beast,
telling them to make an image for the beast who
had been wounded by the sword and revived.
**15** [s]It was then permitted to breathe life into the
beast's image, so that the beast's image could
speak and [could] have anyone who did not
worship it put to death. **16** [t]It forced all the
people, small and great, rich and poor, free and
slave, to be given a stamped image on their right
hands or their foreheads, **17** so that no one
could buy or sell except one who had the
stamped image of the beast's name or the number that stood for its name.
**18** [u]*Wisdom is needed here; one who un-

i Ex 19, 4; Dn 7, 25; 12, 7.
j Gn 3, 15.
k 2 Thes 2, 3-12.
l Dn 7, 3-6.
m Dn 7, 8.11.25; 8, 14; 9, 27; 11, 36; 12, 7.
n Dn 7, 21.
o 3, 5; 17, 8; 20, 12.
p Mt 13, 9.
q Jer 15, 2.
r Dt 13, 2-4; Mt 24, 24; 2 Thes 2, 9-10.
s Dn 3, 5-7.15.
t 14, 9; 16, 2; 19, 20; 20, 4.
u 17, 9.

*

12, 14: *Great eagle:* symbol of the power and swiftness of divine help; cf Ex 19, 4; Dt 32, 11; Is 40, 31.

12, 15: The serpent is depicted as the sea monster; cf 13, 1; Is 27, 1; Ez 32, 2; Ps 74, 13–14.

12, 17: Although the church is protected by God's special providence (16), the individual Christian is to expect persecution and suffering.

12, 18: *It took its position:* many later manuscripts and versions read "I took my position," thus connecting the sentence to the following paragraph.

13, 1–10: This wild beast, combining features of the four beasts in Dn 7, 2–28, symbolizes the Roman empire; the seven heads represent the emperors; see the notes on 17, 10 and 17, 12–14. The blasphemous names are the divine titles assumed by the emperors.

13, 2: Satan (12, 9), the prince of this world (Jn 12, 31), commissioned the beast to persecute the church (5–7).

13, 3: This may be a reference to the popular legend that Nero would come back to life and rule again after his death (which occurred in A.D. 68 from a self-inflicted stab wound in the throat); cf v 14; 17, 8. Domitian (A.D. 81–96) embodied all the cruelty and impiety of Nero. Cf Introduction.

13, 4: *Worshiped the beast:* allusion to emperor worship, which Domitian insisted upon and ruthlessly enforced. *Who can compare with the beast:* perhaps a deliberate parody of the name Michael; see the note on 12, 7.

13, 5–6: Domitian, like Antiochus IV Epiphanes (Dn 7, 8.11.25), demanded that he be called by divine titles such as "our lord and god" and "Jupiter." See the note on 11, 2.

13, 5: *Forty-two months:* this is the same duration as the profanation of the holy city (11, 2), the prophetic mission of the two witnesses (11, 3), and the retreat of the woman into the desert (12, 6.14).

13, 11–18: The second beast is described in terms of the false prophets (cf 16, 13; 19, 20; 20, 10) who accompany the false messiahs (the first beast); cf Mt 24, 24; Mk 13, 22; 2 Thes 2, 9; cf also Dt 13, 2–4. Christians had either to worship the emperor and his image or to suffer martyrdom.

13, 18: Each of the letters of the alphabet in Hebrew as well as in Greek has a numerical value. Many possible combinations of letters will add up to 666, and many candidates have

derstands can calculate the number of the beast,
for it is a number that stands for a person. His
number is six hundred and sixty-six.

## CHAPTER 14

### The Lamb's Companions
1 [v]*Then I
looked and there was the Lamb standing on
Mount Zion, and with him a hundred and forty-four thousand who had his name and his Father's name written on their foreheads. 2 I
heard a sound from heaven like the sound of
rushing water or a loud peal of thunder. The
sound I heard was like that of harpists playing
their harps. 3 [w]They were singing [what
seemed to be] a new hymn before the throne,
before the four living creatures and the elders.
No one could learn this hymn except the hundred and forty-four thousand who had been ransomed from the earth. 4 [x]*These are they who
were not defiled with women; they are virgins
and these are the ones who follow the Lamb
wherever he goes. They have been ransomed as
the firstfruits of the human race for God and the
Lamb. 5 [y]*On their lips no deceit has been
found; they are unblemished.

### The Three Angels
6 *Then I saw another
angel flying high overhead, with everlasting
good news to announce to those who dwell on
earth, to every nation, tribe, tongue, and people. 7 [z]He said in a loud voice, "Fear God and
give him glory, for his time has come to sit in
judgment. Worship him who made heaven and
earth and sea and springs of water."

8 [a]*A second angel followed, saying:
"Fallen, fallen is Babylon the great,
that made all the nations drink
the wine of her licentious passion."

9 A third angel followed them and said in a loud
voice, "Anyone who worships the beast or its
image, or accepts its mark on forehead or hand,
10 *will also drink the wine of God's fury,
poured full strength into the cup of his wrath,
and will be tormented in burning sulfur before
the holy angels and before the Lamb. 11 [b]The
smoke of the fire that torments them will rise
forever and ever, and there will be no relief day
or night for those who worship the beast or its
image or accept the mark of its name."
12 [c]*Here is what sustains the holy ones who
keep God's commandments and their faith in
Jesus.
13 [d]*I heard a voice from heaven say,
"Write this: Blessed are the dead who die in the
Lord from now on." "Yes," said the Spirit,
"let them find rest from their labors, for their
works accompany them."

### The Harvest of the Earth
14 [e]*Then I
looked and there was a white cloud, and sitting
on the cloud one who looked like a son of man,
with a gold crown on his head and a sharp sickle
in his hand. 15 [f]Another angel came out of the
temple, crying out in a loud voice to the one
sitting on the cloud, "Use your sickle and reap
the harvest, for the time to reap has come, because the earth's harvest is fully ripe." 16 So

v Jl 3, 5; Ob 17; Acts 2, 21.
w Pss 33, 3; 96, 1; 98, 1; Is 42, 10.
x Jer 2, 2; Jas 1, 18.
y Zep 3, 13.
z 2, 10; Mt 10, 28.
a 18, 2-3; Is 21, 9; Jer 51, 8 / Is 51, 17; Jer 25, 15-17.
b 19, 3.
c 12, 17.
d Mt 11, 28-29; 2 Thes 1, 7; Heb 4, 10.
e 1, 7; Dn 7, 13.
f Jl 4, 13; Mt 13, 36-43.

* been nominated for this infamous number. The most likely is the emperor Caesar Nero (see the note on 13, 3), the Greek form of whose name in Hebrew letters gives the required sum. (The Latin form of this name equals 616, which is the reading of a few manuscripts.) Nero personifies the emperors who viciously persecuted the church. It has also been observed that "6" represents imperfection, falling short of the perfect number "7," and is represented here in a triple or superlative form.

14, 1–5: Now follows a tender and consoling vision of the Lamb and his companions.

14, 1: *Mount Zion:* in Jerusalem, the traditional place where the true remnant, the Israel of faith, is to be gathered in the messianic reign; cf 2 Kgs 19, 30–31; Jl 3, 5; Ob 17; Mi 4, 6–8; Zep 3, 12–20. *A hundred and forty-four thousand:* see the note on 7, 4–9. *His Father's name . . . foreheads:* in contrast to the pagans who were marked with the name or number of the beast (13, 16–17).

14, 4: *Virgins:* metaphorically, because they never indulged in any idolatrous practices, which are considered in the Old Testament to be adultery and fornication (2, 14–15.20–22; 17, 1–6; cf Ez 16, 1–58; 23, 1–49). The parallel passages (7, 3; 22, 4) indicate that the 144,000 whose foreheads are sealed represent all Christian people.

14, 5: *No deceit:* because they did not deny Christ or do homage to the beast. Lying is characteristic of the opponents of Christ (Jn 8, 44), but the Suffering Servant spoke no falsehood (Is 53, 9; 1 Pt 2, 22). *Unblemished:* a cultic term taken from the vocabulary of sacrificial ritual.

14, 6–13: Three angels proclaim imminent judgment on the pagan world, calling all peoples to worship God the creator. Babylon (Rome) will fall, and its supporters will be tormented forever.

14, 6: *Everlasting good news:* that God's eternal reign is about to begin; see the note on 10, 7.

14, 8: This verse anticipates the lengthy dirge over Babylon (Rome) in 18, 1—19, 4. The oracle of Is 21, 9 to Babylon is applied here.

14, 10–11: *The wine of God's fury:* image taken from Is 51, 17; Jer 25, 15–16; 49, 12; 51, 7; Ez 23, 31–34. Eternal punishment in the fiery pool of burning sulfur (or "fire and brimstone"; cf Gn 19, 24) is also reserved for the Devil, the beast, and the false prophet (19, 20; 20, 10; 21, 8).

14, 12: In addition to *faith in Jesus,* the seer insists upon the necessity and value of works, as in 2, 23; 20, 12–13; 22, 12; cf Mt 16, 27; Rom 2, 6.

14, 13: See the note on 1, 3. According to Jewish thought, people's actions followed them as witnesses before the court of God.

14, 14–20: The reaping of the harvest symbolizes the gathering of the elect in the final judgment, while the reaping and treading of the grapes symbolizes the doom of the ungodly (cf Jl 4, 12–13; Is 63, 1–6) that will come in 19, 11–21.

the one who was sitting on the cloud swung his
sickle over the earth, and the earth was harvested.
17 Then another angel came out of the temple in heaven who also had a sharp sickle.
18 *Then another angel [came] from the altar,
[who] was in charge of the fire, and cried out in
a loud voice to the one who had the sharp sickle,
"Use your sharp sickle and cut the clusters from
the earth's vines, for its grapes are ripe."
19 [g]So the angel swung his sickle over the earth
and cut the earth's vintage. He threw it into the
great wine press of God's fury. 20 *The wine
press was trodden outside the city and blood
poured out of the wine press to the height of a
horse's bridle for two hundred miles.

## CHAPTER 15

**The Seven Last Plagues** 1 *Then I saw
in heaven another sign, great and awe-inspiring:
seven angels with the seven last plagues, for
through them God's fury is accomplished.
2 [h]*Then I saw something like a sea of glass
mingled with fire. On the sea of glass were
standing those who had won the victory over the
beast and its image and the number that signified its name. They were holding God's harps,
3 [i]*and they sang the song of Moses, the servant of God, and the song of the Lamb:

"Great and wonderful are your works,
Lord God almighty.
Just and true are your ways,
O king of the nations.
4 [j]Who will not fear you, Lord,
or glorify your name?
For you alone are holy.
All the nations will come
and worship before you,
for your righteous acts have been
revealed."

5 *After this I had another vision. The temple
that is the heavenly tent of testimony opened,
6 [k]and the seven angels with the seven plagues
came out of the temple. They were dressed in
clean white linen, with a gold sash around their
chests. 7 One of the four living creatures gave
the seven angels seven gold bowls filled with
the fury of God, who lives forever and ever.
8 [l]Then the temple became so filled with the
smoke from God's glory and might that no one
could enter it until the seven plagues of the
seven angels had been accomplished.

## CHAPTER 16

**The Seven Bowls** 1 *I heard a loud voice
speaking from the temple to the seven angels,
"Go and pour out the seven bowls of God's fury
upon the earth."
2 *The first angel went and poured out his
bowl on the earth. Festering and ugly sores
broke out on those who had the mark of the
beast or worshiped its image.
3 *The second angel poured out his bowl on
the sea. The sea turned to blood like that from
a corpse; every creature living in the sea died.
4 [m]The third angel poured out his bowl on
the rivers and springs of water. These also
turned to blood. 5 [n]Then I heard the angel in
charge of the waters say:

"You are just, O Holy One,
who are and who were,
in passing this sentence.
6 [o]For they have shed the blood of the holy
ones and the prophets,
and you [have] given them blood to drink;
it is what they deserve."
7 [p]Then I heard the altar cry out,
"Yes, Lord God almighty,
your judgments are true and just."

8 The fourth angel poured out his bowl on the
sun. It was given the power to burn people with
fire. 9 [q]People were burned by the scorching
heat and blasphemed the name of God who had
power over these plagues, but they did not repent or give him glory.
10 [r]*The fifth angel poured out his bowl on

g 19, 15; Is 63, 1-6.
h 7, 9.14; 13, 15-18.
i Pss 92, 6; 98, 1 / Dt 32, 4; Ps 145, 17.
j Ps 86, 9-10; Jer 10, 7.
k 19, 8.
l 1 Kgs 8, 10; Is 6, 4.
m Ex 7, 14-24.
n 1, 4.
o Ez 35, 6; Mt 23, 34-35.
p Dn 3, 27; Tb 3, 2.
q Am 4, 6.
r Ex 10, 21-23.

*

14, 18: *Altar:* there was only one altar in the heavenly temple; see the notes above on 6, 9; 8, 3; 11, 1.

14, 20: *Two hundred miles:* literally sixteen hundred stades. The *stadion,* a Greek unit of measurement, was about 607 feet in length, approximately the length of a furlong.

15, 1—16, 21: The seven bowls, the third and last group of seven after the seven seals and the seven trumpets, foreshadow the final cataclysm. Again, the series is introduced by a heavenly prelude, in which the victors over the beast sing the canticle of Moses (15, 2–4).

15, 1–4: A vision of the victorious martyrs precedes the vision of woe in 15, 5—16, 21; cf 7, 9–12.

15, 2: *Mingled with fire:* fire symbolizes the sanctity involved in facing God, reflected in the trials that have prepared the victorious Christians or in God's wrath.

15, 3: *The song of Moses:* the song that Moses and the Israelites sang after their escape from the oppression of Egypt (Ex 15, 1–18). The martyrs have escaped from the oppression of the Devil. *Nations:* many other Greek manuscripts and versions read "ages."

15, 5–8: Seven angels receive the bowls of God's wrath.

15, 5: *Tent of testimony:* the name of the meeting tent in the Greek text of Ex 40. Cf 2 Mc 2, 4–7.

16, 1–21: These seven bowls, like the seven seals (6, 1–17; 8, 1) and the seven trumpets (8, 2—9, 21; 11, 15–19), bring on a succession of disasters modeled in part on the plagues of Egypt (Ex 7—12). See the note on 6, 12–14.

16, 2: Like the sixth Egyptian plague (Ex 9, 8–11).

16, 3–4: Like the first Egyptian plague (Ex 7, 20–21). The same woe followed the blowing of the second trumpet (8, 8–9).

16, 10: *The throne of the beast:* symbol of the forces of evil.

the throne of the beast. Its kingdom was plunged
into darkness, and people bit their tongues in
pain **11** [s]and blasphemed the God of heaven
because of their pains and sores. But they did
not repent of their works.

**12** *The sixth angel emptied his bowl on the
great river Euphrates. Its water was dried up to
prepare the way for the kings of the East. **13** [t]*I
saw three unclean spirits like frogs come from
the mouth of the dragon, from the mouth of the
beast, and from the mouth of the false prophet.
**14** [u]These were demonic spirits who performed
signs. They went out to the kings of the whole
world to assemble them for the battle on the
great day of God the almighty. **15** [v]*("Behold,
I am coming like a thief." Blessed is the one
who watches and keeps his clothes ready, so
that he may not go naked and people see him
exposed.) **16** *They then assembled the kings
in the place that is named Armageddon in Hebrew.

**17** [w]The seventh angel poured out his bowl
into the air. A loud voice came out of the temple
from the throne, saying, "It is done."
**18** [x]Then there were lightning flashes, rumblings,
and peals of thunder, and a great earthquake.
It was such a violent earthquake that
there has never been one like it since the human
race began on earth. **19** *The great city was
split into three parts, and the gentile cities fell.
But God remembered great Babylon, giving it
the cup filled with the wine of his fury and
wrath. **20** *Every island fled, and mountains
disappeared. **21** [y]Large hailstones like huge
weights came down from the sky on people, and
they blasphemed God for the plague of hail
because this plague was so severe.

## *V: THE PUNISHMENT OF BABYLON AND THE DESTRUCTION OF PAGAN NATIONS*

### CHAPTER 17

**Babylon the Great** **1** [z]*Then one of the
seven angels who were holding the seven bowls
came and said to me, "Come here. I will show
you the judgment on the great harlot who lives
near the many waters. **2** [a]*The kings of the
earth have had intercourse with her, and the
inhabitants of the earth became drunk on the
wine of her harlotry." **3** [b]*Then he carried me
away in spirit to a deserted place where I saw
a woman seated on a scarlet beast that was
covered with blasphemous names, with seven
heads and ten horns. **4** [c]*The woman was
wearing purple and scarlet and adorned with
gold, precious stones, and pearls. She held in
her hand a gold cup that was filled with the
abominable and sordid deeds of her harlotry.
**5** On her forehead was written a name, which
is a mystery, "Babylon the great, the mother of
harlots and of the abominations of the earth."
**6** *I saw that the woman was drunk on the
blood of the holy ones and on the blood of the
witnesses to Jesus.

**Meaning of the Beast and Harlot** When
I saw her I was greatly amazed. **7** The angel
said to me, "Why are you amazed? I will explain
to you the mystery of the woman and of
the beast that carries her, the beast with the
seven heads and the ten horns. **8** [d]*The beast
that you saw existed once but now exists no
longer. It will come up from the abyss and is
headed for destruction. The inhabitants of the
earth whose names have not been written in the
book of life from the foundation of the world
shall be amazed when they see the beast, because
it existed once but exists no longer, and
yet it will come again. **9** [e]*Here is a clue for
one who has wisdom. The seven heads repre-

s Ex 9, 8-11 / Jer 5, 3.
t Ex 8, 2-3.
u 1 Cor 1, 8.
v Mt 24, 42-44 / 3, 17.
w Is 66, 6.
x Mk 13, 19.
y Ex 9, 22-26.
z Jer 50, 38; 51, 13.
a Jer 51, 7.
b 13, 1.
c 18, 16.
d 13, 3-4 / 3, 5; 13, 8; 20, 12.
e 13, 18.

*

*Darkness:* like the ninth Egyptian plague (Ex 10, 21–23); cf 9, 2.

16, 12: *The kings of the East:* Parthians; see the notes on 6, 2 and 17, 12–13. *East:* literally, "rising of the sun," as in 7, 2.

16, 13: *Frogs:* possibly an allusion to the second Egyptian plague (Ex 7, 26—8, 11). *The false prophet:* identified with the two-horned second beast (13, 11–18 and the note there).

16, 15: *Like a thief:* as in 3, 3 (cf Mt 24, 42–44; 1 Thes 5, 2). *Blessed:* see the note on 1, 3.

16, 16: *Armageddon:* in Hebrew, this means "Mountain of Megiddo." Since Megiddo was the scene of many decisive battles in antiquity (Jgs 5, 19–20; 2 Kgs 9, 27; 2 Chr 35, 20–24), the town became the symbol of the final disastrous rout of the forces of evil.

16, 19: *The great city:* Rome and the empire.

16, 20–21: See the note on 6, 12–14. *Hailstones:* as in the seventh Egyptian plague (Ex 9, 23–24); cf 8, 7. *Like huge weights:* literally, "weighing a talent," about one hundred pounds.

17, 1—19, 10: The punishment of Babylon is now described as a past event and, metaphorically, under the image of the great harlot who leads people astray into idolatry.

17, 1–6: Babylon, the symbolic name (5) of Rome, is graphically described as "the great harlot."

17, 2: *Intercourse . . . harlotry:* see the note on 14, 4. The pagan kings subject to Rome adopted the cult of the emperor.

17, 3: *Scarlet beast:* see the note on 13, 1–10. *Blasphemous names:* divine titles assumed by the Roman emperors; see the note on 13, 5–6.

17, 4: Reference to the great wealth and idolatrous cults of Rome.

17, 6b–18: An interpretation of the vision is here given.

17, 8: Allusion to the belief that the dead Nero would return to power (11); see the note on 13, 3.

17, 9: *Here is a clue:* literally, "Here a mind that has wisdom." *Seven hills:* of Rome.

sent seven hills upon which the woman sits.
They also represent seven kings: **10** *five have
already fallen, one still lives, and the last has not
yet come, and when he comes he must remain
only a short while. **11** *The beast that existed
once but exists no longer is an eighth king, but
really belongs to the seven and is headed for
destruction. **12** [f]*The ten horns that you saw
represent ten kings who have not yet been
crowned; they will receive royal authority along
with the beast for one hour. **13** They are of one
mind and will give their power and authority to
the beast. **14** [g]They will fight with the Lamb,
but the Lamb will conquer them, for he is Lord
of lords and king of kings, and those with him
are called, chosen, and faithful."

**15** Then he said to me, "The waters that you
saw where the harlot lives represent large numbers of peoples, nations, and tongues.
**16** [h]*The ten horns that you saw and the beast
will hate the harlot; they will leave her desolate
and naked; they will eat her flesh and consume
her with fire. **17** For God has put it into their
minds to carry out his purpose and to make them
come to an agreement to give their kingdom to
the beast until the words of God are accomplished. **18** The woman whom you saw represents the great city that has sovereignty over the
kings of the earth."

## CHAPTER 18

### The Fall of Babylon

**1** [i]*After this I saw
another angel coming down from heaven, having great authority, and the earth became illumined by his splendor. **2** [j]*He cried out in a
mighty voice:

"Fallen, fallen is Babylon the great.
She has become a haunt for demons.
She is a cage for every unclean spirit,
a cage for every unclean bird,
[a cage for every unclean] and disgusting
[beast].
**3** [k]*For all the nations have drunk
the wine of her licentious passion.
The kings of the earth had intercourse with
her,
and the merchants of the earth grew rich
from her drive for luxury."

**4** [l]*Then I heard another voice from heaven
say:

"Depart from her, my people,
so as not to take part in her sins
and receive a share in her plagues,
**5** [m]for her sins are piled up to the sky,
and God remembers her crimes.
**6** [n]Pay her back as she has paid others.
Pay her back double for her deeds.
Into her cup pour double what she poured.
**7** [o]To the measure of her boasting and
wantonness
repay her in torment and grief;
for she said to herself,
'I sit enthroned as queen;
I am no widow,
and I will never know grief.'
**8** Therefore, her plagues will come in one
day,
pestilence, grief, and famine;
she will be consumed by fire.
For mighty is the Lord God who judges
her."

**9** The kings of the earth who had intercourse
with her in their wantonness will weep and
mourn over her when they see the smoke of her
pyre. **10** They will keep their distance for fear
of the torment inflicted on her, and they will
say:

"Alas, alas, great city,
Babylon, mighty city.
In one hour your judgment has come."

**11** *The merchants of the earth will weep and
mourn for her, because there will be no more
markets for their cargo: **12** their cargo of gold,
silver, precious stones, and pearls; fine linen,
purple silk, and scarlet cloth; fragrant wood of
every kind, all articles of ivory and all articles
of the most expensive wood, bronze, iron, and

---

f Dn 7, 24.
g 19, 11-21; 2 Mc 13, 4; 1 Tm 6, 15 / Rom 1, 6; 1 Pt 2, 9; Jude 1.
h Ez 16, 37-41; 23, 25-29.
i Ez 43, 2.
j 14, 8; Is 21, 9; Jer 50, 2-3; 51, 8.
k 17, 2; Jer 51, 7.
l Is 48, 20; Jer 50, 8.
m Jer 51, 9.
n Jer 50, 15 / Jer 16, 18.
o Is 47, 8-9.

---

*

17, 10: There is little agreement as to the identity of the Roman emperors alluded to here. The number seven (9) suggests that all the emperors are meant; see the note on 1, 4.

17, 11: *The beast:* Nero; see the note on v 8.

17, 12–13: *Ten kings who have not yet been crowned:* perhaps Parthian satraps who are to accompany the revived Nero (the beast) in his march on Rome to regain power; see the note on 13, 3. In 19, 11–21, the Lamb and his companions will conquer them.

17, 16–18: *The ten horns:* the ten pagan kings (12) who unwittingly fulfill God's will against harlot Rome, the great city; cf Ez 16, 37.

18, 1—19, 4: A stirring dirge over the fall of Babylon-Rome. The perspective is prophetic, as if the fall of Rome had already taken place. The imagery here, as elsewhere in this book, is not to be taken literally. The vindictiveness of some of the language, borrowed from the scathing Old Testament prophecies against Babylon, Tyre, and Nineveh (Is 23; 24; 27; Jer 50–51; Ez 26–27), is meant to portray symbolically the inexorable demands of God's holiness and justice; cf Introduction. The section concludes with a joyous canticle on the future glory of heaven.

18, 2: Many Greek manuscripts and versions omit *a cage for every unclean . . . beast.*

18, 3–24: Rome is condemned for her immorality, symbol of idolatry (see the note on 14, 4), and for persecuting the church; cf 19, 2.

18, 4: *Depart from her:* not evacuation of the city but separation from sinners, as always in apocalyptic literature.

18, 11: Ironically, the merchants weep not so much for Babylon-Rome, but for their lost markets; cf Ez 27, 36.

marble; 13 *cinnamon, spice, incense, myrrh,
and frankincense; wine, olive oil, fine flour,
and wheat; cattle and sheep, horses and chariots, and slaves, that is, human beings.

14 [p]"The fruit you craved
has left you.
All your luxury and splendor are gone,
never again will one find them."

15 The merchants who deal in these goods,
who grew rich from her, will keep their distance
for fear of the torment inflicted on her. Weeping
and mourning, 16 [q]they cry out:

"Alas, alas, great city,
wearing fine linen, purple and scarlet,
adorned [in] gold, precious stones, and
pearls.
17 In one hour this great wealth has been
ruined."

Every captain of a ship, every traveler at sea,
sailors, and seafaring merchants stood at a distance 18 and cried out when they saw the
smoke of her pyre, "What city could compare
with the great city?" 19 [r]They threw dust on
their heads and cried out, weeping and mourning:

"Alas, alas, great city,
in which all who had ships at sea
grew rich from her wealth.
In one hour she has been ruined.
20 [s]Rejoice over her, heaven,
you holy ones, apostles, and prophets.
For God has judged your case against her."

21 [t]A mighty angel picked up a stone like a
huge millstone and threw it into the sea and said:

"With such force will Babylon the great city
be thrown down,
and will never be found again.
22 [u]No melodies of harpists and musicians,
flutists and trumpeters,
will ever be heard in you again.
No craftsmen in any trade
will ever be found in you again.
No sound of the millstone
will ever be heard in you again.
23 [v]No light from a lamp
will ever be seen in you again.
No voices of bride and groom
will ever be heard in you again.
Because your merchants were the great ones
of the world,
all nations were led astray by your magic
potion.
24 [w]In her was found the blood of prophets and
holy ones
and all who have been slain on the
earth."

## CHAPTER 19

1 *After this I heard what sounded like the
loud voice of a great multitude in heaven, saying:

"Alleluia!
Salvation, glory, and might belong to our
God,
2 [x]for true and just are his judgments.
He has condemned the great harlot
who corrupted the earth with her harlotry.
He has avenged on her the blood of his
servants."

3 [y]They said a second time:

"Alleluia! Smoke will rise from her forever
and ever."

4 The twenty-four elders and the four living
creatures fell down and worshiped God who sat
on the throne, saying, "Amen. Alleluia."

### The Victory Song

5 [z]*A voice coming
from the throne said:

"Praise our God, all you his servants,
[and] you who revere him, small and
great."

6 Then I heard something like the sound of a
great multitude or the sound of rushing water or
mighty peals of thunder, as they said:

"Alleluia!
The Lord has established his reign,
[our] God, the almighty.
7 [a]*Let us rejoice and be glad
and give him glory.
For the wedding day of the Lamb has come,
his bride has made herself ready.
8 [b]*She was allowed to wear
a bright, clean linen garment."

p Hos 10, 5 / Am 6, 7.
q 17, 4.
r Ez 27, 27-32.
s 19, 1-2; Dt 32, 43.
t Jer 51, 63-64; Ez 26, 21.
u Is 24, 8; Ez 26, 13.
v Jer 7, 34; 16, 9; 25, 10.
w 16, 6.
x Dn 3, 27 / Jer 51, 48-49.
y 14, 11; Is 34, 10.
z 11, 18; Ps 115, 13.
a Mt 22, 9; Eph 5, 27.
b 15, 6; Is 61, 10; Mt 22, 11-12.

*

18, 13: *Spice:* an unidentified spice plant called in Greek *amōmon.*

19, 1.3.4.6: *Alleluia:* found only here in the New Testament, this frequent exclamation of praise in the Hebrew psalms was important in Jewish liturgy.

19, 5–10: A victory song follows, sung by the entire church, celebrating the marriage of the Lamb, the union of the Messiah with the community of the elect.

19, 7: *The wedding day of the Lamb:* symbol of God's reign about to begin (21, 1—22, 5); see the note on 10, 7. *His bride:* the church; cf 2 Cor 11, 2; Eph 5, 22–27. Marriage is one of the biblical metaphors used to describe the covenant relationship between God and his people; cf Hos 2, 16–22; Is 54, 5–6; 62, 5; Ez 16, 6–14. Hence, idolatry and apostasy are viewed as adultery and harlotry (Hos 2, 4–15; Ez 16, 15–63); see the note on 14, 4.

19, 8: See the note on 14, 12.

(The linen represents the righteous deeds of the
holy ones.)
**9** [c]*Then the angel said to me, "Write this:
Blessed are those who have been called to the
wedding feast of the Lamb." And he said to me,
"These words are true; they come from God."
**10** [d]*I fell at his feet to worship him. But he
said to me, "Don't! I am a fellow servant of
yours and of your brothers who bear witness to
Jesus. Worship God. Witness to Jesus is the
spirit of prophecy."

**The King of Kings** **11** [e]*Then I saw the
heavens opened, and there was a white horse; its
rider was [called] "Faithful and True." He
judges and wages war in righteousness.
**12** [f]*His eyes were [like] a fiery flame, and on
his head were many diadems. He had a name
inscribed that no one knows except himself.
**13** [g]*He wore a cloak that had been dipped in
blood, and his name was called the Word of
God. **14** [h]The armies of heaven followed him,
mounted on white horses and wearing clean
white linen. **15** [i]*Out of his mouth came a
sharp sword to strike the nations. He will rule
them with an iron rod, and he himself will tread
out in the wine press the wine of the fury and
wrath of God the almighty. **16** [j]He has a name
written on his cloak and on his thigh, "King of
kings and Lord of lords."
**17** *Then I saw an angel standing on the sun.
He cried out [in] a loud voice to all the birds
flying high overhead, "Come here. Gather for
God's great feast, **18** [k]to eat the flesh of kings,
the flesh of military officers, and the flesh of
warriors, the flesh of horses and of their riders,
and the flesh of all, free and slave, small and
great." **19** Then I saw the beast and the kings
of the earth and their armies gathered to fight
against the one riding the horse and against his
army. **20** [l]*The beast was caught and with it the
false prophet who had performed in its sight the
signs by which he led astray those who had
accepted the mark of the beast and those who
had worshiped its image. The two were thrown
alive into the fiery pool burning with sulfur.
**21** The rest were killed by the sword that came
out of the mouth of the one riding the horse, and
all the birds gorged themselves on their flesh.

## CHAPTER 20

**The Thousand-year Reign** **1** [m]*Then I
saw an angel come down from heaven, holding
in his hand the key to the abyss and a heavy
chain. **2** [n]*He seized the dragon, the ancient
serpent, which is the Devil or Satan, and tied it
up for a thousand years **3** and threw it into the
abyss, which he locked over it and sealed, so
that it could no longer lead the nations astray
until the thousand years are completed. After
this, it is to be released for a short time.
**4** [o]*Then I saw thrones; those who sat on
them were entrusted with judgment. I also saw
the souls of those who had been beheaded for
their witness to Jesus and for the word of God,
and who had not worshiped the beast or its
image nor had accepted its mark on their foreheads or hands. They came to life and they
reigned with Christ for a thousand years. **5** The
rest of the dead did not come to life until the
thousand years were over. This is the first resurrection. **6** *Blessed and holy is the one who
shares in the first resurrection. The second death
has no power over these; they will be priests of
God and of Christ, and they will reign with him
for [the] thousand years.
**7** *When the thousand years are completed,
Satan will be released from his prison. **8** [p]*He

c Mt 8, 11; Lk 14, 15.
d 22, 8-9.
e Is 11, 4.
f 1, 14-16; 2, 18 / Lk 10, 22.
g Is 63, 1 / Jn 1, 1.
h 15, 6; 19, 8.
i 14, 20; Is 63, 3.
j 17, 14; 2 Mc 13, 4.
k Ez 39, 17-20.
l 14, 10.
m 9, 1.
n Gn 3, 1.
o Mt 19, 28.
p Ez 38, 2.9.16.

*

19, 9: *Blessed:* see the note on 1, 3.

19, 10: *The spirit of prophecy:* as the prophets were inspired to proclaim God's word, so the Christian is called to give witness to the Word of God (13) made flesh; cf 1, 2; 6, 9; 12, 17.

19, 11–16: Symbolic description of the exalted Christ (cf 1, 13–16) who together with the armies of heaven overcomes the beast and its followers; cf 17, 14.

19, 12: *A name:* in Semitic thought, the name conveyed the reality of the person; cf Mt 11, 27; Lk 10, 22.

19, 13: *Had been dipped in:* other Greek manuscripts and versions read "had been sprinkled with"; cf v 15. *The Word of God:* Christ is the revelation of the Father; cf Jn 1, 1.14; 1 Jn 2, 14.

19, 15: The treading of the wine press is a prophetic symbol used to describe the destruction of God's enemies; cf Is 63, 1–6; Jl 4, 13.

19, 17–21: The certainty of Christ's victory is proclaimed by an angel, followed by a reference to the mustering of enemy forces and a fearsome description of their annihilation. The gruesome imagery is borrowed from Ez 39, 4.17–20.

19, 20: *Beast . . . false prophet:* see the notes on ch 13. *The fiery pool . . . sulfur:* symbol of God's punishment (14, 10; 20, 10.14–15), different from the abyss; see the note on 9, 1.

20, 1–6: Like the other numerical values in this book, the thousand years are not to be taken literally; they symbolize the long period of time between the chaining up of Satan (a symbol for Christ's resurrection-victory over death and the forces of evil) and the end of the world. During this time God's people share in the glorious reign of God that is present to them by virtue of their baptismal victory over death and sin; cf Rom 6, 1–8; Jn 5, 24–25; 16, 33; 1 Jn 3, 14; Eph 2, 1.

20, 1: *Abyss:* see the note on 9, 1.

20, 2: *Dragon . . . serpent . . . Satan:* see the notes on 12, 3.9.10.15.

20, 4: *Beast . . . mark:* see ch 13 and its notes.

20, 6: *Blessed:* see the note on 1, 3. *Second death:* see the note on 2, 11. *Priests:* as in 1, 6; 5, 10; cf 1 Pt 2, 9.

20, 7–10: A description of the symbolic battle to take place when Satan is released at the end of time, when the thousand years are over; see the note on vv 1–6.

20, 8: *Gog and Magog:* symbols of all pagan nations; the

will go out to deceive the nations at the four
corners of the earth, Gog and Magog, to gather
them for battle; their number is like the sand of
the sea. **9** [q]*They invaded the breadth of the
earth and surrounded the camp of the holy ones
and the beloved city. But fire came down from
heaven and consumed them. **10** The Devil who
had led them astray was thrown into the pool of
fire and sulfur, where the beast and the false
prophet were. There they will be tormented day
and night forever and ever.

**The Large White Throne** **11** [r]*Next I saw
a large white throne and the one who was sitting
on it. The earth and the sky fled from his presence and there was no place for them. **12** [s]*I
saw the dead, the great and the lowly, standing
before the throne, and scrolls were opened.
Then another scroll was opened, the book of
life. The dead were judged according to their
deeds, by what was written in the scrolls.
**13** *The sea gave up its dead; then Death and
Hades gave up their dead. All the dead were
judged according to their deeds. **14** [t]*Then
Death and Hades were thrown into the pool of
fire. (This pool of fire is the second death.)
**15** Anyone whose name was not found written
in the book of life was thrown into the pool of
fire.

## *VI: THE NEW CREATION*

## CHAPTER 21

### The New Heaven and the New Earth

**1** [u]*Then I saw a new heaven and a new earth.
The former heaven and the former earth had
passed away, and the sea was no more. **2** [v]*I
also saw the holy city, a new Jerusalem, coming
down out of heaven from God, prepared as a
bride adorned for her husband. **3** [w]*I heard a
loud voice from the throne saying, "Behold,
God's dwelling is with the human race. He will
dwell with them and they will be his people and
God himself will always be with them [as their
God]. **4** [x]He will wipe every tear from their
eyes, and there shall be no more death or mourning, wailing or pain, [for] the old order has
passed away."
**5** [y]*The one who sat on the throne said,
"Behold, I make all things new." Then he said,
"Write these words down, for they are trustworthy and true." **6** [z]*He said to me, "They
are accomplished. I [am] the Alpha and the
Omega, the beginning and the end. To the
thirsty I will give a gift from the spring of
life-giving water. **7** [a]*The victor will inherit
these gifts, and I shall be his God, and he will
be my son. **8** [b]*But as for cowards, the unfaithful, the depraved, murderers, the unchaste, sorcerers, idol-worshipers, and deceivers of every
sort, their lot is in the burning pool of fire and
sulfur, which is the second death."

**The New Jerusalem** **9** *One of the seven
angels who held the seven bowls filled with the
seven last plagues came and said to me, "Come
here. I will show you the bride, the wife of the
Lamb." **10** [c]He took me in spirit to a great,
high mountain and showed me the holy city
Jerusalem coming down out of heaven from
God. **11** [d]It gleamed with the splendor of God.
Its radiance was like that of a precious stone,
like jasper, clear as crystal. **12** It had a massive,
high wall, with twelve gates where twelve angels were stationed and on which names were
inscribed, [the names] of the twelve tribes of the
Israelites. **13** [e]There were three gates facing
east, three north, three south, and three west.
**14** [f]*The wall of the city had twelve courses of
stones as its foundation, on which were in-

q Ez 38, 22.
r 2 Pt 3, 7.10.12.
s Rom 2, 6.
t 1 Cor 15, 26.54-55.
u Is 65, 17; 66, 22; Rom 8, 19-23; 2 Pt 3, 13.
v 19, 7-9.
w Ez 37, 27.
x 7, 17; Is 25, 8; 35, 10.
y Is 43, 19; 2 Cor 5, 17.
z 22, 17; Ps 36, 8-9; Is 55, 1.
a 2 Sm 7, 14.
b 22, 15; Rom 1, 29-32.
c Ez 40, 2.
d Heb 11, 10.
e Ez 48, 31-35.
f Eph 2, 20.

*

names are taken from Ez 38, 1—39, 20.

20, 9: *The breadth of the earth:* Palestine. *The beloved city:* Jerusalem; see the note on 14, 1.

20, 11–15: A description of the final judgment. After the intermediate reign of Christ, all the dead are raised and judged, thus inaugurating the new age.

20, 12: *The book of life:* see the note on 3, 5. *Judged . . . scrolls:* see the note on 14, 12.

20, 13: *Hades:* the netherworld; see the note on 1, 18.

20, 14: *Second death:* see the note on 2, 11.

21, 1—22, 5: A description of God's eternal kingdom in heaven under the symbols of a new heaven and a new earth; cf Is 65, 17–25; 66, 22; Mt 19, 28.

21, 1: *Sea . . . no more:* because as home of the dragon it was doomed to disappear; cf Jb 7, 12.

21, 2: *New Jerusalem . . . bride:* symbol of the church (Gal 4, 26); see the note on 19, 7.

21, 3: *People:* other ancient manuscripts read a plural, "peoples."

21, 3–4: Language taken from Ez 37, 27; Is 25, 8; 35, 10; cf 7, 17.

21, 5: *The one . . . on the throne:* God himself; cf 4, 1–11.

21, 6: *They are accomplished:* God's reign has already begun; see the note on 20, 1–6. *Alpha . . . Omega:* see the note on 1, 8. *Life-giving water:* see the note on 7, 17.

21, 7: *The victor:* over the forces of evil; see the conclusions of the seven letters (2, 7.11.17.26; 3, 5.12.21). *He will be my son:* the victorious Christian enjoys divine affiliation by adoption (Gal 4, 4–7; Rom 8, 14–17); see the note on 2, 26–28.

21, 8: *Cowards:* their conviction is so weak that they deny Christ in time of trial and become traitors. *Second death:* see the note on 2, 11.

21, 9—22, 5: Symbolic descriptions of the new Jerusalem, the church. Most of the images are borrowed from Ez 40—48.

21, 9: *The bride, the wife of the Lamb:* the church (2), the new Jerusalem (10); cf 2 Cor 11, 2.

21, 14: *Courses of stones . . . apostles:* literally, "twelve foundations"; cf Eph 2, 19–20.

scribed the twelve names of the twelve apostles
of the Lamb.
**15** *The one who spoke to me held a gold
measuring rod to measure the city, its gates, and
its wall. **16** *The city was square, its length the
same as [also] its width. He measured the city
with the rod and found it fifteen hundred miles
in length and width and height. **17** *He also
measured its wall: one hundred and forty-four
cubits according to the standard unit of measurement the angel used. **18** *The wall was
constructed of jasper, while the city was pure
gold, clear as glass. **19** [g]The foundations of the
city wall were decorated with every precious
stone; the first course of stones was jasper, the
second sapphire, the third chalcedony, the
fourth emerald, **20** the fifth sardonyx, the sixth
carnelian, the seventh chrysolite, the eighth beryl, the ninth topaz, the tenth chrysoprase, the
eleventh hyacinth, and the twelfth amethyst.
**21** The twelve gates were twelve pearls, each of
the gates made from a single pearl; and the street
of the city was of pure gold, transparent as
glass.
**22** [h]*I saw no temple in the city, for its temple is the Lord God almighty and the Lamb.
**23** [i]*The city had no need of sun or moon to
shine on it, for the glory of God gave it light,
and its lamp was the Lamb. **24** [j]*The nations
will walk by its light, and to it the kings of the
earth will bring their treasure. **25** During the
day its gates will never be shut, and there will
be no night there. **26** The treasure and wealth
of the nations will be brought there, **27** [k]but
nothing unclean will enter it, nor any[one] who
does abominable things or tells lies. Only those
will enter whose names are written in the
Lamb's book of life.

## CHAPTER 22

**1** [l]*Then the angel showed me the river of
life-giving water, sparkling like crystal, flowing
from the throne of God and of the Lamb
**2** *down the middle of its street. On either side
of the river grew the tree of life that produces
fruit twelve times a year, once each month; the
leaves of the trees serve as medicine for the
nations. **3** Nothing accursed will be found there
anymore. The throne of God and of the Lamb
will be in it, and his servants will worship him.
**4** *They will look upon his face, and his name
will be on their foreheads. **5** [m]Night will be no
more, nor will they need light from lamp or sun,
for the Lord God shall give them light, and they
shall reign forever and ever.

## *VII: EPILOGUE*

**6** [n]*And he said to me, "These words are
trustworthy and true, and the Lord, the God of
prophetic spirits, sent his angel to show his
servants what must happen soon."
**7** [o]*"Behold, I am coming soon." Blessed is
the one who keeps the prophetic message of this
book.
**8** It is I, John, who heard and saw these
things, and when I heard and saw them I fell
down to worship at the feet of the angel who
showed them to me. **9** [p]But he said to me,
"Don't! I am a fellow servant of yours and of
your brothers the prophets and of those who
keep the message of this book. Worship God."
**10** *Then he said to me, "Do not seal up the
prophetic words of this book, for the appointed
time is near. **11** Let the wicked still act wickedly, and the filthy still be filthy. The righteous
must still do right, and the holy still be holy."
**12** [q]"Behold, I am coming soon. I bring
with me the recompense I will give to each
according to his deeds. **13** [r]*I am the Alpha and

g Is 54, 11-12.
h Jn 2, 19-20.
i Is 60, 1-2.19-20.
j Is 60, 11.
k Is 35, 8; 52, 1; Zec 13, 2 / Rv 3, 5; 20, 12.
l Ez 47, 1-12.
m Is 60, 20.
n 1, 1.
o 12.20 / 1, 3.
p 19, 10.
q 7.20 / Ps 62, 12; 2 Tm 4, 14.
r 1, 8; 21, 6; Is 41, 4; 44, 6.

*

21, 15–17: The city is shaped like a gigantic cube, a symbol of perfection (cf 1 Kgs 6, 19–20). The measurements of the city and its wall are multiples of the symbolic number twelve; see the note on 7, 4–9.

21, 16: *Fifteen hundred miles:* literally, twelve thousand stades, about 12,000 furlongs (see the note on 14, 20); the number is symbolic: twelve (the apostles as leaders of the new Israel) multiplied by 1,000 (the immensity of Christians); cf Introduction. *In length and width and height:* literally, "its length and width and height are the same."

21, 17: *One hundred and forty-four cubits:* the cubit was about eighteen inches in length. *Standard unit of measurement the angel used:* literally, "by a human measure, i.e., an angel's."

21, 18–21: The gold and precious gems symbolize the beauty and excellence of the church; cf Ex 28, 15–21; Tb 13, 16–17; Is 54, 11–12.

21, 22: Christ is present throughout the church; hence, no temple is needed as an earthly dwelling for God; cf Mt 18, 20; 28, 20; Jn 4, 21.

21, 23: *Lamp . . . Lamb:* cf Jn 8, 12.

21, 24–27: All men and women of good will are welcome in the church; cf Is 60, 1.3.5.11. *The . . . book of life:* see the note on 3, 5.

22, 1.17: *Life-giving water:* see the note on 7, 17.

22, 2: *The tree of life:* cf v 14; see the note on 2, 7. *Fruit . . . medicine:* cf Ez 47, 12.

22, 4: *Look upon his face:* cf Mt 5, 8; 1 Cor 13, 12; 1 Jn 3, 2.

22, 6–21: The book ends with an epilogue consisting of a series of warnings and exhortations and forming an inclusion with the prologue by resuming its themes and expressions; see the note on 1, 1–3.

22, 7.12.20: *I am coming soon:* Christ is the speaker; see the note on 1, 3.

22, 7.14: *Blessed:* see the note on 1, 3.

22, 10: *The appointed time:* see the note on 1, 3.

22, 13: Christ applies to himself words used by God in 1, 8.

the Omega, the first and the last, the beginning
and the end."
**14** [s]*Blessed are they who wash their robes
so as to have the right to the tree of life and enter
the city through its gates. **15** [t]Outside are the
dogs, the sorcerers, the unchaste, the murderers, the idol-worshipers, and all who love and
practice deceit.
**16** [u]*"I, Jesus, sent my angel to give you
this testimony for the churches. I am the root
and offspring of David, the bright morning
star."
**17** [v]*The Spirit and the bride say, "Come."
Let the hearer say, "Come." Let the one who
thirsts come forward, and the one who wants it
receive the gift of life-giving water.
**18** I warn everyone who hears the prophetic
words in this book: if anyone adds to them, God
will add to him the plagues described in this
book, **19** [w]and if anyone takes away from the
words in this prophetic book, God will take
away his share in the tree of life and in the holy
city described in this book.
**20** [x]*The one who gives this testimony says,
"Yes, I am coming soon." Amen! Come, Lord
Jesus!
**21** The grace of the Lord Jesus be with all.

s 7, 14-15; 22, 2.
t 21, 8; Rom 1, 29-32.
u 1, 1.11-12; 22, 6 / 2, 28.
v 21, 6; Is 55, 1.
w Dt 4, 2.
x 7.12 / Acts 3, 20-21; 1 Cor 15, 23; 16, 22.

*

22, 14: *The city:* heavenly Jerusalem; see the note on 21, 2.

22, 16: *The root . . . of David:* see the note on 5, 5. *Morning star:* see the note on 2, 26–28.

22, 17: *Bride:* the church; see the note on 21, 2.

22, 20: *Come, Lord Jesus:* a liturgical refrain, similar to the Aramaic expression *Marana tha*—"Our Lord, come!"—in 1 Cor 16, 22; cf the note there. It was a prayer for the coming of Christ in glory at the parousia; see the note on 1, 3.

# Dictionary/Concordance

Dictionary/Concordance
and non-biblical materials

Nihil Obstat: Rev. Richard L. Schaefer
Censor Deputatus

Imprimatur: Most Rev. Jerome Hanus, O.S.B.
Archbishop of Dubuque

# Dictionary/Concordance

## A

**Aaron** older brother of Moses (Ex 6:20; 7:7). He helped Moses free the Israelites from slavery in Egypt (Ex 12:31) and served as first high priest (Ex 28:1). His male descendants became priests of Israel (Ex 29).

**Abba** word for "father" in the Aramaic language (Mk 14:36; Rom 8:15; Gal 4:6).

**Abel** second son of Adam, who was murdered by his older brother, Cain (Gn 4:8). Jesus called him "righteous" (Mt 23:35). The book of Hebrews lists him as one of the Old Testament people who was guided by faith (11:4).

**Abiathar** son of Ahimelech, the chief priest at Nob. He was the only survivor when King Saul killed the priests at Nob for helping David (1 Sm 22:20). He later became King David's priest and advisor. After David's death, he was exiled to Anathoth by Solomon for supporting Adonijah's claim to the throne (1 Kgs 2:26).

**abide** to remain or stay (Ex 23:33; Ps 102:13).

**Abigail** wife of Nabal, a rich man of Carmel whose flocks David and his men protected. She saved her husband from David's anger when Nabal refused to repay David for his protection (1 Sm 25:14-35). After the death of Nabal, she became David's wife (1 Sm 25:39-42).

**Abijah** son of Rehoboam and king of Judah, who reigned 913-910 B.C. (2 Chr 13). Called Abijam in 1 Kings 15:1-8.

**Abimelech** son of Gideon (Jgs 8:31) who became king of Shechem by killing seventy of his brothers (Jgs 9).

**Abishai** David's nephew and brother of Joab and Asahel (1 Chr 2:16). He was a loyal companion of David and a great warrior (1 Sm 26:1-12; 2 Sm 16:9-12; 21:16-17). He became commander of David's "warriors," who were called "the Thirty" (2 Sm 23:1-19).

**Abner** commander of King Saul's army. He made Saul's son, Ishbaal, king of the northern tribes of Israel (2 Sm 2:8-10). After a quarrel with Ishbaal, Abner gave his support to David, who then became king of all Israel (2 Sm 3:6-19). David sang a funeral song in his honor (2 Sm 3:22-38).

**abolish** to do away with or destroy (Mi. 5,11-12).

**abomination** a thing that angers God (Dt 12:31). When Antiochus Epiphanes invaded Jerusalem and plundered the temple, the resulting horror was referred to as the "Abomination" (1 Mc 4:43; 6:7).

**Abraham** father of the Jewish people. He was called by God to leave his home and family and to journey by faith to a new land. God promised to bless him with descendants beyond number and to give them the land of Canaan. To seal the promise, God changed Abram's name to "Abraham," which means "father of many." Abraham's story begins at Genesis 11:26 and ends at Genesis 25:11. In the New Testament, he is an important example of faith (Rom 4; Gal 3:6-18; Heb 11:8-19).

**Absalom** third son of David. His mother was Maacah (2 Sm 3:3). He killed his half brother Amnon. Absalom led a rebellion against David, which ended in Absalom's death. Absalom's story is told in 2 Samuel 13-18.

**abstain** to refrain deliberately from an action or practice (Nm 6:3).

**Achan** man who was put to death for keeping some of the spoils captured at Jericho (Jos 7).

**acknowledge** 1. to recognize or admit as true (Dt 33:9; Jb 40:14); 2. to recognize the authority or standing of another (Is 61:9).

**Adam** first human created by God. The name means "man" or "humankind." Adam and his wife Eve disobeyed God and were thrown out of the garden of Eden. Adam's sin caused all human beings to be cursed and brought about a separation between God and humankind (Gn 1–5; Rom 5:14; 1 Cor 15:22).

**admonish** to warn gently; to encourage someone to do better (Ps 81:9; 1 Thes 5:12, 14).

**Adonijah** fourth son of David. His mother was Haggith (2 Sm 3:4). When David grew old, Adonijah plotted to make himself king, but his plan was foiled by the prophet Nathan and Bathsheba, mother of Solomon (1 Kgs 1–2).

**adultery** having sexual relations with anyone other than one's spouse (Ex 20:14; Dt 5:18; Mt 5:32; 19:9).

**Advocate** the Holy Spirit (Jn 14:16, 26).

**affliction** troubles or pain; a humbling event (Ps 25:18; 2 Cor 2:4).

**Ahab** son of Omri and one of Israel's most wicked kings (869-850 B.C.) He married Jezebel, daughter of a Phoenician king, who led the northern kingdom of Israel to worship Baal instead of God. Elijah the prophet spoke out against Ahab and Baal worship. The record of King Ahab's reign is found in 1 Kings 16:29–22:40.

**Ahaz** evil king of Judah (735-715 B.C.) who burned his son as a human sacrifice (2 Kgs 16; 2 Chr 28). As the prophet Isaiah predicted, Ahaz brought ruin on Judah by putting his trust in the Assyrians rather than in God (Is 7).

**Ahaziah** son of Ahab and king of Israel, 850-849 B.C. (1 Kgs 22:52-54).

**Ahijah** prophet of Shiloh who foretold that Jeroboam would become king of the northern tribes of Israel (1 Kgs 11:29-40; 14:1-18).

**Ahimelech** priest of Nob. He aided David in escaping from King Saul. In anger Saul ordered the execution of all the priests of Nob and their families. Only Abiathar, son of Ahimelech, escaped being killed (1 Sm. 21:1-10; 22:11-23).

**Ai** small city near Bethel, at which Joshua and his troops first met defeat because of the sin of Achan (Jos 7–8).

**alien** stranger or foreigner (Lv 19:33-4; Nm 15:14-15).

**alienate** to make unfriendly; to cause to withdraw or be separated from (Col 1:21).

**Almighty** name used to describe God, meaning "all powerful" (Gn 17:1; Ps 91:1; Rv 1:8).

**alms** giving to the poor; acts of kindness. Almsgiving is praised as a way to express love (Tb 12:8-9; Mt 6:1-4).

**aloes** fragrant wood, probably eaglewood, which came from a tree in India. It was used in incense and perfumes (Prv 7:17). Jesus' body was prepared for burial with a mixture of myrrh and aloes (Jn 19:39).

**altar** raised platform on which a priest offered sacrifices. Altars were made of earth, stone, metal, or wood covered with metal (Gn 8:20; Ex 27:1-4; 1 Kgs. 18:30-38). The altar of sacrifice used by Israel had hornlike projections at each corner, which were called the "horns of the altar" (1 Kgs 1:50-51).

**Amaziah** son of King Jehoash and eighth king of Judah (800-783 B.C.) He began well but then turned away from God. He was murdered at Lachish by members of his own court (2 Kgs 14; 2 Chr 25).

**amen** means "let it be true." It is spoken at the end of a prayer or pronouncement (Dt 27:15-26; Rom 9:5; 1 Pt 4,11; Rv 22:20-21).

**Amon** king of Judah, 642-640 B.C. Amon followed in the sins of his father Manasseh, but his son Josiah became one of Judah's most godly kings (2 Kgs 21:19-26).

**Amos** prophet, herdsman, and tender of fig trees in Tekoa, south of Bethlehem. He spoke out bravely against the wasteful and cold-hearted ways of the wealthy people in Samaria, capital of the northern kingdom of Israel. The book of Amos records several of his sermons and visions. First of the major prophets.

**Ananias** 1. Greek form of the name Hanahiah. The archangel Raphael appeared to Tobit in the form of one of Hanahiah's descendants (Tb 5:13); 2. early Christian in Jerusalem. He and his wife Sapphira were struck dead for lying to God (Acts 5:1-11); 3. Christian in Damascus who healed Paul's blindness (Acts 9:1-18); 4. high priest in Jerusalem before whom Paul was tried (Acts 22:30–24:1).

**Ancient One** name of God, "who has lived for endless years" (Dn 7:9; 13; 22).

**Andrew** one of the twelve disciples and the brother of Peter (Mt 4:18; Jn 1:35-42 Acts 1:13).

**angel** heavenly being who acts as God's messenger (Ex 3:2) or servant (Gn 48:16; Mt 2:13; 28:2-5).

**anguish** suffering; mental or emotional distress (Ps 119:143).

**anoint** to pour oil or ointment on a person or an object. Anointing was used to prepare objects for religious use (Ex 29:36; 40:10) or to prepare people to serve the Lord (Ex 29:7; 1 Kgs 19:16). Kings were also anointed to show they had been chosen by God (1 Sm 10:1; 2 Kgs 9:6).

**antichrist** one who is against Christ (1 Jn 2:18-22; 2 Jn 1:7). The Bible speaks of an antichrist who will appear at the end of history to turn people against God, but who will be defeated when Christ returns.

**Antioch** 1. capital city of Syria where Jesus' followers first became known as Christians (Acts 11:19-29; 13:1-3); 2. city in Phrygia near Pisidia where Paul and Barnabas preached the gospel (Acts 13:14-52).

**Antiochus IV (Epiphanes)** king of Syria who persecuted the Jews and plundered the temple (1 Mc 1:10).

**Apollos** Jew from Alexandria who knew the scriptures well. He became a Christian and a teacher in the church at Corinth (Acts 18:24-28; 1 Cor 1:12; 3:4-6, 22).

**apostle** means "a person sent out"; a chosen messenger. Jesus chose twelve men to be his apostles during his ministry on earth (Mt 10:1-2; Lk 22:14). St. Paul was made an apostle by Christ after he had risen from the dead (Rom 1:1; 1 Cor 9:1-2).

**Aquila** husband of Priscilla. Like Paul, he was a tentmaker. With his wife, he led Apollos to the Lord (Acts 18; Rom 16:3).

**ark, Noah's** huge boat built by Noah at the Lord's command (Gn 6). In the ark Noah and his family together with two of each kind of animal were saved from a flood that covered the earth. The story of Noah's ark is told in Genesis 6–9.

**ark of the covenant, ark of the testimony** box made of wood covered with gold that the Lord told Moses to make (Ex 25:10; 2 Chr 24:6). The box contained the two stone tablets on which the ten commandments were written (Dt 10:2-5). Also kept inside the ark was a jar of manna and Aaron's staff. The ark was the most holy object in the worship of God (Ex 25:22; 1 Sm 4:4).

**Armageddon** the place of conflict between the kings of the earth and the forces of evil (Rv 16:16).

**armor** clothing worn to protect the body against weapons. Goliath wore a bronze helmet on his head, a coat of metal scales over his body, and metal shin guards (1 Sm 17:5-7). A warrior of God wore golden armor when God intervened to protect the temple depository from Heliodorus (2 Mc 3:25).

**armor-bearer** servant who carried armor and weapons for a great warrior or leader (1 Sm 14:1-17; 31:4-6).

**arrogance** pride; conceit (Prv 8:13; Is 13:11).

**Asa** godly third king of Judah who ruled from 913-873 B.C. (1 Kgs 15; 2 Chr 14–16).

**ascend** to go up; to rise (Jn 6:62).

**Asher** one of the twelve tribes of Israel, descended from the second son of Jacob and Zilpah (Gn 35:26; Nm 1:40-41; 1 Chr 7:30-40). The land given to the tribe of Asher was in northwest Canaan along the Mediterranean Sea (Jos 19:24-31; Jgs 1:31-32).

**Ashtaroth** Canaanite goddess, also called Ashtoreth and Astarte. In myth she was the mother of Baal and many other gods. Ashtaroth poles were placed at sites where the goddess was worshipped (Jgs 2:13; 1 Sm 7:3-4; 1 Kgs 11:5).

**assembly** a gathering of people (Prv 5:14; Acts 19:32, 39-41).

**Assyria** ancient and warlike nation in northern Mesopotamia; its main cities were Asshur, Calah, and Nineveh, all located along the Tigris River. The powerful Assyrians conquered Samaria in 722 B.C. and carried away the people of Israel, bringing to an end the northern kingdom of Israel (2 Kgs 17). Babylon defeated the Assyrian army in 609 B.C. and the Assyrians disappeared from history (2 Kgs 18–19).

**Athaliah** evil daughter of Ahab and Jezebel and wife of King Jehoram of Judah. She murdered her own grandchildren and became queen (841-835 B.C.) Her grandson Joash was hidden away, and when Athaliah was executed, he became king at the age of seven (2 Kgs 8:26; 11:1-20).

**atonement** the making of amends; payment for a wrong (Ex 29:36; Nm 5:8).

**authority** right or power to give orders and be obeyed (Mt 21:23-27; Mk 1:22). Human authorities include rulers, judges, and military leaders. God is the highest authority and rules over the whole universe (1 Cor 15:24-25).

## B

**Baal** the name means "lord" or "master" and refers to a number of Canaanite gods. During Israel's history in Canaan, the people often turned away from God to the worship of false gods such as the Baals (Jgs 2:11-13; 6:25-32; 2 Kgs 23:4-5). Under King Ahab and Queen Jezebel, the worship of Baal became the state religion of Israel, and the worship of the Lord was outlawed (1 Kgs 16:29-32). In a contest on Mount Carmel, Elijah the prophet stood up against the prophets of Baal and proved that the Lord was the one true God (1 Kgs 18).

**Babel, Tower of** great building begun by descendants of Adam and Eve. God caused the people there to speak different languages, so they could not understand each other. Unable to work together, the people scattered over the earth as God intended (Gn 11:1-9).

**Babylon** ancient capital city of Babylonia located between the Tigris and Euphrates Rivers (Gn 10:10). In 609 B.C., Babylonian forces defeated the Assyrian army, and Babylon became the center of the most powerful empire in the world (Is 39). King Nebuchadnezzar II (605-562 B.C.) became Babylon's greatest king during biblical times. Nebuchadnezzar captured Jerusalem in 602 B.C. and took many of the leading Israelites into captivity (2 Kgs 24). When Israel rebelled, the Babylonians destroyed Jerusalem and Solomon's Temple, taking the remaining Israelites to Babylon (2 Kgs 25; Jer 39; 52). The Israelites remained in Babylon for seventy years before a small group returned to the Promised Land (Jer 29; Ezr 1:11; 2:1). The Babylonian Empire came to an end as stated in prophecy when Cyrus the Persian took the city of Babylon (Is 13–14; 47–48; Jer 25; 50–51). In the book of Revelation, Babylon is used as a symbol to represent the center of human society that is hostile to God (Rv 17–18).

**Balaam** son of Beor. A seer hired by Barak, king of Moab, to put a curse on the Israelites on their way to the Promised Land (Nm 22–24). Balaam was forced to bless rather than curse Israel, but he later caused Israelites to worship the Moabite god, Baal of Peor, and for this he was put to death (Nm 31:8; 2 Pt 2:15).

**banish** to send a person away by force (2 Sm 14:13-14).

**baptism** one of the sacraments. Romans 6:1-11 sums up what happens in baptism: the sin-bound Christian over whom water is poured is immersed in Christ's redemptive death and comes from the water alive with Christ's new life (Rom 5:5; Col 2:12).

**Barabbas** prisoner the Jews requested Pilate to release rather than Jesus. He was called a revolutionary in one gospel (Jn 18:40), a murderer and leader of revolt in another (Lk 23:19).

**Barak** general who, under Deborah the judge, defeated the Canaanite army of King Jabin (Jgs 4:1-16).

**barley** grain widely grown in Canaan; of less value than wheat. It was harvested in March or April (2 Kgs 7:1; Jn 6:9).

**Barnabas** apostle of the early church and missionary co-worker with St. Paul (Acts 4:36; 13–14). Later they separated over whether Mark should go with them on a missionary journey (Acts 15:36-40).

**Bartholomew** one of the twelve disciples of Jesus (Mt 10:3; Acts 1:13). He may have been the same as Nathanael in John 1:45-51.

**barren** 1. describing a woman who is unable to have children (Prv 30:16); 2. describing land that is unable to produce plant life (Nm 13:20).

**Baruch** scribe of Jeremiah the prophet and author of the book of Baruch (Bar 1:1-3). He wrote down and publicly read Jeremiah's prophecies of the destruction of Jerusalem (Jer 32:12-16; 36; 45).

**Bathsheba** wife of Uriah the Hittite. King David committed adultery with her and later married her. They had four sons together including Solomon (2 Sm 11–12; 1 Kgs 1).

**Beelzebul** ruler of demons; Satan (Mt 10:25; 12:24-29).

**Beer-sheba** chief city in southern Judah. The expression "from Dan to Beer-sheba" means the whole nation of Israel from north to south (2 Sm 17:11). God appeared to Isaac and Jacob here (Gn 21:25-31; 26:23-25; 46:1-5).

**befall** to happen or be done to someone (Gn 42:38).

**behemoth** large beast, possibly the hippopotamus (Jb 40:15-18).

**behold** to see or look upon (Mt. 1,20. 23).

**Bel** name for Marduk, god of the city of Babylonia (Is 46:1; Dan 14:3-22).

**Beliar** name for Satan (2 Cor 6:15).

**believe** to accept as true, to trust, or to have faith (Ex 4:1-9; Mt 21:25, 32). The Bible teaches that to believe in Jesus means to accept Jesus as Lord and to trust in him for the forgiveness of sins. Those who believe in Jesus receive eternal life (Jn 1:12; 3:16; 11:25-27).

**Benjamin** 1. twelfth and youngest son of Jacob. His mother was Rachel (Gn 42-45); 2. one of the twelve tribes of Israel, descended from Jacob's son, Benjamin (1 Sm 9:21). The land given to this tribe lies just north of Jerusalem (Jos 18:11-20).

**bereave** to take away or leave without (Jer 15:7).

**Bethany** village about two miles from Jerusalem. Jesus stayed at the home of Lazarus, Mary, and Martha in Bethany (Jn 11:1-44; 12:1-11).

**Bethel** city about fourteen miles north of Jerusalem, named by Jacob (Gn 28:19). Bethel was located on the border between Judah and the northern kingdom of Israel after the kingdom was divided. Jeroboam I set up an idol at Bethel, which remained until it was destroyed by Josiah (1 Kgs 12:28-33; 13:1-10; 2 Kgs 23:15).

**Bethlehem** birthplace of Jesus located in Judea (Mt 2:1-12). Micah foretold that the Messiah would come from this city (Mi 5:1).

**bishop** church leader; overseer of church affairs (1 Tm 3:1-7; Ti 1:7).

**blasphemy** that which curses or insults God and godly things (Mk 14:64).

**bless** to say or do something good for another (Gn 12:2-3; Rom 12:14). In the Old Testament, God promised to bless the Israelites when they were obedient to his Law (Dt 11:26-28). In his Sermon on the Mount, Jesus taught that people are blessed by anything that draws them closer to God (Mt 5:3-12).

**blood** fluid in the veins and arteries of humans and animals. In the Bible, blood represents the life of a creature (Lv 17,11-14). Jews were forbidden to drink blood or use it in foods (Dt 12:23). The blood of animal sacrifices was splashed on the sides of the altar to atone to the Lord for one's sins or the sins of the Israelites (Lv 7:2; Heb 9:22). Christ shed his blood on the cross to pay for the sins of all humankind (Mt 26:28; Rom 3:23-25; 5:6-9). We remember his sacrifice by the sacrament of Eucharist (Lk 22:19-20).

**boast** to brag or speak with pride about something (Rom 1:30).

**bondman, bondwoman** slave or servant (2 Chr 28:10).

**branch** limb of a tree or shrub. In the Old Testament, branch was used as a symbol of the Messiah, who would come from David's family tree (Is 4:2). Christians are called "branches" of the vine of Christ (John 15:1-6).

**bread** food made of barley meal or wheat flour, usually baked daily for that day's needs. Ceremonial bread and the bread of wealthy people were made from wheat, but the poor ate the cheaper and coarser bread made from barley. Unleavened bread is made without yeast, so it does not rise (Ex 34:18). Bread is sometimes used in scripture to refer to all food (Dt 8:3; Mt 6:11; Jn 6:31-58). Jesus blessed and gave bread to the disciples at the Last Supper as his sacramental body (Mt 26:26; Lk 22:19). Jesus refers to himself and to the Eucharist as life-giving bread.

**breastplate** piece of armor made of leather or metal, worn over the chest of a soldier (Eph 6:14).

**breastpiece** colorful linen covering worn by the high priest. Fastened to its surface were twelve gems representing the twelve tribes of Israel (Ex 28:15-30).

**brethren** brothers; members of a family, a people, or fellow believers (2 Chr 29:34).

**buckler** shield (Ps 35:2).

**bullock** young bull (Lv 4:4).

**burnt offering** sacrifice in which an animal or other offering was burned on the altar (Lv 6:16; Ps 51, 21).

## C

**Caesar** Roman emperor (Mt. 22,17. 21).

**Caesarea** Roman capital of Judea in New Testament times. Herod the Great built this beautiful port city on the shore of the Mediterranean Sea. At Caesarea, Cornelius and his family became the first Gentiles to become Christians (Acts 10,24-49). Paul was later imprisoned in the city for two years while waiting to stand trial (Acts 24–25).

**Caiaphas** high priest at the trial of Jesus (Jn 11:49-50; 18:24).

**Cain** first-born son of Adam and Eve. He murdered his brother, Abel (Gn 4:1-16).

**Caleb** one of the twelve spies sent by Moses to explore the Promised Land (Nm 13:1-6, 17-33). Only he and Joshua showed faith in God's promise to give the land to Israel (Nm 13:30–14:25). For his loyalty to the Lord, Caleb and his descendants were given the region Hebron in southern Judah (Jos 14:6-15; 15:13-19).

**calendar** the Hebrew calendar was based on a lunar month. A month ran from one new moon to the next (29 ½ days). This made the Hebrew year only 354 long days instead of 365 days, requiring a second month of Adar about every three years to keep the seasons regular. Four of the months have alternative Canaanite names which appear in the Old Testament. The month names begin with Nisan (Abib) in March-April, followed by Lyyar (Ziv), Sivan, Tammuz, Ab, Elul, Tishri (Ethanim), Heshvan (Bul), Chislev, Tebeth, Shebat, and Adar (Ex 12:2).

**camel** animal used to serve the people. The camels known in biblical lands had only one hump. They were used to carry people on journeys and to carry goods from one country to another (Gn 12:16; 24:10-65; 2 Kgs 8:9; Mt 19:24; 23:24).

**Cana** village near Nazareth where Jesus performed his first miracle (Jn 2:1-11; 4:46-54).

**Canaan** ancient name of the land promised by God to Abraham and his descendants (Gn 12:5-7; Nm 34:1-12).

**Canaanites** occupants of the land of Canaan, lying between the Jordan and the Mediterranean from Egypt to Syria. When the Israelites arrived at Canaan, they found the Canaanites living in many powerful walled cities. The Canaanites worshiped many gods, and their religion was known for its immorality (Gn 10:19; Ex 13:5; Jgs 1).

**Capernaum** town on the north shore of the Sea of Galilee. It was a fishing harbor and the center of Christ's ministry (Mt 4:13; Mk 2:1).

**carnal** physical or earthly; opposite of spiritual (Rom 7,14).

**carpenter** craftsman who builds things with wood (Is 44:13). Jesus was a carpenter (Mk 6:3).

**centurion** Roman officer in charge of 100 soldiers (Mk 15:39; Lk 7:1-10; Acts 27:43). Cornelius was a Roman centurion who became a Christian (Acts 10). See *legion*.

**chaff** husks and straw that are discarded after being separated from the kernels of grain (Jer 23:28; Mt 3:12). See *thresh*.

**chariot** two-wheeled vehicle pulled by horses, often used in war. A chariot carried two men: a driver and a warrior. Joseph was assigned a royal chariot (Gn 41:43). The Egyptians pursued the Israelites in chariots (Ex 14:28). Solomon built stables for his horses and chariots (1 Kgs 9:17-19).

**charity** love (Sir 34:21).

**cherub, cherubim** type of angel (Ez 10).

**Chinnereth, Sea of** see *Galilee, Sea of*.

**Christ** Greek word that means "anointed one." It refers to the person the Old Testament prophets said would come to save God's people. It is the same as the Hebrew word "Messiah." Jesus was called "Christ" by those who believed he was the Son of God (Mt 1:1; Rom 1:1).

**Christian** believer or follower of Christ Jesus (Acts 11:26; 26:28).

**chronicle** a record of events. The books of 1 and 2 Chronicles record the events in the history of the Hebrew people.

**church** gathering of Christians who meet together to worship God (Acts 8:1; Rom 16:5; Rv 2–3). In the Bible, the church sometimes means all Christians around the world (Eph 5:23; Col 1:24).

**circumcision** cutting off of the male foreskin at the end of the penis. Circumcision was the outward sign of dedication to the Lord (Gn 17:10-14; Lv 12:3; Rom 2:25-29; 4:11).

**cistern** pit dug in rocky ground to collect rainwater (2 Kgs 18:31; Jer 2:13), usually bottle-shaped, 10 to 25 feet wide, 20 feet deep, and covered by one or more large stones. Both Joseph and Jeremiah were kept prisoner in large cisterns (Gn 37:22-29; Jer 38:6).

**cities of asylum** six cities God told Moses to set aside to be places of safety for anyone who killed another person by accident (Nm 35:9-15; Jos 20:7-9).

**City of David** name for Jerusalem, which David captured and made his capital city (2 Sm 5:6-9).

**clean and unclean** people of Israel were allowed to eat clean animals, but unclean animals were not to be eaten (Lv 11:47). Dead bodies and people with certain diseases were also unclean. A person who touched any unclean person or thing became unclean. Special rules for cleansing were needed to make an unclean person or thing clean again (Lv 14:49-53; Nm 19:13, 16-22).

**commandment** order given by God. God carved the ten commandments on two stone tablets and gave them to Moses for everyone in Israel to obey (Dt 4:13). Jesus gave a new commandment to his followers, telling them to "love one another" (Jn.13:34).

**compassion** sympathy or concern for another (1 Pt 3:8).

**conceive** 1. to become pregnant (Sir 42:10). 2. to know or understand (Wis 9:13).

**concubine** woman in Old Testament times who became the property of a man, but who did not have the full rights of a wife (2 Sm 5:13; 1 Kgs 11:1-3; 1 Chr 1:32).

**condemn** to declare guilty and deserving of punishment (Lk 6:37; Jn 3:17).

**confess** 1. to admit sins (Neh 9:2-3); 2. to tell what one believes (Phil 2:11).

**congregation** group of people meeting together, often to worship God (Acts 13:43).

**conscience** sense of right and wrong (Rom 2:15).

**conspire** plotting with others to do evil (1 Sm 22:8, 13).

**consume** to eat, use up, or destroy (Dt 5:25).

**convert** 1. one who has changed his or her beliefs (Acts 6:5). 2. to change a person from one belief to another (2 Chr 24:19).

**Corinth** large Greek seaport and important trade city. The apostle Paul made only one visit there, staying with Aquila and Priscilla (Acts 18:1-18). The books of 1 Corinthians and 2 Corinthians were two letters Paul wrote to the church in Corinth (1 Cor 1:2; 2 Cor 1:1, 23).

**Cornelius** Roman centurion who lived in Caesarea. He and his family were the first Gentiles to be baptized (Acts 10).

**cornerstone** most important stone used in constructing a building, needed to support the whole structure. Jesus is called the cornerstone because the whole church is built upon him (1 Pt 2:6).

**corpse** dead body (Is 37:36).

**corrupt** 1. to make a person or thing bad (Ez 16:47); 2. thing which has turned bad or person who does evil (Gn 6:11-12).

**covenant** binding agreement, like a contract (Gn 6:18; Heb 8:6, 9).

**covet** to desire too much; to want something that doesn't belong to the person (Ex 20:17).

**covetous** greedy (Lk 12:15; 1 Cor 6:10).

**Creator** the one who makes out of nothing. God is the Creator who made the world and everything in it (Eccl 12:1-7; Rom 1:25).

**cross** raised wooden post used by the Romans to put criminals to death. Jesus died on a cross (Mt 27:32-42; Phil 2:8). After Jesus' death, the cross became a symbol of the Christian faith (Gal 6:14; Phil 3:18). Jesus referred to one's burdens as a cross (Mt 10:38).

**crucify** to put to death by binding or nailing a person to a wooden cross (Mk 15:13-20; 1 Cor 1:23).

**curse** a call on God to send evil or injury down on some person or thing (Nm 22:6; Mk 11:21; Lk 6:28; Jas 3:9). It is the opposite of blessing (Dt 28).

**Cyrus** Persian king called Cyrus the Great. In 538 B.C., he conquered Babylonia as Isaiah the prophet had foretold (Ezr 1:1-4; Is 44:28; Dn 6,:29).

## D

**Damascus** important trade city and capital of Syria to the north of Israel. It became the center of an Aramean kingdom that warred with the Israelites (1 Kgs 11:24-25; 2 Chr 16:2-4). Assyria conquered it in 732 B.C. (2 Kgs 16:9). Christ appeared to Paul on the road to Damascus (Acts 9:1-9).

**Dan** 1. fifth son of Jacob. His mother was Bilhah (Gn 30:1-6); 2. one of the twelve tribes of Israel. They were unable to drive the Canaanites from the land given to them (Jos 19:40-48), so they traveled to Laish, a city in northern Palestine. They captured Laish and renamed it Dan (Jgs 18).

**Daniel** young Jewish captive taken to Babylon. Daniel was a prophet and became an important official in the empire. An angel of God protected Daniel after he was thrown into a lions' den for praying (Dn 6). The book of Daniel tells of his life and of the prophecies attributed to him.

**David** second and greatest king of Israel. His story begins at 1 Samuel 16 and ends at 2 Kings 2. As a youth, he killed Goliath the Philistine giant with only a sling (1 Sm 17). When David became king, he brought all the tribes of Israel together under his rule (2 Sm 5:1-5). Jesus was a descendant of David (Mt 1:6).

**deacon** church leader who helps care for the poor and needy (1 Tm 3:8-13). The word is Greek for "servant."

**Deborah** judge who led the tribes of Israel to a great victory against the Canaanites (Jgs 4). She chose Barak as her general to lead the Israelite army. The Canticle of Deborah in Judges 5 is a poem that tells her story.

**debt** something that a person owes another, usually money (Mt 18:25-32).

**deceive** to mislead or fool someone (Is 36:14; Mt 24:4-13).

**decree** order or law made by a ruler (Ezr 6:8-12; Dn 6,8).

**dedicate** to set apart as holy in the service of God (Ez 20:40).

**deed** action (Lk 11:48).

**defile** to make unclean or impure as a result of sinful behavior (Mt 15:11, 18-20).

**defy** to openly resist; to refuse to obey (1 Sm 17:10).

**deliver** 1. to rescue or save (Jgs 2:16; Ps 39:8-9; Mt 6:13); 2. to give over to (Jdt 2:11).

**descend** to go down (Sg 4:8).

**desolate** empty; deserted (Sir 49:6; Ez 6:6).

**despise** to look down on or treat with contempt (Prv 1:7; Rom 14:3).

**detestable** disgusting; something to be hated (Jer 16:18).

**Deuteronomy** name given to the fifth book of the Old Testament. It means "Second Law."

**devil** 1. name for Satan, meaning "accuser." The devil is a powerful angel who rebelled against God and has become the greatest enemy of God and humans (Lk 4:2-13; Eph 4:27; Jas 4:7; 1 Pt 5:8; Rv 12:9); 2. demon or evil spirit. A devil-possessed person is inhabited by an evil spirit, causing pain, disease, and even madness (Mt 12:22; 15:22; Mk 5:2-20). Jesus drove evil spirits out of many people during his time on earth (Mk 1:34; Lk 4:35).

**devout** devoted to one's religion (Lk 2:25; Acts 2:5; 22:12).

**disciple** devoted student or follower of a teacher or movement. The term comes from a Greek word meaning "learner." Followers of Jesus were called his "disciples" (Mt 10:42; 28:7-20; Jn 13:35).

**discipline** to teach through punishment or correction (Wis 6:17; Heb 12:5-11).

**disgrace** to bring dishonor or shame (Jer 14:21).

**dissension** disagreement (Acts 15:2).

**distress** great pain or desperate need (2 Sm 22:7; Is 25:4; Rom 8:35).

**divine** from God or of God (2 Pt 1:3-4).

**divorce** legal ending of a marriage. Although the Bible says God hates divorce (Mal 2:16), Old Testament law did permit divorce (Dt 24:1). Jesus affirmed God's plan for marriage (Mt 19:3-10).

**doctrine** basic teaching or belief, usually about God (Ti 2:1-10).

**dominion** rule; power over (1 Kgs 9:19).

**doubt** to be uncertain or undecided; not to believe (Mt 14:31).

**dragon** in the Old Testament it means either a jackal or a sea-creature (Is 27:1). In the book of Revelation, it refers to a monster and is used as a symbol for Satan (Rv 12,3).

**dross** worthless leftover material (Prv 25:4).

**drought** long period without rain (Jb 12:5). Drought can cause food shortage because crops do not grow. While Ahab was king, Elijah the prophet foretold a terrible drought in Israel that lasted three years (1 Kgs 17:1-7; 18:1).

**dwell** to settle down or live in (Hb 2:8; Col 13:6).

## E

**earthly** of this world, rather than of heaven. Things which are earthly are imperfect, limited, and do not last (Jn 3:31; 2 Cor 5:1).

**Eden** area in Mesopotamia where God created a garden and placed Adam and Eve. They were thrown out of the Garden of Eden after sinning (Gn 2:8, 15).

**Edomites** people who lived in the nation of Edom, south of the Dead Sea. They were descended from Jacob's brother Esau, so the Edomites were distant relatives of the Israelites (Gn 36; Nm 20:14-21). They became enemies of Israel (Ps 137:7; Lam 4:21-22). Many of the prophets announced that God would punish the Edomites for their hatred of Israel (Jer 49:7-22; Am 9:12; Ob 1).

**Egypt** ancient country lying at the southeast corner of the Mediterranean Sea along the Nile River. In Egypt, Joseph rose from being a slave to second only to Pharaoh, the king of Egypt (Gn 39–50). The Israelites spent 400 years in Egypt, where they became slaves (Ex 1). God sent Moses to lead the people out of Egypt to the Promised Land (Ex 2–14).

**Eli** high priest of Israel who raised Samuel. The sins of Eli's sons resulted in the loss of the ark of the covenant (1 Sm 1:9–4:18).

**Elijah** a great prophet of the Lord during the reign of Ahab (874-853 B.C.). He predicted a terrible drought as God's punishment when Queen Jezebel made Baal worship Israel's religion. He won a contest against the prophets of Baal to prove that the Lord was the only true God. His struggle against Queen Jezebel and her Phoenician priests of Baal is told in 1 Kings 17–19 and 21. He was taken up to heaven (2 Kgs 2).

**Elisha** prophet chosen by God to take Elijah's place (1 Kgs 19:19-21). Elisha asked for and received a "double portion" of Elijah's spirit. The Bible records fourteen miracles that Elisha performed, twice as many as the seven performed by Elijah (2 Kgs 2–9; 13:14-20).

**Elizabeth** mother of John the Baptist and relative of Mary the mother of Jesus (Lk 1:5-58).

**embalm** to treat a dead body to preserve it from decay (Gn 50:2-3).

**engrave** to cut letters or images into a surface (Zec 3:9). The gems on the high priest's ephod and breastpiece were engraved with the names of the Israelite tribes (Ex 28:9-21).

**envy** to want what belongs to another (Gal 5:21, 26).

**Ephesus** large and important trade city on the west coast of Asia Minor. St. Paul spent over two years in the city preaching the gospel. His message had such a powerful effect that his enemies started a riot (Acts 19). Paul wrote the Epistle to the Ephesians, a letter to the church in Ephesus.

**ephod** sleeveless vest worn over a priest's robe (1 Sm 22:18; 1 Chr 15:27). The high priest's ephod was made with red, blue, and purple cloth woven with gold (Ex 39:2-7).

**Ephraim** 1. son of Joseph (Gn 41:52); 2. tribe of Ephraim, whose territory lies northwest of the Dead Sea (Jos 16:4-10); 3. name for the northern kingdom of Israel after the tribes were divided because Ephraim was the northern kingdom's leading tribe (Is 7:2-9).

**Esau** first-born son of Isaac and twin brother of Jacob. He sold his birthright to Jacob for a pot of stew (Gn 25:27-34). Jacob tricked Isaac into giving him Esau's blessing, then fled when Esau planned to kill him in revenge (Gn 27). When they were old, Esau and Jacob made peace with each other (Gn 33).

**Esther** Jewish woman who lived in Persia. She was chosen as the queen of Ahasuerus, and her actions ended Haman's plot to wipe out the entire Jewish people. Her story is told in the book of Esther.

**eternal** without end; lasting forever. God is eternal (Bar 4:8-35). Eternal life is given to those who put their faith in Jesus (Jn 3:15-16; 1 Jn 5:11-13).

**eunuch** male servant, usually one whose sex organs have been removed so he cannot father children. Many of these men were important officials (2 Kgs 9:32; Acts 8:26-39).

**Eve** first woman; wife of Adam (Tb 8:6). Eve and Adam disobeyed God and were thrown out of the garden of Eden (Gn 2–3).

**everlasting** continuing on without end; forever (Gn 9:16; Is 55:3).

**evil** wicked or immoral; acts that God has declared are wrong (Dt 4:25; Rom 12:9, 17). Evil is a result of sin's corrupting influence on human nature (Gn 6:5). God's holy nature requires that evil be punished (Is 13:11; 1 Pt 3:10-12).

**exalt** to raise above; to lift up (Sir 15:5; Zep 3:11).

**exhort** to encourage (Acts 14:22).

**exile** to take a person away from his or her home country by force (Is 5:13; Am 5:5); a person who has been taken from his or her home or country (2 Sm 15:19). The people of Judah were taken into exile by the Babylonians after the fall of Jerusalem in 587 B.C. (Is 5:13; Ez 1:2).

**Exodus** name of the second book of the Bible; it means "a going out." The book of Exodus tells the story of the Israelites' release from slavery in Egypt.

**Ezekiel** prophet who lived among the Jewish people exiled to Babylon. The book of Ezekiel tells about his many visions and acts of prophecy.

**Ezra** devout Jewish priest who lived during the reign of Artaxerxes (Ezr 7:1). The book of Ezra tells how he led a group of Jewish exiles back to Jerusalem and helped to restore temple worship.

## F

**faith** firm belief and trust. Christians put their faith in God (Mt 17:20; Rom 1:17; Heb 11; Jas 2:14-26). Salvation comes through faith in Jesus Christ (Lk 7:50; Rom 3:22).

**faithful** reliable; trustworthy (Mt 25:21; 1 Cor 10:13; 1 Jn 1:9). The Lord is "the faithful God who keeps his merciful covenant" (Dt 7:9).

**false prophet, false teacher** person who claims to speak for God but does not (2 Pt 2; Jude 1:5-16). Near history's end, a false prophet will deceive many with miracles (Rv 16:13; 19:20; 20:10). See *prophet.*

**famine** lack of food causing great hunger (Gn 41; Ru 1:1; 2 Kgs 8:1; Lk 4:25-26). Famines in biblical lands were caused by drought, war, insect plagues, and other disasters.

**fast, fasting** going without food and sometimes without water, especially as a religious duty. Some important fasts by individuals are found in 2 Samuel 12:16-23; 1 Kings 21:27; Nehemiah 1:4; Matthew 4:2. There were also fasts undertaken by a whole community (1 Sm 31:13; Acts 13:3).

**father** 1. male parent (Gn 2:24; Ex 20:12); 2. ancestor (Gn 17:5; Jn 8:39); 3. name for God, showing his relationship with his Son, Jesus, and all believers, who are his adopted children (Mt 6:9; Lk 23:34; Jn 14:6; Rom 8:15).

**fear** 1. to be afraid of (Ps 23:4; 1 Jn 4:18); 2. to greatly respect; to be in awe of. To fear God is to greatly respect him, which leads to love and obedience (Ex 18:21; Dt 6:13; Prv 1:7).

**feasts** joyful festivals that were an important part of the religious life of the Jewish people. In the time of Jesus the main feasts were Passover, the Feast of Weeks, and the Feast of Booths. Jews traveled from all over the world to attend these feasts in Jerusalem.

Passover was held in the Hebrew month of Nisan (March-April) and celebrated the Israelites' rescue from Egypt (Ex 12; Lv 23:4-5). The Feast of

Unleavened Bread was celebrated about the same time and lasted for a week (Lv 23:6-14). This feast was also associated with the Israelite's departure from Egypt.

The Feast of Weeks was held in May, fifty days after Passover (Ex 34:22; Lv 23:15-21). It celebrated the end of the wheat harvest and God's giving of the law to Moses. On this same day, fifty days after the death of Jesus Christ, the Holy Spirit came upon Jesus' disciples. For this reason, Pentecost (which means fiftieth) became a Christian holy day (Acts 2:1-4).

The Feast of Booths was a week-long feast celebrated in late September and early October. The feast was held to celebrate the end of the harvest season and to remember Israel's forty years of wandering in the wilderness (Lv 23:33-43; Nm 29:12-39). During the seven days, the Jewish people lived in "booths," (small huts made of tree branches) that they built around Jerusalem.

**fellowship** friendship; close and sharing relationship (1 Jn 1:3, 6-7).

**festivals** see *feasts.*

**figs** valued fruit of a tree common to biblical lands (Jer 24). Dried figs were pressed into cakes. Fig trees were also valued for the shade they provided (Gn 3:7). Jesus cursed a fig tree that failed to produce fruit (Mk 11:13-21).

**first-born** oldest male child. The first-born son had special value in Hebrew families because he would be the next head of the family and would be responsible for the family's welfare (Ex 13:2, 11-15; Nm 18:15; Col 1:15).

**first fruits** first grain or fruit harvested each year and presented as a special offering to God (Ex 23:16, 19).

**flax** long-stemmed plant grown in biblical lands (Ex 9:31). Fibers of the flax plant were used to make linen cloth. Rahab hid the Israelite spies under a pile of drying flax plants on her roof (Jos 2:6).

**flesh** 1. part or all of the physical body of a living person or animal (Ps 109:24; Jn 1:14) 2. family or other relations (Rom 9:3, 8) 3. a person's sinful nature (Rom 8:8; Eph 2:3).

**flock** group of animals herded together, usually sheep or goats (Gn 30:31-40; Mt 26:31). Believers are called God's flock, and Jesus is presented as their shepherd (Lk 12:32; 1 Pt 5:2-3). See *shepherd.*

**flood** great flowing of water over land (Na 1:8; Mt 24,:38-39; Lk 6:48). When God saw the evil of human beings, he sent a great flood to destroy them. God told Noah to build a boat and fill it with every kind of animal. As a result, Noah and his family were saved from the flood (Gn 6–8). See *ark, Noah's.*

**folly** foolishness; lack of wisdom or common sense (Prv 5:23).

**foreknow** to know something before it happens (Rom 8:29).

**forgive** to pardon; to blame a person no longer for what he or she has done (Mt 6:12-15; Lk 23:34; Col 3:13). When we acknowledge our sins to God, "he is faithful and just and will forgive our sins and cleanse us from every wrongdoing" (1 Jn 1:9).

**forsake** to abandon; to leave and not return (1 Kgs 6:13).

**fortified** strengthened against attack (Nu 13:28). A fortified city is protected with a stone wall, gates, and other defenses to provide protection against enemies (2 Chr 26:9). Joshua and the Israelites captured many large fortified cities in Canaan.

**frankincense** incense that smelled sweet when burned. It was also used in perfume (Ex 30:34-38; Sg 3:6). The wise men from the east brought frankincense as a gift for the baby Jesus (Mt 2:11).

**fruitful** productive; producing plenty (Acts 14:17).

**fulfill** to finish or complete; to make a promise or prediction come true (Mt 26:54; Acts 13:27, 33; Rom 13:8).

## G

**Gabriel** angel who appeared to Daniel to explain the prophet's visions of the future (Dn 8:16; 9:21). The angel Gabriel later appeared to announce the births of John the Baptist and Jesus (Lk 1:11-20; 26-38).

**Gad** one of the twelve tribes of Israel, descended from the seventh son of Jacob (Gn 30:11; 46:16). The territory given to the tribe of Gad lay east of the Jordan River, between the Dead Sea and the Sea of Galilee (Nm 32:20-38; Jos 13:24-28).

**Galilee** region in northern Palestine, west of the Jordan River. It had a large Gentile population, so many Jews looked down on people from Galilee. Jesus grew up in Galilee and centered his ministry there. Twenty-five of his thirty-three recorded miracles were performed in Galilee (Mt 4:23-25; 28:16; Jn 7:41-42).

**Galilee, Sea of** also called the Sea of Gennesaret or Chinnereth; a large fresh-water lake in northern Palestine, known for its plentiful fish and violent storms (Mt 14:22-36; Lk 5:1-11). Jesus calmed a storm on the Sea of Galilee (Mk 4:35-41).

**garrison** fort manned by soldiers; soldiers of a fort (1 Mc 4:61; 2 Mc 12:18).

**gate** entryway through a wall or fence (Mt 7:13-14).

**Gehenna** place of punishment prepared for the devil and his angels. Those who do not turn to Christ to be saved will be sentenced to Gehenna on judgment day (Jas 3:6; Mt 5:22).

**genealogy** family tree; list of a person's ancestors and descendants. The promised Messiah was to be a descendant of David. Jesus' genealogies show he was in David's line (Mt 1:1-17; Lk 3:23-38).

**generation** all people born in the same period of time, generally the time between the birth of a man and of his first-born son, about thirty years (Nm 32:13; Ps 145:13; Mt. 1,17; 17,17).

**Genesis** first book of the Bible, named after its first word in the Greek, which means "in the beginning."

**Gentile** non-Jewish person or nation (Rom 9:24).

**Gideon** judge from the tribe of Manasseh. With an army of just 300 men, he led Israel to victory against the Midianites, ending their cruel treatment of the Israelites (Jgs 6–8).

**gift** 1. something given as a sign of love or respect (Acts 2:38; Rom 5:15-17; 6:23); 2. spiritual gift; special ability given to a believer by the Holy Spirit to better serve others (1 Cor 12:4-11).

**gird** to put on; to bind like a belt to hold clothes in place (1 Sm 25:13).

**glean** to gather up; usually gathering of grain dropped during harvesting (Ru 2:2-23).

**glory** 1. honor; praise (1 Chr 16:9-10; Lk 2:14); 2. visible sign of greatness (Ex 24:16-17; 2 Chr 5:14; Ps 19:2; Mt 25:31); 3. source of great pride (1 Cor 10:31; Eph 3:13).

**glutton** person who eats too much (Prv 23:20-21; Mt 11:19).

**God** Creator and ruler of the universe (Gn 1:1; Is 45:18). There is only one true God (Dt 6:4; 1 Kgs 18:24-39). The Bible is God's word, describing his actions in human history, his will for human beings, and his plan to save people through Jesus Christ (Ex 20:1-17; Dt 6:5; Jn 3:16; 1 Jn 4:14-16).

**godly** holy; person who lives in a way that God approves (2 Cor 7:9, 11).

**Goliath** Philistine giant who was killed in battle by young David (1 Sm 17).

**grace** 1. favor or gift that is undeserved (Gn 10:9); 2. God's provision of salvation (Rom 3:24; Eph 2:5).

**grain** see *barley*.

**guilty** having done something wrong; having broken the law or God's commandments (Lv 5:2-26; Ez 22:4).

## H

**Habakkuk** Levite whose prophecies are recorded in the book of Habakkuk.

**Hagar** Egyptian servant of Sarah who was given to Abraham by Sarah to have children. She was the mother of Ishmael (Gn 16; 21:8-21).

**Haggai** prophet who encouraged the Jews struggling to rebuild the temple in Jerusalem. (Ezr 5:1; Hg 1–2).

**hangings** curtain or drape (Ex 27:11-15; Nm 4:26).

**Hannah** wife of Elkanah. She prayed for a son, and God gave her Samuel, who became Israel's last judge (1 Sm 1–2).

**harlot** prostitute (Sir 9:6; Hos 3:3).

**harvest** 1. gathering of a crop (Jn 4:35-38); 2. time of year when a crop is harvested (Jgs 15:1; Prv 6:8).

**haste, hasten** to hurry; to make the effort to get something done quickly (2 Kgs 7:15).

**haughty** proud (Ps 131:1).

**hearken** listen; pay attention (Nm 23:18).

**heart** center of a person's thoughts, desires, and emotions (Dt 6:5; 1 Sm 16:7; Ps 37:4; Prv 3:5; Ez 36:26; Mt 6:21; 2 Tm 2:22).

**heaven** 1. spiritual home of God. Believers who die go to spend eternal life in heaven with God (2 Kgs 2,:11; Ps 11:4; Mt 6:10; 18:1-4; 2 Cor 5:1-2; Rv 21:1). 2. the atmosphere or sky (Gn 1:1).

**Hebrew** 1. language of the Jewish people. The Old Testament was written mostly in Hebrew (Jn 19:13-20; Acts 26:14; Rv 16:16); some was written in the Hebrew dialect Aramaic; 2. Israelite; anyone descended from Abraham (Ex 1:15-22; 7:16; Jon 1:9; 2 Cor 11:22).

**heed** to listen to (Prv 8:6; Sir 3:1).

**heifer** young cow (Nm 19:2-10).

**heir** person who receives the wealth or property of another who has died (Gn 15:3-4; Rom 8:17; Gal 4:7).

**hell** see *Gehenna*.

**Herod** 1. Herod the Great, evil king of Judea who killed the children of Bethlehem in an attempt to take Jesus' life (Mt 2:16-18; Lk 1:5); 2. Herod Antipas, son of Herod the Great, who ruled over Galilee in Jesus' time. He put John the Baptist to death (Mt 14:1-12; Lk 23:6-16); 3. Herod Agrippa I, grandson of Herod the Great. As king of Judea, he put James to death and threw Peter into prison (Acts 12:1-4, 19-24); 4. Herod Agrippa II. He was present at Paul's trial before Festus (Acts 23:35; 25,13–26,32).

**Hezekiah** godly king of Judah who destroyed the idols in Judah and restored the temple in Jerusalem (2 Kgs 18–20; 2 Chr 29–32; Is 36–39).

**high place** place set aside for religious worship. The Canaanites worshiped false gods at high places (Nm 33:52; 1 Kgs 11:7-8).

**high priest** leader of the priests (Nm 35:25; Jn 18:10-24; Acts 4:6; Heb 4:14-16). Once per year the high priest entered the sanctuary and offered a sacrifice for the sins of the people (Lv 16; Heb 9:25).

**hind** female deer (Gn 49:21).

**holy** 1. pure; godly (Lv 11:44-45; 1 Sm 2,2); 2. sacred; set apart for God to be used for serving or worshipping God (Ex 3:5; Rom 1:2; Heb 3:1).

**Holy Spirit** third person of the trinity together with God the Father and God the Son. Those who accept Jesus Christ as their Savior are given the Holy Spirit, who lives in their hearts (Rom 5:5; 2 Cor 3:3). The Holy Spirit helps believers to know God's will and to live holy lives (Jn 14:26; 2 Cor 6:6).

**honor** 1. show of respect or special favor given to a person (Eph 6:21; 1 Tm 5:3); 2. give high regard and respect (1 Tm 5:17; 1 Pt 2:17).

**hope** to eagerly look forward to; to rely on (1 Cor 13:13). Those who put their hope in God believe in his promises and trust God for the future (Ps 31:25; Acts 24:15; Rom 8:24-25; 15:13).

**Hosanna** Hebrew shout of praise, meaning "save" (Mt 21:9; Mk 11:9).

**Hosea** prophet to the northern kingdom of Israel during the reign of Jeroboam II. In the book of Hosea, the prophet uses his unfaithful wife, Gomer, as an illustration of how Israel has been unfaithful to God.

**hospitality** practice of gladly welcoming others into one's home and giving them food and drink. All Christians are to practice hospitality (Rom 12:13; 1 Pt 4:9).

**humble** 1. lower; to reduce someone in importance (Phil 2:7-8); 2. not proud or pretending to be important (Mi 6:8). Christians are to be humble with each other and toward God, relying on God rather than their own power (Phil 2:3-4; Jas 4:6; 1 Pt 3:8; 5:5).

**hymn** song to praise God used in worship (Mt 26:30).

**hypocrite** person who pretends to be what he or she is not (Mt 6:2, 5). Those who pretend to love God but do evil things are hypocrites (Mt 7:5; 23:13; Lk 13:15).

## I

**idol** false god made in the image of a human or animal and used as an object of worship (Ps 115:4; Ez 6:4-8).

**idolatry** 1. worship of idols (Ez 23:49); 2. anything that takes the place of God in a person's life (Gal 5:19-20).

**image** 1. idol or crafted figure (Na 1:14). 2. likeness, looking or acting like something else (Gn 1:26-27; Rom 8:29).

**Immanuel, Emmanuel** name in Isaiah's prophecy about Jesus, meaning "God with us" (Is 7:14; Mt 1:23).

**inheritance** property or possessions given to a person after the owner dies (Ez 46:18). In Old Testament times, sons received an inheritance of the family property after their father died (Ru 4:5-6). The first-born son received a double share. See *heir.*

**iniquity** a wicked act (Ps 38:5; Rom 4:7).

**inspired** influenced, shaped, or guided by God (2 Tm 3:16).

**integrity** having an honest and moral character; guided by good motives (Ps 101:2; Prv 19:1).

**intercede** to plead for another in need of help (Jer 27:18; Rom 8:27).

**intercession** prayer or request for God's help on behalf of someone (Jb 42:9; Heb 7:25).

**Isaac** son God promised to Abraham, to be born when Abraham was 100 years old. Sarah was his mother (Gn 21:3-5). God told Abraham to sacrifice Isaac but stopped him as Isaac lay on the altar (Gn 22:2-19). Isaac married Rebekah. Esau and Jacob were his sons (Gn 24–25).

**Isaiah** prophet called by God to preach to the people of Judah (2 Kgs 19; Is 6). His ministry lasted for over forty years. He warned Judah to rely on God, not other nations. In his prophecies, Isaiah spoke of the fall of Jerusalem, the defeat of Assyria by Cyrus, and the coming of the Messiah (Is 53). His words are recorded in the book of Isaiah.

**Ishmael** son of Abraham and of Hagar, Sarah's servant, who was given to Abraham to have children (Gn 16:15-16).

**Israel** 1. name God gave to Jacob (Gn 32:28-29); 2. nation of Israel made up of the descendants of the twelve sons of Jacob (Ex 1:1; Jgs 19:1; 1 Kgs 9:5); 3. northern kingdom of Israel made up of ten of Israel's twelve tribes after the nation was divided. The remaining two tribes, Judah and Benjamin, formed the southern nation of Judah (1 Kgs 11:31; 12:20-21).

**Isrealites** people of Israel; members of the twelve tribes descended from Jacob's sons (Gn 49; Ex 1:9; 14:22).

**Issachar** one of the twelve tribes of Israel, descended from the son of Jacob and Leah (Gn 30:14-18; Jos 19:17-23).

## J

**Jacob** son of Isaac and Rebekah and younger twin brother of Esau (Gn 25:19-26). He bought Esau's birthright for a pot of stew (Gn 25:29-34). He later tricked Isaac into giving him Esau's blessing (Gn 27:1-30). He had two wives, Rachel and Leah. His twelve sons were the ancestors of the twelve tribes of Israel (Gn 28:13; 49:1-28). Jacob wrestled with God and was given the name "Israel" (Gn 32:23-32; 35:9-15).

**James** 1. son of Zebedee and brother of John (Mt 4:21). He was one of the twelve apostles. Herod Agrippa I put him to death, fulfilling Jesus' prophecy about him (Mk 10:39; Acts 12:2); 2. son of Alphaeus and one of the twelve apostles (Mt 10:3); 3. a relative of Jesus (Mk 6:3). He became a believer and the bishop of the church in Jerusalem (Acts 15:13-21; Gal 1:19; 2,:9). The letter of James is attributed to him.

**jealous** 1. careful to protect or defend (Nu 11:29; Acts 14:45); 2. expecting total commitment (Jos 24:19-20). God is a jealous God who desires that we remain faithful and not turn away from him (Ex 20:5-6).

**Jehoshaphat** godly fourth king of Judah (872-848 B.C.) His father was King Asa. His son Jehoram became king after him (1 Kgs 22; 2 Chr 17–20).

**Jehu** army commander anointed to be king of Israel. He put Queen Jezebel to death and ended Baal worship in Israel (2 Kgs 9–10). Although Jehu followed some of the Lord's commands, he "was not careful to observe wholeheartedly the law of the LORD" (2 Kgs 10,31).

**Jephthah** judge of Israel who rescued his people from the Ammonites (Jgs 10:6–12:7).

**Jeremiah** prophet called by God to warn Judah that the nation would soon be destroyed (Jer 4). His people rejected him, and members of his own family threatened his life (Jer 12:6). Once, he was thrown into a cistern to die (Jer 38). The terrible fate of his people brought Jeremiah much sadness, and he is often called "the weeping prophet." His words are recorded in the books of Jeremiah and Lamentations.

**Jericho** ancient city near the Dead Sea. When Joshua's army shouted and blew their horns, its great walls collapsed (Dt 34:1-3; Jos 6). They captured and destroyed the city, but it was later rebuilt. Jesus healed a blind beggar in Jericho (Mk 10:46-52).

**Jeroboam** official under King Solomon; he was told by a prophet that God would give him ten of Israel's tribes to rule (1 Kgs 11:26–14:20). He rebelled against Rehoboam, Solomon's son, and became king of the northern kingdom of Israel. He built golden calves in Bethel and Dan and led Israel to sin by worshipping them (1 Kgs 12:30).

**Jerusalem** city that David made capital and religious center of Israel (2 Sm 5:6-10). Solomon built the temple there which was to be the only place to worship God (1 Kgs 5–6). After the kingdom was divided, Jerusalem remained the capital of the nation of Judah. It was later destroyed by the Babylonians in 586 B.C. (2 Kgs 25). The temple and city wall were rebuilt in the time of Ezra and Nehemiah (Ezr 3:10-13; Neh 3). Jesus spent the last week of his life in Jerusalem and was crucified outside its walls (Mt 21:10). See *City of David; Zion.*

**Jesus** Son of God in the flesh. He was born in Bethlehem to a virgin named Mary and raised in Nazareth. He was about thirty when he was baptized by John the Baptist (Mk 1:9-11) and began a ministry of preaching and healing. He promised eternal life to those who believed in him (Jn 3:14-19). Each of the four gospels–the books of Matthew, Mark, Luke, and John–report the story of his life, death on the cross, and resurrection. See *Christ; Messiah.*

**Jew** Israelite; descendant of Abraham through Jacob (Est 2:5; Dn 3:8). The term came from the name of the southern Israelite kingdom, Judah.

**Jezebel** evil Phoenician wife of King Ahab. She was responsible for replacing the worship of the Lord with the worship of Baal in the northern kingdom of Israel (1 Kgs 16:29-33; 21:25). She killed many of the Lord's prophets and tried but failed to end the prophet Elijah's life (1 Kgs 18:4, 13; 19:1-2). As Elijah foretold in prophecy, she was eaten by dogs (1 Kgs 21:23; 2 Kgs 9:30-37).

**Joab** cruel leader of David's army. He murdered Abner and Amasa (2 Sm 3:26-27; 20:9-10). He killed David's son Absalom, ending Absalom's rebellion against his father (2 Sm 18:14-15).

**Joash** ninth king of Judah, crowned when he was only seven years old. He repaired the temple under the guidance of Jehoiada the priest (2 Kgs 12). When Jehoiada died, King Joash turned away from God (2 Chr 24:15-27).

**Job** rich man who feared God and avoided evil (Jb 1:1). His story is told in the book of Job. The book tells how God allowed him to suffer many disasters as a test of his righteousness. Through all he suffered, Job remained faithful to God. In the end, God ended his suffering and gave him "twice as much as he had before" (Jb 42:10).

**Joel** prophet who described a great army that would attack Israel at the end of history. His words were interpreted by Peter as foretelling the coming of the Holy Spirit at Pentecost (Acts 2:16-21). His words are recorded in the book of Joel.

**John** 1. John the Baptist, son of Zechariah and Elizabeth (Lk 1:5-6). He prepared the way for Jesus, preaching in the desert about the need to repent (Lk 3:16-18). He baptized Jesus in the Jordan River (Mk 1:9-11). Herod Antipas arrested him and later put him to death (Mk 6:17-29); 2. one of the twelve apostles, the brother of James. He wrote the gospel of John, the letters of 1 John, 2 John, and 3 John, and the book of Revelation; 3. John Mark, see *Mark.*

**Jonah** prophet called by God to preach to the people of Nineveh (Jon 1:1-3). His story is told in the book of Jonah. It tells how he disobeyed God's command and fled. Thrown overboard during a storm, he was swallowed by a great fish and spent three days in its belly (Jon 1:15–2:1). Finally, he submitted to God and went to the city of Nineveh where his preaching led the people to repent (Jon 3:3-5).

**Jonathan** 1. son of King Saul and loyal friend of David (1 Sm 13:16; 18:1). A daring warrior, he was killed in battle against the Philistines (1 Sm 31:2); 2. son of Mattathias and brother of Judas and Simon. He became the leader of the Maccabean revolt after his brother Judas was killed in the battle against Bacchides (1 Mc 9:23–12:54).

**Jordan** river that flows from the north of Palestine into the Sea of Galilee and then south to the Dead Sea (Nm 13:29; Mt 3:5). The Bible recounts how God stopped the flow of the Jordan River so that Joshua and the Israelites could enter the Promised Land (Jos 3:8-17). John the Baptist baptized Jesus in its waters (Mt 3:13).

**Joseph** 1. son of Jacob who was sold into slavery by his jealous brothers (Gn 37). He later became a ruler in Egypt (Gn 39–50); 2. husband of Mary, Jesus' mother. He was a carpenter who lived in Nazareth (Mt 1:16-25; 2:21-23).

**Joshua** righteous son of Nun who was chosen to lead Israel after Moses died (Dt 31). The book of Joshua tells the story of the Israelite conquest of Canaan under his command. Famous battles he won include the attack on Jericho (Jos 6) and the defeat of five Amorite kings on the day that the Bible recounts how the sun stood still (Jos 10).

**Josiah** godly seventeenth king of Judah. After the book of the law was found in the temple, he led Judah to renewed dedication to the Lord (2 Kgs 22–23).

**Jubilee, year of** every fiftieth year, in which no crops were to be planted and all family lands that had been sold were returned to the original owner (Lv 25:8-55; Nm 36:4).

**Judah** 1. one of the twelve tribes of Israel whose members were descended from Jacob's fourth son (Gn 29:35; Jos 15:1-12). David and Jesus belonged to the tribe of Judah; 2. name for the southern kingdom after the tribes of Judah and Benjamin separated from the northern ten tribes (1 Kgs 12:17-24).

**Judas** 1. third son of Mattathias and leader of the revolt against the Seleucid kings who persecuted the Jews (1 Mc 2:4, 66; 2 Mc 8:1–10:8); 2. one of the twelve apostles, possibly the same as Thaddeus (Acts 1:13); 3. relative of Jesus and the one to whom the book of Jude is attributed (Mt 13:54-55); 4. Judas Iscariot, one of the twelve apostles. He betrayed Jesus for thirty pieces of silver and then took his own life (Mt 26:14-25; 47-50; 27:3-10).

**Judea** in New Testament times, the name for the Jewish district around Jerusalem (Acts 1:8; 2:9). It was part of the Roman Empire.

**judge** 1. to decide an issue of law or morality (Ex 18:13-26; 1 Chr 23:4); 2. to punish or condemn (Rom 3:6; Heb 10:30); 3. title for leaders of the Israelites before the time of Israel's kings. They were chosen by God to save the people from their enemies. The stories of the judges are told in the book of Judges.

**judgment day** time at the end of history when God will judge people (Mt 10:15; 11:22-23).

**Judith** brave Jewish heroine who killed the commander of the Assyrian army, leading to the defeat of the Assyrians. Her story is recorded in the book of Judith.

**justice** fairness; righteousness (2 Sm 8:15; Ps 82:3).

**justify** to be given God's approval and be declared free from guilt or blame (Lk 16:15). By dying on the cross for our sins, Christ has justified every person who believes in him (1 Cor 6:11).

## K

**kid** young goat, used in sacrifices and for meat (Gn 27:9).

**Kephas** Aramaic name Jesus gave to Peter (Jn 1:42). It means "rock." See *Peter.*

**kingdom of God, kingdom of heaven** reign of God over the earth and the lives of believers. By choosing to give God rulership of their lives, all who believe in Christ become part of this kingdom (Mt 5:3; 13).

**know, knowledge** understanding or awareness of something. To know God is to acknowledge God for who he is (Hos 4:11).

## L

**Laban** brother of Rebekah and uncle of Jacob (Gn 24:29). He was the father of Leah and Rachel, Jacob's two wives (Gn 29:16). He was greedy and dishonest with Jacob, who served him for twenty years (Gn 29–31).

**Lamb of God** name given to Jesus. In the Old Testament, a lamb was sacrificed on Passover for the sins of the people. Like a sacrificial lamb, Jesus gave his life on Passover to save people from their sins (Is 53:7; Jn 1:29).

**lame** unable to walk (Lk 7:22). Jesus healed many people who were lame.

**lamentation** a prayer or song that expresses grief. The book of Lamentations contains laments about the ruin of Jerusalem and Judah.

**Last Supper** 1. last meal hosted by Jesus; it was for his disciples before he was crucified (Mt 26, 26-30); 2. The commemorative act of Eucharist celebrated by Jesus' followers as a sacrament (1 Cor 11:23-34).

**law** 1. God's rules and commandments to show people right from wrong (Rom 2:12); 2. the "Law" or "Torah" refers to the first five books of the Old Testament attributed to Moses.

**Lazarus** 1. brother of Martha and Mary from Bethany. Jesus raised him from the dead (Jn 11–12). 2. poor man in one of Jesus' parables (Lk 16:19-31).

**Leah** daughter of Laban and older sister of Rachel. She became Jacob's first wife after Laban tricked Jacob into marrying her (Gn 29–31).

**leaven** yeast or other fermenting agent that causes bread to rise (Ex 12:15; Mt 16:12).

**legion** unit of 6,000 soldiers in the Roman army. The word is often used to mean any great number of people or things (Mt 26:53). The evil spirits Jesus cast out of one man called themselves "Legion" because there were so many of them (Mk 5:9, 15).

**leper** person with leprosy (Mt 8:2).

**leprosy** skin disease or infection (Lv 13:9; Mk 1:42).

**Levi** one of the twelve tribes of Israel whose members were descended from the third son of Jacob and Leah. They were set apart to serve God and had no territory of their own (Gn 29:34; Nm 3:6). See *Levites.*

**Leviathan** mythical sea monster used as a symbol of evil (Ps 74:14; Is 27:1).

**Levites** members of the tribe of Levi. The Levites were set apart to serve God as ministers and to care for the temple (Nm 3:39-51). Levites descended from Aaron became priests of Israel (Nm 18:1-7).

**lewd** indecent (Ez 16:27).

**liberty** freedom (Is 61:1).

**light** that which makes things visible; the opposite of darkness. In the Bible, light is often used as a symbol for the goodness and truth of God. Jesus called himself the "light of the world" because he is the light and because he shows people the way to God (Jn 8:12).

**linen** cloth made from the fibers of the flax plant (Ez 44:17-18; Mk 14:51-52).

**locust** a kind of grasshopper. In biblical lands, large swarms of locusts sometimes covered the land, destroying crops and causing famine (Ex 10:12-20; Jl 1:4).

**loins** 1. waist and hips (Jdt 8:5; Jer 13:11); 2. reproductive organs (Heb. 7:5).

**lord** 1. master or owner (Gn 45:8); 2. term of respect (Ru 2:13); 3. a name referring to God (Gn 2:4; Ex 3:15).

**Lot** nephew of Abraham. He unwisely chose to settle in the wealthy but corrupt city of Sodom (Gn 13). After his capture by raiders, he was rescued by Abraham (Gn 14). Later, he was warned by two angels to leave Sodom just before the city was destroyed by God (Gn 19).

**lots** small stones or objects used to make choices, similar to throwing dice. In biblical times, they were sometimes used to find out God's will (Prv 16:33). The Bible says that lots were used to divide up the land of Canaan among the tribes of Israel (Nm 26:55-56; Jos 18:10).

**love** 1. deep affection (Jgs 16:4; Sg 8:6); 2. compassion, commitment, or devotion (Mt 5:44; Rom 13:10; 1 Jn 3:11-23; 4:16). God's love for us is so great that he gave his only Son to die on the cross for our sins (Jn 3,16).

**Luke** the man thought to be a doctor who worked as a missionary with Paul (Col 4:14; 2 Tm 4:11; Phlm 1:24). He wrote the books of Luke and Acts.

**lust** any strong desire, often for what is wrong or in a disproportionate way (Prv 6:25; Sir 18:30; Mt 5:28).

## M

**Maccabees** historical books which tell the story of the wars of the Jews under the leadership of the Maccabees against the Seleucid kings. The name of the books comes from the names of the leaders of the Jewish revolt: Judas the son of Mattathias, and later his brothers Jonathan and Simon.

**Malachi** prophet who wrote the book of Malachi. He encouraged the Jews who returned home from Babylon to remain loyal to God.

**malice** hatred; evil desire to see harm come to another (Ti 3,3).

**mammon** wealth or riches (Lk 16:13).

**Manasseh** 1. one of the tribes of Israel whose members were descended from the first-born son of Joseph (Gn 48; Nm 26:28-34). The tribe was given territory in northern Israel on both sides of the Jordan River (Jos 17:1-13); 2. evil fourteenth king of Judah who sacrificed his son and practiced black magic (2 Chr 33:1-9). After he was taken captive by the Assyrians, Manasseh repented and changed his ways (2 Chr 33:10-20).

**mandrake** plant related to the potato. It produced a small, yellow fruit that was thought to help a woman conceive a child (Gn 30:14-16).

**manger** open box or trough used for feeding animals (Lk 2:7, 12, 16).

**manifest** to make clear; to demonstrate (2 Tm 1:10).

**manna** food God provided for the Israelites in the wilderness after they left Egypt (Ex 16:31-35; Jn 6:31). The sweet, white seed-like manna appeared every morning with the dew. The name the Israelites gave the food means "what is it?"

**mantle** sleeveless outer garment (Ezr 9:3, 5).

**Mark** John Mark, the young cousin of Barnabas (Col 4:10). He went with Paul and Barnabas on their first missionary journey but left the others at Perga (Acts 12:25). Later, Paul and Barnabas parted company over an argument about Mark (Acts 15:37-39). He wrote the gospel of Mark, the story of Jesus' life primarily as told to him by Peter.

**marriage** joining together of a man and woman in a love relationship for life (Heb 13:4).

**Martha** sister of Mary and Lazarus (Lk 10:38-42; Jn 11:1-44). They lived in Bethany and were close friends of Jesus.

**marvel** to be filled with wonder (Jdt 10:19).

**Mary** 1. virgin who became the mother of Jesus (Mt 1–2; Lk 1–3; Jn 19:25-27). She married Joseph and lived in Nazareth; 2. sister of Martha and Lazarus, the man Jesus raised from the dead (Jn 11:1-44; 12:1-3); 3. Mary Magdalene. Jesus cast a demon out of her, and she became one of his disciples. Jesus appeared to her first after his resurrection from the dead (Mt 27:56, 61; Lk 8:2; Jn 20:1, 11-18).

**Mattathias** priest who began a revolt against the persecution of the Jews ordered by Antiochus Epiphanes. His sons continued to lead the rebellion (1 Mc 1–2).

**Matthew** one of the twelve apostles, also known as Levi (Mk 2:13-14; Lk 5:27-29). He was a tax collector before Jesus called him to be an apostle (Mt 9:9-13; 10:3). He is believed to be the author of the gospel of Matthew.

**mediator** one who settles a disagreement or restores a relationship between two people or groups. Jesus is the mediator between God and people (1 Tm 2:5).

**mercy** undeserved love and kindness (Est B:6; Dn 3:89-90); help given out of love (Eph 2:4).

**Messiah** Hebrew word meaning "anointed one." The title was given to the leader that Old Testament prophets said would come to save God's people (Mt 1:16; Mk 15:61; Jn 1:41). See *Christ; Jesus.*

**Micah** prophet in the time of Isaiah who warned the people of Israel and Judah that God would judge their sins. His words are interpreted as foretelling that the Messiah would come from Bethlehem (Mi 5:1-5). His words are recorded in the book of Micah.

**midwife** woman who helps with the birth of a baby (Gn 38:27-29; Ex 1:19-20).

**ministry** service offered to God or to other people; the use of spiritual gifts to serve others (Acts 1:17, 25; 2 Cor 4:1).

**miracle** amazing act or happening done through the power of God (Neh 9:17; Sir 45:19).

**Miriam** a prophetess, the sister of Moses and Aaron (Ex 2; Nm 12). She led the Israelites in praise after God parted the Red Sea (Ex 15:20-21).

**mock** to make fun of; to treat with contempt (Ps 22:8; Gal 6:7).

**moneychanger** businessman who traded in different kinds of money. In Jesus' time, moneychangers in the temple exchanged many kinds of money for a type of coin used to pay temple taxes and buy animals to sacrifice. The moneychangers often cheated their customers. Jesus chased the moneychangers out of the temple because they were turning God's house into "a den of thieves" (Mt 21:12-13).

**Mordecai** cousin of Esther who warned King Ahasuerus of a plot to take the king's life. The story of how Mordecai and Esther stopped Haman's plot to wipe out the Jewish people is told in the book of Esther.

**mortal** one who must someday die (Rom 8:11; 1 Cor 15:53-54).

**Moses** humble hero of Israel, called by God to lead the Israelites out of Egypt to the Promised Land. God gave him the ten commandments at Mount Sinai (Ex 19–20). He instructed the people in the worship of the Lord (Lv 1–27). He was allowed to see Canaan but died without entering it (Dt 34). In the past, Moses was thought to be the author of the first five books of the Bible.

**mourn** to openly show sorrow or grief following the loss of a loved one or time of disaster (Hos 10:5; Mt 5:4).

**myrrh** sap of a plant that was used to make perfume and incense (Ex 30:23; Mt 2:11).

## N

**Nahum** prophet who predicted the destruction of Nineveh, capital of Assyria. His words are recorded in the book of Nahum.

**Naomi** Jewish mother-in-law of Ruth. When her husband and two sons died, she returned home from Moab. The story of how she guided Ruth into a marriage with a relative named Boaz is told in the book of Ruth.

**Naphtali** one of the twelve tribes of Israel whose members were descended from the sixth son of Jacob (Gn. 30,8). The territory given to the tribe lies in northern Palestine west of the Jordan River and Sea of Galilee (Jos 19:32-39; 1 Kgs 15:20).

**Nathan** prophet who announced God's judgment on David for his sin with Bathsheba (2 Sm 12; 1 Kgs 1).

**Nathanael** one of the twelve disciples. Jesus called him a "true Israelite" (Jn 1:45-51). He is probably the same as Bartholomew (Mt 10:3).

**Nazorean** person from the town of Nazareth. This term became one of the names for the early Christians because Christ came from Nazareth (Acts 24:5).

**nazirite** person who has taken a special vow of dedication to the Lord (Nm 6:1-21; 1 Mc 3:49-51). Such people were not allowed to cut their hair, drink wine, or go near a dead body. Samson is the Bible's most famous nazirite (Jgs 13:1-7).

**Nehemiah** Jewish cupbearer of Artaxerxes who became governor of Jerusalem. He led the Jews in rebuilding the walls of Jerusalem after returning from exile (2 Mc 2:13; Sir 49:13). His words are recorded in the book of Nehemiah.

**neighbor** someone who lives nearby. The Old Testament law commanded the Israelites to love their neighbors as themselves (Lv 19:18). A neighbor was understood to mean any fellow Israelite. Jesus told the story of the Good Samaritan to show that all people should be treated as our neighbors (Lk 10:25-37).

**nettles** thorny plants (Jb 30:7).

**Nicodemus** Pharisee who spoke in secret with Jesus (Jn 3; 19:38-42). He became a disciple of Jesus and helped prepare Jesus' body for burial.

**Nineveh** chief city of Assyria located on the bank of the Tigris River. Tobit was exiled there (Tb 1:1-3). Jonah the prophet is said by the Bible to have announced God's judgment in the city, leading its people to repent (Jon 3). In 612 B.C., about 150 years after Jonah's time, the city was destroyed by the Babylonians and Medes. As foretold by Old Testament prophets, the city was left in ruins, never to be rebuilt (Na 2:8-10; Zep 2:13-15).

**Noah** son of Lamech (Gn 5:29-32). According to the Bible, he was told by God to build a boat and fill it with every kind of animal. He obeyed God and saved his family from a flood that covered the earth (Gn 6–9). In the New Testament, he is one of the heroes of faith (Heb 11:7; 2 Pt 2:5).

## O

**oath** unbreakable promise taken in the name of God (Heb 6:16-18).

**Obadiah** prophet who foretold the destruction of Edom. His words are recorded in the book of Obadiah.

**obey** to do what you are told to do; to follow the commands or will of another (1 Sm 15:22; Rom 6:16-17). Christians owe obedience to parents (Eph 6:1), the government (Heb 13:17), and most of all to God (Acts 5:29).

**observe** 1. to see; to watch (Mt 28:20); 2. to honor; to celebrate (Ex 12:24; Lv 19:37).

**offense** 1. sin or crime (Gn 31:36); 2. something done that causes anger or hurt feelings (Sir 31:17; 1 Cor 10:32).

**offering** 1. something given to God as an act of worship (Gn 4:3-5); 2. killing of an animal offered as a sacrifice to God (Lv 17:4; 1 Sm 7:10). See *sacrifice*.

**offspring** children (Jb 5:25). In the Bible, the term can also mean a descendant (Is 44:3).

**oppress** to keep people down by cruel or unfair use of power (2 Kgs 13:4; Ps 9:10; Zec 7:10).

**ordinance** law or command given by one in power (2 Chr 33:8).

**ox** a bull. Oxen were often used in pairs for plowing, threshing grain, and pulling wagons (Nm 7:3; 2 Sm 24:24; 1 Kgs 19:20-21).

## P

**parable** stories that use familiar images to communicate spiritual truth (Mt 13:3-53).

**paradise** a beautiful, perfect place, for example the Garden of Eden or Heaven (Lk 23:43; 2 Cor 12:4).

**pardon** to forgive; to free a guilty person from punishment (2 Chr 30:18-19; Ps 25:11).

**Passover** see *feasts.*

**patient** willing to wait; able to remain calm and self-controlled at times of difficulty (Col 1:11; 1 Thes 5:14).

**patriarch** male ancestor, usually the head of a tribe or clan (Acts 2:29).

**Paul** apostle who preached the Gospel to non-Jews. Also known as Saul, he was a Pharisee and an enemy of the early Christians until he met Jesus on the road to Damascus. His amazing conversion story is told in Acts 9:4-30 and Acts 26:12-18. Acts 13–28 tells about his exciting missionary journeys, his arrest in Jerusalem, and his trip to Rome to stand trial. Letters attributed to Paul make up about one fourth of the New Testament.

**peace** 1. freedom from war or trouble between people (Eccl 3:8; Heb 12:14); 2. inner calm given by God (Jn 14:27; Phil 4:7; Col 3:12-15).

**Pentecost** see *feasts.*

**perfect** 1. complete and without flaw; finished or whole (Jas 3:2); 2. completely mature (Mt 5:48).

**perish** to be lost or destroyed (Jn 3:15-16).

**persecute** to continually mistreat and show hatred for a person or a group. The early Christians were persecuted for their belief in Jesus (Mt 5:11; Rom 12:14).

**pestilence** widespread disease; a plague (Jer 21:6-9).

**Peter** fisherman who became one of the twelve apostles (Mt 4:18-20), also known as Simon. His brother Andrew was also an apostle. He denied Jesus three times, as Jesus said he would (Mt 26:69-75). After the resurrection, Jesus forgave him (Jn 21:15-25). He became a bold leader of the church in Jerusalem (Acts 2). Acts 10 tells the story of a vision he received from God telling him to share the Gospel with a non-Jew named Cornelius. This event showed that God had accepted Gentiles as believers (Acts 11:18). He is listed as the author of 1 and 2 Peter. See *Kephas.*

**Pharaoh** title of the rulers of Egypt (Gn 45:16-17).

**Pharisees** small group of religious Jews who were very careful to follow the laws of God. They also followed many laws which were their particular interpretations of the Law or Torah (Mk 7:1-13). Many Pharisees became enemies of Jesus and plotted his death (Mt 12:12-14). After Jesus rose from the dead, some Pharisees became Christians (Acts 15:5).

**Philip** 1. one of the twelve apostles. He came from the same town as Peter and Andrew (Jn 1:43-44); 2. one of the seven deacons of the Jerusalem church (Acts 6,5). He became an important missionary to the Samaritans and Gentiles (Acts 8:4-13, 26-40; 21:8).

**Philistines** sea people who settled along the coast of Canaan. They were Israel's chief enemy in the time of Samson (Jgs 13:5). As a boy, David defeated a Philistine giant named Goliath (1 Sm 17). As king, David conquered the Philistines (1 Chr 18:1).

**Pilate** Roman governor of Judea from A.D. 26-36. The Bible recounts how he gave in to the Jewish leaders and sentenced Jesus to die on the cross (Mt 27; Lk 23; Jn 18:28–19:37).

**plague** terrible and widespread disease or disaster (Rv. 9,20). God sent ten plagues against Egypt in order to free the Israelites from slavery (Ex 7:14–12:36).

**plowshare** plow blade (Jl 4:10).

**potter** person who makes clay pottery (Jer 19:1). God is called our "potter" because he shapes us the way a potter shapes clay into a pot (Is 29:16; 64:7; Rom 9:20-21).

**poverty** lack of money or belongings of value; the condition of being poor (Prv 10:15; 2 Cor 8:2. 9). Jesus praises the poor and the poor in spirit.

**praise** to worship; to say good things about someone or to give thanks to another (1 Cor 11:2, 17, 22). Many of the psalms and hymns recorded in the Bible are songs of praise to God (Pss 66; 103; 135).

**pray** to speak to God. When we pray to God, we can be sure that he hears us and will answer our prayers (Jn 17:9-21; Jas 5:13-18).

**pride, proud** having too high an opinion of oneself, which leads a person to be unwilling to obey God (2 Chr 32:26; Prv 8:13; Mk 7:21-23).

**Priscilla, Prisca** co-worker with Paul and her husband Aquila. She was instrumental in leading Apollos to the Lord (Acts 18; Rom 16:3).

**priest** 1. one who made sacrifices and offerings to God for the people of Israel (Lv 1:5, 7, 11; 1 Kgs 8:3-11; 2 Chr 17:8; 23:4-18). The priests of Israel were descended from Aaron (Dt 17:9; 18:1). See *high priest;* 2. leader in the worship of a false god (2 Kgs 10:18-19; 23:20).

**profane** unholy thing; act of spoiling a holy thing by using it wrongly (Lv 18:21; 2 Mc 6:2).

**promise** to swear to something; to say what one will or will not do (Heb 10:23). God made promises to Abraham (Gal 3:17-22; Heb 6:13) and to Israel (Jos 23:5, 15). God has promised to give eternal life to those who believe in Jesus (1 Tm 4:8; Heb 10:34-39).

**prophecy** message from God, often about what will happen in the future (2 Chr 9:29; Mt 13:14).

**prophesy** to speak a prophecy; to give a message from God (Jer 14:14-16; Ez 36:3, 6).

**prophet** 1. person chosen by God to bring his consoling and challenging message to the people. In Old Testament times, God used prophets to teach people what was good and true (Dt 18:17-22). When Israel turned away from God, he sent prophets to speak against their sins and lead the people back to worship of the Lord (Jer 1–2; Ez 12). Prophets sometimes performed miracles to show they were from God (2 Kgs 4); 2. one who claimed to speak the truth, but did not (Jer 23:9-37). See *false prophets, false teachers.*

**proverb** wise saying (Lk 4:23). The book of Proverbs is a collection of wise sayings, many attributed to Solomon.

**provoke** to make another angry; to cause another to act out of anger (Dt 4:25; Sir 8:16).

**prudent** cautious; wise (Is 29:14).

**psalm** song or poem. The book of Psalms is a collection of such writings from a variety of writers. Many psalms are attributed to King David.

**purge** to cleanse completely (2 Chr 34:3; Is 4:4).

**purify** to make clean or pure (Mal 3:3; 1 Pt 1:22).

**Purim** Jewish holiday held once a year to celebrate Queen Esther's rescue of the Jews from Haman's plot to destroy them (Esther 9:20-32).

## Q

**quarrel** disagreement or dispute (2 Kgs 5:7; Prv 17:14).

**quiver** a case for holding arrows (Gn 27:3; Ps 127:4-5).

## R

**Rabbi** title of respect when speaking to an expert in the law of Moses (Mt 23:7-8; Jn 1:38). It means "master" or "teacher."

**Rachel** wife of Jacob and sister of Leah (Gn 29:18-30). She was the mother of Joseph and Benjamin (Gn 30:25; 35:16-19).

**Rahab** a prostitute who lived in Jericho and believed in God. She helped protect the Israelite spies sent by Joshua (Jos 2; 6; Heb 11:31).

**ransom** price paid to gain the release of a person or to free someone from some duty or debt (Ex 21:30; Jb 33:24). Jesus gave his life "as a ransom" to free people from their sins (Mt 20:28).

**Raphael** angel who was sent to cure Tobit and accompany his son on the proposed journey to Media (Tb 5–12).

**reap** 1. to gather grain at harvest time (Lv 19:9; 23:10, 22); 2. to receive in return (Ps 126:5; Jer 12:13; 2 Cor 9:6). The person who acts to please God will "reap eternal life" (Gal 6:7-9).

**Rebekah, Rebecca** wife of Isaac and mother of twins Esau and Jacob. She helped Jacob trick his father into giving him the blessing meant for his older brother, Esau (Gn 24: 27; Rom 9:10-12).

**rebel** to refuse to obey; to resist authority (Jos 22:18-19; Dn 9:5, 9).

**rebuke** to scold for the purpose of instructing (Prv 27:5).

**reconcile** to restore a lost friendship or relationship (Mt 5:24; Col 1:20).

**redeem** to make free by paying a price (Lv 25:25-26).

**refine** to remove impurities from metal by heating (1 Chr 28:18). The Bible uses the word as an image of how God purifies his people through suffering (Zec 13:9; Mal 3:3).

**refuge** safe place (Ps 14:6; Jer 16:19).

**Rehoboam** king of Judah from 922 B.C. to 915 B.C. He was Solomon's son, but made unwise decisions, resulting in a split in the kingdom (1 Kgs 12). He is judged as an evil king, for he "had not truly resolved to seek the LORD" (2 Chr 12:14).

**rejoice** to be joyful; to show great happiness (1 Chr 16:31; Mt 5:12; Lk 15:6).

**remnant** portion that remains ( Jer 40:15); the faithful few.

**render** to give (2 Chr 6:30).

**repent** to be sorry and promise to change; to turn away from one's sins (Mt 12:41; Acts 8:22).

**reproach** to find fault or to blame; the reason one is deserving of blame (Neh 1:3; Jb 27:6; Mt 11:20).

**restore** to bring back; to renew or to make something like it was before (Gn 40:13; 2 Sm 9:7; Mt 17:11).

**resurrection** rising from the dead or returning to life. Jesus was resurrected on the third day following his crucifixion (Rom 1:4). Humans will be resurrected to eternal life or eternal negative judgment (Jn 5:28-29).

**Reuben** one of the twelve tribes of Israel. The members of this tribe are descended from the first-born son of Jacob and Leah (Gn 29:32; 37:21-29; Jos 13:15-23).

**revelation** God's revealing of truth about himself to human beings, often through special means. God makes himself known through creation (Rom 1:18-20). He also has revealed himself through words spoken to people in the past such as Abraham. Other kinds of revelations include visions, prophecies, signs, and miracles (2 Cor 12:1). God's greatest revelation of himself to human beings was Jesus Christ who was God in the flesh (Gal 1:12; Eph 3:3-5).

**revile** to verbally abuse; to show contempt for (Mt 27:39).

**reward** 1. to give something to another for what he or she has done; to repay someone for doing good (Jer 17:10); 2. something given in return for what a person has done (Prv 31:31; Mt 5:12).

**righteous** 1. without sin; completely good and moral (Lk 15:7). 2. person who does what is right (Tb 7:7; Jas 5:16); 3. person whose sins are completely forgiven by God. A person who has put his or her faith in Jesus is seen as righteous in God's eyes (Rom 1:17).

**Rome** in New Testament times, a city of about one million people and capital of the Roman Empire. St. Paul wrote the book of Romans to the church at Rome. Later, Paul was taken to Rome and lived there under house arrest (Acts 28).

**Ruth** Moabite widow who returned with her Jewish mother-in-law Naomi to Bethlehem. There, she married her relative Boaz. Her story is told in the book of Ruth.

## S

**sabbath** the seventh day of the Jewish week. Israelites were to rest on the sabbath day (Ex 20:8-11).

**sackcloth** dark, rough cloth made from the hair of goats or camels. It was worn in times of mourning or to show sorrow for one's sins (2 Sm 3:31; 1 Kgs 21:27; Jon 3:5-8).

**sacrifice** killing of an animal as an offering to God. According to the Old Testament law, the life of an animal was required by God to pay for one's sins or for the sins of the people (Lv 17:5-11; Dt 12:11). Animal sacrifices were repeated regularly as a part of worship in Old Testament times. When Jesus died on the cross, his sacrifice was enough to pay for all of our sins (Heb 10:10-18). See *offering.*

**Sadducees** group of priests and leaders in Jerusalem. Unlike the Pharisees, they accepted only the teachings of Moses (the Law or Torah). They also disagreed with the Pharisees' belief in resurrection or angels (Acts 23:8-10). The head of their party was the chief priest and had great power in Jerusalem (Mk 14:60-64; Acts 5:17-18).

**salvation** 1. condition of being rescued from danger or distress (Is 59:11); 2. condition of being rescued from the power of sin and death. Jesus died and rose from the grave to bring salvation to everyone who believes in him (Acts 28;28; 2 Tm 2:10).

**Samaritan** in New Testament times, a person who lived or came from the district of Samaria. They followed only part of the Jewish tradition and did not fully follow proper Old Testament rules for worship of the Lord. Many Jews of the full Jewish tradition hated the Samaritans. Jesus told a parable about a good Samaritan who stopped to help a Jew in need (Lk 10:25-37).

**Samson** judge from the tribe of Dan who fought against the Philistines. God gave him great physical strength, but he was morally weak. A woman named Delilah tricked him and handed him over to the Philistines. In the end, God used Samson to bring a crushing defeat to the Philistines. The story of his life and death are told in Judges 13–16.

**Samuel** prophet and the last judge of Israel. He was born to Hannah in answer to her prayer (1 Sm 1:20). She dedicated him to the Lord, and he was raised by Eli at the temple in Shiloh. He anointed Saul as king of Israel (1 Sm 10:1). Later, he anointed David to take Saul's place after Saul was rejected by God (1 Sm 16:12-13).

**sanctify** to make holy (Eph 5:26).

**sanctuary** holy place where people worship God (Ex 25:8; Heb 8:2).

**Sarah** 1. half-sister and wife of Abraham, also called Sarai. Although she could not have children, God promised she would have a son. As God promised, she gave birth to a son in her old age and named him "Isaac" (Gn 17:15-22; 22); 2. Young Israelite woman who prayed for death because a demon killed any man who wanted to become her husband. God sent his angel Raphael to instruct her new husband Tobiah on driving away the demon. Her story is told in the book of Tobit.

**Satan** devil; powerful angel who is the enemy of God and human beings (Jb 1:6-12; Mk 1:13).

**Saul** 1. first king of Israel and father of Jonathan. He failed to trust and obey God and was replaced by David (1 Sm 9–29; 31); 2. Jewish name of Paul the apostle. See *Paul.*

**savior** one who saves others. Jesus is called "savior" because he died and rose again to save people from their sins (Lk 2:11; 2 Tm 1:10).

**scepter** rod held by a king or queen as a sign of royal authority (Est 4:11).

**scorn** to make fun of; to ridicule (Dt 32:15; Ps 22:7).

**scourge** 1. to whip (Lk 18:33); 2. instrument used to whip someone (Lk 18:33); 3. a term for punishment in general (2 Mc 9:11; Jb 5:21).

**scribe** educated person who wrote down what people said or copied important writings, such as the Scriptures (2 Sm 8:17; 2 Chr 24:11; Mt 8:19). In Jesus' time, the scribes were experts in the law of Moses and taught the people.

**Scripture, Scriptures** when used in the Bible, it means all or part of the Old Testament (Mt 22:29; Jn 19:24, 28). Today, both the Old Testament and New Testament are called the Scriptures.

**scroll** ancient book made of a long strip of leather or paper rolled up on a pair of sticks (Rv 6:14).

**seal** 1. tool with a design carved into it used to stamp an object with the owner's sign (1 Kgs 21:8; Rv 5:1-5); 2. stamp made by pressing a seal into a soft surface, usually wax or soft clay. Scrolls were often sealed to prove they were from a particular person (Sg 8:6; Jn 6:27). A seal could also be used to keep a scroll or jar from being opened until it was time to break the seal (Jer 32:10; Mt 27:66).

**seer** person who receives visions of the future from God; prophet (1 Sm 9:9; 2 Chr 16:7).

**serpent** snake (Prv 23:32). Satan used the form of a serpent to deceive Adam and Eve (Gn 3:4-6). The book of Revelation uses the image of a serpent for Satan (Rv 12:9).

**shame** 1. being dishonored or humiliated (1 Cor 11:6); 2. painful feeling one gets when dishonored or humiliated (Bar 1:15; Hb 2:16).

**shekel** certain weight of silver or silver coin named for the weight of silver it contained (Gn 23:15-16).

**Shem** son of Noah and ancestor of Abraham (Gn 5:32; 9:23-27; 11:10-26).

**shepherd** person who takes care of flocks of sheep (Wis 17:17; Ez 34:5). In the Bible, this term is often used to refer to God (Ps 23:1) and to human leaders who care for the people under them (Is 56:11). Jesus was called "the good shepherd" because he gave his life for his followers, the "sheep" (Jn 10:11).

**sickle** tool with a long curved blade and a short handle. It is used for cutting stalks of grain or weeds (Mk 4:29).

**siege** to surround with an army for the purpose of attacking (Dt 20:12, 19).

**signet** a seal with the name and title of its owner carved into it (Gn 41:42; Hg 2:23). Usually worn by rulers, it was used to seal letters and important papers. See *seal.*

**Silas** leader in the Jerusalem church. He was a missionary companion of Paul and Peter (Acts 15:36–17:15).

**Simeon** one of the twelve tribes of Israel descended from the second son of Jacob and Leah (Gn 29:33). The land given to the tribe lies in the south of Canaan (Jos 19:1-9).

**Simon** 1. second son of Mattathias. He engaged in several military actions against the Seleucids and Nabataeans (1 Mc 9). Later, he became a leader of the Jews (1 Mc 13–16); 2. given name of the apostle Peter (Mt 4:18). See *Peter;* 3. one of the twelve apostles (Mt 10:4); 3. sorcerer who tried to buy the ability to do miracles from Peter and John (Acts 8:9-24).

**sin** 1. doing what is wrong; disobeying God (2 Sm 24:10; Rom 3:23); 2. acts that are wrong or disobedient to God (Rom 6:23; 1 Jn 3:4).

**Sirach** the book of Sirach derives its name from the author, Jesus, son of Eleazar, son of Sirach (Sir 50:27). The author was a sage who lived in Jerusalem.

**slander** 1. to tell hurtful lies or rumors about another person (Ps 101:5); 2. to falsely accuse a person of wrongdoing (2 Sm 19:28).

**sluggard** lazy person (Prv 6:6).

**snare** trap (Eccl 9:12; 2 Tm 2:26).

**Solomon** son of David and Bathsheba (2 Sm 12:24). He became king after his father and became famous for his wealth and wisdom (1 Kgs 1–11). He built the temple in Jerusalem.

**sojourn** journey (Gn 12:10).

**Son of God** see *Christ; Jesus.*

**Son of Man** name for Jesus Christ (Dn 7:13; Mk 14:62; Lk 19:10).

**soul** person's inner self (Dt 4:29; Ps 16:9-10; Mt 10:28).

**sow** to scatter seeds; to plant (Gn 26:12; Mt 6:26).

**spirit** 1. non-physical part of a person that does not die (Lk 1:47; Acts 7:59); 2. spiritual being, angel, or demon (Mt 12:43; Acts 23:9).

**Spirit, Holy** see *Holy Spirit.*

**spiritual** 1. having to do with the spirit; non-physical (Eph 1:3; 2:2); 2. related to God's holy nature (Gal 6:1; 1 Pt 2:5).

**spiritual gifts** abilities given by the Holy Sprit to believers for serving others (Rom 1:11; 1 Cor 12:1-11).

**Stephen** leader in the Jerusalem church who was stoned to death (Acts 6:5–7:60).

**stone, stoning** to kill by throwing stones at someone (Lv 20:2). Blasphemy (Lv 24:16), idolatry (Dt 13:7-11), and adultery (Dt 22:21; Jn 8,5) were offenses punishable by such stoning.

**strife** conflict; quarreling or serious disagreements (Gn 13:8).

**strive** to struggle for; to try or attempt (Lk 13:24).

**stubble** straw (Jl 2:5).

**subdue** to take control of; to overcome (Gn 1:28; 1 Sm 7:13).

**submit** to yield to another's authority (Jas 4:7).

**suffer** to undergo pain or anguish (Acts 3:18; 1 Pt 4:15-16, 19).

**surety** pledge or guarantee (Gn 43:9).

**Susanna** God-fearing Israelite, falsely accused of adultery. Daniel intervened in her behalf, and she was acquitted of any crime (Dan 13).

**sword** weapon with a long blade and a handle (1 Sm 17:50-51; Mt 26:51-52). It is often used in scripture as a symbol for power or warfare (Mt 10:34; Eph 6:17; Heb 4:12).

**synagogue** place where Jewish people gather for study and worship (Mk 1:21, 23, 29).

## T

**tabernacle** portable worship center of the Israelites during the time they wandered between Egypt and the Promised Land (Wis 9:8; Hb 8:2; 5; 9). See *temple.*

**tempest** violent storm (Jb 9:17; Am 1:14).

**temple** place of worship (Zec 6:12-15). In most of Old Testament times after the Babylonian captivity, the temple in Jerusalem was the only place where the Israelites were supposed to offer sacrifices to God (Dt 12:13-14). See *tabernacle.* In the New Testament, Christians are called God's temple because God lives in their hearts (1 Cor 6:19).

**tempt** to try to lure a person into doing wrong (Gal 6:1; Jas 1:13-15); to test (Ps 78:18; Mt 4:1).

**testimony** statement made by a witness offered as proof (Jn 5:34; 2 Thes 1:10).

**tetrarch** ruler of a district or limited area (Lk 3:1).

**thanksgiving** attitude of thankfulness to God for his blessings; gratefulness (2 Cor 9:11-12).

**Thomas** one of the twelve apostles, also called Didymus (meaning "twin") (Jn 11:16). Thomas doubted that Jesus had returned from the dead until he saw Christ with his own eyes (Jn 20:24-29).

**thresh** to separate the edible kernels of grain from the husks and stalks after harvest (Jb 39:12; 1 Cor 9:10). This was done by crushing the stalks then tossing them into the air. The wind would blow the chaff away while the grain, which was heavier, would fall to the floor to be collected. See *chaff.*

**Timothy** young companion of Paul who traveled with the apostle on his missionary journeys (Acts 16:1-3), also called Timotheus. He became a church leader at Ephesus (1 Tm 1:3). The books of 1 and 2 Timothy are two letters Paul wrote to this young man.

**tithe** offering of one tenth to the Lord (Dt 14:22; Mal 3:10).

**Titus** Greek who became a Christian and co-worker with the apostle Paul (Gal 2:1). Paul sent him to solve difficult problems at the churches in Corinth and Crete (2 Cor 7:6; 8:16; Ti 1:4-5). The book of Titus contains Paul's advice to him during his mission in Crete.

**Tobiah** Tobit's son. He traveled to Media to collect his father's money at Tobit's request. He was accompanied and guided by the angel Raphael. While at Ecbatana, Tobiah married Sarah (Tb 4–14).

**Tobit** an Israelite model of piety, obedience, and patience. Tobit's goodness is rewarded by the Lord's intervention in his life. His story is told in the book of Tobit.

**tongue** 1. muscle of the mouth used in producing speech. The Bible uses the tongue as a symbol for what a person says (Ps 5:10; Jas 3:5-8); 2. language (Acts 2:4).

**tradition** rule or practice handed down from one generation to another (Col 2:8). Jesus criticized the Jewish religious leaders for making people follow traditions added to the teachings of God in the Old Testament (Mk 7:3-13).

**trance** dream-like state of mind while awake (Acts 10:10; 22:17).

**transgress** to rebel; to intentionally act against (Jos. 23:16; 2 Mc 7:2).

**tribe** group of people descended from a single ancestor (Nm 1:4). The twelve tribes of Israel were descended from the twelve sons of Jacob (Gn. 49,28; Acts 26,7).

**trust** to believe and have confidence in someone (Is 42:17; Jer 17:5-7; 2 Cor 1:9; 1 Jn 4:1).

**truth** description or state of the way things really are (Jn 8:32; Rom 1:25; 1 Jn 1:6-8).

**tumult** great noisy disturbance (Ps 83:3).

## U

**unbeliever** person who does not believe in Jesus (2 Cor 6:14-15).

**unblemished** without flaws or marks; perfect (Nm 29:29, 36; 1 Pt 1:19).

**unclean** 1. an "unclean spirit" is a demon or evil spirit (Mt 10:1; Mk 1:23-27); 2. see *clean and unclean.*

**unity** joined together as one (Eph 4:3, 13).

**unleavened bread** bread baked from dough made without yeast so that it does not rise (Ex 12:15-20; 2 Kgs 23:9).

**upright** person who is honest and does what is right (Jb 1:1).

**Urim and Thummim** engraved or marked stones kept in the breastplate of the high priest that were used when seeking guidance from God (Ex 28:30; Dt 33:8).

**usury** interest charged on borrowed money (Neh 5:10; Ez 18:8).

**utmost** furthest or end of (2 Mc 15:17).

## V

**vale** valley (Jos 15:7; Eccl 9:11).

**valiant** strong and brave, especially in battle (2 Chr 17:13-17).

**vanity** worthlessness or meaningless (Eccl 1:2).

**vengeance** hurt or punishment done to another for a wrong that person has committed (Jer 50:28; Rom 12:19).

**vile** disgusting; ugly (Lam 1:8).

**viper** poisonous snake (Mt 3:7; Acts 28:3).

**virgin** person who has not had sexual relations (Is 7:14; Mt 1:23; 2 Cor 11:2).

**visions** images from God given to a prophet or seer in a dream-like state (Nm 12:6; Jl 3:1; Acts 26:19).

**vow** promise made to God (Nm 30:2-16; 2 Sm 15:7-8; Acts 18:18).

## W

**wafers** thin cakes of bread made from unleavened dough which are pressed flat and sometimes sweetened with honey (Ex 16:31; Lv 7:12).

**wail** to cry or weep loudly (Is 15:3; Am 5:16-17).

**weaned** descriptive of a child who no longer feeds on his or her mother's milk (Gn 21:8; 1 Sm 1:22-24; Is 28:9).

**wicked** evil; sinful (Gn 13:13; Prv 10:24-32).

**will** desires or choices of a person or of God (Lk 22:42; Rom 9:16, 18; Jas 1:18).

**wine press** stone vat in which grapes are crushed for their juice (Is 63:2-3; Mk 12:1; Rv 14:19-20). The juice flowed out of the vat into large clay containers or wineskins.

**winnow** to separate kernels of grain from the husks and stalks (Ru 3:2).

**wisdom** knowing good from bad and right from wrong (1 Kgs 5:9-14; Prv 4:5-9; 9:10; 1 Cor 1:19-25; 2:5-8; Jas 3:13-17). The book of Wisdom praises the splendor and worth of divine wisdom.

**witness** 1. person who testifies about something he or she saw or knows (Lv 5:1; 1 Sm 12:5; Acts 26,16; Rv 11:3); 2. object that serves as a memorial (Gn 31:44-50; Jos 22:28; Is 19:19-20).

**woe** sorrow (1 Sm 4:7-8).

**Word, the** name for Jesus Christ, the Son of God (Jn 1:1, 14).

**worship** acts of praise and reverence given to God (Ex 24:1; Jn 4:20-24; Rv 22:9).

**worthy** having worth or value; deserving of honor (Rv 4:11; 5:12).

**wrath** great anger. Sin causes the wrath of God, which brings punishment (Ps 38:2; Jer 32:37).

**wrought** made; did (Ps 78:43).

### Y

**yoke** piece of wood that fits over the necks of a pair of work animals so they could pull a wagon or plow together (Nm 19:2; 1 Sm 6:7). It was used as a symbol for bearing a heavy burden (Gn 27:40; Jer 28:10-14; Mt 11:29-30).

### Z

**zeal** devotion or loyalty to a person or belief (Rom 12:11).

**Zebulun** one of the twelve tribes of Israel whose members were descended from the sixth son of Jacob and Leah (Gn 30:20; 46:14). The small territory given to the tribe lay in the Jezreel Valley west of the Sea of Galilee (Jos 19:10-16).

**Zechariah** 1. son of Jehoiada the priest (2 Chr 24:20). He was put to death for prophesying against King Joash; 2. prophet whose visions are recorded in the book of Zechariah. He offered encouragement to the Jews who returned to Jerusalem after the exile; 3. priest, husband of Elizabeth, and father of John the Baptist (Lk 1:5-25).

**Zedekiah** son of Josiah and last king of Judah, 597-586 B.C. (2 Kgs 24:17–25:21; Jer 21; 34; 37:1–39,7). He rebelled against the Babylonians who came and destroyed Jerusalem and took the Jewish people into exile in Babylon.

**Zephaniah** prophet and descendant of King Hezekiah (Zep 1:1). His words are recorded in the book of Zephaniah.

**Zerubbabel** descendant of David who led the first return of the Jewish exiles to Judah (1 Chr 3:19; Ezr 2–5; Mt 1:12-13). He oversaw the rebuilding of the Jerusalem temple.

**Zion** name for the hill on which the city of Jerusalem was first built (2 Sm 5:7; Ps 48:3, 11-12). The word also can mean all of Jerusalem (Is 59:20; Rom 9:33; 1 Pt 2:4-6).

# Notes

# Notes

# Notes

# Notes

# Notes

# Notes

# The Good News Travels

After the coming of the Holy Spirit on the day of Pentecost, the believers in Jerusalem began to preach boldly and increased in numbers daily (Acts 2:1-47). Some Jewish leaders tried to stop them, but in fact helped the young movement to spread (Acts 4:1-31).

Stephen, a leader of the church in Jerusalem, was accused of blasphemy, and some leaders of the Jews had him stoned to death (Acts 6:1-8:2). Believers in Jerusalem were persecuted, and many fled – south into Judea, north to Samaria, and west to the coast and even as far as Cyprus (Acts 8:1-3, 11:19).

Philip set out for Gaza, baptizing an official from Ethiopia, before moving on to preach in the coastal towns (Acts 8:26-40).

Peter traveled to Caesarea, where he was shown in a vision that he should take the gospel to the Gentiles (Acts 10:1-48).

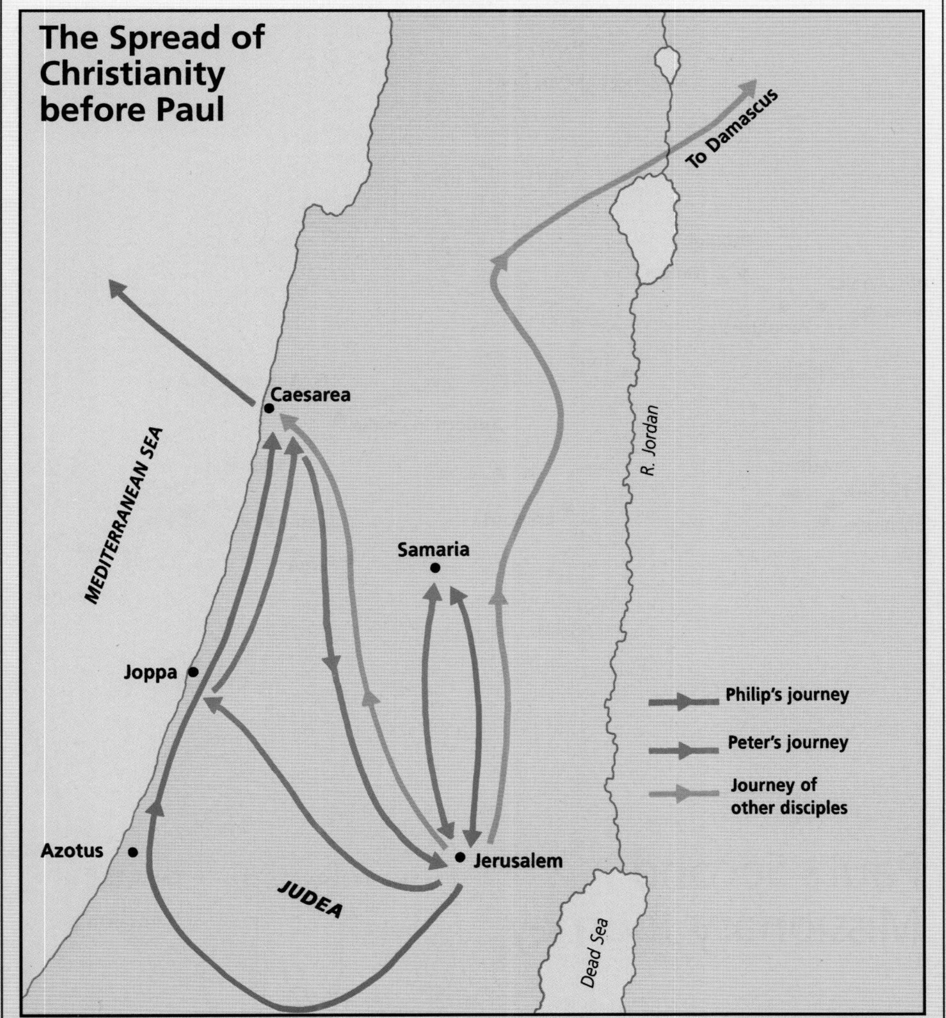

**Paul's First Journey**
Paul traveled with Barnabas. They went first to Cyprus, Barnabas' home, and then to Asia Minor, preaching wherever they went, and leaving communities of believers behind (Acts 13:1-14:28).

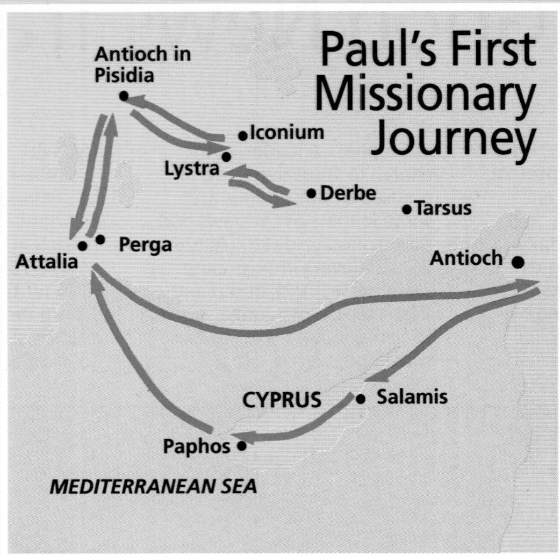

**Paul's Second Journey**

Paul took with him the young man Timothy. He returned to many places he had visited before, but crossed into Greece, bringing the gospel to Europe for the first time. He visited the great cities of Corinth and Athens (Acts 15:36-18:22).

## Paul's First Missionary Journey

Antioch in Pisidia
Iconium
Lystra
Derbe
Tarsus
Attalia
Perga
Antioch
CYPRUS
Salamis
Paphos
MEDITERRANEAN SEA

## Paul's Second Missionary Journey

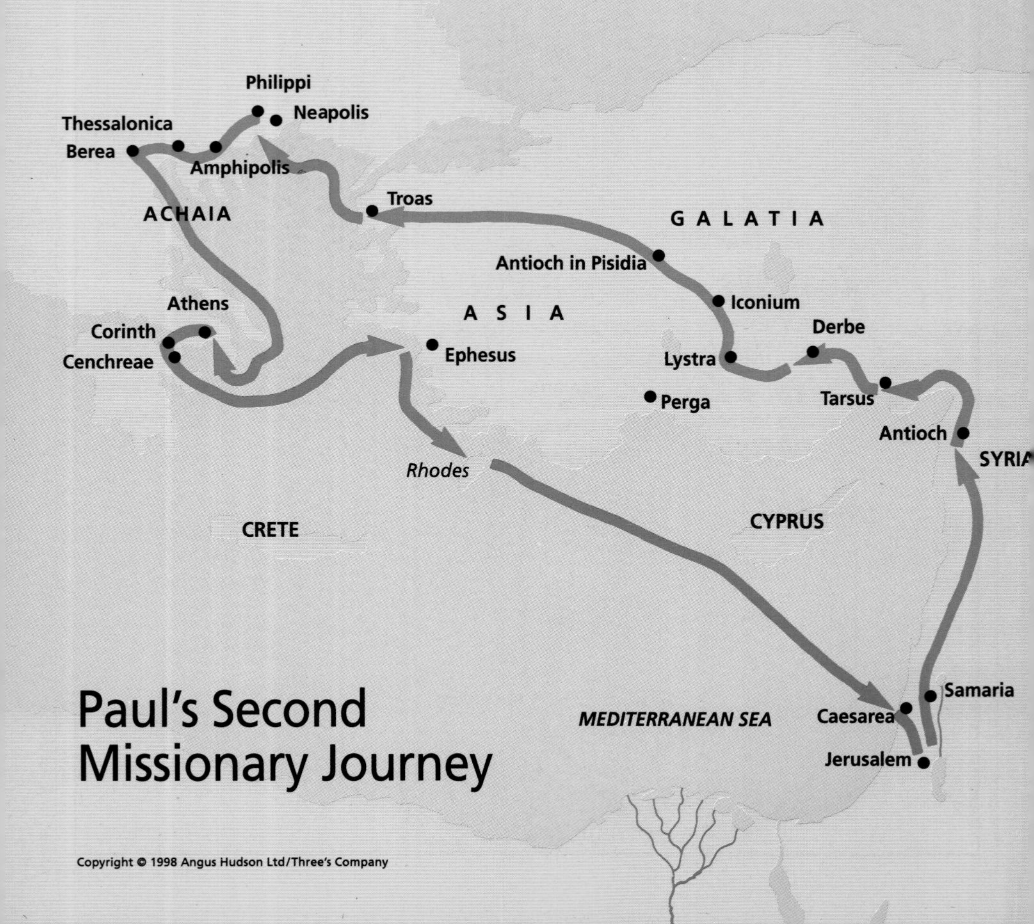

Philippi
Neapolis
Thessalonica
Berea
Amphipolis
Troas
ACHAIA
GALATIA
Antioch in Pisidia
Iconium
Athens
Corinth
Cenchreae
ASIA
Ephesus
Derbe
Lystra
Perga
Tarsus
Antioch
SYRIA
Rhodes
CRETE
CYPRUS
MEDITERRANEAN SEA
Samaria
Caesarea
Jerusalem